**Standard & Poor's®
500 Guide**

# Standard & Poor's®
# 500 Guide

2012 Edition

**Standard & Poor's**

Mc
Graw
Hill

New York   Chicago   San Francisco
Lisbon   London   Madrid   Mexico City
Milan   New Delhi   San Juan   Seoul
Singapore   Sydney   Toronto

**FOR STANDARD & POOR'S**

Managing Director, Equity Research Services
Publisher: Frank LoVaglio

The **McGraw·Hill** Companies

1 2 3 4 5 6 7 8 9 10 11 12 13 14 15   ROV/ROV   1 9 8 7 6 5 4 3 2 1

ISBN      978-0-07-177532-8
MHID      0-07-177532-3

e-ISBN  978-0-07-177615-8
e-MHID      0-07-177615-x

This publication is designed to provide accurate and authoritative information in regard to the subject matter covered. It is sold with the understanding that the publisher is not engaged in rendering legal, accounting, or other professional service. If legal advice or other expert assistance is required, the services of a competent professional person should be sought.

*—From a declaration of principles jointly adopted by a committee of the American Bar Association and a committee of publishers*

The companies contained in this handbook represented the components of the S&P 500 Index as of December 2, 2011.

Additions to or deletions from the Index will cause its composition to change over time.

Company additions and company deletions from the Standard & Poor's equity indexes do not in any way reflect an opinion on the investment merits of the company.

This book is printed on acid-free paper.

## ABOUT THE AUTHOR

Standard & Poor's Financial Services LLC, a subsidiary of The McGraw-Hill Companies, Inc., is the nation's leading securities information company. It provides a broad range of financial services, including the respected Standard & Poor's ratings and stock rankings, advisory services, data guides, and the most closely watched and widely reported gauges of stock market activity—the S&P 500, S&P MidCap 400, S&P SmallCap 600, and the S&P Composite 1500 stock price indexes. Standard & Poor's products are marketed around the world and used extensively by financial professionals and individual investors.

# Introduction

*by* David M. Blitzer, Ph.D.
Managing Director & Chairman of the Index Committee
Standard & Poor's

## The S&P 500

Any Web site, television news program, newspaper, or radio report covering the stock market gives the latest results of a handful of stock indices, including the Dow Industrials, the NASDAQ, and the S&P 500. The Dow is the oldest, extending back over 100 years, and has covered only 30 stocks since shortly before the crash of 1929. The NASDAQ came to fame in the tech boom but ignores all the companies listed on the New York Stock Exchange. The S&P 500 is the index used by market professionals and institutional investors when they need to know what the stock market is doing. While there are several thousand stocks traded in the U.S. market, the S&P 500 covers the most significant ones, representing some three-quarters of the total value of all U.S. equities. Over $1.3 trillion invested through mutual funds, pensions, and exchange-traded funds track the S&P 500. These funds mimic what the index does—if the index rises, so do the funds. Further, when a stock is added to or dropped from the index, these trillions of dollars of funds buy, or sell, the stock. The S&P 500 is also the way the market and its condition is measured—for Wall Street, corporate earnings are the earnings per share calculated for the S&P 500, and the market's valuation is gauged by the price-earnings ratio on the S&P 500.

## The S&P 500 and You, the Investor

If you picked up this book, you are probably interested in the stock market or stocks you might invest in; you may be wondering why institutional investors and market professionals focus so much attention on the 500 or what you can learn from the index. So, what can the index do? It can:

- Give you a benchmark for investment performance
- Tell you what kinds of stocks performed well or poorly in the past
- Let you see if today's valuations are higher or lower than in the past
- Help you compare one company or industry to another

We will look at these in turn before describing what's inside the S&P 500 and how S&P maintains the index.

[*Benchmarks:*] Monitoring investment performance—keeping score—is what separates occasional stock pickers from serious investors. People who chat about stocks with fellow workers or around the backyard barbeque rarely maintain records beyond the minimum level required to file their taxes. For these investors, stocks that go up are good and stocks that go down are disappointing; there is no serious analysis of what makes stocks move. Serious investors, whether institutional investors or individuals committed to managing their investments, know that understanding whether your stock selections work out requires knowing what the market did and how your portfolio compares to the market. This is where an index benchmark is essential.

The first question most investors have about their success is whether they are beating the market. A rough and ready answer can be found by comparing your portfolio's results to the S&P 500. More in-depth answers would either include dividends as well as price changes or would adjust for investment risks, or both. All the necessary data are widely available for the S&P 500 as well as being included in some brokerage statements and most mutual fund reports.

*What went up and what went down:* Simply looking at whether the market—the index—gained or lost can tell you a lot about what happened to your portfolio. For most portfolios and most stocks, the largest factor in their movements is how the overall market did. The second largest factor is often how similar stocks—in the same economic sector or industry—behaved. Because the S&P 500 covers about 75 percent of the total value of the U.S. equity market, it is a very good indication of what the market did. The stocks in the index are all classified into sectors and industries, so you can use these segments of the index to see if your stocks did better or worse than others in the same sector.

There are 10 economic sectors that classify all the stocks in the S&P 500; the table following lists these sectors, and the weight (based on market values) of each sector in the index. The performance of different sectors can be very different. Looking at the period from the recent low on March 9, 2009, to the end of November 2009, the financial sector gained 135%, materials and industrials each rose about 81% while telecommunication services gained "only" 24%. Before someone decides financial stocks are the all-time best remember that from the record high on October 9, 2007, to March 9th financials fell 59%, far more than any other sector. One comment heard from time to time is that no sector holds the leadership in the S&P 500 forever. Indeed, technology and financials have been trading the leadership back and forth for some 20 years. So be wary of anything that seems to overstay its welcome at the top of the list.

There are other classifications of stocks in the S&P 500. Not only are stocks assigned to an economic sector. They are also assigned to an industry group, an industry, and a sub-industry, using a classification standard called GICS® or the Global Industry Classification Standard.[1] There are 10 sectors, 24 industry groups, 68 industries, and 154 sub-industries. Separately from GICS, stocks are classified as growth or value stocks. Traditionally, growth stocks are those with fast-growing earnings, which offer investors the promise of higher earnings in the future. Value stocks are stocks believed to offer unrecognized values that are not reflected in the stock price. The classification is based on a number of financial ratios and measures, including earnings growth, price/earnings ratios, dividend yields, and similar measures. Although most investors hunt for growth stocks, value stocks tend to perform better over the long run. During periods of a few years or less, either one can easily outperform the other. Investors aren't the only people seeking growth; few if any companies want to be known as value stocks, and all want to be called growth stocks.

*Market Valuations:* The last few years certainly proved that there are times when markets go both up and down, sometimes by large amounts. The last 10 years of market moves are likely to be remembered for a long, long time. Through it all, what we really want to know is if stocks are really cheap and the market is likely to rise, or if stocks are overpriced and the market will tumble.

Economics tells us that a stock's value lies in the future earnings and dividends. Two convenient measures of how stock prices compare to earnings and dividends are the ratio of the price to earnings (P/E) and the dividend yield or percentage that the dividend is of the stock's price. Just as these are used for individual stocks, they are also used for the overall market by calculating these measures for the S&P 500. These numbers change as the market rises or falls and as company earnings and dividends change. Up-to-date numbers are published by Standard & Poor's on the Web at www.indices.standardandpoors.com and by various newspapers, magazines, and financial and investing Web sites.

---

[1]GICS(®) is maintained jointly by Standard & Poor's and MSCIBarra. Standard & Poor's Financial Services LLC is a subsidiary of the McGraw-Hill Companies, Inc.

Many investors see a P/E below average as a sign that stocks are undervalued and that there are buying opportunities while a P/E far above the average is a caution sign. Earnings move up and down just as stock prices do, so both can affect the P/E ratio. Corporate earnings tend to fall in recessions and rise in good times, and these movements could distort P/E ratios.

Dividends have dropped out of fashion in the last two decades, and fewer investors seem to watch dividend yields. However, about 368 of the 500 stocks in the S&P 500 pay dividends, so the current dividend yield of 2.3 percent may tell us something about the market. Since the 1950s, the dividend yield on the S&P 500 has almost always been lower than the yield on U.S. treasury or high-grade corporate bonds. The bonds may be attractive for their safety, but they don't offer any opportunity for growth, although companies often raise their dividends as their earnings grow. In late 2008, this pattern reversed for awhile; the dividend yield of 2.3 percent topped the yield on 10-year U.S. treasuries.

Following the gyrations of 2008 another version of the P/E ratio has become popular with some analysts. Instead of looking at one year, the idea is to look at a longer period so that sharp short-term swings don't warp the figures. This approach, originally due to two academic economists[2] is to divide the current price by a 10-year average of earnings after the earnings' figures are adjusted for inflation. This figure gives a sense of the market's long-term relative value and long-run prospects that are less affected by recent economic and market gyrations. In March 2009, when the market made a deep low, this 10-year P/E was about 13 compared to a long-run average around 19 and it suggested stocks were cheap.

Both these measures may give some sense of whether the market is over- or under-priced. However, neither of these is even close to being a fail-safe guide to the stock market in any time period. Moreover, the wide price swings seen in 2007 through 2011 should remind all investors that the market constantly changes and evolves and must be approached with both care and respect.

*Comparing One Company to Another:* Suppose your neighbor or a coworker tells you about a stock you "have to own" because the P/E is only 10, much less than the overall market. Is it a buy? Maybe, or maybe not. The index and its components can tell you a lot about the stocks in the index as well as about the market. Stocks in the same industry or industry group often rise and fall together because the economic events and factors that affect one stock in an industry will affect others as well. When oil prices rise, most oil company stocks tend to do well. Rumors of changes in Medicare and other health care programs may affect all pharmaceutical stocks at once. One can compare data about a stock to the same information for similar stocks, to the industry or economic sector, and to the whole market. The S&P 500 and information about the stocks in it make this possible.

How does this help decide if a stock is cheap? Suppose the market's P/E as measured by the S&P 500 is 15 and the stock's P/E is 20, so it looks to be overpriced. Before forgetting about it, compare the data on the stock—P/E ratios, dividend yields, or other statistics—to similar stocks. The easiest way to find similar stocks is to use the sector and industry classifications from the S&P 500, as shown on the stock reports. As you do this with various stocks, you will begin to see that some sectors or industries seem to always have P/Es higher than the market while other sectors have low P/Es. Some sectors focus on growth stocks, which have high P/Es, while others focus on value stocks. You will notice similar patterns if you compare dividend yields. In fact, even looking for stocks that pay dividends will reveal some patterns.

[2]John Y. Campbell and Robert J. Shiller, "Valuation Ratios and the Long-Run Stock Market Outlook", *Journal of Portfolio Management*, winter 1998. Figures used in the text from www.dshort.com.

The stock market is shifting all the time, with some sectors becoming relatively more expensive and others fading from popularity. Within a sector there are similar movements among stocks as some move up faster while others may fade. It is useful to know how a stock compares to its peers in the same industry or sector as well as to understand how it compares to the entire market. Using the S&P 500 and the data shown on the stock reports, one can see these shifts and comparisons.

## What's in the S&P 500

The S&P 500 Index consists of 500 stocks selected by Standard & Poor's to represent the U.S. stock market and, through the market, the U.S. economy. It is not the 500 "largest" stocks in the market. Rather, it is sometimes described as containing the leading stocks in leading industries. The stocks are selected based on published guidelines; all members of the S&P 500 must be U.S. companies. When they join the index, they must have market values of at least $4 billion, trade with reasonable liquidity, be profitable, and have at least half their shares available to investors. The selection of companies also considers the balance of economic sectors in the market and the index so that the index is a fair representation of the market as a whole.

The S&P 500 index is reported on television, Web sites and newspapers very widely. Data are also published on S&P's Web site at www.indices.standardandpoors.com. Many investors and investment analysts use the S&P 500 to help choose stocks, as described above. However it has many other investment uses: index mutual funds, exchange-traded funds (ETFs), futures, and options. Index mutual funds are mutual funds that track an index. The first funds, and the largest index funds today, track the S&P 500. Exchange-traded funds have grown in popularity in recent years. These are similar to index mutual funds except that they trade on an exchange and can by bought and sold at any time of day whereas mutual funds are only sold at prices based on the market close. The first U.S. ETF was based on the S&P 500; there are two large ETFs based on the S&P 500. In addition, numerous pension funds, endowments, and other institutional investments track the S&P 500. Currently, about $1.3 trillion was invested in various investments that track the S&P 500 as closely as possible. This means that the fund tries to mimic the index, adding stocks when they are added to the index and matching any other adjustments in the index.

There are relatively few changes in the index; most of these changes are caused by mergers, acquisitions, and other corporate actions that remove companies from the index. Over the last several years, the index has seen about 30 changes each year where a "change" is one company added and one dropped. If one thinks of the index as a portfolio, it is amazingly stable compared to most mutual funds—the turnover in the S&P 500 is about 5 to 10 percent of its value each year, whereas mutual funds can see a turnover of over 100 percent in a single year. A typical change in the index occurs when a company is acquired and is dropped from the index and replaced with another company. At times, especially recently with the turmoil in the markets, companies in the index are removed because of bankruptcy.

While changes to the index don't occur every day, they can be important to some traders. Because so much money tracks the index, about 10 percent of the outstanding stock of any company in the index is bought by index funds, ETFs, and other index investors when a stock is added to the index. Further, this buying occurs over a relatively short period of time—a few weeks or less. The result is that stocks added to the S&P 500 often see their prices rise when they go into the index.

The S&P 500 index was created and is maintained by S&P. There is an Index Committee of S&P professional staff who oversee the index and are responsible for making necessary changes to assure that the index will be an accurate reflection of the U.S. equity markets. Because changes in the index can move the market, all the work done by the Index Committee is confidential until any changes to the index are announced. Moreover, because the changes can move the market, the announcements are made available to the public, and no one gets any advance notice before the public announcements on S&P's Web site.

Beyond various kinds of index funds and ETFs, there are other investment uses of the index—futures and options. These are derivatives based on the value of the index that offer investors—mostly institutional investors, but some individuals as well—opportunities to either hedge their positions or to easily establish a leveraged position in the index. Futures and options are usually seen as more complex and often riskier than buying stocks. Just as successful stock investing requires research and understanding, successful use of futures and options demands a solid understanding of how the instruments work and what the risks are. At times these can magnify the impact of shifts in the index. Furthermore, unlike stocks, futures and options have firm expiration dates that must be considered in any investment plan.

## History

The S&P 500 celebrated its fiftieth anniversary in March 2007. However, its forebears go farther back. The S&P 500 is not the oldest index, an honor which goes to the Dow Jones Industrials. The 500 traces its lineage back to an index of 233 companies published weekly by The Standard Statistics Company beginning in 1923. That index was one of the first to have industry classifications to support investment analysis. In 1926, Standard Statistics began a daily index of 90 stocks. A decade and a half later, in 1941, Standard Statistics merged with Poor's Publishing to form S&P. In 1957 the indices were combined and gave us the S&P 500. A small number of companies in the current S&P 500 can trace their membership back to the 1920s, over 50 were members in 1957.

The index has seen various changes over the years as it kept up with the times and with developments in the market. Different industries have come and gone. Some of today's leading sectors were barely present or nonexistent in 1957. Technology is now a much bigger part of the index. Investment banks and brokerage houses were all private partnerships in 1957 and didn't begin to enter the index until the 1970s. In many ways the index's history is the history of the U.S. stock market.

Many investors, especially those who consider mutual funds, have seen data on the history of the U.S. stock market since 1926. That history is the S&P 500 and the 90 stock index that preceded the 500. Mutual funds and other investment products often compare their performance to the market; the market is the S&P 500. You might think that 500 stocks chosen simply to represent the market without any attempt to select "good" stocks that will beat the market might be an easy target to outperform. Actually, it is not; in fact, it is *very* difficult to consistently outperform the S&P 500 or most other broad-based indices. Research by Standard & Poor's and by various others shows that in a typical period of three or more years, fewer than one-third of mutual funds outperform the index. Further, a fund that managed to be in the lucky third that beat the index in the last three years has only a one-in-three chance of beating the index in the next three years. Why? First, index funds and ETFs are cheap, with very low expenses. Second, since it is very hard to know which stocks will go up first, it helps to own a lot of stocks.[3]

Today Standard & Poor's publishes literally hundreds of thousands of indices, covering over 80 stock markets in almost every country where there is a stock market. The largest indices have several times more stocks than the 500, including a global equity index with over 11,000 securities. At the other extreme there are narrow indices focused on a small sub-industry in one country. All these indices are used by investors, often in the same way the 500 can be used, as described here.

[3]On index results vs. mutual funds, see S&P's SPIVA reports on S&P's Web site or books by John Bogle or Burton Malkiel.

## In conclusion

When you want to know how the market did, what went up or down, or whether your stock picks beat the market, the best place to look is the S&P 500.

### S&P 500 Global Industry Classification Standard (GICS) Sectors
*As of December 2, 2011*

|  | Percent of Market Capitalization |
|---|---|
| Consumer Discretionary | 10.70 |
| Consumer Staples | 11.34 |
| Energy | 12.47 |
| Financials | 13.43 |
| Health Care | 11.51 |
| Industrials | 10.70 |
| Information Technology | 19.52 |
| Materials | 3.57 |
| Telecommunication Services | 3.06 |
| Utilities | 3.70 |

## What You'll Find in This Book

In the pages that follow you will find an array of text and statistical data on 500 different companies spanning over 130 sub-industries. This information, dealing with everything from the nature of these companies' basic businesses, recent corporate developments, current outlooks, and select financial information relating to revenues, earnings, dividends, margins, capitalization, and so forth, might initially seem overwhelming. However, it's not that difficult. Just take a few moments to familiarize yourself with what you'll find on these pages.

Following is a glossary of terms and definitions used throughout this book. Please refer to this section as you encounter terms which need further clarification.

### Glossary

**S&P STARS** – Since January 1, 1987, Standard & Poor's Equity Research Services has ranked a universe of U.S. common stocks, ADRs (American Depositary Receipts), and ADSs (American Depositary Shares) based on a given equity's potential for future performance. Similarly, Standard & Poor's Equity Research Services has used STARS® methodology to rank Asian and European equities since June 30, 2002. Under proprietary STARS (Stock Appreciation Ranking System), S&P equity analysts rank equities according to their individual forecast of an equity's future total return potential versus the expected total return of a relevant benchmark (e.g., a regional index (S&P Asia 50 Index, S&P Europe 350® Index or S&P 500® Index)), based on a 12-month time horizon. STARS was designed to meet the needs of investors looking to put their investment decisions in perspective. Data used to assist in determining the STARS ranking may be the result of the analyst's own models as well as internal proprietary models resulting from dynamic data inputs.

**S&P 12-Month Target Price** – The S&P equity analyst's projection of the market price a given security will command 12 months hence, based on a combination of intrinsic, relative, and private market valuation metrics, including S&P fair value.

**Investment Style Classification** – Characterizes the stock as either a growth-or value-oriented investment, and, indicates the market value (size) of the company as large-cap, mid-cap or small-cap. Growth stocks typically have a higher price-to-earnings and price-to-cash flow ratio, that represents the premium that is being paid for the expected higher growth. Value stocks typically have higher dividends and more moderate P/E ratios consistent with their current return policies.

**Qualitative Risk Assessment** – The S&P equity analyst's view of a given company's operational risk, or the risk of a firm's ability to continue as an ongoing concern. The Qualitative Risk Assessment is a relative ranking to the S&P U.S. STARS universe, and should be reflective of risk factors related to a company's operations, as opposed to risk and volatility measures associated with share prices.

**Quantitative Evaluations** – In contrast to our qualitative STARS recommendations, which are assigned by S&P analysts, the quantitative evaluations described below are derived from proprietary arithmetic models. These computer-driven evaluations may at times contradict an analyst's qualitative assessment of a stock. One primary reason for this is that different measures are used to determine each. For instance, when designating STARS, S&P analysts assess many factors that cannot be reflected in a model, such as risks and opportunities, management changes, recent competitive shifts, patent expiration, litigation risk, etc.

**S&P Quality Rankings** (also known as **S&P Earnings & Dividend Rank-ings**) – Growth and stability of earnings and dividends are deemed key elements in establishing S&P's Quality Rankings for common stocks, which are designed to capsulize the nature of this record in a single symbol. It should be noted, however, that the process also takes into consideration certain adjustments and modifications deemed desirable in establishing such rankings. The final score for each stock is measured against a scoring matrix determined by analysis of the scores of a large and representative sample of stocks. The range of scores in the array of this sample has been aligned with the following ladder of rankings:

| | | | |
|----|--------------|----|-----------------|
| A+ | Highest | B− | Lower |
| A | High | C | Lowest |
| A− | Above Average | D | In Reorganization |
| B+ | Average | NR | Not Ranked |
| B | Below Average | | |

**S&P Fair Value Rank** – Using S&P's exclusive proprietary quantitative model, stocks are ranked in one of five groups, ranging from Group 5, listing the most undervalued stocks, to Group 1, the most overvalued issues. Group 5 stocks are expected to generally outperform all others. A positive (+) or negative (−) Timing Index is placed next to the Fair Value ranking to further aid the selection process. A stock with a (+) added to the Fair Value Rank simply means that this stock has a somewhat better chance to outperform other stocks with the same Fair Value Rank. A stock with a (−) has a somewhat lesser chance to outperform other stocks with the same Fair Value Rank. The Fair Value rankings imply the following: 5-Stock is significantly undervalued; 4-Stock is moderately undervalued; 3-Stock is fairly valued; 2-Stock is modestly overvalued; 1-Stock is significantly overvalued.

**S&P Fair Value Calculation** – The price at which a stock should trade at, according to S&P's proprietary quantitative model that incorporates both actual and estimated variables (as opposed to only actual variables in the case of S&P Quality Ranking). Relying heavily on a company's actual return on equity, the S&P Fair Value model places a value on a security based on placing a formula-derived price-to-book multiple on a company's consensus earnings per share estimate.

**Insider Activity** – Gives an insight as to insider sentiment by showing whether directors, officers and key employees who have proprietary information not available to the general public, are buying or selling the company's stock during the most recent six months.

**Investability Quotient (IQ)** – The IQ is a measure of investment desirability. It serves as an indicator of potential medium- to long-term return and as a caution against downside risk. The measure takes into account variables such as technical indicators, earnings estimates, liquidity, financial ratios and selected S&P proprietary measures.

**Volatility** – Rates the volatility of the stock's price over the past year.

**Technical Evaluation** – In researching the past market history of prices and trading volume for each company, S&P's computer models apply special technical methods and formulas to identify and project price trends for the stock.

**Relative Strength Rank** – Shows, on a scale of 1 to 99, how the stock has performed versus all other companies in S&P's universe on a rolling 13-week basis.

**Global Industry Classification Standard (GICS)** – An industry classification standard, developed by Standard & Poor's in collaboration with Morgan Stanley Capital International (MSCI). GICS is currently comprised of 10 sectors, 24 industry groups, 68 industries, and 154 sub-industries.

**S&P EPS Estimates** – Standard & Poor's earnings per share (EPS) estimates reflect analyst projections of future EPS from continuing operations, and generally exclude various items that are viewed as special, non-recurring, or extraordinary. Also, S&P EPS estimates reflect either forecasts of S&P equity analysts; or, the consensus (average) EPS estimate, which are independently compiled by Capital IQ, a data provider to Standard & Poor's Equity Research. Among the items typically excluded from EPS estimates are asset sale gains; impairment, restructuring or merger-related charges; legal and insurance settlements; in process research and development expenses; gains or losses on the extinguishment of debt; the cumulative effect of accounting changes; and earnings related to operations that have been classified by the company as discontinued. The inclusion of some items, such as stock option expense and recurring types of other charges, may vary, and depend on such factors as industry practice, analyst judgment, and the extent to which some types of data is disclosed by companies.

**S&P Core Earnings** – Standard & Poor's Core Earnings is a uniform methodology for adjusting operating earnings by focusing on a company's after-tax earnings generated from its principal businesses. Included in the Standard & Poor's definition are employee stock option grant expenses, pension costs, restructuring charges from ongoing operations, write-downs of depreciable or amortizable operating assets, purchased research and development, M&A related expenses and unrealized gains/losses from hedging activities. Excluded from the definition are pension gains, impairment of goodwill charges, gains or losses from asset sales, reversal of prior-year charges and provision from litigation or insurance settlements.

**S&P Issuer Credit Rating** – A Standard & Poor's Issuer Credit Rating is a current opinion of an obligor's overall financial capacity (its creditworthiness) to pay its financial obligations. This opinion focuses on the obligor's capacity and willingness to meet its financial commitments as they come due. It does not apply to any specific financial obligation, as it does not take into account the nature of and provisions of the obligation, its standing in bankruptcy or liquidation, statutory preferences, or the legality and enforceability of the obligation. In addition, it does not take into account the creditworthiness of the guarantors, insurers, or other forms of credit enhancement on the obligation.

**Standard & Poor's Equity Research Services** – Standard & Poor's Equity Research Services U.S. includes Standard & Poor's Investment Advisory Services LLC; Standard & Poor's Equity Research Services Europe includes McGraw-Hill Financial Research Europe Limited trading as Standard & Poor's; Standard & Poor's Equity Research Services Asia includes Standard & Poor's LLC's offices in Singapore, Standard & Poor's Investment Advisory Services (HK) Limited in Hong Kong, Standard & Poor's Malaysia Sdn Bhd, and Standard & Poor's Information Services (Australia) Pty Ltd.

<u>Abbreviations Used in S&P Equity Research Reports</u>
CAGR – Compound Annual Growth Rate
CAPEX – Capital Expenditures
CY – Calendar Year
DCF – Discounted Cash Flow
EBIT – Earnings Before Interest and Taxes
EBITDA – Earnings Before Interest, Taxes, Depreciation and Amortization
EPS – Earnings Per Share
EV – Enterprise Value
FCF – Free Cash Flow
FFO – Funds From Operations
FY – Fiscal Year
P/E – Price/Earnings
PEG Ratio – P/E-to-Growth Ratio
PV – Present Value
R&D – Research & Development
ROA – Return on Assets
ROE – Return on Equity
ROI – Return on Investment
ROIC – Return on Invested Capital
SG&A – Selling, General & Administrative Expenses
WACC – Weighted Average Cost of Capital
Dividends on American Depository Receipts (ADRs) and American Depository Shares (ADSs) are net of taxes (paid in the country of origin).

## REQUIRED DISCLOSURES

In contrast to the qualitative STARS recommendations covered in this report, which are determined and assigned by S&P equity analysts, S&P's quantitative evaluations are derived from S&P's proprietary Fair Value quantitative model. In particular, the Fair Value Ranking methodology is a relative ranking methodology, whereas the STARS methodology is not. Because the Fair Value model and the STARS methodology reflect different criteria, assumptions and analytical methods, quantitative evaluations may at times differ from (or even contradict) an equity analyst's STARS recommendations. As a quantitative model, Fair Value relies on history and consensus estimates and does not introduce an element of subjectivity as can be the case with equity analysts in assigning STARS recommendations.

### S&P Global STARS Distribution

**In North America**
As of September 30, 2011, research analysts at Standard & Poor's Equity Research Services North America recommended 42.2% of issuers with buy recommendations, 54.2% with hold recommendations and 3.6% with sell recommendations.

### In Europe

As of September 30, 2011, research analysts at Standard & Poor's Equity Research Services Europe recommended 34.4% of issuers with buy recommendations, 49.4% with hold recommendations and 16.2% with sell recommendations.

### In Asia

As of September 30, 2011, research analysts at Standard & Poor's Equity Research Services Asia recommended 48.4% of issuers with buy recommendations, 45.7% with hold recommendations and 5.9% with sell recommendations.

### Globally

As of September 30, 2011, research analysts at Standard & Poor's Equity Research Services globally recommended 41.5% of issuers with buy recommendations, 52.6% with hold recommendations and 5.9% with sell recommendations.

**5-STARS (Strong Buy):** Total return is expected to outperform the total return of a relevant benchmark, by a wide margin over the coming 12 months, with shares rising in price on an absolute basis.

**4-STARS (Buy):** Total return is expected to outperform the total return of a relevant benchmark over the coming 12 months, with shares rising in price on an absolute basis.

**3-STARS (Hold):** Total return is expected to closely approximate the total return of a relevant benchmark over the coming 12 months, with shares generally rising in price on an absolute basis.

**2-STARS (Sell):** Total return is expected to underperform the total return of a relevant benchmark over the coming 12 months, and the share price is not anticipated to show a gain.

**1-STARS (Strong Sell):** Total return is expected to underperform the total return of a relevant benchmark by a wide margin over the coming 12 months, with shares falling in price on an absolute basis.

Relevant benchmarks: In North America, the relevant benchmark is the S&P 500 Index, in Europe and in Asia, the relevant benchmarks are generally the S&P Europe 350 Index and the S&P Asia 50 Index.

### For All Regions:

All of the views expressed in this research report accurately reflect the research analyst's personal views regarding any and all of the subject securities or issuers. No part of analyst compensation was, is, or will be, directly or indirectly, related to the specific recommendations or views expressed in this research report.

### S&P Global Quantitative Recommendations Distribution

### In Europe

As of September 30, 2011, Standard & Poor's Quantitative Services Europe recommended 47.7% of issuers with buy recommendations, 20.8% with hold recommendations and 31.5% with sell recommendations.

### In Asia

As of September 30, 2011, Standard & Poor's Quantitative Services Asia recommended 43.0% of issuers with buy recommendations, 22.2% with hold recommendations and 34.8% with sell recommendations.

**Globally**
As of September 30, 2011, Standard & Poor's Quantitative Services globally recommended 44.7% of issuers with buy recommendations, 21.7% with hold recommendations and 33.6% with sell recommendations.

**Additional information is available upon request.**
**Other Disclosures**

This report has been prepared and issued by Standard & Poor's and/or one of its affiliates. In the United States, research reports are prepared by Standard & Poor's Investment Advisory Services LLC ("SPIAS"). In the United States, research reports are issued by Standard & Poor's ("S&P"); in the United Kingdom by McGraw-Hill Financial Research Europe Limited, which is authorized and regulated by the Financial Services Authority and trades as Standard & Poor's; in Hong Kong by Standard & Poor's Investment Advisory Services (HK) Limited, which is regulated by the Hong Kong Securities Futures Commission; in Singapore by Standard & Poor's LLC, which is regulated by the Monetary Authority of Singapore; in Malaysia by Standard & Poor's Malaysia Sdn Bhd ("S&PM"), which is regulated by the Securities Commission; in Australia by Standard & Poor's Information Services (Australia) Pty Ltd ("SPIS"), which is regulated by the Australian Securities & Investments Commission; and in Korea by SPIAS, which is also registered in Korea as a cross-border investment advisory company.

The research and analytical services performed by SPIAS, McGraw-Hill Financial Research Europe Limited, S&PM, and SPIS are each conducted separately from any other analytical activity of Standard & Poor's.

Standard & Poor's or an affiliate may license certain intellectual property or provide pricing or other services to, or otherwise have a financial interest in, certain issuers of securities, including exchange-traded investments whose investment objective is to substantially replicate the returns of a proprietary Standard & Poor's index, such as the S&P 500. In cases where Standard & Poor's or an affiliate is paid fees that are tied to the amount of assets that are invested in the fund or the volume of trading activity in the fund, investment in the fund will generally result in Standard & Poor's or an affiliate earning compensation in addition to the subscription fees or other compensation for services rendered by Standard & Poor's. A reference to a particular investment or security by Standard & Poor's and/or one of its affiliates is not a recommendation to buy, sell, or hold such investment or security, nor is it considered to be investment advice.

Indexes are unmanaged, statistical composites and their returns do not include payment of any sales charges or fees an investor would pay to purchase the securities they represent. Such costs would lower performance. It is not possible to invest directly in an index.

Standard & Poor's and its affiliates provide a wide range of services to, or relating to, many organizations, including issuers of securities, investment advisers, broker-dealers, investment banks, other financial institutions and financial intermediaries, and accordingly may receive fees or other economic benefits from those organizations, including organizations whose securities or services they may recommend, rate, include in model portfolios, evaluate or otherwise address.

For a list of companies mentioned in this report with whom Standard & Poor's and/or one of its affiliates has had business relationships within the past year, please go to: http://www.standardandpoors.com/products-services/articles/en/us/?assetID=1245187982940

## Disclaimers

With respect to reports issued to clients in Japan and in the case of inconsistencies between the English and Japanese version of a report, the English version prevails. With respect to reports issued to clients in German and in the case of inconsistencies between the English and German version of a report, the English version prevails. Neither S&P nor its affiliates guarantee the accuracy of the translation. Assumptions, opinions and estimates constitute our judgment as of the date of this material and are subject to change without notice. Past performance is not necessarily indicative of future results.

Standard & Poor's, its affiliates, and any third-party providers, as well as their directors, officers, shareholders, employees or agents (collectively S&P Parties) do not guarantee the accuracy, completeness or adequacy of this material, and S&P Parties shall have no liability for any errors, omissions, or interruptions therein, regardless of the cause, or for the results obtained from the use of the information provided by the S&P Parties. S&P PARTIES DISCLAIM ANY AND ALL EXPRESS OR IMPLIED WARRANTIES, INCLUDING, BUT NOT LIMITED TO, ANY WARRANTIES OF MERCHANTABILITY, SUITABILITY OR FITNESS FOR A PARTICULAR PURPOSE OR USE. In no event shall S&P Parties be liable to any party for any direct, indirect, incidental, exemplary, compensatory, punitive, special or consequential damages, costs, expenses, legal fees, or losses (including, without limitation, lost income or lost profits and opportunity costs) in connection with any use of the information contained in this document even if advised of the possibility of such damages. Capital IQ is a business of Standard & Poor's.

Ratings from Standard & Poor's Ratings Services are statements of opinion as of the date they are expressed and not statements of fact or recommendations to purchase, hold, or sell any securities or to make any investment decisions. Standard & Poor's assumes no obligation to update its opinions following publication in any form or format. Standard & Poor's ratings should not be relied on and are not substitutes for the skill, judgment and experience of the user, its management, employees, advisors and/or clients when making investment and other business decisions. Standard & Poor's rating opinions do not address the suitability of any security. Standard & Poor's does not act as a fiduciary. While Standard & Poor's has obtained information from sources it believes to be reliable, Standard & Poor's does not perform an audit and undertakes no duty of due diligence or independent verification of any information it receives.

Standard & Poor's keeps certain activities of its business units separate from each other in order to preserve the independence and objectivity of their respective activities. As a result, certain business units of Standard & Poor's may have information that is not available to other Standard & Poor's business units. Standard & Poor's has established policies and procedures to maintain the confidentiality of certain non-public information received in connection with each analytical process.

Standard & Poor's Ratings Services did not participate in the development of this report. Standard & Poor's may receive compensation for its ratings and certain credit-related analyses, normally from issuers or underwriters of securities or from obligors. Standard & Poor's reserves the right to disseminate its opinions and analyses. Standard & Poor's public ratings and analyses are made available on its Web sites, www.standardandpoors.com (free of charge), and www.ratingsdirect.com and www.globalcreditportal.com (subscription), and may be distributed through other means, including via Standard & Poor's publications and third-party redistributors. Additional information about our ratings fees is available at www.standardandpoors.com/usratingsfees.

This material is not intended as an offer or solicitation for the purchase or sale of any security or other financial instrument. Securities, financial instruments or strategies mentioned herein may not be suitable for all investors. Any opinions expressed herein are given in good faith, are subject to change without notice, and are only current as of the stated date of their issue. Prices, values, or income from any securities or investments mentioned in this report may fall against the interests of the investor and the investor may get back less than the amount invested. Where an investment is described as being likely to yield income, please note that the amount of income that the investor will receive from such an investment may fluctuate. Where an investment or security is denominated in a different currency to the investor's currency of reference, changes in rates of exchange may have an adverse effect on the value, price or income of or from that investment to the investor. The information contained in this report does not constitute advice on the tax consequences of making any particular investment decision. This material is not intended for any specific investor and does not take into account your particular investment objectives, financial situations or needs and is not intended as a recommendation of particular securities, financial instruments or strategies to you. Before acting on any recommendation in this material, you should consider whether it is suitable for your particular circumstances and, if necessary, seek professional advice.

This document does not constitute an offer of services in jurisdictions where Standard & Poor's or its affiliates do not have the necessary licenses.

For residents of the U.K. – This report is only directed at and should only be relied on by persons outside of the United Kingdom or persons who are inside the United Kingdom and who have professional experience in matters relating to investments or who are high net worth persons, as defined in Article 19(5) or Article 49(2) (a) to (d) of the Financial Services and Markets Act 2000 (Financial Promotion) Order 2005, respectively.

For residents of Singapore – Anything herein that may be construed as a recommendation is intended for general circulation and does not take into account the specific investment objectives, financial situation or particular needs of any particular person. Advice should be sought from a financial adviser regarding the suitability of an investment, taking into account the specific investment objectives, financial situation or particular needs of any person in receipt of the recommendation, before the person makes a commitment to purchase the investment product.

For residents of Malaysia – All queries in relation to this report should be referred to Ching Wah Tam and Ahmad Halim.

For residents of Indonesia – This research report does not constitute an offering document and it should not be construed as an offer of securities in Indonesia, and that any such securities will only be offered or sold through a financial institution.

For residents of the Philippines – The securities being offered or sold have not been registered with the Securities and Exchange Commission under the Securities Regulation Code of the Philippines. Any future offer or sale thereof is subject to registration requirements under the Code unless such offer or sale qualifies as an exempt transaction.

Canadian investors should be aware that any specific securities discussed in this research report can only be purchased in Canada through a Canadian registered dealer and, if such securities are not available in the secondary market, they can only be purchased by eligible private placement purchasers on a basis that is exempt from the prospectus requirements of Canadian securities law and will be subject to resale restrictions.

For residents of Australia – This report is distributed by Standard & Poor's Information Services (Australia) Pty Ltd ("SPIS") in Australia.

Any express or implied opinion contained in this report is limited to "General Advice" and based solely on consideration of the investment merits of the financial product(s) alone. The information in this report has not been prepared for use by retail investors and has been prepared without taking account of any particular person's financial or investment objectives, financial situation or needs. Before acting on any advice, any person using the advice should consider its appropriateness having regard to their own or their clients' objectives, financial situation and needs. You should obtain a Product Disclosure Statement relating to the product and consider the statement before making any decision or recommendation about whether to acquire the product. Each opinion must be weighed solely as one factor in any investment decision made by or on behalf of any adviser and any such adviser must accordingly make their own assessment taking into account an individual's particular circumstances.

SPIS holds an Australian Financial Services Licence Number 258896. Please refer to the SPIS Financial Services Guide for more information at www.fundsinsights.com.au.

STANDARD & POOR'S, S&P, S&P 500, S&P Europe 350 and STARS are registered trademarks of Standard & Poor's Financial Services LLC.

This investment analysis was prepared from the following sources: S&P MarketScope, S&P Compustat, S&P Industry Reports, I/B/E/S International, Inc.; Standard & Poor's, 55 Water St., New York, NY 10041.

### Key Stock Statistics

**Market Cap.**—The stock price multiplied by the number of shares outstanding, based on market value calculated at the issue level.

**Institutional Holdings**—Shows the percent of total common shares held by financial institutions. This information covers some 2,500 institutions and is compiled by Vickers Stock Research Corporation, 226 New York Avenue, Huntington, N.Y. 11743

**Value of $10,000 Invested 5 years ago**—The value today of a $10,000 investment in the stock made 5 years ago, assuming year-end reinvestment of dividends.

**Beta**—The beta coefficient is a measure of the volatility of a stock's price relative to the S&P 500 Index (a proxy for the overall market). An issue with a beta of 1.5 for example, tends to move 50% more than the overall market, in the same direction. An issue with a beta of 0.5 tends to move 50% less. If a stock moved exactly as the market moved, it would have a beta of 1.0. A stock with a negative beta tends to move in a direction opposite to that of the overall market.

### Per Share Data ($) Tables

**Cash Flow**—Net income plus depreciation, depletion, and amortization, divided by shares used to calculate earnings per common share. (See also: "Cash Flow" under Industrial Companies.)

**Dividends**—Generally total cash payments per share based on the ex-dividend dates over a 12-month period. May also be reported on a declared basis where this has been established to be a company's payout policy.

**Earnings**—The amount a company reports as having been earned for the year on its common stock based on generally accepted accounting standards. Earnings per share are presented on a "diluted" basis pursuant to FASB 128, which became effective December 15, 1997, and are generally reported from continuing operations, before extraordinary items.

This reflects a change from previously reported *primary earnings per share*. Insurance companies report *operating earnings* before gains/losses on security transactions and *earnings* after such transactions.

**Net Asset Value**—Appears on investment company reports and reflects the market value of stocks, bonds, and net cash divided by outstanding shares. The % difference indicates the percentage premium or discount of the market price over the net asset value.

**Payout Ratio**—Indicates the percentage of earnings paid out in dividends. It is calculated by dividing the annual dividend by the earnings. For insurance companies, *earnings* after gains/losses on security transactions are used.

**P/E Ratio High/Low**—The ratio of market price to earnings—essentially indicates the valuation investors place on a company's earnings. Obtained by dividing the annual earnings into the high and low market price for the year. For insurance companies, *operating earnings* before gains/losses on security transactions are used.

**Portfolio Turnover**—Appears on investment company reports and indicates percentage of total security purchases and sales for the year to overall investment assets. Primarily mirrors trading aggressiveness.

**Prices High/Low**—Shows the calendar year high and low of a stock's market price.

**Tangible Book Value; Book Value** (See also: "Common Equity" under Industrial Companies)—Indicates the theoretical dollar amount per common share one might expect to receive from a company's tangible "book" assets should liquidation take place. Generally, book value is determined by adding the stated value of the common stock, paid-in capital and retained earnings and then subtracting intangible assets (excess cost over equity of acquired companies, goodwill, and patents), preferred stock at liquidating value and unamortized debt discount. Divide that amount by the outstanding shares to get book value per common share.

Income/Balance Sheet Data Tables

*Banks*

**Cash**—Mainly vault cash, interest-bearing deposits placed with banks, reserves required by the Federal Reserve, and items in the process of collection—generally referred to as float.

**Commercial Loans**—Commercial, industrial, financial, agricultural loans and leases, gross.

**Common Equity**—Includes common/capital surplus, undivided profits, reserve for contingencies and other capital reserves.

**Deposits**—Primarily classified as either *demand* (payable at any time upon demand of depositor) or *time* (not payable within 30 days).

**Deposits/Capital Funds**—Average deposits divided by average capital funds. Capital funds include capital notes/debentures, other long-term debt, capital stock, surplus, and undivided profits. May be used as a "leverage" measure.

**Earning Assets**—Assets on which interest is earned.

**Effective Tax Rate**—Actual income tax expense divided by net before taxes.

**Gains/Losses on Securities Transactions**—Realized losses on sales of securities, usually bonds.

**Government Securities**—Includes United States Treasury securities and securities of other U.S. government agencies at book or carrying value. A bank's major "liquid asset."

**Investment Securities**—Federal, state, and local government bonds and other securities.

**Loan Loss Provision**—Amount charged to operating expenses to provide an adequate reserve to cover anticipated losses in the loan portfolio.

**Loans**—All domestic and foreign loans (excluding leases), less unearned discount and reserve for possible losses. Generally considered a bank's principal asset.

**Long-Term Debt**—Total borrowings for terms beyond one year including notes payable, mortgages, debentures, term loans, and capitalized lease obligations.

**Money Market Assets**—Interest-bearing interbank deposits, federal funds sold, trading account securities.

**Net Before Taxes**—Amount remaining after operating expenses are deducted from income, including gains or losses on security transactions.

**Net Income**—The final profit before dividends (common/preferred) from all sources after deduction of expenses, taxes, and fixed charges, but before any discontinued operations or extraordinary items.

**Net Interest Income**—Interest and dividend income, minus interest expense.

**Net Interest Margin**—A percentage computed by dividing net interest income, on a taxable equivalent basis, by average earning assets. Used as an analytical tool to measure profit margins from providing credit services.

**Noninterest Income**—Service fees, trading, and other income, excluding gains/ losses on securities transactions.

**Other Loans**—Gross consumer, real estate and foreign loans.

**% Equity to Assets**—Average common equity divided by average total assets. Used as a measure of capital adequacy.

**% Equity to Loans**—Average common equity divided by average loans. Reflects the degree of equity coverage to loans outstanding.

**% Expenses/Op. Revenues**—Noninterest expense as a percentage of taxable equivalent net interest income plus noninterest income (before securities gains/losses). A measure of cost control.

**% Loan Loss Reserve**—Contra-account to loan assets, built through provisions for loan losses, which serves as a cushion for possible future loan charge-offs.

**% Loans/Deposits**—Proportion of loans funded by deposits. A measure of liquidity and an indication of bank's ability to write more loans.

**% Return on Assets**—Net income divided by average total assets. An analytical measure of asset-use efficiency and industry comparison.

**% Return on Equity**—Net income (minus preferred dividend requirements) divided by average common equity. Generally used to measure performance.

**% Return on Revenues**—Net income divided by gross revenues.

**State and Municipal Securities**—State and municipal securities owned at book value.

**Taxable Equivalent Adjustment**—Increase to render income from tax-exempt loans and securities comparable to fully taxed income.

**Total Assets**—Includes interest-earning financial instruments—principally commercial, real estate, consumer loans and leases; investment securities/ trading accounts; cash/money market investments; other owned assets.

*Industrial Companies*

*Following data is based on Form 10K Annual Report data as filed with SEC.*

**Capital Expenditures**—The sum of additions at cost to property, plant and equipment, and leaseholds, generally excluding amounts arising from acquisitions.

**Cash**—Includes all cash and government and other marketable securities.

**Cash Flow**—Net income (before extraordinary items and discontinued operations, and after preferred dividends) plus depreciation, depletion, and amortization.

**Common Equity** [See also "Tangible Book Value" under Per Share Data($) Tables]—Common stock plus capital surplus and retained earnings, less any difference between the carrying value and liquidating value of preferred stock.

**Current Assets**—Those assets expected to be realized in cash or used up in the production of revenue within one year.

**Current Liabilities**—Generally includes all debts/obligations falling due within one year.

**Current Ratio**—Current assets divided by current liabilities. A measure of liquidity.

**Depreciation**—Includes noncash charges for obsolescence, wear on property, current portion of capitalized expenses (intangibles), and depletion charges.

**Effective Tax Rate**—Actual income tax charges divided by net before taxes.

**Interest Expense**—Includes all interest expense on short/long-term debt, amortization of debt discount/premium, and deferred expenses (e.g., financing costs).

**Long-Term Debt**—Debts/obligations due after one year. Includes bonds, notes payable, mortgages, lease obligations, and industrial revenue bonds. Other long-term debt, when reported as a separate account, is excluded. This account generally includes pension and retirement benefits.

**Net Before Taxes**—Includes operating and nonoperating revenues (including extraordinary items not net of taxes), less all operating and nonoperating expenses, except income taxes and minority interest, but including equity in nonconsolidated subsidiaries.

**Net Income**—Profits derived from all sources after deduction of expenses, taxes, and fixed charges, but before any discontinued operations, extraordinary items, and dividends (preferred/common).

**Operating Income**—Net sales and operating revenues less cost of goods sold and operating expenses (including research and development, profit sharing, exploration and bad debt, but excluding depreciation and amortization).

**% Long-Term Debt of Invested Capital**—Long-term debt divided by total invested capital. Indicates how highly "leveraged" a business might be.

**% Operating Income of Revenues**—Net sales and operating revenues divided into operating income. Used as a measure of operating profitability.

**% Net Income of Revenues**—Net income divided by sales/operating revenues.

**% Return on Assets**—Net income divided by average total assets on a per common share basis. Used in industry analysis and as a measure of asset-use efficiency.

**% Return on Equity**—Net income less preferred dividend requirements divided by average common shareholders' equity on a per common share basis. Generally used to measure performance and industry comparisons.

**Revenues**—Net sales and other operating revenues. Includes franchise/ leased department income for retailers, and royalties for publishers and oil and mining companies. Excludes excise taxes for tobacco, liquor, and oil companies.

**Total Assets**—Current assets plus net plant and other noncurrent assets (intangibles and deferred items).

**Total Invested Capital**—The sum of stockholders' equity plus long-term debt, capital lease obligations, deferred income taxes, investment credits, and minority interest.

*Insurance Companies*

**Life Insurance In Force**—The total value of all life insurance policies including ordinary, group, industrial and credit. Generally the figure is reported before any amounts ceded, or the portions placed with other insurance companies.

**Premium Income**—The amount of premiums earned during the year is generally equal to the net premiums written plus any increase or decrease in earned premiums. The categories are divided into Life, Accident & Health, Annuity and Property & Casualty.

**Net Investment Income**—Income received from investment assets (before taxes) including bonds, stocks, loans and other investments (less related expenses).

**Total Revenues**—Includes premium income, net investment income and other income.

**Property & Casualty Underwriting Ratios**— Includes: Loss Ratio—losses and loss adjustment expenses divided by premiums earned; Expense Ratio—underwriting expenses divided by net premiums written; Combined Loss-Expense Ratio—Measures claims, losses and operating expenses against premiums. The total of losses and loss expenses, before policyholders' dividends, to premiums earned, e.g., at 106.0%, equivalent to a loss of six cents of every premium dollar before investment income and taxes.

**Net Before Taxes**—Total operating income before income taxes and security gains or losses. Generally will include any equity in income of subsidiaries.

**Net Operating Income**—Includes income from operations, before security gains or losses, and before results of discontinued operations and special items.

**Net Income**—Includes income from operations, after security gains or losses, and before results of discontinued operations and special items.

**% Return On Revenues**—Is the net operating income divided by the total revenues.

**% Return On Assets**—Is the net operating income divided by the mean/ average assets.

**% Return On Equity**—Is obtained by dividing the average common equity for the year into the net operating income, less any preferred stock dividend requirements.

**Cash & Equivalent**—Includes cash, accrued investment income and short- term investments (except when classified as investments by the company).

**Premiums Due**—Generally includes premiums owed but uncollected, agent's balances receivable and earned and unbilled premiums receivable.

**Investment Assets**—Includes all investments shown under the company's investment account. Bonds, values at cost, includes bonds and notes, debt obligations and any short-term investments. Stocks, values at market, includes common and preferred stocks in the investment portfolio. Loans, includes mortgage, policy and other loans.

**% Investment Yield**—Is the return received on the company's investment assets, and is obtained by dividing the average investment assets into the net investment income, before applicable income taxes.

**Deferred Policy Costs**—Reflect certain costs of acquiring insurance business which have been deferred. These costs are primarily related to the production of business such as commissions, expenses in issuing policies and certain agency expenses.

**Total Assets**—Includes total investments, cash and cash items, accrued investment income, premiums due, deferred policy acquisition costs, property and equipment, separate accounts and other assets.

**Debt**—Includes bonds, debentures, notes, loans and mortgages payable.

**Common Equity**—Consists of common stock, additional paid in capital, net unrealized capital gains or losses on investments, retained earnings—less treasury stock at cost.

*Investment Companies*

**Total Investment Income**—The sum of income received from dividends and interest on portfolio holdings.

**Net Investment Income**—The amount of income remaining after operating expenses are deducted from total investment income. The per share figure is generally reported by the company, or may be obtained by dividing the net investment income by the shares outstanding. This amount is available for the payment of distributions.

**Realized Capital Gains**—Represents the net gain realized on the sale of investments, as reported by the company in the statement of changes in net assets. Divide amount by shares outstanding to obtain per share figure.

**% Net Investment Income/Net Assets**—Measures return on net assets. Percentage is obtained by dividing net investment income by average net assets.

**% Expenses/Net Assets**—Generally measures cost control. Percentage is obtained by dividing operating expenses by average net assets.

**% Expenses/Investment Income**—Indicates the amount of income absorbed by expenses. Percentage is obtained by dividing operating expenses by total investment income.

**Net Assets**—Represents the total market value of portfolio securities, including net cash, short-term investments, and stocks and bonds at market.

**% Change S&P "500"**—Measures the percentage change in Standard & Poor's 500 stock price index, before reinvestment of dividends, and is a general indicator of overall stock market performance.

**% Change AAA Bonds**—Measures the percentage change in the Standard & Poor's high grade bond index, before reinvestment of interest, and is a measure of AAA bond price movements.

**% Net Asset Distribution**—Indicates the percentage breakdown of net assets in the following categories: a) net cash (cash receivables and other assets, less liabilities); b) short-term obligations (U.S. Government securities, commercial paper and certificates of deposit); c) bonds and preferred stocks; d) common stocks. To calculate the % net asset distribution, divide net assets into each of the above categories.

*Real Estate Investment Trusts and Savings & Loans*

**Rental Income**—Primarily income received from rental property.

**Mortgage Income**—Primarily income derived from mortgages.

**Total Income**—Includes rental and mortgage income, gains on sale of real estate and other.

**General Expenses**—Includes property operating expenses, real estate taxes, depreciation & amortization, administrative expenses and provision for losses.

**Interest Expense**—Includes interest paid on mortgage debt, convertible debentures, other debt obligations and short-term debt.

**% Expenses/Revenues**—Total expenses divided by revenues. The result represents the percentage of revenues (or the number of cents per dollar of income) absorbed by expenses.

**Provision for Losses**—Reserve charged to income for possible real estate losses.

**Net Income**—Profits for the year. This would include any gains/losses on the sale of real estate but exclude extraordinary items.

**% Earnings & Depreciation/Assets**—Obtained by dividing average assets into the sum of net income and depreciation expense (a measure of "cash flow" for REITs).

**Total Assets**—The sum of net investments in real estate and other assets.

**Real Estate Investments**—The sum of gross investments in real estate, construction in process and mortgage loans and notes before allowances for losses and accumulated depreciation.

**Loss Reserve**—Reserves set aside for possible losses on real estate investments.

**Net Investment**—Real estate investments less accumulated depreciation and loss reserves.

**Cash**—Cash on hand, cash in escrow and short-term investments.

**S T Debt**—Short-term obligations due and payable within one year of balance sheet date. This would include the current portion of long-term debt, mortgages and notes, bank loans and commercial paper.

**Debt**—Includes debentures, mortgages and other long-term debt due after one year of balance sheet date.

**Equity**—Represents the sum of shares of beneficial interest or common stock, convertible preferred stock when included as equity, capital surplus and undistributed net income.

**Total Capitalization**—Is the sum of the stated values of a company's total shareholders' equity including preferred, common stock and debt obligations.

**Price Times Book Value Hi Lo**—Indicates the relationship of a stock's market price to book value. Obtained by dividing year-end book values into yearly high/low range.

*Utilities*

**Capital Expenditures**—Represents the amounts spent on capital improvements to plant and funds for construction programs.

**Capitalization Ratios**—Reflect the percentage of each type of debt/equity issues outstanding to total capitalization. % DEBT is obtained by dividing total debt by the sum of debt, preferred, common, paid-in capital and retained earnings. % PREFERRED is obtained by dividing the preferred stocks outstanding by total capitalization. % COMMON, divide the sum of common stocks, paid-in capital and retained earnings by total capitalization.

**Construction Credits**—Credits for interest charged to the cost of constructing new plant. A combination of allowance for equity funds used during construction and allowance for borrowed funds used during construction—credit.

**Depreciation**—Amounts charged to income to compensate for the decline in useful value of plant and equipment.

**Effective Tax Rate**—Actual income tax expense divided by the total of net income and actual income tax expense.

**Fixed Charges Coverage**—The number of times income before interest charges (operating income plus other income) after taxes covers total interest charges and preferred dividend requirements.

**Gross Property**—Includes utility plant at cost, plant work in progress, and nuclear fuel.

**Long-Term Debt**—Debt obligations due beyond one year from balance sheet date.

**Maintenance**—Amounts spent to keep plants in good operating condition.

**Net Income**—Amount of earnings for the year which is available for preferred and common dividend payments.

**Net Property**—Includes items in gross property less provision for depreciation.

**Operating Revenues**—Represents the amount billed to customers by the utility.

**Operating Ratio**—Ratio of operating costs to operating revenues or the proportion of revenues absorbed by expenses. Obtained by dividing operating expenses including depreciation, maintenance, and taxes by revenues.

**% Earned on Net Property**—Percentage obtained by dividing operating income by average net property for the year. A measure of plant efficiency.

**% Return on Common Equity**—Percentage obtained by dividing income available for common stock (net income less preferred dividend requirements) by average common equity.

**% Return on Invested Capital**—Percentage obtained by dividing income available for fixed charges by average total invested capital.

**% Return on Revenues**—Obtained by dividing net income for the year by revenues.

**Total Capitalization**—Combined sum of total common equity, preferred stock and long-term debt.

**Total Invested Capital**—Sum of total capitalization (common-preferred-debt), accumulated deferred income taxes, accumulated investment tax credits, minority interest, contingency reserves, and contributions in aid of construction.

Finally, at the very bottom of the right-hand page, you'll find general information about the company: its address and telephone number, the names of its senior executive officers and directors (usually including the name of the investor contact), and the state in which the company is incorporated.

## How to Use This Book to Select Investments

And so, at last, we come to the $64,000 question: Given this vast array of data, how might a businesswoman seeking to find out about her competition, a marketing manager looking for clients, a job seeker, and an investor use it to best serve their respective purposes?

If you are like one of the first three of these individuals—a businesswoman, a marketing manager, or a job seeker—your task will be arduous, to be sure, but this book will provide you with an excellent starting point and your payoff can make it all worthwhile. You will have to go through this book page by page, looking for those companies that are in the industries in which you are interested, that are of the size and financial strength that appeal to you, that are located geographically in your territory or where you're willing to relocate, that have been profitable and growing, and so forth. And then you will have to read about just what's going on at those companies by referring to the appropriate "Highlights" and "Business Summary" comments in these reports.

Of course, this book won't do it *all* for you. It is, after all, just a starting point, not a conclusive summary of everything you might need to know. It is designed to educate, not to render advice or provide recommendations. But it will get you pointed in the right direction.

Finally, what about an investor who wants to use this book to find good individual investments from among the 500 stocks in the S&P 500 Index? If you fall into that category, what should you do?

Well, you can approach your quest the same way that the businesswoman looking for information about her competitors, the marketing manager, and the job seeker approached theirs—by thumbing through this book page by page, looking for companies with high historical growth rates, generous dividend payout policies, wide profit margins, A+ Standard & Poor's Quality Rankings, or whatever other characteristics you consider desirable in stocks in which you might invest. In this case, however, we have made your job just a little bit easier.

We have already prescreened the 500 companies in this book for several of the stock characteristics in which investors generally are most interested, including Standard & Poor's Quality Rankings, growth records, and dividend payment histories, and we're pleased to present on the next several pages lists of those companies which score highest on the bases of these criteria. So if you, like most investors, find these characteristics important in potential investments, you might want to turn first to the companies on these lists in your search for attractive investments.

Good luck and happy investment returns!

# Companies With Five Consecutive Years of Earnings Increases

This table, compiled from a computer screen of the stocks in this handbook, shows companies that have recorded rising per-share earnings for five consecutive years, have estimated 2011 EPS above those reported for 2010, pay dividends, and have Standard & Poor's Quality Rankings of A– or better.

| Company | Business | S&P Quality Ranking | Fiscal Year End | EPS 2010 Actual $ | EPS 2011 Estimate $ | 5 Yr. EPS % Growth Rate | Price | P/E on 2011 Est. | Yield |
|---|---|---|---|---|---|---|---|---|---|
| Becton, Dickinson | Health care pr:ind'l safety | A | Sep# | 5.49 | 5.62 | 14 | 74.14 | 13.2 | 2.4% |
| Family Dollar Stores | Self-service retail stores | A+ | Aug# | 2.62 | 3.12 | 19 | 59.06 | 18.9 | 1.2% |
| Genl Mills | Consumer foods,restaurants | A+ | May# | 2.24 | 2.70 | 11 | 39.90 | 14.8 | 3.1% |
| Hasbro Inc | Mfrs toys & games | A | Dec | 2.74 | 3.00 | 15 | 35.40 | 11.8 | 3.4% |
| Intl Bus. Machines | Lgst mfr business machines | A+ | Dec | 11.52 | 13.40 | 15 | 189.45 | 14.1 | 1.6% |
| McCormick & Co | Spices, flavoring, tea, mixes | A+ | Nov | 2.75 | 2.79 | 14 | 48.54 | 17.4 | 2.6% |
| Oracle Corp | Mkts database mgmt softwr | A– | May# | 1.21 | 1.67 | 16 | 31.67 | 19.0 | 0.8% |
| Ralph Lauren Corp'A' | Retail apparel/home prd | A– | Mar* | 5.75 | 6.81 | 12 | 143.32 | 21.0 | 0.6% |
| Ross Stores | Apparel,shoes,linen retailer | A+ | Jan* | 4.63 | 5.60 | 28 | 92.28 | 16.5 | 1.0% |
| Sigma-Aldrich | Specialty chem prod | A+ | Dec | 3.12 | 3.76 | 11 | 64.71 | 17.2 | 1.1% |
| TJX Companies | Off-price specialty stores | A+ | Jan* | 3.30 | 3.97 | 20 | 62.56 | 15.8 | 1.2% |
| Wal-Mart Stores | Operates discount stores | A+ | Jan* | 4.47 | 4.54 | 11 | 58.61 | 12.9 | 2.5% |
| Wisconsin Energy Corp | Hdlg:El & gas utility | A | Dec | 1.93 | 2.18 | 10 | 33.26 | 15.3 | 3.1% |
| Yum Brands | Oper family style restaurants | A | Dec | 2.38 | 2.77 | 11 | 56.29 | 20.3 | 2.0% |

\# Actual 2011 EPS; P/E based on actual 2011 EPS.
\* Actual 2011 EPS and estimated 2012 EPS; P/E based on estimated 2012 EPS.
Chart data is as of the close December 1, 2011.
NOTE: All earnings estimates are Standard & Poor's projections.

## S&P 500 STOCK SCREENS

# Stocks With A+ Rankings

**Based on the issues in this handbook, this screen shows stocks of all companies with Standard & Poor's Quality Rankings of A+.**

| Company | Business | Company | Business |
|---|---|---|---|
| Caterpillar Inc | Earthmoving mchy: diesel eng | McCormick & Co | Spices, flavoring, tea, mixes |
| C.H. Robinson Worldwide | Motor freight transportat'n | NIKE, Inc'B' | Athletic footwear |
| Coca-Cola Co | Major soft drink/juice co | Omnicom Group | Major int'l advertising co |
| Colgate-Palmolive | Household & personal care | PepsiCo Inc | Soft drink:snack foods |
| CVS Caremark Corp | Oper drug/health stores | Praxair Inc | Ind'l gases/spcl coatings |
| Danaher Corp | Mfr hand tools,auto parts | Procter & Gamble | Hshld,personal care,food prod |
| Ecolab Inc | Comm'l cleaning&sanitizing | Ross Stores | Apparel,shoes,linen retailer |
| Emerson Electric | Mfr electric/electronic prdts | Sigma-Aldrich | Specialty chem prod |
| Expeditors Intl,Wash | Int'l air freight forward'g | Stryker Corp | Specialty medical devices |
| Exxon Mobil | World's leading oil co | Sysco Corp | Food distr & service systems |
| Family Dollar Stores | Self-service retail stores | Target Corp | Depart/disc/spec stores |
| Genl Dynamics | Armored/space launch vehicles | 3M Co | Scotch tapes: coated abrasives |
| Genl Mills | Consumer foods,restaurants | TJX Companies | Off-price specialty stores |
| Grainger (W.W.) | Natl dstr indus/comm'l prod | United Technologies | Aerospace,climate ctrl sys |
| Hormel Foods | Meat & food processing | UnitedHealth Group | Manages health maint svcs |
| Intl Bus. Machines | Lgst mfr business machines | Wal-Mart Stores | Operates discount stores |
| Johnson & Johnson | Health care products | Walgreen Co | Major retail drug chain |
| Kellogg Co | Convenience food products | | |

Table based on data at the close of December 2, 2011.

**S&P 500 STOCK SCREENS**

xxix

# Rapid Growth Stocks

The stocks below have shown strong and consistent earnings growth. Issues of rapidly growing companies tend to carry high price-earnings ratios and offer potential for substantial appreciation. At the same time, though, the stocks are subject to strong selling pressures should growth in earnings slow. Five-year earnings growth rates have been calculated for fiscal years 2006 through 2010 and the most current 12-month earnings.

| Company | Business | Fiscal Year End | 5 Yr. EPS Growth Rate % | EPS 2010 Actual $ | EPS 2011 Estimate $ | S&P Quality Rank | Price | P/E on 2011 Est. | Yield |
|---|---|---|---|---|---|---|---|---|---|
| Apple Inc | Personal computer systems | Sep# | 62 | 15.15 | 27.68 | B | 387.93 | 14.0 | 0.0% |
| AutoZone Inc | Retail auto parts stores | Aug# | 20 | 14.97 | 19.47 | B+ | 335.30 | 17.2 | 0.0% |
| Biogen Idec | Dvlp stge:immune sys pharma'ls | Dec | 42 | 3.94 | 5.84 | B | 116.48 | 19.9 | 0.0% |
| CA Inc | Dsgn systems software products | Mar* | 40 | 1.61 | 1.81 | B | 21.20 | 11.7 | 0.9% |
| Cognizant Tech Solutions'A' | Computer software & svcs | Dec | 28 | 2.37 | 2.83 | B+ | 67.59 | 23.9 | 0.0% |
| DeVry Inc | Tech'l/MBA degree schools | Jun# | 35 | 3.87 | 4.68 | B+ | 34.71 | 7.4 | 0.9% |
| Intl Bus. Machines | Lgst mfr business machines | Dec | 15 | 11.52 | 13.40 | A+ | 189.45 | 14.1 | 1.6% |
| Medco Health Solutions | Managed pharmac'l svcs | Dec | 26 | 3.16 | 4.10 | NR | 57.29 | 14.0 | 0.0% |
| MetroPCS Communic | Wireless communic svcs | Dec | 37 | 0.54 | 0.77 | NR | 8.30 | 10.8 | 0.0% |
| NetFlix Inc | Online entertainment svcs | Dec | 44 | 2.96 | 4.10 | B | 67.17 | 16.4 | 0.0% |
| Ross Stores | Apparel,shoes,linen retailer | Jan* | 28 | 4.63 | 5.60 | A+ | 92.28 | 16.5 | 1.0% |
| Sigma-Aldrich | Specialty chem prod | Dec | 11 | 3.12 | 3.76 | A+ | 64.71 | 17.2 | 1.1% |
| TJX Companies | Off-price specialty stores | Jan* | 20 | 3.30 | 3.97 | A+ | 62.56 | 15.8 | 1.2% |
| Wisconsin Energy Corp | Hdlg:El & gas utility | Dec | 10 | 1.93 | 2.18 | A | 33.26 | 15.3 | 3.1% |
| Yum Brands | Oper family style restaurants | Dec | 11 | 2.38 | 2.77 | A | 56.29 | 20.3 | 2.0% |

# Actual 2011 EPS; P/E based on actual 2011 EPS.
* Actual 2011 EPS and estimated 2012 EPS; P/E based on estimated 2012 EPS.
Chart based on data at the close of December 1, 2011.
NOTE: All earnings estimates are Standard & Poor's projections.

**S&P 500 STOCK SCREENS**

# Fast-Rising Dividends

Based on the issues in this handbook, the companies below were chosen on the basis of their five-year annual growth rate in dividends to the current 12-month indicated rate. All have increased their dividend payments each calendar year from 2006 to their current 12-month indicated rate.

| Company | Divd. Paid 2006 | Divd. Paid 2010 | *Ind. Divd. Rate | **Divd. Growth Rate | Price | Yield | Company | Divd. Paid 2006 | Divd. Paid 2010 | *Ind. Divd. Rate | **Divd. Growth Rate% | Price | Yield |
|---|---|---|---|---|---|---|---|---|---|---|---|---|---|
| Abbott Laboratories | 1.16 | 1.72 | 1.92 | 10.62 | 54.52 | 3.5% | Leggett & Platt | 0.66 | 1.05 | 1.12 | 11.69 | 22.46 | 5.0% |
| Accenture Plc'A' | 0.35 | 0.82 | 1.13 | 26.65 | 57.97 | 1.9% | Lockheed Martin | 1.25 | 2.64 | 4.00 | 25.03 | 78.98 | 5.1% |
| ACE Limited | 0.96 | 1.28 | 1.88 | 12.20 | 68.60 | 2.7% | Lowe's Cos | 0.16 | 0.40 | 0.56 | 24.31 | 23.87 | 2.3% |
| AFLAC Inc | 0.55 | 1.14 | 1.32 | 17.33 | 43.04 | 3.1% | McCormick & Co | 0.72 | 1.04 | 1.24 | 10.81 | 48.54 | 2.6% |
| Air Products & Chem | 1.34 | 1.92 | 2.32 | 10.76 | 82.64 | 2.8% | McDonald's Corp | 1.00 | 2.26 | 2.80 | 20.79 | 95.50 | 2.9% |
| Airgas Inc | 0.27 | 0.94 | 1.28 | 37.43 | 76.48 | 1.7% | Medtronic, Inc | 0.41 | 0.86 | 0.97 | 19.78 | 36.80 | 2.6% |
| Ameriprise Financial | 0.44 | 0.71 | 0.92 | 13.59 | 45.48 | 2.0% | Microsoft Corp | 0.37 | 0.55 | 0.80 | 14.89 | 25.28 | 3.2% |
| AmerisourceBergen Corp | 0.06 | 0.34 | 0.52 | 50.47 | 37.24 | 1.4% | Monsanto Co | 0.40 | 1.07 | 1.20 | 24.69 | 73.20 | 1.6% |
| Archer-Daniels-Midland | 0.40 | 0.60 | 0.70 | 11.05 | 30.22 | 2.3% | Murphy Oil | 0.53 | 1.05 | 1.10 | 15.88 | 55.35 | 2.0% |
| Assurant Inc | 0.38 | 0.63 | 0.72 | 12.84 | 39.05 | 1.8% | NIKE, Inc'B' | 0.62 | 1.39 | 1.44 | 19.34 | 95.25 | 1.5% |
| Automatic Data Proc | 0.74 | 1.36 | 1.58 | 13.87 | 51.50 | 3.1% | Norfolk Southern | 0.68 | 1.40 | 1.72 | 18.30 | 74.78 | 2.3% |
| Cardinal Health | 0.30 | 0.74 | 0.86 | 22.69 | 42.37 | 2.0% | Northrop Grumman | 1.16 | 1.84 | 2.00 | 10.36 | 57.33 | 3.5% |
| Clorox Co | 1.16 | 2.10 | 2.40 | 15.09 | 64.91 | 3.7% | Occidental Petroleum | 0.76 | 1.42 | 1.84 | 18.32 | 96.83 | 1.9% |
| Colgate-Palmolive | 1.25 | 2.03 | 2.32 | 13.09 | 90.11 | 2.6% | ONEOK Inc | 1.22 | 1.82 | 2.24 | 11.71 | 83.17 | 2.7% |
| ConocoPhillips | 1.44 | 2.15 | 2.64 | 11.66 | 71.76 | 3.7% | Parker-Hannifin | 0.65 | 1.07 | 1.48 | 15.93 | 83.02 | 1.8% |
| Costco Wholesale | 0.51 | 0.80 | 0.96 | 13.23 | 87.09 | 1.1% | PepsiCo Inc | 1.12 | 1.86 | 2.06 | 12.42 | 64.09 | 3.2% |
| CSX Corp | 0.11 | 0.33 | 0.48 | 30.39 | 21.73 | 2.2% | Praxair Inc | 1.00 | 1.80 | 2.00 | 14.52 | 100.85 | 2.0% |
| Cummins Inc | 0.33 | 0.88 | 1.60 | 33.75 | 96.32 | 1.7% | Procter & Gamble | 1.21 | 1.89 | 2.10 | 11.60 | 64.08 | 3.3% |
| CVS Caremark Corp | 0.15 | 0.35 | 0.50 | 23.19 | 38.48 | 1.3% | Raytheon Co | 0.94 | 1.44 | 1.72 | 12.72 | 45.29 | 3.8% |
| Darden Restaurants | 0.43 | 1.14 | 1.72 | 29.61 | 47.45 | 3.6% | Republic Services | 0.39 | 0.77 | 0.88 | 17.19 | 27.35 | 3.2% |
| Deere & Co | 0.78 | 1.16 | 1.64 | 13.72 | 78.73 | 2.1% | Robert Half Intl | 0.32 | 0.52 | 0.56 | 11.06 | 26.39 | 2.1% |
| Dover Corp | 0.71 | 1.07 | 1.26 | 12.04 | 54.76 | 2.3% | Ross Stores | 0.24 | 0.64 | 0.88 | 30.51 | 92.28 | 1.0% |
| Ecolab Inc | 0.40 | 0.62 | 0.80 | 13.51 | 55.62 | 1.4% | Safeway Inc | 0.21 | 0.44 | 0.58 | 21.47 | 20.07 | 2.9% |
| Emerson Electric | 0.93 | 1.35 | 1.60 | 10.31 | 51.84 | 3.1% | Sigma-Aldrich | 0.42 | 0.64 | 0.72 | 11.45 | 64.71 | 1.1% |
| Expeditors Intl,Wash | 0.22 | 0.40 | 0.50 | 16.51 | 42.20 | 1.2% | Stryker Corp | 0.11 | 0.60 | 0.72 | 44.23 | 49.53 | 1.5% |
| Family Dollar Stores | 0.41 | 0.60 | 0.72 | 11.33 | 59.06 | 1.2% | Target Corp | 0.44 | 1.09 | 1.20 | 23.30 | 52.15 | 2.3% |
| Genl Dynamics | 0.89 | 1.64 | 1.88 | 15.50 | 66.50 | 2.8% | Texas Instruments | 0.13 | 0.49 | 0.68 | 32.46 | 30.21 | 2.3% |
| Genl Mills | 0.69 | 1.05 | 1.22 | 11.81 | 39.90 | 3.1% | Tiffany & Co | 0.36 | 0.87 | 1.16 | 24.82 | 66.35 | 1.7% |
| Grainger (W.W.) | 1.11 | 2.08 | 2.64 | 17.99 | 186.30 | 1.4% | TJX Companies | 0.27 | 0.57 | 0.76 | 21.57 | 62.56 | 1.2% |
| Harris Corp | 0.38 | 0.94 | 1.12 | 23.41 | 35.71 | 3.1% | Union Pacific | 0.60 | 1.20 | 2.40 | 28.61 | 102.93 | 2.3% |
| Hasbro Inc | 0.45 | 0.95 | 1.20 | 19.84 | 35.40 | 3.4% | United Technologies | 1.01 | 1.70 | 1.92 | 13.54 | 76.58 | 2.5% |
| Hormel Foods | 0.28 | 0.42 | 0.60 | 14.85 | 29.93 | 2.0% | Wal-Mart Stores | 0.65 | 1.18 | 1.46 | 16.07 | 58.61 | 2.5% |
| Illinois Tool Works | 0.70 | 1.27 | 1.44 | 14.20 | 45.12 | 3.2% | Walgreen Co | 0.28 | 0.63 | 0.90 | 24.67 | 33.88 | 2.7% |
| Intel Corp | 0.40 | 0.63 | 0.84 | 14.51 | 24.92 | 3.4% | Williams Cos | 0.34 | 0.48 | 1.00 | 18.69 | 32.41 | 3.1% |
| Intl Bus. Machines | 1.10 | 2.50 | 3.00 | 21.00 | 189.45 | 1.6% | Wisconsin Energy Corp | 0.46 | 0.80 | 1.04 | 17.73 | 33.26 | 3.1% |
| Kroger Co | 0.20 | 0.39 | 0.46 | 16.14 | 23.37 | 2.0% | Xilinx Inc | 0.34 | 0.64 | 0.76 | 15.85 | 33.06 | 2.3% |
| L-3 Communications Hldgs | 0.75 | 1.60 | 1.80 | 18.50 | 66.01 | 2.7% | Yum Brands | 0.27 | 0.88 | 1.14 | 29.26 | 56.29 | 2.0% |

*12-month indicated rate. ** Five-year compounded annual growth rate. Chart based on data at the close of business December 1, 2011.

## S&P 500 STOCK SCREENS

# Stock Reports

In using the Stock Reports in this handbook, please pay particular attention to the dates attached to each evaluation, recommendation, or analysis section. Opinions rendered are as of that date and may change often. It is strongly suggested that before investing in any security you should obtain the current analysis on that issue.

To order the latest Standard & Poor's Stock Report on a company, for as little as $3.00 per report, please call:

**S&P Reports On-Demand at 1–800–292–0808.**

# Abbott Laboratories

STANDARD
&POOR'S

**S&P Recommendation** BUY ★★★★☆

| | |
|---|---|
| **Price** | **12-Mo. Target Price** |
| $52.05 (as of Nov 25, 2011) | $61.00 |

**Investment Style**
Large-Cap Growth

**GICS Sector** Health Care
**Sub-Industry** Pharmaceuticals

**Summary** This diversified life science company is a leading maker of drugs, nutritional products, diabetes monitoring devices, and diagnostics. In mid-October 2011, Abbott announced plans to split the company.

---

## Key Stock Statistics (Source S&P, Vickers, company reports)

| | | | | | | | |
|---|---|---|---|---|---|---|---|
| 52-Wk Range | $55.61– 45.07 | S&P Oper. EPS 2011**E** | 4.66 | Market Capitalization(B) | $81.083 | Beta | 0.31 |
| Trailing 12-Month EPS | $2.90 | S&P Oper. EPS 2012**E** | 4.95 | Yield (%) | 3.69 | S&P 3-Yr. Proj. EPS CAGR(%) | 10 |
| Trailing 12-Month P/E | 18.0 | P/E on S&P Oper. EPS 2011**E** | 11.2 | Dividend Rate/Share | $1.92 | S&P Credit Rating | AA |
| $10K Invested 5 Yrs Ago | $12,908 | Common Shares Outstg. (M) | 1,557.8 | Institutional Ownership (%) | 64 | | |

---

## Price Performance

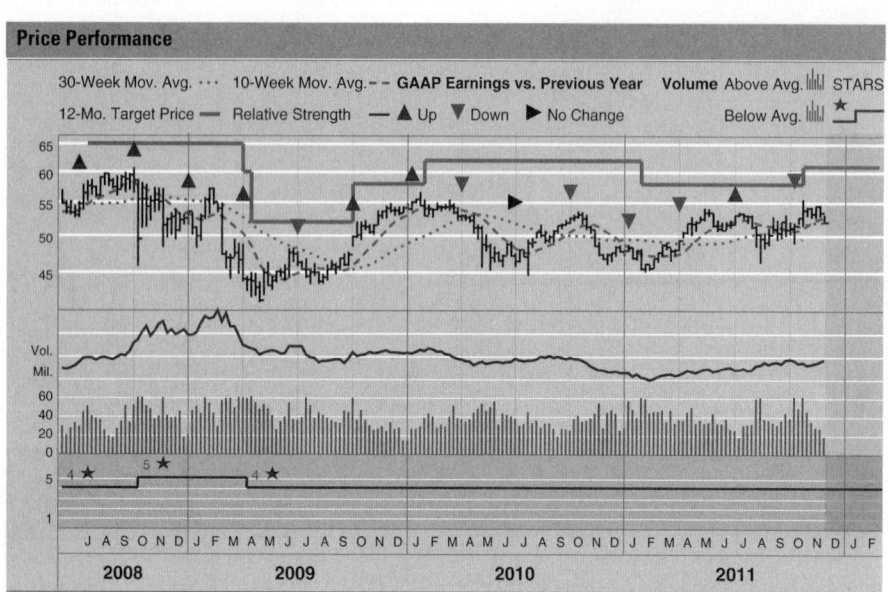

30-Week Mov. Avg. · · · 10-Week Mov. Avg. - - GAAP Earnings vs. Previous Year Volume Above Avg. STARS
12-Mo. Target Price — Relative Strength — ▲ Up ▼ Down ▶ No Change Below Avg.

Options: ASE, CBOE, P, Ph

Analysis prepared by Equity Analyst **Herman Saftlas** on Oct 31, 2011, when the stock traded at **$54.14**.

### Highlights

▶ Based on operations as presently constituted, we project 2012 revenues to rise 4% from the $39 billion that we estimate for 2011. The key pharmaceutical driver, in our opinion, should be Humira, which we expect to soon rank as the world's leading biologic for autoimmune diseases. We also see gains in the Solvay vaccines business. However, sales in ABT's cholesterol franchise are expected to decline, impacted by generic competition. In the medical products area, we see new launches and overseas market expansion powering Abbott's drug-eluting stents, and nutritional and diagnostic products.

▶ We expect adjusted gross margins to expand modestly from the near 60% that we forecast for 2011. Results should also benefit from cost cutting measures, reduced net interest expense and greater accretion from Solvay. These positives should more than offset U.S. healthcare reform and European pricing pressures.

▶ After a projected adjusted tax rate similar to the 16% that we see for 2011, we forecast operating EPS of $4.95 for 2012, up from the $4.66 that we estimate for 2011.

### Investment Rationale/Risk

▶ In mid-October 2011, ABT announced a planned split-up of the company, to be accomplished through the spinoff to shareholders of the research based pharmaceuticals business (estimated sales of $18 billion) as a separate firm to be named. Abbott will retain its legacy medical products operations (sales of $22 billion), comprising diagnostics, devices, nutritional and generic drug operations. We believe this move will result in higher valuations for each company, with investors better able to focus and appreciate the respective growth potentials of each firm. We expect the planned tax-free spinoff, subject to customary approvals, to be completed by the end of 2012.

▶ Risks to our recommendation and target price include failure to successfully execute the planned split-up of the company, as well as more intense competitive pressures, and possible pipeline setbacks.

▶ Our 12-month target price of $61 applies a peer-level multiple of 12.3X to our 2012 EPS estimate. Our discounted cash flow model, which assumes a WACC of about 8.3% and terminal growth of 2%, also implies intrinsic value of $61.

### Qualitative Risk Assessment

| LOW | MEDIUM | HIGH |
|---|---|---|

Our risk assessment reflects Abbott's operations in competitive markets and its exposure to the potential for generic competition. However, we believe the company has a relatively strong new product pipeline, with possible significant launches in medical device and pharmaceutical areas. We see the company financially strong, with a strong balance sheet.

### Quantitative Evaluations

**S&P Quality Ranking** A

| D | C | B- | B | B+ | A- | A | A+ |
|---|---|---|---|---|---|---|---|

**Relative Strength Rank** STRONG

73

LOWEST = 1 HIGHEST = 99

### Revenue/Earnings Data

**Revenue (Million $)**

| | 1Q | 2Q | 3Q | 4Q | Year |
|---|---|---|---|---|---|
| 2011 | 9,041 | 9,616 | 9,817 | -- | -- |
| 2010 | 7,698 | 8,826 | 8,675 | 9,968 | 35,167 |
| 2009 | 6,718 | 7,495 | 7,761 | 8,790 | 30,765 |
| 2008 | 6,766 | 7,314 | 7,498 | 7,950 | 29,528 |
| 2007 | 5,290 | 6,371 | 6,377 | 7,221 | 25,914 |
| 2006 | 5,183 | 5,501 | 5,574 | 6,218 | 22,476 |

**Earnings Per Share ($)**

| | | | | | |
|---|---|---|---|---|---|
| 2011 | 0.55 | 1.23 | 0.19 | E1.45 | E4.66 |
| 2010 | 0.64 | 0.83 | 0.57 | 0.92 | 2.96 |
| 2009 | 0.92 | 0.83 | 0.95 | 0.98 | 3.69 |
| 2008 | 0.60 | 0.85 | 0.69 | 0.89 | 3.03 |
| 2007 | 0.41 | 0.63 | 0.46 | 0.77 | 2.31 |
| 2006 | 0.56 | 0.40 | 0.46 | -0.31 | 1.12 |

Fiscal year ended Dec. 31. Next earnings report expected: NA. EPS Estimates based on S&P Operating Earnings; historical GAAP earnings are as reported.

### Dividend Data (Dates: mm/dd Payment Date: mm/dd/yy)

| Amount ($) | Date Decl. | Ex-Div. Date | Stk. of Record | Payment Date |
|---|---|---|---|---|
| 0.440 | 12/10 | 01/12 | 01/14 | 02/15/11 |
| 0.480 | 02/18 | 04/13 | 04/15 | 05/16/11 |
| 0.480 | 06/10 | 07/13 | 07/15 | 08/15/11 |
| 0.480 | 09/15 | 10/12 | 10/14 | 11/15/11 |

Dividends have been paid since 1926. Source: Company reports.

---

**Please read the Required Disclosures and Analyst Certification on the last page of this report.**

The **McGraw-Hill** Companies

# Abbott Laboratories

STANDARD
&POOR'S

## Business Summary October 31, 2011

CORPORATE OVERVIEW. Abbott Laboratories is a leading player in several growing health care markets. Through acquisitions, product diversification and R&D programs, ABT offers a wide range of prescription pharmaceuticals, infant and adult nutritionals, diagnostics, and medical devices.

During 2010, pharmaceuticals accounted for 56% of operating revenues, while nutritionals represented 16%, diagnostics contributed 11%, and vascular represented 9%. Sales of other products represented 8% of 2010 sales. Foreign sales accounted for 57% of total sales in 2010.

ABT's Pharmaceutical Products Group markets a wide array of human therapeutics. Major products include: Humira to treat rheumatoid arthritis and psoriatic arthritis ($6.5 billion in 2010 sales); Kaletra, an anti-HIV medication ($1.3 billion); TriCor/Trilipix, cholesterol treatments ($1.6 billion); Niaspan, a niacin-based cholesterol treatment ($927 million); and Lupron, a treatment for prostate cancer ($748 million). This division was augmented by the $6.2 billion purchase of the Solvay drug business in February 2010.

Nutritionals fall under U.S.-based Ross Products and Abbott Nutrition International. Products include leading infant formulas sold under the Similac and

Isomil names, as well as adult nutritionals, such as Ensure and ProSure for patients with special dietary needs, including cancer and diabetes patients. ABT also markets enteral feeding items.

Abbott Diabetes Care markets the Precision and FreeStyle lines of hand-held glucose monitors for diabetes patients. This division also markets data management and point-of-care systems, insulin pumps and syringes, and Glucerna shakes and nutrition bars tailored for diabetics.

Abbott Vascular markets coronary and carotid stents, catheters and guide wires, and products used for surgical closure. The principal product is the new Xience drug-eluting stent (DES), which was launched in July 2008 and is presently the leading product in the domestic DES market. Boston Scientific markets the Xience stent manufactured by Abbott under the Promus name, pursuant to an agreement with ABT.

## Company Financials Fiscal Year Ended Dec. 31

| Per Share Data ($) | 2010 | 2009 | 2008 | 2007 | 2006 | 2005 | 2004 | 2003 | 2002 | 2001 |
|---|---|---|---|---|---|---|---|---|---|---|
| Tangible Book Value | NM | 2.17 | 1.51 | 1.24 | NM | 2.89 | 2.22 | 2.90 | 1.93 | 1.14 |
| Cash Flow | 4.66 | 5.04 | 4.21 | 3.50 | 2.13 | 3.02 | 2.84 | 2.56 | 2.52 | 1.74 |
| Earnings | 2.96 | 3.69 | 3.03 | 2.31 | 1.12 | 2.16 | 2.02 | 1.75 | 1.78 | 0.99 |
| S&P Core Earnings | 3.05 | 3.61 | 2.86 | 2.31 | 1.16 | 2.01 | 1.90 | 1.95 | 1.62 | 0.77 |
| Dividends | 1.72 | 1.56 | 1.41 | 1.27 | 1.16 | 1.09 | 1.03 | 0.97 | 0.92 | 0.82 |
| Payout Ratio | 58% | 42% | 46% | 55% | 104% | 50% | 51% | 55% | 51% | 83% |
| Prices:High | 56.79 | 57.39 | 61.09 | 59.50 | 49.87 | 50.00 | 47.63 | 47.15 | 58.00 | 57.17 |
| Prices:Low | 44.59 | 41.27 | 45.75 | 48.75 | 39.18 | 37.50 | 38.26 | 33.75 | 29.80 | 42.00 |
| P/E Ratio:High | 19 | 16 | 20 | 26 | 45 | 23 | 24 | 27 | 33 | 58 |
| P/E Ratio:Low | 15 | 11 | 15 | 21 | 35 | 17 | 19 | 19 | 17 | 42 |

### Income Statement Analysis (Million $)

| | 2010 | 2009 | 2008 | 2007 | 2006 | 2005 | 2004 | 2003 | 2002 | 2001 |
|---|---|---|---|---|---|---|---|---|---|---|
| Revenue | 35,167 | 30,765 | 29,528 | 25,914 | 22,476 | 22,338 | 19,680 | 19,681 | 17,685 | 16,285 |
| Operating Income | 8,954 | 8,698 | 8,316 | 7,378 | 6,419 | 5,738 | 5,187 | 4,597 | 4,815 | 3,062 |
| Depreciation | 2,624 | 2,090 | 1,839 | 1,855 | 1,559 | 1,359 | 1,289 | 1,274 | 1,177 | 1,168 |
| Interest Expense | 448 | 520 | 528 | 593 | 416 | 241 | 200 | 146 | 239 | 307 |
| Pretax Income | 5,713 | 7,194 | 5,856 | 4,479 | 2,276 | 4,620 | 4,126 | 3,734 | 3,673 | 1,883 |
| Effective Tax Rate | NA | 20.1% | 19.2% | 19.3% | 24.6% | 27.0% | 23.0% | 26.3% | 23.9% | 17.7% |
| Net Income | 4,626 | 5,746 | 4,734 | 3,606 | 1,717 | 3,372 | 3,176 | 2,753 | 2,794 | 1,550 |
| S&P Core Earnings | 4,739 | 5,599 | 4,473 | 3,609 | 1,787 | 3,158 | 2,972 | 2,971 | 2,561 | 1,233 |

### Balance Sheet & Other Financial Data (Million $)

| | 2010 | 2009 | 2008 | 2007 | 2006 | 2005 | 2004 | 2003 | 2002 | 2001 |
|---|---|---|---|---|---|---|---|---|---|---|
| Cash | 5,451 | 9,932 | 5,080 | 2,821 | 521 | 2,894 | 1,226 | 995 | 704 | 657 |
| Current Assets | 22,318 | 23,314 | 17,043 | 14,043 | 11,282 | 11,386 | 10,734 | 10,290 | 9,122 | 8,419 |
| Total Assets | 59,462 | 52,417 | 42,419 | 39,714 | 36,178 | 29,141 | 28,767 | 26,715 | 24,259 | 23,296 |
| Current Liabilities | 17,262 | 13,049 | 11,592 | 9,103 | 11,951 | 7,416 | 6,826 | 7,640 | 7,002 | 7,927 |
| Long Term Debt | 12,560 | 11,484 | 8,713 | 9,488 | 7,010 | 4,572 | 4,788 | 3,452 | 4,274 | 4,335 |
| Common Equity | 22,388 | 22,856 | 17,480 | 17,779 | 14,054 | 14,415 | 14,326 | 13,072 | 10,665 | 9,059 |
| Total Capital | 37,169 | 34,594 | 26,193 | 27,266 | 21,064 | 19,570 | 19,334 | 16,525 | 14,939 | 13,395 |
| Capital Expenditures | 1,015 | 1,089 | 1,288 | 1,656 | 1,338 | 1,207 | 1,292 | 1,247 | 1,296 | 1,164 |
| Cash Flow | 7,250 | 7,835 | 6,573 | 5,461 | 3,276 | 4,731 | 4,465 | 4,027 | 3,971 | 2,718 |
| Current Ratio | 1.3 | 1.8 | 1.5 | 1.5 | 0.9 | 1.5 | 1.6 | 1.3 | 1.3 | 1.1 |
| % Long Term Debt of Capitalization | 33.8 | Nil | 33.3 | 34.8 | 33.3 | 23.4 | 24.8 | 20.9 | 28.6 | 32.4 |
| % Net Income of Revenue | 13.2 | 18.7 | 16.0 | 13.9 | 7.6 | 15.1 | 16.1 | 14.0 | 15.8 | 9.5 |
| % Return on Assets | NA | NA | 11.5 | 9.5 | 5.3 | 11.6 | 11.6 | 10.8 | 11.7 | 8.0 |
| % Return on Equity | NA | NA | 26.9 | 22.7 | 12.1 | 23.5 | 23.2 | 23.2 | 28.3 | 17.6 |

Data as orig reptd.; bef. results of disc opers/spec. items. Per share data adj. for stk. divs.; EPS diluted. E-Estimated. NA-Not Available. NM-Not Meaningful. NR-Not Ranked. UR-Under Review.

**Office:** 100 Abbott Park Road, Abbott Park, IL 60064-6400.
**Telephone:** 847-937-6100.
**Website:** http://www.abbott.com
**Chrmn & CEO:** M.D. White

**EVP & CFO:** T.C. Freyman
**EVP, Secy & General Counsel:** L.J. Schumacher
**Chief Acctg Officer & Cntlr:** G.W. Linder
**Treas:** V. Yien

**Investor Contact:** L. Peepo (847-935-6722)
**Board Members:** R. J. Alpern, R. S. Austin, W. J. Farrell, H. L. Fuller, P. N. Novakovic, W. A. Osborn, S. C. Scott, III, G. F. Tilton, M. D. White

**Founded:** 1888
**Domicile:** Illinois
**Employees:** 90,000

The McGraw·Hill Companies

# Abercrombie & Fitch Co.

STANDARD &POOR'S

## S&P Recommendation HOLD ★★★☆☆

| Price | 12-Mo. Target Price | Investment Style |
|---|---|---|
| $44.65 (as of Nov 25, 2011) | $55.00 | Large-Cap Growth |

**GICS Sector** Consumer Discretionary
**Sub-Industry** Apparel Retail

**Summary** This apparel retailer, which specializes in lifestyle branding, operates about 1,100 retail apparel stores across four brands.

### Key Stock Statistics (Source S&P, Vickers, company reports)

| | | | | | | | | | |
|---|---|---|---|---|---|---|---|---|---|
| 52-Wk Range | $78.25– 44.22 | S&P Oper. EPS 2012E | 2.75 | Market Capitalization(B) | $3.882 | Beta | 1.63 |
| Trailing 12-Month EPS | $2.23 | S&P Oper. EPS 2013E | 4.30 | Yield (%) | 1.57 | S&P 3-Yr. Proj. EPS CAGR(%) | 35 |
| Trailing 12-Month P/E | 20.0 | P/E on S&P Oper. EPS 2012E | 16.2 | Dividend Rate/Share | $0.70 | S&P Credit Rating | NA |
| $10K Invested 5 Yrs Ago | $6,866 | Common Shares Outstg. (M) | 86.9 | Institutional Ownership (%) | NM | | |

## Price Performance

30-Week Mov. Avg. ···  10-Week Mov. Avg. - - GAAP Earnings vs. Previous Year   Volume Above Avg. ıllıl STARS
12-Mo. Target Price —  Relative Strength —  ▲ Up ▼ Down ► No Change    Below Avg. ıllıl ★

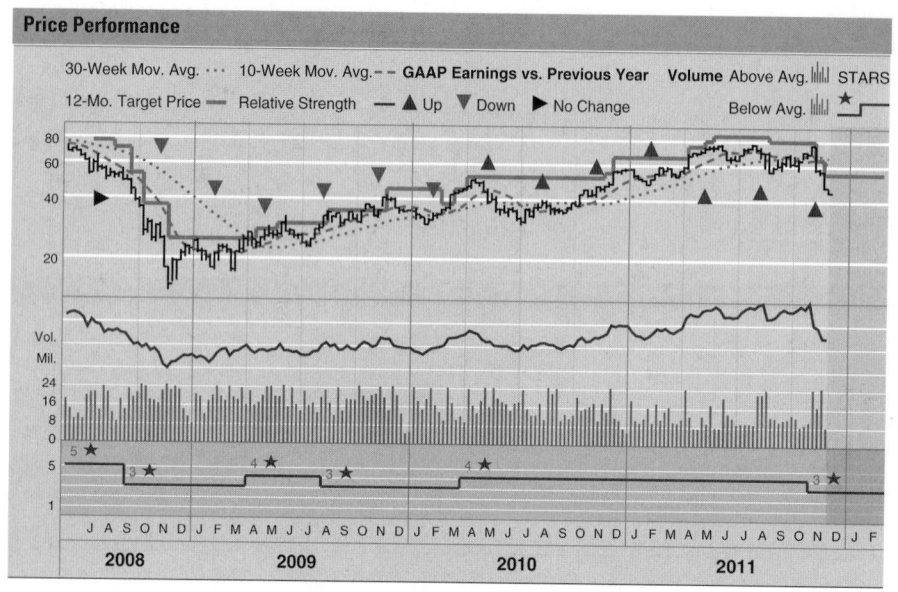

Options: ASE, CBOE, P, Ph

Analysis prepared by Equity Analyst **Jason N. Asaeda** on Nov 17, 2011, when the stock traded at **$49.51**.

## Highlights

➤ We see net sales reaching $4.19 billion in FY 12 (Jan.) and $4.97 billion in FY 13. International expansion is the dominant theme at ANF as it penetrates global markets with 4-5 A&F flagship stores and at least 40 Hollister mall locations annually. We believe the recent opening of Gilly Hicks in London will determine if this young woman's intimate brand has global demand. The company expects to close 55 to 60 U.S. stores as leases expire in FY 12. We project same-store sales growth of 8% in FY 12 and 5% in FY 13, versus FY 11's 7% gain.

➤ Despite promotional activity in U.S. stores and product cost inflation, we project 90 basis points of operating margin expansion in FY 12 to 9.1% on selective price increases, expense leverage, and a more favorable sales mix as ANF's international and e-commerce businesses continue to grow more rapidly than in the U.S. Sales productivity and margins are substantially higher internationally (in FY 11, 35% 4-wall return, versus 20% in the U.S.).

➤ We see opportunity for further margin expansion in FY 13 as product cost pressures ease. We estimate EPS of $2.75 in FY 12 and $4.30 in FY 13.

## Investment Rationale/Risk

➤ We view the shares as appropriately valued at recent levels. ANF reported that business slowed in Europe during the October quarter, including negative same-store sales for flagship stores. While it is still unclear to us whether this is a temporary slowdown or a reflection of a fundamental change in consumer sentiment, we think headwinds in Europe, coupled with ongoing challenges in Japan and Canada, could compromise the company's ability to drive improved operating metrics and margin recovery beyond FY 12. We also think ANF will have a tough time weaning U.S. shoppers off of its highly successful promotional strategy in FY 13.

➤ Risks to our recommendation and target price include weaker global economic growth than we project, a slowing of same-store sales trends in the U.S., and fashion and inventory risk.

➤ Given near-term headwinds for the company in Europe, we think the shares should trade at a discount to their 10-year historical average forward P/E multiple of 16.1X. We arrive at our 12-month target price of $55 by applying a multiple of 12.7X to our FY 13 EPS estimate.

## Qualitative Risk Assessment

| LOW | MEDIUM | HIGH |
|---|---|---|

Our risk assessment reflects our view of ANF's strong balance sheet and cash flows, offset by a consumer base whose tastes change constantly.

## Quantitative Evaluations

**S&P Quality Ranking** B+

| D | C | B- | B | B+ | A- | A | A+ |
|---|---|---|---|---|---|---|---|

**Relative Strength Rank** WEAK

7

LOWEST = 1          HIGHEST = 99

## Revenue/Earnings Data

### Revenue (Million $)

| | 1Q | 2Q | 3Q | 4Q | Year |
|---|---|---|---|---|---|
| 2012 | 836.7 | 916.8 | 1,076 | -- | -- |
| 2011 | 687.8 | 745.8 | 885.8 | 1,149 | 3,469 |
| 2010 | 601.7 | 637.2 | 753.7 | 936.0 | 2,929 |
| 2009 | 800.2 | 845.8 | 896.3 | 998.0 | 3,540 |
| 2008 | 742.4 | 804.5 | 973.9 | 1,229 | 3,750 |
| 2007 | 657.3 | 658.7 | 863.5 | 1,139 | 3,318 |

### Earnings Per Share ($)

| | | | | | |
|---|---|---|---|---|---|
| 2012 | 0.27 | 0.35 | 0.57 | E1.56 | E2.75 |
| 2011 | -0.13 | 0.22 | 0.56 | 1.03 | 1.67 |
| 2010 | -0.26 | -0.09 | 0.55 | 0.68 | 0.89 |
| 2009 | 0.69 | 0.87 | 0.72 | 0.78 | 3.05 |
| 2008 | 0.65 | 0.87 | 1.29 | 2.40 | 5.20 |
| 2007 | 0.62 | 0.72 | 1.11 | 2.14 | 4.59 |

Fiscal year ended Jan. 31. Next earnings report expected: NA. EPS Estimates based on S&P Operating Earnings; historical GAAP earnings are as reported.

## Dividend Data (Dates: mm/dd Payment Date: mm/dd/yy)

| Amount ($) | Date Decl. | Ex-Div. Date | Stk. of Record | Payment Date |
|---|---|---|---|---|
| 0.175 | 02/15 | 02/23 | 02/25 | 03/15/11 |
| 0.175 | 05/17 | 05/25 | 05/27 | 06/14/11 |
| 0.175 | 08/17 | 08/25 | 08/29 | 09/13/11 |
| 0.175 | 11/16 | 11/23 | 11/28 | 12/13/11 |

Dividends have been paid since 2004. Source: Company reports.

---

**Please read the Required Disclosures and Analyst Certification on the last page of this report.**

The McGraw·Hill Companies

# Abercrombie & Fitch Co.

## Business Summary November 17, 2011

CORPORATE OVERVIEW. Abercrombie & Fitch, established in 1892, operates four branded retail concepts: Abercrombie & Fitch (316 domestic, 10 international stores as of November 2011), abercrombie kids (179, four), Hollister Co. (501, 63), and Gilly Hicks (18, one), and e-commerce sites for each concept. Each targets a different age demographic, minimizing cannibalization, and all employ casual luxury positioning.

MARKET PROFILE. The company participates in the specialty apparel retail market targeted at youth, spanning the tween to young adult demographic. While the U.S. apparel market is considered mature, with demand mirroring population growth and a modicum related to fashion, the youth marketplace is generally considered attractive based on its spending clout. According to NPD consumer data, collectively, this group accounts for approximately 35% of total apparel spending, with the "sweet spot" being teenagers, who represent about 20%.

COMPETITIVE LANDSCAPE. The retail landscape is consolidating, with share accruing to the mass merchants and specialty chains while the traditional department store is losing ground. Specialty chains compete on customer knowledge garnered from daily interactions, focus groups and marketing in-

telligence, and this knowledge is often combined with high customer service levels to result in an attractive price/value equation for the consumer. ANF's target demographic is attracted to strong brands, as well as fashion and value, when determining apparel selections. The specialty channel holds the largest share of the apparel market at about 31% according to NPD Group and the sub-segment serving the youth demographic represents about 3% of total retail sales. With barriers to entry minimal (capital investment in merchandise, rent and labor expense) and potential returns on investment high and quick (four wall return on investment exceed 30% in 12 months for many specialty retailers), there was a steady flow of new industry participants through most of this decade, but more recently we've seen more store closures and slowed expansion plans. In addition to competing with other apparel retailers, regardless of channel, for youth discretionary spending, ANF competes with merchandise and services, especially consumer electronics and entertainment services.

## Company Financials Fiscal Year Ended Jan. 31

| Per Share Data ($) | 2011 | 2010 | 2009 | 2008 | 2007 | 2006 | 2005 | 2004 | 2003 | 2002 |
|---|---|---|---|---|---|---|---|---|---|---|
| Tangible Book Value | 21.67 | 20.78 | 21.06 | 23.45 | 19.17 | 11.34 | 7.78 | 9.21 | 7.71 | 6.02 |
| Cash Flow | 4.22 | 3.59 | 5.57 | 7.21 | 6.18 | 5.02 | 3.39 | 2.73 | 2.50 | 2.05 |
| Earnings | 1.67 | 0.89 | 3.05 | 5.20 | 4.59 | 3.66 | 2.28 | 2.06 | 1.94 | 1.65 |
| S&P Core Earnings | 1.64 | 0.96 | 3.15 | 5.20 | 4.59 | 3.38 | 2.32 | 1.81 | 1.70 | 1.45 |
| Dividends | NA | 0.70 | 0.70 | 0.70 | 0.60 | 0.50 | 0.50 | Nil | Nil | Nil |
| Payout Ratio | NA | 79% | 79% | 13% | 13% | 14% | 22% | Nil | Nil | Nil |
| Calendar Year | 2010 | 2009 | 2008 | 2007 | 2006 | 2005 | 2004 | 2003 | 2002 | 2001 |
| Prices:High | 58.50 | 42.31 | 82.06 | 85.77 | 79.42 | 74.10 | 47.45 | 33.65 | 33.85 | 47.50 |
| Prices:Low | 29.88 | 16.95 | 13.66 | 67.72 | 49.98 | 44.17 | 23.07 | 20.65 | 14.97 | 16.21 |
| P/E Ratio:High | 35 | 48 | 27 | 16 | 17 | 20 | 21 | 16 | 17 | 29 |
| P/E Ratio:Low | 18 | 19 | 4 | 13 | 11 | 12 | 10 | 10 | 8 | 10 |
| **Income Statement Analysis** (Million $) | | | | | | | | | | |
| Revenue | 3,469 | 2,929 | 3,540 | 3,750 | 3,318 | 2,785 | 2,021 | 1,708 | 1,596 | 1,365 |
| Operating Income | 506 | 398 | 686 | 912 | 794 | 661 | 453 | 398 | 370 | 313 |
| Depreciation | 229 | 239 | 225 | 184 | 146 | 124 | 106 | 66.6 | 56.9 | 41.2 |
| Interest Expense | 3.36 | 6.60 | 3.40 | Nil | Nil | Nil | Nil | Nil | Nil | Nil |
| Pretax Income | 229 | 120 | 451 | 759 | 672 | 549 | 353 | 335 | 316 | 277 |
| Effective Tax Rate | NA | 33.9% | 39.6% | 37.4% | 37.2% | 39.2% | 38.7% | 38.8% | 38.4% | 39.0% |
| Net Income | 150 | 79.0 | 272 | 476 | 422 | 334 | 216 | 205 | 195 | 169 |
| S&P Core Earnings | 147 | 84.9 | 281 | 476 | 422 | 312 | 220 | 180 | 170 | 148 |
| **Balance Sheet & Other Financial Data** (Million C$) | | | | | | | | | | |
| Cash | 826 | 712 | 522 | 649 | 530 | 462 | 350 | 521 | 401 | 239 |
| Current Assets | 1,433 | 1,260 | 1,085 | 1,140 | 1,092 | 947 | 652 | 753 | 601 | 405 |
| Total Assets | 2,948 | 2,833 | 2,848 | 2,568 | 2,248 | 1,790 | 1,348 | 1,199 | 995 | 771 |
| Current Liabilities | 559 | 449 | 450 | 543 | 511 | 492 | 414 | 280 | 211 | 164 |
| Long Term Debt | 68.6 | 71.2 | 100 | Nil | Nil | Nil | Nil | Nil | Nil | Nil |
| Common Equity | 1,891 | 1,828 | 1,846 | 1,618 | 1,405 | 995 | 669 | 871 | 750 | 595 |
| Total Capital | 1,959 | 1,899 | 1,980 | 1,641 | 1,436 | 1,034 | 725 | 891 | 770 | 597 |
| Capital Expenditures | 161 | 175 | 368 | 403 | 403 | 256 | 185 | 99.1 | 93.0 | 127 |
| Cash Flow | 379 | 318 | 498 | 659 | 568 | 458 | 322 | 272 | 252 | 210 |
| Current Ratio | 2.6 | 2.7 | 2.4 | 2.1 | 2.1 | 1.9 | 1.6 | 2.7 | 2.8 | 2.5 |
| % Long Term Debt of Capitalization | 3.5 | 3.8 | 5.1 | Nil | Nil | Nil | Nil | Nil | Nil | Nil |
| % Net Income of Revenue | 4.3 | 2.7 | 7.7 | 12.7 | 12.7 | 12.0 | 10.7 | 12.0 | 12.2 | 12.4 |
| % Return on Assets | 5.2 | 2.8 | 10.1 | 19.8 | 20.9 | 21.0 | 15.8 | 18.5 | 22.1 | 24.8 |
| % Return on Equity | 8.1 | 4.3 | 15.7 | 31.5 | 35.2 | 40.1 | 28.3 | 25.3 | 29.0 | 33.1 |

Data as orig reptd.; bef. results of disc opers/spec. items. Per share data adj. for stk. divs.; EPS diluted. E-Estimated. NA-Not Available. NM-Not Meaningful. NR-Not Ranked. UR-Under Review.

**Office:** 6301 Fitch Path, New Albany, OH 43054.
**Telephone:** 614-283-6500.
**Email:** investor_relations@abercrombie.com
**Website:** http://www.abercrombie.com

**Chrmn & CEO:** M.S. Jeffries
**EVP, CFO & Chief Acctg Officer:** J.E. Ramsden
**SVP & Treas:** E.E. Gallagher, Jr.
**SVP, Secy & General Counsel:** R.A. Robins, Jr.

**Investor Contact:** T.D. Lennox (614-283-6751)
**Board Members:** J. B. Bachmann, L. J. Brisky, M. E. Greenlees, A. M. Griffin, K. S. Huvane, M. S. Jeffries, J. W. Kessler, E. M. Lee, C. R. Stapleton

**Founded:** 1892
**Domicile:** Delaware
**Employees:** 85,000

# Accenture Plc

**STANDARD &POOR'S**

| S&P Recommendation **BUY** ★★★★☆ | Price<br>$53.70 (as of Nov 25, 2011) | 12-Mo. Target Price<br>$62.00 | Investment Style<br>Large-Cap Growth |
| --- | --- | --- | --- |

**GICS Sector** Information Technology
**Sub-Industry** IT Consulting & Other Services

**Summary** Ireland-based Accenture is a global management consulting, technology services and outsourcing company.

## Key Stock Statistics (Source S&P, Vickers, company reports)

| | | | | | | | |
| --- | --- | --- | --- | --- | --- | --- | --- |
| 52-Wk Range | $63.66– 43.06 | S&P Oper. EPS 2012E | 3.81 | Market Capitalization(B) | $34.417 | Beta | 0.81 |
| Trailing 12-Month EPS | $3.40 | S&P Oper. EPS 2013E | 4.14 | Yield (%) | 2.09 | S&P 3-Yr. Proj. EPS CAGR(%) | 14 |
| Trailing 12-Month P/E | 15.8 | P/E on S&P Oper. EPS 2012E | 14.1 | Dividend Rate/Share | $1.13 | S&P Credit Rating | NA |
| $10K Invested 5 Yrs Ago | $16,994 | Common Shares Outstg. (M) | 640.9 | Institutional Ownership (%) | 85 | | |

## Price Performance

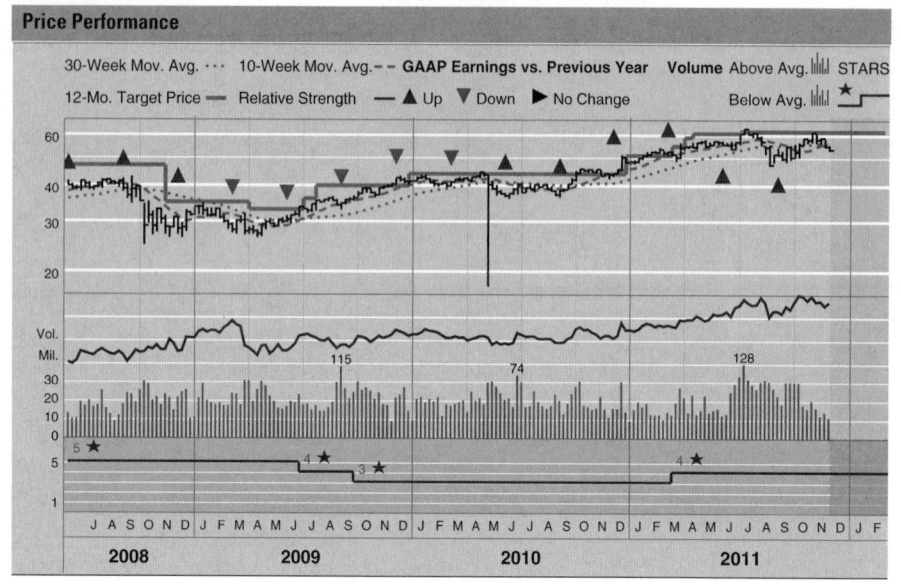

30-Week Mov. Avg. ··· 10-Week Mov. Avg. — **GAAP Earnings vs. Previous Year** Volume Above Avg. STARS
12-Mo. Target Price — Relative Strength — ▲ Up ▼ Down ► No Change Below Avg. ★

Options: ASE, CBOE, P, Ph

Analysis prepared by Equity Analyst **Dylan Cathers** on Sep 30, 2011, when the stock traded at **$52.68**.

## Qualitative Risk Assessment

| LOW | MEDIUM | HIGH |
| --- | --- | --- |

Our risk assessment reflects what we see as the highly competitive nature of the IT consulting and outsourcing market, offset by what we consider ACN's strong balance sheet and widely diversified customer base.

## Quantitative Evaluations

**S&P Quality Ranking**   NR

| D | C | B- | B | B+ | A- | A | A+ |
| --- | --- | --- | --- | --- | --- | --- | --- |

**Relative Strength Rank**   MODERATE

57

LOWEST = 1   HIGHEST = 99

## Revenue/Earnings Data

**Revenue (Million $)**

| | 1Q | 2Q | 3Q | 4Q | Year |
| --- | --- | --- | --- | --- | --- |
| 2011 | 6,478 | 6,496 | 7,204 | 7,174 | 27,353 |
| 2010 | 5,748 | 5,538 | 5,976 | 5,833 | 23,094 |
| 2009 | 6,471 | 5,658 | 5,537 | 5,505 | 23,171 |
| 2008 | 6,102 | 6,058 | 6,593 | 6,561 | 25,314 |
| 2007 | 5,166 | 5,169 | 5,544 | 5,573 | 21,453 |
| 2006 | 4,543 | 4,491 | 4,805 | 4,389 | 18,228 |

**Earnings Per Share ($)**

| | | | | | |
| --- | --- | --- | --- | --- | --- |
| 2011 | 0.75 | 0.75 | 0.93 | 0.91 | 3.40 |
| 2010 | 0.67 | 0.60 | 0.73 | 0.66 | 2.66 |
| 2009 | 0.74 | 0.63 | 0.68 | 0.39 | 2.44 |
| 2008 | 0.60 | 0.64 | 0.74 | 0.67 | 2.65 |
| 2007 | 0.46 | 0.47 | 0.54 | 0.50 | 1.97 |
| 2006 | 0.36 | 0.11 | 0.56 | 0.56 | 1.59 |

Fiscal year ended Aug. 31. Next earnings report expected: NA. EPS Estimates based on S&P Operating Earnings; historical GAAP earnings are as reported.

## Dividend Data (Dates: mm/dd Payment Date: mm/dd/yy)

| Amount ($) | Date Decl. | Ex-Div. Date | Stk. of Record | Payment Date |
| --- | --- | --- | --- | --- |
| 0.450 | 03/24 | 04/13 | 04/15 | 05/13/11 |
| 0.675 | 09/27 | 10/12 | 10/14 | 11/15/11 |

Dividends have been paid since 2005. Source: Company reports.

## Highlights

► We look for revenue growth of 8.0% in FY 12 (Aug.), down from FY 11's 18% gain, as we believe ACN will have less of a currency tailwind. Further, we have some concerns about the weakening economic outlook. Still, the company's total bookings in the August quarter were $8.4 billion. Outsourcing bookings were very strong, at $4.28 billion, and included a large Nokia (NOK 6 Hold) deal. Strength in consulting remained firmly in place. We find it encouraging that the company has been able to quickly convert signed contracts to revenue generators and that customers seem to be interested in longer-term deals, which is the opposite of the way the overall market is trending.

► ACN has been making incremental improvements in operating margins over the past few fiscal years, and we expect this trend to continue in FY 12. We believe solid execution, increased sales of higher-margin consulting services, steady levels of attrition, and cost-containment measures will offset rising wages, the use of subcontractor labor, and continued investments in the business.

► We see EPS of $3.81 in FY 12, aided by fewer shares outstanding, increasing to $4.14 in FY 13.

## Investment Rationale/Risk

► Our buy recommendation on the shares is based on valuation. We believe the company will continue to benefit from robust customer interest in ACN's IT and management consulting services. Additionally, IT outsourcing should be solid, as clients look for help containing costs and improving their operations. Over the long term, we view ACN as well diversified across geographies, verticals and horizontals, which should give it an edge over competitors, in our view.

► Risks to our recommendation and target price include the possibility of increased competition in the IT services and business process outsourcing markets, leading to pressure on pricing and profit margins, and a slowdown in demand for IT services in general.

► Our 12-month target price of $62 is based on a peer-premium P/E of 15.9X our calendar 2012 EPS estimate of $3.90. We think a premium P/E is warranted given what we see as ACN's healthy new bookings and a solid balance sheet that has nearly $5.7 billion in cash and cash equivalents and little total debt.

# Accenture Plc

## Business Summary September 30, 2011

CORPORATE OVERVIEW. Accenture (formerly Andersen Consulting) is a leading global management consulting, technology services and outsourcing enterprise, with operations in 48 countries, serving 17 industries. The company seeks to use its extensive knowledge of industries and business processes to help clients identify new business and technology trends, and to formulate and implement solutions to boost revenue, enter new markets, and deliver products and services more efficiently. Clients include Fortune Global 500 and Fortune 1000 companies, as well as mid-sized enterprises and government entities.

ACN divides its efforts among five operating groups, which together represent 17 industries. The Communications and High Tech group is the largest, and includes the communications, electronics and high tech markets, and media and entertainment. Services, aimed at solutions in these markets, include mo-

bile technology applications, network optimization, broadband, and Internet protocol solutions. Financial Services includes banking, capital markets and insurance. In its Government group, the company works with agencies on all levels in 24 countries, helping transform back-office operations and build Web interfaces and Internet-based functions. The Products group serves a broad array of industries from automotive to health services, to consumer, retail, transportation and pharmaceutical. The Resources group focuses on commodity-based industries, including chemicals, energy, forest products, metals and mining, and utilities.

## Company Financials Fiscal Year Ended Aug. 31

| Per Share Data ($) | 2011 | 2010 | 2009 | 2008 | 2007 | 2006 | 2005 | 2004 | 2003 | 2002 |
|---|---|---|---|---|---|---|---|---|---|---|
| Tangible Book Value | 4.28 | 3.19 | 2.89 | 2.77 | 1.78 | 1.66 | 1.48 | 1.34 | 0.64 | 0.27 |
| Cash Flow | 4.13 | 3.31 | 2.38 | 2.45 | 2.48 | 1.95 | 1.85 | 1.47 | NA | NA |
| Earnings | 3.40 | 2.66 | 2.44 | 2.65 | 1.97 | 1.59 | 1.56 | 1.22 | 1.05 | 0.56 |
| Dividends | 0.90 | 1.50 | 0.50 | 0.50 | 0.35 | 0.30 | Nil | Nil | Nil | Nil |
| Payout Ratio | 26% | 56% | 20% | 19% | 18% | 19% | Nil | Nil | Nil | Nil |
| Prices:High | 63.66 | 51.43 | 43.33 | 43.04 | 44.03 | 38.00 | 29.53 | 28.10 | 26.55 | 30.50 |
| Prices:Low | 47.40 | 36.05 | 26.33 | 24.76 | 33.03 | 25.68 | 21.00 | 21.85 | 13.45 | 11.30 |
| P/E Ratio:High | 19 | 19 | 18 | 16 | 22 | 24 | 19 | 23 | 25 | 54 |
| P/E Ratio:Low | 14 | 14 | 11 | 9 | 17 | 16 | 13 | 18 | 13 | 20 |

| Income Statement Analysis (Million $) | 2011 | 2010 | 2009 | 2008 | 2007 | 2006 | 2005 | 2004 | 2003 | 2002 |
|---|---|---|---|---|---|---|---|---|---|---|
| Revenue | 27,353 | 23,094 | 23,171 | 25,314 | 21,453 | 18,228 | 17,094 | 15,114 | 13,397 | 13,105 |
| Operating Income | 3,985 | 3,399 | 3,172 | 3,353 | 2,963 | 2,402 | 2,304 | 2,045 | 1,788 | -6,646 |
| Depreciation | 513 | 475 | 279 | 319 | 444 | 321 | 282 | 257 | 237 | 285 |
| Interest Expense | NA | NA | 14.1 | 22.7 | 25.0 | 21.1 | 24.0 | 22.0 | 21.0 | 48.9 |
| Pretax Income | 3,512 | 2,914 | 2,678 | 3,108 | 2,619 | 1,924 | 2,206 | 1,799 | 1,613 | 1,068 |
| Effective Tax Rate | NA | NA | 27.6% | 29.3% | 34.2% | 25.5% | 31.6% | 32.0% | 35.1% | 46.0% |
| Net Income | 2,553 | 2,060 | 1,590 | 1,692 | 1,243 | 973 | 940 | 691 | 498 | 245 |

| Balance Sheet & Other Financial Data (Million $) | 2011 | 2010 | 2009 | 2008 | 2007 | 2006 | 2005 | 2004 | 2003 | 2002 |
|---|---|---|---|---|---|---|---|---|---|---|
| Cash | 5,706 | 4,841 | 4,550 | 3,623 | 3,314 | 3,067 | 2,484 | 2,553 | 2,415 | 1,396 |
| Current Assets | NA | NA | 8,991 | 9,159 | 7,971 | 7,354 | 6,685 | 6,096 | 5,037 | 4,061 |
| Total Assets | 15,732 | 12,835 | 12,256 | 12,239 | 10,747 | 9,418 | 8,957 | 7,988 | 6,459 | 5,479 |
| Current Liabilities | NA | NA | 6,151 | 6,848 | 6,963 | 5,816 | 4,862 | 4,413 | 3,351 | 3,327 |
| Long Term Debt | NA | 1.45 | 0.36 | 1.71 | 2.57 | 27.1 | 44.1 | 2.16 | 14.0 | 3.43 |
| Common Equity | 3,879 | 2,836 | 2,887 | 2,541 | 2,063 | 1,894 | 1,697 | 1,472 | 794 | 439 |
| Total Capital | 4,827 | 3,715 | 3,546 | 3,227 | 2,838 | 2,806 | 2,728 | 2,434 | 1,695 | 978 |
| Capital Expenditures | 404 | 238 | 243 | 320 | 364 | 306 | 318 | 282 | 212 | 263 |
| Cash Flow | 3,067 | 2,535 | 1,869 | 2,011 | 1,687 | 1,294 | 1,223 | 948 | 735 | 530 |
| Current Ratio | 1.5 | 1.5 | 1.5 | 1.3 | 1.1 | 1.3 | 1.4 | 1.4 | 1.5 | 1.2 |
| % Long Term Debt of Capitalization | Nil | 0.0 | NM | 0.1 | 0.1 | 1.0 | 1.6 | 0.1 | 0.8 | 0.4 |
| % Net Income of Revenue | 9.3 | 8.9 | 6.9 | 6.7 | 5.8 | 5.3 | 5.5 | 4.6 | 3.7 | 1.9 |
| % Return on Assets | 17.9 | 16.4 | 13.0 | 14.7 | 12.3 | 10.6 | 11.1 | 9.6 | 8.3 | 4.2 |
| % Return on Equity | 76.1 | 72.0 | 58.6 | 73.5 | 62.8 | 54.2 | 59.4 | 60.0 | 80.8 | 67.9 |

Data as orig reptd.; bef. results of disc opers/spec. items. Per share data adj. for stk. divs.; EPS diluted. E-Estimated. NA-Not Available. NM-Not Meaningful. NR-Not Ranked. UR-Under Review.

**Office:** 1 Grand Canal Square, Dublin, Ireland 2.
**Telephone:** 353 1 646 2000.
**Email:** investor.relations@accenture.com
**Website:** www.accenture.com

**Chrmn:** W.D. Green
**Pres:** L. Sherman
**CEO:** P. Nanterme
**COO:** J.G. Deblaere

**CFO:** P.J. Craig
**Investor Contact:** R. Clark (877-226-5659)
**Board Members:** D. Dublon, C. H. Giancarlo, W. D. Green, D. F. Hightower, N. Idei, W. L. Kimsey, R. I. Lipp, M. Magner, B. J. McGarvie, M. Moody-Stuart, P. Nanterme, W. von Schimmelmann

**Founded:** 1995
**Domicile:** Ireland
**Employees:** 236,000

# ACE Ltd

**STANDARD &POOR'S**

| S&P Recommendation **BUY** ★★★★☆ | Price $64.93 (as of Nov 25, 2011) | 12-Mo. Target Price $83.00 | Investment Style Large-Cap Value |
|---|---|---|---|

**GICS Sector** Financials
**Sub-Industry** Property & Casualty Insurance

**Summary** This specialty insurer provides commercial insurance and reinsurance for a diverse group of international clients. In July 2008, ACE redomesticated its holding company to Switzerland from the Cayman Islands.

## Key Stock Statistics (Source S&P, Vickers, company reports)

| | | | | | | | |
|---|---|---|---|---|---|---|---|
| 52-Wk Range | $73.76–56.90 | S&P Oper. EPS 2011**E** | 6.71 | Market Capitalization(B) | $21.870 | Beta | 0.70 |
| Trailing 12-Month EPS | $5.38 | S&P Oper. EPS 2012**E** | 7.54 | Yield (%) | 2.90 | S&P 3-Yr. Proj. EPS CAGR(%) | 1 |
| Trailing 12-Month P/E | 12.1 | P/E on S&P Oper. EPS 2011**E** | 9.7 | Dividend Rate/Share | $1.88 | S&P Credit Rating | BBB+ |
| $10K Invested 5 Yrs Ago | $12,555 | Common Shares Outstg. (M) | 336.8 | Institutional Ownership (%) | 93 | | |

## Price Performance

30-Week Mov. Avg. · · ·   10-Week Mov. Avg. - -   **GAAP Earnings vs. Previous Year**   Volume Above Avg. | STARS
12-Mo. Target Price —   Relative Strength —   ▲ Up  ▼ Down  ► No Change      Below Avg. | ★

Options: ASE, CBOE, P, Ph

Analysis prepared by Equity Analyst **Cathy Seifert** on Nov 10, 2011, when the stock traded at **$70.42**.

## Highlights

➤ We expect earned premiums to increase 5% to 7% in 2011 and 2012. This compares to growth of 2.0% in 2010 and only 0.3% in 2009. Our outlook reflects our view that opportunities for market share gains and contributions from acquisitions are being partly offset by competitive pricing pressure that we believe has begun to abate. Net written premiums rose 3.1% in 2010, reflecting modest growth across most lines of business.

➤ We believe underwriting results in coming periods will remain under pressure amid a projected lower level of favorable prior-year loss development and an increase in the level of catastrophe losses. Nine-month 2011 underwriting profits declined 31%, year to year, largely due to a catastrophe-driven surge in loss costs ($7.2 billion, versus $5.6 billion). The rebound in operating profits expected in 2012 assumes a "normal" level of catastrophe losses.

➤ We see operating EPS of $6.71 in 2011 and $7.54 in 2012, versus $7.79 reported for 2010, $8.17 reported for 2009, $7.72 in 2008, and $8.07 in 2007.

## Investment Rationale/Risk

➤ Our buy recommendation reflects our view that the shares are undervalued versus historical averages, both on a price-to-book and P/E basis. We believe ACE is well positioned to exploit opportunities for growth amid an economic recovery and in light of its ability to garner market share from certain competitors (particularly in certain specialty lines). We also see ACE benefiting from an improved pricing environment for property-casualty insurance -- likely in the aftermath of record industrywide catastrophe losses.

➤ Risks to our opinion and target price include deteriorating claim trends and reserve levels, and deterioration in the credit quality of ACE's investment portfolio.

➤ Our 12-month target price of $83 assumes the shares will trade at a multiple of approximately 11X our 2012 operating EPS estimate. This multiple is a slight premium to the peer group average.

## Qualitative Risk Assessment

| LOW | **MEDIUM** | HIGH |
|---|---|---|

Our risk assessment reflects our view of ACE as an opportunistic underwriter, offset by concerns we have about reserve levels in certain lines of business and the potential that credit quality in ACE's fixed income investment portfolio could deteriorate.

## Quantitative Evaluations

**S&P Quality Ranking** NR

| D | C | B- | B | B+ | A- | A | A+ |
|---|---|---|---|---|---|---|---|

**Relative Strength Rank** MODERATE

67

LOWEST = 1    HIGHEST = 99

## Revenue/Earnings Data

**Revenue (Million $)**

| | 1Q | 2Q | 3Q | 4Q | Year |
|---|---|---|---|---|---|
| 2011 | 3,808 | 4,253 | 4,294 | -- | -- |
| 2010 | 3,949 | 3,760 | 3,888 | 4,409 | 16,006 |
| 2009 | 3,575 | 3,547 | 3,681 | 4,272 | 15,075 |
| 2008 | 3,076 | 3,834 | 3,619 | 3,103 | 13,632 |
| 2007 | 3,549 | 3,468 | 3,642 | 3,495 | 14,154 |
| 2006 | 3,181 | 3,289 | 3,389 | 3,469 | 13,328 |

**Earnings Per Share ($)**

| | | | | | |
|---|---|---|---|---|---|
| 2011 | 0.76 | 1.77 | -0.09 | E1.69 | E6.71 |
| 2010 | 2.22 | 1.98 | 1.98 | 2.92 | 9.11 |
| 2009 | 1.99 | 1.58 | 1.46 | 2.81 | 7.55 |
| 2008 | 1.11 | 2.20 | 0.16 | 0.06 | 3.53 |
| 2007 | 2.10 | 1.93 | 1.95 | 1.69 | 7.66 |
| 2006 | 1.45 | 1.72 | 1.73 | 1.99 | 6.90 |

Fiscal year ended Dec. 31. Next earnings report expected: Early February. EPS Estimates based on S&P Operating Earnings; historical GAAP earnings are as reported.

## Dividend Data (Dates: mm/dd Payment Date: mm/dd/yy)

| Amount ($) | Date Decl. | Ex-Div. Date | Stk. of Record | Payment Date |
|---|---|---|---|---|
| 0.330 | 11/18 | 12/14 | 12/16 | 01/11/11 |
| 0.330 | 02/24 | 03/30 | 04/01 | 04/22/11 |
| 0.470 | 05/18 | 01/06 | 01/10 | 01/31/12 |

Dividends have been paid since 1993. Source: Company reports.

---

**Please read the Required Disclosures and Analyst Certification on the last page of this report.**

**The McGraw·Hill Companies**

# ACE Ltd

**STANDARD &POOR'S**

## Business Summary November 10, 2011

CORPORATE OVERVIEW. ACE Ltd. underwrites an array of insurance and reinsurance, and also provides funds to support underwriting capacity for Lloyd's syndicates managed by Lloyd's managing agencies. Net earned premiums totaled $13.5 billion in 2010 (up 2.3% from $13.2 billion in 2009), with North American Insurance operations accounting for 42%, Overseas General Insurance for 39%, Global Reinsurance for 8%, and Life Insurance and Reinsurance for 11%. Underwriting results deteriorated slightly in 2010, but remained profitable. The combined loss and expense ratio ended the year at 90.2%, versus 88.3% in 2009. Included in these results was the loss ratio, which totaled 59.2% in 2010, versus 58.8% in 2009. The expense ratio also deteriorated a bit, to 31.0% in 2010, from 29.5% in 2009.

Insurance - North America provides property and casualty insurance and reinsurance coverage, including excess liability, professional lines, satellite, excess property and political risk, to a diverse group of industrial, commercial and other enterprises.

Insurance - Overseas General includes the operations of ACE International, which provides property and casualty insurance, accident and health insurance and consumer-oriented products to individuals, mid-sized firms and large commercial clients. It also provides customized and comprehensive insurance policies and services to multinational companies and their cross-border subsidiaries. In addition, the segment includes the insurance operations of ACE Global Markets, which mainly encompasses operations in the Lloyd's market.

Global Reinsurance includes the operations of ACE Tempest Re and several other subsidiaries that mainly provide property catastrophe reinsurance worldwide to insurers of commercial and personal property.

Life Insurance and Reinsurance includes the operations of ACE Tempest Re and ACE International Life and businesses of Combined Insurance. ACE Tempest Re offers traditional life reinsurance products, and an array of other reinsurance products aimed at helping life insurance companies manage their mortality, morbidity, lapse and/or capital market risks. ACE International Life offers individual life and group insurance and savings products in Indonesia, Thailand, Vietnam, Taiwan, UAE, China, Egypt, Europe and Latin America. On April 28, 2004, ACE sold approximately 65% of Assured Guaranty Ltd. (NYSE: AGO) in an initial public offering that netted ACE about $835 million.

## Company Financials Fiscal Year Ended Dec. 31

| Per Share Data ($) | 2010 | 2009 | 2008 | 2007 | 2006 | 2005 | 2004 | 2003 | 2002 | 2001 |
|---|---|---|---|---|---|---|---|---|---|---|
| Tangible Book Value | 59.47 | 51.04 | 29.24 | 42.29 | 35.37 | 28.17 | 25.11 | 21.52 | 13.20 | 12.13 |
| Operating Earnings | NA | NA | NA | NA | NA | NA | NA | NA | NA | NA |
| Earnings | 9.11 | 7.55 | 3.53 | 7.66 | 6.90 | 3.31 | 3.88 | 5.25 | 0.27 | -0.88 |
| Dividends | NA | 1.45 | 1.09 | 1.06 | 0.98 | 0.90 | 0.82 | 0.74 | 0.66 | 0.58 |
| Payout Ratio | NA | 19% | 31% | 14% | 14% | 27% | 21% | 14% | NM | NM |
| Prices:High | 62.63 | 55.64 | 68.00 | 64.32 | 61.90 | 56.85 | 45.98 | 42.80 | 44.98 | 43.19 |
| Prices:Low | 47.09 | 30.92 | 34.90 | 52.79 | 47.81 | 38.36 | 31.80 | 23.59 | 22.01 | 18.10 |
| P/E Ratio:High | 7 | 7 | 19 | 8 | 9 | 17 | NM | NM | NM | NM |
| P/E Ratio:Low | 5 | 4 | 10 | 7 | 7 | 12 | NM | NM | NM | NM |

| Income Statement Analysis (Million $) | 2010 | 2009 | 2008 | 2007 | 2006 | 2005 | 2004 | 2003 | 2002 | 2001 |
|---|---|---|---|---|---|---|---|---|---|---|
| Premium Income | NA | NA | 13,203 | 12,297 | 11,825 | 11,748 | 11,110 | 9,727 | 6,905 | 6,039 |
| Net Investment Income | NA | NA | 2,062 | 1,918 | 1,601 | 1,264 | 1,013 | 901 | 812 | 803 |
| Other Revenue | NA | NA | -1,633 | -61.0 | -98.0 | 76.0 | 198 | 265 | -489 | -58.0 |
| Total Revenue | 16,006 | 15,075 | 13,632 | 14,154 | 13,328 | 13,088 | 12,320 | 10,892 | 7,227 | 6,784 |
| Pretax Income | 3,667 | 3,077 | 1,567 | 3,160 | 2,831 | 1,317 | 1,439 | 1,794 | -11.7 | -247 |
| Net Operating Income | NA | NA | NA | NA | NA | NA | NA | NA | NA | NA |
| Net Income | 3,108 | 2,549 | 1,197 | 2,578 | 2,301 | 1,028 | 1,153 | 1,482 | 100 | -158 |

| Balance Sheet & Other Financial Data (Million $) | 2010 | 2009 | 2008 | 2007 | 2006 | 2005 | 2004 | 2003 | 2002 | 2001 |
|---|---|---|---|---|---|---|---|---|---|---|
| Cash & Equivalent | 772 | 669 | 867 | 926 | 917 | 850 | 807 | 817 | NA | NA |
| Premiums Due | NA | NA | 14,176 | 14,362 | 14,580 | 3,343 | 3,255 | 2,823 | 2,654 | NA |
| Investment Assets:Bonds | NA | NA | 34,015 | 36,171 | 31,587 | 27,361 | 22,891 | 19,312 | NA | NA |
| Investment Assets:Stocks | NA | NA | 2,609 | 1,837 | 1,713 | 1,507 | 1,266 | 562 | NA | NA |
| Investment Assets:Loans | NA | NA | 52.0 | Nil | Nil | Nil | Nil | Nil | NA | NA |
| Investment Assets:Total | 51,767 | 46,515 | 40,547 | 41,779 | 36,601 | 31,922 | 26,925 | 22,555 | 17,555 | 15,197 |
| Deferred Policy Costs | NA | NA | 1,214 | 1,121 | 1,077 | 930 | 944 | 1,005 | 832 | 679 |
| Total Assets | 83,355 | 77,980 | 72,057 | 72,090 | 67,135 | 62,440 | 56,183 | 49,317 | 43,874 | 37,186 |
| Debt | NA | NA | 2,806 | 1,811 | 2,447 | 2,120 | 2,261 | 1,824 | 2,224 | 2,224 |
| Common Equity | 22,974 | 19,667 | 14,446 | 16,675 | 14,276 | 11,810 | 9,843 | 8,821 | 6,269 | 6,010 |
| Property & Casualty:Loss Ratio | NA | NA | 60.6 | 61.6 | 52.3 | 74.5 | 70.6 | 64.6 | 73.7 | 83.9 |
| Property & Casualty:Expense Ratio | NA | NA | 29.0 | 26.3 | 33.9 | 25.1 | 25.8 | 26.4 | 27.5 | 28.5 |
| Property & Casualty Combined Ratio | 90.2 | 88.3 | 89.6 | 87.9 | 86.2 | 99.6 | 96.4 | 91.0 | 101.2 | 112.4 |
| % Return on Revenue | 19.4 | 16.9 | 8.8 | 18.2 | 17.3 | 7.9 | 9.4 | 13.6 | 1.4 | NM |
| % Return on Equity | 14.6 | 14.9 | 7.7 | 16.4 | 17.6 | 9.5 | 11.9 | 19.2 | 1.2 | NM |

Data as orig reptd.; bef. results of disc opers/spec. items. Per share data adj. for stk. divs.; EPS diluted. Data for 2004 and prior years restated based on 2004 SEC Form 10-K/A. E-Estimated. NA-Not Available. NM-Not Meaningful. NR-Not Ranked. UR-Under Review.

**Office:** Barengasse 32, Zurich, Switzerland 8001.
**Telephone:** 41 43 456 76 00.
**Email:** investorrelations@ace.bm
**Website:** www.acelimited.com

**Chrmn, Pres & CEO:** E.G. Greenberg
**Vice Chrmn & COO:** J. Keogh
**CFO:** P.V. Bancroft
**Chief Acctg Officer:** P.B. Medini

**Treas:** K. Koreyva
**Investor Contact:** H.M. Wilson (441-299-9283)
**Board Members:** M. G. Atieh, M. A. Cirillo-Goldberg, M. P. Connors, B. L. Crockett, E. G. Greenberg, R. M. Hernandez, J. Keogh, J. A. Krol, P. Menikoff, L. F. Mullin, T. J. Neff, R. Ripp, E. B. Shanks, Jr., T. E. Shasta, O. Steimer

**Founded:** 1985
**Domicile:** Switzerland
**Employees:** 16,000

The **McGraw·Hill** Companies

# Adobe Systems Inc

**STANDARD &POOR'S**

| S&P Recommendation | HOLD ★★★☆☆ | Price | 12-Mo. Target Price | Investment Style |
|---|---|---|---|---|
| | | $25.83 (as of Nov 25, 2011) | $35.00 | Large-Cap Growth |

**GICS Sector** Information Technology
**Sub-Industry** Application Software

**Summary** This company provides software for multimedia content creation, distribution, and management.

## Key Stock Statistics (Source S&P, Vickers, company reports)

| | | | | | | | |
|---|---|---|---|---|---|---|---|
| 52-Wk Range | $35.99– 22.67 | S&P Oper. EPS 2011**E** | 1.91 | Market Capitalization(B) | $12.680 | Beta | 1.50 |
| Trailing 12-Month EPS | $1.83 | S&P Oper. EPS 2012**E** | 2.15 | Yield (%) | Nil | S&P 3-Yr. Proj. EPS CAGR(%) | 14 |
| Trailing 12-Month P/E | 14.1 | P/E on S&P Oper. EPS 2011**E** | 13.5 | Dividend Rate/Share | Nil | S&P Credit Rating | BBB+ |
| $10K Invested 5 Yrs Ago | $6,218 | Common Shares Outstg. (M) | 490.9 | Institutional Ownership (%) | 89 | | |

## Price Performance

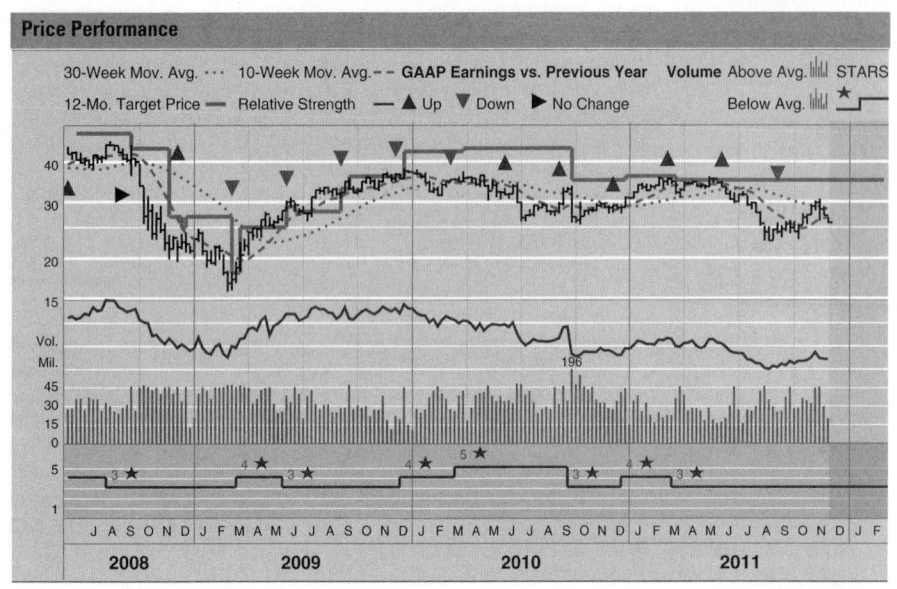

30-Week Mov. Avg. · · · 10-Week Mov. Avg. - - **GAAP Earnings vs. Previous Year**   Volume Above Avg. STARS
12-Mo. Target Price — Relative Strength — ▲ Up ▼ Down ► No Change   Below Avg.

Options: ASE, CBOE, P, Ph

Analysis prepared by Equity Analyst **Zaineb Bokhari** on Sep 26, 2011, when the stock traded at **$24.74**.

## Qualitative Risk Assessment

| LOW | MEDIUM | HIGH |
|---|---|---|

Our risk assessment reflects the regularly changing nature of the software industry and our view that the success of new products will be impacted by the global economic environment. These factors are offset by our view of the company's size and market leadership, strong operating history, and solid balance sheet.

## Quantitative Evaluations

**S&P Quality Ranking**   B+

| D | C | B- | B | B+ | A- | A | A+ |
|---|---|---|---|---|---|---|---|

**Relative Strength Rank**   MODERATE

**54**

LOWEST = 1   HIGHEST = 99

## Revenue/Earnings Data

**Revenue (Million $)**

| | 1Q | 2Q | 3Q | 4Q | Year |
|---|---|---|---|---|---|
| 2011 | 1,028 | 1,023 | 1,013 | -- | -- |
| 2010 | 858.7 | 943.0 | 990.3 | 1,008 | 3,800 |
| 2009 | 786.4 | 704.7 | 697.5 | 757.3 | 2,946 |
| 2008 | 890.5 | 886.9 | 887.3 | 915.3 | 3,580 |
| 2007 | 649.4 | 745.6 | 851.7 | 911.2 | 3,158 |
| 2006 | 655.5 | 635.5 | 602.2 | 682.2 | 2,575 |

**Earnings Per Share ($)**

| | | | | | |
|---|---|---|---|---|---|
| 2011 | 0.46 | 0.45 | 0.39 | E0.50 | E1.91 |
| 2010 | 0.24 | 0.28 | 0.44 | 0.53 | 1.47 |
| 2009 | 0.30 | 0.24 | 0.26 | -0.06 | 0.73 |
| 2008 | 0.38 | 0.41 | 0.35 | 0.46 | 1.59 |
| 2007 | 0.24 | 0.25 | 0.35 | 0.38 | 1.21 |
| 2006 | 0.17 | 0.20 | 0.16 | 0.30 | 0.83 |

Fiscal year ended Nov. 30. Next earnings report expected: Late December. EPS Estimates based on S&P Operating Earnings; historical GAAP earnings are as reported.

## Dividend Data

No cash dividends have been paid since 2005.

## Highlights

► We estimate that sales will rise nearly 10% in FY 11 (Nov.) to $4.16 billion, on our outlook for sales growth from client migration to new versions of existing products such as Creative Suite, and contributions from new versions of Acrobat and from acquisitions such as Day Software. We see global economic conditions influencing the ultimate sales trajectory of Creative Suite 5 and subsequent releases (including 5.5). Recent natural disasters in Japan and ongoing weakness in Europe temper our outlook. We see sales rising 8.5% in FY 12 to approximately $4.5 billion.

► On the projected sales growth, we think FY 11 non-GAAP operating margins will widen modestly to 37.1% from 36.6% in FY 10. We expect the company to benefit from cost containment measures, but expect expenses such as R&D and sales and marketing to trend higher due to hiring as well as added headcount from Day Software. We look for operating margins to widen slightly in FY 12, as ADBE continues to invest in support of new and acquired products.

► We estimate non-GAAP EPS of $1.91 in FY 11 and $2.15 in FY 12, excluding restructuring and amortization.

## Investment Rationale/Risk

► We are encouraged by the recent strength in sales of products such as Acrobat and Creative Suite, and by growth in subscriptions. However, we are concerned about growth in certain regions, including Europe and Japan. We view favorably Adobe's move to release mid cycle versions of Creative Suite, which incorporate more frequent updates amid rapid technological change. We look for strategic acquisitions ahead as ADBE targets higher FY 12 sales, but expect much of ADBE's growth to be organic.

► Risks to our recommendation and target price include weak demand for new products, loss of share to competing products or standards, and lack of support from makers of popular hardware platforms. Prolonged weakness in key markets is also a concern.

► We blend our relative and intrinsic valuation measures to derive our 12-month target price of $35. In our DCF model, we assume a 10.2% WACC and 3% terminal growth, yielding an intrinsic value of $42. In our P/E analysis, we apply a 14X multiple to our forward EPS estimate of $2.03, below the three-year average 18.1X we calculate for the shares, resulting in a $28 value.

---

**Please read the Required Disclosures and Analyst Certification on the last page of this report.**

**The McGraw·Hill Companies**

# Adobe Systems Inc

STANDARD &POOR'S

## Business Summary September 26, 2011

CORPORATE OVERVIEW. Adobe Systems (founded in 1982) is one of the world's largest software companies. It offers creative, business and mobile software and services used by consumers, artistic professionals, designers, knowledge workers, original equipment manufacturers, developers and enterprises for producing, managing, delivering and experiencing content across multiple operating systems, devices and media. Some of the company's core products include: Acrobat (for document creation, distribution and management); Illustrator (to make graphic artwork); and Photoshop (for photo design, enhancement and editing). In December 2005, ADBE acquired Macromedia, a leading developer of software that enables the creation and consumption of digital content, for $3.5 billion in stock and related costs. Through this transaction, the company gained Macromedia's significant products, including Dreamweaver (Web development) and Flash (which provides an environment to produce dynamic digital content).

While acquisition activity had been minor in the two subsequent fiscal years, ADBE acquired Web analytics company Omniture for $1.8 billion in late FY 09 (Nov.). The company reasoned that its products offered the tools to create online content and, with Omniture, it could now help customers measure the efficacy of such content and thus allow them to better monetize it. The company recently (October 2010) completed the purchase of Swiss enterprise content management software provider Day Software, for about $240 million. In January 2011, Demdex, a data management platform company was acquired. How-

ever, the impact on Adobe from this purchase was not considered material.

The company's software runs on Microsoft Windows, Apple Mac OS, Linux, UNIX and other non-PC platforms. ADBE is making a push to provide solutions that can develop content for connected devices such as smartphones. ADBE participates in the Open Screen Project, with the aim of allowing developers of content to deliver their creations across connected devices that use the company's Flash and Adobe Air technologies. Begun in May 2008, the Open Screen Project included many top smartphone manufacturers as participants.

CORPORATE STRATEGY. ADBE's indicated strategy is to address the needs of a variety of customers with offerings that support industry standards and can be deployed in a variety of contexts. We believe ADBE is focused on leveraging its market-leading software franchises with bundles and enhancements. Selling multiple products together has enabled ADBE to gain market share, increase penetration with existing customers, and expand its overall customer base. The Creative Suite is the company's flagship bundled offering. Macromedia was acquired to further this strategy.

## Company Financials  Fiscal Year Ended Nov. 30

| Per Share Data ($) | 2010 | 2009 | 2008 | 2007 | 2006 | 2005 | 2004 | 2003 | 2002 | 2001 |
|---|---|---|---|---|---|---|---|---|---|---|
| Tangible Book Value | 2.04 | 1.50 | 3.74 | 3.67 | 4.25 | 3.54 | 2.68 | 2.08 | 1.24 | 1.23 |
| Cash Flow | 2.03 | 1.26 | 2.09 | 1.74 | 1.33 | 1.31 | 1.03 | 0.65 | 0.52 | 0.53 |
| Earnings | 1.47 | 0.73 | 1.59 | 1.21 | 0.83 | 1.19 | 0.91 | 0.55 | 0.40 | 0.42 |
| S&P Core Earnings | 1.47 | 0.74 | 1.57 | 1.21 | 0.76 | 1.01 | 0.69 | 0.18 | 0.05 | 0.11 |
| Dividends | Nil | Nil | Nil | Nil | Nil | 0.01 | 0.03 | 0.03 | 0.03 | 0.03 |
| Payout Ratio | Nil | Nil | Nil | Nil | Nil | 1% | 3% | 5% | 6% | 6% |
| Prices:High | 37.80 | 38.20 | 46.44 | 48.47 | 43.22 | 39.48 | 32.24 | 23.19 | 21.66 | 30.81 |
| Prices:Low | 25.45 | 15.70 | 19.49 | 37.20 | 25.98 | 25.80 | 17.15 | 12.29 | 8.25 | 11.10 |
| P/E Ratio:High | 26 | 52 | 29 | 40 | 52 | 33 | 35 | 42 | 55 | 74 |
| P/E Ratio:Low | 17 | 22 | 12 | 31 | 31 | 22 | 19 | 22 | 21 | 27 |
| **Income Statement Analysis (Million $)** | | | | | | | | | | |
| Revenue | 3,800 | 2,946 | 3,580 | 3,158 | 2,575 | 1,966 | 1,667 | 1,295 | 1,165 | 1,230 |
| Operating Income | 1,305 | 1,014 | 1,328 | 1,173 | 870 | 793 | 653 | 428 | 368 | 447 |
| Depreciation | 293 | 282 | 268 | 315 | 308 | 64.3 | 60.8 | 49.0 | 63.5 | 56.6 |
| Interest Expense | 57.0 | 3.41 | 10.0 | Nil | Nil | Nil | Nil | Nil | Nil | Nil |
| Pretax Income | 943 | 702 | 1,079 | 947 | 680 | 766 | 609 | 380 | 285 | 307 |
| Effective Tax Rate | NA | 44.9% | 19.2% | 23.5% | 25.6% | 21.3% | 26.0% | 30.0% | 32.8% | 33.0% |
| Net Income | 775 | 387 | 872 | 724 | 506 | 603 | 450 | 266 | 191 | 206 |
| S&P Core Earnings | 777 | 392 | 860 | 721 | 466 | 515 | 343 | 86.7 | 20.6 | 51.7 |
| **Balance Sheet & Other Financial Data (Million $)** | | | | | | | | | | |
| Cash | 2,468 | 1,904 | 2,019 | 946 | 772 | 421 | 376 | 190 | 184 | 219 |
| Current Assets | 3,216 | 2,474 | 2,735 | 2,573 | 2,884 | 2,009 | 1,551 | 1,329 | 814 | 767 |
| Total Assets | 8,141 | 7,256 | 5,822 | 5,714 | 5,963 | 2,440 | 1,959 | 1,555 | 1,052 | 931 |
| Current Liabilities | 1,068 | 845 | 763 | 852 | 677 | 480 | 451 | 437 | 377 | 314 |
| Long Term Debt | 1,514 | 1,000 | 350 | Nil | Nil | Nil | Nil | Nil | Nil | Nil |
| Common Equity | 5,192 | 4,864 | 4,410 | 4,650 | 5,152 | 1,864 | 1,423 | 1,101 | 674 | 617 |
| Total Capital | 6,706 | 5,864 | 4,878 | 4,799 | 5,223 | 1,943 | 1,502 | 1,119 | 674 | 617 |
| Capital Expenditures | 170 | 120 | 112 | 132 | 83.3 | 48.9 | 63.2 | 39.5 | 31.6 | 46.6 |
| Cash Flow | 1,067 | 669 | 1,140 | 1,039 | 814 | 667 | 511 | 315 | 255 | 262 |
| Current Ratio | 3.0 | 2.9 | 3.6 | 3.0 | 4.3 | 4.2 | 3.4 | 3.0 | 2.2 | 2.4 |
| % Long Term Debt of Capitalization | 22.6 | 17.1 | 7.2 | Nil | Nil | Nil | Nil | Nil | Nil | Nil |
| % Net Income of Revenue | 20.4 | 13.1 | 24.4 | 22.9 | 19.6 | 30.7 | 27.0 | 20.6 | 16.4 | 16.7 |
| % Return on Assets | 10.1 | 5.9 | 15.1 | 12.3 | 12.0 | 27.4 | 25.6 | 20.4 | 19.3 | 20.6 |
| % Return on Equity | 15.4 | 8.3 | 19.2 | 14.7 | 14.4 | 36.7 | 35.7 | 30.0 | 29.6 | 30.0 |

Data as orig reptd.; bef. results of disc opers/spec. items. Per share data adj. for stk. divs.; EPS diluted. E-Estimated. NA-Not Available. NM-Not Meaningful. NR-Not Ranked. UR-Under Review.

**Office:** 345 Park Avenue, San Jose, CA, USA 95110-2704.
**Telephone:** 408-536-6000.
**Email:** ir@adobe.com
**Website:** http://www.adobe.com

**Co-Chrmn:** J. Warnock
**Co-Chrmn:** C. Geschke
**Pres & CEO:** S. Narayen
**EVP & CFO:** M. Garrett

**SVP & CTO:** K. Lynch
**Board Members:** E. W. Barnholt, R. K. Burgess, M. R. Cannon, J. E. Daley, C. Geschke, S. Narayen, D. Rosensweig, R. Sedgewick, J. Warnock

**Founded:** 1983
**Domicile:** Delaware
**Employees:** 9,117

# Advanced Micro Devices Inc

STANDARD &POOR'S

| S&P Recommendation | HOLD ★★★★★ | Price $4.99 (as of Nov 25, 2011) | 12-Mo. Target Price $7.00 | Investment Style Large-Cap Value |
|---|---|---|---|---|

**GICS Sector** Information Technology
**Sub-Industry** Semiconductors

**Summary** This company is a leading producer of semiconductors that are used principally in computers and related products.

## Key Stock Statistics (Source S&P, Vickers, company reports)

| | | | | | | | |
|---|---|---|---|---|---|---|---|
| 52-Wk Range | $9.58– 4.31 | S&P Oper. EPS 2011**E** | 0.49 | Market Capitalization(B) | $3.478 | Beta | 2.17 |
| Trailing 12-Month EPS | $1.41 | S&P Oper. EPS 2012**E** | 0.55 | Yield (%) | Nil | S&P 3-Yr. Proj. EPS CAGR(%) | 3 |
| Trailing 12-Month P/E | 3.5 | P/E on S&P Oper. EPS 2011**E** | 10.2 | Dividend Rate/Share | Nil | S&P Credit Rating | B+ |
| $10K Invested 5 Yrs Ago | $2,289 | Common Shares Outstg. (M) | 696.9 | Institutional Ownership (%) | 59 | | |

## Price Performance

30-Week Mov. Avg. ···  10-Week Mov. Avg. - -  **GAAP Earnings vs. Previous Year**  Volume Above Avg. STARS
12-Mo. Target Price —  Relative Strength —  ▲ Up  ▼ Down  ► No Change  Below Avg.  ★

Options: ASE, CBOE, P, Ph

Analysis prepared by Equity Analyst **Angelo Zino, CFA** on Nov 07, 2011, when the stock traded at **$5.58**.

## Qualitative Risk Assessment

| LOW | MEDIUM | HIGH |
|---|---|---|

AMD is subject to the cyclical swings of the semiconductor industry, demand fluctuations for computer end-products, vacillation in average selling prices for chips, and strong competition from Intel, which is a much larger rival in microprocessors.

## Quantitative Evaluations

**S&P Quality Ranking**   B-

| D | C | B- | B | B+ | A- | A | A+ |
|---|---|---|---|---|---|---|---|

**Relative Strength Rank**   WEAK

| 25 |
|---|

LOWEST = 1                                    HIGHEST = 99

## Revenue/Earnings Data

**Revenue (Million $)**

| | 1Q | 2Q | 3Q | 4Q | Year |
|---|---|---|---|---|---|
| 2011 | 1,613 | 1,574 | 1,690 | -- | -- |
| 2010 | 1,574 | 1,653 | 1,618 | 1,649 | 6,494 |
| 2009 | 1,177 | 1,184 | 1,396 | 1,646 | 5,403 |
| 2008 | 1,487 | 1,362 | 1,797 | 1,162 | 5,808 |
| 2007 | 1,233 | 1,378 | 1,632 | 1,770 | 6,013 |
| 2006 | 1,332 | 1,216 | 1,328 | 1,773 | 5,649 |

**Earnings Per Share ($)**

| | | | | | |
|---|---|---|---|---|---|
| 2011 | 0.68 | 0.08 | 0.13 | E0.18 | E0.49 |
| 2010 | 0.35 | -0.06 | -0.17 | 0.50 | 0.64 |
| 2009 | -0.65 | -0.49 | -0.18 | 1.52 | 0.45 |
| 2008 | -0.54 | -1.14 | -0.04 | -2.32 | -3.98 |
| 2007 | -1.11 | -1.09 | -0.71 | -3.06 | -6.06 |
| 2006 | 0.38 | 0.18 | 0.27 | -1.08 | -0.34 |

Fiscal year ended Dec. 31. Next earnings report expected: Late January. EPS Estimates based on S&P Operating Earnings; historical GAAP earnings are as reported.

## Highlights

► We expect revenues to rise around 4.9% in 2012, following a projected 1.9% increase in 2011, reflecting fair PC growth over the next several quarters. Although the company has lost market share in the server and notebook markets, we think new products are likely to gain traction in the coming quarters, bucking this trend. We also see further penetration of the desktop PC and graphics markets.

► We look for AMD's non-GAAP gross margins to remain in the 45% to 47% area through 2012. Although we expect modest changes in margins due to varying sales mix and prices, AMD outsources its manufacturing process, which we see keeping gross margins relatively stable. We positively view AMD's cost optimization strategy, intended to reduce its workforce by 10%, with plans to reinvest the savings into growth opportunities within low power, emerging markets as well as the cloud. Nonetheless, we still expect the non-GAAP operating margin to expand to 8.6% for 2012 from an estimated 8.0% in 2011.

► We think AMD's interest payments will weigh on its bottom line. Our non-GAAP estimates exclude non-recurring charges.

## Investment Rationale/Risk

► Our hold recommendation reflects our view of improving fundamentals, balanced by fair valuations. Although we expect gross margins to remain relatively flat, we believe AMD's revamped product portfolio and more flexible business model will lead to above-industry earnings advances as sales accelerate next year. In addition, we think margins should benefit from better execution of 32 nanometer manufacturing technology. We also see adjusted profits and free cash flows leading to debt reduction, alleviating some financial risks. Based on these anticipated improvements, we think multiples should be above recent historical averages and near the industry average.

► Risks to our recommendation and target price include less-than-anticipated demand for computers, ineffective execution of new products, greater market share losses, and notable financial risk.

► Our 12-month target price of $7 is based on a price-to-earnings (P/E) multiple of 13X, near the industry average to reflect our view of AMD's relative growth, return on equity, and risks, applied to our 2012 EPS estimate.

## Dividend Data

No cash dividends have been paid.

# Advanced Micro Devices Inc

## Business Summary November 07, 2011

CORPORATE OVERVIEW. Advanced Micro Devices designs and sells digital integrated circuits (IC), including x86 microprocessors and chipsets for computers, embedded microprocessors for commercial and consumer applications, and, as a result of the company's acquisition of ATI Technologies in October 2006, graphics processors.

A microprocessor is an IC that serves as the central processing unit, or brain, of a computer. The performance of a processor is a critical factor for the performance of the computer. The main measures for microprocessor performance include: work-per-cycle, or how many instructions per cycle, clock speed, how fast the CPU's internal logic operates as measured by units of hertz, and power consumption. Other factors impacting performance include the number of cores on a microprocessor, bit rating of the microprocessor, memory size, and data access speed. AMD also sells chipsets, which send data between the microprocessor and the computer's input, display, and storage devices.

Embedded microprocessors are used in applications, such as industrial controls, point of sale/self-service kiosks, and casino gaming machines, among others. These chips require moderate-to-high performance and are relatively lower in cost, size, and power. The embedded market has grown at a healthy pace as customers, who generally used to design the embedded chips, are increasingly opting to use industry-standard x86 instruction architecture as a way to reduce costs and speed up time to market.

Graphics processors are used in computers to increase the speed of rendering images and to improve image resolution and color definition. In this business, AMD's discrete graphics processing unit (GPU) includes the relatively popular ATI Radeon products, which are widely utilized to improve graphics for video games and other multimedia functions.

The company has two reportable segments: Computing Solutions and Graphics. The Computing Solutions segment includes sales of microprocessors, chipsets, and embedded processors. The Graphics segment includes graphics, video and multimedia products, as well as revenues from the sale of video game consoles that include its technology.

## Company Financials Fiscal Year Ended Dec. 31

| Per Share Data ($) | 2010 | 2009 | 2008 | 2007 | 2006 | 2005 | 2004 | 2003 | 2002 | 2001 |
|---|---|---|---|---|---|---|---|---|---|---|
| Tangible Book Value | 0.96 | NM | NM | 0.82 | 2.49 | 7.70 | 7.68 | 6.96 | 7.16 | 10.64 |
| Cash Flow | 1.17 | 2.22 | -1.96 | -3.72 | 1.36 | 3.14 | 3.54 | 2.08 | -1.60 | 1.69 |
| Earnings | 0.64 | 0.45 | -3.98 | -6.06 | -0.34 | 0.40 | 0.25 | -0.79 | -3.81 | -0.18 |
| S&P Core Earnings | NA | -1.46 | -2.32 | -6.08 | -0.35 | 0.38 | -0.19 | -1.08 | -4.24 | -0.49 |
| Dividends | Nil | Nil | Nil | Nil | Nil | Nil | Nil | Nil | Nil | Nil |
| Payout Ratio | Nil | Nil | Nil | Nil | Nil | Nil | Nil | Nil | Nil | Nil |
| Prices:High | 10.24 | 10.04 | 8.08 | 20.63 | 42.70 | 31.84 | 24.95 | 18.50 | 20.60 | 34.65 |
| Prices:Low | 5.53 | 1.86 | 1.62 | 7.26 | 16.90 | 14.08 | 10.76 | 4.78 | 3.10 | 7.69 |
| P/E Ratio:High | 16 | 22 | NM | NM | NM | 80 | NM | NM | NM | NM |
| P/E Ratio:Low | 9 | 4 | NM | NM | NM | 35 | NM | NM | NM | NM |

| Income Statement Analysis (Million $) | 2010 | 2009 | 2008 | 2007 | 2006 | 2005 | 2004 | 2003 | 2002 | 2001 |
|---|---|---|---|---|---|---|---|---|---|---|
| Revenue | 6,494 | 5,403 | 5,808 | 6,013 | 5,649 | 5,848 | 5,001 | 3,519 | 2,697 | 3,892 |
| Operating Income | 944 | 615 | 255 | 94.0 | 1,238 | 1,451 | 1,452 | 748 | -139 | 654 |
| Depreciation | 383 | 1,128 | 1,223 | 1,305 | 837 | 1,219 | 1,224 | 996 | 756 | 623 |
| Interest Expense | 199 | 438 | 375 | 390 | 126 | 105 | 112 | 110 | 71.3 | 61.4 |
| Pretax Income | 509 | 408 | -2,313 | -3,321 | -115 | 33.7 | 116 | -316 | -1,258 | -75.0 |
| Effective Tax Rate | NA | 27.5% | NM | NM | NM | NM | 5.05% | NM | NM | NM |
| Net Income | 471 | 213 | -2,414 | -3,379 | -166 | 165 | 91.2 | -274 | -1,303 | -60.6 |
| S&P Core Earnings | 8.70 | -978 | -1,401 | -3,391 | -170 | 155 | -68.2 | -373 | -1,450 | -161 |

| Balance Sheet & Other Financial Data (Million $) | 2010 | 2009 | 2008 | 2007 | 2006 | 2005 | 2004 | 2003 | 2002 | 2001 |
|---|---|---|---|---|---|---|---|---|---|---|
| Cash | 1,789 | 2,676 | 1,096 | 1,889 | 1,380 | 633 | 918 | 968 | 429 | 427 |
| Current Assets | 3,594 | 4,275 | 2,379 | 3,816 | 3,963 | 3,559 | 3,228 | 2,900 | 2,020 | 2,353 |
| Total Assets | 4,964 | 9,078 | 7,675 | 11,550 | 13,147 | 7,288 | 7,844 | 7,094 | 5,619 | 5,647 |
| Current Liabilities | 1,674 | 2,210 | 2,226 | 2,625 | 2,852 | 1,822 | 1,846 | 1,452 | 1,372 | 1,314 |
| Long Term Debt | 2,188 | 4,252 | 4,702 | 5,031 | 3,672 | 1,327 | 1,628 | 1,900 | 1,780 | 673 |
| Common Equity | 1,013 | 648 | -82.0 | 2,990 | 5,785 | 3,352 | 3,010 | 2,438 | 2,467 | 3,555 |
| Total Capital | 3,205 | 6,284 | 4,880 | 8,292 | 9,778 | 5,006 | 5,583 | 5,213 | 4,247 | 4,333 |
| Capital Expenditures | 148 | 466 | 624 | 1,685 | 1,857 | 1,513 | 1,440 | 570 | 705 | 679 |
| Cash Flow | 854 | 1,507 | -1,191 | -2,074 | 671 | 1,385 | 1,315 | 721 | -547 | 562 |
| Current Ratio | 2.2 | 1.9 | 1.1 | 1.5 | 1.4 | 2.0 | 1.7 | 2.0 | 1.5 | 1.8 |
| % Long Term Debt of Capitalization | 68.3 | 67.7 | 96.4 | 60.7 | 37.6 | 26.5 | 29.2 | 36.4 | 41.9 | 15.5 |
| % Net Income of Revenue | 7.3 | 3.9 | NM | NM | NM | 2.8 | 1.8 | NM | NM | NM |
| % Return on Assets | 6.7 | 2.5 | NM | NM | NM | 2.2 | 1.2 | NM | NM | NM |
| % Return on Equity | 56.7 | NM | NM | NM | NM | 5.2 | 3.3 | NM | NM | NM |

Data as orig reptd.; bef. results of disc opers/spec. items. Per share data adj. for stk. divs.; EPS diluted. E-Estimated. NA-Not Available. NM-Not Meaningful. NR-Not Ranked. UR-Under Review.

**Office:** One AMD Place, Sunnyvale, CA 94088-3453.
**Telephone:** 408-749-4000.
**Email:** investor.relations@amd.com
**Website:** http://www.amd.com

**Chrmn:** B.L. Claflin
**Pres & CEO:** R.P. Read
**SVP, CFO & Chief Acctg Officer:** T. Seifert
**SVP & CTO:** M. Papermaster

**SVP, Secy & General Counsel:** H.A. Wolin
**Investor Contact:** R. Cotter (408-749-3887)
**Board Members:** W. A. Al Muhairi, W. M. Barnes, J. E. Caldwell, H. W. Chow, B. L. Claflin, C. A. Conway, N. M. Donofrio, H. P. Eberhart, R. B. Palmer, R. P. Read

**Founded:** 1969
**Domicile:** Delaware
**Employees:** 11,100

The McGraw·Hill Companies

# AES Corporation (The)

**STANDARD &POOR'S**

| S&P Recommendation BUY ★★★★★ | Price $11.09 (as of Nov 25, 2011) | 12-Mo. Target Price $14.00 | Investment Style Large-Cap Growth |
|---|---|---|---|

**GICS Sector** Utilities
**Sub-Industry** Independent Power Producers & Energy Traders

**Summary** The world's largest independent power producer, AES produces and distributes electricity in international and domestic markets.

## Key Stock Statistics (Source S&P, Vickers, company reports)

| | | | | | | | |
|---|---|---|---|---|---|---|---|
| 52-Wk Range | $13.50–9.00 | S&P Oper. EPS 2011E | 1.11 | Market Capitalization(B) | $8.512 | Beta | 1.43 |
| Trailing 12-Month EPS | $-0.21 | S&P Oper. EPS 2012E | 1.26 | Yield (%) | Nil | S&P 3-Yr. Proj. EPS CAGR(%) | 14 |
| Trailing 12-Month P/E | NM | P/E on S&P Oper. EPS 2011E | 10.0 | Dividend Rate/Share | Nil | S&P Credit Rating | BB- |
| $10K Invested 5 Yrs Ago | $4,749 | Common Shares Outstg. (M) | 767.5 | Institutional Ownership (%) | 76 | | |

## Price Performance

30-Week Mov. Avg. · · · 10-Week Mov. Avg. - - GAAP Earnings vs. Previous Year   Volume Above Avg. STARS
12-Mo. Target Price — Relative Strength   ▲ Up ▼ Down ► No Change   Below Avg.

2008    2009    2010    2011

Options: ASE, CBOE, P, Ph

Analysis prepared by Equity Analyst **C. Muir** on Nov 21, 2011, when the stock traded at **$11.49**.

## Highlights

➤ We estimate a 9.3% revenue increase for 2011. We believe 2011 unregulated revenues will be helped by new projects and a weaker U.S. dollar, which makes overseas earnings more valuable. We expect regulated revenues to rise, helped by customer growth. In 2012, we see revenues rising 7.5%, helped by the completion of additional projects.

➤ Our operating margin estimates are 21.5% for 2011 and 23.1% for 2012, versus 21.8% in 2010. For 2011, we expect higher per-revenue cost of sales for the regulated businesses, offset by lower per-revenue unregulated cost of sales and lower per-revenue general and administrative expenses. Our pretax margin estimates are 15.5% for 2011 and 17.3% for 2012, versus 14.8% in 2010. In 2011, we see higher non-operating income partly offset by higher net interest expense.

➤ We estimate 2011 recurring EPS, excluding $0.35 of net mark-to-market and nonrecurring losses, of $1.11, an 18% increase from 2010's $0.94, which excluded $1.05 of net mark-to-market and nonrecurring losses. Our 2012 EPS forecast is $1.26, up 14%.

## Investment Rationale/Risk

➤ On April 20, 2011, AES agreed to acquire DPL Inc. (DPL 30, Hold) for $4.7 billion in cash and assumed debt. We think the purchase will reduce AES's business risk by increasing earnings stability. We believe AES is a superior independent power producer and think it will see above-average earnings growth and an improving balance sheet over the next couple of years, partly due to expansion projects. Results should also be helped by cost controls and strategic growth initiatives. AES has committed to start paying a dividend in the fourth quarter of 2012.

➤ Risks to our recommendation and target price include financial statement revisions, currency fluctuations, political and regulatory uncertainty regarding utility rates and U.S. power margins, and counterparty default risk.

➤ The stock recently traded at 9.1X our 2012 EPS estimate, a 33% discount to independent power producer peers. Our 12-month target price of $14 is 11.1X our 2012 EPS estimate, a discount to peers' valuation, as we see risk related to volatile exchange rates being partly offset by improved earnings stability that is likely as a result of the planned DPL acquisition.

## Qualitative Risk Assessment

| LOW | MEDIUM | HIGH |
|---|---|---|

Our risk assessment reflects the company's relatively large capitalization and mix of lower-risk regulated utility businesses in North America, offset by higher-risk merchant power operations and utility operations in emerging markets in South America, Eastern Europe, Central America and Asia.

## Quantitative Evaluations

**S&P Quality Ranking** B

| D | C | B- | B | B+ | A- | A | A+ |
|---|---|---|---|---|---|---|---|

**Relative Strength Rank** STRONG

76

LOWEST = 1     HIGHEST = 99

## Revenue/Earnings Data

**Revenue (Million $)**

| | 1Q | 2Q | 3Q | 4Q | Year |
|---|---|---|---|---|---|
| 2011 | 4,264 | 4,544 | 4,381 | -- | -- |
| 2010 | 4,071 | 4,021 | 4,151 | 4,404 | 16,647 |
| 2009 | 3,269 | 3,335 | 3,695 | 3,820 | 14,119 |
| 2008 | 4,081 | 4,126 | 4,319 | 3,544 | 16,070 |
| 2007 | 3,121 | 3,344 | 3,471 | 3,673 | 13,588 |
| 2006 | 2,973 | 3,044 | 3,135 | 3,147 | 12,299 |

**Earnings Per Share ($)**

| | | | | | |
|---|---|---|---|---|---|
| 2011 | 0.30 | 0.24 | -0.15 | E0.34 | E1.11 |
| 2010 | 0.26 | 0.17 | 0.05 | -0.56 | -0.11 |
| 2009 | 0.31 | 0.44 | 0.27 | 0.08 | 1.09 |
| 2008 | 0.35 | 1.31 | 0.22 | -0.10 | 1.80 |
| 2007 | 0.18 | 0.41 | 0.14 | 0.01 | 0.73 |
| 2006 | 0.53 | 0.33 | -0.51 | 0.07 | 0.43 |

Fiscal year ended Dec. 31. Next earnings report expected: Early March. EPS Estimates based on S&P Operating Earnings; historical GAAP earnings are as reported.

## Dividend Data

No cash dividends have been paid.

---

**Please read the Required Disclosures and Analyst Certification on the last page of this report.**

# AES Corporation (The)

**STANDARD & POOR'S**

## Business Summary November 21, 2011

**CORPORATE OVERVIEW.** AES Corporation (AES) owns and operates a portfolio of electricity generation and distribution business in 29 countries through its subsidiaries and affiliates. The company has two principal businesses: generation and regulated utilities.

The generation business provides power for sale to utilities and other wholesale customers while the regulated utilities business distributes power to retail, commercial, industrial and governmental customers. In 2010, the generation unit contributed 50% of total revenues. It primarily sells electricity to utilities or other wholesale customers under power purchase agreements that are generally for five years or longer. The generation business also sells electricity to wholesale customers through competitive markets.

The remaining 50% of total revenues in 2010 came from the regulated utilities business. It markets electricity to residential, business, and government customers through integrated transmission and distribution systems.

The company also reports results geographically by segment. Geographically, revenues come from Latin American operations (69% of 2010 revenues), North American operations (19%), European and African operations (8%), Middle Eastern and Asian operations (4%), and corporate activities (<0.1%). The company's largest exposures geographically are to Brazil (39%), the U.S. (16%), Chile (8%), Argentina (5%) and El Salvador (4%).

**CORPORATE STRATEGY.** AES pursues both a global and a local growth strategy to increase its business. The company's global strategy focuses on large-scale projects and pursues strategic initiatives. It concentrates on mergers and acquisitions, exploring opportunities in the climate change business such as the production of greenhouse gas reduction activities and related industries that involve environmental issues. The company also aims to mitigate exposure to price swings. In 2010, 64% of the revenues from its generation business was from plants that operate under PPAs of three years or longer for at least 75% of their output capacity. Additionally, a large portion of its capacity under construction will be subject to PPAs.

## Company Financials Fiscal Year Ended Dec. 31

| Per Share Data ($) | 2010 | 2009 | 2008 | 2007 | 2006 | 2005 | 2004 | 2003 | 2002 | 2001 |
|---|---|---|---|---|---|---|---|---|---|---|
| Tangible Book Value | 5.95 | 4.29 | 2.64 | 1.91 | 1.97 | NM | NM | NM | NM | 2.87 |
| Earnings | -0.11 | 1.09 | 1.80 | 0.73 | 0.43 | 0.95 | 0.57 | 0.56 | -4.81 | 0.87 |
| S&P Core Earnings | 0.16 | 1.10 | 0.53 | 0.65 | 0.78 | 1.04 | 0.51 | 0.94 | -3.66 | 0.74 |
| Dividends | Nil | Nil | Nil | Nil | Nil | Nil | Nil | Nil | Nil | Nil |
| Payout Ratio | Nil | Nil | Nil | Nil | Nil | Nil | Nil | Nil | Nil | Nil |
| Prices:High | 14.24 | 15.44 | 22.48 | 24.24 | 23.85 | 18.13 | 13.71 | 9.50 | 17.92 | 60.15 |
| Prices:Low | 8.82 | 4.80 | 5.80 | 16.69 | 15.63 | 12.53 | 7.56 | 2.63 | 0.92 | 11.60 |
| P/E Ratio:High | NM | 14 | 12 | 33 | 55 | 19 | 24 | 17 | NM | 69 |
| P/E Ratio:Low | NM | 4 | 3 | 23 | 36 | 13 | 13 | 5 | NM | 13 |

| Income Statement Analysis (Million $) | 2010 | 2009 | 2008 | 2007 | 2006 | 2005 | 2004 | 2003 | 2002 | 2001 |
|---|---|---|---|---|---|---|---|---|---|---|
| Revenue | 16,647 | 14,119 | 16,070 | 13,588 | 12,299 | 11,086 | 9,486 | 8,415 | 8,632 | 9,327 |
| Depreciation | 1,126 | 1,049 | 960 | 942 | 933 | 889 | 841 | 781 | 837 | 859 |
| Maintenance | NA | NA | NA | NA | NA | NA | NA | NA | NA | NA |
| Fixed Charges Coverage | NA | 2.56 | 2.12 | 1.90 | 1.94 | 1.73 | 1.30 | 1.38 | 0.34 | 1.42 |
| Construction Credits | NA | NA | NA | NA | NA | NA | NA | NA | NA | NA |
| Effective Tax Rate | 25.0% | 24.6% | 27.8% | 42.4% | 31.0% | 31.9% | 28.2% | 30.3% | NM | 28.7% |
| Net Income | 920 | 729 | 1,216 | 495 | 286 | 632 | 366 | 336 | -2,590 | 467 |
| S&P Core Earnings | 120 | 732 | 344 | 447 | 526 | 693 | 332 | 564 | -1,970 | 394 |

| Balance Sheet & Other Financial Data (Million $) | 2010 | 2009 | 2008 | 2007 | 2006 | 2005 | 2004 | 2003 | 2002 | 2001 |
|---|---|---|---|---|---|---|---|---|---|---|
| Gross Property | 33,794 | 33,217 | 28,908 | 27,522 | 26,053 | 24,741 | 24,141 | 23,098 | 23,050 | 26,748 |
| Capital Expenditures | 2,310 | 2,520 | 2,840 | 2,425 | 1,460 | 1,143 | 892 | 1,228 | 2,116 | 3,173 |
| Net Property | 24,621 | 24,297 | 21,393 | 20,020 | 19,074 | 18,654 | 18,788 | 18,505 | 18,846 | 23,434 |
| Capitalization:Long Term Debt | 16,753 | 18,003 | 16,863 | 16,629 | 14,892 | 36,674 | 16,823 | 16,792 | 17,684 | 20,564 |
| Capitalization:% Long Term Debt | 72.1 | 79.4 | 82.1 | 84.0 | 83.1 | 95.7 | 91.1 | 96.3 | 102.0 | 78.8 |
| Capitalization:Preferred | Nil | Nil | Nil | Nil | Nil | Nil | Nil | Nil | Nil | Nil |
| Capitalization:% Preferred | Nil | Nil | Nil | Nil | Nil | Nil | Nil | Nil | Nil | Nil |
| Capitalization:Common | 6,473 | 4,675 | 3,669 | 3,164 | 3,036 | 1,649 | 1,645 | 645 | -341 | 5,539 |
| Capitalization:% Common | 27.9 | 20.6 | 17.9 | 16.0 | 16.9 | 4.30 | 8.91 | 3.70 | -1.97 | 21.2 |
| Total Capital | 34,506 | 28,856 | 25,082 | 24,282 | 21,818 | 40,655 | 20,758 | 19,293 | 19,142 | 29,537 |
| % Operating Ratio | 80.4 | 81.9 | 84.1 | 83.7 | 83.8 | 85.5 | 84.2 | 84.5 | 88.5 | 89.7 |
| % Earned on Net Property | 14.8 | 13.9 | 16.1 | 15.5 | 23.0 | 20.9 | 18.5 | 17.0 | 14.3 | 13.6 |
| % Return on Revenue | 5.5 | 5.2 | 7.6 | 3.6 | 2.3 | 5.7 | 3.9 | 4.0 | NM | 5.0 |
| % Return on Invested Capital | NA | 12.2 | 12.7 | 16.7 | 16.3 | 7.0 | 13.6 | 13.6 | 21.6 | 7.3 |
| % Return on Common Equity | 16.5 | 17.5 | 35.6 | 15.9 | 12.3 | 48.5 | 33.4 | 221.1 | NM | 8.4 |

Data as orig reptd.; bef. results of disc opers/spec. items. Per share data adj. for stk. divs.; EPS diluted. E-Estimated. NA-Not Available. NM-Not Meaningful. NR-Not Ranked. UR-Under Review.

**Office:** 4300 Wilson Blvd Ste 1100, Arlington, VA 22203-4167.
**Telephone:** 703-522-1315.
**Email:** invest@aes.com
**Website:** http://www.aes.com

**Chrmn:** P.A. Odeen
**Pres & CEO:** A.R. Gluski
**EVP & CFO:** V.D. Harker
**EVP, Secy & General Counsel:** B.A. Miller

**SVP & CIO:** E. Hackenson
**Investor Contact:** A. Pasha (703-682-6552)
**Board Members:** S. W. Bodman, III, A. R. Gluski, K. M. Johnson, T. Khanna, J. A. Koskinen, P. Lader, S. O. Moose, J. B. Morse, Jr., P. A. Odeen, C. O. Rossotti, S. Sandstrom

**Founded:** 1981
**Domicile:** Delaware
**Employees:** 29,000

*The McGraw·Hill Companies*

# Aetna Inc.

STANDARD
&POOR'S

| S&P Recommendation | BUY ★★★★☆ | Price $37.89 (as of Nov 25, 2011) | 12-Mo. Target Price $49.00 | Investment Style Large-Cap Blend |
|---|---|---|---|---|

**GICS Sector** Health Care
**Sub-Industry** Managed Health Care

**Summary** This company offers a broad range of traditional, voluntary and consumer-directed health insurance products and related services.

## Key Stock Statistics (Source S&P, Vickers, company reports)

| | | | | | | |
|---|---|---|---|---|---|---|
| 52-Wk Range | $46.01–29.54 | S&P Oper. EPS 2011**E** | 5.00 | Market Capitalization(B) | $13.728 | Beta | 1.27 |
| Trailing 12-Month EPS | $4.70 | S&P Oper. EPS 2012**E** | 4.85 | Yield (%) | 1.58 | S&P 3-Yr. Proj. EPS CAGR(%) | 13 |
| Trailing 12-Month P/E | 8.1 | P/E on S&P Oper. EPS 2011**E** | 7.6 | Dividend Rate/Share | $0.60 | S&P Credit Rating | A- |
| $10K Invested 5 Yrs Ago | $9,291 | Common Shares Outstg. (M) | 362.3 | Institutional Ownership (%) | 94 | | |

## Price Performance

- 30-Week Mov. Avg. · · · 10-Week Mov. Avg. – – GAAP Earnings vs. Previous Year   Volume Above Avg. STARS
- 12-Mo. Target Price — Relative Strength — ▲ Up ▼ Down ► No Change   Below Avg.

Options: ASE, CBOE, P, Ph

Analysis prepared by Equity Analyst **Phillip Seligman** on Nov 02, 2011, when the stock traded at **$39.33**.

## Qualitative Risk Assessment

| LOW | MEDIUM | HIGH |
|---|---|---|

Our risk assessment reflects AET's leadership in the highly fragmented managed care market. Competition has been intensifying, as consolidation has led the largest companies, including AET, to bump up against one another in more markets and geographies. Still, we believe AET's expanding product, market and geographic diversity will permit stable operating performance over the long term.

## Quantitative Evaluations

**S&P Quality Ranking**                                        B+

| D | C | B- | B | B+ | A- | A | A+ |
|---|---|---|---|---|---|---|---|

**Relative Strength Rank**                          MODERATE

63

LOWEST = 1                                           HIGHEST = 99

## Highlights

▸ We look for Health Care segment operating revenue to decline almost 1% in 2011, and grow by over 7.5% in 2012. We assume 40,000 fewer Medicare Advantage (MA; health plan) and 175,000 fewer stand-alone Medicare Part D (drug plan) members, on Medicare's imposition of a marketing and selling sanction on AET, and a net loss of 260,000 fully insured and 5,000 self-funded commercial members in 2011. For 2012, we forecast modest increases in commercial risk and self-funded enrollment, a recovery of MA and Part D enrollment, on the lifting of the sanctions, and the full-year benefit of the 2011 acquisitions.

▸ We forecast that total medical costs will decline 200 basis points (bps) in 2011 as a percentage of premiums (medical loss ratio, MLR), on moderated medical cost trends and favorable prior-year reserve development (PPRD). In 2012, we expect the MLR to rise by 290 bps, on the absence of favorable PPRD, our assumption of more-normal medical cost trends, and the impact of the health care reform law.

▸ We estimate 2011 operating EPS of $5.00, versus $3.68 in 2010. We look for $4.85 in 2012, aided by additional share buybacks.

## Investment Rationale/Risk

▸ We think AET has the scale, diversity, technology and financial flexibility to perform better than most insurers amid health care reform. We view positively its pricing discipline, cost control initiatives, and increasing diversification, including penetration of the growing Medicaid market and international expansion. We also view AET's cash flow as healthy, providing financial flexibility. In this regard, we see the June 2011 Prodigy acquisition building AET's position in the third-party accounts market, while the October 2011 PayFlex Holdings acquisition provides it with a large foothold in flexible spending account administration. In addition, we see the October 2011 acquisition of the Medicare Supplement business of Genworth Financial (GNW 6, Buy) strengthening its competitive position in the Medicare market.

▸ Risks to our recommendation and target price include intensified competition, a weaker economy, and adverse medical cost trends.

▸ We apply a below-peers multiple of 10.1X, on intensified competition we foresee, to our 2012 EPS estimate to derive our 12-month target price of $49.

## Revenue/Earnings Data

**Revenue (Million $)**

| | 1Q | 2Q | 3Q | 4Q | Year |
|---|---|---|---|---|---|
| 2011 | 8,388 | 8,344 | 8,475 | -- | -- |
| 2010 | 8,622 | 8,546 | 8,539 | 8,540 | 34,246 |
| 2009 | 8,615 | 8,671 | 8,722 | 8,756 | 34,764 |
| 2008 | 7,739 | 7,828 | 7,625 | 7,759 | 30,951 |
| 2007 | 6,700 | 6,794 | 6,961 | 7,144 | 27,600 |
| 2006 | 6,235 | 6,252 | 6,300 | 6,360 | 25,146 |

**Earnings Per Share ($)**

| | | | | | |
|---|---|---|---|---|---|
| 2011 | 1.50 | 1.39 | 1.30 | E0.80 | E5.00 |
| 2010 | 1.28 | 1.14 | 1.19 | 0.54 | 4.18 |
| 2009 | 0.95 | 0.77 | 0.73 | 0.38 | 2.84 |
| 2008 | 0.85 | 0.97 | 0.58 | 0.42 | 2.83 |
| 2007 | 0.81 | 0.85 | 0.95 | 0.87 | 3.47 |
| 2006 | 0.65 | 0.67 | 0.85 | 0.80 | 2.96 |

Fiscal year ended Dec. 31. Next earnings report expected: NA. EPS Estimates based on S&P Operating Earnings; historical GAAP earnings are as reported.

## Dividend Data (Dates: mm/dd Payment Date: mm/dd/yy)

| Amount ($) | Date Decl. | Ex-Div. Date | Stk. of Record | Payment Date |
|---|---|---|---|---|
| 0.040 | 09/24 | 11/10 | 11/15 | 11/30/10 |
| 0.150 | 02/03 | 04/12 | 04/14 | 04/29/11 |
| 0.150 | 05/20 | 07/12 | 07/14 | 07/29/11 |
| 0.150 | 09/23 | 10/11 | 10/13 | 10/28/11 |

Dividends have been paid since 2001. Source: Company reports.

The McGraw-Hill Companies

# Aetna Inc.

STANDARD
&POOR'S

## Business Summary November 02, 2011

CORPORATE OVERVIEW. In December 2000, Aetna sold its financial services and international operations for $5 billion ($35.33 a share, not adjusted) and the assumption of $2.7 billion of debt. AET shareholders received $35.33 a share in cash, plus one share of a new health care company named Aetna. Revenue contributions (excluding net investment and other income) from the company's business operations in 2010 were: Health Care 92.3%; Group Insurance 6.6%; and Large Case Pensions 1.1%.

The Health Care segment offers health maintenance organization (HMO), point-of-service (POS), preferred provider organization (PPO) and indemnity benefit products. The company had total health plan enrollment of 18,230,000 lives as of September 30, 2011, down from 18,468,000 as of December 31, 2010. Commercial risk enrollment was 4,757,000 lives, versus 5,015,000, while commercial administrative services (ASC; fee-based, self-funded accounts) was 11,810,000 lives, versus 11,804,000. Medicare enrollment was 408,000 lives, versus 445,000, while Medicaid enrollment was 1,261,000 lives, versus 1,199,000. The company also provided dental benefits to 13,647,000 members,

versus 13,747,000, and pharmacy benefits to 8,806,000 members, versus 9,417,000.

Group Insurance provides group life, disability and long-term care products. Group life contracts and group conversion policies totaled 41,050,000 at December 31, 2009 (latest available).

Large Case Pensions manages various retirement products, including pension and annuity products, for defined benefit and defined contribution plans. Aetna has not marketed its Large Case Pensions products since 1993, but continues to manage the run-off of existing business. Assets under management totaled $11.2 billion at December 31, 2009 (latest available).

## Company Financials Fiscal Year Ended Dec. 31

| Per Share Data ($) | 2010 | 2009 | 2008 | 2007 | 2006 | 2005 | 2004 | 2003 | 2002 | 2001 |
|---|---|---|---|---|---|---|---|---|---|---|
| Tangible Book Value | 11.05 | 8.74 | 5.33 | 8.46 | 7.46 | 8.57 | 8.42 | 6.15 | 4.69 | 4.51 |
| Cash Flow | NA | NA | 3.61 | 4.08 | 2.96 | 3.04 | 2.22 | 1.79 | 1.14 | 0.54 |
| Earnings | 4.18 | 2.84 | 2.83 | 3.47 | 2.96 | 2.70 | 1.94 | 1.48 | 0.64 | -0.51 |
| S&P Core Earnings | 3.66 | 2.92 | 3.17 | 3.39 | 2.96 | 2.55 | 1.71 | 1.51 | 0.19 | -1.12 |
| Dividends | 0.04 | 0.04 | 0.04 | 0.04 | 0.04 | 0.02 | 0.01 | 0.01 | 0.01 | 0.01 |
| Payout Ratio | 1% | 1% | 1% | 1% | 1% | NM | NM | 1% | 2% | NM |
| Prices:High | 35.96 | 34.91 | 59.80 | 60.00 | 52.48 | 49.68 | 31.89 | 17.56 | 12.98 | 10.67 |
| Prices:Low | 25.00 | 18.66 | 14.21 | 39.02 | 30.94 | 29.93 | 16.41 | 9.98 | 7.48 | 5.75 |
| P/E Ratio:High | 9 | 12 | 21 | 17 | 18 | 18 | 16 | 12 | 20 | NM |
| P/E Ratio:Low | 6 | 7 | 5 | 11 | 10 | 11 | 8 | 7 | 12 | NM |

| Income Statement Analysis (Million $) | | | | | | | | | | |
|---|---|---|---|---|---|---|---|---|---|---|
| Revenue | 34,246 | 34,764 | 30,951 | 27,600 | 25,146 | 22,492 | 19,904 | 17,976 | 19,879 | 25,191 |
| Operating Income | NA | NA | 2,765 | 3,234 | 2,983 | 2,807 | 2,184 | 1,596 | 1,119 | 460 |
| Depreciation | NA | NA | 378 | 322 | 270 | 204 | 182 | 200 | 302 | 598 |
| Interest Expense | 255 | 243 | 236 | 181 | 148 | 123 | 105 | 103 | 120 | 143 |
| Pretax Income | 2,644 | 1,901 | 2,174 | 2,796 | 2,587 | 2,547 | 1,899 | 1,442 | 545 | -379 |
| Effective Tax Rate | NA | 32.9% | 36.3% | 34.5% | 34.8% | 35.8% | 36.0% | 35.2% | 27.8% | NM |
| Net Income | 1,767 | 1,277 | 1,384 | 1,831 | 1,686 | 1,635 | 1,215 | 934 | 393 | -292 |
| S&P Core Earnings | 1,545 | 1,315 | 1,551 | 1,792 | 1,682 | 1,542 | 1,072 | 957 | 140 | -639 |

| Balance Sheet & Other Financial Data (Million $) | | | | | | | | | | |
|---|---|---|---|---|---|---|---|---|---|---|
| Cash | 1,868 | 1,204 | 1,180 | 2,078 | 880 | 1,378 | 1,595 | 1,655 | 2,017 | 1,631 |
| Current Assets | NA | NA | 4,918 | 5,288 | 18,304 | 18,235 | 19,516 | 19,557 | 19,349 | 18,751 |
| Total Assets | 37,739 | 38,550 | 35,853 | 50,725 | 47,626 | 44,365 | 42,134 | 40,950 | 40,048 | 43,255 |
| Current Liabilities | NA | NA | 7,555 | 7,675 | 7,103 | 7,617 | 7,011 | 7,368 | 7,719 | 8,139 |
| Long Term Debt | 3,483 | 3,640 | 3,638 | 3,269 | 2,442 | 1,156 | 1,610 | 1,614 | 1,633 | 1,591 |
| Common Equity | 9,891 | 9,504 | 8,186 | 10,038 | 11,009 | 12,167 | 9,081 | 7,924 | 6,980 | 9,890 |
| Total Capital | NA | NA | 11,825 | 13,323 | 11,587 | 13,338 | 10,691 | 9,538 | 8,613 | 11,481 |
| Capital Expenditures | NA | NA | 447 | 400 | 291 | 272 | 190 | 211 | 156 | 143 |
| Cash Flow | NA | NA | 1,762 | 2,153 | 1,686 | 1,839 | 1,397 | 1,133 | 695 | 306 |
| Current Ratio | 0.8 | 0.8 | 0.7 | 0.7 | 2.6 | 2.4 | 2.8 | 2.7 | 2.5 | 2.3 |
| % Long Term Debt of Capitalization | 24.4 | Nil | 30.8 | 23.8 | 18.2 | 8.7 | 15.1 | 16.9 | 19.0 | 13.9 |
| % Net Income of Revenue | 5.2 | 3.7 | 4.5 | 6.6 | 6.7 | 7.6 | 6.4 | 5.2 | 2.0 | NM |
| % Return on Assets | NA | 3.4 | 3.2 | 3.7 | 3.7 | 3.8 | 2.9 | 2.3 | 0.9 | NM |
| % Return on Equity | NA | NA | 15.2 | 19.1 | 14.5 | 14.0 | 14.3 | 12.5 | 4.7 | NM |

Data as orig reptd.; bef. results of disc opers/spec. items. Per share data adj. for stk. divs.; EPS diluted. E-Estimated. NA-Not Available. NM-Not Meaningful. NR-Not Ranked. UR-Under Review.

**Office:** 151 Farmington Avenue, Hartford, CT 06156.
**Telephone:** 860-273-0123.
**Email:** investorrelations@aetna.com
**Website:** http://www.aetna.com

**Chrmn, Pres & CEO:** M.T. Bertolini
**COO:** M.M. McCarthy
**SVP & General Counsel:** W.J. Casazza
**CFO:** J. Zubretsky

**CTO:** R.J. Leonard
**Investor Contact:** J. Chaffkin (860-273-7830)
**Board Members:** L. Abramson, F. Aguirre, M. T. Bertolini, F. M. Clark, Jr., B. Z. Cohen, M. J. Coye, R. N. Farah, B. H. Franklin, J. E. Garten, E. G. Graves, G. Greenwald, E. M. Hancock, R. J. Harrington, E. J. Ludwig, J. P. Newhouse

**Founded:** 1982
**Domicile:** Pennsylvania
**Employees:** 34,000

# AFLAC Inc

**STANDARD &POOR'S**

| S&P Recommendation | **BUY** ★★★★☆ | Price<br>$40.74 (as of Nov 28, 2011) | 12-Mo. Target Price<br>$48.00 | Investment Style<br>Large-Cap Growth |
|---|---|---|---|---|

**GICS Sector** Financials
**Sub-Industry** Life & Health Insurance

**Summary** AFL provides supplemental health and life insurance in the U.S. and Japan. Products are marketed at work sites and help fill gaps in primary insurance coverage. Approximately 80% of earnings comes from Japan and 20% from the U.S.

## Key Stock Statistics (Source S&P, Vickers, company reports)

| | | | | | | | |
|---|---|---|---|---|---|---|---|
| 52-Wk Range | $59.54– 31.25 | S&P Oper. EPS 2011**E** | 6.34 | Market Capitalization(B) | $19.032 | Beta | 1.85 |
| Trailing 12-Month EPS | $3.94 | S&P Oper. EPS 2012**E** | 6.60 | Yield (%) | 3.24 | S&P 3-Yr. Proj. EPS CAGR(%) | 8 |
| Trailing 12-Month P/E | 10.3 | P/E on S&P Oper. EPS 2011**E** | 6.4 | Dividend Rate/Share | $1.32 | S&P Credit Rating | A- |
| $10K Invested 5 Yrs Ago | $9,909 | Common Shares Outstg. (M) | 467.2 | Institutional Ownership (%) | 60 | | |

## Price Performance

30-Week Mov. Avg. · · · · 10-Week Mov. Avg. - - GAAP Earnings vs. Previous Year   Volume Above Avg. ▌▌▌ STARS
12-Mo. Target Price — Relative Strength — ▲ Up ▼ Down ► No Change   Below Avg. ▌▌▌ ★

Options: ASE, CBOE, Ph

Analysis prepared by Equity Analyst **Cathy Seifert** on Nov 28, 2011, when the stock traded at **$40.98**.

## Highlights

➤ We expect revenues to rise 8% to 10% in 2011, on contributions from new distribution outlets, the launch of new products in Japan, and foreign currency shifts. While we anticipate solid sales at AFL Japan, fueled by strong demand for the company's child endowment policy and new whole life insurance product, we expect sales growth to slow on difficult comps, and due to disruptions caused by the recent earthquake. We forecast that AFL Japan's pretax margins will expand slightly to around 22%, on a decrease in the benefit ratio. While a business mix shift toward less profitable products should adversely affect margin expansion, we think this will be more than offset by an improvement in the overall benefit ratio and stronger premium growth.

➤ We are encouraged that U.S. sales growth turned positive in the first quarter. We expect improved economic conditions, easy comps and a higher agent head count to lead to high single digit sales growth in 2011.

➤ We forecast operating EPS of $6.34 in 2011 and $6.60 in 2012, excluding any realized investment gains or losses.

## Investment Rationale/Risk

➤ Our buy recommendation is based on the steep discount AFL currently trades at versus its historical valuation. While we expect the "de-risking" of its investment portfolio to slow earnings growth over the next few years, we believe the shedding of its holdings of European bank bonds and European sovereign debt will lead to a higher valuation. We view the fundamentals of AFL's Japan operations as strong, and we expect the business to benefit from improved margins and strong premium growth. We believe AFL maintains a strong capital position and generates consistent earnings, which should allow the company to increase its dividend and repurchase its shares.

➤ Risks to our recommendation and target price include investment losses, unfavorable movements in the yen/dollar exchange rate, less organic premium growth than we forecast, and agent recruiting difficulties.

➤ Our 12-month target price is $48, or about 7.3X our 2012 operating EPS estimate , below historical multiples due to our lower earnings growth rate forecast versus AFL's historical average.

## Qualitative Risk Assessment

| LOW | **MEDIUM** | HIGH |
|---|---|---|

Our risk assessment reflects the potential for investment losses given AFL's large exposure to hybrid bonds of financial services companies. Our assessment also takes into account the recent earthquake in Japan, although we think losses will be manageable. This is offset by AFL's strong market share position and solid risk-based capital ratio, and its consistent track record of share repurchases and dividend increases.

## Quantitative Evaluations

**S&P Quality Ranking**   A

| D | C | B- | B | B+ | A- | **A** | A+ |
|---|---|---|---|---|---|---|---|

**Relative Strength Rank**   MODERATE

66

LOWEST = 1   HIGHEST = 99

## Revenue/Earnings Data

**Revenue (Million $)**

| | 1Q | 2Q | 3Q | 4Q | Year |
|---|---|---|---|---|---|
| 2011 | 5,117 | 5,088 | 5,987 | -- | -- |
| 2010 | 5,065 | 4,980 | 5,394 | 5,294 | 20,732 |
| 2009 | 4,818 | 4,313 | 4,526 | 4,597 | 18,254 |
| 2008 | 4,267 | 4,336 | 3,691 | 4,260 | 16,554 |
| 2007 | 3,751 | 3,764 | 3,861 | 4,018 | 15,393 |
| 2006 | 3,559 | 3,697 | 3,672 | 3,687 | 14,616 |

**Earnings Per Share ($)**

| | | | | | |
|---|---|---|---|---|---|
| 2011 | 0.84 | 0.60 | 1.59 | E1.49 | E6.34 |
| 2010 | 1.35 | 1.23 | 1.46 | 0.92 | 4.95 |
| 2009 | 1.22 | 0.67 | 0.77 | 0.53 | 3.19 |
| 2008 | 0.98 | 1.00 | 0.21 | 0.42 | 2.62 |
| 2007 | 0.84 | 0.84 | 0.85 | 0.78 | 3.31 |
| 2006 | 0.90 | 0.81 | 0.73 | 0.67 | 2.95 |

Fiscal year ended Dec. 31. Next earnings report expected: NA. EPS Estimates based on S&P Operating Earnings; historical GAAP earnings are as reported.

## Dividend Data (Dates: mm/dd Payment Date: mm/dd/yy)

| Amount ($) | Date Decl. | Ex-Div. Date | Stk. of Record | Payment Date |
|---|---|---|---|---|
| 0.300 | 02/01 | 02/11 | 02/15 | 03/01/11 |
| 0.300 | 04/27 | 05/16 | 05/18 | 06/01/11 |
| 0.300 | 07/27 | 08/15 | 08/17 | 09/01/11 |
| 0.330 | 10/26 | 11/14 | 11/16 | 12/01/11 |

Dividends have been paid since 1973. Source: Company reports.

**Please read the Required Disclosures and Analyst Certification on the last page of this report.**

# AFLAC Inc

STANDARD &POOR'S

## Business Summary November 28, 2011

CORPORATE OVERVIEW. Aflac provides supplemental health and life insurance in the U.S. and Japan. Most of Aflac's policies are individually underwritten and marketed at work sites through independent agents, with premiums paid by the employee. At of the end of 2010, Aflac believed it was the world's leading underwriter of individually issued policies marketed at work sites.

In 2010, Aflac Japan accounted for 75% of total revenues, compared to 73% in 2009. At December 31, 2010, Aflac Japan accounted for 86% of total company assets, up from 85% at year-end 2009. As of year-end 2010, Aflac Japan ranked first in terms of individual insurance policies in force, surpassing Nippon Life in March 2003. At the end of 2010, AFL exceeded 20 million individual polices in force in Japan. AFL also maintained its position in 2010 as the number one seller of medical insurance policies in Japan.

Aflac Japan's insurance products are designed to help pay for costs that are not reimbursed under Japan's national health insurance system. Products include cancer life plans (22% of total Japanese sales in 2010; 28% in 2009), medical plans (34%: 39%), which include Rider MAX, rider for cancer life policies that provides accident and medical/sickness benefits; and EVER, a stand-

alone whole life medical plan. Aflac Japan also offers ordinary life products (44%; 29%), which include Child Endowment (19%; 9%), a hybrid product called WAYS (9%; 6%), and other ordinary life (12%; 14%). Other products (4%; 4%) include benefit life plans and care products.

During 2010, the number of licensed sales associates at AFL Japan rose to approximately 115,400, from 110,500 at December 31, 2009, primarily reflecting individual agency recruitment. Also, AFL Japan was represented by more than 19,600 sales agencies.

Aflac U.S. sells cancer plans (17% of total U.S. sales in 2010; 18% in 2009) and various types of health insurance, including accident and disability (48%; 48%), fixed-benefit dental (5%; 5%), and hospital indemnity (18%; 18%). Other products include long-term care, short-term disability and ordinary life policies (12%; 11%).

## Company Financials Fiscal Year Ended Dec. 31

| Per Share Data ($) | 2010 | 2009 | 2008 | 2007 | 2006 | 2005 | 2004 | 2003 | 2002 | 2001 |
|---|---|---|---|---|---|---|---|---|---|---|
| Tangible Book Value | 23.54 | 36.20 | 13.78 | 27.97 | 25.32 | 15.89 | 15.03 | 13.03 | 12.41 | 10.39 |
| Operating Earnings | NA | NA | NA | NA | NA | NA | NA | NA | 1.56 | 1.34 |
| Earnings | 4.95 | 3.19 | 2.62 | 3.31 | 2.95 | 2.92 | 2.52 | 1.52 | 1.55 | 1.28 |
| S&P Core Earnings | 5.54 | 4.88 | 3.98 | 3.27 | 2.86 | 2.60 | 2.47 | 1.85 | 1.49 | 1.25 |
| Dividends | 1.14 | 1.12 | 0.96 | 0.80 | 0.55 | 0.44 | 0.38 | 0.30 | 0.23 | 0.19 |
| Payout Ratio | 23% | 35% | 366% | 24% | 19% | 15% | 15% | 20% | 15% | 15% |
| Prices:High | 58.31 | 47.75 | 68.81 | 63.91 | 49.40 | 49.65 | 42.60 | 36.91 | 33.45 | 36.09 |
| Prices:Low | 39.91 | 10.83 | 29.68 | 45.18 | 41.63 | 35.50 | 33.85 | 28.00 | 23.10 | 23.00 |
| P/E Ratio:High | 12 | 15 | 26 | 19 | 17 | 17 | 17 | 24 | 22 | 28 |
| P/E Ratio:Low | 8 | 3 | 11 | 14 | 14 | 12 | 13 | 18 | 15 | 18 |

| Income Statement Analysis (Million $) | 2010 | 2009 | 2008 | 2007 | 2006 | 2005 | 2004 | 2003 | 2002 | 2001 |
|---|---|---|---|---|---|---|---|---|---|---|
| Life Insurance in Force | 149,047 | 128,652 | 123,200 | 98,027 | 87,855 | 80,610 | 80,496 | 69,582 | 56,680 | 46,610 |
| Premium Income:Life | 2,280 | 1,860 | 1,586 | 1,323 | 1,214 | 1,139 | 1,031 | 876 | 761 | 697 |
| Premium Income:A & H | 15,793 | 14,761 | 13,361 | 11,650 | 11,100 | 10,851 | 10,271 | 9,052 | 7,839 | 7,366 |
| Net Investment Income | 3,007 | 2,765 | 2,578 | 2,333 | 2,171 | 2,071 | 1,957 | 1,787 | 1,614 | 1,550 |
| Total Revenue | 20,732 | 18,254 | 16,554 | 15,393 | 14,616 | 14,363 | 13,281 | 11,447 | 10,257 | 9,598 |
| Pretax Income | 3,585 | 2,235 | 1,914 | 2,499 | 2,264 | 2,226 | 1,807 | 1,225 | 1,259 | 1,081 |
| Net Operating Income | NA | NA | NA | NA | NA | NA | NA | NA | 825 | 720 |
| Net Income | 2,344 | 1,497 | 1,254 | 1,634 | 1,483 | 1,483 | 1,299 | 795 | 821 | 687 |
| S&P Core Earnings | 2,624 | 2,290 | 1,903 | 1,616 | 1,438 | 1,321 | 1,274 | 962 | 791 | 670 |

| Balance Sheet & Other Financial Data (Million $) | 2010 | 2009 | 2008 | 2007 | 2006 | 2005 | 2004 | 2003 | 2002 | 2001 |
|---|---|---|---|---|---|---|---|---|---|---|
| Cash & Equivalent | 2,859 | 2,972 | 1,591 | 2,523 | 2,036 | 1,781 | 4,308 | 1,508 | 1,793 | 1,233 |
| Premiums Due | 661 | 764 | 920 | 732 | 535 | 479 | 417 | 547 | 435 | 347 |
| Investment Assets:Bonds | 85,951 | 70,731 | 67,495 | 55,410 | 50,686 | 47,551 | 48,024 | 42,893 | 37,483 | 31,677 |
| Investment Assets:Stocks | 23.0 | 24.0 | 27.0 | 22.0 | 25.0 | 84.0 | 77.0 | 73.0 | 258 | 245 |
| Investment Assets:Loans | Nil | Nil | Nil | Nil | Nil | Nil | Nil | Nil | Nil | Nil |
| Investment Assets:Total | 86,109 | 70,869 | 67,609 | 57,056 | 50,769 | 47,692 | 48,142 | 42,999 | 37,768 | 31,941 |
| Deferred Policy Costs | 9,734 | 8,533 | 8,237 | 6,654 | 6,025 | 5,590 | 5,595 | 5,044 | 4,277 | 3,645 |
| Total Assets | 101,039 | 84,106 | 79,331 | 65,805 | 59,805 | 56,361 | 59,326 | 50,964 | 45,058 | 37,860 |
| Debt | 3,038 | 2,599 | 1,721 | 1,465 | 1,420 | 1,050 | 1,141 | 1,409 | 1,312 | 1,000 |
| Common Equity | 11,056 | 8,417 | 6,639 | 8,795 | 8,341 | 7,927 | 7,573 | 6,646 | 6,394 | 5,425 |
| % Return on Revenue | 11.3 | 8.2 | 7.6 | 10.6 | 10.1 | 10.4 | 9.8 | 6.9 | 8.0 | 7.2 |
| % Return on Assets | 2.5 | 1.8 | 1.7 | 2.6 | 2.6 | 2.6 | 2.4 | 1.7 | 2.0 | 1.8 |
| % Return on Equity | 24.1 | 19.9 | 16.3 | 19.1 | 18.2 | 19.1 | 18.3 | 12.2 | 13.9 | 13.6 |
| % Investment Yield | 3.8 | 4.0 | 4.2 | 4.3 | 4.4 | 4.3 | 4.3 | 4.4 | 4.6 | 4.9 |

Data as orig reptd.; bef. results of disc opers/spec. items. Per share data adj. for stk. divs.; EPS diluted. E-Estimated. NA-Not Available. NM-Not Meaningful. NR-Not Ranked. UR-Under Review.

Office: 1932 Wynnton Road, Columbus, GA 31999.
Telephone: 706-323-3431.
Email: ir@aflac.com
Website: http://www.aflac.com

Chrmn & CEO: D.P. Amos
Pres, EVP, CFO & Treas: K. Cloninger, III
EVP & Chief Admin Officer: R.C. Davis
EVP, Secy & General Counsel: J.M. Loudermilk

Investor Contact: K.S. Janke, Jr. (706-596-3264)
Board Members: D. P. Amos, J. S. Amos, II, P. S. Amos, II, M. H. Armacost, K. Cloninger, III, E. J. Hudson, D. W. Johnson, R. B. Johnson, C. B. Knapp, E. S. Purdom, B. K. Rimer, M. R. Schuster, D. G. Thompson, R. L. Wright, T. Yoshida

Founded: 1973
Domicile: Georgia
Employees: 7,919

The McGraw-Hill Companies

# Agilent Technologies Inc

STANDARD &POOR'S

| S&P Recommendation **BUY** ★★★★☆ | Price $33.83 (as of Nov 25, 2011) | 12-Mo. Target Price $48.00 | Investment Style Large-Cap Blend |
|---|---|---|---|

**GICS Sector** Health Care
**Sub-Industry** Life Sciences Tools & Services

**Summary** This Hewlett-Packard (HPQ) spin-off is a diversified global manufacturer of test and measurement instruments, and life sciences and chemical analysis instruments.

## Key Stock Statistics (Source S&P, Vickers, company reports)

| | | | | | | | |
|---|---|---|---|---|---|---|---|
| 52-Wk Range | $55.33– 28.67 | S&P Oper. EPS 2012**E** | 3.06 | Market Capitalization(B) | $11.746 | Beta | 1.48 |
| Trailing 12-Month EPS | $2.85 | S&P Oper. EPS 2013**E** | NA | Yield (%) | Nil | S&P 3-Yr. Proj. EPS CAGR(%) | 12 |
| Trailing 12-Month P/E | 11.9 | P/E on S&P Oper. EPS 2012**E** | 11.1 | Dividend Rate/Share | Nil | S&P Credit Rating | BBB- |
| $10K Invested 5 Yrs Ago | $10,080 | Common Shares Outstg. (M) | 347.2 | Institutional Ownership (%) | 84 | | |

## Price Performance

30-Week Mov. Avg. · · · · 10-Week Mov. Avg. - - **GAAP Earnings vs. Previous Year** Volume Above Avg. STARS
12-Mo. Target Price — Relative Strength — ▲ Up ▼ Down ▶ No Change Below Avg. ★

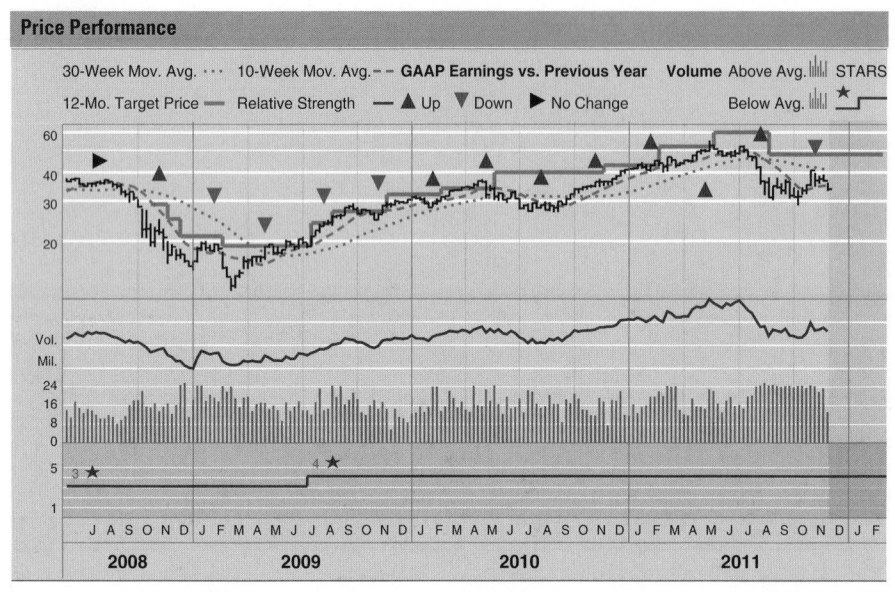

Options: ASE, CBOE, P, Ph

Analysis prepared by Equity Analyst **Angelo Zino** on Aug 17, 2011, when the stock traded at **$36.63**.

## Highlights

▶ We expect sales to rise 6% in FY 12 (Oct.) following our expectation for a 22% rise in FY 11. We see revenues paced by growth in A's more cyclical electronic measurement end markets, with segment sales being driven by opportunities within the communications market. We see the chemical analysis business benefiting from growth in the food safety, petrochemical, and environment and forensic markets. In life sciences, we see sales driven by growth in pharmaceutical and biotech but remain cautious of the uncertain academic and government arena.

▶ We project an annual gross margin of 53% in FY 12, matching our FY 11 margin forecast. Margins should benefit from higher volume and cost-cutting efforts. We view positively prior completed cost-reduction moves, including the restructuring of A's electronic measurement group, as well as synergies from the Varian acquisition. We see R&D expenses absorbing 10% of sales in FY 11 and FY 12.

▶ We estimate operating EPS of $2.90 in FY 11, which excludes $0.16 in projected non-recurring charges, and $3.06 in FY 12. We expect A to expand into high-growth adjacent markets through new product releases.

## Investment Rationale/Risk

▶ We have a favorable view of the company's diversified end-market mix, with exposure to the non-cyclical life sciences and chemical analysis markets as well as cyclical electronic measurement markets. Over the long term, we expect Agilent to focus on expanding aggressively through new product offerings in high-growth industries, complemented by opportunistic acquisitions in core markets. We forecast more stable demand and higher market share in both the chemical analysis and life science end-markets. We view the shares as attractively valued at current levels.

▶ Risks to our recommendation and target price include a weaker-than-expected global economy, narrower margins than we project, and weaker-than-anticipated traction for new product introductions.

▶ Our 12-month target price of $48 is based on our discounted cash flow analysis, which assumes a weighted average cost of capital of 10.9%, beta of 1.3X, and a terminal growth rate of 3%. Our target price is supported by a P/E ratio of 15.7X our FY 12 earnings per share estimate of $3.06, within A's five-year historical average.

## Qualitative Risk Assessment

| LOW | MEDIUM | HIGH |
|---|---|---|

Our risk assessment reflects the volatility of Agilent's results in the past, offset by recent efforts to streamline its businesses and divest parts of its portfolio that contributed to this variability.

## Quantitative Evaluations

**S&P Quality Ranking** B-

| D | C | B- | B | B+ | A- | A | A+ |
|---|---|---|---|---|---|---|---|

**Relative Strength Rank** MODERATE

45

LOWEST = 1 HIGHEST = 99

## Revenue/Earnings Data

**Revenue (Million $)**

| | 1Q | 2Q | 3Q | 4Q | Year |
|---|---|---|---|---|---|
| 2011 | 1,519 | 1,677 | 1,691 | 1,728 | 6,615 |
| 2010 | 1,213 | 1,271 | 1,384 | 1,576 | 5,444 |
| 2009 | 1,166 | 1,091 | 1,057 | 1,167 | 4,481 |
| 2008 | 1,393 | 1,456 | 1,444 | 1,481 | 5,774 |
| 2007 | 1,280 | 1,320 | 1,374 | 1,446 | 5,420 |
| 2006 | 1,167 | 1,239 | 1,239 | 1,328 | 4,973 |

**Earnings Per Share ($)**

| | | | | | |
|---|---|---|---|---|---|
| 2011 | 0.54 | 0.56 | 0.92 | 0.82 | 2.85 |
| 2010 | 0.22 | 0.31 | 0.58 | 0.83 | 1.94 |
| 2009 | 0.18 | -0.29 | -0.06 | 0.07 | -0.09 |
| 2008 | 0.31 | 0.47 | 0.45 | 0.64 | 1.87 |
| 2007 | 0.36 | 0.30 | 0.45 | 0.46 | 1.57 |
| 2006 | 2.03 | 0.28 | 0.51 | 0.31 | 3.26 |

Fiscal year ended Oct. 31. Next earnings report expected: Mid February. EPS Estimates based on S&P Operating Earnings; historical GAAP earnings are as reported.

## Dividend Data

No cash dividends have been paid.

---

**Please read the Required Disclosures and Analyst Certification on the last page of this report.**

The McGraw-Hill Companies

# Agilent Technologies Inc

STANDARD
&POOR'S

## Business Summary August 17, 2011

CORPORATE OVERVIEW. Agilent Technologies, which was spun off from Hewlett-Packard (HPQ) in 1999, provides investors with exposure to the communications, electronics, life sciences and chemical analysis industries. Agilent's revenues during FY 10 (Oct.) came from three business segments: electronic measurement 51% (54% in FY 09), life sciences 27% (27%) and the chemical analysis market 22% (19%).

The company's electronic measurement products provides electronic measurement instruments and systems, software design tools and related services that are used in the design, development, manufacturing, installation, deployment and operation of electronics equipment. A sells its products and services to network equipment manufacturers, handset manufacturers, and communications service providers, including the component manufacturers within the supply chain for these customers.

General purpose test products and services are sold to the electronics industry and other industries with significant electronic content, such as the aerospace and defense, computer and semiconductor industries. A has a suite of fiber optic, broadband and data and wireless communications and microwave network products. It sells electronic measurement products that are used for electronics manufacturing testing, parametric testing, and flat panel

display (FPD) markets. The semiconductor and board test business provides standard and customized measurement instruments and systems that enable customers to develop and test state-of-the-art semiconductors, test and inspect printed circuit boards, perform functional testing, and measure position and distance information to the sub-nanometer level.

Within life sciences, Agilent focuses on the pharmaceutical value chain in the areas of therapeutic research, discovery & development, clinical trials, and manufacturing and quality assurance and quality control. In the pharmaceutical and biopharmaceutical markets, Agilent's instruments help lower the cost of discovering and developing new drugs. It also has exposure to the academic and government market, which includes academic institutions, large government institutes and privately funded organizations. Chemical analysis focuses primarily on the following areas: petrochemical, environmental, homeland security and forensics, bioagriculture and food safety, and material science.

## Company Financials Fiscal Year Ended Oct. 31

| Per Share Data ($) | 2011 | 2010 | 2009 | 2008 | 2007 | 2006 | 2005 | 2004 | 2003 | 2002 |
|---|---|---|---|---|---|---|---|---|---|---|
| Tangible Book Value | NA | 3.75 | 4.86 | 4.81 | 6.75 | 7.79 | 7.39 | 6.42 | 5.09 | 8.44 |
| Cash Flow | 3.56 | 2.34 | 0.38 | 2.35 | 2.04 | 3.64 | 0.65 | 1.31 | -3.02 | -0.62 |
| Earnings | 2.85 | 1.77 | -0.09 | 1.87 | 1.57 | 3.26 | 0.28 | 0.71 | -3.78 | -2.20 |
| S&P Core Earnings | NA | 1.60 | -0.09 | 1.53 | 1.52 | 1.59 | -0.11 | 0.27 | -5.70 | -3.10 |
| Dividends | NA | Nil | Nil | Nil | Nil | Nil | Nil | Nil | Nil | Nil |
| Payout Ratio | Nil | Nil | Nil | Nil | Nil | Nil | Nil | Nil | Nil | Nil |
| Prices:High | 55.33 | 42.08 | 31.77 | 38.00 | 40.42 | 39.54 | 36.10 | 38.80 | 29.42 | 38.00 |
| Prices:Low | 28.67 | 26.68 | 12.02 | 14.76 | 30.26 | 26.96 | 20.11 | 19.51 | 18.35 | 10.50 |
| P/E Ratio:High | 19 | 24 | NM | 20 | 26 | 12 | NM | 55 | NM | NM |
| P/E Ratio:Low | 10 | 15 | NM | 8 | 19 | 8 | NM | 27 | NM | NM |

| Income Statement Analysis (Million $) | 2011 | 2010 | 2009 | 2008 | 2007 | 2006 | 2005 | 2004 | 2003 | 2002 |
|---|---|---|---|---|---|---|---|---|---|---|
| Revenue | 6,615 | 5,444 | 4,481 | 5,774 | 5,420 | 4,973 | 5,139 | 7,181 | 6,056 | 6,010 |
| Operating Income | 1,324 | 768 | 399 | 974 | 775 | 680 | 367 | 678 | -363 | -872 |
| Depreciation | 253 | 202 | 162 | 179 | 191 | 170 | 186 | 292 | 362 | 735 |
| Interest Expense | 86.0 | 96.0 | 88.0 | 123 | 91.0 | 69.0 | 27.0 | 36.0 | Nil | Nil |
| Pretax Income | 1,032 | 692 | 7.00 | 815 | 670 | 1,528 | 306 | 440 | -690 | -1,547 |
| Effective Tax Rate | NA | NA | 542.9% | 15.0% | 4.70% | 5.96% | 50.7% | 20.7% | NM | NM |
| Net Income | 1,012 | 624 | -31.0 | 693 | 638 | 1,437 | 141 | 349 | -1,790 | -1,022 |
| S&P Core Earnings | NA | 565 | -27.9 | 568 | 615 | 701 | -55.1 | 137 | -2,695 | -1,438 |

| Balance Sheet & Other Financial Data (Million $) | 2011 | 2010 | 2009 | 2008 | 2007 | 2006 | 2005 | 2004 | 2003 | 2002 |
|---|---|---|---|---|---|---|---|---|---|---|
| Cash | 3,527 | 2,649 | 2,493 | 1,429 | 1,826 | 2,262 | 2,251 | 2,315 | 1,607 | 1,844 |
| Current Assets | 5,577 | 6,169 | 3,961 | 3,208 | 3,671 | 3,958 | 4,447 | 4,577 | 3,889 | 4,880 |
| Total Assets | 9,057 | 9,644 | 7,612 | 7,437 | 7,554 | 7,369 | 6,751 | 7,056 | 6,297 | 8,203 |
| Current Liabilities | 1,837 | 3,083 | 1,123 | 1,325 | 1,663 | 1,538 | 1,936 | 1,871 | 1,906 | 2,181 |
| Long Term Debt | 1,932 | 2,190 | 2,904 | 2,125 | 2,087 | 1,500 | Nil | 1,150 | 1,150 | 1,150 |
| Common Equity | 4,308 | 3,176 | 2,506 | 2,559 | 3,234 | 3,648 | 4,081 | 3,569 | 2,824 | 4,627 |
| Total Capital | 6,256 | 5,374 | 5,410 | 4,684 | 5,321 | 5,341 | 4,081 | 4,719 | 3,974 | 5,777 |
| Capital Expenditures | 188 | 119 | 128 | 154 | 154 | 185 | 139 | 118 | 205 | 301 |
| Cash Flow | 1,265 | 826 | 131 | 872 | 829 | 1,607 | 327 | 641 | -1,428 | -287 |
| Current Ratio | 3.0 | 2.0 | 3.5 | 2.4 | 2.2 | 2.6 | 2.3 | 2.4 | 2.0 | 2.2 |
| % Long Term Debt of Capitalization | 30.9 | 40.8 | 53.7 | 45.4 | 39.2 | 29.1 | Nil | 24.4 | 28.9 | 19.9 |
| % Net Income of Revenue | 15.3 | 11.5 | NM | 12.0 | 11.7 | 28.9 | 2.7 | 4.9 | NM | NM |
| % Return on Assets | 10.8 | 7.2 | NM | 9.3 | 8.5 | 20.4 | 2.0 | 5.2 | NM | NM |
| % Return on Equity | 26.9 | 22.0 | NM | 23.9 | 18.5 | 37.2 | 3.7 | 10.9 | NM | NM |

Data as orig reptd.; bef. results of disc opers/spec. items. Per share data adj. for stk. divs.; EPS diluted. E-Estimated. NA-Not Available. NM-Not Meaningful. NR-Not Ranked. UR-Under Review.

**Office:** 5301 Stevens Creek Boulevard, Santa Clara, CA 95051.
**Telephone:** 408-345-8886.
**Email:** investor_relations@agilent.com
**Website:** http://www.home.agilent.com

**Chrmn:** J.G. Cullen
**Pres & CEO:** W.P. Sullivan
**COO & EVP:** R.S. Nersesian
**SVP, CFO & Chief Acctg Officer:** D. Hirsch

**SVP, Secy & General Counsel:** M.O. Huber
**Board Members:** P. N. Clark, J. G. Cullen, H. K. Fields, R. J. Herbold, B. Koh, D. M. Lawrence, A. B. Rand, W. P. Sullivan, T. Yamada
**Founded:** 1999
**Domicile:** Delaware
**Employees:** 18,500

The **McGraw·Hill** Companies

# Airgas Inc.

STANDARD
&POOR'S

| S&P Recommendation | HOLD ★ ★ ★ ★ ★ | Price $69.71 (as of Nov 25, 2011) | 12-Mo. Target Price $75.00 | Investment Style Large-Cap Growth |
| --- | --- | --- | --- | --- |

**GICS Sector** Materials
**Sub-Industry** Industrial Gases

**Summary** This leading distributor of industrial, medical and specialty gases and related equipment also distributes safety and other disposable supplies through its network of stores.

## Key Stock Statistics (Source S&P, Vickers, company reports)

| | | | | | | | |
| --- | --- | --- | --- | --- | --- | --- | --- |
| 52-Wk Range | $74.25–58.00 | S&P Oper. EPS 2012**E** | 3.96 | Market Capitalization(B) | $5.292 | Beta | 1.12 |
| Trailing 12-Month EPS | $3.31 | S&P Oper. EPS 2013**E** | 4.57 | Yield (%) | 1.84 | S&P 3-Yr. Proj. EPS CAGR(%) | 10 |
| Trailing 12-Month P/E | 21.1 | P/E on S&P Oper. EPS 2012**E** | 17.6 | Dividend Rate/Share | $1.28 | S&P Credit Rating | BBB |
| $10K Invested 5 Yrs Ago | $17,962 | Common Shares Outstg. (M) | 75.9 | Institutional Ownership (%) | 81 | | |

## Price Performance

30-Week Mov. Avg. · · · 10-Week Mov. Avg. – – GAAP Earnings vs. Previous Year   Volume Above Avg. STARS
12-Mo. Target Price — Relative Strength — ▲ Up ▼ Down ► No Change   Below Avg.

Options: CBOE, Ph

Analysis prepared by Equity Analyst **R. Tortoriello** on Nov 22, 2011, when the stock traded at **$70.91**.

### Highlights

➤ Following a sales decline of 11% in FY 10 (Mar.) and a 10% rise in FY 11, we project FY 12 sales will increase 9%. Our forecast is based on somewhat better pricing, and on greater expected volumes, all leading to higher overall same-store sales growth. We also believe ARG will increase its sales due to the positive effects of continued acquisitions. For FY 13, we project that sales will rise 7%, and we see continued growth in demand for packaged gas.

➤ Following a 70 bps increase in operating margins in FY 11, to 11.0%, we project an increase to 12.0% in FY 12. Our forecast is based on our expectation for greater operating leverage due to higher volumes and pricing. In addition, our forecast assumes lower expenses related to the implementation of customer management software systems. We look for a slight increase in operating margins in FY 13.

➤ We estimate EPS of $3.96 for FY 12, and project $4.57 for FY 13, aided by our expectation of reduced share counts due to share repurchases in both years.

### Investment Rationale/Risk

➤ We believe that ARG's results will continue to improve along with a recovery in the U.S. economy, and we see the company benefiting from better pricing and volumes. In addition, we expect the company to experience higher operating margins, despite continued spending on the rollout of enterprise-wide software systems, due to increased operating leverage. We view the shares as fairly valued.

➤ Risks to our recommendation and target price include a renewed downturn in the economy, weaker-than-expected demand or pricing, and poor implementation of firmwide customer relationship software.

➤ Our 12-month target price of $75 represents an enterprise value multiple of 8.5X our FY 13 EBITDA estimate of $945 million, near ARG's 10-year historical average EV/EBITDA multiple of 8.9X. We view an average multiple as appropriate given the risks and opportunities we see in the current economy.

### Qualitative Risk Assessment

| LOW | MEDIUM | HIGH |
| --- | --- | --- |

Our risk assessment for Airgas reflects the company's acquisition strategy, its significant proportion of sales to the cyclical industrial manufacturing industry, and what we consider to be a relatively high level of debt.

### Quantitative Evaluations

**S&P Quality Ranking**                                         A-

| D | C | B- | B | B+ | A- | A | A+ |
| --- | --- | --- | --- | --- | --- | --- | --- |

**Relative Strength Rank**                              STRONG

87

LOWEST = 1                                              HIGHEST = 99

### Revenue/Earnings Data

**Revenue (Million $)**

| | 1Q | 2Q | 3Q | 4Q | Year |
| --- | --- | --- | --- | --- | --- |
| 2012 | 1,164 | 1,187 | -- | -- | -- |
| 2011 | 1,053 | 1,062 | 1,034 | 1,103 | 4,251 |
| 2010 | 979.3 | 962.3 | 942.1 | 980.4 | 3,864 |
| 2009 | 1,117 | 1,162 | 1,079 | 992.1 | 4,349 |
| 2008 | 915.1 | 1,007 | 1,008 | 1,087 | 4,017 |
| 2007 | 773.0 | 790.8 | 787.4 | 853.9 | 3,205 |

**Earnings Per Share ($)**

| | | | | | |
| --- | --- | --- | --- | --- | --- |
| 2012 | 0.93 | 1.01 | E0.97 | E1.04 | E3.96 |
| 2011 | 0.76 | 0.78 | 0.65 | 0.74 | 2.93 |
| 2010 | 0.66 | 0.65 | 0.56 | 0.47 | 2.34 |
| 2009 | 0.81 | 0.86 | 0.76 | 0.68 | 3.12 |
| 2008 | 0.63 | 0.60 | 0.67 | 0.76 | 2.66 |
| 2007 | 0.48 | 0.49 | 0.40 | 0.54 | 1.92 |

Fiscal year ended Mar. 31. Next earnings report expected: Late January. EPS Estimates based on S&P Operating Earnings; historical GAAP earnings are as reported.

### Dividend Data (Dates: mm/dd Payment Date: mm/dd/yy)

| Amount ($) | Date Decl. | Ex-Div. Date | Stk. of Record | Payment Date |
| --- | --- | --- | --- | --- |
| 0.290 | 01/21 | 03/11 | 03/15 | 03/31/11 |
| 0.290 | 05/17 | 06/13 | 06/15 | 06/30/11 |
| 0.320 | 08/29 | 09/13 | 09/15 | 09/30/11 |
| 0.320 | 11/22 | 12/13 | 12/15 | 12/31/11 |

Dividends have been paid since 2003. Source: Company reports.

---

**Please read the Required Disclosures and Analyst Certification on the last page of this report.**

The McGraw-Hill Companies

# Airgas Inc.

STANDARD
&POOR'S

## Business Summary November 22, 2011

CORPORATE OVERVIEW. Airgas is the largest distributor of industrial, medical, specialty gases, and related hardgoods in the U.S. Since the company's inception in 1986, ARG has completed over 400 acquisitions, helping it become the largest U.S. distributor of packaged gases and welding, safety, and related products, with an average market share of 25%, based on company data. ARG operated an integrated network of over 875 branch locations, 300 gas cylinder fill planters, 61 national/regional specialty gas laboratories, and other gas plants and facilities while marketing its products and services through sales representatives and retail stores while operating electronic, catalog, and tele-sales channels. The company had over 14,000 employees as of March 2011. Competitors in the packaged gas market include independent distributors (about 50% of the market), through a fragmented distribution network, as well as large distributors (25%), including Praxair, Linde AG, Air Liquide, and Air Products. The company operates two reporting segments.

The distribution segment (89% of FY 11 (Mar.) total sales, 89% of earnings before interest and taxes (EBIT), and 7.4% EBIT margins) purchases and distributes industrial, medical and specialty gases sold in packaged and bulk quantities. This segment also sells related hardgoods, which includes welding consumables, welding equipment, safety products, construction supplies, and maintenance/repair/operating supplies. Gas and rent revenues accounted for

59% of segment sales in FY 11, with hardgoods providing the remaining 41%. Industry segments served include repair & maintenance, industrial manufacturing, energy & infrastructure contruction, medical, petrochemical, food & beverage, retail & wholesale operations, and other industries.

The other operations segment (11%, 11%, 7.1%) produces and distributes certain gas products, mainly dry ice, carbon dioxide, nitrous oxide, ammonia, and refrigerant gases. Customers include food processors, food services, pharmaceutical and biotech industries, and wholesale trade and grocery outlets.

ARG has a fairly broad exposure to the overall U.S. economy, and a significant number of customers in multiple industries. Its largest customer accounted for about 0.5% of total company sales. As a percentage of total net sales, ARG estimates sales to the repair & maintenance segment accounted for 29%; industrial manufacturing 26%; energy & infrastructure construction 10%; medical 9%; petrochemical 7%; food products 6%; retail & wholesale trade 3%; analytical 2%; utilities 3%; transportation 2%; and other 3%.

## Company Financials Fiscal Year Ended Mar. 31

| Per Share Data ($) | 2011 | 2010 | 2009 | 2008 | 2007 | 2006 | 2005 | 2004 | 2003 | 2002 |
|---|---|---|---|---|---|---|---|---|---|---|
| Tangible Book Value | 5.28 | 5.69 | 3.59 | 3.59 | 2.93 | 4.59 | 3.76 | 2.22 | 1.84 | 0.95 |
| Cash Flow | 5.87 | 5.15 | 5.75 | 4.90 | 3.66 | 3.14 | 2.64 | 2.25 | 2.05 | 1.74 |
| Earnings | 2.93 | 2.34 | 3.12 | 2.66 | 1.92 | 1.62 | 1.20 | 1.07 | 0.94 | 0.69 |
| S&P Core Earnings | 2.93 | 2.38 | 3.20 | 2.66 | 1.92 | 1.52 | 1.11 | 0.99 | 0.86 | 0.64 |
| Dividends | NA | 0.76 | 0.56 | 0.28 | 0.24 | 0.18 | 0.16 | Nil | Nil | Nil |
| Payout Ratio | NA | 32% | 18% | 11% | 12% | 11% | 13% | Nil | Nil | Nil |
| Calendar Year | 2010 | 2009 | 2008 | 2007 | 2006 | 2005 | 2004 | 2003 | 2002 | 2001 |
| Prices:High | 71.28 | 51.00 | 65.45 | 55.89 | 43.43 | 33.79 | 27.19 | 21.75 | 20.74 | 15.85 |
| Prices:Low | 41.82 | 26.29 | 27.09 | 39.00 | 31.65 | 21.15 | 19.82 | 15.27 | 11.75 | 6.38 |
| P/E Ratio:High | 24 | 22 | 21 | 21 | 22 | 21 | 23 | 20 | 22 | 23 |
| P/E Ratio:Low | 14 | 11 | 9 | 15 | 16 | 13 | 17 | 14 | 13 | 9 |

| Income Statement Analysis (Million $) | | | | | | | | | | |
|---|---|---|---|---|---|---|---|---|---|---|
| Revenue | 4,251 | 3,864 | 4,349 | 4,017 | 3,205 | 2,830 | 2,411 | 1,895 | 1,787 | 1,636 |
| Operating Income | 763 | 658 | 746 | 676 | 489 | 396 | 315 | 255 | 238 | 198 |
| Depreciation | 251 | 235 | 221 | 190 | 147 | 128 | 112 | 88.0 | 79.8 | 72.9 |
| Interest Expense | 60.1 | 63.3 | 87.1 | 61.4 | 62.1 | 55.7 | 52.8 | 43.0 | 47.3 | 48.0 |
| Pretax Income | 406 | 314 | 429 | 371 | 257 | 208 | 148 | 128 | 109 | 78.4 |
| Effective Tax Rate | NA | 37.5% | 39.2% | 38.9% | 38.8% | 37.4% | 36.8% | 37.1% | 37.7% | 38.0% |
| Net Income | 250 | 196 | 261 | 223 | 154 | 128 | 92.0 | 80.2 | 68.1 | 48.6 |
| S&P Core Earnings | 250 | 200 | 268 | 223 | 154 | 119 | 84.9 | 74.2 | 61.8 | 44.5 |

| Balance Sheet & Other Financial Data (Million $) | | | | | | | | | | |
|---|---|---|---|---|---|---|---|---|---|---|
| Cash | 57.2 | 47.0 | 47.2 | 43.1 | 25.9 | 35.0 | 32.6 | Nil | Nil | Nil |
| Current Assets | 1,121 | 711 | 718 | 639 | 550 | 459 | 466 | 327 | 271 | 304 |
| Total Assets | 4,936 | 4,496 | 4,400 | 3,979 | 3,333 | 2,474 | 2,292 | 1,931 | 1,700 | 1,717 |
| Current Liabilities | 564 | 476 | 432 | 506 | 428 | 476 | 333 | 242 | 209 | 221 |
| Long Term Debt | 1,843 | 1,499 | 1,750 | 1,540 | 1,310 | 636 | 802 | 683 | 658 | 764 |
| Common Equity | 1,735 | 1,796 | 1,572 | 1,413 | 1,125 | 947 | 814 | 692 | 597 | 503 |
| Total Capital | 3,588 | 3,305 | 3,888 | 2,993 | 2,866 | 1,968 | 1,934 | 1,668 | 1,464 | 1,465 |
| Capital Expenditures | 256 | 253 | 352 | 267 | 244 | 214 | 168 | 93.7 | 68.0 | 58.3 |
| Cash Flow | 500 | 431 | 482 | 413 | 302 | 255 | 204 | 168 | 148 | 122 |
| Current Ratio | 2.0 | 1.5 | 1.7 | 1.3 | 1.3 | 1.0 | 1.4 | 1.3 | 1.3 | 1.4 |
| % Long Term Debt of Capitalization | 51.4 | 45.4 | 45.0 | 51.4 | 52.6 | 32.3 | 41.4 | 40.9 | 44.9 | 52.1 |
| % Net Income of Revenue | 5.9 | 5.1 | 6.0 | 5.6 | 4.8 | 4.5 | 3.8 | 4.2 | 3.8 | 3.0 |
| % Return on Assets | 5.3 | 4.4 | 6.2 | 6.1 | 5.3 | 5.4 | 4.3 | 4.4 | 4.0 | 2.9 |
| % Return on Equity | 14.2 | 11.7 | 17.5 | 17.6 | 14.9 | 14.5 | 12.2 | 12.4 | 12.4 | 9.7 |

Data as orig reptd.; bef. results of disc opers/spec. items. Per share data adj. for stk. divs.; EPS diluted. E-Estimated. NA-Not Available. NM-Not Meaningful. NR-Not Ranked. UR-Under Review.

**Office:** 259 North Radnor-Chester Road, Radnor, PA 19087-5283.
**Telephone:** 610-687-5253.
**Email:** investor@airgas.com
**Website:** http://www.airgas.com

**Chrmn, Pres & CEO:** P. McCausland
**COO & EVP:** M.L. Molinini
**SVP & CFO:** R.M. McLaughlin
**SVP, Secy & General Counsel:** R.H. Young, Jr.

**SVP & CIO:** R.A. Dougherty
**Investor Contact:** J. Worley (610-902-6206)
**Board Members:** J. P. Clancey, J. W. Hovey, R. L. Lumpkins, P. McCausland, T. B. Miller, Jr., P. A. Sneed, D. M. Stout, L. M. Thomas, J. C. Van Roden, Jr., E. C. Wolf

**Founded:** 1986
**Domicile:** Delaware
**Employees:** 14,000

# Air Products and Chemicals Inc.

**STANDARD &POOR'S**

| S&P Recommendation | HOLD ★★★★★ | Price | 12-Mo. Target Price | Investment Style |
|---|---|---|---|---|
| | | $76.74 (as of Nov 25, 2011) | $90.00 | Large-Cap Blend |

**GICS Sector** Materials
**Sub-Industry** Industrial Gases

**Summary** This major producer of industrial gases and electronics and specialty chemicals also has interests in environmental and energy-related businesses.

## Key Stock Statistics (Source S&P, Vickers, company reports)

| | | | | | | | |
|---|---|---|---|---|---|---|---|
| 52-Wk Range | $98.01– 72.26 | S&P Oper. EPS 2012**E** | 6.14 | Market Capitalization(B) | $16.151 | Beta | 1.15 |
| Trailing 12-Month EPS | $5.63 | S&P Oper. EPS 2013**E** | 6.58 | Yield (%) | 3.02 | S&P 3-Yr. Proj. EPS CAGR(%) | 10 |
| Trailing 12-Month P/E | 13.6 | P/E on S&P Oper. EPS 2012**E** | 12.5 | Dividend Rate/Share | $2.32 | S&P Credit Rating | A |
| $10K Invested 5 Yrs Ago | $12,106 | Common Shares Outstg. (M) | 210.5 | Institutional Ownership (%) | 87 | | |

## Price Performance

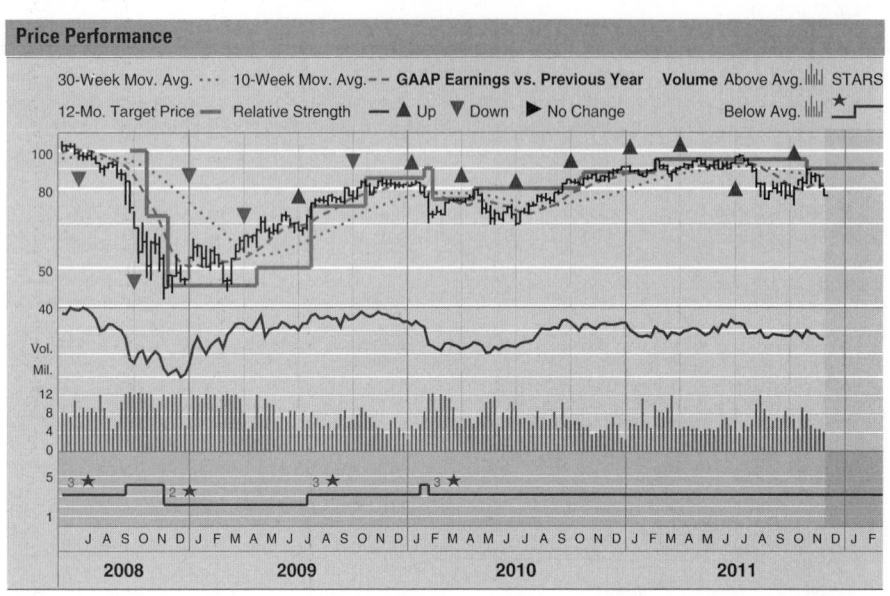

30-Week Mov. Avg. · · · 10-Week Mov. Avg. – – **GAAP Earnings vs. Previous Year** **Volume** Above Avg. STARS
12-Mo. Target Price — Relative Strength — ▲ Up ▼ Down ► No Change Below Avg. ★

Options: CBOE, P, Ph

Analysis prepared by Equity Analyst **Leo J. Larkin** on Nov 11, 2011, when the stock traded at **$86.59**.

## Highlights

➤ Following FY 11's (Sep.) sales increase of 12%, we expect a 5% advance in FY 12, and see EPS rising to $6.14 in FY 12, versus FY 11's operating EPS of $5.73, which excludes $0.14 of costs for a failed merger offer.

➤ We believe the industrial gases businesses will continue to post volume gains in FY 12, reflecting continued growth in global manufacturing activity, led by Asia, and contributions from newer plants. We think merchant gases' margins will rebound from FY 11 levels as APD resolves U.S. operating problems, although the Europe business may continue to struggle. We expect continued volume growth for hydrogen gas, driven by its rising use in petroleum refining. We look for improvement in equipment unit margins in FY 12, but expect some contraction in electronics and materials due to continued weakness in housing and construction.

➤ We see long-term EPS rising on acquisitions, share repurchases and expansion into more rapidly growing markets in Asia and South America.

## Investment Rationale/Risk

➤ We expect APD to continue to expand its core industrial gases businesses, including new on-site projects in Asia, as it plans to increase its total capital spending to $1.9 billion to $2.2 billion in FY 12, from FY 11's total of $1.6 billion. We think this expansion will provide the company with increased exposure to one of the world's fastest-growing economic regions and should bode well for long-term sales and EPS. At the same, we believe that APD will be able to generate enough free cash flow to also buy back shares and increase the dividend.

➤ Risks to our recommendation and target price include weaker-than-expected growth in global industrial activity and in the global electronics materials industry, higher-than-forecast raw material and energy prices, unplanned plant outages, and an inability by APD to achieve planned cost reductions.

➤ Our 12-month target price of $90 assumes a multiple of 14.7X our FY 12 EPS estimate, at the low end of its historical range of the last 10 years. In the context of a slow growth world economy, we think APD will carry a relatively low valuation.

## Qualitative Risk Assessment

| LOW | MEDIUM | HIGH |
|---|---|---|

Our risk assessment reflects the stable growth of the industrial gases industry versus commodity chemicals, and what we see as the company's relatively strong balance sheet, offset by volatile raw material cost exposure in the chemicals segment.

## Quantitative Evaluations

**S&P Quality Ranking**     A

| D | C | B- | B | B+ | A- | A | A+ |
|---|---|---|---|---|---|---|---|

**Relative Strength Rank**     MODERATE

42

LOWEST = 1        HIGHEST = 99

## Revenue/Earnings Data

**Revenue (Million $)**

| | 1Q | 2Q | 3Q | 4Q | Year |
|---|---|---|---|---|---|
| 2011 | 2,392 | 2,501 | 2,578 | 2,611 | 10,082 |
| 2010 | 2,174 | 2,249 | 2,252 | 2,351 | 9,026 |
| 2009 | 2,195 | 1,955 | 1,976 | 2,129 | 8,256 |
| 2008 | 2,474 | 2,605 | 2,808 | 2,715 | 10,415 |
| 2007 | 2,410 | 2,451 | 2,574 | 2,603 | 10,038 |
| 2006 | 2,016 | 2,230 | 2,246 | 2,359 | 8,850 |

**Earnings Per Share ($)**

| | | | | | |
|---|---|---|---|---|---|
| 2011 | 1.23 | 1.39 | 1.46 | 1.51 | 5.59 |
| 2010 | 1.16 | 1.16 | 1.17 | 1.25 | 4.74 |
| 2009 | 0.42 | 0.89 | 0.54 | 1.14 | 3.00 |
| 2008 | 1.16 | 1.16 | 0.23 | 1.26 | 4.98 |
| 2007 | 1.03 | 1.02 | 1.28 | 1.35 | 4.67 |
| 2006 | 0.80 | 0.89 | -- | 0.73 | 3.29 |

Fiscal year ended Sep. 30. Next earnings report expected: Late January. EPS Estimates based on S&P Operating Earnings; historical GAAP earnings are as reported.

## Dividend Data (Dates: mm/dd Payment Date: mm/dd/yy)

| Amount ($) | Date Decl. | Ex-Div. Date | Stk. of Record | Payment Date |
|---|---|---|---|---|
| 0.580 | 03/17 | 03/30 | 04/01 | 05/09/11 |
| 0.580 | 05/18 | 06/29 | 07/01 | 08/08/11 |
| 0.580 | 09/15 | 09/29 | 10/03 | 11/14/11 |
| 0.580 | 11/17 | 12/29 | 01/03 | 02/13/12 |

Dividends have been paid since 1954. Source: Company reports.

---

**Please read the Required Disclosures and Analyst Certification on the last page of this report.**

The **McGraw·Hill** Companies

# Air Products and Chemicals Inc.

STANDARD
&POOR'S

## Business Summary November 11, 2011

CORPORATE OVERVIEW. Air Products & Chemicals is one of the largest global producers of industrial gases, and has a large specialty chemicals business. APD focuses on several areas of growth in industrial gases, including electronics, hydrogen for petroleum refining, health care, and Asia. International operations accounted for 54% of FY 10 (Sep.) sales (latest available data).

The industrial gases businesses consists of nitrogen, oxygen, argon, hydrogen, helium, carbon monoxide, synthesis gas and fluorine compounds for both merchant (40.4% of sales and 45.1% of profits in FY 11) and on-site tonnage (32.9%, 29.8%) customers. APD is the world's leading supplier of hydrogen (15% of total sales) and carbon monoxide products (HYCO) and helium. The company operates packaged gas businesses in Europe, Asia and Brazil. The European health care business is reported as part of the merchant gases segment. APD has leading market positions in Spain, Portugal and the U.K. Beginning in FY 08, the tonnage gases segment has also included the polyurethane intermediates business. The business had sales of $340 million in FY 07.

The electronics and performance materials segment (21.4%, 21.4%) supplies specialty gases (nitrogen trifluoride, silane, phosphine), tonnage gases (nitrogen), specialty chemicals, services and equipment to makers of silicone and semiconductors, displays and photovoltaic devices. Performance materials include epoxy and polyurethane additives, specialty amines, and surfactants for coatings, adhesives, personal care and cleaning products, and polyurethanes.

Equipment and energy (4%, 3.7%) includes cryogenic and gas processing equipment for air separation, natural gas liquefaction (LNG), helium distribution, and hydrogen purification. The segment also includes 50%-owned ventures in power cogeneration and flue gas desulfurization facilities.

## Company Financials Fiscal Year Ended Sep. 30

| Per Share Data ($) | 2011 | 2010 | 2009 | 2008 | 2007 | 2006 | 2005 | 2004 | 2003 | 2002 |
|---|---|---|---|---|---|---|---|---|---|---|
| Tangible Book Value | NA | 20.33 | 17.10 | 18.21 | 22.01 | 17.59 | 16.03 | 15.45 | 12.99 | 13.33 |
| Cash Flow | 9.77 | 8.72 | 6.93 | 8.94 | 8.44 | 6.64 | 6.22 | 5.76 | 4.65 | 4.97 |
| Earnings | 5.59 | 4.74 | 3.00 | 4.98 | 4.67 | 3.29 | 3.08 | 2.64 | 1.79 | 2.36 |
| S&P Core Earnings | 5.21 | 4.84 | 2.74 | 4.56 | 4.65 | 2.94 | 3.01 | 2.63 | 1.66 | 1.67 |
| Dividends | 2.23 | 1.92 | 1.79 | 1.70 | 1.48 | 1.34 | 1.25 | 1.04 | 0.88 | 0.82 |
| Payout Ratio | 40% | 41% | 60% | 34% | 32% | 41% | 41% | 39% | 49% | 35% |
| Prices:High | 98.01 | 91.39 | 85.44 | 106.06 | 105.02 | 72.45 | 65.81 | 59.18 | 53.07 | 53.52 |
| Prices:Low | 72.26 | 64.13 | 43.44 | 41.46 | 68.58 | 58.01 | 53.00 | 46.71 | 36.97 | 40.00 |
| P/E Ratio:High | 18 | 19 | 28 | 21 | 22 | 22 | 21 | 22 | 30 | 23 |
| P/E Ratio:Low | 13 | 14 | 14 | 8 | 15 | 18 | 17 | 18 | 21 | 17 |

| Income Statement Analysis (Million $) | 2011 | 2010 | 2009 | 2008 | 2007 | 2006 | 2005 | 2004 | 2003 | 2002 |
|---|---|---|---|---|---|---|---|---|---|---|
| Revenue | 10,082 | 9,026 | 8,256 | 10,415 | 10,038 | 8,850 | 8,144 | 7,411 | 6,297 | 5,401 |
| Operating Income | 2,545 | 2,354 | 1,995 | 2,360 | 2,179 | 1,777 | 1,700 | 1,567 | 1,218 | 1,319 |
| Depreciation | 874 | 863 | 840 | 869 | 840 | 763 | 728 | 715 | 640 | 581 |
| Interest Expense | 116 | 122 | 144 | 184 | 176 | 119 | 110 | 121 | 124 | 122 |
| Pretax Income | 1,661 | 1,394 | 837 | 1,479 | 1,376 | 1,049 | 998 | 851 | 565 | 784 |
| Effective Tax Rate | NA | NA | 22.2% | 24.7% | 21.9% | 25.8% | 26.4% | 26.6% | 26.0% | 30.7% |
| Net Income | 1,253 | 1,029 | 640 | 1,091 | 1,043 | 748 | 712 | 604 | 400 | 525 |
| S&P Core Earnings | 1,134 | 1,050 | 584 | 1,001 | 1,038 | 670 | 695 | 601 | 369 | 369 |

| Balance Sheet & Other Financial Data (Million $) | 2011 | 2010 | 2009 | 2008 | 2007 | 2006 | 2005 | 2004 | 2003 | 2002 |
|---|---|---|---|---|---|---|---|---|---|---|
| Cash | 423 | 374 | 488 | 104 | 42.3 | 35.2 | 55.8 | 146 | 76.2 | 254 |
| Current Assets | 3,190 | 3,013 | 2,998 | 2,848 | 2,858 | 2,613 | 2,415 | 2,417 | 2,068 | 1,909 |
| Total Assets | 14,291 | 13,486 | 13,080 | 12,490 | 12,660 | 11,181 | 10,409 | 10,040 | 9,432 | 8,495 |
| Current Liabilities | 2,342 | 2,239 | 2,504 | 2,212 | 2,423 | 2,323 | 1,943 | 1,706 | 1,581 | 1,256 |
| Long Term Debt | 3,928 | 3,660 | 3,716 | 3,515 | 2,977 | 2,280 | 2,053 | Nil | 2,169 | 2,041 |
| Common Equity | 5,796 | 5,547 | 4,792 | 5,031 | 5,496 | 4,924 | 4,576 | 4,444 | 3,783 | 3,460 |
| Total Capital | 10,081 | 9,540 | 9,098 | 9,309 | 9,362 | 8,215 | 7,644 | 5,401 | 6,845 | 6,411 |
| Capital Expenditures | 1,352 | 1,031 | 1,179 | 1,085 | 1,055 | 1,261 | 930 | 706 | 613 | 628 |
| Cash Flow | 2,127 | 1,893 | 1,480 | 1,960 | 1,883 | 1,511 | 1,440 | 1,319 | 1,040 | 1,106 |
| Current Ratio | 1.4 | 1.4 | 1.2 | 1.3 | 1.2 | 1.1 | 1.2 | 1.4 | 1.3 | 1.5 |
| % Long Term Debt of Capitalization | 39.0 | 38.4 | 40.8 | 37.8 | 31.8 | 27.8 | 26.9 | Nil | 31.7 | 31.8 |
| % Net Income of Revenue | 12.4 | 11.4 | 7.8 | 10.5 | 10.4 | 8.5 | 8.7 | 8.2 | 6.4 | 9.7 |
| % Return on Assets | 9.0 | 7.8 | 5.0 | 8.7 | 8.8 | 6.9 | 7.0 | 6.2 | 4.5 | 6.3 |
| % Return on Equity | 22.1 | 19.9 | 13.0 | 20.7 | 20.0 | 15.8 | 15.8 | 14.7 | 11.1 | 16.0 |

Data as orig reptd.; bef. results of disc opers/spec. items. Per share data adj. for stk. divs.; EPS diluted. E-Estimated. NA-Not Available. NM-Not Meaningful. NR-Not Ranked. UR-Under Review.

**Office:** 7201 Hamilton Boulevard, Allentown, PA 18195-1501.
**Telephone:** 610-481-4911.
**Website:** http://www.airproducts.com
**Chrmn, Pres & CEO:** J.E. McGlade

**COO:** J.M. Pietrantonio
**SVP & CFO:** P.E. Huck
**SVP & General Counsel:** J.D. Stanley
**Chief Acctg Officer & Cntlr:** M.S. Crocco

**Investor Contact:** S.R. Moore (610-481-7461)
**Board Members:** M. L. Baeza, S. K. Carter, W. L. Davis, III, C. C. Deaton, M. J. Donahue, U. O. Fairbairn, W. D. Ford, E. E. Hagenlocker, E. Henkes, J. E. McGlade, M. G. McGlynn, L. S. Smith

**Founded:** 1940
**Domicile:** Delaware
**Employees:** 18,900

The McGraw-Hill Companies

**STANDARD &POOR'S**

# Akamai Technologies Inc

| S&P Recommendation **BUY** ★★★★☆ | Price $27.74 (as of Nov 29, 2011) | 12-Mo. Target Price $35.00 | Investment Style Large-Cap Growth |
|---|---|---|---|

**GICS Sector** Information Technology
**Sub-Industry** Internet Software & Services

**Summary** This company develops and deploys solutions designed to accelerate and improve the delivery of Internet content and applications.

## Key Stock Statistics (Source S&P, Vickers, company reports)

| | | | | | | | |
|---|---|---|---|---|---|---|---|
| 52-Wk Range | $54.65– 18.25 | S&P Oper. EPS 2011E | 1.05 | Market Capitalization(B) | $4.977 | Beta | 0.64 |
| Trailing 12-Month EPS | $1.02 | S&P Oper. EPS 2012E | 1.25 | Yield (%) | Nil | S&P 3-Yr. Proj. EPS CAGR(%) | 19 |
| Trailing 12-Month P/E | 27.2 | P/E on S&P Oper. EPS 2011E | 26.4 | Dividend Rate/Share | Nil | S&P Credit Rating | NR |
| $10K Invested 5 Yrs Ago | $5,215 | Common Shares Outstg. (M) | 179.4 | Institutional Ownership (%) | 80 | | |

## Price Performance

30-Week Mov. Avg. ···· 10-Week Mov. Avg. – – GAAP Earnings vs. Previous Year   Volume Above Avg. STARS
12-Mo. Target Price — Relative Strength — ▲ Up ▼ Down ► No Change   Below Avg.

Options: ASE, CBOE, P, Ph

Analysis prepared by Equity Analyst **Scott Kessler** on Nov 02, 2011, when the stock traded at **$27.64**.

## Highlights

➤ We project that revenues will increase 12% in 2011 and in 2012, reflecting what we consider solid secular growth, driven by the increasing use and importance of the Internet to distribute content and applications, offset somewhat by cyclical uncertainties and pricing pressures related to volume business.

➤ While we expect annual gross margins to trend slightly lower through 2013, we see operating and net margins improving gradually, reflecting a more favorable revenue mix, scale benefits and efficiencies, despite significant investments.

➤ AKAM has made some $450 million in acquisitions since late 2006, enhancing its capabilities in content and application transmission speeds, rich-media distribution, and peer-to-peer networks. In November 2008, it bought acerno to build a more focused advertising business (in a transaction that cost some $84 million). A $150 million buyback program was authorized in April 2011. As of September 2011, AKAM had roughly $1.2 billion of cash and marketable securities and no debt.

## Investment Rationale/Risk

➤ AKAM has been a pioneer in content and application distribution. We believe these areas will continue to grow. We also see notable demand related to online video, cloud computing, and mobile offerings. Advertising and security are also key opportunities, in our view. We also expect significant international expansion. Despite challenges related to the volume business, we expect contract values to benefit from excess activity over time. We view the stock as attractively valued at recent levels.

➤ Risks to our opinion and target price include the potential for weaker demand and pricing across volume-related offerings, and more significant competition (maybe including new entrants) perhaps related to the value-added services area.

➤ Our DCF analysis, with assumptions including a current WACC of 9.4%, average annual growth in free cash flow of 12% from 2011 to 2015, and a terminal growth rate of 3%, leads to an intrinsic value of $35, which is our 12-month target price. We think DCF analysis is the best way to value AKAM, because certain non-cash items are very material to its results.

## Qualitative Risk Assessment

| LOW | MEDIUM | HIGH |
|---|---|---|

Our risk assessment reflects what we view as rapidly evolving technologies, a large cyclical component to the business, and notable and increasing competition.

## Quantitative Evaluations

**S&P Quality Ranking**   B-

| D | C | B- | B | B+ | A- | A | A+ |
|---|---|---|---|---|---|---|---|

**Relative Strength Rank**   **STRONG**

93

LOWEST = 1   HIGHEST = 99

## Revenue/Earnings Data

**Revenue (Million $)**

| | 1Q | 2Q | 3Q | 4Q | Year |
|---|---|---|---|---|---|
| 2011 | 276.0 | 277.0 | 281.9 | -- | -- |
| 2010 | 240.0 | 245.3 | 253.6 | 284.7 | 1,024 |
| 2009 | 210.4 | 204.6 | 206.5 | 238.3 | 859.8 |
| 2008 | 187.0 | 194.0 | 197.4 | 212.6 | 790.9 |
| 2007 | 139.3 | 152.7 | 161.2 | 183.2 | 636.4 |
| 2006 | 90.83 | 100.7 | 111.5 | 125.7 | 428.7 |

**Earnings Per Share ($)**

| | 1Q | 2Q | 3Q | 4Q | Year |
|---|---|---|---|---|---|
| 2011 | 0.26 | 0.25 | 0.23 | E0.30 | E1.05 |
| 2010 | 0.22 | 0.20 | 0.21 | 0.27 | 0.90 |
| 2009 | 0.20 | 0.19 | 0.17 | 0.21 | 0.77 |
| 2008 | 0.20 | 0.19 | 0.18 | 0.22 | 0.79 |
| 2007 | 0.11 | 0.12 | 0.13 | 0.20 | 0.56 |
| 2006 | 0.07 | 0.07 | 0.08 | 0.12 | 0.34 |

Fiscal year ended Dec. 31. Next earnings report expected: Early February. EPS Estimates based on S&P Operating Earnings; historical GAAP earnings are as reported.

## Dividend Data

No cash dividends have been paid.

---

**Please read the Required Disclosures and Analyst Certification on the last page of this report.**

**The McGraw-Hill Companies**

# Akamai Technologies Inc

STANDARD
&POOR'S

## Business Summary November 02, 2011

CORPORATE OVERVIEW. The Internet plays a crucial role in the way entities conduct business, but it was not designed to accommodate the volume or complexity of today's demands. As a result, online information is often delayed or lost.

Akamai Technologies has developed solutions to accelerate and improve the delivery of Internet content and applications. Its solutions are designed to help customers enhance their revenues and reduce costs by maximizing the performance of their online businesses. Advancing website performance and reliability enable AKAM's clients to improve end-user experiences and promote more effective operations. Specifically, AKAM seeks to address issues related to performance, scalability and security. The company offers solutions focused on digital media distribution and storage, content and application delivery, application performance, on-demand managed services, and website intelligence. Importantly, we believe the company's offerings help clients monetize traffic and save/conserve capital.

CORPORATE STRATEGY. AKAM believes it has deployed the world's largest globally distributed computing platform, which includes over 100,000 servers around the world. The company employs its proprietary solutions and specialized technologies such as advanced routing, load balancing, and data collec-

tion and monitoring to deliver customer content and applications. We perceive this platform and the related intellectual property as notable competitive advantages the company will continue to leverage.

Although competition in this area has increased over the past few years, AKAM's focus on both dynamic (i.e., back and forth) distribution and segments beyond media and entertainment help insulate the company from substantial pricing pressures, in our view. Nonetheless, we believe lower-end business is more at risk given additional players entering the market.

We believe recent acquisitions have bolstered the company's base and breadth of technologies related to streaming rich media, enhancing distribution speeds, peer-to-peer networks, and online advertising. We see these areas contributing to significant growth, and expect AKAM to continue pursuing transactions that are not transformational in nature. We note that value-added services have been growing as a percentage of the company's revenues.

## Company Financials  Fiscal Year Ended Dec. 31

| Per Share Data ($) | 2010 | 2009 | 2008 | 2007 | 2006 | 2005 | 2004 | 2003 | 2002 | 2001 |
|---|---|---|---|---|---|---|---|---|---|---|
| Tangible Book Value | 8.59 | 6.81 | 6.04 | 5.47 | 4.10 | 3.19 | NM | NM | NM | NM |
| Cash Flow | 1.61 | 1.32 | 1.30 | 0.93 | 0.58 | 2.25 | 0.37 | 0.17 | -1.01 | -20.40 |
| Earnings | 0.90 | 0.77 | 0.79 | 0.56 | 0.34 | 2.11 | 0.25 | -0.25 | -1.81 | -23.59 |
| S&P Core Earnings | 0.90 | 0.77 | 0.79 | 0.56 | 0.34 | 1.93 | -0.16 | -0.64 | -2.05 | -12.47 |
| Dividends | Nil | Nil | Nil | Nil | Nil | Nil | Nil | Nil | Nil | Nil |
| Payout Ratio | Nil | Nil | Nil | Nil | Nil | Nil | Nil | Nil | Nil | Nil |
| Prices:High | 54.65 | 26.27 | 40.90 | 59.69 | 56.80 | 22.25 | 18.47 | 14.20 | 6.34 | 37.44 |
| Prices:Low | 24.50 | 12.29 | 9.25 | 27.75 | 19.57 | 10.64 | 10.74 | 1.18 | 0.56 | 2.52 |
| P/E Ratio:High | 61 | 34 | 52 | NM | NM | 11 | 74 | NM | NM | NM |
| P/E Ratio:Low | 27 | 16 | 12 | NM | NM | 5 | 43 | NM | NM | NM |

| Income Statement Analysis (Million $) | 2010 | 2009 | 2008 | 2007 | 2006 | 2005 | 2004 | 2003 | 2002 | 2001 |
|---|---|---|---|---|---|---|---|---|---|---|
| Revenue | 1,024 | 860 | 791 | 636 | 429 | 283 | 210 | 161 | 145 | 163 |
| Operating Income | 390 | 348 | 313 | 217 | 124 | 98.5 | 69.2 | 30.1 | -46.3 | -131 |
| Depreciation | 136 | 116 | 98.1 | 71.9 | 45.6 | 25.2 | 20.2 | 49.7 | 90.4 | 330 |
| Interest Expense | 1.70 | 2.84 | 2.83 | 3.09 | 3.17 | 5.33 | 10.2 | 18.3 | 18.4 | 18.9 |
| Pretax Income | 262 | 237 | 235 | 168 | 98.5 | 70.4 | 35.1 | -28.7 | -204 | -2,434 |
| Effective Tax Rate | NA | 38.5% | 38.1% | 40.0% | 41.7% | NM | 2.20% | NM | NM | NM |
| Net Income | 171 | 146 | 145 | 101 | 57.4 | 328 | 34.4 | -29.3 | -204 | -2,436 |
| S&P Core Earnings | 171 | 144 | 145 | 101 | 57.2 | 300 | -19.9 | -75.6 | -231 | -1,286 |

| Balance Sheet & Other Financial Data (Million $) | 2010 | 2009 | 2008 | 2007 | 2006 | 2005 | 2004 | 2003 | 2002 | 2001 |
|---|---|---|---|---|---|---|---|---|---|---|
| Cash | 607 | 566 | 327 | 546 | 270 | 292 | 70.6 | 165 | 115 | 211 |
| Current Assets | 858 | 761 | 502 | 695 | 375 | 355 | 109 | 202 | 142 | 228 |
| Total Assets | 2,353 | 2,107 | 1,881 | 1,656 | 1,248 | 891 | 183 | 279 | 230 | 421 |
| Current Liabilities | 145 | 327 | 100 | 88.4 | 89.3 | 61.9 | 46.8 | 62.7 | 81.1 | 91.3 |
| Long Term Debt | NA | 200 | 200 | 200 | 200 | 200 | 257 | 386 | 301 | 300 |
| Common Equity | 2,178 | 1,758 | 1,569 | 1,359 | 955 | 624 | -126 | -175 | -168 | 17.2 |
| Total Capital | 2,178 | 1,958 | 1,769 | 1,559 | 1,155 | 824 | 131 | 211 | 133 | 317 |
| Capital Expenditures | 192 | 108 | 115 | 100 | 56.8 | 26.9 | 12.3 | 1.42 | 7.25 | 64.5 |
| Cash Flow | 307 | 248 | 243 | 173 | 103 | 353 | 54.6 | 20.5 | -114 | -2,106 |
| Current Ratio | 5.9 | 6.0 | 5.0 | 7.9 | 4.2 | 5.7 | 2.3 | 3.2 | 1.7 | 2.5 |
| % Long Term Debt of Capitalization | Nil | 10.2 | 11.3 | 12.8 | 17.3 | 24.3 | 196.4 | 183.2 | 226.5 | 94.6 |
| % Net Income of Revenue | 16.7 | 17.0 | 18.4 | 15.9 | 13.4 | 115.9 | 16.4 | NM | NM | NM |
| % Return on Assets | 7.7 | 7.3 | 8.2 | 7.0 | 5.4 | 61.1 | 14.9 | NM | NM | NM |
| % Return on Equity | 8.7 | 8.8 | 9.9 | 8.7 | 7.3 | 131.7 | NM | NM | NM | NM |

Data as orig reptd.; bef. results of disc opers/spec. items. Per share data adj. for stk. divs.; EPS diluted. E-Estimated. NA-Not Available. NM-Not Meaningful. NR-Not Ranked. UR-Under Review.

**Office:** 8 Cambridge Center, Cambridge, MA 02142.
**Telephone:** 617-444-3000.
**Email:** ir@akamai.com
**Website:** http://www.akamai.com

**Chrmn:** G.H. Conrades
**Pres & CEO:** P.L. Sagan
**COO:** R. Blumofe
**SVP, CFO & Chief Acctg Officer:** J.D. Sherman

**SVP & CTO:** M.M. Afergan
**Investor Contact:** S. Smith (617-444-2804)
**Board Members:** G. H. Conrades, M. Coyne, II, P. J. Craig, C. K. Goodwin, J. A. Greenthal, P. J. Kight, F. T. Leighton, G. A. Moore, P. L. Sagan, F. V. Salerno, N. O. Seligman

**Founded:** 1998
**Domicile:** Delaware
**Employees:** 2,200

# AK Steel Holding Corp

**STANDARD &POOR'S**

| S&P Recommendation **BUY** ★★★★☆ | Price $7.04 (as of Nov 25, 2011) | 12-Mo. Target Price $9.00 | Investment Style Large-Cap Blend |
|---|---|---|---|

**GICS Sector** Materials
**Sub-Industry** Steel

**Summary** This company produces flat-rolled carbon, stainless and electrical steels for the automotive, appliance, construction, electrical power generation and distribution markets.

## Key Stock Statistics (Source S&P, Vickers, company reports)

| | | | | | | | |
|---|---|---|---|---|---|---|---|
| 52-Wk Range | $17.88– 5.51 | S&P Oper. EPS 2011E | -0.03 | Market Capitalization(B) | $0.776 | Beta | 2.69 |
| Trailing 12-Month EPS | $-0.54 | S&P Oper. EPS 2012E | 1.02 | Yield (%) | 2.84 | S&P 3-Yr. Proj. EPS CAGR(%) | NM |
| Trailing 12-Month P/E | NM | P/E on S&P Oper. EPS 2011E | NM | Dividend Rate/Share | $0.20 | S&P Credit Rating | BB |
| $10K Invested 5 Yrs Ago | $4,620 | Common Shares Outstg. (M) | 110.3 | Institutional Ownership (%) | 70 | | |

## Price Performance

30-Week Mov. Avg. · · · 10-Week Mov. Avg. – – GAAP Earnings vs. Previous Year   Volume Above Avg. STARS
12-Mo. Target Price — Relative Strength   ▲ Up ▼ Down ► No Change   Below Avg.

Options: ASE, CBOE, P, Ph

Analysis prepared by Equity Analyst **Leo J. Larkin** on Nov 22, 2011, when the stock traded at **$7.85**.

## Highlights

▸ Following a projected sales advance of 6.1% in 2011, we look for a 10.5% rise in 2012, reflecting our expectation for another increase in shipment volume and higher revenue per ton. Our forecast rests on several assumptions. First, S&P forecasts real GDP growth of 1.7% in 2012, versus GDP growth of 1.8% projected in 2011, and we see rising demand for durable goods. Second, S&P projects auto sales of 13.4 million units in 2012, up from 12.7 million units estimated for 2011. Third, we think that distributors will make greater additions to inventories in 2012 compared to 2011. Lastly, we expect that sales will be aided by a better product mix.

▸ We look for improved operating income, aided by higher volume, increased revenue per ton and less raw material cost pressure. After interest expense and taxes, we forecast EPS of $1.02 in 2011, versus an operating loss per share of $0.03 projected for 2011.

▸ Longer term, we think earnings will rise on a gradual decline in pension and health care costs, greater internal sourcing of raw materials, and a more lucrative product mix.

## Investment Rationale/Risk

▸ Long term, we view AKS as a special situation turnaround. AKS has reduced funded debt and underfunded pension and health care liabilities. It also has cut its health care and retiree costs, thereby mitigating a sizable cost disadvantage versus other domestic steel rivals. Thus, we think AKS now has a lower, more competitive cost structure, which should help boost EPS over the course of the business cycle. Also, we believe long-term results will benefit from rising demand for AKS's stainless/electrical steel products. We think the stock is attractively valued, recently trading at about 7.7X our 2012 EPS estimate.

▸ Risks to our recommendation and target price include a decline in the volume of shipments and the average realized price per ton in 2012 instead of the gains we currently project.

▸ Applying a multiple of 8.8X to our 2012 EPS estimate, at the low end of the historical range, we arrive at our 12-month target price of $9. On our projected P/E, AKS would trade at a discount to the peer average P/E of 10.4X. We think a discount is warranted given the company's comparatively high ratio of total liabilities to assets.

## Qualitative Risk Assessment

| LOW | MEDIUM | **HIGH** |
|---|---|---|

Our risk assessment reflects AKS's exposure to the auto industry and other cyclical markets, along with its high ratio of total liabilities to assets versus peers. Partially offsetting these factors are AKS's debt reduction and cost cutting in recent years.

## Quantitative Evaluations

**S&P Quality Ranking**   B-

| D | C | **B-** | B | B+ | A- | A | A+ |
|---|---|---|---|---|---|---|---|

**Relative Strength Rank**   WEAK

15   LOWEST = 1   HIGHEST = 99

## Revenue/Earnings Data

**Revenue (Million $)**

| | 1Q | 2Q | 3Q | 4Q | Year |
|---|---|---|---|---|---|
| 2011 | 1,581 | 1,792 | 1,586 | -- | -- |
| 2010 | 1,406 | 1,596 | 1,576 | 1,391 | 5,968 |
| 2009 | 922.2 | 793.6 | 1,041 | 1,320 | 4,077 |
| 2008 | 1,791 | 2,237 | 2,158 | 1,459 | 7,644 |
| 2007 | 1,720 | 1,870 | 1,722 | 1,692 | 7,003 |
| 2006 | 1,436 | 1,497 | 1,554 | 1,582 | 6,069 |

**Earnings Per Share ($)**

| | 1Q | 2Q | 3Q | 4Q | Year |
|---|---|---|---|---|---|
| 2011 | -0.08 | 0.30 | -0.03 | E-0.43 | E-0.03 |
| 2010 | 0.02 | 0.24 | -0.54 | -0.89 | -1.17 |
| 2009 | -0.67 | -0.43 | -0.06 | 0.36 | -0.68 |
| 2008 | 0.90 | 1.29 | 1.67 | -3.88 | 0.04 |
| 2007 | 0.56 | 0.98 | 0.97 | 0.95 | 3.46 |
| 2006 | 0.06 | 0.26 | 0.23 | -0.45 | 0.11 |

Fiscal year ended Dec. 31. Next earnings report expected: NA. EPS Estimates based on S&P Operating Earnings; historical GAAP earnings are as reported.

## Dividend Data (Dates: mm/dd Payment Date: mm/dd/yy)

| Amount ($) | Date Decl. | Ex-Div. Date | Stk. of Record | Payment Date |
|---|---|---|---|---|
| 0.050 | 01/25 | 02/09 | 02/11 | 03/10/11 |
| 0.050 | 04/26 | 05/11 | 05/13 | 06/10/11 |
| 0.050 | 07/26 | 08/11 | 08/15 | 09/01/11 |
| 0.050 | 10/25 | 11/10 | 11/15 | 12/09/11 |

Dividends have been paid since 2008. Source: Company reports.

**Please read the Required Disclosures and Analyst Certification on the last page of this report.**

The **McGraw-Hill** Companies

# AK Steel Holding Corp

STANDARD
&POOR'S

## Business Summary November 22, 2011

CORPORATE OVERVIEW. AK Steel Holding sells premium quality-coated, cold-rolled and hot-rolled carbon steel to the automotive, appliance and manufacturing markets, as well as to the construction industry and independent steel distributors and service centers. The company also finishes flat-rolled carbon and stainless steel at two tube plants into welded steel tubing used in the automotive, large truck and construction markets.

Sales by market in 2010 were: automotive 36% (36% in 2009), appliance, industrial machinery, construction and manufacturing 25% (31%), and distribution and service centers 39% (33%).

Shipments in 2010 totaled 5,660,900 tons, versus 3,935,500 tons in 2009. In 2010, AKS incurred an operating loss per ton of $11, versus an $18 per ton operating loss in 2009.

CORPORATE STRATEGY. The company seeks to achieve sustained profitability by controlling costs and directing its marketing efforts toward those customers that require the highest quality flat-rolled steel with precise just-in-time delivery and technical support. AKS believes that its enhanced product quality and delivery capabilities, and its emphasis on customer technical support and product planning, are areas in which it excels in serving this market segment.

MARKET PROFILE. The primary factors affecting demand for steel products are economic growth in general and growth in demand for durable goods in particular. The two largest end markets for steel products in the U.S. are autos and construction. In 2010, these two markets accounted for 32% of shipments in the U.S. market. Other end markets include appliances, containers, machinery, and oil and gas. Distributors, also known as service centers, accounted for 26% of industry shipments in the U.S. market in 2010. Distributors are the largest single market for the steel industry in the U.S. Because distributors sell to a wide variety of OEMs, it is difficult to track the final destination of much of the industry's shipments. Consequently, demand for steel from the auto, construction and other industries may be higher than the shipment data would suggest. In terms of shipments, the size of the U.S. market was 83.4 million tons in 2010, and AKS's market share was 6.8%. In the U.S. market, consumption decreased at a compound annual rate of 2.8% from 2001 through 2010. Global steel production was 1.41 billion metric tons in 2010, versus 1.23 billion metric tons in 2009.

## Company Financials Fiscal Year Ended Dec. 31

| Per Share Data ($) | 2010 | 2009 | 2008 | 2007 | 2006 | 2005 | 2004 | 2003 | 2002 | 2001 |
|---|---|---|---|---|---|---|---|---|---|---|
| Tangible Book Value | 5.52 | 7.71 | 8.43 | 7.51 | 3.44 | 1.30 | 0.92 | NM | 3.02 | 7.40 |
| Cash Flow | 0.78 | 1.30 | 1.84 | 5.22 | 1.95 | 1.86 | 2.29 | -3.44 | -2.32 | 1.41 |
| Earnings | -1.17 | -0.68 | 0.04 | 3.46 | 0.11 | 0.01 | 0.28 | -5.48 | -4.42 | -0.87 |
| S&P Core Earnings | -1.49 | -0.88 | 2.41 | 3.43 | 1.00 | 0.84 | 2.70 | -2.71 | -1.06 | -1.89 |
| Dividends | 0.20 | 0.20 | 0.20 | Nil | Nil | Nil | Nil | Nil | Nil | 0.13 |
| Payout Ratio | NM | NM | 500% | Nil | Nil | Nil | Nil | Nil | Nil | NM |
| Prices:High | 26.75 | 24.27 | 73.07 | 53.97 | 17.31 | 18.23 | 16.00 | 8.90 | 14.85 | 15.00 |
| Prices:Low | 15.97 | 5.39 | 5.20 | 16.13 | 7.58 | 6.23 | 3.65 | 1.74 | 6.45 | 7.50 |
| P/E Ratio:High | NM | NM | NM | 16 | NM | NM | 57 | NM | NM | NM |
| P/E Ratio:Low | NM | NM | NM | 5 | NM | NM | 13 | NM | NM | NM |

| Income Statement Analysis (Million $) | | | | | | | | | | |
|---|---|---|---|---|---|---|---|---|---|---|
| Revenue | 5,968 | 4,077 | 7,644 | 7,003 | 6,069 | 5,647 | 5,217 | 4,042 | 4,289 | 3,994 |
| Operating Income | 153 | 147 | 930 | 860 | 409 | 397 | 139 | 155 | 331 | 370 |
| Depreciation | 214 | 217 | 202 | 196 | 204 | 205 | 219 | 222 | 225 | 245 |
| Interest Expense | 33.0 | 37.0 | 50.9 | 68.3 | 89.1 | 86.8 | 110 | 118 | 128 | 133 |
| Pretax Income | -175 | -98.0 | -6.90 | 591 | -3.10 | 38.0 | -193 | -241 | -803 | -147 |
| Effective Tax Rate | NA | 20.4% | NM | 34.4% | NM | NM | NM | NM | NM | NM |
| Net Income | -129 | -74.6 | 4.00 | 388 | 12.0 | -0.80 | 30.5 | -594 | -476 | -92.4 |
| S&P Core Earnings | -163 | -97.0 | 269 | 385 | 110 | 92.4 | 295 | -326 | -125 | -204 |

| Balance Sheet & Other Financial Data (Million $) | | | | | | | | | | |
|---|---|---|---|---|---|---|---|---|---|---|
| Cash | 217 | 462 | 563 | 714 | 519 | 520 | 377 | 54.7 | 283 | 101 |
| Current Assets | 1,404 | 1,630 | 2,003 | 2,427 | 2,548 | 2,246 | 2,107 | 1,358 | 1,700 | 1,548 |
| Total Assets | 4,189 | 4,275 | 4,677 | 5,197 | 5,518 | 5,488 | 5,453 | 5,026 | 5,400 | 5,226 |
| Current Liabilities | 844 | 741 | 734 | 973 | 932 | 903 | 747 | 779 | 860 | 954 |
| Long Term Debt | 651 | 606 | 633 | 653 | 1,115 | 1,115 | 1,110 | 1,198 | 1,260 | 1,325 |
| Common Equity | 645 | 881 | 963 | 875 | 417 | 220 | 197 | -52.8 | 529 | 1,021 |
| Total Capital | 1,292 | 1,487 | 1,596 | 1,527 | 1,532 | 1,335 | 1,307 | 1,145 | 1,789 | 2,358 |
| Capital Expenditures | 266 | 134 | 167 | 104 | 76.2 | 174 | 98.8 | 79.6 | 93.8 | 109 |
| Cash Flow | 85.0 | 142 | 206 | 584 | 216 | 204 | 250 | -373 | -250 | 152 |
| Current Ratio | 1.7 | 2.2 | 2.7 | 2.5 | 2.7 | 2.5 | 2.8 | 1.7 | 2.0 | 1.6 |
| % Long Term Debt of Capitalization | 50.3 | 40.8 | 39.6 | 42.7 | 72.8 | 83.5 | 84.9 | 104.6 | 70.4 | 56.2 |
| % Net Income of Revenue | NM | NM | 0.1 | 5.5 | NM | NM | NM | NM | NM | NM |
| % Return on Assets | NM | NM | 0.1 | 7.2 | NM | NM | NM | NM | NM | NM |
| % Return on Equity | NM | NM | 0.4 | 60.0 | NM | NM | NM | NM | NM | NM |

Data as orig reptd.; bef. results of disc opers/spec. items. Per share data adj. for stk. divs.; EPS diluted. E-Estimated. NA-Not Available. NM-Not Meaningful. NR-Not Ranked. UR-Under Review.

**Office:** 9227 Centre Pointe Drive, West Chester, OH 45069.
**Telephone:** 513-425-5000.
**Website:** http://www.aksteel.com
**Chrmn, Pres & CEO:** J.L. Wainscott

**Chief Acctg Officer & Cntlr:** R.S. Williams
**Secy & General Counsel:** D.C. Horn
**Investor Contact:** A.E. Ferrara, Jr. (513-425-2888)

**Board Members:** R. A. Abdoo, J. S. Brinzo, D. C. Cuneo, W. K. Gerber, B. Hill, R. H. Jenkins, M. Michael, III, S. D. Peterson, J. A. Thomson, J. L. Wainscott

**Founded:** 1900
**Domicile:** Delaware
**Employees:** 6,600

The McGraw-Hill Companies

# Alcoa Inc

STANDARD &POOR'S

| S&P Recommendation | **BUY** ★★★★☆ | Price $8.95 (as of Nov 25, 2011) | 12-Mo. Target Price $13.00 | Investment Style Large-Cap Value |
|---|---|---|---|---|

**GICS Sector** Materials
**Sub-Industry** Aluminum

**Summary** Alcoa is one of the world's largest producers of aluminum and alumina.

## Key Stock Statistics (Source S&P, Vickers, company reports)

| | | | | | | | | |
|---|---|---|---|---|---|---|---|---|
| 52-Wk Range | $18.47– 8.45 | S&P Oper. EPS 2011E | 0.81 | Market Capitalization(B) | $9.526 | Beta | | 2.09 |
| Trailing 12-Month EPS | $0.95 | S&P Oper. EPS 2012E | 0.96 | Yield (%) | 1.34 | S&P 3-Yr. Proj. EPS CAGR(%) | | 38 |
| Trailing 12-Month P/E | 9.4 | P/E on S&P Oper. EPS 2011E | 11.0 | Dividend Rate/Share | $0.12 | S&P Credit Rating | | BBB- |
| $10K Invested 5 Yrs Ago | $3,206 | Common Shares Outstg. (M) | 1,064.3 | Institutional Ownership (%) | 64 | | | |

## Price Performance

30-Week Mov. Avg. ··· 10-Week Mov. Avg. - - GAAP Earnings vs. Previous Year   Volume Above Avg. STARS
12-Mo. Target Price — Relative Strength — ▲ Up ▼ Down ▶ No Change   Below Avg. ★

Options: ASE, CBOE, P, Ph

Analysis prepared by Equity Analyst **Leo J. Larkin** on Oct 13, 2011, when the stock traded at **$10.05**.

## Qualitative Risk Assessment

| LOW | **MEDIUM** | HIGH |
|---|---|---|

Our risk assessment reflects AA's exposure to cyclical markets such as autos and construction, offset by its large shares of the markets it serves.

## Quantitative Evaluations

**S&P Quality Ranking** B-

| D | C | **B-** | B | B+ | A- | A | A+ |
|---|---|---|---|---|---|---|---|

**Relative Strength Rank** WEAK

16

LOWEST = 1     HIGHEST = 99

## Revenue/Earnings Data

**Revenue (Million $)**

| | 1Q | 2Q | 3Q | 4Q | Year |
|---|---|---|---|---|---|
| 2011 | 5,958 | 6,585 | 6,419 | -- | -- |
| 2010 | 4,887 | 5,187 | 5,287 | 5,652 | 21,013 |
| 2009 | 4,147 | 4,244 | 4,615 | 5,433 | 18,439 |
| 2008 | 6,998 | 7,245 | 6,970 | 5,688 | 26,901 |
| 2007 | 7,908 | 8,066 | 7,387 | 7,387 | 30,748 |
| 2006 | 7,244 | 7,959 | 7,631 | 7,840 | 30,379 |

**Earnings Per Share ($)**

| | | | | | |
|---|---|---|---|---|---|
| 2011 | 0.27 | 0.28 | 0.15 | E0.06 | E0.81 |
| 2010 | -0.19 | 0.13 | 0.06 | 0.24 | 0.25 |
| 2009 | -0.59 | -0.32 | -0.07 | -0.27 | -1.06 |
| 2008 | 0.36 | 0.67 | 0.37 | -1.16 | 0.28 |
| 2007 | 0.77 | 0.81 | 0.64 | 0.74 | 2.95 |
| 2006 | 0.70 | 0.86 | 0.62 | 0.29 | 2.47 |

Fiscal year ended Dec. 31. Next earnings report expected: Mid January. EPS Estimates based on S&P Operating Earnings; historical GAAP earnings are as reported.

## Highlights

➤ Following a projected sales rise of 19% in 2011, we forecast a gain of 2.6% in 2012. For 2012, S&P looks for U.S. real GDP growth of 1.9%, versus a projected gain of 1.6% in 2011, and global GDP growth of 3.1%, versus estimated growth of 2.7% in 2011. We look for increased volume and prices for alumina and aluminum in 2012 on another increase in global demand. Also, we think that the aluminum price will be aided by a gradual decline in metal exchange inventories. Finally, we anticipate higher volume in the downstream businesses on a recovery of demand in Europe and further growth in durable goods demand in the rest of the world.

➤ We look for increased operating profit on higher realized prices and volume for aluminum and alumina and production from new lower cost plants. After lower interest expense and taxes, we estimate operating EPS of $0.96 in 2012, versus $0.81 projected for 2011.

➤ Longer term, we think earnings will rise on gradually improving aluminum industry fundamentals and a shift to lower-cost aluminum plants.

## Investment Rationale/Risk

➤ We think AA is attractively valued, recently trading at 10.4X our 2012 EPS estimate. Following what we believe was a cyclical earnings trough in 2010, we look for higher EPS in 2011 and 2012. We view AA as a special situation turnaround and a vehicle to benefit from an expected secular rise in demand for aluminum. In our opinion, AA's cost cutting, together with increased production from new lower-cost facilities, will result in a lower breakeven point, which in turn should lead to greater profitability and generally less volatile earnings over the course of the business cycle. We also note that AA continues to reduce its balance sheet leverage and is placing greater focus on boosting free cash flow.

➤ Risks to our recommendation and target price include a decline in the price of aluminum in 2012 instead of the increase we project.

➤ Our 12-month target price of $13 is based on our view that the stock will trade at 13.5X our 2012 EPS estimate. Based on our target P/E, AA would trade beneath the low end of its historical range of the past 10 years and at 1.6X its tangible book value at the end of 2011's third quarter.

## Dividend Data (Dates: mm/dd Payment Date: mm/dd/yy)

| Amount ($) | Date Decl. | Ex-Div. Date | Stk. of Record | Payment Date |
|---|---|---|---|---|
| 0.030 | 01/21 | 02/02 | 02/04 | 02/25/11 |
| 0.030 | 05/05 | 05/12 | 05/16 | 05/25/11 |
| 0.030 | 07/22 | 08/03 | 08/05 | 08/25/11 |
| 0.030 | 09/30 | 11/02 | 11/04 | 11/25/11 |

Dividends have been paid since 1939. Source: Company reports.

# Alcoa Inc

**STANDARD & POOR'S**

## Business Summary October 13, 2011

CORPORATE OVERVIEW. Alcoa is one of the world's largest producers of primary aluminum as well as one of the world's largest suppliers of alumina, an intermediate raw material used to make aluminum. In 2010, primary aluminum production totaled 3.59 million metric tons, versus 3.56 million metric tons in 2009; and alumina production totaled 15.9 million metric tons, versus 14.3 million metric tons in 2009.

MARKET PROFILE. The primary factor affecting demand for aluminum products is economic growth, in general, and growth in demand for durable goods, in particular. The three largest end markets for aluminum in North America are transportation, containers/packaging, and construction. In 2009 (latest available), these markets accounted for 62% of shipments in North America. In terms of primary production, the size of the world market was 24.3 million metric tons in 2010. Alcoa's market share was 14.8%. From 2001 through 2010, global consumption rose at a compound annual growth rate (CAGR) of 6.0%.

COMPETITIVE LANDSCAPE. Alcoa's direct competitors in the aluminum market are Aleris International, Inc., Aluminum Corp. of China, Century Aluminum,

Kaiser Aluminum, Norsk Hydro, United Company RUSAL and Quanex. Indirect competitors include mining companies that have aluminum and alumina operations, such as Vale, BHP Billiton and Rio Tinto. Led mostly by Alcoa and Alcan (now a subsidiary of Rio Tinto), consolidation of the industry accelerated in the late 1990s and thereafter.

However, the price of aluminum in the last economic expansion that ended in 2008's second half lagged the gains in other base metals such as carbon steel, copper and nickel by a wide margin. In our view, the reason for the less buoyant aluminum price is that exports from China have kept the aluminum market in overall surplus. Beginning in 2002, China became a net exporter of aluminum, and we believe that its production has become a drag on the aluminum price.

## Company Financials Fiscal Year Ended Dec. 31

| Per Share Data ($) | 2010 | 2009 | 2008 | 2007 | 2006 | 2005 | 2004 | 2003 | 2002 | 2001 |
|---|---|---|---|---|---|---|---|---|---|---|
| Tangible Book Value | 7.75 | 6.90 | 7.61 | 12.75 | 8.53 | 6.96 | 6.72 | 5.36 | 3.27 | 4.96 |
| Cash Flow | 1.67 | 0.35 | 1.79 | 4.42 | 3.96 | 2.85 | 2.98 | 2.61 | 3.20 | 2.49 |
| Earnings | 0.25 | -1.06 | 0.28 | 2.95 | 2.47 | 1.40 | 1.60 | 1.20 | 0.58 | 1.05 |
| S&P Core Earnings | 0.28 | -1.09 | -0.26 | 1.74 | 2.46 | 1.05 | 1.52 | 0.92 | -0.17 | 0.17 |
| Dividends | 0.12 | 0.26 | 0.68 | 0.68 | 0.60 | 0.60 | 0.60 | 0.60 | 0.60 | 0.60 |
| Payout Ratio | 48% | NM | 243% | 23% | 24% | 43% | 38% | 50% | 103% | 57% |
| Prices:High | 17.60 | 16.51 | 44.77 | 48.77 | 36.96 | 32.29 | 39.44 | 38.92 | 39.75 | 45.71 |
| Prices:Low | 9.81 | 4.97 | 6.80 | 28.09 | 26.39 | 22.28 | 28.51 | 18.45 | 17.62 | 27.36 |
| P/E Ratio:High | 70 | NM | NM | 17 | 15 | 23 | 25 | 32 | 69 | 44 |
| P/E Ratio:Low | 39 | NM | NM | 10 | 11 | 16 | 18 | 15 | 30 | 26 |

| Income Statement Analysis (Million $) | | | | | | | | | | |
|---|---|---|---|---|---|---|---|---|---|---|
| Revenue | 21,013 | 18,439 | 26,901 | 30,748 | 30,379 | 26,159 | 23,478 | 21,504 | 20,263 | 22,859 |
| Operating Income | 2,705 | 359 | 3,505 | 4,779 | 5,410 | 3,398 | 3,397 | 2,885 | 2,663 | 3,523 |
| Depreciation | 1,451 | 1,311 | 1,234 | 1,268 | 1,280 | 1,267 | 1,212 | 1,202 | 2,224 | 1,253 |
| Interest Expense | 494 | 470 | 574 | 401 | 384 | 339 | 270 | 314 | 350 | 393 |
| Pretax Income | 548 | -1,498 | 792 | 4,491 | 3,432 | 1,933 | 2,204 | 1,669 | 925 | 1,641 |
| Effective Tax Rate | NA | NM | 43.2% | 34.6% | 24.3% | 22.8% | 25.3% | 24.2% | 31.6% | 32.0% |
| Net Income | 262 | -985 | 229 | 2,571 | 2,161 | 1,233 | 1,402 | 1,034 | 498 | 908 |
| S&P Core Earnings | 298 | -1,021 | -210 | 1,511 | 2,154 | 924 | 1,334 | 777 | -143 | 146 |

| Balance Sheet & Other Financial Data (Million $) | | | | | | | | | | |
|---|---|---|---|---|---|---|---|---|---|---|
| Cash | 1,543 | 1,481 | 762 | 483 | 506 | 762 | 457 | 576 | 344 | 512 |
| Current Assets | 6,869 | 7,022 | 8,150 | 8,086 | 9,157 | 8,790 | 7,493 | 6,740 | 6,313 | 6,792 |
| Total Assets | 39,254 | 38,455 | 37,822 | 38,803 | 37,183 | 33,696 | 32,609 | 31,711 | 29,810 | 28,355 |
| Current Liabilities | 5,236 | 5,414 | 7,279 | 7,166 | 7,281 | 7,368 | 6,298 | 5,084 | 4,461 | 5,003 |
| Long Term Debt | 8,842 | 8,974 | 8,509 | 6,371 | 5,910 | 5,279 | 5,346 | 6,692 | 8,365 | 6,388 |
| Common Equity | 13,632 | 12,365 | 11,680 | 15,961 | 14,576 | 13,318 | 13,245 | 12,020 | 9,872 | 10,614 |
| Total Capital | 26,235 | 24,910 | 23,162 | 25,392 | 23,103 | 20,892 | 20,852 | 20,911 | 20,087 | 18,927 |
| Capital Expenditures | 1,015 | 1,617 | 3,438 | 3,636 | 3,201 | 2,124 | 1,142 | 863 | 1,263 | 1,177 |
| Cash Flow | 1,713 | 324 | 1,461 | 3,839 | 3,441 | 2,498 | 2,612 | 2,234 | 2,720 | 2,159 |
| Current Ratio | 1.3 | 1.3 | 1.1 | 1.1 | 1.3 | 1.2 | 1.2 | 1.3 | 1.4 | 1.4 |
| % Long Term Debt of Capitalization | 33.7 | 36.0 | 36.7 | 25.1 | 25.6 | 25.3 | 25.6 | 32.0 | 41.6 | 33.8 |
| % Net Income of Revenue | 1.3 | NM | 0.9 | 8.3 | 7.1 | 4.7 | 6.0 | 4.8 | 2.5 | 4.0 |
| % Return on Assets | 0.7 | NM | 0.6 | 6.7 | 6.1 | 3.7 | 4.4 | 3.4 | 1.7 | 3.0 |
| % Return on Equity | 2.0 | NM | 1.7 | 10.2 | 15.5 | 9.3 | 11.1 | 9.4 | 4.9 | 8.2 |

Data as orig reptd.; bef. results of disc opers/spec. items. Per share data adj. for stk. divs.; EPS diluted. E-Estimated. NA-Not Available. NM-Not Meaningful. NR-Not Ranked. UR-Under Review.

**Office:** 390 Park Ave, New York, NY 10022-4608.
**Telephone:** 212-836-2674.
**Email:** investor.relations@alcoa.com
**Website:** http://www.alcoa.com

**Chrmn & CEO:** K. Kleinfeld
**EVP & CFO:** C.D. McLane, Jr.
**CTO:** R. Kilmer
**Treas:** P. Hong

**Secy:** D.C. Dabney
**Board Members:** A. D. Collins, Jr., K. S. Fuller, J. M. Gueron, K. Kleinfeld, M. G. Morris, E. S. O'Neal, J. W. Owens, P. A. Russo, R. N. Tata, E. Z. de Leon

**Founded:** 1888
**Domicile:** Pennsylvania
**Employees:** 59,000

**STANDARD &POOR'S**

# Allegheny Technologies Inc

| S&P Recommendation **BUY** ★★★★☆ | Price $43.33 (as of Nov 25, 2011) | 12-Mo. Target Price $55.00 | Investment Style Large-Cap Blend |
| --- | --- | --- | --- |

**GICS Sector** Materials
**Sub-Industry** Steel

**Summary** This company is a leading producer of specialty metals for a wide variety of end markets.

## Key Stock Statistics (Source S&P, Vickers, company reports)

| | | | | | | | |
| --- | --- | --- | --- | --- | --- | --- | --- |
| 52-Wk Range | $73.53– 30.79 | S&P Oper. EPS 2011E | 2.45 | Market Capitalization(B) | $4.609 | Beta | 1.84 |
| Trailing 12-Month EPS | $1.88 | S&P Oper. EPS 2012E | 3.98 | Yield (%) | 1.66 | S&P 3-Yr. Proj. EPS CAGR(%) | 65 |
| Trailing 12-Month P/E | 23.1 | P/E on S&P Oper. EPS 2011E | 17.7 | Dividend Rate/Share | $0.72 | S&P Credit Rating | BBB- |
| $10K Invested 5 Yrs Ago | $5,613 | Common Shares Outstg. (M) | 106.4 | Institutional Ownership (%) | 82 | | |

## Price Performance

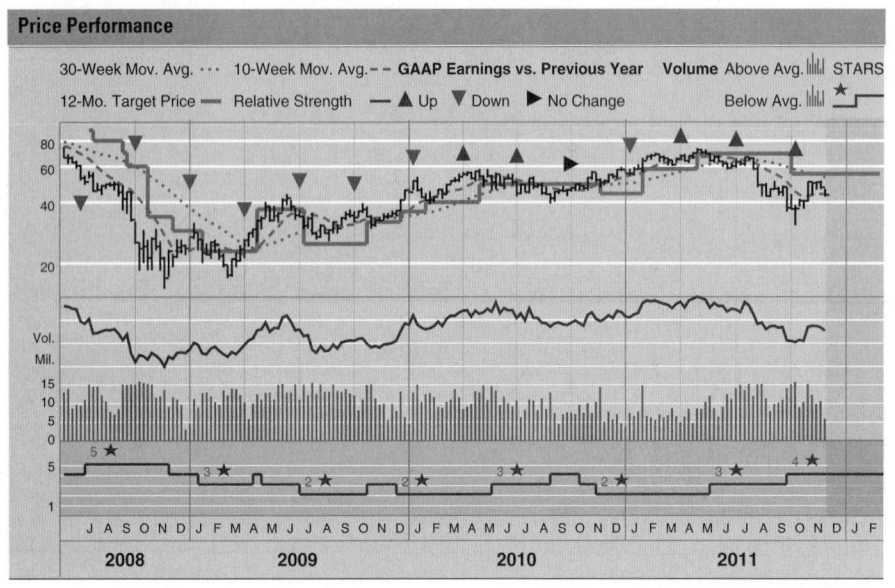

30-Week Mov. Avg. · · · 10-Week Mov. Avg. - - **GAAP Earnings vs. Previous Year**   Volume  Above Avg. |||| STARS
12-Mo. Target Price — Relative Strength — ▲ Up ▼ Down ▶ No Change    Below Avg. |||| ★

Options: ASE, CBOE, P, Ph

Analysis prepared by Equity Analyst **Leo J. Larkin** on Sep 26, 2011, when the stock traded at **$37.44**.

## Highlights

➤ Including Ladish Inc. from its acquisition in early May 2011, we look for a 31% increase in sales in 2011, following 2010's rise of 33%. Our forecast reflects several assumptions. First, S&P estimates U.S. GDP growth of 1.6% in 2011, versus GDP growth of 3.0% in 2010, which we believe will lead to another rise in demand for durable goods and stainless steel. Second, we think distributors will restock stainless steel products in 2011. Third, we expect sales of high-performance metals to rise on increased aircraft output, rebuilding of inventory in the aerospace supply chain, and greater spending by the oil and gas industry.

➤ We look for another sizable increase in operating profit in 2011, mostly from higher volume and prices. After interest expense and taxes, we project operating EPS of $2.85 for 2011, versus 2010's operating EPS of $1.01, which excludes unusual expense items totaling $0.29.

➤ We think that consolidation in the stainless steel industry, along with an upturn in the aerospace industry and other capital goods markets, will boost ATI's long-term earnings.

## Investment Rationale/Risk

➤ We believe the concentration of stainless steel production in fewer hands will lead to better industry pricing discipline and less volatility in sales and profits over the business cycle. In our view, a decline in volatility should ultimately lead to higher valuations for ATI and other stainless steel producers. We also see secular growth in the aerospace industry and other capital goods markets such as oil and gas, mining, and electrical power generation. Following a sharp decline, we think ATI shares are attractively valued at a recent 9.4X our 2012 EPS estimate, with a dividend yield of 1.9%.

➤ Risks to our recommendation and target price include a decline in demand for stainless steel and high performance metals in 2012 instead of the increases we currently project.

➤ Applying a multiple of 13.8X to our 2012 EPS estimate, toward the low end of ATI's range of the past 10 years, our 12-month target price for these volatile shares is $55. On this projected multiple, ATI would trade at a discount to the group average for specialty metals peers.

## Qualitative Risk Assessment

| LOW | MEDIUM | HIGH |
| --- | --- | --- |

Our risk assessment reflects ATI's exposure to cyclical markets such as aerospace and chemical processing, along with volatile raw material costs. Offsetting these factors is our view of the company's solid share of the markets it serves and its moderate balance sheet leverage.

## Quantitative Evaluations

**S&P Quality Ranking**   B

| D | C | B- | **B** | B+ | A- | A | A+ |
| --- | --- | --- | --- | --- | --- | --- | --- |

**Relative Strength Rank**   MODERATE

| 50 |
| --- |

LOWEST = 1                    HIGHEST = 99

## Revenue/Earnings Data

**Revenue (Million $)**

| | 1Q | 2Q | 3Q | 4Q | Year |
| --- | --- | --- | --- | --- | --- |
| 2011 | 1,227 | 1,352 | 1,353 | -- | -- |
| 2010 | 899.4 | 1,052 | 1,059 | 1,038 | 4,048 |
| 2009 | 831.6 | 710.0 | 697.6 | 815.7 | 3,055 |
| 2008 | 1,343 | 1,461 | 1,392 | 1,113 | 5,310 |
| 2007 | 1,373 | 1,471 | 1,335 | 1,274 | 5,453 |
| 2006 | 1,041 | 1,211 | 1,288 | 1,397 | 4,937 |

**Earnings Per Share ($)**

| | | | | | |
| --- | --- | --- | --- | --- | --- |
| 2011 | 0.54 | 0.59 | 0.56 | E0.53 | E2.45 |
| 2010 | 0.18 | 0.36 | 0.01 | 0.15 | 0.72 |
| 2009 | 0.06 | -0.14 | 0.01 | 0.36 | 0.32 |
| 2008 | 1.40 | 1.66 | 1.45 | 1.15 | 5.67 |
| 2007 | 1.92 | 2.00 | 1.88 | 1.45 | 7.26 |
| 2006 | 1.00 | 1.37 | 1.58 | 1.63 | 5.59 |

Fiscal year ended Dec. 31. Next earnings report expected: Late January. EPS Estimates based on S&P Operating Earnings; historical GAAP earnings are as reported.

## Dividend Data (Dates: mm/dd Payment Date: mm/dd/yy)

| Amount ($) | Date Decl. | Ex-Div. Date | Stk. of Record | Payment Date |
| --- | --- | --- | --- | --- |
| 0.180 | 12/10 | 12/17 | 12/21 | 12/30/10 |
| 0.180 | 02/25 | 03/09 | 03/11 | 03/29/11 |
| 0.180 | 04/29 | 05/24 | 05/26 | 06/17/11 |
| 0.180 | 09/09 | 09/16 | 09/20 | 09/28/11 |

Dividends have been paid since 1996. Source: Company reports.

---

**Please read the Required Disclosures and Analyst Certification on the last page of this report.**

*The* **McGraw·Hill** *Companies*

# Allegheny Technologies Inc

**STANDARD &POOR'S**

## Business Summary September 26, 2011

In November 1999, Allegheny Teledyne Inc. spun off all of the common stock of Teledyne Technologies Inc. (TDY 47, NR) and Water Pik Technologies, Inc. to ATI stockholders, and changed its name to Allegheny Technologies Inc.

Following the spin-offs, ATI operates in three segments: Flat-Rolled Products, High Performance Metals, and Engineered Products. Markets for the three units include aerospace, oil and gas, transportation, food, chemical processing, consumer products, medical, and power generation.

The Flat-Rolled Products segment (58% of 2010 sales; 24% of operating profits) consists of Allegheny Ludlum Corp., Rodney Metals, the Allegheny Rodney Strip division of Allegheny Ludlum, and the company's interest in a Chinese joint venture, Shanghai STAL Precision Stainless Steel Ltd. The companies in this segment produce, convert and distribute stainless steel sheet, strip and plate, precision rolled strip products, flat-rolled nickel-based alloys and titanium, silicon electrical steels and tool steels.

Shipments totaled 548,565 tons in 2010, versus 421,073 tons in 2009. The average realized price per ton was $3,888, versus $3,600 in 2009. Operating profits totaled $85.9 million in 2010, versus $71.3 million in 2009.

Competitors in flat-rolled stainless include AK Steel Holding and North American Stainless.

The High Performance Metals segment (33%; 72% of operating profit) consists of Allvac, Allvac Ltd., Oremet-Wah Chang, Titanium Industries, and Rome Metals. These companies produce, convert and distribute nickel- and cobalt-based alloys and superalloys, titanium and titanium-based alloys, zirconium and zirconium chemicals, hafnium and niobium, tantalum and other special metals, primarily in long-product form. The unit's titanium products are sold mostly to aircraft and jet engine manufacturers.

Shipments of titanium mill products totaled 25,457 lbs. in 2010, versus 23,588 lbs. in 2009; shipments of nickel-based alloys were 37,272 lbs. in 2010, versus 32,562 lbs. in 2009; shipments of exotic alloys totaled 4,382 lbs. in 2010, versus 5,067 lbs. in 2009. Operating profits totaled $257.8 million in 2010, versus $234.7 million in 2009.

Competitors in high performance and exotic metals include Titanium Metals Corp., RTI International Metals, Verkhnaya Salda Metallurgical Production Organization and UNITI and certain Japanese producers in the industrial and emerging markets.

## Company Financials Fiscal Year Ended Dec. 31

| Per Share Data ($) | 2010 | 2009 | 2008 | 2007 | 2006 | 2005 | 2004 | 2003 | 2002 | 2001 |
|---|---|---|---|---|---|---|---|---|---|---|
| Tangible Book Value | 18.61 | 18.40 | 18.19 | 19.82 | 12.71 | 6.11 | 2.30 | NM | 3.15 | 9.42 |
| Cash Flow | 2.15 | 1.53 | 6.71 | 8.26 | 6.48 | 4.47 | 1.00 | -2.96 | 0.30 | 0.91 |
| Earnings | 0.72 | 0.32 | 5.67 | 7.26 | 5.59 | 3.59 | 0.22 | -3.87 | -0.82 | -0.31 |
| S&P Core Earnings | 0.90 | 0.73 | 4.42 | 7.12 | 5.92 | 3.76 | 0.26 | -3.19 | -2.17 | -2.09 |
| Dividends | 0.72 | 0.72 | 0.72 | 0.57 | 0.43 | 0.28 | 0.24 | 0.24 | 0.66 | 0.80 |
| Payout Ratio | 100% | NM | 13% | 8% | 8% | 8% | 109% | NM | NM | NM |
| Prices:High | 59.41 | 46.31 | 87.32 | 119.70 | 98.72 | 36.66 | 23.48 | 14.00 | 19.10 | 21.07 |
| Prices:Low | 39.00 | 16.92 | 15.00 | 80.00 | 35.47 | 17.30 | 8.64 | 2.10 | 5.21 | 12.50 |
| P/E Ratio:High | 83 | NM | 15 | 16 | 18 | 10 | NM | NM | NM | NM |
| P/E Ratio:Low | 54 | NM | 3 | 11 | 6 | 5 | NM | NM | NM | NM |

| Income Statement Analysis (Million $) | 2010 | 2009 | 2008 | 2007 | 2006 | 2005 | 2004 | 2003 | 2002 | 2001 |
|---|---|---|---|---|---|---|---|---|---|---|
| Revenue | 4,048 | 3,055 | 5,310 | 5,453 | 4,937 | 3,540 | 2,733 | 1,937 | 1,908 | 2,128 |
| Operating Income | 327 | 211 | 973 | 1,256 | 970 | 452 | 87.7 | -110 | 65.0 | 166 |
| Depreciation | 142 | 133 | 104 | 103 | 84.2 | 77.3 | 76.1 | 74.6 | 90.0 | 98.6 |
| Interest Expense | 62.7 | 21.4 | 38.3 | 4.80 | 23.3 | 38.6 | 35.5 | 27.7 | 34.3 | 29.3 |
| Pretax Income | 126 | 64.9 | 860 | 1,147 | 869 | 307 | 19.8 | -280 | -104 | -36.4 |
| Effective Tax Rate | NA | 41.5% | 34.2% | 34.9% | 34.2% | NM | NM | NM | NM | NM |
| Net Income | 70.7 | 31.7 | 566 | 747 | 572 | 362 | 19.8 | -313 | -65.8 | -25.2 |
| S&P Core Earnings | 88.7 | 71.5 | 441 | 733 | 605 | 378 | 23.3 | -258 | -176 | -168 |

| Balance Sheet & Other Financial Data (Million $) | 2010 | 2009 | 2008 | 2007 | 2006 | 2005 | 2004 | 2003 | 2002 | 2001 |
|---|---|---|---|---|---|---|---|---|---|---|
| Cash | 432 | 709 | 470 | 623 | 502 | 363 | 251 | 79.6 | 59.4 | 33.7 |
| Current Assets | 2,115 | 1,998 | 1,929 | 2,249 | 1,988 | 1,484 | 1,160 | 743 | 812 | 926 |
| Total Assets | 4,494 | 4,346 | 4,170 | 4,096 | 3,282 | 2,732 | 2,316 | 1,885 | 2,093 | 2,643 |
| Current Liabilities | 791 | 625 | 694 | 704 | 646 | 561 | 493 | 395 | 342 | 333 |
| Long Term Debt | 922 | 1,038 | 495 | 507 | 530 | 547 | 553 | 504 | 509 | 573 |
| Common Equity | 2,041 | 2,012 | 1,961 | 2,224 | 1,493 | 800 | 426 | 175 | 449 | 945 |
| Total Capital | 3,193 | 3,161 | 2,524 | 2,731 | 2,023 | 1,347 | 979 | 679 | 958 | 1,671 |
| Capital Expenditures | 219 | 415 | 516 | 447 | 235 | 90.1 | 49.9 | 74.4 | 48.7 | 104 |
| Cash Flow | 212 | 150 | 670 | 850 | 656 | 439 | 95.9 | -239 | 24.2 | 73.4 |
| Current Ratio | 2.7 | 3.2 | 2.8 | 3.2 | 3.1 | 2.6 | 2.4 | 1.9 | 2.4 | 2.8 |
| % Long Term Debt of Capitalization | 28.9 | 32.8 | 19.6 | 18.6 | 26.2 | 40.6 | 56.5 | 74.3 | 53.2 | 34.3 |
| % Net Income of Revenue | 1.8 | 1.0 | 10.7 | 13.7 | 11.6 | 10.2 | 0.7 | NM | NM | NM |
| % Return on Assets | 1.6 | 0.7 | 13.7 | 20.3 | 19.0 | 14.3 | 0.9 | NM | NM | NM |
| % Return on Equity | 3.5 | 1.6 | 27.1 | 40.2 | 49.9 | 59.0 | 6.6 | NM | NM | NM |

Data as orig reptd.; bef. results of disc opers/spec. items. Per share data adj. for stk. divs.; EPS diluted. E-Estimated. NA-Not Available. NM-Not Meaningful. NR-Not Ranked. UR-Under Review.

**Office:** 1000 Six PPG Pl, Pittsburgh, PA 15222-5479.
**Telephone:** 412-394-2800.
**Website:** http://www.alleghenytechnologies.com
**Chrmn, Pres & CEO:** R.J. Harshman

**SVP, Secy & General Counsel:** E.S. Davis
**CFO:** D.G. Reid
**Chief Acctg Officer & Cntlr:** K.D. Schwartz
**Treas:** R.M. Manley

**Investor Contact:** D.L. Greenfield (412-394-3004)
**Board Members:** D. C. Creel, J. C. Diggs, R. J. Harshman, J. B. Harvey, B. S. Jeremiah, M. J. Joyce, J. E. Rohr, L. J. Thomas, J. D. Turner

**Founded:** 1960
**Domicile:** Delaware
**Employees:** 9,200

*The McGraw-Hill Companies*

# Allergan Inc.

**STANDARD &POOR'S**

| S&P Recommendation **BUY** ★★★★☆ | Price $81.38 (as of Nov 29, 2011) | 12-Mo. Target Price $98.00 | Investment Style Large-Cap Growth |
|---|---|---|---|

**GICS Sector** Health Care
**Sub-Industry** Pharmaceuticals

**Summary** This technology-driven global health care company develops and commercializes products in the eye care, neuromodulator, skin care and other specialty markets.

## Key Stock Statistics (Source S&P, Vickers, company reports)

| | | | | | | |
|---|---|---|---|---|---|---|
| 52-Wk Range | $89.25– 66.33 | S&P Oper. EPS 2011**E** | 3.64 | Market Capitalization(B) | $24.824 | Beta 0.82 |
| Trailing 12-Month EPS | $2.93 | S&P Oper. EPS 2012**E** | 4.20 | Yield (%) | 0.25 | S&P 3-Yr. Proj. EPS CAGR(%) 15 |
| Trailing 12-Month P/E | 27.8 | P/E on S&P Oper. EPS 2011**E** | 22.4 | Dividend Rate/Share | $0.20 | S&P Credit Rating A+ |
| $10K Invested 5 Yrs Ago | $13,415 | Common Shares Outstg. (M) | 305.0 | Institutional Ownership (%) | 91 | |

## Price Performance

30-Week Mov. Avg. ··· 10-Week Mov. Avg. - - GAAP Earnings vs. Previous Year   Volume Above Avg. ▮▮▮ STARS
12-Mo. Target Price — Relative Strength — ▲ Up ▼ Down ► No Change   Below Avg. ▮▮▮ ★

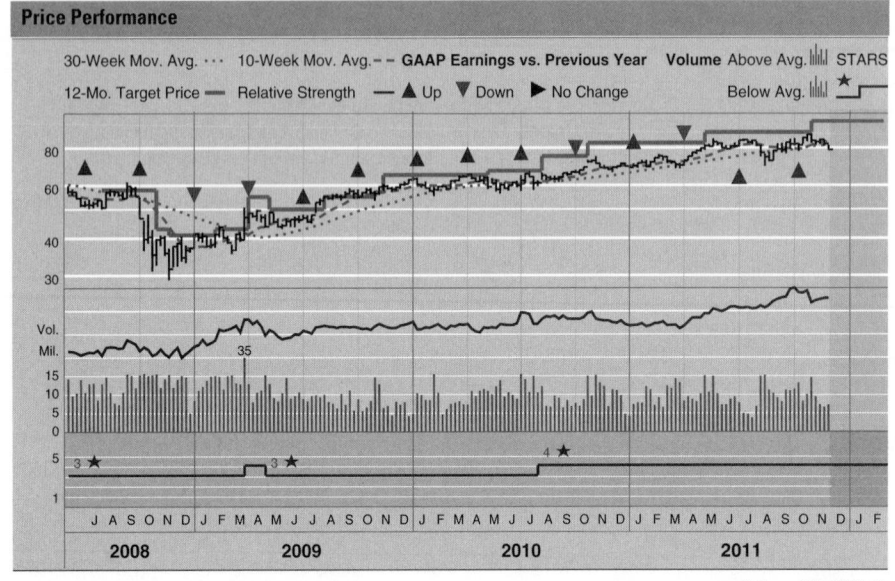

Options: ASE, CBOE, Ph

Analysis prepared by Equity Analyst **Herman Saftlas** on Nov 18, 2011, when the stock traded at **$82.59**.

## Highlights

➤ We see revenues rising about 8% in 2012, from the $5.4 billion that we forecast for 2011. We project a low teens sales gain for Botox, supported by new indications for spasticity, migraine and urinary incontinence in neurological patients, as well as greater penetration of foreign markets. Helped by DTC spending, we see robust gains in sales of Juvederm facial filler and Latisse eyelash thickener. Sales of eye care pharmaceuticals should also rise, in our view, with gains in Lumigan, Restasis and Ozurdex. However, we expect lower sales of urological products.

➤ We expect modest expansion in 2012 gross margins, benefiting from higher volume and manufacturing efficiencies. We look for the SG&A cost ratio to decrease, but for the R&D cost ratio to rise slightly on increased spending on new products. Non-operating expenses are likely to be modestly lower.

➤ After an estimated effective tax rate comparable to the 28% that we forecast for 2011, we project operating EPS to advance to $4.20 in 2012, from the $3.64 that we estimate for 2011. Results exclude amortization and other special items.

## Investment Rationale/Risk

➤ We view Allergan as well positioned in ophthalmic drugs and aesthetics products. Although the soft economy has hurt certain lines, we see growth accelerating this year, helped by greater expansion abroad, firming trends in certain aesthetic markets, and new products. Despite competition from Dysport, we expect Botox sales to approach $1.8 billion in 2012, lifted by greater penetration of foreign markets, and recently approved treatment indications for spasticity, the prevention of chronic migraine headaches, and urinary incontinence in patients with neurological conditions. Other new products should also aid revenues.

➤ Risks to our recommendation and target price include a prolonged economic slump, greater-than-expected competitive pressures, and pipeline setbacks.

➤ Our 12-month target price of $98 applies an above-peers multiple of about 23X to our EPS estimate for 2012. We believe this multiple is reasonable, given the superior EPS growth that we see for AGN. Our DCF model, which assumes a WACC of 9.9% and terminal growth of 1%, also indicates an intrinsic value of about $98.

## Qualitative Risk Assessment

| LOW | MEDIUM | HIGH |
|---|---|---|

Our risk assessment reflects the increased diversity of AGN's aesthetic products and markets via the acquisition of Inamed, our view of its strong focus on R&D, its leading market position in several ophthalmic drugs, and continued strong demand for Botox. However, we view the eye care and aesthetics markets as competitive, with the latter affected by the economic environment. We also note that certain pipeline products may not be successful.

## Quantitative Evaluations

**S&P Quality Ranking** B

| D | C | B- | **B** | B+ | A- | A | A+ |
|---|---|---|---|---|---|---|---|

**Relative Strength Rank** MODERATE

65

LOWEST = 1   HIGHEST = 99

## Revenue/Earnings Data

**Revenue (Million $)**

| | 1Q | 2Q | 3Q | 4Q | Year |
|---|---|---|---|---|---|
| 2011 | 1,271 | 1,417 | 1,328 | -- | -- |
| 2010 | 1,155 | 1,247 | 1,208 | 1,309 | 4,919 |
| 2009 | 1,007 | 1,131 | 1,141 | 1,224 | 4,504 |
| 2008 | 1,077 | 1,172 | 1,098 | 1,057 | 4,403 |
| 2007 | 886.5 | 988.1 | 993.7 | 1,091 | 3,939 |
| 2006 | 625.7 | 801.7 | 806.8 | 829.1 | 3,063 |

**Earnings Per Share ($)**

| | | | | | |
|---|---|---|---|---|---|
| 2011 | 0.51 | 0.79 | 0.81 | E0.99 | E3.64 |
| 2010 | 0.55 | 0.78 | -2.21 | 0.85 | Nil |
| 2009 | 0.15 | 0.58 | 0.59 | 0.72 | 2.03 |
| 2008 | 0.36 | 0.48 | 0.55 | 0.50 | 2.57 |
| 2007 | 0.14 | 0.45 | 0.50 | 0.52 | 1.62 |
| 2006 | -1.65 | 0.25 | 0.35 | 0.45 | -0.44 |

Fiscal year ended Dec. 31. Next earnings report expected: Early February. EPS Estimates based on S&P Operating Earnings; historical GAAP earnings are as reported.

## Dividend Data (Dates: mm/dd Payment Date: mm/dd/yy)

| Amount ($) | Date Decl. | Ex-Div. Date | Stk. of Record | Payment Date |
|---|---|---|---|---|
| 0.050 | 01/31 | 02/16 | 02/18 | 03/11/11 |
| 0.050 | 05/04 | 05/18 | 05/20 | 06/10/11 |
| 0.050 | 08/03 | 08/16 | 08/18 | 09/08/11 |
| 0.050 | 10/26 | 11/08 | 11/10 | 12/01/11 |

Dividends have been paid since 1989. Source: Company reports.

**Please read the Required Disclosures and Analyst Certification on the last page of this report.**

**The McGraw-Hill Companies**

# Allergan Inc.

## Business Summary November 18, 2011

CORPORATE OVERVIEW. Allergan is a leading producer of ophthalmic, neuro-muscular and skin care pharmaceuticals, and, with its March 2006 acquisition of Inamed Corp., aesthetic products. Eye care drugs accounted for 47% of 2010 sales, Botox/neuromodulators 29%, skin care treatments 5%, urologics 1%, breast implants 7%, devices for obesity treatment 5%, and dermal fillers 6%. About 38% of 2010 sales were derived from foreign markets.

Eye care drugs include prescription and nonprescription products to treat eye diseases and disorders, including glaucoma, inflammation, infection, allergy, and dry eye. Important products are Alphagan, Alphagan P, and Combigan (sales of $402 million in 2010, versus $415 million in 2009), Lumigan ($527 million, versus $457 million) treatments, which are used to lower eye pressure in patients with open-angle glaucoma or ocular hypertension, and Restasis ($621 million, versus $523 million) for dry eye disease. Other eye care products include Acular, Alocril and Elestat, for seasonal allergic conjunctivitis; and Zymar and Ocuflox, for bacterial conjunctivitis.

Originally used for ophthalmic movement disorders, Botox (botulinum toxin type A) is also a widely accepted treatment for neuromuscular disorders and related pain. Botox has also garnered a rapidly growing market as a facial cosmetic agent. In 2002, the FDA approved the injectable drug for removing brow furrows and other facial wrinkles. We estimate that Botox sales are

roughly equally divided between therapeutic indications and cosmetic uses. Botox accounts for over 80% of the total global neuromodulator drug market. Botox is also used to treat spasticity, underarm sweating, back spasms, eye disorders, migraines and various other conditions.

Skin care products include Zorac/Tazorac receptor-selective retinoids for acne and psoriasis; Aczone treatment for acne; Prevage and Avage facial aesthetic products; and Latisse, a drug used to produce longer, darker and thicker eyelashes. Aesthetic products include breast implants for aesthetic augmentation and reconstructive surgery following mastectomy, a range of dermal products to correct facial wrinkles, and the Lap-Band and Intragastric Balloon (BIB) systems for obesity treatment.

COMPETITIVE LANDSCAPE. Eye care competitors include Alcon Laboratories, Bausch & Lomb, Pfizer, Novartis, and Merck, while its skin care business competes against Dermik, a division of Sanofi-Aventis, Galderma, a joint venture between Nestle and L'Oreal, Medicis, Connetics, Novartis, Schering-Plough, and Johnson & Johnson.

## Company Financials Fiscal Year Ended Dec. 31

| Per Share Data ($) | 2010 | 2009 | 2008 | 2007 | 2006 | 2005 | 2004 | 2003 | 2002 | 2001 |
|---|---|---|---|---|---|---|---|---|---|---|
| Tangible Book Value | 5.41 | 4.53 | 1.48 | 0.72 | 0.88 | 5.34 | 3.99 | 2.47 | 3.02 | 3.24 |
| Cash Flow | 0.53 | 2.89 | 2.75 | 2.32 | 0.08 | 1.82 | 1.69 | 0.03 | 0.42 | 1.19 |
| Earnings | Nil | 2.03 | 2.57 | 1.62 | -0.44 | 1.51 | 1.41 | -0.20 | 0.25 | 0.85 |
| S&P Core Earnings | 1.93 | 2.00 | 1.85 | 1.64 | -0.42 | 1.36 | 1.26 | -0.33 | 0.45 | 0.70 |
| Dividends | 0.20 | 0.20 | 0.20 | 0.20 | 0.20 | 0.20 | 0.18 | 0.18 | 0.18 | 0.18 |
| Payout Ratio | NM | 10% | 8% | 12% | NM | 13% | 13% | NM | 73% | 21% |
| Prices:High | 74.94 | 64.08 | 70.40 | 69.15 | 61.51 | 55.25 | 46.31 | 40.90 | 37.55 | 49.69 |
| Prices:Low | 55.25 | 35.41 | 28.95 | 52.50 | 46.29 | 34.51 | 33.39 | 35.83 | 24.53 | 29.50 |
| P/E Ratio:High | NM | 32 | 27 | 43 | NM | 37 | 33 | NM | NM | 59 |
| P/E Ratio:Low | NM | 17 | 11 | 32 | NM | 23 | 24 | NM | NM | 35 |

| Income Statement Analysis (Million $) | | | | | | | | | | |
|---|---|---|---|---|---|---|---|---|---|---|
| Revenue | 4,919 | 4,504 | 4,403 | 3,939 | 3,063 | 2,319 | 2,046 | 1,771 | 1,425 | 1,746 |
| Operating Income | 1,408 | 1,338 | 1,170 | 1,060 | 854 | 694 | 603 | 39.1 | 349 | 404 |
| Depreciation | 160 | 262 | 264 | 215 | 152 | 78.9 | 68.3 | 59.6 | 45.0 | 85.5 |
| Interest Expense | 78.7 | 76.9 | 62.0 | 72.7 | 60.2 | 12.4 | 18.1 | 15.6 | 17.4 | 21.4 |
| Pretax Income | 171 | 848 | 1,080 | 688 | -19.5 | 599 | 532 | -29.5 | 89.8 | 336 |
| Effective Tax Rate | 97.1% | 26.5% | 27.0% | 27.1% | NM | 32.1% | 28.9% | NM | 28.0% | 32.4% |
| Net Income | 0.60 | 621 | 786 | 501 | -127 | 404 | 377 | -52.5 | 64.0 | 227 |
| S&P Core Earnings | 591 | 610 | 567 | 507 | -123 | 363 | 339 | -87.3 | 118 | 187 |

| Balance Sheet & Other Financial Data (Million $) | | | | | | | | | | |
|---|---|---|---|---|---|---|---|---|---|---|
| Cash | 2,740 | 1,947 | 1,110 | 1,158 | 1,369 | 1,296 | 895 | 508 | 774 | 782 |
| Current Assets | 3,994 | 3,106 | 2,271 | 2,124 | 2,130 | 1,826 | 1,376 | 928 | 1,200 | 1,325 |
| Total Assets | 8,308 | 7,537 | 6,791 | 6,579 | 5,767 | 2,851 | 2,257 | 1,755 | 1,807 | 2,046 |
| Current Liabilities | 1,528 | 812 | 697 | 716 | 658 | 1,044 | 460 | 383 | 404 | 490 |
| Long Term Debt | 1,534 | 1,491 | 1,635 | 1,630 | 1,606 | 57.5 | 570 | 573 | 526 | 521 |
| Common Equity | 4,758 | 4,823 | 4,010 | 3,739 | 3,143 | 1,567 | 1,116 | 719 | 808 | 977 |
| Total Capital | 7,009 | 6,353 | 5,652 | 5,551 | 4,836 | 1,626 | 1,689 | 1,294 | 1,337 | 1,499 |
| Capital Expenditures | 103 | 95.8 | 190 | 142 | 131 | 78.5 | 96.4 | 110 | 78.8 | 89.9 |
| Cash Flow | 165 | 883 | 843 | 716 | 25.0 | 483 | 445 | 7.10 | 109 | 312 |
| Current Ratio | 2.6 | 3.8 | 3.3 | 3.0 | 3.2 | 1.7 | 3.0 | 2.4 | 3.0 | 2.7 |
| % Long Term Debt of Capitalization | 21.9 | 23.5 | 28.9 | 29.8 | 33.2 | 3.5 | 33.8 | 44.3 | 39.4 | 34.7 |
| % Net Income of Revenue | NM | 13.8 | 17.9 | 12.7 | NM | 17.4 | 18.4 | NM | 4.5 | 13.0 |
| % Return on Assets | NM | 8.7 | 11.8 | 8.1 | NM | 15.8 | 18.8 | NM | 3.3 | 11.3 |
| % Return on Equity | NM | 14.1 | 20.3 | 14.6 | NM | 30.1 | 41.1 | NM | 7.2 | 24.5 |

Data as orig reptd.; bef. results of disc opers/spec. items. Per share data adj. for stk. divs.; EPS diluted. E-Estimated. NA-Not Available. NM-Not Meaningful. NR-Not Ranked. UR-Under Review.

**Office:** 2525 Dupont Drive, Irvine, CA 92612.
**Telephone:** 714-246-4500.
**Email:** corpinfo@allergan.com
**Website:** http://www.alergan.com

**Chrmn, Pres & CEO:** D.E. Pyott
**Vice Chrmn:** H.W. Boyer
**EVP & CSO:** S.M. Whitcup
**EVP & General Counsel:** S.J. Gesten

**SVP, Chief Acctg Officer & Cntlr:** J.F. Barlow
**Investor Contact:** J. Hindman (714-246-4636)
**Board Members:** H. W. Boyer, D. Dunsire, M. R. Gallagher, D. Hudson, R. A. Ingram, T. M. Jones, L. J. Lavigne, Jr., D. E. Pyott, R. T. Ray, S. J. Ryan

**Founded:** 1948
**Domicile:** Delaware
**Employees:** 9,200

# Allstate Corp (The)

**STANDARD &POOR'S**

| S&P Recommendation | HOLD ★★★★★ | Price $24.70 (as of Nov 25, 2011) | 12-Mo. Target Price $30.00 | Investment Style Large-Cap Blend |
|---|---|---|---|---|

**GICS Sector** Financials
**Sub-Industry** Property & Casualty Insurance

**Summary** Allstate, the second largest U.S. personal lines property-casualty insurer, also offers an array of life insurance and retirement savings products.

## Key Stock Statistics (Source S&P, Vickers, company reports)

| | | | | | | | |
|---|---|---|---|---|---|---|---|
| 52-Wk Range | $34.40– 22.27 | S&P Oper. EPS 2011E | 0.79 | Market Capitalization(B) | $12.482 | Beta | 1.48 |
| Trailing 12-Month EPS | $0.68 | S&P Oper. EPS 2012E | 3.97 | Yield (%) | 3.40 | S&P 3-Yr. Proj. EPS CAGR(%) | 1 |
| Trailing 12-Month P/E | 36.3 | P/E on S&P Oper. EPS 2011E | 31.3 | Dividend Rate/Share | $0.84 | S&P Credit Rating | A- |
| $10K Invested 5 Yrs Ago | $4,455 | Common Shares Outstg. (M) | 505.4 | Institutional Ownership (%) | 80 | | |

## Price Performance

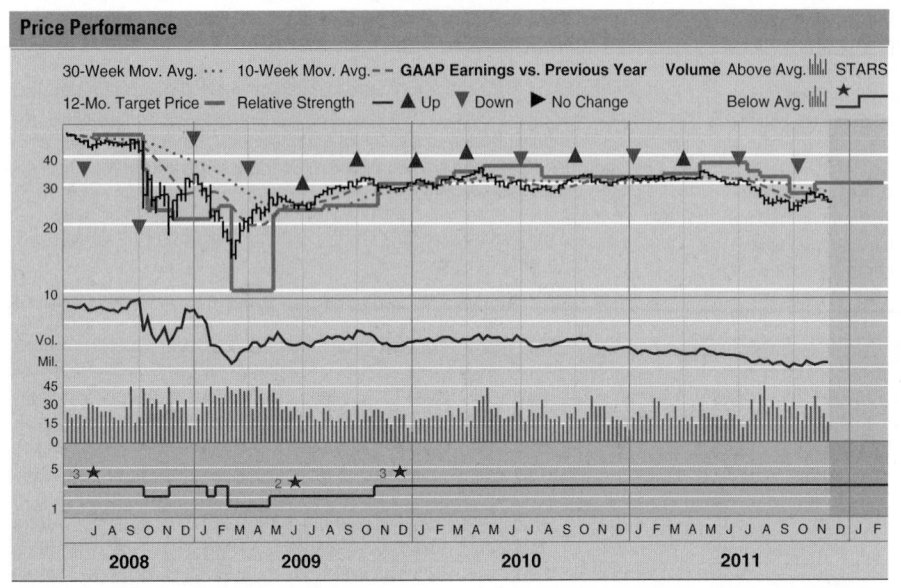

30-Week Mov. Avg. · · · 10-Week Mov. Avg. – – GAAP Earnings vs. Previous Year   Volume Above Avg. ▏▎▍ STARS
12-Mo. Target Price — Relative Strength — ▲ Up ▼ Down ► No Change   Below Avg. ▏▎▍ ★

Options: ASE, CBOE, P, Ph

## Qualitative Risk Assessment

| LOW | MEDIUM | **HIGH** |
|---|---|---|

Our risk assessment reflects our view of ALL's potential exposure to an outsized level of claims from catastrophes, partly offset by ALL's geographically diversified base of business. We also remain concerned about the level of illiquid assets in its investment portfolio.

## Quantitative Evaluations

**S&P Quality Ranking**     B+

| D | C | B- | B | **B+** | A- | A | A+ |
|---|---|---|---|---|---|---|---|

**Relative Strength Rank**     MODERATE

57

LOWEST = 1          HIGHEST = 99

## Highlights

► The 12-month target price for ALL has recently been changed to $30.00 from $27.00. The Highlights section of this Stock Report will be updated accordingly.

## Investment Rationale/Risk

► The Investment Rationale/Risk section of this Stock Report will be updated shortly. For the latest News story on ALL from MarketScope, see below.

► 11/01/11 07:11 am ET ... S&P KEEPS HOLD OPINION ON SHARES OF ALLSTATE CORPORATION (ALL 26.34***): ALL reports Q3 operating EPS of $0.16, vs. $0.83, above our $0.09 estimate, amid better than expected investment results and stable non-catastrophe underwriting results. Still, Q3 catastrophe losses were $1.1B vs. $386M. We raise our 2011 operating EPS forecast $0.05 to $0.79, and still see $3.97 in 2012, which assumes a "normal" level of catastrophe claims. We raise our target price by $3 to $30, which assumes the shares trade at slightly less than 1X estimated 2012 tangible book value, a slight discount to some peers. /C. Seifert

## Revenue/Earnings Data

**Revenue (Million $)**

| | 1Q | 2Q | 3Q | 4Q | Year |
|---|---|---|---|---|---|
| 2011 | 8,095 | 8,081 | 8,242 | -- | -- |
| 2010 | 7,749 | 7,656 | 7,908 | 8,087 | 31,400 |
| 2009 | 7,883 | 8,490 | 7,582 | 8,058 | 32,013 |
| 2008 | 8,087 | 7,418 | 7,320 | 6,569 | 29,394 |
| 2007 | 9,331 | 9,455 | 8,992 | 8,991 | 36,769 |
| 2006 | 9,081 | 8,875 | 8,738 | 9,102 | 35,796 |

**Earnings Per Share ($)**

| | 1Q | 2Q | 3Q | 4Q | Year |
|---|---|---|---|---|---|
| 2011 | 0.97 | -1.19 | 0.32 | E0.94 | E0.79 |
| 2010 | 0.22 | 0.27 | 0.68 | 0.55 | 1.71 |
| 2009 | -0.51 | 0.72 | 0.41 | 0.96 | 1.58 |
| 2008 | 0.62 | 0.05 | -1.71 | -2.11 | -3.07 |
| 2007 | 2.41 | 2.30 | 1.70 | 1.36 | 7.77 |
| 2006 | 2.19 | 1.89 | 1.83 | 1.93 | 7.84 |

Fiscal year ended Dec. 31. Next earnings report expected: Early February. EPS Estimates based on S&P Operating Earnings; historical GAAP earnings are as reported.

## Dividend Data (Dates: mm/dd Payment Date: mm/dd/yy)

| Amount ($) | Date Decl. | Ex-Div. Date | Stk. of Record | Payment Date |
|---|---|---|---|---|
| 0.210 | 02/22 | 03/09 | 03/11 | 04/01/11 |
| 0.210 | 05/17 | 05/26 | 05/31 | 07/01/11 |
| 0.210 | 07/12 | 08/29 | 08/31 | 10/03/11 |
| 0.210 | 11/08 | 11/28 | 11/30 | 01/03/12 |

Dividends have been paid since 1993. Source: Company reports.

# Allstate Corp (The)

STANDARD &POOR'S

## Business Summary September 22, 2011

CORPORATE OVERVIEW. Established in 1931 by Sears, Roebuck & Co., Allstate is the second largest U.S. personal lines property-casualty insurer (based on earned premiums), and the 16th largest life insurer (based on life insurance in force). It writes business mainly through a network of more than 14,000 exclusive agencies. ALL has also implemented a multi-access distribution model designed to allow customers to purchase company products through agents, over the Internet, via telephone, and through The Good Hands Network. ALL became an independent company in June 1995, when Sears, Roebuck & Co. spun off its 80% interest in the company.

The company's primary business is the sale of private passenger automobile and homeowners insurance, and it maintains national market shares of about 11% in each of these lines. ALL is licensed to write policies in all 50 states, the District of Columbia, Puerto Rico, and Canada. In 2010, property-liability net written premiums equaled $25.9 billion, down from $26.0 billion in 2009.. Earned premiums totaled $26.0 billion in 2010, down from $26.2 billion in 2009. Of the 2010 total, standard automobile policies accounted for 64%, nonstandard automobile policies 3%, homeowners' coverage 24%, and other (which includes commercial lines and other personal lines) for the remaining 9%. Underwriting results in 2010 deteriorated amid a 6.7% rise in catastrophe

claims and a deterioration in underlying claim trends. As a improved amid a 38% drop in catastrophe claims, partly offset by an erosion in underlying claim trends. As a result, pretax underwriting profits slumped to $495 million in 2010 from $995 million in 2009. The combined loss and expense ratio ended 2010 at 98.1%, still profitable, but a deterioration from 96.1% in 2009.

Allstate Financial (formerly Allstate Life) offers an array of life insurance, annuity, savings and investment and pension products through Allstate agents, financial institutions, independent agents and brokers, and direct marketing. Premiums and deposits totaled $4.1 billion in 2010, down from $5.1 billion in 2009 (and sharply below the nearly $11 billion in 2008 amid the absence of a $4.2 billion funding agreement). Of the 2010 total, interest-sensitive life insurance products accounted for 36%, traditional life and accident and health insurance for 26%, fixed annuities for 25%, and bank deposits for the remaining 13%.

## Company Financials Fiscal Year Ended Dec. 31

| Per Share Data ($) | 2010 | 2009 | 2008 | 2007 | 2006 | 2005 | 2004 | 2003 | 2002 | 2001 |
|---|---|---|---|---|---|---|---|---|---|---|
| Tangible Book Value | 34.04 | 39.57 | 21.66 | 37.35 | 33.80 | 29.97 | 30.74 | 27.89 | 23.52 | 22.35 |
| Operating Earnings | NA | NA | NA | NA | NA | NA | NA | 3.77 | 2.94 | 2.06 |
| Earnings | 1.71 | 1.58 | -3.07 | 7.77 | 7.84 | 2.64 | 4.79 | 3.85 | 1.13 | 1.61 |
| S&P Core Earnings | 3.02 | 2.06 | 2.52 | 6.56 | 7.91 | 2.21 | 4.33 | 3.82 | 2.64 | 1.66 |
| Dividends | 0.80 | 0.80 | 1.64 | 1.52 | 1.40 | 1.28 | 1.12 | 0.92 | 0.84 | 0.76 |
| Relative Payout | 47% | 51% | NM | 20% | 18% | 48% | 23% | 24% | 74% | 47% |
| Prices:High | 35.51 | 33.50 | 52.90 | 65.85 | 66.14 | 63.22 | 51.99 | 43.27 | 41.95 | 45.90 |
| Prices:Low | 26.86 | 13.77 | 17.72 | 48.90 | 50.22 | 49.66 | 42.55 | 30.05 | 31.03 | 30.00 |
| P/E Ratio:High | 21 | 21 | NM | 8 | 8 | 24 | 11 | 11 | 37 | 29 |
| P/E Ratio:Low | 16 | 9 | NM | 6 | 6 | 19 | 9 | 8 | 27 | 19 |

| Income Statement Analysis (Million $) | | | | | | | | | | |
|---|---|---|---|---|---|---|---|---|---|---|
| Life Insurance in Force | NA | NA | NA | NA | NA | NA | NA | 409,068 | 396,943 | 387,039 |
| Premium Income:Life A & H | 25,957 | 26,194 | 26,967 | 27,233 | 27,369 | 27,039 | 25,989 | 24,677 | 23,361 | 2,230 |
| Premium Income:Casualty/Property. | 2,168 | 1,958 | 1,895 | 1,866 | 1,964 | 2,049 | 2,072 | 2,304 | 2,293 | 22,197 |
| Net Investment Income | 4,102 | 4,444 | 5,622 | 6,435 | 6,177 | 5,746 | 5,284 | 4,972 | 4,854 | 4,796 |
| Total Revenue | 31,400 | 32,013 | 29,394 | 36,769 | 35,796 | 35,383 | 33,936 | 32,149 | 29,579 | 28,865 |
| Pretax Income | 1,126 | 1,248 | -3,025 | 6,653 | 7,178 | 2,088 | 4,586 | 3,566 | 868 | 1,240 |
| Net Operating Income | NA | NA | NA | NA | NA | NA | NA | 2,662 | 2,075 | 1,492 |
| Net Income | 928 | 854 | -1,679 | 4,636 | 4,993 | 1,765 | 3,356 | 2,720 | 803 | 1,167 |
| S&P Core Earnings | 1,643 | 1,115 | 1,372 | 3,915 | 5,040 | 1,487 | 3,028 | 2,692 | 1,879 | 1,201 |

| Balance Sheet & Other Financial Data (Million $) | | | | | | | | | | |
|---|---|---|---|---|---|---|---|---|---|---|
| Cash & Equivalent | 1,371 | 1,476 | 1,299 | 6,113 | 4,935 | 1,387 | 1,428 | 1,434 | 1,408 | 1,146 |
| Premiums Due | 4,839 | 4,839 | 4,842 | 4,879 | 4,789 | 4,739 | 4,721 | 4,386 | 6,958 | 6,674 |
| Investment Assets:Bonds | 79,612 | 78,766 | 68,608 | 94,451 | 98,320 | 98,065 | 95,715 | 87,741 | 77,152 | 65,720 |
| Investment Assets:Stocks | 8,627 | 7,768 | 5,596 | 7,758 | 7,777 | 6,164 | 5,895 | 5,288 | 3,683 | 5,245 |
| Investment Assets:Loans | 6,679 | 7,935 | 10,229 | 10,830 | 9,467 | 8,748 | 7,856 | 6,539 | 6,092 | 5,710 |
| Investment Assets:Total | 100,483 | 99,833 | 95,998 | 118,980 | 119,757 | 118,297 | 115,530 | 103,081 | 90,650 | 79,876 |
| Deferred Policy Costs | 4,769 | 5,470 | 8,542 | 5,768 | 5,332 | 5,802 | 4,968 | 4,842 | 4,385 | 4,421 |
| Total Assets | 130,874 | 132,652 | 134,798 | 156,408 | 157,554 | 156,072 | 149,725 | 134,142 | 117,426 | 109,175 |
| Debt | 5,908 | 5,910 | 5,659 | 5,640 | 4,620 | 4,887 | 5,291 | 5,073 | 4,161 | 3,894 |
| Common Equity | 19,016 | 16,692 | 12,641 | 21,851 | 21,846 | 20,186 | 21,823 | 20,565 | 34,128 | 17,196 |
| Combined Loss-Expense Ratio | 98.1 | 96.2 | 99.4 | 89.6 | 83.6 | 102.4 | 93.0 | 94.6 | 98.9 | 102.9 |
| % Return on Revenue | 3.0 | 2.7 | NM | 12.6 | 13.9 | 5.0 | 9.9 | 8.5 | 2.7 | 4.0 |
| % Return on Equity | 5.2 | 5.8 | NM | 21.2 | 23.8 | 8.4 | 15.8 | 14.3 | 2.4 | 6.7 |
| % Investment Yield | 4.1 | 4.6 | 5.2 | 5.3 | 5.2 | 4.9 | 4.8 | 5.1 | 5.7 | 6.2 |

Data as orig reptd.; bef. results of disc opers/spec. items. Per share data adj. for stk. divs.; EPS diluted. E-Estimated. NA-Not Available. NM-Not Meaningful. NR-Not Ranked. UR-Under Review.

**Office:** 2775 Sanders Road, Northbrook, IL 60062.
**Telephone:** 847-402-5000.
**Website:** http://www.allstate.com
**Chrmn, Pres & CEO:** T.J. Wilson, II

**CFO:** D. Civgin
**Secy:** M.J. McGinn
**General Counsel:** M.C. Mayes
**Cntlr:** S.H. Pilch

**Board Members:** F. D. Ackerman, R. D. Beyer, W. J. Farrell, J. M. Greenberg, R. T. LeMay, A. Redmond, H. J. Riley, Jr., J. I. Smith, J. Sprieser, M. A. Taylor, T. J. Wilson, II

**Founded:** 1953
**Domicile:** Delaware
**Employees:** 35,700

# Alpha Natural Resources Inc

**STANDARD &POOR'S**

| S&P Recommendation HOLD ★★★★★ | Price $18.81 (as of Nov 25, 2011) | 12-Mo. Target Price $28.00 | Investment Style Large-Cap Growth |
|---|---|---|---|

**GICS Sector** Energy
**Sub-Industry** Coal & Consumable Fuels

**Summary** This company is the third largest coal producer in the U.S., with operations in Appalachia and the Powder River Basin.

## Key Stock Statistics (Source S&P, Vickers, company reports)

| | | | | | | | |
|---|---|---|---|---|---|---|---|
| 52-Wk Range | $68.05– 15.49 | S&P Oper. EPS 2011**E** | 0.89 | Market Capitalization(B) | $4.135 | Beta | 1.72 |
| Trailing 12-Month EPS | $0.48 | S&P Oper. EPS 2012**E** | 1.98 | Yield (%) | Nil | S&P 3-Yr. Proj. EPS CAGR(%) | 20 |
| Trailing 12-Month P/E | 39.2 | P/E on S&P Oper. EPS 2011**E** | 21.1 | Dividend Rate/Share | Nil | S&P Credit Rating | BB |
| $10K Invested 5 Yrs Ago | $12,399 | Common Shares Outstg. (M) | 219.8 | Institutional Ownership (%) | 88 | | |

## Price Performance

30-Week Mov. Avg. · · · 10-Week Mov. Avg. - - GAAP Earnings vs. Previous Year    Volume Above Avg. ▍▍▍ STARS
12-Mo. Target Price — Relative Strength — ▲ Up ▼ Down ▶ No Change    Below Avg. ▍▍▍ ★

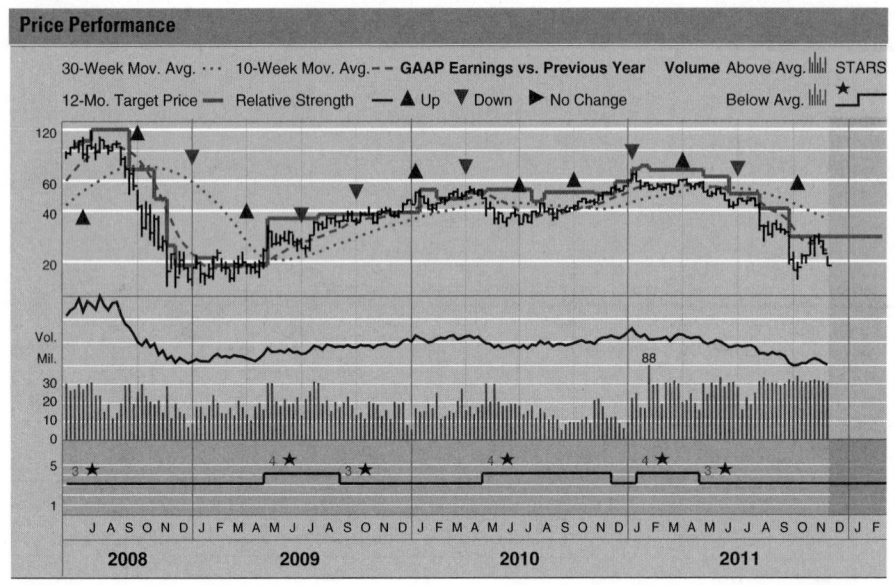

Options: ASE, CBOE, P, Ph

## Qualitative Risk Assessment

| LOW | MEDIUM | **HIGH** |
|---|---|---|

Our risk assessment reflects the cyclicality of the coal market, concentration of the company's coal reserves in the Appalachian region, its acquisition strategy, and heavy regulation of the industry and its utilities end market. These factors are only partially offset by ANR's leading market share in metallurgical coal, and corporate governance practices we view as favorable versus peers.

## Quantitative Evaluations

**S&P Quality Ranking**                               NR

| D | C | B- | B | B+ | A- | A | A+ |
|---|---|---|---|---|---|---|---|

**Relative Strength Rank**                           **WEAK**

7

LOWEST = 1                                    HIGHEST = 99

## Revenue/Earnings Data

**Revenue (Million $)**

| | 1Q | 2Q | 3Q | 4Q | Year |
|---|---|---|---|---|---|
| 2011 | 1,131 | 1,593 | 2,300 | -- | -- |
| 2010 | 922.0 | 1,000 | 1,002 | 993.1 | 3,917 |
| 2009 | 486.7 | 386.2 | 729.3 | 893.3 | 2,496 |
| 2008 | 516.9 | 732.2 | 715.0 | 593.8 | 2,554 |
| 2007 | 427.4 | 434.3 | 507.1 | 508.8 | 1,878 |
| 2006 | 482.3 | 495.7 | 474.7 | 458.0 | 1,911 |

**Earnings Per Share ($)**

| | | | | | |
|---|---|---|---|---|---|
| 2011 | 0.41 | -0.36 | 0.29 | E0.52 | E0.89 |
| 2010 | 0.12 | 0.32 | 0.27 | 0.09 | 0.80 |
| 2009 | 0.66 | 0.24 | -0.19 | 0.17 | 0.73 |
| 2008 | 0.39 | 1.04 | 0.90 | -0.07 | 2.30 |
| 2007 | 0.13 | 0.07 | 0.14 | 0.09 | 0.43 |
| 2006 | 0.43 | 0.36 | 0.23 | 0.98 | 2.00 |

Fiscal year ended Dec. 31. Next earnings report expected: Early February. EPS Estimates based on S&P Operating Earnings; historical GAAP earnings are as reported.

## Dividend Data

No cash dividends have been paid.

## Highlights

➤ The 12-month target price for ANR has recently been changed to $28.00 from $41.00. The Highlights section of this Stock Report will be updated accordingly.

## Investment Rationale/Risk

➤ The Investment Rationale/Risk section of this Stock Report will be updated shortly. For the latest News story on ANR from MarketScope, see below.

➤ 11/03/11 12:10 pm ET ... S&P REITERATES HOLD OPINION ON SHARES OF ALPHA NATURAL RESOURCES (ANR 26.61***): Q3 adjusted EPS of $0.35, vs. $0.27, is above our $0.31 estimate. Results exclude many one-time items related to the acquisition of Massey Energy, which made comparisons difficult. Revenues rose 130%, mainly related to the acqustion, but costs increased at a similar rate. Based on our assumption of slightly lower production volumes at a lower average utilized price, we are cutting our '12 EPS estimate to $1.98 from $3.97. We keep our 12-month target price at $28, above peers on an EV/EBITDA basis, due to our view of ANR's better size and scale. /J. Corridore

# Alpha Natural Resources Inc

**STANDARD &POOR'S**

## Business Summary August 23, 2011

CORPORATE OVERVIEW. Alpha Natural Resources, a leading U.S. producer of both thermal and metallurgical coal, completed its initial public offering on February 18, 2005. As of December 31, 2010, the company operated 38 underground mines, 28 surface mines and 13 preparation plants in Virginia, West Virginia, Kentucky, Pennsylvania, and Wyoming. As of December 31, 2010, ANR owned or leased nearly 2.3 billion tons of proven and probable coal reserves. The majority of the company's coal reserves consist of low-sulfur, high-Btu coal, with approximately 63% of total proven and probable reserves being low-sulfur (sulfur content of 1% or less) and about 64% having a high Btu content (above 12,500 Btu content per pound). This coal typically sells at a premium to lower-Btu, higher-sulfur coal.

In 2010, the company sold 84.9 million tons of produced and processed coal, which included 0.8 million tons purchased from third parties and processed at Alpha's processing plants or loading facilities prior to resale, and 2.2 million

tons of purchased coal that was resold without processing. Approximately 86% of 2010 coal sales volume was accounted for by the sale of steam coal to utilities and industrial customers primarily for electricity generation. The remaining 14% of 2010 coal sales volume consisted of metallurgical coal sales primarily to produce coke, a component of steel making. Metallurgical coal generally sells at a significant premium over steam coal because of its higher quality, energy content, and value in the steel making process. ANR is a significant exporter of metallurgical coal in the U.S. and domestic producer of metallurgical coal. In 2010, around 34% of total company revenue was derived from sales outside the U.S., with sales to Brazil accounting for the largest portion of export sales.

## Company Financials Fiscal Year Ended Dec. 31

| Per Share Data ($) | 2010 | 2009 | 2008 | 2007 | 2006 | 2005 | 2004 | 2003 | 2002 | 2001 |
|---|---|---|---|---|---|---|---|---|---|---|
| Tangible Book Value | 17.52 | 15.25 | 9.95 | 5.34 | 4.80 | 2.84 | 0.76 | 0.74 | NA | NA |
| Cash Flow | 5.85 | 5.02 | 4.85 | 2.88 | 4.14 | 1.47 | NA | 0.74 | NA | NA |
| Earnings | 0.80 | 0.73 | 2.30 | 0.43 | 2.00 | 0.38 | 0.47 | 0.01 | NA | NA |
| S&P Core Earnings | 0.79 | 0.75 | 1.83 | 0.45 | 2.08 | 0.38 | NA | NA | NA | NA |
| Dividends | Nil | Nil | Nil | Nil | Nil | Nil | NA | NA | NA | NA |
| Payout Ratio | Nil | Nil | Nil | Nil | Nil | Nil | NA | NA | NA | NA |
| Prices:High | 61.07 | 46.52 | 119.30 | 35.20 | 27.46 | 32.73 | NA | NA | NA | NA |
| Prices:Low | 32.00 | 14.52 | 13.93 | 12.32 | 14.09 | 18.70 | NA | NA | NA | NA |
| P/E Ratio:High | 76 | 64 | 52 | 82 | 14 | 86 | NA | NA | NA | NA |
| P/E Ratio:Low | 40 | 20 | 6 | 29 | 7 | 49 | NA | NA | NA | NA |

| Income Statement Analysis (Million $) | 2010 | 2009 | 2008 | 2007 | 2006 | 2005 | 2004 | 2003 | 2002 | 2001 |
|---|---|---|---|---|---|---|---|---|---|---|
| Revenue | 3,917 | 2,496 | 2,554 | 1,878 | 1,911 | 1,627 | 1,270 | 903 | 187 | 278 |
| Operating Income | NA | NA | 431 | 234 | 279 | 145 | 123 | 67.4 | NA | NA |
| Depreciation | 616 | 393 | 179 | 160 | 141 | 73.1 | 56.0 | 46.0 | 7.14 | 7.87 |
| Interest Expense | 73.5 | 82.8 | 40.4 | 42.0 | 41.8 | 29.9 | 20.0 | 22.4 | 0.24 | NA |
| Pretax Income | 101 | 33.8 | 200 | 36.2 | 97.6 | 43.3 | 43.8 | 0.33 | -42.5 | 6.82 |
| Effective Tax Rate | NA | NM | 19.5% | 23.9% | NM | 43.8% | 9.04% | NM | 41.3% | NM |
| Net Income | 97.2 | 66.8 | 161 | 27.7 | 128 | 21.4 | 20.0 | 0.54 | -25.0 | 8.32 |
| S&P Core Earnings | 95.6 | 68.5 | 129 | 29.3 | 133 | 21.4 | 20.4 | 2.26 | -29.9 | NA |

| Balance Sheet & Other Financial Data (Million $) | 2010 | 2009 | 2008 | 2007 | 2006 | 2005 | 2004 | 2003 | 2002 | 2001 |
|---|---|---|---|---|---|---|---|---|---|---|
| Cash | 772 | 495 | 676 | 54.4 | 33.3 | 39.6 | NA | 15.8 | 8.44 | NA |
| Current Assets | 1,376 | 1,052 | 992 | 380 | 339 | 319 | NA | 186 | 32.9 | NA |
| Total Assets | 5,179 | 5,109 | 1,728 | 1,211 | 1,146 | 1,014 | 472 | 457 | 108 | NA |
| Current Liabilities | 447 | 435 | 263 | 223 | 222 | 284 | NA | 655 | 45.1 | NA |
| Long Term Debt | 742 | 757 | 521 | 425 | 421 | 424 | 185 | 186 | 14.5 | NA |
| Common Equity | 2,656 | 2,591 | 726 | 381 | 344 | 213 | 67.3 | 66.1 | 23.4 | NA |
| Total Capital | 3,410 | 3,406 | 1,246 | 810 | 766 | 636 | 252 | 252 | 49.1 | NA |
| Capital Expenditures | 309 | 187 | 138 | 126 | 132 | 122 | NA | NA | 22.8 | 10.2 |
| Cash Flow | 713 | 460 | 341 | 187 | 269 | 94.5 | 76.0 | 46.5 | -17.8 | 16.2 |
| Current Ratio | 3.1 | 2.4 | 3.8 | 1.7 | 1.5 | 1.1 | NA | 0.3 | 0.7 | NA |
| % Long Term Debt of Capitalization | 21.8 | 22.4 | 41.8 | 52.5 | 55.1 | 66.6 | 73.3 | 73.8 | 29.5 | Nil |
| % Net Income of Revenue | 2.5 | 2.7 | 6.3 | 1.5 | 6.7 | 1.3 | 1.6 | 0.1 | NM | 3.0 |
| % Return on Assets | 1.9 | 2.0 | 11.0 | 2.4 | 11.9 | 2.9 | NA | NA | NA | NA |
| % Return on Equity | 3.7 | 4.0 | 29.2 | 7.7 | 46.0 | 16.6 | NA | NA | NA | NA |

Data as orig reptd.; bef. results of disc opers/spec. items. Per share data adj. for stk. divs.; EPS diluted. E-Estimated. NA-Not Available. NM-Not Meaningful. NR-Not Ranked. UR-Under Review.

**Office:** PO Box 2345, Abingdon, VA 24212-2345.
**Telephone:** 276-619-4410.
**Email:** ir@alphanr.com
**Website:** http://www.alphanr.com

**Chrmn:** M.J. Quillen
**Pres:** K.D. Kost
**CEO:** K.S. Crutchfield
**EVP & CFO:** F.J. Wood

**EVP & Chief Admin Officer:** R.L. McMillion
**Investor Contact:** T. Pile (276-623-2920)
**Board Members:** W. J. Crowley, Jr., K. S. Crutchfield, E. L. Draper, Jr., G. A. Eisenberg, P. M. Giftos, M. J. Quillen, J. Richards, III, J. F. Roberts, T. G. Wood

**Founded:** 2004
**Domicile:** Delaware
**Employees:** 6,500

# Altera Corp

**STANDARD & POOR'S**

| S&P Recommendation | HOLD ★★★☆☆ | Price $34.12 (as of Nov 25, 2011) | 12-Mo. Target Price $40.00 | Investment Style Large-Cap Growth |
|---|---|---|---|---|

**GICS Sector** Information Technology
**Sub-Industry** Semiconductors

**Summary** This company is one of the largest makers of high-performance, high-density programmable logic devices (PLDs) and associated computer-aided engineering logic development tools.

## Key Stock Statistics (Source S&P, Vickers, company reports)

| | | | | | | | |
|---|---|---|---|---|---|---|---|
| 52-Wk Range | $49.59–30.39 | S&P Oper. EPS 2011**E** | 2.36 | Market Capitalization(B) | $10.948 | Beta | 1.16 |
| Trailing 12-Month EPS | $2.61 | S&P Oper. EPS 2012**E** | 2.44 | Yield (%) | 0.94 | S&P 3-Yr. Proj. EPS CAGR(%) | 2 |
| Trailing 12-Month P/E | 13.1 | P/E on S&P Oper. EPS 2011**E** | 14.5 | Dividend Rate/Share | $0.32 | S&P Credit Rating | A- |
| $10K Invested 5 Yrs Ago | $17,334 | Common Shares Outstg. (M) | 320.9 | Institutional Ownership (%) | 95 | | |

## Price Performance

30-Week Mov. Avg. · · · 10-Week Mov. Avg. - - **GAAP Earnings vs. Previous Year** Volume Above Avg. STARS
12-Mo. Target Price — Relative Strength — ▲ Up ▼ Down ► No Change Below Avg.

Options: ASE, CBOE, P, Ph

Analysis prepared by Equity Analyst **Angelo Zino, CFA** on Oct 24, 2011, when the stock traded at **$38.06**.

## Highlights

▶ We see sales advancing fractionally in 2012, after a projected 8.5% rise in 2011. Near term, customers appear to be sharply reducing inventories given slowing demand in their businesses. However, with the proliferation of semiconductors in electronic devices and the replacement of fixed with programmable logic providing a positive demand backdrop, we see sequential orders rebounding in early 2012 within the automotive, computing, communications and industrial markets. Despite near term challenges, we think ALTR is gaining share through growth from new product releases.

▶ We believe the sequential gross margin will remain in a modestly tight range between 69% and 72% through the end of 2012. ALTR outsources its manufacturing, which contributes to relatively stable gross margins, but we see sales mix, varying yields and pricing causing slight changes in results. We expect R&D expense growth due to new product investments to outpace sales in 2012.

▶ Our 2012 EPS estimate assumes an 11% effective tax rate and a modest increase in the diluted share count.

## Investment Rationale/Risk

▶ Our hold recommendation reflects our view of uncertain end-market demand and valuations. Although we are concerned about elevated inventory in the supply chain and increasing R&D spending dampening near-term earnings, we believe ASIC displacement and market share gains will support healthy, above-peers long-term growth. With our view of relatively high profitability and with some financial leverage from ALTR's capital structure, we think its return on equity will also continue to top the industry's. However, considering the aforementioned risks, we think the fundamentals are largely reflected in the share price.

▶ Risks to our opinion and target price include deteriorating economic conditions, market share losses, limited supply from foundry partners, and excessive inventory buildup.

▶ Our 12-month target price of $40 is based on a price-to-earnings multiple of 16.5X, above the industry average, applied to our 2012 EPS estimate. We believe this multiple is warranted by what we view as ALTR's earnings growth, return on equity and risk compared to other players in the industry.

## Qualitative Risk Assessment

| LOW | MEDIUM | HIGH |
|---|---|---|

Our risk assessment reflects Altera's exposure to the sales swings of the semiconductor industry and competition from a larger rival, offset by the company's participation in a high-growth niche market.

## Quantitative Evaluations

**S&P Quality Ranking** B+

| D | C | B- | B | B+ | A- | A | A+ |
|---|---|---|---|---|---|---|---|

**Relative Strength Rank** MODERATE
45
LOWEST = 1     HIGHEST = 99

## Revenue/Earnings Data

**Revenue (Million $)**

| | 1Q | 2Q | 3Q | 4Q | Year |
|---|---|---|---|---|---|
| 2011 | 535.8 | 548.4 | 522.5 | -- | -- |
| 2010 | 402.3 | 469.3 | 527.5 | 555.4 | 1,954 |
| 2009 | 264.6 | 279.2 | 286.6 | 365.0 | 1,195 |
| 2008 | 336.1 | 359.9 | 356.8 | 314.5 | 1,367 |
| 2007 | 304.9 | 319.7 | 315.8 | 323.2 | 1,264 |
| 2006 | 292.8 | 334.1 | 341.2 | 317.4 | 1,286 |

**Earnings Per Share ($)**

| | | | | | |
|---|---|---|---|---|---|
| 2011 | 0.68 | 0.65 | 0.57 | E0.46 | E2.36 |
| 2010 | 0.50 | 0.58 | 0.69 | 0.72 | 2.49 |
| 2009 | 0.15 | 0.16 | 0.19 | 0.34 | 0.84 |
| 2008 | 0.27 | 0.32 | 0.31 | 0.28 | 1.18 |
| 2007 | 0.21 | 0.22 | 0.20 | 0.20 | 0.82 |
| 2006 | 0.16 | 0.21 | 0.24 | 0.27 | 0.88 |

Fiscal year ended Dec. 31. Next earnings report expected: NA. EPS Estimates based on S&P Operating Earnings; historical GAAP earnings are as reported.

## Dividend Data (Dates: mm/dd Payment Date: mm/dd/yy)

| Amount ($) | Date Decl. | Ex-Div. Date | Stk. of Record | Payment Date |
|---|---|---|---|---|
| 0.060 | 01/25 | 02/08 | 02/10 | 03/01/11 |
| 0.060 | 04/26 | 05/06 | 05/10 | 06/01/11 |
| 0.080 | 07/19 | 08/08 | 08/10 | 09/01/11 |
| 0.080 | 10/20 | 11/08 | 11/10 | 12/01/11 |

Dividends have been paid since 2007. Source: Company reports.

---

**Please read the Required Disclosures and Analyst Certification on the last page of this report.**

The McGraw-Hill Companies

## Business Summary October 24, 2011

CORPORATE OVERVIEW. Altera Corp. is a worldwide supplier of programmable logic devices (PLDs), HardCopy brand structured application specific integrated circuits (ASICs), pre-defined design building blocks known as intellectual property cores, and associated software for logic development.

The company's sales can be segmented by vertical markets. In 2010, The Telecom & Wireless market made up 44% of total revenues, Industrial Automation, Military & Automotive 21%, Networking, Computer & Storage 14%, and Other 21%.

MARKET PROFILE. There are three primary types of integrated circuits used in most digital devices: processors, which are used for control and computing tasks, memory products, which are used to store information, and logic devices, which manage the interchange and manipulation of digital signals within a system. Logic devices can be further split into two categories, fixed and programmable. Fixed logic devices, such as application specific integrated circuits (ASIC) and application specific standard products (ASSP), define the group of logic devices that are manufactured with a permanent set of instructions or functions. Conversely, programmable logic devices, such as field programmable gate arrays (FPGA) and complex programmable devices (CPLD) are not permanent. They are standard products, shipped blank and are programmed at the customer's PC or workstation, using proprietary software.

Since the company's chips are programmed at a desktop and not at a foundry, the customer has the ability to customize designs, an option that is limited in ASICs and ASSPs. Since both fixed and programmable logic devices can be used in the same devices, there is a natural competition between the technologies.

Fixed and programmable logic may perform the same job, but they have distinct differences. The fixed logic chip, which requires relatively high capital during the development stage because it is custom made, is generally a cheaper alternative for high-volume production. The chip tends to be smaller in size, and can be cheaper on a per-unit-basis due to economies of scale. However, the programmable logic chip, which require less capital upfront because it uses standard components and inexpensive software tools, can be more beneficial for low-volume applications. Furthermore, programmable customers enjoy the design flexibility during the development stage and can often develop products faster than with fixed logic, improving time-to-market. Because of these factors, we believe that programmable will grow faster than their fixed logic counterparts.

## Company Financials Fiscal Year Ended Dec. 31

| Per Share Data ($) | 2010 | 2009 | 2008 | 2007 | 2006 | 2005 | 2004 | 2003 | 2002 | 2001 |
|---|---|---|---|---|---|---|---|---|---|---|
| Tangible Book Value | 7.27 | 3.66 | 2.73 | 2.74 | 4.46 | 3.52 | 3.42 | 2.93 | 2.95 | 2.89 |
| Cash Flow | 2.58 | 0.94 | 1.28 | 0.91 | 0.96 | 0.82 | 0.80 | 0.51 | 0.36 | 0.04 |
| Earnings | 2.49 | 0.84 | 1.18 | 0.82 | 0.88 | 0.74 | 0.72 | 0.40 | 0.23 | -0.10 |
| S&P Core Earnings | 2.49 | 0.84 | 1.18 | 0.82 | 0.88 | 0.54 | 0.48 | 0.19 | -0.02 | -0.28 |
| Dividends | 0.22 | 0.20 | NA | 0.12 | Nil | Nil | Nil | Nil | Nil | Nil |
| Payout Ratio | 9% | 24% | 16% | 15% | Nil | Nil | Nil | Nil | Nil | Nil |
| Prices:High | 38.14 | 23.18 | 24.19 | 26.24 | 22.29 | 22.99 | 26.82 | 25.64 | 26.18 | 34.69 |
| Prices:Low | 20.89 | 13.92 | 12.99 | 18.00 | 15.54 | 15.96 | 17.50 | 10.30 | 8.32 | 14.66 |
| P/E Ratio:High | 15 | 28 | 21 | 32 | 25 | 31 | 37 | 64 | NM | NM |
| P/E Ratio:Low | 8 | 17 | 11 | 22 | 18 | 22 | 24 | 26 | NM | NM |

| Income Statement Analysis (Million $) | | | | | | | | | | |
|---|---|---|---|---|---|---|---|---|---|---|
| Revenue | 1,954 | 1,195 | 1,367 | 1,264 | 1,286 | 1,124 | 1,016 | 827 | 712 | 839 |
| Operating Income | 896 | 344 | 452 | 306 | 331 | 352 | 345 | 243 | 146 | 48.8 |
| Depreciation | 27.5 | 29.0 | 30.0 | 31.1 | 29.7 | 29.4 | 30.5 | 45.3 | 48.5 | 54.3 |
| Interest Expense | 3.84 | 5.09 | 15.5 | Nil | Nil | Nil | Nil | Nil | Nil | Nil |
| Pretax Income | 868 | 306 | 419 | 338 | 360 | 357 | 331 | 213 | 123 | -13.0 |
| Effective Tax Rate | NA | 17.8% | 14.2% | 14.1% | 10.1% | 21.9% | 16.8% | 27.0% | 26.0% | NM |
| Net Income | 783 | 251 | 360 | 290 | 323 | 279 | 275 | 155 | 91.3 | -39.8 |
| S&P Core Earnings | 783 | 251 | 360 | 290 | 323 | 204 | 182 | 70.7 | -8.66 | -106 |

| Balance Sheet & Other Financial Data (Million $) | | | | | | | | | | |
|---|---|---|---|---|---|---|---|---|---|---|
| Cash | 2,765 | 1,547 | 1,217 | 1,021 | 738 | 788 | 580 | 259 | 255 | 145 |
| Current Assets | 3,531 | 2,042 | 1,627 | 1,534 | 1,735 | 1,495 | 1,537 | 1,270 | 1,176 | 1,129 |
| Total Assets | 3,760 | 2,293 | 1,880 | 1,770 | 2,215 | 1,823 | 1,747 | 1,488 | 1,372 | 1,361 |
| Current Liabilities | 696 | 490 | 386 | 490 | 598 | 555 | 468 | 385 | 241 | 247 |
| Long Term Debt | 500 | 500 | 503 | 250 | 1.30 | 3.87 | Nil | Nil | Nil | Nil |
| Common Equity | 2,324 | 1,085 | 800 | 861 | 1,608 | 1,326 | 1,279 | 1,102 | 1,131 | 1,115 |
| Total Capital | 2,824 | 1,585 | 1,302 | 1,111 | 1,609 | 1,330 | 1,279 | 1,102 | 1,131 | 1,115 |
| Capital Expenditures | 12.4 | 11.1 | 40.3 | 31.2 | 36.5 | 25.9 | 24.7 | 13.9 | 9.87 | 65.8 |
| Cash Flow | 810 | 280 | 390 | 321 | 353 | 308 | 306 | 200 | 140 | 14.5 |
| Current Ratio | 5.1 | 4.2 | 4.2 | 3.1 | 2.9 | 2.7 | 3.3 | 3.3 | 4.9 | 4.6 |
| % Long Term Debt of Capitalization | 17.7 | 31.5 | 38.6 | 22.5 | 0.1 | 0.3 | Nil | Nil | Nil | Nil |
| % Net Income of Revenue | 40.1 | 21.0 | 26.3 | 23.0 | 25.1 | 24.8 | 27.1 | 18.8 | 12.8 | NM |
| % Return on Assets | 25.9 | 12.0 | 19.7 | 14.6 | 16.0 | 15.5 | 17.1 | 10.9 | 6.7 | NM |
| % Return on Equity | 45.9 | 26.6 | 43.3 | 23.5 | 22.5 | 21.0 | 23.1 | 13.9 | 8.1 | NM |

Data as orig reptd.; bef. results of disc opers/spec. items. Per share data adj. for stk. divs.; EPS diluted. E-Estimated. NA-Not Available. NM-Not Meaningful. NR-Not Ranked. UR-Under Review.

**Office:** 101 Innovation Drive, San Jose, CA 95134.
**Telephone:** 408-544-7000.
**Email:** inv_rel@altera.com
**Website:** http://www.altera.com

**Chrmn, Pres & CEO:** J.P. Daane
**COO:** W.Y. Hata
**SVP, CFO & Chief Acctg Officer:** R.J. Pasek
**Secy & General Counsel:** K.E. Schuelke

**Investor Contact:** S. Wylie (408-544-6996)
**Board Members:** J. P. Daane, E. W. Finney, R. J. Finocchio, Jr., K. McGarity, T. M. Nevens, K. A. Prabhu, J. C. Shoemaker, S. Wang

**Founded:** 1983
**Domicile:** Delaware
**Employees:** 2,666

# Altria Group Inc

STANDARD
&POOR'S

| S&P Recommendation **STRONG BUY** ★★★★★ | Price $27.25 (as of Nov 25, 2011) | 12-Mo. Target Price $30.00 | Investment Style Large-Cap Blend |
|---|---|---|---|

**GICS Sector** Consumer Staples
**Sub-Industry** Tobacco

**Summary** Altria Group (formerly Philip Morris Companies) is the largest U.S. cigarette producer. It spun off Kraft Foods in 2007 and its international cigarette operations in 2008.

## Key Stock Statistics (Source S&P, Vickers, company reports)

| | | | | | | | |
|---|---|---|---|---|---|---|---|
| 52-Wk Range | $28.14– 23.20 | S&P Oper. EPS 2011**E** | 2.02 | Market Capitalization(B) | $56.038 | Beta | 0.41 |
| Trailing 12-Month EPS | $1.67 | S&P Oper. EPS 2012**E** | 2.14 | Yield (%) | 6.02 | S&P 3-Yr. Proj. EPS CAGR(%) | 8 |
| Trailing 12-Month P/E | 16.3 | P/E on S&P Oper. EPS 2011**E** | 13.5 | Dividend Rate/Share | $1.64 | S&P Credit Rating | BBB |
| $10K Invested 5 Yrs Ago | NA | Common Shares Outstg. (M) | 2,056.4 | Institutional Ownership (%) | 59 | | |

## Price Performance

30-Week Mov. Avg. · · · 10-Week Mov. Avg. – – GAAP Earnings vs. Previous Year  Volume Above Avg. STARS
12-Mo. Target Price — Relative Strength ▲ Up ▼ Down ▶ No Change  Below Avg. ★

Options: ASE, CBOE, P, Ph

Analysis prepared by Equity Analyst **Esther Kwon, CFA** on Oct 31, 2011, when the stock traded at **$27.55**.

## Highlights

➤ We see a mid-single digit annual decline in cigarette industry volumes over the next few years, after an accelerated decline in 2009 due to a significant increase in the federal excise tax. We see MO revenues slipping about 2% in 2011, as higher pricing, line extensions and new product introductions are offset by declining consumption. In July 2011, Philip Morris USA raised cigarette prices $0.09 a pack on all brands after raising them $0.08 in late 2010.

➤ Over the next several years, we expect MO's margins to widen on higher pricing and restructuring actions. MO is targeting $400 million in annualized cost savings by the end of 2013 through a reduction of cigarette-related infrastructure.

➤ On a projected effective tax rate of 35.0% and about a 1% decline in shares outstanding, we estimate 2011 EPS of $2.02, up from $1.90 in 2010. In January 2011, Altria announced a new $1 billion share repurchase program, which was completed in the third quarter. In October, directors authorized a new $1 billion program, which MO intends to complete by the end of 2012. For 2012, we forecast EPS of $2.14, on a similar tax rate.

## Investment Rationale/Risk

➤ Although we continue to expect domestic cigarette industry volumes to contract over the long term, we see cigarette companies still having the ability to raise prices, and thus margins. Moreover, we look for more limited commodity input cost pressures than in other industries in the consumer staples sector. Operationally, we think Altria is likely to benefit from several factors over the next several years, including the integration of its 2009 acquisition of smokeless tobacco company UST and various restructuring actions.

➤ Risks to our recommendation and target price include possible pressures on trading multiples as investors remain cautious about court trials, and potential increases in excise taxes and smoking bans at the state and local level.

➤ Our 12-month target price of $30 is based on historical and peer forward P/E multiples. We apply a multiple of 14X, above the average historical forward P/E multiple but a discount to the domestic peer-average forward P/E due to more limited market share opportunities, to our 2012 EPS estimate of $2.14 to calculate our target price. The shares recently provided a dividend yield of nearly 6%.

## Qualitative Risk Assessment

| LOW | MEDIUM | HIGH |
|---|---|---|

MO is a large-cap company in an industry that is operationally very stable. However, the tobacco industry is beset by litigation. The company is subject to several ongoing legal actions, which could have a material impact on future cash flows.

## Quantitative Evaluations

**S&P Quality Ranking** A

| D | C | B- | B | B+ | A- | A | A+ |
|---|---|---|---|---|---|---|---|

**Relative Strength Rank** STRONG

81

LOWEST = 1  HIGHEST = 99

## Revenue/Earnings Data

**Revenue (Million $)**

| | 1Q | 2Q | 3Q | 4Q | Year |
|---|---|---|---|---|---|
| 2011 | 5,643 | 5,920 | 6,108 | -- | -- |
| 2010 | 3,951 | 4,341 | 4,461 | 4,139 | 16,892 |
| 2009 | 3,812 | 4,594 | 4,318 | 4,100 | 16,824 |
| 2008 | 3,604 | 4,179 | 4,341 | 3,833 | 15,957 |
| 2007 | 17,556 | 18,809 | 19,207 | 18,229 | 38,051 |
| 2006 | 24,355 | 25,769 | 25,885 | 25,398 | 101,407 |

**Earnings Per Share ($)**

| | | | | | |
|---|---|---|---|---|---|
| 2011 | 0.45 | 0.21 | 0.57 | E0.48 | E2.02 |
| 2010 | 0.39 | 0.50 | 0.54 | 0.44 | 1.87 |
| 2009 | 0.28 | 0.49 | 0.42 | 0.35 | 1.54 |
| 2008 | 0.29 | 0.43 | 0.42 | 0.33 | 1.48 |
| 2007 | 1.01 | 1.05 | 1.24 | 1.03 | 4.33 |
| 2006 | 1.65 | 1.29 | 1.36 | 1.40 | 5.71 |

Fiscal year ended Dec. 31. Next earnings report expected: Late January. EPS Estimates based on S&P Operating Earnings; historical GAAP earnings are as reported.

## Dividend Data (Dates: mm/dd Payment Date: mm/dd/yy)

| Amount ($) | Date Decl. | Ex-Div. Date | Stk. of Record | Payment Date |
|---|---|---|---|---|
| 0.380 | 12/15 | 12/23 | 12/28 | 01/10/11 |
| 0.380 | 02/24 | 03/11 | 03/15 | 04/11/11 |
| 0.380 | 05/19 | 06/13 | 06/15 | 07/11/11 |
| 0.410 | 08/26 | 09/13 | 09/15 | 10/11/11 |

Dividends have been paid since 1928. Source: Company reports.

---

**Please read the Required Disclosures and Analyst Certification on the last page of this report.**

The McGraw-Hill Companies

# Altria Group Inc

STANDARD
&POOR'S

## Business Summary October 31, 2011

CORPORATE OVERVIEW. Altria Group (formerly Philip Morris Cos., Inc.) is a holding company for wholly owned and majority owned subsidiaries that make and market various consumer products, now primarily including cigarettes. Prior to the March 30, 2007, spinoff of Kraft Foods, Altria Group's reportable segments were domestic tobacco, international tobacco, North American food, international food and financial services. The spinoff of Philip Morris International was completed on March 28, 2008, at a one-for-one exchange rate.

Philip Morris U.S.A. (PM USA) is the largest U.S. tobacco company, with total U.S. cigarette shipments amounting to 140.8 billion units in 2010 (down 5.3% from 2009), accounting for 49.8% of total U.S. cigarette sales (down fractionally from 49.9% in 2009). Focus brands include Marlboro (the largest selling brand in the U.S.), Virginia Slims and Parliament in the premium category, and Basic in the discount category.

In January 2009, Altria completed the acquisition of UST Inc., the largest U.S. manufacturer and marketer of smokeless tobacco products, for $11.7 billion, which included the assumption of about $1.3 billion of debt.

Kraft Foods, the largest packaged food company in North America and sec-

ond largest in the world, was spun off on March 30, 2007, to MO shareholders as a tax-free stock dividend. MO shareholders received approximately 0.68 of a Kraft share per MO share owned as a stock dividend at the end of March 2007, and cash in lieu of fractional shares.

In July 2002, MO sold its Miller Brewing Co. subsidiary to South African Brewers, plc., receiving $3.38 billion worth of shares in the newly formed company, SABMiller. As of December 31, 2010, this stake represented a 27.1% economic and voting interest.

CORPORATE STRATEGY. After considering a number of restructuring alternatives, including the possibility of separating Altria Group, Inc. into two, or potentially three, independent entities, the company in June 2007 announced that cigarette production for international markets would be shifted from U.S. facilities to European plants. It subsequently decided to spin off its international tobacco operations, with an effective date of March 28, 2008.

## Company Financials Fiscal Year Ended Dec. 31

| Per Share Data ($) | 2010 | 2009 | 2008 | 2007 | 2006 | 2005 | 2004 | 2003 | 2002 | 2001 |
|---|---|---|---|---|---|---|---|---|---|---|
| Tangible Book Value | NM | NM | NM | 3.97 | NM | NM | NM | NM | NM | NM |
| Cash Flow | 2.01 | 1.69 | 1.58 | 4.79 | 6.57 | 5.92 | 5.35 | 5.22 | 6.10 | 4.93 |
| Earnings | 1.87 | 1.54 | 1.48 | 4.33 | 5.71 | 5.10 | 4.57 | 4.52 | 5.21 | 3.88 |
| S&P Core Earnings | 1.89 | 1.58 | 1.29 | 4.33 | 5.62 | 5.14 | 4.54 | 4.49 | 4.03 | 3.62 |
| Dividends | 1.46 | 1.32 | 1.68 | 3.05 | 3.32 | 3.06 | 2.82 | 2.64 | 2.44 | 2.22 |
| Payout Ratio | 78% | 86% | 1% | 70% | 58% | 60% | 62% | 58% | 47% | 57% |
| Prices:High | 26.22 | 20.47 | 79.59 | 90.50 | 86.56 | 78.68 | 61.88 | 55.03 | 57.79 | 53.88 |
| Prices:Low | 19.14 | 14.50 | 14.34 | 63.13 | 68.36 | 60.40 | 44.50 | 27.70 | 35.40 | 38.75 |
| P/E Ratio:High | 14 | 13 | 54 | 21 | 15 | 15 | 14 | 12 | 11 | 14 |
| P/E Ratio:Low | 10 | 9 | 10 | 15 | 12 | 12 | 10 | 6 | 7 | 10 |

| Income Statement Analysis (Million $) | | | | | | | | | | |
|---|---|---|---|---|---|---|---|---|---|---|
| Revenue | 16,892 | 16,824 | 15,957 | 38,051 | 70,324 | 68,920 | 63,963 | 60,704 | 62,182 | 72,944 |
| Operating Income | 6,541 | 6,627 | 5,229 | 14,892 | 19,705 | 19,004 | 17,929 | 17,663 | 18,476 | 18,039 |
| Depreciation | 276 | 291 | 215 | 980 | 1,804 | 1,675 | 1,607 | 1,440 | 1,331 | 2,337 |
| Interest Expense | 1,133 | 1,189 | 237 | 653 | 877 | 1,556 | 1,417 | 1,367 | 1,327 | 1,659 |
| Pretax Income | 5,723 | 4,877 | 4,789 | 13,257 | 16,536 | 15,435 | 14,004 | 14,760 | 18,098 | 14,284 |
| Effective Tax Rate | NA | 34.2% | 35.5% | 30.9% | 26.3% | 29.9% | 32.4% | 34.9% | 35.5% | 37.9% |
| Net Income | 3,905 | 3,206 | 3,090 | 9,161 | 12,022 | 10,668 | 9,420 | 9,204 | 11,102 | 8,566 |
| S&P Core Earnings | 3,945 | 3,280 | 2,687 | 9,163 | 11,818 | 10,766 | 9,348 | 9,145 | 8,593 | 7,959 |

| Balance Sheet & Other Financial Data (Million $) | | | | | | | | | | |
|---|---|---|---|---|---|---|---|---|---|---|
| Cash | 2,314 | 1,871 | 7,916 | 6,498 | 5,020 | 6,258 | 5,744 | 3,777 | 565 | 453 |
| Current Assets | 5,981 | 10,576 | 16,527 | 28,919 | 26,152 | 25,781 | 25,901 | 21,382 | 17,441 | 17,275 |
| Total Assets | 37,402 | 36,677 | 27,215 | 57,211 | 104,270 | 107,949 | 101,648 | 96,175 | 87,540 | 84,968 |
| Current Liabilities | 6,840 | 7,992 | 7,642 | 18,782 | 25,427 | 26,158 | 23,574 | 21,393 | 19,082 | 20,141 |
| Long Term Debt | 12,194 | 11,185 | 6,839 | 11,046 | 14,498 | 17,868 | 18,683 | 21,163 | 21,355 | 18,651 |
| Common Equity | 5,195 | 4,072 | 2,828 | 18,554 | 39,619 | 35,707 | 30,714 | 25,077 | 19,478 | 19,620 |
| Total Capital | 17,421 | 16,064 | 14,662 | 33,610 | 68,496 | 71,945 | 67,714 | 64,110 | 56,832 | 52,768 |
| Capital Expenditures | 168 | 273 | 241 | 1,458 | 2,454 | 2,206 | 1,913 | 1,974 | 2,009 | 1,922 |
| Cash Flow | 4,183 | 3,497 | 3,305 | 10,141 | 13,826 | 12,343 | 11,027 | 10,644 | 12,433 | 10,903 |
| Current Ratio | 0.9 | 1.3 | 2.2 | 1.5 | 1.0 | 1.0 | 1.1 | 1.0 | 0.9 | 0.9 |
| % Long Term Debt of Capitalization | 70.0 | 69.6 | 46.6 | 30.0 | 21.2 | 24.8 | 27.6 | 33.0 | 37.6 | 35.3 |
| % Net Income of Revenue | 23.1 | 19.1 | 19.4 | 24.1 | 17.1 | 15.5 | 14.7 | 15.2 | 17.9 | 11.7 |
| % Return on Assets | 10.5 | 10.0 | 7.3 | 11.4 | 11.3 | 10.2 | 9.5 | 10.0 | 12.9 | 10.4 |
| % Return on Equity | 84.3 | 92.9 | 28.9 | 31.5 | 31.9 | 32.1 | 33.8 | 41.3 | 56.8 | 49.5 |

Data as orig reptd.; bef. results of disc opers/spec. items. Per share data adj. for stk. divs.; EPS diluted. E-Estimated. NA-Not Available. NM-Not Meaningful. NR-Not Ranked. UR-Under Review.

**Office:** 6601 W Broad St, Richmond, VA 23230-1723.
**Telephone:** 804-274-2200.
**Website:** http://www.altria.com
**Chrmn & CEO:** M.E. Szymanczyk

**EVP & CFO:** H.A. Willard
**EVP & CTO:** J.R. Nelson, Jr.
**EVP & General Counsel:** D.F. Keane
**Chief Admin Officer:** M.J. Barrington

**Investor Contact:** C.B. Fleet (804-484-8222)
**Board Members:** E. E. Bailey, G. L. Baliles, J. T. Casteen, III, D. S. Devitre, T. F. Farrell, II, T. W. Jones, W. L. Kiely, III, G. Munoz, N. Sakkab, M. E. Szymanczyk

**Founded:** 1919
**Domicile:** Virginia
**Employees:** 10,000

# Amazon.com Inc

**STANDARD &POOR'S**

| S&P Recommendation | HOLD ★ ★ ★ ☆ ☆ | Price $182.40 (as of Nov 25, 2011) | 12-Mo. Target Price $230.00 | Investment Style Large-Cap Growth |
|---|---|---|---|---|

**GICS Sector** Consumer Discretionary
**Sub-Industry** Internet Retail

**Summary** This leading online retailer sells a broad range of items from books to consumer electronics to home and garden products.

## Key Stock Statistics (Source S&P, Vickers, company reports)

| | | | | | | | |
|---|---|---|---|---|---|---|---|
| 52-Wk Range | $246.71– 160.59 | S&P Oper. EPS 2011**E** | 1.35 | Market Capitalization(B) | $82.947 | Beta | 1.13 |
| Trailing 12-Month EPS | $1.90 | S&P Oper. EPS 2012**E** | 2.50 | Yield (%) | Nil | S&P 3-Yr. Proj. EPS CAGR(%) | 30 |
| Trailing 12-Month P/E | 96.0 | P/E on S&P Oper. EPS 2011**E** | NM | Dividend Rate/Share | Nil | S&P Credit Rating | A |
| $10K Invested 5 Yrs Ago | $43,008 | Common Shares Outstg. (M) | 454.8 | Institutional Ownership (%) | 68 | | |

## Price Performance

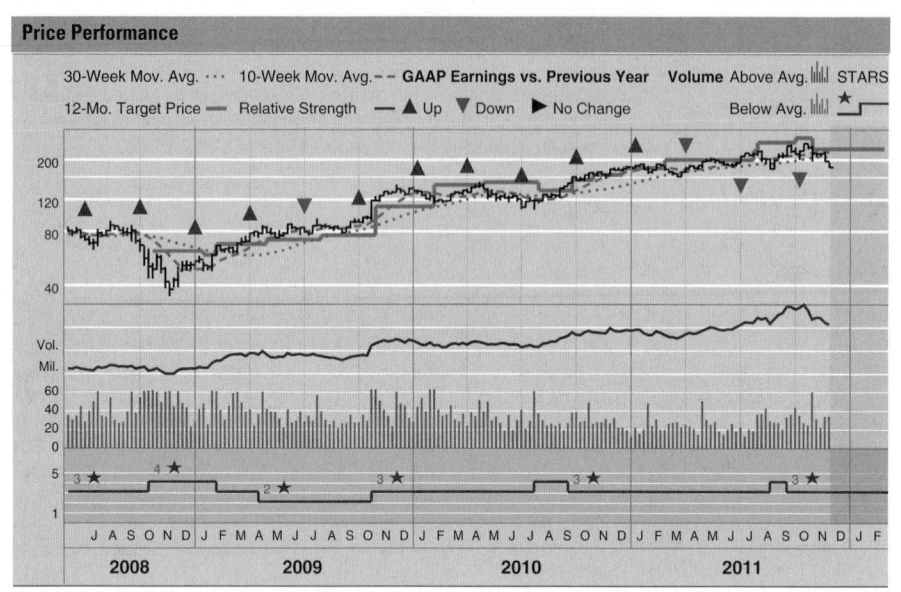

30-Week Mov. Avg. ···    10-Week Mov. Avg. ‑ ‑    **GAAP Earnings vs. Previous Year**    Volume  Above Avg. STARS
12-Mo. Target Price —    Relative Strength ‑ ‑    ▲ Up   ▼ Down   ► No Change    Below Avg.  ★

Options: ASE, CBOE, P, Ph

Analysis prepared by Equity Analyst **Michael Souers** on Nov 09, 2011, when the stock traded at **$217.99**.

## Highlights

➤ We look for net sales to rise 33% in 2012, following our projection of a 43% advance in 2011. We expect this growth to be driven by market share gains from traditional retailers, international expansion, new hardware offerings such as the Kindle Fire tablet, increased digital content and an increase in third-party sellers. Amazon Prime continues to drive increased sales results and build customer loyalty both domestically and abroad. In our view, AMZN's relentless focus on providing value to consumers through selection and price will allow the company to continue to gain notable market share.

➤ In 2012, we expect gross margins to narrow slightly on product mix shift and competitive pressures, partially offset by an increase in third-party sales. We look for operating margins to widen modestly as we expect investments in fulfillment, marketing and technology infrastructure to ease following significant increases in 2011.

➤ After slightly higher net interest income, an effective tax rate of 25.0%, and a flat diluted share count, we project 2012 EPS of $2.50, a significant increase from the $1.35 we project the company to earn in 2011.

## Investment Rationale/Risk

➤ AMZN continues to demonstrate the strength and worldwide potential of its business model, in our view. Continued investments in long-term growth opportunities such as Amazon Prime, hardware such as the Kindle and Kindle Fire and increased digital content should provide new sources of revenue over the next few years. Long term, we expect AMZN's initiatives to result in continued strong sales results and significant margin expansion, as it leverages its leading brand name and position as an Internet retailer. We consider AMZN a best-in-class retailer that generates significant free cash flow. Despite these positives, we think the shares are fairly valued, trading at 85X our 2012 EPS estimate.

➤ Risks to our opinion and target price include a double-dip recession, the potential for lower-than-projected revenues should growth initiatives fail to live up to their potential, and unfavorable currency impacts.

➤ Our 12-month target price of $230 is based on our discounted cash flow analysis, which assumes a weighted average cost of capital of 10.8% and a terminal growth rate of 4%.

## Qualitative Risk Assessment

| LOW | MEDIUM | HIGH |
|---|---|---|

Our risk assessment reflects AMZN's large market capitalization and leading position in the e-commerce industry, offset by increasing competition.

## Quantitative Evaluations

**S&P Quality Ranking**    B-

| D | C | B- | B | B+ | A- | A | A+ |
|---|---|---|---|---|---|---|---|

**Relative Strength Rank**    WEAK

21

LOWEST = 1    HIGHEST = 99

## Revenue/Earnings Data

**Revenue (Million $)**

| | 1Q | 2Q | 3Q | 4Q | Year |
|---|---|---|---|---|---|
| 2011 | 9,857 | 9,913 | 10,876 | -- | -- |
| 2010 | 7,131 | 6,566 | 7,560 | 12,948 | 34,204 |
| 2009 | 4,889 | 4,651 | 5,449 | 9,519 | 24,509 |
| 2008 | 4,135 | 4,063 | 4,264 | 6,704 | 19,166 |
| 2007 | 3,015 | 2,886 | 3,262 | 5,673 | 14,835 |
| 2006 | 2,279 | 2,139 | 2,307 | 3,986 | 10,711 |

**Earnings Per Share ($)**

| | 1Q | 2Q | 3Q | 4Q | Year |
|---|---|---|---|---|---|
| 2011 | 0.44 | 0.41 | 0.14 | E0.36 | E1.35 |
| 2010 | 0.66 | 0.45 | 0.51 | 0.91 | 2.53 |
| 2009 | 0.41 | 0.32 | 0.45 | 0.85 | 2.04 |
| 2008 | 0.34 | 0.37 | 0.27 | 0.52 | 1.49 |
| 2007 | 0.26 | 0.19 | 0.19 | 0.49 | 1.12 |
| 2006 | 0.12 | 0.05 | 0.05 | 0.23 | 0.45 |

Fiscal year ended Dec. 31. Next earnings report expected: Late January. EPS Estimates based on S&P Operating Earnings; historical GAAP earnings are as reported.

## Dividend Data

No cash dividends have been paid.

The **McGraw·Hill** Companies

# Amazon.com Inc

**STANDARD &POOR'S**

## Business Summary November 09, 2011

CORPORATE OVERVIEW. Since opening for business as "Earth's Biggest Bookstore" in July 1995, Amazon.com has expanded into a number of other product categories, including: apparel, shoes and jewelry; electronics and computers; movies, music and games; toys, kids and baby; sports and outdoors; home and garden; tools, auto and industrial; grocery; health and beauty; and digital downloads.

AMZN has virtually unlimited online shelf space, and can offer customers a vast selection of products through an efficient search and retrieval interface. The company personalizes shopping by recommending items which, based on previous purchases, are likely to interest a particular customer. Key Web site features also include editorial and customer reviews, manufacturer product information, secure payment systems, wedding and baby registries, customer wish lists, and the ability to view selected interior pages and search the entire contents of many books.

The company operates the following retail Web sites: www.amazon.com (U.S.), www.amazon.co.uk (U.K.), www.amazon.de (Germany), www.amazon.fr (France), www.amazon.co.jp (Japan), www.amazon.ca (Canada), www.amazon.cn (China), www.joyo.cn, www.shopbop.com, www.endless.com, and www.zappos.com. Amazon also designs, manufac-

tures and sells a wireless e-reading device, the Amazon Kindle. It focuses first and foremost on the customer experience by offering a wide selection of merchandise, low prices and convenience.

In addition to being the seller of record for a broad range of new products, AMZN allows other businesses and individuals to sell new, used and collectible products on its Web sites through its Merchant and Amazon Marketplace programs. The company earns fixed fees, sales commissions, and/or per-unit activity fees under these programs. AMZN also serves developers and enterprises of all sizes through Amazon Web Services, which provides access to technology infrastructure that developers can use to enable virtually any type of business.

Starting in 2003, the company began reporting results for two core segments: North America (55% of 2010 net sales) and International (45%). In 2010, media products accounted for 44% of net sales, electronics and other general merchandise for 54%, and other 3%.

## Company Financials Fiscal Year Ended Dec. 31

| Per Share Data ($) | 2010 | 2009 | 2008 | 2007 | 2006 | 2005 | 2004 | 2003 | 2002 | 2001 |
|---|---|---|---|---|---|---|---|---|---|---|
| Tangible Book Value | 10.47 | 7.35 | 4.44 | 2.30 | 0.58 | 0.15 | NM | NM | NM | NM |
| Cash Flow | 3.77 | 2.51 | 2.28 | 1.76 | 0.93 | 1.07 | 1.56 | 0.27 | -0.16 | -0.80 |
| Earnings | 2.53 | 2.04 | 1.49 | 1.12 | 0.45 | 0.78 | 1.39 | 0.08 | -0.40 | -1.53 |
| S&P Core Earnings | 2.53 | NA | 1.41 | 1.12 | 0.48 | 0.83 | 1.27 | 0.02 | -0.64 | -2.49 |
| Dividends | Nil | Nil | Nil | Nil | Nil | Nil | Nil | Nil | Nil | Nil |
| Payout Ratio | Nil | Nil | Nil | Nil | Nil | Nil | Nil | Nil | Nil | Nil |
| Prices:High | 185.65 | 145.91 | 97.43 | 101.09 | 48.58 | 50.00 | 57.82 | 61.15 | 25.00 | 22.38 |
| Prices:Low | 105.80 | 47.63 | 34.68 | 36.30 | 25.76 | 30.60 | 33.00 | 18.55 | 9.03 | 5.51 |
| P/E Ratio:High | 73 | 72 | 65 | 90 | NM | 64 | 42 | NM | NM | NM |
| P/E Ratio:Low | 42 | 23 | 23 | 32 | NM | 39 | 24 | NM | NM | NM |

| Income Statement Analysis (Million $) | 2010 | 2009 | 2008 | 2007 | 2006 | 2005 | 2004 | 2003 | 2002 | 2001 |
|---|---|---|---|---|---|---|---|---|---|---|
| Revenue | 34,204 | 24,509 | 19,166 | 14,835 | 10,711 | 8,490 | 6,921 | 5,264 | 3,933 | 3,122 |
| Operating Income | 1,974 | 1,386 | 1,129 | 926 | 629 | 553 | 508 | 349 | 193 | 35.1 |
| Depreciation | 568 | 206 | 340 | 271 | 205 | 121 | 75.7 | 78.3 | 87.8 | 266 |
| Interest Expense | 39.0 | 34.0 | 71.0 | 77.0 | 78.0 | 92.0 | 107 | 130 | 143 | 139 |
| Pretax Income | 1,504 | 1,155 | 892 | 660 | 377 | 428 | 356 | 35.3 | -150 | -557 |
| Effective Tax Rate | NA | 21.9% | 27.7% | 27.9% | 49.6% | 22.2% | NM | NM | NM | NM |
| Net Income | 1,152 | 902 | 645 | 476 | 190 | 333 | 588 | 35.3 | -150 | -557 |
| S&P Core Earnings | 1,152 | NA | 609 | 476 | 203 | 354 | 539 | 10.3 | -242 | -910 |

| Balance Sheet & Other Financial Data (Million $) | 2010 | 2009 | 2008 | 2007 | 2006 | 2005 | 2004 | 2003 | 2002 | 2001 |
|---|---|---|---|---|---|---|---|---|---|---|
| Cash | 8,762 | 6,366 | 3,727 | 3,112 | 2,019 | 2,000 | 1,779 | 1,395 | 1,301 | 997 |
| Current Assets | 13,747 | 9,797 | 6,157 | 5,164 | 3,373 | 2,929 | 2,539 | 1,821 | 1,616 | 1,208 |
| Total Assets | 18,797 | 13,813 | 8,314 | 6,485 | 4,363 | 3,696 | 3,249 | 2,162 | 1,990 | 1,638 |
| Current Liabilities | 10,372 | 7,364 | 4,746 | 3,714 | 2,532 | 1,929 | 1,620 | 1,253 | 1,066 | 921 |
| Long Term Debt | 184 | 109 | 533 | 1,282 | 1,247 | 1,521 | 1,855 | 1,945 | 2,277 | 2,156 |
| Common Equity | 6,864 | 5,257 | 2,672 | 1,197 | 431 | 246 | -227 | -1,036 | -1,353 | -1,440 |
| Total Capital | 6,864 | 5,388 | 3,205 | 2,479 | 1,678 | 1,767 | 1,628 | 909 | 924 | 716 |
| Capital Expenditures | 979 | 373 | 333 | 224 | 216 | 204 | 89.1 | 46.0 | 39.2 | 50.3 |
| Cash Flow | 1,720 | 1,108 | 985 | 747 | 395 | 454 | 664 | 114 | -62.2 | -291 |
| Current Ratio | 1.3 | 1.3 | 1.3 | 1.4 | 1.3 | 1.5 | 1.6 | 1.5 | 1.5 | 1.3 |
| % Long Term Debt of Capitalization | Nil | 2.0 | 16.6 | 51.7 | 74.3 | 86.1 | 113.9 | 213.9 | 246.3 | 301.1 |
| % Net Income of Revenue | 3.4 | 3.7 | 3.4 | 3.2 | 1.8 | 3.9 | 8.5 | 0.7 | NM | NM |
| % Return on Assets | 7.1 | 8.2 | 8.7 | 8.8 | 4.7 | 9.6 | 21.8 | 1.7 | NM | NM |
| % Return on Equity | 19.0 | 22.8 | 33.3 | 58.5 | 56.1 | NM | NM | NM | NM | NM |

Data as orig reptd.; bef. results of disc opers/spec. items. Per share data adj. for stk. divs.; EPS diluted. E-Estimated. NA-Not Available. NM-Not Meaningful. NR-Not Ranked. UR-Under Review.

**Office:** 1200 12th Avenue South, Seattle, WA 98144-2734.
**Telephone:** 206-266-1000.
**Email:** ir@amazon.com
**Website:** http://www.amazon.com

**Chrmn, Pres & CEO:** J.P. Bezos
**COO:** M.A. Onetto
**SVP & CFO:** T.J. Szkutak
**SVP, Secy & General Counsel:** L.M. Wilson

**Chief Acctg Officer & Cntlr:** S.L. Reynolds
**Investor Contact:** R. Eldridge (206-266-2171)
**Board Members:** T. A. Alberg, J. P. Bezos, J. S. Brown, W. B. Gordon, B. G. Krikorian, A. Monie, J. J. Rubinstein, T. O. Ryder, P. Stonesifer

**Founded:** 1994
**Domicile:** Delaware
**Employees:** 33,700

*The McGraw-Hill Companies*

# Ameren Corp

**STANDARD &POOR'S**

| S&P Recommendation **HOLD** ★★★☆☆ | Price $31.51 (as of Nov 25, 2011) | 12-Mo. Target Price $32.00 | Investment Style Large-Cap Value |
|---|---|---|---|

**GICS Sector** Utilities
**Sub-Industry** Multi-Utilities

**Summary** Ameren is the holding company for the largest electric utility in the state of Missouri and several utilities in Illinois.

## Key Stock Statistics (Source S&P, Vickers, company reports)

| | | | | | | | |
|---|---|---|---|---|---|---|---|
| 52-Wk Range | $33.49– 25.55 | S&P Oper. EPS 2011E | 2.58 | Market Capitalization(B) | $7.633 | Beta | 0.61 |
| Trailing 12-Month EPS | $2.27 | S&P Oper. EPS 2012E | 2.42 | Yield (%) | 5.08 | S&P 3-Yr. Proj. EPS CAGR(%) | -6 |
| Trailing 12-Month P/E | 13.9 | P/E on S&P Oper. EPS 2011E | 12.2 | Dividend Rate/Share | $1.60 | S&P Credit Rating | BBB- |
| $10K Invested 5 Yrs Ago | $7,800 | Common Shares Outstg. (M) | 242.2 | Institutional Ownership (%) | 60 | | |

## Price Performance

30-Week Mov. Avg. ··· 10-Week Mov. Avg. - - GAAP Earnings vs. Previous Year   Volume Above Avg. STARS
12-Mo. Target Price — Relative Strength — ▲ Up ▼ Down ► No Change   Below Avg.

Options: P, Ph

Analysis prepared by Equity Analyst **Justin McCann** on Nov 15, 2011, when the stock traded at **$32.76**.

## Highlights

➤ We expect operating EPS in 2011 to decline approximately 6% from 2010's $2.75. Operating EPS in the first nine months of 2011 was $0.11 below the year-earlier level, as the impact of lower realized power prices, higher fuel transportation costs in the merchant generation segment, and increased storm-related costs at the utilities, was partially offset by the benefit of electric rate increases in Missouri and Illinois and lower interest expense.

➤ For 2012, we expect operating EPS to decline about 6% from projected results for 2011, on lower merchant generation margins and an assumed return to more normal weather after the warmer than normal summer in 2011. This should be partially offset by expected electric and gas rate increases in Illinois and a full year of the electric rate increase in Missouri.

➤ On July 13, 2011, the Missouri Public Service Commission authorized Ameren Missouri an annual increase of about $173 million (7%) in electric rates, effective as of July 31, 2011. In February 2011, Ameren Illinois filed for an annual increase of $111 million in electric and gas rates. A decision is expected in January 2012, when the new rates would go into effect.

## Investment Rationale/Risk

➤ We believe the recent rise in the shares has reflected the investor shift to the utilities sector due to the extraordinary volatility and often sharp declines in the broader market, the better than expected results in the third quarter, and the above-peers yield from the dividend. Earlier, however, the performance of the stock had been restricted, in our view, by the projected earnings decline for 2011 and 2012, the continuing weakness in the power markets, and the impact of the nuclear crisis in Japan, which affected the shares of virtually all of the nuclear operating utilities in the U.S. We view the stock as appropriately valued at recent levels.

➤ Risks to our recommendation and target price include a much steeper than projected decline in the company's power supply margins, and a substantial drop in the average P/E ratio of AEE's peer group as a whole.

➤ The recent yield from the dividend was about 4.9%, above the recent peer yield of about 4.2%. However, we expect the payout ratio to increase from 56% of operating EPS in 2010 to about 60% of our estimate for 2011. Our target price is $32, a discount-to-peers P/E multiple of 13.2X our operating EPS estimate for 2012.

## Qualitative Risk Assessment

| LOW | MEDIUM | HIGH |
|---|---|---|

Our risk assessment reflects our expectation of steady cash flow from the company's regulated utilities, which have the benefit of fuel costs that are below the industry average, partly offset by the continuing weakness in the power markets and the economy.

## Quantitative Evaluations

**S&P Quality Ranking** B

| D | C | B- | B | B+ | A- | A | A+ |
|---|---|---|---|---|---|---|---|

**Relative Strength Rank** STRONG
86
LOWEST = 1    HIGHEST = 99

## Revenue/Earnings Data

**Revenue (Million $)**

| | 1Q | 2Q | 3Q | 4Q | Year |
|---|---|---|---|---|---|
| 2011 | 1,904 | 1,781 | 2,268 | -- | -- |
| 2010 | 1,916 | 1,704 | 2,254 | 1,706 | 7,638 |
| 2009 | 1,916 | 1,684 | 1,815 | 1,675 | 7,090 |
| 2008 | 2,081 | 1,790 | 2,060 | 1,908 | 7,839 |
| 2007 | 2,019 | 1,723 | 1,997 | 1,807 | 7,546 |
| 2006 | 1,800 | 1,550 | 1,910 | 1,620 | 6,880 |

**Earnings Per Share ($)**

| | | | | | |
|---|---|---|---|---|---|
| 2011 | 0.30 | 0.57 | 1.18 | E0.17 | E2.58 |
| 2010 | 0.43 | 0.64 | -0.70 | 0.22 | 0.58 |
| 2009 | 0.66 | 0.77 | 1.04 | 0.33 | 2.78 |
| 2008 | 0.66 | 0.98 | 0.97 | 0.27 | 2.88 |
| 2007 | 0.59 | 0.69 | 1.18 | 0.52 | 2.98 |
| 2006 | 0.34 | 0.60 | 1.42 | 0.30 | 2.66 |

Fiscal year ended Dec. 31. Next earnings report expected: Late February. EPS Estimates based on S&P Operating Earnings; historical GAAP earnings are as reported.

## Dividend Data (Dates: mm/dd Payment Date: mm/dd/yy)

| Amount ($) | Date Decl. | Ex-Div. Date | Stk. of Record | Payment Date |
|---|---|---|---|---|
| 0.385 | 02/09 | 03/07 | 03/09 | 03/31/11 |
| 0.385 | 04/21 | 06/06 | 06/08 | 06/30/11 |
| 0.385 | 08/12 | 09/06 | 09/08 | 09/30/11 |
| 0.400 | 10/14 | 12/05 | 12/07 | 12/30/11 |

Dividends have been paid since 1906. Source: Company reports.

---

**Please read the Required Disclosures and Analyst Certification on the last page of this report.**

*The McGraw-Hill Companies*

# Ameren Corp

STANDARD &POOR'S

## Business Summary November 15, 2011

CORPORATE OVERVIEW. Ameren Corporation (AEE) is a holding company that operates regulated electric and natural gas utilities and non-regulated businesses, including energy marketing, trading and consulting services, in Missouri and Illinois. AEE's Utility Operations segment is comprised of its electric generation and electric and gas transmission and distribution operations.

The company's utility subsidiaries include: Ameren Missouri - formerly AmerenUE (Union Electric Company) - and, as of October 1, 2010, Ameren Illinois Co., after the merger of AEE's three Illinois utilities - Central Illinois Light Co. (CILCO), Central Illinois Public Service Co. (CIPS) and Illinois Power Co. (IP) - into a single company. Ameren Energy Generating Co. (Genco) is AEE's merchant electric generation business. In 2010, the company's electric services contributed 85.4% of its consolidated operating revenues (83.3% in 2009), while its gas services contributed 14.6% (16.7%).

CORPORATE STRATEGY. Although AEE has attempted to keep its rates low

through disciplined cost control and efficient operations, the costs of nearly every aspect of its business have been rising at a rapid pace. Since new customer rates are usually based on historical costs after an approximate one-year regulatory review, by the time they have been implemented they are already inadequate to fully recover the current costs and to earn a fair return on the company's investment. AEE has determined that in order to deal with this problem more effectively (and to avoid customer shock at a sudden sharp increase in rates), it intends to seek smaller and more frequent rate increases. It also plans to seek automatic cost recovery mechanisms for its most expensive items, such as its fuel costs and environmental investments.

## Company Financials  Fiscal Year Ended Dec. 31

| Per Share Data ($) | 2010 | 2009 | 2008 | 2007 | 2006 | 2005 | 2004 | 2003 | 2002 | 2001 |
|---|---|---|---|---|---|---|---|---|---|---|
| Tangible Book Value | 30.42 | 29.04 | 28.10 | 27.48 | 26.80 | 25.08 | 24.92 | 23.19 | 24.95 | 24.26 |
| Earnings | 0.58 | 2.78 | 2.88 | 2.98 | 2.66 | 3.13 | 2.84 | 3.14 | 2.60 | 3.45 |
| S&P Core Earnings | 2.76 | 2.63 | 2.09 | 3.04 | 2.90 | 3.32 | 3.12 | 3.28 | 2.36 | 2.81 |
| Dividends | 1.54 | 1.54 | 2.54 | 2.54 | 2.54 | 2.54 | 2.54 | 2.54 | 2.54 | 2.54 |
| Payout Ratio | NM | 55% | 88% | 85% | 95% | 81% | 89% | 81% | 98% | 74% |
| Prices:High | 29.89 | 35.35 | 54.29 | 55.00 | 55.24 | 56.77 | 50.36 | 46.50 | 45.25 | 46.00 |
| Prices:Low | 23.09 | 19.51 | 25.51 | 47.10 | 47.96 | 47.51 | 40.55 | 42.55 | 34.72 | 36.53 |
| P/E Ratio:High | 52 | 13 | 19 | 18 | 21 | 18 | 18 | 15 | 17 | 13 |
| P/E Ratio:Low | 40 | 7 | 9 | 16 | 18 | 15 | 14 | 14 | 13 | 11 |
| **Income Statement Analysis** (Million $) | | | | | | | | | | |
| Revenue | 7,638 | 7,090 | 7,839 | 7,546 | 6,880 | 6,780 | 5,160 | 4,593 | 3,841 | 4,506 |
| Depreciation | 837 | 801 | 742 | 681 | 661 | 632 | 557 | 519 | 431 | 406 |
| Maintenance | NA | NA | NA | NA | NA | NA | NA | NA | NA | 382 |
| Fixed Charges Coverage | 1.96 | 2.88 | 3.21 | 3.33 | 3.48 | 4.32 | 3.81 | 3.61 | 4.04 | 4.65 |
| Construction Credits | NA | NA | NA | NA | NA | NA | NA | 4.00 | 11.0 | 20.8 |
| Effective Tax Rate | 68.3% | 34.7% | 33.7% | 33.5% | 32.7% | 35.6% | 34.7% | 37.3% | 38.3% | 38.7% |
| Net Income | 139 | 612 | 605 | 618 | 547 | 628 | 530 | 506 | 382 | 475 |
| S&P Core Earnings | 660 | 578 | 440 | 632 | 597 | 666 | 582 | 530 | 347 | 387 |
| **Balance Sheet & Other Financial Data** (Million $) | | | | | | | | | | |
| Gross Property | 27,047 | 26,397 | 25,066 | 23,484 | 22,013 | 20,800 | 20,291 | 17,511 | 15,745 | 14,962 |
| Capital Expenditures | 1,031 | 1,704 | 1,896 | 1,381 | 992 | 947 | 806 | 682 | 787 | 1,103 |
| Net Property | 17,853 | 17,610 | 16,567 | 15,069 | 14,286 | 13,572 | 13,297 | 10,917 | 8,914 | 8,427 |
| Capitalization:Long Term Debt | 7,313 | 7,943 | 6,749 | 5,902 | 5,498 | 5,568 | 5,236 | 4,273 | 3,626 | 3,071 |
| Capitalization:% Long Term Debt | 48.6 | 50.3 | 49.2 | 46.7 | 45.5 | 46.7 | 47.4 | 49.5 | 48.6 | 47.8 |
| Capitalization:Preferred | Nil | Nil | Nil | Nil | Nil | Nil | Nil | Nil | Nil | Nil |
| Capitalization:% Preferred | Nil | Nil | Nil | Nil | Nil | Nil | Nil | Nil | Nil | Nil |
| Capitalization:Common | 7,730 | 7,853 | 6,963 | 6,752 | 6,583 | 6,364 | 5,800 | 4,354 | 3,842 | 3,349 |
| Capitalization:% Common | 51.4 | 49.7 | 50.8 | 53.3 | 54.5 | 53.3 | 52.6 | 50.5 | 51.4 | 52.2 |
| Total Capital | 15,352 | 16,207 | 15,964 | 14,722 | 14,241 | 14,047 | 13,075 | 10,653 | 9,339 | 8,144 |
| % Operating Ratio | 92.3 | 84.7 | 86.8 | 86.6 | 87.1 | 86.3 | 84.6 | 83.9 | 81.0 | 85.2 |
| % Earned on Net Property | 5.2 | 8.3 | 8.6 | 9.1 | 8.4 | 9.6 | 8.9 | 10.7 | 7.2 | 8.2 |
| % Return on Revenue | 1.8 | 8.6 | 7.7 | 8.4 | 8.0 | 9.3 | 10.3 | 11.0 | 9.9 | 10.6 |
| % Return on Invested Capital | 4.1 | 7.5 | 7.0 | 7.5 | 6.6 | 7.0 | 6.9 | 7.4 | 8.1 | 8.6 |
| % Return on Common Equity | 1.8 | 8.3 | 8.8 | 9.3 | 8.4 | 10.3 | 10.4 | 12.3 | 10.6 | 14.5 |

Data as orig reptd.; bef. results of disc opers/spec. items. Per share data adj. for stk. divs.; EPS diluted. E-Estimated. NA-Not Available. NM-Not Meaningful. NR-Not Ranked. UR-Under Review.

**Office:** 1901 Chouteau Avenue, St. Louis, MO 63103.
**Telephone:** 314-621-3222.
**Email:** invest@ameren.com
**Website:** http://www.ameren.com

**Chrmn, Pres & CEO:** T.R. Voss
**SVP, CFO, Chief Acctg Officer & Cntlr:** M.J. Lyons, Jr.
**SVP & General Counsel:** G.L. Nelson
**Treas:** J.E. Birdsong

**Investor Contact:** D. Fischer (314-554-4859)
**Board Members:** S. F. Brauer, C. S. Brune, E. M. Fitzsimmons, W. J. Galvin, G. P. Jackson, J. C. Johnson, S. H. Lipstein, P. T. Stokes, T. R. Voss, S. R. Wilson, J. D. Woodard

**Founded:** 1881
**Domicile:** Missouri
**Employees:** 9,474

# American Electric Power Co Inc

| S&P Recommendation **STRONG BUY** ★ ★ ★ ★ ★ | Price $37.20 (as of Nov 25, 2011) | 12-Mo. Target Price $42.00 | Investment Style Large-Cap Value |
|---|---|---|---|

**GICS Sector** Utilities
**Sub-Industry** Electric Utilities

**Summary** This electric utility holding company has subsidiaries operating in 11 states in the U.S.

## Key Stock Statistics (Source S&P, Vickers, company reports)

| | | | | | | | |
|---|---|---|---|---|---|---|---|
| 52-Wk Range | $40.08– 33.09 | S&P Oper. EPS 2011E | 3.17 | Market Capitalization(B) | $17.964 | Beta | 0.52 |
| Trailing 12-Month EPS | $3.76 | S&P Oper. EPS 2012E | 3.24 | Yield (%) | 5.05 | S&P 3-Yr. Proj. EPS CAGR(%) | 4 |
| Trailing 12-Month P/E | 9.9 | P/E on S&P Oper. EPS 2011E | 11.7 | Dividend Rate/Share | $1.88 | S&P Credit Rating | BBB |
| $10K Invested 5 Yrs Ago | $11,263 | Common Shares Outstg. (M) | 482.9 | Institutional Ownership (%) | 67 | | |

## Price Performance

30-Week Mov. Avg. ···· 10-Week Mov. Avg. --- GAAP Earnings vs. Previous Year  Volume Above Avg. ▇▇▇ STARS
12-Mo. Target Price — Relative Strength — ▲ Up ▼ Down ▶ No Change  Below Avg. ▇▇▇ ★

Options: ASE, CBOE, P, Ph

Analysis prepared by Equity Analyst **Justin McCann** on Nov 10, 2011, when the stock traded at **$38.84**.

## Highlights

➤ Excluding net one-time gains of $0.67, we expect operating EPS in 2011 to increase more than 4% from 2010's $3.03, which excluded $0.50 of net one-time charges. Operating EPS in the first nine months of 2011 was $0.07 above the $2.65 in the year-earlier period, as higher storm related expenses and the loss of customers to alternate suppliers of generation service nearly offset the benefit of rate increases, higher industrial and off-system sales, and a decline in interest expense.

➤ For 2012, we project EPS to grow about 2% from anticipated results in 2011. We expect results to be aided by a gradual recovery in the economy, an anticipated rate increase in Virginia, and lower interest expense. However, we expect this to be at least partially offset by an assumed return to more normal weather, higher environmental-related operation and maintenance expenses, and a decline in earnings from the generation and marketing operations.

➤ Over the longer term, we expect AEP to realize EPS growth of between 4% and 6%, reflecting its investments in its generation and transmission operations and a recovery in the economy.

## Investment Rationale/Risk

➤ With recent yield from the dividend at a well-above-peers 4.9%, we believe the shares are still attractive for their potential total return. The stock was up approximately 7% in the first 45 weeks of 2011, aided, we believe, by the investor shift to the utilities sector. This followed a 3.4% increase in 2010, in which the shares had rebounded about 27% from their year low. We believe the weak performance had largely reflected the reduced earnings growth rate AEP had projected for 2011 and 2012, while the rebound was aided by the declaration of a 9.5% increase in the company's dividend.

➤ Risks to our recommendation and target price include the potential for weaker than anticipated results from the company's retail and wholesale operations and a sharp decline in the average P/E multiple of the group as a whole.

➤ With the recent declaration of a 2.2% increase in the dividend (effective with the December 2011 payment), the yield (based on recent prices) was lifted to 4.9%, well above the recent average of 4.4% for AEP's peers. Our 12-month target price is $42, which reflects a discount-to-peers P/E of 13X our EPS estimate for 2012.

## Qualitative Risk Assessment

| LOW | MEDIUM | HIGH |
|---|---|---|

Our risk assessment reflects our view of the steady cash flow expected from the regulated utilities, with their low-cost fuel sources and generally supportive regulatory environments. The proceeds from the divestiture of most of AEP's high-risk unregulated energy businesses were used to enhance its balance sheet and financial strength.

## Quantitative Evaluations

**S&P Quality Ranking**        B

| D | C | B- | B | B+ | A- | A | A+ |
|---|---|---|---|---|---|---|---|

**Relative Strength Rank**      MODERATE

65

LOWEST = 1        HIGHEST = 99

## Revenue/Earnings Data

### Revenue (Million $)

| | 1Q | 2Q | 3Q | 4Q | Year |
|---|---|---|---|---|---|
| 2011 | 3,730 | 3,609 | 4,333 | -- | -- |
| 2010 | 3,569 | 3,360 | 4,064 | 3,434 | 14,427 |
| 2009 | 3,458 | 3,202 | 3,547 | 3,282 | 13,489 |
| 2008 | 3,467 | 3,546 | 4,191 | 3,236 | 14,440 |
| 2007 | 3,169 | 3,146 | 3,789 | 3,276 | 13,380 |
| 2006 | 3,108 | 2,936 | 3,594 | 2,984 | 12,622 |

### Earnings Per Share ($)

| | | | | | |
|---|---|---|---|---|---|
| 2011 | 0.73 | 0.73 | 1.35 | E0.45 | E3.17 |
| 2010 | 0.72 | 0.28 | 1.16 | 0.37 | 2.53 |
| 2009 | 0.81 | 0.68 | 0.93 | 0.50 | 2.97 |
| 2008 | 1.43 | 0.70 | 0.93 | 0.34 | 3.39 |
| 2007 | 0.68 | 0.64 | 1.02 | 0.52 | 2.86 |
| 2006 | 0.95 | 0.43 | 0.67 | 0.44 | 2.50 |

Fiscal year ended Dec. 31. Next earnings report expected: Late January. EPS Estimates based on S&P Operating Earnings; historical GAAP earnings are as reported.

## Dividend Data (Dates: mm/dd Payment Date: mm/dd/yy)

| Amount ($) | Date Decl. | Ex-Div. Date | Stk. of Record | Payment Date |
|---|---|---|---|---|
| 0.460 | 01/26 | 02/08 | 02/10 | 03/10/11 |
| 0.460 | 04/26 | 05/06 | 05/10 | 06/10/11 |
| 0.460 | 07/27 | 08/08 | 08/10 | 09/09/11 |
| 0.470 | 10/25 | 11/08 | 11/10 | 12/09/11 |

Dividends have been paid since 1909. Source: Company reports.

---

**Please read the Required Disclosures and Analyst Certification on the last page of this report.**

# American Electric Power Co Inc

STANDARD
&POOR'S

## Business Summary November 10, 2011

CORPORATE OVERVIEW. American Electric Power Co. (AEP) is a holding company that primarily operates electric utility services through its regulated subsidiaries. The utility services include the generation, transmission and distribution of electricity for sale to retail and wholesale customers in the U.S. AEP's non-regulated operations include the AEP River Operations subsidiary (formerly AEP MEMCO). In 2010, utility retail sales accounted for 79.6% of consolidated revenues; wholesale sales 13.8%; and other 6.6%.

CORPORATE STRATEGY. AEP focuses on its core utility operations and seeks to deliver low-cost electric power to the communities it serves. The company plans to improve its efficiency and to maximize the power delivered from its generation facilities. To provide safe and reliable power, AEP will continue to make investments to upgrade its transmission and distribution infrastructure, as well as to be in compliance with the appropriate environmental standards. The company's environmental-related investments in 2010 were $303.8 million, down from $457.2 million in 2009 and $886.8 million in 2008. For the three-year period from 2011 through 2013, AEP has projected nearly $1.242 billion in environmental-related investments, with $223.1 million projected for 2011, $340.3 million for 2012, and $678.5 million for 2013.

MARKET PROFILE. AEP provides electric utility services to about 5.3 million customers in 11 states over a total area of 197,500 square miles. The company derived more than 37% of its consolidated revenues in 2010 from its utilities in Ohio, nearly 23% from the utilities serving portions of Virginia and West Virginia, more than 15% from the one serving portions of Indiana and Michigan, more than 10% from the utility serving portions of Texas, Louisiana and Arkansas, and nearly 9% from the utility serving portions of Oklahoma. In 2010, the residential segment accounted for 44.3% of utility retail revenues, followed by commercial 29.4%; industrial 24.5%; and other 1.8%. Wholesale sales accounted for 14.6% of total utility sales in 2010, up slightly from 14.5% in 2009, while other sales accounted for the remainder. At the end of 2010, AEP had 100% ownership of 224,703 overhead circuit miles of transmission and distribution lines.

## Company Financials  Fiscal Year Ended Dec. 31

| Per Share Data ($) | 2010 | 2009 | 2008 | 2007 | 2006 | 2005 | 2004 | 2003 | 2002 | 2001 |
|---|---|---|---|---|---|---|---|---|---|---|
| Tangible Book Value | 28.17 | 27.31 | 26.09 | 25.17 | 24.88 | 22.87 | 21.31 | 19.74 | 19.67 | 20.92 |
| Earnings | 2.53 | 2.97 | 3.39 | 2.86 | 2.50 | 2.63 | 2.85 | 1.35 | 0.06 | 3.11 |
| S&P Core Earnings | 0.69 | 3.00 | 2.29 | 2.77 | 2.35 | 2.26 | 2.58 | 1.47 | 0.07 | 2.17 |
| Dividends | 1.71 | 1.64 | 1.64 | 1.58 | 1.50 | 1.42 | 1.40 | 1.65 | 2.40 | 2.40 |
| Payout Ratio | 68% | 55% | 48% | 58% | 60% | 54% | 49% | NM | NM | 77% |
| Prices:High | 37.94 | 36.51 | 49.11 | 51.24 | 43.13 | 40.80 | 35.53 | 31.51 | 48.80 | 51.20 |
| Prices:Low | 28.17 | 24.00 | 25.54 | 41.67 | 32.27 | 32.25 | 28.50 | 19.01 | 15.10 | 39.25 |
| P/E Ratio:High | 15 | 12 | 14 | 19 | 17 | 16 | 12 | 23 | NM | 16 |
| P/E Ratio:Low | 11 | 8 | 8 | 15 | 13 | 12 | 10 | 14 | NM | 13 |

| Income Statement Analysis (Million $) | | | | | | | | | | |
|---|---|---|---|---|---|---|---|---|---|---|
| Revenue | 14,427 | 13,489 | 14,440 | 13,380 | 12,622 | 12,111 | 14,057 | 14,545 | 14,555 | 61,257 |
| Depreciation | 1,780 | 1,660 | 1,571 | 1,513 | 1,467 | 1,318 | 1,300 | 1,299 | 1,377 | 1,383 |
| Maintenance | 1,142 | 1,205 | NA | NA | NA | NA | NA | NA | NA | NA |
| Fixed Charges Coverage | 2.84 | 2.98 | 2.81 | 2.96 | 2.96 | 2.80 | 2.60 | 2.97 | 2.84 | 2.64 |
| Construction Credits | 77.0 | 82.0 | 45.0 | 33.0 | 30.0 | 21.0 | NA | NA | NA | NA |
| Effective Tax Rate | 34.6% | 29.6% | 31.9% | 31.0% | 32.7% | 29.4% | 33.7% | 39.8% | 79.3% | 35.9% |
| Net Income | 1,211 | 1,362 | 1,368 | 1,144 | 992 | 1,029 | 1,127 | 522 | 21.0 | 1,003 |
| S&P Core Earnings | 329 | 1,373 | 924 | 1,107 | 934 | 883 | 1,021 | 573 | 21.1 | 698 |

| Balance Sheet & Other Financial Data (Million $) | | | | | | | | | | |
|---|---|---|---|---|---|---|---|---|---|---|
| Gross Property | 53,740 | 51,684 | 49,710 | 46,145 | 42,021 | 39,121 | 37,286 | 36,033 | 37,857 | 40,709 |
| Capital Expenditures | 2,500 | 2,896 | 3,960 | 3,556 | 3,528 | 2,404 | 1,693 | 1,358 | 1,722 | 1,832 |
| Net Property | 35,674 | 34,344 | 32,987 | 29,870 | 26,781 | 24,284 | 22,801 | 22,029 | 21,684 | 24,543 |
| Capitalization:Long Term Debt | 15,562 | 15,818 | 15,597 | 14,263 | 12,490 | 11,073 | 11,069 | 12,459 | 9,329 | 10,230 |
| Capitalization:% Long Term Debt | 53.3 | 54.6 | 59.3 | 58.6 | 57.0 | 54.9 | 56.5 | 61.3 | 56.9 | 55.4 |
| Capitalization:Preferred | Nil | Nil | Nil | Nil | Nil | Nil | Nil | Nil | Nil | Nil |
| Capitalization:% Preferred | Nil | Nil | Nil | Nil | Nil | Nil | Nil | Nil | Nil | Nil |
| Capitalization:Common | 13,622 | 13,140 | 10,693 | 10,079 | 9,412 | 9,088 | 8,515 | 7,874 | 7,064 | 8,229 |
| Capitalization:% Common | 46.7 | 45.4 | 40.7 | 41.4 | 43.0 | 45.1 | 43.5 | 38.7 | 43.1 | 44.6 |
| Total Capital | 30,493 | 30,699 | 31,418 | 29,072 | 26,802 | 25,032 | 24,403 | 24,290 | 21,523 | 24,523 |
| % Operating Ratio | 86.0 | 83.7 | 87.0 | 86.5 | 87.2 | 84.1 | 85.8 | 88.8 | 91.3 | 96.1 |
| % Earned on Net Property | 7.6 | 8.2 | 8.9 | 8.2 | 7.7 | 8.2 | 8.9 | 7.7 | 5.8 | 10.2 |
| % Return on Revenue | 8.4 | 10.1 | 9.5 | 8.6 | 7.9 | 8.5 | 8.0 | 3.6 | 0.1 | 1.6 |
| % Return on Invested Capital | 7.2 | 8.1 | 6.8 | 7.1 | 7.5 | 6.2 | 6.1 | 9.4 | 8.8 | 8.4 |
| % Return on Common Equity | 9.1 | 11.4 | 13.2 | 11.7 | 10.7 | 11.7 | 13.8 | 7.0 | 0.3 | 12.3 |

Data as orig reptd.; bef. results of disc opers/spec. items. Per share data adj. for stk. divs.; EPS diluted. E-Estimated. NA-Not Available. NM-Not Meaningful. NR-Not Ranked. UR-Under Review.

**Office:** 1 Riverside Plz, Columbus , OH 43215-2373.
**Telephone:** 614-716-1000.
**Email:** corpcomm@aep.com
**Website:** http://www.aep.com

**Chrmn:** M.G. Morris
**Pres & CEO:** N.K. Akins
**Vice Chrmn:** C.L. English
**COO & EVP:** R.P. Powers

**EVP & CFO:** B.X. Tierney
**Investor Contact:** B. Rozsa (614-716-2840)
**Board Members:** J. F. Cordes, R. D. Crosby, Jr., C. L. English, L. A. Goodspeed, T. E. Hoaglin, L. A. Hudson, Jr., M. G. Morris, L. L. Nowell, III, R. L. Sandor, S. M. Tucker, J. F. Turner

**Founded:** 1906
**Domicile:** New York
**Employees:** 18,712

# American Express Co

**STANDARD &POOR'S**

| S&P Recommendation | STRONG BUY ★★★★★ | Price $45.00 (as of Nov 25, 2011) | 12-Mo. Target Price $58.00 | Investment Style Large-Cap Growth |

**GICS Sector** Financials
**Sub-Industry** Consumer Finance

**Summary** American Express is a leading global payments and travel services company.

## Key Stock Statistics (Source S&P, Vickers, company reports)

| | | | | | | | |
|---|---|---|---|---|---|---|---|
| 52-Wk Range | $53.80–41.25 | S&P Oper. EPS 2011E | 4.00 | Market Capitalization(B) | $52.267 | Beta | 1.84 |
| Trailing 12-Month EPS | $3.99 | S&P Oper. EPS 2012E | 4.26 | Yield (%) | 1.60 | S&P 3-Yr. Proj. EPS CAGR(%) | 12 |
| Trailing 12-Month P/E | 11.3 | P/E on S&P Oper. EPS 2011E | 11.3 | Dividend Rate/Share | $0.72 | S&P Credit Rating | BBB+ |
| $10K Invested 5 Yrs Ago | $8,261 | Common Shares Outstg. (M) | 1,161.5 | Institutional Ownership (%) | 85 | | |

## Price Performance

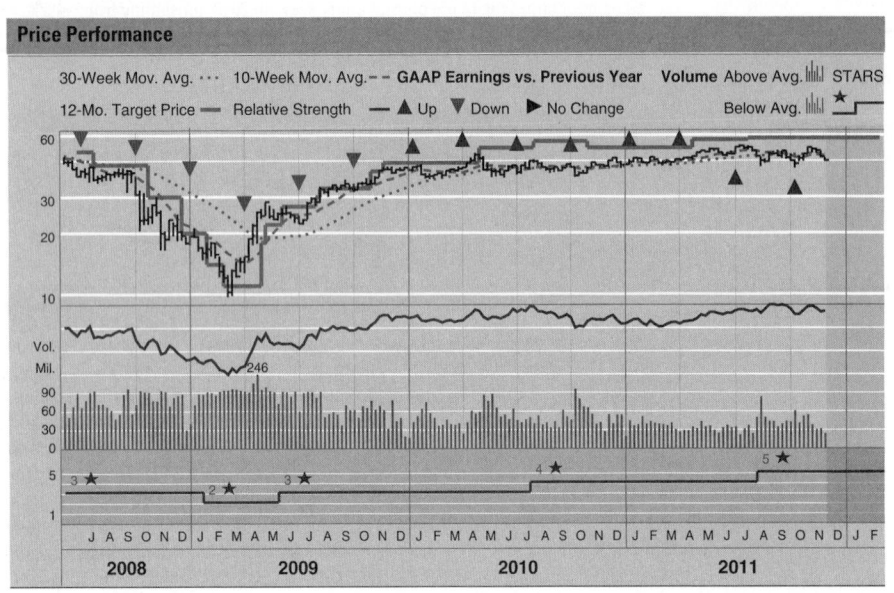

Options: ASE, CBOE, P, Ph

Analysis prepared by Equity Analyst **Robert McMillan** on Oct 21, 2011, when the stock traded at **$48.03**.

## Highlights

► We expect consolidated net revenues (after interest expense) to rise 9% in 2011 and 12% in 2012, reflecting our view that a continued, albeit slow, economic recovery will keep lifting consumer and business spending. We see sales increasing in all of AXP's divisions, driven by the U.S. and international card divisions. We were encouraged by the strength in AXP's international business in the 2011 third quarter amid fears about sovereign debt issues and slowing growth overseas, as well as by a 16% year-over-year gain in AXP's card billed business.

► We project a pickup in expenses in 2011 and 2012, as we anticipate that marketing and promotional costs will increase as AXP attempts to reinforce its brand. We also foresee higher incentive compensation expenses and technology spending as the company invests in growth initiatives. The net writeoff rate (for principal and fees on loans) in the U.S. card division fell to 2.9% in the 2011 third quarter, from 5.7% a year earlier. We anticipate that the write-off rate will gradually rise from historically low levels as management grows the business.

► We forecast EPS of $4.00 for 2011 and $4.26 in 2012.

## Investment Rationale/Risk

► We believe that consumers and businesses will increase their spending in an improving economic environment this year. We think loss provisions in the global commercial, U.S. card and international card businesses will decline, reflecting our outlook for lower delinquencies. In addition, we see AXP taking some of the savings from lower loss provisions and reinvesting them to gain market share.

► Risks to our recommendation and target price include a significant slowdown in consumer and business spending, an increase in loss provisions, a weakening macroeconomic environment, and a decline in credit quality.

► The shares recently traded at 11.2X trailing 12-month EPS. Our 12-month target price of $58 is about 14.4X our forward 12-month EPS estimate of $4.08, reflecting historical levels. Despite the U.S. government's civil antitrust lawsuit against the company over AXP's rules preventing merchants from providing discounts to consumers, we believe that the valuation multiple will likely rise from a relatively low level (by historical standards), driven by continuing growth in consumer spending and receivables growth as well as improving credit metrics.

## Qualitative Risk Assessment

| LOW | MEDIUM | HIGH |

Our risk assessment reflects what we see as solid business fundamentals and a strong customer base. We view AXP as able to withstand a major U.S. or global economic downturn.

## Quantitative Evaluations

**S&P Quality Ranking** A-

| D | C | B- | B | B+ | A- | A | A+ |

**Relative Strength Rank** MODERATE
47
LOWEST = 1    HIGHEST = 99

## Revenue/Earnings Data

**Revenue (Million $)**

| | 1Q | 2Q | 3Q | 4Q | Year |
|---|---|---|---|---|---|
| 2011 | 7,031 | 7,618 | 8,146 | -- | -- |
| 2010 | 7,204 | 7,468 | 7,033 | 7,322 | 30,242 |
| 2009 | 6,481 | 6,639 | 6,559 | 7,051 | 26,730 |
| 2008 | 8,105 | 8,340 | 8,007 | 7,468 | 31,920 |
| 2007 | 7,631 | 8,199 | 7,953 | 7,364 | 31,557 |
| 2006 | 6,319 | 6,850 | 6,759 | 7,208 | 27,136 |

**Earnings Per Share ($)**

| | | | | | |
|---|---|---|---|---|---|
| 2011 | 0.97 | 1.07 | 1.03 | E0.92 | E4.00 |
| 2010 | 0.73 | 0.84 | 0.90 | 0.88 | 3.35 |
| 2009 | 0.32 | 0.09 | 0.54 | 0.59 | 1.55 |
| 2008 | 0.90 | 0.57 | 0.74 | 0.27 | 2.48 |
| 2007 | 0.88 | 0.88 | 0.90 | 0.71 | 3.39 |
| 2006 | 0.70 | 0.78 | 0.78 | 0.76 | 3.01 |

Fiscal year ended Dec. 31. Next earnings report expected: Late January. EPS Estimates based on S&P Operating Earnings; historical GAAP earnings are as reported.

## Dividend Data (Dates: mm/dd Payment Date: mm/dd/yy)

| Amount ($) | Date Decl. | Ex-Div. Date | Stk. of Record | Payment Date |
|---|---|---|---|---|
| 0.180 | 11/22 | 01/05 | 01/07 | 02/10/11 |
| 0.180 | 03/28 | 04/06 | 04/08 | 05/10/11 |
| 0.180 | 05/23 | 06/29 | 07/01 | 08/10/11 |
| 0.180 | 11/22 | 01/04 | 01/06 | 02/10/12 |

Dividends have been paid since 1870. Source: Company reports.

# American Express Co

## Business Summary October 21, 2011

CORPORATE OVERVIEW. American Express is a leading global payments and travel company. Its businesses are organized into two customer-focused groups -- global consumer and global business-to-business. Accordingly, U.S. card services and international card services are aligned within the global consumer group and global commercial services and global network & merchant services are alligned within the global business-to-business group.

U.S. Card Services includes the U.S. proprietary consumer card business, OPEN from American Express, the global Travelers Cheques and Prepaid Services business, and the American Express U.S. Consumer Travel Network.

International Card Services issues proprietary consumer and small business cards outside the U.S.

Global Commercial Services offers global corporate payment and travel-related products and services to large and midsized companies. It offers five primary products and services: Corporate Card, issued to individuals through a corporate account established by their employer and designed primarily for travel and entertainment spending; Corporate Purchasing Solutions, an account established by corporations to pay for everyday business expenses such as office and computer supplies; Buyer Initiated Payment, an electronic

solution for companies looking to streamline their payment processes; vPayment technology, which provides fast and efficient payment for large ticket purchases and permits the processing of large transactions with effective fraud; and American Express Business Travel, which helps businesses manage and optimize their travel expenses through a variety of travel-related products, services and solutions.

Global Network & Merchant Services consists of the merchant services businesses and global network services. Global Network Services develops and manages relationships with third parties that issue American Express branded cards. The Global Merchant Services businesses develop and manage relationships with merchants that accept American Express branded cards; authorize and record transactions; pay merchants; and provide a variety of value-added point of sale and back office services. In addition, in particular emerging markets, issuance of certain proprietary cards is managed within the Global Network Services business.

## Company Financials Fiscal Year Ended Dec. 31

| Per Share Data ($) | 2010 | 2009 | 2008 | 2007 | 2006 | 2005 | 2004 | 2003 | 2002 | 2001 |
|---|---|---|---|---|---|---|---|---|---|---|
| Tangible Book Value | 10.54 | 9.53 | 7.61 | 8.22 | 7.52 | 8.50 | 12.83 | 11.93 | 10.62 | 9.04 |
| Earnings | 3.35 | 1.55 | 2.48 | 3.39 | 3.01 | 2.56 | 2.74 | 2.31 | 2.01 | 0.98 |
| S&P Core Earnings | 2.88 | 0.93 | 2.08 | 2.87 | 2.85 | 2.49 | 2.53 | 2.09 | 1.68 | 0.73 |
| Dividends | 0.72 | 0.72 | 0.72 | 0.60 | 0.54 | 0.48 | 0.32 | 0.38 | 0.32 | 0.32 |
| Payout Ratio | 22% | 46% | 29% | 18% | 18% | 19% | 12% | 16% | 16% | 33% |
| Prices:High | 49.19 | 42.25 | 52.63 | 65.89 | 62.50 | 59.50 | 57.05 | 49.11 | 44.91 | 57.06 |
| Prices:Low | 36.60 | 9.71 | 16.55 | 50.37 | 49.73 | 46.59 | 47.32 | 30.90 | 26.55 | 24.20 |
| P/E Ratio:High | 15 | 27 | 21 | 19 | 21 | 23 | 21 | 21 | 22 | 58 |
| P/E Ratio:Low | 11 | 6 | 7 | 15 | 17 | 18 | 17 | 13 | 13 | 25 |

| Income Statement Analysis (Million $) | 2010 | 2009 | 2008 | 2007 | 2006 | 2005 | 2004 | 2003 | 2002 | 2001 |
|---|---|---|---|---|---|---|---|---|---|---|
| Cards in Force | 91.0 | 87.9 | 92.4 | 86.4 | 78.0 | 71.0 | 65.4 | 60.5 | 57.3 | 55.2 |
| Card Charge Volume | NA | NA | NA | NA | NA | 484,400 | 416,100 | 352,200 | 311,400 | 298,000 |
| Premium Income | Nil | Nil | Nil | Nil | Nil | Nil | 1,525 | 1,366 | 802 | 674 |
| Commissions | 3,810 | 3,372 | 4,317 | 4,343 | 4,333 | 4,236 | 4,079 | 3,484 | 3,521 | 3,969 |
| Interest & Dividends | 7,292 | 5,331 | 7,201 | 6,145 | 4,535 | 3,635 | 3,118 | 3,063 | 2,991 | 3,049 |
| Total Revenue | 30,242 | 26,730 | 31,920 | 31,557 | 27,136 | 24,267 | 29,115 | 25,866 | 23,807 | 22,582 |
| Net Before Taxes | 5,964 | 2,841 | 3,473 | 5,566 | 5,328 | 4,248 | 4,951 | 4,247 | 3,727 | 1,596 |
| Net Income | 4,057 | 2,137 | 2,871 | 4,048 | 3,729 | 3,221 | 3,516 | 3,000 | 2,671 | 1,311 |
| S&P Core Earnings | 3,457 | 1,101 | 2,412 | 3,426 | 3,531 | 3,144 | 3,244 | 2,723 | 2,245 | 986 |

| Balance Sheet & Other Financial Data (Million $) | 2010 | 2009 | 2008 | 2007 | 2006 | 2005 | 2004 | 2003 | 2002 | 2001 |
|---|---|---|---|---|---|---|---|---|---|---|
| Total Assets | 147,000 | 124,000 | 126,000 | 149,830 | 127,853 | 113,960 | 192,638 | 175,001 | 157,253 | 151,100 |
| Cash Items | 17,000 | 16,000 | 21,000 | 14,036 | 11,270 | 7,126 | 9,907 | 5,726 | 10,288 | 7,222 |
| Investment Assets:Bonds | Nil | Nil | Nil | Nil | Nil | Nil | Nil | Nil | Nil | Nil |
| Investment Assets:Stocks | Nil | Nil | Nil | Nil | Nil | Nil | Nil | Nil | Nil | Nil |
| Investment Assets:Loans | 57,616 | 30,010 | 40,659 | 53,436 | 50,248 | 40,801 | 35,942 | 33,421 | 29,003 | 27,401 |
| Investment Assets:Total | 71,626 | 54,347 | 53,185 | 67,472 | 61,518 | 62,135 | 60,809 | 57,067 | 53,638 | 46,488 |
| Accounts Receivable | 40,434 | 38,204 | 36,571 | 95,441 | 89,099 | 35,497 | 34,650 | 31,269 | 29,087 | 29,498 |
| Customer Deposits | 29,727 | 26,289 | 15,486 | 15,397 | 24,656 | 24,579 | 21,091 | 21,250 | 18,317 | 14,557 |
| Travel Cheques Outstanding | 5,526 | 5,975 | 6,433 | 7,197 | 7,215 | 7,175 | 7,287 | 6,819 | 6,623 | 6,190 |
| Debt | 66,416 | 52,338 | 69,034 | 73,047 | 57,909 | 30,781 | 33,061 | 30,809 | 16,819 | 8,288 |
| Common Equity | 16,000 | 14,000 | 12,000 | 11,029 | 10,511 | 10,549 | 16,020 | 15,323 | 13,861 | 12,037 |
| % Return on Assets | 3.0 | 1.7 | 2.0 | 2.9 | 3.1 | 2.1 | 1.9 | 1.8 | 1.7 | 0.9 |
| % Return on Equity | 26.7 | 16.5 | 24.3 | 37.6 | 35.4 | 24.2 | 22.4 | 20.6 | 20.6 | 11.1 |

Data as orig reptd.; bef. results of disc opers/spec. items. Per share data adj. for stk. divs.; EPS diluted. E-Estimated. NA-Not Available. NM-Not Meaningful. NR-Not Ranked. UR-Under Review.

**Office:** World Financial Center, 200 Vesey Street, New York, NY 10285.
**Telephone:** 212-640-2000.
**Website:** http://www.americanexpress.com
**Chrmn & CEO:** K.I. Chenault

**EVP & CFO:** D.T. Henry
**EVP & General Counsel:** L.M. Parent
**EVP & CIO:** T.E. Redshaw
**Chief Acctg Officer & Cntlr:** D. Cornish

**Investor Contact:** R. Stovall (212-640-5574)
**Board Members:** D. F. Akerson, C. Barshefsky, U. M. Burns, K. I. Chenault, P. F. Chernin, E. P. Gilligan, T. J. Leonsis, J. Leschly, R. C. Levin, R. A. McGinn, E. D. Miller, Jr., S. S. Reinemund, R. D. Walter, R. A. Williams

**Founded:** 1868
**Domicile:** New York
**Employees:** 61,000

# American International Group Inc

**STANDARD &POOR'S**

**S&P Recommendation** BUY ★★★★☆

**Price**
$20.07 (as of Nov 25, 2011)

**12-Mo. Target Price**
$28.00

**GICS Sector** Financials
**Sub-Industry** Multi-line Insurance

**Summary** This leading international insurance organization, which was rescued by various government entities in 2008, has been executing a plan to repay its government aid.

## Key Stock Statistics (Source S&P, Vickers, company reports)

| | | | | | | | |
|---|---|---|---|---|---|---|---|
| 52-Wk Range | $62.87– 19.18 | S&P Oper. EPS 2011**E** | 0.97 | Market Capitalization(B) | $38.117 | Beta | 3.55 |
| Trailing 12-Month EPS | $4.41 | S&P Oper. EPS 2012**E** | 2.64 | Yield (%) | Nil | S&P 3-Yr. Proj. EPS CAGR(%) | NM |
| Trailing 12-Month P/E | 4.6 | P/E on S&P Oper. EPS 2011**E** | 20.7 | Dividend Rate/Share | Nil | S&P Credit Rating | A- |
| $10K Invested 5 Yrs Ago | $175 | Common Shares Outstg. (M) | 1,899.2 | Institutional Ownership (%) | 17 | | |

## Price Performance

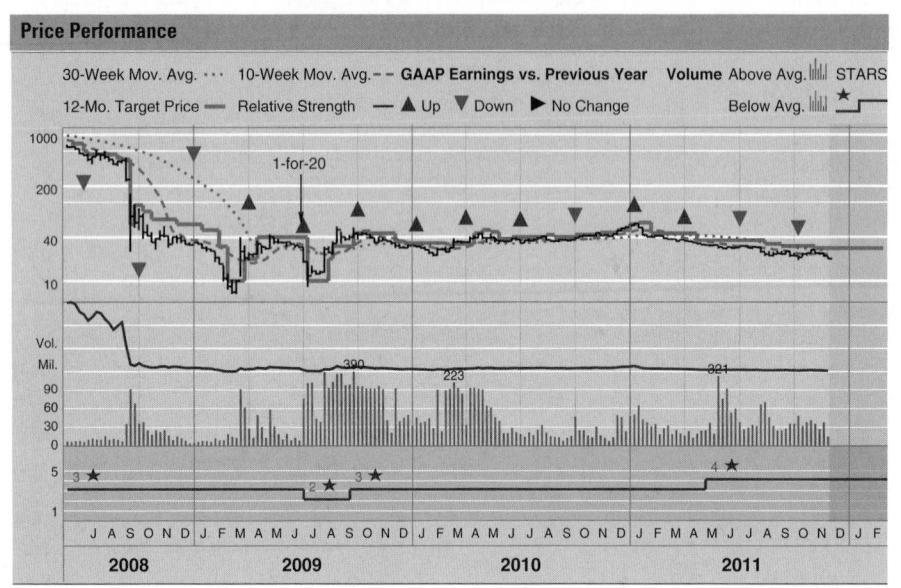

30-Week Mov. Avg. ···· 10-Week Mov. Avg. - - **GAAP Earnings vs. Previous Year**   Volume Above Avg. ⅰⅼⅼ STARS
12-Mo. Target Price — Relative Strength — ▲ Up ▼ Down ► No Change   Below Avg. ⅰⅼⅼ ★

Options: ASE, CBOE, P, Ph

## Qualitative Risk Assessment

| LOW | MEDIUM | HIGH |
|---|---|---|

AIG's outsized exposure (versus peers in the insurance industry) to the mortgage industry and the credit default swap market led to an emergency bailout by the Federal Reserve in 2008 and additional capital infusions in early 2009. AIG's recently unveiled plan to continue to restructure itself and repay the government dilutes common shareholder interests and contains a high degree of execution risk, in our view. We also cannot rule out the need for additional capital infusions.

## Quantitative Evaluations

**S&P Quality Ranking**   C

| D | C | B- | B | B+ | A- | A | A+ |
|---|---|---|---|---|---|---|---|

**Relative Strength Rank**   WEAK

20

LOWEST = 1          HIGHEST = 99

## Highlights

► The 12-month target price for AIG has recently been changed to $28.00 from $30.00. The Highlights section of this Stock Report will be updated accordingly.

## Investment Rationale/Risk

► The Investment Rationale/Risk section of this Stock Report will be updated shortly. For the latest News story on AIG from MarketScope, see below.

► 11/04/11 07:05 am ET ... S&P MAINTAINS BUY OPINION ON SHARES OF AMERICAN INTERNATIONAL GROUP (AIG 24.63****): Q3 operating loss per share of $1.60, vs.$0.84 loss, was wider than our $0.24 loss estimate and the Capital IQ consensus forecast $0.32 loss. Results were impaired by macro head winds that drove mark-to-market write downs. While disappointing, the $1.5B ILFC aircraft writedown better positions unit for a sale, in our view. We cut our 2011 estimate to $0.97 EPS from $2.33, but remain cautious on Q4 catastrophe claims. Our $28 target price assumes the shares trade at 10.6X our $2.64 operating EPS forecast for 2012, a discount to tangible book value and below most peers. /C. Seifert

## Revenue/Earnings Data

### Revenue (Million $)

| | 1Q | 2Q | 3Q | 4Q | Year |
|---|---|---|---|---|---|
| 2011 | 17,436 | 16,676 | 12,716 | -- | -- |
| 2010 | 16,330 | 19,982 | 19,091 | 21,687 | 77,301 |
| 2009 | 20,458 | 29,525 | 26,049 | -- | 96,004 |
| 2008 | 14,031 | 19,933 | 898.0 | -23,758 | 11,104 |
| 2007 | 30,645 | 31,150 | 29,836 | 18,433 | 110,064 |
| 2006 | 27,259 | 26,743 | 29,199 | 29,993 | 113,194 |

### Earnings Per Share ($)

| | | | | | |
|---|---|---|---|---|---|
| 2011 | -1.41 | 1.03 | -2.05 | E0.58 | E0.97 |
| 2010 | -6.48 | 21.21 | -0.81 | -12.67 | 14.24 |
| 2009 | -39.60 | 2.30 | 0.68 | -58.04 | -86.30 |
| 2008 | -61.80 | -41.20 | -181.00 | -459.00 | -756.80 |
| 2007 | 31.60 | 32.80 | 23.80 | -41.40 | 47.80 |
| 2006 | 24.20 | 24.20 | 32.20 | 26.20 | 107.00 |

Fiscal year ended Dec. 31. Next earnings report expected: Late February. EPS Estimates based on S&P Operating Earnings; historical GAAP earnings are as reported.

## Dividend Data (Dates: mm/dd Payment Date: mm/dd/yy)

| Amount ($) | Date Decl. | Ex-Div. Date | Stk. of Record | Payment Date |
|---|---|---|---|---|
| Wrrt | 01/07 | 01/20 | 01/13 | 01/19/11 |

Source: Company reports.

# American International Group Inc

## Business Summary September 06, 2011

American International Group provides an array of insurance and financial services in 130 countries and territories. Investigations several years ago by the New York Attorney General and the SEC into AIG's use of non-traditional insurance products and certain assumed reinsurance transactions culminated in a number of events, including the resignation of AIG's long-time CEO Maurice Greenberg; a write down against earnings from 2000-2004 of nearly $4 billion; and a write down of shareholders' equity of $2.26 billion. During 2005, AIG also incurred after-tax charges totaling $1.15 billion to settle numerous regulatory issues and $1.19 billion to boost loss reserves. During 2007 and 2008, AIG was confronted with the downward spiral of the U.S. residential mortgage market and subsequent deterioration in broader credit market conditions. To help replenish its capital, AIG in May 2008 raised $20 billion of new capital, including the sale of 196,710,525 common shares for $7.47 billion.

These moves proved insufficient, and in late September 2008, AIG was forced to accept an emergency line of credit from the Federal Reserve. To repay the Federal Reserve loan, AIG is undergoing a planned sale of its assets, including the December 2008 sale of Hartford Steam Boiler (HSB) to Munich Re for $742 million in cash and the assumption of $76 million of debt (less than the $1.2 billion AIG paid for HSB in 2000), the January 2009 sale of AIG Life Insurance Co. of Canada to BMO Financial Group for about $308 million in cash, and the

June 2009 sale of 29.9 million shares of Transatlantic Holdings, Inc. (TRH) for gross proceeds of $1.1 billion. As of November 1, 2010, AIG had raised another $36.7 billion (of which nearly $28 billion was in cash) through the sale of its American Life Insurance Co. (ALICO) unit to MetLife for some $16.2 billion; and through the initial public offering of AIA Group Ltd., which yielded gross proceeds of over $20.5 billion. On February 1, 2011, AIG sold AIG Star Life and AIG Edison Life (two Japanese life insurers) to Prudential Financial for $4.8 billion. AIG closed the sale of its Taiwan-based Nan Shan Life Insurance Co. on August 20 for $2.15 billion, and in early September 2011 filed a registration statement with the SEC for the initial public offering of International Lease Finance Corp. (ILFC), its airline leasing unit.

Subsequent revisions and additions to original terms resulted in AIG receiving federal aid valued at approximately $173 billion and in trusts established for the benefit of the U.S. Treasury controlling approximately 77.9% of the voting power of AIG common stock. At December 31, 2010, total authorized and outstanding U.S. government support and assistance equaled $124.1 billion.

## Company Financials Fiscal Year Ended Dec. 31

| Per Share Data ($) | 2010 | 2009 | 2008 | 2007 | 2006 | 2005 | 2004 | 2003 | 2002 | 2001 |
|---|---|---|---|---|---|---|---|---|---|---|
| Tangible Book Value | 50.34 | 256.03 | 347.20 | 683.00 | 759.20 | 602.60 | 554.60 | 487.80 | 406.40 | 398.80 |
| Operating Earnings | NA | NA | NA | NA | NA | NA | NA | NA | NA | NA |
| Earnings | 14.24 | -86.30 | -756.80 | 47.80 | 107.00 | 79.80 | 75.00 | 70.60 | 42.00 | 41.40 |
| S&P Core Earnings | -2.19 | -6.12 | -388.40 | 66.20 | 107.20 | 87.00 | 75.40 | 77.80 | 52.60 | 41.20 |
| Dividends | Nil | Nil | 12.40 | 14.60 | 12.60 | 11.00 | 5.60 | 4.40 | 3.56 | 3.16 |
| Relative Payout | Nil | Nil | NM | 31% | 12% | 14% | 7% | 6% | 8% | 8% |
| Prices:High | 61.68 | 55.90 | 1188 | 1459 | 1459 | 1469 | 1547 | 1327 | 1600 | 1966 |
| Prices:Low | 21.54 | 8.22 | 25.00 | 1017 | 1150 | 998.20 | 1086 | 858.40 | 952.20 | 1320 |
| P/E Ratio:High | 4 | NM | NM | 31 | 14 | 18 | 21 | 19 | 38 | 47 |
| P/E Ratio:Low | 2 | NM | NM | 21 | 11 | 13 | 14 | 12 | 23 | 32 |

| Income Statement Analysis (Million $) | | | | | | | | | | |
|---|---|---|---|---|---|---|---|---|---|---|
| Life Insurance in Force | 892,365 | 2,341,042 | 2,378,314 | 2,312,045 | 2,070,600 | 1,852,833 | 1,858,094 | 1,596,626 | 1,324,451 | 1,228,501 |
| Premium Income:Life A & H | 4,624 | 27,318 | 37,295 | 33,627 | 30,636 | 29,400 | 28,082 | 22,879 | 20,320 | 19,243 |
| Premium Income:Casualty/Property. | 31,612 | 30,664 | 46,222 | 45,682 | 43,451 | 41,872 | 40,607 | 31,734 | 24,269 | 19,365 |
| Net Investment Income | 20,930 | 25,239 | 12,222 | 28,619 | 25,292 | 22,165 | 18,434 | 16,662 | 15,034 | 14,628 |
| Total Revenue | 77,301 | 96,004 | 11,104 | 110,064 | 113,194 | 108,905 | 97,987 | 81,303 | 67,482 | 52,852 |
| Pretax Income | 17,936 | -13,648 | -108,761 | 8,943 | 21,687 | 15,213 | 14,950 | 13,908 | 8,142 | 8,139 |
| Net Operating Income | NA | NA | NA | NA | NA | 105 | NA | NA | NA | NA |
| Net Income | 12,077 | -10,383 | -99,289 | 6,200 | 14,014 | 10,477 | 9,875 | 9,265 | 5,519 | 5,499 |
| S&P Core Earnings | -1,484 | -5,877 | -51,166 | 8,585 | 14,018 | 11,396 | 9,928 | 10,208 | 6,931 | 5,476 |

| Balance Sheet & Other Financial Data (Million $) | | | | | | | | | | |
|---|---|---|---|---|---|---|---|---|---|---|
| Cash & Equivalent | 4,518 | 9,552 | 14,641 | 8,871 | 7,681 | 7,624 | 7,597 | 5,881 | 1,165 | 698 |
| Premiums Due | 15,713 | 16,549 | 17,330 | 18,395 | 17,789 | 15,333 | 15,137 | 14,166 | 13,088 | 11,647 |
| Investment Assets:Bonds | 254,484 | 396,982 | 404,134 | 428,935 | 417,865 | 385,680 | 365,677 | 309,254 | 243,366 | 200,616 |
| Investment Assets:Stocks | 11,233 | 17,840 | 21,143 | 41,646 | 30,222 | 23,588 | 17,851 | 9,584 | 7,066 | 7,937 |
| Investment Assets:Loans | 19,367 | 27,461 | 34,687 | 33,727 | 28,418 | 24,909 | 22,463 | 21,249 | 19,928 | 18,092 |
| Investment Assets:Total | 410,412 | 601,165 | 554,446 | 755,596 | 719,685 | 614,759 | 494,592 | 449,657 | 339,320 | 357,602 |
| Deferred Policy Costs | 14,668 | 40,814 | 45,782 | 43,150 | 37,235 | 33,248 | 29,736 | 26,398 | 22,256 | 17,443 |
| Total Assets | 683,443 | 847,585 | 860,418 | 1,060,505 | 979,414 | 853,370 | 798,660 | 678,346 | 561,229 | 492,982 |
| Debt | 85,476 | 113,298 | 137,054 | 162,935 | 186,866 | 78,625 | 66,850 | 57,877 | 50,076 | 34,503 |
| Common Equity | 13,336 | 40.0 | 52,690 | 95,801 | 101,677 | 86,317 | 80,607 | 71,253 | 59,103 | 52,150 |
| Combined Loss-Expense Ratio | 116.8 | 108.0 | 109.1 | 90.3 | 89.1 | 104.7 | 100.1 | 92.4 | 106.0 | 100.7 |
| % Return on Revenue | 15.6 | NM | NM | 5.6 | 12.4 | 9.6 | 10.1 | 11.4 | 8.2 | 10.5 |
| % Return on Equity | 40.7 | NM | NM | 6.3 | 14.9 | 12.6 | 13.1 | 14.2 | 9.9 | 11.0 |
| % Investment Yield | 4.1 | 4.1 | 2.0 | 3.9 | 3.8 | 3.7 | 3.9 | 4.1 | 4.8 | 4.5 |

Data as orig reptd.; bef. results of disc opers/spec. items. Per share data adj. for stk. divs.; EPS diluted. E-Estimated. NA-Not Available. NM-Not Meaningful. NR-Not Ranked. UR-Under Review.

**Office:** 70 Pine Street, New York, NY 10270-0094.
**Telephone:** 212-770-7000.
**Website:** http://www.aigcorporate.com
**Chrmn, Pres & CEO:** R.H. Benmosche

**EVP & Treas:** B.T. Schreiber
**EVP & General Counsel:** T.A. Russo
**SVP & Chief Admin Officer:** M.R. Cowan
**CFO:** D.L. Herzog

**Investor Contact:** S.J. Bensinger
**Board Members:** R. H. Benmosche, W. D. Cornwell, J. H. Fitzpatrick, S. N. Johnson, L. T. Koellner, D. H. Layton, C. S. Lynch, A. C. Martinez, G. L. Miles, Jr., H. S. Miller, R. S. Miller, Jr., M. W. Offit, R. A. Rittenmeyer, D. M. Steenland

**Founded:** 1967
**Domicile:** Delaware
**Employees:** 63,000

# American Tower Corp

STANDARD &POOR'S

| S&P Recommendation **STRONG BUY** ★★★★★ | Price | 12-Mo. Target Price | Investment Style |
|---|---|---|---|
| | $55.72 (as of Nov 25, 2011) | $74.00 | Large-Cap Blend |

**GICS Sector** Telecommunication Services
**Sub-Industry** Wireless Telecommunication Services

**Summary** This company operates the largest independent portfolio of wireless communications and broadcast towers in North America.

## Key Stock Statistics (Source S&P, Vickers, company reports)

| | | | | | | | |
|---|---|---|---|---|---|---|---|
| 52-Wk Range | $58.60– 45.85 | S&P Oper. EPS 2011**E** | 0.75 | Market Capitalization(B) | $21.899 | Beta | 0.62 |
| Trailing 12-Month EPS | $0.69 | S&P Oper. EPS 2012**E** | 1.36 | Yield (%) | Nil | S&P 3-Yr. Proj. EPS CAGR(%) | 12 |
| Trailing 12-Month P/E | 80.8 | P/E on S&P Oper. EPS 2011**E** | 74.3 | Dividend Rate/Share | Nil | S&P Credit Rating | BB+ |
| $10K Invested 5 Yrs Ago | $14,648 | Common Shares Outstg. (M) | 393.0 | Institutional Ownership (%) | 96 | | |

## Price Performance

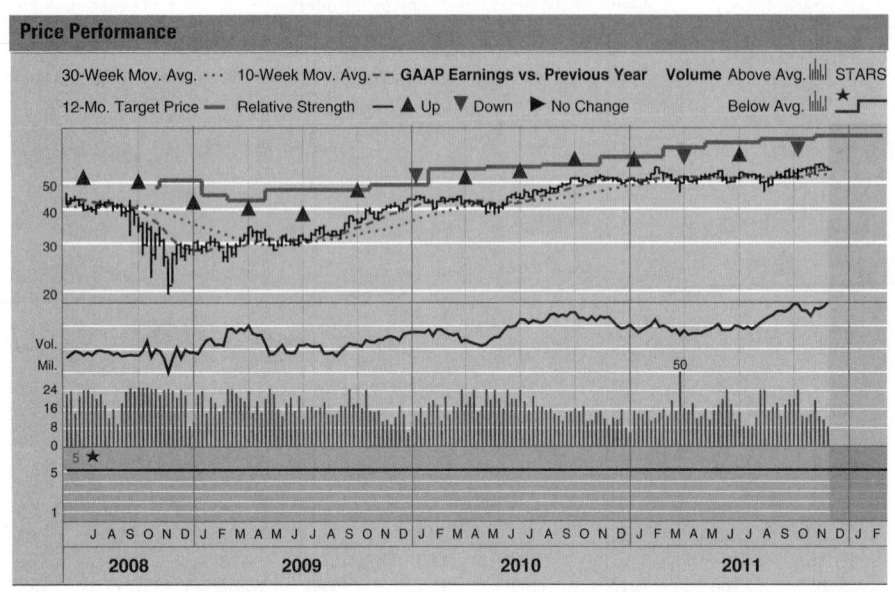

- 30-Week Mov. Avg. ···  10-Week Mov. Avg. - -  GAAP Earnings vs. Previous Year  Volume Above Avg. STARS
- 12-Mo. Target Price —  Relative Strength  ▲ Up ▼ Down ► No Change  Below Avg. ★

2008  2009  2010  2011

Options: ASE, CBOE, P, Ph

## Qualitative Risk Assessment

| LOW | MEDIUM | HIGH |
|---|---|---|

Our risk assessment reflects the company's high total debt to total capitalization ratio, partly offset by our view of its steady cash flow and sufficient cash and investments to meet its working capital, capital expenditure, and debt requirements.

## Quantitative Evaluations

**S&P Quality Ranking**                    B

| D | C | B- | B | B+ | A- | A | A+ |
|---|---|---|---|---|---|---|---|

**Relative Strength Rank**                STRONG

82

LOWEST = 1                    HIGHEST = 99

## Revenue/Earnings Data

**Revenue (Million $)**

| | 1Q | 2Q | 3Q | 4Q | Year |
|---|---|---|---|---|---|
| 2011 | 562.7 | 597.2 | 630.4 | -- | -- |
| 2010 | 454.4 | 469.9 | 513.3 | 547.6 | 1,985 |
| 2009 | 408.7 | 423.4 | 444.1 | 448.0 | 1,724 |
| 2008 | 382.2 | 393.7 | 409.3 | 408.3 | 1,594 |
| 2007 | 352.5 | 358.4 | 367.6 | 378.1 | 1,457 |
| 2006 | 320.4 | 325.9 | 333.5 | 337.7 | 1,317 |

**Earnings Per Share ($)**

| | 1Q | 2Q | 3Q | 4Q | Year |
|---|---|---|---|---|---|
| 2011 | 0.23 | 0.29 | -0.04 | E0.27 | E0.75 |
| 2010 | 0.24 | 0.25 | 0.23 | 0.21 | 0.92 |
| 2009 | 0.14 | 0.13 | 0.17 | 0.16 | 0.59 |
| 2008 | 0.10 | 0.12 | 0.15 | 0.21 | 0.58 |
| 2007 | 0.05 | 0.03 | 0.14 | -0.01 | 0.22 |
| 2006 | -0.01 | 0.02 | 0.01 | 0.04 | 0.06 |

Fiscal year ended Dec. 31. Next earnings report expected: Late February. EPS Estimates based on S&P Operating Earnings; historical GAAP earnings are as reported.

## Dividend Data

No cash dividends have been paid.

## Highlights

- The 12-month target price for AMT has recently been changed to $74.00 from $72.00. The Highlights section of this Stock Report will be updated accordingly.

## Investment Rationale/Risk

- The Investment Rationale/Risk section of this Stock Report will be updated shortly. For the latest News story on AMT from MarketScope, see below.

- 11/01/11 03:10 pm ET ... S&P MAINTAINS STRONG BUY OPINION ON SHARES OF AMERICAN TOWER (AMT 57.33*****): AMT reports Q3 loss per share of $0.04, vs. $0.23 loss, $0.29 below our estimate due to a non-cash loss of $145M due to foreign currency losses. Revenue came in 3.5% better than expected, while EBITDA was 2% below our forecast. We believe that leasing activity will remain strong into 2012. We are reducing our 2011 EPS estimate $0.27 to $0.75, and increasing our 2012 estimate by $0.08 to $1.36. We are raising our 12-month target price by $2 to $74, based on 24X our '12 free cash flow estimate, a slight premium to peers. / James Moorman, CFA

# American Tower Corp

STANDARD
&POOR'S

## Business Summary August 11, 2011

CORPORATE OVERVIEW. American Tower Corp. operates the largest independent portfolio of wireless communications and broadcast towers in North America, based on the number of towers and revenue. The company's primary business is leasing antenna space on multi-tenant communications towers to wireless service providers and radio and television broadcast companies. The tower portfolio provides AMT with a recurring base of leased revenues from its customers and growth potential to add more tenants and equipment to these towers from its unused capacity. AMT also continues to expand its operations in Mexico, Brazil, Peru, Colombia and India. The company completed the purchase of 608 existing towers internationally and 37 sites domestically in the second quarter of 2011 and expects to acquire an additional 1,100 towers in 2011.

PRIMARY BUSINESS DYNAMICS. Rental and management of the antenna sites is AMT's principal business, and accounted for 98% of revenue in the second quarter of 2011. AMT operated a tower portfolio of about 38,048 multi-user sites in the U.S., Mexico, Brazil, Chile, Colombia, India, Peru and South Africa, as of June 30, 2011. The company signs service providers to long-term leases of usually five to 10 years that contain annual lease rate escalations of 3%-5%. Sprint Nextel, AT&T Wireless and Verizon Wireless accounted for roughly 51% of AMT's 2010 tower revenue, putting AMT in a prime position for

further market expansion projects, in our view. AMT could also benefit from increased data usage that will require service providers to add capacity to cell sites, as well as from carriers that expand their networks. Carriers such as Leap Wireless, MetroPCS and Clearwire are currently expanding their networks, and we believe this will boost growth. In addition, U.S. carriers spent close to $20 billion on 700MHz spectrum, and we believe they will use the spectrum to deploy 4G service starting in 2011, continuing for several years.

International growth should benefit AMT in 2011, by our analysis. AMT has about 2,669 wireless towers and approximately 199 broadcast towers in Mexico, about 2,387 wireless towers in Brazil, approximately 8,015 sites in India, 424 sites in Chile, 475 sites in Peru, and 1,139 sites in Colombia. International operations accounted for roughly 19% of revenue in 2010. We expect Mexico and Brazil to conduct 3G spectrum auctions and then to deploy 3G networks in 2011. We think these markets will continue to provide significant growth, as we believe they are also seeing significant data growth, which could lead to additional capacity requirements.

## Company Financials Fiscal Year Ended Dec. 31

| Per Share Data ($) | 2010 | 2009 | 2008 | 2007 | 2006 | 2005 | 2004 | 2003 | 2002 | 2001 |
|---|---|---|---|---|---|---|---|---|---|---|
| Tangible Book Value | NM | NM | NM | 2.41 | 0.88 | 0.74 | NM | 0.28 | NM | 1.94 |
| Cash Flow | 2.06 | 1.60 | 1.83 | 1.41 | 1.28 | 0.92 | 0.40 | 0.34 | 0.01 | -0.05 |
| Earnings | 0.92 | 0.59 | 0.58 | 0.22 | 0.06 | -0.44 | -1.07 | -1.17 | -1.61 | -2.35 |
| S&P Core Earnings | 0.92 | 0.59 | 0.58 | 0.20 | 0.05 | -0.50 | -1.17 | -1.35 | -1.60 | -2.50 |
| Dividends | Nil | Nil | Nil | Nil | Nil | Nil | Nil | Nil | Nil | Nil |
| Payout Ratio | Nil | Nil | Nil | Nil | Nil | Nil | Nil | Nil | Nil | Nil |
| Prices:High | 53.52 | 43.84 | 46.10 | 46.53 | 38.74 | 28.33 | 18.75 | 12.00 | 10.40 | 41.50 |
| Prices:Low | 38.09 | 25.45 | 19.35 | 36.34 | 26.66 | 16.28 | 9.89 | 3.55 | 0.60 | 5.25 |
| P/E Ratio:High | 58 | 74 | 79 | NM | NM | NM | NM | NM | NM | NM |
| P/E Ratio:Low | 41 | 43 | 33 | NM | NM | NM | NM | NM | NM | NM |

| Income Statement Analysis (Million $) | | | | | | | | | | |
|---|---|---|---|---|---|---|---|---|---|---|
| Revenue | 1,985 | 1,724 | 1,594 | 1,457 | 1,317 | 945 | 707 | 715 | 788 | 1,134 |
| Operating Income | NA | NA | 1,020 | 898 | 803 | 589 | 423 | 377 | 312 | 251 |
| Depreciation | 461 | 415 | 527 | 510 | 528 | 411 | 329 | 313 | 317 | 440 |
| Interest Expense | 246 | 250 | 254 | 240 | 217 | 224 | 264 | 280 | 257 | 309 |
| Pretax Income | 556 | 422 | 372 | 153 | 70.9 | -130 | -317 | -305 | -248 | -567 |
| Effective Tax Rate | NA | 43.3% | 36.4% | 39.1% | 58.9% | NM | NM | NM | NM | NM |
| Net Income | 374 | 238 | 236 | 92.7 | 28.3 | -134 | -239 | -242 | -315 | -450 |
| S&P Core Earnings | 373 | 238 | 236 | 85.6 | 24.6 | -154 | -261 | -281 | -313 | -480 |

| Balance Sheet & Other Financial Data (Million $) | | | | | | | | | | |
|---|---|---|---|---|---|---|---|---|---|---|
| Cash | 930 | 257 | 145 | 94.0 | 281 | 113 | 216 | 105 | 127 | 130 |
| Current Assets | 1,401 | 651 | 474 | 246 | 486 | 226 | 309 | 412 | 536 | 522 |
| Total Assets | 10,365 | 8,513 | 8,212 | 8,130 | 8,613 | 8,768 | 5,086 | 5,332 | 5,662 | 6,830 |
| Current Liabilities | 542 | 391 | 303 | 317 | 570 | 453 | 332 | 295 | 670 | 343 |
| Long Term Debt | 5,512 | 4,141 | 4,331 | 4,240 | 3,289 | 3,451 | 3,155 | 3,284 | 3,195 | 3,549 |
| Common Equity | 3,501 | 3,315 | 2,991 | 3,022 | 4,382 | 4,527 | 1,464 | 1,706 | 1,740 | 2,869 |
| Total Capital | 9,095 | 7,530 | 7,326 | 7,309 | 7,678 | 7,988 | 4,626 | 5,008 | 4,950 | 6,433 |
| Capital Expenditures | 347 | 250 | 243 | 154 | 127 | 88.6 | 42.2 | 61.6 | 180 | 568 |
| Cash Flow | 834 | 653 | 763 | 603 | 556 | 277 | 90.2 | 71.0 | 2.11 | -9.72 |
| Current Ratio | 2.6 | 1.7 | 1.6 | 0.8 | 0.9 | 0.5 | 0.9 | 1.4 | 0.8 | 1.5 |
| % Long Term Debt of Capitalization | 60.6 | 55.0 | 59.1 | 58.6 | 42.9 | 43.2 | 68.2 | 65.6 | 64.5 | 55.2 |
| % Net Income of Revenue | 18.8 | 13.8 | 14.8 | 6.4 | 2.2 | NM | NM | NM | NM | NM |
| % Return on Assets | 4.0 | 2.9 | 2.9 | 1.1 | 0.3 | NM | NM | NM | NM | NM |
| % Return on Equity | 11.0 | 7.6 | 7.9 | 2.5 | 0.6 | NM | NM | NM | NM | NM |

Data as orig reptd.; bef. results of disc opers/spec. items. Per share data adj. for stk. divs.; EPS diluted. E-Estimated. NA-Not Available. NM-Not Meaningful. NR-Not Ranked. UR-Under Review.

**Office:** 116 Huntington Avenue, 11th Floor, Boston, MA 02116.
**Telephone:** 617-375-7500.
**Email:** ir@americantower.com
**Website:** http://www.americantower.com

**Chrmn, Pres & CEO:** J.D. Taiclet, Jr.
**COO:** W.H. Hess
**EVP & CFO:** T.A. Bartlett
**EVP, Chief Admin Officer, Secy & General Counsel:** E. DiSanto

**SVP, Chief Acctg Officer & Cntlr:** R.J. Meyer, Jr.
**Investor Contact:** M. Powell (617-375-7500)
**Board Members:** G. L. Cantu, R. P. Dolan, R. Dykes, C. F. Katz, J. A. Reed, P. D. Reeve, D. Sharbutt, J. D. Taiclet, Jr., S. L. Thompson

**Founded:** 1995
**Domicile:** Delaware
**Employees:** 1,729

# Ameriprise Financial Inc

**STANDARD &POOR'S**

| S&P Recommendation HOLD ★★★★★ | Price $41.51 (as of Nov 25, 2011) | 12-Mo. Target Price $53.00 | Investment Style Large-Cap Growth |
|---|---|---|---|

**GICS Sector** Financials
**Sub-Industry** Asset Management & Custody Banks

**Summary** This diversified financial services company, spun off from American Express in September 2005, provides insurance, investment and asset management services.

## Key Stock Statistics (Source S&P, Vickers, company reports)

| | | | | | | | |
|---|---|---|---|---|---|---|---|
| 52-Wk Range | $65.12–36.00 | S&P Oper. EPS 2011**E** | 4.38 | Market Capitalization(B) | $9.392 | Beta | 1.96 |
| Trailing 12-Month EPS | $4.37 | S&P Oper. EPS 2012**E** | 5.20 | Yield (%) | 2.22 | S&P 3-Yr. Proj. EPS CAGR(%) | 24 |
| Trailing 12-Month P/E | 9.5 | P/E on S&P Oper. EPS 2011**E** | 9.5 | Dividend Rate/Share | $0.92 | S&P Credit Rating | A |
| $10K Invested 5 Yrs Ago | $8,464 | Common Shares Outstg. (M) | 226.3 | Institutional Ownership (%) | 91 | | |

## Price Performance

30-Week Mov. Avg. ···· 10-Week Mov. Avg. ─ ─ GAAP Earnings vs. Previous Year   Volume Above Avg. STARS
12-Mo. Target Price ── Relative Strength ── ▲ Up ▼ Down ▶ No Change   Below Avg.

Options: ASE, CBOE, P, Ph

Analysis prepared by Equity Analyst **R. Shepard, CFA** on Nov 02, 2011, when the stock traded at **$45.02**.

## Highlights

▶ Third-quarter operating net revenues were up 8%, year to year, despite volatile financial markets. However, we think a 4% decline in total assets under management could pressure fees in the fourth quarter and 2012. Columbia Management had net outflows for the quarter of $4.1 billion, evenly divided between retail and institutional channels. AMP's Annuities segment has performed relatively well, but a low interest rate environment could reduce profitability in 2012. On the positive side, we expect 2012 revenue growth at the Advice and Wealth Management segment, as the company expands the number of retail advisers.

▶ We expect pretax profit margins to widen in 2012, as the company completes its integration of Columbia Management, acquired in 2010. We think the discontinuation of variable annuity sales through non-Ameriprise channels should also improve the risk/return profile of the Annuities segment, although we expect higher amortization of deferred acquisition costs. Despite recent market volatility, we expect AMP's capital position to remain healthy.

▶ We estimate EPS of $4.38 for 2011 and $5.20 for 2012.

## Investment Rationale/Risk

▶ We like AMP's focus on share repurchases and improving profitability, measured by return on equity. We are encouraged by the increasing share of revenue contribution from wealth management and asset management as well as the increased contribution to earnings from the Annuities segment. We also think that steadily increasing adviser productivity will be a key driver of earnings growth in 2012. Near term, the recent uptick in market volatility has resulted in uneven net asset flows. However, we think the firm's asset management business is benefiting from Columbia Management synergies and positive relative fund performance, which should eventually result in positive revenue and asset growth.

▶ Risks to our recommendation and target price include potential market depreciation, narrower net interest margins on fixed annuity sales due to lower interest rates, and greater regulatory concerns.

▶ Our 12-month target price of $53 is equal to 10.2X our 2012 EPS estimate of $5.20, in line with AMP's historical multiples.

## Qualitative Risk Assessment

| LOW | MEDIUM | HIGH |
|---|---|---|

Our risk assessment reflects our view of the company's significant franchise value, offset by our concerns that the loss of the widely recognized American Express name could negatively affect AMP's ability to raise and retain client assets.

## Quantitative Evaluations

**S&P Quality Ranking**   NR

| D | C | B- | B | B+ | A- | A | A+ |
|---|---|---|---|---|---|---|---|

**Relative Strength Rank**   MODERATE

44

LOWEST = 1   HIGHEST = 99

## Revenue/Earnings Data

**Revenue (Million $)**

| | 1Q | 2Q | 3Q | 4Q | Year |
|---|---|---|---|---|---|
| 2011 | 2,654 | 2,623 | 2,467 | -- | -- |
| 2010 | 2,292 | 2,597 | 2,465 | 2,692 | 10,046 |
| 2009 | 1,716 | 1,874 | 1,946 | 2,269 | 7,946 |
| 2008 | 2,000 | 1,979 | 1,641 | 1,350 | 7,149 |
| 2007 | 2,096 | 2,204 | 2,227 | 2,319 | 8,909 |
| 2006 | 1,949 | 2,053 | 1,977 | 2,161 | 8,140 |

**Earnings Per Share ($)**

| | 1Q | 2Q | 3Q | 4Q | Year |
|---|---|---|---|---|---|
| 2011 | 1.05 | 1.25 | 1.12 | E1.15 | E4.38 |
| 2010 | 0.81 | 0.98 | 1.32 | 1.08 | 4.18 |
| 2009 | 0.58 | 0.41 | 1.00 | 0.90 | 2.95 |
| 2008 | 0.82 | 0.93 | -0.32 | -1.69 | -0.17 |
| 2007 | 0.68 | 0.81 | 0.83 | 1.08 | 3.39 |
| 2006 | 0.57 | 0.57 | 0.71 | 0.69 | 2.54 |

Fiscal year ended Dec. 31. Next earnings report expected: Early February. EPS Estimates based on S&P Operating Earnings; historical GAAP earnings are as reported.

## Dividend Data (Dates: mm/dd Payment Date: mm/dd/yy)

| Amount ($) | Date Decl. | Ex-Div. Date | Stk. of Record | Payment Date |
|---|---|---|---|---|
| 0.180 | 02/02 | 02/09 | 02/11 | 02/25/11 |
| 0.230 | 04/25 | 05/04 | 05/06 | 05/20/11 |
| 0.230 | 07/26 | 08/03 | 08/05 | 08/19/11 |
| 0.230 | 10/24 | 11/02 | 11/04 | 11/18/11 |

Dividends have been paid since 2005. Source: Company reports.

---

**Please read the Required Disclosures and Analyst Certification on the last page of this report.**

The *McGraw·Hill* Companies

# Ameriprise Financial Inc

**STANDARD &POOR'S**

## Business Summary November 02, 2011

CORPORATE OVERVIEW. Ameriprise Financial completed its spinoff from American Express on September 30, 2005, and began trading on the New York Stock Exchange on October 3 under the symbol AMP.

As of September 30, 2011, Ameriprise owned, managed and administered $600 billion of client assets. The company offers a broad assortment of products, including mutual funds, annuities and life insurance products. Ameriprise was originally named Investors Diversified Services before it was acquired by American Express in 1984. American Express spun off the company in 2005. We believe the spinoff and marketing campaign have raised AMP's visibility among prospective clients and may also help attract and retain financial advisers. In terms of corporate governance, we view favorably the high proportion of independent directors on the board, but we would prefer that the company split the roles of chairman and CEO.

Ameriprise has five operating segments. Advice and Wealth Management provides financial advice and full-service brokerage and banking services, primarily to retail clients, through its financial advisers. The Asset Management segment provides investment advice and investment products to retail

and institutional clients. Threadneedle Investments predominantly provides international investment products and services, and RiverSource Investments mainly provides products and services in the U.S. for domestic customers. Its domestic products are primarily distributed through the Advice and Wealth Management segment and third parties, while international products are mostly distributed through third parties. The Annuities segment provides RiverSource Life variable and fixed annuity products to retail clients, primarily through the Advice and Wealth Management segment. The Protection segment offers a variety of protection products to address the identified protection and risk management needs of retail clients including life, disability income and property-casualty insurance. The Corporate and Other segment consists of net investment income on corporate level assets, including unallocated equity and other revenues from various investments as well as unallocated corporate expenses.

## Company Financials Fiscal Year Ended Dec. 31

| Per Share Data ($) | 2010 | 2009 | 2008 | 2007 | 2006 | 2005 | 2004 | 2003 | 2002 | 2001 |
|---|---|---|---|---|---|---|---|---|---|---|
| Tangible Book Value | 37.22 | 30.75 | 22.41 | 34.81 | 31.10 | 30.75 | 6.45 | NA | NA | NA |
| Cash Flow | 5.22 | 3.45 | -0.74 | 4.11 | 3.21 | 2.26 | NA | 4.01 | NA | NA |
| Earnings | 4.18 | 2.95 | -0.17 | 3.39 | 2.54 | 2.26 | 2.80 | 3.00 | NA | NA |
| S&P Core Earnings | 4.11 | 2.92 | 1.98 | 3.26 | 2.41 | 2.37 | 3.02 | 2.46 | NA | NA |
| Dividends | 0.71 | 0.68 | 0.64 | 0.56 | 0.44 | 0.11 | NA | NA | NA | NA |
| Payout Ratio | 17% | 23% | NM | 17% | 17% | 5% | NA | NA | NA | NA |
| Prices:High | 58.17 | 40.00 | 57.55 | 69.25 | 55.79 | 44.78 | NA | NA | NA | NA |
| Prices:Low | 34.68 | 13.50 | 11.74 | 51.31 | 40.30 | 32.00 | NA | NA | NA | NA |
| P/E Ratio:High | 14 | 14 | NM | 20 | 22 | 20 | NA | NA | NA | NA |
| P/E Ratio:Low | 8 | 5 | NM | 15 | 16 | 14 | NA | NA | NA | NA |
| **Income Statement Analysis** (Million $) | | | | | | | | | | |
| Income Interest | 3,961 | 2,704 | 2,899 | 3,238 | 2,204 | 2,241 | 2,125 | NA | NA | NA |
| Income Other | 6,085 | 5,242 | 4,250 | 5,671 | 5,936 | 5,243 | 4,645 | NA | NA | NA |
| Total Income | 10,046 | 7,946 | 7,149 | 8,909 | 8,140 | 7,484 | 6,770 | 6,361 | 5,793 | NA |
| General Expenses | 8,092 | 6,758 | 7,028 | 7,353 | 7,343 | 6,739 | 5,756 | NA | NA | NA |
| Interest Expense | 360 | 268 | 288 | 367 | 116 | 73.0 | 78.0 | NA | NA | NA |
| Depreciation | 110 | 120 | 204 | 173 | 166 | 164 | NA | NA | NA | NA |
| Net Income | 1,097 | 722 | -38.0 | 814 | 631 | 556 | 708 | 738 | 674 | NA |
| S&P Core Earnings | 1,079 | 715 | 440 | 784 | 599 | 588 | 762 | 622 | NA | NA |
| **Balance Sheet & Other Financial Data** (Million $) | | | | | | | | | | |
| Cash | 2,861 | 3,097 | 6,729 | 7,037 | 4,775 | 2,474 | 3,319 | 1,869 | NA | NA |
| Receivables | 5,037 | 4,435 | 3,887 | 7,244 | 6,668 | 2,172 | 2,526 | NA | NA | NA |
| Cost of Investments | 42,497 | 36,974 | 27,522 | 30,625 | 35,553 | 39,100 | 40,157 | NA | NA | NA |
| Total Assets | 131,192 | 113,774 | 95,689 | 109,230 | 104,172 | 93,121 | 90,934 | 85,384 | NA | NA |
| Loss Reserve | Nil | Nil | Nil | Nil | Nil | Nil | Nil | NA | NA | NA |
| Short Term Debt | 397 | Nil | Nil | Nil | Nil | Nil | Nil | NA | NA | NA |
| Capitalization:Debt | 2,317 | 2,249 | 2,027 | 2,018 | 2,225 | 1,833 | 1,878 | NA | NA | NA |
| Capitalization:Equity | 10,725 | 9,273 | 6,191 | 7,810 | 7,925 | 7,687 | 8,058 | 7,288 | NA | NA |
| Capitalization:Total | 13,602 | 12,125 | 8,218 | 9,828 | 10,150 | 9,520 | 9,936 | NA | NA | NA |
| Price Times Book Value:High | 1.6 | 1.3 | 2.6 | 2.0 | 1.7 | 1.5 | NA | NA | NA | NA |
| Price Times Book Value:Low | 0.9 | 0.4 | 0.5 | 1.5 | 1.2 | 1.0 | NA | NA | NA | NA |
| Cash Flow | 1,207 | 842 | 166 | 987 | 759 | 556 | NA | 987 | 855 | NA |
| % Expense/Operating Revenue | 84.1 | 88.4 | 105.2 | 88.6 | 90.2 | 90.0 | 86.2 | NA | NA | NA |
| % Earnings & Depreciation/Assets | 1.0 | 0.8 | 0.2 | 0.9 | 0.1 | 0.1 | NA | NA | NA | NA |

Data as orig reptd.; bef. results of disc opers/spec. items. Per share data adj. for stk. divs.; EPS diluted. E-Estimated. NA-Not Available. NM-Not Meaningful. NR-Not Ranked. UR-Under Review.

**Office:** 55 Ameriprise Financial Center, Minneapolis, MN 55474.
**Telephone:** 612-671-3131.
**Website:** http://www.ameriprise.com
**Chrmn & CEO:** J. Cracchiolo

**EVP & CFO:** W. Berman
**EVP & General Counsel:** J.C. Junek
**SVP, Chief Acctg Officer & Cntlr:** D.K. Stewart
**SVP & Treas:** J. Hamalainen

**Investor Contact:** L. Gagnon (612-671-2080)
**Board Members:** J. Cracchiolo, L. R. Greenberg, W. D. Knowlton, W. W. Lewis, S. S. Marshall, J. Noddle, H. J. Sarles, R. F. Sharpe, Jr., W. H. Turner

**Founded:** 1983
**Domicile:** Delaware
**Employees:** 10,472

The McGraw-Hill Companies

# AmerisourceBergen Corp

**STANDARD &POOR'S**

| S&P Recommendation **BUY** ★★★★☆ | Price $35.98 (as of Nov 25, 2011) | 12-Mo. Target Price $45.00 | Investment Style Large-Cap Blend |
|---|---|---|---|

**GICS Sector** Health Care
**Sub-Industry** Health Care Distributors

**Summary** This distributor of pharmaceutical products and related health care services was formed via the August 2001 merger of Amerisource Health Corp. and Bergen Brunswig Corp.

## Key Stock Statistics (Source S&P, Vickers, company reports)

| | | | | | | | |
|---|---|---|---|---|---|---|---|
| 52-Wk Range | $43.47– 30.56 | S&P Oper. EPS 2012**E** | 2.80 | Market Capitalization(B) | $9.295 | Beta | 0.71 |
| Trailing 12-Month EPS | $2.54 | S&P Oper. EPS 2013**E** | NA | Yield (%) | 1.45 | S&P 3-Yr. Proj. EPS CAGR(%) | 12 |
| Trailing 12-Month P/E | 14.2 | P/E on S&P Oper. EPS 2012**E** | 12.9 | Dividend Rate/Share | $0.52 | S&P Credit Rating | A- |
| $10K Invested 5 Yrs Ago | NA | Common Shares Outstg. (M) | 258.3 | Institutional Ownership (%) | 93 | | |

## Price Performance

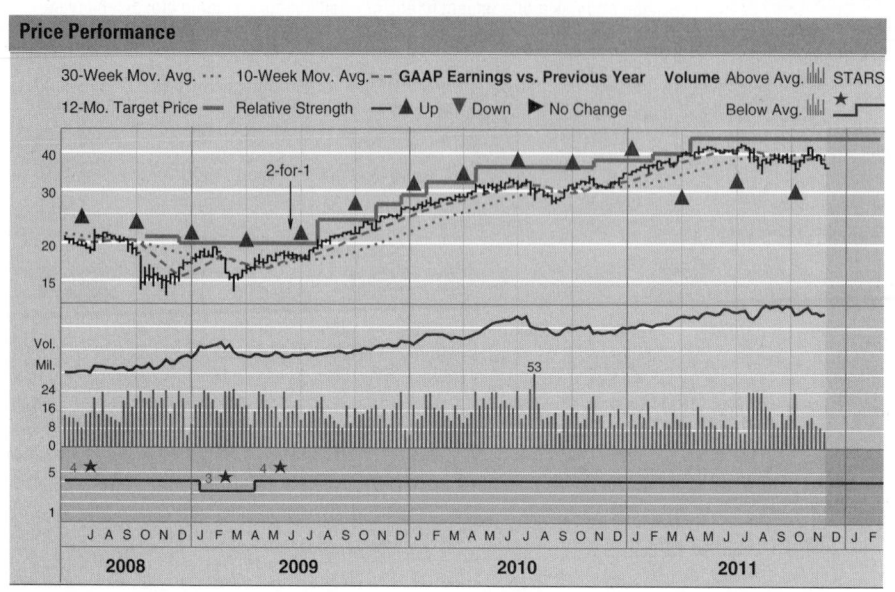

30-Week Mov. Avg. · · · · 10-Week Mov. Avg. – – **GAAP Earnings vs. Previous Year** Volume Above Avg. STARS
12-Mo. Target Price — Relative Strength — ▲ Up ▼ Down ► No Change Below Avg.

Options: ASE, CBOE, P

Analysis prepared by Equity Analyst **Herman Saftlas** on Sep 19, 2011, when the stock traded at **$39.31**.

## Highlights

► We expect revenues in FY 12 (Sep.) to roughly approximate the $80 billion that we forecast for FY 11, with contributions from new generic drugs such as Lipitor and Zyprexa expected to roughly offset lower sales of generic forms of Eloxatin, Gemzar and Taxotere oncology drugs. We expect volume gains from the distribution of other medical products, and contributions from new acquisitions to augment volume. However, an important contract with Duane Reade has not been renewed.

► We see operating margins widening in FY 11, driven mainly by better profitability in the specialty segment of the business. We expect margins in the drug distribution arm to be flat, with positive product mix trends roughly offset by incremental spending on a new information technology platform.

► We estimate FY 11 operating EPS of $2.54, up from FY 10's $2.22 (excluding a $0.05 litigation settlement gain). EPS comparisons should also benefit from share buybacks. We see FY 12 EPS climbing to $2.80, driven by a significant advance in generics sales with patents expiring on Lipitor, Zyprexa and other branded drugs.

## Investment Rationale/Risk

► We believe ABC has shown the resiliency to manage through this period of economic weakness and we expect the company, like its peers, to benefit from health care reform. We also believe it has the wherewithal to hold its own and likely gain share in the competitive drug distribution market over the long term. The company controls costs tightly, in our opinion, and we remain positive about its focus on generic and oncology drugs, which we view as among the fastest-growing and most profitable revenue drivers in the pharmaceutical market. In addition, ABC views acquisitions as a key part of its growth strategy, and we believe it has the cash flow and balance sheet needed for such transactions.

► Risks to our opinion and target price include intensified competition and loss of one or more major clients. Possible changes in Medicare Part D could also affect the business.

► Our 12-month target price of $45 applies a peer-parity P/E multiple of 16.1X to our $2.80 EPS estimate for FY 12. Our target price implies a projected FY 12 EV/EBITDA multiple of about 8.5X, which is comparable to peers.

## Qualitative Risk Assessment

| LOW | MEDIUM | HIGH |
|---|---|---|

Our risk assessment reflects what we view as ABC's improving financial performance, its ability to attract new accounts to more than compensate for account losses, and its healthy operating cash flow. However, we think the drug distribution arena is highly competitive, and that ABC is less diversified than many of its large health care distribution peers.

## Quantitative Evaluations

**S&P Quality Ranking**                    A-

| D | C | B- | B | B+ | A- | A | A+ |
|---|---|---|---|---|---|---|---|

**Relative Strength Rank**          MODERATE

| 45 |
|---|

LOWEST = 1                         HIGHEST = 99

## Revenue/Earnings Data

**Revenue (Million $)**

| | 1Q | 2Q | 3Q | 4Q | Year |
|---|---|---|---|---|---|
| 2011 | 19,889 | 19,760 | 20,161 | 20,408 | 80,218 |
| 2010 | 19,336 | 19,301 | 19,602 | 19,715 | 77,954 |
| 2009 | 17,338 | 17,312 | 18,394 | 18,716 | 71,760 |
| 2008 | 17,279 | 17,756 | 17,997 | 17,158 | 70,190 |
| 2007 | 16,725 | 16,513 | 16,446 | 16,390 | 66,074 |
| 2006 | 14,653 | 15,221 | 15,686 | 15,643 | 61,203 |

**Earnings Per Share ($)**

| | | | | | |
|---|---|---|---|---|---|
| 2011 | 0.57 | 0.77 | 0.66 | 0.54 | 2.54 |
| 2010 | 0.52 | 0.63 | 0.57 | 0.50 | 2.22 |
| 2009 | 0.37 | 0.48 | 0.42 | 0.44 | 1.69 |
| 2008 | 0.33 | 0.41 | 0.35 | 0.37 | 1.45 |
| 2007 | 0.32 | 0.34 | 0.35 | 0.32 | 1.32 |
| 2006 | 0.24 | 0.31 | 0.29 | 0.31 | 1.13 |

Fiscal year ended Sep. 30. Next earnings report expected: Early February. EPS Estimates based on S&P Operating Earnings; historical GAAP earnings are as reported.

## Dividend Data (Dates: mm/dd Payment Date: mm/dd/yy)

| Amount ($) | Date Decl. | Ex-Div. Date | Stk. of Record | Payment Date |
|---|---|---|---|---|
| 0.115 | 05/13 | 05/20 | 05/24 | 06/06/11 |
| 0.115 | 08/11 | 08/18 | 08/22 | 09/06/11 |
| 0.130 | 11/10 | 11/17 | 11/21 | 12/05/11 |
| 0.130 | 11/10 | 11/17 | 11/21 | 12/05/11 |

Dividends have been paid since 2001. Source: Company reports.

---

**Please read the Required Disclosures and Analyst Certification on the last page of this report.**

The **McGraw·Hill** Companies

# AmerisourceBergen Corp

**STANDARD &POOR'S**

## Business Summary September 19, 2011

CORPORATE OVERVIEW. AmerisourceBergen Corp., one of the largest U.S. pharmaceutical distributors, began operation in August 2001, following the merger of Amerisource Health Corp. and Bergen Brunswig Corp. ABC accounted for the merger as an acquisition by Amerisource of Bergen. Pharmaceutical distribution operations consist primarily of AmerisourceBergen Drug Corp. (ABDC) and AmerisourceBergen Specialty Group (ABSG).

ABDC (accounting for an indicated 79% of revenues in FY 10--Sep.) distributes a comprehensive offering of brand-name and generic pharmaceuticals, over-the-counter health care products, home health care supplies and equipment, and related services to a wide variety of health care providers, including acute care hospitals and health systems, retail pharmacies, mail order pharmacies, medical clinics, long-term care and other customers. ABDC also provides pharmacy management, staffing and other consulting services; scalable automated pharmacy dispensing equipment; medication and supply dispensing cabinets; and supply management software to retail and institutional health care providers.

ABSG (21% of revenues) provides pharmaceutical distribution and other services primarily to physicians who specialize in a variety of disease states, especially oncology, and to other health care providers, including dialysis clinics. ABSG also distributes plasma and other blood products, injectable pharmaceuticals and vaccines. In addition, through its specialty services businesses, ABSG provides drug commercialization services, third party logistics, reimbursement consulting, data analytics, and outcomes research, and other services for biotech and other drug companies, practice management, and group purchasing services for physician practices. The company also repackages drugs from bulk to unit dose, unit of use, blister pack and standard bottle sizes.

National and retail drugstore chains, independent community drugstores, and pharmacy departments of supermarkets and mass merchandisers account for its retail market segment (30% of FY 10 total revenue), while the hospital/acute care, mail order and specialty pharmaceuticals markets together comprise its institutional market segment (70%). Revenues generated from sales to pharmacy benefit manager Medco Health Solutions (MHS) accounted for 18% of total revenues in FY 10.

The PharMerica workers' compensation business, which had revenues of about $404 million, was sold in October 2008.

## Company Financials Fiscal Year Ended Sep. 30

| Per Share Data ($) | 2011 | 2010 | 2009 | 2008 | 2007 | 2006 | 2005 | 2004 | 2003 | 2002 |
|---|---|---|---|---|---|---|---|---|---|---|
| Tangible Book Value | NA | 0.39 | NM | NM | 0.03 | 3.96 | 3.69 | 4.31 | 3.61 | 2.61 |
| Cash Flow | 2.93 | 2.52 | 1.99 | 1.70 | 1.59 | 1.36 | 0.87 | 1.18 | 1.10 | 0.90 |
| Earnings | 2.54 | 2.22 | 1.69 | 1.45 | 1.32 | 1.13 | 0.69 | 1.02 | 0.97 | 0.79 |
| S&P Core Earnings | 2.57 | 2.19 | 1.70 | 1.41 | 1.23 | 1.04 | 0.62 | 0.78 | 0.93 | 0.76 |
| Dividends | 0.43 | 0.32 | 0.21 | 0.15 | 0.10 | 0.05 | 0.03 | 0.03 | 0.03 | 0.03 |
| Payout Ratio | 17% | 14% | 12% | 10% | 8% | 4% | 4% | 2% | 3% | 3% |
| Prices:High | 43.47 | 34.72 | 26.58 | 24.30 | 28.28 | 24.48 | 21.09 | 16.00 | 18.36 | 20.71 |
| Prices:Low | 33.91 | 25.66 | 13.75 | 13.33 | 21.11 | 20.08 | 13.24 | 12.44 | 11.41 | 12.55 |
| P/E Ratio:High | 17 | 16 | 16 | 17 | 22 | 22 | 31 | 16 | 19 | 26 |
| P/E Ratio:Low | 13 | 12 | 8 | 9 | 16 | 18 | 19 | 12 | 12 | 16 |

**Income Statement Analysis** (Million $)

| | 2011 | 2010 | 2009 | 2008 | 2007 | 2006 | 2005 | 2004 | 2003 | 2002 |
|---|---|---|---|---|---|---|---|---|---|---|
| Revenue | 80,218 | 77,954 | 71,760 | 70,190 | 66,074 | 61,203 | 54,577 | 53,179 | 49,657 | 45,235 |
| Operating Income | 1,339 | 1,168 | 992 | 919 | 912 | 814 | 723 | 978 | 963 | 804 |
| Depreciation | 108 | 86.5 | 90.0 | 82.1 | 104 | 96.9 | 81.2 | 87.1 | 71.0 | 61.2 |
| Interest Expense | 76.7 | 72.5 | 63.5 | 75.1 | 32.0 | 12.5 | 57.2 | 113 | 145 | 141 |
| Pretax Income | 1,131 | 1,028 | 824 | 761 | 7.85 | 741 | 469 | 760 | 726 | 572 |
| Effective Tax Rate | NA | NA | 37.9% | 38.4% | 37.1% | 36.8% | 37.7% | 38.4% | 39.2% | 39.7% |
| Net Income | 707 | 637 | 512 | 469 | 494 | 468 | 292 | 468 | 441 | 345 |
| S&P Core Earnings | 717 | 625 | 513 | 456 | 462 | 429 | 264 | 356 | 421 | 333 |

**Balance Sheet & Other Financial Data** (Million $)

| | 2011 | 2010 | 2009 | 2008 | 2007 | 2006 | 2005 | 2004 | 2003 | 2002 |
|---|---|---|---|---|---|---|---|---|---|---|
| Cash | 1,826 | 1,658 | 1,009 | 878 | 640 | 1,261 | 1,316 | 871 | 800 | 663 |
| Current Assets | 11,218 | 10,748 | 9,954 | 8,670 | 8,714 | 9,210 | 7,988 | 8,295 | 8,859 | 8,350 |
| Total Assets | 14,983 | 14,435 | 13,573 | 12,153 | 12,310 | 12,784 | 11,381 | 11,654 | 12,040 | 11,213 |
| Current Liabilities | 10,855 | 9,906 | 9,480 | 8,168 | 7,857 | 7,459 | 6,052 | 6,104 | 6,256 | 6,100 |
| Long Term Debt | 973 | 1,343 | 1,177 | 1,187 | 1,227 | 1,094 | 951 | 1,157 | 1,723 | 1,756 |
| Common Equity | 2,869 | 2,954 | 2,716 | 2,710 | 3,100 | 4,141 | 4,280 | 4,339 | 4,005 | 3,316 |
| Total Capital | 4,234 | 4,298 | 3,894 | 3,899 | 4,327 | 5,235 | 5,232 | 5,496 | 5,728 | 5,073 |
| Capital Expenditures | 168 | 185 | 146 | 137 | 118 | 113 | 203 | 189 | 90.6 | 64.2 |
| Cash Flow | 815 | 723 | 602 | 551 | 598 | 565 | 373 | 555 | 512 | 406 |
| Current Ratio | 1.0 | 1.1 | 1.1 | 1.1 | 1.1 | 1.2 | 1.3 | 1.4 | 1.4 | 1.4 |
| % Long Term Debt of Capitalization | 23.0 | 31.3 | 30.2 | 30.5 | 28.3 | 20.9 | 18.2 | 21.1 | 30.1 | 34.6 |
| % Net Income of Revenue | 0.9 | 0.8 | 0.7 | 0.7 | 0.7 | 0.8 | 0.5 | 0.9 | 0.9 | 0.8 |
| % Return on Assets | 4.8 | 4.6 | 4.0 | 3.8 | 3.9 | 3.9 | 2.5 | 4.0 | 3.8 | 3.2 |
| % Return on Equity | 24.3 | 22.5 | 18.9 | 16.2 | 13.6 | 11.1 | 6.8 | 11.2 | 12.1 | 11.2 |

Data as orig reptd.; bef. results of disc opers/spec. items. Per share data adj. for stk. divs.; EPS diluted. E-Estimated. NA-Not Available. NM-Not Meaningful. NR-Not Ranked. UR-Under Review.

**Office:** 1300 Morris Drive, Chesterbrook, PA 19087-5594.
**Telephone:** 610-727-7000.
**Email:** investorrelations@amerisourcebergen.com
**Website:** http://www.amerisourcebergen.com

**Chrmn:** R.C. Gozon
**Pres & CEO:** S.H. Collis
**EVP, CFO & Chief Acctg Officer:** M.D. Dicandilo
**EVP, Secy & General Counsel:** J.G. Chou

**SVP & CIO:** T.H. Murphy
**Board Members:** S. H. Collis, C. H. Cotros, R. W. Gochnauer, R. C. Gozon, E. E. Hagenlocker, J. E. Henney, K. W. Hyle, M. J. Long, H. W. McGee

**Founded:** 1985
**Domicile:** Delaware
**Employees:** 10,300

*The McGraw-Hill Companies*

# Amgen Inc

**STANDARD &POOR'S**

| S&P Recommendation | **BUY** ★★★★☆ | Price $54.65 (as of Nov 25, 2011) | 12-Mo. Target Price $67.00 | Investment Style Large-Cap Growth |
|---|---|---|---|---|

**GICS Sector** Health Care
**Sub-Industry** Biotechnology

**Summary** Amgen is among the world's leading biotech companies and has major treatments for anemia, neutropenia, rheumatoid arthritis, psoriatic arthritis, psoriasis, cancer, and osteoporosis.

## Key Stock Statistics (Source S&P, Vickers, company reports)

| | | | | | | | |
|---|---|---|---|---|---|---|---|
| 52-Wk Range | $61.53– 47.66 | S&P Oper. EPS 2011E | 5.23 | Market Capitalization(B) | $47.903 | Beta | 0.43 |
| Trailing 12-Month EPS | $4.04 | S&P Oper. EPS 2012E | 5.57 | Yield (%) | 2.05 | S&P 3-Yr. Proj. EPS CAGR(%) | 9 |
| Trailing 12-Month P/E | 13.5 | P/E on S&P Oper. EPS 2011E | 10.4 | Dividend Rate/Share | $1.12 | S&P Credit Rating | A+ |
| $10K Invested 5 Yrs Ago | $7,617 | Common Shares Outstg. (M) | 876.5 | Institutional Ownership (%) | 83 | | |

## Price Performance

30-Week Mov. Avg. · · · · 10-Week Mov. Avg. — — GAAP Earnings vs. Previous Year    Volume Above Avg. STARS
12-Mo. Target Price — Relative Strength — ▲ Up ▼ Down ► No Change    Below Avg. ★

Options: ASE, CBOE, P, Ph

Analysis prepared by Equity Analyst **Steven Silver** on Oct 26, 2011, when the stock traded at **$56.95**.

## Highlights

➤ We forecast 2011 revenues of $15.56 billion, 4% above 2010's $15.0 billion, and 2012 revenues of $16.1 billion, which would represent 3% growth. We see growth being driven by the rollout of Prolia/Xgeva, more than offsetting the impact of higher Medicaid rebates resulting from U.S. health care reform and lower utilization of Epogen and Araensp for anemia due to FDA labeling restrictions amid safety concerns.

➤ We expect 2011 and 2012 adjusted operating margins of around 37%, below the 40% in 2010, as AMGN ramps spending related to the launch of Prolia and XGeva. We also expect AMGN to maintain investments in R&D near 20% of sales in both periods, as it recently advanced pipeline candidates AMG 386 for ovarian cancer and AMG 479 for pancreatic cancer to Phase III studies.

➤ We estimate adjusted EPS of $5.23 for 2011 and $5.57 for 2012, excluding acquisition and restructuring costs. We expect AMGN to support EPS growth by deploying more than 40% of net income in share repurchases in the coming years, while paying 20% of net income in dividends.

## Investment Rationale/Risk

➤ Despite near-term headwinds from U.S. health care reform, we expect the market rollout of denosumab for post-menopausal osteoporosis (as Prolia) and cancer indications (as Xgeva) to shift investor focus to AMGN's long-term pipeline and what we view as its attractive valuation. While we forecast more than $3 billion in peak annual sales, we see AMGN being reliant on the drug's commercial success and ultimate expansion into additional cancer indications, given a mature core product roster. However, we see legacy product cash flows supporting dividends and share repurchases, while still enabling R&D investments and acquisitions, like the recently completed purchase of cancer vaccine developer BioVex Group.

➤ Risks to our recommendation and target price include failure to gain market acceptance for Prolia/Xgeva, further regulatory restrictions on AMGN's anemia drug franchise, and increased competition.

➤ Our 12-month target price of $67 applies a 12X multiple to our 2012 adjusted EPS estimate, a discount to the large-cap sector peer target average, on our view of a slower growth profile.

## Qualitative Risk Assessment

| LOW | MEDIUM | **HIGH** |
|---|---|---|

Our risk assessment reflects the highly competitive and regulated markets in which AMGN operates. Changes to government reimbursement policies and drug safety oversight could significantly hurt AMGN's revenues and profitability. We believe that biosimilar versions of several of AMGN's drugs pose a near-term challenge in Europe and a long-term threat in the U.S.

## Quantitative Evaluations

**S&P Quality Ranking**      B+

| D | C | B- | B | **B+** | A- | A | A+ |
|---|---|---|---|---|---|---|---|

**Relative Strength Rank**      MODERATE

66

LOWEST = 1          HIGHEST = 99

## Revenue/Earnings Data

**Revenue (Million $)**

| | 1Q | 2Q | 3Q | 4Q | Year |
|---|---|---|---|---|---|
| 2011 | 3,706 | 3,959 | 3,944 | -- | -- |
| 2010 | 3,592 | 3,804 | 3,816 | 3,841 | 15,053 |
| 2009 | 3,308 | 3,713 | 3,812 | 3,809 | 14,642 |
| 2008 | 3,613 | 3,764 | 3,875 | 3,751 | 15,003 |
| 2007 | 3,687 | 3,728 | 3,611 | 3,745 | 14,771 |
| 2006 | 3,217 | 3,491 | 3,503 | 3,737 | 14,268 |

**Earnings Per Share ($)**

| | | | | | |
|---|---|---|---|---|---|
| 2011 | 1.20 | 1.25 | 0.50 | E1.17 | E5.23 |
| 2010 | 1.18 | 1.25 | 1.29 | 1.08 | 4.79 |
| 2009 | 0.98 | 1.25 | 1.36 | 0.92 | 4.51 |
| 2008 | 1.04 | 0.87 | 1.09 | 0.91 | 3.90 |
| 2007 | 0.94 | 0.90 | 0.18 | 0.77 | 2.82 |
| 2006 | 0.82 | 0.01 | 0.94 | 0.71 | 2.48 |

Fiscal year ended Dec. 31. Next earnings report expected: NA. EPS Estimates based on S&P Operating Earnings; historical GAAP earnings are as reported.

## Dividend Data (Dates: mm/dd Payment Date: mm/dd/yy)

| Amount ($) | Date Decl. | Ex-Div. Date | Stk. of Record | Payment Date |
|---|---|---|---|---|
| 0.280 | 07/29 | 08/16 | 08/18 | 09/08/11 |
| 0.280 | 10/13 | 11/15 | 11/17 | 12/08/11 |

Dividends have been paid since 2011. Source: Company reports.

**Please read the Required Disclosures and Analyst Certification on the last page of this report.**

**The McGraw·Hill Companies**

# Amgen Inc

## Business Summary October 26, 2011

CORPORATE OVERVIEW. Amgen, among the world's largest biotech companies, markets five of the world's best-selling biotech drugs.

Epogen is a genetically engineered version of human erythropoietin (EPO), a hormone that stimulates red blood cell production in bone marrow. Its primary market is dialysis patients suffering from chronic anemia. Epogen sales were $2.52 billion in 2010 ($2.57 billion in 2009). We expect Epogen usage to be pressured by Medicare bundled pricing for patients on dialysis which began in January 2011. However, we expect these impacts to be partially offset by modest patient population expansion and pricing power. Aranesp, a recombinant protein that stimulates the production of red blood cells in pre-dialysis and dialysis patients, is approved to treat anemia associated with chronic renal failure and cancer patients with chemotherapy-induced anemia (CIA).

Aranesp sales declined by 7% to $2.49 billion in 2010 on continuing dosing restrictions. In 2007, Phase III trial data showed a higher rate of death when using Aranesp in treating anemia of cancer (AoC) not associated with chemotherapy, an off-label prescribed use. Medicare removed AoC as a reimbursable use for Aranesp. Several later studies have suggested that Aranesp

may foster tumor growth in several cancers when dosed at or above the approved 12 g/dl dose, which has led to Medicare and FDA dosing and indication restrictions.

Neupogen stimulates neutrophils (white blood cells that defend against bacterial infection) production in cancer patients whose natural neutrophils were destroyed by chemotherapy. In 2002, the FDA approved Neulasta, a long-acting white blood cell stimulant protecting chemo patients from infection. Total Neupogen and Neulasta sales were $4.84 billion in 2010 ($4.64 billion in 2009).

Enbrel, acquired through the purchase of Immunex, (co-marketed with Wyeth) had 2010 sales of $3.53 billion ($3.49 billion in 2009) and is approved to treat rheumatoid arthritis (RA), psoriatic arthritis, and adults with moderate to severe chronic plaque psoriasis.

## Company Financials Fiscal Year Ended Dec. 31

| Per Share Data ($) | 2010 | 2009 | 2008 | 2007 | 2006 | 2005 | 2004 | 2003 | 2002 | 2001 |
|---|---|---|---|---|---|---|---|---|---|---|
| Tangible Book Value | 11.14 | 8.81 | 5.79 | 3.03 | 3.36 | 5.08 | 4.08 | 4.06 | 2.80 | 4.99 |
| Cash Flow | 5.85 | 5.54 | 4.90 | 3.89 | 3.29 | 3.59 | 2.35 | 2.19 | -0.82 | 1.28 |
| Earnings | 4.79 | 4.51 | 3.90 | 2.82 | 2.48 | 2.93 | 1.81 | 1.69 | -1.21 | 1.03 |
| S&P Core Earnings | 4.73 | 4.50 | 4.08 | 2.74 | 2.48 | 2.77 | 1.58 | 1.50 | -1.46 | 0.87 |
| Dividends | Nil | Nil | Nil | Nil | Nil | Nil | Nil | Nil | Nil | Nil |
| Payout Ratio | Nil | Nil | Nil | Nil | Nil | Nil | Nil | Nil | Nil | Nil |
| Prices:High | 61.26 | 64.76 | 66.51 | 76.95 | 81.24 | 86.92 | 66.88 | 72.37 | 62.94 | 75.06 |
| Prices:Low | 50.26 | 44.96 | 39.16 | 46.21 | 63.52 | 56.19 | 52.00 | 48.09 | 30.57 | 45.44 |
| P/E Ratio:High | 13 | 14 | 17 | 27 | 33 | 30 | 37 | 43 | NM | 73 |
| P/E Ratio:Low | 11 | 10 | 10 | 16 | 26 | 19 | 29 | 28 | NM | 44 |

| Income Statement Analysis (Million $) | 2010 | 2009 | 2008 | 2007 | 2006 | 2005 | 2004 | 2003 | 2002 | 2001 |
|---|---|---|---|---|---|---|---|---|---|---|
| Revenue | 15,053 | 14,642 | 15,003 | 14,771 | 14,268 | 12,430 | 10,550 | 8,356 | 5,523 | 4,016 |
| Operating Income | 6,670 | 6,658 | 6,726 | 6,631 | 6,022 | 5,689 | 4,636 | 3,758 | 2,501 | 2,003 |
| Depreciation | 1,017 | 1,049 | 1,073 | 1,202 | 963 | 841 | 734 | 686 | 447 | 266 |
| Interest Expense | 604 | 578 | 338 | 305 | 129 | 99.0 | 38.0 | 31.5 | 44.2 | 13.6 |
| Pretax Income | 5,317 | 5,204 | 5,250 | 3,961 | 4,020 | 4,868 | 3,395 | 3,173 | -684 | 1,686 |
| Effective Tax Rate | NA | 11.5% | 20.1% | 20.1% | 26.6% | 24.5% | 30.4% | 28.8% | NM | 33.6% |
| Net Income | 4,627 | 4,605 | 4,196 | 3,166 | 2,950 | 3,674 | 2,363 | 2,260 | -1,392 | 1,120 |
| S&P Core Earnings | 4,568 | 4,596 | 4,390 | 3,072 | 2,951 | 3,470 | 2,074 | 2,006 | -1,683 | 936 |

| Balance Sheet & Other Financial Data (Million $) | 2010 | 2009 | 2008 | 2007 | 2006 | 2005 | 2004 | 2003 | 2002 | 2001 |
|---|---|---|---|---|---|---|---|---|---|---|
| Cash | 17,422 | 13,442 | 9,552 | 7,151 | 6,277 | 5,255 | 5,808 | 5,123 | 4,664 | 2,662 |
| Current Assets | 23,129 | 18,932 | 15,221 | 13,041 | 11,712 | 9,235 | 9,170 | 7,402 | 6,404 | 3,859 |
| Total Assets | 43,486 | 39,629 | 36,443 | 34,639 | 33,788 | 29,297 | 29,221 | 26,177 | 24,456 | 6,443 |
| Current Liabilities | 6,570 | 3,873 | 4,886 | 6,179 | 7,022 | 3,595 | 4,157 | 2,246 | 1,529 | 1,003 |
| Long Term Debt | 10,874 | 10,601 | 9,176 | 11,177 | 7,134 | 3,957 | 3,937 | 3,080 | 3,048 | 223 |
| Common Equity | 23,944 | 22,667 | 20,386 | 17,869 | 18,964 | 20,451 | 19,705 | 19,389 | 18,286 | 5,217 |
| Total Capital | 37,306 | 33,268 | 29,792 | 27,526 | 26,465 | 25,571 | 24,936 | 23,930 | 22,927 | 5,440 |
| Capital Expenditures | 580 | 530 | 672 | 1,267 | 1,218 | 867 | 1,336 | 1,357 | 658 | 442 |
| Cash Flow | 5,644 | 5,654 | 5,269 | 4,368 | 3,913 | 4,515 | 3,097 | 2,946 | -945 | 1,386 |
| Current Ratio | 3.5 | 4.9 | 3.1 | 2.1 | 1.7 | 2.6 | 2.2 | 3.3 | 4.2 | 3.8 |
| % Long Term Debt of Capitalization | 29.2 | 31.9 | 30.8 | 33.9 | 27.0 | 15.5 | 15.8 | 12.9 | 13.3 | 4.1 |
| % Net Income of Revenue | 30.7 | 31.5 | 28.0 | 21.4 | 20.7 | 29.6 | 22.4 | 27.0 | NM | 27.9 |
| % Return on Assets | 11.1 | 12.1 | 11.8 | 9.3 | 9.4 | 12.6 | 8.5 | 8.9 | NM | 18.9 |
| % Return on Equity | 19.9 | 21.4 | 21.9 | 17.2 | 15.0 | 18.3 | 12.1 | 12.0 | NM | 23.5 |

Data as orig reptd.; bef. results of disc opers/spec. items. Per share data adj. for stk. divs.; EPS diluted. E-Estimated. NA-Not Available. NM-Not Meaningful. NR-Not Ranked. UR-Under Review.

**Office:** One Amgen Center Drive, Thousand Oaks, CA 91320-1799.
**Telephone:** 805-447-1000.
**Email:** investor.relations@amgen.com
**Website:** http://www.amgen.com

**Chrmn & CEO:** K.W. Sharer
**Pres & COO:** R.A. Bradway
**EVP & CFO:** J.M. Peacock
**SVP, Secy & General Counsel:** D.J. Scott

**SVP & CIO:** D. McKenzie
**Investor Contact:** A. Sood (805-447-1060)
**Board Members:** D. Baltimore, F. J. Biondi, Jr., R. A. Bradway, V. D. Coffman, R. M. Henderson, F. C. Herringer, G. S. Omenn, J. C. Pelham, J. P. Reason, L. D. Schaeffer, K. W. Sharer, R. D. Sugar, F. de Carbonnel

**Founded:** 1980
**Domicile:** Delaware
**Employees:** 17,400

# Amphenol Corp

**STANDARD &POOR'S**

| S&P Recommendation | BUY ★★★★☆ | Price $41.58 (as of Nov 25, 2011) | 12-Mo. Target Price $56.00 | Investment Style Large-Cap Growth |
|---|---|---|---|---|

**GICS Sector** Information Technology
**Sub-Industry** Electronic Components

**Summary** This company makes connectors, cable, and interconnect systems for electronics, cable TV, telecommunications, aerospace, transportation, and industrial applications.

## Key Stock Statistics (Source S&P, Vickers, company reports)

| | | | | | | | |
|---|---|---|---|---|---|---|---|
| 52-Wk Range | $59.11– 38.98 | S&P Oper. EPS 2011**E** | 3.05 | Market Capitalization(B) | $6.891 | Beta | 1.36 |
| Trailing 12-Month EPS | $3.10 | S&P Oper. EPS 2012**E** | 3.30 | Yield (%) | 1.01 | S&P 3-Yr. Proj. EPS CAGR(%) | 12 |
| Trailing 12-Month P/E | 13.4 | P/E on S&P Oper. EPS 2011**E** | 13.6 | Dividend Rate/Share | $0.42 | S&P Credit Rating | BBB |
| $10K Invested 5 Yrs Ago | $12,208 | Common Shares Outstg. (M) | 165.7 | Institutional Ownership (%) | NM | | |

## Price Performance

30-Week Mov. Avg. ··· 10-Week Mov. Avg. -- **GAAP Earnings vs. Previous Year** Volume Above Avg. ▮▮▮ STARS
12-Mo. Target Price — Relative Strength — ▲ Up ▼ Down ▶ No Change Below Avg. ▮▮▮ ★

Options: ASE, P, Ph

Analysis prepared by Equity Analyst **Michael Jaffe** on Nov 09, 2011, when the stock traded at **$47.85**.

## Highlights

➤ We forecast an 11% sales increase for 2011, followed by a 6% gain in 2012. Difficult economic conditions in the U.S., Western Europe, and elsewhere limited demand for APH's products in late 2008 and 2009. However, boosted by recoveries in these economies, sales had revived since the early part of 2010, before economic uncertainties caused sales growth to slow to 9% in 2011's third quarter (and for Amphenol to guide towards small sales and EPS declines in 2011's fourth quarter). Although we view this as a soft patch in what we see as an ongoing business recovery at Amphenol, we think less robust global economies will moderate revenue gains in the near-term.

➤ After being aided in recent quarters by stronger sales and aggressive cost controls, we see wider operating margins in 2011, but we see economic and resultant sales challenges causing margins to flatten in 2012. We also expect a negative impact from higher commodity costs in both years.

➤ Our 2011 EPS forecast excludes $0.04 of net credits, and compares with 2010 results that excluded $0.12 of credits.

## Investment Rationale/Risk

➤ Although APH has recently faced moderating trends in its two year old business revival, we think this will prove to be a soft patch. We also are positive about APH's long-term prospects, on what we expect to be an ongoing expansion of the global communications infrastructure, increasing sophistication of military and space systems, and the use of more electronic devices in automobiles and other industrial products. Using relative P/E analysis, we view APH as undervalued.

➤ Risks to our recommendation and target price include a downturn in global economic trends and an extended reduction in demand for APH's products.

➤ The shares recently traded at 14.5X our 2012 EPS estimate, in the lower part of APH's range of the past decade. Based on our belief that the recent sluggishness in APH's business will only last for a short time, we think a higher valuation is merited. Our 12-month target price of $56 is based on a 17X multiple on our 2012 estimate, which is a little closer to the middle of APH's valuation during periods of earnings strength over the past decade.

## Qualitative Risk Assessment

| LOW | MEDIUM | HIGH |
|---|---|---|

Our risk assessment reflects our view of the company's typically solid levels of cash flow and a strong business model, offset by the inherent cyclicality of APH's business.

## Quantitative Evaluations

**S&P Quality Ranking** B+

| D | C | B- | B | B+ | A- | A | A+ |
|---|---|---|---|---|---|---|---|

**Relative Strength Rank** MODERATE

38

LOWEST = 1  HIGHEST = 99

## Revenue/Earnings Data

**Revenue (Million $)**

| | 1Q | 2Q | 3Q | 4Q | Year |
|---|---|---|---|---|---|
| 2011 | 940.6 | 1,018 | 1,033 | -- | -- |
| 2010 | 771.0 | 884.8 | 948.5 | 949.9 | 3,554 |
| 2009 | 660.0 | 685.2 | 716.6 | 758.3 | 2,820 |
| 2008 | 770.7 | 846.8 | 863.7 | 755.3 | 3,236 |
| 2007 | 651.1 | 688.8 | 733.9 | 777.3 | 2,851 |
| 2006 | 569.0 | 606.6 | 636.4 | 659.4 | 2,471 |

**Earnings Per Share ($)**

| | | | | | |
|---|---|---|---|---|---|
| 2011 | 0.72 | 0.85 | 0.79 | E0.73 | E3.05 |
| 2010 | 0.56 | 0.74 | 0.78 | 0.74 | 2.82 |
| 2009 | 0.43 | 0.43 | 0.47 | 0.50 | 1.83 |
| 2008 | 0.54 | 0.61 | 0.63 | 0.56 | 2.34 |
| 2007 | 0.43 | 0.46 | 0.50 | 0.55 | 1.94 |
| 2006 | 0.32 | 0.29 | 0.37 | 0.43 | 1.40 |

Fiscal year ended Dec. 31. Next earnings report expected: Late January. EPS Estimates based on S&P Operating Earnings; historical GAAP earnings are as reported.

## Dividend Data (Dates: mm/dd Payment Date: mm/dd/yy)

| Amount ($) | Date Decl. | Ex-Div. Date | Stk. of Record | Payment Date |
|---|---|---|---|---|
| 0.015 | 01/25 | 03/14 | 03/16 | 04/06/11 |
| 0.015 | 04/27 | 06/13 | 06/15 | 07/06/11 |
| 0.105 | 10/27 | 09/12 | 09/14 | 10/05/11 |
| 0.015 | 10/26 | 12/12 | 12/14 | 01/04/12 |

Dividends have been paid since 2005. Source: Company reports.

---

**Please read the Required Disclosures and Analyst Certification on the last page of this report.**

**The McGraw·Hill Companies**

# Amphenol Corp

STANDARD
&POOR'S

## Business Summary November 09, 2011

CORPORATE OVERVIEW. Amphenol makes electrical, electronic and fiber optic connectors, interconnect systems, and coaxial and high-speed specialty cable. In 2010, APH derived 60% of its revenues from information technology and communications markets, 18% from industrial/automotive, and 22% from commercial aerospace and military. It derived 35% of its sales in the U.S., 24% in China, and 41% in other foreign markets.

APH makes a broad range of interconnect products and assemblies (93% of 2010 revenues) for voice, video and data communications systems, commercial aerospace and military systems, automotive and mass transportation applications, and industrial and factory automation equipment. Its connectors and interconnect systems are mostly used to conduct electrical and optical signals for sophisticated electronic applications.

In communications, the company supplies connector and cable assembly products used in base stations for wireless communication systems and Internet networking equipment; smart card acceptor devices used in mobile telephones; set top boxes and other applications to facilitate reading data from smart cards; fiber optic connectors used in fiber optic transmissions; back-

plane and input/output connectors for servers and data storage devices, and for linking PCs and peripheral equipment; and sculptured flexible circuits for integrating circuit boards.

APH also makes radio frequency connector products and antennas used in telecommunications, computer and office equipment, instrumentation equipment, local area networks and automotive electronics. Radio frequency connectors are also used in base stations, mobile communications devices and other components of cellular and personal communication networks.

The company believes it is the largest supplier of high-performance, military-specification, circular environmental connectors, generally used in sophisticated aerospace, military and industrial equipment. APH also makes industrial interconnect products, used in applications such as factory automation equipment, mass transportation applications and automotive safety products.

## Company Financials Fiscal Year Ended Dec. 31

| Per Share Data ($) | 2010 | 2009 | 2008 | 2007 | 2006 | 2005 | 2004 | 2003 | 2002 | 2001 |
|---|---|---|---|---|---|---|---|---|---|---|
| Tangible Book Value | 3.87 | 1.73 | 0.35 | 1.00 | NM | NM | NM | NM | NM | NM |
| Cash Flow | 3.40 | 2.39 | 2.86 | 2.38 | 1.79 | 1.42 | 1.13 | 0.80 | 0.66 | 0.76 |
| Earnings | 2.82 | 1.83 | 2.34 | 1.94 | 1.40 | 1.14 | 0.91 | 0.59 | 0.46 | 0.49 |
| S&P Core Earnings | 2.86 | 1.87 | 2.27 | 1.97 | 1.43 | 1.14 | 0.90 | 0.57 | 0.35 | 0.36 |
| Dividends | 0.06 | 0.06 | 0.06 | 0.08 | 0.06 | 0.06 | Nil | Nil | Nil | Nil |
| Payout Ratio | 2% | 3% | 3% | 4% | 4% | 5% | Nil | Nil | Nil | Nil |
| Prices:High | 54.07 | 47.14 | 52.28 | 47.24 | 35.25 | 23.10 | 18.76 | 16.03 | 12.94 | 14.50 |
| Prices:Low | 37.78 | 21.55 | 18.38 | 30.61 | 21.94 | 16.62 | 13.95 | 9.25 | 6.87 | 7.08 |
| P/E Ratio:High | 19 | 26 | 22 | 24 | 25 | 20 | 21 | 27 | 28 | 30 |
| P/E Ratio:Low | 13 | 12 | 8 | 16 | 16 | 15 | 15 | 16 | 15 | 15 |

| Income Statement Analysis (Million $) | | | | | | | | | | |
|---|---|---|---|---|---|---|---|---|---|---|
| Revenue | 3,554 | 2,820 | 3,236 | 2,851 | 2,471 | 1,808 | 1,530 | 1,240 | 1,062 | 1,104 |
| Operating Income | 803 | 587 | 724 | 635 | 518 | 394 | 315 | 241 | 209 | 229 |
| Depreciation | 103 | 98.5 | 91.3 | 82.3 | 72.6 | 50.7 | 38.8 | 37.0 | 34.8 | 46.7 |
| Interest Expense | 40.2 | 36.6 | 39.6 | 36.9 | 38.8 | 24.1 | 22.5 | 29.5 | 45.9 | 56.1 |
| Pretax Income | 664 | 447 | 582 | 501 | 373 | 308 | 247 | 158 | 123 | 135 |
| Effective Tax Rate | NA | 26.7% | 28.0% | 29.5% | 31.5% | 33.0% | 34.0% | 34.0% | 34.5% | 38.2% |
| Net Income | 496 | 318 | 419 | 353 | 256 | 206 | 163 | 104 | 80.3 | 83.7 |
| S&P Core Earnings | 505 | 325 | 408 | 359 | 261 | 206 | 161 | 99.8 | 60.0 | 62.0 |

| Balance Sheet & Other Financial Data (Million $) | | | | | | | | | | |
|---|---|---|---|---|---|---|---|---|---|---|
| Cash | 624 | 385 | 215 | 184 | 74.1 | 38.7 | 30.2 | 23.5 | 20.7 | 28.0 |
| Current Assets | 1,992 | 1,420 | 1,336 | 1,224 | 935 | 710 | 529 | 451 | 389 | 370 |
| Total Assets | 4,016 | 3,219 | 2,994 | 2,676 | 2,195 | 1,933 | 1,307 | 1,181 | 1,079 | 1,027 |
| Current Liabilities | 655 | 503 | 635 | 520 | 448 | 336 | 278 | 218 | 236 | 203 |
| Long Term Debt | 800 | 753 | 786 | 722 | 677 | 766 | 432 | 532 | 566 | 661 |
| Common Equity | 2,321 | 1,746 | 1,349 | 1,265 | 903 | 689 | 482 | 323 | 167 | 104 |
| Total Capital | 3,142 | 2,516 | 2,155 | 2,002 | 1,583 | 1,470 | 931 | 866 | 811 | 824 |
| Capital Expenditures | 108 | 59.8 | 107 | 104 | 82.4 | 57.1 | 44.3 | 30.2 | 18.8 | 38.6 |
| Cash Flow | 599 | 416 | 510 | 435 | 328 | 257 | 202 | 141 | 115 | 130 |
| Current Ratio | 3.0 | 2.8 | 2.1 | 2.4 | 2.1 | 2.1 | 1.9 | 2.1 | 1.6 | 1.8 |
| % Long Term Debt of Capitalization | 25.5 | 29.9 | 36.5 | 36.1 | 42.8 | 52.1 | 46.4 | 61.4 | 69.8 | 80.2 |
| % Net Income of Revenue | 14.0 | 11.3 | 13.0 | 12.4 | 10.3 | 11.4 | 10.7 | 8.4 | 7.6 | 7.6 |
| % Return on Assets | 13.7 | 10.2 | 14.8 | 14.5 | 12.4 | 12.7 | 13.1 | 9.2 | 7.6 | 8.2 |
| % Return on Equity | 24.4 | 20.5 | 32.1 | 32.6 | 32.1 | 35.2 | 40.6 | 42.4 | 59.3 | 125.7 |

Data as orig reptd.; bef. results of disc opers/spec. items. Per share data adj. for stk. divs.; EPS diluted. E-Estimated. NA-Not Available. NM-Not Meaningful. NR-Not Ranked. UR-Under Review.

**Office:** 358 Hall Avenue, Wallingford, CT 06492.
**Telephone:** 203-265-8900.
**Email:** aphinfo@amphenol.com
**Website:** http://www.amphenol.com

**Pres & CEO:** R.A. Norwitt
**CFO & Chief Acctg Officer:** D.G. Reardon
**Secy & General Counsel:** E.C. Wetmore
**Investor Contact:** D. Reardon (203-265-8630)

**Cntlr:** C.A. Lampo
**Board Members:** R. P. Badie, S. L. Clark, E. G. Jepsen, A. E. Lietz, M. H. Loeffler, J. R. Lord, R. A. Norwitt, D. H. Secord

**Founded:** 1932
**Domicile:** Delaware
**Employees:** 39,100

# Anadarko Petroleum Corp

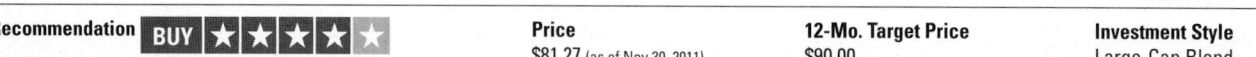

STANDARD
&POOR'S

| S&P Recommendation **BUY** ★★★★★☆ | Price $81.27 (as of Nov 30, 2011) | 12-Mo. Target Price $90.00 | Investment Style Large-Cap Blend |
|---|---|---|---|

**GICS Sector** Energy
**Sub-Industry** Oil & Gas Exploration & Production

**Summary** As one of the largest independent exploration and production companies in the world, this U.S. concern has associated businesses in marketing, trading, and minerals.

## Key Stock Statistics (Source S&P, Vickers, company reports)

| | | | | | | | |
|---|---|---|---|---|---|---|---|
| 52-Wk Range | $85.50– 57.11 | S&P Oper. EPS 2011E | 2.95 | Market Capitalization(B) | $40.470 | Beta | 1.46 |
| Trailing 12-Month EPS | $-4.38 | S&P Oper. EPS 2012E | 3.05 | Yield (%) | 0.44 | S&P 3-Yr. Proj. EPS CAGR(%) | NM |
| Trailing 12-Month P/E | NM | P/E on S&P Oper. EPS 2011E | 27.5 | Dividend Rate/Share | $0.36 | S&P Credit Rating | BBB- |
| $10K Invested 5 Yrs Ago | $17,025 | Common Shares Outstg. (M) | 498.0 | Institutional Ownership (%) | 85 | | |

## Price Performance

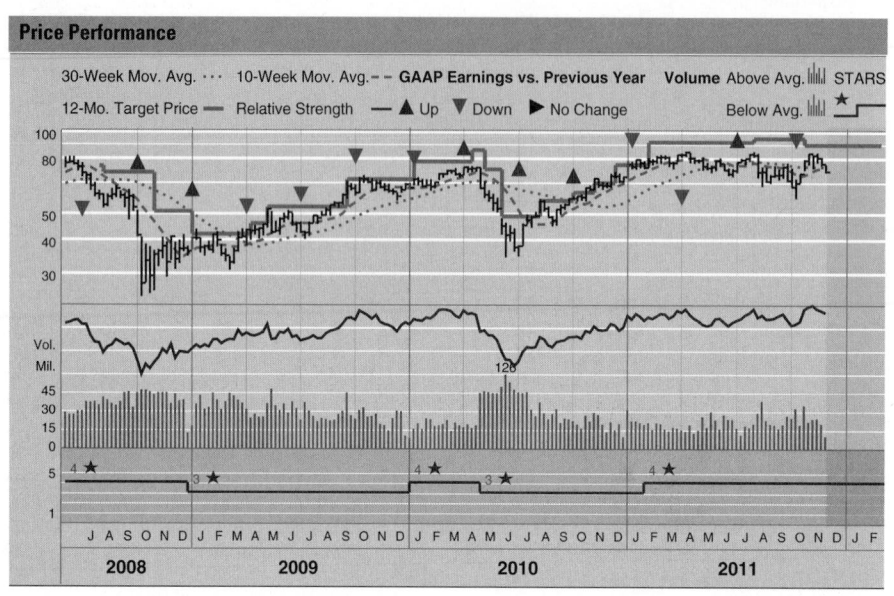

30-Week Mov. Avg. ··· 10-Week Mov. Avg. – – GAAP Earnings vs. Previous Year   Volume Above Avg. STARS
12-Mo. Target Price — Relative Strength  — ▲ Up ▼ Down ▶ No Change     Below Avg.  ★

Options: ASE, CBOE, P, Ph

Analysis prepared by Equity Analyst **Michael Kay** on Nov 30, 2011, when the stock traded at **$80.87**.

## Highlights

▶ Exposure to low-cost resources is expected to yield 7%-9% production growth through 2014 (4%-6% in 2011) and move toward a balanced production mix. We see growth from onshore assets, liquids-rich acreage and APC's 13 "mega-projects," with first oil spurred at Jubilee (Ghana) during the first quarter and Ceasar/Tonga and El Merk expected by 2012. APC is the largest producer at Eagle Ford, and is running a 10-rig program there. APC is also boosting activity in the Permian Basin (Bone Springs) and the DJ Basin (Niobrara Shale).

▶ APC sees 2011 capex of $6.1 billion-$6.4 billion with near-term projects making up 35%, mega-projects 15%, exploration 20%, midstream 20%, and shales 10%. APC formed a $1.6 billion JV with KNOC (Korea National Oil Corp.) in Eagle Ford, where KNOC will fund 100% of drilling in 2011 and 90% through 2013, allowing APC to focus its capex on exploration.

▶ On higher-margin liquids production growth and higher oil prices, we see 2011 and 2012 EPS of $2.95 and $3.05, respectively, versus adjusted EPS of $1.82 in 2010. APC took a $5.36 one-time charge in the third quarter related to the Macondo incident settlement.

## Investment Rationale/Risk

▶ After a $4 billion settlement with BP (BP 44 Hold), we think investor focus has shifted to APC's top-tier E&P portfolio, production ramp, exploration catalysts, and strong balance sheet. APC has cut debt and improved its cash position to $3.5 billion, and will pay the claims via cash and its revolver. APC will not pursue gross negligence, will forfeit interest in the well, and will receive 12.5% of future insurance payments ($1 billion max). Separately, free cash flow at growing U.S. onshore assets, should help fund an active exploration program. APC has expanded its liquids-rich opportunities by assembling a 300,000 gross acreage position in the Utica Shale. Successful well results in Mozambique, where APC has made its biggest gas discovery, have been a recent catalyst.

▶ Risks to our recommendation and target price include unfavorable changes in economic, industry or operating conditions, lower commodity prices and higher-than anticipated Macondo spill liabilities.

▶ Based on our $93 NAV estimate, and our DCF ($105 assuming an 11% WACC and 3% terminal growth) and peer-average relative metrics, we arrive at our 12-month target price of $90.

## Qualitative Risk Assessment

| LOW | MEDIUM | HIGH |
|---|---|---|

Our risk assessment reflects our view of APC's aggressive financial profile, and a business profile limited by participation in the cyclical, competitive, and capital-intensive exploration and production sub-industry, and by U.S. and international oil and gas operations that carry heightened political and operational risk.

## Quantitative Evaluations

**S&P Quality Ranking**                          B+

| D | C | B- | B | B+ | A- | A | A+ |
|---|---|---|---|---|---|---|---|

**Relative Strength Rank**                     STRONG
                                                  90
LOWEST = 1                                  HIGHEST = 99

## Revenue/Earnings Data

**Revenue (Million $)**

| | 1Q | 2Q | 3Q | 4Q | Year |
|---|---|---|---|---|---|
| 2011 | 3,253 | 3,676 | 3,384 | -- | -- |
| 2010 | 3,139 | 2,604 | 2,550 | 2,691 | 10,984 |
| 2009 | 1,796 | 1,913 | 2,874 | 2,417 | 9,000 |
| 2008 | 2,978 | 2,786 | 6,149 | 3,810 | 15,723 |
| 2007 | 2,683 | 3,313 | 3,030 | 3,062 | 11,232 |
| 2006 | 1,701 | 1,809 | 3,498 | 3,179 | 10,187 |

**Earnings Per Share ($)**

| | | | | | |
|---|---|---|---|---|---|
| 2011 | 0.43 | 1.08 | -6.12 | E0.43 | E2.95 |
| 2010 | 1.43 | -0.08 | -0.05 | 0.22 | 1.52 |
| 2009 | -0.73 | -0.48 | -0.40 | 0.46 | -0.28 |
| 2008 | 0.50 | 0.03 | 4.62 | 1.70 | 6.84 |
| 2007 | 0.17 | 1.38 | 1.10 | 0.35 | 8.05 |
| 2006 | 1.22 | 1.43 | 2.98 | 0.40 | 6.02 |

Fiscal year ended Dec. 31. Next earnings report expected: Early February. EPS Estimates based on S&P Operating Earnings; historical GAAP earnings are as reported.

## Dividend Data (Dates: mm/dd Payment Date: mm/dd/yy)

| Amount ($) | Date Decl. | Ex-Div. Date | Stk. of Record | Payment Date |
|---|---|---|---|---|
| 0.090 | 02/15 | 03/07 | 03/09 | 03/23/11 |
| 0.090 | 05/17 | 06/06 | 06/08 | 06/22/11 |
| 0.090 | 08/01 | 09/12 | 09/14 | 09/28/11 |
| 0.090 | 11/09 | 12/12 | 12/14 | 12/28/11 |

Dividends have been paid since 1986. Source: Company reports.

---

**Please read the Required Disclosures and Analyst Certification on the last page of this report.**

The McGraw-Hill Companies

# Anadarko Petroleum Corp

STANDARD
&POOR'S

## Business Summary November 30, 2011

CORPORATE OVERVIEW. APC is one of the largest independent E&P companies in the world engaged in the exploration, development, production, gathering, processing, and marketing of natural gas, crude oil, condensate, and NGLs. Major areas of operation are onshore U.S., deepwater Gulf of Mexico (GOM), and Algeria. APC has expanded deepwater opportunities to include positions in basins located offshore Brazil, East and West Africa, China, Indonesia, and New Zealand.

Proved oil and gas reserves rose 5% to 2,422 billion barrels of oil equivalent (boe) in 2010 (69% developed; 56% natural gas, 44% liquids). Production of 235 MMBOE, or 643,500 BOE/day, was up 7% from 2009. Production was 59% natural gas in 2010.

CORPORATE STRATEGY. In the GOM, APC owns an average 63% working interest in 505 blocks and plans to allocate approximately 15% ($930 million-$990 million) of 2011 capex to the deepwater GOM. As soon as permits are approved, APC is ready to resume drilling. We expect APC to look to settle any liability claims with respect to its 25% interest in the Macondo well, that blew out and exploded in 2010.

APC's international operations are located in Algeria, China, and Ghana and it also has exploration acreage in Ghana, Brazil, Indonesia, Mozambique, Sierra Leone, Cote d'Ivoire, Liberia, New Zealand, and Kenya. These accounted for 11% of both APC's total sales volumes during 2010 and total proved reserves at year-end 2010. APC drilled 45 wells in international areas in 2010 and achieved first oil at the Jubilee field offshore Ghana in 3.5 years from discovery. In 2011, it expects to drill approximately 42 development and 20 exploration wells, allocating approximately 25% ($1.6-$1.7 billion) of 2011 capex to international areas.

APC continues to advance current mega-projects in Ghana (Jubilee) and Algeria (El Merk), and expects each project to remain on schedule and within budget. The Jubilee field in Ghana started producing late in 2010, and in total, the three projects are expected to add more than 60,000 boe/d to APC production by 2012. APC planned to invest $930 million-$990 million, or 15% of expected capex, on mega-projects in 2011.

## Company Financials Fiscal Year Ended Dec. 31

| Per Share Data ($) | 2010 | 2009 | 2008 | 2007 | 2006 | 2005 | 2004 | 2003 | 2002 | 2001 |
|---|---|---|---|---|---|---|---|---|---|---|
| Tangible Book Value | 30.99 | 29.65 | 29.40 | 23.89 | 21.95 | 21.06 | 16.45 | 13.97 | 11.01 | 9.59 |
| Cash Flow | 9.42 | 7.08 | 14.13 | 14.23 | 10.28 | 8.04 | 6.05 | 5.01 | 3.74 | 2.09 |
| Earnings | 1.52 | -0.28 | 6.84 | 8.05 | 6.02 | 5.20 | 3.18 | 2.46 | 1.61 | -0.37 |
| S&P Core Earnings | 1.56 | -0.25 | 5.13 | 1.65 | 6.09 | 5.22 | 3.27 | 2.47 | 1.53 | -0.49 |
| Dividends | 0.36 | 0.36 | 0.36 | 0.36 | 0.36 | 0.36 | 0.28 | 0.22 | 0.16 | 0.11 |
| Payout Ratio | 24% | NM | 5% | 4% | 6% | 7% | 9% | 9% | 10% | NM |
| Prices:High | 78.98 | 69.37 | 81.36 | 68.00 | 56.98 | 50.71 | 35.78 | 25.86 | 29.28 | 36.99 |
| Prices:Low | 34.54 | 30.88 | 24.57 | 38.40 | 39.51 | 30.01 | 24.00 | 20.14 | 18.39 | 21.50 |
| P/E Ratio:High | 52 | NM | 12 | 8 | 9 | 10 | 11 | 11 | 18 | NM |
| P/E Ratio:Low | 23 | NM | 4 | 5 | 7 | 6 | 8 | 8 | 11 | NM |

| Income Statement Analysis (Million $) | | | | | | | | | | |
|---|---|---|---|---|---|---|---|---|---|---|
| Revenue | 10,842 | 8,210 | 14,640 | 15,892 | 10,187 | 7,100 | 6,067 | 5,122 | 3,860 | 8,369 |
| Operating Income | NA | NA | 8,578 | 10,328 | 6,945 | 5,436 | 4,400 | 3,648 | 2,585 | 3,702 |
| Depreciation, Depletion and Amortization | 3,859 | 3,532 | 3,417 | 2,891 | 1,976 | 1,343 | 1,447 | 1,297 | 1,121 | 1,227 |
| Interest Expense | 855 | 702 | 742 | 1,214 | 655 | 201 | 352 | 253 | 203 | 92.0 |
| Pretax Income | 1,641 | -108 | 5,429 | 6,329 | 4,238 | 3,895 | 2,477 | 1,974 | 1,207 | -390 |
| Effective Tax Rate | NA | 4.63% | 40.0% | 40.4% | 34.0% | 36.6% | 35.2% | 36.9% | 31.2% | NM |
| Net Income | 761 | -135 | 3,236 | 3,770 | 2,796 | 2,471 | 1,606 | 1,245 | 831 | -176 |
| S&P Core Earnings | 781 | -121 | 2,400 | 773 | 2,826 | 2,478 | 1,646 | 1,248 | 785 | -243 |

| Balance Sheet & Other Financial Data (Million $) | | | | | | | | | | |
|---|---|---|---|---|---|---|---|---|---|---|
| Cash | 3,680 | 3,531 | 2,360 | 1,268 | 491 | 739 | 874 | 62.0 | 34.0 | 37.0 |
| Current Assets | 6,675 | 6,083 | 5,375 | 4,516 | 4,614 | 2,916 | 2,502 | 1,324 | 1,280 | 1,201 |
| Total Assets | 51,559 | 50,123 | 48,953 | 48,481 | 58,844 | 22,588 | 20,192 | 20,546 | 18,248 | 16,771 |
| Current Liabilities | 4,114 | 3,824 | 5,536 | 5,257 | 16,758 | 2,403 | 1,993 | 1,715 | 1,861 | 1,801 |
| Long Term Debt | 12,722 | 12,748 | 10,867 | 14,747 | 11,520 | 3,555 | 3,671 | 5,058 | 5,171 | 4,638 |
| Common Equity | 20,684 | 19,928 | 18,856 | 16,319 | 15,201 | 10,967 | 9,219 | 8,510 | 6,673 | 6,262 |
| Total Capital | 34,452 | 33,163 | 39,997 | 39,929 | 39,673 | 19,330 | 17,393 | 17,909 | 15,578 | 14,454 |
| Capital Expenditures | 5,008 | 4,352 | 4,801 | 4,246 | 1,086 | 3,408 | 3,064 | 2,772 | 2,388 | 3,316 |
| Cash Flow | 4,680 | 3,397 | 6,614 | 6,658 | 4,769 | 3,809 | 3,048 | 2,537 | 1,946 | 1,044 |
| Current Ratio | 1.6 | 1.6 | 1.0 | 0.9 | 0.3 | 1.2 | 1.3 | 0.8 | 0.7 | 0.7 |
| % Long Term Debt of Capitalization | 36.9 | 39.0 | 27.2 | 44.9 | 28.8 | 18.4 | 21.1 | 28.2 | 33.2 | 32.1 |
| % Return on Assets | 1.5 | NM | 6.6 | 7.0 | 6.9 | 11.5 | 7.9 | 6.4 | 4.7 | NM |
| % Return on Equity | 3.8 | NM | 18.4 | 24.2 | 21.3 | 24.4 | 17.9 | 16.1 | 12.8 | NM |

Data as orig reptd.; bef. results of disc opers/spec. items. Per share data adj. for stk. divs.; EPS diluted. E-Estimated. NA-Not Available. NM-Not Meaningful. NR-Not Ranked. UR-Under Review.

**Office:** 1201 Lake Robbins Drive, The Woodlands, TX 77380-1124.
**Telephone:** 832-636-1000.
**Website:** http://www.anadarko.com
**Chrmn & CEO:** J.T. Hackett

**Pres & COO:** R.A. Walker
**CFO:** R.G. Gwin
**Chief Admin Officer & General Counsel:** R.K. Reeves
**Chief Acctg Officer:** M.C. Douglas

**Investor Contact:** J. Colglazier (832-636-2306)
**Board Members:** R. J. Allison, Jr., J. R. Butler, Jr., K. P. Chilton, L. R. Corbett, H. P. Eberhart, P. J. Fluor, P. M. Geren, III, J. R. Gordon, J. T. Hackett, P. G. Reynolds

**Founded:** 1985
**Domicile:** Delaware
**Employees:** 4,400

The McGraw-Hill Companies

# Analog Devices Inc.

**STANDARD &POOR'S**

| S&P Recommendation HOLD ★★★☆☆ | Price $32.90 (as of Nov 28, 2011) | 12-Mo. Target Price $36.00 | Investment Style Large-Cap Growth |
|---|---|---|---|

**GICS Sector** Information Technology
**Sub-Industry** Semiconductors

**Summary** This company manufactures high-performance integrated circuits (ICs) used in analog and digital signal processing applications.

## Key Stock Statistics (Source S&P, Vickers, company reports)

| | | | | | | | |
|---|---|---|---|---|---|---|---|
| 52-Wk Range | $43.28– 29.23 | S&P Oper. EPS 2012E | 2.40 | Market Capitalization(B) | $9.803 | Beta | 1.04 |
| Trailing 12-Month EPS | $2.81 | S&P Oper. EPS 2013E | NA | Yield (%) | 3.04 | S&P 3-Yr. Proj. EPS CAGR(%) | 2 |
| Trailing 12-Month P/E | 11.7 | P/E on S&P Oper. EPS 2012E | 13.7 | Dividend Rate/Share | $1.00 | S&P Credit Rating | A- |
| $10K Invested 5 Yrs Ago | $10,961 | Common Shares Outstg. (M) | 298.0 | Institutional Ownership (%) | 84 | | |

## Price Performance

30-Week Mov. Avg. ···  10-Week Mov. Avg. - -  **GAAP Earnings vs. Previous Year**  Volume Above Avg. |||| STARS
12-Mo. Target Price —  Relative Strength —  ▲ Up  ▼ Down  ► No Change  Below Avg. |||| ★

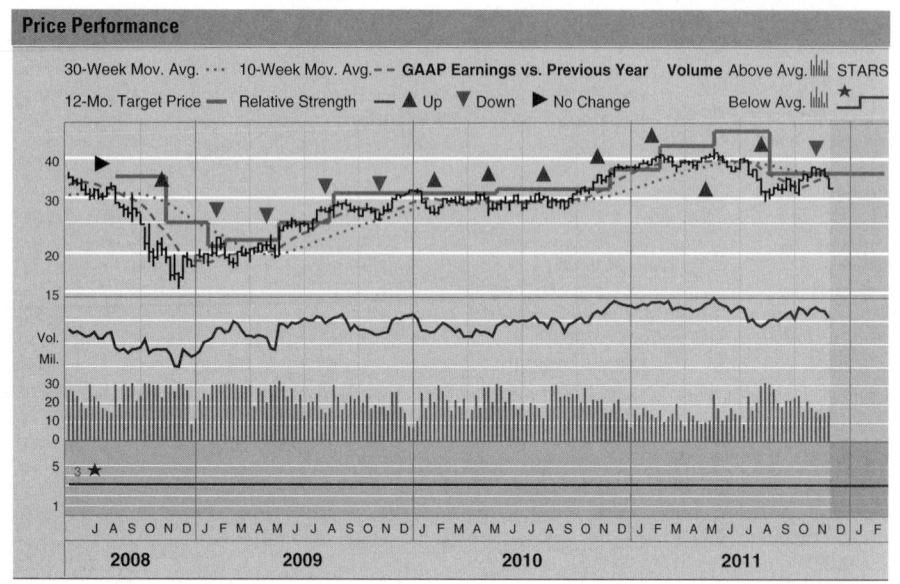

Options: ASE, CBOE, P, Ph

Analysis prepared by Equity Analyst **Angelo Zino, CFA** on Nov 28, 2011, when the stock traded at **$32.28**.

## Highlights

➤ We expect revenues to decline about 3.8% in FY 12 (Oct.), after an 8.4% advance in FY 11. Although we anticipate slow orders over the near term due to the uncertain economic environment, we believe that sequential order growth in calendar year 2012 will be supported by improving economic conditions and the greater usage of analog semiconductors as digital technology expands. We think recent design wins and increasing exposure to the automotive and industrial markets will fuel healthy revenue growth, and we see sales to the communications and consumer markets strengthening from current levels, assuming modest global economic growth in the coming quarters.

➤ We are modeling a gross margin of 63% to 66% over the next several quarters. We believe that ADI will witness modestly lower plant utilization near term, as customers digest existing inventories. However, we think that variable expenses, such as sales-related compensation, will move along at a pace consistent with sales throughout the semiconductor cycle.

➤ Our FY 12 EPS estimate assumes an effective tax rate of around 21% and a modest decline in the diluted share count.

## Investment Rationale/Risk

➤ Our hold recommendation reflects our view of fair growth and valuations. We believe the company has done a good job with design wins for higher-margin products and markets, which could support relatively healthy sales for years to come. With its profitable business model, ADI can continue to post above-industry operating margins and return on equity, in our view. However, we think that ADI and the broader semiconductor industry will experience soft demand over the near term, which, along with anticipated lower plant utilization, could lead to below-industry earnings growth. All told, we believe ADI's multiples should be around the industry average.

➤ Risks to our recommendation and target price include slower traction for new products, worse-than-anticipated economic conditions, and a less favorable sales mix.

➤ Our 12-month target price of $36 is based on a price-to-earnings multiple of approximately 14X, within the peer range to account for our view of ADI's relative growth, return on equity and risk, applied to our 12 months to January 2012 EPS forecast.

## Qualitative Risk Assessment

| LOW | MEDIUM | HIGH |
|---|---|---|

Our risk assessment reflects that ADI is subject to the sales cycles of the semiconductor industry, offset by our view of relatively stable chip pricing owing to high proprietary design content, broad end-markets, a leading market share in key converter and amplifier product categories, and what we consider a low level of debt.

## Quantitative Evaluations

**S&P Quality Ranking**     B+

| D | C | B- | B | B+ | A- | A | A+ |
|---|---|---|---|---|---|---|---|

**Relative Strength Rank**     MODERATE

43

LOWEST = 1           HIGHEST = 99

## Revenue/Earnings Data

**Revenue (Million $)**

| | 1Q | 2Q | 3Q | 4Q | Year |
|---|---|---|---|---|---|
| 2011 | 728.5 | 790.8 | 757.9 | 716.1 | 2,993 |
| 2010 | 603.0 | 668.2 | 720.3 | 770.0 | 2,762 |
| 2009 | 476.6 | 474.8 | 492.0 | 571.6 | 2,015 |
| 2008 | 613.9 | 649.3 | 659.0 | 660.7 | 2,583 |
| 2007 | 645.9 | 614.7 | 637.0 | 648.5 | 2,511 |
| 2006 | 621.3 | 643.9 | 663.7 | 644.3 | 2,573 |

**Earnings Per Share ($)**

| | | | | | |
|---|---|---|---|---|---|
| 2011 | 0.70 | 0.78 | 0.71 | 0.60 | 2.79 |
| 2010 | 0.39 | 0.55 | 0.65 | 0.73 | 2.33 |
| 2009 | 0.08 | 0.18 | 0.22 | 0.36 | 0.85 |
| 2008 | 0.40 | 0.44 | 0.44 | 0.49 | 1.77 |
| 2007 | 0.45 | 0.37 | 0.44 | 0.31 | 1.51 |
| 2006 | 0.32 | 0.39 | 0.39 | 0.39 | 1.48 |

Fiscal year ended Oct. 31. Next earnings report expected: NA. EPS Estimates based on S&P Operating Earnings; historical GAAP earnings are as reported.

## Dividend Data (Dates: mm/dd Payment Date: mm/dd/yy)

| Amount ($) | Date Decl. | Ex-Div. Date | Stk. of Record | Payment Date |
|---|---|---|---|---|
| 0.220 | 02/15 | 03/02 | 03/04 | 03/23/11 |
| 0.250 | 05/17 | 05/25 | 05/27 | 06/15/11 |
| 0.250 | 08/16 | 08/24 | 08/26 | 09/14/11 |
| 0.250 | 11/18 | 11/30 | 12/02 | 12/21/11 |

Dividends have been paid since 2003. Source: Company reports.

---

**Please read the Required Disclosures and Analyst Certification on the last page of this report.**

*The McGraw-Hill Companies*

# Analog Devices Inc.

**STANDARD &POOR'S**

## Business Summary November 28, 2011

**CORPORATE OVERVIEW.** Analog Devices designs, manufactures and markets a broad line of high-performance analog, mixed-signal and digital signal processing (DSP) integrated circuits (ICs) that address a wide range of real-world signal processing applications. The company's analog products are typically general purpose in nature and are used in a wide variety of equipment and systems.

Key markets are industrial, which accounted for approximately 46% of sales in FY 10 (Oct.), communications 22%, consumer 19%, automotive 12%, and computer 2%. The customer base is fairly broad: the 20 largest customers, excluding distributors, accounted for about 32% of sales in FY 10, and the largest customer, excluding distributors, accounted for approximately 4%.

**CORPORATE STRATEGY.** We think that one way Analog Devices is trying to improve profitability is by increasing higher end offerings for applications in fast growing, non-consumer end-markets, such as industrial and automobiles. The company plans to continue to invest heavily in R&D to create new products, but we see the proliferation of products in multiple end-markets helping to stabilize and increase sales and gross margins. The company has also re-duced capacity as a means to improve utilization by closing manufacturing sites and shifting operations to more cost efficient plants.

**MARKET PROFILE.** As more information is digitized, more and more analog chips are required to assist the digital chips that process, transmit, and store information. Analog, or "linear," semiconductors are used to handle continuous signals found in the real world, such as sound, light, heat and pressure. In a common example, a mobile phone utilizes a baseband system for communication, and it relies on a cluster of analog chips to convert the voice signals to digital format for manipulation by the processor, then translate them back to analog format for listening. Analog chips also are needed to manage power usage, which is particularly important for portable electronics, where battery life is a key product feature. The strong push toward wireless capabilities for laptop PCs and smartphones has helped analog sales grow faster than the broader industry over the past few years.

## Company Financials Fiscal Year Ended Oct. 31

| Per Share Data ($) | 2011 | 2010 | 2009 | 2008 | 2007 | 2006 | 2005 | 2004 | 2003 | 2002 |
|---|---|---|---|---|---|---|---|---|---|---|
| Tangible Book Value | 11.77 | 9.85 | 7.78 | 7.46 | 6.71 | 9.17 | 9.61 | 9.66 | 8.42 | 7.50 |
| Cash Flow | 3.18 | 2.72 | 1.32 | 2.28 | 1.97 | 1.95 | 1.49 | 1.84 | 1.22 | 0.90 |
| Earnings | 2.79 | 2.33 | 0.85 | 1.77 | 1.51 | 1.48 | 1.08 | 1.45 | 0.78 | 0.28 |
| S&P Core Earnings | 2.77 | 2.33 | 0.84 | 1.74 | 1.45 | 1.46 | 0.29 | 0.91 | 0.20 | -0.32 |
| Dividends | 0.94 | 0.84 | 0.80 | 0.76 | 0.70 | 0.56 | 0.32 | 0.20 | Nil | Nil |
| Payout Ratio | 34% | 36% | 94% | 43% | 46% | 38% | 30% | 14% | Nil | Nil |
| Prices:High | 43.28 | 38.60 | 31.91 | 36.35 | 41.10 | 41.48 | 41.40 | 52.37 | 50.35 | 48.84 |
| Prices:Low | 29.23 | 26.28 | 17.82 | 15.29 | 30.19 | 26.07 | 31.71 | 31.36 | 22.58 | 17.88 |
| P/E Ratio:High | 16 | 17 | 38 | 21 | 27 | 28 | 38 | 36 | 65 | NM |
| P/E Ratio:Low | 10 | 11 | 21 | 9 | 20 | 18 | 29 | 22 | 29 | NM |

| Income Statement Analysis (Million $) | 2011 | 2010 | 2009 | 2008 | 2007 | 2006 | 2005 | 2004 | 2003 | 2002 |
|---|---|---|---|---|---|---|---|---|---|---|
| Revenue | 2,993 | 2,762 | 2,015 | 2,583 | 2,546 | 2,573 | 2,389 | 2,634 | 2,047 | 1,708 |
| Operating Income | 1,192 | 1,037 | 478 | 782 | 916 | 771 | 703 | 852 | 552 | 405 |
| Depreciation | 118 | 121 | 140 | 153 | 155 | 172 | 156 | 153 | 168 | 238 |
| Interest Expense | 19.2 | 10.4 | 4.09 | Nil | Nil | 0.05 | 0.03 | 0.22 | 32.2 | 44.5 |
| Pretax Income | 1,061 | 902 | 297 | 666 | 659 | 664 | 588 | 733 | 382 | 140 |
| Effective Tax Rate | NA | NA | 16.8% | 21.2% | 24.0% | 17.1% | 29.4% | 22.1% | 21.9% | 25.0% |
| Net Income | 861 | 711 | 247 | 525 | 501 | 549 | 415 | 571 | 298 | 105 |
| S&P Core Earnings | 855 | 710 | 246 | 517 | 481 | 542 | 113 | 364 | 74.2 | -118 |

| Balance Sheet & Other Financial Data (Million $) | 2011 | 2010 | 2009 | 2008 | 2007 | 2006 | 2005 | 2004 | 2003 | 2002 |
|---|---|---|---|---|---|---|---|---|---|---|
| Cash | 3,592 | 2,688 | 1,816 | 1,310 | 425 | 344 | 628 | 519 | 518 | 1,614 |
| Current Assets | 4,386 | 3,479 | 2,491 | 2,090 | 1,979 | 3,011 | 3,732 | 3,529 | 2,886 | 3,624 |
| Total Assets | 5,278 | 4,329 | 3,404 | 3,091 | 2,972 | 3,987 | 4,583 | 4,720 | 4,093 | 4,980 |
| Current Liabilities | 525 | 643 | 387 | 569 | 548 | 491 | 819 | 567 | 463 | 484 |
| Long Term Debt | 872 | 401 | 489 | Nil | Nil | Nil | Nil | Nil | Nil | 1,274 |
| Common Equity | 3,795 | 3,200 | 2,529 | 2,420 | 2,338 | 3,436 | 3,692 | 3,800 | 3,288 | 2,900 |
| Total Capital | 4,682 | 3,600 | 3,018 | 2,435 | 2,348 | 3,439 | 3,692 | 3,810 | 3,305 | 4,197 |
| Capital Expenditures | 123 | 112 | 56.1 | 157 | 142 | 129 | 85.5 | 146 | 67.7 | 57.4 |
| Cash Flow | 979 | 832 | 387 | 679 | 656 | 722 | 570 | 723 | 467 | 343 |
| Current Ratio | 8.4 | 5.4 | 6.4 | 3.7 | 3.6 | 6.1 | 4.6 | 6.2 | 6.2 | 7.5 |
| % Long Term Debt of Capitalization | 18.6 | 11.1 | 12.9 | Nil | Nil | Nil | Nil | Nil | Nil | 30.4 |
| % Net Income of Revenue | 28.8 | 25.8 | 12.3 | 20.3 | 19.6 | 21.4 | 17.4 | 21.7 | 14.6 | 6.2 |
| % Return on Assets | 17.9 | 18.4 | 7.6 | 17.3 | 14.3 | 12.8 | 8.9 | 13.0 | 6.6 | 2.1 |
| % Return on Equity | 24.6 | 24.8 | 10.0 | 22.1 | 17.3 | 15.4 | 11.1 | 16.1 | 9.6 | 3.7 |

Data as orig reptd.; bef. results of disc opers/spec. items. Per share data adj. for stk. divs.; EPS diluted. E-Estimated. NA-Not Available. NM-Not Meaningful. NR-Not Ranked. UR-Under Review.

**Office:** One Technology Way, Norwood, MA 02062-9106.
**Telephone:** 781-329-4700.
**Email:** investor.relations@analog.com
**Website:** http://www.analog.com

**Chrmn:** R. Stata
**Pres & CEO:** J.G. Fishman
**CFO:** D.A. Zinsner
**CTO:** S.H. Fuller

**Chief Acctg Officer:** S. Brennan
**Investor Contact:** M. Kohl (781-461-3759)
**Board Members:** J. A. Champy, J. L. Doyle, J. G. Fishman, J. C. Hodgson, Y. Istel, N. S. Novich, F. G. Saviers, P. J. Severino, K. J. Sicchitano, R. Stata

**Founded:** 1965
**Domicile:** Massachusetts
**Employees:** 9,200

*The McGraw-Hill Companies*

# Aon Corp.

STANDARD
&POOR'S

**S&P Recommendation** `HOLD` ★★★☆☆

| Price | 12-Mo. Target Price | Investment Style |
|---|---|---|
| $44.23 (as of Nov 25, 2011) | $54.00 | Large-Cap Blend |

**GICS Sector** Financials
**Sub-Industry** Insurance Brokers

**Summary** This global provider of insurance brokerage services also offers consulting services and risk and insurance advice.

## Key Stock Statistics (Source S&P, Vickers, company reports)

| | | | | | | | |
|---|---|---|---|---|---|---|---|
| 52-Wk Range | $54.58– 39.68 | S&P Oper. EPS 2011**E** | 3.29 | Market Capitalization(B) | $14.299 | Beta | 0.62 |
| Trailing 12-Month EPS | $2.72 | S&P Oper. EPS 2012**E** | 3.63 | Yield (%) | 1.36 | S&P 3-Yr. Proj. EPS CAGR(%) | 4 |
| Trailing 12-Month P/E | 16.3 | P/E on S&P Oper. EPS 2011**E** | 13.4 | Dividend Rate/Share | $0.60 | S&P Credit Rating | BBB+ |
| $10K Invested 5 Yrs Ago | $13,290 | Common Shares Outstg. (M) | 323.3 | Institutional Ownership (%) | 86 | | |

## Price Performance

30-Week Mov. Avg. ···  10-Week Mov. Avg.·-· **GAAP Earnings vs. Previous Year**  Volume Above Avg.⊪⊪ STARS
12-Mo. Target Price ─ Relative Strength ── ▲ Up ▼ Down ► No Change  Below Avg. ⊪⊪ ★

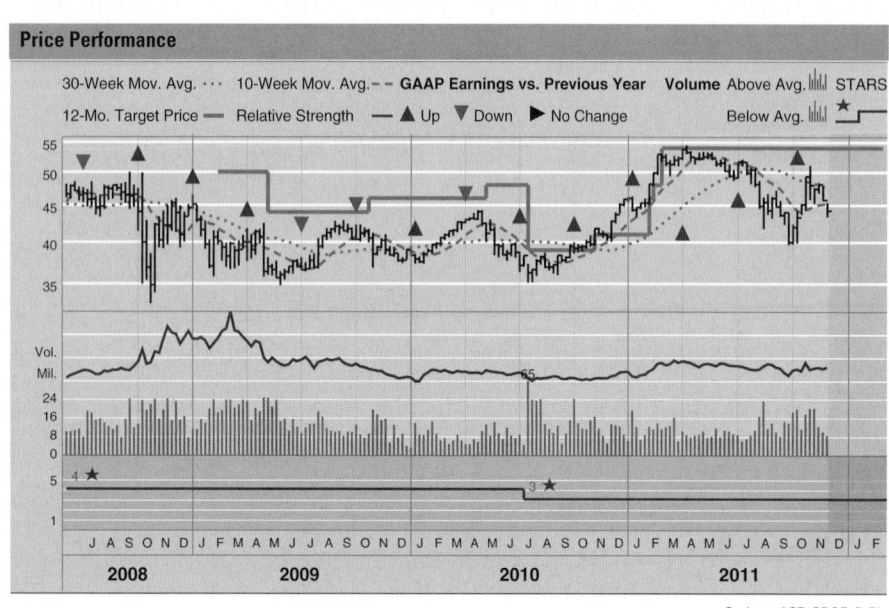

Options: ASE, CBOE, P, Ph

Analysis prepared by Equity Analyst **Robert McMillan** on Nov 07, 2011, when the stock traded at **$46.86**.

## Highlights

➤ After a 12% rise in 2010, we see revenues increasing about 35% in 2011, driven by AON's October 2010 acquisition of Hewitt Associates, Inc., one of the world's leading human resource consulting and outsourcing companies. For 2012, we see revenues rising 4.5%, driven mostly by organic growth. We expect growth of about 5% in Risk Solutions in 2012, as new business production is partially offset by competitive insurance pricing; we see overseas growth offsetting sluggish growth in the U.S. We forecast organic revenues will rise in reinsurance due to an improved pricing environment.

➤ In Aon's HR Solutions business, which includes Hewitt, we look for 2%-3% revenue growth in 2012; we believe the still-weak economy, heightened unemployment and sluggish hiring will restrict growth. Over time, we believe Hewitt Associates will allow AON to generate business wins across multiple product lines and better cross-selling opportunities.

➤ We forecast operating EPS of $3.29 for 2011 and $3.63 for 2012.

## Investment Rationale/Risk

➤ While we think AON's business platform can drive organic revenue growth in an unfavorable environment, we expect the company to face headwinds in Risk Solutions due to flat exposure growth and falling insurance rates. We believe its aggressive cost-cutting initiatives, share buyback program, and earnings contributions from emerging markets will more than offset the impact from a still-challenging operating environment.

➤ Risks to our recommendation and target price include weaker organic revenue growth and margin pressure from a soft property and casualty market; currency risks; and integration risk.

➤ Our 12-month target price of $54 is 15X our four-quarter EPS estimate of $3.59; the shares recently traded at about 13X this estimate. We see the valuation multiple rising back to levels still in line with recent historical levels, which we believe is somewhat reflective of AON's ability to deliver growth in a soft economy and our expectation that an eventual improvement in the economy and jobs growth should generate especially more demand for AON's HR Solutions business.

## Qualitative Risk Assessment

| LOW | MEDIUM | HIGH |
|---|---|---|

Our risk assessment reflects what we see as the company's well-diversified operations and solid balance sheet, business restructuring, a soft insurance pricing environment, lack of exposure growth, potential for elevated amortization of intangible assets, and execution risk related to the acquisition of Hewitt Associates.

## Quantitative Evaluations

**S&P Quality Ranking** B+

| D | C | B- | B | B+ | A- | A | A+ |
|---|---|---|---|---|---|---|---|

**Relative Strength Rank** MODERATE

59

LOWEST = 1                              HIGHEST = 99

## Revenue/Earnings Data

**Revenue (Million $)**

| | 1Q | 2Q | 3Q | 4Q | Year |
|---|---|---|---|---|---|
| 2011 | 2,759 | 2,811 | 2,723 | -- | -- |
| 2010 | 1,904 | 1,898 | 1,801 | 2,909 | 8,512 |
| 2009 | 1,846 | 1,882 | 1,794 | 2,073 | 7,595 |
| 2008 | 1,932 | 1,980 | 1,847 | 1,924 | 7,631 |
| 2007 | 1,798 | 1,866 | 1,775 | 2,032 | 7,471 |
| 2006 | 2,165 | 2,208 | 2,168 | 2,413 | 8,954 |

**Earnings Per Share ($)**

| | | | | | |
|---|---|---|---|---|---|
| 2011 | 0.71 | 0.75 | 0.59 | E0.97 | E3.29 |
| 2010 | 0.63 | 0.63 | 0.51 | 0.67 | 2.46 |
| 2009 | 0.80 | 0.51 | 0.40 | 0.49 | 2.19 |
| 2008 | 0.56 | 0.55 | 0.53 | 0.43 | 2.06 |
| 2007 | 0.51 | 0.57 | 0.42 | 0.11 | 2.10 |
| 2006 | 0.57 | 0.53 | 0.27 | 0.57 | 1.86 |

Fiscal year ended Dec. 31. Next earnings report expected: Early February. EPS Estimates based on S&P Operating Earnings; historical GAAP earnings are as reported.

## Dividend Data (Dates: mm/dd Payment Date: mm/dd/yy)

| Amount ($) | Date Decl. | Ex-Div. Date | Stk. of Record | Payment Date |
|---|---|---|---|---|
| 0.150 | 01/14 | 01/28 | 02/01 | 02/15/11 |
| 0.150 | 04/13 | 04/28 | 05/02 | 05/16/11 |
| 0.150 | 07/15 | 07/28 | 08/01 | 08/15/11 |
| 0.150 | 10/07 | 10/28 | 11/01 | 11/15/11 |

Dividends have been paid since 1950. Source: Company reports.

# Aon Corp.

**STANDARD &POOR'S**

## Business Summary November 07, 2011

CORPORATE OVERVIEW. Aon Corp. is a global provider of insurance broker-age services, insurance products, and risk and insurance advice, as well as other consulting services, conducting business in more than 120 countries and sovereignties. In 2010, AON was recognized by Business Insurance as the world's leading retail agent/broker with revenues in excess of $250 million for the third consecutive year.

AON classifies its businesses into two operating segments: Risk Solutions (formerly known as Risk and Insurance Brokerage Services); and HR Solu-tions (formerly known as Consulting). The Risk Solutions segment accounted for 75% of commission and fees from continuing operations in 2010, and the HR Solutions segment 25%.

CORPORATE STRATEGY. AON employs a growth-through-acquisition strategy, which it believes has been vital in building its network of resources and capa-bilities. Over the past 22 years, AON has completed more than 445 acquisi-tions. In 2008, AON purchased a total of 31 companies, mostly related to its risk and insurance brokerage operations. However, in 2009, due to the chal-lenging economic conditions and turmoil in the financial markets, AON com-pleted only three major acquisitions. In 2010, AON completed two deals, most notably the acquisition of Hewitt Associates, Inc.

IMPACT OF MAJOR DEVELOPMENTS. In October 2010, AON acquired Hewitt Associates for $4.9 billion in cash and stock. The company believes the acqui-sition will be accretive to adjusted EPS in 2011 and to GAAP EPS in 2012. We estimate cost synergies from the deal will exceed $360 million annually until 2013, and result in AON's revenue mix changing to 60% insurance brokerage and 40% consulting.

In August 2008, AON announced plans to acquire Benfield, a leading reinsur-ance intermediary, for $1.75 billion. The transaction closed in November 2008 for $1.43 billion, due to a strengthening of the U.S. dollar versus the British pound. In connection with the transaction, AON announced a global restruc-turing program. AON expects the restructuring program to result in $155 mil-lion in charges, of which $81 million was already recorded in 2009 and 2010. The company projects $19 million in charges to be recorded in future earn-ings. AON believes the acquisition will deliver $122 million of cumulative cost savings in 2011.

## Company Financials Fiscal Year Ended Dec. 31

| Per Share Data ($) | 2010 | 2009 | 2008 | 2007 | 2006 | 2005 | 2004 | 2003 | 2002 | 2001 |
|---|---|---|---|---|---|---|---|---|---|---|
| Tangible Book Value | NM | NM | NM | 4.37 | 2.14 | 2.48 | 0.76 | NM | NM | NM |
| Cash Flow | 3.57 | 3.02 | 2.74 | 2.67 | 2.54 | 2.69 | 2.62 | 3.06 | 2.57 | 1.98 |
| Earnings | 2.46 | 2.19 | 2.06 | 2.10 | 1.86 | 1.89 | 1.72 | 2.08 | 1.64 | 0.73 |
| S&P Core Earnings | 2.67 | 2.19 | 1.22 | 1.66 | 2.03 | 2.10 | 2.29 | 2.05 | 1.00 | -0.06 |
| Dividends | 0.60 | 0.60 | 0.60 | 0.60 | 0.75 | 0.60 | 0.60 | 0.60 | 0.83 | 0.90 |
| Payout Ratio | 24% | 27% | 29% | 29% | 40% | 32% | 35% | 29% | 50% | 123% |
| Prices:High | 46.24 | 46.19 | 50.00 | 51.32 | 42.76 | 37.14 | 29.44 | 26.79 | 39.63 | 44.80 |
| Prices:Low | 35.10 | 34.81 | 32.83 | 34.30 | 31.01 | 20.64 | 18.15 | 17.41 | 13.30 | 29.75 |
| P/E Ratio:High | 19 | 21 | 24 | 24 | 23 | 20 | 17 | 13 | 24 | 61 |
| P/E Ratio:Low | 14 | 16 | 16 | 16 | 17 | 11 | 11 | 8 | 8 | 41 |

| Income Statement Analysis (Million $) | 2010 | 2009 | 2008 | 2007 | 2006 | 2005 | 2004 | 2003 | 2002 | 2001 |
|---|---|---|---|---|---|---|---|---|---|---|
| Revenue | 8,512 | 7,595 | 7,631 | 7,471 | 8,954 | 9,837 | 10,172 | 9,810 | 8,822 | 7,676 |
| Operating Income | 1,637 | 1,263 | 1,536 | 1,437 | 1,426 | 1,530 | 1,545 | 1,511 | 1,195 | 933 |
| Depreciation | 305 | 242 | 204 | 189 | 244 | 277 | 309 | 314 | 263 | 339 |
| Interest Expense | 182 | 122 | 126 | 138 | 129 | 125 | 136 | 137 | 158 | 167 |
| Pretax Income | 1,059 | 949 | 863 | 1,024 | 920 | 965 | 880 | 1,110 | 793 | 399 |
| Effective Tax Rate | NA | 28.2% | 28.0% | 34.4% | 32.0% | 33.5% | 34.4% | 38.3% | 38.6% | 43.5% |
| Net Income | 759 | 636 | 621 | 672 | 626 | 642 | 577 | 663 | 466 | 203 |
| S&P Core Earnings | 798 | 637 | 368 | 531 | 683 | 709 | 765 | 652 | 281 | -19.4 |

| Balance Sheet & Other Financial Data (Million $) | 2010 | 2009 | 2008 | 2007 | 2006 | 2005 | 2004 | 2003 | 2002 | 2001 |
|---|---|---|---|---|---|---|---|---|---|---|
| Cash | 1,131 | 639 | 1,236 | 4,915 | 4,726 | 476 | 570 | 540 | 506 | 439 |
| Current Assets | 14,519 | 13,989 | 14,526 | 17,973 | 13,852 | 14,612 | 15,460 | 14,550 | 14,109 | 11,412 |
| Total Assets | 28,982 | 22,958 | 23,172 | 24,948 | 24,318 | 27,818 | 28,329 | 27,027 | 25,334 | 22,386 |
| Current Liabilities | 12,949 | 12,640 | 12,803 | 14,553 | 12,350 | 14,084 | 15,299 | 15,096 | 14,952 | 12,605 |
| Long Term Debt | 4,014 | 1,998 | 1,872 | 2,145 | 1,588 | 2,105 | 1,523 | 1,787 | 2,064 | 2,363 |
| Common Equity | 8,251 | 5,379 | 5,314 | 6,221 | 5,218 | 5,303 | 5,103 | 4,498 | 3,895 | 3,521 |
| Total Capital | 12,375 | 7,439 | 7,287 | 8,223 | 6,806 | 7,408 | 7,268 | 6,643 | 6,318 | 6,065 |
| Capital Expenditures | 180 | 140 | 103 | 170 | 152 | 126 | 80.0 | 185 | 278 | 281 |
| Cash Flow | 1,064 | 878 | 825 | 861 | 863 | 917 | 883 | 974 | 726 | 539 |
| Current Ratio | 1.1 | 1.1 | 1.1 | 1.2 | 1.1 | 1.0 | 1.0 | 1.0 | 0.9 | 0.9 |
| % Long Term Debt of Capitalization | 32.4 | 26.9 | 25.6 | 23.3 | 23.3 | 28.4 | 21.0 | 26.9 | 32.7 | 39.0 |
| % Net Income of Revenue | 8.9 | 8.4 | 8.1 | 9.0 | 7.0 | 6.5 | 5.7 | 6.8 | 5.3 | 2.6 |
| % Return on Assets | 2.9 | 2.8 | 2.6 | 2.7 | 2.4 | 2.3 | 2.1 | 2.5 | 2.0 | 0.9 |
| % Return on Equity | 11.1 | 11.9 | 10.8 | 11.8 | 11.9 | 12.3 | 12.0 | 15.8 | 12.6 | 5.9 |

Data as orig reptd.; bef. results of disc opers/spec. items. Per share data adj. for stk. divs.; EPS diluted. E-Estimated. NA-Not Available. NM-Not Meaningful. NR-Not Ranked. UR-Under Review.

**Office:** 200 East Randolph Street, Chicago, IL 60601.
**Telephone:** 312-381-1000.
**Website:** http://www.aon.com
**Chrmn:** L.B. Knight, III

**Pres & CEO:** G.C. Case
**EVP & CFO:** C. Davies
**EVP & General Counsel:** P. Lieb
**SVP, Chief Acctg Officer & Cntlr:** L. Meissner

**Investor Contact:** S. Malchow (312-381-3983)
**Board Members:** G. C. Case, F. Conti, C. A. Francis, E. D. Jannotta, P. J. Kalff, L. B. Knight, III, J. M. Losh, R. E. Martin, A. J. McKenna, R. S. Morrison, R. B. Myers, R. C. Notebaert, J. W. Rogers, Jr., G. Santona, C. Y. Woo

**Founded:** 1919
**Domicile:** Delaware
**Employees:** 59,000

*The McGraw-Hill Companies*

# Apache Corp

**STANDARD & POOR'S**

| S&P Recommendation **STRONG BUY** ★★★★★ | Price $86.83 (as of Nov 25, 2011) | 12-Mo. Target Price $145.00 | Investment Style Large-Cap Blend |
|---|---|---|---|

**GICS Sector** Energy
**Sub-Industry** Oil & Gas Exploration & Production

**Summary** Apache is one of the largest independent exploration and production companies in the U.S. The company explores for, develops, and produces natural gas, crude oil, and natural gas liquids.

## Key Stock Statistics (Source S&P, Vickers, company reports)

| | | | | | | | | |
|---|---|---|---|---|---|---|---|---|
| 52-Wk Range | $134.13– 73.04 | S&P Oper. EPS 2011**E** | 11.80 | Market Capitalization(B) | $33.348 | Beta | 1.34 |
| Trailing 12-Month EPS | $10.24 | S&P Oper. EPS 2012**E** | 12.45 | Yield (%) | 0.69 | S&P 3-Yr. Proj. EPS CAGR(%) | 31 |
| Trailing 12-Month P/E | 8.5 | P/E on S&P Oper. EPS 2011**E** | 7.4 | Dividend Rate/Share | $0.60 | S&P Credit Rating | A- |
| $10K Invested 5 Yrs Ago | $13,775 | Common Shares Outstg. (M) | 384.1 | Institutional Ownership (%) | 84 | | |

## Price Performance

- 30-Week Mov. Avg. · · · 10-Week Mov. Avg. – – GAAP Earnings vs. Previous Year   Volume Above Avg. STARS
- 12-Mo. Target Price — Relative Strength ▲ Up ▼ Down ▶ No Change   Below Avg.

Options: ASE, CBOE, P, Ph

Analysis prepared by Equity Analyst **Michael Kay** on Aug 18, 2011, when the stock traded at **$104.89**.

## Qualitative Risk Assessment

| LOW | MEDIUM | **HIGH** |
|---|---|---|

Our risk assessment for APA reflects its participation in a highly capital-intensive industry that derives value based on commodity prices that can be highly volatile. However, APA is a large exploration and production company and is diversified across major producing regions.

## Quantitative Evaluations

**S&P Quality Ranking**   A-

| D | C | B- | B | B+ | **A-** | A | A+ |
|---|---|---|---|---|---|---|---|

**Relative Strength Rank**   MODERATE

30

LOWEST = 1   HIGHEST = 99

## Revenue/Earnings Data

**Revenue (Million $)**

| | 1Q | 2Q | 3Q | 4Q | Year |
|---|---|---|---|---|---|
| 2011 | 3,925 | 4,338 | 4,328 | -- | -- |
| 2010 | 2,673 | 2,972 | 3,013 | 3,434 | 12,092 |
| 2009 | 1,634 | 2,093 | 2,332 | 2,570 | 8,615 |
| 2008 | 3,188 | 3,900 | 3,365 | 1,937 | 12,390 |
| 2007 | 1,997 | 2,468 | 2,499 | 3,014 | 9,978 |
| 2006 | 1,999 | 2,062 | 2,261 | 1,967 | 8,289 |

**Earnings Per Share ($)**

| | | | | | |
|---|---|---|---|---|---|
| 2011 | 2.86 | 3.17 | 2.51 | E2.73 | E11.80 |
| 2010 | 2.08 | 2.53 | 2.12 | 1.77 | 8.46 |
| 2009 | -5.25 | 1.31 | 1.30 | 1.72 | -0.87 |
| 2008 | 3.03 | 4.28 | 3.52 | -8.80 | 2.10 |
| 2007 | 1.47 | 1.89 | 1.83 | 3.19 | 8.39 |
| 2006 | 1.97 | 2.17 | 1.94 | 1.56 | 7.64 |

Fiscal year ended Dec. 31. Next earnings report expected: Mid February. EPS Estimates based on S&P Operating Earnings; historical GAAP earnings are as reported.

## Highlights

▶ We believe a broader portfolio of assets has enlarged APA's opportunity set, providing visible production growth and significant exploration upside. First half 2011 production was up 21%, on track to meet growth targets of 13%-17%, reflecting an 80 rig global program and ramped activity at the U.S. onshore liquids-rich Granite Wash (10 rigs) and Permian Basin (24 rigs) plays. APA is benefiting from widening Brent crude (60% of oil volumes) differentials versus the U.S. WTI benchmark. A resumption of Gulf of Mexico deepwater drilling should allow APA to begin exploiting a deep prospect inventory. No disruptions in Egypt were reported and the Van Gogh field in Australia is back on-line after cyclone activity earlier in the year.

▶ APA's drilling capex budget of $7.5 billion for 2011 is up from $5.3 billion, excluding $12 billion in acquisitions. Under this budget, we expect substantial free cash flow this year.

▶ We see EPS of $12.45 in 2011 and $13.25 in 2012, up from adjusted EPS of $8.92 in 2010, reflecting production and oil price gains. APA's debt-to-capital ratio is 24%, and we view its balance sheet as one of the strongest among peers.

## Investment Rationale/Risk

▶ We believe APA's $11.5 billion of acquisitions in 2010 will add significant future opportunity in core regions. In our view, APA has a proven track record of unlocking value from acquired assets, and it plans to focus much of 2011 on integration and exploiting mature reserves and focusing capital on international development projects. Its portfolio of reserves is balanced between liquids and natural gas (44/56) and is geographically diverse. In 2011, we see Canada and Egypt driving international production, while APA's Granite Wash and Permian Basin program should drive onshore domestic volumes. We expect APA to enhance its top-tier balance sheet with free cash flow in 2011, and we expect about $1 billion in divestments.

▶ Risks to our opinion and target price include unfavorable changes to economic, industry, and operating conditions, including increased costs, and difficulty replacing reserves.

▶ We think APA's large international oil projects provide solid growth visibility. We blend several valuation methods, including NAV ($151), DCF ($149; WACC 11%; terminal growth 3%), and relative metrics to derive our $145 target price.

## Dividend Data (Dates: mm/dd Payment Date: mm/dd/yy)

| Amount ($) | Date Decl. | Ex-Div. Date | Stk. of Record | Payment Date |
|---|---|---|---|---|
| 0.150 | 02/22 | 04/19 | 04/22 | 05/23/11 |
| 0.150 | 05/18 | 07/19 | 07/22 | 08/22/11 |
| 0.150 | 09/20 | 10/19 | 10/21 | 11/22/11 |
| 0.150 | 11/21 | 01/19 | 01/23 | 02/22/12 |

Dividends have been paid since 1965. Source: Company reports.

**Please read the Required Disclosures and Analyst Certification on the last page of this report.**

**The McGraw·Hill Companies**

# Apache Corp

## Business Summary August 18, 2011

CORPORATE OVERVIEW. One of the largest independent exploration and production (E&P) companies in the U.S., Apache Corp. (APA) explores for, develops and produces natural gas, crude oil and natural gas liquids (NGLs). APA has E&P operations in seven countries, the U.S., Canada, Egypt, the U.K., Australia, Argentina and Chile. Acquisitions in 2010 substantially added to its asset base in the U.S., Canada, and Egypt.

In North America, APA's interests are focused on the Gulf of Mexico, the Gulf Coast, Permian and Central regions of the U.S. and Canada. Outside of North America, APA has interests in Egypt, offshore Western Australia, offshore the U.K. in the North Sea, and onshore Argentina and Chile.

APA's North American asset base comprises the U.S. Central region, U.S. Gulf Coast region, the Permian region and Canada region. In 2010 North America assets contributed 48% of production and 70% of estimated proved reserves at year end. APA has 6.3 million net acres across Canada, including approximately 1.3 million net in Western Alberta and British Columbia acquired from BP in 2010. APA and EnCana Corporation (ECA) are 50% partners and control more than 400,000 acres in the Horn River Basin shale-gas play in northeast

British Columbia.

Egypt holds APA's largest acreage position, with more than 11 million gross acres that provide considerable exploration and development opportunities. In addition to being the largest acreage holder in Egypt's Western Desert, APA believes it is also the largest producer of liquid hydrocarbons and natural gas in the Western Desert and the third largest in all of Egypt. In 2010, Egypt contributed 24% of total production and 10% of total estimated proved reserves.

In Australia, exploration activity is focused in the offshore Carnarvon, Exmouth and Browse Basins, where APA holds 12.2 million gross acres. In 2010, the region increased production 40% and accounted for approximately 12% of total production and 11% of year-end estimated proved reserves. Increases reflect the start-up of the Van Gogh field in 2010.

## Company Financials Fiscal Year Ended Dec. 31

| Per Share Data ($) | 2010 | 2009 | 2008 | 2007 | 2006 | 2005 | 2004 | 2003 | 2002 | 2001 |
|---|---|---|---|---|---|---|---|---|---|---|
| Tangible Book Value | 57.84 | 46.34 | 48.63 | 46.49 | 39.30 | 31.06 | 24.18 | 19.25 | 15.33 | 14.69 |
| Cash Flow | 17.25 | 6.57 | 25.68 | 15.41 | 13.19 | 12.22 | 8.81 | 6.67 | 4.55 | 5.30 |
| Earnings | 8.46 | -0.87 | 2.10 | 8.39 | 7.64 | 7.84 | 5.04 | 3.35 | 1.80 | 2.37 |
| S&P Core Earnings | 8.46 | -0.87 | 2.08 | 8.38 | 7.30 | 7.60 | 5.19 | 3.29 | 1.73 | 2.28 |
| Dividends | 0.60 | 0.60 | 0.70 | 0.60 | 0.60 | 0.34 | 0.32 | 0.21 | 0.19 | 0.12 |
| Payout Ratio | 7% | NM | 33% | 7% | 8% | 4% | 6% | 6% | 11% | 5% |
| Prices:High | 120.80 | 106.46 | 149.23 | 109.32 | 76.25 | 78.15 | 55.16 | 41.68 | 28.88 | 31.55 |
| Prices:Low | 81.94 | 51.03 | 57.11 | 63.01 | 56.50 | 47.45 | 36.79 | 26.26 | 21.12 | 16.56 |
| P/E Ratio:High | 14 | NM | 71 | 13 | 10 | 10 | 11 | 12 | 16 | 13 |
| P/E Ratio:Low | 10 | NM | 27 | 8 | 7 | 6 | 7 | 8 | 12 | 7 |

| Income Statement Analysis (Million $) | | | | | | | | | | |
|---|---|---|---|---|---|---|---|---|---|---|
| Revenue | 12,092 | 8,615 | 12,390 | 9,978 | 8,289 | 7,584 | 5,333 | 4,190 | 2,560 | 2,777 |
| Operating Income | NA | NA | 8,988 | 7,224 | 5,753 | 5,792 | 4,119 | 3,241 | 1,048 | 2,146 |
| Depreciation, Depletion and Amortization | 3,194 | 2,500 | 7,952 | 2,348 | 1,816 | 1,416 | 1,222 | 1,073 | 844 | 821 |
| Interest Expense | 229 | 242 | 166 | 312 | 158 | 122 | 120 | 127 | 133 | 132 |
| Pretax Income | 5,206 | 326 | 932 | 4,673 | 4,010 | 4,206 | 2,663 | 1,922 | 899 | 1,199 |
| Effective Tax Rate | NA | 187.1% | 23.6% | 39.8% | 36.3% | 37.6% | 37.3% | 43.0% | 38.3% | 39.7% |
| Net Income | 3,032 | -284 | 712 | 2,812 | 2,552 | 2,624 | 1,670 | 1,095 | 554 | 723 |
| S&P Core Earnings | 3,000 | -292 | 701 | 2,805 | 2,434 | 2,539 | 1,713 | 1,069 | 524 | 681 |

| Balance Sheet & Other Financial Data (Million $) | | | | | | | | | | |
|---|---|---|---|---|---|---|---|---|---|---|
| Cash | 134 | 2,048 | 1,973 | 126 | 141 | 229 | 111 | 33.5 | 51.9 | 35.6 |
| Current Assets | 3,480 | 4,586 | 4,451 | 2,752 | 2,490 | 2,162 | 1,349 | 899 | 767 | 698 |
| Total Assets | 43,425 | 28,186 | 29,186 | 28,635 | 24,308 | 19,272 | 15,502 | 12,416 | 9,460 | 8,934 |
| Current Liabilities | 3,524 | 2,393 | 2,615 | 2,665 | 3,812 | 2,187 | 1,283 | 820 | 532 | 522 |
| Long Term Debt | 8,095 | 4,950 | 4,809 | 4,227 | 2,020 | 2,192 | 2,588 | 2,327 | 2,159 | 2,244 |
| Common Equity | 24,377 | 15,779 | 16,509 | 15,280 | 13,093 | 10,443 | 8,106 | 6,434 | 4,826 | 4,112 |
| Total Capital | 32,472 | 20,839 | 24,484 | 23,315 | 18,830 | 12,733 | 10,793 | 8,860 | 7,083 | 7,655 |
| Capital Expenditures | 4,922 | 3,631 | 5,973 | 5,807 | 3,892 | 3,716 | 2,456 | 1,595 | 1,037 | 1,525 |
| Cash Flow | 6,194 | 2,208 | 8,658 | 5,154 | 4,363 | 4,034 | 2,887 | 2,163 | 1,387 | 1,525 |
| Current Ratio | 1.0 | 1.9 | 1.7 | 1.0 | 0.7 | 1.0 | 1.1 | 1.1 | 1.4 | 1.3 |
| % Long Term Debt of Capitalization | 24.9 | 23.9 | 19.6 | 20.7 | 13.3 | 17.2 | 24.0 | 26.3 | 30.5 | 29.3 |
| % Return on Assets | 8.5 | NM | 2.5 | 10.6 | 11.7 | 15.1 | 12.0 | 10.0 | 6.0 | 8.8 |
| % Return on Equity | 15.1 | NM | 4.5 | 19.8 | 21.6 | 28.2 | 22.9 | 19.4 | 12.2 | 18.6 |

Data as orig reptd.; bef. results of disc opers/spec. items. Per share data adj. for stk. divs.; EPS diluted. E-Estimated. NA-Not Available. NM-Not Meaningful. NR-Not Ranked. UR-Under Review.

**Office:** 2000 Post Oak Blvd Ste 100, Houston, TX 77056-4400.
**Telephone:** 713-296-6000.
**Website:** http://www.apachecorp.com
**Chrmn & CEO:** G.S. Farris

**COO & Co-Pres:** R.J. Eichler
**EVP & CFO:** T.P. Chambers
**Chief Admin Officer & Treas:** M.W. Dundrea
**CTO:** M.S. Bahorich

**Investor Contact:** A. Leon (713-296-6692)
**Board Members:** F. M. Bohen, G. S. Farris, R. M. Ferlic, E. C. Fiedorek, A. D. Frazier, Jr., P. A. Graham, S. D. Josey, C. Joung, J. A. Kocur, G. D. Lawrence, Jr., W. C. Montgomery, R. D. Patton, C. J. Pittman

**Founded:** 1954
**Domicile:** Delaware
**Employees:** 4,449

# Apartment Investment and Management Co

STANDARD
&POOR'S

| S&P Recommendation HOLD ★★★☆☆ | Price<br>$20.56 (as of Nov 25, 2011) | 12-Mo. Target Price<br>$28.00 | Investment Style<br>Large-Cap Value |
|---|---|---|---|

**GICS Sector** Financials
**Sub-Industry** Residential REITS

**Summary** This real estate investment trust is one of the largest U.S. owners and managers of multi-family apartment properties.

## Key Stock Statistics (Source S&P, Vickers, company reports)

| | | | | | | | | |
|---|---|---|---|---|---|---|---|---|
| 52-Wk Range | $28.12– 20.08 | S&P FFO/Sh. 2011E | 1.64 | Market Capitalization(B) | $2.486 | Beta | 2.07 |
| Trailing 12-Month FFO/Share | $1.97 | S&P FFO/Sh. 2012E | 1.75 | Yield (%) | 2.33 | S&P 3-Yr. FFO/Sh. Proj. CAGR(%) | 7 |
| Trailing 12-Month P/FFO | NA | P/FFO on S&P FFO/Sh. 2011E | 12.5 | Dividend Rate/Share | $0.48 | S&P Credit Rating | BB+ |
| $10K Invested 5 Yrs Ago | $6,509 | Common Shares Outstg. (M) | 120.9 | Institutional Ownership (%) | NM | | |

## Price Performance

30-Week Mov. Avg. · · · 10-Week Mov. Avg. - - GAAP Earnings vs. Previous Year Volume Above Avg. STARS
12-Mo. Target Price — Relative Strength — ▲ Up ▼ Down ► No Change Below Avg.

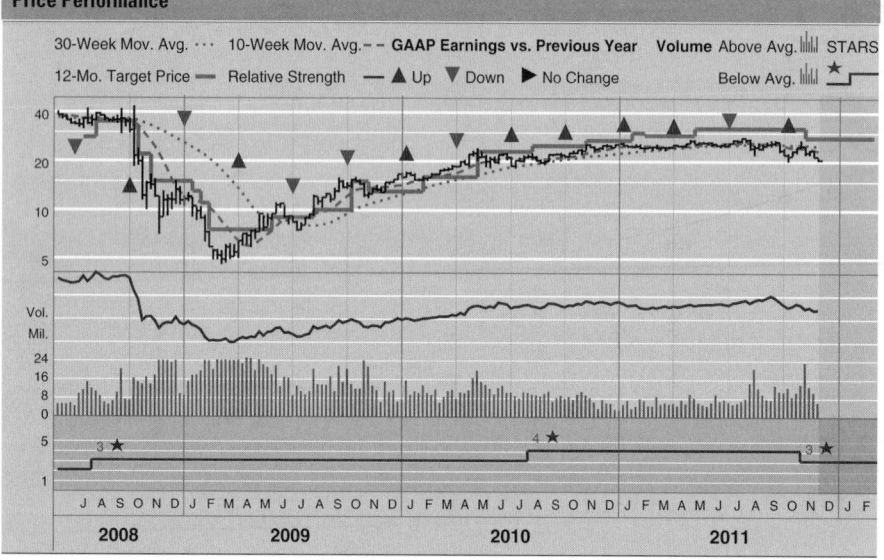

Options: CBOE, P, Ph

Analysis prepared by Equity Analyst **R. Shepard, CFA** on Oct 31, 2011, when the stock traded at **$24.62**.

### Qualitative Risk Assessment

| LOW | MEDIUM | HIGH |
|---|---|---|

Our risk assessment for AIV reflects its high level of financial leverage, offset by what we consider to be a manageable level of near-term debt maturities and improving operating performance.

### Quantitative Evaluations

**S&P Quality Ranking** B-

| D | C | B- | B | B+ | A- | A | A+ |
|---|---|---|---|---|---|---|---|

**Relative Strength Rank** WEAK

25

LOWEST = 1    HIGHEST = 99

### Revenue/FFO Data

**Revenue (Million $)**

| | 1Q | 2Q | 3Q | 4Q | Year |
|---|---|---|---|---|---|
| 2011 | 286.6 | 281.0 | 281.4 | -- | -- |
| 2010 | 279.9 | 285.2 | 286.4 | 293.5 | 1,145 |
| 2009 | 297.5 | 299.1 | 296.4 | 302.8 | 1,196 |
| 2008 | 349.2 | 374.0 | 375.1 | 359.6 | 1,458 |
| 2007 | 413.1 | 426.4 | 426.7 | 455.0 | 1,721 |
| 2006 | 408.5 | 420.0 | 423.9 | 438.6 | 1,691 |

**FFO Per Share ($)**

| | | | | | |
|---|---|---|---|---|---|
| 2011 | 0.49 | 0.35 | 0.47 | E0.42 | E1.64 |
| 2010 | 0.37 | 0.49 | 0.54 | 0.45 | 1.85 |
| 2009 | 0.42 | 0.44 | 0.31 | 0.25 | 1.55 |
| 2008 | 0.79 | 0.83 | 0.82 | -0.34 | 1.45 |
| 2007 | 0.74 | 0.88 | 0.83 | 0.83 | 3.17 |
| 2006 | 0.68 | 0.73 | 0.74 | 0.91 | 3.07 |

Fiscal year ended Dec. 31. Next earnings report expected: NA. FFO Estimates based on S&P Funds From Operations Est..

### Dividend Data (Dates: mm/dd Payment Date: mm/dd/yy)

| Amount ($) | Date Decl. | Ex-Div. Date | Stk. of Record | Payment Date |
|---|---|---|---|---|
| 0.120 | 02/02 | 02/16 | 02/18 | 02/28/11 |
| 0.120 | 04/29 | 05/18 | 05/20 | 05/31/11 |
| 0.120 | 07/28 | 08/17 | 08/19 | 08/31/11 |
| 0.120 | 10/27 | 11/16 | 11/18 | 11/30/11 |

Dividends have been paid since 1994. Source: Company reports.

## Highlights

► AIV has recently reported a slowdown in potential tenants visiting its communities since August. Average occupancy declined 80 basis points during the third quarter of 2011, reflecting, in our view, some pressure on middle-income clientele from a challenging economy. As a result, we expect some moderation in gains on new rental rates in 2012. We estimate total 2012 revenues will gain 3%, also reflecting the divestment of over 6,000 non-core apartment units during 2011.

► We expect AIV to slow its disposition program in 2012 and begin considering new acquisitions in its core markets. We look for new investments to be concentrated in core, coastal markets, which accounted for over 84% of 2010 operating income. We think AIV is less likely to invest capital in the construction of new apartment communities over the next 12 months.

► Our 2012 per-share FFO estimate of $1.75 reflects a moderate increase in forecasted operating income on a same-property basis. The trust raised its 2011 dividend payout by 20%, to $0.48, a level we find adequately covered by available cash flow.

## Investment Rationale/Risk

► AIV holds what we view as a large and diversified portfolio of conventional and affordable residential properties. In our view, AIV's recent revenue growth has lagged peers, primarily due to an active disposition program designed to reposition its portfolio in coastal markets. However, we think a lower home ownership rate and improving local job markets will allow it to maintain positive rent growth in 2012. AIV also has recurring management fees that provide a degree of stability, in our view. We think the shares, recently trading at 15.2X our 2011 FFO estimate of $1.64, fairly reflect earnings growth below the residential REIT average.

► Risks to our opinion and target price include weaker-than-expected employment trends in AIV's markets, higher borrowing rates on floating rate debt, and a significant increase in new construction that creates competitive supply.

► Our 12-month target price of $28 is based on a multiple of 16X our 2012 FFO estimate of $1.75, a moderate discount to peers, incorporating our view of AIV's below-average financial position. We blend in our net asset value model, using estimated 2011 cash flow and a one-year cash yield of 6.50%, leading to intrinsic value of $26.

---

**Please read the Required Disclosures and Analyst Certification on the last page of this report.**

The McGraw-Hill Companies

# Apartment Investment and Management Co

STANDARD &POOR'S

## Business Summary October 31, 2011

CORPORATE OVERVIEW. Apartment Investment and Management Co. is one of the largest U.S. multi-family residential REITs in terms of units. At December 31, 2010, it owned, held an equity interest in, or managed a geographically diversified portfolio of 768 properties, including about 122,694 apartment units, located in 43 states, the District of Columbia, and Puerto Rico.

The trust conducts substantially all its business, and owns all its assets, through AIMCO Properties, L.P., of which AIV owns approximately a 91% interest. AIV operates in two segments: the ownership, operation and management of apartment properties; and the management of apartment properties for third parties and affiliates.

MARKET PROFILE. The U.S. housing market is highly fragmented and is characterized broadly by two types of housing units: multi-family and single-family. At the end of 2010, the U.S. Census Bureau estimated that there were 130.85 million housing units in the country, an increase of 0.5% from the end of 2009. Due to the large stock and the fact that residents have the option of either being owners or tenants (renters), the housing market can be highly competitive. Main demand drivers for apartments are household formation and employ-

ment growth. S&P estimates 0.4 million new households were formed in 2010. Supply is created by new housing unit construction, which could consist of single-family homes or multi-family apartment buildings or condominiums. According the U.S. Department of Housing, 0.59 million total housing units were started in 2010, up about 6% from depressed levels in 2009. Multi-family starts, for structures with more than four units, rose 8.1% in 2010, but remained 60% below the level posted in 2008.

With apartment tenants on relatively short leases compared to those of commercial and industrial properties, apartment REITs are generally more sensitive to changes in market conditions than REITs in other property categories. Results could be hurt by new construction that adds new space in excess of actual demand. Trends in home price affordability also affect both rent levels and the level of new construction, since the relative price attractiveness of owning versus renting is an important factor in consumer decision making.

## Company Financials Fiscal Year Ended Dec. 31

| Per Share Data ($) | 2010 | 2009 | 2008 | 2007 | 2006 | 2005 | 2004 | 2003 | 2002 | 2001 |
|---|---|---|---|---|---|---|---|---|---|---|
| Tangible Book Value | 2.49 | 4.10 | 5.51 | 9.82 | NA | NA | NA | NA | NA | 18.90 |
| Earnings | -1.73 | -2.34 | -1.51 | -1.14 | -1.29 | -1.25 | -0.39 | -0.25 | 0.94 | 0.23 |
| S&P Core Earnings | -1.48 | -1.75 | -1.51 | -1.12 | -1.29 | -1.25 | -0.39 | -0.32 | 0.89 | 0.19 |
| Dividends | 0.30 | 0.40 | 1.20 | 2.40 | NA | NA | NA | NA | NA | 3.12 |
| Payout Ratio | NM | NM | NM | NM | NM | NM | NM | NM | NM | NM |
| Prices:High | 26.24 | 17.09 | 43.67 | 65.79 | 59.17 | 44.14 | 39.25 | 42.05 | 51.46 | 50.13 |
| Prices:Low | 15.01 | 4.57 | 7.01 | 33.97 | 37.76 | 34.17 | 26.45 | 33.00 | 33.90 | 39.25 |
| P/E Ratio:High | NM | NM | 1458 | NM | NM | NM | NM | NM | 55 | NM |
| P/E Ratio:Low | NM | NM | NM | NM | NM | NM | NM | NM | 36 | NM |

| Income Statement Analysis (Million $) | | | | | | | | | | |
|---|---|---|---|---|---|---|---|---|---|---|
| Rental Income | 1,109 | 1,141 | 1,351 | 1,641 | 1,630 | 1,460 | 1,402 | 1,446 | 1,292 | 1,298 |
| Mortgage Income | Nil | Nil | Nil | Nil | Nil | Nil | Nil | Nil | Nil | Nil |
| Total Income | 1,145 | 1,196 | 1,458 | 1,721 | 1,691 | 1,522 | 1,469 | 1,516 | 1,506 | 1,464 |
| General Expenses | 588 | 627 | 795 | 886 | 874 | 816 | 768 | 729 | 664 | 652 |
| Interest Expense | 313 | 324 | 369 | 422 | 408 | 368 | 367 | 373 | 340 | 316 |
| Provision for Losses | 0.95 | 21.5 | 4.18 | 3.95 | 2.78 | 1.37 | Nil | Nil | Nil | Nil |
| Depreciation | 426 | 444 | 459 | 473 | 471 | 412 | 369 | 328 | 289 | 364 |
| Net Income | -148 | -217 | -129 | -48.1 | -42.7 | -27.9 | 55.7 | 70.7 | 175 | 107 |
| S&P Core Earnings | -172 | -200 | -183 | -112 | -124 | -117 | -35.5 | -29.2 | 77.1 | 13.8 |

| Balance Sheet & Other Financial Data (Million $) | | | | | | | | | | |
|---|---|---|---|---|---|---|---|---|---|---|
| Cash | 111 | 81.3 | 300 | 210 | 230 | 330 | 293 | 98.0 | 97.0 | 820 |
| Total Assets | 7,379 | 7,906 | 9,403 | 10,607 | 10,290 | 10,017 | 10,072 | 10,113 | 10,317 | 8,323 |
| Real Estate Investment | 9,468 | 9,663 | 10,885 | 12,384 | 11,982 | 10,990 | 10,800 | 10,601 | 10,227 | 8,416 |
| Loss Reserve | Nil | Nil | Nil | Nil | Nil | Nil | Nil | Nil | Nil | Nil |
| Net Investment | 6,533 | 6,962 | 8,102 | 9,349 | 9,081 | 8,752 | 8,785 | 8,753 | 8,616 | 6,796 |
| Short Term Debt | Nil | Nil | Nil | Nil | Nil | Nil | Nil | Nil | Nil | 214 |
| Capitalization:Debt | 5,505 | 5,690 | 6,777 | 7,532 | 6,873 | 6,284 | 5,734 | 6,198 | 5,529 | 4,670 |
| Capitalization:Equity | 388 | 579 | 722 | 1,026 | 1,516 | 1,706 | 1,967 | 2,005 | 2,218 | 1,592 |
| Capitalization:Total | 6,915 | 7,342 | 8,632 | 9,838 | 9,165 | 9,436 | 9,246 | 9,580 | 9,180 | 7,904 |
| % Earnings & Depreciation/Assets | 3.6 | 2.6 | 3.3 | 4.2 | 4.2 | 3.8 | 4.2 | 3.9 | 5.0 | 5.9 |
| Price Times Book Value:High | 10.5 | 4.2 | 7.9 | 6.7 | 4.0 | 2.5 | 1.9 | 2.0 | 2.3 | 2.7 |
| Price Times Book Value:Low | 6.0 | 1.1 | 1.3 | 3.5 | 2.5 | 1.9 | 1.3 | 1.6 | 1.5 | 2.1 |

Data as orig reptd.; bef. results of disc opers/spec. items. Per share data adj. for stk. divs.; EPS diluted. E-Estimated. NA-Not Available. NM-Not Meaningful. NR-Not Ranked. UR-Under Review.

Office: 4582 S Ulster St Pkwy Ste 1100, Denver, CO 80237-2662.
Telephone: 303-757-8101.
Email: investor@aimco.com
Website: http://www.aimco.com

Chrmn & CEO: T. Considine
EVP & CFO: E.M. Freedman
EVP & Chief Admin Officer: M. Cortez
EVP & Treas: P.K. Fielding

SVP & Chief Acctg Officer: P. Beldin
Investor Contact: J. Martin (303-691-4440)
Board Members: J. N. Bailey, T. Considine, R. S. Ellwood, T. L. Keltner, J. L. Martin, R. A. Miller, K. M. Nelson, M. A. Stein

Founded: 1994
Domicile: Maryland
Employees: 3,100

# Apollo Group Inc

**STANDARD &POOR'S**

| S&P Recommendation | SELL ★★☆☆☆ | Price | 12-Mo. Target Price | Investment Style |
|---|---|---|---|---|
| | | $44.75 (as of Nov 25, 2011) | $35.00 | Large-Cap Growth |

**GICS Sector** Consumer Discretionary
**Sub-Industry** Education Services

**Summary** This provider of higher education programs for working adults offers educational programs and services throughout the U.S. and in a small number of foreign markets.

## Key Stock Statistics (Source S&P, Vickers, company reports)

| | | | | | | | | |
|---|---|---|---|---|---|---|---|---|
| 52-Wk Range | $54.23–33.75 | S&P Oper. EPS 2012**E** | 3.00 | Market Capitalization(B) | $5.822 | Beta | 0.23 |
| Trailing 12-Month EPS | $4.04 | S&P Oper. EPS 2013**E** | 3.05 | Yield (%) | Nil | S&P 3-Yr. Proj. EPS CAGR(%) | -13 |
| Trailing 12-Month P/E | 11.1 | P/E on S&P Oper. EPS 2012**E** | 14.9 | Dividend Rate/Share | Nil | S&P Credit Rating | NA |
| $10K Invested 5 Yrs Ago | $12,338 | Common Shares Outstg. (M) | 130.6 | Institutional Ownership (%) | 95 | | |

## Price Performance

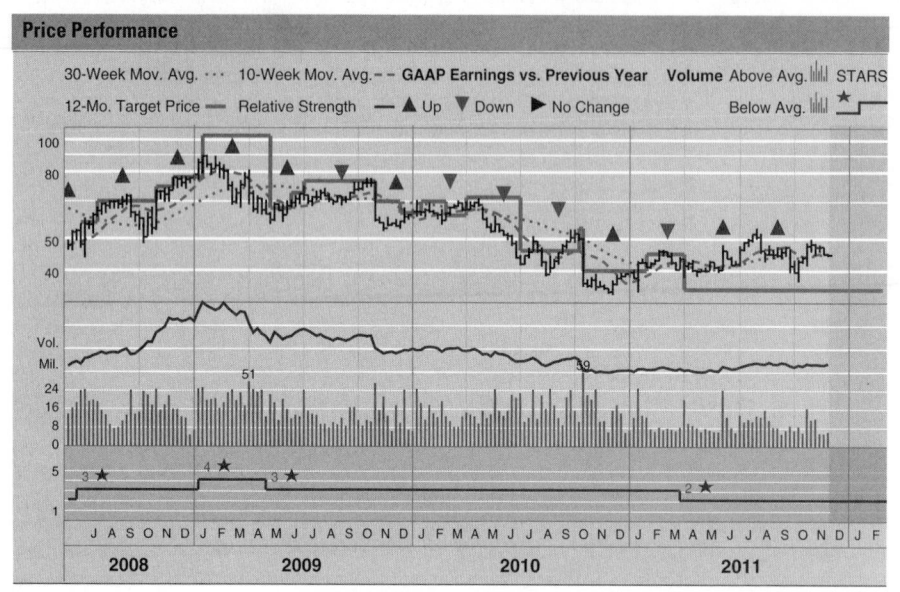

30-Week Mov. Avg. · · · 10-Week Mov. Avg. - - GAAP Earnings vs. Previous Year   Volume Above Avg. STARS
12-Mo. Target Price — Relative Strength — ▲ Up ▼ Down ► No Change   Below Avg.

Options: ASE, CBOE, P, Ph

Analysis prepared by Equity Analyst **Michael Jaffe** on Oct 26, 2011, when the stock traded at **$47.15**.

## Highlights

▸ We expect revenues to decline by 13% in FY 12 (Aug.). This reflects our belief that student counts will be lower following average quarterly declines of 40% in new student enrollments in FY 11. The downturn in new students seems to be related to initiatives to improve student retention and loan repayments. APOL's most aggressive measure, in our view, is its action (effective November 1) to require all prospective students with fewer than 24 credit hours earned to take a free three-week orientation course. On the positive side for APOL, however, is that following the dramatic downturn in new student counts in FY 11, it believes that its business is poised to record modest gains in new students in FY 12.

▸ We expect narrower net margins in FY 12, on the expected major negative near-term impact of APOL's student orientation initiative on enrollments. We see that outweighing Apollo's actions to reduce costs and bad debt expense.

▸ Our FY 12 EPS estimate of $3.00 compares with operating EPS of $4.94 in FY 11, which excluded $0.92 of charges, mostly impairment charges at BPP Holdings.

## Investment Rationale/Risk

▸ Federal student loan usage at APOL's schools has been near the peak allowed in recent years, and we see its need to comply with recently finalized "gainful employment" rules (based on student loan repayment and debt-to-income tests) limiting near-term results. At the same time, the finalized rule was less harsh than originally expected, repayments of APOL's students have been more favorable than at most of its peers, and we think major initiatives being undertaken by APOL will eventually enhance its operating results. However, when combining these factors with our valuation model, we find the shares overvalued.

▸ Risks to our recommendation and target price include major success in recent initiatives, and a limited impact from proposed regulations on government student loans.

▸ APOL traded recently at 17X our calendar 2012 EPS forecast of $2.80, a large premium to peers. We see APOL's current initiatives having a positive long-term effect, but we think they will limit APOL's operating results through at least the coming year. We set our 12-month target price at $35, or 12.5X our calendar 2012 EPS estimate, which is more in line with peers.

## Qualitative Risk Assessment

| LOW | MEDIUM | HIGH |
|---|---|---|

Our risk assessment reflects a lack of consistent conditions in the for-profit education market, and APOL's frequent transformations of its business model. In the corporate governance area, we have a negative view of the nearly 100% voting control held by insiders through separate voting shares. We believe these factors are offset by what we view as APOL's consistently solid levels of cash flow and a healthy balance sheet.

## Quantitative Evaluations

**S&P Quality Ranking**   B+

| D | C | B- | B | B+ | A- | A | A+ |
|---|---|---|---|---|---|---|---|

**Relative Strength Rank**   STRONG

71

LOWEST = 1                HIGHEST = 99

## Revenue/Earnings Data

**Revenue (Million $)**

| | 1Q | 2Q | 3Q | 4Q | Year |
|---|---|---|---|---|---|
| 2011 | 1,326 | 1,049 | 1,236 | 1,122 | 4,733 |
| 2010 | 1,259 | 1,070 | 1,337 | 1,259 | 4,926 |
| 2009 | 971.0 | 876.1 | 1,051 | 1,076 | 3,974 |
| 2008 | 780.7 | 693.6 | 835.2 | 831.4 | 3,141 |
| 2007 | 667.8 | 608.7 | 733.4 | 713.9 | 2,724 |
| 2006 | 628.9 | 569.6 | 653.6 | 624.2 | 2,478 |

**Earnings Per Share ($)**

| | | | | | |
|---|---|---|---|---|---|
| 2011 | 1.61 | -0.47 | 1.51 | 1.37 | 4.02 |
| 2010 | 1.54 | 0.67 | 1.16 | 0.32 | 3.72 |
| 2009 | 1.12 | 0.77 | 1.26 | 0.59 | 3.75 |
| 2008 | 0.83 | -0.19 | 0.85 | 1.43 | 2.87 |
| 2007 | 0.65 | 0.35 | 0.75 | 0.60 | 2.35 |
| 2006 | 0.73 | 0.46 | 0.77 | 0.54 | 2.35 |

Fiscal year ended Aug. 31. Next earnings report expected: Mid January. EPS Estimates based on S&P Operating Earnings; historical GAAP earnings are as reported.

## Dividend Data

No cash dividends have been paid.

---

**Please read the Required Disclosures and Analyst Certification on the last page of this report.**

*The McGraw-Hill Companies*

# Apollo Group Inc

STANDARD
&POOR'S

## Business Summary October 26, 2011

CORPORATE OVERVIEW. Historically, Apollo Group derived most of its revenues by providing higher education programs for working adults, with most of its students attending its University of Phoenix (UOP) unit. UOP offers its programs at campuses, as well as online. They consist largely of programs in business, education, information technology, criminal justice and nursing. At August 31, 2011, APOL offered programs and services in 40 states, the District of Columbia, Puerto Rico, Latin America and Europe. Enrollment at UOP totaled 380,800 at August 31, 2011, down sharply from 470,800 a year earlier, limited mostly by a major downturn in new student starts in FY 11 (Aug.). Operational changes and initiatives implemented by APOL to more effectively support students and improve educational outcomes seem to be the primary reasons for the downturn.

CORPORATE STRATEGY. With growing levels of students at its schools not adequately prepared for college level work, APOL recently developed a student orientation program. Effective November 1, 2010, the company required all prospective students with fewer than 24 credit hours to attend its orientation program. The program lasts three weeks and is provided at no cost. Given the time requirement of the program and the portion of students who will decide

not to attend APOL's schools, the company has experienced a sharp downturn in new student enrollments over the past year (down 42% in FY 11's first quarter, 45% in the second quarter, 40% in the third, and 33% in the fourth). However, it sees its orientation actions ultimately leading to much higher student retention and loan repayment rates among its student base.

Until a few years ago, APOL focused mostly on students who were older than the traditional 18-to-22-year-old college student, chiefly baby boomers. Yet, with the youngest baby boomers now nearing the age of 50, APOL began to seek students in other demographic categories. As a result, it began to place much more focus on associate degrees, targeting younger students (36% of APOL's students were in associates programs at August 31, 2011). Yet, with persistence rates and loan repayment less favorable among its associates population, APOL has again moved back toward a focus on bachelors programs (48% of degreed enrollments at August 31).

## Company Financials Fiscal Year Ended Aug. 31

| Per Share Data ($) | 2011 | 2010 | 2009 | 2008 | 2007 | 2006 | 2005 | 2004 | 2003 | 2002 |
|---|---|---|---|---|---|---|---|---|---|---|
| Tangible Book Value | 7.56 | 5.98 | 44.33 | 4.56 | 3.62 | 3.40 | 3.73 | 4.89 | 5.23 | 3.60 |
| Cash Flow | 4.78 | 4.68 | 4.38 | 3.35 | 2.77 | 2.74 | 2.68 | 1.79 | 1.62 | 1.12 |
| Earnings | 4.02 | 3.72 | 3.75 | 2.87 | 2.35 | 2.35 | 2.39 | 0.77 | 1.30 | 0.87 |
| S&P Core Earnings | 4.98 | 5.42 | 4.08 | 2.87 | 2.35 | 2.42 | 2.30 | 0.72 | 1.22 | 0.79 |
| Dividends | NA | Nil | Nil | Nil | Nil | Nil | Nil | Nil | Nil | Nil |
| Payout Ratio | Nil | Nil | Nil | Nil | Nil | Nil | Nil | Nil | Nil | Nil |
| Prices:High | 54.23 | 66.69 | 90.00 | 81.68 | 80.75 | 63.26 | 84.20 | 98.01 | 73.09 | 46.15 |
| Prices:Low | 34.43 | 33.75 | 52.79 | 37.92 | 39.02 | 33.33 | 57.40 | 62.55 | 40.72 | 28.13 |
| P/E Ratio:High | 13 | 18 | 24 | 28 | 34 | 25 | 35 | NM | 56 | 53 |
| P/E Ratio:Low | 9 | 9 | 14 | 13 | 17 | 13 | 24 | NM | 31 | 32 |
| **Income Statement Analysis** (Million $) | | | | | | | | | | |
| Revenue | 4,733 | 4,926 | 3,974 | 3,141 | 2,724 | 2,478 | 2,251 | 1,798 | 1,340 | 1,009 |
| Operating Income | 1,336 | 1,520 | 1,229 | 829 | 697 | 738 | 767 | 481 | 428 | 293 |
| Depreciation | 144 | 147 | 117 | 79.7 | 71.1 | 67.3 | 54.5 | 43.2 | 40.3 | 35.2 |
| Interest Expense | 8.93 | 11.9 | 4.46 | Nil | Nil | Nil | Nil | Nil | Nil | Nil |
| Pretax Income | 954 | 1,001 | 1,040 | 783 | 657 | 668 | 730 | 456 | 402 | 266 |
| Effective Tax Rate | NA | NA | 42.9% | 39.2% | 37.8% | 37.9% | 39.1% | 39.1% | 38.5% | 39.4% |
| Net Income | 533 | 568 | 129 | 477 | 409 | 415 | 445 | 278 | 247 | 161 |
| S&P Core Earnings | 705 | 829 | 651 | 477 | 409 | 428 | 427 | 131 | 218 | 140 |
| **Balance Sheet & Other Financial Data** (Million $) | | | | | | | | | | |
| Cash | 1,572 | 1,285 | 968 | 486 | 370 | 355 | 595 | 677 | 800 | 610 |
| Current Assets | 2,371 | 2,253 | 1,880 | 1,170 | 925 | 803 | 835 | 855 | 950 | 730 |
| Total Assets | 3,270 | 3,601 | 3,263 | 1,860 | 1,450 | 1,283 | 1,303 | 1,452 | 1,378 | 980 |
| Current Liabilities | 1,655 | 1,794 | 1,755 | 866 | 744 | 596 | 518 | 465 | 335 | 264 |
| Long Term Debt | 180 | 168 | 128 | Nil | Nil | Nil | Nil | Nil | Nil | 15.5 |
| Common Equity | 1,240 | 1,356 | 1,158 | 834 | 634 | 604 | 707 | 957 | 1,027 | 699 |
| Total Capital | 1,427 | 1,557 | 7,966 | 849 | 634 | 604 | 707 | 957 | 1,027 | 715 |
| Capital Expenditures | 163 | 168 | 127 | 105 | 61.2 | 44.6 | 104 | 80.3 | 55.8 | 36.7 |
| Cash Flow | 677 | 715 | 698 | 556 | 480 | 482 | 499 | 321 | 287 | 196 |
| Current Ratio | 1.4 | 1.3 | 1.1 | 1.4 | 1.2 | 1.3 | 1.6 | 1.8 | 2.8 | 2.8 |
| % Long Term Debt of Capitalization | 12.6 | 10.8 | 9.4 | Nil | Nil | Nil | Nil | Nil | Nil | 2.2 |
| % Net Income of Revenue | 11.3 | 11.5 | 15.1 | 15.2 | 15.0 | 16.7 | 19.8 | 15.4 | 18.4 | 16.0 |
| % Return on Assets | 15.5 | 16.6 | 23.4 | 28.8 | 29.9 | 32.4 | 31.8 | 19.6 | 20.9 | 19.4 |
| % Return on Equity | 41.1 | 45.2 | 60.1 | 64.9 | 66.0 | 67.0 | 53.5 | 28.0 | 28.6 | 29.3 |

Data as orig reptd.; bef. results of disc opers/spec. items. Per share data adj. for stk. divs.; EPS diluted. E-Estimated. NA-Not Available. NM-Not Meaningful. NR-Not Ranked. UR-Under Review.

**Office:** 4025 S. Riverpoint Pkwy, Phoenix, AZ 85040.
**Telephone:** 480-966-5394.
**Website:** http://www.apollogrp.edu
**Chrmn:** J.G. Sperling

**Pres & COO:** J.L. D'Amico
**Vice Chrmn:** P.V. Sperling
**Co-CEO:** C.B. Edelstein
**Co-CEO:** G.W. Cappelli

**Investor Contact:** J. Pasinski (800-990-2765)
**Board Members:** T. C. Bishop, G. W. Cappelli, D. J. Deconcini, C. B. Edelstein, R. A. Herberger, A. Kirschner, R. S. Murley, K. S. Redman, M. F. Rivelo, D. E. Shupp, J. G. Sperling, P. V. Sperling, G. A. Zimmer

**Founded:** 1981
**Domicile:** Arizona
**Employees:** 56,743

**STANDARD &POOR'S**

# Apple Inc

| | | | |
|---|---|---|---|
| **S&P Recommendation** BUY ★★★★☆ | **Price** $363.57 (as of Nov 25, 2011) | **12-Mo. Target Price** $500.00 | **Investment Style** Large-Cap Growth |

**GICS Sector** Information Technology
**Sub-Industry** Computer Hardware

**Summary** This company is a prominent provider of hardware and software, including Mac computers, the iPod digital media player, the iPhone smartphone, and the iPad tablet.

## Key Stock Statistics (Source S&P, Vickers, company reports)

| | | | | | | | | |
|---|---|---|---|---|---|---|---|---|
| 52-Wk Range | $426.70– 310.50 | S&P Oper. EPS 2012**E** | 37.00 | Market Capitalization(B) | $337.905 | Beta | 1.28 |
| Trailing 12-Month EPS | $27.68 | S&P Oper. EPS 2013**E** | 40.50 | Yield (%) | Nil | S&P 3-Yr. Proj. EPS CAGR(%) | 35 |
| Trailing 12-Month P/E | 13.1 | P/E on S&P Oper. EPS 2012**E** | 9.8 | Dividend Rate/Share | Nil | S&P Credit Rating | NR |
| $10K Invested 5 Yrs Ago | $39,678 | Common Shares Outstg. (M) | 929.4 | Institutional Ownership (%) | 69 | | |

## Price Performance

30-Week Mov. Avg. · · · 10-Week Mov. Avg. - - GAAP Earnings vs. Previous Year  Volume Above Avg. STARS
12-Mo. Target Price — Relative Strength  ▲ Up ▼ Down ▶ No Change  Below Avg.

Options: ASE, CBOE, P, Ph

Analysis prepared by Equity Analyst **Scott Kessler** on Nov 11, 2011, when the stock traded at **$386.60**.

## Highlights

▶ We estimate sales growth of 31% for FY 12 (Sep.), after a 66% rise in FY 11, reflecting gains in shipments of iPads, iPhones, and MacBooks. We see continuing growth from downloads, as hardware sales enable and promote consumption of apps, music, movies and books. We see iMac shipments rising at an above-industry pace due to product refreshes, but iPod units declining because of market saturation and AAPL's already dominant market share.

▶ We expect the gross margin to continue to widen in FY 12, from 40% in FY 11. We believe margins for the iPhone will improve because of scale and cost-cutting efforts, balancing anticipated price drops for other products as AAPL tries to overcome increasing competition and market saturation. Although we see R&D rising notably, we think the operating margin will expand due to operating leverage.

▶ Our EPS projections assume an effective tax rate around 24% and a modest increase in the share count. We note that AAPL had some $82 billion in cash/investments as of September 2011, but that it does not have a material stock buyback program or pay a dividend.

## Investment Rationale/Risk

▶ Despite somewhat soft demand for computers and consumer electronics, and competitive threats, we think iPhones, iPads and MacBooks will largely gain or retain market share over next year or so. Higher volumes and a focus on common components should lead to better profitability, in our view. With AAPL's earnings growth expected to lead most mega/large-cap technology companies, and considering its large cash position, strong free cash flow generation and relatively high return on equity (ROE), we believe the shares have appeal.

▶ Risks to our recommendation and target price include possible weaker end-market demand, pricing pressures, competitive handset and tablet offerings gaining traction, and less execution success as to product refreshes/innovations.

▶ Our 12-month target price of $500 implies a P/E of 13.5X our FY 12 EPS estimate, accounting for our view of relative growth, risk and ROE. We think AAPL offers a unique and attractive combination of growth and value. We also see the potential for more shareholder-friendly use of the balance sheet.

## Qualitative Risk Assessment

| LOW | MEDIUM | **HIGH** |
|---|---|---|

Our risk assessment reflects our view of a seemingly ever-evolving market for consumer-oriented technology products, potential challenges associated with the company's growing size and offerings, and possible changes to the pace or success of product innovations following recent management changes.

## Quantitative Evaluations

**S&P Quality Ranking**  B

| D | C | B- | **B** | B+ | A- | A | A+ |
|---|---|---|---|---|---|---|---|

**Relative Strength Rank**  MODERATE

49

LOWEST = 1    HIGHEST = 99

## Revenue/Earnings Data

**Revenue (Million $)**

| | 1Q | 2Q | 3Q | 4Q | Year |
|---|---|---|---|---|---|
| 2011 | 26,741 | 24,667 | 28,571 | 28,270 | 108,249 |
| 2010 | 15,683 | 13,499 | 15,700 | 20,343 | 65,225 |
| 2009 | 11,880 | 9,084 | 9,734 | 12,207 | 42,905 |
| 2008 | 9,608 | 7,512 | 7,464 | 7,895 | 32,479 |
| 2007 | 7,115 | 5,264 | 5,410 | 6,217 | 24,006 |
| 2006 | 5,749 | 4,359 | 4,370 | 4,837 | 19,315 |

**Earnings Per Share ($)**

| | | | | | |
|---|---|---|---|---|---|
| 2011 | 6.43 | 6.40 | 7.79 | 7.05 | 27.68 |
| 2010 | 3.67 | 3.33 | 3.51 | 4.64 | 15.15 |
| 2009 | 2.50 | 1.79 | 2.01 | 2.77 | 9.08 |
| 2008 | 1.76 | 1.16 | 1.19 | 1.26 | 5.36 |
| 2007 | 1.14 | 0.87 | 0.92 | 1.01 | 3.93 |
| 2006 | 0.65 | 0.47 | 0.54 | 0.62 | 2.27 |

Fiscal year ended Sep. 30. Next earnings report expected: NA. EPS Estimates based on S&P Operating Earnings; historical GAAP earnings are as reported.

## Dividend Data

No cash dividends have been paid since 1996.

---

**Please read the Required Disclosures and Analyst Certification on the last page of this report.**

The **McGraw·Hill** Companies

# Apple Inc

STANDARD
&POOR'S

## Business Summary November 11, 2011

CORPORATE OVERVIEW. Apple Inc. makes personal computers, smartphones, tablet computers, portable digital media players, and sells a variety of related software, services, peripherals and networking solutions. We look at the company based on its major business lines, including iPhone, Mac, iPad, iPod, and music-related products (iTunes) and others.

AAPL's smartphone, called iPhones, and related items made up 39% of total 2010 revenues, with over 47 million iPhones sold. This has been one AAPL's of the fastest growing businesses over the past couple of years, and while we expect the rate of growth to slow as the business becomes more mature, we still see substantial opportunities over the next couple of years that can make it an even larger portion of total revenues.

Sales of AAPL's computers, commonly known as Macs, made up approximately 24% of total revenues in calendar 2010. The company shipped over 14 million units of desktop and laptop computers, with laptop units selling almost two times desktops. On a unit shipment basis, Macs grew around 28%, much faster than the growth that market researchers have reported for the PC in-

dustry. Mac revenues advanced as greater unit shipments offset deteriorating blended average selling prices, trends we believe will continue over the next couple of years.

Released in April 2010, the iPad has quickly become the best selling tablet computer by far. Before the iPad, unit sales for similar computing devices were less than 200,000 units, according to market researchers. In calendar 2010, the first year of availability, AAPL sold over 14 million iPads, accounting for around 13% of total revenues and making this product line the third largest business for the company. We believe that the tablet form factor will become even more popular for the foreseeable future, and we see new entrants diluting AAPL's overall market share. Nonetheless, we expect AAPL to own the mid-to-high end of this fast-growing computing market for some time.

## Company Financials Fiscal Year Ended Sep. 30

| Per Share Data ($) | 2011 | 2010 | 2009 | 2008 | 2007 | 2006 | 2005 | 2004 | 2003 | 2002 |
|---|---|---|---|---|---|---|---|---|---|---|
| Tangible Book Value | 77.68 | 50.99 | 34.66 | 23.04 | 16.27 | 11.47 | 8.83 | 6.36 | 5.61 | 5.54 |
| Cash Flow | 29.61 | 16.26 | 9.89 | 5.88 | 4.29 | 2.52 | 1.77 | 0.55 | 0.50 | 0.25 |
| Earnings | 27.68 | 15.15 | 9.08 | 5.36 | 3.93 | 2.27 | 1.56 | 0.36 | 0.10 | 0.09 |
| S&P Core Earnings | 27.60 | 15.15 | 9.08 | 5.36 | 3.93 | 2.27 | 1.47 | 0.22 | -0.17 | -0.19 |
| Dividends | NA | Nil | Nil | Nil | Nil | Nil | Nil | Nil | Nil | Nil |
| Payout Ratio | Nil | Nil | Nil | Nil | Nil | Nil | Nil | Nil | Nil | Nil |
| Prices:High | 426.70 | 326.66 | 213.95 | 200.26 | 202.96 | 93.16 | 75.46 | 34.79 | 12.51 | 13.09 |
| Prices:Low | 310.50 | 190.25 | 78.20 | 79.14 | 81.90 | 50.16 | 31.30 | 10.59 | 6.36 | 6.68 |
| P/E Ratio:High | 15 | 22 | 24 | 37 | 52 | 41 | 48 | 98 | NM | NM |
| P/E Ratio:Low | 11 | 13 | 9 | 15 | 21 | 22 | 20 | 30 | NM | NM |

| Income Statement Analysis (Million $) | 2011 | 2010 | 2009 | 2008 | 2007 | 2006 | 2005 | 2004 | 2003 | 2002 |
|---|---|---|---|---|---|---|---|---|---|---|
| Revenue | 108,249 | 65,225 | 42,905 | 32,479 | 24,006 | 19,315 | 13,931 | 8,279 | 6,207 | 5,742 |
| Operating Income | 35,604 | 19,412 | 12,474 | 6,748 | 4,726 | 2,645 | 1,829 | 499 | 138 | 164 |
| Depreciation | 1,814 | 1,027 | 734 | 473 | 317 | 225 | 179 | 150 | 113 | 118 |
| Interest Expense | NA | NA | Nil | Nil | Nil | Nil | Nil | 3.00 | 8.00 | 11.0 |
| Pretax Income | 34,205 | 18,540 | 12,066 | 6,895 | 5,008 | 2,818 | 1,815 | 383 | 92.0 | 87.0 |
| Effective Tax Rate | NA | NA | 31.8% | 29.9% | 30.2% | 29.4% | 26.4% | 27.9% | 26.1% | 25.3% |
| Net Income | 25,922 | 14,013 | 8,235 | 4,834 | 3,496 | 1,989 | 1,335 | 276 | 68.0 | 65.0 |
| S&P Core Earnings | 25,851 | 14,013 | 8,235 | 4,834 | 3,496 | 1,989 | 1,259 | 164 | -119 | -137 |

| Balance Sheet & Other Financial Data (Million $) | 2011 | 2010 | 2009 | 2008 | 2007 | 2006 | 2005 | 2004 | 2003 | 2002 |
|---|---|---|---|---|---|---|---|---|---|---|
| Cash | 25,952 | 25,620 | 23,464 | 24,490 | 9,352 | 6,392 | 3,491 | 2,969 | 3,396 | 2,252 |
| Current Assets | 44,988 | 41,678 | 31,555 | 34,690 | 21,956 | 14,509 | 10,300 | 7,055 | 5,887 | 5,388 |
| Total Assets | 116,371 | 75,183 | 47,501 | 39,572 | 25,347 | 17,205 | 11,551 | 8,050 | 6,815 | 6,298 |
| Current Liabilities | 27,970 | 20,722 | 11,506 | 14,092 | 9,299 | 6,471 | 3,484 | 2,680 | 2,357 | 1,658 |
| Long Term Debt | NA | NA | Nil | Nil | Nil | Nil | Nil | Nil | Nil | 316 |
| Common Equity | 76,615 | 47,791 | 31,640 | 21,030 | 14,532 | 9,984 | 7,466 | 5,076 | 4,223 | 4,095 |
| Total Capital | 76,615 | 47,791 | 31,640 | 21,705 | 15,151 | 10,365 | 7,466 | 5,076 | 4,223 | 4,640 |
| Capital Expenditures | 4,260 | 2,005 | 1,144 | 1,091 | 735 | 657 | 260 | 176 | 164 | 174 |
| Cash Flow | 27,736 | 15,040 | 8,969 | 5,307 | 3,813 | 2,214 | 1,514 | 426 | 181 | 183 |
| Current Ratio | 1.6 | 2.0 | 2.7 | 2.5 | 2.4 | 2.2 | 3.0 | 2.6 | 2.5 | 3.2 |
| % Long Term Debt of Capitalization | Nil | Nil | Nil | Nil | Nil | Nil | Nil | Nil | Nil | 6.8 |
| % Net Income of Revenue | 24.0 | 21.5 | 19.2 | 14.9 | 14.6 | 10.3 | 9.6 | 3.3 | 1.1 | 1.1 |
| % Return on Assets | 27.1 | 21.7 | 19.7 | 14.9 | 16.4 | 13.9 | 13.6 | 3.7 | 1.0 | 1.1 |
| % Return on Equity | 41.7 | 37.1 | 30.5 | 27.2 | 28.5 | 22.8 | 21.3 | 5.9 | 1.6 | 1.6 |

Data as orig reptd.; bef. results of disc opers/spec. items. Per share data adj. for stk. divs.; EPS diluted. 2009 data as amended from SEC Form 10-K/A to reflect application of new accounting principles. E-Estimated. NA-Not Available. NM-Not Meaningful. NR-Not Ranked. UR-Under Review.

**Office:** 1 Infinite Loop, Cupertino, CA 95014.
**Telephone:** 408-996-1010.
**Email:** investor_relations@apple.com
**Website:** http://www.apple.com

**Chrmn:** A.D. Levinson
**CEO:** T.D. Cook
**COO:** J.E. Williams
**Investor Contact:** P. Oppenheimer (408-974-3123)

**SVP & CFO:** P. Oppenheimer
**Board Members:** W. V. Campbell, T. D. Cook, M. S. Drexler, A. A. Gore, Jr., R. A. Iger, A. Jung, A. D. Levinson, R. D. Sugar

**Founded:** 1977
**Domicile:** California
**Employees:** 63,300

# Applied Materials Inc

STANDARD
&POOR'S

| S&P Recommendation | STRONG BUY ★★★★★ | Price $10.16 (as of Nov 25, 2011) | 12-Mo. Target Price $16.00 | Investment Style Large-Cap Blend |
|---|---|---|---|---|

**GICS Sector** Information Technology
**Sub-Industry** Semiconductor Equipment

**Summary** This company is the world's largest manufacturer of wafer fabrication equipment for the semiconductor industry.

## Key Stock Statistics (Source S&P, Vickers, company reports)

| | | | | | | | |
|---|---|---|---|---|---|---|---|
| 52-Wk Range | $16.93–9.70 | S&P Oper. EPS 2012E | 0.80 | Market Capitalization(B) | $13.386 | Beta | 1.10 |
| Trailing 12-Month EPS | $1.45 | S&P Oper. EPS 2013E | 1.17 | Yield (%) | 3.15 | S&P 3-Yr. Proj. EPS CAGR(%) | 2 |
| Trailing 12-Month P/E | 7.0 | P/E on S&P Oper. EPS 2012E | 12.7 | Dividend Rate/Share | $0.32 | S&P Credit Rating | A- |
| $10K Invested 5 Yrs Ago | $6,029 | Common Shares Outstg. (M) | 1,317.5 | Institutional Ownership (%) | 81 | | |

## Price Performance

30-Week Mov. Avg. ··· 10-Week Mov. Avg. – – GAAP Earnings vs. Previous Year   Volume Above Avg. STARS
12-Mo. Target Price — Relative Strength — ▲ Up ▼ Down ► No Change   Below Avg.

Options: ASE, CBOE, P, Ph

Analysis prepared by Equity Analyst **Angelo Zino, CFA** on Nov 21, 2011, when the stock traded at **$10.91**.

## Highlights

▶ We project that sales will decline 15% in FY 12 (Oct.) but rise 15% in FY 13, following a 10% rise in FY 11. Despite a cyclical correction in the semiconductor equipment industry, we think orders have bottomed, and we expect FY 12 results to be aided by the acquisition of Varian Semiconductor Equipment. While we think flat panel display and solar equipment revenues will remain depressed near term, we believe orders for these segments have both troughed, albeit at very low levels. We view flash memory spending as the biggest long term driver to chip equipment sales.

▶ We forecast annual gross margins of 40% in FY 12 and 41% in FY 13, compared to 42% in FY 11. Despite lower expected sales, we think AMAT will try to maintain margins through tight cost controls, and we see restructuring efforts supporting margins. In addition, we expect Varian's better margin profile and potential cost synergies to aid results. We forecast 18% and 22% operating margins in FY 12 and FY 13.

▶ We estimate operating EPS of $0.80 for FY 12 and $1.17 for FY 13, with modest share repurchases aiding results.

## Investment Rationale/Risk

▶ Our strong buy opinion reflects valuation and our view of bottoming fundamentals. Given a more than 80% plunge in both display and solar equipment segment orders in recent quarters, we think orders are likely in a bottoming process. In addition, chip equipment orders have fallen more than 45% over the past two quarters, and we expect improvement in this category as calendar 2012 progresses. Longer term, we see healthy end-demand driving orders for flash memory devices such as tablets and smartphones. We think lower selling prices for solar modules in the coming months will enhance project returns and improve the excess industry supply scenario.

▶ Risks to our recommendation and target price include a slowdown in the global economy, which could weaken demand for chips and increase pricing pressures.

▶ We derive our 12-month target price of $16 by applying a blend of our peer-premium P/E and price/sales (P/S) multiples. We apply a multiple of 16X to our calendar year 2012 EPS estimate of $0.91 to obtain a $15 value. We derive a $17 value by applying a 2.4X multiple to our calendar year 2012 sales per share forecast of $7.14.

## Qualitative Risk Assessment

| LOW | MEDIUM | HIGH |
|---|---|---|

Our risk assessment reflects the historical cyclicality of the semiconductor equipment industry, a lack of visibility in the intermediate term, the dynamic nature of changes in semiconductor technology, and intense competition. This is offset by AMAT's market leadership, size, and what we see as its solid balance sheet.

## Quantitative Evaluations

**S&P Quality Ranking**  B

| D | C | B- | B | B+ | A- | A | A+ |
|---|---|---|---|---|---|---|---|

**Relative Strength Rank**  WEAK

25

LOWEST = 1   HIGHEST = 99

## Revenue/Earnings Data

**Revenue (Million $)**

| | 1Q | 2Q | 3Q | 4Q | Year |
|---|---|---|---|---|---|
| 2011 | 2,686 | 2,862 | 2,787 | 2,182 | 10,517 |
| 2010 | 1,849 | 2,296 | 2,518 | 2,886 | 9,549 |
| 2009 | 1,333 | 1,020 | 1,134 | 1,526 | 5,014 |
| 2008 | 2,087 | 2,150 | 1,848 | 2,044 | 8,129 |
| 2007 | 2,277 | 2,530 | 2,561 | 2,367 | 9,735 |
| 2006 | 1,858 | 2,248 | 2,543 | 2,518 | 9,167 |

**Earnings Per Share ($)**

| | | | | | |
|---|---|---|---|---|---|
| 2011 | 0.38 | 0.37 | 0.36 | 0.34 | 1.45 |
| 2010 | 0.06 | 0.20 | 0.09 | 0.35 | 0.70 |
| 2009 | -0.10 | -0.19 | -0.04 | 0.10 | -0.23 |
| 2008 | 0.19 | 0.22 | 0.12 | 0.17 | 0.70 |
| 2007 | 0.29 | 0.29 | 0.12 | 0.30 | 1.20 |
| 2006 | 0.09 | 0.26 | 0.33 | 0.30 | 0.97 |

Fiscal year ended Oct. 31. Next earnings report expected: Late February. EPS Estimates based on S&P Operating Earnings; historical GAAP earnings are as reported.

## Dividend Data (Dates: mm/dd Payment Date: mm/dd/yy)

| Amount ($) | Date Decl. | Ex-Div. Date | Stk. of Record | Payment Date |
|---|---|---|---|---|
| 0.070 | 12/08 | 02/28 | 03/02 | 03/23/11 |
| 0.080 | 03/08 | 05/27 | 06/01 | 06/22/11 |
| 0.080 | 06/07 | 08/29 | 08/31 | 09/21/11 |
| 0.080 | 09/13 | 11/21 | 11/23 | 12/14/11 |

Dividends have been paid since 2005. Source: Company reports.

---

**Please read the Required Disclosures and Analyst Certification on the last page of this report.**

The McGraw-Hill Companies

# Applied Materials Inc

STANDARD
&POOR'S

## Business Summary November 21, 2011

CORPORATE OVERVIEW. At the end of FY 10 (Oct.), Applied Materials (AMAT) was the worldwide leader in the manufacturing of semiconductor capital equipment. AMAT divides its business into four segments: Silicon Systems Group, Applied Global Services, Display, and Energy and Environmental Solutions. The Silicon Systems Group, which accounted for 55% of FY 10 sales (39% in FY 09), is focused on developing and selling equipment for use in the front end of the semiconductor fabrication process. The silicon segment includes semiconductor capital equipment for etch, rapid thermal processing, deposition, chemical mechanical planarization, and metrology and inspection. AMAT's equipment in the silicon segment addresses most of the primary steps in chip fabrication.

The Applied Global Services segment, which represented 20% (28%) of FY 10 sales, provides solutions to optimize and increase productivity at customers fabs (semiconductor fabrication facilities). The segment includes products and services to improve the efficiency and reduce operating costs at semiconductor, display and solar customer factories. Applied Global Services products consist of spares, services, certain earlier generation products, and remanufactured equipment.

The Display segment, which comprised for 9% (10%) of FY 10 sales, develops equipment for the fabrication of flat panel displays. The segment develops equipment for manufacturing Liquid Crystal Displays (LCD's) for TVs, personal computers and other video-enabled devices. The Display segment also includes the design and manufacture of differentiated stand-alone equipment for the Applied SunFab Thin Film Line.

The Energy and Environmental Solutions segment accounted for 16% (23%) of sales in FY 10, and includes products targeting the solar photovoltaic (PV) cell market and energy efficient glass. AMAT offers manufacturing solutions for both wafer-based crystalline silicon (c-Si) and glass-based thin film applications to enable customers to increase the conversion efficiency and yields of PV devices.

## Company Financials Fiscal Year Ended Oct. 31

| Per Share Data ($) | 2011 | 2010 | 2009 | 2008 | 2007 | 2006 | 2005 | 2004 | 2003 | 2002 |
|---|---|---|---|---|---|---|---|---|---|---|
| Tangible Book Value | NA | 4.45 | 4.19 | 4.50 | 4.65 | 5.80 | 5.30 | 5.33 | 4.62 | 4.67 |
| Cash Flow | 1.63 | 0.92 | -0.01 | 0.93 | 1.39 | 1.14 | 0.91 | 0.99 | 0.14 | 0.39 |
| Earnings | 1.45 | 0.70 | -0.23 | 0.70 | 1.20 | 0.97 | 0.73 | 0.78 | -0.09 | 0.16 |
| S&P Core Earnings | NA | 0.69 | -0.19 | 0.69 | 1.20 | 0.97 | 0.54 | 0.59 | -0.33 | -0.04 |
| Dividends | 0.30 | 0.26 | 0.24 | 0.24 | 0.22 | 0.16 | 0.06 | Nil | Nil | Nil |
| Payout Ratio | 21% | 37% | NM | 34% | 18% | 16% | 8% | Nil | Nil | Nil |
| Prices:High | 16.93 | 14.94 | 14.22 | 21.75 | 23.00 | 21.06 | 19.47 | 24.75 | 25.94 | 27.95 |
| Prices:Low | 9.70 | 10.27 | 8.19 | 7.17 | 17.35 | 14.39 | 14.33 | 15.36 | 11.25 | 10.26 |
| P/E Ratio:High | 12 | 21 | NM | 31 | 19 | 22 | 27 | 32 | NM | NM |
| P/E Ratio:Low | 7 | 15 | NM | 10 | 14 | 15 | 20 | 20 | NM | NM |

| Income Statement Analysis (Million $) | | | | | | | | | | |
|---|---|---|---|---|---|---|---|---|---|---|
| Revenue | 10,517 | 9,549 | 5,014 | 8,129 | 9,735 | 9,167 | 6,992 | 8,013 | 4,477 | 5,062 |
| Operating Income | 2,587 | 1,934 | 53.4 | 1,695 | 2,665 | 2,517 | 1,748 | 2,313 | 440 | 683 |
| Depreciation | 246 | 305 | 291 | 320 | 268 | 270 | 300 | 356 | 382 | 388 |
| Interest Expense | 59.0 | 21.5 | 21.3 | 20.5 | 38.6 | 36.1 | 37.8 | 52.9 | 46.9 | 49.4 |
| Pretax Income | 2,378 | 1,387 | -486 | 1,409 | 2,440 | 2,167 | 1,582 | 1,829 | -212 | 341 |
| Effective Tax Rate | NA | NA | NM | 31.8% | 29.9% | 30.0% | 23.5% | 26.1% | NM | 21.0% |
| Net Income | 1,926 | 938 | -305 | 961 | 1,710 | 1,517 | 1,210 | 1,351 | -149 | 269 |
| S&P Core Earnings | NA | 930 | -256 | 936 | 1,710 | 1,511 | 905 | 1,017 | -562 | -65.2 |

| Balance Sheet & Other Financial Data (Million $) | | | | | | | | | | |
|---|---|---|---|---|---|---|---|---|---|---|
| Cash | 6,243 | 2,585 | 2,215 | 2,101 | 1,203 | 861 | 990 | 2,282 | 1,365 | 1,285 |
| Current Assets | 10,355 | 6,765 | 5,689 | 6,664 | 6,606 | 6,081 | 9,449 | 10,282 | 8,371 | 8,073 |
| Total Assets | 13,861 | 10,943 | 9,574 | 10,906 | 10,654 | 9,481 | 11,269 | 12,093 | 10,312 | 10,225 |
| Current Liabilities | 2,794 | 2,888 | 1,939 | 2,946 | 2,373 | 2,436 | 1,765 | 2,288 | 1,641 | 1,501 |
| Long Term Debt | 1,947 | 204 | 201 | 202 | 202 | 205 | 407 | 410 | 456 | 574 |
| Common Equity | 8,800 | 7,536 | 7,095 | 7,449 | 7,821 | 6,651 | 8,929 | 9,262 | 8,068 | 8,020 |
| Total Capital | 10,747 | 7,742 | 7,297 | 7,808 | 8,023 | 6,856 | 9,336 | 9,672 | 8,524 | 8,594 |
| Capital Expenditures | 209 | 169 | 248 | 288 | 265 | 179 | 200 | 191 | 265 | 417 |
| Cash Flow | 2,172 | 1,242 | -14.1 | 1,281 | 1,978 | 1,787 | 1,510 | 1,707 | 233 | 657 |
| Current Ratio | 3.7 | 2.3 | 2.9 | 2.3 | 2.8 | 2.5 | 5.4 | 4.5 | 5.1 | 5.4 |
| % Long Term Debt of Capitalization | 18.1 | 2.6 | 2.8 | 2.6 | 2.5 | 3.0 | 4.4 | 4.2 | 5.4 | 6.7 |
| % Net Income of Revenue | 18.3 | 9.8 | NM | 11.8 | 17.5 | 16.5 | 17.3 | 16.9 | NM | 5.3 |
| % Return on Assets | 15.5 | 9.1 | NM | 8.9 | 16.9 | 14.6 | 10.4 | 12.1 | NM | 2.7 |
| % Return on Equity | 23.6 | 12.8 | NM | 12.6 | 23.6 | 19.5 | 13.3 | 15.6 | NM | 3.4 |

Data as orig reptd.; bef. results of disc opers/spec. items. Per share data adj. for stk. divs.; EPS diluted. E-Estimated. NA-Not Available. NM-Not Meaningful. NR-Not Ranked. UR-Under Review.

**Office:** 3050 Bowers Avenue, Santa Clara, CA 95054-3299.
**Telephone:** 408-727-5555.
**Email:** investor_relations@appliedmaterials.com
**Website:** http://www.appliedmaterials.com

**Chrmn, Pres & CEO:** M.R. Splinter
**COO:** J.G. Flanagan
**SVP, Secy & General Counsel:** J.J. Sweeney
**CFO:** G.S. Davis

**CTO:** O. Nalamasu
**Auditor:** KPMG
**Board Members:** S. R. Forrest, T. J. Iannotti, S. M. James, A. A. Karsner, G. H. Parker, D. D. Powell, W. P. Roelandts, J. E. Rogers, Jr., M. R. Splinter, R. H. Swan, A. J. de Geus

**Founded:** 1967
**Domicile:** Delaware
**Employees:** 13,045

# Archer-Daniels-Midland Co

**STANDARD &POOR'S**

| S&P Recommendation | HOLD ★★★★★ | Price $27.90 (as of Nov 25, 2011) | 12-Mo. Target Price $31.00 | Investment Style Large-Cap Blend |
|---|---|---|---|---|

**GICS Sector** Consumer Staples
**Sub-Industry** Agricultural Products

**Summary** This company is one of the world's leading agribusiness concerns, with major market positions in agricultural processing and merchandising.

## Key Stock Statistics (Source S&P, Vickers, company reports)

| | | | | | | | |
|---|---|---|---|---|---|---|---|
| 52-Wk Range | $38.02– 23.69 | S&P Oper. EPS 2012**E** | 3.00 | Market Capitalization(B) | $18.637 | Beta | 0.45 |
| Trailing 12-Month EPS | $3.26 | S&P Oper. EPS 2013**E** | NA | Yield (%) | 2.51 | S&P 3-Yr. Proj. EPS CAGR(%) | 6 |
| Trailing 12-Month P/E | 8.6 | P/E on S&P Oper. EPS 2012**E** | 9.3 | Dividend Rate/Share | $0.70 | S&P Credit Rating | A |
| $10K Invested 5 Yrs Ago | $9,111 | Common Shares Outstg. (M) | 668.0 | Institutional Ownership (%) | 70 | | |

## Price Performance

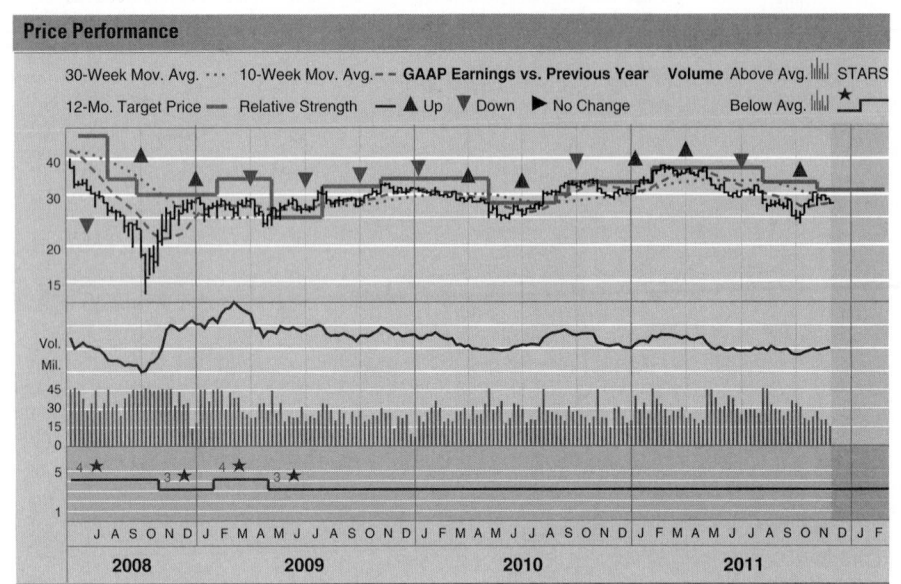

30-Week Mov. Avg. ···· 10-Week Mov. Avg. – – GAAP Earnings vs. Previous Year  Volume Above Avg. ||||| STARS
12-Mo. Target Price — Relative Strength — ▲ Up ▼ Down ▶ No Change  Below Avg. ||||| ★

Options: ASE, CBOE, P, Ph

## Qualitative Risk Assessment

| LOW | MEDIUM | HIGH |
|---|---|---|

Our risk assessment reflects the company's exposure to volatile commodity industry conditions, and moderately aggressive financial policies and leverage levels given the inherent cyclicality of the company's agricultural operations.

## Quantitative Evaluations

**S&P Quality Ranking** A

| D | C | B- | B | B+ | A- | **A** | A+ |
|---|---|---|---|---|---|---|---|

**Relative Strength Rank** STRONG

71

LOWEST = 1          HIGHEST = 99

## Revenue/Earnings Data

**Revenue (Million $)**

| | 1Q | 2Q | 3Q | 4Q | Year |
|---|---|---|---|---|---|
| 2012 | 21,902 | -- | -- | -- | -- |
| 2011 | 16,799 | 20,930 | 20,077 | 22,870 | 80,676 |
| 2010 | 14,921 | 15,913 | 15,145 | 15,703 | 61,682 |
| 2009 | 21,160 | 16,673 | 14,842 | 16,532 | 69,207 |
| 2008 | 12,828 | 16,496 | 18,708 | 21,784 | 69,816 |
| 2007 | 9,447 | 10,976 | 11,381 | 12,214 | 44,018 |

**Earnings Per Share ($)**

| | | | | | |
|---|---|---|---|---|---|
| 2012 | 0.68 | E0.82 | E0.80 | E0.80 | E3.00 |
| 2011 | 0.54 | 1.14 | 0.86 | 0.58 | 3.13 |
| 2010 | 0.77 | 0.88 | 0.65 | 0.69 | 3.00 |
| 2009 | 1.63 | 0.91 | 0.01 | 0.10 | 2.65 |
| 2008 | 0.68 | 0.73 | 0.80 | 0.58 | 2.79 |
| 2007 | 0.61 | 0.67 | 0.56 | 1.47 | 3.30 |

Fiscal year ended Jun. 30. Next earnings report expected: Early February. EPS Estimates based on S&P Operating Earnings; historical GAAP earnings are as reported.

## Highlights

▶ The 12-month target price for ADM has recently been changed to $31.00 from $33.00. The Highlights section of this Stock Report will be updated accordingly.

## Investment Rationale/Risk

▶ The Investment Rationale/Risk section of this Stock Report will be updated shortly. For the latest News story on ADM from MarketScope, see below.

▶ 11/01/11 10:45 am ET ... S&P REITERATES HOLD OPINION ON SHARES OF ARCHER DANIELS MIDLAND (ADM 28.13***): Before some special items, Sep-Q EPS of $0.58, vs. $0.67, is $0.07 below our estimate. The weakest profit comparison was in corn processing; net corn costs more than doubled, including an impact from earlier hedging benefits. Before some special items, we reduce our FY 12 (Jun) EPS forecast to $3.00 from $3.15. Long term, we expect ADM to benefit from growing global demand for global protein meal and vegetable oil, with increased agricultural trade. However, with a lower EPS projection for FY 12, we are cutting our target price to $31 from $33. Indicated dividend yield is 2.3%. /Tom Graves, CFA

## Dividend Data (Dates: mm/dd Payment Date: mm/dd/yy)

| Amount ($) | Date Decl. | Ex-Div. Date | Stk. of Record | Payment Date |
|---|---|---|---|---|
| 0.160 | 05/05 | 05/17 | 05/19 | 06/09/11 |
| 0.160 | 08/04 | 08/16 | 08/18 | 09/08/11 |
| 0.175 | 11/03 | 11/15 | 11/17 | 12/08/11 |
| 0.175 | 11/03 | 11/15 | 11/17 | 12/08/11 |

Dividends have been paid since 1927. Source: Company reports.

# Archer-Daniels-Midland Co

## Business Summary September 19, 2011

Archer Daniels Midland Company engages in procuring, transporting, storing, processing and merchandising agricultural commodities and products.

The company operates in four business segments: Oilseeds Processing (33% of FY 11 (Jun.) net sales and other operating income; 38% of segment operating profit), Corn Processing (12%; 26%), Agricultural Services (47%; 23%), and Other (8%; 13%).

The Oilseeds Processing segment includes activities related to oilseeds such as soybeans, cottonseed, sunflower seeds, canola, rapeseed and flaxseed. This segment produces processed oilseed products as ingredients for the food, feed, energy and other industrial products industries.

Crude vegetable oil is sold 'as is' or is further processed by refining, blending, bleaching and deodorizing into salad oils. Salad oils are sold 'as is' or are further processed by hydrogenating and/or interesterifying into margarine, shortening, and other food products. Partially refined oil is used to produce

biodiesel or is sold to other manufacturers for use in chemicals, paints, and other industrial products.

Oilseed protein meals are principally sold to third parties to be used as ingredients in commercial livestock and poultry feeds. ADM also produces natural health and nutrition products and other specialty food and feed ingredients, produces cottonseed flour that is sold primarily to the pharmaceutical industry, and cotton cellulose pulp that is sold to the chemical, paper and filter markets. In Europe and South America, the Oilseeds Processing segment includes a network of grain elevators, port facilities and transportation assets to buy, store, clean and transport agricultural commodities. In South America, the segment operates fertilizer blending facilities.

## Company Financials Fiscal Year Ended Jun. 30

| Per Share Data ($) | 2011 | 2010 | 2009 | 2008 | 2007 | 2006 | 2005 | 2004 | 2003 | 2002 |
|---|---|---|---|---|---|---|---|---|---|---|
| Tangible Book Value | 26.93 | 22.04 | 20.20 | 20.16 | 17.01 | 14.47 | 12.47 | 11.31 | 10.43 | 10.39 |
| Cash Flow | 4.43 | 4.41 | 3.80 | 3.91 | 4.36 | 3.00 | 2.60 | 1.82 | 1.69 | 1.64 |
| Earnings | 3.13 | 3.00 | 2.65 | 2.79 | 3.30 | 2.00 | 1.59 | 0.76 | 0.70 | 0.78 |
| S&P Core Earnings | 3.17 | 3.03 | 2.50 | 2.64 | 2.31 | 2.02 | 1.53 | 1.14 | 0.61 | 0.55 |
| Dividends | 0.62 | 0.58 | 0.54 | 0.49 | 0.43 | 0.37 | 0.32 | 0.27 | 0.24 | 0.20 |
| Payout Ratio | 20% | 19% | 20% | 18% | 13% | 19% | 20% | 36% | 34% | 25% |
| Prices:High | 38.02 | 34.03 | 33.00 | 48.95 | 47.33 | 46.71 | 25.55 | 22.55 | 15.24 | 14.85 |
| Prices:Low | 23.69 | 24.22 | 23.13 | 13.53 | 30.20 | 24.05 | 17.50 | 14.90 | 10.50 | 10.00 |
| P/E Ratio:High | 12 | 11 | 12 | 18 | 14 | 23 | 16 | 30 | 22 | 19 |
| P/E Ratio:Low | 8 | 8 | 9 | 5 | 9 | 12 | 11 | 20 | 15 | 13 |

| Income Statement Analysis (Million $) | | | | | | | | | | |
|---|---|---|---|---|---|---|---|---|---|---|
| Revenue | 80,676 | 61,682 | 69,207 | 69,816 | 44,018 | 36,596 | 35,944 | 36,151 | 30,708 | 23,454 |
| Operating Income | 3,566 | 3,357 | 3,420 | 3,188 | 2,743 | 2,450 | 2,015 | 1,432 | 1,423 | 1,424 |
| Depreciation | 877 | 912 | 743 | 721 | 701 | 657 | 665 | 686 | 644 | 567 |
| Interest Expense | 482 | 422 | 430 | 529 | Nil | 365 | Nil | Nil | Nil | 356 |
| Pretax Income | 3,015 | 2,585 | 2,534 | 2,624 | 3,154 | 1,855 | 1,516 | 718 | 631 | 719 |
| Effective Tax Rate | NA | NA | 32.6% | 31.3% | 31.5% | 29.3% | 31.1% | 31.1% | 28.5% | 28.9% |
| Net Income | 2,018 | 1,930 | 1,707 | 1,802 | 2,162 | 1,312 | 1,044 | 495 | 451 | 511 |
| S&P Core Earnings | 2,059 | 1,952 | 1,615 | 1,706 | 1,508 | 1,322 | 1,001 | 739 | 397 | 363 |

| Balance Sheet & Other Financial Data (Million $) | | | | | | | | | | |
|---|---|---|---|---|---|---|---|---|---|---|
| Cash | 615 | 1,046 | 1,055 | 1,265 | 2,087 | 2,334 | 1,430 | 1,412 | 765 | 844 |
| Current Assets | 16,339 | 18,134 | 19,408 | 25,455 | 15,122 | 11,826 | 9,711 | 10,339 | 8,422 | 7,363 |
| Total Assets | 31,028 | 23,693 | 23,104 | 25,790 | 25,118 | 21,269 | 18,598 | 19,369 | 17,183 | 15,416 |
| Current Liabilities | 1,875 | 8,573 | 8,885 | 14,621 | 7,868 | 6,165 | 5,367 | 6,750 | 5,147 | 4,719 |
| Long Term Debt | 8,444 | 7,174 | 7,848 | 7,690 | 4,752 | 4,050 | 3,530 | 3,740 | 3,872 | 3,111 |
| Common Equity | 18,838 | 14,631 | 13,499 | 13,490 | 11,253 | 9,807 | 8,433 | 7,698 | 7,069 | 6,755 |
| Total Capital | 27,282 | 21,805 | 21,577 | 21,653 | 16,537 | 14,614 | 12,743 | 12,092 | 11,485 | 10,498 |
| Capital Expenditures | 1,247 | 1,607 | 1,898 | 1,779 | 1,198 | 762 | 624 | 509 | 420 | 350 |
| Cash Flow | 2,895 | 2,842 | 2,450 | 2,523 | 2,863 | 1,969 | 1,709 | 1,180 | 1,095 | 1,078 |
| Current Ratio | 8.7 | 2.1 | 30.7 | 1.7 | 1.9 | 1.9 | 1.8 | 1.5 | 1.6 | 1.6 |
| % Long Term Debt of Capitalization | 31.0 | 32.9 | 36.4 | 35.5 | 28.7 | 27.7 | 27.7 | 30.9 | 33.7 | 29.6 |
| % Net Income of Revenue | 2.5 | 3.1 | 2.5 | 2.6 | 4.9 | 3.6 | 2.9 | 1.4 | 1.5 | 2.2 |
| % Return on Assets | 6.5 | 7.0 | 5.7 | 7.1 | 9.3 | 6.6 | 5.5 | 2.7 | 2.8 | 3.4 |
| % Return on Equity | 12.1 | 13.7 | 12.7 | 14.6 | 20.5 | 14.4 | 12.9 | 6.7 | 6.5 | 7.8 |

Data as orig reptd.; bef. results of disc opers/spec. items. Per share data adj. for stk. divs.; EPS diluted. E-Estimated. NA-Not Available. NM-Not Meaningful. NR-Not Ranked. UR-Under Review.

**Office:** 4666 Faries Parkway, Box 1470, Decatur, IL 62526.
**Telephone:** 217-424-5200.
**Website:** http://www.admworld.com
**Chrmn, Pres & CEO:** P.A. Woertz

**COO & EVP:** J.R. Luciano
**EVP, Secy & General Counsel:** D.J. Smith
**SVP & CFO:** R.G. Young
**Treas:** V. Luthar

**Investor Contact:** D. Grimestad (217-424-4586)
**Board Members:** G. W. Buckley, M. H. Carter, T. K. Crews, P. Dufour, D. E. Felsinger, V. F. Haynes, P. J. Moore, A. M. Neto, T. F. O'Neill, K. R. Westbrook, P. A. Woertz

**Auditor:** ERNST & YOUNG
**Founded:** 1898
**Domicile:** Delaware
**Employees:** 30,700

# Assurant Inc.

**STANDARD &POOR'S**

| S&P Recommendation **HOLD** ★★★★☆ | Price $36.22 (as of Nov 25, 2011) | 12-Mo. Target Price $42.00 | Investment Style Large-Cap Value |
|---|---|---|---|

**GICS Sector** Financials
**Sub-Industry** Multi-line Insurance

**Summary** This company pursues a differentiated strategy of building leading positions in niche insurance markets.

## Key Stock Statistics (Source S&P, Vickers, company reports)

| | | | | | | | |
|---|---|---|---|---|---|---|---|
| 52-Wk Range | $41.90–30.65 | S&P Oper. EPS 2011**E** | 4.23 | Market Capitalization(B) | $3.336 | Beta | 1.34 |
| Trailing 12-Month EPS | $1.97 | S&P Oper. EPS 2012**E** | 5.40 | Yield (%) | 1.99 | S&P 3-Yr. Proj. EPS CAGR(%) | 3 |
| Trailing 12-Month P/E | 18.4 | P/E on S&P Oper. EPS 2011**E** | 8.6 | Dividend Rate/Share | $0.72 | S&P Credit Rating | BBB |
| $10K Invested 5 Yrs Ago | $7,185 | Common Shares Outstg. (M) | 92.1 | Institutional Ownership (%) | 91 | | |

## Price Performance

30-Week Mov. Avg. · · · 10-Week Mov. Avg. - - GAAP Earnings vs. Previous Year  Volume Above Avg. STARS
12-Mo. Target Price — Relative Strength — ▲ Up ▼ Down ► No Change  Below Avg. ★

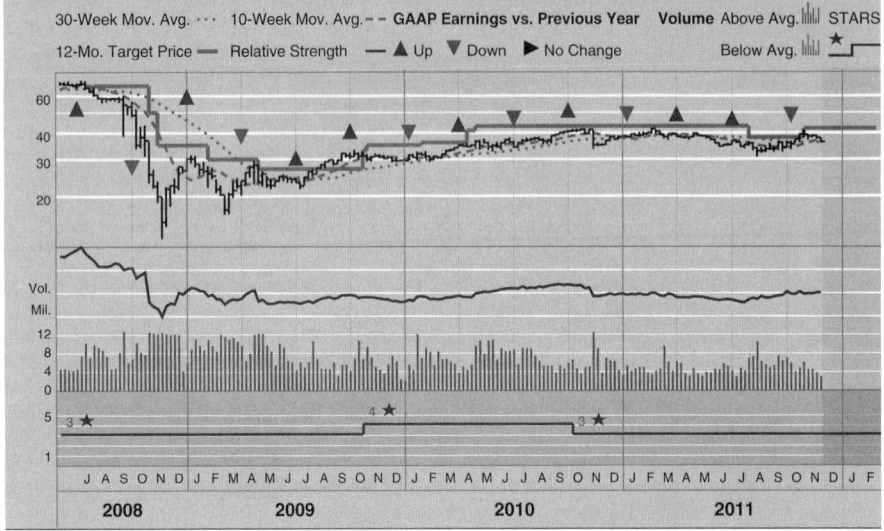

Options: ASE, CBOE, P, Ph

## Qualitative Risk Assessment

| LOW | **MEDIUM** | HIGH |
|---|---|---|

Our risk assessment reflects the difficult operating environment for Assurant's Health and Specialty Property segments. Also, AIZ's Solutions business remains vulnerable to weak consumer spending. However, in our view, AIZ has a solid track record of disciplined capital management, and we believe the company's balance sheet is more conservatively positioned versus peers due to less debt and more conservative investment holdings.

## Quantitative Evaluations

**S&P Quality Ranking** NR

| D | C | B- | B | B+ | A- | A | A+ |
|---|---|---|---|---|---|---|---|

**Relative Strength Rank** MODERATE

70

LOWEST = 1     HIGHEST = 99

## Highlights

> The 12-month target price for AIZ has recently been changed to $42.00 from $38.00. The Highlights section of this Stock Report will be updated accordingly.

## Investment Rationale/Risk

> The Investment Rationale/Risk section of this Stock Report will be updated shortly. For the latest News story on AIZ from MarketScope, see below.

> 10/27/11 03:44 pm ET ... S&P KEEPS HOLD OPINION ON SHARES OF ASSURANT INC. (AIZ 39.92***): AIZ reports Q3 operating EPS of $0.79, vs. $1.27, below our $0.87 estimate, largely due to higher catastrophe claims in its Specialty Property unit. We are lowering our full year 2011 operating EPS forecast to $4.23 from $4.31 to reflect these reuslts. Our $42 target price assumes the shares trade at just under 8X our $5.40 operating EPS estimate for 2012, about the midpoint of its historical average. /C. Seifert

## Revenue/Earnings Data

### Revenue (Million $)

| | 1Q | 2Q | 3Q | 4Q | Year |
|---|---|---|---|---|---|
| 2011 | 2,037 | 2,063 | 2,062 | -- | -- |
| 2010 | 2,168 | 2,140 | 2,114 | 2,106 | 8,528 |
| 2009 | 2,088 | 2,274 | 2,157 | 2,182 | 8,701 |
| 2008 | 2,177 | 2,249 | 1,955 | 2,221 | 8,601 |
| 2007 | 2,057 | 2,065 | 2,148 | 2,183 | 8,454 |
| 2006 | 1,930 | 1,949 | 1,984 | 2,208 | 8,071 |

### Earnings Per Share ($)

| | | | | | |
|---|---|---|---|---|---|
| 2011 | 1.39 | 1.68 | 0.79 | E1.31 | E4.23 |
| 2010 | 1.34 | 1.46 | 1.30 | -1.74 | 2.50 |
| 2009 | 0.68 | 1.63 | 1.22 | 0.10 | 3.63 |
| 2008 | 1.57 | 1.59 | -0.95 | 1.55 | 3.77 |
| 2007 | 1.45 | 1.36 | 1.56 | 1.01 | 5.38 |
| 2006 | 1.22 | 1.16 | 1.18 | 2.01 | 5.56 |

Fiscal year ended Dec. 31. Next earnings report expected: Early February. EPS Estimates based on S&P Operating Earnings; historical GAAP earnings are as reported.

## Dividend Data (Dates: mm/dd Payment Date: mm/dd/yy)

| Amount ($) | Date Decl. | Ex-Div. Date | Stk. of Record | Payment Date |
|---|---|---|---|---|
| 0.160 | 01/14 | 02/24 | 02/28 | 03/14/11 |
| 0.180 | 05/13 | 05/19 | 05/23 | 06/07/11 |
| 0.180 | 07/07 | 08/25 | 08/29 | 09/13/11 |
| 0.180 | 11/11 | 11/23 | 11/28 | 12/12/11 |

Dividends have been paid since 2004. Source: Company reports.

# Assurant Inc.

STANDARD &POOR'S

## Business Summary September 16, 2011

Assurant, Inc. (AIZ) provides specialized insurance products and related services in North America and selected international markets. The company's segments include Assurant Solutions, Assurant Specialty Property, Assurant Health, and Assurant Employee Benefits. Assurant, Inc. was founded in 1969.

The Assurant Solutions Segment targets growth in three key product areas: extended service contracts (ESC) and warranties, both domestically and internationally; preneed life insurance and international credit insurance. In addition, the company offers debt protection/debt deferment services through financial institutions. Through partnerships with retailers, AIZ underwrites and provides administrative services for extended service contracts and warranties. Preneed life insurance allows individuals to prepay for a funeral in a single payment or in multiple payments over a fixed number of years. The company's credit insurance products offer protection from life events and uncertainties that arise in purchasing and borrowing transactions. Credit insurance programs generally offer consumers the option to protect a credit card balance or installment loan in the event of death, involuntary unemployment or disability. Debt protection/debt deferment is coverage offered by a lender with credit card accounts, installment loans and lines of credit. It waives or

defers all or a portion of the monthly payments, monthly interest, or the actual debt for the account holder for a covered event, such as death, disability, unemployment and family leave. The company, in addition to its domestic market, operates in Canada, the United Kingdom, Argentina, Brazil, Puerto Rico, Chile, Germany, Spain, Italy, Mexico and China. In these markets, AIZ primarily sells ESC and credit insurance products through agreements with financial institutions, retailers and wireless service providers.

The Assurant Specialty Property segment also offers manufactured housing insurance on a creditor-placed and voluntary basis. The company offers its manufactured housing insurance programs primarily through three channels: manufactured housing lenders; manufactured housing retailers and independent specialty agents. The independent specialty agents distribute flood products and miscellaneous specialty property products. Renters insurance is distributed primarily through property management companies.

## Company Financials Fiscal Year Ended Dec. 31

| Per Share Data ($) | 2010 | 2009 | 2008 | 2007 | 2006 | 2005 | 2004 | 2003 | 2002 | 2001 |
|---|---|---|---|---|---|---|---|---|---|---|
| Tangible Book Value | 37.74 | 31.11 | 19.06 | NM | 28.46 | 21.01 | 18.90 | 14.76 | NA | NA |
| Operating Earnings | NA | NA | NA | NA | NA | NA | NA | NA | NA | NA |
| Earnings | 2.50 | 3.63 | 3.77 | 5.38 | 5.56 | 3.50 | 2.53 | 1.70 | 31.29 | 11.81 |
| S&P Core Earnings | 4.97 | 4.18 | 5.79 | 5.60 | 4.77 | 3.49 | 2.50 | 1.72 | 38.61 | 15.43 |
| Dividends | 0.63 | 0.74 | 0.54 | 0.46 | 0.38 | 0.31 | 0.21 | NA | NA | NA |
| Relative Payout | 25% | 20% | 14% | 9% | 7% | 9% | 8% | NA | NA | NA |
| Prices:High | 41.87 | 33.37 | 71.31 | 69.77 | 56.78 | 44.68 | 31.29 | NA | NA | NA |
| Prices:Low | 29.08 | 16.34 | 12.52 | 45.27 | 42.72 | 29.70 | 22.00 | NA | NA | NA |
| P/E Ratio:High | 17 | 9 | 19 | 13 | 10 | 13 | 12 | NA | NA | NA |
| P/E Ratio:Low | 12 | 5 | 3 | 8 | 8 | 8 | 9 | NA | NA | NA |

| Income Statement Analysis (Million $) | 2010 | 2009 | 2008 | 2007 | 2006 | 2005 | 2004 | 2003 | 2002 | 2001 |
|---|---|---|---|---|---|---|---|---|---|---|
| Life Insurance in Force | 111,941 | 123,383 | 123,383 | 136,530 | 137,507 | 157,203 | 166,452 | 169,787 | 192,984 | 203,660 |
| Premium Income:Life A & H | 3,426 | 3,460 | 3,828 | 4,061 | 4,203 | 4,595 | 4,789 | 4,565 | 4,385 | 4,215 |
| Premium Income:Casualty/Property. | 3,977 | 4,091 | 4,097 | 3,347 | 2,641 | 1,926 | 1,694 | 1,591 | 1,297 | 1,027 |
| Net Investment Income | 703 | 699 | 774 | 799 | 737 | 687 | 635 | 607 | 632 | 712 |
| Total Revenue | 8,528 | 8,701 | 8,601 | 8,454 | 8,071 | 7,498 | 7,403 | 7,066 | 6,532 | 6,187 |
| Pretax Income | 606 | 710 | 563 | 1,011 | 1,096 | 656 | 536 | 259 | 370 | 206 |
| Net Operating Income | NA | NA | NA | NA | NA | NA | NA | NA | NA | NA |
| Net Income | 279 | 431 | 448 | 654 | 716 | 479 | 351 | 186 | 260 | 98.1 |
| S&P Core Earnings | 542 | 496 | 689 | 680 | 613 | 477 | 345 | 187 | 320 | 128 |

| Balance Sheet & Other Financial Data (Million $) | 2010 | 2009 | 2008 | 2007 | 2006 | 2005 | 2004 | 2003 | 2002 | 2001 |
|---|---|---|---|---|---|---|---|---|---|---|
| Cash & Equivalent | 1,151 | 1,474 | 1,185 | 954 | 1,125 | NA | NA | NA | 550 | 559 |
| Premiums Due | 1,298 | 508 | 513 | 580 | 612 | 455 | 435 | 368 | NA | NA |
| Investment Assets:Bonds | 10,613 | 9,967 | 8,591 | 10,126 | 9,118 | 8,962 | 9,178 | 8,729 | NA | NA |
| Investment Assets:Stocks | 467 | 513 | 475 | 636 | 742 | 693 | 527 | 456 | NA | NA |
| Investment Assets:Loans | 1,377 | 1,484 | 1,565 | 1,491 | 1,325 | 1,273 | 1,119 | 1,001 | NA | NA |
| Investment Assets:Total | 13,505 | 13,158 | 12,067 | 13,747 | 12,429 | 12,516 | 13,472 | 10,924 | 10,029 | 9,601 |
| Deferred Policy Costs | 2,493 | 2,505 | 2,651 | 2,895 | 2,398 | 2,022 | 1,648 | 1,394 | NA | NA |
| Total Assets | 26,397 | 25,842 | 24,515 | 26,750 | 25,165 | 25,365 | 24,504 | 23,728 | 22,924 | 24,450 |
| Debt | 972 | 972 | 972 | 972 | 972 | 972 | 972 | 1,946 | 975 | NA |
| Common Equity | 4,781 | 4,853 | 3,710 | 4,089 | 3,833 | 3,778 | 3,768 | 2,832 | 3,346 | 3,452 |
| Combined Loss-Expense Ratio | 73.3 | 74.7 | 76.4 | 92.0 | 91.4 | 90.8 | 92.4 | 93.3 | NA | NA |
| % Return on Revenue | 3.3 | 5.0 | 5.2 | 7.7 | 8.9 | 6.4 | 4.9 | 2.6 | 4.0 | 1.6 |
| % Return on Equity | 5.8 | 10.1 | 11.5 | 16.5 | 18.7 | 12.8 | 10.6 | 6.7 | NA | NA |
| % Investment Yield | 5.1 | 5.5 | 1.2 | 6.1 | 5.7 | 5.2 | 5.2 | 5.8 | 6.4 | 14.8 |

Data as orig reptd.; bef. results of disc opers/spec. items. Per share data adj. for stk. divs.; EPS diluted. E-Estimated. NA-Not Available. NM-Not Meaningful. NR-Not Ranked. UR-Under Review.

**Office:** One Chase Manhattan Plaza, 41st Floor, New York, NY 10005.
**Telephone:** 212-859-7000.
**Website:** http://www.assurant.com
**Chrmn:** E.D. Rosen

**Pres & CEO:** R.B. Pollock
**EVP & CFO:** M.J. Peninger
**EVP, Secy & General Counsel:** B.R. Schwartz
**SVP, Chief Acctg Officer & Cntlr:** J.A. Sondej

**Investor Contact:** M. Kivett (212-859-7029)
**Board Members:** H. L. Carver, J. N. Cento, E. Douglas, L. V. Jackson, D. B. Kelso, C. J. Koch, H. C. Mackin, R. B. Pollock, P. J. Reilly, E. D. Rosen, R. W. Stein, J. A. Swainson

**Founded:** 1969
**Domicile:** Delaware
**Employees:** 14,000

# AT&T Inc

**STANDARD &POOR'S**

| S&P Recommendation | **STRONG BUY** ★★★★☆ | Price | 12-Mo. Target Price | Investment Style |
|---|---|---|---|---|
| | | $27.41 (as of Nov 25, 2011) | $34.00 | Large-Cap Value |

**GICS Sector** Telecommunication Services
**Sub-Industry** Integrated Telecommunication Services

**Summary** AT&T Inc. (formerly SBC Communications) provides telephone and broadband service and holds full ownership of AT&T Mobility (formerly Cingular Wireless). AT&T plans to acquire T Mobile USA, subject to approvals, in 2012.

## Key Stock Statistics (Source S&P, Vickers, company reports)

| | | | | | | | |
|---|---|---|---|---|---|---|---|
| 52-Wk Range | $31.94–27.20 | S&P Oper. EPS 2011**E** | 2.32 | Market Capitalization(B) | $162.432 | Beta | 0.60 |
| Trailing 12-Month EPS | $1.97 | S&P Oper. EPS 2012**E** | 2.57 | Yield (%) | 6.28 | S&P 3-Yr. Proj. EPS CAGR(%) | 6 |
| Trailing 12-Month P/E | 13.9 | P/E on S&P Oper. EPS 2011**E** | 11.8 | Dividend Rate/Share | $1.72 | S&P Credit Rating | A- |
| $10K Invested 5 Yrs Ago | $10,982 | Common Shares Outstg. (M) | 5,926.0 | Institutional Ownership (%) | 58 | | |

## Price Performance

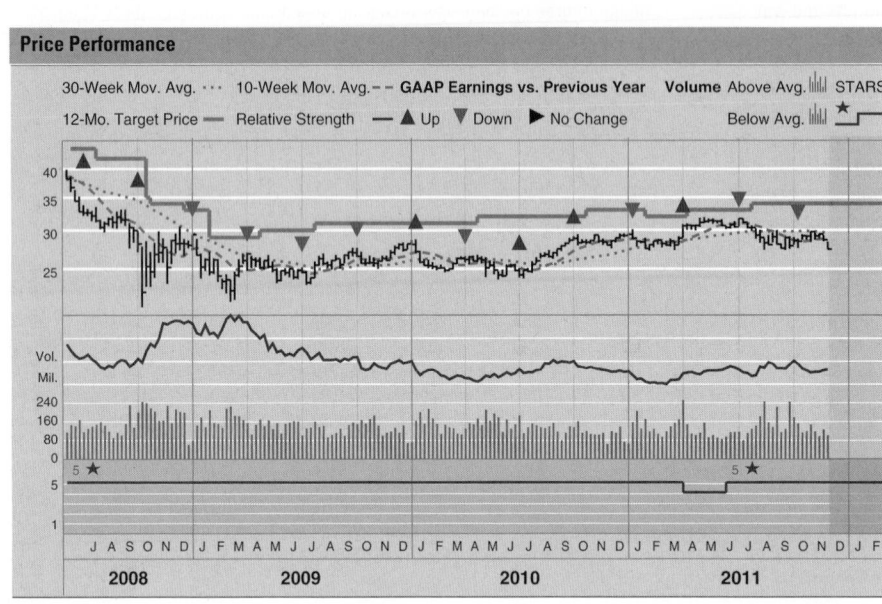

30-Week Mov. Avg. · · ·   10-Week Mov. Avg. – –  **GAAP Earnings vs. Previous Year**   Volume Above Avg. STARS
12-Mo. Target Price —   Relative Strength —   ▲ Up  ▼ Down  ► No Change   Below Avg. ★

2008   2009   2010   2011

Options: ASE, CBOE, P, Ph

Analysis prepared by Equity Analyst **Todd Rosenbluth** on Oct 24, 2011, when the stock traded at **$28.91**.

## Highlights

► We forecast that revenues will rise to $126 billion in 2011 and $128 billion in 2012, from $124 billion in 2010. We look for wireless revenue to advance 7% in 2011 and 4% in 2012, on customer additions and faster growth in wireless data services. Meanwhile, we expect wireline data gains, stemming from U-verse and enterprise operations, to help outweigh pressures in consumer and business voice operations.

► We see operating margins of 19% in 2011 and 20% in 2012. Despite high wireless handset subsidies offered to gain and retain smartphone customers and higher pension-related costs, we believe wireless data and U-verse are generating improved profitability, and we see further benefits from recent work force reductions. We expect capital spending, primarily focused on wireless backhaul, to increase in 2012.

► We estimate EPS of $2.32 for 2011 and $2.57 for 2012, with higher interest expenses. Our estimates do not reflect T's planned acquisition of T-Mobile USA assets that could close in the first half of 2012.

## Investment Rationale/Risk

► We see gains in consumer wireless and broadband continuing to offset some wireline voice pressure. Despite competition, we believe a strong balance sheet, long-term customer relationships and wide operating margins are positives. While we think regulatory objections to T's planned acquisition of T-Mobile USA assets represent a setback, we believe T will move forward and look for potential asset sales to complete the deal, which offers potential synergies. We view T's above-average dividend as secure and adding to total return potential.

► Risks to our recommendation and target price include balance sheet weakness, increased competition that leads to unexpected customer losses, and worse-than-projected wireless services execution.

► We view T as undervalued, recently trading at about 11X our 2012 EPS estimate, a discount to the 14X of telecom peers. Our 12-month target price of $34 is based on our relative analysis, which assumes a multiple of approximately 13X our 2012 EPS estimate to reflect T's strong industry leadership and above-average dividend yield, despite the risks we see.

## Qualitative Risk Assessment

| LOW | **MEDIUM** | HIGH |
|---|---|---|

Our risk assessment reflects our view of the company's strong balance sheet and its power over suppliers, offset by the competitive nature of the telecom business and integration challenges of numerous acquisitions.

## Quantitative Evaluations

**S&P Quality Ranking**                                    B+

| D | C | B- | B | **B+** | A- | A | A+ |
|---|---|---|---|---|---|---|---|

**Relative Strength Rank**                          MODERATE

54

LOWEST = 1                                      HIGHEST = 99

## Revenue/Earnings Data

**Revenue (Million $)**

| | 1Q | 2Q | 3Q | 4Q | Year |
|---|---|---|---|---|---|
| 2011 | 31,247 | 31,495 | 31,478 | -- | -- |
| 2010 | 30,649 | 30,808 | 31,581 | 31,361 | 124,280 |
| 2009 | 30,571 | 30,734 | 30,855 | 30,858 | 123,018 |
| 2008 | 30,744 | 30,866 | 31,342 | 31,076 | 124,028 |
| 2007 | 28,969 | 29,478 | 30,132 | 30,349 | 118,928 |
| 2006 | 15,756 | 15,770 | 15,638 | 15,891 | 63,055 |

**Earnings Per Share ($)**

| | | | | | |
|---|---|---|---|---|---|
| 2011 | 0.57 | 0.60 | 0.61 | E0.53 | E2.32 |
| 2010 | 0.42 | 0.68 | 1.95 | 0.18 | 3.22 |
| 2009 | 0.53 | 0.54 | 0.54 | 0.51 | 2.12 |
| 2008 | 0.57 | 0.63 | 0.55 | 0.41 | 2.16 |
| 2007 | 0.45 | 0.47 | 0.50 | 0.52 | 1.94 |
| 2006 | 0.37 | 0.46 | 0.56 | 0.50 | 1.89 |

Fiscal year ended Dec. 31. Next earnings report expected: Late January. EPS Estimates based on S&P Operating Earnings; historical GAAP earnings are as reported.

## Dividend Data (Dates: mm/dd Payment Date: mm/dd/yy)

| Amount ($) | Date Decl. | Ex-Div. Date | Stk. of Record | Payment Date |
|---|---|---|---|---|
| 0.430 | 12/17 | 01/06 | 01/10 | 02/01/11 |
| 0.430 | 03/25 | 04/06 | 04/08 | 05/02/11 |
| 0.430 | 06/24 | 07/06 | 07/08 | 08/01/11 |
| 0.430 | 09/30 | 10/05 | 10/10 | 11/01/11 |

Dividends have been paid since 1984. Source: Company reports.

---

**Please read the Required Disclosures and Analyst Certification on the last page of this report.**

*The McGraw·Hill Companies*

## Business Summary October 24, 2011

CORPORATE OVERVIEW. The current AT&T Inc. (T) represents the combination of SBC Communications with the assets of AT&T Corp. that were acquired in November 2005. At the end of 2006, T closed on its acquisition of BellSouth (BLS) for $86 billion in stock. As of June 2011, the company had 41.3 million voice connections (down 10.3% from a year earlier) and 16.5 million broadband connections (up 3.3%). With the acquisition of BLS, T took full control of Cingular Wireless, now the second largest U.S. carrier with 100.7 million subscribers (up 8.6% from a year earlier), 69 million of which are post-paid customers, and expanded its wireline presence into the southeastern U.S. In early 2007, Cingular was renamed AT&T Wireless.

IMPACT OF MAJOR DEVELOPMENTS. In 2006, T first launched its new fiber-based network, which offers video and faster-speed broadband services. As of September 2011, the service, called U-verse, had been rolled out in part of T's operating territory with 3.6 million customers, up 31% from a year earlier. T has deployed the service to more than 29 million households, with eligible home penetration of 15.7%. As of September 2011, T said IP revenues, through U-verse and traditional broadband, comprised 51% of consumer wireline revenues. We expect AT&T to increase broadband speeds for non-U-verse homes during 2012 to offset competition and following regulatory clarity on net neutrality rules.

In March 2011, AT&T announced plans to acquire T-Mobile USA assets (34 million subscribers) for approximately $39 billion, subject to necessary approvals, equal to 7.1X 2010 EBITDA. T sees the deal as earnings dilutive in the first two years, but believes there are $3 billion in annual cost synergies plus room for revenue growth through higher smartphone penetration. In August 2011, the U.S. Department of Justice filed to block the deal, citing market concentration concerns and the absence of competition. While this makes deal completion a greater challenge, we expect T will fight to complete the deal and could agree to sell up to one third of T-Mobile assets to avoid a break-up fee. A federal court date is scheduled for early 2012.

In mid-2007, T became the exclusive U.S. provider of the iPhone. Since then, it has launched multiple, faster versions of the product. T has been subsidizing the smartphone to drive customer demand and revenue per user. In 2010 and 2011, T activated more than 25 million iPhones on its network, but in February 2011, Verizon Wireless began to offer a 3G version of the iPhone. While AT&T still had strong iPhone additions in the first nine months of 2011 and churn remained low, overall post-paid subscriber growth slowed.

## Company Financials Fiscal Year Ended Dec. 31

| Per Share Data ($) | 2010 | 2009 | 2008 | 2007 | 2006 | 2005 | 2004 | 2003 | 2002 | 2001 |
|---|---|---|---|---|---|---|---|---|---|---|
| Tangible Book Value | NM | NM | NM | NM | NM | 8.29 | 11.77 | 11.09 | 9.51 | 8.62 |
| Cash Flow | 6.48 | 5.44 | 5.50 | 5.43 | 2.77 | 3.68 | 3.80 | 4.16 | 4.79 | 2.25 |
| Earnings | 3.22 | 2.12 | 2.16 | 1.94 | 1.89 | 1.42 | 1.50 | 1.80 | 2.23 | 2.14 |
| S&P Core Earnings | 3.32 | 2.11 | 1.39 | 1.66 | 1.82 | 1.24 | 1.22 | 1.50 | 1.21 | 1.39 |
| Dividends | 1.68 | 1.64 | 1.60 | 1.42 | 1.33 | 1.29 | 1.25 | 1.37 | 1.07 | 1.02 |
| Payout Ratio | 52% | 77% | 74% | 73% | 70% | 91% | 83% | 76% | 48% | 48% |
| Prices:High | 29.56 | 29.46 | 41.94 | 42.97 | 36.21 | 25.98 | 27.73 | 31.65 | 40.99 | 53.06 |
| Prices:Low | 23.78 | 21.44 | 20.90 | 31.94 | 24.24 | 21.75 | 22.98 | 18.85 | 19.57 | 36.50 |
| P/E Ratio:High | 9 | 14 | 19 | 22 | 19 | 18 | 18 | 18 | 18 | 25 |
| P/E Ratio:Low | 7 | 10 | 10 | 16 | 13 | 15 | 15 | 10 | 9 | 17 |

| Income Statement Analysis (Million $) | | | | | | | | | | |
|---|---|---|---|---|---|---|---|---|---|---|
| Revenue | 124,280 | 123,018 | 124,028 | 118,928 | 63,055 | 43,862 | 40,787 | 40,843 | 43,138 | 45,908 |
| Depreciation | 19,379 | 19,714 | 19,883 | 21,577 | 9,907 | 7,643 | 7,564 | 7,870 | 8,578 | 9,077 |
| Maintenance | NA | NA | NA | NA | NA | NA | NA | NA | NA | NA |
| Construction Credits | NA | NA | NA | NA | NA | 36.0 | 31.0 | 37.0 | 58.0 | 119 |
| Effective Tax Rate | NM | 32.4% | 35.4% | 34.0% | 32.4% | 16.3% | 30.5% | 32.9% | 28.5% | 36.1% |
| Net Income | 19,085 | 12,535 | 12,867 | 11,951 | 7,356 | 4,786 | 4,979 | 5,971 | 7,473 | 7,260 |
| S&P Core Earnings | 19,643 | 12,483 | 8,235 | 10,225 | 7,080 | 4,189 | 4,031 | 5,000 | 4,048 | 4,717 |

| Balance Sheet & Other Financial Data (Million $) | | | | | | | | | | |
|---|---|---|---|---|---|---|---|---|---|---|
| Gross Property | 243,833 | 230,552 | 218,579 | 210,518 | 202,149 | 149,238 | 136,177 | 133,923 | 131,755 | 127,524 |
| Net Property | 103,196 | 100,093 | 99,088 | 95,890 | 94,596 | 58,727 | 50,046 | 52,128 | 48,490 | 49,827 |
| Capital Expenditures | 20,302 | 17,335 | 20,335 | 17,717 | 8,320 | 5,576 | 5,099 | 5,219 | 6,808 | 11,189 |
| Total Capital | 178,117 | 174,406 | 176,415 | 197,561 | 193,009 | 96,727 | 77,544 | 69,607 | 62,705 | 58,476 |
| Fixed Charges Coverage | 6.8 | 6.4 | 6.6 | 6.0 | 5.8 | 4.4 | 6.9 | 7.0 | 6.9 | 6.6 |
| Capitalization:Long Term Debt | 58,971 | 64,720 | 60,872 | 57,255 | 50,063 | 26,115 | 21,231 | 16,060 | 18,536 | 17,133 |
| Capitalization:Preferred | Nil | Nil | Nil | Nil | Nil | Nil | Nil | Nil | Nil | Nil |
| Capitalization:Common | 111,647 | 101,900 | 96,347 | 115,367 | 115,540 | 54,690 | 40,504 | 38,248 | 33,199 | 32,491 |
| % Return on Revenue | 15.4 | 10.2 | 10.4 | 10.0 | 11.7 | 10.9 | 12.2 | 14.6 | 17.3 | 15.8 |
| % Return on Invested Capital | 12.3 | 8.9 | 8.3 | 7.6 | 4.9 | 6.5 | 7.0 | 9.0 | 11.4 | 12.9 |
| % Return on Common Equity | 17.8 | 12.7 | 12.2 | 10.4 | 8.6 | 10.1 | 12.6 | 16.7 | 22.6 | 23.1 |
| % Earned on Net Property | 19.3 | 21.6 | 23.7 | 21.4 | 13.4 | 11.3 | 11.6 | 12.9 | 17.5 | 22.4 |
| % Long Term Debt of Capitalization | 34.6 | 38.8 | 38.7 | 33.2 | 30.3 | 32.3 | 34.4 | 29.6 | 35.8 | 34.5 |
| Capital % Preferred | Nil | Nil | Nil | Nil | Nil | Nil | Nil | Nil | Nil | Nil |
| Capitalization:% Common | 65.4 | 61.2 | 61.3 | 66.8 | 67.8 | 67.7 | 65.6 | 70.4 | 64.2 | 65.5 |

Data as orig reptd.; bef. results of disc opers/spec. items. Per share data adj. for stk. divs.; EPS diluted. E-Estimated. NA-Not Available. NM-Not Meaningful. NR-Not Ranked. UR-Under Review.

**Office:** 2088 S Akard St, Dallas, TX 75202.
**Telephone:** 210-821-4105.
**Website:** http://www.att.com
**Chrmn, Pres & CEO:** R.L. Stephenson

**EVP & General Counsel:** D.W. Watts
**SVP & CFO:** J.J. Stephens
**SVP & Secy:** A.E. Meuleman
**CTO:** J.M. Donovan

**Investor Contact:** D. Cessac (210-351-2058)
**Board Members:** G. F. Amelio, R. V. Anderson, J. H. Blanchard, J. Chico Pardo, J. P. Kelly, J. C. Madonna, M. Martin, J. B. McCoy, C. Pinney, J. M. Roche, M. Rose, R. L. Stephenson, L. D. Tyson

**Auditor:** ERNST & YOUNG
**Founded:** 1983
**Domicile:** Delaware
**Employees:** 266,590

# Autodesk Inc

**STANDARD &POOR'S**

| **S&P Recommendation** HOLD ★★★☆☆ | **Price** $29.80 (as of Nov 25, 2011) | **12-Mo. Target Price** $40.00 | **Investment Style** Large-Cap Growth |
|---|---|---|---|

**GICS Sector** Information Technology
**Sub-Industry** Application Software

**Summary** This company develops, markets and supports computer-aided design and drafting (CAD) software for use on desktop computers and workstations.

## Key Stock Statistics (Source S&P, Vickers, company reports)

| | | | | | | | |
|---|---|---|---|---|---|---|---|
| 52-Wk Range | $46.15– 22.99 | S&P Oper. EPS 2012**E** | 1.38 | Market Capitalization(B) | $6.819 | Beta | 2.09 |
| Trailing 12-Month EPS | $1.17 | S&P Oper. EPS 2013**E** | 1.53 | Yield (%) | Nil | S&P 3-Yr. Proj. EPS CAGR(%) | 15 |
| Trailing 12-Month P/E | 25.5 | P/E on S&P Oper. EPS 2012**E** | 21.6 | Dividend Rate/Share | Nil | S&P Credit Rating | NA |
| $10K Invested 5 Yrs Ago | $7,167 | Common Shares Outstg. (M) | 228.8 | Institutional Ownership (%) | 91 | | |

## Price Performance

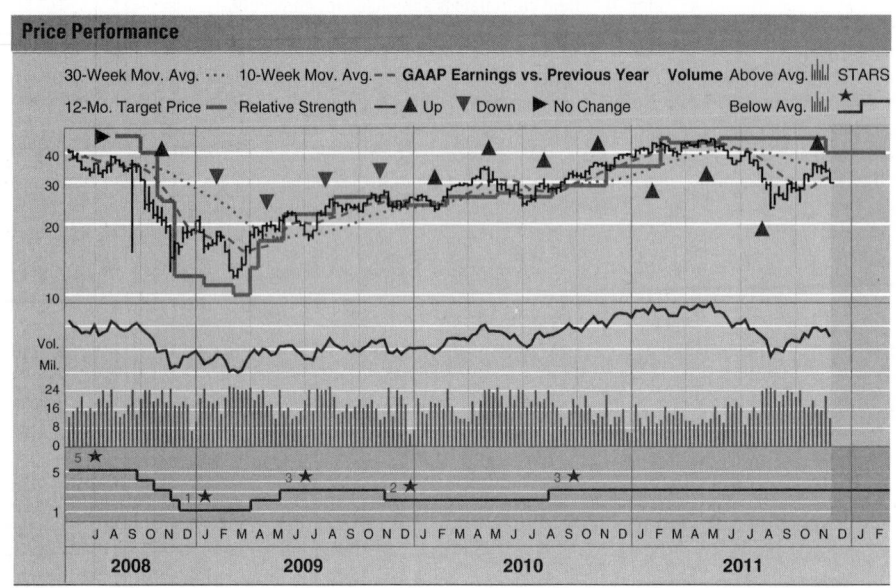

30-Week Mov. Avg. ··· 10-Week Mov. Avg. -- **GAAP Earnings vs. Previous Year** Volume Above Avg. STARS
12-Mo. Target Price — Relative Strength ▲ Up ▼ Down ▶ No Change Below Avg. ★

Options: ASE, CBOE, P, Ph

## Qualitative Risk Assessment

| LOW | MEDIUM | **HIGH** |
|---|---|---|

Our risk assessment reflects our concern about slow economic growth in Europe, the cyclical nature of ADSK's business, and intense competition in the computer-aided design market.

## Quantitative Evaluations

**S&P Quality Ranking** B

| D | C | B- | **B** | B+ | A- | A | A+ |
|---|---|---|---|---|---|---|---|

**Relative Strength Rank** MODERATE

45

LOWEST = 1 HIGHEST = 99

## Revenue/Earnings Data

**Revenue (Million $)**

| | 1Q | 2Q | 3Q | 4Q | Year |
|---|---|---|---|---|---|
| 2012 | 528.3 | 546.3 | 548.6 | -- | -- |
| 2011 | 474.6 | 472.8 | 476.7 | 527.7 | 1,952 |
| 2010 | 425.8 | 414.9 | 416.9 | 456.1 | 1,714 |
| 2009 | 598.8 | 619.5 | 607.1 | 489.8 | 2,315 |
| 2008 | 508.5 | 525.9 | 538.4 | 599.1 | 2,172 |
| 2007 | 436.0 | 449.6 | 456.8 | 497.4 | 1,840 |

**Earnings Per Share ($)**

| | | | | | |
|---|---|---|---|---|---|
| 2012 | 0.29 | 0.30 | 0.32 | E0.35 | E1.38 |
| 2011 | 0.16 | 0.25 | 0.23 | 0.26 | 0.90 |
| 2010 | -0.14 | 0.05 | 0.13 | 0.22 | 0.25 |
| 2009 | 0.41 | 0.39 | 0.45 | -0.47 | 0.80 |
| 2008 | 0.34 | 0.39 | 0.35 | 0.40 | 1.47 |
| 2007 | 0.20 | 0.36 | 0.24 | 0.40 | 1.19 |

Fiscal year ended Jan. 31. Next earnings report expected: Late February. EPS Estimates based on S&P Operating Earnings; historical GAAP earnings are as reported.

## Dividend Data

Quarterly cash dividends were discontinued after April 2005.

## Highlights

▶ The 12-month target price for ADSK has recently been changed to $40.00 from $46.00. The Highlights section of this Stock Report will be updated accordingly.

## Investment Rationale/Risk

▶ The Investment Rationale/Risk section of this Stock Report will be updated shortly. For the latest News story on ADSK from MarketScope, see below.

▶ 11/16/11 03:00 pm ET ... S&P REITERATES HOLD OPINION ON SHARES OF AUTODESK (ADSK 36.54***): ADSK posts adjusted Oct-Q EPS of $0.36 vs. $0.29, $0.04 above our forecast. Revenues rose 15%, exceeding our forecast, reflecting better performance than we expected across licenses and maintenance offerings. We think ADSK has done a good job of diversifying across geographies, verticals and offerings. We are raising our EPS estimates for FY 12 (Jan.) to $1.38 from $1.32 and FY 13 to $1.53 from $1.41, reflecting the business momentum we see. However, based on revised DCF, price-to-sales and P/E-to-growth analyses, we are lowering our 12-month target price to $40 from $46. /S. Kessler

# Autodesk Inc

## Business Summary August 24, 2011

CORPORATE OVERVIEW. Autodesk (ADSK) develops software solutions that enable customers in the architectural, engineering, construction, manufacturing, infrastructure, media and entertainment markets to create, manage and share their data and designs digitally. ADSK's software helps its customers to improve their designs before they actually begin the building process, thus saving time and money. The company is organized into four reportable operating segments: Platform Solutions and Emerging Business, which accounted for 37% of net revenue in FY 11 (Jan.), Architecture, Engineering and Construction (29%), Manufacturing (24%), and the Media and Entertainment segment (10%).

The targeted customers for its Platform Solutions and Emerging Business; Architecture, Engineering and Construction; and Manufacturing segments are those who design, build, manage or own building, manufacturing and infrastructure projects. Key products for these segments include AutoCAD, a general-purpose computer aided design (CAD) tool for design, modeling, drafting, mapping, rendering and facility management tasks; AutoCAD LT, a low-cost CAD package with 2D and basic 3D drafting capabilities; and Au-

todesk Inventor, a software that allows engineers to perform simulation and analysis on 3D models. Other products include Autodesk Mechanical Desktop, Autodesk Civil 3D, and Autodesk Revit products.

The Media and Entertainment segment develops digital systems and software for creating 3D animation, color grading, visual effects compositing, editing and finishing. Its products are used for PC and console game development, animation, film, television, and design visualization. Products include Autodesk 3ds Max, a 3D modeling and animation software package; Autodesk Flame, a digital system used by professionals to create and edit special visual effects in real-time; and Autodesk Inferno, which provides all the features of flame with film tools, and increased image resolution and color control for digital film work.

## Company Financials Fiscal Year Ended Jan. 31

| Per Share Data ($) | 2011 | 2010 | 2009 | 2008 | 2007 | 2006 | 2005 | 2004 | 2003 | 2002 |
|---|---|---|---|---|---|---|---|---|---|---|
| Tangible Book Value | 4.13 | 3.68 | 2.89 | 3.14 | 3.07 | 2.06 | 2.07 | 2.07 | 1.84 | 2.20 |
| Cash Flow | 1.36 | 0.73 | 1.24 | 1.68 | 1.37 | 1.51 | 1.11 | 0.74 | 0.35 | 0.68 |
| Earnings | 0.90 | 0.25 | 0.80 | 1.47 | 1.19 | 1.33 | 0.90 | 0.52 | 0.14 | 0.40 |
| S&P Core Earnings | 0.90 | 0.31 | 1.18 | 1.49 | 1.19 | 1.05 | 0.67 | 0.33 | -0.07 | 0.09 |
| Dividends | NA | Nil | Nil | Nil | 0.02 | 0.06 | 0.06 | 0.06 | 0.06 | 0.06 |
| Payout Ratio | NA | Nil | Nil | Nil | 2% | 5% | 7% | 12% | 43% | 15% |
| Calendar Year | 2010 | 2009 | 2008 | 2007 | 2006 | 2005 | 2004 | 2003 | 2002 | 2001 |
| Prices:High | 39.80 | 27.97 | 49.71 | 51.32 | 44.75 | 48.27 | 38.98 | 12.45 | 11.84 | 10.55 |
| Prices:Low | 22.50 | 11.70 | 12.45 | 36.74 | 29.56 | 26.20 | 12.10 | 6.41 | 5.09 | 6.05 |
| P/E Ratio:High | 44 | NM | 62 | 35 | 38 | 36 | 43 | 24 | 85 | 26 |
| P/E Ratio:Low | 25 | NM | 16 | 25 | 25 | 20 | 13 | 12 | 36 | 15 |

| Income Statement Analysis (Million $) | | | | | | | | | | |
|---|---|---|---|---|---|---|---|---|---|---|
| Revenue | 1,952 | 1,714 | 2,315 | 2,172 | 1,840 | 1,523 | 1,234 | 952 | 825 | 947 |
| Operating Income | 388 | 246 | 543 | 539 | 440 | 414 | 314 | 0.16 | 99.7 | 195 |
| Depreciation | 105 | 112 | 102 | 49.8 | 43.9 | 43.7 | 51.9 | 50.3 | 48.8 | 62.9 |
| Interest Expense | NA | NA | Nil | Nil | 2.10 | Nil | Nil | Nil | Nil | Nil |
| Pretax Income | 272 | 84.7 | 253 | 470 | 367 | 383 | 246 | 117 | 38.5 | 55.1 |
| Effective Tax Rate | NA | 31.5% | 27.3% | 24.2% | 21.0% | 14.1% | 10.1% | NM | 17.1% | NM |
| Net Income | 212 | 58.0 | 184 | 356 | 290 | 329 | 222 | 120 | 31.9 | 90.3 |
| S&P Core Earnings | 212 | 71.7 | 271 | 362 | 292 | 258 | 161 | 74.4 | -16.2 | 19.5 |

| Balance Sheet & Other Financial Data (Million $) | | | | | | | | | | |
|---|---|---|---|---|---|---|---|---|---|---|
| Cash | 1,274 | 1,001 | 981 | 949 | 778 | 369 | 533 | 364 | 247 | 505 |
| Current Assets | 1,714 | 1,380 | 1,388 | 1,482 | 1,190 | 739 | 782 | 597 | 450 | 564 |
| Total Assets | 2,788 | 2,447 | 2,421 | 2,209 | 1,798 | 1,361 | 1,142 | 1,017 | 884 | 902 |
| Current Liabilities | 870 | 704 | 800 | 746 | 574 | 507 | 477 | 385 | 310 | 371 |
| Long Term Debt | NA | NA | Nil | Nil | Nil | Nil | Nil | Nil | Nil | Nil |
| Common Equity | 1,609 | 1,474 | 1,311 | 1,231 | 1,115 | 791 | 648 | 622 | 569 | 529 |
| Total Capital | 1,609 | 1,474 | 1,333 | 1,231 | 1,115 | 791 | 648 | 629 | 571 | 529 |
| Capital Expenditures | 28.3 | 39.0 | 78.4 | 43.3 | 35.3 | 20.5 | 40.8 | 25.9 | 36.1 | 45.1 |
| Cash Flow | 317 | 170 | 286 | 406 | 334 | 373 | 273 | 171 | 80.7 | 153 |
| Current Ratio | 2.0 | 2.0 | 1.7 | 2.0 | 2.1 | 1.5 | 1.6 | 1.6 | 1.5 | 1.5 |
| % Long Term Debt of Capitalization | Nil | Nil | Nil | Nil | Nil | Nil | Nil | Nil | Nil | Nil |
| % Net Income of Revenue | 10.9 | 3.4 | 7.9 | 16.4 | 15.8 | 21.6 | 18.0 | 12.6 | 3.9 | 9.5 |
| % Return on Assets | 8.1 | 2.4 | 7.9 | 17.8 | 18.4 | 26.3 | 20.5 | 12.7 | 3.6 | 10.6 |
| % Return on Equity | 13.8 | 4.2 | 14.5 | 30.4 | 30.4 | 45.7 | 34.9 | 20.2 | 5.8 | 18.3 |

Data as orig reptd.; bef. results of disc opers/spec. items. Per share data adj. for stk. divs.; EPS diluted. E-Estimated. NA-Not Available. NM-Not Meaningful. NR-Not Ranked. UR-Under Review.

**Office:** 111 McInnis Parkway, San Rafael, CA 94903.
**Telephone:** 415-507-5000.
**Email:** investor.relations@autodesk.com
**Website:** http://www.autodesk.com

**Chrmn:** C.W. Beveridge
**Pres & CEO:** C. Bass
**COO & SVP:** M. Chin
**EVP & CFO:** M.J. Hawkins

**CTO:** J.M. Kowalski
**Investor Contact:** S. Pirri (415-507-6467)
**Board Members:** C. Bass, C. W. Beveridge, J. H. Dawson, P. Halvorsen, M. T. McDowell, L. M. Norrington, C. J. Robel, S. J. Smith, S. M. West

**Founded:** 1982
**Domicile:** Delaware
**Employees:** 6,800

# Automatic Data Processing Inc.

**STANDARD &POOR'S**

| S&P Recommendation **BUY** ★★★★☆ | Price $47.93 (as of Nov 25, 2011) | 12-Mo. Target Price $60.00 | Investment Style Large-Cap Growth |
|---|---|---|---|

**GICS Sector** Information Technology
**Sub-Industry** Data Processing & Outsourced Services

**Summary** ADP, one of the world's largest independent computing services companies, provides a broad range of data processing services.

## Key Stock Statistics (Source S&P, Vickers, company reports)

| | | | | | | | |
|---|---|---|---|---|---|---|---|
| 52-Wk Range | $55.12– 44.41 | S&P Oper. EPS 2012**E** | 2.75 | Market Capitalization(B) | $23.423 | Beta | 0.65 |
| Trailing 12-Month EPS | $2.57 | S&P Oper. EPS 2013**E** | 2.99 | Yield (%) | 3.30 | S&P 3-Yr. Proj. EPS CAGR(%) | 10 |
| Trailing 12-Month P/E | 18.7 | P/E on S&P Oper. EPS 2012**E** | 17.4 | Dividend Rate/Share | $1.58 | S&P Credit Rating | AAA |
| $10K Invested 5 Yrs Ago | NA | Common Shares Outstg. (M) | 488.7 | Institutional Ownership (%) | 76 | | |

## Price Performance

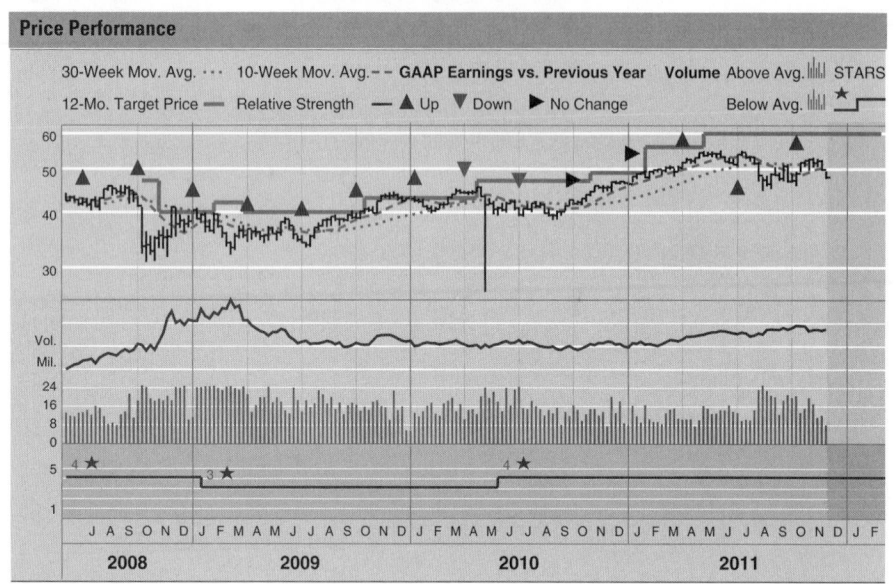

30-Week Mov. Avg. · · · 10-Week Mov. Avg. – – GAAP Earnings vs. Previous Year Volume Above Avg. STARS
12-Mo. Target Price — Relative Strength ▲ Up ▼ Down ► No Change Below Avg. ★

Options: ASE, CBOE, P, Ph

Analysis prepared by Equity Analyst **Dylan Cathers** on Nov 17, 2011, when the stock traded at **$49.88**.

## Highlights

➤ We look for a revenue increase of 8.0% in FY 12 (Jun.), aided by a strong first-quarter gain. Pays per control, which is ADP's version of a same-store sales metric, were up again in the September quarter, albeit modestly, in the face of continued sluggishness in the employment market. This gives us confidence in the company's core Employer Services segment, given increasing average client fund balances and client growth in the small-business space. Additionally, sales in the Dealer Services unit should remain solid. We see low prevailing interest rates reducing income from funds held for clients, but this should be partially offset by lower borrowing costs. In FY 13, we expect 6.0% revenue growth.

➤ We think operating margins will be roughly flat in FY 12. We believe investments in the sales force and in new technologies, as well as acquisitions in FY 11, will approximately offset improving operational metrics and cost controls.

➤ Aided by a modest level of share buybacks, EPS was $2.52 in FY 11. For FY 12, we assume just enough buyback activity to offset share issuance, and expect EPS of $2.75. We forecast EPS of $2.99 in FY 13.

## Investment Rationale/Risk

➤ Our buy opinion on the shares is based on valuation. Despite the major headwinds of continued high levels of unemployment and low prevailing interest rates, we believe conditions are improving. U.S. vehicle sales are gaining strength, despite being below levels of a couple of years ago, which should aid the Dealer Services unit. Over the longer term, we think the market for payroll outsourcing is relatively untapped, especially in the small- and medium-sized business market and overseas, providing opportunities for future growth, by our analysis.

➤ Risks to our recommendation and target price include increased competition in the business process outsourcing market, an area into which ADP is venturing, which could lead to downward pressure on pricing and profit margins; a decrease in payrolls due to a weak economy; and failure of ADP to expand further into small- and mid-sized businesses and international markets.

➤ Our 12-month target price of $60 is based on our relative valuation analysis, applying a roughly peer-average P/E of 20.9X to our calendar 2012 EPS estimate of $2.87.

## Qualitative Risk Assessment

| LOW | MEDIUM | HIGH |
|---|---|---|

Our risk assessment reflects what we see as the company's strong balance sheet, steady cash inflow, and recurring revenue stream, offset by intense competition in payroll processing and the threat of new entrants into the marketplace.

## Quantitative Evaluations

**S&P Quality Ranking**     A

| D | C | B- | B | B+ | A- | A | A+ |
|---|---|---|---|---|---|---|---|

**Relative Strength Rank**     MODERATE

55

LOWEST = 1      HIGHEST = 99

## Revenue/Earnings Data

**Revenue (Million $)**

| | 1Q | 2Q | 3Q | 4Q | Year |
|---|---|---|---|---|---|
| 2012 | 2,523 | -- | -- | -- | -- |
| 2011 | 2,229 | 2,406 | 2,737 | 2,507 | 9,880 |
| 2010 | 2,096 | 2,198 | 2,443 | 2,190 | 8,928 |
| 2009 | 2,182 | 2,203 | 2,375 | 2,108 | 8,867 |
| 2008 | 1,992 | 2,150 | 2,427 | 2,207 | 8,777 |
| 2007 | 1,755 | 1,874 | 2,171 | 2,000 | 7,800 |

**Earnings Per Share ($)**

| | | | | | |
|---|---|---|---|---|---|
| 2012 | 0.61 | E0.67 | E0.91 | E0.56 | E2.75 |
| 2011 | 0.56 | 0.62 | 0.85 | 0.48 | 2.52 |
| 2010 | 0.56 | 0.62 | 0.79 | 0.42 | 2.40 |
| 2009 | 0.54 | 0.59 | 0.80 | 0.69 | 2.63 |
| 2008 | 0.45 | 0.53 | 0.77 | 0.44 | 2.20 |
| 2007 | 0.39 | 0.45 | 0.65 | 0.35 | 1.83 |

Fiscal year ended Jun. 30. Next earnings report expected: Late January. EPS Estimates based on S&P Operating Earnings; historical GAAP earnings are as reported.

## Dividend Data (Dates: mm/dd Payment Date: mm/dd/yy)

| Amount ($) | Date Decl. | Ex-Div. Date | Stk. of Record | Payment Date |
|---|---|---|---|---|
| 0.360 | 02/08 | 03/09 | 03/11 | 04/01/11 |
| 0.360 | 04/28 | 06/08 | 06/10 | 07/01/11 |
| 0.360 | 08/09 | 09/07 | 09/09 | 10/01/11 |
| 0.395 | 11/08 | 12/07 | 12/09 | 01/01/12 |

Dividends have been paid since 1974. Source: Company reports.

---

**Please read the Required Disclosures and Analyst Certification on the last page of this report.**

The McGraw·Hill Companies

# Automatic Data Processing Inc.

STANDARD &POOR'S

## Business Summary November 17, 2011

CORPORATE OVERVIEW. Automatic Data Processing (ADP) is the largest global provider of payroll outsourcing services based on revenue. The company also offers human resources outsourcing, tax filing, and benefits administration, with a broad range of data processing services in two business segments: employer and dealer.

Employer Services provides payroll, human resource, benefits administration, time and attendance, and tax filing and reporting services to more than 570,000 clients in North America, Europe, Australia, Asia and Brazil. Dealer Services provides transaction systems, data products and professional services to automobile and truck dealers and manufacturers worldwide.

MARKET PROFILE. The market for HR management services, which is the largest segment of ADP's Employer Services division, totaled $101.5 billion worldwide in calendar 2010, according to market researcher IDC. Between 2010 and 2015, IDC expects this area to expand at a compound annual growth rate (CAGR) of 4.4%, with the market in the U.S. increasing 3.5%, from $51.0 billion in 2010. For the more narrow processing services market, where ADP is the dominant company, IDC sees a CAGR of 2.5% in the U.S. between 2010 and 2015. In contrast, in the market for business process outsourcing (BPO) services, an area in which we see ADP expanding further, IDC expects a CAGR of

3.4% over the same time frame.

IMPACT OF MAJOR DEVELOPMENTS. In April 2006, ADP completed the sale of its Claims Services business for $975 million in cash, netting $480 million after taxes. In August 2006, ADP announced its intention to spin off its Brokerage Services business. The new public company, Broadridge Financial Services, which began trading on April 2, 2007, had sales of about $2 billion in FY 07 (Jun.), a high level of recurring revenues, and a revenue growth rate in the mid-single digits. This growth rate is below what we think the remaining Employer Services and Dealer Services units are capable of, especially given what we believe are strong overseas prospects. Further, the disposition of the Brokerage business (as well as the Claims sale) allows management to better concentrate on its two remaining businesses, in our opinion. With the Brokerage business spinoff complete, the new company distributed $690 million to ADP, which it used primarily for share buybacks, acquiring 40 million shares at a cost of about $2 billion in FY 07.

## Company Financials Fiscal Year Ended Jun. 30

| Per Share Data ($) | 2011 | 2010 | 2009 | 2008 | 2007 | 2006 | 2005 | 2004 | 2003 | 2002 |
|---|---|---|---|---|---|---|---|---|---|---|
| Tangible Book Value | 4.53 | 5.19 | 4.72 | 3.97 | 3.93 | 5.21 | 4.55 | 4.23 | 4.57 | 5.25 |
| Cash Flow | 3.16 | 3.01 | 3.24 | 2.40 | 2.35 | 5.35 | 2.30 | 2.07 | 2.13 | 2.19 |
| Earnings | 2.52 | 2.40 | 2.63 | 2.20 | 1.83 | 1.85 | 1.79 | 1.56 | 1.68 | 1.75 |
| S&P Core Earnings | 2.45 | 2.37 | 2.58 | 2.11 | 1.78 | 1.85 | 1.60 | 1.38 | 1.42 | 1.49 |
| Dividends | 1.42 | 1.35 | 1.28 | 1.10 | 1.06 | 0.71 | 0.61 | 0.54 | 0.48 | 0.45 |
| Payout Ratio | 56% | 56% | 49% | 50% | 58% | 38% | 34% | 35% | 28% | 26% |
| Prices:High | 55.12 | 47.17 | 44.50 | 45.97 | 51.50 | 49.94 | 48.11 | 47.31 | 40.81 | 59.53 |
| Prices:Low | 44.72 | 26.46 | 32.03 | 30.83 | 43.89 | 42.50 | 40.37 | 38.60 | 27.24 | 31.15 |
| P/E Ratio:High | 22 | 20 | 17 | 21 | 28 | 27 | 27 | 30 | 24 | 34 |
| P/E Ratio:Low | 18 | 11 | 12 | 14 | 24 | 23 | 23 | 25 | 16 | 18 |

| Income Statement Analysis (Million $) | 2011 | 2010 | 2009 | 2008 | 2007 | 2006 | 2005 | 2004 | 2003 | 2002 |
|---|---|---|---|---|---|---|---|---|---|---|
| Revenue | 9,880 | 8,928 | 8,867 | 8,777 | 7,800 | 8,882 | 8,499 | 7,755 | 7,147 | 7,004 |
| Operating Income | 2,144 | 2,081 | 2,138 | 1,832 | 1,795 | 1,967 | 1,948 | 1,745 | 1,793 | 1,952 |
| Depreciation | 318 | 309 | 308 | 106 | 289 | 289 | 304 | 307 | 275 | 279 |
| Interest Expense | 8.60 | 8.60 | 33.3 | 80.5 | 94.9 | 72.8 | 32.3 | Nil | Nil | 21.2 |
| Pretax Income | 1,933 | 1,863 | 1,905 | 1,812 | 1,624 | 3,486 | 1,678 | 1,495 | 1,645 | 1,787 |
| Effective Tax Rate | NA | NA | 30.3% | 35.9% | 37.1% | 19.2% | 37.1% | 37.4% | 38.1% | 38.4% |
| Net Income | 1,254 | 1,207 | 1,328 | 1,162 | 1,021 | 2,815 | 1,055 | 936 | 1,018 | 1,101 |
| S&P Core Earnings | 1,222 | 1,193 | 1,302 | 1,115 | 992 | 1,077 | 940 | 824 | 857 | 940 |

| Balance Sheet & Other Financial Data (Million $) | 2011 | 2010 | 2009 | 2008 | 2007 | 2006 | 2005 | 2004 | 2003 | 2002 |
|---|---|---|---|---|---|---|---|---|---|---|
| Cash | 1,426 | 1,671 | 2,296 | 1,584 | 1,817 | 2,269 | 1,671 | 1,129 | 2,344 | 2,750 |
| Current Assets | 28,584 | 22,317 | 20,704 | 18,809 | 3,364 | 4,760 | 4,441 | 2,762 | 3,676 | 2,817 |
| Total Assets | 34,238 | 26,862 | 25,352 | 23,734 | 26,649 | 27,490 | 27,615 | 21,121 | 19,834 | 18,277 |
| Current Liabilities | 26,787 | 20,052 | 18,756 | 17,342 | 1,791 | 2,593 | 2,801 | 1,768 | 1,999 | 1,411 |
| Long Term Debt | 34.2 | 39.8 | 42.7 | 52.1 | 43.5 | 74.3 | 75.8 | 76.2 | 84.7 | 90.6 |
| Common Equity | 6,010 | 5,479 | 5,323 | 5,087 | 5,148 | 6,012 | 5,784 | 5,418 | 5,371 | 5,114 |
| Total Capital | 6,045 | 5,519 | 5,620 | 5,309 | 5,319 | 6,210 | 6,150 | 5,778 | 5,777 | 5,442 |
| Capital Expenditures | 182 | 103 | 158 | 181 | 173 | 292 | 196 | 196 | 134 | 146 |
| Cash Flow | 1,572 | 1,517 | 1,636 | 1,268 | 1,310 | 3,104 | 1,360 | 1,242 | 1,293 | 1,380 |
| Current Ratio | 1.1 | 1.1 | 1.1 | 1.1 | 1.9 | 1.8 | 1.6 | 1.6 | 1.8 | 2.0 |
| % Long Term Debt of Capitalization | 0.6 | 0.7 | 0.8 | 1.0 | 0.8 | 1.2 | 1.2 | 1.3 | 1.5 | 1.7 |
| % Net Income of Revenue | 12.7 | 13.5 | 15.0 | 13.2 | 13.1 | 31.7 | 12.4 | 12.1 | 14.2 | 15.7 |
| % Return on Assets | 4.1 | 4.6 | 5.4 | 4.6 | 3.8 | 10.2 | 4.3 | 4.6 | 5.3 | 6.1 |
| % Return on Equity | 21.8 | 22.4 | 25.5 | 22.7 | 18.3 | 47.7 | 18.8 | 17.3 | 19.4 | 22.4 |

Data as orig reptd.; bef. results of disc opers/spec. items. Per share data adj. for stk. divs.; EPS diluted. E-Estimated. NA-Not Available. NM-Not Meaningful. NR-Not Ranked. UR-Under Review.

**Office:** 1 Adp Blvd, Roseland, NJ 07068-1728.
**Telephone:** 973-974-5000.
**Website:** http://www.adp.com
**Chrmn:** L.A. Brun

**Pres:** P. Tan
**CEO:** C.A. Rodriguez
**CFO:** C.R. Reidy
**Chief Acctg Officer & Cntlr:** A. Sheiness

**Board Members:** G. D. Brenneman, L. A. Brun, R. T. Clark, E. C. Fast, L. R. Gooden, R. G. Hubbard, J. P. Jones, III, C. A. Rodriguez, E. T. Salem, G. L. Summe

**Founded:** 1949
**Domicile:** Delaware
**Employees:** 51,000

# AutoNation Inc

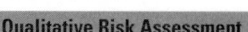

**STANDARD & POOR'S**

| | | | |
|---|---|---|---|
| **S&P Recommendation** HOLD ★★★☆☆ | **Price** $34.06 (as of Nov 25, 2011) | **12-Mo. Target Price** $38.00 | **Investment Style** Large-Cap Blend |

**GICS Sector** Consumer Discretionary
**Sub-Industry** Automotive Retail

**Summary** AutoNation, the largest U.S. retail auto dealer, owns and operates more than 250 new vehicle franchises in 15 states.

## Key Stock Statistics (Source S&P, Vickers, company reports)

| | | | | | | | |
|---|---|---|---|---|---|---|---|
| 52-Wk Range | $41.55–25.43 | S&P Oper. EPS 2011**E** | 1.97 | Market Capitalization(B) | $4.765 | Beta | 1.24 |
| Trailing 12-Month EPS | $1.85 | S&P Oper. EPS 2012**E** | 2.29 | Yield (%) | Nil | S&P 3-Yr. Proj. EPS CAGR(%) | 15 |
| Trailing 12-Month P/E | 18.4 | P/E on S&P Oper. EPS 2011**E** | 17.3 | Dividend Rate/Share | Nil | S&P Credit Rating | BBB- |
| $10K Invested 5 Yrs Ago | $16,510 | Common Shares Outstg. (M) | 139.9 | Institutional Ownership (%) | 83 | | |

## Price Performance

30-Week Mov. Avg. ···· 10-Week Mov. Avg. - - **GAAP Earnings vs. Previous Year** Volume Above Avg. STARS
12-Mo. Target Price — Relative Strength — ▲ Up ▼ Down ▶ No Change Below Avg.

Options: ASE, CBOE, P, Ph

## Highlights

► The 12-month target price for AN has recently been changed to $38.00 from $37.00. The Highlights section of this Stock Report will be updated accordingly.

## Investment Rationale/Risk

► The Investment Rationale/Risk section of this Stock Report will be updated shortly. For the latest News story on AN from MarketScope, see below.

► 10/20/11 02:39 pm ET ... S&P KEEPS HOLD OPINION ON SHARES OF AUTONATION (AN 37.71***): Q3 EPS of $0.48, vs. $0.39, misses our $0.50 estimate. Revenues rose 7% to $3.5B, driven by higher average selling prices. New vehicle unit sales were hurt by the availability of vehicles produced by Japanese manufacturers. While inventory remains constrained, we think sales will improve, reflecting our view of an economic recovery. We expect operating margins to widen as sales trend higher. We keep our '11 EPS forecast at $1.97, but raise '12's by $0.05 to $2.29 on fewer shares outstanding. We lift our target price by $1 to $38, based on historical and peer P/E analysis. /E. Levy, CFA, J. Yin, CFA

## Qualitative Risk Assessment

| LOW | **MEDIUM** | HIGH |
|---|---|---|

Our risk assessment reflects the cyclical nature of the automotive retailing industry, which is affected by interest rates, consumer confidence and personal discretionary spending, offset by the company's highly variable cost structure.

## Quantitative Evaluations

**S&P Quality Ranking** B-

| D | C | **B-** | B | B+ | A- | A | A+ |
|---|---|---|---|---|---|---|---|

**Relative Strength Rank** MODERATE

53

LOWEST = 1 HIGHEST = 99

## Revenue/Earnings Data

**Revenue (Million $)**

| | 1Q | 2Q | 3Q | 4Q | Year |
|---|---|---|---|---|---|
| 2011 | 3,311 | 3,336 | 3,507 | -- | -- |
| 2010 | 2,837 | 3,104 | 3,274 | 3,246 | 12,461 |
| 2009 | 2,412 | 2,615 | 2,916 | 2,815 | 10,758 |
| 2008 | 3,970 | 3,885 | 3,540 | 2,737 | 14,132 |
| 2007 | 4,395 | 4,559 | 4,602 | 4,214 | 17,692 |
| 2006 | 4,612 | 4,959 | 4,945 | 4,473 | 18,989 |

**Earnings Per Share ($)**

| | | | | | |
|---|---|---|---|---|---|
| 2011 | 0.46 | 0.49 | 0.48 | E0.50 | E1.97 |
| 2010 | 0.34 | 0.31 | 0.39 | 0.45 | 1.48 |
| 2009 | 0.30 | 0.30 | 0.36 | 0.36 | 1.32 |
| 2008 | 0.31 | 0.30 | -7.95 | 0.40 | -6.89 |
| 2007 | 0.39 | 0.38 | 0.39 | 0.27 | 1.44 |
| 2006 | 0.37 | 0.33 | 0.40 | 0.35 | 1.45 |

Fiscal year ended Dec. 31. Next earnings report expected: Early February. EPS Estimates based on S&P Operating Earnings; historical GAAP earnings are as reported.

## Dividend Data

No cash dividends have been paid.

---

**Please read the Required Disclosures and Analyst Certification on the last page of this report.**

The **McGraw-Hill** Companies

# AutoNation Inc

## Business Summary September 12, 2011

AutoNation, Inc., through its subsidiaries, operates as an automotive retailer in the United States. As of December 31, 2010, the company owned and operated 242 new vehicle franchises from 206 dealerships located in major metropolitan markets in the United States.

The company offers a range of automotive products and services, including new vehicles, used vehicles, parts and automotive services, and automotive finance and insurance products. It also arranges financing for vehicle purchases through third-party finance sources. The company's stores also provide a range of vehicle maintenance, repair, paint and collision repair services, including warranty work that can be performed only at franchised dealerships and customer-pay service work.

AutoNation offers various financial products and services to its customers. It arranges for its customers to finance vehicles through installment loans or leases with third-party lenders, including the vehicle manufacturers' and distributors' captive finance subsidiaries. It also offers its customers various vehicle protection products, including extended service contracts, maintenance programs, guaranteed auto protection (known as GAP, covering the shortfall

between a customer's loan balance and insurance payoff in the event of a casualty), tire and wheel protection, and theft protection products.

The company's segments include Domestic, Import, and Premium Luxury.

The Domestic segment consists of retail automotive franchises that sell new vehicles manufactured by General Motors, Ford and Chrysler.

The Import segment consists of retail automotive franchises that sell new vehicles manufactured primarily by Toyota, Honda and Nissan.

The Premium Luxury segment consists of retail automotive franchises that sell new vehicles manufactured primarily by Mercedes, BMW and Lexus. The franchises in each segment also sell used vehicles, parts and automotive services, and automotive finance and insurance products.

## Company Financials Fiscal Year Ended Dec. 31

| Per Share Data ($) | 2010 | 2009 | 2008 | 2007 | 2006 | 2005 | 2004 | 2003 | 2002 | 2001 |
|---|---|---|---|---|---|---|---|---|---|---|
| Tangible Book Value | 4.95 | 5.84 | 4.93 | 2.37 | 2.66 | 6.53 | 4.53 | 3.91 | 3.14 | 2.99 |
| Cash Flow | 1.97 | 1.76 | -6.38 | 1.90 | 1.81 | 1.78 | 1.78 | 2.01 | 1.40 | 1.18 |
| Earnings | 1.48 | 1.32 | -6.89 | 1.44 | 1.45 | 1.48 | 1.45 | 1.76 | 1.19 | 0.73 |
| S&P Core Earnings | 1.48 | 1.27 | 1.32 | 1.44 | 1.45 | 1.44 | 1.41 | 1.69 | 1.12 | 0.57 |
| Dividends | Nil | Nil | Nil | Nil | Nil | Nil | Nil | Nil | Nil | Nil |
| Payout Ratio | Nil | Nil | Nil | Nil | Nil | Nil | Nil | Nil | Nil | Nil |
| Prices:High | 28.50 | 21.60 | 19.59 | 23.19 | 22.94 | 22.84 | 19.33 | 19.19 | 18.73 | 13.07 |
| Prices:Low | 17.18 | 7.62 | 3.97 | 14.65 | 18.95 | 17.91 | 15.01 | 11.61 | 9.05 | 4.94 |
| P/E Ratio:High | 19 | 16 | NM | 16 | 16 | 15 | 13 | 11 | 16 | 18 |
| P/E Ratio:Low | 12 | 6 | NM | 10 | 13 | 12 | 10 | 7 | 8 | 7 |

| Income Statement Analysis (Million $) | 2010 | 2009 | 2008 | 2007 | 2006 | 2005 | 2004 | 2003 | 2002 | 2001 |
|---|---|---|---|---|---|---|---|---|---|---|
| Revenue | 12,461 | 10,758 | 14,132 | 17,692 | 18,989 | 19,253 | 19,425 | 19,381 | 19,479 | 19,989 |
| Operating Income | 573 | 464 | 566 | 798 | 879 | 888 | 861 | 805 | 786 | 667 |
| Depreciation | 76.8 | 77.5 | 90.8 | 91.7 | 82.9 | 80.7 | 89.7 | 71.0 | 69.7 | 152 |
| Interest Expense | 98.6 | 78.7 | 177 | 247 | 267 | 191 | 159 | 143 | 125 | 43.7 |
| Pretax Income | 381 | 351 | -1,423 | 459 | 542 | 623 | 607 | 591 | 618 | 401 |
| Effective Tax Rate | NA | 33.3% | NM | 37.3% | 38.9% | 36.5% | 34.7% | 14.4% | 38.3% | 38.9% |
| Net Income | 235 | 234 | -1,225 | 288 | 331 | 396 | 396 | 506 | 382 | 245 |
| S&P Core Earnings | 235 | 225 | 234 | 288 | 331 | 385 | 385 | 486 | 359 | 192 |

| Balance Sheet & Other Financial Data (Million $) | 2010 | 2009 | 2008 | 2007 | 2006 | 2005 | 2004 | 2003 | 2002 | 2001 |
|---|---|---|---|---|---|---|---|---|---|---|
| Cash | 95.1 | 174 | 111 | 32.8 | 52.2 | 244 | 107 | 171 | 176 | 128 |
| Current Assets | 2,629 | 2,251 | 2,554 | 3,238 | 3,386 | 3,880 | 3,678 | 3,990 | 3,629 | 3,153 |
| Total Assets | 5,974 | 5,407 | 6,014 | 8,480 | 8,607 | 8,825 | 8,699 | 8,823 | 8,585 | 8,065 |
| Current Liabilities | 2,399 | 1,863 | 2,456 | 2,902 | 3,031 | 3,412 | 3,411 | 3,810 | 2,981 | 2,578 |
| Long Term Debt | 1,341 | 1,105 | 1,226 | 3,917 | 1,558 | 484 | 798 | 808 | 643 | 647 |
| Common Equity | 2,079 | 2,303 | 2,198 | 3,474 | 3,713 | 4,670 | 4,263 | 3,950 | 3,910 | 3,828 |
| Total Capital | 3,428 | 3,416 | 3,424 | 5,446 | 5,496 | 5,340 | 5,218 | 4,935 | 5,500 | 5,329 |
| Capital Expenditures | 162 | 75.5 | 117 | 160 | 170 | 132 | 133 | 133 | 183 | 164 |
| Cash Flow | 312 | 312 | -1,135 | 380 | 414 | 476 | 486 | 577 | 451 | 397 |
| Current Ratio | 1.1 | 1.2 | 1.0 | 1.1 | 1.1 | 1.1 | 1.1 | 1.0 | 1.2 | 1.2 |
| % Long Term Debt of Capitalization | 39.1 | Nil | 35.8 | 33.5 | 28.3 | 9.1 | 15.3 | 16.4 | 11.7 | 12.1 |
| % Net Income of Revenue | 1.9 | 2.2 | NM | 1.6 | 1.7 | 2.1 | 2.0 | 2.6 | 2.0 | 1.2 |
| % Return on Assets | NA | NA | NM | 3.4 | 3.8 | 4.5 | 4.5 | 5.8 | 4.6 | 2.9 |
| % Return on Equity | NA | NA | NM | 8.0 | 7.9 | 8.9 | 9.7 | 12.9 | 9.9 | 6.4 |

Data as orig reptd.; bef. results of disc opers/spec. items. Per share data adj. for stk. divs.; EPS diluted. E-Estimated. NA-Not Available. NM-Not Meaningful. NR-Not Ranked. UR-Under Review.

Office: 200 SW 1st Ave, Ft. Lauderdale, FL 33301.
Telephone: 954-769-6000.
Website: http://www.autonation.com
Chrmn & CEO: M.J. Jackson

Pres & COO: M.E. Maroone
EVP & CFO: M. Short
Chief Acctg Officer & Cntlr: M.J. Stephan
Treas: J.J. Teufel

Board Members: R. J. Brown, R. L. Burdick, W. C. Crowley, D. B. Edelson, R. R. Grusky, M. J. Jackson, M. Larson, M. E. Maroone, C. A. Migoya, A. H. Rosenthal

Founded: 1991
Domicile: Delaware
Employees: 19,000

# AutoZone Inc

**STANDARD &POOR'S**

**S&P Recommendation** HOLD ★★★★☆

| Price | 12-Mo. Target Price | Investment Style |
|---|---|---|
| $322.96 (as of Nov 25, 2011) | $340.00 | Large-Cap Growth |

**GICS Sector** Consumer Discretionary
**Sub-Industry** Automotive Retail

**Summary** This retailer of automotive parts and accessories operates over 4,600 AutoZone stores throughout most of the U.S. and in Mexico.

## Key Stock Statistics (Source S&P, Vickers, company reports)

| | | | | | | | |
|---|---|---|---|---|---|---|---|
| 52-Wk Range | $341.89– 246.26 | S&P Oper. EPS 2012E | 22.55 | Market Capitalization(B) | $12.882 | Beta | 0.39 |
| Trailing 12-Month EPS | $19.47 | S&P Oper. EPS 2013E | 25.74 | Yield (%) | Nil | S&P 3-Yr. Proj. EPS CAGR(%) | 14 |
| Trailing 12-Month P/E | 16.6 | P/E on S&P Oper. EPS 2012E | 14.3 | Dividend Rate/Share | Nil | S&P Credit Rating | BBB |
| $10K Invested 5 Yrs Ago | $28,103 | Common Shares Outstg. (M) | 39.9 | Institutional Ownership (%) | 90 | | |

## Price Performance

30-Week Mov. Avg. · · · 10-Week Mov. Avg. – – GAAP Earnings vs. Previous Year   Volume Above Avg. STARS
12-Mo. Target Price — Relative Strength   ▲ Up  ▼ Down  ▶ No Change   Below Avg. ★

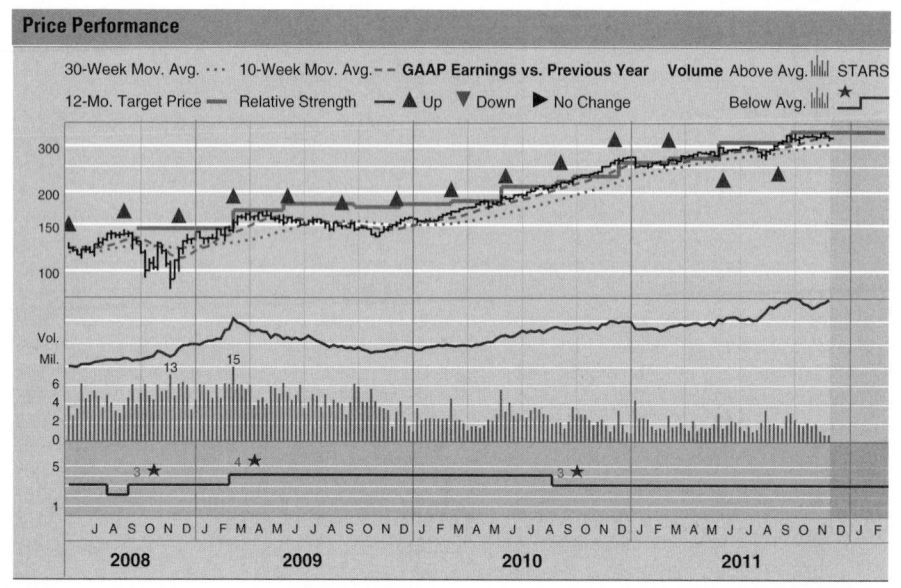

Options: ASE, CBOE, P, Ph

Analysis prepared by Equity Analyst **Michael Souers** on Sep 22, 2011, when the stock traded at **$316.02**.

## Highlights

➤ We see sales growth of 6.2% in FY 12 (Aug.), following a 9.6% advance in FY 11. This reflects our forecast of approximately 200 new stores in the U.S. and Mexico, along with same-store sales growth of about 3%. This follows a 6.3% comp-store-sales increase for FY 11, which may be a tough comp to hurdle despite continued positive business momentum. While macroeconomic pressures have put a financial strain on consumers, we continue to view industry-specific metrics favorably, such as the increased number of vehicles seven years or older on the road.

➤ We look for a 10 basis points widening of operating margins, as supply chain efficiencies are partially offset by an increasing percentage of lower-margin commercial sales in the mix. We expect a slight leveraging of SG&A expenses due to our projected low-single digit comp-store sales gain.

➤ After modestly higher interest expense, taxes at 36%, and about 8% fewer shares due to AZO's active share repurchase program, we forecast that FY 12 operating EPS will increase 16%, to $22.55, from the $19.47 the company earned in FY 11. We see FY 13 EPS of $25.74.

## Investment Rationale/Risk

➤ AutoZone maintains an industry-leading sales-to-square foot ratio, and sports higher gross, operating and net margins than any of its peers in our coverage universe. In addition, we think long-term trends for the automotive aftermarket retail industry are extremely favorable, with an aging vehicle population and pent-up demand from recent maintenance deferrals. We believe AZO's recent comp performance has been impressive, given the macro challenges facing consumers. However, following a strong recent increase in the share price, we view AZO as appropriately valued, and think higher gasoline prices will slow the recent increases in vehicle maintenance.

➤ Risks to our recommendation and target price include a significant decline in consumer spending; a sharp rise in oil prices; a decrease in auto usage and miles driven; and declines in same-store-sales, which would cause expense deleverage.

➤ Our 12-month target price of $340 is based on our DCF analysis. Our DCF model assumes a weighted average cost of capital of 9.2% and a terminal growth rate of 3.0%.

## Qualitative Risk Assessment

| LOW | MEDIUM | HIGH |
|---|---|---|

Our risk assessment reflects the cyclical and seasonal nature of the auto parts retailing industry, which is sensitive to various economic data points, offset by our view of the company's strong financial metrics and margins.

## Quantitative Evaluations

**S&P Quality Ranking** B+

| D | C | B- | B | B+ | A- | A | A+ |
|---|---|---|---|---|---|---|---|

**Relative Strength Rank** STRONG

82

LOWEST = 1    HIGHEST = 99

## Revenue/Earnings Data

**Revenue (Million $)**

| | 1Q | 2Q | 3Q | 4Q | Year |
|---|---|---|---|---|---|
| 2011 | 1,792 | 1,661 | 1,978 | 2,642 | 8,073 |
| 2010 | 1,589 | 1,506 | 1,822 | 2,445 | 7,363 |
| 2009 | 1,478 | 1,448 | 1,658 | 2,232 | 6,817 |
| 2008 | 1,456 | 1,339 | 1,517 | 2,211 | 6,523 |
| 2007 | 1,393 | 1,300 | 1,474 | 2,003 | 6,170 |
| 2006 | 1,338 | 1,254 | 1,417 | 1,939 | 5,948 |

**Earnings Per Share ($)**

| | 1Q | 2Q | 3Q | 4Q | Year |
|---|---|---|---|---|---|
| 2011 | 3.77 | 3.34 | 5.29 | 7.18 | 19.47 |
| 2010 | 2.82 | 2.46 | 4.12 | 5.66 | 14.97 |
| 2009 | 2.23 | 2.03 | 3.13 | 4.43 | 11.73 |
| 2008 | 2.02 | 1.67 | 2.49 | 3.88 | 10.04 |
| 2007 | 1.73 | 1.45 | 2.17 | 3.23 | 8.53 |
| 2006 | 1.48 | 1.25 | 1.89 | 2.92 | 7.50 |

Fiscal year ended Aug. 31. Next earnings report expected: Early December. EPS Estimates based on S&P Operating Earnings; historical GAAP earnings are as reported.

## Dividend Data

No cash dividends have been paid.

---

**Please read the Required Disclosures and Analyst Certification on the last page of this report.**

The **McGraw·Hill** Companies

# AutoZone Inc

**STANDARD &POOR'S**

## Business Summary September 22, 2011

CORPORATE OVERVIEW. AutoZone is the leading specialty retailer in the U.S. and a leading distributor of automotive replacement parts and accessories, focusing primarily on do-it-yourself (DIY) consumers. As of August 28, 2010, the company operated 4,389 U.S. AutoZone stores, in 48 states, the District of Columbia and Puerto Rico, and 238 stores in Mexico. AZO also sells automotive diagnostic equipment and repair software through ALLDATA, and diagnostic and repair information, along with and parts and accessories, online at www.autozone.com.

The company's 4,627 stores represented 30.0 million sq. ft., up from 4,417 stores and 28.6 million sq. ft. a year earlier. Each store's product line includes new and remanufactured automotive hard parts, such as alternators, starters, water pumps, brake shoes and pads, carburetors, clutches and engines; maintenance items, such as oil, antifreeze, transmission, brake and power steering fluids, engine additives, protectants and waxes; and accessories, such as car stereos and floor mats. Parts are carried for domestic and foreign cars, sport utility vehicles, vans, and light trucks.

Stores, generally in high-visibility locations, average 6,490 sq. ft. with a range from about 4,000 sq. ft. to 8,100 sq. ft. New stores are typically built in the larger format. As of August 28, 2010, AutoZone stores were principally in the following locations: 540 stores in Texas, 463 in California, 229 in Ohio, 217 in Florida, 214 in Illinois, 175 in Georgia, 172 in North Carolina, 153 in Tennessee, 149 in Michigan, 141 in Indiana, 123 in New York, 120 in Arizona, 114 in Pennsylvania, 109 in Louisiana and 100 in Missouri, with the rest in other states.

CORPORATE STRATEGY. AZO offers everyday low prices, and attempts to be the price leader in hard parts. Stores generally carry about 21,000 stock-keeping units. In addition to targeting the DIY customer, the company has a commercial sales program in the U.S. (AZ Commercial), which provides commercial credit and delivery of parts and other products to local, regional and national repair garages, dealers and service stations. As of August 28, 2010, 2,597 stores had commercial sales programs. The hub stores provide fast replenishment of key merchandise to support the DIY and commercial sales businesses. AZO does not perform repairs or installations.

## Company Financials Fiscal Year Ended Aug. 31

| Per Share Data ($) | 2011 | 2010 | 2009 | 2008 | 2007 | 2006 | 2005 | 2004 | 2003 | 2002 |
|---|---|---|---|---|---|---|---|---|---|---|
| Tangible Book Value | NM | NM | NM | NM | 1.52 | 2.35 | 1.15 | NM | 0.90 | 3.87 |
| Cash Flow | 23.97 | 18.87 | 14.96 | 12.70 | 10.82 | 9.34 | 8.92 | 7.79 | 6.47 | 5.10 |
| Earnings | 19.47 | 14.98 | 11.73 | 10.04 | 8.53 | 7.50 | 7.18 | 6.56 | 5.34 | 4.00 |
| S&P Core Earnings | 19.63 | 15.04 | 11.58 | 9.91 | 8.53 | 7.50 | 7.03 | 6.40 | 5.09 | 3.87 |
| Dividends | NA | Nil | Nil | Nil | Nil | Nil | Nil | Nil | Nil | Nil |
| Payout Ratio | Nil | Nil | Nil | Nil | Nil | Nil | Nil | Nil | Nil | Nil |
| Prices:High | 341.89 | 276.00 | 169.99 | 143.80 | 140.29 | 120.37 | 103.94 | 92.35 | 103.53 | 89.34 |
| Prices:Low | 246.26 | 152.32 | 125.80 | 84.66 | 103.40 | 83.81 | 77.76 | 70.35 | 58.21 | 59.20 |
| P/E Ratio:High | 18 | 18 | 14 | 14 | 16 | 16 | 14 | 14 | 19 | 22 |
| P/E Ratio:Low | 13 | 10 | 11 | 8 | 12 | 11 | 11 | 11 | 11 | 15 |

| Income Statement Analysis (Million $) | | | | | | | | | | |
|---|---|---|---|---|---|---|---|---|---|---|
| Revenue | 8,073 | 7,363 | 6,817 | 6,523 | 6,170 | 5,948 | 5,711 | 5,637 | 5,457 | 5,326 |
| Operating Income | 1,673 | 1,493 | 1,357 | 1,294 | 1,215 | 1,239 | 1,114 | 1,106 | 1,028 | 889 |
| Depreciation | 196 | 192 | 180 | 170 | 159 | 139 | 138 | 107 | 110 | 118 |
| Interest Expense | 171 | 159 | 148 | 121 | 119 | 110 | 104 | 93.0 | 84.8 | 79.9 |
| Pretax Income | 1,324 | 1,161 | 1,034 | 1,007 | 936 | 902 | 873 | 906 | 833 | 691 |
| Effective Tax Rate | NA | 36.4% | 36.4% | 36.3% | 36.4% | 36.9% | 34.6% | 37.5% | 37.9% | 38.1% |
| Net Income | 849 | 738 | 657 | 642 | 596 | 569 | 571 | 566 | 518 | 428 |
| S&P Core Earnings | 856 | 742 | 649 | 633 | 596 | 569 | 560 | 553 | 492 | 415 |

| Balance Sheet & Other Financial Data (Million $) | | | | | | | | | | |
|---|---|---|---|---|---|---|---|---|---|---|
| Cash | 97.6 | 98.3 | 92.7 | 242 | 86.7 | 91.6 | 74.8 | 76.9 | 6.74 | 6.50 |
| Current Assets | 2,792 | 2,612 | 2,562 | 2,586 | 2,270 | 2,119 | 1,929 | 1,756 | 1,585 | 1,450 |
| Total Assets | 5,870 | 5,572 | 5,318 | 5,257 | 4,805 | 4,526 | 4,245 | 3,913 | 3,680 | 3,478 |
| Current Liabilities | 3,431 | 3,064 | 2,707 | 2,519 | 2,286 | 2,055 | 1,811 | 1,818 | 1,676 | 1,534 |
| Long Term Debt | 3,352 | 2,882 | 2,727 | 2,250 | 1,936 | 1,857 | 1,862 | 1,869 | 1,547 | 1,195 |
| Common Equity | -1,254 | -739 | -433 | 230 | 403 | 470 | 391 | 171 | 374 | 1,378 |
| Total Capital | 2,097 | 2,144 | 2,294 | 2,480 | 2,339 | 2,327 | 2,253 | 2,046 | 1,921 | 2,573 |
| Capital Expenditures | 322 | 315 | 272 | 244 | 224 | 264 | 283 | 185 | 182 | 117 |
| Cash Flow | 1,045 | 930 | 837 | 811 | 755 | 709 | 709 | 673 | 627 | 546 |
| Current Ratio | 0.8 | 0.9 | 1.0 | 1.0 | 1.0 | 1.0 | 1.1 | 1.0 | 0.9 | 0.9 |
| % Long Term Debt of Capitalization | 159.8 | 134.5 | 118.9 | 90.7 | 82.8 | 79.8 | 82.6 | 91.3 | 80.5 | 46.4 |
| % Net Income of Revenue | 10.5 | 10.0 | 9.6 | 9.8 | 9.7 | 9.6 | 10.0 | 10.0 | 9.5 | 8.0 |
| % Return on Assets | 14.8 | 13.6 | 12.4 | 12.8 | 12.8 | 13.0 | 14.0 | 14.7 | 14.5 | 12.4 |
| % Return on Equity | NM | NM | NM | 202.8 | 136.5 | 132.3 | 203.1 | 207.7 | 97.4 | 27.5 |

Data as orig reptd.; bef. results of disc opers/spec. items. Per share data adj. for stk. divs.; EPS diluted. E-Estimated. NA-Not Available. NM-Not Meaningful. NR-Not Ranked. UR-Under Review.

**Office:** 123 South Front Street, Memphis, TN 38103.
**Telephone:** 901-495-6500.
**Email:** investor.relations@autozone.com
**Website:** http://www.autozone.com

**Chrmn, Pres & CEO:** W.C. Rhodes, III
**EVP, CFO & Treas:** W.T. Giles
**EVP, Secy & General Counsel:** H.L. Goldsmith
**SVP, Chief Acctg Officer & Cntlr:** C. Pleas, III

**SVP & CIO:** J.A. Bascom
**Investor Contact:** B. Campbell (901-495-7005)
**Board Members:** W. C. Crowley, S. E. Gove, E. B. Graves, Jr., R. R. Grusky, J. R. Hyde, III, W. A. McKenna, G. R. Mrkonic, Jr., L. P. Nieto, Jr., W. C. Rhodes, III, T. W. Ullyot

**Founded:** 1979
**Domicile:** Nevada
**Employees:** 65,000

# AvalonBay Communities Inc.

**STANDARD &POOR'S**

| | | | |
|---|---|---|---|
| **S&P Recommendation** BUY ★★★★☆ | **Price** $118.10 (as of Nov 25, 2011) | **12-Mo. Target Price** $141.00 | **Investment Style** Large-Cap Blend |

**GICS Sector** Financials
**Sub-Industry** Residential REITS

**Summary** This real estate investment trust, formed via the 1998 merger of Bay Apartment Communities and Avalon Properties, specializes in upscale apartment communities.

## Key Stock Statistics (Source S&P, Vickers, company reports)

| | | | | | | | |
|---|---|---|---|---|---|---|---|
| 52-Wk Range | $139.91– 107.32 | S&P FFO/Sh. 2011**E** | 4.59 | Market Capitalization(B) | $11.229 | Beta | 1.31 |
| Trailing 12-Month FFO/Share | $4.11 | S&P FFO/Sh. 2012**E** | 5.20 | Yield (%) | 3.02 | S&P 3-Yr. FFO/Sh. Proj. CAGR(%) | 10 |
| Trailing 12-Month P/FFO | NA | P/FFO on S&P FFO/Sh. 2011**E** | 25.7 | Dividend Rate/Share | $3.57 | S&P Credit Rating | BBB+ |
| $10K Invested 5 Yrs Ago | $11,127 | Common Shares Outstg. (M) | 95.1 | Institutional Ownership (%) | NM | | |

## Price Performance

30-Week Mov. Avg. · · · 10-Week Mov. Avg. - - **GAAP Earnings vs. Previous Year** Volume Above Avg. STARS
12-Mo. Target Price — Relative Strength — ▲ Up ▼ Down ▶ No Change Below Avg.

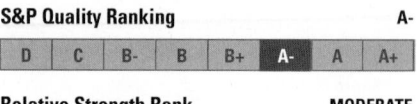

Options: ASE, CBOE, P

Analysis prepared by Equity Analyst **R. Shepard, CFA** on Nov 14, 2011, when the stock traded at **$129.32**.

## Highlights

▶ We think AVB will take advantage of high occupancy levels to lift rental rents over the next 12 months. During the third quarter, average rental rates rose 5.9%, and we estimate a gain of 5% to 6% for 2012. In our opinion, the strong demand reflects a trend away from home ownership, which hit a 10-year low in the third quarter of 2010, according to the U.S. Census Bureau. Also, the competitive supply of new homes is modest, thanks to a sharp drop in 2010 and 2011 multi-family construction starts.

▶ We think new development activities will be an important driver of earnings in 2012. As of September 30, 2011, the trust had 15 communities under construction for an expected total cost of $990 million. We expect seven of these communities with about 1,428 apartment units to be completed by the fourth quarter of 2012. An additional 2,377 units are undergoing capital upgrades at an expect total cost of $407 million.

▶ Our 2011 FFO per share forecast is $4.59, expanding to $5.20 in 2012, reflecting higher revenues from rent increases, initial revenues from recently development properties, and increased equity income from joint venture investments.

## Investment Rationale/Risk

▶ We expect a better balance between supply and demand to lead to renewed rental growth. In our view, AVB's position in urban coastal markets will enable it to raise 2012 rents close to 6% on renewed leases. We also think AVB's large pipeline of development projects holds value and will add incrementally to earnings in 2012. We do not believe the shares, recently selling at 24.1X our 2012 FFO estimate of $5.20, a moderate premium to peers, appropriately reflect its above-average long-term earnings growth profile.

▶ Risks to our recommendation and target price include the potential for slower-than-expected employment growth, increased competition from unsold inventories of single-family homes, and less liquid credit markets that restrict investor demand for AVB's real estate properties and the underlying valuation of its portfolio.

▶ Our 12-month target price of $141 is derived from applying a multiple of 27.1X to our 2012 FFO per share estimate of $5.20, a 20% premium to REIT peers, on average. Our valuation reflects our view of AVB's relatively strong financial position, high quality properties, and large development pipeline.

## Qualitative Risk Assessment

| LOW | MEDIUM | HIGH |
|---|---|---|

Our risk assessment reflects AVB's geographically diverse asset base and strong dividend coverage ratio.

## Quantitative Evaluations

**S&P Quality Ranking** A-

| D | C | B- | B | B+ | A- | A | A+ |
|---|---|---|---|---|---|---|---|

**Relative Strength Rank** MODERATE

50

LOWEST = 1 HIGHEST = 99

## Revenue/FFO Data

**Revenue (Million $)**

| | 1Q | 2Q | 3Q | 4Q | Year |
|---|---|---|---|---|---|
| 2011 | 236.3 | 244.9 | 253.7 | -- | -- |
| 2010 | 215.5 | 220.3 | 227.6 | 231.9 | 895.3 |
| 2009 | 222.9 | 222.1 | 222.2 | 211.7 | 853.0 |
| 2008 | 204.2 | 211.2 | 218.5 | 220.4 | 854.2 |
| 2007 | 192.7 | 199.5 | 208.2 | 212.4 | 812.7 |
| 2006 | 175.2 | 180.7 | 187.7 | 193.8 | 737.3 |

**FFO Per Share ($)**

| | | | | | |
|---|---|---|---|---|---|
| 2011 | 1.08 | 1.13 | 1.17 | E1.21 | E4.59 |
| 2010 | 0.96 | 1.04 | 0.98 | 1.01 | 4.00 |
| 2009 | 1.27 | 0.90 | 1.09 | 0.64 | 3.89 |
| 2008 | 1.24 | 1.26 | 1.28 | 0.30 | 4.07 |
| 2007 | 1.11 | 1.17 | 1.19 | 1.14 | 4.61 |
| 2006 | 1.15 | 1.03 | 1.11 | 1.09 | 4.38 |

Fiscal year ended Dec. 31. Next earnings report expected: Early February. FFO Estimates based on S&P Funds From Operations Est..

## Dividend Data (Dates: mm/dd Payment Date: mm/dd/yy)

| Amount ($) | Date Decl. | Ex-Div. Date | Stk. of Record | Payment Date |
|---|---|---|---|---|
| 0.893 | 02/16 | 03/30 | 04/01 | 04/15/11 |
| 0.893 | 05/12 | 06/28 | 06/30 | 07/15/11 |
| 0.893 | 09/15 | 09/28 | 09/30 | 10/17/11 |
| 0.893 | 11/15 | 12/28 | 12/30 | 01/17/12 |

Dividends have been paid since 1994. Source: Company reports.

---

**Please read the Required Disclosures and Analyst Certification on the last page of this report.**

The McGraw-Hill Companies

# AvalonBay Communities Inc.

**STANDARD &POOR'S**

## Business Summary November 14, 2011

CORPORATE OVERVIEW. AvalonBay Communities (AVB) is a real estate investment trust (REIT) specializing in the ownership of multi-family apartment communities. At December 31, 2010, AVB owned or held an interest in 186 apartment communities containing 54,579 apartment homes in 10 states and the District of Columbia, of which 14 communities were under construction and nine communities were under reconstruction. AVB also owned a direct or indirect ownership interest in rights to develop an additional 26 communities; if developed in the manner expected, these would contain an estimated 7,313 apartment homes.

MARKET PROFILE. The U.S. housing market is highly fragmented and is characterized broadly by two types of housing units: multi-family and single-family. At the end of 2010, the U.S. Census Bureau estimated there were 130.85 million housing units in the country, an increase of 0.5% from the end of 2009. Due to the large stock and the fact that residents have the option of either being owners or tenants (renters), the housing market can be highly competitive. Main demand drivers for apartments are household formation and employment growth. S&P estimates 0.4 million new households were formed in 2010. Supply is created by new housing unit construction, which could consist of

single-family homes or multi-family apartment buildings or condominiums. According the U.S. Department of Housing, 0.59 million total housing units were started in 2010, up about 6% from depressed levels in 2009. Multi-family starts, for structures with more than four units, rose 8.1% in 2010, but remained 60% below the level of 2008.

With apartment tenants on relatively short leases compared to those of commercial and industrial properties, we believe apartment REITs are generally more sensitive to changes in market conditions than REITs in other property categories. Results could be hurt by new construction that adds new space in excess of actual demand. Trends in home price affordability also affect both rent levels and the level of new construction, since the relative price attractiveness of owning versus renting is an important factor in consumer decision making.

## Company Financials Fiscal Year Ended Dec. 31

| Per Share Data ($) | 2010 | 2009 | 2008 | 2007 | 2006 | 2005 | 2004 | 2003 | 2002 | 2001 |
|---|---|---|---|---|---|---|---|---|---|---|
| Tangible Book Value | 38.54 | 37.41 | 37.82 | 37.85 | NA | NA | NA | NA | 31.88 | NA |
| Earnings | 1.17 | 0.97 | 1.34 | 3.00 | 2.27 | 1.34 | 1.09 | 1.30 | 1.48 | 3.12 |
| S&P Core Earnings | 1.16 | 0.95 | 1.34 | 3.00 | 2.12 | 1.34 | 1.09 | 1.27 | 1.22 | 3.07 |
| Dividends | 3.57 | 3.57 | 5.38 | 3.33 | NA | NA | NA | NA | NA | 2.56 |
| Payout Ratio | NM | NM | 401% | 111% | 137% | NM | NM | NM | 188% | 82% |
| Prices:High | 116.09 | 87.82 | 113.07 | 149.94 | 134.60 | 92.99 | 75.93 | 49.71 | 52.65 | 51.90 |
| Prices:Low | 71.75 | 38.34 | 41.43 | 88.94 | 88.95 | 64.98 | 46.72 | 35.24 | 36.38 | 42.45 |
| P/E Ratio:High | 99 | 91 | 84 | 50 | 59 | 69 | 65 | 38 | 35 | 17 |
| P/E Ratio:Low | 61 | 40 | 31 | 30 | 39 | 48 | 40 | 27 | 24 | 14 |

| Income Statement Analysis (Million $) | 2010 | 2009 | 2008 | 2007 | 2006 | 2005 | 2004 | 2003 | 2002 | 2001 |
|---|---|---|---|---|---|---|---|---|---|---|
| Rental Income | 888 | 844 | 848 | 807 | 731 | 666 | 648 | Nil | Nil | 637 |
| Mortgage Income | Nil | Nil | Nil | Nil | Nil | Nil | Nil | Nil | Nil | Nil |
| Total Income | 895 | 852 | 854 | 813 | 737 | 671 | 648 | 610 | 639 | 642 |
| General Expenses | 390 | 374 | 436 | 346 | 236 | 376 | 368 | 192 | 247 | 229 |
| Interest Expense | 175 | 150 | 115 | 97.5 | 111 | 127 | 131 | 135 | 121 | 103 |
| Provision for Losses | Nil | Nil | Nil | Nil | Nil | Nil | Nil | Nil | Nil | Nil |
| Depreciation | 233 | 210 | 194 | 180 | 163 | 159 | 152 | 151 | 144 | 130 |
| Net Income | 96.8 | 77.8 | 114 | 248 | 180 | 108 | 86.3 | 100 | 121 | 249 |
| S&P Core Earnings | 97.9 | 76.1 | 104 | 239 | 159 | 98.9 | 76.7 | 87.6 | 85.7 | 213 |

| Balance Sheet & Other Financial Data (Million $) | 2010 | 2009 | 2008 | 2007 | 2006 | 2005 | 2004 | 2003 | 2002 | 2001 |
|---|---|---|---|---|---|---|---|---|---|---|
| Cash | 306 | 106 | 259 | 210 | 146 | 48.0 | 4,921 | 4,744 | 4,813 | 4,479 |
| Total Assets | 7,821 | 7,458 | 7,173 | 6,736 | 5,813 | 5,165 | 5,068 | 4,910 | 4,952 | 4,664 |
| Real Estate Investment | 8,661 | 8,311 | 5,297 | 5,038 | 5,662 | 5,874 | NA | 5,431 | 5,369 | 4,838 |
| Loss Reserve | Nil | Nil | Nil | Nil | Nil | Nil | NA | Nil | Nil | Nil |
| Net Investment | 6,956 | 6,833 | 6,650 | 6,297 | 4,562 | 4,946 | 4,919 | 4,736 | 4,800 | 4,391 |
| Short Term Debt | 237 | 125 | 310 | 514 | Nil | Nil | Nil | Nil | 165 | 101 |
| Capitalization:Debt | 3,831 | 3,850 | 3,365 | 2,694 | 2,705 | 2,177 | 2,335 | 2,337 | 2,307 | 1,983 |
| Capitalization:Equity | 3,311 | 3,050 | 2,916 | 3,027 | 2,631 | 2,542 | 2,385 | 2,311 | 2,194 | 2,314 |
| Capitalization:Total | 7,161 | 6,906 | 6,290 | 5,534 | 5,194 | 4,738 | 4,741 | 2,336 | 4,579 | 4,353 |
| % Earnings & Depreciation/Assets | 4.3 | 3.9 | 8.7 | 6.8 | 6.2 | 5.2 | NA | 5.1 | 5.5 | 8.4 |
| Price Times Book Value:High | 3.0 | 2.3 | 3.0 | 4.0 | 4.0 | 2.8 | NA | 1.5 | 1.7 | 1.6 |
| Price Times Book Value:Low | 1.9 | 1.0 | 1.1 | 2.3 | 2.7 | 2.0 | NA | 1.1 | 1.1 | 1.3 |

Data as orig reptd.; bef. results of disc opers/spec. items. Per share data adj. for stk. divs.; EPS diluted. E-Estimated. NA-Not Available. NM-Not Meaningful. NR-Not Ranked. UR-Under Review.

**Office:** Ballston Tower, 671 North Glebe Road, Suite 800, Arlington, VA 22203.
**Telephone:** 703-329-6300.
**Email:** investments@avalonbay.com
**Website:** http://www.avalonbay.com

**Chrmn & CEO:** B. Blair
**Pres:** T.J. Naughton
**COO:** L.S. Horey
**EVP & CFO:** T.J. Sargeant

**SVP, Secy & General Counsel:** E.M. Schulman
**Investor Contact:** J. Christie (703-317-4747)
**Board Members:** B. Blair, A. B. Buckelew, B. A. Choate, J. J. Healy, Jr., T. J. Naughton, L. R. Primis, P. S. Rummell, H. J. Sarles, W. E. Walter

**Founded:** 1978
**Domicile:** Maryland
**Employees:** 1,993

The McGraw-Hill Companies

# Avery Dennison Corp

**STANDARD &POOR'S**

**S&P Recommendation** HOLD ★★★☆☆

| Price | 12-Mo. Target Price | Investment Style |
|---|---|---|
| $24.25 (as of Nov 25, 2011) | $28.00 | Large-Cap Blend |

**GICS Sector** Industrials
**Sub-Industry** Office Services & Supplies

**Summary** This company is a leading worldwide manufacturer of pressure-sensitive adhesives and materials, office products, labels, retail systems and specialty chemicals.

## Key Stock Statistics (Source S&P, Vickers, company reports)

| | | | | | | | |
|---|---|---|---|---|---|---|---|
| 52-Wk Range | $43.52–23.52 | S&P Oper. EPS 2011E | 2.25 | Market Capitalization(B) | $2.575 | Beta | 1.47 |
| Trailing 12-Month EPS | $2.64 | S&P Oper. EPS 2012E | 2.60 | Yield (%) | 4.12 | S&P 3-Yr. Proj. EPS CAGR(%) | -2 |
| Trailing 12-Month P/E | 9.2 | P/E on S&P Oper. EPS 2011E | 10.8 | Dividend Rate/Share | $1.00 | S&P Credit Rating | BBB |
| $10K Invested 5 Yrs Ago | $4,210 | Common Shares Outstg. (M) | 106.2 | Institutional Ownership (%) | 87 | | |

## Price Performance

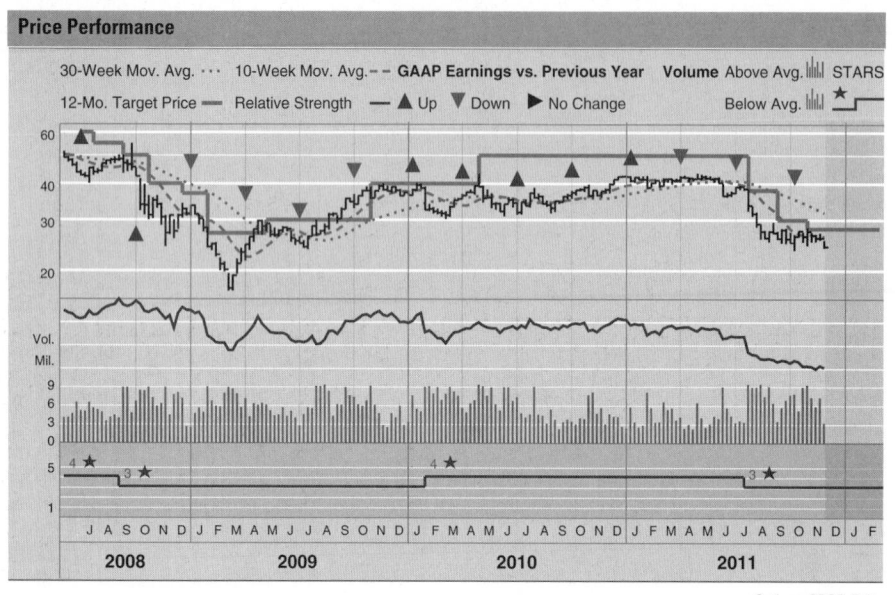

30-Week Mov. Avg. · · · 10-Week Mov. Avg. - - GAAP Earnings vs. Previous Year Volume Above Avg. STARS
12-Mo. Target Price — Relative Strength — ▲ Up ▼ Down ▶ No Change Below Avg.

Options: CBOE, P, Ph

Analysis prepared by Equity Analyst **S. Benway, CFA** on Nov 01, 2011.

## Qualitative Risk Assessment

| LOW | **MEDIUM** | HIGH |
|---|---|---|

Our risk assessment reflects the company's leading market shares in pressure-sensitive adhesives and office products, and our view of above-average growth rates in key end markets and relatively strong cash flow, offset by current sluggish markets.

## Quantitative Evaluations

**S&P Quality Ranking** B

| D | C | B- | **B** | B+ | A- | A | A+ |
|---|---|---|---|---|---|---|---|

**Relative Strength Rank** MODERATE

32

LOWEST = 1    HIGHEST = 99

## Revenue/Earnings Data

**Revenue (Million $)**

| | 1Q | 2Q | 3Q | 4Q | Year |
|---|---|---|---|---|---|
| 2011 | 1,659 | 1,726 | 1,700 | -- | -- |
| 2010 | 1,555 | 1,680 | 1,641 | 1,637 | 6,513 |
| 2009 | 1,426 | 1,455 | 1,549 | 1,522 | 5,953 |
| 2008 | 1,645 | 1,829 | 1,725 | 1,512 | 6,710 |
| 2007 | 1,390 | 1,524 | 1,680 | 1,714 | 6,308 |
| 2006 | 1,337 | 1,410 | 1,418 | 1,411 | 5,576 |

**Earnings Per Share ($)**

| | 1Q | 2Q | 3Q | 4Q | Year |
|---|---|---|---|---|---|
| 2011 | 0.42 | 0.69 | 0.47 | E0.49 | E2.25 |
| 2010 | 0.51 | 0.78 | 0.60 | 1.06 | 2.97 |
| 2009 | -8.99 | 0.38 | 0.59 | 0.47 | -7.21 |
| 2008 | 0.69 | 0.93 | 0.63 | 0.43 | 2.70 |
| 2007 | 0.80 | 0.87 | 0.59 | 0.81 | 3.07 |
| 2006 | 0.69 | 0.96 | 0.85 | 1.01 | 3.51 |

Fiscal year ended Dec. 31. Next earnings report expected: NA. EPS Estimates based on S&P Operating Earnings; historical GAAP earnings are as reported.

## Highlights

➤ We see sales rising 3%-5% in both 2011 and 2012, versus 9% growth in 2010. Much of the sales gain this year is expected to come from positive foreign currency effects, with prices also contributing. However, volume could be flat to down slightly on sluggish demand. In 2012, we expect volume to be stronger on growing demand in emerging markets, and market growth of pressure-sensitive materials.

➤ Margins will likely narrow in 2011 on the slower growth in demand, and as raw material costs continue to increase. We expect additional price increases to narrow the cost gap somewhat in 2012. We forecast higher marketing and development spending next year, especially in office products. EBIT margins are expected to fall 60 basis points to 6.4% in 2011, and remain near that level in 2012.

➤ For 2011, we expect a reduction in pension expense, but we see a higher effective tax rate. Our EPS estimate for 2011 of $2.25 excludes projected restructuring charges of $0.20. For 2012, we forecast EPS of $2.60.

## Investment Rationale/Risk

➤ Recent results at AVY have been disappointing, in our view, due to sudden volume declines. The current uncertain economic environment makes us cautious on near-term growth prospects. However, we believe long-term fundamentals remain sound, with growth driven by market expansion in pressure sensitive labels, and further penetration of emerging markets.

➤ Risks to our recommendation and target price include an inability to introduce new products or raise selling prices in response to higher raw material costs, and unexpected changes in customer order patterns.

➤ Our discounted cash flow model, which assumes a weighted average cost of capital of 10.5%, steady cash flow generation over the next three years, and 3% free cash flow growth in perpetuity, projects an intrinsic value of $31. A peer group of specialty chemical companies recently traded at 11.0X our 2012 EPS estimates. Applying a 10% discount to this valuation, due to our view of AVY's weak near-term prospects, to our 2012 EPS forecast, we derive a value of $26. Our 12-month target price of $28 is a blend of these metrics.

## Dividend Data (Dates: mm/dd Payment Date: mm/dd/yy)

| Amount ($) | Date Decl. | Ex-Div. Date | Stk. of Record | Payment Date |
|---|---|---|---|---|
| 0.250 | 02/02 | 02/28 | 03/02 | 03/16/11 |
| 0.250 | 04/28 | 05/27 | 06/01 | 06/15/11 |
| 0.250 | 07/27 | 09/02 | 09/07 | 09/21/11 |
| 0.250 | 10/27 | 12/05 | 12/07 | 12/21/11 |

Dividends have been paid since 1964. Source: Company reports.

# Avery Dennison Corp

## Business Summary November 01, 2011

Avery Dennison Corporation (AVY) produces pressure-sensitive materials, office products and various tickets, tags, labels and other converted products. Established in 1935, AVY also manufactures and sells various other items not involving pressure-sensitive components, such as binders, organizing systems, markers, fasteners, business forms, as well as radio-frequency identification (RFID) inlays, and imprinting equipment for retail and apparel manufacturers.

AVY's operating segments include: Pressure-sensitive Materials; Retail Branding and Information Solution; and Office and Consumer Products.

The Pressure-sensitive Materials segment (56% of sales and 66% of operating profits in 2010) manufactures and sells Fasson-, JAC-, and Avery Dennison-brand pressure-sensitive label and packaging materials, Avery-brand graphics and graphic films, Avery Dennison-brand reflective products, and performance polymers. Pressure-sensitive materials consist primarily of papers, plastic films, metal foils, and fabrics, which are coated with company-developed and purchased adhesives, and then laminated with specially coated backing papers and films. The company's graphic products consist of various

films and other products sold to the architectural, commercial sign, digital printing, and other related markets. It also sells durable cast and reflective films to the construction, automotive, and fleet transportation markets, scrim-reinforced vinyl material for banner sign applications, and reflective films for traffic and safety applications. The company's performance polymer products include solvent- and emulsion-based acrylic polymer adhesives, protective coatings and other polymer additives.

The Retail Branding and Information Solutions segment (23% and 14%) designs, manufactures and sells various products for retailers, apparel manufacturers, distributors, and industrial customers on a worldwide basis. AVY's brand identification products include woven and printed labels, graphic tags, and barcode tags. Its information management products include price tickets, carton labels, RFID tags, and printing applications.

## Company Financials Fiscal Year Ended Dec. 31

| Per Share Data ($) | 2010 | 2009 | 2008 | 2007 | 2006 | 2005 | 2004 | 2003 | 2002 | 2001 |
|---|---|---|---|---|---|---|---|---|---|---|
| Tangible Book Value | 3.16 | NA | NM | NM | 8.84 | 6.74 | 5.85 | 4.08 | 2.53 | 4.70 |
| Cash Flow | 5.29 | -4.63 | 5.10 | 5.13 | 5.50 | 4.95 | 4.66 | 4.22 | 4.12 | 4.05 |
| Earnings | 2.97 | -7.21 | 2.70 | 3.07 | 3.51 | 2.90 | 2.78 | 2.43 | 2.59 | 2.47 |
| S&P Core Earnings | 3.09 | -1.71 | 2.20 | 2.98 | 3.48 | 2.66 | 2.51 | 2.05 | 2.02 | 1.81 |
| Dividends | 0.80 | 1.22 | 1.65 | 1.61 | 1.57 | 1.53 | 1.49 | 1.45 | 1.35 | 1.23 |
| Payout Ratio | 27% | NM | 61% | 52% | 45% | 53% | 54% | 60% | 52% | 50% |
| Prices:High | 43.33 | 40.14 | 55.00 | 71.35 | 69.31 | 63.58 | 66.60 | 63.75 | 69.70 | 60.50 |
| Prices:Low | 30.22 | 17.02 | 24.30 | 49.69 | 54.95 | 49.60 | 53.50 | 46.25 | 52.06 | 43.25 |
| P/E Ratio:High | 15 | NM | 20 | 23 | 20 | 22 | 24 | 26 | 27 | 24 |
| P/E Ratio:Low | 10 | NM | 9 | 16 | 16 | 17 | 19 | 19 | 20 | 18 |

| Income Statement Analysis (Million $) | | | | | | | | | | |
|---|---|---|---|---|---|---|---|---|---|---|
| Revenue | 6,513 | 5,953 | 6,710 | 6,308 | 5,576 | 5,474 | 5,341 | 4,763 | 4,207 | 3,803 |
| Operating Income | 703 | 585 | 684 | 787 | 683 | 690 | 655 | 602 | 593 | 566 |
| Depreciation | 248 | 267 | 237 | 204 | 199 | 202 | 188 | 179 | 153 | 156 |
| Interest Expense | 76.6 | 85.3 | 122 | 111 | 55.5 | 57.9 | 58.5 | 57.7 | 43.7 | 50.2 |
| Pretax Income | 351 | -791 | 271 | 375 | 426 | 367 | 373 | 335 | 365 | 360 |
| Effective Tax Rate | NA | 5.59% | 1.66% | 19.1% | 17.2% | 20.4% | 25.1% | 27.5% | 29.5% | 32.4% |
| Net Income | 317 | -747 | 266 | 304 | 353 | 292 | 280 | 243 | 257 | 243 |
| S&P Core Earnings | 328 | -178 | 217 | 294 | 348 | 269 | 251 | 205 | 201 | 179 |

| Balance Sheet & Other Financial Data (Million $) | | | | | | | | | | |
|---|---|---|---|---|---|---|---|---|---|---|
| Cash | 128 | 138 | 106 | 71.5 | 58.5 | 98.5 | 84.8 | 29.5 | 22.8 | 19.1 |
| Current Assets | 1,952 | 1,733 | 1,930 | 2,058 | 1,655 | 1,558 | 1,542 | 1,441 | 1,216 | 982 |
| Total Assets | 5,099 | 5,003 | 6,036 | 6,245 | 4,294 | 4,204 | 4,399 | 4,105 | 3,652 | 2,819 |
| Current Liabilities | 1,832 | 1,868 | 2,058 | 2,478 | 1,699 | 1,526 | 1,387 | 1,496 | 1,296 | 951 |
| Long Term Debt | 956 | 1,089 | 1,545 | 1,145 | 502 | 723 | 1,007 | 888 | 837 | 627 |
| Common Equity | 1,646 | 1,363 | 1,750 | 1,989 | 1,681 | 1,512 | 1,549 | 1,319 | 1,056 | 929 |
| Total Capital | 2,602 | 2,451 | 3,295 | 3,376 | 2,261 | 2,235 | 2,647 | 2,274 | 1,968 | 1,647 |
| Capital Expenditures | 83.5 | 72.2 | 129 | 191 | 162 | 163 | 179 | 201 | 152 | 135 |
| Cash Flow | 564 | -479 | 504 | 508 | 552 | 493 | 468 | 422 | 410 | 399 |
| Current Ratio | 1.1 | 0.9 | 0.9 | 0.8 | 1.0 | 1.0 | 1.1 | 1.0 | 0.9 | 1.0 |
| % Long Term Debt of Capitalization | 36.8 | 44.4 | 46.9 | 33.9 | 22.2 | 32.4 | 38.1 | 39.0 | 42.5 | 38.0 |
| % Net Income of Revenue | 4.9 | NM | 4.0 | 4.8 | 6.3 | 5.3 | 5.2 | 5.1 | 6.1 | 6.4 |
| % Return on Assets | 6.3 | NM | 4.3 | 5.8 | 8.3 | 6.8 | 6.6 | 6.3 | 7.8 | 8.8 |
| % Return on Equity | 21.1 | NM | 14.2 | 16.5 | 22.1 | 19.1 | 19.5 | 20.4 | 25.9 | 27.7 |

Data as orig reptd.; bef. results of disc opers/spec. items. Per share data adj. for stk. divs.; EPS diluted. E-Estimated. NA-Not Available. NM-Not Meaningful. NR-Not Ranked. UR-Under Review.

**Office:** 150 North Orange Grove Boulevard, Pasadena, CA 91103.
**Telephone:** 626-304-2000.
**Email:** investorcom@averydennison.com
**Website:** http://www.averydennison.com

**Chrmn, Pres & CEO:** D.A. Scarborough
**SVP & CIO:** R.W. Hoffman
**CFO:** M.R. Butier
**CTO:** D.N. Edwards

**Chief Acctg Officer & Cntlr:** L.J. Bondar
**Investor Contact:** E.M. Leeds (626-304-2029)
**Board Members:** B. A. Alford, P. K. Barker, R. Borjesson, J. T. Cardis, K. C. Hicks, P. W. Mullin, C. H. Noski, D. E. Pyott, D. A. Scarborough, P. T. Siewert, J. A. Stewart

**Founded:** 1935
**Domicile:** Delaware
**Employees:** 32,100

# Avon Products Inc.

**STANDARD &POOR'S**

| S&P Recommendation | HOLD ★★★★☆ | Price | 12-Mo. Target Price | Investment Style |
|---|---|---|---|---|
| | | $16.09 (as of Nov 25, 2011) | $21.00 | Large-Cap Growth |

**GICS Sector** Consumer Staples
**Sub-Industry** Personal Products

**Summary** This company is the world's leading direct marketer of cosmetics, toiletries, fashion jewelry and fragrances, with about 6.5 million sales representatives worldwide.

## Key Stock Statistics (Source S&P, Vickers, company reports)

| | | | | | | | |
|---|---|---|---|---|---|---|---|
| 52-Wk Range | $31.60– 16.09 | S&P Oper. EPS 2011E | 1.78 | Market Capitalization(B) | $6.931 | Beta | 1.40 |
| Trailing 12-Month EPS | $1.70 | S&P Oper. EPS 2012E | 1.81 | Yield (%) | 5.72 | S&P 3-Yr. Proj. EPS CAGR(%) | 5 |
| Trailing 12-Month P/E | 9.5 | P/E on S&P Oper. EPS 2011E | 9.0 | Dividend Rate/Share | $0.92 | S&P Credit Rating | BBB+ |
| $10K Invested 5 Yrs Ago | $5,583 | Common Shares Outstg. (M) | 430.8 | Institutional Ownership (%) | 84 | | |

## Price Performance

- 30-Week Mov. Avg. · · ·
- 10-Week Mov. Avg. - -
- **GAAP Earnings vs. Previous Year**
- Volume Above Avg. ▮▮▮ STARS
- 12-Mo. Target Price —
- Relative Strength —
- ▲ Up ▼ Down ► No Change
- Below Avg. ▮▮▮ ★

Options: ASE, CBOE, P, Ph

Analysis prepared by Equity Analyst **Esther Kwon, CFA** on Oct 31, 2011, when the stock traded at **$18.28**.

## Highlights

➤ We estimate sales growth of approximately 6% for 2011, from 2010's $11 billion, followed by about 6% growth in 2012. On tougher first-half comparisons, we see a slower start followed by acceleration in the second half. We expect growth to be led by Western Europe/Middle East/Africa, Asia Pacific and Latin America. China appears to be having difficulty transitioning from beauty boutiques to the now-permitted direct sales channel, and its sales are now included in the Asia Pacific region.

➤ We expect some cost-savings benefits in 2011 from AVP's 2005 and 2009 multi-year restructuring plans and other cost-reduction programs, following significant savings in 2008 and 2009. Also, the operating margin for 2011 should benefit from better sales leverage and a swing to positive foreign currency translation effects. Currency effects involve not just the U.S. dollar but also the sale of euro-cost product into Central and Eastern Europe and the U.K., for example.

➤ Our 2011 operating EPS estimate is $1.78, down from 2010's operating EPS of $1.80, excluding restructuring charges and one-time charges. For 2012, we forecast EPS of $1.81.

## Investment Rationale/Risk

➤ After withdrawing its target of mid-single digit revenue growth and 50 to 70 basis points of operating margin improvement in 2011, AVP is reviewing operations and will update the financial community in the first quarter of 2012. On top of a Securities and Exchange Commission review of potential violation of Foreign Corrupt Practices Act, the company received a subpoena from the SEC in connection with Regulation Fair Disclosure. Although we see these reviews complicating efforts to turn around the business, we think the shares, which are trading at a significant discount to peers and their historical average, incorporate these risks.

➤ Risks to our recommendation and target price include weakness in the U.S. market, deceleration in high-growth markets, unfavorable movement in foreign exchange rates, worse-than-expected acceptance of new products, and higher-than-expected cost pressures.

➤ Our 12-month target price of $21 is a blend of our historical and peer models. Our historical model uses a P/E of 13.1X our 2011 EPS estimate, a discount to the 10-year average, for a $23 value. Our discount-to-peer average multiple of 11.1X produces a value of $20.

## Qualitative Risk Assessment

| LOW | MEDIUM | HIGH |
|---|---|---|

Our risk assessment reflects that demand for personal care products is usually static and not generally affected by changes in the economy or geopolitical factors. However, certain product categories, such as fragrances, may be more susceptible to adverse factors.

## Quantitative Evaluations

**S&P Quality Ranking** A-

| D | C | B- | B | B+ | A- | A | A+ |
|---|---|---|---|---|---|---|---|

**Relative Strength Rank** WEAK

13

LOWEST = 1  HIGHEST = 99

## Revenue/Earnings Data

**Revenue (Million $)**

| | 1Q | 2Q | 3Q | 4Q | Year |
|---|---|---|---|---|---|
| 2011 | 2,629 | 2,856 | 2,763 | -- | -- |
| 2010 | 2,446 | 2,629 | 2,612 | 3,176 | 10,863 |
| 2009 | 2,180 | 2,470 | 2,551 | 3,181 | 10,383 |
| 2008 | 2,502 | 2,736 | 2,645 | 2,808 | 10,690 |
| 2007 | 2,185 | 2,329 | 2,349 | 3,076 | 9,939 |
| 2006 | 2,003 | 2,080 | 2,059 | 2,623 | 8,764 |

**Earnings Per Share ($)**

| | | | | | |
|---|---|---|---|---|---|
| 2011 | 0.35 | 0.47 | 0.38 | E0.54 | E1.78 |
| 2010 | 0.10 | 0.38 | 0.38 | 0.50 | 1.36 |
| 2009 | 0.27 | 0.19 | 0.36 | 0.62 | 1.45 |
| 2008 | 0.43 | 0.55 | 0.52 | 0.54 | 2.04 |
| 2007 | 0.34 | 0.26 | 0.32 | 0.30 | 1.22 |
| 2006 | 0.12 | 0.34 | 0.19 | 0.41 | 1.06 |

Fiscal year ended Dec. 31. Next earnings report expected: Early February. EPS Estimates based on S&P Operating Earnings; historical GAAP earnings are as reported.

## Dividend Data (Dates: mm/dd Payment Date: mm/dd/yy)

| Amount ($) | Date Decl. | Ex-Div. Date | Stk. of Record | Payment Date |
|---|---|---|---|---|
| 0.230 | 02/03 | 02/15 | 02/17 | 03/01/11 |
| 0.230 | 05/05 | 05/17 | 05/19 | 06/01/11 |
| 0.230 | 08/01 | 08/11 | 08/15 | 09/01/11 |
| 0.230 | 11/02 | 11/10 | 11/15 | 12/01/11 |

Dividends have been paid since 1919. Source: Company reports.

**Please read the Required Disclosures and Analyst Certification on the last page of this report.**

The McGraw-Hill Companies

# Avon Products Inc.

STANDARD &POOR'S

## Business Summary October 31, 2011

CORPORATE OVERVIEW. Avon Products, which began operations in 1886, is a global manufacturer and marketer of beauty and related products. Beginning in the fourth quarter of 2008, AVP changed its product categories from Beauty, Beauty Plus and Beyond Beauty to Beauty, Fashion and Home & Other. Beauty consists of cosmetics, fragrances, skin care and toiletries, and accounted for 71% of sales in 2010. Fashion (19%) consists of fashion jewelry, watches, apparel, footwear and accessories. Home & Other (10%) consists of gift and decorative products, housewares, entertainment & leisure, kids and nutrition. The company has operations in 64 countries and territories, including the U.S., and its products are distributed in 41 more. Geographically, 21% of 2010 sales were derived from North America, while Latin America accounted for 42%, Western Europe, the Middle East & Africa 13%, Central & Eastern Europe 15%, Asia-Pacific 7%, and China 2%. Operations outside North America accounted for 88% of segment operating profits in 2010. Sales are made to the ultimate consumer mainly through a combination of direct selling and marketing by about 6.5 million independent Avon representatives.

In 2010, the number of active representatives fell 3% in North America, rose 8% in Latin America, 12% in Western Europe, the Middle East & Africa, 4% in Central & Eastern Europe and 5% in Asia-Pacific, fell 39% in China (from a low base), and rose 4% overall.

CORPORATE STRATEGY. AVP embarked on a multi-year restructuring plan in November 2005 in an effort to drive revenue and profit growth. The plan entails reorganizing and downsizing the organization, implementing global manufacturing, and increasing supply chain efficiencies. AVP expects restructuring benefits to help fund an increase in consumer research, marketing and product development, which, in turn, is expected to enhance sales and ultimately profits. In fact, we saw an improvement in the year-to-year sales growth rate starting in mid-2006, but savings from the plan were not large enough to offset increases in the expenses mentioned above until 2008. Also in 2005, Avon started to implement a global supply chain strategy, which includes the development of a new common systems platform, known as enterprise resource planning (ERP).

## Company Financials Fiscal Year Ended Dec. 31

| Per Share Data ($) | 2010 | 2009 | 2008 | 2007 | 2006 | 2005 | 2004 | 2003 | 2002 | 2001 |
|---|---|---|---|---|---|---|---|---|---|---|
| Tangible Book Value | 1.10 | 2.16 | 0.76 | 1.66 | 1.79 | 1.68 | 2.02 | 0.79 | NM | NM |
| Cash Flow | 1.81 | 1.88 | 2.41 | 1.55 | 1.42 | 2.10 | 2.05 | 1.63 | 1.34 | 1.10 |
| Earnings | 1.36 | 1.45 | 2.04 | 1.22 | 1.06 | 1.81 | 1.77 | 1.39 | 1.11 | 0.90 |
| S&P Core Earnings | 1.42 | 1.53 | 1.94 | 1.25 | 1.16 | 1.80 | 1.80 | 1.37 | 0.95 | 0.77 |
| Dividends | 0.88 | 0.84 | 0.80 | 0.74 | 0.70 | 0.66 | 0.70 | 0.42 | 0.40 | 0.38 |
| Payout Ratio | 65% | 58% | 39% | 61% | 66% | 36% | 40% | 30% | 36% | 42% |
| Prices:High | 36.20 | 36.39 | 45.34 | 42.51 | 34.25 | 45.66 | 46.65 | 34.88 | 28.55 | 25.06 |
| Prices:Low | 25.00 | 14.40 | 17.45 | 31.95 | 26.16 | 24.33 | 30.81 | 24.47 | 21.75 | 17.78 |
| P/E Ratio:High | 27 | 25 | 22 | 35 | 32 | 25 | 26 | 25 | 26 | 28 |
| P/E Ratio:Low | 18 | 10 | 9 | 26 | 25 | 13 | 17 | 18 | 20 | 20 |

### Income Statement Analysis (Million $)

| | 2010 | 2009 | 2008 | 2007 | 2006 | 2005 | 2004 | 2003 | 2002 | 2001 |
|---|---|---|---|---|---|---|---|---|---|---|
| Revenue | 10,863 | 10,383 | 10,690 | 9,939 | 8,764 | 8,150 | 7,748 | 6,876 | 6,228 | 5,995 |
| Operating Income | 1,430 | 1,370 | 1,558 | 1,176 | 1,146 | 1,289 | 1,361 | 1,162 | 1,029 | 951 |
| Depreciation | 195 | 181 | 158 | 145 | 160 | 140 | 135 | 124 | 125 | 109 |
| Interest Expense | 87.1 | 105 | 105 | 125 | 99.6 | 54.1 | 33.8 | 33.3 | 52.0 | 71.1 |
| Pretax Income | 945 | 926 | 1,238 | 796 | 704 | 1,124 | 1,188 | 994 | 836 | 666 |
| Effective Tax Rate | NA | 32.2% | 29.3% | 33.0% | 31.8% | 24.0% | 27.8% | 32.1% | 35.0% | 34.7% |
| Net Income | 595 | 626 | 875 | 531 | 478 | 848 | 846 | 665 | 535 | 430 |
| S&P Core Earnings | 613 | 654 | 833 | 549 | 518 | 845 | 859 | 652 | 455 | 367 |

### Balance Sheet & Other Financial Data (Million $)

| | 2010 | 2009 | 2008 | 2007 | 2006 | 2005 | 2004 | 2003 | 2002 | 2001 |
|---|---|---|---|---|---|---|---|---|---|---|
| Cash | 1,180 | 1,312 | 1,105 | 963 | 1,199 | 1,059 | 770 | 694 | 607 | 509 |
| Current Assets | 4,184 | 4,189 | 3,557 | 3,515 | 3,334 | 2,921 | 2,506 | 2,226 | 2,048 | 1,889 |
| Total Assets | 7,874 | 6,833 | 6,074 | 5,716 | 5,238 | 4,763 | 4,148 | 3,562 | 3,328 | 3,193 |
| Current Liabilities | 2,956 | 2,275 | 2,912 | 3,053 | 2,550 | 2,502 | 1,526 | 1,588 | 1,976 | 1,461 |
| Long Term Debt | 2,409 | 2,308 | 1,456 | 1,168 | 1,171 | 766 | 866 | 878 | 767 | 1,236 |
| Common Equity | 1,657 | 1,273 | 675 | 712 | 790 | 794 | 950 | 371 | -128 | -74.6 |
| Total Capital | 4,097 | 3,620 | 2,205 | 2,089 | 2,028 | 1,595 | 1,829 | 1,300 | 712 | 1,192 |
| Capital Expenditures | 331 | 297 | 381 | 279 | 175 | 207 | 250 | 163 | 127 | 155 |
| Cash Flow | 790 | 806 | 1,034 | 676 | 637 | 987 | 981 | 788 | 659 | 539 |
| Current Ratio | 1.4 | 1.8 | 1.2 | 1.2 | 1.3 | 1.2 | 1.6 | 1.4 | 1.0 | 1.3 |
| % Long Term Debt of Capitalization | 58.8 | 63.7 | 66.1 | 62.1 | 58.8 | 48.1 | 47.4 | 67.5 | 107.8 | 103.7 |
| % Net Income of Revenue | 5.5 | 6.0 | 8.2 | 5.3 | 5.4 | 10.4 | 10.9 | 9.7 | 8.6 | 7.2 |
| % Return on Assets | 8.1 | 9.7 | 14.9 | 9.7 | 9.6 | 19.0 | 21.9 | 19.3 | 16.4 | 14.3 |
| % Return on Equity | 40.6 | 64.3 | 126.3 | 70.7 | 60.3 | 97.2 | 128.0 | 545.8 | NM | NM |

Data as orig reptd.; bef. results of disc opers/spec. items. Per share data adj. for stk. divs.; EPS diluted. E-Estimated. NA-Not Available. NM-Not Meaningful. NR-Not Ranked. UR-Under Review.

**Office:** 1345 Avenue of the Americas, New York, NY 10105-0196.
**Telephone:** 212-282-5000.
**Email:** individual.investor@avon.com
**Website:** http://www.avoncompany.com

**Chrmn & CEO:** A. Jung
**COO:** J.P. Higson
**EVP & CFO:** K.A. Ross
**SVP, Secy & General Counsel:** K.K. Rucker

**SVP & CIO:** D. Herlihy
**Investor Contact:** A.L. Chasen (212-282-5320)
**Board Members:** W. D. Cornwell, V. A. Hailey, F. Hassan, A. Jung, M. E. Lagomasino, A. S. Moore, P. S. Pressler, G. M. Rodkin, P. Stern, L. A. Weinbach

**Founded:** 1886
**Domicile:** New York
**Employees:** 42,000

# Baker Hughes Inc

**STANDARD &POOR'S**

| **S&P Recommendation** BUY ★★★★☆ | **Price** $48.87 (as of Nov 25, 2011) | **12-Mo. Target Price** $74.00 | **Investment Style** Large-Cap Growth |
|---|---|---|---|

**GICS Sector** Energy
**Sub-Industry** Oil & Gas Equipment & Services

**Summary** This company is one of the world's largest oilfield services companies, providing products and services to the energy industry.

## Key Stock Statistics (Source S&P, Vickers, company reports)

| | | | | | | | |
|---|---|---|---|---|---|---|---|
| 52-Wk Range | $81.00– 41.91 | S&P Oper. EPS 2011**E** | 4.06 | Market Capitalization(B) | $21.330 | Beta | 1.69 |
| Trailing 12-Month EPS | $4.06 | S&P Oper. EPS 2012**E** | 5.47 | Yield (%) | 1.23 | S&P 3-Yr. Proj. EPS CAGR(%) | 59 |
| Trailing 12-Month P/E | 12.0 | P/E on S&P Oper. EPS 2011**E** | 12.0 | Dividend Rate/Share | $0.60 | S&P Credit Rating | A |
| $10K Invested 5 Yrs Ago | $7,330 | Common Shares Outstg. (M) | 436.5 | Institutional Ownership (%) | 84 | | |

## Price Performance

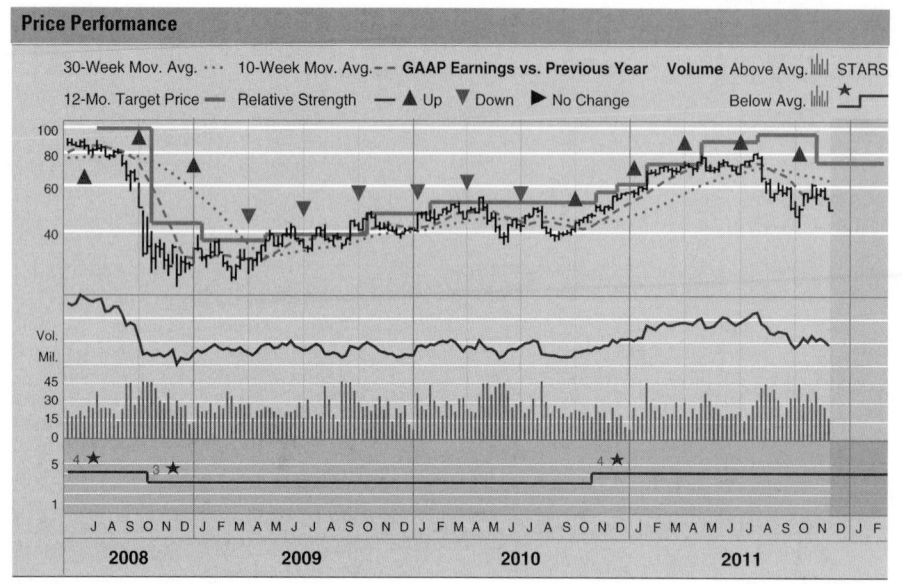

30-Week Mov. Avg. · · · 10-Week Mov. Avg. – – GAAP Earnings vs. Previous Year   Volume Above Avg. ▯▮▯ STARS
12-Mo. Target Price — Relative Strength — ▲ Up ▼ Down ► No Change   Below Avg. ▯▯▯ ★

Options: ASE, CBOE, P, Ph

## Qualitative Risk Assessment

| LOW | **MEDIUM** | HIGH |
|---|---|---|

Our risk assessment reflects BHI's exposure to volatile crude oil and natural gas prices, capital spending decisions by its exploration and production customers, and political risk associated with operating in frontier regions. Offsetting these risks is BHI's strong position in drilling and completion products.

## Quantitative Evaluations

**S&P Quality Ranking** B+

| D | C | B- | B | **B+** | A- | A | A+ |
|---|---|---|---|---|---|---|---|

**Relative Strength Rank** WEAK

23

LOWEST = 1   HIGHEST = 99

## Highlights

► The 12-month target price for BHI has recently been changed to $74.00 from $95.00. The Highlights section of this Stock Report will be updated accordingly.

## Investment Rationale/Risk

► The Investment Rationale/Risk section of this Stock Report will be updated shortly. For the latest News story on BHI from MarketScope, see below.

► 11/01/11 01:46 pm ET ... S&P MAINTAINS BUY OPINION ON SHARES OF BAKER HUGHES (BHI 53.76****): Q3 EPS of $1.18, before net 1X benefits of $0.43, vs. $0.93, is $0.02 below our estimate. Results were led by gains in North America, but international margins were under our model. We think international margin expansion is a case of when, not if, although we do expect gains at some point in '12. We lift our '11 EPS forecast $0.01 to $4.06, but cut '12's by $0.13 to $5.47. Given modestly weaker visbility on timing for international margin gains, however, we trim relative multiples. Blended with our DCF model, we cut our 12-month target price by $21 to $74. /Stewart Glickman, CFA

## Revenue/Earnings Data

### Revenue (Million $)

| | 1Q | 2Q | 3Q | 4Q | Year |
|---|---|---|---|---|---|
| 2011 | 4,525 | 4,741 | 5,178 | -- | -- |
| 2010 | 2,539 | 3,374 | 4,078 | 4,423 | 14,414 |
| 2009 | 2,668 | 2,336 | 2,232 | 2,428 | 9,664 |
| 2008 | 2,670 | 2,998 | 3,010 | 3,186 | 11,864 |
| 2007 | 2,473 | 2,538 | 2,678 | 2,740 | 10,428 |
| 2006 | 2,062 | 2,203 | 2,309 | 2,453 | 9,027 |

### Earnings Per Share ($)

| | | | | | |
|---|---|---|---|---|---|
| 2011 | 0.87 | 0.77 | 1.61 | E1.24 | E4.06 |
| 2010 | 0.41 | 0.23 | 0.59 | 0.77 | 2.06 |
| 2009 | 0.63 | 0.28 | 0.18 | 0.27 | 1.36 |
| 2008 | 1.27 | 1.23 | 1.39 | 1.41 | 5.30 |
| 2007 | 1.17 | 1.09 | 1.22 | 1.26 | 4.73 |
| 2006 | 0.93 | 4.14 | 1.09 | 1.02 | 7.21 |

Fiscal year ended Dec. 31. Next earnings report expected: NA. EPS Estimates based on S&P Operating Earnings; historical GAAP earnings are as reported.

## Dividend Data (Dates: mm/dd Payment Date: mm/dd/yy)

| Amount ($) | Date Decl. | Ex-Div. Date | Stk. of Record | Payment Date |
|---|---|---|---|---|
| 0.150 | 01/27 | 02/03 | 02/07 | 02/18/11 |
| 0.150 | 04/28 | 05/05 | 05/09 | 05/20/11 |
| 0.150 | 07/28 | 08/04 | 08/08 | 08/19/11 |
| 0.150 | 10/28 | 11/03 | 11/07 | 11/18/11 |

Dividends have been paid since 1987. Source: Company reports.

# Baker Hughes Inc

**STANDARD &POOR'S**

## Business Summary September 14, 2011

CORPORATE OVERVIEW. Baker Hughes was formed through the 1987 merger of Baker International Corp. and Hughes Tool Co. In 1998, it acquired seismic and wireline logging company Western Atlas, creating the third largest oilfield services company. BHI has operations in over 90 countries. North America accounted for 46% of total revenues in 2010, followed by the Europe, CIS and Africa region (21%), the Middle East and Asia-Pacific region (16%), and Latin America (11%). The Industrial Services segment accounted for the remaining 6% of 2010 revenues. In 2005, the company reorganized its seven product-line focused divisions into three operating segments: Drilling & Evaluation; Completion & Production; and Western Geco (which provides reservoir imaging, monitoring and development services). In April 2006, however, BHI sold its 30% minority stake in seismic company Western Geco to the majority joint venture partner, Schlumberger, and in 2010, the company further reorganized its operating segments along geographic lines, much like its major competitors. In April 2010, BHI acquired the former BJ Services, adding a significant pressure pumping operation to its completion & production arsenal.

The former Drilling & Evaluation segment consists of a variety of products and services that are typically used in the drilling of crude oil and natural gas wells. Such services include drill bit systems; conventional and rotary steerable systems used to drill wells directionally and horizontally; measurement-while-drilling and logging-while-drilling systems; drilling optimization systems;

coil tubing drilling; open-hole and cased-hole wireline services; reservoir evaluation; fluid characterization; well integrity services; and drilling fluids.

The former Completion & Production segment consists of well completion systems, which are used to control the flow of hydrocarbons; wellbore intervention, which includes remedial stimulation tools; intelligent production systems, which are used to monitor and control the production from individual wells or fields, chemical injection services and artificial lift monitoring; artificial lift, which includes electric submersible pumps, gas lifts and surface pumping systems when a reservoir is no longer capable of lifting large volumes of oil and water on its own; upstream chemicals, which are used for flow assurance for upstream production; and pressure pumping services, which include cementing, stimulation and coil tubing services in the completion of new oil and gas wells and in remedial work on existing wells.

The new Industrial Services segment consists of downstream chemicals, process and pipeline services, stimulation chemicals, reservoir technology, and consulting.

## Company Financials Fiscal Year Ended Dec. 31

| Per Share Data ($) | 2010 | 2009 | 2008 | 2007 | 2006 | 2005 | 2004 | 2003 | 2002 | 2001 |
|---|---|---|---|---|---|---|---|---|---|---|
| Tangible Book Value | 15.65 | 18.18 | 16.89 | 15.14 | 11.58 | 9.42 | 7.35 | 5.87 | 6.05 | 5.69 |
| Cash Flow | 4.78 | NA | 7.35 | 6.36 | 8.85 | 3.68 | 2.69 | 1.59 | 1.56 | 2.32 |
| Earnings | 2.06 | 1.36 | 5.30 | 4.73 | 7.21 | 2.56 | 1.57 | 0.40 | 0.66 | 1.31 |
| S&P Core Earnings | 2.07 | 1.38 | 5.33 | 4.70 | 4.24 | 2.47 | 1.50 | 0.62 | 0.55 | 1.17 |
| Dividends | 0.60 | 0.60 | 0.56 | 0.52 | 0.52 | 0.48 | 0.46 | 0.46 | 0.46 | 0.46 |
| Payout Ratio | 29% | 44% | 11% | 11% | 7% | 19% | 29% | 115% | 70% | 35% |
| Prices:High | 57.45 | 48.19 | 90.81 | 100.29 | 89.30 | 63.13 | 45.30 | 36.15 | 39.95 | 45.29 |
| Prices:Low | 35.62 | 25.69 | 24.40 | 62.26 | 60.60 | 40.73 | 31.56 | 26.90 | 22.60 | 25.76 |
| P/E Ratio:High | 28 | 35 | 17 | 21 | 12 | 25 | 29 | 90 | 61 | 35 |
| P/E Ratio:Low | 17 | 19 | 5 | 13 | 8 | 16 | 20 | 67 | 34 | 20 |

| Income Statement Analysis (Million $) | | | | | | | | | | |
|---|---|---|---|---|---|---|---|---|---|---|
| Revenue | 14,414 | 9,664 | 11,864 | 10,428 | 9,027 | 7,186 | 6,104 | 5,293 | 5,020 | 5,382 |
| Operating Income | NA | NA | 3,075 | 2,799 | 2,417 | 1,616 | 1,195 | 957 | 856 | 1,077 |
| Depreciation, Depletion and Amortization | 1,069 | NA | 637 | 521 | 434 | 382 | 374 | 349 | 302 | 345 |
| Interest Expense | 141 | 131 | 89.0 | 66.1 | 68.9 | 72.3 | 83.6 | 103 | 111 | 126 |
| Pretax Income | 1,282 | 611 | 2,319 | 2,257 | 3,737 | 1,279 | 780 | 328 | 380 | 662 |
| Effective Tax Rate | NA | 31.1% | 29.5% | 32.9% | 35.8% | 31.6% | 32.3% | 45.1% | 41.2% | 33.7% |
| Net Income | 812 | 421 | 1,635 | 1,514 | 2,399 | 874 | 528 | 180 | 224 | 439 |
| S&P Core Earnings | 816 | 427 | 1,645 | 1,504 | 1,393 | 842 | 506 | 209 | 186 | 393 |

| Balance Sheet & Other Financial Data (Million $) | | | | | | | | | | |
|---|---|---|---|---|---|---|---|---|---|---|
| Cash | 1,706 | 1,595 | 1,955 | 1,054 | 750 | 697 | 319 | 98.4 | 144 | 45.4 |
| Current Assets | 8,707 | 6,225 | 7,145 | 5,456 | 4,968 | 3,840 | 2,967 | 2,524 | 2,556 | 2,697 |
| Total Assets | 22,875 | 11,439 | 11,861 | 9,857 | 8,706 | 7,807 | 6,821 | 6,302 | 6,401 | 6,676 |
| Current Liabilities | 3,065 | 1,613 | 2,511 | 1,618 | 1,622 | 1,361 | 1,236 | 1,302 | 1,080 | 1,212 |
| Long Term Debt | 3,554 | 1,785 | 1,775 | 1,069 | 1,074 | 1,078 | 1,086 | 1,133 | 1,424 | 1,682 |
| Common Equity | 14,286 | 7,284 | 6,807 | 6,306 | 5,243 | 4,698 | 3,895 | 3,350 | 3,397 | 3,328 |
| Total Capital | 18,171 | 9,084 | 8,966 | 7,791 | 6,617 | 6,004 | 5,214 | 4,611 | 4,988 | 5,221 |
| Capital Expenditures | 1,491 | NA | 1,303 | 1,127 | 922 | 478 | 348 | 405 | 317 | 319 |
| Cash Flow | 1,888 | NA | 2,272 | 2,035 | 2,832 | 1,257 | 902 | 529 | 525 | 783 |
| Current Ratio | 2.8 | 3.9 | 2.9 | 3.4 | 3.1 | 2.8 | 2.4 | 1.9 | 2.4 | 2.2 |
| % Long Term Debt of Capitalization | 19.6 | 19.7 | 19.8 | 13.7 | 16.2 | 18.0 | 20.8 | 24.6 | 28.6 | 32.2 |
| % Return on Assets | 4.7 | 3.6 | 15.1 | 16.3 | 29.1 | 12.0 | 8.0 | 2.8 | 3.4 | 6.7 |
| % Return on Equity | 7.5 | 6.0 | 24.9 | 26.2 | 48.3 | 20.4 | 14.6 | 5.3 | 6.7 | 13.8 |

Data as orig reptd.; bef. results of disc opers/spec. items. Per share data adj. for stk. divs.; EPS diluted. E-Estimated. NA-Not Available. NM-Not Meaningful. NR-Not Ranked. UR-Under Review.

**Office:** 2929 Allen Pkwy Ste 2100, Houston, TX 77019-2118.
**Telephone:** 713-439-8600.
**Website:** http://www.bakerhughes.com
**Chrmn & CEO:** C.C. Deaton

**Pres & COO:** M. Craighead
**SVP & CFO:** P.A. Ragauss
**CTO:** D. Mathieson
**Chief Acctg Officer & Cntlr:** A.J. Keifer

**Board Members:** L. D. Brady, II, C. P. Cazalot, Jr., M. Craighead, C. C. Deaton, A. G. Fernandes, C. W. Gargalli, P. J. Jungels, I, J. A. Lash, J. L. Nichols, H. J. Riley, Jr., J. W. Stewart, C. L. Watson

**Founded:** 1972
**Domicile:** Delaware
**Employees:** 53,100

*The McGraw-Hill Companies*

# Ball Corp

STANDARD &POOR'S

| S&P Recommendation **BUY** ★★★★☆ | Price<br>$33.18 (as of Nov 25, 2011) | 12-Mo. Target Price<br>$43.00 | Investment Style<br>Large-Cap Blend |
|---|---|---|---|

**GICS Sector** Materials
**Sub-Industry** Metal & Glass Containers

**Summary** One of the largest producers of metal beverage cans in the world, Ball also derives nearly 10% of revenues from sales of hi-tech equipment to the aerospace industry.

## Key Stock Statistics (Source S&P, Vickers, company reports)

| | | | | | | | |
|---|---|---|---|---|---|---|---|
| 52-Wk Range | $40.56–29.69 | S&P Oper. EPS 2011E | 2.80 | Market Capitalization(B) | $5.396 | Beta | 0.67 |
| Trailing 12-Month EPS | $2.67 | S&P Oper. EPS 2012E | 3.15 | Yield (%) | 0.84 | S&P 3-Yr. Proj. EPS CAGR(%) | 13 |
| Trailing 12-Month P/E | 12.4 | P/E on S&P Oper. EPS 2011E | 11.9 | Dividend Rate/Share | $0.28 | S&P Credit Rating | BB+ |
| $10K Invested 5 Yrs Ago | $16,334 | Common Shares Outstg. (M) | 162.6 | Institutional Ownership (%) | 74 | | |

## Price Performance

30-Week Mov. Avg. · · · · 10-Week Mov. Avg. - - GAAP Earnings vs. Previous Year   Volume Above Avg. ▮▮▮ STARS
12-Mo. Target Price — Relative Strength — ▲ Up ▼ Down ▶ No Change   Below Avg. ▮▮▮ ★

Options: ASE, CBOE, P, Ph

Analysis prepared by Equity Analyst **Stewart Scharf** on Nov 07, 2011, when the stock traded at **$34.77**.

## Highlights

➤ We project sales growth of close to 15% in 2011, driven by increased demand for metal beverage packaging in China and Europe, offsetting adverse summer weather in parts of the U.S. and Europe, which impacted beverage can sales. Although we expect sales to grow less rapidly in 2012, we see a gradual pickup in volume in North America along with strength in specialty cans, while food cans and aerospace bookings rebound.

➤ In our view, gross margins (before D&A) will continue to widen somewhat through 2012, up from 18% in 2010, reflecting supply chain initiatives, a better mix, and the elimination of higher-priced metal inventories. We look for EBITDA margins to expand to at least 14% in 2012, based on improved productivity and synergies from plant relocations and acquisitions. Interest expense should decline somewhat in 2012, following a rise in 2011 due to debt related to acquiring AB InBev's plants.

➤ We project a higher effective tax rate of about 31% in 2011, and estimate operating EPS of $2.80, advancing 13% to $3.15 in 2012. A 2-for-1 stock split was effected in mid-February 2011.

## Investment Rationale/Risk

➤ Our buy opinion is based on our valuation metrics, as well as our view of improving global trends for beverage cans, a better cost structure, and strong free cash generation. We expect BLL to focus on its core metal can operations.

➤ Risks to our recommendation and target price include negative foreign currency exchange; a decline in sales of imported beer and, to some extent, domestic soft drinks; cost pressures in Europe and China; supply disruptions due to strikes at facilities; integration problems; and sharply higher raw material costs.

➤ At 11X our 2012 EPS estimate, the stock was recently trading at a modest premium to BLL's closest peers, and at a small discount to our projected P/E for the S&P 500 Index. Based on our relative metrics, including below-peer PEG (P/E-to-growth) and enterprise value-to-EBITDA ratios, we value the stock at $41. Our DCF model, which assumes a 3.5% perpetuity growth rate and a weighted average cost of capital of 8%, derives an intrinsic value of $44. Blending these valuations, our 12-month target price is $43.

## Qualitative Risk Assessment

| LOW | MEDIUM | HIGH |
|---|---|---|

Our risk assessment reflects the seasonality and cyclicality inherent in the beverage can business, volatile raw material prices, and our view of BLL's high debt levels. These factors are offset by BLL's improving balance sheet, with solid credit quality and liquidity, and our expectations for solid cash flow.

## Quantitative Evaluations

**S&P Quality Ranking**   A

| D | C | B- | B | B+ | A- | A | A+ |
|---|---|---|---|---|---|---|---|

**Relative Strength Rank**   MODERATE

62

LOWEST = 1   HIGHEST = 99

## Revenue/Earnings Data

**Revenue (Million $)**

| | 1Q | 2Q | 3Q | 4Q | Year |
|---|---|---|---|---|---|
| 2011 | 2,011 | 2,310 | 2,258 | -- | -- |
| 2010 | 1,592 | 2,008 | 2,035 | 1,995 | 7,630 |
| 2009 | 1,586 | 1,926 | 1,969 | 1,864 | 7,345 |
| 2008 | 1,740 | 2,080 | 2,008 | 1,733 | 7,562 |
| 2007 | 1,694 | 2,033 | 1,992 | 1,756 | 7,475 |
| 2006 | 1,365 | 1,843 | 1,822 | 1,592 | 6,622 |

**Earnings Per Share ($)**

| | 1Q | 2Q | 3Q | 4Q | Year |
|---|---|---|---|---|---|
| 2011 | 0.54 | 0.84 | 0.80 | E0.56 | E2.80 |
| 2010 | 0.44 | 0.77 | 1.22 | 0.53 | 2.96 |
| 2009 | 0.37 | 0.70 | 0.55 | 0.43 | 2.04 |
| 2008 | 0.43 | 0.51 | 0.52 | 0.18 | 1.65 |
| 2007 | 0.39 | 0.52 | 0.29 | 0.17 | 1.37 |
| 2006 | 0.22 | 0.62 | 0.51 | 0.23 | 1.57 |

Fiscal year ended Dec. 31. Next earnings report expected: Late January. EPS Estimates based on S&P Operating Earnings; historical GAAP earnings are as reported.

## Dividend Data (Dates: mm/dd Payment Date: mm/dd/yy)

| Amount ($) | Date Decl. | Ex-Div. Date | Stk. of Record | Payment Date |
|---|---|---|---|---|
| 0.070 | 01/26 | 02/25 | 03/01 | 03/15/11 |
| 0.070 | 04/27 | 05/27 | 06/01 | 06/15/11 |
| 0.070 | 07/27 | 08/30 | 09/01 | 09/15/11 |
| 0.070 | 10/26 | 11/29 | 12/01 | 12/15/11 |

Dividends have been paid since 1958. Source: Company reports.

# Ball Corp

STANDARD
&POOR'S

## Business Summary November 07, 2011

CORPORATE OVERVIEW. Ball Corp. primarily manufactures rigid packaging products for beverages and foods. Two beverage companies account for a substantial part of its packaging sales: SABMiller plc and PepsiCo. BLL is comprised of five segments: Metal Beverage Packaging (Americas/Asia); Metal Beverage Packaging (Europe); Metal Food & Household Packaging (Americas); Plastic Packaging (Americas); and Aerospace and Technologies. The Aerospace and Technologies segment provides products and services to the defense and commercial markets, with U.S. government agencies accounting for 96% of the segment's sales in 2010. In June 2010, the company completed the purchase of the remaining 65% stake in JFP's Sanshui, China, metal beverage can facility for $90 million in cash and assumed debt. The company recorded a $22 million ($0.12 a share, adjusted for split) gain on the transaction. BLL produced more than 43 billion recyclable beverage cans in the U.S., Canada and Brazil in 2010, about 37% of the total market. Aluminum and steel beverage cans accounted for 73% of the company's net sales and 82% of EBIT in 2010.

The company's packaging products include aluminum and steel two-piece beverage cans, and two- and three-piece steel food cans. Metal Beverage Packaging (Americas and Asia) segment net sales represented 50% of the total in 2010 ($418 million of pretax earnings); Metal Beverage Packaging (Europe) 22% ($210 million); Metal Food and Household Packaging (Americas)

18% ($147 million); and Aerospace and Technologies 9.4% ($70 million). Sales volumes of metal food containers in North America tend to be highest from June through October due to seasonal vegetable and salmon packs. BLL believes this accounts for more than 30% of all North American metal beverage can shipments. In the first quarter of 2011, BLL consolidated production at its salmon can plant in British Columbia into other facilities. A $7 million after-tax charge was incurred related to the closure (including $3 million in the third quarter of 2010). In 2010, no customer accounted for more than 10% of sales. Sales outside of the U.S. account for about 30% of the total.

In early October 2009, BLL acquired four U.S. beverage can plants from Anheuser-Busch InBev (AB InBev) for $577 million. The company expected the facilities to generate $680 million in revenues and $94 million in EBITDA in their first year. BLL expected the deal to be accretive to earnings and cash flow in 2010, with $50 million of cash generated annually after the first year. The plants manufacture 10 billion aluminum cans and 10 billion easy-open can ends annually. We view this deal as a good strategic fit for BLL's global beverage can expansion plans.

## Company Financials Fiscal Year Ended Dec. 31

| Per Share Data ($) | 2010 | 2009 | 2008 | 2007 | 2006 | 2005 | 2004 | 2003 | 2002 | 2001 |
|---|---|---|---|---|---|---|---|---|---|---|
| Tangible Book Value | NM | NM | NM | NM | NM | NM | NM | NM | NM | 0.63 |
| Cash Flow | 4.41 | 3.55 | 3.18 | 2.74 | 2.78 | 2.15 | 2.24 | 1.91 | 1.34 | 0.22 |
| Earnings | 2.96 | 2.04 | 1.65 | 1.37 | 1.57 | 1.19 | 1.30 | 1.01 | 0.69 | -0.46 |
| S&P Core Earnings | 2.98 | 1.96 | 1.39 | 1.66 | 1.15 | 1.27 | 1.34 | 1.06 | 0.55 | -0.44 |
| Dividends | 0.20 | 0.20 | 0.20 | 0.20 | 0.20 | 0.20 | 0.18 | 0.12 | 0.09 | 0.08 |
| Payout Ratio | 7% | 10% | 12% | 15% | 13% | 17% | 13% | 12% | 13% | NM |
| Prices:High | 34.85 | 26.23 | 28.10 | 28.03 | 22.50 | 23.23 | 22.60 | 14.94 | 13.62 | 9.02 |
| Prices:Low | 23.35 | 18.25 | 13.69 | 21.76 | 17.08 | 17.53 | 14.13 | 10.58 | 8.15 | 4.76 |
| P/E Ratio:High | 12 | 13 | 17 | 20 | 14 | 20 | 17 | 15 | 20 | NM |
| P/E Ratio:Low | 8 | 9 | 8 | 16 | 11 | 15 | 11 | 11 | 12 | NM |

| Income Statement Analysis (Million $) | | | | | | | | | | |
|---|---|---|---|---|---|---|---|---|---|---|
| Revenue | 7,630 | 7,345 | 7,562 | 7,475 | 6,622 | 5,751 | 5,440 | 4,977 | 3,859 | 3,686 |
| Operating Income | 1,019 | 945 | 926 | 914 | 729 | 697 | 739 | 663 | 458 | 127 |
| Depreciation | 266 | 285 | 297 | 281 | 253 | 214 | 215 | 206 | 149 | 153 |
| Interest Expense | 149 | 117 | 145 | 156 | 134 | 116 | 104 | 126 | 75.6 | 88.3 |
| Pretax Income | 724 | 551 | 467 | 377 | 462 | 362 | 436 | 331 | 245 | -110 |
| Effective Tax Rate | NA | 29.5% | 31.5% | 25.4% | 28.5% | 27.5% | 31.9% | 30.2% | 34.3% | NM |
| Net Income | 543 | 388 | 320 | 281 | 330 | 262 | 296 | 230 | 159 | -99.2 |
| S&P Core Earnings | 546 | 371 | 270 | 340 | 242 | 280 | 304 | 242 | 127 | -96.0 |

| Balance Sheet & Other Financial Data (Million $) | | | | | | | | | | |
|---|---|---|---|---|---|---|---|---|---|---|
| Cash | 152 | 211 | 127 | 152 | 152 | 61.0 | 199 | 36.5 | 259 | 83.1 |
| Current Assets | 2,306 | 1,923 | 2,165 | 1,843 | 1,761 | 1,226 | 1,246 | 924 | 1,225 | 794 |
| Total Assets | 6,928 | 6,488 | 6,369 | 6,021 | 5,841 | 4,343 | 4,478 | 4,070 | 4,132 | 2,314 |
| Current Liabilities | 1,383 | 1,429 | 1,862 | 1,513 | 1,454 | 1,176 | 996 | 861 | 1,069 | 575 |
| Long Term Debt | 2,702 | 2,284 | 2,107 | 2,182 | 2,270 | 1,473 | 1,538 | 1,579 | 1,854 | 949 |
| Common Equity | 1,658 | 1,583 | 1,086 | 1,343 | 1,165 | 835 | 1,087 | 808 | 493 | 504 |
| Total Capital | 4,360 | 3,867 | 3,342 | 3,525 | 3,437 | 2,314 | 2,631 | 2,393 | 2,353 | 1,463 |
| Capital Expenditures | 250 | 187 | 307 | 309 | 280 | 292 | 196 | 137 | 158 | 68.5 |
| Cash Flow | 808 | 673 | 617 | 562 | 582 | 475 | 511 | 435 | 309 | 51.3 |
| Current Ratio | 1.7 | 1.4 | 1.2 | 1.2 | 1.2 | 1.0 | 1.3 | 1.1 | 1.1 | 1.4 |
| % Long Term Debt of Capitalization | 62.0 | 59.1 | 63.0 | 61.9 | 66.1 | 63.7 | 58.5 | 66.0 | 78.8 | 64.9 |
| % Net Income of Revenue | 7.1 | 5.3 | 4.2 | 3.8 | 5.0 | 4.5 | 5.4 | 4.6 | 4.1 | NM |
| % Return on Assets | 8.1 | 6.0 | 5.2 | 4.7 | 6.5 | 5.9 | 6.9 | 5.6 | 4.9 | NM |
| % Return on Equity | 33.5 | 29.1 | 26.3 | 22.4 | 32.7 | 27.2 | 31.2 | 35.4 | 32.0 | NM |

Data as orig reptd.; bef. results of disc opers/spec. items. Per share data adj. for stk. divs.; EPS diluted. E-Estimated. NA-Not Available. NM-Not Meaningful. NR-Not Ranked. UR-Under Review.

**Office:** 10 Longs Peak Drive, PO Box 5000, Broomfield, CO 80021-2510.
**Telephone:** 303-469-3131.
**Website:** http://www.ball.com
**Chrmn:** R.D. Hoover

**Pres & CEO:** J.A. Hayes
**SVP & CFO:** S.C. Morrison
**Treas:** J.A. Knobel
**Secy:** D.A. Westerlund

**Investor Contact:** A.T. Scott (303-460-3537)
**Board Members:** R. W. Alspaugh, H. C. Fiedler, J. A. Hayes, R. D. Hoover, J. F. Lehman, G. R. Nelson, J. Nicholson, G. M. Smart, T. M. Solso, S. A. Taylor, II, E. Van Der Kaay

**Founded:** 1880
**Domicile:** Indiana
**Employees:** 14,000

The McGraw-Hill Companies

# Bank of America Corp

**STANDARD &POOR'S**

| S&P Recommendation | HOLD ★★★☆☆ | Price<br>$5.44 (as of Nov 30, 2011) | 12-Mo. Target Price<br>$8.00 | Investment Style<br>Large-Cap Blend |
|---|---|---|---|---|

**GICS Sector** Financials
**Sub-Industry** Other Diversified Financial Services

**Summary** BAC is the second largest U.S.-based financial holding company, with global assets of $2.22 trillion.

## Key Stock Statistics (Source S&P, Vickers, company reports)

| | | | | | | | |
|---|---|---|---|---|---|---|---|
| 52-Wk Range | $15.31– 5.03 | S&P Oper. EPS 2011**E** | 0.10 | Market Capitalization(B) | $55.139 | Beta | 2.19 |
| Trailing 12-Month EPS | $-0.31 | S&P Oper. EPS 2012**E** | 1.41 | Yield (%) | 0.74 | S&P 3-Yr. Proj. EPS CAGR(%) | NA |
| Trailing 12-Month P/E | NM | P/E on S&P Oper. EPS 2011**E** | 54.4 | Dividend Rate/Share | $0.04 | S&P Credit Rating | A- |
| $10K Invested 5 Yrs Ago | $1,160 | Common Shares Outstg. (M) | 10,135.9 | Institutional Ownership (%) | 58 | | |

## Price Performance

30-Week Mov. Avg. · · ·   10-Week Mov. Avg. - -   GAAP Earnings vs. Previous Year   Volume Above Avg. ▮▮▮ STARS
12-Mo. Target Price —   Relative Strength —   ▲ Up   ▼ Down   ▶ No Change   Below Avg. ▮▮▮

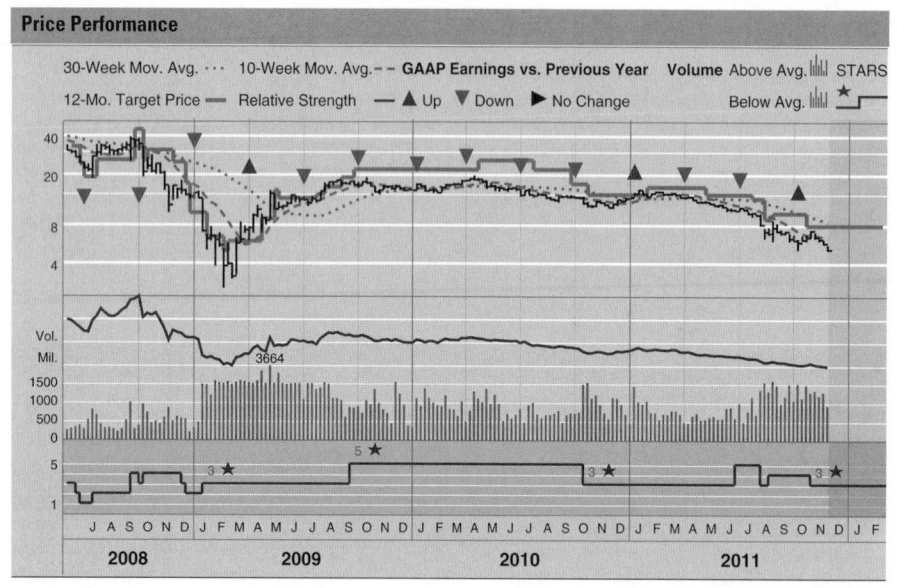

Options: ASE, CBOE, P, Ph

Analysis prepared by Equity Analyst **Erik Oja** on Nov 08, 2011, when the stock traded at **$6.45**.

## Highlights

▶ Third-quarter net interest income fell 17.3% sequentially, as the net interest margin narrowed to 2.31% from 2.49%, interest-earning assets dipped 0.2%, and the loan portfolio fell 0.9%, all about in line with large U.S. banks. For 2011, we expect interest-earning assets to fall 2.5% and the fourth-quarter net interest margin to shrink to 2.25%, from 2.67% a year earlier. We see net interest income declining 14.5% in 2011.

▶ Non-performing loans at September 30 stood at 2.85% of total loans, above the median of large U.S. banks, but 4.1% below the level three months earlier, a decline rate above the median of large U.S. banks. BAC's third-quarter allowance for non-performing loans was nearly 133% of non-performing loans, higher than peers. BAC was able to boost earnings by taking a loan loss provision of only 67% of third-quarter net chargeoffs. We expect 2011 loan loss provisions of $13.8 billion, down from $28.4 billion in 2010. For 2012, we look for provisions to fall to $13.0 billion.

▶ We expect declines in the loan loss provision to drive earnings growth in 2012. We see EPS of $0.10 in 2011 and $1.41 in 2012.

## Investment Rationale/Risk

▶ BAC's primary concern is whether it can raise capital levels fast enough to meet upcoming requirements. Adding to the uncertainty is the timeline of the Basel III capital guidelines, and whether BAC will have to boost beyond Basel III, as a safety buffer against its global size. In the best case scenario, BAC will have until 2019 to raise common equity capital to 9.50% of risk-weighted assets, from the September 30 level of 8.65%. However, BAC could be forced to raise capital to 10.50% as soon as 2013. We think the actual requirement may be something in the middle, such as 10.50% before 2019. We think Berkshire Hathaway's (BRK.B 72, Hold) recent $5.0 billion investment goes a long way toward firming up BAC's capital levels, though at a relatively high price. Despite this clarification of BAC's capital picture, we see heightened risks from global uncertainty.

▶ Risks to our recommendation and target price include a court rejection of the June mortgage settlement, additional foreclosure and mortgage putback costs, and regulatory costs.

▶ Our 12-month target price of $8 equates to a discount to peers 6.0X our forward four quarters EPS estimate of $1.33.

## Qualitative Risk Assessment

| LOW | MEDIUM | HIGH |
|---|---|---|

Our risk assessment reflects weak U.S. consumer trends, exposure to residential lending and credit cards, and a lower-than-historical tangible capital ratio, offset by what we see as a strong U.S. presence with a robust customer base.

## Quantitative Evaluations

**S&P Quality Ranking**                                B-

| D | C | B- | B | B+ | A- | A | A+ |
|---|---|---|---|---|---|---|---|

**Relative Strength Rank**                         WEAK

11

LOWEST = 1                                          HIGHEST = 99

## Revenue/Earnings Data

**Revenue (Million $)**

| | 1Q | 2Q | 3Q | 4Q | Year |
|---|---|---|---|---|---|
| 2011 | 32,620 | 19,038 | 33,816 | -- | -- |
| 2010 | 38,099 | 35,384 | 32,474 | 28,249 | 134,194 |
| 2009 | 45,417 | 40,736 | 33,135 | 31,162 | 150,450 |
| 2008 | 28,871 | 29,721 | 30,175 | 24,176 | 113,106 |
| 2007 | 30,447 | 32,409 | 29,347 | 26,987 | 119,190 |
| 2006 | 27,026 | 28,895 | 30,739 | 30,357 | 117,017 |

**Earnings Per Share ($)**

| | | | | | |
|---|---|---|---|---|---|
| 2011 | 0.17 | -0.90 | 0.56 | E0.27 | E0.10 |
| 2010 | 0.28 | 0.28 | -0.77 | -0.15 | -0.37 |
| 2009 | 0.44 | 0.33 | -0.26 | -0.60 | -0.29 |
| 2008 | 0.23 | 0.72 | 0.15 | -0.48 | 0.55 |
| 2007 | 1.16 | 1.28 | 0.82 | 0.05 | 3.30 |
| 2006 | 1.07 | 1.19 | 1.18 | 1.16 | 4.59 |

Fiscal year ended Dec. 31. Next earnings report expected: Late January. EPS Estimates based on S&P Operating Earnings; historical GAAP earnings are as reported.

## Dividend Data (Dates: mm/dd Payment Date: mm/dd/yy)

| Amount<br>($) | Date<br>Decl. | Ex-Div.<br>Date | Stk. of<br>Record | Payment<br>Date |
|---|---|---|---|---|
| 0.010 | 01/26 | 03/02 | 03/04 | 03/25/11 |
| 0.010 | 05/11 | 06/01 | 06/03 | 06/24/11 |
| 0.010 | 08/22 | 08/31 | 09/02 | 09/23/11 |
| 0.010 | 11/18 | 11/30 | 12/02 | 12/23/11 |

Dividends have been paid since 1903. Source: Company reports.

---

**Please read the Required Disclosures and Analyst Certification on the last page of this report.**

The McGraw-Hill Companies

# Bank of America Corp

STANDARD
&POOR'S

## Business Summary November 08, 2011

CORPORATE OVERVIEW. Bank of America is the second U.S.-based financial holding company, with September 30, 2011, assets of $2.220 trillion, loans of $932.5 billion, and total deposits of $1.041 trillion. BAC's U.S. deposits were $950.4 billion, about 12% of U.S. deposits.

Bank of America was founded in San Francisco in 1904, and, after a series of mergers, assumed its modern name in 1930. In the next few decades, Bank of America expanded its branch network outside its home state of California, and also built an insurance company. In the mid-1950s, Bank of America's bank branches outside of California and its insurance operations were separated into independent companies to comply with changes in federal banking laws. In the late 1950s, Bank of America introduced the BankAmericard, one of the first U.S. credit cards. BankAmericard became Visa (V 93, Hold) in the mid-1970s, and now exists independently of BAC. In the 1980s, Bank of America staggered under the weight of non-performing international loans, particu-

larly in Latin America.

In 1998, Bank of America was acquired by fast-growing NationsBank, of Charlotte, NC. The combined company assumed the name Bank of America, and kept its headquarters in Charlotte. BAC continued to grow rapidly. In October 2003, BAC announced an agreement to merge with aggressive and fast-growing FleetBoston Financial Corp., with year-end 2003 assets of $200.2 billion, in a stock-for-stock transaction worth $46.0 billion. This transformative acquisition added nearly 35% to BAC's assets, which, including FleetBoston, totaled $1.15 trillion at the end of 2004.

## Company Financials Fiscal Year Ended Dec. 31

| Per Share Data ($) | 2010 | 2009 | 2008 | 2007 | 2006 | 2005 | 2004 | 2003 | 2002 | 2001 |
|---|---|---|---|---|---|---|---|---|---|---|
| Tangible Book Value | 12.68 | 11.09 | 7.14 | 11.54 | 12.18 | 13.18 | 12.41 | 12.34 | 12.59 | 11.65 |
| Earnings | -0.37 | -0.29 | 0.55 | 3.30 | 4.59 | 4.04 | 3.69 | 3.57 | 2.96 | 2.09 |
| S&P Core Earnings | 0.89 | -0.29 | 0.35 | 3.26 | 4.47 | 4.06 | 3.75 | 3.54 | 2.70 | 1.96 |
| Dividends | 0.04 | 0.04 | 2.24 | 2.40 | 2.12 | 1.90 | 1.70 | 1.44 | 1.22 | 1.14 |
| Payout Ratio | NM | NM | 407% | 73% | 46% | 47% | 46% | 40% | 41% | 55% |
| Prices:High | 19.86 | 19.10 | 45.08 | 54.21 | 55.08 | 47.44 | 47.47 | 42.45 | 38.54 | 32.77 |
| Prices:Low | 12.96 | 2.53 | 10.01 | 40.61 | 40.93 | 41.13 | 38.51 | 32.13 | 26.98 | 22.50 |
| P/E Ratio:High | NM | NM | 82 | 16 | 12 | 12 | 13 | 12 | 13 | 16 |
| P/E Ratio:Low | NM | NM | 18 | 12 | 9 | 10 | 10 | 9 | 9 | 11 |

| Income Statement Analysis (Million $) | 2010 | 2009 | 2008 | 2007 | 2006 | 2005 | 2004 | 2003 | 2002 | 2001 |
|---|---|---|---|---|---|---|---|---|---|---|
| Net Interest Income | 51,523 | 47,109 | 45,360 | 34,433 | 34,591 | 30,737 | 28,797 | 21,464 | 20,923 | 20,290 |
| Tax Equivalent Adjustment | 1,170 | 1,291 | 1,194 | 1,749 | 1,224 | 832 | 716 | 643 | 588 | 343 |
| Non Interest Income | 58,697 | 72,534 | 27,422 | 31,706 | 38,432 | 26,438 | 20,097 | 16,422 | 13,571 | 14,348 |
| Loan Loss Provision | 28,435 | 48,570 | 26,825 | 8,385 | 5,010 | 4,014 | 2,769 | 2,839 | 3,697 | 4,287 |
| % Expense/Operating Revenue | 75.4% | 55.8% | 57.1% | 56.0% | 47.9% | 50.4% | 54.5% | 52.2% | 63.1% | 59.8% |
| Pretax Income | -1,323 | 4,360 | 4,428 | 20,924 | 31,973 | 24,480 | 21,221 | 15,861 | 12,991 | 10,117 |
| Effective Tax Rate | NM | NM | 9.48% | 28.4% | 33.9% | 32.7% | 33.4% | 31.8% | 28.8% | 32.9% |
| Net Income | -2,238 | 6,276 | 4,008 | 14,982 | 21,133 | 16,465 | 14,143 | 10,810 | 9,249 | 6,792 |
| % Net Interest Margin | 2.65 | 2.65 | 2.98 | 2.60 | 2.82 | 2.84 | 3.26 | 3.36 | 3.75 | 3.68 |
| S&P Core Earnings | 8,737 | -2,239 | 1,656 | 14,615 | 20,568 | 16,499 | 14,308 | 10,708 | 8,452 | 6,384 |

| Balance Sheet & Other Financial Data (Million $) | 2010 | 2009 | 2008 | 2007 | 2006 | 2005 | 2004 | 2003 | 2002 | 2001 |
|---|---|---|---|---|---|---|---|---|---|---|
| Money Market Assets | 390,720 | 396,341 | 251,570 | 303,389 | 302,482 | 294,292 | 197,308 | 153,090 | 115,687 | 81,384 |
| Investment Securities | 338,054 | 311,411 | 277,589 | 214,056 | 192,846 | 221,603 | 195,073 | 68,240 | 69,148 | 85,499 |
| Commercial Loans | NA | 322,564 | 342,767 | 325,143 | 240,785 | 218,334 | 193,930 | 131,304 | 145,170 | 163,898 |
| Other Loans | NA | 577,564 | 588,679 | 551,201 | 465,705 | 355,457 | 327,907 | 240,159 | 197,585 | 165,255 |
| Total Assets | 2,264,909 | 2,223,299 | 1,817,943 | 1,715,746 | 1,459,737 | 1,291,803 | 1,110,457 | 736,445 | 660,458 | 621,764 |
| Demand Deposits | 285,200 | 275,104 | 217,998 | 192,227 | 184,808 | 186,736 | 169,899 | 121,530 | 124,359 | 113,934 |
| Time Deposits | 725,230 | 716,507 | 664,999 | 612,950 | 508,689 | 447,934 | 448,671 | 292,583 | 262,099 | 259,561 |
| Long Term Debt | 448,433 | 438,521 | 268,292 | 197,508 | 146,000 | 100,848 | 98,078 | 75,343 | 67,176 | 68,026 |
| Common Equity | 211,686 | 194,236 | 139,351 | 142,394 | 132,421 | 101,262 | 99,374 | 47,926 | 50,261 | 48,455 |
| % Return on Assets | NM | 0.3 | 0.2 | 0.9 | 1.5 | 1.4 | 1.5 | 1.5 | 1.4 | 1.1 |
| % Return on Equity | NM | 3.8 | 2.9 | 10.8 | 18.1 | 16.3 | 19.2 | 22.0 | 18.7 | 14.1 |
| % Loan Loss Reserve | 4.1 | 3.8 | 2.5 | 1.3 | 0.4 | 1.4 | 1.7 | 1.7 | 2.0 | 2.1 |
| % Loans/Deposits | 101.6 | 99.0 | 105.5 | 105.5 | 304.3 | 87.4 | 84.4 | 89.7 | 88.4 | 97.8 |
| % Equity to Assets | 10.2 | 8.3 | 8.0 | 8.7 | 8.5 | 8.4 | 8.0 | 7.0 | 7.7 | 7.6 |

Data as orig reptd.; bef. results of disc opers/spec. items. Per share data adj. for stk. divs.; EPS diluted. E-Estimated. NA-Not Available. NM-Not Meaningful. NR-Not Ranked. UR-Under Review.

**Office:** 100 N Tryon St, Charlotte, NC 28255.
**Telephone:** 704-386-5681.
**Website:** http://www.bankofamerica.com
**Chrmn:** C.O. Holliday, Jr.

**Pres & CEO:** B.T. Moynihan
**CFO:** B.R. Thompson
**CTO:** M. Gordon
**Chief Acctg Officer:** N.A. Cotty

**Investor Contact:** K. Stitt (704-386-5667)
**Board Members:** M. D. Ambani, S. S. Bies, F. P. Bramble, V. W. Colbert, C. K. Gifford, C. O. Holliday, Jr., D. P. Jones, Jr., M. C. Lozano, T. J. May, B. T. Moynihan, D. E. Powell, C. O. Rossotti, R. W. Scully

**Founded:** 1874
**Domicile:** Delaware
**Employees:** 288,000

The McGraw-Hill Companies

# Bank of New York Mellon Corp (The)

**STANDARD &POOR'S**

| S&P Recommendation HOLD ★★★★★ | Price $19.46 (as of Nov 30, 2011) | 12-Mo. Target Price $21.00 | Investment Style Large-Cap Blend |
|---|---|---|---|

**GICS Sector** Financials
**Sub-Industry** Asset Management & Custody Banks

**Summary** This company is a leader in securities processing, and also provides a complete range of banking, asset management and other financial services.

## Key Stock Statistics (Source S&P, Vickers, company reports)

| | | | | | | |
|---|---|---|---|---|---|---|
| 52-Wk Range | $32.50–17.10 | S&P Oper. EPS 2011**E** | 2.15 | Market Capitalization(B) | $23.598 | Beta | 0.83 |
| Trailing 12-Month EPS | $2.16 | S&P Oper. EPS 2012**E** | 2.33 | Yield (%) | 2.67 | S&P 3-Yr. Proj. EPS CAGR(%) | 10 |
| Trailing 12-Month P/E | 9.0 | P/E on S&P Oper. EPS 2011**E** | 9.1 | Dividend Rate/Share | $0.52 | S&P Credit Rating | AA- |
| $10K Invested 5 Yrs Ago | $5,706 | Common Shares Outstg. (M) | 1,212.6 | Institutional Ownership (%) | 83 | | |

## Price Performance

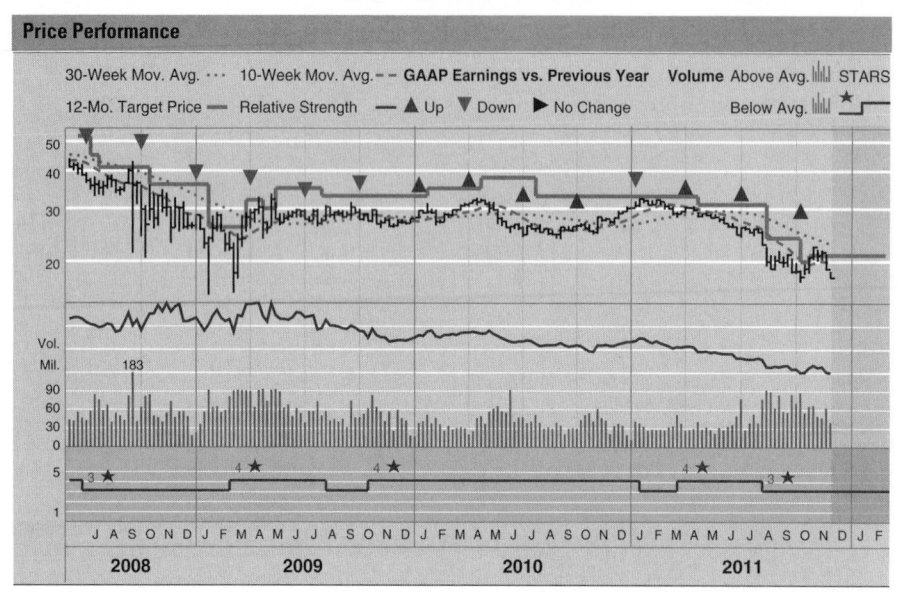

30-Week Mov. Avg. ··· 10-Week Mov. Avg. ‑‑ GAAP Earnings vs. Previous Year Volume Above Avg. STARS
12-Mo. Target Price — Relative Strength ▲ Up ▼ Down ▶ No Change Below Avg.

Options: ASE, CBOE, P, Ph

Analysis prepared by Equity Analyst **Erik Oja** on Nov 28, 2011, when the stock traded at **$18.05**.

## Highlights

➤ Investment Services, about 75% of BK's net revenues, grew steadily in the third quarter, driven by Issuer Services, partly offset by a decline in Asset Servicing fees, as assets under custody and administration fell 2% from the second quarter. We expect total Investment Services revenues to rise 3.1% in 2011 and 6.3% in 2012. Investment Management, about 22% of BK's net revenues, fell steeply in the third quarter, as assets under management fell 6% from second quarter levels. Due to European turmoil, we expect further declines in assets. Our 2011 revenue forecast for Investment Management is for 0.2% growth; for 2012, we expect a 2.0% decline. Our total net revenue forecast for BK is -0.2% in 2011 and 3.3% in 2012.

➤ Expenses have been relatively high and inflexible in the past few quarters, especially for staff, which absorbed 39.5% of core revenues in the third quarter. Despite restructuring efforts, we expect these costs to remain fairly high in 2011 and 2012 as a percentage of net revenues. We expect total expenses, excluding amortization, of 71.0% of core revenues, higher than at many peers.

➤ We see EPS of $2.15 in 2011 and $2.33 in 2012.

## Investment Rationale/Risk

➤ Solid third quarter results in BK's Investment Services unit were offset by a precipitous fall in Investment Management revenues, due to the European financial crisis and the U.S. market plunge in August. We also see BK's share price performance correlated to the spread between the U.S. 10-year Treasury note and the U.S. 30-day Treasury bill; the smaller the interest rate spread, the weaker BK's share price. With European turmoil increasing, and the possibility of increasing use of U.S. bonds as a safe harbor, we think it is more likely than not that U.S. interest rates will fall further. We think this could further pressure BK's net interest margin and total net revenues.

➤ Risks to our opinion and target price include a worsening of the low interest rate environment, a significant decline in capital markets activity, and higher-than-expected operating expenses.

➤ Our 12-month target price of $21 equates to a multiple of 9.4X our forward four quarters EPS estimate of $2.24, a discount to BK's historical multiple, reflecting volatile market conditions and the persistent low interest rate environment.

## Qualitative Risk Assessment

| LOW | MEDIUM | HIGH |
|---|---|---|

Our risk assessment reflects what we view as solid fundamentals, diverse business lines, and progress in raising capital levels, offset by increasing market risk and interest rate risk, due to the global debt crisis.

## Quantitative Evaluations

**S&P Quality Ranking** B

| D | C | B- | B | B+ | A- | A | A+ |
|---|---|---|---|---|---|---|---|

**Relative Strength Rank** MODERATE

38

LOWEST = 1          HIGHEST = 99

## Revenue/Earnings Data

**Revenue (Million $)**

| | 1Q | 2Q | 3Q | 4Q | Year |
|---|---|---|---|---|---|
| 2011 | 3,815 | 4,045 | 3,847 | -- | -- |
| 2010 | 3,497 | 3,498 | 3,580 | 3,944 | 14,483 |
| 2009 | 3,431 | 3,358 | 3,446 | 3,434 | 13,648 |
| 2008 | 3,745 | 4,078 | 4,262 | 3,367 | 16,339 |
| 2007 | 2,496 | 2,893 | 3,600 | 3,044 | 9,031 |
| 2006 | 2,074 | 2,276 | 2,219 | 2,493 | 9,062 |

**Earnings Per Share ($)**

| | | | | | |
|---|---|---|---|---|---|
| 2011 | 0.50 | 0.59 | 0.53 | E0.53 | E2.15 |
| 2010 | 0.49 | 0.55 | 0.51 | 0.55 | 2.11 |
| 2009 | 0.28 | 0.23 | -2.04 | 0.59 | -0.93 |
| 2008 | 0.65 | 0.26 | 0.27 | 0.05 | 1.22 |
| 2007 | 0.60 | 0.59 | 0.56 | 0.61 | 2.38 |
| 2006 | 0.50 | 0.55 | 0.41 | 0.59 | 2.05 |

Fiscal year ended Dec. 31. Next earnings report expected: NA. EPS Estimates based on S&P Operating Earnings; historical GAAP earnings are as reported.

## Dividend Data (Dates: mm/dd Payment Date: mm/dd/yy)

| Amount ($) | Date Decl. | Ex-Div. Date | Stk. of Record | Payment Date |
|---|---|---|---|---|
| 0.090 | 01/19 | 01/27 | 01/31 | 02/09/11 |
| 0.130 | 03/22 | 04/27 | 04/29 | 05/10/11 |
| 0.130 | 07/19 | 07/27 | 07/29 | 08/09/11 |
| 0.130 | 10/19 | 10/27 | 10/31 | 11/09/11 |

Dividends have been paid since 1785. Source: Company reports.

---

**Please read the Required Disclosures and Analyst Certification on the last page of this report.**

*The McGraw·Hill Companies*

# Bank of New York Mellon Corp (The)

STANDARD
&POOR'S

## Business Summary November 28, 2011

CORPORATE OVERVIEW. Bank of New York Mellon provides a comprehensive array of services that enable institutions and individuals to move and manage financial assets in more than 100 markets worldwide. The company specializes in institutional services, private banking and asset management. Key products include advisory and asset management services to support the investment decision, trade execution, clearance and settlement capabilities, custody, securities lending, accounting, and administrative services for investment portfolios, sophisticated risk and performance measurement tools for analyzing portfolios, and services for issuers of equity and debt securities.

Recently, BK realigned its reporting and presentation to focus on its two principal businesses, Investment Management and Investment Services. Investment Management includes the former Asset Management and Wealth Management businesses. Investment Services includes the former Asset Servicing, Issuer Services, Clearing Services, and Cash Management operations.

## Company Financials Fiscal Year Ended Dec. 31

| Per Share Data ($) | 2010 | 2009 | 2008 | 2007 | 2006 | 2005 | 2004 | 2003 | 2002 | 2001 |
|---|---|---|---|---|---|---|---|---|---|---|
| Tangible Book Value | 6.22 | 5.42 | 3.06 | 5.83 | 11.50 | 7.48 | 6.84 | 5.93 | 6.00 | 6.14 |
| Earnings | 2.11 | -0.93 | 1.22 | 2.38 | 2.05 | 2.15 | 1.96 | 1.61 | 1.31 | 1.92 |
| S&P Core Earnings | 2.14 | -0.99 | 1.05 | 2.33 | 2.01 | 2.11 | 1.83 | 1.55 | 1.07 | 1.65 |
| Dividends | 0.36 | 0.51 | 0.96 | 0.95 | 0.91 | 0.87 | 0.84 | 0.81 | 0.81 | 0.76 |
| Payout Ratio | 17% | NM | 79% | 40% | 45% | 40% | 43% | 50% | 61% | 40% |
| Prices:High | 32.65 | 33.62 | 49.90 | 50.26 | 42.98 | 35.71 | 36.94 | 35.50 | 49.29 | 61.61 |
| Prices:Low | 23.78 | 15.44 | 20.49 | 38.30 | 32.66 | 28.55 | 28.88 | 20.40 | 22.10 | 31.53 |
| P/E Ratio:High | 16 | NM | 40 | 21 | 21 | 17 | 19 | 22 | 37 | 32 |
| P/E Ratio:Low | 11 | NM | 17 | 16 | 16 | 13 | 15 | 13 | 17 | 16 |

| Income Statement Analysis (Million $) | | | | | | | | | | |
|---|---|---|---|---|---|---|---|---|---|---|
| Net Interest Income | 2,925 | 2,915 | 2,951 | 2,300 | 1,499 | 1,909 | 1,645 | 1,609 | 1,665 | 1,681 |
| Tax Equivalent Adjustment | 19.0 | 18.0 | 22.0 | 12.0 | NA | 29.0 | 30.0 | 35.0 | 49.0 | 60.0 |
| Non Interest Income | 10,697 | 10,141 | 12,329 | 9,232 | 5,337 | 4,888 | 4,613 | 3,971 | 3,261 | 3,386 |
| Loan Loss Provision | 11.0 | 332 | 131 | -10.0 | 20.0 | 15.0 | 15.0 | 155 | 685 | 375 |
| % Expense/Operating Revenue | 74.5% | 73.2% | 75.8% | 70.4% | 68.6% | 65.7% | 65.6% | 65.9% | 55.3% | 54.4% |
| Pretax Income | 3,694 | -2,208 | 1,939 | 3,225 | 2,170 | 2,367 | 2,199 | 1,762 | 1,372 | 2,058 |
| Effective Tax Rate | 28.3% | NM | 25.6% | 31.0% | 32.0% | 33.6% | 34.5% | 34.3% | 34.3% | 34.7% |
| Net Income | 2,584 | -814 | 1,442 | 2,227 | 1,476 | 1,571 | 1,440 | 1,157 | 902 | 1,343 |
| % Net Interest Margin | 1.70 | 1.82 | 1.92 | 2.08 | 2.01 | 2.36 | 2.07 | 2.22 | 2.62 | 2.57 |
| S&P Core Earnings | 2,625 | -1,179 | 1,217 | 2,179 | 1,452 | 1,536 | 1,350 | 1,097 | 728 | 1,159 |

| Balance Sheet & Other Financial Data (Million $) | | | | | | | | | | |
|---|---|---|---|---|---|---|---|---|---|---|
| Money Market Assets | 73,918 | 65,838 | 52,228 | 49,840 | 23,830 | 16,999 | 18,527 | 18,521 | 13,798 | 19,684 |
| Investment Securities | 66,307 | 56,049 | 39,435 | 48,698 | 21,106 | 27,326 | 23,802 | 22,903 | 18,300 | 12,862 |
| Commercial Loans | NA | 3,797 | 7,205 | 4,766 | 5,925 | 13,252 | 12,624 | 13,646 | 20,335 | 19,034 |
| Other Loans | NA | 32,892 | 35,774 | 43,465 | 31,868 | 27,474 | 23,157 | 21,637 | 11,004 | 16,713 |
| Total Assets | 247,259 | 212,224 | 237,009 | 197,656 | 103,370 | 102,074 | 94,529 | 92,397 | 77,564 | 81,025 |
| Demand Deposits | 38,703 | 33,477 | 55,816 | 32,372 | 19,554 | 18,236 | 17,442 | 14,789 | 13,301 | 12,635 |
| Time Deposits | 106,636 | 101,573 | 103,857 | 85,753 | 45,992 | 46,188 | 41,279 | 41,617 | 42,086 | 43,076 |
| Long Term Debt | 16,517 | 17,234 | 13,991 | 16,873 | 8,773 | Nil | Nil | Nil | Nil | Nil |
| Common Equity | 32,354 | 28,977 | 25,264 | 29,403 | 11,593 | 9,876 | 9,290 | 8,428 | 6,684 | 6,317 |
| % Return on Assets | 1.1 | NM | 0.7 | 1.5 | 1.4 | 1.6 | 1.5 | 1.4 | 1.1 | 1.7 |
| % Return on Equity | 8.4 | NM | 5.3 | 10.9 | 13.7 | 16.4 | 16.3 | 15.3 | 13.9 | 21.5 |
| % Loan Loss Reserve | 1.3 | 1.4 | 0.9 | 0.6 | 0.8 | 1.0 | 1.7 | 1.9 | 2.7 | 1.7 |
| % Loans/Deposits | 26.6 | 27.2 | 29.0 | 49.3 | 60.8 | 63.2 | 60.9 | 62.6 | 56.6 | 64.2 |
| % Equity to Assets | 13.4 | 8.8 | 12.6 | 13.6 | 10.5 | 9.7 | 9.5 | 8.9 | 8.2 | 7.9 |

Data as orig reptd.; bef. results of disc opers/spec. items. Per share data adj. for stk. divs.; EPS diluted. E-Estimated. NA-Not Available. NM-Not Meaningful. NR-Not Ranked. UR-Under Review.

Office: One Wall Street, New York, NY 10286.
Telephone: 212-495-1784.
Email: shareowner-svcs@bankofny.com
Website: http://www.bankofny.com

Chrmn, Pres & CEO: G.L. Hassell
Vice Chrmn: C.Y. Arledge
COO, Chief Admin Officer & CTO: K.D. Woetzel
EVP & Treas: S. Freidenrich

EVP & General Counsel: J. Sherburne
Board Members: C. Y. Arledge, R. E. Bruch, N. M. Donofrio, G. L. Hassell, E. F. Kelly, R. J. Kogan, M. J. Kowalski, J. A. Luke, Jr., M. A. Nordenberg, C. A. Rein, W. C. Richardson, S. C. Scott, III, J. P. Surma, Jr., W. W. von Schack

Founded: 1784
Domicile: Delaware
Employees: 48,000

# Bard (C.R.) Inc

**STANDARD &POOR'S**

| S&P Recommendation **HOLD** ★★★★★ | Price $83.37 (as of Nov 25, 2011) | 12-Mo. Target Price $93.00 | Investment Style Large-Cap Growth |
|---|---|---|---|

**GICS Sector** Health Care
**Sub-Industry** Health Care Equipment

**Summary** This diversified maker of therapeutic and diagnostic medical devices has exposure to the vascular, urology, oncology and specialty surgical markets.

## Key Stock Statistics (Source S&P, Vickers, company reports)

| | | | | | | | |
|---|---|---|---|---|---|---|---|
| 52-Wk Range | $113.84–80.80 | S&P Oper. EPS 2011**E** | 6.38 | Market Capitalization(B) | $7.152 | Beta | 0.32 |
| Trailing 12-Month EPS | $3.89 | S&P Oper. EPS 2012**E** | 7.00 | Yield (%) | 0.91 | S&P 3-Yr. Proj. EPS CAGR(%) | 10 |
| Trailing 12-Month P/E | 21.4 | P/E on S&P Oper. EPS 2011**E** | 13.1 | Dividend Rate/Share | $0.76 | S&P Credit Rating | A |
| $10K Invested 5 Yrs Ago | $10,521 | Common Shares Outstg. (M) | 85.8 | Institutional Ownership (%) | 90 | | |

## Price Performance

30-Week Mov. Avg. · · · 10-Week Mov. Avg. – – GAAP Earnings vs. Previous Year   Volume Above Avg. STARS
12-Mo. Target Price — Relative Strength   ▲ Up ▼ Down ► No Change   Below Avg. ★

Options: ASE, CBOE, P, Ph

Analysis prepared by Equity Analyst **Phillip Seligman** on Nov 01, 2011.

## Qualitative Risk Assessment

| LOW | **MEDIUM** | HIGH |
|---|---|---|

Our risk assessment reflects the highly competitive environment in which BCR operates. In addition, hospital customers generate a large portion of revenues from Medicare, and are therefore subject to reimbursement risks that could reduce prices paid to suppliers. However, we believe BCR's product line is largely focused on areas that have not been subject to intense pricing pressure, and we think management has a solid track record in terms of identifying and integrating acquisitions.

## Quantitative Evaluations

**S&P Quality Ranking** A

| D | C | B- | B | B+ | A- | **A** | A+ |
|---|---|---|---|---|---|---|---|

**Relative Strength Rank** MODERATE

50

LOWEST = 1     HIGHEST = 99

## Highlights

➤ We look for net sales to climb by 6.5% in 2011 and almost 6% on 2012. Drivers we see include growth of high-single to low-double-digit growth in the vascular category, on new products and acquisitions; upper-single-digit oncology growth, on improved sales of PICCs, and ports, mainly in emerging markets; and mid-single-digit growth in surgical specialties, with gains in natural tissue repair and new synthetic hernia fixation products. We expect urology sales to remain soft, on tepid U.S. sales of drainage products amid reduced hospital admissions. Full-year 2011 revenues have also been benefiting in 2011 from favorable currency exchange, but are being hurt by launch delays of some products.

➤ We forecast that gross margins will decline modestly in 2011, partly on pricing pressure and increased amortization from acquisitions, but recover slightly in 2012 on an improving product mix. We expect operating costs to decline as a percentage of sales through 2012.

➤ We look for 2011 EPS of $6.38, versus 2010 adjusted EPS of $5.60, aided by share buybacks that we see supported by $750 million of new debt. We project $7.00 in 2012.

## Investment Rationale/Risk

➤ While we are positive on the recovery we see to 14% EPS growth in 2011, following the slowdown in 2010, we think much of the gain will result from share buybacks. Hence, we think BCR could face tougher EPS comparisons in 2012, unless there is a pickup in surgical procedure rates in the U.S., the cadence of new product launches increases, BCR's new and pending products attract strong demand, and the company continues to make accretive acquisitions, including the pending one of therapeutic cooling products maker, and share buybacks. In this regard, we are encouraged by BCR's product pipeline. We also think its expansion under way in emerging markets holds promise.

➤ Risks to our recommendation and target price include intensified competition, reduced reimbursement, and failure to commercialize new products in a timely fashion.

➤ Given the decelerating net income growth rate we project, we believe a discount to the medical device group's valuation is appropriate. Applying a forward P/E of 13.3X to our 2012 EPS estimate yields our 12-month target price of $93.

## Revenue/Earnings Data

### Revenue (Million $)

| | 1Q | 2Q | 3Q | 4Q | Year |
|---|---|---|---|---|---|
| 2011 | 264.8 | 725.0 | 719.2 | -- | -- |
| 2010 | 650.8 | 673.9 | 678.4 | 717.1 | 2,720 |
| 2009 | 596.4 | 624.6 | 637.0 | 676.9 | 2,535 |
| 2008 | 584.0 | 617.1 | 616.8 | 634.2 | 2,452 |
| 2007 | 528.2 | 545.7 | 544.8 | 583.3 | 2,202 |
| 2006 | 467.5 | 498.2 | 498.9 | 520.9 | 1,986 |

### Earnings Per Share ($)

| | | | | | |
|---|---|---|---|---|---|
| 2011 | 1.49 | -0.55 | 1.46 | E1.68 | E6.38 |
| 2010 | 1.24 | 1.29 | 1.34 | 1.47 | 5.32 |
| 2009 | 1.10 | 1.11 | 1.31 | 1.08 | 4.60 |
| 2008 | 0.76 | 0.76 | 1.09 | 1.47 | 4.06 |
| 2007 | 0.95 | 0.91 | 0.96 | 1.01 | 3.84 |
| 2006 | 0.76 | 0.76 | 0.82 | 0.21 | 2.55 |

Fiscal year ended Dec. 31. Next earnings report expected: Early February. EPS Estimates based on S&P Operating Earnings; historical GAAP earnings are as reported.

## Dividend Data (Dates: mm/dd Payment Date: mm/dd/yy)

| Amount ($) | Date Decl. | Ex-Div. Date | Stk. of Record | Payment Date |
|---|---|---|---|---|
| 0.180 | 12/08 | 01/20 | 01/24 | 02/04/11 |
| 0.180 | 04/20 | 04/28 | 05/02 | 05/13/11 |
| 0.190 | 06/08 | 07/21 | 07/25 | 08/05/11 |
| 0.190 | 10/12 | 10/20 | 10/24 | 11/04/11 |

Dividends have been paid since 1960. Source: Company reports.

---

**Please read the Required Disclosures and Analyst Certification on the last page of this report.**

The McGraw-Hill Companies

# Bard (C.R.) Inc

STANDARD &POOR'S

## Business Summary November 01, 2011

CORPORATE OVERVIEW. C.R. Bard offers a range of medical, surgical, diagnostic and patient care devices. Sales in 2010 came from vascular (28%), urology (26%), oncology (27%), surgical specialties (16%) and other (3%) products.

Bard's vascular products include percutaneous transluminal angioplasty (PTA) catheters, guide wires, introducers and accessories, peripheral stents, vena cava filters and biopsy devices; electrophysiology products such as lab systems and diagnostic therapeutic and temporary pacing electrode catheters; and fabrics, meshes and implantable vascular grafts.

Urological diagnosis and intervention products include Foley catheters, procedure kits and trays, and related urine monitoring and collection systems; urethral stents; and specialty devices for incontinence, endoscopic procedures, and stone removal. Newer products include the Infection Control Foley catheter that reduces the rate of urinary tract infections; a collagen implant and sling materials used to treat urinary incontinence; and brachytherapy services, devices and radioactive seeds to treat prostate cancer.

Oncology products include specialty access catheters, including peripherally

inserted central catheters (PICCs), and ports; gastroenterological products (endoscopic accessories, percutaneous feeding devices and stents); biopsy devices; and a suturing system for gastroesophageal reflux disease.

Surgical specialties products include meshes for hernia and other soft tissue repairs; irrigation devices for orthopedic, laparoscopic and gynecological procedures; and topical hemostatic devices. In January 2003, Bard introduced the VentralexT hernia patch, a simplified intra-abdominal hernia repair technology characterized by minimal suturing, small incisions, and potentially shorter recovery times. In December 2007, Bard entered into a license agreement with Genzyme Corp. to manufacture and market the Sepramesh IP hernia repair product line and incorporate the related Sepra coating technology into the development of future hernia repair applications.

## Company Financials  Fiscal Year Ended Dec. 31

| Per Share Data ($) | 2010 | 2009 | 2008 | 2007 | 2006 | 2005 | 2004 | 2003 | 2002 | 2001 |
|---|---|---|---|---|---|---|---|---|---|---|
| Tangible Book Value | 5.69 | 13.34 | 11.62 | 10.73 | 9.46 | 10.39 | 7.26 | 5.35 | 4.84 | 3.97 |
| Cash Flow | 6.50 | 5.59 | 4.95 | 4.59 | 3.25 | 3.71 | 3.33 | 2.03 | 1.87 | 1.89 |
| Earnings | 5.32 | 4.60 | 4.06 | 3.84 | 2.55 | 3.12 | 2.82 | 1.60 | 1.47 | 1.38 |
| S&P Core Earnings | 5.35 | 4.80 | 3.96 | 3.86 | 2.96 | 2.86 | 2.29 | 1.73 | 1.27 | 1.21 |
| Dividends | 0.70 | 0.66 | 0.62 | 0.58 | 0.54 | 0.50 | 0.47 | 0.45 | 0.43 | 0.42 |
| Payout Ratio | 13% | 14% | 15% | 15% | 21% | 16% | 17% | 28% | 29% | 31% |
| Prices:High | 95.72 | 88.43 | 101.61 | 95.33 | 85.72 | 72.79 | 65.13 | 40.80 | 31.97 | 32.47 |
| Prices:Low | 75.16 | 68.94 | 70.00 | 76.61 | 59.89 | 60.82 | 40.09 | 27.02 | 22.05 | 20.43 |
| P/E Ratio:High | 18 | 19 | 25 | 25 | 34 | 23 | 23 | 25 | 22 | 24 |
| P/E Ratio:Low | 14 | 15 | 17 | 20 | 23 | 19 | 14 | 17 | 15 | 15 |

| Income Statement Analysis (Million $) | 2010 | 2009 | 2008 | 2007 | 2006 | 2005 | 2004 | 2003 | 2002 | 2001 |
|---|---|---|---|---|---|---|---|---|---|---|
| Revenue | 2,720 | 2,535 | 2,452 | 2,202 | 1,986 | 1,771 | 1,656 | 1,433 | 1,274 | 1,181 |
| Operating Income | 870 | 825 | 735 | 638 | 550 | 503 | 418 | 333 | 295 | 266 |
| Depreciation | 105 | 93.5 | 90.9 | 79.8 | 74.9 | 63.8 | 54.7 | 44.7 | 42.3 | 53.2 |
| Interest Expense | 12.7 | 11.8 | 12.1 | 11.9 | 16.9 | 12.2 | 12.7 | 12.5 | 12.6 | 14.2 |
| Pretax Income | 718 | 672 | 550 | 577 | 348 | 450 | 414 | 223 | 211 | 205 |
| Effective Tax Rate | NA | 31.3% | 24.3% | 29.6% | 21.7% | 25.0% | 26.9% | 24.5% | 26.5% | 30.1% |
| Net Income | 509 | 460 | 417 | 406 | 272 | 337 | 303 | 169 | 155 | 143 |
| S&P Core Earnings | 506 | 475 | 407 | 409 | 317 | 309 | 244 | 182 | 134 | 126 |

| Balance Sheet & Other Financial Data (Million $) | 2010 | 2009 | 2008 | 2007 | 2006 | 2005 | 2004 | 2003 | 2002 | 2001 |
|---|---|---|---|---|---|---|---|---|---|---|
| Cash | 641 | 674 | 592 | 571 | 416 | 754 | 541 | 417 | 23.1 | 30.8 |
| Current Assets | 1,529 | 1,492 | 1,354 | 1,242 | 1,134 | 1,264 | 1,054 | 875 | 758 | 647 |
| Total Assets | 3,172 | 2,907 | 2,666 | 2,476 | 2,277 | 2,266 | 2,009 | 1,692 | 1,417 | 1,231 |
| Current Liabilities | 398 | 282 | 273 | 282 | 296 | 641 | 390 | 422 | 317 | 235 |
| Long Term Debt | 897 | 150 | 150 | 150 | 151 | 0.80 | 151 | 152 | 152 | 156 |
| Common Equity | 1,632 | 2,194 | 1,977 | 1,848 | 1,698 | 1,536 | 1,360 | 1,046 | 880 | 789 |
| Total Capital | 2,528 | 2,356 | 2,151 | 2,018 | 1,871 | 1,544 | 1,534 | 1,197 | 1,033 | 945 |
| Capital Expenditures | 51.2 | 48.1 | 50.6 | 50.7 | 70.4 | 97.2 | 74.0 | 72.1 | 41.0 | 27.4 |
| Cash Flow | 614 | 554 | 507 | 486 | 347 | 401 | 358 | 213 | 197 | 196 |
| Current Ratio | 3.9 | 5.3 | 5.0 | 4.4 | 3.8 | 2.0 | 2.7 | 2.1 | 2.4 | 2.8 |
| % Long Term Debt of Capitalization | 35.5 | Nil | 7.0 | 7.4 | 8.1 | 0.1 | 9.9 | 12.7 | 14.7 | 16.5 |
| % Net Income of Revenue | 18.7 | 18.2 | 17.0 | 18.5 | 13.7 | 19.0 | 18.3 | 11.8 | 12.2 | 12.1 |
| % Return on Assets | NA | NA | 16.2 | 17.1 | 12.0 | 15.8 | 16.4 | 10.8 | 11.5 | 12.3 |
| % Return on Equity | NA | NA | 21.8 | 22.9 | 16.8 | 23.3 | 25.2 | 17.5 | 18.6 | 20.4 |

Data as orig reptd.; bef. results of disc opers/spec. items. Per share data adj. for stk. divs.; EPS diluted. E-Estimated. NA-Not Available. NM-Not Meaningful. NR-Not Ranked. UR-Under Review.

Office: 730 Central Avenue, Murray Hill, NJ 07974.
Telephone: 908-277-8000.
Website: http://www.crbard.com
Chrmn & CEO: T.M. Ring

Pres & COO: J.H. Weiland
SVP & CFO: T.C. Schermerhorn
Chief Acctg Officer & Cntlr: F. Lupisella, Jr.
Treas: S.T. Lowry

Investor Contact: E.J. Shick (908-277-8413)
Board Members: D. M. Barrett, M. C. Breslawsky, H. L. Henkel, J. C. Kelly, T. E. Martin, G. Naughton, T. M. Ring, T. G. Thompson, J. H. Weiland, A. Welters, T. L. White

Founded: 1907
Domicile: New Jersey
Employees: 11,700

# Baxter International Inc

**STANDARD &POOR'S**

| S&P Recommendation **BUY** ★★★★☆ | Price $47.72 (as of Nov 25, 2011) | 12-Mo. Target Price $65.00 | Investment Style Large-Cap Growth |
|---|---|---|---|

**GICS Sector** Health Care
**Sub-Industry** Health Care Equipment

**Summary** This global medical products and services company provides critical therapies for people with life-threatening conditions.

## Key Stock Statistics (Source S&P, Vickers, company reports)

| | | | | | | | |
|---|---|---|---|---|---|---|---|
| 52-Wk Range | $62.50– 47.69 | S&P Oper. EPS 2011**E** | 4.30 | Market Capitalization(B) | $26.908 | Beta | 0.51 |
| Trailing 12-Month EPS | $3.78 | S&P Oper. EPS 2012**E** | 4.60 | Yield (%) | 2.81 | S&P 3-Yr. Proj. EPS CAGR(%) | 6 |
| Trailing 12-Month P/E | 12.6 | P/E on S&P Oper. EPS 2011**E** | 11.1 | Dividend Rate/Share | $1.34 | S&P Credit Rating | A+ |
| $10K Invested 5 Yrs Ago | $11,921 | Common Shares Outstg. (M) | 563.9 | Institutional Ownership (%) | 82 | | |

## Price Performance

30-Week Mov. Avg. · · · 10-Week Mov. Avg. - - GAAP Earnings vs. Previous Year   Volume Above Avg. STARS
12-Mo. Target Price — Relative Strength   ▲ Up  ▼ Down  ▶ No Change   Below Avg.

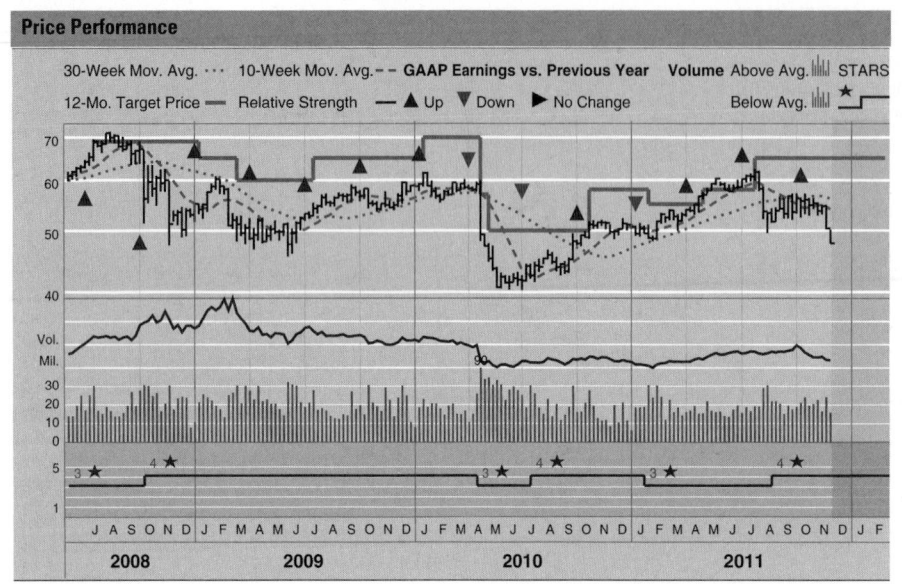

Options: ASE, CBOE, P, Ph

Analysis prepared by Equity Analyst **Herman Saftlas** on Aug 31, 2011, when the stock traded at **$55.74**.

## Qualitative Risk Assessment

| LOW | **MEDIUM** | HIGH |
|---|---|---|

Our risk assessment reflects BAX's operations in a highly competitive business characterized by rapid technological change and new market entrants. In addition, the business entails regulatory and reimbursement risks, as well as liability risk from malfunctioning products. This is offset by our belief that health care products are largely immune to economic cycles, and that long-term demand should benefit from demographic growth of the elderly and a greater penetration of developing global markets.

## Quantitative Evaluations

**S&P Quality Ranking**    A

| D | C | B- | B | B+ | A- | **A** | A+ |
|---|---|---|---|---|---|---|---|

**Relative Strength Rank**    WEAK

28

LOWEST = 1                                      HIGHEST = 99

## Highlights

➤ We see 2011 revenues in constant currencies rising 5% from 2010's adjusted $13.1 billion, despite the May 2011 divestiture of the generic injectables business (annual sales of about $200 million). Key sales drivers we see are projected high-single-digit growth in plasma proteins, and low-teens gains in antibody therapies, and regenerative medicine lines. We expect sales of global injectables and recombinants to increase in the low single digits. Sales of renal care products are also expected to rise, with gains in peritoneal dialysis products offsetting declines in older hemodialysis lines.

➤ We expect gross margins to approximate 2010's 51.1%. Despite headwinds from U.S. health care reform and European austerity pricing, we look for modest improvement in operating margins, helped by cost controls and productivity enhancements. However, we believe non-operating expenses will increase.

➤ After a projected effective tax rate of about 21.5%, versus 2010's 20.1%, we estimate operating EPS of $4.30 in 2011, up from 2010's $3.98. We see further progress to $4.60 in 2012.

## Investment Rationale/Risk

➤ Despite pricing headwinds in the U.S. and Europe, we expect solid growth in key plasma proteins, antibody therapies, and regenerative medicine lines over the coming quarters. We are encouraged by BAX's launch of new products and other strategies designed to grow the plasma business, as well as by greater efforts to expand in emerging markets. We also see promise in Baxter's R&D pipeline, which includes new vaccines, hospital products and drugs. We expect cash flow of about $2.8 billion in 2011, including a $300 million outlay related to a Colleague pump consent order, and a $150 million pension contribution.

➤ Risks to our recommendation and target price include lower-than-expected Advate sales, adverse adjustments to Medicare reimbursement rates, and an inability to further streamline operating costs and resolve regulatory issues.

➤ Our 12-month target price of $65 assumes a parity-to-peers multiple of about 14.1X our 2012 EPS forecast. Our DCF model, which assumes declining cash flow growth, a WACC of 9.2% and a terminal growth rate of 2%, also indicates intrinsic value of about $65.

## Revenue/Earnings Data

**Revenue (Million $)**

| | 1Q | 2Q | 3Q | 4Q | Year |
|---|---|---|---|---|---|
| 2011 | 3,284 | 3,536 | 3,479 | -- | -- |
| 2010 | 2,927 | 3,194 | 3,224 | 3,498 | 12,843 |
| 2009 | 2,824 | 3,123 | 3,145 | 3,470 | 12,562 |
| 2008 | 2,877 | 3,189 | 3,151 | 3,131 | 12,348 |
| 2007 | 2,675 | 2,829 | 2,750 | 3,009 | 11,263 |
| 2006 | 2,409 | 2,649 | 2,557 | 2,763 | 10,378 |

**Earnings Per Share ($)**

| | | | | | |
|---|---|---|---|---|---|
| 2011 | 0.98 | 1.07 | 1.01 | E1.17 | E4.30 |
| 2010 | -0.11 | 0.90 | 0.89 | 0.72 | 2.39 |
| 2009 | 0.83 | 0.96 | 0.87 | 0.94 | 3.59 |
| 2008 | 0.67 | 0.85 | 0.74 | 0.91 | 3.16 |
| 2007 | 0.61 | 0.65 | 0.61 | 0.74 | 2.61 |
| 2006 | 0.43 | 0.47 | 0.57 | 0.66 | 2.13 |

Fiscal year ended Dec. 31. Next earnings report expected: Late January. EPS Estimates based on S&P Operating Earnings; historical GAAP earnings are as reported.

## Dividend Data (Dates: mm/dd Payment Date: mm/dd/yy)

| Amount ($) | Date Decl. | Ex-Div. Date | Stk. of Record | Payment Date |
|---|---|---|---|---|
| 0.310 | 02/15 | 03/08 | 03/10 | 04/01/11 |
| 0.310 | 05/02 | 06/08 | 06/10 | 07/01/11 |
| 0.310 | 07/26 | 09/07 | 09/09 | 10/03/11 |
| 0.335 | 11/15 | 12/07 | 12/09 | 01/04/12 |

Dividends have been paid since 1934. Source: Company reports.

**Please read the Required Disclosures and Analyst Certification on the last page of this report.**

**The McGraw-Hill** Companies

# Baxter International Inc

**STANDARD &POOR'S**

## Business Summary August 31, 2011

CORPORATE OVERVIEW. Founded in 1931 as the first producer of commercially prepared intravenous (IV) solutions, Baxter International makes and distributes medical products and equipment, with a focus on the blood and circulatory system. International sales accounted for about 58% of total sales in 2010. In May 2011, BAX divested its generic injectables business. The Transfusion Therapies unit was divested in March 2007.

The BioSciences unit (43% of 2010 sales) produces plasma-based and recombinant clotting factors for hemophilia, as well as biopharmaceuticals for immune deficiencies, cancer, and other disorders. It also offers biosurgery products for hemostasis, tissue sealing and tissue regeneration, vaccines, and blood processing and storage systems used by hospitals, blood banks and others. In addition, BAX sells a meningitis C vaccine, and is developing cell culture-derived vaccines for influenza, smallpox, Severe Acute Respiratory Syndrome and other diseases. Its most important Biosciences product is Advate, a recombinant blood-clotting agent produced without adding human or animal proteins in the cell culture, purification or final formulation process.

The Medication Delivery unit (38%) makes IV solutions and various specialty products such as intravenous solutions, premixed drugs, pre-filled vials and syringes, IV nutrition products, and inhalation anesthetics. The products work with devices such as drug-reconstitution systems, IV infusion pumps, nutritional compounding equipment, and medication management systems to provide fluid replenishment, general anesthesia, parenteral nutrition, pain management, antibiotic therapy, and chemotherapy.

Renal Care products (18%) comprise dialysis equipment and other products and services provided for kidney failure patients. BAX sells products for peritoneal dialysis (PD), including solutions, container systems and automated machines that cleanse patients' blood overnight while they sleep. The company also makes dialyzers and instrumentation for hemodialysis (HD). Another renal care product is Extraneal (icodextrin) solution, which facilitates increased fluid removal from the bloodstream during dialysis. Revenues related to Transfusion Therapies accounted for 1% of 2010 sales.

## Company Financials Fiscal Year Ended Dec. 31

| Per Share Data ($) | 2010 | 2009 | 2008 | 2007 | 2006 | 2005 | 2004 | 2003 | 2002 | 2001 |
|---|---|---|---|---|---|---|---|---|---|---|
| Tangible Book Value | 6.98 | 8.08 | 6.79 | 7.53 | 6.42 | 3.61 | 2.45 | 1.74 | 1.53 | 3.44 |
| Cash Flow | 3.56 | 4.63 | 4.11 | 3.46 | 3.01 | 2.45 | 1.59 | 2.42 | 2.38 | 1.81 |
| Earnings | 2.39 | 3.59 | 3.16 | 2.61 | 2.13 | 1.52 | 0.62 | 1.52 | 1.67 | 1.09 |
| S&P Core Earnings | 2.56 | 3.66 | 2.99 | 2.68 | 2.24 | 1.38 | 0.52 | 1.25 | 1.30 | 0.53 |
| Dividends | 1.18 | 1.07 | 0.91 | 0.72 | 0.58 | 0.58 | 0.58 | 0.58 | 0.58 | 0.58 |
| Payout Ratio | 49% | 30% | 29% | 28% | 27% | 38% | 94% | 38% | 35% | 53% |
| Prices:High | 61.88 | 60.99 | 71.53 | 61.09 | 48.54 | 41.07 | 34.84 | 31.32 | 59.90 | 55.90 |
| Prices:Low | 40.25 | 45.46 | 47.41 | 46.07 | 35.12 | 33.08 | 27.10 | 18.18 | 24.07 | 40.06 |
| P/E Ratio:High | 26 | 17 | 23 | 23 | 23 | 27 | 56 | 21 | 36 | 51 |
| P/E Ratio:Low | 17 | 13 | 15 | 18 | 16 | 22 | 44 | 12 | 14 | 37 |

| Income Statement Analysis (Million $) | 2010 | 2009 | 2008 | 2007 | 2006 | 2005 | 2004 | 2003 | 2002 | 2001 |
|---|---|---|---|---|---|---|---|---|---|---|
| Revenue | 12,843 | 12,562 | 12,348 | 11,263 | 10,378 | 9,849 | 9,509 | 8,916 | 8,110 | 7,663 |
| Operating Income | 3,505 | 3,594 | 3,333 | 2,913 | 2,479 | 2,110 | 2,039 | 2,161 | 2,168 | 1,934 |
| Depreciation | 685 | 638 | 606 | 558 | 575 | 580 | 601 | 545 | 439 | 441 |
| Interest Expense | 87.0 | 117 | 165 | 136 | 101 | 166 | 99.0 | 118 | 71.0 | 108 |
| Pretax Income | 1,890 | 2,734 | 2,451 | 2,114 | 1,746 | 1,444 | 430 | 1,150 | 1,397 | 964 |
| Effective Tax Rate | NA | 19.0% | 17.8% | 19.3% | 19.9% | 33.7% | 10.9% | 19.8% | 26.1% | 31.1% |
| Net Income | 1,420 | 2,205 | 2,014 | 1,707 | 1,398 | 958 | 383 | 922 | 1,033 | 664 |
| S&P Core Earnings | 1,523 | 2,248 | 1,906 | 1,757 | 1,467 | 864 | 323 | 756 | 794 | 313 |

| Balance Sheet & Other Financial Data (Million $) | 2010 | 2009 | 2008 | 2007 | 2006 | 2005 | 2004 | 2003 | 2002 | 2001 |
|---|---|---|---|---|---|---|---|---|---|---|
| Cash | 2,685 | 2,811 | 2,131 | 2,539 | 2,485 | 841 | 1,109 | 927 | 1,169 | 582 |
| Current Assets | 7,989 | 8,271 | 7,148 | 7,555 | 6,970 | 5,116 | 6,019 | 5,437 | 5,160 | 3,977 |
| Total Assets | 17,489 | 17,354 | 15,405 | 15,294 | 14,686 | 12,727 | 14,147 | 13,779 | 12,478 | 10,343 |
| Current Liabilities | 4,041 | 4,464 | 3,635 | 3,812 | 3,610 | 4,165 | 4,286 | 3,819 | 3,851 | 3,294 |
| Long Term Debt | 4,363 | 3,440 | 3,362 | 2,664 | 2,567 | 2,414 | 3,933 | 4,421 | 4,398 | 2,486 |
| Common Equity | 6,567 | 7,191 | 6,229 | 6,916 | 6,272 | 4,299 | 3,705 | 3,323 | 2,939 | 3,757 |
| Total Capital | 11,397 | 11,542 | 9,597 | 9,580 | 8,839 | 6,713 | 7,638 | 7,744 | 7,366 | 6,461 |
| Capital Expenditures | 963 | 1,014 | 954 | 692 | 526 | 444 | 558 | 789 | 734 | 669 |
| Cash Flow | 2,112 | 2,843 | 2,620 | 2,265 | 1,973 | 1,538 | 984 | 1,467 | 1,472 | 1,105 |
| Current Ratio | 2.0 | 1.9 | 2.0 | 2.0 | 1.9 | 1.2 | 1.4 | 1.4 | 1.3 | 1.2 |
| % Long Term Debt of Capitalization | 38.3 | Nil | 35.1 | 27.8 | 29.0 | 36.0 | 51.5 | 57.1 | 59.7 | 38.5 |
| % Net Income of Revenue | 11.1 | 17.6 | 16.3 | 15.2 | 13.5 | 9.7 | 4.0 | 10.3 | 12.7 | 8.7 |
| % Return on Assets | NA | NA | 13.1 | 11.4 | 10.2 | 7.1 | 2.8 | 7.0 | 9.1 | 7.0 |
| % Return on Equity | NA | NA | 30.6 | 25.9 | 26.4 | 23.9 | 10.8 | 29.4 | 30.9 | 20.7 |

Data as orig reptd.; bef. results of disc opers/spec. items. Per share data adj. for stk. divs.; EPS diluted. E-Estimated. NA-Not Available. NM-Not Meaningful. NR-Not Ranked. UR-Under Review.

**Office:** One Baxter Parkway, Deerfield, IL 60015-4633.
**Telephone:** 847-948-2000.
**Website:** http://www.baxter.com
**Chrmn, Pres & CEO:** R.L. Parkinson, Jr.

**CFO:** R.J. Hombach
**CSO:** N.G. Riedel
**Chief Acctg Officer & Cntlr:** M.J. Baughman
**Treas:** J.K. Saccaro

**Investor Contact:** M. Ladone (847-948-3371)
**Board Members:** W. E. Boomer, B. E. Devitt, J. D. Forsyth, G. D. Fosler, J. Gavin, III, P. S. Hellman, W. T. Hockmeyer, J. Martin, R. L. Parkinson, Jr., C. J. Shapazian, T. T. Stallkamp, K. J. Storm, A. P. Stroucken

**Founded:** 1931
**Domicile:** Delaware
**Employees:** 48,000

The McGraw-Hill Companies

# BB&T Corp

**STANDARD &POOR'S**

| S&P Recommendation | BUY ★★★★☆ | Price $21.17 (as of Nov 25, 2011) | 12-Mo. Target Price $26.00 | Investment Style Large-Cap Blend |
|---|---|---|---|---|

**GICS Sector** Financials
**Sub-Industry** Regional Banks

**Summary** BBT, with September 30 assets of $167.7 billion, is the eighth largest U.S. bank by assets, operating some 1,750 branches, mainly in the Southeast U.S.

## Key Stock Statistics (Source S&P, Vickers, company reports)

| | | | | | | | |
|---|---|---|---|---|---|---|---|
| 52-Wk Range | $29.60–18.92 | S&P Oper. EPS 2011**E** | 1.84 | Market Capitalization(B) | $14.758 | Beta | 1.00 |
| Trailing 12-Month EPS | $1.56 | S&P Oper. EPS 2012**E** | 2.60 | Yield (%) | 3.02 | S&P 3-Yr. Proj. EPS CAGR(%) | 35 |
| Trailing 12-Month P/E | 13.6 | P/E on S&P Oper. EPS 2011**E** | 11.5 | Dividend Rate/Share | $0.64 | S&P Credit Rating | A |
| $10K Invested 5 Yrs Ago | $6,085 | Common Shares Outstg. (M) | 697.1 | Institutional Ownership (%) | 57 | | |

## Price Performance

30-Week Mov. Avg. ···· 10-Week Mov. Avg. – – GAAP Earnings vs. Previous Year   Volume Above Avg. ▮▮▮ STARS
12-Mo. Target Price — Relative Strength — ▲ Up ▼ Down ▶ No Change   Below Avg. ▮▮▮ ★

Options: ASE, CBOE, P, Ph

Analysis prepared by Equity Analyst **Erik Oja** on Nov 10, 2011, when the stock traded at **$23.08**.

### Highlights

➤ For 2011, we look for net interest income to rise 3.1%, on our expectations for 2.6% growth in the loan portfolio and interest-earning assets growth of 5.5%. For 2012, we see loan growth of 2.2%, leading to a 3.4% rise in net interest income. However, we expect total noninterest income to fall 26% in 2011, due to regulatory pressures. We see total revenues decreasing 9.6% in 2011 before advancing 2.6% in 2012.

➤ We expect BBT's earnings in 2011 to be helped by a reduction in loan loss provisions. We are modeling 2011 loan loss provisions of $1.175 billion, down from $2.638 billion in 2010, based on our forecast of $1.45 billion of net chargeoffs, down from $2.530 billion in 2010. For 2012, we project chargeoffs to fall further, to $860 million, and we see loan loss provisions of $820 million. We expect negligible reserve releases in 2012. Despite increased FDIC expenses as well as the cost of holding foreclosed real estate, we expect a 2012 efficiency ratio of 64.1%, lower than our 2011 projection of 65.3%, and in line with 2010's level.

➤ We estimate EPS of $1.84 for 2011, rising to $2.60 in 2012.

### Investment Rationale/Risk

➤ BBT reported strong third-quarter results, with rising loan and investment securities yields, above-peers loan growth, another drop in non-performing loans, relatively low noninterest expenses, and good mortgage banking growth. We expect loan net chargeoffs and loss provisions to decline each quarter in 2011 and 2012, and we believe that the 2010 third quarter was the peak for each. Although BBT's tangible common equity to tangible assets ratio is lower than at some large peers, we expect internally generated capital to boost the ratio to 7.05% by the end of 2011 and 7.80% at year-end 2012.

➤ Risks to our opinion and target price include a downturn in the U.S. economy, and greater than expected declines in mortgage banking, card revenues and insurance.

➤ BBT trades at 9.4X our forward four quarters EPS estimate of $2.45, and 8.9X our 2012 EPS estimate of $2.60, in line with peers. Our 12-month target price of $26 is a premium to peers 10.6X our forward four quarters EPS estimate, and an above-peers multiple of 1.60X our year-end 2011 tangible book value per share estimate of $16.40. The shares yield 2.8%, and our target price assumes a 15% total return.

### Qualitative Risk Assessment

| LOW | MEDIUM | HIGH |
|---|---|---|

Our risk assessment reflects the company's large-cap valuation, our view of the strong credit quality of its loan portfolio, and its history of profitability, offset by exposure to the banking industry's current issues regarding funding and credit quality.

### Quantitative Evaluations

**S&P Quality Ranking**          B+

| D | C | B- | B | B+ | A- | A | A+ |
|---|---|---|---|---|---|---|---|

**Relative Strength Rank**          MODERATE

46

LOWEST = 1          HIGHEST = 99

### Revenue/Earnings Data

**Revenue (Million $)**

| | 1Q | 2Q | 3Q | 4Q | Year |
|---|---|---|---|---|---|
| 2011 | 2,390 | 2,477 | 2,440 | -- | -- |
| 2010 | 2,623 | 2,858 | 2,872 | 2,719 | 11,072 |
| 2009 | 2,740 | 2,633 | 2,685 | 2,790 | 10,818 |
| 2008 | 2,655 | 2,617 | 2,585 | 2,536 | 10,404 |
| 2007 | 2,543 | 2,690 | 2,719 | 2,747 | 10,668 |
| 2006 | 2,165 | 2,319 | 2,463 | 2,468 | 9,414 |

**Earnings Per Share ($)**

| | 1Q | 2Q | 3Q | 4Q | Year |
|---|---|---|---|---|---|
| 2011 | 0.32 | 0.44 | 0.52 | E0.56 | E1.84 |
| 2010 | 0.27 | 0.30 | 0.30 | 0.30 | 1.16 |
| 2009 | 0.48 | 0.20 | 0.23 | 0.27 | 1.15 |
| 2008 | 0.78 | 0.78 | 0.65 | 0.51 | 2.71 |
| 2007 | 0.77 | 0.83 | 0.80 | 0.75 | 3.14 |
| 2006 | 0.79 | 0.79 | 0.77 | 0.46 | 2.81 |

Fiscal year ended Dec. 31. Next earnings report expected: Late January. EPS Estimates based on S&P Operating Earnings; historical GAAP earnings are as reported.

### Dividend Data (Dates: mm/dd Payment Date: mm/dd/yy)

| Amount ($) | Date Decl. | Ex-Div. Date | Stk. of Record | Payment Date |
|---|---|---|---|---|
| .01 Spl. | 03/18 | 04/06 | 04/08 | 05/02/11 |
| 0.160 | 02/22 | 04/06 | 04/08 | 05/02/11 |
| 0.160 | 06/21 | 07/06 | 07/08 | 08/01/11 |
| 0.160 | 08/23 | 10/12 | 10/14 | 11/01/11 |

Dividends have been paid since 1903. Source: Company reports.

---

**Please read the Required Disclosures and Analyst Certification on the last page of this report.**

**The McGraw-Hill Companies**

# BB&T Corp

STANDARD
&POOR'S

## Business Summary November 10, 2011

CORPORATE OVERVIEW. BB&T Corp. has bank operations providing loan, deposit and financial products primarily in the Southeast. BBT has seven reportable business segments: Banking Network, Mortgage Banking, Trust Services, Insurance Services, Investment Banking and Brokerage, Specialized Lending, and Treasury.

MARKET PROFILE. As of June 30, 2011, which is the latest available FDIC branch-level data, BBT had 1,751 branches and $111.4 billion in deposits. BBT's footprint is relatively concentrated, as over 60% of deposits are in Virginia, North Carolina, and Florida. In North Carolina, BBT had 355 branches, $35.1 billion of deposits, and a deposit market share of 11.1%, ranking third. In Virginia, BBT had 387 branches, $20.3 billion of deposits, and a deposit market share of about 8.0%, ranking fifth. In Florida, BBT had 269 branches, $12.6 billion of deposits, and a deposit market share of about 2.8%, ranking fifth, largely due to the 2009 Colonial acquisition.

In Georgia, BBT had 161 branches, $11.3 billion of deposits, and a deposit market share of about 5.6%, ranking fifth. In Maryland, BBT had 127 branches, $6.6 billion of deposits, and a deposit market share of about 5.0%, ranking seventh. In South Carolina, BBT had 114 branches, $6.7 billion of deposits, and a deposit market share of about 8.7%, ranking third. In Alabama, BBT had 87 branches, $4.5 billion of deposits, and a deposit market share of about 4.6%, ranking fourth. Almost all of BBT's current Alabama presence resulted from the Colonial transaction. In addition, BBT had a number one market ranking in West Virginia, was fourth in Kentucky, 9th in DC, and sixth in Tennessee. Finally, BBT had a small presence in Texas and Indiana.

## Company Financials Fiscal Year Ended Dec. 31

| Per Share Data ($) | 2010 | 2009 | 2008 | 2007 | 2006 | 2005 | 2004 | 2003 | 2002 | 2001 |
|---|---|---|---|---|---|---|---|---|---|---|
| Tangible Book Value | 14.29 | 13.77 | 11.86 | 12.73 | 11.04 | 11.76 | 12.26 | 11.66 | 12.04 | 13.50 |
| Earnings | 1.16 | 1.15 | 2.71 | 3.14 | 2.81 | 3.00 | 2.80 | 2.07 | 2.70 | 2.12 |
| S&P Core Earnings | 1.10 | 1.15 | 2.54 | 3.09 | 2.79 | 2.90 | 2.75 | 1.97 | 2.59 | 2.02 |
| Dividends | 0.75 | 1.24 | 1.86 | 1.76 | 1.60 | 1.46 | 1.34 | 1.22 | 1.10 | 0.98 |
| Payout Ratio | 65% | 108% | 67% | 56% | 57% | 49% | 48% | 59% | 41% | 46% |
| Prices:High | 35.72 | 29.81 | 45.31 | 44.30 | 44.74 | 43.92 | 43.25 | 39.69 | 39.47 | 38.84 |
| Prices:Low | 21.72 | 12.90 | 18.71 | 30.36 | 38.24 | 37.04 | 33.02 | 30.66 | 31.03 | 30.24 |
| P/E Ratio:High | 31 | 26 | 17 | 14 | 16 | 15 | 15 | 19 | 15 | 18 |
| P/E Ratio:Low | 19 | 11 | 7 | 10 | 14 | 12 | 12 | 15 | 11 | 14 |

| Income Statement Analysis (Million $) | | | | | | | | | | |
|---|---|---|---|---|---|---|---|---|---|---|
| Net Interest Income | 5,320 | 4,844 | 4,238 | 3,880 | 3,708 | 3,525 | 3,348 | 3,082 | 2,747 | 2,434 |
| Tax Equivalent Adjustment | 10.8 | 119 | 83.0 | 68.0 | NA | 82.7 | NA | 21.2 | 151 | 19.1 |
| Non Interest Income | 3,957 | 3,934 | 3,197 | 2,777 | 2,594 | 2,326 | 2,113 | 1,782 | 1,522 | 1,256 |
| Loan Loss Provision | 2,638 | 2,811 | 1,445 | 448 | 240 | 217 | 249 | 248 | 264 | 224 |
| % Expense/Operating Revenue | 61.1% | 56.2% | 54.4% | 54.6% | 55.8% | 53.4% | 57.6% | 63.6% | 54.0% | 60.1% |
| Pretax Income | 969 | 1,036 | 2,069 | 2,570 | 2,473 | 2,467 | 2,322 | 1,617 | 1,791 | 1,360 |
| Effective Tax Rate | 11.9% | 15.4% | 26.6% | 32.5% | 38.2% | 33.0% | 32.9% | 34.1% | 27.8% | 28.4% |
| Net Income | 816 | 853 | 1,519 | 1,734 | 1,528 | 1,654 | 1,558 | 1,065 | 1,293 | 974 |
| % Net Interest Margin | 4.03 | 3.66 | 3.63 | 3.52 | 3.74 | 3.89 | 4.04 | 4.06 | 4.25 | 4.17 |
| S&P Core Earnings | 776 | 728 | 1,406 | 1,707 | 1,514 | 1,608 | 1,529 | 1,012 | 1,241 | 927 |

| Balance Sheet & Other Financial Data (Million $) | | | | | | | | | | |
|---|---|---|---|---|---|---|---|---|---|---|
| Money Market Assets | 1,259 | 1,065 | 1,101 | 1,067 | 688 | 697 | 1,244 | 604 | 591 | 458 |
| Investment Securities | 23,802 | 34,545 | 33,219 | 23,428 | 22,868 | 20,489 | 19,173 | 16,317 | 17,655 | 16,662 |
| Commercial Loans | 48,886 | 49,820 | 50,480 | 44,870 | 41,300 | 37,655 | 34,321 | 12,429 | 7,061 | 6,551 |
| Other Loans | 585,378 | 56,387 | 48,189 | 46,037 | 41,611 | 36,739 | 33,228 | 49,151 | 44,079 | 38,985 |
| Total Assets | 157,081 | 165,764 | 152,015 | 132,618 | 121,351 | 109,170 | 100,509 | 90,467 | 80,217 | 70,870 |
| Demand Deposits | 24,687 | 22,365 | 16,225 | 14,260 | 14,726 | 13,477 | 12,246 | 11,098 | 7,864 | 6,940 |
| Time Deposits | 82,526 | 92,600 | 82,388 | 72,506 | 66,245 | 60,805 | 55,453 | 48,252 | 43,416 | 37,794 |
| Long Term Debt | 21,730 | 21,376 | 18,032 | 18,693 | 12,604 | 13,119 | 11,420 | 10,808 | 13,588 | 11,721 |
| Common Equity | 16,436 | 16,191 | 16,037 | 448 | 11,745 | 11,129 | 10,874 | 9,935 | 7,388 | 6,150 |
| % Return on Assets | 0.5 | 0.5 | 1.1 | 1.3 | 1.3 | 1.6 | 1.6 | 1.2 | 1.7 | 1.4 |
| % Return on Equity | 5.0 | 5.9 | 10.6 | 14.0 | 13.4 | 15.0 | 15.0 | 12.3 | 19.1 | 16.8 |
| % Loan Loss Reserve | 2.6 | 2.5 | 1.6 | 1.1 | 1.1 | 1.1 | 1.2 | 1.3 | 1.4 | 1.4 |
| % Loans/Deposits | 96.6 | 90.2 | 98.6 | 103.6 | 103.2 | 99.0 | 100.7 | 105.0 | 104.4 | 106.1 |
| % Equity to Assets | 10.1 | 10.1 | 9.0 | 9.6 | 9.9 | 10.5 | 10.9 | 10.1 | 9.0 | 8.4 |

Data as orig reptd.; bef. results of disc opers/spec. items. Per share data adj. for stk. divs.; EPS diluted. E-Estimated. NA-Not Available. NM-Not Meaningful. NR-Not Ranked. UR-Under Review.

**Office:** 200 West Second Street, Winston-Salem, NC 27101.
**Telephone:** 336-733-2000.
**Website:** http://www.bbandt.com
**Chrmn, Pres & CEO:** K.S. King

**COO & EVP:** C.L. Henson
**EVP & CFO:** D.N. Bible
**EVP, Chief Acctg Officer & Cntlr:** C.B. Powell
**Treas:** J. Nichols

**Investor Contact:** T. Gjesdal (336-733-3058)
**Board Members:** J. A. Allison, IV, J. S. Banner, K. D. Boyer, Jr., A. R. Cablik, R. E. Deal, J. L. Glover, Jr., J. P. Helm, J. P. Howe, III, K. S. King, V. L. Lee, J. H. Morrison, N. R. Qubein, T. E. Skains, T. N. Thompson, E. H. Welch, S. T. Williams

**Founded:** 1968
**Domicile:** North Carolina
**Employees:** 31,400

The McGraw-Hill Companies

# Beam Inc

**STANDARD &POOR'S**

| S&P Recommendation HOLD ★★★☆☆ | Price $48.53 (as of Nov 25, 2011) | 12-Mo. Target Price $52.00 | Investment Style Large-Cap Blend |
|---|---|---|---|

**GICS Sector** Consumer Staples
**Sub-Industry** Distillers & Vintners

**Summary** This distilled spirits company is the successor to Fortune Brands, which divested its home improvement and golf-related businesses in October 2011.

## Key Stock Statistics (Source S&P, Vickers, company reports)

| | | | | | | | |
|---|---|---|---|---|---|---|---|
| 52-Wk Range | $65.48– 42.30 | S&P Oper. EPS 2011**E** | 2.13 | Market Capitalization(B) | $7.544 | Beta | 1.41 |
| Trailing 12-Month EPS | $5.79 | S&P Oper. EPS 2012**E** | 2.36 | Yield (%) | 1.57 | S&P 3-Yr. Proj. EPS CAGR(%) | 8 |
| Trailing 12-Month P/E | 8.4 | P/E on S&P Oper. EPS 2011**E** | 22.8 | Dividend Rate/Share | $0.76 | S&P Credit Rating | BBB- |
| $10K Invested 5 Yrs Ago | NA | Common Shares Outstg. (M) | 155.5 | Institutional Ownership (%) | 79 | | |

## Price Performance

30-Week Mov. Avg. · · · 10-Week Mov. Avg. - - GAAP Earnings vs. Previous Year  Volume Above Avg. STARS
12-Mo. Target Price — Relative Strength — ▲ Up ▼ Down ▶ No Change  Below Avg. ★

Options: ASE, CBOE, P, Ph

Analysis prepared by Equity Analyst **Esther Kwon, CFA** on Nov 09, 2011, when the stock traded at **$49.27**.

### Highlights

➤ For 2011, we forecast a pro forma sales increase of about 9%, with good growth in core "Power Brands," such as Jim Beam and Maker's Mark bourbon and Sauza tequila and strength in high growth, high margin "Rising Stars," such as Knob Creek bourbon, Effen vodka and Laphroaig scotch. We expect sales to be boosted by the acquisition of Skinnygirl Cocktails, with minimal lift from higher pricing. For 2012, we project approximately 5% sales growth.

➤ We look for contraction in the operating margin in 2011, reflecting higher commodity costs and continued investment spending in brand building activities and new product launches, although we see investment spending moderating in the second half. Longer term, we expect BEAM to sustain strong brand investment levels at a mid-teens percentage of sales. In 2012, we forecast an improvement in operating margin on economies of scale and cost cuts.

➤ On lower interest expense, our 2011 pro forma EPS estimate is $2.13, compared to EPS of $1.92 in 2010. For 2012, we forecast EPS of $2.36 on a similar tax rate of 26.5%.

### Investment Rationale/Risk

➤ Our hold opinion reflects our view that BEAM's stock price adequately reflects the near-term outlook for the company. In an effort to maximize shareholder value, predecessor Fortune Brands sold its golf business and spun off the Home & Security business in a tax-free transaction to shareholders in 2011. The net proceeds of $1.1 billion from the golf business sale and a $500 million tax-free dividend from the Home & Security spin-off were used to pay down debt. All told, we think the long-term prospects remain bright for the company's strong portfolio of spirits brands, which have growing emerging markets exposure, but we see BEAM's valuation as appropriate.

➤ Risks to our recommendation and target price include a delayed recovery in consumer spending in the U.S. and other major markets, and weak consumer acceptance of new products.

➤ Our 12-month target price of $52 is based on a slight premium to the historical group average of approximately 21X on our 2012 EPS estimate of $2.36. We think potential interest from other large multi-national spirits companies for parts of its brand portfolio could provide support to the shares.

### Qualitative Risk Assessment

| LOW | MEDIUM | HIGH |
|---|---|---|

Demand for BEAM's spirits products tends to be stable and not very sensitive to economic weakness. However, BEAM has only recently been organized as a pure spirits company after other businesses were divested in 2011.

### Quantitative Evaluations

**S&P Quality Ranking** B+

| D | C | B- | B | B+ | A- | A | A+ |
|---|---|---|---|---|---|---|---|

**Relative Strength Rank** MODERATE

49

LOWEST = 1     HIGHEST = 99

### Revenue/Earnings Data

**Revenue (Million $)**

| | 1Q | 2Q | 3Q | 4Q | Year |
|---|---|---|---|---|---|
| 2011 | 1,757 | 1,592 | 1,427 | -- | -- |
| 2010 | 1,499 | 1,771 | 1,594 | 1,707 | 7,142 |
| 2009 | 1,338 | 1,617 | 1,593 | 1,658 | 6,205 |
| 2008 | 1,711 | 1,967 | 1,922 | 1,628 | 7,105 |
| 2007 | 1,909 | 2,293 | 2,145 | 2,215 | 8,563 |
| 2006 | 2,017 | 2,257 | 2,219 | 2,277 | 8,769 |

**Earnings Per Share ($)**

| | 1Q | 2Q | 3Q | 4Q | Year |
|---|---|---|---|---|---|
| 2011 | 0.52 | 0.65 | -0.41 | E0.69 | E2.13 |
| 2010 | 0.47 | 1.48 | 0.67 | 0.55 | 3.16 |
| 2009 | 0.05 | 0.66 | 0.82 | 0.08 | 1.60 |
| 2008 | 0.69 | 0.17 | 2.01 | -1.83 | 1.07 |
| 2007 | 0.78 | 1.47 | 1.33 | 1.22 | 4.79 |
| 2006 | 1.15 | 1.63 | 0.98 | 1.65 | 5.42 |

Fiscal year ended Dec. 31. Next earnings report expected: Early February. EPS Estimates based on S&P Operating Earnings; historical GAAP earnings are as reported.

### Dividend Data (Dates: mm/dd Payment Date: mm/dd/yy)

| Amount ($) | Date Decl. | Ex-Div. Date | Stk. of Record | Payment Date |
|---|---|---|---|---|
| 0.190 | 01/25 | 02/07 | 02/09 | 03/01/11 |
| 0.190 | 04/26 | 05/09 | 05/11 | 06/01/11 |
| 0.190 | 07/26 | 08/08 | 08/10 | 09/01/11 |
| Stk. | 08/25 | 10/04 | 09/20 | 10/03/11 |

Dividends have been paid since 1905. Source: Company reports.

---

**Please read the Required Disclosures and Analyst Certification on the last page of this report.**

**The McGraw·Hill Companies**

# Beam Inc

STANDARD
&POOR'S

## Business Summary November 09, 2011

CORPORATE OVERVIEW. Beam is the world's fourth largest premium spirits company, and the second largest in the United States. It sold 33 million 9-liter cases in 2010.

Leading brands include Jim Beam bourbon whiskey, DeKuyper cordials, Gilbey's gin, Kamchatka vodka, and Maker's Mark bourbon. Principal markets are the U.S., the U.K., Spain, Germany and Australia, with markets outside North America accounting for about 45% of total sales. Approximately 25% of sales are derived from Europe, the Middle East and Africa, and 20% from Asia Pacific/Latin America.

In July 2005, the company acquired various spirits and wine brands from Pernod Ricard, which had in turn been acquired by Pernod from Allied Domecq PLC. This transaction more than doubled the sales of the company's Spirits & Wine segment. In 2007, the U.S. wine businesses were sold; we be-

lieve they had annualized sales of about $225 million. In August 2008, Pernod Ricard, which purchased the Absolut Vodka brand earlier in 2008, agreed to pay BEAM $230 million for early termination of BEAM's distribution agreement for Absolut and other brands. Also, Pernod Ricard agreed to sell the Cruzan Rum brand, already distributed by BEAM, to BEAM for $103 million.

IMPACT OF MAJOR DEVELOPMENTS. On December 8, 2010, Fortune Brands (FO), BEAM's predecessor company, announced its intent to separate its three businesses. As a result, FO became a pure-play spirits company, spun off the Home & Security business to shareholders, sold the Golf business, and changed its name to Beam Inc.

## Company Financials Fiscal Year Ended Dec. 31

| Per Share Data ($) | 2010 | 2009 | 2008 | 2007 | 2006 | 2005 | 2004 | 2003 | 2002 | 2001 |
|---|---|---|---|---|---|---|---|---|---|---|
| Tangible Book Value | NM | NM | NM | NM | NM | NM | NM | NM | NM | 2.06 |
| Cash Flow | 4.80 | 3.27 | 2.74 | 6.58 | 7.37 | 5.35 | 6.70 | 5.14 | 4.57 | 3.89 |
| Earnings | 3.16 | 1.60 | 1.07 | 4.79 | 5.42 | 3.87 | 5.23 | 3.86 | 3.41 | 2.49 |
| S&P Core Earnings | 3.20 | 1.68 | 1.66 | 4.62 | 5.47 | 3.73 | 4.58 | 3.79 | 3.14 | 2.38 |
| Dividends | 0.76 | 1.01 | 1.72 | 1.62 | 1.50 | 1.38 | 1.26 | 1.14 | 1.02 | 0.97 |
| Payout Ratio | 24% | 63% | 161% | 34% | 28% | 36% | 24% | 30% | 30% | 39% |
| Prices:High | 63.51 | 46.77 | 74.44 | 90.80 | 85.96 | 96.18 | 80.50 | 71.80 | 57.86 | 40.54 |
| Prices:Low | 37.05 | 17.67 | 30.24 | 72.13 | 68.45 | 73.50 | 66.10 | 40.60 | 36.85 | 28.38 |
| P/E Ratio:High | 20 | 29 | 70 | 19 | 16 | 25 | 15 | 19 | 17 | 16 |
| P/E Ratio:Low | 12 | 11 | 28 | 15 | 13 | 19 | 13 | 11 | 11 | 11 |

| Income Statement Analysis (Million $) | | | | | | | | | | |
|---|---|---|---|---|---|---|---|---|---|---|
| Revenue | 6,571 | 6,205 | 7,105 | 8,563 | 8,769 | 7,061 | 7,321 | 6,215 | 5,678 | 5,679 |
| Operating Income | 1,054 | 974 | 1,313 | 1,712 | 1,777 | 1,715 | 1,374 | 1,142 | 1,011 | 870 |
| Depreciation | 245 | 255 | 263 | 280 | 298 | 224 | 221 | 193 | 179 | 219 |
| Interest Expense | 214 | 216 | 237 | 294 | 332 | 159 | 87.9 | 73.8 | 74.1 | 96.8 |
| Pretax Income | 588 | 283 | 188 | 1,120 | 1,209 | 926 | 1,086 | 884 | 756 | 492 |
| Effective Tax Rate | NA | 12.8% | 47.6% | 30.9% | 25.7% | 35.0% | 26.1% | 32.7% | 28.3% | 19.2% |
| Net Income | 496 | 243 | 165 | 750 | 830 | 582 | 784 | 579 | 526 | 386 |
| S&P Core Earnings | 493 | 255 | 255 | 722 | 837 | 559 | 684 | 567 | 484 | 367 |

| Balance Sheet & Other Financial Data (Million $) | | | | | | | | | | |
|---|---|---|---|---|---|---|---|---|---|---|
| Cash | 865 | 417 | 163 | 204 | 183 | 93.6 | 165 | 105 | 15.4 | 48.7 |
| Current Assets | 4,343 | 3,872 | 3,468 | 3,781 | 3,930 | 3,193 | 2,642 | 2,282 | 1,903 | 1,970 |
| Total Assets | 12,675 | 12,371 | 12,092 | 13,957 | 14,668 | 13,202 | 7,884 | 7,445 | 5,822 | 5,301 |
| Current Liabilities | 2,107 | 1,464 | 1,190 | 2,094 | 2,515 | 2,818 | 2,036 | 2,134 | 1,515 | 1,258 |
| Long Term Debt | 3,637 | 4,413 | 4,689 | 4,374 | 5,035 | 4,890 | 1,240 | 1,243 | 200 | 950 |
| Common Equity | 5,671 | 5,092 | 4,692 | 5,680 | 4,722 | 3,639 | 3,203 | 2,712 | 2,305 | 2,094 |
| Total Capital | 9,933 | 9,519 | 9,393 | 11,138 | 11,458 | 9,788 | 5,207 | 4,664 | 2,983 | 3,444 |
| Capital Expenditures | 223 | 158 | 176 | 267 | 266 | 222 | 242 | 194 | 194 | 207 |
| Cash Flow | 741 | 497 | 421 | 1,029 | 1,128 | 805 | 1,005 | 772 | 704 | 605 |
| Current Ratio | 2.1 | 2.7 | 2.9 | 1.8 | 1.6 | 1.1 | 1.3 | 1.1 | 1.3 | 1.6 |
| % Long Term Debt of Capitalization | 36.6 | 46.4 | 49.9 | 38.7 | 43.9 | 50.0 | 23.8 | 26.6 | 6.7 | 27.6 |
| % Net Income of Revenue | 7.6 | 3.9 | 2.3 | 8.7 | 9.5 | 8.2 | 10.7 | 9.3 | 9.3 | 6.8 |
| % Return on Assets | 4.0 | 2.0 | 1.3 | 5.2 | 6.0 | 5.5 | 10.2 | 8.7 | 9.5 | 7.0 |
| % Return on Equity | 9.2 | 5.0 | 3.2 | 14.4 | 19.9 | 17.2 | 26.5 | 23.1 | 23.9 | 18.3 |

Data as orig reptd.; bef. results of disc opers/spec. items. Per share data adj. for stk. divs.; EPS diluted. E-Estimated. NA-Not Available. NM-Not Meaningful. NR-Not Ranked. UR-Under Review.

**Office:** 510 Lake Cook Road, Deerfield, IL 60015.
**Telephone:** 847-948-8888.
**Email:** investorrelations@fortunebrands.com
**Website:** http://www.beamglobal.com

**Chrmn:** A.D. MacKay
**Pres & CEO:** M.J. Shattock
**SVP & CFO:** R. Probst
**SVP, Chief Admin Officer & Secy:** K.R. Rose

**SVP, Chief Acctg Officer & Cntlr:** E.A. Wiertel
**Board Members:** R. A. Goldstein, A. F. Hackett, P. E. Leroy, A. D. MacKay, M. J. Shattock, A. M. Tatlock, P. M. Wilson

**Founded:** 1904
**Domicile:** Delaware
**Employees:** 24,600

The **McGraw·Hill** Companies

# Becton, Dickinson and Co

**STANDARD &POOR'S**

| S&P Recommendation HOLD ★★★☆☆ | Price | 12-Mo. Target Price | Investment Style |
|---|---|---|---|
| | $71.11 (as of Nov 25, 2011) | $78.00 | Large-Cap Growth |

**GICS Sector** Health Care
**Sub-Industry** Health Care Equipment

**Summary** This company provides a wide range of medical devices and diagnostic products used in hospitals, doctors' offices, research labs and other settings.

## Key Stock Statistics (Source S&P, Vickers, company reports)

| | | | | | | | |
|---|---|---|---|---|---|---|---|
| 52-Wk Range | $89.75– 69.59 | S&P Oper. EPS 2012**E** | 5.82 | Market Capitalization(B) | $15.463 | Beta | 0.59 |
| Trailing 12-Month EPS | $5.62 | S&P Oper. EPS 2013**E** | 6.46 | Yield (%) | 2.53 | S&P 3-Yr. Proj. EPS CAGR(%) | 10 |
| Trailing 12-Month P/E | 12.7 | P/E on S&P Oper. EPS 2012**E** | 12.2 | Dividend Rate/Share | $1.80 | S&P Credit Rating | A+ |
| $10K Invested 5 Yrs Ago | $10,918 | Common Shares Outstg. (M) | 217.4 | Institutional Ownership (%) | 82 | | |

## Price Performance

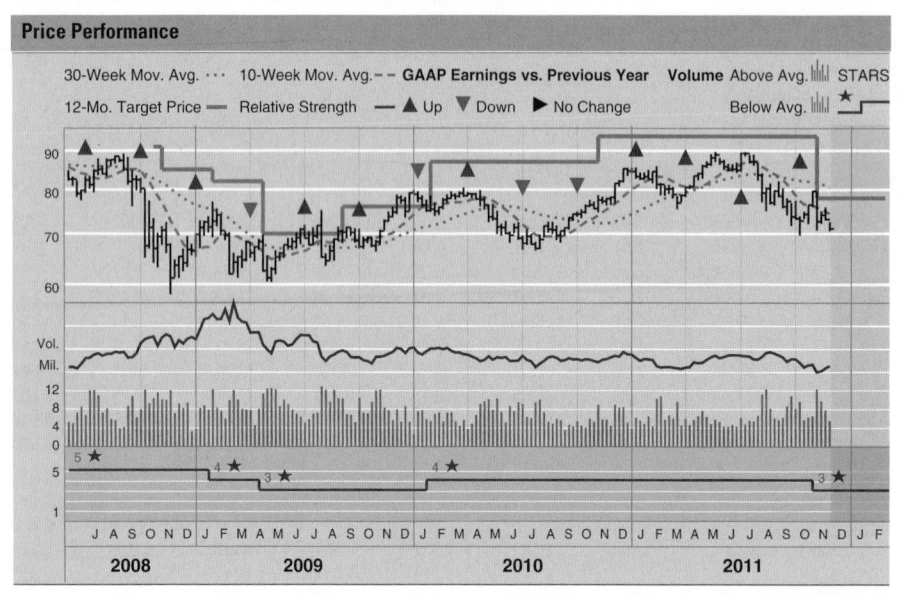

30-Week Mov. Avg. · · · ·   10-Week Mov. Avg. – –   GAAP Earnings vs. Previous Year   Volume Above Avg. STARS
12-Mo. Target Price —   Relative Strength   ▲ Up   ▼ Down   ► No Change   Below Avg.

Analysis prepared by Equity Analyst **Jeffrey Loo, CFA** on Nov 18, 2011, when the stock traded at **$73.15**.

Options: CBOE, P, Ph

## Qualitative Risk Assessment

| LOW | MEDIUM | HIGH |
|---|---|---|

BDX's markets are competitive, and new product introductions by current and future competitors have the potential to significantly affect market dynamics. In addition, changes in domestic and foreign health care industry practices and regulations may result in increased pricing pressures and lower reimbursements for some of its products. However, we believe BDX's product line has more favorable demand and pricing characteristics than those in the medical equipment industry in general.

## Quantitative Evaluations

**S&P Quality Ranking**     A

| D | C | B- | B | B+ | A- | A | A+ |
|---|---|---|---|---|---|---|---|

**Relative Strength Rank**     MODERATE

50

LOWEST = 1     HIGHEST = 99

## Highlights

▶ We expect sales to rise 3% in FY 11 (Sep.), to $8.08 billion, as macroeconomic challenges, lower health care utilization in the U.S. and Europe, and downward pricing pressure adversely impact sales. We see the medical segment growing 2.9% on global demand for diabetes care products, diagnostics revenues rising 3.4% on infectious disease testing products, and biosciences revenues advancing 3.8% on solid cell analysis sales. We forecast that gross margins will decline 70 basis points (bps) on higher raw material prices, and operating margins will narrow 80 bps on higher SG&A costs, primarily related to the acquisitions of Carmel Pharma AB, and higher R&D spending for new product platforms, along with geographic expansion, particularly in emerging markets, which accounted for $1.55 billion (20%) of revenues in FY 10.

▶ Effective October 1, 2011, COO Vincent Forlenza succeeded Edward Ludwig as CEO as part of BDX's succession plan.

▶ BDX indicated it plans to repurchase $1.5 billion in shares in FY 12 through the use of free cash flow and the issuance of debt. Our FY 12 EPS estimate is $5.82.

## Investment Rationale/Risk

▶ We recently downgraded our recommendation on the shares to hold, from buy, as we see macroeconomic challenges limiting sales growth. We believe the shares, recently trading at about 13X FY 12 EPS, below historical levels, are fairly valued as we do not see sufficient near-term catalysts. However, we are encouraged by strong global demand for BDX's safety, diabetes care and disease-testing products, which we view as sustainable for the long term. BDX's international sales account for 56% of sales, and we expect this percentage to rise on continued emerging markets growth. Meanwhile, we view positively recent growth in the biosciences segment, driven by increased demand for cell analysis products in the U.S.

▶ Risks to our opinion and target price include a slower-than-expected recovery in key life science markets, continued cutbacks in spending by the company's hospital customers, and prolonged softness in physician office visits.

▶ Our 12-month target price of $78 is derived by applying a multiple of 13.5X to our FY 12 EPS estimate, slightly below historical levels, as we see limited near-term catalysts.

## Revenue/Earnings Data

**Revenue (Million $)**

| | 1Q | 2Q | 3Q | 4Q | Year |
|---|---|---|---|---|---|
| 2011 | 1,842 | 1,922 | 2,014 | 2,051 | 7,829 |
| 2010 | 1,869 | 1,799 | 1,831 | 1,873 | 7,372 |
| 2009 | 1,734 | 1,741 | 1,820 | 1,898 | 7,161 |
| 2008 | 1,706 | 1,747 | 1,868 | 1,836 | 7,156 |
| 2007 | 1,502 | 1,576 | 1,631 | 1,651 | 6,360 |
| 2006 | 1,414 | 1,449 | 1,484 | 1,488 | 5,835 |

**Earnings Per Share ($)**

| | | | | | |
|---|---|---|---|---|---|
| 2011 | 1.35 | 1.38 | 1.51 | 1.36 | 5.59 |
| 2010 | 1.25 | 1.18 | 1.23 | 1.24 | 4.90 |
| 2009 | 1.26 | 1.06 | 1.38 | 1.25 | 4.92 |
| 2008 | 1.07 | 1.09 | 1.18 | 1.13 | 4.46 |
| 2007 | 0.51 | 0.92 | 0.95 | 0.98 | 3.36 |
| 2006 | 0.85 | 0.61 | 0.81 | 0.69 | 2.95 |

Fiscal year ended Sep. 30. Next earnings report expected: Early February. EPS Estimates based on S&P Operating Earnings; historical GAAP earnings are as reported.

## Dividend Data (Dates: mm/dd Payment Date: mm/dd/yy)

| Amount ($) | Date Decl. | Ex-Div. Date | Stk. of Record | Payment Date |
|---|---|---|---|---|
| 0.410 | 02/01 | 03/08 | 03/10 | 03/31/11 |
| 0.410 | 05/24 | 06/07 | 06/09 | 06/30/11 |
| 0.410 | 07/26 | 09/07 | 09/09 | 09/30/11 |
| 0.450 | 11/22 | 12/08 | 12/12 | 12/30/11 |

Dividends have been paid since 1926. Source: Company reports.

---

**Please read the Required Disclosures and Analyst Certification on the last page of this report.**

*The McGraw·Hill Companies*

# Becton, Dickinson and Co

STANDARD
&POOR'S

## Business Summary November 18, 2011

Becton, Dickinson traces its roots to a concern started by Maxwell Becton and Fairleigh Dickinson in 1897. One of the first companies to sell U.S.-made glass syringes, BDX was also a pioneer in the production of hypodermic needles. The company now manufactures and sells medical supplies, devices, lab equipment and diagnostic products used by health care institutions, life science researchers, clinical laboratories, industry and the general public. In FY 11 (Sep.) 57.1%, (55.4% in FY 10) of the company's sales were generated from non-U.S. markets.

Major products in the core medical systems division (51% of FY 11 revenues) include hypodermic syringes and needles for injection, insulin syringes and pen needles for diabetes care, infusion therapy devices, prefillable drug delivery systems, and surgical blades and scalpels. The segment also markets specialty blades and cannulas for ophthalmic surgery procedures, anesthesia needles, critical care systems, elastic support products, and thermometers.

The diagnostics segment (32%) provides a range of products designed for the safe collection and transport of diagnostic specimens and instrumentation for analysis across a wide range of infectious disease testing, including health care-associated infections (HAIs). Its principal products and services include integrated systems for specimen collection; an extensive line of safety-

engineered blood collection products and systems; plated media; automated blood culturing systems; molecular testing systems for sexually transmitted diseases and HAIs; microorganism identification and drug susceptibility systems; liquid-based cytology systems for cervical cancer screening; and rapid diagnostic assays. The segment also includes consulting services and customized, automated bar-code systems for patient identification and point-of-care data capture.

The biosciences unit (17%) provides research tools and reagents to clinicians and medical researchers studying genes, proteins and cells in order to better understand disease, improve diagnosis and disease management, and facilitate the discovery and development of novel therapeutics. Products include instrument systems for cell sorting and analysis, monoclonal antibody reagents and kits for diagnostic and research use, tools to aid in drug discovery and vaccine development, molecular biology products, fluid handling, cell growth and screening products.

## Company Financials Fiscal Year Ended Sep. 30

| Per Share Data ($) | 2011 | 2010 | 2009 | 2008 | 2007 | 2006 | 2005 | 2004 | 2003 | 2002 |
|---|---|---|---|---|---|---|---|---|---|---|
| Tangible Book Value | NA | 17.49 | 16.52 | 15.38 | 13.41 | 11.96 | 10.28 | 9.28 | 8.82 | 6.06 |
| Cash Flow | NA | 6.99 | 6.39 | 5.89 | 5.09 | 4.52 | 4.36 | 3.57 | 3.54 | 2.92 |
| Earnings | 5.59 | 4.90 | 4.92 | 4.46 | 3.36 | 2.95 | 2.66 | 2.21 | 2.07 | 1.79 |
| S&P Core Earnings | 5.47 | 5.00 | 4.93 | 4.22 | 3.38 | 2.99 | 2.75 | 2.39 | 2.01 | 1.57 |
| Dividends | 1.64 | 1.48 | 1.32 | 1.14 | 0.98 | 0.86 | 0.72 | 0.60 | 0.40 | 0.39 |
| Payout Ratio | 29% | 30% | 27% | 26% | 29% | 29% | 27% | 27% | 19% | 22% |
| Prices:High | 89.75 | 85.50 | 79.97 | 93.24 | 85.89 | 74.25 | 61.17 | 58.18 | 41.82 | 38.60 |
| Prices:Low | 69.59 | 66.47 | 60.40 | 58.14 | 69.30 | 58.08 | 49.71 | 40.90 | 28.82 | 24.70 |
| P/E Ratio:High | 16 | 17 | 16 | 21 | 26 | 25 | 23 | 26 | 20 | 22 |
| P/E Ratio:Low | 12 | 14 | 12 | 13 | 21 | 20 | 19 | 19 | 14 | 14 |

| Income Statement Analysis (Million $) | 2011 | 2010 | 2009 | 2008 | 2007 | 2006 | 2005 | 2004 | 2003 | 2002 |
|---|---|---|---|---|---|---|---|---|---|---|
| Revenue | 7,829 | 7,372 | 7,161 | 7,156 | 6,360 | 5,835 | 5,415 | 4,935 | 4,528 | 4,033 |
| Operating Income | 2,260 | 2,187 | 2,060 | 1,912 | 1,644 | 1,456 | 1,419 | 1,244 | 1,094 | 1,002 |
| Depreciation | NA | 502 | 365 | 360 | 441 | 405 | 387 | 357 | 344 | 305 |
| Interest Expense | 84.0 | 51.3 | 69.8 | 66.2 | 46.0 | 66.0 | 55.7 | 29.6 | 73.1 | 33.3 |
| Pretax Income | 1,716 | 1,661 | 1,639 | 1,554 | 1,204 | 1,035 | 1,005 | 753 | 710 | 629 |
| Effective Tax Rate | NA | NA | 26.0% | 27.4% | 28.8% | 27.0% | 31.1% | 22.6% | 22.9% | 23.6% |
| Net Income | 1,265 | 1,176 | 1,213 | 1,128 | 856 | 756 | 692 | 583 | 547 | 480 |
| S&P Core Earnings | 1,238 | 1,199 | 1,216 | 1,068 | 863 | 766 | 714 | 628 | 523 | 417 |

| Balance Sheet & Other Financial Data (Million $) | 2011 | 2010 | 2009 | 2008 | 2007 | 2006 | 2005 | 2004 | 2003 | 2002 |
|---|---|---|---|---|---|---|---|---|---|---|
| Cash | NA | 1,753 | 1,946 | 1,030 | 511 | 1,000 | 1,043 | 719 | 520 | 243 |
| Current Assets | NA | 4,505 | 4,647 | 3,615 | 3,131 | 3,185 | 2,975 | 2,641 | 2,339 | 1,929 |
| Total Assets | NA | 9,651 | 9,305 | 7,913 | 7,329 | 6,825 | 6,072 | 5,753 | 5,572 | 5,040 |
| Current Liabilities | NA | 1,672 | 1,777 | 1,417 | 1,479 | 1,576 | 1,299 | 1,050 | 1,043 | 1,252 |
| Long Term Debt | NA | 1,495 | 1,488 | 953 | 956 | 957 | 1,061 | 1,172 | 1,184 | 803 |
| Common Equity | NA | 5,435 | 5,143 | 4,936 | 4,362 | 3,836 | 3,284 | 3,037 | 2,863 | 2,450 |
| Total Capital | NA | 6,930 | 6,831 | 5,924 | 5,318 | 4,793 | 4,345 | 4,328 | 4,200 | 3,396 |
| Capital Expenditures | NA | 537 | 591 | 602 | 556 | 459 | 318 | 266 | 261 | 260 |
| Cash Flow | NA | 1,678 | 1,578 | 1,488 | 1,297 | 1,161 | 1,080 | 940 | 889 | 783 |
| Current Ratio | NA | 2.7 | 2.6 | 2.6 | 2.1 | 2.0 | 2.3 | 2.5 | 2.2 | 1.5 |
| % Long Term Debt of Capitalization | NA | 21.6 | 21.8 | 16.1 | 17.9 | 20.0 | 24.4 | 27.1 | 28.2 | 23.6 |
| % Net Income of Revenue | 16.2 | 16.0 | 16.9 | 15.8 | 13.4 | 12.9 | 12.8 | 11.8 | 12.1 | 11.9 |
| % Return on Assets | NA | NA | 14.1 | 14.1 | 12.0 | 11.7 | 11.7 | 10.3 | 10.3 | 9.8 |
| % Return on Equity | NA | NA | 24.1 | 24.3 | 20.8 | 21.2 | 21.9 | 19.7 | 20.5 | 20.2 |

Data as orig reptd.; bef. results of disc opers/spec. items. Per share data adj. for stk. divs.; EPS diluted. E-Estimated. NA-Not Available. NM-Not Meaningful. NR-Not Ranked. UR-Under Review.

**Office:** One Becton Drive, Franklin Lakes, NJ 07417-1880.
**Telephone:** 201-847-6800.
**Email:** investor_relations@bdhq.bd.com
**Website:** http://www.bd.com

**Chrmn:** E.J. Ludwig
**Pres & CEO:** V.A. Forlenza
**EVP & CFO:** D.V. Elkins
**SVP & CTO:** S.P. Bruder

**SVP & General Counsel:** J.S. Sherman
**Investor Contact:** P.A. Spinella (201-847-5453)
**Board Members:** B. L. Anderson, H. P. Becton, Jr., E. F. DeGraan, V. A. Forlenza, C. M. Fraser-Liggett, C. I. Jones, M. O. Larsen, E. J. Ludwig, A. A. Mahmoud, G. A. Mecklenburg, C. E. Minehan, J. F. Orr, W. J. Overlock, Jr., B. L. Scott, A. Sommer

**Founded:** 1897
**Domicile:** New Jersey
**Employees:** 28,803

# Bed Bath & Beyond Inc

**STANDARD &POOR'S**

| **S&P Recommendation** BUY ★★★★☆ | **Price** $57.90 (as of Nov 25, 2011) | **12-Mo. Target Price** $72.00 | **Investment Style** Large-Cap Growth |
|---|---|---|---|

**GICS Sector** Consumer Discretionary
**Sub-Industry** Homefurnishing Retail

**Summary** This company operates a nationwide chain of more than 900 Bed Bath & Beyond superstores selling better-quality domestics merchandise and home furnishings. It also has retail stores under the names Christmas Tree Shops, Harmon and buybuy BABY.

## Key Stock Statistics (Source S&P, Vickers, company reports)

| | | | | | | | |
|---|---|---|---|---|---|---|---|
| 52-Wk Range | $63.83– 43.12 | S&P Oper. EPS 2012**E** | 3.84 | Market Capitalization(B) | $14.165 | Beta | 1.14 |
| Trailing 12-Month EPS | $3.51 | S&P Oper. EPS 2013**E** | 4.38 | Yield (%) | Nil | S&P 3-Yr. Proj. EPS CAGR(%) | 15 |
| Trailing 12-Month P/E | 16.5 | P/E on S&P Oper. EPS 2012**E** | 15.1 | Dividend Rate/Share | Nil | S&P Credit Rating | BBB+ |
| $10K Invested 5 Yrs Ago | $14,752 | Common Shares Outstg. (M) | 244.6 | Institutional Ownership (%) | 89 | | |

## Price Performance

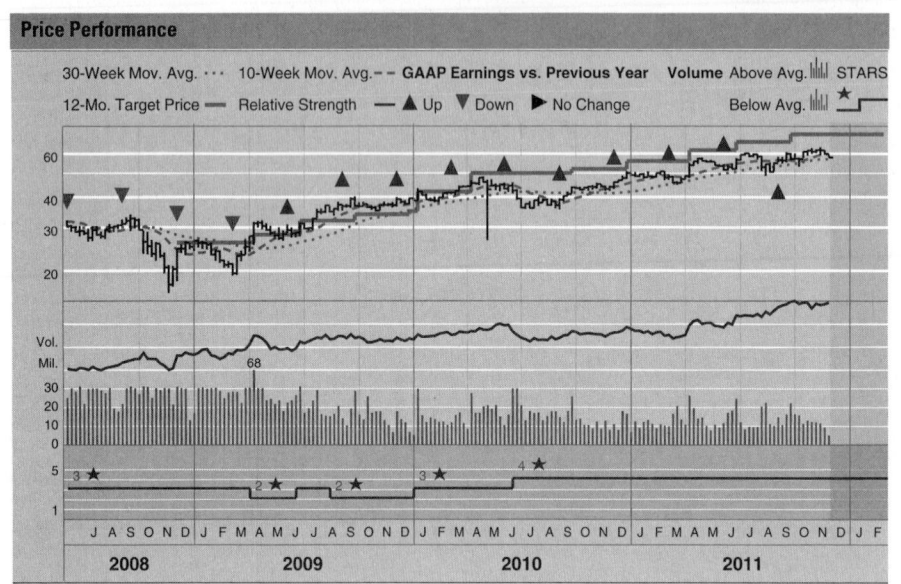

30-Week Mov. Avg. ··· 10-Week Mov. Avg. – – GAAP Earnings vs. Previous Year Volume Above Avg. STARS
12-Mo. Target Price — Relative Strength ▲ Up ▼ Down ▶ No Change Below Avg.

Options: ASE, CBOE, Ph

Analysis prepared by Equity Analyst **Michael Souers** on Sep 23, 2011, when the stock traded at **$56.91**.

## Highlights

➤ We expect sales to rise 7.5% in FY 12 (Feb.), following a 12% advance in FY 11. This reflects the projected addition of about 10-15 new Bed Bath & Beyond stores and a 4%-5% same-store sales increase. We also anticipate the opening of approximately 15 new Christmas Tree Shops and about 15-20 new buybuy BABY stores. We see same-store sales reflecting slight increases in both foot traffic and average ticket.

➤ We look for gross margins to widen slightly in FY 12, driven by a decrease in coupon redemptions and improved inventory management, partially offset by a negative product mix shift. We forecast a 140 basis point increase in operating margins, driven by gross margin improvement and continued cost-cutting efforts in payroll and advertising. In addition, we think BBBY will leverage fixed expenses on a solid expected comp-store sales increase.

➤ After a modest decline in interest income, an anticipated effective tax rate of 38.0%, and a 5% reduction in diluted shares driven by share repurchases, we estimate FY 12 EPS of $3.84, a 25% increase from the $3.07 the company earned in FY 11. We see FY 13 EPS of $4.38.

## Investment Rationale/Risk

➤ We think BBBY shares are attractively priced, trading at about 13X our FY 13 EPS estimate, a modest discount to historical averages. In addition, the company's balance sheet includes over $7 of net cash per share. We expect continued market share gains for BBBY, with better merchandising and execution than peers. Despite continued expected economic malaise, we think sales of soft goods will remain relatively strong as consumers look for ways to spruce up their homes in a low-cost manner. BBBY is about 75% of the way to reaching its long-term goal of 1,300 stores, so we expect square footage growth to slow over the medium term.

➤ Risks to our recommendation and target price include an unexpected decline in consumer spending, an unanticipated shift in spending away from home-centric products, and miscues in BBBY's store expansion strategy.

➤ Our 12-month target price of $72, or about 16X our FY 13 EPS estimate, is based on our discounted cash flow analysis, which assumes a weighted average cost of capital of 10.3% and a terminal growth rate of 3.5%.

## Qualitative Risk Assessment

| LOW | MEDIUM | HIGH |
|---|---|---|

Our risk assessment reflects the cyclical nature of the home furnishings retail industry, which relies heavily on consumer spending, and, to a lesser extent, housing turnover, offset by significant growth we see in major domestic metro markets and Canada.

## Quantitative Evaluations

**S&P Quality Ranking** B+

| D | C | B- | B | B+ | A- | A | A+ |
|---|---|---|---|---|---|---|---|

**Relative Strength Rank** MODERATE

67

LOWEST = 1          HIGHEST = 99

## Revenue/Earnings Data

**Revenue (Million $)**

| | 1Q | 2Q | 3Q | 4Q | Year |
|---|---|---|---|---|---|
| 2012 | 2,110 | 2,314 | -- | -- | -- |
| 2011 | 1,923 | 2,137 | 2,194 | 2,505 | 8,759 |
| 2010 | 1,694 | 1,915 | 1,975 | 2,244 | 7,829 |
| 2009 | 1,648 | 1,854 | 1,783 | 1,923 | 7,208 |
| 2008 | 1,553 | 1,768 | 1,795 | 1,933 | 7,049 |
| 2007 | 1,396 | 1,607 | 1,619 | 1,995 | 6,617 |

**Earnings Per Share ($)**

| | | | | | |
|---|---|---|---|---|---|
| 2012 | 0.72 | 0.93 | E0.88 | E1.31 | E3.84 |
| 2011 | 0.52 | 0.70 | 0.74 | 1.12 | 3.07 |
| 2010 | 0.34 | 0.52 | 0.58 | 0.86 | 2.30 |
| 2009 | 0.30 | 0.46 | 0.34 | 0.55 | 1.64 |
| 2008 | 0.38 | 0.55 | 0.52 | 0.66 | 2.10 |
| 2007 | 0.35 | 0.51 | 0.50 | 0.72 | 2.09 |

Fiscal year ended Feb. 28. Next earnings report expected: Late December. EPS Estimates based on S&P Operating Earnings; historical GAAP earnings are as reported.

## Dividend Data

No cash dividends have been paid.

---

**Please read the Required Disclosures and Analyst Certification on the last page of this report.**

*The McGraw-Hill Companies*

# Bed Bath & Beyond Inc

## Business Summary September 23, 2011

CORPORATE OVERVIEW. Bed Bath & Beyond operates one of the largest U.S. chains of superstores selling domestics merchandise and home furnishings. BBBY stores predominantly range in size from 20,000 sq. ft. to 50,000 sq. ft., with some encompassing 100,000 sq. ft. The company has grown rapidly, from 34 stores at the end of FY 93 (Feb.) to 982 Bed Bath & Beyond stores in 50 states, the District of Columbia, Puerto Rico and Canada at year-end FY 11. BBBY opened 18 net new Bed Bath & Beyond Stores stores in FY 11, after opening 35 stores in FY 09; it expects to open 10-15 new stores in FY 12. During FY 11, total square footage of Bed Bath & Beyond stores grew 4.2%, to 35.1 million sq. ft., from 33.7 million sq. ft. Company stores are principally located in suburban areas of medium- and large-sized cities. These stores are situated in strip and power strip shopping centers, as well as in major off-price and conventional malls, and freestanding buildings.

In March 2002, the company acquired Harmon Stores, Inc., a health and beauty care retailer. The Harmon chain had 46 stores in four states at February 26, 2011, ranging in size from approximately 5,000 to 9,000 sq. ft.

In June 2003, BBBY acquired Christmas Tree Shops, a retailer of home decor, giftware, housewares, food, paper goods and seasonal products, for approximately $194.4 million, net of cash acquired. The company operated 66 Christmas Tree Shops in 18 states at year-end FY 11, ranging in size from 30,000 to 50,000 sq. ft.

In March 2007, BBBY acquired buybuy BABY, a retailer of infant and toddler merchandise, for approximately $67 million, net of cash acquired. The company operated 45 buybuy BABY stores in 20 states at year-end FY 11, ranging in size from 28,000 to 60,000 square feet.

Bed Bath & Beyond is also a partner in a joint venture that operates two stores in the Mexico City market under the name "Home & More".

## Company Financials Fiscal Year Ended Feb. 28

| Per Share Data ($) | 2011 | 2010 | 2009 | 2008 | 2007 | 2006 | 2005 | 2004 | 2003 | 2002 |
|---|---|---|---|---|---|---|---|---|---|---|
| Tangible Book Value | 14.98 | 13.02 | 10.67 | 11.34 | 9.56 | 8.05 | 6.99 | 6.14 | 4.93 | 3.75 |
| Cash Flow | 3.78 | 3.01 | 2.32 | 2.69 | 2.56 | 2.29 | 1.96 | 1.59 | 1.25 | 0.94 |
| Earnings | 3.07 | 2.30 | 1.64 | 2.10 | 2.09 | 1.92 | 1.65 | 1.31 | 1.00 | 0.74 |
| S&P Core Earnings | 3.07 | 2.30 | 1.64 | 2.10 | 2.09 | 1.87 | 1.55 | 1.23 | 0.92 | 0.67 |
| Dividends | Nil | Nil | Nil | Nil | Nil | Nil | Nil | Nil | Nil | Nil |
| Payout Ratio | Nil | Nil | Nil | Nil | Nil | Nil | Nil | Nil | Nil | Nil |
| Calendar Year | 2010 | 2009 | 2008 | 2007 | 2006 | 2005 | 2004 | 2003 | 2002 | 2001 |
| Prices:High | 50.95 | 40.23 | 34.73 | 43.32 | 41.72 | 46.99 | 44.43 | 45.00 | 37.90 | 35.70 |
| Prices:Low | 26.50 | 19.11 | 16.23 | 27.96 | 30.92 | 35.50 | 33.88 | 30.18 | 26.70 | 18.70 |
| P/E Ratio:High | 17 | 17 | 21 | 21 | 20 | 24 | 27 | 34 | 38 | 48 |
| P/E Ratio:Low | 9 | 8 | 10 | 13 | 15 | 18 | 21 | 23 | 27 | 25 |

| Income Statement Analysis (Million $) | | | | | | | | | | |
|---|---|---|---|---|---|---|---|---|---|---|
| Revenue | 8,759 | 7,829 | 7,208 | 7,049 | 6,617 | 5,810 | 5,148 | 4,478 | 3,665 | 2,928 |
| Operating Income | 1,472 | 1,165 | 850 | 996 | 1,026 | 990 | 890 | 724 | 555 | 409 |
| Depreciation | 184 | 184 | 176 | 158 | 136 | 111 | 97.5 | 84.6 | 74.8 | 62.5 |
| Interest Expense | Nil | Nil | Nil | Nil | Nil | Nil | Nil | Nil | Nil | Nil |
| Pretax Income | 1,293 | 985 | 683 | 865 | 933 | 915 | 811 | 650 | 491 | 357 |
| Effective Tax Rate | NA | 39.1% | 37.8% | 35.0% | 36.3% | 37.4% | 37.8% | 38.5% | 38.5% | 38.5% |
| Net Income | 791 | 600 | 425 | 563 | 594 | 573 | 505 | 399 | 302 | 220 |
| S&P Core Earnings | 791 | 600 | 425 | 563 | 594 | 557 | 470 | 370 | 277 | 200 |

| Balance Sheet & Other Financial Data (Million $) | | | | | | | | | | |
|---|---|---|---|---|---|---|---|---|---|---|
| Cash | 1,789 | 1,528 | 670 | 224 | 988 | 652 | 851 | 867 | 617 | 429 |
| Current Assets | 4,074 | 3,563 | 2,563 | 2,080 | 2,699 | 2,072 | 2,097 | 1,969 | 1,594 | 1,227 |
| Total Assets | 5,646 | 5,152 | 4,269 | 3,844 | 3,959 | 3,382 | 3,200 | 2,865 | 2,189 | 1,648 |
| Current Liabilities | 1,322 | 1,150 | 953 | 1,014 | 1,145 | 990 | 874 | 770 | 680 | 511 |
| Long Term Debt | Nil | Nil | Nil | Nil | Nil | Nil | Nil | Nil | Nil | Nil |
| Common Equity | 3,932 | 3,653 | 3,000 | 2,562 | 2,649 | 2,262 | 2,204 | 1,991 | 1,452 | 1,094 |
| Total Capital | 3,932 | 3,653 | 3,000 | 2,562 | 2,649 | 2,262 | 2,204 | 1,991 | 1,452 | 1,094 |
| Capital Expenditures | 183 | 154 | 216 | 358 | 318 | 220 | 191 | 113 | 135 | 121 |
| Cash Flow | 975 | 784 | 601 | 721 | 731 | 684 | 602 | 484 | 377 | 282 |
| Current Ratio | 3.1 | 3.1 | 2.7 | 2.1 | 2.4 | 2.1 | 2.4 | 2.6 | 2.3 | 2.4 |
| % Long Term Debt of Capitalization | Nil | Nil | Nil | Nil | Nil | Nil | Nil | Nil | Nil | Nil |
| % Net Income of Revenue | 9.0 | 7.7 | 5.9 | 8.0 | 9.0 | 9.9 | 9.8 | 8.9 | 8.2 | 7.5 |
| % Return on Assets | 14.7 | 12.7 | 10.5 | 14.4 | 16.2 | 17.4 | 16.7 | 15.8 | 15.8 | 15.4 |
| % Return on Equity | 20.9 | 18.0 | 15.3 | 21.6 | 24.2 | 25.7 | 24.1 | 23.2 | 23.7 | 23.0 |

Data as orig reptd.; bef. results of disc opers/spec. items. Per share data adj. for stk. divs.; EPS diluted. E-Estimated. NA-Not Available. NM-Not Meaningful. NR-Not Ranked. UR-Under Review.

**Office:** 650 Liberty Avenue, Union, NJ 07083.
**Telephone:** 908-688-0888.
**Website:** http://www.bedbathandbeyond.com
**Co-Chrmn:** L. Feinstein

**Co-Chrmn & Secy:** W. Eisenberg
**Pres:** A. Stark
**CEO:** S.H. Temares
**COO & CTO:** K. Wanner

**Investor Contact:** R. Curwin (908-688-0888)
**Board Members:** D. S. Adler, S. F. Barshay, W. Eisenberg, K. Eppler, L. Feinstein, P. R. Gaston, J. Heller, V. A. Morrison, S. H. Temares

**Founded:** 1971
**Domicile:** New York
**Employees:** 45,000

# Bemis Co Inc

**STANDARD &POOR'S**

| S&P Recommendation **HOLD** ★★★☆☆ | Price $27.62 (as of Nov 25, 2011) | 12-Mo. Target Price $31.00 | Investment Style Large-Cap Blend |
|---|---|---|---|

**GICS Sector** Materials
**Sub-Industry** Paper Packaging

**Summary** This company is a leading maker of a broad range of flexible packaging and pressure-sensitive materials.

## Key Stock Statistics (Source S&P, Vickers, company reports)

| | | | | | | | |
|---|---|---|---|---|---|---|---|
| 52-Wk Range | $34.40– 27.21 | S&P Oper. EPS 2011**E** | 1.90 | Market Capitalization(B) | $2.844 | Beta | 0.68 |
| Trailing 12-Month EPS | $1.99 | S&P Oper. EPS 2012**E** | 2.30 | Yield (%) | 3.48 | S&P 3-Yr. Proj. EPS CAGR(%) | 11 |
| Trailing 12-Month P/E | 13.9 | P/E on S&P Oper. EPS 2011**E** | 14.5 | Dividend Rate/Share | $0.96 | S&P Credit Rating | BBB |
| $10K Invested 5 Yrs Ago | $9,522 | Common Shares Outstg. (M) | 103.0 | Institutional Ownership (%) | 78 | | |

## Price Performance

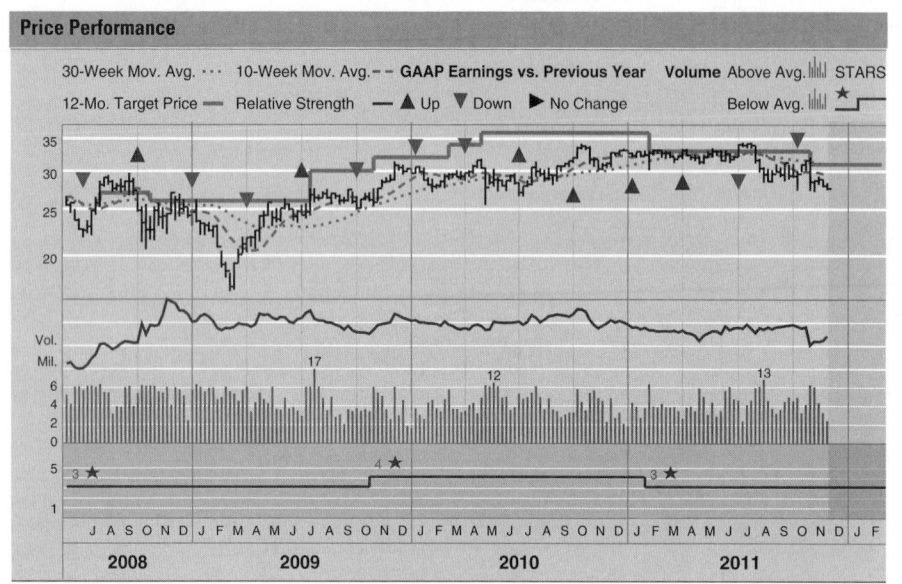

- 30-Week Mov. Avg. ···
- 10-Week Mov. Avg. – –
- **GAAP Earnings vs. Previous Year**
- Volume Above Avg. STARS
- 12-Mo. Target Price —
- Relative Strength
- ▲ Up ▼ Down ► No Change
- Below Avg.

Options: ASE, CBOE, P

Analysis prepared by Equity Analyst **Stewart Scharf** on Nov 04, 2011, when the stock traded at **$28.01**.

## Qualitative Risk Assessment

| LOW | MEDIUM | HIGH |
|---|---|---|

Our risk assessment reflects challenging global economic conditions, volatile raw material prices and possible difficulty integrating acquisitions. BMS has an S&P Quality Ranking of B+, which indicates a record of average long-term earnings and dividend growth.

## Quantitative Evaluations

**S&P Quality Ranking**　　　　B+

| D | C | B- | B | B+ | A- | A | A+ |
|---|---|---|---|---|---|---|---|

**Relative Strength Rank**　　　MODERATE

48

LOWEST = 1　　　　　　　　HIGHEST = 99

## Revenue/Earnings Data

**Revenue (Million $)**

| | 1Q | 2Q | 3Q | 4Q | Year |
|---|---|---|---|---|---|
| 2011 | 1,324 | 1,370 | 1,358 | -- | -- |
| 2010 | 1,022 | 1,270 | 1,294 | 1,249 | 4,835 |
| 2009 | 843.4 | 866.4 | 898.9 | 905.9 | 3,515 |
| 2008 | 947.3 | 980.0 | 984.3 | 867.9 | 3,779 |
| 2007 | 909.1 | 921.8 | 905.7 | 912.7 | 3,649 |
| 2006 | 901.7 | 933.8 | 903.3 | 900.6 | 3,639 |

**Earnings Per Share ($)**

| | | | | | |
|---|---|---|---|---|---|
| 2011 | 0.47 | 0.51 | 0.53 | E0.37 | E1.90 |
| 2010 | 0.27 | 0.52 | 0.56 | 0.48 | 1.83 |
| 2009 | 0.36 | 0.47 | 0.33 | 0.26 | 1.40 |
| 2008 | 0.42 | 0.46 | 0.44 | 0.33 | 1.65 |
| 2007 | 0.45 | 0.47 | 0.40 | 0.42 | 1.74 |
| 2006 | 0.35 | 0.46 | 0.45 | 0.39 | 1.65 |

Fiscal year ended Dec. 31. Next earnings report expected: Early February. EPS Estimates based on S&P Operating Earnings; historical GAAP earnings are as reported.

## Highlights

► We project low single digit organic sales growth for 2011, with modest improvement in 2012, reflecting soft global demand for flexible consumer food packaging products due mainly to inflationary price hikes, while pricing initiatives offset weak pressure-sensitive materials volume. In our view, BMS will continue to roll out innovative flexible packaging products and product line extensions.

► We look for gross margins to narrow in 2011, from 18.4% in 2010, on less fixed-cost absorption due to lower production volumes, offsetting cost pass-throughs stemming from rising raw material costs mainly in the first half, and new higher-margin products. We see stabilizing resin costs, along with price hikes, aiding margins sequentially. Operating margins (EBITDA) should narrow to near 12% in 2011 on higher operating costs, from an adjusted 15% in 2010, but we see some sequential improvement during 2012, reflecting improved operating efficiencies.

► We project a slightly higher effective tax rate of 36% in 2011, with operating EPS of $1.90, advancing to $2.30 in 2012.

## Investment Rationale/Risk

► Our hold opinion is based on our valuation metrics, along with some headwinds from rising raw material costs, due in part to longer-term contracts acquired from Food Americas. Although BMS's debt ratio has risen due to financing related to the Alcan unit acquisition, we believe the deal will be a good strategic fit, with cash generation sufficient to pay down debt.

► Risks to our recommendation and target price include volatile and sharply rising commodity prices, softer global demand for food and other packaging products, and a negative foreign currency effect.

► With the stock's recent dividend yield of 3.4%, versus 2.1% for the S&P 500 Index, and our view of BMS's solid earnings track record, we apply a multiple of 15X, a small premium to BMS's five-year historical average forward P/E, to our 2012 operating EPS estimate to derive a value of $35. Based on our DCF analysis, the stock has an intrinsic value of $27, assuming a 3% terminal growth rate and an 8.3% weighted average cost of capital. Blending these valuations, we arrive at our 12-month target price of $31.

## Dividend Data (Dates: mm/dd Payment Date: mm/dd/yy)

| Amount ($) | Date Decl. | Ex-Div. Date | Stk. of Record | Payment Date |
|---|---|---|---|---|
| 0.240 | 02/04 | 02/11 | 02/15 | 03/01/11 |
| 0.240 | 05/05 | 05/16 | 05/18 | 06/01/11 |
| 0.240 | 08/05 | 08/15 | 08/17 | 09/01/11 |
| 0.240 | 11/03 | 11/10 | 11/15 | 12/01/11 |

Dividends have been paid since 1922. Source: Company reports.

**Please read the Required Disclosures and Analyst Certification on the last page of this report.**

The **McGraw·Hill** Companies

# Bemis Co Inc

STANDARD
&POOR'S

## Business Summary November 04, 2011

CORPORATE OVERVIEW. Bemis Co., a leading North American producer of flexible packaging products, as well as pressure-sensitive materials, focuses primarily on the food industry (about 65% of sales). BMS expects combined food packaging sales going forward following the acquisition of Food Americas to range from 65% to 70% of total sales. Markets also include the chemicals, agribusiness, pharmaceutical, personal care products, electronics, automotive and graphic industries. BMS has 73 flexible packaging manufacturing plants (11 leased) in 18 U.S. states, Puerto Rico, and 11 countries. It also has seven pressure sensitive materials plants in three states and two countries.

Although BMS focuses on marketing its products in the U.S (67% of 2010 net sales), it has broadened its reach to Latin America (21%), as well as Southeast Asia and Mexico, due to strong demand for barrier films to extend the shelf life of perishable foods. Europe accounted for 11% of sales in 2010, while Asia Pacific contributed 1.2%.

The Flexible Packaging Products segment (88% of net sales in 2010; $475 million of operating profits) produces a wide range of consumer and industrial packaging products, including high barrier, polyethylene and paper products.

High barrier products, which comprise more than 50% of net sales, include flexible polymer film structures and barrier laminates for food, medical and personal care products.

The Pressure Sensitive Materials segment (12%; $33 million in operating profits) produces printing products, decorative and sheet products, and technical products.

Flexible packaging competitors include Sealed Air, Sonoco Products, Amcor and Hood Packaging. Pressure-sensitive materials competitors include Avery Dennison, Acucote, Minnesota Mining and Manufacturing (3M), Ricoh, FLEXcon and Spinnaker Industries.

BMS contributed $15 million to its U.S. pension plans in early 2010, reflecting a lower funded status due to lower assets and increased liabilities.

## Company Financials Fiscal Year Ended Dec. 31

| Per Share Data ($) | 2010 | 2009 | 2008 | 2007 | 2006 | 2005 | 2004 | 2003 | 2002 | 2001 |
|---|---|---|---|---|---|---|---|---|---|---|
| Tangible Book Value | 6.18 | 9.90 | 6.72 | 9.70 | 7.31 | 6.29 | 7.48 | 5.81 | 4.11 | 4.39 |
| Cash Flow | 3.72 | 2.96 | 3.26 | 3.28 | 3.08 | 2.98 | 2.88 | 2.56 | 2.65 | 2.49 |
| Earnings | 1.83 | 1.40 | 1.65 | 1.74 | 1.65 | 1.51 | 1.67 | 1.37 | 1.54 | 1.32 |
| S&P Core Earnings | 1.90 | 1.39 | 1.40 | 1.67 | 1.64 | 1.48 | 1.65 | 1.32 | 1.28 | 1.02 |
| Dividends | 0.92 | 0.90 | 0.66 | 0.84 | 0.76 | 0.72 | 0.64 | 0.56 | 0.52 | 0.50 |
| Payout Ratio | 50% | 64% | 40% | 48% | 46% | 48% | 38% | 41% | 34% | 38% |
| Prices:High | 34.25 | 31.41 | 29.70 | 36.53 | 34.99 | 32.50 | 29.49 | 25.58 | 29.12 | 26.24 |
| Prices:Low | 25.50 | 16.85 | 20.62 | 25.53 | 27.86 | 23.20 | 23.24 | 19.67 | 19.70 | 14.34 |
| P/E Ratio:High | 19 | 22 | 18 | 21 | 21 | 22 | 18 | 19 | 19 | 20 |
| P/E Ratio:Low | 14 | 12 | 12 | 15 | 17 | 15 | 14 | 14 | 13 | 11 |

| Income Statement Analysis (Million $) | | | | | | | | | | |
|---|---|---|---|---|---|---|---|---|---|---|
| Revenue | 4,835 | 3,515 | 3,779 | 3,649 | 3,639 | 3,474 | 2,834 | 2,635 | 2,369 | 2,293 |
| Operating Income | 626 | 464 | 443 | 468 | 492 | 472 | 420 | 384 | 401 | 384 |
| Depreciation | 210 | 159 | 163 | 159 | 152 | 151 | 131 | 128 | 119 | 124 |
| Interest Expense | 73.5 | 42.1 | 42.0 | 54.5 | 49.3 | 38.7 | 15.5 | 12.6 | 15.4 | 30.3 |
| Pretax Income | 327 | 245 | 269 | 290 | 289 | 282 | 294 | 240 | 268 | 228 |
| Effective Tax Rate | NA | 36.5% | 35.9% | 36.0% | 37.8% | 40.3% | 38.7% | 38.4% | 37.9% | 38.2% |
| Net Income | 203 | 150 | 166 | 182 | 176 | 163 | 180 | 147 | 166 | 140 |
| S&P Core Earnings | 208 | 144 | 142 | 174 | 176 | 160 | 179 | 142 | 137 | 108 |

| Balance Sheet & Other Financial Data (Million $) | | | | | | | | | | |
|---|---|---|---|---|---|---|---|---|---|---|
| Cash | 60.4 | 1,066 | 48.3 | 147 | 112 | 91.1 | 93.9 | 76.5 | 56.4 | 35.1 |
| Current Assets | 1,467 | 2,005 | 983 | 1,137 | 1,094 | 988 | 874 | 752 | 722 | 587 |
| Total Assets | 4,286 | 3,929 | 2,827 | 3,191 | 3,039 | 2,965 | 2,487 | 2,293 | 2,257 | 1,923 |
| Current Liabilities | 675 | 525 | 422 | 535 | 555 | 474 | 375 | 316 | 326 | 238 |
| Long Term Debt | 1,284 | 1,228 | 660 | 843 | 722 | 790 | 534 | 583 | 718 | 595 |
| Common Equity | 1,880 | 1,807 | 1,342 | 1,562 | 1,472 | 1,349 | 1,308 | 1,139 | 959 | 886 |
| Total Capital | 3,214 | 3,105 | 2,147 | 2,533 | 2,358 | 2,336 | 2,019 | 1,878 | 1,788 | 1,606 |
| Capital Expenditures | 113 | 89.2 | 121 | 179 | 159 | 187 | 135 | 106 | 91.0 | 117 |
| Cash Flow | 413 | 306 | 329 | 341 | 329 | 313 | 311 | 275 | 285 | 264 |
| Current Ratio | 2.2 | 3.9 | 2.3 | 2.1 | 2.0 | 2.1 | 2.3 | 2.4 | 2.2 | 2.5 |
| % Long Term Debt of Capitalization | 39.9 | 39.5 | 30.7 | 32.6 | 30.6 | 33.8 | 26.4 | 31.1 | 40.2 | 37.1 |
| % Net Income of Revenue | 4.2 | 4.3 | 4.4 | 5.0 | 4.8 | 4.7 | 6.3 | 5.6 | 7.0 | 6.1 |
| % Return on Assets | 5.0 | 4.5 | 5.5 | 5.8 | 5.9 | 6.0 | 7.5 | 6.5 | 7.9 | 7.4 |
| % Return on Equity | 11.0 | 9.5 | 11.5 | 12.0 | 12.5 | 12.2 | 14.7 | 14.0 | 17.9 | 16.7 |

Data as orig reptd.; bef. results of disc opers/spec. items. Per share data adj. for stk. divs.; EPS diluted. E-Estimated. NA-Not Available. NM-Not Meaningful. NR-Not Ranked. UR-Under Review.

**Office:** One Neenah Center, 4th Floor PO Box 669, Neenah, WI 54957-0669.
**Telephone:** 920-727-4100.
**Website:** http://www.bemis.com
**Chrmn:** W.J. Bolton

**Pres & CEO:** H.J. Theisen
**CFO:** S.B. Ullem
**CTO:** R. Germonprez
**Investor Contact:** M.E. Miller (920-527-5045)

**Board Members:** W. J. Bolton, J. H. Curler, D. S. Haffner, B. L. Johnson, T. M. Manganello, R. D. O'Shaughnessy, P. S. Peercy, E. N. Perry, H. J. Theisen, H. A. Van Deursen, P. G. Weaver, G. C. Wulf

**Founded:** 1858
**Domicile:** Missouri
**Employees:** 19,796

# Berkshire Hathaway Inc.

STANDARD &POOR'S

| S&P Recommendation HOLD ★★★★★ | Price<br>$75.13 (as of Nov 29, 2011) | 12-Mo. Target Price<br>$80.00 | Investment Style<br>Large-Cap Blend |
|---|---|---|---|

**GICS Sector** Financials
**Sub-Industry** Property & Casualty Insurance

**Summary** This holding company has interests in insurance, railroads, energy, financial services, publishing, retailing and manufacturing. Its investment portfolio included more than $67 billion of marketable equity securities as of September 30, 2011.

## Key Stock Statistics (Source S&P, Vickers, company reports)

| | | | | | | | |
|---|---|---|---|---|---|---|---|
| 52-Wk Range | $87.65– 65.35 | S&P Oper. EPS 2011E | 4.58 | Market Capitalization(B) | $80.160 | Beta | 0.51 |
| Trailing 12-Month EPS | $4.97 | S&P Oper. EPS 2012E | 5.38 | Yield (%) | Nil | S&P 3-Yr. Proj. EPS CAGR(%) | 9 |
| Trailing 12-Month P/E | 15.1 | P/E on S&P Oper. EPS 2011E | 16.4 | Dividend Rate/Share | Nil | S&P Credit Rating | AA+ |
| $10K Invested 5 Yrs Ago | $10,159 | Common Shares Outstg. (M) | 1,067.9 | Institutional Ownership (%) | 58 | | |

## Price Performance

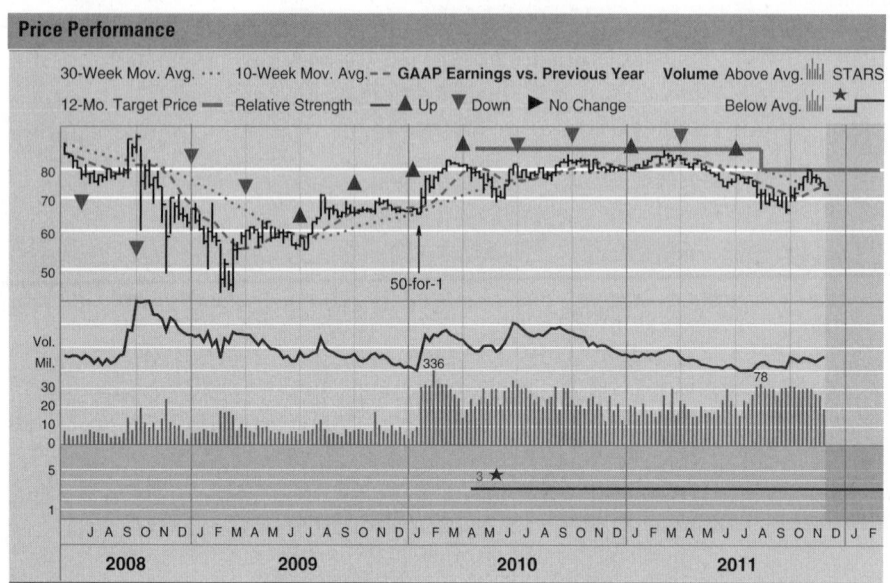

30-Week Mov. Avg. · · · ·   10-Week Mov. Avg. - - -   **GAAP Earnings vs. Previous Year**   Volume Above Avg. |||| STARS
12-Mo. Target Price —   Relative Strength —   ▲ Up  ▼ Down  ▶ No Change   Below Avg. |||| ★

Analysis prepared by Equity Analyst **Cathy Seifert** on Nov 28, 2011, when the stock traded at **$75.00**.

## Highlights

▶ We expect operating revenues to advance 9%-13% in 2011, as contributions from recent acquisitions are offset by economy-driven weakness in other areas, particularly in the first half of the year. We look for revenue growth in the insurance area (Berkshire's largest unit) to be above industry averages, primarily reflecting market share gains at GEICO and increased writings at certain reinsurance units. We estimate segment organic revenue growth in 2012 of 6% to 8%.

▶ We see underwriting margins at GEICO remaining under pressure in 2011, reflecting a higher level of policy acquisition costs and some mixed claim trends. Underwriting margins in catastrophe-exposed lines of business may also come under some pressure amid a resumption of "normal" levels of catastrophe losses. Margin improvements at other units (largely due to cost cuts) will likely enhance operating profits.

▶ We estimate operating EPS of $4.58 in 2011 and $5.38 in 2012, versus the $4.52 a share we calculate the company earned on an operating basis in 2010.

## Investment Rationale/Risk

▶ Our hold opinion reflects our view that the shares are appropriately valued on both a price/earnings and price/tangible book value basis. At recent levels, the shares are trading at a premium to many of the company's closest peers (though peer comparisons are difficult given Berkshire's conglomerate-like business mix) and at the upper end of historical ranges.

▶ Risks to our opinion and target price include significant erosion in claims and premium pricing trends, and a more prolonged economic downturn, which would likely continue to dampen demand for many of Berkshire's products.

▶ Our 12-month target price of $80 assumes that the shares will trade at 15X our 2012 operating EPS forecast. This represents the upper end of Berkshire's historical average multiple, and is a premium to most of the company's insurance and reinsurance peers. We believe this premium is warranted in light of what we see as Berkshire's superior financial strength. Our target price also assumes the shares will trade at just under 2X estimated 2012 tangible book value per share.

## Qualitative Risk Assessment

| LOW | MEDIUM | HIGH |
|---|---|---|

We believe the low risk represented by the company's diversified revenue and earnings base is outweighed by the risks associated with the actions of former executive David Sokol and his purchase of Lubrizol shares before the company acquired Lubrizol. We also view chairman and CEO Warren Buffett's advanced age as a risk factor.

## Quantitative Evaluations

**S&P Quality Ranking**   B+

| D | C | B- | B | B+ | A- | A | A+ |
|---|---|---|---|---|---|---|---|

**Relative Strength Rank**   STRONG

78

LOWEST = 1                    HIGHEST = 99

## Revenue/Earnings Data

**Revenue (Million $)**

| | 1Q | 2Q | 3Q | 4Q | Year |
|---|---|---|---|---|---|
| 2011 | 33,720 | 38,274 | -- | -- | -- |
| 2010 | 32,037 | 31,709 | 36,274 | 36,165 | 136,185 |
| 2009 | 22,784 | 29,607 | 29,904 | 30,198 | 112,493 |
| 2008 | 25,175 | 30,093 | 27,926 | 24,592 | 107,786 |
| 2007 | 32,918 | 27,347 | 25,387 | 28,043 | 118,245 |
| 2006 | 22,763 | 24,185 | 2,536 | 26,231 | 98,539 |

**Earnings Per Share ($)**

| | 1Q | 2Q | 3Q | 4Q | Year |
|---|---|---|---|---|---|
| 2011 | 0.61 | 1.38 | E1.27 | E1.30 | E4.58 |
| 2010 | 1.51 | 0.80 | 1.21 | 1.77 | 5.29 |
| 2009 | -0.66 | 1.42 | 1.39 | 1.31 | 3.46 |
| 2008 | 0.40 | 1.24 | 0.45 | 0.05 | 2.15 |
| 2007 | 1.12 | 1.35 | 1.96 | 1.27 | 5.70 |
| 2006 | 1.00 | 1.01 | 1.20 | 1.55 | 4.76 |

Fiscal year ended Dec. 31. Next earnings report expected: NA. EPS Estimates based on S&P Operating Earnings; historical GAAP earnings are as reported.

## Dividend Data

No cash dividends have been paid.

---

# Berkshire Hathaway Inc.

## STANDARD &POOR'S

## Business Summary November 28, 2011

CORPORATE OVERVIEW. This insurance-based conglomerate's segment operating revenues totaled $133.2 billion in 2010 (up from $110.8 billion in 2009) and were derived as follows: GEICO Corp. 11%, General Re 4%, Berkshire Hathaway Reinsurance Group 7%, investment income 4%, financial products 3%, Burlington Northern SantaFe 11%, Marmon 4%, McLane Company 25%, MidAmerican 8%, and other 23%.

Berkshire has grown through acquisitions. In September 2011, it acquired Lubrizol (LZ) for $9.7 billion ($135 a share in cash). The trading of LZ shares before Berkshire announced the offer by former Berkshire executive David Sokol has raised some controversy, and Mr. Sokol resigned. In February 2010, Berkshire acquired the 77.5% of Burlington Northern Santa Fe it did not already own for $26.5 billion ($100 a share in cash/stock). Berkshire acquired 60% of Marmon Holdings (a private conglomerate) for $4.5 billion in March 2008; and another 4.4% in April 2008 . Berkshire plans to increase its stake in Marmon to 80.2% in 2011, and to acquire the remaining 19.8% during 2013 and 2014.

Berkshire's common equity holdings had a market value of more than $61 billion at year-end 2010. The largest holdings were Coca-Cola (KO 66, Strong Buy) (with a 12/31/10 market value of $13.2 billion), Wells Fargo (WFC 24, Buy)

($11.1 billion), American Express Co. (AXP 46, Strong Buy) ($6.5 billion) and Procter & Gamble (PG 62, Hold) ($4.7 billion). In October 2008, the company paid $8 billion to acquire newly issued 10% perpetual preferred stock of Goldman Sachs Group (GS 89, Hold) and General Electric (GE 15, Buy); and warrants (expiring in October 2013) to acquire up to 43.5 million GS common shares at $115 per share and up to 134.8 million GE common shares at $22.25 a share. On April 18, 2011, Goldman Sachs redeemed the entire 10% preferred investment. In March 2009, Berkshire acquired a 12% convertible perpetual capital instrument without maturity and redemption date, issued by Swiss Re for $2.7 billion that is convertible into 120 million Swiss Re common shares. In April 2009, Berkshire acquired 3 million Series A cumulative convertible perpetual preferred shares of Dow Chemical Co. (DOW 25, Buy) for $3 billion. Each share is convertible into 24.201 DOW common shares, subject to certain conditions. In late August 2011, Berkshire invested $5 billion in Bank of America (BAC 5, Hold) by acquiring 50,000 shares of 6% cumulate preferred stock and warrants to buy 700,000 BAC shares at $7.142857 a share.

## Company Financials Fiscal Year Ended Dec. 31

| Per Share Data ($) | 2010 | 2009 | 2008 | 2007 | 2006 | 2005 | 2004 | 2003 | 2002 | 2001 |
|---|---|---|---|---|---|---|---|---|---|---|
| Tangible Book Value | 41.02 | 41.72 | 32.49 | 37.84 | 32.91 | 29.35 | 27.24 | 23.70 | 18.13 | 15.94 |
| Operating Earnings | NA | NA | NA | NA | NA | NA | NA | NA | NA | NA |
| Earnings | 5.29 | 3.46 | 2.15 | 5.70 | 4.76 | 3.69 | 3.17 | 3.54 | 1.86 | 0.35 |
| S&P Core Earnings | 4.76 | 4.29 | 2.21 | 4.20 | 4.30 | 2.06 | 2.67 | 2.72 | 1.70 | -0.02 |
| Dividends | Nil | Nil | Nil | Nil | Nil | Nil | Nil | Nil | Nil | Nil |
| Payout Ratio | Nil | Nil | Nil | Nil | Nil | Nil | Nil | Nil | Nil | Nil |
| Prices:High | 85.86 | 71.38 | 97.16 | 101.18 | 76.50 | 61.34 | 63.90 | 56.48 | 52.40 | 50.50 |
| Prices:Low | 64.72 | 44.82 | 49.02 | 69.20 | 56.78 | 52.24 | 53.70 | 40.30 | 38.50 | 39.54 |
| P/E Ratio:High | 16 | 21 | 45 | 18 | 16 | 17 | 20 | 16 | 28 | NM |
| P/E Ratio:Low | 12 | 13 | 23 | 12 | 12 | 14 | 17 | 11 | 21 | NM |

| Income Statement Analysis (Million $) | 2010 | 2009 | 2008 | 2007 | 2006 | 2005 | 2004 | 2003 | 2002 | 2001 |
|---|---|---|---|---|---|---|---|---|---|---|
| Premium Income | 30,749 | 27,884 | 25,525 | 31,783 | 23,964 | 21,997 | 21,085 | NA | 19,182 | 17,905 |
| Net Investment Income | 6,898 | 7,131 | 6,756 | 6,696 | NA | NA | NA | 4,191 | NA | 2,765 |
| Other Revenue | 98,538 | 77,478 | 75,505 | 79,766 | 74,575 | 59,666 | 53,297 | 59,668 | 17,984 | 16,998 |
| Total Revenue | 136,185 | 112,493 | 107,786 | 118,245 | 98,539 | 81,663 | 74,382 | 63,859 | 42,353 | 37,668 |
| Pretax Income | 19,101 | 11,979 | 7,574 | 20,161 | 16,778 | 12,791 | 10,936 | 12,020 | 6,435 | 1,469 |
| Net Operating Income | NA | NA | NA | NA | NA | NA | NA | NA | NA | -47.0 |
| Net Income | 12,967 | 8,055 | 4,994 | 13,213 | 11,015 | 8,528 | 7,308 | 8,151 | 4,286 | 795 |
| S&P Core Earnings | 11,675 | 9,990 | 5,127 | 9,739 | 9,954 | 4,767 | 6,148 | 6,275 | 3,919 | -43.1 |

| Balance Sheet & Other Financial Data (Million $) | 2010 | 2009 | 2008 | 2007 | 2006 | 2005 | 2004 | 2003 | 2002 | 2001 |
|---|---|---|---|---|---|---|---|---|---|---|
| Cash & Equivalent | 38,227 | 30,558 | 25,539 | 44,329 | 43,743 | 44,660 | 43,427 | 35,957 | 12,748 | 5,313 |
| Premiums Due | 6,342 | 5,295 | 4,961 | 4,215 | NA | NA | NA | NA | NA | NA |
| Investment Assets:Bonds | 34,883 | 37,131 | 31,632 | 31,571 | 28,312 | 30,855 | 31,305 | 26,116 | NA | 36,509 |
| Investment Assets:Stocks | 59,819 | 56,562 | 49,073 | 74,999 | 61,533 | 46,721 | 37,717 | 35,287 | NA | 28,675 |
| Investment Assets:Loans | 15,226 | 13,989 | 13,942 | 12,359 | NA | NA | NA | NA | NA | Nil |
| Investment Assets:Total | 132,937 | 140,282 | 116,182 | 118,929 | 87,738 | 79,269 | 66,876 | 78,029 | 87,356 | 67,158 |
| Deferred Policy Costs | NA | NA | NA | NA | NA | NA | NA | NA | NA | NA |
| Total Assets | 372,229 | 297,119 | 267,399 | 273,160 | 248,437 | 198,325 | 188,874 | 180,559 | 169,544 | 162,752 |
| Debt | 58,574 | 37,909 | 36,882 | 33,826 | 27,450 | 12,523 | 7,192 | 9,119 | 18,270 | 1,230 |
| Common Equity | 157,318 | 131,102 | 109,267 | 120,733 | 108,419 | 91,484 | 85,900 | 77,596 | 64,037 | 57,950 |
| Property & Casualty:Loss Ratio | 74.4 | 77.0 | 74.8 | 72.2 | NA | NA | NA | NA | NA | 79.9 |
| Property & Casualty:Expense Ratio | 178.0 | 18.2 | 17.9 | 18.4 | NA | NA | NA | NA | NA | 16.5 |
| Property & Casualty Combined Ratio | 92.2 | 95.2 | 92.7 | 90.6 | 88.1 | 87.9 | 89.1 | 94.2 | 93.8 | 96.4 |
| % Return on Revenue | 9.5 | 7.2 | 4.6 | 11.2 | 11.2 | 10.4 | 9.8 | 12.8 | 10.1 | 2.1 |
| % Return on Equity | 9.0 | 6.7 | 4.3 | 11.5 | 11.0 | 9.6 | 8.9 | 11.5 | 7.0 | 1.3 |

Data as orig reptd.; bef. results of disc opers/spec. items. Per share data adj. for stk. divs.; EPS diluted. Tangible book value per share based on combined A & B shares. E-Estimated. NA-Not Available. NM-Not Meaningful. NR-Not Ranked. UR-Under Review.

Office: 3555 Farnam St, Omaha, NE 68131.
Telephone: 402-346-1400.
Website: http://www.berkshirehathaway.com
Chrmn & CEO: W.E. Buffett

Vice Chrmn: C.T. Munger
CFO: M.D. Hamburg
Chief Acctg Officer & Cntlr: D.J. Jaksich
Secy: F.N. Krutter

Investor Contact: M. Hamburg (402-346-1400)
Board Members: H. G. Buffett, W. E. Buffett, S. B. Burke, S. L. Decker, W. H. Gates, III, D. S. Gottesman, C. Guyman, D. R. Keough, C. T. Munger, T. S. Murphy, R. L. Olson, W. Scott, Jr.

Auditor: DELOITTE & TOUCHE
Founded: 1889
Domicile: Delaware
Employees: 260,519

The McGraw·Hill Companies

# Best Buy Co. Inc.

## STANDARD &POOR'S

| S&P Recommendation | BUY ★★★★☆ | Price $25.63 (as of Nov 25, 2011) | 12-Mo. Target Price $31.00 | Investment Style Large-Cap Growth |
|---|---|---|---|---|

**GICS Sector** Consumer Discretionary
**Sub-Industry** Computer & Electronics Retail

**Summary** This leading retailer of consumer electronics and entertainment software operates approximately 4,000 stores in the U.S., Canada, China and Europe.

## Key Stock Statistics (Source S&P, Vickers, company reports)

| | | | | | |
|---|---|---|---|---|---|
| 52-Wk Range | $44.62– 21.79 | S&P Oper. EPS 2012**E** 3.37 | Market Capitalization(B) $9.286 | Beta | 1.28 |
| Trailing 12-Month EPS | $2.93 | S&P Oper. EPS 2013**E** 3.71 | Yield (%) 2.50 | S&P 3-Yr. Proj. EPS CAGR(%) | 8 |
| Trailing 12-Month P/E | 8.8 | P/E on S&P Oper. EPS 2012**E** 7.6 | Dividend Rate/Share $0.64 | S&P Credit Rating | BBB- |
| $10K Invested 5 Yrs Ago | $5,010 | Common Shares Outstg. (M) 362.3 | Institutional Ownership (%) 71 | | |

## Price Performance

30-Week Mov. Avg. · · · 10-Week Mov. Avg. - - GAAP Earnings vs. Previous Year   Volume Above Avg. STARS

12-Mo. Target Price — Relative Strength — ▲ Up ▼ Down ► No Change   Below Avg. ★

Options: ASE, CBOE, P, Ph

Analysis prepared by Equity Analyst **Michael Souers** on Sep 16, 2011, when the stock traded at **$25.68**.

## Qualitative Risk Assessment

| LOW | MEDIUM | HIGH |
|---|---|---|

Our risk assessment reflects what we see as BBY's strong balance sheet, sizable market share, numerous suppliers and buyers, and a history of profitability, offset by a highly competitive environment for consumer electronics retailing, with numerous rivals and strong price competition.

## Quantitative Evaluations

**S&P Quality Ranking**   B+

| D | C | B- | B | B+ | A- | A | A+ |
|---|---|---|---|---|---|---|---|

**Relative Strength Rank**   MODERATE

67

LOWEST = 1   HIGHEST = 99

## Revenue/Earnings Data

**Revenue (Million $)**

| | 1Q | 2Q | 3Q | 4Q | Year |
|---|---|---|---|---|---|
| 2012 | 10,940 | 11,347 | -- | -- | -- |
| 2011 | 10,787 | 11,339 | 11,890 | 16,256 | 50,272 |
| 2010 | 10,095 | 11,022 | 12,024 | 16,553 | 49,694 |
| 2009 | 8,990 | 9,801 | 11,500 | 14,724 | 45,015 |
| 2008 | 7,927 | 8,750 | 9,928 | 13,418 | 40,023 |
| 2007 | 6,959 | 7,603 | 8,473 | 12,899 | 35,934 |

**Earnings Per Share ($)**

| | 1Q | 2Q | 3Q | 4Q | Year |
|---|---|---|---|---|---|
| 2012 | 0.35 | 0.47 | E0.53 | E2.13 | E3.37 |
| 2011 | 0.36 | 0.60 | 0.54 | 1.62 | 3.08 |
| 2010 | 0.36 | 0.37 | 0.53 | 1.82 | 3.10 |
| 2009 | 0.43 | 0.48 | 0.13 | 1.35 | 2.39 |
| 2008 | 0.39 | 0.48 | 0.53 | 1.71 | 3.12 |
| 2007 | 0.47 | 0.47 | 0.31 | 1.55 | 2.79 |

Fiscal year ended Feb. 28. Next earnings report expected: Mid December. EPS Estimates based on S&P Operating Earnings; historical GAAP earnings are as reported.

## Highlights

► We view BBY as the best-of-class U.S. consumer electronics retailer, based on its digital product focus, knowledgeable sales staff, and effective marketing campaigns. We think BBY's focus on advanced TVs, notebook and tablet computers, video gaming devices and mobile phones will support solid revenue growth.

► We project a 2.9% rise in revenues for FY 12 (Feb.), after a 1.2% advance in FY 11, driven by the opening of approximately 10 (net) new Best Buy stores worldwide, 150 Best Buy Mobile standalone stores and 40-50 Five Star stores in China. We look for a 1%-2% decline in comparable-store sales, given our forecast that consumer spending will remain pressured by macroeconomic factors. We see a slight narrowing of operating margins, with an expected increase in promotional activity and a shift toward lower-margin online business.

► After taxes at an effective rate of 36.9%, and 9% fewer shares due to BBY's repurchase program, we estimate FY 12 EPS of $3.37, a decline of 1.7% from the $3.43 the company earned in FY 11, excluding restructuring charges totaling $0.36. We see FY 13 EPS of $3.54.

## Investment Rationale/Risk

► We favor BBY's decision to curb capital spending and strictly manage SG&A expenses. We also expect BBY to maintain its market share leadership over the long term with exclusive products and a customer-centric business model. However, we maintain that the industry is facing a potential saturation of flat-panel TVs, and we think mass adoption of revolutionary products such as 3-D TVs may be a few years away. We are also concerned about the weak near-term economic environment and its potential impact on discretionary spending. Despite these reservations, we think the shares are attractively valued following a significant recent selloff, trading at about 7X our FY 13 EPS estimate, a significant discount to both historical averages and the S&P 500.

► Risks to our recommendation and target price include sharp deterioration in the economic climate and consumer confidence, and failure to successfully execute strategic objectives.

► Our 12-month target price of $31, about 9X our FY 13 EPS projection, is based on our DCF analysis, which assumes a weighted average cost of capital of 10.3% and a terminal growth rate of 3.5%.

## Dividend Data (Dates: mm/dd Payment Date: mm/dd/yy)

| Amount ($) | Date Decl. | Ex-Div. Date | Stk. of Record | Payment Date |
|---|---|---|---|---|
| 0.150 | 12/15 | 12/31 | 01/04 | 01/25/11 |
| 0.150 | 03/25 | 04/12 | 04/14 | 05/05/11 |
| 0.150 | 06/15 | 06/30 | 07/05 | 07/26/11 |
| 0.160 | 06/21 | 09/30 | 10/04 | 10/25/11 |

Dividends have been paid since 2003. Source: Company reports.

---

**Please read the Required Disclosures and Analyst Certification on the last page of this report.**

The **McGraw·Hill** Companies

# Best Buy Co. Inc.

**STANDARD &POOR'S**

## Business Summary September 16, 2011

CORPORATE OVERVIEW. This leading consumer electronics retailer operated, as of February 26, 2011, 1,099 Best Buy stores, 177 Best Buy Mobile stand-alone stores, 35 Pacific Sales showrooms and six Magnolia Audio Video stores in the U.S. BBY also operated 885 Carphone Warehouse and 1,555 The Phone House Stores in Europe, 71 Canada Best Buy stores, 146 Future Shop stores in Canada, 166 Five Star stores in China, eight Best Buy China stores, six Best Buy Mexico stores and two Best Buy Turkey stores as of February 26, 2011. On February 21, 2011, Best Buy announced its decision to exit the Turkey market as well as to close its eight Best Buy China stores in FY 12.

U.S. Best Buy stores average approximately 39,000 retail square feet (although the company plans to reduce square footage over the next few years when lease negotiations are made), and offer products in six revenue categories: consumer electronics (37% of FY 11 (Feb.) revenues), home office (37%), entertainment software (14%), appliances (5%), services (6%), and other (1%). The consumer electronics category includes products such as televisions, digital cameras and accessories, digital camcorders and accessories,

e-readers, DVD players, MP3 players and accessories, musical instruments, navigation products, home theater audio systems and components, and mobile electronics including car stereo and satellite radio products. The home office category includes notebook and desktop computers, tablets, monitors, mobile phones and related subscription service commissions, hard drives, networking equipment and related accessories such as printers.

CORPORATE STRATEGY. BBY's three main strategic priorities are: to capture new growth opportunities and target online opportunities; to improve growth and returns in international markets; and to drive structural opportunities to improve returns. Recent expansion of Best Buy Mobile is likely to continue, and Best Buy also plans to increase market share in appliances and gaming.

## Company Financials Fiscal Year Ended Feb. 28

| Per Share Data ($) | 2011 | 2010 | 2009 | 2008 | 2007 | 2006 | 2005 | 2004 | 2003 | 2002 |
|---|---|---|---|---|---|---|---|---|---|---|
| Tangible Book Value | 9.71 | 8.19 | 4.70 | 7.99 | 10.82 | 9.60 | 7.91 | 5.97 | 4.70 | 3.65 |
| Cash Flow | 5.41 | 5.25 | 4.25 | 4.40 | 3.80 | 3.16 | 2.76 | 2.41 | 1.91 | 1.91 |
| Earnings | 3.08 | 3.10 | 2.39 | 3.12 | 2.79 | 2.27 | 1.86 | 1.63 | 1.27 | 1.18 |
| S&P Core Earnings | 3.07 | 3.10 | 2.77 | 3.12 | 2.76 | 2.27 | 1.77 | 1.45 | 1.11 | 1.08 |
| Dividends | 0.58 | 0.56 | 0.54 | 0.46 | 0.36 | 0.31 | 0.50 | 0.27 | Nil | Nil |
| Payout Ratio | 19% | 18% | 23% | 15% | 13% | 14% | 38% | 17% | Nil | Nil |
| Calendar Year | 2010 | 2009 | 2008 | 2007 | 2006 | 2005 | 2004 | 2003 | 2002 | 2001 |
| Prices:High | 48.83 | 45.55 | 52.98 | 53.90 | 59.50 | 18.03 | 41.47 | 41.80 | 35.83 | 33.42 |
| Prices:Low | 30.90 | 23.97 | 16.42 | 41.85 | 43.32 | 14.84 | 29.25 | 15.77 | 11.33 | 12.36 |
| P/E Ratio:High | 16 | 15 | 22 | 17 | 21 | 14 | 22 | 26 | 28 | 28 |
| P/E Ratio:Low | 10 | 8 | 7 | 13 | 16 | 11 | 16 | 10 | 9 | 10 |

| Income Statement Analysis (Million $) | | | | | | | | | | |
|---|---|---|---|---|---|---|---|---|---|---|
| Revenue | 50,272 | 49,694 | 45,015 | 40,023 | 35,934 | 30,848 | 27,433 | 24,547 | 20,946 | 19,597 |
| Operating Income | 3,311 | 3,213 | 2,807 | 2,746 | 2,508 | 2,100 | 1,901 | 1,699 | 1,320 | 1,246 |
| Depreciation | 978 | 926 | 793 | 585 | 509 | 456 | 459 | 385 | 310 | 309 |
| Interest Expense | 87.0 | 94.0 | 94.0 | 62.0 | Nil | 30.0 | 44.0 | 31.0 | 25.0 | 2.00 |
| Pretax Income | 2,080 | 2,196 | 1,707 | 2,225 | 2,130 | 1,721 | 1,443 | 1,296 | 1,014 | 936 |
| Effective Tax Rate | NA | 36.5% | 39.5% | 36.6% | 35.3% | 33.8% | 35.3% | 38.3% | 38.7% | 39.1% |
| Net Income | 1,277 | 1,317 | 1,003 | 1,407 | 1,377 | 1,140 | 934 | 800 | 622 | 570 |
| S&P Core Earnings | 1,272 | 1,317 | 1,163 | 1,407 | 1,364 | 1,140 | 873 | 704 | 538 | 512 |

| Balance Sheet & Other Financial Data (Million $) | | | | | | | | | | |
|---|---|---|---|---|---|---|---|---|---|---|
| Cash | 1,125 | 1,916 | 498 | 1,438 | 1,205 | 681 | 470 | 2,600 | 1,914 | 1,855 |
| Current Assets | 10,473 | 10,566 | 8,192 | 7,342 | 9,081 | 7,985 | 6,903 | 5,724 | 4,867 | 4,611 |
| Total Assets | 17,849 | 18,302 | 15,826 | 12,758 | 13,570 | 11,864 | 10,294 | 8,652 | 7,663 | 7,375 |
| Current Liabilities | 8,663 | 8,978 | 8,435 | 6,769 | 6,301 | 6,056 | 4,959 | 4,501 | 3,793 | 3,730 |
| Long Term Debt | 711 | 1,104 | 1,126 | 627 | 590 | 178 | 528 | 482 | 828 | 813 |
| Common Equity | 7,292 | 6,964 | 4,643 | 4,484 | 6,201 | 5,257 | 4,449 | 3,422 | 2,730 | 2,521 |
| Total Capital | 8,003 | 8,103 | 6,071 | 5,151 | 6,826 | 5,435 | 4,977 | 3,904 | 3,558 | 3,334 |
| Capital Expenditures | 744 | 615 | 1,303 | 797 | 733 | 648 | 502 | 545 | 725 | 627 |
| Cash Flow | 2,255 | 2,243 | 1,796 | 1,992 | 1,886 | 1,596 | 1,393 | 1,185 | 932 | 925 |
| Current Ratio | 1.2 | 1.2 | 1.0 | 1.1 | 1.4 | 1.3 | 1.4 | 1.3 | 1.3 | 1.2 |
| % Long Term Debt of Capitalization | 8.9 | 13.6 | 18.6 | 12.2 | 8.6 | 3.3 | 10.6 | 12.3 | 23.3 | 24.4 |
| % Net Income of Revenue | 2.5 | 2.7 | 2.2 | 3.5 | 3.8 | 3.7 | 3.4 | 3.3 | 3.0 | 2.9 |
| % Return on Assets | 7.1 | 7.7 | 7.0 | 10.7 | 10.8 | 10.3 | 9.9 | 9.8 | 8.3 | 9.3 |
| % Return on Equity | 17.9 | 22.7 | 22.0 | 26.3 | 24.0 | 23.5 | 23.7 | 26.0 | 23.8 | 26.2 |

Data as orig reptd.; bef. results of disc opers/spec. items. Per share data adj. for stk. divs.; EPS diluted. E-Estimated. NA-Not Available. NM-Not Meaningful. NR-Not Ranked. UR-Under Review.

**Office:** 7601 Penn Avenue South, Richfield, MN 55423-3645.
**Telephone:** 612-291-1000.
**Email:** moneytalk@bestbuy.com
**Website:** http://www.bby.com

**Chrmn:** R.M. Schulze
**CEO:** B.J. Dunn
**EVP & General Counsel:** K.J. Nelsen
**SVP, Chief Acctg Officer & Cntlr:** S.S. Grafton

**CFO:** J.L. Muehlbauer
**Investor Contact:** J. Driscoll (612-291-6110)
**Board Members:** L. M. Caputo, B. J. Dunn, K. J. Higgins, R. James, S. Khosla, G. L. Mikan, III, M. H. Paull, R. M. Rebolledo, R. M. Schulze, H. Tyabji, G. R. Vittecoq

**Founded:** 1966
**Domicile:** Minnesota
**Employees:** 180,000

*The McGraw-Hill Companies*

# Big Lots Inc

STANDARD &POOR'S

| S&P Recommendation **HOLD** ★★★☆☆ | Price $36.82 (as of Nov 25, 2011) | 12-Mo. Target Price $35.00 | Investment Style Large-Cap Blend |
|---|---|---|---|

**GICS Sector** Consumer Discretionary
**Sub-Industry** General Merchandise Stores

**Summary** This leading broadline closeout retailer has about 1,400 Big Lots stores in 48 states.

## Key Stock Statistics (Source S&P, Vickers, company reports)

| | | | | | | | |
|---|---|---|---|---|---|---|---|
| 52-Wk Range | $44.44– 27.82 | S&P Oper. EPS 2012E | 2.90 | Market Capitalization(B) | $2.414 | Beta | 1.04 |
| Trailing 12-Month EPS | $2.89 | S&P Oper. EPS 2013E | 3.15 | Yield (%) | Nil | S&P 3-Yr. Proj. EPS CAGR(%) | 8 |
| Trailing 12-Month P/E | 12.7 | P/E on S&P Oper. EPS 2012E | 12.7 | Dividend Rate/Share | Nil | S&P Credit Rating | BBB |
| $10K Invested 5 Yrs Ago | $15,884 | Common Shares Outstg. (M) | 65.6 | Institutional Ownership (%) | NM | | |

## Price Performance

30-Week Mov. Avg. · · · ·   10-Week Mov. Avg. – – –   **GAAP Earnings vs. Previous Year**   Volume Above Avg. ⅢⅢ STARS
12-Mo. Target Price —   Relative Strength —   ▲ Up   ▼ Down   ▶ No Change   Below Avg. ⅢⅢ ★

Options: P, Ph

Analysis prepared by Equity Analyst **Joseph Agnese** on Aug 31, 2011, when the stock traded at **$34.30**.

## Highlights

➤ In FY 12 (Jan.), we expect BIG to focus on improving its food assortment, an underperforming category in FY 11, and its toy offering, a key traffic driver during the holiday selling season. However, factoring in adverse spring weather, which hurt demand for seasonal categories, and difficult sales comparisons in the furniture and home categories, we see flat same-store sales in FY 12, versus FY 11's 2.5% increase. We project about 3% growth in selling square footage based on the company's plans to open 90 new stores (including 25 to 30 in "A" locations) and to close 45 stores. We believe BIG will focus new store openings in its most successful trade areas in an effort to achieve higher sales productivity. All told, we estimate net sales of $5.1 billion in FY 12.

➤ While we expect the company to leverage expenses off forecasted same-store sales growth, we see operating margins narrowing modestly on higher spring clearance markdowns, added costs for new stores, rising commodity, labor and freight costs, and higher projected debit card fees.

➤ Assuming no share repurchase activity, we estimate EPS of $2.90 in FY 12.

## Investment Rationale/Risk

➤ While same-store sales have weakened over the past six quarters, including a 1.5% decline in the second quarter of FY 12, our long-term company outlook remains positive. We look for BIG to weather a tough retail environment and to maintain strong cash flow, supported by its efforts to raise sales productivity and lower its cost structure by better aligning products with customer preferences, increasing the number of new stores in locations with better co-tenant mixes and/or demographics, and building customer loyalty with the Buzz Club Rewards program, which has over 7 million members. That said, we view the shares as appropriately valued at recent levels.

➤ Risks to our recommendation and target price include sales shortfalls due to changes in customer spending patterns, close-out merchandise availability, increased promotional activity by competitors, and adverse/unseasonable weather.

➤ Our 12-month target price of $35 is based on a peer-average forward P/E multiple of 12.0X applied to our FY 12 EPS estimate.

## Qualitative Risk Assessment

| LOW | MEDIUM | HIGH |
|---|---|---|

Our risk assessment reflects our expectation of improving company fundamentals, supported by BIG's new merchandising and cost reduction initiatives, offset by what we see as a challenging retail environment that could hinder a turnaround.

## Quantitative Evaluations

**S&P Quality Ranking**          B

| D | C | B- | B | B+ | A- | A | A+ |
|---|---|---|---|---|---|---|---|

**Relative Strength Rank**          STRONG

78

LOWEST = 1          HIGHEST = 99

## Revenue/Earnings Data

**Revenue (Million $)**

| | 1Q | 2Q | 3Q | 4Q | Year |
|---|---|---|---|---|---|
| 2012 | 1,227 | 1,167 | -- | -- | -- |
| 2011 | 1,235 | 1,142 | 1,056 | 1,519 | 4,952 |
| 2010 | 1,142 | 1,087 | 1,035 | 1,463 | 4,727 |
| 2009 | 1,152 | 1,105 | 1,022 | 1,367 | 4,645 |
| 2008 | 1,128 | 1,085 | 1,031 | 1,412 | 4,656 |
| 2007 | 1,092 | 1,057 | 1,050 | 1,545 | 4,743 |

**Earnings Per Share ($)**

| | 1Q | 2Q | 3Q | 4Q | Year |
|---|---|---|---|---|---|
| 2012 | 0.70 | 0.50 | E0.23 | E1.51 | E2.90 |
| 2011 | 0.68 | 0.48 | 0.23 | 1.46 | 2.83 |
| 2010 | 0.44 | 0.35 | 0.37 | 1.28 | 2.44 |
| 2009 | 0.42 | 0.32 | 0.15 | 1.00 | 1.89 |
| 2008 | 0.26 | 0.32 | 0.14 | 0.97 | 1.47 |
| 2007 | 0.13 | 0.04 | 0.02 | 0.83 | 1.01 |

Fiscal year ended Jan. 31. Next earnings report expected: Early December. EPS Estimates based on S&P Operating Earnings; historical GAAP earnings are as reported.

## Dividend Data

Proceeds from the sale of rights amounting to $0.01 a share were distributed in 2001.

---

**Please read the Required Disclosures and Analyst Certification on the last page of this report.**

The McGraw·Hill Companies

# Big Lots Inc

**STANDARD &POOR'S**

## Business Summary August 31, 2011

CORPORATE OVERVIEW. Big Lot's strategy is to position itself as a preferred shopping destination for middle-income consumers seeking savings on brand-name closeouts and other value-priced merchandise. The company's product offerings range from everyday essentials such as food and other consumables, to more discretionary-purchase items, including furniture, holiday assortments, electronics, apparel, and small appliances. In our view, FY 07 (Jan.) was a transitional year for BIG, as the company slowed chain expansion in order to better focus on implementing operational changes to reverse a two-year trend of declining operating profits. Since then, we have seen BIG apply successful new merchandising and marketing strategies to further strengthen its financial performance. As of April 30, 2011, the company operated 1,405 Big Lots stores in 48 states.

CORPORATE STRATEGY. BIG's primary growth driver is expansion. The company seeks to build on its leadership position in broadline closeout retailing by expanding its market presence in both existing and new markets. From FY 00 through FY 05, the company increased its selling square footage at a compound annual growth rate (CAGR) of about 6% as it expanded its store count

from 1,230 to 1,502. In FY 06, BIG continued to expand its store base, adding 73 new stores. However, the company also accelerated the closure of underperforming locations as part of its What's Important Now (WIN) turnaround strategy, which was announced in November 2005. BIG closed 174 stores in FY 06, ending the fiscal year with 1,401 stores in 47 states.

WIN is aimed at improving BIG's financial performance via changes in the company's merchandising, cost structure, and real estate. As its first steps, BIG is attempting to raise the productivity of its chain by closing low-volume stores located mainly in small, rural, or weaker performing markets, and by moving from an opportunistic real estate strategy to one focused on its most successful trade areas. These areas include California, Arizona, Washington, New York and New Jersey. Between FY 07 and FY 09, the company closed 101 underperforming stores and opened only 39 new stores.

## Company Financials Fiscal Year Ended Jan. 31

| Per Share Data ($) | 2011 | 2010 | 2009 | 2008 | 2007 | 2006 | 2005 | 2004 | 2003 | 2002 |
|---|---|---|---|---|---|---|---|---|---|---|
| Tangible Book Value | 12.81 | 12.35 | 9.61 | 13.34 | 11.10 | 9.47 | 9.54 | 9.51 | 8.83 | 8.11 |
| Cash Flow | 3.83 | 3.30 | 2.84 | 2.34 | 1.91 | 1.15 | 1.17 | 1.56 | 1.38 | 0.37 |
| Earnings | 2.83 | 2.44 | 1.89 | 1.47 | 1.01 | 0.14 | 0.27 | 0.77 | 0.65 | -0.25 |
| S&P Core Earnings | 2.85 | 2.40 | 1.86 | 1.38 | 1.06 | 0.05 | 0.25 | 0.78 | 0.60 | -0.32 |
| Dividends | NA | Nil | Nil | Nil | Nil | Nil | Nil | Nil | Nil | Nil |
| Payout Ratio | NA | Nil | Nil | Nil | Nil | Nil | Nil | Nil | Nil | Nil |
| Calendar Year | 2010 | 2009 | 2008 | 2007 | 2006 | 2005 | 2004 | 2003 | 2002 | 2001 |
| Prices:High | 41.42 | 29.75 | 35.33 | 36.15 | 26.36 | 14.29 | 15.62 | 18.39 | 19.90 | 15.75 |
| Prices:Low | 27.82 | 12.62 | 12.40 | 15.35 | 11.83 | 10.06 | 11.05 | 9.92 | 9.75 | 7.15 |
| P/E Ratio:High | 15 | 12 | 19 | 25 | 26 | NM | 58 | 24 | 31 | NM |
| P/E Ratio:Low | 10 | 5 | 7 | 10 | 12 | NM | 41 | 13 | 15 | NM |

| Income Statement Analysis (Million $) | | | | | | | | | | |
|---|---|---|---|---|---|---|---|---|---|---|
| Revenue | 4,952 | 4,727 | 4,645 | 4,656 | 4,743 | 4,430 | 4,375 | 4,174 | 3,869 | 3,433 |
| Operating Income | 436 | 388 | 334 | 315 | 276 | 141 | 172 | 222 | 231 | 43.4 |
| Depreciation | 78.6 | 74.9 | 78.6 | 88.5 | 101 | 115 | 104 | 93.7 | 85.7 | 72.0 |
| Interest Expense | 2.57 | 1.84 | 5.28 | 2.51 | 0.68 | 6.27 | 24.8 | 16.4 | 21.0 | 20.5 |
| Pretax Income | 355 | 323 | 250 | 239 | 170 | 20.9 | 43.3 | 113 | 125 | -48.7 |
| Effective Tax Rate | NA | 37.7% | 38.0% | 36.8% | 34.0% | 24.8% | 29.8% | 20.6% | 39.5% | NM |
| Net Income | 223 | 201 | 155 | 151 | 113 | 15.7 | 30.4 | 89.9 | 75.7 | -29.5 |
| S&P Core Earnings | 224 | 198 | 153 | 142 | 118 | 4.93 | 27.8 | 91.6 | 70.7 | -36.7 |

| Balance Sheet & Other Financial Data (Million $) | | | | | | | | | | |
|---|---|---|---|---|---|---|---|---|---|---|
| Cash | 178 | 284 | 34.8 | 37.1 | 282 | 1.71 | 2.52 | 174 | 160 | NA |
| Current Assets | 1,052 | 1,123 | 871 | 891 | 1,149 | 994 | 1,035 | 1,134 | NA | NA |
| Total Assets | 1,620 | 1,669 | 1,432 | 1,444 | 1,721 | 1,625 | 1,734 | 1,801 | 1,656 | 1,470 |
| Current Liabilities | 542 | 543 | 515 | 500 | 474 | 437 | 413 | 416 | NA | NA |
| Long Term Debt | NA | NA | 3.64 | 165 | Nil | 5.50 | 159 | 204 | 204 | 204 |
| Common Equity | 947 | 1,001 | 775 | 638 | 1,130 | 1,167 | 1,075 | 1,109 | 1,020 | 923 |
| Total Capital | 947 | 1,001 | 837 | 804 | 1,130 | 1,173 | 1,235 | 1,313 | 1,224 | 1,127 |
| Capital Expenditures | 108 | 78.7 | 88.7 | 60.4 | 35.9 | 68.5 | 135 | 170 | 110 | NA |
| Cash Flow | 301 | 273 | 233 | 240 | 214 | 130 | 135 | 184 | 161 | 42.5 |
| Current Ratio | 1.9 | 2.1 | 1.7 | 1.8 | 2.4 | 2.3 | 2.5 | 2.7 | NA | NA |
| % Long Term Debt of Capitalization | Nil | Nil | 0.4 | 20.6 | Nil | 0.5 | 12.9 | 15.5 | 16.7 | 18.1 |
| % Net Income of Revenue | 4.5 | 4.3 | 3.3 | 3.3 | 2.4 | 0.4 | 0.7 | 2.2 | 2.0 | NM |
| % Return on Assets | 13.5 | 13.0 | 10.8 | 9.6 | 6.7 | 0.9 | 1.7 | 5.2 | 4.8 | NM |
| % Return on Equity | 22.9 | 22.7 | 21.9 | 17.1 | 10.2 | 1.4 | 2.8 | 8.4 | 7.8 | NM |

Data as orig reptd.; bef. results of disc opers/spec. items. Per share data adj. for stk. divs.; EPS diluted. E-Estimated. NA-Not Available. NM-Not Meaningful. NR-Not Ranked. UR-Under Review.

**Office:** 300 Phillipi Road, P O Box 28512, Columbus, OH 43228-5311.
**Telephone:** 614-278-6800.
**Website:** http://www.biglots.com
**Chrmn, Pres & CEO:** S.S. Fishman

**EVP, CFO & Chief Acctg Officer:** J.R. Cooper
**Investor Contact:** T.A. Johnson (614-278-6622)
**Chief Admin Officer:** J.C. Martin
**Secy & General Counsel:** C.W. Haubiel, II

**Board Members:** J. P. Berger, S. S. Fishman, P. J. Hayes, D. T. Kollat, B. J. Lauderback, P. E. Mallott, R. Solt, J. R. Tener, D. B. Tishkoff

**Founded:** 1983
**Domicile:** Ohio
**Employees:** 35,600

The McGraw-Hill Companies

# Biogen Idec Inc

**STANDARD &POOR'S**

| S&P Recommendation HOLD ★★★☆☆ | Price $109.20 (as of Nov 25, 2011) | 12-Mo. Target Price $120.00 | Investment Style Large-Cap Growth |
|---|---|---|---|

**GICS Sector** Health Care
**Sub-Industry** Biotechnology

**Summary** This major biopharmaceutical concern develops and markets targeted therapies for the treatment of multiple sclerosis, non-Hodgkin's lymphoma and rheumatoid arthritis.

## Key Stock Statistics (Source S&P, Vickers, company reports)

| | | | | | | | |
|---|---|---|---|---|---|---|---|
| 52-Wk Range | $120.66–63.77 | S&P Oper. EPS 2011E | 5.84 | Market Capitalization(B) | $26.527 | Beta | 0.76 |
| Trailing 12-Month EPS | $4.80 | S&P Oper. EPS 2012E | 6.34 | Yield (%) | Nil | S&P 3-Yr. Proj. EPS CAGR(%) | 13 |
| Trailing 12-Month P/E | 22.8 | P/E on S&P Oper. EPS 2011E | 18.7 | Dividend Rate/Share | Nil | S&P Credit Rating | BBB+ |
| $10K Invested 5 Yrs Ago | $21,200 | Common Shares Outstg. (M) | 242.9 | Institutional Ownership (%) | 91 | | |

## Price Performance

30-Week Mov. Avg. · · · 10-Week Mov. Avg. - - GAAP Earnings vs. Previous Year   Volume Above Avg. ▦ STARS
12-Mo. Target Price — Relative Strength — ▲ Up ▼ Down ▶ No Change   Below Avg. ▦ ★

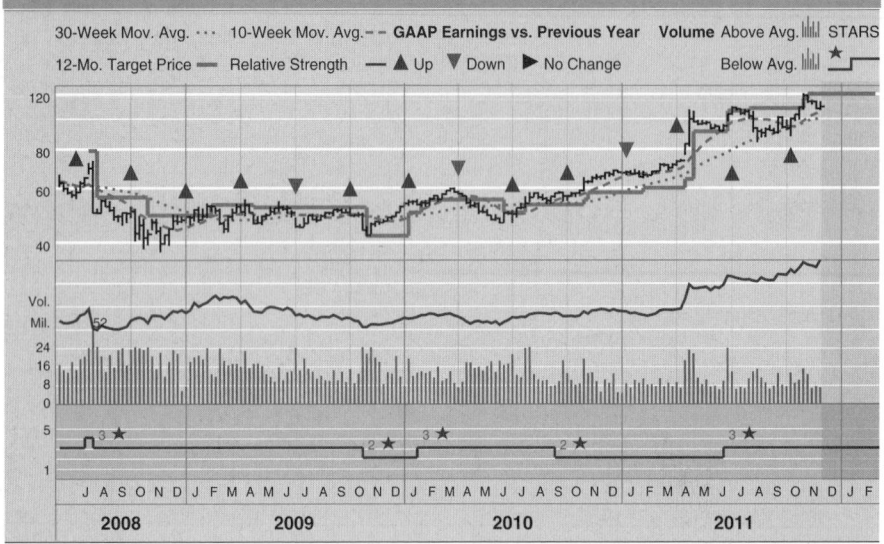

Options: ASE, CBOE, P, Ph

Analysis prepared by Equity Analyst **Steven Silver** on Nov 04, 2011, when the stock traded at **$113.69**.

## Qualitative Risk Assessment

| LOW | MEDIUM | HIGH |
|---|---|---|

Our risk assessment reflects that Biogen Idec sells products in increasingly competitive markets, and its biggest near-term growth driver faces safety concerns, requiring a comprehensive risk monitoring and minimization program.

## Quantitative Evaluations

**S&P Quality Ranking**  B

| D | C | B- | B | B+ | A- | A | A+ |
|---|---|---|---|---|---|---|---|

**Relative Strength Rank**  STRONG
91
LOWEST = 1    HIGHEST = 99

## Revenue/Earnings Data

**Revenue (Million $)**

| | 1Q | 2Q | 3Q | 4Q | Year |
|---|---|---|---|---|---|
| 2011 | 1,203 | 1,209 | 1,310 | -- | -- |
| 2010 | 1,109 | 1,213 | 1,176 | 1,219 | 4,716 |
| 2009 | 1,037 | 1,093 | 1,121 | 1,127 | 4,377 |
| 2008 | 942.2 | 993.4 | 1,093 | 1,069 | 4,098 |
| 2007 | 715.9 | 773.2 | 789.2 | 893.3 | 3,172 |
| 2006 | 611.2 | 660.0 | 703.5 | 708.3 | 2,683 |

**Earnings Per Share ($)**

| | 1Q | 2Q | 3Q | 4Q | Year |
|---|---|---|---|---|---|
| 2011 | 1.20 | 1.18 | 1.43 | E1.48 | E5.84 |
| 2010 | 0.80 | 1.12 | 1.05 | 0.99 | 3.94 |
| 2009 | 0.84 | 0.49 | 0.95 | 1.06 | 3.35 |
| 2008 | 0.54 | 0.70 | 0.70 | 0.70 | 2.65 |
| 2007 | 0.38 | 0.54 | 0.41 | 0.67 | 1.99 |
| 2006 | 0.35 | -0.50 | 0.45 | 0.32 | 0.62 |

Fiscal year ended Dec. 31. Next earnings report expected: Early February. EPS Estimates based on S&P Operating Earnings; historical GAAP earnings are as reported.

## Dividend Data

No cash dividends have been paid.

## Highlights

➤ We see revenue growth of 6% in 2011, to $5.0 billion, and 3.5% in 2012, to $5.18 billion, driven by accelerating Tysabri expansion, which we view as BIIB's key near-term revenue growth driver. We expect recent price increases for both Tysabri and Avonex to support sales in an increasingly competitive multiple sclerosis market. We see Rituxan revenues moderating, and we expect BIIB to recognize $50 million lower revenues on the drug in 2011 due to a royalty dispute with partner Roche.

➤ We expect operating expenses near 44% of total revenues in 2011 and 2012, down from 48% in 2010, after a November 2010 restructuring intended to save $300 million annually, mostly from R&D. We see BIIB aggressively pushing to re-ignite Avonex usage, but we view it as well positioned to contain expense growth by launching new drugs into an established global infrastructure. BIIB had $2.9 billion in cash and securities as of September 30, 2011.

➤ Our adjusted 2011 and 2012 EPS estimates of $5.84 and $6.34, respectively, exclude amortization of intangible assets and acquired in-process R&D costs. BIIB repurchased 40 million of its shares in 2010.

## Investment Rationale/Risk

➤ Our hold recommendation is based on our view that BIIB's current valuation reflects re-accelerating revenue growth prospects with new products from its core multiple sclerosis franchise. We are encouraged by positive Phase III data to date for orally dosed BG-12, which showed robust relapse reduction after two years in two Phase III studies, and we see its safety to date positioning the drug for a 2013 launch and solid market share in a competitive MS market. We also believe that Tysabri sales are likely to continue to grow, despite a rise in cases of PML infection, as progress on an assay to stratify patient risk advances, and as it retains superior efficacy in treating MS. In addition, we are encouraged by progress in BIIB's expanding long-term clinical pipeline.

➤ Risks to our recommendation and target price include slowing Tysabri use due to safety concerns and competition, and delays in regulatory approval of BIIB's oral MS drug BG-12.

➤ Our 12-month target price of $120 applies a 19X multiple to our 2012 adjusted EPS estimate of $6.34, a premium to the large-cap sector peer average to reflect our view of enhanced long-term growth prospects.

---

**Please read the Required Disclosures and Analyst Certification on the last page of this report.**

The McGraw·Hill Companies

# Biogen Idec Inc

## Business Summary November 04, 2011

CORPORATE OVERVIEW. Formed through the 2003 merger of IDEC Pharmaceuticals and Biogen, Biogen Idec researches, develops and markets therapeutics to treat cancer and autoimmune diseases.

BIIB's core franchise has been in autoimmune disorder multiple sclerosis, led by Avonex, approved by the FDA in 1996 to treat relapsing multiple sclerosis (MS), and in Europe in 1997. Avonex sales were $2.52 billion in 2010, up 8% from $2.32 billion in 2009. Recent growth has been largely driven by price increases, as competition has slowed prescription growth. A new Avonex method of use patent issued in 2009 expires in 2026, extending the prior 2013 deadline. In May 2010, BIIB filed a lawsuit against rivals marketing similar beta interferons like Avonex, seeking sales royalties due to patent infringement.

Rituxan is a monoclonal antibody that binds to and eliminates CD-20 protein positive B-cells. The drug is approved for refractory non-Hodgkin's lymphomas (NHL) and rheumatoid arthritis. In November 2010, a co-promotion pact in the U.S. with Roche (via Genentech) was amended to a royalty-based agreement; BIIB eliminated its sales force in order to pare operating expenses on the drug. BIIB already earned royalties from Roche on ex-U.S. sales. Rituxan produced revenues to BIIB of about $1.1 billion in 2010, 2% below 2009 levels as ex-U.S. royalties have begun to expire. Rituxan is being explored for several new uses, but failed in progressive MS and lupus during 2008. A next-generation anti-CD20 candidate under co-development, ocrelizumab, was dis-

continued in May 2010 for rheumatoid arthritis due to safety concerns. In October 2010, BIIB and Roche amended their co-development pact for ocrelizumab, whereby BIIB would receive sales royalties while Roche assumes primary development cost responsibilities in multiple sclerosis.

Tysabri, developed with Elan Corp., was approved for treating relapsing MS in late 2004. However, three cases of progressive multifocal leukoencephalopathy (PML) -- a rare, fatal nervous system disorder -- in 2005 prompted its removal from the market. Following safety evaluations and further data analyses, Tysabri was re-launched in the U.S. and Europe in 2006, with a stringent distribution program. As of September 30, 2011, BIIB cited 63,500 patients on Tysabri worldwide. As of September 2011, there were 159 confirmed cases of PML in Tysabri patients, and the drug's label in the U.S. and Europe reflects higher PML risk as therapy duration passes two years. BIIB and Elan are developing an assay to identify patients with JC virus, which causes PML, which is available in Europe as of June 2011, and could receive FDA approval by early 2012, in our view. BIIB recognized $900 million of Tysabri revenues in 2010, 16% higher than the $776 million in 2009.

## Company Financials Fiscal Year Ended Dec. 31

| Per Share Data ($) | 2010 | 2009 | 2008 | 2007 | 2006 | 2005 | 2004 | 2003 | 2002 | 2001 |
|---|---|---|---|---|---|---|---|---|---|---|
| Tangible Book Value | 10.76 | 11.69 | 8.70 | 6.44 | 9.60 | 8.38 | 7.08 | 6.85 | 7.25 | 6.22 |
| Cash Flow | 4.91 | 4.82 | 4.22 | 3.18 | 1.71 | 1.63 | 1.35 | -4.57 | 0.88 | 0.62 |
| Earnings | 3.94 | 3.35 | 2.65 | 1.99 | 0.62 | 0.47 | 0.07 | -4.92 | 0.85 | 0.59 |
| S&P Core Earnings | 3.95 | 3.32 | 2.76 | 2.01 | 0.69 | 0.16 | -0.06 | -5.13 | 0.54 | 0.34 |
| Dividends | Nil | Nil | Nil | Nil | Nil | Nil | Nil | Nil | Nil | Nil |
| Payout Ratio | Nil | Nil | Nil | Nil | Nil | Nil | Nil | Nil | Nil | Nil |
| Prices:High | 68.60 | 55.34 | 73.59 | 84.75 | 52.72 | 70.00 | 68.13 | 42.15 | 71.40 | 75.00 |
| Prices:Low | 45.96 | 41.75 | 37.21 | 42.86 | 40.24 | 33.18 | 36.60 | 27.80 | 20.76 | 32.63 |
| P/E Ratio:High | 17 | 17 | 28 | 43 | 85 | NM | NM | NM | 84 | NM |
| P/E Ratio:Low | 12 | 12 | 14 | 22 | 65 | NM | NM | NM | 24 | NM |

**Income Statement Analysis** (Million $)

| | 2010 | 2009 | 2008 | 2007 | 2006 | 2005 | 2004 | 2003 | 2002 | 2001 |
|---|---|---|---|---|---|---|---|---|---|---|
| Revenue | 4,716 | 4,377 | 4,098 | 3,172 | 2,683 | 2,423 | 2,212 | 679 | 404 | 273 |
| Operating Income | 1,923 | 1,723 | 1,832 | 1,260 | 1,117 | 756 | 483 | 14.6 | 285 | 137 |
| Depreciation | 354 | 428 | 462 | 380 | 376 | 402 | 439 | 61.3 | 10.2 | 6.31 |
| Interest Expense | 36.1 | 35.8 | 75.2 | 50.6 | Nil | Nil | 18.9 | 15.2 | 16.1 | 7.30 |
| Pretax Income | 1,230 | 1,333 | 1,149 | 852 | 492 | 256 | 64.1 | -881 | 232 | 162 |
| Effective Tax Rate | NA | 26.7% | 31.8% | 32.0% | 56.6% | 37.3% | 60.9% | NM | 36.0% | 37.1% |
| Net Income | 1,005 | 970 | 783 | 638 | 214 | 161 | 25.1 | -875 | 148 | 102 |
| S&P Core Earnings | 1,007 | 961 | 816 | 642 | 237 | 56.6 | -21.6 | -914 | 93.4 | 61.4 |

**Balance Sheet & Other Financial Data** (Million $)

| | 2010 | 2009 | 2008 | 2007 | 2006 | 2005 | 2004 | 2003 | 2002 | 2001 |
|---|---|---|---|---|---|---|---|---|---|---|
| Cash | 1,208 | 1,264 | 1,342 | 1,187 | 2,315 | 851 | 1,058 | 836 | 373 | 426 |
| Current Assets | 2,540 | 2,481 | 2,458 | 2,368 | 1,713 | 1,618 | 1,931 | 1,839 | 978 | 700 |
| Total Assets | 8,092 | 8,552 | 8,479 | 8,629 | 8,553 | 8,367 | 9,166 | 9,504 | 2,060 | 1,141 |
| Current Liabilities | 1,050 | 715 | 923 | 2,189 | 583 | 583 | 1,261 | 405 | 56.2 | 35.3 |
| Long Term Debt | 1,066 | 1,080 | 1,085 | 1,563 | 96.7 | 43.4 | 102 | 887 | 866 | 136 |
| Common Equity | 5,449 | 6,222 | 5,806 | 5,534 | 7,150 | 6,906 | 6,826 | 7,053 | 1,110 | 956 |
| Total Capital | 6,653 | 7,362 | 7,248 | 6,108 | 7,890 | 7,712 | 7,850 | 9,049 | 1,976 | 1,092 |
| Capital Expenditures | 173 | 166 | 276 | 284 | 198 | 318 | 361 | 301 | 166 | 0.07 |
| Cash Flow | 1,251 | 1,396 | 1,244 | 1,017 | 590 | 563 | 465 | -814 | 158 | 108 |
| Current Ratio | 2.4 | 3.5 | 2.7 | 1.1 | 2.9 | 2.8 | 1.5 | 4.5 | 17.4 | 19.8 |
| % Long Term Debt of Capitalization | 16.0 | 14.7 | 15.0 | 0.9 | 1.2 | 0.6 | 1.3 | 9.8 | 43.8 | 12.4 |
| % Net Income of Revenue | 21.3 | 22.2 | 19.1 | 20.1 | 8.0 | 6.6 | 1.1 | NM | 36.6 | 37.3 |
| % Return on Assets | 12.1 | 11.4 | 9.2 | 7.4 | 2.5 | 1.8 | 0.3 | NM | 9.3 | 10.2 |
| % Return on Equity | 17.2 | 16.1 | 13.8 | 10.1 | 3.0 | 2.3 | 0.4 | NM | 14.3 | 12.3 |

Data as orig reptd.; bef. results of disc opers/spec. items. Per share data adj. for stk. divs.; EPS diluted. E-Estimated. NA-Not Available. NM-Not Meaningful. NR-Not Ranked. UR-Under Review.

**Office:** 133 Boston Post Road, Weston, MA 02493.
**Telephone:** 781-464-2000.
**Website:** http://www.biogenidec.com
**Chrmn:** W.D. Young

**CEO:** G.A. Scangos
**COO:** T. Kingsley
**EVP & CFO:** P.J. Clancy
**SVP & CTO:** M.D. Kowolenko

**Investor Contact:** R. Jacobson (617-679-3710)
**Board Members:** A. J. Denner, C. D. Dorsa, N. L. Leaming, R. C. Mulligan, R. W. Pangia, S. Papadopoulos, B. S. Posner, E. K. Rowinsky, G. A. Scangos, L. Schenk, S. A. Sherwin, W. D. Young

**Founded:** 1985
**Domicile:** Delaware
**Employees:** 4,850

The McGraw·Hill Companies

# BlackRock Inc

**STANDARD &POOR'S**

| S&P Recommendation **HOLD** ★★★★☆ | Price $151.27 (as of Nov 25, 2011) | 12-Mo. Target Price $185.00 | Investment Style Large-Cap Growth |

**GICS Sector** Financials
**Sub-Industry** Asset Management & Custody Banks

**Summary** BlackRock is one of the leading investment management companies in the U.S.

## Key Stock Statistics (Source S&P, Vickers, company reports)

| | | | | | | | |
|---|---|---|---|---|---|---|---|
| 52-Wk Range | $209.77– 137.00 | S&P Oper. EPS 2011**E** | 12.13 | Market Capitalization(B) | $27.056 | Beta | 1.55 |
| Trailing 12-Month EPS | $12.67 | S&P Oper. EPS 2012**E** | 14.31 | Yield (%) | 3.64 | S&P 3-Yr. Proj. EPS CAGR(%) | 33 |
| Trailing 12-Month P/E | 11.9 | P/E on S&P Oper. EPS 2011**E** | 12.5 | Dividend Rate/Share | $5.50 | S&P Credit Rating | A+ |
| $10K Invested 5 Yrs Ago | $11,208 | Common Shares Outstg. (M) | 178.9 | Institutional Ownership (%) | 66 | | |

## Price Performance

30-Week Mov. Avg. · · · · 10-Week Mov. Avg. - - **GAAP Earnings vs. Previous Year**   Volume Above Avg. ||||| STARS
12-Mo. Target Price — Relative Strength — ▲ Up ▼ Down ▶ No Change   Below Avg. ||||| ★

Options: CBOE, P, Ph

Analysis prepared by Equity Analyst **Cathy Seifert** on Nov 15, 2011, when the stock traded at **$165.88**.

## Highlights

➤ BLK's assets under management (AUM) of $3.35 trillion at September 30, 2011, were down 3%, year to year. We expect iShares/exchange-traded products, institutional index fixed income products and multi-asset class products to be the largest contributors to AUM growth in the near term. We think an increased level of volatility in markets and choppy economic data are likely to continue in the near term, putting the aforementioned products and services in higher demand. We expect institutional investors to favor fixed income products and alternative assets, which we think will result in a stable investment management fee rate contributing to BLK's earnings growth. We also expect demand for BLK's Solutions business to continue as institutions seek outsourcing and risk management functions.

➤ BLK's compensation ratio increased by 130 basis points sequentially, but the operating margin widened to 35.9%, from 35.6%. We expect focused expense management to lift operating margins to 37% in 2011, from 34.8% in 2010.

➤ We estimate EPS of $12.13 in 2011 and $14.31 in 2012.

## Investment Rationale/Risk

➤ We believe risk appetite is still relatively healthy despite being recently muted by political dysfunction in the U.S. and Europe. We see investment trends evolving in the wake of major concerns such as inflation and U.S. deficit reduction legislation that favor BLK's investment products and advisory services. We think the pace of net inflows will slow near term, but we still see investment advisory fees and robust demand for exchange-traded products supporting top-line growth in 2011. Given our view of decelerating inflows in the near term, we expect organic AUM growth to slow, which may suppress BLK's earnings multiple somewhat. We think BLK's new business pipeline is strong going into 2012, but we remain neutral on BLK shares, as we view them as fairly valued.

➤ Risks to our recommendation and target price include depreciating securities markets and material regulatory changes.

➤ Our 12-month target price of $185 is equal to about 13X our forward EPS estimate of $14.31, a discount to BLK's historical multiple to reflect the uncertain effects of regulatory changes and volatile securities markets.

## Qualitative Risk Assessment

| LOW | **MEDIUM** | HIGH |

Our risk assessment for BlackRock reflects our view of potential integration challenges and the company's exposure to equity markets, offset by our view of its success in expanding its fixed income franchise and strong brand.

## Quantitative Evaluations

**S&P Quality Ranking** B+

| D | C | B- | B | **B+** | A- | A | A+ |

**Relative Strength Rank** MODERATE

55

LOWEST = 1     HIGHEST = 99

## Revenue/Earnings Data

**Revenue (Million $)**

| | 1Q | 2Q | 3Q | 4Q | Year |
|---|---|---|---|---|---|
| 2011 | 2,282 | 2,347 | 2,225 | -- | -- |
| 2010 | 1,995 | 2,032 | 2,092 | 2,493 | 8,612 |
| 2009 | 987.0 | 1,029 | 1,140 | 1,544 | 4,700 |
| 2008 | 1,300 | 1,387 | 1,313 | 1,064 | 5,064 |
| 2007 | 1,005 | 1,097 | 1,298 | 1,444 | 4,845 |
| 2006 | 395.7 | 360.7 | 323.1 | 1,019 | 2,098 |

**Earnings Per Share ($)**

| | | | | | |
|---|---|---|---|---|---|
| 2011 | 2.89 | 3.21 | 3.23 | E3.15 | E12.13 |
| 2010 | 2.17 | 2.21 | 2.83 | 3.35 | 10.55 |
| 2009 | 0.62 | 1.59 | 2.27 | 1.60 | 6.09 |
| 2008 | 1.82 | 2.05 | 1.63 | 0.40 | 5.91 |
| 2007 | 1.48 | 1.69 | 1.94 | 2.43 | 7.53 |
| 2006 | 1.06 | 0.95 | 0.28 | 1.28 | 3.87 |

Fiscal year ended Dec. 31. Next earnings report expected: NA. EPS Estimates based on S&P Operating Earnings; historical GAAP earnings are as reported.

## Dividend Data (Dates: mm/dd Payment Date: mm/dd/yy)

| Amount ($) | Date Decl. | Ex-Div. Date | Stk. of Record | Payment Date |
|---|---|---|---|---|
| 1.375 | 02/24 | 03/03 | 03/07 | 03/23/11 |
| 1.375 | 05/25 | 06/03 | 06/07 | 06/23/11 |
| 1.375 | 06/22 | 08/31 | 09/02 | 09/22/11 |
| 1.375 | 09/27 | 12/01 | 12/05 | 12/23/11 |

Dividends have been paid since 2003. Source: Company reports.

---

**Please read the Required Disclosures and Analyst Certification on the last page of this report.**

The **McGraw·Hill** Companies

# BlackRock Inc

**STANDARD &POOR'S**

## Business Summary November 15, 2011

CORPORATE OVERVIEW. BlackRock is one of the leading investment management companies in the U.S., known for its expertise in fixed income asset management. We think the company has benefited from the globalization of capital markets and the growing demand for more sophisticated risk management tools and solutions. The firm had more than $3.6 trillion of assets under management as of the end of June 2011, and we believe the company has been gaining market share, aided by its significant scale and untarnished reputation in the marketplace. PNC Financial Services Group acquired BLK in 1995 and subsequently consolidated a substantial part of its asset management businesses under the BlackRock name in 1998. PNC subsequently took the company public in October 1999, which we think has increased its visibility and helped it win international mandates.

We are encouraged by the new-look BlackRock, with a more diverse product line of fixed income and equity-oriented funds. At the end of 2010, fixed-income products accounted for 32% of total assets under management, equity products 48%, multi-asset class products 5%, alternative investment products 3%, advisory assets 4%, and cash management 8%. We are impressed with the breadth of BLK's institutional client base, which includes domestic tax-exempt institutions, such as public and private pension plans, foundations and endowments. BLK serves individual investors through its private client and wealth management groups, focusing on high-net-worth individuals and family offices.

We are also pleased with the growth at BlackRock Solutions, and we expect margins for the business to expand slowly following the aggressive addition of head count. BLK Solutions was launched in 2000, consisting of risk management services and enterprise investment system outsourcing targeted at a variety of institutional clients. We see strong demand for BLK's asset and risk management products internationally, particularly in Europe and Asia, aided by the opening of several offices. We also expect further financial markets advisory work to help increase assets under management in the Solutions business. Recent financial market turmoil has caused a number of clients, including the U.S. federal government, to seek out BlackRock to help liquidate troubled asset classes, which should provide another source of income.

## Company Financials Fiscal Year Ended Dec. 31

| Per Share Data ($) | 2010 | 2009 | 2008 | 2007 | 2006 | 2005 | 2004 | 2003 | 2002 | 2001 |
|---|---|---|---|---|---|---|---|---|---|---|
| Tangible Book Value | NM | NM | NM | NM | NM | 6.84 | 9.18 | 8.13 | 6.96 | 4.72 |
| Cash Flow | 12.25 | 7.99 | 7.65 | 9.03 | 4.74 | 3.96 | 2.48 | 2.68 | 2.35 | 2.06 |
| Earnings | 10.55 | 6.09 | 5.91 | 7.53 | 3.87 | 3.50 | 2.17 | 2.36 | 2.04 | 1.65 |
| S&P Core Earnings | 10.55 | 6.11 | 5.93 | 7.49 | 3.86 | 3.38 | 1.90 | 2.13 | 1.91 | 1.55 |
| Dividends | 4.00 | 3.12 | 3.12 | 2.68 | 1.68 | 1.20 | 1.00 | 0.40 | Nil | Nil |
| Payout Ratio | 38% | 51% | 53% | 36% | 43% | 34% | 46% | 17% | Nil | Nil |
| Prices:High | 243.80 | 241.67 | 249.37 | 224.54 | 161.49 | 113.87 | 78.24 | 53.63 | 47.60 | 44.50 |
| Prices:Low | 138.42 | 88.91 | 94.78 | 139.20 | 105.74 | 69.38 | 53.03 | 39.58 | 33.55 | 30.76 |
| P/E Ratio:High | 23 | 40 | 42 | 30 | 42 | 33 | 36 | 23 | 23 | 27 |
| P/E Ratio:Low | 13 | 15 | 16 | 18 | 27 | 20 | 24 | 17 | 16 | 19 |

| Income Statement Analysis (Million $) | | | | | | | | | | |
|---|---|---|---|---|---|---|---|---|---|---|
| Income Interest | 29.0 | NA | 65.0 | 74.5 | 66.3 | 43.1 | 35.5 | 23.3 | 9.50 | 11.6 |
| Income Other | Nil | Nil | Nil | Nil | Nil | Nil | Nil | Nil | Nil | Nil |
| Total Income | 8,612 | 4,700 | 5,064 | 4,845 | 2,098 | 1,191 | 725 | 598 | 577 | 533 |
| General Expenses | 5,454 | 3,275 | 3,325 | 3,421 | 1,699 | 882 | 574 | 391 | 382 | 389 |
| Interest Expense | 150 | 68.0 | 66.0 | 49.4 | 9.92 | 7.92 | 0.84 | 0.72 | 0.68 | 0.76 |
| Depreciation | 310 | 239 | 232 | 197 | 72.8 | 30.9 | 20.7 | 21.4 | 20.2 | 26.0 |
| Net Income | 2,063 | 875 | 786 | 995 | 323 | 234 | 143 | 155 | 133 | 107 |
| S&P Core Earnings | 2,033 | 853 | 789 | 990 | 322 | 226 | 125 | 141 | 125 | 101 |

| Balance Sheet & Other Financial Data (Million $) | | | | | | | | | | |
|---|---|---|---|---|---|---|---|---|---|---|
| Cash | 3,460 | 4,708 | 2,032 | 1,656 | 1,160 | 484 | 458 | 316 | 255 | 186 |
| Receivables | 2,245 | 1,919 | 1,254 | 1,458 | 1,202 | 340 | 165 | 127 | 114 | 96.7 |
| Cost of Investments | 1,540 | 1,049 | 1,415 | 2,000 | 2,098 | 299 | 227 | 235 | 209 | 139 |
| Total Assets | 178,459 | 177,994 | 19,924 | 22,562 | 20,469 | 1,848 | 1,145 | 967 | 864 | 684 |
| Loss Reserve | Nil | Nil | Nil | Nil | Nil | Nil | Nil | Nil | Nil | Nil |
| Short Term Debt | 100 | Nil | Nil | 0.30 | Nil | Nil | Nil | Nil | Nil | Nil |
| Capitalization:Debt | 4,537 | 3,434 | 946 | 947 | 253 | 254 | Nil | Nil | Nil | Nil |
| Capitalization:Equity | 26,094 | 24,329 | 12,066 | 11,597 | 10,782 | 935 | 768 | 713 | 635 | 486 |
| Capitalization:Total | 4,563 | 28,036 | 15,328 | 15,182 | 13,883 | 1,198 | 786 | 715 | 635 | 486 |
| Price Times Book Value:High | NM | NM | NM | NM | NM | 16.6 | 8.5 | 6.6 | 6.8 | 9.4 |
| Price Times Book Value:Low | NM | NM | NM | NM | NM | 10.1 | 5.8 | 4.9 | 4.8 | 6.5 |
| Cash Flow | 2,360 | 1,114 | 1,018 | 1,193 | 395 | 265 | 164 | 177 | 153 | 133 |
| % Expense/Operating Revenue | 65.2 | 72.8 | 68.5 | 73.2 | 81.5 | 74.7 | 79.3 | 65.5 | 66.3 | 73.1 |
| % Earnings & Depreciation/Assets | 1.3 | 1.1 | 4.8 | 5.5 | 3.5 | 17.7 | 15.5 | 19.3 | 19.8 | 21.9 |

Data as orig reptd.; bef. results of disc opers/spec. items. Per share data adj. for stk. divs.; EPS diluted. E-Estimated. NA-Not Available. NM-Not Meaningful. NR-Not Ranked. UR-Under Review.

**Office:** Park Avenue Plaza, 55 East 52nd Street, New York, NY 10055.
**Telephone:** 212-810-5300.
**Email:** invrel@blackrock.com
**Website:** http://www.blackrock.com

**Chrmn & CEO:** L.D. Fink
**Pres:** R.S. Kapito
**COO:** C.S. Hallac
**CFO:** A.M. Petach

**Chief Acctg Officer:** J. Feliciani, Jr.
**Board Members:** A. Y. Al-Hamad, M. Cabiallavetta, M. J. Castellano, D. I. Chen, D. D. Dammerman, W. S. Demchak, R. E. Diamond, Jr., L. D. Fink, M. S. Gerber, J. Grosfeld, R. S. Kapito, D. H. Komansky, D. C. Maughan, T. K. Montag, T. H. O'Brien, Jr., J. E. Rohr, I. G. Seidenberg, M. Slim Domit, J. S. Varley

**Founded:** 1998
**Domicile:** Delaware
**Employees:** 9,127

*The McGraw-Hill Companies*

# BMC Software Inc

**STANDARD &POOR'S**

| S&P Recommendation HOLD ★★★★★ | Price $33.28 (as of Nov 25, 2011) | 12-Mo. Target Price $45.00 | Investment Style Large-Cap Blend |
|---|---|---|---|

**GICS Sector** Information Technology
**Sub-Industry** Systems Software

**Summary** This company provides systems management software that improves the availability, performance and recovery of applications and data.

## Key Stock Statistics (Source S&P, Vickers, company reports)

| | | | | | | | |
|---|---|---|---|---|---|---|---|
| 52-Wk Range | $56.55–32.91 | S&P Oper. EPS 2012**E** | 3.25 | Market Capitalization(B) | $5.663 | Beta | 0.72 |
| Trailing 12-Month EPS | $2.44 | S&P Oper. EPS 2013**E** | 3.50 | Yield (%) | Nil | S&P 3-Yr. Proj. EPS CAGR(%) | 7 |
| Trailing 12-Month P/E | 13.6 | P/E on S&P Oper. EPS 2012**E** | 10.2 | Dividend Rate/Share | Nil | S&P Credit Rating | BBB+ |
| $10K Invested 5 Yrs Ago | $10,261 | Common Shares Outstg. (M) | 170.2 | Institutional Ownership (%) | 96 | | |

## Price Performance

30-Week Mov. Avg. ···  10-Week Mov. Avg.--  GAAP Earnings vs. Previous Year  Volume Above Avg. ▮▮▮ STARS
12-Mo. Target Price —  Relative Strength —  ▲ Up ▼ Down ► No Change  Below Avg. ▮▮▮ ★

Options: ASE, CBOE, P, Ph

Analysis prepared by Equity Analyst **Jim Yin, CFA** on Nov 01, 2011, when the stock traded at **$34.16**.

## Highlights

➤ We expect total revenues to increase 7.3% in FY 12 (Mar.). We project high-single digit growth in the Enterprise Service Management business segment in FY 12, driven by increased interest in cloud computing but hampered by weakness in the public sector, adverse foreign exchange, and longer sales cycles. In the past couple of years, BMC made several acquisitions to strengthen its offerings in this market segment. Meanwhile, we see the Mainframe Service Management business growing at a somewhat slower pace, reflecting a shift in enterprises' spending priorities. In FY 13, we expect 4.7% revenue growth.

➤ We think gross and operating margins this year will be roughly flat versus FY 11. We believe cost-saving initiatives and lower acquisition-related expenses will be offset by investments in sales and services capacity and development costs surrounding cloud computing and software-as-a-service.

➤ We see FY 12 operating EPS of $3.25, up from $2.99 in FY 11, which excludes amortization of intangibles and other one-time charges of $0.49 in FY 11. For FY 13, we forecast EPS of $3.50.

## Investment Rationale/Risk

➤ Our hold recommendation reflects our concern about BMC's modest revenue growth and costs surrounding investment expenses. We think much of the increased IT spending this year will be focused on cloud computing and virtualization because these solutions reduce IT operating costs. We believe BMC will benefit from this trend, somewhat offset by sluggish growth in its mainframe business.

➤ Risks to our recommendation and target price include a weaker-than-expected recovery in the global economy, heightened competition from large platform vendors, a decline in corporate spending on information technology, increased expenses surrounding investments in new technologies, and greater pricing pressures.

➤ Our 12-month target price is based on our relative P/E analysis. We derive a value of $45, using a roughly industry average P/E-to-growth ratio of 1.8X, or 12.9X our FY 13 EPS estimate of $3.50.

## Qualitative Risk Assessment

| LOW | MEDIUM | HIGH |
|---|---|---|

Our risk assessment for BMC Software reflects our concern about slow organic growth in its mainframe business, offset by the company's cost-cutting measures.

## Quantitative Evaluations

**S&P Quality Ranking**   C

| D | C | B- | B | B+ | A- | A | A+ |
|---|---|---|---|---|---|---|---|

**Relative Strength Rank**   WEAK

24

LOWEST = 1                HIGHEST = 99

## Revenue/Earnings Data

**Revenue (Million $)**

| | 1Q | 2Q | 3Q | 4Q | Year |
|---|---|---|---|---|---|
| 2012 | 502.4 | 556.7 | -- | -- | -- |
| 2011 | 460.9 | 502.3 | 539.9 | 562.2 | 2,065 |
| 2010 | 450.0 | 461.8 | 508.1 | 491.3 | 1,911 |
| 2009 | 437.5 | 466.7 | 488.4 | 479.3 | 1,872 |
| 2008 | 385.0 | 420.7 | 459.0 | 466.9 | 1,732 |
| 2007 | 361.4 | 386.7 | 412.9 | 419.4 | 1,580 |

**Earnings Per Share ($)**

| | | | | | |
|---|---|---|---|---|---|
| 2012 | 0.68 | 0.65 | E0.82 | E0.84 | E3.25 |
| 2011 | 0.50 | 0.73 | 0.60 | 0.67 | 2.50 |
| 2010 | 0.44 | 0.50 | 0.59 | 0.64 | 2.17 |
| 2009 | 0.01 | 0.36 | 0.45 | 0.45 | 1.25 |
| 2008 | 0.27 | 0.38 | 0.45 | 0.46 | 1.57 |
| 2007 | 0.15 | 0.28 | 0.30 | 0.30 | 1.03 |

Fiscal year ended Mar. 31. Next earnings report expected: Early February. EPS Estimates based on S&P Operating Earnings; historical GAAP earnings are as reported.

## Dividend Data

No cash dividends have been paid.

# BMC Software Inc

**STANDARD
&POOR'S**

## Business Summary November 01, 2011

CORPORATE OVERVIEW. BMC Software is a leading provider of systems management, service management and automation solutions primarily for large enterprises. The company's software, called Business Service Management (BSM), helps customers increase productivity and reduce costs by automating IT processes and improving IT responses to business decisions and challenges. The company's products and services are used by over 15,000 companies, including 90% of the Fortune 100.

BMC's software business is organized in two segments. The Enterprise Service Management (ESM) business segment targets non-mainframe computing and addresses broad categories of IT management issues including Service Support, Service Assurance and Service Automation. ESM license revenue accounted for 64% of software revenue and 54% of maintenance revenue in FY 11 (Mar.).

The Mainframe Service Management (MSM) segment includes automated tools that enhance the performance and availability of database management systems on mainframe platforms. This segment includes BMC's mainframe performance monitoring and management product line, MAINVIEW. It also includes the management and recovery of IBM's DB2 and IMS databases. MSM license revenue accounted for 36% of software revenue and 46% of maintenance revenue in FY 11.

BMC competes in a highly competitive industry. Its main competitors include International Business Machines Corporation, CA, Inc. and Hewlett-Packard.

BMC sells its software directly through its sales force and indirectly through resellers, distributors and systems integrators. The company also provides maintenance and support, which give customers the right to receive product upgrades. Product license and maintenance revenues accounted for 91% and 93% of total revenues in FY 11 and FY 10, respectively. BMC also provides professional services, which include implementation, integration and education services and contributed 9% and 7% of total revenues in FY 11 and FY 10, respectively.

## Company Financials Fiscal Year Ended Mar. 31

| Per Share Data ($) | 2011 | 2010 | 2009 | 2008 | 2007 | 2006 | 2005 | 2004 | 2003 | 2002 |
|---|---|---|---|---|---|---|---|---|---|---|
| Tangible Book Value | NM | NM | NM | 0.41 | 1.66 | 2.31 | 2.60 | 3.11 | 3.70 | 5.49 |
| Cash Flow | 3.54 | 2.78 | 1.89 | 2.01 | 1.79 | 1.40 | 1.33 | 1.03 | 1.25 | 0.78 |
| Earnings | 2.50 | 2.17 | 1.25 | 1.57 | 1.03 | 0.47 | 0.34 | -0.12 | 0.20 | -0.75 |
| S&P Core Earnings | 2.49 | 2.15 | 1.28 | 1.54 | 1.00 | 0.29 | -0.03 | -0.56 | -0.01 | -0.94 |
| Dividends | NA | Nil | Nil | Nil | Nil | Nil | Nil | Nil | Nil | Nil |
| Payout Ratio | NA | Nil | Nil | Nil | Nil | Nil | Nil | Nil | Nil | Nil |
| Calendar Year | 2010 | 2009 | 2008 | 2007 | 2006 | 2005 | 2004 | 2003 | 2002 | 2001 |
| Prices:High | 49.11 | 40.73 | 40.87 | 37.05 | 33.67 | 21.68 | 21.87 | 19.84 | 23.00 | 33.00 |
| Prices:Low | 34.24 | 24.76 | 20.58 | 24.77 | 19.90 | 14.44 | 13.70 | 13.18 | 10.85 | 11.50 |
| P/E Ratio:High | 20 | 19 | 33 | 24 | 33 | 41 | 64 | NM | NM | NM |
| P/E Ratio:Low | 14 | 11 | 16 | 16 | 19 | 27 | 40 | NM | NM | NM |

| Income Statement Analysis (Million $) | | | | | | | | | | |
|---|---|---|---|---|---|---|---|---|---|---|
| Revenue | 2,065 | 1,911 | 1,872 | 1,732 | 1,580 | 1,498 | 1,463 | 1,419 | 1,327 | 1,289 |
| Operating Income | 737 | 622 | 573 | 464 | 413 | 334 | 264 | 162 | 349 | 400 |
| Depreciation | 190 | 176 | 121 | 88.2 | 161 | 205 | 222 | 259 | 248 | 376 |
| Interest Expense | 19.8 | 21.3 | 18.7 | 16.9 | 1.50 | 1.70 | 2.00 | 1.10 | Nil | 0.40 |
| Pretax Income | 531 | 504 | 364 | 434 | 301 | 204 | 98.2 | -29.4 | 69.3 | -231 |
| Effective Tax Rate | NA | 19.5% | 34.6% | 27.8% | 28.2% | 50.0% | 23.3% | NM | 30.7% | NM |
| Net Income | 456 | 406 | 238 | 314 | 216 | 102 | 75.3 | -26.8 | 48.0 | -184 |
| S&P Core Earnings | 454 | 401 | 243 | 308 | 211 | 63.9 | -5.94 | -128 | -3.42 | -232 |

| Balance Sheet & Other Financial Data (Million $) | | | | | | | | | | |
|---|---|---|---|---|---|---|---|---|---|---|
| Cash | 1,689 | 1,434 | 1,097 | 1,351 | 1,296 | 1,063 | 929 | 909 | 1,015 | 546 |
| Current Assets | 2,267 | 1,905 | 1,561 | 1,803 | 1,790 | 1,506 | 1,440 | 1,425 | 1,098 | 997 |
| Total Assets | 4,485 | 4,138 | 3,698 | 3,346 | 3,260 | 3,211 | 3,298 | 3,045 | 2,846 | 2,676 |
| Current Liabilities | 1,390 | 1,361 | 1,333 | 1,289 | 1,233 | 1,202 | 1,085 | 987 | 839 | 681 |
| Long Term Debt | 336 | 341 | 314 | 6.30 | Nil | Nil | Nil | Nil | Nil | Nil |
| Common Equity | 1,663 | 1,388 | 1,049 | 994 | 1,049 | 1,099 | 1,262 | 1,215 | 1,383 | 1,507 |
| Total Capital | 1,999 | 1,729 | 1,362 | 994 | 1,049 | 1,099 | 1,262 | 1,215 | 1,383 | 1,507 |
| Capital Expenditures | 22.0 | 22.1 | 28.0 | 38.4 | 33.7 | 24.1 | 57.7 | 50.4 | 23.6 | 64.3 |
| Cash Flow | 646 | 519 | 359 | 402 | 377 | 307 | 297 | 233 | 296 | 192 |
| Current Ratio | 1.6 | 1.4 | 1.2 | 1.4 | 1.5 | 1.3 | 1.3 | 1.4 | 1.3 | 1.5 |
| % Long Term Debt of Capitalization | 16.8 | 19.7 | 23.0 | Nil | Nil | Nil | Nil | Nil | Nil | Nil |
| % Net Income of Revenue | 22.1 | 21.3 | 12.7 | 18.1 | 13.7 | 6.8 | 5.1 | NM | 3.6 | NM |
| % Return on Assets | 10.6 | 10.4 | 6.8 | 9.5 | 6.7 | 3.1 | 2.4 | NM | 1.7 | NM |
| % Return on Equity | 29.9 | 33.3 | 23.3 | 30.7 | 20.1 | 8.6 | 6.1 | NM | 3.3 | NM |

Data as orig reptd.; bef. results of disc opers/spec. items. Per share data adj. for stk. divs.; EPS diluted. E-Estimated. NA-Not Available. NM-Not Meaningful. NR-Not Ranked. UR-Under Review.

**Office:** 2101 Citywest Boulevard, Houston, TX 77042-2827.
**Telephone:** 713-918-8800.
**Email:** investor@bmc.com
**Website:** http://www.bmc.com

**Chrmn, Pres & CEO:** R.E. Beauchamp
**COO:** D.S. Goddard, Jr.
**Investor Contact:** S.B. Solcher
**SVP & CFO:** S.B. Solcher

**SVP & CTO:** K. Behnia
**Board Members:** J. E. Barfield, R. E. Beauchamp, G. L. Bloom, M. K. Gafner, M. J. Hawkins, S. A. James, P. T. Jenkins, L. J. Lavigne, Jr., K. O'Neil, T. C. Tinsley

**Founded:** 1980
**Domicile:** Delaware
**Employees:** 6,200

The **McGraw-Hill** Companies

# Boeing Co (The)

STANDARD
&POOR'S

| S&P Recommendation | BUY ★★★★☆ | Price $62.78 (as of Nov 25, 2011) | 12-Mo. Target Price $86.00 | Investment Style Large-Cap Growth |
|---|---|---|---|---|

**GICS Sector** Industrials
**Sub-Industry** Aerospace & Defense

**Summary** This company is the world's second largest manufacturer of commercial jets (behind Airbus) and third largest military weapons maker (behind Lockheed Martin and Britain's BAE Systems).

## Key Stock Statistics (Source S&P, Vickers, company reports)

| | | | | | | | |
|---|---|---|---|---|---|---|---|
| 52-Wk Range | $80.65– 56.01 | S&P Oper. EPS 2011**E** | 4.40 | Market Capitalization(B) | $46.660 | Beta | 1.25 |
| Trailing 12-Month EPS | $5.05 | S&P Oper. EPS 2012**E** | 4.90 | Yield (%) | 2.68 | S&P 3-Yr. Proj. EPS CAGR(%) | 10 |
| Trailing 12-Month P/E | 12.4 | P/E on S&P Oper. EPS 2011**E** | 14.3 | Dividend Rate/Share | $1.68 | S&P Credit Rating | A |
| $10K Invested 5 Yrs Ago | $7,929 | Common Shares Outstg. (M) | 743.2 | Institutional Ownership (%) | 72 | | |

## Price Performance

30-Week Mov. Avg. · · · 10-Week Mov. Avg. - - GAAP Earnings vs. Previous Year   Volume Above Avg. STARS
12-Mo. Target Price — Relative Strength — ▲ Up ▼ Down ► No Change   Below Avg. ★

Options: ASE, CBOE, P, Ph

Analysis prepared by Equity Analyst **R. Tortoriello** on Oct 27, 2011, when the stock traded at **$66.56**.

## Highlights

➤ We estimate sales will rise 6% in 2011. For 2012, we project a 12% sales increase, driven almost entirely by Commercial Airplanes, where we see revenues up 20% on rising deliveries of 737s (increasing to 35 per month in early 2012 from 31.5 currently) and the 747-8 (rising to 2 per month in mid-2012 from 1.5 currently), as well as production increases on the 787, which has just begun to be delivered. On the defense and space side of Boeing's business, we expect 1% revenue growth, held back by U.S. defense budget weakness. However, we note that President Obama's fiscal 2012 defense budget proposal contains additional funds for 41 F/A-18s, and Boeing recently won the KC-X refueling tanker competition.

➤ We estimate 2011 operating margins of 7.9%, up slightly from 7.7% in 2010. For 2012, we project a narrow increase to 8.0%, as declining R&D costs are offset by lower margin initial production of the 787 and 747-8.

➤ We estimate EPS of $4.40 in 2011 and $4.90 in 2012. We expect a significant rise in free cash flow in 2012, as 787s and 747-8s are delivered to customers.

## Investment Rationale/Risk

➤ We see several factors benefiting the shares. We expect emerging economies in Asia and the Middle East to continue to grow strongly, which should sustain demand for narrow-body aircraft, supporting Boeing's total backlog of about 3,500 aircraft as of September 2011. In addition, U.S. airlines continue to take deliveries to improve fuel efficiency of aging fleets. Further, we expect the production ramp of the 787 (first delivery was in September 2011) to act as a catalyst for the stock, with about 820 aircraft recently on order. Finally, we view valuations, which are at or below historical averages, as attractive given our view that current income levels are depressed.

➤ Risks to our opinion and target price include a worsening economic environment, failure to win new military contracts, and manufacturing or operational difficulties on existing programs.

➤ Our 12-month target price of $86 is based on an enterprise value-to-EBITDA multiple of 8.5X our 2012 EBITDA estimate. This compares with BA's 20-year historical average EV-to-EBITDA multiple of 11.5X, and a recent peer average multiple of 7X.

## Qualitative Risk Assessment

| LOW | MEDIUM | HIGH |
|---|---|---|

Our risk assessment reflects BA's participation in highly cyclical, very competitive and capital-intensive businesses, offset by its long-term government contracts and our view of its solid cash position, typically strong free cash flow generation and healthy backlog of business.

## Quantitative Evaluations

**S&P Quality Ranking**   B+

| D | C | B- | B | B+ | A- | A | A+ |
|---|---|---|---|---|---|---|---|

**Relative Strength Rank**   MODERATE

63

LOWEST = 1                HIGHEST = 99

## Revenue/Earnings Data

**Revenue (Million $)**

| | 1Q | 2Q | 3Q | 4Q | Year |
|---|---|---|---|---|---|
| 2011 | 14,910 | 16,543 | 17,727 | -- | -- |
| 2010 | 15,216 | 15,573 | 16,967 | 16,550 | 64,306 |
| 2009 | 16,502 | 14,296 | 16,688 | 17,937 | 68,281 |
| 2008 | 15,990 | 16,962 | 15,293 | 12,664 | 60,909 |
| 2007 | 15,365 | 17,028 | 16,517 | 17,477 | 66,387 |
| 2006 | 14,264 | 14,986 | 14,739 | 17,541 | 61,530 |

**Earnings Per Share ($)**

| | | | | | |
|---|---|---|---|---|---|
| 2011 | 0.78 | 1.25 | 1.46 | E0.91 | E4.40 |
| 2010 | 0.70 | 1.06 | 1.12 | 1.56 | 4.46 |
| 2009 | 0.87 | 1.41 | -2.22 | 1.77 | 1.87 |
| 2008 | 1.61 | 1.16 | 0.94 | -0.12 | 3.65 |
| 2007 | 1.12 | 1.35 | 1.43 | 1.35 | 5.26 |
| 2006 | 0.88 | -0.21 | 0.89 | 1.28 | 2.84 |

Fiscal year ended Dec. 31. Next earnings report expected: Late January. EPS Estimates based on S&P Operating Earnings; historical GAAP earnings are as reported.

## Dividend Data (Dates: mm/dd Payment Date: mm/dd/yy)

| Amount ($) | Date Decl. | Ex-Div. Date | Stk. of Record | Payment Date |
|---|---|---|---|---|
| 0.420 | 12/13 | 02/09 | 02/11 | 03/04/11 |
| 0.420 | 05/02 | 05/11 | 05/13 | 06/03/11 |
| 0.420 | 06/27 | 08/10 | 08/12 | 09/02/11 |
| 0.420 | 10/31 | 11/08 | 11/11 | 12/02/11 |

Dividends have been paid since 1942. Source: Company reports.

# Boeing Co (The)

**STANDARD &POOR'S**

## Business Summary October 27, 2011

CORPORATE OVERVIEW. Boeing is a global aerospace and defense giant that conducts business through three operating segments. Boeing Commercial Airplanes (BCA; 49% of revenues and 50% of operating profits in 2010) and EADS's Airbus division are the world's only makers of 150-plus seat passenger jets. Boeing Defense, Space & Security (50%, 48%) is the world's third largest military contractor behind Lockheed Martin Corp and England's BAE Systems. Boeing Capital Corp. (1%, 2%) primarily finances Boeing aircraft for airlines.

BCA's commercial jet aircraft family includes the 737 Next-Generation narrow body model and the 747, 767, 777 and 787 wide body models. The 787 (Dreamliner) is Boeing's newest model, and is scheduled for first delivery, following a more than three-year delay, in the third quarter of 2011. Boeing's upgraded 747-8 Freighter is also slated for delivery in the middle of 2011, with the passenger version scheduled for year end. BCA also offers aviation support, aircraft modifications, spare parts, training, maintenance documents, and technical advice. Boeing had a commercial aircraft backlog at year-end 2010 of $256 billion.

Defense, Space & Security (BDS) designs, develops and supports military aircraft, including fighters, transports, tankers, intelligence surveillance and re-

connaissance aircraft, and helicopters; unmanned systems; missiles; space systems; missile defense systems; satellites and satellite launch vehicles; and communication, information and battle management systems. BDS contains three business units: Boeing Military Aircraft (46% of BDS sales and 44% of BDS operating income in 2010), Network & Space Systems (30% and 25%), and Global Services & Support (26% and 31%). BDS's primary customer is the U.S. Department of Defense (82% of 2010 sales), but it also sells to NASA, international defense customers, civilian markets, and commercial satellite markets. Major programs include the AH-64 Apache and CH-47 Chinook helicopters, the C-17 Globemaster military transport, the V-22 Osprey tiltrotor aircraft, F/A-18E/F Super Hornet and F-15 Eagle fighter jets, the P-8A Poseiden, as well as commercial and military satellites. In February 2011, Boeing won a $3.5 billion contract to produce KC-X aerial refueling tankers for the Air Force. The total program is expected to be worth about $35 billion for the production of 179 aircraft.

## Company Financials Fiscal Year Ended Dec. 31

| Per Share Data ($) | 2010 | 2009 | 2008 | 2007 | 2006 | 2005 | 2004 | 2003 | 2002 | 2001 |
|---|---|---|---|---|---|---|---|---|---|---|
| Tangible Book Value | NM | NM | NM | 3.78 | NM | 10.33 | 10.08 | 6.17 | 4.53 | 5.23 |
| Cash Flow | 6.77 | 4.21 | 5.26 | 7.18 | 4.76 | 5.08 | 4.00 | 2.68 | 2.46 | 5.52 |
| Earnings | 4.46 | 1.87 | 3.65 | 5.26 | 2.84 | 3.19 | 2.24 | 0.89 | 2.87 | 3.41 |
| S&P Core Earnings | 4.61 | 2.02 | 0.87 | 5.41 | 3.90 | 3.05 | 1.99 | 1.33 | 0.26 | -0.06 |
| Dividends | 2.10 | 1.68 | 1.60 | 1.40 | 1.20 | 1.00 | 0.77 | 0.68 | 0.68 | 0.68 |
| Payout Ratio | 47% | 90% | 44% | 27% | 42% | 31% | 34% | 76% | 24% | 20% |
| Prices:High | 76.00 | 56.56 | 88.29 | 107.83 | 92.05 | 72.40 | 55.48 | 43.37 | 51.07 | 69.85 |
| Prices:Low | 54.80 | 29.05 | 36.17 | 84.60 | 65.90 | 49.52 | 38.04 | 24.73 | 28.53 | 27.60 |
| P/E Ratio:High | 17 | 30 | 24 | 20 | 32 | 23 | 25 | 49 | 18 | 20 |
| P/E Ratio:Low | 12 | 16 | 10 | 16 | 23 | 16 | 17 | 28 | 10 | 8 |

| Income Statement Analysis (Million $) | 2010 | 2009 | 2008 | 2007 | 2006 | 2005 | 2004 | 2003 | 2002 | 2001 |
|---|---|---|---|---|---|---|---|---|---|---|
| Revenue | 64,306 | 68,281 | 60,909 | 66,387 | 61,530 | 54,845 | 52,457 | 50,485 | 54,069 | 58,198 |
| Operating Income | 6,425 | 3,537 | 5,107 | 7,090 | 5,176 | 3,707 | 3,405 | 3,198 | 5,447 | 6,467 |
| Depreciation | 1,727 | 1,666 | 1,179 | 1,486 | 1,545 | 1,503 | 1,509 | 1,450 | 1,497 | 1,750 |
| Interest Expense | 516 | 339 | 524 | 196 | 593 | 653 | 685 | 800 | 730 | 650 |
| Pretax Income | 4,507 | 1,731 | 4,033 | 6,118 | 1,218 | 2,819 | 1,960 | 550 | 1,353 | 3,565 |
| Effective Tax Rate | NA | 22.9% | 33.5% | 33.6% | NM | 9.12% | 7.14% | NM | 63.6% | 20.7% |
| Net Income | 3,311 | 1,335 | 2,684 | 4,058 | 2,206 | 2,562 | 1,820 | 718 | 492 | 2,827 |
| S&P Core Earnings | 3,420 | 1,442 | 619 | 4,177 | 3,042 | 2,450 | 1,616 | 1,074 | 203 | 284 |

| Balance Sheet & Other Financial Data (Million $) | 2010 | 2009 | 2008 | 2007 | 2006 | 2005 | 2004 | 2003 | 2002 | 2001 |
|---|---|---|---|---|---|---|---|---|---|---|
| Cash | 10,517 | 11,223 | 3,279 | 7,042 | 6,118 | 5,412 | 3,204 | 4,633 | 2,333 | 633 |
| Current Assets | 40,572 | 35,275 | 25,964 | 27,280 | 22,983 | 21,968 | 15,100 | 17,258 | 16,855 | 16,206 |
| Total Assets | 68,565 | 62,053 | 53,801 | 58,986 | 51,794 | 60,058 | 53,963 | 53,035 | 52,342 | 48,343 |
| Current Liabilities | 35,395 | 32,883 | 30,925 | 31,538 | 29,701 | 28,188 | 20,835 | 18,448 | 19,810 | 20,486 |
| Long Term Debt | 11,473 | 12,217 | 6,952 | 7,455 | 8,157 | 9,538 | 10,879 | 13,299 | 12,589 | 10,866 |
| Common Equity | 2,766 | 2,128 | -1,264 | 9,004 | 4,739 | 11,059 | 11,286 | 8,139 | 7,696 | 10,825 |
| Total Capital | 15,283 | 15,149 | 5,658 | 17,649 | 12,896 | 22,664 | 23,255 | 21,438 | 20,285 | 21,868 |
| Capital Expenditures | 1,125 | 1,186 | 1,674 | 1,731 | 1,681 | 1,547 | 978 | 741 | 1,001 | 1,068 |
| Cash Flow | 5,038 | 3,001 | 3,833 | 5,544 | 3,751 | 4,065 | 3,329 | 2,168 | 1,989 | 4,577 |
| Current Ratio | 1.2 | 1.1 | 0.8 | 0.9 | 0.8 | 0.8 | 0.7 | 0.9 | 0.9 | 0.8 |
| % Long Term Debt of Capitalization | 75.1 | 80.7 | 122.9 | 42.2 | 63.3 | 42.1 | 46.8 | 62.0 | 62.1 | 49.7 |
| % Net Income of Revenue | 5.2 | 2.0 | 4.4 | 6.1 | 3.6 | 4.7 | 3.5 | 1.4 | 0.9 | 4.9 |
| % Return on Assets | 5.1 | 2.3 | 4.8 | 7.3 | 3.9 | 4.4 | 3.4 | 1.4 | 1.0 | 6.2 |
| % Return on Equity | 135.3 | NM | NM | 59.0 | 27.9 | 22.9 | 18.7 | 9.1 | 5.3 | 25.9 |

Data as orig reptd.; bef. results of disc opers/spec. items. Per share data adj. for stk. divs.; EPS diluted. E-Estimated. NA-Not Available. NM-Not Meaningful. NR-Not Ranked. UR-Under Review.

**Office:** 100 North Riverside Plaza, Chicago, IL 60606-1596.
**Telephone:** 312-544-2000.
**Website:** http://www.boeing.com
**Chrmn, Pres & CEO:** W.J. McNerney, Jr.

**COO & CTO:** J.J. Tracy
**CFO:** J.A. Bell
**Chief Admin Officer:** R.D. Stephens
**Chief Acctg Officer & Cntlr:** G.D. Smith

**Investor Contact:** R. Young (312-544-2140)
**Board Members:** D. L. Calhoun, A. D. Collins, Jr., L. Z. Cook, K. M. Duberstein, E. P. Giambastiani, Jr., L. W. Kellner, E. M. Liddy, J. F. McDonnell, W. J. McNerney, Jr., S. C. Schwab, R. A. Williams, M. S. Zafirovski

**Founded:** 1916
**Domicile:** Delaware
**Employees:** 160,500

# Boston Properties Inc

**STANDARD &POOR'S**

| S&P Recommendation **BUY** ★★★★☆ | Price $89.15 (as of Nov 25, 2011) | 12-Mo. Target Price $110.00 | Investment Style Large-Cap Blend |
|---|---|---|---|

**GICS Sector** Financials
**Sub-Industry** Office REITS

**Summary** This real estate investment trust primarily owns office buildings in the Boston, Washington, DC, New York City, San Francisco and Princeton, NJ, markets.

## Key Stock Statistics (Source S&P, Vickers, company reports)

| | | | | | |
|---|---|---|---|---|---|
| 52-Wk Range | $112.84–81.11 | S&P FFO/Sh. 2011E | 4.82 | Market Capitalization(B) | $13.161 |
| Trailing 12-Month FFO/Share | $4.12 | S&P FFO/Sh. 2012E | 4.85 | Yield (%) | 2.24 |
| Trailing 12-Month P/FFO | NA | P/FFO on S&P FFO/Sh. 2011E | 18.5 | Dividend Rate/Share | $2.00 |
| $10K Invested 5 Yrs Ago | $9,835 | Common Shares Outstg. (M) | 147.6 | Institutional Ownership (%) | NM |

| | |
|---|---|
| Beta | 1.42 |
| S&P 3-Yr. FFO/Sh. Proj. CAGR(%) | 5 |
| S&P Credit Rating | A- |

## Price Performance

30-Week Mov. Avg. ··· 10-Week Mov. Avg. -- **GAAP Earnings vs. Previous Year** Volume Above Avg. STARS
12-Mo. Target Price — Relative Strength — ▲ Up ▼ Down ► No Change Below Avg.

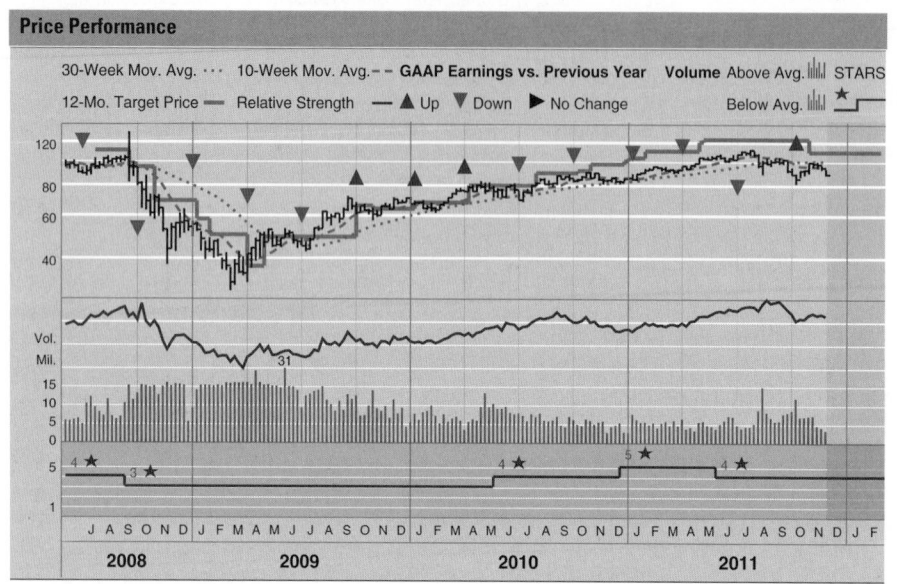

Analysis prepared by Equity Analyst **R. Shepard, CFA** on Oct 27, 2011, when the stock traded at **$97.12**.

Options: ASE, CBOE, P

### Highlights

► We believe BXP will benefit in 2012 from the recent delivery of new development projects. During 2011, initial occupancy commenced for residential units in both Boston and Washington, DC. Also, BXP has opened office space at 2200 Pennsylvania Avenue in Washington, DC, and 510 Madison Avenue in New York City. In 2012, we expect three additional office projects to begin leasing 620,000 square feet of office space. In total, BXP has a pipeline of development projects with a combined estimated investment of $2.2 billion through 2014.

► We expect BXP to maintain occupancy close to 91.5% in 2011, despite the addition of new space. We estimate that total revenues will rise about 3%, reduced by lower lease termination fees and lower expected rents on the rollover of several large office leases.

► Our 2012 FFO per share estimate of $4.85 reflects a modest decline in occupancy, lower rental rates on new leasing activity, and reduced lease termination fees, offset by an initial contribution from newly developed properties and lower financing costs.

### Investment Rationale/Risk

► We think BXP's portfolio is well positioned to capitalize on conditions in U.S. office markets, which we believe are slowly recovering from depressed conditions in 2008 and 2009. In our view, its portfolio, concentrated in urban markets, will outperform peers in suburban markets with lower barriers to entry. We think the trust faces some pressure on rental rates as existing long-term leases expire in 2012. However, we anticipate a positive contribution from newly developed properties. BXP recently traded at 20X our 2012 FFO estimate of $4.85, and we think a significant premium to peers valuation is warranted by what we view as its strong balance sheet and long-term growth potential.

► Risks to our recommendation and target price include national employment growth lagging our expectations, and weaker-than-anticipated economic conditions in BXP's markets.

► Our 12-month target price of $110 primarily reflects our estimate of net asset value (NAV), based on estimated 2012 cash flow and a one-year cash yield of 5.5%. This implies a multiple of 22.7X our 2012 FFO per share estimate, a premium to office REITs serving what we view as less attractive suburban markets.

### Qualitative Risk Assessment

| LOW | MEDIUM | HIGH |
|---|---|---|

Our risk assessment reflects what we see as BXP's large and diverse asset portfolio, its relatively unleveraged balance sheet, and consistent cash distribution.

### Quantitative Evaluations

**S&P Quality Ranking** B

| D | C | B- | B | B+ | A- | A | A+ |
|---|---|---|---|---|---|---|---|

**Relative Strength Rank** MODERATE

45

LOWEST = 1    HIGHEST = 99

### Revenue/FFO Data

**Revenue (Million $)**

| | 1Q | 2Q | 3Q | 4Q | Year |
|---|---|---|---|---|---|
| 2011 | 417.9 | 436.5 | 452.4 | -- | -- |
| 2010 | 386.0 | 396.0 | 388.2 | 402.3 | 1,551 |
| 2009 | 377.5 | 389.5 | 377.3 | 377.9 | 1,522 |
| 2008 | 371.4 | 368.7 | 358.0 | 390.3 | 1,488 |
| 2007 | 360.7 | 372.2 | 368.6 | 380.8 | 1,482 |
| 2006 | 356.1 | 370.4 | 372.5 | 378.7 | 1,502 |

**FFO Per Share ($)**

| | 1Q | 2Q | 3Q | 4Q | Year |
|---|---|---|---|---|---|
| 2011 | 1.28 | 1.40 | 1.45 | E1.19 | E4.82 |
| 2010 | 1.23 | 1.12 | 1.08 | 0.64 | 4.48 |
| 2009 | 1.11 | 1.32 | 1.31 | 1.05 | 4.61 |
| 2008 | 1.18 | 1.19 | 1.13 | 0.05 | 3.49 |
| 2007 | 0.42 | 0.32 | 0.32 | 1.22 | 4.64 |
| 2006 | 0.27 | 0.39 | 0.32 | 0.32 | 4.17 |

Fiscal year ended Dec. 31. Next earnings report expected: Late January. FFO Estimates based on S&P Funds From Operations Est..

### Dividend Data (Dates: mm/dd Payment Date: mm/dd/yy)

| Amount ($) | Date Decl. | Ex-Div. Date | Stk. of Record | Payment Date |
|---|---|---|---|---|
| 0.500 | 12/20 | 12/29 | 12/31 | 01/28/11 |
| 0.500 | 03/18 | 03/29 | 03/31 | 04/29/11 |
| 0.500 | 06/17 | 06/28 | 06/30 | 07/29/11 |
| 0.500 | 09/16 | 09/28 | 09/30 | 10/31/11 |

Dividends have been paid since 1997. Source: Company reports.

# Boston Properties Inc

STANDARD
&POOR'S

## Business Summary October 27, 2011

CORPORATE OVERVIEW. Boston Properties, founded in 1970, is a real estate investment trust (REIT) that develops, acquires, manages, operates, and is one of the largest U.S. owners of, Class A office properties. BXP conducts substantially all of its business through a limited partnership of which it is the sole general partner and in which it holds an 84% economic interest.

At December 31, 2010, the property portfolio consisted of 146 properties, totaling 53.6 million net rentable sq. ft. and structured parking facilities for vehicles containing approximately 13.7 million sq. ft. The properties included 140 in-service office buildings and one hotel in Cambridge, MA. In addition, BXP had six buildings under development totaling 2.4 million sq. ft.

MARKET PROFILE The market for office leases is inherently cyclical. Local economic conditions, particularly employment levels, play an important role in determining competitive dynamics. Non-farm monthly payrolls declined in 2009 and 2010. The unemployment rate in the fourth quarter of 2010 was 9.7%, up from 7.2% in December 2008.

The U.S. office market tends to track the overall economy on a lagged basis. At the end of 2010, we believe the national vacancy rate was about 17.5%, an increase from a cyclical low of about 12.5% at the end of 2007. Going forward,

we believe vacancy levels will begin to decline in 2011 due to a gradually improving economic environment. In our opinion, BXP's principal markets, including Washington, DC, Manhattan, Boston and San Francisco, are among the nation's strongest due to limited new construction activity in recent years. We believe that renewed job growth could lead to renewed market rents rising about 5% in 2011. In total, as of December 31, 2010, BXP had an office occupancy rate at established properties of 93.2%, much better than the national average. Leases will expire on only about 6.9% of existing office space in 2011, limiting the trust's exposure to local market volatility.

Competition for leasing real estate is high. In addition, we believe that competition for the acquisition of new properties is intensifying from other REITs, private real estate funds, financial institutions, insurance companies and others. Even so, we think BXP's strong financial position will allow it to effectively bid on new assets. During 2010, the trust completed five transactions at a total investment of $1.3 billion.

## Company Financials  Fiscal Year Ended Dec. 31

| Per Share Data ($) | 2010 | 2009 | 2008 | 2007 | 2006 | 2005 | 2004 | 2003 | 2002 | 2001 |
|---|---|---|---|---|---|---|---|---|---|---|
| Tangible Book Value | 31.19 | 32.01 | 29.14 | 30.72 | 27.45 | 25.92 | 26.61 | 22.51 | 20.79 | 19.34 |
| Earnings | 1.14 | 1.76 | 1.03 | 9.06 | 7.46 | 3.46 | 2.35 | 2.94 | 4.40 | 2.26 |
| S&P Core Earnings | 1.14 | 1.76 | 1.03 | 9.06 | 7.46 | 3.46 | 2.34 | 2.88 | 4.37 | 2.20 |
| Dividends | 2.00 | 2.18 | 1.52 | 2.72 | 2.72 | 5.19 | 2.58 | 2.50 | 2.41 | 2.27 |
| Payout Ratio | 175% | 124% | NM | 30% | 36% | 150% | 110% | 85% | 55% | 100% |
| Prices:High | 91.45 | 72.23 | 50.63 | 133.02 | 118.22 | 76.67 | 64.90 | 48.47 | 41.55 | 43.88 |
| Prices:Low | 61.50 | 29.30 | 19.69 | 87.78 | 72.98 | 56.66 | 42.99 | 34.80 | 32.95 | 34.00 |
| P/E Ratio:High | 80 | 41 | 60 | 15 | 16 | 22 | 28 | 16 | 9 | 19 |
| P/E Ratio:Low | 54 | 17 | 23 | 10 | 10 | 16 | 18 | 12 | 7 | 15 |

| Income Statement Analysis (Million $) | | | | | | | | | | |
|---|---|---|---|---|---|---|---|---|---|---|
| Rental Income | 1,477 | 1,453 | 1,402 | 1,334 | 1,344 | 1,339 | 1,293 | 1,219 | 1,174 | 1,008 |
| Mortgage Income | Nil | Nil | Nil | Nil | Nil | Nil | Nil | Nil | Nil | Nil |
| Total Income | 1,551 | 1,522 | 1,488 | 1,482 | 1,502 | 1,438 | 1,400 | 1,310 | 1,235 | 1,033 |
| General Expenses | 607 | 601 | 588 | 554 | 557 | 545 | 528 | 498 | 464 | 351 |
| Interest Expense | 378 | 323 | 272 | 286 | 298 | 308 | 306 | 299 | 272 | 223 |
| Provision for Losses | Nil | Nil | Nil | Nil | Nil | Nil | Nil | Nil | Nil | Nil |
| Depreciation | 338 | 322 | 304 | 286 | 277 | 267 | 252 | 210 | 186 | 150 |
| Net Income | 159 | 231 | 125 | 1,098 | 874 | 393 | 255 | 290 | 420 | 215 |
| S&P Core Earnings | 159 | 231 | 125 | 1,094 | 874 | 393 | 254 | 284 | 413 | 203 |

| Balance Sheet & Other Financial Data (Million $) | | | | | | | | | | |
|---|---|---|---|---|---|---|---|---|---|---|
| Cash | 479 | 1,449 | 242 | 1,716 | 752 | 377 | 345 | 133 | 199 | 201 |
| Total Assets | 13,348 | 12,349 | 10,912 | 11,193 | 9,695 | 8,902 | 9,063 | 8,551 | 8,427 | 7,254 |
| Real Estate Investment | 12,765 | 11,100 | 10,618 | 10,250 | 9,552 | 9,151 | 9,291 | 8,983 | 8,671 | 7,458 |
| Loss Reserve | Nil | Nil | Nil | Nil | Nil | Nil | Nil | Nil | Nil | Nil |
| Net Investment | 10,441 | 9,066 | 8,850 | 8,718 | 8,160 | 7,886 | 8,148 | 7,981 | 7,848 | 6,738 |
| Short Term Debt | 439 | 310 | 100 | Nil | Nil | Nil | Nil | Nil | Nil | 282 |
| Capitalization:Debt | 7,348 | 6,608 | 6,172 | 5,492 | 4,559 | 4,679 | 4,733 | 5,005 | 3,336 | 4,033 |
| Capitalization:Equity | 4,373 | 4,446 | 3,531 | 3,669 | 3,223 | 2,917 | 2,936 | 2,400 | 2,160 | 1,754 |
| Capitalization:Total | 12,368 | 11,732 | 10,302 | 9,216 | 8,406 | 8,335 | 8,455 | 8,235 | 6,340 | 6,732 |
| % Earnings & Depreciation/Assets | 3.9 | 4.8 | 3.9 | 13.3 | 12.3 | 7.3 | 5.8 | 5.9 | 7.7 | 5.4 |
| Price Times Book Value:High | 2.9 | 2.3 | 4.5 | 4.3 | 4.3 | 3.0 | 2.4 | 2.1 | 2.0 | 2.3 |
| Price Times Book Value:Low | 2.0 | 0.9 | 1.3 | 2.9 | 2.7 | 2.2 | 1.6 | 1.5 | 1.6 | 1.8 |

Data as orig reptd.; bef. results of disc opers/spec. items. Per share data adj. for stk. divs.; EPS diluted. E-Estimated. NA-Not Available. NM-Not Meaningful. NR-Not Ranked. UR-Under Review.

**Office:** 800 Boylston St Ste 1900, Boston, MA 02199-8103.
**Telephone:** 617-236-3300.
**Email:** investor_relations@bostonproperties.com
**Website:** http://www.bostonproperties.com

**Chrmn & CEO:** M.B. Zuckerman
**Pres:** D.T. Linde
**SVP, Secy & General Counsel:** F.D. Burt
**CFO & Treas:** M.E. LaBelle

**Chief Acctg Officer & Cntlr:** A.S. Flashman
**Investor Contact:** M. Walsh (617-236-3300)
**Board Members:** L. S. Bacow, Z. B. Budinger, C. B. Einiger, J. A. Frenkel, D. T. Linde, M. J. Lustig, A. J. Patricof, M. Turchin, D. A. Twardock, M. B. Zuckerman

**Founded:** 1970
**Domicile:** Delaware
**Employees:** 680

# Boston Scientific Corp

**STANDARD &POOR'S**

| S&P Recommendation **HOLD** ★★★★☆ | Price $5.90 (as of Nov 30, 2011) | 12-Mo. Target Price $6.50 | Investment Style Large-Cap Growth |
|---|---|---|---|

**GICS Sector** Health Care
**Sub-Industry** Health Care Equipment

**Summary** This manufacturer of minimally invasive medical devices acquired its device rival Guidant Corp. in April 2006 for $27 billion in cash and stock.

## Key Stock Statistics (Source S&P, Vickers, company reports)

| | | | | | | | |
|---|---|---|---|---|---|---|---|
| 52-Wk Range | $7.96–5.26 | S&P Oper. EPS 2011**E** | 0.46 | Market Capitalization(B) | $8.741 | Beta | 1.16 |
| Trailing 12-Month EPS | $0.38 | S&P Oper. EPS 2012**E** | 0.52 | Yield (%) | Nil | S&P 3-Yr. Proj. EPS CAGR(%) | 13 |
| Trailing 12-Month P/E | 15.5 | P/E on S&P Oper. EPS 2011**E** | 12.8 | Dividend Rate/Share | Nil | S&P Credit Rating | BBB- |
| $10K Invested 5 Yrs Ago | $3,722 | Common Shares Outstg. (M) | 1,481.5 | Institutional Ownership (%) | 91 | | |

## Price Performance

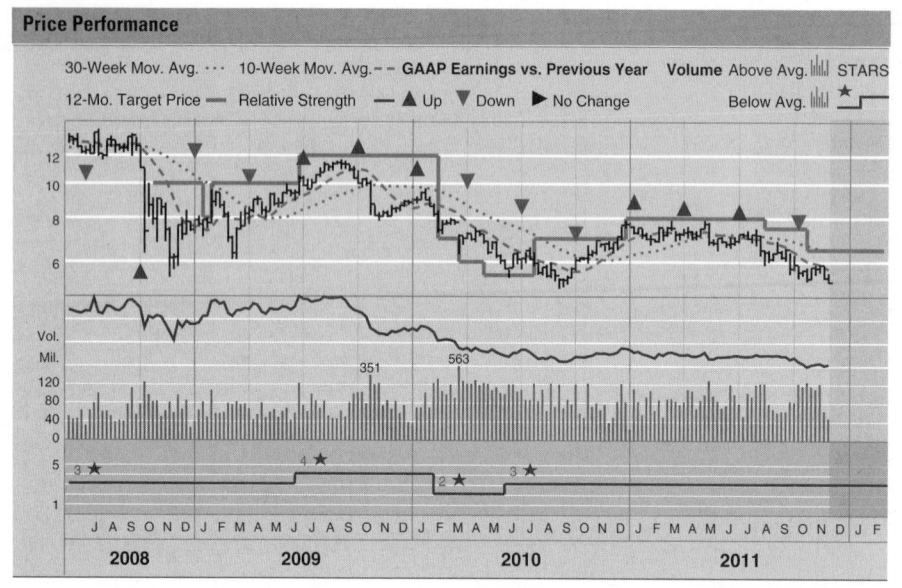

- 30-Week Mov. Avg. ···· 10-Week Mov. Avg. — **GAAP Earnings vs. Previous Year**   Volume Above Avg. STARS
- 12-Mo. Target Price — Relative Strength — ▲ Up ▼ Down ▶ No Change   Below Avg.

Options: ASE, CBOE, P, Ph

Analysis prepared by Equity Analyst **Phillip Seligman** on Oct 26, 2011, when the stock traded at **$5.45**.

## Qualitative Risk Assessment

| LOW | MEDIUM | **HIGH** |
|---|---|---|

Our risk assessment reflects the company's operations within intensely competitive areas of the health care industry, and its dependence for growth on the development and commercialization of new products. In addition, a large percentage of customers are reimbursed by the federal Medicare program, and we believe the government is likely to reduce the pace of expenditure growth by lowering reimbursement rates for expensive medical devices such as defibrillators and cardiac stents.

## Quantitative Evaluations

**S&P Quality Ranking**                                C

| D | **C** | B- | B | B+ | A- | A | A+ |
|---|---|---|---|---|---|---|---|

**Relative Strength Rank**                     **MODERATE**

67

LOWEST = 1                                        HIGHEST = 99

## Highlights

➤ We look for revenues to decline by 1.7% in 2011, assuming gains from new products are outweighed by the sale of BSX's neurovascular business, the weak ICD market, and significant pricing pressures and some volume softness in the drug-eluting stent (DES) market. For 2012, we expect growth to recover, albeit in the low single digits, on the lapping of the divestiture, new products and easier comparisons. Pending new products include next-generation ICDs that BSX launched in international markets and is poised to launch shortly in the U.S. We also expect its DES sales to benefit from new stents and from Johnson & Johnson's (JNJ 64, Buy) decision to exit the market. However, we do not see a recovery in the U.S. ICD and DES markets any time soon.

➤ We expect gross margins to narrow in 2011, as a less favorable product mix on the neurovascular unit's sale outweighs gains from new products, but to then recover. We think operating costs will decline slightly as a percentage of sales in 2011 and remain stable in 2012.

➤ We see adjusted EPS, after amortization, of $0.46 in 2011, versus 2010's $0.40, and $0.52 in 2012.

## Investment Rationale/Risk

➤ We expect continued pressure on the U.S. ICD market from a medical journal article on, and a U.S. Justice Dept. probe of, improper ICD implantations. But while BSX saw an encouraging volume pickup in September/early October, and we think its new ICDs hold promise, we see no signs yet that markets will stabilize in the near term. Meantime, we are encouraged by its recent share gains in DES markets, and we believe its new Promus Element will improve the sales mix, but we expect sustained pricing pressure on rivals' pending new stents. Elsewhere, we are encouraged by gains by BSX's endoscopy and peripheral segments, but we expect continued sluggishness in women's health and electrophysiology amid a still tough economy. On a positive note, we view as promising BSX's new products and pipeline, acquisitions, and emerging markets expansion.

➤ Risks to our recommendation and target price include intensified competition, slow commercialization of new products, and product recalls.

➤ Our 12-month target price of $6.50 reflects a below-peers multiple of 8.5X our 2012 cash EPS estimate of $0.76, before amortization of $0.24.

## Revenue/Earnings Data

**Revenue (Million $)**

| | 1Q | 2Q | 3Q | 4Q | Year |
|---|---|---|---|---|---|
| 2011 | 1,925 | 1,975 | 1,874 | -- | -- |
| 2010 | 1,960 | 1,928 | 1,916 | 2,002 | 7,806 |
| 2009 | 2,010 | 2,074 | 2,025 | 2,079 | 8,188 |
| 2008 | 2,046 | 2,024 | 1,978 | 2,002 | 8,050 |
| 2007 | 2,086 | 2,071 | 2,048 | 2,152 | 8,357 |
| 2006 | 1,620 | 2,110 | 2,206 | 2,065 | 7,821 |

**Earnings Per Share ($)**

| | | | | | |
|---|---|---|---|---|---|
| 2011 | 0.01 | 0.10 | 0.09 | E0.10 | E0.46 |
| 2010 | -1.05 | 0.06 | 0.12 | 0.15 | -0.70 |
| 2009 | -0.01 | 0.10 | 0.13 | -0.71 | -0.68 |
| 2008 | 0.22 | 0.07 | -0.04 | -1.62 | -1.38 |
| 2007 | 0.08 | 0.08 | -0.18 | -0.31 | -0.33 |
| 2006 | 0.40 | -3.21 | 0.05 | 0.19 | -2.81 |

Fiscal year ended Dec. 31. Next earnings report expected: Early February. EPS Estimates based on S&P Operating Earnings; historical GAAP earnings are as reported.

## Dividend Data

No cash dividends have been paid.

---

**Please read the Required Disclosures and Analyst Certification on the last page of this report.**

*The McGraw-Hill Companies*

# Boston Scientific Corp

STANDARD
&POOR'S

## Business Summary October 26, 2011

CORPORATE OVERVIEW. Boston Scientific develops and markets minimally invasive medical devices that are used in a broad range of interventional medical specialties, including interventional cardiology, cardiac rhythm management, peripheral intervention, electrophysiology, gynecology, oncology, urology and neuromodulation.

Within the cardiovascular market, the company sells products used to treat coronary vessel disease known as arteriosclerosis. The majority of BSX's cardiovascular products are used in percutaneous transluminal coronary angioplasty (PTCA) and percutaneous transluminal coronary rotational atherectomy. These products include PTCA balloon catheters, rotational atherectomy systems, guide wires, guide catheters, diagnostic catheters, and, more recently, a cutting balloon catheter. Other products include thrombectomy catheters, peripheral vascular stents, embolic protection filters, blood clot fil-

ter systems, and electrophysiology products.

BSX also sells balloon-expandable and self-expanding coronary stent systems. In early 2004, BSX launched Taxus, an Express stent coated with a polymer embedded with the anticancer compound paclitaxel. In January 2005, BSX launched its next-generation Taxus Liberte paclitaxel-eluting coronary stent in 18 Inter-Continental countries and in Europe. Taxus Liberte was launched in the U.S. in 2008. Through an agreement with Abbott Labs, BSX also sells the PROMUS everolimus-eluting stent system in the U.S. During 2010, drug-coated coronary stents accounted for 20% of total revenues.

## Company Financials Fiscal Year Ended Dec. 31

| Per Share Data ($) | 2010 | 2009 | 2008 | 2007 | 2006 | 2005 | 2004 | 2003 | 2002 | 2001 |
|---|---|---|---|---|---|---|---|---|---|---|
| Tangible Book Value | NM | NM | NM | NM | NM | 0.67 | 0.82 | 0.49 | 0.12 | NM |
| Cash Flow | -0.16 | -0.13 | -0.78 | 0.30 | -1.90 | 1.12 | 1.60 | 0.79 | 0.64 | 0.22 |
| Earnings | -0.70 | -0.68 | -1.38 | -0.33 | -2.81 | 0.75 | 1.24 | 0.56 | 0.45 | -0.07 |
| S&P Core Earnings | 0.32 | 0.49 | -0.16 | 0.16 | -2.75 | 1.39 | 1.27 | 0.50 | 0.33 | -0.10 |
| Dividends | Nil | Nil | Nil | Nil | Nil | Nil | Nil | Nil | Nil | Nil |
| Payout Ratio | Nil | Nil | Nil | Nil | Nil | Nil | Nil | Nil | Nil | Nil |
| Prices:High | 9.79 | 11.77 | 14.22 | 18.69 | 26.56 | 35.50 | 46.10 | 36.85 | 22.15 | 13.95 |
| Prices:Low | 5.04 | 6.08 | 5.41 | 11.27 | 14.43 | 22.80 | 31.25 | 19.10 | 10.24 | 6.63 |
| P/E Ratio:High | NM | NM | NM | NM | NM | 47 | 37 | 66 | 49 | NM |
| P/E Ratio:Low | NM | NM | NM | NM | NM | 30 | 25 | 34 | 23 | NM |

### Income Statement Analysis (Million $)

| | 2010 | 2009 | 2008 | 2007 | 2006 | 2005 | 2004 | 2003 | 2002 | 2001 |
|---|---|---|---|---|---|---|---|---|---|---|
| Revenue | 7,806 | 8,188 | 8,050 | 8,357 | 7,821 | 6,283 | 5,624 | 3,476 | 2,919 | 2,673 |
| Operating Income | 1,849 | 2,141 | 2,159 | 2,158 | -2,383 | 2,338 | 1,989 | 945 | 757 | 614 |
| Depreciation | 816 | 834 | 864 | 939 | 781 | 314 | 275 | 196 | 161 | 232 |
| Interest Expense | 393 | 407 | 468 | 570 | 435 | 90.0 | 64.0 | 46.0 | 43.0 | 59.0 |
| Pretax Income | -1,063 | -1,308 | -2,062 | -569 | -3,535 | 891 | 1,494 | 643 | 549 | 44.0 |
| Effective Tax Rate | NA | 21.6% | NM | NM | NM | 29.5% | 28.9% | 26.6% | 32.1% | NM |
| Net Income | -1,065 | -1,025 | -2,072 | -495 | -3,577 | 628 | 1,062 | 472 | 373 | -54.0 |
| S&P Core Earnings | 467 | 744 | -231 | 240 | -3,498 | 1,162 | 1,082 | 423 | 269 | -77.0 |

### Balance Sheet & Other Financial Data (Million $)

| | 2010 | 2009 | 2008 | 2007 | 2006 | 2005 | 2004 | 2003 | 2002 | 2001 |
|---|---|---|---|---|---|---|---|---|---|---|
| Cash | 213 | 864 | 1,641 | 1,452 | 1,688 | 848 | 1,640 | 671 | 277 | 180 |
| Current Assets | 3,615 | 4,061 | 5,452 | 5,921 | 4,901 | 2,631 | 3,289 | 1,880 | 1,208 | 1,106 |
| Total Assets | 22,128 | 25,177 | 27,080 | 31,197 | 31,096 | 8,196 | 8,170 | 5,699 | 4,450 | 3,974 |
| Current Liabilities | 2,609 | 3,022 | 3,233 | 3,250 | 2,630 | 1,479 | 2,605 | 1,393 | 923 | 831 |
| Long Term Debt | 4,934 | 5,915 | 6,743 | 8,161 | 8,895 | 1,864 | 1,139 | 1,172 | 847 | 973 |
| Common Equity | 11,296 | 12,301 | 13,138 | 15,097 | 15,298 | 4,282 | 4,025 | 2,862 | 2,467 | 2,015 |
| Total Capital | 16,230 | 18,216 | 22,143 | 25,314 | 26,977 | 6,408 | 5,423 | 4,185 | 3,414 | 2,988 |
| Capital Expenditures | 272 | 312 | 362 | 363 | 341 | 341 | 274 | 188 | 112 | 121 |
| Cash Flow | -249 | -191 | -1,172 | 444 | -2,796 | 942 | 1,337 | 668 | 534 | 178 |
| Current Ratio | 1.4 | 1.3 | 1.7 | 1.8 | 1.9 | 1.8 | 1.3 | 1.3 | 1.3 | 1.3 |
| % Long Term Debt of Capitalization | 30.4 | 32.5 | 30.5 | 34.5 | 33.0 | 29.1 | 21.0 | 28.0 | 24.8 | 32.6 |
| % Net Income of Revenue | NM | NM | NM | NM | NM | 10.0 | 18.9 | 13.6 | 12.8 | NM |
| % Return on Assets | NM | NM | NM | NM | NM | 7.7 | 15.3 | 9.3 | 8.9 | NM |
| % Return on Equity | NM | NM | NM | NM | NM | 15.1 | 30.8 | 17.7 | 16.6 | NM |

Data as orig reptd.; bef. results of disc opers/spec. items. Per share data adj. for stk. divs.; EPS diluted. E-Estimated. NA-Not Available. NM-Not Meaningful. NR-Not Ranked. UR-Under Review.

**Office:** One Boston Scientific Place, Natick, MA 01760-1537.
**Telephone:** 508-650-8000.
**Email:** investor_relations@bsci.com
**Website:** http://www.bostonscientific.com

**Chrmn:** P.M. Nicholas
**Pres:** M.F. Mahoney
**CEO:** W.H. Kucheman
**COO & EVP:** S.R. Leno

**EVP & CFO:** J.D. Capello
**Board Members:** K. T. Bartlett, B. L. Byrnes, N. J. Connors, J. R. Elliott, K. M. Johnson, W. H. Kucheman, E. Mario, P. M. Nicholas, N. J. Nicholas, Jr., U. E. Reinhardt, J. E. Sununu

**Founded:** 1979
**Domicile:** Delaware
**Employees:** 25,000

The McGraw-Hill Companies

# Bristol-Myers Squibb Co

**STANDARD &POOR'S**

| S&P Recommendation **BUY** ★★★★☆ | Price $31.50 (as of Nov 29, 2011) | 12-Mo. Target Price $36.00 | Investment Style Large-Cap Value |
| --- | --- | --- | --- |

**GICS Sector** Health Care
**Sub-Industry** Pharmaceuticals

**Summary** Bristol-Myers Squibb is a leading global drugmaker, with strengths in cardiovascular, anti-infective and anticancer therapeutics.

## Key Stock Statistics (Source S&P, Vickers, company reports)

| | | | | | | | |
| --- | --- | --- | --- | --- | --- | --- | --- |
| 52-Wk Range | $33.27– 24.97 | S&P Oper. EPS 2011**E** | 2.30 | Market Capitalization(B) | $53.378 | Beta | 0.51 |
| Trailing 12-Month EPS | $1.94 | S&P Oper. EPS 2012**E** | 2.06 | Yield (%) | 4.19 | S&P 3-Yr. Proj. EPS CAGR(%) | 5 |
| Trailing 12-Month P/E | 16.2 | P/E on S&P Oper. EPS 2011**E** | 13.7 | Dividend Rate/Share | $1.32 | S&P Credit Rating | A+ |
| $10K Invested 5 Yrs Ago | $15,581 | Common Shares Outstg. (M) | 1,694.5 | Institutional Ownership (%) | 67 | | |

## Price Performance

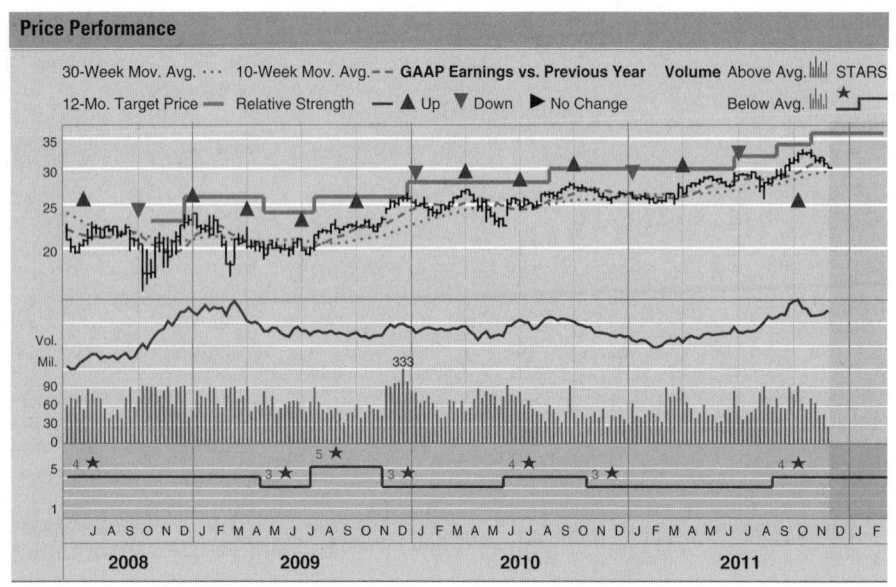

30-Week Mov. Avg. ···  10-Week Mov. Avg. – –  GAAP Earnings vs. Previous Year  Volume Above Avg. STARS
12-Mo. Target Price —  Relative Strength  ▲ Up  ▼ Down  ► No Change  Below Avg.

Options: ASE, CBOE, P, Ph

Analysis prepared by Equity Analyst **Herman Saftlas** on Nov 07, 2011, when the stock traded at **$31.34**.

## Qualitative Risk Assessment

| LOW | **MEDIUM** | HIGH |
| --- | --- | --- |

In common with other large capitalization drugmakers, BMY is subject to generic challenges to its branded drugs, as well as risks associated with new drug development and regulatory approval. While we see promise in BMY's recent efforts to expand its pharmaceutical portfolio, we remain unsure if new products will be sufficient to offset the loss of patent protection on several key drugs over the 2012-2015 period. However, cost restructurings should help the bottom line.

## Quantitative Evaluations

**S&P Quality Ranking** B+

| D | C | B- | B | **B+** | A- | A | A+ |
| --- | --- | --- | --- | --- | --- | --- | --- |

**Relative Strength Rank** STRONG

83

LOWEST = 1    HIGHEST = 99

## Highlights

➤ We expect sales from continuing operations in 2012 to decline about 14% from the $21.3 billion that we forecast for 2011. The decline should largely reflect a projected over 50% drop in sales of Plavix, whose U.S. patent expires in mid-May 2012. We estimate U.S. Plavix sales at about $6.8 billion in 2011. On the plus side, we see strong sales uptakes for newer products such as Yervoy for the treatment for metastatic melanoma, Sprycel for leukemia, Orencia for arthritis and Onglyza for type 2 diabetes. We also see much potential for Eliquis, a novel anti-coagulant now under FDA review.

➤ Gross margins in 2012 are likely to be similar to the 73.5% that we projected for 2011. We expect SG&A expenses to decline, aided by cost efficiencies. However, R&D spending is likely to hold relatively steady with the $3.6 billion that we forecast for 2011, reflecting continued aggressive investment in new drugs.

➤ After estimated effective taxes modestly lower than the 26% indicated for 2011, we project non-GAAP EPS of $2.06 for 2012, versus the $2.30 that we estimate for 2011.

## Investment Rationale/Risk

➤ Preparing for looming U.S. and European patent expirations over the next four years on key products such as Plavix, Avapro, Sustiva and Abilify, BMY has become more active in recent years in expanding its new product portfolio through acquisitions and in-licensed products. In March 2011, the FDA approved Yervoy (formerly ipilimumab), a novel treatment for advanced melanoma that we think has over $1.5 billion in sales potential by 2015. Another key R&D drug that we think has significant potential is Eliquis, a blood-thinning agent for stroke prevention that BMY is co-developing with Pfizer (PFE 20, Buy). Supported by strong clinical data, sales of Eliquis should exceed $3.5 billion by 2015, in our estimation.

➤ Risks to our recommendation and target price include increased competitive pressures in key product lines, and possible pipeline setbacks.

➤ Our 12-month target price of $36 is derived by applying a premium-to-peers P/E of 15.6X to our 2011 EPS estimate. Our DCF model, which assumes a WACC of 9.1% and terminal growth of 1%, also indicates intrinsic value near $36. The indicated dividend yield was recently 4.1%.

## Revenue/Earnings Data

**Revenue (Million $)**

| | 1Q | 2Q | 3Q | 4Q | Year |
| --- | --- | --- | --- | --- | --- |
| 2011 | 5,011 | 5,434 | 5,345 | -- | -- |
| 2010 | 4,807 | 4,768 | 4,798 | 5,111 | 19,484 |
| 2009 | 4,322 | 4,665 | 4,788 | 5,033 | 18,808 |
| 2008 | 4,891 | 5,203 | 5,254 | 5,249 | 20,597 |
| 2007 | 4,317 | 4,757 | 4,893 | 5,381 | 19,348 |
| 2006 | 4,676 | 4,871 | 4,154 | 4,213 | 17,914 |

**Earnings Per Share ($)**

| | | | | | |
| --- | --- | --- | --- | --- | --- |
| 2011 | 0.57 | 0.52 | 0.56 | E0.55 | E2.30 |
| 2010 | 0.43 | 0.53 | 0.55 | 0.28 | 1.79 |
| 2009 | 0.33 | 0.44 | 0.45 | 0.41 | 1.63 |
| 2008 | 0.32 | 0.36 | 0.30 | 0.61 | 1.59 |
| 2007 | 0.33 | 0.33 | 0.41 | -0.07 | 0.99 |
| 2006 | 0.36 | 0.34 | 0.17 | -0.07 | 0.81 |

Fiscal year ended Dec. 31. Next earnings report expected: Late January. EPS Estimates based on S&P Operating Earnings; historical GAAP earnings are as reported.

## Dividend Data (Dates: mm/dd Payment Date: mm/dd/yy)

| Amount ($) | Date Decl. | Ex-Div. Date | Stk. of Record | Payment Date |
| --- | --- | --- | --- | --- |
| 0.330 | 12/14 | 01/05 | 01/07 | 02/01/11 |
| 0.330 | 03/01 | 03/30 | 04/01 | 05/02/11 |
| 0.330 | 06/22 | 06/29 | 07/01 | 08/01/11 |

Dividends have been paid since 1900. Source: Company reports.

# Bristol-Myers Squibb Co

STANDARD &POOR'S

## Business Summary November 07, 2011

CORPORATE OVERVIEW. Bristol-Myers Squibb is a major global drugmaker, offering a wide range of prescription drugs. With the late 2009 split-off of the Mead Johnson nutritional products business, BMY is now solely a biopharmaceuticals company. In recent years, BMY also divested other non-core operations, including beauty care, orthopedic devices and imaging products. Foreign operations accounted for 35% of sales from continuing operations in 2010, down from 36% in 2009.

The company's largest selling drug is Plavix (sales of $6.7 billion in 2010), a platelet aggregation inhibitor for the prevention of stroke, heart attack and vascular disease. Plavix is produced through a joint venture with French drugmaker Sanofi-Aventis SA. Another important heart drug is Avapro/Avalide ($1.2 billion), an angiotensin II receptor blocker for hypertension.

The company's second biggest drug is Abilify ($2.6 billion), a psychotic agent used to treat schizophrenia and bipolar disorder. It is also used to treat major depression in combination with antidepressants. Principal oncology drugs are Erbitux ($662 million), a treatment for colorectal and head & neck cancers; Sprycel ($576 million) for leukemia; and Ixempra ($117 million), a drug for advanced breast cancer.

Key anti-infective drugs are HIV/AIDS treatments such as Reyataz ($1.5 billion), Sustiva ($1.4 billion) and Baraclude ($931 million). BMY also offers Cefzil, Tequin, Maxipime, and other antibiotics. Other important drugs are Orencia, a treatment for rheumatoid arthritis ($733 million); Onglyza, a drug for type 2 diabetes; and Sinemet for Parkinson's disease.

In late December 2009, BMY completed the split-off of its Mead Johnson subsidiary (MJN 71, Hold) to BMY shareholders. Under terms of the deal, BMY's remaining 170 million MJN shares (an 83% interest) were exchanged for some 269 million BMY shares. BMY sold an initial 17% interest in Mead Johnson through an IPO, raising close to $1 billion.

During 2008, BMY sold its ConvaTec ostomy and wound care and its medical imaging businesses for a combined total of $4.5 billion in cash.

## Company Financials Fiscal Year Ended Dec. 31

| Per Share Data ($) | 2010 | 2009 | 2008 | 2007 | 2006 | 2005 | 2004 | 2003 | 2002 | 2001 |
|---|---|---|---|---|---|---|---|---|---|---|
| Tangible Book Value | 5.30 | 4.80 | 3.17 | 2.14 | 1.68 | 2.28 | 1.76 | 1.62 | 0.88 | 1.70 |
| Cash Flow | 3.00 | 1.93 | 1.94 | 1.39 | 1.28 | 1.98 | 1.66 | 1.99 | 1.43 | 1.68 |
| Earnings | 1.79 | 1.63 | 1.59 | 0.99 | 0.81 | 1.52 | 1.21 | 1.59 | 1.05 | 1.29 |
| S&P Core Earnings | 1.87 | 1.59 | 1.24 | 1.02 | 0.88 | 1.43 | 1.24 | 1.57 | 1.07 | 0.67 |
| Dividends | 0.96 | 1.25 | 1.24 | 1.12 | 1.12 | 1.12 | 1.12 | 1.12 | 1.12 | 1.10 |
| Payout Ratio | 54% | 77% | 27% | 113% | 138% | 74% | 93% | 70% | 107% | 85% |
| Prices:High | 28.00 | 26.62 | 27.37 | 32.35 | 26.41 | 26.60 | 31.30 | 29.21 | 51.95 | 73.50 |
| Prices:Low | 22.24 | 17.23 | 16.00 | 25.73 | 20.08 | 20.70 | 22.22 | 21.00 | 19.49 | 48.50 |
| P/E Ratio:High | 16 | 16 | 17 | 33 | 33 | 17 | 26 | 18 | 49 | 57 |
| P/E Ratio:Low | 12 | 11 | 10 | 26 | 25 | 14 | 18 | 13 | 19 | 38 |

| Income Statement Analysis (Million $) | 2010 | 2009 | 2008 | 2007 | 2006 | 2005 | 2004 | 2003 | 2002 | 2001 |
|---|---|---|---|---|---|---|---|---|---|---|
| Revenue | 19,484 | 18,808 | 20,597 | 19,348 | 17,914 | 19,207 | 19,380 | 20,894 | 18,119 | 19,423 |
| Operating Income | 6,996 | 5,819 | 5,152 | 4,309 | 3,483 | 4,880 | 5,373 | 5,726 | 4,851 | 7,034 |
| Depreciation | 672 | 647 | 728 | 776 | 927 | 929 | 909 | 779 | 735 | 781 |
| Interest Expense | 145 | 184 | 333 | 457 | 498 | 349 | 310 | 277 | 410 | 182 |
| Pretax Income | 6,071 | 5,602 | 5,471 | 3,534 | 2,635 | 4,516 | 4,418 | 4,694 | 2,647 | 2,986 |
| Effective Tax Rate | NA | 21.1% | 24.1% | 22.7% | 23.1% | 20.6% | 34.4% | 25.9% | 16.4% | 15.4% |
| Net Income | 3,102 | 3,239 | 3,155 | 1,968 | 1,585 | 2,992 | 2,378 | 3,106 | 2,034 | 2,527 |
| S&P Core Earnings | 3,225 | 3,149 | 2,465 | 2,024 | 1,727 | 2,808 | 2,448 | 3,043 | 2,076 | 1,321 |

| Balance Sheet & Other Financial Data (Million $) | 2010 | 2009 | 2008 | 2007 | 2006 | 2005 | 2004 | 2003 | 2002 | 2001 |
|---|---|---|---|---|---|---|---|---|---|---|
| Cash | 7,301 | 8,514 | 8,265 | 2,225 | 4,013 | 5,799 | 7,474 | 5,457 | 3,989 | 5,654 |
| Current Assets | 13,273 | 13,958 | 14,763 | 10,348 | 10,302 | 12,283 | 14,801 | 11,918 | 9,975 | 12,349 |
| Total Assets | 31,076 | 31,008 | 29,552 | 26,172 | 25,575 | 28,138 | 30,435 | 27,471 | 24,874 | 27,057 |
| Current Liabilities | 6,739 | 6,313 | 6,710 | 8,644 | 6,496 | 6,890 | 9,843 | 7,530 | 8,220 | 8,826 |
| Long Term Debt | 5,328 | 6,130 | 6,585 | 4,381 | 7,248 | 8,364 | 8,463 | 8,522 | 6,261 | 6,237 |
| Common Equity | 15,713 | 14,843 | 12,241 | 10,562 | 9,991 | 11,208 | 10,202 | 19,572 | 8,967 | 10,736 |
| Total Capital | 20,891 | 20,915 | 18,885 | 14,943 | 17,307 | 19,572 | 18,665 | 28,094 | 15,228 | 16,973 |
| Capital Expenditures | 424 | 730 | 941 | 843 | 762 | 738 | 676 | 937 | 997 | 1,023 |
| Cash Flow | 5,185 | 3,817 | 3,883 | 2,744 | 2,512 | 3,921 | 3,287 | 3,885 | 2,769 | 3,308 |
| Current Ratio | 2.0 | 2.2 | 2.2 | 1.2 | 1.6 | 1.8 | 1.5 | 1.6 | 1.2 | 1.4 |
| % Long Term Debt of Capitalization | 25.5 | Nil | 34.9 | 29.3 | 42.0 | 42.7 | 45.3 | 30.3 | 41.1 | 36.7 |
| % Net Income of Revenue | 15.9 | 17.2 | 15.3 | 10.2 | 8.8 | 15.6 | 12.3 | 14.9 | 11.2 | 13.0 |
| % Return on Assets | NA | NA | 11.4 | 7.6 | 5.9 | 10.2 | 8.2 | 11.8 | 7.7 | 11.3 |
| % Return on Equity | NA | NA | 27.7 | 19.2 | 15.0 | 27.9 | 23.8 | 16.8 | 22.5 | 25.4 |

Data as orig reptd.; bef. results of disc opers/spec. items. Per share data adj. for stk. divs.; EPS diluted. E-Estimated. NA-Not Available. NM-Not Meaningful. NR-Not Ranked. UR-Under Review.

**Office:** 345 Park Ave , New York, NY 10154-0037.
**Telephone:** 212-546-4000.
**Website:** http://www.bms.com
**Chrmn:** J.M. Cornelius

**CEO:** L. Andreotti
**EVP & CFO:** C. Bancroft
**SVP, Secy & General Counsel:** S. Leung
**SVP & CIO:** P. Von Autenried

**Investor Contact:** J. Elicker (212-546-3775)
**Board Members:** L. Andreotti, L. B. Campbell, J. M. Cornelius, L. J. Freeh, L. H. Glimcher, M. Grobstein, A. J. Lacy, V. L. Sato, E. Sigal, T. D. West, Jr., R. S. Williams

**Founded:** 1887
**Domicile:** Delaware
**Employees:** 27,000

# Broadcom Corp

**STANDARD &POOR'S**

| S&P Recommendation | HOLD ★★★☆☆ | Price $29.58 (as of Nov 25, 2011) | 12-Mo. Target Price $40.00 | Investment Style Large-Cap Blend |
|---|---|---|---|---|

**GICS Sector** Information Technology
**Sub-Industry** Semiconductors

**Summary** This company provides semiconductors for broadband communications markets, including cable set-top boxes, cable modems, office networks, and home networking.

## Key Stock Statistics (Source S&P, Vickers, company reports)

| | | | | | | | |
|---|---|---|---|---|---|---|---|
| 52-Wk Range | $47.39– 29.51 | S&P Oper. EPS 2011**E** | 1.59 | Market Capitalization(B) | $14.376 | Beta | 1.21 |
| Trailing 12-Month EPS | $1.66 | S&P Oper. EPS 2012**E** | 2.12 | Yield (%) | 1.22 | S&P 3-Yr. Proj. EPS CAGR(%) | 3 |
| Trailing 12-Month P/E | 17.8 | P/E on S&P Oper. EPS 2011**E** | 18.6 | Dividend Rate/Share | $0.36 | S&P Credit Rating | A- |
| $10K Invested 5 Yrs Ago | $8,391 | Common Shares Outstg. (M) | 539.0 | Institutional Ownership (%) | 88 | | |

## Price Performance

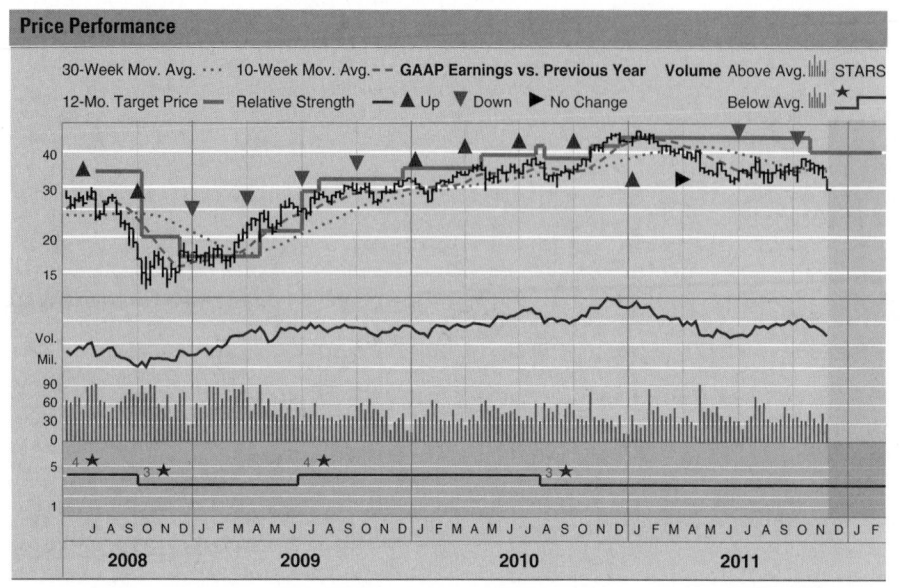

30-Week Mov. Avg. ···· 10-Week Mov. Avg. - - GAAP Earnings vs. Previous Year   Volume Above Avg. STARS
12-Mo. Target Price — Relative Strength  — ▲ Up  ▼ Down  ▶ No Change   Below Avg.

Options: ASE, CBOE, P, Ph

Analysis prepared by Equity Analyst **Angelo Zino, CFA** on Oct 26, 2011, when the stock traded at **$35.66**.

## Qualitative Risk Assessment

| LOW | MEDIUM | HIGH |
|---|---|---|

Our risk assessment reflects Broadcom's exposure to the sales cycles of the semiconductor industry, dependence on foundry partners for production, and greater reliance than most companies on stock-based compensation. This is partially offset by our view of a lack of debt and a broadening base of end users.

## Quantitative Evaluations

**S&P Quality Ranking**   B-

| D | C | B- | B | B+ | A- | A | A+ |
|---|---|---|---|---|---|---|---|

**Relative Strength Rank**   WEAK

21

LOWEST = 1                                        HIGHEST = 99

## Revenue/Earnings Data

**Revenue (Million $)**

| | 1Q | 2Q | 3Q | 4Q | Year |
|---|---|---|---|---|---|
| 2011 | 1,816 | 1,796 | 1,957 | -- | -- |
| 2010 | 1,462 | 1,604 | 1,806 | 1,946 | 6,818 |
| 2009 | 853.4 | 1,040 | 1,254 | 1,343 | 4,490 |
| 2008 | 1,032 | 1,201 | 1,298 | 1,127 | 4,658 |
| 2007 | 901.5 | 897.9 | 950.0 | 1,027 | 3,776 |
| 2006 | 900.7 | 941.1 | 902.6 | 923.5 | 3,668 |

**Earnings Per Share ($)**

| | 1Q | 2Q | 3Q | 4Q | Year |
|---|---|---|---|---|---|
| 2011 | 0.40 | 0.31 | 0.48 | E0.40 | E1.59 |
| 2010 | 0.40 | 0.52 | 0.60 | 0.47 | 1.99 |
| 2009 | -0.19 | 0.03 | 0.16 | 0.11 | 0.13 |
| 2008 | 0.14 | 0.25 | 0.31 | -0.32 | 0.41 |
| 2007 | 0.10 | 0.06 | 0.05 | 0.16 | 0.37 |
| 2006 | 0.20 | 0.18 | 0.19 | 0.08 | 0.64 |

Fiscal year ended Dec. 31. Next earnings report expected: Early February. EPS Estimates based on S&P Operating Earnings; historical GAAP earnings are as reported.

## Highlights

➤ We anticipate sales will rise 7.3% in 2012, after a projected 7.6% advance in 2011. Near term, we expect sales to be hindered by customers digesting inventories as well as plans to exit its Digital TV/Blu-Ray business. Generally, we believe BRCM has a well-diversified and innovative product portfolio, which has expanded its served available market and should lead to higher market share. We look for recent design wins for various combination wireless and mobile handset products to boost mobile and wireless networking sales. We also see expansion of broadband services and IT spending providing growth opportunities for BRCM's broadband communication and networking businesses.

➤ We see gross margins of 50% to 51% over the next few quarters. Although a variable sales mix could affect results, we believe BRCM's fabless structure will help keep gross margins relatively stable. We expect the operating margin to widen to 15% in 2012, from an anticipated 12% in 2011, largely on fewer non-recurring charges as well as operating leverage benefits.

➤ Our 2012 EPS projection includes about $0.80 per share in stock-based compensation.

## Investment Rationale/Risk

➤ Our hold recommendation reflects our view of healthy long term fundamentals balanced by fair valuations. We believe that BRCM, through its focus on making integrated and multifunctional chips, is taking market share in relatively fast-growing markets, which should lead to above-industry growth over the next few years. Although non-recurring and stock-based compensation hinder profitability, the sales advances should still provide operating leverage and lead to improving profitability, in our opinion. Consequently, we think relative multiples deserve to be above the industry average, which is already the case.

➤ Risks to our recommendation and target price include lower than anticipated enterprise spending, slower than anticipated orders for handset chips, and rising operating expenses.

➤ Our 12-month target price of $40 is based on a P/E multiple of 19X, above the peer average to account for our view of BRCM's relative earnings growth, return metrics, and risk, applied to our 2012 EPS estimate. We note that without the inclusion of stock-based compensation, the P/E multiple would be notably closer to the industry average.

## Dividend Data (Dates: mm/dd Payment Date: mm/dd/yy)

| Amount ($) | Date Decl. | Ex-Div. Date | Stk. of Record | Payment Date |
|---|---|---|---|---|
| 0.090 | 01/31 | 02/16 | 02/18 | 03/07/11 |
| 0.090 | 05/05 | 05/18 | 05/20 | 06/06/11 |
| 0.090 | 08/11 | 08/24 | 08/26 | 09/12/11 |
| 0.090 | 11/09 | 11/30 | 12/02 | 12/19/11 |

Dividends have been paid since 2010. Source: Company reports.

**Please read the Required Disclosures and Analyst Certification on the last page of this report.**

The **McGraw·Hill** Companies

# Broadcom Corp

## Business Summary October 26, 2011

CORPORATE OVERVIEW. Founded in 1991, Broadcom is a global provider of semiconductors for wired and wireless communications. The company's products enable the delivery of voice, video, data and multimedia to and throughout the home, the office and the mobile environment. Broadcom's diverse product portfolio includes solutions for digital cable, satellite and Internet Protocol (IP) set-top boxes and media servers; high definition television (HDTV); high definition DVD players and personal video recording (PVR) devices; cable and DSL modems and residential gateways; high-speed transmission and switching for local, metropolitan, wide area and storage networking; System I/O server solutions; broadband network and security processors; wireless and personal area networking; cellular communications; global positioning system (GPS) applications; mobile multimedia and applications processors; mobile power management; and Voice over Internet Protocol (VoIP) gateway and telephony systems.

Revenues can be separated into three main target markets: Broadband Communications, Infrastructure and Networking, and Mobile and Wireless Networking. Broadband Communication products offer manufacturers a range of

broadband communications and consumer electronics systems-on-a-chip (SoCs) that enable voice, video, data and multimedia services over residential wired and wireless networks. Infrastructure and Networking produces silicon and software solutions for service providers, data centers, enterprise and small-to-medium-sized business, or SMB, markets. Its solutions aim to enable these networks to offer faster, "greener" and more cost-efficient transport and processing of voice, data and video traffic across wired and wireless networks. Mobile and Wireless Networking allows manufacturers to develop leading-edge portable devices, enabling end-to-end wireless opportunities for the home, business and mobile markets. In 2010, net revenue by major target market was 31% broadband communications; 24% infrastructure and networking; and 41% mobile and wireless, with All Other making up the remainder.

## Company Financials Fiscal Year Ended Dec. 31

| Per Share Data ($) | 2010 | 2009 | 2008 | 2007 | 2006 | 2005 | 2004 | 2003 | 2002 | 2001 |
|---|---|---|---|---|---|---|---|---|---|---|
| Tangible Book Value | 7.13 | 4.97 | 4.63 | 4.86 | 5.43 | 3.79 | 2.59 | 1.43 | 0.94 | 2.19 |
| Cash Flow | 2.24 | 0.33 | 0.60 | 0.48 | 0.73 | 0.85 | 0.59 | -1.98 | -5.20 | -4.87 |
| Earnings | 1.99 | 0.13 | 0.41 | 0.37 | 0.64 | 0.73 | 0.42 | -2.19 | -5.57 | -7.19 |
| S&P Core Earnings | 2.05 | 0.19 | 0.62 | 0.37 | 0.64 | -0.04 | -0.70 | -2.31 | -5.07 | -6.87 |
| Dividends | 0.32 | Nil | Nil | Nil | Nil | Nil | Nil | Nil | Nil | Nil |
| Payout Ratio | 16% | Nil | Nil | Nil | Nil | Nil | Nil | Nil | Nil | Nil |
| Prices:High | 47.00 | 32.29 | 29.91 | 43.07 | 50.00 | 33.28 | 31.37 | 25.10 | 35.57 | 93.00 |
| Prices:Low | 26.40 | 15.31 | 12.98 | 25.70 | 21.98 | 18.25 | 16.83 | 7.91 | 6.35 | 12.27 |
| P/E Ratio:High | 24 | NM | 73 | NM | 78 | 46 | 75 | NM | NM | NM |
| P/E Ratio:Low | 13 | NM | 32 | NM | 34 | 25 | 40 | NM | NM | NM |

| Income Statement Analysis (Million $) | 2010 | 2009 | 2008 | 2007 | 2006 | 2005 | 2004 | 2003 | 2002 | 2001 |
|---|---|---|---|---|---|---|---|---|---|---|
| Revenue | 6,612 | 4,490 | 4,658 | 3,776 | 3,668 | 2,671 | 2,401 | 1,610 | 1,083 | 962 |
| Operating Income | 1,094 | 265 | 490 | 148 | 309 | 557 | 450 | -30.4 | -442 | -573 |
| Depreciation | 137 | 105 | 97.5 | 62.0 | 47.6 | 68.5 | 91.7 | 90.9 | 147 | 889 |
| Interest Expense | NA | NA | Nil | Nil | Nil | Nil | Nil | Nil | 3.60 | 5.00 |
| Pretax Income | 1,097 | 72.2 | 222 | 219 | 367 | 392 | 294 | -935 | -1,939 | -2,799 |
| Effective Tax Rate | NA | 9.60% | 3.38% | 2.70% | NM | NM | 25.7% | NM | NM | NM |
| Net Income | 1,082 | 65.3 | 215 | 213 | 379 | 412 | 219 | -960 | -2,237 | -2,742 |
| S&P Core Earnings | 1,114 | 97.5 | 319 | 215 | 379 | -25.7 | -330 | -1,011 | -2,039 | -2,617 |

| Balance Sheet & Other Financial Data (Million $) | 2010 | 2009 | 2008 | 2007 | 2006 | 2005 | 2004 | 2003 | 2002 | 2001 |
|---|---|---|---|---|---|---|---|---|---|---|
| Cash | 2,658 | 1,929 | 1,898 | 2,329 | 2,680 | 1,733 | 1,183 | 606 | 503 | 540 |
| Current Assets | 4,184 | 2,914 | 2,751 | 3,054 | 3,352 | 2,336 | 1,584 | 996 | 722 | 674 |
| Total Assets | 7,944 | 5,127 | 4,393 | 4,838 | 4,877 | 3,752 | 2,886 | 2,018 | 2,216 | 3,623 |
| Current Liabilities | 1,271 | 1,148 | 717 | 758 | 679 | 595 | 497 | 504 | 534 | 412 |
| Long Term Debt | 697 | NA | Nil | Nil | Nil | Nil | Nil | Nil | 1.21 | 4.01 |
| Common Equity | 5,826 | 3,892 | 3,607 | 4,036 | 4,192 | 3,145 | 2,366 | 1,490 | 1,645 | 3,207 |
| Total Capital | 6,523 | 3,892 | 3,607 | 4,036 | 4,192 | 3,145 | 2,366 | 1,490 | 1,646 | 3,211 |
| Capital Expenditures | 109 | 66.6 | 82.8 | 160 | 92.5 | 41.8 | 49.9 | 47.9 | 75.2 | 71.4 |
| Cash Flow | 1,219 | 170 | 312 | 275 | 427 | 480 | 310 | -869 | -2,090 | -1,853 |
| Current Ratio | 3.3 | 2.5 | 3.8 | 4.0 | 4.9 | 3.9 | 3.2 | 2.0 | 1.4 | 1.6 |
| % Long Term Debt of Capitalization | 10.7 | Nil | Nil | Nil | Nil | Nil | Nil | Nil | 0.1 | 0.1 |
| % Net Income of Revenue | 16.4 | 1.5 | 4.6 | 5.6 | 10.3 | 15.4 | 9.1 | NM | NM | NM |
| % Return on Assets | 16.6 | 1.4 | 4.7 | 4.3 | 8.8 | 12.4 | 8.9 | NM | NM | NM |
| % Return on Equity | 22.3 | 1.7 | 5.6 | 5.1 | 10.3 | 14.9 | 11.3 | NM | NM | NM |

Data as orig reptd.; bef. results of disc opers/spec. items. Per share data adj. for stk. divs.; EPS diluted. E-Estimated. NA-Not Available. NM-Not Meaningful. NR-Not Ranked. UR-Under Review.

**Office:** 5300 California Avenue, Buildings 1-8, Irvine, CA 92617.
**Telephone:** 949-926-5000.
**Email:** investorinfo@broadcom.com
**Website:** http://www.broadcom.com

**Chrmn:** J.E. Major
**Pres & CEO:** S.A. McGregor
**COO:** N.Y. Kim
**CFO:** E.K. Brandt

**CTO:** H. Samueli
**Investor Contact:** T.P. Andrew (949-926-5663)
**Board Members:** N. H. Handel, E. Hartenstein, M. M. Klawe, J. E. Major, S. A. McGregor, W. T. Morrow, H. Samueli, J. A. Swainson, R. E. Switz

**Founded:** 1991
**Domicile:** California
**Employees:** 8,950

# Brown-Forman Corp

**STANDARD &POOR'S**

| S&P Recommendation | BUY ★★★★☆ | Price<br>$73.86 (as of Nov 25, 2011) | 12-Mo. Target Price<br>$79.00 | Investment Style<br>Large-Cap Growth |
|---|---|---|---|---|

**GICS Sector** Consumer Staples
**Sub-Industry** Distillers & Vintners

**Summary** This leading distiller and importer of alcoholic beverages markets Jack Daniel's, Southern Comfort, Finlandia, Korbel, and Bolla brands.

## Key Stock Statistics (Source S&P, Vickers, company reports)

| | | | | | | | |
|---|---|---|---|---|---|---|---|
| 52-Wk Range | $77.56– 62.14 | S&P Oper. EPS 2012**E** | 3.68 | Market Capitalization(B) | $6.472 | Beta | 0.70 |
| Trailing 12-Month EPS | $3.95 | S&P Oper. EPS 2013**E** | 4.01 | Yield (%) | 1.90 | S&P 3-Yr. Proj. EPS CAGR(%) | 9 |
| Trailing 12-Month P/E | 18.7 | P/E on S&P Oper. EPS 2012**E** | 20.1 | Dividend Rate/Share | $1.40 | S&P Credit Rating | A |
| $10K Invested 5 Yrs Ago | $14,854 | Common Shares Outstg. (M) | 144.1 | Institutional Ownership (%) | 55 | | |

## Price Performance

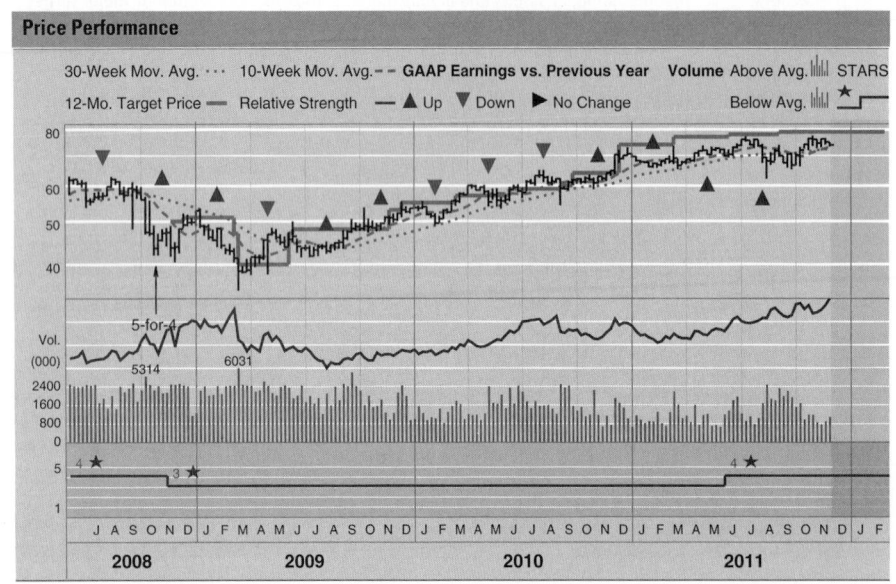

30-Week Mov. Avg. ···  10-Week Mov. Avg. --  **GAAP Earnings vs. Previous Year**  Volume Above Avg. STARS
12-Mo. Target Price —  Relative Strength  ▲ Up  ▼ Down  ► No Change  Below Avg.

Analysis prepared by Equity Analyst **Esther Kwon, CFA** on Sep 02, 2011, when the stock traded at **$70.34**.

## Highlights

► We forecast net sales growth (before excise taxes) of over 8% in FY 12 (Apr.), an acceleration of growth from the nearly 5% rise in FY 11, to approximately $2.8 billion, on new products and further growth from key brand Jack Daniel's. In constant currency, we see Jack Daniel's branded product sales rising, but we expect continued softness in Southern Comfort. Long term, with over 50% of net sales from outside the U.S., we think growth prospects remain bright for the company's brands.

► We look for lower gross margins on higher commodity costs, lower-margin product and geographic mix, and a continued high level of value added pack promotions, partially offset by operating efficiencies. We forecast improved operating leverage as BF benefits from investments made to build out its own distribution in certain international markets in FY 11 offset somewhat by higher media and advertising costs as the company supports new product launches.

► We estimate FY 12 EPS of $3.68, up from operating EPS of $3.41 in FY 11. A $1 a share special dividend was paid to stockholders of record December 10, 2010.

## Investment Rationale/Risk

► Long term, we look for continued strength in the global market, and we think spirits will continue to make successful inroads in the 21- to 27-year-old demographic. BF should continue to capitalize on what we see as positive industry trends with its strong portfolio of spirits and international reach, particularly with its Jack Daniel's brand. In the near term, while we see the domestic market remaining challenging in the face of competition in the brown spirits category stemming from new product launches and line extensions, we think BF's own new product introductions will be a boost.

► Risks to our recommendation and target price include an unexpected slowdown in the growth of top-performing brands. Also, we view BF's dual-class structure and the majority representation of insiders on its board of directors as corporate governance concerns.

► Our 12-month target price of $79 is supported by our P/E analysis, which applies a multiple of 19.6X, in line with the stock's historical average and a premium to peers and the S&P 500, to our FY 13 EPS estimate of $4.01. We think a premium is appropriate given the company's greater international exposure.

## Qualitative Risk Assessment

| LOW | MEDIUM | HIGH |
|---|---|---|

Brown-Forman is a large-cap competitor in an industry that has historically demonstrated relative stability. However, we believe the company's dual-class structure and the majority representation of insiders on its board of directors pose corporate governance concerns.

## Quantitative Evaluations

**S&P Quality Ranking**     A

| D | C | B- | B | B+ | A- | A | A+ |
|---|---|---|---|---|---|---|---|

**Relative Strength Rank**     STRONG

84

LOWEST = 1        HIGHEST = 99

## Revenue/Earnings Data

**Revenue (Million $)**

| | 1Q | 2Q | 3Q | 4Q | Year |
|---|---|---|---|---|---|
| 2012 | 637.8 | -- | -- | -- | -- |
| 2011 | 745.0 | 906.0 | 962.0 | 791.0 | 3,404 |
| 2010 | 738.0 | 893.0 | 862.0 | 733.0 | 3,326 |
| 2009 | 790.0 | 935.0 | 784.0 | 683.0 | 3,192 |
| 2008 | 739.0 | 893.0 | 877.0 | 772.0 | 3,282 |
| 2007 | 633.0 | 727.0 | 754.8 | 690.8 | 2,218 |

**Earnings Per Share ($)**

| | 1Q | 2Q | 3Q | 4Q | Year |
|---|---|---|---|---|---|
| 2012 | 0.81 | E1.14 | E1.04 | E0.70 | E3.68 |
| 2011 | 0.76 | 1.05 | 0.96 | 1.13 | 3.90 |
| 2010 | 0.81 | 0.99 | 0.73 | 0.49 | 3.02 |
| 2009 | 0.58 | 0.94 | 0.81 | 0.53 | 2.87 |
| 2008 | 0.58 | 0.83 | 0.74 | 0.65 | 2.85 |
| 2007 | 0.61 | 0.80 | 0.72 | 0.45 | 2.58 |

Fiscal year ended Apr. 30. Next earnings report expected: NA. EPS Estimates based on S&P Operating Earnings; historical GAAP earnings are as reported.

## Dividend Data (Dates: mm/dd Payment Date: mm/dd/yy)

| Amount ($) | Date Decl. | Ex-Div. Date | Stk. of Record | Payment Date |
|---|---|---|---|---|
| 0.320 | 01/27 | 03/07 | 03/09 | 04/01/11 |
| 0.320 | 05/26 | 06/06 | 06/08 | 07/01/11 |
| 0.320 | 07/28 | 09/01 | 09/06 | 10/03/11 |
| 0.350 | 11/17 | 12/02 | 12/06 | 12/27/11 |

Dividends have been paid since 1960. Source: Company reports.

*The McGraw-Hill Companies*

# Brown-Forman Corp

STANDARD
&POOR'S

## Business Summary September 02, 2011

CORPORATE OVERVIEW. Brown-Forman Corp.'s origins date back to 1870. It is the world's fourth largest producer of distilled spirits. With a portfolio of well known brands, the company is best known for its popular Jack Daniel's Tennessee Whiskey, which continues to be its largest sales and profit producer.

Although many alcoholic beverage companies have moved in recent years to reduce their dependence on the highly mature brown spirits market, BF has remained whiskey-oriented. Its product line is stocked with well known whiskies, bourbons, vodkas, tequilas, rums, and liqueurs. Brands include Jack Daniel's, Southern Comfort, Tequila Herradura, el Jimador Tequila, and Canadian Mist. Global depletions of Jack Daniel's in FY 10 (Apr.) increased 2%, compared to 1% in FY 09. Statistics based on case sales rank Jack Daniel's as the largest selling American whiskey in the world, Canadian Mist as the second largest selling Canadian whiskey in the U.S. and the third largest in the world, and Southern Comfort as the largest selling domestic proprietary liqueur in the U.S. Other major alcoholic beverage lines include Fetzer and Bolla wines, Finlandia vodka, Chambord liqueur, and Korbel Champagnes.

International sales, consisting principally of exports of wines and spirits, in-

creased to 53% of total net revenues in FY 10 from 52% in FY 09. Beverage growth in recent years has come primarily from international markets for the company's spirits brands. The key export markets for brands include the U.K., Australia, Mexico, Poland, Germany, France, Spain, Italy, South Africa, China, Japan, Canada and Russia.

Until year-end FY 05, the consumer durables segment consisted of the Lenox Inc. subsidiary, which produced and marketed china, crystal and giftware under the Lenox and Gorham trademarks. The segment also included Dansk, a producer of tableware and giftware, Gorham, Kirk Steiff, and Hartmann Luggage. In July 2005, following a strategic review, the company agreed to sell Lenox. On September 1, 2005, BF consummated the sale of substantially all of Lenox to Department 56 for $196 million. Consumer durables was eliminated as a segment, and in May 2007, the sale of substantially all of the assets of Hartmann to Clarion Capital Partners was completed.

## Company Financials  Fiscal Year Ended Apr. 30

| Per Share Data ($) | 2011 | 2010 | 2009 | 2008 | 2007 | 2006 | 2005 | 2004 | 2003 | 2002 |
|---|---|---|---|---|---|---|---|---|---|---|
| Tangible Book Value | 5.28 | 3.81 | 3.03 | 2.24 | 1.42 | 6.79 | 4.55 | 3.43 | 1.93 | 6.17 |
| Cash Flow | 3.94 | 3.06 | 3.23 | 3.18 | 2.89 | 2.88 | 2.38 | 1.83 | 1.76 | 1.64 |
| Earnings | 3.90 | 3.02 | 2.87 | 2.85 | 2.58 | 2.56 | 2.02 | 1.69 | 1.45 | 1.33 |
| S&P Core Earnings | 3.72 | 3.03 | 2.62 | 2.62 | 2.82 | 2.54 | 2.52 | 1.90 | 1.66 | 1.24 | 1.11 |
| Dividends | NA | 1.17 | 0.81 | 2.25 | 0.62 | 0.73 | 0.64 | 0.58 | 0.58 | 0.54 |
| Payout Ratio | NA | 30% | 28% | 79% | 24% | 29% | 32% | 34% | 40% | 41% |
| Calendar Year | 2010 | 2009 | 2008 | 2007 | 2006 | 2005 | 2004 | 2003 | 2002 | 2001 |
| Prices:High | 73.00 | 55.47 | 63.02 | 63.90 | 66.04 | 57.92 | 40.07 | 38.05 | 32.22 | 28.80 |
| Prices:Low | 48.93 | 34.97 | 40.46 | 50.54 | 52.22 | 37.30 | 34.24 | 24.10 | 23.48 | 23.06 |
| P/E Ratio:High | 19 | 18 | 22 | 22 | 26 | 23 | 20 | 23 | 22 | 22 |
| P/E Ratio:Low | 13 | 12 | 14 | 18 | 20 | 15 | 17 | 14 | 16 | 17 |

| Income Statement Analysis (Million $) | | | | | | | | | | |
|---|---|---|---|---|---|---|---|---|---|---|
| Revenue | 2,587 | 2,469 | 2,481 | 3,282 | 2,806 | 2,444 | 2,729 | 2,577 | 2,378 | 1,958 |
| Operating Income | 860 | 715 | 730 | 735 | 627 | 560 | 513 | 473 | 429 | 408 |
| Depreciation | 5.10 | 5.00 | 55.0 | 52.0 | 44.0 | 44.0 | 58.0 | 56.0 | 55.0 | 55.0 |
| Interest Expense | 26.4 | 28.0 | 37.0 | 49.0 | 34.0 | 18.0 | 21.0 | 21.0 | 8.00 | 8.00 |
| Pretax Income | 829 | 682 | 630 | 644 | 586 | 559 | 476 | 388 | 373 | 348 |
| Effective Tax Rate | NA | NA | 31.1% | 31.7% | 31.7% | 29.3% | 35.3% | 33.5% | 34.3% | 34.5% |
| Net Income | 572 | 449 | 434 | 440 | 400 | 395 | 308 | 258 | 245 | 228 |
| S&P Core Earnings | 544 | 450 | 397 | 438 | 393 | 389 | 289 | 252 | 209 | 190 |

| Balance Sheet & Other Financial Data (Million $) | | | | | | | | | | |
|---|---|---|---|---|---|---|---|---|---|---|
| Cash | 567 | 232 | 340 | 119 | 283 | 475 | 295 | 68.0 | 72.0 | 116 |
| Current Assets | 1,976 | 1,527 | 1,574 | 1,456 | 1,635 | 1,610 | 1,317 | 1,083 | 1,068 | 1,029 |
| Total Assets | 3,712 | 3,383 | 3,475 | 3,405 | 3,551 | 2,728 | 2,624 | 2,376 | 2,264 | 2,016 |
| Current Liabilities | 707 | 546 | 836 | 984 | 1,347 | 569 | 638 | 369 | 548 | 495 |
| Long Term Debt | 504 | 508 | 509 | 417 | 422 | 351 | 352 | 630 | 629 | 40.0 |
| Common Equity | 2,060 | 1,895 | 1,816 | 1,725 | 1,672 | 1,563 | 1,310 | 1,085 | 840 | 1,311 |
| Total Capital | 2,819 | 2,406 | 2,405 | 2,231 | 2,150 | 2,047 | 1,794 | 1,837 | 1,547 | 1,409 |
| Capital Expenditures | 39.0 | 34.0 | 49.0 | 41.0 | 58.0 | 52.0 | 49.0 | 56.0 | 119 | 71.0 |
| Cash Flow | 577 | 454 | 490 | 492 | 444 | 439 | 366 | 314 | 300 | 283 |
| Current Ratio | 2.8 | 2.8 | 1.9 | 1.5 | 1.2 | 2.8 | 2.1 | 2.9 | 1.9 | 2.1 |
| % Long Term Debt of Capitalization | 17.9 | 21.1 | 21.2 | 18.7 | 19.6 | 17.1 | 19.6 | 34.3 | 40.7 | 2.8 |
| % Net Income of Revenue | 22.1 | 18.2 | 17.5 | 13.4 | 14.3 | 16.2 | 11.3 | 10.0 | 10.3 | 11.6 |
| % Return on Assets | 16.1 | 13.1 | 12.6 | 12.7 | 12.7 | 14.7 | 12.3 | 11.1 | 11.4 | 11.5 |
| % Return on Equity | 28.9 | 24.2 | 24.5 | 26.7 | 24.7 | 27.5 | 25.6 | 26.8 | 22.8 | 18.3 |

Data as orig reptd.; bef. results of disc opers/spec. items. Per share data adj. for stk. divs.; EPS diluted. E-Estimated. NA-Not Available. NM-Not Meaningful. NR-Not Ranked. UR-Under Review.

**Office:** 850 Dixie Highway, Louisville, KY 40210.
**Telephone:** 502-585-1100.
**Website:** http://www.brown-forman.com
**Co-Chrmn:** G.G. Brown, IV

**Co-Chrmn & CEO:** P.C. Varga
**Vice Chrmn & SVP:** J.S. Welch, Jr.
**COO & EVP:** M.I. McCallum
**EVP & CFO:** D.C. Berg

**Investor Contact:** B. Marmor (502-774-6691)
**Board Members:** J. L. Amble, P.
Bousquet-Chavanne, G. G. Brown, IV, M. S. Brown, Jr., B. L. Byrnes, J. D. Cook, S. A. Frazier, R. P. Mayer, W. E. Mitchell, D. B. Stubbs, P. C. Varga, J. S. Welch, Jr.

**Founded:** 1870
**Domicile:** Delaware
**Employees:** 3,900

The **McGraw·Hill** Companies

# Cablevision Systems Corp

**STANDARD
&POOR'S**

| S&P Recommendation | HOLD ★★★★★ | Price<br>$14.48 (as of Nov 25, 2011) | 12-Mo. Target Price<br>$16.00 | Investment Style<br>Large-Cap Growth |
|---|---|---|---|---|

**GICS Sector** Consumer Discretionary
**Sub-Industry** Cable & Satellite

**Summary** This mid-sized U.S. cable multiple system operator (MSO), which offers Optimum-branded cable, Internet and voice services to mostly residential (and increasingly commercial) subscribers, recently spun off its Rainbow Media programming unit.

## Key Stock Statistics (Source S&P, Vickers, company reports)

| | | | | | | | |
|---|---|---|---|---|---|---|---|
| 52-Wk Range | $38.08–14.18 | S&P Oper. EPS 2011**E** | 0.90 | Market Capitalization(B) | $3.263 | Beta | 1.44 |
| Trailing 12-Month EPS | $1.19 | S&P Oper. EPS 2012**E** | 1.07 | Yield (%) | 4.14 | S&P 3-Yr. Proj. EPS CAGR(%) | 13 |
| Trailing 12-Month P/E | 12.2 | P/E on S&P Oper. EPS 2011**E** | 16.1 | Dividend Rate/Share | $0.60 | S&P Credit Rating | BB |
| $10K Invested 5 Yrs Ago | NA | Common Shares Outstg. (M) | 279.5 | Institutional Ownership (%) | 87 | | |

## Price Performance

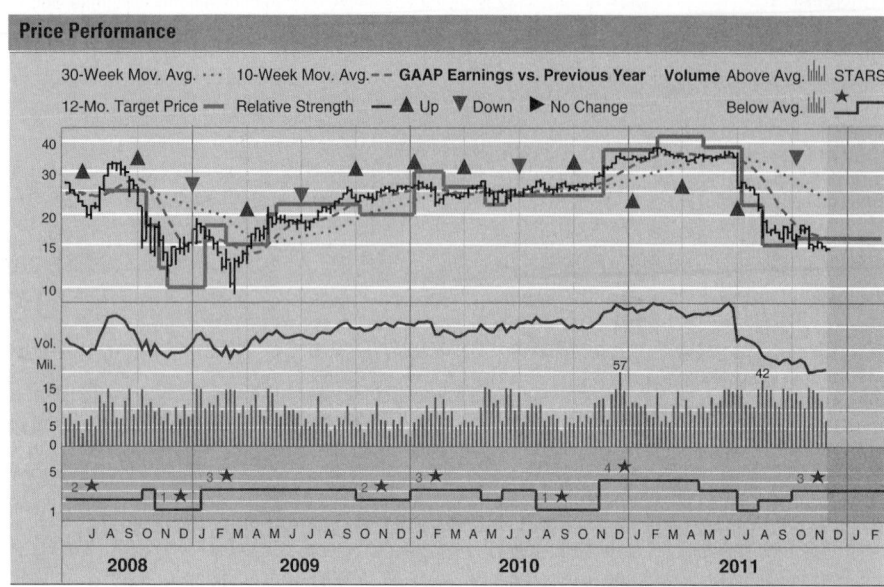

30-Week Mov. Avg. · · · 10-Week Mov. Avg. – – **GAAP Earnings vs. Previous Year** Volume Above Avg. STARS
12-Mo. Target Price — Relative Strength — ▲ Up ▼ Down ► No Change Below Avg. ★

Options: ASE, CBOE, P, Ph

Analysis prepared by Equity Analyst **T. Amobi, CFA CPA** on Oct 31, 2011, when the stock traded at **$14.50**.

## Highlights

► We project telecom revenues to rise 9.5% in 2011, to nearly $6.28 billion, and 3.4% in 2012, to $6.49 billion, with moderate growth from 11.6 million 2010 year-end RGUs -- including about 880,000 subscribers from the December 2010 Bresnan acquisition -- and higher ARPU on rate hikes and HD DVR offerings, and lower churn on bundled high-speed data and voice services for residential and business customers, versus video subscriber losses.

► Assuming high single-digit to low double-digit growth for the Lightpath (Ethernet-based) unit, and relatively stagnant growth to further declines at Newsday and other smaller businesses, we see 2011 and 2012 consolidated revenues declining 3.6% and 0.9%, respectively, to $6.97 billion and $6.91 billion.

► With further margin expansion for Lightpath, and some narrowing of the margin differential for the Bresnan systems, after higher programming costs and lingering challenges for NY Newsday, we project consolidated adjusted EBITDA of about $2.31 billion and $2.39 billion in 2011 and 2012, respectively, and after interest and taxes, EPS of $0.90 and $1.07.

## Investment Rationale/Risk

► CVC reported what we saw as generally lackluster results for the first nine months of 2011, as difficult economic and competitive conditions weighed on the core residential business, while the enterprise unit held up well. Amid an ensuing sharp sell-off in the months since the AMC Networks (AMCX 33 NR) spinoff, we think the latest results also call into question the longer-term financial targets for the Bresnan deal, for which we nonetheless remain somewhat cautiously optimistic. Still, we are more wary of CVC's financial flexibility for continued share buybacks and dividends.

► Risks to our recommendation and target price include increased competition from satellite TV and telcos as well as online video providers ("cord-cutting"); sizable earnings dilution on the Bresnan deal; adverse shifts in capital allocation; and governance concerns with the Dolan family's voting control and dual-class shares.

► Our $17 12-month target price reflects a 6.4X EV/EBITDA multiple on our 2012 estimate, or $4,100 per subscriber, which we view as ample relative to pure-play cable peers. We note a 4.1% dividend yield, and $1.6 billion of NOLs.

## Qualitative Risk Assessment

| LOW | MEDIUM | HIGH |
|---|---|---|

Our risk assessment reflects governance issues related to the controlling shareholders, and our view of CVC's highly leveraged balance sheet and relatively inconsistent capital allocation, partly offset by a potential increase in scale efficiencies (including the Bresnan acquisition), plus what we see as a relatively clustered footprint concentration in the New York metro area.

## Quantitative Evaluations

**S&P Quality Ranking**      B-

| D | C | B- | B | B+ | A- | A | A+ |
|---|---|---|---|---|---|---|---|

**Relative Strength Rank**      WEAK

19

LOWEST = 1          HIGHEST = 99

## Revenue/Earnings Data

**Revenue (Million $)**

| | 1Q | 2Q | 3Q | 4Q | Year |
|---|---|---|---|---|---|
| 2011 | 1,922 | -- | -- | -- | -- |
| 2010 | 1,752 | 1,802 | 1,808 | 1,869 | 7,231 |
| 2009 | 1,913 | 1,876 | 1,840 | 2,145 | 7,773 |
| 2008 | 1,721 | 1,712 | 1,745 | 2,052 | 7,230 |
| 2007 | 1,586 | 1,568 | 1,512 | 1,842 | 6,484 |
| 2006 | 1,409 | 1,424 | 1,409 | 1,685 | 5,927 |

**Earnings Per Share ($)**

| | | | | | |
|---|---|---|---|---|---|
| 2011 | 0.36 | 0.24 | 0.14 | E0.16 | E0.90 |
| 2010 | 0.26 | 0.20 | 0.37 | 0.38 | 1.21 |
| 2009 | 0.07 | 0.29 | 0.33 | 0.26 | 0.96 |
| 2008 | -0.11 | 0.34 | 0.09 | -1.11 | -0.78 |
| 2007 | -0.11 | -0.43 | -0.27 | 0.03 | -0.08 |
| 2006 | -0.20 | -0.09 | -0.21 | -0.03 | -0.47 |

Fiscal year ended Dec. 31. Next earnings report expected: NA. EPS Estimates based on S&P Operating Earnings; historical GAAP earnings are as reported.

## Dividend Data (Dates: mm/dd Payment Date: mm/dd/yy)

| Amount ($) | Date Decl. | Ex-Div. Date | Stk. of Record | Payment Date |
|---|---|---|---|---|
| 0.150 | 05/04 | 05/12 | 05/16 | 06/06/11 |
| Stk. | 06/06 | 07/01 | 06/16 | 06/30/11 |
| 0.150 | 08/05 | 08/17 | 08/19 | 09/09/11 |
| 0.150 | 10/28 | 11/08 | 11/11 | 12/02/11 |

Dividends have been paid since 2006. Source: Company reports.

# Cablevision Systems Corp

## Business Summary October 31, 2011

CORPORATE OVERVIEW. Cablevision Systems Corp. (CVC) is the fifth largest U.S. cable operator. The company had nearly 11.6 million revenue-generating units (RGUs) as of December 31, 2010, with more than 3.3 million basic video subscribers (63.2% penetration of residential homes passed), over 3.1 million iO Digital Video customers (93.9%), nearly 2.9 million Optimum Online high-speed data subscribers (52.3%), and 2.3 million Optimum Voice telephone customers (41.0%). CVC's Lightpath unit also provides advanced broadband (data and voice) services mainly to medium to large business customers.

On July 1, 2011, CVC completed the spinoff of its Rainbow Media programming unit as AMC Networks (AMCX 33, NR) -- an entity that includes cable networks AMC, WE tv, IFC, Sundance Channel and Wedding Central, as well as IFC Entertainment (independent film producer) and Rainbow Network Communications (a programming origination and distribution company).

Following the Rainbow spinoff, CVC is mainly comprised of the core cable sys-

tems and telecom operations, as well as NY Newsday -- a 97%-owned Long Island, NY-based newspaper acquired in May 2008 for $650 million in cash (with Tribune retaining a 3% stake), as well as News 12 Networks, MSG Varsity and Clearview Cinemas.

COMPETITIVE LANDSCAPE. In addition to facing competition from over-builders such as RCN Corp., CVC also competes with DISH Network and DirecTV -- the two major satellite TV providers currently representing over 30% of U.S. pay TV homes. CVC also competes in residential data and voice services with incumbent telephone companies such as Verizon and AT&T; in addition to DSL services, both telcos have a growing base of fiber-based video and broadband customers.

## Company Financials Fiscal Year Ended Dec. 31

| Per Share Data ($) | 2010 | 2009 | 2008 | 2007 | 2006 | 2005 | 2004 | 2003 | 2002 | 2001 |
|---|---|---|---|---|---|---|---|---|---|---|
| Tangible Book Value | NM | NM | NM | NM | NM | NM | NM | NM | NM | NM |
| Cash Flow | 4.47 | 4.58 | 2.98 | 3.88 | 3.51 | 3.42 | 2.35 | 2.72 | 1.05 | 12.14 |
| Earnings | 1.21 | 0.96 | -0.78 | -0.08 | -0.47 | -0.43 | -2.32 | -0.99 | -1.91 | 3.71 |
| S&P Core Earnings | 1.00 | 0.95 | 0.32 | 0.14 | -1.20 | -0.31 | -2.65 | -1.54 | -0.28 | -1.52 |
| Dividends | 0.48 | 0.40 | 0.20 | Nil | Nil | Nil | Nil | Nil | Nil | Nil |
| Payout Ratio | 39% | 42% | Nil | Nil | Nil | Nil | Nil | Nil | Nil | Nil |
| Prices:High | 36.10 | 26.43 | 33.00 | 39.75 | 28.80 | 33.90 | 27.70 | 24.01 | 48.25 | 91.50 |
| Prices:Low | 21.53 | 9.34 | 11.00 | 23.58 | 18.00 | 22.50 | 16.13 | 15.42 | 4.67 | 32.50 |
| P/E Ratio:High | 30 | 28 | NM | NM | NM | NM | NM | NM | NM | 25 |
| P/E Ratio:Low | 18 | 10 | NM | NM | NM | NM | NM | NM | NM | 9 |

| Income Statement Analysis (Million $) | | | | | | | | | | |
|---|---|---|---|---|---|---|---|---|---|---|
| Revenue | 7,231 | 7,773 | 7,230 | 6,484 | 5,927 | 5,176 | 5,029 | 4,177 | 4,003 | 4,405 |
| Operating Income | 2,520 | 2,510 | 2,247 | 2,035 | 1,713 | 1,586 | 1,282 | 1,094 | 1,058 | 939 |
| Depreciation | 994 | 1,084 | 1,092 | 1,119 | 1,129 | 1,084 | 1,342 | 1,061 | 911 | 1,141 |
| Interest Expense | 784 | 757 | 797 | 941 | 928 | 765 | 721 | 616 | 510 | 544 |
| Pretax Income | 591 | 521 | -317 | 103 | -258 | -195 | -909 | -125 | -477 | 1,580 |
| Effective Tax Rate | 38.1% | 45.2% | NM | 77.2% | NM | NM | NM | NM | NM | 11.9% |
| Net Income | 366 | 286 | -227 | 23.7 | -133 | -121 | -667 | -283 | -561 | 1,008 |
| S&P Core Earnings | 298 | 281 | 93.4 | 42.1 | -340 | -88.2 | -765 | -436 | -24.4 | -408 |

| Balance Sheet & Other Financial Data (Million $) | | | | | | | | | | |
|---|---|---|---|---|---|---|---|---|---|---|
| Cash | 394 | 355 | 323 | 615 | 549 | 397 | 867 | 327 | 126 | 108 |
| Current Assets | 1,640 | 2,055 | 1,859 | 1,744 | 1,667 | 2,131 | 2,375 | 1,062 | 920 | 939 |
| Total Assets | 8,841 | 9,326 | 9,383 | 9,141 | 9,845 | 9,845 | 11,393 | 11,189 | 10,488 | 10,217 |
| Current Liabilities | 2,162 | 2,070 | 2,297 | 2,352 | 2,431 | 2,558 | 2,127 | 1,620 | 1,611 | 1,520 |
| Long Term Debt | 12,249 | 10,991 | 11,286 | 11,561 | 11,710 | 8,953 | 10,368 | 8,455 | 9,221 | 8,521 |
| Common Equity | -6,297 | -5,156 | -5,362 | -5,099 | -5,339 | -2,469 | -2,630 | -1,990 | -1,724 | -1,585 |
| Total Capital | 6,663 | 6,388 | 6,568 | 6,014 | 6,549 | 6,540 | 8,424 | 8,879 | 7,497 | 7,868 |
| Capital Expenditures | 840 | 810 | 909 | 781 | 886 | 769 | 776 | 888 | 1,340 | 1,385 |
| Cash Flow | 1,350 | 1,366 | 865 | 1,142 | 996 | 963 | 675 | 778 | 350 | 2,149 |
| Current Ratio | 0.8 | 1.0 | 0.8 | 0.7 | 0.7 | 0.8 | 1.1 | 0.7 | 0.6 | 0.6 |
| % Long Term Debt of Capitalization | 183.8 | 172.1 | 171.8 | 189.6 | 180.3 | 136.9 | 123.1 | 95.2 | 123.0 | 108.3 |
| % Net Income of Revenue | 5.1 | 3.7 | NM | 0.4 | NM | NM | NM | NM | NM | 22.9 |
| % Return on Assets | 4.0 | 3.1 | NM | 0.3 | NM | NM | NM | NM | NM | 10.9 |
| % Return on Equity | NM | NM | NM | NM | NM | NM | NM | NM | NM | NM |

Data as orig reptd.; bef. results of disc opers/spec. items. Per share data adj. for stk. divs.; EPS diluted. E-Estimated. NA-Not Available. NM-Not Meaningful. NR-Not Ranked. UR-Under Review.

**Office:** 1111 Stewart Avenue, Bethpage, NY 11714.
**Telephone:** 516-803-2300.
**Website:** http://www.cablevision.com
**Chrmn:** C.F. Dolan

**Pres & CEO:** J.L. Dolan
**Vice Chrmn:** H.J. Ratner
**COO:** T.M. Rutledge
**EVP & General Counsel:** J.D. Schwartz

**Investor Contact:** P. Armstrong (516-803-2300)
**Board Members:** R. V. Araskog, F. J. Biondi, Jr., G. C. Brown, Z. W. Carter, C. F. Dolan, J. L. Dolan, K. M. Dolan, K. A. Dolan, P.F. Dolan, D. A. Dolan-Sweeney, B. Dorsogna, C. D. Ferris, R. H. Hochman, V. Oristano, H. J. Ratner, T. V. Reifenheiser, J. R. Ryan, B. G. Sweeney, V. Tese, L. Tow, M. D. Weber

**Founded:** 1985
**Domicile:** Delaware
**Employees:** 18,138

# Cabot Oil & Gas Corp

**STANDARD &POOR'S**

| S&P Recommendation HOLD ★★★☆☆ | Price $76.69 (as of Nov 25, 2011) | 12-Mo. Target Price $78.00 | Investment Style Large-Cap Growth |
|---|---|---|---|

**GICS Sector** Energy
**Sub-Industry** Oil & Gas Exploration & Production

**Summary** Cabot is an independent oil and gas company engaged in development, exploration and production in North America.

## Key Stock Statistics (Source S&P, Vickers, company reports)

| | | | | | | | |
|---|---|---|---|---|---|---|---|
| 52-Wk Range | $90.00– 34.34 | S&P Oper. EPS 2011**E** | 1.28 | Market Capitalization(B) | $8.014 | Beta | 1.18 |
| Trailing 12-Month EPS | $1.37 | S&P Oper. EPS 2012**E** | 2.00 | Yield (%) | 0.16 | S&P 3-Yr. Proj. EPS CAGR(%) | 5 |
| Trailing 12-Month P/E | 56.0 | P/E on S&P Oper. EPS 2011**E** | 59.9 | Dividend Rate/Share | $0.12 | S&P Credit Rating | NA |
| $10K Invested 5 Yrs Ago | $26,011 | Common Shares Outstg. (M) | 104.5 | Institutional Ownership (%) | 100 | | |

## Price Performance

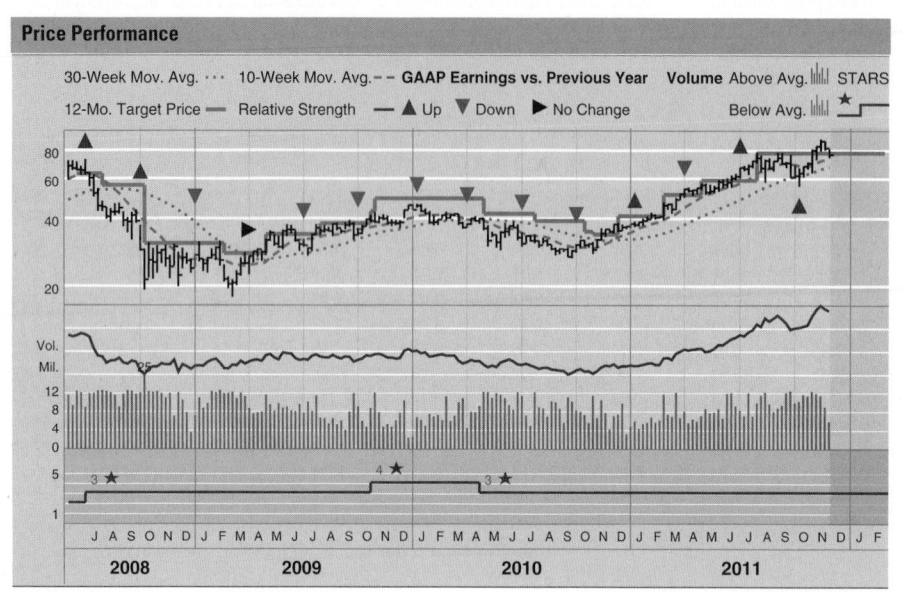

- 30-Week Mov. Avg. ···
- 10-Week Mov. Avg. – –
- 12-Mo. Target Price —
- Relative Strength —
- GAAP Earnings vs. Previous Year
- ▲ Up ▼ Down ▶ No Change
- Volume Above Avg. ▦ Below Avg. ▦
- STARS ★

Options: ASE, CBOE, P, Ph

Analysis prepared by Equity Analyst **Michael Kay** on Aug 18, 2011, when the stock traded at **$69.18**.

## Highlights

- COG has set a production growth midpoint target of 38%, following production growth of 27% in 2010, on success in the Marcellus Shale, where COG is operating five rigs. COG plans to drill 54 Marcellus wells in 2011, and will direct a majority of capex there. COG has begun to de-risk some of its Haynesville acreage, and has been leasing acreage in the Eagle Ford oil window. Drilling capex in Haynesville/Bossier is being carried by JV proceeds, and excess proceeds are being redirected to Eagle Ford, where margins on liquids production are strong. COG has sold Rocky Mountain assets and has entered a JV in East Texas expected to provide over $340 million in proceeds in 2011.

- We think a realigned asset base has lowered portfolio risk and improved drilling success. Total production costs per unit fell for the third year in a row in 2010, by 17%. Second quarter production costs per unit fell 31% sequentially.

- We see adjusted EPS of $1.45 in 2011 and $2.30 in 2012, on production growth and cost cutting resulting from drilling efficiencies, versus adjusted 2010 EPS of $0.99. COG has set 2011 capex at $600 million, down from $829 million (with $132 million for acquisitions) in 2010.

## Investment Rationale/Risk

- COG's core operating areas are performing well, with horizontal drilling programs at Marcellus, Haynesville and Eagle Ford shales moving ahead nicely. Recent Marcellus wells have outperformed flow rate expectations. COG believes an infrastructure buildout will resolve any takeaway capacity issues it has had at the play, but it has a large backlog of completions. COG plans to close on three separate Haynesville JVs in 2011. On growing production, we expect COG to drill close to within its cash flow constraints in 2011 ($600 million), and we see accelerating cash flow growth going forward. We expect about 58% of capex to be allocated to Marcellus and 42% to Eagle Ford.

- Risks to our recommendation and target price include declining oil and gas prices, difficulty replacing reserves, and production declines.

- Based on our proved reserve NAV estimate ($75), a target multiple of 10X EV to 2012 EBITDA ($80), a premium to peers on expected double digit production growth, and other metrics, we arrive at our 12-month target price of $78. Despite weak gas markets, COG shares have benefited along with peer Marcellus operators thus far in 2011.

## Qualitative Risk Assessment

| LOW | MEDIUM | HIGH |
|---|---|---|

Our risk assessment reflects COG's operations in a very capital-intensive industry that is cyclical and derives value from producing a commodity whose price is extremely volatile.

## Quantitative Evaluations

**S&P Quality Ranking**    B+

| D | C | B- | B | B+ | A- | A | A+ |
|---|---|---|---|---|---|---|---|

**Relative Strength Rank**    STRONG

90

LOWEST = 1        HIGHEST = 99

## Revenue/Earnings Data

**Revenue (Million $)**

| | 1Q | 2Q | 3Q | 4Q | Year |
|---|---|---|---|---|---|
| 2011 | 209.0 | 240.7 | 262.1 | -- | -- |
| 2010 | 212.6 | 195.5 | 219.1 | 216.9 | 844.0 |
| 2009 | 233.9 | 204.8 | 207.0 | 233.5 | 879.3 |
| 2008 | 219.7 | 248.9 | 244.8 | 232.5 | 945.8 |
| 2007 | 191.6 | 175.8 | 170.9 | 193.9 | 732.2 |
| 2006 | 214.8 | 190.8 | 184.7 | 171.7 | 762.0 |

**Earnings Per Share ($)**

| | | | | | |
|---|---|---|---|---|---|
| 2011 | 0.12 | 0.52 | 0.27 | E0.33 | E1.28 |
| 2010 | 0.28 | 0.21 | 0.04 | 0.47 | 1.00 |
| 2009 | 0.46 | 0.24 | 0.37 | 0.34 | 1.42 |
| 2008 | 0.46 | 0.55 | 0.64 | 0.42 | 2.10 |
| 2007 | 0.50 | 0.42 | 0.36 | 0.43 | 1.71 |
| 2006 | 0.50 | 0.41 | 1.92 | 0.33 | 3.32 |

Fiscal year ended Dec. 31. Next earnings report expected: Late February. EPS Estimates based on S&P Operating Earnings; historical GAAP earnings are as reported.

## Dividend Data (Dates: mm/dd Payment Date: mm/dd/yy)

| Amount ($) | Date Decl. | Ex-Div. Date | Stk. of Record | Payment Date |
|---|---|---|---|---|
| 0.030 | 01/13 | 01/26 | 01/28 | 02/04/11 |
| 0.030 | 05/03 | 05/13 | 05/17 | 05/24/11 |
| 0.030 | 07/29 | 08/10 | 08/12 | 08/19/11 |
| 0.030 | 10/28 | 11/09 | 11/14 | 11/21/11 |

Dividends have been paid since 1990. Source: Company reports.

# Cabot Oil & Gas Corp

STANDARD &POOR'S

## Business Summary August 18, 2011

CORPORATE OVERVIEW. Cabot Oil & Gas Corp. is an independent oil and gas company engaged in the development, exploitation and exploration of oil and gas properties in North America. In 2009, COG restructured operations, combining Rocky Mountain and Appalachia areas to form the North Region, and combining the Anadarko Basin with the Texas and Louisiana areas to form the South Region. In 2009, COG sold substantially all of its Canadian properties.

In the North Region, activity is concentrated in northeast Pennsylvania and West Virginia in Appalachia, in the Green River and Washakie Basins in Wyoming, and the Paradox Basin in Colorado. COG spent $604 million, or 68% of 2010 capex, on the North Region, and has budgeted $350 million for 2011, down from 2010 when spending was driven by an expanded program to hold acreage. Average daily production from the region in 2010 was 223.4 MMcfe, up from 136.6 MMcfe, or 62% of total COG production.

The South Region is concentrated in east and south Texas, and Oklahoma and Louisiana, with principal producing intervals in the Cotton Valley, Haynesville Shale, Pettet and James Lime formations. COG spent $280 million, or 32% of 2010 capex, on the South Region, and has budgeted $250 million for 2011 for the Eagle Ford Shale. Average daily production from the region in 2009 was 134.4 MMcfe, down from 145.5 MMcfe in 2009, or 38% of total COG production.

CORPORATE STRATEGY. In 2010, COG drilled 113 gross wells, with a success

rate of 98%, compared to 143 gross wells with a success rate of 95% in 2009. COG's proved reserves totaled 2,701 Bcfe at December 31, 2010, of which 98% was natural gas, up 31% from year-end 2009 on additions at the Marcellus Shale. In 2010, capital and exploration spending was $892 million, compared to $640 million of total capex in 2009. At the end of 2010, 64% of total proved reserves were developed, and we estimate COG's reserve life to be 21 years. Production increased 27% in 2010, to 131 Bcfe, from 103 Bcfe in 2009, due to increased production from the Marcellus Shale. We estimate COG's reserve replacement rate in 2010 to be 603%, compared to a three-year reserve replacement rate of 448%. We calculate 2010 finding and development costs of $1.05/Mcf, versus a three-year F&D cost of $1.74/Mcf.

COG's interests are held mainly under customary mineral leases. These leases generally allow for the development of oil and gas on the properties, with terms ranging from 3-10 years. COG owns leasehold rights on about 2.3 million gross acres. COG's largest field is Dimock in Susquehanna County, PA, which accounts for 46% of total proved reserves.

## Company Financials Fiscal Year Ended Dec. 31

| Per Share Data ($) | 2010 | 2009 | 2008 | 2007 | 2006 | 2005 | 2004 | 2003 | 2002 | 2001 |
|---|---|---|---|---|---|---|---|---|---|---|
| Tangible Book Value | 18.01 | 17.49 | NA | 11.60 | 9.83 | 6.18 | 4.69 | 3.78 | 3.67 | 3.66 |
| Cash Flow | 4.54 | 3.99 | 4.31 | 3.36 | 4.57 | 2.58 | 1.94 | 1.27 | 1.18 | 1.41 |
| Earnings | 1.00 | 1.42 | 2.10 | 1.71 | 3.32 | 1.50 | 0.90 | 0.29 | 0.17 | 0.51 |
| S&P Core Earnings | 0.46 | 1.47 | 1.76 | 1.63 | 1.74 | 1.49 | 0.88 | 0.20 | 0.15 | 0.49 |
| Dividends | 0.22 | 0.12 | 0.12 | 0.11 | 0.08 | 0.07 | 0.05 | 0.05 | 0.05 | 0.05 |
| Payout Ratio | 22% | 8% | 6% | 6% | 2% | 5% | 6% | 18% | 32% | 10% |
| Prices:High | 46.46 | 46.26 | 72.92 | 42.50 | 33.26 | 26.75 | 16.30 | 10.17 | 8.85 | 11.45 |
| Prices:Low | 26.62 | 17.84 | 19.18 | 27.87 | 19.13 | 13.72 | 9.57 | 7.50 | 5.92 | 5.42 |
| P/E Ratio:High | 47 | 33 | 35 | 25 | 10 | 18 | 18 | 35 | 53 | 22 |
| P/E Ratio:Low | 27 | 13 | 9 | 16 | 6 | 9 | 11 | 26 | 36 | 11 |

| Income Statement Analysis (Million $) | | | | | | | | | | |
|---|---|---|---|---|---|---|---|---|---|---|
| Revenue | 844 | 879 | 946 | 732 | 762 | 683 | 530 | 509 | 354 | 447 |
| Operating Income | NA | NA | 550 | 423 | 436 | 380 | 278 | 252 | 182 | 191 |
| Depreciation, Depletion and Amortization | 368 | 269 | 227 | 162 | 129 | 108 | 103 | 94.9 | 96.5 | 80.6 |
| Interest Expense | 67.9 | 59.0 | 36.4 | 17.2 | 18.4 | 22.5 | 22.0 | 23.5 | 25.3 | 20.8 |
| Pretax Income | 199 | 223 | 336 | 258 | 511 | 236 | 139 | 43.0 | 23.8 | 74.5 |
| Effective Tax Rate | NA | 33.6% | 37.1% | 35.0% | 37.1% | 37.2% | 36.2% | 35.0% | 32.3% | 36.8% |
| Net Income | 103 | 148 | 211 | 167 | 321 | 148 | 88.4 | 28.0 | 16.1 | 47.1 |
| S&P Core Earnings | 49.3 | 153 | 178 | 159 | 172 | 148 | 87.2 | 19.1 | 14.4 | 45.1 |

| Balance Sheet & Other Financial Data (Million $) | | | | | | | | | | |
|---|---|---|---|---|---|---|---|---|---|---|
| Cash | 56.0 | 40.2 | 28.1 | 30.1 | 41.9 | 10.6 | 10.0 | 0.72 | 2.56 | 5.71 |
| Current Assets | 203 | 282 | 461 | 221 | 316 | 230 | 195 | 121 | 93.1 | 85.0 |
| Total Assets | 4,005 | 3,683 | 3,702 | 2,209 | 1,834 | 1,495 | 1,211 | 1,024 | 1,055 | 1,069 |
| Current Liabilities | 304 | 309 | 379 | 252 | 251 | 219 | 197 | 155 | 123 | 110 |
| Long Term Debt | 975 | 805 | 831 | 350 | 220 | 320 | 250 | 270 | 365 | 393 |
| Common Equity | 1,873 | 1,813 | 1,791 | 1,070 | 945 | 600 | 456 | 365 | 351 | 347 |
| Total Capital | 2,848 | 2,618 | 3,221 | 1,882 | 1,513 | 1,210 | 953 | 815 | 916 | 940 |
| Capital Expenditures | 857 | 611 | 1,454 | 557 | 467 | 351 | 207 | 122 | 103 | 127 |
| Cash Flow | 471 | 417 | 438 | 329 | 450 | 257 | 192 | 123 | 113 | 128 |
| Current Ratio | 0.7 | 0.9 | 1.2 | 0.9 | 1.3 | 1.1 | 1.0 | 0.8 | 0.8 | 0.8 |
| % Long Term Debt of Capitalization | 34.2 | 30.8 | 25.8 | 23.6 | 14.5 | 26.5 | 26.2 | 33.1 | 39.9 | 41.8 |
| % Return on Assets | 2.7 | 4.0 | 7.2 | 8.3 | 19.3 | 11.0 | 7.8 | 2.7 | 1.5 | 5.2 |
| % Return on Equity | 5.6 | 8.2 | 14.8 | 16.6 | 41.6 | 28.1 | 21.5 | 7.8 | 4.6 | 16.0 |

Data as orig reptd.; bef. results of disc opers/spec. items. Per share data adj. for stk. divs.; EPS diluted. E-Estimated. NA-Not Available. NM-Not Meaningful. NR-Not Ranked. UR-Under Review.

**Office:** 840 Gessner Rd Ste 1400, Houston, TX 77024.
**Telephone:** 281-589-4600.
**Website:** http://www.cabotog.com
**Chrmn, Pres & CEO:** D.O. Dinges

**Investor Contact:** S.C. Schroeder (281-589-4993)
**CFO & Treas:** S.C. Schroeder
**CTO:** S.W. Lindeman
**Chief Acctg Officer & Cntlr:** T.M. Roemer

**Board Members:** R. J. Best, D. M. Carmichael, D. O. Dinges, J. R. Gibbs, R. L. Keiser, R. Kelley, P. D. Peacock, W. M. Ralls, W. P. Vititoe

**Founded:** 1989
**Domicile:** Delaware
**Employees:** 409

# Cameron International Corp

**STANDARD &POOR'S**

| | | | |
|---|---|---|---|
| **S&P Recommendation** HOLD ★★★☆☆ | **Price** $48.78 (as of Nov 28, 2011) | **12-Mo. Target Price** $59.00 | **Investment Style** Large-Cap Growth |

**GICS Sector** Energy
**Sub-Industry** Oil & Gas Equipment & Services

**Summary** This company is a leading international manufacturer of oil and gas blowout preventers, flow control valves, surface and subsea production systems, and related oilfield services products.

## Key Stock Statistics (Source S&P, Vickers, company reports)

| | | | | | | | |
|---|---|---|---|---|---|---|---|
| 52-Wk Range | $63.16–38.77 | S&P Oper. EPS 2011E | 2.67 | Market Capitalization(B) | $11.961 | Beta | 1.54 |
| Trailing 12-Month EPS | $2.35 | S&P Oper. EPS 2012E | 3.73 | Yield (%) | Nil | S&P 3-Yr. Proj. EPS CAGR(%) | 18 |
| Trailing 12-Month P/E | 20.8 | P/E on S&P Oper. EPS 2011E | 18.3 | Dividend Rate/Share | Nil | S&P Credit Rating | BBB+ |
| $10K Invested 5 Yrs Ago | $17,428 | Common Shares Outstg. (M) | 245.2 | Institutional Ownership (%) | 90 | | |

## Price Performance

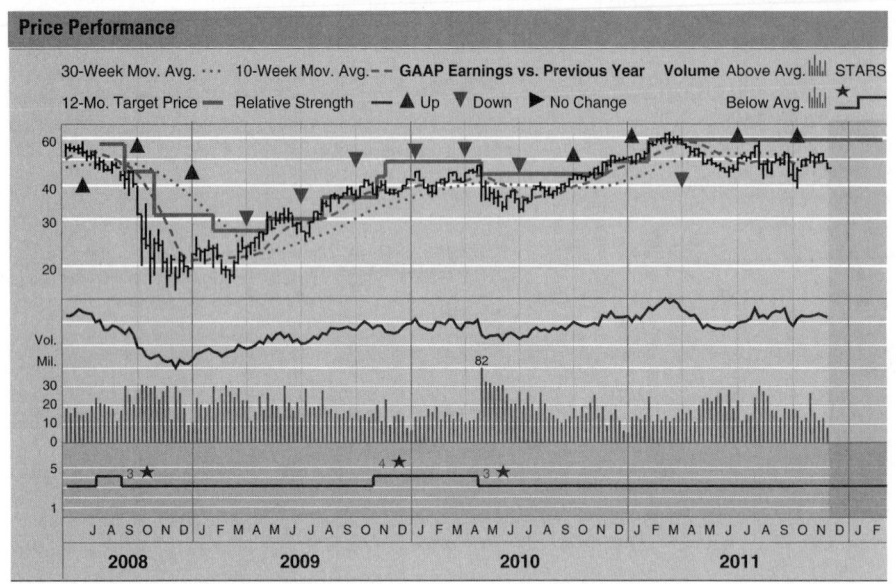

30-Week Mov. Avg. ··· 10-Week Mov. Avg. -- **GAAP Earnings vs. Previous Year**   Volume Above Avg. STARS
12-Mo. Target Price — Relative Strength — ▲ Up ▼ Down ► No Change   Below Avg.

Options: ASE, CBOE, P, Ph

Analysis prepared by Equity Analyst **S. Glickman, CFA** on Nov 28, 2011, when the stock traded at **$46.29**.

## Highlights

➤ The Obama administration ended the offshore drilling ban in October 2010. Most contractors have subsequently obtained NTL-5 certifications for their U.S.-based offshore rigs, which attest to their corresponding blowout preventers (BOPs) meeting current regulatory requirements. However, we also note a relative lack of new deepwater drilling permits issued by federal regulators since the end of the ban, although the pace has improved modestly year to date in 2011. We think CAM may benefit from increased BOP upgrade demand, and/or refurbishments, and we expect greater interest by operators in arranging for CAM after-market support on installed BOPs. We think CAM has a sizable market share of BOPs globally.

➤ Third-quarter orders were $2.0 billion, an increase of about 35% year over year. While Brazil looms as a potential catalyst for CAM, the timing of project awards remains uncertain.

➤ We project operating EPS of $2.67 in 2011, rising to $3.73 in 2012 on higher sales and slightly wider margins.

## Investment Rationale/Risk

➤ We see some potential tailwinds for CAM. First, regulatory changes could spur annuity-like demand for BOP aftermarket services. Second, rising U.S. land activity is boosting demand for short-cycle businesses. Third, Brazil demand remains a catalyst, perhaps longer-term. Still, we see ongoing legal risk. A third-party review of the BOP installed on the Deepwater Horizon hypothesized that the explosion caused the drill pipe to move off-center, rendering the shear rams non-functioning, but CAM has challenged that hypothesis and notes that it is based on computer simulations rather than a physical analysis of the BOP.

➤ Risks to our recommendation and target price include lower oil and natural gas prices; new regulatory requirements that may affect CAM's manufacturing processes; and legal risk associated with the Deepwater Horizon accident.

➤ Our DCF model, with terminal growth of 3% and a WACC of 12.9%, shows intrinsic value of $71. Using peer-premium multiples of 10X enterprise value to forecast 2012 EBITDA, 11X projected 2012 operating cash flow, and blending with our DCF model, our 12-month target price is $59.

## Qualitative Risk Assessment

| LOW | MEDIUM | HIGH |
|---|---|---|

Our risk assessment reflects CAM's exposure to volatile crude oil and natural gas prices, capital spending decisions made by its oil and gas producing customers, political risk associated with operating in frontier regions, an unclear regulatory environment, and legal risk associated with the U.S. Gulf of Mexico oil spill.

## Quantitative Evaluations

**S&P Quality Ranking**     B+

| D | C | B- | B | B+ | A- | A | A+ |
|---|---|---|---|---|---|---|---|

**Relative Strength Rank**     STRONG

71

LOWEST = 1      HIGHEST = 99

## Revenue/Earnings Data

**Revenue (Million $)**

| | 1Q | 2Q | 3Q | 4Q | Year |
|---|---|---|---|---|---|
| 2011 | 1,501 | 1,741 | 1,686 | -- | -- |
| 2010 | 1,347 | 1,453 | 1,527 | 1,808 | 6,135 |
| 2009 | 1,257 | 1,270 | 1,232 | 1,464 | 5,223 |
| 2008 | 1,339 | 1,481 | 1,505 | 1,524 | 5,849 |
| 2007 | 997.0 | 1,139 | 1,186 | 1,344 | 4,666 |
| 2006 | 829.7 | 857.8 | 978.8 | 1,077 | 3,743 |

**Earnings Per Share ($)**

| | | | | | |
|---|---|---|---|---|---|
| 2011 | 0.43 | 0.59 | 0.67 | E0.80 | E2.67 |
| 2010 | 0.48 | 0.52 | 0.61 | 0.66 | 2.27 |
| 2009 | 0.52 | 0.63 | 0.56 | 0.41 | 2.11 |
| 2008 | 0.55 | 0.65 | 0.73 | 0.67 | 2.60 |
| 2007 | 0.44 | 0.54 | 0.66 | 0.54 | 2.17 |
| 2006 | 0.24 | 0.32 | 0.39 | 0.42 | 1.36 |

Fiscal year ended Dec. 31. Next earnings report expected: Early February. EPS Estimates based on S&P Operating Earnings; historical GAAP earnings are as reported.

## Dividend Data

No cash dividends have been paid.

*The McGraw-Hill Companies*

# Cameron International Corp

STANDARD
&POOR'S

## Business Summary November 28, 2011

CORPORATE OVERVIEW. Cameron International, an international provider of oil and gas pressure control equipment, is organized into three business segments: Drilling & Production Systems (DPS), Valves & Measurement (V&M), and Process & Compression Systems (PCS). Primary customers of DPS, V&M and PCS are major and independent oil and gas exploration companies, foreign national oil and gas companies, drilling contractors, pipeline companies, refiners, and other industrial and petrochemical processing companies. The company serves customers in North America (41% of 2010 revenues), Africa (19%), Asia/Middle East (19%), Europe (11%), South America (8.6%) and Other (1.7%).

Drilling & Production Systems (DPS; 61% of 2010 revenues and 68% of 2010 segment pretax income) manufactures pressure control equipment used at the wellhead in drilling, production and transmission of oil and gas, both onshore and offshore. Primary products include wellheads, drilling valves, blowout preventers, and control systems, marketed under the brand names Cameron, W-K-M, McEvoy, Willis, and Ingram Cactus. The segment also makes subsea production systems, which tend to be highly sophisticated technically. The company believes subsea capacity additions at manufactur-

ing plants in England, Brazil and Germany provide support for increased completions of subsea trees and associated manifolds, production controls and other equipment in the future.

Valves & Measurement (VMS; 21%, 19%), split out from the DPS division as a separately managed business in 1995, provides a full range of ball valves, gate valves, butterfly valves, and accessories used primarily to control pressures and direct oil and gas as they are moved from individual wellheads through transmission systems to refineries, petrochemical plants, and other processing centers. In September 2005, CAM announced an agreement to acquire substantially all of the flow control businesses of Dresser Inc.; the acquisition was completed in January 2006. The acquisition, which expanded the company's valve product line, totaled $217.5 million in cash and assumed debt. The acquired businesses were added to the company's V&M segment.

## Company Financials Fiscal Year Ended Dec. 31

| Per Share Data ($) | 2010 | 2009 | 2008 | 2007 | 2006 | 2005 | 2004 | 2003 | 2002 | 2001 |
|---|---|---|---|---|---|---|---|---|---|---|
| Tangible Book Value | 10.91 | 9.04 | 6.88 | 6.67 | 5.11 | 4.40 | 3.83 | 3.81 | 3.39 | 2.92 |
| Cash Flow | 3.09 | 2.81 | 3.03 | 2.52 | 1.79 | 1.11 | 0.83 | 0.59 | 0.58 | 0.78 |
| Earnings | 2.27 | 2.11 | 2.60 | 2.17 | 1.36 | 0.76 | 0.44 | 0.26 | 0.28 | 0.44 |
| S&P Core Earnings | 2.31 | 2.12 | 2.63 | 2.27 | 1.43 | 0.73 | 0.34 | 0.17 | 0.12 | 0.21 |
| Dividends | Nil | Nil | Nil | Nil | Nil | Nil | Nil | Nil | Nil | Nil |
| Payout Ratio | Nil | Nil | Nil | Nil | Nil | Nil | Nil | Nil | Nil | Nil |
| Prices:High | 51.71 | 42.49 | 58.53 | 53.83 | 28.91 | 21.55 | 14.19 | 13.90 | 14.90 | 18.25 |
| Prices:Low | 31.42 | 17.19 | 16.15 | 24.30 | 19.04 | 12.76 | 10.01 | 10.25 | 8.98 | 7.21 |
| P/E Ratio:High | 23 | 20 | 23 | 25 | 21 | 28 | 32 | 53 | 54 | 42 |
| P/E Ratio:Low | 14 | 8 | 6 | 11 | 14 | 17 | 23 | 39 | 33 | 16 |

| Income Statement Analysis (Million $) | | | | | | | | | | |
|---|---|---|---|---|---|---|---|---|---|---|
| Revenue | 6,135 | 5,223 | 5,849 | 4,666 | 3,743 | 2,518 | 2,093 | 1,634 | 1,538 | 1,564 |
| Operating Income | NA | NA | 1,023 | 814 | 605 | 340 | 232 | 164 | 196 | 251 |
| Depreciation, Depletion and Amortization | 202 | 157 | 98.7 | 81.5 | 101 | 78.4 | 82.8 | 83.6 | 77.9 | 83.1 |
| Interest Expense | 82.2 | 92.4 | 49.7 | 23.3 | 20.7 | 12.0 | 17.8 | 8.16 | 7.98 | 5.62 |
| Pretax Income | 733 | 643 | 872 | 708 | 489 | 263 | 133 | 77.6 | 85.1 | 143 |
| Effective Tax Rate | NA | 26.0% | 31.9% | 29.3% | 35.0% | 34.9% | 29.0% | 26.2% | 29.0% | 31.0% |
| Net Income | 563 | 476 | 594 | 501 | 318 | 171 | 94.4 | 57.2 | 60.5 | 98.3 |
| S&P Core Earnings | 574 | 478 | 601 | 527 | 333 | 167 | 73.1 | 37.5 | 23.3 | 44.0 |

| Balance Sheet & Other Financial Data (Million $) | | | | | | | | | | |
|---|---|---|---|---|---|---|---|---|---|---|
| Cash | 1,833 | 1,861 | 1,621 | 740 | 1,034 | 362 | 227 | 292 | 274 | 112 |
| Current Assets | 4,933 | 4,714 | 4,056 | 3,072 | 2,908 | 1,728 | 1,205 | 1,148 | 1,018 | 965 |
| Total Assets | 8,005 | 7,725 | 5,902 | 4,731 | 4,351 | 3,099 | 2,356 | 2,141 | 1,998 | 1,875 |
| Current Liabilities | 2,574 | 2,296 | 2,112 | 1,693 | 1,628 | 922 | 528 | 680 | 375 | 378 |
| Long Term Debt | 773 | 1,232 | 1,256 | 742 | 745 | 444 | 458 | 204 | 463 | 459 |
| Common Equity | 4,392 | 3,920 | 2,320 | 2,095 | 1,741 | 1,595 | 1,228 | 1,137 | 1,041 | 976 |
| Total Capital | 5,685 | 5,174 | 3,662 | 2,909 | 2,577 | 2,078 | 1,727 | 1,387 | 1,550 | 1,477 |
| Capital Expenditures | 201 | 241 | 272 | 246 | 185 | 77.5 | 53.5 | 64.7 | 82.1 | 125 |
| Cash Flow | 764 | 632 | 692 | 582 | 419 | 250 | 177 | 141 | 138 | 181 |
| Current Ratio | 1.9 | 2.1 | 1.9 | 1.8 | 1.8 | 1.9 | 2.3 | 1.7 | 2.7 | 2.6 |
| % Long Term Debt of Capitalization | 13.6 | 23.8 | 34.3 | 26.2 | 28.9 | 21.4 | 26.5 | 14.7 | 29.9 | 31.1 |
| % Return on Assets | 7.2 | 7.0 | 11.2 | 11.0 | 8.5 | 6.3 | 4.2 | 2.8 | 3.1 | 5.8 |
| % Return on Equity | 13.5 | 15.2 | 26.9 | 26.1 | 19.1 | 12.1 | 8.0 | 5.3 | 6.2 | 10.6 |

Data as orig reptd.; bef. results of disc opers/spec. items. Per share data adj. for stk. divs.; EPS diluted. E-Estimated. NA-Not Available. NM-Not Meaningful. NR-Not Ranked. UR-Under Review.

**Office:** 1333 W Loop S Ste 1700, Houston, TX 77027-9118.
**Telephone:** 713-513-3300.
**Website:** http://www.c-a-m.com
**Chrmn, Pres & CEO:** J.B. Moore

**COO & EVP:** J.D. Carne
**SVP & CFO:** C.M. Sledge
**SVP & General Counsel:** W.C. Lemmer
**CTO:** J.C. Bartos

**Investor Contact:** R.S. Amann (713-513-3344)
**Board Members:** C. B. Cunningham, S. R. Erikson, P. J. Fluor, D. L. Foshee, R. Landim, J. B. Moore, M. E. Patrick, J. E. Reinhardsen, D. W. Ross, III, B. W. Wilkinson

**Founded:** 1994
**Domicile:** Delaware
**Employees:** 19,500

# Campbell Soup Co

**STANDARD &POOR'S**

| S&P Recommendation | HOLD ★★★★★ | Price $31.85 (as of Nov 25, 2011) | 12-Mo. Target Price $34.00 | Investment Style Large-Cap Growth |
| --- | --- | --- | --- | --- |

**GICS Sector** Consumer Staples
**Sub-Industry** Packaged Foods & Meats

**Summary** This company is a major producer of branded soups and other grocery food products.

## Key Stock Statistics (Source S&P, Vickers, company reports)

| | | | | | | | |
| --- | --- | --- | --- | --- | --- | --- | --- |
| 52-Wk Range | $35.66– 29.69 | S&P Oper. EPS 2012**E** | 2.38 | Market Capitalization(B) | $10.199 | Beta | 0.27 |
| Trailing 12-Month EPS | $2.41 | S&P Oper. EPS 2013**E** | 2.55 | Yield (%) | 3.64 | S&P 3-Yr. Proj. EPS CAGR(%) | 1 |
| Trailing 12-Month P/E | 13.2 | P/E on S&P Oper. EPS 2012**E** | 13.4 | Dividend Rate/Share | $1.16 | S&P Credit Rating | A- |
| $10K Invested 5 Yrs Ago | $9,831 | Common Shares Outstg. (M) | 320.2 | Institutional Ownership (%) | 80 | | |

## Price Performance

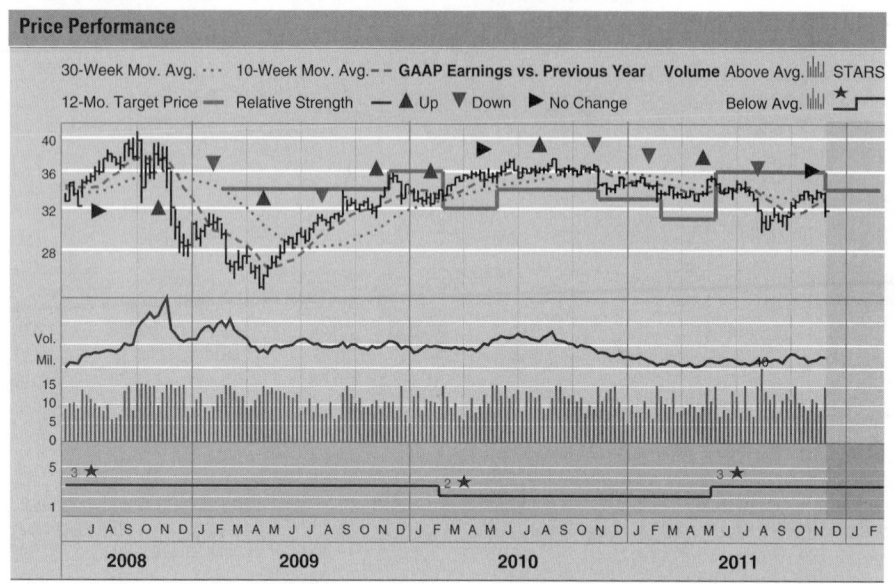

- 30-Week Mov. Avg. · · ·
- 10-Week Mov. Avg. – –
- **GAAP Earnings vs. Previous Year**
- Volume Above Avg. STARS
- 12-Mo. Target Price —
- Relative Strength · · ·
- ▲ Up  ▼ Down  ► No Change
- Below Avg.

Options: ASE, CBOE, P, Ph

## Highlights

► The 12-month target price for CPB has recently been changed to $34.00 from $36.00. The Highlights section of this Stock Report will be updated accordingly.

## Investment Rationale/Risk

► The Investment Rationale/Risk section of this Stock Report will be updated shortly. For the latest News story on CPB from MarketScope, see below.

► 11/22/11 11:50 am ET ... S&P REITERATES HOLD OPINION ON SHARES OF CAMPBELL SOUP (CPB 31.49***): Oct-Q EPS of $0.82, vs. $0.82, is $0.01 above our estimate and $0.03 above Capital IQ consensus. However, we view 0.5% sales decline and the extent of the gross margin decline as disappointing. Marketing and selling expense was down, but we expect an increase in the remainder of FY 12 (Jul), and for sales comparisons to improve somewhat. We are lowering our FY 12 EPS estimate to $2.38 from $2.39, and initiating FY 13's at $2.55. With a more cautious view on sales, we are reducing our target price to $34 from $36. The stock has an indicated dividend yield of 3.7%. /Tom Graves, CFA

## Qualitative Risk Assessment

| LOW | MEDIUM | HIGH |
| --- | --- | --- |

Our risk assessment reflects the relatively stable nature of the company's end markets, our view of its strong cash flow, and corporate governance practices that we see as favorable relative to peers.

## Quantitative Evaluations

**S&P Quality Ranking**          A-

| D | C | B- | B | B+ | A- | A | A+ |
| --- | --- | --- | --- | --- | --- | --- | --- |

**Relative Strength Rank**          MODERATE

64

LOWEST = 1          HIGHEST = 99

## Revenue/Earnings Data

**Revenue (Million $)**

| | 1Q | 2Q | 3Q | 4Q | Year |
| --- | --- | --- | --- | --- | --- |
| 2012 | 2,161 | -- | | | |
| 2011 | 2,172 | 2,127 | 1,813 | 1,607 | 7,719 |
| 2010 | 2,203 | 2,153 | 1,802 | 1,518 | 7,676 |
| 2009 | 2,250 | 2,122 | 1,686 | 1,528 | 7,586 |
| 2008 | 2,185 | 2,218 | 1,880 | 1,715 | 7,998 |
| 2007 | 2,153 | 2,252 | 1,868 | 1,594 | 7,867 |

**Earnings Per Share ($)**

| | 1Q | 2Q | 3Q | 4Q | Year |
| --- | --- | --- | --- | --- | --- |
| 2012 | 0.82 | E0.68 | E0.53 | E0.35 | E2.38 |
| 2011 | 0.82 | 0.71 | 0.57 | 0.29 | 2.42 |
| 2010 | 0.87 | 0.74 | 0.49 | 0.33 | 2.42 |
| 2009 | 0.71 | 0.63 | 0.49 | 0.20 | 2.04 |
| 2008 | 0.69 | 0.67 | 0.14 | 0.24 | 1.76 |
| 2007 | 0.66 | 0.72 | 0.55 | 0.24 | 2.08 |

Fiscal year ended Jul. 31. Next earnings report expected: Late February. EPS Estimates based on S&P Operating Earnings; historical GAAP earnings are as reported.

## Dividend Data (Dates: mm/dd Payment Date: mm/dd/yy)

| Amount ($) | Date Decl. | Ex-Div. Date | Stk. of Record | Payment Date |
| --- | --- | --- | --- | --- |
| 0.290 | 03/24 | 04/07 | 04/11 | 05/02/11 |
| 0.290 | 06/23 | 07/07 | 07/11 | 08/01/11 |
| 0.290 | 09/22 | 10/06 | 10/11 | 10/31/11 |
| 0.290 | 11/16 | 12/22 | 12/27 | 01/30/12 |

Dividends have been paid since 1902. Source: Company reports.

# Campbell Soup Co

## Business Summary October 12, 2011

Campbell Soup Company engages in the manufacture and marketing of branded convenience food products.

In FY 11 (Jul.), operations outside the U.S. accounted for 31% of net sales. CPB's largest customer, Wal-Mart Stores, Inc., and its affiliates accounted for about 17% of CPB's overall net sales in FY 11.

The company now reports results based on the following segments: U.S. Simple Meals (36% of FY 11 sales, 45% of segment profits); U.S. Beverages (10%, 12%); Global Baking and Snacking (28%, 24%), International Simple Meals and Beverages (19%, 13%); and North America Foodservice (8%, 6%).

The U.S. Simple Meals segment includes the U.S. Soup retail business, with such products as Campbell's condensed and ready-to-serve soups, and Swanson broth and stocks; and the U.S. Sauces retail business, with such products as Prego pasta sauce, Pace Mexican sauce, Swanson canned poultry, and Campbell's canned gravies, pasta, and beans.

The U.S. Beverages segment includes such retail products as V8 juices and beverages and Campbell's tomato juice. The Global Baking and Snacking segment includes such products as Pepperidge Farm cookies, crackers, bakery

and frozen products in U.S. retail; and Arnott's biscuits in Australia and Asia Pacific.

The International Simple Meals and Beverages segment includes Erasco and Heisse Tasse soups in Germany, Liebig and Royco soups in France, Devos Lemmens mayonnaise and cold sauces and Campbell's and Royco soups in Belgium, and Bla Band soups and sauces in Sweden. In Asia Pacific, operations include Campbell's soup and stock, Swanson broths, V8 beverages and Prego pasta sauce. In Canada, operations include Habitant and Campbell's soups, Prego pasta sauce, Pace Mexican sauce, V8 beverages and certain Pepperidge Farm products.

The North America Foodservice segment includes the distribution of products such as soup, specialty entrees, beverage products, other prepared foods and Pepperidge Farm products through various food service channels in the United States and Canada.

## Company Financials Fiscal Year Ended Jul. 31

| Per Share Data ($) | 2011 | 2010 | 2009 | 2008 | 2007 | 2006 | 2005 | 2004 | 2003 | 2002 |
|---|---|---|---|---|---|---|---|---|---|---|
| Tangible Book Value | NM | NM | NM | NM | NM | NM | NM | NM | NM | NM |
| Cash Flow | 3.24 | 3.19 | 2.78 | 2.47 | 2.79 | 2.52 | 2.39 | 2.20 | 2.11 | 2.05 |
| Earnings | 2.42 | 2.42 | 2.04 | 1.76 | 2.08 | 1.82 | 1.71 | 1.57 | 1.52 | 1.28 |
| S&P Core Earnings | 2.46 | 2.44 | 1.78 | 1.52 | 1.95 | 1.81 | 1.63 | 1.47 | 1.46 | 1.00 |
| Dividends | 1.15 | 1.08 | 1.00 | 0.88 | 0.80 | 0.72 | 0.68 | 0.63 | 0.63 | 0.63 |
| Payout Ratio | 47% | 45% | 49% | 50% | 38% | 40% | 40% | 40% | 41% | 49% |
| Prices:High | 35.66 | 37.59 | 35.80 | 40.85 | 42.65 | 39.98 | 31.60 | 30.52 | 27.90 | 30.00 |
| Prices:Low | 29.69 | 32.18 | 24.63 | 27.35 | 34.17 | 28.88 | 27.35 | 25.03 | 19.95 | 19.65 |
| P/E Ratio:High | 15 | 16 | 18 | 23 | 21 | 22 | 18 | 19 | 18 | 23 |
| P/E Ratio:Low | 12 | 13 | 12 | 16 | 16 | 16 | 16 | 16 | 13 | 15 |

| Income Statement Analysis (Million $) | | | | | | | | | | |
|---|---|---|---|---|---|---|---|---|---|---|
| Revenue | 7,719 | 7,676 | 7,586 | 7,998 | 7,867 | 7,343 | 7,548 | 7,109 | 6,678 | 6,133 |
| Operating Income | 1,614 | 1,611 | 1,532 | 1,564 | 1,541 | 1,445 | 1,483 | 1,394 | 1,376 | 1,442 |
| Depreciation | 265 | 251 | 264 | 271 | 23.0 | 289 | 279 | 260 | 243 | 319 |
| Interest Expense | 111 | 106 | 114 | 171 | 163 | 165 | 184 | 174 | 186 | 190 |
| Pretax Income | 1,168 | 1,242 | 1,079 | 939 | 1,149 | 1,001 | 1,030 | 947 | 924 | 798 |
| Effective Tax Rate | NA | NA | 32.2% | 28.5% | 28.4% | 24.6% | 31.4% | 31.7% | 32.3% | 34.2% |
| Net Income | 802 | 844 | 732 | 671 | 823 | 755 | 707 | 647 | 626 | 525 |
| S&P Core Earnings | 806 | 838 | 640 | 579 | 772 | 751 | 675 | 603 | 604 | 413 |

| Balance Sheet & Other Financial Data (Million $) | | | | | | | | | | |
|---|---|---|---|---|---|---|---|---|---|---|
| Cash | 484 | 254 | 51.0 | 81.0 | 71.0 | 657 | 40.0 | 32.0 | 32.0 | 21.0 |
| Current Assets | 1,963 | 1,687 | 1,551 | 1,693 | 1,578 | 2,112 | 1,512 | 1,481 | 1,290 | 1,199 |
| Total Assets | 6,862 | 6,276 | 6,056 | 6,474 | 6,445 | 7,870 | 6,776 | 6,675 | 6,205 | 5,721 |
| Current Liabilities | 1,989 | 2,065 | 1,628 | 2,403 | 2,030 | 2,962 | 2,002 | 2,339 | 2,783 | 2,678 |
| Long Term Debt | 2,427 | 1,945 | 2,246 | 1,633 | 2,074 | 2,116 | 2,542 | 2,543 | 2,249 | 2,449 |
| Common Equity | 1,096 | 929 | 728 | 1,318 | 1,295 | 1,768 | 1,270 | 874 | 387 | -114 |
| Total Capital | 4,180 | 2,874 | 2,974 | 3,251 | 3,369 | 3,884 | 3,812 | 3,417 | 2,636 | 2,335 |
| Capital Expenditures | 272 | 315 | 345 | 298 | 334 | 309 | 332 | 288 | 283 | 269 |
| Cash Flow | 1,067 | 1,095 | 996 | 942 | 1,106 | 1,044 | 986 | 907 | 869 | 844 |
| Current Ratio | 1.0 | 0.8 | 1.0 | 0.7 | 0.8 | 0.7 | 0.8 | 0.6 | 0.5 | 0.4 |
| % Long Term Debt of Capitalization | 58.1 | 67.7 | 75.5 | 49.4 | 61.6 | 54.5 | 66.7 | 74.4 | 85.3 | 104.9 |
| % Net Income of Revenue | 10.4 | 11.0 | 9.7 | 8.4 | 10.5 | 10.3 | 9.4 | 9.1 | 9.4 | 8.6 |
| % Return on Assets | 12.2 | 13.7 | 11.7 | 10.4 | 11.5 | 10.3 | 10.5 | 10.0 | 10.5 | 9.0 |
| % Return on Equity | 79.3 | 101.9 | 71.6 | 51.4 | 53.7 | 49.7 | 66.0 | 102.6 | 458.6 | NM |

Data as orig reptd.; bef. results of disc opers/spec. items. Per share data adj. for stk. divs.; EPS diluted. E-Estimated. NA-Not Available. NM-Not Meaningful. NR-Not Ranked. UR-Under Review.

**Office:** 1 Campbell Place, Camden, NJ 08103-1701.
**Telephone:** 856-342-4800.
**Website:** http://www.campbellsoupcompany.com
**Chrmn:** P.R. Charron

**Pres & CEO:** D.M. Morrison
**SVP, CFO & Chief Admin Officer:** B.C. Owens
**SVP & Chief Acctg Officer:** A.P. DiSilvestro
**SVP & CIO:** J. Spagnoletti

**Investor Contact:** L.F. Griehs (856-342-6427)
**Board Members:** E. M. Carpenter, P. R. Charron, B. Dorrance, L. C. Karlson, R. W. Larrimore, M. A. Malone, S. Mathew, D. M. Morrison, W. D. Perez, C. R. Perrin, A. B. Rand, N. Shreiber, T. T. Travis, L. C. Vinney, C. C. Weber, A. D. van Beuren

**Founded:** 1869
**Domicile:** New Jersey
**Employees:** 17,500

# CA Inc

**STANDARD &POOR'S**

| S&P Recommendation | HOLD ★★★★☆ | Price $19.80 (as of Nov 25, 2011) | 12-Mo. Target Price $26.00 | Investment Style Large-Cap Blend |
| --- | --- | --- | --- | --- |

**GICS Sector** Information Technology
**Sub-Industry** Systems Software

**Summary** This company (formerly Computer Associates International) develops systems software, database management systems, and applications software.

## Key Stock Statistics (Source S&P, Vickers, company reports)

| | | | | | | | |
| --- | --- | --- | --- | --- | --- | --- | --- |
| 52-Wk Range | $25.68– 18.61 | S&P Oper. EPS 2012E | 1.81 | Market Capitalization(B) | $9.769 | Beta | 0.95 |
| Trailing 12-Month EPS | $1.70 | S&P Oper. EPS 2013E | 1.98 | Yield (%) | 1.01 | S&P 3-Yr. Proj. EPS CAGR(%) | 7 |
| Trailing 12-Month P/E | 11.7 | P/E on S&P Oper. EPS 2012E | 10.9 | Dividend Rate/Share | $0.20 | S&P Credit Rating | BBB+ |
| $10K Invested 5 Yrs Ago | $9,276 | Common Shares Outstg. (M) | 493.4 | Institutional Ownership (%) | 74 | | |

## Price Performance

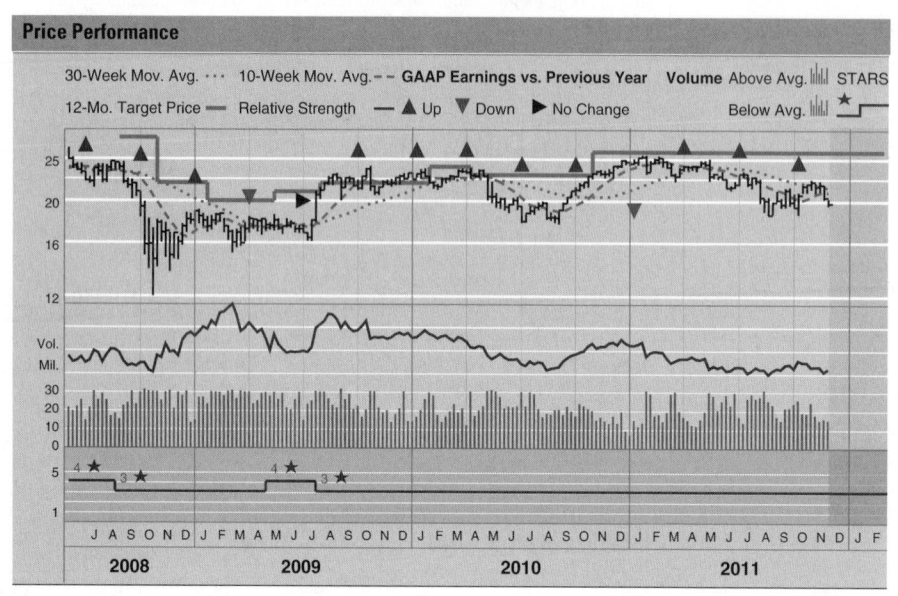

30-Week Mov. Avg. · · · ·  10-Week Mov. Avg. – –  GAAP Earnings vs. Previous Year  Volume Above Avg. STARS
12-Mo. Target Price —  Relative Strength —  ▲ Up  ▼ Down  ► No Change  Below Avg.

Options: ASE, CBOE, P, Ph

Analysis prepared by Equity Analyst **Jim Yin, CFA** on Nov 17, 2011, when the stock traded at **$21.20**.

## Qualitative Risk Assessment

| LOW | MEDIUM | HIGH |
| --- | --- | --- |

Our risk assessment for the company reflects our concern about the financial crisis in Europe, weak spending in enterprise software, and modest underlying growth.

## Quantitative Evaluations

**S&P Quality Ranking**  B

| D | C | B- | B | B+ | A- | A | A+ |
| --- | --- | --- | --- | --- | --- | --- | --- |

**Relative Strength Rank**  MODERATE

48

LOWEST = 1    HIGHEST = 99

## Revenue/Earnings Data

**Revenue (Million $)**

| | 1Q | 2Q | 3Q | 4Q | Year |
| --- | --- | --- | --- | --- | --- |
| 2012 | 1,163 | 1,200 | -- | -- | -- |
| 2011 | 1,069 | 1,088 | 1,144 | 1,128 | 4,429 |
| 2010 | 1,050 | 1,072 | 1,128 | 1,103 | 4,353 |
| 2009 | 1,087 | 110.7 | 1,042 | 1,035 | 4,271 |
| 2008 | 1,025 | 1,067 | 1,100 | 1,085 | 4,277 |
| 2007 | 949.0 | 987.0 | 1,002 | 1,005 | 3,943 |

**Earnings Per Share ($)**

| | 1Q | 2Q | 3Q | 4Q | Year |
| --- | --- | --- | --- | --- | --- |
| 2012 | 0.45 | 0.47 | E0.43 | E0.42 | E1.81 |
| 2011 | 0.43 | 0.43 | 0.38 | 0.37 | 1.60 |
| 2010 | 0.37 | 0.41 | 0.49 | 0.19 | 1.47 |
| 2009 | 0.37 | 0.39 | 0.40 | 0.13 | 1.29 |
| 2008 | 0.24 | 0.26 | 0.31 | 0.14 | 0.93 |
| 2007 | 0.06 | 0.09 | 0.10 | -0.04 | 0.22 |

Fiscal year ended Mar. 31. Next earnings report expected: NA. EPS Estimates based on S&P Operating Earnings; historical GAAP earnings are as reported.

## Highlights

➤ We look for revenue growth of 5.7% in FY 12 (Mar.), aided by a favorable foreign currency exchange impact. Although CA will likely continue to see solid gains in its North American operations, we have ongoing concerns about its sales performance in the EMEA region. Also, the company expects its renewal rate to decline. We note, however, that CA's revenue backlog was up a solid 10% in the June period. For FY 13, we project a 3.9% revenue gain.

➤ We expect operating margins to widen modestly this fiscal year, primarily reflecting better management of the company's cost structure and operational improvements. Still, we see these positives being somewhat offset by expected investments in the Enterprise Solutions business and $35 million to $45 million of expenses related to upcoming layoffs of 500 employees in that division.

➤ We estimate EPS of $1.81 in FY 12, up from $1.60 in FY 11, assuming a modest level of share repurchases. In FY 13, we forecast $1.98.

## Investment Rationale/Risk

➤ Our hold recommendation is based on valuation. We are also concerned about CA's modest revenue growth. We believe most of the growth in the IT industry will be focused on cloud computing. Thus, we think CA will recover slower than other software companies because it has a small presence in that market. We also project a decline in the mainframe business. On the positive side, CA has controlled its operating expenses by streamlining operations and cutting its workforce, offsetting sluggish revenue growth.

➤ Risks to our opinion and target price include significant declines in corporate spending on enterprise software from current levels, pricing pressure from increased competition, and the weak global economy.

➤ Our 12-month target price of $26 is based on a blend of our discounted cash flow (DCF) and P/E analyses. Our DCF model assumes a 12.2% weighted average cost of capital and 3% terminal growth rate, yielding an intrinsic value of $29. From our P/E analysis, we derive a value of $23 based on an industry average P/E-to-growth ratio of 1.8X, or 12.7X our FY 12 EPS estimate.

## Dividend Data (Dates: mm/dd Payment Date: mm/dd/yy)

| Amount ($) | Date Decl. | Ex-Div. Date | Stk. of Record | Payment Date |
| --- | --- | --- | --- | --- |
| 0.040 | 02/02 | 02/10 | 02/14 | 03/14/11 |
| 0.050 | 05/12 | 05/19 | 05/23 | 06/16/11 |
| 0.050 | 08/03 | 08/12 | 08/16 | 09/14/11 |
| 0.050 | 11/09 | 11/18 | 11/22 | 12/14/11 |

Dividends have been paid since 1990. Source: Company reports.

---

**Please read the Required Disclosures and Analyst Certification on the last page of this report.**

The McGraw-Hill Companies

# CA Inc

**STANDARD &POOR'S**

## Business Summary November 17, 2011

CORPORATE OVERVIEW. CA Inc. provides information technology (IT) management software, which helps customers better manage their IT infrastructure. The company has a broad portfolio of software products and services that span the areas of infrastructure management, IT security management, storage management, application performance management and business service optimization. The company's products and services include both mainframe and distributed solutions, each of which we estimate contribute about half of CA's revenues.

CORPORATE STRATEGY. In April 2007, CA announced a new strategy, Enterprise IT Management (EITM), for transforming the way companies manage their IT. The goal of EITM is to unify disparate elements of IT, including hardware, processes and people, so customers can have better control and manage these resources rather than replace existing IT investments. For example, CA's Unicenter Advanced Systems Management provides centralized management for virtualized and clustered server environments, enabling customers to assess and optimize network resources.

Key parts of CA's EITM strategy include:

Internal Product Development - CA plans to ship new versions of every major product, including those products obtained through acquisitions. The company has added headcount in India and Czech Republic research centers.

Strengthening Partner Relationships - CA intends to strengthen its global distribution by recruiting and educating channel partners on CA products and services. The company formed a Mid-Market and Storage organization that targets enterprises with 500-5,000 employees.

International Expansion - CA plans to invest in regions outside the U.S., especially in emerging markets such as China and India to increase the volume of enterprise sales. The company has also pursued small- and medium-sized customers in the Europe, Middle East and Africa (EMEA) region. International revenue comprised nearly 43% of total sales in FY 11 (Mar.), down from 45% in FY 10.

## Company Financials Fiscal Year Ended Mar. 31

| Per Share Data ($) | 2011 | 2010 | 2009 | 2008 | 2007 | 2006 | 2005 | 2004 | 2003 | 2002 |
|---|---|---|---|---|---|---|---|---|---|---|
| Tangible Book Value | NM | NM | NM | NM | NM | NM | 0.50 | 8.09 | NM | NM |
| Cash Flow | 2.17 | 2.01 | 1.56 | 1.21 | 0.47 | 1.22 | 0.24 | 0.17 | 0.60 | -0.01 |
| Earnings | 1.60 | 1.47 | 1.29 | 0.93 | 0.22 | 0.26 | 0.02 | -0.06 | -0.46 | -1.91 |
| S&P Core Earnings | 1.58 | 1.48 | 1.31 | 0.97 | 0.23 | 0.26 | 0.22 | 0.02 | -0.53 | -2.05 |
| Dividends | NA | 0.16 | 0.16 | 0.16 | 0.16 | 0.08 | 0.08 | 0.08 | 0.08 | 0.08 |
| Payout Ratio | NA | 11% | 12% | 17% | 73% | 31% | NM | NM | NM | NM |
| Calendar Year | 2010 | 2009 | 2008 | 2007 | 2006 | 2005 | 2004 | 2003 | 2002 | 2001 |
| Prices:High | 25.08 | 24.15 | 26.68 | 28.46 | 29.50 | 31.35 | 31.71 | 29.29 | 38.74 | 39.03 |
| Prices:Low | 17.70 | 15.13 | 12.00 | 22.86 | 18.97 | 26.04 | 22.37 | 12.39 | 7.47 | 18.31 |
| P/E Ratio:High | 16 | 16 | 21 | 31 | NM | NM | NM | NM | NM | NM |
| P/E Ratio:Low | 11 | 10 | 9 | 25 | NM | NM | NM | NM | NM | NM |

| Income Statement Analysis (Million $) | 2011 | 2010 | 2009 | 2008 | 2007 | 2006 | 2005 | 2004 | 2003 | 2002 |
|---|---|---|---|---|---|---|---|---|---|---|
| Revenue | 4,429 | 4,353 | 4,271 | 4,277 | 3,943 | 3,796 | 3,530 | 3,276 | 3,116 | 2,964 |
| Operating Income | 1,636 | 1,631 | 1,377 | 1,137 | 560 | 836 | 504 | 417 | 421 | -62.0 |
| Depreciation | 275 | 301 | 149 | 156 | 148 | 583 | 130 | 134 | 612 | 1,096 |
| Interest Expense | 45.0 | 76.0 | 95.0 | 370 | 126 | 41.0 | 106 | Nil | 172 | 227 |
| Pretax Income | 1,209 | 1,171 | 1,102 | 808 | 154 | 121 | 11.0 | -54.0 | -363 | -1,385 |
| Effective Tax Rate | NA | 34.2% | 37.0% | 38.1% | 21.4% | NM | NM | NM | NM | NM |
| Net Income | 823 | 771 | 694 | 500 | 121 | 156 | 13.0 | -36.0 | -267 | -1,102 |
| S&P Core Earnings | 802 | 768 | 704 | 522 | 122 | 155 | 136 | 7.10 | -301 | -1,185 |

| Balance Sheet & Other Financial Data (Million $) | 2011 | 2010 | 2009 | 2008 | 2007 | 2006 | 2005 | 2004 | 2003 | 2002 |
|---|---|---|---|---|---|---|---|---|---|---|
| Cash | 3,124 | 2,583 | 2,713 | 2,796 | 2,280 | 1,865 | 3,125 | 1,902 | 1,512 | 1,180 |
| Current Assets | 4,371 | 3,990 | 4,180 | 4,468 | 3,101 | 2,648 | 3,954 | 3,358 | 3,565 | 3,061 |
| Total Assets | 12,414 | 11,838 | 11,252 | 11,756 | 10,585 | 10,438 | 11,082 | 10,679 | 11,054 | 12,226 |
| Current Liabilities | 3,924 | 3,588 | 4,078 | 4,278 | 3,714 | 3,377 | 3,664 | 2,455 | 2,974 | 2,321 |
| Long Term Debt | 1,282 | 1,530 | 1,287 | 2,221 | 2,572 | 1,810 | 1,810 | 2,298 | 2,298 | 3,334 |
| Common Equity | 5,620 | 4,983 | 4,344 | 3,709 | 3,690 | 4,680 | 4,840 | 4,718 | 4,363 | 4,617 |
| Total Capital | 7,171 | 6,528 | 5,767 | 6,291 | 6,282 | 6,536 | 6,822 | 7,634 | 7,525 | 9,218 |
| Capital Expenditures | 92.0 | 79.0 | 83.0 | 117 | 150 | 143 | 69.0 | 30.0 | 30.0 | 25.0 |
| Cash Flow | 1,098 | 1,072 | 843 | 656 | 269 | 739 | 143 | 98.0 | 345 | -6.00 |
| Current Ratio | 1.1 | 1.1 | 1.0 | 1.0 | 0.8 | 0.8 | 1.1 | 1.4 | 1.2 | 1.3 |
| % Long Term Debt of Capitalization | 17.9 | 23.4 | 22.3 | 36.2 | 41.1 | 27.7 | 26.5 | 30.1 | 30.5 | 36.2 |
| % Net Income of Revenue | 18.6 | 17.7 | 16.3 | 11.7 | 3.1 | 4.1 | 0.4 | NM | NM | NM |
| % Return on Assets | 6.8 | 6.7 | 6.0 | 4.5 | 1.2 | 1.4 | 0.1 | NM | NM | NM |
| % Return on Equity | 15.5 | 16.5 | 17.2 | 13.5 | 2.9 | 3.2 | 0.3 | NM | NM | NM |

Data as orig reptd.; bef. results of disc opers/spec. items. Per share data adj. for stk. divs.; EPS diluted. E-Estimated. NA-Not Available. NM-Not Meaningful. NR-Not Ranked. UR-Under Review.

**Office:** One CA Plaza, Islandia, NY 11749.
**Telephone:** 800-225-5224.
**Email:** cainvestor@ca.com
**Website:** http://www.ca.com

**Chrmn:** A.F. Weinbach
**CEO:** W.E. McCracken
**EVP & Chief Admin Officer:** P.J. Harrington, Jr.
**EVP & CTO:** D.F. Ferguson

**SVP & Secy:** C.H. DuPree
**Investor Contact:** K. Doherty (212-415-6844)
**Board Members:** J. Alder, R. J. Bromark, G. J. Fernandes, R. Kapoor, K. Koplovitz, C. B. Lofgren, W. E. McCracken, R. Sulpizio, L. S. Unger, A. F. Weinbach, R. Zambonini

**Founded:** 1974
**Domicile:** Delaware
**Employees:** 13,400

**The McGraw-Hill Companies**

# Capital One Financial Corp.

**STANDARD &POOR'S**

| | | | |
|---|---|---|---|
| **S&P Recommendation** BUY ★★★★☆ | **Price** $40.02 (as of Nov 25, 2011) | **12-Mo. Target Price** $54.00 | **Investment Style** Large-Cap Blend |

**GICS Sector** Financials
**Sub-Industry** Consumer Finance

**Summary** This diversified consumer finance company is one of the largest issuers of Visa and MasterCard credit cards in the world.

## Key Stock Statistics (Source S&P, Vickers, company reports)

| | | | | | | | |
|---|---|---|---|---|---|---|---|
| 52-Wk Range | $56.26– 35.94 | S&P Oper. EPS 2011E | 7.68 | Market Capitalization(B) | $18.253 | Beta | 1.72 |
| Trailing 12-Month EPS | $7.47 | S&P Oper. EPS 2012E | 6.08 | Yield (%) | 0.50 | S&P 3-Yr. Proj. EPS CAGR(%) | -2 |
| Trailing 12-Month P/E | 5.4 | P/E on S&P Oper. EPS 2011E | 5.2 | Dividend Rate/Share | $0.20 | S&P Credit Rating | BBB |
| $10K Invested 5 Yrs Ago | $5,722 | Common Shares Outstg. (M) | 456.1 | Institutional Ownership (%) | 92 | | |

## Price Performance

30-Week Mov. Avg. · · · · 10-Week Mov. Avg. -- **GAAP Earnings vs. Previous Year** Volume Above Avg. STARS
12-Mo. Target Price — Relative Strength — ▲ Up ▼ Down ► No Change Below Avg. ★

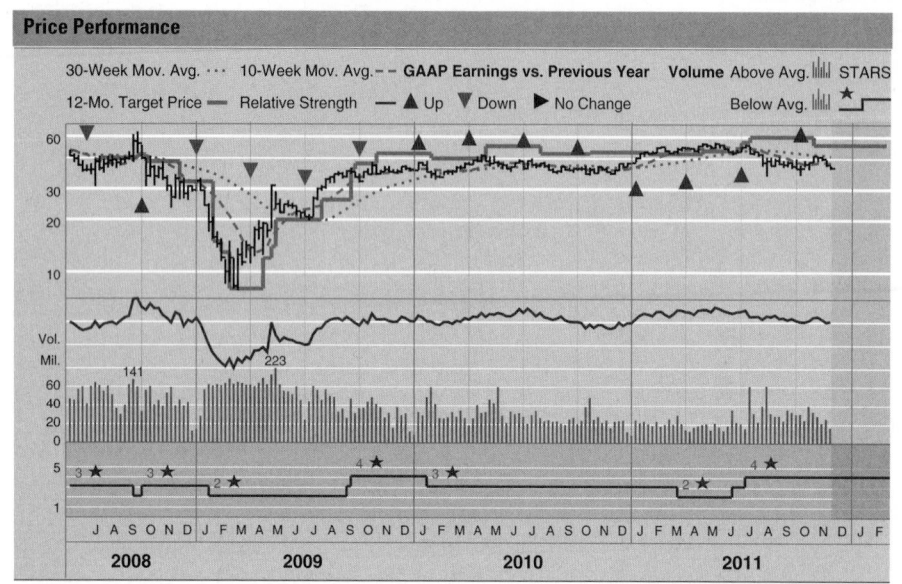

Options: ASE, CBOE, P, Ph

Analysis prepared by Equity Analyst **Robert McMillan** on Oct 24, 2011, when the stock traded at **$44.49**.

## Highlights

► COF's results have been volatile over the past five years, reflecting the economic climate, which has resulted in consumers being more cautious with credit card debt. Coupled with added government regulations, growth will be restricted, in our view. However, after several years of decline, we now expect COF revenues to rise 1.0% in 2011 and 4.3% in 2012, on growth in the portfolio tied to rising loan balances. Although new regulations covering its U.S. credit card business will likely hurt revenue due to a mandated change in minimum payment policies, we think COF will come up with alternative means to make up for some, but not all, of the lost revenue.

► After steep declines, we expect loan loss provisions and charge-offs to rise in tandem with growth in the portfolio. Nevertheless, we see charge-offs remaining under control even if they do rise from historically low levels. We were encouraged that the charge-off rate in the 2011 third quarter fell to 2.52%, from 4.82% in the year-earlier period.

► We estimate operating EPS of $7.68 in 2011 and $6.08 in 2012, versus $6.68 in 2010, excluding one-time items.

## Investment Rationale/Risk

► We believe COF shares are poised to move higher as uncertainty regarding the impact of recent credit card regulation wanes, consumers return to using their credit cards more often and credit trends continue to improve. We also think COF's planned purchase of the U.S. business of ING Direct from ING Groep (ING 9, Hold) for about $9 billion in cash and stock will help bolster COF's funding sources and present the company with attractive cross-selling opportunities.

► Risks to our recommendation and target price include a sustained decrease in consumer confidence, as well as a pickup in unemployment levels that leads to higher charge-off and delinquency rates.

► The shares recently traded at less than 6X trailing 12-month EPS, reflecting, in our view, deep pessimism about the global economy and the company's prospects. Our 12-month target price of $54 is 8.8X our forward 12-month EPS estimate of $6.13, well below the five-year historical P/E multiple. We expect the valuation multiple to widen on expected improvements in operations as well as contributions from acquisitions.

## Qualitative Risk Assessment

| LOW | MEDIUM | HIGH |
|---|---|---|

Our risk assessment reflects what we perceive as the company's solid financial position. Although we expect the credit card business to be hit by falling receivables as households reduce their debt burden, we also see improving credit metrics and strong capital levels.

## Quantitative Evaluations

**S&P Quality Ranking** A-

| D | C | B- | B | B+ | A- | A | A+ |
|---|---|---|---|---|---|---|---|

**Relative Strength Rank** MODERATE

41

LOWEST = 1    HIGHEST = 99

## Revenue/Earnings Data

**Revenue (Million $)**

| | 1Q | 2Q | 3Q | 4Q | Year |
|---|---|---|---|---|---|
| 2011 | 4,694 | 4,556 | 4,706 | -- | -- |
| 2010 | 5,091 | 4,642 | 4,722 | 4,613 | 19,067 |
| 2009 | 3,740 | 3,949 | 4,255 | 4,007 | 15,951 |
| 2008 | 4,936 | 4,269 | 4,469 | 4,137 | 17,856 |
| 2007 | 4,598 | 4,719 | 4,917 | 5,119 | 19,132 |
| 2006 | 3,737 | 3,607 | 2,826 | 4,021 | 15,191 |

**Earnings Per Share ($)**

| | | | | | |
|---|---|---|---|---|---|
| 2011 | 2.24 | 2.04 | 1.88 | E1.52 | E7.68 |
| 2010 | 1.58 | 1.78 | 1.79 | 1.53 | 6.68 |
| 2009 | -0.38 | -0.64 | 0.96 | 0.89 | 0.98 |
| 2008 | 1.70 | 1.24 | 1.03 | -3.67 | 0.14 |
| 2007 | 1.62 | 1.89 | -2.09 | 0.85 | 6.55 |
| 2006 | 2.86 | 1.78 | 1.89 | 1.14 | 7.62 |

Fiscal year ended Dec. 31. Next earnings report expected: Late January. EPS Estimates based on S&P Operating Earnings; historical GAAP earnings are as reported.

## Dividend Data (Dates: mm/dd Payment Date: mm/dd/yy)

| Amount ($) | Date Decl. | Ex-Div. Date | Stk. of Record | Payment Date |
|---|---|---|---|---|
| 0.050 | 01/27 | 02/09 | 02/11 | 02/22/11 |
| 0.050 | 05/11 | 05/19 | 05/23 | 06/03/11 |
| 0.050 | 07/28 | 08/10 | 08/12 | 08/22/11 |
| 0.050 | 11/11 | 11/17 | 11/21 | 12/02/11 |

Dividends have been paid since 1995. Source: Company reports.

**The McGraw-Hill Companies**

# Capital One Financial Corp.

STANDARD
&POOR'S

## Business Summary October 24, 2011

Capital One Financial Corporation operates as a diversified financial services company. The company focuses primarily on consumer and commercial lending and deposit origination.

The company's principal subsidiaries are Capital One Bank (USA), National Association (COBNA), which offers credit and debit card products, other lending products, and deposit products; and Capital One, National Association (CONA), which offers a spectrum of banking products and financial services to consumers, small businesses and commercial clients.

The company offers its products throughout the United States. It also offers its products outside of the United States principally through Capital One Bank (Europe) plc, an indirect subsidiary of COBNA organized and located in the United Kingdom (the U.K. Bank), and through a branch of COBNA in Canada. The company's U.K. Bank has authority to accept deposits and provide credit card and installment loans. Its branch of COBNA in Canada has the authority to provide credit card loans.

The company's principal business segments are divided into three main segments: 1) the Credit Card segment includes the company's domestic consumer and small business card lending, domestic national small business lending, national closed end installment lending and the international card lending businesses in Canada and the United Kingdom; 2) the Commercial Banking segment includes the company's lending, deposit gathering and treasury management services to commercial real estate and middle market customers, and the financial results of a national portfolio of small ticket commercial real estate loans that are in run-off mode; and 3) the Consumer Banking segment includes the company's branch-based lending and deposit gathering activities for small business customers, as well as its branch-based consumer deposit gathering and lending activities, national deposit gathering, national automobile lending, consumer mortgage lending, and servicing activities.

## Company Financials Fiscal Year Ended Dec. 31

| Per Share Data ($) | 2010 | 2009 | 2008 | 2007 | 2006 | 2005 | 2004 | 2003 | 2002 | 2001 |
|---|---|---|---|---|---|---|---|---|---|---|
| Tangible Book Value | 27.05 | 26.90 | 27.28 | 27.89 | 28.30 | 33.99 | 33.98 | 25.75 | 20.44 | 15.33 |
| Earnings | 6.68 | 0.98 | 0.14 | 6.55 | 7.62 | 6.73 | 6.21 | 4.92 | 3.93 | 2.91 |
| S&P Core Earnings | 6.67 | 0.87 | 1.83 | 6.55 | 7.61 | 6.61 | 5.72 | 4.41 | 3.37 | 2.55 |
| Dividends | 0.20 | 0.52 | 1.50 | 0.11 | 0.11 | 0.11 | 0.11 | 0.11 | 0.11 | 0.11 |
| Payout Ratio | 3% | 54% | NM | 2% | 1% | 2% | 2% | 2% | 3% | 4% |
| Prices:High | 47.73 | 42.90 | 63.50 | 83.84 | 90.04 | 88.56 | 84.45 | 64.25 | 66.50 | 72.58 |
| Prices:Low | 34.03 | 7.80 | 23.28 | 44.40 | 69.30 | 69.09 | 60.04 | 24.91 | 24.05 | 36.40 |
| P/E Ratio:High | 7 | 44 | NM | 13 | 12 | 13 | 14 | 13 | 17 | 25 |
| P/E Ratio:Low | 5 | 8 | NM | 7 | 9 | 10 | 10 | 5 | 6 | 13 |

| Income Statement Analysis (Million $) | | | | | | | | | | |
|---|---|---|---|---|---|---|---|---|---|---|
| Net Interest Income | 12,457 | 7,697 | 7,149 | 6,530 | 5,100 | 3,680 | 3,003 | 2,785 | 2,719 | 1,663 |
| Non Interest Income | 3,714 | 5,286 | 6,692 | 8,054 | 6,997 | 6,358 | 5,900 | 5,416 | 5,467 | 4,420 |
| Loan Loss Provision | 3,907 | 4,230 | 5,101 | 2,637 | 1,476 | 1,491 | 1,221 | 1,517 | 2,149 | 990 |
| Non Interest Expenses | 7,934 | 7,417 | 8,210 | 8,078 | 6,967 | 5,718 | 5,322 | 4,857 | 4,586 | 4,058 |
| % Expense/Operating Revenue | 49.1% | 57.1% | 59.3% | 55.4% | 57.6% | 57.0% | 59.8% | 59.2% | 56.0% | 66.7% |
| Pretax Income | 4,330 | 1,336 | 582 | 3,870 | 3,653 | 2,829 | 2,360 | 1,827 | 1,451 | 1,035 |
| Effective Tax Rate | 29.6% | 26.2% | 85.5% | 33.0% | 33.9% | 36.1% | 34.6% | 37.0% | 38.0% | 38.0% |
| Net Income | 3,050 | 987 | 84.5 | 2,592 | 2,414 | 1,809 | 1,543 | 1,151 | 900 | 642 |
| % Net Interest Margin | 7.09 | 5.30 | 5.38 | 6.46 | 6.03 | 6.63 | 6.44 | 7.45 | 8.73 | 8.03 |
| S&P Core Earnings | 3,045 | 374 | 691 | 2,591 | 2,412 | 1,792 | 1,431 | 1,012 | 742 | 545 |

| Balance Sheet & Other Financial Data (Million $) | | | | | | | | | | |
|---|---|---|---|---|---|---|---|---|---|---|
| Money Market Assets | 3,182 | 5,585 | 5,444 | 2,444 | 1,843 | 2,049 | 1,084 | 1,598 | 641 | 352 |
| Investment Securities | 41,537 | 38,910 | 31,003 | 19,782 | 15,452 | 14,350 | 9,300 | 5,867 | 4,424 | 3,116 |
| Earning Assets:Total Loans | 125,947 | 90,619 | 101,342 | 98,842 | 106,947 | 59,848 | 38,216 | 32,850 | 27,854 | 20,921 |
| Total Assets | 197,503 | 169,400 | 165,981 | 150,590 | 149,739 | 88,701 | 53,747 | 46,284 | 37,382 | 28,184 |
| Demand Deposits | 15,048 | 13,439 | 11,294 | 11,047 | 11,648 | 4,841 | NA | Nil | Nil | Nil |
| Time Deposits | 107,162 | 102,370 | 97,327 | 71,944 | 74,123 | 43,092 | NA | 22,416 | 17,326 | 12,839 |
| Long Term Debt | 28,690 | 15,438 | 16,735 | 20,237 | 20,217 | 14,863 | Nil | 14,813 | 8,124 | Nil |
| Common Equity | 26,541 | 26,589 | 23,516 | 24,294 | 25,235 | 14,129 | 8,388 | 6,052 | 4,623 | 3,324 |
| % Return on Assets | 1.7 | 0.6 | 0.1 | 1.7 | 2.0 | 2.5 | 3.1 | 2.8 | 2.7 | 2.7 |
| % Return on Equity | 11.5 | 3.9 | 0.4 | 10.5 | 12.3 | 16.1 | 21.4 | 21.6 | 22.6 | 24.3 |
| % Loan Loss Reserve | 4.5 | 4.6 | 4.5 | 2.9 | 2.0 | 3.0 | 3.9 | 4.9 | 6.2 | 4.0 |
| % Loans/Deposits | 103.1 | 78.3 | 93.0 | 114.5 | 124.7 | 124.8 | 149.1 | 146.5 | 160.8 | 162.9 |
| % Loans/Assets | 59.0 | 57.2 | 63.2 | 64.2 | 70.0 | 68.8 | 71.0 | 71.9 | 74.4 | 74.3 |
| % Equity to Assets | 14.5 | 14.9 | 15.1 | 16.5 | 16.5 | 15.8 | 14.4 | 12.8 | 12.1 | 11.2 |

Data as orig reptd.; bef. results of disc opers/spec. items. Per share data adj. for stk. divs.; EPS diluted. E-Estimated. NA-Not Available. NM-Not Meaningful. NR-Not Ranked. UR-Under Review.

**Office:** 1680 Capital One Drive, McLean, VA 22102-3407.
**Telephone:** 703-720-1000.
**Email:** investor.relations@capitalone.com
**Website:** http://www.capitalone.com

**Chrmn, Pres & CEO:** R.D. Fairbank
**SVP, Chief Acctg Officer & Cntlr:** R.S. Blackley
**SVP & Treas:** S. Linehan
**CFO:** G.L. Perlin

**Secy & General Counsel:** J.G. Finneran, Jr.
**Investor Contact:** M. Rowen (703-720-2455)
**Board Members:** E. R. Campbell, W. R. Dietz, R. D. Fairbank, P. W. Gross, A. F. Hackett, L. Hay, III, P. E. Leroy, M. A. Shattuck, III, B. H. Warner

**Founded:** 1993
**Domicile:** Delaware
**Employees:** 27,826

The *McGraw-Hill* Companies

# Cardinal Health Inc

STANDARD
&POOR'S

| S&P Recommendation | BUY ★★★★☆ | Price $40.29 (as of Nov 25, 2011) | 12-Mo. Target Price $51.00 | Investment Style Large-Cap Blend |
|---|---|---|---|---|

**GICS Sector** Health Care
**Sub-Industry** Health Care Distributors

**Summary** This company is one of the leading wholesale distributors of pharmaceuticals, medical/surgical supplies and related products to a broad range of health care customers.

## Key Stock Statistics (Source S&P, Vickers, company reports)

| | | | | | | | |
|---|---|---|---|---|---|---|---|
| 52-Wk Range | $47.06– 35.07 | S&P Oper. EPS 2012**E** | 3.13 | Market Capitalization(B) | $13.920 | Beta | 0.75 |
| Trailing 12-Month EPS | $2.56 | S&P Oper. EPS 2013**E** | 3.45 | Yield (%) | 2.13 | S&P 3-Yr. Proj. EPS CAGR(%) | 11 |
| Trailing 12-Month P/E | 15.7 | P/E on S&P Oper. EPS 2012**E** | 12.9 | Dividend Rate/Share | $0.86 | S&P Credit Rating | A- |
| $10K Invested 5 Yrs Ago | NA | Common Shares Outstg. (M) | 345.5 | Institutional Ownership (%) | 86 | | |

## Price Performance

30-Week Mov. Avg. · · · 10-Week Mov. Avg. - - GAAP Earnings vs. Previous Year   Volume Above Avg. STARS
12-Mo. Target Price — Relative Strength — ▲ Up ▼ Down ► No Change   Below Avg. ★

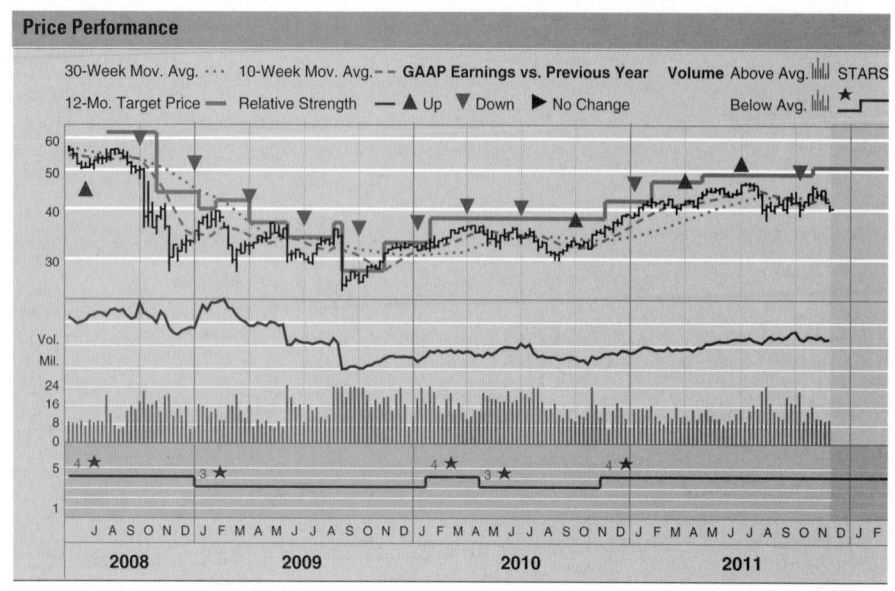

Options: ASE, CBOE, P, Ph

Analysis prepared by Equity Analyst **Herman Saftlas** on Nov 08, 2011, when the stock traded at **$44.16**.

### Qualitative Risk Assessment

| LOW | MEDIUM | HIGH |
|---|---|---|

Our risk assessment reflects CAH's diversified products and services and what we believe are good growth prospects for its contract drugmaking and drug dispensing systems. However, we also see intense competition in the drug distribution market, and we believe that future drugmaker-distributor contract negotiations could be less favorable to distributors.

### Quantitative Evaluations

**S&P Quality Ranking**                               B+

| D | C | B- | B | B+ | A- | A | A+ |
|---|---|---|---|---|---|---|---|

**Relative Strength Rank**                    MODERATE

52

LOWEST = 1                              HIGHEST = 99

### Highlights

➤ We forecast a rise in revenues for FY 12 (Jun.) of 4%, from FY 11's $102.6 billion. The gain should be paced by projected mid-single digit growth in the Pharmaceutical segment, supported by strong customer retention, new contracts, and benefits from an indicated rise in new generic launches. We also see mid-single digit growth for the Medical segment, lifted by expected higher sales to existing customers and new customers. The recent acquisitions of Healthcare Solutions, an oncology services firm, and Kinray and Yong Yu distributors should also augment volume. However, we see slowing trends in the nuclear low energy cardiac imaging business.

➤ We expect gross margins to improve in FY 12, reflecting higher volume, a more profitable revenue mix and expense controls. We see improvement in the EBITDA ratio, aided by tight control of SG&A costs. Although depreciation is expected to decline, interest expense will probably rise.

➤ After an estimated adjusted tax rate slightly higher than the 37.2% rate of FY 11, we see non-GAAP cash EPS of $3.13 for FY 12, up from an adjusted $2.80 in FY 11.

### Investment Rationale/Risk

➤ One of three major drug distribution companies in the U.S., Cardinal appears to us to be well situated in its industry, with relationships with two major retail pharmacy chains generating over 40% of its revenues. We are also encouraged by three recent acquisitions: Healthcare Solutions, an oncology services firm; Kinray, a drug distributor serving over 2,000 independent retail pharmacies in the NYC metropolitan area; and Yong Yu, a leading pharmaceutical distributor in China. We expect these deals to contribute importantly to EPS growth over the coming years. We also view CAH's cash flow as healthy, providing financial flexibility for business expansion, dividends and common share buybacks.

➤ Risks to our recommendation and target price include intensified competition, the loss of major accounts, consolidation trends in the U.S. retail pharmacy industry reducing the customer base, and unfavorable changes in contracts with drugmakers or retailers.

➤ Our 12-month target price of $51 is based on a peer-level multiple of 16.3X applied to our EPS estimate of $3.13 for FY 12.

### Revenue/Earnings Data

#### Revenue (Million $)

| | 1Q | 2Q | 3Q | 4Q | Year |
|---|---|---|---|---|---|
| 2012 | 26,792 | -- | -- | -- | -- |
| 2011 | 24,438 | 25,372 | 26,071 | 26,764 | 102,644 |
| 2010 | 24,781 | 24,920 | 24,343 | 24,460 | 98,503 |
| 2009 | 24,321 | 25,075 | 24,918 | 25,199 | 99,512 |
| 2008 | 21,973 | 23,283 | 22,910 | 22,926 | 91,091 |
| 2007 | 20,938 | 21,785 | 21,867 | 22,263 | 86,852 |

#### Earnings Per Share ($)

| | | | | | |
|---|---|---|---|---|---|
| 2012 | 0.68 | E0.79 | E0.86 | E0.75 | E3.13 |
| 2011 | 0.84 | 0.61 | 0.71 | 0.58 | 2.74 |
| 2010 | -0.17 | 0.64 | 0.62 | 0.54 | 1.62 |
| 2009 | 0.68 | 0.88 | 0.87 | 0.74 | 3.16 |
| 2008 | 0.82 | 0.89 | 1.02 | 0.89 | 3.62 |
| 2007 | 0.71 | 0.77 | -0.01 | 0.61 | 2.08 |

Fiscal year ended Jun. 30. Next earnings report expected: Early February. EPS Estimates based on S&P Operating Earnings; historical GAAP earnings are as reported.

### Dividend Data (Dates: mm/dd Payment Date: mm/dd/yy)

| Amount ($) | Date Decl. | Ex-Div. Date | Stk. of Record | Payment Date |
|---|---|---|---|---|
| 0.195 | 02/01 | 03/30 | 04/01 | 04/15/11 |
| 0.215 | 05/04 | 06/29 | 07/01 | 07/15/11 |
| 0.215 | 08/03 | 09/28 | 10/01 | 10/15/11 |
| 0.215 | 11/02 | 12/28 | 01/01 | 01/15/12 |

Dividends have been paid since 1983. Source: Company reports.

# Cardinal Health Inc

STANDARD
&POOR'S

## Business Summary November 08, 2011

CORPORATE OVERVIEW. Cardinal Health ranks as one of the nation's largest wholesalers of pharmaceuticals and medical products. On August 31, 2009, the company spun off to its shareholders stock in CareFusion Corp., a company formed from Cardinal's previous device businesses designed to prevent hospital medication errors and infections. CareFusion's stock trades on the NYSE under the symbol CFN.

The Pharmaceutical segment (91% of revenues in FY 11 (Jun.)) distributes pharmaceutical and related health care products to independent and chain drug stores, hospitals, alternate care centers, and supermarket and mass merchandiser pharmacies. The company also provides pharmaceutical repackaging and distribution for retail and mail order customers. Cardinal also offers third-party logistics support services, distributes therapeutic plasma to hospitals, clinics and other providers located in the U.S.

The company manufactures and markets generic pharmaceutical products for sale to hospitals, clinics and pharmacies in the United Kingdom. CAH also has a specialty pharmacy that provides prescription fulfillment and clinical care services directly to individual patients requiring highly intensive therapies. In July 2010, the company acquired Healthcare Solutions, a provider of data and services for oncology and specialty customers, for $517 million in cash, plus

an additional $150 million in future contingent payments.

Cardinal operates the world's largest network of nuclear pharmacies and is expanding its positron emission tomography (PET) agent manufacturing capabilities to support new drug development and the future of personalized medicine. This unit prepares and delivers radiopharmaceuticals for use in nuclear imaging and other procedures in hospitals and clinics. In addition, about 200 hospitals across the U.S. outsource the management of their inpatient pharmacy to Cardinal.

The Medical segment (9% of revenues) distributes medical-surgical products to ambulatory care centers, physician offices, clinical laboratories and hospitals across the U.S. and Canada. This unit also produces gloves, gowns, surgical drapes, scrubs and fluid management products. In addition, this segment conducts surgical and procedural kitting operations that assemble all necessary single-use surgical products and apparel for specific procedures into one kit, allowing clinicians to focus on the patient.

## Company Financials  Fiscal Year Ended Jun. 30

| Per Share Data ($) | 2011 | 2010 | 2009 | 2008 | 2007 | 2006 | 2005 | 2004 | 2003 | 2002 |
|---|---|---|---|---|---|---|---|---|---|---|
| Tangible Book Value | 4.53 | 8.48 | 7.30 | 4.26 | 4.12 | 8.52 | 8.20 | 7.05 | 12.10 | 11.50 |
| Cash Flow | 3.63 | 2.33 | 4.27 | 4.65 | 2.87 | 3.82 | 3.34 | 4.15 | 3.70 | 2.98 |
| Earnings | 2.74 | 1.62 | 3.16 | 3.62 | 2.07 | 2.90 | 2.40 | 3.47 | 3.12 | 2.45 |
| S&P Core Earnings | 2.55 | 1.39 | 3.16 | 3.64 | 3.08 | 2.88 | 2.16 | 3.14 | 2.78 | 2.26 |
| Dividends | 0.80 | 0.72 | 0.60 | 0.50 | 0.39 | 0.27 | 0.15 | 0.12 | 0.11 | 0.10 |
| Payout Ratio | 29% | 44% | 19% | 14% | 19% | 9% | 6% | 3% | 4% | 4% |
| Prices:High | 47.06 | 39.29 | 39.87 | 62.25 | 76.15 | 75.74 | 69.64 | 76.54 | 67.96 | 73.70 |
| Prices:Low | 37.53 | 29.69 | 24.87 | 27.79 | 56.41 | 61.15 | 52.85 | 36.08 | 50.00 | 46.60 |
| P/E Ratio:High | 17 | 24 | 13 | 17 | 37 | 26 | 29 | 22 | 22 | 30 |
| P/E Ratio:Low | 14 | 18 | 8 | 8 | 27 | 21 | 22 | 10 | 16 | 19 |

| Income Statement Analysis (Million $) | | | | | | | | | | |
|---|---|---|---|---|---|---|---|---|---|---|
| Revenue | 102,644 | 98,503 | 99,512 | 91,091 | 86,852 | 81,364 | 74,911 | 65,054 | 50,467 | 44,394 |
| Operating Income | 1,881 | 1,627 | 2,488 | 2,594 | 2,485 | 2,474 | 2,555 | 2,694 | 3,723 | 2,216 |
| Depreciation | 313 | 254 | 399 | 375 | 322 | 393 | 410 | 299 | 266 | 244 |
| Interest Expense | 92.8 | 114 | 219 | 171 | 121 | 132 | 134 | 98.9 | 115 | 133 |
| Pretax Income | 1,518 | 1,212 | 1,667 | 1,957 | 1,252 | 1,835 | 1,629 | 2,238 | 2,127 | 1,701 |
| Effective Tax Rate | NA | NA | 31.5% | 32.3% | 32.9% | 32.2% | 35.8% | 31.9% | 33.6% | 33.8% |
| Net Income | 966 | 587 | 1,143 | 1,325 | 840 | 1,245 | 1,047 | 1,525 | 1,412 | 1,126 |
| S&P Core Earnings | 898 | 503 | 1,142 | 1,326 | 1,247 | 1,236 | 936 | 1,369 | 1,266 | 1,045 |

| Balance Sheet & Other Financial Data (Million $) | | | | | | | | | | |
|---|---|---|---|---|---|---|---|---|---|---|
| Cash | 1,929 | 2,755 | 1,848 | 1,291 | 1,309 | 1,321 | 1,412 | 1,096 | 1,724 | 1,382 |
| Current Assets | 16,316 | 14,919 | 15,799 | 14,184 | 14,545 | 14,777 | 13,443 | 13,058 | 13,250 | 11,907 |
| Total Assets | 22,846 | 19,990 | 25,119 | 23,448 | 23,154 | 23,374 | 22,059 | 21,369 | 18,521 | 16,438 |
| Current Liabilities | 13,370 | 11,538 | 11,400 | 10,376 | 11,460 | 11,373 | 10,105 | 9,369 | 7,314 | 6,810 |
| Long Term Debt | 2,175 | 1,896 | 3,280 | 3,687 | 3,457 | 2,600 | 2,320 | 2,835 | 2,472 | 2,207 |
| Common Equity | 5,849 | 5,276 | 8,725 | 7,756 | 7,377 | 8,491 | 8,593 | 7,976 | 7,758 | 6,393 |
| Total Capital | 8,351 | 7,405 | 12,005 | 11,444 | 10,834 | 11,090 | 10,913 | 12,000 | 11,207 | 8,600 |
| Capital Expenditures | 291 | 256 | 533 | 376 | 1,630 | 443 | 572 | 410 | 423 | 285 |
| Cash Flow | 1,280 | 841 | 1,542 | 1,691 | 1,162 | 1,637 | 1,456 | 1,824 | 1,678 | 1,370 |
| Current Ratio | 1.2 | 1.3 | 1.4 | 1.4 | 1.3 | 1.3 | 1.3 | 1.4 | 1.8 | 1.7 |
| % Long Term Debt of Capitalization | 26.1 | 25.6 | 27.3 | 32.2 | 31.9 | 23.4 | 21.3 | 23.6 | 22.1 | 25.7 |
| % Net Income of Revenue | 0.9 | 0.6 | 1.2 | 1.5 | 1.0 | 1.5 | 1.4 | 2.3 | 2.8 | 2.5 |
| % Return on Assets | 4.5 | 2.6 | 4.7 | 5.7 | 3.6 | 5.5 | 4.8 | 7.7 | 8.1 | 7.2 |
| % Return on Equity | 17.4 | 8.4 | 13.9 | 17.5 | 10.6 | 14.6 | 12.6 | 19.5 | 20.0 | 19.0 |

Data as orig reptd.; bef. results of disc opers/spec. items. Per share data adj. for stk. divs.; EPS diluted. E-Estimated. NA-Not Available. NM-Not Meaningful. NR-Not Ranked. UR-Under Review.

**Office:** 7000 Cardinal Place, Dublin, OH 43017.
**Telephone:** 614-757-5000.
**Website:** http://www.cardinalhealth.com
**Chrmn & CEO:** G.S. Barrett

**EVP & CIO:** P. Morrison
**SVP & Chief Acctg Officer:** S.G. Laws
**SVP & Treas:** J.M. Gomez
**CFO:** J.W. Henderson

**Board Members:** C. F. Arnold, G. S. Barrett, G. A. Britt, C. S. Cox, C. Darden, B. L. Downey, J. F. Finn, G. B. Kenny, D. P. King, R. C. Notebaert, D. W. Raisbeck, J. G. Spaulding
**Founded:** 1979
**Domicile:** Ohio
**Employees:** 31,900

# CareFusion Corp

## STANDARD &POOR'S

**S&P Recommendation** HOLD ★★★☆☆

| Price | 12-Mo. Target Price | Investment Style |
|---|---|---|
| $23.20 (as of Nov 25, 2011) | $28.00 | Large-Cap Growth |

**GICS Sector** Health Care
**Sub-Industry** Health Care Equipment

**Summary** This leading maker of infusion pumps, dispensing systems, and respiratory and infection prevention products was spun off from Cardinal Health on August 31, 2009.

## Key Stock Statistics (Source S&P, Vickers, company reports)

| | | | | | | | |
|---|---|---|---|---|---|---|---|
| 52-Wk Range | $29.97– 22.01 | S&P Oper. EPS 2012E | 1.85 | Market Capitalization(B) | $5.206 | Beta | NA |
| Trailing 12-Month EPS | $1.20 | S&P Oper. EPS 2013E | 2.07 | Yield (%) | Nil | S&P 3-Yr. Proj. EPS CAGR(%) | 12 |
| Trailing 12-Month P/E | 19.3 | P/E on S&P Oper. EPS 2012E | 12.5 | Dividend Rate/Share | Nil | S&P Credit Rating | BBB- |
| $10K Invested 5 Yrs Ago | NA | Common Shares Outstg. (M) | 224.4 | Institutional Ownership (%) | 87 | | |

## Price Performance

30-Week Mov. Avg. · · · 10-Week Mov. Avg. - - **GAAP Earnings vs. Previous Year** Volume Above Avg. STARS
12-Mo. Target Price — Relative Strength — ▲ Up ▼ Down ▶ No Change Below Avg.

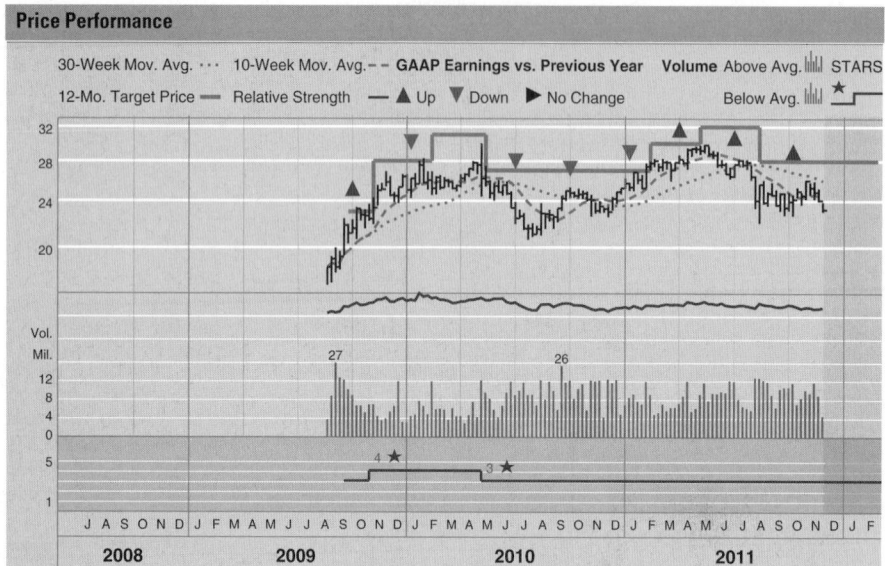

Analysis prepared by Equity Analyst **Phillip Seligman** on Nov 11, 2011, when the stock traded at **$24.82**.

## Highlights

▶ We expect CFN's revenues to grow 4.2% in FY 12 (Jun.), led by mid- to high single digit growth in dispensing, aided by an acquisition in Europe, and high single digit growth in infection prevention products, on demand for Chloraprep and expansion into new markets. While we forecast double digit volume growth for infusion pumps, mainly as hospitals convert from Baxter's (BAX 54, Buy) recalled infusion pump, we see heavily discounted pumps yielding mid-single digit revenue growth. We also expect flat respiratory revenues as stabilization in the U.S. offsets some softness in Europe, and we see a small impact from the April 2011 divestiture of a business that contributed $32 million in FY 11.

▶ We see gross margins expanding slightly in FY 12 on an improved product mix. We also expect G&A expenses to contract as a percentage of revenue, mainly on cost control and a restructuring, while the R&D cost ratio rises on the company's plans to build R&D scale.

▶ We estimate EPS from continuing operations of $1.85 in FY 12, versus $1.65 in FY 11. We look for $2.07 in FY 13.

## Investment Rationale/Risk

▶ We are positive on CFN's plans to achieve long-term revenue growth above the 3%-5% range and 11%-15% operating earnings growth. In the process, it realigned its businesses into capital equipment and consumables segments. It also seeks to boost R&D spending, penetrate emerging markets and improve efficiencies. Meantime, while CFN gained infusion pump market share, which we also view positively, it resorted to price discounting. However, on a positive note, it should garner years of recurring revenues in infusion pump-related disposables. Separately, we do not expect a meaningful improvement in consumables and disposables sales until procedure volumes recover. Separately, we see some share-price volatility amid the federal government's investigation of ChloraPrep marketing.

▶ Risks to our recommendation and target price include further declines in hospital capital spending, intensified competition, product recalls, and increased health care regulation.

▶ Our 12-month target price of $28 reflects a multiple of 14X our calendar 2012 EPS estimate of $2.01, near medical device group peers.

## Qualitative Risk Assessment

| LOW | MEDIUM | HIGH |
|---|---|---|

Our risk assessment reflects our belief that U.S. hospital capital spending will remain under pressure over the long term, limiting the sales growth of CFN's capital equipment, which represents about 40% of its business. Still, we expect these and CFN's disposables products to benefit from hospitals seeking to improve patient safety.

## Quantitative Evaluations

**S&P Quality Ranking** NR

| D | C | B- | B | B+ | A- | A | A+ |
|---|---|---|---|---|---|---|---|

**Relative Strength Rank** MODERATE
49
LOWEST = 1          HIGHEST = 99

## Revenue/Earnings Data

**Revenue (Million $)**

| | 1Q | 2Q | 3Q | 4Q | Year |
|---|---|---|---|---|---|
| 2012 | 844.0 | -- | -- | -- | -- |
| 2011 | 811.0 | 886.0 | 867.0 | 964.0 | 3,528 |
| 2010 | 923.0 | 1,019 | 952.0 | 1,035 | 3,929 |
| 2009 | 1,167 | 1,167 | 1,076 | 1,091 | 4,501 |
| 2008 | 1,060 | 1,060 | 1,150 | 1,248 | 4,518 |
| 2007 | -- | -- | -- | -- | 3,478 |

**Earnings Per Share ($)**

| | 1Q | 2Q | 3Q | 4Q | Year |
|---|---|---|---|---|---|
| 2012 | 0.30 | E0.46 | E0.47 | E0.59 | E1.85 |
| 2011 | 0.17 | 0.32 | 0.38 | 0.43 | 1.29 |
| 2010 | 0.25 | 0.33 | -0.04 | 0.23 | 0.77 |
| 2009 | 0.14 | 0.49 | -- | 0.44 | 2.57 |
| 2008 | -- | -- | -- | -- | -- |
| 2007 | -- | -- | -- | -- | -- |

Fiscal year ended Jun. 30. Next earnings report expected: Early February. EPS Estimates based on S&P Operating Earnings; historical GAAP earnings are as reported.

## Dividend Data

No cash dividends have been paid.

The McGraw·Hill Companies

# CareFusion Corp

**STANDARD &POOR'S**

## Business Summary November 11, 2011

CORPORATE OVERVIEW. CareFusion Corp. is a global medical technology company with leading products and services designed to improve the safety and quality of health care. In 2008, Cardinal Health reorganized and consolidated the businesses comprising the majority of CareFusion into Cardinal Health's Clinical and Medical Products segment. CareFusion was incorporated in Delaware on January 14, 2009, for the purpose of holding the segment in connection with its planned spinoff, and transferred the equity interests of the entities that hold the assets and liabilities of the clinical and medical products businesses to CareFusion. Approximately 81% of the equity of CareFusion was spun off to Cardinal Health shareholders after the close of trading on August 31, 2009, and Cardinal divested its remaining stake by September 2010.

In July 2011, CFN realigned its organization into two new global operating segments. Medical Systems, which comprises capital equipment, and Procedural Solutions. The Medical Systems segment consists of dispensing technologies, infusion systems (infusion pumps and dedicated disposables), respiratory technologies (ventilators and dedicated disposables) and other (including the MedMined Data Mining Surveillance service). The Procedural Solutions segment consists of infection prevention (ChloraPrep products, legacy prep products, and non-dedicated infusion disposables), medical specialties (surgical instruments and interventional specialties), specialty disposables (respiratory disposables), and other (Neurocare and respiratory diagnostics). CFN's primary customers include hospitals, ambulatory surgical centers, clinics, long-term care facilities and physician offices in the U.S., and hospitals in more than 130 countries worldwide.

Primary product brands include: (1) Alaris IV infusion systems that feature proprietary software, Guardrails, an application that alerts the clinician when a parameter is outside the institution's pre-established limitations for that medication, thereby helping to reduce IV medication errors; (2) Pyxis automated medication dispensing systems that provide medication management and Pyxis automated medical supply dispensing systems; (3) AVEA and Pulmonetic Systems ventilation and respiratory products, and Jaeger and SensorMedics pulmonary products; (4) ChloraPrep products that help prevent vascular and surgical-site infections and MedMined software and services that help target and reduce hospital-acquired infections (HAIs); and (5) V. Mueller surgical instruments and related products and services.

## Company Financials Fiscal Year Ended Jun. 30

| Per Share Data ($) | 2011 | 2010 | 2009 | 2008 | 2007 | 2006 | 2005 | 2004 | 2003 | 2002 |
|---|---|---|---|---|---|---|---|---|---|---|
| Tangible Book Value | 5.60 | 3.63 | 4.73 | NA | NA | NA | NA | NA | NA | NA |
| Cash Flow | 2.13 | 1.54 | 3.45 | NA | NA | NA | NA | NA | NA | NA |
| Earnings | 1.29 | 0.77 | 2.57 | NA | NA | NA | NA | NA | NA | NA |
| S&P Core Earnings | 1.25 | 0.77 | 2.51 | 2.93 | 2.23 | NA | NA | NA | NA | NA |
| Dividends | NA | Nil | Nil | NA | NA | NA | NA | NA | NA | NA |
| Payout Ratio | Nil | Nil | Nil | NA | NA | NA | NA | NA | NA | NA |
| Prices:High | 29.97 | 30.08 | 26.99 | NA | NA | NA | NA | NA | NA | NA |
| Prices:Low | 22.01 | 20.63 | 17.25 | NA | NA | NA | NA | NA | NA | NA |
| P/E Ratio:High | 23 | 39 | 11 | NA | NA | NA | NA | NA | NA | NA |
| P/E Ratio:Low | 17 | 27 | 7 | NA | NA | NA | NA | NA | NA | NA |

| Income Statement Analysis (Million $) | | | | | | | | | | |
|---|---|---|---|---|---|---|---|---|---|---|
| Revenue | 3,528 | 3,929 | 4,501 | 4,518 | 3,478 | 3,052 | NA | NA | NA | NA |
| Operating Income | 790 | 714 | 856 | 945 | 691 | 573 | NA | NA | NA | NA |
| Depreciation | 188 | 173 | 194 | 165 | 117 | 109 | NA | NA | NA | NA |
| Interest Expense | 81.0 | 93.0 | 92.0 | 22.3 | 37.0 | 57.5 | NA | NA | NA | NA |
| Pretax Income | 415 | 357 | 719 | 847 | 619 | 567 | NA | NA | NA | NA |
| Effective Tax Rate | NA | NA | 21.0% | 21.8% | 18.8% | 18.8% | NA | NA | NA | NA |
| Net Income | 291 | 171 | 568 | 663 | 502 | 460 | NA | NA | NA | NA |
| S&P Core Earnings | 283 | 172 | 568 | 663 | 502 | NA | NA | NA | NA | NA |

| Balance Sheet & Other Financial Data (Million $) | | | | | | | | | | |
|---|---|---|---|---|---|---|---|---|---|---|
| Cash | 1,371 | 1,019 | 783 | 607 | 677 | NA | NA | NA | NA | NA |
| Current Assets | 2,868 | 2,508 | 2,390 | 2,322 | NA | NA | NA | NA | NA | NA |
| Total Assets | 8,221 | 7,943 | 8,349 | 8,329 | 7,876 | NA | NA | NA | NA | NA |
| Current Liabilities | 619 | 753 | 762 | 762 | NA | NA | NA | NA | NA | NA |
| Long Term Debt | 1,387 | 1,386 | 1,159 | 1,539 | 1,268 | NA | NA | NA | NA | NA |
| Common Equity | 5,093 | 4,704 | 5,451 | 5,048 | 4,887 | NA | NA | NA | NA | NA |
| Total Capital | 6,481 | 6,094 | 6,740 | 6,657 | 6,167 | NA | NA | NA | NA | NA |
| Capital Expenditures | 124 | 127 | 129 | 188 | 115 | 105 | NA | NA | NA | NA |
| Cash Flow | 479 | 344 | 762 | 828 | 620 | 569 | NA | NA | NA | NA |
| Current Ratio | 4.6 | 3.3 | 3.1 | 2.9 | 3.2 | NA | NA | NA | NA | NA |
| % Long Term Debt of Capitalization | 21.4 | 22.7 | 17.2 | 23.1 | 20.6 | Nil | NA | NA | NA | NA |
| % Net Income of Revenue | 8.3 | 4.4 | 12.6 | 14.7 | 14.5 | 15.1 | NA | NA | NA | NA |
| % Return on Assets | NA | NA | 6.8 | 8.2 | NA | NA | NA | NA | NA | NA |
| % Return on Equity | NA | NA | 10.8 | 13.3 | NA | NA | NA | NA | NA | NA |

Data as orig reptd.; bef. results of disc opers/spec. items. Per share data adj. for stk. divs.; EPS diluted. E-Estimated. NA-Not Available. NM-Not Meaningful. NR-Not Ranked. UR-Under Review.

**Office:** 3750 Torrey View Court, San Diego, CA 92130.
**Telephone:** 858-617-2000.
**Website:** http://www.carefusion.com
**Chrmn & CEO:** K.T. Gallahue

**EVP, Secy & General Counsel:** J. Stafslien
**SVP, Chief Acctg Officer & Cntlr:** J. Maschal
**CFO:** J.F. Hinrichs
**Investor Contact:** C. Cox (858-617-2020)

**Board Members:** P. L. Francis, R. F. Friel, K. T. Gallahue, J. B. Kosecoff, J. M. Losh, G. T. Lucier, E. D. Miller, M. D. O'Halleran, R. P. Wayman

**Employees:** 14,000

**The McGraw-Hill Companies**

# CarMax Inc

**STANDARD &POOR'S**

| S&P Recommendation | HOLD ★★★☆☆ | Price<br>$27.02 (as of Nov 25, 2011) | 12-Mo. Target Price<br>$27.00 | Investment Style<br>Large-Cap Growth |
|---|---|---|---|---|

**GICS Sector** Consumer Discretionary
**Sub-Industry** Automotive Retail

**Summary** CarMax, the largest U.S. retailer of used vehicles, owns and operates more than 100 used car superstores in about 50 markets. It also sells new vehicles at five locations.

## Key Stock Statistics (Source S&P, Vickers, company reports)

| | | | | | | | |
|---|---|---|---|---|---|---|---|
| 52-Wk Range | $37.02– 22.77 | S&P Oper. EPS 2012**E** | 1.83 | Market Capitalization(B) | $6.118 | Beta | 1.34 |
| Trailing 12-Month EPS | $1.78 | S&P Oper. EPS 2013**E** | 1.95 | Yield (%) | Nil | S&P 3-Yr. Proj. EPS CAGR(%) | 10 |
| Trailing 12-Month P/E | 15.2 | P/E on S&P Oper. EPS 2012**E** | 14.8 | Dividend Rate/Share | Nil | S&P Credit Rating | NA |
| $10K Invested 5 Yrs Ago | $11,730 | Common Shares Outstg. (M) | 226.4 | Institutional Ownership (%) | 97 | | |

## Price Performance

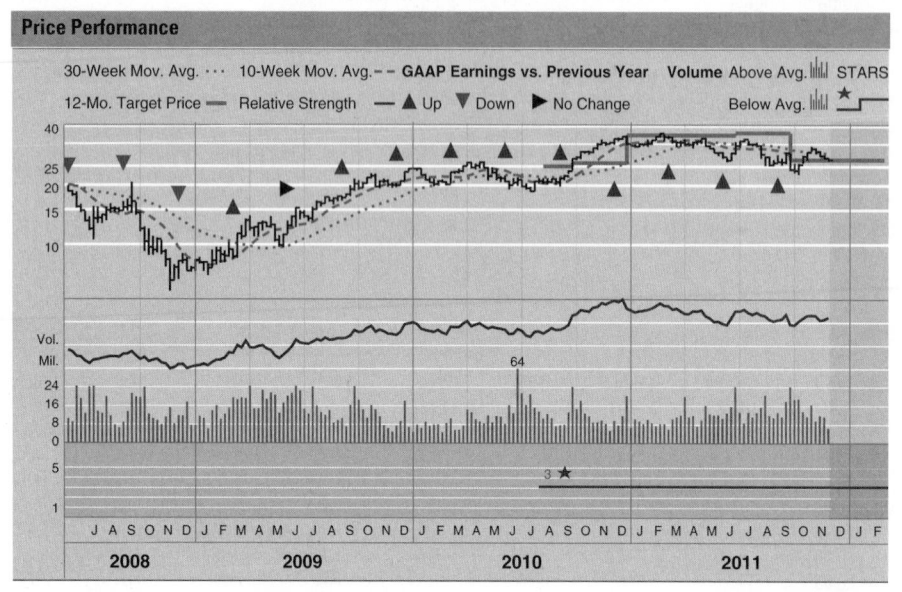

30-Week Mov. Avg. · · · 10-Week Mov. Avg. - - GAAP Earnings vs. Previous Year  Volume Above Avg. STARS
12-Mo. Target Price — Relative Strength — ▲ Up ▼ Down ► No Change  Below Avg.

Options: ASE, CBOE, P, Ph

Analysis prepared by Equity Analyst **Efraim Levy, CFA** on Sep 26, 2011, when the stock traded at **$24.44**.

## Highlights

▸ We estimate that revenues will rise 9.7% in FY 12 (Feb.) and about 6% in FY 13, via a combination of comparable-store sales growth, new store additions and increased credit availability. Sales volume has been improving, and average transaction price has been rising. The company has opened three new stores so far in FY 12. Even as we expect SG&A expenses will rise as demand expands, we believe operating margins will increase during the fiscal year. In addition to its core used car superstores, CarMax owns several new vehicle dealerships for selling a variety of automaker brands.

▸ For calendar 2011, we project that higher industry volume and macroeconomic factors will bolster new and used vehicle sales. The company plans to open five used vehicle stores in FY 12 and between eight and 10 in FY 13. As a result, we expect to see rising capital spending and depreciation and amortization charges.

▸ We forecast EPS of $1.83 for FY 12 and $1.95 for FY 13. The balance sheet, with limited long-term debt, excluding non-recourse loans payable, should support an increase in debt as the company resumes the addition of new stores to its portfolio.

## Investment Rationale/Risk

▸ Based on our calendar 2011 P/E and price-to-free cash flow and total enterprise value-to-EBITDA estimates, KMX recently traded at a premium to the average of publicly traded automobile retailers in our analytical coverage. We believe the premium is warranted given KMX's better-than-peers net margins. We estimate adjusted free cash flow per share of $1.13 for FY 12 and $1.16 for FY 13, compared to $1.60 in FY 11. Rising investment in new facilities will likely limit capital available for other purposes.

▸ Risks to our recommendation and target price include a decrease in multiples for automotive retailers. In addition, demand for and pricing of used vehicles could be less than we expect, and credit for dealers and consumers could be more costly or difficult to obtain.

▸ We expect CarMax Auto Finance (CAF) to help deliver sales by providing financing for consumers, and we think CAF will make a solid profit contribution on its own. Based on historical and peer P/E comparisons, our 12-month target price is $27, or about 13.8X our FY 12 EPS estimate of $1.95, within its historical range and above publicly traded automotive retailing peers.

## Qualitative Risk Assessment

| LOW | **MEDIUM** | HIGH |
|---|---|---|

Our risk assessment reflects the cyclical nature of the automotive retailing industry, which is affected by interest rates, consumer confidence and personal discretionary spending, offset by the company's variable cost structure.

## Quantitative Evaluations

**S&P Quality Ranking**  B+

| D | C | B- | B | **B+** | A- | A | A+ |
|---|---|---|---|---|---|---|---|

**Relative Strength Rank**  MODERATE

58

LOWEST = 1          HIGHEST = 99

## Revenue/Earnings Data

**Revenue (Million $)**

| | 1Q | 2Q | 3Q | 4Q | Year |
|---|---|---|---|---|---|
| 2012 | 2,679 | 2,588 | -- | -- | -- |
| 2011 | 2,319 | 2,394 | 2,175 | 2,307 | 9,196 |
| 2010 | 1,813 | 2,149 | 1,792 | 1,892 | 7,645 |
| 2009 | 2,219 | 1,832 | 1,440 | 1,498 | 6,989 |
| 2008 | 2,184 | 2,156 | 1,902 | 2,044 | 8,285 |
| 2007 | 1,918 | 1,966 | 1,800 | 1,915 | 7,598 |

**Earnings Per Share ($)**

| | | | | | |
|---|---|---|---|---|---|
| 2012 | 0.55 | 0.49 | E0.39 | E0.41 | E1.83 |
| 2011 | 0.44 | 0.48 | 0.36 | 0.39 | 1.67 |
| 2010 | 0.13 | 0.46 | 0.33 | 0.33 | 1.26 |
| 2009 | 0.13 | 0.06 | -0.10 | 0.17 | 0.27 |
| 2008 | 0.30 | 0.29 | 0.14 | 0.10 | 0.83 |
| 2007 | 0.27 | 0.25 | 0.21 | 0.19 | 0.92 |

Fiscal year ended Feb. 28. Next earnings report expected: NA. EPS Estimates based on S&P Operating Earnings; historical GAAP earnings are as reported.

## Dividend Data

No cash dividends have been paid.

---

**Please read the Required Disclosures and Analyst Certification on the last page of this report.**

**The McGraw·Hill Companies**

# CarMax Inc

STANDARD &POOR'S

## Business Summary September 26, 2011

CORPORATE OVERVIEW. CarMax, Inc., is the largest U.S. retailer of used cars, based on data for FY 10 (Feb.). As of September 22, 2011, CarMax owned and operated 106 used car superstores. It also sells new vehicles at five locations under franchise agreements with four new car manufacturers. The company also provides financial services to customers through CarMax Auto Finance (CAF).

MARKET PROFILE. The automotive retailing industry is the largest retail trade sector in the U.S. It generates approximately $1.0 trillion in annual sales, comprising roughly 7% of GDP. The industry is highly fragmented, and we estimate that the 100 largest automotive retailers produce approximately 15% of industry revenues.

While CarMax is the largest used auto retailer, it still represented only about 2% of the total late model used units sold.

During the past few years, Internet marketing has taken on great significance for the used vehicle and vehicle financing markets.

Our fundamental outlook for the automotive retailers sub-industry is positive, reflecting our view of improving sales prospects. We see an expanding economy, higher consumer confidence and an improving credit environment helping demand. The emergence of Chrysler and General Motors from bankruptcy should also help their remaining dealers, as should GM's November IPO and Chrysler's government debt repayment. We believe we will see increased year-over-year new vehicle sales volume in 2011. On the negative side, reduced new vehicle sales in recent years should, over time, hurt parts and services revenue, and recent oil & gas price increases could hurt sales if they continue, as well as alter the mix of vehicles.

In 2010, U.S. light vehicle sales volume rebounded 11%, to nearly 11.6 million, and we estimate further improvement to 12.9 million in 2011 and 14.2 million in 2012. With expected higher sales, we look for dealer profits to improve in 2011.

## Company Financials Fiscal Year Ended Feb. 28

| Per Share Data ($) | 2011 | 2010 | 2009 | 2008 | 2007 | 2006 | 2005 | 2004 | 2003 | 2002 |
|---|---|---|---|---|---|---|---|---|---|---|
| Tangible Book Value | 10.10 | 8.62 | 7.18 | 6.76 | 5.77 | 4.57 | 3.84 | 3.28 | 2.69 | 6.56 |
| Cash Flow | 1.93 | 1.53 | 0.52 | 1.04 | 1.08 | 0.82 | 0.63 | 0.63 | 0.52 | 0.65 |
| Earnings | 1.67 | 1.26 | 0.27 | 0.83 | 0.92 | 0.70 | 0.54 | 0.55 | 0.46 | 0.41 |
| S&P Core Earnings | 1.67 | 1.24 | 0.23 | 0.83 | 0.93 | 0.64 | 0.49 | 0.52 | 0.43 | 0.41 |
| Dividends | NA | Nil | Nil | Nil | Nil | Nil | Nil | Nil | Nil | Nil |
| Payout Ratio | NA | Nil | Nil | Nil | Nil | Nil | Nil | Nil | Nil | Nil |
| Calendar Year | 2010 | 2009 | 2008 | 2007 | 2006 | 2005 | 2004 | 2003 | 2002 | 2001 |
| Prices:High | 36.00 | 24.75 | 23.00 | 29.45 | 27.60 | 17.40 | 18.55 | 19.65 | 17.00 | 12.00 |
| Prices:Low | 18.62 | 6.92 | 5.76 | 18.57 | 13.87 | 12.32 | 9.02 | 6.23 | 6.45 | 1.94 |
| P/E Ratio:High | 22 | 20 | 85 | 35 | 30 | 25 | 35 | 36 | 37 | 29 |
| P/E Ratio:Low | 11 | 5 | 21 | 22 | 15 | 18 | 17 | 11 | 14 | 5 |

**Income Statement Analysis** (Million $)

| | 2011 | 2010 | 2009 | 2008 | 2007 | 2006 | 2005 | 2004 | 2003 | 2002 |
|---|---|---|---|---|---|---|---|---|---|---|
| Revenue | 9,196 | 7,645 | 6,989 | 8,285 | 7,598 | 6,260 | 5,260 | 4,598 | 3,970 | 3,518 |
| Operating Income | 676 | 514 | 156 | 347 | 362 | 165 | 124 | 119 | 90.7 | 168 |
| Depreciation | 59.4 | 58.3 | 54.7 | 46.6 | 34.6 | 26.7 | 20.1 | 16.2 | 14.9 | 16.3 |
| Interest Expense | 3.11 | 3.46 | 7.99 | 9.96 | 5.37 | 4.09 | 2.81 | 1.14 | 2.26 | 4.96 |
| Pretax Income | 613 | 453 | 96.8 | 297 | 323 | 240 | 185 | 189 | 157 | 146 |
| Effective Tax Rate | NA | 37.8% | 38.8% | 38.7% | 38.6% | 38.3% | 38.8% | 38.5% | 39.5% | 38.0% |
| Net Income | 381 | 282 | 59.2 | 182 | 199 | 148 | 113 | 116 | 94.8 | 90.8 |
| S&P Core Earnings | 380 | 275 | 50.2 | 181 | 200 | 135 | 102 | 109 | 90.2 | 27.4 |

**Balance Sheet & Other Financial Data** (Million $)

| | 2011 | 2010 | 2009 | 2008 | 2007 | 2006 | 2005 | 2004 | 2003 | 2002 |
|---|---|---|---|---|---|---|---|---|---|---|
| Cash | 41.1 | 18.3 | 141 | 13.0 | 19.5 | 21.8 | 29.1 | 61.6 | 34.6 | 3.29 |
| Current Assets | 1,410 | 1,556 | 1,288 | 1,357 | 1,151 | 942 | 865 | 773 | 709 | 578 |
| Total Assets | 6,840 | 2,556 | 2,379 | 2,333 | 1,886 | 1,489 | 1,293 | 1,037 | 918 | 720 |
| Current Liabilities | 508 | 477 | 491 | 490 | 512 | 363 | 329 | 242 | 248 | 223 |
| Long Term Debt | 3,881 | 27.4 | 178 | 227 | 33.7 | 135 | 128 | 100 | 100 | 14.1 |
| Common Equity | 2,292 | 1,934 | 1,593 | 1,489 | 1,247 | 960 | 801 | 681 | 555 | 485 |
| Total Capital | 6,306 | 2,083 | 1,901 | 1,716 | 1,281 | 1,095 | 934 | 781 | 659 | 502 |
| Capital Expenditures | 76.6 | 22.4 | 186 | 253 | 192 | 194 | 230 | 181 | 122 | 41.4 |
| Cash Flow | 440 | 340 | 114 | 229 | 233 | 175 | 133 | 133 | 110 | 44.3 |
| Current Ratio | 2.8 | 3.3 | 2.6 | 2.8 | 2.2 | 2.6 | 2.6 | 3.2 | 2.9 | 2.6 |
| % Long Term Debt of Capitalization | 61.6 | 1.3 | 9.2 | 13.2 | 2.6 | 12.3 | 13.7 | 12.8 | 15.2 | 2.8 |
| % Net Income of Revenue | 4.1 | 3.7 | 0.9 | 2.2 | 2.6 | 2.4 | 2.1 | 2.5 | 2.4 | 2.6 |
| % Return on Assets | 8.1 | 11.4 | 2.5 | 8.6 | 11.7 | 10.6 | 9.6 | 11.9 | 11.6 | 12.7 |
| % Return on Equity | 18.0 | 16.0 | 3.8 | 13.3 | 17.8 | 16.8 | 15.2 | 18.9 | 18.2 | 20.7 |

Data as orig reptd.; bef. results of disc opers/spec. items. Per share data adj. for stk. divs.; EPS diluted. E-Estimated. NA-Not Available. NM-Not Meaningful. NR-Not Ranked. UR-Under Review.

**Office:** 12800 Tuckahoe Creek Pkwy, Richmond, VA 23238-1124.
**Telephone:** 804-747-0422.
**Website:** http://www.carmax.com
**Chrmn:** W.R. Tiefel

**Pres & CEO:** T.J. Folliard
**EVP & Chief Admin Officer:** M.K. Dolan
**SVP & CFO:** T.W. Reedy
**SVP, Secy & General Counsel:** E.M. Margolin

**Investor Contact:** K.D. Browning (804-747-0422)
**Board Members:** R. E. Blaylock, T. J. Folliard, R. Gangwal, J. E. Garten, S. D. Goodman, W. R. Grafton, E. H. Grubb, M. D. Steenrod, T. G. Stemberg, V. M. Stephenson, B. A. Stewart, W. R. Tiefel

**Founded:** 1996
**Domicile:** Virginia
**Employees:** 15,565

The McGraw-Hill Companies

# Carnival Corp

**STANDARD &POOR'S**

**S&P Recommendation** BUY ★★★★☆

| Price | 12-Mo. Target Price | Investment Style |
|---|---|---|
| $30.47 (as of Nov 25, 2011) | $40.00 | Large-Cap Blend |

**GICS Sector** Consumer Discretionary
**Sub-Industry** Hotels, Resorts & Cruise Lines

**Summary** Carnival Corp. and Carnival plc own businesses that operate about 100 cruise ships, as well as tour companies in Alaska and Canada.

## Key Stock Statistics (Source S&P, Vickers, company reports)

| | | | | | | | |
|---|---|---|---|---|---|---|---|
| 52-Wk Range | $48.14– 28.52 | S&P Oper. EPS 2011**E** | 2.35 | Market Capitalization(B) | $23.828 | Beta | 1.47 |
| Trailing 12-Month EPS | $2.45 | S&P Oper. EPS 2012**E** | 2.85 | Yield (%) | 3.28 | S&P 3-Yr. Proj. EPS CAGR(%) | NA |
| Trailing 12-Month P/E | 12.4 | P/E on S&P Oper. EPS 2011**E** | 13.0 | Dividend Rate/Share | $1.00 | S&P Credit Rating | BBB+ |
| $10K Invested 5 Yrs Ago | $6,825 | Common Shares Outstg. (M) | 782.0 | Institutional Ownership (%) | 57 | | |

## Price Performance

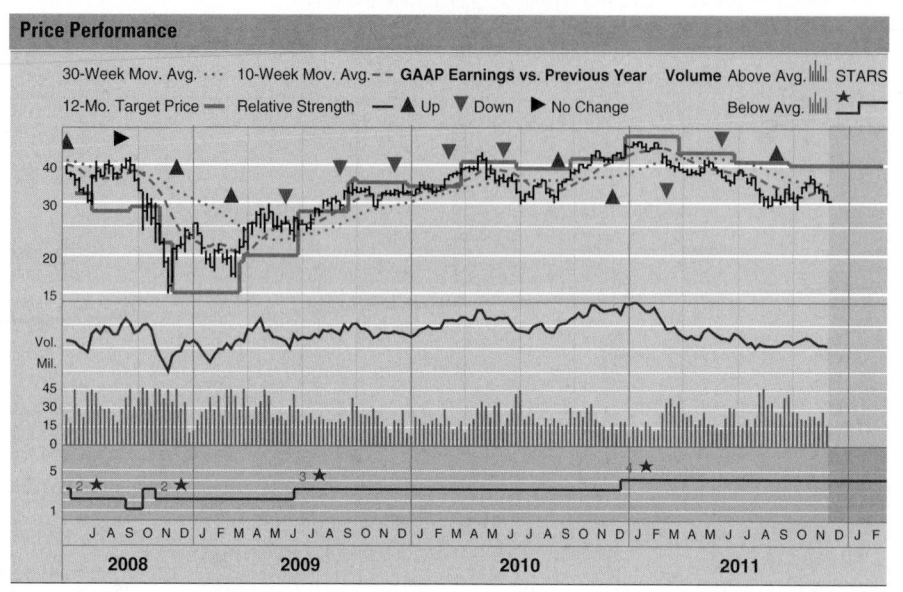

30-Week Mov. Avg. · · · 10-Week Mov. Avg. – – GAAP Earnings vs. Previous Year    Volume Above Avg. STARS
12-Mo. Target Price — Relative Strength — ▲ Up ▼ Down ▶ No Change    Below Avg.

Options: ASE, CBOE, P, Ph

Analysis prepared by Equity Analyst **Preeti Rambhiya** on Sep 27, 2011, when the stock traded at **$33.01**.

## Highlights

▶ We believe a recent slowdown in bookings momentum in the European Economic Area amid the political turmoil is cause for concern. On the other hand, the booking and pricing environment in North America has appeared to be developing strongly. All told, we look for CCL to have about 10% sales growth in FY 12 (Nov.), following a projected 9.3% rise in FY 11. The key factor to monitor will be whether Carnival can continue to maintain pricing in the current weak economic environment.

▶ In FY 12, we look for an EBIT profit margin of 14.9%, following a projected decline to 13.9% in FY 11. We expect strong operating leverage in the business to bolster margins, as should economies of scale from new capacity additions.

▶ Given the current economic environment, we think the lure of all-inclusive packages and the value appeal of cruises will prove rather enticing to consumers, and we see the prospect of sizable cash generation for the company. We forecast EPS of $2.85 in FY 12, following an estimated $2.35 in FY 11.

## Investment Rationale/Risk

▶ We believe macro-economic uncertainty clouds near-term visibility, but we see the share valuation as attractive. We also see a robust financial position. We think slowing capital expenditures and strong cash flow generation should lead to higher returns on capital and higher shareholder payouts.

▶ Risks to our recommendation and target price include material disappointments on pricing and advance bookings, a significant deterioration in consumer confidence, and terrorism concerns. Rising oil prices are a key risk, in our opinion, particularly as Carnival does not hedge its fuel exposure.

▶ Our 12-month target price of $40 is based on an equal blend of EV/EBITDA, P/E and DCF valuations. Based on our FY 11 estimated EBITDA of $3.7 billion, we apply a multiple of 11.5X, a 5% discount to the 10-year average given somewhat limited visibility, yielding a value of about $42. Our DCF analysis (WACC 8.2%, terminal growth rate of 2.5%) indicates an intrinsic value of about $41. Our P/E approach implies a value of about $37.

## Qualitative Risk Assessment

| LOW | MEDIUM | HIGH |
|---|---|---|

Our risk assessment reflects the capital intensity of the cruise sector and its sensitivity to economic cycles. This is offset by our view of Carnival's premier position in a consolidated industry with high barriers to entry, economies of scale, and Carnival's strong operating profile.

## Quantitative Evaluations

**S&P Quality Ranking**                         NR

| D | C | B- | B | B+ | A- | A | A+ |
|---|---|---|---|---|---|---|---|

**Relative Strength Rank**                    MODERATE

41

LOWEST = 1                                    HIGHEST = 99

## Revenue/Earnings Data

**Revenue (Million $)**

| | 1Q | 2Q | 3Q | 4Q | Year |
|---|---|---|---|---|---|
| 2011 | 3,419 | 3,620 | 5,058 | -- | -- |
| 2010 | 3,095 | 3,195 | 4,426 | 3,497 | 14,469 |
| 2009 | 2,864 | 2,948 | 4,139 | 3,206 | 13,157 |
| 2008 | 3,152 | 3,378 | 4,814 | 3,302 | 14,646 |
| 2007 | 2,688 | 2,900 | 4,321 | 3,124 | 13,033 |
| 2006 | 2,463 | 2,662 | 3,905 | 2,809 | 11,839 |

**Earnings Per Share ($)**

| | | | | | |
|---|---|---|---|---|---|
| 2011 | 0.19 | 0.26 | 1.69 | E0.22 | E2.35 |
| 2010 | 0.22 | 0.31 | 1.62 | 0.31 | 2.47 |
| 2009 | 0.32 | 0.33 | 1.33 | 0.24 | 2.23 |
| 2008 | 0.30 | 0.49 | 1.64 | 0.46 | 2.86 |
| 2007 | 0.35 | 0.48 | 1.64 | 0.44 | 2.95 |
| 2006 | 0.31 | 0.46 | 1.49 | 0.51 | 2.77 |

Fiscal year ended Nov. 30. Next earnings report expected: Late December. EPS Estimates based on S&P Operating Earnings; historical GAAP earnings are as reported.

## Dividend Data (Dates: mm/dd Payment Date: mm/dd/yy)

| Amount ($) | Date Decl. | Ex-Div. Date | Stk. of Record | Payment Date |
|---|---|---|---|---|
| 0.100 | 10/19 | 11/17 | 11/19 | 12/10/10 |
| 0.250 | 01/20 | 02/16 | 02/18 | 03/11/11 |
| 0.250 | 04/13 | 05/18 | 05/20 | 06/10/11 |
| 0.250 | 10/11 | 11/22 | 11/25 | 12/16/11 |

Dividends have been paid since 2010. Source: Company reports.

# Carnival Corp

STANDARD
&POOR'S

## Business Summary September 27, 2011

CORPORATE OVERVIEW. Carnival Corp. is part of the world's largest cruise ship business, which has grown significantly through acquisitions and the addition of new ships. In 2003, Carnival Corp. merged with P&O Princess Cruises plc, which was renamed Carnival plc (CUK 32, Buy). As of early 2011, the combined Carnival had 98 cruise ships with capacity for some 191,464 passengers (based on two passengers per cabin, even though some cabins could accommodate more). In addition, Carnival has tour operations in Alaska and the Canadian Yukon. In terms of capacity, Carnival is more than double the size of its biggest competitor -- Royal Caribbean Cruises Ltd. (RCL 22, Buy) -- which in 2010 operated 40 ships and had about 92,300 berths.

The global cruise industry is already consolidated, we believe, with the top three companies controlling around 80% of the market. Based on the Cruise Line International Association's (CLIA) estimates, CCL was the global market leader with a 50% share, followed by RCL with 25%. NCL Corp., equally owned by Asian company Star Cruises Ltd and Apollo Management L.P., controls about 8% of the market. We see further major consolidation as unlikely given that we think it would raise anti-trust concerns.

CORPORATE GOVERNANCE. With Carnival's dual listing company (DLC) for-

mat, there are separate stocks trading under the Carnival Corp. and Carnival plc names. Each company has retained its separate legal identity, but the two share a single senior executive management team, have identical boards of directors, and are run as if they were a single economic enterprise. In valuing the Carnival shares, we look at the combined financial results and equity base of the Carnival entities.

MARKET PROFILE. In our view, cruising represents a small but growing sector of the overall holiday market, competing with other vacation alternatives such as land-based resort hotels and sightseeing destinations for consumers' leisure time and discretionary income. We expect demand for cruise ship vacations to grow. In the U.S., we believe that most people have never taken a multi-night cruise ship vacation, and we expect that an aging U.S. population will lead to more interest in cruises. Also, we think that continued industry emphasis on providing ships with more features and the addition of more local ports will bolster passenger demand.

## Company Financials Fiscal Year Ended Nov. 30

| Per Share Data ($) | 2010 | 2009 | 2008 | 2007 | 2006 | 2005 | 2004 | 2003 | 2002 | 2001 |
|---|---|---|---|---|---|---|---|---|---|---|
| Tangible Book Value | 23.28 | 21.90 | 18.52 | 19.01 | 17.10 | 15.47 | 13.96 | 11.83 | 11.48 | 10.13 |
| Cash Flow | 4.22 | 3.85 | 4.39 | 4.24 | 3.89 | 3.91 | 3.13 | 2.46 | 2.38 | 2.21 |
| Earnings | 2.47 | 2.23 | 2.86 | 2.95 | 2.77 | 2.70 | 2.24 | 1.66 | 1.73 | 1.58 |
| Dividends | 0.40 | Nil | 1.60 | 1.38 | 1.03 | 0.80 | 0.52 | 0.44 | 0.42 | 0.42 |
| Payout Ratio | 16% | Nil | 56% | 47% | 37% | 30% | 23% | 27% | 24% | 27% |
| Prices:High | 47.22 | 34.95 | 45.22 | 52.73 | 56.14 | 58.98 | 58.75 | 39.84 | 34.64 | 34.94 |
| Prices:Low | 29.68 | 16.80 | 14.85 | 41.70 | 36.40 | 45.78 | 39.75 | 20.34 | 22.07 | 16.95 |
| P/E Ratio:High | 19 | 16 | 6 | 18 | 20 | 22 | 26 | 24 | 20 | 22 |
| P/E Ratio:Low | 12 | 8 | 2 | 14 | 13 | 17 | 18 | 12 | 13 | 11 |

| Income Statement Analysis (Million $) | | | | | | | | | | |
|---|---|---|---|---|---|---|---|---|---|---|
| Revenue | 14,469 | 13,157 | 14,646 | 13,033 | 11,839 | 11,087 | 9,727 | 6,718 | 4,368 | 4,536 |
| Operating Income | 3,746 | 3,463 | 3,921 | 3,826 | 3,601 | 3,541 | 2,985 | 1,968 | 1,444 | 1,448 |
| Depreciation | 1,416 | 1,309 | 1,249 | 1,101 | 988 | 902 | 812 | 585 | 382 | 372 |
| Interest Expense | 378 | 380 | 466 | 367 | 312 | 330 | 284 | 195 | 111 | 121 |
| Pretax Income | 1,979 | 1,806 | 2,377 | 2,424 | 2,240 | 2,184 | 1,901 | 1,223 | 959 | 948 |
| Effective Tax Rate | NM | 0.89% | 1.98% | 0.10% | NM | NM | 2.47% | 2.37% | NM | 2.34% |
| Net Income | 1,978 | 1,790 | 2,330 | 2,408 | 2,279 | 2,257 | 1,854 | 1,194 | 1,016 | 926 |

| Balance Sheet & Other Financial Data (Million $) | | | | | | | | | | |
|---|---|---|---|---|---|---|---|---|---|---|
| Cash | 429 | 538 | 650 | 943 | 1,163 | 1,178 | 643 | 1,070 | 667 | 1,421 |
| Current Assets | 1,244 | 1,518 | 1,650 | 1,976 | 1,995 | 2,215 | 1,728 | 2,132 | 1,132 | 1,959 |
| Total Assets | 37,490 | 36,835 | 33,400 | 34,181 | 30,552 | 28,432 | 27,636 | 24,491 | 12,335 | 11,564 |
| Current Liabilities | 5,755 | 4,967 | 5,781 | 7,260 | 5,415 | 5,192 | 5,034 | 3,315 | 1,620 | 1,480 |
| Long Term Debt | 8,011 | 9,097 | 7,735 | 6,313 | 6,355 | 5,727 | 6,291 | 6,918 | 3,012 | 2,955 |
| Common Equity | 23,031 | 22,035 | 19,098 | 19,963 | 18,210 | 16,972 | 15,760 | 13,793 | 7,418 | 6,591 |
| Total Capital | 31,655 | 31,947 | 27,914 | 26,276 | 24,565 | 22,699 | 22,051 | 20,711 | 10,430 | 9,546 |
| Capital Expenditures | 3,579 | 3,380 | 3,353 | 3,312 | 2,480 | 1,977 | 3,586 | 2,516 | 1,986 | 827 |
| Cash Flow | 3,394 | 3,099 | 3,579 | 3,509 | 3,267 | 3,159 | 2,666 | 1,779 | 1,398 | 1,298 |
| Current Ratio | 0.2 | 0.3 | 0.3 | 0.3 | 0.4 | 0.4 | 0.3 | 0.6 | 0.7 | 1.3 |
| % Long Term Debt of Capitalization | 25.3 | 28.5 | 27.7 | 24.0 | 25.9 | 25.2 | 28.5 | 33.4 | 28.9 | 31.0 |
| % Net Income of Revenue | 13.7 | 13.6 | 15.9 | 18.4 | 19.2 | 20.4 | 19.1 | 17.8 | 23.3 | 20.4 |
| % Return on Assets | 5.3 | 5.1 | 6.9 | 7.4 | 7.7 | 8.1 | 7.1 | 6.5 | 8.5 | 8.7 |
| % Return on Equity | 8.8 | 8.7 | 11.9 | 12.6 | 13.0 | 13.8 | 12.5 | 11.3 | 14.5 | 14.9 |

Data as orig reptd.; bef. results of disc opers/spec. items. Per share data adj. for stk. divs.; EPS diluted. E-Estimated. NA-Not Available. NM-Not Meaningful. NR-Not Ranked. UR-Under Review.

**Office:** 3655 NorthWest 87th Avenue, Miami, FL 33178-2428.
**Telephone:** 305-599-2600.
**Website:** http://www.carnivalcorp.com
**Chrmn & CEO:** M.M. Arison

**Vice Chrmn & COO:** H.S. Frank
**SVP, Secy & General Counsel:** A. Perez
**CFO:** D. Bernstein
**CTO:** T. Strang

**Investor Contact:** B. Roberts (305-406-4832)
**Board Members:** M. M. Arison, J. Band, R. H. Dickinson, A. W. Donald, P. L. Foschi, H. S. Frank, R. J. Glasier, M. A. Maidique, J. Parker, P. G. Ratcliffe, S. Subotnick, L. A. Weil, R. J. Weisenburger, U. Zucker

**Founded:** 1974
**Domicile:** Panama
**Employees:** 89,200

The McGraw-Hill Companies

# Caterpillar Inc

STANDARD &POOR'S

| S&P Recommendation BUY ★★★★☆ | Price $86.72 (as of Nov 25, 2011) | 12-Mo. Target Price $129.00 | Investment Style Large-Cap Blend |

**GICS Sector** Industrials
**Sub-Industry** Construction & Farm Machinery & Heavy Trucks

**Summary** CAT is the world's largest producer of earthmoving equipment, and a big maker of electric power generators and engines used in petroleum markets, and mining equipment.

## Key Stock Statistics (Source S&P, Vickers, company reports)

| | | | | | |
|---|---|---|---|---|---|
| 52-Wk Range | $116.55– 67.54 | S&P Oper. EPS 2011E | 7.35 | Market Capitalization(B) | $56.075 | Beta | 1.85 |
| Trailing 12-Month EPS | $6.55 | S&P Oper. EPS 2012E | 9.20 | Yield (%) | 2.12 | S&P 3-Yr. Proj. EPS CAGR(%) | 35 |
| Trailing 12-Month P/E | 13.2 | P/E on S&P Oper. EPS 2011E | 11.8 | Dividend Rate/Share | $1.84 | S&P Credit Rating | A |
| $10K Invested 5 Yrs Ago | $15,721 | Common Shares Outstg. (M) | 646.6 | Institutional Ownership (%) | 66 | | |

## Price Performance

30-Week Mov. Avg. ···  10-Week Mov. Avg.- - GAAP Earnings vs. Previous Year   Volume Above Avg. STARS
12-Mo. Target Price— Relative Strength  — ▲ Up ▼ Down ► No Change   Below Avg.

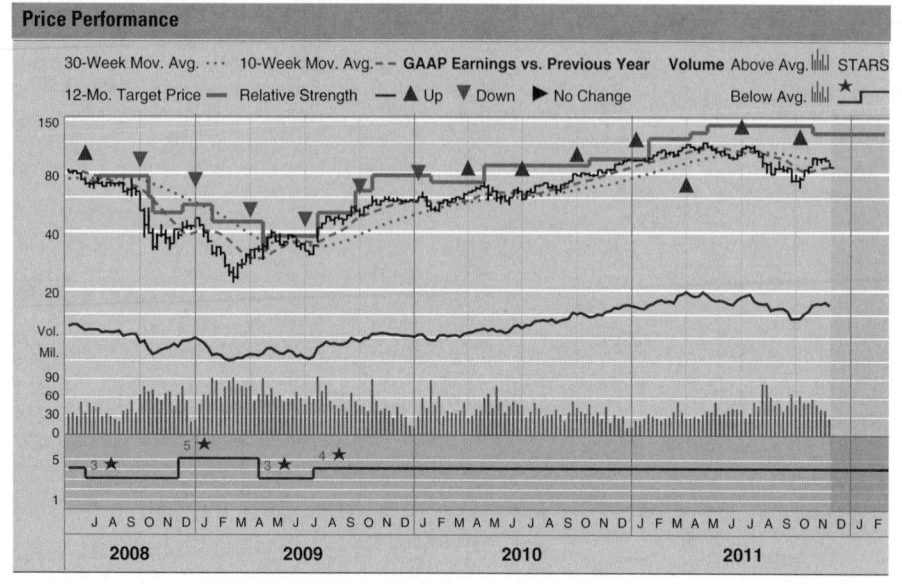

Options: ASE, CBOE, P, Ph

Analysis prepared by Equity Analyst **Michael Jaffe** on Oct 27, 2011, when the stock traded at **$91.57**.

## Highlights

► We expect revenues to rise 19% in 2012, as a better global economy seems to have CAT's machinery and power system businesses in the midst of robust recoveries. We see results aided by further economic growth (especially in developing nations), ongoing robust construction growth in emerging nations, the need to replace aging and worn out construction equipment in North America and Europe, and strong demand for resource equipment as a result of strong commodity markets. We also see CAT's top line aided by the full-year inclusion of Bucyrus International, a mining equipment company that was purchased in July 2011.

► We forecast wider margins in 2012, on leverage from the better sales trends that we see. We also expect margins to be aided by improved operating efficiencies, and synergies from the Bucyrus acquisition (about $50 million to $100 million expected in 2012, compared with $25 million seen in 2011).

► Our forecast for 2012 compares with operating results for 2011 that exclude $0.50 a share of expected net costs related to the Bucyrus acquisition, including $0.46 recorded in the first nine months of the year.

## Investment Rationale/Risk

► Aided by global government stimulus packages, CAT is in the midst of a robust business recovery, and we see growth going on for an extended period. We also have a very positive view of its July 2011 purchase of Bucyrus International, which expanded CAT's footprint in what we view as a robust market. Based on these factors and our valuation model, we find CAT shares undervalued.

► Risks to our opinion and target price include a resumed downturn in global economies, and worse-than-expected conditions in global credit markets.

► The shares recently traded at 10X our 2012 EPS forecast of $9.20, which is at the low-end of CAT's typical valuation range as it moved further into business recoveries. Based on our belief that better economic conditions and CAT's aggressive streamlining actions will allow revenues and earnings in the current cycle to far exceed prior records, we view the shares as undervalued. We set our 12-month target price at $129, which is 14X our 2012 EPS forecast, or the top end of CAT's range at a similar stage of its last business revival.

## Qualitative Risk Assessment

| LOW | MEDIUM | HIGH |

Our risk assessment reflects CAT's leading position in many of the end markets it serves, offset by the highly cyclical nature of the construction equipment, mining equipment and engine businesses.

## Quantitative Evaluations

### S&P Quality Ranking    A+

| D | C | B- | B | B+ | A- | A | A+ |

### Relative Strength Rank    MODERATE

63

LOWEST = 1    HIGHEST = 99

## Revenue/Earnings Data

### Revenue (Million $)

| | 1Q | 2Q | 3Q | 4Q | Year |
|---|---|---|---|---|---|
| 2011 | 12,949 | 14,230 | 15,716 | -- | -- |
| 2010 | 8,238 | 10,409 | 11,134 | 12,807 | 42,588 |
| 2009 | 9,225 | 7,975 | 7,298 | 7,898 | 32,396 |
| 2008 | 11,796 | 13,624 | 12,981 | 12,923 | 51,324 |
| 2007 | 10,016 | 11,356 | 11,442 | 12,144 | 44,958 |
| 2006 | 9,392 | 10,605 | 10,517 | 11,003 | 41,517 |

### Earnings Per Share ($)

| | 1Q | 2Q | 3Q | 4Q | Year |
|---|---|---|---|---|---|
| 2011 | 1.84 | 1.52 | 1.71 | E1.86 | E7.35 |
| 2010 | 0.36 | 1.09 | 1.22 | 1.47 | 4.15 |
| 2009 | -0.19 | 0.60 | 0.64 | 0.36 | 1.43 |
| 2008 | 1.45 | 1.74 | 1.39 | 1.08 | 5.66 |
| 2007 | 1.23 | 1.24 | 1.40 | 1.50 | 5.37 |
| 2006 | 1.20 | 1.52 | 1.14 | 1.32 | 5.17 |

Fiscal year ended Dec. 31. Next earnings report expected: Late January. EPS Estimates based on S&P Operating Earnings; historical GAAP earnings are as reported.

## Dividend Data (Dates: mm/dd Payment Date: mm/dd/yy)

| Amount ($) | Date Decl. | Ex-Div. Date | Stk. of Record | Payment Date |
|---|---|---|---|---|
| 0.440 | 12/08 | 01/18 | 01/20 | 02/19/11 |
| 0.440 | 04/13 | 04/20 | 04/25 | 05/20/11 |
| 0.460 | 06/08 | 07/18 | 07/20 | 08/20/11 |
| 0.460 | 10/12 | 10/20 | 10/24 | 11/19/11 |

Dividends have been paid since 1914. Source: Company reports.

The McGraw-Hill Companies

# Caterpillar Inc

**STANDARD
&POOR'S**

## Business Summary October 27, 2011

CORPORATE OVERVIEW. Caterpillar's distinctive yellow machines are in service in nearly every country in the world, with 62% of the company's revenues derived outside of North America in 2010 (62% in 2009). CAT previously operated in three principal lines of business: Machinery, Engines and Financial Products. However, in 2011, it shifted its segment breakup to Construction Industries, Resource Industries, Power Systems, Other, and Financial Products.

Under its previous division of segments, CAT's largest operating segment was its Machinery unit (65% of revenues and 48% of operating profit in 2010), which made earthmoving equipment. Operations included the design, manufacture, marketing and sale of construction, mining and forestry machinery including track and wheel tractors, track and wheel loaders, pipelayers, motor graders, wheel tractor-scrapers, track and wheel excavators, backhoe loaders, log skidders, log loaders, off-highway trucks, articulated trucks, paving products, skid steer loaders, underground mining equipment, boring equipment and related parts. This segment also included logistics services for other companies, the production of diesel-electric locomotives and the design, manufacture, remanufacture, maintenance and servicing of rail-related products. The division's products were used mostly in heavy construction (including infrastructure), general construction, mining, and quarry/aggregates markets. These end markets are very cyclical and competitive.

The Engine segment (28% and 43%) made diesel, heavy fuel and natural gas reciprocating engines for both CAT's own earthmoving equipment and third-party customers. This segment designed, manufactured, marketed and sold engines for Caterpillar machinery; electric power generation systems; marine, petroleum, construction, industrial, agricultural and other applications; and related parts. This area also included the remanufacture of Caterpillar engines and a variety of Caterpillar machine and engine components and remanufacturing services for other companies. The division's major end markets were petroleum, electric power generation, industrial and marine.

The Financial Products segment (6% and 9%) primarily provides equipment financing to CAT dealers and customers. The division consists primarily of Caterpillar Financial Services Corporation (Cat Financial) and Caterpillar Insurance Holdings, Inc. (Cat Insurance) and their respective subsidiaries. Cat Financial provides a wide range of financing alternatives, including loans to customers and dealers for Caterpillar products. Cat Insurance provides various forms of insurance to customers and dealers to help support the purchase and lease of equipment.

## Company Financials Fiscal Year Ended Dec. 31

| Per Share Data ($) | 2010 | 2009 | 2008 | 2007 | 2006 | 2005 | 2004 | 2003 | 2002 | 2001 |
|---|---|---|---|---|---|---|---|---|---|---|
| Tangible Book Value | 11.62 | 9.61 | 5.51 | 14.88 | 7.07 | 9.77 | 8.34 | 6.48 | 5.51 | 5.75 |
| Cash Flow | 7.68 | 4.02 | 8.80 | 8.09 | 7.52 | 6.14 | 4.85 | 3.48 | 2.91 | 2.85 |
| Earnings | 4.15 | 1.43 | 5.66 | 5.37 | 5.17 | 4.04 | 2.88 | 1.57 | 1.15 | 1.16 |
| S&P Core Earnings | 4.53 | 2.03 | 4.56 | 5.46 | 5.48 | 4.05 | 2.76 | 1.50 | 0.20 | 0.16 |
| Dividends | 2.16 | 1.68 | 1.68 | 1.32 | 1.10 | 0.91 | 0.78 | 0.71 | 0.70 | 0.69 |
| Payout Ratio | 52% | 117% | 30% | 25% | 21% | 23% | 27% | 45% | 61% | 59% |
| Prices:High | 94.89 | 61.28 | 85.96 | 87.00 | 82.03 | 59.88 | 49.36 | 42.48 | 30.00 | 28.42 |
| Prices:Low | 50.50 | 21.71 | 31.95 | 57.98 | 57.05 | 41.31 | 34.25 | 20.62 | 16.88 | 19.88 |
| P/E Ratio:High | 23 | 43 | 15 | 16 | 16 | 15 | 17 | 27 | 26 | 24 |
| P/E Ratio:Low | 12 | 15 | 6 | 11 | 11 | 10 | 12 | 13 | 15 | 17 |

| Income Statement Analysis (Million $) | 2010 | 2009 | 2008 | 2007 | 2006 | 2005 | 2004 | 2003 | 2002 | 2001 |
|---|---|---|---|---|---|---|---|---|---|---|
| Revenue | 42,588 | 32,396 | 51,324 | 44,958 | 41,517 | 36,339 | 30,251 | 22,763 | 20,152 | 20,450 |
| Operating Income | 6,259 | 2,928 | 7,569 | 7,850 | 7,634 | 6,029 | 4,650 | 3,505 | 3,060 | 3,137 |
| Depreciation | 2,296 | 2,336 | 1,968 | 1,797 | 1,602 | 1,477 | 1,397 | 1,347 | 1,220 | 1,169 |
| Interest Expense | 343 | 389 | 1,427 | 1,420 | 1,297 | 1,028 | 750 | 716 | 800 | 942 |
| Pretax Income | 3,726 | 557 | 4,510 | 5,026 | 4,942 | 3,974 | 2,766 | 1,497 | 1,110 | 1,172 |
| Effective Tax Rate | NA | NM | 21.1% | 29.6% | 28.4% | 28.2% | 26.4% | 26.6% | 28.1% | 31.3% |
| Net Income | 2,700 | 895 | 3,557 | 3,541 | 3,537 | 2,854 | 2,035 | 1,099 | 798 | 805 |
| S&P Core Earnings | 2,950 | 1,277 | 2,867 | 3,604 | 3,748 | 2,860 | 1,951 | 1,052 | 133 | 98.7 |

| Balance Sheet & Other Financial Data (Million $) | 2010 | 2009 | 2008 | 2007 | 2006 | 2005 | 2004 | 2003 | 2002 | 2001 |
|---|---|---|---|---|---|---|---|---|---|---|
| Cash | 1,825 | 2,239 | 1,517 | 1,122 | 530 | 1,108 | 445 | 342 | 309 | 400 |
| Current Assets | 31,810 | 26,789 | 31,633 | 25,477 | 23,093 | 22,790 | 20,856 | 16,791 | 14,628 | 13,400 |
| Total Assets | 64,020 | 60,038 | 67,782 | 56,132 | 50,879 | 47,069 | 43,091 | 36,465 | 32,851 | 30,657 |
| Current Liabilities | 22,020 | 19,292 | 26,069 | 22,245 | 19,252 | 19,092 | 16,210 | 12,621 | 11,344 | 10,276 |
| Long Term Debt | 4,505 | 5,652 | 22,834 | 17,829 | 17,680 | 15,677 | 15,837 | 14,078 | 11,596 | 11,291 |
| Common Equity | 10,824 | 8,740 | 6,087 | 8,883 | 6,859 | 8,432 | 7,467 | 6,078 | 5,472 | 5,611 |
| Total Capital | 16,325 | 15,254 | 29,575 | 26,712 | 24,539 | 24,109 | 23,304 | 20,156 | 17,068 | 16,902 |
| Capital Expenditures | 2,586 | 2,316 | 4,011 | 3,040 | 2,675 | 2,415 | 2,114 | 1,765 | 1,773 | 1,968 |
| Cash Flow | 4,996 | 2,518 | 5,525 | 5,338 | 5,139 | 4,331 | 3,432 | 2,446 | 2,018 | 1,974 |
| Current Ratio | 1.4 | 1.4 | 1.2 | 1.2 | 1.2 | 1.2 | 1.3 | 1.3 | 1.3 | 1.3 |
| % Long Term Debt of Capitalization | 27.6 | 37.1 | 77.2 | 66.7 | 72.0 | 65.0 | 68.0 | 69.8 | 67.9 | 66.8 |
| % Net Income of Revenue | 6.3 | 2.8 | 6.9 | 7.9 | 8.5 | 7.9 | 6.7 | 4.8 | 4.0 | 3.9 |
| % Return on Assets | 4.4 | 1.4 | 5.7 | 6.6 | 7.2 | 6.3 | 5.1 | 3.2 | 2.5 | 2.7 |
| % Return on Equity | 27.6 | 12.1 | 47.5 | 45.0 | 46.3 | 35.9 | 30.0 | 19.0 | 14.4 | 14.4 |

Data as orig reptd.; bef. results of disc opers/spec. items. Per share data adj. for stk. divs.; EPS diluted. E-Estimated. NA-Not Available. NM-Not Meaningful. NR-Not Ranked. UR-Under Review.

**Office:** 100 North East Adams Street, Peoria, IL 61629.
**Telephone:** 309-675-1000.
**Email:** catir@cat.com
**Website:** http://www.caterpillar.com

**Chrmn & CEO:** D.R. Oberhelman
**Pres:** L.C. Calil
**SVP & General Counsel:** J.B. Buda
**CFO:** E.J. Rapp

**CTO:** T.L. Utley
**Investor Contact:** M. DeWalt (309-675-4549)
**Board Members:** D. L. Calhoun, D. M. Dickinson, E. V. Fife, J. Gallardo, D. R. Goode, J. J. Greene, Jr., P. A. Magowan, D. A. Muilenburg, D. R. Oberhelman, W. A. Osborn, C. D. Powell, E. B. Rust, Jr., S. C. Schwab, J. I. Smith, M. D. White

**Founded:** 1925
**Domicile:** Delaware
**Employees:** 0

*The McGraw-Hill Companies*

# CBRE Group Inc

**STANDARD &POOR'S**

| S&P Recommendation **BUY** ★★★★☆ | Price $14.62 (as of Nov 25, 2011) | 12-Mo. Target Price $22.00 | Investment Style Large-Cap Growth |
|---|---|---|---|

**GICS Sector** Financials
**Sub-Industry** Real Estate Services

**Summary** CBRE Group (formerly CB Richard Ellis Group) is a global commercial real estate services company.

## Key Stock Statistics (Source S&P, Vickers, company reports)

| | | | | | | | |
|---|---|---|---|---|---|---|---|
| 52-Wk Range | $29.88–12.30 | S&P Oper. EPS 2011**E** | 1.00 | Market Capitalization(B) | $4.662 | Beta | 2.53 |
| Trailing 12-Month EPS | $0.79 | S&P Oper. EPS 2012**E** | 1.40 | Yield (%) | Nil | S&P 3-Yr. Proj. EPS CAGR(%) | 44 |
| Trailing 12-Month P/E | 18.5 | P/E on S&P Oper. EPS 2011**E** | 14.6 | Dividend Rate/Share | Nil | S&P Credit Rating | NA |
| $10K Invested 5 Yrs Ago | $4,483 | Common Shares Outstg. (M) | 318.9 | Institutional Ownership (%) | 96 | | |

## Price Performance

30-Week Mov. Avg. · · · · 10-Week Mov. Avg. – – **GAAP Earnings vs. Previous Year** Volume Above Avg. STARS
12-Mo. Target Price — Relative Strength — ▲ Up ▼ Down ▶ No Change Below Avg. ★

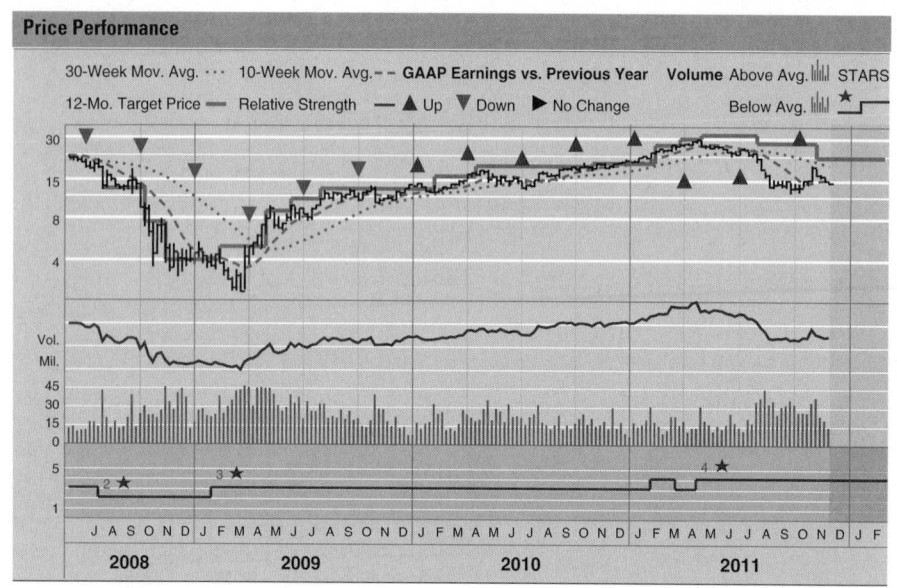

Options: ASE, CBOE, P, Ph

Analysis prepared by Equity Analyst **R. Shepard, CFA** on Nov 01, 2011, when the stock traded at **$17.59**.

## Highlights

➤ We forecast revenues will gain 22% in 2012, after a 21% increase in 2011. We think CBG is taking advantage of a rebound in demand for commercial real estate and related transaction activity. We also look for CBG's property management and investment management businesses to benefit from recent acquisitions, including the July 1, 2011 purchase of ING Clarion Real Estate Securities. Overall, we think the continuing but gradual thawing of the credit markets and more prudent underwriting will contribute to a sustained pickup in the property sales and leasing business.

➤ We expect operating margins to widen to 11.1% in 2012, from 9.6% in 2010. Our outlook reflects lower acquisition related costs in 2012 as well as reduced reserves for insurance claims and legal expenses. We also expect increased returns from third-party development services. In our view, net earnings will benefit from lower interest rates on refinancing debt obligations.

➤ We see EPS of $1.40 in 2012, up from $1.00 in 2011, driven by strong revenue growth and operating margin expansion.

## Investment Rationale/Risk

➤ We expect the company to benefit over the long term from its large size and broad array of products and services relative to peers. We think the global reach of CBG's operations helps generate economies of scale that few other real estate firms can match, helping to create sustainable barriers to entry. Although turbulence in the capital markets in the U.S. and Europe may cause a near-term pause in transaction activity, we expect any such pause to be short-lived. Nevertheless, we see the shares remaining volatile.

➤ Risks to our recommendation and target price include lower-than-expected demand for office and industrial space, greater competition, and declines in financing availability for commercial real estate transactions.

➤ The stock recently traded at 17.6X our 2011 EPS estimate. Our 12-month target price of $22 reflects a multiple of 15.7X our 2012 EPS forecast, a modest discount to historical levels. We think the shares have meaningful upside potential on strong momentum in the commercial real estate recovery.

## Qualitative Risk Assessment

| LOW | MEDIUM | HIGH |
|---|---|---|

Our risk assessment reflects CBG's position as one of the world's largest commercial real estate services firms, which should benefit from a worldwide rebound in demand for commercial real estate space and services.

## Quantitative Evaluations

**S&P Quality Ranking** NR

| D | C | B- | B | B+ | A- | A | A+ |
|---|---|---|---|---|---|---|---|

**Relative Strength Rank** MODERATE

36

LOWEST = 1     HIGHEST = 99

## Revenue/Earnings Data

**Revenue (Million $)**

| | 1Q | 2Q | 3Q | 4Q | Year |
|---|---|---|---|---|---|
| 2011 | 1,185 | 1,422 | -- | -- | -- |
| 2010 | 1,026 | 1,172 | 1,266 | 1,651 | -- |
| 2009 | 890.5 | 955.7 | 1,023 | 1,297 | 4,166 |
| 2008 | 1,231 | 1,315 | 1,300 | 1,283 | 5,129 |
| 2007 | 1,214 | 1,490 | 1,493 | 1,837 | 6,034 |
| 2006 | 903.5 | 751.3 | 967.9 | 1,409 | 4,032 |

**Earnings Per Share ($)**

| | 1Q | 2Q | 3Q | 4Q | Year |
|---|---|---|---|---|---|
| 2011 | 0.11 | 0.19 | 0.20 | E0.46 | E1.00 |
| 2010 | -0.02 | 0.15 | 0.17 | 0.30 | 0.60 |
| 2009 | -0.14 | -0.02 | 0.04 | 0.21 | 0.12 |
| 2008 | 0.10 | 0.08 | 0.15 | 0.03 | 0.34 |
| 2007 | 0.05 | 0.59 | 0.48 | 0.53 | 1.65 |
| 2006 | 0.16 | 0.27 | 0.39 | 0.53 | 1.35 |

Fiscal year ended Dec. 31. Next earnings report expected: Early February. EPS Estimates based on S&P Operating Earnings; historical GAAP earnings are as reported.

## Dividend Data

No cash dividends have been paid.

# CBRE Group Inc

STANDARD &POOR'S

## Business Summary November 01, 2011

CBRE Group (formerly CB Richard Ellis Group), Inc. is one of the largest global commercial real estate services companies in the world. The company's business is focused on several service competencies, including strategic advice and execution assistance for property leasing and sales, forecasting, valuations, origination and servicing of commercial mortgage loans, facilities and project management, and real estate investment management. CBG's primary business objective is to leverage its integrated global platform to garner an increasing share of industry revenues relative to competitors. CBG believes this will enable the company to maximize and sustain its long-term cash flow and increase long-term stockholder value. Management's strategy to achieve these business objectives consists of several elements: increasing revenues from large clients; capitalizing on cross-selling opportunities; continuing to grow the investment management business; expanding through fill-in acquisitions; and focusing on improving operating efficiency.

CBG's advisory services (35.0% of 2010 total consolidated revenues) include occupier/tenant and investor/owner services that meet a broad range of client needs, including real estate services, capital markets and valuation. The real estate services business offers a broad spectrum of services to oc-

cupiers/tenants and investors/owners. Real estate services include strategic advice and execution for owners, investors and occupiers of real estate in connection with the leasing, disposition and acquisition of property. With economies around the world improving, we expect commercial real estate activity around the world to accelerate over the next 12-18 months as still stringent lending and credit conditions ease somewhat. Through its capital markets business, CBG offers comprehensive capital markets solutions, rather than separate sales and financing transactions. During 2010, this unit concluded more than $38.6 billion of capital markets transactions in the Americas, including $24.1 billion of investment sales transactions and $14.5 billion of mortgage loan originations. The valuation business provides valuation services that include market value appraisals, litigation support, discounted cash flow analyses, and feasibility and fairness opinions. During 2010, CBG completed over 31,000 valuation, appraisal and advisory assignments.

## Company Financials Fiscal Year Ended Dec. 31

| Per Share Data ($) | 2010 | 2009 | 2008 | 2007 | 2006 | 2005 | 2004 | 2003 | 2002 | 2001 |
|---|---|---|---|---|---|---|---|---|---|---|
| Tangible Book Value | NM | NM | NM | NM | NM | NM | NM | NM | NA | NA |
| Cash Flow | 0.92 | 0.47 | 0.84 | 2.09 | 1.64 | 1.14 | 0.56 | 0.38 | 0.34 | 0.54 |
| Earnings | 0.60 | 0.12 | 0.34 | 1.65 | 1.35 | 0.95 | 0.30 | -0.11 | 0.15 | 0.32 |
| S&P Core Earnings | 0.69 | 0.21 | -1.30 | 1.71 | 1.33 | 0.94 | 0.30 | -0.24 | 0.11 | NA |
| Dividends | Nil | Nil | Nil | Nil | Nil | Nil | Nil | Nil | NA | NA |
| Payout Ratio | Nil | Nil | Nil | Nil | Nil | Nil | Nil | Nil | NA | NA |
| Prices:High | 21.53 | 14.14 | 24.50 | 42.74 | 34.26 | 19.92 | 11.36 | NA | NA | NA |
| Prices:Low | 12.05 | 2.34 | 3.00 | 17.49 | 19.46 | 10.40 | 6.03 | NA | NA | NA |
| P/E Ratio:High | 36 | NM | 72 | 26 | 25 | 21 | 37 | NA | NA | NA |
| P/E Ratio:Low | 20 | NM | 9 | 11 | 14 | 11 | 20 | NA | NA | NA |

| Income Statement Analysis (Million $) | | | | | | | | | | |
|---|---|---|---|---|---|---|---|---|---|---|
| Revenue | 5,115 | 4,166 | 5,129 | 6,034 | 4,032 | 2,911 | 2,365 | 1,949 | 1,170 | 675 |
| Operating Income | NA | NA | NA | 879 | 618 | 418 | 251 | 155 | NA | NA |
| Depreciation | 109 | NA | 91.3 | 103 | 67.6 | 45.5 | 54.9 | 92.6 | 24.6 | 14.6 |
| Interest Expense | 209 | 218 | 167 | 179 | 45.0 | 54.3 | 65.4 | 87.2 | 60.5 | 35.7 |
| Pretax Income | 272 | -0.64 | 134 | 592 | 523 | 358 | 108 | -41.0 | 48.8 | 42.5 |
| Effective Tax Rate | NA | NM | 85.4% | 32.5% | 37.9% | 38.8% | 40.2% | NM | 61.7% | 50.8% |
| Net Income | 186 | 33.3 | 73.7 | 388 | 319 | 217 | 64.7 | -34.7 | 18.7 | 20.9 |
| S&P Core Earnings | 219 | 58.5 | -272 | 403 | 314 | 216 | 64.0 | -37.5 | 13.8 | NA |

| Balance Sheet & Other Financial Data (Million $) | | | | | | | | | | |
|---|---|---|---|---|---|---|---|---|---|---|
| Cash | 507 | 742 | 159 | 392 | 244 | 449 | 257 | 164 | 79.7 | 57.5 |
| Current Assets | NA | NA | NA | 2,361 | 2,212 | 1,293 | 864 | 839 | NA | NA |
| Total Assets | 5,122 | 5,039 | 5,818 | 6,243 | 5,945 | 2,816 | 2,272 | 2,213 | 1,325 | 1,359 |
| Current Liabilities | NA | 1,883 | 1,937 | 2,428 | 1,906 | 1,138 | 809 | 833 | NA | NA |
| Long Term Debt | 2,056 | 2,672 | 2,287 | 2,792 | 2,067 | 549 | 601 | 791 | 511 | 522 |
| Common Equity | 908 | 629 | 1,211 | 989 | 1,182 | 794 | 560 | 333 | 251 | 257 |
| Total Capital | NA | 3,157 | 3,465 | 3,244 | 3,573 | 1,622 | 1,321 | 1,394 | 779 | 794 |
| Capital Expenditures | NA | NA | 51.5 | 93.0 | 55.3 | 37.8 | 53.0 | 27.0 | 14.3 | 60.9 |
| Cash Flow | 295 | 133 | -919 | 490 | 386 | 263 | 120 | 57.9 | 43.3 | 35.6 |
| Current Ratio | 1.1 | 1.4 | 1.0 | 1.0 | 1.2 | 1.1 | 1.1 | 1.0 | 0.9 | 0.9 |
| % Long Term Debt of Capitalization | 65.9 | 80.9 | 65.2 | 61.4 | 60.7 | 40.7 | 51.8 | 70.0 | 65.6 | 65.8 |
| % Net Income of Revenue | 3.6 | NA | 1.4 | 6.4 | 7.9 | 7.5 | 2.7 | NM | 1.6 | 3.1 |
| % Return on Assets | 3.7 | 0.7 | 1.2 | 6.4 | 7.3 | 8.5 | 2.9 | NM | 1.4 | NA |
| % Return on Equity | 24.2 | 9.0 | 6.7 | 35.8 | 32.3 | 32.1 | 14.5 | NM | 7.4 | NA |

Data as orig reptd.; bef. results of disc opers/spec. items. Per share data adj. for stk. divs.; EPS diluted. E-Estimated. NA-Not Available. NM-Not Meaningful. NR-Not Ranked. UR-Under Review.

**Office:** 11150 Santa Monica Boulevard, Suite 1600, Los Angeles, CA 90025.
**Telephone:** 310-405-8900.
**Website:** http://www.cbre.com
**Investor Contact:** N. Kormeluk (949-809-4308)

**Founded:** 2001

**Board Members:** R. C. Blum, B. White, R. Wirta

**Founded:** 2001
**Domicile:** Delaware
**Employees:** 31,000

The McGraw·Hill Companies

# CBS Corp

**STANDARD &POOR'S**

| S&P Recommendation **BUY** ★★★★☆ | Price<br>$23.55 (as of Nov 25, 2011) | 12-Mo. Target Price<br>$32.00 | Investment Style<br>Large-Cap Value |
|---|---|---|---|

**GICS Sector** Consumer Discretionary
**Sub-Industry** Broadcasting & Cable TV

**Summary** This major media and entertainment company has diversified ownership interests in broadcast and cable TV networks and studio, TV and radio stations, outdoor properties, book publishing and interactive businesses.

## Key Stock Statistics (Source S&P, Vickers, company reports)

| | | | | | | |
|---|---|---|---|---|---|---|
| 52-Wk Range | $29.68– 15.99 | S&P Oper. EPS 2011**E** | 1.87 | Market Capitalization(B) | $14.388 | Beta | 2.21 |
| Trailing 12-Month EPS | $1.76 | S&P Oper. EPS 2012**E** | 2.36 | Yield (%) | 1.70 | S&P 3-Yr. Proj. EPS CAGR(%) | 18 |
| Trailing 12-Month P/E | 13.4 | P/E on S&P Oper. EPS 2011**E** | 12.6 | Dividend Rate/Share | $0.40 | S&P Credit Rating | BBB |
| $10K Invested 5 Yrs Ago | $9,240 | Common Shares Outstg. (M) | 654.4 | Institutional Ownership (%) | 90 | | |

## Price Performance

30-Week Mov. Avg. ···  10-Week Mov. Avg. -- **GAAP Earnings vs. Previous Year**  Volume Above Avg. STARS
12-Mo. Target Price —  Relative Strength  — ▲ Up  ▼ Down  ► No Change  Below Avg.

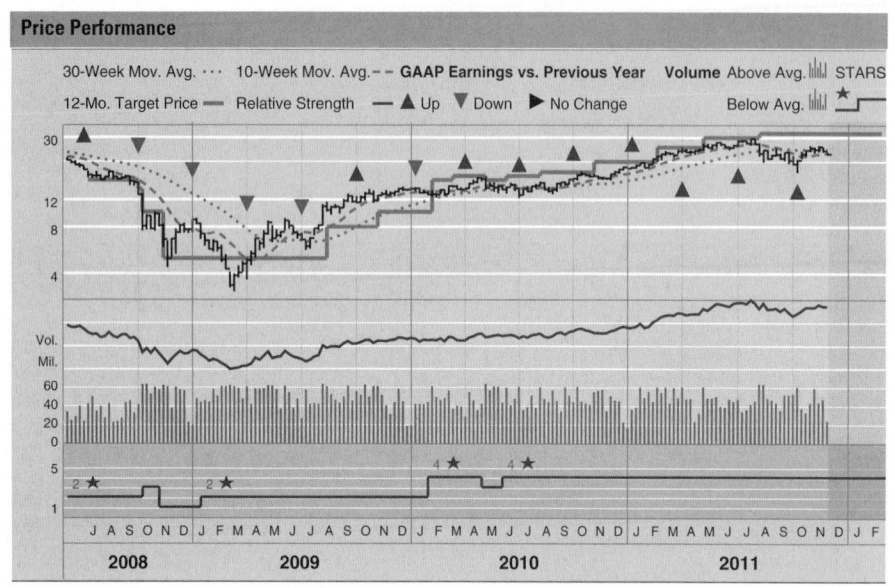

Options: ASE, CBOE, P

Analysis prepared by Equity Analyst **T. Amobi, CFA CPA** on Nov 07, 2011, when the stock traded at **$25.24**.

## Qualitative Risk Assessment

| LOW | MEDIUM | HIGH |
|---|---|---|

Our risk assessment reflects what we view as CBS's steady free cash flow-generating businesses, as well as increased opportunities from digital distribution and economies of scale on continued diversification into higher-growth international markets, offset by exposure to cyclical advertising-dependent businesses, some of which may increasingly face structural and/or secular challenges.

## Quantitative Evaluations

**S&P Quality Ranking**  B-

| D | C | B- | B | B+ | A- | A | A+ |
|---|---|---|---|---|---|---|---|

**Relative Strength Rank**  MODERATE

64

LOWEST = 1    HIGHEST = 99

## Highlights

➤ We estimate consolidated revenue growth of about 3% and 6% in 2011 and 2012, respectively, to $14.5 billion and $15.3 billion, led by the Entertainment and Cable Networks segments, as well as the Local Broadcasting (TV/radio stations) and global Outdoor divisions. We see continued healthy growth in predominant advertising sales (local and national), as well as TV licensing, subscriptions and, increasingly, retransmission and digital revenues, while noting difficult 2011 comparisons against last year's Super Bowl game, political ads and pared-down NCAA games on CBS.

➤ We expect significant margin expansion over the next two years on operating leverage, combined with a ramp-up of higher-margin revenues from digital streaming and TV retransmission. We project about 33% and 16% growth in adjusted EBIT in 2011 and 2012, respectively, to $2.7 billion in 2011 and $3.3 billion in 2012.

➤ After D&A and reduced interest cost (versus 2010), using a 39% tax rate, we estimate 2011 and 2012 operating EPS of $1.87 and $2.36, respectively, with ramping share buybacks (of which about $2.1 billion recently remained).

## Investment Rationale/Risk

➤ Amid fundamental momentum through the first nine months of 2011, we see steady progress on de-risking the business model, as CBS increasingly taps emerging and/or under-exploited revenue opportunities away from its highly cyclical advertising base. In particular, we see TV stations steadily transitioning to a dual revenue model through a ramp-up of retransmission payments, while digital streaming deals with providers such as Netflix, Amazon and Hulu are also becoming a major factor. We see ample financial flexibility on free cash flow acceleration, for share buybacks and dividends.

➤ Risks to our opinion and target price include vulnerability to a sharp macroeconomic slowdown and heavy dependence on ad revenues; corporate governance concerns related to voting control, dual class shares and board independence; and foreign currency exposure.

➤ Our 12-month target price of $32 reflects a blend of 7.0X EV/EBITDA and 0.8X P/E-to-growth, using 2012 estimates, which we see as attractively discounted to less ad-dependent entertainment peers. We note the stock's recent dividend yield of 1.6%.

## Revenue/Earnings Data

**Revenue (Million $)**

| | 1Q | 2Q | 3Q | 4Q | Year |
|---|---|---|---|---|---|
| 2011 | 3,510 | 3,586 | 3,365 | -- | -- |
| 2010 | 3,531 | 3,331 | 3,298 | 3,900 | 14,060 |
| 2009 | 3,160 | 3,006 | 3,350 | 3,498 | 13,015 |
| 2008 | 3,654 | 3,394 | 3,376 | 3,527 | 13,950 |
| 2007 | 3,658 | 3,375 | 3,281 | 3,759 | 14,073 |
| 2006 | 3,575 | 3,483 | 3,379 | 3,883 | 14,320 |

**Earnings Per Share ($)**

| | | | | | |
|---|---|---|---|---|---|
| 2011 | 0.29 | 0.58 | 0.50 | E0.50 | E1.87 |
| 2010 | -0.04 | 0.22 | 0.46 | 0.41 | 1.04 |
| 2009 | -0.08 | 0.02 | 0.30 | 0.09 | 0.33 |
| 2008 | 0.36 | 0.61 | -18.53 | 0.20 | -17.43 |
| 2007 | 0.28 | 0.55 | 0.48 | 0.40 | 1.70 |
| 2006 | 0.31 | 0.64 | 0.42 | 0.43 | 1.79 |

Fiscal year ended Dec. 31. Next earnings report expected: Mid February. EPS Estimates based on S&P Operating Earnings; historical GAAP earnings are as reported.

## Dividend Data (Dates: mm/dd Payment Date: mm/dd/yy)

| Amount ($) | Date Decl. | Ex-Div. Date | Stk. of Record | Payment Date |
|---|---|---|---|---|
| 0.050 | 02/23 | 03/09 | 03/11 | 04/01/11 |
| 0.100 | 05/03 | 06/08 | 06/10 | 07/01/11 |
| 0.100 | 08/09 | 09/07 | 09/09 | 10/01/11 |
| 0.100 | 11/22 | 12/07 | 12/09 | 01/01/12 |

Dividends have been paid since 2003. Source: Company reports.

---

**Please read the Required Disclosures and Analyst Certification on the last page of this report.**

*The McGraw-Hill Companies*

# CBS Corp

**STANDARD &POOR'S**

## Business Summary November 07, 2011

CORPORATE OVERVIEW. In its current form, the company is one of the two independent public entities created after the early 2006 separation of the "old" Viacom (which was renamed CBS Corp., while the other entity adopted the "Viacom" name). Pursuant to the separation, each Class A and B shareholder of the "old" Viacom received 0.5 of a share of corresponding A or B stock of each of the new entities. We believe that CBS Corp. was the lower-growth entity resulting from the separation, and that it was targeted to value-oriented investors.

The company is organized into five business reporting segments. The Entertainment segment (52% of 2010 revenue and 34% of adjusted EBIT) includes the CBS networks, CBS TV production and syndication, CBS Films and CBS Interactive. Cable Networks (10% and 25%) comprises the Showtime Networks and CBS College Sports Network. Publishing (5% and 3%) comprises Simon & Schuster book publishers. The Local Broadcasting segment (20% and 36%) includes 30 owned and operated (O&O) TV stations, as well as 130 radio stations in 29 U.S. markets. The Outdoor unit (13% and 2%) operates billboards and out-of-home displays in the U.S. and abroad. In 2006, CBS sold its Paramount Parks unit for $1.24 billion in cash.

CORPORATE STRATEGY. CBS recently outlined plans to mitigate its business model risk, in part through increased exploitation of non-advertising dependent revenue streams (e.g., local TV station retransmission consent revenues) and emerging digital distribution platforms such as a recent two-year deal with Netflix -- combined with increasingly aggressive cultivation of international licensing opportunities. The breakdown of 2010 revenue contributions by type were advertising, 65%; content licensing and distribution, 22%; affiliate and subscription fees, 11%; and other, 2%.

In June 2008, CBS paid $1.8 billion in cash to acquire CNET, which is now part of CBS Interactive unit -- an online audience network. In recent years, the company has divested several dozen radio stations (and some TV stations) in smaller markets. In May 2007, CBS acquired Last.fm, a music-based social network with nearly 20 million users in more than 200 countries, for $280 million in cash. In January 2006, CBS acquired College Sports Network cable channel for about $325 million in stock.

## Company Financials Fiscal Year Ended Dec. 31

| Per Share Data ($) | 2010 | 2009 | 2008 | 2007 | 2006 | 2005 | 2004 | 2003 | 2002 | 2001 |
|---|---|---|---|---|---|---|---|---|---|---|
| Tangible Book Value | NM | NM | NM | NM | NM | NM | NM | NM | NM | NM |
| Cash Flow | 1.85 | 1.18 | -16.64 | 2.34 | 2.36 | -9.91 | -16.62 | 2.77 | 3.55 | 3.31 |
| Earnings | 1.04 | 0.33 | -17.43 | 1.70 | 1.79 | -5.27 | -17.56 | 1.62 | 2.48 | -0.26 |
| S&P Core Earnings | 1.04 | 0.49 | -7.03 | 1.72 | 1.90 | 1.10 | 2.92 | 2.40 | 2.08 | -0.76 |
| Dividends | 0.20 | 0.20 | 1.06 | 0.94 | 0.68 | 0.56 | 0.50 | 0.24 | Nil | Nil |
| Payout Ratio | 19% | 61% | NM | 55% | NM | NM | NM | 15% | Nil | Nil |
| Prices:High | 19.65 | 14.56 | 27.18 | 35.75 | 32.04 | 77.98 | 90.10 | 99.50 | 103.78 | 119.00 |
| Prices:Low | 12.26 | 3.06 | 4.36 | 25.57 | 23.85 | 59.86 | 60.18 | 66.22 | 59.50 | 56.50 |
| P/E Ratio:High | 19 | 44 | NM | 21 | 18 | NM | NM | 61 | 42 | NM |
| P/E Ratio:Low | 12 | 9 | NM | 15 | 13 | NM | NM | 41 | 24 | NM |

| Income Statement Analysis (Million $) | | | | | | | | | | |
|---|---|---|---|---|---|---|---|---|---|---|
| Revenue | NA | 13,015 | 13,950 | 14,073 | 14,320 | 14,536 | 22,526 | 26,585 | 24,606 | 23,223 |
| Operating Income | NA | NA | 2,691 | 3,078 | 3,135 | 3,165 | 5,838 | 5,957 | 5,542 | 4,667 |
| Depreciation | 562 | 582 | 532 | 456 | 440 | 499 | 810 | 1,000 | 946 | 3,087 |
| Interest Expense | 529 | 542 | 547 | 571 | 566 | 720 | 719 | 776 | 848 | 963 |
| Pretax Income | 1,187 | 409 | -12,593 | 2,052 | 2,036 | -7,513 | -13,676 | 2,861 | 3,695 | 656 |
| Effective Tax Rate | NA | 44.7% | NM | 40.0% | 32.0% | NM | NM | 55.9% | 39.2% | NM |
| Net Income | 724 | 227 | -11,673 | 1,231 | 1,383 | -8,322 | -15,060 | 1,435 | 2,207 | -220 |
| S&P Core Earnings | 725 | 329 | -4,713 | 1,247 | 1,468 | 871 | 2,497 | 2,087 | 1,845 | -656 |

| Balance Sheet & Other Financial Data (Million $) | | | | | | | | | | |
|---|---|---|---|---|---|---|---|---|---|---|
| Cash | 480 | 717 | 420 | 1,347 | 3,075 | 1,655 | 928 | 851 | 631 | 727 |
| Current Assets | 5,335 | 5,637 | 5,193 | 6,031 | 8,144 | 6,796 | 7,494 | 7,736 | 7,167 | 7,206 |
| Total Assets | 26,143 | 26,962 | 26,889 | 40,430 | 43,509 | 43,030 | 68,002 | 89,849 | 89,754 | 90,810 |
| Current Liabilities | 4,026 | 4,747 | 4,801 | 4,405 | 4,400 | 5,379 | 6,880 | 7,585 | 7,341 | 7,562 |
| Long Term Debt | 5,974 | 6,553 | 6,975 | 6,979 | 7,027 | 7,153 | 9,649 | 9,683 | 10,205 | 10,824 |
| Common Equity | 9,821 | 9,019 | 8,597 | 21,472 | 24,153 | 21,737 | 59,862 | 63,205 | 62,488 | 62,717 |
| Total Capital | 15,821 | 16,016 | 15,593 | 30,490 | 32,862 | 31,007 | 70,879 | 73,812 | 74,337 | 75,884 |
| Capital Expenditures | 284 | 262 | 474 | 469 | 394 | 376 | 415 | 534 | 537 | 515 |
| Cash Flow | 1,287 | 809 | -11,142 | 1,687 | 1,822 | -7,823 | -14,250 | 2,435 | 3,152 | 2,867 |
| Current Ratio | 1.3 | 1.2 | 1.1 | 1.4 | 1.9 | 1.3 | 1.1 | 1.0 | 1.0 | 1.0 |
| % Long Term Debt of Capitalization | 37.8 | 40.9 | 44.7 | 24.8 | 21.0 | 23.1 | 13.6 | 13.1 | 13.7 | 14.3 |
| % Net Income of Revenue | NM | 1.7 | NM | 8.8 | 9.7 | NM | NM | 5.4 | 9.0 | NM |
| % Return on Assets | 2.7 | 0.8 | NM | 2.9 | 3.2 | NM | NM | 1.6 | 2.4 | NM |
| % Return on Equity | 7.7 | 2.6 | NM | 5.5 | 5.9 | NM | NM | 2.3 | 3.5 | NM |

Data as orig reptd.; bef. results of disc opers/spec. items. Per share data adj. for stk. divs.; EPS diluted. Data as orig. reptd., for "old" Viacom through third qtr. 2005. E-Estimated. NA-Not Available. NM-Not Meaningful. NR-Not Ranked. UR-Under Review.

**Office:** 51 West 52nd Street, New York, NY 10019.
**Telephone:** 212-975-4321.
**Website:** http://www.cbscorporation.com
**Chrmn:** S.M. Redstone

**Pres & CEO:** L. Moonves
**Vice Chrmn:** S.E. Redstone
**EVP & CFO:** J.R. Ianniello
**EVP & General Counsel:** L.J. Briskman

**Board Members:** D. R. Andelman, J. A. Califano, Jr., W. S. Cohen, G. L. Countryman, C. K. Gifford, L. Goldberg, B. S. Gordon, L. M. Griego, A. Kopelson, L. Moonves, D. Morris, S. E. Redstone, S. M. Redstone, F. V. Salerno

**Founded:** 1986
**Domicile:** Delaware
**Employees:** 25,380

The McGraw-Hill Companies

# Celgene Corp

STANDARD &POOR'S

| S&P Recommendation | **STRONG BUY** ★★★★★ | Price $60.24 (as of Nov 25, 2011) | 12-Mo. Target Price $89.00 | Investment Style Large-Cap Growth |
|---|---|---|---|---|

**GICS Sector** Health Care
**Sub-Industry** Biotechnology

**Summary** This company primarily develops and commercializes small molecule drugs for the treatment of bloodborne and solid tumor cancers and inflammatory disease.

## Key Stock Statistics (Source S&P, Vickers, company reports)

| | | | | | | |
|---|---|---|---|---|---|---|
| 52-Wk Range | $68.25– 48.92 | S&P Oper. EPS 2011**E** | 3.43 | Market Capitalization(B) | $26.742 | Beta | 0.57 |
| Trailing 12-Month EPS | $2.38 | S&P Oper. EPS 2012**E** | 4.05 | Yield (%) | Nil | S&P 3-Yr. Proj. EPS CAGR(%) | 22 |
| Trailing 12-Month P/E | 25.3 | P/E on S&P Oper. EPS 2011**E** | 17.6 | Dividend Rate/Share | Nil | S&P Credit Rating | BBB+ |
| $10K Invested 5 Yrs Ago | $10,923 | Common Shares Outstg. (M) | 443.9 | Institutional Ownership (%) | 86 | | |

## Price Performance

30-Week Mov. Avg. ···· 10-Week Mov. Avg. ── **GAAP Earnings vs. Previous Year**    **Volume** Above Avg. ▌▊▐ STARS
12-Mo. Target Price ── Relative Strength ── ▲ Up ▼ Down ▶ No Change    Below Avg. ▖▌▎ ★

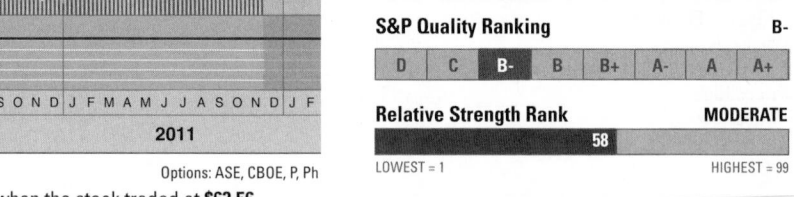

Options: ASE, CBOE, P, Ph

Analysis prepared by Equity Analyst **Steven Silver** on Nov 01, 2011, when the stock traded at **$63.56**.

## Qualitative Risk Assessment

| LOW | MEDIUM | **HIGH** |
|---|---|---|

Our risk assessment reflects the strong competition we see in the blood cancer treatment markets, particularly from Velcade in multiple myeloma. Further, in Thalomid and Revlimid, the company currently depends on two products in the same markets for the majority of its revenues. We also see inherent risk in CELG's drugs maintaining a competitive safety profile, including a higher incidence of secondary cancers, as seen in some Revlimid studies.

## Quantitative Evaluations

**S&P Quality Ranking**                                    B-

| D | C | **B-** | B | B+ | A- | A | A+ |
|---|---|---|---|---|---|---|---|

**Relative Strength Rank**                          MODERATE

58

LOWEST = 1                                         HIGHEST = 99

## Highlights

➤ We see 2011 revenues rising 34%, to $4.84 billion, with 30% growth in Revlimid sales, to $3.2 billion, and 2012 revenues gaining 11%, to $5.35 billion, with 15% Revlimid growth, to $3.68 billion. We see potential for significant additional Revlimid growth, with new uses being studied and its global expansion still in early stages. We expect Vidaza and recently acquired Abraxane to provide revenue diversification.

➤ We expect 2011 and 2012 gross margins of over 93%, up from 92.4% in 2010, as CELG improves manufacturing efficiencies and has discontinued the sale of lower-margin drugs. We estimate operating margins of 41% for 2011 and 42% in 2012, up from 40% in 2010, despite what we view as robust investments in CELG's late-stage pipeline and international expansion. We view R&D investments favorably, as CELG advances more than 20 late-stage studies.

➤ We project adjusted EPS of $3.43 in 2011 and $4.05 in 2012, excluding amortization of intangibles but including $0.34 in after-tax stock option expense in both periods. We expect CELG to maintain a below-industry-average effective tax rate between 18% and 20%, on higher sales in lower tax jurisdictions.

## Investment Rationale/Risk

➤ In our view, CELG holds the brightest growth prospects among large-cap biotech companies. We expect Revlimid to drive near-term revenue growth, given its oral formulation and robust survival benefits seen in first-line multiple myeloma studies. We see recent European affirmation of a positive risk/benefit profile easing concerns over a link to secondary cancers seen in some of these studies. Over the longer term, we look for CELG's inflammation/immunology and cellular therapeutics pipelines to complement core hematology/oncology franchises. We view favorably CELG's $2.6 billion cash balance at September 30, 2011, for pipeline investment and share repurchases.

➤ Risks to our opinion and target price include slowing Revlimid sales growth and failure to expand its approved uses, reimbursement issues for the drug, unsuccessful defense of patents, and clinical failure of CELG's earlier pipeline candidates.

➤ Our 12-month target price of $89 applies a 22X multiple to our 2012 adjusted EPS estimate of $4.05, a premium to large-cap peers on what we view as a superior earnings growth and pipeline outlook.

## Revenue/Earnings Data

### Revenue (Million $)

| | 1Q | 2Q | 3Q | 4Q | Year |
|---|---|---|---|---|---|
| 2011 | 1,125 | 1,183 | 1,250 | -- | -- |
| 2010 | 791.3 | 852.7 | 910.1 | 1,066 | 3,620 |
| 2009 | 605.1 | 628.7 | 695.1 | 761.0 | 2,690 |
| 2008 | 462.6 | 571.5 | 592.5 | 628.3 | 2,255 |
| 2007 | 293.4 | 347.9 | 349.9 | 414.6 | 1,406 |
| 2006 | 181.8 | 197.2 | 244.8 | 275.0 | 898.9 |

### Earnings Per Share ($)

| | 1Q | 2Q | 3Q | 4Q | Year |
|---|---|---|---|---|---|
| 2011 | 0.54 | 0.59 | 0.81 | E0.97 | E3.43 |
| 2010 | 0.50 | 0.33 | 0.60 | 0.45 | 1.88 |
| 2009 | 0.35 | 0.31 | 0.46 | 0.54 | 1.66 |
| 2008 | -3.98 | 0.26 | 0.29 | -0.33 | -3.46 |
| 2007 | 0.14 | 0.13 | 0.09 | 0.18 | 0.54 |
| 2006 | 0.04 | 0.03 | 0.05 | 0.06 | 0.18 |

Fiscal year ended Dec. 31. Next earnings report expected: Late January. EPS Estimates based on S&P Operating Earnings; historical GAAP earnings are as reported.

## Dividend Data

No cash dividends have been paid.

# Celgene Corp

STANDARD &POOR'S

## Business Summary November 01, 2011

CORPORATE OVERVIEW. Celgene is a biopharmaceutical company focusing on the discovery, development and commercialization of products for the treatment of cancer and other severe, immune, inflammatory conditions. Its primary areas of expertise have been on hematological and solid tumor cancers, including multiple myeloma, myelodysplastic syndromes, chronic lymphocyte leukemia (CLL), non-Hodgkin's lymphoma (NHL), glioblastoma, and ovarian, pancreatic and prostate cancers.

CORPORATE STRATEGY. CELG uses its small molecule technology to develop Immunomodulatory Drugs (IMiDs) and Selective Cytokine Inhibitory Drugs (SelCIDs), potent, orally available agents to fight acute and chronic diseases. Its primary focus to date has been treating multiple myeloma (MM), the second most commonly diagnosed blood cancer. According to the International Myeloma Foundation, there are an estimated 100,000 people in the U.S. with multiple myeloma and nearly 20,000 new cases diagnosed each year, representing 1% of all cancers and 2% of cancer deaths.

Celgene's core marketed products have been Thalomid ($387 million sales in 2010) and Revlimid ($2.47 billion). Thalomid is CELG's version of thalidomide, an antiangiogenic agent capable of inhibiting blood vessel growth and down-regulating TNFa. In 1998, Thalomid was approved by the FDA to treat leprosy-related conditions and in 2006 to treat relapsed/refractory multiple myeloma. European rights to Thalomid were re-acquired in the March 2008 acquisition of Pharmion, and the drug was approved in Europe for first-line multiple myeloma in April 2008.

In December 2005, the FDA approved Revlimid, a successor analogue version of Thalomid, to treat blood disorder myelodysplastic syndrome (MDS). Revlimid has since been approved in the U.S., Europe and Japan, and other countries, for relapsed/refractory multiple myeloma, which has become its most lucrative indication. Revlimid is also being studied for amyloidosis, non-Hodgkin's lymphoma, and solid tumors including prostate, renal cell carcinoma, pancreatic and colorectal cancers. In 2009, a pivotal Phase III study, MM-015, showed a 50% reduction in progression-free survival in patients receiving Revlimid with melphalan and prednisone (MP) versus patients receiving MP alone as a multiple myeloma maintenance regimen after autologous stem cell transplant, and patients saw 75% progression-free survival benefits beyond nine treatment cycles.

## Company Financials Fiscal Year Ended Dec. 31

| Per Share Data ($) | 2010 | 2009 | 2008 | 2007 | 2006 | 2005 | 2004 | 2003 | 2002 | 2001 |
|---|---|---|---|---|---|---|---|---|---|---|
| Tangible Book Value | 1.78 | 7.55 | 5.37 | 6.80 | 4.83 | 1.48 | 1.06 | 0.93 | 0.85 | 1.03 |
| Cash Flow | 2.22 | 1.93 | -3.13 | 0.60 | 0.23 | 0.23 | 0.18 | 0.06 | -0.31 | 0.01 |
| Earnings | 1.88 | 1.66 | -3.46 | 0.54 | 0.18 | 0.18 | 0.16 | 0.04 | -0.33 | -0.01 |
| S&P Core Earnings | 1.88 | 1.66 | -3.45 | 0.55 | 0.19 | 0.05 | 0.08 | -0.04 | -0.33 | -0.09 |
| Dividends | Nil | Nil | Nil | Nil | Nil | Nil | Nil | Nil | Nil | Nil |
| Payout Ratio | Nil | Nil | Nil | Nil | Nil | Nil | Nil | Nil | Nil | Nil |
| Prices:High | 65.79 | 58.31 | 77.39 | 75.44 | 60.12 | 32.68 | 16.29 | 12.22 | 8.05 | 9.72 |
| Prices:Low | 48.02 | 36.90 | 45.44 | 41.26 | 31.51 | 12.35 | 9.37 | 5.04 | 2.83 | 3.60 |
| P/E Ratio:High | 35 | 35 | NM | NM | NM | NM | NM | NM | NM | NM |
| P/E Ratio:Low | 26 | 22 | NM | NM | NM | NM | NM | NM | NM | NM |

| Income Statement Analysis (Million $) | | | | | | | | | | |
|---|---|---|---|---|---|---|---|---|---|---|
| Revenue | 3,620 | 2,690 | 2,255 | 1,406 | 899 | 537 | 378 | 271 | 136 | 114 |
| Operating Income | 1,202 | 968 | 742 | 457 | 200 | 97.9 | 52.4 | 5.38 | -31.0 | -19.9 |
| Depreciation | 163 | 126 | 149 | 31.5 | 25.7 | 14.3 | 9.69 | 8.03 | 5.18 | 5.09 |
| Interest Expense | 12.6 | 1.97 | 4.44 | 11.1 | 9.42 | 9.50 | 9.55 | 5.67 | 0.03 | 0.08 |
| Pretax Income | 1,017 | 976 | -1,369 | 517 | 203 | 84.2 | 63.2 | 12.0 | -101 | -4.14 |
| Effective Tax Rate | NA | 20.4% | NM | 56.2% | 66.0% | 24.4% | 16.5% | NM | NM | NM |
| Net Income | 884 | 777 | -1,534 | 226 | 69.0 | 63.7 | 52.8 | 12.8 | -101 | -2.90 |
| S&P Core Earnings | 881 | 777 | -1,528 | 230 | 71.5 | 10.8 | 25.0 | -13.0 | -88.6 | -26.5 |

| Balance Sheet & Other Financial Data (Million $) | | | | | | | | | | |
|---|---|---|---|---|---|---|---|---|---|---|
| Cash | 2,601 | 2,997 | 2,222 | 2,739 | 1,982 | 724 | 749 | 667 | 261 | 310 |
| Current Assets | 4,343 | 3,845 | 2,841 | 3,084 | 2,311 | 973 | 850 | 730 | 296 | 336 |
| Total Assets | 10,177 | 5,389 | 4,445 | 3,611 | 2,736 | 1,247 | 1,107 | 791 | 327 | 354 |
| Current Liabilities | 1,070 | 495 | 527 | 433 | 240 | 136 | 141 | 71.8 | 44.3 | 30.0 |
| Long Term Debt | 1,268 | 21.1 | 22.2 | 22.6 | 400 | 400 | 400 | 400 | 0.04 | 11.8 |
| Common Equity | 5,984 | 4,395 | 3,491 | 2,844 | 1,976 | 636 | 477 | 310 | 277 | 310 |
| Total Capital | 7,275 | 4,420 | 3,514 | 2,877 | 2,376 | 1,036 | 877 | 710 | 277 | 322 |
| Capital Expenditures | 98.6 | 93.4 | 77.4 | 64.4 | 46.1 | 35.9 | 36.0 | 11.2 | 11.1 | 7.87 |
| Cash Flow | 1,043 | 903 | -1,385 | 258 | 94.7 | 77.9 | 62.4 | 20.8 | -95.8 | 2.18 |
| Current Ratio | 4.1 | 7.8 | 5.4 | 7.1 | 9.6 | 7.2 | 6.0 | 10.2 | 6.7 | 11.2 |
| % Long Term Debt of Capitalization | 17.4 | Nil | 0.6 | 0.8 | 16.8 | 38.6 | 45.6 | 56.3 | 0.0 | 3.7 |
| % Net Income of Revenue | 24.4 | 28.9 | NM | 16.1 | 7.7 | 11.9 | 14.0 | 4.7 | NM | NM |
| % Return on Assets | NA | NA | NM | 7.1 | 3.5 | 5.4 | 5.5 | 2.3 | NM | NM |
| % Return on Equity | NA | NA | NM | 9.4 | 5.3 | 11.4 | 13.0 | 4.3 | NM | NM |

Data as orig reptd.; bef. results of disc opers/spec. items. Per share data adj. for stk. divs.; EPS diluted. E-Estimated. NA-Not Available. NM-Not Meaningful. NR-Not Ranked. UR-Under Review.

**Office:** 86 Morris Avenue, Summit, NJ 07901.
**Telephone:** 908-673-9000.
**Email:** info@celgene.com
**Website:** http://www.celgene.com

**Chrmn, Pres, CEO & Secy:** R.J. Hugin
**COO:** P.A. Karsen
**SVP & CFO:** J.A. Fouse
**Chief Acctg Officer & Cntlr:** A.V. Hoek

**Investor Contact:** B.P. Gill (908-673-9530)
**Board Members:** M. D. Casey, C. S. Cox, R. L. Drake, M. A. Friedman, R. J. Hugin, G. Kaplan, J. J. Loughlin, E. Mario

**Founded:** 1986
**Domicile:** Delaware
**Employees:** 4,182

# CenterPoint Energy Inc.

**STANDARD &POOR'S**

| S&P Recommendation | HOLD ★★★★★ | Price | 12-Mo. Target Price | Investment Style |
|---|---|---|---|---|
| | | $18.59 (as of Nov 25, 2011) | $22.00 | Large-Cap Value |

**GICS Sector** Utilities
**Sub-Industry** Multi-Utilities

**Summary** This Houston-based energy company (formerly Reliant Energy) is one of the largest electric and natural gas delivery companies in the U.S.

## Key Stock Statistics (Source S&P, Vickers, company reports)

| | | | | | | | |
|---|---|---|---|---|---|---|---|
| 52-Wk Range | $21.47– 15.09 | S&P Oper. EPS 2011**E** | 1.18 | Market Capitalization(B) | $7.918 | Beta | 0.66 |
| Trailing 12-Month EPS | $3.18 | S&P Oper. EPS 2012**E** | 1.23 | Yield (%) | 4.25 | S&P 3-Yr. Proj. EPS CAGR(%) | -2 |
| Trailing 12-Month P/E | 5.9 | P/E on S&P Oper. EPS 2011**E** | 15.8 | Dividend Rate/Share | $0.79 | S&P Credit Rating | BBB+ |
| $10K Invested 5 Yrs Ago | $14,803 | Common Shares Outstg. (M) | 425.9 | Institutional Ownership (%) | 73 | | |

## Price Performance

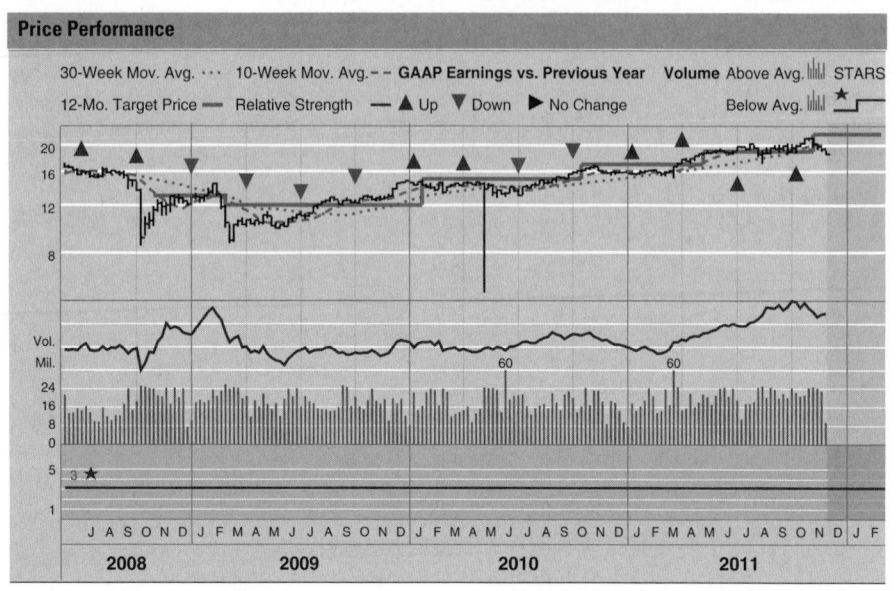

30-Week Mov. Avg. ···  10-Week Mov. Avg. --  **GAAP Earnings vs. Previous Year**  **Volume** Above Avg. STARS
12-Mo. Target Price —  Relative Strength —  ▲ Up  ▼ Down  ► No Change  Below Avg. ★

Options: ASE, CBOE, P, Ph

Analysis prepared by Equity Analyst **Justin McCann** on Nov 03, 2011, when the stock traded at **$20.30**.

### Highlights

► We expect operating EPS in 2011 to increase about 10% from 2010's $1.07. Despite 5% more shares than in the year-ago period, operating EPS in the first nine months of 2011 benefited from higher income at the electric transmission and distribution segment, the natural gas distribution segment, and especially at the field services operations. This was partially offset by declines at the interstate pipelines and the competitive natural gas business.

► For 2012, we project operating EPS to increase about 4% from anticipated results in 2011, with higher operating margins in nearly all of CNP's segments and an expected gradual recovery in the economy being partially offset by a lower than expected return on equity authorization for CNP's Houston Electric subsidiary (CEHE), and an assumed return to more normal weather.

► On October 13, 2011, the Texas Utility Commission issued a final order authorizing CEHE to recover an additional balance of $1.695 billion related to the utility's stranded-cost-true-up proceeding. Then, on October 27, 2011, the Commission authorized the issuance of transition bonds by CEHE to securitize the additional $1.695 billion it had authorized for recovery.

### Investment Rationale/Risk

► The stock was up around 30% in the first 10 months of 2011. We believe the gain has largely reflected the Texas Supreme Court's favorable ruling on CEHE's stranded-cost-true-up proceeding, which was remanded back to the Texas PUC, and then the subsequent PUC authorization, on October 13, for the recovery of the true-up balance of $1.695 billion. The strong gain has also reflected the company's improved financial strength and the recovery in the utilities sector. We believe the stock is appropriately valued at recent levels.

► Risks to our recommendation and target price include a potential significant economic decline in the company's service territories, unfavorable regulatory rulings or political legislation, and/or a large decline in the average P/E of the company's electric and gas utility peers.

► Despite the sharp rise in the shares, the dividend yield, recently at 3.9%, was only slightly below the recent electric and gas utility peer average of about 4.2%. Given the estimated 67% payout ratio on our EPS estimate for 2011, we believe the dividend is secure. Our 12-month target price is $22, reflecting a premium-to-peers P/E of 17.9X our 2012 estimate.

## Qualitative Risk Assessment

| LOW | MEDIUM | HIGH |
|---|---|---|

Our risk assessment reflects the strong and steady cash flow we expect from the Houston electric operations, which have a growing service territory; a low commodity risk profile; a generally supportive regulatory environment; and the gas purchase adjustment clauses that reduce the commodity risks related to the company's more diversified gas distribution operations.

## Quantitative Evaluations

**S&P Quality Ranking**                     **B**

| D | C | B- | B | B+ | A- | A | A+ |
|---|---|---|---|---|---|---|---|

**Relative Strength Rank**          **MODERATE**

50

LOWEST = 1                          HIGHEST = 99

## Revenue/Earnings Data

**Revenue (Million $)**

| | 1Q | 2Q | 3Q | 4Q | Year |
|---|---|---|---|---|---|
| 2011 | 2,587 | 1,837 | 1,881 | -- | -- |
| 2010 | 3,023 | 1,756 | 1,908 | 2,098 | 8,785 |
| 2009 | 2,766 | 1,640 | 1,576 | 2,299 | 8,281 |
| 2008 | 3,363 | 2,670 | 2,515 | 2,774 | 11,322 |
| 2007 | 3,106 | 2,033 | 1,882 | 2,602 | 9,623 |
| 2006 | 3,077 | 1,843 | 1,935 | 2,464 | 9,319 |

**Earnings Per Share ($)**

| | | | | | |
|---|---|---|---|---|---|
| 2011 | 0.35 | 0.28 | 0.90 | E0.24 | E1.18 |
| 2010 | 0.29 | 0.20 | 0.29 | 0.29 | 1.07 |
| 2009 | 0.19 | 0.24 | 0.31 | 0.27 | 1.01 |
| 2008 | 0.36 | 0.30 | 0.39 | 0.25 | 1.30 |
| 2007 | 0.38 | 0.20 | 0.27 | 0.32 | 1.17 |
| 2006 | 0.28 | 0.61 | 0.26 | 0.20 | 1.33 |

Fiscal year ended Dec. 31. Next earnings report expected: Early March. EPS Estimates based on S&P Operating Earnings; historical GAAP earnings are as reported.

## Dividend Data (Dates: mm/dd Payment Date: mm/dd/yy)

| Amount ($) | Date Decl. | Ex-Div. Date | Stk. of Record | Payment Date |
|---|---|---|---|---|
| 0.198 | 01/20 | 02/14 | 02/16 | 03/10/11 |
| 0.198 | 04/21 | 05/12 | 05/16 | 06/10/11 |
| 0.198 | 07/19 | 08/12 | 08/16 | 09/09/11 |
| 0.198 | 10/27 | 11/14 | 11/16 | 12/09/11 |

Dividends have been paid since 1922. Source: Company reports.

---

**Please read the Required Disclosures and Analyst Certification on the last page of this report.**

**The McGraw·Hill Companies**

# CenterPoint Energy Inc.

STANDARD &POOR'S

## Business Summary November 03, 2011

CORPORATE OVERVIEW. CenterPoint Energy (formerly Reliant Energy) is a Houston-based energy delivery company with operations that include electric transmission and distribution (45.4% of operating income in 2010), interstate pipelines (21.6%), natural gas distribution (18.5%), field services (12.1%), competitive natural gas sales and services (1.3%), and other (1.1%).

MARKET PROFILE. The CenterPoint Energy Houston Electric (CEHE) utility serves more than 2 million customers in a 5,000 square mile territory that includes the cities of Houston and Galveston, TX, and (with the exception of Texas City), nearly all of the Houston/Galveston metropolitan area. Following the deregulation of the industry in Texas, wholesale and retail suppliers pay the company to deliver the electricity over its transmission lines. The natural gas subsidiary, CenterPoint Energy Resources Corp. (CERC), serves about 3.2 million residential, commercial and industrial customers in Arkansas, Louisiana, Minnesota, Mississippi, Oklahoma and Texas. In 2010, approximately 42% of total demand was accounted for by residential customers, and

about 58% was from commercial and industrial customers.

CERC's interstate pipeline business owns and operates approximately 8,000 miles of gas transmission lines primarily located in Arkansas, Illinois, Louisiana, Missouri, Oklahoma and Texas. It also owns and operates six natural gas storage fields with a combined daily volume of about 1.3 billion cubic feet per day. CERC's field services business owns and operates around 3,800 miles of gathering pipelines and processing plants that collect, treat and process natural gas primarily from three regions located in major producing fields in Arkansas, Oklahoma, Louisiana and Texas. CNP's other operations include office buildings and other real estate that are used in support of all of its business operations.

## Company Financials Fiscal Year Ended Dec. 31

| Per Share Data ($) | 2010 | 2009 | 2008 | 2007 | 2006 | 2005 | 2004 | 2003 | 2002 | 2001 |
|---|---|---|---|---|---|---|---|---|---|---|
| Tangible Book Value | 3.53 | 2.41 | 0.99 | NM | NM | NM | NM | NM | NM | 13.05 |
| Earnings | 1.07 | 1.01 | 1.30 | 1.17 | 1.33 | 0.67 | 0.61 | 1.37 | 1.29 | 3.14 |
| S&P Core Earnings | 1.07 | 1.05 | 1.31 | 1.31 | 1.18 | 0.75 | 0.65 | 1.28 | 2.17 | 3.00 |
| Dividends | 0.78 | 0.76 | 0.73 | 0.68 | 0.60 | 0.40 | 0.40 | 0.40 | 1.07 | 1.50 |
| Payout Ratio | 73% | 75% | 56% | 58% | 45% | 60% | 66% | 29% | 83% | 48% |
| Prices:High | 17.00 | 14.87 | 17.35 | 20.20 | 16.87 | 15.14 | 12.32 | 10.49 | 27.10 | 50.45 |
| Prices:Low | 5.67 | 8.66 | 8.48 | 14.70 | 11.62 | 10.55 | 9.66 | 4.35 | 4.24 | 23.27 |
| P/E Ratio:High | 16 | 15 | 13 | 17 | 13 | 23 | 20 | 8 | 21 | 16 |
| P/E Ratio:Low | 5 | 9 | 7 | 13 | 9 | 16 | 16 | 3 | 3 | 7 |

### Income Statement Analysis (Million $)

| | 2010 | 2009 | 2008 | 2007 | 2006 | 2005 | 2004 | 2003 | 2002 | 2001 |
|---|---|---|---|---|---|---|---|---|---|---|
| Revenue | 8,785 | 8,281 | 11,322 | 9,623 | 9,319 | 9,722 | 8,510 | 9,760 | 7,923 | 46,226 |
| Depreciation | 864 | 743 | 708 | 631 | 599 | 541 | 490 | 625 | 616 | 911 |
| Maintenance | NA | NA | NA | NA | NA | NA | NA | NA | NA | NA |
| Fixed Charges Coverage | NA | 1.80 | 2.14 | 1.95 | 1.80 | 1.35 | 1.15 | 1.37 | 1.80 | 3.33 |
| Construction Credits | NA | NA | NA | NA | NA | NA | NA | NA | NA | NA |
| Effective Tax Rate | NA | 32.1% | 38.3% | 32.8% | 12.6% | 40.5% | NM | 35.6% | 35.0% | 33.3% |
| Net Income | 442 | 372 | 447 | 399 | 432 | 225 | 206 | 420 | 386 | 919 |
| S&P Core Earnings | 442 | 386 | 451 | 444 | 384 | 254 | 224 | 390 | 642 | 868 |

### Balance Sheet & Other Financial Data (Million $)

| | 2010 | 2009 | 2008 | 2007 | 2006 | 2005 | 2004 | 2003 | 2002 | 2001 |
|---|---|---|---|---|---|---|---|---|---|---|
| Gross Property | NA | 14,770 | 14,006 | 13,250 | 12,567 | 11,558 | 10,963 | 11,812 | 11,409 | 24,214 |
| Capital Expenditures | 1,509 | 1,160 | 1,020 | 1,114 | 1,007 | 693 | 530 | 648 | 854 | 2,053 |
| Net Property | NA | 10,788 | 10,296 | 9,740 | 9,204 | 8,492 | 8,186 | 11,812 | 11,409 | 15,857 |
| Capitalization:Long Term Debt | NA | 9,119 | 10,181 | 8,364 | 7,802 | 8,568 | 7,193 | 10,783 | 9,194 | 6,448 |
| Capitalization:% Long Term Debt | 71.3 | 77.6 | 83.3 | 82.2 | 83.4 | 86.9 | 86.7 | 86.0 | 71.0 | 48.4 |
| Capitalization:Preferred | NA | Nil | Nil | Nil | Nil | Nil | Nil | Nil | Nil | Nil |
| Capitalization:% Preferred | NA | Nil | Nil | Nil | Nil | Nil | Nil | Nil | Nil | Nil |
| Capitalization:Common | 3,198 | 2,639 | 2,037 | 1,810 | 1,556 | 1,296 | 1,106 | 1,761 | 3,756 | 6,881 |
| Capitalization:% Common | NA | 22.4 | 16.7 | 17.8 | 16.6 | 13.1 | 13.3 | 14.0 | 29.0 | 51.6 |
| Total Capital | 12,627 | 12,661 | 14,851 | 12,440 | 12,036 | 12,769 | 10,767 | 12,934 | 13,180 | 16,970 |
| % Operating Ratio | NA | 88.6 | 91.2 | 89.7 | 89.5 | 91.9 | 91.5 | 85.8 | 85.8 | 96.6 |
| % Earned on Net Property | NA | 10.7 | 12.7 | 12.5 | 11.8 | 11.3 | 10.6 | 21.8 | 17.2 | 12.8 |
| % Return on Revenue | 5.0 | 4.5 | 4.0 | 4.1 | 2.8 | 1.4 | 2.4 | 4.3 | 4.9 | 2.0 |
| % Return on Invested Capital | NA | 7.8 | 7.3 | 8.5 | 8.3 | 7.9 | 7.6 | 11.1 | 14.7 | 11.2 |
| % Return on Common Equity | 15.1 | 15.9 | 23.2 | 23.7 | 30.3 | 18.7 | 14.4 | 26.4 | 10.3 | 14.8 |

Data as orig reptd.; bef. results of disc opers/spec. items. Per share data adj. for stk. divs.; EPS diluted. E-Estimated. NA-Not Available. NM-Not Meaningful. NR-Not Ranked. UR-Under Review.

**Office:** 1111 Louisiana Street, Houston, TX 77002-5230.
**Telephone:** 713-207-1111.
**Email:** info@reliantenergy.nl
**Website:** http://www.centerpointenergy.com

**Chrmn:** M. Carroll
**Pres & CEO:** D.M. McClanahan
**EVP & CFO:** G.L. Whitlock
**EVP, Secy & General Counsel:** S.E. Rozzell

**SVP & Chief Acctg Officer:** W.L. Fitzgerald
**Investor Contact:** M. Paulsen (713-207-6500)
**Board Members:** D. R. Campbell, M. Carroll, O. H. Crosswell, M. P. Johnson, J. M. Longoria, D. M. McClanahan, S. O. Rheney, R. A. Walker, P. S. Wareing, S. M. Wolff

**Founded:** 1882
**Domicile:** Texas
**Employees:** 8,843

# CenturyLink Inc

STANDARD
&POOR'S

| S&P Recommendation **HOLD** ★★★★★ | Price<br>$35.70 (as of Nov 25, 2011) | 12-Mo. Target Price<br>$37.00 | Investment Style<br>Large-Cap Blend |
|---|---|---|---|

**GICS Sector** Telecommunication Services
**Sub-Industry** Integrated Telecommunication Services

**Summary** CTL acquired larger telecom peer Qwest Communications in a stock deal in April 2011. Combined, the company provides voice service to 15 million customers and Internet service to 5 million customers in rural towns as well as larger cities such as Denver.

## Key Stock Statistics (Source S&P, Vickers, company reports)

| | | | | | | |
|---|---|---|---|---|---|---|
| 52-Wk Range | $46.87–31.16 | S&P Oper. EPS 2011**E** | 2.68 | Market Capitalization(B) | $22.049 | Beta | 0.74 |
| Trailing 12-Month EPS | $1.51 | S&P Oper. EPS 2012**E** | 2.61 | Yield (%) | 8.12 | S&P 3-Yr. Proj. EPS CAGR(%) | 5 |
| Trailing 12-Month P/E | 23.6 | P/E on S&P Oper. EPS 2011**E** | 13.3 | Dividend Rate/Share | $2.90 | S&P Credit Rating | BB |
| $10K Invested 5 Yrs Ago | $11,571 | Common Shares Outstg. (M) | 617.6 | Institutional Ownership (%) | 76 | | |

## Price Performance

30-Week Mov. Avg. ··· 10-Week Mov. Avg. -- **GAAP Earnings vs. Previous Year** Volume Above Avg. STARS
12-Mo. Target Price — Relative Strength — ▲ Up ▼ Down ► No Change Below Avg. ★

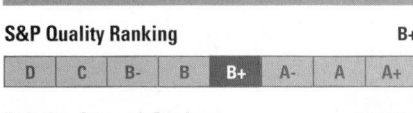

Options: Cycle P, Ph

Analysis prepared by Equity Analyst **Todd Rosenbluth** on Nov 21, 2011, when the stock traded at **$37.26**.

## Highlights

► On a pro forma basis, we expect CTL to generate revenues of $18.7 billion in 2011 and $18.4 billion in 2012, inclusive of the 2011 acquisitions Qwest Communications and Savvis, down from $19.4 billion in 2010. We expect continued pressure on voice services as ongoing access line losses outweigh gains we expect from data services such as DSL and more stability in enterprise assets.

► We forecast EBITDA margins of 41% in the fourth quarter of 2011 and 42% in 2012. We see cost synergies from billing and network integration of the Qwest assets along with corporate savings from the Savvis deal in 2012, partially offset by high costs to deploy IPTV in new markets. On a pro forma basis, we expect EBITDA to edge down from $7.84 billion in 2011 to $7.77 billion in 2012.

► On a GAAP basis, depreciation should be higher in 2011 and 2012 due to non-cash valuation of assets, but our adjusted EPS normalizes these charges. We look for EPS of $2.61 in 2012, down modestly from the pro forma $2.68 we forecast for 2011.

## Investment Rationale/Risk

► Despite volatility in earnings, due to non-cash charges, we believe CTL's financial profile remains sound. We think free cash flow will be strong enough to easily support the dividend, and we think merger integration efforts will limit the EBITDA pressure in 2012. However, we see risks as CenturyLink has increased in size over a short period of time and looks to realign business in the midst of a slow macroeconomy. In addition, the company's debt leverage has increased.

► Risks to our recommendation and target price include regulatory changes that could pressure revenues; lower-than-expected merger benefits; and an increase in line losses.

► We think the shares, supported by a recent dividend yield of about 7.8%, are fairly valued. Our 12-month target price of $37 is based on a multiple of 5.6X applied to our 2012 EBITDA forecast estimate, a discount to the multiple we use for peers. At our target price, CTL would also trade at a slight discount on a P/E basis, using pro forma estimates.

## Qualitative Risk Assessment

| LOW | MEDIUM | HIGH |
|---|---|---|

Our risk assessment reflects what we see as CTL's relatively strong cash flow generation, offset by the competitive nature of its markets and integration of a large acquisition.

## Quantitative Evaluations

**S&P Quality Ranking** B+

| D | C | B- | B | B+ | A- | A | A+ |
|---|---|---|---|---|---|---|---|

**Relative Strength Rank** STRONG

79

LOWEST = 1      HIGHEST = 99

## Revenue/Earnings Data

### Revenue (Million $)

| | 1Q | 2Q | 3Q | 4Q | Year |
|---|---|---|---|---|---|
| 2011 | 1,696 | 4,406 | 4,596 | -- | -- |
| 2010 | 1,800 | 1,772 | 1,747 | 1,722 | 7,042 |
| 2009 | 636.4 | 634.5 | 1,874 | 1,829 | 4,974 |
| 2008 | 648.6 | 658.1 | 650.1 | 643.0 | 2,600 |
| 2007 | 600.9 | 690.0 | 708.8 | 656.6 | 2,656 |
| 2006 | 611.3 | 608.9 | 619.8 | 607.7 | 2,448 |

### Earnings Per Share ($)

| | | | | | |
|---|---|---|---|---|---|
| 2011 | 0.69 | 0.17 | 0.23 | E0.61 | E2.68 |
| 2010 | 0.84 | 0.88 | 0.76 | 0.74 | 3.13 |
| 2009 | 0.67 | 0.69 | 0.50 | 0.76 | 2.55 |
| 2008 | 0.83 | 0.88 | 0.84 | 1.01 | 3.56 |
| 2007 | 0.68 | 1.00 | 1.01 | 1.05 | 3.72 |
| 2006 | 0.55 | 1.26 | 0.64 | 0.62 | 3.07 |

Fiscal year ended Dec. 31. Next earnings report expected: Mid February. EPS Estimates based on S&P Operating Earnings; historical GAAP earnings are as reported.

## Dividend Data (Dates: mm/dd Payment Date: mm/dd/yy)

| Amount ($) | Date Decl. | Ex-Div. Date | Stk. of Record | Payment Date |
|---|---|---|---|---|
| 0.725 | 01/24 | 02/16 | 02/18 | 02/25/11 |
| 0.725 | 05/18 | 06/02 | 06/06 | 06/16/11 |
| 0.725 | 08/23 | 09/01 | 09/06 | 09/16/11 |
| 0.725 | 11/15 | 12/02 | 12/06 | 12/16/11 |

Dividends have been paid since 1974. Source: Company reports.

---

**Please read the Required Disclosures and Analyst Certification on the last page of this report.**

The McGraw-Hill Companies

# CenturyLink Inc

STANDARD
&POOR'S

## Business Summary November 21, 2011

CORPORATE OVERVIEW. As of September 2011, CenturyLink Inc (formerly CenturyTel) operated 14.8 million telephone access lines, following the acquisition of Embarq in July 2009 and Qwest Communications in April 2011. The company also provided DSL broadband to 5.5 million customers and had partnered to offer wholesale satellite services to customers through CTL's product bundles.

In July 2011, CTL acquired data center and cloud computing company Savvis in a stock and cash deal valued at $2.5 billion. CTL expects the deal to be free cash flow accretive in the first year excluding integration costs. In the second quarter of 2011, Savvis generated $264 million of revenues.

In April 2011, CTL closed on the acquisition of wireline carrier Qwest Communications (Q) in a $22 billion deal, including $11.8 billion in assumed net debt. We see room for synergies following the deal's closing, but we believe it will take three years before CTL can achieve its annual operating cost savings goal of $575 million. CTL aims to exit 2011 with an annual savings run rate of $200 million; as of September 2011, the company had achieved $160 million in savings.

In early July 2009, CTL completed the planned acquisition of its larger fellow telco Embarq Corp. (EQ). The deal involved a swap of 1.37 CTL shares per EQ

share and the assumption of $6 billion of debt. CTL believes it finished the second quarter of 2011 with a $350 million annualized synergy run rate and sees an additional $25 million in such savings.

COMPETITIVE LANDSCAPE. We believe CTL faces challenges from technology substitution to cable telephony and to wireless. The penetration of the necessary broadband connection is smaller in the Tier II and Tier III markets in which CTL previously operated. However, Embarq's operations included larger cities in Florida and Nevada, while Qwest's included larger cities in Colorado and Washington that faced greater competition and were hurt by weakness in the housing market. In the third quarter of 2011, CTL's access lines were down 7.1% from a year earlier.

CORPORATE STRATEGY. We believe CTL's management has a history of wringing cost savings from its operations, with the integration of traffic largely onto one network, and it completed the billing integration of EQ assets in July 2011. In addition to cost savings, we look for CTL to focus on growing the DSL customer base in the new markets to stem the line losses.

## Company Financials Fiscal Year Ended Dec. 31

| Per Share Data ($) | 2010 | 2009 | 2008 | 2007 | 2006 | 2005 | 2004 | 2003 | 2002 | 2001 |
|---|---|---|---|---|---|---|---|---|---|---|
| Tangible Book Value | NM | NM | NM | NM | NM | 1.41 | NM | 0.37 | NM | NM |
| Cash Flow | 7.91 | 7.46 | 8.64 | 8.44 | 7.31 | 6.37 | 5.90 | 5.63 | 4.21 | 5.73 |
| Earnings | 3.13 | 2.55 | 3.56 | 3.72 | 3.07 | 2.49 | 2.41 | 2.38 | 1.33 | 2.41 |
| S&P Core Earnings | 3.04 | 2.77 | 3.33 | 3.37 | 2.52 | 2.30 | 2.36 | 2.35 | 1.08 | 1.21 |
| Dividends | 2.90 | 2.80 | 1.61 | 0.26 | 0.25 | 0.24 | 0.23 | 0.22 | 0.21 | 0.20 |
| Payout Ratio | 93% | 110% | 45% | 7% | 8% | 10% | 10% | 9% | 16% | 8% |
| Prices:High | 46.87 | 37.16 | 42.00 | 49.94 | 44.11 | 36.50 | 35.54 | 36.76 | 35.50 | 39.88 |
| Prices:Low | 14.16 | 23.41 | 20.45 | 39.91 | 32.54 | 29.55 | 26.20 | 25.25 | 21.13 | 25.45 |
| P/E Ratio:High | 15 | 15 | 12 | 13 | 14 | 15 | 15 | 15 | 27 | 17 |
| P/E Ratio:Low | 5 | 9 | 6 | 11 | 11 | 12 | 11 | 11 | 16 | 11 |

| Income Statement Analysis (Million $) | | | | | | | | | | |
|---|---|---|---|---|---|---|---|---|---|---|
| Revenue | 7,042 | 4,974 | 2,600 | 2,656 | 2,448 | 2,479 | 2,407 | 2,381 | 1,972 | 2,117 |
| Depreciation | 1,434 | 975 | 524 | 536 | 524 | 532 | 501 | 471 | 412 | 473 |
| Maintenance | NA | NA | NA | NA | NA | NA | NA | NA | NA | NA |
| Construction Credits | NA | NA | NA | NA | NA | NA | NA | NA | NA | NA |
| Effective Tax Rate | NA | 37.1% | 34.7% | 32.4% | 37.4% | 37.8% | 38.4% | 35.2% | 35.3% | 37.2% |
| Net Income | 949 | 511 | 3,294 | 418 | 370 | 334 | 337 | 345 | 190 | 343 |
| S&P Core Earnings | 917 | 551 | 342 | 377 | 302 | 307 | 330 | 339 | 153 | 171 |

| Balance Sheet & Other Financial Data (Million $) | | | | | | | | | | |
|---|---|---|---|---|---|---|---|---|---|---|
| Gross Property | NA | 15,557 | 8,869 | 8,666 | 7,894 | 7,801 | 7,431 | 3,455 | 6,668 | 5,839 |
| Net Property | NA | 9,097 | 2,896 | 3,108 | 3,109 | 3,304 | 3,341 | 3,455 | 3,532 | 3,000 |
| Capital Expenditures | 864 | 755 | 287 | 326 | 314 | 415 | 385 | 378 | 386 | 507 |
| Total Capital | 16,975 | 17,221 | 7,311 | 6,962 | 5,604 | 5,993 | 6,172 | 6,588 | 6,666 | 4,425 |
| Fixed Charges Coverage | NA | 3.2 | 3.8 | 3.9 | 4.4 | 3.6 | 3.6 | 3.4 | 2.3 | 3.4 |
| Capitalization:Long Term Debt | NA | 7,254 | 3,294 | 2,734 | 2,413 | 2,376 | 2,762 | 3,109 | 3,578 | 2,088 |
| Capitalization:Preferred | NA | 0.24 | 0.24 | 6.97 | 7.45 | 7.85 | 7.98 | 7.98 | 7.98 | 7.98 |
| Capitalization:Common | 9,647 | 9,461 | 3,163 | 3,402 | 3,184 | 3,609 | 3,402 | 3,471 | 3,080 | 2,329 |
| % Return on Revenue | 13.5 | 10.3 | 14.1 | 15.8 | 15.1 | 13.5 | 14.0 | 14.5 | 9.6 | 16.2 |
| % Return on Invested Capital | NA | 7.5 | 7.5 | 9.5 | 9.8 | 8.8 | 8.6 | 8.6 | 7.4 | 12.2 |
| % Return on Common Equity | 9.9 | 8.1 | 11.1 | 12.7 | 10.9 | 9.5 | 9.8 | 10.5 | 7.0 | 15.7 |
| % Earned on Net Property | NA | 20.6 | 24.2 | 25.5 | 20.8 | 38.2 | 36.9 | 35.0 | 31.5 | 34.6 |
| % Long Term Debt of Capitalization | 43.1 | 43.4 | 51.0 | 44.5 | 43.1 | 39.6 | 44.8 | 47.2 | 53.7 | 47.2 |
| Capital % Preferred | NA | Nil | Nil | 0.1 | 0.1 | 0.1 | 0.1 | 0.1 | 0.1 | 0.2 |
| Capitalization:% Common | NA | 56.6 | 49.0 | 55.4 | 56.8 | 60.2 | 55.1 | 52.7 | 46.2 | 52.6 |

Data as orig reptd.; bef. results of disc opers/spec. items. Per share data adj. for stk. divs.; EPS diluted. E-Estimated. NA-Not Available. NM-Not Meaningful. NR-Not Ranked. UR-Under Review.

**Office:** 100 CenturyLink Drive, Monroe, LA 71203.
**Telephone:** 318-388-9000.
**Website:** http://www.centurylink.com
**Chrmn:** W.A. Owens

**Pres & CEO:** G.F. Post, III
**Vice Chrmn:** H.P. Perry
**COO & EVP:** K.A. Puckett
**EVP & CFO:** R.S. Ewing, Jr.

**Investor Contact:** T. Davis (800-833-1188)
**Board Members:** C. L. Biggs, V. Boulet, P. C. Brown, R. A. Gephardt, W. B. Hanks, G. J. McCray, III, C. G. Melville, Jr., E. A. Mueller, F. R. Nichols, W. A. Owens, H. P. Perry, G. F. Post, III, M. J. Roberts, L. A. Siegel, J. A. Unruh, J. R. Zimmel

**Founded:** 1968
**Domicile:** Louisiana
**Employees:** 20,300

The McGraw·Hill Companies

# Cerner Corp

STANDARD
&POOR'S

| S&P Recommendation | STRONG BUY ★★★★★ | Price $57.02 (as of Nov 25, 2011) | 12-Mo. Target Price $80.00 | Investment Style Large-Cap Growth |
|---|---|---|---|---|

**GICS Sector** Health Care
**Sub-Industry** Health Care Technology

**Summary** This company is a leading supplier of health care information technology (HCIT) solutions, health care devices and related services.

## Key Stock Statistics (Source S&P, Vickers, company reports)

| | | | | | | | |
|---|---|---|---|---|---|---|---|
| 52-Wk Range | $74.39– 43.48 | S&P Oper. EPS 2011**E** | 1.75 | Market Capitalization(B) | $9.660 | Beta | 0.93 |
| Trailing 12-Month EPS | $1.65 | S&P Oper. EPS 2012**E** | 2.16 | Yield (%) | Nil | S&P 3-Yr. Proj. EPS CAGR(%) | 24 |
| Trailing 12-Month P/E | 34.6 | P/E on S&P Oper. EPS 2011**E** | 32.6 | Dividend Rate/Share | Nil | S&P Credit Rating | NA |
| $10K Invested 5 Yrs Ago | $23,660 | Common Shares Outstg. (M) | 169.4 | Institutional Ownership (%) | 85 | | |

## Price Performance

30-Week Mov. Avg. · · · 10-Week Mov. Avg. – – GAAP Earnings vs. Previous Year   Volume Above Avg. STARS
12-Mo. Target Price — Relative Strength — ▲ Up ▼ Down ▶ No Change   Below Avg. ★

Options: ASE, CBOE, P, Ph

Analysis prepared by Equity Analyst **Jeffrey Loo, CFA** on Oct 31, 2011, when the stock traded at **$63.43**.

## Highlights

➤ We expect sales to rise 18% in 2011 to $2.18 billion, and 13% in 2012 to $2.46 billion, as we see the benefit of accelerating industry growth due to the American Recovery and Reinvestment Act of 2009 (ARRA) and the HITECH Act, which incentivizes hospitals and clinicians to adopt health care information technology. We believe the release of the final "meaningful use" rules provides flexibility and will lead to broader adoption of health care IT, positively affecting the industry and CERN. "Meaningful Use" incentive payments begin in 2011 and progressing stages of meaningful use will continue to drive sales as companies need to meet various requirements. We look for ARRA to drive solid bookings throughout the year, aided by new clients. We believe over 30% of bookings in 2011 will be from new clients and we see this trend continuing in 2012.

➤ We project gross margins to narrow 250 basis points as system sales outweigh higher support and maintenance margins. But we see operating margins improving 150 bps on leverage.

➤ Inclusive of stock compensation costs estimated at $0.11, our 2011 and 2012 EPS forecasts are $1.75 and $2.16, respectively.

## Investment Rationale/Risk

➤ We recently upgraded our recommendation on the shares to strong buy, from buy. We see continued robust growth throughout 2011 and 2012 as health care firms seek to meet meaningful use requirements along with other regulatory issues such as health care reform and the pending transition to ICD 10 codes. As a result, bookings have been robust and we expect continued strong bookings into 2012. Bookings of $650 million in the third quarter were the second highest in company history driving backlog up 21% from a year ago to $5.66 billion as of September 30. However, we note that implementation many be more complex and time-consuming than anticipated, thereby slowing the recognition of revenue.

➤ Risks to our recommendation and target price include increased competition for CERN's core HCIT products, and further slowdowns in hospital capital spending.

➤ Our 12-month target price of $80 is based on a PEG ratio of 1.5X, a premium to peers, based on our 2012 EPS estimate of $2.16 and a projected three-year EPS growth rate of 24%. We believe a premium valuation is warranted based on CERN's robust growth and market share.

## Qualitative Risk Assessment

| LOW | MEDIUM | HIGH |
|---|---|---|

Our risk assessment reflects CERN's established market position in the HCIT market and its broad customer base, weighed against a highly competitive environment for its products and services as well as the risk of technological obsolescence.

## Quantitative Evaluations

**S&P Quality Ranking** B+

| D | C | B- | B | B+ | A- | A | A+ |
|---|---|---|---|---|---|---|---|

**Relative Strength Rank** MODERATE

31

LOWEST = 1     HIGHEST = 99

## Revenue/Earnings Data

**Revenue (Million $)**

| | 1Q | 2Q | 3Q | 4Q | Year |
|---|---|---|---|---|---|
| 2011 | 491.7 | 524.2 | 571.6 | -- | -- |
| 2010 | 431.3 | 456.0 | 462.7 | 500.2 | 1,850 |
| 2009 | 392.3 | 403.8 | 409.4 | 466.3 | 1,672 |
| 2008 | 384.8 | 402.8 | 422.7 | 465.7 | 1,676 |
| 2007 | 365.9 | 386.6 | 372.9 | 394.5 | 1,520 |
| 2006 | 321.2 | 330.6 | 345.5 | 380.8 | 1,378 |

**Earnings Per Share ($)**

| | | | | | |
|---|---|---|---|---|---|
| 2011 | 0.38 | 0.42 | 0.45 | E0.50 | E1.75 |
| 2010 | 0.29 | 0.33 | 0.36 | 0.41 | 1.39 |
| 2009 | 0.25 | 0.26 | 0.29 | 0.36 | 1.16 |
| 2008 | 0.22 | 0.21 | 0.27 | 0.43 | 1.13 |
| 2007 | 0.17 | 0.16 | 0.19 | 0.25 | 0.77 |
| 2006 | 0.13 | 0.15 | 0.17 | 0.24 | 0.67 |

Fiscal year ended Dec. 31. Next earnings report expected: Early February. EPS Estimates based on S&P Operating Earnings; historical GAAP earnings are as reported.

## Dividend Data (Dates: mm/dd Payment Date: mm/dd/yy)

| Amount ($) | Date Decl. | Ex-Div. Date | Stk. of Record | Payment Date |
|---|---|---|---|---|
| 2-for-1 | 05/27 | 06/27 | 06/15 | 06/24/11 |

Source: Company reports.

---

**Please read the Required Disclosures and Analyst Certification on the last page of this report.**

The McGraw-Hill Companies

# Cerner Corp

**STANDARD
&POOR'S**

## Business Summary October 31, 2011

CORPORATE OVERVIEW. Cerner Corp. is the largest standalone health care information technology (HCIT) company providing health care information technology solutions and devices and related services to health care organizations and consumers. Domestic (U.S.) revenues accounted for 84% of the total in 2010 (84% in 2009).

Revenues are derived from system sales, support, maintenance, and services. System sales (30% of revenues in 2010; 30% in 2009) includes sales of software, deployment period upgrade rights, installation fees, content subscriptions, transaction processing and hardware and sublicensed software. Support, maintenance and services (68%; 68%) includes ongoing support and services provided to clients. Services includes professional services excluding installation, and managed services. Reimbursed travel, which includes reimbursable out-of-pocket expenses related to client service activities, accounted for the remaining 2% (2%).

CORPORATE STRATEGY. Cerner intends to increase its market share by providing innovative solutions and services to existing and new clients as well as by capturing some potential clients who wish to upgrade their systems to

avail themselves of the incentives offered by the Health Information Technology for Economic and Clinical Health Act (HITECH) provisions of the American Recovery and Reinvestment Act (ARRA). We believe HCIT is in its nascent stages in the U.S., based on a recent article in FT Health magazine that estimated only about 20% of doctors' offices and 10% of hospitals currently utilize "some form" of HCIT.

Cerner, currently operating in over 25 countries, plans to increase its sales outside the U.S. as other countries realize the importance of HCIT. It also expects to increase its market share by making its offerings affordable to smaller community hospitals, critical access hospitals and physician practices, as well as by selling software as a service. It also plans to offer solutions beyond the HCIT market, similar to its current offerings, in the form of clinic, pharmacy and wellness services provided directly to employers.

## Company Financials Fiscal Year Ended Dec. 31

| Per Share Data ($) | 2010 | 2009 | 2008 | 2007 | 2006 | 2005 | 2004 | 2003 | 2002 | 2001 |
|---|---|---|---|---|---|---|---|---|---|---|
| Tangible Book Value | 8.77 | 7.11 | 5.57 | 4.63 | 4.69 | 3.72 | 3.53 | 2.95 | 2.62 | 2.49 |
| Cash Flow | 2.12 | 1.91 | 1.71 | 1.36 | 1.44 | 1.28 | 1.03 | 0.77 | 0.72 | 0.04 |
| Earnings | 1.39 | 1.16 | 1.13 | 0.77 | 0.67 | 0.55 | 0.43 | 0.29 | 0.33 | -0.30 |
| S&P Core Earnings | 1.39 | 1.16 | 1.16 | 0.77 | 0.67 | 0.48 | 0.37 | 0.20 | 0.24 | 0.19 |
| Dividends | Nil | Nil | Nil | Nil | Nil | Nil | Nil | Nil | Nil | Nil |
| Payout Ratio | Nil | Nil | Nil | Nil | Nil | Nil | Nil | Nil | Nil | Nil |
| Prices:High | 48.88 | 42.99 | 29.91 | 33.09 | 25.29 | 24.63 | 13.48 | 11.63 | 14.26 | 15.38 |
| Prices:Low | 36.03 | 16.69 | 15.19 | 22.06 | 16.25 | 11.80 | 8.97 | 4.09 | 6.83 | 7.00 |
| P/E Ratio:High | 35 | 37 | 26 | 43 | 38 | 45 | 31 | 39 | 43 | NM |
| P/E Ratio:Low | 26 | 14 | 13 | 29 | 24 | 21 | 21 | 14 | 21 | NM |

| Income Statement Analysis (Million $) | | | | | | | | | | |
|---|---|---|---|---|---|---|---|---|---|---|
| Revenue | 1,850 | 1,672 | 1,676 | 1,520 | 1,378 | 1,161 | 926 | 840 | 752 | 543 |
| Operating Income | 480 | 418 | 412 | 303 | 291 | 261 | 202 | 147 | 148 | 109 |
| Depreciation | 124 | 126 | 96.7 | 153 | 125 | 114 | 90.8 | 69.3 | 57.3 | 47.3 |
| Interest Expense | 6.91 | 8.49 | 10.6 | 11.9 | 0.70 | 5.86 | 6.15 | 7.02 | 5.56 | 4.43 |
| Pretax Income | 362 | 293 | 281 | 204 | 52.2 | 135 | 108 | 71.2 | 80.6 | -63.3 |
| Effective Tax Rate | NA | 33.9% | 33.0% | 37.7% | NM | 36.2% | 40.1% | 39.9% | 39.5% | NM |
| Net Income | 237 | 193 | 189 | 127 | 110 | 86.3 | 64.6 | 42.8 | 48.8 | -42.4 |
| S&P Core Earnings | 237 | 193 | 194 | 127 | 110 | 75.3 | 54.9 | 29.4 | 35.2 | 24.9 |

| Balance Sheet & Other Financial Data (Million $) | | | | | | | | | | |
|---|---|---|---|---|---|---|---|---|---|---|
| Cash | 571 | 559 | 309 | 345 | 163 | 113 | 190 | 122 | 143 | 108 |
| Current Assets | 1,146 | 1,146 | 859 | 819 | 746 | 652 | 509 | 429 | 448 | 348 |
| Total Assets | 2,423 | 2,149 | 1,881 | 1,690 | 1,491 | 1,304 | 982 | 859 | 779 | 712 |
| Current Liabilities | 306 | 358 | 341 | 288 | 301 | 260 | 199 | 177 | 166 | 158 |
| Long Term Debt | 67.9 | 95.5 | 111 | 178 | 187 | 194 | 109 | 125 | 137 | 92.1 |
| Common Equity | 1,905 | 1,581 | 1,311 | 1,132 | 918 | 761 | 597 | 495 | 441 | 395 |
| Total Capital | 1,998 | 1,701 | 1,454 | 1,326 | 1,176 | 1,029 | 777 | 680 | 578 | 549 |
| Capital Expenditures | 102 | 131 | 108 | 181 | 131 | 64.8 | 44.2 | 26.8 | 33.2 | 25.7 |
| Cash Flow | 362 | 319 | 285 | 226 | 235 | 200 | 155 | 112 | 106 | 4.94 |
| Current Ratio | 3.8 | 3.2 | 2.5 | 2.8 | 2.5 | 2.5 | 2.6 | 2.4 | 2.7 | 2.2 |
| % Long Term Debt of Capitalization | 3.4 | 5.6 | 7.7 | 13.4 | 15.9 | 18.9 | 14.0 | 18.3 | 23.7 | 16.8 |
| % Net Income of Revenue | 12.8 | 11.6 | 11.3 | 8.4 | 8.0 | 7.4 | 7.0 | 5.1 | 6.5 | NM |
| % Return on Assets | 10.4 | 9.6 | 10.6 | 8.0 | 7.9 | 7.5 | 7.0 | 5.2 | 6.5 | NM |
| % Return on Equity | 13.6 | 13.4 | 15.4 | 12.4 | 13.1 | 12.7 | 11.8 | 9.1 | 11.7 | NM |

Data as orig reptd.; bef. results of disc opers/spec. items. Per share data adj. for stk. divs.; EPS diluted. E-Estimated. NA-Not Available. NM-Not Meaningful. NR-Not Ranked. UR-Under Review.

**Office:** 2800 Rockcreek Parkway, North Kansas City, MO 64117.
**Telephone:** 816-201-1024.
**Email:** invrelations@cerner.com
**Website:** http://www.cerner.com

**Chrmn & CEO:** N. Patterson
**Vice Chrmn:** C. Illig
**COO:** M.R. Nill
**CFO & Treas:** M.G. Naughton

**Chief Acctg Officer:** M.R. Battaglioli
**Investor Contact:** A. Kells (816-201-2445)
**Board Members:** G. E. Bisbee, Jr., D. A. Cortese, J. C. Danforth, L. M. Dillman, C. Illig, W. B. Neaves, N. Patterson, W. D. Zollars

**Founded:** 1980
**Domicile:** Delaware
**Employees:** 8,200

*The McGraw-Hill Companies*

# CF Industries Holdings Inc

STANDARD
&POOR'S

| S&P Recommendation | HOLD ★★★☆☆ | Price $139.75 (as of Nov 25, 2011) | 12-Mo. Target Price $184.00 | Investment Style Large-Cap Value |
|---|---|---|---|---|

**GICS Sector** Materials
**Sub-Industry** Fertilizers & Agricultural Chemicals

**Summary** This company is a major manufacturer and distributor of nitrogen and phosphate fertilizer products in North America.

## Key Stock Statistics (Source S&P, Vickers, company reports)

| | | | | | | | |
|---|---|---|---|---|---|---|---|
| 52-Wk Range | $192.70– 115.34 | S&P Oper. EPS 2011E | 21.96 | Market Capitalization(B) | $9.269 | Beta | 1.09 |
| Trailing 12-Month EPS | $18.18 | S&P Oper. EPS 2012E | 22.31 | Yield (%) | 1.14 | S&P 3-Yr. Proj. EPS CAGR(%) | 28 |
| Trailing 12-Month P/E | 7.7 | P/E on S&P Oper. EPS 2011E | 6.4 | Dividend Rate/Share | $1.60 | S&P Credit Rating | NA |
| $10K Invested 5 Yrs Ago | $62,518 | Common Shares Outstg. (M) | 66.3 | Institutional Ownership (%) | NM | | |

## Price Performance

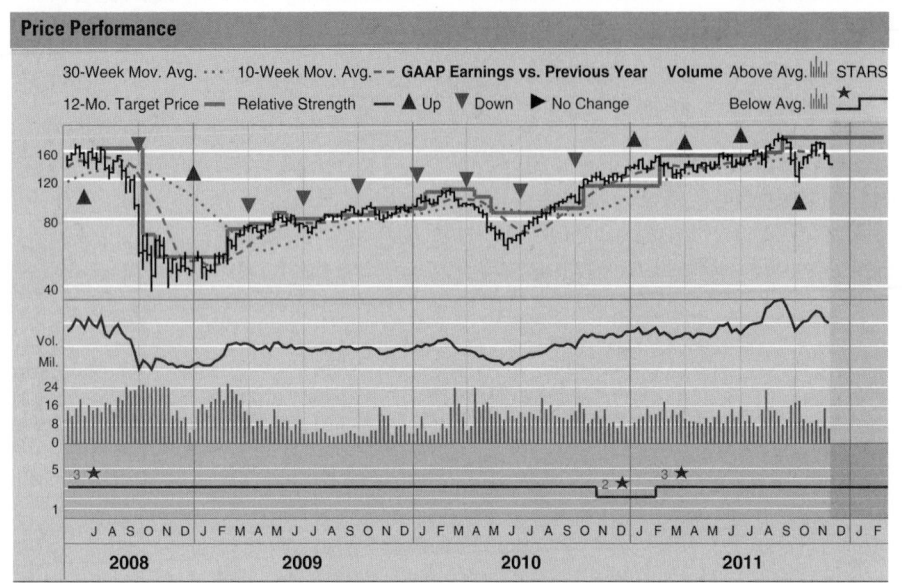

Options: ASE, CBOE, Ph

Analysis prepared by Equity Analyst **Kevin Kirkeby** on Sep 06, 2011, when the stock traded at **$181.89**.

## Qualitative Risk Assessment

| LOW | MEDIUM | HIGH |
|---|---|---|

Our risk assessment reflects the cyclical and seasonal nature of the agriculture industry and the company's reliance on the volatile natural gas industry for much of its raw materials, partly offset by the competitive advantage of having many overseas suppliers.

## Quantitative Evaluations

**S&P Quality Ranking** NR

| D | C | B- | B | B+ | A- | A | A+ |
|---|---|---|---|---|---|---|---|

**Relative Strength Rank** WEAK

28

LOWEST = 1          HIGHEST = 99

## Revenue/Earnings Data

**Revenue (Million $)**

| | 1Q | 2Q | 3Q | 4Q | Year |
|---|---|---|---|---|---|
| 2011 | 1,174 | 1,802 | 1,404 | -- | -- |
| 2010 | 502.4 | 1,308 | 917.1 | 1,238 | 3,965 |
| 2009 | 680.6 | 991.0 | 430.1 | 506.7 | 2,608 |
| 2008 | 667.3 | 1,161 | 1,021 | 1,072 | 3,921 |
| 2007 | 447.7 | 848.9 | 582.9 | 852.5 | 2,757 |
| 2006 | 400.5 | 664.8 | 378.0 | 506.2 | 1,950 |

**Earnings Per Share ($)**

| | | | | | |
|---|---|---|---|---|---|
| 2011 | 3.91 | 6.75 | 4.73 | E6.36 | E21.96 |
| 2010 | -0.09 | 1.54 | 0.67 | 2.78 | 5.34 |
| 2009 | 1.28 | 4.33 | 0.78 | 1.04 | 7.42 |
| 2008 | 2.77 | 5.02 | 0.82 | 3.59 | 12.14 |
| 2007 | 1.02 | 1.65 | 1.52 | 2.38 | 6.57 |
| 2006 | -0.45 | 0.77 | 0.13 | 0.14 | 0.60 |

Fiscal year ended Dec. 31. Next earnings report expected: NA. EPS Estimates based on S&P Operating Earnings; historical GAAP earnings are as reported.

## Dividend Data (Dates: mm/dd Payment Date: mm/dd/yy)

| Amount ($) | Date Decl. | Ex-Div. Date | Stk. of Record | Payment Date |
|---|---|---|---|---|
| 0.100 | 02/02 | 02/10 | 02/14 | 03/01/11 |
| 0.100 | 04/29 | 05/12 | 05/16 | 05/27/11 |
| 0.400 | 08/04 | 08/11 | 08/15 | 08/29/11 |
| 0.400 | 10/21 | 11/09 | 11/14 | 11/29/11 |

Dividends have been paid since 2005. Source: Company reports.

## Highlights

➤ We are looking for CF to achieve 2011 revenues of $6.2 billion, up 57%. The additional three months of contribution from the Terra Industries acquisition, by our calculations, adds about 10 percentage points to growth. Still, we think the primary driver of revenues will be higher average selling prices, reflecting rising grain prices and tight fertilizer supplies around the globe. We believe CF's scope to expand overall production is limited due to capacity constraints and are forecasting relatively flat pro-forma volumes in both 2011 and 2012. We look for revenues to increase less than 1% in 2012 as average selling prices stabilize.

➤ We expect margins to widen in 2011 and 2012 due to higher selling prices, as well as cost-saving initiatives tied to combining CF's operations with Terra's. CF has taken $110 million in annualized costs out of the operations and has at least $25 million more to be realized in the next year. We expect natural gas costs to be relatively stable, as rising shale gas production covers increases in demand into 2012.

➤ Excluding a $0.14 net benefit from asset sales and mark-to-market adjustments, our EPS estimate for 2011 is $20.65.

## Investment Rationale/Risk

➤ Following its April 2010 acquisition of Terra Industries, CF is now among the largest global producers of phosphate and nitrogen. Because the U.S. is a net importer of nitrogen fertilizer, we believe CF, as a domestic producer, benefits from a generally lower cost base, especially during periods of rising demand and selling prices. Market fundamentals appear favorable, but we think this is already reflected in above-average valuations.

➤ Risks to our recommendation and target price include a sharp rise in key input prices such as natural gas or sulfur, a decrease in grain prices that reduces the incentive to seek more yield through added fertilizer usage, a lowering of Chinese tariffs on fertilizer exports, and stricter environmental regulations, especially those targeting carbon dioxide emissions.

➤ Our discounted cash flow model assumes free cash flow averaging $1.5 billion over the next three years, a 9.8% WACC and 2.0% terminal growth, and calculates intrinsic value of $169. We apply a multiple of 9.9X, above the historical average of 9.0X, to our four-quarter forward EPS estimate for a $200 value. Blending the two, we arrive at our target price of $184.

# CF Industries Holdings Inc

STANDARD
&POOR'S

## Business Summary September 06, 2011

CORPORATE OVERVIEW. CF Industries is a major manufacturer and distributor of nitrogen and phosphate fertilizer products in North America. In April 2010, CF completed the $4.7 billion acquisition of Terra Industries, boosting its revenue base by about 60%, based on 2009 figures. Principal products of the combined entity are ammonia, urea, urea ammonium nitrate solution (UAN), diammonium phosphate (DAP) and monoammonium phosphate (MAP). Revenues in 2010 for CF, including about nine months' contribution from Terra Industries, were $4.0 billion. This is based on sales of 11.5 million tons of nitrogen-related fertilizers and 1.9 million tons of phosphate fertilizers. Core markets and distribution facilities for the company are concentrated in the midwestern U.S. grain-producing states.

PRIMARY BUSINESS DYNAMICS. Nitrogen, phosphates and potash are the three primary plant nutrients that are essential for proper crop nutrition and maximum yields. There are no substitutes for them, and they are generally not substitutable for each other. Each of these fertilizers is actively traded in the global marketplace, with price being the primary means of differentiation. The U.S. is a net exporter of phosphate fertilizers, while it tends to import a significant amount of nitrogen-based product. Producers typically build their inventories ahead of the spring planting season when demand is the highest, and over the summer in advance of post-harvest fertilizer applications.

In 2010, natural gas purchases accounted for about 45% of the combined company's total cost of sales of nitrogen fertilizers and a substantially higher percentage of cash costs. CF uses, and plans to continue using, a combination of spot and term purchases of varied duration from a number of suppliers to maintain a reliable, competitively priced natural gas supply, and also uses certain financial instruments to hedge natural gas prices. It has developed a forward pricing program under which it traditionally sells about half of its nitrogen fertilizer, and this system provides some margin certainty.

CORPORATE STRATEGY. CF's manufacturing facilities are competitive, due, in our view, to their large scale and a modular configuration that allows it to adjust production to changing market conditions. Its distribution system is flexible and strategically located to serve its midwestern customers. The company's Donaldsonville, LA, nitrogen fertilizer facility is the largest in North America, and its Medicine Hat, Alberta, plant is the second largest, which gives it significant economies-of-scale advantages over its competitors. Through the purchase of Terra Industries, CF acquired interests in six nitrogen facilities in the U.S., as well as joint ventures in Trinidad and the United Kingdom.

## Company Financials Fiscal Year Ended Dec. 31

| Per Share Data ($) | 2010 | 2009 | 2008 | 2007 | 2006 | 2005 | 2004 | 2003 | 2002 | 2001 |
|---|---|---|---|---|---|---|---|---|---|---|
| Tangible Book Value | 26.77 | 35.58 | 27.72 | 21.09 | 13.88 | 13.73 | 12.96 | NA | NA | NA |
| Cash Flow | 11.24 | 9.48 | 13.93 | 8.06 | 2.32 | 1.11 | 3.21 | 1.57 | 2.14 | 0.77 |
| Earnings | 5.34 | 7.42 | 12.14 | 6.57 | 0.60 | -0.66 | 1.23 | -0.33 | -0.51 | -1.35 |
| S&P Core Earnings | 5.11 | 7.30 | 11.91 | 6.56 | 0.63 | -0.68 | 1.22 | -0.35 | NA | NA |
| Dividends | 0.40 | 0.40 | 0.40 | 0.08 | 0.08 | 0.02 | NA | NA | NA | NA |
| Payout Ratio | 8% | 5% | 3% | 1% | 13% | NM | NA | NA | NA | NA |
| Prices:High | 138.74 | 95.13 | 172.99 | 118.88 | 26.60 | 18.00 | NA | NA | NA | NA |
| Prices:Low | 57.56 | 42.30 | 37.71 | 25.70 | 12.91 | 11.19 | NA | NA | NA | NA |
| P/E Ratio:High | 26 | 13 | 14 | 18 | 44 | NM | NA | NA | NA | NA |
| P/E Ratio:Low | 11 | 6 | 3 | 4 | 22 | NM | NA | NA | NA | NA |

| Income Statement Analysis (Million $) | | | | | | | | | | |
|---|---|---|---|---|---|---|---|---|---|---|
| Revenue | 3,965 | 2,608 | 3,921 | 2,757 | 1,950 | 1,908 | 1,651 | 1,370 | 1,014 | 1,160 |
| Operating Income | 1,220 | 838 | 1,313 | 686 | 166 | 236 | 258 | 99.4 | 89.6 | -32.1 |
| Depreciation | 294 | 101 | 101 | 84.5 | 94.6 | 97.5 | 109 | 105 | 108 | 102 |
| Interest Expense | 221 | 1.50 | 1.60 | 1.70 | 2.90 | 14.0 | 22.7 | 23.9 | 23.6 | 31.8 |
| Pretax Income | 714 | 694 | 1,180 | 627 | 81.8 | 110 | 132 | -25.0 | -38.3 | -151 |
| Effective Tax Rate | NA | 35.4% | 32.1% | 31.8% | 24.1% | NM | 31.3% | NM | NM | NM |
| Net Income | 441 | 366 | 685 | 373 | 33.3 | -36.2 | 67.7 | -18.4 | -28.1 | -59.7 |
| S&P Core Earnings | 334 | 360 | 671 | 372 | 34.9 | -37.1 | 67.5 | -19.7 | NA | NA |

| Balance Sheet & Other Financial Data (Million $) | | | | | | | | | | |
|---|---|---|---|---|---|---|---|---|---|---|
| Cash | 801 | 882 | 625 | 861 | 25.4 | 37.4 | 72.8 | 169 | NA | NA |
| Current Assets | 1,341 | 1,283 | 1,433 | 1,279 | 633 | 576 | NA | 526 | NA | NA |
| Total Assets | 8,759 | 2,495 | 2,388 | 2,013 | 1,290 | 1,228 | 1,149 | 1,405 | NA | NA |
| Current Liabilities | 947 | 480 | 818 | 629 | 353 | 341 | NA | 350 | NA | NA |
| Long Term Debt | 1,954 | 4.70 | Nil | 4.90 | 4.20 | 4.20 | 4.01 | 255 | NA | NA |
| Common Equity | 4,050 | 1,729 | 1,338 | 1,187 | 767 | 756 | 720 | -0.79 | NA | NA |
| Total Capital | 6,775 | 1,750 | 1,357 | 1,241 | 785 | 782 | 724 | 1,038 | NA | NA |
| Capital Expenditures | 258 | 236 | 142 | 105 | 59.3 | 69.4 | 33.7 | 28.7 | 26.3 | 41.7 |
| Cash Flow | 735 | 467 | 785 | 457 | 128 | 61.3 | 176 | 86.6 | 118 | 42.3 |
| Current Ratio | 1.4 | 2.7 | 1.8 | 2.0 | 1.8 | 1.7 | NA | 1.5 | NA | NA |
| % Long Term Debt of Capitalization | 28.8 | 0.3 | Nil | 0.4 | 0.5 | 0.5 | 0.6 | 24.6 | Nil | NA |
| % Net Income of Revenue | 11.1 | 14.0 | 17.5 | 13.5 | 1.7 | NM | 4.1 | NM | NM | NM |
| % Return on Assets | 7.8 | 15.0 | 31.1 | 22.6 | 2.6 | NM | NA | NA | NA | NA |
| % Return on Equity | 15.3 | 23.8 | 54.2 | 38.2 | 4.4 | NM | NA | NA | NA | NA |

Data as orig reptd.; bef. results of disc opers/spec. items. Per share data adj. for stk. divs.; EPS diluted. 2004 pro forma as adjusted; bal. sheet and book val. as of Jun. 30, 2005. Prior to 2005, per sh. data based on pro forma shs. E-Estimated. NA-Not Available. NM-Not Meaningful. NR-Not Ranked. UR-Under Review.

**Office:** 4 Parkway North, Suite 400, Deerfield, IL 60015-2590.
**Telephone:** 847-405-2400.
**Website:** http://www.cfindustries.com
**Chrmn, Pres & CEO:** S.R. Wilson

**SVP & CFO:** D.P. Kelleher
**Treas:** S.C. Munsell
**Secy & General Counsel:** D.C. Barnard
**Investor Contact:** T. Huch (847-405-2515)

**Board Members:** R. C. Arzbaecher, W. W. Creek, W. Davisson, S. A. Furbacher, S. J. Hagge, D. R. Harvey, J. D. Johnson, R. G. Kuhbach, E. A. Schmitt, S. R. Wilson

**Founded:** 1946
**Domicile:** Delaware
**Employees:** 2,500

The McGraw-Hill Companies

# Chesapeake Energy Corp

**STANDARD &POOR'S**

| S&P Recommendation **BUY** ★★★★☆ | Price<br>$23.78 (as of Nov 29, 2011) | 12-Mo. Target Price<br>$38.00 | Investment Style<br>Large-Cap Blend |
|---|---|---|---|

**GICS Sector** Energy
**Sub-Industry** Oil & Gas Exploration & Production

**Summary** One of the largest independent exploration and production companies in the U.S., CHK focuses on U.S. onshore natural gas production east of the Rocky Mountains.

## Key Stock Statistics (Source S&P, Vickers, company reports)

| | | | | | | |
|---|---|---|---|---|---|---|
| 52-Wk Range | $35.95– 21.11 | S&P Oper. EPS 2011E | 2.88 | Market Capitalization(B) | $15.210 | Beta | 1.30 |
| Trailing 12-Month EPS | $1.99 | S&P Oper. EPS 2012E | 2.73 | Yield (%) | 1.47 | S&P 3-Yr. Proj. EPS CAGR(%) | 2 |
| Trailing 12-Month P/E | 12.0 | P/E on S&P Oper. EPS 2011E | 8.3 | Dividend Rate/Share | $0.35 | S&P Credit Rating | BB+ |
| $10K Invested 5 Yrs Ago | $7,272 | Common Shares Outstg. (M) | 639.6 | Institutional Ownership (%) | 78 | | |

## Price Performance

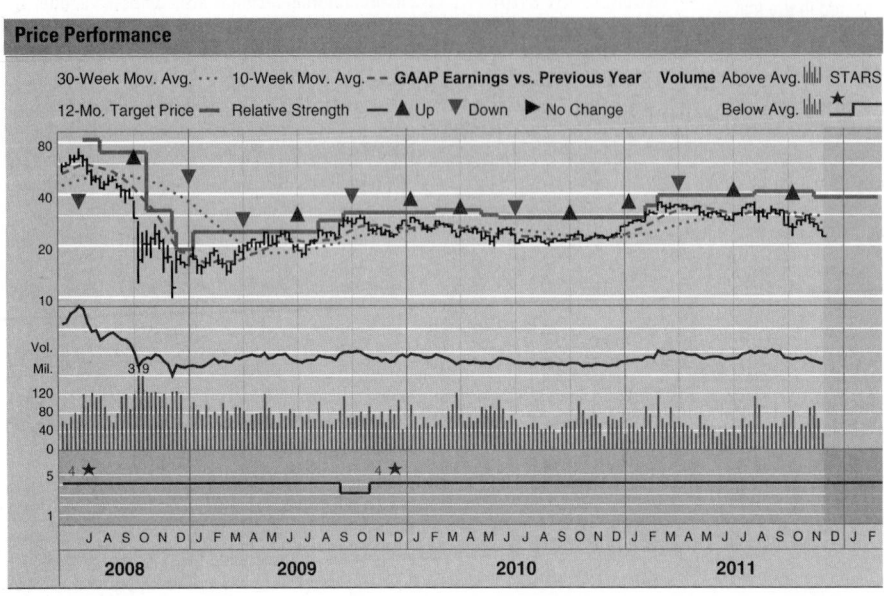

Options: ASE, CBOE, P, Ph

Analysis prepared by Equity Analyst **Michael Kay** on Nov 29, 2011, when the stock traded at **$23.36**.

## Qualitative Risk Assessment

| LOW | MEDIUM | HIGH |
|---|---|---|

Our risk assessment reflects CHK's business profile in a volatile, cyclical and capital-intensive segment of the energy industry. We believe CHK's financial strategy is aggressive, as it has been one of the most active acquirers in exploration and production, and one of the most active users of commodity hedges. This is partly offset by what we see as strong volume growth and good drilling prospects.

## Quantitative Evaluations

**S&P Quality Ranking**   B-

| D | C | B- | B | B+ | A- | A | A+ |
|---|---|---|---|---|---|---|---|

**Relative Strength Rank**   WEAK
20
LOWEST = 1     HIGHEST = 99

## Highlights

► CHK recently updated strategic and financial plans for 2011-2012. Its "25/25" plan sets two-year production growth targets at 25% (recently raised to 30%) while targeting debt reduction of 25%, through asset monetizations, asset sales, and reduced leasehold spending. Also, on an increased focus on higher-margin liquids plays, CHK expects liquids production during this span to grow over 190%, versus 6% for gas, and to increase its liquids mix to 20%-25% of production (15% currently). Production was up 14% in 2010 (10% in 2009). CHK has announced several liquids-rich opportunities and has core acreage in most major U.S. shales. CHK is running 171 operated rigs and about 105 non-operated rigs, with 50% of 2011 capex and 75% of 2012's being allocated to liquids drilling.

► CHK has entered seven JV asset monetizations. Most recently it entered into a letter of intent for a $2.1 billion Utica Shale JV, selling a 25% stake in 570,000 net acres. It currently operates 5 rigs at Utica and plans to reach 20 rigs by the end of 2012.

► Adjusted 2010 EPS grew 16% to $2.97 on rising oil prices and mix. We see EPS of $2.88 in 2011 and $2.73 in 2012, reflecting weak gas prices.

## Investment Rationale/Risk

► From 2006-2009, CHK was at the center of a major land grab for shale gas assets. As gas fundamentals have weakened, and conversely strengthened for liquids, the focus has switched to higher-margin unconventional liquids. CHK has built a solid position at more than 12 liquids-rich plays with 5.5 million net acres. It sees drilling capex of $6 billion to $6.5 billion in 2011, versus $5.6 billion in 2010, and $6.2 billion to $6.8 billion in 2012. Organic production growth is guided at 24% and 16% for 2011 and 2012. We expect proceeds from the sale of Fayetteville assets and the Niobrara JV to be allocated toward debt reduction and improving liquidity, and we see the possibility of JVs at Granite Wash and Permian Basin acreage. CHK thinks Utica could be a major catalyst in 2012.

► Risks to our recommendation and target price include weaker economic and operating conditions, a sustained decline in natural gas prices, and difficulty replacing reserves.

► Our 12-month target price is $38, based on our proved NAV ($41), DCF ($42, assuming an 8.8% WACC and 3% terminal growth) and peer-average relative metrics, reflecting solid growth, most notably at oil-rich plays.

## Revenue/Earnings Data

**Revenue (Million $)**

| | 1Q | 2Q | 3Q | 4Q | Year |
|---|---|---|---|---|---|
| 2011 | 1,612 | 3,318 | 3,977 | -- | -- |
| 2010 | 2,798 | 2,012 | 2,581 | 1,975 | 9,366 |
| 2009 | 1,995 | 1,673 | 1,811 | 2,222 | 7,702 |
| 2008 | 1,611 | 3,372 | 7,491 | 2,981 | 11,629 |
| 2007 | 1,580 | 2,105 | 2,027 | 2,089 | 7,800 |
| 2006 | 1,945 | 1,584 | 1,929 | 1,868 | 7,326 |

**Earnings Per Share ($)**

| | | | | | |
|---|---|---|---|---|---|
| 2011 | -0.32 | 0.68 | 1.23 | E0.65 | E2.88 |
| 2010 | 1.14 | 0.37 | 0.75 | 0.28 | 2.51 |
| 2009 | -9.63 | 0.39 | 0.30 | -0.84 | -9.57 |
| 2008 | -0.29 | -3.16 | 5.61 | -1.51 | 1.14 |
| 2007 | 0.50 | 1.01 | 0.72 | 0.27 | 2.62 |
| 2006 | 1.44 | 0.82 | 1.13 | 0.96 | 4.35 |

Fiscal year ended Dec. 31. Next earnings report expected: Early January. EPS Estimates based on S&P Operating Earnings; historical GAAP earnings are as reported.

## Dividend Data (Dates: mm/dd Payment Date: mm/dd/yy)

| Amount ($) | Date Decl. | Ex-Div. Date | Stk. of Record | Payment Date |
|---|---|---|---|---|
| 0.075 | 12/20 | 12/30 | 01/03 | 01/18/11 |
| 0.075 | 03/07 | 03/30 | 04/01 | 04/15/11 |
| 0.088 | 06/13 | 06/29 | 07/01 | 07/15/11 |
| 0.088 | 08/01 | 09/29 | 10/03 | 10/17/11 |

Dividends have been paid since 2002. Source: Company reports.

# Chesapeake Energy Corp

STANDARD
&POOR'S

## Business Summary November 29, 2011

CORPORATE OVERVIEW. The second largest producer of natural gas in the U.S., Chesapeake Energy Corp. (CHK) is focused on discovering, acquiring and developing unconventional natural gas and oil reserves onshore in the U.S., primarily in the Barnett Shale in the Fort Worth Basin of Texas, the Haynesville/Bossier Shales in Louisiana and East Texas and the Marcellus Shale in the Appalachian Basin of West Virginia and Pennsylvania. CHK also has operations in the liquids-rich plays of the Eagle Ford Shale in South Texas, the Granite Wash, Cleveland, Tonkawa and Mississippian plays in the Anadarko Basin, the Niobrara Shale, Frontier and Codell plays in the Powder River and Denver Julesburg (DJ) Basins of Wyoming and Colorado, and the Avalon, Bone Spring, Wolfcamp and Wolfberry plays in the Permian and Delaware Basins of West Texas and New Mexico, as well as various other plays, both conventional and unconventional, in the Mid-Continent, Williston Basin, Appalachian Basin, South Texas, Texas Gulf Coast and Ark-La-Tex regions of the U.S.

CHK operations are concentrated in six U.S. operating areas: Mid-Continent, Barnett Shale, Appalachian Basin, Permian and Delaware Basin, Ark-La-Tex, and South Texas and Texas Gulf Coast. Proved oil and gas reserves rose 20% in 2010, to 17.1 trillion cubic feet equivalent (Tcfe; 90% natural gas, 54% developed). Oil and gas production rose 15%, to 1,059 billion cubic feet equivalent

(89% natural gas). We estimate CHK's 2010 organic reserve replacement at 510%, versus a three-year rate of 400%. During 2010, CHK drilled 1,445 gross (938 net) operated wells and participated in 1,586 gross (211 net) wells operated by other companies. CHK's drilling success rate was 98% for company-operated wells. During 2010, CHK invested $4.6 billion in operated wells (using an average of 131 operated rigs) and $815 million in non-operated wells (using an average of 123 non-operated rigs) for total drilling, completing and equipping costs of $5.4 billion.

IMPACT OF MAJOR DEVELOPMENTS. In July 2008, CHK and Plains Exploration & Production Company (PXP) announced a Haynesville Shale JV. PXP acquired a 20% interest in CHK's Haynesville Shale leasehold for $1.65 billion in cash. In addition, PXP agreed to fund 50% of CHK's 80% share of drilling and completion costs for future Haynesville Shale JV wells over a several year period until an additional $1.65 billion has been paid. PXP will have the right to a 20% participation in any additional acquired leasehold in the Haynesville Shale.

## Company Financials Fiscal Year Ended Dec. 31

| Per Share Data ($) | 2010 | 2009 | 2008 | 2007 | 2006 | 2005 | 2004 | 2003 | 2002 | 2001 |
|---|---|---|---|---|---|---|---|---|---|---|
| Tangible Book Value | 19.28 | 17.47 | 26.00 | 21.87 | 20.32 | 12.42 | 8.57 | 5.45 | 3.99 | 3.75 |
| Cash Flow | 4.64 | 11.26 | 5.21 | 6.87 | 7.36 | 5.05 | 3.56 | 2.61 | 1.54 | 2.52 |
| Earnings | 2.51 | -9.57 | 1.14 | 2.62 | 4.35 | 2.51 | 1.53 | 1.20 | 0.17 | 1.51 |
| S&P Core Earnings | 2.29 | -9.36 | 1.35 | 2.51 | 4.19 | 2.48 | 1.50 | 1.19 | 0.17 | 1.36 |
| Dividends | 0.30 | 0.30 | 0.29 | 0.26 | 0.23 | 0.20 | 0.17 | 0.14 | 0.06 | Nil |
| Payout Ratio | 12% | NM | 26% | 10% | 5% | 8% | 11% | 11% | 35% | Nil |
| Prices:High | 29.22 | 30.00 | 74.00 | 41.19 | 35.57 | 40.20 | 18.31 | 14.00 | 8.55 | 11.06 |
| Prices:Low | 19.62 | 13.27 | 9.84 | 27.27 | 26.81 | 15.06 | 11.70 | 7.27 | 4.50 | 4.50 |
| P/E Ratio:High | 12 | NM | 65 | 16 | 8 | 16 | 12 | 12 | 50 | 7 |
| P/E Ratio:Low | 8 | NM | 9 | 10 | 6 | 6 | 8 | 6 | 26 | 3 |

| Income Statement Analysis (Million $) | | | | | | | | | | |
|---|---|---|---|---|---|---|---|---|---|---|
| Revenue | 9,366 | 7,702 | 11,629 | 7,800 | 7,326 | 4,665 | 2,709 | 1,717 | 738 | 969 |
| Operating Income | NA | NA | 3,631 | 4,638 | 3,413 | 1,773 | 992 | 675 | 191 | 597 |
| Depreciation, Depletion and Amortization | 1,614 | 12,745 | 2,147 | 1,989 | 1,463 | 945 | 611 | 386 | 235 | 178 |
| Interest Expense | 99.0 | 113 | 314 | 675 | 301 | 220 | 167 | 154 | 111 | 98.3 |
| Pretax Income | 2,884 | -9,288 | 1,186 | 2,341 | 3,255 | 1,493 | 805 | 501 | 67.1 | 438 |
| Effective Tax Rate | NA | 37.5% | 39.0% | 38.0% | 38.5% | 36.5% | 36.0% | 38.0% | 40.0% | 39.9% |
| Net Income | 1,774 | -5,830 | 723 | 1,451 | 2,003 | 948 | 515 | 311 | 40.3 | 263 |
| S&P Core Earnings | 1,506 | -5,723 | 737 | 1,178 | 1,831 | 871 | 431 | 283 | 29.9 | 235 |

| Balance Sheet & Other Financial Data (Million $) | | | | | | | | | | |
|---|---|---|---|---|---|---|---|---|---|---|
| Cash | 102 | 307 | 1,749 | 1.00 | 2.52 | 60.0 | 6.90 | 40.6 | 248 | 125 |
| Current Assets | 3,266 | 2,446 | 4,292 | 1,396 | 1,154 | 1,183 | 568 | 342 | 435 | 361 |
| Total Assets | 37,179 | 29,914 | 38,444 | 30,734 | 24,417 | 16,118 | 8,245 | 4,572 | 2,876 | 2,287 |
| Current Liabilities | 4,490 | 2,688 | 3,621 | 2,761 | 1,890 | 1,964 | 964 | 513 | 266 | 173 |
| Long Term Debt | 12,640 | 12,295 | 14,184 | 10,950 | 7,376 | 5,490 | 3,075 | 2,058 | 1,651 | 1,329 |
| Common Equity | 15,264 | 11,444 | 16,297 | 11,170 | 9,293 | 4,598 | 2,672 | 1,180 | 758 | 617 |
| Total Capital | 27,904 | 24,636 | 34,244 | 27,046 | 21,944 | 13,469 | 7,172 | 3,982 | 2,559 | 2,097 |
| Capital Expenditures | 12,630 | 5,226 | 9,177 | 9,705 | 986 | 484 | 127 | 71.5 | 33.6 | 24.9 |
| Cash Flow | 3,277 | 6,892 | 2,837 | 3,346 | 3,377 | 1,851 | 1,087 | 674 | 265 | 439 |
| Current Ratio | 0.7 | 0.9 | 1.2 | 0.5 | 0.6 | 0.6 | 0.6 | 0.7 | 1.6 | 2.1 |
| % Long Term Debt of Capitalization | 45.3 | 51.8 | 41.4 | 47.4 | 33.6 | 40.8 | 42.9 | 51.7 | 64.5 | 63.4 |
| % Return on Assets | 5.3 | NM | 4.5 | 4.9 | 9.9 | 7.8 | 8.0 | 8.3 | 1.6 | 14.1 |
| % Return on Equity | 13.5 | NM | 5.3 | 13.3 | 27.6 | 24.9 | 24.7 | 29.7 | 4.4 | 58.1 |

Data as orig reptd.; bef. results of disc opers/spec. items. Per share data adj. for stk. divs.; EPS diluted. E-Estimated. NA-Not Available. NM-Not Meaningful. NR-Not Ranked. UR-Under Review.

**Office:** 6100 North Western Avenue, Oklahoma City, OK 73118.
**Telephone:** 405-848-8000.
**Website:** http://www.chk.com
**Chrmn & CEO:** A.K. McClendon

**COO & EVP:** S.C. Dixon
**EVP & CFO:** D.J. Dell'Osso, Jr.
**SVP, Chief Acctg Officer & Cntlr:** M.A. Johnson
**SVP, Treas & Secy:** J.M. Grigsby

**Investor Contact:** J.L. Mobley (405-767-4763)
**Board Members:** R. K. Davidson, K. Eisbrenner, V. B. Hargis, F. A. Keating, C. T. Maxwell, A. K. McClendon, M. A. Miller, Jr., D. L. Nickles, L. A. Simpson

**Auditor:** PRICEWATERHOUSECOOPERS
**Founded:** 1989
**Domicile:** Oklahoma
**Employees:** 10,000

# Chevron Corp

**STANDARD &POOR'S**

| S&P Recommendation | STRONG BUY ★★★★★ | Price $95.77 (as of Nov 28, 2011) | 12-Mo. Target Price $132.00 | Investment Style Large-Cap Blend |
| --- | --- | --- | --- | --- |

**GICS Sector** Energy
**Sub-Industry** Integrated Oil & Gas

**Summary** This global integrated oil company (formerly ChevronTexaco) has interests in exploration, production, refining and marketing, and petrochemicals.

## Key Stock Statistics (Source S&P, Vickers, company reports)

| | | | | | | | |
| --- | --- | --- | --- | --- | --- | --- | --- |
| 52-Wk Range | $110.01–80.47 | S&P Oper. EPS 2011**E** | 14.20 | Market Capitalization(B) | $190.724 | Beta | 0.80 |
| Trailing 12-Month EPS | $13.50 | S&P Oper. EPS 2012**E** | 13.65 | Yield (%) | 3.38 | S&P 3-Yr. Proj. EPS CAGR(%) | 41 |
| Trailing 12-Month P/E | 7.1 | P/E on S&P Oper. EPS 2011**E** | 6.7 | Dividend Rate/Share | $3.24 | S&P Credit Rating | AA |
| $10K Invested 5 Yrs Ago | $15,796 | Common Shares Outstg. (M) | 1,991.5 | Institutional Ownership (%) | 64 | | |

## Price Performance

30-Week Mov. Avg. · · · 10-Week Mov. Avg. – – **GAAP Earnings vs. Previous Year** Volume Above Avg. STARS
12-Mo. Target Price — Relative Strength — ▲ Up ▼ Down ► No Change Below Avg.

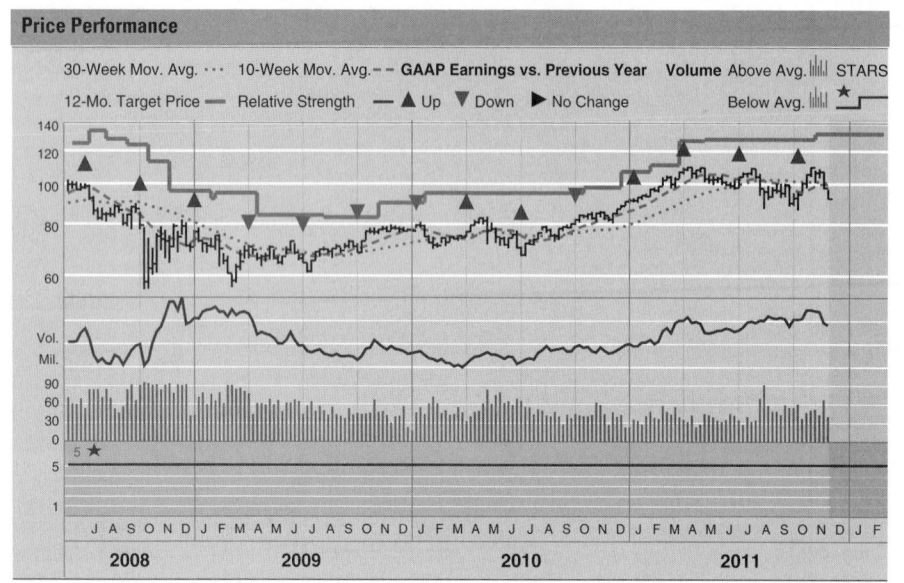

Options: ASE, CBOE, P, Ph

Analysis prepared by Equity Analyst **Michael Kay** on Nov 28, 2011, when the stock traded at **$96.08**.

### Highlights

➤ Production in the first nine months of 2011 was down 2.5%, reflecting a pipeline incident in Thailand and the impact of high prices on production-sharing contracts (about 39,000 b/d). Still, CVX sees new field developments fueling production growth of 1%-2% per year during 2011-2014 and 4%-5% between 2014 and 2017. We see CVX funding mega-projects internally, and we believe it has the capability to pursue strategic acquisitions. The Jack (50% stake)/St. Malo (51%) and the Tahiti 2 projects in the deepwater GOM are currently under development and expected to start up by 2014.

➤ CVX is restructuring its downstream to make it smaller and less complex. Divestment efforts have allowed it to exit 21 countries and build exposure to Asia. It is in the process of exiting Spain, Africa and Caribbean downstream.

➤ We see higher oil prices lifting EPS by 51% in 2011, to $14.20, but on our expectation for more modest refining margins, we see 2012 EPS of $13.65. We expect dividend growth and share buybacks. Capex in 2011 is planned at $26 billion, up from $21.8 billion, with 87% for E&P, focused on Australia LNG, the GOM, and deepwater projects.

### Investment Rationale/Risk

➤ CVX is reducing its refining footprint and focusing on large upstream projects with higher margin potential, while also being aided by a heavy oil-weighted mix at start-ups. We view positively its aim to develop LNG projects and build a top gas supply position in Asia-Pacific. The Atlas Energy deal provides an industry-leading position in the Marcellus Shale, and it has solid acreage at the Wolfcamp and Utica shales. It will begin drilling for Polish shale gas in 2011. CVX suspended drilling offshore Brazil after it became aware of oil seep lines in the ocean floor. CVX has stopped the primary source of oil and does not expect production to be affected by the suspension (36,000 b/d).

➤ Risks to our opinion and target price include weaker economic, industry and operating conditions, a decline in oil prices, an inability to replace production, and geopolitical risk.

➤ On our DCF ($131; WACC 7.0%, terminal growth 3%) and relative market valuations, currently discounted versus peer integrateds, our 12-month target price is $132. We view discounts as unwarranted given CVX's liquids-to-gas production weighting near 70%.

## Qualitative Risk Assessment

| LOW | MEDIUM | HIGH |
| --- | --- | --- |

Our risk assessment reflects our view of Chevron's diversified and strong business profile in volatile, cyclical and capital-intensive segments of the energy industry. We view its corporate governance practices as generally sound and its earnings as stable.

## Quantitative Evaluations

**S&P Quality Ranking**     A

| D | C | B- | B | B+ | A- | A | A+ |
| --- | --- | --- | --- | --- | --- | --- | --- |

**Relative Strength Rank**     MODERATE

48

LOWEST = 1     HIGHEST = 99

## Revenue/Earnings Data

**Revenue (Million $)**

| | 1Q | 2Q | 3Q | 4Q | Year |
| --- | --- | --- | --- | --- | --- |
| 2011 | 58,412 | 66,671 | 61,261 | -- | -- |
| 2010 | 46,741 | 51,051 | 48,554 | 51,852 | 198,198 |
| 2009 | 34,987 | 39,647 | 45,180 | 47,588 | 167,402 |
| 2008 | 65,903 | 78,310 | 73,615 | 43,145 | 264,958 |
| 2007 | 46,302 | 54,344 | 53,545 | 59,900 | 203,970 |
| 2006 | 54,624 | 53,536 | 54,212 | 47,746 | 210,118 |

**Earnings Per Share ($)**

| | 1Q | 2Q | 3Q | 4Q | Year |
| --- | --- | --- | --- | --- | --- |
| 2011 | 3.09 | 3.85 | 3.92 | E3.34 | E14.20 |
| 2010 | 2.27 | 2.70 | 1.88 | 2.64 | 9.48 |
| 2009 | 0.92 | 0.87 | 1.92 | 1.53 | 5.24 |
| 2008 | 2.48 | 2.89 | 3.86 | 2.43 | 11.67 |
| 2007 | 2.18 | 2.52 | 1.75 | 2.32 | 8.77 |
| 2006 | 1.80 | 1.97 | 2.29 | 1.74 | 7.80 |

Fiscal year ended Dec. 31. Next earnings report expected: Late January. EPS Estimates based on S&P Operating Earnings; historical GAAP earnings are as reported.

## Dividend Data (Dates: mm/dd Payment Date: mm/dd/yy)

| Amount ($) | Date Decl. | Ex-Div. Date | Stk. of Record | Payment Date |
| --- | --- | --- | --- | --- |
| 0.720 | 01/26 | 02/14 | 02/16 | 03/10/11 |
| 0.780 | 04/27 | 05/17 | 05/19 | 06/10/11 |
| 0.780 | 07/28 | 08/17 | 08/19 | 09/12/11 |
| 0.810 | 10/26 | 11/16 | 11/18 | 12/12/11 |

Dividends have been paid since 1912. Source: Company reports.

---

**Please read the Required Disclosures and Analyst Certification on the last page of this report.**

The McGraw-Hill Companies

# Chevron Corp

STANDARD
&POOR'S

## Business Summary November 28, 2011

CORPORATE OVERVIEW. In October 2001, Chevron Corp. (CHV) and Texaco Inc. (TX) merged, creating the second largest U.S.-based oil company at the time, ChevronTexaco Corp. (CVX). In May 2005, the company changed its name to Chevron Corp. CVX is the second largest U.S. oil company and the fifth largest publicly traded oil company in the world.

CVX separately manages its upstream (or exploration and production; 28% of 2010 revenues and 88% of 2010 segment income), downstream (or refining, marketing and transportation; 72% and 12%), chemicals and other businesses, which includes its mining operations for coal and molybdenum, power generation, Chevron Energy Solutions (CES), and energy technology such as Chevron Technology Ventures (CTV) companies.

Net production of crude oil, natural gas liquids (NGLs) and natural gas rose 2.2%, to 2.763 million barrels of oil equivalent (boe) per day (70% liquids), in 2010, reflecting production increases in Brazil, China, Kazakhstan and Thailand, and declines in the U.S. Net proved oil and gas reserves, including equi-

ty share in affiliates, fell 7%, to 10.55 billion boe (62% liquids, 63% developed) in 2010. The decline is attributable to an unfavorable effect of higher crude oil prices on certain production-sharing contracts. As of December 31, 2010, CVX owned eight refineries and one asphalt plant (which has been idled since 2008, and is being operated as a terminal), and had interests in eight international refineries, for a total operable capacity of 2.160 million b/d (50% North America). CVX processes imported (84% of 2010 refinery inputs) and domestic (16%) crude oil in its U.S. refining operations. As of year-end 2010, it had a network of about 19,550 (42% U.S.) branded retail sites worldwide.

CVX's chemical segment includes the company's Oronite subsidiary and the 50%-owned Chevron Phillips Chemical Co. LLC (CPChem).

## Company Financials Fiscal Year Ended Dec. 31

| Per Share Data ($) | 2010 | 2009 | 2008 | 2007 | 2006 | 2005 | 2004 | 2003 | 2002 | 2001 |
|---|---|---|---|---|---|---|---|---|---|---|
| Tangible Book Value | 50.04 | 43.48 | 40.93 | 34.66 | 29.71 | 25.99 | 21.47 | 16.98 | 14.80 | 15.92 |
| Cash Flow | 16.04 | 11.29 | 16.32 | 12.67 | 11.38 | 8.96 | 8.53 | 5.99 | 2.98 | 5.17 |
| Earnings | 9.48 | 5.24 | 11.67 | 8.77 | 7.80 | 6.54 | 6.14 | 3.57 | 0.54 | 1.85 |
| S&P Core Earnings | 9.31 | 5.04 | 10.90 | 8.34 | 7.88 | 6.62 | 5.88 | 3.50 | 1.22 | 1.66 |
| Dividends | 2.84 | 2.66 | 2.53 | 2.26 | 2.01 | 1.75 | 1.53 | 1.43 | 1.40 | 1.33 |
| Payout Ratio | 30% | 51% | 22% | 26% | 26% | 27% | 25% | 40% | NM | 72% |
| Prices:High | 92.39 | 79.82 | 104.63 | 95.50 | 76.20 | 65.98 | 56.07 | 43.50 | 45.80 | 49.25 |
| Prices:Low | 66.83 | 56.12 | 55.50 | 64.99 | 53.76 | 49.81 | 42.00 | 30.66 | 32.71 | 39.22 |
| P/E Ratio:High | 10 | 15 | 9 | 11 | 10 | 10 | 9 | 12 | 86 | 27 |
| P/E Ratio:Low | 7 | 11 | 5 | 7 | 7 | 8 | 7 | 9 | 61 | 21 |

| Income Statement Analysis (Million $) | 2010 | 2009 | 2008 | 2007 | 2006 | 2005 | 2004 | 2003 | 2002 | 2001 |
|---|---|---|---|---|---|---|---|---|---|---|
| Revenue | 198,198 | 167,402 | 264,958 | 214,091 | 204,892 | 193,641 | 150,865 | 120,032 | 98,691 | 104,409 |
| Operating Income | NA | NA | 45,238 | 33,936 | 35,748 | 27,129 | 21,542 | 49,336 | 28,848 | 16,031 |
| Depreciation, Depletion and Amortization | 13,063 | 12,110 | 9,528 | 8,309 | 7,506 | 5,913 | 4,935 | 5,384 | 5,231 | 7,059 |
| Interest Expense | 50.0 | 28.0 | 2.00 | 468 | 451 | 482 | 406 | 474 | 565 | 833 |
| Pretax Income | 32,055 | 18,528 | 43,057 | 32,274 | 32,046 | 25,293 | 20,636 | 12,850 | 4,213 | 8,412 |
| Effective Tax Rate | NA | 43.0% | 44.2% | 41.8% | 46.3% | 43.9% | 36.4% | 41.6% | 71.8% | 51.8% |
| Net Income | 19,024 | 10,483 | 23,931 | 18,688 | 17,138 | 14,099 | 13,034 | 7,426 | 1,132 | 3,931 |
| S&P Core Earnings | 18,684 | 10,080 | 22,346 | 17,772 | 17,310 | 14,277 | 12,471 | 7,454 | 2,590 | 3,518 |

| Balance Sheet & Other Financial Data (Million $) | 2010 | 2009 | 2008 | 2007 | 2006 | 2005 | 2004 | 2003 | 2002 | 2001 |
|---|---|---|---|---|---|---|---|---|---|---|
| Cash | 17,070 | 8,822 | 9,560 | 8,094 | 11,446 | 11,144 | 10,742 | 5,267 | 3,781 | 3,150 |
| Current Assets | 48,841 | 37,216 | 36,470 | 39,377 | 36,304 | 34,336 | 28,503 | 19,426 | 17,776 | 18,327 |
| Total Assets | 184,769 | 164,621 | 161,165 | 148,786 | 132,628 | 125,833 | 93,208 | 81,470 | 77,359 | 77,572 |
| Current Liabilities | 29,012 | 26,211 | 32,023 | 33,798 | 28,409 | 25,011 | 18,795 | 16,111 | 19,876 | 20,654 |
| Long Term Debt | 11,003 | 9,829 | 6,083 | 6,753 | 7,679 | 12,131 | 10,456 | 10,894 | 10,911 | 8,989 |
| Common Equity | 105,081 | 91,914 | 86,648 | 77,088 | 73,684 | 66,722 | 48,575 | 40,022 | 36,176 | 37,120 |
| Total Capital | 117,577 | 102,456 | 104,739 | 95,532 | 93,219 | 90,315 | 66,471 | 57,601 | 53,009 | 52,524 |
| Capital Expenditures | 19,612 | 19,843 | 19,666 | 16,678 | 13,813 | 8,701 | 6,310 | 5,625 | 7,597 | 9,713 |
| Cash Flow | 32,199 | 22,593 | 33,459 | 26,997 | 24,644 | 20,012 | 17,969 | 12,810 | 6,363 | 10,990 |
| Current Ratio | 1.7 | 1.4 | 1.1 | 1.2 | 1.3 | 1.4 | 1.5 | 1.2 | 0.9 | 0.9 |
| % Long Term Debt of Capitalization | 9.4 | Nil | 5.8 | 7.3 | 8.2 | 13.4 | 15.7 | 18.9 | 20.6 | 17.1 |
| % Return on Assets | NA | 6.4 | 15.4 | 13.3 | 13.3 | 12.9 | 14.9 | 9.4 | 1.5 | 5.1 |
| % Return on Equity | NA | NA | 29.2 | 25.6 | 24.4 | 24.5 | 29.4 | 19.5 | 3.1 | 10.7 |

Data as orig reptd.; bef. results of disc opers/spec. items. Per share data adj. for stk. divs.; EPS diluted. Quarterly revs. incl. other inc. E-Estimated. NA-Not Available. NM-Not Meaningful. NR-Not Ranked. UR-Under Review.

**Office:** 6001 Bollinger Canyon Road, San Ramon, CA 94583-2324.
**Telephone:** 925-842-1000.
**Email:** invest@chevrontexaco.com
**Website:** http://www.chevron.com

**Chrmn & CEO:** J.S. Watson
**Vice Chrmn:** G.L. Kirkland
**CFO & Chief Acctg Officer:** P.E. Yarrington
**CTO:** J.W. McDonald

**Treas:** P.V. Bennett
**Board Members:** L. F. Deily, R. E. Denham, R. J. Eaton, C. T. Hagel, E. Hernandez, Jr., G. L. Kirkland, D. B. Rice, K. W. Sharer, C. R. Shoemate, J. G. Stumpf, R. D. Sugar, C. Ware, J. S. Watson

**Founded:** 1901
**Domicile:** Delaware
**Employees:** 62,000

The McGraw-Hill Companies

# Chipotle Mexican Grill Inc

**STANDARD & POOR'S**

| S&P Recommendation | HOLD ★★★☆☆ | Price $300.75 (as of Nov 25, 2011) | 12-Mo. Target Price $345.00 | Investment Style Large-Cap Growth |

**GICS Sector** Consumer Discretionary
**Sub-Industry** Restaurants

**Summary** This expansion-minded company operates fast casual Mexican food restaurants with over 1,100 locations throughout the United States, as well as its first overseas in London.

## Key Stock Statistics (Source S&P, Vickers, company reports)

| | | | | | |
|---|---|---|---|---|---|
| 52-Wk Range | $347.94– 212.58 | S&P Oper. EPS 2011**E** | 6.75 | Market Capitalization(B) | $9.412 |
| Trailing 12-Month EPS | $6.42 | S&P Oper. EPS 2012**E** | 8.22 | Yield (%) | Nil |
| Trailing 12-Month P/E | 46.9 | P/E on S&P Oper. EPS 2011**E** | 44.6 | Dividend Rate/Share | Nil |
| $10K Invested 5 Yrs Ago | $49,295 | Common Shares Outstg. (M) | 31.3 | Institutional Ownership (%) | NM |

| | |
|---|---|
| Beta | 1.04 |
| S&P 3-Yr. Proj. EPS CAGR(%) | 18 |
| S&P Credit Rating | NA |

## Price Performance

30-Week Mov. Avg. ···· 10-Week Mov. Avg. – – **GAAP Earnings vs. Previous Year**   Volume Above Avg. ▥ STARS
12-Mo. Target Price — Relative Strength — ▲ Up ▼ Down ▶ No Change   Below Avg. ▥ ★

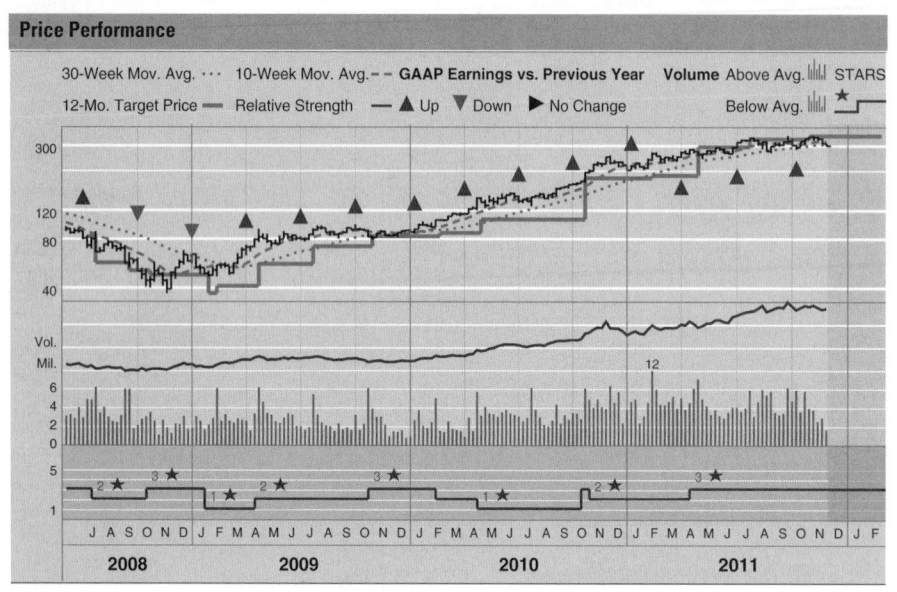

Options: ASE, P, Ph

Analysis prepared by Equity Analyst **Jim Yin, CFA** on Oct 26, 2011, when the stock traded at **$334.51**.

## Qualitative Risk Assessment

| LOW | **MEDIUM** | HIGH |

Our risk assessment reflects our view that free cash flow is likely to grow faster than sales or profits, on the company's growing base of restaurants in operation, even as expansion has stayed about level on an absolute basis, but dipped as a percentage of the base. However, even as the company continues to expand, average restaurant sales have weakened, possibly due to the recession and greater market saturation.

## Quantitative Evaluations

**S&P Quality Ranking**                                         NR

| D | C | B- | B | B+ | A- | A | A+ |

**Relative Strength Rank**                          MODERATE

| 52 |

LOWEST = 1                                      HIGHEST = 99

## Highlights

➤ We believe revenues will rise 20% in 2012, following a 24% advance projected for 2011. We estimate same-store sales growth of 11% and 7% for 2011 and 2012, respectively. We believe CMG will continue to post same-restaurant sales growth above peers, given the perception of its higher-quality food and the overall newness of the concept. In addition, we expect the company to open about 140 new restaurants in both 2011 and 2012. We think CMG has significant growth opportunity in international markets as well as further penetration in the U.S.

➤ We look for restaurant margins of 26% for both 2011 and 2012, down from 27% in 2010, hurt by higher food and other commodity costs. However, we think this factor will be partially offset by restrained labor costs and lower occupancy costs as a percentage of revenues. We see operating margins remaining steady in the 15%-16% range for 2011 and 2012.

➤ We project EPS of $6.75 and $8.22 in 2011 and 2012, respectively, compared to $5.64 in 2010. The estimated increases reflect our outlook for strong revenue growth despite a sluggish economic recovery.

## Investment Rationale/Risk

➤ We think CMG's revenues and earnings will remain on a positive trajectory through 2012, and the shares currently trade roughly in line with our near-term expectations. New restaurant openings and strong same-store sales growth will likely drive results. We see further growth in new store openings, given that the company has slightly more than 1,160 restaurants at the end of September 2011. We think CMG's niche casual Mexican restaurants remain attractive with consumers, including both those trading up as well as those moving down.

➤ Risks to our recommendation and target price include a weaker economy than S&P's outlook for a 2.4% increase in real GDP in 2011. Also, a meaningful decrease in housing and downside surprises to our forecasts for consumer income and jobs growth could lead to a weaker economic outlook.

➤ Our 12-month target price of $345 is based on our relative analysis. We apply a P/E multiple of 42X, which is above peers and near the high-end of CMG's historical range, to our 2012 EPS estimate of $8.22.

## Revenue/Earnings Data

**Revenue (Million $)**

| | 1Q | 2Q | 3Q | 4Q | Year |
|---|---|---|---|---|---|
| 2011 | 509.4 | 571.6 | 591.9 | -- | -- |
| 2010 | 409.7 | 466.8 | 476.9 | 482.5 | 1,836 |
| 2009 | 354.5 | 388.8 | 387.5 | 387.5 | 1,518 |
| 2008 | 305.3 | 340.8 | 340.5 | 345.3 | 1,332 |
| 2007 | 236.1 | 274.3 | 286.4 | 289.0 | 1,086 |
| 2006 | 187.0 | 204.9 | 211.3 | 219.7 | 822.9 |

**Earnings Per Share ($)**

| | | | | | |
|---|---|---|---|---|---|
| 2011 | 1.46 | 1.59 | 1.90 | E1.79 | E6.75 |
| 2010 | 1.19 | 1.46 | 1.52 | 1.47 | 5.64 |
| 2009 | 0.78 | 1.10 | 1.08 | 0.99 | 3.95 |
| 2008 | 0.52 | 0.74 | 0.59 | 0.52 | 2.36 |
| 2007 | 0.38 | 0.60 | 0.62 | 0.53 | 2.13 |
| 2006 | 0.26 | 0.33 | 0.36 | 0.33 | 1.28 |

Fiscal year ended Dec. 31. Next earnings report expected: Mid February. EPS Estimates based on S&P Operating Earnings; historical GAAP earnings are as reported.

## Dividend Data

No cash dividends have been paid.

---

**Please read the Required Disclosures and Analyst Certification on the last page of this report.**

The McGraw-Hill Companies

# Chipotle Mexican Grill Inc

## Business Summary October 26, 2011

**CORPORATE OVERVIEW.** Chipotle Mexican Grill operates fast casual restaurants serving a menu of tacos, burritos, salads and burrito bowls made with fresh ingredients that are prepared using classic cooking methods. The company emphasizes the use of raw ingredients that are raised without the use of animal byproducts, antibiotics or hormones, as well as produce that is grown using sustainable farming methods. As of December 31, 2010, Chipotle operated 1,084 locations, versus 956 a year earlier.

Based on the geographic data as of December 31, 2010, there were 1,081 restaurants throughout the United States, two in Toronto, Canada, and one in London, England. Most restaurants are located in shopping centers, although a number are free-standing and a small number are in enclosed malls.

**CORPORATE STRATEGY.** The company has grown rapidly in recent years, but we think it may be difficult to maintain the rate of expansion. It opened 138 new restaurants in 2010 -- a 15% growth rate -- and plans to open 135-145 new units in 2011, or roughly a 13% rate. Based on company statements, future expansion into France is planned, and its first London location opened in 2010.

Of new units opened in 2010, 36 were the new "Type A" design, featuring a smaller footprint and lower upfront costs, which will enable the company to enter new locations where the return on investment of a traditional unit would not warrant expansion. The average investment cost of these units was under $700,000, and with lower operating and occupancy costs, CMG believes the return potential on these units is much higher. Roughly one third of new openings in 2011 are expected to use the "Type A" format.

In the aggregate, capital expenditures were $113 million in 2010, versus $117 million in 2009, $152 million in 2008 and $139 million in 2007. Funding sources include cash on hand from the company's January 2006 initial public offering, as well as cash from operations. The company had no debt as of December 31, 2010.

## Company Financials Fiscal Year Ended Dec. 31

| Per Share Data ($) | 2010 | 2009 | 2008 | 2007 | 2006 | 2005 | 2004 | 2003 | 2002 | 2001 |
|---|---|---|---|---|---|---|---|---|---|---|
| Tangible Book Value | 25.39 | 21.65 | 39.66 | 16.47 | 14.02 | 11.10 | 12.43 | NA | NA | NA |
| Cash Flow | 7.81 | 5.86 | 3.95 | 3.44 | 2.33 | 2.49 | 0.50 | 0.47 | -0.46 | NA |
| Earnings | 5.64 | 3.95 | 2.36 | 2.13 | 1.28 | 1.43 | 0.24 | -0.50 | -1.32 | NA |
| S&P Core Earnings | 5.77 | 4.07 | 2.54 | 2.25 | 1.36 | 1.51 | 0.29 | -0.14 | NA | NA |
| Dividends | Nil | Nil | Nil | Nil | Nil | Nil | NA | NA | NA | NA |
| Payout Ratio | Nil | Nil | Nil | Nil | Nil | Nil | NA | NA | NA | NA |
| Prices:High | 262.78 | 98.66 | 150.00 | 155.49 | 67.77 | NA | NA | NA | NA | NA |
| Prices:Low | 86.00 | 46.46 | 36.86 | 54.61 | 22.00 | NA | NA | NA | NA | NA |
| P/E Ratio:High | 47 | 25 | 64 | 73 | 53 | NA | NA | NA | NA | NA |
| P/E Ratio:Low | 15 | 12 | 16 | 26 | 17 | NA | NA | NA | NA | NA |

| Income Statement Analysis (Million $) | 2010 | 2009 | 2008 | 2007 | 2006 | 2005 | 2004 | 2003 | 2002 | 2001 |
|---|---|---|---|---|---|---|---|---|---|---|
| Revenue | 1,836 | 1,518 | 1,332 | 1,086 | 823 | 628 | 471 | 316 | 205 | NA |
| Operating Income | 363 | 271 | 186 | 158 | 100 | 62.1 | 29.6 | 11.7 | -4.88 | NA |
| Depreciation | 68.9 | 61.3 | 52.8 | 43.6 | 34.3 | 28.0 | 21.8 | 15.1 | 11.3 | NA |
| Interest Expense | 0.27 | 0.41 | 0.30 | 0.30 | 0.27 | 0.79 | 0.20 | 0.03 | 0.10 | NA |
| Pretax Income | 289 | 204 | 127 | 114 | 68.3 | 30.2 | 6.10 | -7.71 | -17.3 | NA |
| Effective Tax Rate | NA | 37.9% | 38.5% | 38.1% | 39.3% | NM | Nil | NA | NA | NA |
| Net Income | 179 | 127 | 78.2 | 70.6 | 41.4 | 37.7 | 6.10 | -7.71 | -17.3 | NA |
| S&P Core Earnings | 183 | 131 | 84.3 | 74.6 | 44.0 | 39.7 | 7.28 | -3.64 | NA | NA |

| Balance Sheet & Other Financial Data (Million $) | 2010 | 2009 | 2008 | 2007 | 2006 | 2005 | 2004 | 2003 | 2002 | 2001 |
|---|---|---|---|---|---|---|---|---|---|---|
| Cash | 350 | 270 | 188 | 171 | 154 | 0.06 | 119 | NA | NA | NA |
| Current Assets | 406 | 297 | 211 | 202 | 179 | 17.8 | 131 | 7.83 | NA | NA |
| Total Assets | 1,122 | 962 | 825 | 722 | 604 | 392 | 489 | 249 | NA | NA |
| Current Liabilities | 123 | 102 | 76.8 | 73.3 | 61.2 | 42.0 | 32.8 | 38.3 | NA | NA |
| Long Term Debt | 3.66 | 3.78 | 3.88 | 0.08 | Nil | 3.48 | Nil | NA | NA | NA |
| Common Equity | 811 | 703 | 623 | 562 | 474 | 309 | 420 | 191 | NA | NA |
| Total Capital | 815 | 707 | 627 | 583 | 493 | 313 | 263 | 192 | NA | NA |
| Capital Expenditures | 113 | 117 | 152 | 141 | 97.3 | 83.0 | 95.6 | 86.1 | 48.6 | NA |
| Cash Flow | 248 | 188 | 131 | 114 | 75.7 | 65.7 | 27.9 | 7.38 | -6.03 | NA |
| Current Ratio | 3.3 | 2.9 | 2.8 | 2.8 | 2.9 | 0.4 | 4.0 | 0.2 | NA | NA |
| % Long Term Debt of Capitalization | 0.5 | 0.5 | Nil | 0.7 | Nil | 1.1 | Nil | Nil | NA | NA |
| % Net Income of Revenue | 9.8 | 8.4 | 5.9 | 6.5 | 5.0 | 6.0 | 1.3 | NM | NM | NA |
| % Return on Assets | 17.2 | 14.2 | 10.1 | 10.6 | 8.3 | 10.4 | NM | NA | NA | NA |
| % Return on Equity | 23.6 | 19.1 | 13.2 | 13.6 | 10.6 | 13.2 | NM | NA | NA | NA |

Data as orig reptd.; bef. results of disc opers/spec. items. Per share data adj. for stk. divs.; EPS diluted. E-Estimated. NA-Not Available. NM-Not Meaningful. NR-Not Ranked. UR-Under Review.

**Chrmn & Co-CEO:** M.S. Ells
**Co-CEO & Secy:** M.F. Moran
**CFO & Chief Acctg Officer:** J.R. Hartung
**Investor Contact:** C. Arnold (303-222-5912)

**Board Members:** A. S. Baldocchi, J. S. Charlesworth, M. S. Ells, N. Flanzraich, P. J. Flynn, D. J. Friedman, M. F. Moran

**Auditor:** ERNST & YOUNG
**Founded:** 1993
**Domicile:** Delaware
**Employees:** 26,500

# C.H. Robinson Worldwide Inc

**STANDARD &POOR'S**

| S&P Recommendation | BUY ★★★★☆ | Price $63.63 (as of Nov 25, 2011) | 12-Mo. Target Price $95.00 | Investment Style Large-Cap Growth |

**GICS Sector** Industrials
**Sub-Industry** Air Freight & Logistics

**Summary** This global provider of multimodal transportation and logistics solutions has a network of over 230 offices in North America, South America, Europe, and Asia.

## Key Stock Statistics (Source S&P, Vickers, company reports)

| | | | | | | | |
|---|---|---|---|---|---|---|---|
| 52-Wk Range | $82.61–62.30 | S&P Oper. EPS 2011E | 2.61 | Market Capitalization(B) | $10.447 | Beta | 0.79 |
| Trailing 12-Month EPS | $2.57 | S&P Oper. EPS 2012E | 3.09 | Yield (%) | 1.82 | S&P 3-Yr. Proj. EPS CAGR(%) | 14 |
| Trailing 12-Month P/E | 24.8 | P/E on S&P Oper. EPS 2011E | 24.4 | Dividend Rate/Share | $1.16 | S&P Credit Rating | NA |
| $10K Invested 5 Yrs Ago | $16,225 | Common Shares Outstg. (M) | 164.2 | Institutional Ownership (%) | 83 | | |

## Price Performance

30-Week Mov. Avg. · · · 10-Week Mov. Avg. – – GAAP Earnings vs. Previous Year Volume Above Avg. STARS
12-Mo. Target Price — Relative Strength — ▲ Up ▼ Down ► No Change Below Avg. ★

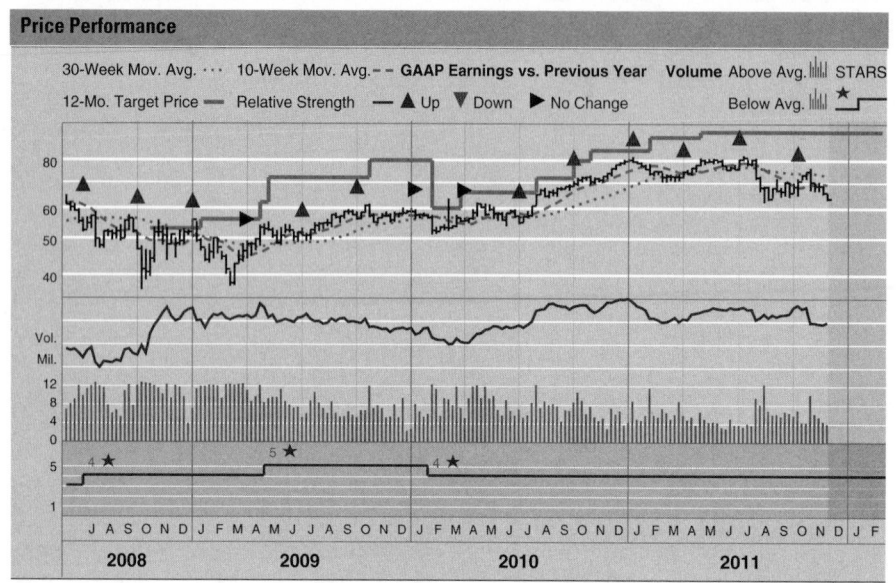

Options: ASE, CBOE, P, Ph

Analysis prepared by Equity Analyst **Jim Corridore** on Oct 31, 2011, when the stock traded at **$70.40**.

## Highlights

► We see gross revenues rising about 11% in 2011 and 10% in 2012, after a 22% increase in 2010. While comparisons to prior periods are more difficult, we see improving demand related to a slowly strengthening U.S. economy. We believe CHRW will continue to gain market share as it increases penetration into existing accounts and adds new ones. Gross revenues declined 12% in 2009, reflecting decreased volume and pricing for truck, intermodal, ocean and air shipping services related to the weak U.S. economy.

► We expect operating margins in 2011 and 2012 to be aided by lower SG&A and personnel costs as a percentage of revenues as well as a modest improvement in purchased transportation costs, driven by likely capacity increases among the trucking companies CHRW hires to transport goods. We see operating margins of 6.8% in 2011 and 7.3% in 2012, up from 6.7% in 2010.

► Our 2011 EPS estimate is $2.61, representing 12% growth over 2010 EPS of $2.33. For 2012, we see EPS rising 18%, to $3.09. We believe the quality of CHRW's earnings is high relative to most transportation companies that we cover.

## Investment Rationale/Risk

► We are positive on CHRW's history of strong returns on assets and equity relative to most other transportation companies. Also, CHRW has no long-term debt and has been a generator of cash over the past few years. We think the quality of its reported earnings is high relative to peers, as the company does not have a defined benefit pension plan or high capital requirements. CHRW has shown an ability to leverage its non-asset model to generate profits during periods of declining demand, which has allowed it to financially outperform most peers during the current difficult economic climate.

► Risks to our recommendation and target price include the possibility of investor rotation out of transportation stocks, a weakening of transport volumes, and sharply lower pricing related to excess industry transportation capacity.

► Our 12-month target price of $95 values the stock at 31X our 2012 EPS estimate of $3.15. Our valuation is above peer levels, but within CHRW's historical P/E range for the past five years of 17.5X to 36.1X earnings.

## Qualitative Risk Assessment

| LOW | MEDIUM | HIGH |

Our risk assessment reflects CHRW's lack of long-term debt and our favorable view of its high quality of earnings and non-asset-based structure. This is only partially offset, in our view, by exposure to cyclical economic slowdowns and volatile transportation costs.

## Quantitative Evaluations

**S&P Quality Ranking** A+

| D | C | B- | B | B+ | A- | A | A+ |

**Relative Strength Rank** MODERATE

39

LOWEST = 1    HIGHEST = 99

## Revenue/Earnings Data

**Revenue (Million $)**

| | 1Q | 2Q | 3Q | 4Q | Year |
|---|---|---|---|---|---|
| 2011 | 2,365 | 2,708 | 2,695 | -- | -- |
| 2010 | 2,075 | 2,454 | 2,420 | 2,325 | 9,274 |
| 2009 | 1,688 | 1,926 | 1,955 | 2,008 | 7,577 |
| 2008 | 1,985 | 2,322 | 2,317 | 1,955 | 8,579 |
| 2007 | 1,619 | 1,880 | 1,865 | 1,952 | 7,316 |
| 2006 | 1,499 | 1,701 | 1,713 | 1,643 | 6,556 |

**Earnings Per Share ($)**

| | | | | | |
|---|---|---|---|---|---|
| 2011 | 0.59 | 0.67 | 0.70 | E0.65 | E2.61 |
| 2010 | 0.50 | 0.59 | 0.62 | 0.62 | 2.33 |
| 2009 | 0.50 | 0.54 | 0.57 | 0.52 | 2.13 |
| 2008 | 0.50 | 0.52 | 0.54 | 0.52 | 2.08 |
| 2007 | 0.42 | 0.47 | 0.48 | 0.49 | 1.86 |
| 2006 | 0.33 | 0.38 | 0.40 | 0.42 | 1.53 |

Fiscal year ended Dec. 31. Next earnings report expected: Early February. EPS Estimates based on S&P Operating Earnings; historical GAAP earnings are as reported.

## Dividend Data (Dates: mm/dd Payment Date: mm/dd/yy)

| Amount ($) | Date Decl. | Ex-Div. Date | Stk. of Record | Payment Date |
|---|---|---|---|---|
| 0.290 | 02/12 | 08/31 | 09/02 | 10/03/11 |

Dividends have been paid since 1997. Source: Company reports.

---

**Please read the Required Disclosures and Analyst Certification on the last page of this report.**

The **McGraw·Hill** Companies

# C.H. Robinson Worldwide Inc

STANDARD &POOR'S

## Business Summary October 31, 2011

CORPORATE OVERVIEW. With 2010 gross revenues of about $9.3 billion, C.H. Robinson Worldwide is one of the largest third-party logistics companies in North America. At February 1, 2011, the company provided multimodal transportation services and logistics solutions through a network of 231 offices in North America, South America, Europe and Asia. In 2010, gross profits were divided as follows: 87% from transportation, 9% from sourcing, and 4% from information services. Within the transportation segment, CHRW offers several modes of service, including trucks (85% of gross profits in the transportation segment in 2010), intermodal (3%), ocean (5%), air (3%), and miscellaneous (4%).

Through contracts with about 50,000 transportation companies, including motor carriers, railroads, and air freight and ocean carriers, the company maintains the largest network of motor carrier capacity in North America. One of the largest third-party providers of intermodal services in the U.S., it also provides air, ocean and customs services. In addition, CHRW operates value-added logistics services, including fresh produce sourcing, freight consolida-

tion and cross-docking. In 2010, the company handled about 9.2 million shipments for more than 36,000 customers.

CORPORATE STRATEGY. CHRW has historically grown through internal growth, by expanding current offices, opening new branch offices and hiring additional sales people. Growth has also been augmented through selective acquisitions, though in recent years CHRW has slowed the pace of acquisitions. In 2009, the company acquired Walker, an international freight forwarding company, for $9.0 million; ITC, a customs brokerage, for $7.0 million; and Rosemont Farms, a produce marketing company, for $29.0 million. In 2008, the company acquired Transera International, a forwarding company, for $52.7 million.

## Company Financials Fiscal Year Ended Dec. 31

| Per Share Data ($) | 2010 | 2009 | 2008 | 2007 | 2006 | 2005 | 2004 | 2003 | 2002 | 2001 |
|---|---|---|---|---|---|---|---|---|---|---|
| Tangible Book Value | 4.92 | 4.14 | 4.46 | 4.47 | 3.86 | 3.11 | 2.60 | 2.09 | 1.59 | 1.23 |
| Cash Flow | 2.51 | 2.31 | 2.24 | 2.00 | 1.66 | 1.27 | 0.86 | 0.73 | 0.64 | 0.60 |
| Earnings | 2.33 | 2.13 | 2.08 | 1.86 | 1.53 | 1.16 | 0.80 | 0.67 | 0.56 | 0.49 |
| S&P Core Earnings | 2.33 | 2.13 | 2.08 | 1.86 | 1.53 | 1.16 | 0.79 | 0.63 | 0.56 | 0.47 |
| Dividends | Nil | 0.25 | 0.90 | 0.75 | 0.57 | 0.36 | 0.26 | 0.18 | 0.13 | 0.11 |
| Payout Ratio | Nil | 12% | 43% | 0% | 37% | 31% | 32% | 27% | 23% | 21% |
| Prices:High | 81.02 | 61.69 | 67.36 | 58.19 | 55.18 | 41.70 | 28.20 | 21.50 | 17.70 | 16.13 |
| Prices:Low | 51.16 | 37.36 | 36.50 | 42.11 | 35.55 | 23.60 | 18.30 | 13.50 | 12.92 | 11.41 |
| P/E Ratio:High | 35 | 29 | 32 | 31 | 36 | 36 | 35 | 32 | 32 | 33 |
| P/E Ratio:Low | 22 | 18 | 18 | 23 | 23 | 20 | 23 | 20 | 23 | 23 |

### Income Statement Analysis (Million $)

| | 2010 | 2009 | 2008 | 2007 | 2006 | 2005 | 2004 | 2003 | 2002 | 2001 |
|---|---|---|---|---|---|---|---|---|---|---|
| Revenue | 9,274 | 7,577 | 8,579 | 7,316 | 6,556 | 5,689 | 4,342 | 3,614 | 3,294 | 3,090 |
| Operating Income | 652 | 615 | 598 | 534 | 439 | 345 | 235 | 195 | 171 | 153 |
| Depreciation | 29.4 | 30.5 | 26.9 | 24.1 | 23.9 | 18.5 | 11.8 | 11.0 | 14.0 | 19.1 |
| Interest Expense | NA | NA | Nil | Nil | Nil | Nil | Nil | Nil | Nil | Nil |
| Pretax Income | 624 | 587 | 578 | 524 | 430 | 333 | 226 | 186 | 158 | 138 |
| Effective Tax Rate | NA | 38.5% | 37.9% | 38.1% | 37.9% | 38.9% | 39.3% | 38.7% | 39.0% | 39.3% |
| Net Income | 387 | 361 | 359 | 324 | 267 | 203 | 137 | 114 | 96.3 | 84.0 |
| S&P Core Earnings | 387 | 361 | 359 | 324 | 267 | 203 | 136 | 107 | 94.9 | 79.8 |

### Balance Sheet & Other Financial Data (Million $)

| | 2010 | 2009 | 2008 | 2007 | 2006 | 2005 | 2004 | 2003 | 2002 | 2001 |
|---|---|---|---|---|---|---|---|---|---|---|
| Cash | 408 | 386 | 497 | 455 | 349 | 231 | 166 | 199 | 133 | 116 |
| Current Assets | 1,482 | 1,307 | 1,348 | 1,389 | 1,256 | 1,085 | 846 | 717 | 589 | 503 |
| Total Assets | 1,996 | 1,834 | 1,816 | 1,811 | 1,632 | 1,395 | 1,081 | 908 | 778 | 683 |
| Current Liabilities | 772 | 732 | 698 | 758 | 687 | 612 | 453 | 381 | 343 | 324 |
| Long Term Debt | NA | NA | Nil | Nil | Nil | Nil | Nil | Nil | Nil | Nil |
| Common Equity | 1,204 | 1,080 | 1,107 | 1,042 | 944 | 780 | 621 | 517 | 426 | 356 |
| Total Capital | 1,204 | 1,080 | 1,107 | 1,042 | 944 | 782 | 621 | 524 | 432 | 359 |
| Capital Expenditures | 17.7 | 34.5 | 23.8 | 43.7 | 43.2 | 21.8 | 34.7 | 8.57 | 17.3 | 17.1 |
| Cash Flow | 416 | 391 | 386 | 348 | 291 | 222 | 149 | 125 | 110 | 103 |
| Current Ratio | 1.9 | 1.8 | 1.9 | 1.8 | 1.8 | 1.8 | 1.9 | 1.9 | 1.7 | 1.6 |
| % Long Term Debt of Capitalization | Nil | Nil | Nil | Nil | Nil | Nil | Nil | Nil | Nil | Nil |
| % Net Income of Revenue | 4.2 | 4.8 | 4.2 | 4.4 | 4.1 | 3.6 | 3.2 | 3.2 | 2.9 | 2.7 |
| % Return on Assets | 20.2 | 19.8 | 19.8 | 18.8 | 17.6 | 16.4 | 13.8 | 13.5 | 13.2 | 12.7 |
| % Return on Equity | 33.9 | 33.0 | 33.4 | 32.7 | 31.0 | 29.0 | 24.1 | 24.2 | 24.6 | 25.7 |

Data as orig reptd.; bef. results of disc opers/spec. items. Per share data adj. for stk. divs.; EPS diluted. E-Estimated. NA-Not Available. NM-Not Meaningful. NR-Not Ranked. UR-Under Review.

**Office:** 14701 Charlson Rd, Eden Prairie, MN 55347-5076.
**Telephone:** 952-937-8500.
**Website:** http://www.chrobinson.com
**Chrmn, Pres & CEO:** J.P. Wiehoff

**CFO & Chief Acctg Officer:** C.M. Lindbloom
**Treas:** T.A. Renner
**Secy & General Counsel:** B.G. Campbell
**Investor Contact:** A. Freeman (952-937-7847)

**Board Members:** R. Ezrilov, W. M. Fortun, D. W. MacLennan, R. K. Roloff, B. Short, J. B. Stake, M. W. Wickham, J. P. Wiehoff

**Founded:** 1905
**Domicile:** Delaware
**Employees:** 7,628

# Chubb Corp (The)

**STANDARD &POOR'S**

| S&P Recommendation | BUY ★★★★☆ | Price $63.82 (as of Nov 25, 2011) | 12-Mo. Target Price $75.00 | Investment Style Large-Cap Blend |

**GICS Sector** Financials
**Sub-Industry** Property & Casualty Insurance

**Summary** One of the largest U.S. property-casualty insurers, Chubb has carved out a number of niches, including high-end personal lines and specialty liability lines coverage.

## Key Stock Statistics (Source S&P, Vickers, company reports)

| | | | | | | | |
|---|---|---|---|---|---|---|---|
| 52-Wk Range | $70.07– 55.39 | S&P Oper. EPS 2011E | 5.15 | Market Capitalization(B) | $17.747 | Beta | 0.48 |
| Trailing 12-Month EPS | $6.20 | S&P Oper. EPS 2012E | 6.00 | Yield (%) | 2.44 | S&P 3-Yr. Proj. EPS CAGR(%) | 2 |
| Trailing 12-Month P/E | 10.3 | P/E on S&P Oper. EPS 2011E | 12.4 | Dividend Rate/Share | $1.56 | S&P Credit Rating | A+ |
| $10K Invested 5 Yrs Ago | $13,991 | Common Shares Outstg. (M) | 278.1 | Institutional Ownership (%) | 89 | | |

## Price Performance

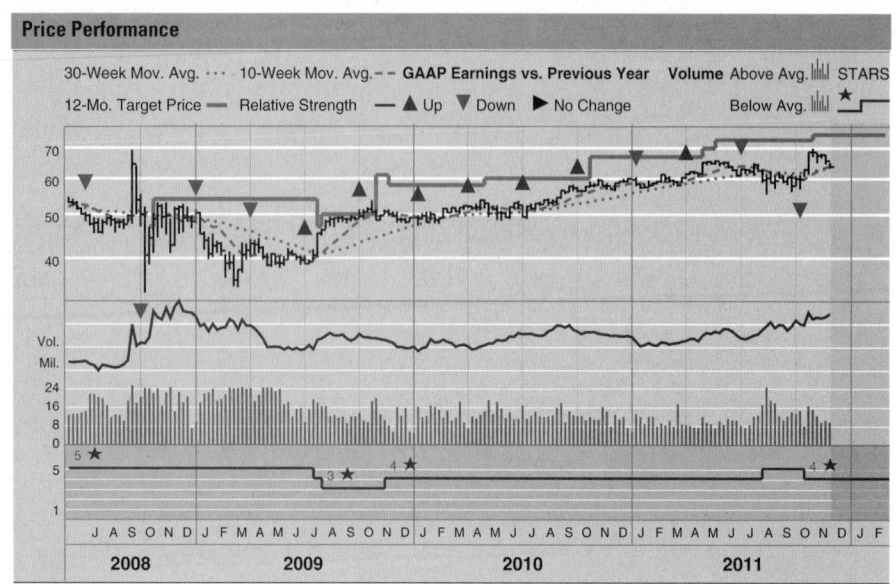

30-Week Mov. Avg. · · · 10-Week Mov. Avg. - - GAAP Earnings vs. Previous Year   Volume Above Avg. STARS
12-Mo. Target Price — Relative Strength — ▲ Up ▼ Down ► No Change   Below Avg. ★

Options: ASE, CBOE, P, Ph

Analysis prepared by Equity Analyst **Cathy Seifert** on Nov 21, 2011, when the stock traded at **$64.43**.

## Highlights

➤ We expect earned premiums to be modestly higher in 2011, with further gains expected in 2012. This is compared with the 1.0% decline reported in 2010 and the 4.2% decrease in 2009. We look for Chubb to leverage its financial strength and gain market share as some of its competitors experience financial stress. Pricing across many lines of business may also begin to firm in the aftermath of heavy catastrophe claims experienced so far in 2011. We think these two factors will aid premium growth relative to some of CB's peers in 2012.

➤ We see investment income inching up slightly in 2011, versus a rise of less than 1% in 2010 and a 4.5% decline in 2009, as still relatively low investment yields are being offset by relatively favorable cash flow trends. EPS results will likely be aided by share buybacks, such as the 37.7 million shares repurchased during 2010 at a cost of $2.0 billion.

➤ We estimate operating EPS of $5.15 for 2011 and $6.00 for 2012, versus the $5.90 reported for 2010. Our estimates reflect our view that underwriting margins will narrow amid a higher level of catastrophe claims, but that CB will not incur any large reserve boosts.

## Investment Rationale/Risk

➤ Our buy recommendation reflects our view that the shares of this prudent underwriter are undervalued at recent levels. We believe concerns over the adequacy of loss reserves in the professional liability unit may be eased by relatively favorable year-to-date underwriting results in that line. We also think CB has a superior personal lines franchise and a wider-margin mix of business and a higher-quality balance sheet than many of its peers.

➤ Risks to our recommendation and target price include deterioration in claim trends and loss reserves, and greater-than-expected deterioration in the company's investment portfolio. There is also a risk that competitive pricing pressures may not ease as much as expected in the aftermath of a period of heavy catastrophe losses.

➤ Our 12-month target price of $75 assumes that the stock's forward P/E multiple will increase to 12.5X our operating EPS estimate for 2012. This multiple is a slight premium to some of CB's closest peers, and is a little above the mid-point of the historical range.

## Qualitative Risk Assessment

| LOW | MEDIUM | HIGH |

Our risk assessment reflects our view that CB is a superior underwriter with sound capital and risk management practices and an attractive mix of business. This is offset by our concerns over the company's exposure to catastrophe and professional liability claims.

## Quantitative Evaluations

**S&P Quality Ranking** A

| D | C | B- | B | B+ | A- | A | A+ |

**Relative Strength Rank** STRONG

76

LOWEST = 1   HIGHEST = 99

## Revenue/Earnings Data

**Revenue (Million $)**

| | 1Q | 2Q | 3Q | 4Q | Year |
|---|---|---|---|---|---|
| 2011 | 3,420 | 3,400 | 3,420 | -- | -- |
| 2010 | 3,323 | 3,318 | 3,267 | -3,411 | 13,319 |
| 2009 | 2,965 | 3,266 | 3,320 | -3,465 | 13,016 |
| 2008 | 3,489 | 3,354 | 3,303 | 3,075 | 13,221 |
| 2007 | 3,519 | 3,521 | 3,549 | 3,518 | 14,107 |
| 2006 | 3,506 | 3,445 | 3,451 | 3,601 | 14,003 |

**Earnings Per Share ($)**

| | 1Q | 2Q | 3Q | 4Q | Year |
|---|---|---|---|---|---|
| 2011 | 1.70 | 1.42 | 1.04 | E1.66 | E5.15 |
| 2010 | 1.39 | 1.59 | 1.80 | 2.02 | 6.76 |
| 2009 | 0.95 | 1.54 | 1.69 | 2.03 | 6.18 |
| 2008 | 1.77 | 1.27 | 0.73 | 1.13 | 4.92 |
| 2007 | 1.71 | 1.75 | 1.87 | 1.68 | 7.01 |
| 2006 | 1.58 | 1.41 | 1.43 | 1.56 | 5.98 |

Fiscal year ended Dec. 31. Next earnings report expected: Late January. EPS Estimates based on S&P Operating Earnings; historical GAAP earnings are as reported.

## Dividend Data (Dates: mm/dd Payment Date: mm/dd/yy)

| Amount ($) | Date Decl. | Ex-Div. Date | Stk. of Record | Payment Date |
|---|---|---|---|---|
| 0.370 | 12/09 | 12/21 | 12/23 | 01/11/11 |
| 0.390 | 02/24 | 03/16 | 03/18 | 04/05/11 |
| 0.390 | 06/09 | 06/22 | 06/24 | 07/12/11 |
| 0.390 | 09/08 | 09/21 | 09/23 | 10/11/11 |

Dividends have been paid since 1902. Source: Company reports.

---

**Please read the Required Disclosures and Analyst Certification on the last page of this report.**

The **McGraw·Hill** Companies

# Chubb Corp (The)

**STANDARD
&POOR'S**

## Business Summary November 21, 2011

CORPORATE OVERVIEW. Chubb Corp.'s property-casualty operations are divided into three strategic business units: Personal Lines (34% of net written insurance premiums in 2010); Commercial Insurance (42%); and Specialty Insurance (24%). Net written premiums totaled $11.2 billion in 2010, up slightly from net written premiums of $11.1 billion recorded in 2009. During 2010, 72% of CB's written premiums originated in the United States, while 28% was derived from overseas.

The Personal Lines division offers primarily automobile and homeowners insurance coverage. The company's products are typically targeted to individuals with upscale homes and automobiles, requiring more coverage choices and higher policy limits than are offered under standard insurance policies. Net written premiums totaled $3.83 billion in 2010 (up from $3.66 billion in 2009), and were divided as follows: homeowners 62%, automobile 17%, and other (mainly personal article coverage) 21%.

Chubb Commercial Insurance underwrites an array of commercial insurance

policies, including those for multiple peril, casualty, workers' compensation, and property and marine coverage. Net written premiums totaled $4.68 billion in 2010 (up fractionally from $4.66 billion in 2009) and were divided as follows: commercial casualty 33%, commercial multi-peril 23%, property and marine 28%, and workers' compensation 16%.

Chubb Specialty Insurance offers a variety of specialized executive protection and professional liability products for privately and publicly owned companies, financial institutions, professional firms, and health care organizations. Net written premiums totaled $2.73 billion in 2010 (down from $2.74 billion in 2009), and were divided as follows: professional liability 88%, and surety 12%. Reinsurance assumed totaled $8 million in 2010, down from $21 million in 2009.

## Company Financials Fiscal Year Ended Dec. 31

| Per Share Data ($) | 2010 | 2009 | 2008 | 2007 | 2006 | 2005 | 2004 | 2003 | 2002 | 2001 |
|---|---|---|---|---|---|---|---|---|---|---|
| Tangible Book Value | 50.67 | 50.03 | 36.63 | 37.31 | 32.57 | 28.56 | 25.06 | 21.50 | 18.67 | 17.81 |
| Operating Earnings | NA | NA | NA | NA | NA | NA | NA | NA | 0.58 | 0.31 |
| Earnings | 6.76 | 6.18 | 4.92 | 7.01 | 5.98 | 4.47 | 4.01 | 2.23 | 0.65 | 0.32 |
| S&P Core Earnings | 5.90 | 6.14 | 5.58 | 6.41 | 5.63 | 3.87 | 3.63 | 2.08 | 0.42 | 0.19 |
| Dividends | 1.48 | 1.40 | 1.32 | 1.45 | 1.00 | 1.08 | 0.78 | 0.72 | 0.70 | 0.68 |
| Payout Ratio | 22% | 23% | 27% | 21% | 17% | 24% | 19% | 32% | 109% | NM |
| Prices:High | 60.23 | 53.79 | 69.39 | 55.99 | 54.73 | 49.73 | 38.73 | 34.65 | 39.32 | 43.31 |
| Prices:Low | 47.10 | 34.44 | 33.47 | 45.65 | 46.61 | 36.51 | 31.50 | 20.89 | 25.96 | 27.77 |
| P/E Ratio:High | 9 | 9 | 14 | 8 | 9 | 11 | 10 | 16 | 61 | NM |
| P/E Ratio:Low | 7 | 6 | 7 | 7 | 8 | 8 | 8 | 9 | 40 | NM |

| Income Statement Analysis (Million $) | | | | | | | | | | |
|---|---|---|---|---|---|---|---|---|---|---|
| Premium Income | 11,215 | 11,331 | 11,828 | 11,946 | 11,958 | 12,176 | 11,636 | 10,183 | 8,035 | 6,656 |
| Net Investment Income | 1,665 | 1,649 | 1,732 | 1,738 | 1,580 | 1,408 | 1,256 | 1,118 | 997 | 983 |
| Other Revenue | 439 | 36.0 | -339 | 423 | 465 | 12,675 | 286 | 93.2 | 57.7 | 115 |
| Total Revenue | 13,319 | 13,016 | 13,221 | 14,107 | 14,003 | 14,082 | 13,177 | 11,394 | 9,140 | 7,754 |
| Pretax Income | 2,839 | 2,954 | 2,537 | 3,937 | 3,525 | 2,447 | 2,068 | 934 | 168 | -66.0 |
| Net Operating Income | NA | NA | NA | NA | NA | NA | NA | NA | 201 | 111 |
| Net Income | 2,174 | 2,183 | 1,804 | 2,807 | 2,528 | 1,826 | 1,548 | 809 | 223 | 112 |
| S&P Core Earnings | 1,897 | 2,168 | 2,045 | 2,564 | 2,378 | 1,578 | 1,402 | 754 | 146 | 65.2 |

| Balance Sheet & Other Financial Data (Million $) | | | | | | | | | | |
|---|---|---|---|---|---|---|---|---|---|---|
| Cash & Equivalent | 517 | 511 | 491 | 489 | 449 | 427 | 392 | 1,044 | 1,644 | 691 |
| Premiums Due | 2,098 | 2,101 | 2,201 | 2,227 | 2,314 | 2,319 | 2,336 | 2,188 | 6,112 | 6,198 |
| Investment Assets:Bonds | 36,519 | 36,578 | 32,755 | 33,871 | 31,966 | 30,523 | 28,009 | 22,412 | 18,263 | 16,117 |
| Investment Assets:Stocks | 1,550 | 1,433 | 1,479 | 2,320 | 1,957 | 2,212 | 1,841 | 1,514 | 795 | 710 |
| Investment Assets:Loans | Nil | Nil | Nil | Nil | Nil | Nil | Nil | Nil | Nil | Nil |
| Investment Assets:Total | 42,213 | 42,004 | 38,738 | 40,081 | 37,693 | 34,893 | 31,504 | 26,934 | 21,279 | 17,784 |
| Deferred Policy Costs | 1,562 | 1,533 | 1,532 | 1,556 | 1,480 | 1,445 | 1,435 | 1,343 | 1,150 | 929 |
| Total Assets | 50,249 | 50,449 | 48,429 | 50,574 | 50,277 | 48,061 | 44,260 | 38,361 | 34,114 | 29,449 |
| Debt | 3,975 | 3,975 | 3,975 | 3,460 | 1,791 | 2,467 | 2,814 | 2,814 | 1,959 | 2,901 |
| Common Equity | 15,530 | 15,634 | 13,432 | 14,445 | 13,863 | 12,407 | 10,126 | 8,522 | 6,859 | 6,525 |
| Property & Casualty:Loss Ratio | 58.1 | 55.4 | 58.5 | 52.8 | 55.2 | 64.3 | 63.1 | 67.6 | 75.4 | 80.8 |
| Property & Casualty:Expense Ratio | 31.2 | 30.6 | 30.2 | 30.1 | 29.0 | 28.0 | 29.2 | 30.4 | 31.3 | 32.6 |
| Property & Casualty Combined Ratio | 89.3 | 86.0 | 88.7 | 82.9 | 84.2 | 92.3 | 92.3 | 98.0 | 106.7 | 113.4 |
| % Return on Revenue | 16.3 | 16.8 | 13.6 | 19.8 | 18.1 | 13.0 | 11.8 | 7.1 | 2.4 | 1.4 |
| % Return on Equity | 14.0 | NA | 12.9 | 19.8 | 19.2 | 16.2 | 16.6 | 10.5 | 3.3 | 1.7 |

Data as orig reptd.; bef. results of disc opers/spec. items. Per share data adj. for stk. divs.; EPS diluted. E-Estimated. NA-Not Available. NM-Not Meaningful. NR-Not Ranked. UR-Under Review.

**Office:** 15 Mountain View Road, Warren, NJ 07059.
**Telephone:** 908-903-2000.
**Email:** info@chubb.com
**Website:** http://www.chubb.com
**Chrmn, Pres & CEO:** J.D. Finnegan
**EVP & CFO:** R.G. Spiro
**EVP & General Counsel:** M.A. Brundage
**SVP & Chief Acctg Officer:** J.J. Kennedy
**Chief Admin Officer:** H.L. Morrison, Jr.
**Investor Contact:** G.A. Montgomery (908-903-2365)
**Board Members:** Z. B. Budinger, S. P. Burke, J. I. Cash, Jr., J. S. Derberg, J. D. Finnegan, L. W. Kellner, M. G. McGuinn, S. R. Pozzi, L. M. Small, D. E. Somers, J. M. Zimmerman, A. W. Zollar
**Founded:** 1967
**Domicile:** New Jersey
**Employees:** 10,100

The McGraw-Hill Companies

# Cigna Corp

**STANDARD &POOR'S**

**S&P Recommendation** BUY ★★★★☆

| | |
|---|---|
| **Price** $40.92 (as of Nov 25, 2011) | |
| **12-Mo. Target Price** $54.00 | |
| **Investment Style** Large-Cap Growth | |

**GICS Sector** Health Care
**Sub-Industry** Managed Health Care

**Summary** CIGNA is one of the largest investor-owned employee benefits organizations in the U.S. Its subsidiaries are major workplace providers of employee benefits.

## Key Stock Statistics (Source S&P, Vickers, company reports)

| | | | | | | | |
|---|---|---|---|---|---|---|---|
| 52-Wk Range | $52.95–35.63 | S&P Oper. EPS 2011E | 5.30 | Market Capitalization(B) | $11.058 | Beta | 1.48 |
| Trailing 12-Month EPS | $5.50 | S&P Oper. EPS 2012E | 5.75 | Yield (%) | 0.10 | S&P 3-Yr. Proj. EPS CAGR(%) | 10 |
| Trailing 12-Month P/E | 7.4 | P/E on S&P Oper. EPS 2011E | 7.7 | Dividend Rate/Share | $0.04 | S&P Credit Rating | BBB |
| $10K Invested 5 Yrs Ago | $9,913 | Common Shares Outstg. (M) | 270.2 | Institutional Ownership (%) | 85 | | |

## Price Performance

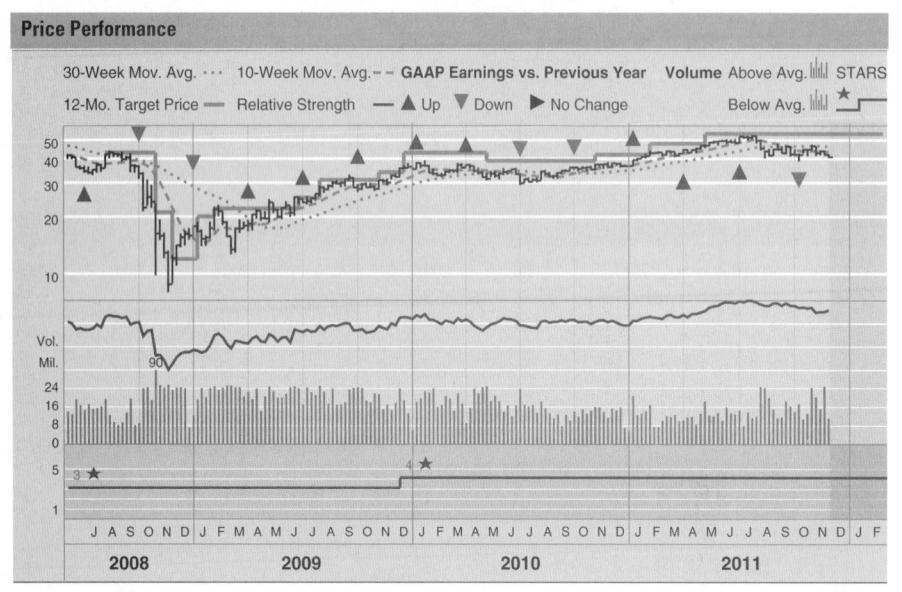

Options: ASE, CBOE, P, Ph

Analysis prepared by Equity Analyst **Phillip Seligman** on Nov 07, 2011, when the stock traded at **$41.88**.

### Highlights

► We look for companywide premium and fee revenue to rise more than 3% in 2011, after a nearly 15% advance in 2010, and we forecast almost 6% growth in 2012. In the health care segment, we expect enrollment losses in 2011, mainly on the elimination of the Medicare Advantage (MA) Private Fee-for-Service (PFFS) business and fewer national accounts. We expect enrollment in 2012 to rise, mainly on strong gains in commercial ASO markets.

► We expect commercial medical costs to decline in 2011 as a percentage of premiums (MCR: medical cost ratio), on the moderated cost trends. But we assume the trends will start to rise to more normalized levels in the fourth quarter of 2011. We look for the group disability and life results to be stable in 2011 and rise in 2012, and for the international segment to expand through 2012.

► We estimate adjusted EPS of $5.30 for 2011, versus $4.64 in 2010, and we look for $5.75 in 2012. Our model excludes future acquisitions and a pending 2012 accounting change in the international segment that if applied retroactively would reduce 2011 EPS by $0.22-$0.26.

### Investment Rationale/Risk

► We view CI's target of 10%-13% annual three- to five-year EPS growth as achievable. The company has been enjoying healthy member-ship gains in the individual/small-group, select and middle markets. We think this is partly due to a strong customer service focus, and its self-insured health plan with a stop-loss option. We are also positive on CI's international initiatives, which we believe will help attract national ac-counts. Our model excludes the planned $3.8 billion acquisition of HealthSpring Inc. (HS 54, Hold) in the first half of 2012. CI believes that the deal, which should boost its Medicare en-rollment, will be accretive to EPS in its first 12 months, despite its plan to fund the acquisition partly via new equity and debt. We think CI's existing commercial and MA businesses will benefit from the adoption of HS's physician en-gagement and health clinic models.

► Risks to our recommendation and target price include intensified competition and higher-than-expected medical costs.

► Our 12-month target price of $54 assumes a be-low-peers 9.4X forward multiple, in line with CI's historical discount, on our 2012 EPS esti-mate.

## Qualitative Risk Assessment

| LOW | MEDIUM | HIGH |
|---|---|---|

Our risk assessment reflects our view of CI's improving cost structure, strong cash flow, diversity, and wide range of products. However, competition has been intensifying in the managed care market, and CI's focus on maintaining pricing discipline in a weak economy has contributed to declines in enrollment.

## Quantitative Evaluations

**S&P Quality Ranking** B+

| D | C | B- | B | B+ | A- | A | A+ |
|---|---|---|---|---|---|---|---|

**Relative Strength Rank** MODERATE

46

LOWEST = 1    HIGHEST = 99

## Revenue/Earnings Data

**Revenue (Million $)**

| | 1Q | 2Q | 3Q | 4Q | Year |
|---|---|---|---|---|---|
| 2011 | 5,413 | 5,509 | 5,613 | -- | -- |
| 2010 | 5,205 | 5,353 | 5,266 | 5,429 | 21,253 |
| 2009 | 4,773 | 4,488 | 4,517 | 4,636 | 18,414 |
| 2008 | 4,569 | 4,863 | 4,852 | 4,817 | 19,101 |
| 2007 | 4,374 | 4,381 | 4,413 | 4,455 | 17,623 |
| 2006 | 4,107 | 4,098 | 4,137 | 4,205 | 16,547 |

**Earnings Per Share ($)**

| | | | | | |
|---|---|---|---|---|---|
| 2011 | 1.57 | 1.50 | 0.74 | E1.20 | E5.30 |
| 2010 | 1.02 | 1.06 | 1.13 | 1.69 | 4.89 |
| 2009 | 0.76 | 1.58 | 1.19 | 1.19 | 4.73 |
| 2008 | 0.20 | 0.98 | 0.62 | -0.78 | 1.04 |
| 2007 | 0.93 | 0.75 | 1.28 | 0.93 | 3.88 |
| 2006 | 0.96 | 0.78 | 0.93 | 0.76 | 3.44 |

Fiscal year ended Dec. 31. Next earnings report expected: Early February. EPS Estimates based on S&P Operating Earnings; historical GAAP earnings are as reported.

## Dividend Data (Dates: mm/dd Payment Date: mm/dd/yy)

| Amount ($) | Date Decl. | Ex-Div. Date | Stk. of Record | Payment Date |
|---|---|---|---|---|
| 0.040 | 02/24 | 03/09 | 03/11 | 04/11/11 |

Dividends have been paid since 1867. Source: Company reports.

---

**Please read the Required Disclosures and Analyst Certification on the last page of this report.**

**The McGraw-Hill Companies**

# Cigna Corp

**STANDARD &POOR'S**

## Business Summary November 07, 2011

CORPORATE OVERVIEW. CIGNA Corp., one of the largest U.S. employee benefits organizations, provides health care products and services and group life, accident and disability insurance.

Health Care offers group medical, dental, behavioral health and pharmacy services products. Medical products include consumer directed health plans (CDHPs), HMOs, network only, point-of-service (POS) plans, preferred provider organizations (PPOs), and traditional indemnity coverage. The health care products and services are offered through guaranteed cost, retrospectively experience-rated, administrative services only (ASO) and minimum premium funding arrangements. Under ASO, the employer or other plan sponsor self-funds all of its claims and assumes the risk for claim costs incurred. CI's CDHPs offer a modular product portfolio that provides a choice of benefits network and various funding, medical management, consumerism and health advocacy options for employers and consumers.

Medical covered lives as of September 30, 2011, totaled 11,471,000 (versus 11,437,000 as of December 31, 2010): 1,128,000 (1,177,000) guaranteed cost (commercial HMO and voluntary/limited benefits); 785,000 (761,000) experience-related indemnity; 44,000 (145,000) Medicare; and 9,514,000 (9,266,000) ASO. Restated in terms of covered lives by market segment: 3,811,000

(3,949,000) national accounts (multi-site employers with more than 5,000 employees); 6,761,000 (6,525,000) regional (multi-site employers with more than 250 but fewer than 5,000 employees, and single-site employers with more than 250 employees); 706,000 (620,000) select (employers with more than 50 but fewer than 250 employees); 120,000 (105,000) individual; 44,000 (54,000) Medicare HMO and Medicare Group Private Fee-for-Service (PFFS); 29,000 (184,000) other (small business, which includes employers with 2-50 employees, Medicare individual PFFS and student health business. CI has made a strategic business decision to de-emphasize these markets.

Disability and Life, which provides employer-paid and voluntary life, accident and disability products, held group life insurance policies covering 5.1 million lives at year-end 2010, up from 4.7 million at year-end 2009. International operates in selected markets outside the U.S., providing individual and group life, accident and health, health care and pension products. CI's invested assets under management at year-end 2010 totaled $20.9 billion, versus $19.8 billion at year-end 2009.

## Company Financials Fiscal Year Ended Dec. 31

| Per Share Data ($) | 2010 | 2009 | 2008 | 2007 | 2006 | 2005 | 2004 | 2003 | 2002 | 2001 |
|---|---|---|---|---|---|---|---|---|---|---|
| Tangible Book Value | 9.80 | 10.35 | 0.21 | 13.93 | 8.73 | 10.30 | 9.05 | 6.85 | 2.74 | 7.62 |
| Operating Earnings | NA | NA | NA | NA | NA | NA | NA | NA | NA | 2.45 |
| Earnings | 4.89 | 4.73 | 1.04 | 3.88 | 3.44 | 3.28 | 3.81 | 1.47 | -0.94 | 2.20 |
| S&P Core Earnings | 4.67 | 4.76 | 1.21 | 4.10 | 3.34 | 2.80 | 2.62 | 1.21 | -0.24 | 1.77 |
| Dividends | 0.04 | 0.04 | NA | 0.04 | 0.03 | 0.03 | 0.14 | 0.44 | 0.44 | 0.43 |
| Relative Payout | 1% | 1% | NA | 1% | 1% | 1% | 4% | 30% | NM | 19% |
| Prices:High | 39.26 | 38.12 | NA | 57.61 | 44.59 | 39.94 | 27.76 | 19.53 | 37.00 | 44.98 |
| Prices:Low | 29.12 | 12.68 | NA | 42.33 | 29.35 | 26.04 | 17.63 | 13.03 | 11.38 | 23.29 |
| P/E Ratio:High | 8 | 8 | NA | 15 | 13 | 12 | 7 | 13 | NM | 20 |
| P/E Ratio:Low | 6 | 3 | NA | 11 | 9 | 8 | 5 | 9 | NM | 11 |

### Income Statement Analysis (Million $)

| | 2010 | 2009 | 2008 | 2007 | 2006 | 2005 | 2004 | 2003 | 2002 | 2001 |
|---|---|---|---|---|---|---|---|---|---|---|
| Life Insurance in Force | 576,575 | 615,794 | NA | 475,346 | NA | NA | NA | 459,995 | 516,661 | 609,970 |
| Premium Income:Life A & H | 18,393 | 16,041 | NA | 15,008 | 13,641 | 13,695 | 14,236 | 15,441 | 15,737 | 15,367 |
| Premium Income:Casualty/Property. | Nil | Nil | NA | Nil | Nil | Nil | Nil | Nil | Nil | Nil |
| Net Investment Income | 1,105 | 1,014 | NA | 1,114 | 1,195 | 1,359 | 1,643 | 2,594 | 2,716 | 2,843 |
| Total Revenue | 21,253 | 18,414 | 19,101 | 17,623 | 16,547 | 16,684 | 18,176 | 18,808 | 19,348 | 19,115 |
| Pretax Income | 1,345 | 1,301 | 288 | 1,631 | 1,731 | 1,793 | 2,375 | 903 | -569 | 1,497 |
| Net Operating Income | NA | NA | NA | NA | NA | NA | NA | NA | NA | 1,101 |
| Net Income | 1,345 | 1,301 | 288 | 1,120 | 1,159 | 1,276 | 1,577 | 620 | -397 | 989 |
| S&P Core Earnings | 1,283 | 1,309 | 335 | 1,180 | 1,127 | 1,090 | 1,082 | 509 | -99.2 | 794 |

### Balance Sheet & Other Financial Data (Million $)

| | 2010 | 2009 | 2008 | 2007 | 2006 | 2005 | 2004 | 2003 | 2002 | 2001 |
|---|---|---|---|---|---|---|---|---|---|---|
| Cash & Equivalent | 1,840 | 1,162 | 1,439 | 2,203 | 1,647 | 1,991 | 2,804 | 1,860 | 2,079 | 2,455 |
| Premiums Due | 7,813 | 7,958 | NA | 8,736 | 9,501 | 8,616 | 16,223 | 9,421 | 9,981 | 2,832 |
| Investment Assets:Bonds | 14,709 | 13,443 | NA | 12,081 | 12,155 | 14,947 | 16,136 | 17,121 | 27,803 | 23,401 |
| Investment Assets:Stocks | 127 | 113 | NA | 132 | 131 | 135 | 33.0 | 11,300 | 295 | 404 |
| Investment Assets:Loans | 5,067 | 5,071 | NA | 4,727 | 5,393 | 5,271 | 5,123 | 10,227 | 11,134 | 12,694 |
| Investment Assets:Total | 20,948 | 19,839 | 17,921 | 17,530 | 18,303 | 21,376 | 21,919 | 39,658 | 40,362 | 38,261 |
| Deferred Policy Costs | 1,122 | 943 | NA | 816 | 707 | 618 | 544 | 580 | 494 | 448 |
| Total Assets | 45,682 | 43,013 | 41,406 | 40,065 | 42,399 | 44,863 | 81,059 | 90,953 | 88,950 | 91,589 |
| Debt | 2,288 | 2,436 | NA | 1,790 | 1,294 | 1,338 | 1,438 | 1,500 | 1,500 | 1,627 |
| Common Equity | 6,645 | 5,417 | 3,592 | 4,748 | 4,330 | 5,360 | 5,203 | 4,465 | 3,665 | 5,055 |
| Combined Loss-Expense Ratio | NA | NA | NA | NA | NA | NA | NA | NA | NA | NA |
| % Return on Revenue | 6.3 | 7.1 | 1.5 | 6.4 | 7.0 | 7.6 | 8.7 | 3.3 | NM | 5.2 |
| % Return on Equity | NA | 28.9 | NA | 24.7 | 23.9 | 24.2 | 32.2 | 15.3 | NM | 18.9 |
| % Investment Yield | 5.4 | 5.4 | 6.0 | 6.3 | 6.0 | 6.3 | 5.3 | 6.5 | 6.9 | 7.3 |

Data as orig reptd.; bef. results of disc opers/spec. items. Per share data adj. for stk. divs.; EPS diluted. E-Estimated. NA-Not Available. NM-Not Meaningful. NR-Not Ranked. UR-Under Review.

**Office:** 900 Cottage Grove Road, Bloomfield, CT 06002.
**Telephone:** 860-226-6000.
**Website:** http://www.cigna.com
**Chrmn:** I. Harris, Jr.

**Pres & CEO:** D.M. Cordani
**EVP & CFO:** R.J. Nicoletti
**EVP & General Counsel:** N.S. Jones
**Chief Acctg Officer:** M.T. Hoeltzel

**Investor Contact:** T. Detrick (215-761-1414)
**Board Members:** D. M. Cordani, E. J. Foss, I. Harris, Jr., J. E. Henney, R. Martinez, IV, J. Partridge, J. E. Rogers, Jr., J. P. Sullivan, C. C. Wait, E. C. Wiseman, D. F. Zarcone, W. D. Zollars

**Founded:** 1792
**Domicile:** Delaware
**Employees:** 30,600

*The McGraw-Hill Companies*

# Cincinnati Financial Corp

**STANDARD &POOR'S**

| S&P Recommendation | HOLD ★★★★☆ | Price $27.48 (as of Nov 25, 2011) | 12-Mo. Target Price $30.00 | Investment Style Large-Cap Blend |

**GICS Sector** Financials
**Sub-Industry** Property & Casualty Insurance

**Summary** This insurance holding company primarily markets property and casualty coverage. It also conducts life insurance and asset management operations.

## Key Stock Statistics (Source S&P, Vickers, company reports)

| | | | | | | | |
|---|---|---|---|---|---|---|---|
| 52-Wk Range | $34.33– 23.65 | S&P Oper. EPS 2011E | 0.38 | Market Capitalization(B) | $4.454 | Beta | 0.73 |
| Trailing 12-Month EPS | $0.98 | S&P Oper. EPS 2012E | 1.75 | Yield (%) | 5.86 | S&P 3-Yr. Proj. EPS CAGR(%) | 1 |
| Trailing 12-Month P/E | 28.0 | P/E on S&P Oper. EPS 2011E | 72.3 | Dividend Rate/Share | $1.61 | S&P Credit Rating | BBB |
| $10K Invested 5 Yrs Ago | $7,840 | Common Shares Outstg. (M) | 162.1 | Institutional Ownership (%) | 65 | | |

## Price Performance

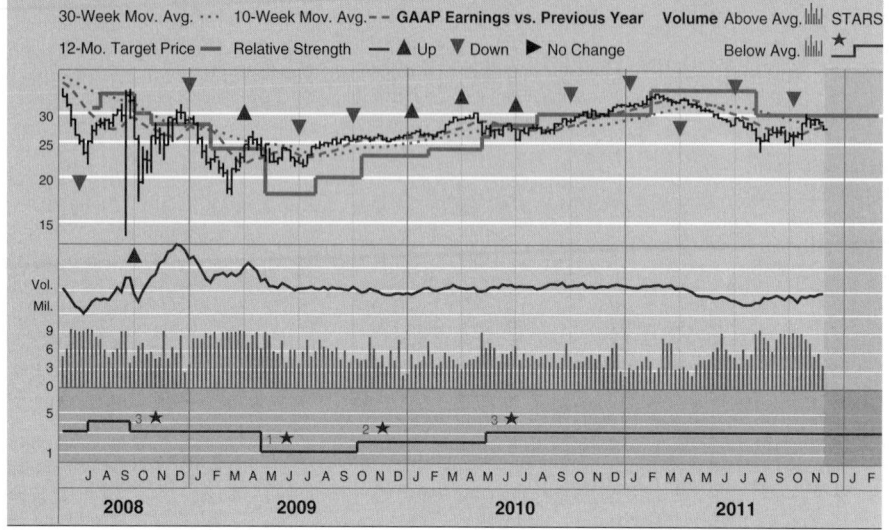

30-Week Mov. Avg. · · · 10-Week Mov. Avg. - - GAAP Earnings vs. Previous Year   Volume Above Avg. STARS
12-Mo. Target Price — Relative Strength — ▲ Up ▼ Down ► No Change   Below Avg. ★

Options: CBOE, P

Analysis prepared by Equity Analyst **Cathy Seifert** on Nov 01, 2011, when the stock traded at **$28.30**.

## Highlights

► We expect property-casualty earned premiums to advance modestly (2% to 4%) in 2011 and 2012, following a 1% rise in 2010 and a 2.6% drop in 2009. We see the effects of CINF's expansion being partly offset by price competition that may begin to ease. Underwriting margins should narrow in coming periods, particularly if catastrophe losses remain elevated. This impact may be offset, however, by cost-cutting initiatives CINF has undertaken.

► We estimate that net investment income will advance modestly in 2011 and 2012, after rising 3% in 2010 and declining 6.8% in 2009. The turnaround in investment results experienced in 2010 partly reflected steps CINF has taken in recent periods to shift its invested asset mix. However, CINF still has a greater exposure to equities than many of its peers. As of December 31, 2010, 26% of CINF's invested assets were in equity securities (versus 25% at December 31, 2009). This compares to an industry average that we estimate at less than 15%.

► We estimate operating EPS of $0.38 in 2011 and $1.75 in 2012, versus $1.68 in 2010, $1.32 in 2009 and $2.10 in 2008.

## Investment Rationale/Risk

► We view the shares, trading at a premium to most peers, as fairly valued, particularly on a price to operating earnings basis. Our outlook reflects what we see as the dual challenges of continued price competition in many of CINF's core lines of business and a challenging investment environment. We believe CINF's results on both of those fronts lag many peers. We also see a high degree of execution risk in a number of the company's expansion strategies. We note that the $1.61 indicated annual dividend exceeded 95% of 2010 reported operating earnings per share.

► Risks to our opinion and target price include a significant downturn in underwriting results (including an erosion in earned premiums and a significant narrowing of underwriting margins), and a greater-than-anticipated deterioration in investment results.

► Our 12-month target price of $30 assumes the shares will trade at approximately 17.1X our 2012 operating EPS estimate, a premium of more than 50% to most of the company's peers, and at the upper end of CINF's historical range.

## Qualitative Risk Assessment

| LOW | **MEDIUM** | HIGH |

Our risk assessment reflects our view of the company as a fairly conservative underwriter with sound risk and capital management policies. However, CINF's investment allocation is more heavily weighted than peers toward equity holdings, although the company has taken steps to re-balance its investments.

## Quantitative Evaluations

**S&P Quality Ranking**  A-

| D | C | B- | B | B+ | **A-** | A | A+ |

**Relative Strength Rank**  STRONG

LOWEST = 1   71   HIGHEST = 99

## Revenue/Earnings Data

### Revenue (Million $)

| | 1Q | 2Q | 3Q | 4Q | Year |
|---|---|---|---|---|---|
| 2011 | 929.0 | 975.0 | 944.0 | -- | -- |
| 2010 | 887.0 | 878.0 | 1,071 | 936.0 | 3,772 |
| 2009 | 890.0 | 874.0 | 1,007 | 1,133 | 3,903 |
| 2008 | 704.0 | 917.0 | 1,186 | 1,018 | 3,824 |
| 2007 | 1,031 | 1,270 | 982.0 | 983.0 | 4,259 |
| 2006 | 1,607 | 981.0 | 967.0 | 995.0 | 4,550 |

### Earnings Per Share ($)

| | 1Q | 2Q | 3Q | 4Q | Year |
|---|---|---|---|---|---|
| 2011 | 0.38 | -0.30 | 0.12 | E0.49 | E0.38 |
| 2010 | 0.42 | 0.17 | 0.95 | 0.77 | 2.31 |
| 2009 | 0.22 | -0.12 | 1.05 | 1.50 | 2.65 |
| 2008 | -0.25 | 0.38 | 1.50 | 0.99 | 2.63 |
| 2007 | 1.11 | 2.02 | 0.72 | 1.11 | 4.97 |
| 2006 | 3.13 | 0.76 | 0.66 | 0.75 | 5.30 |

Fiscal year ended Dec. 31. Next earnings report expected: Early February. EPS Estimates based on S&P Operating Earnings; historical GAAP earnings are as reported.

## Dividend Data (Dates: mm/dd Payment Date: mm/dd/yy)

| Amount ($) | Date Decl. | Ex-Div. Date | Stk. of Record | Payment Date |
|---|---|---|---|---|
| 0.400 | 01/28 | 03/21 | 03/23 | 04/15/11 |
| 0.400 | 05/23 | 06/20 | 06/22 | 07/15/11 |
| 0.403 | 08/15 | 09/19 | 09/21 | 10/17/11 |
| 0.403 | 11/21 | 12/19 | 12/21 | 01/17/12 |

Dividends have been paid since 1954. Source: Company reports.

# Cincinnati Financial Corp

STANDARD &POOR'S

## Business Summary November 01, 2011

CORPORATE OVERVIEW. Cincinnati Financial Corp. (CINF) underwrites and sells property-casualty insurance primarily in the Midwest and Southeast, through a network of independent agents. Operations as of year-end 2010 were conducted in 39 states. The company is licensed in all 50 states, the District of Columbia, and Puerto Rico. An ongoing geographical expansion plan is being implemented. Ten states accounted for about 67% of earned premium volume in 2010: Ohio (21%), Illinois (8%), Indiana (7%), Pennsylvania (6%), North Carolina (5%), Georgia (5%), Michigan (4%), Virginia (4%), Kentucky (4%), and Tennessee (3%).

Property-casualty net earned premiums totaled $2.9 billion in 2010, with commercial lines accounting for 75% and personal lines for 25% and excess and surplus lines for less than 1%. During 2010, commercial casualty lines of coverage accounted for 32% of commercial lines earned premiums, while commercial property lines coverage accounted for 23%, commercial auto for 18%, workers' compensation for 14%, special package coverages for 7%, surety and executive risk for 4%, and other for 2%. Personal auto accounted for 47% of personal lines earned premiums in 2010, homeowners' coverage for 40%, and other personal lines for 13%.

Underwriting results improved modestly in 2010 (amid lower catastrophe claims), but remained unprofitable. The loss ratio in 2010 equaled 68.9% (including 5.1 points of catastrophe losses), versus 71.7% in 2009 (including 5.7 points of catastrophe losses). The expense ratio inched upward, to 32.9%, from 32.7%. Taken together, the combined ratio (before policyholder dividends) equaled 101.8% in 2010, a slight improvement from 2009's combined ratio of 104.4%. (A combined ratio of under 100% indicates an underwriting profit, while one in excess of 100% signals an underwriting loss.)

Life, accident and health insurance is marketed through property-casualty agents and independent life insurance agents. This unit has been expanding its work site marketing activities, introducing a new product line and exploring expansion opportunities. During 2010, four lines of business -- term insurance, universal life insurance, work site products and whole life insurance -- accounted for nearly 97% of this unit's revenues. Life insurance earned premiums totaled $204 million in 2010, up from $143 million in 2009.

## Company Financials  Fiscal Year Ended Dec. 31

| Per Share Data ($) | 2010 | 2009 | 2008 | 2007 | 2006 | 2005 | 2004 | 2003 | 2002 | 2001 |
|---|---|---|---|---|---|---|---|---|---|---|
| Tangible Book Value | 30.87 | 29.38 | 22.67 | 32.94 | 39.38 | 34.88 | 35.60 | 35.10 | 31.42 | 33.62 |
| Operating Earnings | NA | NA | NA | NA | 2.82 | 3.02 | 2.93 | NA | 1.67 | 1.17 |
| Earnings | 2.31 | 2.65 | 2.63 | 4.97 | 5.30 | 3.40 | 3.28 | 2.10 | 1.32 | 1.08 |
| S&P Core Earnings | 1.69 | 1.28 | 2.16 | 3.49 | 2.78 | 3.10 | 2.87 | 2.09 | 1.55 | 1.06 |
| Dividends | 1.99 | 1.57 | 1.56 | 1.42 | 1.34 | 1.21 | 1.04 | 0.91 | 0.81 | 0.76 |
| Relative Payout | 86% | 59% | 59% | 29% | 25% | 35% | 32% | 43% | 61% | 71% |
| Prices:High | 32.27 | 29.66 | 40.24 | 48.45 | 49.19 | 45.95 | 43.52 | 38.01 | 42.90 | 38.94 |
| Prices:Low | 25.25 | 17.84 | 13.68 | 36.00 | 41.21 | 38.38 | 36.57 | 30.00 | 29.42 | 30.84 |
| P/E Ratio:High | 14 | 11 | 15 | 10 | 9 | 14 | 13 | 18 | 32 | 36 |
| P/E Ratio:Low | 11 | 7 | 5 | 7 | 8 | 11 | 11 | 14 | 22 | 29 |

| Income Statement Analysis (Million $) | 2010 | 2009 | 2008 | 2007 | 2006 | 2005 | 2004 | 2003 | 2002 | 2001 |
|---|---|---|---|---|---|---|---|---|---|---|
| Life Insurance in Force | 74,123 | 69,814 | 65,887 | 61,873 | 56,971 | 51,493 | 44,921 | 48,492 | 32,486 | 27,534 |
| Premium Income:Life A & H | 158 | 143 | 126 | 125 | 115 | 106 | 101 | 95.0 | 87.0 | 81.0 |
| Premium Income:Casualty/Property. | 2,924 | 2,911 | 3,010 | 3,125 | 3,163 | 3,058 | 2,919 | 2,653 | 2,391 | 2,071 |
| Net Investment Income | 518 | 501 | 537 | 608 | 570 | 526 | 492 | 465 | 445 | 421 |
| Total Revenue | 3,772 | 3,903 | 3,824 | 4,259 | 4,550 | 3,767 | 3,614 | 3,181 | 2,843 | 2,561 |
| Pretax Income | 501 | 582 | 540 | 1,192 | 1,329 | 823 | 800 | 480 | 279 | 221 |
| Net Operating Income | NA | NA | NA | NA | 496 | 562 | 524 | 286 | 300 | 210 |
| Net Income | 377 | 432 | 429 | 855 | 930 | 602 | 584 | 374 | 238 | 193 |
| S&P Core Earnings | 275 | 208 | 354 | 602 | 487 | 549 | 512 | 372 | 279 | 189 |

| Balance Sheet & Other Financial Data (Million $) | 2010 | 2009 | 2008 | 2007 | 2006 | 2005 | 2004 | 2003 | 2002 | 2001 |
|---|---|---|---|---|---|---|---|---|---|---|
| Cash & Equivalent | 385 | 557 | 1,009 | 226 | 202 | 119 | 306 | 91.0 | 112 | 93.0 |
| Premiums Due | 1,587 | 1,670 | 1,818 | 1,861 | 1,811 | 1,797 | 1,799 | 1,677 | 1,483 | 732 |
| Investment Assets:Bonds | 8,383 | 7,855 | 5,827 | 5,848 | 5,805 | 5,476 | 5,141 | 3,925 | 3,305 | 3,010 |
| Investment Assets:Stocks | 3,041 | 2,701 | 2,896 | 6,249 | 7,799 | 7,106 | 7,498 | 8,524 | 7,884 | 8,495 |
| Investment Assets:Loans | Nil | Nil | Nil | Nil | Nil | Nil | Nil | Nil | Nil | Nil |
| Investment Assets:Total | 11,508 | 10,643 | 8,890 | 12,261 | 13,759 | 12,702 | 12,677 | 12,527 | 11,257 | 11,571 |
| Deferred Policy Costs | 488 | 481 | 509 | 461 | 453 | 429 | 400 | 372 | 343 | 286 |
| Total Assets | 15,095 | 14,440 | 13,369 | 16,637 | 17,222 | 16,003 | 16,107 | 15,509 | 14,059 | 13,959 |
| Debt | 839 | 838 | 840 | 860 | 840 | 791 | 791 | 603 | 420 | 609 |
| Common Equity | 5,032 | 4,760 | 4,182 | 5,929 | 6,808 | 4,145 | 6,249 | 6,204 | 5,998 | 5,998 |
| Combined Loss-Expense Ratio | 101.7 | 104.5 | 100.6 | 90.3 | 94.3 | 89.2 | 89.8 | 94.7 | 98.4 | 104.9 |
| % Return on Revenue | 10.0 | 11.1 | 11.2 | 20.1 | 23.4 | 16.0 | 16.2 | 11.8 | 8.4 | 7.5 |
| % Return on Equity | 7.7 | 9.7 | 8.5 | 13.4 | 14.4 | 15.4 | 8.0 | 5.4 | 3.6 | 3.2 |
| % Investment Yield | 4.7 | 5.1 | 5.3 | 4.7 | 4.3 | 4.1 | 3.9 | 3.9 | 3.9 | 3.7 |

Data as orig reptd.; bef. results of disc opers/spec. items. Per share data adj. for stk. divs.; EPS diluted. E-Estimated. NA-Not Available. NM-Not Meaningful. NR-Not Ranked. UR-Under Review.

**Office:** 6200 South Gilmore Road, Fairfield, OH 45014-5141.
**Telephone:** 513-870-2000.
**Email:** investor_inquiries@cinfin.com
**Website:** http://www.cinfin.com

**Chrmn:** K.W. Stecher
**Pres & CEO:** S.J. Johnston
**SVP, CFO & Treas:** M. Sewell
**SVP, Secy & General Counsel:** L.A. Love

**Chief Acctg Officer:** E.N. Mathews
**Investor Contact:** H.J. Wietzel (513-870-2768)
**Board Members:** W. F. Bahl, G. T. Bier, L. W. Clement-Holmes, K. C. Lichtendahl, W. R. McMullen, G. W. Price, J. J. Schiff, T. R. Schiff, D. S. Skidmore, K. W. Stecher, J. F. Steele, Jr., L. R. Webb, E. A. Woods

**Founded:** 1950
**Domicile:** Ohio
**Employees:** 4,060

# Cintas Corp

**STANDARD &POOR'S**

| S&P Recommendation | BUY ★★★★☆ | Price $27.63 (as of Nov 25, 2011) | 12-Mo. Target Price $39.00 | Investment Style Large-Cap Growth |
|---|---|---|---|---|

**GICS Sector** Industrials
**Sub-Industry** Diversified Support Services

**Summary** A leader in the corporate identity uniform business, Cintas also provides entrance mats, cleaning services and supplies, first aid products, and document management and shredding services.

## Key Stock Statistics (Source S&P, Vickers, company reports)

| | | | | | | | |
|---|---|---|---|---|---|---|---|
| 52-Wk Range | $34.54–26.39 | S&P Oper. EPS 2012E | 2.05 | Market Capitalization(B) | $3.584 | Beta | 0.90 |
| Trailing 12-Month EPS | $1.80 | S&P Oper. EPS 2013E | 2.27 | Yield (%) | 1.95 | S&P 3-Yr. Proj. EPS CAGR(%) | 15 |
| Trailing 12-Month P/E | 15.4 | P/E on S&P Oper. EPS 2012E | 13.5 | Dividend Rate/Share | $0.54 | S&P Credit Rating | BBB+ |
| $10K Invested 5 Yrs Ago | $7,197 | Common Shares Outstg. (M) | 129.7 | Institutional Ownership (%) | 73 | | |

## Price Performance

30-Week Mov. Avg. · · · 10-Week Mov. Avg. - - GAAP Earnings vs. Previous Year   Volume Above Avg.||||| STARS
12-Mo. Target Price — Relative Strength — ▲ Up ▼ Down ► No Change   Below Avg.||||| ★

Options: ASE, CBOE, P, Ph

Analysis prepared by Equity Analyst **Kevin Kirkeby** on Oct 19, 2011, when the stock traded at **$29.38**.

### Highlights

► We look for revenues to rise 7% in FY 12 (May), driven by an expected recovery in CTAS's rental unit. Price competition was aggressive during much of FY 11, but we think it will lessen in the coming year as the number of workers in industries served by CTAS rises. The sales team is generating new clients for the rental operations and making notable progress in cross-selling services, in our view.

► We see margins widening slightly during FY 12 as cost savings from facility closures and route consolidations offset higher garment expenses as well as rising diesel and natural gas prices. Further, we think the improved sales performance will benefit margins as the relatively high fixed costs associated with CTAS's laundry facilities and fleet of delivery trucks are spread across a greater number of uniforms.

► In the last 12 months, CTAS repurchased 15.8 million shares, or approximately 11% of its shares outstanding. Our EPS estimate for FY 12 of $2.05 reflects an average share count of 130.6 million.

### Investment Rationale/Risk

► Valuations compressed steadily over the past decade as CTAS's revenue growth slowed, which we attribute mostly to declines in headcount at many of its manufacturing customers. Still, the company has been actively investing during this time in its non-uniform service offerings. We believe CTAS is set to achieve faster revenue growth and a widening in margins across its business segments as the economy improves and employment levels rise. This is supportive of a P/E valuation in the top quartile of the five-year range, in our view.

► Risks to our recommendation and target price include a rise in fuel prices that slows business activity at CTAS's customers, declines in the prices CTAS receives for recycled paper, and regulatory changes that raise labor costs.

► Applying a 20X multiple to our forward four-quarter EPS estimate, we calculate a value of $41. Our DCF model yields an intrinsic value of approximately $37, assuming a 10.9% average cost of equity, 11% annual free cash flow growth over the next five years, and 3% growth in perpetuity. Blending these valuation models results in our 12-month target price of $39.

## Qualitative Risk Assessment

| LOW | MEDIUM | HIGH |
|---|---|---|

Our risk assessment reflects the company's leading position in its core business, other related services that we believe are showing growth, and what we view as a strong balance sheet and cash flow.

## Quantitative Evaluations

**S&P Quality Ranking**   A-

| D | C | B- | B | B+ | A- | A | A+ |
|---|---|---|---|---|---|---|---|

**Relative Strength Rank**   MODERATE

48

LOWEST = 1                    HIGHEST = 99

## Revenue/Earnings Data

**Revenue (Million $)**

| | 1Q | 2Q | 3Q | 4Q | Year |
|---|---|---|---|---|---|
| 2012 | 1,017 | -- | -- | -- | -- |
| 2011 | 923.9 | 936.6 | 937.8 | 1,012 | 3,810 |
| 2010 | 891.6 | 884.5 | 861.8 | 909.5 | 3,547 |
| 2009 | 1,002 | 985.2 | 908.6 | 878.7 | 3,775 |
| 2008 | 969.1 | 983.9 | 976.0 | 1,009 | 3,938 |
| 2007 | 914.2 | 923.3 | 905.4 | 964.1 | 3,707 |

**Earnings Per Share ($)**

| | | | | | |
|---|---|---|---|---|---|
| 2012 | 0.52 | E0.50 | E0.48 | E0.55 | E2.05 |
| 2011 | 0.40 | 0.38 | 0.41 | 0.49 | 1.68 |
| 2010 | 0.35 | 0.37 | 0.32 | 0.36 | 1.40 |
| 2009 | 0.51 | 0.47 | 0.47 | 0.03 | 1.48 |
| 2008 | 0.51 | 0.53 | 0.53 | 0.58 | 2.15 |
| 2007 | 0.53 | 0.51 | 0.48 | 0.57 | 2.09 |

Fiscal year ended May 31. Next earnings report expected: Late December. EPS Estimates based on S&P Operating Earnings; historical GAAP earnings are as reported.

## Dividend Data (Dates: mm/dd Payment Date: mm/dd/yy)

| Amount ($) | Date Decl. | Ex-Div. Date | Stk. of Record | Payment Date |
|---|---|---|---|---|
| 0.490 | 10/26 | 11/09 | 11/12 | 12/15/10 |
| 0.540 | 10/18 | 11/08 | 11/11 | 12/14/11 |

Dividends have been paid since 1984. Source: Company reports.

---

**Please read the Required Disclosures and Analyst Certification on the last page of this report.**

**The McGraw-Hill Companies**

# Cintas Corp

STANDARD
&POOR'S

## Business Summary October 19, 2011

CORPORATE OVERVIEW. Cintas Corp. is North America's leading supplier of corporate uniforms, as well as a significant provider of related services. The company operates through four segments: Rental Uniforms and Ancillary Products; Uniform Direct Sales; First Aid, Safety and Fire Protection Services; and Document Management Services.

The Rental operating segment (71% of total revenues in FY 11 (May) and 72% of gross profits) designs and manufactures corporate uniforms that it rents to its customers. Services provided to the rental markets by the company also include the cleaning of uniforms, as well as the provision of ongoing replacements as required by each customer. The company also offers ancillary products, including the rental or sale of entrance and special-purpose mats, towels, mops, and linen products, as well as sanitation supplies and services and cleanroom supplies. It operates through 166 rental processing plants, 105 rental branches and about 7,700 local delivery routes (down from about 8,400 at the end of FY 08 following route restructuring initiatives). The company also operates six garment manufacturing plants.

The Uniform Direct Sales segment (11%, 8%) includes the design, manufac-

ture and direct sale of uniforms to CTAS's national account customers. In recent years, there has been an effort to offer more branded items in its catalogs alongside the traditional propriety uniform and apparel lines. This segment generally has less recurring business than the rental operations.

The First Aid, Safety and Fire Protection segment (10%, 10%) provides first aid equipment, inspection, repair and recharging of portable fire extinguishers, fire suppression systems, and emergency and exit lights. In a short period of time, CTAS believes it has become the second-largest fire protection services company in the U.S., with capabilities in at least 42 of the top 50 cities. Although the company estimated the market for first aid and fire protection services to be about $4.5 billion a year, the recession and declines in non-residential construction prompted the company to re-evaluate its goals for this segment and cease providing fire protection services in certain smaller markets. As of May 2011, the unit operated through 60 dedicated facilities.

## Company Financials Fiscal Year Ended May 31

| Per Share Data ($) | 2011 | 2010 | 2009 | 2008 | 2007 | 2006 | 2005 | 2004 | 2003 | 2002 |
|---|---|---|---|---|---|---|---|---|---|---|
| Tangible Book Value | 5.09 | 6.93 | 5.83 | 4.92 | 4.73 | 4.73 | 6.15 | 6.32 | 5.42 | 4.39 |
| Cash Flow | 2.71 | 2.41 | 2.50 | 3.10 | 2.96 | 2.78 | 2.43 | 2.26 | 2.12 | 1.95 |
| Earnings | 1.68 | 1.40 | 1.48 | 2.15 | 2.09 | 1.94 | 1.74 | 1.58 | 1.45 | 1.36 |
| S&P Core Earnings | 1.68 | 1.49 | 1.48 | 2.15 | 2.09 | 1.92 | 1.69 | 1.54 | 1.43 | 1.33 |
| Dividends | NA | 0.48 | 0.46 | 0.39 | 0.35 | 0.32 | 0.32 | 0.29 | 0.27 | 0.25 |
| Payout Ratio | NA | 34% | 31% | 18% | 17% | 16% | 18% | 18% | 19% | 18% |
| Calendar Year | 2010 | 2009 | 2008 | 2007 | 2006 | 2005 | 2004 | 2003 | 2002 | 2001 |
| Prices:High | 29.72 | 30.85 | 33.89 | 42.89 | 44.30 | 45.50 | 50.35 | 50.68 | 56.62 | 53.25 |
| Prices:Low | 23.10 | 18.09 | 19.51 | 31.14 | 34.57 | 37.51 | 39.51 | 30.60 | 39.15 | 33.75 |
| P/E Ratio:High | 18 | 22 | 23 | 20 | 21 | 23 | 29 | 32 | 42 | 39 |
| P/E Ratio:Low | 14 | 13 | 13 | 14 | 17 | 19 | 23 | 19 | 29 | 25 |

### Income Statement Analysis (Million $)

| | 2011 | 2010 | 2009 | 2008 | 2007 | 2006 | 2005 | 2004 | 2003 | 2002 |
|---|---|---|---|---|---|---|---|---|---|---|
| Revenue | 3,810 | 3,547 | 3,775 | 3,938 | 3,707 | 3,404 | 3,067 | 2,814 | 2,687 | 2,271 |
| Operating Income | 591 | 564 | 653 | 726 | 713 | 674 | 614 | 602 | 539 | 478 |
| Depreciation | 151 | 152 | 158 | 149 | 135 | 127 | 120 | 117 | 115 | 101 |
| Interest Expense | 49.7 | 48.6 | 52.5 | 16.6 | 50.3 | 31.8 | 24.4 | 25.1 | 30.9 | 11.0 |
| Pretax Income | 393 | 344 | 362 | 531 | 534 | 522 | 477 | 432 | 396 | 372 |
| Effective Tax Rate | NA | NA | 37.4% | 36.8% | 37.3% | 37.3% | 37.0% | 37.0% | 37.0% | 37.0% |
| Net Income | 247 | 216 | 226 | 335 | 335 | 327 | 301 | 272 | 249 | 234 |
| S&P Core Earnings | 246 | 228 | 226 | 335 | 335 | 324 | 293 | 265 | 245 | 229 |

### Balance Sheet & Other Financial Data (Million $)

| | 2011 | 2010 | 2009 | 2008 | 2007 | 2006 | 2005 | 2004 | 2003 | 2002 |
|---|---|---|---|---|---|---|---|---|---|---|
| Cash | 525 | 566 | 250 | 192 | 155 | 241 | 309 | 254 | 57.7 | 85.1 |
| Current Assets | 1,701 | 1,525 | 1,270 | 1,282 | 1,157 | 1,178 | 1,167 | 1,034 | 878 | 853 |
| Total Assets | 4,352 | 3,970 | 3,695 | 3,809 | 3,570 | 3,425 | 3,060 | 2,810 | 2,583 | 2,519 |
| Current Liabilities | 434 | 384 | 317 | 367 | 403 | 412 | 356 | 326 | 305 | 313 |
| Long Term Debt | 1,285 | 785 | 786 | 943 | 877 | 794 | 465 | 474 | 535 | 703 |
| Common Equity | 2,303 | 2,534 | 2,367 | 2,254 | 2,168 | 2,088 | 2,104 | 1,888 | 1,646 | 1,424 |
| Total Capital | 3,589 | 3,320 | 3,154 | 3,198 | 3,167 | 3,013 | 2,703 | 2,485 | 2,278 | 2,207 |
| Capital Expenditures | 183 | 111 | 160 | 190 | 181 | 157 | 141 | 113 | 115 | 170 |
| Cash Flow | 398 | 368 | 384 | 484 | 470 | 454 | 420 | 389 | 365 | 335 |
| Current Ratio | 3.9 | 4.0 | 4.0 | 3.5 | 2.9 | 2.9 | 3.3 | 3.2 | 2.9 | 2.7 |
| % Long Term Debt of Capitalization | 35.8 | 23.7 | 24.9 | 28.4 | 27.7 | 26.4 | 17.2 | 19.1 | 23.5 | 31.9 |
| % Net Income of Revenue | 6.5 | 6.1 | 6.0 | 8.5 | 9.0 | 9.6 | 9.8 | 44.4 | 9.3 | 10.3 |
| % Return on Assets | 5.9 | 5.6 | 6.0 | 9.1 | 9.6 | 10.1 | 10.2 | 10.1 | 9.8 | 11.0 |
| % Return on Equity | 10.2 | 8.8 | 9.8 | 15.2 | 15.7 | 15.6 | 15.1 | 15.4 | 16.2 | 17.6 |

Data as orig reptd.; bef. results of disc opers/spec. items. Per share data adj. for stk. divs.; EPS diluted. E-Estimated. NA-Not Available. NM-Not Meaningful. NR-Not Ranked. UR-Under Review.

Office: 6800 Cintas Boulevard, PO Box 625737, Cincinnati, OH 45262-5737.
Telephone: 513-459-1200.
Website: http://www.cintas-corp.com
Chrmn: R.J. Kohlhepp

Pres & COO: J.P. Holloman
CEO: S.D. Farmer
Investor Contact: W.C. Gale (513-459-1200)
SVP, CFO & Chief Acctg Officer: W.C. Gale

Board Members: G. S. Adolph, M. W. Barstad, R. T. Farmer, S. D. Farmer, J. J. Johnson, R. J. Kohlhepp, D. C. Phillips, J. M. Scaminace, R. W. Tysoe

Founded: 1968
Domicile: Washington
Employees: 30,000

# Cisco Systems Inc

STANDARD &POOR'S

| S&P Recommendation | HOLD ★★★☆☆ | Price<br>$18.01 (as of Nov 28, 2011) | 12-Mo. Target Price<br>$21.00 | Investment Style<br>Large-Cap Growth |
|---|---|---|---|---|

**GICS Sector** Information Technology
**Sub-Industry** Communications Equipment

**Summary** This company offers a complete line of routers and switching products that connect and manage communications among local and wide area computer networks employing a variety of protocols.

## Key Stock Statistics (Source S&P, Vickers, company reports)

| | | | | | | | |
|---|---|---|---|---|---|---|---|
| 52-Wk Range | $22.34– 13.30 | S&P Oper. EPS 2012E | 1.60 | Market Capitalization(B) | $96.819 | Beta | 1.14 |
| Trailing 12-Month EPS | $1.16 | S&P Oper. EPS 2013E | 1.73 | Yield (%) | 1.33 | S&P 3-Yr. Proj. EPS CAGR(%) | 8 |
| Trailing 12-Month P/E | 15.5 | P/E on S&P Oper. EPS 2012E | 11.3 | Dividend Rate/Share | $0.24 | S&P Credit Rating | A+ |
| $10K Invested 5 Yrs Ago | $6,593 | Common Shares Outstg. (M) | 5,375.9 | Institutional Ownership (%) | 67 | | |

## Price Performance

30-Week Mov. Avg. · · · 10-Week Mov. Avg. - - GAAP Earnings vs. Previous Year   Volume Above Avg. STARS
12-Mo. Target Price — Relative Strength — ▲ Up ▼ Down ▶ No Change   Below Avg.

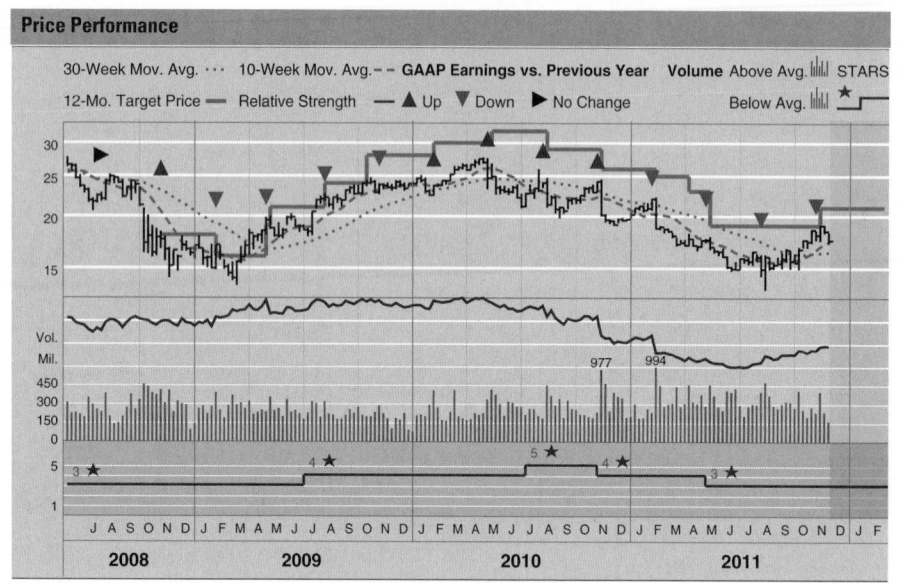

Options: ASE, CBOE, P, Ph

Analysis prepared by Equity Analyst **J. Moorman, CFA** on Nov 28, 2011, when the stock traded at **$17.98**.

## Highlights

➤ Following a 7.9% increase in FY 11 (Jul.), we see sales advancing 5.7% in FY 12 and 6.2% in FY 13, driven by higher new product demand, particularly for data center and collaboration solutions, and solid routing growth. We expect switching sales to lag the corporate average, however, as the company works through several new product transitions. CSCO is reorganizing its field sales, services and engineering operations to better focus on growth areas directly related to its core networking competency.

➤ Despite the expected higher sales volume, we see FY 12 gross margins narrowing about 160 basis points, to 61.7%, owing to an unfavorable sales mix shift toward new products and intensifying pricing pressure. As a result of a $1 billion cost reduction program announced in May, we expect FY 12 operating expenses to decline from the prior year. All told, we see FY 12 operating margins widening modestly to 26.9%.

➤ After taxes at a 20% effective rate, we project operating EPS of $1.60 in FY 12 and $1.73 in FY 13, versus $1.44 in FY 11. Estimates for both periods include $0.20 of projected stock option expense.

## Investment Rationale/Risk

➤ While we see CSCO benefiting from a rapid rise in bandwidth usage, we expect product transition issues, public spending weakness and pricing pressure to persist for the next several quarters. The company recently dropped its long-term 12% to 17% revenue growth outlook to a range of 5% to 7%. Although the stock is trading well below peers on a P/E and price-to-EBITDA basis, we think valuation multiples will remain depressed until CSCO proves it can maintain gross margins despite slowing revenue and a competitive environment. We think CSCO is performing well in a difficult environment, but remain cautious given today's macroeconomy.

➤ Risks to our recommendation and target price include a downturn in enterprise and telecom spending, increased competition, and delays related to the company's organizational realignment.

➤ Our 12-month target price of $21 equals 12X our FY 13 EPS estimate of $1.73, below peers, warranted by what we view as the company's below industry-average sales growth profile.

## Qualitative Risk Assessment

| LOW | MEDIUM | HIGH |
|---|---|---|

Our risk assessment reflects the highly competitive nature of the industry in which CSCO operates, balanced by our view of the company's strong financials, including $45 billion of cash and investments, and its dominant market position.

## Quantitative Evaluations

**S&P Quality Ranking**   B+

| D | C | B- | B | B+ | A- | A | A+ |
|---|---|---|---|---|---|---|---|

**Relative Strength Rank**   STRONG
89
LOWEST = 1   HIGHEST = 99

## Revenue/Earnings Data

**Revenue (Million $)**

| | 1Q | 2Q | 3Q | 4Q | Year |
|---|---|---|---|---|---|
| 2012 | 11,256 | -- | -- | -- | -- |
| 2011 | 10,750 | 10,407 | 10,866 | 11,195 | 43,218 |
| 2010 | 9,021 | 9,815 | 10,368 | 10,836 | 40,040 |
| 2009 | 10,331 | 9,089 | 8,162 | 8,535 | 36,117 |
| 2008 | 9,554 | 9,831 | 9,791 | 10,364 | 39,540 |
| 2007 | 8,184 | 8,439 | 8,866 | 9,433 | 34,922 |

**Earnings Per Share ($)**

| | | | | | |
|---|---|---|---|---|---|
| 2012 | 0.33 | E0.39 | E0.40 | E0.43 | E1.60 |
| 2011 | 0.34 | 0.27 | 0.33 | 0.22 | 1.17 |
| 2010 | 0.30 | 0.32 | 0.37 | 0.33 | 1.33 |
| 2009 | 0.37 | 0.26 | 0.23 | 0.19 | 1.05 |
| 2008 | 0.35 | 0.33 | 0.29 | 0.33 | 1.31 |
| 2007 | 0.26 | 0.31 | 0.30 | 0.33 | 1.17 |

Fiscal year ended Jul. 31. Next earnings report expected: Early February. EPS Estimates based on S&P Operating Earnings; historical GAAP earnings are as reported.

## Dividend Data (Dates: mm/dd Payment Date: mm/dd/yy)

| Amount ($) | Date Decl. | Ex-Div. Date | Stk. of Record | Payment Date |
|---|---|---|---|---|
| 0.060 | 03/18 | 03/29 | 03/31 | 04/20/11 |
| 0.060 | 06/08 | 07/05 | 07/07 | 07/27/11 |
| 0.060 | 09/20 | 10/04 | 10/06 | 10/26/11 |

Dividends have been paid since 2011. Source: Company reports.

# Cisco Systems Inc

STANDARD &POOR'S

## Business Summary November 28, 2011

CORPORATE OVERVIEW. Cisco Systems is the world's largest supplier of high-performance computer internetworking systems. The company's sales strategy is primarily based on distribution channel partners, with over 40,000 reseller partner sales representatives around the world. Geographically, FY 11 (Jul.) sales were distributed to the following regions: the U.S. and Canada (54%), Europe (20%), emerging markets (11%), and Asia-Pacific (15%).

Product families are categorized into four segments: switches (39% of total FY 11 product sales), routers (21%), new products (38%), and other (3%). The advanced technologies segment (moved in FY 11 to the new products segment) consisted of home networking, unified communications, security, storage area networking, wireless, application networking services, and video systems. The company also has a broad range of service offerings, including technical support services and advanced services.

In our view, the primary driver of company sales growth will be the new products segment. CSCO distinguishes its new products sub-segments as industry segments with the potential to become billion dollar businesses. We see the company continuing to identify additional advanced technology sub-segments in markets that build on its networking expertise. During FY 11, the company revised the categorization of certain products, with the new product segment replacing the prior advanced technologies segment. The new product category consists of collaboration, data center, security, wireless, and video connected home solutions.

MARKET PROFILE. With a dominant market share of approximately 60.3% of the overall Ethernet switching market, according to IDC, we believe CSCO has become the de facto choice for Ethernet switches. We view the company's large installed base as a significant competitive advantage over peers. In early 2008, the company introduced its new Nexus series of switches that aims to unify storage and computing in data centers.

## Company Financials Fiscal Year Ended Jul. 31

| Per Share Data ($) | 2011 | 2010 | 2009 | 2008 | 2007 | 2006 | 2005 | 2004 | 2003 | 2002 |
|---|---|---|---|---|---|---|---|---|---|---|
| Tangible Book Value | 5.13 | 4.30 | 4.15 | 3.37 | 2.76 | 2.07 | 2.74 | 3.16 | 3.35 | 3.33 |
| Cash Flow | 1.61 | 1.68 | 1.35 | 1.59 | 1.40 | 1.10 | 1.02 | 0.91 | 0.72 | 0.52 |
| Earnings | 1.17 | 1.33 | 1.05 | 1.31 | 1.17 | 0.89 | 0.87 | 0.70 | 0.50 | 0.25 |
| S&P Core Earnings | 1.16 | 1.31 | 1.06 | 1.30 | 1.15 | 0.88 | 0.70 | 0.52 | 0.28 | 0.12 |
| Dividends | 0.12 | Nil | Nil | Nil | Nil | Nil | Nil | Nil | Nil | Nil |
| Payout Ratio | 10% | Nil | Nil | Nil | Nil | Nil | Nil | Nil | Nil | Nil |
| Prices:High | 22.34 | 27.74 | 24.83 | 27.72 | 34.24 | 27.96 | 20.25 | 29.39 | 24.60 | 21.84 |
| Prices:Low | 13.30 | 19.00 | 13.61 | 14.20 | 24.82 | 17.10 | 16.83 | 17.53 | 12.33 | 12.24 |
| P/E Ratio:High | 19 | 21 | 24 | 21 | 29 | 31 | 23 | 42 | 49 | 87 |
| P/E Ratio:Low | 11 | 14 | 13 | 11 | 21 | 19 | 19 | 25 | 25 | 49 |

| Income Statement Analysis (Million $) | 2011 | 2010 | 2009 | 2008 | 2007 | 2006 | 2005 | 2004 | 2003 | 2002 |
|---|---|---|---|---|---|---|---|---|---|---|
| Revenue | 43,218 | 40,040 | 36,117 | 39,540 | 34,922 | 28,484 | 24,801 | 22,045 | 18,878 | 18,915 |
| Operating Income | 11,146 | 11,194 | 9,153 | 11,189 | 10,034 | 8,380 | 8,451 | 7,738 | 6,477 | 4,941 |
| Depreciation | 2,486 | 2,030 | 1,768 | 1,744 | 1,413 | 1,293 | 1,009 | 1,443 | 1,591 | 1,957 |
| Interest Expense | 628 | 623 | 346 | 319 | Nil | Nil | Nil | Nil | Nil | Nil |
| Pretax Income | 7,825 | 9,415 | 7,693 | 10,255 | 9,461 | 7,633 | 8,036 | 6,992 | 5,013 | 2,710 |
| Effective Tax Rate | NA | NA | 20.3% | 21.5% | 22.5% | 26.9% | 28.6% | 28.9% | 28.6% | 30.1% |
| Net Income | 6,490 | 7,767 | 6,134 | 8,052 | 7,333 | 5,580 | 5,741 | 4,968 | 3,578 | 1,893 |
| S&P Core Earnings | 6,393 | 7,622 | 6,186 | 7,985 | 7,197 | 5,499 | 4,645 | 3,652 | 2,051 | 931 |

| Balance Sheet & Other Financial Data (Million $) | 2011 | 2010 | 2009 | 2008 | 2007 | 2006 | 2005 | 2004 | 2003 | 2002 |
|---|---|---|---|---|---|---|---|---|---|---|
| Cash | 44,585 | 39,861 | 35,001 | 26,235 | 3,728 | 3,297 | 4,742 | 3,722 | 3,925 | 9,484 |
| Current Assets | 57,231 | 51,421 | 44,177 | 35,699 | 31,574 | 25,676 | 13,031 | 14,343 | 13,415 | 17,433 |
| Total Assets | 87,095 | 81,130 | 68,128 | 58,734 | 53,340 | 43,315 | 33,883 | 35,594 | 37,107 | 37,795 |
| Current Liabilities | 17,506 | 19,233 | 13,655 | 13,858 | 13,358 | 11,313 | 9,511 | 8,703 | 8,294 | 8,375 |
| Long Term Debt | 16,234 | 12,188 | 10,295 | 6,393 | 6,408 | 6,332 | Nil | Nil | Nil | Nil |
| Common Equity | 47,259 | 44,285 | 38,647 | 34,353 | 31,480 | 23,912 | 23,174 | 25,826 | 28,029 | 28,656 |
| Total Capital | 64,081 | 59,569 | 48,972 | 40,875 | 37,898 | 30,250 | 23,184 | 25,916 | 28,039 | 28,671 |
| Capital Expenditures | 1,174 | 1,008 | 1,005 | 1,268 | 1,251 | 772 | 692 | 613 | 717 | 2,641 |
| Cash Flow | 8,976 | 9,797 | 7,902 | 9,796 | 8,746 | 6,873 | 6,750 | 6,411 | 5,169 | 3,850 |
| Current Ratio | 3.3 | 2.7 | 3.2 | 2.6 | 2.4 | 2.3 | 1.4 | 1.6 | 1.6 | 2.1 |
| % Long Term Debt of Capitalization | 25.3 | 20.5 | 21.0 | 15.6 | 16.9 | 20.9 | Nil | Nil | Nil | Nil |
| % Net Income of Revenue | 15.0 | 19.4 | 17.0 | 20.4 | 21.0 | 19.6 | 23.1 | 22.5 | 19.0 | 10.0 |
| % Return on Assets | 7.7 | 10.4 | 9.7 | 14.4 | 15.2 | 14.5 | 16.5 | 13.7 | 9.6 | 5.2 |
| % Return on Equity | 14.2 | 18.7 | 16.8 | 24.5 | 26.5 | 23.7 | 23.4 | 18.4 | 12.6 | 6.8 |

Data as orig reptd.; bef. results of disc opers/spec. items. Per share data adj. for stk. divs.; EPS diluted. E-Estimated. NA-Not Available. NM-Not Meaningful. NR-Not Ranked. UR-Under Review.

**Office:** 170 West Tasman Drive, San Jose, CA 95134-1706.
**Telephone:** 408-526-4000.
**Email:** investor-relations@cisco.com
**Website:** http://www.cisco.com

**Chrmn & CEO:** J.T. Chambers
**COO & EVP:** G.B. Moore
**EVP & CFO:** F.A. Calderoni
**SVP, Secy & General Counsel:** M. Chandler

**SVP & CIO:** R.J. Jacoby
**Investor Contact:** L. Graves (408-526-6521)
**Board Members:** M. M. Burns, M. D. Capellas, L. R. Carter, J. T. Chambers, B. L. Halla, J. L. Hennessy, R. M. Kovacevich, R. C. Mcgeary, A. Sarin, J. Yang

**Founded:** 1984
**Domicile:** California
**Employees:** 71,825

The McGraw-Hill Companies

# Citigroup Inc

**STANDARD &POOR'S**

| S&P Recommendation | **HOLD** ★★★★★ | Price $27.48 (as of Nov 30, 2011) | 12-Mo. Target Price $35.00 | Investment Style Large-Cap Blend |
|---|---|---|---|---|

**GICS Sector** Financials
**Sub-Industry** Other Diversified Financial Services

**Summary** This diversified financial services company provides a wide range of financial services to consumers and corporate customers in more than 100 countries and territories.

## Key Stock Statistics (Source S&P, Vickers, company reports)

| | | | | | | | |
|---|---|---|---|---|---|---|---|
| 52-Wk Range | $51.50– 21.40 | S&P Oper. EPS 2011E | 4.20 | Market Capitalization(B) | $80.344 | Beta | 2.55 |
| Trailing 12-Month EPS | $3.75 | S&P Oper. EPS 2012E | 4.70 | Yield (%) | 0.15 | S&P 3-Yr. Proj. EPS CAGR(%) | 17 |
| Trailing 12-Month P/E | 7.3 | P/E on S&P Oper. EPS 2011E | 6.5 | Dividend Rate/Share | $0.04 | S&P Credit Rating | A- |
| $10K Invested 5 Yrs Ago | $613 | Common Shares Outstg. (M) | 2,923.7 | Institutional Ownership (%) | 60 | | |

## Price Performance

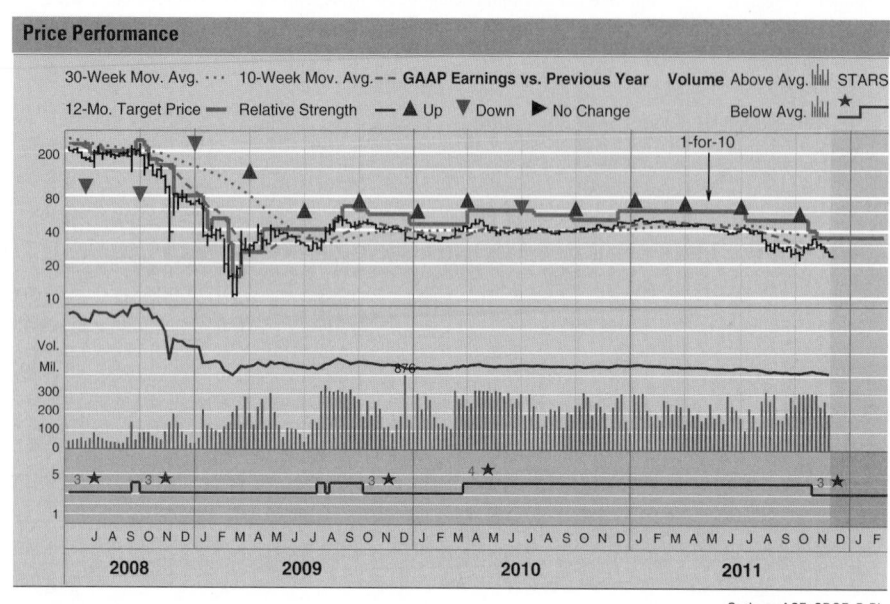

- 30-Week Mov. Avg. ···
- 10-Week Mov. Avg. - -
- **GAAP Earnings vs. Previous Year**
- Volume Above Avg. STARS
- 12-Mo. Target Price —
- Relative Strength —
- ▲ Up ▼ Down ▶ No Change
- Below Avg. ★

1-for-10

Options: ASE, CBOE, P, Ph

Analysis prepared by Equity Analyst **Erik Oja** on Nov 02, 2011, when the stock traded at **$29.83**.

## Highlights

➤ We expect C's total net revenues to fall 6.3% in 2011, and rise 1.6% in 2012. We see net interest income falling 10.5% in 2011, and rising 0.8% in 2012. However, we expect core noninterest revenues to rebound 9.1% in 2011, driven by principal transactions, which received a boost from valuation adjustments. For 2012, we expect core noninterest income to rise 3.0%.

➤ In the third quarter, Citigroup released $2.31 billion of reserves, contributing $0.57 to third quarter earnings of $1.26. C's total allowance for credit losses now stands at $32.1 billion, equal to 2.65X nonperforming loans, and 5.0% of total loans, much higher than peers levels. Third quarter net chargeoffs of $5.359 billion were slightly down from second quarter levels, non-performing loans fell 8.4% to $12.1 billion, or 1.9% of total loans, and new nonperforming loans were $3.4 billion, in line with previous quarterly trends. We see credit quality continuing to improve, and we expect the pace of reserve releases to decline. We see total provisions of $12.2 billion in 2011, down from $25.2 billion in 2010. For 2012, we see provisions of $13.1 billion.

➤ We see EPS of $4.20 in 2011 and $4.70 in 2012.

## Investment Rationale/Risk

➤ Citigroup's earnings have benefited from management's decision to lower reserves to $32.1 billion at September 30, down from a high of $48.7 billion at March 31, 2010. In these six quarters, C released $15.6 billion of reserves, which we calculate contributed nearly $4.50, or 75%, to GAAP earnings per share of $6.00 in that time period. We expect reserve releases to taper off to a total of $8.0 billion through the end of 2012, contributing about $2.00, or 35%, to our next five quarters EPS estimate of $5.60. Despite this, we think C is on track with building capital ratios, shedding non-core assets, and growing internationally.

➤ Risks to our recommendation and target price include higher FDIC fees on the largest banks, costs of U.S. financial regulatory reform, and foreclosure and mortgage putback issues.

➤ Our 12-month target price of $35 is based on a peer-level multiple of 8.0X our forward four quarters EPS estimate of $4.40, equal to 0.70X tangible book value per share, a 35% discount to peer JPMorgan Chase (JPM 34, Hold), and a 27% premium to peer Bank of America (BAC 7, Hold).

## Qualitative Risk Assessment

| LOW | **MEDIUM** | HIGH |
|---|---|---|

Our risk assessment reflects our view of C's exposure to risky assets on its balance sheet and to uncertain credit in domestic and international markets, offset by the many improvements C has made to capital levels, credit quality and earnings stability over the past two years.

## Quantitative Evaluations

**S&P Quality Ranking**    **B**

| D | C | B- | **B** | B+ | A- | A | A+ |
|---|---|---|---|---|---|---|---|

**Relative Strength Rank**    **MODERATE**

35

LOWEST = 1    HIGHEST = 99

## Revenue/Earnings Data

**Revenue (Million $)**

| | 1Q | 2Q | 3Q | 4Q | Year |
|---|---|---|---|---|---|
| 2011 | 25,702 | 27,060 | 26,862 | -- | -- |
| 2010 | 31,460 | 8,032 | 74,880 | 24,440 | 111,465 |
| 2009 | 32,178 | 36,811 | 27,070 | 11,947 | 108,006 |
| 2008 | 29,696 | 32,392 | 29,456 | 16,253 | 105,782 |
| 2007 | 43,021 | 45,802 | 43,197 | 27,209 | 159,229 |
| 2006 | 34,290 | 35,899 | 36,323 | 40,046 | 146,558 |

**Earnings Per Share ($)**

| | | | | | |
|---|---|---|---|---|---|
| 2011 | 10.00 | 1.07 | 1.24 | E0.90 | E4.20 |
| 2010 | 1.40 | 0.90 | 0.80 | 0.40 | 3.50 |
| 2009 | -1.60 | 5.10 | -2.30 | -3.40 | -7.60 |
| 2008 | -10.40 | -5.10 | -7.10 | -41.20 | -47.20 |
| 2007 | 10.10 | 12.40 | 4.40 | -19.90 | 7.20 |
| 2006 | 11.10 | 10.50 | 10.60 | 10.30 | 42.50 |

Fiscal year ended Dec. 31. Next earnings report expected: NA. EPS Estimates based on S&P Operating Earnings; historical GAAP earnings are as reported.

## Dividend Data (Dates: mm/dd Payment Date: mm/dd/yy)

| Amount ($) | Date Decl. | Ex-Div. Date | Stk. of Record | Payment Date |
|---|---|---|---|---|
| 1-for-10 REV. | -- | 05/06 | -- | 05/06/11 |
| 0.010 | 05/13 | 05/25 | 05/27 | 06/17/11 |
| 0.010 | 07/18 | 07/28 | 08/01 | 08/26/11 |
| 0.010 | 10/19 | 11/03 | 11/07 | 11/23/11 |

Dividends have been paid since 2011. Source: Company reports.

---

**Please read the Required Disclosures and Analyst Certification on the last page of this report.**

*The McGraw·Hill Companies*

# Citigroup Inc

STANDARD &POOR'S

## Business Summary November 02, 2011

CORPORATE OVERVIEW. Citigroup (C) consists of Citicorp, Citi Holdings, and Corporate / Other. Citicorp consists of core banking operations for consumers and businesses, and includes Regional Consumer Banking, Securities and Banking, and Transaction Services. Citi Holdings contains businesses and assets that the company no longer considers part of its core business, including its Brokerage and Asset Management, Local Consumer Lending and Special Asset Pool units. Its Corporate and Other segment includes global staff functions and other corporate expenses.

The Regional Consumer Banking unit offers traditional banking services to retail customers, as well as its branded cards business and a small commercial banking business. Securities and Banking includes securities and banking and transaction services units that provide corporate, institutional and high-net-worth clients with a wide range of banking and investment services and products.

Citi Holdings contains a number of businesses and assets that the company intends to exit as quickly as practicable through divestitures, portfolio run-off and asset sales. C has completed more than 30 divestiture transactions since the beginning of 2009, including Smith Barney, Nikko Cordial Securities, Nikko Asset Management, Primerica Financial Services, various credit card businesses, Diners Club North America, and The Student Loan Corporation. Citi Holdings' assets, at September 30, 2011, were $289 billion (about 14.9% of C's total assets), down from $359 billion (about 19% of C's total assets) at December 31, 2010, and $487 billion (26%) at December 31, 2009.

## Company Financials Fiscal Year Ended Dec. 31

| Per Share Data ($) | 2010 | 2009 | 2008 | 2007 | 2006 | 2005 | 2004 | 2003 | 2002 | 2001 |
|---|---|---|---|---|---|---|---|---|---|---|
| Tangible Book Value | 44.60 | 41.50 | 44.10 | 99.50 | 141.40 | 127.60 | 117.20 | 107.50 | 97.00 | 154.90 |
| Earnings | 3.50 | -7.60 | -47.20 | 7.20 | 42.50 | 38.20 | 32.60 | 34.20 | 25.90 | 27.50 |
| S&P Core Earnings | 3.50 | -15.30 | -49.70 | 4.30 | 40.90 | 36.90 | 40.20 | 33.50 | 23.30 | 25.10 |
| Dividends | Nil | 0.10 | 11.20 | 21.60 | 19.60 | 17.60 | 16.00 | 11.00 | 7.00 | 6.00 |
| Payout Ratio | Nil | NM | NM | NM | 46% | 46% | 49% | 32% | 27% | 22% |
| Prices:High | 50.70 | 75.85 | 298.90 | 562.80 | 570.00 | 499.90 | 528.80 | 491.50 | 522.00 | 573.75 |
| Prices:Low | 31.10 | 32.60 | 30.50 | 288.00 | 448.10 | 429.10 | 421.00 | 302.50 | 244.80 | 345.10 |
| P/E Ratio:High | 15 | NM | NM | 78 | 13 | 13 | 16 | 14 | 20 | 21 |
| P/E Ratio:Low | 9 | NM | NM | 40 | 11 | 11 | 13 | 9 | 9 | 13 |

| Income Statement Analysis (Million $) | 2010 | 2009 | 2008 | 2007 | 2006 | 2005 | 2004 | 2003 | 2002 | 2001 |
|---|---|---|---|---|---|---|---|---|---|---|
| Premium Income | 2,684 | 3,020 | 3,221 | 3,132 | 3,202 | 3,132 | 3,993 | 3,749 | 3,410 | 13,460 |
| Investment Income | NA | 29,178 | 44,319 | 58,273 | 41,409 | 28,833 | 22,728 | 18,937 | 21,036 | 26,949 |
| Other Revenue | NA | 75,808 | 58,242 | 126,392 | 109,179 | 88,353 | 81,555 | 72,027 | 68,110 | 71,613 |
| Total Revenue | 111,465 | 108,006 | 105,782 | 159,229 | 146,558 | 120,318 | 108,276 | 94,713 | 92,556 | 112,022 |
| Interest Expense | 24,864 | 27,721 | 52,963 | 77,531 | 56,943 | 36,676 | 22,086 | 17,271 | 21,248 | 31,965 |
| % Expense/Operating Revenue | NA | 71.1% | 117.3% | 87.3% | 74.3% | 75.5% | 77.6% | 72.2% | 77.8% | 80.5% |
| Pretax Income | 13,184 | -7,799 | -43,113 | 1,701 | 29,639 | 29,433 | 24,182 | 26,333 | 20,537 | 21,897 |
| Effective Tax Rate | 16.9% | NM | 45.6% | NM | 27.3% | 30.8% | 28.6% | 31.1% | 34.1% | 34.4% |
| Net Income | 10,670 | -1,161 | -23,125 | 3,617 | 21,249 | 19,806 | 17,046 | 17,853 | 13,448 | 14,284 |
| S&P Core Earnings | 10,464 | -17,737 | -26,217 | 2,154 | 20,311 | 19,114 | 20,934 | 17,424 | 12,000 | 12,943 |

| Balance Sheet & Other Financial Data (Million $) | 2010 | 2009 | 2008 | 2007 | 2006 | 2005 | 2004 | 2003 | 2002 | 2001 |
|---|---|---|---|---|---|---|---|---|---|---|
| Receivables | 31,213 | 33,634 | 44,278 | 57,359 | 44,445 | 42,823 | 44,056 | 31,053 | 29,714 | 47,528 |
| Cash & Investment | 755,005 | 757,681 | 763,760 | 242,663 | 300,105 | 208,970 | 236,799 | 204,041 | 186,839 | 179,352 |
| Loans | 648,794 | 591,504 | 694,216 | 777,993 | 679,192 | 583,503 | 548,829 | 478,006 | 447,805 | 391,933 |
| Total Assets | 1,913,902 | 1,856,164 | 1,945,263 | 2,187,631 | 1,884,318 | 1,494,037 | 1,484,101 | 1,264,032 | 1,097,190 | 1,051,450 |
| Capitalization:Debt | 381,183 | 364,019 | 359,593 | 427,112 | 288,494 | 217,499 | 207,910 | 168,759 | 133,079 | 128,756 |
| Capitalization:Equity | 163,156 | 152,388 | 80,110 | 113,598 | 118,783 | 111,412 | 108,166 | 96,889 | 85,318 | 79,722 |
| Capitalization:Total | 546,972 | 518,992 | 501,223 | 540,710 | 408,277 | 330,036 | 317,201 | 284,251 | 219,797 | 210,003 |
| Price Times Book Value:High | 1.1 | 1.8 | 6.8 | 5.7 | 4.0 | 3.9 | 4.5 | 4.6 | 5.4 | 3.7 |
| Price Times Book Value:Low | 0.7 | 0.8 | 0.7 | 2.9 | 3.2 | 3.4 | 3.5 | 2.8 | 2.5 | 2.2 |
| % Return on Revenue | 9.6 | NM | NM | 2.3 | 22.0 | 16.5 | 15.7 | 18.8 | 14.5 | 12.8 |
| % Return on Assets | 0.6 | NM | NM | 0.2 | 1.3 | 1.3 | 1.2 | 1.5 | 1.3 | 1.5 |
| % Return on Equity | 6.8 | NM | NM | 3.1 | 18.5 | 18.0 | 16.6 | 19.5 | 11.6 | 19.7 |
| Loans/Equity | 3.9 | 5.8 | 8.0 | 6.3 | 5.5 | 5.2 | 5.1 | 5.1 | 3.6 | 5.3 |

Data as orig reptd.; bef. results of disc opers/spec. items. Per share data adj. for stk. divs.; EPS diluted. E-Estimated. NA-Not Available. NM-Not Meaningful. NR-Not Ranked. UR-Under Review.

**Office:** 399 Park Avenue, New York, NY, USA 10043.
**Telephone:** 212-559-1000.
**Website:** http://www.citigroup.com
**Chrmn:** R.D. Parsons

**Pres & COO:** J. Havens
**CEO:** V.S. Pandit
**CFO:** J.C. Gerspach
**Chief Admin Officer & CTO:** D. Callahan

**Board Members:** A. J. Belda, T. C. Collins, R. L. Joss, M. E. O'Neill, V. S. Pandit, R. D. Parsons, L. R. Ricciardi, J. Rodin, R. L. Ryan, A. M. Santomero, D. Taylor, W. S. Thompson, Jr., E. Z. de Leon
**Founded:** 1901
**Domicile:** Delaware
**Employees:** 260,000

# Citrix Systems Inc

**STANDARD &POOR'S**

| S&P Recommendation | HOLD ★★★☆☆ | Price<br>$64.47 (as of Nov 25, 2011) | 12-Mo. Target Price<br>$85.00 | Investment Style<br>Large-Cap Growth |
| --- | --- | --- | --- | --- |

**GICS Sector** Information Technology
**Sub-Industry** Application Software

**Summary** This company is a leading developer and supplier of access infrastructure software and services.

## Key Stock Statistics (Source S&P, Vickers, company reports)

| | | | | | | | |
| --- | --- | --- | --- | --- | --- | --- | --- |
| 52-Wk Range | $88.49– 50.21 | S&P Oper. EPS 2011**E** | 2.12 | Market Capitalization(B) | $12.024 | Beta | 1.11 |
| Trailing 12-Month EPS | $1.80 | S&P Oper. EPS 2012**E** | 2.55 | Yield (%) | Nil | S&P 3-Yr. Proj. EPS CAGR(%) | 18 |
| Trailing 12-Month P/E | 35.8 | P/E on S&P Oper. EPS 2011**E** | 30.4 | Dividend Rate/Share | Nil | S&P Credit Rating | NR |
| $10K Invested 5 Yrs Ago | $21,014 | Common Shares Outstg. (M) | 186.5 | Institutional Ownership (%) | 95 | | |

## Price Performance

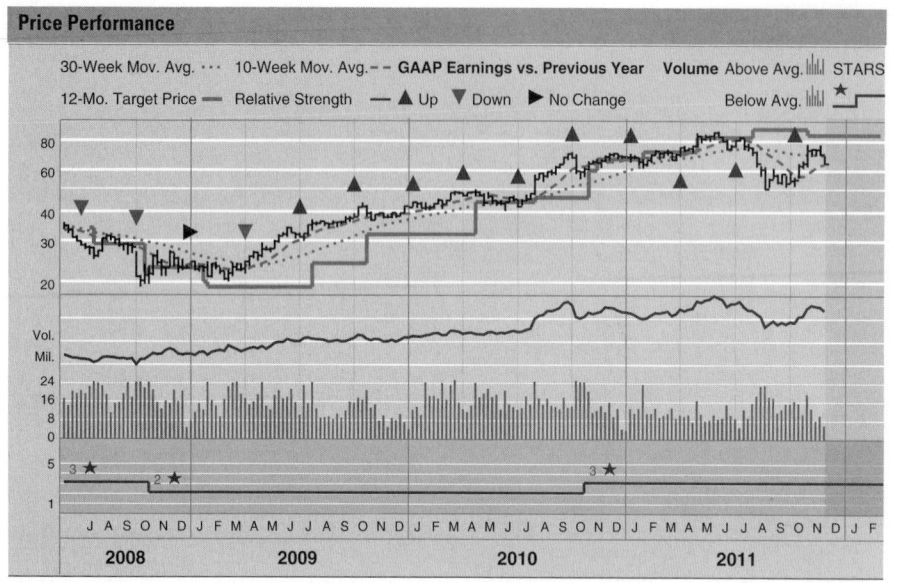

30-Week Mov. Avg. ···· 10-Week Mov. Avg. --- **GAAP Earnings vs. Previous Year** Volume Above Avg. STARS
12-Mo. Target Price — Relative Strength — ▲ Up ▼ Down ► No Change Below Avg. ★

Options: ASE, CBOE, P, Ph

### Qualitative Risk Assessment

| LOW | MEDIUM | **HIGH** |
| --- | --- | --- |

Our risk assessment reflects rapidly changing technology and the competitive nature of the enterprise software market.

### Quantitative Evaluations

**S&P Quality Ranking** **B+**

| D | C | B- | B | **B+** | A- | A | A+ |
| --- | --- | --- | --- | --- | --- | --- | --- |

**Relative Strength Rank** **MODERATE**

63

LOWEST = 1     HIGHEST = 99

### Revenue/Earnings Data

**Revenue (Million $)**

| | 1Q | 2Q | 3Q | 4Q | Year |
| --- | --- | --- | --- | --- | --- |
| 2011 | 490.9 | 530.8 | 565.4 | -- | -- |
| 2010 | 414.3 | 458.4 | 472.2 | 529.7 | 1,875 |
| 2009 | 369.1 | 392.8 | 401.0 | 451.2 | 1,614 |
| 2008 | 377.0 | 391.7 | 398.9 | 415.7 | 1,583 |
| 2007 | 308.1 | 334.4 | 349.9 | 399.6 | 1,392 |
| 2006 | 260.0 | 275.5 | 277.9 | 321.0 | 1,134 |

**Earnings Per Share ($)**

| | | | | | |
| --- | --- | --- | --- | --- | --- |
| 2011 | 0.38 | 0.43 | 0.49 | E0.66 | E2.12 |
| 2010 | 0.25 | 0.25 | 0.46 | 0.49 | 1.46 |
| 2009 | 0.04 | 0.23 | 0.29 | 0.47 | 1.03 |
| 2008 | 0.18 | 0.18 | 0.26 | 0.33 | 0.96 |
| 2007 | 0.20 | 0.29 | 0.33 | 0.33 | 1.14 |
| 2006 | 0.22 | 0.23 | 0.23 | 0.29 | 0.97 |

Fiscal year ended Dec. 31. Next earnings report expected: Late January. EPS Estimates based on S&P Operating Earnings; historical GAAP earnings are as reported.

### Dividend Data

No cash dividends have been paid.

## Highlights

► The 12-month target price for CTXS has recently been changed to $85.00 from $90.00. The Highlights section of this Stock Report will be updated accordingly.

## Investment Rationale/Risk

► The Investment Rationale/Risk section of this Stock Report will be updated shortly. For the latest News story on CTXS from MarketScope, see below.

► 10/27/11 12:52 pm ET ... S&P REITERATES HOLD OPINION ON SHARES OF CITRIX SYSTEMS (CTXS 74.65***): CTXS posts adjusted Q3 EPS of $0.53, vs. $0.46, $0.02 below our estimate, reflecting strong revenue outperformance, but lower margins than we expected. Revenues rose 20%, well above the 15% we projected, with product license revenues rising 28%. Company growth and margins seems to reflect demand related to secular trends including cloud computing and virtualization. We are keeping our '11 EPS forecast of $2.12, but increasing our '12 outlook to $2.55 from $2.48. Based on revised DCF and P/E-to-growth analyses, we are trimming our 12-month target price to $85 from $90. /S. Kessler

# Citrix Systems Inc

**STANDARD
&POOR'S**

## Business Summary August 12, 2011

CORPORATE OVERVIEW. Citrix Systems (CTXS) designs, develops and markets server and desktop virtualization software solutions that enable users to access and share applications and files on-demand with a higher performance and level of security. CTXS's solutions help people conduct business in remote and mobile locations as they move from location to location, use multiple devices, and connect with a wide range of heterogeneous applications over wired, wireless and Internet networks.

CTXS organizes its products into three groups: Citrix Delivery Center, Online Services and Technical Services.

Citrix Delivery Center is focused on application virtualization, application networking and desktop virtualization. It includes Server Virtualization products, which allow servers to run multiple operating systems, thus enabling them to process multiple business applications. As a result, enterprises can reduce infrastructure costs by aggregating servers and data storage into pools of shared resources. The key product is Citrix XenServer, which was obtained through the acquisition of XenSource. CTXS and Microsoft entered into patent cross license and source code licensing agreements related to Microsoft's operating systems.

Another key application in Citrix Delivery Center is Citrix XenApp, previously

called Citrix Presentation Server, which runs the business logic of applications on a central server and displays the video on the users' computers. By keeping applications under a centralized control, it improves data security and reduces the costs of managing many different applications on every user's desktop. Other products include Citrix NetScaler and Citrix Repeater, which optimize the performance of a network by balancing the load and providing firewall protection.

Online Services are Web-based access and collaboration software and services. GoToMyPC allows users to remotely access PCs via the Internet. GoToMeeting enables online meetings, training sessions and collaborative gatherings. GoToAssist is an online solution that enables businesses to provide customer support over the Internet. GoToWebinar helps organizations conduct online events, such as large marketing events.

Technical Services include consulting, support and training to help ensure that customers are achieving the maximum value of CTXS's products and services.

## Company Financials Fiscal Year Ended Dec. 31

| Per Share Data ($) | 2010 | 2009 | 2008 | 2007 | 2006 | 2005 | 2004 | 2003 | 2002 | 2001 |
|---|---|---|---|---|---|---|---|---|---|---|
| Tangible Book Value | 7.75 | 5.89 | 4.13 | 3.59 | 3.92 | 2.68 | 2.80 | 3.24 | 2.57 | 2.48 |
| Cash Flow | 2.18 | 1.78 | 1.62 | 1.60 | 1.32 | 1.06 | 0.95 | 0.94 | 0.75 | 0.95 |
| Earnings | 1.46 | 1.03 | 0.96 | 1.14 | 0.97 | 0.93 | 0.75 | 0.74 | 0.52 | 0.54 |
| S&P Core Earnings | 1.45 | 1.02 | 0.99 | 1.14 | 0.97 | 0.74 | 0.48 | 0.23 | -0.34 | -0.19 |
| Dividends | Nil | Nil | Nil | Nil | Nil | Nil | Nil | Nil | Nil | Nil |
| Payout Ratio | Nil | Nil | Nil | Nil | Nil | Nil | Nil | Nil | Nil | Nil |
| Prices:High | 71.93 | 43.78 | 38.95 | 43.90 | 45.50 | 29.46 | 26.00 | 27.86 | 24.70 | 37.19 |
| Prices:Low | 40.33 | 20.00 | 19.00 | 26.10 | 26.62 | 20.70 | 15.02 | 10.48 | 4.70 | 16.88 |
| P/E Ratio:High | 49 | 43 | 41 | 39 | 47 | 32 | 35 | 38 | 47 | 69 |
| P/E Ratio:Low | 28 | 19 | 20 | 23 | 27 | 22 | 20 | 14 | 9 | 31 |

| Income Statement Analysis (Million $) | | | | | | | | | | |
|---|---|---|---|---|---|---|---|---|---|---|
| Revenue | 1,875 | 1,614 | 1,583 | 1,392 | 1,134 | 909 | 741 | 589 | 527 | 592 |
| Operating Income | 460 | 344 | 295 | 297 | 267 | 233 | 212 | 189 | 145 | 216 |
| Depreciation | 138 | 139 | 124 | 85.2 | 63.6 | 22.0 | 33.6 | 34.3 | 41.4 | 79.6 |
| Interest Expense | 0.46 | 0.43 | 0.44 | 0.74 | 0.93 | 2.23 | 4.37 | 18.3 | 18.2 | 20.6 |
| Pretax Income | 334 | 194 | 197 | 251 | 243 | 226 | 164 | 161 | 113 | 153 |
| Effective Tax Rate | NA | 1.48% | 9.47% | 14.5% | 24.7% | 26.2% | 20.0% | 21.0% | 17.0% | 31.0% |
| Net Income | 277 | 191 | 178 | 214 | 183 | 166 | 132 | 127 | 93.9 | 105 |
| S&P Core Earnings | 275 | 190 | 184 | 214 | 183 | 131 | 83.5 | 39.3 | -60.5 | -36.2 |

| Balance Sheet & Other Financial Data (Million $) | | | | | | | | | | |
|---|---|---|---|---|---|---|---|---|---|---|
| Cash | 894 | 600 | 575 | 580 | 349 | 484 | 73.5 | 359 | 143 | 140 |
| Current Assets | 1,470 | 1,039 | 940 | 934 | 812 | 726 | 427 | 809 | 375 | 346 |
| Total Assets | 3,704 | 3,091 | 2,694 | 2,535 | 2,024 | 1,682 | 1,286 | 1,345 | 1,162 | 1,208 |
| Current Liabilities | 1,020 | 834 | 731 | 654 | 536 | 426 | 342 | 626 | 189 | 193 |
| Long Term Debt | NA | NA | Nil | Nil | Nil | 31.0 | Nil | Nil | 334 | 346 |
| Common Equity | 2,561 | 2,189 | 1,918 | 1,838 | 1,464 | 1,203 | 925 | 707 | 622 | 647 |
| Total Capital | 2,561 | 2,189 | 1,918 | 1,838 | 1,464 | 1,234 | 925 | 707 | 955 | 994 |
| Capital Expenditures | 75.4 | 76.3 | 181 | 85.9 | 52.1 | 26.4 | 24.4 | 11.1 | 19.1 | 60.6 |
| Cash Flow | 415 | 330 | 302 | 300 | 247 | 188 | 165 | 161 | 135 | 185 |
| Current Ratio | 1.4 | 1.3 | 1.3 | 1.4 | 1.5 | 1.7 | 1.2 | 1.3 | 2.0 | 1.8 |
| % Long Term Debt of Capitalization | Nil | Nil | Nil | Nil | Nil | 2.5 | Nil | Nil | 34.9 | 34.8 |
| % Net Income of Revenue | 14.8 | 11.8 | 11.3 | 15.4 | 16.1 | 18.3 | 17.7 | 21.6 | 17.8 | 17.8 |
| % Return on Assets | 8.2 | 6.6 | 6.8 | 9.4 | 9.8 | 11.2 | 10.0 | 10.1 | 7.9 | 9.1 |
| % Return on Equity | 11.7 | 9.3 | 9.5 | 13.0 | 13.7 | 15.6 | 16.1 | 19.1 | 14.6 | 17.0 |

Data as orig reptd.; bef. results of disc opers/spec. items. Per share data adj. for stk. divs.; EPS diluted. E-Estimated. NA-Not Available. NM-Not Meaningful. NR-Not Ranked. UR-Under Review.

**Office:** 851 West Cypress Creek Road, Fort Lauderdale, FL 33309.
**Telephone:** 954-267-3000.
**Email:** investor@citrix.com
**Website:** http://www.citrix.com

**Chrmn:** T.F. Bogan
**Pres & CEO:** M.B. Templeton
**COO, CFO & Chief Acctg Officer:** D.J. Henshall
**Treas:** K. Leopardi

**Secy:** A.G. Gomes
**Investor Contact:** E. Fleites (954-267-3000)
**Board Members:** T. F. Bogan, N. E. Caldwell, M. J. Demo, S. M. Dow, A. S. Hirji, G. E. Morin, G. Sullivan, M. B. Templeton

**Founded:** 1989
**Domicile:** Delaware
**Employees:** 5,637

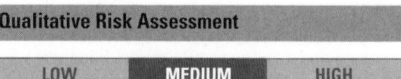

# Cliffs Natural Resources Inc

**STANDARD &POOR'S**

| S&P Recommendation **STRONG BUY** ★ ★ ★ ★ ☆ | Price $59.72 (as of Nov 25, 2011) | 12-Mo. Target Price $115.00 | Investment Style Large-Cap Growth |
| --- | --- | --- | --- |

**GICS Sector** Materials
**Sub-Industry** Steel

**Summary** CLF is the largest supplier of iron ore pellets to the North American steel industry.

## Key Stock Statistics (Source S&P, Vickers, company reports)

| | | | | | | | |
| --- | --- | --- | --- | --- | --- | --- | --- |
| 52-Wk Range | $102.48– 47.31 | S&P Oper. EPS 2011**E** | 12.99 | Market Capitalization(B) | $8.541 | Beta | 2.50 |
| Trailing 12-Month EPS | $12.95 | S&P Oper. EPS 2012**E** | 13.51 | Yield (%) | 1.88 | S&P 3-Yr. Proj. EPS CAGR(%) | 19 |
| Trailing 12-Month P/E | 4.6 | P/E on S&P Oper. EPS 2011**E** | 4.6 | Dividend Rate/Share | $1.12 | S&P Credit Rating | BBB- |
| $10K Invested 5 Yrs Ago | $26,185 | Common Shares Outstg. (M) | 143.0 | Institutional Ownership (%) | 85 | | |

## Price Performance

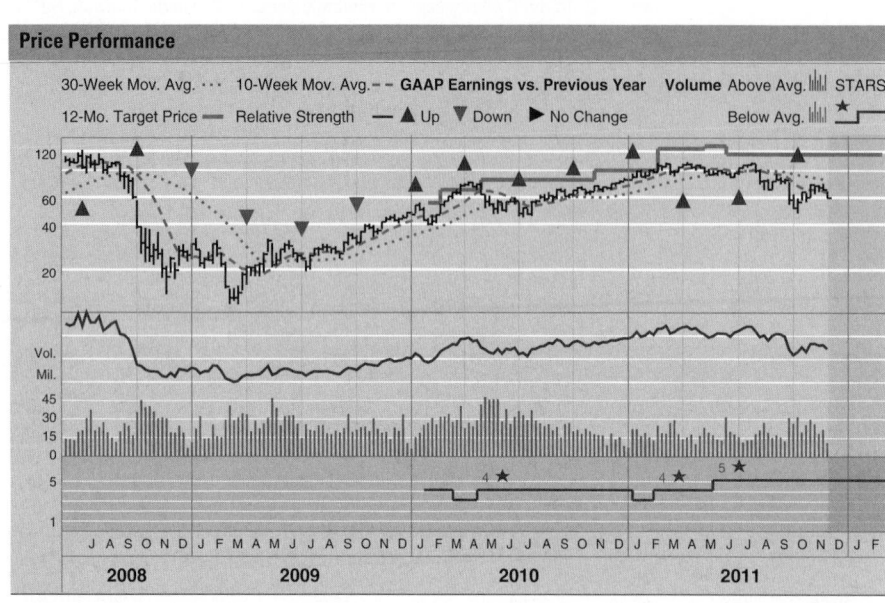

30-Week Mov. Avg. · · · 10-Week Mov. Avg. – – GAAP Earnings vs. Previous Year Volume Above Avg. STARS
12-Mo. Target Price — Relative Strength — ▲ Up ▼ Down ► No Change Below Avg. ★

Options: ASE, CBOE, P, Ph

Analysis prepared by Equity Analyst **Leo J. Larkin** on Sep 13, 2011, when the stock traded at **$77.29**.

## Highlights

➤ Excluding the acquisition of Consolidated Thompson Iron Mines Limited, we look for a 38% sales gain in 2011 on another increase in volume and prices along with the inclusion of INR Energy for a full year. Our forecast rests on several assumptions. First, we look for U.S. GDP growth of 1.7% and global GDP growth of 2.8% in 2011. Second, we see another increase in steel production both in the U.S and the world in 2011, leading to increased demand for iron ore and metallurgical coal. Third, we believe that supplies of iron ore and metallurgical coal were tight going into 2011, which we think will support higher prices.

➤ We look for higher operating income in 2011, reflecting increased prices and volume. After interest expense, taxes, and equity income, we estimate EPS of $12.28 for 2011, versus operating EPS of $7.29 in 2010, which excludes special credits totaling $0.20.

➤ Longer term, we see earnings rising on acquisitions, market share gains, consolidation of the iron ore mining industry, and a secular rise in steel consumption in Asia.

## Investment Rationale/Risk

➤ In our view, consolidation of the iron ore mining industry will result in generally firmer pricing and less volatile sales and profits over the course of the business cycle. Also, we think the company's strong market position in North America's iron ore market provides it with a solid platform for expansion in Asia and the ability to enter new markets such as ferrochrome. For the long term, we believe CLF's sales and earnings will rise on a combination of acquisitions, continued consolidation of the global iron ore mining industry, and a secular increase in steel consumption in most of Asia. We think the shares are very attractively valued, recently trading at about 5.8X our 2012 EPS estimate.

➤ Risks to our recommendation and target price include declines in iron ore and metallurgical coal prices in 2012 instead of the increases that we project.

➤ Our 12-month target price of $115 is 8.7X our 2012 EPS estimate of $13.20. On this projected multiple, the shares would trade toward the low end of their range of the past 10 years and at a small premium to the P/E we apply to CLF's main iron ore mining peer.

## Qualitative Risk Assessment

| LOW | **MEDIUM** | HIGH |
| --- | --- | --- |

Our risk assessment reflects the company's exposure to the highly cyclical demand for iron ore and metallurgical coal, offset by its large market share in iron ore.

## Quantitative Evaluations

**S&P Quality Ranking** B

| D | C | B- | **B** | B+ | A- | A | A+ |
| --- | --- | --- | --- | --- | --- | --- | --- |

**Relative Strength Rank** WEAK

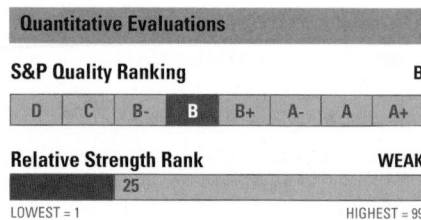

25

LOWEST = 1 HIGHEST = 99

## Revenue/Earnings Data

**Revenue (Million $)**

| | 1Q | 2Q | 3Q | 4Q | Year |
| --- | --- | --- | --- | --- | --- |
| 2011 | 1,183 | 1,806 | 2,143 | -- | -- |
| 2010 | 727.7 | 1,184 | 1,346 | 1,424 | 4,682 |
| 2009 | 464.8 | 390.3 | 666.4 | 820.5 | 2,342 |
| 2008 | 494.4 | 1,009 | 1,190 | 916.3 | 3,609 |
| 2007 | 325.5 | 547.6 | 619.6 | 782.5 | 2,275 |
| 2006 | 306.4 | 486.2 | 580.1 | 549.0 | 1,922 |

**Earnings Per Share ($)**

| | 1Q | 2Q | 3Q | 4Q | Year |
| --- | --- | --- | --- | --- | --- |
| 2011 | 3.11 | 2.92 | 4.19 | E2.77 | E12.99 |
| 2010 | 0.57 | 1.92 | 2.18 | 2.82 | 7.49 |
| 2009 | -0.07 | 0.36 | 0.45 | 0.82 | 1.63 |
| 2008 | 0.16 | 2.57 | 1.61 | 0.47 | 4.76 |
| 2007 | 0.31 | 0.83 | 0.54 | 0.88 | 2.57 |
| 2006 | 0.34 | 0.77 | 0.84 | 0.67 | 2.60 |

Fiscal year ended Dec. 31. Next earnings report expected: Mid February. EPS Estimates based on S&P Operating Earnings; historical GAAP earnings are as reported.

## Dividend Data (Dates: mm/dd Payment Date: mm/dd/yy)

| Amount ($) | Date Decl. | Ex-Div. Date | Stk. of Record | Payment Date |
| --- | --- | --- | --- | --- |
| 0.140 | 01/11 | 02/11 | 02/15 | 03/01/11 |
| 0.140 | 04/13 | 04/27 | 04/29 | 06/01/11 |
| 0.280 | 07/11 | 08/11 | 08/15 | 09/01/11 |
| 0.280 | 11/08 | 11/16 | 11/18 | 12/01/11 |

Dividends have been paid since 2004. Source: Company reports.

---

**Please read the Required Disclosures and Analyst Certification on the last page of this report.**

*The McGraw-Hill Companies*

# Cliffs Natural Resources Inc

## Business Summary September 13, 2011

CORPORATE OVERVIEW. Cliffs Natural Resources, the largest producer of iron ore pellets in North America, primarily sells to integrated steel companies in the United States and Canada. The company manages and operates six North American iron ore mines located in Michigan, Minnesota and Eastern Canada that currently have a rated capacity of 38.4 million tons of iron ore pellet production annually, representing approximately 45.3% of total North American pellet production capacity. CLF is also a major supplier of direct-shipping lump and fines iron ore out of Australia and a significant producer of metallurgical coal.

Based on its percentage ownership of the North American mines CLF currently operates, its share of the rated pellet production capacity is currently 29.9 million tons annually, representing some 35.3% of total North American annual pellet capacity. In 2010, production totaled 32 million tons of iron ore pellets, including 25.4 million tons for the company's account and 6.6 million tons on behalf of steel company owners of the mines.

In 2010, the North American Iron Ore segment accounted for 62% of sales and had $922 million of operating profit; North American Coal accounted for 9% of

sales and incurred an operating loss of $28.6 million; Asia Pacific Iron Ore accounted for 24% of sales and had an operating profit of $566.2 million; and other operations accounted for 5% of sales and had $63.9 million of operating profit.

In 2010, the United States accounted for 42% of revenues, China 27%, Canada 15%, Japan 6%, and other countries 10%.

CORPORATE STRATEGY. The company seeks to achieve scale in the mining industry and focuses on serving the world's largest and fastest-growing steel markets. CLF plans to increase its business and presence as an international mining company by expanding both geographically and through the minerals it mines and markets. The company also intends to make acquisitions in minerals other than iron ore, such as metallurgical coal.

## Company Financials Fiscal Year Ended Dec. 31

| Per Share Data ($) | 2010 | 2009 | 2008 | 2007 | 2006 | 2005 | 2004 | 2003 | 2002 | 2001 |
|---|---|---|---|---|---|---|---|---|---|---|
| Tangible Book Value | 25.64 | 17.97 | 14.20 | 13.35 | 9.12 | 7.28 | 4.76 | 2.72 | 0.98 | 4.63 |
| Cash Flow | 9.86 | 3.51 | 6.61 | 3.54 | 3.24 | 0.00 | 3.14 | -0.10 | -0.51 | -0.21 |
| Earnings | 7.49 | 1.63 | 4.76 | 2.57 | 2.60 | 2.45 | 2.92 | -0.43 | -0.82 | -0.40 |
| S&P Core Earnings | 7.47 | 1.85 | 4.48 | 2.38 | 2.67 | 2.40 | 2.16 | -0.18 | -1.07 | -0.60 |
| Dividends | 0.51 | 0.25 | 0.35 | 0.25 | 0.24 | 0.15 | 0.03 | Nil | Nil | 0.05 |
| Payout Ratio | 7% | 16% | 7% | 10% | 9% | 6% | 1% | Nil | Nil | NM |
| Prices:High | 80.40 | 48.41 | 121.95 | 53.15 | 27.59 | 24.81 | 13.51 | 6.80 | 4.03 | 2.81 |
| Prices:Low | 39.13 | 11.80 | 13.73 | 23.00 | 15.70 | 11.70 | 4.85 | 1.84 | 1.96 | 1.71 |
| P/E Ratio:High | 11 | 30 | 26 | 21 | 10 | 10 | 5 | NM | NM | NM |
| P/E Ratio:Low | 5 | 7 | 3 | 9 | 6 | 5 | 2 | NM | NM | NM |

### Income Statement Analysis (Million $)

| | 2010 | 2009 | 2008 | 2007 | 2006 | 2005 | 2004 | 2003 | 2002 | 2001 |
|---|---|---|---|---|---|---|---|---|---|---|
| Revenue | 4,682 | 2,342 | 3,609 | 2,275 | 1,933 | 1,753 | 1,207 | 825 | 599 | 374 |
| Operating Income | 1,655 | 589 | 1,201 | 473 | 445 | 403 | 146 | -17.7 | 17.6 | -33.8 |
| Depreciation | 322 | 237 | 201 | 107 | 73.9 | 48.6 | 29.3 | 26.7 | 25.5 | 15.4 |
| Interest Expense | 69.7 | 39.0 | 39.8 | 21.8 | 3.60 | 4.50 | 0.80 | 4.60 | 6.60 | 9.30 |
| Pretax Income | 1,312 | 225 | 681 | 370 | 388 | 368 | 286 | -35.2 | -57.3 | -53.6 |
| Effective Tax Rate | NA | 9.24% | 21.2% | 22.8% | 23.4% | 23.0% | NM | NM | NM | NM |
| Net Income | 1,020 | 205 | 516 | 270 | 280 | 273 | 321 | -34.9 | -66.4 | -32.2 |
| S&P Core Earnings | 1,017 | 233 | 485 | 245 | 282 | 262 | 231 | -14.8 | -86.2 | -48.4 |

### Balance Sheet & Other Financial Data (Million $)

| | 2010 | 2009 | 2008 | 2007 | 2006 | 2005 | 2004 | 2003 | 2002 | 2001 |
|---|---|---|---|---|---|---|---|---|---|---|
| Cash | 1,567 | 503 | 179 | 157 | 352 | 213 | 400 | 265 | 61.8 | 184 |
| Current Assets | 2,584 | 1,161 | 862 | 755 | 782 | 636 | 734 | 313 | 301 | 363 |
| Total Assets | 7,778 | 4,639 | 4,111 | 3,076 | 1,940 | 1,747 | 1,161 | 895 | 730 | 825 |
| Current Liabilities | 1,029 | 570 | 845 | 400 | 375 | 363 | 257 | 226 | 205 | 190 |
| Long Term Debt | 1,713 | 525 | 525 | 440 | Nil | Nil | Nil | Nil | 35.0 | 70.0 |
| Common Equity | 3,846 | 2,543 | 1,751 | 1,164 | 746 | 652 | 424 | 228 | 79.3 | 374 |
| Total Capital | 5,545 | 3,062 | 2,346 | 2,045 | 1,122 | 1,012 | 626 | 283 | 134 | 470 |
| Capital Expenditures | 267 | 116 | 183 | 200 | 120 | 97.8 | 60.7 | 20.1 | 8.60 | 9.20 |
| Cash Flow | 1,342 | 442 | 716 | 372 | 348 | 316 | 345 | -8.20 | -40.9 | -16.8 |
| Current Ratio | 2.5 | 2.0 | 1.0 | 1.9 | 2.1 | 1.8 | 2.9 | 1.4 | 1.5 | 1.9 |
| % Long Term Debt of Capitalization | 30.9 | 17.2 | 22.4 | 21.5 | Nil | Nil | Nil | Nil | 26.1 | 14.9 |
| % Net Income of Revenue | 21.8 | 8.8 | 14.3 | 11.9 | 14.5 | 15.6 | 26.6 | NM | NM | NM |
| % Return on Assets | 16.4 | 4.7 | 14.4 | 10.6 | 15.2 | 18.3 | 31.4 | NM | NM | NM |
| % Return on Equity | 31.9 | 9.6 | 35.4 | 27.7 | 39.2 | 49.8 | 96.7 | NM | NM | NM |

Data as orig reptd.; bef. results of disc opers/spec. items. Per share data adj. for stk. divs.; EPS diluted. E-Estimated. NA-Not Available. NM-Not Meaningful. NR-Not Ranked. UR-Under Review.

**Office:** 200 Public Square, Suite 3300, Cleveland, OH 44114-2315.
**Telephone:** 216-694-5700.
**Website:** http://www.cliffsnaturalresources.com
**Chrmn, Pres & CEO:** J.A. Carrabba

**COO & EVP:** D.P. Price
**EVP & General Counsel:** P.K. Tompkins
**SVP & Treas:** S.M. Raguz
**CFO & Chief Admin Officer:** L. Brlas

**Auditor:** DELOITTE & TOUCHE
**Board Members:** J. A. Carrabba, S. M. Cunningham, B. Eldridge, A. R. Gluski, S. M. Green, J. K. Henry, J. F. Kirsch, F. R. McAllister, R. Phillips, R. K. Riederer, R. A. Ross, A. G. Schwartz

**Founded:** 1920
**Domicile:** Ohio
**Employees:** 6,567

# Clorox Co (The)

**STANDARD &POOR'S**

| **S&P Recommendation** HOLD ★★★☆☆ | **Price** $63.97 (as of Nov 25, 2011) | **12-Mo. Target Price** $70.00 | **Investment Style** Large-Cap Growth |
|---|---|---|---|

**GICS Sector** Consumer Staples
**Sub-Industry** Household Products

**Summary** This diversified producer of household cleaning, grocery and specialty food products is also a leading producer of natural personal care products.

## Key Stock Statistics (Source S&P, Vickers, company reports)

| | | | | | | | |
|---|---|---|---|---|---|---|---|
| 52-Wk Range | $75.44– 60.56 | S&P Oper. EPS 2012**E** | 4.05 | Market Capitalization(B) | $8.438 | Beta | 0.39 |
| Trailing 12-Month EPS | $3.48 | S&P Oper. EPS 2013**E** | 4.41 | Yield (%) | 3.75 | S&P 3-Yr. Proj. EPS CAGR(%) | 6 |
| Trailing 12-Month P/E | 18.4 | P/E on S&P Oper. EPS 2012**E** | 15.8 | Dividend Rate/Share | $2.40 | S&P Credit Rating | BBB+ |
| $10K Invested 5 Yrs Ago | $11,565 | Common Shares Outstg. (M) | 131.9 | Institutional Ownership (%) | 70 | | |

## Price Performance

30-Week Mov. Avg. · · · 10-Week Mov. Avg. - - GAAP Earnings vs. Previous Year   Volume Above Avg. STARS
12-Mo. Target Price — Relative Strength — ▲ Up ▼ Down ► No Change   Below Avg.

Options: ASE, CBOE, P, Ph

Analysis prepared by Equity Analyst **Tom Graves, CFA** on Nov 14, 2011, when the stock traded at **$65.98**.

## Highlights

▸ For FY 12 (Jun.), we look for sales to increase 2.5%, to $5.36 billion, from the $5.2 billion reported for FY 11. We expect the fastest growth from the Lifestyle and International segments, although results from the latter could be adversely affected by currency fluctuation.

▸ In FY 12's first quarter, we saw a lower-than-expected tax rate largely offsetting $0.06 a share of advisory fees related to a withdrawn proxy contest. For the remainder of FY 12, we look for cost savings and price increases to continue bolstering gross margins, helping CLX to at least largely offset commodity cost pressure and a 250 basis point gross margin decline in the first quarter. We estimate FY 12 EPS of $4.05, up from $3.93 in FY 11, excluding goodwill impairment charges. For FY 13, we estimate $4.41.

▸ In September 2011, High River Limited Partnership, an affiliate of Icahn Enterprises L.P., withdrew its slate of nominees for CLX's board of directors. By so doing, we think Carl Icahn was signaling that an effort to gain control of CLX and/or have it sold to a third party did not seem practical.

## Investment Rationale/Risk

▸ In recent years, CLX's performance has been positive but somewhat erratic, in our view. We attribute this partly to the categories in which CLX operates, and the timing of new product introductions. However, we think the company's level of product innovation is respectable, and bolsters its pricing power and competitive stance. We view positively CLX's increased presence in the natural home/personal care products arena through Burt's Bees and Green Works.

▸ Risks to our recommendation and target price include increased competition and promotional activity that would affect profitability, poor consumer acceptance of new products, unfavorable foreign exchange, and potential challenges in the implementation of new enterprise resource planning system software.

▸ Our 12-month target price of $70 blends our historical and peer analyses. We apply a P/E multiple close to the 10-year historical mean to our calendar 2012 EPS estimate for a $77 value. Our peer analysis suggests a $63 value, using a P/E that is close to the recent peer average. CLX shares recently had an indicated dividend yield of 3.6%.

## Qualitative Risk Assessment

| LOW | MEDIUM | HIGH |
|---|---|---|

Our risk assessment reflects our view of stable demand for household and personal care products, which is generally not affected by changes in the economy or geopolitical factors.

## Quantitative Evaluations

**S&P Quality Ranking** A

| D | C | B- | B | B+ | A- | A | A+ |
|---|---|---|---|---|---|---|---|

**Relative Strength Rank** MODERATE

60

LOWEST = 1   HIGHEST = 99

## Revenue/Earnings Data

**Revenue (Million $)**

| | 1Q | 2Q | 3Q | 4Q | Year |
|---|---|---|---|---|---|
| 2012 | 1,305 | -- | -- | -- | -- |
| 2011 | 1,266 | 1,179 | 1,304 | 1,482 | 5,231 |
| 2010 | 1,372 | 1,279 | 1,366 | 1,517 | 5,534 |
| 2009 | 1,384 | 1,216 | 1,350 | 1,500 | 5,450 |
| 2008 | 1,239 | 1,186 | 1,353 | 1,495 | 5,273 |
| 2007 | 1,161 | 1,101 | 1,241 | 1,344 | 4,847 |

**Earnings Per Share ($)**

| | 1Q | 2Q | 3Q | 4Q | Year |
|---|---|---|---|---|---|
| 2012 | 0.98 | E0.68 | E1.10 | E1.35 | E4.05 |
| 2011 | 0.98 | -1.17 | 1.02 | 1.26 | 2.07 |
| 2010 | 1.11 | 0.77 | 1.17 | 1.20 | 4.24 |
| 2009 | 0.91 | 1.08 | 1.09 | 1.20 | 3.81 |
| 2008 | 0.76 | 0.65 | 0.71 | 1.13 | 3.25 |
| 2007 | 0.73 | 0.59 | 0.84 | 1.07 | 3.22 |

Fiscal year ended Jun. 30. Next earnings report expected: Early February. EPS Estimates based on S&P Operating Earnings; historical GAAP earnings are as reported.

## Dividend Data (Dates: mm/dd Payment Date: mm/dd/yy)

| Amount ($) | Date Decl. | Ex-Div. Date | Stk. of Record | Payment Date |
|---|---|---|---|---|
| 0.550 | 02/15 | 04/25 | 04/27 | 05/13/11 |
| 0.600 | 05/18 | 07/25 | 07/27 | 08/12/11 |
| 0.600 | 09/13 | 10/24 | 10/26 | 11/14/11 |
| 0.600 | 11/15 | 01/24 | 01/26 | 02/13/12 |

Dividends have been paid since 1968. Source: Company reports.

---

**Please read the Required Disclosures and Analyst Certification on the last page of this report.**

The **McGraw·Hill** Companies

# Clorox Co (The)

## Business Summary November 14, 2011

CORPORATE OVERVIEW. Since it divestiture from The Procter & Gamble Company in 1969, Clorox has expanded into a company with approximately $5.5 billion in annual sales, by focusing on building big-share brands in mid-sized categories. Clorox's products are manufactured in more than two dozen countries and marketed in more than 100 countries. In FY 11(Jun.), 79% of CLX's net sales were from the U.S.

In FY 11, Clorox had four segments for reporting purposes: Cleaning (31% of net sales); Household (31%); Lifestyle (17%); and International (21%). Liquid bleach represented about 14% of total net sales, trash bags 13%, and charcoal 11%. In FY 11, Wal-Mart Stores and its affiliated companies accounted for 26% of consolidated net sales.

The Cleaning segment consists of laundry, home-care and professional products marketed and sold in the United States. Products comprise laundry additives, including bleaches under the Clorox brand and Clorox 2 stain fighter and color booster; home-care products, primarily under the Clorox, Formula 409, Liquid-Plumr, Pine-Sol, S.O.S and Tilex brands; and natural cleaning and laundry products under the Green Works brand.

The Household segment consists of charcoal, cat litter and plastic bags, wraps and container products marketed and sold in the United States. Prod-

ucts include plastic bags, wraps and containers under the Glad brand; cat litter products under the Fresh Step, Scoop Away and Ever Clean brands; and charcoal products under the Kingsford and Match Light brands.

The Lifestyle segment consists of food products, water filtration systems and filters marketed and sold in the United States, and natural personal care products. Products include dressings and sauces, primarily under the Hidden Valley and K C Masterpiece brands; water-filtration systems and filters under the Brita brand; and natural personal care products under the Burt's Bees brand.

The International segment consists of products sold outside the United States, excluding natural personal care products. These products include home care, laundry, water filtration, charcoal and cat litter products, dressings and sauces, plastic bags, wraps and containers, and insecticides, primarily under the Clorox, Javex, Glad, PinoLuz, Ayudin, Limpido, Clorinda, Poett, Mistolin, Lestoil, Bon Bril, Nevex, Brita, Green Works, Pine-Sol, Agua Jane, Chux, Kingsford, Fresh Step, Scoop Away, Ever Clean, K C Masterpiece and Hidden Valley brands.

## Company Financials Fiscal Year Ended Jun. 30

| Per Share Data ($) | 2011 | 2010 | 2009 | 2008 | 2007 | 2006 | 2005 | 2004 | 2003 | 2002 |
|---|---|---|---|---|---|---|---|---|---|---|
| Tangible Book Value | NM | NM | NM | NM | NM | NM | NM | 0.77 | NM | 0.24 |
| Cash Flow | 3.33 | 5.57 | 5.16 | 4.61 | 4.47 | 4.12 | 3.95 | 3.47 | 3.19 | 2.18 |
| Earnings | 2.07 | 4.24 | 3.81 | 3.25 | 3.22 | 2.89 | 2.88 | 2.55 | 2.33 | 1.37 |
| S&P Core Earnings | 3.92 | 4.26 | 3.70 | 3.15 | 3.26 | 2.94 | 2.73 | 2.43 | 2.26 | 1.63 |
| Dividends | 2.20 | 2.00 | 1.84 | 1.60 | 1.20 | 1.14 | 1.10 | 1.08 | 0.88 | 0.84 |
| Payout Ratio | 106% | 47% | 48% | 49% | 37% | 39% | 38% | 42% | 38% | 61% |
| Prices:High | 75.44 | 69.00 | 63.10 | 65.25 | 69.36 | 66.00 | 66.04 | 59.45 | 49.16 | 47.95 |
| Prices:Low | 60.56 | 58.96 | 45.67 | 47.48 | 56.22 | 56.17 | 52.50 | 46.50 | 37.40 | 31.92 |
| P/E Ratio:High | 36 | 16 | 17 | 20 | 22 | 23 | 23 | 23 | 21 | 35 |
| P/E Ratio:Low | 29 | 14 | 12 | 15 | 17 | 19 | 18 | 18 | 16 | 23 |

### Income Statement Analysis (Million $)

| | 2011 | 2010 | 2009 | 2008 | 2007 | 2006 | 2005 | 2004 | 2003 | 2002 |
|---|---|---|---|---|---|---|---|---|---|---|
| Revenue | 5,231 | 5,534 | 5,450 | 5,273 | 4,847 | 4,644 | 4,388 | 4,324 | 4,144 | 4,061 |
| Operating Income | 1,094 | 1,291 | 1,208 | 1,116 | 1,059 | 967 | 1,011 | 1,069 | 1,046 | 942 |
| Depreciation | 173 | 185 | 190 | 193 | 192 | 188 | 190 | 197 | 191 | 190 |
| Interest Expense | 123 | 139 | 161 | 168 | 113 | 127 | 79.0 | 30.0 | 28.0 | 39.0 |
| Pretax Income | 563 | 925 | 811 | 693 | 743 | 653 | 731 | 840 | 802 | 498 |
| Effective Tax Rate | NA | NA | 33.8% | 33.5% | 33.2% | 32.2% | 29.3% | 35.0% | 35.9% | 35.3% |
| Net Income | 287 | 603 | 537 | 461 | 496 | 443 | 517 | 546 | 514 | 322 |
| S&P Core Earnings | 541 | 602 | 521 | 448 | 501 | 450 | 489 | 521 | 496 | 383 |

### Balance Sheet & Other Financial Data (Million $)

| | 2011 | 2010 | 2009 | 2008 | 2007 | 2006 | 2005 | 2004 | 2003 | 2002 |
|---|---|---|---|---|---|---|---|---|---|---|
| Cash | 259 | 87.0 | 206 | 214 | 182 | 192 | 293 | 232 | 172 | 177 |
| Current Assets | 1,279 | 1,124 | 1,180 | 1,249 | 1,032 | 1,007 | 1,090 | 1,043 | 951 | 1,002 |
| Total Assets | 4,163 | 4,555 | 4,576 | 4,708 | 3,666 | 3,616 | 3,617 | 3,834 | 3,652 | 3,630 |
| Current Liabilities | 1,365 | 1,647 | 1,937 | 1,661 | 1,427 | 1,130 | 1,348 | 1,268 | 1,451 | 1,225 |
| Long Term Debt | 2,125 | 2,124 | 2,151 | 2,720 | 1,462 | 1,966 | 2,122 | 475 | 495 | 678 |
| Common Equity | -86.0 | 83.0 | -175 | -370 | 171 | -156 | -553 | 1,540 | 1,215 | 1,354 |
| Total Capital | 2,039 | 2,507 | 1,999 | 2,447 | 1,723 | 1,939 | 1,651 | 2,189 | 1,825 | 2,174 |
| Capital Expenditures | 228 | 203 | 197 | 170 | 147 | 180 | 151 | 172 | 205 | 177 |
| Cash Flow | 460 | 788 | 727 | 654 | 688 | 631 | 707 | 743 | 705 | 512 |
| Current Ratio | 0.9 | 0.7 | 0.6 | 0.8 | 0.7 | 0.9 | 0.8 | 0.8 | 0.7 | 0.8 |
| % Long Term Debt of Capitalization | 104.2 | 84.7 | 107.6 | 111.2 | 84.9 | 101.4 | 128.5 | 21.7 | 27.1 | 31.2 |
| % Net Income of Revenue | 5.5 | 10.9 | 9.9 | 8.7 | 10.2 | 9.5 | 11.8 | 12.6 | 12.4 | 7.9 |
| % Return on Assets | 6.6 | 13.2 | 11.6 | 11.0 | 13.6 | 12.2 | 13.9 | 14.6 | 14.3 | 8.4 |
| % Return on Equity | NM | NM | NM | NM | 6613.3 | NM | 104.8 | 39.6 | 39.8 | 19.8 |

Data as orig reptd.; bef. results of disc opers/spec. items. Per share data adj. for stk. divs.; EPS diluted. E-Estimated. NA-Not Available. NM-Not Meaningful. NR-Not Ranked. UR-Under Review.

Office: 1221 Broadway, Oakland, CA 94612-1888.
Telephone: 510-271-7000.
Email: investor_relations@clorox.com
Website: http://www.thecloroxcompany.com

Chrmn & CEO: D.R. Knauss
COO & EVP: L.S. Peiros
SVP & CFO: S.M. Robb
SVP & General Counsel: L. Stein

Chief Acctg Officer & Cntlr: S.A. Gentile
Investor Contact: S. Austenfeld
Board Members: D. Boggan, Jr., R. H. Carmona, T. M. Friedman, G. J. Harad, D. R. Knauss, R. W. Matschullat, G. G. Michael, E. A. Mueller, J. L. Murley, P. A. Thomas-Graham, C. M. Ticknor

Founded: 1913
Domicile: Delaware
Employees: 8,100

# CME Group Inc

**STANDARD &POOR'S**

## S&P Recommendation  BUY ★★★★☆

| | | |
|---|---|---|
| **Price** $237.89 (as of Nov 25, 2011) | **12-Mo. Target Price** $323.00 | **Investment Style** Large-Cap Growth |

**GICS Sector** Financials
**Sub-Industry** Specialized Finance

**Summary** The CME Group, a combination of the Chicago Mercantile Exchange and CBOT Holdings, is the world's largest futures exchange.

### Key Stock Statistics (Source S&P, Vickers, company reports)

| | | | | | | | |
|---|---|---|---|---|---|---|---|
| 52-Wk Range | $328.00– 235.23 | S&P Oper. EPS 2011**E** | 18.13 | Market Capitalization(B) | $15.793 | Beta | 1.09 |
| Trailing 12-Month EPS | $18.86 | S&P Oper. EPS 2012**E** | 19.26 | Yield (%) | 2.35 | S&P 3-Yr. Proj. EPS CAGR(%) | 11 |
| Trailing 12-Month P/E | 12.6 | P/E on S&P Oper. EPS 2011**E** | 13.1 | Dividend Rate/Share | $5.60 | S&P Credit Rating | AA |
| $10K Invested 5 Yrs Ago | $4,648 | Common Shares Outstg. (M) | 66.4 | Institutional Ownership (%) | 68 | | |

## Price Performance

30-Week Mov. Avg. · · · 10-Week Mov. Avg. - - GAAP Earnings vs. Previous Year   Volume Above Avg. STARS
12-Mo. Target Price — Relative Strength — ▲ Up ▼ Down ► No Change   Below Avg.

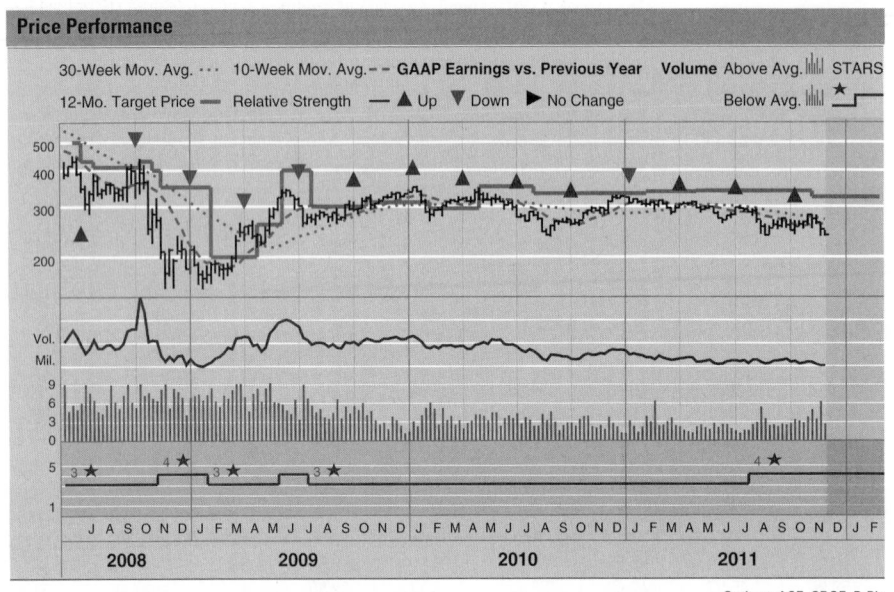

Options: ASE, CBOE, P, Ph

Analysis prepared by Equity Analyst **Robert McMillan** on Nov 03, 2011, when the stock traded at **$262.23**.

## Highlights

➤ We think trading volumes in 2011 will improve, driven by concerns about the economy and increased volatility in the markets stemming from sovereign risk fears. In 2011, we foresee strength in domestic products and expansion into new international markets. Uncertainty about the direction of interest rates and the price of oil and gas should lead to a pickup in hedging and speculative activity, although extreme volatility in the market may dampen the pickup in trading activity. In the 2011 third quarter, average daily trading volume across CME's product lines rose 27% from a year earlier and 8.9% sequentially; average price per contract declined in both periods, reflecting the volume gains.

➤ After increasing 15% in 2010, revenues should advance about 14% this year and 11% in 2012, by our analysis. Although we look for staffing levels to increase on growth in CME's business, we expect management to focus on keeping expenses under control, with expense growth of 5% or less near term.

➤ We forecast operating EPS of $18.13 in 2011 and $19.26 in 2012.

## Investment Rationale/Risk

➤ In July 2011, the Commodity Futures Trading Commission began finalizing the rules mandated or authorized by the Dodd-Frank Act. We expect the legislation to have minimal impact on near-term trading volume, reflecting our outlook for a long implementation period for any new approved rules.

➤ Risks to our recommendation and target price include intensified price competition, increased regulation that curbs speculative trading, significantly lower trading volume, and deterioration in the macroeconomic environment.

➤ Our 12-month target price of $323 is about 17.0X our forward four-quarter EPS estimate of $19.01; the shares recently traded at about 13.8X our forward four-quarter estimate. We believe the valuation multiple will expand from recent levels as operations improve, while remaining below recent historical levels as increasing competition in the clearing business pressures revenues and margins.

## Qualitative Risk Assessment

| LOW | **MEDIUM** | HIGH |
|---|---|---|

Our risk assessment reflects potential volatility in results due to changes in futures trading volumes, recent acquisition activity in the sector, and a changing regulatory environment.

## Quantitative Evaluations

**S&P Quality Ranking**   B+

| D | C | B- | B | **B+** | A- | A | A+ |
|---|---|---|---|---|---|---|---|

**Relative Strength Rank**   MODERATE

38

LOWEST = 1                HIGHEST = 99

## Revenue/Earnings Data

### Revenue (Million $)

| | 1Q | 2Q | 3Q | 4Q | Year |
|---|---|---|---|---|---|
| 2011 | 831.6 | 838.3 | 874.2 | -- | -- |
| 2010 | 693.2 | 813.9 | 733.4 | 763.2 | 3,004 |
| 2009 | 647.1 | 647.8 | 650.4 | 667.5 | 2,613 |
| 2008 | 625.1 | 563.2 | 681.0 | 691.8 | 2,561 |
| 2007 | 332.3 | 329.0 | 565.2 | 529.5 | 1,756 |
| 2006 | 251.7 | 282.2 | 274.7 | 281.3 | 1,090 |

### Earnings Per Share ($)

| | | | | | |
|---|---|---|---|---|---|
| 2011 | 6.81 | 4.38 | 4.74 | E4.65 | E18.13 |
| 2010 | 3.62 | 4.11 | 3.66 | 2.93 | 14.31 |
| 2009 | 3.00 | 3.33 | 3.04 | 3.04 | 12.41 |
| 2008 | 5.25 | 3.67 | 2.81 | 0.93 | 12.13 |
| 2007 | 3.69 | 3.57 | 3.87 | 3.75 | 14.93 |
| 2006 | 2.61 | 3.12 | 2.95 | 2.91 | 11.60 |

Fiscal year ended Dec. 31. Next earnings report expected: NA. EPS Estimates based on S&P Operating Earnings; historical GAAP earnings are as reported.

## Dividend Data (Dates: mm/dd Payment Date: mm/dd/yy)

| Amount ($) | Date Decl. | Ex-Div. Date | Stk. of Record | Payment Date |
|---|---|---|---|---|
| 1.150 | 11/03 | 12/08 | 12/10 | 12/27/10 |
| 1.400 | 02/23 | 03/08 | 03/10 | 03/25/11 |
| 1.400 | 06/09 | 06/16 | 06/20 | 06/27/11 |
| 1.400 | 08/03 | 09/07 | 09/09 | 09/26/11 |

Dividends have been paid since 2003. Source: Company reports.

# CME Group Inc

**STANDARD
&POOR'S**

## Business Summary November 03, 2011

CORPORATE OVERVIEW. The largest futures exchange in the world, CME Group was formed in July 2007 from the merger of the Chicago Mercantile Exchange and CBOT Holdings. CME serves the risk management needs of clients worldwide through a diverse range of futures and options-on-futures products on its CME Globex electronic trading platform and on its trading floors. CME offers futures and options on futures primarily in four product areas: interest rates, stock indexes, foreign exchange, and commodities. CME is the leading exchange for trading Eurodollar futures, the world's most actively traded futures contract and a benchmark for measuring the relative value of U.S. dollar-denominated short-term fixed income securities.

CME operates its own clearing house, which clears, settles and guarantees every contract traded through its exchange. We view CME's internal clearing capabilities as a key competitive advantage as CME is able to capture the revenue associated with both the trading and clearing of its products. We expect CME to expand its clearing business by partnering with other exchanges, both domestically and abroad, and clearing over-the-counter (OTC) transactions.

In 2010, CME derived 83% of its revenue from fees associated with trading and clearing its products. These fees include per contract charges for trade execution, clearing and CME Globex fees. Within trading and clearing, the different products include commodities, equities, energy, foreign exchange, interest rates, and metals. CME Globex is the company's electronic platform through which it conducts more than 75% of CME's trading volume. Fees are charged at various rates based on the product traded, the method of trade, and the exchange trading privileges of the customer making the trade. Generally, members are charged lower fees than non-members. Certain customers benefit from volume discounts and limits on fees to encourage increased liquidity.

## Company Financials Fiscal Year Ended Dec. 31

| Per Share Data ($) | 2010 | 2009 | 2008 | 2007 | 2006 | 2005 | 2004 | 2003 | 2002 | 2001 |
|---|---|---|---|---|---|---|---|---|---|---|
| Tangible Book Value | NM | NM | NM | NM | 42.91 | 32.38 | 23.83 | 17.10 | 13.71 | 12.39 |
| Cash Flow | 18.20 | 16.19 | 16.08 | 18.00 | 13.67 | 10.71 | 7.93 | 5.16 | 4.76 | 3.61 |
| Earnings | 14.31 | 12.41 | 12.13 | 14.93 | 11.60 | 8.81 | 6.38 | 3.60 | 3.13 | 2.33 |
| S&P Core Earnings | 14.62 | 12.92 | 15.26 | 14.96 | 11.59 | 8.80 | 6.37 | 3.61 | 3.23 | 2.30 |
| Dividends | 4.60 | 4.60 | 9.60 | 3.44 | 2.52 | 1.84 | 1.04 | 0.63 | Nil | NA |
| Payout Ratio | 32% | 37% | 79% | 23% | 22% | 21% | 16% | 18% | Nil | NA |
| Prices:High | 353.03 | 346.24 | 686.43 | 714.48 | 557.97 | 396.90 | 229.80 | 79.30 | 45.50 | NA |
| Prices:Low | 234.50 | 155.06 | 155.49 | 497.00 | 354.50 | 163.80 | 72.50 | 41.35 | 35.00 | NA |
| P/E Ratio:High | 25 | 28 | 57 | 48 | 48 | 45 | 36 | 22 | 15 | NA |
| P/E Ratio:Low | 16 | 12 | 13 | 33 | 31 | 19 | 11 | 11 | 11 | NA |

| Income Statement Analysis (Million $) | 2010 | 2009 | 2008 | 2007 | 2006 | 2005 | 2004 | 2003 | 2002 | 2001 |
|---|---|---|---|---|---|---|---|---|---|---|
| Revenue | 3,004 | 2,613 | 2,561 | 1,756 | 1,090 | 977 | 753 | 545 | 469 | 397 |
| Operating Income | 2,089 | 1,846 | 1,946 | 1,258 | 694 | 631 | 464 | 290 | NA | NA |
| Depreciation | 258 | 251 | 233 | 136 | 72.8 | 66.0 | 53.0 | 53.0 | 48.5 | 37.6 |
| Interest Expense | 140 | 134 | 56.5 | 115 | 92.1 | 57.0 | 19.0 | 8.74 | 15.9 | 9.48 |
| Pretax Income | 1,722 | 1,438 | 1,248 | 1,096 | 672 | 508 | 368 | 206 | 154 | 114 |
| Effective Tax Rate | NA | 42.6% | 42.7% | 39.9% | 39.4% | 39.6% | 40.2% | 40.7% | 39.0% | 40.3% |
| Net Income | 952 | 826 | 715 | 659 | 407 | 307 | 220 | 122 | 94.1 | 68.3 |
| S&P Core Earnings | 972 | 859 | 900 | 660 | 407 | 307 | 219 | 123 | 97.2 | 67.5 |

| Balance Sheet & Other Financial Data (Million $) | 2010 | 2009 | 2008 | 2007 | 2006 | 2005 | 2004 | 2003 | 2002 | 2001 |
|---|---|---|---|---|---|---|---|---|---|---|
| Cash | 905 | 303 | 608 | 4,744 | 3,872 | 904 | 660 | 442 | 339 | 292 |
| Current Assets | 5,388 | 6,699 | 19,112 | 4,987 | 4,030 | 3,783 | 2,695 | 4,723 | 3,215 | 2,818 |
| Total Assets | 35,045 | 35,651 | 48,133 | 20,306 | 4,307 | 3,969 | 2,857 | 4,873 | 3,355 | 2,958 |
| Current Liabilities | 4,781 | 6,524 | 18,643 | 4,076 | 2,755 | 2,830 | 2,026 | 4,288 | 2,889 | 2,544 |
| Long Term Debt | 2,105 | 2,015 | 2,966 | Nil | Nil | Nil | Nil | Nil | 2.33 | 8.22 |
| Common Equity | 20,059 | 19,301 | 18,689 | 12,306 | 1,519 | 1,119 | 813 | 563 | 446 | 394 |
| Total Capital | 22,300 | 21,316 | 29,383 | 16,154 | 1,519 | 1,119 | 813 | 563 | 448 | 402 |
| Capital Expenditures | 160 | 158 | 200 | 164 | 87.8 | 85.6 | 67.0 | 63.0 | 56.3 | 16.3 |
| Cash Flow | 1,210 | 1,077 | 948 | 794 | 480 | 373 | 273 | 175 | 143 | 106 |
| Current Ratio | 1.1 | 1.0 | 1.0 | 1.2 | 1.5 | 1.3 | 1.3 | 1.1 | 1.1 | 1.1 |
| % Long Term Debt of Capitalization | 9.4 | 9.5 | 10.1 | Nil | Nil | Nil | Nil | Nil | 0.5 | 2.0 |
| % Net Income of Revenue | 31.7 | 31.6 | 27.9 | 37.5 | 37.4 | 31.4 | 29.2 | 22.5 | 20.1 | 17.2 |
| % Return on Assets | 2.7 | 2.0 | 2.1 | 5.4 | 9.8 | 8.9 | 5.6 | 3.0 | 3.5 | 5.6 |
| % Return on Equity | 4.8 | 4.4 | 4.6 | 9.5 | 30.9 | 31.7 | 31.9 | 24.2 | 27.1 | 33.0 |

Data as orig reptd.; bef. results of disc opers/spec. items. Per share data adj. for stk. divs.; EPS diluted. E-Estimated. NA-Not Available. NM-Not Meaningful. NR-Not Ranked. UR-Under Review.

**Office:** 20 South Wacker Drive, Chicago, IL 60606-7499.
**Telephone:** 312-930-1000.
**Email:** info@cme.com
**Website:** http://www.cme.com

**Chrmn:** T.A. Duffy
**Pres:** P.S. Gill
**CEO:** C.S. Donohue
**COO:** B.T. Durkin

**CFO:** J.E. Parisi
**Investor Contact:** J. Peschier (312-930-8491)
**Board Members:** J. M. Bernacchi, T. Bitsberger, C. P. Carey, M. Cermak, D. H. Chookaszian, J. Clegg, R. F. Corvino, J. A. Donaldson, C. S. Donohue, T. A. Duffy, M. J. Gepsman, L. G. Gerdes, J. S. Ginsburg, D. R. Glickman, J. D. Hastert, G. J. Heraty, B. F. Johnson, G. M. Katler, L. Melamed, W. Miller, II, C. C. Odom, II, J. Oliff, R. A. Pankau, J. L. Pietrzak, E. Pinto, A. J. Pollock, J. F. Sandner, T. L. Savage, W. R. Shepard, H. J. Siegel, C. Stewart, D. A. Suskind, D. J. Wescott

**Founded:** 1898
**Domicile:** Delaware
**Employees:** 2,570

The McGraw-Hill Companies

# CMS Energy Corp

**STANDARD &POOR'S**

| S&P Recommendation HOLD ★★★★★ | Price<br>$19.71 (as of Nov 25, 2011) | 12-Mo. Target Price<br>$21.00 | Investment Style<br>Large-Cap Value |
|---|---|---|---|

**GICS Sector** Utilities
**Sub-Industry** Multi-Utilities

**Summary** This energy holding company's principal subsidiary is Consumers Energy, the largest utility in Michigan and the sixth largest gas and 13th largest electric utility in the U.S.

## Key Stock Statistics (Source S&P, Vickers, company reports)

| | | | | | | | |
|---|---|---|---|---|---|---|---|
| 52-Wk Range | $21.58–16.96 | S&P Oper. EPS 2011E | 1.47 | Market Capitalization(B) | $4.998 | Beta | 0.54 |
| Trailing 12-Month EPS | $1.52 | S&P Oper. EPS 2012E | 1.56 | Yield (%) | 4.26 | S&P 3-Yr. Proj. EPS CAGR(%) | 7 |
| Trailing 12-Month P/E | 13.0 | P/E on S&P Oper. EPS 2011E | 13.4 | Dividend Rate/Share | $0.84 | S&P Credit Rating | BBB- |
| $10K Invested 5 Yrs Ago | $15,189 | Common Shares Outstg. (M) | 253.6 | Institutional Ownership (%) | 94 | | |

## Price Performance

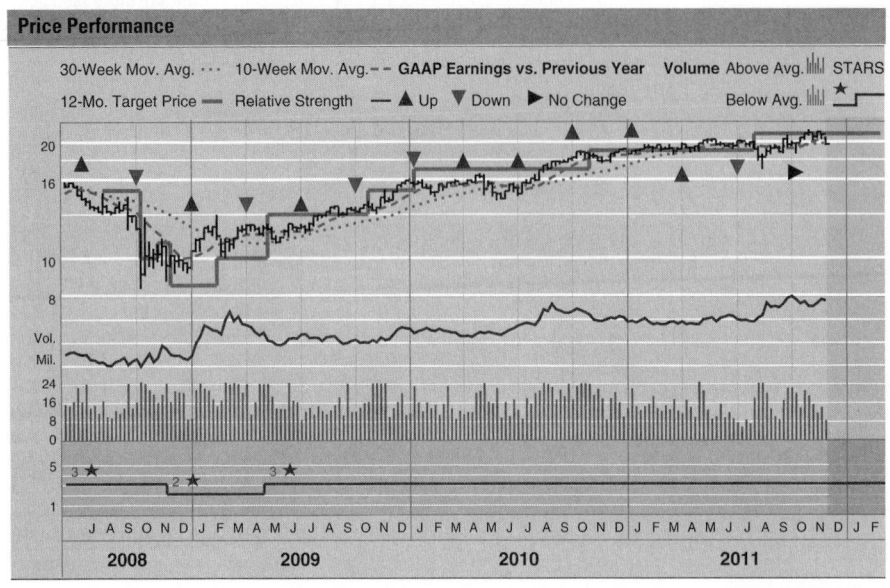

30-Week Mov. Avg. ···· 10-Week Mov. Avg. – – GAAP Earnings vs. Previous Year Volume Above Avg. STARS
12-Mo. Target Price — Relative Strength ▲ Up ▼ Down ► No Change Below Avg. ★

Options: ASE, CBOE, P, Ph

Analysis prepared by Equity Analyst **Justin McCann** on Nov 09, 2011, when the stock traded at **$20.54**.

## Highlights

➤ We expect operating EPS in 2011 to grow 8% from 2010's $1.36. In the first nine months of 2011, operating EPS of $1.30 was $0.14 above the year-earlier level. Results benefited from higher electric rates, a lower tax rate, a decline in interest expense, and higher gas deliveries as the abnormally cold weather in the first quarter contrasted with the much milder weather in the first quarter of 2010. This was partially offset by 9.7% more shares and higher O&M expenses as storm restoration costs were more than twice that of the year-ago period.

➤ For 2012, we expect operating EPS to increase approximately 6% from anticipated results in 2011, driven by the company's rate base investments and an improving local economy. Over the next couple of years, we look for weather-adjusted electric deliveries to grow at an annual rate of about 1.5%, but for gas deliveries to decline at an annual rate of about 1%.

➤ CMS plans to invest $650 million in renewable energy projects over the next five years, mainly for wind power. Michigan law requires 10% of power to come from renewables by 2015, and the company expects to have about 5% obtained through purchased power contracts.

## Investment Rationale/Risk

➤ The stock was up about 13% in the first 45 weeks of 2011, aided, we believe, by an investor shift into the utility sector given the often sharp declines in the broader market. This followed a 19% gain in 2010 that reflected, in our view, a sharp hike in the dividend and the favorable outlook for CMS's long-term earnings growth. CMS plans to invest more than $6 billion in its Consumers Energy utility over the next five years, which should significantly add to its rate base and enable it to grow EPS at an average annual rate of 5% to 7%. We do not expect CMS to issue any new equity through 2015.

➤ Risks to our recommendation and target price include a slower-than-expected recovery in the Michigan economy, as well as a decrease in the average P/E multiple of the utility sector.

➤ After years of having a below-peers dividend yield, CMS's yield (recently about 4%) has become more competitive with its peers (about 4.2%) after a 40% dividend hike in November 2010. The increase was made possible after CMS reduced its five-year capital investment plan by about $1 billion. Our 12-month target price is $21, reflecting an approximate peer P/E of 13.5X our operating EPS estimate for 2012.

## Qualitative Risk Assessment

| LOW | MEDIUM | HIGH |
|---|---|---|

Our risk assessment reflects the steady cash flow from the regulated electric and gas utility businesses, which operate within a generally supportive regulatory environment, and our view of a substantially improved financial risk profile.

## Quantitative Evaluations

**S&P Quality Ranking** B

| D | C | B- | B | B+ | A- | A | A+ |
|---|---|---|---|---|---|---|---|

**Relative Strength Rank** MODERATE

67

LOWEST = 1     HIGHEST = 99

## Revenue/Earnings Data

**Revenue (Million $)**

| | 1Q | 2Q | 3Q | 4Q | Year |
|---|---|---|---|---|---|
| 2011 | 2,055 | 1,364 | 1,464 | -- | -- |
| 2010 | 1,967 | 1,340 | 1,443 | 1,682 | 6,432 |
| 2009 | 2,104 | 1,225 | 1,263 | 1,613 | 6,205 |
| 2008 | 2,184 | 1,365 | 1,428 | 1,844 | 6,821 |
| 2007 | 2,237 | 1,319 | 1,282 | 1,674 | 6,464 |
| 2006 | 2,032 | 1,396 | 1,462 | 1,920 | 6,810 |

**Earnings Per Share ($)**

| | | | | | |
|---|---|---|---|---|---|
| 2011 | 0.51 | 0.38 | 0.53 | E0.17 | E1.47 |
| 2010 | 0.35 | 0.39 | 0.53 | 0.11 | 1.36 |
| 2009 | 0.31 | 0.21 | 0.29 | 0.03 | 0.83 |
| 2008 | 0.44 | 0.20 | 0.33 | 0.27 | 1.23 |
| 2007 | -0.16 | -0.26 | 0.34 | -0.56 | -0.62 |
| 2006 | -0.13 | 0.30 | -0.47 | -0.16 | -0.44 |

Fiscal year ended Dec. 31. Next earnings report expected: Late February. EPS Estimates based on S&P Operating Earnings; historical GAAP earnings are as reported.

## Dividend Data (Dates: mm/dd Payment Date: mm/dd/yy)

| Amount ($) | Date Decl. | Ex-Div. Date | Stk. of Record | Payment Date |
|---|---|---|---|---|
| 0.210 | 01/28 | 02/03 | 02/07 | 02/28/11 |
| 0.210 | 04/19 | 05/04 | 05/06 | 05/31/11 |
| 0.210 | 07/22 | 08/03 | 08/05 | 08/31/11 |
| 0.210 | 10/21 | 11/02 | 11/04 | 11/30/11 |

Dividends have been paid since 2007. Source: Company reports.

# CMS Energy Corp

STANDARD
&POOR'S

## Business Summary November 09, 2011

CORPORATE OVERVIEW. CMS Energy (CMS) is the energy holding company for Consumers Energy (formerly Consumers Power Co.), a regulated electric and gas utility serving Michigan's lower peninsula, and CMS Enterprises, which is engaged in U.S. and international energy-related businesses. CMS operates in three business segments: electric utility, gas utility, and enterprises. CMS's electric utility operations include generation, purchase, distribution and sale of electricity. CMS's gas utility purchases, transports, stores, distributes and sells natural gas. The Enterprises segment, through its various subsidiaries and equity investments, is engaged in diversified energy businesses, including independent power production, electric distribution, and natural gas transmission, storage and processing.

MARKET PROFILE. CMS's electric utility provides electricity to more than 1.7 million customers in 61 of the 68 counties in the lower peninsula of Michigan. In 2010, the electric utility had total electric deliveries of 38 billion kWh. Consumers' electric utility customer base includes a mix of residential, commercial and diversified industrial customers, the largest segment of which is the automotive industry, which accounted for about 6% of total electric revenues

in 2010. In April 2007, CMS completed the sale of the 798-megawatt Palisades nuclear power plant to Entergy (ETR) for $363 million. The transaction included a 15-year power purchase agreement with ETR. In May 2010, the company announced that due to projected surplus generating capacity in its market, it was indefinitely deferring the development of an 830-megawatt clean coal power plant it planned to have operational in 2017.

The company's gas utility serves nearly 1.7 million customers in 54 of the 68 counties in Michigan's lower peninsula. The gas utility also owned 1,664 miles of transmission lines at the end of 2010, and 15 gas storage fields in Michigan, with a storage capacity of 307 bcf. The electric utility segment accounted for 59.1% of the company's consolidated revenues in 2010 (54.9% in 2009); the gas utility segment for 36.6% (41.2%); Enterprises for 3.7% (3.5%); and other for 0.6% (0.4%).

## Company Financials Fiscal Year Ended Dec. 31

| Per Share Data ($) | 2010 | 2009 | 2008 | 2007 | 2006 | 2005 | 2004 | 2003 | 2002 | 2001 |
|---|---|---|---|---|---|---|---|---|---|---|
| Tangible Book Value | 11.19 | 11.42 | 10.88 | 9.46 | 9.90 | 10.53 | 10.51 | 9.69 | 7.47 | 8.11 |
| Earnings | 1.36 | 0.83 | 1.23 | -0.62 | -0.44 | -0.51 | 0.67 | -0.30 | -2.99 | -2.53 |
| S&P Core Earnings | 1.57 | 1.08 | 1.01 | -0.65 | -0.16 | -0.44 | 0.36 | 0.25 | -3.75 | -3.29 |
| Dividends | 0.66 | 0.50 | 0.36 | 0.20 | Nil | Nil | Nil | Nil | 1.09 | 1.46 |
| Payout Ratio | 49% | 60% | 29% | NM | Nil | Nil | Nil | Nil | NM | NM |
| Prices:High | 19.25 | 16.13 | 17.47 | 19.55 | 17.00 | 16.80 | 10.65 | 10.74 | 24.80 | 31.80 |
| Prices:Low | 14.09 | 9.98 | 8.33 | 14.98 | 12.09 | 9.70 | 7.81 | 3.41 | 5.45 | 19.49 |
| P/E Ratio:High | 14 | 19 | 14 | NM | NM | NM | 16 | NM | NM | NM |
| P/E Ratio:Low | 10 | 12 | 7 | NM | NM | NM | 12 | NM | NM | NM |

| Income Statement Analysis (Million $) | | | | | | | | | | |
|---|---|---|---|---|---|---|---|---|---|---|
| Revenue | 6,432 | 6,205 | 6,821 | 6,464 | 6,810 | 6,288 | 5,472 | 5,513 | 8,687 | 9,597 |
| Depreciation | 597 | 590 | 629 | 540 | 576 | 525 | 431 | 428 | 403 | 530 |
| Maintenance | NA | 220 | 193 | 201 | 326 | 249 | 256 | 226 | 211 | 263 |
| Fixed Charges Coverage | 2.25 | 1.70 | 2.05 | 3.38 | 1.18 | -0.56 | 1.01 | 1.23 | 0.12 | 1.26 |
| Construction Credits | NA | NA | NA | NA | NA | NA | NA | NA | NA | NA |
| Effective Tax Rate | 38.0% | 34.3% | 31.6% | 63.3% | NM | NM | NM | NM | NM | NM |
| Net Income | 363 | 209 | 300 | -126 | -85.0 | -98.0 | 127 | -43.0 | -416 | -331 |
| S&P Core Earnings | 403 | 260 | 238 | -145 | -31.0 | -93.1 | 63.4 | 40.6 | -522 | -431 |

| Balance Sheet & Other Financial Data (Million $) | | | | | | | | | | |
|---|---|---|---|---|---|---|---|---|---|---|
| Gross Property | 14,715 | 14,222 | 13,618 | 12,894 | 13,293 | 12,448 | 14,751 | 11,790 | 11,344 | 15,195 |
| Capital Expenditures | 821 | 818 | 792 | 1,263 | 670 | 593 | 525 | 535 | 747 | 1,262 |
| Net Property | 10,069 | 9,682 | 9,190 | 8,728 | 7,976 | 7,325 | 8,636 | 6,944 | 5,234 | 8,362 |
| Capitalization:Long Term Debt | 6,636 | 6,092 | 6,287 | 5,832 | 6,466 | 7,286 | 7,307 | 8,652 | 6,399 | 6,983 |
| Capitalization:% Long Term Debt | 70.4 | 68.2 | 69.9 | 71.0 | 72.2 | 73.8 | 75.8 | 84.5 | 85.0 | 78.7 |
| Capitalization:Preferred | Nil | 239 | 243 | 250 | 261 | 261 | 261 | Nil | Nil | Nil |
| Capitalization:% Preferred | Nil | 2.70 | 2.70 | 3.00 | 2.91 | 2.64 | 2.71 | Nil | Nil | Nil |
| Capitalization:Common | 2,793 | 2,602 | 2,463 | 2,130 | 2,234 | 2,322 | 2,072 | 1,585 | 1,133 | 1,890 |
| Capitalization:% Common | 29.6 | 29.1 | 27.4 | 25.9 | 24.9 | 23.5 | 21.5 | 15.5 | 15.0 | 21.3 |
| Total Capital | 10,223 | 9,724 | 9,145 | 8,323 | 9,234 | 10,566 | 11,123 | 11,010 | 8,058 | 9,834 |
| % Operating Ratio | 89.1 | 90.8 | 90.6 | 100.4 | 92.8 | 84.8 | 88.2 | 91.5 | 92.1 | 89.6 |
| % Earned on Net Property | 9.3 | 7.3 | 8.9 | 8.8 | NM | NM | 7.6 | 8.1 | 1.8 | 3.7 |
| % Return on Revenue | 5.6 | 3.4 | 4.4 | NM | NM | NM | 2.3 | NM | NM | NM |
| % Return on Invested Capital | 7.8 | 6.7 | 7.9 | 4.4 | 8.1 | 11.0 | 9.5 | 6.7 | 7.9 | 9.4 |
| % Return on Common Equity | 12.9 | 8.3 | 13.1 | NM | NM | NM | 6.3 | NM | NM | NM |

Data as orig reptd.; bef. results of disc opers/spec. items. Per share data adj. for stk. divs.; EPS diluted. E-Estimated. NA-Not Available. NM-Not Meaningful. NR-Not Ranked. UR-Under Review.

**Office:** One Energy Plaza, Jackson, MI 49201-2357.
**Telephone:** 517-788-0550.
**Email:** invest@cmsenergy.com
**Website:** http://www.cmsenergy.com

**Chrmn:** D.W. Joos
**Pres & CEO:** J.G. Russell
**CFO:** T.J. Webb
**Chief Acctg Officer & Cntlr:** G.P. Barba

**Investor Contact:** L.L. Mountcastle (517-788-2590)
**Board Members:** M. S. Ayres, J. E. Barfield, S. E. Ewing, R. M. Gabrys, D. W. Joos, P. R. Lochner, Jr., M. T. Monahan, J. G. Russell, K. L. Way, J. B. Yasinsky

**Founded:** 1987
**Domicile:** Michigan
**Employees:** 7,822

The McGraw·Hill Companies

# Coach Inc.

## STANDARD &POOR'S

| S&P Recommendation | STRONG BUY ★★★★★ | Price<br>$58.25 (as of Nov 25, 2011) | 12-Mo. Target Price<br>$77.00 | Investment Style<br>Large-Cap Growth |
|---|---|---|---|---|

**GICS Sector** Consumer Discretionary
**Sub-Industry** Apparel, Accessories & Luxury Goods

**Summary** COH designs, makes and markets fine accessories for women and men, including handbags, weekend and travel accessories, outerwear, footwear, and business cases.

## Key Stock Statistics (Source S&P, Vickers, company reports)

| | | | | | | | |
|---|---|---|---|---|---|---|---|
| 52-Wk Range | $69.20–45.70 | S&P Oper. EPS 2012**E** | 3.43 | Market Capitalization(B) | $16.999 | Beta | 1.57 |
| Trailing 12-Month EPS | $3.02 | S&P Oper. EPS 2013**E** | 3.92 | Yield (%) | 1.55 | S&P 3-Yr. Proj. EPS CAGR(%) | 15 |
| Trailing 12-Month P/E | 19.3 | P/E on S&P Oper. EPS 2012**E** | 17.0 | Dividend Rate/Share | $0.90 | S&P Credit Rating | NA |
| $10K Invested 5 Yrs Ago | $14,034 | Common Shares Outstg. (M) | 291.8 | Institutional Ownership (%) | 91 | | |

## Price Performance

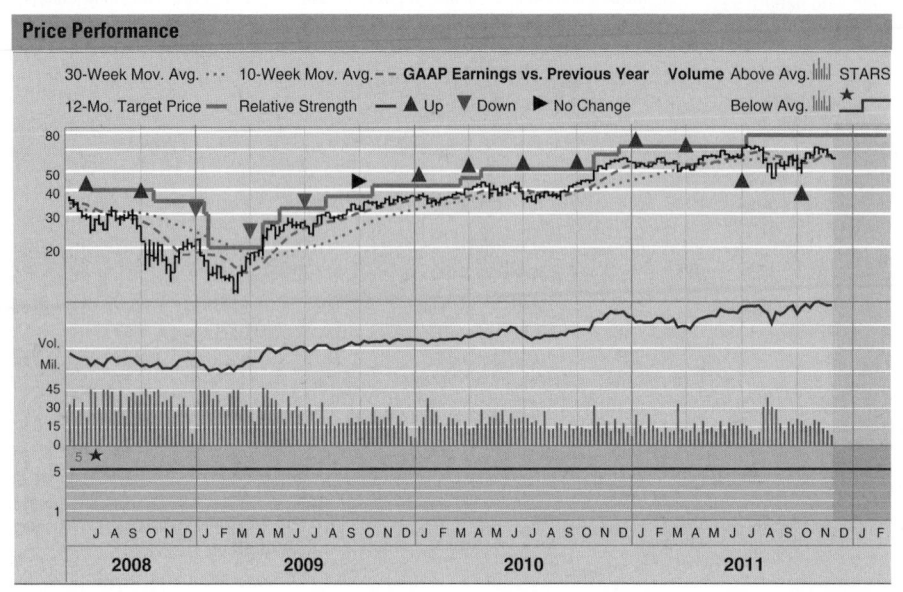

30-Week Mov. Avg. ···   10-Week Mov. Avg. - -   GAAP Earnings vs. Previous Year   Volume Above Avg. STARS
12-Mo. Target Price —   Relative Strength —   ▲ Up  ▼ Down  ► No Change   Below Avg.

Options: ASE, CBOE, P, Ph

Analysis prepared by Equity Analyst **Jason N. Asaeda** on Nov 02, 2011, when the stock traded at **$62.89**.

## Highlights

> In FY 11 (Jun.), COH estimates the U.S. addressable market for women's accessories and handbags grew to 10%, to $9.3 billion; the company grew more rapidly, expanding its domestic market share. A re-emphasis on Coach Men's also doubled the business to about $200 million, and a focus on expanding Asian distribution increased COH's market share in China to 6%, or $185 million. The company is targeting a 10% share, or approximately $500 million of a projected $5 billion market, by FY 14.

> We see sales reaching $4.73 billion in FY 12. COH intends to expand global retail square footage 12%, concentrating on China, where it projects sales of over $300 million. We expect EBIT margins to widen 50 bps, to 31.9%, driven by higher-margin sales in China and Japan, and SG&A expense leverage despite ongoing infrastructure investments and planned spending on a global media campaign highlighting the company's 70th anniversary. COH will also anniversary higher sourcing costs (mainly reflecting wage inflation in China) in the second half of FY 12.

> Assuming share repurchases, we estimate EPS of $3.43 in FY 12.

## Investment Rationale/Risk

> We see favorable long-term sales and earnings prospects for COH, as much based on management's acumen as on global brand potential. In the September quarter, North American comparable-store sales rose 9.2%, reflecting momentum in both full-price and factory channels. The return of the global luxury shopper and compelling assortments also drove penetration of $400+ handbags in the September quarter to 22%, from 16% in the year-ago period. The celebration of Coach's 70th anniversary is a vehicle to highlight the brand's New York City heritage and quality, which we see attracting new customers globally in FY 12. We also see further development of Coach Men's expanding the company's market opportunity while enhancing its luxury positioning.

> Risks to our recommendation and target price include a sharp drop in consumer spending; sourcing, fashion and inventory risks; and international expansion difficulties.

> Our 12-month target price of $77 is 20.7X our calendar 2012 EPS estimate of $3.74, in line with COH's broad peer group of specialty apparel retailers and luxury brands.

## Qualitative Risk Assessment

| LOW | MEDIUM | HIGH |
|---|---|---|

Our risk assessment reflects our view of COH's strong brand equity and rising cash flow, offset by a highly competitive market amid retail consolidation.

## Quantitative Evaluations

**S&P Quality Ranking**  B+

| D | C | B- | B | B+ | A- | A | A+ |
|---|---|---|---|---|---|---|---|

**Relative Strength Rank**  MODERATE

62

LOWEST = 1      HIGHEST = 99

## Revenue/Earnings Data

**Revenue (Million $)**

| | 1Q | 2Q | 3Q | 4Q | Year |
|---|---|---|---|---|---|
| 2012 | 1,050 | -- | -- | -- | -- |
| 2011 | 911.7 | 1,264 | 950.7 | 1,032 | 4,159 |
| 2010 | 761.4 | 1,065 | 830.7 | 950.5 | 3,608 |
| 2009 | 752.5 | 960.3 | 739.9 | 777.7 | 3,230 |
| 2008 | 676.7 | 978.0 | 744.5 | 781.5 | 3,181 |
| 2007 | 529.4 | 805.6 | 625.3 | 652.1 | 2,612 |

**Earnings Per Share ($)**

| | 1Q | 2Q | 3Q | 4Q | Year |
|---|---|---|---|---|---|
| 2012 | 0.73 | E1.12 | E0.75 | E0.83 | E3.43 |
| 2011 | 0.63 | 1.00 | 0.62 | 0.68 | 2.92 |
| 2010 | 0.44 | 0.75 | 0.50 | 0.64 | 2.33 |
| 2009 | 0.44 | 0.67 | 0.36 | 0.46 | 1.91 |
| 2008 | 0.41 | 0.69 | 0.46 | 0.62 | 2.17 |
| 2007 | 0.31 | 0.57 | 0.39 | 0.42 | 1.69 |

Fiscal year ended Jun. 30. Next earnings report expected: NA. EPS Estimates based on S&P Operating Earnings; historical GAAP earnings are as reported.

## Dividend Data (Dates: mm/dd Payment Date: mm/dd/yy)

| Amount ($) | Date Decl. | Ex-Div. Date | Stk. of Record | Payment Date |
|---|---|---|---|---|
| 0.150 | 02/28 | 03/03 | 03/07 | 04/04/11 |
| 0.225 | 05/19 | 06/02 | 06/06 | 07/05/11 |
| 0.225 | 08/17 | 09/01 | 09/06 | 10/03/11 |
| 0.225 | 11/17 | 12/01 | 12/05 | 01/03/12 |

Dividends have been paid since 2009. Source: Company reports.

---

**Please read the Required Disclosures and Analyst Certification on the last page of this report.**

The McGraw-Hill Companies

# Coach Inc.

STANDARD
&POOR'S

## Business Summary November 02, 2011

CORPORATE OVERVIEW. Coach is a leading U.S. designer and marketer of high-quality accessories. Founded in 1941, COH has over the past several years transformed the Coach brand, building on its popular core categories by introducing new products in a broader array of materials, styles and categories. The company has also implemented a flexible sourcing and manufacturing model, which it believes enables it to bring a broader range of products to market more rapidly and efficiently.

MARKET PROFILE. Coach is the number one luxury accessories brand in the U.S., with an estimated 20% share of this estimated $9.3 billion market ($100+ handbags). In FY 11 (Jun.), the category grew an estimated 10% (up from an estimated 3%-5% pace in FY 10), which COH easily outpaced with its 17% gain in its own stores. This sub-segment of the handbag/accessories market remains one of the best-performing categories at retail. COH has been able to outpace industry growth as it executed its multi-channel growth strategy, and we believe COH has an estimated 20%+ U.S. handbag market share entering FY 12. The Japanese consumer makes up about 40% of the global luxury handbag market; COH estimates it holds 16% of the domestic Japanese market,

and aims to leverage its brand there by entering the men's small leather goods market. Developing markets represent the next leg of growth, supporting a global market projected at $24 billion in 2011. With a total of 66 locations in Greater China, COH currently holds an estimated 6% share of that market.

PRIMARY BUSINESS DYNAMICS. COH sells its products through direct-to-consumer and indirect channels, with the former accounting for 87% of total sales in FY 11 and FY 10, up from 84% in FY 09 and 55% in FY 05 via store expansion and comp-store sales gains. As of July 2, 2011, direct-to-consumer channels included the Internet, direct mail catalogs, 345 North American retail stores, 142 North American factory stores, and 176 department store shop-in-shops, retail stores and factory stores in Japan. Indirect channels include an estimated 900 U.S. department store locations and 140 international department store, retail store and duty-free shop locations in 18 countries.

## Company Financials Fiscal Year Ended Jun. 30

| Per Share Data ($) | 2011 | 2010 | 2009 | 2008 | 2007 | 2006 | 2005 | 2004 | 2003 | 2002 |
|---|---|---|---|---|---|---|---|---|---|---|
| Tangible Book Value | 4.41 | 4.01 | 4.41 | 3.73 | 4.52 | 2.57 | 2.07 | 2.00 | 1.11 | 0.67 |
| Cash Flow | 3.34 | 2.73 | 2.29 | 2.45 | 1.90 | 1.44 | 1.14 | 0.79 | 0.48 | 0.31 |
| Earnings | 2.92 | 2.33 | 1.91 | 2.17 | 1.69 | 1.27 | 1.00 | 0.68 | 0.40 | 0.24 |
| S&P Core Earnings | 2.92 | 2.33 | 1.91 | 2.17 | 1.69 | 1.26 | 0.91 | 0.61 | 0.35 | 0.21 |
| Dividends | 0.68 | 0.38 | 0.08 | Nil | Nil | Nil | Nil | Nil | Nil | Nil |
| Payout Ratio | 23% | 16% | 4% | Nil | Nil | Nil | Nil | Nil | Nil | Nil |
| Prices:High | 69.20 | 58.55 | 37.36 | 37.64 | 54.00 | 44.99 | 36.84 | 28.85 | 20.42 | 8.93 |
| Prices:Low | 45.70 | 32.96 | 11.41 | 13.19 | 29.22 | 25.18 | 24.51 | 16.88 | 7.26 | 4.30 |
| P/E Ratio:High | 24 | 25 | 20 | 17 | 32 | 35 | 37 | 42 | 52 | 38 |
| P/E Ratio:Low | 16 | 14 | 6 | 6 | 17 | 20 | 25 | 25 | 18 | 18 |

| Income Statement Analysis (Million $) | | | | | | | | | | |
|---|---|---|---|---|---|---|---|---|---|---|
| Revenue | 4,159 | 3,608 | 3,230 | 3,181 | 2,612 | 2,112 | 1,710 | 1,321 | 953 | 719 |
| Operating Income | 1,430 | 1,276 | 1,095 | 1,280 | 1,074 | 830 | 679 | 487 | 274 | 163 |
| Depreciation | 125 | 127 | 123 | 101 | 80.9 | 65.1 | 57.0 | 42.9 | 30.2 | 25.5 |
| Interest Expense | NA | NA | NA | NA | Nil | Nil | 1.22 | 0.81 | 0.70 | 1.12 |
| Pretax Income | 1,301 | 1,152 | 977 | 1,195 | 1,035 | 797 | 638 | 448 | 245 | 133 |
| Effective Tax Rate | NA | NA | 36.2% | 34.5% | 38.5% | 38.0% | 36.9% | 37.5% | 37.0% | 35.5% |
| Net Income | 881 | 735 | 623 | 783 | 637 | 494 | 389 | 262 | 147 | 85.8 |
| S&P Core Earnings | 881 | 735 | 625 | 783 | 637 | 492 | 356 | 236 | 129 | 74.9 |

| Balance Sheet & Other Financial Data (Million $) | | | | | | | | | | |
|---|---|---|---|---|---|---|---|---|---|---|
| Cash | 702 | 696 | 800 | 699 | 557 | 143 | 155 | 263 | 229 | 94.0 |
| Current Assets | 1,452 | 1,303 | 1,396 | 1,386 | 1,740 | 974 | 709 | 706 | 449 | 288 |
| Total Assets | 2,635 | 2,467 | 2,564 | 2,274 | 2,450 | 1,627 | 1,347 | 1,029 | 618 | 441 |
| Current Liabilities | 593 | 529 | 460 | 451 | 408 | 342 | 266 | 182 | 161 | 159 |
| Long Term Debt | 23.4 | 24.2 | 25.1 | 2.58 | 2.87 | 3.10 | 3.27 | 3.42 | 3.54 | 3.62 |
| Common Equity | 1,613 | 1,505 | 1,696 | 1,516 | 1,910 | 1,189 | 1,033 | 782 | 427 | 260 |
| Total Capital | 1,637 | 1,530 | 1,721 | 1,545 | 1,950 | 1,223 | 1,041 | 842 | 453 | 279 |
| Capital Expenditures | 148 | 81.1 | 240 | 175 | 141 | 134 | 94.6 | 67.7 | 57.1 | 42.8 |
| Cash Flow | 1,006 | 862 | 746 | 884 | 717 | 559 | 446 | 305 | 177 | 111 |
| Current Ratio | 2.5 | 2.5 | 3.0 | 3.1 | 4.3 | 2.9 | 2.7 | 3.9 | 2.8 | 1.8 |
| % Long Term Debt of Capitalization | 1.4 | 1.6 | 1.5 | 0.2 | 0.1 | 0.3 | 0.3 | 0.4 | 0.8 | 1.3 |
| % Net Income of Revenue | 21.2 | 20.4 | 19.3 | 24.6 | 24.4 | 23.4 | 22.7 | 19.8 | 15.4 | 11.9 |
| % Return on Assets | 34.5 | 29.2 | 25.8 | 33.2 | 31.2 | 33.0 | 32.5 | 31.8 | 27.7 | 24.5 |
| % Return on Equity | 56.5 | 45.9 | 38.8 | 45.7 | 41.1 | 44.0 | 42.8 | 43.3 | 42.7 | 42.0 |

Data as orig reptd.; bef. results of disc opers/spec. items. Per share data adj. for stk. divs.; EPS diluted. E-Estimated. NA-Not Available. NM-Not Meaningful. NR-Not Ranked. UR-Under Review.

Office: 516 West 34th Street, New York, NY 10001.
Telephone: 212-594-1850.
Email: info@coach.com
Website: http://www.coach.com

Chrmn & CEO: L. Frankfort
COO & Co-Pres: J. Stritzke
EVP, CFO & Chief Acctg Officer: J. Nielsen
EVP, Secy & General Counsel: T. Kahn

Treas: N. Walsh
Investor Contact: M. Devine (212-594-1850)
Board Members: L. Frankfort, S. J. Kropf, G. W. Loveman, I. M. Menezes, I. R. Miller, M. E. Murphy, J. J. Zeitlin

Founded: 1941
Domicile: Maryland
Employees: 0

The McGraw-Hill Companies

# Coca-Cola Co (The)

**STANDARD**
**&POOR'S**

| S&P Recommendation | STRONG BUY ★★★★★ | Price $64.74 (as of Nov 25, 2011) | 12-Mo. Target Price $77.00 | Investment Style Large-Cap Growth |
|---|---|---|---|---|

**GICS Sector** Consumer Staples
**Sub-Industry** Soft Drinks

**Summary** The world's largest soft drink company, KO also has a sizable fruit juice business.

## Key Stock Statistics (Source S&P, Vickers, company reports)

| | | | | | | | |
|---|---|---|---|---|---|---|---|
| 52-Wk Range | $71.77– 61.29 | S&P Oper. EPS 2011**E** | 3.87 | Market Capitalization(B) | $147.040 | Beta | 0.59 |
| Trailing 12-Month EPS | $5.44 | S&P Oper. EPS 2012**E** | 4.27 | Yield (%) | 2.90 | S&P 3-Yr. Proj. EPS CAGR(%) | 9 |
| Trailing 12-Month P/E | 11.9 | P/E on S&P Oper. EPS 2011**E** | 16.7 | Dividend Rate/Share | $1.88 | S&P Credit Rating | A+ |
| $10K Invested 5 Yrs Ago | $15,972 | Common Shares Outstg. (M) | 2,271.2 | Institutional Ownership (%) | 63 | | |

## Price Performance

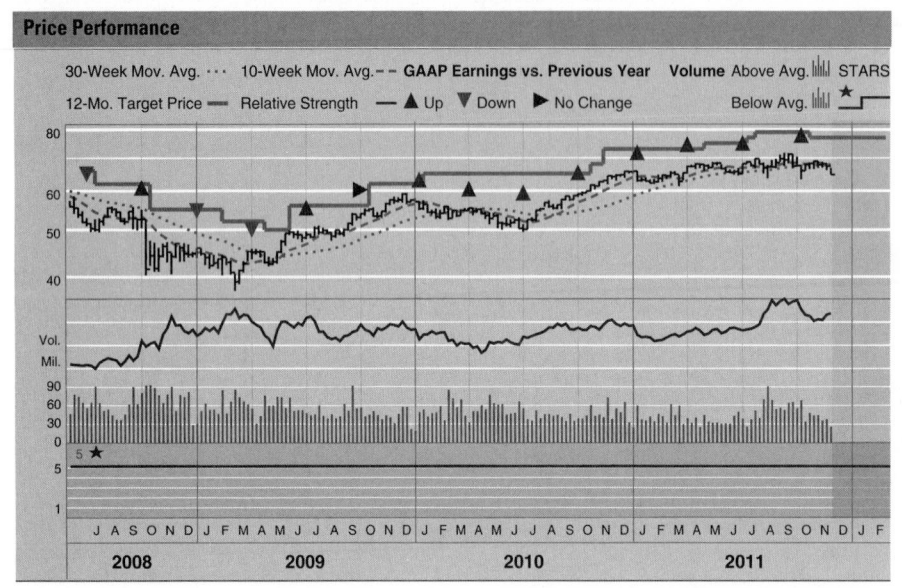

- 30-Week Mov. Avg. ···· 10-Week Mov. Avg. - - GAAP Earnings vs. Previous Year   Volume Above Avg. STARS
- 12-Mo. Target Price — Relative Strength   ▲ Up ▼ Down ► No Change   Below Avg.

Options: ASE, CBOE, P, Ph

Analysis prepared by Equity Analyst **Esther Kwon, CFA** on Oct 18, 2011, when the stock traded at **$67.00**.

## Highlights

► For 2011, we project that sales will rise over 30% from 2010's $35 billion, on a full year's results from North American operations of Coca-Cola Enterprises and, to a lesser extent, higher prices, international volume growth, and positive foreign exchange. We look for mid-single digit growth in volumes, with carbonated volumes increasing at a low single-digit rate and non-carbonated volumes rising at a high single-digit rate. In 2010, sales rose over 13% on about one quarter's worth of results from the North American operations of Coca-Cola Enterprises. For 2012, we forecast 4% sales growth.

► We expect operating profit to grow at a slower rate than sales as cost-cutting initiatives are more than outweighed by an unfavorable mix, with a larger proportion of profit derived from bottling due to the transaction with Coca-Cola Enterprises and lower-margin emerging markets recovering faster than developed ones, and higher commodity costs.

► Assuming a higher effective tax rate of 24%, compared to about 23% in 2010, we estimate EPS of $3.87 for 2011, up from operating EPS of $3.49 in 2010, before one-time charges. For 2012, we forecast EPS of $4.27.

## Investment Rationale/Risk

► In October 2010, KO completed the purchase of the North American bottling operations from Coca-Cola Enterprises' (CCE 26, Hold) for a total value of approximately $12.3 billion, and KO sold its bottling operations in Norway and Sweden to CCE for $822 million. While we have an unfavorable view of the reduction in international exposure, we still see KO having an attractive relative international footprint, particularly in faster-growing emerging markets, and capability to generate strong free cash flow, which we believe will be returned to shareholders through dividends and stock repurchases. We also see an opportunity to improve execution and reduce costs in North America.

► Risks to our recommendation and target price include adverse foreign currency movements, and unfavorable weather conditions in the company's markets.

► Our 12-month target price of $77 is based on an analysis of historical and comparative peer P/E multiples. KO's forward P/E has ranged between 16X and 40X over the past few years. Given a more challenging economic environment, we think a multiple in the lower half of that range is appropriate.

## Qualitative Risk Assessment

| LOW | MEDIUM | HIGH |
|---|---|---|

Our risk assessment for Coca-Cola Company reflects the relatively stable nature of the company's end markets, its dominant market share positions around the world, and our view of its strong balance sheet and cash flow.

## Quantitative Evaluations

**S&P Quality Ranking**                    A+

| D | C | B- | B | B+ | A- | A | A+ |
|---|---|---|---|---|---|---|---|

**Relative Strength Rank**          MODERATE

59

LOWEST = 1                    HIGHEST = 99

## Revenue/Earnings Data

**Revenue (Million $)**

| | 1Q | 2Q | 3Q | 4Q | Year |
|---|---|---|---|---|---|
| 2011 | 10,517 | 12,737 | 12,248 | -- | -- |
| 2010 | 7,525 | 8,674 | 8,426 | 10,494 | 35,119 |
| 2009 | 7,169 | 8,267 | 8,044 | 7,510 | 30,990 |
| 2008 | 7,379 | 9,046 | 8,393 | 7,126 | 31,944 |
| 2007 | 6,103 | 7,733 | 7,690 | 7,331 | 28,857 |
| 2006 | 5,226 | 6,476 | 6,454 | 5,932 | 24,088 |

**Earnings Per Share ($)**

| | 1Q | 2Q | 3Q | 4Q | Year |
|---|---|---|---|---|---|
| 2011 | 0.82 | 1.20 | 0.95 | E0.81 | E3.87 |
| 2010 | 0.69 | 1.02 | 0.88 | 2.46 | 5.06 |
| 2009 | 0.58 | 0.88 | 0.81 | 0.66 | 2.93 |
| 2008 | 0.64 | 0.61 | 0.81 | 0.43 | 2.49 |
| 2007 | 0.54 | 0.80 | 0.71 | 0.52 | 2.57 |
| 2006 | 0.47 | 0.78 | 0.62 | 0.29 | 2.16 |

Fiscal year ended Dec. 31. Next earnings report expected: Early February. EPS Estimates based on S&P Operating Earnings; historical GAAP earnings are as reported.

## Dividend Data (Dates: mm/dd Payment Date: mm/dd/yy)

| Amount ($) | Date Decl. | Ex-Div. Date | Stk. of Record | Payment Date |
|---|---|---|---|---|
| 0.470 | 02/17 | 03/11 | 03/15 | 04/01/11 |
| 0.470 | 04/28 | 06/13 | 06/15 | 07/01/11 |
| 0.470 | 07/21 | 09/13 | 09/15 | 10/01/11 |
| 0.470 | 10/20 | 11/29 | 12/01 | 12/15/11 |

Dividends have been paid since 1893. Source: Company reports.

**Please read the Required Disclosures and Analyst Certification on the last page of this report.**

The **McGraw·Hill** Companies

# Coca-Cola Co (The)

**STANDARD &POOR'S**

## Business Summary October 18, 2011

CORPORATE OVERVIEW. The Coca-Cola Company is the world's largest producer of soft drink concentrates and syrups, as well as the world's biggest producer of juice and juice-related products. Finished soft drink products bearing the company's trademarks have been sold in the U.S. since 1886, and are now sold in more than 200 countries. It owns or licenses more than 500 brands. Sales by operating segment in 2010 were derived as follows: North America (31.7% of revenues); Bottling Investments (23.4%); Europe (12.6%); Pacific (14.1%); Latin America (11.0%); Eurasia and Africa (6.9%); and Corporate (0.3%)

The company's business encompasses the production and sale of soft drink and non-carbonated beverage concentrates and syrups. These products are sold to the company's authorized independent and company-owned bottling/canning operations, and fountain wholesalers. These customers then either combine the syrup with carbonated water, or combine the concentrate with sweetener, water and carbonated water to produce finished soft drinks. The finished soft drinks are packaged in containers bearing the company's well-known trademarks, which include Coca-Cola, caffeine free Coca-Cola, Diet

Coke (sold as Coke Light in many markets outside the U.S.), Cherry Coke, Coca-Cola Zero (sold as Coke Zero in some markets), Fanta, Full Throttle, Sprite, Diet Sprite/Sprite Zero, Barq's, Pi bb Xtra, Mello Yello, Tab, Fresca, Powerade, Aquarius, and other products developed for specific markets. Other beverage products included enhanced water brands such as glaceau vitaminwater and smartwater. The company also markets Schweppes, Canada Dry, Crush and Dr. Pepper brands outside of the U.S. In 2010, trademark Cola-Cola beverages accounted for approximately 50% of worldwide case volume with sparkling beverages representing about 76% of volumes. Trademark Coca-Cola beverages accounted for 51% of U.S. unit case volume while sparkling beverages represented 71% of total U.S. case volume.

In 2010, concentrate operations comprised 51% of total revenue and finished product operations were 49%.

## Company Financials Fiscal Year Ended Dec. 31

| Per Share Data ($) | 2010 | 2009 | 2008 | 2007 | 2006 | 2005 | 2004 | 2003 | 2002 | 2001 |
|---|---|---|---|---|---|---|---|---|---|---|
| Tangible Book Value | 1.79 | 5.20 | 3.45 | 8.53 | 5.08 | 5.29 | 5.02 | 4.14 | 3.34 | 3.53 |
| Cash Flow | 5.70 | 3.46 | 2.94 | 3.00 | 2.56 | 2.43 | 2.36 | 2.11 | 1.93 | 1.92 |
| Earnings | 5.06 | 2.93 | 2.49 | 2.57 | 2.16 | 2.04 | 2.00 | 1.77 | 1.60 | 1.60 |
| S&P Core Earnings | 3.59 | 2.94 | 2.40 | 2.51 | 2.04 | 2.03 | 2.08 | 1.77 | 1.62 | 1.46 |
| Dividends | 1.76 | 1.64 | 1.52 | 1.36 | 1.24 | 1.12 | 1.00 | 0.88 | 0.80 | 0.72 |
| Payout Ratio | 35% | 56% | 61% | 53% | 57% | 55% | 50% | 50% | 50% | 45% |
| Prices:High | 65.88 | 59.45 | 65.59 | 64.32 | 49.35 | 45.26 | 53.50 | 50.90 | 57.91 | 62.19 |
| Prices:Low | 49.47 | 37.44 | 40.29 | 45.56 | 39.36 | 40.31 | 38.30 | 37.01 | 42.90 | 42.37 |
| P/E Ratio:High | 13 | 20 | 26 | 25 | 23 | 22 | 27 | 29 | 36 | 39 |
| P/E Ratio:Low | 10 | 13 | 16 | 18 | 18 | 20 | 19 | 21 | 27 | 26 |

| Income Statement Analysis (Million $) | 2010 | 2009 | 2008 | 2007 | 2006 | 2005 | 2004 | 2003 | 2002 | 2001 |
|---|---|---|---|---|---|---|---|---|---|---|
| Revenue | 35,119 | 30,990 | 31,944 | 28,857 | 24,088 | 23,104 | 21,962 | 21,044 | 19,564 | 20,092 |
| Operating Income | 10,780 | 9,780 | 9,862 | 8,532 | 7,246 | 7,017 | 6,591 | 6,071 | 6,264 | 6,155 |
| Depreciation | 1,443 | 1,236 | 1,066 | 1,012 | 938 | 932 | 893 | 850 | 806 | 803 |
| Interest Expense | 733 | 355 | 438 | 456 | 220 | 240 | 196 | 178 | 199 | 289 |
| Pretax Income | 14,243 | 8,946 | 7,439 | 7,873 | 6,578 | 6,690 | 6,222 | 5,495 | 5,499 | 5,670 |
| Effective Tax Rate | NA | 22.8% | 21.9% | 24.0% | 22.8% | 27.2% | 22.1% | 20.9% | 27.7% | 29.8% |
| Net Income | 11,809 | 6,824 | 5,807 | 5,981 | 5,080 | 4,872 | 4,847 | 4,347 | 3,976 | 3,979 |
| S&P Core Earnings | 8,363 | 6,842 | 5,595 | 5,827 | 4,797 | 4,854 | 5,063 | 4,350 | 4,021 | 3,654 |

| Balance Sheet & Other Financial Data (Million $) | 2010 | 2009 | 2008 | 2007 | 2006 | 2005 | 2004 | 2003 | 2002 | 2001 |
|---|---|---|---|---|---|---|---|---|---|---|
| Cash | 11,337 | 9,213 | 4,979 | 4,308 | 2,590 | 4,767 | 6,768 | 3,482 | 2,345 | 1,934 |
| Current Assets | 21,579 | 17,551 | 12,176 | 12,105 | 8,441 | 10,250 | 12,094 | 8,396 | 7,352 | 7,171 |
| Total Assets | 72,921 | 48,671 | 40,519 | 43,269 | 29,963 | 29,427 | 31,327 | 27,342 | 24,501 | 22,417 |
| Current Liabilities | 18,508 | 13,721 | 12,988 | 13,225 | 8,890 | 9,836 | 10,971 | 7,886 | 7,341 | 8,429 |
| Long Term Debt | 14,041 | 5,059 | 2,781 | 9,329 | 1,314 | 1,154 | 1,157 | 2,517 | 2,701 | 1,219 |
| Common Equity | 31,003 | 24,799 | 20,472 | 21,744 | 16,920 | 16,355 | 15,935 | 14,090 | 11,800 | 11,366 |
| Total Capital | 46,948 | 30,456 | 24,130 | 27,269 | 18,842 | 17,861 | 17,542 | 16,944 | 14,900 | 13,027 |
| Capital Expenditures | 2,215 | 1,993 | 1,968 | 1,648 | 1,407 | 899 | 755 | 812 | 851 | 769 |
| Cash Flow | 13,302 | 8,060 | 6,873 | 6,993 | 6,018 | 5,804 | 5,740 | 5,197 | 4,782 | 4,782 |
| Current Ratio | 1.2 | 1.3 | 0.9 | 0.9 | 0.9 | 1.0 | 1.1 | 1.1 | 1.0 | 0.9 |
| % Long Term Debt of Capitalization | 29.9 | 16.6 | 11.5 | 12.9 | 7.0 | 6.5 | 6.6 | 14.9 | 18.1 | 9.4 |
| % Net Income of Revenue | 33.6 | 22.0 | 18.2 | 20.7 | 21.1 | 21.1 | 22.1 | 20.7 | 20.3 | 19.8 |
| % Return on Assets | 19.5 | 15.3 | 13.9 | 16.3 | 17.1 | 16.0 | 16.5 | 16.8 | 16.9 | 18.4 |
| % Return on Equity | 42.5 | 30.2 | 27.5 | 30.9 | 30.5 | 30.2 | 32.3 | 33.6 | 34.3 | 38.5 |

Data as orig reptd.; bef. results of disc opers/spec. items. Per share data adj. for stk. divs.; EPS diluted. E-Estimated. NA-Not Available. NM-Not Meaningful. NR-Not Ranked. UR-Under Review.

**Office:** 1 Coca Cola Plz NW, Atlanta, GA 30313-2499.
**Telephone:** 404-676-2121.
**Website:** http://www.coca-cola.com
**Chrmn & CEO:** M. Kent

**Investor Contact:** G.P. Fayard
**EVP & CFO:** G.P. Fayard
**EVP & Chief Admin Officer:** A.B. Cummings, Jr.
**SVP & CTO:** G. Wollaert

**Board Members:** H. A. Allen, R. W. Allen, H. G. Buffett, B. Diller, E. G. Greenberg, A. Herman, M. Kent, D. R. Keough, D. McHenry, S. A. Nunn, J. D. Robinson, III, P. V. Ueberroth, J. Wallenberg, J. B. Williams

**Founded:** 1886
**Domicile:** Delaware
**Employees:** 139,600

The McGraw-Hill Companies

# Coca-Cola Enterprises Inc

**STANDARD &POOR'S**

| S&P Recommendation **HOLD** ★★★★★ | Price $24.22 (as of Nov 25, 2011) | 12-Mo. Target Price $30.00 | Investment Style Large-Cap Blend |
|---|---|---|---|

**GICS Sector** Consumer Staples
**Sub-Industry** Soft Drinks

**Summary** Formerly the world's largest bottler of Coca-Cola beverage products, CCE sold its North American operations to Coca-Cola Co. in 2010 and is now Coca-Cola's strategic bottling partner in Western Europe and the third largest independent bottler globally.

## Key Stock Statistics (Source S&P, Vickers, company reports)

| | | | | | |
|---|---|---|---|---|---|
| 52-Wk Range | $29.99– 23.03 | S&P Oper. EPS 2011E | 2.18 | Market Capitalization(B) | $7.557 | Beta | 1.20 |
| Trailing 12-Month EPS | $2.19 | S&P Oper. EPS 2012E | 2.36 | Yield (%) | 2.15 | S&P 3-Yr. Proj. EPS CAGR(%) | 9 |
| Trailing 12-Month P/E | 11.1 | P/E on S&P Oper. EPS 2011E | 11.1 | Dividend Rate/Share | $0.52 | S&P Credit Rating | BBB+ |
| $10K Invested 5 Yrs Ago | $12,722 | Common Shares Outstg. (M) | 312.0 | Institutional Ownership (%) | 85 | | |

## Price Performance

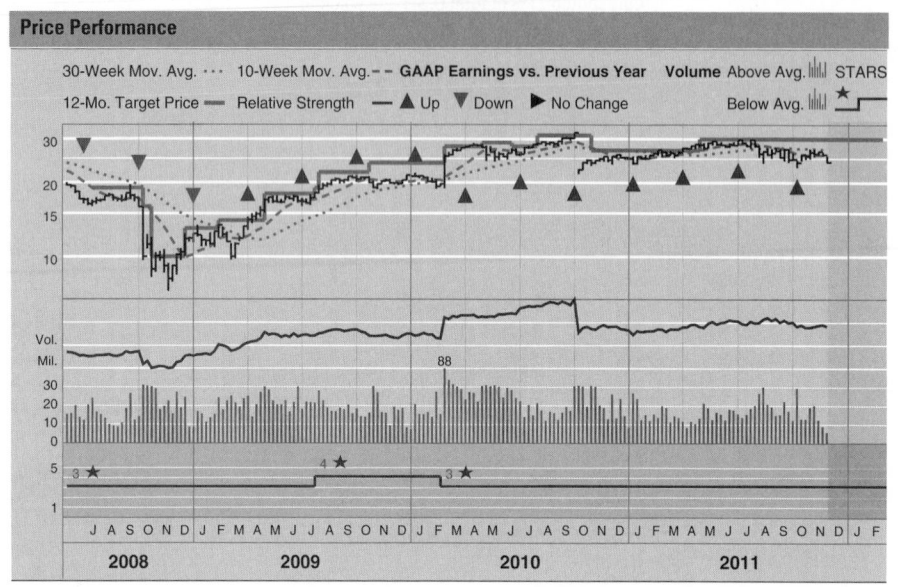

- 30-Week Mov. Avg. · · · 10-Week Mov. Avg. - - GAAP Earnings vs. Previous Year  Volume Above Avg. STARS
- 12-Mo. Target Price — Relative Strength — ▲ Up ▼ Down ▶ No Change  Below Avg.

Options: ASE, CBOE, P, Ph

Analysis prepared by Equity Analyst **Esther Kwon, CFA** on Oct 31, 2011, when the stock traded at **$26.62**.

## Highlights

➤ In 2011, we project about a 12% gain in revenue, boosted by foreign exchange, after a drop of over 60% in 2010 due to CCE's sale of its North American bottling operations to Coca-Cola Co. (KO 69, Strong Buy). We project higher pricing in Europe, with a low to mid-single digit volume gain there. We look for a low single digit volume rise in carbonated beverages, while we expect non-carbonated volumes to climb at a high single digit rate or better. For 2012, we see revenues rising about 2%.

➤ We see 2011 gross margins down, with higher pricing and cost savings more than offset by higher commodity costs. We think SG&A expenses will be down as a percentage of sales.

➤ On an effective tax rate of about 26%, down from 2010's effective rate just under 28%, we see 2011 EPS of $2.18, up from 2010's pro forma $1.78, which excludes restructuring charges, transaction costs and the mark-to-market of commodity hedges. For 2012, we forecast EPS of $2.36. CCE plans to repurchase approximately $1 billion worth of shares by the end of the first quarter of 2012, and pay an annual dividend of $0.50 per share.

## Investment Rationale/Risk

➤ In February 2010, Coca-Cola Co. agreed to acquire CCE's North America bottling business for $10 and one new CCE share for each existing CCE share. In turn, CCE purchased Coca-Cola Co.'s bottling operations in Norway and Sweden for $822 million and has the right to acquire its 83% equity stake in its German bottling operations for fair value 18 to 36 months after the close of the deal. The deal was completed at the beginning of October 2010. We like the deal for CCE shareholders, as we believe the new business will be higher growth with higher profitability, but we see the shares as fairly valued.

➤ Risks to our recommendation and target price include sustained turmoil in the European economy and more rapid commodity cost inflation than we expect. In terms of corporate governance, a majority of the board of directors are insiders and affiliated outsiders, which we view unfavorably.

➤ Our 12-month target price of $30 is based on a multiple of less than 13X our 2012 EPS estimate of $2.36, a discount to the concentrate companies and to Dr Pepper Snapple Group (DPS 37, Hold), which also has high exposure to bottling.

## Qualitative Risk Assessment

| LOW | MEDIUM | HIGH |
|---|---|---|

Our risk assessment for Coca-Cola Enterprises reflects our view of the relatively stable nature of the company's end markets, its strong cash flow, and its relationship with corporate partner Coca-Cola Co.

## Quantitative Evaluations

**S&P Quality Ranking**  B-

| D | C | B- | B | B+ | A- | A | A+ |
|---|---|---|---|---|---|---|---|

**Relative Strength Rank**  MODERATE

46

LOWEST = 1  HIGHEST = 99

## Revenue/Earnings Data

**Revenue (Million $)**

| | 1Q | 2Q | 3Q | 4Q | Year |
|---|---|---|---|---|---|
| 2011 | 1,844 | 2,407 | 2,140 | -- | -- |
| 2010 | 4,968 | 5,884 | 1,681 | 1,794 | 6,714 |
| 2009 | 5,050 | 5,909 | 5,569 | 5,117 | 21,645 |
| 2008 | 4,892 | 5,935 | 5,743 | 5,237 | 21,807 |
| 2007 | 4,567 | 5,665 | 5,405 | 5,299 | 20,936 |
| 2006 | 4,333 | 5,467 | 5,218 | 4,786 | 19,804 |

**Earnings Per Share ($)**

| | | | | | |
|---|---|---|---|---|---|
| 2011 | 0.31 | 0.74 | 0.88 | E0.36 | E2.18 |
| 2010 | 0.21 | 0.69 | 0.61 | 0.28 | 1.83 |
| 2009 | 0.13 | 0.64 | 0.50 | 0.22 | 1.48 |
| 2008 | 0.02 | -6.52 | 0.44 | -2.99 | -9.05 |
| 2007 | 0.03 | 0.56 | 0.55 | 0.32 | 1.46 |
| 2006 | 0.03 | 0.71 | 0.44 | -3.59 | -2.41 |

Fiscal year ended Dec. 31. Next earnings report expected: Mid February. EPS Estimates based on S&P Operating Earnings; historical GAAP earnings are as reported.

## Dividend Data (Dates: mm/dd Payment Date: mm/dd/yy)

| Amount ($) | Date Decl. | Ex-Div. Date | Stk. of Record | Payment Date |
|---|---|---|---|---|
| 0.120 | 02/08 | 03/09 | 03/11 | 03/24/11 |
| 0.130 | 04/26 | 06/08 | 06/10 | 06/23/11 |
| 0.130 | 07/26 | 09/07 | 09/09 | 09/22/11 |
| 0.130 | 11/10 | 11/22 | 11/25 | 12/08/11 |

Dividends have been paid since 1986. Source: Company reports.

# Coca-Cola Enterprises Inc

STANDARD &POOR'S

## Business Summary October 31, 2011

CORPORATE OVERVIEW. Coca-Cola Enterprises is the world's third largest bottler of Coca-Cola beverage products, following the sale of its North American operations to The Coca-Cola Co. (KO) in 2010 and the purchase of KO's bottling operations in Norway and Sweden. CCE's product line also includes other nonalcoholic beverages, such as still and sparkling waters, juices, isotonics and teas. In 2010, including volumes from Norway and Sweden from their acquisition at the beginning of the fourth quarter, the company sold approximately 11 billion bottles and cans (or 560 million cases) throughout its territories. More than 90% of this volume consisted of beverages produced and sold under licenses from KO and its affiliates and joint ventures. CCE also distributes Dr Pepper and several other beverage brands.

Based on net operating revenues in 2010, Great Britain accounted for 38% of the total, France for 31%, Belgium for 18%, the Netherlands for 10%, Norway for 2% and Sweden for 1%. CCE operates in Belgium, France, Great Britain, Luxembourg, Monaco, the Netherlands, Norway and Sweden and serves a market of approximately 165 million consumers. The company's five leading brands in 2010 were Coca-Cola, Diet Coke/Coca-Cola Light, Fanta, Coca-Cola Zero, and Capri Sun.

During 2010, the company's package mix was as follows: 40% cans, 44% PET plastic and 16% glass and other, while multi-serve accounted for 60% of the company's mix and single-serve was 40%. By brand type, Coca-Cola trademark was 69% of total volume; sparkling flavors and energy was 17.5%; juices, isotonics and other were 10.5%, and water was 3%.

In addition to concentrates, sweeteners, juices and finished product, CCE purchases carbon dioxide, PET preforms, glass and plastic bottles, cans, closures, packaging such as plastic bags and cardboard boxes, and other packaging materials. The beverage agreements with The Coca-Cola Co. provide that all authorized containers, closures, cases, cartons and other packages, and labels for the products of The Coca-Cola Co. must be purchased from manufacturers approved by The Coca-Cola Co.

## Company Financials Fiscal Year Ended Dec. 31

| Per Share Data ($) | 2010 | 2009 | 2008 | 2007 | 2006 | 2005 | 2004 | 2003 | 2002 | 2001 |
|---|---|---|---|---|---|---|---|---|---|---|
| Tangible Book Value | NM | NM | NM | NM | NM | NM | NM | NM | NM | 6.25 |
| Cash Flow | 2.61 | 3.60 | -6.90 | 3.64 | -0.28 | 3.27 | 3.52 | 3.88 | 3.35 | 3.08 |
| Earnings | 1.83 | 1.48 | -9.05 | 1.46 | -2.41 | 1.08 | 1.26 | 1.48 | 1.07 | -0.05 |
| S&P Core Earnings | 1.82 | 1.54 | 0.83 | 1.45 | -2.34 | 1.01 | 1.19 | 1.22 | 0.78 | -0.34 |
| Dividends | 0.39 | 0.30 | 0.28 | 0.24 | 0.24 | 0.16 | 0.16 | 0.16 | 0.16 | 0.12 |
| Payout Ratio | 21% | 20% | NM | 16% | NM | 15% | 13% | 11% | 15% | NM |
| Prices:High | 31.80 | 21.53 | 26.99 | 27.09 | 22.49 | 23.92 | 29.34 | 23.30 | 24.50 | 23.90 |
| Prices:Low | 18.84 | 9.70 | 7.25 | 19.78 | 18.83 | 18.52 | 18.45 | 16.85 | 15.94 | 13.46 |
| P/E Ratio:High | 17 | 15 | NM | 19 | NM | 22 | 23 | 16 | 23 | NM |
| P/E Ratio:Low | 10 | 7 | NM | 14 | NM | 17 | 15 | 11 | 15 | NM |

| Income Statement Analysis (Million $) | | | | | | | | | | |
|---|---|---|---|---|---|---|---|---|---|---|
| Revenue | 6,714 | 21,645 | 21,807 | 20,936 | 19,804 | 18,706 | 18,158 | 17,330 | 16,889 | 15,700 |
| Operating Income | 1,087 | 2,684 | 2,510 | 2,537 | 2,439 | 2,475 | 2,504 | 2,674 | 2,409 | 1,954 |
| Depreciation | 264 | 1,043 | 1,050 | 1,067 | 1,012 | 1,044 | 1,068 | 1,097 | 1,045 | 1,353 |
| Interest Expense | 63.0 | 574 | 587 | 629 | 633 | 633 | 619 | 607 | 662 | 753 |
| Pretax Income | 746 | 963 | -6,901 | 841 | -2,118 | 790 | 818 | 972 | 705 | -150 |
| Effective Tax Rate | NA | 24.1% | NM | 15.4% | NM | 34.9% | 27.1% | 30.5% | 29.9% | NM |
| Net Income | 624 | 731 | -4,394 | 711 | -1,143 | 514 | 596 | 676 | 494 | -19.0 |
| S&P Core Earnings | 622 | 760 | 405 | 708 | -1,110 | 478 | 563 | 563 | 356 | -147 |

| Balance Sheet & Other Financial Data (Million $) | | | | | | | | | | |
|---|---|---|---|---|---|---|---|---|---|---|
| Cash | 321 | 1,057 | 722 | 170 | 184 | 107 | 155 | 80.0 | 68.0 | 284 |
| Current Assets | 2,230 | 5,170 | 4,583 | 4,092 | 3,691 | 3,395 | 3,264 | 3,000 | 2,844 | 2,876 |
| Total Assets | 8,596 | 16,416 | 15,589 | 24,046 | 23,225 | 25,357 | 26,354 | 25,700 | 24,375 | 23,719 |
| Current Liabilities | 1,942 | 4,588 | 5,074 | 5,343 | 3,818 | 3,846 | 3,431 | 3,941 | 3,455 | 4,522 |
| Long Term Debt | 2,124 | 7,804 | 7,247 | 7,391 | 9,218 | 9,165 | 10,523 | 10,552 | 11,236 | 10,365 |
| Common Equity | 3,143 | 859 | -31.0 | 5,689 | 4,526 | 5,643 | 5,378 | 4,365 | 3,310 | 2,783 |
| Total Capital | 5,429 | 9,406 | 8,324 | 19,048 | 17,801 | 19,914 | 21,139 | 19,882 | 19,122 | 17,521 |
| Capital Expenditures | 291 | 916 | 981 | 938 | 882 | 914 | 946 | 1,099 | 1,029 | 972 |
| Cash Flow | 888 | 1,774 | -3,344 | 1,178 | -131 | 1,558 | 1,664 | 1,771 | 1,536 | 1,331 |
| Current Ratio | 1.2 | 1.1 | 0.9 | 0.8 | 1.0 | 0.9 | 1.0 | 0.8 | 0.8 | 0.6 |
| % Long Term Debt of Capitalization | 39.1 | 83.0 | 87.1 | 38.8 | 51.8 | 46.0 | 49.8 | 53.1 | 58.8 | 59.2 |
| % Net Income of Revenue | 9.3 | 3.4 | NM | 3.3 | NM | 2.7 | 3.3 | 3.9 | 2.9 | NM |
| % Return on Assets | 7.5 | 4.6 | NM | 3.0 | NM | 2.0 | 2.3 | 2.7 | 2.1 | NM |
| % Return on Equity | 19.7 | NM | NM | 13.9 | NM | 9.3 | 12.2 | 17.6 | 16.1 | NM |

Data as orig reptd.; bef. results of disc opers/spec. items. Per share data adj. for stk. divs.; EPS diluted. E-Estimated. NA-Not Available. NM-Not Meaningful. NR-Not Ranked. UR-Under Review.

**Office:** 2500 Windy Ridge Parkway, Atlanta, GA 30339.
**Telephone:** 678-260-3000.
**Website:** http://www.cokecce.com
**Chrmn & CEO:** J.F. Brock, III

**SVP & General Counsel:** J.R. Parker, Jr.
**SVP & CIO:** E. Sezer
**CFO:** W.W. Douglas, III
**Chief Acctg Officer & Cntlr:** S.D. Patterson

**Investor Contact:** T. Erickson (770-989-3110)
**Board Members:** J. Bennink, J. F. Brock, III, C. Darden, M. J. Herb, L. P. Humann, J. Hunter, O. H. Ingram, II, D. A. James, T. H. Johnson, S. B. Labarge, V. Morali, G. Watts, C. R. Welling, P. A. Wood

**Founded:** 1944
**Domicile:** Delaware
**Employees:** 13,500

# Cognizant Technology Solutions Corp

STANDARD &POOR'S

**S&P Recommendation** HOLD ★★★☆☆

| Price | 12-Mo. Target Price | Investment Style |
|---|---|---|
| $62.48 (as of Nov 25, 2011) | $76.00 | Large-Cap Growth |

**GICS Sector** Information Technology
**Sub-Industry** IT Consulting & Other Services

**Summary** This company offers full life-cycle solutions to complex software development and maintenance problems.

## Key Stock Statistics (Source S&P, Vickers, company reports)

| | | | | | | | |
|---|---|---|---|---|---|---|---|
| 52-Wk Range | $83.48–53.54 | S&P Oper. EPS 2011E | 2.83 | Market Capitalization(B) | $18.876 | Beta | 1.08 |
| Trailing 12-Month EPS | $2.73 | S&P Oper. EPS 2012E | 3.40 | Yield (%) | Nil | S&P 3-Yr. Proj. EPS CAGR(%) | 24 |
| Trailing 12-Month P/E | 22.9 | P/E on S&P Oper. EPS 2011E | 22.1 | Dividend Rate/Share | Nil | S&P Credit Rating | NA |
| $10K Invested 5 Yrs Ago | $15,677 | Common Shares Outstg. (M) | 302.1 | Institutional Ownership (%) | 94 | | |

## Price Performance

30-Week Mov. Avg. · · · 10-Week Mov. Avg. - - GAAP Earnings vs. Previous Year Volume Above Avg. STARS
12-Mo. Target Price — Relative Strength — ▲ Up ▼ Down ► No Change Below Avg. ★

Options: ASE, CBOE, P, Ph

Analysis prepared by Equity Analyst **Dylan Cathers** on Nov 10, 2011, when the stock traded at **$67.58**.

## Highlights

► Although revenue growth in 2011 will likely not duplicate last year's 40% gain, we look for still strong growth of 34% this year and 25% in 2012. Despite many of the uncertainties in the economy, we still believe companies are looking to initiate growth-oriented projects as conditions improve. As evidence, we point to the company's 36% growth within application development in the September quarter. Within individual verticals, we look for the biggest gains from retail, manufacturing and logistics, which is benefiting from demand for consulting services, and healthcare, which is seeing increasing traction in cloud-based CRM, mobile, and business process as a service.

► We expect operating margins, including stock option expense, to be down slightly in 2011 with a further small narrowing in 2012. All of the outsourcers with significant labor pools in India are dealing with wage inflation and attrition. CTSH has had some success with selective price increases, and we think improving leverage and a recent strengthening of the U.S. dollar relative to the rupee should help margins.

► We look for EPS of $2.83 in 2011 and $3.40 in 2012.

## Investment Rationale/Risk

► Our hold recommendation is based on valuation. Nonetheless, we view the company positively, given what we see as its strong balance sheet, with over $7.55 per share in cash and short-term investments and no debt, and its U.S. incorporation. Also, we think CTSH's revenue growth will be faster than that of many peers, and we believe it has done a good job of moving into high-growth verticals. However, we think visibility is becoming a bit more cloudy, given the current economic backdrop.

► Risks to our recommendation and target price include increasing competition in offshore outsourcing, with consequent margin pressures; rising wages of Indian employees; appreciation of the rupee; and immigration restrictions that could affect personnel. Our corporate governance concerns center around a classified board of directors and a "poison pill" that is in place.

► We apply a slight peer premium P/E of 22.4X to our 2012 EPS estimate to arrive at our 12-month target price of $76. At that level, the stock's P/E-to-growth ratio would be about 0.95X, assuming an expected three-year growth rate of 24%.

## Qualitative Risk Assessment

| LOW | MEDIUM | HIGH |
|---|---|---|

Our risk assessment reflects what we see as CTSH's strong balance sheet, steady cash inflows, and rapid revenue growth, offset by intense competition in the IT services peer group from companies domiciled in India as well as multinationals.

## Quantitative Evaluations

**S&P Quality Ranking** B+

| D | C | B- | B | B+ | A- | A | A+ |
|---|---|---|---|---|---|---|---|

**Relative Strength Rank** MODERATE

41

LOWEST = 1    HIGHEST = 99

## Revenue/Earnings Data

**Revenue (Million $)**

| | 1Q | 2Q | 3Q | 4Q | Year |
|---|---|---|---|---|---|
| 2011 | 1,371 | 1,485 | 1,601 | -- | -- |
| 2010 | 959.7 | 1,105 | 1,217 | 1,311 | 4,592 |
| 2009 | 745.9 | 776.6 | 853.5 | 902.7 | 3,279 |
| 2008 | 643.1 | 685.4 | 734.7 | 753.0 | 2,816 |
| 2007 | 460.3 | 516.5 | 558.8 | 600.0 | 2,136 |
| 2006 | 285.5 | 336.8 | 377.5 | 424.4 | 1,424 |

**Earnings Per Share ($)**

| | | | | | |
|---|---|---|---|---|---|
| 2011 | 0.67 | 0.67 | 0.73 | E0.76 | E2.83 |
| 2010 | 0.49 | 0.56 | 0.66 | 0.66 | 2.37 |
| 2009 | 0.38 | 0.47 | 0.45 | 0.47 | 1.78 |
| 2008 | 0.34 | 0.35 | 0.38 | 0.38 | 1.44 |
| 2007 | 0.25 | 0.27 | 0.32 | 0.32 | 1.15 |
| 2006 | 0.16 | 0.19 | 0.20 | 0.23 | 0.78 |

Fiscal year ended Dec. 31. Next earnings report expected: Early February. EPS Estimates based on S&P Operating Earnings; historical GAAP earnings are as reported.

## Dividend Data

No cash dividends have been paid.

---

**Please read the Required Disclosures and Analyst Certification on the last page of this report.**

The McGraw-Hill Companies

# Cognizant Technology Solutions Corp

**STANDARD &POOR'S**

## Business Summary November 10, 2011

CORPORATE OVERVIEW. Cognizant Technology Solutions began operations in 1994 as an in-house technology development center for Dun & Bradstreet Corp. and its operating units. In its June 1998 IPO, 2,917,000 common shares were sold at $10 each.

The company's objective is to be a leading provider of full life-cycle e-business and application development projects, take full responsibility for on-going management of a client's software systems, and help clients move legacy transformation projects through to completion. The company's solutions include application development and integration, application management, and re-engineering services.

Applications development services are provided using a full life-cycle application development approach in which the company assumes total start to finish responsibility and accountability for analysis, design, implementation, testing and integration of systems, or through cooperative development, in which CTSH employees work with the customer's in-house IT personnel. In either case, the company's on-site team members work closely with end users

of the application to develop specifications and define requirements.

CTSH applications management services seeks to ensure that a customer's core operational systems are free of defects and responsive to end-users' changing needs. The company is often able to introduce product and process enhancements and improve service levels.

Through its re-engineering services, the company works with customers to migrate systems based on legacy computing environments to newer, open systems-based platforms and client/server architectures, often in response to the more stringent demands of e-business. CTSH's re-engineering tools automate many processes required to implement advanced client/server technologies.

## Company Financials Fiscal Year Ended Dec. 31

| Per Share Data ($) | 2010 | 2009 | 2008 | 2007 | 2006 | 2005 | 2004 | 2003 | 2002 | 2001 |
|---|---|---|---|---|---|---|---|---|---|---|
| Tangible Book Value | 10.78 | 8.02 | 6.05 | 4.42 | 3.60 | 2.44 | 1.61 | 0.98 | 0.62 | 0.42 |
| Cash Flow | 2.73 | 2.07 | 1.69 | 1.33 | 0.89 | 0.64 | 0.41 | 0.26 | 0.17 | 0.12 |
| Earnings | 2.37 | 1.78 | 1.44 | 1.15 | 0.78 | 0.57 | 0.35 | 0.21 | 0.14 | 0.09 |
| S&P Core Earnings | 2.37 | 1.78 | 1.44 | 1.15 | 0.78 | 0.51 | 0.30 | 0.16 | 0.09 | 0.07 |
| Dividends | Nil | Nil | Nil | Nil | Nil | Nil | Nil | Nil | Nil | Nil |
| Payout Ratio | Nil | Nil | Nil | Nil | Nil | Nil | Nil | Nil | Nil | Nil |
| Prices:High | 74.79 | 46.61 | 37.10 | 47.78 | 41.25 | 26.24 | 21.47 | 12.40 | 6.38 | 4.48 |
| Prices:Low | 42.08 | 17.26 | 14.38 | 29.44 | 24.26 | 17.79 | 9.80 | 4.28 | 2.70 | 1.48 |
| P/E Ratio:High | 32 | 26 | 26 | 42 | 53 | 46 | 61 | 59 | 47 | 49 |
| P/E Ratio:Low | 18 | 10 | 10 | 26 | 31 | 31 | 28 | 20 | 20 | 16 |

| Income Statement Analysis (Million $) | 2010 | 2009 | 2008 | 2007 | 2006 | 2005 | 2004 | 2003 | 2002 | 2001 |
|---|---|---|---|---|---|---|---|---|---|---|
| Revenue | 4,592 | 3,279 | 2,816 | 2,136 | 1,424 | 886 | 587 | 368 | 229 | 178 |
| Operating Income | 969 | 708 | 591 | 435 | 293 | 199 | 134 | 84.2 | 106 | 42.0 |
| Depreciation | 110 | 89.4 | 74.8 | 53.9 | 34.2 | 21.4 | 16.4 | 11.9 | 7.84 | 6.37 |
| Interest Expense | NA | NA | Nil | Nil | Nil | Nil | Nil | Nil | Nil | Nil |
| Pretax Income | 879 | 637 | 515 | 414 | 278 | 185 | 122 | 72.2 | 45.1 | 35.4 |
| Effective Tax Rate | NA | 16.0% | 16.4% | 15.5% | 16.2% | 10.3% | 17.9% | 20.6% | 23.4% | 37.4% |
| Net Income | 734 | 535 | 431 | 350 | 233 | 166 | 100 | 57.4 | 34.6 | 22.2 |
| S&P Core Earnings | 733 | 534 | 431 | 350 | 233 | 148 | 85.1 | 42.4 | 23.0 | 16.3 |

| Balance Sheet & Other Financial Data (Million $) | 2010 | 2009 | 2008 | 2007 | 2006 | 2005 | 2004 | 2003 | 2002 | 2001 |
|---|---|---|---|---|---|---|---|---|---|---|
| Cash | 2,226 | 1,399 | 763 | 670 | 266 | 197 | 293 | 194 | 126 | 85.0 |
| Current Assets | 3,518 | 2,308 | 1,468 | 1,242 | 1,040 | 663 | 454 | 278 | 176 | 117 |
| Total Assets | 4,583 | 3,338 | 2,375 | 1,838 | 1,326 | 870 | 573 | 361 | 231 | 145 |
| Current Liabilities | 931 | 647 | 388 | 341 | 250 | 156 | 115 | 62.6 | 41.5 | 21.7 |
| Long Term Debt | NA | NA | Nil | Nil | Nil | Nil | Nil | Nil | Nil | Nil |
| Common Equity | 3,584 | 2,653 | 1,966 | 1,468 | 1,073 | 714 | 454 | 274 | 165 | 98.8 |
| Total Capital | 3,584 | 2,653 | 1,973 | 1,483 | 1,073 | 714 | 458 | 298 | 190 | 123 |
| Capital Expenditures | 186 | 76.6 | 169 | 182 | 105 | 71.8 | 46.6 | 30.0 | 22.3 | 15.0 |
| Cash Flow | 844 | 624 | 506 | 404 | 267 | 188 | 117 | 69.3 | 42.4 | 28.5 |
| Current Ratio | 3.8 | 3.6 | 3.8 | 3.7 | 4.2 | 4.3 | 3.9 | 4.4 | 4.2 | 5.4 |
| % Long Term Debt of Capitalization | Nil | Nil | Nil | Nil | Nil | Nil | Nil | Nil | Nil | Nil |
| % Net Income of Revenue | 16.0 | 16.3 | 15.3 | 16.4 | 16.3 | 18.8 | 17.1 | 15.6 | 15.1 | 12.5 |
| % Return on Assets | 18.5 | 18.7 | 20.5 | 22.1 | 21.2 | 23.1 | 21.4 | 19.4 | 18.4 | 17.4 |
| % Return on Equity | 23.5 | 23.2 | 25.1 | 27.6 | 26.0 | 28.5 | 27.6 | 26.1 | 26.2 | 26.9 |

Data as orig reptd.; bef. results of disc opers/spec. items. Per share data adj. for stk. divs.; EPS diluted. E-Estimated. NA-Not Available. NM-Not Meaningful. NR-Not Ranked. UR-Under Review.

**Office:** 500 Glenpointe Ctr W Ste, Teaneck, NJ 07666.
**Telephone:** 201-801-0233.
**Website:** http://www.cognizant.com
**Chrmn:** J. Klein

**Pres & CEO:** F. D'Souza
**Vice Chrmn:** L. Narayanan
**COO, CFO, Chief Acctg Officer & Treas:** G.J. Coburn
**Secy & General Counsel:** S.E. Schwartz

**Investor Contact:** G. Coburn (201-678-2712)
**Board Members:** M. Breakiron-Evans, F. D'Souza, J. N. Fox, Jr., R. W. Howe, J. Klein, L. Narayanan, R. E. Weissman, T. M. Wendel

**Founded:** 1988
**Domicile:** Delaware
**Employees:** 104,000

# Colgate-Palmolive Co

STANDARD
&POOR'S

| S&P Recommendation HOLD ★★★★☆ | Price $86.73 (as of Nov 25, 2011) | 12-Mo. Target Price $89.00 | Investment Style Large-Cap Growth |
|---|---|---|---|

**GICS Sector** Consumer Staples
**Sub-Industry** Household Products

**Summary** This major consumer products company markets oral, personal and household care and pet nutrition products in more than 200 countries and territories.

## Key Stock Statistics (Source S&P, Vickers, company reports)

| | | | | | | | |
|---|---|---|---|---|---|---|---|
| 52-Wk Range | $94.89–74.86 | S&P Oper. EPS 2011E | 5.06 | Market Capitalization(B) | $41.977 | Beta | 0.43 |
| Trailing 12-Month EPS | $4.98 | S&P Oper. EPS 2012E | 5.57 | Yield (%) | 2.67 | S&P 3-Yr. Proj. EPS CAGR(%) | 8 |
| Trailing 12-Month P/E | 17.4 | P/E on S&P Oper. EPS 2011E | 17.1 | Dividend Rate/Share | $2.32 | S&P Credit Rating | AA- |
| $10K Invested 5 Yrs Ago | $14,819 | Common Shares Outstg. (M) | 484.0 | Institutional Ownership (%) | 74 | | |

## Price Performance

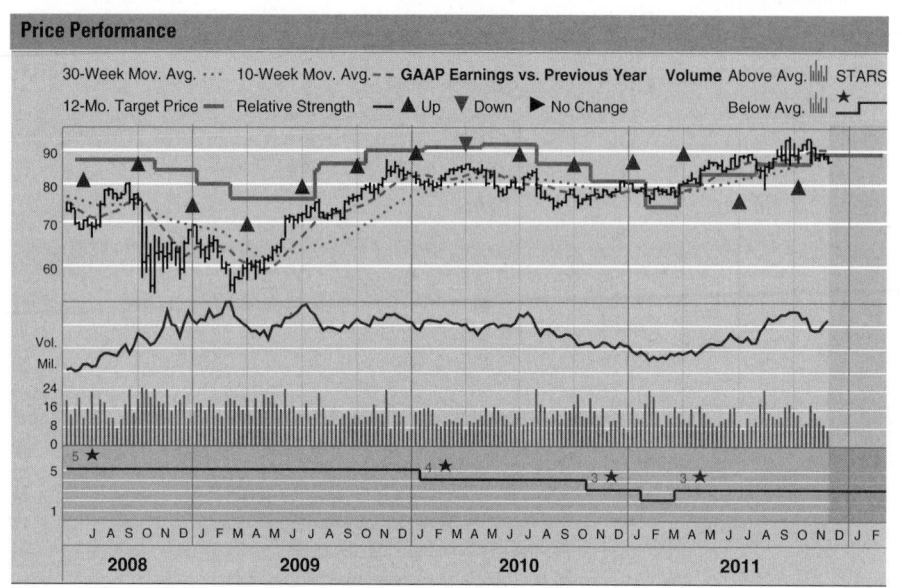

30-Week Mov. Avg. ··· 10-Week Mov. Avg. -- GAAP Earnings vs. Previous Year  Volume Above Avg. STARS
12-Mo. Target Price — Relative Strength — ▲ Up ▼ Down ► No Change  Below Avg. ★

Options: ASE, CBOE, P

Analysis prepared by Equity Analyst **Tom Graves, CFA** on Nov 03, 2011, when the stock traded at **$88.68**.

## Highlights

➤ In 2012, we look for sales to increase about 5%, to $17.7 billion, from the $16.8 billion we estimate for 2011, including roughly a half-year's benefit in both years from a June 2011 acquisition. However, we anticipate that currency fluctuation will have a less favorable impact on reported sales than we think it will in 2011. Within the company's Oral, Personal and Home Care business, we anticipate that Latin America will again be CL's largest geographic segment by sales.

➤ We expect margin pressure from raw material costs to ease in 2012, with profit margins to be bolstered by higher prices and by cost savings elsewhere.

➤ Before special items, we estimate 2012 EPS of $5.57, up from the $5.06 that we project for 2011. In 2011's first nine months, special items included a gain on the sale of laundry detergent brands in Colombia, which offset other items, including charges related to business realignment and other cost-saving initiatives.

## Investment Rationale/Risk

➤ Over time, we expect the company to continue to invest in R&D and marketing, with more resources to be allocated to faster-growing markets. More than 60% of CL's sales come from outside the U.S. Looking ahead, especially in less mature international markets, we believe CL will have opportunities to benefit from rising incomes and changing lifestyles.

➤ Risks to our recommendation and target price include increased competition in the global oral care market, more-than-anticipated commodity cost pressure, unfavorable currency translation, and weaker-than-expected consumer acceptance of new products.

➤ Our 12-month target price of $89 reflects a blend of three valuation models. Our DCF model assumes a terminal WACC of 9.0% and a terminal growth rate of 2.8%, which leads to a value of $93. A peer P/E of 16.2X leads to a value of about $82, while our historical analysis uses a P/E of 18X, below the 10-year average, to value the stock at about $91. We expect additional stock repurchases by CL in 2011.

## Qualitative Risk Assessment

| LOW | MEDIUM | HIGH |
|---|---|---|

Our risk assessment reflects our view that demand for household and personal care products is relatively static, and, in mature markets, not likely to be affected much by economic conditions. In developing economies, there is likely to be more growth opportunity, but also more risk.

## Quantitative Evaluations

**S&P Quality Ranking** A+

| D | C | B- | B | B+ | A- | A | A+ |
|---|---|---|---|---|---|---|---|

**Relative Strength Rank** MODERATE

67

LOWEST = 1    HIGHEST = 99

## Revenue/Earnings Data

**Revenue (Million $)**

| | 1Q | 2Q | 3Q | 4Q | Year |
|---|---|---|---|---|---|
| 2011 | 3,994 | 4,185 | 4,383 | -- | -- |
| 2010 | 3,829 | 3,814 | 3,943 | 3,978 | 15,564 |
| 2009 | 3,503 | 3,745 | 3,998 | 4,081 | 15,327 |
| 2008 | 3,713 | 3,965 | 3,988 | 3,664 | 15,330 |
| 2007 | 3,214 | 3,405 | 3,528 | 3,642 | 13,790 |
| 2006 | 2,871 | 3,014 | 3,144 | 3,209 | 12,238 |

**Earnings Per Share ($)**

| | 1Q | 2Q | 3Q | 4Q | Year |
|---|---|---|---|---|---|
| 2011 | 1.16 | 1.26 | 1.31 | E1.33 | E5.06 |
| 2010 | 0.69 | 1.15 | 1.22 | 1.25 | 4.31 |
| 2009 | 0.97 | 1.07 | 1.12 | 1.21 | 4.37 |
| 2008 | 0.87 | 0.92 | 0.94 | 0.94 | 3.66 |
| 2007 | 0.89 | 0.76 | 0.77 | 0.77 | 3.20 |
| 2006 | 0.59 | 0.51 | 0.63 | 0.73 | 2.46 |

Fiscal year ended Dec. 31. Next earnings report expected: Late January. EPS Estimates based on S&P Operating Earnings; historical GAAP earnings are as reported.

## Dividend Data (Dates: mm/dd Payment Date: mm/dd/yy)

| Amount ($) | Date Decl. | Ex-Div. Date | Stk. of Record | Payment Date |
|---|---|---|---|---|
| 0.530 | 01/13 | 01/21 | 01/25 | 02/15/11 |
| 0.580 | 02/24 | 04/21 | 04/26 | 05/16/11 |
| 0.580 | 07/14 | 07/22 | 07/26 | 08/15/11 |
| 0.580 | 10/13 | 10/21 | 10/25 | 11/15/11 |

Dividends have been paid since 1895. Source: Company reports.

**Please read the Required Disclosures and Analyst Certification on the last page of this report.**

The McGraw-Hill Companies

# Colgate-Palmolive Co

STANDARD
&POOR'S

## Business Summary November 03, 2011

CORPORATE OVERVIEW. Colgate-Palmolive Co. is a leading global consumer products company that operates in the oral, personal and household care and pet food markets. Its products are marketed in more than 200 countries and territories worldwide. The company's Oral, Personal and Home Care segment accounted for 87% of total worldwide sales in 2010. The balance of revenues was derived from the Pet Foods segment. The company's oral care products include toothbrushes, toothpaste and pharmaceutical products for oral health professionals. CL's personal care products include bar and liquid soaps, shampoos, conditioners, deodorants, antiperspirants, and shave products. The home care business produces major brands such as Palmolive and Ajax soaps. Within the Oral, Personal and Home Care area, North America represented 22% of 2010 sales, Latin America accounted for 32%, Europe/South Pacific represented 24% and Greater Asia/Africa accounted for 22%.

CORPORATE STRATEGY. We think CL follows a business strategy to develop and increase market leadership in key product categories. These categories are prioritized based on their capacity to maximize the use of the organization's core competencies and strong global equities and to deliver sustainable

long-term growth. Operationally, CL is organized along geographic lines, with specific regional management teams having responsibility for the financial results in each region. We think that on an ongoing basis, management focuses on a variety of key indicators to monitor business health and performance, including: market share; sales (including volume, pricing and foreign exchange components); gross profit margins; operating profits; net income; and EPS. We also think CL focuses on measures to optimize the management of working capital, capital expenditures, cash flow, and return on capital.

To enhance its global leadership position in its core businesses, in December 2004, CL commenced a four-year restructuring and business-building program. It included a workforce reduction, the closing of some factories, and an increased focus on faster-growing markets. Looking ahead, we expect further cost saving efforts by the company.

## Company Financials Fiscal Year Ended Dec. 31

| Per Share Data ($) | 2010 | 2009 | 2008 | 2007 | 2006 | 2005 | 2004 | 2003 | 2002 | 2001 |
|---|---|---|---|---|---|---|---|---|---|---|
| Tangible Book Value | NM | NM | NM | NM | NM | NM | NM | NM | NM | NM |
| Cash Flow | 5.05 | 4.98 | 4.26 | 3.76 | 3.06 | 2.97 | 2.86 | 3.15 | 2.65 | 2.40 |
| Earnings | 4.31 | 4.37 | 3.66 | 3.20 | 2.46 | 2.43 | 2.33 | 2.46 | 2.19 | 1.89 |
| S&P Core Earnings | 4.37 | 4.48 | 3.51 | 3.22 | 2.42 | 2.21 | 2.26 | 2.31 | 2.00 | 1.71 |
| Dividends | 2.03 | 1.72 | 1.56 | 1.40 | 1.25 | 1.11 | 0.96 | 0.90 | 0.72 | 0.68 |
| Payout Ratio | 47% | 39% | 43% | 44% | 51% | 46% | 41% | 37% | 33% | 36% |
| Prices:High | 86.15 | 87.39 | 81.98 | 81.27 | 67.08 | 57.15 | 59.04 | 60.99 | 58.86 | 64.75 |
| Prices:Low | 73.12 | 54.51 | 54.36 | 63.75 | 53.41 | 48.25 | 42.89 | 48.56 | 44.05 | 48.50 |
| P/E Ratio:High | 20 | 20 | 22 | 25 | 27 | 24 | 25 | 25 | 27 | 34 |
| P/E Ratio:Low | 17 | 12 | 15 | 20 | 22 | 20 | 18 | 20 | 20 | 26 |
| **Income Statement Analysis** (Million $) | | | | | | | | | | |
| Revenue | 15,564 | 15,327 | 15,330 | 13,790 | 12,238 | 11,397 | 10,584 | 9,903 | 9,294 | 9,428 |
| Operating Income | 3,865 | 4,004 | 3,673 | 3,108 | 2,674 | 2,613 | 2,540 | 2,467 | 2,333 | 2,198 |
| Depreciation | 376 | 351 | 348 | 334 | 329 | 329 | 328 | 316 | 297 | 336 |
| Interest Expense | 59.0 | 88.0 | 115 | 173 | 159 | 143 | 124 | 124 | 151 | 192 |
| Pretax Income | 3,430 | 3,538 | 2,925 | 2,564 | 2,002 | 2,134 | 2,050 | 2,042 | 1,870 | 1,709 |
| Effective Tax Rate | NA | 32.3% | 33.1% | 29.6% | 32.4% | 34.1% | 32.9% | 30.4% | 31.1% | 30.6% |
| Net Income | 2,203 | 2,291 | 1,957 | 1,737 | 1,353 | 1,351 | 1,327 | 1,421 | 1,288 | 1,147 |
| S&P Core Earnings | 2,202 | 2,320 | 1,848 | 1,718 | 1,306 | 1,207 | 1,262 | 1,309 | 1,152 | 1,011 |
| **Balance Sheet & Other Financial Data** (Million $) | | | | | | | | | | |
| Cash | 564 | 641 | 567 | 451 | 490 | 341 | 320 | 265 | 168 | 173 |
| Current Assets | 3,730 | 3,810 | 3,710 | 3,619 | 3,301 | 2,757 | 2,740 | 2,497 | 2,228 | 2,203 |
| Total Assets | 11,172 | 11,134 | 9,979 | 10,112 | 9,138 | 8,507 | 8,673 | 7,479 | 7,087 | 6,985 |
| Current Liabilities | 3,119 | 3,599 | 2,953 | 3,163 | 3,469 | 2,743 | 2,731 | 2,445 | 2,149 | 2,124 |
| Long Term Debt | 3,424 | 3,182 | 3,585 | 3,508 | 2,720 | 2,918 | 3,090 | 2,685 | 3,211 | 2,812 |
| Common Equity | 2,675 | 3,116 | 1,922 | 2,308 | 1,188 | 1,380 | 971 | 594 | 27.3 | 505 |
| Total Capital | 6,241 | 6,439 | 5,711 | 5,882 | 4,441 | 5,106 | 4,845 | 4,028 | 4,050 | 4,139 |
| Capital Expenditures | 550 | 575 | 684 | 583 | 476 | 389 | 348 | 302 | 344 | 340 |
| Cash Flow | 2,579 | 2,612 | 2,276 | 2,043 | 1,682 | 1,653 | 1,629 | 1,736 | 1,563 | 1,461 |
| Current Ratio | 1.2 | 1.2 | 1.3 | 1.1 | 1.0 | 1.0 | 1.0 | 1.0 | 1.0 | 1.0 |
| % Long Term Debt of Capitalization | 54.9 | 49.4 | 62.8 | 57.4 | 61.3 | 57.1 | 63.8 | 66.7 | 79.3 | 67.9 |
| % Net Income of Revenue | 14.2 | 15.0 | 12.8 | 12.6 | 11.1 | 11.9 | 12.5 | 14.4 | 13.9 | 12.2 |
| % Return on Assets | 19.8 | 21.7 | 19.5 | 17.8 | 15.3 | 15.7 | 16.4 | 19.5 | 18.3 | 16.1 |
| % Return on Equity | 78.4 | 94.3 | 97.6 | 91.2 | 118.5 | 99.5 | 166.2 | 457.2 | 475.7 | 139.0 |

Data as orig reptd.; bef. results of disc opers/spec. items. Per share data adj. for stk. divs.; EPS diluted. E-Estimated. NA-Not Available. NM-Not Meaningful. NR-Not Ranked. UR-Under Review.

Office: 300 Park Avenue, New York, NY 10022.
Telephone: 212-310-2000.
Email: investor_relations@colpal.com
Website: http://www.colgate.com

Chrmn, Pres & CEO: I.M. Cook
CFO: D.J. Hickey
CTO: P. Verduin
Chief Acctg Officer & Cntlr: V.L. Dolan

Treas: E. Paik
Investor Contact: B. Thompson (212-310-3072)
Board Members: J. T. Cahill, I. M. Cook, H. D. Gayle, E. M. Hancock, J. Jimenez, R. J. Kogan, D. Lewis, J. P. Reinhard, S. I. Sadove

Founded: 1806
Domicile: Delaware
Employees: 39,200

# Comcast Corp

| S&P Recommendation **BUY** ★★★★☆ | Price<br>$21.00 (as of Nov 25, 2011) | 12-Mo. Target Price<br>$29.00 | Investment Style<br>Large-Cap Blend |
|---|---|---|---|

**GICS Sector** Consumer Discretionary
**Sub-Industry** Cable & Satellite

**Summary** After the 2011 combination with NBC Universal, this media and entertainment conglomerate has diversified interests in cable, broadcasting, film and theme parks.

## Key Stock Statistics (Source S&P, Vickers, company reports)

| | | | | | | | |
|---|---|---|---|---|---|---|---|
| 52-Wk Range | $27.16–19.19 | S&P Oper. EPS 2011**E** | 1.55 | Market Capitalization(B) | $57.023 | Beta | 1.03 |
| Trailing 12-Month EPS | $1.39 | S&P Oper. EPS 2012**E** | 1.90 | Yield (%) | 2.14 | S&P 3-Yr. Proj. EPS CAGR(%) | 15 |
| Trailing 12-Month P/E | 15.1 | P/E on S&P Oper. EPS 2011**E** | 13.5 | Dividend Rate/Share | $0.45 | S&P Credit Rating | BBB |
| $10K Invested 5 Yrs Ago | $8,478 | Common Shares Outstg. (M) | 2,724.8 | Institutional Ownership (%) | 64 | | |

## Price Performance

Options: ASE, CBOE, P, Ph

Analysis prepared by Equity Analyst **T. Amobi, CFA CPA** on Nov 04, 2011, when the stock traded at **$22.64**.

## Qualitative Risk Assessment

| LOW | MEDIUM | HIGH |
|---|---|---|

Our risk assessment reflects lingering merger execution risk on the Comcast/NBCU integration, intensifying competition in a relatively saturated U.S. pay-TV market, and potential threats from new online video services, offset by potentially significant economies of scale on the vertical combination of some of the industry's leading content and distribution assets.

## Quantitative Evaluations

**S&P Quality Ranking**      B+

| D | C | B- | B | B+ | A- | A | A+ |
|---|---|---|---|---|---|---|---|

**Relative Strength Rank**      MODERATE

47

LOWEST = 1      HIGHEST = 99

## Highlights

➤ We see consolidated pro forma revenues up 5.3% and 7.0% in 2011 and 2012, respectively, to about $58.0 billion and $62.1 billion, mainly on higher penetration and pricing of bundled video, data and voice services to residential (and increasingly business) cable customers, and continued solid gains in advertising and affiliate revenues for NBCU's cable networks.

➤ The NBCU broadcast division should reflect difficult 2011 revenue comparisons with last winter's Vancouver Olympics, with projected 2012 revenues aided by next summer's London Olympics, but again likely to incur sizable losses. But difficult 2011 revenue comparisons for NBCU's filmed entertainment business should ease in 2012, while assuming continued strong contributions from the Universal theme parks business (recently acquired from a JV partner).

➤ With only moderate margin expansion seen after higher programming costs for the cable distribution and NBCU's content businesses, we project 2011 and 2012 consolidated pro forma EBITDA up 7.1% and 8.0%, respectively, to $18.5 billion and $19.9 billion. After D&A, interest expense and taxes, we estimate EPS of $1.55 and $1.90 for the respective years.

## Investment Rationale/Risk

➤ After relatively encouraging results thus far in 2011 for the months since the NBCU acquisition, we remain cautiously optimistic on the longer-term prospects of a potentially transformational vertical combination that could deliver some economies of scale for the integrated cable distribution and programming businesses, aside from sizable upside on NBCU's retransmission revenues. We believe the combined company has ample financial flexibility for continued share buybacks and recurring dividends, as well as potential future redemptions of GE's (GE 16, Buy) NBCU stake.

➤ Risks to our recommendation and target price include persistent severe turnaround challenges for NBC network; a sharp macroeconomic slowdown; increased pay-TV competition; and governance issues on dual class shares and voting control by the Roberts family.

➤ Our 12-month target price of $29 implies 5.5X 2012E EV/EBITDA, which we view as attractive relative to the average of media and entertainment peers, in light of potential scale economies on the combination. CMCSA recently yielded 2.0%.

## Revenue/Earnings Data

### Revenue (Million $)

| | 1Q | 2Q | 3Q | 4Q | Year |
|---|---|---|---|---|---|
| 2011 | 12,128 | 14,333 | 14,339 | -- | -- |
| 2010 | 9,202 | 9,525 | 9,489 | 9,721 | 37,937 |
| 2009 | 8,866 | 8,978 | 8,845 | 9,067 | 35,756 |
| 2008 | 8,389 | 8,553 | 8,549 | 8,765 | 34,256 |
| 2007 | 7,388 | 7,712 | 7,781 | 8,014 | 30,895 |
| 2006 | 5,595 | 5,908 | 6,432 | 7,031 | 24,966 |

### Earnings Per Share ($)

| | | | | | |
|---|---|---|---|---|---|
| 2011 | 0.34 | 0.37 | 0.33 | E0.46 | E1.55 |
| 2010 | 0.31 | 0.31 | 0.31 | 0.36 | 1.29 |
| 2009 | 0.27 | 0.33 | 0.33 | 0.33 | 1.26 |
| 2008 | 0.24 | 0.21 | 0.26 | 0.14 | 0.86 |
| 2007 | 0.26 | 0.19 | 0.18 | 0.20 | 0.83 |
| 2006 | 0.15 | 0.13 | 0.31 | 0.14 | 0.70 |

Fiscal year ended Dec. 31. Next earnings report expected: NA. EPS Estimates based on S&P Operating Earnings; historical GAAP earnings are as reported.

## Dividend Data (Dates: mm/dd Payment Date: mm/dd/yy)

| Amount<br>($) | Date<br>Decl. | Ex-Div.<br>Date | Stk. of<br>Record | Payment<br>Date |
|---|---|---|---|---|
| 0.113 | 05/11 | 07/01 | 07/06 | 07/27/11 |
| 0.113 | 07/21 | 09/28 | 10/02 | 10/26/11 |
| 0.113 | 07/21 | 10/03 | 10/05 | 10/26/11 |
| 0.113 | 10/27 | 12/30 | 01/04 | 01/25/12 |

Dividends have been paid since 2008. Source: Company reports.

**Please read the Required Disclosures and Analyst Certification on the last page of this report.**

# Comcast Corp

STANDARD
&POOR'S

## Business Summary November 04, 2011

CORPORATE OVERVIEW. In January 2011, Comcast, the largest U.S. cable operator, acquired a 51% controlling stake in NBC Universal, a media and entertainment conglomerate, in a $30 billion transaction that created a vertically integrated entity with diversified interests in content and distribution. Following the combination, the company plans to improve the customer experience and execute on efficiency initiatives, as well as maintain momentum in NBCU's cable channels and establish a foundation for an NBC broadcast turnaround.

Cable Communications (65% of 2010 consolidated pro forma revenues and 82% of OCF) -- which serves mainly residential (and increasingly business) customers, recently offered its services to nearly 22.8 million video subscribers (over 20.0 million for digital video -- on advanced services such as HD and DVR), over 17.4 million for high-speed Internet service, and almost 8.9 million for digital phone. Also included is Comcast Interactive Media

(Comcast.net, Fancast, thePlatform and Fandango).

NBCU (35% of 2010 consolidated pro forma revenues and 18% of OCF) comprises the following: cable networks (40% of NBCU's total 2010 revenues), broadcast television (35%), filmed entertainment (23%) and theme parks (2%). The segment includes several leading cable networks (USA, E!, CNBC, MSNBC, Bravo, Oxygen, Syfy, Versus, Golf Channel, G4, Style) as well as 12 regional sports and news networks; two broadcast networks (NBC and Telemundo) plus owned-and-operated TV stations; a major film studio (with a 4,000+ title library); and Universal Orlando theme parks.

## Company Financials Fiscal Year Ended Dec. 31

| Per Share Data ($) | 2010 | 2009 | 2008 | 2007 | 2006 | 2005 | 2004 | 2003 | 2002 | 2001 |
|---|---|---|---|---|---|---|---|---|---|---|
| Tangible Book Value | NM | NM | NM | NM | NM | NM | NM | NM | NM | NM |
| Cash Flow | 3.64 | 3.51 | 3.03 | 2.81 | 2.22 | 1.79 | 1.69 | 0.24 | 1.05 | 0.99 |
| Earnings | 1.29 | 1.26 | 0.86 | 0.83 | 0.70 | 0.28 | 0.29 | -0.07 | -0.17 | -0.89 |
| S&P Core Earnings | 1.09 | 1.04 | 0.84 | 0.74 | 0.48 | 0.33 | 0.14 | -0.30 | 0.47 | -1.03 |
| Dividends | 0.38 | 0.26 | 0.19 | Nil | Nil | Nil | Nil | Nil | Nil | Nil |
| Payout Ratio | 29% | 21% | 22% | Nil | Nil | Nil | Nil | Nil | Nil | Nil |
| Prices:High | 22.40 | 18.10 | 22.86 | 30.18 | 28.94 | 23.00 | 24.33 | 23.23 | 25.03 | 30.54 |
| Prices:Low | 15.10 | 11.10 | 9.20 | 17.37 | 16.90 | 17.20 | 17.50 | 15.61 | 11.37 | 21.23 |
| P/E Ratio:High | 17 | 14 | 27 | 36 | 41 | 82 | 85 | NM | NM | NM |
| P/E Ratio:Low | 12 | 9 | 11 | 21 | 24 | 61 | 61 | NM | NM | NM |

### Income Statement Analysis (Million $)

| | 2010 | 2009 | 2008 | 2007 | 2006 | 2005 | 2004 | 2003 | 2002 | 2001 |
|---|---|---|---|---|---|---|---|---|---|---|
| Revenue | 37,937 | 35,756 | 34,256 | 30,895 | 24,966 | 22,255 | 20,307 | 18,348 | 12,460 | 19,697 |
| Operating Income | 14,596 | 13,714 | 13,132 | 11,786 | 9,442 | 8,493 | 7,531 | 6,392 | 3,691 | 1,576 |
| Depreciation | 6,616 | 6,500 | 6,400 | 6,208 | 4,823 | 4,803 | 4,623 | 4,438 | 2,032 | 6,345 |
| Interest Expense | 2,156 | 2,348 | 2,439 | 2,289 | 2,064 | 1,796 | 1,876 | 2,018 | 884 | 2,341 |
| Pretax Income | 6,104 | 5,106 | 4,058 | 4,349 | 3,594 | 1,880 | 1,810 | -137 | 70.0 | -5,927 |
| Effective Tax Rate | 39.9% | 29.0% | 37.8% | 41.4% | 37.5% | 49.6% | 45.6% | NM | NM | NM |
| Net Income | 3,635 | 3,638 | 2,547 | 2,587 | 2,235 | 928 | 970 | -218 | -276 | -3,021 |
| S&P Core Earnings | 3,063 | 3,000 | 2,484 | 2,313 | 1,541 | 1,090 | 465 | -979 | 792 | -1,482 |

### Balance Sheet & Other Financial Data (Million $)

| | 2010 | 2009 | 2008 | 2007 | 2006 | 2005 | 2004 | 2003 | 2002 | 2001 |
|---|---|---|---|---|---|---|---|---|---|---|
| Cash | 6,065 | 721 | 1,254 | 1,061 | 1,239 | 693 | 452 | 1,550 | 781 | 558 |
| Current Assets | 8,886 | 3,223 | 3,716 | 3,667 | 5,202 | 2,594 | 3,535 | 5,403 | 7,076 | 4,944 |
| Total Assets | 118,534 | 112,733 | 113,017 | 113,417 | 110,405 | 103,146 | 104,694 | 109,159 | 113,105 | 109,319 |
| Current Liabilities | 8,234 | 7,249 | 8,939 | 7,952 | 7,440 | 6,269 | 8,635 | 9,654 | 15,383 | 12,489 |
| Long Term Debt | 29,615 | 27,940 | 30,178 | 29,828 | 27,992 | 21,682 | 20,093 | 23,835 | 27,957 | 27,528 |
| Common Equity | 44,354 | 42,721 | 40,450 | 41,340 | 41,167 | 40,219 | 41,422 | 41,662 | 38,329 | 38,451 |
| Total Capital | 75,992 | 72,073 | 73,203 | 98,298 | 96,489 | 89,928 | 88,798 | 91,689 | 92,070 | 94,758 |
| Capital Expenditures | 4,961 | 5,117 | 5,750 | 6,158 | 4,395 | 3,621 | 3,660 | 4,161 | 1,975 | NA |
| Cash Flow | 10,251 | 10,138 | 8,947 | 8,795 | 7,058 | 5,731 | 5,593 | 4,220 | 1,756 | 3,324 |
| Current Ratio | 1.1 | 0.4 | 0.4 | 0.5 | 0.7 | 0.4 | 0.4 | 0.6 | 0.5 | 0.4 |
| % Long Term Debt of Capitalization | 39.0 | 38.9 | 41.2 | 30.3 | 29.0 | 24.1 | 22.6 | 26.0 | 30.4 | 29.1 |
| % Net Income of Revenue | 9.6 | 10.2 | 7.4 | 8.4 | 9.0 | 4.2 | 4.8 | NM | NM | NM |
| % Return on Assets | 3.2 | 3.2 | 2.3 | 2.3 | 2.1 | 0.9 | 0.9 | NM | NM | NM |
| % Return on Equity | 8.4 | 8.8 | 6.2 | 6.3 | 5.5 | 2.3 | 2.3 | NM | NM | NM |

Data as orig reptd.; bef. results of disc opers/spec. items. Per share data adj. for stk. divs.; EPS diluted. E-Estimated. NA-Not Available. NM-Not Meaningful. NR-Not Ranked. UR-Under Review.

**Office:** 1701 John F. Kennedy Boulevard, One Comcast Center, Philadelphia, PA 19103.
**Telephone:** 215-286-1700.
**Website:** http://www.comcast.com
**Chrmn, Pres & CEO:** B.L. Roberts

**SVP & Treas:** W.E. Dordelman
**SVP, Secy & General Counsel:** A.R. Block
**CFO:** M.J. Angelakis
**Chief Admin Officer:** K.D. Buchholz

**Investor Contact:** M. Dooner (866-281-2100)
**Board Members:** K. J. Bacon, S. M. Bonovitz, J. J. Collins, J. M. Cook, G. L. Hassell, J. A. Honickman, E. G. Mestre, B. L. Roberts, R. J. Roberts, J. A. Rodgers, J. Rodin

**Founded:** 1969
**Domicile:** Pennsylvania
**Employees:** 102,000

# Comerica Inc

**STANDARD &POOR'S**

| S&P Recommendation **BUY** ★★★★☆ | Price $23.02 (as of Nov 25, 2011) | 12-Mo. Target Price $30.00 | Investment Style Large-Cap Value |
|---|---|---|---|

**GICS Sector** Financials
**Sub-Industry** Diversified Banks

**Summary** This bank holding company, based in Dallas, operates in Texas, Michigan, California, Arizona and Florida.

## Key Stock Statistics (Source S&P, Vickers, company reports)

| | | | | | | | |
|---|---|---|---|---|---|---|---|
| 52-Wk Range | $43.53– 21.48 | S&P Oper. EPS 2011E | 2.18 | Market Capitalization(B) | $4.574 | Beta | 1.17 |
| Trailing 12-Month EPS | $2.14 | S&P Oper. EPS 2012E | 2.41 | Yield (%) | 1.74 | S&P 3-Yr. Proj. EPS CAGR(%) | 49 |
| Trailing 12-Month P/E | 10.8 | P/E on S&P Oper. EPS 2011E | 10.6 | Dividend Rate/Share | $0.40 | S&P Credit Rating | A- |
| $10K Invested 5 Yrs Ago | $4,613 | Common Shares Outstg. (M) | 198.7 | Institutional Ownership (%) | 83 | | |

## Price Performance

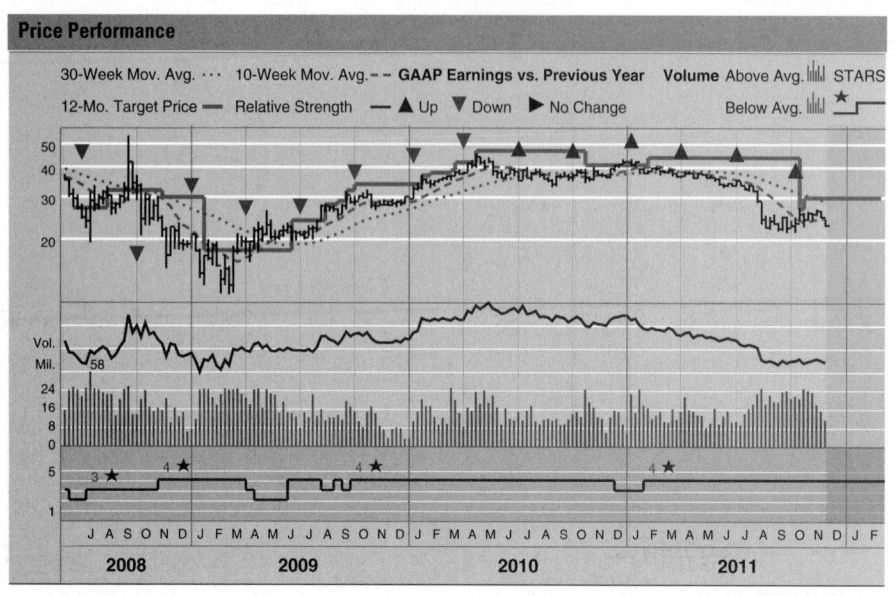

30-Week Mov. Avg. · · · · 10-Week Mov. Avg. – – **GAAP Earnings vs. Previous Year** Volume Above Avg. STARS
12-Mo. Target Price — Relative Strength — ▲ Up ▼ Down ▶ No Change Below Avg.

Options: ASE, CBOE, P, Ph

Analysis prepared by Equity Analyst **Erik Oja** on Nov 21, 2011, when the stock traded at **$24.20**.

## Highlights

➤ We see CMA's loan portfolio shrinking 2.0% organically in 2011, before growing 3.8% in 2012. We see interest-earning assets growing 2.5% organically in 2011 and 3.0% in 2012. We expect CMA's net interest margin to shrink in 2011, but rebound slightly in 2012. We expect net interest income to fall 0.7% in 2011, including the Sterling Bancshares acquisition, but rise 5.8% in 2012. We see core fee income falling 4.0% in 2011, due to regulatory pressures, but rising 3.9% in 2012. We expect total net revenues to rise 0.1% in 2011 and 4.5% in 2012.

➤ We expect 2011 and 2012 earnings to reflect a reduction in the loan loss provision. We look for provisions to fall to $170 million in 2011, from $480 million in 2010, covering only 52% of our forecasted net chargeoffs of $329 million. For 2012, we expect $150 million of provisions. CMA's allowance for loan losses was $767 million at September 30, equal to 82.6% of nonperforming loans, below the peer median of 100%. However, in our estimation, CMA's allowance, with respect to the credit quality of its loan portfolio, is high enough to allow for additional significant reserve releases.

➤ We see EPS of $2.18 in 2011 and $2.41 in 2012.

## Investment Rationale/Risk

➤ We see meaningful improvement in CMA's credit quality, with decreasing net chargeoffs and fewer new nonperforming loans, on an organic basis. Third quarter results, including the Sterling Bancshares acquisition, showed solid commercial loan growth, which was enough to offset shrinkage in real estate construction lending and residential mortgages. Since CMA's deposits are at much lower rates than at peers, the net interest margin proved to be resilient. In 2011, we expect the loan pipeline to grow, particularly from middle-market lending, small business, and auto dealers. We expect revenue growth to begin in earnest by late 2011, and to reach 4.5% in 2012.

➤ Risks to our recommendation and target price include a slower-than-expected economic recovery, and continued high unemployment.

➤ Our 12-month target price of $30 is an above peers 12.5X our forward four quarters EPS estimate of $2.40, equal to a discount to peers 0.82X our year-end tangible book value per share estimate of $37.00. Our target multiple reflects our view of CMA's balance sheet strength, capital levels and credit quality, relative to peers, as well as CMA's historical valuation trends.

## Qualitative Risk Assessment

| LOW | MEDIUM | HIGH |
|---|---|---|

Our risk assessment reflects CMA's long history of profitability and relatively high capital ratios, tempered by its exposure to the Michigan and California residential real estate markets.

## Quantitative Evaluations

**S&P Quality Ranking** B

| D | C | B- | B | B+ | A- | A | A+ |
|---|---|---|---|---|---|---|---|

**Relative Strength Rank** MODERATE

34

LOWEST = 1     HIGHEST = 99

## Revenue/Earnings Data

**Revenue (Million $)**

| | 1Q | 2Q | 3Q | 4Q | Year |
|---|---|---|---|---|---|
| 2011 | 641.0 | 633.0 | 664.0 | -- | -- |
| 2010 | 670.0 | 670.0 | 642.0 | 660.0 | 2,642 |
| 2009 | 762.0 | 866.0 | 819.0 | 685.0 | 3,155 |
| 2008 | 1,100 | 979.0 | 975.0 | 890.0 | 3,944 |
| 2007 | 1,104 | 1,158 | 1,182 | 1,174 | 4,618 |
| 2006 | 967.0 | 1,048 | 1,088 | 1,174 | 4,277 |

**Earnings Per Share ($)**

| | | | | | |
|---|---|---|---|---|---|
| 2011 | 0.57 | 0.53 | 0.51 | E0.56 | E2.18 |
| 2010 | -0.57 | 0.39 | 0.33 | 0.53 | 0.78 |
| 2009 | -0.16 | -0.11 | -0.10 | -0.41 | -0.78 |
| 2008 | 0.73 | 0.37 | 0.18 | 0.01 | 1.29 |
| 2007 | 1.19 | 1.25 | 1.17 | 0.77 | 4.40 |
| 2006 | 1.26 | 1.19 | 1.20 | 1.16 | 4.81 |

Fiscal year ended Dec. 31. Next earnings report expected: NA. EPS Estimates based on S&P Operating Earnings; historical GAAP earnings are as reported.

## Dividend Data (Dates: mm/dd Payment Date: mm/dd/yy)

| Amount ($) | Date Decl. | Ex-Div. Date | Stk. of Record | Payment Date |
|---|---|---|---|---|
| 0.100 | 01/25 | 03/11 | 03/15 | 04/01/11 |
| 0.100 | 04/26 | 06/13 | 06/15 | 07/01/11 |
| 0.100 | 07/26 | 09/13 | 09/15 | 10/01/11 |
| 0.100 | 11/15 | 12/13 | 12/15 | 01/01/12 |

Dividends have been paid since 1936. Source: Company reports.

---

**Please read the Required Disclosures and Analyst Certification on the last page of this report.**

The **McGraw·Hill** Companies

# Comerica Inc

## Business Summary November 21, 2011

CORPORATE OVERVIEW. Comerica is a Dallas-headquartered bank holding company that operates banking units in Michigan, California, Texas, Arizona and Florida. It also has international banking subsidiaries in Canada and Mexico.

Operations are divided into three major lines of business: the Business Bank, the Retail Bank (formerly known as Small Business and Personal Financial Services), and Wealth & Institutional Management. The Business Bank is primarily comprised of middle market, commercial real estate, national dealer services, global finance, large corporate, leasing, financial services, and technology and life sciences. This business segment offers various products and services, including commercial loans and lines of credit, deposits, cash management, capital market products, international trade finance, letters of credit, foreign exchange management services and loan syndication services.

CORPORATE STRATEGY. Comerica has positioned itself to deliver financial services in its four primary geographic markets: Midwest & Other, West, Texas, and Florida.

CMA's goal is to deliver attractive returns to its shareholders over time by ex-

porting its expertise to higher-growth markets, continuing its investments to grow the Retail Bank and Wealth & Institutional Management, building and enhancing customer relationships, and improving risk management processes.

MARKET PROFILE. As of June 30, 2011, which is the latest available FDIC branch-level data, CMA had 500 branches, and $45.2 billion in deposits, including, on a pro forma basis, the acquisition of Sterling Bancshares. About 48% of deposits were concentrated in Michigan, where CMA had 218 branches, about $21.8 billion in deposits, and a deposit market share of about 11.4%, ranking second. In California, CMA had 103 branches and $12.5 billion in deposits, with a deposit market share of about 1.3%, ranking 13th. In Texas, CMA had 151 branches, $10.4 billion in deposits, and a deposit market share of about 1.7%, ranking seventh. CMA also has 17 offices in Arizona and 11 offices in Florida.

## Company Financials Fiscal Year Ended Dec. 31

| Per Share Data ($) | 2010 | 2009 | 2008 | 2007 | 2006 | 2005 | 2004 | 2003 | 2002 | 2001 |
|---|---|---|---|---|---|---|---|---|---|---|
| Tangible Book Value | 32.82 | 32.26 | 32.57 | 34.12 | 32.82 | 33.01 | 29.85 | 29.20 | 28.31 | 27.15 |
| Earnings | 0.78 | -0.78 | 1.29 | 4.40 | 4.81 | 5.11 | 4.36 | 3.75 | 3.40 | 3.88 |
| S&P Core Earnings | 0.81 | -0.72 | 0.86 | 4.48 | 4.71 | 4.90 | 4.27 | 3.72 | 3.30 | 3.27 |
| Dividends | 0.25 | 0.20 | 0.20 | 2.56 | 2.36 | 2.20 | 2.08 | 2.00 | 1.92 | 1.76 |
| Payout Ratio | 32% | NM | 16% | 58% | 49% | 43% | 48% | 53% | 56% | 45% |
| Prices:High | 45.85 | 32.30 | 54.00 | 63.89 | 60.10 | 63.38 | 63.80 | 56.34 | 66.09 | 65.15 |
| Prices:Low | 29.68 | 11.72 | 15.05 | 39.62 | 50.12 | 53.17 | 50.45 | 37.10 | 35.20 | 44.02 |
| P/E Ratio:High | 59 | NM | 42 | 15 | 12 | 12 | 15 | 15 | 19 | 17 |
| P/E Ratio:Low | 38 | NM | 12 | 9 | 10 | 10 | 12 | 10 | 10 | 11 |

| Income Statement Analysis (Million $) | | | | | | | | | | |
|---|---|---|---|---|---|---|---|---|---|---|
| Net Interest Income | 1,646 | 1,567 | 1,815 | 2,003 | 1,983 | 1,956 | 1,810 | 1,926 | 2,132 | 2,102 |
| Tax Equivalent Adjustment | 5.00 | 8.00 | 6.00 | 3.00 | NA | 4.00 | 3.00 | 3.00 | 4.00 | 4.00 |
| Non Interest Income | 789 | 1,050 | 893 | 881 | 855 | 942 | 857 | 837 | 819 | 784 |
| Loan Loss Provision | 480 | 1,082 | 686 | 212 | 37.0 | -47.0 | 64.0 | 377 | 635 | 236 |
| % Expense/Operating Revenue | 67.4% | 63.0% | 66.2% | 58.6% | 59.0% | 57.4% | 55.9% | 53.6% | 51.3% | 53.9% |
| Pretax Income | 315 | -115 | 271 | 988 | 1,127 | 1,279 | 1,110 | 953 | 882 | 1,111 |
| Effective Tax Rate | 17.5% | NM | 21.8% | 31.0% | 30.6% | 32.7% | 31.8% | 30.6% | 31.9% | 36.1% |
| Net Income | 260 | 16.0 | 212 | 682 | 782 | 861 | 757 | 661 | 601 | 710 |
| % Net Interest Margin | 3.24 | 2.72 | 3.02 | 3.66 | 3.79 | 4.06 | 3.86 | 3.95 | 4.55 | 4.61 |
| S&P Core Earnings | 140 | -107 | 131 | 694 | 766 | 826 | 744 | 657 | 584 | 587 |

| Balance Sheet & Other Financial Data (Million $) | | | | | | | | | | |
|---|---|---|---|---|---|---|---|---|---|---|
| Money Market Assets | 1,415 | 4,843 | 2,510 | 36.0 | 2,632 | 1,159 | 3,230 | 4,013 | 2,446 | 1,079 |
| Investment Securities | 7,560 | 7,416 | 9,201 | 6,296 | 3,989 | 5,399 | 7,173 | 8,502 | 5,499 | 5,370 |
| Commercial Loans | 31,912 | 32,147 | 38,488 | 38,271 | 35,924 | 33,707 | 31,540 | 32,153 | 33,732 | 32,660 |
| Other Loans | 7,423 | 9,029 | 11,247 | 12,472 | 11,507 | 9,540 | 9,303 | 7,274 | 8,549 | 8,536 |
| Total Assets | 53,667 | 59,263 | 67,548 | 62,331 | 58,001 | 53,013 | 51,766 | 52,592 | 53,301 | 50,732 |
| Demand Deposits | 15,538 | 15,871 | 11,701 | 27,181 | 29,151 | 15,666 | 15,164 | 14,104 | 16,335 | 12,596 |
| Time Deposits | 24,933 | 23,794 | 17,817 | 17,097 | 15,776 | 26,765 | 25,772 | 27,359 | 25,440 | 24,974 |
| Long Term Debt | 6,138 | 11,060 | 15,053 | 8,821 | 5,949 | 3,961 | 4,286 | 4,801 | 5,216 | 5,503 |
| Common Equity | 5,793 | 4,878 | 5,023 | 5,126 | 5,153 | 5,068 | 5,105 | 5,110 | 4,947 | 4,807 |
| % Return on Assets | 0.5 | 0.0 | 0.3 | 1.1 | 1.4 | 1.6 | 1.5 | 1.2 | 1.2 | 1.4 |
| % Return on Equity | 4.9 | 0.3 | 4.2 | 13.3 | 15.3 | 16.9 | 14.8 | 13.1 | 12.3 | 15.4 |
| % Loan Loss Reserve | 2.2 | 2.3 | 1.5 | 1.1 | 1.0 | 1.2 | -1.6 | 2.0 | 1.9 | -1.6 |
| % Loans/Deposits | 99.4 | 106.3 | 120.4 | 110.1 | 105.6 | 101.9 | 99.8 | 99.3 | 101.2 | 109.7 |
| % Equity to Assets | 9.4 | 7.8 | 7.8 | 8.5 | 9.2 | 9.7 | 9.8 | 9.5 | 9.4 | 9.0 |

Data as orig reptd.; bef. results of disc opers/spec. items. Per share data adj. for stk. divs.; EPS diluted. E-Estimated. NA-Not Available. NM-Not Meaningful. NR-Not Ranked. UR-Under Review.

**Office:** Comerica Bank Tower, 1717 Main Street, MC 6404, Dallas, TX 75201.
**Telephone:** 214-462-6831.
**Website:** http://www.comerica.com
**Chrmn, Pres & CEO:** R.W. Babb, Jr.

**Vice Chrmn:** L.C. Anderson
**EVP & Treas:** J.J. Herzog
**EVP, Secy & General Counsel:** J.W. Bilstrom
**EVP & CIO:** P.R. Obermeyer

**Investor Contact:** D.P. Persons (313-222-2840)
**Board Members:** L. C. Anderson, R. W. Babb, Jr., R. A. Cregg, K. T. DeNicola, J. P. Kane, R. Lindner, K. L. Parkhill, A. A. Piergallini, R. S. Taubman, R. M. Turner, Jr., N. G. VacaHumrichouse

**Founded:** 1849
**Domicile:** Delaware
**Employees:** 9,001

# Computer Sciences Corp

STANDARD &POOR'S

| S&P Recommendation | HOLD ★★★☆☆ | Price | 12-Mo. Target Price | Investment Style |
|---|---|---|---|---|
| | | $22.93 (as of Nov 25, 2011) | $30.00 | Large-Cap Blend |

**GICS Sector** Information Technology
**Sub-Industry** Data Processing & Outsourced Services

**Summary** This leading computer services company provides consulting, systems integration and outsourcing services.

## Key Stock Statistics (Source S&P, Vickers, company reports)

| | | | | | | | |
|---|---|---|---|---|---|---|---|
| 52-Wk Range | $56.61– 22.80 | S&P Oper. EPS 2012E | 4.05 | Market Capitalization(B) | $3.556 | Beta | 1.14 |
| Trailing 12-Month EPS | $-14.75 | S&P Oper. EPS 2013E | 4.12 | Yield (%) | 3.49 | S&P 3-Yr. Proj. EPS CAGR(%) | -9 |
| Trailing 12-Month P/E | NM | P/E on S&P Oper. EPS 2012E | 5.7 | Dividend Rate/Share | $0.80 | S&P Credit Rating | A- |
| $10K Invested 5 Yrs Ago | $4,556 | Common Shares Outstg. (M) | 155.1 | Institutional Ownership (%) | 81 | | |

## Price Performance

30-Week Mov. Avg. ··· 10-Week Mov. Avg. – GAAP Earnings vs. Previous Year   Volume Above Avg. |||| STARS
12-Mo. Target Price — Relative Strength — ▲ Up ▼ Down ▶ No Change   Below Avg. |||| ★

Options: ASE, CBOE, P, Ph

Analysis prepared by Equity Analyst **Dylan Cathers** on Nov 11, 2011, when the stock traded at **$26.04**.

## Highlights

▶ We look for revenue growth of 2.0% in FY 12 (Mar.), aided somewhat by the iSoft acquisition, and 3.0% in FY 13. Larger iSoft dividends are likely in FY 13. We think the company will continue to see disruptions to its North American Public Sector (NPS) business, given the budget issues facing the U.S. CSC has managed to post healthy bookings numbers, but converting those contracts into revenue may take a while, in our view. The Business Solutions & Services (BSS) sector should show good growth, but weakness overseas is affecting results, as are contract issues with the U.K.'s National Health Service (NHS).

▶ The Managed Services Sector (MSS) business continues to be a drag on operating margins. Overall, we think operating margins will narrow again this fiscal year, reflecting additional costs from SEC investigations and shareholder lawsuits. Also affecting margins will be dilution from the addition of iSoft. We expect to see a rebound in FY 13, however.

▶ We expect operating EPS of $4.05 in FY 12, aided by a large tax benefit, but excluding numerous one-time charges. We see $4.12 in FY 13.

## Investment Rationale/Risk

▶ Our hold recommendation on the shares is based on our concerns about the pace of contract signings within the NPS business and about reduced income from the important NHS deal. We believe that overall revenue growth for the company is likely to remain lackluster. We are also concerned about another SEC investigation, this one pertaining to possible intentional misconduct in Australia. While the shares recently traded at a low P/E relative to peers, we view the quality of earnings as poor.

▶ Risks to our recommendation and target price include increased competition for large long-term contracts in the IT outsourcing arena, further delays of contracts in the government segment, and a formal SEC investigation into CSC's accounting. We also have concerns regarding corporate governance, including the combination of the chairman, president and CEO roles.

▶ Our 12-month target price of $30 is based on a peer-discount P/E of 7.8X using our calendar 2012 EPS estimate of $3.83. Our peer group is comprised of other U.S.-based multinational IT outsourcing companies.

## Qualitative Risk Assessment

| LOW | MEDIUM | HIGH |
|---|---|---|

Our risk assessment reflects the highly competitive nature of the IT consulting and outsourcing market, offset by our view of CSC's strong balance sheet and the stability afforded the company by the numerous long-term contracts it has signed with customers.

## Quantitative Evaluations

**S&P Quality Ranking**                     B+

| D | C | B- | B | B+ | A- | A | A+ |
|---|---|---|---|---|---|---|---|

**Relative Strength Rank**                  WEAK

| 11 | |
|---|---|
| LOWEST = 1 | HIGHEST = 99 |

## Revenue/Earnings Data

**Revenue (Million $)**

| | 1Q | 2Q | 3Q | 4Q | Year |
|---|---|---|---|---|---|
| 2012 | 4,033 | 3,966 | -- | -- | -- |
| 2011 | 3,910 | 3,935 | 3,995 | 4,202 | 16,042 |
| 2010 | 3,898 | 4,041 | 3,953 | 4,236 | 16,128 |
| 2009 | 4,437 | 4,239 | 3,952 | 4,112 | 16,740 |
| 2008 | 3,838 | 4,017 | 4,160 | 4,484 | 16,500 |
| 2007 | 3,561 | 3,609 | 3,641 | 4,046 | 14,857 |

**Earnings Per Share ($)**

| | | | | | |
|---|---|---|---|---|---|
| 2012 | 1.18 | -18.56 | E0.58 | E1.35 | E4.05 |
| 2011 | 0.89 | 1.05 | 1.55 | 1.01 | 4.51 |
| 2010 | 0.86 | 1.40 | 1.36 | 1.66 | 5.28 |
| 2009 | 0.79 | 2.95 | 1.06 | 2.51 | 7.31 |
| 2008 | 0.61 | 0.43 | 1.05 | 1.15 | 3.20 |
| 2007 | -0.31 | 0.51 | 0.62 | 1.42 | 2.16 |

Fiscal year ended Mar. 31. Next earnings report expected: Early February. EPS Estimates based on S&P Operating Earnings; historical GAAP earnings are as reported.

## Dividend Data (Dates: mm/dd Payment Date: mm/dd/yy)

| Amount ($) | Date Decl. | Ex-Div. Date | Stk. of Record | Payment Date |
|---|---|---|---|---|
| 0.200 | 12/13 | 12/21 | 12/23 | 01/13/11 |
| 0.200 | 02/28 | 03/11 | 03/15 | 04/15/11 |
| 0.200 | 05/20 | 06/10 | 06/14 | 07/12/11 |
| 0.200 | 08/08 | 09/02 | 09/07 | 10/04/11 |

Dividends have been paid since 2010. Source: Company reports.

**Please read the Required Disclosures and Analyst Certification on the last page of this report.**

The McGraw-Hill Companies

# Computer Sciences Corp

**STANDARD &POOR'S**

## Business Summary November 11, 2011

CORPORATE OVERVIEW. Computer Sciences offers what it believes is a broad array of services to clients in the global commercial and government markets. The company specializes in the application of complex information technology (IT) to achieve the strategic objectives of its customers. Offerings include IT and business process outsourcing, and IT and professional services.

Outsourcing involves operating all or a portion of a customer's technology infrastructure, including systems analysis, applications development, network operations, desktop computing, and data center management. CSC also provides business process outsourcing, which involves managing key functions for clients such as claims processing, credit checking, logistics, and customer call centers.

IT and professional services includes systems integration, consulting, and professional services. Systems integration encompasses designing, developing, implementing, and integrating complete information systems. Consulting

and professional services includes advising clients on the strategic acquisition and utilization of IT, and on business strategy, security, modeling, engineering, and business process re-engineering. CSC also licenses sophisticated software systems for health care and financial services markets, and provides a broad array of end-to-end e-business solutions to meet the needs of large commercial and government clients.

The company provides services to clients in global commercial industries and to the U.S. federal government. In the global commercial segment, offerings are marketed to clients in a wide variety of industries. In the U.S. federal government market, CSC provides traditional systems integration and outsourcing for complex project management and technical services.

## Company Financials Fiscal Year Ended Mar. 31

| Per Share Data ($) | 2011 | 2010 | 2009 | 2008 | 2007 | 2006 | 2005 | 2004 | 2003 | 2002 |
|---|---|---|---|---|---|---|---|---|---|---|
| Tangible Book Value | 17.69 | 13.44 | 8.25 | 6.35 | 19.51 | 23.85 | 21.71 | 15.44 | 11.78 | 11.58 |
| Cash Flow | 11.91 | 12.49 | 15.08 | 9.26 | 8.95 | 9.42 | 8.56 | 8.29 | 6.95 | 7.02 |
| Earnings | 4.51 | 5.28 | 7.31 | 3.20 | 2.16 | 3.07 | 2.59 | 2.75 | 2.54 | 2.01 |
| S&P Core Earnings | 4.73 | 5.19 | 6.24 | 2.95 | 2.14 | 3.00 | 2.59 | 2.68 | 1.84 | 1.48 |
| Dividends | NA | Nil | Nil | Nil | Nil | Nil | Nil | Nil | Nil | Nil |
| Payout Ratio | NA | Nil | Nil | Nil | Nil | Nil | Nil | Nil | Nil | Nil |
| Calendar Year | 2010 | 2009 | 2008 | 2007 | 2006 | 2005 | 2004 | 2003 | 2002 | 2001 |
| Prices:High | 58.00 | 58.36 | 50.52 | 63.76 | 60.39 | 59.90 | 58.00 | 44.99 | 53.47 | 66.71 |
| Prices:Low | 39.61 | 31.11 | 23.93 | 46.95 | 46.23 | 42.31 | 38.07 | 26.52 | 24.30 | 28.99 |
| P/E Ratio:High | 13 | 11 | 7 | 20 | 28 | 20 | 22 | 16 | 21 | 33 |
| P/E Ratio:Low | 9 | 6 | 3 | 15 | 21 | 14 | 15 | 10 | 10 | 14 |

| Income Statement Analysis (Million $) | | | | | | | | | | |
|---|---|---|---|---|---|---|---|---|---|---|
| Revenue | 16,042 | 16,128 | 16,740 | 16,500 | 14,857 | 14,616 | 14,059 | 14,768 | 11,347 | 11,426 |
| Operating Income | 2,219 | 2,359 | 2,396 | 2,205 | 2,211 | 2,149 | 1,845 | 1,968 | 1,609 | 1,497 |
| Depreciation | 1,140 | 1,116 | 1,186 | 1,032 | 1,162 | 1,188 | 1,146 | 1,038 | 858 | 858 |
| Interest Expense | 168 | 252 | 261 | 106 | 175 | 104 | 157 | 170 | 143 | 155 |
| Pretax Income | 968 | 1,038 | 949 | 918 | 607 | 821 | 715 | 747 | 612 | 497 |
| Effective Tax Rate | NA | NA | NM | 40.7% | 35.9% | 29.7% | 30.6% | 30.5% | 28.0% | 30.7% |
| Net Income | 725 | 817 | 1,115 | 545 | 389 | 577 | 496 | 519 | 440 | 344 |
| S&P Core Earnings | 740 | 803 | 954 | 502 | 385 | 565 | 495 | 507 | 319 | 254 |

| Balance Sheet & Other Financial Data (Million $) | | | | | | | | | | |
|---|---|---|---|---|---|---|---|---|---|---|
| Cash | 1,837 | 2,784 | 2,297 | 699 | 1,050 | 1,291 | 1,010 | 610 | 300 | 149 |
| Current Assets | 7,557 | 8,422 | 7,707 | 6,923 | 6,706 | 6,306 | 5,690 | 4,867 | 4,088 | 3,304 |
| Total Assets | 16,120 | 16,455 | 15,619 | 15,775 | 13,731 | 12,943 | 12,634 | 11,804 | 10,433 | 8,611 |
| Current Liabilities | 4,178 | 4,122 | 4,016 | 5,590 | 5,260 | 4,141 | 3,878 | 3,253 | 2,987 | 2,708 |
| Long Term Debt | 2,409 | 3,494 | 4,173 | 2,506 | 1,412 | 1,377 | 1,303 | 2,306 | 2,205 | 1,873 |
| Common Equity | 7,560 | 6,446 | 5,510 | 5,462 | 5,886 | 6,772 | 6,495 | 5,504 | 4,606 | 3,624 |
| Total Capital | 9,969 | 10,017 | 9,683 | 7,968 | 7,298 | 8,149 | 7,798 | 7,810 | 6,811 | 5,497 |
| Capital Expenditures | 663 | 578 | 699 | 877 | 686 | 827 | 855 | 725 | 638 | 672 |
| Cash Flow | 1,865 | 1,933 | 2,301 | 1,576 | 1,551 | 1,765 | 1,642 | 1,558 | 1,298 | 1,202 |
| Current Ratio | 1.8 | 2.0 | 1.9 | 1.2 | 1.3 | 1.5 | 1.5 | 1.5 | 1.4 | 1.2 |
| % Long Term Debt of Capitalization | 24.2 | 34.9 | 43.1 | 31.5 | 19.4 | 16.9 | 16.7 | 29.5 | 32.4 | 34.1 |
| % Net Income of Revenue | 4.5 | 5.1 | 6.7 | 3.3 | 2.6 | 3.9 | 3.5 | 3.5 | 3.9 | 3.0 |
| % Return on Assets | 4.5 | 5.1 | 7.1 | 3.7 | 2.9 | 4.5 | 4.1 | 4.7 | 4.6 | 4.1 |
| % Return on Equity | 10.4 | 13.7 | 20.3 | 9.6 | 6.3 | 8.7 | 8.3 | 10.3 | 10.7 | 10.1 |

Data as orig reptd.; bef. results of disc opers/spec. items. Per share data adj. for stk. divs.; EPS diluted. E-Estimated. NA-Not Available. NM-Not Meaningful. NR-Not Ranked. UR-Under Review.

**Office:** 3170 Fairview Park Drive, Falls Church, VA 22042.
**Telephone:** 703-876-1000.
**Email:** investorrelations@csc.com
**Website:** http://www.csc.com

**Chrmn, Pres & CEO:** M.W. Laphen
**COO:** P. Lavatelli
**CFO:** M.J. Mancuso
**CTO:** P. Gross

**Chief Acctg Officer & Cntlr:** D.G. DeBuck
**Investor Contact:** B. Lackey (310-615-1700)
**Board Members:** I. W. Bailey, II, D. J. Barram, S. L. Baum, E. Brynjolfsson, R. F. Chase, J. R. Haberkorn, M. W. Laphen, F. W. McFarlan, C. S. Park, T. H. Patrick

**Founded:** 1959
**Domicile:** Nevada
**Employees:** 91,000

# Compuware Corp

**STANDARD &POOR'S**

## S&P Recommendation  HOLD ★★★☆☆

| Price | 12-Mo. Target Price | Investment Style |
|---|---|---|
| $7.61 (as of Nov 25, 2011) | $9.00 | Large-Cap Blend |

**GICS Sector** Information Technology
**Sub-Industry** Application Software

**Summary** This company provides software products and professional services designed to increase the productivity of information systems departments.

### Key Stock Statistics (Source S&P, Vickers, company reports)

| | | | | | | | | |
|---|---|---|---|---|---|---|---|---|
| 52-Wk Range | $12.25– 6.97 | S&P Oper. EPS 2012**E** | 0.48 | Market Capitalization(B) | $1.662 | Beta | 1.33 |
| Trailing 12-Month EPS | $0.49 | S&P Oper. EPS 2013**E** | 0.56 | Yield (%) | Nil | S&P 3-Yr. Proj. EPS CAGR(%) | 8 |
| Trailing 12-Month P/E | 15.5 | P/E on S&P Oper. EPS 2012**E** | 15.9 | Dividend Rate/Share | Nil | S&P Credit Rating | NR |
| $10K Invested 5 Yrs Ago | $8,839 | Common Shares Outstg. (M) | 218.4 | Institutional Ownership (%) | 83 | | |

## Price Performance

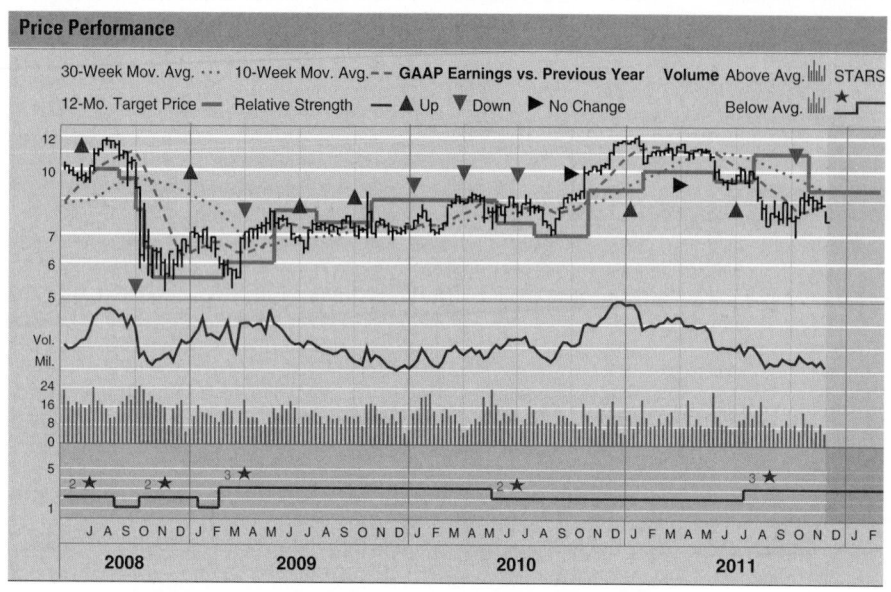

- 30-Week Mov. Avg. · · ·    10-Week Mov. Avg. - - -    **GAAP Earnings vs. Previous Year**    Volume Above Avg. STARS
- 12-Mo. Target Price — Relative Strength — ▲ Up ▼ Down ► No Change    Below Avg. ★

2008  2009  2010  2011

Options: CBOE, P

Analysis prepared by Equity Analyst **Jim Yin, CFA** on Nov 02, 2011, when the stock traded at **$8.44**.

## Highlights

➤ We estimate that total revenues will increase 11.2% in FY 12 (Mar.), following a 4.1% rise in FY 11, before slowing to 6.1% growth in FY 13. We believe the Mainframe business will grow at a mid-single digit rate in FY 12. Despite a gradual shift toward cloud computing, the company closed several large deals recently, and we believe its pipeline is ramping up. We think revenue growth will also be driven by sales of new services, and we note that renewal rates remain above 90%. We project 15% growth for its newer businesses in FY 12.

➤ We forecast that gross margins this fiscal year will decline to 67%, from FY 11's 69%. We anticipate that operating margins, excluding one-time gains and restructuring charges, will stay at FY 11's 16%, as economies of scale, strong profitability at the Mainframe unit and an expected move to profitability at Covisint are offset by investments in the business.

➤ Our FY 12 EPS estimate is $0.48, the same as in FY 11. For FY 13, our EPS forecast is $0.56.

## Investment Rationale/Risk

➤ Our hold opinion is based on valuation and our concerns about weakness in CPWR's legacy business. We view the company's mainframe business as mature, and we project a decline as enterprises shift their spending toward distributed computing. We think CPWR will recover more slowly than many other software companies in our coverage universe due to its heavy reliance on that market segment. We believe these negative factors offset the growth opportunity we see in the application performance management market segment.

➤ Risks to our opinion and target price include a slower recovery in the global economy, fewer revenue and cost synergies from the Gomez acquisition, and steeper sales declines for mainframes.

➤ Our 12-month target price of $9.00 is based on a blend of our discounted cash flow (DCF) and P/E analyses. Our DCF model assumes a weighted average cost of capital of 10% and a terminal growth rate of 3%, yielding an intrinsic value of $9.50. From our P/E analysis, we derive a value of $8.00, based on an industry P/E-to-growth ratio of 1.8X, or 14.3X our FY 13 EPS estimate of $0.56.

## Qualitative Risk Assessment

| LOW | MEDIUM | HIGH |
|---|---|---|

Our risk assessment reflects our concern about the maturity of CPWR's core businesses. Absent a meaningful pickup in revenue growth, we expect future earnings growth to be driven by ongoing cost reductions and share repurchases.

## Quantitative Evaluations

**S&P Quality Ranking**  NR

| D | C | B- | B | B+ | A- | A | A+ |
|---|---|---|---|---|---|---|---|

**Relative Strength Rank**  MODERATE

35

LOWEST = 1    HIGHEST = 99

## Revenue/Earnings Data

**Revenue (Million $)**

| | 1Q | 2Q | 3Q | 4Q | Year |
|---|---|---|---|---|---|
| 2012 | 230.0 | 260.7 | -- | -- | -- |
| 2011 | 206.5 | 225.9 | 247.0 | 249.6 | 928.9 |
| 2010 | 214.4 | 217.9 | 229.9 | 230.0 | 892.2 |
| 2009 | 298.6 | 269.9 | 268.7 | 253.4 | 1,090 |
| 2008 | 279.4 | 302.0 | 309.3 | 338.9 | 1,230 |
| 2007 | 296.3 | 288.5 | 315.2 | 313.0 | 1,213 |

**Earnings Per Share ($)**

| | 1Q | 2Q | 3Q | 4Q | Year |
|---|---|---|---|---|---|
| 2012 | 0.08 | 0.10 | E0.15 | E0.16 | E0.48 |
| 2011 | 0.06 | 0.12 | 0.15 | 0.16 | 0.48 |
| 2010 | 0.21 | 0.12 | 0.11 | 0.16 | 0.60 |
| 2009 | 0.13 | 0.08 | 0.14 | 0.20 | 0.55 |
| 2008 | Nil | 0.13 | 0.13 | 0.23 | 0.47 |
| 2007 | 0.08 | 0.07 | 0.11 | 0.21 | 0.45 |

Fiscal year ended Mar. 31. Next earnings report expected: Late January. EPS Estimates based on S&P Operating Earnings; historical GAAP earnings are as reported.

## Dividend Data

No cash dividends have been paid.

# Compuware Corp

## Business Summary November 02, 2011

CORPORATE OVERVIEW. Originally founded as a professional services company, Compuware provides software, maintenance and professional services intended to increase the productivity of the information technology (IT) departments of businesses. The company has two main product lines: mainframe products and distributed products. CPWR's mainframe software products help customers maintain their IBM OS/390 and z/Series IT infrastructure. Key mainframe products include File-AID, Xpeditor, Hiperstation, Abend-AID and Strobe. These products facilitate application analysis, testing, defect detection and remediation, fault management, file and data management. Mainframe product revenues accounted for 44% of total revenue in FY 11 (Mar.).

CPWR's distributed software products help customers maximize the performance of their corporate IT infrastructure, which include multiple hardware, software and network platforms. The company's distributed products support requirements management (Changepoint), application development (Uniface), and application performance analysis (Vantage). Distributed product revenue accounted for 23% of total revenue in FY 11.

CPWR launched its Compuware 2.0 initiative in FY 09 with the main objective of delivering value-added high end-to-end application performance to meet the growing and ever-more critical demand from enterprises that application systems deliver value to their business. As part of this initiative, the company acquired Gomez in FY 10 for $295 million in cash. Gomez is a leading provider of web application performance services, which enable organizations to test and monitor web applications from outside their firewall. We believe this acquisition complements CPWR's Vantage products. To better focus on the faster growth, higher margined segment of the market, the company has divested its Quality and DevPartner software products.

CPWR also provides applications services, which are marketed under the brand name "Covisint." Covisint provides a secure, collaborative platform that enables trading partners, customers, and vendors to share vital business information and process transactions across disparate systems. Application services revenue accounted for about 5.9% of total revenue in FY 11, up from 4.5% in FY 10.

## Company Financials Fiscal Year Ended Mar. 31

| Per Share Data ($) | 2011 | 2010 | 2009 | 2008 | 2007 | 2006 | 2005 | 2004 | 2003 | 2002 |
|---|---|---|---|---|---|---|---|---|---|---|
| Tangible Book Value | 1.20 | 1.24 | 2.09 | 1.95 | 2.57 | 3.33 | 3.15 | 3.11 | 2.93 | 2.60 |
| Cash Flow | 0.70 | 0.79 | 0.67 | 0.58 | 0.70 | 0.51 | 0.34 | 0.27 | 0.41 | -0.40 |
| Earnings | 0.48 | 0.60 | 0.55 | 0.47 | 0.45 | 0.37 | 0.20 | 0.13 | 0.27 | -0.66 |
| S&P Core Earnings | 0.48 | 0.39 | 0.49 | 0.43 | 0.41 | 0.33 | 0.12 | 0.03 | 0.14 | -0.15 |
| Dividends | NA | Nil | Nil | Nil | Nil | Nil | Nil | Nil | Nil | Nil |
| Payout Ratio | NA | Nil | Nil | Nil | Nil | Nil | Nil | Nil | Nil | Nil |
| Calendar Year | 2010 | 2009 | 2008 | 2007 | 2006 | 2005 | 2004 | 2003 | 2002 | 2001 |
| Prices:High | 11.99 | 8.95 | 11.91 | 12.56 | 9.55 | 9.99 | 8.95 | 6.52 | 14.00 | 14.50 |
| Prices:Low | 6.99 | 5.18 | 5.08 | 7.32 | 6.02 | 5.51 | 4.35 | 3.22 | 2.35 | 6.25 |
| P/E Ratio:High | 25 | 15 | 22 | 27 | NM | 27 | 45 | 50 | 52 | NM |
| P/E Ratio:Low | 15 | 9 | 9 | 16 | NM | 15 | 22 | 25 | 9 | NM |

| Income Statement Analysis (Million $) | 2011 | 2010 | 2009 | 2008 | 2007 | 2006 | 2005 | 2004 | 2003 | 2002 |
|---|---|---|---|---|---|---|---|---|---|---|
| Revenue | 929 | 892 | 1,090 | 1,230 | 1,213 | 1,205 | 1,232 | 1,265 | 1,375 | 1,729 |
| Operating Income | 201 | 184 | 220 | 224 | 188 | 198 | 143 | 90.5 | 188 | 264 |
| Depreciation | 50.3 | 45.0 | 30.4 | 32.8 | 55.0 | 50.2 | 56.4 | 55.2 | 53.8 | 98.2 |
| Interest Expense | NA | NA | NA | 31.3 | Nil | Nil | Nil | Nil | 6.10 | 7.43 |
| Pretax Income | 155 | 209 | 213 | 180 | 193 | 191 | 106 | 56.0 | 156 | -245 |
| Effective Tax Rate | NA | NA | 34.4% | 25.5% | 18.1% | 25.3% | 28.0% | 11.0% | 34.0% | NM |
| Net Income | 107 | 141 | 140 | 134 | 158 | 143 | 76.5 | 49.8 | 103 | -245 |
| S&P Core Earnings | 107 | 93.3 | 124 | 124 | 143 | 126 | 46.1 | 9.72 | 51.2 | -55.3 |

| Balance Sheet & Other Financial Data (Million $) | 2011 | 2010 | 2009 | 2008 | 2007 | 2006 | 2005 | 2004 | 2003 | 2002 |
|---|---|---|---|---|---|---|---|---|---|---|
| Cash | 180 | 150 | 278 | 286 | 261 | 612 | 498 | 455 | 319 | 233 |
| Current Assets | 743 | 705 | 859 | 919 | 921 | 1,445 | 1,358 | 1,143 | 1,050 | 1,063 |
| Total Assets | 2,038 | 2,013 | 1,875 | 2,019 | 2,029 | 2,511 | 2,478 | 2,234 | 2,123 | 1,994 |
| Current Liabilities | 599 | 613 | 562 | 645 | 529 | 545 | 578 | 493 | 469 | 556 |
| Long Term Debt | NA | NA | Nil | Nil | Nil | Nil | Nil | Nil | Nil | Nil |
| Common Equity | 953 | 914 | 881 | 927 | 1,132 | 1,579 | 1,516 | 1,414 | 1,332 | 1,170 |
| Total Capital | 953 | 914 | 905 | 955 | 1,167 | 1,605 | 1,516 | 1,418 | 1,332 | 1,170 |
| Capital Expenditures | 19.1 | 9.58 | 17.9 | 10.5 | 18.6 | 14.5 | 134 | 74.6 | 225 | 90.4 |
| Cash Flow | 158 | 186 | 170 | 167 | 213 | 193 | 133 | 105 | 157 | -147 |
| Current Ratio | 1.2 | 1.2 | 1.5 | 1.4 | 1.7 | 2.6 | 2.3 | 2.3 | 2.2 | 1.9 |
| % Long Term Debt of Capitalization | Nil | Nil | Nil | Nil | Nil | Nil | Nil | Nil | Nil | Nil |
| % Net Income of Revenue | 11.6 | 15.8 | 12.8 | 10.9 | 13.0 | 11.9 | 6.2 | 3.9 | 7.5 | NM |
| % Return on Assets | 5.3 | 7.2 | 7.2 | 6.6 | 7.0 | 5.7 | 3.2 | 2.3 | 5.0 | NM |
| % Return on Equity | 11.5 | 15.7 | 15.5 | 13.1 | 11.7 | 9.2 | 5.2 | 3.6 | 8.2 | NM |

Data as orig reptd.; bef. results of disc opers/spec. items. Per share data adj. for stk. divs.; EPS diluted. E-Estimated. NA-Not Available. NM-Not Meaningful. NR-Not Ranked. UR-Under Review.

Office: One Campus Martius, Detroit, MI 48226-5099.
Telephone: 313-227-7300.
Email: investor.relations@compuware.com
Website: http://www.compuware.com

Chrmn: P. Karmanos, Jr.
Pres & COO: J. Angileri
CEO: R.C. Paul
EVP & Chief Admin Officer: D.A. Knobblock

EVP & CTO: P.A. Czarnik
Investor Contact: L. Elkin (248-737-7345)
Board Members: D. W. Archer, G. S. Bedi, W. O. Grabe, F. A. Henderson, P. Karmanos, Jr., F. A. Nelson, R. C. Paul, G. D. Price, W. J. Prowse, G. S. Romney, R. J. Szygenda

Founded: 1973
Domicile: Michigan
Employees: 4,396

# ConAgra Foods Inc.

**STANDARD &POOR'S**

| S&P Recommendation | HOLD ★★★☆☆ | Price $23.95 (as of Nov 25, 2011) | 12-Mo. Target Price $27.00 | Investment Style Large-Cap Value |
|---|---|---|---|---|

**GICS Sector** Consumer Staples
**Sub-Industry** Packaged Foods & Meats

**Summary** This company is one of the largest U.S. packaged food processors.

## Key Stock Statistics (Source S&P, Vickers, company reports)

| | | | | | | | |
|---|---|---|---|---|---|---|---|
| 52-Wk Range | $26.60– 21.43 | S&P Oper. EPS 2012E | 1.80 | Market Capitalization(B) | $9.927 | Beta | 0.70 |
| Trailing 12-Month EPS | $1.76 | S&P Oper. EPS 2013E | 1.94 | Yield (%) | 4.01 | S&P 3-Yr. Proj. EPS CAGR(%) | 6 |
| Trailing 12-Month P/E | 13.6 | P/E on S&P Oper. EPS 2012E | 13.3 | Dividend Rate/Share | $0.96 | S&P Credit Rating | BBB |
| $10K Invested 5 Yrs Ago | $11,449 | Common Shares Outstg. (M) | 414.5 | Institutional Ownership (%) | 70 | | |

## Price Performance

30-Week Mov. Avg. · · · 10-Week Mov. Avg. - - **GAAP Earnings vs. Previous Year** Volume Above Avg. STARS
12-Mo. Target Price — Relative Strength — ▲ Up ▼ Down ► No Change  Below Avg.

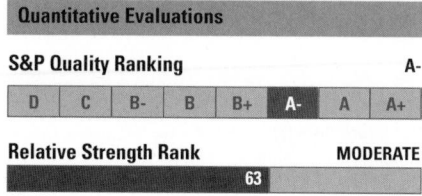

Options: ASE, CBOE, P

Analysis prepared by Equity Analyst **Tom Graves, CFA** on Oct 21, 2011, when the stock traded at **$25.52**.

## Qualitative Risk Assessment

| LOW | MEDIUM | HIGH |
|---|---|---|

Our risk assessment reflects the relatively stable nature of the company's end markets, and what we view as relatively strong expected cash flows.

## Quantitative Evaluations

**S&P Quality Ranking**                                          A-

| D | C | B- | B | B+ | A- | A | A+ |
|---|---|---|---|---|---|---|---|

**Relative Strength Rank**                                  MODERATE

63

LOWEST = 1                                              HIGHEST = 99

## Revenue/Earnings Data

**Revenue (Million $)**

| | 1Q | 2Q | 3Q | 4Q | Year |
|---|---|---|---|---|---|
| 2012 | 3,072 | -- | -- | -- | -- |
| 2011 | 2,804 | 3,148 | 3,141 | 3,210 | 12,303 |
| 2010 | 2,886 | 3,100 | 3,031 | 3,063 | 12,079 |
| 2009 | 3,066 | 3,252 | 3,125 | 3,298 | 12,731 |
| 2008 | 2,956 | 3,511 | 3,528 | 3,078 | 11,606 |
| 2007 | 2,689 | 3,089 | 2,918 | 3,333 | 12,028 |

**Earnings Per Share ($)**

| | 1Q | 2Q | 3Q | 4Q | Year |
|---|---|---|---|---|---|
| 2012 | 0.20 | E0.43 | E0.55 | E0.53 | E1.80 |
| 2011 | 0.32 | 0.45 | 0.52 | 0.62 | 1.90 |
| 2010 | 0.37 | 0.53 | 0.49 | 0.27 | 1.67 |
| 2009 | 0.23 | 0.38 | 0.43 | 0.39 | 1.42 |
| 2008 | 0.23 | 0.50 | 0.63 | -0.43 | 1.06 |
| 2007 | 0.21 | 0.39 | 0.37 | 0.38 | 1.35 |

Fiscal year ended May 31. Next earnings report expected: NA. EPS Estimates based on S&P Operating Earnings; historical GAAP earnings are as reported.

## Highlights

► In September 2011, Ralcorp Holdings, Inc. (RAH 80, Hold) said that RAH's board of directors had unanimously reiterated its rejection of a ConAgra proposal to acquire RAH for $94 a share, and determined not to enter into negotiations with respect to that proposal. While we think CAG has withdrawn its proposal to acquire RAH, we expect possible acquisition activity to be part of CAG's future growth strategy.

► We look for CAG's FY 12 (May) revenue from continuing operations to increase about 6% from the $12.3 billion reported for FY 11, largely due to higher prices. We expect profit margins to be bolstered by cost reduction efforts, and we think that price increases, including some expected after completion of the first quarter, will at least partly offset commodity cost pressures.

► Before some special items, we estimate FY 12 EPS from continuing operations of $1.80, up from $1.75 in FY 11. For FY 13, we estimate EPS of $1.94. In FY 12's first quarter, there was a $0.09 negative impact from special items. In FY 11, CAG's reported EPS of $1.90 included about a $0.15 (net) benefit from special items.

## Investment Rationale/Risk

► We had a generally favorable view of CAG's proposal to acquire Ralcorp, but it appears that opposition from Ralcorp has kept the deal from occurring. In our view, CAG's proposal to acquire Ralcorp included a focus on expanding CAG's private label (store-brand) business. Meanwhile, we expect CAG to be a strong cash generator in FY 12, with operating cash flow of at least $1.2 billion.

► Risks to our recommendation and target price include competitive pressures on CAG's businesses, higher-than-anticipated commodity cost inflation, and the company's ability to generate interest income and achieve cost savings and efficiency targets.

► Our 12-month target price of $27 reflects our view that the stock warrants a P/E that is at a discount to a group of other packaged food stocks, partly due to our expectation that CAG will have lower profit margins than some other major food companies. Based on a recently raised dividend, payable December 1, the stock recently had an indicated dividend yield of 3.8%.

## Dividend Data (Dates: mm/dd Payment Date: mm/dd/yy)

| Amount ($) | Date Decl. | Ex-Div. Date | Stk. of Record | Payment Date |
|---|---|---|---|---|
| 0.230 | 11/30 | 01/27 | 01/31 | 03/02/11 |
| 0.230 | 04/01 | 04/27 | 04/29 | 06/01/11 |
| 0.230 | 07/12 | 07/27 | 07/29 | 09/01/11 |
| 0.240 | 09/23 | 10/27 | 10/31 | 12/01/11 |

Dividends have been paid since 1976. Source: Company reports.

# ConAgra Foods Inc.

**STANDARD & POOR'S**

## Business Summary October 21, 2011

CORPORATE OVERVIEW. ConAgra Foods is one of the largest food companies in North America. The company's continuing operations businesses are now being presented in two reporting segments: consumer foods, which provided 65% of total sales in FY 11 (May); and commercial foods (35%). In June 2008, CAG sold its trading and merchandising segment (12% of FY 07 sales), which was treated as a discontinued operation for FY 08 and FY 09.

The consumer foods segment includes branded, private label and customized food products. CAG's brands include Hunt's, Healthy Choice, Chef Boyardee, Peter Pan, Wesson, Blue Bonnet, Orville Redenbacher's, Slim Jim, PAM, Swiss Miss, Van Camp's, Banquet, Marie Callender's, Hebrew National, Egg Beaters, and Reddi-wip. In FY 11, what CAG calls Convenient Meals accounted for 35% of segment sales, while Specialty Foods represented 21%, Specialty International accounted for 8.9%, Snacks represented 22%, and Meal Enhancers accounted for 13%.

CAG's commercial foods segment includes branded foods and ingredients, which are sold principally to foodservice, food manufacturing, and industrial customers. This segment's primary products include specialty potato products, milled grain ingredients, a variety of vegetable products, seasonings, blends, and flavors. Products are sold under brands such as ConAgra Mills,

Lamb Weston, and Spicetec Flavors and Seasonings. In FY 11, what CAG calls Specialty Potatoes accounted for 55% of segment sales, while Milled Products represented 35%, and Seasonings, Blends and Flavors accounted for 9.4%.

In FY 11, CAG's largest customer, Wal-Mart Stores, Inc., and its affiliates, accounted for about 18% of consolidated net sales.

CORPORATE STRATEGY. In recent years, CAG has been pursuing an acquisition and divestiture strategy, which has included shifting its focus toward its core branded and value-added food products, while exiting commodity-related businesses. In September 2011, Ralcorp Holdings, Inc. (RAH), said that RAH's board of directors had unanimously reiterated its rejection of a ConAgra proposal to acquire RAH for $94 a share, and determined not to enter into negotiations with respect to that proposal. In our view, CAG's proposal to acquire Ralcorp included a focus on expanding CAG's private label (store-brand) business.

## Company Financials Fiscal Year Ended May 31

| Per Share Data ($) | 2011 | 2010 | 2009 | 2008 | 2007 | 2006 | 2005 | 2004 | 2003 | 2002 |
|---|---|---|---|---|---|---|---|---|---|---|
| Tangible Book Value | 0.38 | 1.12 | 0.89 | 2.14 | 0.73 | 0.79 | 0.47 | 0.41 | NM | NM |
| Cash Flow | 2.74 | 2.40 | 2.12 | 1.66 | 2.10 | 1.74 | 1.95 | 2.16 | 2.30 | 2.39 |
| Earnings | 1.90 | 1.67 | 1.42 | 1.06 | 1.35 | 1.15 | 1.27 | 1.50 | 1.58 | 1.47 |
| S&P Core Earnings | 1.73 | 1.56 | 1.20 | 1.05 | 1.29 | 0.91 | 1.14 | 1.39 | 1.42 | 1.27 |
| Dividends | NA | 0.79 | 0.75 | 0.72 | 0.72 | 1.08 | 1.03 | 0.98 | NA | 0.88 |
| Payout Ratio | NA | 42% | 53% | 68% | 53% | 94% | 81% | 65% | NA | 60% |
| Calendar Year | 2010 | 2009 | 2008 | 2007 | 2006 | 2005 | 2004 | 2003 | 2002 | 2001 |
| Prices:High | 26.32 | 23.67 | 24.87 | 27.73 | 28.35 | 30.24 | 29.65 | 26.41 | 27.65 | 26.00 |
| Prices:Low | 21.02 | 14.00 | 13.52 | 22.81 | 18.85 | 19.99 | 25.38 | 17.75 | 20.90 | 17.50 |
| P/E Ratio:High | 14 | 14 | 18 | 26 | 21 | 26 | 23 | 18 | 18 | 18 |
| P/E Ratio:Low | 11 | 8 | 10 | 22 | 14 | 17 | 20 | 12 | 14 | 12 |

| Income Statement Analysis (Million $) | | | | | | | | | | |
|---|---|---|---|---|---|---|---|---|---|---|
| Revenue | 12,303 | 12,079 | 12,731 | 11,606 | 12,028 | 11,579 | 14,567 | 14,522 | 19,839 | 27,630 |
| Operating Income | 1,763 | 1,572 | 1,519 | 1,317 | 1,577 | 1,184 | 1,618 | 1,735 | 1,123 | 2,144 |
| Depreciation | 361 | 327 | 319 | 297 | 346 | 311 | 351 | 352 | 392 | 474 |
| Interest Expense | 178 | 160 | 268 | 467 | 226 | 307 | 341 | 275 | 276 | 402 |
| Pretax Income | 1,251 | 1,107 | 984 | 746 | 1,050 | 906 | 1,133 | 1,151 | 1,276 | 1,268 |
| Effective Tax Rate | NA | NA | 34.3% | 30.5% | 34.8% | 34.2% | 41.5% | 30.9% | 34.2% | 38.1% |
| Net Income | 830 | 747 | 646 | 519 | 684 | 596 | 663 | 796 | 840 | 785 |
| S&P Core Earnings | 754 | 691 | 547 | 512 | 657 | 470 | 589 | 740 | 750 | 668 |

| Balance Sheet & Other Financial Data (Million $) | | | | | | | | | | |
|---|---|---|---|---|---|---|---|---|---|---|
| Cash | 972 | 953 | 243 | 141 | 735 | 332 | 208 | 589 | 629 | 158 |
| Current Assets | 3,899 | 3,960 | 3,337 | 6,082 | 5,006 | 4,790 | 4,524 | 5,145 | 6,060 | 6,434 |
| Total Assets | 11,409 | 11,738 | 11,073 | 13,683 | 11,836 | 11,970 | 12,792 | 14,230 | 15,071 | 15,496 |
| Current Liabilities | 2,126 | 2,036 | 1,575 | 3,651 | 2,681 | 2,965 | 2,389 | 3,002 | 3,803 | 4,313 |
| Long Term Debt | 2,870 | 3,226 | 3,461 | 3,387 | 3,420 | 3,155 | 4,349 | 5,281 | 5,570 | 5,919 |
| Common Equity | 4,709 | 4,929 | 4,721 | 5,337 | 4,583 | 4,650 | 4,859 | 4,840 | 4,622 | 4,308 |
| Total Capital | 7,942 | 8,416 | 8,234 | 8,739 | 8,003 | 7,805 | 9,209 | 10,120 | 10,192 | 10,227 |
| Capital Expenditures | 466 | 483 | 442 | 490 | 425 | 263 | 453 | 352 | 390 | 531 |
| Cash Flow | 1,191 | 1,074 | 965 | 815 | 1,030 | 907 | 1,014 | 1,148 | 1,232 | 1,259 |
| Current Ratio | 1.8 | 1.9 | 2.1 | 1.7 | 1.9 | 1.6 | 1.9 | 1.7 | 1.6 | 1.5 |
| % Long Term Debt of Capitalization | 36.1 | 38.3 | 42.0 | 38.7 | 42.7 | 40.4 | 47.2 | 52.2 | 54.7 | 57.9 |
| % Net Income of Revenue | 6.8 | 6.2 | 5.1 | 4.5 | 5.7 | 5.1 | 4.6 | 5.5 | 4.2 | 2.8 |
| % Return on Assets | 7.2 | 6.6 | 5.2 | 4.1 | 5.7 | 4.8 | 4.9 | 5.4 | 5.5 | 4.9 |
| % Return on Equity | 17.2 | 15.5 | 12.9 | 10.5 | 14.8 | 12.5 | 13.7 | 16.8 | 18.8 | 18.9 |

Data as orig reptd.; bef. results of disc opers/spec. items. Per share data adj. for stk. divs.; EPS diluted. E-Estimated. NA-Not Available. NM-Not Meaningful. NR-Not Ranked. UR-Under Review.

**Office:** One ConAgra Drive, Omaha, NE 68102-5001.
**Telephone:** 402-240-4000.
**Website:** http://www.conagrafoods.com
**Chrmn:** S.F. Goldstone

**Pres & CEO:** G.M. Rodkin
**EVP & CFO:** J.F. Gehring
**EVP & Chief Admin Officer:** B.L. Keck
**EVP, Secy & General Counsel:** C.R. Batcheler

**Investor Contact:** C.W. Klinefelter (402-595-4154)
**Board Members:** M. C. Bay, S. G. Butler, S. F. Goldstone, J. A. Gregor, R. Johri, W. G. Jurgensen, R. H. Lenny, R. A. Marshall, G. M. Rodkin, A. J. Schindler, K. E. Stinson

**Founded:** 1919
**Domicile:** Delaware
**Employees:** 23,200

**The McGraw-Hill Companies**

# ConocoPhillips

**STANDARD &POOR'S**

| S&P Recommendation **BUY** ★★★★☆ | Price $66.14 (as of Nov 25, 2011) | 12-Mo. Target Price $93.00 | Investment Style Large-Cap Blend |
|---|---|---|---|

**GICS Sector** Energy
**Sub-Industry** Integrated Oil & Gas

**Summary** ConocoPhillips, formed via the 2002 merger of Phillips Petroleum and Conoco, is the fourth largest integrated oil company in the world, and second largest in the U.S.

## Key Stock Statistics (Source S&P, Vickers, company reports)

| | | | | | | | |
|---|---|---|---|---|---|---|---|
| 52-Wk Range | $81.80–58.65 | S&P Oper. EPS 2011**E** | 8.65 | Market Capitalization(B) | $87.817 | Beta | 1.17 |
| Trailing 12-Month EPS | $7.80 | S&P Oper. EPS 2012**E** | 8.40 | Yield (%) | 3.99 | S&P 3-Yr. Proj. EPS CAGR(%) | 32 |
| Trailing 12-Month P/E | 8.5 | P/E on S&P Oper. EPS 2011**E** | 7.6 | Dividend Rate/Share | $2.64 | S&P Credit Rating | A |
| $10K Invested 5 Yrs Ago | $12,154 | Common Shares Outstg. (M) | 1,327.7 | Institutional Ownership (%) | 73 | | |

## Price Performance

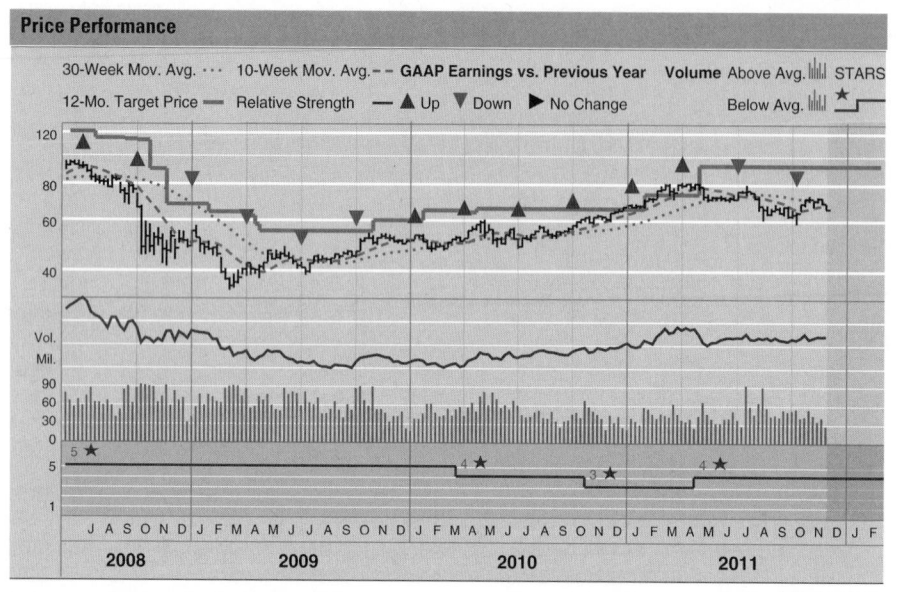

30-Week Mov. Avg. · · · · 10-Week Mov. Avg. - - GAAP Earnings vs. Previous Year  Volume Above Avg. STARS
12-Mo. Target Price — Relative Strength — ▲ Up ▼ Down ▶ No Change  Below Avg.

Options: ASE, CBOE, P, Ph

Analysis prepared by Equity Analyst **Michael Kay** on Aug 25, 2011, when the stock traded at **$65.22**.

## Qualitative Risk Assessment

| LOW | MEDIUM | HIGH |
|---|---|---|

Our risk assessment reflects our view of the company's diversified and solid business profile in volatile, cyclical and capital-intensive segments of the energy industry. While COP has a history of aggressive acquisition activity, we believe its earnings stability is good and its corporate governance practices are sound.

## Quantitative Evaluations

**S&P Quality Ranking**  B

| D | C | B- | B | B+ | A- | A | A+ |
|---|---|---|---|---|---|---|---|

**Relative Strength Rank**  MODERATE

59

LOWEST = 1  HIGHEST = 99

## Revenue/Earnings Data

**Revenue (Million $)**

| | 1Q | 2Q | 3Q | 4Q | Year |
|---|---|---|---|---|---|
| 2011 | 58,247 | 66,961 | 63,629 | -- | -- |
| 2010 | 44,821 | 45,686 | 47,208 | 51,726 | 175,752 |
| 2009 | 30,741 | 35,448 | 40,173 | 42,979 | 149,341 |
| 2008 | 54,883 | 71,411 | 70,044 | 44,504 | 240,842 |
| 2007 | 41,320 | 47,370 | 46,062 | 52,685 | 187,437 |
| 2006 | 46,906 | 47,149 | 48,076 | 41,519 | 183,650 |

**Earnings Per Share ($)**

| | 1Q | 2Q | 3Q | 4Q | Year |
|---|---|---|---|---|---|
| 2011 | 2.09 | 2.41 | 1.91 | E1.90 | E8.65 |
| 2010 | 1.40 | 2.77 | 2.05 | 1.39 | 7.62 |
| 2009 | 0.56 | 0.87 | 1.00 | 0.81 | 3.24 |
| 2008 | 2.62 | 3.50 | 3.39 | -21.37 | -11.16 |
| 2007 | 2.12 | 0.18 | 2.23 | 2.71 | 7.22 |
| 2006 | 2.34 | 3.09 | 2.31 | 1.91 | 9.66 |

Fiscal year ended Dec. 31. Next earnings report expected: Late January. EPS Estimates based on S&P Operating Earnings; historical GAAP earnings are as reported.

## Highlights

▶ Unexpected downtime and asset disposals depressed first-half 2011 production of 1.7 MM-boe/day by 6%. While COP's field decline rates have been higher than anticipated, new production may accelerate future cash flow given the liquids nature of future growth. We look for a production drop in 2011, on asset sales, before a gain of about 3% per year during 2012-15, driven by the expected addition of 800 MBOE/d by 2015 from Canadian oil sands, unconventional North America activity, the North Sea, and LNG projects. Non-core asset sales should allow COP to allocate resources to these higher-margin projects. In November 2010, COP began shipping LNG from its Qatargas 3 project. We see 2011 capex of about $13 billion, up from $10.7 billion in 2010.

▶ In the downstream, fuel demand has improved, and light-heavy crude price differentials and U.S. refining margins have widened, but unplanned downtime hurt U.S. utilization, not allowing COP to capture all the benefits of improved market opportunities.

▶ On higher oil prices and improved downstream and chemicals, we see a 41% rise in 2011 adjusted EPS, to $8.50, and 8% in 2012, to $9.20.

## Investment Rationale/Risk

▶ In July, COP announced plans to split its upstream and downstream operations via a tax-free spinoff of the refining and marketing business to shareholders by the first half of 2012. This will allow each entity to pursue individual strategies. COP had been reshaping its portfolio through a multi-year strategic repositioning, to focus on higher growth and profit upstream assets in an attempt to boost returns and cut debt. COP will keep its strategy to repurchase over $10 billion of stock and raise $5-$10 billion in asset sales in 2011-2012. About 60%-80% of the divestment is expected from North America E&P, and 20%-40% from downstream assets. We think the asset repositioning has placed COP in better position to improve future return rates.

▶ Risks to our recommendation and target price include unfavorable changes in economic, industry and operating conditions, which include COP's ability to replace its reserves; geopolitical risk; and operational risk.

▶ Based on our DCF analysis ($90; WACC 9.0%; terminal growth 3%) and relative market valuations, including a target enterprise value to 2011 EBITDA forecast of 5.5X, above peer averages, our 12-month target price is $93.

## Dividend Data (Dates: mm/dd Payment Date: mm/dd/yy)

| Amount ($) | Date Decl. | Ex-Div. Date | Stk. of Record | Payment Date |
|---|---|---|---|---|
| 0.660 | 02/11 | 02/17 | 02/22 | 03/01/11 |
| 0.660 | 05/11 | 05/19 | 05/23 | 06/01/11 |
| 0.660 | 07/13 | 07/21 | 07/25 | 09/01/11 |
| 0.660 | 10/05 | 10/13 | 10/17 | 12/01/11 |

Dividends have been paid since 1934. Source: Company reports.

**Please read the Required Disclosures and Analyst Certification on the last page of this report.**

*The McGraw-Hill Companies*

# ConocoPhillips

## Business Summary August 25, 2011

CORPORATE OVERVIEW. On August 30, 2002, Phillips Petroleum and Conoco merged, creating ConocoPhillips (COP). Today, we estimate COP is the second largest publicly integrated oil company in the U.S., based on a blend of its oil and gas reserves and production capacity. COP operates in six segments: exploration and production (E&P; 23% of 2010 sales, 81% of 2010 net income); refining and marketing (R&M; 73%, 2%); midstream (4%, 3%); 20% stake in the Russian oil company Lukoil (NA; 22%); chemicals (NA; 4%); and emerging businesses. As of the end of February 2011, COP had sold its 20% stake in Lukoil and received about $9.5 billion in proceeds from the sale of its shares. In July 2011, COP announced its intention to split its upstream and downstream businesses by the first half of 2012.

Including Lukoil, and COP's share of equity affiliates, net oil and gas production fell 6% in 2010, to 1.75 million barrels of oil equivalent per day (boe/d), reflecting field declines, the impact of higher prices on production-sharing arrangements, and the sale of the Syncrude oil sands mining operation. Proved oil and gas reserves (including Lukoil, bitumen, synthetic oil, and equity affiliates) fell 20%, to 8.3 billion barrels (66% liquids, 77% developed), in 2010, on asset divestments.

Using data from John S. Herold, we estimate COP's three-year (2008-10) finding and development costs at $45.21 per boe, above the peer average; three-year proved acquisition costs at $30.86 per boe, above the peer average; three-year reserve replacement costs at $44.94 per boe, above the peer average; and three-year reserve replacement at 29%, below the peer average. We estimate COP's 2010 organic reserve replacement at 138%.

As of December 31, 2010, COP owned or had interests in 12 U.S. refineries (net crude throughput capacity of 2.0 million barrels per day, b/d), four European refineries (610,000 b/d), and one refinery in Malaysia (61,000 b/d). At year-end 2010, fuel was sold through wholesale and retail operations in the U.S. (under Phillips 66, Conoco and 76 brands) and Europe (under the JET and Coop brands).

## Company Financials Fiscal Year Ended Dec. 31

| Per Share Data ($) | 2010 | 2009 | 2008 | 2007 | 2006 | 2005 | 2004 | 2003 | 2002 | 2001 |
|---|---|---|---|---|---|---|---|---|---|---|
| Tangible Book Value | 44.82 | 39.03 | 34.15 | 36.40 | 29.69 | 25.49 | 18.53 | 12.85 | 9.91 | 14.07 |
| Cash Flow | 13.69 | 9.48 | -3.86 | 12.54 | 14.19 | 12.63 | 8.49 | 5.90 | 5.31 | 5.14 |
| Earnings | 7.62 | 3.24 | -11.16 | 7.22 | 9.66 | 9.63 | 5.79 | 3.53 | 0.74 | 2.79 |
| S&P Core Earnings | 5.23 | 3.36 | 4.96 | 7.49 | 9.59 | 9.72 | 5.88 | 3.43 | 0.64 | 2.60 |
| Dividends | 2.15 | 1.91 | 1.88 | 1.64 | 1.44 | 1.18 | 0.90 | 0.82 | 0.74 | 0.70 |
| Payout Ratio | 28% | 59% | NM | 23% | 15% | 12% | 15% | 23% | 101% | 25% |
| Prices:High | 68.58 | 57.44 | 95.96 | 90.84 | 74.89 | 71.48 | 45.61 | 33.02 | 32.05 | 34.00 |
| Prices:Low | 46.63 | 34.12 | 41.27 | 61.59 | 54.90 | 41.40 | 32.15 | 26.80 | 22.02 | 25.00 |
| P/E Ratio:High | 9 | 18 | NM | 13 | 8 | 7 | 8 | 9 | 44 | 12 |
| P/E Ratio:Low | 6 | 11 | NM | 9 | 6 | 4 | 6 | 8 | 30 | 9 |

| Income Statement Analysis (Million $) | | | | | | | | | | |
|---|---|---|---|---|---|---|---|---|---|---|
| Revenue | 175,752 | 149,341 | 240,842 | 187,437 | 183,650 | 179,442 | 135,076 | 104,196 | 56,748 | 26,868 |
| Operating Income | NA | NA | 36,158 | 31,164 | 37,433 | 24,691 | 17,033 | 11,866 | 4,571 | 8,393 |
| Depreciation, Depletion and Amortization | 9,060 | 9,346 | 11,116 | 8,740 | 7,284 | 4,253 | 3,798 | 3,485 | 4,446 | 1,391 |
| Interest Expense | 1,187 | 1,289 | 935 | 1,801 | 1,087 | 497 | 546 | 864 | 614 | 391 |
| Pretax Income | 19,750 | 10,032 | -3,523 | 23,359 | 28,409 | 23,580 | 14,401 | 8,337 | 2,164 | 3,302 |
| Effective Tax Rate | NA | 50.8% | NM | 48.7% | 45.0% | 42.0% | 43.5% | 44.9% | 67.0% | 50.2% |
| Net Income | 11,358 | 4,858 | -16,998 | 11,891 | 15,550 | 13,640 | 8,107 | 4,593 | 714 | 1,643 |
| S&P Core Earnings | 7,786 | 5,032 | 7,569 | 12,317 | 15,442 | 13,753 | 8,241 | 4,697 | 618 | 1,533 |

| Balance Sheet & Other Financial Data (Million $) | | | | | | | | | | |
|---|---|---|---|---|---|---|---|---|---|---|
| Cash | 11,521 | 542 | 755 | 1,456 | 817 | 2,214 | 1,387 | 490 | 307 | 142 |
| Current Assets | 34,660 | 21,167 | 20,843 | 24,735 | 25,066 | 19,612 | 15,021 | 11,192 | 10,903 | 4,363 |
| Total Assets | 156,314 | 152,588 | 142,865 | 177,757 | 164,781 | 106,999 | 92,861 | 82,455 | 76,836 | 35,217 |
| Current Liabilities | 27,419 | 23,695 | 21,780 | 26,882 | 26,431 | 21,359 | 15,586 | 14,011 | 12,816 | 4,542 |
| Long Term Debt | 26,943 | 31,912 | 32,754 | 26,583 | 23,091 | 10,758 | 14,370 | 16,340 | 19,267 | 9,295 |
| Common Equity | 68,562 | 62,467 | 55,165 | 88,983 | 82,646 | 52,731 | 42,723 | 34,366 | 29,517 | 14,340 |
| Total Capital | 98,218 | 97,348 | 107,186 | 137,757 | 106,939 | 76,137 | 68,583 | 60,113 | 57,796 | 27,650 |
| Capital Expenditures | 9,761 | 10,861 | 19,099 | 11,791 | 15,596 | 11,620 | 9,496 | 6,169 | 4,388 | 3,085 |
| Cash Flow | 20,418 | 14,204 | -5,882 | 20,631 | 22,834 | 17,893 | 11,905 | 8,078 | 5,160 | 3,034 |
| Current Ratio | 1.3 | 0.9 | 1.0 | 0.9 | 0.9 | 0.9 | 1.0 | 0.8 | 0.9 | 1.0 |
| % Long Term Debt of Capitalization | 27.4 | Nil | 30.6 | 19.3 | 21.6 | 14.1 | 21.0 | 27.2 | 33.3 | 33.6 |
| % Return on Assets | NA | 3.3 | NM | 6.9 | 11.4 | 13.6 | 9.2 | 5.8 | 1.3 | 5.9 |
| % Return on Equity | NA | NA | NM | 13.9 | 23.0 | 28.6 | 21.0 | 14.4 | 3.3 | 16.1 |

Data as orig reptd.; bef. results of disc opers/spec. items. Per share data adj. for stk. divs.; EPS diluted. E-Estimated. NA-Not Available. NM-Not Meaningful. NR-Not Ranked. UR-Under Review.

**Office:** 600 N Dairy Ashford St, Houston, TX 77079-1175.
**Telephone:** 281-293-1000.
**Website:** http://www.conocophillips.com
**Chrmn & CEO:** J.J. Mulva

**SVP & CFO:** J.W. Sheets
**SVP & Chief Admin Officer:** E.L. Batchelder
**SVP, Secy & General Counsel:** J.L. Kelly
**Chief Acctg Officer & Cntlr:** G.M. Schwarz

**Investor Contact:** G. Russell (212-207-1996)
**Board Members:** R. L. Armitage, R. H. Auchinleck, J. E. Copeland, Jr., K. M. Duberstein, R. R. Harkin, H. McGraw, III, J. J. Mulva, R. A. Niblock, H. J. Norvik, W. K. Reilly, V. J. Tschinkel, K. C. Turner, W. E. Wade, Jr.

**Founded:** 1917
**Domicile:** Delaware
**Employees:** 29,700

# Consolidated Edison Inc.

**STANDARD &POOR'S**

| S&P Recommendation **HOLD** ★★★★★ | Price $57.16 (as of Nov 25, 2011) | 12-Mo. Target Price $58.00 | Investment Style Large-Cap Value |
|---|---|---|---|

**GICS Sector** Utilities
**Sub-Industry** Multi-Utilities

**Summary** This electric and gas utility holding company serves parts of New York, New Jersey and Pennsylvania.

## Key Stock Statistics (Source S&P, Vickers, company reports)

| | | | | | | |
|---|---|---|---|---|---|---|
| 52-Wk Range | $59.89– 47.51 | S&P Oper. EPS 2011**E** | 3.61 | Market Capitalization(B) | $16.742 | Beta | 0.26 |
| Trailing 12-Month EPS | $3.71 | S&P Oper. EPS 2012**E** | 3.74 | Yield (%) | 4.20 | S&P 3-Yr. Proj. EPS CAGR(%) | 6 |
| Trailing 12-Month P/E | 15.4 | P/E on S&P Oper. EPS 2011**E** | 15.8 | Dividend Rate/Share | $2.40 | S&P Credit Rating | A- |
| $10K Invested 5 Yrs Ago | $15,490 | Common Shares Outstg. (M) | 292.9 | Institutional Ownership (%) | 44 | | |

## Price Performance

30-Week Mov. Avg. · · · 10-Week Mov. Avg. – – **GAAP Earnings vs. Previous Year** Volume Above Avg. STARS
12-Mo. Target Price — Relative Strength ▲ Up ▼ Down ▶ No Change Below Avg.

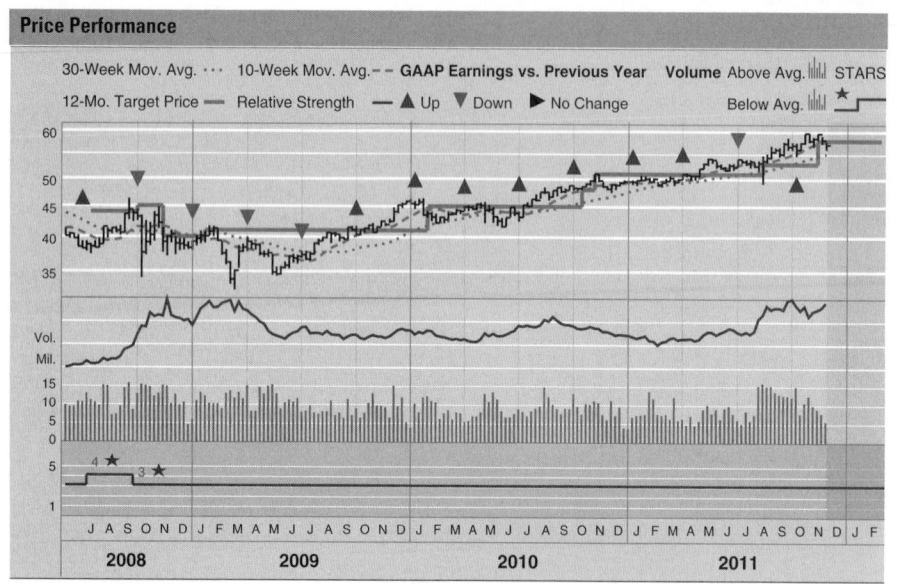

Options: ASE, CBOE, P, Ph

Analysis prepared by Equity Analyst **Justin McCann** on Nov 10, 2011, when the stock traded at **$58.85**.

## Highlights

► Excluding $0.05 of net one-time gains, we expect operating EPS in 2011 to increase more than 4% from 2010's $3.45, which grew 11.7% from 2009's $3.09. Operating EPS in the first nine months of 2011 was $0.12 above the year-earlier level, mainly reflecting rate increases, partially offset by higher depreciation and property taxes, and 3.7% more shares outstanding.

► For 2012, we expect operating EPS to reflect the benefit of the rate increases Consolidated Edison Company of New York (CECONY) was authorized in its three-year rate plan and a gradual recovery in the New York City economy. ED had not and did not expect to issue any long term debt in 2011 and expects to meet its equity needs by issuing shares through its dividend reinvestment and employee stock plans.

► In September 2010, the New York Public Service Commission authorized CECONY annual natural gas rate increases of $47.1 million, $47.9 million and $46.7 million for the three-year period that began on October 1, 2010. In March 2010, CECONY had been authorized annual electric rate increases of $420 million for the three-year period through March 31, 2013.

## Investment Rationale/Risk

► The shares advanced approximately 17% in the first 45 weeks of 2011, aided, in our view, by the extraordinarily volatile and often sharp declines in the broader market. The shares were up 9.1% in 2010, which, although slightly underperforming ED's gas distribution peers, substantially outperformed its electric utility peers. We believe the solid performance reflected the expectation and then the realization of additional rate increases, the appeal of ED's above-peers dividend yield, and the recovery in the broader market. We think the stock had earlier been restricted by the slowdown in the economy and the dilutive effect of new equity issuances.

► Risks to our recommendation and target price include extended weakness in ED's service territory economy, unfavorable regulatory rulings, and a sharp decline in the utility sector.

► We believe the shares will be supported by a dividend yield (recently 4.1%) slightly below the industry average (about 4.3%). We expect the dividend to continue to be increased at an annual rate of slightly less than 1%. Our 12-month target price is $58, a premium-to-peers P/E multiple of 15.5X our EPS estimate for 2012.

## Qualitative Risk Assessment

| LOW | MEDIUM | HIGH |
|---|---|---|

Our risk assessment reflects our view of the company's strong and steady cash flows from regulated electric and gas utility operations, its solid balance sheet and A- credit rating, a relatively healthy economy in its service territory, and a historically supportive regulatory environment.

## Quantitative Evaluations

**S&P Quality Ranking** B+

| D | C | B- | B | B+ | A- | A | A+ |
|---|---|---|---|---|---|---|---|

**Relative Strength Rank** STRONG

78

LOWEST = 1          HIGHEST = 99

## Revenue/Earnings Data

**Revenue (Million $)**

| | 1Q | 2Q | 3Q | 4Q | Year |
|---|---|---|---|---|---|
| 2011 | 3,349 | 2,993 | 3,629 | -- | -- |
| 2010 | 3,462 | 3,017 | 3,707 | 3,139 | 13,325 |
| 2009 | 3,423 | 2,845 | 3,489 | 3,273 | 13,032 |
| 2008 | 3,577 | 3,149 | 3,858 | 2,999 | 13,583 |
| 2007 | 3,357 | 2,956 | 3,579 | 3,228 | 13,120 |
| 2006 | 3,317 | 2,555 | 3,441 | 2,824 | 12,137 |

**Earnings Per Share ($)**

| | 1Q | 2Q | 3Q | 4Q | Year |
|---|---|---|---|---|---|
| 2011 | 1.06 | 0.56 | 1.30 | E0.72 | E3.61 |
| 2010 | 0.80 | 0.64 | 1.23 | 0.80 | 3.47 |
| 2009 | 0.66 | 0.55 | 1.22 | 0.73 | 3.14 |
| 2008 | 1.10 | 1.02 | 0.66 | 0.58 | 3.36 |
| 2007 | 0.99 | 0.58 | 1.15 | 0.76 | 3.46 |
| 2006 | 0.74 | 0.51 | 0.92 | 0.78 | 2.95 |

Fiscal year ended Dec. 31. Next earnings report expected: NA. EPS Estimates based on S&P Operating Earnings; historical GAAP earnings are as reported.

## Dividend Data (Dates: mm/dd Payment Date: mm/dd/yy)

| Amount ($) | Date Decl. | Ex-Div. Date | Stk. of Record | Payment Date |
|---|---|---|---|---|
| 0.600 | 01/20 | 02/14 | 02/16 | 03/15/11 |
| 0.600 | 04/21 | 05/16 | 05/18 | 06/15/11 |
| 0.600 | 07/21 | 08/15 | 08/17 | 09/15/11 |
| 0.600 | 10/28 | 11/14 | 11/16 | 12/15/11 |

Dividends have been paid since 1885. Source: Company reports.

---

**Please read the Required Disclosures and Analyst Certification on the last page of this report.**

*The McGraw-Hill Companies*

# Consolidated Edison Inc.

**STANDARD
&POOR'S**

## Business Summary November 10, 2011

CORPORATE OVERVIEW. Consolidated Edison is a holding company with electric and gas utilities serving a territory that includes New York City (except part of Queens), most of Westchester County, southeastern New York state, northern New Jersey, and northeastern Pennsylvania. Although the company also has some competitive subsidiaries that participate in energy-related businesses, we expect the two regulated utilities to provide substantially all of ED's earnings over the next few years.

MARKET PROFILE. The company's principal business operations are the regulated electric, gas and steam utility operations of Consolidated Edison Co. of New York (CECONY), and the regulated electric and gas utility operations of Orange and Rockland Utilities (O&R). In 2010, electric revenues accounted for 68.0% of consolidated sales (63.8% in 2009); non-utility revenues 13.8% (16.2%); gas revenues 13.2% (14.9%); and steam revenues 4.9% (5.1%). At December 31, 2010, the distribution system of CECONY had about 36,781 miles of overhead distribution lines and around 96,324 miles of underground distribution lines. The distribution system of O&R had about 3,774 miles of overhead distribution lines, and 1,727 miles of underground distribution lines.

The company's CECONY unit provides electric service (79.2% of CENY's operating revenues in 2010) to about 3.3 million customers and gas service (14.6%) to around 1.1 million customers in New York City and Westchester County. It also provides steam service (6.2%) in parts of Manhattan to around 1,760 customers (mostly large office buildings, apartment houses and hospitals). Most of the electricity sold by CECONY in 2010 was purchased under firm power contracts (primarily with non-utility generators) or through the wholesale electricity market administered by the New York Independent System Operator (NYISO). We expect this to continue for the foreseeable future.

The company's O&R unit provides electric and gas service in southeastern New York and adjacent areas of eastern Pennsylvania, and electric service in areas of New Jersey adjacent to its New York service territory. In 2010, electric sales accounted for 76.0% of operating revenues, and gas sales 24.0%.

## Company Financials  Fiscal Year Ended Dec. 31

| Per Share Data ($) | 2010 | 2009 | 2008 | 2007 | 2006 | 2005 | 2004 | 2003 | 2002 | 2001 |
|---|---|---|---|---|---|---|---|---|---|---|
| Tangible Book Value | 36.45 | 34.96 | 37.05 | 34.83 | 32.13 | 30.69 | 29.86 | 29.09 | 25.40 | 24.23 |
| Earnings | 3.47 | 3.14 | 3.36 | 3.46 | 2.95 | 2.99 | 2.32 | 2.36 | 3.13 | 3.21 |
| S&P Core Earnings | 3.62 | 3.23 | 1.19 | 2.99 | 2.54 | 2.54 | 1.78 | 1.66 | 0.50 | 0.66 |
| Dividends | 2.38 | 2.36 | 2.34 | 2.32 | 2.30 | 2.28 | 2.26 | 2.24 | 2.22 | 2.20 |
| Payout Ratio | 69% | 75% | 70% | 67% | 78% | 76% | 97% | 95% | 71% | 69% |
| Prices:High | 51.03 | 46.35 | 49.30 | 52.90 | 49.28 | 49.29 | 45.59 | 46.02 | 45.40 | 43.37 |
| Prices:Low | 41.52 | 32.56 | 34.11 | 43.10 | 41.17 | 41.10 | 37.23 | 36.55 | 32.65 | 31.44 |
| P/E Ratio:High | 15 | 15 | 15 | 15 | 17 | 16 | 20 | 20 | 15 | 14 |
| P/E Ratio:Low | 12 | 10 | 10 | 12 | 14 | 14 | 16 | 15 | 10 | 10 |
| **Income Statement Analysis** (Million $) | | | | | | | | | | |
| Revenue | 13,325 | 13,032 | 13,583 | 13,120 | 12,137 | 11,690 | 9,758 | 9,827 | 8,482 | 9,634 |
| Depreciation | 840 | 791 | 717 | 645 | 621 | 584 | 551 | 529 | 495 | 526 |
| Maintenance | NA | NA | NA | NA | NA | NA | NA | 353 | 387 | 430 |
| Fixed Charges Coverage | 3.48 | 3.10 | 3.14 | 3.49 | 2.97 | 3.19 | 2.64 | 3.13 | 3.25 | 3.46 |
| Construction Credits | 24.0 | 23.0 | 16.0 | 18.0 | 12.0 | 16.0 | 43.0 | 27.0 | 14.0 | 9.00 |
| Effective Tax Rate | 35.6% | 33.6% | 36.2% | 31.8% | 34.6% | 34.6% | 33.1% | 37.5% | 35.6% | 38.9% |
| Net Income | 992 | 868 | 922 | 925 | 738 | 732 | 549 | 525 | 680 | 696 |
| S&P Core Earnings | 1,035 | 893 | 329 | 800 | 635 | 621 | 421 | 370 | 106 | 141 |
| **Balance Sheet & Other Financial Data** (Million $) | | | | | | | | | | |
| Gross Property | 29,722 | 27,921 | 25,993 | 24,698 | 23,028 | 21,467 | 20,394 | 19,294 | 18,000 | 16,630 |
| Capital Expenditures | 2,014 | 2,179 | 2,318 | 1,928 | 1,847 | 1,617 | 1,359 | 1,292 | 1,216 | 1,104 |
| Net Property | 23,863 | 22,464 | 20,874 | 19,914 | 18,445 | 17,112 | 16,106 | 15,225 | 13,330 | 12,136 |
| Capitalization:Long Term Debt | 10,891 | 10,081 | 9,462 | 7,846 | 8,537 | 7,641 | 6,807 | 6,769 | 6,206 | 5,542 |
| Capitalization:% Long Term Debt | 49.6 | 49.6 | 49.4 | 46.4 | 51.6 | 51.1 | 49.1 | 51.3 | 50.3 | 48.3 |
| Capitalization:Preferred | Nil | Nil | Nil | Nil | Nil | Nil | Nil | Nil | Nil | 250 |
| Capitalization:% Preferred | Nil | Nil | Nil | Nil | Nil | Nil | Nil | Nil | Nil | 2.18 |
| Capitalization:Common | 11,061 | 10,249 | 9,698 | 9,076 | 8,004 | 7,310 | 7,054 | 6,423 | 5,921 | 5,690 |
| Capitalization:% Common | 50.4 | 50.4 | 50.6 | 53.6 | 48.4 | 48.9 | 50.9 | 48.7 | 48.0 | 49.6 |
| Total Capital | 21,957 | 21,061 | 24,159 | 21,430 | 20,677 | 18,637 | 17,626 | 16,406 | 15,037 | 13,835 |
| % Operating Ratio | 88.2 | 88.8 | 91.6 | 89.4 | 89.5 | 90.3 | 90.3 | 88.8 | 74.1 | 88.1 |
| % Earned on Net Property | 9.2 | 8.8 | 8.1 | 9.6 | 7.1 | 7.0 | 5.9 | 6.4 | 8.3 | 9.4 |
| % Return on Revenue | 7.4 | 6.7 | 6.8 | 7.1 | 6.1 | 6.3 | 5.6 | 5.3 | 8.0 | 7.2 |
| % Return on Invested Capital | 7.5 | 7.3 | 5.3 | 6.9 | 6.6 | 6.7 | 5.9 | 7.3 | 7.8 | 8.3 |
| % Return on Common Equity | 9.3 | 8.7 | 9.8 | 11.0 | 9.4 | 10.0 | 7.9 | 8.5 | 11.5 | 12.2 |

Data as orig reptd.; bef. results of disc opers/spec. items. Per share data adj. for stk. divs.; EPS diluted. E-Estimated. NA-Not Available. NM-Not Meaningful. NR-Not Ranked. UR-Under Review.

**Office:** 4 Irving Place, New York, NY 10003-3502.
**Telephone:** 212-460-4600.
**Email:** corpcom@coned.com
**Website:** http://www.coned.com

**Chrmn, Pres & CEO:** K. Burke
**CFO:** R.N. Hoglund
**Treas:** S. Sanders
**Secy:** C. Sobin

**General Counsel:** E.D. Moore
**Board Members:** K. Burke, V. A. Calarco, G. Campbell, Jr., G. J. Davis, M. J. Del Giudice, E. Futter, J. F. Hennessy, III, S. Hernandez-Pinero, J. F. Killian, E. R. McGrath, M. W. Ranger, L. F. Sutherland

**Founded:** 1884
**Domicile:** New York
**Employees:** 15,180

# CONSOL Energy Inc.

**STANDARD &POOR'S**

| S&P Recommendation HOLD ★★★★★ | Price $35.29 (as of Nov 25, 2011) | 12-Mo. Target Price $49.00 | Investment Style Large-Cap Blend |
|---|---|---|---|

**GICS Sector** Energy
**Sub-Industry** Coal & Consumable Fuels

**Summary** The leading diversified fuel producer in the Appalachian Basin, CONSOL has 11 bituminous coal mining complexes in five states, with coal reserves of 4.5 billion tons, and is also the leading Appalachian gas producer, with proved reserves of 2.9 trillion cubic feet.

## Key Stock Statistics (Source S&P, Vickers, company reports)

| | | | | | |
|---|---|---|---|---|---|
| 52-Wk Range | $56.32– 30.56 | S&P Oper. EPS 2011**E** | 3.13 | Market Capitalization(B) | $8.006 | Beta | 1.52 |
| Trailing 12-Month EPS | $2.38 | S&P Oper. EPS 2012**E** | 4.15 | Yield (%) | 1.42 | S&P 3-Yr. Proj. EPS CAGR(%) | 20 |
| Trailing 12-Month P/E | 14.8 | P/E on S&P Oper. EPS 2011**E** | 11.3 | Dividend Rate/Share | $0.50 | S&P Credit Rating | BB |
| $10K Invested 5 Yrs Ago | $10,589 | Common Shares Outstg. (M) | 226.9 | Institutional Ownership (%) | 92 | | |

## Price Performance

30-Week Mov. Avg. · · ·   10-Week Mov. Avg. - -   ▬ GAAP Earnings vs. Previous Year   Volume Above Avg. STARS
12-Mo. Target Price ▬   Relative Strength —   ▲ Up   ▼ Down   ▶ No Change   Below Avg.

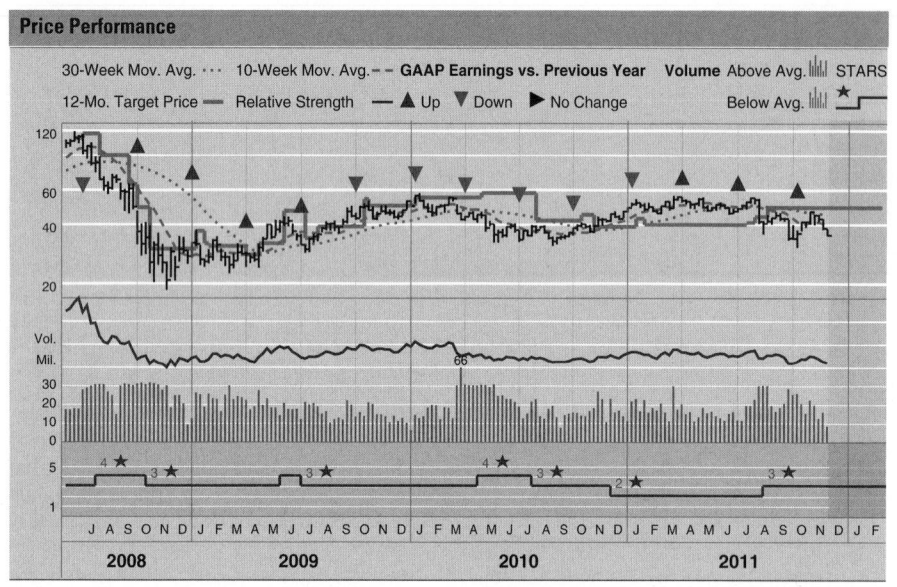

2008   2009   2010   2011

Options: ASE, CBOE, P, Ph

Analysis prepared by Equity Analyst **Jim Corridore** on Aug 29, 2011, when the stock traded at **$44.36**.

## Highlights

➤ Following a 13% advance in 2010, we look for 2011 sales to rise more than 12%. This forecast is based on our expectation for a 1% decline in coal volumes, led by a 6% projected decline in thermal coal. This volume decline is more than offset by a projected 15% rise in pricing. In addition, our sales projection is based on an expected increase in gas production but a nearly 15% decline in realized gas pricing. For 2012, we project about an 11% rise in revenue on both higher volume and pricing across CNX's platform.

➤ Following a 140 basis points (bps) decline in 2010, we think that the operating margin will widen this year on higher operating leverage resulting from better pricing at the company's coal operations and lower overhead expenses as a percentage of sales. In 2012, we see a wider operating margin on better pricing and volume.

➤ Assuming an effective tax rate of 26% in 2011 and 25% in 2012, we estimate EPS of $2.93 for 2011 and $4.06 for 2012.

## Investment Rationale/Risk

➤ Our hold recommendation reflects a positive view of the cash flow CNX is likely to receive from the agreed sale of a 50% interest in its Marcellus Shale acreage to Noble Energy (NBL 88, Hold) for $3.4 billion. This is offset by concerns we have about CNX's 2011 gas production schedule. Although we think that higher pricing will lead to better coal segment results, we also believe that the large natural gas exposure will offset some of this benefit.

➤ Risks to our recommendation and target price include lower-than-expected coal/natural gas pricing and volumes, a decline in CNX's productivity, and worse-than-forecast U.S. economic activity leading to lower-than-expected volume.

➤ Our 12-month target price of $49 is based on an EV/EBITDA multiple of 7X applied to our 2012 EBITDA estimate. This multiple is in line with coal and natural gas peers, reflecting our positive view of CNX's stated intention to use the cash from the Marcellus sale for dividends, debt paydown and stock repurchases.

## Qualitative Risk Assessment

| LOW | MEDIUM | HIGH |
|---|---|---|

Our risk assessment reflects the cyclical nature of the coal market, our view of unfavorable corporate governance practices related to takeover defenses, and the heavily regulated nature of the industry and its utilities end market, notwithstanding expected benefits from the pricing cycle and a rising market share.

## Quantitative Evaluations

**S&P Quality Ranking**                  **B**

| D | C | B- | B | B+ | A- | A | A+ |
|---|---|---|---|---|---|---|---|

**Relative Strength Rank**                  **WEAK**

21

LOWEST = 1                                          HIGHEST = 99

## Revenue/Earnings Data

**Revenue (Million $)**

| | 1Q | 2Q | 3Q | 4Q | Year |
|---|---|---|---|---|---|
| 2011 | 1,465 | 1,588 | 1,522 | -- | -- |
| 2010 | 1,218 | 1,264 | 1,319 | 1,337 | 5,138 |
| 2009 | 1,195 | 1,031 | 1,069 | 1,214 | 4,509 |
| 2008 | 951.1 | 1,200 | 1,137 | 1,198 | 4,486 |
| 2007 | 890.1 | 938.8 | 847.7 | 888.9 | 3,565 |
| 2006 | 944.3 | 884.4 | 808.4 | 907.2 | 3,544 |

**Earnings Per Share ($)**

| | | | | | |
|---|---|---|---|---|---|
| 2011 | 0.84 | 0.34 | 0.73 | E0.72 | E3.13 |
| 2010 | 0.54 | 0.29 | 0.33 | 0.46 | 1.60 |
| 2009 | 1.08 | 0.62 | 0.48 | 0.77 | 2.95 |
| 2008 | 0.41 | 0.54 | 0.49 | 0.97 | 2.40 |
| 2007 | 0.61 | 0.83 | -0.03 | 0.04 | 1.45 |
| 2006 | 0.67 | 0.57 | 0.27 | 0.69 | 2.20 |

Fiscal year ended Dec. 31. Next earnings report expected: Mid January. EPS Estimates based on S&P Operating Earnings; historical GAAP earnings are as reported.

## Dividend Data (Dates: mm/dd Payment Date: mm/dd/yy)

| Amount ($) | Date Decl. | Ex-Div. Date | Stk. of Record | Payment Date |
|---|---|---|---|---|
| 0.100 | 01/28 | 02/04 | 02/08 | 02/18/11 |
| 0.100 | 04/29 | 05/11 | 05/13 | 05/24/11 |
| 0.100 | 07/29 | 08/08 | 08/10 | 08/22/11 |
| 0.125 | 10/27 | 11/08 | 11/11 | 11/25/11 |

Dividends have been paid since 1999. Source: Company reports.

---

**Please read the Required Disclosures and Analyst Certification on the last page of this report.**

**The McGraw·Hill Companies**

# CONSOL Energy Inc.

STANDARD
&POOR'S

## Business Summary August 29, 2011

CORPORATE OVERVIEW. Through expansion projects and acquisitions, CONSOL Energy has grown from a single fuel mining company formed in 1860 into a multi-energy producer of coal and natural gas. CNX produces high Btu coal and natural gas, two fuels that collectively generate two-thirds of all U.S. electric power, from reserves located mainly east of the Mississippi River.

The company's coal operations (CNX Coal) includes 13 active mining complexes in the U.S., selling steam coal to power generators and metallurgical coal to metal and coke producers. The company had an estimated 4.4 billion tons of proven and probable coal reserves at the end of 2010, nearly all of which was located east of the Mississippi River. About 63% of CNX's reserves are in Northern Appalachia, with 18% in the Midwest, 12.5% in Central Appalachia, 4.5% in the western U.S., and 2% in western Canada. In addition, about 13% of reserves are metallurgical quality, while 87% are steam coal grade reserves. The company is a major fuel supplier to the electric power industry in the northeast quadrant of the U.S. Coal produced at CNX's mines is transported to customers via railroad cars, barges, trucks and conveyor belts, or by a combination of such methods. In 2010, the company sold 63.7 million produced tons of coal, up from 58.1 million tons in 2009, but lower than the 66.1 million tons in 2008. Approximately 89% of coal produced in 2010 was sold under contracts with terms of one year or more. The average sales price per produced ton sold in 2010 was $61.21, versus $58.42 realized in 2009. No cus-

tomer accounted for more than 10% of revenue in 2010.

As of the end of December 2010, CNX's natural gas operations controlled over 3.7 trillion cubic feet of proven developed and undeveloped natural gas resources. This is up from 1.9 trillion cubic feet in 2009 and is a result of the purchase of the remaining CNX Gas that was not already owned and the natural gas assets of Dominion Resources, both completed in April 2010. In addition, CNX also controlled over 5 million proven and unproven acres and more than 12,500 producing natural gas wells. The company's natural gas growth strategy focuses on well development in the Marcellus Shale basin, located in Pennsylvania and West Virginia. CNX also has natural gas acreage in Kentucky, Indiana and Illinois. Lastly, CNX also has coalbed methane (CBM) operations. CBM produces pipeline quality gas that is found in coal seams, usually in formations at depths of less than 2,500 feet, versus conventional natural gas fields with depths of up to 15,000 feet. In 2010, CNX produced over 127 Bcf of gas at an average price of $4.53 per Mcf, versus 94.4 Bcf at $4.15 per Mcf in 2009.

## Company Financials Fiscal Year Ended Dec. 31

| Per Share Data ($) | 2010 | 2009 | 2008 | 2007 | 2006 | 2005 | 2004 | 2003 | 2002 | 2001 |
|---|---|---|---|---|---|---|---|---|---|---|
| Tangible Book Value | 13.02 | 9.86 | 8.10 | 6.77 | 5.84 | 5.54 | 2.59 | NM | 1.03 | 2.23 |
| Cash Flow | 4.23 | 5.37 | 4.53 | 3.24 | 3.80 | 4.54 | 2.17 | 1.40 | 1.74 | 2.71 |
| Earnings | 1.60 | 2.95 | 2.40 | 1.45 | 2.20 | 3.13 | 0.64 | -0.05 | 0.08 | 1.17 |
| S&P Core Earnings | 1.78 | 2.97 | 2.05 | 1.02 | 1.88 | 2.05 | 0.69 | 0.04 | 0.03 | 0.98 |
| Dividends | 0.40 | 0.40 | 0.40 | 0.31 | 0.28 | 0.28 | 0.28 | 0.28 | 0.42 | 0.56 |
| Payout Ratio | 25% | 14% | 17% | 21% | 13% | 9% | 44% | NM | NM | 48% |
| Prices:High | 58.00 | 53.50 | 119.10 | 74.18 | 49.09 | 39.91 | 21.95 | 13.40 | 14.16 | 21.24 |
| Prices:Low | 31.08 | 22.47 | 18.50 | 29.15 | 28.07 | 18.58 | 10.12 | 7.28 | 4.90 | 9.15 |
| P/E Ratio:High | 36 | 18 | 50 | 51 | 22 | 13 | 35 | NM | NM | 18 |
| P/E Ratio:Low | 19 | 8 | 8 | 20 | 13 | 6 | 16 | NM | NM | 8 |

| Income Statement Analysis (Million $) | | | | | | | | | | |
|---|---|---|---|---|---|---|---|---|---|---|
| Revenue | 5,139 | 4,509 | 4,486 | 3,565 | 3,544 | 3,378 | 2,690 | 2,157 | 2,138 | 2,298 |
| Operating Income | NA | 1,180 | 1,008 | 628 | 743 | 511 | 308 | 181 | 222 | 347 |
| Depreciation | 572 | 441 | 394 | 329 | 296 | 262 | 280 | 242 | 263 | 243 |
| Interest Expense | 205 | 31.4 | 36.2 | 45.4 | 25.1 | 27.3 | 31.4 | 34.5 | 46.2 | 57.6 |
| Pretax Income | 468 | 788 | 726 | 429 | 551 | 655 | 82.6 | -33.5 | -40.4 | 240 |
| Effective Tax Rate | NA | 28.1% | 33.1% | 31.7% | 20.4% | 9.83% | NM | NM | NM | 23.6% |
| Net Income | 347 | 540 | 442 | 268 | 409 | 581 | 115 | -12.6 | 11.7 | 184 |
| S&P Core Earnings | 387 | 544 | 377 | 190 | 349 | 381 | 125 | 6.95 | 3.70 | 154 |

| Balance Sheet & Other Financial Data (Million $) | | | | | | | | | | |
|---|---|---|---|---|---|---|---|---|---|---|
| Cash | 32.8 | 65.6 | 139 | 41.7 | 224 | 341 | 6.42 | 6.51 | 11.5 | 16.6 |
| Current Assets | 1,115 | 941 | 984 | 683 | 914 | 998 | 470 | 471 | 623 | 566 |
| Total Assets | 12,071 | 7,725 | 7,370 | 6,208 | 5,663 | 5,088 | 4,196 | 4,319 | 4,293 | 3,895 |
| Current Liabilities | 1,665 | 1,429 | 1,512 | 1,016 | 740 | 804 | 705 | 825 | 814 | 934 |
| Long Term Debt | 3,129 | 423 | 468 | 489 | 493 | 438 | 426 | 442 | 488 | 231 |
| Common Equity | 2,944 | 1,786 | 1,462 | 1,214 | 984 | 1,025 | 469 | 291 | 162 | 352 |
| Total Capital | 6,090 | 2,447 | 2,143 | 1,866 | 1,612 | 1,557 | 895 | 733 | 650 | 583 |
| Capital Expenditures | 1,154 | 920 | 1,062 | 743 | 659 | 523 | 411 | 291 | 295 | 214 |
| Cash Flow | 919 | 981 | 837 | 597 | 705 | 843 | 396 | 230 | 275 | 427 |
| Current Ratio | 0.7 | 0.7 | 0.7 | 0.7 | 1.2 | 1.2 | 0.7 | 0.6 | 0.8 | 0.6 |
| % Long Term Debt of Capitalization | 51.4 | 17.3 | 21.9 | 26.2 | 30.6 | 28.2 | 47.6 | 60.3 | 75.1 | 39.6 |
| % Net Income of Revenue | 6.8 | 12.0 | 9.9 | 7.5 | 12.1 | 17.2 | 4.3 | NM | 0.5 | 8.0 |
| % Return on Assets | 3.5 | 7.2 | 6.5 | 4.5 | 7.6 | 12.5 | 2.7 | NM | NM | 4.7 |
| % Return on Equity | 14.7 | 33.2 | 33.1 | 23.5 | 40.7 | 77.7 | 30.3 | NM | NM | 60.6 |

Data as orig reptd.; bef. results of disc opers/spec. items. Per share data adj. for stk. divs.; EPS diluted. E-Estimated. NA-Not Available. NM-Not Meaningful. NR-Not Ranked. UR-Under Review.

**Office:** 1000 Consol Energy Dr, Canonsburg, PA 15317-6506.
**Telephone:** 724-485-4000.
**Website:** http://www.consolenergy.com
**Chrmn & CEO:** J.B. Harvey

**Pres:** N.J. Deluliis
**Vice Chrmn:** J.L. Whitmire, III
**Investor Contact:** W.J. Lyons
**EVP, CFO & Chief Acctg Officer:** W.J. Lyons

**Board Members:** J. E. Altmeyer, W. E. Davis, R. K. Gupta, P. A. Hammick, D. C. Hardesty, Jr., J. B. Harvey, J. T. Mills, W. P. Powell, J. L. Whitmire, III, J. T. Williams

**Founded:** 1991
**Domicile:** Delaware
**Employees:** 8,630

The McGraw-Hill Companies

# Constellation Brands Inc

STANDARD &POOR'S

| S&P Recommendation | **BUY** ★★★★☆ | Price $17.98 (as of Nov 25, 2011) | 12-Mo. Target Price $24.00 | Investment Style Large-Cap Growth |

**GICS Sector** Consumer Staples
**Sub-Industry** Distillers & Vintners

**Summary** This leading international producer and marketer of alcoholic beverages has a broad portfolio of wine, imported beer, and distilled spirits brands.

## Key Stock Statistics (Source S&P, Vickers, company reports)

| | | | | | | | |
|---|---|---|---|---|---|---|---|
| 52-Wk Range | $23.19–16.42 | S&P Oper. EPS 2012E | 2.05 | Market Capitalization(B) | $3.216 | Beta | 1.01 |
| Trailing 12-Month EPS | $3.08 | S&P Oper. EPS 2013E | 2.21 | Yield (%) | Nil | S&P 3-Yr. Proj. EPS CAGR(%) | 6 |
| Trailing 12-Month P/E | 5.8 | P/E on S&P Oper. EPS 2012E | 8.8 | Dividend Rate/Share | Nil | S&P Credit Rating | BB+ |
| $10K Invested 5 Yrs Ago | $6,507 | Common Shares Outstg. (M) | 202.4 | Institutional Ownership (%) | 91 | | |

## Price Performance

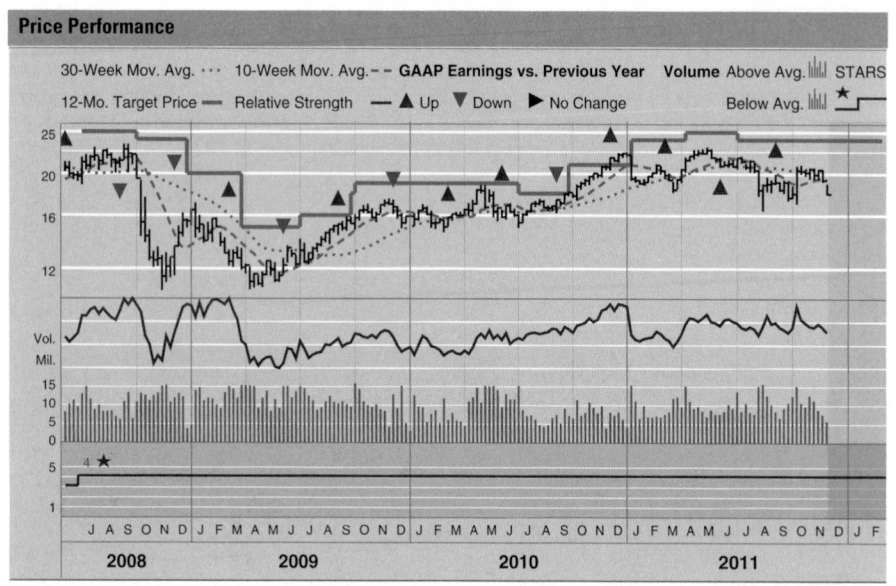

30-Week Mov. Avg. ··· 10-Week Mov. Avg. -- GAAP Earnings vs. Previous Year   Volume Above Avg. STARS
12-Mo. Target Price — Relative Strength — ▲ Up ▼ Down ▶ No Change   Below Avg. ★

Options: ASE, CBOE, P, Ph

Analysis prepared by Equity Analyst **Esther Kwon, CFA** on Oct 06, 2011, when the stock traded at **$20.22**.

## Highlights

▶ Following about a 1% sales decline in FY 11 (Feb.), on divestitures of the U.K. cider and Australian and U.K. wine business, we see FY 12 net revenues from continuing operations flat to up slightly as focus brands' volumes rise with modest pricing gains. Including the divesture of the Australian and U.K. wine business, we project revenues will fall approximately 19%. We forecast widening gross margins on a more favorable product mix.

▶ In FY 11, STZ's 50/50 joint venture with Grupo Modelo, Crown Imports, continued to face softness on market share losses, but improved in the second half, resulting in equity earnings rising slightly for the year. For FY 12, while we expect continued momentum in volumes and market share gains, we project the joint venture's earnings will be flat to down slightly on increased investment spending.

▶ On projected lower interest expense and an effective tax rate of about 27%, versus 31% in FY 11, we see FY 12 EPS of $2.05, up from FY 10's operating EPS of $1.87. In November 2010, STZ completed its $300 million accelerated share buyback, and in April 2011, its board authorized a new $500 million share repurchase program.

## Investment Rationale/Risk

▶ We view STZ's actions to move away from acquisitions, reduce debt, and focus on premium wines favorably. In December 2010, STZ entered into an agreement to sell its struggling Australian and U.K. wine business to a private equity firm for cash proceeds of about $230 million and a 20% equity stake. The transaction closed at the end of January 2011. With STZ's move away from acquisitions and a focus on debt reduction, we see free cash flow of between $600 million and $650 million for FY 12. Moreover, we see STZ as a beneficiary of a resumption of consumer trade-up to premium wines and an improvement in sales in the on-premise channel (restaurants, bars, etc.). We view the shares' valuation as attractive at a significant discount to peers.

▶ Risks to our recommendation and target price include higher commodity costs, increased discounting, and weakness in consumer demand.

▶ Our 12-month target price of $24 is based on a multiple of approximately 11X our FY 13 EPS estimate of $2.21. We think a discount to the historical average of over 13X and current forward peer average of over 17X is appropriate amid a backdrop of slow economic growth.

## Qualitative Risk Assessment

| LOW | MEDIUM | HIGH |

STZ operates in an industry that we believe has demonstrated stable revenue streams. This is offset by our corporate governance concerns relating to STZ's dual class stock structure with unequal voting rights.

## Quantitative Evaluations

**S&P Quality Ranking** B-

| D | C | B- | B | B+ | A- | A | A+ |

**Relative Strength Rank** MODERATE

39

LOWEST = 1   HIGHEST = 99

## Revenue/Earnings Data

**Revenue (Million $)**

| | 1Q | 2Q | 3Q | 4Q | Year |
|---|---|---|---|---|---|
| 2012 | 635.3 | 690.2 | -- | -- | -- |
| 2011 | 787.5 | 862.8 | 966.4 | 715.3 | 3,332 |
| 2010 | 791.6 | 876.8 | 987.7 | 708.7 | 3,365 |
| 2009 | 931.8 | 956.5 | 1,031 | 735.1 | 3,655 |
| 2008 | 901.2 | 1,168 | 1,406 | 884.4 | 3,773 |
| 2007 | 1,156 | 1,418 | 1,501 | 1,142 | 5,216 |

**Earnings Per Share ($)**

| | | | | | |
|---|---|---|---|---|---|
| 2012 | 0.35 | 0.76 | E0.53 | E0.36 | E2.05 |
| 2011 | 0.22 | 0.43 | 0.65 | 1.19 | 2.62 |
| 2010 | 0.03 | 0.45 | 0.20 | -0.23 | 0.45 |
| 2009 | 0.20 | -0.11 | 0.38 | -1.88 | -1.40 |
| 2008 | 0.13 | 0.34 | 0.55 | -3.92 | -2.83 |
| 2007 | 0.36 | 0.28 | 0.45 | 0.29 | 1.38 |

Fiscal year ended Feb. 28. Next earnings report expected: Early January. EPS Estimates based on S&P Operating Earnings; historical GAAP earnings are as reported.

## Dividend Data

No cash dividends have been paid.

# Constellation Brands Inc

## Business Summary October 06, 2011

Constellation Brands, Inc. (STZ) engages in the production and marketing of beverage alcohol with a portfolio of brands across the wine, spirits, and imported beer categories in the United States, Canada, the United Kingdom, Australia, and New Zealand. The company operates in two business divisions, Constellation Wines (branded wine, spirits and other) and Crown Imports (imported beer).

The Constellation Wines segment produces and markets wine worldwide. It sells various wine brands across various categories (table wine, sparkling wine and dessert wine) and price points (popular, premium, super-premium, and fine wine). The portfolio of super-premium and fine wines is supported by vineyard holdings in the U.S., Canada, Australia, and New Zealand. Constellation Wines produces and markets wine in the U.S., Canada, Australia and New Zealand and markets wine in the U.K. Wine produced by the company in the U.S. is primarily marketed domestically and in the U.K. and Canada. Wine

produced in Australia and New Zealand is primarily marketed domestically and in the U.S., Canada and U.K., while wine produced in Canada is primarily marketed domestically. In addition, Constellation Wines exports its wine products to other major wine consuming markets of the world.

Constellation Wines' primary wine brands include Robert Mondavi Brands, Franciscan Estate, Wild Horse, Simi, Toasted Head, Estancia, Clos du Bois, Blackstone, Ravenswood, Black Box, Vendange, Arbor Mist, Inniskillin, Kim Crawford, Ruffino, Nobilo, Jackson-Triggs, Alice White, Hardys, Banrock Station, Stowells, and Kumala. Constellation Wines also produces and sells Paul Masson Grande Amber Brandy, a brand in the brandy/cognac category.

## Company Financials Fiscal Year Ended Feb. 28

| Per Share Data ($) | 2011 | 2010 | 2009 | 2008 | 2007 | 2006 | 2005 | 2004 | 2003 | 2002 |
|---|---|---|---|---|---|---|---|---|---|---|
| Tangible Book Value | NM | NM | NM | NM | NM | NM | NM | NM | 0.39 | NM |
| Cash Flow | 3.24 | 1.26 | -0.69 | -2.07 | 1.95 | 1.86 | 1.59 | 1.39 | 1.42 | 1.08 |
| Earnings | 2.62 | 0.45 | -1.40 | -2.83 | -1.38 | 1.36 | 1.19 | 1.03 | 1.10 | 0.79 |
| S&P Core Earnings | 2.79 | 0.87 | -0.04 | 1.13 | 1.41 | 1.24 | 1.02 | 0.96 | 0.97 | 0.66 |
| Dividends | NA | Nil | Nil | Nil | Nil | Nil | Nil | Nil | Nil | Nil |
| Payout Ratio | NA | Nil | Nil | Nil | Nil | Nil | Nil | Nil | Nil | Nil |
| Calendar Year | 2010 | 2009 | 2008 | 2007 | 2006 | 2005 | 2004 | 2003 | 2002 | 2001 |
| Prices:High | 22.52 | 17.56 | 23.81 | 29.17 | 29.14 | 31.60 | 23.91 | 17.33 | 16.00 | 11.63 |
| Prices:Low | 14.60 | 10.72 | 10.66 | 18.83 | 23.32 | 21.15 | 14.65 | 10.95 | 10.53 | 6.63 |
| P/E Ratio:High | 9 | 39 | NM | NM | 22 | 23 | 20 | 17 | 15 | 15 |
| P/E Ratio:Low | 6 | 24 | NM | NM | 18 | 16 | 12 | 11 | 10 | 8 |

### Income Statement Analysis (Million $)

| | 2011 | 2010 | 2009 | 2008 | 2007 | 2006 | 2005 | 2004 | 2003 | 2002 |
|---|---|---|---|---|---|---|---|---|---|---|
| Revenue | 3,332 | 3,365 | 3,655 | 3,773 | 5,216 | 4,603 | 4,088 | 3,552 | 2,732 | 2,821 |
| Operating Income | 668 | 721 | 711 | 704 | 895 | 840 | 689 | 601 | 470 | 394 |
| Depreciation | 134 | 156 | 150 | 160 | 140 | 128 | 104 | 82.0 | 60.1 | 51.9 |
| Interest Expense | 195 | 266 | 316 | 342 | 269 | 190 | 138 | 145 | 105 | 114 |
| Pretax Income | 551 | 259 | -107 | -441 | 535 | 477 | 432 | 344 | 335 | 230 |
| Effective Tax Rate | NA | 61.7% | NM | NM | 38.0% | 31.8% | 36.0% | 36.0% | 39.3% | 40.0% |
| Net Income | 560 | 99.3 | -301 | -613 | 332 | 325 | 276 | 220 | 203 | 138 |
| S&P Core Earnings | 594 | 190 | -10.7 | 243 | 334 | 288 | 230 | 199 | 181 | 115 |

### Balance Sheet & Other Financial Data (Million $)

| | 2011 | 2010 | 2009 | 2008 | 2007 | 2006 | 2005 | 2004 | 2003 | 2002 |
|---|---|---|---|---|---|---|---|---|---|---|
| Cash | 9.20 | 43.5 | 13.1 | 20.5 | 33.5 | 10.9 | 17.6 | 37.1 | 13.8 | 8.96 |
| Current Assets | 2,083 | 2,589 | 2,535 | 3,199 | 3,023 | 2,701 | 2,734 | 2,071 | 1,330 | 1,231 |
| Total Assets | 7,168 | 8,094 | 8,037 | 10,053 | 9,438 | 7,401 | 7,804 | 5,559 | 3,196 | 3,069 |
| Current Liabilities | 663 | 1,373 | 1,326 | 1,718 | 1,591 | 1,298 | 1,138 | 1,030 | 585 | 595 |
| Long Term Debt | 3,137 | 3,277 | 3,971 | 4,649 | 3,715 | 2,516 | 3,205 | 1,779 | 1,192 | 1,293 |
| Common Equity | 2,552 | 2,576 | 1,908 | 2,766 | 3,418 | 2,975 | 2,780 | 2,378 | 1,207 | 956 |
| Total Capital | 5,705 | 6,041 | 6,423 | 7,950 | 7,607 | 5,862 | 6,375 | 4,344 | 2,544 | 2,412 |
| Capital Expenditures | 89.1 | 108 | 129 | 144 | 192 | 132 | 120 | 105 | 71.6 | 71.1 |
| Cash Flow | 693 | 249 | -151 | -454 | 467 | 444 | 370 | 297 | 263 | 190 |
| Current Ratio | 3.1 | 1.9 | 1.9 | 1.9 | 1.9 | 2.1 | 2.4 | 2.0 | 2.3 | 2.1 |
| % Long Term Debt of Capitalization | 55.0 | 54.3 | 61.8 | 58.5 | 48.8 | 42.9 | 50.3 | 41.0 | 46.8 | 53.6 |
| % Net Income of Revenue | 16.8 | 3.0 | NM | NM | 6.4 | 7.1 | 6.8 | 6.2 | 7.4 | 4.9 |
| % Return on Assets | 7.3 | 1.2 | NM | NM | 3.9 | 4.3 | 4.1 | 5.0 | 6.5 | 4.9 |
| % Return on Equity | 21.8 | 4.4 | NM | NM | 10.2 | 11.0 | 10.3 | 12.1 | 18.5 | 17.5 |

Data as orig reptd.; bef. results of disc opers/spec. items. Per share data adj. for stk. divs.; EPS diluted. E-Estimated. NA-Not Available. NM-Not Meaningful. NR-Not Ranked. UR-Under Review.

**Office:** 207 High Point Drive, Building 100, Victor, NY 14564.
**Telephone:** 585-678-7100.
**Website:** http://www.cbrands.com
**Chrmn:** R. Sands

**Pres & CEO:** R. Sands
**COO & EVP:** J. Wright
**EVP, CFO & Chief Acctg Officer:** R.P. Ryder
**EVP & Chief Admin Officer:** W.K. Wilson

**Investor Contact:** P. Yahn-Urlaub (585-218-3838)
**Board Members:** J. S. Fowden, B. A. Fromberg, J. K. Hauswald, J. A. Locke, III, R. Sands, R. Sands, P. L. Smith, K. E. Wandell, M. Zupan

**Founded:** 1972
**Domicile:** Delaware
**Employees:** 4,300

# Constellation Energy Group Inc.

**STANDARD &POOR'S**

| S&P Recommendation HOLD ★★★☆☆ | Price $37.97 (as of Nov 25, 2011) | 12-Mo. Target Price $40.00 | Investment Style Large-Cap Blend |
|---|---|---|---|

**GICS Sector** Utilities
**Sub-Industry** Independent Power Producers & Energy Traders

**Summary** This company, one of the largest wholesale power suppliers in the U.S. and the parent of Baltimore Gas and Electric, has agreed to be acquired by Exelon Corporation.

## Key Stock Statistics (Source S&P, Vickers, company reports)

| | | | | | | | |
|---|---|---|---|---|---|---|---|
| 52-Wk Range | $40.97–27.64 | S&P Oper. EPS 2011**E** | 3.06 | Market Capitalization(B) | $7.653 | Beta | 1.00 |
| Trailing 12-Month EPS | $2.01 | S&P Oper. EPS 2012**E** | 2.48 | Yield (%) | 2.53 | S&P 3-Yr. Proj. EPS CAGR(%) | -9 |
| Trailing 12-Month P/E | 18.9 | P/E on S&P Oper. EPS 2011**E** | 12.4 | Dividend Rate/Share | $0.96 | S&P Credit Rating | BBB- |
| $10K Invested 5 Yrs Ago | $6,585 | Common Shares Outstg. (M) | 201.6 | Institutional Ownership (%) | 72 | | |

## Price Performance

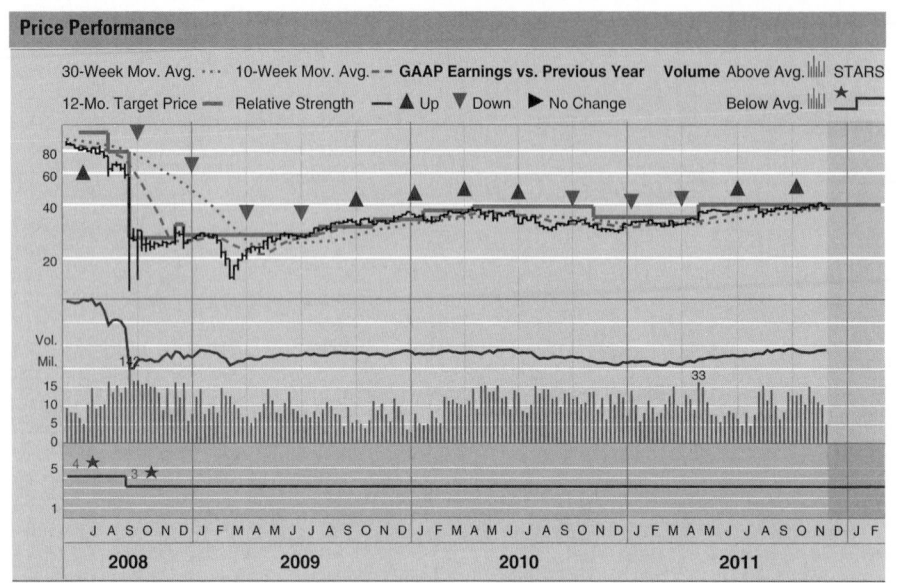

Options: ASE, CBOE, P, Ph

Analysis prepared by Equity Analyst **Justin McCann** on Oct 07, 2011, when the stock traded at **$37.07**.

### Highlights

➤ Subject to required approvals, the agreed-to merger with Exelon Corporation (EXC 41, Buy) is expected to close in the first quarter of 2012 and result in a company that would be the largest competitive energy producer in the U.S., and the second largest electric and gas distributor, with 6.6 million customers in three states. We expect the merger to be neutral to operating earnings in 2012 and more than 5% accretive to projected earnings for 2013.

➤ Operating EPS of $1.39 in the first half of 2011 was $0.75 below the year-earlier level, hurt by the impact of two severe ice storms in Texas that resulted in extended outages at the joint venture nuclear facilities, as well as by the timing of certain contract assignments at New Energy, where quarterly earnings are expected to have timing issues.

➤ For the second half of 2011, we expect results to reflect stronger earnings at New Energy, partially offset by the ongoing weakness in the power markets. While we look for standalone earnings to decline sharply in 2012 due to much lower generation margins, we expect a gradual recovery in 2013.

### Investment Rationale/Risk

➤ We believe the planned merger would, if approved, provide the scale and financial strength for the expansion of the combined company's presence in the competitive energy markets that neither company would have on its own, and leave it well positioned for a potential recovery in the power markets and/or regulations requiring a significant reduction in power generation emissions considered harmful by the EPA. The merger agreement's exchange ratio of 0.93 EXC shares for each CEG share represented an 18% premium to the 30-day average of their closing stock prices as of April 27.

➤ Risks to our recommendation and target price include the potential termination of the planned merger, prolonged weakness in the economy and power markets, and a sharp decline in the average P/E multiple of the group as a whole.

➤ Based on Exelon's current annual dividend of $2.10 per share, CEG shareholders would receive an approximate 103% increase over the current Constellation dividend. Given the uncertainties related to the successful completion of the merger, our target price of $40 reflects a 12% discount to our target price for Exelon, based on the terms of the merger agreement.

### Qualitative Risk Assessment

| LOW | MEDIUM | HIGH |
|---|---|---|

Our risk assessment reflects our view that the stability of earnings provided by CEG's regulated electric and gas utility operations is more than offset by the cyclical and volatile earnings of the unregulated merchant energy business, including power generation, energy, and energy-related marketing and trading.

### Quantitative Evaluations

**S&P Quality Ranking**    B

| D | C | B- | B | B+ | A- | A | A+ |
|---|---|---|---|---|---|---|---|

**Relative Strength Rank**    MODERATE

70

LOWEST = 1     HIGHEST = 99

### Revenue/Earnings Data

**Revenue (Million $)**

| | 1Q | 2Q | 3Q | 4Q | Year |
|---|---|---|---|---|---|
| 2011 | 3,570 | 3,360 | 3,521 | -- | -- |
| 2010 | 3,587 | 3,310 | 3,969 | 3,475 | 14,340 |
| 2009 | 4,303 | 3,864 | 4,028 | 3,404 | 15,599 |
| 2008 | 4,827 | 5,077 | 5,324 | 4,926 | 19,818 |
| 2007 | 5,111 | 4,876 | 5,856 | 5,349 | 21,193 |
| 2006 | 4,859 | 4,379 | 5,393 | 4,644 | 19,285 |

**Earnings Per Share ($)**

| | | | | | |
|---|---|---|---|---|---|
| 2011 | 0.35 | 0.49 | 0.36 | E0.86 | E3.06 |
| 2010 | 0.95 | 0.36 | -6.99 | 0.79 | -4.90 |
| 2009 | -0.62 | 0.04 | 0.69 | 21.96 | 22.18 |
| 2008 | 0.81 | 0.95 | -1.26 | -7.75 | -7.34 |
| 2007 | 1.08 | 0.64 | 1.37 | 1.42 | 4.51 |
| 2006 | 0.56 | 0.41 | 1.69 | 1.46 | 4.12 |

Fiscal year ended Dec. 31. Next earnings report expected: Early February. EPS Estimates based on S&P Operating Earnings; historical GAAP earnings are as reported.

### Dividend Data (Dates: mm/dd Payment Date: mm/dd/yy)

| Amount ($) | Date Decl. | Ex-Div. Date | Stk. of Record | Payment Date |
|---|---|---|---|---|
| 0.240 | 05/27 | 06/08 | 06/10 | 07/01/11 |
| 0.240 | 07/22 | 09/08 | 09/12 | 10/03/11 |
| 0.240 | 10/21 | 12/08 | 12/12 | 01/03/12 |
| 0.240 | 10/21 | 03/08 | 03/12 | 04/02/12 |

Dividends have been paid since 1910. Source: Company reports.

# Constellation Energy Group Inc.

**STANDARD**
**&POOR'S**

## Business Summary October 07, 2011

CORPORATE OVERVIEW. Constellation Energy is a major U.S. wholesale power seller and one of the largest competitive suppliers of electricity to large commercial and industrial customers in North America. It is also the holding company for Baltimore Gas & Electric Company, a regulated utility.

IMPACT OF MAJOR DEVELOPMENTS. On April 28, 2011, Constellation Energy announced a definitive merger agreement with Exelon (EXC 41, Buy), the largest nuclear operator in the U.S., and the utility holding company for Chicago-based Commonwealth Edison and Philadelphia-based PECO Energy. Under the terms of the stock-for-stock agreement, Constellation Energy shareholders would receive 0.93 of an EXC share for each CEG share. Upon the close of the merger, which is subject to approvals, CEG shareholders would have an approximate 22% interest in the combined company, which would maintain the Exelon name, and CEG would have four directors on the 16-member board. CEG's chairman, president and CEO, Mayo A. Shattuck III, would become executive chairman of the combined company, and Christopher M. Crane, Exelon's president and COO, would be the president and CEO.

On November 3, 2010, Constellation Energy completed the $140 million sale (agreed to on October 26, 2010) of its 50% interest in the UniStar Nuclear Energy joint venture to its partner EDF Development, Inc., a wholly owned subsidiary of Electricite de France. UniStar Nuclear Energy was created for the development of new nuclear sites, and the agreement included the transfer of both the existing site at Calvert Cliffs 3 and the potential new sites at their other jointly held nuclear facilities. Under the terms of their agreement, Constellation terminated its rights to the asset put option EDF had provided for CEG to sell to EDF its non-nuclear generation assets for an amount up to $2 billion, and EDF transferred to Constellation 3.5 million of the shares it had in CEG and relinquished its seat on Constellation's board.

On November 6, 2009, CEG completed a transaction (agreed to on December 17, 2008) with EDF, in which EDF acquired a 49.99% interest in the Constellation Energy Nuclear Group (CENG) for $4.5 billion. The agreement was announced on the same day that CEG and MidAmerican Energy Holdings, a privately held subsidiary of Berkshire Hathaway, announced that they had jointly agreed to terminate their merger agreement of September 19, 2008. The agreement with EDF (84%-owned by the French state and with a 9.5% stake in CEG) included an immediate $1 billion cash investment in the form of nonconvertible preferred stock, which was surrendered to Constellation Energy upon the completion of the transaction and credited against the $4.5 billion purchase price. EDF had also provided CEG with a two-year asset put option to sell to EDF its non-nuclear generation assets with a value of up to $2 billion.

## Company Financials Fiscal Year Ended Dec. 31

| Per Share Data ($) | 2010 | 2009 | 2008 | 2007 | 2006 | 2005 | 2004 | 2003 | 2002 | 2001 |
|---|---|---|---|---|---|---|---|---|---|---|
| Tangible Book Value | 38.25 | 40.14 | 15.08 | 27.46 | 24.66 | 26.76 | 25.99 | 23.81 | 22.71 | 23.44 |
| Earnings | -4.90 | 22.18 | -7.34 | 4.51 | 4.12 | 3.38 | 3.40 | 2.85 | 3.20 | 0.52 |
| S&P Core Earnings | -5.85 | -0.40 | -7.77 | 4.26 | 3.93 | 3.31 | 3.33 | 2.66 | 1.75 | 0.34 |
| Dividends | 0.96 | 0.96 | 1.91 | 1.74 | 1.51 | 1.34 | 1.14 | 1.04 | 0.96 | 0.48 |
| Payout Ratio | NM | 4% | NM | 39% | 37% | 40% | 34% | 36% | 30% | 92% |
| Prices:High | 38.73 | 36.55 | 107.97 | 104.29 | 70.20 | 62.60 | 44.90 | 39.61 | 32.38 | 50.14 |
| Prices:Low | 27.64 | 15.05 | 13.00 | 68.78 | 50.55 | 43.01 | 35.89 | 25.17 | 19.30 | 20.90 |
| P/E Ratio:High | NM | 2 | NM | 23 | 17 | 19 | 13 | 14 | 10 | 96 |
| P/E Ratio:Low | NM | 1 | NM | 15 | 12 | 13 | 11 | 9 | 6 | 40 |

| Income Statement Analysis (Million $) | 2010 | 2009 | 2008 | 2007 | 2006 | 2005 | 2004 | 2003 | 2002 | 2001 |
|---|---|---|---|---|---|---|---|---|---|---|
| Revenue | 14,340 | 15,599 | 19,818 | 21,193 | 19,285 | 17,132 | 12,550 | 9,703 | 4,703 | 3,928 |
| Depreciation | 660 | 1,258 | 560 | 558 | 524 | 542 | 526 | 479 | 481 | 419 |
| Maintenance | NA | NA | NA | NA | NA | NA | NA | NA | NA | NA |
| Fixed Charges Coverage | NA | 3.29 | 2.52 | 4.96 | 4.01 | 3.50 | 3.40 | 3.12 | 2.90 | 3.01 |
| Construction Credits | NA | NA | NA | NA | NA | NA | NA | NA | NA | NA |
| Effective Tax Rate | NM | 39.9% | NM | 33.9% | 31.9% | 25.2% | 22.6% | 36.2% | 37.1% | 31.5% |
| Net Income | -932 | 4,443 | -1,314 | 822 | 749 | 607 | 589 | 476 | 526 | 82.4 |
| S&P Core Earnings | -1,174 | -81.3 | -1,391 | 777 | 714 | 594 | 578 | 444 | 290 | 54.9 |

| Balance Sheet & Other Financial Data (Million $) | 2010 | 2009 | 2008 | 2007 | 2006 | 2005 | 2004 | 2003 | 2002 | 2001 |
|---|---|---|---|---|---|---|---|---|---|---|
| Gross Property | 13,589 | 12,535 | 15,729 | 14,513 | 13,680 | 14,403 | 14,315 | 13,580 | 12,354 | 11,862 |
| Capital Expenditures | 996 | 1,530 | 1,934 | 1,296 | 963 | 760 | 704 | 658 | 850 | 1,318 |
| Net Property | 9,279 | 8,454 | 10,717 | 9,767 | 9,222 | 10,067 | 10,087 | 9,602 | 7,957 | 7,700 |
| Capitalization:Long Term Debt | 4,639 | 5,004 | 5,289 | 4,851 | 4,222 | 4,559 | 5,003 | 5,229 | 4,804 | 2,903 |
| Capitalization:% Long Term Debt | 37.2 | 36.5 | 62.4 | 47.6 | 47.8 | 48.1 | 51.4 | 55.8 | 55.4 | 43.0 |
| Capitalization:Preferred | Nil | Nil | Nil | Nil | Nil | Nil | Nil | Nil | Nil | Nil |
| Capitalization:% Preferred | Nil | Nil | Nil | Nil | Nil | Nil | Nil | Nil | Nil | Nil |
| Capitalization:Common | 7,829 | 8,697 | 3,181 | 5,340 | 4,609 | 4,916 | 4,727 | 4,141 | 3,862 | 3,844 |
| Capitalization:% Common | 62.8 | 63.5 | 37.6 | 52.4 | 52.2 | 51.9 | 48.6 | 44.2 | 44.6 | 57.0 |
| Total Capital | 13,141 | 13,833 | 9,211 | 11,849 | 10,419 | 10,720 | 11,105 | 10,833 | 10,083 | 8,271 |
| % Operating Ratio | 105.9 | 110.9 | 94.7 | 95.6 | 94.7 | 94.5 | 92.2 | 91.6 | 87.2 | 78.3 |
| % Earned on Net Property | NM | 13.5 | 9.4 | 14.3 | 13.1 | 10.5 | 17.0 | 17.1 | 17.8 | 5.0 |
| % Return on Revenue | NM | 28.5 | NM | 3.9 | 3.9 | 3.5 | 4.7 | 4.9 | 11.2 | 2.1 |
| % Return on Invested Capital | NA | NM | 9.4 | 9.7 | 11.4 | 9.2 | 9.0 | 8.2 | 9.8 | 10.5 |
| % Return on Common Equity | NM | 74.8 | NM | 16.5 | 15.7 | 12.6 | 13.3 | 11.9 | 13.6 | 2.3 |

Data as orig reptd.; bef. results of disc opers/spec. items. Per share data adj. for stk. divs.; EPS diluted. E-Estimated. NA-Not Available. NM-Not Meaningful. NR-Not Ranked. UR-Under Review.

**Office:** 100 Constellation Way, Baltimore, MD 21202.
**Telephone:** 410-470-2800.
**Website:** http://www.constellation.com
**Chrmn, Pres & CEO:** M.A. Shattuck, III

**CFO:** J.W. Thayer
**Chief Acctg Officer & Cntlr:** B.P. Wright
**Treas:** J.E. Lowry
**Secy & General Counsel:** C.A. Berardesco

**Investor Contact:** K. Hadlock (410-864-6440)
**Board Members:** A. C. Berzin, J. T. Brady, J. R. Curtiss, F. A. Hrabowski, III, N. Lampton, R. J. Lawless, M. A. Shattuck, III, J. L. Skolds, M. D. Sullivan, Y. C. de Balmann

**Founded:** 1906
**Domicile:** Maryland
**Employees:** 7,600

The McGraw-Hill Companies

# Cooper Industries Plc

**STANDARD &POOR'S**

| S&P Recommendation HOLD ★★★☆☆ | Price $51.96 (as of Nov 25, 2011) | 12-Mo. Target Price $57.00 | Investment Style Large-Cap Growth |
| --- | --- | --- | --- |

**GICS Sector** Industrials
**Sub-Industry** Electrical Components & Equipment

**Summary** This company is a diversified worldwide manufacturer of electrical products, tools and hardware.

## Key Stock Statistics (Source S&P, Vickers, company reports)

| | | | | | |
| --- | --- | --- | --- | --- | --- |
| 52-Wk Range | $70.00–41.15 | S&P Oper. EPS 2011E | 3.81 | Market Capitalization(B) | $8.215 |
| Trailing 12-Month EPS | $4.87 | S&P Oper. EPS 2012E | 4.31 | Yield (%) | 2.23 |
| Trailing 12-Month P/E | 10.7 | P/E on S&P Oper. EPS 2011E | 13.6 | Dividend Rate/Share | $1.16 |
| $10K Invested 5 Yrs Ago | $12,536 | Common Shares Outstg. (M) | 158.1 | Institutional Ownership (%) | 84 |

| | |
| --- | --- |
| Beta | 1.55 |
| S&P 3-Yr. Proj. EPS CAGR(%) | 19 |
| S&P Credit Rating | NA |

## Price Performance

- 30-Week Mov. Avg. · · ·
- 10-Week Mov. Avg. – –
- GAAP Earnings vs. Previous Year
- Volume Above Avg. STARS
- 12-Mo. Target Price —
- Relative Strength —
- ▲ Up ▼ Down ▶ No Change
- Below Avg.

Options: ASE, CBOE, P, Ph

Analysis prepared by Equity Analyst **Efraim Levy, CFA** on Oct 28, 2011, when the stock traded at **$54.82**.

## Highlights

► Revenues in 2011 will not be directly comparable with those of 2010 because the tools segment was deconsolidated after the second quarter of last year. However, higher volume from continuing operations and restructuring and cost improvements should boost margins despite rising raw material costs and a higher effective tax rate. Our EPS estimates reflect the relatively low tax rates CBE enjoys from its transition to being an Irish corporation, as well as 2011's reduced share count. We expect sales to advance 6% in 2012.

► We expect EPS to rise to $3.81 in 2011, from $3.20 in 2010, excluding costs for the establishment of the tools joint venture. In 2012, we see EPS advancing to $4.31. Our estimates exclude any residual income that may be received from Belden Inc., as well as special items.

► Greater investment should make it more difficult to achieve free cash flow exceeding net income in 2011. Still, we think that cash flow will allow for share repurchases and acquisitions. Long-term debt, including current maturities, amounted to nearly 31% of total capital at the end of 2010. We believe its low debt level positions the company for potential acquisitions.

## Investment Rationale/Risk

► Based on our 2012 estimates, Cooper's P/E multiple, price-to-free cash flow ratio and projected net margin of 12.2% are in the middle to upper portion of peer group ranges. Possible exposure to asbestos liabilities stemming from the 2001 Federal-Mogul (FMO) bankruptcy filing remains a concern to us, but to a lesser degree than in the past. FMO has since emerged from bankruptcy protection.

► Risks to our recommendation and target price include weaker-than-expected industrial and economic demand, greater-than-expected raw material cost increases, and a higher tax rate than we forecast.

► Applying a multiple of about 12.5X to our 2012 EPS estimate of $4.31, which reflects peer and historical P/E multiple comparisons and our view of slowing economic growth, implies a value of about $54. Our DCF model, which assumes a weighted average cost of capital of 10.3%, a compound annual growth rate of 5.0% over the next 15 years, and a terminal growth rate of 3.0%, calculates intrinsic value of $60. Based on a combination of our P/E and DCF analyses, our 12-month target price is $57.

## Qualitative Risk Assessment

| LOW | MEDIUM | HIGH |
| --- | --- | --- |

Our risk assessment reflects our view of favorable growth prospects in markets CBE serves, and what we consider to be good corporate governance and a healthy balance sheet, offset by vulnerability to weaker-than-expected real GDP growth in the U.S. and abroad.

## Quantitative Evaluations

**S&P Quality Ranking** NR

| D | C | B- | B | B+ | A- | A | A+ |
| --- | --- | --- | --- | --- | --- | --- | --- |

**Relative Strength Rank** STRONG

81

LOWEST = 1   HIGHEST = 99

## Revenue/Earnings Data

### Revenue (Million $)

| | 1Q | 2Q | 3Q | 4Q | Year |
| --- | --- | --- | --- | --- | --- |
| 2011 | 1,278 | 1,369 | 1,390 | -- | -- |
| 2010 | 1,229 | 1,337 | 1,241 | 1,229 | 5,066 |
| 2009 | 1,257 | 1,270 | 1,286 | 1,257 | 5,070 |
| 2008 | 1,546 | 1,724 | 1,728 | 1,523 | 6,521 |
| 2007 | 1,394 | 1,464 | 1,501 | 1,544 | 5,903 |
| 2006 | 1,241 | 1,288 | 1,315 | 1,341 | 5,185 |

### Earnings Per Share ($)

| | | | | | |
| --- | --- | --- | --- | --- | --- |
| 2011 | 0.93 | 0.96 | 0.98 | E0.94 | E3.81 |
| 2010 | 0.70 | 0.25 | 0.85 | 0.72 | 2.64 |
| 2009 | 0.48 | 0.53 | 0.68 | 0.76 | 2.46 |
| 2008 | 0.86 | 0.92 | 1.08 | 0.65 | 3.51 |
| 2007 | 0.71 | 1.12 | 0.93 | 0.98 | 3.73 |
| 2006 | 0.57 | 0.64 | 0.69 | 0.69 | 2.58 |

Fiscal year ended Dec. 31. Next earnings report expected: Late January. EPS Estimates based on S&P Operating Earnings; historical GAAP earnings are as reported.

## Dividend Data (Dates: mm/dd Payment Date: mm/dd/yy)

| Amount ($) | Date Decl. | Ex-Div. Date | Stk. of Record | Payment Date |
| --- | --- | --- | --- | --- |
| 0.290 | 02/16 | 11/28 | 11/30 | 01/03/12 |

Dividends have been paid since 1947. Source: Company reports.

---

**Please read the Required Disclosures and Analyst Certification on the last page of this report.**

*The McGraw-Hill Companies*

# Cooper Industries Plc

## Business Summary October 28, 2011

**CORPORATE OVERVIEW.** Cooper Industries, a diversified, worldwide manufacturer of electrical products, tools and hardware, focuses on leveraging its strong brand name recognition by broadening its product line; strengthening its manufacturing and distribution systems to lower costs and improve customer service; expanding globally via acquisitions and joint ventures to participate in growing economies; and improving working capital efficiency and increasing cash flow to fuel future growth.

About 39% of sales in 2010 were outside the U.S.

The countries that generate the most international revenues for CBE are Canada, Germany, Mexico and the U.K. The company has several small joint ventures with operations in China.

Adjusted cash flow from operations in 2010 was $701 million, down from 2009's $752 million.

**CORPORATE STRATEGY.** The company's acquisition program resumed in 2006, with four acquisitions for approximately $280 million. CBE spent $336 million on acquisitions in 2007, $297 million in 2008, $61 million in 2009, and $113 million in 2010.

Capital spending totaled more than $115 million in 2007 and reached $137 million in 2008 before dipping to $127 million in 2009 and $99 million in 2010.

**IMPACT OF MAJOR DEVELOPMENTS.** In June 2010, Cooper and Danaher Corporation (DHR 45, Hold) formed a joint venture combining Cooper's tools business with certain tools businesses from Danaher's Tools and Components segment. The venture is called Apex Tool Group, LLC. Under the joint venture agreement, Cooper and Danaher each own a 50% share of the new company and have equal representation on the venture's board of directors.

Beginning in the third quarter of 2010, the tools segment was deconsolidated on Cooper's consolidated financial statements and reflected as an equity investment on Cooper's balance sheet. Its income was included as equity earnings from a joint venture on Cooper's consolidated income statement.

In October 2008, a U.S. bankruptcy court did not approve the Plan A settlement whereby Pneumo-Abex asbestos claims would be settled through the Federal Mogul Corp. Asbestos Trust. Previously, the court had approved Plan B, which called for Cooper to receive $138 million from the Federal Mogul bankruptcy estate, and cases would continue through the court system.

## Company Financials Fiscal Year Ended Dec. 31

| Per Share Data ($) | 2010 | 2009 | 2008 | 2007 | 2006 | 2005 | 2004 | 2003 | 2002 | 2001 |
|---|---|---|---|---|---|---|---|---|---|---|
| Tangible Book Value | 3.14 | 1.92 | 0.24 | 1.98 | 0.76 | 0.66 | 0.77 | 0.33 | 0.04 | 0.63 |
| Cash Flow | 3.47 | 3.32 | 4.32 | 4.37 | 3.27 | 2.74 | 2.40 | 2.11 | 1.79 | 2.36 |
| Earnings | 2.64 | 2.46 | 3.51 | 3.73 | 2.58 | 2.06 | 1.79 | 1.46 | 1.14 | 1.38 |
| Dividends | 1.08 | 0.50 | 1.00 | 0.84 | 0.74 | 0.74 | 0.70 | 0.70 | 0.70 | 0.70 |
| Payout Ratio | 41% | 20% | 28% | 23% | 29% | 36% | 39% | 48% | 61% | 51% |
| Prices:High | 59.65 | 44.99 | 53.25 | 59.05 | 48.06 | 37.88 | 34.22 | 29.43 | 23.51 | 30.23 |
| Prices:Low | 41.01 | 18.86 | 19.32 | 40.00 | 36.02 | 31.04 | 25.67 | 16.93 | 13.57 | 15.81 |
| P/E Ratio:High | 23 | 18 | 15 | 16 | 19 | 18 | 19 | 20 | 21 | 22 |
| P/E Ratio:Low | 16 | 8 | 6 | 11 | 14 | 15 | 14 | 12 | 12 | 11 |

| Income Statement Analysis (Million $) | 2010 | 2009 | 2008 | 2007 | 2006 | 2005 | 2004 | 2003 | 2002 | 2001 |
|---|---|---|---|---|---|---|---|---|---|---|
| Revenue | 5,066 | 5,070 | 6,521 | 5,903 | 5,185 | 4,730 | 4,463 | 4,061 | 3,961 | 4,210 |
| Operating Income | 839 | 720 | 1,073 | 971 | 811 | 671 | 614 | 516 | 516 | 662 |
| Depreciation | 140 | 146 | 143 | 118 | 112 | 111 | 118 | 121 | 122 | 186 |
| Interest Expense | 49.4 | 61.4 | 70.4 | 51.0 | 51.5 | 64.8 | 68.1 | 74.1 | 74.5 | 84.7 |
| Pretax Income | 530 | 483 | 807 | 826 | 648 | 495 | 429 | 347 | 280 | 316 |
| Effective Tax Rate | 16.3% | 14.3% | 23.7% | 16.2% | 25.2% | 21.0% | 20.7% | 20.8% | 23.7% | 17.4% |
| Net Income | 444 | 414 | 616 | 692 | 484 | 391 | 340 | 274 | 214 | 261 |

| Balance Sheet & Other Financial Data (Million $) | 2010 | 2009 | 2008 | 2007 | 2006 | 2005 | 2004 | 2003 | 2002 | 2001 |
|---|---|---|---|---|---|---|---|---|---|---|
| Cash | 1,035 | 382 | 281 | 327 | 424 | 453 | 653 | 464 | 302 | 11.5 |
| Current Assets | 2,491 | 1,902 | 2,198 | 2,303 | 2,194 | 2,131 | 2,219 | 1,961 | 1,689 | 1,651 |
| Total Assets | 6,669 | 5,984 | 6,165 | 6,134 | 5,375 | 5,215 | 5,341 | 4,965 | 4,688 | 4,611 |
| Current Liabilities | 1,026 | 955 | 1,462 | 1,635 | 1,499 | 1,161 | 1,828 | 1,022 | 960 | 1,106 |
| Long Term Debt | 1,420 | 923 | 932 | 910 | 703 | 1,003 | 699 | 1,337 | 1,281 | 1,107 |
| Common Equity | 3,206 | 2,963 | 2,607 | 2,842 | 2,475 | 2,205 | 2,287 | 2,118 | 2,002 | 2,023 |
| Total Capital | 4,627 | 3,888 | 3,815 | 3,752 | 3,178 | 3,208 | 2,985 | 3,455 | 3,283 | 3,130 |
| Capital Expenditures | 98.5 | 127 | 137 | 116 | 85.3 | 96.7 | 103 | 79.9 | 73.8 | 115 |
| Cash Flow | 584 | 559 | 759 | 810 | 596 | 502 | 457 | 396 | 335 | 448 |
| Current Ratio | 2.4 | 2.0 | 1.5 | 1.4 | 1.5 | 1.8 | 1.2 | 1.9 | 1.8 | 1.5 |
| % Long Term Debt of Capitalization | 30.7 | 23.7 | 24.4 | 24.3 | 22.1 | 31.3 | 23.4 | 38.7 | 39.0 | 35.4 |
| % Net Income of Revenue | 8.8 | 8.2 | 9.4 | 11.7 | 9.3 | 8.3 | 7.6 | 6.8 | 5.4 | 6.2 |
| % Return on Assets | 7.0 | 6.8 | 10.0 | 12.0 | 9.1 | 7.4 | 6.6 | 5.7 | 4.6 | 5.6 |
| % Return on Equity | 14.4 | 14.8 | 22.6 | 26.0 | 20.7 | 17.4 | 15.4 | 13.3 | 10.6 | 13.3 |

Data as orig reptd.; bef. results of disc opers/spec. items. Per share data adj. for stk. divs.; EPS diluted. E-Estimated. NA-Not Available. NM-Not Meaningful. NR-Not Ranked. UR-Under Review.

**Office:** 5 Fitzwilliam Square, Dublin, Ireland 2.
**Telephone:** 713-209-8400.
**Email:** info@cooperindustries.com
**Website:** http://www.cooperindustries.com

**Chrmn, Pres & CEO:** K.S. Hachigian
**COO:** L. Ulz
**SVP & CFO:** D.A. Barta
**SVP & General Counsel:** B.M. Taten

**Chief Acctg Officer & Cntlr:** R.L. Johnson
**Investor Contact:** T.A. Klebe
**Board Members:** S. G. Butler, I. J. Evans, K. S. Hachigian, L. A. Hill, L. D. Kingsley, J. J. Postl, D. F. Smith, G. B. Smith, M. S. Thompson

**Founded:** 1833
**Domicile:** Ireland
**Employees:** 24,795

# Corning Inc

**STANDARD &POOR'S**

| S&P Recommendation **BUY** ★★★★☆ | Price $13.27 (as of Nov 30, 2011) | 12-Mo. Target Price $16.00 | Investment Style Large-Cap Blend |
| --- | --- | --- | --- |

**GICS Sector** Information Technology
**Sub-Industry** Electronic Components

**Summary** GLW, once an old-line housewares company, is now a leading maker of glass substrates used by the electronics industry and fiber optic equipment used by the telecommunications industry.

## Key Stock Statistics (Source S&P, Vickers, company reports)

| | | | | | | | |
| --- | --- | --- | --- | --- | --- | --- | --- |
| 52-Wk Range | $23.43– 11.51 | S&P Oper. EPS 2011**E** | 1.82 | Market Capitalization(B) | $20.855 | Beta | 1.43 |
| Trailing 12-Month EPS | $2.12 | S&P Oper. EPS 2012**E** | 1.80 | Yield (%) | 2.26 | S&P 3-Yr. Proj. EPS CAGR(%) | 7 |
| Trailing 12-Month P/E | 6.3 | P/E on S&P Oper. EPS 2011**E** | 7.3 | Dividend Rate/Share | $0.30 | S&P Credit Rating | BBB+ |
| $10K Invested 5 Yrs Ago | $6,502 | Common Shares Outstg. (M) | 1,571.6 | Institutional Ownership (%) | 82 | | |

## Price Performance

30-Week Mov. Avg. ···  10-Week Mov. Avg. – –  **GAAP Earnings vs. Previous Year**  **Volume** Above Avg. STARS
12-Mo. Target Price —  Relative Strength —  ▲ Up  ▼ Down  ► No Change  Below Avg. ★

Options: ASE, CBOE, P, Ph

## Qualitative Risk Assessment

| LOW | **MEDIUM** | HIGH |
| --- | --- | --- |

Our risk assessment reflects Corning's exposure to intense competition in its major businesses, offset by its market leadership and positive cash flow, and our view of its strong balance sheet.

## Quantitative Evaluations

**S&P Quality Ranking**     B

| D | C | B- | **B** | B+ | A- | A | A+ |
| --- | --- | --- | --- | --- | --- | --- | --- |

**Relative Strength Rank**     WEAK

25

LOWEST = 1            HIGHEST = 99

## Revenue/Earnings Data

### Revenue (Million $)

| | 1Q | 2Q | 3Q | 4Q | Year |
| --- | --- | --- | --- | --- | --- |
| 2011 | 1,923 | 2,005 | 2,075 | -- | -- |
| 2010 | 1,553 | 1,712 | 1,602 | 1,765 | 6,632 |
| 2009 | 989.0 | 1,395 | 1,479 | 1,532 | 5,395 |
| 2008 | 1,617 | 1,692 | 1,555 | 1,084 | 5,948 |
| 2007 | 1,307 | 1,418 | 1,553 | 1,582 | 5,860 |
| 2006 | 1,262 | 1,261 | 1,282 | 1,369 | 5,174 |

### Earnings Per Share ($)

| | | | | | |
| --- | --- | --- | --- | --- | --- |
| 2011 | 0.47 | 0.47 | 0.51 | E0.39 | E1.82 |
| 2010 | 0.52 | 0.58 | 0.50 | 0.66 | 2.25 |
| 2009 | 0.01 | 0.39 | 0.41 | 0.47 | 1.28 |
| 2008 | 0.64 | 2.01 | 0.49 | 0.16 | 3.32 |
| 2007 | 0.20 | 0.30 | 0.38 | 0.45 | 1.34 |
| 2006 | 0.16 | 0.32 | 0.27 | 0.41 | 1.16 |

Fiscal year ended Dec. 31. Next earnings report expected: NA. EPS Estimates based on S&P Operating Earnings; historical GAAP earnings are as reported.

## Highlights

➤ The 12-month target price for GLW has recently been changed to $16.00 from $18.00. The Highlights section of this Stock Report will be updated accordingly.

## Investment Rationale/Risk

➤ The Investment Rationale/Risk section of this Stock Report will be updated shortly. For the latest News story on GLW from MarketScope, see below.

➤ 11/29/11 10:50 am ET ... S&P MAINTAINS BUY OPINION ON SHARES OF CORNING (GLW 13.25****): GLW revised lower its Q4 outlook for its LCD glass volume growth, which we think will put some pressure on Q4 revenues, and now expects equity earnings to be lower than previously forecast due to greater industry supply than demand. We are lowering our '11 EPS estimate by $0.05 to $1.82 and our '12 estimate by $0.20 to $1.80, reflecting these developments. Based on revised P/E analysis, we cut our 12-month target price by $2 to $16. But reflecting a recently increased dividend, an ongoing share buyback plan and diversified operations, we still see the shares as attractive. / Todd Rosenbluth

## Dividend Data (Dates: mm/dd Payment Date: mm/dd/yy)

| Amount ($) | Date Decl. | Ex-Div. Date | Stk. of Record | Payment Date |
| --- | --- | --- | --- | --- |
| 0.050 | 02/02 | 02/24 | 02/28 | 03/31/11 |
| 0.050 | 04/27 | 05/26 | 05/31 | 06/30/11 |
| 0.050 | 07/20 | 08/29 | 08/31 | 09/30/11 |
| 0.075 | 10/05 | 11/14 | 11/16 | 12/16/11 |

Dividends have been paid since 2007. Source: Company reports.

**Please read the Required Disclosures and Analyst Certification on the last page of this report.**

The McGraw·Hill Companies

# Corning Inc

**STANDARD &POOR'S**

## Business Summary November 08, 2011

CORPORATE OVERVIEW. Corning (GLW) is a maker of high-technology fiber optics for the global telecom industry and high-performance glass components for the personal computer and television manufacturing industries. Results are reported in the following primary business segments: display technologies (40% of sales in the first half of 2011), telecommunications (26%), specialty materials (14%), environmental technologies (13%), and life sciences (8%).

PRIMARY BUSINESS DYNAMICS. The display technologies segment manufactures glass substrates for active matrix liquid crystal displays (LCDs), which are used primarily in notebook computers, flat panel desktop monitors and LCD televisions. Large substrates (Generation 5 and higher) allow LCD manufacturers to produce a greater number of larger panels from each substrate. The larger size leads to economies of scale for LCD manufacturers and has enabled lower display prices for consumers, which may continue in the future. During the second quarter of 2010, volumes rose more than 10% from a strong first quarter, but GLW experienced some pressure in the second half of 2010 as capacity utilization at key customers slowed. Strong demand helped support GLW's gross margin expansion in 2009 and the first half of 2010, but margins narrowed in the second half of 2010. In the first half of 2011, display sales declined 4%, hurt by temporary curtailment of LCD production by Sharp,

but GLW expects glass volume to be stable in the third quarter at its wholly owned business relative to the second quarter, but that there will be pressure at its joint venture.

The telecom segment produces optical fiber and cable, and hardware and equipment products, including cable assemblies, fiber optic hardware and components. We believe demand for fiber-to-the-premise product in 2009 and 2010 was being driven by demand from China and the U.S., but we see greater growth occurring in new markets such as Australia in 2011. We are encouraged by the 27% revenue growth achieved in the first half of 2011.

The environmental technologies segment includes solutions for emissions and pollution control. Although sales are to the emission control systems manufacturers, substrates and filters are also required by the automotive and diesel engine manufacturers following new regulations in the U.S., Europe and Japan.

## Company Financials Fiscal Year Ended Dec. 31

| Per Share Data ($) | 2010 | 2009 | 2008 | 2007 | 2006 | 2005 | 2004 | 2003 | 2002 | 2001 |
|---|---|---|---|---|---|---|---|---|---|---|
| Tangible Book Value | 11.95 | 9.57 | 8.49 | 5.97 | 4.43 | 3.43 | 2.38 | 2.65 | 2.14 | 3.39 |
| Cash Flow | 2.79 | 1.79 | 3.76 | 1.72 | 1.56 | 0.71 | -1.20 | 0.23 | -1.04 | -4.74 |
| Earnings | 2.25 | 1.28 | 3.32 | 1.34 | 1.16 | 0.38 | -1.57 | -0.18 | -1.85 | -5.89 |
| S&P Core Earnings | 2.00 | 1.31 | 3.29 | 1.33 | 1.17 | 0.34 | -1.03 | -0.37 | -1.89 | -3.11 |
| Dividends | 0.20 | 0.20 | 0.20 | 0.10 | Nil | Nil | Nil | Nil | Nil | 0.12 |
| Payout Ratio | 9% | 16% | 6% | 7% | Nil | Nil | Nil | Nil | Nil | NM |
| Prices:High | 21.10 | 19.55 | 28.07 | 27.25 | 29.61 | 21.95 | 13.89 | 12.34 | 11.15 | 72.19 |
| Prices:Low | 15.45 | 8.97 | 7.36 | 18.12 | 17.50 | 10.61 | 9.29 | 3.34 | 1.10 | 6.92 |
| P/E Ratio:High | 9 | 15 | 8 | 20 | 26 | 58 | NM | NM | NM | NM |
| P/E Ratio:Low | 7 | 7 | 2 | 14 | 15 | 28 | NM | NM | NM | NM |

| Income Statement Analysis (Million $) | 2010 | 2009 | 2008 | 2007 | 2006 | 2005 | 2004 | 2003 | 2002 | 2001 |
|---|---|---|---|---|---|---|---|---|---|---|
| Revenue | 6,632 | 5,395 | 5,948 | 5,860 | 5,174 | 4,579 | 3,854 | 3,090 | 3,164 | 6,272 |
| Operating Income | 2,280 | 1,435 | 1,894 | 1,869 | 1,489 | 1,284 | 892 | 386 | 21.0 | 805 |
| Depreciation | 854 | 792 | 695 | 607 | 591 | 512 | 523 | 517 | 661 | 1,080 |
| Interest Expense | 109 | 82.0 | 90.0 | 101 | 76.0 | 116 | 141 | 154 | 179 | 153 |
| Pretax Income | 3,845 | 1,934 | 2,851 | 2,233 | 2,421 | 1,170 | -1,137 | -550 | -2,604 | -5,963 |
| Effective Tax Rate | NA | NM | NM | 3.58% | 22.9% | 49.4% | NM | NM | NM | NM |
| Net Income | 3,558 | 2,008 | 5,257 | 2,150 | 1,855 | 585 | -2,185 | -223 | -1,780 | -5,498 |
| S&P Core Earnings | 3,176 | 2,048 | 5,200 | 2,134 | 1,865 | 520 | -1,442 | -463 | -1,947 | -2,908 |

| Balance Sheet & Other Financial Data (Million $) | 2010 | 2009 | 2008 | 2007 | 2006 | 2005 | 2004 | 2003 | 2002 | 2001 |
|---|---|---|---|---|---|---|---|---|---|---|
| Cash | 6,350 | 3,583 | 2,816 | 3,516 | 1,157 | 1,342 | 1,009 | 833 | 1,471 | 1,037 |
| Current Assets | 8,859 | 5,521 | 4,619 | 5,294 | 4,798 | 3,860 | 3,281 | 2,694 | 3,825 | 4,107 |
| Total Assets | 25,833 | 21,295 | 19,256 | 15,215 | 13,065 | 11,175 | 9,710 | 10,752 | 11,548 | 12,793 |
| Current Liabilities | 1,986 | 1,539 | 2,052 | 2,512 | 2,319 | 2,216 | 2,336 | 1,553 | 1,680 | 1,994 |
| Long Term Debt | 2,262 | 1,930 | 1,527 | 1,514 | 1,696 | 1,789 | 2,214 | 2,668 | 3,963 | 4,461 |
| Common Equity | 19,375 | 15,543 | 13,443 | 9,496 | 7,246 | 5,609 | 3,752 | 5,379 | 4,536 | 5,414 |
| Total Capital | 21,745 | 17,599 | 15,034 | 11,077 | 8,987 | 7,441 | 6,059 | 8,168 | 8,713 | 10,001 |
| Capital Expenditures | 1,007 | 890 | 1,921 | 1,262 | 1,182 | 1,553 | 857 | 366 | 357 | 1,800 |
| Cash Flow | 4,412 | 2,800 | 5,952 | 2,757 | 2,446 | 1,097 | -1,662 | 294 | -1,247 | -4,418 |
| Current Ratio | 4.5 | 3.6 | 2.3 | 2.1 | 2.1 | 1.7 | 1.4 | 1.7 | 2.3 | 2.1 |
| % Long Term Debt of Capitalization | 10.4 | 11.0 | 10.2 | 13.7 | 18.9 | 24.0 | 36.5 | 32.7 | 45.5 | 44.6 |
| % Net Income of Revenue | 53.7 | 37.2 | 88.4 | 36.7 | 35.9 | 12.8 | NM | NM | NM | NM |
| % Return on Assets | 15.1 | 9.9 | 30.5 | 15.2 | 15.3 | 5.6 | NM | NM | NM | NM |
| % Return on Equity | 20.4 | 13.9 | 45.8 | 25.7 | 29.1 | 12.5 | NM | NM | NM | NM |

Data as orig reptd.; bef. results of disc opers/spec. items. Per share data adj. for stk. divs.; EPS diluted. E-Estimated. NA-Not Available. NM-Not Meaningful. NR-Not Ranked. UR-Under Review.

**Office:** One Riverfront Plaza, Corning, NY 14831-0001.
**Telephone:** 607-974-9000.
**Email:** info@corning.com
**Website:** http://www.corning.com

**Chrmn, Pres & CEO:** W.P. Weeks
**Vice Chrmn & CFO:** J.B. Flaws
**EVP & Chief Admin Officer:** K.P. Gregg
**EVP & CTO:** J.A. Miller, Jr.

**SVP, Chief Acctg Officer & Cntlr:** R.T. Tripeny
**Board Members:** J. S. Brown, J. A. Canning, Jr., R. F. Cummings, Jr., J. B. Flaws, G. Gund, K. M. Landgraf, D. Rieman, H. O. Ruding, W. D. Smithburg, G. F. Tilton, H. E. Tookes, II, W. P. Weeks, M. S. Wrighton

**Founded:** 1851
**Domicile:** New York
**Employees:** 26,200

*The McGraw-Hill Companies*

# Costco Wholesale Corp

## STANDARD &POOR'S

| S&P Recommendation | HOLD ★★★☆☆ | Price $80.82 (as of Nov 25, 2011) | 12-Mo. Target Price $81.00 | Investment Style Large-Cap Blend |
|---|---|---|---|---|

**GICS Sector** Consumer Staples
**Sub-Industry** Hypermarkets & Super Centers

**Summary** This company operates over 590 membership warehouses in the U.S., Puerto Rico, Canada, the U.K., Taiwan, Japan, Korea, Mexico and Australia.

### Key Stock Statistics (Source S&P, Vickers, company reports)

| | | | | | | | |
|---|---|---|---|---|---|---|---|
| 52-Wk Range | $86.34–66.33 | S&P Oper. EPS 2012E | 3.85 | Market Capitalization(B) | $35.025 | Beta | 0.66 |
| Trailing 12-Month EPS | $3.30 | S&P Oper. EPS 2013E | NA | Yield (%) | 1.19 | S&P 3-Yr. Proj. EPS CAGR(%) | 14 |
| Trailing 12-Month P/E | 24.5 | P/E on S&P Oper. EPS 2012E | 21.0 | Dividend Rate/Share | $0.96 | S&P Credit Rating | A+ |
| $10K Invested 5 Yrs Ago | $16,019 | Common Shares Outstg. (M) | 433.4 | Institutional Ownership (%) | 78 | | |

## Price Performance

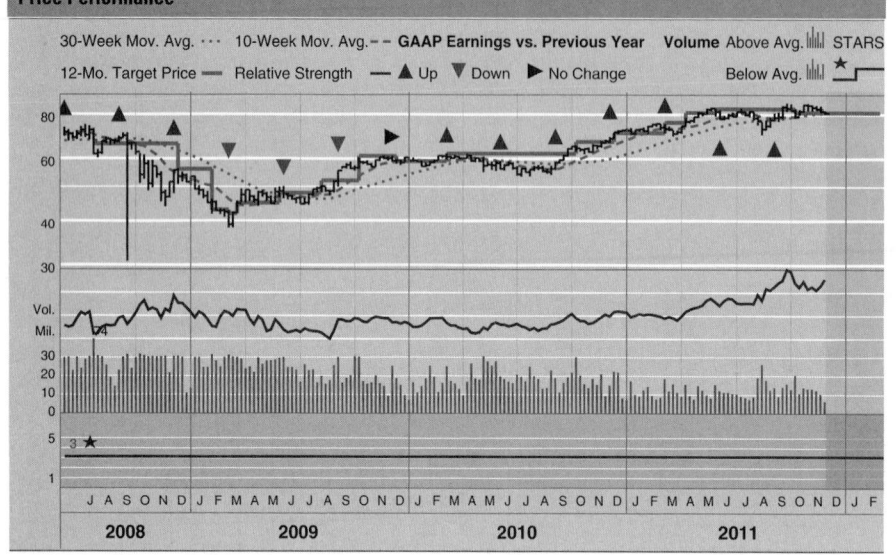

- 30-Week Mov. Avg. · · · 10-Week Mov. Avg. - - GAAP Earnings vs. Previous Year   Volume Above Avg. STARS
- 12-Mo. Target Price — Relative Strength — ▲ Up ▼ Down ► No Change   Below Avg. ★

2008   2009   2010   2011

Options: ASE, CBOE, P, Ph

Analysis prepared by Equity Analyst **Joseph Agnese** on Oct 06, 2011, when the stock traded at **$79.15**.

## Highlights

➤ We see revenues increasing 10.1% in FY 12 (Aug.), reflecting a same-store sales rise of about 5.0%, excluding fuel and foreign exchange rates, and square footage growth of about 3.5% (reflecting the expected opening of about 20 net new clubs). We believe comparable store sales will be driven mostly by increased average transaction sizes, reflecting low to mid-single digit food inflation. We expect membership fee income to rise significantly, reflecting company plans to raise the price of U.S. and Canada memberships beginning with renewing memberships as of November 2011.

➤ We project that margins will widen in FY 12, reflecting increased sales leverage and rising demand for discretionary goods, partially offset by increasing gross margin pressures from rising food cost inflation and a shift in mix toward narrower margin ancillary products. We see pre-opening expenses rising significantly as the company accelerates the opening of new club stores.

➤ Following benefits from fewer shares outstanding due to an active share repurchase program, we estimate that FY 12 EPS will rise 17%, to $3.85, from $3.30 in FY 11.

## Investment Rationale/Risk

➤ We expect COST to increase its market share in the near term, as we see it pricing aggressively as it maintains a strong value proposition and a relatively upscale product mix that appeals to a more affluent customer base. We think the company is well positioned to generate long-term earnings growth due to new store expansion in both domestic and international markets and what we view as a strong balance sheet.

➤ Risks to our recommendation and target price include a slowdown in sales due to weakness in the economy, more difficult foreign currency comparisons, and increased cannibalization from new store expansion.

➤ We believe the stock's valuation will be supported by the company's strong balance sheet and expectations for increased traffic and average transaction gains as consumers continue to seek value as they increase discretionary goods purchases in a more stable economic environment. We apply a P/E of about 21X to our FY 12 EPS estimate of $3.85, in line with its 11-year historical average, to arrive at our 12-month target price of $81.

## Qualitative Risk Assessment

| LOW | MEDIUM | HIGH |
|---|---|---|

Our risk assessment for Costco Wholesale incorporates our view of its strong balance sheet, its market leadership position, and our expectation that consistent earnings and dividend growth will continue.

## Quantitative Evaluations

**S&P Quality Ranking**   A-

| D | C | B- | B | B+ | A- | A | A+ |
|---|---|---|---|---|---|---|---|

**Relative Strength Rank**   STRONG

71

LOWEST = 1   HIGHEST = 99

## Revenue/Earnings Data

**Revenue (Million $)**

| | 1Q | 2Q | 3Q | 4Q | Year |
|---|---|---|---|---|---|
| 2011 | 19,239 | 20,875 | 20,623 | 28,178 | 88,915 |
| 2010 | 17,299 | 18,742 | 17,780 | 24,125 | 77,946 |
| 2009 | 16,395 | 16,843 | 15,806 | 22,378 | 71,422 |
| 2008 | 15,810 | 16,960 | 16,614 | 23,100 | 72,483 |
| 2007 | 14,152 | 15,112 | 14,659 | 20,477 | 64,400 |
| 2006 | 12,933 | 14,059 | 13,284 | 19,875 | 60,151 |

**Earnings Per Share ($)**

| | 1Q | 2Q | 3Q | 4Q | Year |
|---|---|---|---|---|---|
| 2011 | 0.71 | 0.79 | 0.73 | 1.08 | 3.30 |
| 2010 | 0.60 | 0.67 | 0.68 | 0.97 | 2.92 |
| 2009 | 0.60 | 0.55 | 0.48 | 0.85 | 2.47 |
| 2008 | 0.59 | 0.74 | 0.67 | 0.90 | 2.89 |
| 2007 | 0.51 | 0.54 | 0.49 | 0.83 | 2.37 |
| 2006 | 0.45 | 0.62 | 0.49 | 0.75 | 2.30 |

Fiscal year ended Aug. 31. Next earnings report expected: Early December. EPS Estimates based on S&P Operating Earnings; historical GAAP earnings are as reported.

## Dividend Data (Dates: mm/dd Payment Date: mm/dd/yy)

| Amount ($) | Date Decl. | Ex-Div. Date | Stk. of Record | Payment Date |
|---|---|---|---|---|
| 0.205 | 01/27 | 02/09 | 02/11 | 02/25/11 |
| 0.240 | 04/26 | 05/11 | 05/13 | 05/27/11 |
| 0.240 | 07/17 | 08/03 | 08/05 | 08/19/11 |
| 0.240 | 10/25 | 11/08 | 11/11 | 11/25/11 |

Dividends have been paid since 2004. Source: Company reports.

---

**Please read the Required Disclosures and Analyst Certification on the last page of this report.**

The **McGraw·Hill** Companies

# Costco Wholesale Corp

## Business Summary October 06, 2011

CORPORATE OVERVIEW. Costco Wholesale (formerly Costco Companies, Inc., and prior to that, Price/Costco, Inc.) began the pioneering "I can get it for you wholesale" membership warehouse concept in 1976, in San Diego, CA. The company operated 592 warehouses worldwide as of October 2011, mainly in the U.S. and Canada. COST also operates an e-commerce Web site, costco.com.

A typical warehouse format averages about 143,000 sq. ft. Floor plans are designed for economy and efficiency in the use of selling space, in the handling of merchandise, and in the control of inventory. Merchandise is generally stored on racks above the sales floor, and is displayed on pallets containing large quantities of each item, reducing the labor required for handling and stocking. Specific items in each product line are limited to fast-selling models, sizes and colors. COST carries an average of about 4,000 stock keeping units (SKUs) per warehouse, well below the 45,000 to 60,000 SKUs of a typical discount store or supermarket. By using a membership format, and strictly controlling entrances and exits, the company limits inventory losses (shrinkage) to well below the average of discount competitors.

COST has two primary types of memberships: Gold Star (individual) and Business members. Individual memberships are available to employees of federal, state and local governments; financial institutions; corporations; utility and transportation companies; public and private educational institutions; and other organizations. As of October 2011, Gold Star membership is $50 annually. There were 22.5 million Gold Star memberships as of September 2010, up from 21.5 million as of September 2009.

Businesses, including individuals with retail sales or business licenses, may become Business members by paying an annual $50 fee, with add-on membership cards raised to an annual fee of $50 from $40 starting with renewals after March 2011. As of September 2010, there were 5.8 million Business memberships, compared to 5.7 million in September 2009. Executive memberships, available for a $100 annual fee, offer business and individual members savings on services such as merchant credit card processing and small business loans, as well as a 2% annual reward, up to a maximum of $500 annually, on qualified purchases. Executive members made up approximately one third of the primary membership base in FY 10 (Aug.), up from 29% and 26% in FY 09 and FY 08, respectively.

## Company Financials Fiscal Year Ended Aug. 31

| Per Share Data ($) | 2011 | 2010 | 2009 | 2008 | 2007 | 2006 | 2005 | 2004 | 2003 | 2002 |
|---|---|---|---|---|---|---|---|---|---|---|
| Tangible Book Value | 27.47 | 24.82 | 23.27 | 21.08 | 19.73 | 19.78 | 18.80 | 16.48 | 14.33 | 12.51 |
| Cash Flow | 5.41 | 4.70 | 4.12 | 4.36 | 3.60 | 3.37 | 3.13 | 2.74 | 2.32 | 2.17 |
| Earnings | 3.30 | 2.92 | 2.47 | 2.89 | 2.37 | 2.30 | 2.18 | 1.85 | 1.53 | 1.48 |
| S&P Core Earnings | 3.30 | 2.91 | 2.53 | 2.89 | 2.37 | 2.30 | 2.12 | 1.76 | 1.40 | 1.32 |
| Dividends | 0.89 | 0.77 | 0.68 | 0.61 | 0.55 | 0.49 | 0.43 | 0.20 | Nil | Nil |
| Payout Ratio | 27% | 26% | 28% | 21% | 23% | 21% | 20% | 11% | Nil | Nil |
| Prices:High | 86.34 | 73.16 | 61.25 | 75.23 | 72.68 | 57.94 | 51.21 | 50.46 | 39.02 | 46.90 |
| Prices:Low | 69.54 | 53.41 | 38.17 | 30.70 | 51.52 | 46.00 | 39.48 | 35.05 | 27.00 | 27.09 |
| P/E Ratio:High | 26 | 25 | 25 | 26 | 31 | 25 | 23 | 27 | 26 | 32 |
| P/E Ratio:Low | 21 | 18 | 15 | 11 | 22 | 20 | 18 | 19 | 18 | 18 |

| Income Statement Analysis (Million $) | | | | | | | | | | |
|---|---|---|---|---|---|---|---|---|---|---|
| Revenue | 88,915 | 77,946 | 71,422 | 72,483 | 64,400 | 60,151 | 52,935 | 48,107 | 42,546 | 38,763 |
| Operating Income | 3,224 | 2,817 | 2,522 | 2,622 | 2,189 | 2,146 | 1,969 | 1,827 | 1,567 | 1,494 |
| Depreciation | 855 | 795 | 728 | 653 | 566 | 515 | 478 | 441 | 391 | 342 |
| Interest Expense | 116 | 111 | 108 | 103 | 64.1 | 12.6 | 34.4 | 36.7 | 36.9 | 29.1 |
| Pretax Income | 2,383 | 2,054 | 1,714 | 1,999 | 1,710 | 1,751 | 1,549 | 1,401 | 1,158 | 1,138 |
| Effective Tax Rate | NA | NA | 36.6% | 35.8% | 36.7% | 37.0% | 31.4% | 37.0% | 37.8% | 38.5% |
| Net Income | 1,542 | 1,303 | 1,086 | 1,283 | 1,083 | 1,103 | 1,063 | 882 | 721 | 700 |
| S&P Core Earnings | 1,461 | 1,300 | 1,114 | 1,283 | 1,082 | 1,104 | 1,044 | 837 | 660 | 624 |

| Balance Sheet & Other Financial Data (Million $) | | | | | | | | | | |
|---|---|---|---|---|---|---|---|---|---|---|
| Cash | 5,613 | 4,749 | 3,727 | 3,275 | 2,780 | 1,511 | 2,063 | 2,823 | 1,545 | 806 |
| Current Assets | 13,706 | 11,708 | 10,337 | 9,462 | 9,324 | 8,232 | 8,086 | 7,269 | 5,712 | 4,631 |
| Total Assets | 26,761 | 23,815 | 21,979 | 20,682 | 19,607 | 17,495 | 16,514 | 15,093 | 13,192 | 11,620 |
| Current Liabilities | 12,050 | 10,063 | 9,281 | 8,874 | 8,582 | 7,819 | 6,609 | 6,171 | 5,011 | 4,450 |
| Long Term Debt | 1,253 | 2,141 | 2,135 | 2,206 | 2,108 | 215 | 711 | 994 | 1,290 | 1,211 |
| Common Equity | 12,002 | 10,829 | 10,018 | 9,192 | 8,623 | 9,143 | 8,881 | 7,625 | 6,555 | 5,694 |
| Total Capital | 14,397 | 13,071 | 12,319 | 11,480 | 10,801 | 9,422 | 9,650 | 8,922 | 8,181 | 7,025 |
| Capital Expenditures | 1,290 | 1,055 | 1,250 | 1,599 | 1,386 | 1,213 | 995 | 706 | 811 | 1,039 |
| Cash Flow | 2,397 | 2,098 | 1,814 | 1,936 | 1,649 | 1,619 | 1,541 | 1,323 | 1,112 | 1,042 |
| Current Ratio | 1.1 | 1.2 | 1.1 | 1.1 | 1.1 | 1.1 | 1.2 | 1.2 | 1.1 | 1.0 |
| % Long Term Debt of Capitalization | 8.7 | 16.4 | 17.3 | 19.2 | 19.5 | 2.3 | 7.4 | 11.1 | 15.8 | 17.2 |
| % Net Income of Revenue | 1.7 | 1.7 | 1.5 | 1.8 | 1.7 | 1.8 | 2.0 | 1.8 | 1.7 | 1.8 |
| % Return on Assets | 6.1 | 5.7 | 5.1 | 6.4 | 5.8 | 6.5 | 6.7 | 6.2 | 5.8 | 6.4 |
| % Return on Equity | 13.5 | 12.5 | 11.3 | 14.4 | 12.2 | 12.2 | 12.9 | 12.4 | 11.8 | 13.2 |

Data as orig reptd.; bef. results of disc opers/spec. items. Per share data adj. for stk. divs.; EPS diluted. E-Estimated. NA-Not Available. NM-Not Meaningful. NR-Not Ranked. UR-Under Review.

**Office:** 999 Lake Drive, Issaquah, WA 98027.
**Telephone:** 425-313-8100.
**Email:** investor@costco.com
**Website:** http://www.costco.com

**Chrmn:** J.H. Brotman
**Pres & COO:** W.C. Jelinek
**CEO:** J.D. Sinegal
**Investor Contact:** R.A. Galanti (425-313-8203)

**EVP & CFO:** R.A. Galanti
**Board Members:** J. H. Brotman, B. S. Carson, S. L. Decker, D. J. Evans, R. A. Galanti, W. H. Gates, H. E. James, W. C. Jelinek, R. M. Libenson, J. W. Meisenbach, C. T. Munger, J. S. Raikes, J. S. Ruckelshaus, J. D. Sinegal.

**Founded:** 1976
**Domicile:** Washington
**Employees:** 164,000

The McGraw-Hill Companies

# Coventry Health Care Inc.

**STANDARD &POOR'S**

**S&P Recommendation** HOLD ★★★★★

| Price | 12-Mo. Target Price | Investment Style |
|---|---|---|
| $29.29 (as of Nov 25, 2011) | $36.00 | Large-Cap Growth |

**GICS Sector** Health Care
**Sub-Industry** Managed Health Care

**Summary** This national managed health care company operates health plans, insurance companies, network rental/managed care services companies, and workers' compensation services companies.

## Key Stock Statistics (Source S&P, Vickers, company reports)

| | | | | | | | |
|---|---|---|---|---|---|---|---|
| 52-Wk Range | $37.86– 25.21 | S&P Oper. EPS 2011**E** | 3.00 | Market Capitalization(B) | $4.226 | Beta | 1.85 |
| Trailing 12-Month EPS | $4.10 | S&P Oper. EPS 2012**E** | 3.30 | Yield (%) | Nil | S&P 3-Yr. Proj. EPS CAGR(%) | -5 |
| Trailing 12-Month P/E | 7.1 | P/E on S&P Oper. EPS 2011**E** | 9.8 | Dividend Rate/Share | Nil | S&P Credit Rating | BBB- |
| $10K Invested 5 Yrs Ago | $6,387 | Common Shares Outstg. (M) | 144.3 | Institutional Ownership (%) | 91 | | |

## Price Performance

30-Week Mov. Avg. · · · 10-Week Mov. Avg. – – **GAAP Earnings vs. Previous Year** Volume Above Avg. STARS

12-Mo. Target Price — Relative Strength — ▲ Up ▼ Down ▶ No Change Below Avg.

Options: ASE, CBOE, P, Ph

Analysis prepared by Equity Analyst **Phillip Seligman** on Nov 04, 2011, when the stock traded at **$31.26**.

### Highlights

➤ We expect revenues to rise 4.7% in 2011, driven by premium price hikes, stable commercial and Medicare Advantage (MA) HMO enrollment and 275,000 additional Medicaid members mostly via the Kentucky contract starting November 1, but 83,000 fewer commercial self-funded accounts and 480,000 fewer Medicare Part D members. For 2012, we see revenues up by over 11% on modestly higher commercial enrollment, strong MA and Part D enrollment growth, and the Kentucky Medicaid contract.

➤ We project medical costs will increase as a percentage of total premiums (MLR; medical loss ratio), on more-normalized medical cost trends and a lower level of favorable prior-period reserve development (PPRD; via the release of reserves from the defunct MA PFFS program), and in 2012, the absence of favorable PPRD. We expect the SG&A cost ratio to decline through 2012 on revenue leverage.

➤ We estimate operating EPS of $3.00 in 2011 (including $0.11 from the reserve release), versus $4.15 in 2010 (including $0.45 from the reserve release). We look for EPS of $3.30 in 2012.

### Investment Rationale/Risk

➤ We view CVH's cost management focus and diversity as notable. However, we believe it has more challenges under health care reform than some peers, given its focus on individual and small group plans, many with MLRs well below the health care reform law's mandated MLR floors. We think it will need to provide additional benefits, put more resources into the medical delivery system, and/or rebate some of the premiums to meet the mandated floors. We also think it needs to continue to improve SG&A cost efficiencies to help compensate for the higher MLRs. We look for CVH to seek more acquisitions, including the planned purchase of Family Health Partners, a Medicaid health plan, and we believe its $1.15 billion in deployable cash as of September 30, 2011, gives it financial flexibility. We also expect it to bid for additional Medicaid contracts.

➤ Risks to our recommendation and target price include intensified competition, sharply higher medical costs, and a weak economy.

➤ Our 12-month target price of $36 is based on a peer-level forward multiple of 11X applied to our 2011 EPS estimate.

## Qualitative Risk Assessment

| LOW | MEDIUM | HIGH |
|---|---|---|

Our risk assessment reflects CVH's increasingly diversified operations and its January 2005 acquisition of First Health, which spurred growth. Even so, we think competition amid the soft economy and our view of high unemployment is taking a toll on commercial enrollment, although we see gains in Medicare and Medicaid enrollment.

## Quantitative Evaluations

**S&P Quality Ranking** B+

| D | C | B- | B | B+ | A- | A | A+ |
|---|---|---|---|---|---|---|---|

**Relative Strength Rank** MODERATE

52

LOWEST = 1 HIGHEST = 99

## Revenue/Earnings Data

### Revenue (Million $)

| | 1Q | 2Q | 3Q | 4Q | Year |
|---|---|---|---|---|---|
| 2011 | 3,049 | 3,033 | 2,976 | -- | -- |
| 2010 | 2,859 | 2,868 | 2,836 | 3,025 | 11,588 |
| 2009 | 3,574 | 3,537 | 3,444 | 3,428 | 13,904 |
| 2008 | 2,941 | 2,978 | 2,975 | 3,020 | 11,914 |
| 2007 | 2,237 | 2,332 | 2,523 | 2,788 | 9,880 |
| 2006 | 1,939 | 1,945 | 1,909 | 1,941 | 7,734 |

### Earnings Per Share ($)

| | | | | | |
|---|---|---|---|---|---|
| 2011 | 0.74 | 1.51 | 0.84 | E0.59 | E3.00 |
| 2010 | 0.66 | 0.01 | 1.29 | 1.01 | 2.97 |
| 2009 | 0.30 | 0.13 | 0.68 | 0.74 | 2.14 |
| 2008 | 0.81 | 0.55 | 0.58 | 0.60 | 2.54 |
| 2007 | 0.76 | 0.96 | 1.08 | 1.18 | 3.98 |
| 2006 | 0.74 | 0.84 | 0.92 | 0.97 | 3.47 |

Fiscal year ended Dec. 31. Next earnings report expected: Early February. EPS Estimates based on S&P Operating Earnings; historical GAAP earnings are as reported.

## Dividend Data

No cash dividends have been paid.

The **McGraw·Hill** Companies

# Coventry Health Care Inc.

STANDARD
&POOR'S

## Business Summary November 04, 2011

CORPORATE OVERVIEW. Coventry Health Care is a diversified national managed care company. It traditionally offered individual and employer groups a full range of commercial risk products, including health maintenance organization (HMO), preferred provider organization (PPO) and point-of service (POS) products. Through its January 2005 acquisition of First Health Group (FH), it gained a nationwide provider network and high-margin, fee-based service businesses, such as network rental, clinical programs, workers' compensation administration, Medicaid health care management services, and pharmacy benefit management. CVH also gained additional PPO members, including the Federal Employee Health Benefit program, the largest employer-sponsored group health program in the U.S., and an administrative services only (ASO, or non-risk) product for large employers with locations in several states that self-insure. Starting in 2007, CVH combined the enrollment of its existing business with that of FH.

As of September 30, 2011, the company had a total of 3,409,000 members (versus 3,490,000 at December 31, 2010), excluding stand-alone Medicare prescription drug program members.

The Health Plan division is comprised of Health Plan Commercial Risk members (1,636,000, versus 1,641,000), Health Plan Commercial ASO (710,000, versus 698,000), Medicare Advantage Coordinated Care Plans (220,000, versus 224,000), and Medicaid Risk (467,000, versus 468,000). Health Plan Commercial Risk membership includes the Individual business (under 65 years of age).

Other medical membership consists of other National ASO (376,000, versus 459,000). In the ASO businesses, CVH offers management services and access to its provider networks to employers that self-insure their employee health benefits. The Other National ASO membership includes active National Accounts and Federal Employees Health Benefits Plan (FEHBP) administrative services business. Medicare Part D (Prescription Drug Program) had 1,148,000 members (versus 1,628,000). (The Medicare Advantage Private Fee-for-Service (PFFS) program had 329,000 members when it ended as of December 31, 2009.)

## Company Financials Fiscal Year Ended Dec. 31

| Per Share Data ($) | 2010 | 2009 | 2008 | 2007 | 2006 | 2005 | 2004 | 2003 | 2002 | 2001 |
|---|---|---|---|---|---|---|---|---|---|---|
| Tangible Book Value | 8.14 | 4.81 | 1.28 | 1.15 | 5.92 | 3.21 | 6.60 | 4.57 | 2.85 | 2.89 |
| Cash Flow | NA | NA | 3.54 | 4.89 | 4.17 | 3.63 | 2.61 | 1.97 | 1.24 | 0.72 |
| Earnings | 2.97 | 2.14 | 2.54 | 3.98 | 3.47 | 3.10 | 2.48 | 1.83 | 1.06 | 0.55 |
| S&P Core Earnings | 4.12 | 2.09 | 2.69 | 3.98 | 3.47 | 3.01 | 2.41 | 1.80 | 1.03 | 0.52 |
| Dividends | Nil | Nil | Nil | Nil | Nil | Nil | Nil | Nil | Nil | Nil |
| Payout Ratio | Nil | Nil | Nil | Nil | Nil | Nil | Nil | Nil | Nil | Nil |
| Prices:High | 27.44 | 25.78 | 63.89 | 64.00 | 61.88 | 60.31 | 36.20 | 29.46 | 16.89 | 12.22 |
| Prices:Low | 16.61 | 7.97 | 9.44 | 48.78 | 44.33 | 34.21 | 24.66 | 10.80 | 8.67 | 5.78 |
| P/E Ratio:High | 9 | 12 | 25 | 16 | 18 | 19 | 15 | 16 | 16 | 22 |
| P/E Ratio:Low | 6 | 4 | 4 | 12 | 13 | 11 | 10 | 6 | 8 | 11 |

| Income Statement Analysis (Million $) | | | | | | | | | | |
|---|---|---|---|---|---|---|---|---|---|---|
| Revenue | 11,588 | 13,904 | 11,914 | 9,880 | 7,734 | 6,611 | 5,312 | 4,535 | 3,577 | 3,147 |
| Operating Income | NA | NA | 770 | 1,075 | 954 | 878 | 514 | 384 | 220 | 117 |
| Depreciation | NA | NA | 150 | 143 | 113 | 86.2 | 17.6 | 18.2 | 18.9 | 25.9 |
| Interest Expense | 80.4 | 84.9 | 96.4 | 73.1 | 52.4 | 58.4 | 14.3 | 15.1 | 13.4 | Nil |
| Pretax Income | 687 | 505 | 606 | 995 | 896 | 799 | 527 | 393 | 226 | 135 |
| Effective Tax Rate | NA | 37.5% | 37.0% | 37.1% | 37.5% | 37.3% | 36.0% | 36.4% | 35.5% | 38.0% |
| Net Income | 439 | 315 | 382 | 626 | 560 | 502 | 337 | 250 | 146 | 83.5 |
| S&P Core Earnings | 609 | 308 | 404 | 627 | 560 | 485 | 328 | 245 | 143 | 78.5 |

| Balance Sheet & Other Financial Data (Million $) | | | | | | | | | | |
|---|---|---|---|---|---|---|---|---|---|---|
| Cash | 1,854 | 1,419 | 1,123 | 1,101 | 1,371 | 392 | 418 | 253 | 187 | 312 |
| Current Assets | NA | NA | 2,410 | 1,847 | 2,134 | 1,326 | 973 | 534 | 424 | 579 |
| Total Assets | 8,496 | 8,167 | 7,727 | 7,159 | 5,665 | 4,895 | 2,341 | 1,982 | 1,643 | 1,451 |
| Current Liabilities | NA | NA | 2,026 | 1,750 | 1,652 | 1,270 | 932 | 855 | 801 | 752 |
| Long Term Debt | 1,599 | 1,599 | 1,902 | 1,662 | 750 | 760 | 171 | 171 | 175 | Nil |
| Common Equity | 4,199 | 3,713 | 3,431 | 3,301 | 2,953 | 2,555 | 1,212 | 929 | 646 | 689 |
| Total Capital | NA | NA | 5,551 | 5,193 | 3,704 | 3,315 | 1,383 | 1,099 | 821 | 689 |
| Capital Expenditures | NA | NA | 69.4 | 61.3 | 72.6 | 71.4 | 15.0 | 13.4 | 13.0 | 11.9 |
| Cash Flow | NA | NA | 532 | 769 | 673 | 588 | 355 | 268 | 164 | 109 |
| Current Ratio | 1.3 | 1.2 | 1.2 | 1.1 | 1.3 | 1.0 | 1.0 | 0.6 | 0.5 | 0.8 |
| % Long Term Debt of Capitalization | 27.6 | 30.1 | 34.3 | 33.5 | 20.3 | 22.9 | 12.3 | 15.5 | 21.3 | Nil |
| % Net Income of Revenue | 3.8 | 2.3 | 3.2 | 6.3 | 7.2 | 7.6 | 6.3 | 5.5 | 4.1 | 2.7 |
| % Return on Assets | 5.3 | 4.0 | 5.1 | 9.8 | 10.6 | 13.9 | 15.6 | 13.8 | 9.4 | 6.2 |
| % Return on Equity | 11.1 | 8.8 | 11.4 | 20.0 | 20.3 | 26.6 | 31.5 | 31.8 | 21.8 | 13.0 |

Data as orig reptd.; bef. results of disc opers/spec. items. Per share data adj. for stk. divs.; EPS diluted. E-Estimated. NA-Not Available. NM-Not Meaningful. NR-Not Ranked. UR-Under Review.

**Office:** 6705 Rockledge Drive, Bethesda, MD 20817.
**Telephone:** 301-581-0600.
**Email:** investor-relations@cvty.com
**Website:** http://www.coventryhealth.com

**EVP, CFO & Treas:** R. Giles
**SVP & CIO:** M. Fitzpatrick
**Secy:** S.R. Smith
**General Counsel:** T.C. Zielinski

**Cntlr:** J.J. Ruhlmann
**Board Members:** J. Ackerman, L. D. Crandall, L. N. Kugelman, D. N. Mendelson, R. W. Moorhead, III, M. A. Stocker, J. R. Swedish, E. E. Tallett, T. T. Weglicki, A. F. Wise

**Founded:** 1986
**Domicile:** Delaware
**Employees:** 14,000

# Covidien Plc

STANDARD
&POOR'S

| S&P Recommendation | STRONG BUY ★★★★★ | Price $45.55 (as of Nov 30, 2011) | 12-Mo. Target Price $64.00 | Investment Style Large-Cap Growth |
|---|---|---|---|---|

**GICS Sector** Health Care
**Sub-Industry** Health Care Equipment

**Summary** Formerly a wholly owned division of Tyco International, Covidien develops, manufactures and distributes medical devices and supplies, diagnostic imaging agents, pharmaceuticals and other health care products used in clinical and home settings.

## Key Stock Statistics (Source S&P, Vickers, company reports)

| | | | | | |
|---|---|---|---|---|---|
| 52-Wk Range | $57.65–41.35 | S&P Oper. EPS 2012**E** | 4.34 | Market Capitalization(B) | $21.975 | Beta | 0.81 |
| Trailing 12-Month EPS | $3.76 | S&P Oper. EPS 2013**E** | 4.70 | Yield (%) | 1.98 | S&P 3-Yr. Proj. EPS CAGR(%) | 9 |
| Trailing 12-Month P/E | 12.1 | P/E on S&P Oper. EPS 2012**E** | 10.5 | Dividend Rate/Share | $0.90 | S&P Credit Rating | NA |
| $10K Invested 5 Yrs Ago | NA | Common Shares Outstg. (M) | 482.4 | Institutional Ownership (%) | 88 | | |

## Price Performance

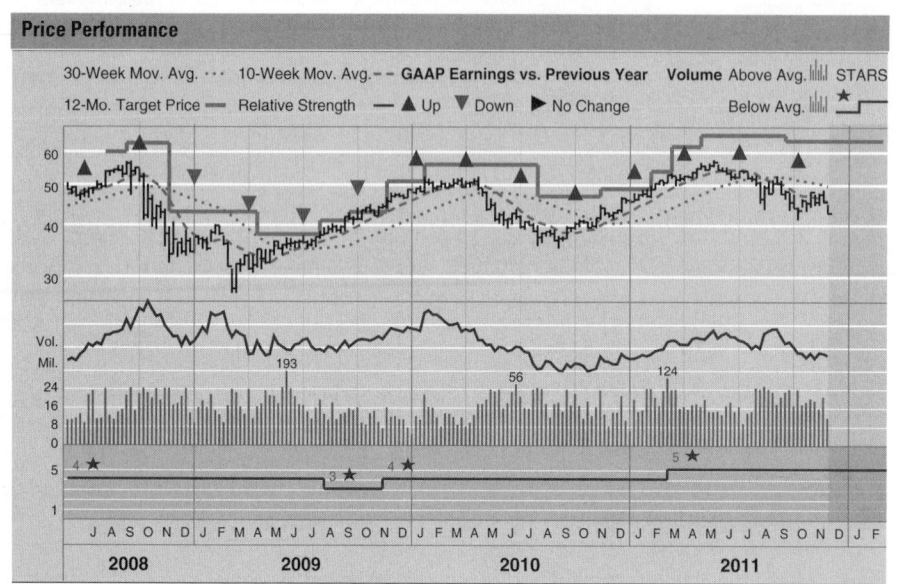

30-Week Mov. Avg. ···· 10-Week Mov. Avg. – – GAAP Earnings vs. Previous Year   Volume Above Avg. STARS
12-Mo. Target Price — Relative Strength   — ▲ Up ▼ Down ► No Change   Below Avg. ★

Options: ASE, CBOE, P

Analysis prepared by Equity Analyst **Phillip Seligman** on Nov 30, 2011, when the stock traded at **$45.45**.

## Qualitative Risk Assessment

| LOW | MEDIUM | HIGH |
|---|---|---|

COV operates in a highly competitive industry subject to pricing pressures and loss of sales due to patent expirations and the introduction of new and potentially disruptive technologies or products. However, we believe COV is a global leader in many health care products and supplies markets and has competitive advantages as a large player in the industry.

## Quantitative Evaluations

**S&P Quality Ranking**   NR

| D | C | B- | B | B+ | A- | A | A+ |
|---|---|---|---|---|---|---|---|

**Relative Strength Rank**   MODERATE

45

LOWEST = 1   HIGHEST = 99

## Highlights

► We look for sales to increase 4.7% in FY 12 (Sep.), following the 11% growth we saw in FY 11. We forecast COV's medical device sales to rise at a mid-single digits pace, down from mid-teens growth in FY 11, on the lapping of large acquisitions. We expect its pharmaceutical sales to grow in the low to mid-single digits, on gains by branded drugs, following a low-single-digit decline in FY 11, due to a divestiture. Lastly, we see flat medical supplies sales on continued procedure softness. The firmwide revenue growth we see in FY 12, supported by a continued slew of new products, would be higher if not for FY 11's additional week of sales and our assumption of a smaller boost from foreign exchange.

► We expect gross margins to continue to expand on an improving product mix and cost control. We look for operating expenses to decline slightly as a percentage of sales in FY 12, as the benefits of revenue leverage and restructuring activities outweigh increased R&D investment.

► Our FY 12 EPS estimate is $4.34, aided by share buybacks, versus an adjusted $3.97 in FY 11. We look for FY 13 EPS of $4.70.

## Investment Rationale/Risk

► We see double digit EPS growth over the long term, led by COV's portfolio optimization (comprising acquisitions, licensing deals, and the divestiture of underperforming units), with emphasis on the device segment, accelerated new product launches and cost control. We expect COV to also benefit from aging global populations and its emerging markets penetration, where it expects sales to double to $2 billion over the next five to six years. Moreover, we view free cash flow as strong, providing financial flexibility. We would not be surprised if COV seeks acquisitions in addition to its planned purchase of BARRX Medical, a leader in the treatment of Barrett's esophagus syndrome.

► Risks to our recommendation and target price include lower-than-expected sales in the device and imaging categories, intensified competition, and raw material cost spikes.

► Our 12-month target price of $64 is derived by applying a multiple of 14.4X our calendar 2012 EPS estimate of $4.43. This multiple is slightly above the average P/E of the five years ended FY 11, on our view of COV's improved top-line growth and margin expansion prospects.

## Revenue/Earnings Data

**Revenue (Million $)**

| | 1Q | 2Q | 3Q | 4Q | Year |
|---|---|---|---|---|---|
| 2011 | 2,769 | 2,801 | 2,926 | 3,078 | 11,574 |
| 2010 | 2,644 | 2,551 | 2,564 | 2,670 | 10,429 |
| 2009 | 2,564 | 2,798 | 2,618 | 2,697 | 10,677 |
| 2008 | 2,316 | 2,426 | 2,595 | 2,573 | 9,910 |
| 2007 | 2,451 | 2,539 | 2,579 | 2,601 | 10,170 |
| 2006 | 2,294 | 2,408 | 2,473 | 2,473 | 9,647 |

**Earnings Per Share ($)**

| | | | | | |
|---|---|---|---|---|---|
| 2011 | 0.87 | 0.92 | 1.06 | 0.93 | 3.79 |
| 2010 | 0.82 | 0.80 | 0.70 | 0.77 | 3.10 |
| 2009 | 0.75 | 0.37 | 0.56 | 0.11 | 1.79 |
| 2008 | 0.89 | 0.49 | 0.65 | 0.82 | 2.86 |
| 2007 | 0.69 | 0.79 | -2.23 | 0.07 | -0.68 |
| 2006 | -- | -- | -- | -- | 2.57 |

Fiscal year ended Sep. 30. Next earnings report expected: Early February. EPS Estimates based on S&P Operating Earnings; historical GAAP earnings are as reported.

## Dividend Data (Dates: mm/dd Payment Date: mm/dd/yy)

| Amount ($) | Date Decl. | Ex-Div. Date | Stk. of Record | Payment Date |
|---|---|---|---|---|
| 0.200 | 07/22 | 01/27 | 01/31 | 02/22/11 |
| 0.200 | 03/15 | 04/05 | 04/07 | 05/06/11 |
| 0.225 | 07/20 | 10/11 | 10/13 | 11/04/11 |

Dividends have been paid since 2007. Source: Company reports.

**Please read the Required Disclosures and Analyst Certification on the last page of this report.**

The McGraw·Hill Companies

# Covidien Plc

## Business Summary November 30, 2011

CORPORATE OVERVIEW. Covidien (COV) is a global leader in the development, manufacture and sale of medical devices and supplies, diagnostic imaging agents, pharmaceuticals and other health care products used in both clinical and home settings. During FY 11 (Sep.), about 45% of sales were generated in non-U.S. markets. The company was separated from parent Tyco International in July 2007.

The medical devices division (68% of FY 11 sales) develops, makes and sells endomechanical instruments, including laparoscopic instruments and surgical staplers; soft tissue repair products, such as sutures, mesh, biosurgery products and hernia mechanical devices; energy devices, including vessel sealing, electrosurgical and ablation products and related capital equipment; oximetry and monitoring products, such as sensors, monitors and temperature management products; airway and ventilation products, encompassing devices like airway products, ventilator, breathing systems and inhalation therapy products; and vascular products such as vascular therapy and compression products.

The pharmaceuticals division (17%) includes the development, manufacture and distribution of specialty pharmaceuticals, active pharmaceutical ingredients, specialty chemicals and contrast products. Specialty pharmaceuticals delivers branded and generic pharmaceuticals, including pain and addiction treatment products; active pharmaceutical ingredients (API) is a producer of medicinal narcotics and acetaminophen and a supplier of other active pharmaceutical ingredients, such as peptides, generic APIs, stearates and phosphates to the pharmaceutical industry; specialty chemicals manufactures high purity chemicals and related products; contrast products includes contrast delivery systems and contrast agents; and radiopharmaceuticals includes radioactive isotopes and associated pharmaceuticals used for the diagnosis and treatment of disease.

## Company Financials Fiscal Year Ended Sep. 30

| Per Share Data ($) | 2011 | 2010 | 2009 | 2008 | 2007 | 2006 | 2005 | 2004 | 2003 | 2002 |
|---|---|---|---|---|---|---|---|---|---|---|
| Tangible Book Value | NM | NM | 0.79 | 1.41 | NM | NM | NA | NA | NA | NA |
| Cash Flow | 4.99 | 4.07 | 2.66 | 3.65 | 0.14 | 3.23 | NA | NA | NA | NA |
| Earnings | 3.79 | 3.10 | 1.79 | 2.86 | -0.68 | 2.57 | NA | NA | NA | NA |
| Dividends | 0.40 | 0.20 | 0.48 | 0.48 | Nil | NA | NA | NA | NA | NA |
| Payout Ratio | 11% | 6% | 27% | 22% | Nil | NA | NA | NA | NA | NA |
| Prices:High | 57.65 | 52.48 | 49.13 | 57.00 | 49.70 | NA | NA | NA | NA | NA |
| Prices:Low | 41.35 | 35.12 | 27.27 | 32.27 | 36.90 | NA | NA | NA | NA | NA |
| P/E Ratio:High | 15 | 17 | 27 | 20 | NM | NA | NA | NA | NA | NA |
| P/E Ratio:Low | 11 | 11 | 15 | 11 | NM | NA | NA | NA | NA | NA |

| Income Statement Analysis (Million $) | 2011 | 2010 | 2009 | 2008 | 2007 | 2006 | 2005 | 2004 | 2003 | 2002 |
|---|---|---|---|---|---|---|---|---|---|---|
| Revenue | 11,574 | 10,429 | 10,677 | 9,910 | 10,170 | 9,647 | 9,543 | 9,110 | NA | NA |
| Operating Income | 3,155 | 2,637 | 2,540 | 2,485 | 2,397 | 2,476 | 2,767 | 2,614 | NA | NA |
| Depreciation | 599 | 489 | 440 | 398 | 409 | 333 | 320 | 318 | NA | NA |
| Interest Expense | NA | NA | 175 | 209 | 188 | NA | NA | NA | NA | NA |
| Pretax Income | 2,216 | 1,926 | 1,851 | 1,979 | 151 | 1,858 | 1,751 | 1,990 | NA | NA |
| Effective Tax Rate | NA | NA | 51.3% | 27.1% | NM | 29.8% | 29.6% | 29.2% | NA | NA |
| Net Income | 1,883 | 1,563 | 902 | 1,443 | -337 | 1,304 | 1,232 | 1,409 | NA | NA |

| Balance Sheet & Other Financial Data (Million $) | 2011 | 2010 | 2009 | 2008 | 2007 | 2006 | 2005 | 2004 | 2003 | 2002 |
|---|---|---|---|---|---|---|---|---|---|---|
| Cash | 1,503 | 1,565 | 1,467 | 1,208 | 872 | 800 | 141 | NA | NA | NA |
| Current Assets | NA | NA | 5,462 | 5,289 | 7,556 | 7,308 | NA | NA | NA | NA |
| Total Assets | 20,374 | 20,387 | 17,139 | 16,003 | 18,328 | 17,895 | 14,784 | NA | NA | NA |
| Current Liabilities | NA | NA | 2,239 | 2,098 | 5,367 | 8,740 | NA | NA | NA | NA |
| Long Term Debt | 4,154 | 4,415 | 2,961 | 2,986 | 3,565 | 148 | 2,544 | NA | NA | NA |
| Common Equity | 9,817 | 8,974 | 8,001 | 7,747 | 6,742 | 6,803 | 8,116 | NA | NA | NA |
| Total Capital | 13,976 | 13,639 | 11,438 | 11,067 | 10,879 | 6,951 | 11,123 | NA | NA | NA |
| Capital Expenditures | 467 | 401 | 412 | 409 | 388 | NA | 331 | 251 | NA | NA |
| Cash Flow | 2,482 | 2,052 | 1,342 | 1,841 | 72.0 | 1,637 | 1,552 | 1,727 | NA | NA |
| Current Ratio | 2.4 | 1.8 | 2.4 | 2.5 | 1.4 | 0.8 | 1.9 | NA | NA | NA |
| % Long Term Debt of Capitalization | 29.7 | 32.4 | 25.9 | 27.0 | 32.7 | 2.1 | 22.9 | Nil | NA | NA |
| % Net Income of Revenue | 16.3 | 15.0 | 8.5 | 14.6 | NM | 13.5 | 12.9 | 15.5 | NA | NA |
| % Return on Assets | NA | NA | 5.4 | 8.4 | NM | NA | NA | NA | NA | NA |
| % Return on Equity | NA | NA | 11.5 | 19.9 | NM | NA | NA | NA | NA | NA |

Data as orig reptd.; bef. results of disc opers/spec. items. Per share data adj. for stk. divs.; EPS diluted. Pro forma data in 2006, bal. sheet & book val. as of March 30, 2007. E-Estimated. NA-Not Available. NM-Not Meaningful. NR-Not Ranked. UR-Under Review.

**Office:** 20 On Hatch, Lower Hatch Street, Dublin, Ireland 2.
**Telephone:** 353 1 438 1700.
**Website:** http://www.covidien.com
**Chrmn:** R.J. Meelia

**Pres & CEO:** J.E. Almeida
**EVP & CFO:** C.J. Dockendorff
**SVP & General Counsel:** J.H. Masterson
**Chief Acctg Officer & Cntlr:** R.G. Brown, Jr.

**Investor Contact:** C.N. Lannum (508-452-4343)
**Board Members:** J. E. Almeida, C. Arnold, R. H. Brust, J. M. Connors, Jr., C. J. Coughlin, T. M. Donahue, K. J. Herbert, R. J. Hogan, III, R. J. Meelia, D. H. Reilley, J. A. Zaccagnino

**Founded:** 2000
**Domicile:** Bermuda
**Employees:** 41,300

# CSX Corp

STANDARD &POOR'S

| S&P Recommendation | BUY ★★★★☆ | Price $20.00 (as of Nov 25, 2011) | 12-Mo. Target Price $27.00 | Investment Style Large-Cap Value |
|---|---|---|---|---|

**GICS Sector** Industrials
**Sub-Industry** Railroads

**Summary** CSX operates a major U.S. rail network, transporting bulk commodities, industrial products, and intermodal containers over its network of approximately 21,000 route miles.

## Key Stock Statistics (Source S&P, Vickers, company reports)

| | | | | | | | |
|---|---|---|---|---|---|---|---|
| 52-Wk Range | $27.06–17.69 | S&P Oper. EPS 2011E | 1.67 | Market Capitalization(B) | $20.999 | Beta | 1.25 |
| Trailing 12-Month EPS | $1.62 | S&P Oper. EPS 2012E | 1.84 | Yield (%) | 2.40 | S&P 3-Yr. Proj. EPS CAGR(%) | 17 |
| Trailing 12-Month P/E | 12.4 | P/E on S&P Oper. EPS 2011E | 12.0 | Dividend Rate/Share | $0.48 | S&P Credit Rating | BBB |
| $10K Invested 5 Yrs Ago | $18,058 | Common Shares Outstg. (M) | 1,050.0 | Institutional Ownership (%) | 72 | | |

## Price Performance

30-Week Mov. Avg. · · · 10-Week Mov. Avg. - - GAAP Earnings vs. Previous Year  Volume Above Avg. STARS
12-Mo. Target Price — Relative Strength — ▲ Up ▼ Down ► No Change  Below Avg. ★

Options: ASE, CBOE, P, Ph

Analysis prepared by Equity Analyst **Kevin Kirkeby** on Nov 23, 2011, when the stock traded at **$20.26**.

## Highlights

➤ Following an expected 10% increase in 2011, we forecast revenues to increase another 5.3% in 2012. This is based on a 3% improvement in volumes and 2.2% increase in price/mix during 2012. We anticipate fuel surcharges to be relatively flat. The increase in carloadings will be driven, in our view, by gains in intermodal containers and metals-related shipments, plus strength in export coal and auto shipments. Domestic coal appears likely to remain under pressure due to historically low natural gas prices.

➤ We see margins widening during 2012 due to increased volumes and ongoing productivity efforts. However, we anticipate that labor costs will rise due to increases in average employee count and health care expenses. Reflecting a step-up in spending on its track infrastructure and fleet of rail cars, we expect depreciation expenses will rise over the coming year.

➤ As of September 30, 2011, CSX had $734 million remaining on its stock repurchase plan in effect through the end of 2012. At a recent price of $21 per share, this represents about 3% of the shares outstanding.

## Investment Rationale/Risk

➤ We believe CSX will benefit from economic recovery in the U.S., given its role in transporting many of the basic materials required in manufacturing and construction. We also think the recession forced a more intense focus on operating efficiencies, which should support wider margins during a period of rising volumes. In our view, a valuation above the historical average is warranted as we weigh CSX's solid cash flow generation against elevated regulatory risk.

➤ Risks to our opinion and target price include renewed deterioration in global economic growth, softness in export coal shipments that we believe generate wider margins than most other shipments, and greater-than-expected regulatory oversight.

➤ Our discounted cash flow model, assuming a 10.9% cost of equity and a 3.5% terminal growth rate, derives an intrinsic value of about $29. Applying an enterprise value-to-EBITDA multiple of 7.6X, which is modestly above the five-year average, to our four-quarter forward EBITDA forecast, we derive a value of $25. Blending these models, we arrive at our 12-month target price of $27.

## Qualitative Risk Assessment

| LOW | MEDIUM | HIGH |
|---|---|---|

Our risk assessment reflects CSX's exposure to economic cycles, freight demand and pricing, offset by its consistently positive cash flow generation and diverse customer base.

## Quantitative Evaluations

**S&P Quality Ranking**  A-

| D | C | B- | B | B+ | A- | A | A+ |
|---|---|---|---|---|---|---|---|

**Relative Strength Rank**  MODERATE
45
LOWEST = 1    HIGHEST = 99

## Revenue/Earnings Data

**Revenue (Million $)**

| | 1Q | 2Q | 3Q | 4Q | Year |
|---|---|---|---|---|---|
| 2011 | 2,810 | 3,019 | 2,963 | -- | -- |
| 2010 | 2,491 | 2,663 | 2,666 | 2,816 | 10,636 |
| 2009 | 2,247 | 2,185 | 2,289 | 2,320 | 9,041 |
| 2008 | 2,713 | 2,907 | 2,961 | 2,674 | 11,255 |
| 2007 | 2,422 | 2,530 | 2,501 | 2,577 | 10,030 |
| 2006 | 2,331 | 2,421 | 2,418 | 2,396 | 9,566 |

**Earnings Per Share ($)**

| | 1Q | 2Q | 3Q | 4Q | Year |
|---|---|---|---|---|---|
| 2011 | 0.35 | 0.46 | 0.43 | E0.43 | E1.67 |
| 2010 | 0.26 | 0.36 | 0.36 | 0.38 | 1.35 |
| 2009 | 0.21 | 0.24 | 0.25 | 0.26 | 0.96 |
| 2008 | 0.28 | 0.31 | 0.31 | 0.21 | 1.11 |
| 2007 | 0.17 | 0.24 | 0.22 | 0.29 | 0.91 |
| 2006 | 0.18 | 0.28 | 0.24 | 0.25 | 0.94 |

Fiscal year ended Dec. 31. Next earnings report expected: NA. EPS Estimates based on S&P Operating Earnings; historical GAAP earnings are as reported.

## Dividend Data (Dates: mm/dd Payment Date: mm/dd/yy)

| Amount ($) | Date Decl. | Ex-Div. Date | Stk. of Record | Payment Date |
|---|---|---|---|---|
| 0.360 | 05/04 | 05/26 | 05/31 | 06/15/11 |
| 3-for-1 | 05/04 | 06/16 | 05/31 | 06/15/11 |
| 0.120 | 07/13 | 08/25 | 08/31 | 09/15/11 |
| 0.120 | 10/04 | 11/28 | 11/30 | 12/15/11 |

Dividends have been paid since 1922. Source: Company reports.

**Please read the Required Disclosures and Analyst Certification on the last page of this report.**

The McGraw-Hill Companies

# CSX Corp

## Business Summary November 23, 2011

**CORPORATE OVERVIEW.** CSX operates the largest rail network in the eastern U.S., with a 21,000-mile rail network linking commercial markets in 23 states and two Canadian provinces, and owns companies providing intermodal and rail-to-truck transload services. In 1997, the company purchased a 42% stake in Conrail, bringing CSX's system into New York City, Boston, Philadelphia and Buffalo; in 2004, CSX gained direct ownership and control of Conrail's New York Central Lines. With these routes, the company was able to offer shippers broader geographic coverage, access more ports, and expand its share of north-south traffic.

**MARKET PROFILE.** We consider railroads to be a mature industry, and expect 1.5% annualized U.S. rail tonnage growth between 2010 and 2022. We believe CSX's growth opportunities are slightly ahead of the industry average, as we see above-average future growth in intermodal traffic, but average prospects in coal and chemicals shipments. We believe growth in CSX's intermodal business, representing 12% of 2010 revenue, will be above the peer average. This, in our view, will be driven by the overall level of economic activity and population density in the Eastern markets it serves. Its initiatives, like the National Gateway project, are designed to capitalize on highway congestion along a key East Coast freight corridors, by converting truck traffic over to rail containers. Still, these types of intermodal shipments, having a length of haul

under 750 miles, are more susceptible to price competition from trucks than transcontinental moves.

Coal accounted for 31% of 2010 revenues. Most of this traffic originates from the Appalachian coal fields (84%) and is primarily delivered to power utilities. We expect CSX's domestic coal tonnage to experience average growth as its customers balance the high sulfur content of coal against using natural gas or other fuel alternatives. Coal shipments directed to export markets, which we calculate to be 17% of total coal volumes, is expected to be more volatile than the domestic business, and be somewhat correlated to exchange rate fluctuations. CSX's merchandise freight provided 47% of freight revenues in 2010, and includes chemical, forest products, metals, and agricultural products. We believe this business is sensitive to U.S. GDP trends, and faces average long-term volume growth prospects. We think automotive freight, at 8% of revenues in 2010, has an average volume growth outlook. Following the partial recovery in 2010, we see production improving further in 2011 and beyond, as the average age of vehicles in use rises and consumer finances improve.

## Company Financials Fiscal Year Ended Dec. 31

| Per Share Data ($) | 2010 | 2009 | 2008 | 2007 | 2006 | 2005 | 2004 | 2003 | 2002 | 2001 |
|---|---|---|---|---|---|---|---|---|---|---|
| Tangible Book Value | 7.75 | 7.44 | 6.81 | 7.05 | 6.81 | 6.08 | 5.26 | 5.00 | 4.84 | 4.77 |
| Cash Flow | 2.18 | 1.72 | 1.85 | 1.57 | 1.56 | 1.14 | 0.85 | 0.65 | 0.87 | 0.72 |
| Earnings | 1.35 | 0.96 | 1.11 | 0.91 | 0.94 | 0.53 | 0.31 | 0.15 | 0.37 | 0.23 |
| S&P Core Earnings | 1.36 | 0.96 | 1.14 | 0.91 | 0.86 | 0.53 | 0.30 | 0.22 | 0.28 | 0.20 |
| Dividends | 0.33 | 0.29 | 0.26 | 0.18 | 0.21 | 0.07 | 0.07 | 0.07 | 0.07 | 0.13 |
| Payout Ratio | 24% | 31% | 23% | 20% | 22% | 14% | 21% | 45% | 18% | 58% |
| Prices:High | 21.60 | 16.93 | 23.57 | 17.29 | 12.77 | 8.60 | 6.74 | 6.05 | 6.90 | 6.88 |
| Prices:Low | 14.02 | 6.90 | 10.00 | 11.17 | 8.10 | 6.15 | 4.80 | 4.25 | 4.18 | 4.14 |
| P/E Ratio:High | 16 | 18 | 21 | 19 | 14 | 16 | 22 | 41 | 19 | 30 |
| P/E Ratio:Low | 10 | 7 | 9 | 12 | 9 | 12 | 15 | 29 | 11 | 18 |

| Income Statement Analysis (Million $) | 2010 | 2009 | 2008 | 2007 | 2006 | 2005 | 2004 | 2003 | 2002 | 2001 |
|---|---|---|---|---|---|---|---|---|---|---|
| Revenue | 10,636 | 9,041 | 11,255 | 10,030 | 9,566 | 8,618 | 8,020 | 7,793 | 8,152 | 8,110 |
| Operating Income | 4,018 | 3,193 | 3,667 | 3,112 | 2,837 | 2,345 | 1,730 | 1,269 | 1,776 | 1,579 |
| Depreciation | 947 | 908 | 904 | 883 | 867 | 833 | 730 | 643 | 649 | 622 |
| Interest Expense | 557 | 558 | 519 | 417 | 392 | 423 | 435 | 418 | 445 | 518 |
| Pretax Income | 2,546 | 1,761 | 2,146 | 1,932 | 1,841 | 1,036 | 637 | 265 | 723 | 448 |
| Effective Tax Rate | NA | 35.4% | 36.4% | 36.5% | 28.8% | 30.5% | 34.4% | 28.7% | 35.4% | 34.6% |
| Net Income | 1,563 | 1,137 | 1,365 | 1,226 | 1,310 | 720 | 418 | 189 | 467 | 293 |
| S&P Core Earnings | 1,576 | 1,142 | 1,392 | 1,228 | 1,194 | 729 | 405 | 280 | 363 | 249 |

| Balance Sheet & Other Financial Data (Million $) | 2010 | 2009 | 2008 | 2007 | 2006 | 2005 | 2004 | 2003 | 2002 | 2001 |
|---|---|---|---|---|---|---|---|---|---|---|
| Cash | 1,346 | 1,090 | 745 | 714 | 461 | 309 | 859 | 368 | 264 | 618 |
| Current Assets | 2,855 | 2,570 | 2,391 | 2,491 | 2,672 | 2,372 | 2,987 | 1,903 | 1,789 | 2,074 |
| Total Assets | 28,141 | 27,036 | 26,288 | 25,534 | 25,129 | 24,232 | 24,581 | 21,760 | 20,951 | 20,801 |
| Current Liabilities | 2,537 | 1,865 | 2,404 | 2,671 | 2,522 | 2,979 | 3,317 | 2,210 | 2,454 | 3,303 |
| Long Term Debt | 8,051 | 7,895 | 7,512 | 6,470 | 5,362 | 5,093 | 6,234 | 6,886 | 6,519 | 5,839 |
| Common Equity | 8,700 | 8,846 | 8,048 | 8,685 | 9,863 | 8,918 | 7,858 | 7,569 | 7,091 | 7,060 |
| Total Capital | 17,364 | 16,868 | 21,816 | 21,272 | 21,335 | 20,093 | 20,071 | 18,207 | 17,177 | 16,520 |
| Capital Expenditures | 1,825 | 1,447 | 1,740 | 1,773 | 1,639 | 1,136 | 1,030 | 1,059 | 1,080 | 930 |
| Cash Flow | 2,510 | 2,045 | 2,269 | 2,109 | 2,177 | 1,553 | 1,148 | 832 | 1,116 | 915 |
| Current Ratio | 1.1 | 1.4 | 1.0 | 0.9 | 1.1 | 0.8 | 0.9 | 0.9 | 0.7 | 0.6 |
| % Long Term Debt of Capitalization | 46.4 | 46.8 | 34.4 | 30.4 | 25.1 | 25.3 | 31.1 | 37.8 | 38.0 | 35.3 |
| % Net Income of Revenue | 14.7 | 12.6 | 12.1 | 12.2 | 13.7 | 8.4 | 5.2 | 2.4 | 5.7 | 3.6 |
| % Return on Assets | 5.7 | 4.3 | 5.3 | 4.8 | 5.3 | 2.9 | 1.8 | 0.9 | 2.2 | 1.4 |
| % Return on Equity | 17.8 | 13.5 | 16.3 | 13.9 | 14.0 | 8.6 | 5.4 | 2.6 | 6.6 | 4.2 |

Data as orig reptd.; bef. results of disc opers/spec. items. Per share data adj. for stk. divs.; EPS diluted. E-Estimated. NA-Not Available. NM-Not Meaningful. NR-Not Ranked. UR-Under Review.

**Office:** 500 Water Street , Jacksonville , FL 32202.
**Telephone:** 904-359-3200.
**Website:** http://www.csx.com
**Chrmn, Pres & CEO:** M.J. Ward

**COO:** D.A. Brown
**SVP & Chief Admin Officer:** L. Mancini
**CFO:** O. Munoz
**Chief Acctg Officer & Cntlr:** C.T. Sizemore

**Investor Contact:** D. Baggs (904-359-4812)
**Auditor:** ERNST & YOUNG
**Board Members:** D. M. Alvarado, J. B. Breaux, P. L. Carter, S. T. Halverson, E. J. Kelly, III, G. H. Lamphere, J. D. McPherson, T. T. O'Toole, D. M. Ratcliffe, D. J. Shepard, M. J. Ward, J. C. Watts, Jr., J. S. Whisler

**Founded:** 1978
**Domicile:** Virginia
**Employees:** 30,000

# Cummins Inc.

**STANDARD &POOR'S**

| S&P Recommendation | STRONG BUY ★★★★★ | Price $86.04 (as of Nov 25, 2011) | 12-Mo. Target Price $145.00 | Investment Style Large-Cap Value |
|---|---|---|---|---|

**GICS Sector** Industrials
**Sub-Industry** Construction & Farm Machinery & Heavy Trucks

**Summary** This leading manufacturer of truck engines also makes stand-by power equipment and industrial filters.

## Key Stock Statistics (Source S&P, Vickers, company reports)

| | | | | | | | |
|---|---|---|---|---|---|---|---|
| 52-Wk Range | $121.49–79.53 | S&P Oper. EPS 2011E | 8.78 | Market Capitalization(B) | $16.593 | Beta | 1.97 |
| Trailing 12-Month EPS | $8.54 | S&P Oper. EPS 2012E | 9.98 | Yield (%) | 1.86 | S&P 3-Yr. Proj. EPS CAGR(%) | 30 |
| Trailing 12-Month P/E | 10.1 | P/E on S&P Oper. EPS 2011E | 9.8 | Dividend Rate/Share | $1.60 | S&P Credit Rating | A |
| $10K Invested 5 Yrs Ago | $29,752 | Common Shares Outstg. (M) | 192.9 | Institutional Ownership (%) | 86 | | |

## Price Performance

30-Week Mov. Avg. · · · 10-Week Mov. Avg. - - GAAP Earnings vs. Previous Year Volume Above Avg. STARS
12-Mo. Target Price — Relative Strength — ▲ Up ▼ Down ▶ No Change Below Avg.

Options: ASE, CBOE, P, Ph

Analysis prepared by Equity Analyst **Jim Corridore** on Oct 28, 2011, when the stock traded at **$102.75**.

## Highlights

▶ We expect revenues to rise about 36% in 2011 and 15% in 2012, after a 22% increase in 2010. North American truck engine sales should continue to pick up into 2012 on pent-up demand and as customers become more comfortable with new engines being sold to meet more stringent EPA emissions. We project strong growth in engine sales in India, China, and Brazil, fueled by GDP growth and infrastructure projects in those regions. We expect improvement in North American class 8 truck demand in 2011, due to an aging national truck fleet and an improving U.S. economy.

▶ We look for EBIT margins of 14% for 2011, in line with guidance, versus 12.2% in 2010. We see 14.2% in 2012. We expect CMI to benefit from cost reductions and strong improvements in productivity at several of its plants. We also expect top-line growth to aid EBIT margins on fixed cost leverage and better capacity utilization.

▶ We estimate that operating EPS will improve to $8.78 in 2011, which would represent 66% growth over 2010 EPS of $5.28. For 2012, we see EPS growing 14%, to $9.98.

## Investment Rationale/Risk

▶ For the long term, with over 50% of its sales derived from outside North America, we believe CMI should benefit from its leading-edge technology in truck engines, helping it gain market share in emerging market countries and infrastructure-related power generation equipment. We think CMI will continue to use technology and its strong balance sheet to increase market share. Although the pace of the economic recovery has slowed, we still expect improving investor sentiment on signs of stronger economic growth.

▶ Risks to our recommendation and target price include weaker-than-projected demand in the truck manufacturing and/or power generation markets; slower-than-anticipated economic growth and/or industrial production; adverse forex volatility; and lower-than-estimated savings from expense reduction initiatives.

▶ Our 12-month target price of $145 values the shares at 14.5X our 2012 EPS estimate of $9.98, in the middle of CMI's five-year historical P/E range of 4.3X-23.9X. We think we are still in the early stages of a new earnings upcycle that we expect to last for several years.

## Qualitative Risk Assessment

| LOW | MEDIUM | HIGH |
|---|---|---|

Our risk assessment reflects the highly cyclical nature of the North America medium (class 5-7) and heavy-duty (class 8) truck markets and significant pension and post-retirement benefit obligations, offset by a geographically diverse mix of business and the low leverage of CMI's balance sheet.

## Quantitative Evaluations

**S&P Quality Ranking** B+

| D | C | B- | B | B+ | A- | A | A+ |
|---|---|---|---|---|---|---|---|

**Relative Strength Rank** MODERATE

36

LOWEST = 1 HIGHEST = 99

## Revenue/Earnings Data

**Revenue (Million $)**

| | 1Q | 2Q | 3Q | 4Q | Year |
|---|---|---|---|---|---|
| 2011 | 3,860 | 4,641 | 4,626 | -- | -- |
| 2010 | 2,478 | 3,208 | 3,401 | 4,139 | 13,226 |
| 2009 | 2,439 | 2,431 | 2,530 | 3,400 | 10,800 |
| 2008 | 3,474 | 3,887 | 3,693 | 3,288 | 14,342 |
| 2007 | 2,817 | 3,343 | 3,372 | 3,516 | 13,048 |
| 2006 | 2,678 | 2,842 | 2,809 | 3,033 | 11,362 |

**Earnings Per Share ($)**

| | | | | | |
|---|---|---|---|---|---|
| 2011 | 1.75 | 2.60 | 2.35 | E2.23 | E8.78 |
| 2010 | 0.75 | 1.25 | 1.44 | 1.84 | 5.28 |
| 2009 | 0.04 | 0.28 | 0.48 | 1.36 | 2.16 |
| 2008 | 0.97 | 1.49 | 1.17 | 0.45 | 4.08 |
| 2007 | 0.71 | 1.06 | 0.92 | 1.00 | 3.70 |
| 2006 | 0.68 | 1.10 | 0.84 | 0.94 | 3.55 |

Fiscal year ended Dec. 31. Next earnings report expected: Early February. EPS Estimates based on S&P Operating Earnings; historical GAAP earnings are as reported.

## Dividend Data (Dates: mm/dd Payment Date: mm/dd/yy)

| Amount ($) | Date Decl. | Ex-Div. Date | Stk. of Record | Payment Date |
|---|---|---|---|---|
| 0.263 | 02/08 | 02/16 | 02/18 | 03/01/11 |
| 0.263 | 05/10 | 05/18 | 05/20 | 06/01/11 |
| 0.400 | 07/12 | 08/18 | 08/22 | 09/01/11 |
| 0.400 | 10/17 | 11/17 | 11/21 | 12/01/11 |

Dividends have been paid since 1948. Source: Company reports.

# Cummins Inc.

STANDARD &POOR'S

## Business Summary October 28, 2011

CORPORATE OVERVIEW. This global equipment company makes and services diesel and natural gas engines, electric power generation systems and engine-related component products.

Cummins (CMI), founded in 1919, has long-standing relationships with many of the customers it serves, including Chrysler LLC, Daimler AG, Volvo AB, PACCAR Inc., International Truck and Engine Corp. (a unit of Navistar), CNH Global N.V., Komatsu, Scania AB, Ford Motor Corp., and Volkswagen. CMI has over 500 company-owned and independent distributor locations and about 5,200 dealer locations in over 190 countries and territories. CMI's key markets are the on-highway, construction, and general industrial markets.

The company believes that its competitive strengths include a group of leading brand names, alliances it has established with customers and partners, its global presence (international sales accounted for 64% of total sales in 2010), and its leading technology. In particular, Cummins' technology addresses the

reduction of diesel engine emissions. CMI's engines met the EPA's heavy-duty on-highway emission standards that went into effect in January 2010.

The engine segment (49% of sales in 2010) manufactures and markets a broad range of diesel and natural-gas powered engines under the Cummins brand name for the heavy- and medium-duty truck, bus, recreational vehicle (RV), light-duty automotive, agricultural, construction, mining, marine, oil and gas, rail and governmental equipment markets. CMI manufactures engines with displacements from 1.4 to 91 liters and horsepower ranging from 31 to 3,500. In addition, it provides new parts and service, as well as remanufactured parts and engines, through its extensive distribution network.

## Company Financials Fiscal Year Ended Dec. 31

| Per Share Data ($) | 2010 | 2009 | 2008 | 2007 | 2006 | 2005 | 2004 | 2003 | 2002 | 2001 |
|---|---|---|---|---|---|---|---|---|---|---|
| Tangible Book Value | 20.85 | 16.04 | 13.48 | 14.20 | 11.12 | 7.56 | 5.18 | 2.79 | 2.42 | 4.06 |
| Cash Flow | 6.90 | 3.80 | 5.44 | 5.15 | 4.96 | 4.54 | 3.38 | 1.75 | 1.79 | 0.85 |
| Earnings | 5.28 | 2.16 | 4.08 | 3.70 | 3.55 | 2.75 | 1.85 | 0.34 | 0.52 | -0.67 |
| S&P Core Earnings | 5.15 | 2.21 | 3.20 | 3.73 | 3.62 | 2.85 | 2.00 | 0.40 | -0.39 | -1.44 |
| Dividends | 0.87 | 0.70 | 0.60 | 0.43 | 0.33 | 0.30 | 0.30 | 0.30 | 0.30 | 0.30 |
| Payout Ratio | 17% | 32% | 15% | 12% | 9% | 11% | 16% | 88% | 58% | NM |
| Prices:High | 111.87 | 51.65 | 75.98 | 71.73 | 34.80 | 23.47 | 21.17 | 13.08 | 12.57 | 11.38 |
| Prices:Low | 44.84 | 18.34 | 17.70 | 28.16 | 22.17 | 15.90 | 12.03 | 5.43 | 4.90 | 7.00 |
| P/E Ratio:High | 21 | 24 | 19 | 19 | 10 | 9 | 11 | 38 | 24 | NM |
| P/E Ratio:Low | 9 | 8 | 4 | 8 | 6 | 6 | 7 | 16 | 10 | NM |

**Income Statement Analysis (Million $)**

| | 2010 | 2009 | 2008 | 2007 | 2006 | 2005 | 2004 | 2003 | 2002 | 2001 |
|---|---|---|---|---|---|---|---|---|---|---|
| Revenue | 13,226 | 10,800 | 14,342 | 13,048 | 11,362 | 9,918 | 8,438 | 6,296 | 5,853 | 5,681 |
| Operating Income | 1,571 | 887 | 1,382 | 1,221 | 1,287 | 1,058 | 696 | 316 | 327 | 304 |
| Depreciation | 320 | 326 | 314 | 290 | 296 | 295 | 272 | 223 | 219 | 231 |
| Interest Expense | 40.0 | 35.0 | 60.0 | 59.0 | 96.0 | 109 | 113 | 101 | 82.0 | 87.0 |
| Pretax Income | 1,617 | 640 | 1,251 | 1,169 | 1,083 | 798 | 432 | 80.0 | 57.0 | -129 |
| Effective Tax Rate | NA | 24.4% | 30.9% | 32.6% | 29.9% | 27.1% | 13.0% | 15.0% | NM | NM |
| Net Income | 1,040 | 428 | 801 | 739 | 715 | 550 | 350 | 54.0 | 79.0 | -102 |
| S&P Core Earnings | 1,016 | 438 | 631 | 744 | 729 | 570 | 380 | 62.8 | -61.4 | -221 |

**Balance Sheet & Other Financial Data (Million $)**

| | 2010 | 2009 | 2008 | 2007 | 2006 | 2005 | 2004 | 2003 | 2002 | 2001 |
|---|---|---|---|---|---|---|---|---|---|---|
| Cash | 1,362 | 1,120 | 503 | 697 | 935 | 840 | 690 | 195 | 298 | 92.0 |
| Current Assets | 6,289 | 5,003 | 4,713 | 4,815 | 4,488 | 3,916 | 3,273 | 2,130 | 1,982 | 1,635 |
| Total Assets | 10,402 | 8,816 | 8,491 | 8,195 | 7,465 | 6,885 | 6,527 | 5,126 | 4,837 | 4,335 |
| Current Liabilities | 3,260 | 2,432 | 2,639 | 2,711 | 2,399 | 2,218 | 2,197 | 1,391 | 1,329 | 970 |
| Long Term Debt | 709 | 637 | 629 | 555 | 647 | 1,213 | 1,299 | 1,380 | 1,290 | 1,206 |
| Common Equity | 4,670 | 3,773 | 3,277 | 3,409 | 2,802 | 1,864 | 2,802 | 949 | 841 | 1,025 |
| Total Capital | 5,705 | 4,657 | 4,139 | 4,257 | 3,703 | 3,302 | 4,309 | 2,452 | 2,223 | 2,314 |
| Capital Expenditures | 364 | 310 | 543 | 353 | 249 | 186 | 151 | 111 | 90.0 | 206 |
| Cash Flow | 1,360 | 752 | 1,069 | 1,029 | 1,011 | 845 | 622 | 277 | 298 | 129 |
| Current Ratio | 1.9 | 2.1 | 1.8 | 1.8 | 1.9 | 1.8 | 1.5 | 1.5 | 1.5 | 1.7 |
| % Long Term Debt of Capitalization | 12.4 | 13.7 | 15.1 | 13.0 | 17.5 | 36.7 | 30.1 | 56.3 | 58.0 | 52.1 |
| % Net Income of Revenue | 7.9 | 4.0 | 5.6 | 5.7 | 6.3 | 5.5 | 4.1 | 0.9 | 1.3 | NM |
| % Return on Assets | 10.8 | 4.9 | 9.6 | 9.4 | 10.0 | 8.2 | 6.0 | 1.1 | 1.7 | NM |
| % Return on Equity | 24.6 | 12.2 | 24.0 | 23.8 | 30.6 | 33.7 | 14.9 | 6.0 | 8.7 | NM |

Data as orig reptd.; bef. results of disc opers/spec. items. Per share data adj. for stk. divs.; EPS diluted. E-Estimated. NA-Not Available. NM-Not Meaningful. NR-Not Ranked. UR-Under Review.

Office: 500 Jackson Street, PO Box 3005, Columbus, IN 47202-3005.
Telephone: 812-377-5000.
Email: investor_relations@cummins.com
Website: http://www.cummins.com

Chrmn & CEO: T.M. Solso
Pres & COO: N.T. Linebarger
CFO: P.J. Ward
Chief Admin Officer: M. Gerstle

CTO: J. Wall
Investor Contact: D.A. Cantrell (812-377-3121)
Board Members: R. J. Bernhard, F. R. Chang-Diaz, S. B. Dobbs, R. K. Herdman, A. Herman, N. T. Linebarger, W. I. Miller, II, G. R. Nelson, T. M. Solso, C. Ware

Founded: 1919
Domicile: Indiana
Employees: 39,200

# CVS Caremark Corp

**STANDARD &POOR'S**

| S&P Recommendation | STRONG BUY ★★★★★ | Price $36.85 (as of Nov 25, 2011) | 12-Mo. Target Price $45.00 | Investment Style Large-Cap Blend |
|---|---|---|---|---|

**GICS Sector** Consumer Staples
**Sub-Industry** Drug Retail

**Summary** This company is a leading operator of retail drug stores and pharmacy benefit management services in the U.S.

## Key Stock Statistics (Source S&P, Vickers, company reports)

| | | | | | |
|---|---|---|---|---|---|
| 52-Wk Range | $39.50–30.73 | S&P Oper. EPS 2011**E** 2.82 | Market Capitalization(B) $47.965 | Beta | 0.80 |
| Trailing 12-Month EPS | $2.51 | S&P Oper. EPS 2012**E** 3.25 | Yield (%) 1.36 | S&P 3-Yr. Proj. EPS CAGR(%) | 13 |
| Trailing 12-Month P/E | 14.7 | P/E on S&P Oper. EPS 2011**E** 13.1 | Dividend Rate/Share $0.50 | S&P Credit Rating | BBB+ |
| $10K Invested 5 Yrs Ago | $13,828 | Common Shares Outstg. (M) 1,301.6 | Institutional Ownership (%) 88 | | |

## Price Performance

30-Week Mov. Avg. ···   10-Week Mov. Avg. – –   GAAP Earnings vs. Previous Year   Volume Above Avg. STARS
12-Mo. Target Price —   Relative Strength —   ▲ Up   ▼ Down   ► No Change   Below Avg. ★

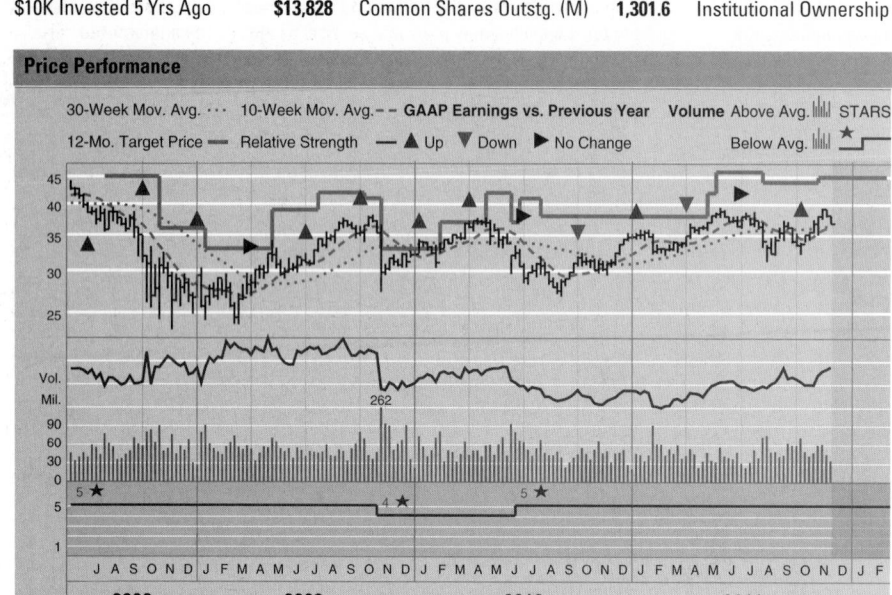

Options: ASE, CBOE, P, Ph

Analysis prepared by Equity Analyst **Joseph Agnese** on Nov 09, 2011, when the stock traded at **$39.04**.

## Highlights

➤ We expect total sales in 2012 to rise 6.1%, to $114.4 billion, from our estimate of $107.8 billion in 2011, reflecting the signing of new pharmacy benefit management (PBM) clients, 2.5% retail drug store comparable store sales growth, and about 2.5% net new square footage growth. Our 2011 estimate includes an estimated $900 million associated with acquisition of Universal American Corp. in April 2011.

➤ We see margins widening in 2012, reflecting increased sales of wider margin generic drugs, improved sales leverage, and improved results from in-store health clinics, despite increased pharmacy drug reimbursement pressures, significant costs related to efforts to streamline the PBM segment, and a change in business mix within the PBM segment.

➤ After benefits from a reduction in the share count due to an active share repurchase program, we project that 2012 operating EPS will rise 15%, to $3.25, from estimated operating EPS of $2.82 in 2011 (excluding amortization of intangibles in both periods).

## Investment Rationale/Risk

➤ We believe CVS is well positioned to benefit over the next few years from pharmacy benefit management market share gains, as favorable demographics result in increased customer drug utilization and as a significant increase in generic drug offerings that we expect by 2012 lead to margin expansion. This is despite what we see an unfavorable near-term environment characterized by a lull in new generic drug offerings and decreased consumer drug utilization in a weak economic environment.

➤ Risks to our recommendation and target price include a greater-than-expected decline in drug reimbursements from federal and state governments, as well as a loss of market share within the PBM services or retail pharmacy businesses.

➤ Due to our expectation of a more favorable environment in 2012, we believe CVS is undervalued on a P/E basis when compared to the S&P 500, its historical range and its closest peers. Assuming that the shares trade at 13.8X our 2012 EPS estimate of $3.25, we arrive at our 12-month target price of $45.

## Qualitative Risk Assessment

| LOW | **MEDIUM** | HIGH |
|---|---|---|

Our risk assessment reflects our view of the company's leadership position and strong market share position in the relatively stable U.S. retail drug industry, offset by acquisition-integration risk and the growth of non-traditional competitors.

## Quantitative Evaluations

**S&P Quality Ranking**                          A+

| D | C | B- | B | B+ | A- | A | **A+** |
|---|---|---|---|---|---|---|---|

**Relative Strength Rank**                       **STRONG**

84

LOWEST = 1                              HIGHEST = 99

## Revenue/Earnings Data

**Revenue (Million $)**

| | 1Q | 2Q | 3Q | 4Q | Year |
|---|---|---|---|---|---|
| 2011 | 25,880 | 26,629 | 26,674 | -- | -- |
| 2010 | 23,760 | 24,007 | 23,875 | 24,771 | 96,413 |
| 2009 | 23,394 | 24,871 | 24,642 | 25,822 | 98,729 |
| 2008 | 21,326 | 21,140 | 20,863 | 24,142 | 87,472 |
| 2007 | 13,189 | 20,703 | 20,495 | 21,942 | 76,330 |
| 2006 | 9,979 | 10,561 | 11,207 | 12,066 | 43,814 |

**Earnings Per Share ($)**

| | | | | | |
|---|---|---|---|---|---|
| 2011 | 0.52 | 0.60 | 0.65 | E0.91 | E2.82 |
| 2010 | 0.55 | 0.60 | 0.60 | 0.75 | 2.50 |
| 2009 | 0.51 | 0.60 | 0.71 | 0.74 | 2.56 |
| 2008 | 0.51 | 0.56 | 0.56 | 0.65 | 2.27 |
| 2007 | 0.43 | 0.47 | 0.45 | 0.55 | 1.92 |
| 2006 | 0.39 | 0.40 | 0.33 | 0.49 | 1.60 |

Fiscal year ended Dec. 31. Next earnings report expected: Early February. EPS Estimates based on S&P Operating Earnings; historical GAAP earnings are as reported.

## Dividend Data (Dates: mm/dd Payment Date: mm/dd/yy)

| Amount ($) | Date Decl. | Ex-Div. Date | Stk. of Record | Payment Date |
|---|---|---|---|---|
| 0.125 | 01/11 | 01/19 | 01/21 | 02/02/11 |
| 0.125 | 03/09 | 04/19 | 04/22 | 05/03/11 |
| 0.125 | 07/06 | 07/20 | 07/22 | 08/02/11 |
| 0.125 | 09/21 | 10/19 | 10/21 | 11/01/11 |

Dividends have been paid since 1916. Source: Company reports.

---

**Please read the Required Disclosures and Analyst Certification on the last page of this report.**

The McGraw·Hill Companies

# CVS Caremark Corp

STANDARD
&POOR'S

## Business Summary November 09, 2011

CORPORATE OVERVIEW. CVS Caremark Corporation operates one of the largest drug store chains and pharmacy benefit managers in the U.S., based on revenues, net income and store count. Drug stores offer prescription drugs and a wide assortment of general merchandise, including OTC drugs, beauty products and cosmetics, film and photo finishing services, seasonal merchandise, greeting cards and convenience foods. Pharmacy benefit management offerings include mail order pharmacy service, specialty pharmacy services, plan design and administration, formulary management and claims processing.

MARKET PROFILE. CVS operated about 7,200 stores as of December 2010, in 41 states, Puerto Rico and the District of Columbia. As of December 2010, the company had stores in 92 of the top 100 U.S. drug store markets, holding the number one or number two market share in 72 of these markets. It filled more than 636 million prescriptions in 2010, accounting for about 18% of the U.S. retail pharmacy market. Pharmacy operations are critical to CVS's success, in our view, accounting for 68% of retail store sales in 2010. Payments by third-party managed care providers under prescription drug plans accounted for 97% of pharmacy sales in 2010. CVS's pharmacy benefit management (PBM) business generated $47.8 billion of sales in 2010, or 45% of total company sales (excluding intersegment eliminations). The company's specialty phar-

macy business operates 44 retail specialty pharmacy stores and 18 specialty mail order pharmacies.

CVS is also the largest operator of retail health care clinics in the U.S. As of December 2010, it operated 560 retail health care clinics in 26 states under the MinuteClinic name. The clinics diagnose and treat minor health conditions, perform health screenings, monitor chronic conditions and deliver vaccinations. The company plans to open 100 new clinics annually over the next five years.

CORPORATE STRATEGY. Through its retail and pharmacy services segments, the company plans to benefit from favorable industry trends, which include an aging U.S. population, increased generic drug utilization, the discovery of new drugs, growth of specialty pharmacy services, and health care reform. CVS's long-term strategy focuses on expanding its retail drug store business in high-growth markets and increasing the size and product offerings of its PBM business. Historically, the company has grown, in large part, through acquisitions.

## Company Financials Fiscal Year Ended Dec. 31

| Per Share Data ($) | 2010 | 2009 | 2008 | 2007 | 2006 | 2005 | 2004 | 2003 | 2002 | 2001 |
|---|---|---|---|---|---|---|---|---|---|---|
| Tangible Book Value | 1.65 | NM | NM | NM | 6.29 | 6.77 | 4.98 | 5.98 | 5.05 | 4.45 |
| Cash Flow | 3.56 | 3.52 | 3.13 | 2.71 | 2.45 | 2.14 | 1.69 | 1.46 | 1.25 | 0.88 |
| Earnings | 2.50 | 2.56 | 2.27 | 1.92 | 1.60 | 1.45 | 1.10 | 1.03 | 0.88 | 0.50 |
| S&P Core Earnings | 2.50 | 2.56 | 2.27 | 1.92 | 1.61 | 1.41 | 1.06 | 0.98 | 0.80 | 0.41 |
| Dividends | 0.35 | 0.30 | 0.26 | 0.23 | 0.16 | 0.15 | 0.13 | 0.12 | 0.12 | 0.12 |
| Payout Ratio | 14% | 12% | 11% | 12% | 10% | 10% | 12% | 11% | 13% | 23% |
| Prices:High | 37.82 | 38.27 | 44.29 | 42.60 | 36.14 | 31.60 | 23.67 | 18.78 | 17.85 | 31.88 |
| Prices:Low | 26.84 | 23.74 | 23.19 | 30.45 | 26.06 | 22.02 | 16.87 | 10.92 | 11.52 | 11.45 |
| P/E Ratio:High | 15 | 15 | 20 | 22 | 23 | 22 | 22 | 18 | 20 | 64 |
| P/E Ratio:Low | 11 | 9 | 10 | 16 | 16 | 15 | 15 | 11 | 13 | 23 |

| Income Statement Analysis (Million $) | 2010 | 2009 | 2008 | 2007 | 2006 | 2005 | 2004 | 2003 | 2002 | 2001 |
|---|---|---|---|---|---|---|---|---|---|---|
| Revenue | 96,413 | 98,729 | 87,472 | 76,330 | 43,814 | 37,006 | 30,594 | 26,588 | 24,182 | 22,241 |
| Operating Income | 7,634 | 7,827 | 7,343 | 5,970 | 3,175 | 2,609 | 1,952 | 1,765 | 1,517 | 1,091 |
| Depreciation | 1,469 | 1,389 | 1,274 | 1,095 | 733 | 589 | 497 | 342 | 310 | 321 |
| Interest Expense | 536 | 530 | 558 | 492 | 216 | 111 | 58.3 | 48.0 | 50.4 | 61.0 |
| Pretax Income | 5,629 | 5,913 | 5,537 | 4,359 | 2,226 | 1,909 | 1,396 | 1,376 | 1,156 | 710 |
| Effective Tax Rate | NA | 37.3% | 39.6% | 39.5% | 38.5% | 35.8% | 34.2% | 38.4% | 38.0% | 41.8% |
| Net Income | 3,439 | 3,708 | 3,344 | 2,637 | 1,369 | 1,225 | 919 | 847 | 717 | 413 |
| S&P Core Earnings | 3,442 | 3,708 | 3,330 | 2,623 | 1,365 | 1,171 | 869 | 785 | 635 | 323 |

| Balance Sheet & Other Financial Data (Million $) | 2010 | 2009 | 2008 | 2007 | 2006 | 2005 | 2004 | 2003 | 2002 | 2001 |
|---|---|---|---|---|---|---|---|---|---|---|
| Cash | 1,431 | 1,091 | 1,352 | 1,084 | 531 | 513 | 392 | 843 | 700 | 236 |
| Current Assets | 17,706 | 17,537 | 16,526 | 14,149 | 10,392 | 8,393 | 7,920 | 6,497 | 5,982 | 5,454 |
| Total Assets | 62,169 | 61,641 | 60,960 | 54,722 | 20,570 | 15,283 | 14,547 | 10,543 | 9,645 | 8,628 |
| Current Liabilities | 11,070 | 12,300 | 13,490 | 10,766 | 7,001 | 4,584 | 4,859 | 3,489 | 3,106 | 3,066 |
| Long Term Debt | 8,652 | 8,756 | 8,057 | 8,350 | 2,870 | 1,594 | 1,926 | 753 | 1,076 | 810 |
| Common Equity | 37,700 | 35,768 | 34,383 | 31,163 | 9,704 | 8,109 | 6,759 | 6,022 | 4,991 | 4,306 |
| Total Capital | 47,525 | 46,665 | 46,333 | 43,048 | 12,788 | 9,925 | 8,913 | 6,817 | 6,318 | 12,706 |
| Capital Expenditures | 2,005 | 2,548 | 2,180 | 1,805 | 1,769 | 1,495 | 1,348 | 1,122 | 1,109 | 714 |
| Cash Flow | 4,908 | 5,097 | 4,604 | 3,717 | 2,088 | 1,800 | 1,401 | 1,189 | 1,012 | 719 |
| Current Ratio | 1.6 | 1.4 | 1.2 | 1.3 | 1.5 | 1.8 | 1.6 | 1.9 | 1.9 | 1.8 |
| % Long Term Debt of Capitalization | 18.2 | 18.8 | 17.4 | 19.4 | 22.4 | 16.1 | 21.6 | 11.0 | 17.0 | 63.8 |
| % Net Income of Revenue | 3.6 | 3.8 | 3.8 | 3.5 | 3.1 | 3.3 | 3.0 | 3.2 | 3.0 | 1.9 |
| % Return on Assets | 5.6 | 6.1 | 5.8 | 7.0 | 7.6 | 8.2 | 7.3 | 8.4 | 7.8 | 5.0 |
| % Return on Equity | 9.4 | 10.6 | 10.2 | 12.8 | 15.2 | 16.3 | 14.4 | 15.4 | 15.1 | 9.6 |

Data as orig reptd.; bef. results of disc opers/spec. items. Per share data adj. for stk. divs.; EPS diluted. E-Estimated. NA-Not Available. NM-Not Meaningful. NR-Not Ranked. UR-Under Review.

Office: One CVS Drive, Woonsocket, RI 02895-6184.
Telephone: 401-765-1500.
Email: investorinfo@cvs.com
Website: http://www.cvs.com

Chrmn: D.W. Dorman
Pres & CEO: L.J. Merlo
EVP & CFO: D.M. Denton
SVP, Chief Acctg Officer & Cntlr: L.K. Daniels

SVP & Treas: C.A. Denale
Investor Contact: N.R. Christal (914-722-4704)
Auditor: ERNST & YOUNG
Board Members: E. M. Banks, C. D. Brown, II, D. W. Dorman, A. M. Finucane, M. L. Heard, L. J. Merlo, J. Millon, T. Murray, C. A. Piccolo, R. J. Swift, T. L. White, K. E. Williams

Founded: 1892
Domicile: Delaware
Employees: 280,000

The McGraw-Hill Companies

# Danaher Corp

STANDARD &POOR'S

| S&P Recommendation **HOLD** ★★★★☆ | Price $44.56 (as of Nov 25, 2011) | 12-Mo. Target Price $54.00 | Investment Style Large-Cap Growth |

**GICS Sector** Industrials
**Sub-Industry** Industrial Conglomerates

**Summary** This company is a leading maker of tools, including Sears Craftsman hand tools, and process/environmental controls and telecommunications equipment.

## Key Stock Statistics (Source S&P, Vickers, company reports)

| | | | | | | | |
|---|---|---|---|---|---|---|---|
| 52-Wk Range | $56.09– 39.34 | S&P Oper. EPS 2011E | 2.84 | Market Capitalization(B) | $30.584 | Beta | 0.91 |
| Trailing 12-Month EPS | $3.00 | S&P Oper. EPS 2012E | 3.29 | Yield (%) | 0.22 | S&P 3-Yr. Proj. EPS CAGR(%) | 16 |
| Trailing 12-Month P/E | 14.9 | P/E on S&P Oper. EPS 2011E | 15.7 | Dividend Rate/Share | $0.10 | S&P Credit Rating | A+ |
| $10K Invested 5 Yrs Ago | $12,067 | Common Shares Outstg. (M) | 686.3 | Institutional Ownership (%) | 76 | | |

## Price Performance

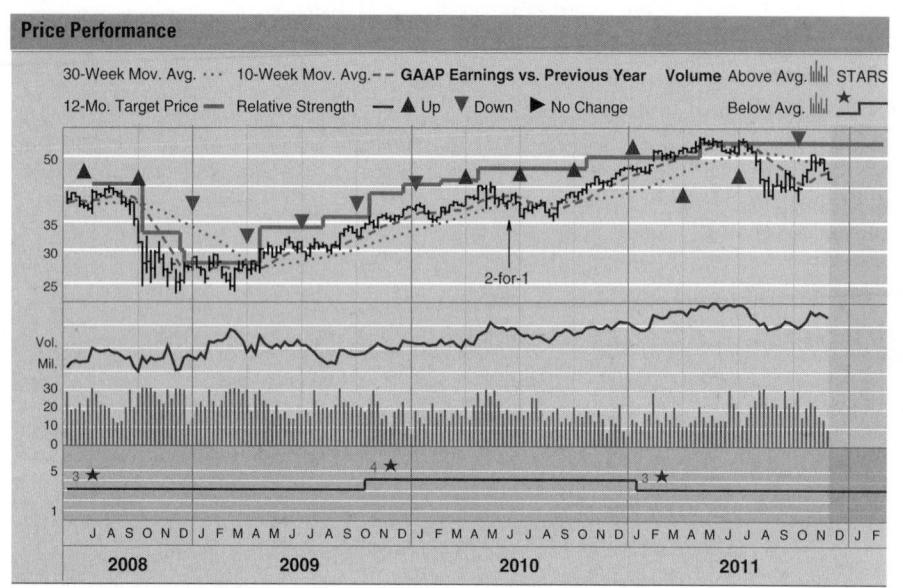

- 30-Week Mov. Avg. ···· 10-Week Mov. Avg. ── GAAP Earnings vs. Previous Year  Volume Above Avg. STARS
- 12-Mo. Target Price ── Relative Strength ▲ Up ▼ Down ▶ No Change  Below Avg. ★

2-for-1

2008 2009 2010 2011

Options: ASE, CBOE, P, Ph

Analysis prepared by Equity Analyst **Efraim Levy, CFA** on Oct 28, 2011, when the stock traded at **$50.56**.

### Highlights

▸ We estimate that Danaher's revenues will advance about 22% in 2011, as acquisitions, including that of Beckman Coulter, and global economic growth outweigh the Pacific Scientific divestiture. With acquisitions likely to slow in 2012, we estimate sales will expand just 11%. DHR is focusing its expansion on faster-growing, high technology businesses and new and rapidly growing geographic markets.

▸ We see streamlining activities aiding margins. The company will focus on restraining SG&A growth, but plans to expand research and development investment. We expect the Beckman Coulter acquisition to be accretive to EPS starting in the fourth quarter.

▸ For the long term, we see sales increases driven by internal growth, supplemented by acquisitions. We anticipate that a steady flow of new and enhanced products, as well as greater sales of traditional tool lines, will aid comparisons. We expect margins to widen over time, as DHR consolidates acquisitions and likely benefits from higher capacity utilization, productivity gains and cost-cutting efforts. In addition, the company has targeted acquisitions of companies with gross margins above 50%.

### Investment Rationale/Risk

▸ We view DHR's balance sheet as strong. Based on several valuation measures, the shares trade at a premium to some peers, which we believe reflects DHR's wider net margins and faster growth. Its earnings quality appears high to us, as we expect free cash flow in 2011 and 2012 to exceed net income. We view positively DHR's 10 million share buyback program. Although we consider its balance sheet to be strong, we expect the company's acquisition pace to slow, as it works to replenish its liquidity.

▸ Risks to our recommendation and target price include slowing demand for DHR's products and unfavorable changes in foreign exchange rates. Also, we are concerned about some of Danaher's corporate governance practices, particularly its classified board of directors with staggered terms, which may allow certain policies to remain entrenched longer despite shareholders' possible desire to change them.

▸ Our 12-month target price of $54 is derived by applying a multiple of 16.4X to our 2012 EPS estimate of $3.29, reflecting relative historical multiples, peer multiples, and brighter prospects for global GDP.

### Qualitative Risk Assessment

| LOW | MEDIUM | HIGH |

Our risk assessment reflects our view of favorable growth prospects in most of the company's markets, good corporate leadership and a solid balance sheet, offset by corporate governance issues.

### Quantitative Evaluations

**S&P Quality Ranking**                    A+

| D | C | B- | B | B+ | A- | A | A+ |

**Relative Strength Rank**              MODERATE

57

LOWEST = 1                              HIGHEST = 99

### Revenue/Earnings Data

**Revenue (Million $)**

| | 1Q | 2Q | 3Q | 4Q | Year |
|---|---|---|---|---|---|
| 2011 | 3,346 | 3,712 | 518.1 | -- | -- |
| 2010 | 3,092 | 3,311 | 3,190 | 3,609 | 13,203 |
| 2009 | 2,628 | 2,674 | 2,751 | 3,133 | 11,185 |
| 2008 | 3,029 | 3,284 | 3,208 | 3,177 | 12,697 |
| 2007 | 2,556 | 2,671 | 2,731 | 3,141 | 11,026 |
| 2006 | 2,144 | 2,350 | 2,443 | 2,660 | 9,596 |

**Earnings Per Share ($)**

| | | | | | |
|---|---|---|---|---|---|
| 2011 | 0.61 | 0.65 | 0.74 | E0.81 | E2.84 |
| 2010 | 0.45 | 0.55 | 0.95 | 0.69 | 2.64 |
| 2009 | 0.36 | 0.45 | 0.52 | 0.40 | 1.73 |
| 2008 | 0.42 | 0.55 | 0.56 | 0.46 | 1.96 |
| 2007 | 0.39 | 0.48 | 0.52 | 0.49 | 1.86 |
| 2006 | 0.34 | 0.49 | 0.42 | 0.50 | 1.74 |

Fiscal year ended Dec. 31. Next earnings report expected: Late January. EPS Estimates based on S&P Operating Earnings; historical GAAP earnings are as reported.

### Dividend Data (Dates: mm/dd Payment Date: mm/dd/yy)

| Amount ($) | Date Decl. | Ex-Div. Date | Stk. of Record | Payment Date |
|---|---|---|---|---|
| 0.020 | 12/07 | 12/29 | 12/31 | 01/28/11 |
| 0.020 | 02/23 | 03/23 | 03/25 | 04/29/11 |
| 0.020 | 05/11 | 06/22 | 06/24 | 07/29/11 |
| 0.025 | 09/13 | 09/28 | 09/30 | 10/28/11 |

Dividends have been paid since 1993. Source: Company reports.

# Danaher Corp

STANDARD
&POOR'S

## Business Summary October 28, 2011

CORPORATE OVERVIEW. Danaher Corp. is a leading maker of hand tools and process and environmental controls. The company has five reporting segments: test and measurement (22% of 2010 sales), environmental (21%), life sciences and diagnostics (17%), dental (14%), and industrial technologies 24%. The Apex joint venture contributed 2% of revenues.

The test and measurement segment offers electronic measurement instruments, monitoring, management and optimization tools for communications networks.

The environmental segment provides products that help protect the water supply and air quality and serves two primary markets: water quality and retail/commercial petroleum.

The life sciences businesses provide research and clinical tools that are used by scientists to study cells and their components to gain a better understanding of complex biological matters.

The dental business provides a range of equipment and consumables for the dental market, focused on developing, manufacturing and marketing innovative solutions for dental professionals around the world.

The industrial technologies segment manufactures products and sub-systems

that are typically incorporated by customers and systems integrators into production and packaging lines as well as by original equipment manufacturers into various end-products.

In 2010, Danaher and Cooper Industries plc formed a joint venture named Apex Tool Group LLC. Each company contributed its respective tools business to, and received a 50% interest in, the joint venture.

Sales in 2010 by geographic destination were: U.S. 45%, Europe 28%, Asia/Australia 17%, and other regions 10%.

CORPORATE STRATEGY. The company seeks to expand revenues through a combination of internal growth and acquisitions. We expect the company to continue its tradition of successful acquisition integrations. During 2010, the company acquired 19 businesses for an aggregate of about $1.1 billion, versus 15 businesses for an aggregate of $704 million in 2009, and 17 businesses for about $423 million in 2008.

## Company Financials Fiscal Year Ended Dec. 31

| Per Share Data ($) | 2010 | 2009 | 2008 | 2007 | 2006 | 2005 | 2004 | 2003 | 2002 | 2001 |
|---|---|---|---|---|---|---|---|---|---|---|
| Tangible Book Value | NM | NM | NM | NM | NM | NM | NM | 0.50 | 0.00 | NM |
| Cash Flow | 3.21 | 1.11 | 2.46 | 2.25 | 2.06 | 1.64 | 1.38 | 1.04 | 0.94 | 0.78 |
| Earnings | 2.64 | 1.73 | 1.96 | 1.86 | 1.74 | 1.38 | 1.15 | 0.84 | 0.75 | 0.50 |
| S&P Core Earnings | 2.65 | 1.66 | 1.87 | 1.86 | 1.74 | 1.35 | 1.10 | 0.78 | 0.60 | 0.42 |
| Dividends | 0.08 | 0.07 | 0.06 | 0.06 | 0.04 | 0.03 | 0.03 | 0.03 | 0.02 | 0.02 |
| Payout Ratio | 3% | 4% | 3% | 3% | 2% | 2% | 2% | 4% | 3% | 4% |
| Prices:High | 47.59 | 38.28 | 44.10 | 44.61 | 37.64 | 29.20 | 29.45 | 23.09 | 18.87 | 17.17 |
| Prices:Low | 35.24 | 23.87 | 23.60 | 34.56 | 27.02 | 24.16 | 21.91 | 14.89 | 13.15 | 10.98 |
| P/E Ratio:High | 18 | 22 | 23 | 24 | 22 | 21 | 26 | 27 | 25 | 34 |
| P/E Ratio:Low | 13 | 14 | 12 | 19 | 16 | 18 | 19 | 18 | 18 | 22 |

| Income Statement Analysis (Million $) | | | | | | | | | | |
|---|---|---|---|---|---|---|---|---|---|---|
| Revenue | 13,203 | 11,185 | 12,697 | 11,026 | 9,596 | 7,985 | 6,889 | 5,294 | 4,577 | 3,782 |
| Operating Income | 2,541 | 2,037 | 2,350 | 2,055 | 1,719 | 1,446 | 1,253 | 957 | 824 | 750 |
| Depreciation | 397 | 342 | 339 | 268 | 217 | 177 | 156 | 133 | 130 | 178 |
| Interest Expense | 121 | 123 | 130 | 110 | 79.8 | 44.9 | 55.0 | 59.0 | 43.7 | 25.7 |
| Pretax Income | 2,343 | 1,425 | 1,749 | 1,637 | 1,446 | 1,234 | 1,058 | 797 | 657 | 476 |
| Effective Tax Rate | NA | 19.2% | 24.7% | 25.9% | 22.4% | 27.3% | 29.5% | 32.6% | 29.4% | 37.5% |
| Net Income | 1,793 | 1,152 | 1,318 | 1,214 | 1,122 | 898 | 746 | 537 | 464 | 298 |
| S&P Core Earnings | 1,802 | 1,105 | 1,243 | 1,215 | 1,121 | 876 | 715 | 491 | 373 | 249 |

| Balance Sheet & Other Financial Data (Million $) | | | | | | | | | | |
|---|---|---|---|---|---|---|---|---|---|---|
| Cash | 1,633 | 1,722 | 393 | 239 | 318 | 316 | 609 | 1,230 | 810 | 707 |
| Current Assets | 5,730 | 5,221 | 4,187 | 4,050 | 3,395 | 2,945 | 2,919 | 2,942 | 2,387 | 1,875 |
| Total Assets | 22,217 | 19,595 | 17,458 | 17,472 | 12,864 | 9,163 | 8,494 | 6,890 | 6,029 | 4,820 |
| Current Liabilities | 3,305 | 2,761 | 2,745 | 2,900 | 2,460 | 2,269 | 2,202 | 1,380 | 1,265 | 1,017 |
| Long Term Debt | 2,784 | 2,889 | 2,553 | 3,396 | 2,423 | 858 | 926 | 1,284 | 1,197 | 1,119 |
| Common Equity | 13,711 | 11,630 | 9,809 | 9,086 | 6,645 | 5,080 | 4,620 | 3,647 | 3,010 | 2,229 |
| Total Capital | 16,597 | 14,563 | 12,428 | 12,481 | 9,068 | 5,938 | 5,545 | 4,931 | 4,207 | 3,348 |
| Capital Expenditures | 217 | 189 | 194 | 162 | 138 | 121 | 116 | 80.3 | 65.4 | 80.6 |
| Cash Flow | 2,190 | 1,493 | 1,657 | 1,482 | 1,339 | 1,075 | 902 | 670 | 594 | 476 |
| Current Ratio | 1.7 | 1.9 | 1.5 | 1.4 | 1.4 | 1.3 | 1.3 | 2.1 | 1.9 | 1.8 |
| % Long Term Debt of Capitalization | 16.8 | 19.8 | 20.5 | 27.2 | 26.7 | 14.4 | 16.7 | 26.0 | 28.5 | 33.4 |
| % Net Income of Revenue | 13.6 | 10.3 | 10.4 | 11.0 | 11.7 | 11.2 | 10.8 | 10.1 | 10.1 | 7.9 |
| % Return on Assets | 8.6 | 6.2 | 7.5 | 8.0 | 10.2 | 10.2 | 9.7 | 8.3 | 8.6 | 6.7 |
| % Return on Equity | 14.2 | 10.7 | 14.0 | 15.4 | 19.1 | 18.5 | 18.0 | 16.1 | 17.7 | 14.3 |

Data as orig reptd.; bef. results of disc opers/spec. items. Per share data adj. for stk. divs.; EPS diluted. E-Estimated. NA-Not Available. NM-Not Meaningful. NR-Not Ranked. UR-Under Review.

**Office:** 2200 Pennsylvania Avenue NW, Suite 800 West, Washington, DC 20037-1701.
**Telephone:** 202-828-0850.
**Email:** ir@danaher.com
**Website:** http://www.danaher.com

**Chrmn:** S.M. Rales
**Pres & CEO:** H.L. Culp, Jr.
**EVP & CFO:** D.L. Comas
**SVP & Chief Acctg Officer:** R.S. Lutz

**SVP & General Counsel:** J.P. Graham
**Board Members:** M. M. Caplin, H. L. Culp, Jr., D. J. Ehrlich, L. Hefner, W. G. Lohr, Jr., M. P. Rales, S. M. Rales, J. T. Schwieters, A. G. Spoon, E. Z. Zerhouni

**Founded:** 1969
**Domicile:** Delaware
**Employees:** 48,200

# Darden Restaurants Inc.

STANDARD &POOR'S

**S&P Recommendation** HOLD ★★★☆☆

| | | |
|---|---|---|
| **Price** $44.60 (as of Nov 25, 2011) | **12-Mo. Target Price** $52.00 | **Investment Style** Large-Cap Growth |

**GICS Sector** Consumer Discretionary
**Sub-Industry** Restaurants

**Summary** This restaurant company operates the Red Lobster, Olive Garden, Bahama Breeze and Seasons 52 chains, as well as the LongHorn Steakhouse and Capital Grille chains, which it acquired in October 2007.

## Key Stock Statistics (Source S&P, Vickers, company reports)

| | | | | | | | |
|---|---|---|---|---|---|---|---|
| 52-Wk Range | $53.81– 40.69 | S&P Oper. EPS 2012**E** | 3.68 | Market Capitalization(B) | $5.879 | Beta | 0.87 |
| Trailing 12-Month EPS | $3.38 | S&P Oper. EPS 2013**E** | 4.10 | Yield (%) | 3.86 | S&P 3-Yr. Proj. EPS CAGR(%) | 11 |
| Trailing 12-Month P/E | 13.2 | P/E on S&P Oper. EPS 2012**E** | 12.1 | Dividend Rate/Share | $1.72 | S&P Credit Rating | BBB |
| $10K Invested 5 Yrs Ago | $12,603 | Common Shares Outstg. (M) | 131.8 | Institutional Ownership (%) | 79 | | |

## Price Performance

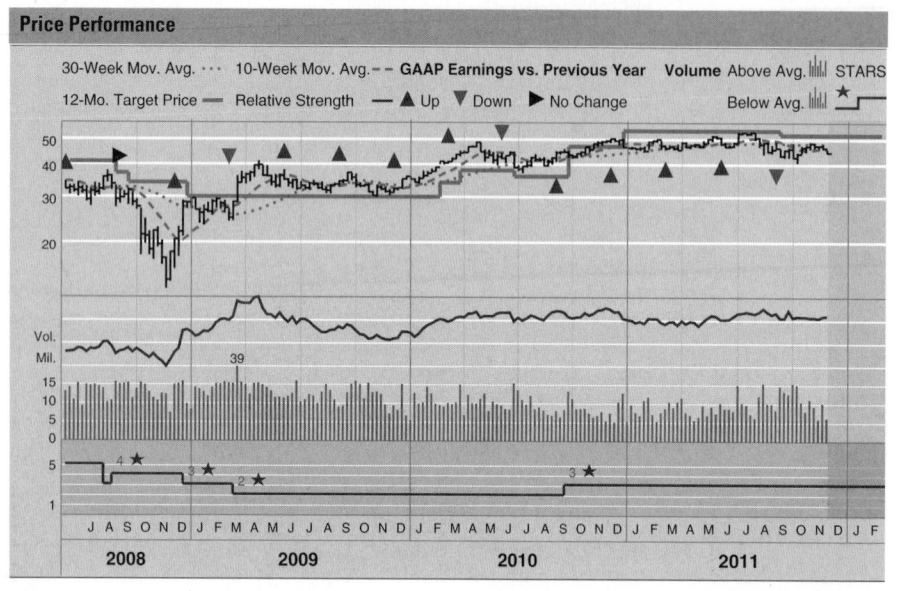

30-Week Mov. Avg. · · · · 10-Week Mov. Avg. – – GAAP Earnings vs. Previous Year Volume Above Avg. STARS
12-Mo. Target Price — Relative Strength — ▲ Up ▼ Down ▶ No Change Below Avg. ★

Options: ASE, CBOE, P, Ph

Analysis prepared by Equity Analyst **Jim Yin, CFA** on Oct 12, 2011, when the stock traded at **$46.86**.

## Highlights

► We see total sales rising about 6.5% in FY 12 (May), with the number of restaurants increasing 4.5% and same-store sales advancing about 2.0%. We believe most of the gain in same-store sales comps will be the result of higher menu prices, as DRI plans to raise its prices between 2% and 3% per year. We think traffic will be relatively flat, given the sluggish economy and the decline in consumer confidence. We also think Olive Garden will continue to underperform due to changes in consumers' preference, and promotional spending may not generate the anticipated traction.

► We think operating margins will narrow to 9.4% in FY 12, from 9.9% in FY 11, due to higher food prices. We also believe a shift in the menu mix, as some consumers trade down to lower-priced items, will hurt margins. We think interest payments in FY 12 will be about $84 million now that debt levels have stabilized.

► We estimate EPS of $3.68 for FY 12, up from $3.41 in FY 11, on 4.1% fewer shares outstanding. For FY 13, we forecast EPS of $4.10.

## Investment Rationale/Risk

► Our hold recommendation reflects our cautious outlook on the U.S. economy. It has slowed considerably in the first half of 2011, and we expect growth to remain sluggish in 2012. We think consumers will become more wary about their future and reduce the number of times they would dine out. Recent results for Olive Garden have been relatively weak, and we are concerned that the brand is losing appeal with customers. Still, we think DRI is taking steps to improve its operations such as controlling its costs.

► Risks to our recommendation and target price include an unexpected acceleration in food cost inflation. Also, consumers may be less resilient than we expect, leading to lower traffic than we anticipate, possibly exacerbated by higher unemployment and ongoing economic uncertainty.

► Our 12-month target price of $52 is based on our relative P/E analysis. We apply a multiple of 14.1X to our FY 12 EPS estimate of $3.68, well within the range for DRI's peer group.

## Qualitative Risk Assessment

| LOW | MEDIUM | HIGH |
|---|---|---|

DRI competes in the casual dining industry, and we believe that its Red Lobster and Olive Garden concepts have among the strongest brand name recognition in the industry. However, the casual dining segment over-expanded in recent years, in our opinion, with an industry consolidation being accelerated by the recession. A slow recovery for the industry is likely.

## Quantitative Evaluations

**S&P Quality Ranking**      A

| D | C | B- | B | B+ | A- | A | A+ |
|---|---|---|---|---|---|---|---|

**Relative Strength Rank**     MODERATE

58

LOWEST = 1          HIGHEST = 99

## Revenue/Earnings Data

**Revenue (Million $)**

| | 1Q | 2Q | 3Q | 4Q | Year |
|---|---|---|---|---|---|
| 2012 | 1,942 | -- | -- | -- | -- |
| 2011 | 1,807 | 1,726 | 1,977 | 1,990 | 7,500 |
| 2010 | 1,734 | 1,641 | 1,874 | 1,864 | 7,113 |
| 2009 | 1,774 | 1,669 | 1,799 | 1,976 | 7,218 |
| 2008 | 1,468 | 1,522 | 1,811 | 1,826 | 6,627 |
| 2007 | 1,360 | 1,298 | 1,450 | 1,460 | 5,567 |

**Earnings Per Share ($)**

| | | | | | |
|---|---|---|---|---|---|
| 2012 | 0.78 | E0.78 | E1.05 | E1.08 | E3.68 |
| 2011 | 0.80 | 0.54 | 1.08 | 1.00 | 3.41 |
| 2010 | 0.67 | 0.43 | 0.95 | 0.81 | 2.86 |
| 2009 | 0.58 | 0.42 | 0.78 | 0.87 | 2.65 |
| 2008 | 0.58 | 0.30 | 0.80 | 0.72 | 2.55 |
| 2007 | 0.62 | 0.45 | 0.79 | 0.67 | 2.53 |

Fiscal year ended May 31. Next earnings report expected: Late December. EPS Estimates based on S&P Operating Earnings; historical GAAP earnings are as reported.

## Dividend Data (Dates: mm/dd Payment Date: mm/dd/yy)

| Amount ($) | Date Decl. | Ex-Div. Date | Stk. of Record | Payment Date |
|---|---|---|---|---|
| 0.320 | 12/20 | 01/06 | 01/10 | 02/01/11 |
| 0.320 | 03/24 | 04/06 | 04/08 | 05/02/11 |
| 0.430 | 06/30 | 07/07 | 07/11 | 08/01/11 |
| 0.430 | 09/28 | 10/06 | 10/11 | 11/01/11 |

Dividends have been paid since 1995. Source: Company reports.

---

**Please read the Required Disclosures and Analyst Certification on the last page of this report.**

The McGraw-Hill Companies

# Darden Restaurants Inc.

## Business Summary October 12, 2011

CORPORATE OVERVIEW. With systemwide sales from continuing operations of more than $7.5 billion in FY 11 (May), Darden Restaurants is the world's largest publicly held casual dining restaurant company. As of May 29, 2011, it operated 1,894 restaurants in the U.S. and Canada, including 698 Red Lobster units, 754 Olive Garden units, 354 LongHorn Steakhouse locations, and 88 other restaurants divided among The Capital Grille, Bahama Breeze and Seasons 52 chains.

Olive Garden is the largest full service dining Italian restaurant operator in the United States. Olive Garden's menu includes a variety of authentic Italian foods featuring fresh ingredients and a wine list that includes a broad selection of wines imported from Italy. Most dinner menu entree prices range from $9.25 - $24.50, and most lunch menu entree prices range from $6.95 - $16.25. For FY 11, the average check per person was $16.00 to $16.50.

Red Lobster, founded by William Darden in 1968, is the largest full service dining seafood specialty restaurant operator in the United States. It offers an extensive menu featuring fresh fish, shrimp, crab, lobster, scallops and other seafood in a casual atmosphere. Most dinner entree prices range from $10.00 - $33.25, and most lunch entree prices range from $6.99 - $12.99. During FY 11, the average check per person was approximately $19.75 to $20.25.

On October 1, 2007, DRI acquired RARE Hospitality International, Inc., in a cash tender offer for all RARE common shares at $38.15 per share, or total consideration of $1.41 billion in cash. Financing was obtained under a $1.2 billion senior interim credit facility and a $700 million senior revolver. Most members of RARE management agreed to join DRI in roles generally similar to those they had at RARE.

RARE operations included the LongHorn Steakhouse chain. LongHorn Steakhouse restaurants are full service establishments serving both lunch and dinner in an attractive and inviting atmosphere reminiscent of the classic American West. Its menu items include signature fresh steaks, as well as salmon, shrimp, chicken, ribs, pork chops, burgers and prime rib. Most dinner menu entree prices range from $12.00 - $23.00, and most lunch menu entree prices range from $8.00 - $15.00. During FY 11, the average check per person was approximately $18.50 to $19.00.

## Company Financials Fiscal Year Ended May 31

| Per Share Data ($) | 2011 | 2010 | 2009 | 2008 | 2007 | 2006 | 2005 | 2004 | 2003 | 2002 |
|---|---|---|---|---|---|---|---|---|---|---|
| Tangible Book Value | 6.54 | 5.92 | 3.89 | 2.45 | 7.57 | 8.20 | 8.25 | 7.86 | 7.03 | 6.56 |
| Cash Flow | 5.67 | 4.97 | 4.61 | 4.19 | 3.88 | 3.57 | 3.08 | 2.60 | 2.43 | 2.20 |
| Earnings | 3.41 | 2.86 | 2.65 | 2.55 | 2.53 | 2.16 | 1.78 | 1.36 | 1.31 | 1.30 |
| S&P Core Earnings | 3.44 | 2.82 | 2.56 | 2.56 | 2.54 | 2.53 | 2.10 | 1.68 | 1.27 | 1.18 | 1.16 |
| Dividends | NA | 1.00 | 0.72 | 0.46 | 0.40 | 0.08 | 0.08 | 0.08 | 0.05 | 0.05 |
| Payout Ratio | NA | 29% | 27% | 18% | 16% | 4% | 4% | 6% | 4% | 4% |
| Calendar Year | 2010 | 2009 | 2008 | 2007 | 2006 | 2005 | 2004 | 2003 | 2002 | 2001 |
| Prices:High | 50.84 | 41.21 | 37.83 | 47.60 | 44.43 | 39.53 | 28.54 | 23.01 | 29.76 | 24.98 |
| Prices:Low | 33.72 | 23.32 | 13.21 | 26.90 | 32.91 | 25.78 | 18.48 | 16.50 | 18.00 | 12.67 |
| P/E Ratio:High | 15 | 14 | 14 | 19 | 18 | 18 | 16 | 17 | 23 | 19 |
| P/E Ratio:Low | 10 | 8 | 5 | 11 | 13 | 12 | 10 | 12 | 14 | 10 |

| Income Statement Analysis (Million $) | | | | | | | | | | |
|---|---|---|---|---|---|---|---|---|---|---|
| Revenue | 7,500 | 7,113 | 7,218 | 6,627 | 5,567 | 5,721 | 5,278 | 5,003 | 4,655 | 4,369 |
| Operating Income | 1,063 | 945 | 895 | 878 | 774 | 757 | 685 | 636 | 588 | 563 |
| Depreciation | 317 | 301 | 275 | 238 | 200 | 221 | 213 | 210 | 198 | 166 |
| Interest Expense | 93.6 | 93.9 | 118 | 35.2 | 40.7 | 43.1 | 43.1 | 43.7 | 44.1 | 37.8 |
| Pretax Income | 648 | 544 | 513 | 515 | 531 | 483 | 424 | 340 | 348 | 363 |
| Effective Tax Rate | NA | NA | 27.5% | 28.2% | 29.0% | 29.9% | 31.4% | 31.9% | 33.2% | 34.5% |
| Net Income | 479 | 407 | 372 | 370 | 377 | 338 | 291 | 231 | 232 | 238 |
| S&P Core Earnings | 482 | 402 | 360 | 367 | 378 | 330 | 274 | 214 | 208 | 212 |

| Balance Sheet & Other Financial Data (Million $) | | | | | | | | | | |
|---|---|---|---|---|---|---|---|---|---|---|
| Cash | 70.5 | 249 | 62.9 | 43.2 | 30.2 | 42.3 | 42.8 | 36.7 | 48.6 | 153 |
| Current Assets | 664 | 678 | 555 | 468 | 545 | 378 | 407 | 346 | 326 | 450 |
| Total Assets | 5,467 | 5,247 | 5,025 | 4,731 | 2,881 | 3,010 | 2,938 | 2,780 | 2,665 | 2,530 |
| Current Liabilities | 1,287 | 1,255 | 1,096 | 1,136 | 1,074 | 1,026 | 1,045 | 683 | 640 | 601 |
| Long Term Debt | 1,407 | 1,409 | 1,632 | 1,634 | 492 | 495 | 350 | 653 | 658 | 663 |
| Common Equity | 1,936 | 1,894 | 1,606 | 1,409 | 1,115 | 1,230 | 1,273 | 1,246 | 1,196 | 1,129 |
| Total Capital | 3,344 | 3,528 | 3,238 | 3,043 | 1,633 | 1,815 | 1,738 | 2,075 | 2,005 | 1,909 |
| Capital Expenditures | 548 | 432 | 535 | 429 | 345 | 338 | 329 | 354 | 423 | 318 |
| Cash Flow | 796 | 708 | 646 | 608 | 578 | 560 | 504 | 441 | 430 | 404 |
| Current Ratio | 0.5 | 0.5 | 0.5 | 0.4 | 0.5 | 0.4 | 0.4 | 0.5 | 0.5 | 0.7 |
| % Long Term Debt of Capitalization | 42.1 | 39.9 | 50.4 | 53.6 | 30.1 | 27.3 | 20.2 | 31.5 | 32.8 | 34.7 |
| % Net Income of Revenue | 6.4 | 5.7 | 5.2 | 5.6 | 6.8 | 5.9 | 5.5 | 4.6 | 5.0 | 5.4 |
| % Return on Assets | 8.9 | 7.9 | 7.6 | 9.7 | 12.8 | 11.4 | 10.2 | 8.5 | 8.9 | 10.0 |
| % Return on Equity | 25.0 | 23.3 | 24.7 | 29.5 | 31.6 | 27.0 | 23.7 | 19.0 | 20.0 | 22.0 |

Data as orig reptd.; bef. results of disc opers/spec. items. Per share data adj. for stk. divs.; EPS diluted. E-Estimated. NA-Not Available. NM-Not Meaningful. NR-Not Ranked. UR-Under Review.

**Office:** 5900 Lake Ellenor Drive, Orlando, FL 32809-4634.
**Telephone:** 407-245-4000.
**Email:** irinfo@darden.com
**Website:** http://www.darden.com

**Chrmn & CEO:** C. Otis, Jr.
**Pres & COO:** A.H. Madsen
**Investor Contact:** C.B. Richmond (407-245-4000)
**SVP, CFO & Chief Acctg Officer:** C.B. Richmond

**SVP, Secy & General Counsel:** T.M. Sebastian
**Board Members:** L. L. Berry, O. C. Donald, C. J. Fraleigh, V. D. Harker, D. H. Hughes, C. A. Ledsinger, Jr., W. M. Lewis, Jr., C. Mack, III, A. H. Madsen, C. Otis, Jr., M. D. Rose, M. A. Sastre

**Founded:** 1968
**Domicile:** Florida
**Employees:** 178,380

The McGraw-Hill Companies

# DaVita Inc

## STANDARD &POOR'S

| S&P Recommendation **BUY** ★★★★☆ | Price $72.85 (as of Nov 25, 2011) | 12-Mo. Target Price $96.00 | Investment Style Large-Cap Growth |
|---|---|---|---|

**GICS Sector** Health Care
**Sub-Industry** Health Care Services

**Summary** This company is one of the largest worldwide providers of integrated dialysis services for patients suffering from chronic kidney failure.

### Key Stock Statistics (Source S&P, Vickers, company reports)

| | | | | | | |
|---|---|---|---|---|---|---|
| 52-Wk Range | $89.76– 59.14 | S&P Oper. EPS 2011**E** | 5.06 | Market Capitalization(B) | $6.811 | Beta | 0.36 |
| Trailing 12-Month EPS | $4.10 | S&P Oper. EPS 2012**E** | 6.20 | Yield (%) | Nil | S&P 3-Yr. Proj. EPS CAGR(%) | 13 |
| Trailing 12-Month P/E | 17.8 | P/E on S&P Oper. EPS 2011**E** | 14.4 | Dividend Rate/Share | Nil | S&P Credit Rating | BB- |
| $10K Invested 5 Yrs Ago | $13,694 | Common Shares Outstg. (M) | 93.5 | Institutional Ownership (%) | 94 | | |

## Price Performance

30-Week Mov. Avg. · · · 10-Week Mov. Avg. – – GAAP Earnings vs. Previous Year   Volume Above Avg. ▥ STARS
12-Mo. Target Price — Relative Strength — ▲ Up ▼ Down ► No Change   Below Avg. ▥ ★

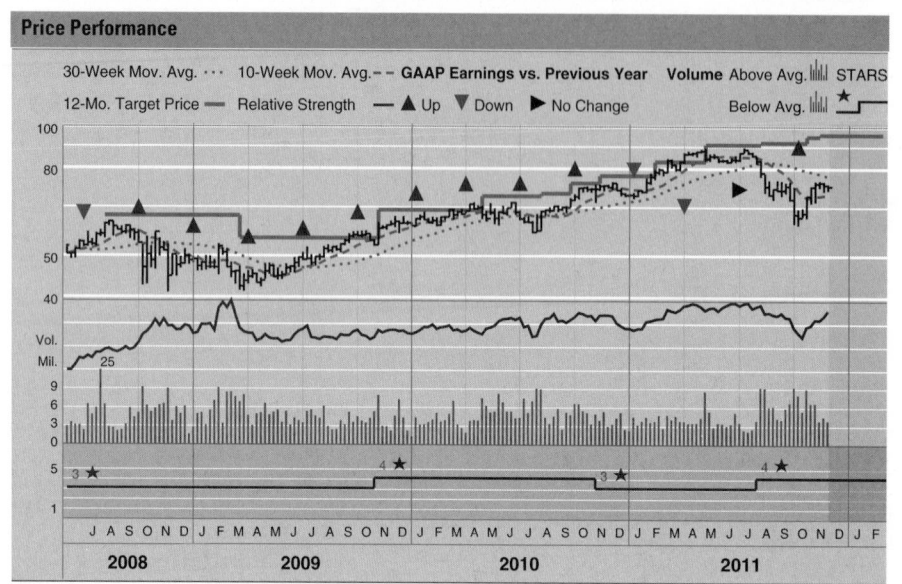

Options: CBOE, P, Ph

Analysis prepared by Equity Analyst **Steven Silver** on Nov 08, 2011, when the stock traded at **$73.85**.

### Highlights

➤ We see sales rising 8% in 2011 and 9% in 2012, with results being boosted by the acquisition of DSI Renal, which closed in September 2011. We expect long-term revenue growth to be supported by an aging U.S. population, stable demand for dialysis services, and a robust acquisition environment. Although we see DVA facing a declining payor mix toward Medicare and Medicaid, which are less profitable than commercial insurers, we are encouraged by stable commercial pricing trends.

➤ We forecast EBITDA margins of 20.1% in 2011 and 20.8% in 2012, with near-term margins impacted by international dialysis market expansion investments, which we view as being in an early stage. Longer term, we project margin expansion as bundled dialysis pricing lowers DVA's drug supply costs, particularly for erythropoietin (EPO). We see bad debt provisions stabilizing, partially given more patients from Medicare and Medicaid.

➤ We estimate adjusted EPS of $5.06 in 2011 and $6.20 in 2012. Our estimates assume 97 million shares outstanding in 2011 and 95 million in 2012.

### Investment Rationale/Risk

➤ Our buy recommendation reflects a positive outlook for DVA to benefit from a stable near-term reimbursement environment, with a 1.8% Medicare rate increase scheduled for fiscal 2012. However, we expect Medicare reimbursement to remain challenging over the longer term. We view DVA's fundamentals as favorable, with strong cash flows supporting acquisitions geared toward expanding its patient base and driving efficiencies through economies of scale. We expect DVA to secure long-term contracts with managed care companies to stabilize its revenues, as it is dependent on commercial pricing, which is sharply above Medicare rates, for most of its profits.

➤ Risks to our recommendation and target price include risk of restrictions over EPO utilization, unfavorable Medicare rule changes, heightened competition, and reduced reimbursement.

➤ Our 12-month target price of $96 assumes a multiple of 15.5X our 2012 EPS estimate, in line with DVA's long-term forward average P/E, which reflects favorable demographic trends tempered by long-term reimbursement uncertainties.

### Qualitative Risk Assessment

| LOW | MEDIUM | HIGH |
|---|---|---|

Our risk assessment reflects our view of stable demand for dialysis services, driven by a rising senior population in the U.S., offset by DVA's dependence on third-party payments, including Medicare and Medicaid.

### Quantitative Evaluations

**S&P Quality Ranking**   B+

| D | C | B- | B | B+ | A- | A | A+ |
|---|---|---|---|---|---|---|---|

**Relative Strength Rank**   STRONG

86

LOWEST = 1                    HIGHEST = 99

### Revenue/Earnings Data

**Revenue (Million $)**

| | 1Q | 2Q | 3Q | 4Q | Year |
|---|---|---|---|---|---|
| 2011 | 1,606 | 1,712 | 1,808 | -- | -- |
| 2010 | 1,559 | 1,587 | 1,652 | 1,649 | 6,447 |
| 2009 | 1,448 | 1,519 | 1,574 | 1,568 | 6,109 |
| 2008 | 1,345 | 1,407 | 1,447 | 1,461 | 5,660 |
| 2007 | 1,278 | 1,313 | 1,318 | 1,355 | 5,264 |
| 2006 | 1,163 | 1,208 | 1,237 | 1,273 | 4,881 |

**Earnings Per Share ($)**

| | 1Q | 2Q | 3Q | 4Q | Year |
|---|---|---|---|---|---|
| 2011 | 0.96 | 1.03 | 1.45 | E1.48 | E5.06 |
| 2010 | 1.04 | 1.03 | 1.15 | 0.70 | 3.94 |
| 2009 | 0.92 | 1.02 | 1.06 | 1.06 | 4.06 |
| 2008 | 0.80 | 0.90 | 0.89 | 0.94 | 3.53 |
| 2007 | 0.72 | 1.17 | 0.88 | 0.79 | 3.55 |
| 2006 | 0.55 | 0.61 | 0.88 | 0.70 | 2.73 |

Fiscal year ended Dec. 31. Next earnings report expected: Mid February. EPS Estimates based on S&P Operating Earnings; historical GAAP earnings are as reported.

### Dividend Data

No cash dividends have been paid.

The **McGraw·Hill** Companies

# DaVita Inc

STANDARD
&POOR'S

## Business Summary November 08, 2011

CORPORATE OVERVIEW. Da Vita is a leading U.S. provider of dialysis and related services for patients suffering from chronic kidney failure, also known as end-stage renal disease (ESRD). As of December 31, 2010, DVA provided dialysis and ancillary services to about 125,000 patients through a network of 1,612 outpatient dialysis facilities. In addition, the company provided acute inpatient dialysis services at over 700 hospitals.

As a result of DVA's growth through acquisitions, it has occasionally become highly leveraged, in our opinion. In 2005, DVA acquired 492 centers through the Gambro acquisition, as well as 12 independent centers. In 2010, the company acquired 41 centers, opened 65 new centers, sold six and closed 21. As of December 31, 2010, the company had a debt leverage ratio of 2.72X, up from 2.56X at the end of 2009, within its 4.25X-1.0X approved range.

Hemodialysis uses an artificial kidney, called a dialyze, to remove certain toxins, fluids and salt from the patient's blood, together with a machine to control external blood flow and to monitor certain vital signs of the patient. Peritoneal dialysis uses the patient's peritoneal (abdominal) cavity to eliminate fluid and toxins.

MARKET PROFILE. ESRD is a state of advanced renal impairment that is irreversible and requires routine dialysis treatments (three times per week) or kidney transplantation to sustain life. Treatment options for ESRD include hemodialysis, peritoneal dialysis, and kidney transplantation.

## Company Financials Fiscal Year Ended Dec. 31

| Per Share Data ($) | 2010 | 2009 | 2008 | 2007 | 2006 | 2005 | 2004 | 2003 | 2002 | 2001 |
|---|---|---|---|---|---|---|---|---|---|---|
| Tangible Book Value | NM | NM | NM | NM | NM | NM | NM | NM | NM | NM |
| Cash Flow | 6.97 | 6.26 | 5.43 | 5.36 | 4.37 | 3.14 | 3.00 | 2.20 | 1.85 | 1.56 |
| Earnings | 3.94 | 4.06 | 3.53 | 3.55 | 2.73 | 1.99 | 2.16 | 1.66 | 1.52 | 1.01 |
| S&P Core Earnings | 3.94 | 4.06 | 3.53 | 3.48 | 2.73 | 1.89 | 2.07 | 1.59 | 1.41 | 0.89 |
| Dividends | Nil | Nil | Nil | Nil | Nil | Nil | Nil | Nil | Nil | Nil |
| Payout Ratio | Nil | Nil | Nil | Nil | Nil | Nil | Nil | Nil | Nil | Nil |
| Prices:High | 74.61 | 61.97 | 60.23 | 67.44 | 60.70 | 53.90 | 41.10 | 26.94 | 17.63 | 16.33 |
| Prices:Low | 56.58 | 41.21 | 40.96 | 50.75 | 46.70 | 38.87 | 25.23 | 12.77 | 12.67 | 9.33 |
| P/E Ratio:High | 19 | 15 | 17 | 19 | 22 | 27 | 19 | 16 | 12 | 16 |
| P/E Ratio:Low | 14 | 10 | 12 | 14 | 17 | 20 | 12 | 8 | 8 | 9 |

| Income Statement Analysis (Million $) | 2010 | 2009 | 2008 | 2007 | 2006 | 2005 | 2004 | 2003 | 2002 | 2001 |
|---|---|---|---|---|---|---|---|---|---|---|
| Revenue | 6,447 | 6,109 | 5,660 | 5,264 | 4,881 | 2,974 | 2,299 | 2,016 | 1,855 | 1,651 |
| Operating Income | 1,222 | 1,167 | 1,069 | 1,046 | 911 | 607 | 510 | 461 | 456 | 423 |
| Depreciation | 234 | 229 | 201 | 193 | 173 | 120 | 86.7 | 74.7 | 64.7 | 105 |
| Interest Expense | 182 | 186 | 229 | 257 | 277 | 140 | 52.4 | 66.8 | 71.6 | 71.7 |
| Pretax Income | 744 | 758 | 656 | 628 | 512 | 353 | 376 | 296 | 325 | 250 |
| Effective Tax Rate | NA | 36.7% | 35.9% | 39.2% | 36.4% | 35.0% | 37.2% | 38.1% | 39.8% | 41.8% |
| Net Income | 484 | 423 | 374 | 382 | 289 | 207 | 222 | 176 | 187 | 136 |
| S&P Core Earnings | 406 | 423 | 374 | 374 | 289 | 197 | 213 | 167 | 175 | 118 |

| Balance Sheet & Other Financial Data (Million $) | 2010 | 2009 | 2008 | 2007 | 2006 | 2005 | 2004 | 2003 | 2002 | 2001 |
|---|---|---|---|---|---|---|---|---|---|---|
| Cash | 883 | 566 | 446 | 487 | 310 | 432 | 252 | 61.7 | 96.5 | 36.7 |
| Current Assets | 2,623 | 2,303 | 2,128 | 1,976 | 1,709 | 1,654 | 869 | 605 | 545 | 475 |
| Total Assets | 8,114 | 7,558 | 7,286 | 6,944 | 6,492 | 6,280 | 2,512 | 1,946 | 1,776 | 1,663 |
| Current Liabilities | 924 | 1,047 | 1,163 | 1,087 | 1,112 | 990 | 442 | 363 | 293 | 299 |
| Long Term Debt | 4,234 | 3,532 | 3,618 | 3,684 | 3,730 | 4,085 | 1,322 | 1,117 | 1,311 | 811 |
| Common Equity | 1,978 | 2,135 | 1,952 | 1,732 | 1,246 | 851 | 523 | 307 | 70.3 | 504 |
| Total Capital | 7,171 | 6,158 | 5,808 | 5,733 | 5,224 | 5,100 | 2,048 | 1,563 | 1,474 | 1,359 |
| Capital Expenditures | 274 | 275 | 318 | 272 | 263 | 161 | 128 | 100 | 103 | 51.2 |
| Cash Flow | 719 | 652 | 575 | 575 | 463 | 327 | 309 | 250 | 251 | 242 |
| Current Ratio | 2.8 | 2.2 | 1.8 | 1.8 | 1.5 | 1.7 | 2.0 | 1.7 | 1.9 | 1.6 |
| % Long Term Debt of Capitalization | 59.0 | 57.4 | 60.5 | 66.2 | 71.4 | 80.1 | 64.6 | 71.4 | 89.0 | 59.7 |
| % Net Income of Revenue | 7.5 | 6.9 | 6.6 | 7.3 | 5.9 | 7.0 | 9.7 | 8.7 | 10.1 | 8.3 |
| % Return on Assets | 6.2 | 5.7 | 5.3 | 5.7 | 4.5 | 4.7 | 10.0 | 9.4 | 10.9 | 8.4 |
| % Return on Equity | 23.5 | 20.7 | 20.3 | 25.6 | 27.6 | 30.2 | 53.6 | 93.2 | 65.1 | 32.0 |

Data as orig reptd.; bef. results of disc opers/spec. items. Per share data adj. for stk. divs.; EPS diluted. E-Estimated. NA-Not Available. NM-Not Meaningful. NR-Not Ranked. UR-Under Review.

**Office:** 1551 Wewatta Street, Denver, CO 80202.
**Telephone:** 303-405-2100.
**Email:** ir@davita.com
**Website:** http://www.davita.com

**Chrmn & CEO:** K.J. Thiry
**COO:** D. Kogod
**CFO:** L.A. Borgen
**Chief Acctg Officer & Cntlr:** J.K. Hilger

**Secy & General Counsel:** K.M. Rivera
**Investor Contact:** L. Zumwalt (800-310-4872)
**Board Members:** P. M. Arway, C. G. Berg, W. W. Brittain, Jr., W. W. Brittian, Jr., C. A. Davidson, P. J. Diaz, P. T. Grauer, J. M. Nehra, W. L. Roper, K. J. Thiry, R. J. Valine

**Founded:** 1994
**Domicile:** Delaware
**Employees:** 36,500

# Dean Foods Co

**STANDARD &POOR'S**

## S&P Recommendation SELL ★ ★ ★ ★ ★

| | | |
|---|---|---|
| **Price** $9.28 (as of Nov 25, 2011) | **12-Mo. Target Price** $9.00 | **Investment Style** Large-Cap Blend |

**GICS Sector** Consumer Staples
**Sub-Industry** Packaged Foods & Meats

**Summary** This leading U.S. dairy processor and distributor was formed in December 2001 when Suiza Foods, the largest U.S. dairy, acquired Dean Foods and adopted the Dean Foods name.

## Key Stock Statistics (Source S&P, Vickers, company reports)

| | | | | | | | |
|---|---|---|---|---|---|---|---|
| 52-Wk Range | $13.90–7.13 | S&P Oper. EPS 2011E | 0.72 | Market Capitalization(B) | $1.705 | Beta | 0.72 |
| Trailing 12-Month EPS | $-8.66 | S&P Oper. EPS 2012E | 0.92 | Yield (%) | Nil | S&P 3-Yr. Proj. EPS CAGR(%) | 14 |
| Trailing 12-Month P/E | NM | P/E on S&P Oper. EPS 2011E | 12.9 | Dividend Rate/Share | Nil | S&P Credit Rating | B+ |
| $10K Invested 5 Yrs Ago | $3,158 | Common Shares Outstg. (M) | 183.7 | Institutional Ownership (%) | 75 | | |

## Price Performance

30-Week Mov. Avg. · · · · 10-Week Mov. Avg. – – **GAAP Earnings vs. Previous Year** Volume Above Avg. STARS
12-Mo. Target Price — Relative Strength — ▲ Up ▼ Down ► No Change Below Avg. ★

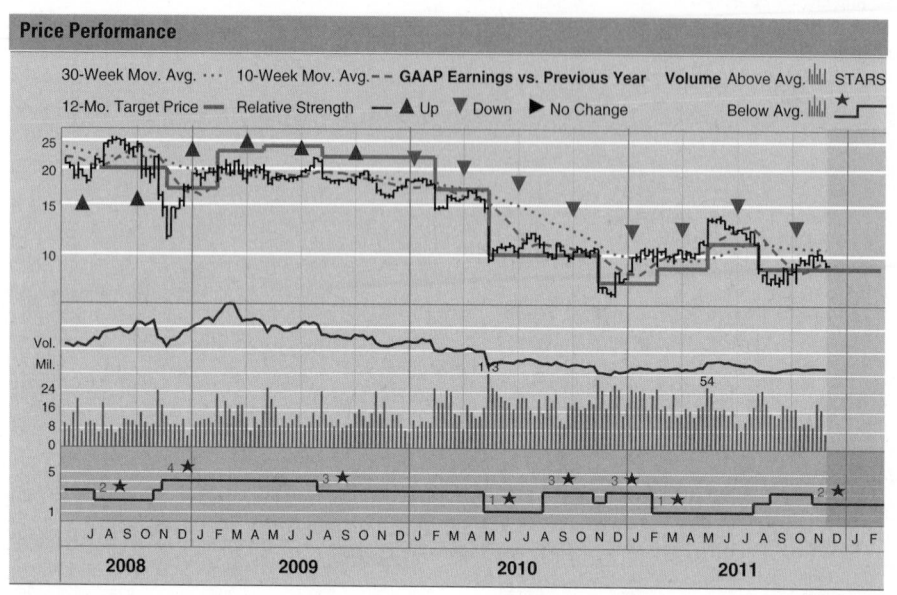

Options: CBOE, P, Ph

## Qualitative Risk Assessment

| LOW | **MEDIUM** | HIGH |
|---|---|---|

Our risk assessment reflects our view of DF's leading position in the U.S. milk market, and our expectation of future free cash flow. However, milk prices can be volatile, and some products are likely to enjoy stronger demand and growth than others.

## Quantitative Evaluations

**S&P Quality Ranking** B-

| D | C | **B-** | B | B+ | A- | A | A+ |
|---|---|---|---|---|---|---|---|

**Relative Strength Rank** MODERATE

62

LOWEST = 1          HIGHEST = 99

## Highlights

➤ The STARS recommendation for DF has recently been changed to 2 (sell) from 3 (hold). The Highlights section of this Stock Report will be updated accordingly.

## Investment Rationale/Risk

➤ The Investment Rationale/Risk section of this Stock Report will be updated shortly. For the latest News story on DF from MarketScope, see below.

➤ 11/09/11 12:13 pm ET ... S&P LOWERS OPINION ON SHARES OF DEAN FOODS TO SELL FROM HOLD (DF 9.94**): Before special items, Q3 EPS of $0.18, vs. $0.13, is $0.03 above our estimate, with lower-than-anticipated effective tax rate. Before special items, we raise our '11 EPS forecast to $0.72 from $0.70, and '12's to $0.92 from $0.88, partly due to tax rates. However, we view the extent of DF goodwill impairment charge (more than $8/share) as a concern. Ahead, we expect additional benefits from cost reductions. However, we think DF is more of a commodity-type business than some other food companies, which we expect will limit the stock's valuation. Our target price stays at $9.00. /Tom Graves, CFA

## Revenue/Earnings Data

### Revenue (Million $)

| | 1Q | 2Q | 3Q | 4Q | Year |
|---|---|---|---|---|---|
| 2011 | 3,050 | 3,299 | 3,411 | -- | -- |
| 2010 | 2,972 | 2,955 | 3,054 | 3,153 | 12,123 |
| 2009 | 2,703 | 2,681 | 2,774 | 3,001 | 11,158 |
| 2008 | 3,077 | 3,103 | 3,195 | 3,080 | 12,455 |
| 2007 | 2,630 | 2,844 | 3,117 | 3,232 | 11,822 |
| 2006 | 2,509 | 2,478 | 2,518 | 2,594 | 10,099 |

### Earnings Per Share ($)

| | 1Q | 2Q | 3Q | 4Q | Year |
|---|---|---|---|---|---|
| 2011 | 0.14 | -0.28 | -8.41 | E0.23 | E0.72 |
| 2010 | 0.23 | 0.25 | 0.11 | -0.11 | 0.47 |
| 2009 | 0.48 | 0.38 | 0.27 | 0.27 | 1.38 |
| 2008 | 0.21 | 0.31 | 0.24 | 0.43 | 1.21 |
| 2007 | 0.47 | 0.21 | 0.05 | 0.24 | 0.95 |
| 2006 | 0.37 | 0.53 | 0.54 | 0.56 | 2.01 |

Fiscal year ended Dec. 31. Next earnings report expected: Mid February. EPS Estimates based on S&P Operating Earnings; historical GAAP earnings are as reported.

## Dividend Data

A special cash dividend of $15 a share was paid in April 2007.

**The McGraw·Hill** Companies

# Dean Foods Co

## Business Summary August 29, 2011

CORPORATE OVERVIEW. Dean Foods Co. is a leading U.S. processor and distributor of milk and other dairy products. In December 2001, Suiza Foods Corp., the largest U.S. dairy, acquired Dean Foods Co. Suiza subsequently changed its name to Dean Foods Co. The company has grown partly through an acquisition strategy and by realizing regional economies of scale and operating efficiencies by consolidating manufacturing and distribution operations. Some of DF's products are sold under licensed brand names.

In 2010, DF changed its presentation of business segments. Fresh Dairy Direct-Morningstar is DF's largest segment, accounting for 84% of 2010 sales. Its products include milk, ice cream, cultured dairy products, creamers, ice cream mix and other dairy products, which are distributed under regional brands such as Country Fresh, Dean's, Garelick Farms, Mayfield and Oak Farms, as well as familiar local brands and private labels. Products are delivered through what the company believes to be one of the most extensive refrigerated direct-store-delivery (DSD) systems in the U.S., as well as through customer warehouse delivery systems.

DF's WhiteWave-Alpro segment, which accounted for the remaining 16% of 2010 sales, includes the WhiteWave business, which manufactures and sells a variety of nationally branded soy, dairy and dairy-related products, such as

Horizon Organic milk and other dairy products, Silk soy milk and cultured soy products, The Organic Cow dairy products, International Delight coffee creamers, and LAND O LAKES creamers and fluid dairy products.

DF's Alpro business manufactures and sells branded soy beverages and soy-based food products across Europe under the Alpro and Provamel brand names. In July 2009, DF acquired the Alpro division of Vandemoortele N.V. for about EUR315 million, excluding transaction costs. Also, with its Hero/WhiteWave joint venture, which was formed in 2008, DF expanded into the chilled fruit-based beverage area with the introduction of Fruit2Day. DF's partner in the joint venture is Hero Group, a producer of international fruit and infant nutrition brands Hero and Beech-Nut.

In August 2010, DF completed the sale of the business operations of its Rachel's Dairy companies, which provided dairy-related products primarily in the U.K. Rachel's was reclassified as discontinued operations.

## Company Financials Fiscal Year Ended Dec. 31

| Per Share Data ($) | 2010 | 2009 | 2008 | 2007 | 2006 | 2005 | 2004 | 2003 | 2002 | 2001 |
|---|---|---|---|---|---|---|---|---|---|---|
| Tangible Book Value | NM | NM | NM | NM | NM | NM | NM | NM | NM | NM |
| Cash Flow | 0.49 | 2.85 | 2.74 | 2.64 | 3.63 | 3.22 | 1.58 | 3.41 | 2.71 | 2.44 |
| Earnings | 0.47 | 1.38 | 1.21 | 0.95 | 2.01 | 1.78 | 1.78 | 2.27 | 1.77 | 1.23 |
| S&P Core Earnings | 0.61 | 1.45 | 1.15 | 0.92 | 2.00 | 1.66 | 1.58 | 1.85 | 1.57 | 0.91 |
| Dividends | Nil | Nil | Nil | Nil | Nil | Nil | Nil | Nil | Nil | Nil |
| Payout Ratio | Nil | Nil | Nil | Nil | Nil | Nil | Nil | Nil | Nil | Nil |
| Prices:High | 18.79 | 22.09 | 29.23 | 50.50 | 43.55 | 42.10 | 38.00 | 33.75 | 27.03 | 24.16 |
| Prices:Low | 7.13 | 15.74 | 11.20 | 24.11 | 34.66 | 31.60 | 28.25 | 24.60 | 18.05 | 14.00 |
| P/E Ratio:High | 40 | 16 | 24 | 53 | 22 | 24 | 21 | 15 | 15 | 20 |
| P/E Ratio:Low | 15 | 11 | 9 | 25 | 17 | 18 | 16 | 11 | 10 | 11 |

| Income Statement Analysis (Million $) | 2010 | 2009 | 2008 | 2007 | 2006 | 2005 | 2004 | 2003 | 2002 | 2001 |
|---|---|---|---|---|---|---|---|---|---|---|
| Revenue | 12,123 | 11,158 | 12,455 | 11,822 | 10,099 | 10,506 | 10,822 | 9,185 | 8,991 | 6,230 |
| Operating Income | 474 | 939 | 869 | 810 | 903 | 867 | 919 | 889 | 856 | 542 |
| Depreciation | 11.3 | 9.64 | 236 | 232 | 228 | 221 | 224 | 192 | 174 | 155 |
| Interest Expense | 248 | 246 | 310 | 322 | 195 | 169 | 205 | 195 | 231 | 135 |
| Pretax Income | 151 | 380 | 300 | 214 | 456 | 439 | 462 | 574 | 421 | 231 |
| Effective Tax Rate | NA | 40.0% | 38.3% | 39.2% | 38.5% | 37.9% | 38.3% | 38.0% | 36.4% | 36.3% |
| Net Income | 77.7 | 240 | 185 | 130 | 280 | 272 | 285 | 356 | 268 | 116 |
| S&P Core Earnings | 112 | 252 | 175 | 126 | 278 | 254 | 253 | 288 | 236 | 79.2 |

| Balance Sheet & Other Financial Data (Million $) | 2010 | 2009 | 2008 | 2007 | 2006 | 2005 | 2004 | 2003 | 2002 | 2001 |
|---|---|---|---|---|---|---|---|---|---|---|
| Cash | 92.0 | 47.6 | 36.0 | 32.6 | 31.1 | 25.1 | 27.6 | 47.1 | 45.9 | 78.3 |
| Current Assets | 1,816 | 1,629 | 1,481 | 1,532 | 1,379 | 1,477 | 1,596 | 1,401 | 1,311 | 1,482 |
| Total Assets | 7,957 | 7,844 | 7,040 | 7,033 | 6,770 | 7,051 | 7,756 | 6,993 | 6,582 | 6,732 |
| Current Liabilities | 1,267 | 1,479 | 1,427 | 933 | 1,337 | 1,137 | 1,106 | 1,170 | 1,268 | 1,175 |
| Long Term Debt | 4,068 | 4,229 | 4,174 | 5,271 | 2,872 | 3,329 | 3,116 | 2,611 | 3,140 | 3,556 |
| Common Equity | 1,500 | 1,352 | 558 | 51.3 | 1,809 | 1,872 | 2,661 | 2,543 | 1,643 | 1,476 |
| Total Capital | 5,596 | 5,596 | 5,201 | 5,781 | 5,186 | 5,688 | 6,308 | 5,542 | 5,077 | 5,313 |
| Capital Expenditures | 302 | 268 | 257 | 241 | 237 | 307 | 356 | 292 | 242 | 137 |
| Cash Flow | 89.0 | 495 | 421 | 362 | 508 | 494 | 509 | 548 | 442 | 270 |
| Current Ratio | 1.4 | 1.3 | 1.0 | 1.6 | 1.0 | 1.3 | 1.4 | 1.2 | 1.0 | 1.3 |
| % Long Term Debt of Capitalization | 72.7 | 75.6 | 80.3 | 99.0 | 55.4 | 58.5 | 49.4 | 47.1 | 61.8 | 66.9 |
| % Net Income of Revenue | 0.6 | 2.2 | 1.5 | 1.1 | 2.8 | 2.6 | 2.6 | 3.9 | 3.0 | 1.9 |
| % Return on Assets | 1.0 | 3.2 | 2.6 | 1.9 | 4.1 | 3.7 | 3.9 | 5.2 | 4.0 | 2.2 |
| % Return on Equity | 5.5 | 25.2 | 60.7 | 14.0 | 15.1 | 12.0 | 11.0 | 17.0 | 17.2 | 11.1 |

Data as orig reptd.; bef. results of disc opers/spec. items. Per share data adj. for stk. divs.; EPS diluted. E-Estimated. NA-Not Available. NM-Not Meaningful. NR-Not Ranked. UR-Under Review.

**Office:** 2711 North Haskell Avenue, Suite 3400, Dallas, TX 75204.
**Telephone:** 214-303-3400.
**Website:** http://www.deanfoods.com
**Chrmn & CEO:** G.L. Engles

**SVP & CIO:** B. Carlini
**CFO:** S.P. Mara
**Chief Acctg Officer & Cntlr:** S. Vopni
**Treas:** T.A. Smith

**Investor Contact:** B. Sievert (214-303-3437)
**Board Members:** H. M. Costa, T. C. Davis, G. L. Engles, S. L. Green, J. S. Hardin, Jr., V. J. Hill, J. W. Mailloux, J. R. Muse, J. L. Turner, D. A. Wright

**Founded:** 1925
**Domicile:** Delaware
**Employees:** 25,780

# Deere & Co

**STANDARD &POOR'S**

| S&P Recommendation | BUY ★★★★☆ | Price | 12-Mo. Target Price | Investment Style |
|---|---|---|---|---|
| | | $73.64 (as of Nov 25, 2011) | $99.00 | Large-Cap Blend |

**GICS Sector** Industrials
**Sub-Industry** Construction & Farm Machinery & Heavy Trucks

**Summary** Deere, the world's biggest producer of farm equipment, is also a large maker of construction machinery and lawn and garden equipment.

## Key Stock Statistics (Source S&P, Vickers, company reports)

| | | | | | | | |
|---|---|---|---|---|---|---|---|
| 52-Wk Range | $99.80–59.92 | S&P Oper. EPS 2011E | 6.40 | Market Capitalization(B) | $30.481 | Beta | 1.54 |
| Trailing 12-Month EPS | $6.08 | S&P Oper. EPS 2012E | 8.60 | Yield (%) | 2.23 | S&P 3-Yr. Proj. EPS CAGR(%) | 10 |
| Trailing 12-Month P/E | 12.1 | P/E on S&P Oper. EPS 2011E | 11.5 | Dividend Rate/Share | $1.64 | S&P Credit Rating | A |
| $10K Invested 5 Yrs Ago | $16,728 | Common Shares Outstg. (M) | 413.9 | Institutional Ownership (%) | 68 | | |

## Price Performance

30-Week Mov. Avg. ···  10-Week Mov. Avg. – – **GAAP Earnings vs. Previous Year**   Volume Above Avg. STARS
12-Mo. Target Price — Relative Strength   ▲ Up  ▼ Down  ► No Change   Below Avg.

Options: ASE, CBOE, Ph

Analysis prepared by Equity Analyst **Michael Jaffe** on Aug 25, 2011, when the stock traded at **$75.10**.

## Highlights

➤ Revenues have been reviving since FY 10's (Oct.) second quarter. On our outlook for an ongoing pickup in demand, we expect revenues in FY 12 to increase by 10%. We see these gains being driven by an ongoing recovery of global economies (despite what we view as a current soft patch), and its likely impact on the markets that DE serves. We are also forecasting higher average crop prices in both years. We see resultant strong levels of U.S. farm cash receipts boosting demand for agricultural equipment, and somewhat better residential construction markets lifting demand for construction equipment. Moreover, we see these generally positive overall trends allowing Deere to benefit from improved price realization.

➤ We project wider net margins in FY 12, on our outlook for better business trends, and incremental benefits from DE's cost cuts of the past few years. We see these factors outweighing what we expect to be still-high raw materials costs.

➤ Our FY 11 and FY 12 EPS estimates of $6.40 and $7.60, respectively, compare with operating EPS of $4.65 in FY 10.

## Investment Rationale/Risk

➤ After a sharp downturn in its business between late 2008 and late 2009, we believe modest improvement in global economic trends is allowing the large majority of Deere's end markets to start recoveries across most of its geographies. We see these conditions bringing an extended upturn in DE's operating results, with streamlining actions taken during the business downturn also likely to aid its bottom line. Based on these factors and our valuation model, we believe the stock is undervalued.

➤ Risks to our recommendation and target price include a global economic downturn, and an extended downturn in crop prices.

➤ The stock recently traded at 9.5X our calendar 2012 EPS forecast of $7.67. We believe it is undervalued, as this falls into the low-end of DE's valuation during the lengthy business upturn it experienced over much of the past decade. Based on these views, our 12-month target price is $99, or 12.9X our calendar 2012 forecast, which is a little closer to the middle of DE's valuation during its prior business upcycle. Our target price incorporates our positive outlook for DE, but growing uncertainties about the economy.

## Qualitative Risk Assessment

| LOW | MEDIUM | HIGH |
|---|---|---|

Our risk assessment reflects Deere's leading position in many of the markets it serves, and a balance sheet that typically carries large cash balances. On the other hand, the company's businesses are highly cyclical.

## Quantitative Evaluations

**S&P Quality Ranking**   A-

| D | C | B- | B | B+ | A- | A | A+ |
|---|---|---|---|---|---|---|---|

**Relative Strength Rank**   STRONG

75

LOWEST = 1                HIGHEST = 99

## Revenue/Earnings Data

**Revenue (Million $)**

| | 1Q | 2Q | 3Q | 4Q | Year |
|---|---|---|---|---|---|
| 2011 | 6,119 | 8,910 | 8,372 | -- | -- |
| 2010 | 4,835 | 7,131 | 6,837 | 7,202 | 26,005 |
| 2009 | 5,146 | 6,748 | 5,884 | 5,334 | 23,112 |
| 2008 | 5,201 | 8,097 | 7,739 | 7,401 | 28,438 |
| 2007 | 4,425 | 6,883 | 6,634 | 6,141 | 24,082 |
| 2006 | 4,202 | 6,562 | 6,267 | 5,118 | 22,148 |

**Earnings Per Share ($)**

| | | | | | |
|---|---|---|---|---|---|
| 2011 | 1.20 | 2.12 | 1.69 | E1.39 | E6.40 |
| 2010 | 0.57 | 1.28 | 1.44 | 1.07 | 4.35 |
| 2009 | 0.48 | 1.11 | 0.99 | -0.53 | 2.06 |
| 2008 | 0.83 | 1.74 | 1.32 | 0.81 | 4.70 |
| 2007 | 0.52 | 1.36 | 1.32 | 0.94 | 4.00 |
| 2006 | 0.47 | 1.09 | 0.93 | 0.93 | 3.08 |

Fiscal year ended Oct. 31. Next earnings report expected: Late November. EPS Estimates based on S&P Operating Earnings; historical GAAP earnings are as reported.

## Dividend Data (Dates: mm/dd Payment Date: mm/dd/yy)

| Amount ($) | Date Decl. | Ex-Div. Date | Stk. of Record | Payment Date |
|---|---|---|---|---|
| 0.350 | 12/01 | 12/29 | 12/31 | 02/01/11 |
| 0.350 | 02/23 | 03/29 | 03/31 | 05/02/11 |
| 0.410 | 05/24 | 06/28 | 06/30 | 08/01/11 |
| 0.410 | 08/31 | 09/28 | 09/30 | 11/01/11 |

Dividends have been paid since 1937. Source: Company reports.

# Deere & Co

**STANDARD &POOR'S**

## Business Summary August 25, 2011

CORPORATE OVERVIEW. Deere & Co. is the world's largest maker of farm tractors and combines, and a leading producer of construction equipment. During FY 10 (Oct.), the company derived 37% of its equipment sales outside of North America.

Effective May 1, 2009, DE combined its agricultural equipment and commercial and consumer equipment segments to form the agriculture and turf division. This streamlining action was an attempt by Deere to act on global market opportunities, leverage its global scale, optimize global product line results, standardize processes, share resources and reduce costs.

The agricultural and turf segment (76% of FY 10 revenues; 14.0% operating margin) makes tractors, loaders, combines, and cotton and sugar cane harvesters; tillage, seeding and soil preparation machinery; and hay and forage equipment for the global farming industry. It also manufactures and distrib-

utes equipment and service parts for commercial and residential uses. These products include small tractors for lawn, garden, commercial and utility purposes; lawn mowers; golf course equipment; utility vehicles; landscape and irrigation equipment; and other outdoor products.

The construction and forestry segment (14%; 3.2%) manufactures and distributes a broad range of machines and service parts used in construction, earth moving, material handling and timber harvesting. Products include backhoe loaders; crawler dozers and loaders; four-wheel-drive loaders; excavators; motor graders; articulated dump trucks; landscape loaders; skid-steer loaders; and log skidders, feller bunchers, harvesters and related attachments.

## Company Financials Fiscal Year Ended Oct. 31

| Per Share Data ($) | 2010 | 2009 | 2008 | 2007 | 2006 | 2005 | 2004 | 2003 | 2002 | 2001 |
|---|---|---|---|---|---|---|---|---|---|---|
| Tangible Book Value | 12.27 | 8.61 | 12.19 | 13.17 | 13.92 | 12.13 | 10.93 | 5.91 | 4.75 | 6.57 |
| Cash Flow | 6.49 | 4.12 | 6.61 | 5.64 | 4.55 | 4.23 | 4.00 | 2.62 | 2.17 | 1.39 |
| Earnings | 4.35 | 2.06 | 4.70 | 4.00 | 3.08 | 2.94 | 2.78 | 1.32 | 0.67 | -0.14 |
| S&P Core Earnings | 4.89 | 2.81 | 3.55 | 4.22 | 3.25 | 3.02 | 2.84 | 1.54 | -0.19 | -0.82 |
| Dividends | 1.16 | 1.12 | 1.06 | 0.91 | 0.78 | 0.61 | 0.53 | 0.44 | 0.44 | 0.44 |
| Payout Ratio | 27% | 54% | 23% | 23% | 22% | 21% | 19% | 33% | 66% | NM |
| Prices:High | 84.85 | 56.87 | 94.89 | 93.74 | 50.70 | 37.21 | 37.47 | 33.71 | 25.80 | 23.06 |
| Prices:Low | 48.33 | 24.51 | 28.50 | 45.12 | 33.45 | 28.50 | 28.36 | 18.78 | 18.75 | 16.75 |
| P/E Ratio:High | 20 | 28 | 20 | 23 | 14 | 13 | 13 | 26 | 39 | NM |
| P/E Ratio:Low | 11 | 12 | 6 | 11 | 9 | 10 | 10 | 14 | 28 | NM |

| Income Statement Analysis (Million $) | | | | | | | | | | |
|---|---|---|---|---|---|---|---|---|---|---|
| Revenue | 26,005 | 23,112 | 28,438 | 24,082 | 22,148 | 21,931 | 19,986 | 15,535 | 13,947 | 13,293 |
| Operating Income | 3,967 | 2,731 | 4,774 | 4,571 | 3,883 | 3,553 | 2,976 | 2,231 | 1,696 | 1,274 |
| Depreciation | 915 | 873 | 829 | 744 | 691 | 636 | 621 | 631 | 725 | 718 |
| Interest Expense | 817 | 1,057 | 1,163 | 1,151 | 1,018 | 761 | 592 | 1,257 | 637 | 766 |
| Pretax Income | 3,036 | 1,334 | 3,164 | 2,676 | 2,195 | 2,162 | 2,115 | 980 | 578 | -46.3 |
| Effective Tax Rate | 38.3% | 34.5% | 35.1% | 33.0% | 33.8% | 33.1% | 33.5% | 34.4% | 44.7% | NM |
| Net Income | 1,865 | 874 | 2,053 | 1,822 | 1,453 | 1,447 | 1,406 | 643 | 319 | -64.0 |
| S&P Core Earnings | 2,097 | 1,187 | 1,556 | 1,917 | 1,534 | 1,483 | 1,430 | 743 | -94.8 | -385 |

| Balance Sheet & Other Financial Data (Million $) | | | | | | | | | | |
|---|---|---|---|---|---|---|---|---|---|---|
| Cash | 3,348 | 3,690 | 1,834 | 3,902 | 3,504 | 4,708 | 3,428 | 4,616 | 3,004 | 1,206 |
| Current Assets | 32,362 | 29,124 | 27,837 | 27,840 | 27,987 | 27,530 | 23,040 | 19,370 | 16,919 | 16,191 |
| Total Assets | 43,267 | 41,133 | 38,735 | 38,576 | 34,720 | 33,637 | 28,754 | 26,258 | 23,768 | 22,663 |
| Current Liabilities | 14,016 | 12,549 | 14,927 | 15,605 | 12,790 | 11,494 | 7,612 | 7,679 | 7,667 | 9,340 |
| Long Term Debt | 16,815 | 17,392 | 13,899 | 11,798 | 11,584 | 11,739 | 11,090 | 10,404 | 8,950 | 6,561 |
| Common Equity | 6,290 | 4,819 | 6,533 | 7,156 | 7,565 | 6,825 | 6,350 | 2,834 | 1,797 | 3,992 |
| Total Capital | 23,105 | 22,211 | 20,603 | 19,137 | 19,214 | 18,564 | 17,441 | 13,238 | 10,772 | 10,566 |
| Capital Expenditures | 1,313 | 1,308 | 1,608 | 1,023 | 766 | 513 | 364 | 310 | 359 | 491 |
| Cash Flow | 2,780 | 1,747 | 2,882 | 2,566 | 2,145 | 2,083 | 2,027 | 1,275 | 1,045 | 654 |
| Current Ratio | 2.3 | 2.3 | 1.9 | NA | 2.2 | 2.4 | 3.0 | 2.5 | 2.2 | 1.7 |
| % Long Term Debt of Capitalization | 72.8 | 78.3 | 67.5 | 61.6 | 60.3 | 63.2 | 63.6 | 78.6 | 83.1 | 62.1 |
| % Net Income of Revenue | 7.2 | 3.8 | 7.2 | 7.5 | 6.6 | 6.6 | 7.0 | 4.2 | 2.4 | NM |
| % Return on Assets | 4.4 | 2.2 | 5.3 | 4.9 | 4.3 | 4.6 | 5.1 | 2.6 | 1.4 | NM |
| % Return on Equity | 33.6 | 15.4 | 30.0 | 24.7 | 20.2 | 22.0 | 30.6 | 27.8 | 11.8 | NM |

Data as orig reptd.; bef. results of disc opers/spec. items. Per share data adj. for stk. divs.; EPS diluted. E-Estimated. NA-Not Available. NM-Not Meaningful. NR-Not Ranked. UR-Under Review.

**Office:** One John Deere Place, Moline, IL 61265-8098.
**Telephone:** 309-765-8000.
**Email:** stockholder@deere.com
**Website:** http://www.deere.com

**Chrmn & CEO:** S.R. Allen
**SVP, CFO & Chief Acctg Officer:** J.M. Field
**SVP & General Counsel:** J.R. Jenkins
**CTO:** J.H. Gilles

**Treas:** M.Z. Ziegler
**Investor Contact:** M. Ziegler (309-765-4491)
**Board Members:** S. R. Allen, C. C. Bowles, V. D. Coffman, C. O. Holliday, Jr., D. Jain, C. Jones, J. Milberg, R. B. Myers, T. H. Patrick, A. L. Peters, D. B. Speer

**Founded:** 1837
**Domicile:** Delaware
**Employees:** 55,650

The *McGraw-Hill* Companies

# Dell Inc

**STANDARD &POOR'S**

| S&P Recommendation | **STRONG BUY** ★★★★★ | Price | 12-Mo. Target Price | Investment Style |
|---|---|---|---|---|
| | | $14.22 (as of Nov 25, 2011) | $19.00 | Large-Cap Growth |

**GICS Sector** Information Technology
**Sub-Industry** Computer Hardware

**Summary** One of the world's 10 leading manufacturers of personal computers, Dell also offers server and storage products and provides IT services.

## Key Stock Statistics (Source S&P, Vickers, company reports)

| | | | | | | | |
|---|---|---|---|---|---|---|---|
| 52-Wk Range | $17.60– 12.99 | S&P Oper. EPS 2012E | 2.15 | Market Capitalization(B) | $25.943 | Beta | 1.39 |
| Trailing 12-Month EPS | $1.94 | S&P Oper. EPS 2013E | 2.03 | Yield (%) | Nil | S&P 3-Yr. Proj. EPS CAGR(%) | 12 |
| Trailing 12-Month P/E | 7.3 | P/E on S&P Oper. EPS 2012E | 6.6 | Dividend Rate/Share | Nil | S&P Credit Rating | A- |
| $10K Invested 5 Yrs Ago | $5,203 | Common Shares Outstg. (M) | 1,824.4 | Institutional Ownership (%) | 71 | | |

## Price Performance

30-Week Mov. Avg. · · · ·   10-Week Mov. Avg. - - -  **GAAP Earnings vs. Previous Year**   Volume Above Avg. STARS
12-Mo. Target Price —  Relative Strength —  ▲ Up  ▼ Down  ▶ No Change   Below Avg.

Options: ASE, CBOE, P, Ph

Analysis prepared by Equity Analyst **Dylan Cathers** on Nov 17, 2011, when the stock traded at **$15.13**.

## Highlights

► We project revenues will rise 1.0% in FY 12 (Jan.) and 2.5% in FY 13. The modest increases we look for reflect the current general economic weakness, as well as an ongoing shift in DELL's focus away from certain lower-margin market segments. We also think near-term revenue growth will be affected by hard disk drive supply shortages related to the flooding in Thailand. Longer term, we think that the current PC refresh cycle is not over, and we expect steady growth for services and acquisitions to add to growth.

► We expect overall margin improvement going forward, as a richer product mix (including a increased percentage of services sales) and potential savings from improved supply chain management outweigh pressure on PC selling prices. New facilities in China should help distribution efficiencies. More overseas business should help reduce the overall tax burden, in our view.

► We estimate FY 12 operating EPS of $2.15, excluding restructuring and acquisition-related expenses. For FY 13, we project EPS of $2.03, aided by a modest pace of share buybacks.

## Investment Rationale/Risk

► We believe DELL's multi-year effort to move into new markets and seek operational efficiencies is leading to a more favorable margin profile. The addition of the Perot Systems service operations in November 2009 and, more recently, expansion in the servers, networking and software areas should lift sales and margin potential, in our view. A cyclical rebound in demand for IT spending that we expect to continue through late calendar 2012 should also aid results, despite soft demand in the consumer PC area in the near term. All told, we view the shares as compellingly valued, based on our P/E analysis.

► Risks to our recommendation and target price include the potential for weaker PC market share and margin performance than we project. Acquisition integration might prove less effective than we expect.

► Applying a target multiple of 9.4X, a discount to Information Technology sector peers in the S&P 500 Index and toward the low end of DELL's historical range to reflect competitive challenges in the PC markets, to our 2012 EPS estimate of $2.03, we arrive at our 12-month target price of $19.

## Qualitative Risk Assessment

| LOW | **MEDIUM** | HIGH |
|---|---|---|

Our risk assessment reflects our view of Dell's economies of scale and strong execution in asset management, offset by what we see as competitive pressures on product design and pricing, industry cyclicality, and a shift to greater reliance on retail partners around the world.

## Quantitative Evaluations

**S&P Quality Ranking**                                   B+

| D | C | B- | B | **B+** | A- | A | A+ |
|---|---|---|---|---|---|---|---|

**Relative Strength Rank**                         MODERATE

45

LOWEST = 1                                    HIGHEST = 99

## Revenue/Earnings Data

### Revenue (Million $)

| | 1Q | 2Q | 3Q | 4Q | Year |
|---|---|---|---|---|---|
| 2012 | 15,017 | 15,658 | 15,365 | -- | -- |
| 2011 | 14,874 | 15,534 | 15,394 | 15,692 | 61,494 |
| 2010 | 12,342 | 12,764 | 12,896 | 14,900 | 52,902 |
| 2009 | 16,077 | 16,434 | 15,162 | 13,428 | 61,101 |
| 2008 | 14,722 | 14,776 | 15,646 | 15,989 | 61,133 |
| 2007 | 14,320 | 14,211 | 14,419 | 14,470 | 57,420 |

### Earnings Per Share ($)

| | 1Q | 2Q | 3Q | 4Q | Year |
|---|---|---|---|---|---|
| 2012 | 0.49 | 0.48 | 0.49 | E0.52 | E2.15 |
| 2011 | 0.17 | 0.28 | 0.42 | 0.48 | 1.35 |
| 2010 | 0.15 | 0.24 | 0.17 | 0.17 | 0.73 |
| 2009 | 0.38 | 0.31 | 0.37 | 0.18 | 1.25 |
| 2008 | 0.34 | 0.31 | 0.34 | 0.31 | 1.31 |
| 2007 | 0.34 | 0.21 | 0.27 | 0.32 | 1.14 |

Fiscal year ended Jan. 31. Next earnings report expected: Mid February. EPS Estimates based on S&P Operating Earnings; historical GAAP earnings are as reported.

## Dividend Data

No cash dividends have been paid.

# Dell Inc

STANDARD &POOR'S

## Business Summary November 17, 2011

CORPORATE OVERVIEW. Dell Inc. is a key player in the personal computer markets that is diversifying into information technology services and data center products. It was number three in global PC unit shipments in 2010, with about a 12.0% market share according to research firm Gartner, down slightly from a 12.1% share in 2009 despite unit shipment growth of 12.8% in 2010. In the fourth quarter of 2010, DELL was number two by PC unit shipments in the U.S. market, with about a 22.1% market share.

The majority of DELL's sales are from PCs (55% of FY 11 (Jan.) total revenue), with 24% from Desktop PCs and 31% from Mobility. Other categories include Software and Peripherals (17%), Servers and Networking (12%), Services (12%), and Storage (4%). Within the PC category, sales of Mobility (mainly notebook PCs) are rising faster than sales of Desktop PCs. Revenue from notebooks pulled approximately even with desktop revenue for the first time in the FY 08 third quarter, and we expect notebooks to lead in the future.

Broken out by global segment, Large Enterprise represented 29% of DELL's FY 11 total revenue (27% in FY 10), Public 27% (27%), Small and Medium Business 24% (23%), and Consumer 20% (23%).

The customer base is broad. The company is expanding in rapid-growth emerging markets including Brazil, Russia, India and China (BRIC), and DELL's revenue from the BRIC countries rose to represent 13% of fourth quarter revenue in FY 11, up from 11% in the prior-year quarter and 9% in the fourth quarter of FY 09. Revenues derived from outside the U.S. represented 50% of total revenue in FY 11, up from 47% in FY 10. Most of the company's long-lived assets are located in the U.S.

IMPACT OF MAJOR DEVELOPMENTS. In January 2007, Michael Dell reassumed his role as CEO, while retaining his duties as chairman of the board. We believe this development reinvigorated the corporate culture and streamlined the decision-making process.

## Company Financials Fiscal Year Ended Jan. 31

| Per Share Data ($) | 2011 | 2010 | 2009 | 2008 | 2007 | 2006 | 2005 | 2004 | 2003 | 2002 |
|---|---|---|---|---|---|---|---|---|---|---|
| Tangible Book Value | 0.99 | NM | 0.95 | 1.03 | 1.60 | 1.77 | 2.61 | 2.46 | 1.89 | 1.80 |
| Cash Flow | 1.84 | 1.16 | 1.64 | 1.58 | 1.34 | 1.62 | 1.32 | 1.11 | 0.88 | 0.54 |
| Earnings | 1.35 | 0.73 | 1.25 | 1.31 | 1.14 | 1.46 | 1.18 | 1.01 | 0.80 | 0.46 |
| S&P Core Earnings | 1.38 | 0.73 | 1.23 | 1.28 | 1.13 | 1.03 | 0.88 | 0.68 | 0.49 | 0.28 |
| Dividends | NA | Nil | Nil | Nil | Nil | Nil | Nil | Nil | Nil | Nil |
| Payout Ratio | NA | Nil | Nil | Nil | Nil | Nil | Nil | Nil | Nil | Nil |
| Calendar Year | 2010 | 2009 | 2008 | 2007 | 2006 | 2005 | 2004 | 2003 | 2002 | 2001 |
| Prices:High | 17.52 | 17.26 | 26.04 | 30.77 | 30.77 | 42.30 | 42.57 | 37.18 | 31.06 | 31.32 |
| Prices:Low | 11.34 | 7.84 | 8.72 | 21.61 | 21.61 | 28.62 | 31.14 | 22.59 | 21.90 | 16.01 |
| P/E Ratio:High | 13 | 24 | 21 | 23 | 27 | 29 | 36 | 37 | 39 | 68 |
| P/E Ratio:Low | 8 | 11 | 7 | 16 | 19 | 20 | 26 | 22 | 27 | 35 |

### Income Statement Analysis (Million $)

| | 2011 | 2010 | 2009 | 2008 | 2007 | 2006 | 2005 | 2004 | 2003 | 2002 |
|---|---|---|---|---|---|---|---|---|---|---|
| Revenue | 61,494 | 52,902 | 61,101 | 61,133 | 57,420 | 55,908 | 49,205 | 41,444 | 35,404 | 31,168 |
| Operating Income | 4,460 | 3,620 | 4,193 | 4,344 | 3,541 | 4,740 | 4,588 | 3,807 | 3,055 | 2,510 |
| Depreciation | 970 | 852 | 769 | 599 | 471 | 393 | 334 | 263 | 211 | 239 |
| Interest Expense | 155 | 160 | 93.0 | 45.0 | 45.0 | 28.0 | 16.0 | 14.0 | 17.0 | 29.0 |
| Pretax Income | 3,350 | 2,024 | 3,324 | 3,856 | 3,345 | 4,574 | 4,445 | 3,724 | 3,027 | 1,731 |
| Effective Tax Rate | NA | 29.2% | 25.5% | 22.8% | 22.8% | 21.9% | 31.5% | 29.0% | 29.9% | 28.0% |
| Net Income | 2,635 | 1,433 | 2,478 | 2,947 | 2,583 | 3,572 | 3,043 | 2,645 | 2,122 | 1,246 |
| S&P Core Earnings | 2,675 | 1,432 | 2,445 | 2,871 | 2,563 | 2,494 | 2,227 | 1,806 | 1,356 | 781 |

### Balance Sheet & Other Financial Data (Million $)

| | 2011 | 2010 | 2009 | 2008 | 2007 | 2006 | 2005 | 2004 | 2003 | 2002 |
|---|---|---|---|---|---|---|---|---|---|---|
| Cash | 14,365 | 11,008 | 9,092 | 7,972 | 9,546 | 7,042 | 4,747 | 4,317 | 4,232 | 3,641 |
| Current Assets | 29,021 | 24,245 | 20,151 | 19,880 | 19,939 | 17,706 | 16,897 | 10,633 | 8,924 | 7,877 |
| Total Assets | 38,599 | 33,652 | 26,500 | 27,561 | 25,635 | 23,109 | 23,215 | 19,311 | 15,470 | 13,535 |
| Current Liabilities | 19,483 | 18,960 | 14,859 | 18,526 | 17,791 | 15,927 | 14,136 | 10,896 | 8,933 | 7,519 |
| Long Term Debt | 5,146 | 3,417 | 1,898 | 362 | 569 | 504 | 505 | 505 | 506 | 520 |
| Common Equity | 7,766 | 5,641 | 4,271 | 3,735 | 4,328 | 4,129 | 6,485 | 6,280 | 4,873 | 4,694 |
| Total Capital | 12,912 | 9,058 | 6,169 | 4,191 | 5,008 | 4,633 | 6,990 | 6,785 | 5,379 | 5,214 |
| Capital Expenditures | 444 | 367 | 440 | 831 | 896 | 728 | 525 | 329 | 305 | 303 |
| Cash Flow | 3,605 | 2,285 | 3,247 | 3,546 | 3,054 | 3,965 | 3,377 | 2,908 | 2,333 | 1,485 |
| Current Ratio | 1.5 | 1.3 | 1.4 | 1.1 | 1.1 | 1.1 | 1.2 | 1.0 | 1.0 | 1.0 |
| % Long Term Debt of Capitalization | 39.9 | 37.7 | 30.8 | 8.6 | 11.4 | 10.9 | 7.2 | 7.4 | 9.4 | 10.0 |
| % Net Income of Revenue | 4.3 | 2.7 | 4.1 | 4.8 | 4.5 | 6.4 | 6.2 | 6.4 | 6.0 | 4.0 |
| % Return on Assets | 7.3 | 4.8 | 9.2 | 11.1 | 10.6 | 15.4 | 14.3 | 15.2 | 14.6 | 9.2 |
| % Return on Equity | 39.3 | 28.9 | 61.9 | 73.1 | 61.1 | 67.3 | 47.7 | 47.4 | 44.4 | 24.2 |

Data as orig reptd.; bef. results of disc opers/spec. items. Per share data adj. for stk. divs.; EPS diluted. E-Estimated. NA-Not Available. NM-Not Meaningful. NR-Not Ranked. UR-Under Review.

**Office:** One Dell Way, Round Rock, TX 78682.
**Telephone:** 512-338-4400.
**Email:** investor_relations_fulfillment@dell.com
**Website:** http://www.dell.com

**Chrmn & CEO:** M.S. Dell
**COO & CTO:** J.R. Clarke
**SVP & CFO:** B.T. Gladden
**SVP, Secy & General Counsel:** L.P. Tu

**Chief Acctg Officer:** T.W. Sweet
**Investor Contact:** L.A. Tyson (512-723-1130)
**Board Members:** J. W. Breyer, D. J. Carty, J. Clark, L. C. Conigliaro, M. S. Dell, K. M. Duberstein, W. H. Gray, III, G. J. Kleisterlee, T. W. Luce, III, K. S. Luft, A. J. Mandl, S. Narayen, H. R. Perot, Jr.

**Founded:** 1984
**Domicile:** Delaware
**Employees:** 103,300

# Denbury Resources Inc.

**STANDARD & POOR'S**

| S&P Recommendation HOLD ★★★☆☆ | Price $14.32 (as of Nov 25, 2011) | 12-Mo. Target Price $19.00 | Investment Style Large-Cap Growth |
|---|---|---|---|

**GICS Sector** Energy
**Sub-Industry** Oil & Gas Exploration & Production

**Summary** This independent oil and gas company acquires, develops, exploits and produces oil and gas in the U.S., primarily in Mississippi and the Barnett Shale in Texas. DNR owns the largest reserves of $CO_2$ used for tertiary oil recovery east of the Mississippi River.

## Key Stock Statistics (Source S&P, Vickers, company reports)

| | | | | | | | |
|---|---|---|---|---|---|---|---|
| 52-Wk Range | $26.03– 10.20 | S&P Oper. EPS 2011E | 1.27 | Market Capitalization(B) | $5.714 | Beta | 1.33 |
| Trailing 12-Month EPS | $1.32 | S&P Oper. EPS 2012E | 1.27 | Yield (%) | Nil | S&P 3-Yr. Proj. EPS CAGR(%) | 23 |
| Trailing 12-Month P/E | 10.9 | P/E on S&P Oper. EPS 2011E | 11.3 | Dividend Rate/Share | Nil | S&P Credit Rating | BB |
| $10K Invested 5 Yrs Ago | $10,415 | Common Shares Outstg. (M) | 399.0 | Institutional Ownership (%) | 96 | | |

## Price Performance

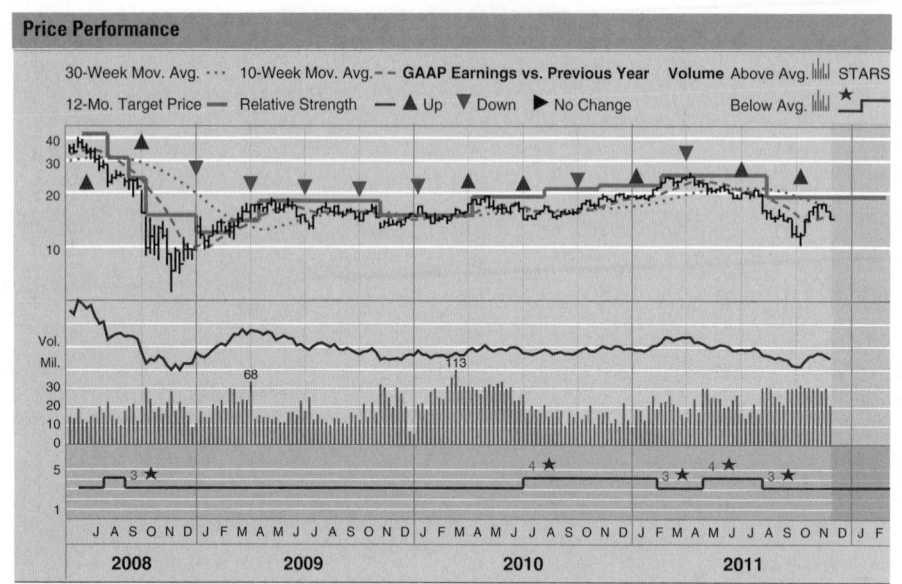

30-Week Mov. Avg. · · · 10-Week Mov. Avg. - - GAAP Earnings vs. Previous Year Volume Above Avg. STARS
12-Mo. Target Price — Relative Strength — ▲ Up ▼ Down ▶ No Change Below Avg. ★

Options: ASE, CBOE, P, Ph

Analysis prepared by Equity Analyst **Michael Kay** on Aug 22, 2011, when the stock traded at **$14.32**.

## Highlights

▶ DNR spent much of 2010 integrating acquired assets, and we see it leveraging its strong platform into future growth. Aided by acquisitions, DNR saw a 42% production boost in 2010. Excluding sold assets, we see organic production growth of 5% in 2011, and with the expected addition of new projects at tertiary fields, Hastings and Oyster Bayou, in late 2011, we are forecasting 17% growth in 2012. DNR has ramped up activity at the Bakken Shale, where it holds about 266,000 net acres and runs five rigs, will add two more rigs in the second half of 2011 and where production is now 12% of its total oil volumes. DNR sees a 13%-15% production CAGR at tertiary fields through 2015. DNR is benefiting from 40% of production priced as Louisiana light sweet crude, which currently trades at a premium to WTI.

▶ DNR recently raised 2011 its capex budget by $200 million to $1.35 billion, modestly above cash flow forecasts, with 35% for tertiary floods and 30% for Bakken. DNR has hedged 80% of forecasted 2011 and 2012 production.

▶ On volume and price gains, we see EPS of $1.25 in 2011 and $1.55 in 2012, up from $0.59 in 2010.

## Investment Rationale/Risk

▶ In 2010, DNR closed its acquisition of EAC for $4.5 billion, including $1.6 billion in debt, $830 million in cash, and 134 million new shares. The acquisition more than doubled DNR's production and reserve base and added a new core region in the Rockies. EAC's enhanced recovery program in the Rockies should complement Gulf Coast tertiary operations, and we view positively its entry into the Bakken Shale. DNR believes its returns on investment are higher at tertiary fields than at Bakken, as finding and development costs are lower. However, Bakken operating costs are lower. DNR believes tertiary potential in the Gulf Coast and Rockies could reach 4.7-10.7 billion BOE, and it sees 350 million BOE potential from Bakken.

▶ Risks to our opinion and target price include a sustained decline in oil and gas prices, and inability to replace reserves at a reasonable cost.

▶ Our 12-month target price of $19 blends an 8.5X enterprise value multiple of our 2011 EBITDA forecast and our proved NAV view of $20. We view higher oil exposure versus peers as attractive, but are cautious as its production has been below forecast.

## Qualitative Risk Assessment

| LOW | MEDIUM | **HIGH** |
|---|---|---|

Our risk assessment reflects the company's operations in a capital-intensive industry that derives value from producing commodities whose price is very volatile.

## Quantitative Evaluations

**S&P Quality Ranking** **B**

| D | C | B- | **B** | B+ | A- | A | A+ |
|---|---|---|---|---|---|---|---|

**Relative Strength Rank** **MODERATE**

**41**

LOWEST = 1     HIGHEST = 99

## Revenue/Earnings Data

**Revenue (Million $)**

| | 1Q | 2Q | 3Q | 4Q | Year |
|---|---|---|---|---|---|
| 2011 | 511.1 | 596.4 | 572.1 | -- | -- |
| 2010 | 335.4 | 492.7 | 465.4 | 519.0 | 1,813 |
| 2009 | 171.2 | 214.4 | 225.0 | 269.5 | 880.1 |
| 2008 | 317.3 | 416.6 | 405.6 | 222.6 | 1,361 |
| 2007 | 174.2 | 222.5 | 253.5 | 321.8 | 972.0 |
| 2006 | 178.9 | 193.3 | 192.0 | 167.3 | 731.5 |

**Earnings Per Share ($)**

| | 1Q | 2Q | 3Q | 4Q | Year |
|---|---|---|---|---|---|
| 2011 | -0.04 | 0.64 | 0.68 | E0.27 | E1.27 |
| 2010 | 0.32 | 0.34 | 0.07 | 0.03 | 0.72 |
| 2009 | -0.07 | -0.35 | 0.11 | 0.01 | -0.30 |
| 2008 | 0.29 | 0.45 | 0.63 | 0.18 | 1.54 |
| 2007 | 0.07 | 0.25 | 0.27 | 0.42 | 1.00 |
| 2006 | 0.19 | 0.18 | 0.24 | 0.23 | 0.82 |

Fiscal year ended Dec. 31. Next earnings report expected: Early February. EPS Estimates based on S&P Operating Earnings; historical GAAP earnings are as reported.

## Dividend Data

No cash dividends have been paid.

# Denbury Resources Inc.

STANDARD &POOR'S

## Business Summary August 22, 2011

CORPORATE OVERVIEW. Denbury Resources, Inc. (DNR) engages in the acquisition, development, operation and exploitation of oil and natural gas properties in the Gulf Coast region of the U.S., primarily in Louisiana, Mississippi, Alabama and Texas, and the Rocky Mountains. DNR is the largest oil and natural gas operator in Mississippi and also owns the rights to a natural source of carbon dioxide ($CO_2$) reserves that it uses for injection in its tertiary oil recovery operations. In March 2010, DNR acquired Encore Acquisition Company (EAC) for $4.5 billion, including $1.6 billion in debt, $830 in cash and the issuance of about 134 million new shares.

With the completion of the EAC acquisition, DNR more than doubled its proved reserve base. As of December 31, 2010, DNR had estimated proved reserves (including tertiary-related reserves) of 398 MMBOE (85% oil, 60% developed), up from 208 MMBOE (93% oil, 62% developed) at year-end 2009. We estimate DNR's 2010 organic reserve replacement at 328%, and reserve replacement cost at $15.42 per BOE. This compares to a three-year organic reserve replacement of 176% and three-year reserve replacement cost of $14.82 per BOE. Total reserve replacement was 1,301% on acquired reserves. Oil and gas production rose 42%, to 68,532 b/d (62,558 b/d organic), in 2010, on acquired EAC properties, and growth at tertiary fields.

CORPORATE STRATEGY. After repositioning its portfolio in 2009, and integrating it in 2010 with the acquisition of Encore, the purchase of two additional enhanced oil recovery fields (Conroe and Hastings) and the sale of 100% of its

Barnett Shale, Haynesville and East Texas assets, we think DNR is now positioned to execute on its plan of tertiary oil growth. DNR added a new core area with EAC's enhanced oil recovery projects in the Rockies, where it sees significant similarities to its own fields, and now has one of the largest positions in the prolific Bakken Shale. DNR sees a 13%-15% production compound annual growth rate (CAGR) on tertiary flood fields through 2015. The company has issued pro forma production guidance of around 65,600 MBOE/day for 2011, up about 5% organically from 62,558 b/d in 2010, on a capital budget of $1.35 billion.

DNR has invested significantly to expand its $CO_2$ pipeline network from Louisiana to Texas and to implement and expand additional tertiary floods, as part of its strategic plan. If oil prices remain at their current levels, DNR believes most of this can be funded with internally generated cash flow, but if needed, it can tap into other resources. DNR's biggest project recently was the construction of the $700 million Green Pipeline, a $CO_2$ pipeline that was completed around year-end 2009. DNR believes this project will create the backbone for a $CO_2$ gathering and distribution system in the southern Gulf Coast region.

## Company Financials Fiscal Year Ended Dec. 31

| Per Share Data ($) | 2010 | 2009 | 2008 | 2007 | 2006 | 2005 | 2004 | 2003 | 2002 | 2001 |
|---|---|---|---|---|---|---|---|---|---|---|
| Tangible Book Value | 7.92 | 6.89 | 7.50 | 5.75 | 4.61 | 3.20 | 2.40 | 1.94 | 1.71 | 1.65 |
| Cash Flow | 1.94 | 0.66 | 2.42 | 1.77 | 1.42 | 1.11 | 0.79 | 0.67 | 0.65 | 0.63 |
| Earnings | 0.72 | -0.30 | 1.54 | 1.00 | 0.82 | 0.70 | 0.36 | 0.24 | 0.22 | 0.28 |
| S&P Core Earnings | 0.55 | -0.30 | 1.54 | 1.00 | 0.82 | 0.68 | 0.35 | 0.23 | 0.21 | 0.27 |
| Dividends | Nil | Nil | Nil | Nil | Nil | Nil | Nil | Nil | Nil | Nil |
| Payout Ratio | Nil | Nil | Nil | Nil | Nil | Nil | Nil | Nil | Nil | Nil |
| Prices:High | 20.00 | 18.84 | 40.32 | 30.56 | 18.30 | 12.86 | 7.33 | 3.56 | 2.99 | 3.08 |
| Prices:Low | 13.41 | 9.61 | 5.59 | 12.98 | 11.79 | 6.18 | 3.32 | 2.55 | 1.55 | 1.46 |
| P/E Ratio:High | 28 | NM | 26 | 31 | 22 | 18 | 20 | 15 | 14 | 11 |
| P/E Ratio:Low | 19 | NM | 4 | 13 | 14 | 9 | 9 | 10 | 7 | 5 |

| Income Statement Analysis (Million $) | | | | | | | | | | |
|---|---|---|---|---|---|---|---|---|---|---|
| Revenue | 1,813 | 880 | 1,361 | 972 | 732 | 560 | 383 | 333 | 285 | 266 |
| Operating Income | NA | NA | 699 | 636 | 482 | 393 | 254 | 276 | 190 | 156 |
| Depreciation, Depletion and Amortization | 444 | 238 | 222 | 193 | 149 | 98.8 | 97.5 | 94.7 | 94.2 | 71.3 |
| Interest Expense | 176 | 47.4 | 32.6 | 51.2 | 23.6 | 18.0 | 19.5 | 23.2 | 26.8 | 22.3 |
| Pretax Income | 479 | -122 | 624 | 393 | 330 | 248 | 122 | 80.2 | 70.3 | 81.4 |
| Effective Tax Rate | NA | 38.5% | 37.8% | 35.7% | 38.6% | 32.9% | 32.3% | 32.7% | 33.4% | 30.5% |
| Net Income | 286 | -75.2 | 388 | 253 | 202 | 166 | 82.4 | 53.9 | 46.8 | 56.6 |
| S&P Core Earnings | 209 | -75.2 | 388 | 253 | 202 | 161 | 79.7 | 49.8 | 43.9 | 53.8 |

| Balance Sheet & Other Financial Data (Million $) | | | | | | | | | | |
|---|---|---|---|---|---|---|---|---|---|---|
| Cash | 475 | 20.6 | 17.1 | 60.1 | 53.9 | 165 | 33.0 | 24.2 | 23.9 | 23.5 |
| Current Assets | 864 | 256 | 415 | 240 | 183 | 299 | 173 | 108 | 128 | 103 |
| Total Assets | 9,065 | 4,270 | 3,590 | 2,771 | 2,140 | 1,505 | 993 | 983 | 895 | 790 |
| Current Liabilities | 579 | 394 | 386 | 265 | 200 | 154 | 82.9 | 127 | 95.9 | 79.9 |
| Long Term Debt | 2,416 | 1,301 | 853 | 675 | 514 | 379 | 0.23 | 298 | 345 | 335 |
| Common Equity | 4,381 | 1,972 | 1,840 | 1,404 | 1,106 | 734 | 542 | 421 | 374 | 353 |
| Total Capital | 6,805 | 3,279 | 3,126 | 2,432 | 1,856 | 1,284 | 639 | 788 | 790 | 707 |
| Capital Expenditures | 998 | 1,463 | 1,086 | 834 | 826 | 379 | 178 | 147 | 156 | 172 |
| Cash Flow | 729 | 163 | 610 | 446 | 352 | 265 | 180 | 149 | 141 | 128 |
| Current Ratio | 1.5 | 0.7 | 1.1 | 0.9 | 0.9 | 1.9 | 2.1 | 0.9 | 1.3 | 1.3 |
| % Long Term Debt of Capitalization | 35.5 | Nil | 27.3 | 32.6 | 27.7 | 29.6 | 0.0 | 37.8 | 43.6 | 47.4 |
| % Return on Assets | NA | NM | 12.2 | 10.3 | 11.1 | 13.3 | 8.3 | 5.7 | 5.6 | 9.1 |
| % Return on Equity | NA | NA | 23.9 | 20.2 | 22.0 | 26.1 | 17.1 | 13.7 | 12.9 | 19.8 |

Data as orig reptd.; bef. results of disc opers/spec. items. Per share data adj. for stk. divs.; EPS diluted. E-Estimated. NA-Not Available. NM-Not Meaningful. NR-Not Ranked. UR-Under Review.

**Office:** 5320 Legacy Drive, Plano, TX 75024.
**Telephone:** 972-673-2000.
**Website:** http://www.denbury.com
**Chrmn:** W.F. Wettstein

**Pres & CEO:** P. Rykhoek
**SVP, CFO & Treas:** M.C. Allen
**Secy & General Counsel:** H.R. Dubuisson
**Investor Contact:** L. Burkes (972-673-2166)

**Board Members:** M. L. Beatty, M. B. Decker, R. G. Greene, D. I. Heather, G. L. McMichael, K. O. Meyers, G. Roberts, P. Rykhoek, R. Stein, W. F. Wettstein

**Founded:** 1951
**Domicile:** Delaware
**Employees:** 1,195

# DENTSPLY International Inc

**STANDARD &POOR'S**

| S&P Recommendation | **BUY** ★★★★☆ | Price | 12-Mo. Target Price | Investment Style |
|---|---|---|---|---|
| | | $32.80 (as of Nov 25, 2011) | $44.00 | Large-Cap Growth |

**GICS Sector** Health Care
**Sub-Industry** Health Care Supplies

**Summary** This company is a designer, developer, manufacturer and marketer of a broad range of products for the dental market.

## Key Stock Statistics (Source S&P, Vickers, company reports)

| | | | | | | | |
|---|---|---|---|---|---|---|---|
| 52-Wk Range | $40.37– 28.35 | S&P Oper. EPS 2011E | 2.07 | Market Capitalization(B) | $4.643 | Beta | 1.08 |
| Trailing 12-Month EPS | $1.89 | S&P Oper. EPS 2012E | 2.31 | Yield (%) | 0.61 | S&P 3-Yr. Proj. EPS CAGR(%) | 13 |
| Trailing 12-Month P/E | 17.4 | P/E on S&P Oper. EPS 2011E | 15.8 | Dividend Rate/Share | $0.20 | S&P Credit Rating | BBB+ |
| $10K Invested 5 Yrs Ago | $10,546 | Common Shares Outstg. (M) | 141.6 | Institutional Ownership (%) | 90 | | |

## Price Performance

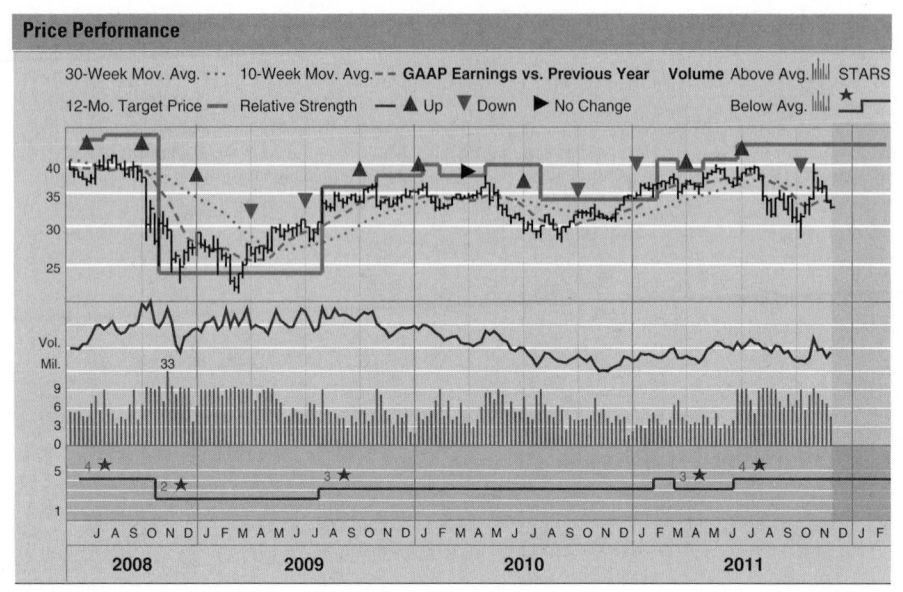

30-Week Mov. Avg. · · · · 10-Week Mov. Avg. – – GAAP Earnings vs. Previous Year   Volume Above Avg. STARS
12-Mo. Target Price — Relative Strength — ▲ Up ▼ Down ► No Change   Below Avg. ★

Options: CBOE, P, Ph

Analysis prepared by Equity Analyst **Phillip Seligman** on Nov 02, 2011, when the stock traded at **$35.55**.

## Qualitative Risk Assessment

| LOW | MEDIUM | HIGH |
|---|---|---|

Our risk assessment reflects XRAY's long-term trend of relative earnings stability and its broad product and geographic diversification, which we believe limits the impact of competition. We also believe XRAY's relatively low long-term debt to capitalization ratio provides some degree of protection from financial difficulties.

## Quantitative Evaluations

**S&P Quality Ranking**   A-

| D | C | B- | B | B+ | A- | A | A+ |
|---|---|---|---|---|---|---|---|

**Relative Strength Rank**   MODERATE

55

LOWEST = 1   HIGHEST = 99

## Revenue/Earnings Data

**Revenue (Million $)**

| | 1Q | 2Q | 3Q | 4Q | Year |
|---|---|---|---|---|---|
| 2011 | 570.5 | 609.4 | 619.8 | -- | -- |
| 2010 | 545.9 | 565.1 | 541.8 | 568.2 | 2,221 |
| 2009 | 507.0 | 553.2 | 531.0 | 568.7 | 2,160 |
| 2008 | 560.8 | 594.9 | 530.0 | 508.1 | 2,194 |
| 2007 | 472.9 | 507.4 | 488.1 | 541.5 | 2,010 |
| 2006 | 431.0 | 472.4 | 435.7 | 471.3 | 1,811 |

**Earnings Per Share ($)**

| | | | | | |
|---|---|---|---|---|---|
| 2011 | 0.48 | 0.52 | 0.42 | E0.54 | E2.07 |
| 2010 | 0.41 | 0.49 | 0.44 | 0.47 | 1.82 |
| 2009 | 0.41 | 0.47 | 0.45 | 0.50 | 1.83 |
| 2008 | 0.45 | 0.52 | 0.44 | 0.47 | 1.87 |
| 2007 | 0.38 | 0.42 | 0.42 | 0.45 | 1.68 |
| 2006 | 0.31 | 0.37 | 0.31 | 0.42 | 1.41 |

Fiscal year ended Dec. 31. Next earnings report expected: Early February. EPS Estimates based on S&P Operating Earnings; historical GAAP earnings are as reported.

## Dividend Data (Dates: mm/dd Payment Date: mm/dd/yy)

| Amount ($) | Date Decl. | Ex-Div. Date | Stk. of Record | Payment Date |
|---|---|---|---|---|
| 0.050 | 09/30 | 12/27 | 12/29 | 01/07/11 |
| 0.050 | 02/11 | 03/29 | 03/31 | 04/08/11 |
| 0.050 | 05/26 | 06/28 | 06/30 | 07/08/11 |
| 0.050 | 07/27 | 09/23 | 09/27 | 10/06/11 |

Dividends have been paid since 1994. Source: Company reports.

## Highlights

► We forecast that 2011 net sales, excluding precious metal content, will grow by 13.7%, to $2.3 billion, and 19.6% in 2012, to $2.8 billion, led by the August 31 acquisition of Astra Tech, a major dental implants maker. We also believe demand for XRAY's new products will help outweigh the loss of sales of an orthodontics product line provided by a key Japanese supplier located in the evacuation zone following the tsunami and nuclear reactor difficulties. The supplier commenced production at alternate sites, but supplies should grow slowly through 2012. Other than this issue, we see a slow recovery in the dental market in the U.S. and softness in Europe, but low double-digit gains in emerging markets.

► We expect gross margins to widen through 2012, on Astra Tech's higher gross margins, higher pricing of existing products, and an improved product mix. But we also look for the SG&A cost ratio to expand, on the acquisition, lower orthodontics sales (while retaining the cost infrastructure in place) and investments in key product launches.

► We estimate operating EPS of $2.07 in 2011 and $2.31 in 2012, versus $1.90 in 2010.

## Investment Rationale/Risk

► We have a favorable view of XRAY's improved growth prospects following the Astra Tech acquisition, which we think will strengthen its already well performing dental implants business and improve its diversity with the expansion of its non-dental business. Astra Tech should add $200 million to XRAY's 2011 top line and about $600 million to 2012's. Meantime, while we see uncertainty surrounding the resumption of full production by a key Japanese supplier, we are positive on the strong market acceptance of XRAY's new products. We are also encouraged by signs of a U.S. dental consumables market recovery, although growth has not reverted to the historical pattern seen before the recession. Long-term fundamentals of the dental products business look favorable to us, and we view XRAY's cash flow as healthy, providing financial flexibility.

► Risks to our recommendation and target price include intensified competition and persistent weakness in the dental care business in the U.S. and Europe.

► Applying a multiple of 19X, near XRAY's historical midpoint, to our 2012 EPS estimate, we derive our 12-month target price of $44.

# DENTSPLY International Inc

STANDARD
&POOR'S

## Business Summary November 02, 2011

CORPORATE OVERVIEW. Dentsply International, Inc. (XRAY) was created by a merger of a predecessor Dentsply International Inc. and Gendex Corp. in 1993. The predecessor Dentsply, founded in 1899, manufactured and distributed artificial teeth, dental equipment and dental consumable products. Gendex, founded in 1983, manufactured dental x-ray equipment and handpieces. In early 2004, the company divested the dental X-ray equipment business. Dentsply believes it is the world's largest developer and manufacturer of a broad range of products for the dental market.

Dental consumables (35% of net sales in 2010 and 35% in 2009, excluding precious metal content) include dental sundries, such as dental anesthetics, prophylaxis paste, dental sealants, impression materials, restorative materials, bone grafting materials, tooth whiteners, and topical fluoride; and small equipment products, such as high and low speed handpieces, intraoral curing light systems, dental diagnostic systems, and ultrasonic scalers and polishers.

Dental laboratory products (16%; 17%) are used in dental laboratories in the preparation of dental appliances. Products include dental prosthetics, including artificial teeth, precious metal dental alloys, dental ceramics, crown and bridge materials, computer aided machining (CAM) ceramics systems, and porcelain furnaces.

Dental specialty products (46%; 45%) include specialized treatment products, such as endodontic (root canal) instruments and materials, implants and related products, bone grafting materials, and orthodontic appliances and accessories.

In addition to the U.S., Dentsply conducts its business in over 120 foreign countries, principally through its foreign subsidiaries. In 2010 and 2009, net sales, excluding precious metal content, to customers outside the U.S., including export sales, accounted for approximately 63% and 62%, respectively, of net sales.

During 2010 and 2009, one customer, Henry Schein Incorporated, a dental distributor, accounted for 11% and 11%, respectively, of the company's net sales.

## Company Financials Fiscal Year Ended Dec. 31

| Per Share Data ($) | 2010 | 2009 | 2008 | 2007 | 2006 | 2005 | 2004 | 2003 | 2002 | 2001 |
|---|---|---|---|---|---|---|---|---|---|---|
| Tangible Book Value | 3.23 | 2.93 | 1.39 | 2.07 | 1.39 | 1.52 | 1.17 | NM | NM | NM |
| Cash Flow | 2.29 | 2.26 | 2.25 | 2.00 | 1.71 | 0.59 | 1.58 | 1.34 | 1.20 | 1.11 |
| Earnings | 1.82 | 1.83 | 1.87 | 1.67 | 1.41 | 0.28 | 1.28 | 1.05 | 0.93 | 0.77 |
| S&P Core Earnings | 1.81 | 1.84 | 1.92 | 1.72 | 1.41 | 0.20 | 1.21 | 0.95 | 0.84 | 0.60 |
| Dividends | 0.20 | 0.20 | 0.19 | 0.17 | 0.15 | 0.13 | 0.11 | 0.10 | 0.09 | 0.09 |
| Payout Ratio | 11% | 11% | 10% | 10% | 10% | 45% | 8% | 9% | 10% | 12% |
| Prices:High | 38.15 | 36.80 | 47.06 | 47.84 | 33.76 | 29.22 | 28.42 | 23.70 | 21.75 | 17.34 |
| Prices:Low | 27.76 | 21.80 | 22.85 | 29.44 | 26.07 | 25.37 | 20.88 | 16.05 | 15.63 | 10.83 |
| P/E Ratio:High | 21 | 20 | 25 | 29 | 24 | NM | 22 | 22 | 24 | 23 |
| P/E Ratio:Low | 15 | 12 | 12 | 18 | 18 | NM | 16 | 15 | 17 | 14 |

| Income Statement Analysis (Million $) | 2010 | 2009 | 2008 | 2007 | 2006 | 2005 | 2004 | 2003 | 2002 | 2001 |
|---|---|---|---|---|---|---|---|---|---|---|
| Revenue | 2,221 | 2,160 | 2,194 | 2,010 | 1,810 | 1,715 | 1,694 | 1,571 | 1,514 | 1,129 |
| Operating Income | 458 | 453 | 469 | 416 | 370 | 356 | 352 | 317 | 298 | 238 |
| Depreciation | 66.3 | 65.2 | 56.6 | 50.3 | 47.4 | 50.6 | 49.3 | 45.7 | 43.9 | 54.3 |
| Interest Expense | 22.6 | 21.9 | 32.5 | 23.8 | 10.8 | 17.8 | 25.1 | 26.1 | 29.2 | 21.7 |
| Pretax Income | 357 | 363 | 355 | 358 | 315 | 71.0 | 274 | 251 | 221 | 185 |
| Effective Tax Rate | NA | 24.5% | 20.1% | 27.5% | 28.9% | 36.1% | 23.3% | 32.4% | 33.0% | 34.4% |
| Net Income | 267 | 274 | 284 | 260 | 224 | 45.4 | 210 | 170 | 148 | 121 |
| S&P Core Earnings | 265 | 276 | 292 | 265 | 223 | 32.0 | 198 | 153 | 134 | 94.6 |

| Balance Sheet & Other Financial Data (Million $) | 2010 | 2009 | 2008 | 2007 | 2006 | 2005 | 2004 | 2003 | 2002 | 2001 |
|---|---|---|---|---|---|---|---|---|---|---|
| Cash | 540 | 450 | 204 | 169 | 65.1 | 435 | 506 | 164 | 25.7 | 33.7 |
| Current Assets | 1,315 | 1,218 | 950 | 982 | 718 | 1,030 | 1,056 | 727 | 541 | 484 |
| Total Assets | 3,258 | 3,088 | 2,830 | 2,676 | 2,181 | 2,407 | 2,798 | 2,446 | 2,087 | 1,798 |
| Current Liabilities | 360 | 445 | 360 | 312 | 311 | 741 | 405 | 338 | 366 | 359 |
| Long Term Debt | 604 | 387 | 424 | 482 | 367 | 270 | 780 | 790 | 770 | 724 |
| Common Equity | 1,839 | 1,832 | 1,588 | 1,516 | 1,274 | 1,242 | 1,444 | 1,122 | 836 | 610 |
| Total Capital | 2,584 | 2,294 | 2,152 | 2,060 | 1,694 | 1,555 | 2,283 | 1,964 | 1,634 | 1,366 |
| Capital Expenditures | 44.2 | 56.5 | 76.4 | 64.2 | 50.6 | 45.3 | 56.3 | 76.6 | 3.31 | 49.3 |
| Cash Flow | 334 | 339 | 340 | 310 | 271 | 96.0 | 260 | 216 | 192 | 176 |
| Current Ratio | 3.7 | 2.7 | 2.6 | 3.1 | 2.3 | 1.4 | 2.6 | 2.2 | 1.5 | 1.4 |
| % Long Term Debt of Capitalization | 23.4 | 16.9 | 19.7 | 23.4 | 21.7 | 17.4 | 34.2 | 40.2 | 47.1 | 53.0 |
| % Net Income of Revenue | 12.0 | 12.7 | 12.9 | 12.9 | 12.4 | 2.6 | 12.4 | 10.8 | 9.8 | 10.8 |
| % Return on Assets | 8.4 | 9.3 | 10.3 | 10.7 | 9.7 | 1.7 | 8.0 | 7.5 | 7.6 | 9.1 |
| % Return on Equity | 14.6 | 16.0 | 18.3 | 18.6 | 17.8 | 3.4 | 16.4 | 17.3 | 20.5 | 21.5 |

Data as orig reptd.; bef. results of disc opers/spec. items. Per share data adj. for stk. divs.; EPS diluted. E-Estimated. NA-Not Available. NM-Not Meaningful. NR-Not Ranked. UR-Under Review.

**Office:** 221 W. Philadelphia St., York, PA 17405.
**Website:** http://www.dentsply.com
**Chrmn & CEO:** B.W. Wise
**Pres & COO:** C.T. Clark

**SVP, CFO & Chief Acctg Officer:** W.R. Jellison
**Investor Contact:** D. Leckow (717-849-7863)
**CTO:** S.R. Jeffries

**Board Members:** M. C. Alfano, E. K. Brandt, P. H. Cholmondeley, M. Coleman, W. A. Deese, W. F. Hecht, L. A. Jones, F. J. Lunger, J. Miclot, J. C. Miles, II, B. W. Wise

**Founded:** 1983
**Domicile:** Delaware
**Employees:** 9,700

# Devon Energy Corp

**STANDARD &POOR'S**

**S&P Recommendation** BUY ★★★★☆

| | | |
|---|---|---|
| **Price** $58.58 (as of Nov 25, 2011) | **12-Mo. Target Price** $84.00 | **Investment Style** Large-Cap Blend |

**GICS Sector** Energy
**Sub-Industry** Oil & Gas Exploration & Production

**Summary** Devon Energy is one of the largest independent oil and gas exploration and production companies in the U.S.

## Key Stock Statistics (Source S&P, Vickers, company reports)

| | | | | | | | |
|---|---|---|---|---|---|---|---|
| 52-Wk Range | $93.56– 50.74 | S&P Oper. EPS 2011E | 6.00 | Market Capitalization(B) | $23.660 | Beta | 1.14 |
| Trailing 12-Month EPS | $11.27 | S&P Oper. EPS 2012E | 6.60 | Yield (%) | 1.16 | S&P 3-Yr. Proj. EPS CAGR(%) | 21 |
| Trailing 12-Month P/E | 5.2 | P/E on S&P Oper. EPS 2011E | 9.8 | Dividend Rate/Share | $0.68 | S&P Credit Rating | BBB+ |
| $10K Invested 5 Yrs Ago | $8,675 | Common Shares Outstg. (M) | 403.9 | Institutional Ownership (%) | 81 | | |

## Price Performance

30-Week Mov. Avg. · · · 10-Week Mov. Avg. – – **GAAP Earnings vs. Previous Year** Volume Above Avg. ▯▯▯ STARS
12-Mo. Target Price — Relative Strength — ▲ Up ▼ Down ▶ No Change Below Avg. ▯▯▯ ★

Options: ASE, CBOE, P

Analysis prepared by Equity Analyst **Michael Kay** on Nov 22, 2011, when the stock traded at **$62.09**.

## Highlights

> DVN sees 2011 production growth of 7%-8%, with liquids up about 16%-18%, after asset sales led to a 7% decline in 2010. In Canadian oil sands, Jackfish is in full-scale operation and Jackfish 2 has begun to ramp and will reach peak production by year-end 2012. It will begin construction of Jackfish 3 in 2012. At Barnett Shale, where it is the largest producer (1.3 Bcfe/d), DVN plans to drill 375 wells in 2011. DVN expects to raise activity at the liquids-rich Cana-Woodford Shale, planning 225 wells in 2011. It is running four rigs in the Granite Wash and 19 rigs in the liquids-rich Permian Basin, where it sees 20% production growth on capex of $650 million in 2011.

> Cash flow from Barnett should aid development funding of new prospects. DVN's acreage position in Canada could provide more exposure to oil and liquids as the focus shifts there.

> We see EPS of $6.00 in 2011 and $6.60 in 2012, versus $6.53, before items, in 2010. Through November 2, DVN had repurchased 3.4 billion shares as part of a $3.5 billion program it expects to complete this year. In July, DVN raised capex plans by $1 billion to $5.5-$5.9 billion in 2011, within cash flows.

## Investment Rationale/Risk

> DVN has sold $10 billion of assets in deepwater GOM, the GOM shelf, Brazil, and Azerbaijan, and sees after-tax proceeds of about $8 billion to fund onshore drilling, buy back shares, reduce debt and fund acreage acquisitions. It is running about 70 rigs, 59 in the U.S. and 11 in Canada. DVN recently formed a JV with BP plc in the Kirby Oil Sands adjacent to its Jackfish project, boosting Canadian oil sands exposure, where it sees a 20% production compound annual growth rate to 2020. DVN is adding acreage at Kirby, Cana-Woodford Shale and the Permian Basin. We believe DVN's acreage at the Wolfberry, Avalon and Bone Springs plays in the Permian Basin will act as catalysts in 2012, given the liquids-rich nature of the assets. We favor DVN's repositioning as a high-growth onshore E&P company and believe the stock does not fully reflect its growth potential.

> Risks to our opinion and target price include negative changes in economic, industry and operating conditions.

> On our proved reserve NAV estimate of $103 and our DCF ($76; WACC 9.2%; terminal growth 3%) and relative peer E&P metrics, we arrive at our 12-month target price of $84.

## Qualitative Risk Assessment

| LOW | MEDIUM | HIGH |
|---|---|---|

Our risk assessment reflects our view of DVN's position as a large independent oil and gas exploration and production company in a highly capital-intensive industry that derives value from producing commodities with very volatile prices.

## Quantitative Evaluations

**S&P Quality Ranking** B

| D | C | B- | B | B+ | A- | A | A+ |
|---|---|---|---|---|---|---|---|

**Relative Strength Rank** MODERATE
35
LOWEST = 1 HIGHEST = 99

## Revenue/Earnings Data

**Revenue (Million $)**

| | 1Q | 2Q | 3Q | 4Q | Year |
|---|---|---|---|---|---|
| 2011 | 2,147 | 3,220 | 2,764 | -- | -- |
| 2010 | 2,600 | 2,232 | 2,353 | 2,198 | 9,129 |
| 2009 | 1,900 | 1,822 | 2,098 | 2,251 | 7,631 |
| 2008 | 3,763 | 4,763 | 4,386 | 2,453 | 15,365 |
| 2007 | 2,473 | 2,929 | 2,763 | 3,197 | 11,362 |
| 2006 | 2,684 | 2,589 | 2,696 | 2,609 | 10,578 |

**Earnings Per Share ($)**

| | | | | | |
|---|---|---|---|---|---|
| 2011 | 0.91 | 0.43 | 2.50 | E1.41 | E6.00 |
| 2010 | 2.40 | 0.79 | 0.98 | 1.10 | 5.29 |
| 2009 | -8.74 | 0.42 | 0.86 | 1.25 | -6.20 |
| 2008 | 1.45 | 1.31 | 5.63 | -15.46 | -6.95 |
| 2007 | 1.27 | 1.82 | 1.43 | 2.45 | 6.97 |
| 2006 | 1.56 | 1.92 | 1.57 | 1.26 | 6.29 |

Fiscal year ended Dec. 31. Next earnings report expected: Mid February. EPS Estimates based on S&P Operating Earnings; historical GAAP earnings are as reported.

## Dividend Data (Dates: mm/dd Payment Date: mm/dd/yy)

| Amount ($) | Date Decl. | Ex-Div. Date | Stk. of Record | Payment Date |
|---|---|---|---|---|
| 0.160 | 12/01 | 03/11 | 03/15 | 03/31/11 |
| 0.170 | 03/03 | 06/13 | 06/15 | 06/30/11 |
| 0.170 | 06/08 | 09/13 | 09/15 | 09/30/11 |
| 0.170 | 09/14 | 12/13 | 12/15 | 12/30/11 |

Dividends have been paid since 1993. Source: Company reports.

# Devon Energy Corp

STANDARD
&POOR'S

## Business Summary November 22, 2011

CORPORATE OVERVIEW. Devon Energy Corp. (DVN) is an independent exploration and production company primarily engaged in the exploration, development and production of oil and natural gas; the acquisition of producing properties; the transportation of oil, natural gas and natural gas liquids (NGLs); and the processing of natural gas.

DVN's operations are focused in the U.S. and Canada. In 2010, DVN sold over $10 billion in assets, mainly in the Gulf of Mexico (GOM), Brazil and Azerbaijan, transforming the company into a pure-play onshore North American E&P company. After recent asset dispositions, U.S. activities are concentrated in four regions: the Mid-Continent, the Permian Basin, the Rocky Mountains, and onshore areas of the Gulf Coast. Canadian operations are located in the provinces of Alberta, British Columbia and Saskatchewan. DVN also has marketing and midstream operations that perform various activities to support its oil and gas operations.

Proved oil and gas reserves rose 5.1%, to 17.2 Tcfe (59% natural gas, 75% developed), in 2010. We estimate DVN has exhibited a three-year reserve compound annual growth rate (CAGR) of 7%. About 74% of DVN proved reserves are located in the U.S. and 26% in Canada. We calculate DVN's 2010 organic

reserve replacement at 204%, and reserve replacement cost at $2.33 per Mcf. This compares to a three-year reserve replacement of 179% and three-year reserve replacement cost of $2.59 per Mcf. Oil and gas production declined 7.1%, to 3.74 Bcfe per day (68% natural gas), in 2010, reflecting asset sales.

CORPORATE STRATEGY. Like many E&P's in 2010, DVN shifted its strategy to increase its exposure to oil or NGL production, given the higher margins in liquids versus natural gas. DVN expects its liquids production to rise 16%-18% in 2011, reflecting the expected start-up of Jackfish 2 and a ramp at Cana-Woodford Shale. DVN has guided total production growth of 6%-8% for 2011. In July, DVN raised its 2011 E&P capex budget $1 billion to between $5.5 billion-$5.9 billion, up from $5.3 billion in 2010. DVN also spent about $1.2 billion on acquisitions during 2010. About 87% of its budget is slated for development, 7% for acreage capture, and 6% for emerging play evaluation. DVN expects about $8 billion in proceeds from its 2010 asset sales, funding share buybacks, debt reduction and E&P capex.

## Company Financials Fiscal Year Ended Dec. 31

| Per Share Data ($) | 2010 | 2009 | 2008 | 2007 | 2006 | 2005 | 2004 | 2003 | 2002 | 2001 |
|---|---|---|---|---|---|---|---|---|---|---|
| Tangible Book Value | 30.53 | 21.58 | NA | 35.31 | 26.09 | 20.31 | 16.30 | 11.50 | 3.20 | 4.32 |
| Cash Flow | 9.88 | 13.13 | 1.15 | 13.32 | 11.73 | 10.87 | 8.95 | 8.10 | 4.04 | 3.54 |
| Earnings | 5.29 | -6.20 | -6.95 | 6.97 | 6.29 | 6.26 | 4.38 | 4.00 | 0.16 | 0.17 |
| S&P Core Earnings | 5.33 | -6.09 | -7.24 | 6.99 | 6.29 | 6.01 | 4.30 | 3.99 | 0.47 | 0.09 |
| Dividends | 0.64 | 0.64 | NA | 0.56 | 0.45 | 0.30 | 0.20 | 0.10 | 0.10 | 0.10 |
| Payout Ratio | 12% | NM | NA | 8% | 7% | 5% | 5% | 3% | 63% | 59% |
| Prices:High | 78.86 | 75.05 | NA | 94.75 | 74.75 | 70.35 | 41.64 | 29.40 | 26.55 | 33.38 |
| Prices:Low | 58.58 | 38.55 | NA | 62.80 | 48.94 | 36.48 | 25.90 | 21.23 | 16.94 | 15.28 |
| P/E Ratio:High | 15 | NM | NA | 14 | 12 | 11 | 10 | 7 | NM | NM |
| P/E Ratio:Low | 11 | NM | NA | 9 | 8 | 6 | 6 | 5 | NM | NM |

| Income Statement Analysis (Million $) | | | | | | | | | | |
|---|---|---|---|---|---|---|---|---|---|---|
| Revenue | 9,129 | 7,631 | 15,365 | 11,362 | 10,578 | 10,741 | 9,189 | 7,352 | 4,316 | 3,075 |
| Operating Income | NA | NA | -153 | 7,380 | 6,938 | 7,290 | 6,038 | 4,589 | 2,403 | 2,350 |
| Depreciation, Depletion and Amortization | 2,022 | 8,516 | 3,595 | 2,858 | 2,442 | 2,191 | 2,290 | 1,793 | 1,211 | 876 |
| Interest Expense | 363 | 349 | 329 | 532 | 421 | 533 | 475 | 504 | 533 | 220 |
| Pretax Income | 3,568 | -4,526 | -4,033 | 4,224 | 4,012 | 4,552 | 3,293 | 2,245 | -134 | 84.0 |
| Effective Tax Rate | NA | 39.2% | 23.7% | 25.5% | 29.6% | 35.6% | 33.6% | 22.9% | NM | 35.7% |
| Net Income | 2,333 | -2,753 | -3,079 | 3,146 | 2,823 | 2,930 | 2,186 | 1,731 | 59.0 | 54.0 |
| S&P Core Earnings | 2,324 | -2,671 | -3,210 | 3,144 | 2,815 | 2,801 | 2,136 | 1,715 | 147 | 22.9 |

| Balance Sheet & Other Financial Data (Million $) | | | | | | | | | | |
|---|---|---|---|---|---|---|---|---|---|---|
| Cash | 2,866 | 646 | 379 | 1,736 | 739 | 1,606 | 2,119 | 1,273 | 292 | 193 |
| Current Assets | 5,555 | 2,992 | 2,684 | 3,914 | 3,212 | 4,206 | 3,583 | 2,364 | 1,064 | 1,081 |
| Total Assets | 32,927 | 29,686 | 31,908 | 41,456 | 35,063 | 30,273 | 29,736 | 27,162 | 16,225 | 13,184 |
| Current Liabilities | 4,583 | 3,802 | 3,135 | 3,657 | 4,645 | 2,934 | 3,100 | 2,071 | 1,042 | 919 |
| Long Term Debt | 3,819 | 5,847 | 5,661 | 7,928 | 5,568 | 5,957 | 7,031 | 8,635 | 7,562 | 6,589 |
| Common Equity | 19,253 | 15,570 | 17,060 | 22,005 | 17,441 | 14,999 | 13,673 | 11,055 | 4,652 | 3,258 |
| Total Capital | 24,883 | 22,849 | 26,400 | 34,972 | 28,660 | 26,362 | 25,505 | 24,061 | 14,842 | 11,990 |
| Capital Expenditures | 6,476 | 4,879 | 9,375 | 6,158 | 7,551 | 4,090 | 3,103 | 2,587 | 3,426 | 5,326 |
| Cash Flow | 4,355 | 5,763 | 511 | 5,994 | 5,255 | 5,111 | 4,466 | 3,514 | 1,260 | 920 |
| Current Ratio | 1.2 | 0.8 | 0.9 | 1.1 | 0.7 | 1.4 | 1.2 | 1.1 | 1.0 | 1.2 |
| % Long Term Debt of Capitalization | 15.4 | 25.6 | 21.4 | 23.9 | 19.4 | 22.6 | 27.6 | 35.9 | 51.0 | 55.0 |
| % Return on Assets | 7.5 | NM | NM | 8.2 | 8.6 | 9.7 | 7.7 | 8.0 | NM | 0.5 |
| % Return on Equity | 13.4 | NM | NM | 15.9 | 17.4 | 20.3 | 17.6 | 21.9 | NM | 1.3 |

Data as orig reptd.; bef. results of disc opers/spec. items. Per share data adj. for stk. divs.; EPS diluted. E-Estimated. NA-Not Available. NM-Not Meaningful. NR-Not Ranked. UR-Under Review.

**Office:** 20 N Broadway, Oklahoma City, OK 73102-8260.
**Telephone:** 405-235-3611.
**Website:** http://www.devonenergy.com
**Chrmn:** J.L. Nichols

**Pres & CEO:** J. Richels
**EVP & CFO:** J.A. Agosta
**Chief Admin Officer:** R.A. Marcum
**Chief Acctg Officer:** J. Humphers

**Investor Contact:** V. White (405-552-4526)
**Board Members:** R. H. Henry, J. A. Hill, M. M. Kanovsky, R. A. Mosbacher, Jr., J. L. Nichols, D. C. Radtke, M. P. Ricciardello, J. Richels

**Auditor:** KPMG
**Founded:** 1988
**Domicile:** Delaware
**Employees:** 5,000

The McGraw-Hill Companies

# DeVry Inc

**STANDARD &POOR'S**

| S&P Recommendation **HOLD** ★★★☆☆ | Price $33.01 (as of Nov 25, 2011) | 12-Mo. Target Price $43.00 | Investment Style Large-Cap Growth |
| --- | --- | --- | --- |

**GICS Sector** Consumer Discretionary
**Sub-Industry** Education Services

**Summary** DeVry offers career-oriented degree programs, preparatory coursework for the CPA and CFA exams, and medical, veterinary and nursing education.

## Key Stock Statistics (Source S&P, Vickers, company reports)

| | | | | | | | |
| --- | --- | --- | --- | --- | --- | --- | --- |
| 52-Wk Range | $66.85–32.97 | S&P Oper. EPS 2012**E** | 3.80 | Market Capitalization(B) | $2.221 | Beta | 0.67 |
| Trailing 12-Month EPS | $4.49 | S&P Oper. EPS 2013**E** | 4.15 | Yield (%) | 0.91 | S&P 3-Yr. Proj. EPS CAGR(%) | -2 |
| Trailing 12-Month P/E | 7.4 | P/E on S&P Oper. EPS 2012**E** | 8.7 | Dividend Rate/Share | $0.30 | S&P Credit Rating | NA |
| $10K Invested 5 Yrs Ago | $12,872 | Common Shares Outstg. (M) | 67.3 | Institutional Ownership (%) | 85 | | |

## Price Performance

30-Week Mov. Avg. · · · 10-Week Mov. Avg. - - GAAP Earnings vs. Previous Year  Volume Above Avg.||||| STARS
12-Mo. Target Price — Relative Strength — ▲ Up ▼ Down ► No Change  Below Avg.|||||

Options: CBOE, P, Ph

Analysis prepared by Equity Analyst **Michael Jaffe** on Nov 09, 2011, when the stock traded at **$36.63**.

## Highlights

➤ We think revenues will fall by 4% in FY 12 (Jun.), hurt mostly by likely declines in undergraduate enrollment at DeVry University and total enrollment at Carrington Colleges. We believe that new entrants to for-profit schools are likely to be limited by the recent negative publicity about private sector education, and regulatory challenges. We see these factors mostly offset by a larger number of campuses, with new campuses at Chamberlain College of Nursing, and the August 2011 acquisition of a medical school in St. Maarten.

➤ We forecast narrower net margins in FY 12, on the challenging demand environment and the expected resultant decline in enrollment at existing campuses. We also see profitability being affected by costs of investments to improve academic quality at DV's schools. We see these factors partly offset by favorable results in the Medical and Healthcare area (outside of Carrington), and cost controls.

➤ We expect bad debt expense to fall a little below DV's historical range of 2.5% to 3%, on DeVry's focus on receivable collections.

## Investment Rationale/Risk

➤ Recent regulatory matters and negative publicity about for-profit educators have started to hurt DV's new student enrollments (and those at nearly all of its peers), and we see this continuing for a while. At the same time, we are positive about DV's ongoing strategy of moving away from its previous dominant focus on technology programs, and we see a solid performance at its Medical and Healthcare campuses. Based on these factors and our valuation model, we view DV shares as fairly valued.

➤ Risks to our recommendation and target price include a major impact from proposed new industry regulations and an extended downturn in new undergraduate enrollment.

➤ The stock recently traded at about 10X our calendar 2012 EPS forecast of $3.94, which is a small discount to DV's peer group. We have mixed views on DV's prospects, as negative industry trends have started to greatly impact undergraduate enrollments, while trends at DV's medical and nursing schools appear favorable. Regulatory uncertainties also will likely pose a challenge. Applying a multiple of 10.9X to our calendar 2012 EPS estimate results in our 12-month target price of $43.

## Qualitative Risk Assessment

| LOW | MEDIUM | HIGH |
| --- | --- | --- |

Our risk assessment reflects DV's operating struggles for a few years in the middle part of the decade and current challenges in its business, offset by what we consider positive turnaround initiatives.

## Quantitative Evaluations

**S&P Quality Ranking**  B+

| D | C | B- | B | B+ | A- | A | A+ |
| --- | --- | --- | --- | --- | --- | --- | --- |

**Relative Strength Rank**  WEAK

15

LOWEST = 1  HIGHEST = 99

## Revenue/Earnings Data

**Revenue (Million $)**

| | 1Q | 2Q | 3Q | 4Q | Year |
| --- | --- | --- | --- | --- | --- |
| 2012 | 519.0 | -- | -- | -- | -- |
| 2011 | 521.4 | 551.5 | 562.7 | 546.8 | 2,182 |
| 2010 | 431.1 | 473.0 | 504.4 | 506.7 | 1,915 |
| 2009 | 303.7 | 369.6 | 391.9 | 396.2 | 1,461 |
| 2008 | 250.3 | 273.7 | 291.0 | 276.8 | 1,092 |
| 2007 | 219.2 | 235.6 | 245.8 | 232.8 | 933.5 |

**Earnings Per Share ($)**

| | | | | | |
| --- | --- | --- | --- | --- | --- |
| 2012 | 0.83 | E0.99 | E1.05 | E0.93 | E3.80 |
| 2011 | 1.03 | 1.25 | 1.32 | 1.08 | 4.68 |
| 2010 | 0.76 | 1.00 | 1.12 | 0.99 | 3.87 |
| 2009 | 0.48 | 0.59 | 0.70 | 0.51 | 2.28 |
| 2008 | 0.37 | 0.49 | 0.53 | 0.34 | 1.73 |
| 2007 | 0.29 | 0.23 | 0.32 | 0.22 | 1.07 |

Fiscal year ended Jun. 30. Next earnings report expected: Late January. EPS Estimates based on S&P Operating Earnings; historical GAAP earnings are as reported.

## Dividend Data (Dates: mm/dd Payment Date: mm/dd/yy)

| Amount ($) | Date Decl. | Ex-Div. Date | Stk. of Record | Payment Date |
| --- | --- | --- | --- | --- |
| 0.120 | 11/10 | 12/08 | 12/10 | 01/10/11 |
| 0.120 | 05/23 | 06/16 | 06/20 | 07/12/11 |
| 0.150 | 11/03 | 12/06 | 12/08 | 01/10/12 |
| 0.150 | 11/03 | 12/06 | 12/08 | 01/10/12 |

Dividends have been paid since 2007. Source: Company reports.

---

**Please read the Required Disclosures and Analyst Certification on the last page of this report.**

**The McGraw·Hill Companies**

# DeVry Inc

**STANDARD &POOR'S**

## Business Summary November 09, 2011

CORPORATE OVERVIEW. DeVry offers associate, undergraduate and graduate degree programs through its DeVry University institute. It also operates Becker Professional Education, which provides preparatory coursework for certification exams in accounting and finance; Ross University, which offers medical and veterinary education; American University of the Caribbean, a 1,000-student medical campus in St. Maarten, which was acquired in August 2011 for $235 million in cash; Chamberlain College of Nursing, which offers nursing programs; Carrington Colleges Group (formerly U.S. Education, purchased in September 2008 for $290 million in cash), which operates Carrington College and Carrington College California in the western U.S. (names changed from Apollo College and Western Career College, respectively, on June 30), offering certificate and associate degree programs in health care; DeVry Brasil (formerly Fanor; 82% stake purchased on April 1, 2009), a post-secondary education provider in Brazil; and Advanced Academics, which provides online secondary education to school districts throughout the U.S.

In August 2009, DV reported that it had reorganized into four segments: Business, Technology and Management (comprised of DeVry University), Medical and Healthcare (Ross University, Chamberlain College of Nursing, and Carrington Colleges Group; with American University of the Caribbean added following its acquisition), Professional Education (Becker Professional Education), and Other Educational Services (Advanced Academics and DeVry Brasil). During FY 11 (Jun.), DV combined its Other Educational Services units into a segment with Becker and DeVry's international business development effort (with the combined segments now called International, K-12 and Professional Education). In FY 11, the Business, Technology and Management segment accounted for 67% of DV's revenues and 72% of operating profits; Medical and Healthcare schools accounted for 26% of revenues and 21% of operating profits; and the International, K-12 and Professional Education segment contributed 8% and 7%, respectively.

## Company Financials Fiscal Year Ended Jun. 30

| Per Share Data ($) | 2011 | 2010 | 2009 | 2008 | 2007 | 2006 | 2005 | 2004 | 2003 | 2002 |
|---|---|---|---|---|---|---|---|---|---|---|
| Tangible Book Value | 9.77 | 6.62 | 2.96 | 5.40 | 4.13 | 2.96 | 2.06 | 1.53 | 0.45 | 3.94 |
| Cash Flow | 5.60 | 4.73 | 2.98 | 2.28 | 1.69 | 1.29 | 1.19 | 1.62 | 1.45 | 1.42 |
| Earnings | 4.68 | 3.87 | 2.28 | 1.73 | 1.07 | 0.61 | 0.38 | 0.82 | 0.87 | 0.95 |
| S&P Core Earnings | 4.68 | 3.86 | 2.34 | 1.76 | 0.89 | 0.61 | 0.29 | 0.77 | 0.83 | 0.91 |
| Dividends | 0.24 | 0.20 | 0.16 | 0.12 | 0.10 | Nil | Nil | Nil | Nil | Nil |
| Payout Ratio | 5% | 5% | 7% | 7% | 9% | Nil | Nil | Nil | Nil | Nil |
| Prices:High | 66.85 | 74.36 | 64.69 | 61.57 | 59.97 | 28.75 | 24.84 | 32.38 | 30.15 | 34.76 |
| Prices:Low | 32.97 | 36.34 | 38.19 | 39.25 | 26.10 | 18.50 | 15.45 | 13.00 | 15.90 | 12.10 |
| P/E Ratio:High | 14 | 19 | 28 | 36 | 56 | 47 | 65 | 39 | 35 | 37 |
| P/E Ratio:Low | 7 | 9 | 17 | 23 | 24 | 30 | 41 | 16 | 18 | 13 |

| Income Statement Analysis (Million $) | | | | | | | | | | |
|---|---|---|---|---|---|---|---|---|---|---|
| Revenue | 2,182 | 1,915 | 1,461 | 1,092 | 933 | 843 | 781 | 785 | 680 | 648 |
| Operating Income | 559 | 473 | 2,994 | 206 | 132 | 116 | 101 | 139 | 128 | 144 |
| Depreciation | 64.6 | 62.2 | 50.5 | 39.7 | 44.0 | 48.1 | 57.6 | 55.6 | 40.3 | 33.5 |
| Interest Expense | 1.28 | 1.59 | 2.78 | 0.52 | 4.78 | 10.2 | 9.05 | 7.80 | 1.28 | 0.81 |
| Pretax Income | 494 | 413 | 237 | 172 | 105 | 57.5 | 34.7 | 81.4 | 86.5 | 111 |
| Effective Tax Rate | NA | NA | 30.2% | 27.1% | 27.4% | 25.1% | 23.1% | 28.6% | 29.3% | 39.4% |
| Net Income | 331 | 280 | 166 | 126 | 76.2 | 43.1 | 26.7 | 58.1 | 61.1 | 67.1 |
| S&P Core Earnings | 330 | 279 | 170 | 128 | 63.5 | 42.8 | 20.2 | 54.6 | 58.4 | 64.4 |

| Balance Sheet & Other Financial Data (Million $) | | | | | | | | | | |
|---|---|---|---|---|---|---|---|---|---|---|
| Cash | 450 | 323 | 225 | 220 | 129 | 131 | 162 | 160 | 123 | 78.9 |
| Current Assets | 625 | 500 | 385 | 326 | 219 | 228 | 242 | 209 | 170 | 118 |
| Total Assets | 1,851 | 1,628 | 1,434 | 1,018 | 844 | 872 | 910 | 884 | 857 | 468 |
| Current Liabilities | 316 | 344 | 392 | 211 | 166 | 211 | 187 | 156 | 139 | 104 |
| Long Term Debt | NA | NA | 20.0 | Nil | 0.01 | 65.0 | 175 | 215 | 275 | Nil |
| Common Equity | 1,390 | 1,179 | 927 | 756 | 642 | 565 | 508 | 478 | 416 | 354 |
| Total Capital | 1,403 | 1,184 | 999 | 778 | 660 | 642 | 704 | 711 | 704 | 354 |
| Capital Expenditures | 136 | 131 | 74.0 | 62.8 | 38.6 | 25.3 | 42.9 | 42.8 | 43.8 | 85.9 |
| Cash Flow | 395 | 342 | 216 | 165 | 120 | 91.2 | 84.3 | 114 | 101 | 101 |
| Current Ratio | 2.0 | 1.5 | 1.0 | 1.6 | 1.3 | 1.1 | 1.3 | 1.3 | 1.2 | 1.1 |
| % Long Term Debt of Capitalization | Nil | Nil | 2.0 | Nil | 0.0 | 10.1 | 24.8 | 30.2 | 39.1 | Nil |
| % Net Income of Revenue | 15.2 | 14.6 | 11.3 | 11.5 | 8.2 | 5.1 | 3.4 | 7.4 | 9.0 | 10.4 |
| % Return on Assets | 19.0 | 18.3 | 13.5 | 13.5 | 8.9 | 4.8 | 3.0 | 6.7 | 9.2 | 15.6 |
| % Return on Equity | 25.8 | 26.6 | 19.7 | 18.0 | 12.6 | 8.0 | 5.4 | 13.0 | 15.9 | 21.0 |

Data as orig reptd.; bef. results of disc opers/spec. items. Per share data adj. for stk. divs.; EPS diluted. E-Estimated. NA-Not Available. NM-Not Meaningful. NR-Not Ranked. UR-Under Review.

**Office:** 3005 Highland Parkway, Downers Grove, IL 60515.
**Telephone:** 630-515-7700.
**Website:** http://www.devryinc.com
**Chrmn:** H.T. Shapiro

**Pres & CEO:** D.M. Hamburger
**SVP, CFO, Chief Acctg Officer & Treas:** R.M. Gunst
**SVP, Secy & General Counsel:** G.S. Davis
**SVP & CIO:** E.P. Dirst

**Investor Contact:** J. Bates (630-574-1949)
**Board Members:** C. B. Begley, D. S. Brown, C. R. Curran, D. M. Hamburger, D. R. Huston, W. T. Keevan, L. Logan, J. A. McGee, L. W. Pickrum, F. Ruiz, H. T. Shapiro, R. L. Taylor

**Founded:** 1931
**Domicile:** Delaware
**Employees:** 12,599

# Diamond Offshore Drilling Inc.

**STANDARD &POOR'S**

| S&P Recommendation **HOLD** ★★★☆☆ | Price $58.05 (as of Nov 25, 2011) | 12-Mo. Target Price $77.00 | Investment Style Large-Cap Blend |
|---|---|---|---|

**GICS Sector** Energy
**Sub-Industry** Oil & Gas Drilling

**Summary** This company provides offshore contract drilling services to the oil and gas industry, and owns one of the world's largest fleets of semisubmersible rigs.

## Key Stock Statistics (Source S&P, Vickers, company reports)

| | | | | | | |
|---|---|---|---|---|---|---|
| 52-Wk Range | $81.19– 51.16 | S&P Oper. EPS 2011**E** | 6.91 | Market Capitalization(B) | $8.071 | Beta | 0.86 |
| Trailing 12-Month EPS | $7.31 | S&P Oper. EPS 2012**E** | 6.09 | Yield (%) | 0.86 | S&P 3-Yr. Proj. EPS CAGR(%) | -15 |
| Trailing 12-Month P/E | 7.9 | P/E on S&P Oper. EPS 2011**E** | 8.4 | Dividend Rate/Share | $0.50 | S&P Credit Rating | A- |
| $10K Invested 5 Yrs Ago | $10,670 | Common Shares Outstg. (M) | 139.0 | Institutional Ownership (%) | 95 | | |

## Price Performance

30-Week Mov. Avg. · · · 10-Week Mov. Avg. – – GAAP Earnings vs. Previous Year   Volume Above Avg. STARS
12-Mo. Target Price — Relative Strength   ▲ Up ▼ Down ► No Change   Below Avg.

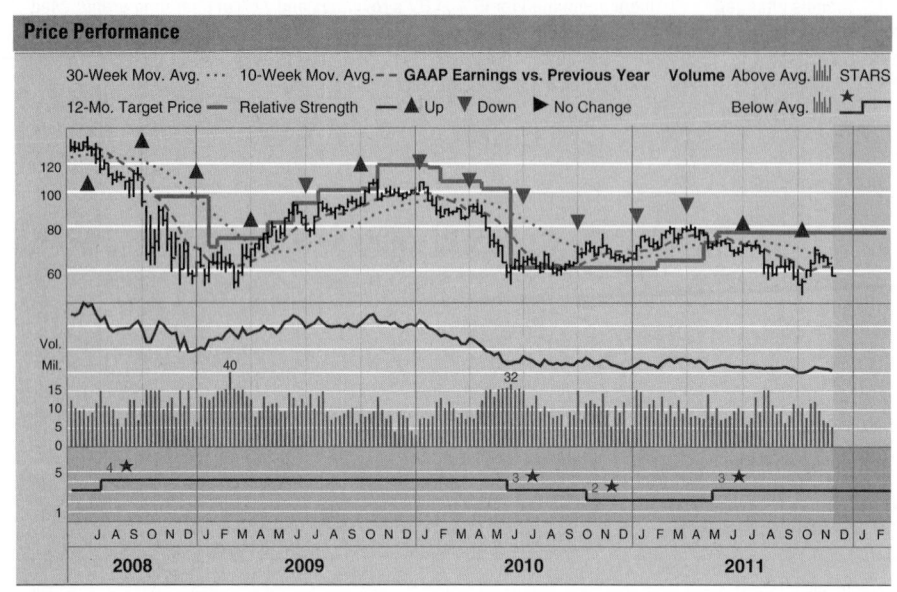

Options: ASE, CBOE, P

Analysis prepared by Equity Analyst **S. Glickman, CFA** on Sep 14, 2011, when the stock traded at **$63.00**.

### Highlights

➤ In May, DO said it had contracted two newbuild drillships under construction, the Ocean Blackhawk and the Ocean Black Hornet, to Anadarko Petroleum (APC 73, Buy). The two units are contracted for five years each with total contract backlog of $1.8 billion, or about $493,000 per day. We think this is a solid combination of dayrate and term and bodes well for DO's longer-term cash flow visibility, with the rigs slated for delivery in mid- to late 2013. We remain concerned near term about industry competition between deepwater and midwater units, which we think is disadvantageous for DO's dayrate prospects on contract rollovers, particularly for the midwater units.

➤ With special and intermediate survey work (which takes rigs off dayrate) projected to be lower for DO in 2011 than in 2009 or 2010, and with most of its potential fleet upgrades completed, we think a strategy that maximizes utilization at the expense of lower dayrates is reasonable.

➤ We look for EPS of $6.59 in 2011, falling 7.6% to $6.09 in 2012, when we see lower dayrates more than offsetting improved utilization.

### Investment Rationale/Risk

➤ We harbor some concern about competition between deepwater and midwater units, although tendering activity appears to be on the rise. To the extent that such competition is heightened, we see this as disadvantageous to DO given its relatively older fleet (albeit one that it continues to modernize via acquisitions). We think DO will consider further divestments of older, midwater units to raise capital for newer, high-specification units.

➤ Risks to our recommendation and target price include lower deepwater drilling activity; lower oil and natural gas prices; slower-than-expected return to normalcy for the U.S. drilling permit issuance process; higher-than-expected idle time for active units; and cuts in special quarterly dividends.

➤ We apply peer average multiples, as we see greater midwater exposure offset to some extent by above-average projected ROIC. Using multiples of 7.5X enterprise value to our 2011 EBITDA estimate and 8.5X our projected 2011 operating cash flow, and blending with our NAV model, our 12-month target price is $77.

### Qualitative Risk Assessment

| LOW | MEDIUM | HIGH |
|---|---|---|

Our risk assessment reflects DO's exposure to volatile crude oil and natural gas prices, capital spending decisions made by its oil and gas producing customers, risks associated with operating in frontier regions, and an uncertain domestic regulatory regime.

### Quantitative Evaluations

**S&P Quality Ranking**                B

| D | C | B- | B | B+ | A- | A | A+ |
|---|---|---|---|---|---|---|---|

**Relative Strength Rank**        MODERATE

43

LOWEST = 1                HIGHEST = 99

### Revenue/Earnings Data

**Revenue (Million $)**

| | 1Q | 2Q | 3Q | 4Q | Year |
|---|---|---|---|---|---|
| 2011 | 806.4 | 889.5 | 878.2 | -- | -- |
| 2010 | 859.7 | 822.6 | 799.7 | 841.0 | 3,323 |
| 2009 | 885.7 | 946.4 | 908.4 | 890.8 | 3,631 |
| 2008 | 786.1 | 954.4 | 900.4 | 903.2 | 3,544 |
| 2007 | 608.2 | 648.9 | 644.0 | 666.7 | 2,568 |
| 2006 | 447.7 | 512.2 | 514.5 | 578.2 | 2,053 |

**Earnings Per Share ($)**

| | | | | | |
|---|---|---|---|---|---|
| 2011 | 1.80 | 1.92 | 1.85 | E1.34 | E6.91 |
| 2010 | 2.09 | 1.61 | 1.43 | 1.74 | 6.87 |
| 2009 | 2.51 | 2.79 | 2.62 | 1.98 | 9.89 |
| 2008 | 2.09 | 2.99 | 2.23 | 2.11 | 9.43 |
| 2007 | 1.64 | 1.81 | 1.48 | 1.19 | 6.12 |
| 2006 | 1.06 | 1.27 | 1.19 | 1.60 | 5.12 |

Fiscal year ended Dec. 31. Next earnings report expected: Early February. EPS Estimates based on S&P Operating Earnings; historical GAAP earnings are as reported.

### Dividend Data (Dates: mm/dd Payment Date: mm/dd/yy)

| Amount ($) | Date Decl. | Ex-Div. Date | Stk. of Record | Payment Date |
|---|---|---|---|---|
| .75 Spl. | 07/21 | 07/28 | 08/01 | 09/01/11 |
| 0.125 | 07/21 | 07/28 | 08/01 | 09/01/11 |
| .75 Spl. | 10/20 | 10/28 | 11/01 | 12/01/11 |
| 0.125 | 10/20 | 10/28 | 11/01 | 12/01/11 |

Dividends have been paid since 1997. Source: Company reports.

---

**Please read the Required Disclosures and Analyst Certification on the last page of this report.**

*The McGraw-Hill Companies*

# Diamond Offshore Drilling Inc.

**STANDARD
&POOR'S**

## Business Summary September 14, 2011

CORPORATE OVERVIEW. Diamond Offshore Drilling is engaged in contract drilling of offshore oil and gas wells, with a focus on deepwater drilling. As of January 2011, the company owned 46 mobile offshore drilling rigs: 32 semi-submersible rigs (including 13 high-specification units and 19 intermediate units), 13 jackup rigs, and one drillship. DO is also constructing two newbuild drillships, due for delivery in 2013. The rigs are located in a number of offshore basins around the world, including the Gulf of Mexico (GOM), the North Sea, South America, Africa, Australia and Southeast Asia. About 81% of 2010 revenues came from outside the United States. DO served 46 customers in 2010, with two customers in Brazil accounting for 38% of total revenues.

Semisubmersible rigs, or floaters (92% of 2010 contract drilling revenues and 96% of segment operating income), operate in a semisubmerged position, afloat off the bottom, with the lower hull 55 ft. to 90 ft. below the water line, and the upper deck well above the surface. Floaters are typically anchored in position, but three company floaters are held in position by computer-controlled thrusters (dynamically positioned, or DP). Of DO's 33 floaters, 14 are high specification rigs (44%, 45%) capable of working in harsh environments and water depths of up to 7,500 ft. The other 19 semisubmersibles (48%, 51%) operate in maximum water depths of 4,000 ft.

Jackup rigs (8%, 4%) are mobile, self-elevating drilling platforms equipped with legs that are lowered to the ocean floor until a foundation is established to support the rig. DO's 13 jackup rigs are used extensively for drilling in water depths from 20 ft. to 350 ft. Of the 13 jackups, four are cold-stacked, with the remaining nine units mostly in international regions.

Drillships, typically self-propelled, are positioned over a drillsite through the use of either an anchoring or DP system. The company owns one drillship, the Ocean Clipper, operating offshore Brazil, but is in the process of building two new drillships, due in mid- to late 2013. The two newbuild drillships were signed to long-term contracts in May 2011.

## Company Financials Fiscal Year Ended Dec. 31

| Per Share Data ($) | 2010 | 2009 | 2008 | 2007 | 2006 | 2005 | 2004 | 2003 | 2002 | 2001 |
|---|---|---|---|---|---|---|---|---|---|---|
| Tangible Book Value | 27.78 | 26.11 | 24.09 | 20.72 | 17.95 | 14.38 | 12.64 | 12.91 | 13.68 | 13.74 |
| Cash Flow | 9.70 | 12.38 | 11.49 | 7.79 | 6.54 | 3.14 | 1.33 | 0.98 | 1.71 | 2.35 |
| Earnings | 6.87 | 9.89 | 9.43 | 6.12 | 5.12 | 1.91 | -0.06 | -0.37 | 0.47 | 1.31 |
| S&P Core Earnings | 6.71 | 9.85 | 9.41 | 6.07 | 5.13 | 1.84 | -0.07 | -0.35 | 0.30 | 1.15 |
| Dividends | 5.15 | 0.50 | 4.13 | 0.50 | 0.50 | 0.38 | 0.25 | 0.44 | 0.50 | 0.50 |
| Payout Ratio | 75% | 5% | 44% | 8% | 10% | 20% | NM | NM | 106% | 38% |
| Prices:High | 107.12 | 108.78 | 147.77 | 149.30 | 97.90 | 71.97 | 40.47 | 23.80 | 34.99 | 45.65 |
| Prices:Low | 54.70 | 53.30 | 54.52 | 73.50 | 62.26 | 37.91 | 20.00 | 17.06 | 17.30 | 22.83 |
| P/E Ratio:High | 16 | 11 | 16 | 24 | 19 | 38 | NM | NM | 74 | 35 |
| P/E Ratio:Low | 8 | 5 | 6 | 12 | 12 | 20 | NM | NM | 37 | 17 |

| Income Statement Analysis (Million $) | 2010 | 2009 | 2008 | 2007 | 2006 | 2005 | 2004 | 2003 | 2002 | 2001 |
|---|---|---|---|---|---|---|---|---|---|---|
| Revenue | 3,323 | 3,631 | 3,544 | 2,568 | 2,053 | 1,221 | 815 | 681 | 753 | 885 |
| Operating Income | NA | NA | 2,233 | 1,454 | 1,141 | 510 | 213 | 138 | 229 | 395 |
| Depreciation, Depletion and Amortization | 393 | 346 | 287 | 235 | 201 | 184 | 179 | 176 | 177 | 170 |
| Interest Expense | 90.7 | 49.6 | 10.1 | 28.5 | 24.1 | 41.8 | 30.3 | 23.9 | 23.6 | 26.2 |
| Pretax Income | 1,336 | 1,868 | 1,848 | 1,247 | 966 | 356 | -3.53 | -54.2 | 96.2 | 272 |
| Effective Tax Rate | NA | 26.3% | 29.0% | 32.1% | 26.9% | 27.0% | NM | NM | 35.0% | 33.3% |
| Net Income | 955 | 1,376 | 1,311 | 847 | 707 | 260 | -7.24 | -48.4 | 62.5 | 182 |
| S&P Core Earnings | 933 | 1,371 | 1,308 | 841 | 707 | 250 | -10.5 | -45.5 | 36.9 | 157 |

| Balance Sheet & Other Financial Data (Million $) | 2010 | 2009 | 2008 | 2007 | 2006 | 2005 | 2004 | 2003 | 2002 | 2001 |
|---|---|---|---|---|---|---|---|---|---|---|
| Cash | 1,077 | 777 | 737 | 639 | 826 | 843 | 266 | 610 | 813 | 1,147 |
| Current Assets | 1,864 | 1,723 | 1,467 | 1,265 | 1,482 | 1,282 | 1,196 | 835 | 1,034 | 1,427 |
| Total Assets | 6,727 | 6,264 | 4,939 | 4,341 | 4,133 | 3,607 | 3,379 | 3,135 | 3,259 | 3,503 |
| Current Liabilities | 626 | 413 | 509 | 453 | 334 | 269 | 614 | 100 | 118 | 335 |
| Long Term Debt | 1,496 | 1,495 | 503 | 507 | 964 | 978 | 709 | 928 | 924 | 921 |
| Common Equity | 3,862 | 3,631 | 3,349 | 2,877 | 2,320 | 1,853 | 1,626 | 1,680 | 1,808 | 1,853 |
| Total Capital | 5,357 | 5,130 | 4,311 | 3,778 | 3,284 | 3,276 | 2,705 | 2,993 | 3,107 | 3,150 |
| Capital Expenditures | 434 | 1,362 | 667 | 647 | 551 | 294 | 89.2 | 209 | 274 | 269 |
| Cash Flow | 1,349 | 1,723 | 1,598 | 1,082 | 907 | 444 | 172 | 127 | 240 | 352 |
| Current Ratio | 3.0 | 4.2 | 2.9 | 2.8 | 4.4 | 4.8 | 1.9 | 8.4 | 8.7 | 4.3 |
| % Long Term Debt of Capitalization | 27.9 | 29.2 | 11.7 | 14.9 | 29.4 | 29.8 | 26.2 | 31.0 | 29.8 | 29.2 |
| % Return on Assets | 14.7 | 24.6 | 28.3 | 20.0 | 18.3 | 7.5 | NM | NM | 1.8 | 5.5 |
| % Return on Equity | 25.5 | 39.4 | 42.1 | 32.6 | 33.9 | 15.0 | NM | NM | 3.4 | 10.0 |

Data as orig reptd.; bef. results of disc opers/spec. items. Per share data adj. for stk. divs.; EPS diluted. E-Estimated. NA-Not Available. NM-Not Meaningful. NR-Not Ranked. UR-Under Review.

**Office:** 15415 Katy Freeway, Houston, TX 77094-1803.
**Telephone:** 281-492-5300.
**Website:** http://www.diamondoffshore.com
**Chrmn:** J.S. Tisch

**Pres & CEO:** L.R. Dickerson
**SVP & CFO:** G.T. Krenek
**SVP, Secy & General Counsel:** W.C. Long
**Chief Acctg Officer & Cntlr:** B.G. Gordon

**Investor Contact:** L. Van Dyke (281-492-5370)
**Board Members:** J. R. Bolton, L. R. Dickerson, C. L. Fabrikant, P. G. Gaffney, II, E. Grebow, H. C. Hofmann, A. L. Rebell, C. M. Sobel, J. S. Tisch, R. S. Troubh

**Founded:** 1989
**Domicile:** Delaware
**Employees:** 5,300

The **McGraw-Hill** Companies

# DIRECTV

STANDARD &POOR'S

| S&P Recommendation **HOLD** ★★★☆☆ | Price $45.08 (as of Nov 25, 2011) | 12-Mo. Target Price $52.00 | Investment Style Large-Cap Blend |
| --- | --- | --- | --- |

**GICS Sector** Consumer Discretionary
**Sub-Industry** Cable & Satellite

**Summary** The larger of the two major satellite TV providers -- with 19.8 million subscribers across the U.S. and 11.1 million in Latin America (including Brazil, Mexico and the PanAmericana regions) -- DIRECTV merged with Liberty Media Entertainment in late 2009.

## Key Stock Statistics (Source S&P, Vickers, company reports)

| | | | | | | | |
| --- | --- | --- | --- | --- | --- | --- | --- |
| 52-Wk Range | $53.40–39.12 | S&P Oper. EPS 2011**E** | 3.45 | Market Capitalization(B) | $31.808 | Beta | 0.87 |
| Trailing 12-Month EPS | $3.02 | S&P Oper. EPS 2012**E** | 4.26 | Yield (%) | Nil | S&P 3-Yr. Proj. EPS CAGR(%) | 17 |
| Trailing 12-Month P/E | 14.9 | P/E on S&P Oper. EPS 2011**E** | 13.1 | Dividend Rate/Share | Nil | S&P Credit Rating | BBB- |
| $10K Invested 5 Yrs Ago | $19,965 | Common Shares Outstg. (M) | 705.6 | Institutional Ownership (%) | 89 | | |

## Price Performance

30-Week Mov. Avg. ··· 10-Week Mov. Avg. - - **GAAP Earnings vs. Previous Year**   Volume Above Avg. ▮▮▮ STARS
12-Mo. Target Price — Relative Strength — ▲ Up ▼ Down ▶ No Change   Below Avg. ▮▮▮ ★

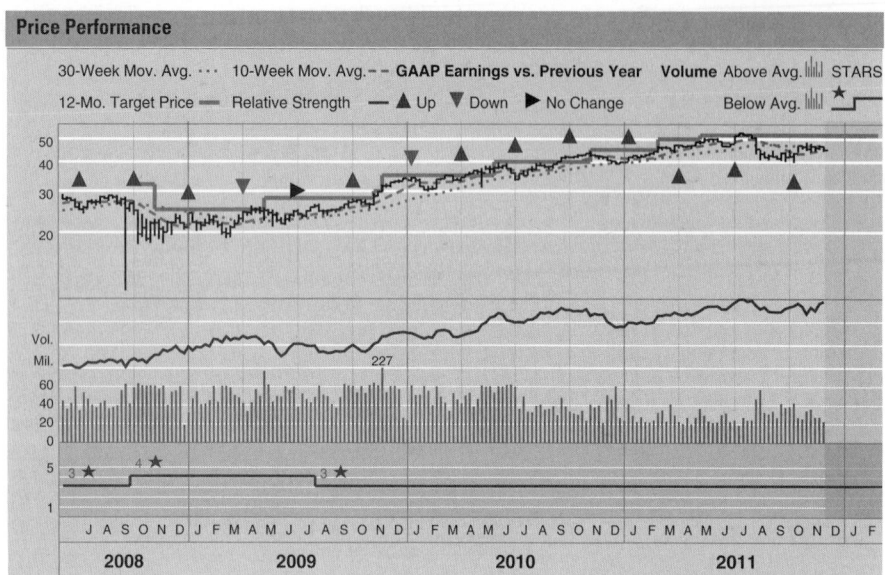

Options: ASE, CBOE, P, Ph

Analysis prepared by Equity Analyst **T. Amobi, CFA CPA** on Nov 08, 2011, when the stock traded at **$46.24**.

## Highlights

➤ We project approximately 4.4 million U.S. gross subscriber additions per year in 2011 and 2012, on gains in the direct sales and independent retail channels, noting a new bundling pact with some telco partners to provide fiber-based broadband offerings. Assuming relatively stable to modestly higher average monthly churn of about 1.6%, we see net additions of 500,000 to 600,000 per year, reaching more than 20.5 million customers by the end of 2012.

➤ With more robust subscriber growth at the DTV Latin America unit, higher ARPU on high take rates for advanced services, and a healthy advertising rebound, we see consolidated revenue up 12.9% and 8.5% in 2011 and 2012, respectively, to more than $27.2 billion and nearly $29.5 billion, with growing contributions from nascent PPV/VOD and commercial businesses.

➤ After significantly higher U.S. programming costs, versus some SAC savings, we see consolidated EBITDA up 10.4% and 8.1% in 2011 and 2012, respectively, to over $7.0 billion and $7.3 billion, and after D&A and interest expense, EPS of $3.45 and $4.26, with ramped-up share buybacks under a $6 billion plan.

## Investment Rationale/Risk

➤ While what we view as DTV's encouraging third quarter U.S. subscriber growth eased concerns with a sharp second quarter deceleration, we note sustained momentum at the Latin America division, with virtually all key operating metrics recently at or near all-time record levels. We see several newer features and product enhancements (e.g., multi-room viewing, broadband connectivity, home media center), and note DTV's early push into potential new business opportunities such as local/addressable ads, VOD/Cinema, and the enterprise market. We see sizable capacity for share buybacks.

➤ Risks to our recommendation and target price include stiffer competition on bundled offerings from pay TV rivals; a sharp macroeconomic slowdown; and currency exposure (including a major currency devaluation in Venezuela).

➤ Our 12-month target price is $52, or 6.4X our 2012 EV/EBITDA (nearly $2,300 per subscriber) estimate, which we view as justifiably higher than peer DISH Network (DISH 24, Buy) given the rapidly growing Latin America business, as well as about $1.7 billion of foreign NOLs.

## Qualitative Risk Assessment

| LOW | MEDIUM | HIGH |
| --- | --- | --- |

Our risk assessment reflects potentially sustainable pay TV market share gains (both for the U.S. and Latin America operations), combined with potential competitive advantages from ample financial flexibility, offset by relatively limited product offerings against competitively bundled services (video, broadband and voice) from cable providers and the telcos.

## Quantitative Evaluations

**S&P Quality Ranking**   B-

| D | C | **B-** | B | B+ | A- | A | A+ |
| --- | --- | --- | --- | --- | --- | --- | --- |

**Relative Strength Rank**   STRONG

73

LOWEST = 1   HIGHEST = 99

## Revenue/Earnings Data

**Revenue (Million $)**

| | 1Q | 2Q | 3Q | 4Q | Year |
| --- | --- | --- | --- | --- | --- |
| 2011 | 6,319 | 6,600 | -- | -- | -- |
| 2010 | 5,608 | 5,848 | 6,025 | 6,621 | 24,102 |
| 2009 | 4,901 | 5,218 | 5,465 | 5,981 | 21,565 |
| 2008 | 4,591 | 4,807 | 4,981 | 5,314 | 19,693 |
| 2007 | 3,908 | 4,135 | 4,327 | 4,876 | 17,246 |
| 2006 | 3,386 | 3,520 | 3,667 | 4,183 | 14,756 |

**Earnings Per Share ($)**

| | | | | | |
| --- | --- | --- | --- | --- | --- |
| 2011 | 0.85 | 0.91 | 0.70 | E0.99 | E3.45 |
| 2010 | 0.59 | 0.42 | 0.55 | 0.74 | 2.30 |
| 2009 | 0.20 | 0.40 | 0.38 | -0.03 | 0.95 |
| 2008 | 0.32 | 0.40 | 0.33 | 0.31 | 1.36 |
| 2007 | 0.27 | 0.36 | 0.27 | 0.30 | 1.19 |
| 2006 | 0.17 | 0.36 | 0.30 | 0.29 | 1.12 |

Fiscal year ended Dec. 31. Next earnings report expected: Late February. EPS Estimates based on S&P Operating Earnings; historical GAAP earnings are as reported.

## Dividend Data

No cash dividends have been paid since 1997.

# DIRECTV

STANDARD
&POOR'S

## Business Summary November 08, 2011

CORPORATE OVERVIEW. The DIRECTV Group (formerly Hughes Electronics) is a leading provider of direct broadcast satellite (DBS) television service, providing hundreds of digital video and audio channels to nearly 18.9 million monthly subscribers in the U.S., and a selection of local and international programming to almost 8.2 million subscribers in Latin America -- mostly through Sky Brazil (74% equity stake), Sky Mexico (41%) and PanAmericana (100%), including Venezuela, Puerto Rico and Argentina. DTV distributes its services mainly through direct sales and retail channels, and through co-branding partnerships with three of the four RBOCs.

In November 2009, DTV completed its merger with Liberty Entertainment (LEI), and named Michael White, retiring CEO of PepsiCo International, as its CEO effective January 1, 2010.

CORPORATE STRATEGY. DTV offers over 160 national HD channels, and local HD covering nearly 90% of U.S. TV homes. DTV also aims for differentiation on plans to launch new features such as whole-home functionality and broadband connectivity (for VOD, TV and multi-media applications), as well as a search functionality, a movie service, and three 3D TV channels. DTV also offers NFL Sunday Ticket sports programming (under a contract through the

2014 season) -- for which it recently launched a mobile offering. The company recently outlined a plan to capture about $750 million incremental revenue opportunities through the launch of VOD/Cinema and addressable advertising products, and increased targeting of the commercial segments. Under its "Connected Home" initiative, DTV plans to foster broadband connectivity to 40% of its subscriber base by 2013.

In July 2008, DTV acquired 180 Connect Inc., a major installation service provider, which it estimates fulfills 15%-20% of its work orders. In June 2007, DTV and DISH Network unveiled distribution pacts to offer WiMax-based wireless high-speed broadband service from Clearwire, which in turn will offer their DBS video services, with both DBS companies offering data, video and voice services in CLWR's markets starting in 2007. Earlier, in 2004, DTV divested assets such as Hughes Networks Systems and PanAmSat, and DTV Latin America emerged from a bankruptcy reorganization.

## Company Financials Fiscal Year Ended Dec. 31

| Per Share Data ($) | 2010 | 2009 | 2008 | 2007 | 2006 | 2005 | 2004 | 2003 | 2002 | 2001 |
|---|---|---|---|---|---|---|---|---|---|---|
| Tangible Book Value | NM | NM | NM | 0.92 | 1.10 | 2.17 | 1.61 | 4.36 | 2.76 | NM |
| Cash Flow | 5.41 | 3.61 | 3.44 | 2.59 | 1.93 | 0.83 | -0.16 | 0.27 | 0.88 | 0.50 |
| Earnings | 2.48 | 0.95 | 1.36 | 1.19 | 1.12 | 0.22 | -0.77 | -0.27 | -0.21 | -0.55 |
| S&P Core Earnings | 2.45 | 0.98 | 1.35 | 1.18 | 1.05 | 0.20 | -0.96 | -0.32 | -0.78 | -0.86 |
| Dividends | Nil | Nil | Nil | Nil | Nil | Nil | Nil | Nil | Nil | Nil |
| Payout Ratio | Nil | Nil | Nil | Nil | Nil | Nil | Nil | Nil | Nil | Nil |
| Prices:High | 44.61 | 34.25 | 29.10 | 27.73 | 25.57 | 17.01 | 18.81 | 16.91 | 17.55 | 28.00 |
| Prices:Low | 29.83 | 18.81 | 19.40 | 20.73 | 13.28 | 13.17 | 14.70 | 9.40 | 8.00 | 11.50 |
| P/E Ratio:High | 18 | 36 | 21 | 23 | 23 | 77 | NM | NM | NM | NM |
| P/E Ratio:Low | 12 | 20 | 14 | 17 | 12 | 60 | NM | NM | NM | NM |

| Income Statement Analysis (Million $) | | | | | | | | | | |
|---|---|---|---|---|---|---|---|---|---|---|
| Revenue | NA | NA | 19,693 | 17,246 | 14,756 | 13,165 | 11,360 | 9,372 | 8,935 | 8,262 |
| Operating Income | NA | NA | 5,029 | 4,145 | 3,274 | 1,441 | -1,281 | 617 | 668 | 390 |
| Depreciation | NA | NA | 2,320 | 1,684 | 1,034 | 853 | 838 | 755 | 1,067 | 1,148 |
| Interest Expense | 557 | 423 | 360 | 286 | 246 | 238 | 132 | 156 | 336 | 196 |
| Pretax Income | 3,514 | 1,834 | 2,471 | 2,388 | 542 | 480 | -1,734 | -478 | -140 | -990 |
| Effective Tax Rate | NA | 45.1% | 35.0% | 39.5% | NM | 36.1% | NM | NM | NM | NM |
| Net Income | 2,312 | 942 | 1,515 | 1,434 | 1,420 | 305 | -1,056 | -375 | -213 | -614 |
| S&P Core Earnings | 2,158 | 976 | 1,498 | 1,410 | 1,336 | 279 | -1,312 | -439 | -862 | -923 |

| Balance Sheet & Other Financial Data (Million $) | | | | | | | | | | |
|---|---|---|---|---|---|---|---|---|---|---|
| Cash | 1,502 | 2,605 | 2,005 | 1,098 | 2,499 | 3,701 | 2,830 | 1,720 | 1,129 | 700 |
| Current Assets | NA | NA | 4,044 | 3,146 | 4,556 | 6,096 | 4,771 | 10,356 | 3,656 | 3,341 |
| Total Assets | 17,909 | 18,260 | 16,539 | 15,063 | 15,141 | 15,630 | 14,324 | 18,978 | 17,885 | 19,210 |
| Current Liabilities | NA | NA | 3,585 | 3,434 | 3,323 | 2,828 | 2,695 | 5,840 | 3,203 | 4,407 |
| Long Term Debt | 10,472 | 6,500 | 6,267 | 3,347 | 3,395 | 3,405 | 2,410 | 2,435 | 2,390 | 989 |
| Common Equity | -194 | 2,911 | 4,853 | 6,302 | 6,681 | 7,940 | 7,507 | 9,631 | 9,063 | 9,574 |
| Total Capital | NA | NA | 11,205 | 10,227 | 10,138 | 11,395 | 9,965 | 12,305 | 12,590 | 13,339 |
| Capital Expenditures | NA | NA | 2,229 | 2,692 | 1,754 | 889 | 1,023 | 444 | 566 | 799 |
| Cash Flow | 4,794 | 3,582 | 3,835 | 3,118 | 2,455 | 1,158 | -218 | 380 | 808 | 438 |
| Current Ratio | 1.0 | 0.9 | 1.1 | 0.9 | 1.4 | 2.2 | 1.8 | 1.8 | 1.1 | 0.8 |
| % Long Term Debt of Capitalization | 99.4 | 59.5 | 55.9 | 32.7 | 33.5 | 29.9 | 24.2 | 19.8 | 19.0 | 7.4 |
| % Net Income of Revenue | NA | NA | 7.7 | 8.3 | 9.6 | 2.3 | NM | NM | NM | NM |
| % Return on Assets | 12.8 | 5.4 | 9.6 | 9.5 | 9.2 | 2.0 | NM | NM | NM | NM |
| % Return on Equity | NM | 24.3 | 27.2 | 22.1 | 19.4 | 3.9 | NM | NM | NM | NM |

Data as orig reptd.; bef. results of disc opers/spec. items. Per share data adj. for stk. divs.; EPS diluted. E-Estimated. NA-Not Available. NM-Not Meaningful. NR-Not Ranked. UR-Under Review.

**Office:** 2230 East Imperial Highway, El Segundo, CA 90245.
**Telephone:** 310-535-5000.
**Website:** http://www.directv.com
**Chrmn, Pres & CEO:** M. White

**COO:** M.W. Palkovic
**EVP & CTO:** R.C. Pontual
**SVP, Chief Acctg Officer & Cntlr:** J.F. Murphy
**CFO:** P.T. Doyle

**Investor Contact:** J. Rubin (212-462-5200)
**Board Members:** N. R. Austrian, R. F. Boyd, Jr., S. A. DiPiazza, Jr., D. B. Dillon, D. R. Doll, C. R. Lee, P. A. Lund, N. S. Newcomb, L. M. Norrington, M. White

**Founded:** 1977
**Domicile:** Delaware
**Employees:** 25,100

The McGraw-Hill Companies

# Discover Financial Services Inc

**STANDARD &POOR'S**

| S&P Recommendation **BUY** ★★★★☆ | Price<br>$22.96 (as of Nov 25, 2011) | 12-Mo. Target Price<br>$32.00 | Investment Style<br>Large-Cap Growth |
|---|---|---|---|

**GICS Sector** Financials
**Sub-Industry** Consumer Finance

**Summary** This leading U.S. credit card issuer and payment services company offers credit and prepaid cards and provides payment processing services to merchants and financial institutions.

## Key Stock Statistics (Source S&P, Vickers, company reports)

| | | | | | | | |
|---|---|---|---|---|---|---|---|
| 52-Wk Range | $27.92– 17.84 | S&P Oper. EPS 2011**E** | 3.95 | Market Capitalization(B) | $12.620 | Beta | 1.54 |
| Trailing 12-Month EPS | $3.75 | S&P Oper. EPS 2012**E** | 3.58 | Yield (%) | 1.05 | S&P 3-Yr. Proj. EPS CAGR(%) | 40 |
| Trailing 12-Month P/E | 6.1 | P/E on S&P Oper. EPS 2011**E** | 5.8 | Dividend Rate/Share | $0.24 | S&P Credit Rating | BBB- |
| $10K Invested 5 Yrs Ago | NA | Common Shares Outstg. (M) | 549.6 | Institutional Ownership (%) | 89 | | |

## Price Performance

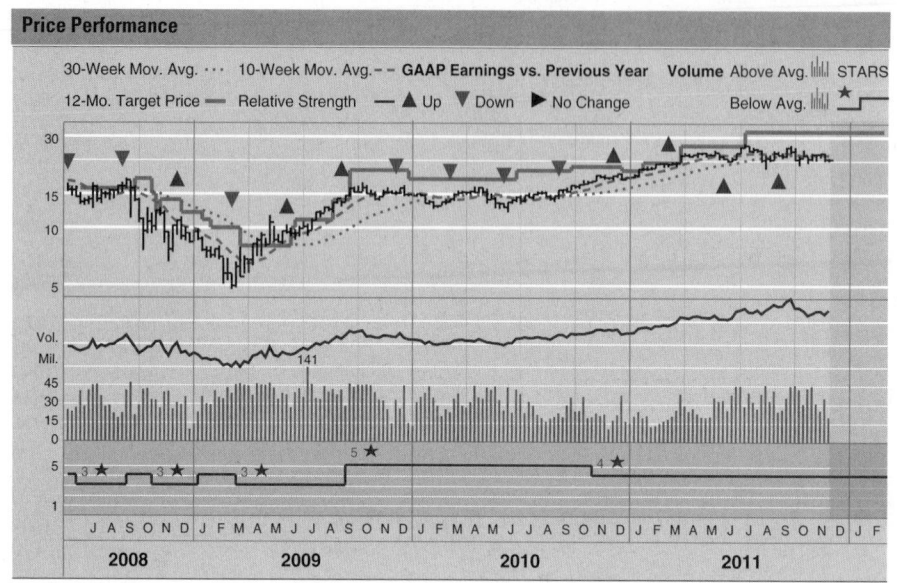

30-Week Mov. Avg. · · · 10-Week Mov. Avg. - - **GAAP Earnings vs. Previous Year** Volume Above Avg. STARS
12-Mo. Target Price — Relative Strength — ▲ Up ▼ Down ► No Change Below Avg.

Options: ASE, CBOE, P

Analysis prepared by Equity Analyst **Robert McMillan** on Sep 22, 2011, when the stock traded at **$25.27**.

## Highlights

➤ We believe that the outlook for DFS has improved significantly since the financial crisis, driven by a rebound in consumer spending and still historically low interest rates. After a drop of 1% in FY 10 (Nov.), we look for revenues to climb 4.3% in FY 11 and 4.6% in FY 12, helped by a rebound in receivables as consumer spending remains resilient despite households continuing to trim their credit card debt. We also see lower funding costs, especially given the Federal Reserve's efforts to stimulate economic growth.

➤ Better credit performance should also benefit DFS. In the FY 11 third quarter, the net principal chargeoff rate for credit cards fell to 3.85%, from 7.73% in the year-ago period. We believe DFS's loss provisions will decline further over the next 12-18 months. We note that DFS's managed chargeoff rate in FY 10 was 7.6%, below the historical industry average of 9.8%. We see expenses on an absolute dollar basis increasing in FY 11 and FY 12, reflecting our expectation for higher employee compensation costs.

➤ We see EPS of $3.95 in FY 11 and $3.58 in FY 12.

## Investment Rationale/Risk

➤ We see DFS benefiting from its strategy of issuing credit cards on its proprietary network primarily in the U.S., and we see its managed chargeoffs continuing to trend below peers, reflecting what we see as its conservative customer base and solid credit risk management. We also see the expanding international presence of Diners Club International contributing to DFS's overall growth.

➤ Risks to our recommendation and target price include a slowdown in the economic environment, a significant decline in credit quality, and higher-than-expected loan loss provisions.

➤ DFS shares recently traded at 6.7X trailing 12-month EPS. Our 12-month target price of $32 is 9.0X our forward 12-month EPS estimate of $3.55, which represents a discount to DFS's historical levels. Although the level of economic uncertainty will likely result in continued volatility in the shares, we believe that the valuation will improve as DFS demonstrates that its operations continue to improve. We consider the continuing declines in charge-offs as well as the resiliency of consumer spending (on DFS's cards) as positive factors in our valuation.

## Qualitative Risk Assessment

| LOW | MEDIUM | HIGH |
|---|---|---|

Our risk assessment reflects what we see as solid business fundamentals and an expanding merchant base, tempered somewhat by DFS's exposure to consumer spending habits and the U.S. economy.

## Quantitative Evaluations

**S&P Quality Ranking** NR

| D | C | B- | B | B+ | A- | A | A+ |
|---|---|---|---|---|---|---|---|

**Relative Strength Rank** MODERATE

58

LOWEST = 1 HIGHEST = 99

## Revenue/Earnings Data

**Revenue (Million $)**

| | 1Q | 2Q | 3Q | 4Q | Year |
|---|---|---|---|---|---|
| 2011 | 2,116 | 2,117 | 2,151 | -- | -- |
| 2010 | 2,105 | 2,065 | 2,100 | 1,971 | 8,241 |
| 2009 | 2,006 | 1,939 | 2,149 | 1,892 | 7,986 |
| 2008 | 1,638 | 1,457 | 1,557 | 2,305 | 6,957 |
| 2007 | 1,506 | 1,575 | 1,601 | 1,752 | 6,434 |
| 2006 | -- | -- | -- | -- | 6,211 |

**Earnings Per Share ($)**

| | | | | | |
|---|---|---|---|---|---|
| 2011 | 0.84 | 1.09 | 1.18 | E0.84 | E3.95 |
| 2010 | -0.22 | 0.33 | 0.47 | 0.64 | 1.22 |
| 2009 | 0.25 | 0.43 | 1.07 | 0.60 | 2.39 |
| 2008 | 0.50 | 0.42 | 0.37 | 0.92 | 2.20 |
| 2007 | 0.55 | 0.44 | 0.42 | -0.18 | 1.23 |
| 2006 | -- | 0.72 | 0.51 | 0.39 | 1.89 |

Fiscal year ended Nov. 30. Next earnings report expected: NA. EPS Estimates based on S&P Operating Earnings; historical GAAP earnings are as reported.

## Dividend Data (Dates: mm/dd Payment Date: mm/dd/yy)

| Amount ($) | Date Decl. | Ex-Div. Date | Stk. of Record | Payment Date |
|---|---|---|---|---|
| 0.020 | 12/16 | 12/27 | 12/29 | 01/20/11 |
| 0.060 | 03/22 | 04/05 | 04/07 | 04/21/11 |
| 0.060 | 06/15 | 07/05 | 07/07 | 07/21/11 |
| 0.060 | 09/14 | 10/04 | 10/06 | 10/20/11 |

Dividends have been paid since 2007. Source: Company reports.

**The McGraw·Hill** Companies

# Discover Financial Services Inc

**STANDARD &POOR'S**

## Business Summary September 22, 2011

CORPORATE OVERVIEW. Discover Financial Services (DFS), formerly a business segment of Morgan Stanley, is a credit card issuer and electronic payment services company. DFS offers credit and prepaid cards and other financial products and services to qualified customers in the United States, and provides payment processing and related services to merchants and financial institutions across the globe. DFS manages its operations through two business segments: Direct Banking and Payments Services. The Direct Banking segment is the major contributor to the company, in terms of income before income taxes. The Payments Services segment is modestly profitable but continues to comprise a growing portion of DFS's income stream.

The Direct Banking segment offers Discover Card-branded credit cards issued to more than 50 million individuals and small businesses over the Discover Network, which is the company's proprietary credit card network in the United States. The segment also includes DFS's other consumer products and services businesses, including prepaid and other consumer lending and deposit products offered primarily through the company's Discover Bank subsidiary. The company entered the debit card business in 2006, allowing banks to offer Discover-branded debit cards.

In addition to credit cards, DFS offers installment loan products, including personal loans and student loans. It offers installment loan products to existing

cardmembers as well as to new customers. DFS accepts applications for installment loans online, by phone or by mail.

DFS offers money market accounts and certificates of deposit directly to its cardmembers using proprietary models to execute targeted statement insert, e-mail, and direct mail campaigns. Aside from direct-to-consumer deposits, DFS obtains deposits through third-party securities brokers that offer DFS's certificates of deposit to their customers. DFS uses deposits to finance its credit card and installment loan businesses. In the long-term, it expects to increase its direct-to-consumer deposit business.

The Payment Services segment includes the Discover network, PULSE and the Diners Club International business. PULSE, an automated teller machine (ATM), debit and electronic funds transfer network, serves more than 4,400 financial institutions and includes more than 289,000 ATMs, as well as point-of-sale terminals nationwide. The Diners Club International network is in over 185 countries. Diners Club International's 79 licensees issues credit cards and provide card acceptance services.

## Company Financials Fiscal Year Ended Nov. 30

| Per Share Data ($) | 2010 | 2009 | 2008 | 2007 | 2006 | 2005 | 2004 | 2003 | 2002 | 2001 |
|---|---|---|---|---|---|---|---|---|---|---|
| Tangible Book Value | 10.94 | 12.48 | 11.37 | 10.98 | NA | NA | NA | NA | NA | NA |
| Earnings | 1.22 | 2.39 | 2.20 | 1.23 | 1.89 | NA | NA | NA | NA | NA |
| S&P Core Earnings | 1.19 | 0.10 | 1.00 | 1.23 | 2.26 | 1.21 | NA | NA | NA | NA |
| Dividends | 0.08 | 0.12 | 0.24 | 0.06 | Nil | NA | NA | NA | NA | NA |
| Payout Ratio | 7% | 5% | 11% | 5% | NA | NA | NA | NA | NA | NA |
| Prices:High | 19.45 | 17.36 | 19.87 | 32.17 | NA | NA | NA | NA | NA | NA |
| Prices:Low | 12.11 | 4.73 | 6.59 | 14.81 | NA | NA | NA | NA | NA | NA |
| P/E Ratio:High | 16 | 7 | 9 | 26 | NA | NA | NA | NA | NA | NA |
| P/E Ratio:Low | 10 | 2 | 3 | 12 | NA | NA | NA | NA | NA | NA |

| Income Statement Analysis (Million $) | | | | | | | | | | |
|---|---|---|---|---|---|---|---|---|---|---|
| Net Interest Income | NA | 1,894 | 1,405 | 1,506 | 1,459 | NA | NA | NA | NA | NA |
| Tax Equivalent Adjustment | NA | NA | NA | NA | NA | NA | NA | NA | NA | NA |
| Non Interest Income | NA | 4,841 | 4,264 | 3,546 | 3,539 | NA | NA | NA | NA | NA |
| Loan Loss Provision | NA | 2,362 | 1,596 | 950 | 756 | NA | NA | NA | NA | NA |
| % Expense/Operating Revenue | NA | 33.4% | NA | 49.0% | 55.5% | NA | NA | NA | NA | NA |
| Pretax Income | 1,269 | 2,150 | 1,658 | 945 | 1,467 | 924 | 1,219 | NA | NA | NA |
| Effective Tax Rate | NA | 39.8% | 35.9% | 37.7% | 31.8% | 37.5% | 36.3% | NA | NA | NA |
| Net Income | 765 | 1,294 | 1,063 | 589 | 1,001 | 578 | 776 | NA | NA | NA |
| % Net Interest Margin | 7.18 | 4.74 | 4.20 | 4.76 | NA | 5.88 | 5.88 | NA | NA | NA |
| S&P Core Earnings | 649 | 47.2 | 485 | 587 | 1,078 | 578 | NA | NA | NA | NA |

| Balance Sheet & Other Financial Data (Million $) | | | | | | | | | | |
|---|---|---|---|---|---|---|---|---|---|---|
| Money Market Assets | NA | 1,350 | 9,378 | 8,416 | Nil | NA | NA | NA | NA | NA |
| Investment Securities | NA | 5,035 | 1,228 | 526 | 86.0 | NA | NA | NA | NA | NA |
| Commercial Loans | NA | 404 | 466 | 234 | 111 | NA | NA | NA | NA | NA |
| Other Loans | NA | 19,826 | 24,751 | 23,720 | 21,707 | NA | NA | NA | NA | NA |
| Total Assets | 60,785 | 46,021 | 39,892 | 37,376 | 32,403 | 26,944 | NA | NA | NA | NA |
| Demand Deposits | 104 | 64.5 | 78.4 | 82.0 | 86.0 | 98.8 | NA | NA | NA | NA |
| Time Deposits | NA | 32,029 | 28,452 | 24,644 | 21,042 | NA | NA | NA | NA | NA |
| Long Term Debt | NA | 1,804 | 1,330 | 2,134 | 1,706 | NA | NA | NA | NA | NA |
| Common Equity | 6,457 | 7,277 | 5,916 | 5,599 | 5,425 | 4,600 | NA | NA | NA | NA |
| % Return on Assets | NA | 3.0 | 2.8 | 1.8 | NM | NA | NA | NA | NA | NA |
| % Return on Equity | NA | 19.6 | 18.5 | 10.4 | NM | NA | NA | NA | NA | NA |
| % Loan Loss Reserve | NA | 8.0 | NA | 3.8 | 3.5 | NA | NA | NA | NA | NA |
| % Loans/Deposits | NA | 80.6 | NA | 96.8 | NM | NA | NA | NA | NA | NA |
| % Equity to Assets | NA | 15.4 | 14.9 | 17.1 | NM | NA | NA | NA | NA | NA |

Data as orig reptd.; bef. results of disc opers/spec. items. Per share data adj. for stk. divs.; EPS diluted. 2006 data pro forma; bal. sheet as of Feb. 28 '07. E-Estimated. NA-Not Available. NM-Not Meaningful. NR-Not Ranked. UR-Under Review.

**Office:** 2500 Lake Cook Road, Riverwoods, IL 60015.
**Telephone:** 224-405-0900.
**Website:** http://www.discover.com
**Chrmn & CEO:** D.W. Nelms

**Pres & COO:** R. Hochschild
**SVP & CIO:** G. Schneider
**CFO & Chief Acctg Officer:** R.M. Graf
**Secy & General Counsel:** K.M. Corley

**Board Members:** J. S. Aronin, M. K. Bush, G. C. Case, R. M. Devlin, C. A. Glassman, R. H. Lenny, T. G. Maheras, M. H. Moskow, D. W. Nelms, E. F. Smith, L. A. Weinbach
**Founded:** 1960
**Domicile:** Delaware
**Employees:** 10,300

*The McGraw-Hill Companies*

# Discovery Communications Inc

**STANDARD &POOR'S**

| S&P Recommendation **STRONG BUY** ★★★★★ | Price $39.22 (as of Nov 25, 2011) | 12-Mo. Target Price $50.00 | Investment Style Large-Cap Growth |
|---|---|---|---|

**GICS Sector** Consumer Discretionary
**Sub-Industry** Broadcasting & Cable TV

**Summary** This pure-play cable networks company, with brands such as Discovery, Animal Planet, and TLC, is a leading global provider of non-fiction entertainment through 115 networks in 180 countries broadcasting in 35 languages.

## Key Stock Statistics (Source S&P, Vickers, company reports)

| | | | | | | | |
|---|---|---|---|---|---|---|---|
| 52-Wk Range | $45.81– 34.75 | S&P Oper. EPS 2011E | 2.39 | Market Capitalization(B) | $5.535 | Beta | 1.22 |
| Trailing 12-Month EPS | $2.42 | S&P Oper. EPS 2012E | 3.00 | Yield (%) | Nil | S&P 3-Yr. Proj. EPS CAGR(%) | 23 |
| Trailing 12-Month P/E | 16.2 | P/E on S&P Oper. EPS 2011E | 16.4 | Dividend Rate/Share | Nil | S&P Credit Rating | NA |
| $10K Invested 5 Yrs Ago | NA | Common Shares Outstg. (M) | 264.3 | Institutional Ownership (%) | NM | | |

## Price Performance

30-Week Mov. Avg. · · · · 10-Week Mov. Avg. - - - **GAAP Earnings vs. Previous Year** Volume Above Avg. ▏▎▍ STARS
12-Mo. Target Price —— Relative Strength —— ▲ Up ▼ Down ► No Change Below Avg. ▏▎▍ ★

Options: CBOE, Ph

Analysis prepared by Equity Analyst **T. Amobi, CFA CPA** on Nov 22, 2011, when the stock traded at **$40.52**.

## Highlights

➤ We expect total revenues (pro forma for a deconsolidated Discovery Health) to grow 15.5% in 2011 to $4.27 billion, and 8.8% in 2012 to $4.65 billion. We see stronger double-digit growth in advertising and affiliate revenues for the international networks, vs. high single- to low double-digit growth in U.S. networks' comparable dual revenue streams. In both years, we also anticipate some meaningful improvement for a relatively small education segment.

➤ The international networks seem poised for continued robust margin expansion, thanks to increased operating leverage and economies of scale. U.S. networks margins should also benefit significantly from a new licensing pact with Netflix (NFLX 72, Hold) starting in the 2011 second half, as well as SG&A cost control, partly constrained by increased content amortization (on programming investments).

➤ We project total adjusted EBITDA growth (pro forma) of 16.4% in 2011 to $1.94 billion, and 13.5% in 2012 to $2.21 billion, and after D&A, interest expense and taxes, EPS of $2.39 and $3.00, respectively, with continued share buybacks under a $2 billion plan.

## Investment Rationale/Risk

➤ After relatively strong results for the first nine months of 2011, we see DISCA well positioned to further exploit a ratings resurgence across its core and emerging networks, with a vast global affiliate footprint reflecting an aggressive multi-year pursuit of international expansion. We think the Netflix pact underscores a potentially significant upside to digital revenues as the company leverages its vast content library in the years ahead. We note DISCA's strong management, a relatively balanced asset mix, and strong balance sheet that provides very ample financial flexibility.

➤ Risks to our recommendation and target price include a weaker-than-expected macroeconomic rebound, sharp ratings declines, lingering uncertainties with OWN and The Hub rebranding, potential governance issues on multiple classes of shares, and currency exposure.

➤ Projecting a FCF ramp-up of more than $2 billion in the next two years, our 12-month target price is $50, on a blend of 10X our 2012 EV/EBITDA view and a 0.8X P/E-to-growth ratio, which we find attractive vs. peers and the S&P 500 given a unique position in non-fiction programming.

## Qualitative Risk Assessment

| LOW | **MEDIUM** | HIGH |
|---|---|---|

Our risk assessment reflects the company's leading position as a provider of niche programming with global appeal, combined with business and geographic diversification and a strong balance sheet, offset by some concerns with the corporate governance framework, such as the company's multi-class stock structure.

## Quantitative Evaluations

**S&P Quality Ranking** NR

| D | C | B- | B | B+ | A- | A | A+ |
|---|---|---|---|---|---|---|---|

**Relative Strength Rank** MODERATE

57

LOWEST = 1                    HIGHEST = 99

## Revenue/Earnings Data

**Revenue (Million $)**

| | 1Q | 2Q | 3Q | 4Q | Year |
|---|---|---|---|---|---|
| 2011 | 951.0 | 1,067 | 1,095 | -- | -- |
| 2010 | 879.0 | 963.0 | 926.0 | 1,015 | 3,773 |
| 2009 | 817.0 | 881.0 | 854.0 | 964.0 | 3,516 |
| 2008 | 189.3 | 194.5 | 845.0 | 904.0 | 3,443 |
| 2007 | 173.9 | 177.2 | 177.9 | 178.2 | 707.2 |
| 2006 | 153.6 | 165.8 | 169.9 | 198.9 | 688.1 |

**Earnings Per Share ($)**

| | | | | | |
|---|---|---|---|---|---|
| 2011 | 0.74 | 0.62 | 0.59 | E0.69 | E2.39 |
| 2010 | 0.39 | 0.25 | 0.37 | 0.48 | 1.49 |
| 2009 | 0.28 | 0.43 | 0.22 | 0.36 | 1.30 |
| 2008 | 0.24 | 0.32 | 0.31 | 0.25 | 0.85 |
| 2007 | 0.14 | 0.52 | 0.06 | -1.22 | -0.48 |
| 2006 | 0.08 | 0.10 | -0.54 | 0.04 | -0.32 |

Fiscal year ended Dec. 31. Next earnings report expected: Mid February. EPS Estimates based on S&P Operating Earnings; historical GAAP earnings are as reported.

## Dividend Data

No cash dividends have been paid.

---

**Please read the Required Disclosures and Analyst Certification on the last page of this report.**

**The McGraw·Hill Companies**

# Discovery Communications Inc

**STANDARD &POOR'S**

## Business Summary November 22, 2011

CORPORATE OVERVIEW. Discovery Communications, Inc. (DISCA) is a leading global media and entertainment company (and a pure-play cable networks operator) reaching 368 million households and over 1.5 billion total subscribers, through 115 networks in 173 countries broadcasting in 35 languages. DISCA primarily provides nonfiction programming through networks such as Discovery Channel, TLC, Animal Planet, Science Channel, Planet Green, Investigation Discovery and HD Theater. DISCA also provides consumer and educational products and services, and owns a portfolio of digital media services (e.g., HowStuffWorks.com).

In 2010, revenues and adjusted EBITDA contributions from the company's three divisions were: U.S. Networks, 63% and 71%, respectively; International Networks, 33% and 28%; and Commerce, Education and Other, 4% and 1%. Three networks (Discovery Channel, TLC and Animal Planet) account for more than 75% of U.S. revenues. Total revenues in 2010 by categories were: distribution fees (50%); advertising (45%); and other (5%).

CORPORATE STRATEGY. To modernize its underdeveloped networks, DISCA rebranded Discovery Home Channel as Planet Green (April 2007) and Discovery Times Channel as ID: Investigation Discovery (November 2007). Recent re-

brandings include OWN: The Oprah Winfrey Network (a 50/50 JV launched January 2011 -- formerly Discovery Health Channel); The Hub (a 50/50 JV with Hasbro launched October 2010 -- formerly Discovery Kids); and Velocity (to be launched September 2011 -- formerly HD Theater). Domestically, DISCA focuses on improving the visibility and image of some of its less profitable networks through 50/50 joint ventures with known brands such as Hasbro Inc. and Oprah Winfrey

In January 2010, as part of a three-member consortium that also includes Sony Corp. and IMAX Corp., the company announced plans for a joint venture to launch a linear 3D television channel in 2011. Meanwhile, the company also wants to get onto new distribution platforms such as brand-aligned Web properties, mobile devices and broadband channels. Internationally, growth is mostly focused on new subscription contracts and boosting the company's advertising business (which lacks the strength it has in the U.S.).

## Company Financials Fiscal Year Ended Dec. 31

| Per Share Data ($) | 2010 | 2009 | 2008 | 2007 | 2006 | 2005 | 2004 | 2003 | 2002 | 2001 |
|---|---|---|---|---|---|---|---|---|---|---|
| Tangible Book Value | NM | NM | NM | NA | 17.66 | 17.42 | NM | NM | NM | NA |
| Cash Flow | 1.84 | 1.68 | 3.35 | NA | 0.16 | 0.78 | 1.02 | 0.12 | -0.30 | NA |
| Earnings | 1.49 | 1.30 | 0.85 | -0.48 | -0.32 | 0.24 | 0.48 | -0.38 | -0.78 | NA |
| S&P Core Earnings | 1.49 | 0.89 | 0.85 | 0.24 | 0.34 | 0.18 | 0.44 | -0.40 | NA | NA |
| Dividends | Nil | Nil | Nil | NA | Nil | Nil | Nil | Nil | Nil | NA |
| Payout Ratio | Nil | Nil | Nil | NA | Nil | Nil | Nil | Nil | Nil | NA |
| Prices:High | 45.42 | 32.69 | 53.66 | NA | 33.92 | 32.60 | NA | NA | NA | NA |
| Prices:Low | 27.69 | 12.46 | 10.02 | NA | 25.62 | 27.02 | NA | NA | NA | NA |
| P/E Ratio:High | 31 | 25 | 63 | NA | NM | NM | NA | NA | NA | NA |
| P/E Ratio:Low | 19 | 10 | 12 | NA | NM | NM | NA | NA | NA | NA |

| Income Statement Analysis (Million $) | | | | | | | | | | |
|---|---|---|---|---|---|---|---|---|---|---|
| Revenue | 3,773 | 3,516 | 3,443 | 707 | 688 | 695 | 631 | 506 | 539 | NA |
| Operating Income | NA | NA | 1,965 | NA | 56.2 | 74.2 | 94.6 | 72.2 | 89.0 | NA |
| Depreciation | 132 | 155 | 804 | 67.7 | 67.9 | 76.4 | 77.6 | 70.5 | 67.3 | NA |
| Interest Expense | 203 | 250 | 258 | NA | Nil | Nil | Nil | 72.2 | 64.8 | NA |
| Pretax Income | 935 | 1,031 | 754 | -9.23 | -2.07 | 82.1 | 101 | -34.5 | -141 | NA |
| Effective Tax Rate | NA | 45.8% | 46.7% | NM | NM | 59.5% | 34.6% | NM | NM | NA |
| Net Income | 658 | 560 | 274 | -68.4 | -46.0 | 33.3 | 66.1 | -52.4 | -109 | NA |
| S&P Core Earnings | 637 | 378 | 274 | 34.1 | 46.1 | 24.2 | 62.2 | -54.4 | NA | NA |

| Balance Sheet & Other Financial Data (Million $) | | | | | | | | | | |
|---|---|---|---|---|---|---|---|---|---|---|
| Cash | 466 | 623 | 100 | 209 | 155 | 250 | 34.4 | 8.60 | NA | NA |
| Current Assets | 1,729 | 1,680 | 1,109 | 372 | 317 | 400 | 212 | 131 | NA | NA |
| Total Assets | 11,013 | 10,965 | 10,484 | 5,866 | 5,871 | 5,819 | 5,565 | 5,397 | NA | NA |
| Current Liabilities | 785 | 790 | 1,070 | 120 | 122 | 89.9 | 109 | 60.6 | NA | NA |
| Long Term Debt | 3,598 | 3,457 | 3,331 | NA | Nil | Nil | Nil | Nil | NA | NA |
| Common Equity | 6,236 | 6,206 | 5,534 | 4,494 | 4,549 | 4,575 | 4,347 | 4,260 | NA | NA |
| Total Capital | 9,870 | 9,763 | 9,325 | 4,494 | 5,724 | 5,707 | 5,431 | 5,313 | NA | NA |
| Capital Expenditures | 49.0 | 57.0 | 102 | 47.1 | 77.5 | 90.5 | 49.3 | 25.9 | 56.4 | NA |
| Cash Flow | 790 | 715 | 1,078 | -0.66 | 21.9 | 110 | 144 | 18.1 | -41.7 | NA |
| Current Ratio | 2.2 | 2.1 | 1.0 | 3.1 | 2.6 | 4.5 | 2.0 | 2.2 | NA | NA |
| % Long Term Debt of Capitalization | 36.5 | 35.6 | 36.4 | Nil | Nil | Nil | Nil | Nil | Nil | NA |
| % Net Income of Revenue | 17.4 | 15.9 | 8.0 | NM | NM | 4.8 | 10.5 | NM | NM | NA |
| % Return on Assets | 6.0 | 5.2 | 3.4 | NM | NM | 0.6 | 1.2 | NM | NM | NA |
| % Return on Equity | 10.6 | 9.5 | 5.5 | NM | NM | 0.7 | 1.5 | NM | NM | NA |

Data as orig reptd.; bef. results of disc opers/spec. items. Per share data adj. for stk. divs.; EPS diluted. E-Estimated. NA-Not Available. NM-Not Meaningful. NR-Not Ranked. UR-Under Review.

**Office:** One Discovery Place, Silver Spring, MD 20910.
**Telephone:** 240-662-2000.
**Website:** http://corporate.discovery.com
**Chrmn:** J.S. Hendricks

**Pres & CEO:** D. Zaslav
**COO & EVP:** P. Liguori
**EVP, CFO & Treas:** B.E. Singer
**EVP & Chief Acctg Officer:** T.R. Colan

**Board Members:** R. R. Beck, R. R. Bennett, P. A. Gould, J. S. Hendricks, L. Kramer, J. C. Malone, R. J. Miron, S. A. Miron, M. L. Robison, J. D. Wargo, D. Zaslav

**Founded:** 2005
**Domicile:** Delaware
**Employees:** 4,200

The **McGraw·Hill** Companies

# Walt Disney Co (The)

**STANDARD &POOR'S**

| S&P Recommendation | STRONG BUY ★★★★★ | Price $35.85 (as of Nov 30, 2011) | 12-Mo. Target Price $45.00 | Investment Style Large-Cap Growth |
|---|---|---|---|---|

**GICS Sector** Consumer Discretionary
**Sub-Industry** Movies & Entertainment

**Summary** This media and entertainment conglomerate has diversified global operations in theme parks, filmed entertainment, television broadcasting and merchandise licensing.

## Key Stock Statistics (Source S&P, Vickers, company reports)

| | | | | | | | |
|---|---|---|---|---|---|---|---|
| 52-Wk Range | $44.34– 28.19 | S&P Oper. EPS 2012E | 2.93 | Market Capitalization(B) | $64.405 | Beta | 1.18 |
| Trailing 12-Month EPS | $2.52 | S&P Oper. EPS 2013E | 3.40 | Yield (%) | 1.67 | S&P 3-Yr. Proj. EPS CAGR(%) | 15 |
| Trailing 12-Month P/E | 14.2 | P/E on S&P Oper. EPS 2012E | 12.2 | Dividend Rate/Share | $0.60 | S&P Credit Rating | A |
| $10K Invested 5 Yrs Ago | NA | Common Shares Outstg. (M) | 1,796.5 | Institutional Ownership (%) | 66 | | |

## Price Performance

30-Week Mov. Avg. · · · 10-Week Mov. Avg. - - GAAP Earnings vs. Previous Year  Volume Above Avg. STARS
12-Mo. Target Price — Relative Strength — ▲ Up ▼ Down ► No Change  Below Avg. ★

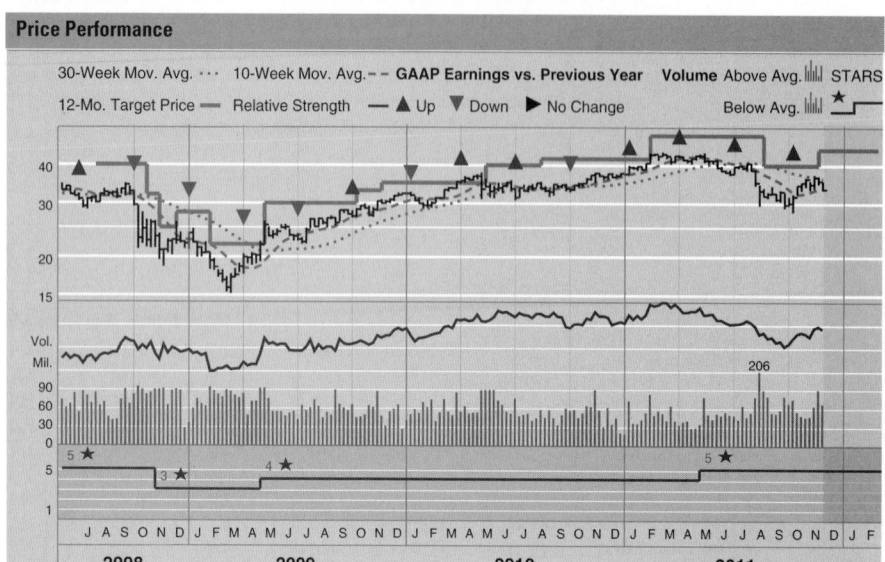

Options: ASE, CBOE, P, Ph

Analysis prepared by Equity Analyst **T. Amobi, CFA CPA** on Nov 15, 2011, when the stock traded at **$36.80**.

## Highlights

➤ We project about 6.5% annual consolidated revenue growth in FY 12 (Sep.) and FY 13, to about $43.6 billion and $46.4 billion in the respective years. This assumes broad-based gains from the cable and broadcast properties (ESPN, ABC, Disney Channel) and worldwide theme parks, as well as the film division (Disney/Pixar/Marvel) and the predominantly royalties-based consumer products businesses, with contributions from the relatively small interactive segment.

➤ Further margin expansion should reflect improved operating leverage on recent restructuring steps; increased higher-margin revenues from Marvel's licensing, TV retransmission and digital streaming deals; further cost savings at the theme parks; and reduced losses in the interactive segment. We project FY 12 and FY 13 adjusted EBIT growth of 11% and 12%, respectively, to nearly $9.8 billion and $10.9 billion.

➤ After interest and taxes, we forecast EPS of $2.93 and $3.40 for FY 12 and FY 13, respectively -- assuming consistent execution of share buybacks under a current authorization to repurchase up to 400 million shares (set ahead of the December 2009 Marvel acquisition).

## Investment Rationale/Risk

➤ After DIS's broad-based FY 11 fourth quarter gains that eased any concerns of a consumer spending slowdown at the theme parks and advertising businesses, we see other near-term catalysts for the shares. These include an expected ramp-up of broadcast TV retransmission revenues, as well as a consumer products business that seems poised for increased global exploitation of a growing franchise trove of film/TV-based characters. Separately, we believe DIS has ample financial flexibility for continued share buybacks, and some potential "tuck-in" acquisitions in the interactive space.

➤ Risks to our recommendation and target price include a double-dip recession or severe slowdown in consumer spending; potential disruption on heightened geopolitical anxieties; inherent volatility of film results; potentially dilutive acquisitions; and foreign currency exposure.

➤ Our 12-month target price is $45, blending relative valuation on FY 12E 9.0X EV/EBITDA and 1.0X P/E-to-growth with sum-of-the-parts methodology. At current levels, we view the shares as attractive (versus the larger-media peer group and the S&P 500), also noting a recent 1.1% dividend yield.

## Qualitative Risk Assessment

| LOW | MEDIUM | HIGH |
|---|---|---|

Our risk assessment reflects scale-related multi-platform benefits from the company's content stable of popular entertainment brands and franchises, offset by vulnerability of the company's core businesses to a macroeconomic slowdown.

## Quantitative Evaluations

**S&P Quality Ranking**  A

| D | C | B- | B | B+ | A- | A | A+ |
|---|---|---|---|---|---|---|---|

**Relative Strength Rank**  STRONG

82

LOWEST = 1    HIGHEST = 99

## Revenue/Earnings Data

**Revenue (Million $)**

| | 1Q | 2Q | 3Q | 4Q | Year |
|---|---|---|---|---|---|
| 2011 | 10,716 | 9,077 | 10,675 | 10,425 | 40,893 |
| 2010 | 9,739 | 8,580 | 10,002 | 9,742 | 38,063 |
| 2009 | 9,599 | 8,087 | 8,956 | 9,867 | 36,149 |
| 2008 | 10,452 | 8,710 | 9,236 | 9,445 | 37,843 |
| 2007 | 9,581 | 7,954 | 9,045 | 8,930 | 35,510 |
| 2006 | 8,854 | 8,027 | 8,620 | 8,784 | 34,285 |

**Earnings Per Share ($)**

| | | | | | |
|---|---|---|---|---|---|
| 2011 | 0.68 | 0.49 | 0.77 | 0.58 | 2.52 |
| 2010 | 0.44 | 0.48 | 0.67 | 0.43 | 2.03 |
| 2009 | 0.45 | 0.33 | 0.51 | 0.47 | 1.76 |
| 2008 | 0.63 | 0.58 | 0.66 | 0.40 | 2.28 |
| 2007 | 0.79 | 0.43 | 0.58 | 0.44 | 2.24 |
| 2006 | 0.37 | 0.37 | 0.53 | 0.36 | 1.64 |

Fiscal year ended Sep. 30. Next earnings report expected: Early February. EPS Estimates based on S&P Operating Earnings; historical GAAP earnings are as reported.

## Dividend Data (Dates: mm/dd Payment Date: mm/dd/yy)

| Amount ($) | Date Decl. | Ex-Div. Date | Stk. of Record | Payment Date |
|---|---|---|---|---|
| 0.400 | 12/01 | 12/09 | 12/13 | 01/18/11 |
| 0.600 | 11/30 | 12/14 | 12/16 | 01/18/12 |

Dividends have been paid since 1957. Source: Company reports.

---

**Please read the Required Disclosures and Analyst Certification on the last page of this report.**

The McGraw-Hill Companies

# Walt Disney Co (The)

## Business Summary November 15, 2011

**CORPORATE OVERVIEW.** The Walt Disney Co. is a leading media conglomerate with key operations in theme parks, television, filmed entertainment and merchandise licensing. Theme Parks and Resorts (28% of FY 11 (Sep.) revenues and 18% of EBIT) includes the company's best known assets: Disney World and Disneyland parks in Orlando, FL, and Anaheim, CA, respectively; the Disney Cruise Line; Euro Disney, Paris (39%-owned); and Hong Kong Disneyland (43%-owned). The company plans to open another park in mainland China (Shanghai) by 2016.

Media Networks (46% of revenues and 70% of EBIT) includes the ABC broadcast network; 10 TV stations; and cable networks ESPN (80%-owned), The Disney Channel and ABC Family. Studio entertainment (16% of revenues and 7% of EBIT) includes the film, television and home video businesses under the Walt Disney, Touchstone and Miramax brands. Consumer products (7% of revenues and 9% of EBIT) includes merchandise licensing, children's book publishing, video game development, as well as over 200 retail stores in North America, over 100 in Europe, and over 50 in Japan. Interactive (2% of revenues and -4% of EBIT) primarily includes the video games production businesses, web sites and online virtual worlds.

**CORPORATE STRATEGY.** As a content-oriented company, DIS's top strategic priorities include creativity and innovation, international expansion, and leveraging new technology applications. Under CEO Robert Iger, DIS has been making its content available across various digital platforms (broadband, wireless/mobile -- including iTunes, iPhone and iPad -- as well as video games).

Over the past few years, DIS has made a number of key acquisitions and divested some non-core assets. In 2009, DIS acquired Marvel Entertainment -- a film studio with a library of over 5,000 comic book characters -- for about $4 billion in cash and stock. Earlier, in 2006, it had acquired Pixar, a CGI animation studio, for $7.4 billion in stock. In 2010, DIS acquired Playdom, an online social gaming platform, for up to $763 million, as well as Tapulous, a developer of mobile games/apps (for an undisclosed price). In 2007, it acquired kids-oriented social networking site Club Penguin for $350 million in cash (plus another $350 million on certain performance targets). In 2010, it sold Miramax film for about $660 million, and earlier, in 2007, it sold ABC radio assets (22 stations plus the ABC radio network) for $2.7 billion.

## Company Financials Fiscal Year Ended Sep. 30

| Per Share Data ($) | 2011 | 2010 | 2009 | 2008 | 2007 | 2006 | 2005 | 2004 | 2003 | 2002 |
|---|---|---|---|---|---|---|---|---|---|---|
| Tangible Book Value | 4.49 | 4.40 | 5.27 | 4.18 | 3.15 | 3.10 | 3.24 | 3.15 | 2.01 | 1.78 |
| Cash Flow | 3.72 | 2.91 | 2.63 | 3.09 | 3.08 | 2.40 | 1.93 | 1.69 | 1.17 | 1.11 |
| Earnings | 2.52 | 2.03 | 1.76 | 2.28 | 2.24 | 1.64 | 1.24 | 1.12 | 0.65 | 0.60 |
| S&P Core Earnings | 2.54 | 2.05 | 1.58 | 2.16 | 1.97 | 1.70 | 1.27 | 1.04 | 0.49 | 0.29 |
| Dividends | 0.40 | 0.35 | 0.35 | 0.35 | 0.31 | 0.27 | 0.24 | 0.21 | 0.21 | 0.21 |
| Payout Ratio | 16% | 17% | 20% | 15% | 14% | 16% | 19% | 19% | 32% | 35% |
| Prices:High | 44.34 | 38.00 | 32.75 | 35.02 | 36.79 | 34.89 | 29.99 | 28.41 | 23.80 | 25.17 |
| Prices:Low | 28.19 | 28.71 | 15.14 | 18.60 | 30.68 | 23.77 | 22.89 | 20.88 | 14.84 | 13.48 |
| P/E Ratio:High | 18 | 19 | 19 | 15 | 16 | 21 | 24 | 25 | 37 | 42 |
| P/E Ratio:Low | 11 | 14 | 9 | 8 | 14 | 14 | 18 | 19 | 23 | 22 |

| Income Statement Analysis (Million $) | 2011 | 2010 | 2009 | 2008 | 2007 | 2006 | 2005 | 2004 | 2003 | 2002 |
|---|---|---|---|---|---|---|---|---|---|---|
| Revenue | 40,893 | 38,063 | 36,149 | 37,843 | 35,510 | 34,285 | 31,944 | 30,752 | 27,061 | 25,329 |
| Operating Income | 9,622 | 8,439 | 7,328 | 8,986 | 8,272 | 6,914 | 5,446 | 5,258 | 3,790 | 3,426 |
| Depreciation | 1,841 | 1,713 | 1,631 | 1,582 | 1,491 | 1,436 | 1,339 | 1,210 | 1,077 | 1,042 |
| Interest Expense | 435 | 456 | 645 | 774 | 593 | 592 | 605 | 629 | 666 | 453 |
| Pretax Income | 8,043 | 6,627 | 5,658 | 7,402 | 7,725 | 5,447 | 3,987 | 3,739 | 2,254 | 2,190 |
| Effective Tax Rate | NA | NA | 36.2% | 36.1% | 37.2% | 34.7% | 31.1% | 32.0% | 35.0% | 38.9% |
| Net Income | 5,258 | 3,963 | 3,307 | 4,427 | 4,674 | 3,374 | 2,569 | 2,345 | 1,338 | 1,236 |
| S&P Core Earnings | 4,827 | 4,010 | 2,975 | 4,209 | 4,091 | 3,500 | 2,635 | 2,201 | 1,006 | 606 |

| Balance Sheet & Other Financial Data (Million $) | 2011 | 2010 | 2009 | 2008 | 2007 | 2006 | 2005 | 2004 | 2003 | 2002 |
|---|---|---|---|---|---|---|---|---|---|---|
| Cash | 3,185 | 2,722 | 3,417 | 3,001 | 3,670 | 2,411 | 1,723 | 2,042 | 1,583 | 1,239 |
| Current Assets | 13,757 | 12,225 | 11,889 | 11,666 | 11,314 | 9,562 | 8,845 | 9,369 | 8,314 | 7,849 |
| Total Assets | 72,124 | 69,206 | 63,117 | 62,497 | 60,928 | 59,998 | 53,158 | 53,902 | 49,988 | 50,045 |
| Current Liabilities | 12,088 | 11,000 | 8,934 | 11,591 | 11,391 | 10,210 | 9,168 | 11,059 | 8,669 | 7,819 |
| Long Term Debt | 10,922 | 10,130 | 11,495 | 11,351 | 11,892 | 10,843 | 10,157 | 9,395 | 10,643 | 12,467 |
| Common Equity | 37,385 | 37,519 | 33,734 | 32,323 | 30,753 | 31,820 | 26,210 | 26,081 | 23,791 | 23,445 |
| Total Capital | 55,498 | 51,822 | 48,126 | 47,368 | 45,218 | 46,657 | 40,045 | 39,224 | 37,574 | 38,943 |
| Capital Expenditures | 3,559 | 2,110 | 1,753 | 1,586 | 1,566 | 1,299 | 1,823 | 1,427 | 1,049 | 1,086 |
| Cash Flow | 7,099 | 5,676 | 4,938 | 6,009 | 6,165 | 4,810 | 3,908 | 3,555 | 2,415 | 2,278 |
| Current Ratio | 1.1 | 1.1 | 1.3 | 1.0 | 1.0 | 0.9 | 1.0 | 0.8 | 1.0 | 1.0 |
| % Long Term Debt of Capitalization | 19.7 | 19.6 | 23.9 | 24.0 | 26.2 | 23.2 | 25.4 | 24.0 | 28.3 | 32.0 |
| % Net Income of Revenue | 12.9 | 10.4 | 9.2 | 11.7 | 13.1 | 9.8 | 8.0 | 7.6 | 4.9 | 4.9 |
| % Return on Assets | 7.4 | 6.0 | 5.3 | 7.2 | 7.7 | 6.0 | 4.8 | 4.5 | 2.7 | 2.6 |
| % Return on Equity | 14.0 | 11.1 | 10.0 | 14.0 | 14.9 | 11.6 | 9.8 | 9.4 | 5.7 | 5.4 |

Data as orig reptd.; bef. results of disc opers/spec. items. Per share data adj. for stk. divs.; EPS diluted. E-Estimated. NA-Not Available. NM-Not Meaningful. NR-Not Ranked. UR-Under Review.

**Office:** 500 South Buena Vista Street, Burbank, CA 91521.
**Telephone:** 818-560-1000.
**Website:** http://www.disney.com
**Chrmn:** J. Pepper, Jr.

**Pres & CEO:** R.A. Iger
**EVP & CFO:** J.A. Rasulo
**EVP & Treas:** C.M. McCarthy
**EVP, Secy & General Counsel:** A.N. Braverman

**Investor Contact:** L. Singer (818-560-6601)
**Board Members:** S. E. Arnold, J. S. Chen, J. L. Estrin, R. A. Iger, F. H. Langhammer, A. B. Lewis, M. C. Lozano, R. W. Matschullat, J. Pepper, Jr., S. Sandberg, O. C. Smith
**Founded:** 1936
**Domicile:** Delaware
**Employees:** 156,000

*The McGraw-Hill Companies*

# Dominion Resources Inc.

**STANDARD &POOR'S**

| S&P Recommendation **SELL** ★☆☆☆☆ | Price<br>$49.51 (as of Nov 25, 2011) | 12-Mo. Target Price<br>$47.00 | Investment Style<br>Large-Cap Blend |
|---|---|---|---|

**GICS Sector** Utilities
**Sub-Industry** Multi-Utilities

**Summary** One of the largest producers and transporters of energy in the U.S., Dominion also operates the largest natural gas storage system and serves retail energy customers in 15 states.

## Key Stock Statistics (Source S&P, Vickers, company reports)

| | | | | | | | |
|---|---|---|---|---|---|---|---|
| 52-Wk Range | $52.68– 41.13 | S&P Oper. EPS 2011E | 3.15 | Market Capitalization(B) | $28.201 | Beta | 0.53 |
| Trailing 12-Month EPS | $2.61 | S&P Oper. EPS 2012E | 3.35 | Yield (%) | 3.98 | S&P 3-Yr. Proj. EPS CAGR(%) | 1 |
| Trailing 12-Month P/E | 19.0 | P/E on S&P Oper. EPS 2011E | 15.7 | Dividend Rate/Share | $1.97 | S&P Credit Rating | A- |
| $10K Invested 5 Yrs Ago | $15,060 | Common Shares Outstg. (M) | 569.6 | Institutional Ownership (%) | 59 | | |

## Price Performance

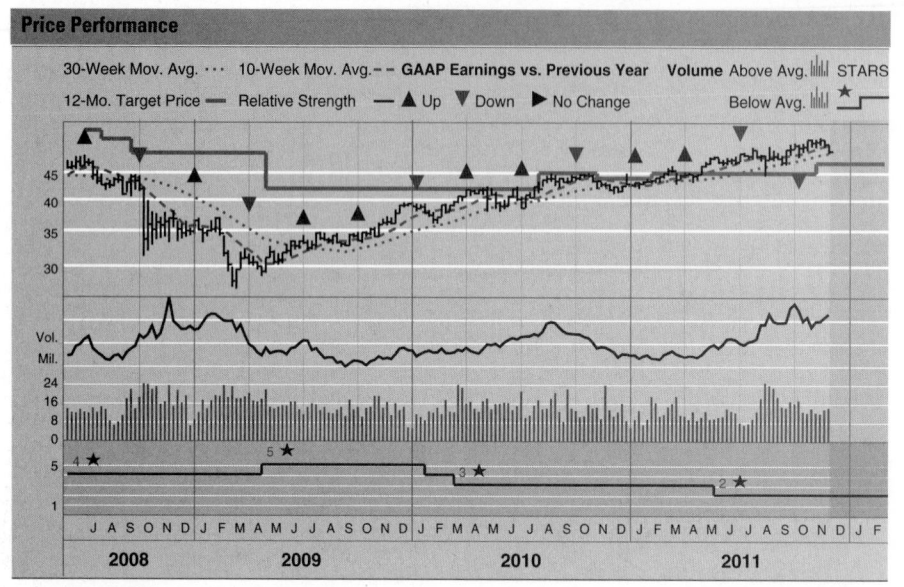

30-Week Mov. Avg. ··· 10-Week Mov. Avg. - - GAAP Earnings vs. Previous Year Volume Above Avg. STARS
12-Mo. Target Price — Relative Strength — ▲ Up ▼ Down ▶ No Change Below Avg.

Options: ASE, CBOE, P, Ph

## Qualitative Risk Assessment

| LOW | MEDIUM | HIGH |
|---|---|---|

Our risk assessment reflects our view of Dominion's relatively large capitalization and geographically balanced sources of earnings, which include low-risk regulated electric and gas distribution, electric generation and pipeline operations.

## Quantitative Evaluations

**S&P Quality Ranking** A-

| D | C | B- | B | B+ | A- | A | A+ |
|---|---|---|---|---|---|---|---|

**Relative Strength Rank** MODERATE

70

LOWEST = 1          HIGHEST = 99

## Highlights

➤ The 12-month target price for D has recently been changed to $47.00 from $45.00. The Highlights section of this Stock Report will be updated accordingly.

## Investment Rationale/Risk

➤ The Investment Rationale/Risk section of this Stock Report will be updated shortly. For the latest News story on D from MarketScope, see below.

➤ 10/28/11 09:30 am ET ... S&P MAINTAINS SELL OPINION ON SHARES OF DOMINION RESOURCES (D 52.04**): Q3 recurring EPS of $0.95, vs. $1.03, misses our estimate by $0.01, but beats the $0.94 Capital IQ consensus forecast. Revenues were lower and per-revenue cost of fuel & purchased power, depreciation charges and operating taxes were higher than we expected, but were partly offset by operating & maintenance expenses that were lower. We see near average EPS growth and think the balance sheet is more levered than many peers. We keep our '11 and '12 EPS estimates at $3.15 and $3.35, but boost our target price by $2 to $47, on higher peer valuations. The shares are yielding 3.8%. /CBMuir

## Revenue/Earnings Data

**Revenue (Million $)**

| | 1Q | 2Q | 3Q | 4Q | Year |
|---|---|---|---|---|---|
| 2011 | 4,057 | 3,341 | 3,803 | -- | -- |
| 2010 | 4,168 | 3,333 | 3,950 | 3,746 | 15,197 |
| 2009 | 4,778 | 3,450 | 3,648 | 3,255 | 15,131 |
| 2008 | 4,389 | 3,452 | 4,231 | 4,173 | 16,290 |
| 2007 | 4,661 | 3,730 | 3,589 | 3,694 | 15,674 |
| 2006 | 4,951 | 3,548 | 4,016 | 3,967 | 16,482 |

**Earnings Per Share ($)**

| | 1Q | 2Q | 3Q | 4Q | Year |
|---|---|---|---|---|---|
| 2011 | 0.82 | 0.58 | 0.69 | E0.68 | E3.15 |
| 2010 | 0.54 | 2.98 | 0.98 | 0.53 | 5.02 |
| 2009 | 0.42 | 0.76 | 1.00 | -0.01 | 2.17 |
| 2008 | 1.18 | 0.52 | 0.87 | 0.60 | 3.16 |
| 2007 | 0.68 | -0.56 | 3.63 | 0.52 | 4.13 |
| 2006 | 0.78 | 0.24 | 0.93 | 0.28 | 2.23 |

Fiscal year ended Dec. 31. Next earnings report expected: Late January. EPS Estimates based on S&P Operating Earnings; historical GAAP earnings are as reported.

## Dividend Data (Dates: mm/dd Payment Date: mm/dd/yy)

| Amount ($) | Date Decl. | Ex-Div. Date | Stk. of Record | Payment Date |
|---|---|---|---|---|
| 0.493 | 01/21 | 03/02 | 03/04 | 03/20/11 |
| 0.493 | 05/12 | 05/25 | 05/27 | 06/20/11 |
| 0.493 | 08/05 | 08/24 | 08/26 | 09/20/11 |
| 0.493 | 10/21 | 11/30 | 12/02 | 12/20/11 |

Dividends have been paid since 1925. Source: Company reports.

---

**Please read the Required Disclosures and Analyst Certification on the last page of this report.**

The *McGraw-Hill* Companies

# Dominion Resources Inc.

STANDARD
&POOR'S

## Business Summary October 04, 2011

CORPORATE OVERVIEW. Dominion Resources is a fully integrated gas and electric holding company. The company operates in three primary segments: Virginia Power, Energy, and Generation. The Virginia Power segment (23.8% of 2010 operating segment revenue) operates regulated electric transmission and distribution business in Virginia and northeastern North Carolina. The Generation segment (52.7%) is involved in generation for the electric utility and merchant power along with energy marketing and risk management activities. The Energy segment (15.4%) operates a regulated natural gas distribution company in Ohio, regulated gas transmission pipeline and storage operations, and regulated LNG operations. The Energy segment includes a producer services business, which engages in natural gas supply aggregation, gas transportation, market-based storage services, and gas trading and marketing. Other operations make up the remainder of revenues.

CORPORATE STRATEGY. D focuses its efforts mainly on the Northeast, Mid-Atlantic and Midwest regions of the U.S. D believes that focusing on its core businesses will reduce earnings volatility and help to grow EPS at rates above 6% annually after 2010. It has a proactive risk management strategy, and has entered into commodity derivative agreements to hedge against commodity price risks.

MARKET PROFILE. As of December 31, 2010, D had total power generation capacity of 27,615 MW, with 16,557 MW of utility generation, 1,861 MW of utility power purchase agreements, and 9,197 MW of merchant generation. The Virginia Power segment served a total of 2.43 million regulated electric customers. Additionally, it had 2.1 million unregulated customer accounts (37% electricity, 27% natural gas and 36% products and services). The Energy segment serves 261,000 gas sales and 1.0 million gas transportation customers in Ohio and has about 11,000 miles of natural gas transmission, gathering and storage pipelines, and 947 Bcf of storage capacity. This division also operates a liquefied natural gas (LNG) terminal at Cove Point, MD, which was recently expanded to a sendout capacity of 1.8 Bcfd, with a storage capacity of 14.6 Bcf.

## Company Financials Fiscal Year Ended Dec. 31

| Per Share Data ($) | 2010 | 2009 | 2008 | 2007 | 2006 | 2005 | 2004 | 2003 | 2002 | 2001 |
|---|---|---|---|---|---|---|---|---|---|---|
| Tangible Book Value | 14.14 | 11.92 | 10.05 | 9.21 | 11.45 | 8.79 | 16.37 | 9.60 | 9.09 | 7.85 |
| Earnings | 5.02 | 2.17 | 3.16 | 4.13 | 2.22 | 1.50 | 1.91 | 1.49 | 2.41 | 1.08 |
| S&P Core Earnings | 2.42 | 2.12 | 2.97 | 0.50 | 2.21 | 1.47 | 1.90 | 1.58 | 1.92 | 0.66 |
| Dividends | 1.83 | 1.75 | 1.58 | 2.25 | 0.35 | 1.34 | 1.30 | 1.29 | 1.29 | 1.29 |
| Payout Ratio | 36% | 81% | 50% | 54% | 16% | 89% | 68% | 87% | 54% | 120% |
| Prices:High | 45.12 | 39.79 | 48.50 | 49.38 | 42.22 | 43.49 | 34.43 | 32.97 | 33.53 | 35.00 |
| Prices:Low | 36.12 | 27.15 | 31.26 | 39.84 | 34.36 | 33.26 | 30.39 | 25.87 | 17.70 | 27.57 |
| P/E Ratio:High | 9 | 18 | 15 | 12 | 19 | 29 | 18 | 22 | 14 | 33 |
| P/E Ratio:Low | 7 | 13 | 10 | 10 | 15 | 22 | 16 | 17 | 7 | 26 |

| Income Statement Analysis (Million $) | 2010 | 2009 | 2008 | 2007 | 2006 | 2005 | 2004 | 2003 | 2002 | 2001 |
|---|---|---|---|---|---|---|---|---|---|---|
| Revenue | 15,197 | 15,131 | 16,290 | 15,674 | 16,482 | 18,041 | 13,972 | 12,078 | 10,218 | 10,558 |
| Depreciation | 1,258 | 1,319 | 1,191 | 1,368 | 1,606 | 1,412 | 1,305 | 1,216 | 1,258 | 1,245 |
| Maintenance | NA | NA | NA | NA | NA | NA | NA | NA | NA | NA |
| Fixed Charges Coverage | 4.09 | 3.14 | 4.23 | 4.82 | 3.42 | 2.63 | 3.09 | 2.63 | 3.15 | 2.02 |
| Construction Credits | NA | NA | NA | Nil | Nil | Nil | Nil | Nil | Nil | Nil |
| Effective Tax Rate | 40.8% | 31.9% | 32.4% | 39.5% | 37.0% | 36.0% | 35.6% | 38.6% | 33.3% | 40.5% |
| Net Income | 2,963 | 1,287 | 1,836 | 2,705 | 1,563 | 1,034 | 1,264 | 949 | 1,362 | 544 |
| S&P Core Earnings | 1,432 | 1,256 | 1,729 | 324 | 1,555 | 1,010 | 1,254 | 1,004 | 1,088 | 331 |

| Balance Sheet & Other Financial Data (Million $) | 2010 | 2009 | 2008 | 2007 | 2006 | 2005 | 2004 | 2003 | 2002 | 2001 |
|---|---|---|---|---|---|---|---|---|---|---|
| Gross Property | 39,855 | 39,036 | 35,448 | 33,331 | 43,575 | 42,063 | 38,663 | 37,107 | 32,631 | 33,105 |
| Capital Expenditures | 3,422 | 3,817 | 3,519 | 3,972 | 4,052 | 1,683 | 1,451 | 2,138 | 2,828 | 1,224 |
| Net Property | 26,713 | 25,592 | 23,274 | 21,352 | 29,382 | 28,940 | 26,716 | 25,850 | 20,257 | 18,681 |
| Capitalization:Long Term Debt | 16,015 | 15,738 | 15,213 | 13,492 | 15,048 | 14,910 | 15,764 | 16,033 | 13,714 | 12,119 |
| Capitalization:% Long Term Debt | 57.2 | 58.5 | 60.2 | 58.9 | 53.8 | 58.9 | 58.0 | 60.3 | 57.3 | 58.1 |
| Capitalization:Preferred | Nil | Nil | Nil | Nil | Nil | Nil | Nil | Nil | Nil | Nil |
| Capitalization:% Preferred | Nil | Nil | Nil | Nil | Nil | Nil | Nil | Nil | Nil | Nil |
| Capitalization:Common | 11,997 | 11,185 | 10,077 | 9,406 | 12,913 | 10,397 | 11,426 | 10,538 | 10,213 | 8,368 |
| Capitalization:% Common | 42.8 | 41.5 | 39.8 | 41.1 | 46.2 | 41.1 | 42.0 | 39.7 | 42.7 | 40.1 |
| Total Capital | 28,509 | 28,061 | 29,427 | 27,179 | 33,842 | 30,291 | 32,689 | 31,134 | 28,136 | 24,811 |
| % Operating Ratio | 92.3 | 86.7 | 82.9 | 75.9 | 85.3 | 89.7 | 85.6 | 83.7 | 78.5 | 85.6 |
| % Earned on Net Property | 12.4 | 10.8 | 16.4 | 21.9 | 11.5 | 8.8 | 10.3 | 10.6 | 21.4 | 10.6 |
| % Return on Revenue | 19.5 | 8.5 | 11.3 | 17.3 | 9.5 | 5.7 | 9.0 | 7.9 | 13.3 | 5.2 |
| % Return on Invested Capital | 4.8 | 8.2 | 9.5 | 12.7 | 8.1 | 6.4 | 6.5 | 6.5 | 8.5 | 7.2 |
| % Return on Common Equity | 25.6 | 12.1 | 18.2 | 24.2 | 13.4 | 9.5 | 11.5 | 9.1 | 14.7 | 7.1 |

Data as orig reptd.; bef. results of disc opers/spec. items. Per share data adj. for stk. divs.; EPS diluted. E-Estimated. NA-Not Available. NM-Not Meaningful. NR-Not Ranked. UR-Under Review.

**Office:** 120 Tredegar Street, Richmond, VA 23219.
**Telephone:** 804-819-2000.
**Email:** investor_relations@domres.com
**Website:** http://www.dom.com

**Chrmn, Pres & CEO:** T.F. Farrell, II
**SVP & CIO:** M.E. McDermid
**CFO:** M.F. McGettrick
**Chief Admin Officer:** S.A. Rogers

**Chief Acctg Officer & Cntlr:** A. Sawhney
**Investor Contact:** J. O'Hare (804-819-2156)
**Board Members:** W. P. Barr, P. W. Brown, G. A. Davidson, Jr., H. E. Dragas, T. F. Farrell, II, J. W. Harris, R. S. Jepson, Jr., M. J. Kington, M. A. McKenna, F. S. Royal, R. H. Spilman, Jr., D. A. Wollard

**Founded:** 1909
**Domicile:** Virginia
**Employees:** 15,800

The McGraw-Hill Companies

STANDARD
&POOR'S

# R.R. Donnelley & Sons Co

| S&P Recommendation HOLD ★★★☆☆ | Price $13.49 (as of Nov 25, 2011) | 12-Mo. Target Price $19.00 | Investment Style Large-Cap Value |
|---|---|---|---|

**GICS Sector** Industrials
**Sub-Industry** Commercial Printing

**Summary** R.R. Donnelley, the largest U.S. commercial printer, specializes in the production of catalogs, inserts, magazines, books, directories, and financial and computer documentation.

## Key Stock Statistics (Source S&P, Vickers, company reports)

| | | | | | | | |
|---|---|---|---|---|---|---|---|
| 52-Wk Range | $21.34– 12.90 | S&P Oper. EPS 2011**E** | 1.71 | Market Capitalization(B) | $2.532 | Beta | 1.95 |
| Trailing 12-Month EPS | $1.14 | S&P Oper. EPS 2012**E** | 1.99 | Yield (%) | 7.71 | S&P 3-Yr. Proj. EPS CAGR(%) | 5 |
| Trailing 12-Month P/E | 11.8 | P/E on S&P Oper. EPS 2011**E** | 7.9 | Dividend Rate/Share | $1.04 | S&P Credit Rating | BB+ |
| $10K Invested 5 Yrs Ago | $4,999 | Common Shares Outstg. (M) | 187.8 | Institutional Ownership (%) | NM | | |

## Price Performance

30-Week Mov. Avg. · · · 10-Week Mov. Avg. - - GAAP Earnings vs. Previous Year   Volume Above Avg. ▮▮▮ STARS
12-Mo. Target Price — Relative Strength — ▲ Up ▼ Down ▶ No Change   Below Avg. ▮▮▮ ★

Options: CBOE, P, Ph

Analysis prepared by Equity Analyst **Jim Corridore** on Nov 14, 2011, when the stock traded at **$15.94**.

### Highlights

➤ We project that revenues will rise 6% in 2011, reflecting our forecast of a 3% increase in the U.S. along with 6% growth in international markets. We believe growth will be spurred by increasing volumes, partly offset by continuing price erosion in line with the long-term trend in financial printing. We see revenues rising about 3% in 2012. RRD expects to generate $600 million of free cash in 2011, after generating $558 million in 2010 and $1.4 billion in 2009.

➤ We expect operating margins in 2011 to be hurt by pressure on pricing along with higher material costs. Offsetting this, we see benefits from productivity increases, cost synergies from recent acquisitions, and fixed cost leverage from a modestly higher revenue base. We see operating margins of 6.7% in 2011, improving to 7.7% in 2012.

➤ After higher interest expense and a lower share count, we forecast 2011 EPS of $1.71, versus 2010 operating EPS of $1.76. For 2012, we estimate EPS of $1.99, up 16% from our 2011 EPS estimate.

### Investment Rationale/Risk

➤ We expect RRD to gain market share by leveraging its geographic and product breadth, but we think its business model is undergoing a long-term secular shift as increased use of electronic media reduces the demand for financial and other printing. We see headwinds from what we view as a highly leveraged balance sheet and digestion of recent acquisitions. However, we think improving investor sentiment will likely lend support to the shares as the U.S. economy starts to show growth.

➤ Risks to our recommendation and target price include substantially higher raw material costs, negative forex translation charges, further sharp deterioration in the company's end-markets, and a greater-than-expected increase in the amount of information disseminated electronically, which would lead to lower publishing demand.

➤ Our 12-month target price of $19 values the shares at 9.5X our 2012 EPS estimate of $1.99, toward the low end of RRD's five-year historical P/E range, reflecting our concerns about the maturation of RRD's business segments and its high balance sheet risk.

### Qualitative Risk Assessment

| LOW | MEDIUM | HIGH |
|---|---|---|

Our risk assessment reflects economies of scale that the company realizes as the largest U.S. commercial printer in a fragmented print industry, offset by industry pricing pressure and the increasingly electronic nature of communication.

### Quantitative Evaluations

**S&P Quality Ranking**                 B-

| D | C | B- | B | B+ | A- | A | A+ |
|---|---|---|---|---|---|---|---|

**Relative Strength Rank**              WEAK

25

LOWEST = 1                          HIGHEST = 99

### Revenue/Earnings Data

**Revenue (Million $)**

| | 1Q | 2Q | 3Q | 4Q | Year |
|---|---|---|---|---|---|
| 2011 | 2,584 | 2,623 | 2,683 | -- | -- |
| 2010 | 2,415 | 2,409 | 2,488 | 2,707 | 10,019 |
| 2009 | 2,456 | 2,356 | 2,463 | 2,583 | 9,857 |
| 2008 | 2,997 | 2,924 | 2,865 | 2,796 | 11,582 |
| 2007 | 2,793 | 2,796 | 2,910 | 3,088 | 11,587 |
| 2006 | 2,267 | 2,274 | 2,309 | 2,467 | 9,317 |

**Earnings Per Share ($)**

| | | | | | |
|---|---|---|---|---|---|
| 2011 | 0.16 | 0.06 | 0.83 | E0.52 | E1.71 |
| 2010 | 0.25 | 0.42 | 0.25 | 0.13 | 1.06 |
| 2009 | 0.07 | 0.12 | 0.06 | -0.39 | -0.13 |
| 2008 | 0.85 | 0.68 | 0.80 | -3.35 | -0.91 |
| 2007 | 0.63 | -0.32 | 0.80 | -1.37 | -0.22 |
| 2006 | 0.52 | 0.57 | 0.75 | -0.01 | 1.84 |

Fiscal year ended Dec. 31. Next earnings report expected: Late February. EPS Estimates based on S&P Operating Earnings; historical GAAP earnings are as reported.

### Dividend Data (Dates: mm/dd Payment Date: mm/dd/yy)

| Amount ($) | Date Decl. | Ex-Div. Date | Stk. of Record | Payment Date |
|---|---|---|---|---|
| 0.260 | 01/13 | 01/26 | 01/28 | 03/01/11 |
| 0.260 | 04/07 | 04/19 | 04/22 | 06/01/11 |
| 0.260 | 07/21 | 08/03 | 08/05 | 09/01/11 |
| 0.260 | 10/26 | 11/08 | 11/10 | 12/01/11 |

Dividends have been paid since 1911. Source: Company reports.

**Please read the Required Disclosures and Analyst Certification on the last page of this report.**

The McGraw·Hill Companies

# R.R. Donnelley & Sons Co

STANDARD
&POOR'S

## Business Summary November 14, 2011

CORPORATE OVERVIEW. R.R. Donnelley & Sons (RRD) is the largest printing company in North America, serving customers in the publishing, health care, advertising, retail, telecommunications, technology, financial services and other industries. The company provides solutions in long- and short-run commercial printing, direct mail, financial printing, print fulfillment, forms and labels, logistics, digital printing, call centers, transactional print-and-mail, print management, online services, digital photography, color services, and content and database management.

The company has two reportable segments: U.S. Print and Related Services, and International. R.R. Donnelley management changed its reportable segments in the third quarter of 2007 to reflect changes in management reporting structure and the manner in which management assesses information for decision-making purposes.

The U.S. Print and Related Services segment (75% of revenues in 2010 and 2009) consists of the following U.S. businesses: magazine, catalog and retail,

which includes print services to consumer magazine and catalog publishers as well as retailers; book, which serves the consumer, religious, educational and specialty book and telecommunications sectors; directories, which serves the printing needs of yellow and white pages directory publishers; logistics, which delivers company and third-party printed products and distributes time-sensitive and secure material, and performs warehousing and fulfillment services; direct mail, which offers content creation, database management, printing, personalization finishing and distribution services to direct marketing companies; financial print; direct mail; and short-run commercial print, which provides print and print related services to a diversified customer base.

## Company Financials Fiscal Year Ended Dec. 31

| Per Share Data ($) | 2010 | 2009 | 2008 | 2007 | 2006 | 2005 | 2004 | 2003 | 2002 | 2001 |
|---|---|---|---|---|---|---|---|---|---|---|
| Tangible Book Value | NM | NM | NM | NM | 0.54 | NM | 3.81 | 5.14 | 4.51 | 3.92 |
| Cash Flow | 3.61 | 2.60 | 2.02 | 2.52 | 3.96 | 2.40 | 5.07 | 4.43 | 4.32 | 3.41 |
| Earnings | 1.06 | -0.13 | -0.91 | -0.22 | 1.84 | 0.44 | 0.88 | 1.54 | 1.24 | 0.21 |
| S&P Core Earnings | 1.20 | 0.01 | 0.61 | 1.48 | 1.97 | 1.27 | 1.20 | 1.18 | 0.18 | -0.65 |
| Dividends | 1.04 | 1.04 | 1.04 | 1.04 | 1.04 | 1.04 | 1.04 | 1.02 | 0.98 | 0.94 |
| Payout Ratio | 98% | NM | NM | NM | 57% | NM | 118% | 66% | 79% | NM |
| Prices:High | 23.20 | 22.78 | 38.19 | 45.25 | 36.00 | 38.27 | 35.37 | 30.15 | 32.10 | 31.90 |
| Prices:Low | 14.87 | 5.54 | 9.53 | 32.59 | 28.50 | 29.54 | 27.62 | 16.94 | 18.50 | 24.30 |
| P/E Ratio:High | 22 | NM | NM | NM | 20 | 87 | 40 | 20 | 26 | NM |
| P/E Ratio:Low | 14 | NM | NM | NM | 15 | 67 | 31 | 11 | 15 | NM |

| Income Statement Analysis (Million $) | 2010 | 2009 | 2008 | 2007 | 2006 | 2005 | 2004 | 2003 | 2002 | 2001 |
|---|---|---|---|---|---|---|---|---|---|---|
| Revenue | 10,019 | 9,857 | 11,582 | 11,587 | 9,317 | 8,430 | 7,156 | 4,787 | 4,755 | 5,298 |
| Operating Income | 1,253 | 1,288 | 1,761 | 1,752 | 1,420 | 1,295 | 952 | 617 | 686 | 722 |
| Depreciation | 539 | 579 | 617 | 598 | 463 | 425 | 771 | 329 | 352 | 379 |
| Interest Expense | 223 | 245 | 241 | 231 | 139 | 111 | 85.9 | 50.4 | 62.8 | 71.2 |
| Pretax Income | 323 | 93.1 | -269 | 91.4 | 601 | 332 | 357 | 208 | 176 | 74.9 |
| Effective Tax Rate | NA | 123.0% | NM | NM | 32.6% | 71.5% | 26.0% | 15.3% | 19.1% | 66.6% |
| Net Income | 217 | -27.3 | -192 | -48.4 | 403 | 95.6 | 265 | 177 | 142 | 25.0 |
| S&P Core Earnings | 252 | 1.17 | 129 | 322 | 430 | 275 | 243 | 136 | 21.3 | -78.3 |

| Balance Sheet & Other Financial Data (Million $) | 2010 | 2009 | 2008 | 2007 | 2006 | 2005 | 2004 | 2003 | 2002 | 2001 |
|---|---|---|---|---|---|---|---|---|---|---|
| Cash | 519 | 499 | 324 | 443 | 211 | 367 | 642 | 60.8 | 60.5 | 48.6 |
| Current Assets | 3,167 | 2,961 | 3,281 | 3,521 | 2,517 | 2,622 | 2,601 | 1,000 | 866 | 940 |
| Total Assets | 9,083 | 8,748 | 9,494 | 12,087 | 9,636 | 9,374 | 8,554 | 3,189 | 3,152 | 3,400 |
| Current Liabilities | 1,973 | 2,040 | 2,487 | 2,765 | 1,612 | 1,814 | 1,487 | 884 | 955 | 984 |
| Long Term Debt | 3,399 | 2,983 | 3,203 | 3,602 | 2,359 | 2,365 | 1,581 | 752 | 753 | 881 |
| Common Equity | 2,224 | 2,134 | 2,319 | 3,907 | 4,125 | 3,724 | 3,987 | 983 | 915 | 888 |
| Total Capital | 5,797 | 5,144 | 5,783 | 8,382 | 7,087 | 6,686 | 6,144 | 1,970 | 1,882 | 1,982 |
| Capital Expenditures | 229 | 195 | 323 | 482 | 374 | 471 | 265 | 203 | 242 | 273 |
| Cash Flow | 756 | 534 | 425 | 550 | 866 | 521 | 1,036 | 506 | 495 | 404 |
| Current Ratio | 1.6 | 1.5 | 1.3 | 1.3 | 1.6 | 1.4 | 1.7 | 1.1 | 0.9 | 1.0 |
| % Long Term Debt of Capitalization | 58.6 | 58.0 | 55.4 | 43.0 | 33.3 | 35.4 | 25.7 | 38.2 | 40.0 | 44.5 |
| % Net Income of Revenue | 2.2 | NM | NM | NM | 4.3 | 1.1 | 3.7 | 3.7 | 3.0 | 0.5 |
| % Return on Assets | 2.4 | NM | NM | NM | 4.2 | 1.1 | 4.5 | 5.5 | 4.4 | 0.7 |
| % Return on Equity | 10.0 | NM | NM | NM | 10.3 | 2.5 | 10.7 | 18.6 | 15.8 | 2.4 |

Data as orig reptd.; bef. results of disc opers/spec. items. Per share data adj. for stk. divs.; EPS diluted. E-Estimated. NA-Not Available. NM-Not Meaningful. NR-Not Ranked. UR-Under Review.

**Office:** 111 South Wacker Drive, Chicago, IL 60606-4301.
**Telephone:** 312-326-8000.
**Email:** investor.info@rrd.com
**Website:** http://www.rrdonnelley.com

**Chrmn:** S.M. Wolf
**Pres & CEO:** T.J. Quinlan, III
**COO:** J.R. Paloian
**EVP, Secy & General Counsel:** S.S. Bettman

**SVP, Chief Acctg Officer & Cntlr:** A.B. Coxhead
**Investor Contact:** D. Leib (312-326-7710)
**Board Members:** L. A. Chaden, J. Hamilton, S. M. Ivey, T. S. Johnson, J. C. Pope, T. J. Quinlan, III, M. T. Riordan, O. R. Sockwell, Jr., S. M. Wolf

**Founded:** 1864
**Domicile:** Delaware
**Employees:** 58,700

# Dover Corp

**STANDARD &POOR'S**

## S&P Recommendation  BUY ★★★★☆

| Price | 12-Mo. Target Price | Investment Style |
|---|---|---|
| $50.26 (as of Nov 25, 2011) | $72.00 | Large-Cap Growth |

**GICS Sector** Industrials
**Sub-Industry** Industrial Machinery

**Summary** This company manufactures a broad range of specialized industrial products and sophisticated manufacturing equipment.

### Key Stock Statistics (Source S&P, Vickers, company reports)

| | | | | | | | |
|---|---|---|---|---|---|---|---|
| 52-Wk Range | $70.15–43.64 | S&P Oper. EPS 2011**E** | 4.41 | Market Capitalization(B) | $9.317 | Beta | 1.32 |
| Trailing 12-Month EPS | $4.30 | S&P Oper. EPS 2012**E** | 5.01 | Yield (%) | 2.51 | S&P 3-Yr. Proj. EPS CAGR(%) | 14 |
| Trailing 12-Month P/E | 11.7 | P/E on S&P Oper. EPS 2011**E** | 11.4 | Dividend Rate/Share | $1.26 | S&P Credit Rating | A |
| $10K Invested 5 Yrs Ago | $11,027 | Common Shares Outstg. (M) | 185.4 | Institutional Ownership (%) | 87 | | |

## Price Performance

- 30-Week Mov. Avg. ····
- 10-Week Mov. Avg. ---
- 12-Mo. Target Price —
- Relative Strength —
- GAAP Earnings vs. Previous Year
- ▲ Up ▼ Down ▶ No Change
- Volume Above Avg. | Below Avg. |
- STARS ★

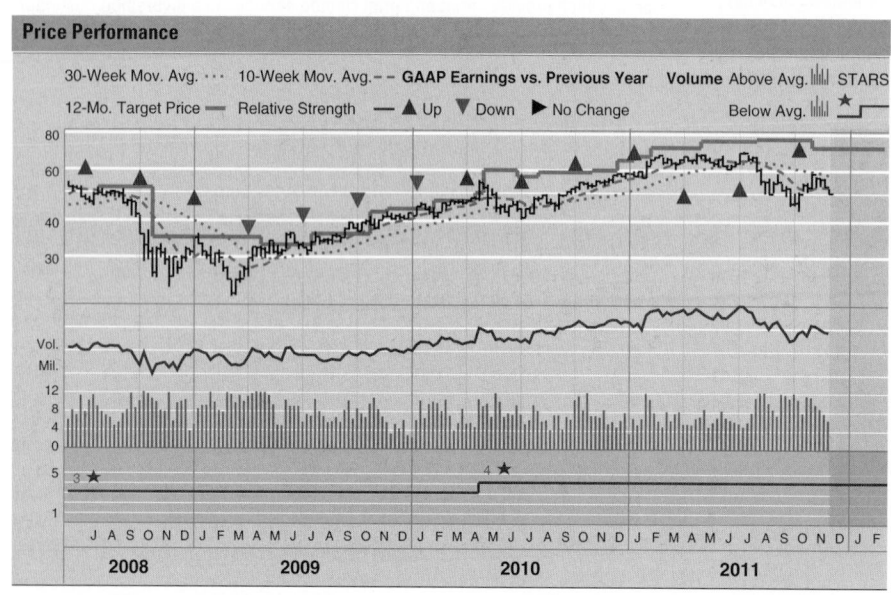

Options: CBOE, P, Ph

Analysis prepared by Equity Analyst **Kevin Kirkeby** on Nov 01, 2011, when the stock traded at **$54.24**.

### Highlights

➤ We anticipate a 20% improvement in revenue during 2011, with acquisitions completed through September adding about 7 percentage points of the growth. Looking to 2012, our forecast is for another 13% improvement in revenues, with each of DOV's four segments contributing to the gain. We think the businesses serving the oil and gas industries face stronger prospects than DOV's units selling into the semiconductor and solar markets.

➤ We expect operating margins to improve in 2012 due to greater leverage from higher volumes and an improved product mix, much like in 2011. We also think the consolidation of certain business functions and cost rationalizations will help to offset rises in input costs. The effective tax rate we are using in our model for 2012 is 27%.

➤ Our EPS estimate for 2011 of $4.41 includes $0.17 per share in discrete tax benefits booked during the first nine months of the year.

### Investment Rationale/Risk

➤ We expect DOV, as a result of exiting over 20 low-margin, capital-intensive businesses over the past two years, and replacing them with what we see as steady-growth, higher-margin units, to drive both top- and bottom-line growth over the long term, and we think the company will produce rising free cash flow. In addition, we believe the company's procurement strategy is contributing to higher margins, as was evident in recent quarterly results and improving year-over-year margins. However, we think valuations near the historical average are warranted currently by broader economic uncertainties.

➤ Risks to our recommendation and target price include weaker-than-expected economic growth, reduced industrial activity, and potential value-diminishing acquisitions.

➤ Our 12-month target price of $72 is a blend of valuation metrics. Our discounted cash flow model, which assumes 3% perpetual growth and a 10.3% discount rate, indicates intrinsic value of $73. For our relative valuation, we apply an P/E multiple of 15.2X, which is the 10-year average, to our four-quarter forward EPS estimate, implying a value of $71.

### Qualitative Risk Assessment

| LOW | MEDIUM | HIGH |
|---|---|---|

Our risk assessment reflects the company's acquisition strategy, its model of operating numerous different businesses as stand-alone entities, its strategic shift to manage numerous aspects of the business using a more top-down approach, and exposure to several cyclical end markets.

### Quantitative Evaluations

**S&P Quality Ranking**  A

| D | C | B- | B | B+ | A- | A | A+ |
|---|---|---|---|---|---|---|---|

**Relative Strength Rank**  MODERATE
44
LOWEST = 1    HIGHEST = 99

### Revenue/Earnings Data

**Revenue (Million $)**

| | 1Q | 2Q | 3Q | 4Q | Year |
|---|---|---|---|---|---|
| 2011 | 1,959 | 2,157 | 2,203 | -- | -- |
| 2010 | 1,583 | 1,787 | 1,887 | 1,876 | 7,133 |
| 2009 | 1,379 | 1,390 | 1,500 | 1,507 | 5,776 |
| 2008 | 1,865 | 2,011 | 1,966 | 1,727 | 7,569 |
| 2007 | 1,780 | 1,859 | 1,844 | 1,860 | 7,226 |
| 2006 | 1,500 | 1,650 | 1,647 | 1,715 | 6,512 |

**Earnings Per Share ($)**

| | 1Q | 2Q | 3Q | 4Q | Year |
|---|---|---|---|---|---|
| 2011 | 0.96 | 1.31 | 1.21 | E0.98 | E4.41 |
| 2010 | 0.65 | 0.91 | 1.18 | 1.01 | 3.74 |
| 2009 | 0.33 | 0.54 | 0.58 | 0.55 | 1.99 |
| 2008 | 0.77 | 0.98 | 1.01 | 0.91 | 3.67 |
| 2007 | 0.67 | 0.85 | 0.88 | 0.86 | 3.22 |
| 2006 | 0.64 | 0.77 | 0.77 | 0.76 | 2.94 |

Fiscal year ended Dec. 31. Next earnings report expected: Late January. EPS Estimates based on S&P Operating Earnings; historical GAAP earnings are as reported.

### Dividend Data (Dates: mm/dd Payment Date: mm/dd/yy)

| Amount ($) | Date Decl. | Ex-Div. Date | Stk. of Record | Payment Date |
|---|---|---|---|---|
| 0.275 | 02/10 | 02/24 | 02/28 | 03/15/11 |
| 0.275 | 05/06 | 05/26 | 05/31 | 06/15/11 |
| 0.315 | 08/04 | 08/29 | 08/31 | 09/15/11 |
| 0.315 | 11/04 | 11/28 | 11/30 | 12/15/11 |

Dividends have been paid since 1947. Source: Company reports.

**Please read the Required Disclosures and Analyst Certification on the last page of this report.**

The **McGraw-Hill** Companies

# Dover Corp

**STANDARD &POOR'S**

## Business Summary November 01, 2011

CORPORATE OVERVIEW. Dover Corporation (DOV) is a diversified manufacturer of a broad range of specialized industrial products and manufacturing equipment. The company has evolved largely through acquisitions, with 91 deals costing approximately $4.4 billion completed between January 2000 and December 2010. The company operates through four operating segments: Industrial Products; Engineered Systems; Fluid Management; and Electronic Technologies.

Industrial Products (26% of 2010 sales; 19.4% of operating profit; with 12.3% operating margin) manufactures a diverse mix of equipment and components for use in the waste handling, bulk transport and automotive service industries. Its two sub-units are Material Handling and Mobile Equipment. Major units include Paladin, PDQ Manufacturing, Heil Environmental, Rotary Lift, Heil Trailer International, Chief Automotive, and Marathon Equipment. In 2010, segment orders increased nearly 30%, and the book-to-bill ratio was 1X.

Engineered Systems (31%; 25.9%; 13.5%) manufactures food equipment (refrigeration systems, display cases, walk-in coolers, etc.) and packaging machinery. It is composed of two primary sub-groups -- Product Identification and Engineered Products. The food equipment businesses (Hill Phoenix and Unified Brands) sell to the institutional and commercial foodservice markets. The packaging machinery businesses sell to the beverage and food processing industries. Orders in 2010 rose more than 25%, and the book-to-bill ratio was greater than 1X.

Fluid Management (23%; 33.3%; 23.7%) manufactures products primarily for the oil and gas, automotive fueling, fluid handling, engineered components, material handling and chemical equipment industries. This segment consists of two primary sub-units -- Energy and Fluid Solutions. The book-to-bill ratio in 2010 was 1X, as new orders gained nearly 32%.

Electronic Technologies (20%; 21.5%; 17.6%) manufactures an array of specialized electronic, electromechanical and plastic components for OEMs in multiple end markets, including hearing aids, telecom, micro-acoustics, speciality electronics, defense and aerospace electronics, and life sciences. It also supplies ATM hardware and software for retail applications and financial institutions, and chemical proportioning and dispensing systems for janitorial/ sanitation applications. In 2010, new orders increased 45%, and the book-to-bill ratio was 1.1X.

## Company Financials Fiscal Year Ended Dec. 31

| Per Share Data ($) | 2010 | 2009 | 2008 | 2007 | 2006 | 2005 | 2004 | 2003 | 2002 | 2001 |
|---|---|---|---|---|---|---|---|---|---|---|
| Tangible Book Value | 1.35 | NM | NM | NM | NM | NM | 2.16 | 2.71 | 2.66 | 1.97 |
| Cash Flow | 5.16 | 3.37 | 5.05 | 4.43 | 3.92 | 3.18 | 2.78 | 2.14 | 1.83 | 1.89 |
| Earnings | 3.74 | 1.99 | 3.67 | 3.22 | 2.94 | 2.32 | 2.00 | 1.40 | 1.04 | 0.82 |
| S&P Core Earnings | 3.79 | 2.00 | 3.55 | 3.28 | 2.98 | 2.25 | 1.92 | 1.31 | 0.90 | 0.68 |
| Dividends | 1.07 | 1.02 | 0.90 | 0.77 | 0.71 | 0.66 | 0.62 | 0.57 | 0.54 | 0.52 |
| Payout Ratio | 29% | 51% | 25% | 24% | 24% | 28% | 31% | 41% | 52% | 63% |
| Prices:High | 59.20 | 43.10 | 54.57 | 54.59 | 51.92 | 42.11 | 44.13 | 40.45 | 43.55 | 43.55 |
| Prices:Low | 40.50 | 21.79 | 23.39 | 44.34 | 40.30 | 34.11 | 35.12 | 22.85 | 23.54 | 26.40 |
| P/E Ratio:High | 16 | 22 | 15 | 17 | 18 | 18 | 22 | 29 | 42 | 53 |
| P/E Ratio:Low | 11 | 11 | 6 | 14 | 14 | 15 | 18 | 16 | 23 | 32 |

| Income Statement Analysis (Million $) | | | | | | | | | | |
|---|---|---|---|---|---|---|---|---|---|---|
| Revenue | 7,133 | 5,776 | 7,569 | 7,226 | 6,512 | 6,078 | 5,488 | 4,413 | 4,184 | 4,460 |
| Operating Income | 1,303 | 918 | 1,311 | 1,220 | 1,113 | 876 | 773 | 595 | 503 | 518 |
| Depreciation | 268 | 258 | 261 | 245 | 202 | 176 | 161 | 151 | 161 | 219 |
| Interest Expense | 106 | 116 | 96.0 | 89.0 | 77.0 | 72.2 | 61.3 | 62.2 | 70.0 | 91.2 |
| Pretax Income | 925 | 492 | 946 | 888 | 823 | 644 | 552 | 372 | 270 | 238 |
| Effective Tax Rate | NA | 24.4% | 26.6% | 26.4% | 26.7% | 26.3% | 25.9% | 23.3% | 21.7% | 30.0% |
| Net Income | 708 | 372 | 695 | 653 | 603 | 474 | 409 | 285 | 211 | 167 |
| S&P Core Earnings | 716 | 373 | 672 | 667 | 613 | 460 | 392 | 267 | 182 | 138 |

| Balance Sheet & Other Financial Data (Million $) | | | | | | | | | | |
|---|---|---|---|---|---|---|---|---|---|---|
| Cash | 1,309 | 938 | 827 | 602 | 374 | 191 | 358 | 370 | 295 | 177 |
| Current Assets | 3,262 | 2,523 | 2,614 | 2,544 | 2,272 | 1,976 | 2,150 | 1,850 | 1,658 | 1,655 |
| Total Assets | 8,563 | 7,808 | 7,867 | 8,070 | 7,627 | 6,573 | 5,792 | 5,134 | 4,437 | 4,602 |
| Current Liabilities | 1,042 | 969 | 1,238 | 1,681 | 1,434 | 1,207 | 1,356 | 911 | 697 | 819 |
| Long Term Debt | 1,791 | 1,825 | 1,861 | 1,452 | 1,480 | 1,344 | 753 | 1,004 | 1,030 | 1,033 |
| Common Equity | 4,527 | 4,084 | 3,793 | 3,946 | 3,811 | 3,330 | 3,119 | 2,743 | 2,395 | 2,520 |
| Total Capital | 6,319 | 5,944 | 5,968 | 5,714 | 5,656 | 5,046 | 4,168 | 3,980 | 3,561 | 3,656 |
| Capital Expenditures | 183 | 120 | 176 | 174 | 195 | 152 | 107 | 96.4 | 102 | 167 |
| Cash Flow | 976 | 630 | 956 | 898 | 805 | 650 | 570 | 437 | 372 | 386 |
| Current Ratio | 3.1 | 2.7 | 2.1 | 1.5 | 1.6 | 1.6 | 1.6 | 2.0 | 2.4 | 2.0 |
| % Long Term Debt of Capitalization | 28.3 | 30.7 | 31.2 | 25.4 | 26.2 | 26.6 | 18.1 | 25.2 | 28.9 | 28.3 |
| % Net Income of Revenue | 9.9 | 6.4 | 9.2 | 9.0 | 9.3 | 7.8 | 7.5 | 6.5 | 5.0 | 3.7 |
| % Return on Assets | 8.6 | 4.8 | 8.7 | 8.3 | 8.5 | 7.7 | 7.5 | 6.0 | 4.7 | 3.5 |
| % Return on Equity | 16.4 | 9.4 | 18.0 | 16.8 | 16.9 | 14.7 | 14.0 | 11.1 | 8.6 | 6.7 |

Data as orig reptd.; bef. results of disc opers/spec. items. Per share data adj. for stk. divs.; EPS diluted. E-Estimated. NA-Not Available. NM-Not Meaningful. NR-Not Ranked. UR-Under Review.

**Office:** 3005 Highland Parkway, Suite 200, Downers Grove, IL 60515.
**Telephone:** 630-541-1540.
**Website:** http://www.dovercorporation.com
**Chrmn:** R.W. Cremin

**Pres & CEO:** R.A. Livingston
**SVP & CFO:** B.M. Cerepak
**SVP, Secy & General Counsel:** J.W. Schmidt
**Chief Acctg Officer & Cntlr:** R.T. McKay, Jr.

**Investor Contact:** P.E. Goldberg (212-922-1640)
**Board Members:** D. H. Benson, R. W. Cremin, J. P. Ergas, P. T. Francis, K. C. Graham, R. A. Livingston, R. K. Lochridge, B. G. Rethore, M. B. Stubbs, S. M. Todd, S. K. Wagner, M. A. Winston

**Founded:** 1947
**Domicile:** Delaware
**Employees:** 32,000

# Dow Chemical Co (The)

| S&P Recommendation **BUY** ★★★★☆ | Price $24.47 (as of Nov 25, 2011) | 12-Mo. Target Price $39.00 | Investment Style Large-Cap Blend |
|---|---|---|---|

**GICS Sector** Materials
**Sub-Industry** Diversified Chemicals

**Summary** Dow Chemical, the largest U.S. chemical company, provides chemical, plastic, and agricultural products and services to many consumer markets.

## Key Stock Statistics (Source S&P, Vickers, company reports)

| | | | | | | | |
|---|---|---|---|---|---|---|---|
| 52-Wk Range | $42.23–20.61 | S&P Oper. EPS 2011**E** | 2.80 | Market Capitalization(B) | $28.919 | Beta | 2.31 |
| Trailing 12-Month EPS | $2.44 | S&P Oper. EPS 2012**E** | 3.09 | Yield (%) | 4.09 | S&P 3-Yr. Proj. EPS CAGR(%) | 15 |
| Trailing 12-Month P/E | 10.0 | P/E on S&P Oper. EPS 2011**E** | 8.7 | Dividend Rate/Share | $1.00 | S&P Credit Rating | BBB |
| $10K Invested 5 Yrs Ago | $7,371 | Common Shares Outstg. (M) | 1,181.8 | Institutional Ownership (%) | 69 | | |

## Price Performance

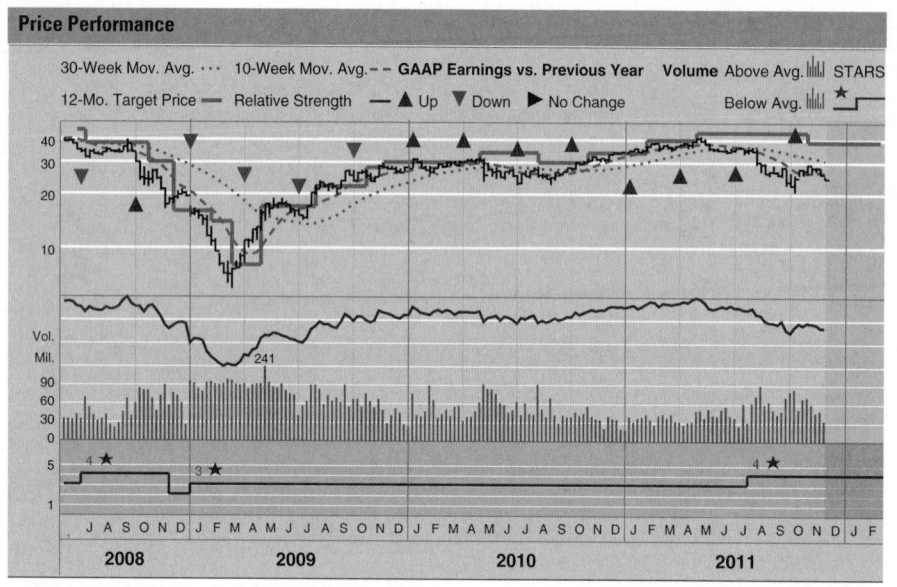

30-Week Mov. Avg. · · · 10-Week Mov. Avg. ‒ ‒ GAAP Earnings vs. Previous Year   Volume Above Avg. ▮▮▮ STARS
12-Mo. Target Price ‒ Relative Strength ‒ ▲ Up ▼ Down ► No Change   Below Avg. ▮▮▮ ★

Options: ASE, CBOE, P, Ph

### Qualitative Risk Assessment

| LOW | MEDIUM | HIGH |
|---|---|---|

Our risk assessment reflects our view of the highly leveraged post-merger balance sheet and integration risks and the cyclical nature of the commodity chemical industry, partly offset by Dow's diverse business and geographic sales mix and manufacturing integration.

### Quantitative Evaluations

**S&P Quality Ranking**  B

| D | C | B- | B | B+ | A- | A | A+ |
|---|---|---|---|---|---|---|---|

**Relative Strength Rank**  MODERATE

31

LOWEST = 1   HIGHEST = 99

### Revenue/Earnings Data

**Revenue (Million $)**

| | 1Q | 2Q | 3Q | 4Q | Year |
|---|---|---|---|---|---|
| 2011 | 14,733 | 16,046 | 15,109 | -- | -- |
| 2010 | 13,417 | 13,618 | 12,868 | 13,771 | 53,674 |
| 2009 | 9,041 | 11,322 | 12,046 | 12,466 | 44,875 |
| 2008 | 14,824 | 16,380 | 15,411 | 10,899 | 57,514 |
| 2007 | 12,432 | 13,265 | 13,589 | 14,227 | 53,513 |
| 2006 | 12,020 | 12,509 | 12,359 | 12,236 | 49,124 |

**Earnings Per Share ($)**

| | | | | | |
|---|---|---|---|---|---|
| 2011 | 0.54 | 0.84 | 0.69 | E0.51 | E2.80 |
| 2010 | 0.41 | 0.50 | 0.45 | 0.37 | 1.72 |
| 2009 | 0.03 | -0.57 | -0.64 | 0.08 | 0.22 |
| 2008 | 0.99 | 0.81 | 0.46 | -1.68 | 0.62 |
| 2007 | 1.00 | 1.07 | 0.24 | 0.49 | 2.99 |
| 2006 | 1.24 | 1.05 | 0.53 | 1.00 | 3.82 |

Fiscal year ended Dec. 31. Next earnings report expected: Early February. EPS Estimates based on S&P Operating Earnings; historical GAAP earnings are as reported.

## Highlights

➤ The 12-month target price for DOW has recently been changed to $39.00 from $44.00. The Highlights section of this Stock Report will be updated accordingly.

## Investment Rationale/Risk

➤ The Investment Rationale/Risk section of this Stock Report will be updated shortly. For the latest News story on DOW from MarketScope, see below.

➤ 10/27/11 05:49 pm ET ... S&P MAINTAINS BUY OPINION ON SHARES OF DOW CHEMICAL (DOW 29.1****): DOW posts Q3 operating EPS of $0.62, vs. operating EPS of $0.54, on a 17% sales rise, below our $0.68 estimate and the $0.64 Capital IQ consensus forecast. The shortfall occurred as higher than expected sales were offset by margin erosion. We cut our '11 estimate to $2.80 from $3.00 and reduce '12's estimate to $3.09 from $3.40 on more conservative margin assumptions. Based on the lower '12 estimate and concerns over global growth, we cut our 12-month target price to $39 from $44. We think DOW is attractive trading at 9.4X '12's estimate, with a dividend yield of 3.4%. /L. Larkin

### Dividend Data (Dates: mm/dd Payment Date: mm/dd/yy)

| Amount ($) | Date Decl. | Ex-Div. Date | Stk. of Record | Payment Date |
|---|---|---|---|---|
| 0.150 | 12/09 | 12/29 | 12/31 | 01/28/11 |
| 0.150 | 02/10 | 03/29 | 03/31 | 04/29/11 |
| 0.250 | 04/14 | 06/28 | 06/30 | 07/29/11 |
| 0.250 | 09/15 | 09/28 | 09/30 | 10/28/11 |

Dividends have been paid since 1911. Source: Company reports.

# Dow Chemical Co (The)

## Business Summary August 08, 2011

CORPORATE OVERVIEW. Dow Chemical is the largest U.S. chemical company. Foreign operations accounted for 67% of 2010 sales.

Electronic and specialty materials (9% of sales and 19% of profits in 2010) consists of photoresists, coatings, CMP slurries and pads, and plating products for electronics; water and process solutions (ion exchange resins, membranes); biocides; cellulosics; and home and personal care ingredients. The segment also includes results of the Dow Corning joint venture.

Coatings and infrastructure (10%, 8%) includes coatings materials (acrylics, opaque polymers, rheology modifiers, epoxy resins, surfactants, and solvents), building and construction products (insulation products (STYROFOAM), weather barrier products, foams, sealants, roofing adhesives, and POWER-HOUSE solar shingle), and adhesives and coatings.

Performance systems (13%, 10%) consists of automotive products (engineering plastics, adhesives, films, foams, and fluids); elastomers, resins, films, and plastic additives; polyolefins and flame retardants for wire and cable insulation; and polyurethanes foams and systems. Performance products (20%, 15%) consists of amines; epoxy resins and intermediates (phenol and acetone); glycols, surfactants, and fluids (lubricants, heat transfer, deicing, and coolants); polyurethanes (isocyanates, propylene oxide/glycol, polyols); solvents; acrylic acid, dispersants, and methyl methacrylate; and custom manufacturing.

Dow AgroSciences (9%, 7%) is a leading global maker of herbicides (Clincher, Starane), insecticides (Lorsban, Sentricon termite colony elimination system, Tracer) and fungicides for crop protection and industrial/commercial pest control. It also provides crop seeds (Mycogen), traits (Herculex) and value-added grains.

The company, a major producer of plastics (22%, 34%), is the world's largest producer of polyethylene; it also makes polypropylene and offers technology licensing (UNIPOL for polyethylene and polypropylene). In June 2010, Dow sold its polystyrene and polycarbonate and compounds businesses. Chemicals and energy (7%, 7%) includes chlor-alkali (chlorine, caustic soda, ethylene dichloride and vinyl chloride); chlorinated solvents; ethylene oxide/glycol, used primarily as raw materials in the manufacture of customer products; technology licensing (Meteor for ethylene oxide/glycol); and supplies power and steam. The hydrocarbons business (10%, nil) procures fuels and raw materials and produces ethylene, propylene, aromatics, and styrene.

## Company Financials Fiscal Year Ended Dec. 31

| Per Share Data ($) | 2010 | 2009 | 2008 | 2007 | 2006 | 2005 | 2004 | 2003 | 2002 | 2001 |
|---|---|---|---|---|---|---|---|---|---|---|
| Tangible Book Value | NM | NM | 10.05 | 17.00 | 14.50 | 12.14 | 9.01 | 5.79 | 4.19 | 7.59 |
| Cash Flow | 4.32 | 2.90 | 2.86 | 5.09 | 5.83 | 6.83 | 5.12 | 3.93 | 4.57 | 1.55 |
| Earnings | 1.72 | 0.22 | 0.62 | 2.99 | 3.82 | 4.64 | 2.93 | 1.88 | -0.44 | -0.46 |
| S&P Core Earnings | 1.78 | -0.28 | 0.05 | 2.82 | 3.73 | 4.04 | 2.34 | 1.58 | -1.41 | -1.43 |
| Dividends | 0.60 | 0.60 | 1.68 | 1.64 | 1.50 | 1.34 | 1.34 | 1.34 | 1.34 | 1.30 |
| Payout Ratio | 35% | NM | 271% | 55% | 39% | 29% | 46% | 71% | NM | NM |
| Prices:High | 34.50 | 29.50 | 43.42 | 47.96 | 45.15 | 56.75 | 51.34 | 42.00 | 37.00 | 39.67 |
| Prices:Low | 22.42 | 5.89 | 14.93 | 38.89 | 33.00 | 40.18 | 36.35 | 24.83 | 23.66 | 25.06 |
| P/E Ratio:High | 20 | NM | 70 | 16 | 12 | 12 | 18 | 22 | NM | NM |
| P/E Ratio:Low | 13 | NM | 24 | 13 | 9 | 9 | 12 | 13 | NM | NM |

| Income Statement Analysis (Million $) | | | | | | | | | | |
|---|---|---|---|---|---|---|---|---|---|---|
| Revenue | 53,674 | 44,875 | 57,514 | 53,513 | 49,124 | 46,307 | 40,161 | 32,632 | 27,609 | 27,805 |
| Operating Income | 6,109 | 4,443 | 4,482 | 5,903 | 6,675 | 7,437 | 5,466 | 3,922 | 2,925 | 2,953 |
| Depreciation | 2,962 | 2,827 | 2,108 | 2,031 | 1,954 | 2,134 | 2,088 | 1,903 | 1,825 | 1,815 |
| Interest Expense | 1,473 | 1,571 | 745 | 669 | 689 | 702 | 747 | 828 | 774 | 733 |
| Pretax Income | 2,802 | 469 | 1,321 | 4,229 | 4,972 | 6,399 | 3,796 | 1,751 | -622 | -613 |
| Effective Tax Rate | NA | NM | 50.5% | 29.4% | 23.2% | 27.8% | 23.1% | NM | NM | NM |
| Net Income | 2,321 | 538 | 579 | 2,887 | 3,724 | 4,535 | 2,797 | 1,739 | -405 | -417 |
| S&P Core Earnings | 2,024 | -312 | 29.0 | 2,734 | 3,638 | 3,956 | 2,236 | 1,462 | -1,295 | -1,303 |

| Balance Sheet & Other Financial Data (Million $) | | | | | | | | | | |
|---|---|---|---|---|---|---|---|---|---|---|
| Cash | 6,894 | 2,846 | 2,800 | 1,737 | 2,910 | 3,838 | 3,192 | 2,434 | 1,573 | 264 |
| Current Assets | 23,781 | 19,560 | 16,060 | 18,654 | 17,209 | 17,404 | 15,890 | 13,002 | 11,681 | 10,308 |
| Total Assets | 69,588 | 65,937 | 45,474 | 48,801 | 45,581 | 45,934 | 45,885 | 41,891 | 39,562 | 35,515 |
| Current Liabilities | 13,896 | 13,106 | 13,108 | 12,445 | 10,601 | 10,663 | 10,506 | 9,534 | 8,856 | 8,125 |
| Long Term Debt | 20,605 | 19,152 | 8,042 | 7,581 | 8,036 | 10,186 | 12,629 | 12,763 | 12,659 | 10,266 |
| Common Equity | 17,839 | 16,555 | 13,511 | 19,389 | 17,065 | 15,324 | 12,270 | 9,175 | 7,626 | 9,993 |
| Total Capital | 45,805 | 41,358 | 22,868 | 29,238 | 27,465 | 27,241 | 26,649 | 23,438 | 21,645 | 21,376 |
| Capital Expenditures | 2,175 | 2,396 | 2,339 | 2,075 | 1,775 | 1,597 | 1,333 | 1,100 | 1,623 | 1,587 |
| Cash Flow | 4,943 | 3,053 | 2,687 | 4,918 | 5,678 | 6,669 | 4,885 | 3,642 | 1,420 | 1,398 |
| Current Ratio | 1.7 | 1.5 | 1.2 | 1.5 | 1.6 | 1.6 | 1.5 | 1.4 | 1.3 | 1.3 |
| % Long Term Debt of Capitalization | 45.0 | 46.3 | 35.2 | 25.9 | 30.4 | 37.4 | 47.4 | 54.5 | 58.5 | 48.0 |
| % Net Income of Revenue | 4.3 | 1.2 | 1.0 | 5.4 | 7.6 | 9.8 | 7.0 | 5.3 | NM | NM |
| % Return on Assets | 3.4 | 1.0 | 1.2 | 6.1 | 8.1 | 9.9 | 6.4 | 4.3 | NM | NM |
| % Return on Equity | 13.5 | 3.6 | 3.5 | 15.8 | 23.0 | 32.9 | 26.1 | 20.7 | NM | NM |

Data as orig reptd.; bef. results of disc opers/spec. items. Per share data adj. for stk. divs.; EPS diluted. E-Estimated. NA-Not Available. NM-Not Meaningful. NR-Not Ranked. UR-Under Review.

**Office:** 2030 Dow Center, Midland, MI 48674.
**Telephone:** 989-636-1000.
**Website:** http://www.dow.com
**Chrmn, Pres & CEO:** A.N. Liveris

**COO:** N. Parakh
**EVP & CFO:** W.H. Weideman
**Investor Contact:** H. Ungerleider (989-636-1463)
**CTO:** W.F. Banholzer

**Board Members:** A. A. Allemang, J. K. Barton, J. A. Bell, J. M. Fettig, B. H. Franklin, J. B. Hess, A. N. Liveris, P. Polman, D. H. Reilley, J. M. Ringler, R. G. Shaw, P. G. Stern

**Founded:** 1897
**Domicile:** Delaware
**Employees:** 49,505

# D.R. Horton Inc.

**STANDARD &POOR'S**

| S&P Recommendation | HOLD ★★★★★ | Price $10.86 (as of Nov 25, 2011) | 12-Mo. Target Price $12.00 | Investment Style Large-Cap Blend |
| --- | --- | --- | --- | --- |

**GICS Sector** Consumer Discretionary
**Sub-Industry** Homebuilding

**Summary** This company is one of the largest homebuilders in the U.S., based on number of homes sold and its nationwide presence.

## Key Stock Statistics (Source S&P, Vickers, company reports)

| | | | | | | | |
| --- | --- | --- | --- | --- | --- | --- | --- |
| 52-Wk Range | $13.50– 8.03 | S&P Oper. EPS 2012**E** | 0.50 | Market Capitalization(B) | $3.432 | Beta | 1.02 |
| Trailing 12-Month EPS | $0.23 | S&P Oper. EPS 2013**E** | 0.75 | Yield (%) | 1.38 | S&P 3-Yr. Proj. EPS CAGR(%) | 13 |
| Trailing 12-Month P/E | 47.2 | P/E on S&P Oper. EPS 2012**E** | 21.7 | Dividend Rate/Share | $0.15 | S&P Credit Rating | BB- |
| $10K Invested 5 Yrs Ago | $4,689 | Common Shares Outstg. (M) | 316.1 | Institutional Ownership (%) | 86 | | |

## Price Performance

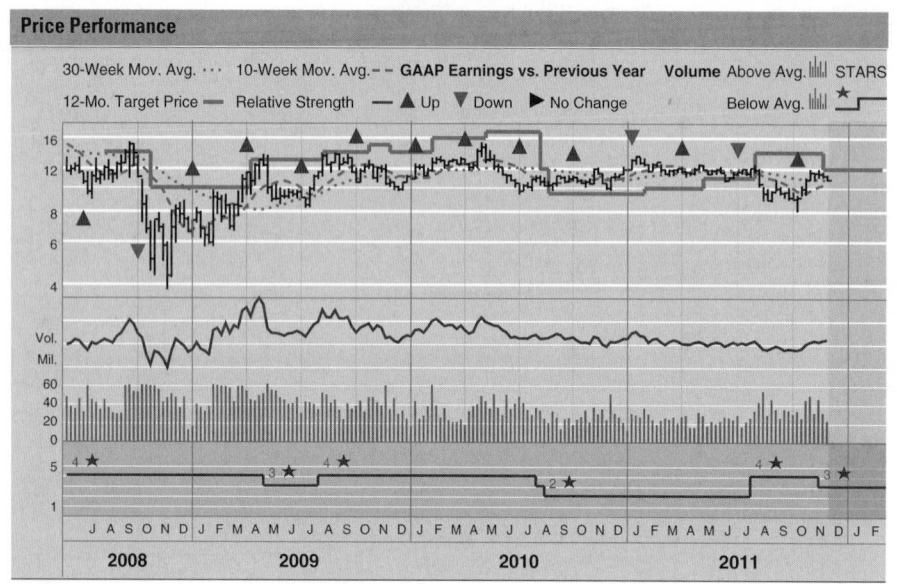

30-Week Mov. Avg. · · ·   10-Week Mov. Avg. - -   **GAAP Earnings vs. Previous Year**   **Volume** Above Avg. ⅄⅄⅄ STARS
12-Mo. Target Price —   Relative Strength · · ·   ▲ Up   ▼ Down   ▶ No Change   Below Avg. ⅄⅄⅄ ★

2008    2009    2010    2011

Options: ASE, CBOE, P, Ph

Analysis prepared by Equity Analyst **Kenneth Leon, CPA** on Nov 16, 2011, when the stock traded at **$11.66.**

## Qualitative Risk Assessment

| LOW | MEDIUM | HIGH |
| --- | --- | --- |

Our risk assessment reflects DHI's exposure to an extended downturn in the housing market, partly offset by its focus on reducing debt with free cash flow from operations. As the second largest U.S. homebuilder, DHI has scale advantages to reduce labor and material costs, but a slow recovery in the housing market may restrict earnings and cash flow.

## Quantitative Evaluations

**S&P Quality Ranking**     B

| D | C | B- | B | B+ | A- | A | A+ |
| --- | --- | --- | --- | --- | --- | --- | --- |

**Relative Strength Rank**     **STRONG**

84

LOWEST = 1                                      HIGHEST = 99

## Highlights

➤ Following a 20% sales decrease in FY 11 (Sep.), we forecast 10% growth in both FY 12 and FY 13, assuming an expected modest housing recovery. DHI suffered a 23% drop in its contract backlog in FY 10, to $850 million, and backlog declined further to $795 million at the end of the FY 11 first quarter, before recovering to $1 billion at the end of FY 11.

➤ We think net new orders and contract backlog will show seasonal weakness in the first two quarters of FY 12 before improving. In our view, demand for new homes will benefit from record affordability of new homes, more stable employment levels, and low mortgage rates for households that qualify. We believe DHI can maintain gross margins in the 17% to 18% range in FY 12 and FY 13 with added cost controls, compared to 16.7% in FY 11. DHI realized peak gross margins of 24% in FY 06.

➤ We believe SG&A costs will decline as a percentage of total revenues as sales volumes increase. Following operating EPS of $0.23 in FY 11, we forecast operating EPS of $0.50 for FY 12 and $0.75 for FY 13.

## Investment Rationale/Risk

➤ DHI is one of the largest U.S. homebuilders, and we see low mortgage rates raising affordability in its target market for first-time buyers. With a balance sheet we view as strong ($1.0 billion in cash), we believe the company can be opportunistic in reducing debt and making select new land acquisitions to expand new home communities. While we assume higher community count in FY 12, DHI maintains conservative business practices in how it competes and uses capital.

➤ Risks to our recommendation and target price include the possibility of a further weakening economy and weaker employment data. A decrease in demand from first-time homebuyers would hurt the company more than many peers since it concentrates primarily on this category.

➤ Our 12-month target price of $12 reflects a narrower risk premium on a target price-to-book multiple just above 1.4X applied to our forward book value estimate of $8.30. Our target multiple is near the middle of the historical range for DHI and near most peers, supported by its strong cash position and operating scale advantages, as well as sales growth expected in FY 12.

## Revenue/Earnings Data

**Revenue (Million $)**

| | 1Q | 2Q | 3Q | 4Q | Year |
| --- | --- | --- | --- | --- | --- |
| 2011 | 788.2 | 751.1 | 999.2 | 1,098 | 3,637 |
| 2010 | 1,132 | 913.5 | 1,406 | 948.4 | 4,400 |
| 2009 | 918.0 | 778.0 | 932.9 | 1,029 | 3,658 |
| 2008 | 1,708 | 1,624 | 1,464 | 1,782 | 6,646 |
| 2007 | 3,172 | 2,598 | 2,658 | 2,868 | 11,297 |
| 2006 | 2,903 | 3,598 | 3,668 | 4,883 | 15,051 |

**Earnings Per Share ($)**

| | | | | | |
| --- | --- | --- | --- | --- | --- |
| 2011 | -0.06 | 0.09 | 0.09 | 0.11 | 0.23 |
| 2010 | 0.56 | 0.04 | 0.16 | -0.03 | 0.77 |
| 2009 | -0.20 | -0.34 | -0.45 | -0.73 | -1.72 |
| 2008 | -0.41 | -4.14 | -1.26 | -2.53 | -8.34 |
| 2007 | 0.35 | 0.16 | -2.62 | -0.16 | -2.27 |
| 2006 | 0.98 | 1.11 | 0.93 | 0.88 | 3.90 |

Fiscal year ended Sep. 30. Next earnings report expected: NA. EPS Estimates based on S&P Operating Earnings; historical GAAP earnings are as reported.

## Dividend Data (Dates: mm/dd Payment Date: mm/dd/yy)

| Amount ($) | Date Decl. | Ex-Div. Date | Stk. of Record | Payment Date |
| --- | --- | --- | --- | --- |
| 0.038 | 01/27 | 02/08 | 02/10 | 02/18/11 |
| 0.038 | 04/29 | 05/10 | 05/12 | 05/24/11 |
| 0.038 | 07/28 | 08/10 | 08/12 | 08/24/11 |
| 0.038 | 11/11 | 11/30 | 12/02 | 12/13/11 |

Dividends have been paid since 1997. Source: Company reports.

**Please read the Required Disclosures and Analyst Certification on the last page of this report.**

The McGraw·Hill Companies

# D.R. Horton Inc.

**STANDARD & POOR'S**

## Business Summary November 16, 2011

**CORPORATE OVERVIEW.** D.R. Horton was founded in 1978 by Donald Horton, now chairman. In 1992, it went public to gain broader access to capital markets, which has helped fuel its subsequent growth beyond its base in the Dallas/Fort Worth area. With operating divisions in 25 states and 73 markets, D.R. Horton is the second largest domestic homebuilder by number of homes closed in FY 11, and the most geographically diversified.

The company was the first U.S. builder to sell 50,000 homes in a single year (FY 05), and it aims to be the first to eclipse the 100,000 unit mark, although market conditions may have pushed back that target for a few years, in our opinion. By emphasizing entry level and first-time move-up buyers, it targets the broadest segments of the population. In FY 11, DHI closed on 16,695 homes with a contract value of approximately $3.5 billion, compared to $4.3 billion in FY 10. DHI's homes are among the most affordable of all public builders.

**CORPORATE STRATEGY.** Most of D.R. Horton's growth in the past 15 to 20 years has been the result of organic initiatives, in our opinion. Generally, the company has established satellite operations in new markets located in rela-

tively close proximity to existing markets. We think the company has been successful at quickly ramping up volumes in these satellite operations -- often at the expense of smaller competitors -- aided by materials purchasing agreements struck at the regional level and relatively favorable access to capital markets.

Complementing this organic growth has been an aggressive takeover program, with close to 20 acquisitions since DHI went public. Most of these deals have occurred in new markets in an effort to either create a platform for future growth in a locale or to expand an existing satellite operation there. The majority of these acquisitions have been focused on a single market and have been asset-based transactions, rather than purchases of companies. However, in 2002, DHI bought Schuler Homes for about $1.8 billion, in a deal that increased its revenue base about 25%.

## Company Financials Fiscal Year Ended Sep. 30

| Per Share Data ($) | 2011 | 2010 | 2009 | 2008 | 2007 | 2006 | 2005 | 2004 | 2003 | 2002 |
|---|---|---|---|---|---|---|---|---|---|---|
| Tangible Book Value | 8.24 | 8.15 | 7.07 | 8.90 | 17.64 | 18.75 | 15.28 | 10.87 | 7.93 | 5.77 |
| Cash Flow | 0.29 | 0.82 | -1.64 | -8.17 | -2.06 | 4.10 | 4.87 | 3.24 | 2.16 | 1.54 |
| Earnings | 0.23 | 0.77 | -1.72 | -8.34 | -2.27 | 3.90 | 4.62 | 3.08 | 2.05 | 1.44 |
| S&P Core Earnings | 0.23 | 0.77 | -1.72 | -8.18 | -1.29 | 3.90 | 4.61 | 3.07 | 2.04 | 1.44 |
| Dividends | 0.15 | 0.15 | 0.15 | 0.33 | 0.60 | 0.44 | 0.31 | 0.22 | 0.14 | 0.10 |
| Payout Ratio | 65% | 19% | NM | NM | NM | 11% | 7% | 7% | 7% | 7% |
| Prices:High | 13.50 | 15.44 | 13.90 | 17.95 | 31.13 | 41.66 | 42.82 | 31.41 | 22.69 | 14.58 |
| Prices:Low | 8.03 | 9.41 | 5.72 | 3.79 | 10.15 | 19.52 | 26.83 | 18.47 | 8.48 | 8.02 |
| P/E Ratio:High | 59 | 20 | NM | NM | NM | 11 | 9 | 10 | 11 | 10 |
| P/E Ratio:Low | 35 | 12 | NM | NM | NM | 5 | 6 | 6 | 4 | 6 |

| Income Statement Analysis (Million $) | | | | | | | | | | |
|---|---|---|---|---|---|---|---|---|---|---|
| Revenue | 3,637 | 4,400 | 3,658 | 6,646 | 11,297 | 15,051 | 13,864 | 10,841 | 8,728 | 6,739 |
| Operating Income | 131 | 263 | -457 | -2,474 | -420 | 2,036 | 2,402 | 1,430 | 1,049 | 693 |
| Depreciation | 19.9 | 17.2 | 25.7 | 53.2 | 64.4 | 61.7 | 52.8 | 49.6 | 41.8 | 32.8 |
| Interest Expense | 50.5 | 86.3 | 198 | 240 | 328 | 55.0 | 21.2 | 9.30 | 12.6 | 11.5 |
| Pretax Income | 12.1 | 99.5 | -552 | -2,632 | -951 | 1,987 | 2,379 | 1,583 | 1,008 | 648 |
| Effective Tax Rate | NA | NA | NM | NM | 25.1% | 37.9% | 38.2% | 38.4% | 37.9% | 37.5% |
| Net Income | 71.8 | 245 | -545 | -2,634 | -712 | 1,233 | 1,471 | 975 | 626 | 405 |
| S&P Core Earnings | 71.7 | 245 | -545 | -2,582 | -404 | 1,233 | 1,463 | 969 | 622 | 406 |

| Balance Sheet & Other Financial Data (Million $) | | | | | | | | | | |
|---|---|---|---|---|---|---|---|---|---|---|
| Cash | 1,013 | 1,580 | 1,923 | 1,356 | 275 | 588 | 1,150 | 518 | 583 | 104 |
| Current Assets | 4,836 | 5,380 | 6,517 | 7,101 | 10,137 | 13,202 | 10,995 | 7,709 | 6,151 | 4,912 |
| Total Assets | 5,358 | 5,939 | 6,757 | 7,710 | 11,556 | 14,821 | 12,515 | 8,985 | 7,279 | 6,018 |
| Current Liabilities | 1,147 | 1,230 | 823 | 1,510 | 2,127 | 3,591 | 3,288 | 1,627 | 1,297 | 1,091 |
| Long Term Debt | 1,588 | 2,085 | 2,969 | 2,968 | 3,746 | 4,861 | 3,660 | 3,032 | 2,665 | 2,636 |
| Common Equity | 2,621 | 2,613 | 2,260 | 2,834 | 5,587 | 6,453 | 5,360 | 3,961 | 3,031 | 2,270 |
| Total Capital | 4,215 | 4,708 | 5,477 | 6,410 | 9,644 | 11,419 | 9,224 | 7,159 | 5,832 | 4,927 |
| Capital Expenditures | 16.3 | 19.2 | 6.20 | 6.60 | 39.8 | 83.3 | 68.2 | 55.2 | 48.7 | 39.8 |
| Cash Flow | 91.7 | 262 | -520 | -2,580 | -648 | 1,295 | 1,523 | 1,025 | 668 | 437 |
| Current Ratio | 4.2 | 4.4 | 7.9 | 4.7 | 4.8 | 3.7 | 3.3 | 4.7 | 4.7 | 4.5 |
| % Long Term Debt of Capitalization | 37.7 | 44.3 | 54.2 | 46.3 | 39.1 | 42.6 | 39.7 | 42.4 | 45.7 | 53.5 |
| % Net Income of Revenue | 2.0 | 5.6 | NM | NM | NM | 8.2 | 10.6 | 8.9 | 7.2 | 6.0 |
| % Return on Assets | 1.3 | 3.9 | NM | NM | NM | 9.0 | 13.7 | 12.0 | 9.4 | 8.4 |
| % Return on Equity | 2.7 | 10.1 | NM | NM | NM | 20.9 | 31.5 | 27.9 | 23.6 | 23.0 |

Data as orig reptd.; bef. results of disc opers/spec. items. Per share data adj. for stk. divs.; EPS diluted. E-Estimated. NA-Not Available. NM-Not Meaningful. NR-Not Ranked. UR-Under Review.

**Office:** 301 Commerce St Ste 500, Fort Worth, TX 76102-4178.
**Telephone:** 817-390-8200.
**Website:** http://www.drhorton.com
**Chrmn:** D.R. Horton

**Pres, Vice Chrmn & CEO:** D.J. Tomnitz
**EVP, CFO & Chief Acctg Officer:** B.W. Wheat
**Investor Contact:** S.H. Dwyer (817-390-8200)
**EVP & Treas:** S.H. Dwyer

**Board Members:** B. S. Anderson, M. R. Buchanan, M. W. Hewatt, D. R. Horton, B. G. Scott, D. J. Tomnitz, B. W. Wheat

**Founded:** 1978
**Domicile:** Delaware
**Employees:** 3,010

**The McGraw-Hill Companies**

# Dr Pepper Snapple Group Inc

**STANDARD &POOR'S**

| S&P Recommendation | HOLD ★★★★★ | Price $36.53 (as of Nov 30, 2011) | 12-Mo. Target Price $40.00 | Investment Style Large-Cap Growth |
|---|---|---|---|---|

**GICS Sector** Consumer Staples
**Sub-Industry** Soft Drinks

**Summary** Spun off from Cadbury Schweppes in May 2008, DPS is the third largest marketer, bottler and distributor of non-alcoholic beverages in North America.

## Key Stock Statistics (Source S&P, Vickers, company reports)

| | | | | | |
|---|---|---|---|---|---|
| 52-Wk Range | $43.13– 33.68 | S&P Oper. EPS 2011**E** | 2.71 | Market Capitalization(B) | $7.831 |
| Trailing 12-Month EPS | $2.46 | S&P Oper. EPS 2012**E** | 2.84 | Yield (%) | 3.50 |
| Trailing 12-Month P/E | 14.9 | P/E on S&P Oper. EPS 2011**E** | 13.5 | Dividend Rate/Share | $1.28 |
| $10K Invested 5 Yrs Ago | NA | Common Shares Outstg. (M) | 214.4 | Institutional Ownership (%) | 98 |

| | |
|---|---|
| Beta | 0.86 |
| S&P 3-Yr. Proj. EPS CAGR(%) | 8 |
| S&P Credit Rating | BBB |

## Price Performance

30-Week Mov. Avg. · · · 10-Week Mov. Avg. – – GAAP Earnings vs. Previous Year   Volume Above Avg. STARS
12-Mo. Target Price — Relative Strength   ▲ Up  ▼ Down  ▶ No Change   Below Avg.

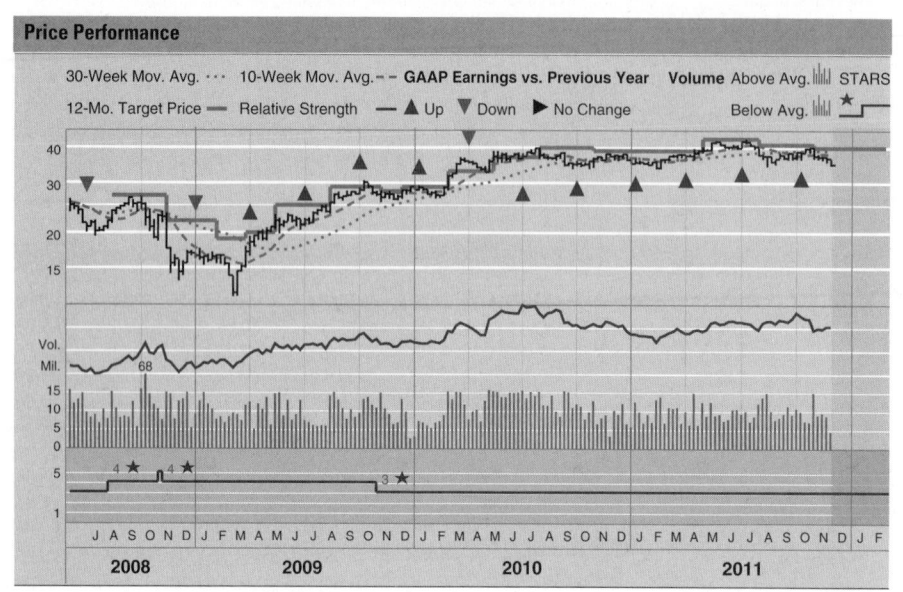

Options: CBOE, P, Ph

Analysis prepared by Equity Analyst **Esther Kwon, CFA** on Oct 27, 2011, when the stock traded at **$37.20**.

## Highlights

> In 2011, we see revenues rising over 4%, to approximately $5.9 billion, on modest price increases and flat to slightly higher volume, paced by flavored carbonated soft drink share gains. We think growth will continue to be driven by single-serve wins in fountain and continued expansion of the cold drink program. For 2012, we forecast revenue growth of 3%.

> We project operating margin contraction in 2011, as higher raw material and fuel costs are only partially offset by a full year's inclusion of Coca-Cola's $715 million payment (25-year amortization), which commenced in the third quarter of 2010; efficiencies at its Victorville, CA facility; and a full year's inclusion of PepsiCo's $900 million payment (also a 25-year amortization), which began in the back half of the first quarter of 2010. We see packaging and ingredient costs rising 9%, partially offset by net price increases of 2% to 3%.

> On fewer shares outstanding and a lower effective tax rate of approximately 35% due to initial treatment of the PepsiCo and Coca-Cola payments, we estimate 2011 EPS of $2.71, up from 2010 operating EPS of $2.40. For 2012, we forecast EPS of $2.84.

## Investment Rationale/Risk

> Excluding recognition of the Coca-Cola Co. payment, we think DPS could have more limited margin expansion in the near term as commodity costs rise and higher oil prices likely squeeze bottling operation profits. In addition, while we still expect DPS's flavored carbonated brands to outperform the industry, we think the rollout of Sun Drop could fall short of the impressive performance of the Crush brand, which boosted results over the past two years. We expect a less robust recovery overall due to what we see as a weaker portfolio of non-carbonated brands compared to beverage peers.

> Risks to our recommendation and target price include more rapid commodity cost inflation than expected, consumer reluctance to accept new products, and unfavorable weather conditions in the company's markets.

> Our 12-month target price of $40 is derived from our peer multiple analysis. We apply a multiple of 14X to our 2012 EPS estimate of $2.84, a discount to our blended peer average multiple of bottling and concentrate companies. We think a discount is appropriate considering the company's market position and greater reliance on bottling operations.

## Qualitative Risk Assessment

| LOW | MEDIUM | HIGH |
|---|---|---|

Our risk assessment for Dr Pepper Snapple Group reflects our view of the relatively stable nature of the company's end markets and its strong cash flow generation ability.

## Quantitative Evaluations

**S&P Quality Ranking** NR

| D | C | B- | B | B+ | A- | A | A+ |
|---|---|---|---|---|---|---|---|

**Relative Strength Rank** MODERATE

44

LOWEST = 1   HIGHEST = 99

## Revenue/Earnings Data

**Revenue (Million $)**

| | 1Q | 2Q | 3Q | 4Q | Year |
|---|---|---|---|---|---|
| 2011 | 1,331 | 1,582 | 1,529 | -- | -- |
| 2010 | 1,248 | 1,519 | 1,457 | 1,412 | 5,636 |
| 2009 | 1,260 | 1,481 | 1,434 | 1,356 | 5,531 |
| 2008 | 1,295 | 1,545 | 1,494 | 1,376 | 5,710 |
| 2007 | 1,269 | 1,543 | 1,535 | 1,401 | 5,748 |
| 2006 | 990.0 | 990.0 | 1,378 | 1,378 | 4,735 |

**Earnings Per Share ($)**

| | | | | | |
|---|---|---|---|---|---|
| 2011 | 0.50 | 0.77 | 0.71 | E0.74 | E2.71 |
| 2010 | 0.35 | 0.74 | 0.60 | 0.49 | 2.17 |
| 2009 | 0.52 | 0.62 | 0.59 | 0.45 | 2.18 |
| 2008 | 0.38 | 0.42 | 0.41 | -2.44 | -1.23 |
| 2007 | -- | 0.54 | -- | 0.54 | 1.79 |
| 2006 | -- | -- | -- | -- | -- |

Fiscal year ended Dec. 31. Next earnings report expected: Mid February. EPS Estimates based on S&P Operating Earnings; historical GAAP earnings are as reported.

## Dividend Data (Dates: mm/dd Payment Date: mm/dd/yy)

| Amount ($) | Date Decl. | Ex-Div. Date | Stk. of Record | Payment Date |
|---|---|---|---|---|
| 0.250 | 02/10 | 03/17 | 03/21 | 04/08/11 |
| 0.320 | 05/18 | 06/16 | 06/20 | 07/08/11 |
| 0.320 | 08/11 | 09/15 | 09/19 | 10/07/11 |
| 0.320 | 11/17 | 12/15 | 12/19 | 01/06/12 |

Dividends have been paid since 2010. Source: Company reports.

**Please read the Required Disclosures and Analyst Certification on the last page of this report.**

*The McGraw-Hill Companies*

# Dr Pepper Snapple Group Inc

**STANDARD &POOR'S**

## Business Summary October 27, 2011

CORPORATE OVERVIEW. Dr Pepper Snapple Group is the third largest marketer, bottler and distributor of non-alcoholic beverages in North America and the leading flavored carbonated soft drink (CSD) company in the United States. Its CSD brands include Dr Pepper, 7UP, Sunkist, A&W, Canada Dry, Crush, Schweppes, Squirt and Penafiel. DPS's non-CSD brands include Snapple, Mott's, Hawaiian Punch and Clamato. The company also distributes FIJI mineral water and AriZona tea. A small portion of bottling group sales comes from fees paid by private label owners and others for bottling beverages and other products, with 87% of manufactured volumes related to company brands and the remainder to third-party and private-label products. Some 71% of Dr Pepper volumes are distributed through PepsiCo and Coca-Cola bottlers affiliated with PepsiCo Inc. and Coca-Cola Co., the two largest customers of the beverage concentrates segment, accounting for 30% and 21%, respectively, of net sales of that segment in 2010.

The company has three main operating segments: beverage concentrates (20.5% of 2010 sales, with an operating profit margin of 64.4%), packaged beverages (72.7% of sales, with a 13.1% operating margin), and Latin America beverages (6.8%, with a 10.5% operating margin).

In 2010, DPS generated 89% of its sales in the United States, 4% in Canada, and 7% in Mexico and the Caribbean.

CORPORATE STRATEGY. DPS's growth strategies include leveraging key brands through line extensions, such as launching Snapple super premium teas and antioxidant waters with functional benefits through its Snapple line. DPS is also targeting opportunities in high-growth and high-margin categories, including ready-to-drink teas, energy drinks and other functional beverages, and plans to increase its presence in higher-margin channels and packages. These channels include convenience stores, vending machines and small independent retail outlets, most often offering higher-margin single-serve packages. With the lackluster economy and continuing high unemployment, however, Standard & Poor's remains cautious on this segment, which is particularly sensitive to changes in discretionary income. The company may also selectively enter into distribution agreements for high-growth, third-party brands that can use DPS's bottling and distribution network.

## Company Financials Fiscal Year Ended Dec. 31

| Per Share Data ($) | 2010 | 2009 | 2008 | 2007 | 2006 | 2005 | 2004 | 2003 | 2002 | 2001 |
|---|---|---|---|---|---|---|---|---|---|---|
| Tangible Book Value | NM | NM | NM | NM | NA | NA | NA | NA | NA | NA |
| Cash Flow | 3.10 | 2.92 | -0.56 | 2.19 | NA | NA | NA | NA | NA | NA |
| Earnings | 2.17 | 2.18 | -1.23 | 1.79 | NA | NA | NA | NA | NA | NA |
| S&P Core Earnings | 2.17 | 2.15 | 1.51 | 1.76 | 1.92 | NA | NA | NA | NA | NA |
| Dividends | 0.90 | 0.15 | Nil | NA | NA | NA | NA | NA | NA | NA |
| Payout Ratio | 42% | 7% | Nil | NA | NA | NA | NA | NA | NA | NA |
| Prices:High | 40.24 | 30.65 | 30.00 | NA | NA | NA | NA | NA | NA | NA |
| Prices:Low | 26.38 | 11.83 | 13.45 | NA | NA | NA | NA | NA | NA | NA |
| P/E Ratio:High | 19 | 14 | NM | NA | NA | NA | NA | NA | NA | NA |
| P/E Ratio:Low | 12 | 5 | NM | NA | NA | NA | NA | NA | NA | NA |

| Income Statement Analysis (Million $) | 2010 | 2009 | 2008 | 2007 | 2006 | 2005 | 2004 | 2003 | 2002 | 2001 |
|---|---|---|---|---|---|---|---|---|---|---|
| Revenue | 5,636 | 5,531 | 5,710 | 5,748 | 4,735 | 3,205 | 3,065 | NA | NA | NA |
| Operating Income | 1,248 | 1,235 | 1,134 | 1,113 | 1,152 | 959 | 953 | NA | NA | NA |
| Depreciation | 223 | 207 | 169 | 100 | 139 | 79.0 | 84.0 | NA | NA | NA |
| Interest Expense | 128 | 243 | 241 | 250 | 257 | 210 | 177 | NA | NA | NA |
| Pretax Income | 822 | 870 | -373 | 774 | 808 | 808 | 716 | NA | NA | NA |
| Effective Tax Rate | NA | 36.2% | NM | 41.2% | 36.9% | 39.7% | 37.7% | NA | NA | NA |
| Net Income | 528 | 555 | -312 | 455 | 510 | 487 | 446 | NA | NA | NA |
| S&P Core Earnings | 527 | 549 | 385 | 446 | 487 | NA | NA | NA | NA | NA |

| Balance Sheet & Other Financial Data (Million $) | 2010 | 2009 | 2008 | 2007 | 2006 | 2005 | 2004 | 2003 | 2002 | 2001 |
|---|---|---|---|---|---|---|---|---|---|---|
| Cash | 315 | 280 | 214 | 100 | 35.0 | 28.0 | NA | NA | NA | NA |
| Current Assets | 1,309 | 1,279 | 1,237 | 1,179 | 1,632 | 1,331 | NA | NA | NA | NA |
| Total Assets | 8,859 | 8,776 | 8,638 | 9,598 | 9,346 | 7,433 | NA | NA | NA | NA |
| Current Liabilities | 1,338 | 854 | 801 | 2,764 | 1,691 | 1,136 | NA | NA | NA | NA |
| Long Term Debt | 1,687 | 2,960 | 3,505 | 1,999 | 3,084 | 2,858 | NA | NA | NA | NA |
| Common Equity | 2,459 | 3,187 | 2,607 | 2,922 | 3,250 | 2,426 | NA | NA | NA | NA |
| Total Capital | 4,550 | 6,147 | 6,112 | 6,245 | 7,042 | 5,688 | NA | NA | NA | NA |
| Capital Expenditures | 246 | 317 | 304 | 230 | 158 | 44.0 | 71.0 | NA | NA | NA |
| Cash Flow | 751 | 744 | -143 | 555 | 649 | 566 | 530 | NA | NA | NA |
| Current Ratio | 1.0 | 1.5 | 1.5 | 0.4 | 1.0 | 1.2 | NA | NA | NA | NA |
| % Long Term Debt of Capitalization | 37.1 | 48.2 | 57.3 | 32.0 | 43.8 | 50.3 | Nil | NA | NA | NA |
| % Net Income of Revenue | 9.4 | 10.0 | NM | 7.9 | 10.8 | 15.2 | 14.6 | NA | NA | NA |
| % Return on Assets | 6.0 | 6.4 | NM | NA | 6.1 | NA | NA | NA | NA | NA |
| % Return on Equity | 18.7 | 19.2 | NM | NA | 18.0 | NA | NA | NA | NA | NA |

Data as orig reptd.; bef. results of disc opers/spec. items. Per share data adj. for stk. divs.; EPS diluted. Pro forma data in 2007. E-Estimated. NA-Not Available. NM-Not Meaningful. NR-Not Ranked. UR-Under Review.

**Office:** 5301 Legacy Drive, Plano, TX 75024.
**Telephone:** 972-673-7000.
**Website:** http://www.drpeppersnapplegroup.com
**Chrmn:** W.R. Sanders

**Pres & CEO:** L.D. Young
**EVP & CFO:** M.M. Ellen
**EVP, Secy & General Counsel:** J.L. Baldwin, Jr.
**SVP, Chief Acctg Officer & Cntlr:** A.A. Stephens

**Investor Contact:** A. Noormohamed (972-673-6050)
**Board Members:** J. L. Adams, D. E. Alexander, T. D. Martin, P. H. Patsley, J. M. Roche, R. G. Rogers, W. R. Sanders, J. L. Stahl, M. A. Szostak, M. F. Weinstein, L. D. Young

**Founded:** 2007
**Domicile:** Delaware
**Employees:** 19,000

**The McGraw-Hill Companies**

# DTE Energy Co

| S&P Recommendation | HOLD ★★★☆☆ | Price | 12-Mo. Target Price |
|---|---|---|---|
| | | $49.43 (as of Nov 25, 2011) | $51.00 |

**GICS Sector** Utilities
**Sub-Industry** Multi-Utilities

**Summary** This diversified energy company is involved in the development and management of energy-related businesses and services nationwide.

## Key Stock Statistics (Source S&P, Vickers, company reports)

| | | | | | | | |
|---|---|---|---|---|---|---|---|
| 52-Wk Range | $52.82–43.22 | S&P Oper. EPS 2011E | 3.68 | Market Capitalization(B) | $8.366 | Beta | 0.65 |
| Trailing 12-Month EPS | $4.20 | S&P Oper. EPS 2012E | 3.77 | Yield (%) | 4.75 | S&P 3-Yr. Proj. EPS CAGR(%) | 5 |
| Trailing 12-Month P/E | 11.8 | P/E on S&P Oper. EPS 2011E | 13.4 | Dividend Rate/Share | $2.35 | S&P Credit Rating | BBB+ |
| $10K Invested 5 Yrs Ago | $13,636 | Common Shares Outstg. (M) | 169.3 | Institutional Ownership (%) | 57 | | |

## Price Performance

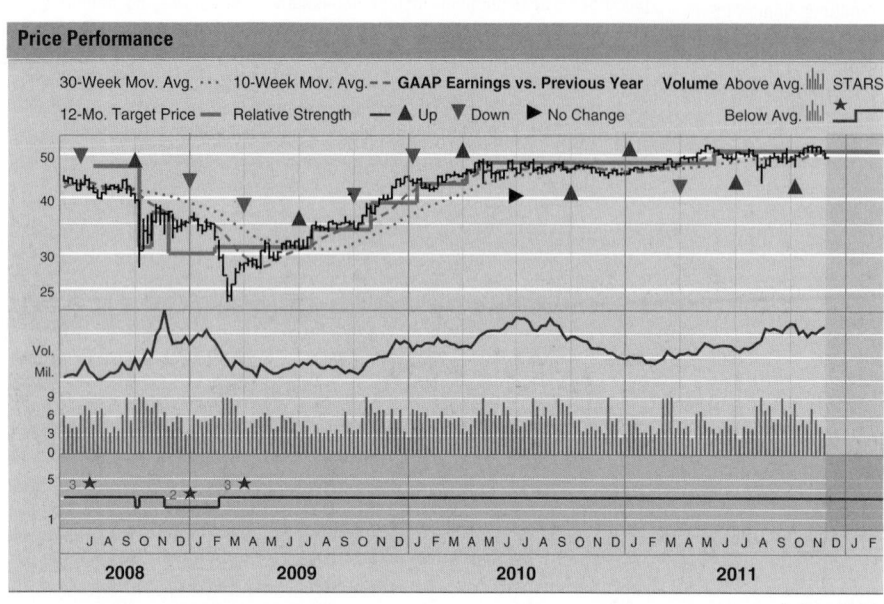

30-Week Mov. Avg. ··· 10-Week Mov. Avg. -- GAAP Earnings vs. Previous Year    Volume Above Avg. STARS
12-Mo. Target Price — Relative Strength — ▲ Up ▼ Down ► No Change    Below Avg. ★

Options: ASE, Ph

Analysis prepared by Equity Analyst **Justin McCann** on Aug 26, 2011, when the stock traded at **$49.51**.

## Qualitative Risk Assessment

| LOW | MEDIUM | HIGH |
|---|---|---|

Our risk assessment reflects a balance between the steady cash flow that we expect from the regulated utilities, which operate within a generally supportive regulatory environment, and most of the unregulated operations, which continue to contribute a significant portion of DTE's consolidated cash flow. While we expect DTE to benefit from the modification of Michigan's Electric Choice program, we remain concerned about the weak outlook for the state's economy.

## Quantitative Evaluations

**S&P Quality Ranking** B+

| D | C | B- | B | B+ | A- | A | A+ |
|---|---|---|---|---|---|---|---|

**Relative Strength Rank** MODERATE

68

LOWEST = 1    HIGHEST = 99

## Highlights

► We expect operating EPS in 2011 to increase about 2% from 2010's $3.60. We expect earnings to be moderately higher at the utilities (aided by a self-implemented rate increase at Detroit Edison), relatively stable at the Gas Storage and Pipelines segment, and improved at Energy Trading. However, this should be nearly offset by a sharp decline at the Power & Industrial Projects segment due to lower coke sales and the absence of a steel industry fuel tax credit that inflated results in 2010. For 2012, we expect operating EPS to increase about 2% from anticipated results for 2011.

► Detroit Edison self-implemented a $107 million rate increase on April 28, 2011. It will remain in place until a final order is issued by the MPSC, which is expected in October 2011. Should the authorized increase be less than the one self-implemented, the utility would have to refund the difference to its customers.

► In August 2011, DTE announced that Gerard M. Anderson, its president and CEO, would also become chairman, effective September 12, 2011. He would replace Anthony F. Earley, Jr., who will become chairman, president and CEO of PG&E Corp., effective September 13, 2011.

## Investment Rationale/Risk

► While the stock has been very volatile over the past few weeks, reflecting, we think, the volatility in the broader market, it was still up about 9% in the first 34 weeks of 2011. This has reflected, we believe, increased investor awareness that the expansion of Detroit Edison's rate base will result in higher earnings growth over the next few years. We believe DTE has benefited from the energy legislation that modified Michigan's electric choice program and ensured a more efficient rate case process.

► Risks to our recommendation and target price include a slower-than-expected recovery in the Michigan economy, a decline in non-utility earnings, and a sharp decrease in the average P/E of the peer group as a whole.

► With the 4.9% increase in the dividend (effective with the July 15 payment), the recent yield was a slightly above peers 4.8%. The increase lifted the payout ratio from 61% to 65% of DTE's operating EPS for 2010 and to 64% of our estimate for 2011, and we believe the company has the financial flexibility to maintain the new level. Our 12-month target price is $51, reflecting a premium-to-peers P/E of 14.2X our operating EPS estimate for 2011.

## Revenue/Earnings Data

**Revenue (Million $)**

| | 1Q | 2Q | 3Q | 4Q | Year |
|---|---|---|---|---|---|
| 2011 | 2,431 | 2,028 | 2,265 | -- | -- |
| 2010 | 2,453 | 1,792 | 2,139 | 2,173 | 8,557 |
| 2009 | 2,255 | 1,688 | 1,961 | 2,121 | 8,014 |
| 2008 | 2,570 | 2,251 | 2,338 | 2,170 | 9,329 |
| 2007 | 2,463 | 1,692 | 2,140 | 2,211 | 8,506 |
| 2006 | 2,635 | 1,895 | 2,196 | 2,296 | 9,022 |

**Earnings Per Share ($)**

| | | | | | |
|---|---|---|---|---|---|
| 2011 | 1.04 | 1.19 | 1.07 | E0.87 | E3.68 |
| 2010 | 1.38 | 0.51 | 0.96 | 0.90 | 3.74 |
| 2009 | 1.09 | 0.51 | 0.92 | 0.72 | 3.24 |
| 2008 | 1.23 | 0.17 | 1.03 | 0.80 | 3.23 |
| 2007 | 0.54 | 1.99 | 0.92 | 1.17 | 4.62 |
| 2006 | 0.76 | -0.18 | 1.07 | 0.81 | 2.45 |

Fiscal year ended Dec. 31. Next earnings report expected: Early February. EPS Estimates based on S&P Operating Earnings; historical GAAP earnings are as reported.

## Dividend Data (Dates: mm/dd Payment Date: mm/dd/yy)

| Amount ($) | Date Decl. | Ex-Div. Date | Stk. of Record | Payment Date |
|---|---|---|---|---|
| 0.560 | 02/03 | 03/17 | 03/21 | 04/15/11 |
| 0.588 | 05/05 | 06/16 | 06/20 | 07/15/11 |
| 0.588 | 06/23 | 09/15 | 09/19 | 10/15/11 |
| 0.588 | 11/16 | 12/15 | 12/19 | 01/15/12 |

Dividends have been paid since 1909. Source: Company reports.

---

**Please read the Required Disclosures and Analyst Certification on the last page of this report.**

The McGraw-Hill Companies

# DTE Energy Co

**STANDARD &POOR'S**

## Business Summary August 26, 2011

CORPORATE OVERVIEW. DTE Energy, formed on January 1, 1996, is the holding company for The Detroit Edison Company and Michigan Consolidated Gas (MichCon), regulated electric and gas utilities serving customers within the state of Michigan, and four non-utility operations engaged in a variety of energy-related businesses in various portions of the United States. The electric utility business accounted for 58.3% of consolidated revenues in 2010; the gas utility business 19.3%; power and industrial projects, 13.4%; and other non-utility operations 9.0%.

MARKET PROFILE. Detroit Edison is a regulated electric utility serving approximately 2.1 million customers in southeastern Michigan. In 2010, residential customers accounted for 42.3% of the utility's revenues; commercial customers 33.6%; industrial customers 14.2%; and other 9.9%. With its high percentage of commercial and industrial customers, the utility had been hurt by the state's Customer Choice program, losing about 10% of retail sales in 2010, 3% in 2009 and 2008, 4% in 2007, 6% in 2006, 12% in 2005, and 18% in 2004. Recent energy legislation in Michigan and orders by the Michigan Public Service Commission (MPSC) placed a 10% cap on the total potential migration. When market conditions are favorable, Detroit Edison will sell excess power into the wholesale market. The utility's generating capability is heavily dependent on the availability of coal, and the majority of its coal needs are obtained through long-term contracts, with the remainder purchased through short-term agreements or purchases in the spot market.

MichCon is a regulated natural gas utility serving about 1.2 million residential, commercial and industrial customers in the state of Michigan. It also has subsidiaries involved in the gathering and transmission of natural gas in northern Michigan, and operates one of the largest natural gas distribution and transmission systems in the U.S., with connections to interstate pipelines providing access to most of the major natural gas producing regions in the Gulf Coast, Mid-Continent and Canadian regions. The company purchases its natural gas supplies on the open market through a diversified portfolio of supply contracts, and, given its storage capacity, should be able to meet its supply requirements.

## Company Financials Fiscal Year Ended Dec. 31

| Per Share Data ($) | 2010 | 2009 | 2008 | 2007 | 2006 | 2005 | 2004 | 2003 | 2002 | 2001 |
|---|---|---|---|---|---|---|---|---|---|---|
| Tangible Book Value | 27.36 | 25.39 | 23.99 | 23.22 | 21.02 | 20.88 | 20.01 | 19.05 | 14.61 | 16.06 |
| Earnings | 3.74 | 3.24 | 3.23 | 4.62 | 2.45 | 3.27 | 2.55 | 2.85 | 3.83 | 2.14 |
| S&P Core Earnings | 4.25 | 3.84 | 1.69 | 1.55 | 2.88 | 2.13 | 1.97 | 3.22 | 2.80 | 2.09 |
| Dividends | 2.18 | 2.12 | 2.12 | 2.12 | 2.08 | 2.06 | 2.06 | 2.06 | 2.06 | 2.06 |
| Payout Ratio | 58% | 65% | 66% | 46% | 85% | 63% | 81% | 72% | 54% | 96% |
| Prices:High | 49.06 | 44.96 | 45.34 | 54.74 | 49.24 | 48.31 | 45.49 | 49.50 | 47.70 | 47.13 |
| Prices:Low | 41.25 | 23.32 | 27.82 | 43.96 | 38.77 | 41.39 | 37.88 | 34.00 | 33.05 | 33.13 |
| P/E Ratio:High | 13 | 14 | 14 | 12 | 20 | 15 | 18 | 17 | 12 | 22 |
| P/E Ratio:Low | 11 | 7 | 9 | 10 | 16 | 13 | 15 | 12 | 9 | 15 |

| Income Statement Analysis (Million $) | | | | | | | | | | |
|---|---|---|---|---|---|---|---|---|---|---|
| Revenue | 8,557 | 8,014 | 9,329 | 8,506 | 9,022 | 9,022 | 7,114 | 7,041 | 6,749 | 7,849 |
| Depreciation | 1,027 | 954 | 899 | 932 | 1,014 | 869 | 744 | 687 | 759 | 795 |
| Maintenance | NA | NA | NA | NA | NA | NA | NA | NA | NA | NA |
| Fixed Charges Coverage | 2.73 | 2.43 | 2.37 | 1.55 | 1.82 | 1.21 | 1.35 | 1.49 | 2.00 | 2.04 |
| Construction Credits | NA | NA | NA | NA | NA | NA | NA | NA | NA | NA |
| Effective Tax Rate | 32.7% | 31.6% | 35.2% | 31.5% | NM | NM | NM | 24.0% | NM | NM |
| Net Income | 630 | 532 | 526 | 787 | 437 | 576 | 443 | 480 | 632 | 329 |
| S&P Core Earnings | 717 | 631 | 275 | 266 | 512 | 374 | 344 | 542 | 463 | 322 |

| Balance Sheet & Other Financial Data (Million $) | | | | | | | | | | |
|---|---|---|---|---|---|---|---|---|---|---|
| Gross Property | 21,574 | 20,588 | 20,065 | 18,809 | 19,224 | 18,660 | 18,011 | 17,679 | 17,862 | 17,067 |
| Capital Expenditures | 1,099 | 1,035 | 1,373 | 1,299 | 1,403 | 1,065 | 904 | 751 | 984 | 1,096 |
| Net Property | 12,992 | 12,431 | 12,231 | 11,408 | 11,451 | 10,830 | 10,491 | 10,324 | 9,813 | 9,543 |
| Capitalization:Long Term Debt | 7,089 | 7,370 | 7,741 | 6,971 | 7,474 | 7,080 | 7,606 | 7,669 | 7,785 | 7,928 |
| Capitalization:% Long Term Debt | 51.3 | 54.0 | 56.4 | 54.4 | 56.1 | 55.1 | 57.8 | 59.2 | 63.0 | 63.0 |
| Capitalization:Preferred | Nil | Nil | Nil | Nil | Nil | Nil | Nil | Nil | Nil | Nil |
| Capitalization:% Preferred | Nil | Nil | Nil | Nil | Nil | Nil | Nil | Nil | Nil | Nil |
| Capitalization:Common | 6,722 | 6,278 | 5,995 | 5,853 | 5,849 | 5,769 | 5,548 | 5,287 | 4,565 | 4,657 |
| Capitalization:% Common | 48.7 | 46.0 | 43.6 | 45.6 | 43.9 | 44.9 | 42.2 | 40.8 | 37.0 | 37.0 |
| Total Capital | 14,781 | 14,357 | 15,833 | 14,804 | 14,950 | 14,468 | 13,429 | 14,256 | 13,434 | 14,063 |
| % Operating Ratio | 86.6 | 87.7 | 91.0 | 95.2 | 91.2 | 96.1 | 93.4 | 91.1 | 82.8 | 86.3 |
| % Earned on Net Property | 11.4 | 10.0 | 9.5 | 6.8 | 7.4 | 8.9 | 8.1 | 7.2 | 11.4 | 8.2 |
| % Return on Revenue | 7.4 | 6.6 | 5.6 | 9.3 | 4.8 | 6.4 | 6.2 | 6.8 | 9.4 | 4.2 |
| % Return on Invested Capital | 8.2 | 7.6 | 5.8 | 3.1 | 5.4 | 6.0 | 6.1 | 7.5 | 9.1 | 8.9 |
| % Return on Common Equity | 9.7 | 8.7 | 8.9 | 13.5 | 7.5 | 10.2 | 8.2 | 9.7 | 13.8 | 7.6 |

Data as orig reptd.; bef. results of disc opers/spec. items. Per share data adj. for stk. divs.; EPS diluted. E-Estimated. NA-Not Available. NM-Not Meaningful. NR-Not Ranked. UR-Under Review.

**Office:** One Energy Plaza, Detroit, MI 48226-1279.
**Telephone:** 313-235-4000.
**Email:** shareholdersvcs@dteenergy.com
**Website:** http://www.dteenergy.com

**Chrmn, Pres & CEO:** G.M. Anderson
**EVP & CFO:** D.E. Meador
**SVP & General Counsel:** B.D. Peterson
**Chief Acctg Officer & Cntlr:** P.B. Oleksiak

**Treas:** N. Khouri
**Investor Contact:** L. Muschong (313-235-8505)
**Board Members:** G. M. Anderson, L. Bauder, D. A. Brandon, W. F. Fountain, F. M. Hennessey, J. E. Lobbia, G. J. McGovern, E. A. Miller, M. A. Murray, C. W. Pryor, Jr., J. Robles, Jr., J. H. Vandenberghe

**Founded:** 1995
**Domicile:** Michigan
**Employees:** 9,800

*The McGraw-Hill Companies*

# Duke Energy Corp

**STANDARD &POOR'S**

| S&P Recommendation **HOLD** ★★★★★ | Price $19.79 (as of Nov 25, 2011) | 12-Mo. Target Price $20.00 | Investment Style Large-Cap Value |

**GICS Sector** Utilities
**Sub-Industry** Electric Utilities

**Summary** DUK provides service to 3.9 million electric customers in North Carolina, South Carolina, Indiana, Ohio and Kentucky, and 500,000 gas customers in Kentucky and Ohio.

## Key Stock Statistics (Source S&P, Vickers, company reports)

| | | | | | |
|---|---|---|---|---|---|
| 52-Wk Range | $21.02–16.87 | S&P Oper. EPS 2011**E** 1.43 | Market Capitalization(B) $26.375 | Beta | 0.35 |
| Trailing 12-Month EPS | $1.38 | S&P Oper. EPS 2012**E** 1.47 | Yield (%) 5.05 | S&P 3-Yr. Proj. EPS CAGR(%) | 2 |
| Trailing 12-Month P/E | 14.3 | P/E on S&P Oper. EPS 2011**E** 13.8 | Dividend Rate/Share $1.00 | S&P Credit Rating | A- |
| $10K Invested 5 Yrs Ago | NA | Common Shares Outstg. (M) 1,332.7 | Institutional Ownership (%) 49 | | |

## Price Performance

30-Week Mov. Avg. · · · 10-Week Mov. Avg. - - GAAP Earnings vs. Previous Year Volume Above Avg. STARS
12-Mo. Target Price — Relative Strength — ▲ Up ▼ Down ▶ No Change Below Avg. ★

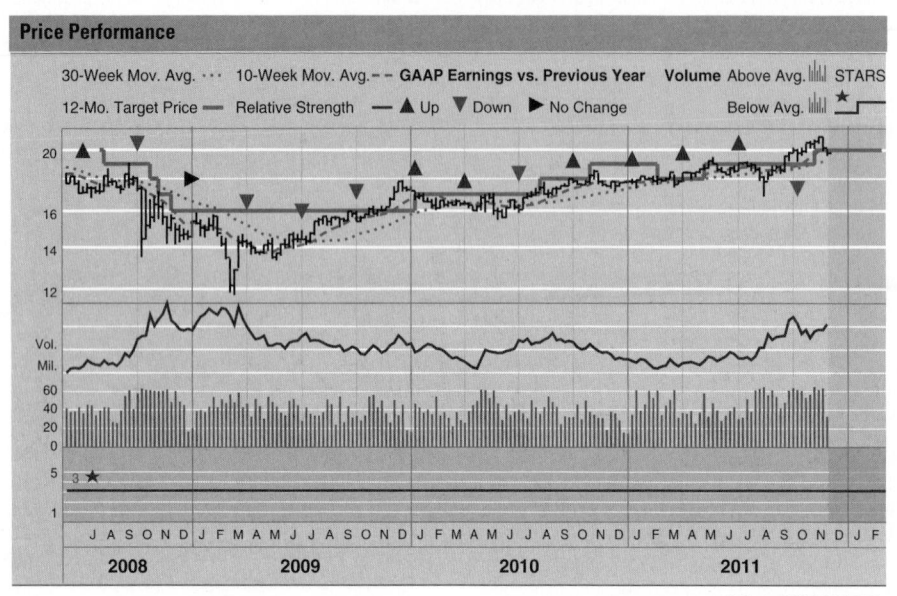

Options: ASE, CBOE, P, Ph

## Qualitative Risk Assessment

| LOW | MEDIUM | HIGH |

Our risk assessment reflects DUK's large market capitalization and a balanced portfolio of businesses that include lower-risk regulated electric and gas utility services, partly offset by higher-risk unregulated businesses, which contribute less than 25% of the company's earnings.

## Quantitative Evaluations

**S&P Quality Ranking** B

| D | C | B- | B | B+ | A- | A | A+ |

**Relative Strength Rank** STRONG

75

LOWEST = 1 HIGHEST = 99

## Highlights

▶ The 12-month target price for DUK has recently been changed to $20.00 from $19.00. The Highlights section of this Stock Report will be updated accordingly.

## Investment Rationale/Risk

▶ The Investment Rationale/Risk section of this Stock Report will be updated shortly. For the latest News story on DUK from MarketScope, see below.

▶ 11/03/11 10:24 am ET ... S&P MAINTAINS HOLD OPINION ON SHARES OF DUKE ENERGY (DUK 20.48***): Q3 recurring EPS of $0.50, vs. $0.51, beats our $0.47 estimate and the $0.46 Capital IQ consensus forecast. Revenues were lower and interest cost higher than we expected, but these items were more than offset by higher operating margin percentage. We believe that DUK's EPS will benefit from several rate cases underway. Progress continues on the proposed acquisition, with a settlement in North Carolina and conditional FERC approval. We are raising our '11 and '12 EPS estimates by $0.03 to $1.43 and $1.47 and initiate '13's at $1.51. We are lifting our target price by $1 to $20. /CBMuir

## Revenue/Earnings Data

**Revenue (Million $)**

| | 1Q | 2Q | 3Q | 4Q | Year |
|---|---|---|---|---|---|
| 2011 | 3,585 | 3,534 | 3,964 | -- | -- |
| 2010 | 3,594 | 3,287 | 3,946 | 3,445 | 14,272 |
| 2009 | 3,312 | 2,913 | 3,396 | 3,110 | 12,731 |
| 2008 | 3,337 | 3,229 | 3,508 | 3,133 | 13,207 |
| 2007 | 3,035 | 2,966 | 3,688 | 3,031 | 12,443 |
| 2006 | 3,106 | 3,865 | 4,143 | 4,070 | 15,184 |

**Earnings Per Share ($)**

| | 1Q | 2Q | 3Q | 4Q | Year |
|---|---|---|---|---|---|
| 2011 | 0.38 | 0.33 | 0.35 | E0.21 | E1.43 |
| 2010 | 0.34 | -0.17 | 0.51 | 0.32 | 1.00 |
| 2009 | 0.27 | 0.22 | 0.09 | 0.26 | 0.82 |
| 2008 | 0.37 | 0.27 | 0.17 | 0.21 | 1.01 |
| 2007 | 0.27 | 0.24 | 0.48 | 0.21 | 1.20 |
| 2006 | 0.50 | 0.34 | 0.60 | 0.31 | 1.70 |

Fiscal year ended Dec. 31. Next earnings report expected: Mid February. EPS Estimates based on S&P Operating Earnings; historical GAAP earnings are as reported.

## Dividend Data (Dates: mm/dd Payment Date: mm/dd/yy)

| Amount ($) | Date Decl. | Ex-Div. Date | Stk. of Record | Payment Date |
|---|---|---|---|---|
| 0.245 | 01/06 | 02/09 | 02/11 | 03/16/11 |
| 0.245 | 05/05 | 05/18 | 05/20 | 06/16/11 |
| 0.250 | 06/21 | 08/10 | 08/12 | 09/16/11 |
| 0.250 | 10/25 | 11/16 | 11/18 | 12/16/11 |

Dividends have been paid since 1926. Source: Company reports.

---

**Please read the Required Disclosures and Analyst Certification on the last page of this report.**

The McGraw-Hill Companies

# Duke Energy Corp

STANDARD &POOR'S

## Business Summary August 30, 2011

CORPORATE OVERVIEW. Duke provides electric and gas utility services, sells wholesale power, and has investments in various South American generation plants. Its Franchised Electric and Gas (E&G) segment generates, transmits, distributes and sells electricity in central and western North Carolina, western South Carolina, southwestern Ohio, central, north central and southern Indiana, and northern Kentucky. The Commercial Power segment owns, operates and manages power plants and engages in the wholesale marketing and procurement of electric power, fuel and emission allowances related to these plants as well as other contractual positions. The International Energy segment (IE) owns, operates and manages power generation facilities, and engages in sales and marketing of electric power and natural gas outside the U.S. The Other segment includes unallocated corporate costs and investments in other businesses.

Franchised Electric and Gas serves about 4 million electric customers over 50,000 square miles in North Carolina, South Carolina, Indiana, Ohio and Kentucky, and about 500,000 gas customers in Kentucky and Ohio, and owns generating assets totaling 27,150 MW (50% coal; 20% natural gas, oil or other; 19% nuclear; 12% hydro; and <1% solar) as of December 2010. Electric sales in 2010 were 30% residential, 32% commercial, 26% industrial, and 12% other.

The Power segment consists of 8,555 MW, mostly supporting regulated operations in Ohio. There are 5,813 MW located in Ohio, 690 MW in Pennsylvania, 640 MW in Illinois, 509 MW in Texas, 480 MW in Indiana, 370 MW in Wyoming, 51 MW in Colorado, and 2 MW in North Carolina. Commercial Power's fuel mix includes 44% natural gas, 41% coal, 12% wind, 3% fuel oil, and <1% solar. The IE segment primarily consists of power generation (4,203 MW) in Central and South America.

CORPORATE STRATEGY. In recent years, Duke has focused on utility spending in an effort to increase its rate base, which can lead to rate increases. The Power segment has focused on increasing renewable generation assets, and IE aims to take advantage of any opportunities that may arise. In June 2009, IE purchased the remaining 24% of its Aguaytia Integrated Energy Project subsidiary in Peru.

## Company Financials Fiscal Year Ended Dec. 31

| Per Share Data ($) | 2010 | 2009 | 2008 | 2007 | 2006 | 2005 | 2004 | 2003 | 2002 | 2001 |
|---|---|---|---|---|---|---|---|---|---|---|
| Tangible Book Value | 13.69 | 12.84 | 12.25 | 12.55 | 13.54 | 13.65 | 12.54 | 10.74 | 12.51 | 14.11 |
| Earnings | 1.00 | 0.82 | 1.01 | 1.20 | 1.70 | 2.61 | 1.27 | -1.13 | 1.22 | 2.56 |
| S&P Core Earnings | 1.23 | 1.11 | 0.82 | 1.22 | 1.80 | 1.29 | 1.24 | -1.10 | 1.01 | 2.29 |
| Dividends | 0.97 | 0.94 | 0.90 | 0.86 | 0.95 | 1.17 | 1.10 | 1.10 | 1.10 | 1.10 |
| Payout Ratio | 97% | 115% | 89% | 70% | 56% | 45% | 87% | NM | 90% | 43% |
| Prices:High | 18.60 | 17.94 | 20.60 | 21.30 | 34.50 | 30.55 | 26.16 | 21.57 | 40.00 | 47.74 |
| Prices:Low | 15.47 | 11.72 | 13.50 | 16.91 | 26.94 | 24.37 | 18.85 | 12.21 | 16.42 | 32.22 |
| P/E Ratio:High | 19 | 22 | 20 | 17 | 20 | 12 | 21 | NM | 33 | 19 |
| P/E Ratio:Low | 16 | 14 | 13 | 14 | 16 | 9 | 15 | NM | 13 | 13 |

| Income Statement Analysis (Million $) | | | | | | | | | | |
|---|---|---|---|---|---|---|---|---|---|---|
| Revenue | 14,272 | 12,731 | 13,207 | 12,720 | 15,184 | 16,746 | 22,503 | 22,529 | 15,663 | 59,503 |
| Depreciation | 1,786 | 1,656 | 1,670 | 1,746 | 2,049 | 1,728 | 1,851 | 1,803 | 1,571 | 1,336 |
| Maintenance | NA | NA | NA | NA | NA | NA | NA | NA | NA | NA |
| Fixed Charges Coverage | 3.19 | 3.32 | 3.72 | 4.03 | 2.77 | 2.91 | 2.40 | 1.96 | 2.46 | 5.33 |
| Construction Credits | NA | NA | NA | NA | NA | NA | NA | NA | NA | 53.0 |
| Effective Tax Rate | 40.3% | 41.4% | 32.6% | 31.8% | 28.8% | 29.5% | 27.5% | NM | 35.1% | 33.1% |
| Net Income | 1,320 | 1,063 | 1,279 | 1,522 | 2,019 | 2,533 | 1,232 | -1,005 | 1,034 | 1,994 |
| S&P Core Earnings | 1,626 | 1,423 | 1,041 | 1,551 | 2,131 | 1,249 | 1,199 | -994 | 908 | 1,777 |

| Balance Sheet & Other Financial Data (Million $) | | | | | | | | | | |
|---|---|---|---|---|---|---|---|---|---|---|
| Gross Property | 58,539 | 55,362 | 50,304 | 46,056 | 58,330 | 40,574 | 46,806 | 47,157 | 48,677 | 39,464 |
| Capital Expenditures | 4,855 | 4,557 | 4,922 | 3,125 | 3,381 | 2,309 | 2,055 | 2,470 | 4,924 | 5,930 |
| Net Property | 40,344 | 37,950 | 34,036 | 31,110 | 41,447 | 29,200 | 33,506 | 34,986 | 36,219 | 28,415 |
| Capitalization:Long Term Debt | 17,935 | 16,113 | 13,250 | 9,498 | 18,118 | 14,547 | 16,932 | 20,622 | 21,629 | 13,728 |
| Capitalization:% Long Term Debt | 44.3 | 42.6 | 38.7 | 30.9 | 41.0 | 46.9 | 50.5 | 59.8 | 58.9 | 51.5 |
| Capitalization:Preferred | Nil | Nil | Nil | Nil | Nil | Nil | 134 | 134 | 157 | 234 |
| Capitalization:% Preferred | Nil | Nil | Nil | Nil | Nil | Nil | 0.40 | 0.39 | 0.43 | 0.88 |
| Capitalization:Common | 22,522 | 21,750 | 20,988 | 21,199 | 26,102 | 16,439 | 16,441 | 13,748 | 14,944 | 12,689 |
| Capitalization:% Common | 55.7 | 57.4 | 61.3 | 69.1 | 59.0 | 53.1 | 49.1 | 39.8 | 40.7 | 47.6 |
| Total Capital | 40,878 | 38,905 | 39,666 | 35,790 | 52,203 | 36,988 | 40,375 | 40,490 | 43,644 | 33,393 |
| % Operating Ratio | 90.1 | 88.6 | 85.5 | 86.0 | 87.6 | 89.6 | 88.6 | 85.4 | 87.1 | 95.0 |
| % Earned on Net Property | 5.9 | 6.2 | 7.8 | 6.9 | 9.0 | 11.5 | 8.9 | NM | 7.6 | 15.5 |
| % Return on Revenue | 9.3 | 8.4 | 9.7 | 12.0 | 13.3 | 15.1 | 5.5 | NM | 6.6 | 3.4 |
| % Return on Invested Capital | 4.5 | 4.4 | 5.7 | 4.7 | 7.5 | 11.1 | 7.0 | 8.7 | 6.3 | 10.5 |
| % Return on Common Equity | 6.0 | 5.0 | 6.1 | 6.4 | 9.5 | 15.3 | 8.1 | NM | 7.4 | 17.4 |

Data as orig reptd.; bef. results of disc opers/spec. items. Per share data adj. for stk. divs.; EPS diluted. E-Estimated. NA-Not Available. NM-Not Meaningful. NR-Not Ranked. UR-Under Review.

**Office:** 526 South Church Street, Charlotte, NC 28202-1904.
**Telephone:** 704-594-6200.
**Website:** http://www.duke-energy.com
**Chrmn, Pres & CEO:** J.E. Rogers, Jr.

**EVP & CIO:** A.R. Mullinax
**Investor Contact:** S.G. De May ()
**SVP & Treas:** S.G. De May
**CFO:** L.J. Good

**Board Members:** W. Barnet, III, G. A. Bernhardt, M. G. Browning, D. R. DiMicco, J. H. Forsgren, Jr., A. M. Gray, J. H. Hance, Jr., E. J. Reinsch, J. T. Rhodes, J. E. Rogers, Jr., P. R. Sharp

**Founded:** 1917
**Domicile:** Delaware
**Employees:** 18,440

The McGraw-Hill Companies

# Dun & Bradstreet Corp (The)

**STANDARD &POOR'S**

| S&P Recommendation | HOLD ★★★★★ | Price $65.14 (as of Nov 25, 2011) | 12-Mo. Target Price $83.00 | Investment Style Large-Cap Growth |
|---|---|---|---|---|

**GICS Sector** Industrials
**Sub-Industry** Research & Consulting Services

**Summary** This company is a worldwide provider of business information and related decision support services and commercial receivables management services.

## Key Stock Statistics (Source S&P, Vickers, company reports)

| | | | | | | | |
|---|---|---|---|---|---|---|---|
| 52-Wk Range | $87.08–58.50 | S&P Oper. EPS 2011**E** | 6.10 | Market Capitalization(B) | $3.166 | Beta | 0.60 |
| Trailing 12-Month EPS | $5.21 | S&P Oper. EPS 2012**E** | 6.58 | Yield (%) | 2.21 | S&P 3-Yr. Proj. EPS CAGR(%) | 6 |
| Trailing 12-Month P/E | 12.5 | P/E on S&P Oper. EPS 2011**E** | 10.7 | Dividend Rate/Share | $1.44 | S&P Credit Rating | A- |
| $10K Invested 5 Yrs Ago | $8,549 | Common Shares Outstg. (M) | 48.6 | Institutional Ownership (%) | 87 | | |

## Price Performance

30-Week Mov. Avg. ··· 10-Week Mov. Avg. - - GAAP Earnings vs. Previous Year   Volume Above Avg. ⅢⅢ STARS
12-Mo. Target Price — Relative Strength — ▲ Up ▼ Down ► No Change   Below Avg. ⅢⅢ ★

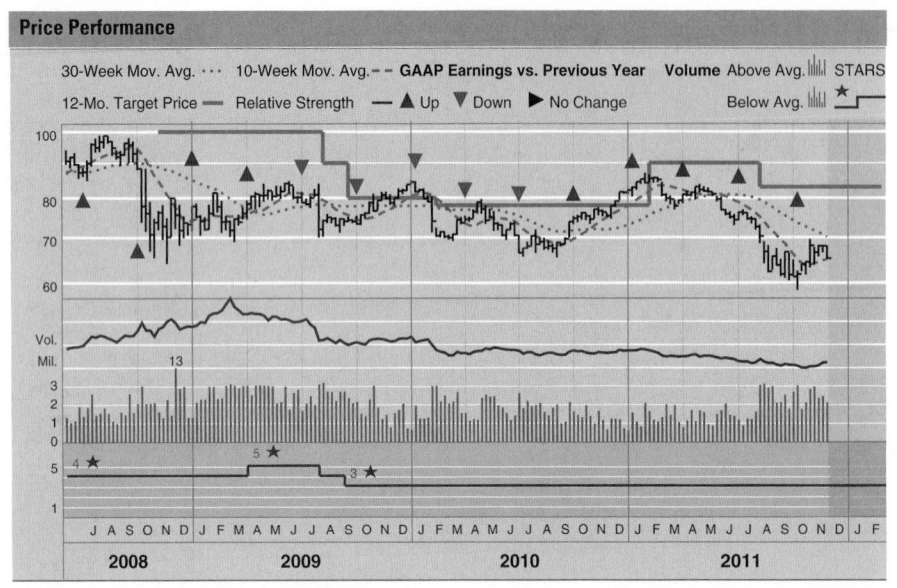

Options: Ph

Analysis prepared by Equity Analyst **Robert McMillan** on Oct 31, 2011, when the stock traded at **$67.32**.

### Highlights

➤ After falling 2.2% in 2009 and fractionally in 2010, sales should increase about 9% in 2011 and 12% in 2012, in our view, driven primarily by growth in international sales. Although we see a recovery in the key North America division on a projected recovery in spending by corporations and small businesses in the key U.S. market, we think the recovery will be slow and erratic as continued concerns about the economy and unemployment levels restrict spending. We believe International division sales will advance sharply in 2011 and 2012, on our view of strength in emerging markets and our outlook for incremental revenues from recently acquired D&B Australia Holdings.

➤ We expect higher expenses in 2011, primarily stemming from DNB's technology investment program, which we think will enhance business productivity and help lower expenses in the long term. However, we believe the company will keep tight control over other expenses. As a result, we see operating margins at 26.1% in 2011 and 26.9% in 2012, compared to 29.0% in 2010.

➤ Our operating EPS estimates are $6.10 for 2011 and $6.58 for 2012.

### Investment Rationale/Risk

➤ Although we expect a gradual recovery in DNB's North American business, we remain concerned about the relatively high level of U.S. unemployment. We see DNB continuing to increase its presence internationally through investments, joint ventures and partnerships. We also expect the company to continue deploying free cash flow toward acquisitions, stock repurchases and dividends.

➤ Risks to our recommendation and target price include a stronger U.S. dollar depressing overseas profits, a deteriorating outlook for DNB's U.K. operations, and an inability by the company to realize operating efficiencies from the company's business rationalization program.

➤ The shares recently traded at 11.0X trailing 12-month EPS. Our 12-month target price of $83 is equal to 12.9X our forward 12-month EPS projection of $6.44, which represents a discount to the recent historical average. We believe the valuation multiple will expand from recent levels based on our outlook for continued robust international sales, a recovery in the company's key North American market and investment in a technology program.

## Qualitative Risk Assessment

| LOW | MEDIUM | HIGH |
|---|---|---|

Our risk assessment reflects DNB's global business database and proprietary identification system, which we think provides a competitive advantage, and its notable record of long-term EPS growth, notwithstanding a slightly uncertain regulatory outlook for its ability to collect and use data.

## Quantitative Evaluations

**S&P Quality Ranking**     B+

| D | C | B- | B | B+ | A- | A | A+ |
|---|---|---|---|---|---|---|---|

**Relative Strength Rank**     **STRONG**

72

LOWEST = 1      HIGHEST = 99

## Revenue/Earnings Data

### Revenue (Million $)

| | 1Q | 2Q | 3Q | 4Q | Year |
|---|---|---|---|---|---|
| 2011 | 403.6 | 416.8 | 439.4 | -- | -- |
| 2010 | 397.2 | 397.3 | 400.4 | 481.7 | 1,677 |
| 2009 | 407.4 | 416.9 | 399.0 | 463.7 | 1,687 |
| 2008 | 414.7 | 427.7 | 409.2 | 474.7 | 1,726 |
| 2007 | 379.0 | 380.8 | 374.7 | 464.7 | 1,599 |
| 2006 | 367.2 | 367.4 | 359.2 | 437.5 | 1,531 |

### Earnings Per Share ($)

| | | | | | |
|---|---|---|---|---|---|
| 2011 | 1.00 | 1.18 | 1.19 | E2.04 | E6.10 |
| 2010 | 0.92 | 1.11 | 1.12 | 1.85 | 4.98 |
| 2009 | 1.93 | 1.43 | 1.02 | 1.61 | 5.99 |
| 2008 | 1.05 | 1.51 | 1.18 | 1.85 | 5.58 |
| 2007 | 0.86 | 1.44 | 0.93 | 1.68 | 4.90 |
| 2006 | 0.75 | 0.79 | 0.72 | 1.46 | 3.70 |

Fiscal year ended Dec. 31. Next earnings report expected: NA. EPS Estimates based on S&P Operating Earnings; historical GAAP earnings are as reported.

## Dividend Data (Dates: mm/dd Payment Date: mm/dd/yy)

| Amount ($) | Date Decl. | Ex-Div. Date | Stk. of Record | Payment Date |
|---|---|---|---|---|
| 0.360 | 02/02 | 02/24 | 02/28 | 03/16/11 |
| 0.360 | 05/03 | 05/25 | 05/27 | 06/15/11 |
| 0.360 | 08/03 | 08/29 | 08/31 | 09/15/11 |
| 0.360 | 10/18 | 11/23 | 11/28 | 12/13/11 |

Dividends have been paid since 2007. Source: Company reports.

**Please read the Required Disclosures and Analyst Certification on the last page of this report.**

The **McGraw·Hill** Companies

# Dun & Bradstreet Corp (The)

**STANDARD &POOR'S**

## Business Summary October 31, 2011

CORPORATE OVERVIEW. Dun & Bradstreet (DNB) is a leading worldwide provider of business information and related decision support services. DNB believes it has the world's largest global business database, with over 150 million business records.

DNB operates its business through four customer solution sets: Risk Management Solutions (63% of 2010) (Risk Management includes Supply Management as of January 1, 2008), Sales and Marketing Solutions (30%), and Internet Solutions (7%). Sales in North America accounted for 75% of 2010 revenues, while the remaining 25% came from DNB's overseas presence, including strategic partner relationships and minority equity investments.

Risk Management Solutions helps clients extend commercial credit, set credit limits, and determine total credit risk exposure. It aims to help clients increase cash flow and profitability while minimizing operational, credit, and regulatory risk. Within this customer solution set, DNB offers traditional and what it considers value-added products. Traditional products consist of reports from DNB's database used primarily for making decisions about new credit applications. Value-added products generally support automated decision making and portfolio management through the use of scoring and integrated software solutions.

The Supply Management Solutions set helps customers understand their supplier base, rationalize their supplier rosters, leverage buying power, minimize supply-related risks, and identify and evaluate new sources of supply. Starting in January 2008, DNB started managing its Supply Management business as part of its Risk Management Solutions business.

Sales and Marketing Solutions helps customers conduct market segmentation, maintain updated customer relationship management systems, and offers client profiling, prospect selection and marketing list development. Traditional products generally consist of marketing lists, labels and customized data files used by DNB's customers in their direct mail and marketing activities. Value-added products primarily include decision making and customer information management solutions.

Internet Solutions represents the results of Hoover's, Inc., which DNB acquired in 2003, and AllBusiness.com. Hoover's provides information on public and private companies, primarily to senior executives and sales professionals, using a proprietary database.

## Company Financials Fiscal Year Ended Dec. 31

| Per Share Data ($) | 2010 | 2009 | 2008 | 2007 | 2006 | 2005 | 2004 | 2003 | 2002 | 2001 |
|---|---|---|---|---|---|---|---|---|---|---|
| Tangible Book Value | NM | NM | NM | NM | NM | NM | NM | NM | NM | NM |
| Cash Flow | 6.33 | 7.14 | 5.93 | 5.19 | 4.21 | 3.71 | 3.54 | 3.15 | 2.96 | 3.02 |
| Earnings | 4.98 | 5.99 | 5.58 | 4.90 | 3.70 | 3.19 | 2.90 | 2.30 | 1.87 | 1.88 |
| S&P Core Earnings | 4.57 | 5.69 | 4.28 | 4.66 | 3.69 | 2.83 | 2.14 | 1.97 | 0.63 | 0.07 |
| Dividends | 1.40 | 1.36 | 1.20 | 1.00 | Nil | Nil | Nil | Nil | Nil | Nil |
| Payout Ratio | 28% | 23% | 22% | 20% | Nil | Nil | Nil | Nil | Nil | Nil |
| Prices:High | 84.61 | 84.95 | 98.90 | 108.45 | 84.98 | 68.00 | 60.80 | 50.81 | 43.40 | 36.90 |
| Prices:Low | 65.34 | 68.97 | 64.00 | 81.50 | 65.03 | 54.90 | 47.85 | 32.31 | 28.26 | 20.99 |
| P/E Ratio:High | 17 | 14 | 18 | 22 | 23 | 21 | 21 | 22 | 23 | 20 |
| P/E Ratio:Low | 13 | 12 | 11 | 17 | 18 | 17 | 16 | 14 | 15 | 11 |

| Income Statement Analysis (Million $) | | | | | | | | | | |
|---|---|---|---|---|---|---|---|---|---|---|
| Revenue | 1,677 | 1,687 | 1,726 | 1,599 | 1,531 | 1,444 | 1,414 | 1,386 | 1,276 | 1,309 |
| Operating Income | 488 | 546 | 521 | 469 | 461 | 431 | 398 | 373 | 371 | 344 |
| Depreciation | 68.1 | 58.1 | 19.6 | 17.9 | 33.3 | 36.1 | 47.3 | 64.0 | 84.2 | 94.5 |
| Interest Expense | 46.0 | 45.7 | 47.4 | 28.3 | 20.3 | 21.1 | 18.9 | 18.6 | 19.5 | 16.4 |
| Pretax Income | 389 | 434 | 440 | 428 | 389 | 355 | 341 | 281 | 238 | 260 |
| Effective Tax Rate | NA | 25.8% | 29.1% | 31.8% | 37.7% | 37.7% | 37.9% | 37.8% | 39.6% | 38.9% |
| Net Income | 251 | 319 | 310 | 293 | 241 | 221 | 212 | 175 | 143 | 153 |
| S&P Core Earnings | 231 | 302 | 238 | 278 | 240 | 197 | 156 | 151 | 48.5 | 6.51 |

| Balance Sheet & Other Financial Data (Million $) | | | | | | | | | | |
|---|---|---|---|---|---|---|---|---|---|---|
| Cash | 78.5 | 223 | 164 | 176 | 138 | 305 | 336 | 239 | 192 | 145 |
| Current Assets | 668 | 760 | 696 | 718 | 645 | 759 | 762 | 731 | 614 | 580 |
| Total Assets | 1,906 | 1,749 | 1,586 | 1,659 | 1,360 | 1,613 | 1,636 | 1,625 | 1,528 | 1,431 |
| Current Liabilities | 928 | 859 | 908 | 910 | 806 | 1,029 | 714 | 736 | 718 | 663 |
| Long Term Debt | 972 | 962 | 904 | 725 | 459 | 0.10 | 300 | 300 | 300 | 300 |
| Common Equity | -654 | -746 | -856 | -440 | -399 | 77.6 | 54.2 | 48.4 | -18.8 | -20.9 |
| Total Capital | 337 | 230 | 53.7 | 288 | 62.4 | 77.7 | 354 | 348 | 281 | 280 |
| Capital Expenditures | 9.50 | 9.20 | 11.8 | 13.7 | 11.6 | 5.70 | 12.1 | 11.0 | 15.8 | 16.2 |
| Cash Flow | 319 | 378 | 329 | 311 | 274 | 257 | 259 | 239 | 228 | 248 |
| Current Ratio | 0.7 | 0.9 | 0.8 | 0.8 | 0.8 | 0.7 | 1.1 | 1.0 | 0.9 | 0.9 |
| % Long Term Debt of Capitalization | 288.7 | Nil | NM | 251.4 | NM | 0.1 | 84.7 | 86.1 | 106.7 | 107.0 |
| % Net Income of Revenue | 15.0 | 18.9 | 17.9 | 18.3 | 15.7 | 15.3 | 15.0 | 12.6 | 11.2 | 11.7 |
| % Return on Assets | NA | NA | 19.1 | 19.4 | 16.2 | 13.6 | 13.0 | 11.1 | 9.6 | 10.7 |
| % Return on Equity | NA | NA | NM | NM | NM | 335.7 | 412.9 | 1179.1 | NM | NM |

Data as orig reptd.; bef. results of disc opers/spec. items. Per share data adj. for stk. divs.; EPS diluted. E-Estimated. NA-Not Available. NM-Not Meaningful. NR-Not Ranked. UR-Under Review.

**Office:** 103 JFK Parkway, Short Hills, NJ 07078.
**Telephone:** 973-921-5500.
**Website:** http://www.dnb.com
**Chrmn, Pres & CEO:** S. Mathew

**CFO:** R.H. Veldran
**Chief Admin Officer:** E.A. Conti
**CTO & CIO:** W.S. Hauck, III
**Chief Acctg Officer & Cntlr:** A. Pietrontone, Jr.

**Investor Contact:** R. Veldran (973-921-5863)
**Board Members:** A. A. Adams, J. W. Alden, C. J. Coughlin, J. N. Fernandez, D. A. Kehring, S. Mathew, S. E. Peterson, M. R. Quinlan, N. O. Seligman, M. J. Winkler

**Founded:** 2000
**Domicile:** Delaware
**Employees:** 5,200

*The McGraw-Hill Companies*

# E. I. du Pont de Nemours and Co

STANDARD
&POOR'S

**S&P Recommendation** BUY ★ ★ ★ ★ ☆

| Price | 12-Mo. Target Price | Investment Style |
|---|---|---|
| $43.86 (as of Nov 25, 2011) | $60.00 | Large-Cap Value |

**GICS Sector** Materials
**Sub-Industry** Diversified Chemicals

**Summary** This broadly diversified company is the second largest U.S. chemicals manufacturer.

## Key Stock Statistics (Source S&P, Vickers, company reports)

| | | | | | | | |
|---|---|---|---|---|---|---|---|
| 52-Wk Range | $57.00–37.10 | S&P Oper. EPS 2011E | 4.00 | Market Capitalization(B) | $40.523 | Beta | 1.46 |
| Trailing 12-Month EPS | $3.68 | S&P Oper. EPS 2012E | 4.35 | Yield (%) | 3.74 | S&P 3-Yr. Proj. EPS CAGR(%) | 10 |
| Trailing 12-Month P/E | 11.9 | P/E on S&P Oper. EPS 2011E | 11.0 | Dividend Rate/Share | $1.64 | S&P Credit Rating | A |
| $10K Invested 5 Yrs Ago | $11,101 | Common Shares Outstg. (M) | 923.9 | Institutional Ownership (%) | 63 | | |

## Price Performance

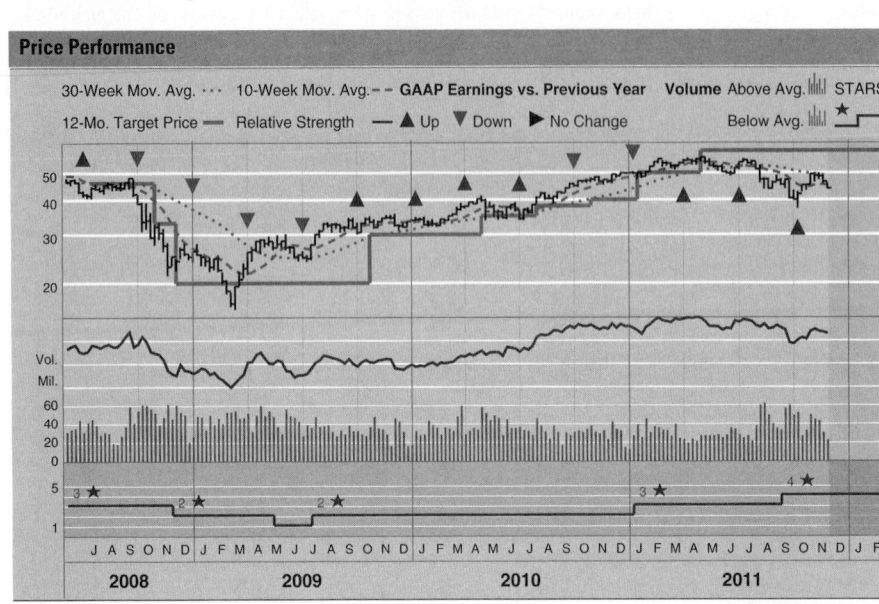

- 30-Week Mov. Avg. ···· 10-Week Mov. Avg. – – GAAP Earnings vs. Previous Year   Volume Above Avg. ▮▮▮ STARS
- 12-Mo. Target Price — Relative Strength   — ▲ Up ▼ Down ▶ No Change   Below Avg. ▮▮▮ ★

2008   2009   2010   2011

Options: ASE, CBOE, P, Ph

Analysis prepared by Equity Analyst **Leo J. Larkin** on Sep 14, 2011, when the stock traded at **$45.94**.

## Highlights

➤ We expect 2011 sales growth of about 12%, after a 21% increase in 2010, assuming steady global growth in demand in DD's chemicals-related segments, increasing selling prices (including pass-throughs of higher metal prices), and favorable exchange rates. We expect raw material and energy costs to average 11% higher in 2011, after a 6% increase in 2010.

➤ We assume the agriculture segment's sales will grow about 12% in 2011, amid continued strong agricultural industry conditions, and see profits up about 17.5%. Pharmaceutical profits projected at about $230 million for 2011 would be almost 80% lower than in 2009, as a result of the April 2010 expiration of U.S. patents for Cozaar/Hyzaar.

➤ We expect DD to achieve further productivity gains in 2011, but we expect a base tax rate (excluding impact of exchange gains and losses) of 21.0%, up from 18.8% in 2010. Our operating EPS estimate of $3.95 excludes merger costs of up to $0.34 related to the purchase of Danisco A/S for $7.0 billion.

## Investment Rationale/Risk

➤ Our buy recommendation is based on valuation. Following a sharp decline in the stock price, we think that the shares are attractive, recently trading at about 10.6X our estimate for 2012, and with a dividend yield of over 3.5%. Thanks to its expansion in its agricultural products segment and with the majority of its revenues derived from overseas, we believe DD is well positioned to benefit from what we believe is a secular increase in agriculture and greater global economic growth.

➤ Risks to our recommendation and target price include lower-than-expected global industrial activity, higher raw material costs than we assume, a loss in market share for corn and soybean seeds, a greater-than-projected decline in pharmaceutical profits, and an inability to successfully develop and launch new products.

➤ Applying a 13.8X P/E multiple to our $4.35 EPS estimate for 2012, we derive a target price of $60. On our projected P/E, the shares would trade the low end of the historical range of the last 10 years. Despite our positive secular outlook for DD and its high return on equity, we think its high ratio of liabilities to assets will limit the extent to which the P/E can expand.

## Qualitative Risk Assessment

| LOW | MEDIUM | HIGH |
|---|---|---|

Our risk assessment reflects the company's diverse business and geographic sales mix and its leadership positions in key products, offset by the cyclical nature of the chemical industry and the volatility of raw material costs.

## Quantitative Evaluations

**S&P Quality Ranking**   B+

| D | C | B- | B | B+ | A- | A | A+ |
|---|---|---|---|---|---|---|---|

**Relative Strength Rank**   MODERATE

52

LOWEST = 1   HIGHEST = 99

## Revenue/Earnings Data

**Revenue (Million $)**

| | 1Q | 2Q | 3Q | 4Q | Year |
|---|---|---|---|---|---|
| 2011 | 10,059 | 10,493 | 9,399 | -- | -- |
| 2010 | 8,484 | 8,616 | 7,067 | 7,404 | 31,505 |
| 2009 | 6,871 | 6,858 | 5,961 | 6,419 | 26,109 |
| 2008 | 8,575 | 8,837 | 7,297 | 5,820 | 30,529 |
| 2007 | 7,845 | 7,875 | 6,675 | 6,983 | 29,378 |
| 2006 | 7,394 | 7,442 | 6,309 | 6,276 | 27,421 |

**Earnings Per Share ($)**

| | | | | | |
|---|---|---|---|---|---|
| 2011 | 1.52 | 1.29 | 0.48 | E0.50 | E4.00 |
| 2010 | 1.24 | 1.26 | 0.25 | 0.40 | 3.28 |
| 2009 | 0.54 | 0.46 | 0.45 | 0.48 | 1.92 |
| 2008 | 1.31 | 1.18 | 0.40 | -0.70 | 2.20 |
| 2007 | 1.01 | 1.04 | 0.56 | 0.60 | 3.22 |
| 2006 | 0.88 | 1.04 | 0.52 | 0.94 | 3.38 |

Fiscal year ended Dec. 31. Next earnings report expected: NA. EPS Estimates based on S&P Operating Earnings; historical GAAP earnings are as reported.

## Dividend Data (Dates: mm/dd Payment Date: mm/dd/yy)

| Amount ($) | Date Decl. | Ex-Div. Date | Stk. of Record | Payment Date |
|---|---|---|---|---|
| 0.410 | 01/24 | 02/11 | 02/15 | 03/14/11 |
| 0.410 | 04/27 | 05/11 | 05/13 | 06/10/11 |
| 0.410 | 07/15 | 08/11 | 08/15 | 09/12/11 |
| 0.410 | 10/20 | 11/10 | 11/15 | 12/14/11 |

Dividends have been paid since 1904. Source: Company reports.

# E. I. du Pont de Nemours and Co

STANDARD
&POOR'S

## Business Summary September 14, 2011

E.I. du Pont de Nemours and Company, the second largest domestic chemicals producer, has made several major changes in recent years, including expanding its life sciences businesses (now crop pesticides and nutrition). Foreign sales accounted for 64% of the total in 2010.

The Agricultural segment (24% of sales in 2010, and 27% of pretax operating income) consists of Pioneer Hi-Bred (68% of segment sales), the world's largest seed company, including corn (66% of seed sales) and soybeans; DuPont is also a major global supplier of crop protection chemicals. Segment sales rose 11% in 2010, including 14% in seeds, and profits climbed 11%.

The Nutrition and Health segment (4%, 1%) includes the Solae soy protein business and microbial diagnostic testing products, and beginning in 2011 the Danisco food ingredients business.

The Electronic and Communication Technologies segment (9%, 9%) includes electronic, advanced display and photovoltaic materials and products (photoresists, slurries, films, laminants, metallization pastes), and flexographic printing and proofing systems and inks.

Performance Chemicals (20%, 22%) is the world's largest maker of titanium dioxide pigments (44% of sales in 2010) used in coatings and paper, a leading

producer of fluorochemicals (refrigerants, blowing agents, aerosols) and fluoropolymers (Teflon resins and coatings), and makes specialty and intermediate chemicals.

The Performance Coatings unit (12%, 5%) is one of the largest global auto paint suppliers (including OEM and refinish markets) and also provides liquid and powder coatings for industrial applications.

Performance Materials (20%, 21%) includes engineering polymers and elastomers for auto, electrical, consumer and industrial uses; packaging and industrial polymers and films (including interlayers for laminated safety glass); and polyester films.

Safety & Protection (10%, 9%) consists of Kevlar and Nomex aramid fibers and Tyvek and Sontara nonwovens for industrial, construction, packaging, automotive, military, and personal safety uses; solid surfaces (Corian products); and safety consulting services.

## Company Financials Fiscal Year Ended Dec. 31

| Per Share Data ($) | 2010 | 2009 | 2008 | 2007 | 2006 | 2005 | 2004 | 2003 | 2002 | 2001 |
|---|---|---|---|---|---|---|---|---|---|---|
| Tangible Book Value | 4.06 | 2.53 | 2.26 | 6.64 | 4.56 | 4.24 | 6.25 | 4.63 | 4.54 | 7.30 |
| Cash Flow | 4.79 | 3.57 | 3.79 | 4.70 | 4.49 | 3.45 | 3.11 | 2.58 | 3.35 | 5.83 |
| Earnings | 3.28 | 1.92 | 2.20 | 3.22 | 3.38 | 2.07 | 1.77 | 0.99 | 1.84 | 4.15 |
| S&P Core Earnings | 3.39 | 1.69 | 0.74 | 2.93 | 2.98 | 1.98 | 2.00 | 1.14 | 0.40 | -1.04 |
| Dividends | 1.64 | 1.64 | 1.64 | 1.52 | 1.48 | 1.46 | 1.40 | 1.40 | 1.40 | 1.40 |
| Payout Ratio | 50% | 85% | 75% | 47% | 44% | 71% | 79% | 141% | 76% | 34% |
| Prices:High | 50.17 | 35.62 | 52.49 | 53.90 | 49.68 | 54.90 | 49.39 | 46.00 | 49.80 | 49.88 |
| Prices:Low | 31.88 | 16.05 | 21.32 | 42.25 | 38.52 | 37.60 | 39.88 | 38.60 | 35.02 | 32.64 |
| P/E Ratio:High | 15 | 19 | 24 | 17 | 15 | 27 | 28 | 46 | 27 | 12 |
| P/E Ratio:Low | 10 | 8 | 10 | 13 | 11 | 18 | 23 | 39 | 19 | 8 |

| Income Statement Analysis (Million $) | | | | | | | | | | |
|---|---|---|---|---|---|---|---|---|---|---|
| Revenue | 31,505 | 26,109 | 30,529 | 29,378 | 27,421 | 26,639 | 27,340 | 26,996 | 24,006 | 24,726 |
| Operating Income | 4,419 | 3,086 | 2,904 | 4,269 | 3,612 | 3,507 | 3,574 | 3,176 | 4,263 | 4,130 |
| Depreciation | 1,380 | 1,503 | 1,444 | 1,371 | 1,384 | 1,358 | 1,347 | 1,584 | 1,515 | 1,754 |
| Interest Expense | 590 | 408 | 425 | 430 | 460 | 518 | 362 | 347 | 359 | 590 |
| Pretax Income | 3,711 | 2,184 | 2,391 | 3,743 | 3,329 | 3,558 | 1,442 | 143 | 2,124 | 6,844 |
| Effective Tax Rate | NA | 19.0% | 15.9% | 20.0% | 5.89% | 41.3% | NM | NM | 8.71% | 36.0% |
| Net Income | 3,031 | 1,755 | 2,007 | 2,988 | 3,148 | 2,053 | 1,780 | 1,002 | 1,841 | 4,328 |
| S&P Core Earnings | 3,112 | 1,543 | 677 | 2,713 | 2,768 | 1,965 | 2,008 | 1,132 | 398 | -1,087 |

| Balance Sheet & Other Financial Data (Million $) | | | | | | | | | | |
|---|---|---|---|---|---|---|---|---|---|---|
| Cash | 6,801 | 6,137 | 3,704 | 1,436 | 1,893 | 1,851 | 3,536 | 3,298 | 4,143 | 5,848 |
| Current Assets | 19,059 | 17,288 | 15,311 | 13,160 | 12,870 | 12,422 | 15,211 | 18,462 | 13,459 | 14,801 |
| Total Assets | 40,410 | 38,185 | 36,209 | 34,131 | 31,777 | 33,250 | 35,632 | 37,039 | 34,621 | 40,319 |
| Current Liabilities | 9,389 | 9,390 | 9,710 | 8,541 | 7,940 | 7,463 | 7,939 | 13,043 | 7,096 | 8,067 |
| Long Term Debt | 10,137 | 9,528 | 7,638 | 5,955 | 6,013 | 6,783 | 5,548 | 4,301 | 5,647 | 5,350 |
| Common Equity | 9,041 | 6,978 | 6,888 | 10,899 | 9,185 | 8,670 | 11,140 | 9,544 | 8,826 | 14,215 |
| Total Capital | 19,880 | 17,179 | 15,330 | 18,335 | 16,145 | 17,346 | 19,001 | 15,087 | 18,755 | 24,916 |
| Capital Expenditures | 1,508 | 1,308 | 1,978 | 1,585 | 1,532 | 1,340 | 1,232 | 1,713 | 1,280 | 1,494 |
| Cash Flow | 4,411 | 3,248 | 3,441 | 4,349 | 4,532 | 3,411 | 3,117 | 2,576 | 3,346 | 6,072 |
| Current Ratio | 2.0 | 1.8 | 1.6 | 1.5 | 1.6 | 1.7 | 1.9 | 1.4 | 1.9 | 1.8 |
| % Long Term Debt of Capitalization | 51.0 | 55.5 | 49.8 | 32.5 | 37.2 | 39.1 | 29.2 | 28.5 | 30.1 | 21.5 |
| % Net Income of Revenue | 9.6 | 6.7 | 6.6 | 10.2 | 11.5 | 7.7 | 6.5 | 3.7 | 7.7 | 17.5 |
| % Return on Assets | 7.7 | 4.7 | 5.7 | 9.1 | 9.7 | 6.0 | 4.9 | 2.8 | 4.9 | 10.9 |
| % Return on Equity | 37.8 | 25.3 | 22.6 | 29.7 | 35.2 | 20.6 | 17.1 | 10.8 | 15.9 | 31.7 |

Data as orig reptd.; bef. results of disc opers/spec. items. Per share data adj. for stk. divs.; EPS diluted. Beginning in 2008, revenues include other income. E-Estimated. NA-Not Available. NM-Not Meaningful. NR-Not Ranked. UR-Under Review.

**Office:** 1007 Market Street, Wilmington, DE 19898.
**Telephone:** 302-774-1000.
**Email:** info@dupont.com
**Website:** http://www.dupont.com

**Chrmn & CEO:** E. Kullman
**SVP, CSO & CTO:** D. Muzyka
**CFO & Chief Acctg Officer:** N.C. Fanandakis
**Treas:** S.M. Stalnecker

**Secy:** M.E. Bowler
**Investor Contact:** K. Fletcher (800-441-7515)
**Board Members:** R. H. Brown, R. A. Brown, B. Collomb, C. J. Crawford, A. M. Cutler, M. A. Hewson, L. D. Juliber, E. Kullman, W. K. Reilly, E. I. du Pont, II

**Founded:** 1802
**Domicile:** Delaware
**Employees:** 60,000

The McGraw-Hill Companies

# Eastman Chemical Co

**STANDARD &POOR'S**

| S&P Recommendation **BUY** ★★★★☆ | Price $35.47 (as of Nov 25, 2011) | 12-Mo. Target Price $50.00 | Investment Style Large-Cap Value |
|---|---|---|---|

**GICS Sector** Materials
**Sub-Industry** Diversified Chemicals

**Summary** This global company manufactures and markets chemicals, fibers and plastics used in consumer and industrial products.

## Key Stock Statistics (Source S&P, Vickers, company reports)

| | | | | | | | |
|---|---|---|---|---|---|---|---|
| 52-Wk Range | $55.36–32.45 | S&P Oper. EPS 2011**E** | 4.65 | Market Capitalization(B) | $4.880 | Beta | 1.95 |
| Trailing 12-Month EPS | $4.24 | S&P Oper. EPS 2012**E** | 5.00 | Yield (%) | 2.93 | S&P 3-Yr. Proj. EPS CAGR(%) | 10 |
| Trailing 12-Month P/E | 8.4 | P/E on S&P Oper. EPS 2011**E** | 7.6 | Dividend Rate/Share | $1.04 | S&P Credit Rating | BBB |
| $10K Invested 5 Yrs Ago | $13,816 | Common Shares Outstg. (M) | 137.6 | Institutional Ownership (%) | 86 | | |

## Price Performance

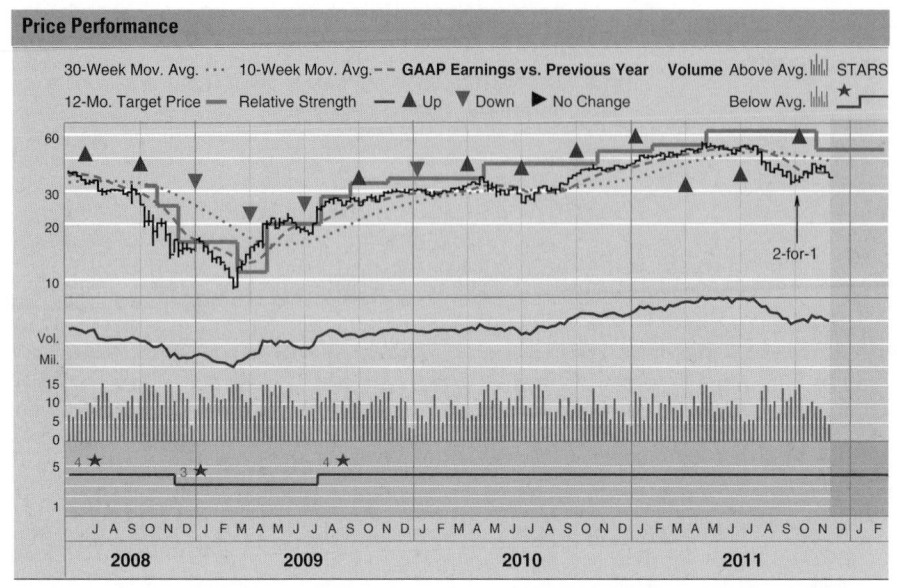

30-Week Mov. Avg. ···   10-Week Mov. Avg. - -   **GAAP Earnings vs. Previous Year**   Volume Above Avg. |ıllı| STARS
12-Mo. Target Price —   Relative Strength —   ▲ Up   ▼ Down   ▶ No Change   Below Avg. |ıllı| ★

Options: ASE, CBOE, P, Ph

Analysis prepared by Equity Analyst **S. Benway, CFA** on Nov 14, 2011, when the stock traded at **$40.09**.

## Highlights

▶ Following the early 2011 sale of EMN's PET business, we expect sales from continuing operations to increase strongly for the year, rising 23% on top of the 33% growth posted in 2010, reflecting strengthened packaging and durable goods markets and higher prices. We look for slower but still solid revenue growth of 8%-10% in 2012 due partly to increased capacity.

▶ We project record annual profits for the fibers, coatings and adhesives, and performance chemicals segments in 2011. Profits for the capacity-constrained specialty plastics unit most likely will be up by more than 20%, as the new copolyester resin plant is now sold out. Results in 2011 will reflect a full-year contribution from a new acetate tow facility and additional supply from a restarted cost-advantaged propylene plant. However, raw material costs are higher. Several sizable capacity projects and a pending small acquisition should contribute to profits beginning in 2012.

▶ We see solid growth in EPS in 2011 to $4.65, up from $3.48 in 2010. We project a further increase in 2012 to $5.00 per share.

## Investment Rationale/Risk

▶ Our buy opinion on the shares reflects our favorable outlook for EMN's ongoing businesses and its healthy balance sheet and strong cash flow. We expect record operating earnings in 2011 following the sale of the unprofitable polyester (PET) resin business for about $615 million. We look for the coatings, specialty plastics and fibers segments to grow over the long term, aided by new capacity in specialty polyesters and acetate tow.

▶ Risks to our recommendation and target price include reduced demand for the company's products, unplanned production outages and interruptions, higher-than-expected raw material costs, and possible greater-than-estimated asbestos liabilities.

▶ Our discounted cash flow model, which projects a weighted average cost of capital of 9.8% and growth in perpetuity of 3%, calculates a value for the shares of $53. A peer group of diversified chemical producers, was recently trading at 9.5X our 2012 EPS estimates. Applying this forward P/E to our 2012 forecast for EMN values the shares at $48. Our 12-month target price of $50 is a blend of these metrics.

## Qualitative Risk Assessment

| LOW | **MEDIUM** | HIGH |
|---|---|---|

Our risk assessment reflects the company's diverse business and geographic sales mix, offset by the cyclical nature of the chemicals industry and volatility of raw material costs.

## Quantitative Evaluations

**S&P Quality Ranking**          B

| D | C | B- | **B** | B+ | A- | A | A+ |
|---|---|---|---|---|---|---|---|

**Relative Strength Rank**          MODERATE

36

LOWEST = 1                    HIGHEST = 99

## Revenue/Earnings Data

**Revenue (Million $)**

| | 1Q | 2Q | 3Q | 4Q | Year |
|---|---|---|---|---|---|
| 2011 | 1,758 | 1,885 | 1,812 | -- | -- |
| 2010 | 1,370 | 1,502 | 1,507 | 1,463 | 5,842 |
| 2009 | 1,129 | 1,253 | 1,337 | 1,328 | 5,047 |
| 2008 | 1,727 | 1,834 | 1,819 | 1,346 | 6,726 |
| 2007 | 1,795 | 1,895 | 1,813 | 1,737 | 6,830 |
| 2006 | 1,803 | 1,929 | 1,966 | 1,752 | 7,450 |

**Earnings Per Share ($)**

| | | | | | |
|---|---|---|---|---|---|
| 2011 | 1.26 | 1.45 | 1.16 | E0.82 | E4.65 |
| 2010 | 0.70 | 0.96 | 1.11 | 0.12 | 2.88 |
| 2009 | 0.02 | 0.45 | 0.69 | -0.22 | 0.93 |
| 2008 | 0.73 | 0.75 | 0.67 | -0.02 | 2.16 |
| 2007 | 0.46 | 0.61 | 0.12 | 0.63 | 1.92 |
| 2006 | 0.64 | 0.69 | 0.58 | 0.56 | 2.46 |

Fiscal year ended Dec. 31. Next earnings report expected: Early February. EPS Estimates based on S&P Operating Earnings; historical GAAP earnings are as reported.

## Dividend Data (Dates: mm/dd Payment Date: mm/dd/yy)

| Amount ($) | Date Decl. | Ex-Div. Date | Stk. of Record | Payment Date |
|---|---|---|---|---|
| 0.470 | 02/17 | 03/11 | 03/15 | 04/01/11 |
| 0.470 | 05/05 | 06/13 | 06/15 | 07/01/11 |
| 0.520 | 08/05 | 09/13 | 09/15 | 10/03/11 |
| 2-for-1 | 08/05 | 10/04 | 09/15 | 10/03/11 |

Dividends have been paid since 1994. Source: Company reports.

# Eastman Chemical Co

**STANDARD &POOR'S**

## Business Summary November 14, 2011

CORPORATE OVERVIEW. Eastman Chemical Co. is a large global maker of a broad range of chemicals, plastics and fibers. International operations accounted for 52% of sales in 2010. It reports results in four segments. The coatings, adhesive, specialty polymers and inks segment (27% of 2010 sales, operating profits of $293 million) is a leading supplier of alcohols and solvents (45% of segment sales), hydrocarbon and rosin resins and dispersions (35%), and specialty polymers (20%) used in paints and coatings, inks, adhesives, and other formulated products. Performance chemicals and intermediates (36%, $224 million) includes oxo chemicals, acetyls, plasticizers and glycols used for polymers, photographic and home care products, agricultural chemicals and pharmaceutical intermediates; and additives for food and beverage ingredients. Beginning in 2010, the segment includes intermediates capacity that EMN retained following the sale in January 2011 of the discontinued polyethylene terephthalate (PET) resin business. About 65% of annual segment sales is generated in North America.

In the fibers business (19%, $323 million), EMN is one of the world's two largest suppliers of acetate cigarette filter tow (annual capacity of 463 million lbs. at end of 2010) and the leader in acetate yarn for use in apparel, home furnishings and industrial fabrics. The business reported record profits in 2010. The company projects global growth in demand for filter tow of 1%-2% annually over the next several years, with Asia accounting for over 50% of global growth. In 2010, production began at a new acetate tow facility in South Korea to support customer demand in Asia. The business also includes acetyl chemicals (acetate flake, acetic anhydride). Specialty plastics (18%, $88 million) includes modified copolyesters (80% of segment sales) and cellulosic (20%) plastics for specialty packaging, consumer, medical and durable goods, and specialty applications, including in-store fixtures, optical films, fibers/nonwovens, and liquid crystal displays (LCD). EMN's copolyesters compete with alternative polymers, primarily acrylic and polycarbonate. Segment sales in 2010 increased by 39% from strengthened end-use demand and the positive impact of growth initiatives for copolyesters and the Tritan copolyester product lines, while earnings rose from $9 million in 2009.

## Company Financials Fiscal Year Ended Dec. 31

| Per Share Data ($) | 2010 | 2009 | 2008 | 2007 | 2006 | 2005 | 2004 | 2003 | 2002 | 2001 |
|---|---|---|---|---|---|---|---|---|---|---|
| Tangible Book Value | 8.06 | 7.84 | 7.76 | 13.32 | 10.21 | 7.93 | 5.35 | 4.50 | 4.53 | 4.96 |
| Cash Flow | 4.77 | 2.72 | 3.84 | 3.49 | 4.32 | 5.25 | 3.11 | 0.61 | 3.09 | 1.67 |
| Earnings | 2.88 | 0.93 | 2.16 | 1.92 | 2.46 | 3.41 | 1.09 | -1.77 | 0.51 | -1.17 |
| S&P Core Earnings | 2.91 | 0.89 | 1.65 | 1.90 | 2.21 | 2.82 | 1.12 | -1.73 | 0.13 | -1.53 |
| Dividends | 0.90 | 0.88 | 0.88 | 0.88 | 0.88 | 0.88 | 0.88 | 0.88 | 0.88 | 0.88 |
| Payout Ratio | 31% | 95% | 41% | 46% | 36% | 26% | 81% | NM | 173% | NM |
| Prices:High | 42.29 | 30.98 | 39.15 | 36.22 | 30.65 | 30.90 | 29.09 | 19.79 | 24.78 | 27.83 |
| Prices:Low | 25.55 | 8.88 | 12.94 | 28.77 | 23.65 | 22.05 | 19.00 | 13.78 | 17.27 | 14.52 |
| P/E Ratio:High | 15 | 33 | 18 | 19 | 12 | 9 | 27 | NM | 49 | NM |
| P/E Ratio:Low | 9 | 10 | 6 | 15 | 10 | 6 | 17 | NM | 34 | NM |

| Income Statement Analysis (Million $) | | | | | | | | | | |
|---|---|---|---|---|---|---|---|---|---|---|
| Revenue | 5,842 | 5,047 | 6,726 | 6,830 | 7,450 | 7,059 | 6,580 | 5,800 | 5,320 | 5,384 |
| Operating Income | 1,171 | 800 | 805 | 929 | 981 | 1,092 | 696 | 590 | 610 | 755 |
| Depreciation | 280 | 274 | 256 | 264 | 308 | 304 | 322 | 367 | 397 | 435 |
| Interest Expense | 99.0 | 85.0 | 106 | 113 | 80.0 | 100 | 115 | 124 | 128 | 140 |
| Pretax Income | 636 | 226 | 429 | 470 | 576 | 783 | 64.0 | -381 | 84.0 | -297 |
| Effective Tax Rate | NA | 39.8% | 23.5% | 31.7% | 29.0% | 28.9% | NM | NM | 5.95% | NM |
| Net Income | 425 | 136 | 328 | 321 | 409 | 557 | 170 | -273 | 79.0 | -179 |
| S&P Core Earnings | 430 | 131 | 252 | 316 | 368 | 459 | 173 | -266 | 20.4 | -236 |

| Balance Sheet & Other Financial Data (Million $) | | | | | | | | | | |
|---|---|---|---|---|---|---|---|---|---|---|
| Cash | 516 | 793 | 387 | 888 | 939 | 524 | 325 | 558 | 77.0 | 66.0 |
| Current Assets | 2,047 | 1,735 | 1,423 | 2,293 | 2,422 | 1,924 | 1,768 | 2,010 | 1,529 | 1,458 |
| Total Assets | 6,023 | 5,515 | 5,281 | 6,009 | 6,173 | 5,773 | 5,872 | 6,230 | 6,273 | 6,086 |
| Current Liabilities | 1,070 | 800 | 832 | 1,122 | 1,059 | 1,051 | 1,099 | 1,477 | 1,224 | 958 |
| Long Term Debt | 1,598 | 1,604 | 1,442 | 1,613 | 1,589 | 1,621 | 2,061 | 2,089 | 2,054 | 2,143 |
| Common Equity | 1,627 | 1,513 | 1,553 | 2,082 | 2,029 | 1,612 | 1,184 | 1,913 | 1,271 | 1,378 |
| Total Capital | 3,231 | 3,117 | 3,008 | 3,917 | 3,618 | 3,550 | 3,455 | 4,318 | 3,809 | 3,973 |
| Capital Expenditures | 243 | 310 | 634 | 518 | 389 | 343 | 248 | 230 | 427 | 234 |
| Cash Flow | 705 | 399 | 584 | 585 | 717 | 861 | 492 | 94.0 | 476 | 256 |
| Current Ratio | 1.9 | 2.2 | 1.7 | 2.0 | 2.3 | 1.8 | 1.6 | 1.4 | 1.2 | 1.5 |
| % Long Term Debt of Capitalization | 49.5 | 51.5 | 47.9 | 42.4 | 43.9 | 45.7 | 59.7 | 48.4 | 53.9 | 53.9 |
| % Net Income of Revenue | 7.3 | 2.7 | 4.9 | 4.7 | 5.5 | 7.9 | 2.6 | NM | 1.5 | NM |
| % Return on Assets | 7.4 | 2.5 | 5.8 | 5.3 | 6.8 | 9.6 | 2.8 | NM | 1.3 | NM |
| % Return on Equity | 27.1 | 8.9 | 18.1 | 15.6 | 22.5 | 39.8 | 15.3 | NM | 6.0 | NM |

Data as orig reptd.; bef. results of disc opers/spec. items. Per share data adj. for stk. divs.; EPS diluted. E-Estimated. NA-Not Available. NM-Not Meaningful. NR-Not Ranked. UR-Under Review.

**Office:** 200 S Wilcox Dr, Kingsport, TN, USA 37660-5147.
**Telephone:** 423-229-2000.
**Website:** http://www.eastman.com
**Chrmn & CEO:** J.P. Rogers

**SVP, Chief Admin Officer & General Counsel:** T.K. Lee
**SVP & CTO:** G.W. Nelson
**CFO:** C.E. Espeland
**Chief Acctg Officer & Cntlr:** S.V. King

**Investor Contact:** G. Riddle (212-835-1620)
**Board Members:** H. P. Alfonso, G. E. Anderson, B. D. Begemann, M. P. Connors, S. R. Demeritt, R. M. Hernandez, R. Hornbaker, L. M. Kling, H. L. Lance, T. H. McLain, D. W. Raisbeck, J. P. Rogers

**Founded:** 1920
**Domicile:** Delaware
**Employees:** 10,000

# Eaton Corp

**STANDARD &POOR'S**

**S&P Recommendation** BUY ★★★★☆

| | | |
|---|---|---|
| **Price** $40.55 (as of Nov 25, 2011) | **12-Mo. Target Price** $55.00 | **Investment Style** Large-Cap Blend |

**GICS Sector** Industrials
**Sub-Industry** Industrial Machinery

**Summary** This diversified industrial manufacturer's products include electrical systems and components for power management, truck transmissions and fluid power systems, and services for industrial, mobile and aircraft equipment.

## Key Stock Statistics (Source S&P, Vickers, company reports)

| | | | | | | | |
|---|---|---|---|---|---|---|---|
| 52-Wk Range | $56.49– 33.09 | S&P Oper. EPS 2011**E** | 4.01 | Market Capitalization(B) | $13.552 | Beta | 1.51 |
| Trailing 12-Month EPS | $3.69 | S&P Oper. EPS 2012**E** | 4.55 | Yield (%) | 3.35 | S&P 3-Yr. Proj. EPS CAGR(%) | 22 |
| Trailing 12-Month P/E | 11.0 | P/E on S&P Oper. EPS 2011**E** | 10.1 | Dividend Rate/Share | $1.36 | S&P Credit Rating | A- |
| $10K Invested 5 Yrs Ago | $12,257 | Common Shares Outstg. (M) | 334.2 | Institutional Ownership (%) | 83 | | |

## Price Performance

30-Week Mov. Avg. ···· 10-Week Mov. Avg. – – GAAP Earnings vs. Previous Year   Volume Above Avg. ▎▍▏ STARS
12-Mo. Target Price —   Relative Strength —   ▲ Up   ▼ Down   ▶ No Change   Below Avg. ▎▍▏ ★

Options: ASE, CBOE, P, Ph

Analysis prepared by Equity Analyst **Stewart Scharf** on Oct 26, 2011, when the stock traded at **$43.20**.

## Highlights

➤ We expect total revenues to climb about 18% in 2011 (low-single digits organically), driven by strength in the hydraulics and trucking segments, and growth in electrical, automotive and aerospace. Although we see more modest growth during 2012 due to softer global economic conditions, especially in the first half and in Europe, emerging markets should remain strong and bookings should pick up in most regions later in the year, by our analysis. In our view, revenues will advance in the high single digits, with growth in all segments.

➤ We forecast that operating margins (EBITDA) will continue to expand through 2012, reaching about 15.5%, up nearly 100 basis points from our 2011 projection, as better pricing, well-controlled costs and more stabilized metals prices aid results. We see margins widening in most segments, driven by electrical, hydraulics, truck and automotive.

➤ We estimate a tax rate of near 16.5% in 2011, and operating EPS of $4.01 in 2011 (excluding $0.04 of restructuring charges), advancing to $4.55 in 2012.

## Investment Rationale/Risk

➤ Based on our valuation metrics, and our view that global markets will gradually rebound during 2012 once sovereign debt issues are resolved in Europe and budgets are finalized in the U.S., we keep our buy opinion on the shares. We expect ETN to continue to generate strong cash for share buybacks, annual dividend hikes and selective acquisitions. In addition, we see more demand in mid-cycle businesses, which comprise about one-third of total revenue.

➤ Risks to our recommendation and target price include softer global economic markets, an inability to offset volatile commodity costs with hedging programs, adverse foreign currency exchange, and pension plans headwinds leading to higher pension costs.

➤ Our 12-month target price of $55 blends two valuation metrics. Our discounted cash flow model, which assumes 3% perpetuity growth and a 10% discount rate, indicates an intrinsic value of $52. As for relative peer valuations, we apply a multiple of near 13X, above the peer forward average, to our 2012 operating EPS estimate, implying a $58 valuation.

## Qualitative Risk Assessment

| LOW | MEDIUM | HIGH |
|---|---|---|

Our risk assessment reflects our view that ETN has good geographic and product diversification, offset by the highly cyclical nature of the company's various end markets, and significant pension and other post-retirement benefit obligations.

## Quantitative Evaluations

**S&P Quality Ranking**     A

| D | C | B- | B | B+ | A- | A | A+ |
|---|---|---|---|---|---|---|---|

**Relative Strength Rank**     MODERATE

**51**

LOWEST = 1                                    HIGHEST = 99

## Revenue/Earnings Data

**Revenue (Million $)**

| | 1Q | 2Q | 3Q | 4Q | Year |
|---|---|---|---|---|---|
| 2011 | 3,803 | 4,090 | 4,123 | -- | -- |
| 2010 | 3,103 | 3,378 | 3,571 | 3,663 | 13,715 |
| 2009 | 2,813 | 2,901 | 3,028 | 3,131 | 11,873 |
| 2008 | 3,496 | 4,279 | 4,114 | 3,487 | 15,376 |
| 2007 | 3,153 | 3,248 | 3,298 | 3,374 | 13,033 |
| 2006 | 2,991 | 3,162 | 3,115 | 3,102 | 12,370 |

**Earnings Per Share ($)**

| | | | | | |
|---|---|---|---|---|---|
| 2011 | 0.83 | 0.97 | 1.07 | E1.13 | E4.01 |
| 2010 | 0.46 | 0.67 | 0.79 | 0.82 | 2.73 |
| 2009 | -0.15 | 0.09 | 0.57 | 0.63 | 1.14 |
| 2008 | 0.81 | 1.02 | 0.94 | 0.49 | 3.25 |
| 2007 | 0.77 | 0.80 | 0.80 | 0.84 | 3.19 |
| 2006 | 0.68 | 0.82 | 0.70 | 0.80 | 2.99 |

Fiscal year ended Dec. 31. Next earnings report expected: NA. EPS Estimates based on S&P Operating Earnings; historical GAAP earnings are as reported.

## Dividend Data (Dates: mm/dd Payment Date: mm/dd/yy)

| Amount ($) | Date Decl. | Ex-Div. Date | Stk. of Record | Payment Date |
|---|---|---|---|---|
| 2-for-1 | 01/27 | 03/01 | 02/07 | 02/28/11 |
| 0.340 | 04/27 | 05/05 | 05/09 | 05/27/11 |
| 0.340 | 07/27 | 08/04 | 08/08 | 08/26/11 |
| 0.340 | 10/26 | 11/03 | 11/07 | 11/25/11 |

Dividends have been paid since 1923. Source: Company reports.

---

**Please read the Required Disclosures and Analyst Certification on the last page of this report.**

The **McGraw·Hill** Companies

# Eaton Corp

## Business Summary October 26, 2011

CORPORATE OVERVIEW. Eaton Corp., a diversified industrial equipment and parts manufacturer with $13.7 billion in revenues in 2010, conducts business through six diversified business segments.

ETN separates its electrical product results into two units -- Electrical Americas (27% of 2010 sales, with 14.4% operating margins, excluding one-time items) and Electrical Rest of World (20%, 10.8%). The two units make a wide range of power distribution and control equipment, such as switchboards, circuit boards, circuit breakers, starters, AC and DC Uninterruptible Power Systems (UPS) and power management software. They also produce electronic sensors that control industrial machinery, as well as electricity quality-monitoring systems. Both units' primary competitors include GE, Germany-based Siemens and Schneider Electric. Demand for ETN's electrical equipment and components mainly reflects the health of the non-residential, power quality, industrial, residential construction and telecom industries.

The Hydraulics segment (16%; 12.7%) makes products including, but not limited to, pumps, motors, valves, cylinders, hydraulic power units, control and sensing products, fluid conveyance products, hoses and assemblies. The principal markets for the segment's products include various energy industries, and the marine, agriculture, construction, mining, forestry, utilities, ma-

terial handling, automotive, machine tool, metals and entertainment industries.

The Aerospace segment (11%; 14.6%) is a global provider of pumps, motors, hydraulic power units and other equipment, valves, cylinders, hoses and fittings, control and sensing products, fluid conveyance products, sensors, actuators and other products used in the aviation industry. The segment's products are sold to after-market customers as well as to manufacturers of commercial and military aviation products.

ETN's Truck unit (15%; 12.3%) is the world's largest maker of medium- and heavy-duty truck transmissions. The unit's products include transmissions and transmission components such as drive trains, clutches, gearboxes and shafts along with brake clutch products. The segment's primary competitors are Germany-based ZF Friedrichshafen AG and Wabco. Demand for ETN's truck components is mainly driven by the health of the medium- and heavy-duty truck market globally.

## Company Financials Fiscal Year Ended Dec. 31

| Per Share Data ($) | 2010 | 2009 | 2008 | 2007 | 2006 | 2005 | 2004 | 2003 | 2002 | 2001 |
|---|---|---|---|---|---|---|---|---|---|---|
| Tangible Book Value | NM | NM | NM | NM | 1.15 | 0.05 | 1.73 | 1.57 | NM | 0.14 |
| Cash Flow | 4.38 | 2.85 | 5.07 | 4.75 | 4.40 | 4.04 | 3.34 | 2.59 | 2.25 | 1.89 |
| Earnings | 2.73 | 1.14 | 3.25 | 3.19 | 2.99 | 2.62 | 2.07 | 1.28 | 0.98 | 0.60 |
| S&P Core Earnings | 2.94 | 1.45 | 3.05 | 3.43 | 3.23 | 2.70 | 2.08 | 1.22 | 0.49 | -0.09 |
| Dividends | 1.08 | 1.00 | 1.00 | 0.86 | 0.74 | 0.62 | 0.54 | 0.46 | 0.44 | 0.44 |
| Payout Ratio | 40% | 88% | 31% | 27% | 24% | 24% | 26% | 36% | 45% | 74% |
| Prices:High | 51.35 | 33.53 | 49.07 | 52.06 | 39.99 | 36.35 | 36.32 | 27.35 | 22.17 | 20.36 |
| Prices:Low | 30.42 | 15.01 | 18.84 | 35.96 | 31.19 | 28.33 | 26.37 | 16.50 | 14.78 | 13.78 |
| P/E Ratio:High | 19 | 30 | 15 | 16 | 13 | 14 | 18 | 21 | 23 | 34 |
| P/E Ratio:Low | 11 | 13 | 6 | 11 | 10 | 11 | 13 | 13 | 15 | 23 |

| Income Statement Analysis (Million $) | 2010 | 2009 | 2008 | 2007 | 2006 | 2005 | 2004 | 2003 | 2002 | 2001 |
|---|---|---|---|---|---|---|---|---|---|---|
| Revenue | 13,715 | 11,873 | 15,376 | 13,033 | 12,370 | 11,115 | 9,817 | 8,061 | 7,209 | 7,299 |
| Operating Income | 1,722 | 1,281 | 1,847 | 1,646 | 1,487 | 1,468 | 1,287 | 984 | 870 | 703 |
| Depreciation | 551 | 573 | 592 | 469 | 434 | 409 | 400 | 394 | 353 | 355 |
| Interest Expense | 136 | 150 | 157 | 147 | 104 | 90.0 | 78.0 | 87.0 | 104 | 142 |
| Pretax Income | 1,036 | 303 | 1,128 | 1,041 | 989 | 996 | 781 | 508 | 399 | 278 |
| Effective Tax Rate | NA | NM | 6.47% | 7.88% | 7.79% | 19.2% | 17.0% | 24.0% | 29.6% | 39.2% |
| Net Income | 929 | 383 | 1,055 | 959 | 912 | 805 | 648 | 386 | 281 | 169 |
| S&P Core Earnings | 998 | 488 | 989 | 1,031 | 985 | 832 | 651 | 367 | 141 | -25.0 |

| Balance Sheet & Other Financial Data (Million $) | 2010 | 2009 | 2008 | 2007 | 2006 | 2005 | 2004 | 2003 | 2002 | 2001 |
|---|---|---|---|---|---|---|---|---|---|---|
| Cash | 1,171 | 773 | 530 | 646 | 114 | 110 | 85.0 | 61.0 | 75.0 | 112 |
| Current Assets | 5,506 | 4,524 | 4,795 | 4,767 | 4,408 | 3,578 | 3,182 | 3,093 | 2,457 | 2,387 |
| Total Assets | 17,252 | 16,282 | 16,655 | 13,430 | 11,417 | 10,218 | 9,075 | 8,223 | 7,138 | 7,646 |
| Current Liabilities | 3,233 | 2,689 | 3,745 | 3,659 | 3,407 | 2,968 | 2,262 | 2,126 | 1,734 | 1,669 |
| Long Term Debt | 3,382 | 3,349 | 3,190 | 3,417 | 1,774 | 1,830 | Nil | 1,651 | 1,887 | 2,252 |
| Common Equity | 7,362 | 6,777 | 6,317 | 5,172 | 4,106 | 3,778 | 3,606 | 3,117 | 2,302 | 2,475 |
| Total Capital | 10,789 | 10,172 | 9,776 | 7,604 | 5,880 | 5,608 | 3,606 | 4,768 | 4,752 | 5,307 |
| Capital Expenditures | 394 | 195 | 448 | 354 | 360 | 363 | 330 | 2,733 | 228 | 295 |
| Cash Flow | 1,488 | 956 | 1,647 | 1,428 | 1,346 | 1,214 | 1,048 | 780 | 634 | 524 |
| Current Ratio | 1.7 | 1.7 | 1.3 | 1.3 | 1.3 | 1.2 | 1.4 | 1.5 | 1.4 | 1.4 |
| % Long Term Debt of Capitalization | 31.4 | 32.9 | 31.7 | 32.0 | 30.2 | 32.6 | Nil | 34.6 | 39.7 | 42.4 |
| % Net Income of Revenue | 6.8 | 3.2 | 6.9 | 7.4 | 7.4 | 7.2 | 6.6 | 4.8 | 3.9 | 2.3 |
| % Return on Assets | 5.5 | 2.3 | 7.0 | 7.7 | 8.4 | 8.3 | 7.5 | 5.0 | 3.8 | 2.1 |
| % Return on Equity | 13.1 | 5.9 | 18.4 | 20.7 | 23.1 | 21.8 | 19.3 | 14.2 | 11.8 | 6.9 |

Data as orig reptd.; bef. results of disc opers/spec. items. Per share data adj. for stk. divs.; EPS diluted. E-Estimated. NA-Not Available. NM-Not Meaningful. NR-Not Ranked. UR-Under Review.

**Office:** Eaton Center 1111 Superior Ave, Cleveland, OH 44114-2584.
**Telephone:** 216-523-5000.
**Website:** http://www.eaton.com
**Chrmn, Pres & CEO:** A.M. Cutler

**EVP & CTO:** L. Jonsson
**EVP & General Counsel:** M.M. McGuire
**SVP, Chief Acctg Officer & Cntlr:** B.K. Rawot
**SVP & Secy:** T.E. Moran

**Investor Contact:** B. Hartman (216-523-4501)
**Auditor:** ERNST & YOUNG
**Board Members:** G. S. Barrett, T. M. Bluedorn, C. M. Connor, M. J. Critelli, A. M. Cutler, C. E. Golden, A. E. Johnson, N. C. Lautenbach, D. L. McCoy, G. R. Page, G. L. Tooker

**Founded:** 1916
**Domicile:** Ohio
**Employees:** 70,000

# eBay Inc

**STANDARD &POOR'S**

| S&P Recommendation | HOLD ★★★★★ | Price $28.23 (as of Nov 25, 2011) | 12-Mo. Target Price $37.00 | Investment Style Large-Cap Growth |
|---|---|---|---|---|

**GICS Sector** Information Technology
**Sub-Industry** Internet Software & Services

**Summary** EBAY owns one of the world's most popular e-commerce destinations, which bears its name, as well as PayPal (an online payments company) and other online business interests.

## Key Stock Statistics (Source S&P, Vickers, company reports)

| | | | | | | | |
|---|---|---|---|---|---|---|---|
| 52-Wk Range | $35.35–26.86 | S&P Oper. EPS 2011**E** | 1.75 | Market Capitalization(B) | $36.443 | Beta | 1.52 |
| Trailing 12-Month EPS | $1.37 | S&P Oper. EPS 2012**E** | 2.05 | Yield (%) | Nil | S&P 3-Yr. Proj. EPS CAGR(%) | 17 |
| Trailing 12-Month P/E | 20.6 | P/E on S&P Oper. EPS 2011**E** | 16.1 | Dividend Rate/Share | Nil | S&P Credit Rating | A |
| $10K Invested 5 Yrs Ago | $8,455 | Common Shares Outstg. (M) | 1,290.9 | Institutional Ownership (%) | 81 | | |

## Price Performance

30-Week Mov. Avg. · · · 10-Week Mov. Avg. — **GAAP Earnings vs. Previous Year**   **Volume** Above Avg. ▥▥▥   STARS
12-Mo. Target Price — Relative Strength — ▲ Up ▼ Down ► No Change    Below Avg. ▥▥▥ ★

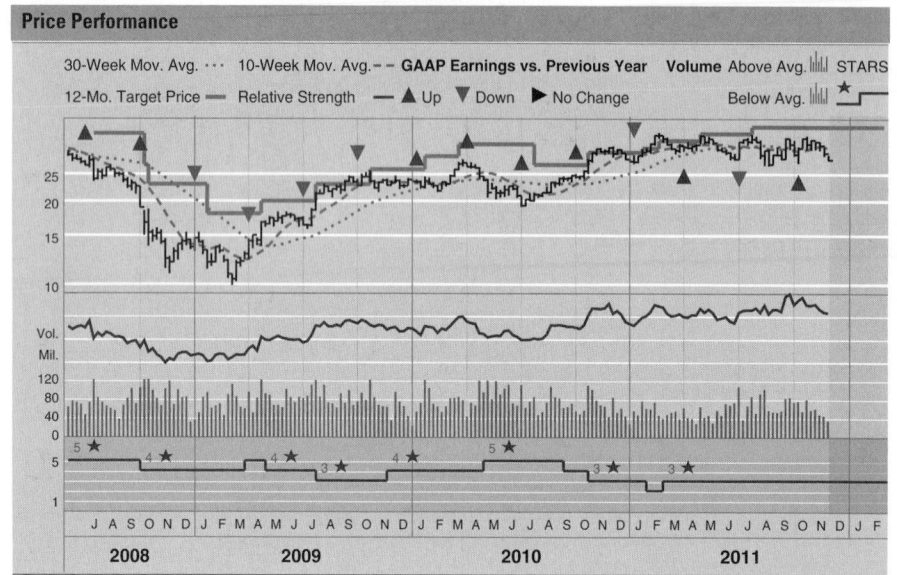

Options: ASE, CBOE, P, Ph

Analysis prepared by Equity Analyst **Scott Kessler** on Oct 21, 2011, when the stock traded at **$32.01**.

## Highlights

➤ We project that net revenues excluding Skype (70% of which was sold in 2009 and the rest of which was sold in 2011) will increase 24% in 2011 and 18% in 2012. We believe EBAY will report annual growth of 16% in its Marketplaces segment (including eBay.com and the mid-2009-acquired Gmarket) and 28% in the Payments business (PayPal) in 2011. The last year Marketplaces grew more than 10% was 2007.

➤ We think EBAY's annual non-GAAP operating margins bottomed in 2009, reflecting economic difficulties, notable retooling of and investment in the core marketplaces businesses around the world, and a less favorable revenue mix. We foresee a negative impact from acquisitions in 2011 before improvement in 2012.

➤ In June 2011, EBAY acquired GSI Commerce in a transaction valued at $2.4 billion. GSI provides e-commerce solutions and interactive marketing services to larger online vendors, and is operating as a subsidiary of EBAY. A $2 billion stock buyback program was announced in October 2010.

## Investment Rationale/Risk

➤ We see EBAY as a leader in online auctions, a mainstream Internet retail destination, a facilitator of large transactions involving cars and real estate, and having a growing international presence. We are optimistic about its payment segments and mobile opportunities, but we have concerns about the sustainability of growth in the Marketplaces segment and the possibility of increasing state taxes on Internet sales. Additionally, we see potential issues related to regulatory and legal matters (such as oversight of PayPal and a lawsuit involving craigslist).

➤ Risks to our opinion and target price include the potential for weakening consumer sentiment/spending, an increase in competition in the marketplaces and/or payments areas, and issues related to the GSI acquisition.

➤ Our DCF model, with assumptions that include a WACC of 10.7%, average annual free cash flow growth of 12% from 2011 to 2015, and a terminal growth rate of 3%, yields an intrinsic value of $37, which is our 12-month target price.

## Qualitative Risk Assessment

| LOW | MEDIUM | **HIGH** |
|---|---|---|

Our risk assessment reflects our view that the company operates in fast-changing areas and faces notable competition. Over the past few years, we have viewed EBAY's quarterly results, financial outlook, strategic decisions and management changes as disappointing at times. This is only partially offset by our view of EBAY as a well-established leader in the Internet segment, with a business model that we see as attractive, and a strong balance sheet.

## Quantitative Evaluations

**S&P Quality Ranking** B+

| D | C | B- | B | **B+** | A- | A | A+ |
|---|---|---|---|---|---|---|---|

**Relative Strength Rank** MODERATE

35

LOWEST = 1    HIGHEST = 99

## Revenue/Earnings Data

**Revenue (Million $)**

| | 1Q | 2Q | 3Q | 4Q | Year |
|---|---|---|---|---|---|
| 2011 | 2,546 | 2,760 | 2,966 | -- | -- |
| 2010 | 2,196 | 2,215 | 2,249 | 2,495 | 9,156 |
| 2009 | 2,021 | 2,098 | 2,238 | 2,371 | 8,727 |
| 2008 | 2,192 | 2,196 | 2,118 | 2,036 | 8,541 |
| 2007 | 1,768 | 1,418 | 1,889 | 2,181 | 7,672 |
| 2006 | 1,390 | 1,411 | 1,449 | 1,720 | 5,970 |

**Earnings Per Share ($)**

| | | | | | |
|---|---|---|---|---|---|
| 2011 | 0.36 | 0.22 | 0.37 | E0.50 | E1.75 |
| 2010 | 0.30 | 0.31 | 0.33 | 0.42 | 1.36 |
| 2009 | 0.28 | 0.25 | 0.27 | 1.02 | 1.83 |
| 2008 | 0.34 | 0.35 | 0.38 | 0.29 | 1.36 |
| 2007 | 0.27 | 0.27 | -0.69 | 0.39 | 0.25 |
| 2006 | 0.17 | 0.17 | 0.20 | 0.25 | 0.79 |

Fiscal year ended Dec. 31. Next earnings report expected: NA. EPS Estimates based on S&P Operating Earnings; historical GAAP earnings are as reported.

## Dividend Data

No cash dividends have been paid.

# eBay Inc

**STANDARD &POOR'S**

## Business Summary October 21, 2011

CORPORATE OVERVIEW. eBay operates the world's largest online trading community. As of September 2011, the Marketplaces segment had 98.7 million active users (compared with 93.2 million a year earlier), who accounted for total gross merchandise volume (including vehicles) of $16.8 billion ($14.7 billion) in the third quarter of 2011. Following acquisitions in recent years, the company also owns Bill Me Later (online payments), GSI Commerce (enterprise commerce and marketing solutions), PayPal (online payments), Rent.com (home and apartment rentals), Shopping.com (comparison shopping), StubHub (online ticket sales), and Gmarket (Asia-focused e-commerce). As of October 2011, PayPal had 100.3 million active registered accounts (87.2 million). In November 2009, EBAY sold 70% of Skype to a group of investors in a transaction valuing the business at $2.75 billion. In October 2011, Skype was sold to Microsoft (MSFT 27, Buy) for $8.5 billion, and EBAY netted $1.7 billion in pre-tax proceeds for its 30% stake.

EBAY and its affiliates have websites directed toward the following geographies: Argentina, Australia, Austria, Belgium, Brazil, Canada, China, France, Germany, Hong Kong, India, Ireland, Italy, Malaysia, Mexico, the Netherlands, New Zealand, the Philippines, Poland, Singapore, South Korea, Spain, Sweden, Switzerland, Taiwan, Thailand, Turkey, the U.K. and Vietnam. In December 2006, EBAY announced it would contribute its China operations to a joint venture with Internet portal and wireless services company TOM Online.

EBAY owns a 49% stake in the venture, which was created in February 2007. In May 2010, EBAY and Gmarket's founder announced a joint venture to expand Gmarket's offerings in Japan and Singapore. In April 2011, EBAY announced the pending acquisition of GittiGidiyor, a leading online marketplace in Turkey, for an undisclosed sum.

CORPORATE STRATEGY. EBAY's stated goal is to become the world's most efficient and abundant marketplace by expanding its community of users, delivering value to buyers and sellers, creating a global marketplace, and providing a faster, easier and safer trading experience. EBAY has increasingly employed acquisitions to fulfill the aforementioned goal, with a focus on international expansion and offering more choices and services to its buyers and sellers. In our view, PayPal was an extremely successful acquisition because it dramatically enhanced the user experience. Moreover, we think the combination accelerated the benefits the companies already derived from the "network effect" (whereby a product/service becomes more valuable to its users as its number of users increases).

## Company Financials Fiscal Year Ended Dec. 31

| Per Share Data ($) | 2010 | 2009 | 2008 | 2007 | 2006 | 2005 | 2004 | 2003 | 2002 | 2001 |
|---|---|---|---|---|---|---|---|---|---|---|
| Tangible Book Value | 6.60 | 5.30 | 2.59 | 3.90 | 2.69 | 2.21 | 2.73 | 2.23 | 1.46 | 1.11 |
| Cash Flow | 1.93 | 2.45 | 1.90 | 0.69 | 1.17 | 1.05 | 0.75 | 0.46 | 0.28 | 0.16 |
| Earnings | 1.36 | 1.83 | 1.36 | 0.25 | 0.79 | 0.78 | 0.57 | 0.34 | 0.21 | 0.08 |
| S&P Core Earnings | 1.35 | 1.01 | 1.36 | 1.26 | 0.79 | 0.61 | 0.43 | 0.21 | 0.04 | -0.00 |
| Dividends | Nil | Nil | Nil | Nil | Nil | Nil | Nil | Nil | Nil | Nil |
| Payout Ratio | Nil | Nil | Nil | Nil | Nil | Nil | Nil | Nil | Nil | Nil |
| Prices:High | 31.64 | 25.80 | 33.53 | 40.73 | 47.86 | 58.89 | 59.21 | 32.40 | 17.71 | 18.19 |
| Prices:Low | 19.06 | 9.91 | 10.91 | 28.60 | 22.83 | 30.78 | 31.30 | 16.88 | 12.21 | 7.11 |
| P/E Ratio:High | 23 | 14 | 25 | NM | 61 | 75 | NM | 95 | 83 | NM |
| P/E Ratio:Low | 14 | 5 | 8 | NM | 29 | 39 | NM | 50 | 57 | NM |

| Income Statement Analysis (Million $) | | | | | | | | | | |
|---|---|---|---|---|---|---|---|---|---|---|
| Revenue | 9,156 | 8,727 | 8,541 | 7,672 | 5,970 | 4,552 | 3,271 | 2,165 | 1,214 | 749 |
| Operating Income | 2,837 | 2,649 | 2,845 | 2,606 | 1,968 | 1,820 | 1,313 | 828 | 431 | 227 |
| Depreciation | 762 | 811 | 711 | 602 | 545 | 378 | 254 | 159 | 76.6 | 86.6 |
| Interest Expense | NA | NA | 8.04 | 16.6 | 5.92 | 3.48 | 8.88 | 4.31 | 1.49 | 2.85 |
| Pretax Income | 2,098 | 2,879 | 2,184 | 751 | 1,547 | 1,549 | 1,128 | 662 | 398 | 163 |
| Effective Tax Rate | NA | 17.0% | 18.5% | 53.6% | 27.2% | 30.2% | 30.5% | 31.3% | 36.7% | 49.1% |
| Net Income | 1,801 | 2,389 | 1,779 | 348 | 1,126 | 1,082 | 778 | 447 | 250 | 90.4 |
| S&P Core Earnings | 1,787 | 1,325 | 1,779 | 1,739 | 1,126 | 853 | 589 | 270 | 52.2 | -4.04 |

| Balance Sheet & Other Financial Data (Million $) | | | | | | | | | | |
|---|---|---|---|---|---|---|---|---|---|---|
| Cash | 6,623 | 4,944 | 3,353 | 5,984 | 2,663 | 1,314 | 1,330 | 1,382 | 1,109 | 524 |
| Current Assets | 11,065 | 8,460 | 6,287 | 7,123 | 4,971 | 3,183 | 2,911 | 2,146 | 1,468 | 884 |
| Total Assets | 22,004 | 18,408 | 15,592 | 15,366 | 13,494 | 11,789 | 7,991 | 5,820 | 4,124 | 1,679 |
| Current Liabilities | 4,517 | 3,642 | 3,705 | 3,100 | 2,518 | 1,485 | 1,085 | 647 | 386 | 180 |
| Long Term Debt | 1,494 | NA | Nil | Nil | Nil | Nil | 0.08 | 124 | 13.8 | 12.0 |
| Common Equity | 15,302 | 13,788 | 11,084 | 11,705 | 10,905 | 10,048 | 6,728 | 4,896 | 3,556 | 1,429 |
| Total Capital | 16,796 | 13,788 | 11,084 | 11,705 | 10,905 | 10,264 | 6,868 | 5,139 | 3,715 | 1,479 |
| Capital Expenditures | 724 | 567 | 566 | 454 | 515 | 338 | 293 | 365 | 139 | 57.4 |
| Cash Flow | 2,563 | 3,200 | 2,490 | 950 | 1,670 | 1,460 | 1,032 | 606 | 326 | 177 |
| Current Ratio | 2.5 | 2.3 | 1.7 | 2.3 | 2.0 | 2.1 | 2.7 | 3.3 | 3.8 | 4.9 |
| % Long Term Debt of Capitalization | 8.9 | Nil | Nil | Nil | Nil | Nil | NM | 2.4 | 0.4 | 0.8 |
| % Net Income of Revenue | 19.7 | 27.4 | 20.8 | 4.5 | 18.9 | 23.8 | 23.8 | 20.7 | 20.6 | 12.1 |
| % Return on Assets | 8.9 | 14.1 | 11.5 | 2.4 | 8.9 | 10.9 | 11.3 | 9.1 | 8.6 | 6.3 |
| % Return on Equity | 12.4 | 19.2 | 15.6 | 3.1 | 10.7 | 12.9 | 13.4 | 10.6 | 10.0 | 7.4 |

Data as orig reptd.; bef. results of disc opers/spec. items. Per share data adj. for stk. divs.; EPS diluted. E-Estimated. NA-Not Available. NM-Not Meaningful. NR-Not Ranked. UR-Under Review.

**Office:** 2145 Hamilton Avenue, San Jose, CA 95125.
**Telephone:** 408-376-7400.
**Email:** investor_relations@ebay.com
**Website:** http://www.ebayinc.com

**Chrmn:** P.M. Omidyar
**Pres & CEO:** J.J. Donahoe
**SVP & CFO:** R.H. Swan
**SVP & CTO:** M. Carges

**SVP, Secy & General Counsel:** M.R. Jacobson
**Investor Contact:** T. Ford (408-376-7205)
**Board Members:** F. D. Anderson, M. L. Andreessen, E. W. Barnholt, S. D. Cook, J. J. Donahoe, W. C. Ford, Jr., D. G. Lepore, K. C. Mitic, D. M. Moffett, P. M. Omidyar, R. T. Schlosberg, III, T. J. Tierney

**Founded:** 1995
**Domicile:** Delaware
**Employees:** 17,700

**The McGraw·Hill Companies**

# Ecolab Inc.

STANDARD &POOR'S

| S&P Recommendation **HOLD** ★★★☆☆ | Price $53.51 (as of Nov 25, 2011) | 12-Mo. Target Price $55.00 | Investment Style Large-Cap Growth |
|---|---|---|---|

**GICS Sector** Materials
**Sub-Industry** Specialty Chemicals

**Summary** This company is the leading worldwide marketer of cleaning, sanitizing and maintenance products and services for the hospitality, institutional and industrial markets.

## Key Stock Statistics (Source S&P, Vickers, company reports)

| | | | | | | | |
|---|---|---|---|---|---|---|---|
| 52-Wk Range | $57.19– 43.81 | S&P Oper. EPS 2011**E** | 2.55 | Market Capitalization(B) | $12.420 | Beta | 0.69 |
| Trailing 12-Month EPS | $2.13 | S&P Oper. EPS 2012**E** | 3.00 | Yield (%) | 1.31 | S&P 3-Yr. Proj. EPS CAGR(%) | 15 |
| Trailing 12-Month P/E | 25.1 | P/E on S&P Oper. EPS 2011**E** | 21.0 | Dividend Rate/Share | $0.70 | S&P Credit Rating | A |
| $10K Invested 5 Yrs Ago | $12,402 | Common Shares Outstg. (M) | 232.1 | Institutional Ownership (%) | 83 | | |

## Price Performance

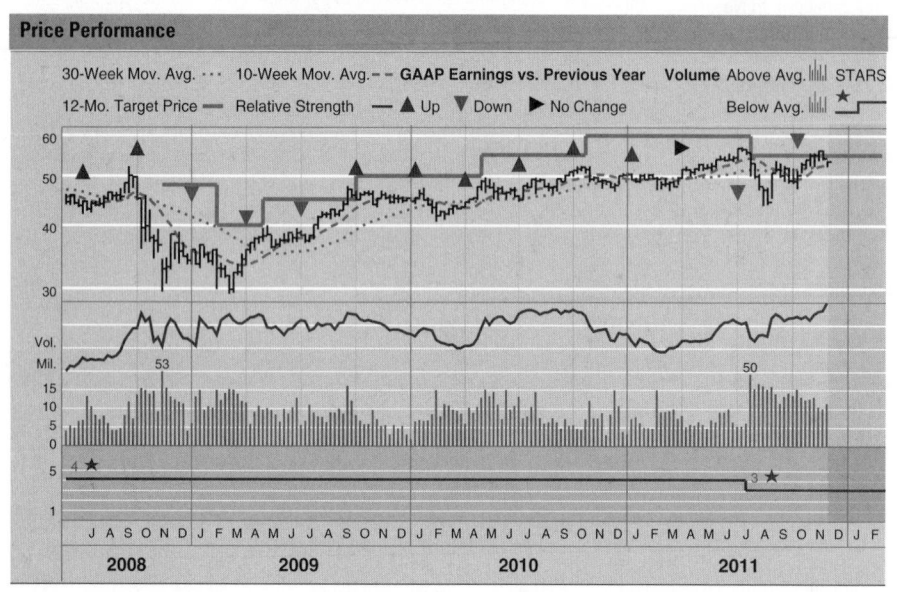

30-Week Mov. Avg. · · · 10-Week Mov. Avg. – – GAAP Earnings vs. Previous Year   Volume Above Avg. STARS
12-Mo. Target Price — Relative Strength   ▲ Up  ▼ Down  ► No Change   Below Avg.

Options: CBOE, P, Ph

Analysis prepared by Equity Analyst **R. O'Reilly, CFA** on Jul 21, 2011, when the stock traded at **$52.21**.

## Qualitative Risk Assessment

| LOW | MEDIUM | HIGH |
|---|---|---|

Our risk assessment reflects the company's leading share positions in its core businesses, the relatively stable nature of its end markets and customers, and our view of its strong balance sheet and cash generation. The stock's S&P Quality Ranking of A+, the highest possible, indicates a superior 10-year historical record of earnings and dividend growth.

## Quantitative Evaluations

**S&P Quality Ranking**  A+

| D | C | B- | B | B+ | A- | A | A+ |
|---|---|---|---|---|---|---|---|

**Relative Strength Rank**  STRONG

84

LOWEST = 1     HIGHEST = 99

## Revenue/Earnings Data

**Revenue (Million $)**

| | 1Q | 2Q | 3Q | 4Q | Year |
|---|---|---|---|---|---|
| 2011 | 1,518 | 1,699 | 1,736 | -- | -- |
| 2010 | 1,432 | 1,520 | 1,562 | 1,576 | 6,090 |
| 2009 | 1,348 | 1,442 | 1,546 | 1,565 | 5,901 |
| 2008 | 1,458 | 1,570 | 1,626 | 1,483 | 6,138 |
| 2007 | 1,254 | 1,362 | 1,413 | 1,440 | 5,470 |
| 2006 | 1,120 | 1,226 | 1,279 | 1,271 | 4,896 |

**Earnings Per Share ($)**

| | 1Q | 2Q | 3Q | 4Q | Year |
|---|---|---|---|---|---|
| 2011 | 0.40 | 0.53 | 0.65 | E0.73 | E2.55 |
| 2010 | 0.40 | 0.55 | 0.74 | 0.56 | 2.23 |
| 2009 | 0.24 | 0.41 | 0.60 | 0.48 | 1.74 |
| 2008 | 0.41 | 0.55 | 0.50 | 0.33 | 1.80 |
| 2007 | 0.35 | 0.44 | 0.46 | 0.45 | 1.70 |
| 2006 | 0.30 | 0.36 | 0.43 | 0.34 | 1.43 |

Fiscal year ended Dec. 31. Next earnings report expected: Mid February. EPS Estimates based on S&P Operating Earnings; historical GAAP earnings are as reported.

## Highlights

► We expect sales to grow about 7% in 2011. Organic sales, which resumed growth in 2010, should be aided by improving global end markets and benefits from new products and customers, forecasted price increases of 1%-2%, and favorable exchange rates, while recent acquisitions are seen adding to reported growth.

► We look for the domestic units to continue to expand in 2011, and institutional and pest elimination sales to rebound. We believe international sales will continue to grow as well, including a modest gain in Europe. We project that operating margins in 2011 will again widen slightly, helped by improving sales and price gains, partly offset by higher raw material and delivery costs mostly in the first half and continued sales force and market development spending. A newly announced European restructuring should boost the region's margins over the next three years.

► Our EPS estimate for 2011 excludes expected restructuring charges of about $0.25. We believe the planned purchase of Nalco, expected to be completed by the end of 2011, will expand ECL's annual sales to about $11 billion and be accretive to EPS in 2012.

## Investment Rationale/Risk

► We recently lowered our opinion on the shares to hold, from buy, due to strategic risks, after ECL agreed to buy Nalco Holdings (NLC 36, Hold) for a total of $8.1 billion. The planned purchase would expand ECL's annual sales to about $11 billion. A restructuring program announced in early 2011 should boost margins of ECL's lagging European business over the next three years.

► Risks to our recommendation and target price include merger-related problems, unexpected slowdowns in the hospitality, travel, food and foodservice industries, an inability to continue to successfully introduce new products and services, and higher-than-projected raw material and delivery costs.

► ECL has historically traded at a higher P/E multiple than the S&P 500, owing, in our view, to investors' willingness to pay a premium for growth and stability. However, the purchase of Nalco would boost ECL's interest in the water treatment sector and in cyclical industrial markets, where it traditionally has had little exposure. Our 12-month target price of $55 is 22X our 2011 EPS forecast of $2.55, at the low end of the stock's historical range.

## Dividend Data (Dates: mm/dd Payment Date: mm/dd/yy)

| Amount ($) | Date Decl. | Ex-Div. Date | Stk. of Record | Payment Date |
|---|---|---|---|---|
| 0.175 | 12/02 | 12/17 | 12/21 | 01/18/11 |
| 0.175 | 02/25 | 03/04 | 03/08 | 04/15/11 |
| 0.175 | 05/05 | 06/17 | 06/21 | 07/15/11 |
| 0.175 | 08/04 | 09/16 | 09/20 | 10/17/11 |

Dividends have been paid since 1936. Source: Company reports.

---

**Please read the Required Disclosures and Analyst Certification on the last page of this report.**

The McGraw-Hill Companies

# Ecolab Inc.

## Business Summary July 21, 2011

CORPORATE OVERVIEW. Ecolab is a global supplier of cleaning, sanitizing and maintenance products and services for hospitality, institutional and industrial markets. In the U.S. cleaning and sanitizing business (45% of 2010 sales, 61% of profits), the institutional division (24% of total sales) is the leading provider of cleaners and sanitizers for warewashing, on-premise laundry, kitchen cleaning, food safety and general housekeeping, product dispensing equipment and dishwashing racks and related kitchen sundries to the foodservice, lodging and health care industries. It also provides pool and spa treatment products. In addition, the division includes professional janitorial products (detergents, floor care, disinfectants, odor control) sold under the Airkem brand name.

The Kay division (6%) is the largest supplier of cleaning and sanitizing products (surface cleaners, degreasers, sanitizers and hand care products) for the quick-service restaurant, convenience store and food retail markets. The Food and Beverage division (9%) offers cleaning and sanitizing products and services to farms, dairy plants, food and beverage processors, and pharmaceutical plants; and water treatment products to institutional, laundry, food and beverage and processing markets for boilers and cooling and waste treatment systems.

ECL also sells health care products (skin care, disinfectants, sterilants, surgical drapes and fluid control products; 4%) under the Ecolab and Microtek names; textile care products (1%) for large institutional and commercial laundries; and vehicle care products (soaps, polishes, wheel treatments) for rental, fleet and retail car washes (1%).

Other U.S. services (7%, 9%) include institutional and commercial pest elimination and prevention services (5%) and GCS Services, a provider of commercial kitchen equipment repair and maintenance services (2%). ECL bought GCS in 1998, and has added to this business through small acquisitions; this business had operating losses for the eight years through 2010.

The International business (48%, 30%) provides services similar to those offered in the U.S. to Canada (3%) and about 71 countries in Europe (30%), Latin America (5%) and the Asia/Pacific region (10%). The institutional and food & beverage businesses constitute a larger portion of the international business than in the U.S.

## Company Financials Fiscal Year Ended Dec. 31

| Per Share Data ($) | 2010 | 2009 | 2008 | 2007 | 2006 | 2005 | 2004 | 2003 | 2002 | 2001 |
|---|---|---|---|---|---|---|---|---|---|---|
| Tangible Book Value | 2.23 | 1.16 | NM | 1.33 | 1.67 | 2.00 | 1.33 | 1.14 | 0.83 | 0.41 |
| Cash Flow | 3.70 | 3.13 | 3.14 | 2.85 | 2.48 | 2.22 | 2.13 | 1.93 | 1.67 | 1.35 |
| Earnings | 2.23 | 1.74 | 1.80 | 1.70 | 1.43 | 1.23 | 1.19 | 1.06 | 0.81 | 0.73 |
| S&P Core Earnings | 2.24 | 1.77 | 1.52 | 1.69 | 1.46 | 1.46 | 1.24 | 1.10 | 0.64 | 0.61 |
| Dividends | 0.64 | 0.57 | 0.53 | 0.48 | 0.42 | 0.36 | 0.33 | 0.30 | 0.28 | 0.26 |
| Payout Ratio | 29% | 33% | 29% | 28% | 29% | 29% | 28% | 28% | 34% | 36% |
| Prices:High | 52.46 | 47.88 | 52.35 | 52.78 | 46.40 | 37.15 | 35.59 | 27.92 | 25.20 | 22.09 |
| Prices:Low | 40.66 | 29.27 | 29.56 | 37.01 | 33.64 | 30.68 | 26.12 | 23.08 | 18.27 | 14.25 |
| P/E Ratio:High | 24 | 28 | 29 | 31 | 32 | 30 | 30 | 26 | 31 | 30 |
| P/E Ratio:Low | 18 | 17 | 16 | 22 | 24 | 25 | 22 | 22 | 23 | 20 |

| Income Statement Analysis (Million $) | | | | | | | | | | |
|---|---|---|---|---|---|---|---|---|---|---|
| Revenue | 6,090 | 5,901 | 6,138 | 5,470 | 4,896 | 4,535 | 4,185 | 3,762 | 3,404 | 2,355 |
| Operating Income | 1,160 | 1,095 | 1,073 | 978 | 880 | 799 | 786 | 713 | 656 | 482 |
| Depreciation | 348 | 334 | 335 | 291 | 269 | 257 | 247 | 230 | 223 | 163 |
| Interest Expense | 59.1 | 67.5 | 70.8 | 58.9 | 51.3 | 49.8 | 45.3 | 45.3 | 43.9 | 28.4 |
| Pretax Income | 748 | 620 | 651 | 616 | 567 | 498 | 489 | 448 | 354 | 306 |
| Effective Tax Rate | NA | 32.5% | 31.2% | 30.7% | 35.0% | 35.9% | 36.5% | 38.1% | 39.6% | 38.4% |
| Net Income | 531 | 417 | 448 | 427 | 369 | 319 | 310 | 277 | 214 | 188 |
| S&P Core Earnings | 533 | 424 | 378 | 424 | 376 | 322 | 283 | 260 | 167 | 157 |

| Balance Sheet & Other Financial Data (Million $) | | | | | | | | | | |
|---|---|---|---|---|---|---|---|---|---|---|
| Cash | 242 | 73.6 | 66.7 | 137 | 484 | 104 | 71.2 | 85.6 | 49.2 | 41.8 |
| Current Assets | 1,870 | 1,814 | 1,691 | 1,717 | 1,854 | 1,422 | 1,279 | 1,150 | 1,016 | 930 |
| Total Assets | 4,872 | 5,021 | 4,757 | 4,723 | 4,419 | 3,797 | 3,716 | 3,229 | 2,878 | 2,525 |
| Current Liabilities | 1,325 | 1,250 | 1,442 | 1,518 | 1,503 | 1,119 | 940 | 851 | 866 | 828 |
| Long Term Debt | 656 | 869 | 799 | 600 | 557 | 519 | Nil | 604 | 540 | 512 |
| Common Equity | 2,129 | 2,001 | 1,572 | 1,936 | 1,680 | 1,649 | 1,563 | 1,295 | 1,100 | 880 |
| Total Capital | 2,793 | 2,878 | 2,376 | 2,536 | 2,237 | 2,169 | 1,563 | 1,900 | 1,639 | 1,393 |
| Capital Expenditures | 261 | 253 | 327 | 362 | 288 | 269 | 276 | 212 | 213 | 158 |
| Cash Flow | 879 | 752 | 783 | 718 | 637 | 576 | 558 | 507 | 437 | 351 |
| Current Ratio | 1.4 | 1.5 | 1.2 | 1.1 | 1.2 | 1.3 | 1.4 | 1.4 | 1.2 | 1.1 |
| % Long Term Debt of Capitalization | 23.5 | 30.2 | 33.7 | 23.7 | 24.9 | 23.9 | Nil | 31.8 | 32.9 | 36.8 |
| % Net Income of Revenue | 8.7 | 7.1 | 7.3 | 7.8 | 7.5 | 7.0 | 7.4 | 7.4 | 6.3 | 8.0 |
| % Return on Assets | 10.7 | 8.5 | 9.5 | 9.3 | 9.0 | 8.5 | 8.9 | 9.1 | 7.9 | 8.9 |
| % Return on Equity | 25.7 | 23.4 | 25.6 | 23.6 | 22.1 | 19.7 | 21.7 | 23.2 | 21.6 | 23.0 |

Data as orig reptd.; bef. results of disc opers/spec. items. Per share data adj. for stk. divs.; EPS diluted. E-Estimated. NA-Not Available. NM-Not Meaningful. NR-Not Ranked. UR-Under Review.

Office: Ecolab Center, 370 Wabasha Street North, St. Paul, MN 55102.
Telephone: 651-293-2233.
Email: investor.info@ecolab.com
Website: http://www.ecolab.com

Chrmn, Pres & CEO: D.M. Baker, Jr.
CFO: S.L. Fritze
CTO: L.L. Berger
Chief Acctg Officer & Cntlr: J.J. Corkrean

Secy & General Counsel: J.J. Seifert
Investor Contact: M.J. Monahan (651-293-2809)
Board Members: D. M. Baker, Jr., B. J. Beck, L. S. Biller, J. A. Grundhofer, A. J. Higgins, J. W. Johnson, J. W. Levin, R. L. Lumpkins, C. S. O'Hara, V. J. Reich, J. Zillmer

Founded: 1924
Domicile: Delaware
Employees: 26,494

# Edison International

**STANDARD &POOR'S**

## S&P Recommendation HOLD ★★★★☆

| Price | 12-Mo. Target Price | Investment Style |
|---|---|---|
| $37.85 (as of Nov 25, 2011) | $39.00 | Large-Cap Blend |

**GICS Sector** Utilities
**Sub-Industry** Electric Utilities

**Summary** EIX is the holding company for Southern California Edison. Other businesses include electric power generation, financial investments, and real estate development.

### Key Stock Statistics (Source S&P, Vickers, company reports)

| | | | | | | | |
|---|---|---|---|---|---|---|---|
| 52-Wk Range | $41.57– 32.64 | S&P Oper. EPS 2011**E** | 2.96 | Market Capitalization(B) | $12.332 | Beta | 0.67 |
| Trailing 12-Month EPS | $2.95 | S&P Oper. EPS 2012**E** | 2.67 | Yield (%) | 3.38 | S&P 3-Yr. Proj. EPS CAGR(%) | -6 |
| Trailing 12-Month P/E | 12.8 | P/E on S&P Oper. EPS 2011**E** | 12.8 | Dividend Rate/Share | $1.28 | S&P Credit Rating | BBB- |
| $10K Invested 5 Yrs Ago | $9,625 | Common Shares Outstg. (M) | 325.8 | Institutional Ownership (%) | 77 | | |

## Price Performance

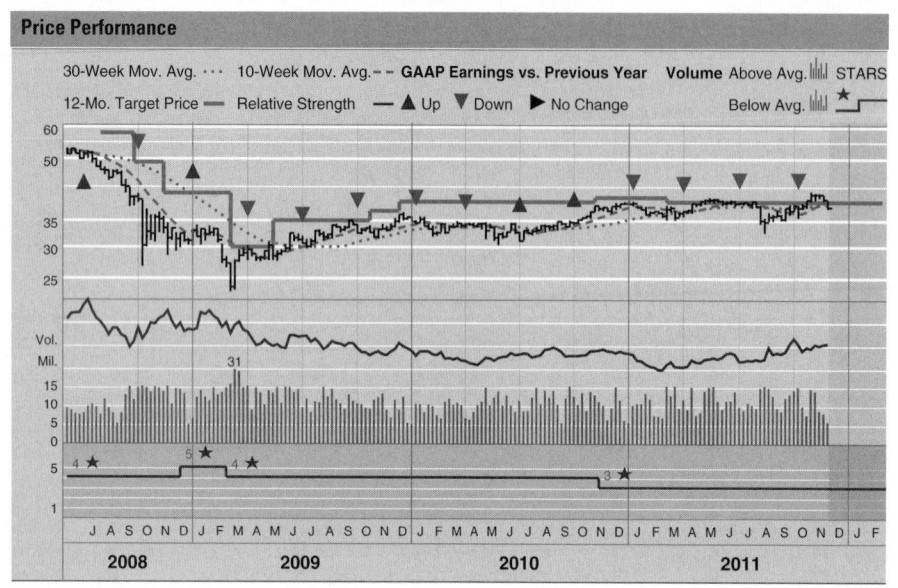

- 30-Week Mov. Avg. ···· 10-Week Mov. Avg. ─ ─ **GAAP Earnings vs. Previous Year** **Volume** Above Avg. STARS
- 12-Mo. Target Price ─ Relative Strength ─ ▲ Up ▼ Down ► No Change Below Avg. ★

Options: ASE, CBOE, P

Analysis prepared by Equity Analyst **Justin McCann** on Sep 13, 2011, when the stock traded at **$35.86**.

### Highlights

➤ We expect operating EPS in 2011 to decline about 18% from 2010's $3.48. In the first half of 2011, operating EPS was $0.28 below the year-earlier period, on a sharp decline at Edison Mission Group (EMG), due to lower generation and realized power prices, and higher O&M costs, as well as the absence of a tax benefit for Southern California Edison (SCE) in the 2010 period. This was partially offset by increased income due to rate base growth at SCE.

➤ Our full-year 2011 estimate reflects a projected sharp drop in EMG earnings, partially offset by higher earnings at SCE, on rate increases related to rate base growth. We expect SCE to earn $3.15 a share in 2011 (up from $3.01 in 2010), with EMG posting a loss of $0.18 (EPS of $0.59), and the holding company a loss of $0.13 (a loss of $0.12). For 2012, we expect operating EPS to decline nearly 10% from anticipated results in 2011, reflecting lower power margins at EMG.

➤ We see earnings growth at SCE being driven by its four-year infrastructure development plan, which is expected to result in annual rate base growth of 8% to 11% through 2014, from between $18 billion and $18.2 billion in 2011 to between $22.8 billion and $24.7 billion in 2014.

### Investment Rationale/Risk

➤ The shares, which have underperformed the company's peers this year, were down about 7% year to date through mid-September. We believe the underperformance has reflected the expectation of a worse than previously projected decline in EMG's earnings, as well as the below-peers yield from the dividend. The decline follows an 11% gain in 2010, which reflected, we think, the recovery in the broader market. We believe the stock, recently trading at an approximate peers P/E of around 14.0X our EPS estimate for 2011, is fairly valued, but think EIX is well positioned for an eventual recovery in the power markets.

➤ Risks to our recommendation and target price include extended weakness in the economy and power markets, a sharp drop in the P/E of the electric utility sector, and the potential for unfavorable regulatory or legislative actions.

➤ Despite the 1.6% hike in the January dividend payment, the recent yield of 3.6% remained well below the level of peers (recently about 4.7%). We do not expect a change in EIX's dividend policy in the near future. Our 12-month target price is $39, reflecting a premium-to-peers P/E of about 15.2X our EPS estimate for 2012.

### Qualitative Risk Assessment

| LOW | MEDIUM | HIGH |
|---|---|---|

Our risk assessment reflects our view that the strong and steady earnings and cash flow we expect from the regulated Southern California Edison utility, with its large and expanding service territory and generally supportive regulatory environment, are offset by the cyclical and volatile earnings of the unregulated independent power operations of Edison Mission Group.

### Quantitative Evaluations

**S&P Quality Ranking** B

| D | C | B- | B | B+ | A- | A | A+ |
|---|---|---|---|---|---|---|---|

**Relative Strength Rank** MODERATE

67

LOWEST = 1     HIGHEST = 99

### Revenue/Earnings Data

**Revenue (Million $)**

| | 1Q | 2Q | 3Q | 4Q | Year |
|---|---|---|---|---|---|
| 2011 | 2,782 | 2,983 | 3,981 | -- | -- |
| 2010 | 2,810 | 2,741 | 3,788 | 3,069 | 12,409 |
| 2009 | 2,812 | 2,834 | 3,664 | 3,050 | 12,361 |
| 2008 | 3,113 | 3,477 | 4,295 | 3,228 | 14,112 |
| 2007 | 2,912 | 3,047 | 3,942 | 3,211 | 13,113 |
| 2006 | 2,751 | 3,001 | 3,802 | 3,067 | 12,622 |

**Earnings Per Share ($)**

| | | | | | |
|---|---|---|---|---|---|
| 2011 | 0.62 | 0.54 | 1.30 | E0.48 | E2.96 |
| 2010 | 0.70 | 1.05 | 1.56 | 0.51 | 3.81 |
| 2009 | 0.75 | -0.03 | 1.22 | 0.65 | 2.60 |
| 2008 | 0.92 | 0.79 | 1.31 | 0.66 | 3.68 |
| 2007 | 1.00 | 0.28 | 1.40 | 0.65 | 3.32 |
| 2006 | 0.56 | 0.53 | 1.39 | 0.80 | 3.28 |

Fiscal year ended Dec. 31. Next earnings report expected: Early March. EPS Estimates based on S&P Operating Earnings; historical GAAP earnings are as reported.

### Dividend Data (Dates: mm/dd Payment Date: mm/dd/yy)

| Amount ($) | Date Decl. | Ex-Div. Date | Stk. of Record | Payment Date |
|---|---|---|---|---|
| 0.320 | 12/09 | 12/29 | 12/31 | 01/31/11 |
| 0.320 | 02/24 | 03/29 | 03/31 | 04/30/11 |
| 0.320 | 04/28 | 06/28 | 06/30 | 07/31/11 |
| 0.320 | 09/01 | 09/28 | 09/30 | 10/31/11 |

Dividends have been paid since 2004. Source: Company reports.

---

**Please read the Required Disclosures and Analyst Certification on the last page of this report.**

*The McGraw-Hill Companies*

# Edison International

STANDARD &POOR'S

## Business Summary September 13, 2011

CORPORATE OVERVIEW. Edison International (EIX) is the holding company for the regulated Southern California Edison (SCE) utility and several non-regulated subsidiaries. The principal non-utility companies, held by Edison Mission Group (EMG), are Edison Mission Energy (EME), an independent power-er producer that also conducts price risk management and energy trading activities, and Edison Capital, which holds equity investments in energy and infrastructure projects. In 2010, SCE accounted for 80.4% of EIX's consolidated revenues, and the non-utility power generation business 19.6%. The utility's retail operations are regulated by the California Public Utilities Commission (CPUC), while its wholesale operations fall under the oversight of the Federal Energy Regulatory Commission (FERC).

CORPORATE STRATEGY. The company seeks to establish a balanced approach for growth, dividends, and balance sheet strength. It has taken steps

to rebalance its capital structure and to further reduce its debt, and is working to reduce administration expenses in the non-utility companies and to establish a multi-year productivity effort at the utility. SCE is working on new projects that should expand its transmission and distribution systems, and has scheduled the installment of advanced electricity meters with more than 5 million customer accounts by the end of 2012. Given the weakness in the economy and power markets, it has also worked to manage the liquidity of its independent power business through disciplined cost-cutting initiatives. However, to diversify EME's concentration in coal-fired generation, it is also making selective investments in renewable energy projects.

## Company Financials Fiscal Year Ended Dec. 31

| Per Share Data ($) | 2010 | 2009 | 2008 | 2007 | 2006 | 2005 | 2004 | 2003 | 2002 | 2001 |
|---|---|---|---|---|---|---|---|---|---|---|
| Tangible Book Value | 32.48 | 30.06 | 28.99 | 25.92 | 23.65 | 20.30 | 18.56 | 13.86 | 11.59 | 8.10 |
| Earnings | 3.81 | 2.60 | 3.68 | 3.32 | 3.28 | 3.34 | 0.68 | 2.37 | 3.46 | 7.36 |
| S&P Core Earnings | 3.82 | 2.73 | 2.93 | 3.26 | 3.28 | 3.35 | 0.60 | 2.45 | 2.81 | 6.78 |
| Dividends | 1.27 | 1.24 | 1.23 | 1.17 | 1.10 | 1.02 | 1.05 | Nil | Nil | Nil |
| Payout Ratio | 33% | 48% | 33% | 35% | 34% | 31% | 154% | Nil | Nil | Nil |
| Prices:High | 39.37 | 36.72 | 55.70 | 60.26 | 47.15 | 49.16 | 32.52 | 22.07 | 19.60 | 16.12 |
| Prices:Low | 30.37 | 23.09 | 26.73 | 42.76 | 37.90 | 30.43 | 21.24 | 10.57 | 7.80 | 6.25 |
| P/E Ratio:High | 10 | 14 | 15 | 18 | 14 | 15 | 48 | 9 | 6 | 2 |
| P/E Ratio:Low | 8 | 9 | 7 | 13 | 12 | 9 | 31 | 4 | 2 | 1 |

| Income Statement Analysis (Million $) | 2010 | 2009 | 2008 | 2007 | 2006 | 2005 | 2004 | 2003 | 2002 | 2001 |
|---|---|---|---|---|---|---|---|---|---|---|
| Revenue | 12,409 | 12,361 | 14,112 | 13,113 | 12,622 | 11,852 | 10,199 | 12,135 | 11,488 | 11,436 |
| Depreciation | 1,640 | 1,538 | 1,419 | 1,264 | 1,181 | 1,061 | 1,022 | 1,184 | 1,030 | 973 |
| Maintenance | NA | NA | NA | NA | NA | NA | NA | NA | NA | NA |
| Fixed Charges Coverage | 2.99 | 1.97 | 3.42 | 3.38 | 3.18 | 3.28 | 2.20 | 1.73 | 1.91 | 3.38 |
| Construction Credits | NA | NA | NA | NA | NA | NA | NA | NA | NA | NA |
| Effective Tax Rate | 22.1% | NM | 31.5% | 27.4% | 32.3% | 26.4% | NM | 21.5% | 25.6% | 40.7% |
| Net Income | 1,252 | 856 | 1,215 | 1,100 | 1,083 | 1,108 | 226 | 779 | 1,135 | 2,402 |
| S&P Core Earnings | 1,248 | 894 | 955 | 1,065 | 1,082 | 1,111 | 199 | 808 | 921 | 2,211 |

| Balance Sheet & Other Financial Data (Million $) | 2010 | 2009 | 2008 | 2007 | 2006 | 2005 | 2004 | 2003 | 2002 | 2001 |
|---|---|---|---|---|---|---|---|---|---|---|
| Gross Property | 38,368 | 35,265 | 31,932 | 29,248 | 25,090 | 24,775 | 23,214 | 24,674 | 23,264 | 22,396 |
| Capital Expenditures | 4,543 | 3,282 | 2,824 | 2,826 | 2,536 | 1,868 | 1,733 | 1,288 | 1,590 | 933 |
| Net Property | 30,184 | 27,113 | 24,343 | 22,309 | 20,269 | 18,588 | 17,397 | 20,288 | 15,170 | 14,427 |
| Capitalization:Long Term Debt | 13,278 | 11,344 | 11,857 | 9,931 | 10,016 | 9,552 | 9,807 | 12,221 | 12,915 | 14,007 |
| Capitalization:% Long Term Debt | 55.6 | 53.5 | 55.5 | 54.0 | 56.5 | 59.1 | 61.3 | 69.4 | 74.4 | 81.1 |
| Capitalization:Preferred | Nil | Nil | Nil | Nil | Nil | Nil | Nil | 9.00 | Nil | Nil |
| Capitalization:% Preferred | Nil | Nil | Nil | Nil | Nil | Nil | Nil | 0.05 | Nil | Nil |
| Capitalization:Common | 10,583 | 9,841 | 9,517 | 8,444 | 7,709 | 6,615 | 6,049 | 5,383 | 4,437 | 3,272 |
| Capitalization:% Common | 44.4 | 46.5 | 44.5 | 46.0 | 43.5 | 40.9 | 37.8 | 30.6 | 25.6 | 18.9 |
| Total Capital | 23,913 | 21,820 | 27,485 | 23,980 | 23,415 | 21,854 | 21,688 | 24,246 | 23,786 | 24,163 |
| % Operating Ratio | 85.3 | 80.7 | 86.4 | 84.6 | 84.7 | 80.7 | 80.6 | 75.2 | 82.8 | 93.2 |
| % Earned on Net Property | 7.6 | 8.9 | 10.8 | 13.1 | 12.8 | 6.9 | 6.6 | 9.1 | 16.0 | 36.9 |
| % Return on Revenue | 10.1 | 6.9 | 8.6 | 8.8 | 8.6 | 9.3 | 2.2 | 6.4 | 9.9 | 21.0 |
| % Return on Invested Capital | 8.3 | 7.5 | 7.7 | 9.4 | 10.2 | 12.2 | 10.4 | 14.9 | 10.9 | 4.8 |
| % Return on Common Equity | 12.3 | 8.8 | 13.5 | 13.6 | 15.1 | 17.1 | 3.8 | 15.9 | 29.4 | 84.4 |

Data as orig reptd.; bef. results of disc opers/spec. items. Per share data adj. for stk. divs.; EPS diluted. E-Estimated. NA-Not Available. NM-Not Meaningful. NR-Not Ranked. UR-Under Review.

**Office:** 2244 Walnut Grove Avenue, Rosemead, CA 91770-3714.
**Telephone:** 877-379-9515.
**Website:** http://www.edison.com
**Chrmn, Pres & CEO:** T.F. Craver, Jr.

**EVP & General Counsel:** R.L. Adler
**CFO & Treas:** W.J. Scilacci, Jr.
**Chief Acctg Officer & Cntlr:** M.C. Clarke
**Secy:** B.E. Mathews

**Investor Contact:** S. Cunningham (877-379-9515)
**Board Members:** J. S. Bindra, V. C. Chang, F. A. Cordova, T. F. Craver, Jr., C. B. Curtis, B. M. Freeman, L. G. Nogales, R. L. Olson, J. M. Rosser, R. T. Schlosberg, III, T. C. Sutton, W. B. White

**Founded:** 1886
**Domicile:** California
**Employees:** 20,117

# Edwards Lifesciences Corp

**STANDARD &POOR'S**

| S&P Recommendation **BUY** ★★★★☆ | Price $62.50 (as of Nov 25, 2011) | 12-Mo. Target Price $85.00 | Investment Style Large-Cap Growth |
|---|---|---|---|

**GICS Sector** Health Care
**Sub-Industry** Health Care Equipment

**Summary** This company makes and markets a comprehensive line of products and services to treat late-stage cardiovascular disease.

## Key Stock Statistics (Source S&P, Vickers, company reports)

| | | | | | | | |
|---|---|---|---|---|---|---|---|
| 52-Wk Range | $91.82– 61.59 | S&P Oper. EPS 2011**E** | 2.00 | Market Capitalization(B) | $7.130 | Beta | 0.52 |
| Trailing 12-Month EPS | $1.99 | S&P Oper. EPS 2012**E** | 2.80 | Yield (%) | Nil | S&P 3-Yr. Proj. EPS CAGR(%) | 25 |
| Trailing 12-Month P/E | 31.4 | P/E on S&P Oper. EPS 2011**E** | 31.3 | Dividend Rate/Share | Nil | S&P Credit Rating | NA |
| $10K Invested 5 Yrs Ago | $27,821 | Common Shares Outstg. (M) | 114.1 | Institutional Ownership (%) | 87 | | |

## Price Performance

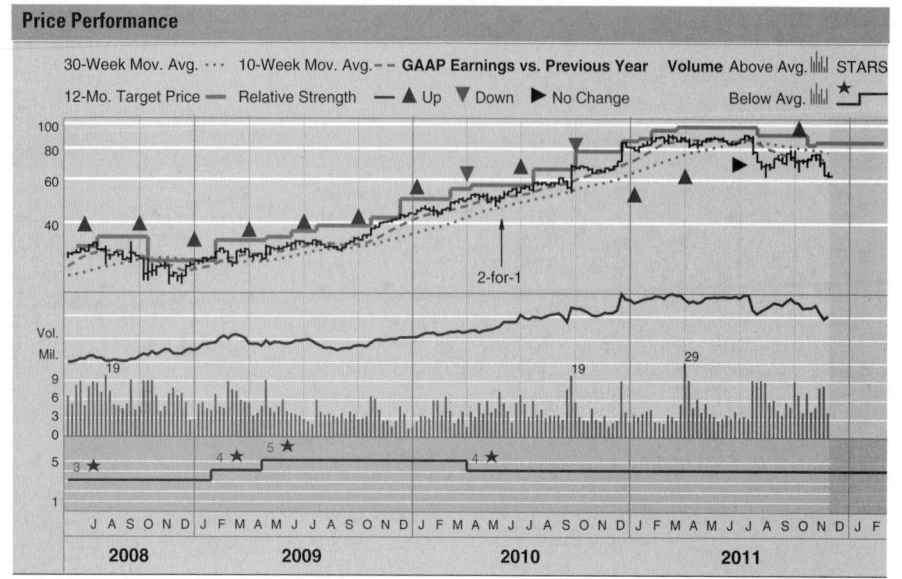

30-Week Mov. Avg. ··· 10-Week Mov. Avg. - - GAAP Earnings vs. Previous Year  Volume Above Avg. |ılıl| STARS
12-Mo. Target Price — Relative Strength — ▲ Up ▼ Down ► No Change  Below Avg. |ılıl| ★

2-for-1

Options: CBOE, P, Ph

Analysis prepared by Equity Analyst **Phillip Seligman** on Nov 03, 2011, when the stock traded at **$76.19**.

## Qualitative Risk Assessment

| LOW | **MEDIUM** | HIGH |
|---|---|---|

Our risk assessment reflects the company's operations in a highly competitive industry characterized by technological innovation and new market entrants ranging from start-up enterprises to well-established medical product developers. Consequently, the company must consistently enhance current products and develop new ones to maintain its competitive standing. In our view, however, demand for the company's products is immune to economic cycles and tends to exhibit stable long-term unit pricing.

## Quantitative Evaluations

**S&P Quality Ranking**      B

| D | C | B- | **B** | B+ | A- | A | A+ |
|---|---|---|---|---|---|---|---|

**Relative Strength Rank**      WEAK

25

LOWEST = 1          HIGHEST = 99

## Highlights

➤ We forecast revenue growth of 18% in 2011 and an additional 18% in 2012. Drivers include a 23% increase we see in heart valve sales in 2011 and faster growth in 2012. These sales are fueled by strong demand for the second-generation SAPIEN XT transcatheter aortic valve (TAV) that was launched in Europe in early 2010. We also assume a late-2011 U.S. launch of the SAPIEN TAV, on the FDA's November 2 approval. We also see demand for minimally invasive products generating over 9% growth in the cardiac surgery category in 2011, and we see more than 12% growth in the critical care segment, on hospitals' demand for improved monitoring products. We expect sales growth in both product lines to slow in 2012, as each will be coming off an expanded base.

➤ We expect gross margins to decline slightly in 2011, owing to a foreign exchange headwind, but we see a recovery in 2012, mainly on the U.S. SAPIEN launch. We also expect operating costs to rise as a percentage of sales in 2011 on new product initiatives and U.S. SAPIEN launch costs, and to decline afterward.

➤ We see adjusted EPS of $2.00 in 2011, versus $1.84 in 2010, and we look for $2.80 in 2012.

## Investment Rationale/Risk

➤ We view EW's core surgical valve and valve repair businesses as defensive lines that should continue to post solid results despite current economic weakness. We believe EW has gained share in the E.U. TAV space and will have a substantial time-to-market advantage in the U.S., assuming FDA approval. We view EW's other new products and growing pipeline as promising. We expect EPS to improve to 20%-plus growth starting in 2012, assuming strong TAV uptake in the U.S. despite a higher risk for stroke and other complications than traditional valve surgery, an improving sales mix, and revenue leverage. But given SAPIEN's risks, we see tight FDA and Medicare oversight of its implantation in the U.S.

➤ Risks to our recommendation and target price include market share losses in key product categories and an inability to successfully commercialize products in the pipeline, including SAPIEN in the U.S.

➤ Our 12-month target price of $85 assumes EW will trade at an above-peers P/E-to-growth ratio of 1.7X applied to our 2011 EPS estimate, given the resurgence in EPS growth we anticipate after 2011.

## Revenue/Earnings Data

**Revenue (Million $)**

| | 1Q | 2Q | 3Q | 4Q | Year |
|---|---|---|---|---|---|
| 2011 | 404.5 | 431.2 | 412.7 | -- | -- |
| 2010 | 340.5 | 365.2 | 348.9 | 392.4 | 1,447 |
| 2009 | 313.5 | 335.5 | 325.7 | 346.7 | 1,321 |
| 2008 | 296.8 | 327.6 | 303.6 | 309.7 | 1,238 |
| 2007 | 264.1 | 272.6 | 261.4 | 293.0 | 1,091 |
| 2006 | 256.7 | 267.3 | 247.4 | 265.6 | 1,037 |

**Earnings Per Share ($)**

| | 1Q | 2Q | 3Q | 4Q | Year |
|---|---|---|---|---|---|
| 2011 | 0.53 | 0.48 | 0.43 | E0.61 | E2.00 |
| 2010 | 0.40 | 0.48 | 0.40 | 0.54 | 1.83 |
| 2009 | 0.52 | 0.41 | 0.63 | 0.40 | 1.95 |
| 2008 | 0.16 | 0.34 | 0.28 | 0.33 | 1.10 |
| 2007 | 0.27 | 0.29 | 0.24 | 0.14 | 0.94 |
| 2006 | 0.37 | 0.29 | 0.23 | 0.17 | 1.05 |

Fiscal year ended Dec. 31. Next earnings report expected: Early February. EPS Estimates based on S&P Operating Earnings; historical GAAP earnings are as reported.

## Dividend Data

No cash dividends have been paid.

---

**Please read the Required Disclosures and Analyst Certification on the last page of this report.**

**The McGraw·Hill Companies**

# Edwards Lifesciences Corp

**STANDARD & POOR'S**

## Business Summary November 03, 2011

CORPORATE OVERVIEW. Edwards Lifesciences Corp. develops, manufactures and markets products and technologies that are designed to treat advanced stage cardiovascular disease. In 2010, 61% of revenues were generated in markets outside the U.S.

In heart valve therapy (58% of 2010 net sales), the company manufactures tissue heart valves, including the Carpentier-Edwards Perimount pericardial valve. In January 2004, EW launched the new Perimount Magna aortic pericardial bioprosthesis in the U.S. This FDA-approved, premium-priced device is designed to enhance blood flow. Other valve lines include Carpentier-Edwards porcine valves, Prima Plus stentless tissue valves, Edwards MIRA bileaflet mechanical valves, and Starr-Edwards silastic ball valves. In valve repair, the company sells annuloplasty rings and systems. The company also sells cardiac surgery systems (7%), including cannulae to facilitate vacuum-assisted venous drainage during perfusion, products to facilitate beating heart coronary artery bypass surgery, and a product used to capture material such as blood clots or tissue fragments that might be released during open-heart surgery procedures. EW also develops, makes and sells disposable per-

fusion products for customers outside the U.S. and Western Europe. Products include oxygenators, blood containers, filters, and related devices used during the practice of bypassing the heart and lungs during stopped-heart procedures.

In critical care (31%), EW sells hemodynamic monitoring systems that are used to measure a patient's heart function in surgical and intensive care settings. These products are often deployed before, during and after open heart, major vascular, major abdominal, neurological and orthopedic surgical procedures. The company also sells disposable pressure monitoring devices, a line of innovative products enabling closed-loop arterial blood sampling to protect both patients and clinicians from infection, and products used to help perform hemofiltration.

## Company Financials Fiscal Year Ended Dec. 31

| Per Share Data ($) | 2010 | 2009 | 2008 | 2007 | 2006 | 2005 | 2004 | 2003 | 2002 | 2001 |
|---|---|---|---|---|---|---|---|---|---|---|
| Tangible Book Value | 8.05 | 6.66 | 4.17 | 4.06 | 2.56 | 1.80 | 1.16 | 1.92 | 1.22 | 1.01 |
| Cash Flow | 2.30 | 2.45 | 1.55 | 1.34 | 1.47 | 1.09 | 0.46 | 1.02 | 0.79 | 0.40 |
| Earnings | 1.83 | 1.95 | 1.10 | 0.94 | 1.05 | 0.64 | 0.02 | 0.65 | 0.46 | -0.09 |
| S&P Core Earnings | 1.87 | 1.50 | 1.14 | 1.02 | 0.88 | 0.44 | -0.12 | 0.57 | 0.26 | 0.29 |
| Dividends | Nil | Nil | Nil | Nil | Nil | Nil | Nil | Nil | Nil | Nil |
| Payout Ratio | Nil | Nil | Nil | Nil | Nil | Nil | Nil | Nil | Nil | Nil |
| Prices:High | 85.47 | 44.13 | 33.50 | 26.48 | 24.24 | 23.45 | 21.15 | 16.80 | 14.80 | 14.58 |
| Prices:Low | 42.31 | 26.43 | 20.85 | 22.78 | 20.50 | 19.28 | 14.74 | 12.20 | 9.20 | 8.38 |
| P/E Ratio:High | 47 | 23 | 31 | 28 | 23 | 37 | NM | 26 | 33 | NM |
| P/E Ratio:Low | 23 | 14 | 19 | 24 | 20 | 30 | NM | 19 | 20 | NM |

| Income Statement Analysis (Million $) | | | | | | | | | | |
|---|---|---|---|---|---|---|---|---|---|---|
| Revenue | 1,447 | 1,321 | 1,238 | 1,091 | 1,037 | 998 | 932 | 860 | 704 | 692 |
| Operating Income | 339 | 297 | 254 | 227 | 230 | 232 | 210 | 184 | 152 | 164 |
| Depreciation | 56.5 | 58.7 | 55.6 | 54.8 | 56.8 | 56.2 | 55.7 | 45.6 | 40.0 | 57.0 |
| Interest Expense | 1.50 | 2.70 | 7.20 | 9.10 | 10.5 | 9.70 | 14.2 | 13.2 | 12.0 | 23.0 |
| Pretax Income | 268 | 304 | 164 | 150 | 172 | 117 | 30.1 | 92.8 | 56.0 | -9.00 |
| Effective Tax Rate | NA | 24.7% | 21.6% | 24.6% | 24.3% | 32.0% | 94.4% | 14.9% | NM | NM |
| Net Income | 218 | 229 | 129 | 113 | 131 | 79.3 | 1.70 | 79.0 | 56.0 | -10.0 |
| S&P Core Earnings | 223 | 176 | 134 | 123 | 109 | 54.3 | -13.9 | 69.5 | 32.2 | 33.5 |

| Balance Sheet & Other Financial Data (Million $) | | | | | | | | | | |
|---|---|---|---|---|---|---|---|---|---|---|
| Cash | 396 | 334 | 227 | 191 | 183 | 179 | 48.9 | 61.1 | 34.0 | 48.0 |
| Current Assets | 1,033 | 889 | 692 | 582 | 532 | 514 | 368 | 360 | 326 | 293 |
| Total Assets | 1,767 | 1,616 | 1,400 | 1,345 | 1,247 | 1,229 | 1,113 | 1,101 | 1,008 | 973 |
| Current Liabilities | 338 | 291 | 259 | 375 | 226 | 194 | 195 | 167 | 198 | 184 |
| Long Term Debt | NA | 90.3 | 176 | 212 | 236 | 316 | 267 | 256 | 246 | 310 |
| Common Equity | 1,308 | 1,158 | 879 | 835 | 749 | 690 | 628 | 635 | 538 | 459 |
| Total Capital | 1,350 | 1,248 | 1,054 | 897 | 985 | 1,006 | 895 | 891 | 784 | 769 |
| Capital Expenditures | 61.8 | 64.0 | 50.6 | 57.0 | 57.4 | 48.5 | 42.5 | 37.9 | 41.0 | 38.0 |
| Cash Flow | 275 | 288 | 185 | 168 | 187 | 136 | 57.4 | 125 | 96.0 | 47.0 |
| Current Ratio | 3.1 | 3.1 | 2.7 | 1.6 | 2.4 | 2.6 | 1.9 | 2.1 | 1.6 | 1.6 |
| % Long Term Debt of Capitalization | Nil | 7.2 | 16.7 | 6.9 | 23.9 | 31.4 | 29.8 | 28.7 | 31.3 | 40.3 |
| % Net Income of Revenue | 15.1 | 17.3 | 10.4 | 10.4 | 12.6 | 7.9 | 0.2 | 9.2 | 7.9 | NM |
| % Return on Assets | 12.9 | 15.2 | 9.4 | 8.7 | 10.5 | 6.8 | 0.2 | 7.5 | 5.7 | NM |
| % Return on Equity | 17.7 | 22.5 | 15.0 | 14.3 | 18.1 | 12.0 | 0.3 | 13.5 | 11.2 | NM |

Data as orig reptd.; bef. results of disc opers/spec. items. Per share data adj. for stk. divs.; EPS diluted. E-Estimated. NA-Not Available. NM-Not Meaningful. NR-Not Ranked. UR-Under Review.

**Office:** 1 Edwards Way, Irvine, CA 92614-5688.
**Telephone:** 949-250-2500.
**Email:** investor_relations@edwards.com
**Website:** http://www.edwards.com

**Chrmn & CEO:** M.A. Mussallem
**CFO & Chief Acctg Officer:** T.M. Abate
**CSO:** S.J. Rowe
**Secy:** D.E. Botticelli

**General Counsel:** A.S. Weisner
**Investor Contact:** D. Erickson (949-250-2806)
**Board Members:** M. R. Bowlin, J. T. Cardis, R. A. Ingram, W. J. Link, B. J. McNeil, M. A. Mussallem, D. E. Pyott, W. W. von Schack

**Founded:** 1999
**Domicile:** Delaware
**Employees:** 7,000

*The McGraw·Hill Companies*

# Electronic Arts Inc

**STANDARD & POOR'S**

| S&P Recommendation **SELL** ★★☆☆☆ | Price $20.83 (as of Nov 25, 2011) | 12-Mo. Target Price $17.00 | Investment Style Large-Cap Growth |

**GICS Sector** Information Technology
**Sub-Industry** Home Entertainment Software

**Summary** This company produces entertainment software for PCs, home video game consoles and mobile gaming devices.

## Key Stock Statistics (Source S&P, Vickers, company reports)

| | | | | | |
|---|---|---|---|---|---|
| 52-Wk Range | $26.13–14.67 | S&P Oper. EPS 2012**E** | 0.43 | Market Capitalization(B) | $6.904 | Beta | 1.25 |
| Trailing 12-Month EPS | $-0.87 | S&P Oper. EPS 2013**E** | 0.88 | Yield (%) | Nil | S&P 3-Yr. Proj. EPS CAGR(%) | 10 |
| Trailing 12-Month P/E | NM | P/E on S&P Oper. EPS 2012**E** | 48.4 | Dividend Rate/Share | Nil | S&P Credit Rating | NA |
| $10K Invested 5 Yrs Ago | $3,566 | Common Shares Outstg. (M) | 331.4 | Institutional Ownership (%) | 93 | | |

## Price Performance

30-Week Mov. Avg. · · · · 10-Week Mov. Avg. – – GAAP Earnings vs. Previous Year Volume Above Avg. STARS
12-Mo. Target Price — Relative Strength — ▲ Up ▼ Down ► No Change Below Avg.

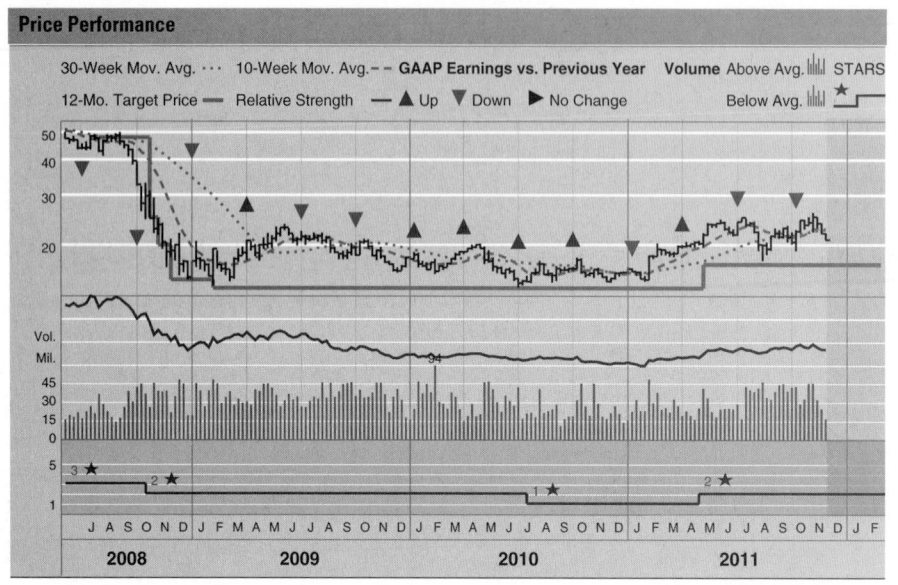

Options: ASE, CBOE, P, Ph

Analysis prepared by Equity Analyst **Jim Yin, CFA** on Nov 17, 2011, when the stock traded at **$22.69**.

## Highlights

► We see non-GAAP revenues, which include changes in deferred revenues, rising 7.3% in FY 12 (Mar.), following an 8.0% decline in FY 11. We expect most of the gains will come from growth in digital revenues, such as revenues generated from online and mobile games. However, we project a mid-single digit decline in sales through retail stores, as sales of video game consoles continue to decline, reflecting weak consumer confidence. We also see a shift in consumer buying behavior, resulting in a greater focus on top-selling titles at the expense of older titles.

► We forecast a non-GAAP gross margin of 60% in FY 12, down from 61% in FY 11. We see operating expenses declining as a percentage of revenues in FY 12, as the company plans to reduce the number of game titles. We project that FY 12 non-GAAP operating margins will improve to 10%, from 8.2% in FY 11.

► We estimate non-GAAP operating EPS of $0.43 in FY 12, compared to $0.32 in FY 11. These figures exclude amortization of intangibles and other one-time charges of $1.16 and $0.06 in FY 11 and FY 12, respectively.

## Investment Rationale/Risk

► Our sell recommendation reflects our view of weak consumer spending and deteriorating industry fundamentals. We think consumers, in addition to buying fewer titles, are focusing their purchases on top-rated games. As a result, development costs on these titles have increased significantly. Although its multiplayer online role-playing game, Star Wars: The Old Republic, has been receiving praise during beta-testing, we think it will have difficulty displacing the dominant market leader, World of Warcraft.

► Risks to our recommendation and target price include a stronger-than-expected economic recovery, rising consumer spending, and further cost reductions.

► Our 12-month target price of $17 is based on a blend of our discounted cash flow (DCF) and enterprise value (EV) to sales analyses. Our DCF model assumes a 12.8% weighted average cost of capital and 3% terminal growth, yielding an intrinsic value of $16. We derive a value of $19 based on an EV/sales multiple of 1.1X our FY 12 revenue estimate, a discount to the industry average of 1.3X due to ERTS's low profitability.

## Qualitative Risk Assessment

| LOW | MEDIUM | **HIGH** |

Our risk assessment takes into account weak consumer spending, the volatile nature of the home entertainment software industry, and declining sales of video game consoles.

## Quantitative Evaluations

**S&P Quality Ranking** B+

| D | C | B- | B | **B+** | A- | A | A+ |

**Relative Strength Rank** MODERATE

39

LOWEST = 1    HIGHEST = 99

## Revenue/Earnings Data

**Revenue (Million $)**

| | 1Q | 2Q | 3Q | 4Q | Year |
|---|---|---|---|---|---|
| 2012 | 999.0 | 715.0 | -- | -- | -- |
| 2011 | 815.0 | 631.0 | 1,053 | 1,090 | 3,589 |
| 2010 | 644.0 | 788.0 | 1,243 | 979.0 | 3,654 |
| 2009 | 804.0 | 894.0 | 1,654 | 860.0 | 4,212 |
| 2008 | 395.0 | 640.0 | 1,503 | 1,127 | 3,665 |
| 2007 | 413.0 | 784.0 | 1,281 | 613.0 | 3,091 |

**Earnings Per Share ($)**

| | | | | | |
|---|---|---|---|---|---|
| 2012 | -0.66 | -1.03 | E0.66 | E0.28 | E0.43 |
| 2011 | 0.29 | -0.61 | -0.97 | 0.45 | -0.84 |
| 2010 | -0.72 | -1.21 | -0.25 | 0.09 | -2.08 |
| 2009 | -0.52 | -0.97 | -2.00 | -0.13 | -3.40 |
| 2008 | -0.42 | -0.62 | -0.10 | -0.29 | -1.45 |
| 2007 | -0.26 | 0.07 | 0.50 | -0.08 | 0.24 |

Fiscal year ended Mar. 31. Next earnings report expected: Early February. EPS Estimates based on S&P Operating Earnings; historical GAAP earnings are as reported.

## Dividend Data

No cash dividends have been paid.

# Electronic Arts Inc

## Business Summary November 17, 2011

CORPORATE OVERVIEW. ERTS is one of the largest third-party developers of video games, which can be played on a variety of platforms including Sony PlayStation, Microsoft Xbox 360, Nintendo Wii, personal computers, and mobile devices. ERTS owns many of today's most popular video game franchises, including Madden NFL, The Sims, and Need for Speed. The company organizes its business into four labels: EA SPORTS, EA Games, EA Play, and EA Interactive. Each label operates with dedicated studio and marketing teams.

ERTS publishes titles across all major platforms, including consoles, PCs, and handheld gaming devices. The company has a diversified video game portfolio. In FY 10 (Mar.), the company produced 48 titles for mobile devices, 22 titles for Xbox 360, 21 for PlayStation 3, 19 for Nintendo Wii, 16 for PCs, and 16 for Nintendo DS. No title accounted for more than 10% of its total revenue in FY 10.

ERTS publishes and distributes games in over 35 countries throughout the world. Sales in North America were $2.0 billion in FY 10, or 55% of total revenue, while international revenue accounted for $1.6 billion, or 45%.

MARKET PROFILE. Video game sales grew at a low-teens compound annual growth rate (CAGR) from 2004 to 2008. However, sales declined about 10% in 2009 due to the economic recession. Although the economy is recovering, we expect video game sales to remain weak given the lack of job growth. We also think that most of the growth will be in mobile games, which have much lower barriers to entry than console games because they have lower design requirements such as graphic display. Thus, we expect pricing pressure to be more intense in this market segment. International Development Group (IDG), an independent research firm, forecasts that the annual sales of video game software in North America, Europe, and Japan will decline from $27.7 billion in 2008 to an estimated $16.7 billion in 2013 due to the shift in the consumer buying behavior. Thus, we believe future growth opportunity will come mostly from casual gamers rather than "hardcore" gamers, who already devote a large portion of their leisure time to playing video games.

## Company Financials Fiscal Year Ended Mar. 31

| Per Share Data ($) | 2011 | 2010 | 2009 | 2008 | 2007 | 2006 | 2005 | 2004 | 2003 | 2002 |
|---|---|---|---|---|---|---|---|---|---|---|
| Tangible Book Value | 3.94 | 4.34 | 6.52 | 9.19 | 9.93 | 8.29 | 10.66 | 8.52 | 11.62 | 3.92 |
| Cash Flow | -0.29 | -1.49 | -2.81 | -0.85 | 0.70 | 1.05 | 1.82 | 2.12 | 2.79 | 0.74 |
| Earnings | -0.84 | -2.08 | -3.40 | -1.45 | 0.24 | 0.75 | 1.59 | 1.87 | 1.09 | 0.36 |
| S&P Core Earnings | -0.92 | -2.03 | -2.51 | -1.22 | 0.24 | 0.49 | 1.35 | 1.59 | 0.82 | 0.10 |
| Dividends | NA | Nil | Nil | Nil | Nil | Nil | Nil | Nil | Nil | Nil |
| Payout Ratio | NA | Nil | Nil | Nil | Nil | Nil | Nil | Nil | Nil | Nil |
| Calendar Year | 2010 | 2009 | 2008 | 2007 | 2006 | 2005 | 2004 | 2003 | 2002 | 2001 |
| Prices:High | 20.24 | 23.76 | 58.35 | 61.62 | 59.85 | 71.16 | 63.71 | 52.89 | 36.22 | 33.46 |
| Prices:Low | 14.06 | 14.24 | 14.79 | 46.27 | 39.99 | 47.45 | 43.38 | 23.76 | 24.74 | 17.25 |
| P/E Ratio:High | NM | NM | NM | NM | NM | 95 | 40 | 28 | 33 | 94 |
| P/E Ratio:Low | NM | NM | NM | NM | NM | 63 | 27 | 13 | 23 | 49 |

| Income Statement Analysis (Million $) | | | | | | | | | | |
|---|---|---|---|---|---|---|---|---|---|---|
| Revenue | 3,589 | 3,654 | 4,212 | 3,665 | 3,091 | 2,951 | 3,129 | 2,957 | 2,482 | 1,725 |
| Operating Income | 12.0 | -352 | -128 | -60.0 | 204 | 454 | 759 | 863 | 629 | 267 |
| Depreciation | 180 | 192 | 189 | 186 | 147 | 95.0 | 75.0 | 77.5 | 91.6 | 111 |
| Interest Expense | NA | NA | Nil | Nil | Nil | Nil | Nil | Nil | Nil | Nil |
| Pretax Income | -279 | -706 | -855 | -507 | 138 | 389 | 725 | 797 | 461 | 148 |
| Effective Tax Rate | NA | 4.11% | NM | NM | 47.8% | 37.8% | 30.5% | 27.5% | 30.9% | 31.0% |
| Net Income | -276 | -677 | -1,088 | -454 | 76.0 | 236 | 504 | 577 | 317 | 102 |
| S&P Core Earnings | -302 | -660 | -805 | -382 | 76.0 | 153 | 425 | 482 | 239 | 28.0 |

| Balance Sheet & Other Financial Data (Million $) | | | | | | | | | | |
|---|---|---|---|---|---|---|---|---|---|---|
| Cash | 2,237 | 1,996 | 2,520 | 3,016 | 1,712 | 1,402 | 1,410 | 2,151 | 951 | 804 |
| Current Assets | 3,032 | 2,585 | 3,120 | 3,925 | 3,597 | 3,012 | 3,706 | 2,911 | 1,911 | 1,153 |
| Total Assets | 4,928 | 4,646 | 4,678 | 6,059 | 5,146 | 4,386 | 4,370 | 3,401 | 2,360 | 1,699 |
| Current Liabilities | 2,001 | 1,574 | 1,136 | 1,299 | 1,026 | 869 | 828 | 722 | 571 | 453 |
| Long Term Debt | NA | NA | Nil | Nil | Nil | Nil | Nil | Nil | Nil | Nil |
| Common Equity | 2,564 | 2,729 | 3,134 | 4,339 | 4,032 | 3,408 | 3,498 | 2,678 | 1,785 | 1,243 |
| Total Capital | 2,564 | 2,729 | 3,176 | 4,339 | 4,040 | 3,449 | 3,509 | 2,678 | 1,789 | 1,246 |
| Capital Expenditures | 59.0 | 305 | 115 | 84.0 | 178 | 123 | 126 | 89.6 | 59.1 | 51.5 |
| Cash Flow | -96.0 | -485 | -899 | -268 | 223 | 331 | 579 | 655 | 409 | 212 |
| Current Ratio | 1.5 | 1.6 | 2.8 | 3.0 | 3.5 | 3.5 | 4.5 | 4.0 | 3.3 | 2.5 |
| % Long Term Debt of Capitalization | Nil | Nil | Nil | Nil | Nil | Nil | Nil | Nil | Nil | Nil |
| % Net Income of Revenue | NM | NM | NM | NM | 2.5 | 8.0 | 16.1 | 19.5 | 12.8 | 5.9 |
| % Return on Assets | NM | NM | NM | NM | 1.6 | 5.4 | 12.9 | 20.0 | 15.6 | 6.6 |
| % Return on Equity | NM | NM | NM | NM | 2.0 | 6.8 | 16.3 | 25.9 | 20.9 | 8.9 |

Data as orig reptd.; bef. results of disc opers/spec. items. Per share data adj. for stk. divs.; EPS diluted. E-Estimated. NA-Not Available. NM-Not Meaningful. NR-Not Ranked. UR-Under Review.

**Office:** 209 Redwood Shores Parkway, Redwood City, CA 94065-1175.
**Telephone:** 650-628-1500.
**Email:** investorrelations@ea.com
**Website:** http://www.ea.com

**Chrmn:** L.F. Probst, III
**CEO:** J.S. Riccitiello
**COO:** P.R. Moore
**EVP & CFO:** E.F. Brown

**SVP & Chief Acctg Officer:** K.A. Barker
**Investor Contact:** J. Brown (650-628-7922)
**Board Members:** L. S. Coleman, Jr., J. C. Hoag, J. T. Huber, G. B. Laybourne, G. B. Maffei, V. Paul, L. F. Probst, III, J. S. Riccitiello, R. Simonson, L. J. Srere, L. A. Ubinas, R. V. Whitworth

**Founded:** 1982
**Domicile:** Delaware
**Employees:** 7,645

**STANDARD &POOR'S**

# El Paso Corp

| S&P Recommendation | HOLD ★★★★★ | Price $24.84 (as of Nov 25, 2011) | 12-Mo. Target Price $27.00 | Investment Style Large-Cap Value |
|---|---|---|---|---|

**GICS Sector** Energy
**Sub-Industry** Oil & Gas Storage & Transportation

**Summary** This provider of natural gas and related energy products has agreed to be acquired by Kinder Morgan for cash and stock.

## Key Stock Statistics (Source S&P, Vickers, company reports)

| | | | | | | | |
|---|---|---|---|---|---|---|---|
| 52-Wk Range | $25.73– 13.07 | S&P Oper. EPS 2011**E** | 1.01 | Market Capitalization(B) | $19.157 | Beta | 1.19 |
| Trailing 12-Month EPS | $0.04 | S&P Oper. EPS 2012**E** | 1.14 | Yield (%) | 0.16 | S&P 3-Yr. Proj. EPS CAGR(%) | 17 |
| Trailing 12-Month P/E | NM | P/E on S&P Oper. EPS 2011**E** | 24.6 | Dividend Rate/Share | $0.04 | S&P Credit Rating | BB |
| $10K Invested 5 Yrs Ago | $19,128 | Common Shares Outstg. (M) | 771.2 | Institutional Ownership (%) | 78 | | |

## Price Performance

30-Week Mov. Avg. · · · · 10-Week Mov. Avg. - - GAAP Earnings vs. Previous Year Volume Above Avg. ⅢⅢ STARS
12-Mo. Target Price — Relative Strength — ▲ Up ▼ Down ► No Change Below Avg. ⅢⅢ ★

Analysis prepared by Equity Analyst **Tanjila Shafi** on Oct 25, 2011, when the stock traded at **$25.51**.

Options: ASE, CBOE, P

## Highlights

➤ EP has earmarked $1.8 billion in capital expenditures for its pipeline segment, including $0.4 billion for integrity and maintenance expenditures. EP has completed three of the five major projects that it planned to place into service in 2011. We expect throughput volumes to experience single digit growth this year.

➤ This year, we see total production between 830 million and 860 million cubic feet of natural gas equivalents per day, compared to 782 million cubic feet of natural gas equivalents per day in 2010. EP plans to operate 12 to 14 rigs for the remainder of the year. We are encouraged with EP's drilling activities in liquid rich plays such as the Eagle Ford and Wolfcamp. The company has budgeted $1.6 billion for capital expenditures for its E&P segment.

➤ We see asset dropdowns and attractive hedges improving future cash flows and the balance sheet. Our 2011 EPS forecast is $1.10, compared to 2010's adjusted EPS of $0.98.

## Investment Rationale/Risk

➤ On October 16, 2011, EP announced that Kinder Morgan, Inc. (KMI 30, NR) had signed a definitive agreement to acquire all of its outstanding shares for a total purchase price of $38 billion (including assumption of debt). We believe the combined footprint offers growth opportunities. Subject to regulatory approval, the transaction is expected to close in the second quarter of 2012.

➤ Risks to our recommendation and target price include lower natural gas prices, weaker-than-expected economic conditions, and difficulties obtaining approval for the KMI acquisition.

➤ Our 12-month target price of $27 is based on terms of the KMI offer, which is comprised of $14.65 per share in cash, 0.4187 of a KMI share (recently valued at $12.56 per EP share) and 0.64 of a KMI five-year warrant ($40 exercise price; current value about $1). EP holders may instead elect to receive $25.91 in cash or 0.9635 of a KMI share, subject to proration, plus 0.64 of the KMI warrant.

## Qualitative Risk Assessment

| LOW | MEDIUM | HIGH |
|---|---|---|

Our risk assessment reflects EP's increased focus on volatile exploration and production (E&P) activities and our view of its highly leveraged balance sheet, given the capital intensity of its operations. Partly offsetting these risks is EP's involvement in regulated pipelines.

## Quantitative Evaluations

**S&P Quality Ranking** B-

| D | C | B- | B | B+ | A- | A | A+ |
|---|---|---|---|---|---|---|---|

**Relative Strength Rank** STRONG

96

LOWEST = 1    HIGHEST = 99

## Revenue/Earnings Data

**Revenue (Million $)**

| | 1Q | 2Q | 3Q | 4Q | Year |
|---|---|---|---|---|---|
| 2011 | 989.0 | 1,236 | 1,403 | -- | -- |
| 2010 | 1,401 | 1,018 | 1,213 | 984.0 | 4,616 |
| 2009 | 1,484 | 973.0 | 981.0 | 1,193 | 4,631 |
| 2008 | 1,269 | 1,153 | 1,598 | 1,343 | 5,363 |
| 2007 | 1,022 | 1,198 | 1,166 | 1,262 | 4,648 |
| 2006 | 1,337 | 1,089 | 942.0 | 913.0 | 4,281 |

**Earnings Per Share ($)**

| | | | | | |
|---|---|---|---|---|---|
| 2011 | 0.08 | 0.34 | -0.48 | E0.28 | E1.01 |
| 2010 | 0.51 | 0.21 | 0.19 | 0.09 | 1.00 |
| 2009 | -1.41 | 0.11 | 0.08 | 0.36 | -0.83 |
| 2008 | 0.33 | 0.25 | 0.58 | -2.43 | -1.24 |
| 2007 | -0.08 | 0.22 | 0.20 | 0.20 | 0.57 |
| 2006 | 0.42 | 0.19 | 0.15 | -0.30 | 0.72 |

Fiscal year ended Dec. 31. Next earnings report expected: Late January. EPS Estimates based on S&P Operating Earnings; historical GAAP earnings are as reported.

## Dividend Data (Dates: mm/dd Payment Date: mm/dd/yy)

| Amount ($) | Date Decl. | Ex-Div. Date | Stk. of Record | Payment Date |
|---|---|---|---|---|
| 0.010 | 02/08 | 03/02 | 03/04 | 04/01/11 |
| 0.010 | 04/01 | 06/01 | 06/03 | 07/01/11 |
| 0.010 | 07/14 | 08/31 | 09/02 | 10/03/11 |
| 0.010 | 10/06 | 11/30 | 12/02 | 01/03/12 |

Dividends have been paid since 1992. Source: Company reports.

**The McGraw-Hill Companies**

# El Paso Corp

## Business Summary October 25, 2011

CORPORATE OVERVIEW. Founded in 1928, El Paso Corp. originally served as a regional natural gas pipeline company that ultimately expanded geographically and into complementary business lines. By 2001, its total assets exceeded $44 billion and included natural gas production, power generation, trading operations and its traditional natural gas pipeline businesses. In late 2001 through 2003, various industry and company-specific events led to a substantial decline in EP's fundamentals. In late 2003, EP announced a long-term business strategy principally focused on core pipeline and production businesses. During the past several years, EP has sold off non-core assets to reduce debt and improve liquidity. In 2007, EP formed El Paso Pipeline Partners, L.P. (EPB 36, NR), a master limited partnership. As of December 31, 2010, EP's ownership interest in EPB was 51%, including its 2% general partner interest.

PRIMARY BUSINESS DYNAMICS. Operations are conducted through two primary segments: Pipelines; and Exploration and Production. EP also has a smaller Marketing segment, whose focus is to market its exploration and production segment's natural gas and oil production, and to manage EP's overall price risk.

The Pipelines segment is the largest U.S. owner of interstate natural gas

pipelines, owning or with interests in 43,100 miles of pipeline, with eight separate wholly or majority owned pipeline systems and two partially owned systems. The division also has 240 Bcf of natural gas storage capacity and two liquefied natural gas terminalling facilities, one of which is under construction and the other is located at Elba Island, GA. Each pipeline system and storage facility operates under the Federal Energy Regulatory Commission (FERC).

EP's strategy in this segment is to expand systems into new markets while leveraging existing assets; recontract or contract available or expiring capacity and resolve open rate cases; leverage its coast-to-coast scale economies; and invest in maintenance and pipeline integrity projects to maintain the value and ensure the safety of its pipeline systems and assets. During 2009, EP placed several pipeline expansion projects into service, obtained a 50% partner on its Ruby project and secured financing for a portion of its remaining pipeline backlog. In 2010, EP placed five growth projects into service.

## Company Financials Fiscal Year Ended Dec. 31

| Per Share Data ($) | 2010 | 2009 | 2008 | 2007 | 2006 | 2005 | 2004 | 2003 | 2002 | 2001 |
|---|---|---|---|---|---|---|---|---|---|---|
| Tangible Book Value | 4.50 | 3.50 | 4.70 | 6.47 | 6.00 | 3.38 | 4.68 | 5.36 | 11.70 | 17.65 |
| Cash Flow | 2.43 | 3.47 | 0.50 | 2.25 | 2.09 | 0.61 | 0.45 | 0.99 | 0.21 | 2.76 |
| Earnings | 1.00 | -0.83 | -1.24 | 0.57 | 0.72 | -1.13 | -1.25 | -1.03 | -2.30 | 0.13 |
| S&P Core Earnings | 0.94 | -0.79 | -1.46 | 0.54 | 0.69 | -1.07 | -0.84 | -0.68 | -1.95 | -0.37 |
| Dividends | 0.04 | 0.16 | 0.18 | 0.16 | 0.16 | 0.16 | 0.16 | 0.16 | 0.87 | 0.85 |
| Payout Ratio | 4% | NM | NM | 28% | 22% | NM | NM | NM | NM | NM |
| Prices:High | 14.08 | 11.37 | 22.47 | 18.56 | 16.39 | 14.16 | 11.85 | 10.30 | 46.89 | 75.30 |
| Prices:Low | 9.55 | 5.22 | 5.32 | 13.71 | 11.80 | 9.30 | 6.57 | 3.33 | 4.39 | 36.00 |
| P/E Ratio:High | 14 | NM | NM | 33 | 23 | NM | NM | NM | NM | NM |
| P/E Ratio:Low | 10 | NM | NM | 24 | 16 | NM | NM | NM | NM | NM |

| Income Statement Analysis (Million $) | | | | | | | | | | |
|---|---|---|---|---|---|---|---|---|---|---|
| Revenue | 4,616 | 4,631 | 5,363 | 4,648 | 4,281 | 4,017 | 5,874 | 6,711 | 12,194 | 57,475 |
| Operating Income | NA | NA | 3,579 | 2,904 | 1,427 | 934 | 2,386 | 2,907 | 2,872 | 4,391 |
| Depreciation | 967 | 2,990 | 1,205 | 1,176 | 1,047 | 1,121 | 1,088 | 1,207 | 1,405 | 1,359 |
| Interest Expense | 1,031 | 1,008 | 914 | 1,044 | 1,228 | 1,389 | 1,632 | 1,839 | 1,400 | 1,155 |
| Pretax Income | 1,310 | -873 | -1,034 | 664 | 523 | -991 | -777 | -1,200 | -1,567 | 466 |
| Effective Tax Rate | NA | 45.7% | NM | 33.4% | NM | NM | NM | NM | NM | 39.1% |
| Net Income | 924 | -539 | -823 | 436 | 531 | -702 | -802 | -616 | -1,289 | 67.0 |
| S&P Core Earnings | 672 | -543 | -1,021 | 375 | 471 | -696 | -531 | -401 | -1,096 | -194 |

| Balance Sheet & Other Financial Data (Million $) | | | | | | | | | | |
|---|---|---|---|---|---|---|---|---|---|---|
| Cash | 347 | 641 | 1,024 | 285 | 537 | 2,132 | 2,117 | 1,429 | 1,591 | 1,139 |
| Current Assets | 1,552 | 2,008 | 3,051 | 1,712 | 7,167 | 6,185 | 5,632 | 8,922 | 11,924 | 12,659 |
| Total Assets | 25,270 | 22,505 | 23,668 | 24,579 | 27,261 | 31,838 | 31,383 | 37,084 | 46,224 | 48,171 |
| Current Liabilities | 2,565 | 2,686 | 3,243 | 2,413 | 6,151 | 5,712 | 4,572 | 7,074 | 10,350 | 13,565 |
| Long Term Debt | 13,517 | 13,391 | 12,818 | 12,483 | 13,260 | 17,054 | 18,608 | 20,722 | 19,727 | 14,109 |
| Common Equity | 3,167 | 2,456 | 3,285 | 4,530 | 3,436 | 2,639 | 3,439 | 4,474 | 8,377 | 9,356 |
| Total Capital | 23,613 | 18,004 | 17,979 | 19,485 | 18,396 | 21,850 | 23,358 | 25,196 | 31,680 | 31,012 |
| Capital Expenditures | 4,073 | 2,810 | 2,757 | 2,495 | 2,164 | 1,718 | 1,782 | 2,452 | 3,716 | 4,079 |
| Cash Flow | 1,854 | 2,414 | 345 | 1,575 | 1,541 | 392 | 286 | 591 | 116 | 1,426 |
| Current Ratio | 0.6 | 0.8 | 0.9 | 0.7 | 1.2 | 1.1 | 1.2 | 1.3 | 1.2 | 0.9 |
| % Long Term Debt of Capitalization | 57.2 | Nil | 71.3 | 64.1 | 72.1 | 78.1 | 79.7 | 82.2 | 62.3 | 45.5 |
| % Net Income of Revenue | 20.0 | NM | NM | 9.4 | 12.4 | NM | NM | NM | NM | 0.1 |
| % Return on Assets | 3.9 | NM | NM | 1.7 | 1.8 | NM | NM | NM | NM | 0.1 |
| % Return on Equity | 32.9 | NA | NM | 10.0 | 16.3 | NM | NM | NM | NM | 0.8 |

Data as orig reptd.; bef. results of disc opers/spec. items. Per share data adj. for stk. divs.; EPS diluted. E-Estimated. NA-Not Available. NM-Not Meaningful. NR-Not Ranked. UR-Under Review.

**Office:** El Paso Building, 1001 Louisiana Street, Houston, TX 77002.
**Telephone:** 713-420-2600.
**Email:** investorrelations@epenergy.com
**Website:** http://www.elpaso.com

**Chrmn, Pres & CEO:** D.L. Foshee
**COO:** B. Neskora
**EVP & General Counsel:** R.W. Baker
**CFO:** J.R. Sult

**Chief Acctg Officer & Cntlr:** F.C. Olmsted, III
**Investor Contact:** B. Connery (713-420-5855)
**Board Members:** J. C. Braniff Hierro, D. Crane, D. L. Foshee, R. W. Goldman, A. W. Hall, Jr., T. R. Hix, F. P. McClean, T. J. Probert, S. J. Shapiro, J. M. Talbert, R. F. Vagt, J. L. Whitmire, III

**Founded:** 1928
**Domicile:** Delaware
**Employees:** 4,937

The McGraw-Hill Companies

# EMC Corp

**STANDARD &POOR'S**

| S&P Recommendation **HOLD** ★★★☆☆ | Price $21.88 (as of Nov 25, 2011) | 12-Mo. Target Price $27.00 | Investment Style Large-Cap Blend |
|---|---|---|---|

**GICS Sector** Information Technology
**Sub-Industry** Computer Storage & Peripherals

**Summary** This company is one of the world's largest suppliers of enterprise storage systems. It owns 80% of VMware, the largest provider of server virtualization software.

## Key Stock Statistics (Source S&P, Vickers, company reports)

| | | | | | | | |
|---|---|---|---|---|---|---|---|
| 52-Wk Range | $28.73– 19.84 | S&P Oper. EPS 2011**E** | 1.22 | Market Capitalization(B) | $44.634 | Beta | 1.04 |
| Trailing 12-Month EPS | $1.01 | S&P Oper. EPS 2012**E** | 1.34 | Yield (%) | Nil | S&P 3-Yr. Proj. EPS CAGR(%) | 8 |
| Trailing 12-Month P/E | 21.7 | P/E on S&P Oper. EPS 2011**E** | 17.9 | Dividend Rate/Share | Nil | S&P Credit Rating | A- |
| $10K Invested 5 Yrs Ago | $16,728 | Common Shares Outstg. (M) | 2,040.0 | Institutional Ownership (%) | 88 | | |

## Price Performance

30-Week Mov. Avg. · · · 10-Week Mov. Avg. - - GAAP Earnings vs. Previous Year  Volume Above Avg. STARS
12-Mo. Target Price — Relative Strength — ▲ Up ▼ Down ► No Change  Below Avg. ★

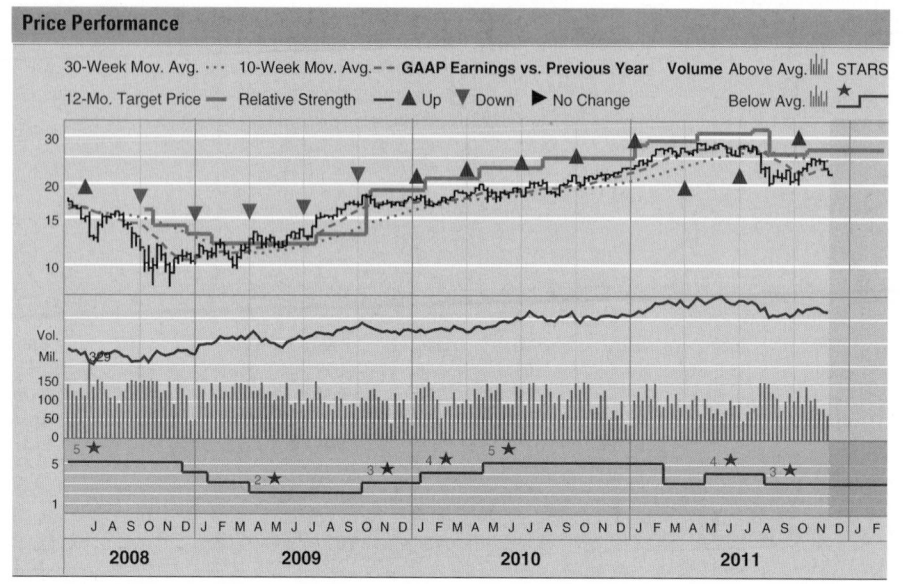

Options: ASE, CBOE, P, Ph

Analysis prepared by Equity Analyst **Jim Yin, CFA** on Nov 03, 2011, when the stock traded at **$24.68**.

## Highlights

➤ We expect revenues to increase 17% in 2011. We think the Information Infrastructure business will grow at a low-teens rate in 2011, driven by growing interest in cloud computing. We look for EMC to gain market share due to its broad hardware/software offerings and increased presence in the small- and medium-sized business segment with the acquisition of Isilon Systems. We believe revenues from its VMware Virtual Infrastructure business will rise 31%. However, we are cautious in our outlook for 2012, given recent data of a sluggish economy. We see overall revenues rising only 7.3% in 2012.

➤ We look for overall gross margins of about 60% in both 2011 and 2012, up from 59% in 2010. We believe expenses will decrease as a percentage of revenues this year due to cost savings and economies of scale. We think GAAP operating margins will widen to 17% and 18% in 2011 and 2012, respectively, from 16% in 2010.

➤ We forecast operating EPS of $1.22 and $1.34 in 2011 and 2012, respectively, up from $1.04 in 2010. Our estimates exclude acquisition-related and one-time charges that we see of $0.14 in 2011 and $0.08 in 2012.

## Investment Rationale/Risk

➤ We believe long-term demand for data storage will remain strong, driven by several positive trends, including higher usage of video and electronic record keeping. We think sales should benefit from growing interest in cloud computing and virtualization software. We also believe EMC is gaining market share, particularly in small and medium-sized businesses, with new products in unified storage and data backup. However, we are concerned about weaker growth of IT spending in 2012, due to a slowing global economy and uncertainties about sovereign debt issues.

➤ Risks to our recommendation and target price include a weaker-than-expected economic recovery, lower corporate IT spending, increased competition, unfavorable foreign currency exchange due to a rapid rise in the U.S. dollar, and a significant loss of market share.

➤ Our 12-month target price of $27 is based on our DCF analysis. Our DCF model assumes an 11% weighted average cost of capital, 18.0% operating margins, an 8.0% revenue growth rate for the next 10 years, and 3% terminal growth.

## Qualitative Risk Assessment

| LOW | MEDIUM | HIGH |
|---|---|---|

Our risk assessment reflects our view that EMC is a market leader, generates consistent free cash flow, and has a strong balance sheet. However, we see the storage segment as somewhat cyclical, highly competitive, and often typified by pricing pressure.

## Quantitative Evaluations

**S&P Quality Ranking**  B

| D | C | B- | **B** | B+ | A- | A | A+ |
|---|---|---|---|---|---|---|---|

**Relative Strength Rank**  MODERATE
**46**
LOWEST = 1    HIGHEST = 99

## Revenue/Earnings Data

**Revenue (Million $)**

| | 1Q | 2Q | 3Q | 4Q | Year |
|---|---|---|---|---|---|
| 2011 | 4,608 | 4,845 | 4,980 | -- | -- |
| 2010 | 3,891 | 4,024 | 4,212 | 4,889 | 17,015 |
| 2009 | 3,151 | 3,257 | 3,518 | 4,100 | 14,026 |
| 2008 | 3,470 | 3,674 | 3,716 | 4,017 | 14,876 |
| 2007 | 2,975 | 3,125 | 3,300 | 3,831 | 13,230 |
| 2006 | 2,551 | 2,575 | 2,815 | 3,215 | 11,155 |

**Earnings Per Share ($)**

| | | | | | |
|---|---|---|---|---|---|
| 2011 | 0.21 | 0.24 | 0.27 | E0.38 | E1.22 |
| 2010 | 0.18 | 0.20 | 0.22 | 0.29 | 0.88 |
| 2009 | 0.10 | 0.10 | 0.14 | 0.19 | 0.53 |
| 2008 | 0.13 | 0.18 | 0.20 | 0.14 | 0.64 |
| 2007 | 0.15 | 0.16 | 0.23 | 0.24 | 0.77 |
| 2006 | 0.12 | 0.12 | 0.13 | 0.18 | 0.54 |

Fiscal year ended Dec. 31. Next earnings report expected: NA. EPS Estimates based on S&P Operating Earnings; historical GAAP earnings are as reported.

## Dividend Data

No cash dividends have been paid.

# EMC Corp

STANDARD &POOR'S

## Business Summary November 03, 2011

CORPORATE OVERVIEW. EMC is a leading provider of data storage solutions for enterprises and government entities around the world. The company's products and services are used in conjunction with a variety of computing platforms that support key business processes, including transaction processing, data warehousing, electronic commerce and content management. Due to the growing complexity of its customers' infrastructure, EMC not only helps customers manage and secure their vast and ever-increasing quantities of information, but also automate their data centers and reduce their operational costs.

The company divides its operations into two major businesses, Information Infrastructure and VMware Virtual Infrastructure. Information Infrastructure business is comprised of three reporting segments - Information Storage, Content Management and Archiving and RSA Information Security. The company offers a wide range of storage systems designed to fulfill customers' needs in terms of performance, functionality, scalability, data availability and cost. Its key product line, Symmetrix, can scale to hundreds of thousands of terabytes of storage and 10s of millions of IOPS (input/output per second) supporting hundreds of thousands of virtual machines in a single federated storage infrastructure. EMC also has other product lines - CLARiiON, Celerra, and Centera - that target the mid-tier and the low end of the markets. Information Storage accounted for 76% of total revenues in 2009. Sales in this business unit fell 8.3% in 2009, reflecting lower IT spending, in particular for hardware. Content Management and Archiving helps companies manage, backup, and restore their data, while RSA Information Security helps to safeguard the integrity and confidentiality of information throughout its lifecycle. Revenues from these two business units accounted 9.6% of total revenues in 2009.

VMware Virtual Infrastructure provides software solutions that help companies cut costs in their data center operations. Virtualization software can reduce the number of servers by consolidating many different types of workloads and operating systems onto virtual environments, thus enabling servers to run multiple applications. Revenues from its VMware Virtual Infrastructure business unit grew 7.7% in 2009, and accounted for 14% of total revenues.

## Company Financials Fiscal Year Ended Dec. 31

| Per Share Data ($) | 2010 | 2009 | 2008 | 2007 | 2006 | 2005 | 2004 | 2003 | 2002 | 2001 |
|---|---|---|---|---|---|---|---|---|---|---|
| Tangible Book Value | 1.68 | 2.51 | 2.37 | 2.42 | 4.39 | 3.20 | 3.22 | 3.19 | 3.05 | 3.31 |
| Cash Flow | 1.43 | 1.05 | 0.92 | 1.02 | 0.87 | 0.73 | 0.61 | 0.45 | 0.24 | 0.07 |
| Earnings | 0.88 | 0.53 | 0.64 | 0.77 | 0.54 | 0.47 | 0.36 | 0.22 | -0.05 | -0.23 |
| S&P Core Earnings | 0.88 | 0.54 | 0.63 | 0.73 | 0.55 | 0.35 | 0.21 | 0.04 | -0.23 | -0.33 |
| Dividends | Nil | Nil | Nil | Nil | Nil | Nil | Nil | Nil | Nil | Nil |
| Payout Ratio | Nil | Nil | Nil | Nil | Nil | Nil | Nil | Nil | Nil | Nil |
| Prices:High | 23.20 | 18.44 | 18.60 | 25.47 | 14.75 | 15.09 | 15.80 | 14.66 | 17.97 | 82.00 |
| Prices:Low | 16.45 | 9.61 | 8.25 | 12.74 | 9.44 | 11.10 | 9.24 | 5.98 | 3.67 | 10.01 |
| P/E Ratio:High | 26 | 35 | 29 | 33 | 27 | 32 | 44 | 67 | NM | NM |
| P/E Ratio:Low | 19 | 18 | 13 | 17 | 17 | 24 | 26 | 27 | NM | NM |

| Income Statement Analysis (Million $) | 2010 | 2009 | 2008 | 2007 | 2006 | 2005 | 2004 | 2003 | 2002 | 2001 |
|---|---|---|---|---|---|---|---|---|---|---|
| Revenue | 17,015 | 14,026 | 14,876 | 13,230 | 11,155 | 9,664 | 8,229 | 6,237 | 5,438 | 7,091 |
| Operating Income | 3,934 | 2,595 | 2,459 | 2,302 | 2,170 | 2,222 | 1,716 | 988 | 310 | 355 |
| Depreciation | 1,168 | 1,073 | 561 | 530 | 764 | 640 | 616 | 521 | 654 | 655 |
| Interest Expense | 178 | 183 | 73.8 | 72.9 | 34.1 | 7.99 | 7.52 | 3.03 | 11.4 | 11.3 |
| Pretax Income | 2,608 | 1,375 | 1,703 | 2,060 | 1,390 | 1,652 | 1,185 | 571 | -296 | -577 |
| Effective Tax Rate | NA | 18.4% | 18.4% | 18.4% | 11.7% | 31.4% | 26.5% | 13.1% | NM | NM |
| Net Income | 1,900 | 1,088 | 1,346 | 1,666 | 1,227 | 1,133 | 871 | 496 | -119 | -508 |
| S&P Core Earnings | 1,898 | 1,124 | 1,312 | 1,569 | 1,241 | 839 | 504 | 84.2 | -477 | -720 |

| Balance Sheet & Other Financial Data (Million $) | 2010 | 2009 | 2008 | 2007 | 2006 | 2005 | 2004 | 2003 | 2002 | 2001 |
|---|---|---|---|---|---|---|---|---|---|---|
| Cash | 5,375 | 6,695 | 6,807 | 6,127 | 1,828 | 2,322 | 1,477 | 1,869 | 1,687 | 2,129 |
| Current Assets | 9,783 | 10,538 | 10,665 | 10,053 | 6,521 | 6,574 | 4,831 | 4,687 | 4,217 | 4,923 |
| Total Assets | 30,833 | 26,812 | 23,875 | 22,285 | 18,566 | 16,790 | 15,423 | 14,093 | 9,590 | 9,890 |
| Current Liabilities | 9,378 | 5,148 | 5,148 | 4,408 | 3,881 | 3,674 | 2,949 | 2,547 | 2,042 | 2,179 |
| Long Term Debt | 235 | 3,100 | 3,450 | 3,450 | 3,450 | 127 | 128 | 130 | Nil | Nil |
| Common Equity | 17,404 | 15,550 | 13,042 | 12,521 | 10,326 | 12,065 | 11,523 | 10,885 | 7,226 | 7,601 |
| Total Capital | 21,617 | 18,650 | 17,038 | 16,448 | 13,776 | 12,368 | 11,793 | 11,015 | 7,226 | 7,601 |
| Capital Expenditures | 745 | 412 | 696 | 699 | 718 | 601 | 371 | 369 | 391 | 889 |
| Cash Flow | 3,068 | 2,161 | 1,907 | 2,196 | 1,992 | 1,773 | 1,488 | 1,017 | 535 | 147 |
| Current Ratio | 1.0 | 2.1 | 2.0 | 2.3 | 1.7 | 1.8 | 1.6 | 1.8 | 2.1 | 2.3 |
| % Long Term Debt of Capitalization | 1.1 | 16.6 | 20.3 | 21.4 | 25.0 | 1.0 | 1.1 | 1.2 | Nil | Nil |
| % Net Income of Revenue | 11.2 | 7.8 | 9.1 | 12.6 | 11.0 | 11.7 | 10.6 | 8.0 | NM | NM |
| % Return on Assets | 6.6 | 4.3 | 5.8 | 8.2 | 6.9 | 7.0 | 5.9 | 4.2 | NM | NM |
| % Return on Equity | 11.5 | 7.5 | 10.5 | 14.6 | 11.0 | 9.6 | 7.8 | 5.5 | NM | NM |

Data as orig reptd.; bef. results of disc opers/spec. items. Per share data adj. for stk. divs.; EPS diluted. E-Estimated. NA-Not Available. NM-Not Meaningful. NR-Not Ranked. UR-Under Review.

**Office:** 176 South Street, Hopkinton, MA 01748.
**Telephone:** 508-435-1000.
**Email:** emc_ir@emc.com
**Website:** http://www.emc.com

**Chrmn, Pres & CEO:** J.M. Tucci
**SVP & CTO:** J.M. Nick
**CFO:** D.I. Goulden
**Chief Acctg Officer & Cntlr:** D.G. Cashman

**Secy:** T.J. Dougherty
**Board Members:** M. W. Brown, R. L. Cowen, G. Deegan, J. S. DiStasio, J. R. Egan, E. F. Kelly, W. B. Priem, P. L. Sagan, D. N. Strohm, J. M. Tucci

**Founded:** 1979
**Domicile:** Massachusetts
**Employees:** 48,500

The McGraw-Hill Companies

# Emerson Electric Co.

**STANDARD &POOR'S**

| | | | |
|---|---|---|---|
| **S&P Recommendation** HOLD ★★★☆☆ | **Price** $47.11 (as of Nov 25, 2011) | **12-Mo. Target Price** $53.00 | **Investment Style** Large-Cap Blend |

**GICS Sector** Industrials
**Sub-Industry** Electrical Components & Equipment

**Summary** This company designs and supplies product technology, and delivers engineering services and solutions to a wide range of industrial, commercial, and consumer markets around the world.

## Key Stock Statistics (Source S&P, Vickers, company reports)

| | | | | | | | | |
|---|---|---|---|---|---|---|---|---|
| 52-Wk Range | $62.24– 39.50 | S&P Oper. EPS 2012**E** | 3.68 | Market Capitalization(B) | $34.661 | Beta | | 1.24 |
| Trailing 12-Month EPS | $3.28 | S&P Oper. EPS 2013**E** | NA | Yield (%) | 3.40 | S&P 3-Yr. Proj. EPS CAGR(%) | | 14 |
| Trailing 12-Month P/E | 14.4 | P/E on S&P Oper. EPS 2012**E** | 12.8 | Dividend Rate/Share | $1.60 | S&P Credit Rating | | A |
| $10K Invested 5 Yrs Ago | $12,199 | Common Shares Outstg. (M) | 735.8 | Institutional Ownership (%) | 74 | | | |

## Price Performance

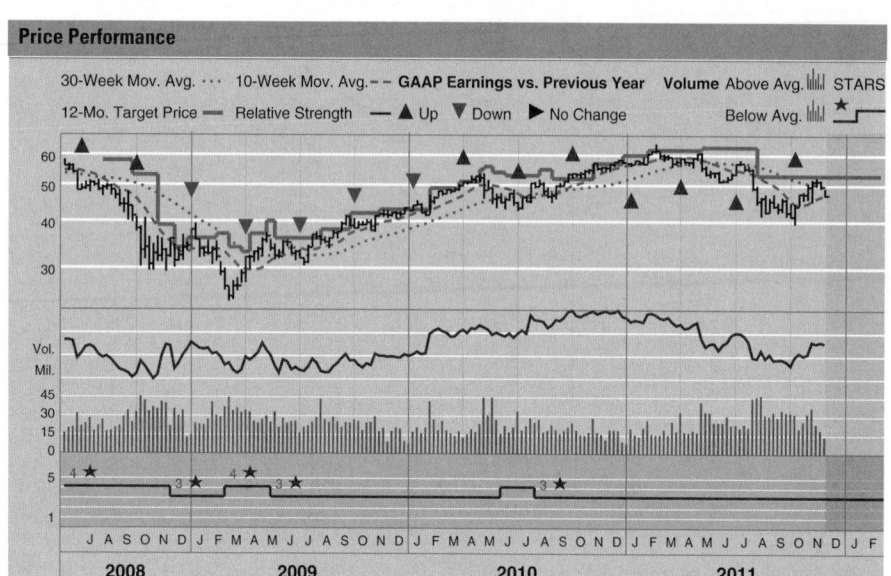

30-Week Mov. Avg. · · · 10-Week Mov. Avg. - - **GAAP Earnings vs. Previous Year** Volume Above Avg. STARS
12-Mo. Target Price — Relative Strength — ▲ Up ▼ Down ► No Change Below Avg. ★

Options: ASE, CBOE, P, Ph

Analysis prepared by Equity Analyst **Kevin Kirkeby** on Nov 22, 2011, when the stock traded at **$48.92**.

### Highlights

➤ Following organic revenue growth of 11% in FY 11 (Sep.), we forecast a slowing to 5% growth in FY 12 due to ongoing economic uncertainty. We think spending by EMR's industrial and commercial customers will improve as they perform necessary maintenance work, as well as begin facility upgrades. Likewise, we see favorable order trends from the customers in the oil and gas markets. However, the domestic construction markets will start the year weak, before improving into year-end, in our view. Flooding in Thailand is causing near-term supply disruptions for EMR, and will likely reduce December-quarter revenues by about $350 million, or nearly 6%.

➤ We think operating margins will widen modestly during FY 12 due to the positive impact from greater operating leverage and further benefits of cost realignments. Between recent pullbacks in price and EMR's hedging activity, we think raw material costs will have limited impact on margins in the coming year.

➤ With taxes at a projected effective rate of 30.5% in FY 12, we estimate EPS of $3.68.

### Investment Rationale/Risk

➤ We think EMR is well positioned to benefit from any strengthening in the global economy, particularly from spending on infrastructure. However, orders rates across EMR's business units have slowed over the past few quarters. Still, backlog in the later-cycle segments, like process management, continue to expand. Based on these factors, we think a valuation near the historical average is warranted.

➤ Risks to our recommendation and target price include weaker-than-expected global economic growth, softer industrial, energy, and electronics markets, potential value-diminishing acquisitions, and availability and cost of product components and commodities.

➤ Our 12-month target price of $53 represents a blend of two valuation metrics. Our discounted cash flow model, which assumes a 3% perpetuity growth rate and an 11.4% discount rate, indicates an intrinsic value near $50. Our P/E valuation applies a 15.8X multiple, near the historical average but ahead of the peer average, to our forward 12-months EPS estimate, indicating a $56 value.

## Qualitative Risk Assessment

| LOW | MEDIUM | HIGH |
|---|---|---|

Our risk assessment reflects the cyclical nature of several of the company's major end markets, its acquisition strategy, and corporate governance practices that we view as unfavorable versus peers. This is offset by our view of its strong competitive position in major product categories.

## Quantitative Evaluations

**S&P Quality Ranking** A+

| D | C | B- | B | B+ | A- | A | A+ |
|---|---|---|---|---|---|---|---|

**Relative Strength Rank** MODERATE

68

LOWEST = 1 HIGHEST = 99

## Revenue/Earnings Data

**Revenue (Million $)**

| | 1Q | 2Q | 3Q | 4Q | Year |
|---|---|---|---|---|---|
| 2011 | 5,535 | 5,854 | 6,288 | 6,545 | 24,222 |
| 2010 | 4,828 | 4,953 | 5,417 | 5,841 | 21,039 |
| 2009 | 5,415 | 5,087 | 5,091 | 5,322 | 20,915 |
| 2008 | 5,520 | 6,023 | 6,568 | 6,696 | 24,807 |
| 2007 | 5,051 | 5,513 | 5,874 | 6,134 | 22,572 |
| 2006 | 4,548 | 4,852 | 5,217 | 5,516 | 20,133 |

**Earnings Per Share ($)**

| | | | | | |
|---|---|---|---|---|---|
| 2011 | 0.63 | 0.73 | 0.90 | 0.98 | 3.24 |
| 2010 | 0.56 | 0.55 | 0.78 | 0.76 | 2.60 |
| 2009 | 0.60 | 0.49 | 0.51 | 0.67 | 2.27 |
| 2008 | 0.65 | 0.75 | 0.82 | 0.88 | 3.11 |
| 2007 | 0.55 | 0.61 | 0.72 | 0.78 | 2.66 |
| 2006 | 0.48 | 0.52 | 0.59 | 0.65 | 2.24 |

Fiscal year ended Sep. 30. Next earnings report expected: Early February. EPS Estimates based on S&P Operating Earnings; historical GAAP earnings are as reported.

## Dividend Data (Dates: mm/dd Payment Date: mm/dd/yy)

| Amount ($) | Date Decl. | Ex-Div. Date | Stk. of Record | Payment Date |
|---|---|---|---|---|
| 0.345 | 02/01 | 02/09 | 02/11 | 03/10/11 |
| 0.345 | 05/03 | 05/11 | 05/13 | 06/10/11 |
| 0.345 | 08/02 | 08/10 | 08/12 | 09/09/11 |
| 0.400 | 11/01 | 11/08 | 11/11 | 12/09/11 |

Dividends have been paid since 1947. Source: Company reports.

---

**Please read the Required Disclosures and Analyst Certification on the last page of this report.**

*The McGraw-Hill Companies*

# Emerson Electric Co.

## Business Summary November 22, 2011

CORPORATE OVERVIEW. Emerson Electric is an industrial conglomerate operating in five primary business segments: Process Management, Industrial Automation, Network Power, Climate Technologies, and Tools and Storage.

The company's Process Management segment, which accounted for 30% of FY 11 (Sep.) total sales and 39% of earnings, and had 22.3% margins, produces process management software and systems, analytical instrumentation, valves, control systems for measurement and control of fluid flow, and integrated solutions for process and industrial applications. In FY 10 (latest available), 33% of segment sales were made within the U.S., 23% in Europe, 23% in Asia, and 21% from the rest of the world. Segment sales are mainly conducted via a direct sales force while segment brands include Emerson Process Management, AMS Suite, Baumann, Bettis, Bristol, PlantWeb, CSI, DeltaV, and Fisher, to name a few.

The Industrial Automation segment (21%, 18%, 14.8%) primarily makes industrial motors and drives, transmissions, alternators and controls for automated equipment. Products in this segment are sold predominantly to manufacturing firms via a direct sales force or independent resellers. Geographic distribution of segment sales during FY 10 (latest available): 37% U.S., 38% Europe, 16% Asia, and 9% other regions. Segment brands include Emerson Industrial Automation, Appleton, Trident, McGill, and ASCO.

The Network Power segment (27%, 21%, 13.5%) mainly makes power systems and precision cooling products used in computer, telecommunications and Internet infrastructure sold mainly to large data centers. In FY 10 (latest available), 40% of segment sales were generated in the U.S., 16% in Europe, 34% in Asia, and 10% elsewhere. Product distribution is mainly through Emerson's direct sales force in Europe and Asia and independent resellers domestically. Segment brands include Emerson Network Power, Aperture, ASCO Power Technologies, Astec, Liebert, Netsure, Stratos, Chloride, and Avocent.

The Climate Technologies segment (15%, 14%, 17.0%) makes home and building thermostats and compressors (cooling components used in heating and air conditioning units and refrigerators). Geographic distribution of FY 10 (latest available) segment sales: 54% U.S., 13% Europe, 23% Asia, and 10% other regions. Segment brands: Emerson Climate Technologies, Computer Process Controls, Dixell, and Emerson Retail Services.

## Company Financials Fiscal Year Ended Sep. 30

| Per Share Data ($) | 2011 | 2010 | 2009 | 2008 | 2007 | 2006 | 2005 | 2004 | 2003 | 2002 |
|---|---|---|---|---|---|---|---|---|---|---|
| Tangible Book Value | NA | NM | 0.44 | 2.25 | 2.99 | 2.67 | 2.34 | 2.36 | 1.81 | 0.99 |
| Cash Flow | 4.47 | 3.69 | 3.13 | 3.92 | 3.47 | 3.04 | 2.41 | 4.37 | 1.84 | 1.90 |
| Earnings | 3.24 | 2.61 | 2.27 | 3.11 | 2.66 | 2.24 | 1.70 | 1.49 | 1.21 | 1.26 |
| S&P Core Earnings | 3.11 | 2.65 | 2.08 | 2.94 | 2.67 | 2.24 | 1.70 | 1.49 | 1.13 | 0.94 |
| Dividends | 1.38 | 1.34 | 1.32 | 1.20 | 1.05 | 0.89 | 0.83 | 0.80 | 0.79 | 0.78 |
| Payout Ratio | 43% | 51% | 58% | 39% | 39% | 40% | 49% | 54% | 65% | 62% |
| Prices:High | 62.24 | 58.74 | 43.71 | 58.72 | 59.05 | 45.21 | 38.92 | 35.44 | 32.50 | 33.04 |
| Prices:Low | 39.50 | 41.22 | 24.39 | 29.26 | 41.26 | 36.78 | 30.35 | 28.11 | 21.89 | 20.87 |
| P/E Ratio:High | 19 | 23 | 19 | 19 | 22 | 20 | 23 | 24 | 27 | 26 |
| P/E Ratio:Low | 12 | 16 | 11 | 9 | 16 | 16 | 18 | 19 | 18 | 17 |

| Income Statement Analysis (Million $) | | | | | | | | | | |
|---|---|---|---|---|---|---|---|---|---|---|
| Revenue | 24,222 | 21,039 | 20,915 | 24,807 | 22,572 | 20,133 | 17,305 | 15,615 | 13,958 | 13,824 |
| Operating Income | 5,096 | 4,325 | 3,710 | 4,639 | 4,174 | 3,676 | 3,150 | 2,842 | 2,497 | 2,443 |
| Depreciation | 867 | 816 | 651 | 638 | 656 | 607 | 562 | 557 | 534 | 541 |
| Interest Expense | 223 | 261 | 244 | 244 | 261 | 225 | 243 | 234 | 246 | 250 |
| Pretax Income | 3,631 | 2,879 | 2,417 | 3,591 | 3,107 | 2,684 | 2,149 | 3,704 | 1,414 | 1,565 |
| Effective Tax Rate | NA | NA | 28.7% | 31.7% | 31.3% | 31.3% | 33.8% | 16.1% | 28.4% | 32.3% |
| Net Income | 2,504 | 1,978 | 1,724 | 2,454 | 2,136 | 1,845 | 1,422 | 3,109 | 1,013 | 1,060 |
| S&P Core Earnings | 2,341 | 2,001 | 1,580 | 2,321 | 2,145 | 1,846 | 1,424 | 1,250 | 951 | 784 |

| Balance Sheet & Other Financial Data (Million $) | | | | | | | | | | |
|---|---|---|---|---|---|---|---|---|---|---|
| Cash | 2,052 | 1,592 | 1,560 | 1,777 | 1,008 | 810 | 1,233 | 1,346 | 696 | 381 |
| Current Assets | 9,345 | 8,363 | 7,653 | 9,331 | 8,065 | 7,330 | 6,837 | 6,416 | 5,500 | 4,961 |
| Total Assets | 23,861 | 22,843 | 19,763 | 21,040 | 19,680 | 18,672 | 17,227 | 16,361 | 15,194 | 14,545 |
| Current Liabilities | 6,465 | 5,849 | 4,956 | 6,573 | 5,546 | 5,374 | 4,931 | 4,339 | 3,417 | 4,400 |
| Long Term Debt | 4,324 | 4,586 | 3,998 | 3,297 | 3,372 | 3,128 | 3,128 | 3,136 | 3,733 | 2,990 |
| Common Equity | 10,551 | 9,952 | 8,555 | 9,113 | 8,772 | 7,848 | 7,400 | 12,266 | 6,460 | 5,741 |
| Total Capital | 14,875 | 14,538 | 12,553 | 13,131 | 12,144 | 10,976 | 10,528 | 15,402 | 10,193 | 8,731 |
| Capital Expenditures | 647 | 524 | 531 | 714 | 681 | 601 | 518 | 400 | 337 | 384 |
| Cash Flow | 3,371 | 2,794 | 2,375 | 3,092 | 2,792 | 2,452 | 1,984 | 3,666 | 1,547 | 1,601 |
| Current Ratio | 1.5 | 1.4 | 1.5 | 1.4 | 1.5 | 1.4 | 1.4 | 1.5 | 1.6 | 1.1 |
| % Long Term Debt of Capitalization | 29.1 | 31.5 | 31.9 | 25.1 | 27.8 | 28.5 | 29.7 | 20.4 | 36.6 | 34.2 |
| % Net Income of Revenue | 10.3 | 9.4 | 8.2 | 9.9 | 9.5 | 9.2 | 8.2 | 19.9 | 7.3 | 7.7 |
| % Return on Assets | 10.7 | 9.3 | 8.5 | 12.1 | 11.1 | 10.3 | 8.5 | 19.7 | 6.8 | 7.2 |
| % Return on Equity | 24.6 | 21.4 | 19.5 | 27.4 | 25.7 | 24.1 | 19.4 | 26.1 | 16.6 | 17.9 |

Data as orig reptd.; bef. results of disc opers/spec. items. Per share data adj. for stk. divs.; EPS diluted. E-Estimated. NA-Not Available. NM-Not Meaningful. NR-Not Ranked. UR-Under Review.

**Office:** 8000 West Florissant Avenue, PO Box 4100, St Louis, MO 63136.
**Telephone:** 314-553-2000.
**Website:** http://www.emersonelectric.com
**Chrmn & CEO:** D.N. Farr

**Pres & COO:** E.L. Monser
**Vice Chrmn:** W.J. Galvin
**EVP, Secy & General Counsel:** F.L. Steeves
**SVP & CFO:** F.J. Dellaquila

**Investor Contact:** C. Tucker (314-553-2197)
**Board Members:** C. A. Boersig, A. A. Busch, III, D. N. Farr, C. G. Fernandez, W. J. Galvin, A. F. Golden, H. Green, W. R. Johnson, J. B. Menzer, C. A. Peters, J. W. Prueher, R. L. Ridgway, R. L. Stephenson

**Founded:** 1890
**Domicile:** Missouri
**Employees:** 133,200

# Entergy Corp.

STANDARD &POOR'S

**S&P Recommendation** HOLD ★★★☆☆

| | |
|---|---|
| **Price** | **12-Mo. Target Price** | **Investment Style** |
| $66.54 (as of Nov 25, 2011) | $71.00 | Large-Cap Blend |

**GICS Sector** Utilities
**Sub-Industry** Electric Utilities

**Summary** This electric utility holding company serves 2.6 million customers in Arkansas, Louisiana, Mississippi and Texas, and has non-utility, nuclear operations in several states.

## Key Stock Statistics (Source S&P, Vickers, company reports)

| | | | | | | | |
|---|---|---|---|---|---|---|---|
| 52-Wk Range | $74.50– 57.60 | S&P Oper. EPS 2011**E** | 7.68 | Market Capitalization(B) | $11.719 | Beta | 0.57 |
| Trailing 12-Month EPS | $7.92 | S&P Oper. EPS 2012**E** | 6.18 | Yield (%) | 4.99 | S&P 3-Yr. Proj. EPS CAGR(%) | -2 |
| Trailing 12-Month P/E | 8.4 | P/E on S&P Oper. EPS 2011**E** | 8.7 | Dividend Rate/Share | $3.32 | S&P Credit Rating | BBB |
| $10K Invested 5 Yrs Ago | $8,959 | Common Shares Outstg. (M) | 176.1 | Institutional Ownership (%) | 83 | | |

## Price Performance

30-Week Mov. Avg. ···    10-Week Mov. Avg. - - **GAAP Earnings vs. Previous Year**    Volume Above Avg. STARS
12-Mo. Target Price —    Relative Strength    — ▲ Up ▼ Down ► No Change    Below Avg. ★

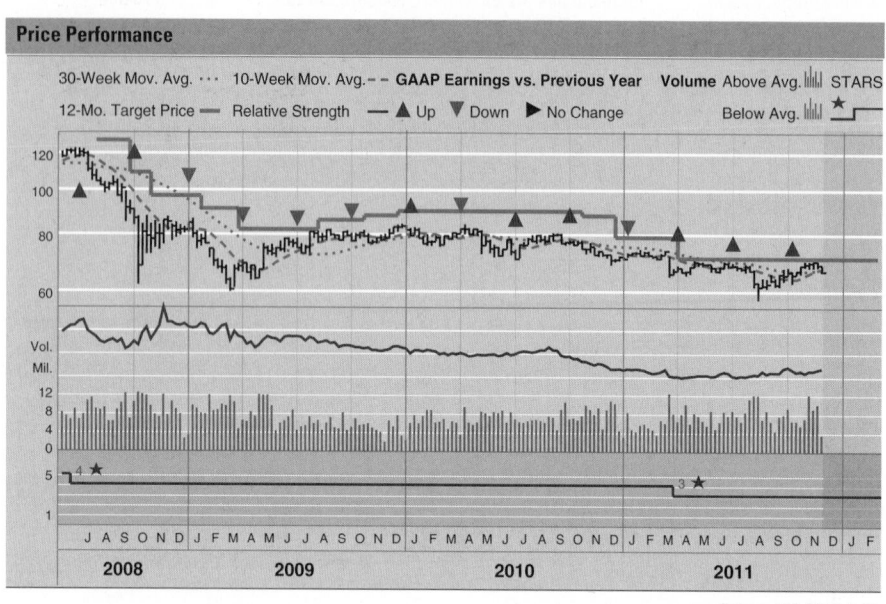

Options: ASE, CBOE, P, Ph

Analysis prepared by Equity Analyst **Justin McCann** on Oct 20, 2011, when the stock traded at **$67.20**.

## Highlights

▸ We expect operating EPS in 2011 to increase about 8% from 2010's $7.10. Operating EPS in the first half of 2011 was $0.11 above the $3.03 in the year-earlier period, as lower power prices and unplanned outages at a nuclear plant were more than offset by rate increases at the utilities and around 6% fewer shares.

▸ For the second half of 2011, we believe the projected increase in operating EPS will reflect a third quarter tax settlement that will significantly reduce income tax expense, partially offset by the ongoing weakness in the power markets. For 2012, we expect operating EPS to decline nearly 20% from anticipated results in 2011, reflecting lower-margin power contracts and the absence of the tax settlement benefit.

▸ On September 14, 2011, the U.S. District Court in Vermont completed its hearing of Entergy's suit aimed at preventing the state from closing its Vermont Yankee nuclear plant on the March 21, 2012, expiration of the current license. ETR noted that the Nuclear Regulatory Commission had, on March 21, 2011, renewed the plant's operating license for an additional 20 years beyond its 2012 expiration. The Court's decision is expected during the fourth quarter of 2011.

## Investment Rationale/Risk

▸ We see limited upside to the shares until the uncertainties regarding the Vermont Yankee nuclear plant are resolved. In addition to the ongoing weakness in the power markets, the stock has been restricted by the impact of the nuclear crisis in Japan, which intensified the opposition to the renewal of ETR's operating licenses for its plants in Vermont and New York. Given the problems related to ETR's management of its plant in Vermont, which is the only state with the power to reject an NRC approval, it was thought that a sale to another owner could resolve the matter. However, the opposition to the plant deterred potential buyers.

▸ Risks to our recommendation and target price include extended weakness in the power markets, further problems with obtaining license renewals for ETR's nuclear facilities, and a sharp decline in the average P/E of the group.

▸ The recent 5.0% yield from the dividend was well above the electric utility average of 4.4% and slightly above the approximate 4.8% yield from utility holding companies with large wholesale power operations. Our 12-month target price of $71 reflects a discount-to-peers P/E multiple of about 11.5X our 2012 EPS estimate.

## Qualitative Risk Assessment

| LOW | MEDIUM | HIGH |
|---|---|---|

Our risk assessment reflects the steady cash flow we expect from most of the regulated utilities and the nuclear operations, offset by uncertainties related to the recovery of the economy and the wholesale power markets.

## Quantitative Evaluations

**S&P Quality Ranking**  A

| D | C | B- | B | B+ | A- | A | A+ |
|---|---|---|---|---|---|---|---|

**Relative Strength Rank**  STRONG

73

LOWEST = 1    HIGHEST = 99

## Revenue/Earnings Data

**Revenue (Million $)**

| | 1Q | 2Q | 3Q | 4Q | Year |
|---|---|---|---|---|---|
| 2011 | 2,541 | 2,803 | 3,396 | -- | -- |
| 2010 | 2,759 | 2,863 | 3,332 | 2,533 | 11,488 |
| 2009 | 2,789 | 2,521 | 2,937 | 2,499 | 10,746 |
| 2008 | 2,865 | 3,264 | 3,964 | 3,001 | 13,094 |
| 2007 | 2,600 | 2,769 | 3,289 | 2,825 | 11,484 |
| 2006 | 2,568 | 2,629 | 3,255 | 2,481 | 10,932 |

**Earnings Per Share ($)**

| | 1Q | 2Q | 3Q | 4Q | Year |
|---|---|---|---|---|---|
| 2011 | 1.38 | 1.76 | 3.53 | E1.01 | E7.68 |
| 2010 | 1.12 | 1.65 | 2.63 | 1.26 | 6.66 |
| 2009 | 1.19 | 1.14 | 2.32 | 1.64 | 6.30 |
| 2008 | 1.56 | 1.37 | 2.41 | 0.89 | 6.23 |
| 2007 | 1.03 | 1.32 | 2.30 | 0.96 | 5.60 |
| 2006 | 0.93 | 1.27 | 1.83 | 1.32 | 5.36 |

Fiscal year ended Dec. 31. Next earnings report expected: Early February. EPS Estimates based on S&P Operating Earnings; historical GAAP earnings are as reported.

## Dividend Data (Dates: mm/dd Payment Date: mm/dd/yy)

| Amount ($) | Date Decl. | Ex-Div. Date | Stk. of Record | Payment Date |
|---|---|---|---|---|
| 0.830 | 01/28 | 02/08 | 02/10 | 03/01/11 |
| 0.830 | 04/06 | 05/10 | 05/12 | 06/01/11 |
| 0.830 | 07/29 | 08/09 | 08/11 | 09/01/11 |
| 0.830 | 10/28 | 11/08 | 11/10 | 12/01/11 |

Dividends have been paid since 1988. Source: Company reports.

# Entergy Corp.

## Business Summary October 20, 2011

CORPORATE OVERVIEW. Entergy is an integrated energy company primarily engaged in electric power production and retail electric distribution operations. It owns and operates power plants with about 30,000 megawatts (MW) of electric generating capacity, and is the second largest nuclear power generator in the U.S. As the holding company for Entergy Arkansas, Entergy Gulf States Louisiana, Entergy Louisiana, Entergy Mississippi, Entergy New Orleans, and Entergy Texas, Entergy Corp. provides electricity to more than 2.7 million U.S. retail customers, and gas service to 191,000 customers in portions of Louisiana and New Orleans. ETR also owns System Energy Resources, which has a 90% interest in the Grand Gulf 1 nuclear plant. The non-utility nuclear business owns and operates six nuclear plants (located in New York, Massachusetts, Michigan and Vermont), which sell power mainly to wholesale customers.

MARKET PROFILE. In 2010, Entergy's utility segment accounted for 78% of consolidated revenues (75% in 2009), 65% of net income (57%), and 80% of assets (80%); and the Entergy Wholesale Commodities segment (which includes both the nuclear and non-nuclear non-utility operations) accounted for 22% of revenues (25%), 39% of net income (51%), and 26% of assets (30%). ETR's electric sales by customer class in 2010 were: residential (38.6% of revenue, 33.5% of volume); commercial (26.5%, 25.8%); industrial (25.3%, 34.6%); wholesale and other (7.2%, 3.9%); and governmental (2.4%, 2.2%). With the industrial

segment accounting for more than 25% of total electricity sales, a distinct weakening in a service territory's economy would have a significant impact on earnings.

Fuel sources for the five utilities and System Energy Resources in 2010 were: nuclear, 36% (34% in 2009); purchased power, 29% (35%); natural gas, 22% (19%); and coal, 13% (12%). Hydroelectric provided less than 1% of Entergy Arkansas's generation in 2010, and is expected to provide about 1% of it in 2011. ETR expects nuclear to account for 34% of its fuel supply in 2011; purchased power 30%; natural gas 23%; and coal 13%. Based on currently planned fuel cycles, the company believes that the nuclear units in its utility and non-utility wholesale commodity segments have a diversified portfolio of contracts and inventory that provide substantially adequate nuclear fuel materials and services. In April 2007, the company completed the $380 million purchase of the 798-megawatt Palisades nuclear plant from Michigan-based Consumers Energy. Under the terms of the purchase agreement, ETR is to sell 100% of the plant's output back to Consumers Energy for a 15-year period.

## Company Financials Fiscal Year Ended Dec. 31

| Per Share Data ($) | 2010 | 2009 | 2008 | 2007 | 2006 | 2005 | 2004 | 2003 | 2002 | 2001 |
|---|---|---|---|---|---|---|---|---|---|---|
| Tangible Book Value | 45.42 | 43.55 | 40.08 | 38.76 | 38.59 | 35.49 | 36.43 | 36.38 | 33.61 | 33.74 |
| Earnings | 6.66 | 6.30 | 6.23 | 5.60 | 5.36 | 4.40 | 3.93 | 3.42 | 2.64 | 3.13 |
| S&P Core Earnings | 6.73 | 6.72 | 5.64 | 5.74 | 5.54 | 4.49 | 3.99 | 3.70 | 2.14 | 2.21 |
| Dividends | 3.24 | 3.00 | 3.00 | 2.58 | 2.16 | 2.16 | 1.89 | 1.60 | 1.34 | 1.28 |
| Payout Ratio | 49% | 48% | 48% | 46% | 40% | 49% | 48% | 47% | 51% | 41% |
| Prices:High | 84.33 | 86.61 | 127.48 | 125.00 | 94.03 | 79.22 | 68.67 | 57.24 | 46.85 | 44.67 |
| Prices:Low | 68.65 | 59.87 | 61.93 | 89.60 | 66.78 | 64.48 | 50.64 | 42.26 | 32.12 | 32.56 |
| P/E Ratio:High | 13 | 14 | 20 | 22 | 18 | 18 | 17 | 17 | 18 | 14 |
| P/E Ratio:Low | 10 | 10 | 10 | 16 | 12 | 15 | 13 | 12 | 12 | 10 |

| Income Statement Analysis (Million $) | | | | | | | | | | |
|---|---|---|---|---|---|---|---|---|---|---|
| Revenue | 11,488 | 10,746 | 13,094 | 11,484 | 10,932 | 10,106 | 10,124 | 9,195 | 8,305 | 9,621 |
| Depreciation | 1,494 | 1,083 | 1,031 | 1,132 | 888 | 856 | 896 | 851 | 839 | 721 |
| Maintenance | NA | NA | NA | NA | NA | NA | NA | NA | NA | NA |
| Fixed Charges Coverage | 4.14 | 4.17 | 3.92 | 3.49 | 3.36 | 3.69 | 3.54 | 2.66 | 2.23 | 2.25 |
| Construction Credits | 94.4 | 92.8 | 69.8 | 67.8 | 63.8 | 75.1 | 65.3 | 75.9 | 57.0 | 48.0 |
| Effective Tax Rate | 33.1% | 34.0% | 33.1% | 30.7% | 28.1% | 36.6% | 28.2% | 37.6% | 32.1% | 38.5% |
| Net Income | 1,250 | 1,231 | 1,221 | 1,135 | 1,133 | 969 | 933 | 813 | 623 | 727 |
| S&P Core Earnings | 1,262 | 1,311 | 1,108 | 1,162 | 1,171 | 961 | 922 | 856 | 487 | 495 |

| Balance Sheet & Other Financial Data (Million $) | | | | | | | | | | |
|---|---|---|---|---|---|---|---|---|---|---|
| Gross Property | 41,581 | 40,503 | 38,591 | 36,302 | 33,366 | 32,437 | 32,055 | 31,181 | 32,964 | 32,403 |
| Capital Expenditures | 1,915 | 1,872 | 2,435 | 1,578 | 1,586 | 1,458 | 1,411 | 1,569 | 1,580 | 1,380 |
| Net Property | 24,106 | 23,637 | 22,660 | 21,194 | 19,651 | 19,426 | 18,915 | 18,561 | 20,657 | 20,597 |
| Capitalization:Long Term Debt | 11,359 | 10,706 | 11,174 | 9,728 | 8,809 | 8,838 | 7,034 | 7,498 | 7,458 | 7,536 |
| Capitalization:% Long Term Debt | 56.3 | 54.5 | 57.4 | 54.3 | 50.8 | 53.2 | 44.5 | 45.2 | 47.6 | 49.1 |
| Capitalization:Preferred | 311 | 311 | 311 | 311 | 345 | Nil | 365 | 334 | 359 | 361 |
| Capitalization:% Preferred | 1.50 | 1.60 | 1.60 | 1.70 | 1.99 | Nil | 2.31 | 2.01 | 2.29 | 2.35 |
| Capitalization:Common | 8,496 | 8,613 | 7,967 | 7,863 | 8,198 | 7,761 | 8,400 | 8,773 | 7,839 | 7,456 |
| Capitalization:% Common | 42.1 | 43.9 | 41.0 | 44.0 | 47.2 | 46.8 | 53.2 | 52.8 | 50.1 | 48.6 |
| Total Capital | 20,859 | 20,342 | 26,343 | 24,625 | 23,531 | 22,399 | 21,266 | 21,805 | 20,355 | 19,399 |
| % Operating Ratio | 85.6 | 84.6 | 87.2 | 87.1 | 88.7 | 63.3 | 87.6 | 89.4 | 85.8 | 88.6 |
| % Earned on Net Property | 9.5 | 9.9 | 10.4 | 10.3 | 9.2 | 9.3 | 8.8 | 8.1 | 5.8 | 8.1 |
| % Return on Revenue | 10.9 | 11.5 | 9.3 | 9.9 | 10.4 | 9.6 | 9.2 | 8.8 | 7.5 | 7.6 |
| % Return on Invested Capital | 9.0 | 9.1 | 7.3 | 7.7 | 7.0 | 6.6 | 6.5 | 2.4 | 7.7 | 7.6 |
| % Return on Common Equity | 14.6 | 14.9 | 15.4 | 14.1 | 14.2 | 11.7 | 10.6 | 9.5 | 7.8 | 9.7 |

Data as orig reptd.; bef. results of disc opers/spec. items. Per share data adj. for stk. divs.; EPS diluted. E-Estimated. NA-Not Available. NM-Not Meaningful. NR-Not Ranked. UR-Under Review.

**Office:** 639 Loyola Ave, New Orleans, LA 70113-3125.
**Telephone:** 504-576-4000.
**Website:** http://www.entergy.com
**Chrmn & CEO:** J.W. Leonard

**COO:** M.T. Savoff
**EVP & CFO:** L.P. Denault
**EVP & Chief Admin Officer:** R.K. West
**SVP & Chief Acctg Officer:** T. Bunting, Jr.

**Investor Contact:** N. Morovich (504-576-5506)
**Board Members:** M. S. Bateman, G. W. Edwards, A. Herman, D. C. Hintz, J. W. Leonard, S. L. Levenick, B. L. Lincoln, S. C. Myers, W. A. Percy, II, W. J. Tauzin, S. V. Wilkinson

**Founded:** 1989
**Domicile:** Delaware
**Employees:** 14,958

# EOG Resources Inc.

**STANDARD &POOR'S**

| S&P Recommendation | BUY ★★★★☆ | Price $90.87 (as of Nov 25, 2011) | 12-Mo. Target Price $117.00 | Investment Style Large-Cap Growth |
|---|---|---|---|---|

**GICS Sector** Energy
**Sub-Industry** Oil & Gas Exploration & Production

**Summary** One of the largest independent exploration and production companies in the world, this U.S. company focuses on onshore natural gas production in North America.

## Key Stock Statistics (Source S&P, Vickers, company reports)

| | | | | | | | |
|---|---|---|---|---|---|---|---|
| 52-Wk Range | $121.44– 66.81 | S&P Oper. EPS 2011**E** | 3.43 | Market Capitalization(B) | $24.430 | Beta | 1.00 |
| Trailing 12-Month EPS | $3.90 | S&P Oper. EPS 2012**E** | 4.68 | Yield (%) | 0.70 | S&P 3-Yr. Proj. EPS CAGR(%) | 16 |
| Trailing 12-Month P/E | 23.3 | P/E on S&P Oper. EPS 2011**E** | 26.5 | Dividend Rate/Share | $0.64 | S&P Credit Rating | A- |
| $10K Invested 5 Yrs Ago | $13,485 | Common Shares Outstg. (M) | 268.9 | Institutional Ownership (%) | 96 | | |

## Price Performance

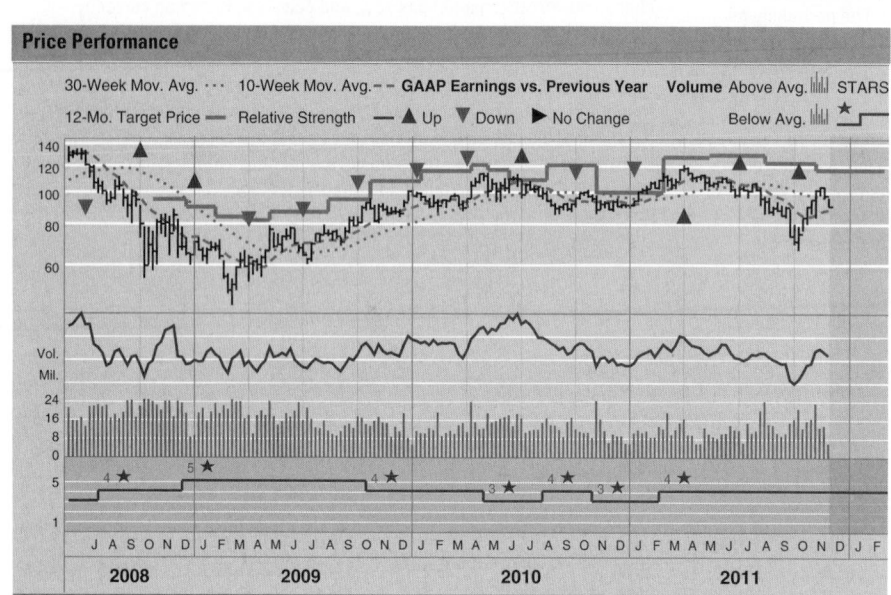

30-Week Mov. Avg. ···· 10-Week Mov. Avg. — **GAAP Earnings vs. Previous Year** **Volume** Above Avg. ▍▍▍ STARS
12-Mo. Target Price — Relative Strength ▲ Up ▼ Down ► No Change Below Avg. ▍▍▍ ★

Options: ASE, CBOE, P, Ph

Analysis prepared by Equity Analyst **Michael Kay** on Nov 23, 2011, when the stock traded at **$91.61**.

## Highlights

► EOG has sharpened its focus on unconventional liquids, shifting its portfolio mix to limit exposure to gas volatility. It sees stronger returns in Bakken, Eagle Ford and Barnett Shale Combo horizontal oil prospects versus those at deepwater plays or Canadian oil sands. EOG is currently running about 22 rigs at Eagle Ford, where it sees a resource potential of 900 MM-BOE. In the Bakken, EOG's largest crude asset, it plans a seven-rig program on its 600,000 net acres. EOG is running about eight rigs in the Barnett Combo, focused on liquids, a two-rig Niobrara program, two rigs at Wolfcamp (Permian), and one at Leonard Shale.

► EOG is targeting 2011 production growth of 9%. It has stated a goal of raising the liquids weighting of its production portfolio, targeting 47% liquids growth in 2011 and 27% in 2012. EOG plans 2011 capex of $6.8-$7 billion and sees at least flat 2012 capex should WTI crude average over $85/bbl.

► On growing higher-margin crude oil production, we see EPS of $3.43 and $4.68 in 2011 and 2012, respectively, up from adjusted EPS of $1.18 in 2010. EOG aims to divest $1.6 billion of non-core midstream assets in 2011.

## Investment Rationale/Risk

► EOG plans to focus 80% of 2011-2012 capex on liquids-rich plays such as the Barnett Combo and Eagle Ford Shale in Texas, the Bakken and Niobrara in the Rockies, the Leonard Shale in New Mexico, and a recently announced position at the Wolfcamp Shale in the Permian Basin. About 20% of capex will focus on holding leases at gas-rich plays, but EOG will not look to grow gas. We think expertise in horizontal drilling will aid onshore growth. Unlike others, EOG can shift its focus from liquids to gas should fundamentals require, and it expects liquids to represent 70% of production by year-end 2011, up from 20% in 2006. EOG has a debt-to-total capitalization target of 30% to fund oil projects, higher than its previous target of 25%.

► Risks to our recommendation and target price include adverse changes in economic conditions, lower oil and gas prices, increased costs, and difficulty replacing reserves.

► Our 12-month target price of $117 is based on a blend of our NAV estimate of $129, DCF ($119; WACC 10%, terminal growth 3%) and above-peer relative metrics, warranted, in our view, by strong resource potential at oil-rich plays, production growth and financial flexibility.

## Qualitative Risk Assessment

| LOW | MEDIUM | HIGH |
|---|---|---|

Our risk assessment is based on EOG's participation in a very competitive, capital-intensive and cyclical industry, partly offset by our view of its significant net acreage position, active drilling program, and history of relatively low operating costs.

## Quantitative Evaluations

**S&P Quality Ranking** **B+**

| D | C | B- | B | B+ | A- | A | A+ |
|---|---|---|---|---|---|---|---|

**Relative Strength Rank** **STRONG**

72

LOWEST = 1 HIGHEST = 99

## Revenue/Earnings Data

**Revenue (Million $)**

| | 1Q | 2Q | 3Q | 4Q | Year |
|---|---|---|---|---|---|
| 2011 | 1,892 | 2,570 | 2,886 | -- | -- |
| 2010 | 1,371 | 1,358 | 1,582 | 1,789 | 6,100 |
| 2009 | 1,158 | 861.0 | 1,007 | 1,761 | 4,787 |
| 2008 | 1,101 | 1,875 | 3,220 | 1,105 | 6,529 |
| 2007 | 875.2 | 1,055 | 990.5 | 1,251 | 4,191 |
| 2006 | 1,085 | 919.1 | 968.3 | 932.5 | 3,904 |

**Earnings Per Share ($)**

| | 1Q | 2Q | 3Q | 4Q | Year |
|---|---|---|---|---|---|
| 2011 | 0.52 | 1.10 | 2.01 | E0.81 | E3.43 |
| 2010 | 0.46 | 0.24 | -0.28 | 0.21 | 0.63 |
| 2009 | 0.63 | -0.07 | 0.02 | 1.58 | 2.17 |
| 2008 | 0.96 | 0.71 | 6.20 | 1.85 | 9.72 |
| 2007 | 0.88 | 1.24 | 0.82 | 1.44 | 4.37 |
| 2006 | 1.73 | 1.34 | 1.21 | 0.96 | 5.24 |

Fiscal year ended Dec. 31. Next earnings report expected: Late February. EPS Estimates based on S&P Operating Earnings; historical GAAP earnings are as reported.

## Dividend Data (Dates: mm/dd Payment Date: mm/dd/yy)

| Amount ($) | Date Decl. | Ex-Div. Date | Stk. of Record | Payment Date |
|---|---|---|---|---|
| 0.155 | 12/14 | 01/12 | 01/14 | 01/31/11 |
| 0.160 | 02/17 | 04/13 | 04/15 | 04/29/11 |
| 0.160 | 05/04 | 07/13 | 07/15 | 07/29/11 |
| 0.160 | 09/07 | 10/13 | 10/17 | 10/31/11 |

Dividends have been paid since 1990. Source: Company reports.

---

**Please read the Required Disclosures and Analyst Certification on the last page of this report.**

**The McGraw·Hill Companies**

# EOG Resources Inc.

## Business Summary November 23, 2011

CORPORATE OVERVIEW. EOG Resources, Inc. (EOG), a Delaware corporation organized in 1985, together with its subsidiaries, explores for, develops, produces and markets natural gas and crude oil primarily in major producing basins in the U.S., Canada, offshore Trinidad, the U.K. North Sea, China and other select regions.

Proved oil and gas reserves rose 7% in 2010, to 11.6 trillion cubic feet equivalent (Tcfe; 73% natural gas, 53% developed). EOG had 76% of reserves classified as proved developed at year-end 2008, exhibiting the addition of significant undeveloped acreage for future drilling inventory. Also, we estimate EOG has exhibited a three-year reserve CAGR (compound annual growth rate) of 14%. About 81% of EOG's 2010 proved reserves were in the U.S., 11% in Canada, and 7% in Trinidad. We estimate EOG's 2010 organic reserve replacement at 231%, and reserve replacement cost at $2.74 per Mcf. This compares to a three-year reserve replacement of 263% and three-year reserve replacement cost of $2.09 per Mcf. Oil and gas production rose 10%, to 2.317 billion cubic feet equivalent (Bcfe) per day (73% natural gas), in 2010. Production growth came from a 36% boost in oil volumes due to the development of EOG's Bakken properties, a 30% rise in NGL volumes, and a 3% rise in natural gas production.

CORPORATE STRATEGY. One of the largest independent exploration and production companies in the world, EOG has focused on onshore natural gas operations, primarily in the U.S. and Canada. Substantial portions of its reserves are in long-lived fields with well established production characteristics. EOG's business strategy is to maximize the rate of return on investment of capital by controlling operating and capital costs and maximizing reserve recoveries. This strategy is intended to enhance the generation of cash flow and earnings from each unit of production on a cost-effective basis.

In the U.S., EOG has interests in the Barnett Shale play of the Fort Worth Basin; the Upper Gulf Coast area covering East Texas, Louisiana and Mississippi; the Permian Basin; the Rocky Mountain area, including the Uinta Basin, Williston Basin and Bakken play in North Dakota; the Mid-Continent area; South Texas and the Gulf of Mexico; and the Marcellus Shale in Pennsylvania.

In Canada, EOG operates through its subsidiary, EOG Resources Canada, Inc. (EOGRC), with operations focused in the Southeast Alberta/Southwest Saskatchewan shallow natural gas trends; the Pembina/Highvale area of Central Alberta; the Grand Prairie/Wapiti area of Northwest Alberta; the Waskada area in Southwest Manitoba; and the Horn River Basin in northeastern British Columbia.

## Company Financials Fiscal Year Ended Dec. 31

| Per Share Data ($) | 2010 | 2009 | 2008 | 2007 | 2006 | 2005 | 2004 | 2003 | 2002 | 2001 |
|---|---|---|---|---|---|---|---|---|---|---|
| Tangible Book Value | 40.27 | 39.59 | 36.11 | 28.68 | 22.76 | 17.21 | 11.97 | 8.95 | 6.64 | 6.47 |
| Cash Flow | 8.26 | 9.53 | 15.79 | 9.27 | 8.56 | 7.81 | 4.69 | 3.73 | 2.02 | 3.32 |
| Earnings | 0.63 | 2.17 | 9.72 | 4.37 | 5.24 | 5.13 | 2.58 | 1.83 | 0.33 | 1.65 |
| S&P Core Earnings | 0.06 | 0.79 | 9.39 | 4.37 | 5.21 | 5.08 | 2.54 | 1.77 | 0.26 | 1.60 |
| Dividends | 0.61 | 0.57 | 0.47 | 0.33 | 0.22 | 0.15 | 0.12 | 0.09 | 0.08 | 0.08 |
| Payout Ratio | 97% | 26% | 5% | 8% | 4% | 3% | 5% | 5% | 25% | 5% |
| Prices:High | 114.95 | 101.76 | 144.99 | 91.63 | 86.91 | 82.00 | 38.25 | 23.76 | 22.08 | 27.75 |
| Prices:Low | 85.42 | 45.03 | 54.42 | 59.21 | 56.31 | 32.05 | 21.23 | 17.85 | 15.01 | 12.90 |
| P/E Ratio:High | NM | 47 | 15 | 21 | 17 | 16 | 15 | 13 | 68 | 17 |
| P/E Ratio:Low | NM | 21 | 6 | 14 | 11 | 6 | 8 | 10 | 46 | 8 |

| Income Statement Analysis (Million $) | | | | | | | | | | |
|---|---|---|---|---|---|---|---|---|---|---|
| Revenue | 5,814 | 3,820 | 6,529 | 4,191 | 3,904 | 3,620 | 2,271 | 1,745 | 1,095 | 1,655 |
| Operating Income | NA | NA | 5,144 | 2,802 | 1,895 | 1,992 | 979 | 697 | 648 | 1,181 |
| Depreciation, Depletion and Amortization | 1,942 | 1,855 | 1,520 | 1,213 | 817 | 654 | 504 | 442 | 398 | 392 |
| Interest Expense | 130 | 101 | 51.7 | 76.1 | 43.2 | 62.5 | 63.1 | 58.7 | 59.7 | 45.1 |
| Pretax Income | 408 | 872 | 3,747 | 1,631 | 1,913 | 1,965 | 926 | 654 | 120 | 631 |
| Effective Tax Rate | NA | 37.3% | 35.0% | 33.2% | 32.0% | 35.9% | 32.5% | 33.1% | 27.2% | 36.9% |
| Net Income | 161 | 547 | 2,437 | 1,090 | 1,300 | 1,260 | 625 | 437 | 87.2 | 399 |
| S&P Core Earnings | 15.4 | 199 | 2,353 | 1,083 | 1,281 | 1,238 | 605 | 412 | 62.4 | 376 |

| Balance Sheet & Other Financial Data (Million $) | | | | | | | | | | |
|---|---|---|---|---|---|---|---|---|---|---|
| Cash | 789 | 686 | 331 | 54.2 | 218 | 644 | 21.0 | 4.44 | 9.85 | 2.51 |
| Current Assets | 2,527 | 1,840 | 2,108 | 1,292 | 1,350 | 1,563 | 587 | 396 | 395 | 272 |
| Total Assets | 21,624 | 18,119 | 15,951 | 12,089 | 9,402 | 7,753 | 5,799 | 4,749 | 3,814 | 3,414 |
| Current Liabilities | 2,220 | 1,346 | 1,765 | 1,474 | 1,255 | 1,172 | 632 | 477 | 276 | 311 |
| Long Term Debt | 5,003 | 2,760 | 1,860 | 1,185 | 733 | 859 | 1,078 | 1,109 | 1,145 | 856 |
| Common Equity | 10,232 | 9,998 | 9,015 | 6,985 | 5,547 | 4,217 | 2,847 | 2,098 | 1,524 | 1,495 |
| Total Capital | 15,455 | 12,795 | 13,688 | 10,246 | 7,846 | 6,298 | 4,925 | 4,125 | 3,478 | 3,050 |
| Capital Expenditures | 5,581 | 3,503 | 5,195 | 3,679 | 2,819 | 1,725 | 1,417 | 1,204 | 714 | 974 |
| Cash Flow | 2,103 | 2,402 | 3,956 | 2,296 | 2,106 | 1,906 | 1,118 | 868 | 474 | 780 |
| Current Ratio | 1.1 | 1.4 | 1.2 | 0.9 | 1.1 | 1.3 | 0.9 | 0.8 | 1.4 | 0.9 |
| % Long Term Debt of Capitalization | 32.4 | 21.6 | 13.6 | 14.5 | 9.3 | 13.6 | 21.9 | 26.9 | 32.9 | 28.1 |
| % Return on Assets | 0.8 | 3.2 | 17.4 | 10.1 | 15.2 | 18.6 | 11.8 | 10.2 | 2.4 | 12.4 |
| % Return on Equity | 1.6 | 5.8 | 30.5 | 17.3 | 26.4 | 35.5 | 24.9 | 23.4 | 5.0 | 28.4 |

Data as orig reptd.; bef. results of disc opers/spec. items. Per share data adj. for stk. divs.; EPS diluted. E-Estimated. NA-Not Available. NM-Not Meaningful. NR-Not Ranked. UR-Under Review.

**Office:** 1111 Bagby, Sky Lobby 2, Houston, TX 77002. 
**Telephone:** 713-651-7000. 
**Email:** ir@eogresources.com 
**Website:** http://www.eogresources.com

**Chrmn & CEO:** M.G. Papa 
**Pres:** W.R. Thomas 
**COO:** G.L. Thomas 
**SVP & General Counsel:** F.J. Plaeger, II

**CFO:** T.K. Driggers 
**Investor Contact:** M.A. Baldwin (713-651-6364) 
**Board Members:** G. A. Alcorn, C. R. Crisp, J. C. Day, M. G. Papa, H. L. Steward, D. F. Textor, F. G. Wisner

**Founded:** 1985 
**Domicile:** Delaware 
**Employees:** 2,290

# E TRADE Financial Corporation

**STANDARD &POOR'S**

| S&P Recommendation **BUY** ★★★★☆ | Price $8.14 (as of Nov 25, 2011) | 12-Mo. Target Price $15.00 | Investment Style Large-Cap Growth |
|---|---|---|---|

**GICS Sector** Financials
**Sub-Industry** Investment Banking & Brokerage

**Summary** This company provides online discount brokerage, mortgage and banking services, primarily to retail customers.

## Key Stock Statistics (Source S&P, Vickers, company reports)

| | | | | | | | |
|---|---|---|---|---|---|---|---|
| 52-Wk Range | $18.13– 7.74 | S&P Oper. EPS 2011E | 0.81 | Market Capitalization(B) | $2.310 | Beta | 2.11 |
| Trailing 12-Month EPS | $0.51 | S&P Oper. EPS 2012E | 0.88 | Yield (%) | Nil | S&P 3-Yr. Proj. EPS CAGR(%) | NM |
| Trailing 12-Month P/E | 16.0 | P/E on S&P Oper. EPS 2011E | 10.0 | Dividend Rate/Share | Nil | S&P Credit Rating | B- |
| $10K Invested 5 Yrs Ago | $321 | Common Shares Outstg. (M) | 283.8 | Institutional Ownership (%) | 76 | | |

## Price Performance

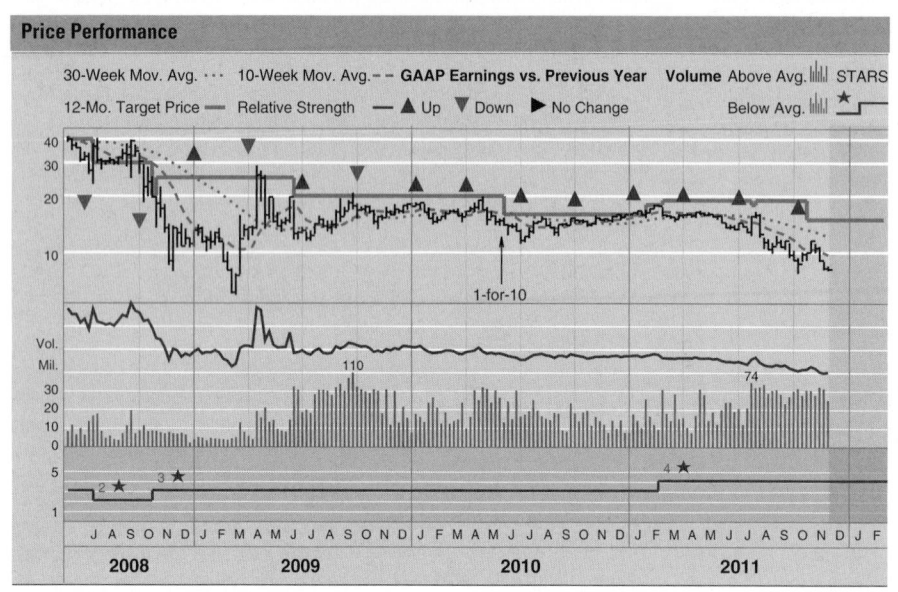

30-Week Mov. Avg. ···  10-Week Mov. Avg. - -  **GAAP Earnings vs. Previous Year**  Volume Above Avg. STARS
12-Mo. Target Price —  Relative Strength —  ▲ Up  ▼ Down  ▶ No Change  Below Avg.

1-for-10

Options: ASE, CBOE, P, Ph

Analysis prepared by Equity Analyst **Erik Oja** on Nov 09, 2011, when the stock traded at **$10.13**.

## Qualitative Risk Assessment

| LOW | MEDIUM | **HIGH** |
|---|---|---|

Our risk assessment reflects our concerns about significant industry volatility and ETFC's exposure to residential mortgage and home equity loans, partially offset by our view of its strong client relationships.

## Quantitative Evaluations

**S&P Quality Ranking**  **C**

| D | **C** | B- | B | B+ | A- | A | A+ |
|---|---|---|---|---|---|---|---|

**Relative Strength Rank**  **WEAK**

13

LOWEST = 1      HIGHEST = 99

## Revenue/Earnings Data

**Revenue (Million $)**

| | 1Q | 2Q | 3Q | 4Q | Year |
|---|---|---|---|---|---|
| 2011 | 121.0 | 124.1 | 122.9 | -- | -- |
| 2010 | 536.5 | 534.0 | 489.4 | 517.9 | 2,078 |
| 2009 | 497.3 | 620.9 | 575.3 | 529.1 | 2,217 |
| 2008 | 529.1 | 532.3 | 377.7 | 486.4 | 1,926 |
| 2007 | 645.0 | 663.5 | 321.2 | -2,008 | -378.0 |
| 2006 | 598.4 | 611.4 | 581.8 | 628.9 | 2,420 |

**Earnings Per Share ($)**

| | | | | | |
|---|---|---|---|---|---|
| 2011 | 0.16 | 0.16 | 0.24 | E0.24 | E0.81 |
| 2010 | -0.20 | 0.12 | 0.03 | -0.11 | -0.13 |
| 2009 | -4.10 | -2.20 | -6.70 | -0.40 | -11.80 |
| 2008 | -2.00 | -2.40 | -6.00 | -5.00 | -15.90 |
| 2007 | 3.90 | 3.70 | -1.40 | -39.80 | -34.00 |
| 2006 | 3.30 | 3.60 | 3.40 | 4.00 | 14.40 |

Fiscal year ended Dec. 31. Next earnings report expected: Late January. EPS Estimates based on S&P Operating Earnings; historical GAAP earnings are as reported.

## Dividend Data

No cash dividends have been paid.

## Highlights

➤ Third quarter results support our view that ETFC is making progress repairing its balance sheet. With total delinquencies down 8.6% from the prior quarter, ETFC lowered its loan loss provision by $53.6 million from the year-earlier quarter. We also see ETFC continuing to grow brokerage accounts, which increased by 9,300 during the third quarter, and benefiting from its strong brand recognition. Despite recent weakness in broad equity trading volumes, we expect to see improving client engagement and margin debt growth for ETFC in 2012, as political issues are resolved. Low interest rates will likely keep pressure on net interest income until short-term rates rise, but we expect revenues to increase modestly in 2012 and loan loss provisions to decrease.

➤ Total operating expenses increased 11.1%, year to year, in the first nine months of 2011, as compared to a 27.7% increase in net revenues. We expect disciplined expense management along with a gradual decrease in loan loss provisions to lead to wider operating margins in 2011.

➤ We see EPS of $0.81 in 2011 and $0.88 in 2012.

## Investment Rationale/Risk

➤ We view ETFC's client asset growth trends and improving credit profile as strong positives. In addition, we think there is increased potential for M&A activity given recent activist shareholder actions requesting that ETFC consider the sale of the company to maximize shareholder value. ETFC has responded by saying the optimal means of maximizing shareholder value is to continue executing its business model, as opposed to selling the company. Despite recent weakness in trading volumes, we expect ETFC to grow earnings given increasing customer accounts and assets in addition to an improving credit profile. We remain positive on ETFC given a combination of healthy customer account growth, an improving credit portfolio, and increased likelihood of M&A activity. All told, we think the stock is undervalued.

➤ Risks to our opinion and target price include greater-than-expected declines in retail trading volume and client assets, and larger write-downs in the remaining mortgage portfolio.

➤ Our target price of $15 is based on a premium to peers multiple of 16.7X our forward four quarters EPS estimate of $0.90.

---

The McGraw-Hill Companies

# E TRADE Financial Corporation

**STANDARD &POOR'S**

## Business Summary November 09, 2011

CORPORATE OVERVIEW. E Trade Financial Corporation is one of the industry's leading online financial services concerns. The company provides online discount brokerage and banking services, primarily to retail customers. Although most of the company's business is done over the Internet, ETFC also serves customers through branches, automated and live telephone service, and Internet-enabled wireless devices. Retail customers can move money electronically between brokerage, banking and lending accounts.

Brokerage customers can buy and sell stocks, bonds, options, futures, and over 7,000 non-proprietary mutual funds. Customers can also obtain streaming quotes and charts, access real-time market commentary and research reports, and perform personalized portfolio tracking. Brokerage customers can obtain margin loans collateralized by their securities. The company uses sophisticated proprietary transaction-enabling technology to automate traditionally labor-intensive transactions. The brokerage business continues to be the primary point of introduction for the majority of ETFC's customers, which are typically self-directed investors.

Through its Banking segment, the company has historically offered residential mortgage products, home equity loans and home equity lines of credit (HELOCs). However, in view of the housing-led recession, ETFC made the decision to exit all loan origination channels in 2008.

In 2003, the Banking segment began sweeping Brokerage customer money market balances into an FDIC-insured Sweep Deposit Account (SDA) product, which lowered its cost of funds. At the end of 2009, ETFC had $12.5 billion in the SDA product, up from $4.3 billion at the end of 2003. ETFC's loan portfolio consists of first mortgages, the majority of which are adjustable-rate, home equity lines of credit, second mortgage loan products, and consumer loans for RVs, marine, automobile, and credit card loans. Going forward, we expect the asset composition of this segment to change significantly as ETFC completes its restructuring plan announced in September 2007 and realigns its focus on its core retail business.

## Company Financials Fiscal Year Ended Dec. 31

| Per Share Data ($) | 2010 | 2009 | 2008 | 2007 | 2006 | 2005 | 2004 | 2003 | 2002 | 2001 |
|---|---|---|---|---|---|---|---|---|---|---|
| Tangible Book Value | 7.36 | 6.70 | 4.70 | 10.10 | 38.70 | 20.70 | 45.80 | 37.30 | 26.80 | 25.40 |
| Cash Flow | 1.24 | -10.80 | -14.30 | -31.00 | 16.06 | 13.55 | 10.70 | 5.53 | 12.00 | -2.76 |
| Earnings | -0.13 | -11.80 | -15.90 | -34.00 | 14.40 | 11.60 | 9.20 | 5.50 | 3.00 | -8.10 |
| S&P Core Earnings | -0.17 | -11.80 | -14.50 | -32.60 | 13.30 | 8.80 | 6.60 | 2.70 | 2.70 | -8.60 |
| Dividends | Nil | Nil | Nil | Nil | Nil | Nil | Nil | Nil | Nil | Nil |
| Payout Ratio | Nil | Nil | Nil | Nil | Nil | Nil | Nil | Nil | Nil | Nil |
| Prices:High | 19.90 | 29.00 | 54.80 | 260.80 | 277.60 | 217.10 | 154.00 | 129.10 | 126.40 | 153.75 |
| Prices:Low | 11.15 | 5.90 | 7.90 | 31.50 | 188.10 | 105.30 | 95.10 | 36.50 | 28.10 | 40.70 |
| P/E Ratio:High | NM | NM | NM | NM | 19 | 19 | 17 | 23 | 42 | NM |
| P/E Ratio:Low | NM | NM | NM | NM | 13 | 9 | 10 | 7 | 9 | NM |

| Income Statement Analysis (Million $) | 2010 | 2009 | 2008 | 2007 | 2006 | 2005 | 2004 | 2003 | 2002 | 2001 |
|---|---|---|---|---|---|---|---|---|---|---|
| Commissions | 431 | 548 | 516 | 694 | 625 | 459 | 350 | 337 | 302 | 407 |
| Interest Income | 1,547 | 1,833 | 2,470 | 3,570 | 2,775 | 1,650 | 1,146 | 893 | 946 | 1,160 |
| Total Revenue | 2,398 | 2,789 | 3,128 | 2,223 | 3,840 | 2,537 | 2,077 | 2,009 | 1,903 | 2,062 |
| Interest Expense | 488 | 855 | 1,202 | 2,133 | 1,527 | 853 | 558 | 532 | 609 | 832 |
| Pretax Income | -3.14 | -1,835 | -1,279 | -2,178 | 929 | 676 | 514 | 310 | 194 | -310 |
| Effective Tax Rate | NM | 548.0% | 36.7% | 33.8% | 32.5% | 34.0% | 31.6% | 36.2% | 43.9% | NM |
| Net Income | -28.5 | -1,298 | -809 | -1,442 | 627 | 446 | 351 | 203 | 107 | -271 |
| S&P Core Earnings | -36.1 | -1,297 | -742 | -1,378 | 580 | 339 | 247 | 101 | 96.1 | -291 |

| Balance Sheet & Other Financial Data (Million $) | 2010 | 2009 | 2008 | 2007 | 2006 | 2005 | 2004 | 2003 | 2002 | 2001 |
|---|---|---|---|---|---|---|---|---|---|---|
| Total Assets | 46,373 | 47,366 | 48,538 | 56,846 | 53,739 | 44,568 | 31,033 | 26,049 | 21,534 | 18,172 |
| Cash Items | 3,046 | 5,067 | 5,051 | 2,243 | 1,672 | 1,601 | 2,257 | 2,566 | 2,223 | 1,601 |
| Receivables | 5,121 | 3,827 | 2,791 | 7,179 | 7,636 | 7,174 | 3,035 | 2,298 | 1,500 | 2,139 |
| Securities Owned | 17,268 | 13,320 | 10,806 | 11,255 | 13,922 | 12,763 | 12,589 | 9,876 | 8,702 | 4,726 |
| Securities Borrowed | Nil | Nil | Nil | Nil | Nil | Nil | Nil | Nil | Nil | Nil |
| Due Brokers & Customers | 5,020 | 5,234 | 3,753 | 5,515 | 7,825 | 7,316 | 3,619 | 3,696 | 2,792 | 2,700 |
| Other Liabilities | 32,423 | 33,177 | 35,090 | 38,033 | NA | NA | NA | NA | NA | NA |
| Capitalization:Debt | 4,878 | 5,206 | 7,104 | 10,469 | 7,166 | 6,189 | 586 | 695 | 907 | 605 |
| Capitalization:Equity | 4,052 | 3,750 | 2,592 | 2,829 | 4,196 | 3,400 | 2,228 | 1,918 | 1,506 | 1,571 |
| Capitalization:Total | 8,930 | 8,956 | 9,696 | 13,298 | 11,363 | 9,589 | 2,814 | 2,614 | 2,412 | 2,175 |
| % Return on Revenue | NM | NM | NM | NM | 20.7 | 68.4 | 18.0 | 11.8 | 5.4 | NM |
| % Return on Assets | NM | NM | NM | NM | 1.3 | 1.2 | 1.2 | 0.9 | 0.5 | NM |
| % Return on Equity | NM | NM | NM | NM | 16.5 | 15.9 | 16.9 | 11.9 | 7.0 | NM |

Data as orig reptd.; bef. results of disc opers/spec. items. Per share data adj. for stk. divs.; EPS diluted. Total net revenues reported in quarterly table. E-Estimated. NA-Not Available. NM-Not Meaningful. NR-Not Ranked. UR-Under Review.

**Office:** 1271 Avenue of the Americas, 14th Floor, New York, NY 10020-1302.
**Telephone:** 646-521-4300.
**Email:** ir@etrade.com
**Website:** http://www.etrade.com

**Chrmn & CEO:** S.J. Freiberg
**Vice Chrmn:** S.H. Willard
**COO & EVP:** G.A. Framke
**EVP, CFO & Cntlr:** M.J. Audette

**EVP, Secy & General Counsel:** K.A. Roessner
**Board Members:** R. D. Fisher, S. J. Freiberg, K. C. Griffin, F. W. Kanner, M. K. Parks, L. E. Randall, J. L. Sclafani, J. M. Velli, D. Weaver, S. H. Willard

**Founded:** 1982
**Domicile:** Delaware
**Employees:** 2,962

*The McGraw·Hill Companies*

# EQT Corp

**STANDARD &POOR'S**

| S&P Recommendation | **BUY** ★★★★☆ | Price $55.35 (as of Nov 25, 2011) | 12-Mo. Target Price $74.00 | Investment Style Large-Cap Growth |
| --- | --- | --- | --- | --- |

**GICS Sector** Energy
**Sub-Industry** Oil & Gas Exploration & Production

**Summary** This energy company focuses on natural gas production, transmission and distribution, and energy management services.

## Key Stock Statistics (Source S&P, Vickers, company reports)

| | | | | | | | |
| --- | --- | --- | --- | --- | --- | --- | --- |
| 52-Wk Range | $73.10– 39.53 | S&P Oper. EPS 2011**E** | 2.21 | Market Capitalization(B) | $8.271 | Beta | 0.88 |
| Trailing 12-Month EPS | $3.09 | S&P Oper. EPS 2012**E** | 2.65 | Yield (%) | 1.59 | S&P 3-Yr. Proj. EPS CAGR(%) | 21 |
| Trailing 12-Month P/E | 17.9 | P/E on S&P Oper. EPS 2011**E** | 25.0 | Dividend Rate/Share | $0.88 | S&P Credit Rating | BBB |
| $10K Invested 5 Yrs Ago | $14,072 | Common Shares Outstg. (M) | 149.4 | Institutional Ownership (%) | 80 | | |

## Price Performance

30-Week Mov. Avg. · · · 10-Week Mov. Avg. - - **GAAP Earnings vs. Previous Year** Volume Above Avg. STARS
12-Mo. Target Price — Relative Strength — ▲ Up ▼ Down ▶ No Change Below Avg. ★

Options: ASE, CBOE, P, Ph

Analysis prepared by Equity Analyst **C. Muir** on Nov 22, 2011, when the stock traded at **$56.98**.

## Qualitative Risk Assessment

| LOW | MEDIUM | HIGH |
| --- | --- | --- |

Our risk assessment is based on our view that the company's riskier exploration and production and energy marketing operations are balanced by its regulated gas businesses.

## Quantitative Evaluations

**S&P Quality Ranking** B+

| D | C | B- | B | B+ | A- | A | A+ |
| --- | --- | --- | --- | --- | --- | --- | --- |

**Relative Strength Rank** MODERATE

41

LOWEST = 1 HIGHEST = 99

## Revenue/Earnings Data

**Revenue (Million $)**

| | 1Q | 2Q | 3Q | 4Q | Year |
| --- | --- | --- | --- | --- | --- |
| 2011 | 455.7 | 349.0 | 336.7 | -- | -- |
| 2010 | 436.6 | 257.5 | 257.3 | 371.2 | 1,323 |
| 2009 | 469.4 | 238.0 | 218.4 | 344.0 | 1,270 |
| 2008 | 535.8 | 334.0 | 297.8 | 408.9 | 1,576 |
| 2007 | 456.6 | 293.2 | 226.8 | 384.8 | 1,361 |
| 2006 | 430.1 | 251.2 | 232.8 | 353.8 | 1,268 |

**Earnings Per Share ($)**

| | 1Q | 2Q | 3Q | 4Q | Year |
| --- | --- | --- | --- | --- | --- |
| 2011 | 0.82 | 0.58 | 1.19 | E0.58 | E2.21 |
| 2010 | 0.65 | 0.20 | 0.24 | 0.49 | 1.57 |
| 2009 | 0.55 | 0.20 | 0.02 | 0.42 | 1.19 |
| 2008 | 0.57 | 0.42 | 0.73 | 0.26 | 2.00 |
| 2007 | 0.46 | 0.87 | 0.27 | 0.49 | 2.10 |
| 2006 | 0.59 | 0.36 | 0.26 | 0.56 | 1.77 |

Fiscal year ended Dec. 31. Next earnings report expected: Late January. EPS Estimates based on S&P Operating Earnings; historical GAAP earnings are as reported.

## Highlights

► We expect 2011 revenues to rise 18.6%, helped by higher volumes during the year at EQT's exploration and production business as well as its midstream business, partly offset by lower average realized commodity prices. We see revenues from these unregulated businesses rising 30%. In 2012, we forecast that revenues will rise 10%, as we anticipate slightly higher commodity prices and increasing volumes. We see lower 2011 utility revenues on lower gas prices, and higher 2012 revenues on higher volumes and gas prices.

► We expect operating margins to increase to 40.7% in 2011 and 42.6% in 2012 from 35.6% in 2010, on wider gross margins and lower per-revenue operations & maintenance expenses and general & administrative costs, partly offset by depreciation & depletion charges in 2011. We see pretax margins rising to 32.9% in 2011, and to 35.7% in 2012, from 26.7% in 2010. We expect higher interest expense in both years.

► We project 2011 EPS, excluding $0.96 in nonrecurring gains, of $2.21, up 43% from $1.55, which excludes a penny nonrecurring gain, in 2010. Our 2012 EPS estimate is $2.65, up 20%.

## Investment Rationale/Risk

► We are positive about EQT's horizontal drilling program, which includes re-entry wells into existing fields. We believe results have been positive in the program so far. We expect EQT to use cash generated by recent non-core asset sales for additional investment in E&P operations. Much of the company's expansion has been in the Huron shale, but we think it also has opportunities and has shown good early results in the Berea Sandstone wells, in the Devonian shale re-entry wells, and in the Marcellus shale.

► Risks to our opinion and target price include lower-than-expected E&P production growth, energy prices and utility income, as well as higher-than-expected interest rates.

► EQT's shares recently traded at 21.6X our 2012 EPS estimate, a 33% premium to gas distribution peers. Our 12-month target price of $74 is 27.9X our 2012 EPS estimate, also a substantial premium to peers. We believe this premium is warranted by our expectation for superior EPS growth driven by EQT's unregulated businesses, partly offset by the riskier nature of its unregulated businesses.

## Dividend Data (Dates: mm/dd Payment Date: mm/dd/yy)

| Amount ($) | Date Decl. | Ex-Div. Date | Stk. of Record | Payment Date |
| --- | --- | --- | --- | --- |
| 0.220 | 01/19 | 02/02 | 02/04 | 03/01/11 |
| 0.220 | 05/10 | 05/16 | 05/18 | 06/01/11 |
| 0.220 | 07/14 | 08/03 | 08/05 | 09/01/11 |
| 0.220 | 10/12 | 11/02 | 11/04 | 12/01/11 |

Dividends have been paid since 1950. Source: Company reports.

---

**Please read the Required Disclosures and Analyst Certification on the last page of this report.**

*The McGraw-Hill Companies*

# EQT Corp

**STANDARD &POOR'S**

## Business Summary November 22, 2011

CORPORATE OVERVIEW. EQT Corp. is a vertically integrated energy company operating through three business segments: EQT Production (EP), EQT Midstream (EM) and EQT Distribution (ED). The EP unit (46% of 2010 operating income before unallocated expenses) is engaged in exploration and production of natural gas and oil, chiefly in the Appalachian Basin. The EM unit (37%) provides gathering, processing, transmission and storage services to EP and independent third parties. Its transmission system is located throughout north central West Virginia and southwestern Pennsylvania, and its gas gathering assets are located in Kentucky, West Virginia, Virginia and Pennsylvania. The ED unit (17%) operates a regulated natural gas utility in southwestern Pennsylvania and a small gathering system in Pennsylvania, and provides off-system sales activities.

CORPORATE STRATEGY. The ED unit is focused on earning a competitive return on its asset base through regulatory mechanisms and operational efficiency. ED believes it can achieve earnings growth by establishing a reputation for excellent customer service, effectively managing its capital spending, improving the efficiency of its work force through superior work management, and continuing to leverage technology throughout its operations. In 2008, ED filed a base rate case in Pennsylvania and agreed to a settlement of the rate case that requested a $38 million increase in revenues. In January 2009, the settlement was approved by an administrative law judge. In West Virginia, a base rate increase settlement was approved in the second half of 2010.

The EP unit's business strategy is to focus on increased drilling and development in the Appalachian basin. EP also plans to create additional reserve potential through emerging development investments. To achieve maximum value from its existing assets, EP drills multilateral and stacked multilateral horizontal wells, refracs existing wells and drills re-entry wells where low pressured vertical shale wells were previously drilled.

The EM unit's strategy focuses on building a long-term growth platform to facilitate the development of EP's growing reserve base in the Huron play, and provides opportunities to sell capacity to third parties by connecting wells to existing midstream infrastructure in an effort to fill existing capacity.

## Company Financials Fiscal Year Ended Dec. 31

| Per Share Data ($) | 2010 | 2009 | 2008 | 2007 | 2006 | 2005 | 2004 | 2003 | 2002 | 2001 |
|---|---|---|---|---|---|---|---|---|---|---|
| Tangible Book Value | 20.64 | 16.43 | 15.67 | 11.52 | 7.78 | 2.96 | 6.75 | 7.33 | 5.83 | 6.18 |
| Cash Flow | 3.43 | 2.68 | 3.06 | 2.99 | 2.59 | 2.94 | 2.88 | 3.40 | 1.72 | 1.70 |
| Earnings | 1.57 | 1.19 | 2.00 | 2.10 | 1.77 | 2.09 | 2.22 | 1.37 | 1.18 | 1.15 |
| S&P Core Earnings | 1.56 | 1.20 | 2.08 | 1.45 | 1.79 | 1.59 | 1.33 | 1.35 | 1.11 | 1.09 |
| Dividends | 0.88 | 0.88 | 0.88 | 0.88 | 0.87 | 0.82 | 0.72 | 0.49 | 0.34 | 0.31 |
| Payout Ratio | 56% | 74% | 44% | 42% | 49% | 39% | 32% | 35% | 28% | 27% |
| Prices:High | 47.43 | 46.80 | 76.14 | 56.75 | 44.48 | 41.18 | 30.59 | 21.71 | 18.78 | 20.25 |
| Prices:Low | 32.23 | 27.39 | 20.71 | 39.26 | 31.59 | 27.89 | 21.05 | 17.22 | 14.34 | 13.00 |
| P/E Ratio:High | 30 | 39 | 38 | 27 | 25 | 20 | 14 | 16 | 16 | 18 |
| P/E Ratio:Low | 21 | 23 | 10 | 19 | 18 | 13 | 9 | 13 | 12 | 11 |

| Income Statement Analysis (Million $) | 2010 | 2009 | 2008 | 2007 | 2006 | 2005 | 2004 | 2003 | 2002 | 2001 |
|---|---|---|---|---|---|---|---|---|---|---|
| Revenue | 1,323 | 1,270 | 1,576 | 1,361 | 1,268 | 1,254 | 1,192 | 1,047 | 1,069 | 1,764 |
| Operating Income | NA | NA | 602 | 432 | 470 | 445 | 388 | 380 | 352 | 328 |
| Depreciation | 270 | 196 | 137 | 110 | 100 | 93.5 | 83.1 | 78.1 | 69.4 | 73.2 |
| Interest Expense | 128 | 112 | 58.4 | 54.4 | 47.1 | 44.4 | 49.2 | 45.8 | 38.8 | 41.1 |
| Pretax Income | 355 | 254 | 411 | 402 | 326 | 412 | 424 | 257 | 235 | 240 |
| Effective Tax Rate | NA | 38.1% | 37.7% | 35.9% | 33.7% | 37.2% | 33.7% | 31.9% | 33.0% | 36.6% |
| Net Income | 228 | 157 | 256 | 257 | 216 | 259 | 280 | 174 | 151 | 152 |
| S&P Core Earnings | 227 | 158 | 266 | 177 | 219 | 197 | 168 | 170 | 141 | 143 |

| Balance Sheet & Other Financial Data (Million $) | 2010 | 2009 | 2008 | 2007 | 2006 | 2005 | 2004 | 2003 | 2002 | 2001 |
|---|---|---|---|---|---|---|---|---|---|---|
| Cash | NA | NA | Nil | 81.7 | Nil | 75.0 | Nil | 37.3 | 17.7 | 92.6 |
| Current Assets | 828 | 695 | 927 | 742 | 701 | 1,097 | 653 | 550 | 430 | 613 |
| Total Assets | 7,098 | 5,957 | 5,330 | 3,937 | 3,257 | 3,342 | 3,197 | 2,940 | 2,437 | 2,519 |
| Current Liabilities | 597 | 613 | 1,043 | 1,519 | 1,080 | 2,092 | 1,015 | 703 | 552 | 612 |
| Long Term Debt | 1,943 | 1,949 | 1,249 | 754 | 754 | 763 | 618 | 681 | 586 | 396 |
| Common Equity | 3,079 | 2,151 | 2,050 | 1,097 | 946 | 354 | 875 | 965 | 779 | 846 |
| Total Capital | 5,028 | 4,100 | 3,304 | 2,252 | 2,038 | 1,142 | 1,990 | 2,118 | 1,728 | 1,621 |
| Capital Expenditures | 1,251 | 952 | 1,344 | 777 | 405 | 276 | 202 | 222 | 218 | 133 |
| Cash Flow | 498 | 353 | 392 | 367 | 316 | 352 | 363 | 430 | 220 | 225 |
| Current Ratio | 1.4 | 1.1 | 0.9 | 0.5 | 0.6 | 0.5 | 0.6 | 0.8 | 0.8 | 1.0 |
| % Long Term Debt of Capitalization | 38.7 | Nil | 37.8 | 33.5 | 37.0 | 66.9 | 31.0 | 32.2 | 33.9 | 24.4 |
| % Net Income of Revenue | 17.2 | 12.4 | 16.2 | 18.9 | 17.0 | 20.6 | 23.5 | 16.6 | 14.1 | 8.6 |
| % Return on Assets | NA | 2.8 | 5.5 | 7.2 | 6.5 | 7.9 | 9.1 | 6.5 | 6.1 | 6.1 |
| % Return on Equity | NA | NA | 16.2 | 25.2 | 33.2 | 42.1 | 30.4 | 19.9 | 18.5 | 19.7 |

Data as orig reptd.; bef. results of disc opers/spec. items. Per share data adj. for stk. divs.; EPS diluted. E-Estimated. NA-Not Available. NM-Not Meaningful. NR-Not Ranked. UR-Under Review.

**Office:** EQT Plaza 625 Liberty Avenue, Suite 1700, Pittsburgh, PA 15222.
**Telephone:** 412-553-5700.
**Website:** http://www.eqt.com
**Chrmn, Pres, CEO & COO:** D.L. Porges

**SVP & CFO:** P.P. Conti
**Chief Acctg Officer & Cntlr:** T.Z. Bone
**Secy:** K.L. Sachse
**General Counsel:** L.B. Gardner

**Investor Contact:** P.J. Kane (412-553-7833)
**Board Members:** V. A. Bailey, P. G. Behrman, A. B. Cary, Jr., M. S. Gerber, B. S. Jeremiah, G. L. Miles, Jr., D. L. Porges, J. E. Rohr, D. S. Shapira, S. A. Thorington, L. T. Todd, Jr.

**Founded:** 1926
**Domicile:** Pennsylvania
**Employees:** 1,815

The McGraw·Hill Companies

# Equifax Inc.

**STANDARD &POOR'S**

| S&P Recommendation | HOLD ★★★☆☆ | Price $33.56 (as of Nov 25, 2011) | 12-Mo. Target Price $38.00 | Investment Style Large-Cap Growth |
|---|---|---|---|---|

**GICS Sector** Industrials
**Sub-Industry** Research & Consulting Services

**Summary** This company is a leading worldwide source of consumer and commercial credit information.

## Key Stock Statistics (Source S&P, Vickers, company reports)

| | | | | | | | |
|---|---|---|---|---|---|---|---|
| 52-Wk Range | $39.90– 28.59 | S&P Oper. EPS 2011E | 2.50 | Market Capitalization(B) | $4.063 | Beta | 1.07 |
| Trailing 12-Month EPS | $1.78 | S&P Oper. EPS 2012E | 2.80 | Yield (%) | 1.91 | S&P 3-Yr. Proj. EPS CAGR(%) | 10 |
| Trailing 12-Month P/E | 18.9 | P/E on S&P Oper. EPS 2011E | 13.4 | Dividend Rate/Share | $0.64 | S&P Credit Rating | BBB+ |
| $10K Invested 5 Yrs Ago | $9,174 | Common Shares Outstg. (M) | 121.1 | Institutional Ownership (%) | 81 | | |

## Price Performance

30-Week Mov. Avg. · · · 10-Week Mov. Avg. - - GAAP Earnings vs. Previous Year   Volume Above Avg. ▁▃▅ STARS
12-Mo. Target Price — Relative Strength — ▲ Up ▼ Down ▶ No Change   Below Avg. ▁▃▅ ★

Options: ASE, P, Ph

Analysis prepared by Equity Analyst **Stewart Scharf** on Nov 07, 2011, when the stock traded at **$36.04**.

## Highlights

▶ We forecast sales growth of at least 6% for 2011, with similar growth projected for 2012, as we believe demand will continue to be driven by strength in international markets (excluding Brazil, which was deconsolidated in the second quarter of 2011), as well as the Personal Solutions and Commercial Solutions businesses in North America, despite weakness in the mortgage market. In our view, the company's TALX and USCIS operations will also grow, albeit less rapidly.

▶ We expect the company to continue to focus on realigning its organizational structure and operations, while paying down debt and buying back stock. As market conditions improve, we expect EFX to increase investments in international markets, especially in India and the United Kingdom. As a result, we see operating margins (EBITDA) widening to about 32.5% in 2011, from 32.1% in 2010, with further expansion likely in 2012 to above 33%.

▶ We forecast a higher effective tax rate of near 42% in 2011, and estimate operating EPS of $2.50 in 2011 (before amortization of acquisition-related intangibles), rising to $2.80 in 2012.

## Investment Rationale/Risk

▶ Our hold opinion in based on the company's ability to execute in a difficult economic environment, along with our valuation metrics. We see favorable trends in international markets, while EFX's largest and most profitable segment, U.S. Consumer Information Solutions (USCIS), has begun to rebound following an extended period of decline since late 2007. We expect acquisitions to aid this segment's growth, while marketing activity picks up for consumer products. We are also optimistic about settlement and analytical tools and services, which we view as counter-cyclical.

▶ Risks to our recommendation and target price include increasing competition from the other major credit bureaus and data providers, a negative foreign exchange effect, prolonged softness in the housing market, and a significant downturn in the global economy.

▶ Our 12-month target price of $38 is derived by applying a multiple of 13.5X to our 2012 operating EPS estimate of $2.80, above the midpoint of the shares' three-year P/E range of 10.2X-15.3X, amid signs of a slowly improving business climate.

## Qualitative Risk Assessment

| LOW | MEDIUM | HIGH |
|---|---|---|

Our risk assessment reflects our view that a majority of the company's domestic operations have exposure to consumer financial services. We are also concerned global economic conditions, particularly in Europe, offset by our positive outlook for the company's Latin American operations, which we see expanding faster than its domestic operations.

## Quantitative Evaluations

**S&P Quality Ranking**    B+

| D | C | B- | B | B+ | A- | A | A+ |
|---|---|---|---|---|---|---|---|

**Relative Strength Rank**    STRONG

74

LOWEST = 1          HIGHEST = 99

## Revenue/Earnings Data

**Revenue (Million $)**

| | 1Q | 2Q | 3Q | 4Q | Year |
|---|---|---|---|---|---|
| 2011 | 472.6 | 487.1 | 490.4 | -- | -- |
| 2010 | 443.0 | 460.7 | 473.8 | 482.0 | 1,860 |
| 2009 | 452.9 | 455.4 | 451.9 | 464.3 | 1,825 |
| 2008 | 503.1 | 501.9 | 484.1 | 446.6 | 1,936 |
| 2007 | 405.1 | 454.5 | 492.5 | 490.9 | 1,843 |
| 2006 | 374.0 | 387.7 | 394.6 | 390.0 | 1,546 |

**Earnings Per Share ($)**

| | | | | | |
|---|---|---|---|---|---|
| 2011 | 0.46 | 0.28 | 0.54 | E0.65 | E2.50 |
| 2010 | 0.42 | 0.45 | 0.49 | 0.50 | 1.86 |
| 2009 | 0.43 | 0.47 | 0.47 | 0.47 | 1.83 |
| 2008 | 0.50 | 0.54 | 0.56 | 0.50 | 2.09 |
| 2007 | 0.54 | 0.51 | 0.48 | 0.49 | 2.02 |
| 2006 | 0.48 | 0.53 | 0.61 | 0.50 | 2.12 |

Fiscal year ended Dec. 31. Next earnings report expected: Early February. EPS Estimates based on S&P Operating Earnings; historical GAAP earnings are as reported.

## Dividend Data (Dates: mm/dd Payment Date: mm/dd/yy)

| Amount ($) | Date Decl. | Ex-Div. Date | Stk. of Record | Payment Date |
|---|---|---|---|---|
| 0.160 | 02/11 | 02/17 | 02/22 | 03/15/11 |
| 0.160 | 05/05 | 05/23 | 05/25 | 06/15/11 |
| 0.160 | 08/15 | 08/23 | 08/25 | 09/15/11 |
| 0.160 | 11/03 | 11/21 | 11/24 | 12/15/11 |

Dividends have been paid since 1914. Source: Company reports.

---

**Please read the Required Disclosures and Analyst Certification on the last page of this report.**

**The McGraw-Hill Companies**

# Equifax Inc.

**STANDARD &POOR'S**

## Business Summary November 07, 2011

CORPORATE OVERVIEW. Equifax is one of three global providers of consumer and commercial credit information. Equifax collects, organizes and manages credit, financial, demographic and marketing information regarding individuals and businesses, which the company collects from various sources. These sources include financial or credit granting institutions (which provide accounts receivable information), government organizations and consumers. The company maintains information in proprietary databases regarding consumers and businesses worldwide. EFX amasses and processes this data using proprietary systems, and makes the data available to customers in various formats.

Products and services include consumer credit information, information database management, marketing information, business credit information, decisioning and analytical tools, and identity verification services that enable businesses to make informed decisions about extending credit or providing services, managing portfolio risk, and developing marketing strategies. According to the company, EFX allows consumers to manage and protect their financial affairs through products that the company sells directly to individuals using the Internet.

Equifax derived a majority of operating revenue from North America in 2010 and 2009. The U.S. accounted for 73% of operating revenues in 2010, unchanged from 2009, while EFX's Canadian Consumer business accounted for 7% of total revenues in 2010 (7%). The company's largest segment, U.S. Consumer Information Solutions (40% of revenues in 2010, down from 41.5% in 2009), includes Consumer Information Solutions (credit information regarding individuals; 26% of 2010 revenues, down from 29% in 2009), Mortgage Reporting Solutions (credit loan origination information; 6%, 6%), and Credit Marketing Services (8%, 6%). Other North American operating segments include Personal Solutions (credit information sales to consumers; 9%, 9%) and Commercial Solutions (credit information concerning businesses; 4%, 4%). TALX, acquired in May 2007 (employment, income verification and human resources outsourcing services) accounted for 21% of revenues in 2010 (20%).

## Company Financials Fiscal Year Ended Dec. 31

| Per Share Data ($) | 2010 | 2009 | 2008 | 2007 | 2006 | 2005 | 2004 | 2003 | 2002 | 2001 |
|---|---|---|---|---|---|---|---|---|---|---|
| Tangible Book Value | NM | NM | NM | NM | NM | NM | NM | NM | NM | NM |
| Cash Flow | 3.25 | 3.07 | 2.60 | 2.48 | 2.76 | 2.49 | 2.39 | 2.00 | 1.96 | 1.61 |
| Earnings | 1.86 | 1.83 | 2.09 | 2.02 | 2.12 | 1.86 | 1.78 | 1.31 | 1.39 | 0.84 |
| S&P Core Earnings | 1.87 | 1.83 | 1.90 | 2.02 | 2.07 | 1.88 | 1.59 | 1.18 | 1.04 | 0.52 |
| Dividends | 0.28 | 0.16 | 0.16 | 0.16 | 0.16 | 0.15 | 0.11 | 0.08 | 0.08 | 0.25 |
| Payout Ratio | 15% | 9% | 8% | 8% | 8% | 8% | 6% | 6% | 6% | 29% |
| Prices:High | 36.63 | 31.64 | 39.95 | 46.30 | 41.64 | 39.00 | 28.46 | 27.59 | 31.30 | 38.76 |
| Prices:Low | 27.64 | 19.63 | 19.38 | 35.22 | 30.15 | 26.97 | 22.60 | 17.84 | 18.95 | 18.60 |
| P/E Ratio:High | 20 | 17 | 19 | 23 | 20 | 21 | 16 | 21 | 23 | 46 |
| P/E Ratio:Low | 15 | 11 | 9 | 17 | 14 | 14 | 13 | 14 | 14 | 22 |

| Income Statement Analysis (Million $) | 2010 | 2009 | 2008 | 2007 | 2006 | 2005 | 2004 | 2003 | 2002 | 2001 |
|---|---|---|---|---|---|---|---|---|---|---|
| Revenue | 1,860 | 1,825 | 1,936 | 1,843 | 1,546 | 1,443 | 1,273 | 1,225 | 1,109 | 1,139 |
| Operating Income | 598 | 591 | 560 | 548 | 519 | 504 | 459 | 438 | 432 | 420 |
| Depreciation | 168 | 159 | 66.3 | 62.0 | 82.8 | 82.2 | 81.1 | 95.3 | 80.5 | 106 |
| Interest Expense | 56.1 | 57.0 | 71.3 | 58.5 | 31.9 | 35.6 | 34.9 | 39.6 | 41.2 | 47.8 |
| Pretax Income | 375 | 357 | 412 | 431 | 420 | 396 | 388 | 286 | 317 | 205 |
| Effective Tax Rate | NA | 32.6% | 32.3% | 35.3% | 33.6% | 36.5% | 38.1% | 36.5% | 39.0% | 41.7% |
| Net Income | 243 | 234 | 273 | 273 | 275 | 247 | 237 | 179 | 191 | 117 |
| S&P Core Earnings | 236 | 234 | 247 | 273 | 268 | 248 | 211 | 162 | 146 | 73.6 |

| Balance Sheet & Other Financial Data (Million $) | 2010 | 2009 | 2008 | 2007 | 2006 | 2005 | 2004 | 2003 | 2002 | 2001 |
|---|---|---|---|---|---|---|---|---|---|---|
| Cash | 119 | 103 | 58.2 | 81.6 | 67.8 | 37.5 | 52.1 | 39.3 | 30.5 | 33.2 |
| Current Assets | 429 | 417 | 354 | 425 | 345 | 280 | 300 | 286 | 286 | 358 |
| Total Assets | 3,434 | 3,551 | 3,260 | 3,524 | 1,791 | 1,832 | 1,557 | 1,553 | 1,507 | 1,423 |
| Current Liabilities | 320 | 492 | 318 | 547 | 582 | 295 | 457 | 355 | 428 | 276 |
| Long Term Debt | 979 | 991 | 1,187 | 1,165 | 174 | 464 | 399 | 663 | 691 | 694 |
| Common Equity | 1,691 | 1,601 | 1,312 | 1,399 | 838 | 820 | 524 | 372 | 221 | 244 |
| Total Capital | 2,725 | 2,606 | 2,715 | 2,842 | 1,083 | 1,410 | 961 | 1,079 | 938 | 1,026 |
| Capital Expenditures | 99.8 | 70.7 | 111 | 119 | 52.0 | 17.2 | 16.5 | 14.6 | 12.8 | 13.0 |
| Cash Flow | 411 | 393 | 339 | 335 | 357 | 329 | 318 | 274 | 272 | 224 |
| Current Ratio | 1.3 | 0.9 | 1.1 | 0.8 | 0.6 | 1.0 | 0.7 | 0.8 | 0.7 | 1.3 |
| % Long Term Debt of Capitalization | 35.9 | 38.0 | 43.7 | 41.0 | 16.1 | 32.9 | 41.5 | 61.5 | 73.7 | 67.6 |
| % Net Income of Revenue | 13.1 | 12.8 | 14.1 | 14.8 | 17.8 | 17.1 | 18.6 | 14.6 | 17.2 | 10.3 |
| % Return on Assets | 7.0 | 6.9 | 8.0 | 10.3 | 15.2 | 14.5 | 15.3 | 11.7 | 13.1 | 7.1 |
| % Return on Equity | 14.8 | 16.1 | 20.1 | 24.4 | 33.1 | 36.7 | 53.0 | 60.3 | 82.4 | 37.4 |

Data as orig reptd.; bef. results of disc opers/spec. items. Per share data adj. for stk. divs.; EPS diluted. E-Estimated. NA-Not Available. NM-Not Meaningful. NR-Not Ranked. UR-Under Review.

**Office:** 1550 Peachtree Street NW, Atlanta, GA 30309.
**Telephone:** 404-885-8000.
**Email:** investor@equifax.com
**Website:** http://www.equifax.com

**Chrmn & CEO:** R.F. Smith
**COO:** A.S. Bodea
**CFO:** L. Adrean
**Chief Acctg Officer:** N.M. King

**Secy:** D.C. Arvidson
**Auditor:** ERNST & YOUNG
**Board Members:** J. E. Copeland, Jr., R. D. Daleo, W. W. Driver, Jr., M. L. Feidler, L. P. Humann, S. S. Marshall, J. A. McKinley, Jr., R. F. Smith, M. B. Templeton

**Founded:** 1913
**Domicile:** Georgia
**Employees:** 6,500

# Equity Residential

STANDARD &POOR'S

| S&P Recommendation HOLD ★★★☆☆ | Price $52.63 (as of Nov 25, 2011) | 12-Mo. Target Price $63.00 | Investment Style Large-Cap Value |

**GICS Sector** Financials
**Sub-Industry** Residential REITS

**Summary** This equity real estate investment trust owns and operates a nationally diversified portfolio of apartment properties.

## Key Stock Statistics (Source S&P, Vickers, company reports)

| | | | | | | | |
|---|---|---|---|---|---|---|---|
| 52-Wk Range | $63.86– 48.46 | S&P FFO/Sh. 2011E | 2.45 | Market Capitalization(B) | $15.612 | Beta | 1.26 |
| Trailing 12-Month FFO/Share | $2.17 | S&P FFO/Sh. 2012E | 2.60 | Yield (%) | 2.57 | S&P 3-Yr. FFO/Sh. Proj. CAGR(%) | 6 |
| Trailing 12-Month P/FFO | NA | P/FFO on S&P FFO/Sh. 2011E | 21.5 | Dividend Rate/Share | $1.35 | S&P Credit Rating | BBB+ |
| $10K Invested 5 Yrs Ago | $12,224 | Common Shares Outstg. (M) | 296.6 | Institutional Ownership (%) | NM | | |

## Price Performance

30-Week Mov. Avg. ···· 10-Week Mov. Avg. ─ ─ **GAAP Earnings vs. Previous Year**   Volume Above Avg. STARS
12-Mo. Target Price ─ Relative Strength   ─ ▲ Up ▼ Down ▶ No Change   Below Avg. ★

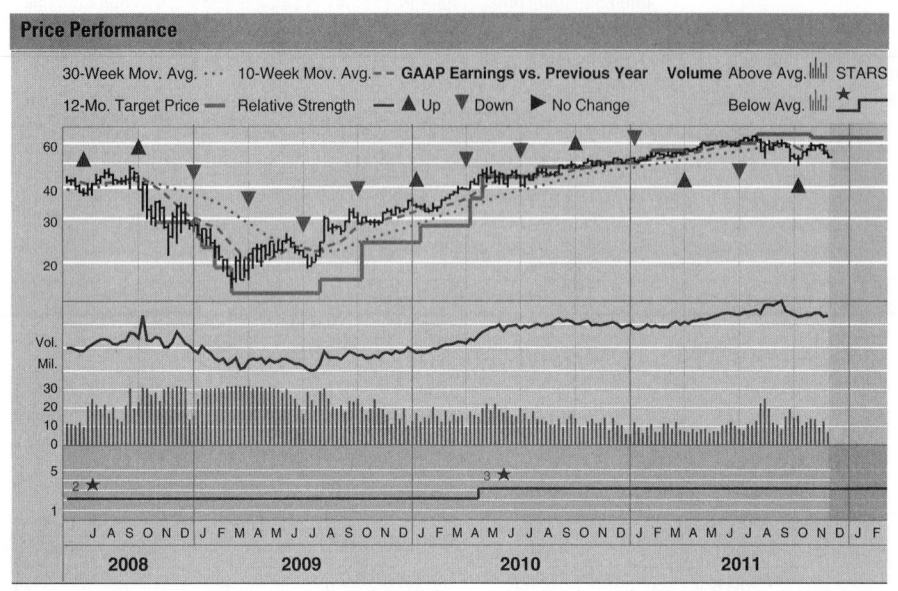

Options: ASE, CBOE, Ph

Analysis prepared by Equity Analyst **R. Shepard, CFA** on Oct 28, 2011, when the stock traded at **$58.49**.

## Highlights

➤ We think EQR will take advantage of high occupancy levels to accelerate rental rate increases in 2012. During the third quarter of 2011, occupancy averaged 95.4% and average rents rose 4.9%. As existing leases renew, we forecast average rent hikes will move up to about 6% in 2012.

➤ EQR is accelerating the disposition of non-core properties to fund new acquisitions. It closed on the sale of $1.4 billion million in assets in the first nine months of 2011 and we expect the trust to take advantage of favorable transaction market conditions again in 2012. Net proceeds will go toward acquisitions, including ten new properties for an aggregate price of $702 million in the first nine months of 2011. Due to a decline in construction costs, EQR could also accelerate its investment in new development. As of September 30, 2011, it had four communities under way at a total budgeted cost of $237 million.

➤ We forecast 2012 FFO of $2.60 per share, excluding gains from debt buybacks or asset sales. EQR has established a new dividend policy, targeting a payout ratio of 65% of recurring FFO. Based on our 2011 projection, the 2011 dividend should be $1.59.

## Investment Rationale/Risk

➤ We like EQR's long-term focus on coastal markets, which we believe have favorable demographic trends and a limited supply of new units. We think a gradually improving economic environment has begun to bolster operating results, including higher occupancy levels and accelerating rent hikes on lease renewals. We expect that dilution from recent asset sales will be roughly offset by an active acquisition program and renewed development activities in 2011 and 2012. Recently at about 23X our 2012 FFO per share outlook, EQR is trading modestly above apartment REIT peers.

➤ Risks to our recommendation and target price include slower-than-anticipated job growth, increased competition from excess inventories of unsold single-family homes and condominiums, and a decline in property values.

➤ Our 12-month target price of $63 is based primarily on a multiple of 24.2X our 2012 FFO outlook, a moderate premium to peers based on what we see as EQR's superior capital structure and its focus on geographic markets that are leading the apartment sector recovery.

## Qualitative Risk Assessment

| LOW | MEDIUM | HIGH |

Our risk assessment reflects our view that EQR is one of the largest, most diversified residential REITs and has below-average financial leverage and strong coverage of fixed charges.

## Quantitative Evaluations

**S&P Quality Ranking**     B

| D | C | B- | B | B+ | A- | A | A+ |

**Relative Strength Rank**    MODERATE
46
LOWEST = 1     HIGHEST = 99

## Revenue/FFO Data

### Revenue (Million $)

| | 1Q | 2Q | 3Q | 4Q | Year |
|---|---|---|---|---|---|
| 2011 | 520.6 | 498.1 | 512.0 | -- | -- |
| 2010 | 488.7 | 510.9 | 527.4 | 517.1 | 1,996 |
| 2009 | 515.1 | 505.2 | 492.8 | 483.0 | 1,944 |
| 2008 | 507.4 | 525.6 | 536.9 | 533.3 | 2,103 |
| 2007 | 483.2 | 507.2 | 522.6 | 528.1 | 2,038 |
| 2006 | 470.5 | 490.6 | 511.5 | 517.9 | 1,990 |

### FFO Per Share ($)

| | 1Q | 2Q | 3Q | 4Q | Year |
|---|---|---|---|---|---|
| 2011 | 0.56 | 0.58 | 0.63 | E0.69 | E2.45 |
| 2010 | 0.52 | 0.58 | 0.55 | 0.48 | 2.20 |
| 2009 | 0.57 | 0.63 | 0.56 | 0.46 | 2.12 |
| 2008 | 0.59 | 0.64 | 0.65 | 0.29 | 2.18 |
| 2007 | 0.55 | 0.60 | 0.58 | 0.67 | 2.39 |
| 2006 | 0.56 | 0.61 | 0.62 | 0.49 | 2.27 |

Fiscal year ended Dec. 31. Next earnings report expected: NA. FFO Estimates based on S&P Funds From Operations Est..

## Dividend Data (Dates: mm/dd Payment Date: mm/dd/yy)

| Amount ($) | Date Decl. | Ex-Div. Date | Stk. of Record | Payment Date |
|---|---|---|---|---|
| 0.458 | 12/09 | 12/16 | 12/20 | 01/14/11 |
| 0.338 | 03/11 | 03/17 | 03/21 | 04/08/11 |
| 0.338 | 06/10 | 06/16 | 06/20 | 07/08/11 |
| 0.338 | 09/09 | 09/16 | 09/20 | 10/14/11 |

Dividends have been paid since 1993. Source: Company reports.

---

**Please read the Required Disclosures and Analyst Certification on the last page of this report.**

The McGraw-Hill Companies

# Equity Residential

**STANDARD &POOR'S**

## Business Summary October 28, 2011

CORPORATE OVERVIEW. Equity Residential is one of the largest publicly held owners of multi-family properties. Structured as a real estate investment trust (REIT), it owns, manages and operates properties through its 93.4% interest in its operating limited partnership. At December 31, 2010, EQR owned or had interests in 451 multi-family properties with 129,604 units in 17 states. The trust adopted its current name in May 2002.

During 2006, EQR sold a majority of its ranch style properties, leaving a focus on garden and mid-rise/high-rise assets. Garden-style properties have two or three floors, while mid-rise/high-rise properties have more than three floors. At the end of December 2010, the trust's largest geographic markets as measured by net operating income were the New York Metro Area (12.7%), Washington DC/N. Virginia (12.1%), South Florida (9.9%), Los Angeles (6.4%), and Boston (4.4%). Average occupancy during the fourth quarter of 2010 was 94.6%, ahead of 93.9% for the same period in 2009.

MARKET PROFILE. The U.S. housing market is highly fragmented, and is characterized broadly by two types of housing units: multi-family and single-family. At the end of 2010, the U.S. Census Bureau estimated that there were 130.85 million housing units in the country, an increase of 0.5% from the end of 2009. Due to the large stock and the fact that residents have the option of either being owners or tenants (renters), the housing market can be highly competitive.

Main demand drivers for apartments are household formation and employment growth. S&P estimates 0.4 million new households were formed in 2010. Supply is created by new housing unit construction, which could consist of single-family homes or multi-family apartment buildings or condominiums. According the U.S. Department of Housing, 0.59 million total housing units were started in 2010, up about 6% from depressed levels in 2009. Multi-family starts, for structures with more than four units, rose 8.1% in 2010, but remained 60% below their level in 2008.

With apartment tenants on relatively short leases compared to those of commercial and industrial properties, we believe apartment REITs are generally more sensitive to changes in market conditions than REITs in other property categories. Results could be hurt by new construction that adds new space in excess of actual demand. Trends in home price affordability also affect both rent levels and the level of new construction, since the relative price attractiveness of owning versus renting is an important factor in consumer decision making.

## Company Financials Fiscal Year Ended Dec. 31

| Per Share Data ($) | 2010 | 2009 | 2008 | 2007 | 2006 | 2005 | 2004 | 2003 | 2002 | 2001 |
|---|---|---|---|---|---|---|---|---|---|---|
| Tangible Book Value | 16.85 | 17.28 | 17.55 | 17.79 | 18.58 | 16.65 | 15.28 | 15.43 | 15.57 | 16.20 |
| Earnings | -0.16 | -0.02 | 0.09 | 0.23 | 0.20 | 0.51 | 0.37 | 0.43 | 0.78 | 1.36 |
| S&P Core Earnings | -0.12 | 0.05 | 0.10 | 0.21 | 0.20 | 0.51 | 0.34 | 0.41 | 0.72 | 1.38 |
| Dividends | 1.47 | 1.64 | 1.93 | 1.87 | 1.79 | 1.74 | 1.73 | 1.73 | 1.73 | 1.68 |
| Payout Ratio | NM | NM | NM | NM | NM | NM | NM | NM | 222% | 124% |
| Prices:High | 52.64 | 36.38 | 49.00 | 56.46 | 61.50 | 42.17 | 36.75 | 30.30 | 30.96 | 30.45 |
| Prices:Low | 31.40 | 15.68 | 21.27 | 33.79 | 38.84 | 30.70 | 26.65 | 23.12 | 21.55 | 24.80 |
| P/E Ratio:High | NM | NM | NM | NM | NM | 83 | 99 | 70 | 40 | 22 |
| P/E Ratio:Low | NM | NM | NM | NM | NM | 60 | 72 | 54 | 28 | 18 |

| Income Statement Analysis (Million $) | 2010 | 2009 | 2008 | 2007 | 2006 | 2005 | 2004 | 2003 | 2002 | 2001 |
|---|---|---|---|---|---|---|---|---|---|---|
| Rental Income | 1,986 | 1,933 | 2,092 | 2,029 | 1,981 | 1,944 | 1,878 | 1,809 | 1,970 | 2,075 |
| Mortgage Income | Nil | Nil | Nil | Nil | Nil | Nil | Nil | Nil | Nil | 8.79 |
| Total Income | 1,996 | 1,944 | 2,103 | 2,038 | 1,990 | 1,955 | 1,890 | 1,823 | 1,994 | 2,171 |
| General Expenses | 852 | 821 | 890 | 883 | 881 | 925 | 870 | 802 | 841 | 924 |
| Interest Expense | 481 | 504 | 489 | 495 | 436 | 391 | 349 | 333 | 343 | 361 |
| Provision for Losses | Nil | Nil | Nil | Nil | Nil | Nil | Nil | Nil | Nil | Nil |
| Depreciation | 657 | 582 | 591 | 588 | 563 | 508 | 484 | 444 | 462 | 457 |
| Net Income | -32.2 | 8.27 | 40.9 | 93.0 | 101 | 152 | 135 | 212 | 302 | 474 |
| S&P Core Earnings | -36.0 | 13.3 | 26.4 | 58.3 | 59.5 | 98.5 | 74.5 | 86.4 | 194 | 374 |

| Balance Sheet & Other Financial Data (Million $) | 2010 | 2009 | 2008 | 2007 | 2006 | 2005 | 2004 | 2003 | 2002 | 2001 |
|---|---|---|---|---|---|---|---|---|---|---|
| Cash | 431 | 193 | 891 | 71.0 | 260 | 88.8 | 83.5 | 49.6 | 540 | 449 |
| Total Assets | 16,184 | 15,418 | 16,535 | 15,690 | 15,062 | 14,099 | 12,645 | 11,467 | 11,811 | 12,236 |
| Real Estate Investment | 19,702 | 18,465 | 18,690 | 18,333 | 17,235 | 16,597 | 14,864 | 12,874 | 13,046 | 13,016 |
| Loss Reserve | Nil | Nil | Nil | Nil | Nil | Nil | Nil | Nil | Nil | Nil |
| Net Investment | 15,365 | 14,588 | 15,129 | 15,163 | 14,217 | 13,709 | 12,264 | 10,578 | 10,934 | 11,297 |
| Short Term Debt | 1,666 | 602 | 863 | 680 | 921 | NA | NA | NA | 334 | 699 |
| Capitalization:Debt | 8,282 | 8,790 | 9,638 | 8,829 | 7,136 | 7,032 | 5,642 | 4,836 | 5,050 | 5,044 |
| Capitalization:Equity | 4,890 | 4,839 | 4,789 | 4,853 | 5,498 | 4,891 | 4,436 | 4,345 | 4,251 | 4,447 |
| Capitalization:Total | 13,875 | 14,223 | 14,954 | 14,929 | 13,432 | 12,850 | 10,714 | 10,452 | 10,858 | 11,094 |
| % Earnings & Depreciation/Assets | 4.0 | 3.7 | 3.9 | 4.4 | 4.5 | 4.9 | 5.1 | 5.6 | 6.4 | 7.6 |
| Price Times Book Value:High | 3.1 | 2.1 | 2.8 | 3.2 | 3.3 | 2.5 | 2.4 | 2.0 | 2.0 | 1.9 |
| Price Times Book Value:Low | 1.9 | 0.9 | 1.2 | 1.9 | 2.1 | 1.8 | 1.7 | 1.5 | 1.4 | 1.5 |

Data as orig reptd.; bef. results of disc opers/spec. items. Per share data adj. for stk. divs.; EPS diluted. E-Estimated. NA-Not Available. NM-Not Meaningful. NR-Not Ranked. UR-Under Review.

# Exelon Corp

**STANDARD &POOR'S**

| **S&P Recommendation** BUY ★★★★☆ | **Price** $41.93 (as of Nov 25, 2011) | **12-Mo. Target Price** $49.00 | **Investment Style** Large-Cap Blend |
|---|---|---|---|

**GICS Sector** Utilities
**Sub-Industry** Electric Utilities

**Summary** Exelon, the holding company for Philadelphia-based PECO Energy and Chicago-based ComEd, is the largest nuclear operator in the U.S.

## Key Stock Statistics (Source S&P, Vickers, company reports)

| | | | | | | |
|---|---|---|---|---|---|---|
| 52-Wk Range | $45.45– 39.05 | S&P Oper. EPS 2011**E** | 4.24 | Market Capitalization(B) | $27.800 | Beta | 0.58 |
| Trailing 12-Month EPS | $3.63 | S&P Oper. EPS 2012**E** | 3.17 | Yield (%) | 5.01 | S&P 3-Yr. Proj. EPS CAGR(%) | -1 |
| Trailing 12-Month P/E | 11.6 | P/E on S&P Oper. EPS 2011**E** | 9.9 | Dividend Rate/Share | $2.10 | S&P Credit Rating | BBB |
| $10K Invested 5 Yrs Ago | $8,535 | Common Shares Outstg. (M) | 663.0 | Institutional Ownership (%) | 66 | | |

## Price Performance

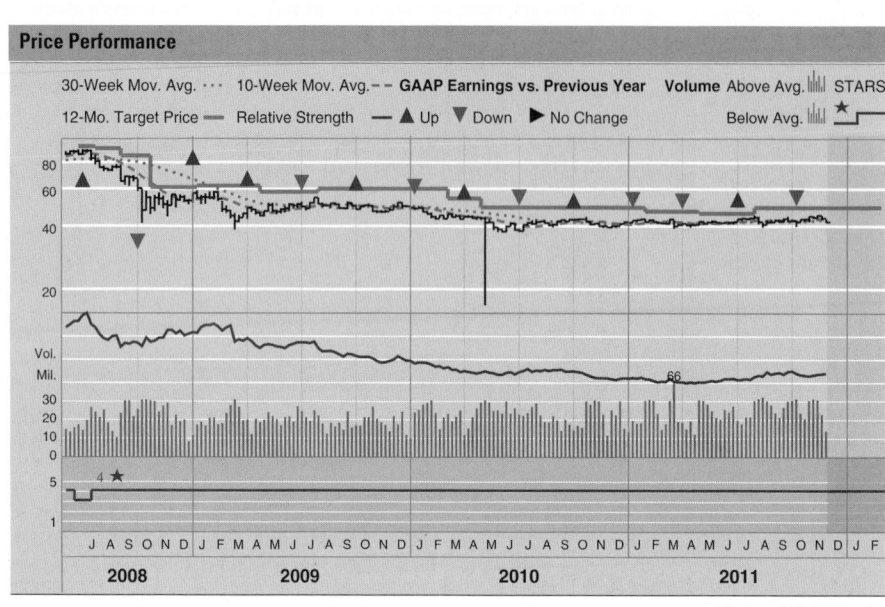

30-Week Mov. Avg. · · · · 10-Week Mov. Avg. – – 12-Mo. Target Price — Relative Strength — ▲ Up ▼ Down ► No Change    GAAP Earnings vs. Previous Year    Volume Above Avg. STARS ★ Below Avg.

Options: ASE, CBOE, P, Ph

Analysis prepared by Equity Analyst **Justin McCann** on Nov 08, 2011, when the stock traded at **$45.17**.

## Highlights

➤ Subject to required approvals, the agreed-to merger with Constellation Energy (CEG 40 Hold) is expected close in the first quarter of 2012 and to result in a company that would be the largest competitive energy producer in the U.S., and the second largest electric and gas distributor, with 6.6 million customers in three states. We expect the merger to be breakeven to operating earnings in 2012 and more than 5% accretive to earnings for 2013.

➤ We expect operating EPS to rise more than 4% in 2011. In the first nine months of 2011, operating EPS of $3.34 was $0.24 above the year-ago period. Despite six nuclear refueling outages, earnings for the generation segment benefited from the strong weather-aided first and third quarters, and higher-margin power contracts with PECO Energy. This was partially offset by reduced earnings at ComEd, due to higher O&M costs, and lower earnings at PECO, as the benefit of rate hikes were offset by the absence of special customer charges realized in 2010.

➤ For 2012, we expect to see a steep decline in stand-alone earnings, reflecting the replacement of expired higher-margin power contracts with sharply lower-margin contracts.

## Investment Rationale/Risk

➤ While the shares have been restricted by the weakness in the economy and power prices, we believe the planned merger with Constellation Energy would, if approved, give it the scale and financial strength to expand its presence in the competitive energy markets and leave it well positioned for a potential recovery in the power markets and/or regulations requiring a significant reduction in power generation emissions considered harmful by the EPA.

➤ Risks to our opinion and target price include unexpected problems in the regulatory approval process, an extended recession, sharply reduced wholesale power margins, and a drop in the average peer P/E of the sub-industry.

➤ The recent dividend yield of 4.7% is above the recent 4.2% average yield of electric utility peers primarily involved in power distribution, and well above that of other utility holding companies with major operations in the wholesale power markets. Our 12-month target price is $49, a premium-to-peers P/E of 15.5X our EPS estimate for 2012. Given the above-peers dividend yield and Exelon's leading position in the nuclear power industry, we believe the stock is attractive for total return potential.

## Qualitative Risk Assessment

| LOW | MEDIUM | HIGH |
|---|---|---|

Our risk assessment reflects our view of Exelon's strong and steady cash flow from the regulated PECO Energy and ComEd utilities, as well as the healthy earnings and cash flow from very profitable but higher-risk power generating and energy marketing operations.

## Quantitative Evaluations

**S&P Quality Ranking**     B+

| D | C | B- | B | B+ | A- | A | A+ |
|---|---|---|---|---|---|---|---|

**Relative Strength Rank**     MODERATE

65

LOWEST = 1     HIGHEST = 99

## Revenue/Earnings Data

**Revenue (Million $)**

| | 1Q | 2Q | 3Q | 4Q | Year |
|---|---|---|---|---|---|
| 2011 | 5,052 | 4,587 | 5,295 | -- | -- |
| 2010 | 4,461 | 4,398 | 5,291 | 4,494 | 18,644 |
| 2009 | 4,722 | 4,141 | 4,339 | 4,116 | 17,318 |
| 2008 | 4,517 | 4,622 | 5,228 | 4,493 | 18,859 |
| 2007 | 4,829 | 4,501 | 5,032 | 4,554 | 18,916 |
| 2006 | 3,861 | 3,697 | 4,401 | 3,696 | 15,655 |

**Earnings Per Share ($)**

| | | | | | |
|---|---|---|---|---|---|
| 2011 | 1.01 | 0.96 | 0.90 | E0.80 | E4.24 |
| 2010 | 1.13 | 0.67 | 1.27 | 0.79 | 3.87 |
| 2009 | 1.08 | 0.99 | 1.14 | 0.88 | 4.09 |
| 2008 | 0.88 | 1.13 | 1.06 | 1.04 | 4.10 |
| 2007 | 1.01 | 1.03 | 1.15 | 0.84 | 4.03 |
| 2006 | 0.59 | 0.95 | -0.07 | 0.87 | 2.35 |

Fiscal year ended Dec. 31. Next earnings report expected: Late January. EPS Estimates based on S&P Operating Earnings; historical GAAP earnings are as reported.

## Dividend Data (Dates: mm/dd Payment Date: mm/dd/yy)

| Amount ($) | Date Decl. | Ex-Div. Date | Stk. of Record | Payment Date |
|---|---|---|---|---|
| 0.525 | 05/03 | 05/12 | 05/16 | 06/10/11 |
| 0.525 | 07/26 | 08/11 | 08/15 | 09/09/11 |
| 0.525 | 10/25 | 11/10 | 11/15 | 12/09/11 |
| 0.525 | 10/25 | 02/13 | 02/15 | 03/09/12 |

Dividends have been paid since 1902. Source: Company reports.

**Please read the Required Disclosures and Analyst Certification on the last page of this report.**

*The McGraw·Hill Companies*

# Exelon Corp

## Business Summary November 08, 2011

CORPORATE OVERVIEW. Exelon Corp. was formed in October 2000 through the acquisition by Philadelphia-based PECO Energy of Chicago-based Unicom Corp. The company, along with its subsidiaries, is engaged in the energy delivery, generation and other businesses. Exelon operates in three business segments: Generation, PECO, and ComEd (Commonwealth Edison). Segment contributions to consolidated net income in 2010 were: Generation, $1,972 million ($2,122 million in 2009); ComEd, $337 million ($374 million); PECO, $324 million ($353 million), and other, a loss of $70 million (a loss of $142 million).

IMPACT OF MAJOR DEVELOPMENTS. On April 28, 2011, Exelon announced a definitive merger agreement with Constellation Energy (CEG 39 Hold), a leading competitive supplier of power and natural gas, and the holding company for Baltimore Gas & Electric Company. Under the terms of the stock-for-stock agreement, Constellation Energy shareholders would receive 0.93 EXC shares for each CEG share. Upon the close of the merger, which is subject to required approvals, Exelon would have about a 78% interest in the combined company, which would maintain the Exelon name, and 12 members on the 16-member board. CEG's chairman, president and CEO, Mayo A. Shattuck III,

would become executive chairman of the combined company, and Christopher M. Crane, Exelon's president and COO, would be the president and CEO. John W. Rowe, Exelon's current chairman and CEO, would retire upon the completion of the transaction.

On December 9, 2010, Exelon Generation acquired all of the equity interests of John Deere Renewables, LLC (subsequently renamed Exelon Wind), a leading operator and developer of wind power for approximately $893 million in cash. The business had 735 megawatts of installed, operating wind capacity located in eight states, with about 75% of the operating portfolio's expected output already sold under long-term power purchase arrangements. Additionally, Generation will pay up to $40 million related to three projects with a capacity of 230 megawatts which are currently in advanced stages of development.

## Company Financials Fiscal Year Ended Dec. 31

| Per Share Data ($) | 2010 | 2009 | 2008 | 2007 | 2006 | 2005 | 2004 | 2003 | 2002 | 2001 |
|---|---|---|---|---|---|---|---|---|---|---|
| Tangible Book Value | 16.52 | 15.06 | 12.58 | 11.86 | 11.08 | 8.48 | 7.10 | 5.77 | 4.26 | 4.51 |
| Earnings | 3.87 | 4.09 | 4.10 | 4.03 | 2.35 | 1.40 | 2.75 | 1.20 | 2.58 | 2.20 |
| S&P Core Earnings | 4.08 | 4.33 | 3.32 | 3.92 | 3.49 | 3.01 | 2.79 | 1.74 | 1.64 | 1.49 |
| Dividends | 2.10 | 2.10 | 2.02 | 1.76 | 2.00 | 1.60 | 1.53 | 0.96 | 0.88 | 0.91 |
| Payout Ratio | 54% | 51% | 49% | 44% | 85% | 114% | 56% | 80% | 34% | 41% |
| Prices:High | 49.88 | 58.98 | 92.13 | 86.83 | 63.62 | 57.46 | 44.90 | 33.31 | 28.50 | 35.13 |
| Prices:Low | 16.78 | 38.41 | 41.23 | 58.74 | 51.13 | 41.77 | 30.92 | 23.04 | 18.92 | 19.38 |
| P/E Ratio:High | 13 | 14 | 22 | 22 | 27 | 41 | 16 | 28 | 11 | 16 |
| P/E Ratio:Low | 4 | 9 | 10 | 15 | 22 | 30 | 11 | 19 | 7 | 9 |

| Income Statement Analysis (Million $) | 2010 | 2009 | 2008 | 2007 | 2006 | 2005 | 2004 | 2003 | 2002 | 2001 |
|---|---|---|---|---|---|---|---|---|---|---|
| Revenue | 18,644 | 17,318 | 18,859 | 18,916 | 15,655 | 15,357 | 14,515 | 15,812 | 14,955 | 15,140 |
| Depreciation | 2,943 | 2,601 | 2,308 | 1,520 | 1,487 | 1,334 | 1,305 | 1,126 | 1,340 | 1,449 |
| Maintenance | NA | NA | NA | NA | NA | NA | NA | NA | NA | NA |
| Fixed Charges Coverage | 6.17 | 7.08 | 5.88 | 6.03 | 5.19 | 4.88 | 3.94 | 2.19 | 3.56 | 2.98 |
| Construction Credits | NA | NA | NA | NA | NA | NA | NA | NA | NA | NA |
| Effective Tax Rate | 39.3% | 38.8% | 32.7% | 34.7% | 43.1% | 49.8% | 27.5% | 29.4% | 37.4% | 39.7% |
| Net Income | 2,563 | 2,706 | 2,717 | 2,726 | 1,590 | 951 | 1,841 | 793 | 1,670 | 1,416 |
| S&P Core Earnings | 2,700 | 2,865 | 2,197 | 2,656 | 2,358 | 2,035 | 1,865 | 1,142 | 1,062 | 962 |

| Balance Sheet & Other Financial Data (Million $) | 2010 | 2009 | 2008 | 2007 | 2006 | 2005 | 2004 | 2003 | 2002 | 2001 |
|---|---|---|---|---|---|---|---|---|---|---|
| Gross Property | 40,005 | 36,364 | 34,055 | 31,964 | 30,025 | 29,853 | 28,711 | 27,578 | 25,904 | 21,526 |
| Capital Expenditures | 3,326 | 3,273 | 3,117 | 2,674 | 2,418 | 2,165 | 1,921 | 1,954 | 2,150 | 2,041 |
| Net Property | 29,941 | 27,341 | 25,813 | 24,153 | 22,775 | 21,981 | 21,482 | 20,630 | 17,134 | 13,742 |
| Capitalization:Long Term Debt | 12,091 | 11,472 | 12,679 | 12,052 | 11,998 | 11,760 | 12,235 | 13,576 | 14,580 | 13,492 |
| Capitalization:% Long Term Debt | 47.1 | 47.6 | 53.5 | 54.3 | 54.6 | 56.3 | 56.5 | 61.5 | 65.3 | 62.1 |
| Capitalization:Preferred | Nil | Nil | Nil | Nil | Nil | Nil | Nil | Nil | Nil | Nil |
| Capitalization:% Preferred | Nil | Nil | Nil | Nil | Nil | Nil | Nil | Nil | Nil | Nil |
| Capitalization:Common | 13,560 | 12,640 | 11,047 | 10,137 | 9,973 | 9,125 | 9,423 | 8,503 | 7,742 | 8,230 |
| Capitalization:% Common | 52.9 | 52.4 | 46.6 | 45.7 | 45.4 | 43.7 | 43.5 | 38.5 | 34.7 | 37.9 |
| Total Capital | 26,253 | 25,166 | 24,074 | 27,270 | 27,395 | 25,964 | 26,463 | 26,724 | 26,325 | 26,341 |
| % Operating Ratio | 83.5 | 82.5 | 78.9 | 83.0 | 80.3 | 80.5 | 81.1 | 82.2 | 73.1 | 83.9 |
| % Earned on Net Property | 16.5 | 17.9 | 21.2 | 19.9 | 15.7 | 12.5 | 16.3 | 11.4 | 21.3 | 25.2 |
| % Return on Revenue | 13.8 | 15.6 | 14.4 | 14.4 | 10.2 | 6.2 | 12.7 | 5.0 | 11.2 | 9.4 |
| % Return on Invested Capital | 13.1 | 14.1 | 15.1 | 13.5 | 12.1 | 11.4 | 10.3 | 10.2 | 10.2 | 9.8 |
| % Return on Common Equity | 19.6 | 22.9 | 25.7 | 27.1 | 16.7 | 10.2 | 20.5 | 9.8 | 21.1 | 18.3 |

Data as orig reptd.; bef. results of disc opers/spec. items. Per share data adj. for stk. divs.; EPS diluted. E-Estimated. NA-Not Available. NM-Not Meaningful. NR-Not Ranked. UR-Under Review.

**Office:** 10 South Dearborn Street 48th Floor, PO Box 805398, Chicago, IL 60680-5398.
**Telephone:** 312-394-7398.
**Website:** http://www.exeloncorp.com
**Chrmn & CEO:** J.W. Rowe

**Pres & COO:** C.M. Crane
**SVP, CFO & Treas:** M.F. Hilzinger
**SVP & General Counsel:** D.M. Bradford
**SVP & CIO:** D. Hill

**Investor Contact:** C.M. Patterson (312-394-7234)
**Board Members:** J. A. Canning, Jr., M. W. D'Alessio, N. DeBenedictis, N. A. Diaz, S. L. Gin, R. B. Greco, P. L. Joskow, R. W. Mies, J. M. Palms, W. C. Richardson, T. J. Ridge, J. W. Rogers, Jr., J. W. Rowe, S. D. Steinour, D. Thompson

**Founded:** 1887
**Domicile:** Pennsylvania
**Employees:** 19,214

# Expedia Inc

**STANDARD &POOR'S**

| **S&P Recommendation** | **BUY** ★★★★☆ | **Price** $26.11 (as of Nov 25, 2011) | **12-Mo. Target Price** $40.00 | **Investment Style** Large-Cap Blend |
|---|---|---|---|---|

**GICS Sector** Consumer Discretionary
**Sub-Industry** Internet Retail

**Summary** Expedia is one of the world's largest online travel-services companies. Businesses include Expedia, Hotels.com, Hotwire and TripAdvisor. In April 2011, Expedia announced plans to spin off TripAdvisor as a publicly traded company.

## Key Stock Statistics (Source S&P, Vickers, company reports)

| | | | | | | | |
|---|---|---|---|---|---|---|---|
| 52-Wk Range | $32.89– 19.61 | S&P Oper. EPS 2011**E** | 1.85 | Market Capitalization(B) | $6.304 | Beta | 1.84 |
| Trailing 12-Month EPS | $1.69 | S&P Oper. EPS 2012**E** | 2.15 | Yield (%) | 1.07 | S&P 3-Yr. Proj. EPS CAGR(%) | 14 |
| Trailing 12-Month P/E | 15.5 | P/E on S&P Oper. EPS 2011**E** | 14.1 | Dividend Rate/Share | $0.28 | S&P Credit Rating | BBB- |
| $10K Invested 5 Yrs Ago | $14,575 | Common Shares Outstg. (M) | 267.0 | Institutional Ownership (%) | 86 | | |

## Price Performance

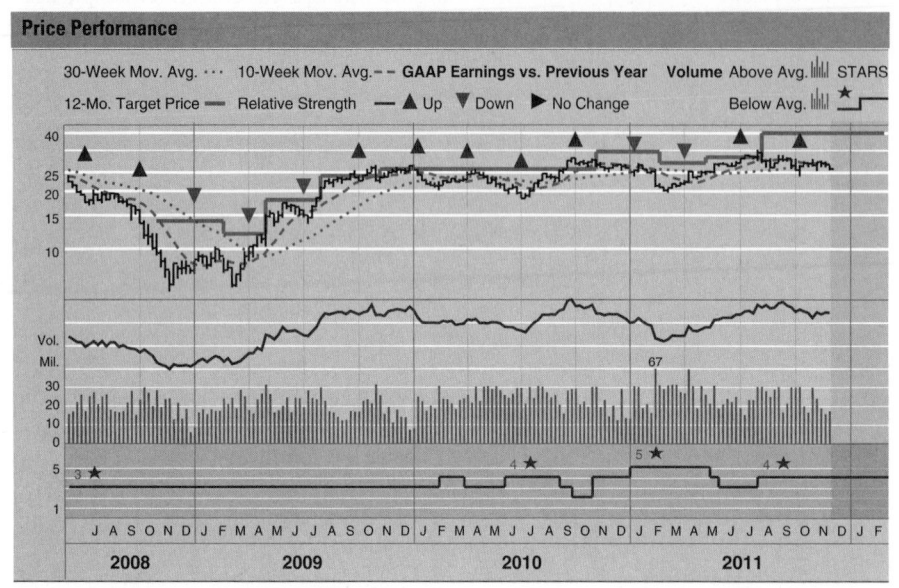

30-Week Mov. Avg. · · · 10-Week Mov. Avg.- - **GAAP Earnings vs. Previous Year** Volume Above Avg. STARS
12-Mo. Target Price — Relative Strength ▲ Up ▼ Down ► No Change Below Avg. ★

Options: ASE, CBOE, P, Ph

Analysis prepared by Equity Analyst **Scott Kessler** on Nov 22, 2011, when the stock traded at **$26.07**.

## Highlights

➤ We believe EXPE is among the worldwide leaders in the Internet travel segment and will benefit from the continuing migration of associated purchases online. While we have concerns related to economic uncertainty in and substantial exposure to Europe, we estimate that revenues will rise 16% in 2011 and 11% in 2012, given what we see as intact secular growth trends and likely market share gains.

➤ We estimate that annual operating income before amortization (OIBA) and net margins bottomed in 2006, partly due to considerable sales and marketing expenses and technology investments, which yielded benefits. We expect investment in new offerings and expansion to negatively affect margins in 2011.

➤ EXPE had $2.0 billion in cash and investments as of September 2011, and $1.6 billion of long-term debt. In February 2010, EXPE announced its first dividend. In April 2011, EXPE announced plans to spin off TripAdvisor as a publicly traded company, and we expect the transaction to be completed by December 2011, subject to approvals.

## Investment Rationale/Risk

➤ We believe EXPE has some of the Internet's best-known travel franchises (including Expedia, Hotels.com and TripAdvisor), some well positioned and strong international operations, and a healthy domestic business. Over the past few years, EXPE has seized upon opportunities and executed relatively well, in our view. We think EXPE is well positioned to benefit from favorable secular trends. We view the shares as attractively valued at recent levels.

➤ Risks to our opinion and target price include possible notable weakening of global or domestic consumer sentiment or spending, and increasing competitive and/or pricing pressures, perhaps related to recent indications of tensions between airlines and travel distributors.

➤ Our DCF model assumes a weighted average cost of capital of 10.9%, annual free cash flow growth averaging 9% over the next five years, and a perpetuity growth rate of 3%. These inputs yield an intrinsic value of $40, which is our 12-month target price. We think the planned spinoff of TripAdvisor could be a positive catalyst for EXPE.

## Qualitative Risk Assessment

| LOW | MEDIUM | **HIGH** |
|---|---|---|

Our risk assessment reflects what we believe is a maturing online travel market in the U.S., substantial competition and pricing pressure, and relatively low barriers to entry.

## Quantitative Evaluations

**S&P Quality Ranking** NR

| D | C | B- | B | B+ | A- | A | A+ |
|---|---|---|---|---|---|---|---|

**Relative Strength Rank** MODERATE

49

LOWEST = 1      HIGHEST = 99

## Revenue/Earnings Data

**Revenue (Million $)**

| | 1Q | 2Q | 3Q | 4Q | Year |
|---|---|---|---|---|---|
| 2011 | 822.2 | 1,024 | 1,141 | -- | -- |
| 2010 | 717.9 | 834.0 | 987.9 | 808.4 | 3,348 |
| 2009 | 635.7 | 769.8 | 852.4 | 697.5 | 2,955 |
| 2008 | 687.8 | 795.1 | 833.3 | 620.8 | 2,937 |
| 2007 | 550.5 | 689.9 | 759.6 | 665.3 | 2,665 |
| 2006 | 493.9 | 598.5 | 613.9 | 531.3 | 2,238 |

**Earnings Per Share ($)**

| | | | | | |
|---|---|---|---|---|---|
| 2011 | 0.19 | 0.50 | 0.75 | E0.39 | E1.85 |
| 2010 | 0.20 | 0.40 | 0.62 | 0.25 | 1.46 |
| 2009 | 0.14 | 0.14 | 0.40 | 0.35 | 1.03 |
| 2008 | 0.17 | 0.33 | 0.33 | -9.60 | -8.63 |
| 2007 | 0.11 | 0.30 | 0.32 | 0.22 | 0.94 |
| 2006 | 0.06 | 0.27 | 0.17 | 0.20 | 0.70 |

Fiscal year ended Dec. 31. Next earnings report expected: NA. EPS Estimates based on S&P Operating Earnings; historical GAAP earnings are as reported.

## Dividend Data (Dates: mm/dd Payment Date: mm/dd/yy)

| Amount ($) | Date Decl. | Ex-Div. Date | Stk. of Record | Payment Date |
|---|---|---|---|---|
| 0.070 | 02/09 | 03/09 | 03/11 | 03/31/11 |
| 0.070 | 04/27 | 05/25 | 05/27 | 06/17/11 |
| 0.070 | 07/28 | 08/24 | 08/26 | 09/16/11 |
| 0.070 | 10/25 | 11/16 | 11/18 | 12/09/11 |

Dividends have been paid since 2010. Source: Company reports.

---

**Please read the Required Disclosures and Analyst Certification on the last page of this report.**

The **McGraw·Hill** Companies

# Expedia Inc

**STANDARD &POOR'S**

## Business Summary November 22, 2011

CORPORATE OVERVIEW. Expedia, Inc. leverages its portfolio of brands to target a broad range of travelers interested in different travel options. EXPE provides a wide selection of travel products and services, from simple discounted travel to more complex luxury trips. The company's offerings primarily include airline tickets, hotel reservations, car rentals, cruise arrangements, and destination services.

The company's localized Expedia-branded websites (focused on 20 countries around the world) offer a large variety of travel products and services. Hotels.com provides a multitude of lodging options to travelers, from traditional hotels to vacation rentals. Part of Hotels.com's strategy is to position itself as a hotel expert offering premium content about lodging properties. Hotwire.com is a discount travel website that offers deals to travelers willing to make purchases without knowing certain itinerary details such as brand, time of departure, and hotel address. Egencia (formerly known as Expedia Corporate Travel) is a full-service travel management firm available to corporate travelers in 39 countries in North America, Europe and Asia. eLong (LONG 15, NR) is a majority-owned online travel services company based in and focused on China (see below for more details).

TripAdvisor is an online travel content destination, with search and directory features, guidebook reviews, and user opinions. We believe TripAdvisor has been an extremely valuable asset for EXPE, not only because we believe it constitutes the Internet's largest and most active travel-related social networking property, but also because it diversifies EXPE's operations away from transactions and into media and advertising. Expansion in China has been a major focus of TripAdvisor, with entry into the market in April 2009 with the launch of DaoDao.com (a localized reviews and community website for Chinese travelers), and acquisition of Kuxun.cn (the second-largest online travel-related website in China) in late 2009.

In December 2004, IAC/InterActiveCorp (IACI 40, Hold) announced a plan to spin off what became EXPE. In August 2005, EXPE was spun off as a separate publicly traded company.

## Company Financials Fiscal Year Ended Dec. 31

| Per Share Data ($) | 2010 | 2009 | 2008 | 2007 | 2006 | 2005 | 2004 | 2003 | 2002 | 2001 |
|---|---|---|---|---|---|---|---|---|---|---|
| Tangible Book Value | NM | NM | NM | NM | NM | NM | NA | NA | NA | NA |
| Cash Flow | 2.02 | 1.29 | -8.13 | 1.38 | 1.40 | 1.82 | NA | NA | NA | NA |
| Earnings | 1.46 | 1.03 | -8.63 | 0.94 | 0.70 | 0.65 | 0.37 | NA | NA | NA |
| S&P Core Earnings | 1.47 | 1.19 | -2.48 | 0.94 | 0.79 | 0.69 | 0.48 | 0.27 | 0.26 | -1.04 |
| Dividends | 0.28 | Nil | Nil | Nil | Nil | Nil | NA | NA | NA | NA |
| Payout Ratio | 19% | Nil | Nil | Nil | Nil | Nil | NA | NA | NA | NA |
| Prices:High | 29.85 | 27.51 | 31.88 | 35.28 | 27.55 | 27.50 | NA | NA | NA | NA |
| Prices:Low | 18.30 | 6.31 | 6.00 | 19.97 | 12.87 | 18.49 | NA | NA | NA | NA |
| P/E Ratio:High | 20 | 27 | NM | 38 | 39 | 42 | NA | NA | NA | NA |
| P/E Ratio:Low | 13 | 6 | NM | 21 | 18 | 28 | NA | NA | NA | NA |

| Income Statement Analysis (Million $) | 2010 | 2009 | 2008 | 2007 | 2006 | 2005 | 2004 | 2003 | 2002 | 2001 |
|---|---|---|---|---|---|---|---|---|---|---|
| Revenue | 3,348 | 2,955 | 2,937 | 2,665 | 2,238 | 2,119 | 1,843 | 2,340 | 1,499 | NA |
| Operating Income | 893 | 751 | 713 | 666 | 648 | 678 | 397 | 364 | 257 | NA |
| Depreciation | 156 | 140 | 146 | 137 | 249 | 407 | 157 | 104 | 61.4 | NA |
| Interest Expense | 101 | 84.2 | 72.0 | 52.9 | 17.3 | Nil | 7.45 | 2.90 | NA | NA |
| Pretax Income | 621 | 458 | -2,515 | 497 | 385 | 414 | 219 | 256 | 209 | NA |
| Effective Tax Rate | NA | 33.7% | NM | 40.9% | 36.2% | 44.9% | 40.0% | 38.0% | 39.4% | NA |
| Net Income | 426 | 300 | -2,518 | 296 | 245 | 229 | 131 | 111 | 76.7 | NA |
| S&P Core Earnings | 425 | 347 | -722 | 296 | 275 | 244 | 163 | 92.3 | 34.2 | -98.1 |

| Balance Sheet & Other Financial Data (Million $) | 2010 | 2009 | 2008 | 2007 | 2006 | 2005 | 2004 | 2003 | 2002 | 2001 |
|---|---|---|---|---|---|---|---|---|---|---|
| Cash | 1,230 | 688 | 758 | 634 | 853 | 297 | 232 | 882 | NA | NA |
| Current Assets | 1,702 | 1,225 | 1,199 | 1,046 | 1,183 | 590 | 569 | 1,680 | NA | NA |
| Total Assets | 6,651 | 5,937 | 5,894 | 8,295 | 8,269 | 7,757 | 7,803 | 8,755 | NA | NA |
| Current Liabilities | 1,889 | 1,835 | 1,566 | 1,774 | 1,400 | 1,438 | 1,515 | 825 | NA | NA |
| Long Term Debt | 1,645 | 895 | 1,545 | 1,085 | 500 | Nil | NA | NA | NA | NA |
| Common Equity | 2,673 | 2,683 | 2,328 | 4,818 | 5,904 | 5,734 | 5,820 | 7,554 | NA | NA |
| Total Capital | 4,446 | 3,645 | 4,115 | 6,316 | 6,835 | 6,174 | 8,171 | 7,554 | NA | NA |
| Capital Expenditures | 155 | 92.0 | 160 | 86.7 | 92.6 | 52.3 | 53.4 | 46.2 | 46.5 | NA |
| Cash Flow | 581 | 377 | -2,372 | 433 | 494 | 636 | 320 | 215 | 138 | NA |
| Current Ratio | 0.9 | 0.7 | 0.8 | 0.6 | 0.8 | 0.4 | 0.4 | 2.0 | NA | NA |
| % Long Term Debt of Capitalization | 37.0 | 24.6 | 37.5 | 17.2 | 7.3 | Nil | Nil | Nil | Nil | NA |
| % Net Income of Revenue | 12.7 | 10.1 | NM | 11.1 | 10.9 | 10.8 | 7.1 | 4.8 | 5.1 | NA |
| % Return on Assets | 6.8 | 5.1 | NM | 3.6 | 3.1 | 2.6 | 1.8 | NA | NA | NA |
| % Return on Equity | 15.9 | 12.0 | NM | 5.5 | 4.2 | 3.3 | 2.1 | NA | NA | NA |

Data as orig reptd.; bef. results of disc opers/spec. items. Per share data adj. for stk. divs.; EPS diluted. E-Estimated. NA-Not Available. NM-Not Meaningful. NR-Not Ranked. UR-Under Review.

**Office:** 333 108th Avenue NE, Bellevue, WA 98004.
**Telephone:** 425-679-7200.
**Website:** http://www.expediainc.com
**Chrmn:** B. Diller

**Pres & CEO:** D. Khosrowshahi
**Vice Chrmn:** V.A. Kaufman
**EVP & CFO:** M. Okerstrom
**EVP & CTO:** P.V. Samec

**Investor Contact:** A. Pickerill (425-679-7973)
**Board Members:** A. G. Battle, B. Diller, J. L. Dolgen, W. R. Fitzgerald, C. A. Jacobson, V. A. Kaufman, P. Kern, D. Khosrowshahi, J. C. Malone, D. C. Marriott, J. Miller, J. A. Tazon

**Founded:** 1996
**Domicile:** Delaware
**Employees:** 8,900

*The McGraw-Hill Companies*

# Expeditors International of Washington Inc

**STANDARD &POOR'S**

**S&P Recommendation** BUY ★★★★☆

| Price | 12-Mo. Target Price | Investment Style |
|---|---|---|
| $40.00 (as of Nov 25, 2011) | $60.00 | Large-Cap Growth |

**GICS Sector** Industrials
**Sub-Industry** Air Freight & Logistics

**Summary** This company is a global air and ocean freight forwarder and customs broker.

## Key Stock Statistics (Source S&P, Vickers, company reports)

| | | | | | | | |
|---|---|---|---|---|---|---|---|
| 52-Wk Range | $57.15– 38.25 | S&P Oper. EPS 2011**E** | 1.80 | Market Capitalization(B) | $8.481 | Beta | 0.83 |
| Trailing 12-Month EPS | $1.81 | S&P Oper. EPS 2012**E** | 1.98 | Yield (%) | 1.25 | S&P 3-Yr. Proj. EPS CAGR(%) | 16 |
| Trailing 12-Month P/E | 22.1 | P/E on S&P Oper. EPS 2011**E** | 22.2 | Dividend Rate/Share | $0.50 | S&P Credit Rating | NA |
| $10K Invested 5 Yrs Ago | $8,911 | Common Shares Outstg. (M) | 212.0 | Institutional Ownership (%) | 93 | | |

## Price Performance

30-Week Mov. Avg. · · ·   10-Week Mov. Avg. – – **GAAP Earnings vs. Previous Year**   Volume Above Avg. ▮▮▮ STARS
12-Mo. Target Price —   Relative Strength — ▲ Up ▼ Down ► No Change   Below Avg. ▮▮▮ ★

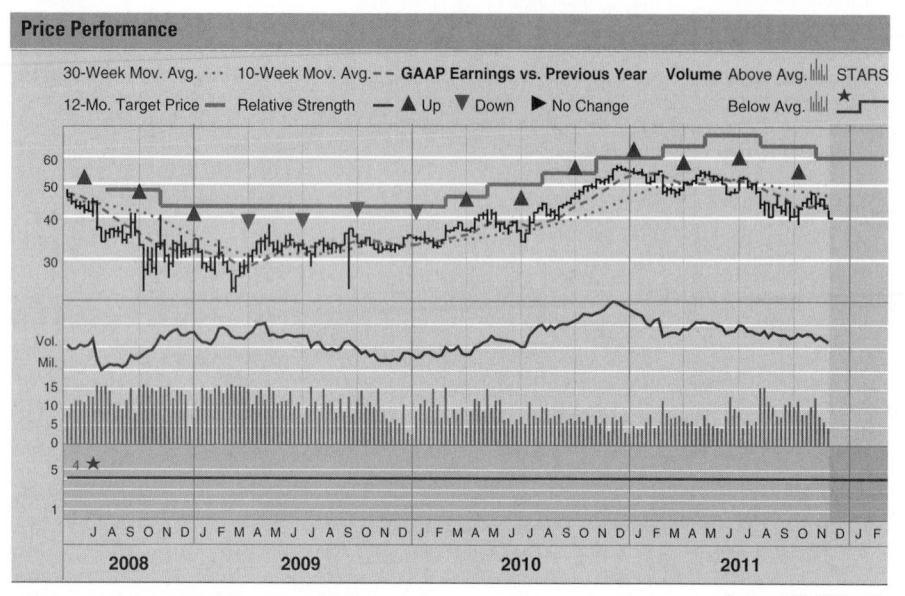

Options: ASE, CBOE, P, Ph

Analysis prepared by Equity Analyst **Jim Corridore** on Nov 10, 2011, when the stock traded at **$44.01**.

## Qualitative Risk Assessment

| LOW | MEDIUM | HIGH |
|---|---|---|

Our risk assessment reflects that EXPD operates in a highly cyclical industry and is exposed to currency and global economic risk. We see its communication style as an additional risk. However, we think EXPD has a diversified stream of air, ocean, and customs businesses, and we also believe the balance sheet is strong, with no debt and a relatively large amount of cash.

## Quantitative Evaluations

**S&P Quality Ranking**     **A+**

| D | C | B- | B | B+ | A- | A | A+ |
|---|---|---|---|---|---|---|---|

**Relative Strength Rank**     **MODERATE**

36

LOWEST = 1      HIGHEST = 99

## Revenue/Earnings Data

**Revenue (Million $)**

| | 1Q | 2Q | 3Q | 4Q | Year |
|---|---|---|---|---|---|
| 2011 | 1,461 | 1,581 | 1,606 | -- | -- |
| 2010 | 1,201 | 1,517 | 1,668 | 1,582 | 5,968 |
| 2009 | 912.7 | 895.4 | 1,037 | 1,247 | 4,092 |
| 2008 | 1,307 | 1,454 | 1,565 | 1,307 | 5,634 |
| 2007 | 1,119 | 1,259 | 1,411 | 1,447 | 5,235 |
| 2006 | 1,025 | 1,129 | 1,230 | 1,242 | 4,626 |

**Earnings Per Share ($)**

| | 1Q | 2Q | 3Q | 4Q | Year |
|---|---|---|---|---|---|
| 2011 | 0.42 | 0.44 | 0.50 | E0.44 | E1.80 |
| 2010 | 0.28 | 0.42 | 0.44 | 0.45 | 1.59 |
| 2009 | 0.27 | 0.25 | 0.27 | 0.32 | 1.11 |
| 2008 | 0.30 | 0.32 | 0.39 | 0.36 | 1.37 |
| 2007 | 0.27 | 0.30 | 0.34 | 0.32 | 1.21 |
| 2006 | 0.24 | 0.25 | 0.29 | 0.28 | 1.06 |

Fiscal year ended Dec. 31. Next earnings report expected: Late February. EPS Estimates based on S&P Operating Earnings; historical GAAP earnings are as reported.

## Highlights

➤ We expect net revenues to rise about 5% in 2011 and 7% in 2012, after 46% growth in 2010 and a 27% decline in 2009. Net revenue growth should see modest growth in volumes on strengthening global transportation demand. We look for strengthening air and ocean volumes with yield expansion in 2012. Volumes and pricing in the U.S. showed strong improvement in 2010, which created challenging comparisons in 2011. In addition, Ocean and air freight demand decelerated in the first nine months of 2011.

➤ We project operating margins to be aided by improving volumes and reductions in ocean and air transportation rates, reflecting new ocean freight capacity that has recently come on line, as well as excess ocean and air shipping capacity. We think continued legal costs related to a Department of Justice investigation into potential anti-competitive practices, as well as some pressure on SG&A expenses, will partially offset the benefits.

➤ We forecast 2011 EPS of $1.80, a 13% advance over 2010's EPS of $1.59. For 2012, we see EPS rising 10% to $1.98.

## Investment Rationale/Risk

➤ While the overall logistics sector is likely to see a recovery in volumes related to strengthening in the U.S. and global economies, we believe EXPD's diversified revenue base, geographical reach, and shipping mode will allow it to outperform peers. A debt-free balance sheet and what we view as strong long-term earnings and cash flow growth potential are additional positives. We also expect improved investor sentiment for EXPD and other logistics stocks on good economic news that points to improvement in the U.S. economy.

➤ Risks to our recommendation and target price include any worsening of the global economy. We also see management's communication style, in which it mainly answers questions through 8-K filings, as a risk, in that it may not allow investors to react quickly enough to potentially important news. Also, the company could potentially be hit with a large judgment related to the current Department of Justice investigation into anti-competitive practices.

➤ Our 12-month target price of $60 values the stock at 30X our 2012 EPS estimate of $1.98, compared to a five-year historical P/E range of 17.6X-45.0X EPS.

## Dividend Data (Dates: mm/dd Payment Date: mm/dd/yy)

| Amount ($) | Date Decl. | Ex-Div. Date | Stk. of Record | Payment Date |
|---|---|---|---|---|
| 0.200 | 11/02 | 11/29 | 12/01 | 12/15/10 |
| 0.250 | 05/05 | 05/27 | 06/01 | 06/15/11 |
| 0.250 | 11/02 | 11/29 | 12/01 | 12/15/11 |

Dividends have been paid since 1993. Source: Company reports.

---

**Please read the Required Disclosures and Analyst Certification on the last page of this report.**

# Expeditors International of Washington Inc

STANDARD
&POOR'S

## Business Summary November 10, 2011

CORPORATE OVERVIEW. With an international network supporting the movement and strategic positioning of goods, Expeditors International of Washington is engaged in the business of providing global logistics services to customers diversified in terms of industry specialization and geographic location. In each of its U.S. offices, and in many international offices, the company acts as a customs broker, and also provides additional services, including distribution management, vendor consolidation, cargo insurance, purchase order management, and customized logistics information. EXPD does not compete for domestic freight, overnight courier, or small parcel business, and does not own aircraft or steamships. The company has historically pursued a strategy emphasizing organic growth supplemented by strategic acquisitions. As of February 2011, EXPD had a network of 184 full-service offices, 65 satellite locations, and two international service centers located on six continents.

Shipments of computer components, other electronic equipment, housewares, sporting goods, machine parts and toys comprise a significant percentage of the company's business. Import customers include computer retailers and distributors of consumer electronics, department store chains, clothing and shoe wholesalers. Historically, no single customer has accounted for over 5% of revenues.

Air freight services accounted for 47% of total revenues in 2010. EXPD typically acts either as a freight consolidator (purchasing cargo space on airlines and reselling it to customers at lower rates than the airline would charge customers directly), or as an agent for the airlines (receiving shipments from suppliers, and consolidating and forwarding them to the airlines). Shipments are usually characterized by a high value-to-weight ratio, a need for rapid delivery, or both. The company estimates that its average air freight consolidation weighs 3,500 lbs. to 4,500 lbs. Because shipping by air is relatively expensive compared with ocean transportation, air shipments are generally categorized by a high value-to-weight ratio, the need for rapid delivery, or both.

The company's strategy to not own aircraft is based on its view that the ownership of aircraft would subject EXPD to undue business risks, including large capital outlays, increased fixed operating costs, problems of fully utilizing aircraft and competition with airlines. EXPD relies on commercial aircraft to transport its shipments.

## Company Financials Fiscal Year Ended Dec. 31

| Per Share Data ($) | 2010 | 2009 | 2008 | 2007 | 2006 | 2005 | 2004 | 2003 | 2002 | 2001 |
|---|---|---|---|---|---|---|---|---|---|---|
| Tangible Book Value | 8.16 | 7.26 | 6.38 | 5.69 | 4.95 | 4.21 | 3.70 | 2.98 | 2.49 | 2.01 |
| Cash Flow | 1.76 | 1.30 | 1.56 | 1.39 | 1.27 | 1.12 | 0.82 | 0.67 | 0.62 | 0.55 |
| Earnings | 1.59 | 1.11 | 1.37 | 1.21 | 1.06 | 0.98 | 0.71 | 0.56 | 0.52 | 0.45 |
| S&P Core Earnings | 1.59 | 1.11 | 1.37 | 1.21 | 1.06 | 0.85 | 0.59 | 0.46 | 0.44 | 0.39 |
| Dividends | 0.40 | 0.38 | 0.32 | 0.28 | 0.22 | 0.15 | 0.11 | 0.08 | 0.06 | 0.04 |
| Payout Ratio | 25% | 34% | 23% | 23% | 21% | 15% | 16% | 14% | 12% | 10% |
| Prices:High | 57.15 | 38.10 | 49.92 | 54.46 | 58.32 | 36.37 | 29.20 | 20.42 | 17.22 | 16.48 |
| Prices:Low | 32.36 | 23.86 | 24.05 | 38.31 | 32.83 | 23.59 | 17.85 | 14.81 | 12.47 | 10.49 |
| P/E Ratio:High | 36 | 34 | 36 | 45 | 55 | 37 | 41 | 36 | 33 | 37 |
| P/E Ratio:Low | 20 | 21 | 18 | 32 | 31 | 24 | 25 | 26 | 24 | 24 |

| Income Statement Analysis (Million $) | | | | | | | | | | |
|---|---|---|---|---|---|---|---|---|---|---|
| Revenue | 5,968 | 4,092 | 5,634 | 5,235 | 4,626 | 3,902 | 3,318 | 2,625 | 2,297 | 1,653 |
| Operating Income | 584 | 427 | 515 | 463 | 411 | 337 | 268 | 211 | 194 | 170 |
| Depreciation | 36.9 | 40.0 | 41.6 | 40.0 | 35.4 | 32.3 | 26.7 | 24.4 | 22.7 | 23.5 |
| Interest Expense | 0.58 | 0.50 | 0.18 | Nil | 0.20 | 0.31 | 0.04 | 0.19 | 0.18 | 0.52 |
| Pretax Income | 564 | 403 | 500 | 450 | 396 | 320 | 250 | 196 | 178 | 154 |
| Effective Tax Rate | NA | 40.3% | 39.4% | 40.0% | 40.6% | 29.6% | 35.4% | 36.4% | 36.8% | 37.0% |
| Net Income | 344 | 240 | 301 | 269 | 235 | 219 | 156 | 122 | 113 | 97.2 |
| S&P Core Earnings | 344 | 240 | 301 | 269 | 235 | 187 | 130 | 98.4 | 92.7 | 83.8 |

| Balance Sheet & Other Financial Data (Million $) | | | | | | | | | | |
|---|---|---|---|---|---|---|---|---|---|---|
| Cash | 1,085 | 927 | 742 | 575 | 511 | 464 | 409 | 296 | 212 | 219 |
| Current Assets | 2,140 | 1,788 | 1,573 | 1,535 | 1,342 | 1,202 | 1,046 | 762 | 605 | 511 |
| Total Assets | 2,679 | 2,324 | 2,101 | 2,069 | 1,822 | 1,566 | 1,364 | 1,041 | 880 | 688 |
| Current Liabilities | 862 | 708 | 670 | 770 | 709 | 613 | 524 | 392 | 356 | 274 |
| Long Term Debt | NA | NA | Nil | Nil | Nil | Nil | Nil | Nil | Nil | Nil |
| Common Equity | 1,741 | 1,553 | 1,366 | 1,227 | 1,070 | 914 | 807 | 646 | 524 | 415 |
| Total Capital | 1,755 | 1,561 | 1,430 | 1,299 | 1,113 | 954 | 840 | 649 | 524 | 415 |
| Capital Expenditures | 42.4 | 34.7 | 59.7 | 82.8 | 141 | 90.8 | 66.2 | 20.7 | 81.4 | 37.4 |
| Cash Flow | 381 | 282 | 343 | 309 | 271 | 251 | 183 | 146 | 135 | 121 |
| Current Ratio | 2.5 | 2.5 | 2.4 | 2.0 | 1.9 | 2.0 | 2.0 | 1.9 | 1.7 | 1.9 |
| % Long Term Debt of Capitalization | Nil | Nil | Nil | Nil | Nil | Nil | Nil | Nil | Nil | Nil |
| % Net Income of Revenue | 5.8 | 5.9 | 5.3 | 5.1 | 5.1 | 5.6 | 4.7 | 4.6 | 4.9 | 5.9 |
| % Return on Assets | 13.8 | 10.9 | 14.4 | 13.8 | 13.9 | 14.9 | 13.0 | 12.7 | 14.3 | 14.4 |
| % Return on Equity | 20.9 | 16.5 | 23.2 | 23.4 | 23.6 | 25.4 | 21.5 | 20.9 | 24.0 | 25.0 |

Data as orig reptd.; bef. results of disc opers/spec. items. Per share data adj. for stk. divs.; EPS diluted. E-Estimated. NA-Not Available. NM-Not Meaningful. NR-Not Ranked. UR-Under Review.

**Office:** 1015 Third Avenue, 12th Floor, Seattle, WA 98104.
**Telephone:** 206-674-3400.
**Website:** http://www.expeditors.com
**Chrmn & CEO:** P.J. Rose

**Pres & COO:** R. Gates
**SVP & Cntlr:** C.J. Lynch
**CFO & Chief Acctg Officer:** B.S. Powell
**Secy & General Counsel:** A.J. Tangeman

**Investor Contact:** R.J. Gates (206-674-3400)
**Board Members:** M. A. Emmert, R. Gates, D. P. Kourkoumelis, M. J. Malone, J. W. Meisenbach, P. J. Rose, L. Wang, R. R. Wright

**Founded:** 1979
**Domicile:** Washington
**Employees:** 12,880

# Express Scripts Inc

**STANDARD &POOR'S**

| S&P Recommendation **STRONG BUY** ★★★★★ | Price $42.15 (as of Nov 25, 2011) | 12-Mo. Target Price $52.00 | Investment Style Large-Cap Growth |
|---|---|---|---|

**GICS Sector** Health Care
**Sub-Industry** Health Care Services

**Summary** This company offers prescription benefits and disease state management services.

## Key Stock Statistics (Source S&P, Vickers, company reports)

| | | | | | | | |
|---|---|---|---|---|---|---|---|
| 52-Wk Range | $60.89–34.47 | S&P Oper. EPS 2011**E** | 3.03 | Market Capitalization(B) | $20.506 | Beta | 0.98 |
| Trailing 12-Month EPS | $2.54 | S&P Oper. EPS 2012**E** | 3.70 | Yield (%) | Nil | S&P 3-Yr. Proj. EPS CAGR(%) | 18 |
| Trailing 12-Month P/E | 16.6 | P/E on S&P Oper. EPS 2011**E** | 13.9 | Dividend Rate/Share | Nil | S&P Credit Rating | BBB+ |
| $10K Invested 5 Yrs Ago | $25,160 | Common Shares Outstg. (M) | 486.5 | Institutional Ownership (%) | NM | | |

## Price Performance

30-Week Mov. Avg. ··· 10-Week Mov. Avg. – – **GAAP Earnings vs. Previous Year** **Volume** Above Avg. STARS
12-Mo. Target Price — Relative Strength — ▲ Up ▼ Down ► No Change Below Avg. ★

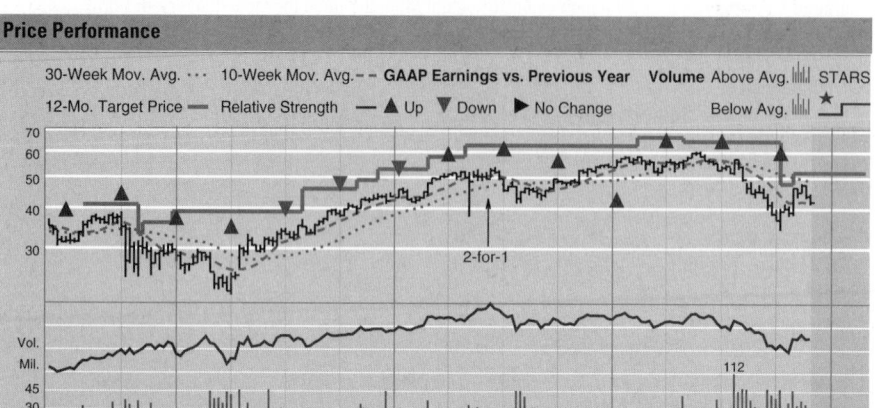

Options: ASE, CBOE, P

Analysis prepared by Equity Analyst **Herman Saftlas** on Nov 08, 2011, when the stock traded at **$48.12**.

## Highlights

➤ For ESRX alone (excluding the planned acquisition of Medco), we see 2012 revenues rising modestly from the $45.6 billion we estimate for 2011. Despite a challenging macro-economic environment, we see 2012 claims growing about 2% from the 740 million adjusted claims we forecast for 2011. Growth should reflect a 97%+ customer retention rate, and new client additions.

➤ We expect EBITDA per adjusted claim to exceed $4.15 in 2012, up from $3.72 in the third quarter of 2011. Key profit drivers, in our opinion, will include a new wave of generics resulting from major branded patent expirations, and a higher proportion of high-margin mail order prescriptions in the total mix. We see cash flow from operations exceeding the $2.3 billion indicated for 2011.

➤ After an effective tax rate in 2012 similar to the 37% that we forecast for 2011, we project non-GAAP EPS of $3.70 for 2012, up from the $3.03 that we estimate for 2011, before amortization and one-time items. We also expect per share profits to benefit from fewer shares outstanding.

## Investment Rationale/Risk

➤ In mid-July 2011, ESRX agreed to acquire rival PBM Medco (MHS 55, Hold) for a combination of cash and stock currently valued at about $26 billion. Terms call for ESRX to pay $28.80 in cash, plus 0.81 of a share of ESRX common stock, for each Medco share outstanding. MHS earned $1.4 billion on revenues of about $66 billion in 2010. We believe a merger with Medco could significantly enhance ESRX's market position, yield more than $1 billion in operating synergies, and enable ESRX to generate over $4 billion in cash flow. Despite antitrust concerns, we think the FTC is likely to approve the merger, with the deal likely to be completed in the first half of 2012.

➤ Risks to our recommendation and target price include failure to complete the Medco acquisition, and the possible loss of key clients.

➤ We derive our 12-month target price of $52 by applying a below-peers multiple of 14X to our $3.70 EPS estimate for 2012, which is near the low end of ESRX's recent P/E range. Our DCF model, which assumes a WACC of 10.4% and terminal growth of 1%, also indicates intrinsic value of $52.

## Qualitative Risk Assessment

| LOW | MEDIUM | HIGH |
|---|---|---|

Our risk assessment reflects our view of rising drug demand, and the company's improving financial performance and healthy operating cash flow. However, we believe intense competition and increased government regulation of pharmacy benefits managers (PBMs), which we view as likely, could result in changes in industry conditions.

## Quantitative Evaluations

**S&P Quality Ranking** A-

| D | C | B- | B | B+ | A- | A | A+ |
|---|---|---|---|---|---|---|---|

**Relative Strength Rank** MODERATE

56

LOWEST = 1 HIGHEST = 99

## Revenue/Earnings Data

**Revenue (Million $)**

| | 1Q | 2Q | 3Q | 4Q | Year |
|---|---|---|---|---|---|
| 2011 | 11,095 | 11,361 | 11,571 | -- | -- |
| 2010 | 11,138 | 11,289 | 11,252 | 11,294 | 44,973 |
| 2009 | 5,423 | 5,503 | 5,619 | 8,203 | 24,749 |
| 2008 | 5,491 | 5,530 | 5,451 | 5,506 | 21,978 |
| 2007 | 4,540 | 4,600 | 4,519 | 4,694 | 18,274 |
| 2006 | 4,380 | 4,421 | 4,330 | 4,529 | 17,660 |

**Earnings Per Share ($)**

| | | | | | |
|---|---|---|---|---|---|
| 2011 | 0.61 | 0.66 | 0.66 | E0.87 | E3.03 |
| 2010 | 0.47 | 0.56 | 0.57 | 0.62 | 2.21 |
| 2009 | 0.43 | 0.37 | 0.36 | 0.40 | 1.56 |
| 2008 | 0.35 | 0.38 | 0.41 | 0.42 | 1.55 |
| 2007 | 0.24 | 0.29 | 0.28 | 0.33 | 1.14 |
| 2006 | 0.18 | 0.19 | 0.21 | 0.27 | 0.84 |

Fiscal year ended Dec. 31. Next earnings report expected: Mid February. EPS Estimates based on S&P Operating Earnings; historical GAAP earnings are as reported.

## Dividend Data

No cash dividends have been paid.

# Express Scripts Inc

STANDARD
&POOR'S

## Business Summary November 08, 2011

CORPORATE OVERVIEW. Express Scripts is one of the largest U.S. pharmacy benefits managers (PBMs). Its PBM services (97% of 2010 revenue, versus 95% in 2009) include retail network pharmacy management, home delivery services, specialty pharmacy services patient care contact centers, benefit plan design and consultation, drug formulary management, compliance and therapy management programs, and various other programs.

Clients include health insurers, third-party administrators, employers, union-sponsored benefit plans, government health programs, office-based oncologists, renal dialysis clinics, ambulatory surgery centers, primary care physicians and others. In November 2009, it implemented a new contract with the U.S. Dept. of Defense (DoD). While it has provided services to the DoD since 2003, this new contract combines the pharmacy network services, home delivery, and specialty pharmacy, as well as additional services.

Through its Emerging Markets Services (EM) segment, it provides services including distribution of pharmaceuticals and medical supplies to providers and clinics, distribution of fertility pharmaceuticals requiring special handling or packaging, distribution of sample units to physicians, verification of practitioner licensure, healthcare account administration, and implementation of consumer-directed health care solutions. During 2010, 3% of ESRX's revenue was derived from EM services, compared to 5% during 2009.

Revenues are generated primarily from the delivery of prescription drugs through 60,000 contracted retail pharmacies, three home delivery fulfillment pharmacies, and eight specialty drug pharmacies, as of December 31, 2010. Revenues from the delivery of prescription drugs to members represented 98.9% of revenues in 2010, versus 98.8% in 2009. Revenues from services, such as the administration of some clients' retail pharmacy networks, medication counseling services, specialty distribution services, and sample fulfillment and sample accountability services comprised the remainder.

The five largest clients accounted for 55% of revenues in 2010, compared to 24% in 2009. Two clients -- WellPoint and the Department of Defense -- accounted for 29% of 2010 revenues. ESRX processed 602 million network pharmacy claims and 54.1 million home delivery and specialty pharmacy claims in 2010, versus 404.3 million and 41 million, respectively, in 2009.

## Company Financials Fiscal Year Ended Dec. 31

| Per Share Data ($) | 2010 | 2009 | 2008 | 2007 | 2006 | 2005 | 2004 | 2003 | 2002 | 2001 |
|---|---|---|---|---|---|---|---|---|---|---|
| Tangible Book Value | NM | NM | NM | NM | NM | NM | NM | NM | NM | NM |
| Cash Flow | 2.62 | 1.72 | 1.74 | 1.32 | 1.01 | 0.81 | 0.56 | 0.48 | 0.45 | 0.32 |
| Earnings | 2.21 | 1.56 | 1.55 | 1.14 | 0.84 | 0.67 | 0.45 | 0.40 | 0.32 | 0.20 |
| S&P Core Earnings | 2.21 | 1.57 | 1.56 | 1.12 | 0.84 | 0.65 | 0.43 | 0.38 | 0.30 | 0.18 |
| Dividends | Nil | Nil | Nil | Nil | Nil | Nil | Nil | Nil | Nil | Nil |
| Payout Ratio | Nil | Nil | Nil | Nil | Nil | Nil | Nil | Nil | Nil | Nil |
| Prices:High | 55.68 | 44.94 | 39.55 | 37.20 | 23.75 | 22.70 | 10.15 | 9.43 | 8.24 | 7.68 |
| Prices:Low | 37.75 | 21.38 | 24.19 | 16.16 | 14.70 | 9.13 | 7.29 | 5.79 | 4.83 | 4.36 |
| P/E Ratio:High | 25 | 29 | 26 | 33 | 28 | 34 | 23 | 24 | 26 | 39 |
| P/E Ratio:Low | 17 | 14 | 16 | 14 | 18 | 14 | 16 | 15 | 15 | 22 |

| Income Statement Analysis (Million $) | 2010 | 2009 | 2008 | 2007 | 2006 | 2005 | 2004 | 2003 | 2002 | 2001 |
|---|---|---|---|---|---|---|---|---|---|---|
| Revenue | 44,973 | 24,749 | 21,978 | 18,274 | 17,660 | 16,266 | 15,115 | 13,295 | 12,261 | 9,329 |
| Operating Income | 2,415 | 1,668 | 1,390 | 1,177 | 925 | 727 | 563 | 503 | 454 | 317 |
| Depreciation | 222 | 110 | 97.7 | 97.5 | 101 | 84.0 | 70.0 | 54.0 | 82.0 | 80.1 |
| Interest Expense | 167 | 194 | 77.6 | 108 | 95.7 | 37.0 | 41.7 | 41.4 | 42.2 | 34.2 |
| Pretax Income | 1,909 | 1,309 | 1,214 | 945 | 740 | 615 | 451 | 405 | 330 | 208 |
| Effective Tax Rate | NA | 36.9% | 35.8% | 36.5% | 35.9% | 35.0% | 38.3% | 38.2% | 38.2% | 39.9% |
| Net Income | 1,205 | 826 | 780 | 600 | 474 | 400 | 278 | 251 | 204 | 125 |
| S&P Core Earnings | 1,204 | 837 | 784 | 592 | 474 | 389 | 270 | 239 | 192 | 115 |

| Balance Sheet & Other Financial Data (Million $) | 2010 | 2009 | 2008 | 2007 | 2006 | 2005 | 2004 | 2003 | 2002 | 2001 |
|---|---|---|---|---|---|---|---|---|---|---|
| Cash | 524 | 1,070 | 539 | 437 | 131 | 478 | 166 | 396 | 191 | 178 |
| Current Assets | 2,941 | 4,144 | 2,044 | 1,968 | 1,772 | 2,257 | 1,443 | 1,560 | 1,394 | 1,213 |
| Total Assets | 10,558 | 11,931 | 5,509 | 5,256 | 5,108 | 5,493 | 3,600 | 3,409 | 3,207 | 2,500 |
| Current Liabilities | 3,917 | 5,457 | 2,722 | 2,475 | 2,429 | 2,394 | 1,813 | 1,626 | 1,544 | 1,246 |
| Long Term Debt | 2,494 | 2,493 | 1,340 | 1,760 | 1,270 | 1,401 | 412 | 455 | 563 | 346 |
| Common Equity | 3,607 | 3,552 | 1,078 | 696 | 1,125 | 1,465 | 1,196 | 1,194 | 1,003 | 832 |
| Total Capital | 6,100 | 7,384 | 2,732 | 2,735 | 2,395 | 2,866 | 1,608 | 1,649 | 1,565 | 1,178 |
| Capital Expenditures | 120 | 149 | 85.8 | 75.0 | 66.8 | 60.0 | 51.5 | 53.1 | 61.3 | 57.3 |
| Cash Flow | 1,426 | 914 | 877 | 698 | 575 | 484 | 348 | 305 | 286 | 205 |
| Current Ratio | 0.8 | 0.8 | 0.8 | 0.8 | 0.7 | 0.9 | 0.8 | 1.0 | 0.9 | 1.0 |
| % Long Term Debt of Capitalization | 40.9 | 33.8 | 49.1 | 64.4 | 53.0 | 48.9 | 25.6 | 27.6 | 35.9 | 29.4 |
| % Net Income of Revenue | 2.7 | 3.3 | 3.6 | 3.3 | 2.7 | 2.5 | 1.8 | 1.9 | 1.7 | 1.3 |
| % Return on Assets | 10.7 | 9.5 | 14.5 | 11.6 | 8.9 | 8.8 | 7.9 | 7.6 | 7.1 | 5.2 |
| % Return on Equity | 33.7 | 35.7 | 87.9 | 65.9 | 36.6 | 30.1 | 23.3 | 22.8 | 22.2 | 16.3 |

Data as orig reptd.; bef. results of disc opers/spec. items. Per share data adj. for stk. divs.; EPS diluted. E-Estimated. NA-Not Available. NM-Not Meaningful. NR-Not Ranked. UR-Under Review.

**Office:** One Express Way, St. Louis, MO 63121.
**Telephone:** 314-996-0900.
**Email:** investor.relations@express-scripts.com
**Website:** http://www.express-scripts.com

**Chrmn, Pres & CEO:** G. Paz
**COO & EVP:** P. McNamee
**EVP & CFO:** J.L. Hall
**EVP, Secy & General Counsel:** K.J. Ebling

**SVP & CIO:** G. Wimberly
**Investor Contact:** D. Myers (314-810-3115)
**Board Members:** G. G. Benanav, M. Breen, W. J. DeLaney, III, N. J. LaHowchic, T. P. Mac Mahon, F. Mergenthaler, W. A. Myers, Jr., J. O. Parker, Jr., G. Paz, S. K. Skinner, S. Sternberg

**Founded:** 1986
**Domicile:** Delaware
**Employees:** 13,170

# Exxon Mobil Corp

## STANDARD &POOR'S

| S&P Recommendation | STRONG BUY ★★★★★ | Price $73.90 (as of Nov 25, 2011) | 12-Mo. Target Price $103.00 | Investment Style Large-Cap Blend |
|---|---|---|---|---|

**GICS Sector** Energy
**Sub-Industry** Integrated Oil & Gas

**Summary** XOM, formed through the merger of Exxon and Mobil in late 1999, is the world's largest publicly owned integrated oil company.

## Key Stock Statistics (Source S&P, Vickers, company reports)

| | | | | | | | |
|---|---|---|---|---|---|---|---|
| 52-Wk Range | $88.23– 67.03 | S&P Oper. EPS 2011E | 8.55 | Market Capitalization(B) | $354.218 | Beta | 0.51 |
| Trailing 12-Month EPS | $8.28 | S&P Oper. EPS 2012E | 8.55 | Yield (%) | 2.54 | S&P 3-Yr. Proj. EPS CAGR(%) | 29 |
| Trailing 12-Month P/E | 8.9 | P/E on S&P Oper. EPS 2011E | 8.6 | Dividend Rate/Share | $1.88 | S&P Credit Rating | AAA |
| $10K Invested 5 Yrs Ago | $11,393 | Common Shares Outstg. (M) | 4,793.2 | Institutional Ownership (%) | 49 | | |

## Price Performance

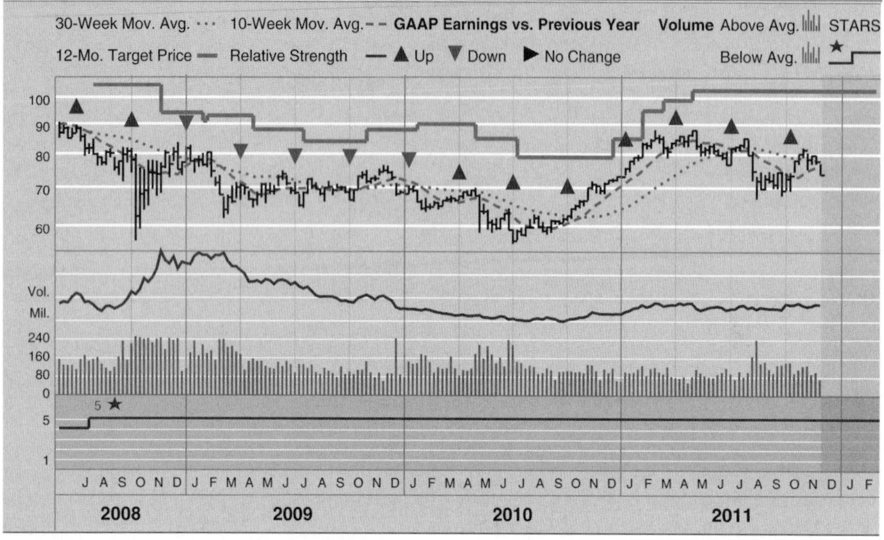

30-Week Mov. Avg. ···· 10-Week Mov. Avg. -- GAAP Earnings vs. Previous Year   Volume Above Avg. � STARS
12-Mo. Target Price — Relative Strength — ▲ Up ▼ Down ► No Change   Below Avg. III ★

Options: ASE, CBOE, P, Ph

Analysis prepared by Equity Analyst **Michael Kay** on Aug 18, 2011, when the stock traded at **$70.83**.

## Highlights

➤ Second quarter production of 4.4 MMboe/day was up 10% annually, driven by XTO, Qatar and Iraq project rampups, but was down 9% sequentially as OPEC quotas and production sharing negatively affected volumes. The start-up of 11 major projects through 2013 in Qatar, the U.S., the U.K., Canada, Australia, Russia, Angola and Nigeria should boost output by 600,000 boe/day (80% oil). XOM sees production growth of 3%-4% in 2011 and 4%-5% a year through 2014. As of July, XOM was running 65-70 rigs in U.S. unconventional plays. Only about 6% of output is from the Gulf of Mexico, where drilling remains delayed. XOM believes it is developing 26 Bboe, with heavy oil sands, LNG and unconventional projects representing 57%.

➤ We see refining and chemical conditions pressured as new capacity affects global supply/demand balances, although U.S. and Asia refining margins recently widened. XOM's history of rationalizing refinery units has provided a top-tier cost structure.

➤ On higher prices and volumes, we see EPS of $8.75 in 2011 and $9.70 in 2012. XOM sees $5 billion per quarter in stock repurchases and capex of $33-$37 billion through 2015.

## Investment Rationale/Risk

➤ XOM has enjoyed superior earnings and dividend growth and stability (as evidenced by its S&P Quality Ranking of A+). We believe it will benefit from "big-pocket" upstream growth opportunities in the deepwater, LNG, onshore unconventional, and ventures with state-owned companies. We think XOM's advanced technology permits project development in a timely and cost-efficient manner. In addition, we see its upstream business benefiting from a strong pipeline of long-lived assets (2010 reserve replacement of 211%) with an improving decline rate of 3%, and the downstream unit should benefit over the long term from its complex refineries, which offer feedstock and product flexibility. We see further expansion of activities in global LNG and frontier regions.

➤ Risks to our recommendation and target price include deterioration in economic, industry and operating conditions, such as difficulty replacing reserves and increased production costs.

➤ On our DCF ($102; WACC 5.9%, terminal growth 3%) and relative valuations, including a target enterprise value of 6X our 2011 EBITDA estimate, a premium to the supermajor oil peer average of 4.4X, our 12-month target price is $103.

## Qualitative Risk Assessment

| LOW | MEDIUM | HIGH |
|---|---|---|

Our risk assessment reflects our view of the company's diversified and strong business profile in volatile, cyclical and capital-intensive segments of the energy industry. We consider ExxonMobil's earnings stability and corporate governance practices to be above average.

## Quantitative Evaluations

**S&P Quality Ranking**          A+

| D | C | B- | B | B+ | A- | A | A+ |
|---|---|---|---|---|---|---|---|

**Relative Strength Rank**          MODERATE

60

LOWEST = 1          HIGHEST = 99

## Revenue/Earnings Data

**Revenue (Million $)**

| | 1Q | 2Q | 3Q | 4Q | Year |
|---|---|---|---|---|---|
| 2011 | 114,000 | 125,486 | 125,330 | -- | -- |
| 2010 | 90,250 | 92,490 | 95,300 | 105,190 | 383,221 |
| 2009 | 64,028 | 74,457 | 82,260 | 89,841 | 310,586 |
| 2008 | 116,854 | 138,072 | 137,737 | 84,696 | 477,359 |
| 2007 | 87,223 | 98,350 | 102,337 | 116,642 | 404,552 |
| 2006 | 86,317 | 96,024 | 96,268 | 86,858 | 377,635 |

**Earnings Per Share ($)**

| | | | | | |
|---|---|---|---|---|---|
| 2011 | 2.14 | 2.18 | 2.13 | E2.10 | E8.55 |
| 2010 | 1.33 | 1.60 | 1.44 | 1.85 | 6.22 |
| 2009 | 0.92 | 0.81 | 0.98 | 1.27 | 3.98 |
| 2008 | 2.03 | 2.22 | 2.86 | 1.55 | 8.69 |
| 2007 | 1.62 | 1.83 | 1.70 | 2.14 | 7.28 |
| 2006 | 1.37 | 1.72 | 1.77 | 1.76 | 6.62 |

Fiscal year ended Dec. 31. Next earnings report expected: Early February. EPS Estimates based on S&P Operating Earnings; historical GAAP earnings are as reported.

## Dividend Data (Dates: mm/dd Payment Date: mm/dd/yy)

| Amount ($) | Date Decl. | Ex-Div. Date | Stk. of Record | Payment Date |
|---|---|---|---|---|
| 0.440 | 01/26 | 02/08 | 02/10 | 03/10/11 |
| 0.470 | 04/27 | 05/11 | 05/13 | 06/10/11 |
| 0.470 | 07/27 | 08/10 | 08/12 | 09/09/11 |
| 0.470 | 10/26 | 11/08 | 11/10 | 12/09/11 |

Dividends have been paid since 1882. Source: Company reports.

**Please read the Required Disclosures and Analyst Certification on the last page of this report.**

The McGraw·Hill Companies

# Exxon Mobil Corp

**STANDARD**
**&POOR'S**

## Business Summary August 18, 2011

CORPORATE OVERVIEW. In late 1999, the FTC allowed Exxon and Mobil to re-unite, creating Exxon Mobil Corp. ExxonMobil's businesses include oil and natural gas exploration and production (74% of 2010 segment earnings); refining and marketing (11%); chemicals (15%); and other operations, such as electric power generation, coal and minerals.

Including non-consolidated equity interest, proved oil and gas reserves grew 8% in 2010, to 24.8 billion barrels of oil equivalent (boe; 47% petroleum liquids, including oil sands; 69% developed) in 2010. Oil and gas production rose 13%, to 4.45 million boe/day (54% petroleum liquids), in 2010. Rising production and reserves primarily reflected the completion of the XTO Energy acquisition. Using data from John S. Herold, we estimate XOM's three-year (2006-2008) reserve replacement at 128%, above the peer average; three-year finding and development cost at $8.68 per boe, below the peer average; proved acquisition costs at $0.44 per boe, below the peer average; and its reserve replacement costs at $7.63 per boe, below the peer average.

At year-end 2010, the company had an ownership interest in 36 refineries with 6.26 million barrels per day (b/d) of atmospheric distillation capacity (U.S. 31%, Europe 28%, Asia Pacific 27%, Canada 8%, and Middle East/Latin America/Other 6%).

MANAGEMENT. We believe XOM is one of the best managed companies in the energy sector. In January 2006, Lee R. Raymond retired, and Rex W. Tillerson became chairman and CEO. We expect Mr. Tillerson to benefit from the strategic plans made by Mr. Raymond, and we see Mr. Tillerson's diplomatic skills as playing an important role in enhancing those plans.

## Company Financials Fiscal Year Ended Dec. 31

| Per Share Data ($) | 2010 | 2009 | 2008 | 2007 | 2006 | 2005 | 2004 | 2003 | 2002 | 2001 |
|---|---|---|---|---|---|---|---|---|---|---|
| Tangible Book Value | 29.49 | 23.39 | 22.70 | 22.62 | 19.87 | 18.13 | 15.90 | 13.69 | 11.13 | 10.74 |
| Cash Flow | 9.43 | 6.44 | 11.08 | 9.48 | 8.89 | 7.34 | 5.38 | 4.50 | 2.84 | 3.32 |
| Earnings | 6.22 | 3.98 | 8.69 | 7.28 | 6.62 | 5.71 | 3.89 | 3.15 | 1.61 | 2.18 |
| S&P Core Earnings | 6.48 | 4.36 | 8.64 | 7.40 | 6.75 | 5.72 | 4.01 | 3.03 | 1.52 | 2.03 |
| Dividends | 1.74 | 1.66 | 1.55 | 1.37 | 1.28 | 1.14 | 1.06 | 0.98 | 0.92 | 0.91 |
| Payout Ratio | 28% | 42% | 18% | 19% | 19% | 20% | 27% | 31% | 57% | 42% |
| Prices:High | 73.69 | 82.73 | 96.12 | 95.27 | 79.00 | 65.96 | 52.05 | 41.13 | 44.58 | 45.84 |
| Prices:Low | 55.94 | 61.86 | 56.51 | 69.02 | 56.42 | 49.25 | 39.91 | 31.58 | 29.75 | 35.01 |
| P/E Ratio:High | 12 | 21 | 11 | 13 | 12 | 12 | 13 | 13 | 28 | 21 |
| P/E Ratio:Low | 9 | 16 | 7 | 9 | 9 | 9 | 10 | 10 | 18 | 16 |

| Income Statement Analysis (Million $) | 2010 | 2009 | 2008 | 2007 | 2006 | 2005 | 2004 | 2003 | 2002 | 2001 |
|---|---|---|---|---|---|---|---|---|---|---|
| Revenue | 383,221 | 310,586 | 477,359 | 404,552 | 377,635 | 370,680 | 298,035 | 246,738 | 204,506 | 213,488 |
| Operating Income | NA | NA | 78,669 | 156,810 | 150,107 | 59,255 | 45,639 | 32,230 | 23,280 | 29,602 |
| Depreciation, Depletion and Amortization | 14,760 | 11,917 | 12,379 | 12,250 | 11,416 | 10,253 | 9,767 | 9,047 | 8,310 | 7,944 |
| Interest Expense | 259 | 548 | 673 | 957 | 654 | 496 | 638 | 207 | 398 | 293 |
| Pretax Income | 52,959 | 34,777 | 81,750 | 71,479 | 68,453 | 60,231 | 42,017 | 32,660 | 17,719 | 24,688 |
| Effective Tax Rate | NA | 43.5% | 44.7% | 41.8% | 40.8% | 38.7% | 37.9% | 33.7% | 36.7% | 36.5% |
| Net Income | 30,460 | 19,280 | 45,220 | 40,610 | 39,500 | 36,130 | 25,330 | 20,960 | 11,011 | 15,105 |
| S&P Core Earnings | 31,732 | 21,109 | 44,959 | 41,250 | 40,263 | 36,164 | 26,089 | 20,214 | 10,418 | 14,042 |

| Balance Sheet & Other Financial Data (Million $) | 2010 | 2009 | 2008 | 2007 | 2006 | 2005 | 2004 | 2003 | 2002 | 2001 |
|---|---|---|---|---|---|---|---|---|---|---|
| Cash | 7,827 | 10,862 | 32,007 | 34,500 | 32,848 | 28,671 | 18,531 | 10,626 | 7,229 | 6,547 |
| Current Assets | 58,984 | 55,235 | 72,266 | 85,963 | 75,777 | 73,342 | 60,377 | 45,960 | 38,291 | 35,681 |
| Total Assets | 302,510 | 233,323 | 228,052 | 242,082 | 219,015 | 208,335 | 195,256 | 174,278 | 152,644 | 143,174 |
| Current Liabilities | 62,633 | 52,061 | 49,100 | 58,312 | 48,817 | 46,307 | 42,981 | 38,386 | 33,175 | 30,114 |
| Long Term Debt | 11,923 | 6,761 | 7,025 | 7,183 | 6,645 | 6,220 | 5,013 | 4,756 | 6,655 | 7,099 |
| Common Equity | 146,839 | 110,569 | 112,965 | 121,762 | 113,844 | 111,186 | 101,756 | 89,915 | 74,597 | 73,161 |
| Total Capital | 170,787 | 123,037 | 144,274 | 156,126 | 141,340 | 138,284 | 131,813 | 118,171 | 100,504 | 99,444 |
| Capital Expenditures | 26,871 | 22,491 | 19,318 | 15,387 | 15,462 | 13,839 | 11,986 | 12,859 | 11,437 | 9,989 |
| Cash Flow | 46,158 | 31,197 | 57,599 | 52,860 | 50,916 | 46,383 | 35,097 | 30,007 | 19,321 | 23,049 |
| Current Ratio | 0.9 | 1.1 | 1.5 | 1.5 | 1.6 | 1.6 | 1.4 | 1.2 | 1.2 | 1.2 |
| % Long Term Debt of Capitalization | 7.0 | Nil | 4.9 | 4.6 | 4.7 | 4.4 | 3.8 | 4.0 | 6.6 | 7.1 |
| % Return on Assets | NA | 8.4 | 19.2 | 17.6 | 18.5 | 17.9 | 13.7 | 12.8 | 7.4 | 10.3 |
| % Return on Equity | NA | NA | 38.5 | 34.5 | 35.1 | 33.9 | 26.4 | 25.5 | 14.9 | 21.0 |

Data as orig reptd.; bef. results of disc opers/spec. items. Per share data adj. for stk. divs.; EPS diluted. E-Estimated. NA-Not Available. NM-Not Meaningful. NR-Not Ranked. UR-Under Review.

**Office:** 5959 Las Colinas Boulevard, Irving, TX 75039-2298.
**Telephone:** 972-444-1000.
**Website:** http://www.exxonmobil.com
**Chrmn, Pres & CEO:** R.W. Tillerson

**CFO:** D. Humphreys
**Chief Acctg Officer & Cntlr:** P.T. Mulva
**Treas:** R.N. Schleckser
**Secy:** D.S. Rosenthal

**Board Members:** M. J. Boskin, P. Brabeck-Letmathe, L. R. Faulkner, J. S. Fishman, K. C. Frazier, W. W. George, M. C. Nelson, S. J. Palmisano, S. S. Reinemund, R. W. Tillerson, E. E. Whitacre, Jr.

**Founded:** 1870
**Domicile:** New Jersey
**Employees:** 83,600

# Family Dollar Stores Inc.

STANDARD
&POOR'S

| | | | | |
|---|---|---|---|---|
| **S&P Recommendation** HOLD ★★★☆☆ | | **Price** $55.80 (as of Nov 25, 2011) | **12-Mo. Target Price** $58.00 | **Investment Style** Large-Cap Blend |

**GICS Sector** Consumer Discretionary
**Sub-Industry** General Merchandise Stores

**Summary** This company operates a chain of over 7,000 retail discount stores in 44 states across the U.S.

## Key Stock Statistics (Source S&P, Vickers, company reports)

| | | | | | | | |
|---|---|---|---|---|---|---|---|
| 52-Wk Range | $60.53–41.31 | S&P Oper. EPS 2012**E** | 3.74 | Market Capitalization(B) | $6.550 | Beta | 0.22 |
| Trailing 12-Month EPS | $3.12 | S&P Oper. EPS 2013**E** | NA | Yield (%) | 1.29 | S&P 3-Yr. Proj. EPS CAGR(%) | 17 |
| Trailing 12-Month P/E | 17.9 | P/E on S&P Oper. EPS 2012**E** | 14.9 | Dividend Rate/Share | $0.72 | S&P Credit Rating | BBB- |
| $10K Invested 5 Yrs Ago | $21,419 | Common Shares Outstg. (M) | 117.4 | Institutional Ownership (%) | 90 | | |

## Price Performance

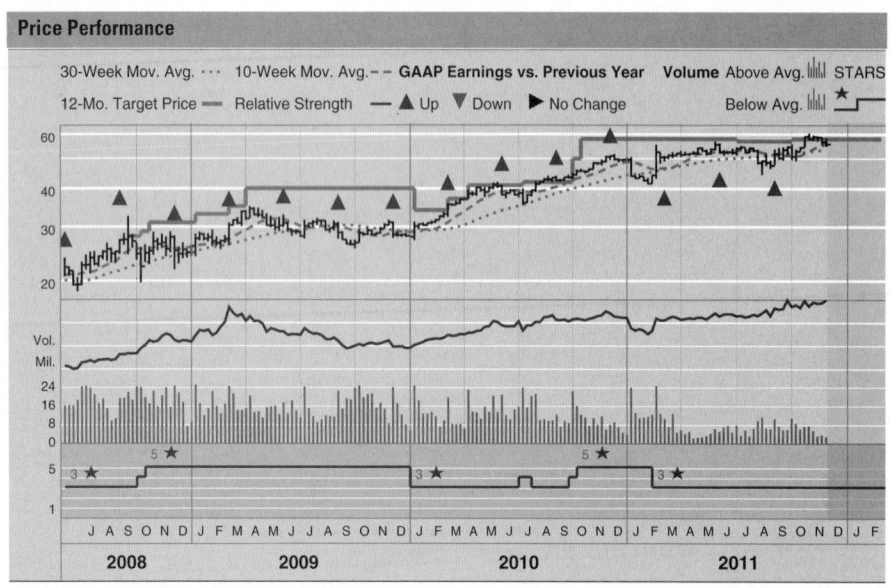

30-Week Mov. Avg. · · · 10-Week Mov. Avg. - - **GAAP Earnings vs. Previous Year** Volume Above Avg. STARS
12-Mo. Target Price — Relative Strength — ▲ Up ▼ Down ▶ No Change Below Avg.

Options: ASE, CBOE, P, Ph

Analysis prepared by Equity Analyst **Joseph Agnese** on Oct 07, 2011, when the stock traded at **$52.17**.

## Highlights

➤ We expect net sales to increase 9.9%, to $9.40 billion, in FY 12 (Aug.), from $8.55 billion in FY 11. We look for growth to be driven by mid-single digit same-store sales increases, as well as an accelerated pace of expansion and an aggressive store remodel program. We see FDO attracting cost-conscious consumers with its value-priced assortment of everyday necessities, and planned improvements in the quality and packaging of private-label consumables.

➤ We expect sales to be weighted toward lower-margin consumables and foresee higher freight costs and incremental expenses in support of new stores, store renovations, and longer store operating hours. However, we project modest operating margin expansion on lower markdowns and shrinkage, reflecting effective inventory management, increased penetration of private-label goods, higher initial mark-ups through global sourcing, and expense leverage off of projected same-store sales growth.

➤ Factoring in higher interest expense for debt-funded share buybacks, we see EPS of $3.74 in FY 12, up 20% from $3.12 in FY 11.

## Investment Rationale/Risk

➤ We view the shares as appropriately valued at recent levels. With lower-income households curbing spending due to financial constraints, we see FDO's core customers shopping close to need over the near term. However, we believe the company is well positioned to drive increases in both customer traffic and average customer transaction value with its growing food assortment and new easier-to-shop store layout. Longer term, we look for FDO to focus on tailoring product assortments by store to drive higher sales productivity. We also view the company's finances and balance sheet as healthy, and expect FDO to generate free cash that it could use for expansion and store renovations, dividends and/or share repurchases.

➤ Risks to our recommendation and target price include sales shortfalls due to changes in customer spending patterns, merchandise availability and/or aggressive pricing by competitors.

➤ Our 12-month target price of $58 reflects a multiple of about 18X, the average of FDO's 10-year historical multiple range, applied to our calendar 2011 EPS estimate of $3.24.

## Qualitative Risk Assessment

| LOW | MEDIUM | HIGH |
|---|---|---|

Our risk assessment reflects FDO's top S&P Quality Ranking of A+ for growth and stability of earnings and dividends, and our view of a healthy balance sheet and strong cash flow generation. We also believe demand for the company's merchandise is generally stable and not affected by changes in the economy, except for more discretionary categories.

## Quantitative Evaluations

**S&P Quality Ranking** A+

| D | C | B- | B | B+ | A- | A | A+ |
|---|---|---|---|---|---|---|---|

**Relative Strength Rank** STRONG

81

LOWEST = 1          HIGHEST = 99

## Revenue/Earnings Data

**Revenue (Million $)**

| | 1Q | 2Q | 3Q | 4Q | Year |
|---|---|---|---|---|---|
| 2011 | 1,997 | 2,263 | 2,153 | 2,134 | 8,548 |
| 2010 | 1,823 | 2,090 | 1,997 | 1,957 | 7,867 |
| 2009 | 1,754 | 1,992 | 1,843 | 1,811 | 7,401 |
| 2008 | 1,683 | 1,833 | 1,702 | 1,766 | 6,984 |
| 2007 | 1,600 | 1,947 | 1,655 | 1,632 | 6,834 |
| 2006 | 1,511 | 1,736 | 1,570 | 1,578 | 6,395 |

**Earnings Per Share ($)**

| | | | | | |
|---|---|---|---|---|---|
| 2011 | 0.58 | 0.98 | 0.91 | 0.66 | 3.12 |
| 2010 | 0.49 | 0.81 | 0.77 | 0.56 | 2.62 |
| 2009 | 0.42 | 0.60 | 0.62 | 0.43 | 2.07 |
| 2008 | 0.37 | 0.45 | 0.46 | 0.38 | 1.66 |
| 2007 | 0.36 | 0.60 | 0.40 | 0.26 | 1.62 |
| 2006 | 0.32 | 0.35 | 0.37 | 0.21 | 1.26 |

Fiscal year ended Aug. 31. Next earnings report expected: Early January. EPS Estimates based on S&P Operating Earnings; historical GAAP earnings are as reported.

## Dividend Data (Dates: mm/dd Payment Date: mm/dd/yy)

| Amount ($) | Date Decl. | Ex-Div. Date | Stk. of Record | Payment Date |
|---|---|---|---|---|
| 0.180 | 01/20 | 03/11 | 03/15 | 04/15/11 |
| 0.180 | 05/11 | 06/13 | 06/15 | 07/15/11 |
| 0.180 | 08/12 | 09/13 | 09/15 | 10/14/11 |
| 0.180 | 11/15 | 12/13 | 12/15 | 01/13/12 |

Dividends have been paid since 1976. Source: Company reports.

# Family Dollar Stores Inc.

STANDARD
&POOR'S

## Business Summary October 07, 2011

CORPORATE OVERVIEW. Family Dollar Stores Inc. (FDO) operates a chain of over 7,000 retail discount stores in 44 states. The company describes its typical customer as a woman in her mid-40s who is the head of her household and has an annual income of under $30,000. Family Dollar stores carry an assortment of hardlines and softlines priced from under $1 to $10 and are operated on a self-service basis, with limited advertising support and promotional activity. The once cash-only stores now accept PIN-based debit card payments in most locations. Food stamp and credit card acceptance is also being rolled out. In our view, broader tender options offer the company an opportunity to improve its share of customer wallet as shopping is more convenient and available cash does not limit basket size.

Store inventory is comprised of both regularly available merchandise, which provides consistency in product offerings, and a frequently changing selection of brands and products that FDO acquires through closeouts and manufacturer overruns at discounted wholesale prices. Low product costs and store overhead enable the company to sell its value-priced merchandise profitably.

PRIMARY BUSINESS DYNAMICS. FDO's primary growth drivers are same-store sales and chain expansion. In FY 10 (Aug.), same-store sales rose 4.8%, reflecting flat average customer transaction value and higher customer traffic, as measured by the company in number of register transactions. In our opinion, FDO is attracting customers with an expanded assortment of consumables and "treasure hunt" items that add an element of excitement and interest to the shopping experience. The company has also increased its marketing efforts to emphasize the value and shopping convenience it offers.

While core customers are spending more per store visit, they are also shopping less often due to macroeconomic concerns. However, we think FDO is gaining incremental business from middle-income customers trading down from higher-priced retailers for everyday basics.

## Company Financials Fiscal Year Ended Aug. 31

| Per Share Data ($) | 2011 | 2010 | 2009 | 2008 | 2007 | 2006 | 2005 | 2004 | 2003 | 2002 |
|---|---|---|---|---|---|---|---|---|---|---|
| Tangible Book Value | 9.26 | 10.90 | 10.38 | 8.98 | 8.19 | 8.04 | 8.64 | 8.13 | 7.61 | 6.66 |
| Cash Flow | 4.59 | 3.88 | 3.21 | 2.72 | 2.59 | 2.13 | 1.99 | 2.10 | 1.94 | 1.69 |
| Earnings | 3.12 | 2.62 | 2.07 | 1.66 | 1.62 | 1.26 | 1.30 | 1.53 | 1.43 | 1.25 |
| S&P Core Earnings | 3.12 | 2.55 | 2.07 | 1.66 | 1.71 | 1.44 | 1.21 | 1.45 | 1.39 | 1.22 |
| Dividends | 0.67 | 0.58 | 0.52 | 0.48 | 0.44 | 0.40 | 0.36 | 0.32 | 0.28 | 0.25 |
| Payout Ratio | 21% | 22% | 25% | 29% | 27% | 31% | 28% | 21% | 20% | 20% |
| Prices:High | 60.53 | 51.81 | 35.00 | 32.50 | 35.42 | 30.91 | 35.25 | 39.66 | 44.13 | 37.25 |
| Prices:Low | 41.31 | 27.15 | 24.02 | 14.62 | 17.95 | 21.57 | 19.40 | 25.09 | 25.46 | 23.75 |
| P/E Ratio:High | 19 | 20 | 17 | 20 | 22 | 24 | 27 | 26 | 31 | 30 |
| P/E Ratio:Low | 13 | 10 | 12 | 9 | 11 | 17 | 15 | 16 | 18 | 19 |

| Income Statement Analysis (Million $) | | | | | | | | | | |
|---|---|---|---|---|---|---|---|---|---|---|
| Revenue | 8,548 | 7,867 | 7,401 | 6,984 | 6,834 | 6,395 | 5,825 | 5,282 | 4,750 | 4,163 |
| Operating Income | 821 | 748 | 617 | 515 | 532 | 452 | 458 | 512 | 478 | 419 |
| Depreciation | 182 | 172 | 160 | 150 | 144 | 135 | 115 | 97.9 | 88.3 | 77.0 |
| Interest Expense | 22.5 | 13.3 | 14.1 | 15.4 | 17.0 | 13.1 | Nil | Nil | Nil | Nil |
| Pretax Income | 617 | 564 | 451 | 362 | 382 | 311 | 343 | 414 | 390 | 342 |
| Effective Tax Rate | NA | NA | 35.4% | 35.6% | 36.4% | 37.3% | 36.5% | 36.6% | 36.5% | 36.5% |
| Net Income | 388 | 358 | 291 | 233 | 243 | 195 | 218 | 263 | 247 | 217 |
| S&P Core Earnings | 388 | 349 | 291 | 233 | 257 | 223 | 202 | 250 | 241 | 213 |

| Balance Sheet & Other Financial Data (Million $) | | | | | | | | | | |
|---|---|---|---|---|---|---|---|---|---|---|
| Cash | 237 | 503 | 445 | 159 | 87.0 | 79.7 | 105 | 150 | 207 | 220 |
| Current Assets | 1,534 | 1,660 | 1,599 | 1,344 | 1,537 | 1,419 | 1,355 | 1,225 | 1,156 | 1,056 |
| Total Assets | 2,996 | 2,982 | 2,843 | 2,662 | 2,624 | 2,523 | 2,410 | 2,167 | 1,986 | 1,755 |
| Current Liabilities | 1,017 | 1,054 | 1,060 | 1,069 | 1,130 | 986 | 895 | 714 | 595 | 531 |
| Long Term Debt | 532 | 250 | 250 | 250 | 250 | 250 | Nil | Nil | Nil | Nil |
| Common Equity | 1,087 | 1,422 | 1,440 | 1,254 | 1,175 | 1,208 | 2,187 | 1,360 | 1,533 | 1,245 |
| Total Capital | 1,636 | 1,672 | 1,690 | 1,555 | 1,494 | 1,537 | 2,274 | 1,454 | 1,612 | 1,314 |
| Capital Expenditures | 345 | 212 | 155 | 168 | 132 | 192 | 229 | 218 | 220 | 187 |
| Cash Flow | 571 | 530 | 451 | 383 | 387 | 330 | 332 | 361 | 336 | 294 |
| Current Ratio | 1.5 | 1.6 | 1.5 | 1.3 | 1.4 | 1.4 | 1.5 | 1.7 | 1.9 | 2.0 |
| % Long Term Debt of Capitalization | 32.6 | 15.0 | 14.8 | 16.1 | 16.7 | 16.2 | Nil | Nil | Nil | Nil |
| % Net Income of Revenue | 4.5 | 4.6 | 3.9 | 3.3 | 3.5 | 3.1 | 3.7 | 5.0 | 5.2 | 5.2 |
| % Return on Assets | 13.0 | 12.3 | 10.6 | 8.8 | 9.4 | 7.9 | 9.4 | 12.7 | 13.2 | 13.8 |
| % Return on Equity | 31.0 | 25.0 | 21.6 | 19.2 | 20.3 | 8.9 | 10.6 | 19.7 | 17.8 | 18.9 |

Data as orig reptd.; bef. results of disc opers/spec. items. Per share data adj. for stk. divs.; EPS diluted. E-Estimated. NA-Not Available. NM-Not Meaningful. NR-Not Ranked. UR-Under Review.

**Office:** 10401 Monroe Road, Matthews, NC 28105.
**Telephone:** 704-847-6961.
**Website:** http://www.familydollar.com
**Chrmn & CEO:** H.R. Levine

**Pres & COO:** M. Bloom
**Vice Chrmn:** R.J. Kelly
**Vice Chrmn & Chief Admin Officer:** D.K. Flur
**SVP, CFO & Chief Acctg Officer:** K.T. Smith

**Investor Contact:** K.F. Rawlins (704-849-7496)
**Board Members:** M. R. Bernstein, P. L. Davies, S. A. Decker, E. C. Dolby, G. A. Eisenberg, D. K. Flur, E. P. Garden, R. J. Kelly, H. R. Levine, G. R. Mahoney, Jr., J. G. Martin, P. W. May, H. Morgan, N. Peltz, D. Pond

**Founded:** 1959
**Domicile:** Delaware
**Employees:** 52,000

# Fastenal Company

**STANDARD &POOR'S**

| S&P Recommendation **STRONG BUY** ★★★★★ | Price $38.42 (as of Nov 25, 2011) | 12-Mo. Target Price $48.00 | Investment Style Large-Cap Growth |
| --- | --- | --- | --- |

**GICS Sector** Industrials
**Sub-Industry** Trading Companies & Distributors

**Summary** This company distributes fasteners and other industrial and construction supplies through nearly 2,600 stores throughout the U.S. and in a few foreign countries.

## Key Stock Statistics (Source S&P, Vickers, company reports)

| | | | | | | |
| --- | --- | --- | --- | --- | --- | --- |
| 52-Wk Range | $41.65–26.50 | S&P Oper. EPS 2011**E** | 1.22 | Market Capitalization(B) | $11.342 | Beta | 0.96 |
| Trailing 12-Month EPS | $1.13 | S&P Oper. EPS 2012**E** | 1.45 | Yield (%) | 1.35 | S&P 3-Yr. Proj. EPS CAGR(%) | 25 |
| Trailing 12-Month P/E | 34.0 | P/E on S&P Oper. EPS 2011**E** | 31.5 | Dividend Rate/Share | $0.52 | S&P Credit Rating | NA |
| $10K Invested 5 Yrs Ago | $22,740 | Common Shares Outstg. (M) | 295.2 | Institutional Ownership (%) | 87 | | |

## Price Performance

30-Week Mov. Avg. · · · 10-Week Mov. Avg. - - **GAAP Earnings vs. Previous Year** Volume Above Avg. ⅢⅢ STARS
12-Mo. Target Price — Relative Strength — ▲ Up ▼ Down ► No Change Below Avg. ⅢⅢ ★

Options: ASE, CBOE, P

Analysis prepared by Equity Analyst **Michael Jaffe** on Oct 27, 2011, when the stock traded at **$38.57**.

## Qualitative Risk Assessment

| LOW | MEDIUM | HIGH |
| --- | --- | --- |

Our risk assessment for FAST reflects our view of its consistent generation of solid levels of free cash flow, a healthy balance sheet with no long-term debt, and a very well run business model, with a strong focus on growth and cost controls. This is offset by the cyclical nature of the markets that FAST serves.

## Quantitative Evaluations

**S&P Quality Ranking** A

| D | C | B- | B | B+ | A- | A | A+ |
| --- | --- | --- | --- | --- | --- | --- | --- |

**Relative Strength Rank** STRONG

92

LOWEST = 1 HIGHEST = 99

## Revenue/Earnings Data

**Revenue (Million $)**

| | 1Q | 2Q | 3Q | 4Q | Year |
| --- | --- | --- | --- | --- | --- |
| 2011 | 640.6 | 701.7 | 726.7 | -- | -- |
| 2010 | 520.8 | 571.2 | 603.8 | 573.8 | 2,269 |
| 2009 | 489.3 | 474.9 | 489.3 | 476.8 | 1,930 |
| 2008 | 566.2 | 604.2 | 625.0 | 545.0 | 2,340 |
| 2007 | 489.2 | 519.7 | 533.8 | 519.2 | 2,062 |
| 2006 | 431.7 | 458.8 | 470.1 | 448.7 | 1,809 |

**Earnings Per Share ($)**

| | | | | | |
| --- | --- | --- | --- | --- | --- |
| 2011 | 0.27 | 0.32 | 0.33 | E0.30 | E1.22 |
| 2010 | 0.19 | 0.24 | 0.26 | 0.22 | 0.90 |
| 2009 | 0.17 | 0.15 | 0.16 | 0.15 | 0.62 |
| 2008 | 0.23 | 0.26 | 0.25 | 0.21 | 0.94 |
| 2007 | 0.18 | 0.20 | 0.21 | 0.19 | 0.78 |
| 2006 | 0.16 | 0.17 | 0.18 | 0.15 | 0.66 |

Fiscal year ended Dec. 31. Next earnings report expected: NA. EPS Estimates based on S&P Operating Earnings; historical GAAP earnings are as reported.

## Highlights

➤ We forecast that sales will increase 19% in 2012, after a projected 22% rise in 2011. After turning very soft in 2009, FAST's sales have been staging a recovery since the early part of 2010, and we expect this trend to continue. The company's positive shift in operating performance is related to the start of an economic recovery in the U.S., in our view. We see the expected growth coming from both FAST's manufacturing and non-residential construction client bases. We also look for FAST's top line to be assisted by store openings and market share gains. We see the latter aided in part by incremental revenues from FAST's initiative to put vending machines at customer sites, which has seen great success in its early stages.

➤ We expect FAST's sales details to shift in coming periods, under its strategy (announced in July 2007) of slowing its rate of store growth while increasing sales-related resources.

➤ We see slightly wider net margins in 2012 versus 2011, on the expected sales improvement. We also see margins aided by FAST's likely ongoing focus on controlling operating expenses, assisted in part by a higher proportion of variable costs under its revised business model.

## Investment Rationale/Risk

➤ We expect FAST's business revival to go on for an extended period. Sales to manufacturing customers have rebounded solidly since the start of 2010. Non-residential construction sales took longer to bounce back, but the category has recorded double-digit growth since 2010's final quarter. We also favor FAST's strategy of the past few years, which focuses on larger stores, greater sales resources and fewer store openings. Combined with valuation considerations, we view FAST as undervalued.

➤ Risks to our recommendation and target price include a resumption of a downturn in the U.S. economy, and unsuccessful results from the company's change in business strategy.

➤ The shares recently traded at about 25X our 2012 EPS estimate, a large premium to the S&P 500, but at the low end of FAST's valuation at a similar stage of its last business recovery. Given our outlook for an ongoing rebound in FAST's business, and our very positive views of its mid-2007 strategy change and its management effort, we think a higher P/E multiple is merited. Our 12-month target price is $48, or 33.1X our 2012 EPS forecast, in the middle of FAST's multiple range over the past decade.

## Dividend Data (Dates: mm/dd Payment Date: mm/dd/yy)

| Amount ($) | Date Decl. | Ex-Div. Date | Stk. of Record | Payment Date |
| --- | --- | --- | --- | --- |
| .26 Spl. | 04/11 | 04/13 | 04/12 | 04/28/11 |
| 2-for-1 | 04/19 | 05/24 | 05/02 | 05/20/11 |
| 0.130 | 07/11 | 07/21 | 07/25 | 08/22/11 |
| 0.140 | 10/12 | 10/24 | 10/26 | 11/22/11 |

Dividends have been paid since 1991. Source: Company reports.

---

**Please read the Required Disclosures and Analyst Certification on the last page of this report.**

The **McGraw-Hill** Companies

# Fastenal Company

STANDARD
&POOR'S

## Business Summary October 27, 2011

CORPORATE OVERVIEW. Fastenal, which sells industrial and construction supplies, began operations in 1967, with a plan to supply threaded fasteners in small- to medium-size cities. It later changed its business plan to include some sites in large cities. At the end of 2010, FAST had 2,490 stores in all 50 states, Puerto Rico, the Dominican Republic, Canada, Mexico, Panama, Singapore, China, Malaysia, the Netherlands, Hungary and the United Kingdom (but with the large majority in the U.S.), up 5.1% from 2,369 sites a year earlier; there were 2,566 sites at September 30, 2011. FAST distributes products to its store sites from 14 distribution centers, with 11 located throughout the U.S., two in Canada and one in Mexico. Threaded fasteners accounted for 46% of 2010 sales.

The company offered 11 product lines at the end of 2010, after adding the product category of office supplies over the past year. Its original product line now consists of about 456,000 different types of threaded fasteners and supplies. Other product lines offered include 147,000 different types of tools and equipment; 276,000 different cutting tool blades and abrasives; 86,000 types of fluid transfer components and accessories for hydraulic and pneumatic power, plumbing, and heating, ventilating and air-conditioning; 19,000 types of material handling, storage and packaging products; 17,000 kinds of janitorial sup-

plies, chemicals and paint; 28,000 types of electrical supplies; 39,000 welding supply items; 37,000 different safety supplies; 13,000 types of metals, alloys and materials; and 3,000 office supply items. FAST sells mostly to customers in the manufacturing market for both OEMs and maintenance and repair operations, and to construction markets. Its construction customers serve general construction, electrical, plumbing, sheet metal, and road contractor markets.

Most products sold are made by other companies. No supplier accounted for over 5% of FAST's 2010 purchases. No customer accounts for a significant portion of total sales.

COMPETITIVE LANDSCAPE. Fastenal's business is highly competitive. Competition includes both large distributors located primarily in large cities and smaller distributors located in many of the cities in which the company has stores. FAST believes that the principal competitive factors affecting the markets for its products are customer service, price and convenience.

## Company Financials Fiscal Year Ended Dec. 31

| Per Share Data ($) | 2010 | 2009 | 2008 | 2007 | 2006 | 2005 | 2004 | 2003 | 2002 | 2001 |
|---|---|---|---|---|---|---|---|---|---|---|
| Tangible Book Value | 4.35 | 4.04 | 3.84 | 3.38 | 3.05 | 2.60 | 2.26 | 1.90 | 1.65 | 1.40 |
| Cash Flow | 1.04 | 0.76 | 1.07 | 0.90 | 0.77 | 0.65 | 0.51 | 0.34 | 0.30 | 0.28 |
| Earnings | 0.90 | 0.62 | 0.94 | 0.78 | 0.66 | 0.55 | 0.43 | 0.28 | 0.25 | 0.23 |
| S&P Core Earnings | 0.90 | 0.62 | 0.96 | 0.78 | 0.66 | 0.55 | 0.43 | 0.27 | 0.23 | 0.23 |
| Dividends | 0.62 | 0.36 | 0.40 | 0.22 | 0.20 | 0.16 | 0.10 | 0.05 | 0.01 | 0.01 |
| Payout Ratio | 69% | 58% | 42% | 28% | 30% | 28% | 23% | 19% | 5% | 5% |
| Prices:High | 30.20 | 21.14 | 28.24 | 26.47 | 24.66 | 20.98 | 16.13 | 12.75 | 10.84 | 9.13 |
| Prices:Low | 20.49 | 12.94 | 15.04 | 16.53 | 16.59 | 12.77 | 10.97 | 6.88 | 6.65 | 5.87 |
| P/E Ratio:High | 34 | 34 | 30 | 30 | 37 | 38 | 37 | 46 | 44 | 40 |
| P/E Ratio:Low | 23 | 21 | 16 | 21 | 25 | 23 | 26 | 25 | 27 | 26 |

| Income Statement Analysis (Million $) | 2010 | 2009 | 2008 | 2007 | 2006 | 2005 | 2004 | 2003 | 2002 | 2001 |
|---|---|---|---|---|---|---|---|---|---|---|
| Revenue | 2,269 | 1,930 | 2,340 | 2,062 | 1,809 | 1,523 | 1,238 | 995 | 905 | 818 |
| Operating Income | 470 | 337 | 498 | 414 | 354 | 297 | 231 | 156 | 131 | 127 |
| Depreciation | 40.8 | 40.1 | 39.3 | 37.4 | 33.5 | 29.0 | 23.6 | 20.4 | 16.9 | 15.0 |
| Interest Expense | NA | NA | Nil | Nil | Nil | Nil | Nil | Nil | Nil | Nil |
| Pretax Income | 431 | 297 | 451 | 378 | 321 | 269 | 208 | 136 | 121 | 114 |
| Effective Tax Rate | NA | 38.0% | 38.0% | 38.4% | 38.0% | 38.0% | 37.1% | 38.3% | 38.3% | 38.3% |
| Net Income | 265 | 184 | 280 | 233 | 199 | 167 | 131 | 84.1 | 74.8 | 70.7 |
| S&P Core Earnings | 265 | 185 | 284 | 233 | 199 | 167 | 131 | 82.6 | 68.5 | 70.3 |

| Balance Sheet & Other Financial Data (Million $) | 2010 | 2009 | 2008 | 2007 | 2006 | 2005 | 2004 | 2003 | 2002 | 2001 |
|---|---|---|---|---|---|---|---|---|---|---|
| Cash | 170 | 189 | 86.7 | 57.4 | 33.9 | 70.1 | 74.5 | 95.6 | 51.4 | 68.5 |
| Current Assets | 1,086 | 982 | 975 | 881 | 768 | 649 | 538 | 454 | 396 | 341 |
| Total Assets | 1,468 | 1,330 | 1,304 | 1,163 | 1,039 | 890 | 1,308 | 652 | 559 | 475 |
| Current Liabilities | 162 | 120 | 148 | 138 | 104 | 91.5 | 71.2 | 60.9 | 47.1 | 40.6 |
| Long Term Debt | NA | NA | Nil | Nil | Nil | Nil | Nil | Nil | Nil | Nil |
| Common Equity | 1,283 | 1,191 | 1,142 | 1,010 | 922 | 784 | 684 | 577 | 504 | 425 |
| Total Capital | 1,283 | 1,191 | 1,156 | 1,025 | 935 | 798 | 699 | 591 | 516 | 435 |
| Capital Expenditures | 73.6 | 52.5 | 95.3 | 55.8 | 77.6 | 65.9 | 52.7 | 50.2 | 42.7 | 45.3 |
| Cash Flow | 306 | 224 | 319 | 270 | 233 | 196 | 155 | 105 | 91.8 | 85.1 |
| Current Ratio | 6.7 | 8.2 | 6.6 | 6.4 | 7.4 | 7.1 | 7.6 | 7.5 | 8.4 | 8.4 |
| % Long Term Debt of Capitalization | Nil | Nil | Nil | Nil | Nil | Nil | Nil | Nil | Nil | Nil |
| % Net Income of Revenue | 11.7 | 9.6 | 12.0 | 11.3 | 11.0 | 11.0 | 10.6 | 8.5 | 8.3 | 8.6 |
| % Return on Assets | 19.0 | 14.0 | 22.7 | 21.1 | 20.6 | 20.0 | 10.9 | 13.9 | 14.5 | 16.0 |
| % Return on Equity | 21.5 | 15.8 | 26.0 | 24.1 | 23.3 | 22.7 | 20.8 | 15.6 | 16.1 | 17.9 |

Data as orig reptd.; bef. results of disc opers/spec. items. Per share data adj. for stk. divs.; EPS diluted. E-Estimated. NA-Not Available. NM-Not Meaningful. NR-Not Ranked. UR-Under Review.

**Office:** 2001 Theurer Blvd, Winona, MN 55987-1500.
**Telephone:** 507-454-5374.
**Email:** info@fastenal.com
**Website:** http://www.fastenal.com

**Chrmn:** R.A. Kierlin
**Pres & CEO:** W.D. Oberton
**COO:** J.C. Jansen
**EVP, CFO, Chief Acctg Officer & Treas:** D.L. Florness

**Board Members:** M. J. Ancius, M. J. Dolan, M. M. Gostomski, R. A. Kierlin, H. L. Miller, W. D. Oberton, S. A. Satterlee, S. M. Slaggie, R. K. Wisecup

**Founded:** 1968
**Domicile:** Minnesota
**Employees:** 13,285

# Federated Investors Inc.

**STANDARD &POOR'S**

| S&P Recommendation HOLD ★★★☆☆ | Price $15.12 (as of Nov 25, 2011) | 12-Mo. Target Price $22.00 | Investment Style Large-Cap Growth |
|---|---|---|---|

**GICS Sector** Financials
**Sub-Industry** Asset Management & Custody Banks

**Summary** This leading U.S. investment management company has a strong market share in money market products.

## Key Stock Statistics (Source S&P, Vickers, company reports)

| | | | | | | | |
|---|---|---|---|---|---|---|---|
| 52-Wk Range | $28.57–15.05 | S&P Oper. EPS 2011E | 1.51 | Market Capitalization(B) | $1.569 | Beta | 0.84 |
| Trailing 12-Month EPS | $1.55 | S&P Oper. EPS 2012E | 1.71 | Yield (%) | 6.35 | S&P 3-Yr. Proj. EPS CAGR(%) | -4 |
| Trailing 12-Month P/E | 9.8 | P/E on S&P Oper. EPS 2011E | 10.0 | Dividend Rate/Share | $0.96 | S&P Credit Rating | NA |
| $10K Invested 5 Yrs Ago | $6,042 | Common Shares Outstg. (M) | 103.8 | Institutional Ownership (%) | 80 | | |

## Price Performance

- 30-Week Mov. Avg. ··· 10-Week Mov. Avg. – – GAAP Earnings vs. Previous Year  Volume Above Avg. STARS
- 12-Mo. Target Price — Relative Strength — ▲ Up ▼ Down ▶ No Change  Below Avg.

Options: ASE, CBOE

Analysis prepared by Equity Analyst **Cathy Seifert** on Nov 21, 2011, when the stock traded at **$16.13**.

## Qualitative Risk Assessment

| LOW | MEDIUM | HIGH |
|---|---|---|

Our risk assessment reflects the company's relatively narrow product offering and significant competition from larger, more diversified fund management companies.

## Quantitative Evaluations

**S&P Quality Ranking**  B+

| D | C | B- | B | B+ | A- | A | A+ |
|---|---|---|---|---|---|---|---|

**Relative Strength Rank**  WEAK

18

LOWEST = 1  HIGHEST = 99

## Revenue/Earnings Data

**Revenue (Million $)**

| | 1Q | 2Q | 3Q | 4Q | Year |
|---|---|---|---|---|---|
| 2011 | 238.9 | 225.8 | 214.1 | -- | -- |
| 2010 | 233.0 | 231.5 | 242.2 | 245.3 | 951.9 |
| 2009 | 310.6 | 306.9 | 293.6 | 264.8 | 1,176 |
| 2008 | 305.7 | 310.3 | 305.9 | 301.8 | 1,224 |
| 2007 | 264.4 | 276.5 | 286.0 | 300.3 | 1,128 |
| 2006 | 238.8 | 236.4 | 243.9 | 259.7 | 978.9 |

**Earnings Per Share ($)**

| | 1Q | 2Q | 3Q | 4Q | Year |
|---|---|---|---|---|---|
| 2011 | 0.32 | 0.41 | 0.37 | E0.41 | E1.51 |
| 2010 | 0.38 | 0.46 | 0.42 | 0.45 | 1.73 |
| 2009 | 0.34 | 0.52 | 0.56 | 0.51 | 1.92 |
| 2008 | 0.55 | 0.55 | 0.56 | 0.54 | 2.20 |
| 2007 | 0.50 | 0.54 | 0.57 | 0.52 | 2.12 |
| 2006 | 0.43 | 0.44 | 0.43 | 0.51 | 1.80 |

Fiscal year ended Dec. 31. Next earnings report expected: NA. EPS Estimates based on S&P Operating Earnings; historical GAAP earnings are as reported.

## Highlights

- We think FII's revenue in coming periods will remain under pressure, due to a trend of mediocre net asset inflows and our expectation that low interest rates will remain in place for an extended period of time. Revenues for the nine months ended September 30, 2011, declined 4%, year to year, amid weakness across the board, including a 6% drop in investment advisory fees. Assets under management at September 30, 2011, totaled $351.7 billion, of which more than 77% were money market funds. We think that persistent low interest rates will limit FII's ability to derive revenue growth from those assets. Furthermore, at the end of the third quarter, FII's assets under management had grown by only 3.0%, year over year.

- We expect expenses, primarily marketing and distribution and compensation, to increase moderately as a percentage of sales. We also think that money market fund waivers will continue to be a drag on earnings.

- We estimate EPS of $1.51 in 2011 and $1.71 in 2012.

## Investment Rationale/Risk

- We view the company's capital position favorably, and we think FII's niche in the money market fund business will be very profitable when the interest rate outlook improves. While we see FII diversifying its business somewhat toward equity and fixed income funds, we think the majority of the company's asset mix will remain money market funds. We expect that the company will have to continue waiving money market fees, and we think this will prove to be a headwind to earnings growth. All told, we think the stock's current valuation reflects the aforementioned risks, and we see the shares as appropriately valued at recent levels.

- Risks to our recommendation and target price include increased competition, low short-term interest rates persisting longer than we expect, and weaker equity fund performance. From a corporate governance perspective, we think there should be a greater percentage of independent directors on the board.

- Our 12-month target price of $22 is 12.9X our forward earnings per share forecast, a discount to the historical multiple that we think is warranted by our outlook for money market fee waivers to drag on FII's earnings.

## Dividend Data (Dates: mm/dd Payment Date: mm/dd/yy)

| Amount ($) | Date Decl. | Ex-Div. Date | Stk. of Record | Payment Date |
|---|---|---|---|---|
| 0.240 | 01/27 | 02/04 | 02/08 | 02/15/11 |
| 0.240 | 04/28 | 05/04 | 05/06 | 05/13/11 |
| 0.240 | 07/28 | 08/04 | 08/08 | 08/15/11 |
| 0.240 | 10/27 | 11/04 | 11/08 | 11/15/11 |

Dividends have been paid since 1998. Source: Company reports.

---

**Please read the Required Disclosures and Analyst Certification on the last page of this report.**

**The McGraw·Hill Companies**

# Federated Investors Inc.

STANDARD
&POOR'S

## Business Summary November 21, 2011

Federated Investors, Inc. was founded in 1955 as a provider of investment management products and related financial services in the United States. The company sponsors, markets and provides investment-related services for various investment products such as mutual funds, money market funds, and separately managed accounts as well as sub-advised funds, both variable annuity and other. The company markets these funds to banks, broker/dealers and other financial intermediaries, which use them to meet the needs of their customers, including retail investors, corporations and retirement plans.

The company provides investment advisory services for separate account assets. These separate accounts (together with the Federated Funds, 'Managed Assets') represent assets from high net worth individuals, government entities, and pension and other employee benefit plans, along with corporations, trusts, foundations, endowments, and other products sponsored by third parties. The company also provides various services to support the operation and administration of the Federated Funds. These services include administrative services, shareholder servicing and general support.

FII offers various products, including money market, equity and fixed-income investments. The company also manages retail money market products that are distributed through broker/dealers. The company manages money market funds in various asset classes, including prime corporate, government and tax free. Equity assets are managed across various styles including small-mid cap growth; core equity; large-cap value; flexible; equity income; international/global; and mid-large cap growth. FII also manages assets in equity index funds and balanced and asset allocation funds. These asset allocation funds include fixed-income assets. The company's fixed-income assets are managed in various sectors including multi-sector; mortgage-backed; municipal; U.S. corporate; high-yield; U.S. government; and international/global. The company's fixed-income products offer fiduciaries and others various products designed to meet many of their investment needs.

## Company Financials Fiscal Year Ended Dec. 31

| Per Share Data ($) | 2010 | 2009 | 2008 | 2007 | 2006 | 2005 | 2004 | 2003 | 2002 | 2001 |
|---|---|---|---|---|---|---|---|---|---|---|
| Tangible Book Value | NM | NM | NM | 0.53 | 0.39 | 1.59 | 1.36 | 2.05 | 1.46 | 0.79 |
| Cash Flow | 2.10 | 2.21 | 2.44 | 2.37 | 2.07 | 1.75 | 1.79 | 1.95 | 1.90 | 1.65 |
| Earnings | 1.73 | 1.92 | 2.20 | 2.12 | 1.80 | 1.51 | 1.62 | 1.71 | 1.74 | 1.44 |
| S&P Core Earnings | 1.56 | 1.91 | 2.23 | 2.16 | 1.80 | 1.67 | 1.70 | 1.67 | 1.69 | 1.46 |
| Dividends | 1.98 | 0.96 | 0.93 | 0.81 | 0.69 | 0.58 | 0.41 | 0.30 | 0.22 | 0.22 |
| Payout Ratio | 115% | 50% | 42% | 38% | 38% | 38% | 26% | 17% | 12% | 15% |
| Prices:High | 28.14 | 28.31 | 45.01 | 43.35 | 40.17 | 38.11 | 33.79 | 31.90 | 36.18 | 32.80 |
| Prices:Low | 20.01 | 16.10 | 15.80 | 30.31 | 29.56 | 26.99 | 26.72 | 23.85 | 23.43 | 23.31 |
| P/E Ratio:High | 16 | 15 | 20 | 20 | 22 | 25 | 21 | 19 | 21 | 23 |
| P/E Ratio:Low | 12 | 8 | 7 | 14 | 16 | 18 | 16 | 14 | 13 | 16 |

| Income Statement Analysis (Million $) | | | | | | | | | | |
|---|---|---|---|---|---|---|---|---|---|---|
| Income Interest | NA | NA | NA | NA | NA | NA | NA | NA | NA | 9.74 |
| Income Other | 952 | 1,176 | 1,224 | 1,128 | 979 | 909 | 847 | 823 | 711 | 706 |
| Total Income | 952 | 1,176 | 1,224 | 1,128 | 979 | 909 | 847 | 823 | 711 | 716 |
| General Expenses | 642 | 847 | 863 | 770 | 694 | 634 | 530 | 531 | 399 | 388 |
| Interest Expense | 15.5 | 5.71 | 5.20 | 5.40 | 8.19 | 17.9 | 21.0 | 4.71 | 4.79 | 29.7 |
| Depreciation | 21.1 | 23.8 | 24.5 | 25.6 | 24.1 | 24.0 | 19.0 | 20.6 | 19.2 | 26.0 |
| Net Income | 179 | 197 | 222 | 217 | 191 | 163 | 179 | 191 | 204 | 173 |
| S&P Core Earnings | 155 | 191 | 225 | 222 | 191 | 181 | 188 | 187 | 199 | 175 |

| Balance Sheet & Other Financial Data (Million $) | | | | | | | | | | |
|---|---|---|---|---|---|---|---|---|---|---|
| Cash | 199 | 90.5 | 45.4 | 146 | 119 | 246 | 258 | 234 | 151 | 73.5 |
| Receivables | 21.2 | 10.7 | 24.0 | 37.3 | 23.3 | 45.8 | 33.8 | 38.3 | 31.2 | 32.6 |
| Cost of Investments | 135 | 31.5 | 13.2 | 25.9 | 16.2 | 38.4 | 2.10 | 1.53 | 1.00 | 4.60 |
| Total Assets | 1,154 | 912 | 847 | 841 | 810 | 897 | 955 | 879 | 530 | 432 |
| Loss Reserve | Nil | Nil | Nil | Nil | Nil | Nil | Nil | Nil | Nil | 0.32 |
| Short Term Debt | 42.5 | 21.0 | 51.1 | Nil | Nil | Nil | Nil | Nil | Nil | Nil |
| Capitalization:Debt | 366 | 119 | 157 | 63.0 | 113 | 160 | 285 | 328 | 59.2 | 55.0 |
| Capitalization:Equity | 493 | 528 | 423 | 574 | 529 | 540 | 458 | 396 | 341 | 237 |
| Capitalization:Total | 860 | 662 | 613 | 667 | 671 | 723 | 767 | 744 | 416 | 299 |
| Price Times Book Value:High | NM | NM | NM | 81.8 | 103 | 24.0 | 24.8 | 15.6 | 24.8 | 41.5 |
| Price Times Book Value:Low | NM | NM | NM | 57.2 | 76.0 | 17.0 | 19.6 | 11.6 | 16.0 | 29.5 |
| Cash Flow | 200 | 221 | 246 | 243 | 215 | 187 | 198 | 212 | 223 | 199 |
| % Expense/Operating Revenue | 67.4 | 72.0 | 70.5 | 68.3 | 71.7 | 71.7 | 65.1 | 65.1 | 56.7 | 58.4 |
| % Earnings & Depreciation/Assets | 19.4 | 25.1 | 29.1 | 29.4 | 25.2 | 20.2 | 19.5 | 25.3 | 46.4 | 35.0 |

Data as orig reptd.; bef. results of disc opers/spec. items. Per share data adj. for stk. divs.; EPS diluted. E-Estimated. NA-Not Available. NM-Not Meaningful. NR-Not Ranked. UR-Under Review.

**Office:** Federated Investors Tower, 1001 Liberty Avenue, Pittsburgh, PA 15222-3779.
**Telephone:** 412-288-1900.
**Email:** investors@federatedinv.com
**Website:** http://www.federatedinvestors.com

**Chrmn:** J.F. Donahue
**Pres & CEO:** J.C. Donahue
**Vice Chrmn, EVP, Secy & General Counsel:** J.W. McGonigle
**CFO & Treas:** T.R. Donahue

**Chief Acctg Officer:** D. McAuley, III
**Investor Contact:** R. Hanley (412-288-1920)
**Board Members:** L. E. Auriana, J. C. Donahue, J. F. Donahue, M. J. Farrell, D. M. Kelly, J. W. McGonigle, E. G. O'Connor

**Founded:** 1955
**Domicile:** Pennsylvania
**Employees:** 1,334

# FedEx Corp.

STANDARD &POOR'S

| S&P Recommendation | STRONG BUY ★★★★★ | Price $76.08 (as of Nov 25, 2011) | 12-Mo. Target Price $111.00 | Investment Style Large-Cap Growth |
|---|---|---|---|---|

**GICS Sector** Industrials
**Sub-Industry** Air Freight & Logistics

**Summary** This company provides guaranteed domestic and international air express, residential and business ground package delivery, heavy freight and logistics services.

## Key Stock Statistics (Source S&P, Vickers, company reports)

| | | | | | | | |
|---|---|---|---|---|---|---|---|
| 52-Wk Range | $98.66– 64.07 | S&P Oper. EPS 2012E | 6.51 | Market Capitalization(B) | $24.134 | Beta | 1.20 |
| Trailing 12-Month EPS | $4.83 | S&P Oper. EPS 2013E | NA | Yield (%) | 0.68 | S&P 3-Yr. Proj. EPS CAGR(%) | 15 |
| Trailing 12-Month P/E | 15.8 | P/E on S&P Oper. EPS 2012E | 11.7 | Dividend Rate/Share | $0.52 | S&P Credit Rating | BBB |
| $10K Invested 5 Yrs Ago | $6,668 | Common Shares Outstg. (M) | 317.2 | Institutional Ownership (%) | 78 | | |

## Price Performance

30-Week Mov. Avg. ···· 10-Week Mov. Avg. - - GAAP Earnings vs. Previous Year   Volume Above Avg. |||| STARS
12-Mo. Target Price — Relative Strength   ▲ Up   ▼ Down   ► No Change   Below Avg. |||| ★

Options: ASE, CBOE, P, PH

Analysis prepared by Equity Analyst **Jim Corridore** on Oct 12, 2011, when the stock traded at **$74.62**.

## Highlights

➤ We see revenues rising 10% in FY 12 (May) after a 13% increase in FY 11. We think FedEx Ground is likely to benefit from market share gains and increased penetration of its home delivery business. We see Express revenues in FY 12 up 9%, Ground up 10%, and Freight up 9%. FDX announced a 5.9% general rate increase for calendar 2011 and 3.9% for 2012, and we think the company will be able to get better traction on these price increases than in recent years.

➤ We believe improving volumes are likely to aid capacity utilization and productivity in FY 12, as FDX pushes more packages through its network. Partly offsetting this should be rising personnel costs due to changes related to disputes over the independent contractor model. In addition, FDX faces pension cost headwinds and rising maintenance costs to bring idled planes back into service. Reinstatement of bonuses and 401(k) matching should lead to higher compensation expense.

➤ We forecast FY 12 operating EPS of $6.51, which represents potential 33% growth from FY 11 operating EPS of $4.90.

## Investment Rationale/Risk

➤ While the U.S. and global economies remain weak, we expect to see some improvement over the next 12 months. We believe an improving U.S. and global economy would lead to increased volumes across FDX's entire network. This would drive improved capacity utilization and likely margin expansion in FY 12. We believe the shares will benefit from increased investor interest in logistics stocks on concrete signs of economic improvement. As we believe that EPS will increase faster than the overall market in the next three to five years, we think the shares deserve to trade at a premium valuation to the S&P 500.

➤ Risks to our recommendation and target price include a possible price war on excess industry capacity. If recent challenges to the company's independent contractor model bear fruit, or attempts to overturn the U.S. Railway Labor Act succeed, the company would likely incur higher labor costs.

➤ Our 12-month target price of $111 values the shares at about 17X our FY 12 EPS estimate of $6.51, toward the low end of the company's five-year historical P/E range of 13.7X-27.6X.

## Qualitative Risk Assessment

| LOW | MEDIUM | HIGH |
|---|---|---|

Our risk assessment reflects our view of the company's strong and stable balance sheet, healthy cash flow generation and strong earnings growth potential in an inherently cyclical business.

## Quantitative Evaluations

**S&P Quality Ranking**      B+

| D | C | B- | B | B+ | A- | A | A+ |
|---|---|---|---|---|---|---|---|

**Relative Strength Rank**      MODERATE

61

LOWEST = 1      HIGHEST = 99

## Revenue/Earnings Data

**Revenue (Million $)**

| | 1Q | 2Q | 3Q | 4Q | Year |
|---|---|---|---|---|---|
| 2012 | 10,521 | -- | -- | -- | -- |
| 2011 | 9,457 | 9,632 | 9,663 | 10,552 | 39,304 |
| 2010 | 8,009 | 8,596 | 8,701 | 9,428 | 34,734 |
| 2009 | 9,970 | 9,538 | 8,137 | 7,852 | 35,497 |
| 2008 | 9,199 | 9,451 | 9,437 | 9,866 | 37,953 |
| 2007 | 8,545 | 8,926 | 8,592 | 9,151 | 35,214 |

**Earnings Per Share ($)**

| | | | | | |
|---|---|---|---|---|---|
| 2012 | 1.46 | E1.55 | E1.21 | E2.29 | E6.51 |
| 2011 | 1.20 | 0.89 | 0.73 | 1.75 | 4.57 |
| 2010 | 0.58 | 1.10 | 0.76 | 1.33 | 3.76 |
| 2009 | 1.23 | 1.58 | 0.31 | -2.82 | 0.31 |
| 2008 | 1.23 | 1.54 | 1.26 | -0.78 | 3.60 |
| 2007 | 1.53 | 1.64 | 1.35 | 1.96 | 6.48 |

Fiscal year ended May 31. Next earnings report expected: Mid December. EPS Estimates based on S&P Operating Earnings; historical GAAP earnings are as reported.

## Dividend Data (Dates: mm/dd Payment Date: mm/dd/yy)

| Amount ($) | Date Decl. | Ex-Div. Date | Stk. of Record | Payment Date |
|---|---|---|---|---|
| 0.120 | 02/28 | 03/16 | 03/18 | 04/01/11 |
| 0.130 | 06/06 | 06/15 | 06/17 | 07/01/11 |
| 0.130 | 08/19 | 09/08 | 09/12 | 10/03/11 |
| 0.130 | 11/18 | 12/09 | 12/13 | 01/03/12 |

Dividends have been paid since 2002. Source: Company reports.

Stock Report | November 26, 2011 | NYS Symbol: **FDX**

# FedEx Corp.

**STANDARD
&POOR'S**

## Business Summary October 12, 2011

CORPORATE OVERVIEW. FedEx Corp. provides global time-definite air express services for packages, documents and freight in more than 220 countries, and ground-based delivery of small packages in North America. In addition, the company offers expedited critical shipment delivery, customs brokerage solutions, less-than-truckload (LTL) freight transportation, and customized logistics. In February 2004, FDX paid $2.4 billion in cash for Kinko's, which operates about 1,200 copy centers that also provide business services. This business was subsequently renamed FedEx Office.

CORPORATE STRATEGY. The company intends to leverage and extend the FedEx brand and to provide customers with seamless access to its entire portfolio of integrated transportation services. Sales and marketing activities

are coordinated among operating companies. Advanced information technology makes it convenient for customers to use the full range of FedEx services and provides a single point of contact for customers to access shipment tracking, customer service and invoicing information. The company intends to continue to operate independent express, ground and freight networks, but has increased its emphasis on having the individual business units work together to compete more effectively.

## Company Financials Fiscal Year Ended May 31

| Per Share Data ($) | 2011 | 2010 | 2009 | 2008 | 2007 | 2006 | 2005 | 2004 | 2003 | 2002 |
|---|---|---|---|---|---|---|---|---|---|---|
| Tangible Book Value | 40.55 | 36.98 | 36.15 | 35.92 | 29.73 | 28.39 | 22.36 | 17.45 | 21.03 | 18.38 |
| Cash Flow | 10.80 | 10.01 | 6.64 | 9.84 | 12.20 | 10.83 | 9.48 | 7.28 | 7.20 | 6.89 |
| Earnings | 4.57 | 3.76 | 0.31 | 3.60 | 6.48 | 5.83 | 4.72 | 2.76 | 2.74 | 2.39 |
| S&P Core Earnings | 4.68 | 3.55 | -0.16 | 2.77 | 6.32 | 5.60 | 4.48 | 2.61 | 1.38 | 0.95 |
| Dividends | NA | 0.44 | 0.44 | 0.36 | 0.36 | 0.32 | 0.28 | 0.22 | 0.20 | Nil |
| Payout Ratio | NA | 12% | 142% | 10% | 6% | 5% | 6% | 8% | 7% | Nil |
| Calendar Year | 2010 | 2009 | 2008 | 2007 | 2006 | 2005 | 2004 | 2003 | 2002 | 2001 |
| Prices:High | 97.75 | 92.59 | 99.46 | 121.42 | 120.01 | 105.82 | 100.92 | 78.05 | 61.35 | 53.48 |
| Prices:Low | 69.78 | 34.02 | 53.90 | 89.01 | 96.50 | 76.81 | 64.84 | 47.70 | 42.75 | 33.15 |
| P/E Ratio:High | 21 | 25 | NM | 34 | 19 | 18 | 21 | 28 | 22 | 22 |
| P/E Ratio:Low | 15 | 9 | NM | 25 | 15 | 13 | 14 | 17 | 16 | 14 |

### Income Statement Analysis (Million $)

| | 2011 | 2010 | 2009 | 2008 | 2007 | 2006 | 2005 | 2004 | 2003 | 2002 |
|---|---|---|---|---|---|---|---|---|---|---|
| Revenue | 39,304 | 34,734 | 35,497 | 37,953 | 35,214 | 32,294 | 29,363 | 24,710 | 22,487 | 20,607 |
| Operating Income | 4,506 | 3,974 | 3,926 | 4,903 | 5,018 | 4,564 | 3,933 | 3,250 | 2,822 | 2,804 |
| Depreciation | 1,973 | 1,958 | 1,975 | 1,946 | 1,742 | 1,550 | 1,462 | 1,375 | 1,351 | 1,364 |
| Interest Expense | 77.0 | 71.0 | 156 | 182 | 136 | 142 | 160 | 136 | 118 | 139 |
| Pretax Income | 2,265 | 1,894 | 677 | 2,016 | 3,215 | 2,899 | 2,313 | 1,319 | 1,338 | 1,160 |
| Effective Tax Rate | NA | NA | 85.5% | 44.2% | 37.3% | 37.7% | 37.4% | 36.5% | 38.0% | 37.5% |
| Net Income | 1,452 | 1,184 | 98.0 | 1,125 | 2,016 | 1,806 | 1,449 | 838 | 830 | 725 |
| S&P Core Earnings | 1,482 | 1,115 | -49.6 | 868 | 1,966 | 1,733 | 1,376 | 790 | 415 | 286 |

### Balance Sheet & Other Financial Data (Million $)

| | 2011 | 2010 | 2009 | 2008 | 2007 | 2006 | 2005 | 2004 | 2003 | 2002 |
|---|---|---|---|---|---|---|---|---|---|---|
| Cash | 2,328 | 1,952 | 2,292 | 1,539 | 1,569 | 1,937 | 1,039 | 1,046 | 538 | 331 |
| Current Assets | 8,285 | 7,284 | 7,116 | 7,244 | 6,629 | 6,464 | 5,269 | 4,970 | 3,941 | 3,665 |
| Total Assets | 27,385 | 24,902 | 24,244 | 25,633 | 24,000 | 22,690 | 20,404 | 19,134 | 15,385 | 13,812 |
| Current Liabilities | 4,882 | 4,645 | 4,524 | 5,368 | 5,428 | 5,473 | 4,734 | 4,732 | 3,335 | 2,942 |
| Long Term Debt | 1,667 | 1,668 | 1,930 | 1,506 | 2,662 | 1,592 | 2,427 | 2,837 | 1,709 | 1,800 |
| Common Equity | 15,220 | 13,811 | 13,626 | 14,526 | 12,656 | 11,511 | 9,588 | 8,036 | 7,288 | 6,545 |
| Total Capital | 16,905 | 15,741 | 16,209 | 16,534 | 16,215 | 14,470 | 13,221 | 12,054 | 9,879 | 8,944 |
| Capital Expenditures | 3,434 | 2,816 | 2,459 | 2,947 | 2,882 | 2,518 | 2,236 | 1,271 | 1,511 | 1,615 |
| Cash Flow | 3,425 | 3,142 | 2,073 | 3,071 | 3,758 | 3,356 | 2,911 | 2,213 | 2,181 | 2,089 |
| Current Ratio | 1.7 | 1.6 | 1.6 | 1.4 | 1.2 | 1.2 | 1.1 | 1.1 | 1.2 | 1.2 |
| % Long Term Debt of Capitalization | 9.9 | 10.6 | 11.9 | 8.7 | 16.4 | 11.0 | 18.3 | 23.5 | 17.2 | 20.1 |
| % Net Income of Revenue | 3.7 | 3.4 | 0.3 | 3.0 | 5.7 | 5.6 | 4.9 | 3.4 | 3.7 | 3.5 |
| % Return on Assets | 5.6 | 4.8 | 0.4 | 4.5 | 8.6 | 8.4 | 7.3 | 4.9 | 5.7 | 5.3 |
| % Return on Equity | 10.0 | 8.6 | 0.7 | 8.3 | 16.7 | 17.1 | 16.4 | 10.9 | 11.8 | 11.7 |

Data as orig reptd.; bef. results of disc opers/spec. items. Per share data adj. for stk. divs.; EPS diluted. E-Estimated. NA-Not Available. NM-Not Meaningful. NR-Not Ranked. UR-Under Review.

**Office:** 942 South Shady Grove Road, Memphis, TN 38120-4117.
**Telephone:** 901-818-7500.
**Website:** http://www.fedex.com
**Chrmn, Pres & CEO:** F.W. Smith

**COO & EVP:** K. Dixon
**Investor Contact:** A.B. Graf, Jr. (901-818-7388)
**EVP & CFO:** A.B. Graf, Jr.
**EVP, Secy & General Counsel:** C.P. Richards

**Board Members:** J. L. Barksdale, J. A. Edwardson, S. A. Jackson, S. R. Loranger, G. W. Loveman, R. B. Martin, J. C. Ramo, S. C. Schwab, F. W. Smith, J. I. Smith, D. P. Steiner, P. S. Walsh

**Founded:** 1971
**Domicile:** Delaware
**Employees:** 143,000

# F5 Networks Inc

**STANDARD &POOR'S**

| S&P Recommendation **BUY** ★★★★☆ | Price $97.62 (as of Nov 25, 2011) | 12-Mo. Target Price $124.00 |
|---|---|---|

**GICS Sector** Information Technology
**Sub-Industry** Communications Equipment

**Summary** This company focuses on application delivery networking products that help manage Internet traffic to servers and network devices.

## Key Stock Statistics (Source S&P, Vickers, company reports)

| | | | | | | | |
|---|---|---|---|---|---|---|---|
| 52-Wk Range | $145.76– 69.01 | S&P Oper. EPS 2012**E** | 3.50 | Market Capitalization(B) | $7.759 | Beta | 1.30 |
| Trailing 12-Month EPS | $2.96 | S&P Oper. EPS 2013**E** | 4.30 | Yield (%) | Nil | S&P 3-Yr. Proj. EPS CAGR(%) | 23 |
| Trailing 12-Month P/E | 33.0 | P/E on S&P Oper. EPS 2012**E** | 27.9 | Dividend Rate/Share | Nil | S&P Credit Rating | NA |
| $10K Invested 5 Yrs Ago | $26,705 | Common Shares Outstg. (M) | 79.5 | Institutional Ownership (%) | 91 | | |

## Price Performance

30-Week Mov. Avg. · · · 10-Week Mov. Avg. - - GAAP Earnings vs. Previous Year    Volume Above Avg. ╟╫╢ STARS
12-Mo. Target Price — Relative Strength — ▲ Up ▼ Down ► No Change    Below Avg. ╟╫╢ ★

Options: ASE, CBOE, P, Ph

Analysis prepared by Equity Analyst **Todd Rosenbluth** on Nov 02, 2011, when the stock traded at **$104.63**.

## Highlights

► Following a 31% increase in FY 11 (Sep.), we see sales advancing 18% in FY 12, on strong demand for application delivery controlling (ADC) solutions, aided by recent product upgrades. We think application traffic management tools are becoming a critical customer requirement, due to their compelling return on investment by virtue of making networks less costly to manage and more efficient in traffic flow. But with continued macroeconomic uncertainty in North America and EMEA, we expect more modest growth than in the recent past.

► We see FY 12 gross margins narrowing modestly, to 82%, reflecting increasing industry pricing pressure. We expect FFIV to continue to display good cost management execution, and we see FY 12 operating margin at 38%, which remains higher than communications equipment peers.

► After interest income, taxes at 34%, and modest share repurchases, we look for FY 12 EPS of $3.50, up from the $2.96 earned in FY 11. Our FY 12 estimate includes projected stock option expense of $0.85.

## Investment Rationale/Risk

► While near-term results could experience some choppiness due to a weak macroeconomic climate in Europe, we believe positive industry trends toward server virtualization and data consolidation will provide FFIV with strong underlying growth drivers for the next several years. Operationally, we view the company's sales (FY 12 estimated revenue growth of 18%) and profitability profile as among the best in the industry. Despite a recovery in October, in our view, the shares still do not adequately reflect the growth opportunity that we see available for FFIV.

► Risks to our recommendation and target price include lower network spending, increased pricing pressure, and the loss of a major customer.

► We value the shares on a P/E-to-growth basis, which we think best incorporates the company's above industry average sales and earnings growth profile. On that metric, using our three-year EPS growth estimate of 23% applied to our FY 12 EPS estimate of $3.50, our 12-month target price of $124 equates to a PEG multiple of about 1.5X, in line with the industry average.

## Qualitative Risk Assessment

| LOW | MEDIUM | **HIGH** |
|---|---|---|

Our risk assessment reflects the highly competitive nature of the industry, and our view of weak corporate governance policies, including the lack of cumulative shareholder voting rights in director elections and stock-based incentive plans that have been adopted without shareholder approval.

## Quantitative Evaluations

**S&P Quality Ranking** B+

| D | C | B- | B | **B+** | A- | A | A+ |
|---|---|---|---|---|---|---|---|

**Relative Strength Rank** STRONG

86

LOWEST = 1    HIGHEST = 99

## Revenue/Earnings Data

**Revenue (Million $)**

| | 1Q | 2Q | 3Q | 4Q | Year |
|---|---|---|---|---|---|
| 2011 | 268.9 | 277.6 | 290.7 | 314.6 | 1,152 |
| 2010 | 191.2 | 206.1 | 230.5 | 254.3 | 882.0 |
| 2009 | 165.6 | 154.2 | 158.2 | 175.1 | 653.1 |
| 2008 | 154.2 | 159.1 | 165.6 | 171.3 | 650.2 |
| 2007 | 120.0 | 127.6 | 132.4 | 145.6 | 525.7 |
| 2006 | 88.09 | 94.12 | 100.1 | 111.7 | 394.1 |

**Earnings Per Share ($)**

| | | | | | |
|---|---|---|---|---|---|
| 2011 | 0.68 | 0.68 | 0.77 | 0.84 | 2.96 |
| 2010 | 0.36 | 0.41 | 0.50 | 0.59 | 1.86 |
| 2009 | 0.27 | 0.24 | 0.29 | 0.36 | 1.14 |
| 2008 | 0.21 | 0.21 | 0.23 | 0.24 | 0.89 |
| 2007 | 0.26 | 0.24 | 0.26 | 0.15 | 0.90 |
| 2006 | 0.19 | 0.20 | 0.21 | 0.22 | 0.80 |

Fiscal year ended Sep. 30. Next earnings report expected: NA. EPS Estimates based on S&P Operating Earnings; historical GAAP earnings are as reported.

## Dividend Data

No cash dividends have been paid.

---

**Please read the Required Disclosures and Analyst Certification on the last page of this report.**

**The McGraw·Hill Companies**

# F5 Networks Inc

STANDARD
&POOR'S

## Business Summary November 02, 2011

CORPORATE OVERVIEW. F5 Networks focuses on application delivery networking products intended to help manage Internet traffic to servers and network devices in order to improve the scalability and availability of the network components and applications that run on them. The company markets and sells products primarily through multiple indirect sales channels to enterprise customers across the technology, telecommunications, financial services, government, transportation, education, manufacturing, and health care industries. During FY 10 (Sep.), global distributors Avnet Technology Solutions and Tech Data accounted for 14.5% and 10.2% of total sales, respectively. International revenue represented 41% of FY 10 sales, down from 45% in FY 09.

The majority of revenue is derived from the company's flagship BIG-IP application delivery controller (ADC) solution. This product sits in front of web and application servers, balancing traffic and performing compute-intensive functions such as encryption, security screening, traffic management and acceleration, and a variety of other functions. The VIPRION solutions is a chassis-based ADC that scales from one to four blades, each equipped with two dual-core processors. In January 2010, FFIV introduced the PB 200 blade, which doubles the performance of the previous blade. During FY 11, FFIV plans to roll-out a mid-range 4 slot chassis-based ADC solution called Victoria.

Other products include the ARX product family, a series of enterprise-class intelligent file virtualization devices that aim to simplify and lower the cost of file storage management and the FirePass systems that provide SSL VPN access for remote users of IP networks and any applications connected to those networks from any standard Web browser on any device.

The core of the company's software technology is the Traffic Management Operating System, or TM/OS. During 2009, the company rolled out TM/OS version 10, its first major upgrade from the version 9 specification that came out in 2004. TM/OS employs a full proxy architecture that enables it to inspect, modify, and direct both inbound and outbound traffic flows across multiple packets. FFIV believes that these features enable the system to direct, optimize, and secure application traffic in ways not available in competing products on the market.

## Company Financials Fiscal Year Ended Sep. 30

| Per Share Data ($) | 2011 | 2010 | 2009 | 2008 | 2007 | 2006 | 2005 | 2004 | 2003 | 2002 |
|---|---|---|---|---|---|---|---|---|---|---|
| Tangible Book Value | NA | 9.73 | 7.06 | 5.93 | 6.36 | 6.56 | 5.37 | 3.71 | 1.58 | 1.82 |
| Cash Flow | 3.22 | 2.16 | 1.45 | 1.17 | 1.09 | 0.93 | 0.76 | 0.53 | 0.16 | -0.06 |
| Earnings | 2.96 | 1.86 | 1.14 | 0.89 | 0.90 | 0.80 | 0.67 | 0.46 | 0.07 | -0.17 |
| S&P Core Earnings | 2.96 | 1.87 | 1.15 | 0.89 | 0.90 | 0.80 | 0.58 | 0.20 | -0.37 | -0.35 |
| Dividends | NA | Nil | Nil | Nil | Nil | Nil | Nil | Nil | Nil | Nil |
| Payout Ratio | Nil | Nil | Nil | Nil | Nil | Nil | Nil | Nil | Nil | Nil |
| Prices:High | 145.76 | 143.75 | 53.59 | 35.85 | 46.94 | 39.28 | 29.56 | 24.90 | 13.73 | 13.62 |
| Prices:Low | 69.01 | 47.11 | 18.41 | 17.70 | 25.91 | 20.28 | 17.67 | 10.70 | 5.35 | 3.20 |
| P/E Ratio:High | 49 | 77 | 47 | 40 | 52 | 49 | 44 | 54 | NM | NM |
| P/E Ratio:Low | 23 | 25 | 16 | 20 | 29 | 26 | 26 | 23 | NM | NM |

| Income Statement Analysis (Million $) | 2011 | 2010 | 2009 | 2008 | 2007 | 2006 | 2005 | 2004 | 2003 | 2002 |
|---|---|---|---|---|---|---|---|---|---|---|
| Revenue | 1,152 | 882 | 653 | 650 | 526 | 394 | 281 | 171 | 116 | 108 |
| Operating Income | 372 | 254 | 152 | 128 | 129 | 102 | 78.7 | 31.7 | 9.35 | -0.66 |
| Depreciation | 20.9 | 23.8 | 24.7 | 23.4 | 15.9 | 11.6 | 6.80 | 5.36 | 5.16 | 5.61 |
| Interest Expense | NA | NA | Nil | Nil | Nil | Nil | Nil | Nil | Nil | Nil |
| Pretax Income | 361 | 238 | 132 | 118 | 128 | 108 | 80.0 | 29.1 | 4.94 | -8.12 |
| Effective Tax Rate | NA | NA | 30.5% | 37.2% | 39.7% | 38.6% | 35.3% | NM | 17.3% | NM |
| Net Income | 241 | 151 | 91.5 | 74.3 | 77.0 | 66.0 | 51.7 | 33.0 | 4.09 | -8.61 |
| S&P Core Earnings | 241 | 152 | 92.4 | 74.3 | 77.0 | 66.0 | 44.7 | 14.1 | -19.2 | -17.4 |

| Balance Sheet & Other Financial Data (Million $) | 2011 | 2010 | 2009 | 2008 | 2007 | 2006 | 2005 | 2004 | 2003 | 2002 |
|---|---|---|---|---|---|---|---|---|---|---|
| Cash | 543 | 429 | 317 | 190 | 54.3 | 37.7 | 51.9 | 24.9 | 45.0 | 26.8 |
| Current Assets | 764 | 606 | 468 | 323 | 387 | 463 | 294 | 175 | 69.7 | 106 |
| Total Assets | 1,569 | 1,362 | 1,069 | 939 | 944 | 730 | 537 | 363 | 148 | 126 |
| Current Liabilities | 372 | 287 | 223 | 187 | 153 | 99.6 | 63.3 | 50.6 | 36.0 | 31.3 |
| Long Term Debt | NA | NA | Nil | Nil | Nil | Nil | 9.96 | Nil | Nil | Nil |
| Common Equity | 1,105 | 1,004 | 799 | 718 | 771 | 616 | 464 | 308 | 110 | 93.7 |
| Total Capital | 1,105 | 1,004 | 799 | 718 | 771 | 66.5 | 474 | 310 | 111 | 93.7 |
| Capital Expenditures | 30.4 | 12.6 | 11.7 | 27.9 | 16.5 | 21.4 | 9.29 | 5.78 | 2.58 | 3.20 |
| Cash Flow | 262 | 175 | 116 | 97.7 | 92.9 | 77.6 | 58.5 | 38.3 | 9.25 | -3.00 |
| Current Ratio | 2.1 | 2.1 | 2.1 | 1.7 | 2.5 | 4.6 | 4.6 | 3.5 | 1.9 | 3.4 |
| % Long Term Debt of Capitalization | Nil | Nil | Nil | Nil | Nil | Nil | 2.1 | Nil | Nil | Nil |
| % Net Income of Revenue | 21.0 | 17.1 | 14.0 | 11.4 | 14.7 | 16.8 | 18.4 | 19.2 | 3.5 | NM |
| % Return on Assets | 16.5 | 12.4 | 9.1 | 7.9 | 9.2 | 10.4 | 11.5 | 12.9 | 3.0 | NM |
| % Return on Equity | 22.9 | 16.8 | 12.1 | 10.0 | 11.1 | 12.3 | 13.4 | 15.8 | 4.0 | NM |

Data as orig reptd.; bef. results of disc opers/spec. items. Per share data adj. for stk. divs.; EPS diluted. E-Estimated. NA-Not Available. NM-Not Meaningful. NR-Not Ranked. UR-Under Review.

**Office:** 401 Elliott Avenue West, Seattle, WA 98119.
**Telephone:** 206-272-5555.
**Website:** http://www.f5.com
**Chrmn:** A.J. Higginson

**Pres & CEO:** J. McAdam
**SVP & CFO:** A. Reinland
**SVP & CTO:** K.D. Triebes
**SVP & Chief Acctg Officer:** J. Rodriguez

**Board Members:** G. Ames, D. L. Bevier, J. C. Chadwick, J. H. Chapple, K. D. Guelich, A. J. Higginson, J. McAdam, S. Thompson

**Founded:** 1996
**Domicile:** Washington
**Employees:** 2,488

The McGraw-Hill Companies

# Fidelity National Information Services Inc

STANDARD
&POOR'S

| S&P Recommendation **HOLD** ★★★☆☆ | Price $22.79 (as of Nov 29, 2011) | 12-Mo. Target Price $30.00 | Investment Style Large-Cap Growth |
|---|---|---|---|

**GICS Sector** Information Technology
**Sub-Industry** Data Processing & Outsourced Services

**Summary** This company is a leading provider of core processing services and products to financial institutions.

## Key Stock Statistics (Source S&P, Vickers, company reports)

| | | | | | | | |
|---|---|---|---|---|---|---|---|
| 52-Wk Range | $33.76–22.53 | S&P Oper. EPS 2011**E** | 2.30 | Market Capitalization(B) | $6.825 | Beta | 0.68 |
| Trailing 12-Month EPS | $1.50 | S&P Oper. EPS 2012**E** | 2.55 | Yield (%) | 0.88 | S&P 3-Yr. Proj. EPS CAGR(%) | 12 |
| Trailing 12-Month P/E | 15.2 | P/E on S&P Oper. EPS 2011**E** | 9.9 | Dividend Rate/Share | $0.20 | S&P Credit Rating | BB |
| $10K Invested 5 Yrs Ago | NA | Common Shares Outstg. (M) | 299.5 | Institutional Ownership (%) | 83 | | |

## Price Performance

30-Week Mov. Avg. ···· 10-Week Mov. Avg. - - **GAAP Earnings vs. Previous Year**   Volume Above Avg. ⅢⅢ STARS
12-Mo. Target Price — Relative Strength — ▲ Up ▼ Down ▶ No Change   Below Avg. ⅢⅢ ★

[Price performance chart showing years 2008, 2009, 2010, 2011 with J A S O N D monthly markers]

Options: ASE, CBOE, P, Ph

Analysis prepared by Equity Analyst **Dylan Cathers** on Nov 29, 2011, when the stock traded at **$22.93**.

## Highlights

▶ We expect 9.0% revenue growth in 2011, aided by what we anticipate will be greater investment in technology by FIS's financial clients and by the purchase of Capco (December 2010), and a 5.5% increase in 2012. We look for organic growth to accelerate into early 2012 despite a slow recovery in the global economy, and we see ample opportunity for FIS to cross-sell add-on services to its large base of core processing customers. We also expect good gains overseas, including in Asia, Brazil and northern Europe. Partly offsetting some of our optimism is the ongoing decline in FIS's check processing business reflecting declining usage of checks, the potential for business disruption due to ongoing industry consolidation, and pricing pressure.

▶ We look for modestly wider operating margins in 2011 and 2012, on a higher mix of services as well as the addition of Capco.

▶ Our 2011 adjusted EPS estimate is $2.30, and we see a rise to $2.55 in 2012. Our estimates exclude projected M&A and restructuring charges and purchase price amortization.

## Investment Rationale/Risk

▶ We expect FIS to continue cost-cutting efforts as it targets post-M&A efficiencies. The purchase of Capco will aid revenue growth, although we expect organic growth to improve as well. We see strategic benefit from the purchase as FIS expands its professional services capabilities. Existing contracts should allow FIS to generate the vast majority of revenues on a recurring basis, and new core deals should drive a ramp-up in revenues as clients "go live." We are concerned about higher debt levels after FIS executed a leveraged recapitalization to buy back shares. Despite this, we view the shares as fairly valued at recent levels, noting the company's strong adjusted cash flow.

▶ Risks to our recommendation and target price include ongoing consolidation among financial services clients that may lead to business loss or disruption. We are also concerned about higher interest expense after a recent debt issuance to fund a large share buyback.

▶ We apply an 11.8X multiple to our 2012 EPS estimate to derive our 12-month target price of $30, a discount to the recent mean for data processing peers of 14.5X.

## Qualitative Risk Assessment

| LOW | **MEDIUM** | HIGH |
|---|---|---|

Our risk assessment reflects the company's exposure to the financial services industry and ongoing acquisition integration risks, offset by the high base of recurring revenue from the company's transaction processing business.

## Quantitative Evaluations

**S&P Quality Ranking**   NR

| D | C | B- | B | B+ | A- | A | A+ |
|---|---|---|---|---|---|---|---|

**Relative Strength Rank**   WEAK

24

LOWEST = 1   HIGHEST = 99

## Revenue/Earnings Data

**Revenue (Million $)**

| | 1Q | 2Q | 3Q | 4Q | Year |
|---|---|---|---|---|---|
| 2011 | 1,383 | 1,442 | 1,426 | -- | -- |
| 2010 | 1,250 | 1,286 | 1,367 | 1,396 | 5,270 |
| 2009 | 797.8 | 834.8 | 850.7 | 1,301 | 3,770 |
| 2008 | 1,291 | 1,339 | 893.8 | 862.0 | 3,446 |
| 2007 | 1,124 | 1,176 | 1,168 | 1,330 | 4,758 |
| 2006 | 900.9 | 1,022 | 1,081 | 1,129 | 4,133 |

**Earnings Per Share ($)**

| | 1Q | 2Q | 3Q | 4Q | Year |
|---|---|---|---|---|---|
| 2011 | 0.31 | 0.42 | 0.47 | E0.64 | E2.30 |
| 2010 | 0.25 | 0.24 | 0.40 | 0.40 | 1.27 |
| 2009 | 0.18 | 0.31 | 0.35 | -0.15 | 0.42 |
| 2008 | 0.35 | 0.38 | 0.24 | 0.26 | 0.61 |
| 2007 | 0.30 | 0.75 | 1.02 | 0.55 | 2.60 |
| 2006 | 0.23 | 0.34 | 0.41 | 0.39 | 1.37 |

Fiscal year ended Dec. 31. Next earnings report expected: Early February. EPS Estimates based on S&P Operating Earnings; historical GAAP earnings are as reported.

## Dividend Data (Dates: mm/dd Payment Date: mm/dd/yy)

| Amount ($) | Date Decl. | Ex-Div. Date | Stk. of Record | Payment Date |
|---|---|---|---|---|
| 0.050 | 01/26 | 03/15 | 03/17 | 03/31/11 |
| 0.050 | 04/26 | 06/14 | 06/16 | 06/30/11 |
| 0.050 | 07/19 | 09/14 | 09/16 | 09/30/11 |
| 0.050 | 10/18 | 12/14 | 12/16 | 12/30/11 |

Dividends have been paid since 2006. Source: Company reports.

---

**Please read the Required Disclosures and Analyst Certification on the last page of this report.**

The **McGraw·Hill** Companies

# Fidelity National Information Services Inc

STANDARD
&POOR'S

## Business Summary November 29, 2011

CORPORATE OVERVIEW. Fidelity National Information Services, Inc. (FIS) was formed via the combination, on February 1, 2006, of the information processing subsidiary of Fidelity National Financial (FNF) and Certegy, a provider of card and check processing services. As a result of the combination, the company became a leading provider of technology solutions, processing services, and information-based services to the financial industry. Until 2008, FIS operated in two main business segments: Transaction Processing Services (TPS) and Lender Processing Services (LPS). On July 2, 2008, FIS completed the spin-off of Lender Processing Services to shareholders. In October 2009, FIS acquired Metavante Technologies in a stock transaction valued at $4.2 billion. After these transactions, FIS served more than 14,000 financial institution customers in more than 100 countries, at December 31, 2010.

The company's segments were recast in late 2008 as Financial Solutions, Payment Solutions and International Solutions. The Financial Solutions segment includes products and services that address the core processing needs of clients such as banks, credit unions, commercial and automotive lenders, and independent community banks. Core processing solutions include applications used to process deposits, loans, and other central services provided to customers of a financial institution. Channel solutions, which include applications that improve customer interaction are also included in this segment.

These include customer-facing channels through which customers access an institution's products and services, such as ATMs, and the Internet, as well as call centers. Other solutions offered include decision management solutions, which aid in the management of accounts throughout their lifecycle, applications that support wholesale and commercial banking, and assist in the evaluation and management of auto loans. Other solutions offered through this segment support risk management and fraud detection, branch automation and compliance. In 2010, the Financial Solutions segment accounted for almost 36% of total revenues.

Through its Payment Solutions segment, FIS offers payment and electronic funds services to banks, credit unions and other financial institutions. Segment offerings include: debit and electronic funds transfer processing, Internet banking and bill payment, merchant processing, item processing, credit card production and activation, fraud management, check authorization and pre-paid card management and administration services. Revenues from this segment comprised 47% of 2010 revenues.

## Company Financials Fiscal Year Ended Dec. 31

| Per Share Data ($) | 2010 | 2009 | 2008 | 2007 | 2006 | 2005 | 2004 | 2003 | 2002 | 2001 |
|---|---|---|---|---|---|---|---|---|---|---|
| Tangible Book Value | NM | NM | NM | NM | NM | 3.53 | 0.55 | NA | NA | NA |
| Cash Flow | 2.90 | 2.03 | 2.03 | 4.04 | 3.66 | 2.48 | 2.40 | NA | NA | NA |
| Earnings | 1.27 | 0.42 | 0.61 | 2.60 | 1.37 | 1.66 | 0.92 | NA | NA | NA |
| S&P Core Earnings | 1.25 | 0.42 | 0.70 | 1.72 | 1.37 | 0.98 | 0.94 | 1.00 | NA | NA |
| Dividends | 0.20 | 0.20 | 0.20 | 0.20 | 0.20 | Nil | Nil | NA | NA | NA |
| Payout Ratio | 16% | 48% | 33% | 8% | 15% | Nil | Nil | NA | NA | NA |
| Prices:High | 30.78 | 26.00 | 43.83 | 57.80 | 42.62 | NA | NA | NA | NA | NA |
| Prices:Low | 22.13 | 15.20 | 11.15 | 39.99 | 33.50 | NA | NA | NA | NA | NA |
| P/E Ratio:High | 24 | 62 | 72 | 22 | 31 | NA | NA | NA | NA | NA |
| P/E Ratio:Low | 17 | 36 | 18 | 15 | 24 | NA | NA | NA | NA | NA |

| Income Statement Analysis (Million $) | 2010 | 2009 | 2008 | 2007 | 2006 | 2005 | 2004 | 2003 | 2002 | 2001 |
|---|---|---|---|---|---|---|---|---|---|---|
| Revenue | 5,270 | 3,770 | 3,446 | 4,758 | 4,133 | 1,117 | 1,040 | 1,945 | 654 | 418 |
| Operating Income | 1,699 | 833 | 710 | 1,030 | 1,025 | 248 | 227 | 518 | 116 | 64.4 |
| Depreciation | 620 | 434 | 276 | 284 | 434 | 51.9 | 47.4 | 144 | 18.6 | 9.45 |
| Interest Expense | 173 | 134 | 148 | 201 | 193 | 12.8 | 12.9 | 2.83 | 2.32 | 1.33 |
| Pretax Income | 616 | 156 | 179 | 813 | 409 | 174 | 168 | 362 | 106 | 53.8 |
| Effective Tax Rate | NA | 33.4% | 32.2% | 37.0% | 36.7% | 39.5% | 37.0% | 38.8% | 37.3% | 40.9% |
| Net Income | 401 | 101 | 117 | 510 | 259 | 106 | 106 | 207 | 58.2 | 31.0 |
| S&P Core Earnings | 441 | 101 | 135 | 338 | 259 | 196 | 189 | 200 | NA | NA |

| Balance Sheet & Other Financial Data (Million $) | 2010 | 2009 | 2008 | 2007 | 2006 | 2005 | 2004 | 2003 | 2002 | 2001 |
|---|---|---|---|---|---|---|---|---|---|---|
| Cash | 338 | 431 | 221 | 355 | 212 | 138 | 86.7 | 100 | 56.5 | NA |
| Current Assets | 1,673 | 1,666 | 1,180 | 1,830 | 1,301 | 445 | 409 | 503 | 260 | NA |
| Total Assets | 14,162 | 13,998 | 7,490 | 9,795 | 7,631 | 972 | 922 | 2,371 | 556 | NA |
| Current Liabilities | 1,286 | 1,235 | 852 | 1,254 | 881 | 234 | 290 | 370 | 168 | NA |
| Long Term Debt | 4,935 | 3,017 | 2,409 | 4,275 | 2,948 | 228 | 274 | 10.5 | 18.9 | NA |
| Common Equity | 6,403 | 8,309 | 3,538 | 3,781 | 3,548 | 459 | 300 | 1,904 | 295 | NA |
| Total Capital | 11,912 | 11,772 | 6,212 | 8,194 | 6,892 | 716 | 614 | 1,958 | 392 | NA |
| Capital Expenditures | 133 | 52.5 | 76.7 | 114 | 122 | 63.6 | 40.9 | 57.3 | 3.35 | 0.50 |
| Cash Flow | 1,020 | 486 | 393 | 795 | 693 | 157 | 153 | 351 | 76.8 | 40.5 |
| Current Ratio | 1.3 | 1.4 | 1.4 | 1.5 | 1.5 | 1.9 | 1.4 | 1.4 | 1.6 | NA |
| % Long Term Debt of Capitalization | 41.4 | 25.6 | 37.3 | 51.3 | 42.8 | 31.8 | 44.6 | 0.5 | 4.8 | Nil |
| % Net Income of Revenue | 7.6 | 2.7 | 3.4 | 10.7 | 6.3 | 9.4 | 10.2 | 10.6 | 8.9 | 7.4 |
| % Return on Assets | 2.9 | 0.9 | 1.4 | 5.9 | 4.4 | 11.1 | 12.4 | 14.1 | NA | NA |
| % Return on Equity | 5.5 | 1.7 | 3.2 | 14.8 | 12.2 | 27.5 | 37.7 | 18.8 | NA | NA |

Data as orig reptd.; bef. results of disc opers/spec. items. Per share data adj. for stk. divs.; EPS diluted. E-Estimated. NA-Not Available. NM-Not Meaningful. NR-Not Ranked. UR-Under Review.

**Office:** 601 Riverside Avenue, Jacksonville, FL 32204.
**Telephone:** 904-854-5000.
**Website:** http://www.fisglobal.com
**Chrmn:** W.P. Foley, II

**Pres & CEO:** F. Martire
**COO:** G. Norcross
**EVP & CFO:** M.D. Hayford
**EVP, Secy & General Counsel:** M.L. Gravelle

**Board Members:** W. P. Foley, II, T. M. Hagerty, K. W. Hughes, D. K. Hunt, S. A. James, F. Martire, R. N. Massey, J. Neary

**Founded:** 2001
**Domicile:** Georgia
**Employees:** 33,000

The McGraw·Hill Companies

# Fifth Third Bancorp

STANDARD
&POOR'S

| S&P Recommendation | BUY ★★★★☆ | Price | 12-Mo. Target Price | Investment Style |
|---|---|---|---|---|
| | | $10.97 (as of Nov 25, 2011) | $15.00 | Large-Cap Blend |

**GICS Sector** Financials
**Sub-Industry** Regional Banks

**Summary** This diversified financial services company, based in Cincinnati, operates more than 1,300 branches in Ohio, Michigan, and several other states.

## Key Stock Statistics (Source S&P, Vickers, company reports)

| | | | | | | | | |
|---|---|---|---|---|---|---|---|---|
| 52-Wk Range | $15.75–9.13 | S&P Oper. EPS 2011**E** | 1.21 | Market Capitalization(B) | $10.090 | Beta | 2.20 |
| Trailing 12-Month EPS | $1.19 | S&P Oper. EPS 2012**E** | 1.35 | Yield (%) | 2.92 | S&P 3-Yr. Proj. EPS CAGR(%) | 28 |
| Trailing 12-Month P/E | 9.2 | P/E on S&P Oper. EPS 2011**E** | 9.1 | Dividend Rate/Share | $0.32 | S&P Credit Rating | BBB |
| $10K Invested 5 Yrs Ago | $3,139 | Common Shares Outstg. (M) | 919.8 | Institutional Ownership (%) | 78 | | |

## Price Performance

- 30-Week Mov. Avg. · · · 10-Week Mov. Avg. – · – GAAP Earnings vs. Previous Year Volume Above Avg. STARS
- 12-Mo. Target Price — Relative Strength ▲ Up ▼ Down ► No Change Below Avg. ★

2008    2009    2010    2011

Options: ASE, CBOE, P, Ph

Analysis prepared by Equity Analyst **Erik Oja** on Nov 22, 2011, when the stock traded at **$11.35**.

## Highlights

➤ For 2011, we project fee income, excluding gains and losses, of $2.15 billion, down 5.0% from $2.26 billion in 2010, as we expect the mortgage refinancing boom to wind down, and we see lower service charges on deposits. Further downward pressure is being exerted by the Fed's debit interchange pricing rules, effective October 1. For 2012, we expect a 0.1% decline in fee income. We forecast a 2.4% decrease in net interest income in 2011, to $3.52 billion, on a lower net interest margin, offsetting improving loan growth. We expect a 1.4% decline in 2012. We see a 4.7% decline in total revenues in 2011, followed by a 1.1% decline in 2012. We expect 3.7% growth in 2013.

➤ Our 2011 net chargeoff estimate is $1.16 billion, and our 2012 forecast is $800 million, down sharply from $2.328 billion in 2010. We look for loan loss provisions to fall faster than net chargeoffs, given FITB's higher-than-peers allowance of $2.439 billion (a higher-than-peers 215% of nonperforming loans). Our provisioning forecasts are $480 million for 2011 and $600 million for 2012, down from $1.538 billion in 2010.

➤ We see EPS of $1.21 in 2011 and $1.35 in 2012.

## Investment Rationale/Risk

➤ Recent results show continuing improvement in loan credit quality and stability in FITB's higher-than-peers capital levels. We think FITB should be able to generate enough internal capital through 2011 to continue to raise capital levels by year end. In our view, FITB has a balance sheet that is stronger than many of its large regional banking peers in terms of its large allowance for loan losses, relatively high capital level, and a large and stable base of core deposits. We also think financial reform will affect FITB less than larger banking peers. Our main concern is that earnings growth has been relatively slow, and that earnings quality has been low compared to peers, due to a large portion of earnings coming from releases of reserves for nonperforming loans.

➤ Risks to our recommendation and target price include worsening unemployment, declining loan growth, an SEC investigation, and the costs of a possible foreclosure and mortgage servicing settlement.

➤ Our 12-month target price of $15 equals 10.9X our forward four quarters EPS estimate of $1.38, above peers.

## Qualitative Risk Assessment

| LOW | MEDIUM | HIGH |
|---|---|---|

We have a positive view of the many steps FITB has taken over the past three years to rebuild capital levels and credit quality, but numerous credit challenges remain in its Florida and Michigan loan portfolios.

## Quantitative Evaluations

**S&P Quality Ranking**      B

| D | C | B- | B | B+ | A- | A | A+ |
|---|---|---|---|---|---|---|---|

**Relative Strength Rank**      MODERATE

61

LOWEST = 1      HIGHEST = 99

## Revenue/Earnings Data

**Revenue (Million $)**

| | 1Q | 2Q | 3Q | 4Q | Year |
|---|---|---|---|---|---|
| 2011 | 1,644 | 1,701 | 1,720 | -- | -- |
| 2010 | 1,770 | 1,736 | 1,953 | 676.0 | 7,218 |
| 2009 | 1,875 | 3,762 | 2,020 | 1,794 | 9,450 |
| 2008 | 2,311 | 1,929 | 2,265 | 2,048 | 8,554 |
| 2007 | 2,108 | 2,202 | 2,251 | 2,126 | 8,479 |
| 2006 | 2,015 | 2,132 | 2,196 | 1,765 | 8,108 |

**Earnings Per Share ($)**

| | 1Q | 2Q | 3Q | 4Q | Year |
|---|---|---|---|---|---|
| 2011 | 0.10 | 0.35 | 0.40 | E0.36 | E1.21 |
| 2010 | -0.09 | 0.16 | 0.22 | 0.33 | 0.63 |
| 2009 | -0.04 | 1.15 | -0.20 | -0.20 | 0.67 |
| 2008 | 0.54 | -0.37 | -0.14 | -3.82 | -3.94 |
| 2007 | 0.65 | 0.69 | 0.61 | 0.07 | 1.99 |
| 2006 | 0.65 | 0.69 | 0.68 | 0.12 | 2.12 |

Fiscal year ended Dec. 31. Next earnings report expected: Late January. EPS Estimates based on S&P Operating Earnings; historical GAAP earnings are as reported.

## Dividend Data (Dates: mm/dd Payment Date: mm/dd/yy)

| Amount ($) | Date Decl. | Ex-Div. Date | Stk. of Record | Payment Date |
|---|---|---|---|---|
| 0.060 | 03/22 | 03/30 | 04/01 | 04/21/11 |
| 0.060 | 06/21 | 06/29 | 07/01 | 07/21/11 |
| 0.080 | 09/20 | 09/28 | 09/30 | 10/20/11 |
| 0.080 | 09/20 | 09/28 | 09/30 | 10/20/11 |

Dividends have been paid since 1952. Source: Company reports.

---

**Please read the Required Disclosures and Analyst Certification on the last page of this report.**

The McGraw·Hill Companies

# Fifth Third Bancorp

STANDARD
&POOR'S

## Business Summary November 22, 2011

CORPORATE OVERVIEW. Fifth Third Bancorp (FITB) operates in four segments: commercial banking, branch banking, consumer lending, and investment advisers. Processing solutions, which was sold in mid-2009, had been a fifth segment.

Commercial banking provides a comprehensive range of financial services and products to large and middle-market businesses, governments and professional customers. Branch banking offers depository and loan products, such as checking and savings accounts, home equity lines of credit, credit cards, and loans for automobiles and other personal financing needs. Consumer lending includes mortgage and home equity lending activities and other indirect lending activities. Mortgage and home equity lending activities include the origination, retention and servicing of mortgage and home equity loans or lines of credit, sales and securitizations of those loans or pools of loans or lines of credit and all associated hedging activities. Investment advisers provides a full range of investment alternatives for individuals, companies and not-for-profit organizations.

MARKET PROFILE. As of June 30, 2011, which is the latest available FDIC

branch-level data, FITB had 1,336 branches and $77.5 billion in deposits, with 41% of its deposits concentrated in Ohio and 17% in Michigan. In Ohio, FITB had 370 branches, $31.7 billion of deposits, and a deposit market share of about 12.6%, ranking first. In Michigan, FITB had 239 branches, $13.1 billion of deposits, and a deposit market share of about 6.8%, ranking fifth. In Illinois, FITB had 162 branches, $8.0 billion of deposits, and a deposit market share of about 2.1%, ranking 10th. In Florida, FITB had 168 branches, $8.0 billion of deposits, and a deposit market share of about 1.8%, ranking ninth. In Indiana, FITB had 139 branches, $6.6 billion of deposits, and a deposit market share of about 5.7%, ranking third. In Kentucky, FITB had 107 branches, $4.9 billion of deposits, and a deposit market share of about 6.5%, ranking second. In addition, FITB had a total of $5.2 billion in deposits and 151 offices in Tennessee, North Carolina, Georgia, West Virginia, Pennsylvania and Missouri.

## Company Financials Fiscal Year Ended Dec. 31

| Per Share Data ($) | 2010 | 2009 | 2008 | 2007 | 2006 | 2005 | 2004 | 2003 | 2002 | 2001 |
|---|---|---|---|---|---|---|---|---|---|---|
| Tangible Book Value | 9.94 | 9.26 | 7.87 | 11.11 | 13.78 | 12.72 | 13.33 | 13.46 | 13.12 | 13.09 |
| Earnings | 0.63 | 0.67 | -3.94 | 1.99 | 2.12 | 2.77 | 2.68 | 2.97 | 2.76 | 1.86 |
| S&P Core Earnings | 0.52 | -0.87 | -2.36 | 2.19 | 2.14 | 2.78 | 2.69 | 2.84 | 2.56 | 1.63 |
| Dividends | 0.04 | 0.04 | 0.04 | 1.70 | 1.58 | 1.46 | 1.31 | 1.13 | 0.98 | 0.83 |
| Payout Ratio | 6% | 6% | NM | 85% | 75% | 53% | 49% | 38% | 36% | 45% |
| Prices:High | 15.95 | 11.20 | 28.58 | 43.32 | 41.57 | 48.12 | 60.00 | 62.15 | 69.70 | 64.77 |
| Prices:Low | 9.81 | 1.01 | 6.32 | 24.82 | 35.86 | 35.04 | 45.32 | 47.05 | 55.26 | 45.69 |
| P/E Ratio:High | 25 | 17 | NM | 22 | 20 | 17 | 22 | 21 | 25 | 35 |
| P/E Ratio:Low | 16 | 2 | NM | 12 | 17 | 13 | 17 | 16 | 20 | 25 |

### Income Statement Analysis (Million $)

| | 2010 | 2009 | 2008 | 2007 | 2006 | 2005 | 2004 | 2003 | 2002 | 2001 |
|---|---|---|---|---|---|---|---|---|---|---|
| Net Interest Income | 3,604 | 3,354 | 3,514 | 3,009 | 2,873 | 2,965 | 3,012 | 2,905 | 2,700 | 2,433 |
| Tax Equivalent Adjustment | 18.0 | 19.0 | 22.0 | 24.0 | 26.0 | 31.0 | 36.0 | 39.0 | 39.5 | 45.5 |
| Non Interest Income | 2,729 | 4,782 | 2,870 | 2,494 | 1,657 | 2,461 | 2,502 | 2,399 | 2,047 | 1,626 |
| Loan Loss Provision | 1,538 | 3,543 | 4,560 | 628 | 343 | 330 | 268 | 399 | 247 | 236 |
| % Expense/Operating Revenue | 60.9% | 47.0% | 55.5% | 55.3% | 67.1% | 53.6% | 53.5% | 46.0% | 51.9% | 57.7% |
| Pretax Income | 940 | 767 | -2,664 | 1,537 | 1,627 | 2,208 | 2,237 | 2,547 | 2,432 | 1,653 |
| Effective Tax Rate | 19.9% | 3.91% | NM | 30.0% | 27.2% | 29.8% | 31.8% | 31.6% | 31.2% | 33.3% |
| Net Income | 753 | 737 | -2,113 | 1,076 | 1,184 | 1,549 | 1,525 | 1,722 | 1,635 | 1,101 |
| % Net Interest Margin | 3.66 | 3.32 | 3.54 | 3.36 | 3.06 | 3.23 | 3.48 | 3.62 | 3.96 | 3.82 |
| S&P Core Earnings | 411 | -617 | -1,301 | 1,183 | 1,191 | 1,555 | 1,529 | 1,650 | 1,513 | 965 |

### Balance Sheet & Other Financial Data (Million $)

| | 2010 | 2009 | 2008 | 2007 | 2006 | 2005 | 2004 | 2003 | 2002 | 2001 |
|---|---|---|---|---|---|---|---|---|---|---|
| Money Market Assets | 294 | 355 | 1,191 | 171 | 187 | 117 | 77.0 | 55.0 | 312 | 225 |
| Investment Securities | 15,767 | 18,568 | 13,088 | 11,032 | 12,218 | 22,471 | 25,474 | 29,402 | 25,828 | 20,748 |
| Commercial Loans | 43,462 | 44,805 | 50,479 | 40,412 | 36,114 | 33,214 | 30,601 | 28,242 | 22,614 | 10,839 |
| Other Loans | 34,029 | 28,225 | 30,877 | 39,841 | 39,485 | 38,024 | 29,207 | 25,493 | 23,314 | 30,709 |
| Total Assets | 111,007 | 113,380 | 119,764 | 110,962 | 100,669 | 105,225 | 94,456 | 91,143 | 80,894 | 71,026 |
| Demand Deposits | 39,973 | 39,346 | 29,113 | 36,179 | 36,908 | 39,020 | 37,288 | 31,899 | 11,139 | 10,595 |
| Time Deposits | 41,675 | 44,959 | 49,500 | 39,266 | 32,472 | 13,656 | 20,938 | 25,196 | 41,069 | 35,259 |
| Long Term Debt | 9,558 | 10,507 | 13,585 | 12,857 | 12,558 | 15,227 | 13,983 | 9,063 | 8,179 | 7,030 |
| Common Equity | 10,397 | 9,888 | 7,836 | 9,152 | 10,013 | 9,437 | 8,915 | 8,516 | 8,466 | 7,630 |
| % Return on Assets | 0.7 | 0.6 | NM | 1.0 | 1.2 | 1.6 | 1.6 | 2.0 | 2.2 | 1.6 |
| % Return on Equity | 7.4 | 8.3 | NM | 11.2 | 12.2 | 16.9 | 17.3 | 20.3 | 20.3 | 15.4 |
| % Loan Loss Reserve | 3.9 | 4.9 | 3.3 | 1.1 | 1.0 | 1.0 | 1.2 | 1.4 | 1.4 | 1.4 |
| % Loans/Deposits | 94.9 | 91.1 | 107.0 | 106.8 | 108.8 | 105.6 | 103.7 | 94.9 | 94.4 | 95.4 |
| % Equity to Assets | 9.1 | 7.6 | 7.4 | 9.1 | 9.4 | 9.2 | 9.5 | 9.9 | 10.6 | 10.2 |

Data as orig reptd.; bef. results of disc opers/spec. items. Per share data adj. for stk. divs.; EPS diluted. E-Estimated. NA-Not Available. NM-Not Meaningful. NR-Not Ranked. UR-Under Review.

**Office:** 38 Fountain Square Plaza, Fifth Third Center, Cincinnati, OH 45263.
**Telephone:** 800-972-3030.
**Website:** http://www.53.com
**Chrmn:** W.M. Isaac

**Pres & CEO:** K.T. Kabat
**COO & EVP:** G.D. Carmichael
**EVP & CFO:** D.T. Poston
**SVP, Chief Acctg Officer & Cntlr:** M.D. Hazel

**Investor Contact:** C.G. Marshall
**Board Members:** D. F. Allen, E. Bayh, III, U. L. Bridgeman, Jr., E. L. Brumback, J. P. Hackett, G. R. Heminger, J. D. Hoover, W. M. Isaac, K. T. Kabat, M. D. Livingston, H. G. Meijer, J. J. Schiff, M. C. Williams

**Founded:** 1862
**Domicile:** Ohio
**Employees:** 21,613

# FirstEnergy Corp.

**STANDARD &POOR'S**

| S&P Recommendation | HOLD ★★★☆☆ | Price $41.94 (as of Nov 25, 2011) | 12-Mo. Target Price $46.00 | Investment Style Large-Cap Blend |
|---|---|---|---|---|

**GICS Sector** Utilities
**Sub-Industry** Electric Utilities

**Summary** This electric utility holding company, which serves about 4.5 million customers in portions of Ohio, Pennsylvania and New Jersey, recently acquired Allegheny Energy.

## Key Stock Statistics (Source S&P, Vickers, company reports)

| | | | | | | | |
|---|---|---|---|---|---|---|---|
| 52-Wk Range | $46.51–35.02 | S&P Oper. EPS 2011E | 3.45 | Market Capitalization(B) | $17.540 | Beta | 0.47 |
| Trailing 12-Month EPS | $2.49 | S&P Oper. EPS 2012E | 3.38 | Yield (%) | 5.25 | S&P 3-Yr. Proj. EPS CAGR(%) | -4 |
| Trailing 12-Month P/E | 16.8 | P/E on S&P Oper. EPS 2011E | 12.2 | Dividend Rate/Share | $2.20 | S&P Credit Rating | BBB- |
| $10K Invested 5 Yrs Ago | $8,893 | Common Shares Outstg. (M) | 418.2 | Institutional Ownership (%) | 71 | | |

## Price Performance

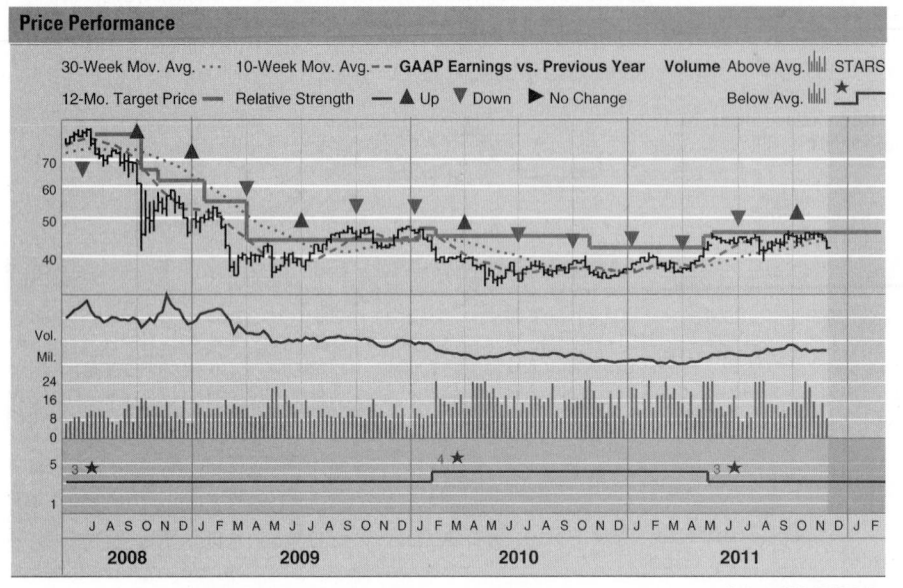

30-Week Mov. Avg. ···· 10-Week Mov. Avg. – – GAAP Earnings vs. Previous Year  Volume Above Avg. STARS
12-Mo. Target Price — Relative Strength  ▲ Up ▼ Down ► No Change  Below Avg.

Options: ASE, CBOE, P, Ph

Analysis prepared by Equity Analyst **Justin McCann** on Nov 21, 2011, when the stock traded at **$43.67**.

## Qualitative Risk Assessment

| LOW | MEDIUM | HIGH |
|---|---|---|

Our risk assessment reflects the strong and steady cash flow we expect from the company's regulated electric utility subsidiaries; its low-cost baseload power generation in Ohio and Pennsylvania; its low-risk transmission distribution operations in New Jersey and Pennsylvania; and its rate certainty in Ohio. This is partially offset by the company's below-average production performance from nuclear operations and our view of its high level of debt and environmental spending.

## Quantitative Evaluations

**S&P Quality Ranking** A-

| D | C | B- | B | B+ | A- | A | A+ |
|---|---|---|---|---|---|---|---|

**Relative Strength Rank** MODERATE

53

LOWEST = 1    HIGHEST = 99

## Highlights

▶ Excluding $0.82 of net one-time charges, we expect operating EPS in 2011 to decline about 4% from 2010's $3.61. Operating EPS of $1.34 in the third of quarter of 2011 was up $0.06 from the year-ago quarter, driven by higher power margins (aided by the hottest July in decades) and a $0.32 contribution from Allegheny Energy. However, this was substantially offset by nearly 38% more shares related to the Allegheny acquisition, which reduced EPS by $0.35.

▶ For 2012, we expect operating EPS to decline about 2% from anticipated results for 2011, as the Allegheny Energy synergies and a gradual improvement in the economy are more than offset by a decline in power margins and an assumed return to more normal weather.

▶ The acquisition of Allegheny Energy increased FirstEnergy's customer base by approximately 33% and its generating capacity by more than 65%. We expect the acquisition to be accretive to earnings by the end of the first quarter of 2012. The company said that the merger had realized, through September 30, 2011, about $165 million of pretax savings, or nearly 79% of its annual target of $210 million.

## Investment Rationale/Risk

▶ While the shares have retreated from their recent high, reflecting, we believe, the decline and volatility of the broader market, they were still up more that 18% year-to-date through mid-November. With this advance, the yield from the dividend declined from around 5.9% to the recent 5.0%. The strong performance in 2011 follows a 20% decline in 2010, when the stock was hurt, in our view, by the weakness in the economy and power markets, and by concerns that the planned merger could encounter difficulties during the regulatory approval process.

▶ Risks to our recommendation and target price include the possibility of a slower than expected recovery in the economy, and/or extended weakness in the power markets.

▶ While we do not expect dividend increases during the economic slowdown, we believe FE will still target future annual increases of 4% to 5%. The targeted growth rate is above both the industry's expected dividend growth rate and FE's own expected long-term EPS growth rate of 3% to 4%. Our 12-month target price of $46 reflects a modest discount-to-peers P/E of about 13.6X our 2012 EPS estimate.

## Revenue/Earnings Data

**Revenue (Million $)**

| | 1Q | 2Q | 3Q | 4Q | Year |
|---|---|---|---|---|---|
| 2011 | 3,457 | 3,944 | 4,582 | -- | -- |
| 2010 | 3,299 | 3,128 | 3,693 | 3,219 | 13,339 |
| 2009 | 3,334 | 3,271 | 3,408 | 2,954 | 12,967 |
| 2008 | 3,277 | 3,245 | 3,904 | 3,201 | 13,627 |
| 2007 | 2,973 | 3,109 | 3,641 | 3,079 | 12,802 |
| 2006 | 2,705 | 2,751 | 3,365 | 2,680 | 11,501 |

**Earnings Per Share ($)**

| | 1Q | 2Q | 3Q | 4Q | Year |
|---|---|---|---|---|---|
| 2011 | 0.15 | 0.43 | 1.22 | E0.74 | E3.45 |
| 2010 | 0.51 | 0.87 | 0.59 | 0.61 | 2.57 |
| 2009 | 0.39 | 1.36 | 0.77 | 0.78 | 3.29 |
| 2008 | 0.90 | 0.85 | 1.54 | 1.09 | 4.38 |
| 2007 | 0.92 | 1.10 | 1.34 | 0.87 | 4.22 |
| 2006 | 0.67 | 0.93 | 1.40 | 0.84 | 3.82 |

Fiscal year ended Dec. 31. Next earnings report expected: Mid February. EPS Estimates based on S&P Operating Earnings; historical GAAP earnings are as reported.

## Dividend Data (Dates: mm/dd Payment Date: mm/dd/yy)

| Amount ($) | Date Decl. | Ex-Div. Date | Stk. of Record | Payment Date |
|---|---|---|---|---|
| 0.025 | 02/15 | 03/01 | 02/25 | 03/07/11 |
| 0.550 | 02/15 | 05/04 | 05/06 | 06/01/11 |
| 0.550 | 07/19 | 08/03 | 08/05 | 09/01/11 |
| 0.550 | 09/20 | 11/03 | 11/07 | 12/01/11 |

Dividends have been paid since 1930. Source: Company reports.

**Please read the Required Disclosures and Analyst Certification on the last page of this report.**

The **McGraw-Hill** Companies

# FirstEnergy Corp.

## Business Summary November 21, 2011

CORPORATE OVERVIEW. FirstEnergy (FE) is a diversified energy company involved in the generation, transmission and distribution of electricity as well as energy management and related services. The company operates primarily through two core business segments: Regulated Services, which is comprised of seven electric utility operating companies and provides transmission and distribution services, and Power Supply Management Services, which owns and operates the generation assets and wholesale purchase of electricity, energy management and other energy-related services. In 2010, the electric utilities accounted for 93.9% of consolidated revenues, and the unregulated businesses 6.1%.

IMPACT OF MAJOR DEVELOPMENTS. On February 25, 2011, FirstEnergy completed the merger (announced on February 11, 2010) of Allegheny Energy, Inc., a Pennsylvania-headquartered electric utility holding company serving 1.6 million customers in portions of Pennsylvania, Maryland and West Virginia. Under the terms of the transaction (which included the assumption of approximately $3.8 billion of Allegheny net debt), Allegheny shareholders received 0.667 of a share of FirstEnergy for each Allegheny share. Upon the completion

of the transaction, FE shareholders had an approximate 73% interest in the combined company and Allegheny shareholders 27%. We believe the merger could result in potential synergies of about $180 million by the end of the first year and $350 million by the second, with about half occurring in the competitive generation business.

MARKET PROFILE. FirstEnergy's utility subsidiaries serves approximately six million customers within an area of 67,000 square miles in Ohio, Pennsylvania, New Jersey, New York, Maryland and West Virginia. Upon the completion of the merger with Allegheny Energy, the company's power generating facilities had demonstrated net capacity of about 23,260 megawatts (MW) of electricity, with coal plants expected to account for approximately 63.1% of the total; nuclear 17.2%; oil and natural gas peaking units 9.4%; hydroelectric 7.9; wind 1.6%; and other 1.9%.

## Company Financials Fiscal Year Ended Dec. 31

| Per Share Data ($) | 2010 | 2009 | 2008 | 2007 | 2006 | 2005 | 2004 | 2003 | 2002 | 2001 |
|---|---|---|---|---|---|---|---|---|---|---|
| Tangible Book Value | 9.30 | 9.79 | 8.88 | 11.06 | 9.83 | 9.63 | 7.70 | 6.55 | 4.11 | 6.04 |
| Earnings | 2.57 | 3.29 | 4.38 | 4.22 | 3.82 | 2.65 | 2.66 | 1.39 | 2.33 | 2.84 |
| S&P Core Earnings | 2.63 | 3.00 | 3.28 | 3.80 | 3.71 | 2.56 | 2.77 | 1.61 | 1.69 | 2.36 |
| Dividends | 2.20 | 2.20 | 2.20 | 2.00 | 1.80 | 1.67 | 1.50 | 1.50 | 1.50 | 1.13 |
| Payout Ratio | 86% | 67% | 50% | 47% | 47% | 63% | 56% | 108% | 64% | 40% |
| Prices:High | 47.09 | 53.63 | 84.00 | 74.98 | 61.70 | 53.36 | 43.41 | 38.90 | 39.12 | 36.98 |
| Prices:Low | 33.57 | 35.26 | 41.20 | 57.77 | 47.75 | 37.70 | 35.24 | 25.82 | 24.85 | 25.10 |
| P/E Ratio:High | 18 | 16 | 19 | 18 | 16 | 20 | 16 | 28 | 17 | 13 |
| P/E Ratio:Low | 13 | 11 | 9 | 14 | 13 | 14 | 13 | 19 | 11 | 9 |

| Income Statement Analysis (Million $) | | | | | | | | | | |
|---|---|---|---|---|---|---|---|---|---|---|
| Revenue | 13,339 | 12,967 | 13,627 | 12,802 | 11,501 | 11,989 | 12,453 | 12,307 | 12,152 | 7,999 |
| Depreciation | 914 | 736 | 789 | 1,657 | 1,457 | 1,870 | 1,756 | 1,282 | 1,106 | 890 |
| Maintenance | NA | NA | NA | NA | NA | NA | NA | NA | NA | NA |
| Fixed Charges Coverage | 2.83 | 2.46 | 4.02 | 3.95 | 3.78 | 3.39 | 3.25 | 1.88 | 2.25 | 2.85 |
| Construction Credits | NA | NA | NA | NA | NA | NA | NA | NA | 24.5 | 35.5 |
| Effective Tax Rate | 38.8% | 19.8% | 36.7% | 40.3% | 38.7% | 46.3% | 43.4% | 49.0% | 44.5% | 42.0% |
| Net Income | 784 | 1,006 | 1,342 | 1,309 | 1,258 | 873 | 874 | 422 | 686 | 655 |
| S&P Core Earnings | 800 | 920 | 1,005 | 1,177 | 1,211 | 841 | 911 | 492 | 496 | 546 |

| Balance Sheet & Other Financial Data (Million $) | | | | | | | | | | |
|---|---|---|---|---|---|---|---|---|---|---|
| Gross Property | 30,968 | 30,561 | 28,544 | 25,731 | 24,722 | 23,790 | 22,892 | 22,374 | 21,231 | 20,589 |
| Capital Expenditures | 1,963 | 2,203 | 2,888 | 1,633 | 1,315 | 1,208 | 846 | 856 | 998 | 852 |
| Net Property | 19,788 | 19,164 | 17,723 | 15,383 | 14,667 | 13,998 | 13,478 | 13,269 | 12,680 | 12,428 |
| Capitalization:Long Term Debt | 12,579 | 11,908 | 9,100 | 8,869 | 8,535 | 8,339 | 10,348 | 9,789 | 11,636 | 12,508 |
| Capitalization:% Long Term Debt | 59.5 | 58.2 | 52.3 | 49.7 | 48.6 | 47.1 | 53.7 | 53.1 | 62.0 | 62.8 |
| Capitalization:Preferred | Nil | Nil | Nil | Nil | Nil | 184 | 335 | 352 | Nil | Nil |
| Capitalization:% Preferred | Nil | Nil | Nil | Nil | Nil | 1.04 | 1.74 | 1.91 | Nil | Nil |
| Capitalization:Common | 8,545 | 8,559 | 8,283 | 8,977 | 9,035 | 9,188 | 8,589 | 8,289 | 7,120 | 7,399 |
| Capitalization:% Common | 40.5 | 41.8 | 47.7 | 50.3 | 51.4 | 51.9 | 44.6 | 45.0 | 38.0 | 37.2 |
| Total Capital | 22,578 | 22,299 | 19,546 | 20,517 | 20,310 | 20,437 | 21,597 | 20,608 | 21,360 | 22,852 |
| % Operating Ratio | 90.1 | 87.4 | 85.4 | 84.9 | 84.3 | 89.0 | 87.3 | 90.4 | 86.6 | 50.8 |
| % Earned on Net Property | 9.3 | 10.2 | 16.7 | 18.7 | 18.2 | 15.0 | 16.5 | 11.2 | 17.4 | 16.8 |
| % Return on Revenue | 5.9 | 7.8 | 9.8 | 10.2 | 10.9 | 7.3 | 7.0 | 3.4 | 5.6 | 8.2 |
| % Return on Invested Capital | 6.4 | 8.7 | 10.2 | 10.1 | 9.6 | 7.3 | 7.4 | 6.5 | 7.4 | 21.8 |
| % Return on Common Equity | 9.2 | 12.0 | 15.6 | 14.5 | 13.8 | 9.8 | 10.4 | 5.5 | 9.5 | 10.9 |

Data as orig reptd.; bef. results of disc opers/spec. items. Per share data adj. for stk. divs.; EPS diluted. E-Estimated. NA-Not Available. NM-Not Meaningful. NR-Not Ranked. UR-Under Review.

Office: 76 South Main Street, Akron, OH 44308-1890.
Telephone: 800-736-3402.
Website: http://www.firstenergycorp.com
Chrmn: G.M. Smart

Pres & CEO: A.J. Alexander
CFO: M.T. Clark
Chief Acctg Officer & Cntlr: H.L. Wagner
Treas: J.F. Pearson

Investor Contact: R.E. Seeholzer (800-736-3402)
Board Members: P. T. Addison, A. J. Alexander, M. Anderson, C. A. Cartwright, W. T. Cottle, R. B. Heisler, Jr., J. L. Johnson, T. J. Kleisner, E. J. Novak, Jr., C. D. Pappas, C. A. Rein, G. M. Smart, W. M. Taylor, J. T. Williams

Founded: 1996
Domicile: Ohio
Employees: 13,330

# First Horizon National Corp

STANDARD &POOR'S

| S&P Recommendation | HOLD ★★★☆☆ | Price $6.79 (as of Nov 25, 2011) | 12-Mo. Target Price $7.00 | Investment Style Large-Cap Blend |
|---|---|---|---|---|

**GICS Sector** Financials
**Sub-Industry** Regional Banks

**Summary** Memphis, Tennessee-based First Horizon National Corp. owns First Tennessee Bank and First Horizon Home Loan Corporation, and has assets of $25.6 billion.

## Key Stock Statistics (Source S&P, Vickers, company reports)

| | | | | | | | | |
|---|---|---|---|---|---|---|---|---|
| 52-Wk Range | $12.67– 5.38 | S&P Oper. EPS 2011E | 0.58 | Market Capitalization(B) | $1.790 | Beta | | 0.74 |
| Trailing 12-Month EPS | $0.16 | S&P Oper. EPS 2012E | 0.53 | Yield (%) | 0.59 | S&P 3-Yr. Proj. EPS CAGR(%) | | NM |
| Trailing 12-Month P/E | 42.4 | P/E on S&P Oper. EPS 2011E | 11.7 | Dividend Rate/Share | $0.04 | S&P Credit Rating | | BBB- |
| $10K Invested 5 Yrs Ago | $2,255 | Common Shares Outstg. (M) | 263.6 | Institutional Ownership (%) | 87 | | | |

## Price Performance

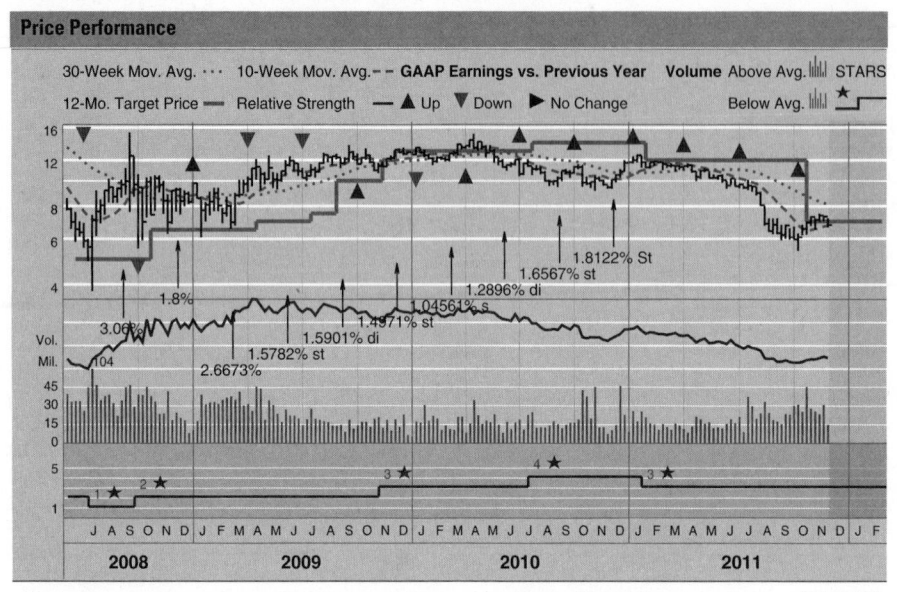

30-Week Mov. Avg. · · · 10-Week Mov. Avg. – – GAAP Earnings vs. Previous Year   Volume Above Avg. ▫▫▫ STARS
12-Mo. Target Price — Relative Strength — ▲ Up ▼ Down ► No Change   Below Avg. ▫▫▫ ★

Options: P, Ph

Analysis prepared by Equity Analyst **Erik Oja** on Oct 31, 2011, when the stock traded at **$7.08**.

### Highlights

► We expect loans outstanding to decline 2.9% in 2011, versus a 12.3% drop in 2010, followed by a 3.8% increase in 2012. Our net interest income forecast is $690 million for 2011, a decline of 5.6%, followed by a 4.1% decline in 2012. We forecast a 17.5% reduction in core fee income in 2011, due to a drop-off in mortgage banking. For 2012, we expect a 2.9% increase in core fee income. We see revenues declining 10.7% in 2011 and 3.9% in 2012.

► We expect 2011 earnings growth to be driven mostly by reductions of loan loss provisions. Our net chargeoff forecasts for 2011 and 2012 are $305 million and $85 million, respectively, down from $502 million in 2010. We expect 2011 and 2012 loan loss provisions of $42.5 million and $67 million, respectively, with 2011 at only 14% of our net chargeoff forecast, a lower than peers level of provisions, which we think will be made possible by FHN's relatively high allowance for loan losses.

► We project EPS of $0.58 for 2011 and $0.53 for 2012.

### Investment Rationale/Risk

► We think FHN's recovery is on track, with capital levels and allowances high and stable. Even with a third quarter rise in net chargeoffs, credit quality has improved greatly in the past two years. Although FHN appears inexpensive on a price to book value basis, at 0.74X September 30 tangible book value per share, we think the shares are fully valued on a price to earnings basis, currently at 13.5X our forward four quarters EPS estimate of $0.54. We expect very low EPS growth over the foreseeable future, due to our expectation that loan loss provisions will rise in 2012, that revenues will fall each year through 2013, and also due to FHN's relatively high non-interest expense levels.

► Risks to our recommendation and target price include greater than expected loan and balance sheet shrinkage, lower non-interest income, and elevated national unemployment.

► Our 12-month target price of $7 is based on an above-peers 13X multiple of our forward four quarters EPS estimate of $0.54, a multiple that reflects recovering earnings, and 0.7X our 2011 year-end tangible book value per share estimate of $9.90, a multiple in line with peer banks having similar credit quality.

## Qualitative Risk Assessment

| LOW | MEDIUM | HIGH |
|---|---|---|

Our risk assessment reflects FHN's ongoing recovery from credit losses, offset by its relatively high capital levels and good prospects for fee income growth.

## Quantitative Evaluations

**S&P Quality Ranking** B

| D | C | B- | B | B+ | A- | A | A+ |
|---|---|---|---|---|---|---|---|

**Relative Strength Rank** MODERATE

61

LOWEST = 1          HIGHEST = 99

## Revenue/Earnings Data

**Revenue (Million $)**

| | 1Q | 2Q | 3Q | 4Q | Year |
|---|---|---|---|---|---|
| 2011 | 399.4 | 395.5 | 429.3 | -- | -- |
| 2010 | 467.8 | 468.6 | 471.4 | 428.3 | 1,836 |
| 2009 | 669.4 | 547.8 | 540.2 | 246.2 | 2,226 |
| 2008 | 925.5 | 814.5 | 688.4 | 669.6 | 3,098 |
| 2007 | 866.4 | 875.2 | 786.1 | 638.5 | 3,166 |
| 2006 | 731.0 | 913.6 | 930.4 | 921.0 | 3,496 |

**Earnings Per Share ($)**

| | 1Q | 2Q | 3Q | 4Q | Year |
|---|---|---|---|---|---|
| 2011 | 0.15 | 0.06 | 0.12 | E0.14 | E0.58 |
| 2010 | -0.09 | 0.01 | 0.07 | -0.20 | -0.22 |
| 2009 | -0.35 | -0.53 | -0.19 | -0.29 | -1.37 |
| 2008 | -0.05 | -0.10 | -0.53 | -0.27 | -0.97 |
| 2007 | 0.46 | 0.14 | -0.09 | -1.67 | -1.16 |
| 2006 | 0.03 | 0.68 | 0.44 | 0.50 | 3.01 |

Fiscal year ended Dec. 31. Next earnings report expected: NA. EPS Estimates based on S&P Operating Earnings; historical GAAP earnings are as reported.

## Dividend Data (Dates: mm/dd Payment Date: mm/dd/yy)

| Amount ($) | Date Decl. | Ex-Div. Date | Stk. of Record | Payment Date |
|---|---|---|---|---|
| 0.010 | 01/19 | 03/09 | 03/11 | 04/01/11 |
| 0.010 | 04/19 | 06/08 | 06/10 | 07/01/11 |
| 0.010 | 07/19 | 09/14 | 09/16 | 10/01/11 |
| 0.010 | 10/18 | 12/14 | 12/16 | 01/01/12 |

Dividends have been paid since 2011. Source: Company reports.

# First Horizon National Corp

STANDARD &POOR'S

## Business Summary October 31, 2011

CORPORATE OVERVIEW. First Horizon National Corporation (FHN) operates as the holding company for First Tennessee Bank National Association, which provides various financial services in the United States and internationally.

FHN's services include general banking services for consumers, businesses, financial institutions, and governments; through FTN Financial - fixed income sales and trading, underwriting of bank-eligible securities and other fixed-income securities eligible for underwriting by financial subsidiaries, equity sales, trading, and research, loan sales, advisory services, correspondent banking, and derivative sales; transaction processing, including nationwide check clearing services and remittance processing; mortgage banking services; trust, fiduciary, and agency services; credit card products; discount brokerage and full-service brokerage; equipment finance; investment and financial advisory services; mutual fund sales as agent; retail and commercial insurance sales as agent; private mortgage reinsurance; and services related to health savings accounts.

FHN's loan portfolio includes commercial loans, such as commercial, financial, industrial, real estate commercial, and real estate construction loans; and retail loans, such as real estate residential, real estate construction, and other retail loans.

FHN's investment portfolio includes government agency issued mortgage-backed securities & collateralized mortgage obligations; U.S. treasuries; other U.S. government agencies; and states and municipalities.

FHN has 180 branch locations in four states: 169 branches in Tennessee counties, with a deposit market share of 12.8%, ranking second. FHN has seven branches in Mississippi, two branches in North Carolina, and two in Georgia.

## Company Financials Fiscal Year Ended Dec. 31

| Per Share Data ($) | 2010 | 2009 | 2008 | 2007 | 2006 | 2005 | 2004 | 2003 | 2002 | 2001 |
|---|---|---|---|---|---|---|---|---|---|---|
| Tangible Book Value | 8.31 | 8.49 | 8.08 | 12.44 | 14.17 | 12.66 | 12.28 | 11.19 | 9.93 | 8.56 |
| Earnings | -0.22 | -1.37 | -0.97 | -1.16 | 3.01 | 2.85 | 2.95 | 3.02 | 2.41 | 2.09 |
| S&P Core Earnings | -0.22 | -1.35 | -1.18 | -0.85 | 1.70 | 2.72 | 2.84 | 2.77 | 2.16 | 1.57 |
| Dividends | Nil | Nil | 0.33 | 1.50 | 1.50 | 1.45 | 1.36 | 1.08 | 0.88 | 0.76 |
| Payout Ratio | Nil | Nil | NM | NM | 50% | 51% | 46% | 36% | 36% | 36% |
| Prices:High | 15.13 | 13.73 | 18.70 | 37.87 | 35.89 | 37.34 | 40.54 | 40.42 | 34.17 | 31.24 |
| Prices:Low | 9.15 | 6.08 | 3.77 | 14.71 | 30.92 | 28.99 | 33.99 | 29.65 | 24.80 | 22.61 |
| P/E Ratio:High | NM | NM | NM | NM | 12 | 13 | 14 | 13 | 14 | 15 |
| P/E Ratio:Low | NM | NM | NM | NM | 10 | 10 | 12 | 10 | 10 | 11 |

| Income Statement Analysis (Million $) | | | | | | | | | | |
|---|---|---|---|---|---|---|---|---|---|---|
| Net Interest Income | 731 | 776 | 895 | 941 | 997 | 984 | 856 | 806 | 753 | 686 |
| Tax Equivalent Adjustment | 2.80 | 1.06 | 1.35 | 0.69 | NA | 1.17 | 1.10 | 1.26 | 1.50 | 2.10 |
| Non Interest Income | 974 | 1,234 | 1,491 | 861 | 1,233 | 1,400 | 1,342 | 1,638 | 1,550 | 1,321 |
| Loan Loss Provision | 270 | 880 | 1,080 | 273 | 83.1 | 67.7 | 48.3 | 86.7 | 92.2 | 93.5 |
| % Expense/Operating Revenue | 80.2% | 77.2% | 69.4% | 102.3% | 78.2% | 70.1% | 68.4% | 67.1% | 71.3% | 67.7% |
| Pretax Income | 49.4 | -421 | -350 | -316 | 338 | 645 | 667 | 719 | 558 | 494 |
| Effective Tax Rate | NM | NM | NM | NM | 25.8% | 31.6% | 31.9% | 34.2% | 32.5% | 33.2% |
| Net Income | 57.1 | -257 | -193 | -175 | 251 | 441 | 454 | 473 | 376 | 330 |
| % Net Interest Margin | 3.20 | 3.06 | 2.95 | 2.82 | 2.93 | 3.08 | 3.62 | 3.78 | 4.33 | 4.27 |
| S&P Core Earnings | -51.4 | -316 | -244 | -128 | 261 | 423 | 438 | 434 | 337 | 248 |

| Balance Sheet & Other Financial Data (Million $) | | | | | | | | | | |
|---|---|---|---|---|---|---|---|---|---|---|
| Money Market Assets | 1,712 | 1,692 | 1,926 | 2,898 | 3,415 | 3,629 | NA | NA | NA | NA |
| Investment Securities | 3,032 | 2,694 | 3,125 | 3,033 | 3,890 | 2,912 | 2,681 | 2,470 | 2,700 | 2,526 |
| Commercial Loans | 7,338 | 7,159 | 7,864 | 8,435 | 8,338 | 9,899 | 7,730 | 6,904 | 5,723 | 5,598 |
| Other Loans | 9,445 | 10,965 | 13,414 | 13,669 | 13,767 | 10,702 | 8,698 | 7,087 | 5,622 | 4,685 |
| Total Assets | 24,699 | 26,069 | 31,022 | 37,015 | 37,918 | 36,579 | 29,772 | 24,507 | 23,823 | 20,617 |
| Demand Deposits | 4,376 | 4,394 | 3,957 | 5,055 | 5,448 | 10,027 | 4,995 | 4,540 | 5,149 | 4,010 |
| Time Deposits | 10,832 | 10,473 | 10,285 | 11,977 | 14,766 | 13,411 | 14,788 | 11,140 | 10,564 | 9,596 |
| Long Term Debt | 3,228 | 2,891 | 4,768 | 6,825 | 6,132 | 3,733 | 2,617 | 1,117 | 1,074 | 3,066 |
| Common Equity | 2,383 | 2,209 | 2,497 | 2,136 | 2,462 | 2,312 | 2,041 | 1,850 | 1,691 | 1,478 |
| % Return on Assets | 0.2 | NM | NM | NM | 0.7 | 1.3 | 1.7 | 2.0 | 1.7 | 1.7 |
| % Return on Equity | NM | NM | NM | NM | 10.4 | 20.3 | 23.1 | 26.7 | 23.8 | 23.0 |
| % Loan Loss Reserve | 4.0 | 5.0 | 4.0 | 1.5 | 0.9 | 0.8 | 0.7 | 0.9 | 0.9 | 1.1 |
| % Loans/Deposits | 110.4 | 121.9 | 149.4 | 118.7 | 123.6 | 106.8 | 109.2 | 108.2 | 102.7 | 100.6 |
| % Equity to Assets | 9.0 | 8.2 | 6.8 | 6.1 | 6.5 | 6.6 | 7.2 | 7.3 | 7.1 | 7.3 |

Data as orig reptd.; bef. results of disc opers/spec. items. Per share data adj. for stk. divs.; EPS diluted. E-Estimated. NA-Not Available. NM-Not Meaningful. NR-Not Ranked. UR-Under Review.

Office: 165 Madison Avenue, Memphis, TN 38103.
Telephone: 901-523-4444.
Website: http://www.fhnc.com
Chrmn: M.D. Rose

Pres & CEO: B. Jordan
EVP & CFO: W.C. Losch, III
EVP & Chief Acctg Officer: J.F. Keen
EVP & Treas: T.C. Adams, Jr.

Investor Contact: D. Miller (901-523-4162)
Board Members: R. B. Carter, J. C. Compton, M. A. Emkes, V. B. Gregg, J. A. Haslam, III, B. Jordan, R. B. Martin, S. M. Niswonger, V. R. Palmer, C. V. Reed, M. D. Rose, W. B. Sansom, L. Yancy, III

Founded: 1968
Domicile: Tennessee
Employees: 5,435

The McGraw-Hill Companies

# First Solar Inc

**STANDARD &POOR'S**

| S&P Recommendation | SELL ★ ★ ★ ★ ★ | Price | 12-Mo. Target Price | Investment Style |
|---|---|---|---|---|
| | | $40.32 (as of Nov 25, 2011) | $40.00 | Large-Cap Blend |

**GICS Sector** Information Technology
**Sub-Industry** Semiconductors

**Summary** This company produces solar modules using a proprietary thin film semiconductor technology.

## Key Stock Statistics (Source S&P, Vickers, company reports)

| | | | | | | | | |
|---|---|---|---|---|---|---|---|---|
| 52-Wk Range | $175.45– 40.05 | S&P Oper. EPS 2011**E** | 6.96 | Market Capitalization(B) | $3.485 | Beta | 1.62 |
| Trailing 12-Month EPS | $6.09 | S&P Oper. EPS 2012**E** | 6.60 | Yield (%) | Nil | S&P 3-Yr. Proj. EPS CAGR(%) | -10 |
| Trailing 12-Month P/E | 6.6 | P/E on S&P Oper. EPS 2011**E** | 5.8 | Dividend Rate/Share | Nil | S&P Credit Rating | NA |
| $10K Invested 5 Yrs Ago | $14,530 | Common Shares Outstg. (M) | 86.4 | Institutional Ownership (%) | 81 | | |

## Price Performance

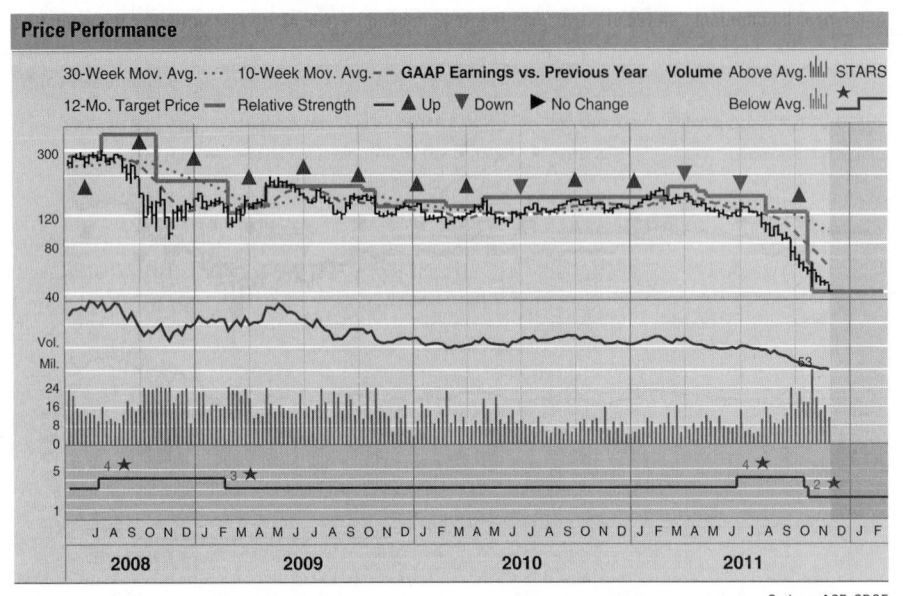

30-Week Mov. Avg. · · · 10-Week Mov. Avg. – – **GAAP Earnings vs. Previous Year** Volume Above Avg. STARS
12-Mo. Target Price — Relative Strength — ▲ Up ▼ Down ► No Change   Below Avg. ★

Options: ASE, CBOE

Analysis prepared by Equity Analyst **Angelo Zino, CFA** on Nov 08, 2011, when the stock traded at **$47.10**.

## Qualitative Risk Assessment

| LOW | MEDIUM | HIGH |
|---|---|---|

Our risk assessment reflects our view of the highly competitive nature of First Solar's business, the relatively early stages of the business cycle for alternative energy sources, and a high degree of execution risk in the company's aggressive capacity expansion plans. We also have concerns that a substantial amount of the company's common stock is held by the estate of John T. Walton and affiliates, which have considerable control over operation of the company's business.

## Quantitative Evaluations

**S&P Quality Ranking**                          NR

| D | C | B- | B | B+ | A- | A | A+ |
|---|---|---|---|---|---|---|---|

**Relative Strength Rank**                     WEAK

5

LOWEST = 1                                  HIGHEST = 99

## Highlights

➤ We expect sales to rise 9% in 2012, following our expectation for a 25% increase in 2011, on higher solar module volume and greater revenue from the systems business. Despite higher volume, we anticipate that revenues will be hurt by sharply lower prices, as solar companies are forced to reduce prices given lower government subsidies and aggressive competition from China-based silicon module makers. In addition, we expect inventories to remain at high levels, and we are more wary of order levels in Europe, as large project financing appears to be more challenging.

➤ We forecast an annual gross margin of 33% in 2012, compared to our 39% outlook for 2011, as lower selling prices more than offset higher volume and reduced manufacturing costs. We think FSLR can lower its cost per watt from $0.74 currently to $0.68 by the end of 2012 through scale and efficiencies. FSLR's modules had an average conversion efficiency ratio of 11.8% as of September 30, 2011.

➤ We believe FSLR will grow capacity to 2.8 gigawatts by the end of 2012. We positively view its scale, balance sheet, and intent to diversify into new emerging solar markets.

## Investment Rationale/Risk

➤ Our sell opinion reflects our view of deteriorating fundamentals, downside to consensus estimates, and recent management turnover. Near term, we expect the supply of solar modules to remain at unhealthy levels, as government incentive reductions and more challenging financing conditions impact end-demand. We expect margins to trend sharply lower, as we think a weaker pricing environment will persist given competitive forces and the need to stimulate consumer demand. Although we think plans to tame capacity expansion and focus on improving conversion efficiency are prudent, we believe that this is unlikely to prevent margin erosion. In addition, we expect cost per watt improvements to be far less than China-based competitors in the coming quarters. Our 2012 EPS estimate implies more than 15% downside to the consensus Capital IQ forecast.

➤ Risks to our opinion and target price include more stable than projected margins, steeper cost per watt reductions than anticipated, and more favorable government incentives.

➤ Our 12-month target price of $40 is based on a multiple of 6.1X our 2012 EPS projection, within the peer range.

## Revenue/Earnings Data

**Revenue (Million $)**

| | 1Q | 2Q | 3Q | 4Q | Year |
|---|---|---|---|---|---|
| 2011 | 567.3 | 532.8 | 1,006 | -- | -- |
| 2010 | 568.0 | 587.9 | 797.9 | 609.8 | 2,564 |
| 2009 | 418.2 | 525.9 | 480.9 | 641.3 | 2,066 |
| 2008 | 196.9 | 267.0 | 348.7 | 433.7 | 1,246 |
| 2007 | 66.95 | 77.22 | 159.0 | 200.8 | 504.0 |
| 2006 | 13.62 | 27.86 | 40.79 | 52.70 | 135.0 |

**Earnings Per Share ($)**

| | | | | | |
|---|---|---|---|---|---|
| 2011 | 1.33 | 0.70 | 2.25 | E2.67 | E6.96 |
| 2010 | 2.00 | 1.84 | 2.04 | 1.80 | 7.68 |
| 2009 | 1.99 | 2.11 | 1.79 | 1.65 | 7.53 |
| 2008 | 0.57 | 0.85 | 1.20 | 1.61 | 4.24 |
| 2007 | 0.07 | 0.58 | 0.58 | 0.77 | 2.03 |
| 2006 | -0.12 | -0.05 | 0.07 | 0.12 | 0.07 |

Fiscal year ended Dec. 31. Next earnings report expected: Late February. EPS Estimates based on S&P Operating Earnings; historical GAAP earnings are as reported.

## Dividend Data

No cash dividends have been paid.

# First Solar Inc

**STANDARD
&POOR'S**

## Business Summary November 08, 2011

CORPORATE OVERVIEW. First Solar designs and manufactures solar modules using a proprietary thin film semiconductor technology. The company's solar modules employ a thin layer of cadmium telluride semiconductor material to convert sunlight into electricity. In less than three hours, FSLR is able to transform a two foot by four foot sheet of glass into a complete solar module, using about 1% of the semiconductor material needed to produce crystalline silicon solar modules. Its production process eliminates the multiple supply chain operators, and expensive and time-consuming batch processing steps that are used to make a crystalline silicon solar module. In 2010, we believe the company derived a substantial portion of its revenues from customers headquartered in the European Union (with Germany accounting for the greatest percentage by region).

As of year-end 2010, FSLR manufactured its solar modules and conducted its research and development activities at production lines in locations including Perrysburg, OH, Frankfurt/Oder, Germany, and Kulim, Malaysia. During 2010, FSLR produced 1.4 gigawatts of solar modules, including 395 megawatts in the fourth quarter. We believe FSLR currently has plans to grow capacity from 1.43 gigawatts in 2010 to 2.25 gigawatts in 2011 and 2.88 gigawatts in 2012. At

the end of 2010, FSLR had 66% of its total capacity in Malaysia, 17% in Germany, and 17% in Ohio.

CORPORATE STRATEGY. FSLR aims to reduce PV system costs in three primary areas: module manufacturing, Balance of System (BoS) costs (costs unrelated to the module, including inverters, mounting hardware, grid interconnection equipment, wiring and other devices, and installation labor costs), and cost of capital. FSLR's manufacturing costs totaled $0.75 per watt in 2010's fourth quarter, down 14% from the year-earlier level. The company's average manufacturing cost for the full year was $0.77 per watt, versus $0.87 in 2009, an 11% reduction. We believe FSLR's cost lead advantage will allow it to be the first solar-module manufacturer to offer a product that competes on a non-subsidized basis with the price of retail electricity in key markets in North America, Europe and Asia.

## Company Financials Fiscal Year Ended Dec. 31

| Per Share Data ($) | 2010 | 2009 | 2008 | 2007 | 2006 | 2005 | 2004 | 2003 | 2002 | 2001 |
|---|---|---|---|---|---|---|---|---|---|---|
| Tangible Book Value | 35.20 | 28.14 | 18.12 | 13.54 | 5.69 | NM | NA | NA | NA | NA |
| Cash Flow | 9.48 | 9.05 | 4.99 | 2.35 | 0.21 | -0.07 | -0.34 | -0.74 | NA | NA |
| Earnings | 7.68 | 7.53 | 4.24 | 2.03 | 0.07 | -0.13 | -0.39 | -0.78 | NA | NA |
| S&P Core Earnings | 7.65 | 7.53 | 4.24 | 2.03 | 0.06 | -0.09 | NA | NA | NA | NA |
| Dividends | Nil | Nil | Nil | Nil | Nil | Nil | NA | NA | NA | NA |
| Payout Ratio | Nil | Nil | Nil | Nil | Nil | Nil | NA | NA | NA | NA |
| Prices:High | 153.30 | 207.51 | 317.00 | 283.00 | 30.00 | NA | NA | NA | NA | NA |
| Prices:Low | 98.71 | 100.90 | 85.28 | 27.54 | 20.00 | NA | NA | NA | NA | NA |
| P/E Ratio:High | 20 | 28 | 75 | NM | NM | NA | NA | NA | NA | NA |
| P/E Ratio:Low | 13 | 13 | 20 | NM | NM | NA | NA | NA | NA | NA |

| Income Statement Analysis (Million $) | | | | | | | | | | |
|---|---|---|---|---|---|---|---|---|---|---|
| Revenue | 2,564 | 2,066 | 1,246 | 504 | 135 | 48.1 | 13.5 | 3.21 | NA | NA |
| Operating Income | 899 | 832 | 501 | 162 | 13.0 | -1.41 | -14.8 | -22.6 | NA | NA |
| Depreciation | 156 | 130 | 61.5 | 24.8 | 10.2 | 3.38 | 1.94 | 1.50 | NA | NA |
| Interest Expense | 0.01 | 5.26 | 7.39 | 6.07 | 4.36 | 0.42 | 0.10 | 3.97 | NA | NA |
| Pretax Income | 762 | 686 | 464 | 156 | 9.18 | -6.55 | -16.8 | -28.0 | NA | NA |
| Effective Tax Rate | NA | 6.73% | 24.9% | NM | 56.7% | NM | NA | NA | NA | NA |
| Net Income | 664 | 640 | 348 | 158 | 3.97 | -6.55 | -16.8 | -28.0 | NA | NA |
| S&P Core Earnings | 662 | 640 | 348 | 158 | 3.97 | -6.55 | NA | NA | NA | NA |

| Balance Sheet & Other Financial Data (Million $) | | | | | | | | | | |
|---|---|---|---|---|---|---|---|---|---|---|
| Cash | 934 | 785 | 792 | 637 | 308 | 17.0 | 3.77 | NA | NA | NA |
| Current Assets | 1,584 | 1,351 | 1,077 | 803 | 389 | 26.6 | 12.3 | NA | NA | NA |
| Total Assets | 4,380 | 3,350 | 2,115 | 1,371 | 579 | 102 | 41.8 | NA | NA | NA |
| Current Liabilities | 470 | 395 | 382 | 186 | 52.1 | 33.9 | 5.35 | NA | NA | NA |
| Long Term Debt | 211 | 146 | 164 | 68.9 | 61.1 | 28.6 | 13.7 | NA | NA | NA |
| Common Equity | 3,455 | 2,653 | 1,513 | 1,097 | 411 | 13.1 | 22.6 | NA | NA | NA |
| Total Capital | 3,692 | 2,828 | 1,712 | 1,166 | 523 | 41.7 | 36.3 | NA | NA | NA |
| Capital Expenditures | 589 | 280 | 459 | 242 | 153 | 42.5 | 7.73 | 14.9 | NA | NA |
| Cash Flow | 820 | 770 | 410 | 183 | 14.2 | -3.18 | -14.8 | -26.5 | NA | NA |
| Current Ratio | 3.4 | 3.4 | 2.8 | 4.3 | 7.5 | 0.8 | 2.3 | NA | NA | NA |
| % Long Term Debt of Capitalization | 5.7 | 5.2 | 9.6 | 5.9 | 11.7 | 68.5 | 37.7 | NA | NA | NA |
| % Net Income of Revenue | 25.9 | 31.0 | 28.0 | 31.4 | 2.9 | NM | NM | NM | NA | NA |
| % Return on Assets | 17.2 | 23.4 | 20.0 | 16.2 | 1.2 | NM | NA | NA | NA | NA |
| % Return on Equity | 21.8 | 30.7 | 26.7 | 21.0 | 1.9 | NM | NA | NA | NA | NA |

Data as orig reptd.; bef. results of disc opers/spec. items. Per share data adj. for stk. divs.; EPS diluted. E-Estimated. NA-Not Available. NM-Not Meaningful. NR-Not Ranked. UR-Under Review.

**Office:** 350 West Washington Street, Suite 600, Tempe, AZ 85281.
**Telephone:** 602-414-9300.
**Email:** info@firstsolar.com
**Website:** http://www.firstsolar.com

**Chrmn & CEO:** M.J. Ahearn
**COO:** T. DeJong
**CFO:** M.R. Widmar
**CTO:** D. Eaglesham

**Chief Acctg Officer:** J. Zhu
**Investor Contact:** L. Polizzotto (602-414-9315)
**Board Members:** M. J. Ahearn, C. Kennedy, J. F. Nolan, W. J. Post, J. T. Presby, P. H. Stebbins, M. T. Sweeney, J. H. Villarreal

**Founded:** 1999
**Domicile:** Delaware
**Employees:** 6,100

*The McGraw-Hill Companies*

# Fiserv Inc

**STANDARD &POOR'S**

| S&P Recommendation HOLD ★★★☆☆ | Price<br>$54.12 (as of Nov 25, 2011) | 12-Mo. Target Price<br>$61.00 | Investment Style<br>Large-Cap Growth |
|---|---|---|---|

**GICS Sector** Information Technology
**Sub-Industry** Data Processing & Outsourced Services

**Summary** This company provides account processing and integrated information management systems for financial institutions.

## Key Stock Statistics (Source S&P, Vickers, company reports)

| | | | | | | | |
|---|---|---|---|---|---|---|---|
| 52-Wk Range | $65.41– 48.75 | S&P Oper. EPS 2011**E** | 4.55 | Market Capitalization(B) | $7.623 | Beta | 1.04 |
| Trailing 12-Month EPS | $3.05 | S&P Oper. EPS 2012**E** | 5.05 | Yield (%) | Nil | S&P 3-Yr. Proj. EPS CAGR(%) | 11 |
| Trailing 12-Month P/E | 17.7 | P/E on S&P Oper. EPS 2011**E** | 11.9 | Dividend Rate/Share | Nil | S&P Credit Rating | BBB- |
| $10K Invested 5 Yrs Ago | $10,398 | Common Shares Outstg. (M) | 140.9 | Institutional Ownership (%) | 84 | | |

## Price Performance

30-Week Mov. Avg. · · · 10-Week Mov. Avg. – – **GAAP Earnings vs. Previous Year** Volume Above Avg.▐▌▌ STARS
12-Mo. Target Price — Relative Strength — ▲ Up ▼ Down ► No Change Below Avg.▐▌▌

Options: ASE, CBOE, Ph

## Highlights

► The 12-month target price for FISV has recently been changed to $61.00 from $66.00. The Highlights section of this Stock Report will be updated accordingly.

## Investment Rationale/Risk

► The Investment Rationale/Risk section of this Stock Report will be updated shortly. For the latest News story on FISV from MarketScope, see below.

► 11/02/11 12:00 pm ET ... S&P REITERATES HOLD OPINION ON SHARES OF FISERV (FISV 56.90***): FISV reports adjusted Q3 EPS of $1.16, vs. $1.04, $0.04 above our forecast and $0.02 better than the S&P Capital IQ consensus estimate. Adjusted internal revenues growth was 2%, paced by the Payments segment with 4%, but offset somewhat by lacking growth from the Financials unit. FISV won a number of key deals in Q3, with large and small institutions, across multiple offerings. We are raising our '11 EPS estimate to $4.55 from $4.52 and leaving our '12 forecast at $5.05. Based on revised P/E and P/E-to-growth analyses, we are lowering our 12-month target price to $61 from $66. /S. Kessler

## Qualitative Risk Assessment

| LOW | MEDIUM | HIGH |
|---|---|---|

Our risk assessment reflects our view of FISV's notable size and market position, offset by what we consider its relatively modest internal growth rate and active acquisition strategy.

## Quantitative Evaluations

**S&P Quality Ranking**　　　　　　　B+

| D | C | B- | B | B+ | A- | A | A+ |
|---|---|---|---|---|---|---|---|

**Relative Strength Rank**　　　　MODERATE

59

LOWEST = 1　　　　　　　　　　　HIGHEST = 99

## Revenue/Earnings Data

**Revenue (Million $)**

| | 1Q | 2Q | 3Q | 4Q | Year |
|---|---|---|---|---|---|
| 2011 | 1,048 | 1,065 | 1,063 | -- | -- |
| 2010 | 1,008 | 1,022 | 1,025 | 1,078 | 4,133 |
| 2009 | 1,044 | 1,032 | 992.0 | 1,062 | 4,077 |
| 2008 | 1,310 | 1,295 | 1,080 | 1,061 | 4,739 |
| 2007 | 1,219 | 1,180 | 1,174 | 1,110 | 3,922 |
| 2006 | 1,097 | 1,093 | 1,157 | 1,198 | 4,544 |

**Earnings Per Share ($)**

| | | | | | |
|---|---|---|---|---|---|
| 2011 | 0.77 | 0.67 | 0.89 | E1.19 | E4.55 |
| 2010 | 0.80 | 0.85 | 0.89 | 0.80 | 3.34 |
| 2009 | 0.65 | 0.73 | 0.80 | 0.83 | 3.04 |
| 2008 | 0.59 | 0.60 | 0.45 | 0.45 | 2.12 |
| 2007 | 0.66 | 0.62 | 0.72 | 0.54 | 2.42 |
| 2006 | 0.64 | 0.63 | 0.63 | 0.61 | 2.49 |

Fiscal year ended Dec. 31. Next earnings report expected: Early February. EPS Estimates based on S&P Operating Earnings; historical GAAP earnings are as reported.

## Dividend Data

No cash dividends have been paid.

# Fiserv Inc

**STANDARD &POOR'S**

## Business Summary July 28, 2011

CORPORATE OVERVIEW. Fiserv is a leading provider of financial technology solutions including transaction processing, bill payment, item processing, check imaging and related software and services. The company generates the majority of its revenue from account and transaction processing services, which are provided under three- and five-year contracts. In 2010, 83% of reported revenue was considered recurring. FISV derived 6% of revenue from countries outside the U.S. (5% in 2009), including Australia, China, India, Mexico, and the United Kingdom, to name a few. The company primarily serves mid-sized and small banks in the U.S., a market which has been consolidating due to financial, regulatory and market pressures. The company's largest client accounted for 6% of revenue, while its top fifty clients represented less than 25%.

The Financial segment (accounting for 47% of revenues in 2010 and 47% in 2009) provides solutions to thousands of financial institutions, including banks, credit unions, leasing and finance companies, and savings institutions. Many offerings are sold as an integrated suite to clients, and could include core processing (allowing for account servicing and management information functionality for banks, thrifts and credit unions), lending and item processing (providing for the clearing of paper and imaged checks), payments processing (enabling FISV clients to provide their customers with services such as home-

banking and bill payment offerings), and a variety of industry-specific products and services.

In December 2007, FISV acquired CheckFree for $4.4 billion, and thus created the Payments unit (53%, 53%). The segment's financial e-commerce products enable consumers to review bank accounts and receive and pay bills electronically. Fiserv also provides ATM and point-of-sale pin debit and signature debit transaction processing, investment account processing and fraud and risk management products and services. In 2010, the business processed 1.4 billion transactions (up from 1.3 billion in 2009) and delivered 330 million electronic bills (320 million in 2009). We believe the CheckFree acquisition has bolstered FISV's base of offerings, technology and customers, and we see notable cross-selling potential.

We note that a $1 billion class action lawsuit was filed against FISV in April 2009, related to its custodial relationship with Madoff Securities. FISV has publicly stated it believes the suit is meritless and will vigorously defend itself.

## Company Financials Fiscal Year Ended Dec. 31

| Per Share Data ($) | 2010 | 2009 | 2008 | 2007 | 2006 | 2005 | 2004 | 2003 | 2002 | 2001 |
|---|---|---|---|---|---|---|---|---|---|---|
| Tangible Book Value | NM | NM | NM | NM | NM | NM | 0.96 | NM | 2.60 | 2.60 |
| Cash Flow | 5.57 | 4.90 | 2.85 | 2.88 | 3.62 | 3.62 | 2.94 | 2.48 | 2.09 | 1.86 |
| Earnings | 3.34 | 3.04 | 2.12 | 2.42 | 2.49 | 2.68 | 2.00 | 1.61 | 1.37 | 1.09 |
| S&P Core Earnings | 3.34 | 3.04 | 2.47 | 2.42 | 2.50 | 2.28 | 1.91 | 1.47 | 1.26 | 1.00 |
| Dividends | Nil | Nil | Nil | Nil | Nil | Nil | Nil | Nil | Nil | Nil |
| Payout Ratio | Nil | Nil | Nil | Nil | Nil | Nil | Nil | Nil | Nil | Nil |
| Prices:High | 60.64 | 50.91 | 56.80 | 59.85 | 53.60 | 46.89 | 41.01 | 40.77 | 47.24 | 44.61 |
| Prices:Low | 44.80 | 29.46 | 27.75 | 44.16 | 40.29 | 36.33 | 32.20 | 27.23 | 22.50 | 29.08 |
| P/E Ratio:High | 18 | 17 | 27 | 25 | 21 | 17 | 21 | 25 | 34 | 41 |
| P/E Ratio:Low | 13 | 10 | 13 | 18 | 16 | 14 | 16 | 17 | 16 | 27 |

| Income Statement Analysis (Million $) | 2010 | 2009 | 2008 | 2007 | 2006 | 2005 | 2004 | 2003 | 2002 | 2001 |
|---|---|---|---|---|---|---|---|---|---|---|
| Revenue | 4,133 | 4,077 | 4,739 | 3,922 | 4,544 | 4,059 | 3,730 | 3,034 | 2,569 | 1,890 |
| Operating Income | 1,346 | 1,234 | 1,046 | 836 | 943 | 925 | 845 | 704 | 734 | 501 |
| Depreciation | 339 | 333 | 119 | 78.0 | 199 | 179 | 185 | 172 | 141 | 148 |
| Interest Expense | 188 | 220 | 260 | 76.0 | 41.0 | 27.8 | 24.9 | 22.9 | 17.8 | 12.1 |
| Pretax Income | 807 | 746 | 625 | 661 | 710 | 818 | 641 | 516 | 436 | 347 |
| Effective Tax Rate | NA | 36.6% | 44.6% | 38.3% | 37.6% | 37.5% | 38.4% | 39.0% | 39.0% | 40.0% |
| Net Income | 506 | 473 | 346 | 408 | 443 | 511 | 395 | 315 | 266 | 208 |
| S&P Core Earnings | 506 | 473 | 403 | 408 | 443 | 435 | 377 | 288 | 246 | 191 |

| Balance Sheet & Other Financial Data (Million $) | 2010 | 2009 | 2008 | 2007 | 2006 | 2005 | 2004 | 2003 | 2002 | 2001 |
|---|---|---|---|---|---|---|---|---|---|---|
| Cash | 563 | 363 | 232 | 309 | 185 | 184 | 516 | 203 | 227 | 136 |
| Current Assets | 1,417 | 1,277 | 2,145 | 4,204 | 963 | 844 | 3,806 | 2,681 | 2,427 | 1,982 |
| Total Assets | 8,281 | 8,378 | 9,331 | 11,846 | 6,208 | 6,040 | 8,383 | 7,214 | 6,439 | 5,322 |
| Current Liabilities | 891 | 1,161 | 2,047 | 3,754 | 619 | 626 | 759 | 2,866 | 2,398 | 1,791 |
| Long Term Debt | 3,353 | 3,382 | 3,850 | 5,405 | 747 | 595 | 505 | 699 | 483 | 343 |
| Common Equity | 3,229 | 3,026 | 2,594 | 2,467 | 2,426 | 2,466 | 2,564 | 2,200 | 1,828 | 1,605 |
| Total Capital | 6,585 | 6,667 | 6,974 | 7,933 | 3,173 | 3,227 | 3,204 | 2,990 | 2,357 | 1,948 |
| Capital Expenditures | 175 | 198 | 199 | 160 | 187 | 165 | 161 | 143 | 142 | 68.0 |
| Cash Flow | 845 | 761 | 465 | 486 | 642 | 691 | 580 | 487 | 407 | 356 |
| Current Ratio | 1.6 | 1.1 | 1.1 | 1.1 | 1.6 | 1.4 | 5.0 | 0.9 | 1.0 | 1.1 |
| % Long Term Debt of Capitalization | 50.9 | 50.7 | 55.2 | 66.5 | 23.6 | 18.4 | 15.8 | 23.4 | 20.5 | 17.6 |
| % Net Income of Revenue | 12.2 | 11.6 | 7.3 | 10.4 | 9.8 | 12.6 | 10.6 | 10.4 | 10.4 | 11.0 |
| % Return on Assets | 6.1 | 5.3 | 3.3 | 4.5 | 7.2 | 7.1 | 5.1 | 4.6 | 4.5 | 3.8 |
| % Return on Equity | 16.2 | 16.8 | 13.7 | 16.7 | 18.1 | 20.3 | 16.6 | 15.6 | 15.5 | 14.6 |

Data as orig reptd.; bef. results of disc opers/spec. items. Per share data adj. for stk. divs.; EPS diluted. E-Estimated. NA-Not Available. NM-Not Meaningful. NR-Not Ranked. UR-Under Review.

**Office:** 255 Fiserv Drive, Brookfield, WI 53045-5815.
**Telephone:** 262-879-5000.
**Email:** general_info@fiserv.com
**Website:** http://www.fiserv.com

**Chrmn:** D.F. Dillon
**Pres & CEO:** J. Yabuki
**COO & EVP:** M. Ernst
**EVP, CFO, Chief Acctg Officer & Treas:** T.J. Hirsch

**EVP, Secy & General Counsel:** C.W. Sprague
**Investor Contact:** P. Holbrook (1-800-425-3478)
**Board Members:** D. F. Dillon, D. P. Kearney, P. J. Kight, D. J. O'Leary, G. M. Renwick, K. M. Robak, D. R. Simons, T. Wertheimer, J. Yabuki

**Founded:** 1984
**Domicile:** Wisconsin
**Employees:** 19,000

# FLIR Systems Inc

**STANDARD &POOR'S**

| S&P Recommendation | HOLD ★★★★★ | Price | 12-Mo. Target Price | Investment Style |
|---|---|---|---|---|
| | | $24.20 (as of Nov 25, 2011) | $31.00 | Large-Cap Growth |

**GICS Sector** Information Technology
**Sub-Industry** Electronic Equipment Manufacturers

**Summary** This company designs, manufactures and markets thermal imaging and broadcast camera systems for use in commercial and government markets.

## Key Stock Statistics (Source S&P, Vickers, company reports)

| | | | | | | | |
|---|---|---|---|---|---|---|---|
| 52-Wk Range | $37.29–21.86 | S&P Oper. EPS 2011**E** | 1.53 | Market Capitalization(B) | $3.775 | Beta | 0.86 |
| Trailing 12-Month EPS | $1.33 | S&P Oper. EPS 2012**E** | 1.74 | Yield (%) | 0.99 | S&P 3-Yr. Proj. EPS CAGR(%) | 7 |
| Trailing 12-Month P/E | 18.2 | P/E on S&P Oper. EPS 2011**E** | 15.8 | Dividend Rate/Share | $0.24 | S&P Credit Rating | BBB- |
| $10K Invested 5 Yrs Ago | $14,559 | Common Shares Outstg. (M) | 156.0 | Institutional Ownership (%) | NM | | |

## Price Performance

30-Week Mov. Avg. · · · 10-Week Mov. Avg. - - **GAAP Earnings vs. Previous Year** Volume Above Avg. STARS
12-Mo. Target Price — Relative Strength — ▲ Up ▼ Down ► No Change Below Avg.

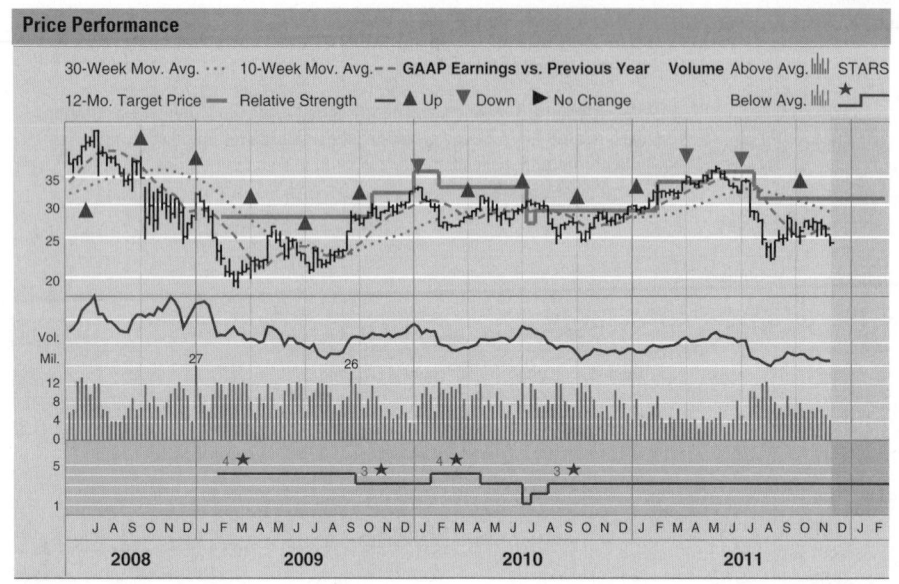

Options: ASE, CBOE, P, Ph

Analysis prepared by Equity Analyst **Dylan Cathers** on Oct 24, 2011, when the stock traded at **$27.18**.

## Qualitative Risk Assessment

| LOW | **MEDIUM** | HIGH |
|---|---|---|

Our risk assessment reflects the uncertainty of government spending on infrared-related technologies balanced by the long nature of government contracts, helping to reduce business risk. The company carries long-term debt, but has also exhibited healthy profitability and cash flows that we think balance the financial risk.

## Quantitative Evaluations

### S&P Quality Ranking                                          B+

| D | C | B- | B | **B+** | A- | A | A+ |
|---|---|---|---|---|---|---|---|

### Relative Strength Rank                              MODERATE

39

LOWEST = 1                                                    HIGHEST = 99

## Revenue/Earnings Data

### Revenue (Million $)

| | 1Q | 2Q | 3Q | 4Q | Year |
|---|---|---|---|---|---|
| 2011 | 373.5 | 390.0 | 371.3 | -- | -- |
| 2010 | 287.3 | 331.1 | 332.5 | 434.4 | 1,385 |
| 2009 | 272.0 | 278.0 | 285.6 | 311.6 | 1,147 |
| 2008 | 236.9 | 261.0 | 276.7 | 302.4 | 1,077 |
| 2007 | 161.4 | 184.3 | 191.1 | 242.6 | 779.4 |
| 2006 | 117.3 | 138.6 | 133.2 | 185.9 | 575.0 |

### Earnings Per Share ($)

| | | | | | |
|---|---|---|---|---|---|
| 2011 | 0.32 | 0.18 | 0.40 | E0.43 | E1.53 |
| 2010 | 0.35 | 0.37 | 0.39 | 0.43 | 1.54 |
| 2009 | 0.33 | 0.35 | 0.38 | 0.37 | 1.45 |
| 2008 | 0.24 | 0.29 | 0.35 | 0.41 | 1.28 |
| 2007 | 0.18 | 0.19 | 0.23 | 0.30 | 0.89 |
| 2006 | 0.09 | 0.14 | 0.18 | 0.26 | 0.66 |

Fiscal year ended Dec. 31. Next earnings report expected: Early February. EPS Estimates based on S&P Operating Earnings; historical GAAP earnings are as reported.

## Highlights

➤ We look for revenue growth of 14.5% in 2011 and 9% in 2012. We expect FLIR's Commercial Systems division, as well as last year's acquisitions of Raymarine and ICx Technologies, to aid growth. There, we expect gains from thermography and point to 20% order growth in the third quarter. That said, there has been some shift towards uncooled cameras in Core and Components, and Security, which aids volumes but pressures sales dollars. We think FLIR's Government Systems division will likely continue to be adversely affected by delays in contract awards and the uncertainty surrounding the entire federal budget process.

➤ We look for operating margins to contract for the second straight year. The main culprit we see is the addition of the lower-margin acquisitions. Also adversely affecting margins should be an unfavorable mix shift within Government Systems and unfavorable currency effects. We think cost controls and improving leverage will help offset some of these issues in 2012.

➤ We estimate operating EPS of $1.53 in 2011 and $1.74 in 2012.

## Investment Rationale/Risk

➤ Our hold recommendation is based on valuation. We believe that the difficulties in Government Systems and the integration of the two 2010 acquisitions (ICx in particular) will adversely affect the company in the near term. Longer term, we think FLIR is well positioned to benefit from increasing demand for various detection devices, both for commercial and government use. Furthermore, we are positive on the company's balance sheet, despite the recent addition of nearly $250 million in debt. The company had $375 million in cash at the end of the September quarter.

➤ Risks to our recommendation and target price include a sharper-than-anticipated decrease in military spending on infrared related technology, formidable competition, economic headwinds, and financial and integration risks.

➤ Our 12-month target price of $31 is based on our relative valuation analysis. We arrive at our target price using a peer-premium P/E ratio of 17.8X our 2012 EPS estimate, which is toward the low end of FLIR's range of 14.3X-22.6X over the past two years.

## Dividend Data (Dates: mm/dd Payment Date: mm/dd/yy)

| Amount ($) | Date Decl. | Ex-Div. Date | Stk. of Record | Payment Date |
|---|---|---|---|---|
| 0.060 | 02/09 | 02/17 | 02/22 | 03/10/11 |
| 0.060 | 04/29 | 05/18 | 05/20 | 06/10/11 |
| 0.060 | 07/22 | 08/18 | 08/22 | 09/09/11 |
| 0.060 | 10/20 | 11/17 | 11/21 | 12/09/11 |

Dividends have been paid since 2011. Source: Company reports.

# FLIR Systems Inc

STANDARD
&POOR'S

## Business Summary October 24, 2011

CORPORATE OVERVIEW. A leading infrared technology company, FLIR Systems, Inc. (FLIR) uses its expertise in product design, infrared imagers, optics, lasers, image processing, systems integration and other technologies, to develop and produce sophisticated thermal and multi-sensor imaging systems used in various applications in commercial, industrial, and government markets. In addition to offering a variety of systems configurations to suit customers' requirements, the company also sells more general, commercial applications.

FLIR's business until 2010 was organized in three divisions. Subsequently, operations were reorganized into two divisions -- Commercial Systems and Government Systems. In 2010, Government Systems accounted for 48% of total sales, Thermography 23%, Commercial Vision Systems 18%, and 2010 acquisitions ICx Technologies and Raymarine accounted for 11%.

The Government Systems division is focused on government contracts and markets where high performance is required. Products are often customized for specific applications, and frequently incorporate additional sensors, including visible light cameras, low light cameras, laser rangefinders, laser illuminators and laser designators. These products are used in applications such as surveillance, force protection, drug interdiction, search and rescue, spe-

cial operations and target designation. Prices range from $30,000 for hand-held and fixed security systems to over $1 million for advanced stabilized laser designation systems.

The Thermography division sells products for commercial and industrial applications where imaging and temperature together are required, and include specialized cameras with analytical and image processing capabilities to less expensive cameras for less demanding applications. Prices for these cameras range from $3,000 to $150,000.

The Commercial Vision Systems division is focused on emerging commercial markets for infrared imaging technology where the primary need is to see at night or in adverse conditions. The company notes that demand from markets, such as commercial security and automotive, has grown rapidly as the cost of infrared technology has declined. CVS products range in price from under $2,000 for an OEM imaging core to more than $450,000 for a high definition airborne electronic news gathering broadcast system.

## Company Financials Fiscal Year Ended Dec. 31

| Per Share Data ($) | 2010 | 2009 | 2008 | 2007 | 2006 | 2005 | 2004 | 2003 | 2002 | 2001 |
|---|---|---|---|---|---|---|---|---|---|---|
| Tangible Book Value | 5.42 | 5.65 | 3.95 | 2.88 | 1.51 | 1.18 | 0.85 | 1.13 | 1.13 | 0.67 |
| Cash Flow | 1.92 | 1.69 | 1.50 | 1.02 | 0.92 | 0.77 | 0.53 | 0.39 | 0.33 | 0.26 |
| Earnings | 1.54 | 1.45 | 1.28 | 0.89 | 0.66 | 0.58 | 0.47 | 0.32 | 0.29 | 0.20 |
| S&P Core Earnings | 1.56 | 1.45 | 1.28 | 0.89 | 0.66 | 0.51 | 0.38 | 0.27 | 0.19 | 0.16 |
| Dividends | Nil | Nil | Nil | Nil | Nil | Nil | Nil | Nil | Nil | Nil |
| Payout Ratio | Nil | Nil | Nil | Nil | Nil | Nil | Nil | Nil | Nil | Nil |
| Prices:High | 33.22 | 33.35 | 45.49 | 36.43 | 17.02 | 18.18 | 16.67 | 9.25 | 7.44 | 6.19 |
| Prices:Low | 24.00 | 18.81 | 23.68 | 14.81 | 10.73 | 10.23 | 8.74 | 5.13 | 3.42 | 0.52 |
| P/E Ratio:High | 22 | 23 | 36 | 41 | 26 | 31 | 35 | 29 | 26 | 31 |
| P/E Ratio:Low | 16 | 13 | 19 | 17 | 16 | 18 | 19 | 16 | 12 | 3 |

| Income Statement Analysis (Million $) | 2010 | 2009 | 2008 | 2007 | 2006 | 2005 | 2004 | 2003 | 2002 | 2001 |
|---|---|---|---|---|---|---|---|---|---|---|
| Revenue | 1,385 | 1,147 | 1,077 | 779 | 575 | 509 | 483 | 312 | 261 | 214 |
| Operating Income | 413 | 390 | 324 | 218 | 158 | 142 | 124 | 69.8 | 56.4 | 44.8 |
| Depreciation | 61.3 | 42.4 | 40.0 | 25.9 | 20.6 | 15.6 | 14.8 | 6.26 | 6.20 | 7.50 |
| Interest Expense | 2.88 | 6.88 | 8.99 | 10.2 | 8.96 | 7.92 | 8.09 | 4.86 | 1.68 | 9.42 |
| Pretax Income | 363 | 340 | 295 | 191 | 133 | 122 | 99.9 | 63.8 | 48.9 | 28.7 |
| Effective Tax Rate | NA | 32.4% | 30.9% | 28.5% | 23.9% | 25.7% | 28.4% | 30.0% | 15.0% | 9.77% |
| Net Income | 249 | 230 | 204 | 137 | 101 | 90.8 | 71.5 | 44.7 | 41.6 | 25.9 |
| S&P Core Earnings | 252 | 231 | 204 | 137 | 101 | 78.4 | 57.6 | 38.4 | 27.6 | 20.5 |

| Balance Sheet & Other Financial Data (Million $) | 2010 | 2009 | 2008 | 2007 | 2006 | 2005 | 2004 | 2003 | 2002 | 2001 |
|---|---|---|---|---|---|---|---|---|---|---|
| Cash | 193 | 422 | 289 | 204 | 139 | 107 | 121 | 198 | 46.6 | 15.5 |
| Current Assets | 955 | 971 | 812 | 656 | 486 | 406 | 367 | 382 | 174 | 140 |
| Total Assets | 1,857 | 1,485 | 1,244 | 1,024 | 798 | 694 | 619 | 450 | 234 | 185 |
| Current Liabilities | 250 | 178 | 172 | 166 | 170 | 90.1 | 88.7 | 70.3 | 52.6 | 71.0 |
| Long Term Debt | NA | 58.0 | 190 | 227 | 207 | 206 | 205 | 204 | Nil | Nil |
| Common Equity | 1,523 | 1,204 | 840 | 623 | 399 | 369 | 313 | 165 | 172 | 105 |
| Total Capital | 1,523 | 1,262 | 1,036 | 833 | 608 | 586 | 519 | 369 | 172 | 105 |
| Capital Expenditures | 66.0 | 41.9 | 27.6 | 44.1 | 43.0 | 34.0 | 13.9 | 14.6 | 6.60 | 4.24 |
| Cash Flow | 310 | 273 | 244 | 163 | 121 | 106 | 86.3 | 51.0 | 47.8 | 33.4 |
| Current Ratio | 3.8 | 5.5 | 4.7 | 4.0 | 2.9 | 4.5 | 4.1 | 5.4 | 3.3 | 2.0 |
| % Long Term Debt of Capitalization | Nil | 4.6 | 18.4 | 25.0 | 34.0 | 35.2 | 39.6 | 55.4 | Nil | Nil |
| % Net Income of Revenue | 18.0 | 20.1 | 18.9 | 17.5 | 17.5 | 17.8 | 14.8 | 14.3 | 15.9 | 12.1 |
| % Return on Assets | 14.9 | 16.9 | 18.0 | 15.0 | 13.6 | 13.7 | 13.4 | 13.1 | 19.8 | 14.7 |
| % Return on Equity | 18.2 | 22.5 | 27.8 | 26.8 | 26.7 | 26.6 | 29.9 | 26.5 | 30.0 | 38.7 |

Data as orig reptd.; bef. results of disc opers/spec. items. Per share data adj. for stk. divs.; EPS diluted. E-Estimated. NA-Not Available. NM-Not Meaningful. NR-Not Ranked. UR-Under Review.

**Office:** 27700 SW Parkway Ave Ste A, Wilsonville, OR 97070-8238.
**Telephone:** 503-498-3547.
**Email:** investor@flir.com
**Website:** http://www.flir.com

**Chrmn, Pres & CEO:** E.R. Lewis
**Investor Contact:** A.L. Trunzo (503-498-3547)
**SVP & CFO:** A.L. Trunzo
**SVP, Secy & General Counsel:** W.W. Davis

**Chief Acctg Officer & Cntlr:** D.A. Muessle
**Board Members:** J. D. Carter, W. W. Crouch, E. R. Lewis, A. L. MacDonald, M. T. Smith, J. W. Wood, Jr., S. E. Wynne

**Founded:** 1978
**Domicile:** Oregon
**Employees:** 3,215

# Flowserve Corp.

STANDARD &POOR'S

| S&P Recommendation | STRONG BUY ★ ★ ★ ★ ★ | Price $90.10 (as of Nov 25, 2011) | 12-Mo. Target Price $130.00 | Investment Style Large-Cap Growth |
|---|---|---|---|---|

**GICS Sector** Industrials
**Sub-Industry** Industrial Machinery

**Summary** This company is a global manufacturer of industrial pumps and related equipment for the chemical, oil and gas and power industries.

## Key Stock Statistics (Source S&P, Vickers, company reports)

| | | | | | | | |
|---|---|---|---|---|---|---|---|
| 52-Wk Range | $135.72– 66.84 | S&P Oper. EPS 2011**E** | 7.85 | Market Capitalization(B) | $5.006 | Beta | 1.60 |
| Trailing 12-Month EPS | $7.39 | S&P Oper. EPS 2012**E** | 9.10 | Yield (%) | 1.42 | S&P 3-Yr. Proj. EPS CAGR(%) | 12 |
| Trailing 12-Month P/E | 12.2 | P/E on S&P Oper. EPS 2011**E** | 11.5 | Dividend Rate/Share | $1.28 | S&P Credit Rating | BB+ |
| $10K Invested 5 Yrs Ago | $17,600 | Common Shares Outstg. (M) | 55.6 | Institutional Ownership (%) | 88 | | |

## Price Performance

30-Week Mov. Avg. · · · 10-Week Mov. Avg. - - GAAP Earnings vs. Previous Year Volume Above Avg. STARS
12-Mo. Target Price — Relative Strength — ▲ Up ▼ Down ▶ No Change Below Avg.

Options: ASE, CBOE, Ph

Analysis prepared by Equity Analyst **Stewart Scharf** on Nov 01, 2011, when the stock traded at **$90.20**.

## Qualitative Risk Assessment

| LOW | MEDIUM | HIGH |
|---|---|---|

Our risk assessment reflects the company's exposure to cyclical end markets and foreign exchange swings based on its significant proportion of foreign sales. We think these factors are offset by its leading position in many markets, significant aftermarket business, strong cash flows, and favorable leverage ratio.

## Quantitative Evaluations

**S&P Quality Ranking** — B

| D | C | B- | B | B+ | A- | A | A+ |
|---|---|---|---|---|---|---|---|

**Relative Strength Rank** — STRONG

71

LOWEST = 1   HIGHEST = 99

## Revenue/Earnings Data

**Revenue (Million $)**

| | 1Q | 2Q | 3Q | 4Q | Year |
|---|---|---|---|---|---|
| 2011 | 997.2 | 1,126 | 1,122 | -- | -- |
| 2010 | 958.9 | 961.1 | 971.7 | 1,140 | 4,032 |
| 2009 | 1,025 | 1,090 | 1,051 | 1,199 | 4,365 |
| 2008 | 993.3 | 1,158 | 1,154 | 1,169 | 4,473 |
| 2007 | 803.4 | 930.7 | 919.2 | 1,109 | 3,763 |
| 2006 | 653.9 | 752.9 | 770.8 | 883.5 | 3,061 |

**Earnings Per Share ($)**

| | | | | | |
|---|---|---|---|---|---|
| 2011 | 1.72 | 1.76 | 1.92 | E2.21 | E7.85 |
| 2010 | 1.42 | 1.62 | 1.84 | 1.99 | 6.88 |
| 2009 | 1.64 | 1.92 | 2.07 | 1.96 | 7.59 |
| 2008 | 1.53 | 2.13 | 2.04 | 2.03 | 7.74 |
| 2007 | 0.59 | 1.11 | 1.10 | 1.67 | 4.47 |
| 2006 | 0.32 | 0.58 | 0.49 | 0.58 | 2.00 |

Fiscal year ended Dec. 31. Next earnings report expected: Late February. EPS Estimates based on S&P Operating Earnings; historical GAAP earnings are as reported.

## Highlights

➤ We expect sales to advance about 10% in 2011, with similar growth likely in 2012, reflecting strength in the aftermarket and short-cycle OEM businesses led by growth in the Middle East, Asia/Pacific and Latin America. Despite long-cycle large project delays, we see bookings picking up in oil & gas, chemicals and general industrials, while foreign exchange remains positive.

➤ In our view, gross margins should widen sequentially to about 35% in 2012, based on supply chain efficiencies, better pricing and stabilizing commodity costs, and a better mix of higher-margin aftermarket sales. Adjusted EBITDA margins should expand by at least 100 basis points to above 17% in 2012, driven by cost-cutting initiatives related to FLS optimizing certain non-strategic facilities, short-cycle volume leverage and synergies from Valbart.

➤ We project an effective tax rate of near 27% in 2011, and see operating EPS of $7.85 (before at least $0.22 of charges, including $0.15 from realignments, but after $0.03 dilutive effect from Lawrence Pumps acquisition), advancing 16% to $9.10 in 2012.

## Investment Rationale/Risk

➤ We recently upgraded our recommendation on the shares to strong buy, from hold, based on our valuation metrics, along with our view that a short-cycle original equipment recovery and improving long-cycle small project work will gradually extend into the unsettled long-cycle large project business.

➤ Risks to our recommendation and target price include significant project delays or cancellations; geopolitical issues in developing regions; competitive pricing pressures; and a negative foreign exchange effect from weakness in the euro and other currencies. We also note past financial reporting problems.

➤ The shares trade at a modest discount to our projected P/E for S&P's Industrial Machinery group, which we attribute to FLS's cyclical project business and exposure to volatile markets. Our DCF model, which assumes a terminal growth rate of 4.0% and a weighted average cost of capital of 12.5%, indicates intrinsic value of $121. Our relative metrics, including enterprise value to EBITDA and P/E-to-EPS growth, suggest a value of $138. Blending these valuations, we arrive at our 12-month target price of $130.

## Dividend Data (Dates: mm/dd Payment Date: mm/dd/yy)

| Amount ($) | Date Decl. | Ex-Div. Date | Stk. of Record | Payment Date |
|---|---|---|---|---|
| 0.290 | 12/15 | 12/29 | 12/31 | 01/14/11 |
| 0.320 | 02/21 | 03/29 | 03/31 | 04/14/11 |
| 0.320 | 08/12 | 09/28 | 09/30 | 10/14/11 |
| 0.320 | 11/18 | 12/28 | 12/30 | 01/13/12 |

Dividends have been paid since 2007. Source: Company reports.

---

**Please read the Required Disclosures and Analyst Certification on the last page of this report.**

The **McGraw·Hill** Companies

# Flowserve Corp.

STANDARD
&POOR'S

## Business Summary November 01, 2011

CORPORATE OVERVIEW. Flowserve Corp., which was formed through the 1997 merger of Durco International Inc. and BW/IP, Inc., is one of the world's leading providers of fluid motion and control products and services. Customers use fluid motion and control products to regulate the movement of liquids or gases through processing systems in their facilities. As of January 1, 2010, in an effort to drive business growth and further leverage its operations, FLS combined its pump and flow solutions divisions into a new Flow Solutions Group (FSG), which will be reported in two segments: FSG Engineered Product division (highly engineered pump product operations of the former pump division and all the mechanical seal operations of the former flow solutions division) and FSG Industrial Product division (general purpose pump operations of the former pump division). Pump systems and components are produced at 30 plants worldwide. FLS manufactures over 150 different pump models, ranging from simple fractional horsepower industrial pumps to high horsepower engineered pumps (over 30,000 horsepower). Aftermarket services through the company's global network are provided in about 80 service centers in 30 countries.

Principal markets for the company's products are oil & gas (42% of bookings

in 2010), general industrial (20%), chemical (16%), power generation (17%) and water treatment (5%). On a geographic basis, 2010 revenue broke down as follows: North America 31%; Europe 26%; Middle East and Africa 15%; Asia Pacific 18%; and Latin America 10%. FLS exported 7.4% of its sales in 2010.

The FSG Engineered Product division (53% of sales in 2010; includes intersegment sales) manufactures engineered pumps, vertical circulation and other pumps, seals, repair and service, and integrated solutions primarily used by companies in the oil & gas, power and water treatment (desalination) markets. The FSG Industrial Product division (20% of sales) manufactures industrial, water and vertical turbine pumps for the oil & gas, water and general industrial sectors. The Flow Control division (30%) provides manual valves, control valves and other aftermarket parts and services for the power generation, oil & gas, chemical and general industrial markets. These products are typically utilized to control the flow of liquids or gases.

## Company Financials Fiscal Year Ended Dec. 31

| Per Share Data ($) | 2010 | 2009 | 2008 | 2007 | 2006 | 2005 | 2004 | 2003 | 2002 | 2001 |
|---|---|---|---|---|---|---|---|---|---|---|
| Tangible Book Value | 17.13 | 14.68 | 7.56 | 5.42 | 0.47 | NM | NM | NM | NM | NM |
| Cash Flow | 8.69 | 9.29 | 9.12 | 5.82 | 3.30 | 2.07 | 1.68 | 2.36 | 2.29 | 2.29 |
| Earnings | 6.88 | 7.59 | 7.74 | 4.47 | 2.00 | 0.82 | 0.36 | 0.96 | 1.16 | 0.42 |
| S&P Core Earnings | 6.92 | 7.72 | 7.44 | 4.39 | 2.14 | 0.87 | 0.41 | 0.95 | 0.82 | -0.08 |
| Dividends | 1.16 | 1.08 | 1.00 | 0.60 | Nil | Nil | Nil | Nil | Nil | Nil |
| Payout Ratio | 17% | 14% | 13% | 13% | Nil | Nil | Nil | Nil | Nil | Nil |
| Prices:High | 119.83 | 108.85 | 145.45 | 102.74 | 61.06 | 39.75 | 28.18 | 22.93 | 35.09 | 33.30 |
| Prices:Low | 81.35 | 43.23 | 37.18 | 48.73 | 39.63 | 23.69 | 18.64 | 10.40 | 7.58 | 18.70 |
| P/E Ratio:High | 17 | 14 | 19 | 23 | 31 | 48 | 78 | 24 | 30 | 79 |
| P/E Ratio:Low | 12 | 6 | 5 | 11 | 20 | 29 | 52 | 11 | 7 | 45 |

### Income Statement Analysis (Million $)

| | 2010 | 2009 | 2008 | 2007 | 2006 | 2005 | 2004 | 2003 | 2002 | 2001 |
|---|---|---|---|---|---|---|---|---|---|---|
| Revenue | 4,032 | 4,365 | 4,473 | 3,763 | 3,061 | 2,695 | 2,638 | 2,404 | 2,251 | 1,918 |
| Operating Income | 687 | 785 | 675 | 488 | 296 | 260 | 229 | 260 | 274 | 204 |
| Depreciation | 101 | 95.4 | 79.1 | 77.7 | 71.0 | 69.9 | 73.2 | 77.6 | 65.3 | 73.9 |
| Interest Expense | 34.3 | 40.0 | 51.3 | 60.1 | 65.7 | 74.1 | 81.0 | 84.2 | 92.9 | 118 |
| Pretax Income | 530 | 585 | 590 | 360 | 187 | 83.3 | 59.6 | 73.8 | 92.1 | 25.6 |
| Effective Tax Rate | NA | 26.8% | 25.0% | 29.0% | 39.1% | 44.5% | 66.2% | 28.4% | 34.4% | 36.2% |
| Net Income | 389 | 428 | 442 | 256 | 114 | 46.2 | 20.2 | 52.9 | 60.4 | 16.4 |
| S&P Core Earnings | 391 | 435 | 425 | 252 | 122 | 48.9 | 22.5 | 52.4 | 42.7 | -3.30 |

### Balance Sheet & Other Financial Data (Million $)

| | 2010 | 2009 | 2008 | 2007 | 2006 | 2005 | 2004 | 2003 | 2002 | 2001 |
|---|---|---|---|---|---|---|---|---|---|---|
| Cash | 558 | 654 | 472 | 371 | 67.0 | 92.9 | 63.8 | 53.5 | 49.3 | 21.5 |
| Current Assets | 2,524 | 2,499 | 2,332 | 1,897 | 1,303 | 1,071 | 1,050 | 1,091 | 1,031 | 898 |
| Total Assets | 4,460 | 4,249 | 4,024 | 3,520 | 2,869 | 2,576 | 2,634 | 2,801 | 2,608 | 2,052 |
| Current Liabilities | 1,456 | 1,458 | 1,608 | 1,250 | 884 | 695 | 708 | 633 | 492 | 417 |
| Long Term Debt | 475 | 539 | 546 | 550 | 557 | 653 | 658 | 880 | 1,056 | 996 |
| Common Equity | 2,103 | 1,796 | 1,368 | 1,293 | 1,021 | 832 | 870 | 821 | 756 | 411 |
| Total Capital | 2,625 | 2,368 | 1,924 | 1,856 | 1,577 | 1,485 | 1,528 | 1,701 | 1,811 | 1,407 |
| Capital Expenditures | 102 | 108 | 127 | 89.0 | 73.5 | 49.3 | 45.2 | 28.8 | 30.9 | 35.2 |
| Cash Flow | 490 | 523 | 522 | 333 | 185 | 116 | 93.3 | 130 | 126 | 90.2 |
| Current Ratio | 1.7 | 1.7 | 1.5 | 1.5 | 1.5 | 1.5 | 1.5 | 1.7 | 2.1 | 2.2 |
| % Long Term Debt of Capitalization | 18.1 | 22.8 | 28.3 | 29.6 | 35.3 | 44.0 | 43.0 | 51.7 | 58.3 | 70.8 |
| % Net Income of Revenue | 9.6 | 9.8 | 9.9 | 6.8 | 3.7 | 1.7 | 0.8 | 2.2 | 2.7 | 0.9 |
| % Return on Assets | 8.9 | 10.3 | 11.7 | 8.0 | 4.2 | 1.8 | 0.8 | 2.0 | 2.6 | 0.8 |
| % Return on Equity | 19.9 | 27.1 | 33.3 | 22.1 | 12.2 | 5.4 | 2.4 | 6.9 | 10.4 | 4.6 |

Data as orig reptd.; bef. results of disc opers/spec. items. Per share data adj. for stk. divs.; EPS diluted. E-Estimated. NA-Not Available. NM-Not Meaningful. NR-Not Ranked. UR-Under Review.

**Office:** 5215 N O Connor Blvd Ste 2300, Irving, TX, USA 75039-3726.
**Telephone:** 972-443-6500.
**Website:** http://www.flowserve.com
**Chrmn:** J.O. Rollans

**Pres & CEO:** M.A. Blinn
**SVP & CFO:** M.S. Taff
**SVP & Chief Admin Officer:** M.D. Dailey
**SVP, Chief Acctg Officer & Cntlr:** R.J. Guiltinan, Jr.

**Investor Contact:** P. Fehlman (972-443-6517)
**Board Members:** M. A. Blinn, G. J. Delly, R. L. Fix, J. R. Friedery, J. E. Harlan, M. F. Johnston, R. J. Mills, C. M. Rampacek, D. E. Roberts, Jr., J. O. Rollans, W. C. Rusnack

**Founded:** 1912
**Domicile:** New York
**Employees:** 15,000

# Fluor Corp.

STANDARD &POOR'S

| S&P Recommendation | BUY ★★★★☆ | Price | 12-Mo. Target Price | Investment Style |
|---|---|---|---|---|
| | | $49.51 (as of Nov 25, 2011) | $70.00 | Large-Cap Blend |

**GICS Sector** Industrials
**Sub-Industry** Construction & Engineering

**Summary** Fluor is one of the world's largest engineering, procurement and construction companies, with more than 70% of its backlog derived from outside the U.S.

## Key Stock Statistics (Source S&P, Vickers, company reports)

| | | | | | | | | |
|---|---|---|---|---|---|---|---|---|
| 52-Wk Range | $75.76–44.16 | S&P Oper. EPS 2011E | 3.45 | Market Capitalization(B) | $8.400 | Beta | | 1.33 |
| Trailing 12-Month EPS | $3.16 | S&P Oper. EPS 2012E | 4.00 | Yield (%) | 1.01 | S&P 3-Yr. Proj. EPS CAGR(%) | | 13 |
| Trailing 12-Month P/E | 15.7 | P/E on S&P Oper. EPS 2011E | 14.4 | Dividend Rate/Share | $0.50 | S&P Credit Rating | | A- |
| $10K Invested 5 Yrs Ago | $12,256 | Common Shares Outstg. (M) | 169.7 | Institutional Ownership (%) | 89 | | | |

## Price Performance

30-Week Mov. Avg. ···   10-Week Mov. Avg. – –   **GAAP Earnings vs. Previous Year**   **Volume** Above Avg. STARS
12-Mo. Target Price —   Relative Strength   — ▲ Up ▼ Down ▶ No Change   Below Avg.

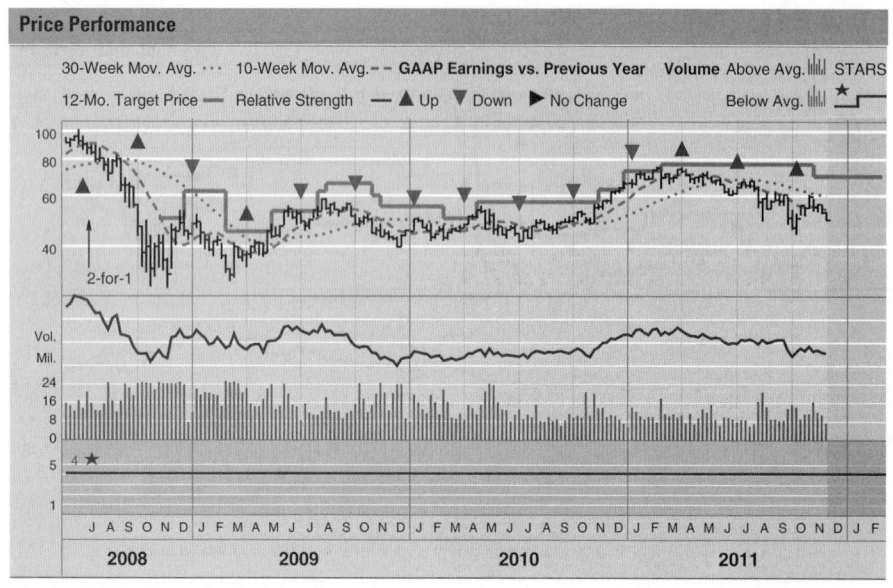

Options: ASE, CBOE, P, Ph

Analysis prepared by Equity Analyst **Stewart Scharf** on Nov 10, 2011, when the stock traded at **$54.00**.

### Qualitative Risk Assessment

| LOW | MEDIUM | HIGH |
|---|---|---|

Our risk assessment reflects still uncertain global markets along with geopolitical issues as more projects are in unstable regions of the world. This is offset by our view of FLR's strong balance sheet, modest debt levels, and diverse project mix and customer base.

### Quantitative Evaluations

**S&P Quality Ranking**      B+

| D | C | B- | B | B+ | A- | A | A+ |
|---|---|---|---|---|---|---|---|

**Relative Strength Rank**      MODERATE

32

LOWEST = 1        HIGHEST = 99

### Revenue/Earnings Data

**Revenue (Million $)**

| | 1Q | 2Q | 3Q | 4Q | Year |
|---|---|---|---|---|---|
| 2011 | 5,058 | 6,034 | 6,038 | -- | -- |
| 2010 | 4,919 | 5,152 | 5,511 | 5,267 | 20,849 |
| 2009 | 5,798 | 5,293 | 5,420 | 5,479 | 21,990 |
| 2008 | 4,807 | 5,574 | 5,674 | 6,072 | 22,326 |
| 2007 | 3,642 | 4,222 | 4,155 | 4,712 | 16,691 |
| 2006 | 3,625 | 3,456 | 3,364 | 3,633 | 14,079 |

**Earnings Per Share ($)**

| | 1Q | 2Q | 3Q | 4Q | Year |
|---|---|---|---|---|---|
| 2011 | 0.78 | 0.94 | 0.78 | E0.80 | E3.45 |
| 2010 | 0.76 | 0.87 | -0.30 | 0.65 | 1.98 |
| 2009 | 1.12 | 0.93 | 0.89 | 0.82 | 3.75 |
| 2008 | 0.75 | 1.13 | 1.01 | 1.04 | 3.93 |
| 2007 | 0.47 | 0.52 | 0.51 | 1.42 | 2.93 |
| 2006 | 0.50 | 0.37 | 0.16 | 0.45 | 1.48 |

Fiscal year ended Dec. 31. Next earnings report expected: Late February. EPS Estimates based on S&P Operating Earnings; historical GAAP earnings are as reported.

## Highlights

➤ We project near 15% revenue growth through 2012, driven by further strength in the Government segment, and mining and metals projects in the Industrial and Infrastructure segment. Bookings should rebound in 2012 for Oil & Gas projects, while the Power segment remains weak. We see favorable long-term trends but, in our view, timing issues for new awards will likely continue to affect quarterly results.

➤ We look for gross margins to widen in 2011, reflecting cost controls and stabilizing commodity costs, but mix issues based on more lower-margin mining projects in backlog and a rise in CFM (client-furnished materials) work may limit expansion in 2012. We expect operating margins (EBITDA) to expand modestly in 2011, from 6% (before special charges) in 2010, on cost-reduction initiatives, while mix issues and costs related to the NuScale investment could pressure margins somewhat in 2012.

➤ We forecast lower interest expense but a higher effective tax rate of at least 32% through 2012 (21% in 2010), and we estimate operating EPS of $3.45, advancing 16%, to $4.00, in 2012.

## Investment Rationale/Risk

➤ Our buy recommendation is based on our valuation models, along with our view of FLR's favorable long-term prospects, especially in the Americas and Asia-Pacific, and its strong balance sheet. Despite volatile markets and geopolitical issues, we see stronger bookings as customers gradually resume long-term capital spending plans.

➤ Risks to our recommendation and target price include additional project delays and/or cancellations, political unrest, labor shortages, project disruptions, negative foreign currency effect, credit market issues, sharply lower oil prices, and timing and pricing issues for new awards.

➤ Our 12-month target price of $70 is derived from a blend of our relative and discounted cash flow (DCF) metrics. Based on various relative metrics, we use a premium-to-peers P/E of 17X our 2012 operating EPS estimate, reflecting FLR's strong global prospect list and diversified business model, resulting in a value of $68. Our DCF model, which assumes a 3.5% terminal growth rate and an 8.3% weighted average cost of capital, suggests the stock's intrinsic value is $72.

### Dividend Data (Dates: mm/dd Payment Date: mm/dd/yy)

| Amount ($) | Date Decl. | Ex-Div. Date | Stk. of Record | Payment Date |
|---|---|---|---|---|
| 0.125 | 02/03 | 03/02 | 03/04 | 04/04/11 |
| 0.125 | 05/05 | 06/01 | 06/03 | 07/05/11 |
| 0.125 | 08/04 | 08/31 | 09/02 | 10/04/11 |
| 0.125 | 11/03 | 11/30 | 12/02 | 01/04/12 |

Dividends have been paid since 1974. Source: Company reports.

---

**Please read the Required Disclosures and Analyst Certification on the last page of this report.**

The McGraw·Hill Companies

# Fluor Corp.

STANDARD &POOR'S

## Business Summary November 10, 2011

CORPORATE OVERVIEW. Fluor Corp. is one of the world's largest engineering, procurement, construction and maintenance companies. It has five principal operating segments. The Oil and Gas segment provides services to oil, gas, refining, chemical, polymer and petrochemical customers. Industrial and Infrastructure provides EPC services to businesses, including industrial, commercial, telecommunications, mining and technology. Global Services provides operations and maintenance support, and equipment and outsourcing, through TRS Staffing Solutions. Government provides support services to the federal government and other government entities. In the Power segment, Fluor provides a full range of services to the gas fueled, solid fueled, renewables, nuclear and plant betterment markets.

Contributions to revenues and operating profits in 2010 were as follows: Oil and Gas, 37% of revenues and operating profits of $344 million; Industrial and Infrastructure, 33% and a loss of $170 million; Global Services, 7.2% and $133 million; Government, 15% and $142 million; and Power, 8.1% and $171 million.

Backlog at September 30, 2011, was up 27%, year to year, to over $41.8 billion. The backlog was divided by segment as follows: Oil and Gas $14.6 billion (35%

of total backlog), up 25% from a year earlier; Industrial and Infrastructure $22.3 billion (53%), up 29%; Global Services $2.0 billion (5%), down 6%; Government $1.8 billion (4%), up 73%, and Power $1.1 billion (3%), up 26%. Backlog by geographic region was: U.S. 20%; the Americas 30%; Europe, Africa and the Middle East 22%; and Asia-Pacific (including Australia) 28%.

Backlog includes a long cycle of larger projects that tend to take three to five years to complete, versus earlier smaller projects, which had an 18-to-36-month cycle. Historically, the backlog burn rate has been 60% to 65%, with FLR projecting about 55% for 2011, with a rampup during 2012. At September 30, 2011, FLR's percentage of fixed price work in its backlog was 14%, down from 24% at the end of the preceding quarter, and 29% at 2010 year end, with most in infrastructure and power, while oil and gas is primarily cost reimbursable. In the first nine months of 2011, new awards climbed 12%, year to year, to $22.6 billion.

## Company Financials  Fiscal Year Ended Dec. 31

| Per Share Data ($) | 2010 | 2009 | 2008 | 2007 | 2006 | 2005 | 2004 | 2003 | 2002 | 2001 |
|---|---|---|---|---|---|---|---|---|---|---|
| Tangible Book Value | 19.32 | 17.99 | 14.23 | 12.39 | 9.39 | 8.92 | 7.45 | 6.26 | 5.38 | 4.79 |
| Cash Flow | 3.48 | 4.79 | 4.82 | 3.74 | 2.18 | 1.91 | 1.68 | 1.61 | 1.55 | 1.26 |
| Earnings | 1.98 | 3.75 | 3.93 | 2.93 | 1.48 | 1.31 | 1.13 | 1.12 | 1.07 | 0.81 |
| S&P Core Earnings | 2.37 | 3.86 | 3.49 | 2.93 | 1.50 | 1.31 | 1.04 | 1.17 | 0.90 | 0.57 |
| Dividends | 0.50 | 0.50 | 0.50 | 0.40 | 0.22 | 0.32 | 0.32 | 0.32 | 0.32 | 0.32 |
| Payout Ratio | 25% | 13% | 13% | 14% | 15% | 24% | 28% | 29% | 30% | 40% |
| Prices:High | 67.31 | 58.62 | 101.37 | 86.08 | 51.93 | 39.55 | 27.60 | 20.41 | 22.48 | 31.60 |
| Prices:Low | 41.20 | 30.21 | 28.60 | 37.61 | 36.76 | 25.06 | 18.05 | 13.33 | 10.03 | 15.60 |
| P/E Ratio:High | 34 | 16 | 26 | 29 | 35 | 30 | 25 | 18 | 21 | 39 |
| P/E Ratio:Low | 21 | 8 | 7 | 13 | 25 | 19 | 16 | 12 | 9 | 19 |
| **Income Statement Analysis (Million $)** | | | | | | | | | | |
| Revenue | 20,849 | 21,990 | 22,326 | 16,691 | 14,079 | 13,161 | 9,380 | 8,806 | 9,959 | 8,972 |
| Operating Income | 738 | 1,305 | 1,160 | 755 | 504 | 396 | 370 | 344 | 332 | 258 |
| Depreciation | 189 | 182 | 163 | 147 | 126 | 104 | 91.9 | 79.7 | 78.0 | 71.9 |
| Interest Expense | 10.6 | 10.1 | 11.9 | 24.0 | 23.0 | 16.3 | 15.4 | 10.1 | 8.93 | 25.0 |
| Pretax Income | 560 | 1,137 | 1,114 | 649 | 382 | 300 | 281 | 268 | 261 | 185 |
| Effective Tax Rate | NA | 35.5% | 35.4% | 17.8% | 31.0% | 24.1% | 33.6% | 33.0% | 34.8% | 31.1% |
| Net Income | 357 | 685 | 720 | 533 | 263 | 227 | 187 | 180 | 170 | 128 |
| S&P Core Earnings | 428 | 700 | 640 | 533 | 267 | 226 | 171 | 188 | 143 | 90.2 |
| **Balance Sheet & Other Financial Data (Million $)** | | | | | | | | | | |
| Cash | 2,607 | 2,291 | 2,108 | 1,714 | 976 | 789 | 605 | 497 | 753 | 573 |
| Current Assets | 5,563 | 5,122 | 4,669 | 4,060 | 3,324 | 3,108 | 2,723 | 2,214 | 1,941 | 1,851 |
| Total Assets | 7,615 | 7,178 | 6,424 | 5,796 | 4,875 | 4,574 | 3,970 | 3,449 | 3,142 | 3,091 |
| Current Liabilities | 3,523 | 3,301 | 3,163 | 2,860 | 2,406 | 2,339 | 1,764 | 1,829 | 1,756 | 1,811 |
| Long Term Debt | 17.8 | 17.7 | 17.7 | 325 | 187 | 92.0 | 348 | 44.7 | 17.6 | 17.6 |
| Common Equity | 3,497 | 3,306 | 2,671 | 2,274 | 1,730 | 1,631 | 1,336 | 1,082 | 884 | 789 |
| Total Capital | 3,612 | 3,461 | 2,689 | 2,292 | 1,918 | 1,723 | 1,683 | 1,126 | 901 | 807 |
| Capital Expenditures | 265 | 233 | 300 | 284 | 274 | 213 | 104 | 79.2 | 63.0 | 148 |
| Cash Flow | 630 | 867 | 884 | 680 | 390 | 331 | 279 | 259 | 248 | 200 |
| Current Ratio | 1.6 | 1.6 | 1.5 | 1.4 | 1.4 | 1.3 | 1.5 | 1.2 | 1.1 | 1.0 |
| % Long Term Debt of Capitalization | 0.5 | 0.5 | 0.7 | 0.8 | 9.8 | 5.3 | 20.7 | 4.0 | 2.0 | 2.2 |
| % Net Income of Revenue | 1.7 | 3.1 | 3.2 | 3.2 | 1.9 | 1.7 | 2.0 | 2.0 | 1.7 | 1.4 |
| % Return on Assets | NA | 10.1 | 11.8 | 10.0 | 5.6 | 5.3 | 5.0 | 5.4 | 5.4 | 4.4 |
| % Return on Equity | NA | 22.9 | 29.1 | 26.6 | 15.7 | 15.3 | 15.4 | 18.3 | 20.3 | 18.0 |

Data as orig reptd.; bef. results of disc opers/spec. items. Per share data adj. for stk. divs.; EPS diluted. E-Estimated. NA-Not Available. NM-Not Meaningful. NR-Not Ranked. UR-Under Review.

**Office:** 6700 Las Colinas Blvd, Irving, TX 75039-2902.
**Telephone:** 469-398-7000.
**Email:** investor@fluor.com
**Website:** http://www.fluor.com

**Chrmn:** A.L. Boeckmann
**CEO:** D.T. Seaton
**SVP, CFO & Chief Acctg Officer:** D.M. Steuert
**SVP, Secy & General Counsel:** C.M. Hernandez

**Chief Admin Officer:** G.C. Gilkey
**Investor Contact:** K. Lockwood (469-398-7220)
**Board Members:** P. K. Barker, A. M. Bennett, R. T. Berkery, P. J. Fluor, J. T. Hackett, K. Kresa, D. R. O'Hare, J. W. Prueher, D. T. Seaton, N. H. Sultan, S. H. Woolsey

**Founded:** 1924
**Domicile:** Delaware
**Employees:** 39,229

# FMC Corp.

**STANDARD &POOR'S**

**S&P Recommendation** HOLD ★★★☆☆

| Price | 12-Mo. Target Price | Investment Style |
|---|---|---|
| $76.79 (as of Nov 25, 2011) | $85.00 | Large-Cap Value |

**GICS Sector** Materials
**Sub-Industry** Diversified Chemicals

**Summary** This company is a diversified producer of industrial, specialty and agricultural chemicals.

## Key Stock Statistics (Source S&P, Vickers, company reports)

| | | | | | | | |
|---|---|---|---|---|---|---|---|
| 52-Wk Range | $93.00–63.81 | S&P Oper. EPS 2011E | 5.74 | Market Capitalization(B) | $5.408 | Beta | 1.07 |
| Trailing 12-Month EPS | $3.28 | S&P Oper. EPS 2012E | 6.50 | Yield (%) | 0.78 | S&P 3-Yr. Proj. EPS CAGR(%) | 10 |
| Trailing 12-Month P/E | 23.4 | P/E on S&P Oper. EPS 2011E | 13.4 | Dividend Rate/Share | $0.60 | S&P Credit Rating | BBB+ |
| $10K Invested 5 Yrs Ago | $22,395 | Common Shares Outstg. (M) | 70.4 | Institutional Ownership (%) | 96 | | |

## Price Performance

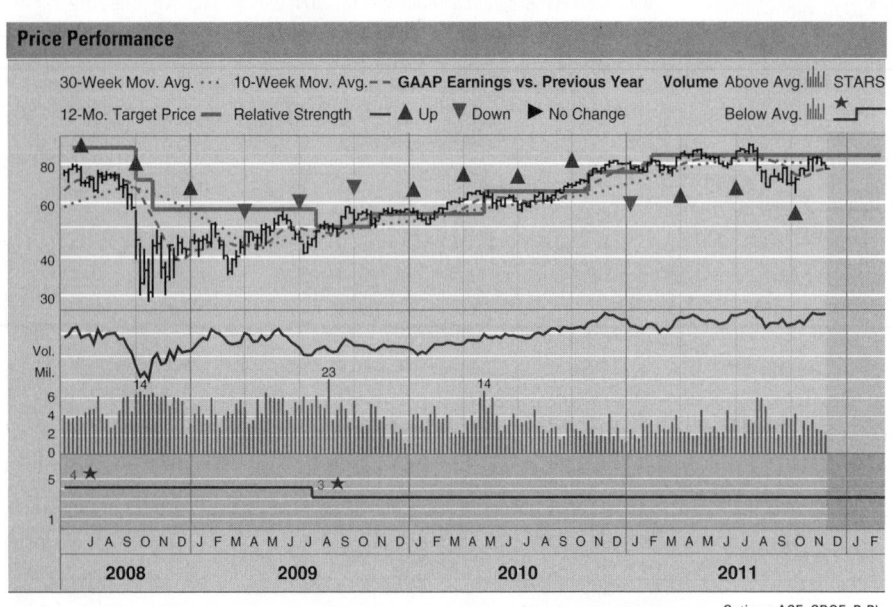

30-Week Mov. Avg. · · · 10-Week Mov. Avg. – – GAAP Earnings vs. Previous Year    Volume Above Avg. STARS
12-Mo. Target Price — Relative Strength    — ▲ Up ▼ Down ► No Change    Below Avg.    ★

Options: ASE, CBOE, P, Ph

Analysis prepared by Equity Analyst **R. O'Reilly, CFA** on Aug 03, 2011, when the stock traded at **$82.07.**

## Highlights

➤ We expect operating EPS of $5.70 in 2011, versus $4.84 in 2010. We believe industrial chemicals profits will continue to recover in 2011, up about 30%, after a 55% decline in 2009, on a continued recovery in demand and higher prices for soda ash and peroxygens due to stronger glass, paper and pulp markets, and tight supply capacities. The recent restart of soda ash capacity will likely begin to benefit earnings in late 2011; the closure of the European phosphate business at the end of 2010 should reduce earnings volatility.

➤ Specialty chemicals profits in 2011 should increase about 10% on expected modest sales growth for both lithium and biopolymer products, and despite higher materials costs. We look for profits at the pesticide unit to grow for the eighth consecutive year, up about 10% in 2011, reflecting sales increases in most regions on new product introductions, limited by increased development spending.

➤ We see interest expense in 2011 of about $40 million, similar to 2010, and expect the effective tax rate to remain at about 29%. Reported EPS for 2010 includes restructuring charges totaling $2.02.

## Investment Rationale/Risk

➤ Our hold opinion is based on our belief that the shares are fairly valued. We project further profit gains in pesticides and specialty chemicals into 2011. Industrial chemicals should show a continued recovery in profitability, reflecting better demand and higher prices for soda ash and peroxygens. We believe FMC's balance sheet and cash flow will allow it to make bolt-on acquisitions in the specialty businesses while continuing stock buybacks.

➤ Risks to our recommendation and target price include higher-than-expected raw material and energy costs, unplanned production outages and interruptions, adverse weather conditions, adverse economic conditions in Brazil (18% of annual sales), and the company's inability to maintain or increase industrial chemicals selling prices and receive approvals for new specialty chemical and pesticide products.

➤ Based on our 2011 estimates, the stock recently traded at P/E and cash flow multiples at discounts to those of comparable-sized chemical companies. Our 12-month target price of $85 is based on a multiple of 15.0X our 2011 EPS estimate, still a discount to the company's peer group.

## Qualitative Risk Assessment

| LOW | MEDIUM | HIGH |
|---|---|---|

Our risk assessment reflects the company's diversified product mix and leading domestic market positions in many product lines, offset by the cyclical nature of the industrial chemicals business and exposure to the Brazilian farm economy.

## Quantitative Evaluations

**S&P Quality Ranking** — B-

| D | C | B- | B | B+ | A- | A | A+ |
|---|---|---|---|---|---|---|---|

**Relative Strength Rank** — STRONG

71

LOWEST = 1    HIGHEST = 99

## Revenue/Earnings Data

**Revenue (Million $)**

| | 1Q | 2Q | 3Q | 4Q | Year |
|---|---|---|---|---|---|
| 2011 | 795.0 | 812.2 | 862.1 | -- | -- |
| 2010 | 756.5 | 776.8 | 772.5 | 810.5 | 3,116 |
| 2009 | 690.5 | 700.3 | 713.3 | 722.1 | 2,826 |
| 2008 | 750.2 | 806.6 | 820.8 | 737.7 | 3,115 |
| 2007 | 674.1 | 657.9 | 626.6 | 674.3 | 2,633 |
| 2006 | 594.1 | 592.3 | 572.2 | 588.4 | 2,347 |

**Earnings Per Share ($)**

| | | | | | |
|---|---|---|---|---|---|
| 2011 | 1.41 | 1.61 | 1.30 | E1.33 | E5.74 |
| 2010 | 1.13 | 1.16 | 1.14 | -0.63 | 2.82 |
| 2009 | 1.00 | 1.01 | 0.46 | 0.88 | 3.37 |
| 2008 | 1.31 | 1.20 | 1.13 | 0.69 | 4.35 |
| 2007 | 0.71 | 0.19 | 0.54 | 0.60 | 2.02 |
| 2006 | 0.48 | 0.44 | 0.49 | 0.43 | 1.84 |

Fiscal year ended Dec. 31. Next earnings report expected: Early February. EPS Estimates based on S&P Operating Earnings; historical GAAP earnings are as reported.

## Dividend Data (Dates: mm/dd Payment Date: mm/dd/yy)

| Amount ($) | Date Decl. | Ex-Div. Date | Stk. of Record | Payment Date |
|---|---|---|---|---|
| 0.125 | 12/17 | 12/29 | 12/31 | 01/20/11 |
| 0.150 | 02/18 | 03/29 | 03/31 | 04/21/11 |
| 0.150 | 04/26 | 06/28 | 06/30 | 07/21/11 |
| 0.150 | 07/22 | 09/28 | 09/30 | 10/20/11 |

Dividends have been paid since 2006. Source: Company reports.

# FMC Corp.

## Business Summary August 03, 2011

CORPORATE OVERVIEW. FMC Corp. is a diversified chemicals company that produces pesticides, and industrial and specialty chemicals. International operations provided 65% of 2010 sales; Brazil alone accounted for 18% of sales.

Industrial chemicals accounted for 34% of sales and 20% of profits in 2010. FMC is North America's largest producer of natural soda ash (about 59% of annual segment sales in 2010) and a large North American producer of peroxygens (26%, consisting of hydrogen peroxide (two-thirds of sales) and specialties). The company is a major European producer of zeolites and silicates through Foret, S.A. (4%). At the end of 2010, FMC ceased operations of its European phosphorus business (11%); reported earnings for the fourth quarter of 2010 include a related pretax charge of $110.4 million. The segment's profits fell 55% in 2009 on lower volumes due to the recession. Profits rebounded 37% in 2010 on a strong recovery in demand and lower raw material and energy costs, more than offsetting lower selling prices.

Agricultural products (40%, 50%) consist of insecticides, herbicides, and fungicides for crop protection and pest control. The segment achieved its sev-

enth consecutive year of record profits in 2010, growing 7%, as sales rose 18%. Insecticides (including Founce, Furadan and Capture) account for about 48% of annual segment sales; about 80% of segment sales are derived outside the U.S. Herbicide sales (43%) have grown significantly over the past several years. FMC's herbicides primarily target niche uses and include two product lines (sulfentrazone and carfentrazone) introduced in the late 1990s.

In the specialty chemicals segment (26%, 30%), FMC BioPolymer (about 74% of segment sales) is the world's leading producer of carrageenan, alginate, and microcrystalline cellulose (over 50% share), used for pharmaceutical ingredients, food stabilizers and thickeners, and personal care products. FMC believes that carrageenan and microcrystalline cellulose are growing faster than the overall food ingredients market.

## Company Financials Fiscal Year Ended Dec. 31

| Per Share Data ($) | 2010 | 2009 | 2008 | 2007 | 2006 | 2005 | 2004 | 2003 | 2002 | 2001 |
|---|---|---|---|---|---|---|---|---|---|---|
| Tangible Book Value | 12.09 | 11.00 | 9.19 | 15.24 | 11.17 | 10.53 | 9.55 | 6.12 | 3.94 | 1.64 |
| Cash Flow | 4.82 | 5.10 | 5.75 | 3.49 | 3.50 | 3.21 | 4.19 | 2.33 | 2.68 | -2.79 |
| Earnings | 2.82 | 3.37 | 4.35 | 2.02 | 1.84 | 1.42 | 2.35 | 0.56 | 1.01 | -4.93 |
| S&P Core Earnings | 3.06 | 3.58 | 3.42 | 1.79 | 1.99 | 0.97 | 2.22 | 0.30 | 0.40 | -4.94 |
| Dividends | 0.50 | 0.50 | 0.48 | 0.41 | 0.36 | Nil | Nil | Nil | Nil | Nil |
| Payout Ratio | 18% | 15% | 11% | 20% | 20% | Nil | Nil | Nil | Nil | Nil |
| Prices:High | 82.03 | 58.13 | 80.23 | 59.00 | 38.99 | 31.94 | 25.25 | 17.43 | 21.15 | 42.00 |
| Prices:Low | 50.75 | 34.90 | 28.53 | 35.63 | 25.87 | 21.63 | 16.48 | 7.11 | 11.45 | 22.83 |
| P/E Ratio:High | 29 | 17 | 18 | 29 | 21 | 23 | 11 | 31 | 21 | NM |
| P/E Ratio:Low | 18 | 10 | 7 | 18 | 14 | 15 | 7 | 13 | 11 | NM |

| Income Statement Analysis (Million $) | | | | | | | | | | |
|---|---|---|---|---|---|---|---|---|---|---|
| Revenue | 3,116 | 2,826 | 3,115 | 2,633 | 2,347 | 2,150 | 2,051 | 1,921 | 1,853 | 1,943 |
| Operating Income | 650 | 577 | 656 | 507 | 461 | 416 | 363 | 321 | 306 | 323 |
| Depreciation | 134 | 127 | 106 | 114 | 132 | 136 | 134 | 125 | 119 | 132 |
| Interest Expense | 39.3 | 27.2 | 38.6 | 41.4 | 42.0 | 62.3 | 80.9 | 96.1 | 73.0 | 63.0 |
| Pretax Income | 351 | 310 | 472 | 195 | 153 | 201 | 135 | 40.9 | 89.9 | -471 |
| Effective Tax Rate | NA | 17.1% | 26.6% | 14.9% | NM | 41.0% | NM | NM | 19.4% | NM |
| Net Income | 219 | 247 | 330 | 157 | 145 | 111 | 176 | 39.8 | 69.1 | -306 |
| S&P Core Earnings | 222 | 261 | 259 | 139 | 157 | 75.9 | 166 | 21.4 | 27.4 | -307 |

| Balance Sheet & Other Financial Data (Million $) | | | | | | | | | | |
|---|---|---|---|---|---|---|---|---|---|---|
| Cash | 162 | 76.6 | 52.4 | 75.5 | 166 | 206 | 212 | 57.0 | 364 | 23.4 |
| Current Assets | 1,646 | 1,488 | 1,433 | 1,194 | 1,068 | 1,067 | 1,073 | 1,010 | 1,176 | 820 |
| Total Assets | 3,320 | 3,136 | 2,976 | 2,733 | 2,735 | 2,740 | 2,978 | 2,829 | 2,872 | 2,477 |
| Current Liabilities | 963 | 709 | 759 | 751 | 702 | 659 | 820 | 728 | 875 | 1,079 |
| Long Term Debt | 503 | 588 | 593 | 420 | 524 | 640 | 822 | 1,033 | 1,036 | 652 |
| Common Equity | 1,189 | 1,133 | 903 | 1,064 | 1,056 | 1,026 | 942 | 654 | 406 | 219 |
| Total Capital | 1,809 | 1,744 | 1,561 | 1,542 | 1,638 | 1,717 | 1,816 | 1,736 | 1,487 | 915 |
| Capital Expenditures | 142 | 161 | 175 | 115 | 116 | 93.5 | 85.4 | 87.0 | 83.9 | 146 |
| Cash Flow | 352 | 374 | 436 | 271 | 277 | 247 | 310 | 164 | 188 | -175 |
| Current Ratio | 1.7 | 2.1 | 1.9 | 1.6 | 1.5 | 1.6 | 1.3 | 1.4 | 1.3 | 0.8 |
| % Long Term Debt of Capitalization | 27.8 | 33.7 | 38.0 | 27.2 | 32.0 | 37.3 | 45.3 | 59.5 | 69.7 | 71.2 |
| % Net Income of Revenue | 7.0 | 8.7 | 10.6 | 6.0 | 6.2 | 5.2 | 8.6 | 2.1 | 3.7 | NM |
| % Return on Assets | 6.8 | 8.1 | 11.5 | 5.7 | 5.3 | 3.9 | 6.0 | 1.4 | 2.6 | NM |
| % Return on Equity | 19.3 | 24.2 | 33.5 | 15.0 | 13.9 | 11.3 | 22.0 | 7.0 | 22.1 | NM |

Data as orig reptd.; bef. results of disc opers/spec. items. Per share data adj. for stk. divs.; EPS diluted. E-Estimated. NA-Not Available. NM-Not Meaningful. NR-Not Ranked. UR-Under Review.

Office: 1735 Market St, Philadelphia, PA 19103-7597.
Telephone: 215-299-6000.
Email: investor-info@fmc.com
Website: http://www.fmc.com

Chrmn, Pres & CEO: P.R. Brondeau
CFO: W.K. Foster
Chief Acctg Officer & Cntlr: G.R. Wood
Treas: T.C. Deas, Jr.

Secy & General Counsel: A.E. Utecht
Investor Contact: B. Arndt (215-299-6266)
Board Members: P. R. Brondeau, E. E. Cordeiro, G. P. D'Aloia, C. S. Greer, D. A. Kempthorne, E. J. Mooney, P. Norris, R. C. Pallash, W. H. Powell, E. J. Sosa, V. R. Volpe, Jr.

Founded: 1884
Domicile: Delaware
Employees: 4,900

# FMC Technologies Inc

**STANDARD &POOR'S**

| **S&P Recommendation** HOLD ★★★☆☆ | **Price** $46.37 (as of Nov 25, 2011) | **12-Mo. Target Price** $47.00 | **Investment Style** Large-Cap Growth |

**GICS Sector** Energy
**Sub-Industry** Oil & Gas Equipment & Services

**Summary** This company is a leading provider of oilfield services capital equipment, particularly for subsea equipment used in deepwater energy exploration and development.

## Key Stock Statistics (Source S&P, Vickers, company reports)

| | | | | | |
|---|---|---|---|---|---|
| 52-Wk Range | $50.33– 34.46 | S&P Oper. EPS 2011E | 1.76 | Market Capitalization(B) | $11.049 | Beta | 1.28 |
| Trailing 12-Month EPS | $1.64 | S&P Oper. EPS 2012E | 2.29 | Yield (%) | Nil | S&P 3-Yr. Proj. EPS CAGR(%) | 17 |
| Trailing 12-Month P/E | 28.3 | P/E on S&P Oper. EPS 2011E | 26.3 | Dividend Rate/Share | Nil | S&P Credit Rating | NA |
| $10K Invested 5 Yrs Ago | NA | Common Shares Outstg. (M) | 238.3 | Institutional Ownership (%) | NM | | |

## Price Performance

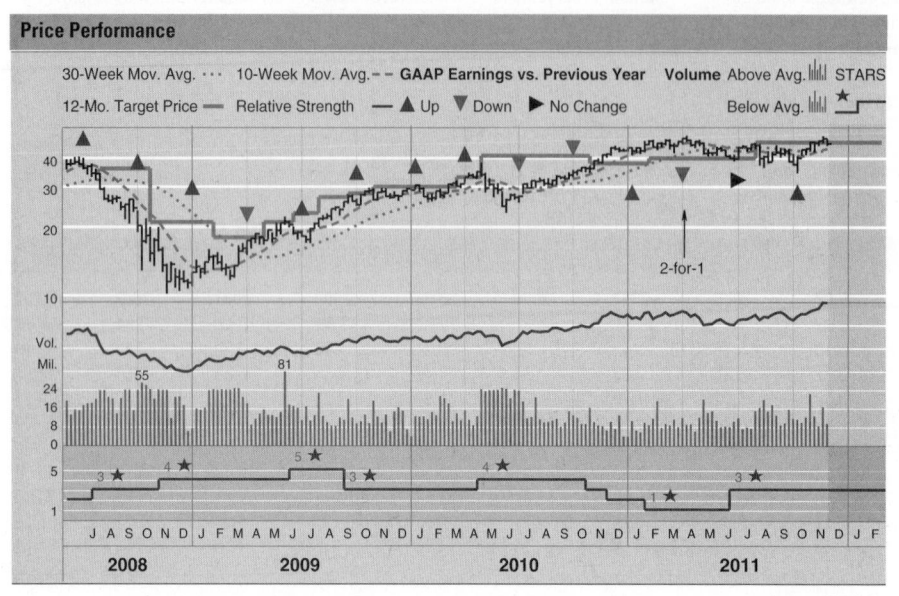

30-Week Mov. Avg. · · ·   10-Week Mov. Avg. - - -   **GAAP Earnings vs. Previous Year**   Volume Above Avg. STARS
12-Mo. Target Price ——   Relative Strength ——   ▲ Up   ▼ Down   ► No Change   Below Avg.   ★

Options: ASE, P, Ph

Analysis prepared by Equity Analyst **S. Glickman, CFA** on Aug 15, 2011, when the stock traded at **$40.71**.

## Highlights

➤ Energy Production Systems segment backlog at the end of June was $4.4 billion, up from $2.3 billion at the end of 2009, with subsea backlog comprising the vast majority. The book-to-bill ratio at Energy Production Systems doubled to 1.47 in 2010, after averaging 0.73 in 2009; we project an average of 1.26 for 2011. The end of the drilling moratorium in the U.S. Gulf of Mexico is a necessary, but not sufficient, condition for a recovery there as the drilling permit process remains sluggish and is likely to impede U.S. Gulf subsea activity until resolved, although we note that 18 deepwater permits have now been issued since February. The Gulf accounted for just 11% of FTI's revenues in 2010, and will likely be relatively lower in 2011.

➤ Fundamentals continue to improve, in our view. Subsea order flow is likely to be dictated by deepwater drilling demand, which looks promising to us for 2011-12 as newbuild floaters go to work. We also see strong demand for fluid control products, given the intensity of U.S. shale plays.

➤ We see EPS of $1.65 in 2011 rising to $2.20 in 2012 on widening Energy Production Systems margins.

## Investment Rationale/Risk

➤ After a recent pullback, we no longer find that shares overextended. The stock was recently trading at about the average of its 10-year historical forward multiples of EBITDA, cash flow and earnings. We think FTI has done a good job at increasing dollar value per subsea tree installed. With oil prices remaining stubbornly high in the $80/barrel to $100/barrel range, we think customer confidence to undertake major subsea projects will be sustained as well.

➤ Risks to our recommendation and target price include reduced subsea activity, lower energy prices, changes in forex, and a slower than expected return to normalcy in the U.S. Gulf drilling permit process.

➤ Our DCF model, assuming free cash flow growth of 15%, terminal growth of 3%, and a WACC of 11%, shows intrinsic value of $48. Applying premium multiples of 15X enterprise value to estimated 2012 EBITDA and 17X projected 2012 cash flow (merited, in our view, by deepwater exposure and above-average projected ROIC), and blending these values with our DCF model, our 12-month target price is $47.

## Qualitative Risk Assessment

| LOW | **MEDIUM** | HIGH |

Our risk assessment reflects the company's exposure to crude oil and natural gas prices and capital spending decisions by oil and gas producers, and its commitment to technological innovation in oilfield services, offset by a longer-term trend toward deepwater development.

## Quantitative Evaluations

**S&P Quality Ranking** **B+**

| D | C | B- | B | **B+** | A- | A | A+ |

**Relative Strength Rank** **STRONG**
**92**
LOWEST = 1          HIGHEST = 99

## Revenue/Earnings Data

**Revenue (Million $)**

| | 1Q | 2Q | 3Q | 4Q | Year |
|---|---|---|---|---|---|
| 2011 | 1,082 | 1,229 | 1,287 | -- | -- |
| 2010 | 1,050 | 1,013 | 960.0 | 1,103 | 4,126 |
| 2009 | 1,053 | 1,104 | 1,088 | 1,160 | 4,405 |
| 2008 | 1,294 | 1,454 | 1,128 | 1,205 | 4,551 |
| 2007 | 979.9 | 1,153 | 1,136 | 1,364 | 4,615 |
| 2006 | 826.6 | 949.2 | 938.3 | 1,077 | 3,791 |

**Earnings Per Share ($)**

| | | | | | |
|---|---|---|---|---|---|
| 2011 | 0.35 | 0.39 | 0.50 | E0.51 | E1.76 |
| 2010 | 0.40 | 0.39 | 0.33 | 0.41 | 1.53 |
| 2009 | 0.28 | 0.42 | 0.37 | 0.38 | 1.44 |
| 2008 | 0.31 | 0.41 | 0.36 | 0.37 | 1.36 |
| 2007 | 0.23 | 0.28 | 0.30 | 0.35 | 1.15 |
| 2006 | 0.17 | 0.23 | 0.22 | 0.24 | 0.75 |

Fiscal year ended Dec. 31. Next earnings report expected: Mid February. EPS Estimates based on S&P Operating Earnings; historical GAAP earnings are as reported.

## Dividend Data (Dates: mm/dd Payment Date: mm/dd/yy)

| Amount ($) | Date Decl. | Ex-Div. Date | Stk. of Record | Payment Date |
|---|---|---|---|---|
| 2-for-1 | 02/25 | 04/01 | 03/14 | 03/31/11 |

Source: Company reports.

# FMC Technologies Inc

**STANDARD
&POOR'S**

## Business Summary August 15, 2011

CORPORATE OVERVIEW. FMC Technologies is a global provider of high technology solutions for the energy industry. The company designs, manufactures and services advanced systems and products such as subsea production and processing systems, surface wellhead production systems, high pressure fluid control equipment, measurement solutions and marine loading systems for the oil and gas industry. Operations are separated into two reportable segments: Energy Production Systems and Energy Processing Systems. Approximately 23% of total 2010 revenues were derived in the United States, followed by Norway, with 17%. In July 2008, the company spun off its former FoodTech and Airport Systems segments to John Bean Technologies (JBT 19, Not Ranked), rendering the remainder of FTI as a pure-play energy services company that specializes in capital equipment. These former segments are now classified under discontinued operations.

The Energy Production Systems segment (81% of 2010 revenues and 79% of 2010 segment operating profits) is a global leader in production systems that control the flow of oil and gas from producing wells. Approximately 70% of this segment's revenue base is derived from sales of subsea systems. Subsea systems are placed on the seafloor, and are used to control the flow of oil or gas from the reservoir to a host facility (such as floating production facility, a fixed platform, or an onshore facility). Many systems that the company provides are used in exploration, development and production of crude oil and

natural gas reserves located in deepwater environments, with water depths greater than 1,000 ft. The remaining 30% of this segment's revenue base is derived from surface production systems. The company is also involved in subsea separation systems, which help separate the flow of oil, gas and water more efficiently. Lastly, FTI is advancing the development of subsea processing, an emerging technology that enables separation at the seabed and is thus more cost-efficient for customers. This technology was introduced commercially in the North Sea in 2007.

The Energy Processing Systems segment (19%, 21%) designs, manufactures and supplies technologically advanced high pressure valves and fittings for oilfield services customers. FTI also builds and supplies liquid and gas measurement and transportation equipment and systems to customers involved in upstream, midstream and downstream operations. Products include the WECO/Chiksan line of flowline products, which pump fracturing fluids into a well during the well servicing process, or that pump cement during the completion of new wells. Other product lines include flow meters, fluid loading and transfer systems, material handling systems, and blending and transfer systems.

## Company Financials Fiscal Year Ended Dec. 31

| Per Share Data ($) | 2010 | 2009 | 2008 | 2007 | 2006 | 2005 | 2004 | 2003 | 2002 | 2001 |
|---|---|---|---|---|---|---|---|---|---|---|
| Tangible Book Value | 3.64 | 2.66 | 1.89 | 2.90 | 2.59 | 1.91 | 1.72 | 0.91 | 0.70 | 0.27 |
| Cash Flow | 1.96 | 1.81 | 1.61 | 1.43 | 1.01 | 0.61 | 0.65 | 0.50 | 0.42 | 0.37 |
| Earnings | 1.53 | 1.44 | 1.36 | 1.15 | 0.75 | 0.38 | 0.42 | 0.28 | 0.24 | 0.15 |
| S&P Core Earnings | 1.52 | 1.46 | 1.26 | 1.10 | 0.74 | 0.28 | 0.29 | 0.26 | 0.14 | 0.08 |
| Dividends | Nil | Nil | Nil | Nil | Nil | Nil | Nil | Nil | Nil | Nil |
| Payout Ratio | Nil | Nil | Nil | Nil | Nil | Nil | Nil | Nil | Nil | Nil |
| Prices:High | 45.40 | 29.78 | 41.59 | 33.89 | 17.97 | 11.06 | 8.63 | 6.15 | 5.96 | 5.62 |
| Prices:Low | 23.08 | 11.68 | 10.14 | 13.78 | 10.85 | 7.16 | 5.49 | 4.49 | 3.58 | 2.75 |
| P/E Ratio:High | 30 | 21 | 31 | 29 | 24 | 29 | 21 | 22 | 25 | 37 |
| P/E Ratio:Low | 15 | 8 | 7 | 12 | 14 | 19 | 13 | 16 | 15 | 18 |

| Income Statement Analysis (Million $) | | | | | | | | | | |
|---|---|---|---|---|---|---|---|---|---|---|
| Revenue | 4,126 | 4,405 | 4,551 | 4,615 | 3,791 | 3,227 | 2,768 | 2,307 | 2,072 | 1,928 |
| Operating Income | NA | NA | 596 | 524 | 375 | 198 | 174 | 174 | 154 | 149 |
| Depreciation | 101 | 93.0 | 64.9 | 73.4 | 70.8 | 65.9 | 63.5 | 57.7 | 48.6 | 57.8 |
| Interest Expense | 8.80 | 9.50 | 1.50 | 21.5 | 11.8 | 9.00 | Nil | 10.1 | 14.1 | 14.1 |
| Pretax Income | 538 | 518 | 506 | 465 | 299 | 165 | 160 | 108 | 92.5 | 63.5 |
| Effective Tax Rate | NA | 30.0% | 30.0% | 33.7% | 28.3% | 34.1% | 26.4% | 28.8% | 28.3% | 38.0% |
| Net Income | 378 | 361 | 353 | 308 | 212 | 106 | 117 | 75.6 | 64.1 | 39.4 |
| S&P Core Earnings | 373 | 366 | 327 | 294 | 208 | 78.3 | 81.3 | 68.3 | 36.1 | 21.6 |

| Balance Sheet & Other Financial Data (Million $) | | | | | | | | | | |
|---|---|---|---|---|---|---|---|---|---|---|
| Cash | 316 | 461 | 340 | 130 | 79.5 | 153 | 124 | 29.0 | 32.4 | 28.0 |
| Current Assets | 2,345 | 2,226 | 2,444 | 2,104 | 1,690 | 1,428 | 1,217 | 949 | 813 | 755 |
| Total Assets | 3,644 | 3,510 | 3,586 | 3,211 | 2,488 | 2,096 | 1,894 | 1,591 | 1,363 | 1,438 |
| Current Liabilities | 1,495 | 1,679 | 1,963 | 1,785 | 1,208 | 1,058 | 995 | 845 | 728 | 681 |
| Long Term Debt | 351 | 392 | 472 | 122 | 213 | 253 | 160 | 201 | 175 | 194 |
| Common Equity | 1,312 | 1,103 | 696 | 1,022 | 886 | 706 | 669 | 442 | 322 | 418 |
| Total Capital | 1,684 | 1,504 | 1,181 | 1,151 | 1,107 | 965 | 835 | 650 | 502 | 616 |
| Capital Expenditures | 113 | 110 | 165 | 203 | 139 | 91.8 | 50.2 | 65.2 | 68.1 | 67.6 |
| Cash Flow | 480 | 454 | 418 | 381 | 282 | 172 | 180 | 133 | 113 | 97.2 |
| Current Ratio | 1.6 | 1.3 | 1.3 | 1.2 | 1.4 | 1.3 | 1.2 | 1.1 | 1.1 | 1.1 |
| % Long Term Debt of Capitalization | 20.9 | 26.2 | 40.0 | 10.6 | 19.2 | 26.2 | 19.2 | 30.9 | 34.9 | 31.5 |
| % Net Income of Revenue | 9.2 | 8.2 | 7.8 | 6.7 | 5.6 | 3.3 | 4.2 | 3.3 | 3.1 | 2.0 |
| % Return on Assets | 10.6 | 10.2 | 10.4 | 10.8 | 9.2 | 5.3 | 6.7 | 5.1 | 4.6 | 2.8 |
| % Return on Equity | 31.3 | 40.2 | 41.1 | 32.2 | 26.7 | 15.4 | 20.7 | 19.8 | 16.8 | 7.5 |

Data as orig reptd.; bef. results of disc opers/spec. items. Per share data adj. for stk. divs.; EPS diluted. E-Estimated. NA-Not Available. NM-Not Meaningful. NR-Not Ranked. UR-Under Review.

**Office:** 1803 Gears Rd, Houston, TX 77067-4003.
**Telephone:** 281-591-4000.
**Website:** http://www.fmctechnologies.com
**Chrmn, Pres & CEO:** J.T. Gremp

**EVP & CFO:** W.H. Schumann, III
**Chief Admin Officer:** M.J. Scott
**CTO:** B.D. Beitler
**Chief Acctg Officer & Cntlr:** J.A. Nutt

**Investor Contact:** R. Cherry (281-591-4560)
**Board Members:** M. R. Bowlin, P. J. Burguieres, C. M. Devine, T. Enger, C. S. Farley, J. T. Gremp, T. Hamilton, P. D. Kinnear, E. J. Mooney, J. H. Netherland, Jr., R. A. Pattarozzi, J. M. Ringler, E. de Carvalho Filho

**Founded:** 2000
**Domicile:** Delaware
**Employees:** 11,500

*The McGraw-Hill Companies*

# Ford Motor Co

**STANDARD &POOR'S**

| S&P Recommendation **BUY** ★★★★☆ | Price<br>$9.75 (as of Nov 25, 2011) | 12-Mo. Target Price<br>$17.00 | Investment Style<br>Large-Cap Value |
|---|---|---|---|

**GICS Sector** Consumer Discretionary
**Sub-Industry** Automobile Manufacturers

**Summary** The world's third largest producer of cars and trucks, Ford also has automotive financing and insurance operations.

## Key Stock Statistics (Source S&P, Vickers, company reports)

| | | | | | | | |
|---|---|---|---|---|---|---|---|
| 52-Wk Range | $18.97– 9.05 | S&P Oper. EPS 2011**E** | 2.02 | Market Capitalization(B) | $36.360 | Beta | 2.39 |
| Trailing 12-Month EPS | $1.67 | S&P Oper. EPS 2012**E** | 1.94 | Yield (%) | Nil | S&P 3-Yr. Proj. EPS CAGR(%) | 11 |
| Trailing 12-Month P/E | 5.8 | P/E on S&P Oper. EPS 2011**E** | 4.8 | Dividend Rate/Share | Nil | S&P Credit Rating | BB+ |
| $10K Invested 5 Yrs Ago | $11,444 | Common Shares Outstg. (M) | 3,800.1 | Institutional Ownership (%) | 56 | | |

## Price Performance

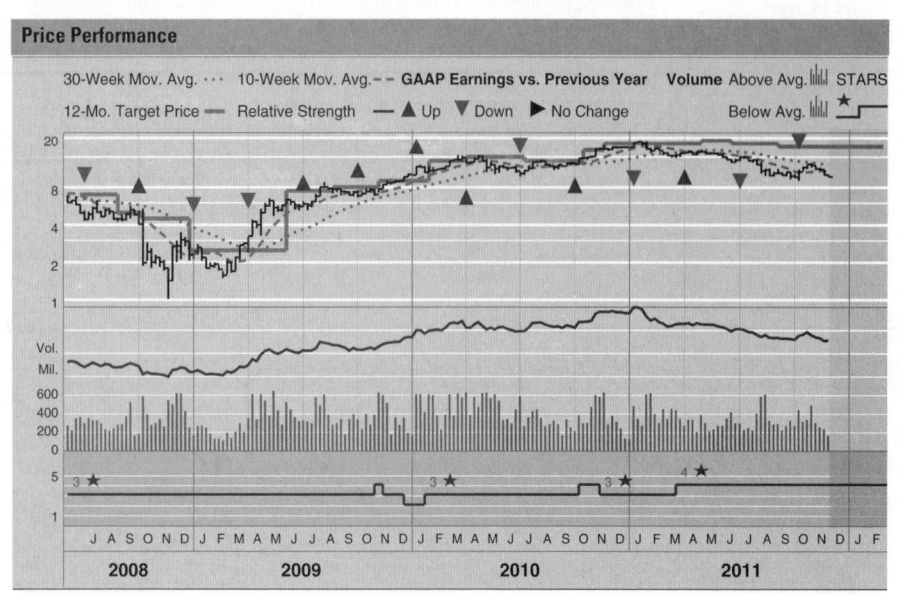

30-Week Mov. Avg. · · · 10-Week Mov. Avg. - - **GAAP Earnings vs. Previous Year** Volume Above Avg. STARS
12-Mo. Target Price — Relative Strength — ▲ Up ▼ Down ► No Change Below Avg. ★

Options: ASE, CBOE, P, Ph

Analysis prepared by Equity Analyst **Efraim Levy, CFA** on Nov 01, 2011, when the stock traded at **$11.10**.

## Qualitative Risk Assessment

| LOW | MEDIUM | **HIGH** |
|---|---|---|

Our risk assessment reflects the highly cyclical nature of Ford's markets and our view of the current and long-term challenges it faces, including weak industry demand, intensifying competition, high fixed and legacy costs, and a weak, albeit improving, balance sheet.

## Quantitative Evaluations

**S&P Quality Ranking**      **B-**

| D | C | **B-** | B | B+ | A- | A | A+ |
|---|---|---|---|---|---|---|---|

**Relative Strength Rank**      **WEAK**

27

LOWEST = 1           HIGHEST = 99

## Revenue/Earnings Data

**Revenue (Million $)**

| | 1Q | 2Q | 3Q | 4Q | Year |
|---|---|---|---|---|---|
| 2011 | 33,114 | 35,527 | 33,047 | -- | -- |
| 2010 | 31,566 | 31,300 | 29,893 | 32,428 | 128,954 |
| 2009 | 24,778 | 27,189 | 30,892 | 35,449 | 118,308 |
| 2008 | 43,513 | 38,600 | 32,100 | 29,200 | 139,300 |
| 2007 | 43,019 | 44,200 | 41,100 | 44,100 | 172,455 |
| 2006 | 41,055 | 41,965 | 37,110 | 40,318 | 160,123 |

**Earnings Per Share ($)**

| | | | | | |
|---|---|---|---|---|---|
| 2011 | 0.61 | 0.59 | 0.41 | E0.32 | E2.02 |
| 2010 | 0.50 | 0.61 | 0.43 | 0.07 | 1.66 |
| 2009 | -0.60 | 0.69 | 0.29 | 0.25 | 0.86 |
| 2008 | 0.05 | -3.88 | -0.06 | -2.46 | -6.41 |
| 2007 | -0.15 | 0.30 | -0.19 | -1.33 | -1.40 |
| 2006 | -0.64 | -0.14 | -2.79 | -2.98 | -6.72 |

Fiscal year ended Dec. 31. Next earnings report expected: Late January. EPS Estimates based on S&P Operating Earnings; historical GAAP earnings are as reported.

## Dividend Data

No cash dividends have been paid since 2006.

## Highlights

► We see Ford's total revenues rising at a mid-single digit pace in 2011, due to gains in the U.S., China, and most non-European regions, partly offset by the absence of Volvo and Mercury brand sales. The financial services segment has historically been an important sales and earnings contributor, but we expect a segment profit decline in 2011. Total revenues should rise 9% in 2012.

► Margins should benefit from more rapid product introduction, improved volume, more efficient capacity utilization, and cost-cutting efforts, partly offset by higher raw material costs and greater investment actions. In our view, Ford's brand benefited from not tapping government financial aid, and from various new products. Also, we believe Ford has taken advantage of Toyota's difficulties and that the Japan crisis has given Ford a brief opportunity to enhance margins and improve market share.

► Ford should benefit from improved perception of and buyer interest in its vehicles. The termination of the Mercury brand should help it revive the Lincoln brand. While we expect pretax profit to advance in 2012, after expected higher tax rates, EPS could fall.

## Investment Rationale/Risk

► We think Ford's president and CEO has made a noticeable positive difference in the company's improvement efforts. Also, we have become more confident in Ford's ability to bring successful vehicles to market -- one of the company's most important challenges, in our view -- and we see progress in bolstering the company's image. However, we think competitive and economic challenges remain.

► Risks to our opinion and target price include increased competition, less-than-expected demand and production, weaker-than-projected financial services income, higher raw material costs, and an unfavorable shift in cash balances. As for corporate governance, we are concerned about Ford family members having greater voting rights than other shareholders.

► Improved consumer perception of Ford products and rising vehicle demand should outweigh the potential negative volume and mix effects from higher gas and commodity prices, in our view. Our 12-month target price of $17 is equal to 8.8X our 2012 EPS estimate of $1.94, based on historical and peer P/E analysis. We believe the company will reinstate a quarterly dividend payment in early 2012.

---

**Please read the Required Disclosures and Analyst Certification on the last page of this report.**

**The McGraw-Hill Companies**

# Ford Motor Co

**STANDARD &POOR'S**

## Business Summary November 01, 2011

CORPORATE OVERVIEW. Ford is the second largest U.S. motor vehicle manufacturer. It produces cars and trucks, and many of the vehicles' plastic, glass and electronic components, and replacement parts. It also owns a 3.5% stake in Mazda Motor Corp. Financial services include Ford Motor Credit (automotive financing and insurance) and American Road Insurance Co.

In recent years, Ford's margins have been pressured by an increase in competition -- primarily from Asian companies -- and a shift away from the more profitable large pickup truck and SUV segments to smaller, less profitable crossover utility vehicles (CUVs). However, in 2009 and 2010, competitors' bankruptcy filings and recall issues and its own new products helped it gain market share, in our view.

CORPORATE STRATEGY. Challenged by a shrinking U.S. market share and more recently by lower industry volume, the company has announced restructuring plans in recent years in an attempt to lower its costs. Also, even as global demand begins what we expect to be a multi-year uptrend, the company has worked to prune it product portfolio to focus on its Ford and Lincoln

brands. Most recently, the company announced plans to discontinue production of Mercury brand vehicles.

The company sold its Volvo unit to China's Zhejiang Geely Holding Group Co. Ltd. for $1.8 billion in the third quarter of 2010.

The company's business and product portfolio has changed several times in recent years, as Ford sought to optimize its financial health and performance. In 2000, Ford acquired Land Rover from BMW Group for $1.9 billion. In June 2008, the company sold Jaguar and Land Rover to Tata Motors for $2.3 billion, but used about $600 million of the proceeds to fund the Jaguar and Land Rover pension plans. In late 2008, the company reduced its stake in Mazda from 33% to 13.8% (now 3.5%).

## Company Financials Fiscal Year Ended Dec. 31

| Per Share Data ($) | 2010 | 2009 | 2008 | 2007 | 2006 | 2005 | 2004 | 2003 | 2002 | 2001 |
|---|---|---|---|---|---|---|---|---|---|---|
| Tangible Book Value | NM | NM | NM | 0.70 | NM | 3.68 | 4.60 | 2.30 | NM | NM |
| Cash Flow | 2.91 | 2.91 | 2.49 | 5.26 | -6.71 | 7.62 | 9.12 | 8.31 | 8.45 | 5.78 |
| Earnings | 1.66 | 0.86 | -6.41 | -1.40 | -6.72 | 1.14 | 1.80 | 0.50 | 0.15 | -3.02 |
| S&P Core Earnings | 1.54 | 0.84 | -7.69 | -0.94 | -5.58 | 0.64 | 1.80 | 1.03 | -1.16 | -4.56 |
| Dividends | Nil | Nil | Nil | Nil | 0.35 | 0.40 | 0.40 | 0.40 | 0.40 | 1.05 |
| Payout Ratio | Nil | Nil | Nil | Nil | NM | 35% | 22% | 80% | NM | NM |
| Prices:High | 17.42 | 10.37 | 8.79 | 9.70 | 9.48 | 14.75 | 17.34 | 17.33 | 18.23 | 31.42 |
| Prices:Low | 9.75 | 1.50 | 1.01 | 6.65 | 1.06 | 7.57 | 12.61 | 6.58 | 6.90 | 14.70 |
| P/E Ratio:High | 11 | 12 | NM | NM | NM | 13 | 10 | 35 | NM | NM |
| P/E Ratio:Low | 6 | 2 | NM | NM | NM | 7 | 7 | 13 | NM | NM |

| Income Statement Analysis (Million $) | 2010 | 2009 | 2008 | 2007 | 2006 | 2005 | 2004 | 2003 | 2002 | 2001 |
|---|---|---|---|---|---|---|---|---|---|---|
| Revenue | 128,954 | 118,300 | 139,300 | 172,455 | 160,123 | 177,089 | 171,652 | 164,196 | 163,420 | 162,412 |
| Operating Income | 14,476 | 10,935 | 16,199 | 21,189 | 8,286 | 21,052 | 24,945 | 24,770 | 25,034 | 22,941 |
| Depreciation | 5,584 | 6,931 | 20,329 | 13,158 | 16,453 | 14,042 | 13,052 | 14,297 | 15,177 | 15,922 |
| Interest Expense | 1,807 | 1,515 | 9,682 | 10,927 | 8,783 | 7,643 | 7,071 | 7,690 | 8,824 | 10,848 |
| Pretax Income | 7,149 | 3,008 | -14,303 | -3,746 | -15,051 | 1,996 | 4,853 | 1,370 | 953 | -7,584 |
| Effective Tax Rate | 8.30% | 2.29% | NM | NM | NM | NM | 19.3% | 9.85% | 31.7% | NM |
| Net Income | 6,557 | 2,694 | -14,580 | -2,764 | -12,615 | 2,228 | 3,634 | 921 | 284 | -5,453 |
| S&P Core Earnings | 6,102 | 2,631 | -17,458 | -1,866 | -10,472 | 1,146 | 3,637 | 1,905 | -2,202 | -8,266 |

| Balance Sheet & Other Financial Data (Million $) | 2010 | 2009 | 2008 | 2007 | 2006 | 2005 | 2004 | 2003 | 2002 | 2001 |
|---|---|---|---|---|---|---|---|---|---|---|
| Cash | 20,307 | 31,696 | 15,181 | 50,031 | 50,366 | 39,082 | 33,018 | 33,642 | 30,521 | 15,028 |
| Total Assets | 164,687 | 194,850 | 218,328 | 279,264 | 278,554 | 269,476 | 292,654 | 304,594 | 289,357 | 276,543 |
| Long Term Debt | 88,733 | 114,727 | 90,534 | 107,478 | 144,373 | 94,428 | 106,540 | 119,751 | 125,806 | 121,430 |
| Total Debt | 103,988 | 132,441 | 154,196 | 168,530 | 172,049 | 154,332 | 172,973 | 179,804 | 167,892 | 168,009 |
| Common Equity | -673 | -7,820 | -17,311 | 5,628 | -3,465 | 12,957 | 16,045 | 11,651 | 5,590 | 7,786 |
| Capital Expenditures | 4,092 | 4,561 | 6,696 | 6,022 | 6,848 | 7,517 | 6,745 | 7,749 | 7,278 | 7,008 |
| Cash Flow | 12,141 | 9,625 | 5,648 | 10,394 | -12,615 | 16,270 | 16,686 | 15,218 | 15,446 | 10,454 |
| % Return on Assets | 3.7 | 1.3 | NM | NM | NM | 0.8 | 1.2 | 0.3 | 0.1 | NM |
| % Return on Equity | NM | NM | NM | NM | NM | 15.4 | 26.2 | 10.7 | 4.0 | NM |
| % Long Term Debt of Capitalization | 100.7 | 106.0 | 111.7 | 93.9 | 106.0 | 82.9 | 82.2 | 87.5 | 87.8 | 87.2 |

Data as orig reptd.; bef. results of disc opers/spec. items. Per share data adj. for stk. divs.; EPS diluted. E-Estimated. NA-Not Available. NM-Not Meaningful. NR-Not Ranked. UR-Under Review.

**Office:** 1 American Rd, Dearborn, MI 48126-2798.
**Telephone:** 313-322-3000.
**Website:** http://www.ford.com
**Chrmn:** W.C. Ford, Jr.

**Pres & CEO:** A.R. Mulally
**CFO:** L.W. Booth
**CTO:** P.A. Mascarenas
**Chief Acctg Officer & Cntlr:** R.L. Shanks

**Investor Contact:** L. Heck (313-594-0613)
**Board Members:** S. G. Butler, K. A. Casiano, A. F. Earley, Jr., E. B. Ford, II, W. C. Ford, Jr., R. A. Gephardt, J. H. Hance, Jr., W. W. Helman, IV, I. O. Hockaday, Jr., R. A. Manoogian, E. R. Marram, A. R. Mulally, H. A. Neal, G. L. Shaheen, J. L. Thornton

**Founded:** 1903
**Domicile:** Delaware
**Employees:** 164,000

# Forest Laboratories Inc

**STANDARD &POOR'S**

| **S&P Recommendation** STRONG SELL ★ ☆ ☆ ☆ ☆ | **Price** $29.96 (as of Nov 30, 2011) | **12-Mo. Target Price** $25.00 | **Investment Style** Large-Cap Growth |
|---|---|---|---|

**GICS Sector** Health Care
**Sub-Industry** Pharmaceuticals

**Summary** This company develops and makes branded and generic ethical drug products, sold primarily in the U.S., Puerto Rico, and Western and Eastern Europe.

## Key Stock Statistics (Source S&P, Vickers, company reports)

| | | | | | | | |
|---|---|---|---|---|---|---|---|
| 52-Wk Range | $40.52– 28.56 | S&P Oper. EPS 2012**E** | 3.60 | Market Capitalization(B) | $8.004 | Beta | 0.70 |
| Trailing 12-Month EPS | $4.05 | S&P Oper. EPS 2013**E** | 1.15 | Yield (%) | Nil | S&P 3-Yr. Proj. EPS CAGR(%) | -25 |
| Trailing 12-Month P/E | 7.4 | P/E on S&P Oper. EPS 2012**E** | 8.3 | Dividend Rate/Share | Nil | S&P Credit Rating | NA |
| $10K Invested 5 Yrs Ago | $6,152 | Common Shares Outstg. (M) | 267.2 | Institutional Ownership (%) | NM | | |

## Price Performance

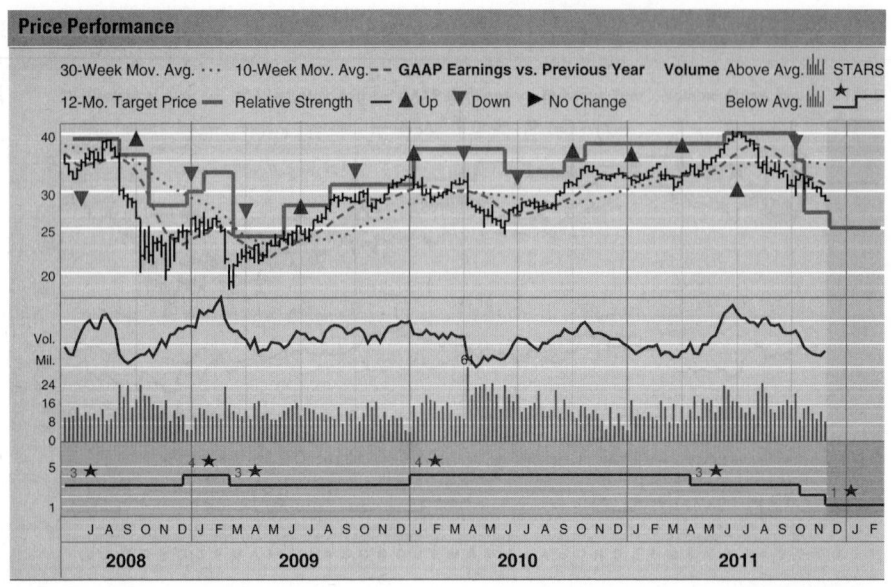

30-Week Mov. Avg. · · · 10-Week Mov. Avg. - - GAAP Earnings vs. Previous Year  Volume Above Avg. STARS
12-Mo. Target Price — Relative Strength — ▲ Up ▼ Down ► No Change  Below Avg.

Options: ASE, CBOE, P, Ph

## Qualitative Risk Assessment

| LOW | MEDIUM | HIGH |
|---|---|---|

Our risk assessment reflects our view of the company's recent successes on the new product front, with the launches of Bystolic cardiovascular, Savella treatment for COPD, and Teflaro novel antibiotic. We also see several additional important pipeline launches in the years ahead. On the other hand, Forest's relatively small size among big pharma competitors, and impending patent expirations on Lexapro and Namenda, are significant risk factors.

## Quantitative Evaluations

**S&P Quality Ranking**                                B

| D | C | B- | B | B+ | A- | A | A+ |
|---|---|---|---|---|---|---|---|

**Relative Strength Rank**                      MODERATE

36

LOWEST = 1                                      HIGHEST = 99

## Highlights

► The STARS recommendation for FRX has recently been changed to 1 (strong sell) from 2 (sell) and the 12-month target price has recently been changed to $25.00 from $27.00. The Highlights section of this Stock Report will be updated accordingly.

## Investment Rationale/Risk

► The Investment Rationale/Risk section of this Stock Report will be updated shortly. For the latest News story on FRX from MarketScope, see below.

► 11/30/11 03:01 pm ET ... S&P DOWNGRADES OPINION ON SHARES OF FOREST LABORATORIES TO STRONG SELL FROM SELL (FRX 29.73*): Reflecting the impending March '12 patent expiration on Lexapro (accounting for 53% of total sales in the Sep-Q), we expect FY 13 (Mar.) EPS to drop 68%, to $1.15, down from our previous estimate of $1.28. We believe recent prescription trends for several of Forest's newer products such as Daliresp for COPD, Viibyrd antidepressant and Savella for fibromyalgia have been disappointing, leading us to doubt that FRX will be able to achieve its $1.20 EPS guidance for FY 13. We are lowering our target price by $2, to $25, based on revised forward P/E and DCF assumptions. /H. Saftlas

## Revenue/Earnings Data

### Revenue (Million $)

| | 1Q | 2Q | 3Q | 4Q | Year |
|---|---|---|---|---|---|
| 2012 | 1,152 | 1,164 | -- | -- | -- |
| 2011 | 1,060 | 1,080 | 1,126 | 1,131 | 4,420 |
| 2010 | 1,008 | 1,013 | 1,065 | 1,050 | 4,193 |
| 2009 | 947.9 | 972.8 | 972.4 | 951.9 | 3,845 |
| 2008 | 928.3 | 919.0 | 998.2 | 990.9 | 3,718 |
| 2007 | 816.3 | 847.0 | 893.0 | 885.4 | 3,442 |

### Earnings Per Share ($)

| | 1Q | 2Q | 3Q | 4Q | Year |
|---|---|---|---|---|---|
| 2012 | 0.90 | 0.91 | E0.95 | E0.70 | E3.60 |
| 2011 | 0.39 | 1.00 | 1.11 | 1.12 | 3.59 |
| 2010 | 0.87 | 0.61 | 0.69 | 0.07 | 2.25 |
| 2009 | 0.79 | 0.80 | 0.62 | 0.31 | 2.52 |
| 2008 | 0.83 | 0.71 | 0.96 | 0.55 | 3.06 |
| 2007 | 0.62 | 0.75 | 0.78 | -0.75 | 1.41 |

Fiscal year ended Mar. 31. Next earnings report expected: NA. EPS Estimates based on S&P Operating Earnings; historical GAAP earnings are as reported.

## Dividend Data

No cash dividends have been paid.

# Forest Laboratories Inc

**STANDARD &POOR'S**

## Business Summary November 07, 2011

CORPORATE OVERVIEW. Forest Laboratories is a leading producer of niche-oriented branded and generic prescription pharmaceuticals. Most of Forest's products were developed in collaboration with licensing partners. Product sales accounted for 95% of total revenues in FY 11 (Mar.), contract revenues for 4%, and other income for 1%.

Lexapro antidepressant is FRX's single most important product. A single enanitomer version of Celexa (an older, off-patent FRX antidepressant), Lexapro is an advanced selective serotonin reuptake inhibitor (SSRI) indicated for both depression and generalized anxiety disorder. Lexapro had sales of $2.3 billion in FY 11, unchanged from FY 10. As of March 2011, Lexapro accounted for about 13% of the U.S. prescription antidepressant market. FRX in-licensed Lexapro from H. Lundbeck A/S, a Danish drug firm. FRX's Lexapro patent expires in March 2012.

FRX's second most important product is Namenda (licensed from Merz Pharmaceuticals of Germany), a treatment for moderate to severe Alzheimer's disease. Sales of Namenda were $1.3 billion in FY 11, up from $1.1 billion in FY 10. Namenda is believed to account for over one third of the Alzheimer's prescription drug market.

In January 2008, FRX launched Bystolic, a novel beta blocker antihypertensive

that was in-licensed from Mylan Laboratories. Bystolic had sales of $264 million in FY 11, up from $179 million in FY 10. Launched in April 2009, Savella, a treatment for fibromyalgia, had sales of $90 million in FY 11, up from $53 million in FY 10. In October 2010, the FDA approved Teflaro, a broad-spectrum injectible antibiotic. Other products include Tiazac antihypertensive, Aerobid asthma drug, Campral for alcohol addiction, Combunox for severe pain, and other drugs. FRX also books contract income from sales of Benicar, an antihypertensive co-promoted with Sankyo.

COMPETITIVE LANDSCAPE. The U.S. antidepressant drug market totaled about $11.6 billion in 2010, based on data from IMS Health. We expect this market to shrink in terms of dollar sales over the coming years, reflecting the impact of inexpensive generic versions of many patent-expired branded antidepressants. Pfizer's Zoloft antidepressant lost patent protection in 2006, and Wyeth's patent on Effexor antidepressant expired in 2008. Generics now largely comprise previously branded Prozac and Paxil antidepressant markets.

## Company Financials Fiscal Year Ended Mar. 31

| Per Share Data ($) | 2011 | 2010 | 2009 | 2008 | 2007 | 2006 | 2005 | 2004 | 2003 | 2002 |
|---|---|---|---|---|---|---|---|---|---|---|
| Tangible Book Value | 16.63 | 14.58 | 11.94 | 10.19 | 8.93 | 7.69 | 8.21 | 8.03 | 5.66 | 3.75 |
| Cash Flow | 3.85 | 2.50 | 2.84 | 3.34 | 1.55 | 2.20 | 2.32 | 2.01 | 1.80 | 1.06 |
| Earnings | 3.59 | 2.25 | 2.52 | 3.06 | 1.41 | 2.08 | 2.25 | 1.95 | 1.66 | 0.91 |
| S&P Core Earnings | 3.96 | 2.26 | 2.53 | 3.01 | 1.41 | 1.97 | 2.15 | 1.85 | 1.58 | 0.74 |
| Dividends | NA | Nil | Nil | Nil | Nil | Nil | Nil | Nil | Nil | Nil |
| Payout Ratio | NA | Nil | Nil | Nil | Nil | Nil | Nil | Nil | Nil | Nil |
| Calendar Year | 2010 | 2009 | 2008 | 2007 | 2006 | 2005 | 2004 | 2003 | 2002 | 2001 |
| Prices:High | 34.17 | 32.76 | 42.76 | 57.97 | 54.70 | 45.21 | 78.81 | 63.23 | 54.99 | 41.60 |
| Prices:Low | 24.17 | 18.37 | 19.23 | 34.89 | 36.18 | 32.46 | 36.10 | 41.85 | 32.12 | 23.25 |
| P/E Ratio:High | 10 | 15 | 17 | 19 | 39 | 22 | 35 | 32 | 33 | 46 |
| P/E Ratio:Low | 7 | 8 | 8 | 11 | 26 | 16 | 16 | 21 | 19 | 26 |
| **Income Statement Analysis** (Million $) | | | | | | | | | | |
| Revenue | 4,390 | 4,112 | 3,845 | 3,718 | 3,442 | 2,962 | 3,114 | 2,650 | 2,207 | 1,567 |
| Operating Income | 1,373 | 1,027 | 989 | 1,179 | 754 | 701 | 1,164 | 929 | 833 | 490 |
| Depreciation | 73.0 | 76.5 | 96.5 | 86.7 | 45.4 | 40.7 | 25.4 | 22.2 | 51.6 | 54.6 |
| Interest Expense | NA | NA | Nil | Nil | Nil | Nil | Nil | Nil | Nil | Nil |
| Pretax Income | 1,338 | 951 | 971 | 1,210 | 709 | 870 | 1,185 | 937 | 821 | 470 |
| Effective Tax Rate | NA | 28.2% | 20.9% | 20.0% | 35.9% | 18.5% | 29.2% | 21.5% | 24.2% | 28.1% |
| Net Income | 1,047 | 682 | 768 | 968 | 454 | 709 | 839 | 736 | 622 | 338 |
| S&P Core Earnings | 1,154 | 686 | 771 | 953 | 454 | 673 | 800 | 697 | 589 | 272 |
| **Balance Sheet & Other Financial Data** (Million $) | | | | | | | | | | |
| Cash | 3,851 | 3,322 | 2,581 | 1,777 | 1,353 | 1,323 | 1,619 | 2,131 | 1,556 | 893 |
| Current Assets | 5,260 | 4,579 | 3,786 | 2,908 | 2,423 | 2,207 | 2,708 | 2,916 | 2,255 | 1,195 |
| Total Assets | 6,922 | 6,224 | 5,197 | 4,525 | 3,653 | 3,120 | 3,705 | 3,863 | 2,918 | 1,952 |
| Current Liabilities | 938 | 980 | 818 | 611 | 628 | 421 | 564 | 605 | 564 | 325 |
| Long Term Debt | NA | NA | Nil | Nil | Nil | Nil | Nil | Nil | Nil | Nil |
| Common Equity | 5,499 | 4,890 | 4,115 | 3,715 | 3,025 | 2,698 | 3,132 | 3,256 | 2,352 | 1,625 |
| Total Capital | 5,499 | 4,890 | 4,115 | 3,716 | 3,026 | 2,699 | 3,141 | 3,258 | 2,354 | 1,627 |
| Capital Expenditures | 38.5 | 32.3 | 40.6 | 34.9 | 30.0 | 55.0 | 89.0 | 102 | 79.6 | 36.4 |
| Cash Flow | 1,120 | 759 | 864 | 1,055 | 500 | 749 | 864 | 758 | 674 | 393 |
| Current Ratio | 5.6 | 4.7 | 4.6 | 4.8 | 3.9 | 5.2 | 4.8 | 4.8 | 4.0 | 3.7 |
| % Long Term Debt of Capitalization | Nil | Nil | Nil | Nil | Nil | Nil | Nil | Nil | Nil | Nil |
| % Net Income of Revenue | 23.8 | 16.6 | 20.0 | 26.0 | 13.5 | 24.3 | 26.9 | 27.8 | 28.2 | 21.6 |
| % Return on Assets | NA | NA | 15.8 | 23.7 | 13.4 | 20.8 | 22.2 | 21.7 | 25.5 | 19.9 |
| % Return on Equity | NA | NA | 19.6 | 28.7 | 15.9 | 24.3 | 26.3 | 26.2 | 31.3 | 23.7 |

Data as orig reptd.; bef. results of disc opers/spec. items. Per share data adj. for stk. divs.; EPS diluted. E-Estimated. NA-Not Available. NM-Not Meaningful. NR-Not Ranked. UR-Under Review.

**Office:** 909 3rd Ave, New York, NY 10022-4748.
**Telephone:** 212-421-7850.
**Email:** investor.relations@frx.com
**Website:** http://www.frx.com

**Chrmn, Pres & CEO:** H. Solomon
**CFO & Chief Admin Officer:** F.I. Perier, Jr.
**Chief Acctg Officer & Cntlr:** R. Weinberger
**Secy:** H.S. Weinstein

**Investor Contact:** F.J. Murdolo (212-224-6714)
**Board Members:** N. Basgoz, C. J. Coughlin, D. L. Goldwasser, K. E. Goodman, G. M. Lieberman, L. S. Olanoff, L. B. Salans, B. L. Saunders, H. Solomon, P. J. Zimetbaum

**Founded:** 1956
**Domicile:** Delaware
**Employees:** 5,600

# Franklin Resources Inc

**STANDARD &POOR'S**

| S&P Recommendation **BUY** ★★★★☆ | Price $91.63 (as of Nov 25, 2011) | 12-Mo. Target Price $128.00 | Investment Style Large-Cap Growth |
|---|---|---|---|

**GICS Sector** Financials
**Sub-Industry** Asset Management & Custody Banks

**Summary** This company is one of the world's largest asset managers, serving retail, institutional and high-net-worth clients.

## Key Stock Statistics (Source S&P, Vickers, company reports)

| | | | | | | | |
|---|---|---|---|---|---|---|---|
| 52-Wk Range | $137.56– 87.71 | S&P Oper. EPS 2012**E** | 9.40 | Market Capitalization(B) | $19.920 | Beta | 1.48 |
| Trailing 12-Month EPS | $8.62 | S&P Oper. EPS 2013**E** | NA | Yield (%) | 1.09 | S&P 3-Yr. Proj. EPS CAGR(%) | 15 |
| Trailing 12-Month P/E | 10.6 | P/E on S&P Oper. EPS 2012**E** | 9.7 | Dividend Rate/Share | $1.00 | S&P Credit Rating | AA- |
| $10K Invested 5 Yrs Ago | $9,134 | Common Shares Outstg. (M) | 217.4 | Institutional Ownership (%) | 53 | | |

## Price Performance

30-Week Mov. Avg. · · · 10-Week Mov. Avg. – – GAAP Earnings vs. Previous Year  Volume Above Avg. STARS
12-Mo. Target Price — Relative Strength — ▲ Up ▼ Down ► No Change  Below Avg.

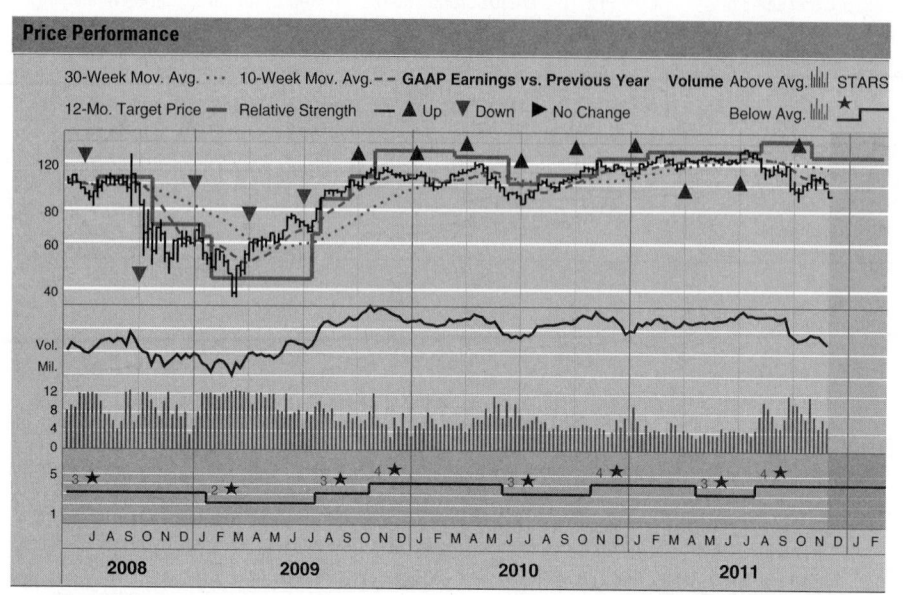

Options: ASE, CBOE, P, Ph

Analysis prepared by Equity Analyst **R. Shepard, CFA** on Nov 03, 2011, when the stock traded at **$105.79**.

## Highlights

► We expect BEN's expanding stable of international funds to produce 3% revenue growth in FY 12 (Sep.), despite pressure on asset inflows from volatile financial markets. We think that assets under management (AUM) will be superior to peers given BEN's strong fund performance and increasing presence in key growth markets in Asia. We also expect additional acquisitions as a means of expanding AUM and international diversification. Moreover, we believe the overall pace of asset inflows will quicken once a resolution is found to the European debt crisis. We expect net flows to remain strongest into global taxable fixed income funds, but see choppy equity inflows.

► Top-line growth coupled with disciplined expense management should allow for margin improvement in FY 12, in our view. We expect operating margins of 38.2% in FY 12, up from 37.3% in FY 10. In FY 12, we see a positive revenue and earnings contribution from the purchase of Balanced Equity Management, an Australian equity manager with $10.9 billion in AUM.

► We estimate EPS of $9.40 in FY 12, up from $8.62 in FY 11, aided by share repurchases.

## Investment Rationale/Risk

► We think BEN is one of the best-managed asset gatherers, and believe its balance sheet is characterized by limited debt and ample cash on hand. We have a favorable view of its strong operating free cash flow, and think its earnings power relative to peers is increasing given industry shifts toward fixed income assets, in which BEN has a strong track record of solid fund performance. BEN's results reflect strong relative fund performance, consistent revenues, and strategic cost management. We see BEN's inflows primarily coming from taxable fixed income products, while recent equity outflows are a potential concern. BEN continues to repurchase shares as a means of redeploying capital to shareholders. All told, we view the shares as undervalued at recent levels.

► Risks to our recommendation include potential depreciation in global equity and bond markets and slower asset inflows.

► Our 12-month target price of $128 is equal to 13.6X our 2012 EPS estimate of $9.40, in line with the historical multiple but a slight premium to peers that we think is warranted given BEN's organic growth trends.

## Qualitative Risk Assessment

| LOW | MEDIUM | HIGH |
|---|---|---|

Our risk assessment reflects our view of the company's strong operating margins, well-capitalized balance sheet and international exposure, offset by concerns about uneven client flow trends and recent declines in relative investment performance.

## Quantitative Evaluations

**S&P Quality Ranking** B+

| D | C | B- | B | B+ | A- | A | A+ |
|---|---|---|---|---|---|---|---|

**Relative Strength Rank** WEAK

24

LOWEST = 1   HIGHEST = 99

## Revenue/Earnings Data

**Revenue (Million $)**

| | 1Q | 2Q | 3Q | 4Q | Year |
|---|---|---|---|---|---|
| 2011 | 1,700 | 1,750 | 1,853 | 1,837 | 7,140 |
| 2010 | 1,377 | 1,413 | 1,534 | 1,528 | 5,853 |
| 2009 | 969.3 | 912.3 | 1,074 | 1,239 | 4,194 |
| 2008 | 1,686 | 1,504 | 1,522 | 1,321 | 6,032 |
| 2007 | 1,428 | 1,509 | 1,640 | 1,629 | 6,206 |
| 2006 | 1,181 | 1,255 | 1,317 | 1,297 | 5,051 |

**Earnings Per Share ($)**

| | | | | | |
|---|---|---|---|---|---|
| 2011 | 2.23 | 2.25 | 2.26 | 1.88 | 8.62 |
| 2010 | 1.54 | 1.56 | 1.58 | 1.66 | 6.33 |
| 2009 | 0.52 | 0.48 | 1.29 | 1.60 | 3.87 |
| 2008 | 2.12 | 1.54 | 1.71 | 1.28 | 6.67 |
| 2007 | 1.67 | 1.73 | 1.86 | 1.76 | 7.03 |
| 2006 | 1.21 | 0.74 | 1.41 | 1.49 | 4.86 |

Fiscal year ended Sep. 30. Next earnings report expected: Late January. EPS Estimates based on S&P Operating Earnings; historical GAAP earnings are as reported.

## Dividend Data (Dates: mm/dd Payment Date: mm/dd/yy)

| Amount ($) | Date Decl. | Ex-Div. Date | Stk. of Record | Payment Date |
|---|---|---|---|---|
| 0.250 | 12/16 | 12/29 | 12/31 | 01/07/11 |
| 0.250 | 03/15 | 03/29 | 03/31 | 04/15/11 |
| 0.250 | 06/14 | 06/28 | 06/30 | 07/15/11 |
| 0.250 | 09/15 | 09/28 | 09/30 | 10/14/11 |

Dividends have been paid since 1981. Source: Company reports.

---

**Please read the Required Disclosures and Analyst Certification on the last page of this report.**

The **McGraw·Hill** Companies

# Franklin Resources Inc

STANDARD
&POOR'S

## Business Summary November 03, 2011

CORPORATE OVERVIEW. Franklin Resources is one of the largest U.S. money managers, with $659.9 billion in assets under management at the end of FY 11 (Sep.), up from $644.9 billion at the end of FY 10. At the end of FY 11, equity-based investments accounted for 39% of assets under management, fixed income investments 45%, hybrid funds 15%, and money funds 1%. We think that a decline in the dollar relative to other major currencies would aid BEN, due to the high percentage of assets invested globally. Conversely, the company's results may be challenged by a rising U.S. dollar relative to major currencies. At the end of FY 11, about 33% of assets under management were held by investors domiciled outside the U.S.

The company's sponsored investment products are distributed under five distinct names: Franklin, Templeton, Mutual Series, Bissett and Fiduciary. The Franklin family of funds is best known for its bond funds, although it includes a range of equity and balanced products. The Templeton family of funds is known for its global investment strategies and value style. Mutual Series funds are primarily known for their value-oriented equity focus. The Bissett family of mutual funds operates in Canada, and serves a broad range of clients, primarily institutions. We are impressed with BEN's broad range of investment products, but we think the company lacks a compelling roster of

growth equity products.

The company generates the majority of its revenue from investment management and related services provided to its retail and institutional mutual funds, and to its institutional, high-net-worth and separately managed accounts. Investment management and related services include fund administration, shareholder services, transfer agency, underwriting, distribution, custodial, trustee, and other fiduciary services. Investment management fees depend on the level of client assets under management, and it earns higher revenues and income from equity assets, generally, and a shift in assets from equity to fixed income or balanced funds reduces revenue. Underwriting and distribution fees consist of sales charges and commissions derived from sales of sponsored investment products and distribution fees. It also generates fees from investment management services for high-net-worth individuals and families through Fiduciary Trust.

## Company Financials Fiscal Year Ended Sep. 30

| Per Share Data ($) | 2011 | 2010 | 2009 | 2008 | 2007 | 2006 | 2005 | 2004 | 2003 | 2002 |
|---|---|---|---|---|---|---|---|---|---|---|
| Tangible Book Value | 29.91 | 25.54 | 24.54 | 21.72 | 21.49 | 18.57 | 14.39 | 12.23 | 9.31 | 8.69 |
| Cash Flow | 9.77 | 7.54 | 4.66 | 7.57 | 7.82 | 5.86 | 5.02 | 3.51 | 2.67 | 2.35 |
| Earnings | 8.62 | 6.36 | 3.87 | 6.67 | 7.03 | 4.86 | 4.06 | 2.78 | 1.97 | 1.65 |
| S&P Core Earnings | 8.32 | 6.18 | 3.96 | 6.77 | 6.64 | 4.72 | 3.97 | 2.47 | 1.70 | 1.56 |
| Dividends | 1.00 | 4.09 | 0.83 | 0.75 | 0.57 | 0.36 | 0.40 | 0.33 | 0.29 | 0.28 |
| Payout Ratio | 12% | 64% | 21% | 11% | 8% | 7% | 10% | 12% | 15% | 17% |
| Prices:High | 137.56 | 125.00 | 116.39 | 129.08 | 145.59 | 114.98 | 98.86 | 71.45 | 52.25 | 44.48 |
| Prices:Low | 87.71 | 84.00 | 37.11 | 45.52 | 108.46 | 80.16 | 63.56 | 46.85 | 29.99 | 27.90 |
| P/E Ratio:High | 16 | 20 | 30 | 19 | 21 | 24 | 24 | 26 | 27 | 27 |
| P/E Ratio:Low | 10 | 13 | 10 | 7 | 15 | 16 | 16 | 17 | 15 | 17 |

| Income Statement Analysis (Million $) | 2011 | 2010 | 2009 | 2008 | 2007 | 2006 | 2005 | 2004 | 2003 | 2002 |
|---|---|---|---|---|---|---|---|---|---|---|
| Income Interest | Nil | Nil | Nil | Nil | Nil | NA | NA | NA | NA | NA |
| Income Other | Nil | Nil | Nil | Nil | Nil | NA | NA | NA | NA | NA |
| Total Income | 7,140 | 5,853 | 4,194 | 6,032 | 6,206 | 5,051 | 4,310 | 3,438 | 2,624 | 2,519 |
| General Expenses | 4,480 | 3,894 | 2,991 | 3,933 | 4,138 | 3,417 | 3,004 | NA | NA | NA |
| Interest Expense | 37.4 | 119 | 3.77 | 15.8 | 23.2 | 29.2 | 34.0 | 30.7 | 19.9 | 12.3 |
| Depreciation | 244 | 267 | 181 | 215 | 199 | 215 | 17.5 | NA | NA | NA |
| Net Income | 1,924 | 1,446 | 897 | 1,588 | 1,773 | 1,268 | 1,058 | 702 | 503 | 433 |
| S&P Core Earnings | 1,849 | 1,403 | 917 | 1,612 | 1,674 | 1,229 | 1,033 | 622 | 432 | 410 |

| Balance Sheet & Other Financial Data (Million $) | 2011 | 2010 | 2009 | 2008 | 2007 | 2006 | 2005 | 2004 | 2003 | 2002 |
|---|---|---|---|---|---|---|---|---|---|---|
| Cash | NA | 4,508 | 5,269 | 2,528 | 3,584 | 3,613 | 3,152 | 2,917 | 1,054 | 981 |
| Receivables | 772 | 684 | NA | 1,062 | 1,106 | 711 | 549 | 444 | 441 | 393 |
| Cost of Investments | NA | NA | NA | 916 | 1,065 | NA | 1,566 | NA | NA | NA |
| Total Assets | 13,776 | 10,708 | 9,468 | 9,177 | 9,943 | 9,500 | 8,894 | 8,228 | 6,971 | 6,423 |
| Loss Reserve | Nil | Nil | Nil | Nil | Nil | NA | Nil | NA | NA | NA |
| Short Term Debt | 84.6 | 30.0 | 79.2 | 41.8 | 661 | 400 | 407 | NA | 0.29 | 7.80 |
| Capitalization:Debt | 2,084 | 950 | 42.0 | 227 | 162 | 628 | 1,208 | 1,196 | 1,109 | 595 |
| Capitalization:Equity | 8,525 | 7,727 | 7,632 | 7,074 | 7,332 | 6,685 | 5,684 | 5,107 | 4,310 | 4,267 |
| Capitalization:Total | 11,188 | 8,680 | 7,742 | 7,379 | 7,750 | 7,620 | 7,204 | 6,615 | 5,622 | 5,037 |
| Price Times Book Value:High | 4.6 | 4.9 | 4.7 | 5.9 | 6.8 | 6.2 | 6.9 | NA | 5.5 | 5.1 |
| Price Times Book Value:Low | 2.9 | 3.3 | 1.5 | 2.1 | 5.2 | 4.3 | 4.4 | NA | 3.2 | 3.2 |
| Cash Flow | 2,168 | 1,713 | 1,078 | 1,803 | 1,972 | 1,483 | 1,075 | 885 | 680 | 616 |
| % Expense/Operating Revenue | 62.7 | 66.5 | 71.3 | 65.2 | 66.7 | 67.7 | 70.1 | NA | NA | NA |
| % Earnings & Depreciation/Assets | 16.9 | 17.0 | 11.6 | 18.9 | 20.3 | 16.1 | 12.6 | NA | NA | NA |

Data as orig reptd.; bef. results of disc opers/spec. items. Per share data adj. for stk. divs.; EPS diluted. E-Estimated. NA-Not Available. NM-Not Meaningful. NR-Not Ranked. UR-Under Review.

**Office:** One Franklin Parkway, Building 970 1st Floor, San Mateo, CA 94403.
**Telephone:** 650-312-2000.
**Website:** http://www.franklinresources.com
**Chrmn:** C.B. Johnson

**Pres & CEO:** G.E. Johnson
**Vice Chrmn:** R.H. Johnson, Jr.
**COO:** J.M. Johnson
**SVP & Chief Admin Officer:** N.R. Frisbie, Jr.

**Board Members:** S. H. Armacost, C. Crocker, J. R. Hardiman, C. B. Johnson, G. E. Johnson, R. H. Johnson, Jr., M. C. Pigott, C. Ratnathicam, P. M. Sacerdote, L. Stein, G. Y. Yang

**Founded:** 1947
**Domicile:** Delaware
**Employees:** 8,453

The McGraw-Hill Companies

# Freeport-McMoran Copper & Gold Inc.

**STANDARD &POOR'S**

**S&P Recommendation** BUY ★★★★☆

| | | |
|---|---|---|
| **Price** | | **12-Mo. Target Price** |
| $33.82 (as of Nov 25, 2011) | | $48.00 |

**GICS Sector** Materials
**Sub-Industry** Diversified Metals & Mining

**Summary** FCX is the world's second largest copper producer and a major producer of gold and molybdenum.

## Key Stock Statistics (Source S&P, Vickers, company reports)

| | | | | | | | |
|---|---|---|---|---|---|---|---|
| 52-Wk Range | $61.35–28.85 | S&P Oper. EPS 2011**E** | 5.16 | Market Capitalization(B) | $32.058 | Beta | 1.96 |
| Trailing 12-Month EPS | $5.72 | S&P Oper. EPS 2012**E** | 5.38 | Yield (%) | 2.96 | S&P 3-Yr. Proj. EPS CAGR(%) | 13 |
| Trailing 12-Month P/E | 5.9 | P/E on S&P Oper. EPS 2011**E** | 6.6 | Dividend Rate/Share | $1.00 | S&P Credit Rating | BBB |
| $10K Invested 5 Yrs Ago | $12,310 | Common Shares Outstg. (M) | 947.9 | Institutional Ownership (%) | 76 | | |

## Price Performance

30-Week Mov. Avg. · · · 10-Week Mov. Avg. – – **GAAP Earnings vs. Previous Year** Volume Above Avg. ▮▮ STARS
12-Mo. Target Price — Relative Strength — ▲ Up ▼ Down ▶ No Change Below Avg. ▮▮ ★

Options: ASE, CBOE, P, Ph

Analysis prepared by Equity Analyst **Leo J. Larkin** on Nov 01, 2011, when the stock traded at **$38.76**.

## Qualitative Risk Assessment

| LOW | MEDIUM | HIGH |
|---|---|---|

Our risk assessment reflects the company's exposure to cyclical demand for copper and gold and the challenges posed to reserve growth by a flat production profile. However, we think FCX's large share of the global copper market acts as an offset.

## Quantitative Evaluations

**S&P Quality Ranking** B-

| D | C | B- | B | B+ | A- | A | A+ |
|---|---|---|---|---|---|---|---|

**Relative Strength Rank** WEAK

22

LOWEST = 1 HIGHEST = 99

## Revenue/Earnings Data

**Revenue (Million $)**

| | 1Q | 2Q | 3Q | 4Q | Year |
|---|---|---|---|---|---|
| 2011 | 5,709 | 5,814 | 5,195 | -- | -- |
| 2010 | 4,363 | 3,864 | 5,152 | 5,603 | 18,982 |
| 2009 | 2,602 | 3,684 | 4,144 | 4,610 | 15,040 |
| 2008 | 5,672 | 5,441 | 4,616 | 2,067 | 17,796 |
| 2007 | 2,303 | 5,807 | 5,066 | 4,184 | 16,939 |
| 2006 | 1,086 | 1,426 | 1,636 | 1,642 | 5,791 |

**Earnings Per Share ($)**

| | | | | | |
|---|---|---|---|---|---|
| 2011 | 1.57 | 1.43 | 1.10 | E1.05 | E5.16 |
| 2010 | 1.00 | 0.70 | 1.25 | 1.63 | 4.57 |
| 2009 | 0.06 | 0.69 | 1.04 | 0.99 | 2.93 |
| 2008 | 1.32 | 1.12 | 0.66 | -18.38 | -14.86 |
| 2007 | 1.01 | 1.31 | 0.93 | 0.54 | 3.71 |
| 2006 | 0.62 | 0.87 | 0.84 | 1.00 | 3.32 |

Fiscal year ended Dec. 31. Next earnings report expected: Late January. EPS Estimates based on S&P Operating Earnings; historical GAAP earnings are as reported.

## Highlights

➤ Following a projected sales gain of 13.7% in 2011, we expect a 2% sales rise in 2012, as we think higher prices for copper, gold and molybdenum, along with a slight rise in copper output, will offset another drop in gold production. Our copper price outlook is based on our forecast for continued growth in global copper demand. Our estimate for higher copper demand is based on the IHS Global Insight forecast for world economic growth of 2.6% in 2012, versus estimated growth of 2.7% in 2011. Our expectation for a higher gold price in 2012 assumes continued low short-term interest rates globally, increased currency volatility and lingering concerns over sovereign debt. We think another rise in global steel production in 2012 will support a higher price for molybdenum.

➤ We look for a small rise in operating profit in 2011, reflecting higher prices and the absence of strike-related disruptions. After interest expense and taxes, we project EPS of $5.38 in 2012, versus 2011's estimated EPS of $5.16.

➤ For the longer term, we expect earnings and reserves to increase on a secular rise in copper demand, a higher gold price and expansions at existing mines.

## Investment Rationale/Risk

➤ Longer term, we think rising secular demand for durable goods in China and India, along with less rapid increases in the supply of copper, will support generally higher prices, sales, EPS and reserves. We believe that the depletion of existing mines will offset production from new mines and keep copper supply tight over the course of the business cycle. As the world's second largest copper producer, FCX is well positioned, in our view, to capitalize on rising demand and prices for copper, with expansion projects in Africa and further development of existing mines. We view the shares as attractively valued, recently trading at about 7.2X our 2012 EPS estimate and with a dividend yield of over 2.5%.

➤ Risks to our opinion and target price include a decline in the price of copper in 2012 instead of the increase we project.

➤ Our 12-month target price of $48 assumes that FCX will trade at about 9X our 2012 EPS estimate, which is toward the low end of the stock's historical range of the past 10 years, and a discount to the group average P/E for base metal companies.

## Dividend Data (Dates: mm/dd Payment Date: mm/dd/yy)

| Amount ($) | Date Decl. | Ex-Div. Date | Stk. of Record | Payment Date |
|---|---|---|---|---|
| 0.250 | 03/31 | 04/13 | 04/15 | 05/01/11 |
| 0.500 | 04/20 | 05/11 | 05/15 | 06/01/11 |
| 0.250 | 06/30 | 07/13 | 07/15 | 08/01/11 |
| 0.250 | 09/29 | 10/12 | 10/15 | 11/01/11 |

Dividends have been paid since 2010. Source: Company reports.

The **McGraw·Hill** Companies

# Freeport-McMoran Copper & Gold Inc.

## Business Summary November 01, 2011

CORPORATE OVERVIEW. Freeport-McMoRan Copper & Gold is the world's second largest copper producer and is a major producer of gold and molybdenum. FCX has producing mines located in Indonesia, North America, South America and Africa.

Copper production totaled 3.9 billion pounds in 2010, versus 4.1 billion pounds in 2009; and gold production totaled 1.9 million oz., versus 2.7 million oz. in 2009. Molybdenum production was 72 million pounds in 2010, versus 54 million pounds in 2009.

In 2010, North America accounted for 28% of copper output, versus 28% in 2009; South America 34% versus 34%; Indonesia 31% versus 34%; and Africa 7% versus 4%.

At year-end 2010, consolidated proven and probable reserves totaled 120.5

billion pounds of copper, 35.5 million ounces of gold, 3.39 billion pounds of molybdenum and 325 million ounces of silver. Some 27% of FCX's copper reserves were in Indonesia, 31% in South America, 35% in North America, and 7% in Africa. About 95% of FCX's gold reserves were in Indonesia, with the balance in South America. Some 81% of molybdenum reserves were in North America, with the remainder in South America.

In 2010, copper accounted for 78.4% of sales, gold 12.5%, molybdenum 6.0% and other 3.1%.

## Company Financials Fiscal Year Ended Dec. 31

| Per Share Data ($) | 2010 | 2009 | 2008 | 2007 | 2006 | 2005 | 2004 | 2003 | 2002 | 2001 |
|---|---|---|---|---|---|---|---|---|---|---|
| Tangible Book Value | 12.88 | 6.86 | 2.21 | 14.28 | 3.42 | 1.99 | 0.18 | 2.12 | NM | NM |
| Cash Flow | 5.70 | 3.91 | -12.51 | 5.02 | 3.67 | 2.69 | 0.98 | 1.26 | 1.33 | 1.24 |
| Earnings | 4.57 | 2.93 | -14.86 | 3.71 | 3.32 | 2.34 | 0.43 | 0.54 | 0.45 | 0.26 |
| S&P Core Earnings | 4.59 | 3.00 | -7.07 | 3.63 | 3.28 | 2.32 | 0.24 | 0.52 | 0.42 | 0.25 |
| Dividends | 0.95 | Nil | 0.91 | 0.63 | 0.63 | 0.63 | 0.43 | 0.14 | Nil | Nil |
| Payout Ratio | 21% | Nil | NM | 17% | 19% | 27% | 100% | 25% | Nil | Nil |
| Prices:High | 60.39 | 43.68 | 63.62 | 60.10 | 36.10 | 28.18 | 22.45 | 23.37 | 10.42 | 8.58 |
| Prices:Low | 28.36 | 10.58 | 7.85 | 24.43 | 21.55 | 15.76 | 13.88 | 8.01 | 4.98 | 4.16 |
| P/E Ratio:High | 13 | 15 | NM | 16 | 11 | 12 | 53 | 44 | 23 | 32 |
| P/E Ratio:Low | 6 | 4 | NM | 7 | 7 | 7 | 33 | 15 | 11 | 16 |

| Income Statement Analysis (Million $) | 2010 | 2009 | 2008 | 2007 | 2006 | 2005 | 2004 | 2003 | 2002 | 2001 |
|---|---|---|---|---|---|---|---|---|---|---|
| Revenue | 18,982 | 15,040 | 17,796 | 16,939 | 5,791 | 4,179 | 2,372 | 2,212 | 1,910 | 1,839 |
| Operating Income | 10,196 | 7,736 | -4,711 | 7,801 | 3,096 | 2,429 | 823 | 1,054 | 901 | 827 |
| Depreciation | 1,128 | 1,137 | 1,782 | 1,246 | 228 | 252 | 206 | 231 | 260 | 284 |
| Interest Expense | 462 | 586 | 706 | 660 | 75.6 | 132 | 148 | 197 | 171 | 174 |
| Pretax Income | 8,527 | 5,841 | -13,294 | 6,133 | 2,826 | 2,037 | 574 | 584 | 450 | 359 |
| Effective Tax Rate | NA | 39.5% | NM | 39.1% | 42.5% | 44.9% | 57.6% | 57.9% | 54.6% | 56.6% |
| Net Income | 4,336 | 2,749 | -11,067 | 2,942 | 1,457 | 995 | 202 | 197 | 168 | 113 |
| S&P Core Earnings | 4,287 | 2,595 | -5,396 | 2,672 | 1,381 | 919 | 77.7 | 167 | 123 | 70.8 |

| Balance Sheet & Other Financial Data (Million $) | 2010 | 2009 | 2008 | 2007 | 2006 | 2005 | 2004 | 2003 | 2002 | 2001 |
|---|---|---|---|---|---|---|---|---|---|---|
| Cash | 3,738 | 2,656 | 872 | 1,626 | 907 | 764 | 551 | 464 | 7.84 | 7.59 |
| Current Assets | 9,851 | 7,433 | 5,233 | 5,903 | 2,151 | 2,022 | 1,460 | 1,100 | 638 | 548 |
| Total Assets | 29,386 | 25,871 | 23,271 | 40,661 | 5,390 | 5,550 | 5,087 | 4,718 | 4,192 | 4,212 |
| Current Liabilities | 3,763 | 3,002 | 3,158 | 3,869 | 972 | 1,369 | 698 | 632 | 538 | 628 |
| Long Term Debt | 4,660 | 6,330 | 7,284 | 7,180 | 661 | 1,003 | 1,874 | 2,076 | 1,961 | 2,133 |
| Common Equity | 12,504 | 6,259 | 2,083 | 14,259 | 1,345 | 743 | 63.6 | 776 | -83.2 | -246 |
| Total Capital | 19,315 | 17,118 | 16,643 | 33,953 | 4,119 | 3,971 | 4,189 | 3,925 | 3,514 | 3,464 |
| Capital Expenditures | 1,412 | 1,587 | 2,708 | 1,755 | 251 | 143 | 141 | 139 | 188 | 167 |
| Cash Flow | 5,401 | 3,664 | -9,559 | 3,980 | 1,624 | 1,186 | 363 | 401 | 391 | 360 |
| Current Ratio | 2.6 | 2.5 | 1.7 | 1.5 | 2.2 | 1.5 | 2.1 | 1.7 | 1.2 | 0.9 |
| % Long Term Debt of Capitalization | 24.1 | 37.0 | 43.8 | 26.9 | 16.0 | 25.2 | 44.7 | 52.9 | 55.8 | 61.6 |
| % Net Income of Revenue | 22.8 | 18.3 | NM | 17.4 | 25.2 | 23.8 | 8.5 | 8.9 | 8.8 | 6.1 |
| % Return on Assets | 15.7 | 11.2 | NM | 11.9 | 26.6 | 18.7 | 4.1 | 4.4 | 4.0 | 2.8 |
| % Return on Equity | 46.3 | 66.0 | NM | 35.0 | 133.7 | 231.7 | 37.3 | 49.0 | NM | NM |

Data as orig reptd.; bef. results of disc opers/spec. items. Per share data adj. for stk. divs.; EPS diluted. E-Estimated. NA-Not Available. NM-Not Meaningful. NR-Not Ranked. UR-Under Review.

**Office:** 333 North Central Avenue, Phoenix, AZ 85004.
**Telephone:** 602-366-8100.
**Email:** ir@fmi.com
**Website:** http://www.fcx.com

**Chrmn:** J.R. Moffett
**Vice Chrmn:** B.M. Rankin, Jr.
**CEO:** R.C. Adkerson
**EVP & Chief Admin Officer:** M.J. Arnold

**SVP & General Counsel:** L.R. McMillan
**Investor Contact:** K.L. Quirk
**Board Members:** R. C. Adkerson, R. J. Allison, Jr., R. A. Day, G. J. Ford, H. D. Graham, Jr., C. C. Krulak, B. L. Lackey, J. C. Madonna, D. E. McCoy, J. R. Moffett, B. M. Rankin, Jr., S. H. Siegele

**Founded:** 1987
**Domicile:** Delaware
**Employees:** 29,875

# Frontier Communications Corp

**STANDARD &POOR'S**

**S&P Recommendation** HOLD ★★★★★

| Price | 12-Mo. Target Price | Investment Style |
|---|---|---|
| $5.39 (as of Nov 25, 2011) | $7.50 | Large-Cap Value |

**GICS Sector** Telecommunication Services
**Sub-Industry** Integrated Telecommunication Services

**Summary** After acquiring wireline assets from Verizon Communications in mid-2010 that more than doubled its size, FTR provides wireline communications services, including voice services to 5.5 million customers in rural areas and small and medium-sized cities in the U.S.

## Key Stock Statistics (Source S&P, Vickers, company reports)

| | | | | | | | |
|---|---|---|---|---|---|---|---|
| 52-Wk Range | $9.84–5.22 | S&P Oper. EPS 2011E | 0.27 | Market Capitalization(B) | $5.364 | Beta | 0.80 |
| Trailing 12-Month EPS | $0.16 | S&P Oper. EPS 2012E | 0.23 | Yield (%) | 13.91 | S&P 3-Yr. Proj. EPS CAGR(%) | 4 |
| Trailing 12-Month P/E | 33.7 | P/E on S&P Oper. EPS 2011E | 20.0 | Dividend Rate/Share | $0.75 | S&P Credit Rating | BB |
| $10K Invested 5 Yrs Ago | $5,571 | Common Shares Outstg. (M) | 995.1 | Institutional Ownership (%) | 48 | | |

## Price Performance

30-Week Mov. Avg. · · · 10-Week Mov. Avg. - - - GAAP Earnings vs. Previous Year   Volume Above Avg. STARS
12-Mo. Target Price — Relative Strength — ▲ Up ▼ Down ► No Change   Below Avg.

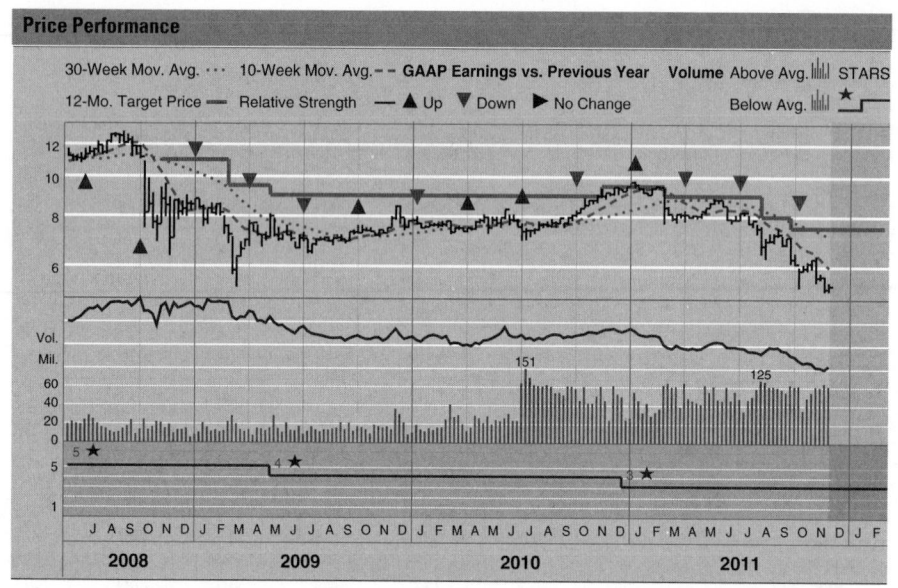

Analysis prepared by Equity Analyst **Todd Rosenbluth** on Sep 21, 2011, when the stock traded at **$6.49**.

Options: CBOE, P, Ph

## Qualitative Risk Assessment

| LOW | **MEDIUM** | HIGH |
|---|---|---|

Our risk assessment for Frontier Communications reflects the rural, less competitive nature of its operations, and what we see as the strong and stable cash flow that supports its dividend policy, offset by sensitivity to the U.S. economy and the company's acquisition strategy.

## Quantitative Evaluations

**S&P Quality Ranking**   B-

| D | C | **B-** | B | B+ | A- | A | A+ |
|---|---|---|---|---|---|---|---|

**Relative Strength Rank**   WEAK

26

LOWEST = 1   HIGHEST = 99

## Revenue/Earnings Data

**Revenue (Million $)**

| | 1Q | 2Q | 3Q | 4Q | Year |
|---|---|---|---|---|---|
| 2011 | 1,347 | 1,322 | 1,291 | -- | -- |
| 2010 | 519.9 | 516.1 | 1,403 | 1,359 | 3,798 |
| 2009 | 538.0 | 532.1 | 526.8 | 521.0 | 2,118 |
| 2008 | 569.2 | 562.6 | 557.9 | 547.4 | 2,237 |
| 2007 | 556.2 | 578.8 | 575.8 | 577.2 | 2,288 |
| 2006 | 506.9 | 506.9 | 507.2 | 504.4 | 2,025 |

**Earnings Per Share ($)**

| | 1Q | 2Q | 3Q | 4Q | Year |
|---|---|---|---|---|---|
| 2011 | 0.06 | 0.03 | 0.02 | E0.07 | E0.27 |
| 2010 | 0.14 | 0.11 | 0.03 | 0.05 | 0.23 |
| 2009 | 0.12 | 0.09 | 0.17 | 0.01 | 0.38 |
| 2008 | 0.14 | 0.15 | 0.15 | 0.11 | 0.57 |
| 2007 | 0.21 | 0.12 | 0.14 | 0.18 | 0.65 |
| 2006 | 0.13 | 0.29 | 0.16 | 0.20 | 0.78 |

Fiscal year ended Dec. 31. Next earnings report expected: NA. EPS Estimates based on S&P Operating Earnings; historical GAAP earnings are as reported.

## Highlights

➤ In 2011 and 2012, we see revenues of $5.3 billion and $5.1 billion, respectively, down from $5.7 billion on a pro forma basis achieved in 2010. In both legacy Frontier markets and in the acquired assets, we see pressure on voice services from access line losses, but we look for partial offsets from DSL and video penetration. We expect Frontier to have some success in new properties with service bundles and as the economy improves.

➤ We expect integration of the new assets to take some time and look for EBITDA margins to widen modestly to 46.4% in 2011 and 47.5% in 2012, from a pro forma 45.5% in 2010, below the 50% that was common for legacy FTR operations. We believe benefits from work force cuts, along with billing and network integration, will help margins on a pro forma basis, but we see this being partially offset by increased promotional activities and delay in sales until systems conversions take place in late 2011.

➤ We forecast higher interest costs related to the merger. We estimate EPS of $0.27 in 2011 and $0.23 in 2012 before certain one-time merger-related expenses.

## Investment Rationale/Risk

➤ We think FTR generates sufficient cash flow to support its dividend, despite limited cushion, but we believe the initial integration of the Verizon asset combination has been hurt by high line losses and the timing of systems conversions that should limit EBITDA. We anticipate FTR will have additional opportunities for cost savings, broadband growth and deleveraging, although we see risks given expected pressure on margins, as it will likely need to spend to retain and expand its voice and broadband customer base. We believe FTR has a strong track record in small deal integration and in generating high revenues per household.

➤ Risks to our recommendation and target price include failure to smoothly integrate the Verizon assets in a timely manner; not retaining customers in legacy and acquired markets; and a further dividend reduction.

➤ Our 12-month target price of $7.50 is based on an EV/EBITDA multiple of 6.4X, in line with mid-size wireline telecom peers. At our target price, FTR's dividend yield, even following the recent reduction in payment, would be above average.

## Dividend Data (Dates: mm/dd Payment Date: mm/dd/yy)

| Amount ($) | Date Decl. | Ex-Div. Date | Stk. of Record | Payment Date |
|---|---|---|---|---|
| 0.188 | 02/17 | 03/07 | 03/09 | 03/31/11 |
| 0.188 | 05/11 | 06/07 | 06/09 | 06/30/11 |
| 0.188 | 08/01 | 09/07 | 09/09 | 09/30/11 |
| 0.188 | 11/02 | 12/07 | 12/09 | 12/30/11 |

Dividends have been paid since 2004. Source: Company reports.

# Frontier Communications Corp

STANDARD &POOR'S

## Business Summary September 21, 2011

CORPORATE OVERVIEW. Frontier Communications (formerly Citizens Communications) provides wireline services to rural areas and small and medium-sized towns and cities across the country including in Arizona, California, New York and West Virginia. In July 2010, FTR completed a combination of wireline assets that were spun out by Verizon Communications in a stock and debt assumption deal valued originally at $8.6 billion. We believe the agreed-on price was then equal to a fair 4.5X trailing EBITDA multiple. The Verizon properties, in 14 states, included 4.0 million access lines, and 1.06 million DSL and FiOS customers as of June 2010. On a pro forma basis, the combined company would have had $6 billion in revenues during 2009. FTR, which expects $600 million in expense savings in 2012, issued new stock and assumed $3.5 billion of debt to complete the deal.

As of June 2011, FTR had 5.5 million access lines, down 8.6% from the prior year on a pro forma basis. Residential lines comprised 63% of the total and were under greater pressure in the past year, while FTR had 1.7 million high-speed Internet customers, mostly through DSL offerings. Consumer average revenue per customer was $58 a month. Meanwhile, average revenue from business customers improved in the second quarter of 2011.

CORPORATE STRATEGY. In the first half of 2010, FTR focused on expanding by providing rural local residential phone customers with enhanced services as

well as long distance, DSL and satellite video to offset access line pressure. But since the deal closed, FTR has focused on deploying broadband to new customers, rebranding itself in new markets and integrating the new assets, with expense reduction efforts. In early 2011, FTR increased its promotional activities in both legacy assets and the newly acquired ones to drive higher non-voice service penetration. In addition, the company made broadband available to approximately 460,000 additional homes since the deal's closing, expanding its potential pool of customers. During the fourth quarter of 2011, FTR expects to complete the integration of its services in four new states, representing a third of the recently acquired lines. We believe revenues in the third quarter of 2011 will be negatively impacted by this timing.

COMPETITIVE LANDSCAPE. We believe FTR faced challenges from cable telephony and wireless that led to access line erosion in 2010 and early 2011. In new and old markets, FTR competes with cable providers such as Time Warner and Comcast, which began to offer telephony services in 2006. As of late 2010, approximately 70% of FTR's operating territory faced cable telephony competition.

## Company Financials Fiscal Year Ended Dec. 31

| Per Share Data ($) | 2010 | 2009 | 2008 | 2007 | 2006 | 2005 | 2004 | 2003 | 2002 | 2001 |
|---|---|---|---|---|---|---|---|---|---|---|
| Tangible Book Value | NM | NM | NM | NM | NM | NM | NM | NM | NM | NM |
| Cash Flow | 1.61 | 1.93 | 2.34 | 2.30 | 2.25 | 2.26 | 2.09 | 2.37 | -0.24 | 2.08 |
| Earnings | 0.23 | 0.38 | 0.57 | 0.65 | 0.78 | 0.59 | 0.23 | 0.42 | -2.93 | -0.28 |
| S&P Core Earnings | 0.25 | 0.45 | 0.46 | 0.52 | 0.64 | 0.59 | 0.19 | 0.68 | -2.89 | -0.58 |
| Dividends | 0.87 | 1.00 | 1.00 | 1.00 | 1.00 | 1.00 | 0.50 | Nil | Nil | Nil |
| Payout Ratio | NM | NM | 175% | 154% | 128% | 169% | NM | Nil | Nil | Nil |
| Prices:High | 9.78 | 8.87 | 12.94 | 16.05 | 14.95 | 14.05 | 14.80 | 13.40 | 11.52 | 15.88 |
| Prices:Low | 6.96 | 5.32 | 6.35 | 12.03 | 11.97 | 12.08 | 11.37 | 8.81 | 2.51 | 8.20 |
| P/E Ratio:High | 43 | 23 | 23 | 25 | 19 | 24 | 62 | 32 | NM | NM |
| P/E Ratio:Low | 30 | 14 | 11 | 19 | 15 | 20 | 47 | 21 | NM | NM |

| Income Statement Analysis (Million $) | | | | | | | | | | |
|---|---|---|---|---|---|---|---|---|---|---|
| Revenue | 3,798 | 2,118 | 2,237 | 2,288 | 2,025 | 2,162 | 2,193 | 2,445 | 2,669 | 2,457 |
| Operating Income | NA | NA | 1,214 | 1,251 | 1,121 | 1,149 | 1,148 | 1,173 | 1,179 | 927 |
| Depreciation | 894 | 476 | 562 | 546 | 476 | 542 | 573 | 595 | 756 | 632 |
| Interest Expense | 522 | 378 | 363 | 384 | 336 | 339 | 379 | 423 | 478 | 386 |
| Pretax Income | 271 | 193 | 289 | 343 | 390 | 285 | 85.5 | 189 | -1,238 | -78.7 |
| Effective Tax Rate | NA | 36.2% | 36.8% | 37.4% | 35.0% | 29.6% | 15.6% | 35.5% | NM | NM |
| Net Income | 156 | 121 | 183 | 215 | 254 | 200 | 72.2 | 122 | -823 | -63.9 |
| S&P Core Earnings | 157 | 139 | 146 | 171 | 206 | 201 | 57.7 | 198 | -811 | -164 |

| Balance Sheet & Other Financial Data (Million $) | | | | | | | | | | |
|---|---|---|---|---|---|---|---|---|---|---|
| Cash | 251 | 359 | 164 | 226 | 1,041 | 266 | 167 | 584 | 393 | 57.7 |
| Current Assets | 1,128 | 680 | 468 | 524 | 1,273 | 542 | 450 | 896 | 1,201 | 2,533 |
| Total Assets | 17,890 | 6,878 | 6,889 | 7,256 | 6,791 | 6,412 | 6,668 | 7,689 | 8,147 | 10,554 |
| Current Liabilities | 1,439 | 393 | 383 | 446 | 426 | 617 | 418 | 536 | 771 | 1,567 |
| Long Term Debt | 7,984 | 4,794 | 4,722 | 4,739 | 4,461 | 3,999 | 4,267 | 4,397 | 5,159 | 5,736 |
| Common Equity | 5,210 | 339 | 519 | 998 | 1,058 | 1,042 | 1,362 | 1,415 | 1,172 | 1,946 |
| Total Capital | 13,473 | 5,140 | 5,245 | 6,446 | 6,033 | 5,366 | 5,629 | 6,259 | 6,468 | 8,112 |
| Capital Expenditures | 578 | 256 | 288 | 316 | 269 | 268 | 276 | 278 | 469 | 531 |
| Cash Flow | 1,049 | 597 | 744 | 761 | 730 | 742 | 645 | 717 | -67.5 | 568 |
| Current Ratio | 0.8 | 1.7 | 1.2 | 1.2 | 3.0 | 0.9 | 1.1 | 1.7 | 1.6 | 1.6 |
| % Long Term Debt of Capitalization | 59.3 | 93.3 | 90.0 | 82.6 | 73.9 | 74.5 | 75.8 | 70.2 | 79.8 | 70.7 |
| % Net Income of Revenue | 4.1 | 5.7 | 8.2 | 9.4 | 12.5 | 9.3 | 3.3 | 5.0 | NM | NM |
| % Return on Assets | 1.3 | 1.8 | 2.6 | 3.1 | 3.8 | 3.1 | 1.0 | 1.5 | NM | NM |
| % Return on Equity | 5.6 | 28.2 | 24.1 | 20.9 | 24.2 | 16.7 | 5.2 | 9.4 | NM | NM |

Data as orig reptd.; bef. results of disc opers/spec. items. Per share data adj. for stk. divs.; EPS diluted. E-Estimated. NA-Not Available. NM-Not Meaningful. NR-Not Ranked. UR-Under Review.

**Office:** 3 High Ridge Park, Stamford, CT 06905-1390.
**Telephone:** 203-614-5600.
**Email:** citizens@cnz.com
**Website:** http://www.frontier.com

**Chrmn, Pres & CEO:** M.A. Wilderotter
**COO:** D.J. McCarthy
**EVP & CFO:** D.R. Shassian
**EVP & General Counsel:** K.Q. Abernathy

**SVP, Chief Acctg Officer & Cntlr:** S. D'emic
**Board Members:** L. T. Barnes, Jr., P. C. Bynoe, J. B. Finard, E. D. Fraioli, J. S. Kahan, P. D. Reeve, H. L. Schrott, L. D. Segil, M. S. Shapiro, M. Wick, III, M. A. Wilderotter

**Founded:** 1927
**Domicile:** Delaware
**Employees:** 14,798

# GameStop Corp.

**STANDARD &POOR'S**

| S&P Recommendation | BUY ★★★★☆ | Price $21.51 (as of Nov 25, 2011) | 12-Mo. Target Price $30.00 | Investment Style Large-Cap Growth |
|---|---|---|---|---|

**GICS Sector** Consumer Discretionary
**Sub-Industry** Computer & Electronics Retail

**Summary** This company is the largest U.S. video game and PC entertainment software specialty retailer, and operates over 6,500 stores worldwide.

## Key Stock Statistics (Source S&P, Vickers, company reports)

| | | | | | |
|---|---|---|---|---|---|
| 52-Wk Range | $28.66–18.34 | S&P Oper. EPS 2012E | 2.86 | Market Capitalization(B) | $2.992 | Beta | 1.04 |
| Trailing 12-Month EPS | $2.79 | S&P Oper. EPS 2013E | 3.14 | Yield (%) | Nil | S&P 3-Yr. Proj. EPS CAGR(%) | 8 |
| Trailing 12-Month P/E | 7.7 | P/E on S&P Oper. EPS 2012E | 7.5 | Dividend Rate/Share | Nil | S&P Credit Rating | NA |
| $10K Invested 5 Yrs Ago | $7,594 | Common Shares Outstg. (M) | 139.1 | Institutional Ownership (%) | NM | | |

## Price Performance

- 30-Week Mov. Avg. ···· 10-Week Mov. Avg. - - GAAP Earnings vs. Previous Year   Volume Above Avg. ▒▒▒ STARS
- 12-Mo. Target Price — Relative Strength   — ▲ Up ▼ Down ▶ No Change   Below Avg. ▒▒▒ ★

Options: ASE, CBOE, Ph

Analysis prepared by Equity Analyst **Michael Souers** on Nov 21, 2011, when the stock traded at **$22.46**.

## Highlights

➤ We see FY 13 (Jan.) revenues rising 3.3%, following our projection of a 3.0% advance in FY 12. We expect this growth to be driven by the opening of about 50 net new stores internationally and comp-store sales growth of 1%-2%. We continue to project that GME's used game business will thrive in the current economic environment, aided by GME's loyalty program, PowerUp Rewards, which encourages trade-in activity. We favor recent strength in downloadable content and e-commerce growth given the evolution of the gaming industry, and project continued rapid growth in FY 13.

➤ We forecast that gross margins will widen slightly in FY 12 on product mix shift and an increase in digital downloads. We see a slight increase in operating margins, driven by gross margin improvement and strong expense control, partially offset by continued strategic investments in digital offerings and e-commerce.

➤ We project taxes at 36.0% and see about 4% fewer shares as a result of GME's share repurchase program. We estimate FY 13 EPS of $3.14, a 9.8% increase from the $2.86 we project the company to earn in FY 12.

## Investment Rationale/Risk

➤ We think the video game industry will benefit from motion-based accessories and 3D gaming re-energizing growth in the space, and expect near-term earnings growth from GME. Long term, we believe the electronic game industry will benefit from hardware platform technology evolution, a growing used video game market, and broadening demographic appeal, but we have concerns that online gaming will take significant share from the retail market. Nonetheless, we consider the shares' valuation to be attractive, with GME recently trading at about 7X our FY 13 EPS estimate, a significant discount to the S&P 500.

➤ Risks to our opinion and target price include a slowdown in consumer spending, inventory shortages, an inability to successfully manage new store openings or merger integration, the threat of online gaming emerging as a viable alternative for gamers, and corporate governance issues including the existence of a non-shareholder-approved "poison pill."

➤ Our 12-month target price of $30, about 10X our FY 13 EPS estimate, is based on our DCF analysis, which assumes a weighted average cost of capital of 11.4% and terminal growth of 2.0%.

## Qualitative Risk Assessment

| LOW | MEDIUM | HIGH |
|---|---|---|

Our risk assessment reflects the company's leading market share position, offset by industry cyclicality, as growth is partly dependent on the timing of new hardware and software releases.

## Quantitative Evaluations

**S&P Quality Ranking**   B+

| D | C | B- | B | B+ | A- | A | A+ |
|---|---|---|---|---|---|---|---|

**Relative Strength Rank**   MODERATE

31

LOWEST = 1   HIGHEST = 99

## Revenue/Earnings Data

**Revenue (Million $)**

| | 1Q | 2Q | 3Q | 4Q | Year |
|---|---|---|---|---|---|
| 2012 | 2,281 | 1,744 | 1,947 | -- | -- |
| 2011 | 2,083 | 1,799 | 1,899 | 3,693 | 9,474 |
| 2010 | 1,981 | 1,739 | 1,835 | 3,524 | 9,078 |
| 2009 | 1,814 | 1,804 | 1,696 | 3,492 | 8,806 |
| 2008 | 1,279 | 1,338 | 1,611 | 2,866 | 7,094 |
| 2007 | 1,040 | 963.4 | 1,012 | 2,304 | 5,319 |

**Earnings Per Share ($)**

| | | | | | |
|---|---|---|---|---|---|
| 2012 | 0.56 | 0.22 | 0.39 | E1.73 | E2.86 |
| 2011 | 0.48 | 0.26 | 0.36 | 1.56 | 2.65 |
| 2010 | 0.42 | 0.23 | 0.31 | 1.29 | 2.25 |
| 2009 | 0.37 | 0.34 | 0.28 | 1.39 | 2.38 |
| 2008 | 0.15 | 0.34 | 0.31 | 1.14 | 1.75 |
| 2007 | 0.08 | 0.02 | 0.09 | 0.81 | 1.00 |

Fiscal year ended Jan. 31. Next earnings report expected: Late March. EPS Estimates based on S&P Operating Earnings; historical GAAP earnings are as reported.

## Dividend Data

No cash dividends have been paid.

---

**Please read the Required Disclosures and Analyst Certification on the last page of this report.**

**The McGraw·Hill Companies**

# GameStop Corp.

STANDARD
&POOR'S

## Business Summary November 21, 2011

CORPORATE OVERVIEW. GameStop is the world's largest retailer of video game products and PC entertainment software. The company sells new and used video game hardware, video game software and accessories, as well as PC entertainment software, related accessories and other merchandise. GME also publishes Game Informer magazine, which is the industry's largest multi-platform video game magazine in the U.S. based on circulation, with approximately 5.7 million subscribers, and operates the online video gaming website www.kongregate.com. As of January 29, 2011, GameStop operated 6,670 stores in the U.S., Australia, Canada and Europe, primarily under the names GameStop, EB Games and Micromania. Of the total store count, 4,536 stores are located in the U.S., with the remaining 2,134 located internationally.

In October 2005, GameStop acquired close peer Electronics Boutique Holding Corp., which essentially doubled the company's market share in video game retailing. In November 2008, GME purchased Micromania, the leading retailer of video and computer games in France, which currently has 379 locations.

MARKET PROFILE. According to NPD Group, Inc., a market research firm, the U.S. electronic games industry generated approximately $18.5 billion in 2010,

and, according to the International Development Group, retail sales of video game hardware and software and PC entertainment software totaled $14.3 billion in Europe. The NPD Group also estimated that video game retail sales were approximately $1.7 billion in Canada in 2010, and independent market research firm GfK Group estimated that the Australian market was also approximately $1.7 billion in 2010. Based on GME estimates compiled from a variety of third-party sources, the North American market for digital mobile, social, console and PC games was approximately $6 billion in 2010 and is expected to double to approximately $12 billion by 2015. The Entertainment Software Association (ESA) estimates that 65% of all American head of households play video or computer games, and that the average game player is 34 years old. We believe that trends such as hardware platform technology evolution and a broadening demographic appeal will continue to propel growth in this industry.

## Company Financials Fiscal Year Ended Jan. 31

| Per Share Data ($) | 2011 | 2010 | 2009 | 2008 | 2007 | 2006 | 2005 | 2004 | 2003 | 2002 |
|---|---|---|---|---|---|---|---|---|---|---|
| Tangible Book Value | 4.43 | 3.26 | 1.17 | 2.80 | NM | NM | 2.19 | 2.41 | 2.02 | NM |
| Cash Flow | 3.79 | 3.22 | 3.24 | 2.54 | 1.69 | 1.34 | 0.85 | 0.77 | 0.62 | 0.47 |
| Earnings | 2.65 | 2.25 | 2.38 | 1.75 | 1.00 | 0.81 | 0.53 | 0.53 | 0.44 | 0.09 |
| S&P Core Earnings | 2.65 | 2.25 | 2.33 | 1.75 | 1.00 | 0.76 | 0.46 | 0.47 | 0.37 | 0.09 |
| Dividends | NA | NA | Nil | Nil | Nil | Nil | Nil | Nil | Nil | Nil |
| Payout Ratio | NA | Nil | Nil | Nil | Nil | Nil | Nil | Nil | Nil | Nil |
| Calendar Year | 2010 | 2009 | 2008 | 2007 | 2006 | 2005 | 2004 | 2003 | 2002 | 2001 |
| Prices:High | 25.75 | 32.82 | 62.29 | 63.77 | 29.21 | 19.21 | 11.76 | 9.52 | 12.15 | NA |
| Prices:Low | 17.12 | 20.02 | 16.91 | 24.95 | 15.57 | 9.27 | 7.19 | 3.75 | 4.46 | NA |
| P/E Ratio:High | 10 | 15 | 26 | 36 | 29 | 24 | 22 | 18 | 28 | NA |
| P/E Ratio:Low | 6 | 9 | 7 | 14 | 16 | 12 | 14 | 7 | 10 | NA |

| Income Statement Analysis (Million $) | 2011 | 2010 | 2009 | 2008 | 2007 | 2006 | 2005 | 2004 | 2003 | 2002 |
|---|---|---|---|---|---|---|---|---|---|---|
| Revenue | 9,474 | 9,078 | 8,806 | 7,094 | 5,319 | 3,092 | 1,843 | 1,579 | 1,353 | 1,121 |
| Operating Income | 837 | 801 | 825 | 632 | 450 | 273 | 163 | 133 | 110 | 64.4 |
| Depreciation | 177 | 164 | 145 | 130 | 110 | 66.7 | 37.0 | 28.9 | 22.6 | 30.3 |
| Interest Expense | 35.2 | 43.2 | 50.5 | 61.6 | 84.7 | 37.9 | 2.16 | 0.66 | 1.37 | 19.6 |
| Pretax Income | 621 | 589 | 634 | 441 | 254 | 160 | 98.9 | 105 | 87.7 | 14.6 |
| Effective Tax Rate | NA | 36.2% | 37.2% | 34.6% | 37.8% | 37.0% | 38.4% | 39.7% | 40.2% | 52.4% |
| Net Income | 407 | 377 | 398 | 288 | 158 | 101 | 60.9 | 63.5 | 52.4 | 6.96 |
| S&P Core Earnings | 408 | 377 | 390 | 288 | 158 | 94.1 | 53.2 | 55.6 | 44.1 | 6.76 |

| Balance Sheet & Other Financial Data (Million $) | 2011 | 2010 | 2009 | 2008 | 2007 | 2006 | 2005 | 2004 | 2003 | 2002 |
|---|---|---|---|---|---|---|---|---|---|---|
| Cash | 711 | 905 | 578 | 857 | 652 | 402 | 171 | 205 | 232 | 80.8 |
| Current Assets | 2,155 | 2,127 | 1,818 | 1,795 | 1,440 | 1,121 | 424 | 473 | 416 | 237 |
| Total Assets | 5,064 | 4,955 | 4,513 | 3,776 | 3,350 | 3,015 | 915 | 899 | 804 | 607 |
| Current Liabilities | 1,748 | 1,656 | 1,563 | 1,261 | 1,087 | 888 | 314 | 284 | 247 | 206 |
| Long Term Debt | 249 | 447 | 546 | 574 | 844 | 963 | 24.3 | Nil | Nil | 400 |
| Common Equity | 2,897 | 2,723 | 2,300 | 1,862 | 1,376 | 1,115 | 543 | 594 | 549 | -3.99 |
| Total Capital | 3,144 | 3,170 | 2,845 | 2,437 | 2,220 | 2,091 | 588 | 612 | 554 | 399 |
| Capital Expenditures | 198 | 164 | 183 | 176 | 134 | 111 | 98.3 | 63.0 | 39.5 | 20.5 |
| Cash Flow | 584 | 541 | 543 | 419 | 268 | 167 | 97.9 | 92.4 | 75.0 | 37.3 |
| Current Ratio | 1.2 | 1.3 | 1.2 | 1.4 | 1.3 | 1.3 | 1.4 | 1.7 | 1.7 | 1.2 |
| % Long Term Debt of Capitalization | 7.9 | 14.1 | 19.2 | 23.6 | 38.0 | 46.1 | 4.1 | Nil | Nil | 100.2 |
| % Net Income of Revenue | 4.3 | 4.2 | 4.5 | 4.1 | 3.0 | 3.3 | 3.3 | 4.0 | 3.9 | 0.6 |
| % Return on Assets | 8.1 | 8.0 | 9.6 | 8.1 | 5.0 | 5.1 | 6.7 | 7.5 | 7.4 | 1.2 |
| % Return on Equity | 14.5 | 15.0 | 19.1 | 17.8 | 12.7 | 12.2 | 10.7 | 11.1 | 19.2 | NM |

Data as orig reptd.; bef. results of disc opers/spec. items. Per share data adj. for stk. divs.; EPS diluted. E-Estimated. NA-Not Available. NM-Not Meaningful. NR-Not Ranked. UR-Under Review.

**Office:** 625 Westport Parkway, Grapevine, TX 76051.
**Telephone:** 817-424-2000.
**Email:** investorrelations@gamestop.com
**Website:** http://www.gamestop.com

**Chrmn:** D.A. Dematteo
**Pres:** T.D. Bartel
**CEO:** J.P. Raines
**EVP & CFO:** R.A. Lloyd

**SVP & Chief Acctg Officer:** T.W. Crawford
**Investor Contact:** M. Hodges (817-424-2000)
**Board Members:** J. L. Davis, D. A. Dematteo, R. R. Fontaine, S. Kim, S. Koonin, M. N. Rosen, S. M. Shern, S. Steinberg, G. R. Szczepanski, E. A. Volkwein, L. S. Zilavy

**Founded:** 1994
**Domicile:** Delaware
**Employees:** 68,000

# Gannett Co Inc.

**STANDARD &POOR'S**

| S&P Recommendation | BUY ★★★★☆ | Price | 12-Mo. Target Price | Investment Style |
|---|---|---|---|---|
| | | $10.50 (as of Nov 25, 2011) | $13.00 | Large-Cap Blend |

**GICS Sector** Consumer Discretionary
**Sub-Industry** Publishing

**Summary** Gannett publishes 82 daily U.S. newspapers, more than 600 non-daily publications in the U.S., and more than 200 U.K. titles, and operates 23 TV stations in the U.S.

## Key Stock Statistics (Source S&P, Vickers, company reports)

| | | | | | | | |
|---|---|---|---|---|---|---|---|
| 52-Wk Range | $18.93– 8.28 | S&P Oper. EPS 2011E | 2.18 | Market Capitalization(B) | $2.502 | Beta | 2.45 |
| Trailing 12-Month EPS | $2.11 | S&P Oper. EPS 2012E | 2.21 | Yield (%) | 3.05 | S&P 3-Yr. Proj. EPS CAGR(%) | 3 |
| Trailing 12-Month P/E | 5.0 | P/E on S&P Oper. EPS 2011E | 4.8 | Dividend Rate/Share | $0.32 | S&P Credit Rating | BB |
| $10K Invested 5 Yrs Ago | $2,126 | Common Shares Outstg. (M) | 238.3 | Institutional Ownership (%) | 100 | | |

## Price Performance

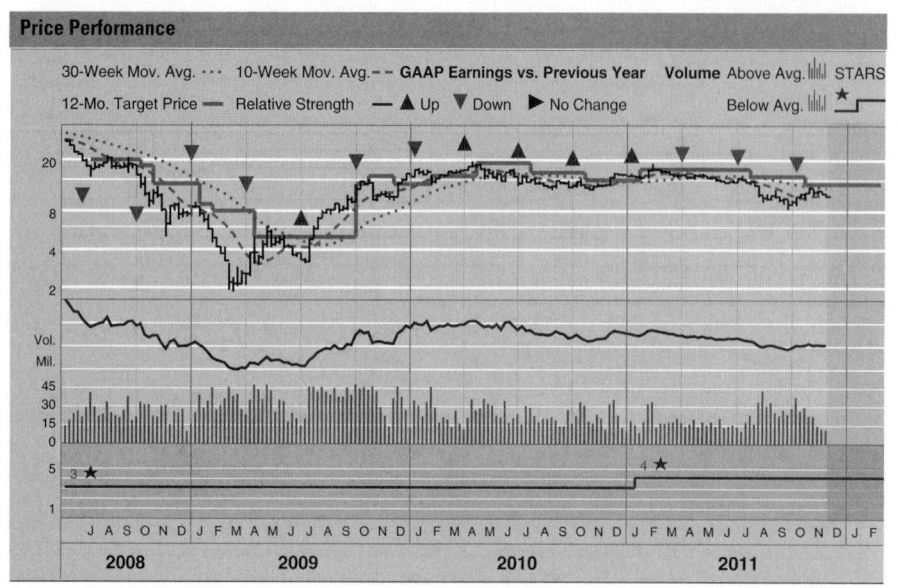

30-Week Mov. Avg. ···  10-Week Mov. Avg.- -  **GAAP Earnings vs. Previous Year**  Volume Above Avg. STARS
12-Mo. Target Price —  Relative Strength —  ▲ Up  ▼ Down  ► No Change  Below Avg.

Options: ASE, CBOE, P, Ph

Analysis prepared by Equity Analyst **Joseph Agnese** on Oct 27, 2011, when the stock traded at **$12.24**.

### Highlights

➤ We look for a contraction in print publishing revenues in 2011 and 2012, although at a slowing rate given a recovering economy in the U.S. We project broadcast revenue growth to decelerate in 2011 on difficult comparisons. However, we see broadcast revenues rising significantly in 2012 due to the U.S. presidential election and 2012 Summer Olympics. Overall, we forecast revenues to decline 5.5% in 2011, before rising 23% in 2012. GCI continues to take preemptive action to deal with weakening demand, including reduced hard copy circulation for some subscribers, but is expanding 24/7 digital channels.

➤ We forecast EBIT margins will widen to 19.0% in 2012, from our estimate of 18.1% in 2011. We see the benefits from strong broadcasting demand in 2012, staff and cost reduction initiatives and lower newsprint usage offsetting negative operating leverage from lower publishing revenues.

➤ Following a rise in interest expense due to higher interest rates, we estimate operating EPS of $2.21 for 2012, up from a projected $2.18 in 2011 (excluding $0.07 in facility consolidation and workforce reduction charges).

### Investment Rationale/Risk

➤ We believe GCI's valuation will benefit over the next 12 months from more stable advertising industry trends and benefits we see from potentially strong political and Olympic advertising demand in 2012. With a high free cash flow/equity yield, we think there is long-term value in what we see as GCI's strong free cash flow generating capabilities. However, our optimism is constrained by what we view as a secular decline in newspaper advertising, especially as only about 21% of the company's revenues are currently generated by digital operations.

➤ Risks to our recommendation and target price include weaker-than-expected U.S. GDP, lower audience ratings at network-affiliated TV stations, and a weakening of the British pound versus the U.S. dollar.

➤ Our 12-month target price of $13 is derived by applying an enterprise value-to-EBITDA ratio of 4.25X, near the low end of its historical range, to our 2012 EBITDA estimate of $1.21 billion. We consider a historically low valuation multiple appropriate given unfavorable impacts from significant negative secular challenges we believe the company is facing.

## Qualitative Risk Assessment

| LOW | MEDIUM | HIGH |
|---|---|---|

Our risk assessment reflects a highly competitive and weak advertising environment along with significant industry upheaval as consumers increasingly opt to get their news online and for free. This is only partly offset, in our view, by GCI's strong free cash flow and profitability as well as its relatively low cost of capital.

## Quantitative Evaluations

**S&P Quality Ranking**    B+

| D | C | B- | B | B+ | A- | A | A+ |
|---|---|---|---|---|---|---|---|

**Relative Strength Rank**    MODERATE

54

LOWEST = 1    HIGHEST = 99

## Revenue/Earnings Data

**Revenue (Million $)**

| | 1Q | 2Q | 3Q | 4Q | Year |
|---|---|---|---|---|---|
| 2011 | 1,251 | 1,335 | 1,266 | -- | -- |
| 2010 | 1,322 | 1,365 | 1,312 | 1,462 | 5,439 |
| 2009 | 1,378 | 1,413 | 1,337 | 1,485 | 5,613 |
| 2008 | 1,677 | 1,718 | 1,637 | 1,735 | 6,768 |
| 2007 | 1,871 | 1,928 | 1,756 | 1,897 | 7,439 |
| 2006 | 1,883 | 2,028 | 1,915 | 2,208 | 8,033 |

**Earnings Per Share ($)**

| | | | | | |
|---|---|---|---|---|---|
| 2011 | 0.37 | 0.62 | 0.41 | E0.76 | E2.18 |
| 2010 | 0.49 | 0.73 | 0.42 | 0.72 | 2.35 |
| 2009 | 0.34 | 0.30 | 0.31 | 0.56 | 1.51 |
| 2008 | 0.84 | -10.03 | 0.69 | 0.69 | -29.11 |
| 2007 | 0.90 | 1.24 | 1.01 | 1.06 | 4.17 |
| 2006 | 0.99 | 1.31 | 1.11 | 1.51 | 4.90 |

Fiscal year ended Dec. 31. Next earnings report expected: Early February. EPS Estimates based on S&P Operating Earnings; historical GAAP earnings are as reported.

## Dividend Data (Dates: mm/dd Payment Date: mm/dd/yy)

| Amount ($) | Date Decl. | Ex-Div. Date | Stk. of Record | Payment Date |
|---|---|---|---|---|
| 0.040 | 02/23 | 03/02 | 03/04 | 04/01/11 |
| 0.040 | 05/03 | 06/01 | 06/03 | 07/01/11 |
| 0.080 | 07/18 | 09/07 | 09/09 | 10/03/11 |
| 0.080 | 10/24 | 12/07 | 12/09 | 01/03/12 |

Dividends have been paid since 1929. Source: Company reports.

**Please read the Required Disclosures and Analyst Certification on the last page of this report.**

The McGraw-Hill Companies

# Gannett Co Inc.

**STANDARD & POOR'S**

## Business Summary October 27, 2011

CORPORATE OVERVIEW. Gannett Co. is the largest newspaper publisher in the U.S. The company publishes newspapers, operates broadcasting stations, runs Web sites in connection with its newspaper and broadcast operations, and is engaged in marketing, commercial printing, a newswire service, data services, and news programming.

The newspaper publishing segment (74% of 2010 revenues) consists of the operations of 82 daily newspapers and about 600 non-daily publications. The segment includes the publication of USA TODAY, the nation's largest selling daily newspaper. The company's strategy for non-daily publications is to target these products at communities of interest, defined by geography, demographics or lifestyle. In the U.K., the company is the second largest regional publisher via its wholly owned subsidiary, Newsquest plc, generating $525 million in 2010 revenues. Newspaper publishing revenues are derived principally from the sale of advertising (67% of 2010 publishing revenues), circulation revenues (27%) and commercial printing revenues (6.3%). Within the advertising category, revenues were derived from retail (51%), national (18%) and classified (30%) advertising.

In 2008, with the purchase of a controlling interest in Careerbuilder, GCI began reporting a separate digital segment (11% of 2010 revenues). The segment al-

so includes PointRoll, an Internet ad services business, Planet Discover, a provider of local, integrated online search and advertising technology, commercial printing, newswire, marketing and data services operations. GCI's Online Internet Audience in December 2010 was 52 million unique visitors, about 24% of the Internet audience as measured by comScore Media Metrix.

The broadcast segment (14% of 2010 revenues) consists of 23 network-affiliated TV stations, including 12 NBC, six CBS, three ABC affiliates and two MyNetworkTV affiliates, and Captivate Network, a national news and entertainment network that delivers programming and full-motion video advertising through video screens located in office tower elevators across North America. The principal sources of GCI's television revenues are: local advertising focusing on the immediate geographic area of the stations; national advertising; compensation paid by the networks for carrying commercial network programs; advertising on the stations' Web sites; and payments by advertisers to television stations for other services, such as the production of advertising material. Captivate derives its revenue principally from national advertising.

## Company Financials Fiscal Year Ended Dec. 31

| Per Share Data ($) | 2010 | 2009 | 2008 | 2007 | 2006 | 2005 | 2004 | 2003 | 2002 | 2001 |
|---|---|---|---|---|---|---|---|---|---|---|
| Tangible Book Value | NM | NM | NM | NM | NM | NM | NM | NM | NM | NM |
| Cash Flow | 3.38 | 2.53 | -27.96 | 5.38 | 6.07 | 6.24 | 6.14 | 5.30 | 5.13 | 4.78 |
| Earnings | 2.35 | 1.51 | -29.11 | 4.17 | 4.90 | 4.92 | 4.92 | 4.46 | 4.31 | 3.12 |
| S&P Core Earnings | 2.41 | 1.54 | -0.17 | 4.01 | 4.86 | 4.43 | 4.45 | 4.23 | 3.70 | 2.39 |
| Dividends | 0.16 | 0.16 | 1.60 | 1.42 | 1.20 | 1.12 | 1.04 | 0.98 | 0.94 | 0.90 |
| Payout Ratio | 7% | 11% | NM | 34% | 24% | 23% | 21% | 22% | 22% | 29% |
| Prices:High | 19.69 | 15.99 | 39.00 | 63.50 | 64.97 | 82.41 | 91.38 | 89.63 | 79.90 | 71.14 |
| Prices:Low | 11.65 | 1.85 | 5.00 | 34.34 | 51.65 | 58.37 | 78.84 | 66.70 | 62.76 | 53.00 |
| P/E Ratio:High | 8 | 11 | NM | 15 | 13 | 17 | 19 | 20 | 19 | 23 |
| P/E Ratio:Low | 5 | 1 | NM | 8 | 11 | 12 | 16 | 15 | 15 | 17 |

| Income Statement Analysis (Million $) | | | | | | | | | | |
|---|---|---|---|---|---|---|---|---|---|---|
| Revenue | 5,439 | 5,613 | 6,768 | 7,439 | 8,033 | 7,599 | 7,381 | 6,711 | 6,422 | 6,344 |
| Operating Income | 1,285 | 1,101 | 1,477 | 2,005 | 2,275 | 2,322 | 2,392 | 2,213 | 2,149 | 2,034 |
| Depreciation | 215 | 243 | 262 | 282 | 277 | 274 | 244 | 232 | 215 | 444 |
| Interest Expense | 173 | 176 | 191 | 260 | 288 | 211 | 141 | 139 | 146 | 222 |
| Pretax Income | 846 | 576 | -1,715 | 1,449 | 1,719 | 1,818 | 1,995 | 1,840 | 1,765 | 1,371 |
| Effective Tax Rate | NA | 33.6% | NM | 32.7% | 32.5% | 33.4% | 34.0% | 34.2% | 34.3% | 39.4% |
| Net Income | 567 | 355 | -1,783 | 976 | 1,161 | 1,211 | 1,317 | 1,211 | 1,160 | 831 |
| S&P Core Earnings | 583 | 363 | -40.6 | 939 | 1,151 | 1,092 | 1,191 | 1,150 | 998 | 638 |

| Balance Sheet & Other Financial Data (Million $) | | | | | | | | | | |
|---|---|---|---|---|---|---|---|---|---|---|
| Cash | 183 | 98.8 | 99.0 | 77.3 | 94.3 | 163 | 136 | 67.2 | 90.4 | 141 |
| Current Assets | 1,139 | 1,049 | 1,246 | 1,343 | 1,532 | 1,462 | 1,371 | 1,223 | 1,133 | 1,178 |
| Total Assets | 6,817 | 7,148 | 7,797 | 15,888 | 16,224 | 15,743 | 15,399 | 14,706 | 13,733 | 13,096 |
| Current Liabilities | 893 | 900 | 1,153 | 962 | 1,117 | 1,096 | 1,005 | 962 | 959 | 1,128 |
| Long Term Debt | 2,352 | 3,062 | 3,817 | 4,098 | 5,210 | 5,438 | 4,608 | 3,835 | 4,547 | 5,080 |
| Common Equity | 2,164 | 1,604 | 1,056 | 9,017 | 8,382 | 7,571 | 8,164 | 8,423 | 6,912 | 5,736 |
| Total Capital | 5,025 | 4,888 | 5,083 | 13,832 | 14,319 | 13,897 | 13,685 | 13,094 | 12,138 | 11,319 |
| Capital Expenditures | 69.1 | 67.7 | 165 | 171 | 201 | 263 | 280 | 281 | 275 | 325 |
| Cash Flow | 817 | 598 | -6,385 | 1,258 | 1,438 | 1,486 | 1,561 | 1,443 | 1,375 | 1,275 |
| Current Ratio | 1.3 | 1.2 | 1.1 | 1.4 | 1.4 | 1.3 | 1.4 | 1.3 | 1.2 | 1.0 |
| % Long Term Debt of Capitalization | 46.8 | Nil | 75.1 | 29.6 | 36.4 | 39.1 | 33.7 | 29.3 | 37.5 | 44.9 |
| % Net Income of Revenue | 10.4 | 6.3 | NM | 13.1 | 14.4 | 15.9 | 17.8 | 18.0 | 18.1 | 13.1 |
| % Return on Assets | NA | NA | NM | 6.1 | 7.3 | 7.8 | 8.8 | 8.5 | 8.6 | 6.4 |
| % Return on Equity | NA | NA | NM | 11.2 | 14.6 | 15.4 | 15.9 | 15.8 | 18.3 | 15.3 |

Data as orig reptd.; bef. results of disc opers/spec. items. Per share data adj. for stk. divs.; EPS diluted. E-Estimated. NA-Not Available. NM-Not Meaningful. NR-Not Ranked. UR-Under Review.

**Office:** 7950 Jones Branch Dr, McLean, VA 22107-0910.
**Telephone:** 703-854-6000.
**Email:** gcishare@gannett.com
**Website:** http://www.gannett.com

**Chrmn:** M. Magner
**Pres & CEO:** G.C. Martore
**SVP & CFO:** P.N. Saleh
**SVP, Secy & General Counsel:** T.A. Mayman

**Chief Acctg Officer & Cntlr:** G.R. Gavagan
**Investor Contact:** J. Heinz (703-854-6917)
**Board Members:** J. E. Cody, H. Elias, A. H. Harper, J. J. Louis, M. Magner, G. C. Martore, S. K. McCune, D. M. McFarland, S. P. Ness, N. Shapiro

**Founded:** 1906
**Domicile:** Delaware
**Employees:** 32,600

**The McGraw-Hill Companies**

# Gap Inc. (The)

**STANDARD &POOR'S**

## S&P Recommendation  HOLD ★★★☆☆

| Price | 12-Mo. Target Price | Investment Style |
|---|---|---|
| $17.62 (as of Nov 25, 2011) | $20.00 | Large-Cap Blend |

**GICS Sector** Consumer Discretionary
**Sub-Industry** Apparel Retail

**Summary** This specialty apparel retailer operates Gap, Banana Republic and Old Navy stores, offering casual clothing to moderate, upscale and value-oriented market segments.

### Key Stock Statistics (Source S&P, Vickers, company reports)

| | | | | | | | |
|---|---|---|---|---|---|---|---|
| 52-Wk Range | $23.73– 15.08 | S&P Oper. EPS 2012**E** | 1.48 | Market Capitalization(B) | $8.990 | Beta | 1.17 |
| Trailing 12-Month EPS | $1.74 | S&P Oper. EPS 2013**E** | 1.75 | Yield (%) | 2.55 | S&P 3-Yr. Proj. EPS CAGR(%) | 8 |
| Trailing 12-Month P/E | 10.1 | P/E on S&P Oper. EPS 2012**E** | 11.9 | Dividend Rate/Share | $0.45 | S&P Credit Rating | BB+ |
| $10K Invested 5 Yrs Ago | $10,080 | Common Shares Outstg. (M) | 510.2 | Institutional Ownership (%) | 63 | | |

## Price Performance

30-Week Mov. Avg. · · · 10-Week Mov. Avg. - - GAAP Earnings vs. Previous Year   Volume Above Avg. STARS
12-Mo. Target Price — Relative Strength — ▲ Up ▼ Down ► No Change   Below Avg. ★

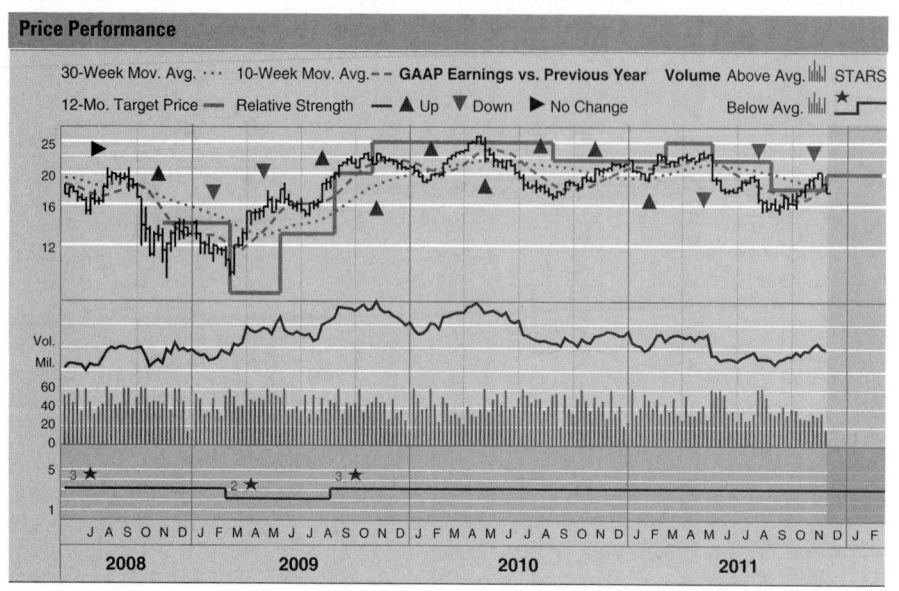

Options: ASE, CBOE, P, Ph

Analysis prepared by Equity Analyst **Jason N. Asaeda** on Nov 22, 2011, when the stock traded at **$18.30**.

## Qualitative Risk Assessment

| LOW | MEDIUM | HIGH |
|---|---|---|

Our risk assessment reflects our view of GPS's strong cash flow and balance sheet, offset by weakness at the Gap brand.

## Quantitative Evaluations

**S&P Quality Ranking**   A

| D | C | B- | B | B+ | A- | A | A+ |
|---|---|---|---|---|---|---|---|

**Relative Strength Rank**   MODERATE

60

LOWEST = 1    HIGHEST = 99

## Revenue/Earnings Data

**Revenue (Million $)**

| | 1Q | 2Q | 3Q | 4Q | Year |
|---|---|---|---|---|---|
| 2012 | 3,295 | 3,386 | 3,585 | -- | -- |
| 2011 | 3,329 | 3,317 | 3,654 | 4,364 | 14,664 |
| 2010 | 3,127 | 3,245 | 3,589 | 4,236 | 14,197 |
| 2009 | 3,384 | 3,499 | 3,561 | 4,082 | 14,526 |
| 2008 | 3,549 | 3,685 | 3,854 | 4,675 | 15,763 |
| 2007 | 3,441 | 3,716 | 3,856 | 4,930 | 15,943 |

**Earnings Per Share ($)**

| | | | | | |
|---|---|---|---|---|---|
| 2012 | 0.40 | 0.35 | 0.38 | E0.35 | E1.48 |
| 2011 | 0.45 | 0.36 | 0.48 | 0.60 | 1.88 |
| 2010 | 0.31 | 0.33 | 0.44 | 0.51 | 1.58 |
| 2009 | 0.34 | 0.32 | 0.35 | 0.34 | 1.34 |
| 2008 | 0.25 | 0.32 | 0.30 | 0.35 | 1.09 |
| 2007 | 0.28 | 0.15 | 0.23 | 0.27 | 0.93 |

Fiscal year ended Jan. 31. Next earnings report expected: NA. EPS Estimates based on S&P Operating Earnings; historical GAAP earnings are as reported.

## Highlights

➤ We project net sales of $14.4 billion in FY 12 (Jan.) and $14.8 in FY 13. In FY 11, GPS "went global" and began shipping to 90 countries while opening stores in China, Italy, the U.K. and Japan, ending FY 11 in 23 countries (including franchised locations). We see Gap International entering new markets annually via e-commerce, franchises and company stores.

➤ Domestically, GPS remains focused driving customer traffic and conversion through sharper merchandising and more impactful marketing. We look for assortments designed by Gap's new merchant team to start flowing into stores in the fourth quarter of FY 12. Continued pruning of underperforming Gap locations and the re-modeling of Old Navy locations also bodes well for improved productivity, in our view.

➤ We see EBIT margins contracting annually on promotional pricing and significant product cost inflation, mitigated by selective price increases and aggressive expense controls. We expect product costs to ease in the second half of FY 13. Factoring in share buybacks, we estimate EPS of $1.48 in FY 12 and $1.75 in FY 13.

## Investment Rationale/Risk

➤ Our hold opinion largely reflects lackluster performance of GPS's mature domestic businesses in the highly promotional value channel. That said, we note that the company is pursuing a number of aggressive growth initiatives in FY 12 that we see providing profitable long-term growth. Most promising, in our view, is international expansion. Gap International represented 13% of FY 11 sales, and we see this business expanding rapidly. We also view Athleta as an incremental growth opportunity for GPS in North America. The company plans to open over 50 Athleta stores by the end of FY 14.

➤ Risks to our recommendation and target price include worse than expected same-store sales trends, a substantially slower than expected global economic recovery, and higher than expected inflationary cost pressures.

➤ Based on projected weak sales and earnings trends, we think the stock should trade at a discount to its five-year historical average forward P/E multiple of 13.7X. Applying a peer-average multiple of 11.5X to our FY 13 EPS estimate, we arrive at our 12-month target price of $20.

## Dividend Data (Dates: mm/dd Payment Date: mm/dd/yy)

| Amount ($) | Date Decl. | Ex-Div. Date | Stk. of Record | Payment Date |
|---|---|---|---|---|
| 0.113 | 02/24 | 04/04 | 04/06 | 04/27/11 |
| 0.113 | 05/18 | 07/01 | 07/06 | 07/27/11 |
| 0.113 | 08/17 | 10/07 | 10/12 | 10/26/11 |
| 0.113 | 11/08 | 12/30 | 01/04 | 01/25/12 |

Dividends have been paid since 1976. Source: Company reports.

---

**Please read the Required Disclosures and Analyst Certification on the last page of this report.**

**The McGraw·Hill Companies**

# Gap Inc. (The)

STANDARD
&POOR'S

## Business Summary November 22, 2011

CORPORATE OVERVIEW. Gap, Inc. is a specialty retailer that operates stores selling casual apparel, accessories, and personal care products for men, women and children. As of October 29, 2011, it operated 3,065 stores: 1,086 Gap North America; 586 Republic North America; 1,022 Old Navy North America; 191 Gap Europe,141 Gap Asia; 29 Banana Republic Asia; nine Banana Republic Europe and four Athleta North America, with 37.6 million sq. ft. of total retail space. Another 211 stores are franchised.

MARKET PROFILE. GPS participates in the men's, women's and children's apparel market, which generated approximately $193 billion at U.S. retail in 2010 (a 1.9% increase from 2009), according to NPD Fashionworld consumer estimated data. The apparel market is fragmented, with national brands marketed by 20 companies accounting for about 30% of total apparel sales, and the remaining 70% comprised of smaller and/or private label "store" brands. The market is mature, in our view, with demand largely mirroring population growth, and fashion trends accounting for a modicum of incremental volume.

Deflationary pricing pressure is a function of channel competition and production steadily moving offshore to low-cost producers in India, Asia and China, in our view. S&P forecasts a 2%-3% increase in 2011 apparel sales.

COMPETITIVE LANDSCAPE. By channel, specialty stores account for the largest share of apparel sales, at 32% in 2010 and added one market share point, according to NPD. Mass merchants (e.g., Wal-mart and Target) came in second, at 20% (vs. 22% in 2009), and department stores and national chains (e.g., Sears and JC Penney) captured 13% each of 2010 apparel sales, and off-price retailers (e.g., TJX and Ross Stores) were at 9%. Factory outlets, direct and e-mail pure plays and other captured the remaining 12%. GPS is the largest U.S. specialty retailer, with an estimated 20% of the channel's volume.

## Company Financials Fiscal Year Ended Jan. 31

| Per Share Data ($) | 2011 | 2010 | 2009 | 2008 | 2007 | 2006 | 2005 | 2004 | 2003 | 2002 |
|---|---|---|---|---|---|---|---|---|---|---|
| Tangible Book Value | 6.64 | 6.96 | 6.04 | 11.50 | 9.58 | 6.33 | 5.73 | 5.33 | 4.12 | 3.48 |
| Cash Flow | 2.76 | 2.51 | 2.25 | 1.89 | 1.57 | 1.93 | 1.79 | 1.71 | 1.43 | 0.93 |
| Earnings | 1.88 | 1.58 | 1.34 | 1.09 | 0.93 | 1.24 | 1.21 | 1.09 | 0.54 | -0.01 |
| S&P Core Earnings | 1.88 | 1.58 | 1.34 | 1.09 | 0.93 | 1.15 | 1.13 | 1.03 | 0.50 | -0.10 |
| Dividends | NA | 0.34 | 0.34 | 0.32 | 0.20 | 0.09 | 0.09 | 0.09 | 0.09 | 0.09 |
| Payout Ratio | NA | 22% | 22% | 29% | 22% | 7% | 7% | 8% | 17% | NM |
| Calendar Year | 2010 | 2009 | 2008 | 2007 | 2006 | 2005 | 2004 | 2003 | 2002 | 2001 |
| Prices:High | 26.34 | 23.36 | 21.89 | 22.02 | 21.39 | 22.70 | 25.72 | 23.47 | 17.14 | 34.98 |
| Prices:Low | 16.62 | 9.56 | 9.41 | 15.20 | 15.91 | 15.90 | 18.12 | 12.01 | 8.35 | 11.12 |
| P/E Ratio:High | 14 | 15 | 16 | 20 | 23 | 18 | 21 | 22 | 32 | NM |
| P/E Ratio:Low | 9 | 6 | 7 | 14 | 17 | 13 | 15 | 11 | 15 | NM |

| Income Statement Analysis (Million $) | | | | | | | | | | |
|---|---|---|---|---|---|---|---|---|---|---|
| Revenue | 14,664 | 14,197 | 14,526 | 15,763 | 15,943 | 16,023 | 16,267 | 15,854 | 14,455 | 13,848 |
| Operating Income | 2,530 | 2,484 | 2,199 | 1,984 | 1,701 | 2,370 | 2,705 | 2,543 | 1,794 | 1,148 |
| Depreciation | 562 | 573 | 651 | 635 | 530 | 625 | 620 | 664 | 781 | 810 |
| Interest Expense | NA | 6.00 | 9.00 | 36.0 | 49.0 | 45.0 | 167 | 234 | 249 | 109 |
| Pretax Income | 1,982 | 1,816 | 1,584 | 1,406 | 1,264 | 1,793 | 1,872 | 1,683 | 801 | 242 |
| Effective Tax Rate | NA | 39.3% | 39.0% | 38.3% | 38.5% | 37.9% | 38.6% | 38.8% | 40.4% | NM |
| Net Income | 1,204 | 1,102 | 967 | 867 | 778 | 1,113 | 1,150 | 1,030 | 477 | -7.76 |
| S&P Core Earnings | 1,204 | 1,102 | 967 | 867 | 776 | 1,033 | 1,073 | 978 | 439 | -89.1 |

| Balance Sheet & Other Financial Data (Million $) | | | | | | | | | | |
|---|---|---|---|---|---|---|---|---|---|---|
| Cash | 1,661 | 2,573 | 1,715 | 1,939 | 2,644 | 2,987 | 7,139 | 2,261 | 3,389 | 1,036 |
| Current Assets | 3,926 | 4,664 | 4,005 | 4,086 | 5,029 | 5,239 | 6,304 | 6,689 | 5,740 | 3,045 |
| Total Assets | 7,065 | 7,985 | 7,564 | 7,838 | 8,544 | 8,821 | 10,048 | 10,343 | 9,902 | 7,591 |
| Current Liabilities | 2,095 | 2,131 | 2,158 | 2,433 | 2,272 | 1,942 | 2,242 | 2,492 | 2,727 | 2,056 |
| Long Term Debt | NA | NA | Nil | 50.0 | 188 | 513 | 1,886 | 2,487 | 2,896 | 1,961 |
| Common Equity | 4,080 | 4,891 | 4,387 | 4,274 | 5,174 | 5,425 | 4,936 | 4,783 | 3,658 | 3,010 |
| Total Capital | 4,080 | 4,891 | 4,437 | 4,324 | 5,362 | 5,938 | 6,822 | 7,270 | 6,554 | 4,971 |
| Capital Expenditures | 557 | 334 | 431 | 682 | 572 | 600 | 442 | 272 | 303 | 940 |
| Cash Flow | 1,766 | 1,757 | 1,618 | 1,502 | 1,308 | 1,738 | 1,770 | 1,694 | 1,258 | 803 |
| Current Ratio | 1.9 | 2.2 | 1.9 | 1.7 | 2.2 | 2.7 | 2.8 | 2.7 | 2.1 | 1.5 |
| % Long Term Debt of Capitalization | Nil | Nil | Nil | 1.2 | 3.5 | 8.6 | 27.6 | 34.2 | 44.2 | 39.5 |
| % Net Income of Revenue | 8.2 | 7.8 | 6.7 | 5.5 | 4.9 | 6.9 | 7.1 | 6.5 | 3.3 | NM |
| % Return on Assets | 16.0 | 14.2 | 12.6 | 10.6 | 9.0 | 11.8 | 11.1 | 10.2 | 5.4 | NM |
| % Return on Equity | 26.8 | 23.8 | 22.3 | 18.4 | 14.7 | 21.5 | 24.0 | 24.4 | 14.3 | NM |

Data as orig reptd.; bef. results of disc opers/spec. items. Per share data adj. for stk. divs.; EPS diluted. E-Estimated. NA-Not Available. NM-Not Meaningful. NR-Not Ranked. UR-Under Review.

Office: 2 Folsom St, San Francisco, CA 94105-1205.
Telephone: 650-952-4400 .
Email: investor_relations@gap.com
Website: http://www.gapinc.com

Chrmn & CEO: G.K. Murphy
EVP, CFO & Chief Acctg Officer: S.L. Simmons
EVP & CIO: J.T. Keiser
Secy: M.A. Banks

Investor Contact: E. Price (415-427-2360)
Board Members: A. D. Bellamy, D. De Sole, R. J. Fisher, W. S. Fisher, I. D. Goren, B. L. Martin, J. P. Montoya, G. K. Murphy, M. A. Shattuck, III, K. Tsang, K. C. Youngblood

Founded: 1969
Domicile: Delaware
Employees: 134,000

The McGraw-Hill Companies

# General Dynamics Corp

**STANDARD &POOR'S**

| S&P Recommendation | HOLD ★★★★★ | Price $61.13 (as of Nov 25, 2011) | 12-Mo. Target Price $75.00 | Investment Style Large-Cap Growth |
|---|---|---|---|---|

**GICS Sector** Industrials
**Sub-Industry** Aerospace & Defense

**Summary** General Dynamics is the world's fifth largest military contractor and also one of the world's biggest makers of corporate jets.

## Key Stock Statistics (Source S&P, Vickers, company reports)

| | | | | | | | |
|---|---|---|---|---|---|---|---|
| 52-Wk Range | $78.27– 53.95 | S&P Oper. EPS 2011**E** | 7.25 | Market Capitalization(B) | $21.769 | Beta | 1.26 |
| Trailing 12-Month EPS | $7.10 | S&P Oper. EPS 2012**E** | 7.70 | Yield (%) | 3.08 | S&P 3-Yr. Proj. EPS CAGR(%) | 6 |
| Trailing 12-Month P/E | 8.6 | P/E on S&P Oper. EPS 2011**E** | 8.4 | Dividend Rate/Share | $1.88 | S&P Credit Rating | A |
| $10K Invested 5 Yrs Ago | $9,263 | Common Shares Outstg. (M) | 356.1 | Institutional Ownership (%) | 79 | | |

## Price Performance

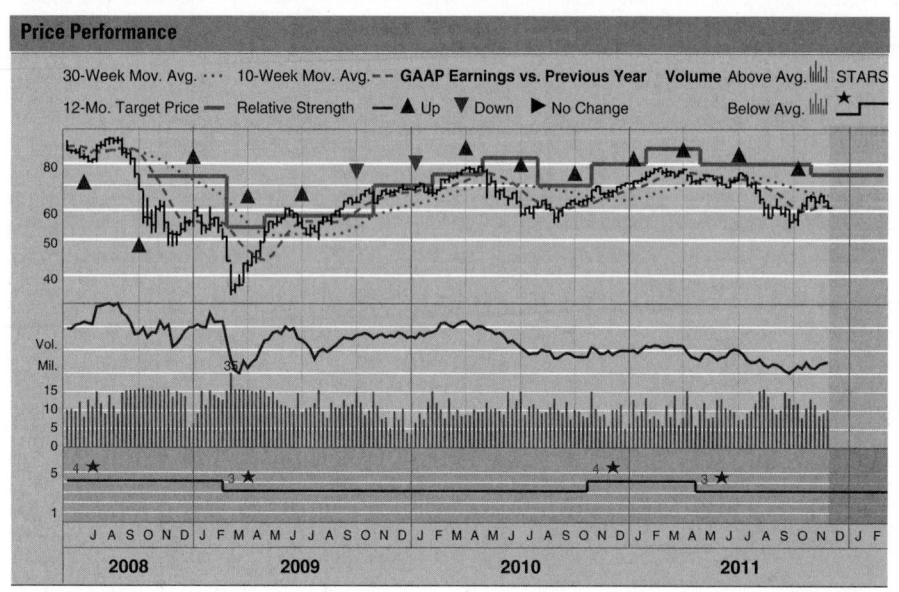

- 30-Week Mov. Avg. · · ·   10-Week Mov. Avg. - -   GAAP Earnings vs. Previous Year   Volume Above Avg. STARS
- 12-Mo. Target Price —   Relative Strength —   ▲ Up  ▼ Down  ► No Change   Below Avg.

2008  2009  2010  2011

Options: ASE, CBOE, Ph

Analysis prepared by Equity Analyst **R. Tortoriello** on Oct 31, 2011, when the stock traded at **$65.38**.

## Highlights

➤ We estimate revenue growth of just over 1% in 2011, as strong business jet growth is offset by weakness in defense. For 2012, we project revenue growth of over 4%, with continued strong growth in Aerospace (about 15%) and defense revenues that are improved versus 2010. We project overall defense growth of about 2.5%, supported by recent and anticipated backlog additions. In Combat systems, GD recently received a $1 billion order to upgrade Canadian LAVs, and it expects a few large foreign military vehicle orders and increased Stryker volume. In the third quarter for Marine, GD received $2.4 billion for three destroyers. In addition, IS&T saw total backlog rise 29% in the third quarter, particularly in IT services.

➤ We estimate operating margins of 12.1% in 2011, down slightly from 12.2% in 2010. For 2012, we are modeling flat operating margins, as we expect higher pension expense to offset potential margin improvement.

➤ We estimate EPS of $7.25 in 2011, and project growth to $7.70 for 2012. We see free cash flow (cash from operating activities less capital expenditures) per share of about $5.50 in 2011.

## Investment Rationale/Risk

➤ We expect improving results in Aerospace to drive GD's growth over the next two years. Specifically, we note that book to bill was 1.5X in the third quarter, that about 70% of orders year to date came from international customers, and that service revenue grew 19% year to date. We see Aerospace being driven by emerging market demand, new product introductions (the G650 and G280, with the G650 expected to be FAA certified by year end and the G280 by early 2012), and rising service volume. We expect GD's defense business to remain a slow growth business, at best.

➤ Risks to our recommendation and target price include potential future cuts in military budgets, failure of GD to perform well on existing contracts or to win new contracts, and a slower-than-expected recovery in business aviation.

➤ Our 12-month target price of $75 is based on an enterprise value to estimated 2012 EBITDA multiple of about 6X, below GD's 20-year historical average of 8X. Given our view of U.S. defense budget pressure, we view a below-average multiple as appropriate for the shares.

## Qualitative Risk Assessment

| LOW | MEDIUM | HIGH |
|---|---|---|

Our risk assessment for GD is based on the company's long-term record of consistent earnings and dividend growth, as reflected in its S&P Quality Ranking of A+. In addition, we view the company's capitalization as conservative, with a total debt to capital ratio of 23% as of September 2011.

## Quantitative Evaluations

**S&P Quality Ranking**   A+

| D | C | B- | B | B+ | A- | A | A+ |
|---|---|---|---|---|---|---|---|

**Relative Strength Rank**   MODERATE

64

LOWEST = 1   HIGHEST = 99

## Revenue/Earnings Data

**Revenue (Million $)**

| | 1Q | 2Q | 3Q | 4Q | Year |
|---|---|---|---|---|---|
| 2011 | 7,798 | 7,879 | 7,853 | -- | -- |
| 2010 | 7,750 | 8,104 | 8,011 | 8,601 | 32,466 |
| 2009 | 8,264 | 8,100 | 7,719 | 7,898 | 31,981 |
| 2008 | 7,005 | 7,303 | 7,140 | 7,852 | 29,300 |
| 2007 | 6,300 | 6,591 | 6,834 | 7,515 | 27,240 |
| 2006 | 5,546 | 5,934 | 6,069 | 6,514 | 24,063 |

**Earnings Per Share ($)**

| | 1Q | 2Q | 3Q | 4Q | Year |
|---|---|---|---|---|---|
| 2011 | 1.64 | 1.79 | 1.83 | E1.99 | E7.25 |
| 2010 | 1.54 | 1.68 | 1.70 | 1.91 | 6.82 |
| 2009 | 1.53 | 1.61 | 1.54 | 1.58 | 6.20 |
| 2008 | 1.42 | 1.60 | 1.59 | 1.62 | 6.22 |
| 2007 | 1.07 | 1.27 | 1.34 | 1.42 | 5.10 |
| 2006 | 0.95 | 1.03 | 1.08 | 1.13 | 4.20 |

Fiscal year ended Dec. 31. Next earnings report expected: Late January. EPS Estimates based on S&P Operating Earnings; historical GAAP earnings are as reported.

## Dividend Data (Dates: mm/dd Payment Date: mm/dd/yy)

| Amount ($) | Date Decl. | Ex-Div. Date | Stk. of Record | Payment Date |
|---|---|---|---|---|
| 0.470 | 03/02 | 04/06 | 04/08 | 05/06/11 |
| 0.470 | 06/01 | 06/29 | 07/01 | 08/05/11 |
| 0.470 | 08/03 | 10/05 | 10/07 | 11/10/11 |
| 0.470 | 08/03 | 10/05 | 10/07 | 11/11/11 |

Dividends have been paid since 1979. Source: Company reports.

# General Dynamics Corp

## Business Summary October 31, 2011

CORPORATE OVERVIEW. General Dynamics is the world's fifth largest defense contractor and the second largest maker of corporate jets by revenues. The company conducts business through four segments.

Information Systems & Technology (IS&T; 36% of sales and 30% of operating profits in 2010) primarily makes sophisticated electronics for land-, sea- and air-based weapons systems. Customers also include federal civilian agencies and commercial customers. The segment was created in 1998, and has grown through numerous acquisitions and internal development. The group's three principal markets are tactical and strategic mission systems (44% of segment revenue in 2010; secure communications systems, command-and-control systems); information technology services (37%), which provides mission-critical wireless and wire-line networks, network modernization, and mission support services; and intelligence, surveillance and reconnaissance systems (19%), which includes signals processing, imagery solutions, sensors/cameras, and cyber security products and services. In 2010, 72% of revenues were from the U.S. government, 8% from international defense, and the remainder from commercial customers.

Combat Systems (27% of sales and 32% of operating profit) makes, repairs and supports wheeled and tracked armored vehicles and munitions. Product lines include wheeled combat and tactical vehicles (44% of segment sales); main battle tanks and tracked infantry vehicles (18%); munitions and propellant (18%); rockets and gun systems (7%); and drivetrain components, aftermarket parts, and other (13%). Reflecting the U.S. Army's desire to transform itself into a highly agile fighting force, demand is expected to slow for tanks, but to accelerate for its various wheeled combat vehicles. Major current programs include the Abrams main battle tank (upgrade programs) and the Stryker wheeled combat vehicle. The group makes M2 heavy machine guns, MK19 and MK47 grenade launchers, and high-speed Gatling guns and Hydra-70 rockets for aircraft. It is also the U.S. military's principal second source for small-caliber ammunition needs.

## Company Financials Fiscal Year Ended Dec. 31

| Per Share Data ($) | 2010 | 2009 | 2008 | 2007 | 2006 | 2005 | 2004 | 2003 | 2002 | 2001 |
|---|---|---|---|---|---|---|---|---|---|---|
| Tangible Book Value | NM | NM | NM | 0.46 | 0.25 | 1.40 | NM | NM | 2.81 | 1.92 |
| Cash Flow | 8.30 | 7.65 | 6.97 | 5.78 | 5.16 | 4.48 | 3.57 | 3.20 | 3.14 | 2.99 |
| Earnings | 6.82 | 6.20 | 6.22 | 5.10 | 4.20 | 3.63 | 2.99 | 2.50 | 2.59 | 2.33 |
| S&P Core Earnings | 6.73 | 6.08 | 5.16 | 4.90 | 4.08 | 3.34 | 2.81 | 2.34 | 1.62 | 1.57 |
| Dividends | 1.64 | 1.49 | 1.34 | 1.10 | 0.66 | 0.78 | 0.70 | 0.63 | 0.59 | 0.55 |
| Payout Ratio | 24% | 24% | 22% | 22% | 16% | 22% | 23% | 25% | 23% | 24% |
| Prices:High | 79.00 | 70.84 | 95.13 | 94.55 | 77.98 | 61.14 | 54.99 | 45.40 | 55.59 | 48.00 |
| Prices:Low | 55.46 | 35.28 | 47.81 | 70.61 | 56.68 | 48.80 | 42.48 | 25.00 | 36.63 | 30.25 |
| P/E Ratio:High | 12 | 11 | 15 | 19 | 19 | 17 | 18 | 18 | 21 | 21 |
| P/E Ratio:Low | 8 | 6 | 8 | 14 | 13 | 13 | 14 | 10 | 14 | 13 |

| Income Statement Analysis (Million $) | | | | | | | | | | |
|---|---|---|---|---|---|---|---|---|---|---|
| Revenue | 32,466 | 31,981 | 29,300 | 27,240 | 24,063 | 21,244 | 19,178 | 16,617 | 13,829 | 12,163 |
| Operating Income | 4,514 | 4,237 | 3,954 | 3,391 | 3,009 | 2,539 | 2,173 | 1,744 | 1,795 | 1,756 |
| Depreciation | 569 | 562 | 301 | 278 | 384 | 342 | 232 | 277 | 213 | 271 |
| Interest Expense | 157 | 171 | 133 | 131 | 101 | 154 | 157 | 98.0 | 45.0 | 56.0 |
| Pretax Income | 3,790 | 3,513 | 3,604 | 3,047 | 2,527 | 2,100 | 1,785 | 1,372 | 1,584 | 1,424 |
| Effective Tax Rate | NA | 31.5% | 31.2% | 31.7% | 32.3% | 30.1% | 32.6% | 27.3% | 33.6% | 33.8% |
| Net Income | 2,628 | 2,407 | 2,478 | 2,080 | 1,710 | 1,468 | 1,203 | 997 | 1,051 | 943 |
| S&P Core Earnings | 2,594 | 2,362 | 2,054 | 1,999 | 1,663 | 1,354 | 1,130 | 931 | 658 | 636 |

| Balance Sheet & Other Financial Data (Million $) | | | | | | | | | | |
|---|---|---|---|---|---|---|---|---|---|---|
| Cash | 2,613 | 2,263 | 1,621 | 3,155 | 1,604 | 2,331 | 976 | 860 | 328 | 442 |
| Current Assets | 14,186 | 13,249 | 11,950 | 12,298 | 9,880 | 9,173 | 7,287 | 6,394 | 5,098 | 4,893 |
| Total Assets | 32,545 | 31,077 | 28,373 | 25,733 | 22,376 | 19,591 | 17,544 | 16,183 | 11,731 | 11,069 |
| Current Liabilities | 11,177 | 10,371 | 10,360 | 9,164 | 7,824 | 6,907 | 5,374 | 5,616 | 4,582 | 4,579 |
| Long Term Debt | 2,430 | 3,159 | 3,113 | 2,118 | 2,774 | 2,781 | 3,291 | 3,296 | 718 | 724 |
| Common Equity | 13,316 | 12,423 | 10,053 | 11,768 | 9,827 | 8,145 | 7,189 | 5,921 | 5,199 | 4,528 |
| Total Capital | 16,519 | 16,287 | 13,265 | 13,886 | 12,601 | 10,926 | 10,480 | 9,217 | 5,917 | 5,252 |
| Capital Expenditures | 370 | 385 | 490 | 474 | 334 | 279 | 266 | 224 | 264 | 356 |
| Cash Flow | 3,197 | 2,969 | 2,779 | 2,358 | 2,094 | 1,810 | 1,435 | 1,274 | 1,264 | 1,214 |
| Current Ratio | 1.3 | 1.3 | 1.2 | 1.3 | 1.3 | 1.3 | 1.4 | 1.1 | 1.1 | 1.1 |
| % Long Term Debt of Capitalization | 14.7 | 19.4 | 23.5 | 15.3 | 22.0 | 25.5 | 31.4 | 35.8 | 12.1 | 13.8 |
| % Net Income of Revenue | 8.1 | 7.5 | 8.5 | 7.6 | 7.1 | 6.9 | 6.3 | 6.0 | 7.6 | 7.8 |
| % Return on Assets | 8.3 | 8.1 | 9.2 | 8.6 | 8.1 | 7.9 | 7.1 | 7.1 | 9.2 | 9.9 |
| % Return on Equity | 20.4 | 21.4 | 22.7 | 19.3 | 19.0 | 19.1 | 18.4 | 17.9 | 21.6 | 22.6 |

Data as orig reptd.; bef. results of disc opers/spec. items. Per share data adj. for stk. divs.; EPS diluted. E-Estimated. NA-Not Available. NM-Not Meaningful. NR-Not Ranked. UR-Under Review.

**Office:** 2941 Fairview Park Dr Ste 100, Falls Church, VA 22042-4513.
**Telephone:** 703-876-3000.
**Website:** http://www.generaldynamics.com
**Chrmn & CEO:** J.L. Johnson

**SVP & CFO:** L.H. Redd
**SVP, Secy & General Counsel:** G.S. Gallopoulos
**Chief Admin Officer:** W. Oliver
**CTO:** G.J. Demuro

**Investor Contact:** A. Gilliland (703-876-3748)
**Board Members:** M. T. Barra, N. D. Chabraja, J. S. Crown, W. P. Fricks, J. L. Johnson, J. L. Jones, G. A. Joulwan, P. G. Kaminski, J. M. Keane, L. L. Lyles, W. A. Osborn, R. Walmsley

**Founded:** 1899
**Domicile:** Delaware
**Employees:** 90,000

# General Electric Co

## STANDARD &POOR'S

| S&P Recommendation BUY ★★★★☆ | Price $14.70 (as of Nov 25, 2011) | 12-Mo. Target Price $20.00 | Investment Style Large-Cap Blend |
|---|---|---|---|

**GICS Sector** Industrials
**Sub-Industry** Industrial Conglomerates

**Summary** This conglomerate sells products ranging from jet engines and gas turbines to consumer appliances, railroad locomotives and medical equipment. It also owns 49% of a joint venture with Comcast that includes NBC Universal, and is a leading provider of consumer and commercial financing.

## Key Stock Statistics (Source S&P, Vickers, company reports)

| | | | | | | | |
|---|---|---|---|---|---|---|---|
| 52-Wk Range | $21.65– 14.02 | S&P Oper. EPS 2011E | 1.27 | Market Capitalization(B) | $155.193 | Beta | 1.64 |
| Trailing 12-Month EPS | $1.31 | S&P Oper. EPS 2012E | 1.45 | Yield (%) | 4.08 | S&P 3-Yr. Proj. EPS CAGR(%) | 12 |
| Trailing 12-Month P/E | 11.2 | P/E on S&P Oper. EPS 2011E | 11.6 | Dividend Rate/Share | $0.60 | S&P Credit Rating | AA+ |
| $10K Invested 5 Yrs Ago | $4,992 | Common Shares Outstg. (M) | 10,557.4 | Institutional Ownership (%) | 53 | | |

## Price Performance

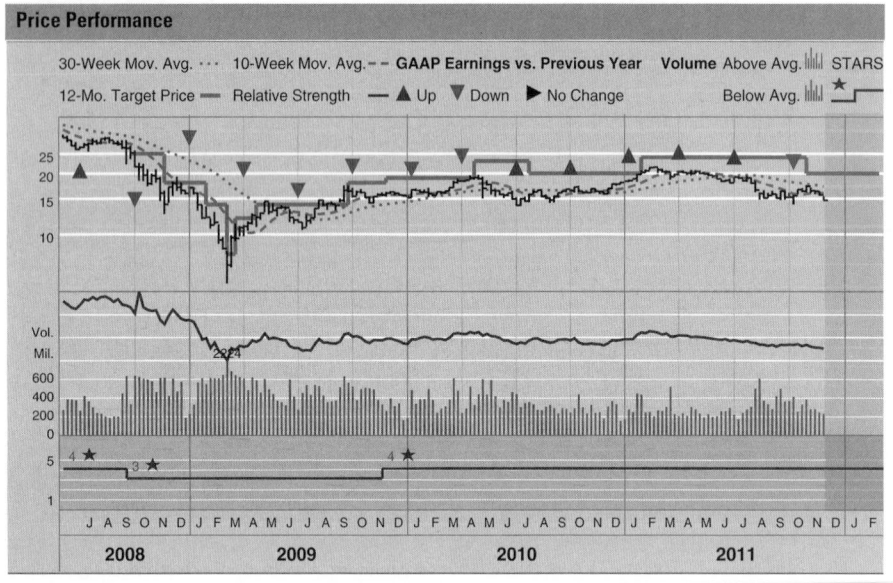

30-Week Mov. Avg. · · · · 10-Week Mov. Avg. – – GAAP Earnings vs. Previous Year Volume Above Avg. STARS
12-Mo. Target Price — Relative Strength — ▲ Up ▼ Down ► No Change Below Avg.

Options: ASE, CBOE, P, Ph

Analysis prepared by Equity Analyst **R. Tortoriello** on Oct 24, 2011, when the stock traded at **$16.56**.

## Qualitative Risk Assessment

| LOW | **MEDIUM** | HIGH |
|---|---|---|

Our risk assessment reflects our view of GE's long-term record of earnings, cash flow and dividends, which we attribute to good management of a diversified portfolio of profitable businesses, offset by risk we see inherent in GE's financial business as it is subject to new regulations and supervision by the Federal Reserve, which began in July 2011.

## Quantitative Evaluations

**S&P Quality Ranking** A-

| D | C | B- | B | B+ | A- | A | A+ |
|---|---|---|---|---|---|---|---|

**Relative Strength Rank** MODERATE

37

LOWEST = 1                                    HIGHEST = 99

## Revenue/Earnings Data

**Revenue (Million $)**

| | 1Q | 2Q | 3Q | 4Q | Year |
|---|---|---|---|---|---|
| 2011 | 38,448 | 35,625 | 35,367 | -- | -- |
| 2010 | 36,605 | 37,444 | 35,888 | 41,377 | 150,211 |
| 2009 | 38,411 | 39,082 | 37,799 | 41,438 | 156,783 |
| 2008 | 42,243 | 46,891 | 47,234 | 46,213 | 182,515 |
| 2007 | 39,200 | 42,384 | 42,534 | 48,588 | 172,738 |
| 2006 | 37,370 | 39,243 | 40,286 | 44,621 | 163,391 |

**Earnings Per Share ($)**

| | | | | | |
|---|---|---|---|---|---|
| 2011 | 0.31 | 0.33 | 0.22 | E0.41 | E1.27 |
| 2010 | 0.21 | 0.30 | 0.29 | 0.36 | 1.15 |
| 2009 | 0.26 | 0.25 | 0.22 | 0.28 | 1.03 |
| 2008 | 0.44 | 0.54 | 0.45 | 0.36 | 1.78 |
| 2007 | 0.44 | 0.52 | 0.50 | 0.68 | 2.20 |
| 2006 | 0.40 | 0.48 | 0.48 | 0.64 | 1.99 |

Fiscal year ended Dec. 31. Next earnings report expected: NA. EPS Estimates based on S&P Operating Earnings; historical GAAP earnings are as reported.

## Highlights

➤ We estimate that sales will rise 12% in 2011, driven by strong growth in energy and technology operations. For 2012, we expect sales to continue to be driven by growth in long-cycle energy and technology businesses, including aviation, gas turbines, oil & gas, transportation, and alternative energy. We also see continued good growth in health care, on emerging market demand, and modest growth in GE Capital revenues, as new originations begin to outpace portfolio reductions and runoff.

➤ We estimate that, excluding a $3.6 billion gain on the NBCU joint venture, operating margins will rise to 11.7% in 2011, from 10.8% in 2010, driven by improvement at GE Capital. For 2012, we project modest continued improvement to 12.1%, on improved pricing in developed markets, partially offset by continued price competition in emerging markets.

➤ We project EPS of $1.27 in 2011, rising to $1.45 in 2012. The formation of the Comcast/NBC Universal joint venture on January 28 resulted in a $0.04 a share gain in the first quarter of 2011.

## Investment Rationale/Risk

➤ We see two major trends buoying GE's stock price over the next 12 months. The first is our view of continued improvement in credit markets, including declining credit loss ratios, modestly better demand, and favorable lending spreads. Given GE's more disciplined credit origination process, we expect these variables to result in increased 2012 profitability at GE Capital. The second is our belief that GE's industrial operations will see improvement in longer-cycle businesses, including industrial gas turbines and jet engines, in 2012.

➤ Risks to our recommendation and target price include the potential for a weaker-than-expected global economic recovery, as well as increased credit losses at GE Capital.

➤ Our 12-month target price of $20 reflects an enterprise value to estimated 2012 EBITDA multiple of 7X. This level is in line with a recent peer average of 6.9X (which includes diversified industrial companies in our coverage universe, excluding GE), reflecting our expectation of little multiple expansion as economic growth remains slow.

## Dividend Data (Dates: mm/dd Payment Date: mm/dd/yy)

| Amount ($) | Date Decl. | Ex-Div. Date | Stk. of Record | Payment Date |
|---|---|---|---|---|
| 0.140 | 12/10 | 12/22 | 12/27 | 01/25/11 |
| 0.140 | 02/11 | 02/24 | 02/28 | 04/25/11 |
| 0.150 | 04/21 | 06/16 | 06/20 | 07/25/11 |
| 0.150 | 09/02 | 09/15 | 09/19 | 10/25/11 |

Dividends have been paid since 1899. Source: Company reports.

---

**Please read the Required Disclosures and Analyst Certification on the last page of this report.**

The McGraw·Hill Companies

# General Electric Co

**STANDARD &POOR'S**

## Business Summary October 24, 2011

CORPORATE OVERVIEW. This multi-industry, heavy-equipment, media and financing giant does business through six segments: Energy Infrastructure, Aviation, Healthcare, Transportation, GE Capital, and Home & Business Solutions. Revenue by geographic region in 2010: U.S. 47%, Europe 21%, Pacific Basin 14%, Americas 9%, Middle East and Africa 6%, and Other 3%.

The Energy Infrastructure segment (28% of segment sales and 42% of segment operating profits in 2010) consists of GE's Energy and Oil & Gas businesses. Major products include gas turbines and generators, wind turbines, solar technology, integrated coal gasification systems, water treatment solutions for industrial and municipal water systems, and nuclear power plants, through joint ventures with Hitachi and Toshiba (the Energy business line); surface and subsea drilling and production systems, equipment for floating production platforms, compressors, turbines, turboexpanders, pressure control equipment, and industrial power generation (Oil & Gas). GE provides extensive aftermarket services for its equipment.

Aviation (13% of sales and 19% of operating profits) makes, sells and services jet engines, turboprop and turbo shaft engines, and replacement parts for use in military and commercial aircraft. Military applications include fighters, bombers, tankers, helicopters, surveillance aircraft and marine applications. Commercial applications include large commercial, regional and executive

jets. GE also makes engines through CFM International (the CFM56 engine line), a joint venture with France's Snecma, and Engine Alliance LLC (the GP7000 line), a joint venture with Pratt & Whitney. Aviation also produces airborne platform computing systems, power generation and distribution products, mechanical actuation products and landing gear, and various engine components.

Healthcare (13% of sales and 16% of operating profits) makes and services a wide variety of medical imaging products, including magnetic resonance (MR), computed tomography (CT), positron emission tomography (PET) scanner, X-ray, nuclear imaging, digital mammography and molecular imaging technologies. Other products include patient and resident monitoring, diagnostic cardiology, ultrasound, bone densitometry, anesthesiology and oxygen therapy, and neonatal and critical care devices. Medical diagnostics and life sciences products include diagnostic imaging agents used in medical scanning procedures, drug discovery, biopharmaceutical manufacturing and purification, and tools for protein and cellular analysis for pharmaceutical and academic research.

## Company Financials Fiscal Year Ended Dec. 31

| Per Share Data ($) | 2010 | 2009 | 2008 | 2007 | 2006 | 2005 | 2004 | 2003 | 2002 | 2001 |
|---|---|---|---|---|---|---|---|---|---|---|
| Tangible Book Value | 4.37 | 4.06 | 0.75 | 2.38 | 2.52 | 2.64 | 2.55 | 2.40 | 1.76 | 2.34 |
| Cash Flow | 2.31 | 1.55 | 2.92 | 3.21 | 2.90 | 2.53 | 2.39 | 2.24 | 2.11 | 2.11 |
| Earnings | 1.15 | 1.03 | 1.78 | 2.20 | 1.99 | 1.72 | 1.59 | 1.55 | 1.51 | 1.41 |
| S&P Core Earnings | 1.20 | 1.03 | 1.57 | 2.07 | 1.90 | 1.66 | 1.54 | 1.41 | 1.10 | 0.98 |
| Dividends | 0.46 | 0.61 | 1.24 | 1.15 | 1.03 | 0.91 | 0.82 | 0.77 | 0.73 | 0.66 |
| Payout Ratio | 40% | 59% | 70% | 52% | 52% | 53% | 52% | 50% | 48% | 47% |
| Prices:High | 19.70 | 17.52 | 38.52 | 42.15 | 38.49 | 37.34 | 37.75 | 32.42 | 41.84 | 53.55 |
| Prices:Low | 13.75 | 5.73 | 12.58 | 33.90 | 32.06 | 32.67 | 28.88 | 21.30 | 21.40 | 28.50 |
| P/E Ratio:High | 17 | 17 | 22 | 19 | 19 | 22 | 24 | 21 | 28 | 38 |
| P/E Ratio:Low | 12 | 6 | 7 | 15 | 16 | 19 | 18 | 14 | 14 | 20 |

| Income Statement Analysis (Million $) | | | | | | | | | | |
|---|---|---|---|---|---|---|---|---|---|---|
| Revenue | 150,211 | 156,783 | 182,515 | 172,738 | 163,391 | 149,702 | 152,363 | 134,187 | 131,698 | 125,913 |
| Operating Income | 26,930 | 17,022 | 57,897 | 69,594 | 53,972 | 46,840 | 40,262 | 36,792 | 35,431 | 38,200 |
| Depreciation | 11,762 | 5,557 | 11,492 | 10,278 | 9,158 | 8,538 | 8,385 | 6,956 | 5,998 | 7,089 |
| Interest Expense | 1,600 | 1,478 | 26,209 | 23,787 | 19,286 | 15,187 | 11,907 | 10,432 | 10,216 | 11,062 |
| Pretax Income | 14,208 | 10,344 | 19,782 | 27,514 | 25,528 | 23,115 | 21,034 | 20,194 | 19,217 | 20,049 |
| Effective Tax Rate | NA | NM | 5.32% | 15.0% | 15.5% | 16.7% | 16.7% | 21.4% | 19.6% | 27.8% |
| Net Income | 12,623 | 11,218 | 18,089 | 22,468 | 20,666 | 18,275 | 16,593 | 15,589 | 15,133 | 14,128 |
| S&P Core Earnings | 12,775 | 10,780 | 15,939 | 21,155 | 19,701 | 17,548 | 16,138 | 14,195 | 11,038 | 9,889 |

| Balance Sheet & Other Financial Data (Million $) | | | | | | | | | | |
|---|---|---|---|---|---|---|---|---|---|---|
| Cash | 122,900 | 124,200 | 12,300 | 17,578 | 14,275 | 9,011 | 150,864 | 133,388 | 125,772 | 110,099 |
| Current Assets | 505,300 | 445,634 | 463,602 | 451,859 | 391,095 | 383,745 | 358,286 | 294,775 | 271,784 | 239,691 |
| Total Assets | 751,200 | 781,000 | 797,800 | 795,337 | 697,239 | 673,342 | 750,330 | 647,483 | 575,244 | 495,023 |
| Current Liabilities | 156,074 | 167,284 | 236,074 | 236,228 | 215,266 | 200,471 | 206,280 | 176,530 | 181,827 | 198,904 |
| Long Term Debt | 478,600 | 510,200 | 330,067 | 319,015 | 260,804 | 212,281 | 213,161 | 170,004 | 140,632 | 79,806 |
| Common Equity | 118,900 | 117,300 | 104,700 | 115,559 | 112,314 | 109,354 | 110,284 | 79,180 | 63,706 | 54,824 |
| Total Capital | 601,600 | 633,300 | 448,263 | 454,722 | 394,867 | 346,019 | 354,242 | 267,611 | 222,328 | 148,975 |
| Capital Expenditures | 9,800 | 8,634 | 16,010 | 17,870 | 16,650 | 14,441 | 13,118 | 9,767 | 13,351 | 15,520 |
| Cash Flow | 24,620 | 16,475 | 29,506 | 32,746 | 29,824 | 26,813 | 24,978 | 22,545 | 21,131 | 21,217 |
| Current Ratio | 3.0 | 2.7 | 2.0 | 1.9 | 1.8 | 1.9 | 1.7 | 1.7 | 1.5 | 1.2 |
| % Long Term Debt of Capitalization | 79.6 | 80.6 | 73.6 | 70.2 | 66.0 | 61.3 | 60.2 | 63.5 | 63.3 | 53.6 |
| % Net Income of Revenue | 8.4 | 7.2 | 9.9 | 13.2 | 12.8 | 12.2 | 10.8 | 11.6 | 11.5 | 11.2 |
| % Return on Assets | 1.7 | 1.4 | 2.3 | 3.0 | 3.0 | 2.6 | 2.4 | 2.5 | 2.8 | 3.0 |
| % Return on Equity | 10.7 | 10.1 | 16.4 | 19.7 | 18.6 | 16.6 | 17.5 | 21.8 | 25.5 | 26.8 |

Data as orig reptd.; bef. results of disc opers/spec. items. Per share data adj. for stk. divs.; EPS diluted. E-Estimated. NA-Not Available. NM-Not Meaningful. NR-Not Ranked. UR-Under Review.

**Office:** 3135 Easton Turnpike, Fairfield, CT 06828-0001.
**Telephone:** 203-373-2211.
**Website:** http://www.ge.com
**Chrmn & CEO:** J.R. Immelt

**Vice Chrmn:** J.G. Rice
**Vice Chrmn:** J. Krenicki, Jr.
**Vice Chrmn:** M.A. Neal
**Vice Chrmn & CFO:** K.S. Sherin

**Investor Contact:** D. Janki
**Board Members:** W. G. Beattie, J. I. Cash, Jr., A. M. Fudge, S. Hockfield, J. R. Immelt, A. Jung, A. G. Lafley, R. W. Lane, R. S. Larsen, R. B. Lazarus, J. J. Mulva, S. A. Nunn, R. S. Penske, R. J. Swieringa, J. S. Tisch, D. A. Warner

**Founded:** 1892
**Domicile:** New York
**Employees:** 287,000

**The McGraw-Hill Companies**

# General Mills Inc.

**STANDARD
&POOR'S**

| S&P Recommendation | STRONG BUY ★ ★ ★ ★ ★ | Price $38.23 (as of Nov 25, 2011) | 12-Mo. Target Price $44.00 | Investment Style Large-Cap Blend |
|---|---|---|---|---|

**GICS Sector** Consumer Staples
**Sub-Industry** Packaged Foods & Meats

**Summary** This company is a major producer of packaged consumer food products, including Big G cereals and Betty Crocker desserts/baking mixes.

## Key Stock Statistics (Source S&P, Vickers, company reports)

| | | | | | | | | |
|---|---|---|---|---|---|---|---|---|
| 52-Wk Range | $40.25– 34.54 | S&P Oper. EPS 2012**E** | 2.61 | Market Capitalization(B) | $24.599 | Beta | | 0.19 |
| Trailing 12-Month EPS | $2.61 | S&P Oper. EPS 2013**E** | 2.81 | Yield (%) | 3.19 | S&P 3-Yr. Proj. EPS CAGR(%) | | 7 |
| Trailing 12-Month P/E | 14.7 | P/E on S&P Oper. EPS 2012**E** | 14.6 | Dividend Rate/Share | $1.22 | S&P Credit Rating | | BBB+ |
| $10K Invested 5 Yrs Ago | $15,598 | Common Shares Outstg. (M) | 643.5 | Institutional Ownership (%) | 71 | | | |

## Price Performance

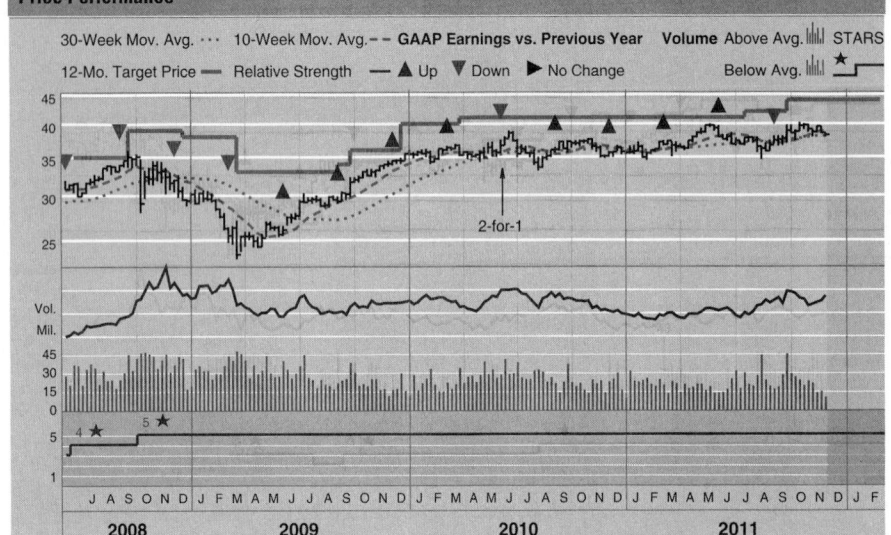

- 30-Week Mov. Avg. · · · 10-Week Mov. Avg. - - **GAAP Earnings vs. Previous Year**   **Volume** Above Avg. STARS
- 12-Mo. Target Price — Relative Strength — ▲ Up ▼ Down ► No Change   Below Avg.

2008  2009  2010  2011

Options: ASE, CBOE, P, Ph

Analysis prepared by Equity Analyst **Tom Graves, CFA** on Nov 21, 2011, when the stock traded at **$38.40**.

## Highlights

- Including about $1.0 billion of sales related to the July 2011 acquisition of a controlling interest in the Yoplait yogurt business, we look for FY 12 (May) net sales to reach about $16.6 billion, up approximately 12% from the $14.9 billion reported for FY 11.

- In FY 12, we anticipate that higher prices and productivity gains will at least partly offset profit margin pressure from increased input costs. Before some special items, but including some possible restructuring costs, we estimate FY 12 EPS of $2.61, up from $2.48 in FY 11. Our EPS estimate for FY 12 excludes integration and transaction costs related to the Yoplait acquisition, but includes a prospective $0.01 dilutive impact from other factors related to the acquisition. For FY 13, we estimate EPS of $2.81. In FY 11, the $2.48 excluded a net favorable impact of about $0.22 from some special items.

- In FY 11, GIS repurchased 32 million of its common shares for $1.164 billion. However, in FY 12, we expect that funding the Yoplait acquisition will be a preferred use of cash.

## Investment Rationale/Risk

- We have a generally favorable view of GIS acquiring a controlling interest in the Yoplait yogurt business. GIS markets Yoplait yogurt in the U.S. Also, we like GIS's overall brand strength, which we think will provide some protection from competitive pressure presented by less expensive private label products. We believe that GIS has opportunities to bolster long-term profit margins through a focus on areas such as manufacturing and spending efficiency, global sourcing, and sales mix.

- Risks to our recommendation and target price include competitive pressures, disappointing consumer acceptance of new products, higher-than-expected commodity cost inflation, and an inability to achieve sales and earnings growth forecasts.

- Our 12-month target price of $44 reflects a moderate P/E premium, based on estimated calendar 2012 EPS, to a recent average P/E for a group of other packaged food stocks. We like GIS's strong brands, good profitability, and its consistency and growth of earnings and dividends. GIS shares recently had an indicated yield of 3.2%.

## Qualitative Risk Assessment

| LOW | MEDIUM | HIGH |
|---|---|---|

Our risk assessment reflects the relatively stable nature of the company's end markets, strong cash flows, and a top S&P Quality Ranking of A+. For the S&P Quality Ranking system, long-term growth and stability of earnings and dividends are key elements.

## Quantitative Evaluations

**S&P Quality Ranking**  A+

| D | C | B- | B | B+ | A- | A | A+ |
|---|---|---|---|---|---|---|---|

**Relative Strength Rank**  STRONG

74

LOWEST = 1  HIGHEST = 99

## Revenue/Earnings Data

**Revenue (Million $)**

| | 1Q | 2Q | 3Q | 4Q | Year |
|---|---|---|---|---|---|
| 2012 | 3,848 | -- | -- | -- | -- |
| 2011 | 3,533 | 4,067 | 3,646 | 3,634 | 14,880 |
| 2010 | 3,519 | 4,078 | 3,629 | 3,570 | 14,797 |
| 2009 | 3,497 | 4,011 | 3,537 | 3,646 | 14,691 |
| 2008 | 3,072 | 3,703 | 3,406 | 3,471 | 13,652 |
| 2007 | 2,860 | 3,467 | 3,054 | 3,061 | 12,442 |

**Earnings Per Share ($)**

| | | | | | |
|---|---|---|---|---|---|
| 2012 | 0.61 | E0.80 | E0.63 | E0.57 | E2.61 |
| 2011 | 0.70 | 0.92 | 0.59 | 0.48 | 2.70 |
| 2010 | 0.63 | 0.83 | 0.49 | 0.31 | 2.24 |
| 2009 | 0.40 | 0.55 | 0.43 | 0.54 | 1.90 |
| 2008 | 0.40 | 0.57 | 0.62 | 0.26 | 1.85 |
| 2007 | 0.37 | 0.54 | 0.37 | 0.31 | 1.59 |

Fiscal year ended May 31. Next earnings report expected: Mid December. EPS Estimates based on S&P Operating Earnings; historical GAAP earnings are as reported.

## Dividend Data (Dates: mm/dd Payment Date: mm/dd/yy)

| Amount ($) | Date Decl. | Ex-Div. Date | Stk. of Record | Payment Date |
|---|---|---|---|---|
| 0.280 | 12/13 | 01/06 | 01/10 | 02/01/11 |
| 0.280 | 03/15 | 04/07 | 04/11 | 05/02/11 |
| 0.305 | 06/28 | 07/07 | 07/11 | 08/01/11 |
| 0.305 | 09/26 | 10/05 | 10/10 | 11/01/11 |

Dividends have been paid since 1898. Source: Company reports.

---

**Please read the Required Disclosures and Analyst Certification on the last page of this report.**

*The McGraw-Hill Companies*

# General Mills Inc.

## Business Summary November 21, 2011

CORPORATE OVERVIEW. General Mills (GIS) is one of the largest U.S. producers of ready-to-eat breakfast cereals, and a leading producer of other well-known packaged consumer foods. The U.S. Retail segment, which accounted for 68% of net sales in FY 11 (May), includes cereals, refrigerated yogurt, soup, dry dinners, vegetables, dough products, baking products, snacks, and organic products. The Bakeries and Foodservice segment (12%) includes products sold to distributors, convenience stores, restaurant operators and cafeterias. The International segment (19%) includes products manufactured in the U.S. for export, mainly to Caribbean and Latin American markets, as well as products manufactured for sale to GIS international joint ventures.

Cereal brands include Cheerios, Wheaties, Lucky Charms, Total, Trix, Golden Grahams, Chex, Kix, and Fiber One. Other consumer packaged food products include baking mixes (e.g., Betty Crocker, Bisquick); dry dinners; Progresso ready-to-serve soups, Green Giant canned and frozen vegetables; snacks; Pillsbury refrigerated and frozen dough products, frozen pizza; Yoplait refrigerated yogurt; Haagen-Dazs ice cream; and Cascadian Farm and Muir Glen organic products. Some products may be marketed under licensing arrange-

ments with other parties. GIS also has a grain merchandising operation that holds inventories carried at fair market value, and uses derivatives to hedge its net inventory position and minimize its market exposures.

During FY 11, Wal-Mart Stores, Inc., and affiliates accounted for 23% of GIS's consolidated net sales.

GIS joint ventures include a 50% equity interest in Cereal Partners Worldwide (CPW), a joint venture with Nestle S.A. that manufactures and markets cereal products outside the U.S. and Canada; a 50% equity interest in Haagen-Dazs Japan, Inc., which manufactures, distributes and markets Haagen-Dazs ice cream products and frozen novelties; and a 51% interest in Yoplait S.A.S., acquired in 2011.

## Company Financials Fiscal Year Ended May 31

| Per Share Data ($) | 2011 | 2010 | 2009 | 2008 | 2007 | 2006 | 2005 | 2004 | 2003 | 2002 |
|---|---|---|---|---|---|---|---|---|---|---|
| Tangible Book Value | NM | NM | NM | NM | NM | NM | NM | NM | NM | NM |
| Cash Flow | 3.42 | 2.91 | 2.56 | 2.53 | 2.30 | 2.00 | 2.06 | 1.89 | 1.70 | 1.11 |
| Earnings | 2.70 | 2.24 | 1.90 | 1.85 | 1.59 | 1.45 | 1.54 | 1.38 | 1.22 | 0.68 |
| S&P Core Earnings | 2.62 | 2.09 | 1.44 | 1.65 | 1.52 | 1.36 | 1.09 | 1.22 | 0.87 | 0.28 |
| Dividends | NA | 0.96 | 0.86 | 0.78 | 0.72 | 0.67 | 0.62 | 0.55 | 0.55 | 0.55 |
| Payout Ratio | NA | 36% | 41% | 42% | 42% | 46% | 40% | 40% | 45% | 81% |
| Calendar Year | 2010 | 2009 | 2008 | 2007 | 2006 | 2005 | 2004 | 2003 | 2002 | 2001 |
| Prices:High | 38.98 | 36.04 | 36.01 | 30.76 | 29.62 | 26.95 | 24.98 | 24.83 | 25.87 | 26.43 |
| Prices:Low | 33.11 | 23.19 | 25.50 | 27.09 | 23.53 | 22.34 | 21.51 | 20.72 | 18.69 | 18.63 |
| P/E Ratio:High | 14 | 16 | 19 | 17 | 19 | 19 | 16 | 18 | 21 | 39 |
| P/E Ratio:Low | 12 | 10 | 14 | 15 | 15 | 15 | 14 | 15 | 15 | 28 |

### Income Statement Analysis (Million $)

| | 2011 | 2010 | 2009 | 2008 | 2007 | 2006 | 2005 | 2004 | 2003 | 2002 |
|---|---|---|---|---|---|---|---|---|---|---|
| Revenue | 14,880 | 14,797 | 14,691 | 13,652 | 12,442 | 11,640 | 11,244 | 11,070 | 10,506 | 7,949 |
| Operating Income | 3,234 | 3,095 | 2,727 | 2,687 | 2,515 | 2,420 | 2,435 | 2,442 | 2,290 | 1,569 |
| Depreciation | 473 | 457 | 454 | 459 | 418 | 424 | 443 | 399 | 365 | 296 |
| Interest Expense | 346 | 402 | 417 | 422 | 427 | 427 | 488 | 537 | 589 | 445 |
| Pretax Income | 2,525 | 2,306 | 2,025 | 1,917 | 1,704 | 1,631 | 1,904 | 1,583 | 1,377 | 700 |
| Effective Tax Rate | NA | NA | 35.6% | 32.5% | 32.9% | 33.2% | 34.9% | 33.4% | 33.4% | 34.1% |
| Net Income | 1,804 | 1,531 | 1,304 | 1,295 | 1,144 | 1,090 | 1,240 | 1,055 | 917 | 461 |
| S&P Core Earnings | 1,750 | 1,429 | 988 | 1,142 | 1,089 | 1,024 | 863 | 931 | 652 | 189 |

### Balance Sheet & Other Financial Data (Million $)

| | 2011 | 2010 | 2009 | 2008 | 2007 | 2006 | 2005 | 2004 | 2003 | 2002 |
|---|---|---|---|---|---|---|---|---|---|---|
| Cash | 620 | 673 | 750 | 674 | 417 | 647 | 573 | 751 | 703 | 975 |
| Current Assets | 3,902 | 3,480 | 3,535 | 3,620 | 3,054 | 3,176 | 3,055 | 3,215 | 3,179 | 3,437 |
| Total Assets | 18,675 | 17,679 | 17,875 | 19,042 | 18,184 | 18,207 | 18,066 | 18,448 | 18,227 | 16,540 |
| Current Liabilities | 3,659 | 3,769 | 3,606 | 4,856 | 5,845 | 6,138 | 4,184 | 2,757 | 3,444 | 5,747 |
| Long Term Debt | 5,543 | 5,269 | 5,755 | 4,349 | 3,218 | 2,415 | 4,255 | 7,410 | 7,516 | 5,591 |
| Common Equity | 6,366 | 5,403 | 5,175 | 6,216 | 5,319 | 5,772 | 5,676 | 5,248 | 4,175 | 3,576 |
| Total Capital | 13,433 | 11,024 | 11,680 | 12,261 | 11,109 | 11,145 | 12,915 | 14,730 | 13,652 | 9,727 |
| Capital Expenditures | 649 | 650 | 563 | 522 | 460 | 360 | 414 | 628 | 711 | 506 |
| Cash Flow | 2,276 | 1,988 | 1,758 | 1,754 | 1,562 | 1,514 | 1,683 | 1,454 | 1,282 | 757 |
| Current Ratio | 1.1 | 0.9 | 1.0 | 0.8 | 0.5 | 0.5 | 0.7 | 1.2 | 0.9 | 0.6 |
| % Long Term Debt of Capitalization | 41.3 | 47.8 | 49.3 | 35.4 | 28.9 | 21.7 | 32.9 | 50.3 | 55.1 | 57.5 |
| % Net Income of Revenue | 12.1 | 10.3 | 8.9 | 9.5 | 9.2 | 9.4 | 11.0 | 9.5 | 8.7 | 5.8 |
| % Return on Assets | 9.9 | 8.6 | 7.1 | 7.0 | 6.3 | 6.0 | 6.8 | 5.8 | 5.3 | 4.3 |
| % Return on Equity | 30.7 | 28.9 | 22.9 | 22.5 | 20.6 | 18.7 | 22.7 | 22.4 | 23.7 | 25.4 |

Data as orig reptd.; bef. results of disc opers/spec. items. Per share data adj. for stk. divs.; EPS diluted. E-Estimated. NA-Not Available. NM-Not Meaningful. NR-Not Ranked. UR-Under Review.

**Office:** Number One General Mills Boulevard, Minneapolis, MN 55426.
**Telephone:** 763-764-7600.
**Website:** http://www.generalmills.com
**Chrmn & CEO:** K.J. Powell

**EVP & CFO:** D.L. Mulligan
**EVP, Secy & General Counsel:** R.A. Palmore
**CTO:** P.C. Erickson
**Chief Acctg Officer & Cntlr:** J.A. Young

**Investor Contact:** K. Wenker (800-245-5703)
**Board Members:** B. H. Anderson, R. K. Clark, P. Danos, W. T. Esrey, R. V. Gilmartin, J. R. Hope, H. G. Miller, H. M. Ochoa-Brillembourg, S. Odland, K. J. Powell, M. D. Rose, R. L. Ryan, D. A. Terrell

**Founded:** 1928
**Domicile:** Delaware
**Employees:** 35,000

# Genuine Parts Co

| S&P Recommendation **HOLD** ★★★☆☆ | Price<br>$54.18 (as of Nov 25, 2011) | 12-Mo. Target Price<br>$62.00 | Investment Style<br>Large-Cap Blend |
|---|---|---|---|

**GICS Sector** Consumer Discretionary
**Sub-Industry** Distributors

**Summary** This company is a leading wholesale distributor of automotive replacement parts, industrial parts and supplies, and office products.

## Key Stock Statistics (Source S&P, Vickers, company reports)

| | | | | | | | |
|---|---|---|---|---|---|---|---|
| 52-Wk Range | $59.40–46.10 | S&P Oper. EPS 2011**E** | 3.57 | Market Capitalization(B) | $8.433 | Beta | 0.74 |
| Trailing 12-Month EPS | $3.47 | S&P Oper. EPS 2012**E** | 3.82 | Yield (%) | 3.32 | S&P 3-Yr. Proj. EPS CAGR(%) | 11 |
| Trailing 12-Month P/E | 15.6 | P/E on S&P Oper. EPS 2011**E** | 15.2 | Dividend Rate/Share | $1.80 | S&P Credit Rating | NA |
| $10K Invested 5 Yrs Ago | $13,840 | Common Shares Outstg. (M) | 155.7 | Institutional Ownership (%) | 74 | | |

## Price Performance

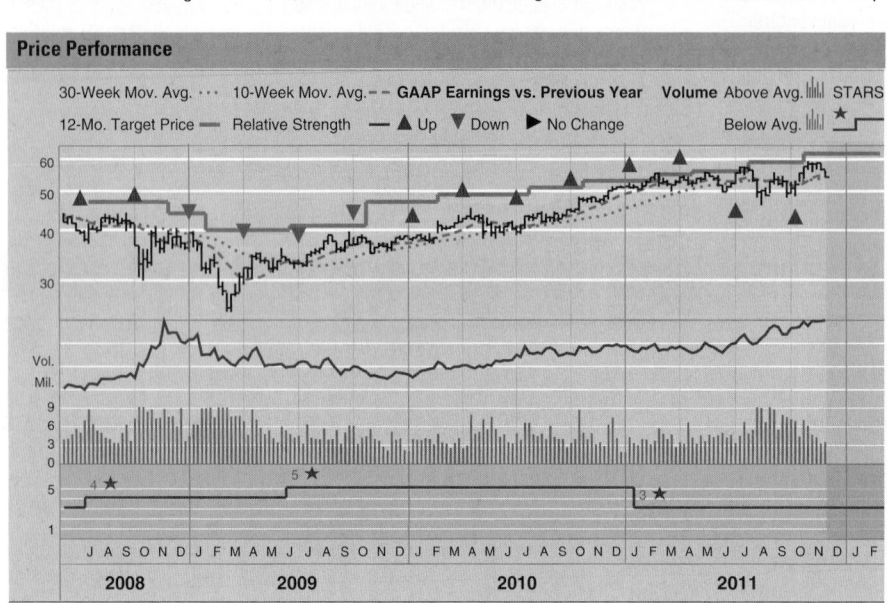

30-Week Mov. Avg. · · · 10-Week Mov. Avg. – – **GAAP Earnings vs. Previous Year** Volume Above Avg. STARS
12-Mo. Target Price — Relative Strength — ▲ Up ▼ Down ▶ No Change Below Avg. ★

Options: ASE, P, Ph

Analysis prepared by Equity Analyst **Efraim Levy, CFA** on Oct 25, 2011, when the stock traded at **$57.12**.

## Highlights

➤ We estimate a sales increase of 11.5% for 2011, as we think all GPC's segments will enjoy growth as the U.S. economy strengthens. Margins should benefit from higher volume and cost-cutting efforts, despite price pressures. We expect EPS to rise to $3.57 in 2011. We see further sales and margin gains in 2012, with EPS of $3.82, as the U.S. economy improves further. We forecast sales to increase 8.3% in 2012.

➤ We expect long-term prospects for GPC's auto parts segment to be enhanced by the rising number of and increasing complexity of vehicles. The median vehicle age in the U.S. is currently more than ten years. We believe GPC will benefit from an expanding market share, as long-term industry consolidation continues to drive out smaller participants. We also think GPC will use its distribution strength to leverage sales of acquired parts companies.

➤ We think what we view as the company's solid balance sheet, low debt and strong cash flow provide the ability and resources to help accelerate earnings growth over the long term. We see GPC using cash flow to repurchase shares, invest in the business, make modest-sized acquisitions, and increase the dividend.

## Investment Rationale/Risk

➤ Results in 2012 should benefit from GDP growth, which S&P forecasts at 1.5%. Based on our 2012 EPS estimate, the stock's recent P/E of about 15.0X is above the average for peers. We think a premium multiple for GPC is warranted by the company's greater earnings stability. We view GPC as financially strong. Earnings quality appears high to us, and an above-average dividend yield adds to GPC's total return potential.

➤ Risks to our recommendation and target price include weaker-than-expected demand for the company's products and a slower-than-anticipated improvement in operating margins.

➤ Our 12-month target price of $62 is based on a weighted blend of our relative valuation and discounted cash flow (DCF) metrics. On a relative basis, we apply a multiple of 15.5X to our 2012 EPS estimate of $3.87 (including $0.05 of expected acquisitions), reflecting historical and peer comparisons, leading to a value of $60. Our DCF model, which assumes a weighted average cost of capital of 9.0%, a compound annual growth rate of 3.5% over the next 15 years, and a terminal growth rate of 3%, calculates an intrinsic value of about $63.

## Qualitative Risk Assessment

| LOW | MEDIUM | HIGH |
|---|---|---|

Our risk assessment reflects GPC's long-term record of rising sales and earnings and what we view as strong corporate leadership and a healthy balance sheet.

## Quantitative Evaluations

**S&P Quality Ranking** A

| D | C | B- | B | B+ | A- | A | A+ |
|---|---|---|---|---|---|---|---|

**Relative Strength Rank** MODERATE

69

LOWEST = 1 HIGHEST = 99

## Revenue/Earnings Data

**Revenue (Million $)**

| | 1Q | 2Q | 3Q | 4Q | Year |
|---|---|---|---|---|---|
| 2011 | 2,974 | 3,185 | 3,286 | -- | -- |
| 2010 | 2,602 | 2,847 | 2,951 | 2,808 | 11,208 |
| 2009 | 2,445 | 2,535 | 2,607 | 2,471 | 10,058 |
| 2008 | 2,739 | 2,873 | 2,882 | 2,520 | 11,015 |
| 2007 | 2,649 | 2,770 | 2,798 | 2,627 | 10,843 |
| 2006 | 2,554 | 2,662 | 2,700 | 2,543 | 10,458 |

**Earnings Per Share ($)**

| | | | | | |
|---|---|---|---|---|---|
| 2011 | 0.80 | 0.96 | 0.97 | E0.85 | E3.57 |
| 2010 | 0.63 | 0.78 | 0.83 | 0.75 | 3.00 |
| 2009 | 0.56 | 0.65 | 0.67 | 0.62 | 2.50 |
| 2008 | 0.75 | 0.81 | 0.81 | 0.55 | 2.92 |
| 2007 | 0.71 | 0.76 | 0.76 | 0.75 | 2.98 |
| 2006 | 0.66 | 0.70 | 0.71 | 0.70 | 2.76 |

Fiscal year ended Dec. 31. Next earnings report expected: Late February. EPS Estimates based on S&P Operating Earnings; historical GAAP earnings are as reported.

## Dividend Data (Dates: mm/dd Payment Date: mm/dd/yy)

| Amount<br>($) | Date<br>Decl. | Ex-Div.<br>Date | Stk. of<br>Record | Payment<br>Date |
|---|---|---|---|---|
| 0.450 | 02/21 | 03/09 | 03/11 | 04/01/11 |
| 0.450 | 04/18 | 06/08 | 06/10 | 07/01/11 |
| 0.450 | 08/15 | 09/07 | 09/09 | 10/03/11 |
| 0.450 | 11/21 | 12/07 | 12/09 | 01/03/12 |

Dividends have been paid since 1948. Source: Company reports.

# Genuine Parts Co

## Business Summary October 25, 2011

CORPORATE OVERVIEW. Genuine Parts is the leading independent U.S. distributor of automotive replacement parts. It operates 58 NAPA warehouse distribution centers in the U.S., about 1,000 company-owned jobbing stores, four Rayloc auto parts rebuilding plants, four Balkamp distribution centers, two Altrom import parts distribution centers, and 16 heavy vehicle parts distribution centers and facilities. It also has operations in Canada and Mexico. The company has been expanding via a combination of internal growth and acquisitions.

The automotive parts segment (50% of 2010 revenues, 50% of profits) serves about 5,800 NAPA Auto Parts stores, including about 1,000 company-owned stores, selling to garages, service stations, car and truck dealers, fleet operators, leasing companies, bus and truck lines, etc.

The industrial parts segment (31%, 30%) distributes around three million industrial replacement parts and related supply items, including bearings, power transmission equipment replacement parts, including hydraulic and pneumatic products, material handling components, agricultural and irrigation

equipment, and related items from locations in the U.S. and Canada.

Through S. P. Richards Co., the office products group (15%, 16%) distributes more than 40,000 office product items, including information processing supplies and office furniture, machines and supplies to office suppliers, from facilities in the U.S. and Canada.

The EIS electrical/electronics materials group (4%, 4%) was formed via the 1998 acquisition of EIS, Inc., for $200 million. EIS is a wholesale distributor of material and supplies to the electrical and electronic industries.

The U.S. accounted for 87% of sales in 2010. Canada contributed 12%, and Mexico represented less than 1%.

## Company Financials Fiscal Year Ended Dec. 31

| Per Share Data ($) | 2010 | 2009 | 2008 | 2007 | 2006 | 2005 | 2004 | 2003 | 2002 | 2001 |
|---|---|---|---|---|---|---|---|---|---|---|
| Tangible Book Value | 16.39 | 15.42 | 13.58 | 15.86 | 4.82 | 15.21 | 14.21 | 12.95 | 11.88 | 10.97 |
| Cash Flow | 3.56 | 3.07 | 3.46 | 3.49 | 3.18 | 2.87 | 2.61 | 2.42 | 2.50 | 2.21 |
| Earnings | 3.00 | 2.50 | 2.92 | 2.98 | 2.76 | 2.50 | 2.25 | 2.03 | 2.10 | 1.71 |
| S&P Core Earnings | 3.04 | 2.47 | 2.54 | 2.98 | 2.76 | 2.40 | 2.22 | 1.95 | 1.80 | 1.53 |
| Dividends | 1.64 | 1.60 | 1.56 | 1.46 | 1.35 | 1.25 | 1.20 | 1.18 | 1.16 | 1.14 |
| Payout Ratio | 55% | 64% | 53% | 49% | 49% | 50% | 53% | 58% | 55% | 67% |
| Prices:High | 51.61 | 39.82 | 46.28 | 51.68 | 48.34 | 46.64 | 44.32 | 33.75 | 38.80 | 37.94 |
| Prices:Low | 36.94 | 24.93 | 29.92 | 46.00 | 40.00 | 40.75 | 32.03 | 27.20 | 27.10 | 23.91 |
| P/E Ratio:High | 17 | 16 | 16 | 17 | 18 | 19 | 20 | 17 | 18 | 22 |
| P/E Ratio:Low | 12 | 10 | 10 | 15 | 14 | 16 | 14 | 13 | 13 | 14 |

| Income Statement Analysis (Million $) | 2010 | 2009 | 2008 | 2007 | 2006 | 2005 | 2004 | 2003 | 2002 | 2001 |
|---|---|---|---|---|---|---|---|---|---|---|
| Revenue | 11,208 | 10,058 | 11,015 | 10,843 | 10,458 | 9,783 | 9,097 | 8,449 | 8,259 | 8,221 |
| Operating Income | 878 | 761 | 889 | 926 | 870 | 804 | 698 | 641 | 676 | 656 |
| Depreciation | 89.3 | 90.4 | 88.7 | 87.7 | 73.4 | 65.5 | 62.2 | 69.0 | 70.2 | 85.8 |
| Interest Expense | 26.6 | 27.9 | 31.7 | 31.3 | 31.6 | 29.6 | Nil | Nil | Nil | Nil |
| Pretax Income | 762 | 644 | 768 | 822 | 771 | 709 | 636 | 572 | 606 | 496 |
| Effective Tax Rate | NA | 38.0% | 38.1% | 37.8% | 38.3% | 38.3% | 37.8% | 38.1% | 39.3% | 40.1% |
| Net Income | 476 | 400 | 475 | 506 | 475 | 437 | 396 | 354 | 368 | 297 |
| S&P Core Earnings | 482 | 395 | 414 | 506 | 475 | 420 | 388 | 339 | 316 | 265 |

| Balance Sheet & Other Financial Data (Million $) | 2010 | 2009 | 2008 | 2007 | 2006 | 2005 | 2004 | 2003 | 2002 | 2001 |
|---|---|---|---|---|---|---|---|---|---|---|
| Cash | 530 | 337 | 67.8 | 232 | 136 | 189 | 135 | 15.4 | 20.0 | 85.8 |
| Current Assets | 4,415 | 4,033 | 3,871 | 4,053 | 3,835 | 3,807 | 3,633 | 3,418 | 3,336 | 3,146 |
| Total Assets | 5,465 | 5,005 | 4,786 | 4,774 | 4,497 | 4,772 | 4,455 | 4,116 | 4,020 | 4,207 |
| Current Liabilities | 1,972 | 1,408 | 1,287 | 1,548 | 1,199 | 1,249 | 1,133 | 1,017 | 1,070 | 919 |
| Long Term Debt | 250 | 500 | 500 | 250 | 500 | 500 | 500 | 625 | 675 | 836 |
| Common Equity | 2,794 | 2,621 | 2,324 | 2,717 | 2,550 | 2,694 | 2,544 | 2,312 | 2,130 | 2,345 |
| Total Capital | 3,312 | 3,129 | 2,893 | 3,033 | 3,111 | 3,408 | 3,212 | 3,100 | 2,950 | 3,287 |
| Capital Expenditures | 85.4 | 142 | 105 | 116 | 126 | 85.7 | 72.1 | 73.9 | 64.8 | 41.9 |
| Cash Flow | 565 | 490 | 564 | 594 | 549 | 503 | 458 | 423 | 438 | 383 |
| Current Ratio | 2.2 | 2.9 | 3.0 | 2.6 | 3.2 | 3.0 | 3.2 | 3.4 | 3.1 | 3.4 |
| % Long Term Debt of Capitalization | 7.6 | 16.0 | 17.3 | 8.2 | 16.1 | 14.7 | 15.6 | 20.2 | 22.9 | 25.4 |
| % Net Income of Revenue | 4.2 | 4.0 | 4.3 | 4.7 | 4.5 | 4.5 | 4.3 | 4.2 | 4.4 | 3.6 |
| % Return on Assets | 9.1 | 8.2 | 10.0 | 10.9 | 10.3 | 9.5 | 9.2 | 8.6 | 8.9 | 7.1 |
| % Return on Equity | 17.6 | 16.2 | 18.9 | 19.2 | 18.1 | 16.7 | 16.3 | 15.9 | 16.4 | 12.9 |

Data as orig reptd.; bef. results of disc opers/spec. items. Per share data adj. for stk. divs.; EPS diluted. E-Estimated. NA-Not Available. NM-Not Meaningful. NR-Not Ranked. UR-Under Review.

**Office:** 2999 Cir 75 Pkwy, Atlanta, GA 30339.
**Telephone:** 770-953-1700.
**Website:** http://www.genpt.com
**Chrmn, Pres & CEO:** T. Gallagher

**Vice Chrmn, EVP, CFO & Chief Acctg Officer:** J.W. Nix
**COO:** M.D. Orr
**SVP & Treas:** F.M. Howard
**SVP & Secy:** C.B. Yancey

**Board Members:** M. B. Bullock, T. Gallagher, G. C. Guynn, J. R. Holder, J. D. Johns, M. M. Johns, J. H. Lanier, R. C. Loudermilk, Jr., W. B. Needham, J. W. Nix, G. W. Rollins

**Founded:** 1928
**Domicile:** Georgia
**Employees:** 29,500

# Genworth Financial Inc

STANDARD
&POOR'S

| S&P Recommendation | BUY ★★★★☆ | Price $5.39 (as of Nov 25, 2011) | 12-Mo. Target Price $9.00 | Investment Style Large-Cap Blend |
|---|---|---|---|---|

**GICS Sector** Financials
**Sub-Industry** Multi-line Insurance

**Summary** This insurance holding company serves lifestyle protection, retirement income and investment and mortgage insurance needs around the world.

## Key Stock Statistics (Source S&P, Vickers, company reports)

| | | | | | | | |
|---|---|---|---|---|---|---|---|
| 52-Wk Range | $14.77– 4.80 | S&P Oper. EPS 2011E | 0.52 | Market Capitalization(B) | $2.646 | Beta | 3.16 |
| Trailing 12-Month EPS | $-0.29 | S&P Oper. EPS 2012E | 1.35 | Yield (%) | Nil | S&P 3-Yr. Proj. EPS CAGR(%) | NM |
| Trailing 12-Month P/E | NM | P/E on S&P Oper. EPS 2011E | 10.4 | Dividend Rate/Share | Nil | S&P Credit Rating | BBB |
| $10K Invested 5 Yrs Ago | $1,700 | Common Shares Outstg. (M) | 490.9 | Institutional Ownership (%) | NM | | |

## Price Performance

30-Week Mov. Avg. · · · 10-Week Mov. Avg. – – GAAP Earnings vs. Previous Year   Volume Above Avg. STARS

12-Mo. Target Price — Relative Strength — ▲ Up ▼ Down ► No Change   Below Avg.

Options: ASE, CBOE, P, Ph

Analysis prepared by Equity Analyst **Cathy Seifert** on Nov 14, 2011, when the stock traded at **$6.73**.

## Highlights

➤ We believe GNW's earnings will benefit from lower losses at U.S. Mortgage Insurance and double-digit earnings growth in International. We believe Retirement and Protection earnings will rise modestly due to higher account values and new product introductions, but we expect weak fixed annuity sales. We forecast 10% to 12% earnings growth in life insurance on better pricing, strong long-term care sales, partially offset by higher funding costs, and lower persistency in term life.

➤ We look for loan modifications and higher cure rates to reduce losses at U.S. Mortgage Insurance. However, we expect that segment's results to be volatile, although we think another reserve strengthening is unlikely. We expect double-digit earnings growth in International mortgage insurance on stable housing markets in Canada and Australia. We believe sales growth will be sluggish in lifestyle protection due to a lack of consumer lending in Europe, but higher pricing and increased market penetration should accelerate earnings growth.

➤ We forecast operating EPS of $0.52 in 2011 and $1.35 in 2012. Our estimates exclude any realized investment gains or losses.

## Investment Rationale/Risk

➤ Our buy recommendation reflects the steep valuation discount for GNW versus peers, and our belief that the valuation does not properly reflect improving fundamentals and a strengthened balance sheet. While the U.S. Mortgage Insurance unit will likely remain unprofitable until late 2012, we expect losses to narrow. We think better results in Retirement and Protection and international mortgage insurance will improve ROE. We view GNW's capital and liquidity positions as weak versus peers, but its financial position has improved with better credit markets and capital raises. We think GNW's top-line trends will generally improve in 2011, but sales and flows should remain below historical levels.

➤ Risks to our recommendation and target price include a continued low interest rate environment; increased investment portfolio risks; elevated lapses in term life products; compressed long-term care margins; and a prolonged slowdown in the housing market.

➤ Our 12-month target price of $9.00 assumes the shares trade at 6.7X our 2012 operating EPS estimate and at a discount to book value. These multiples are still below peer averages.

## Qualitative Risk Assessment

| LOW | MEDIUM | HIGH |
|---|---|---|

Our risk assessment reflects the significant exposure of the mortgage insurance business to the volatile U.S. housing market. Also, we think GNW is vulnerable to investment losses and has a weaker capital position than peers, but its financial health continues to improve. Our assessment also reflects our view of the lower return on equity prospects for GNW's life insurance subsidiaries.

## Quantitative Evaluations

**S&P Quality Ranking**   NR

| D | C | B- | B | B+ | A- | A | A+ |
|---|---|---|---|---|---|---|---|

**Relative Strength Rank**   WEAK

18

LOWEST = 1          HIGHEST = 99

## Revenue/Earnings Data

### Revenue (Million $)

| | 1Q | 2Q | 3Q | 4Q | Year |
|---|---|---|---|---|---|
| 2011 | 2,568 | 2,655 | 2,521 | -- | -- |
| 2010 | 2,421 | 2,410 | 2,667 | 2,591 | 10,089 |
| 2009 | 1,734 | 2,483 | 2,391 | 2,461 | 9,069 |
| 2008 | 2,753 | 2,398 | 2,168 | 2,629 | 9,948 |
| 2007 | 2,710 | 2,765 | 2,875 | 2,775 | 11,125 |
| 2006 | 2,625 | 2,754 | 2,804 | 2,846 | 11,029 |

### Earnings Per Share ($)

| | | | | | |
|---|---|---|---|---|---|
| 2011 | 0.17 | -0.20 | 0.06 | E0.26 | E0.52 |
| 2010 | 0.36 | 0.08 | 0.17 | -0.33 | 0.29 |
| 2009 | -1.08 | -0.11 | 0.04 | 0.08 | -0.88 |
| 2008 | 0.27 | -0.25 | -0.60 | -0.74 | -1.32 |
| 2007 | 0.69 | 0.70 | 0.76 | 0.41 | 2.58 |
| 2006 | 0.69 | 0.68 | 0.65 | 0.81 | 2.83 |

Fiscal year ended Dec. 31. Next earnings report expected: Early February. EPS Estimates based on S&P Operating Earnings; historical GAAP earnings are as reported.

## Dividend Data

The most recent payment was $0.10 a share in October 2008.

# Genworth Financial Inc

**STANDARD &POOR'S**

## Business Summary November 14, 2011

CORPORATE OVERVIEW. Genworth Financial, Inc., carved out from General Electric (GE) in May 2004, is a U.S. insurance company with an expanding international presence. As of February 2011, GNW had operations in 25 countries and offered products and services to over 15 million consumers. The company believed it was one of the largest providers of private mortgage insurance outside the U.S. based on new insurance written. In addition, GNW believed that in the U.S. it was the largest individual provider of long-term care insurance, and also one of the largest providers of mortgage insurance, based on new insurance written. GNW was a leading provider of fixed immediate annuities in 2008, but lost a considerable amount of market share after the financial crisis, mainly given capital constraints at the company.

The company conducts its business through three major segments. The Retirement and Protection segment (67% of 2010 total revenues, 62% of 2009 total revenues) is comprised of wealth management (3.5%, 3.1%); retirement income (14%, 13%); life insurance (18%, 16%); and long-term care (32%, 30%). The International segment (25%, 28%) consists of the company's international

mortgage insurance business in Canada, Australia and Europe, in addition to proposals for other target countries for mortgage insurance. The segment also includes lifestyle protection, which provides payment protection insurance intended to help consumers meet their payment obligations in the event of illness, involuntary unemployment, disability or death. The third segment is U.S. Mortgage Insurance (7.5%, 9.1%), which facilitates home ownership by enabling borrowers to buy homes with low down payment mortgages. These products also help financial institutions manage their capital efficiently by reducing the capital required for low down payment mortgages. The company also has a Corporate and Other segment (0.1%, 0.2%), which includes unallocated corporate income and expenses, results of a small, non-core business, and most interest and other financing expenses.

## Company Financials Fiscal Year Ended Dec. 31

| Per Share Data ($) | 2010 | 2009 | 2008 | 2007 | 2006 | 2005 | 2004 | 2003 | 2002 | 2001 |
|---|---|---|---|---|---|---|---|---|---|---|
| Tangible Book Value | 24.25 | 20.77 | 15.71 | 10.98 | 24.20 | 24.51 | 21.69 | 20.18 | NA | NA |
| Operating Earnings | NA | NA | NA | NA | NA | NA | NA | NA | NA | NA |
| Earnings | 0.29 | -0.88 | -1.32 | 2.58 | 2.83 | 2.52 | 2.34 | 1.82 | NA | NA |
| S&P Core Earnings | 0.47 | 0.44 | 1.45 | 3.04 | 2.92 | 2.52 | 2.29 | 1.96 | NA | NA |
| Dividends | Nil | Nil | 0.40 | 0.37 | 0.32 | 0.27 | 0.07 | NA | NA | NA |
| Relative Payout | Nil | Nil | NM | 14% | 11% | 11% | 3% | NA | NA | NA |
| Prices:High | 19.36 | 13.68 | 25.57 | 37.16 | 36.47 | 35.25 | 27.84 | NA | NA | NA |
| Prices:Low | 10.26 | 0.78 | 0.70 | 23.26 | 31.00 | 25.72 | 18.75 | NA | NA | NA |
| P/E Ratio:High | 67 | NM | NM | 14 | 13 | 14 | 12 | NA | NA | NA |
| P/E Ratio:Low | 35 | NM | NM | 9 | 11 | 10 | 8 | NA | NA | NA |

| Income Statement Analysis (Million $) | | | | | | | | | | |
|---|---|---|---|---|---|---|---|---|---|---|
| Life Insurance in Force | 694,782 | 673,719 | 677 | 670 | NA | NA | NA | NA | NA | NA |
| Premium Income:Life A & H | NA | NA | NA | NA | NA | NA | NA | 6,252 | NA | NA |
| Premium Income:Casualty/Property. | NA | NA | NA | NA | NA | NA | NA | Nil | NA | NA |
| Net Investment Income | 3,266 | 3,033 | 3,730 | 4,135 | 3,837 | 3,536 | 3,648 | 2,928 | NA | NA |
| Total Revenue | 10,089 | 9,069 | 9,948 | 11,125 | 11,029 | 10,504 | 11,057 | 9,775 | 11,229 | 11,101 |
| Pretax Income | 76.0 | -792 | -942 | 1,606 | 1,918 | 1,798 | 1,638 | 1,263 | 1,791 | 1,821 |
| Net Operating Income | NA | NA | NA | NA | NA | NA | NA | NA | NA | NA |
| Net Income | 285 | -460 | -572 | 1,154 | 1,324 | 1,221 | 1,145 | 892 | 1,380 | 1,231 |
| S&P Core Earnings | 232 | 198 | 624 | 1,359 | 1,369 | 1,221 | 1,126 | 956 | NA | NA |

| Balance Sheet & Other Financial Data (Million $) | | | | | | | | | | |
|---|---|---|---|---|---|---|---|---|---|---|
| Cash & Equivalent | 3,865 | 5,693 | 8,064 | 3,864 | 3,222 | 2,608 | 2,125 | 1,630 | 1,569 | 881 |
| Premiums Due | 17,191 | 17,332 | 17,212 | 16,483 | NA | NA | NA | NA | NA | NA |
| Investment Assets:Bonds | 55,183 | 49,752 | 42,871 | 55,154 | 55,448 | 53,791 | 52,424 | 50,081 | NA | NA |
| Investment Assets:Stocks | 332 | 159 | 234 | 366 | NA | 367 | 374 | 387 | NA | NA |
| Investment Assets:Loans | 8,696 | 8,902 | 10,096 | 10,604 | 9,985 | 8,908 | 7,275 | 6,794 | NA | NA |
| Investment Assets:Total | 68,437 | 63,515 | 60,612 | 70,800 | 68,573 | 66,548 | 65,176 | 61,749 | 72,080 | 62,977 |
| Deferred Policy Costs | 7,256 | 7,341 | 7,786 | 7,034 | NA | 5,586 | 5,020 | 4,421 | NA | NA |
| Total Assets | 112,395 | 108,187 | 107,201 | 114,315 | 110,871 | 105,292 | 103,878 | 100,216 | 117,357 | 103,998 |
| Debt | 8,883 | 8,014 | 8,849 | 7,558 | 3,921 | 3,336 | 3,042 | 3,016 | NA | NA |
| Common Equity | 13,861 | 12,276 | 8,926 | 13,478 | 13,330 | 13,310 | 12,866 | 12,258 | 16,752 | 14,165 |
| Combined Loss-Expense Ratio | 69.0 | 243.0 | 198.0 | 93.0 | 49.0 | 48.0 | 50.0 | 51.0 | 39.0 | 50.0 |
| % Return on Revenue | 2.8 | NM | NM | 10.4 | 12.0 | 11.6 | 10.4 | 9.1 | 12.3 | 11.1 |
| % Return on Equity | 2.2 | NM | NM | 8.6 | 2.2 | 9.3 | 8.0 | 6.0 | 8.9 | NA |
| % Investment Yield | 4.3 | 5.2 | 6.0 | 5.9 | 5.7 | 5.4 | 5.2 | 5.4 | 5.9 | 12.4 |

Data as orig reptd.; bef. results of disc opers/spec. items. Per share data adj. for stk. divs.; EPS diluted. E-Estimated. NA-Not Available. NM-Not Meaningful. NR-Not Ranked. UR-Under Review.

**Office:** 6620 West Broad Street, Richmond, VA 23230.
**Telephone:** 804-281-6000.
**Email:** investorinfo@genworth.com
**Website:** http://www.genworth.com

**Chrmn, Pres & CEO:** M.D. Fraizer
**SVP & CFO:** M.P. Klein
**SVP, Secy & General Counsel:** L. Roday
**Chief Acctg Officer & Cntlr:** A.R. Corbin

**Investor Contact:** C. English (804-662-2614)
**Board Members:** S. W. Alesio, W. H. Bolinder, M. D. Fraizer, N. J. Karch, J. R. Kerrey, R. J. Lavizzo-Mourey, C. B. Mead, T. E. Moloney, J. A. Parke, J. S. Riepe

**Founded:** 2003
**Domicile:** Delaware
**Employees:** 6,500

# Gilead Sciences Inc

**STANDARD &POOR'S**

| S&P Recommendation | BUY ★★★★☆ | Price<br>$39.28 (as of Nov 25, 2011) | 12-Mo. Target Price<br>$52.00 | Investment Style<br>Large-Cap Growth |
| --- | --- | --- | --- | --- |

**GICS Sector** Health Care
**Sub-Industry** Biotechnology

**Summary** This biopharmaceutical company is engaged in the discovery, development and commercialization of treatments to fight viral, bacterial and fungal infections, respiratory disorders, and cardiovascular conditions.

## Key Stock Statistics (Source S&P, Vickers, company reports)

| | | | | | | | | |
| --- | --- | --- | --- | --- | --- | --- | --- | --- |
| 52-Wk Range | $43.49–34.45 | S&P Oper. EPS 2011E | 3.73 | Market Capitalization(B) | $29.505 | Beta | | 0.39 |
| Trailing 12-Month EPS | $3.42 | S&P Oper. EPS 2012E | 4.32 | Yield (%) | Nil | S&P 3-Yr. Proj. EPS CAGR(%) | | 13 |
| Trailing 12-Month P/E | 11.5 | P/E on S&P Oper. EPS 2011E | 10.5 | Dividend Rate/Share | Nil | S&P Credit Rating | | A- |
| $10K Invested 5 Yrs Ago | $11,876 | Common Shares Outstg. (M) | 751.1 | Institutional Ownership (%) | 90 | | | |

## Price Performance

30-Week Mov. Avg. · · · 10-Week Mov. Avg. – – GAAP Earnings vs. Previous Year   Volume Above Avg. ▮▮▮ STARS
12-Mo. Target Price — Relative Strength — ▲ Up ▼ Down ► No Change   Below Avg. ▮▮▮ ★

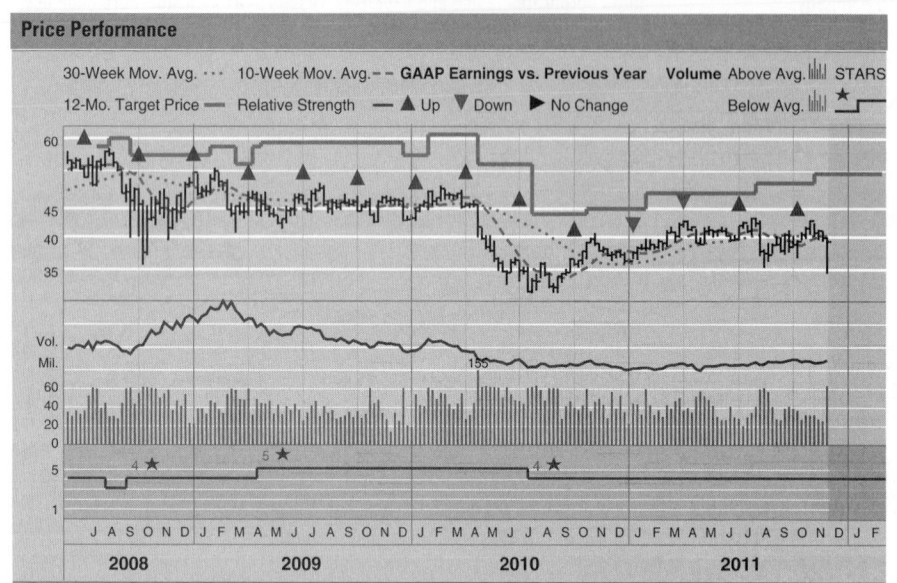

Options: ASE, CBOE, P, Ph

Analysis prepared by Equity Analyst **Steven Silver** on Nov 02, 2011, when the stock traded at **$40.98**.

## Qualitative Risk Assessment

| LOW | MEDIUM | HIGH |
| --- | --- | --- |

Our risk assessment reflects Gilead's dependence on its HIV drug franchise, and we see the company as subject to increasing pricing and reimbursement sensitivity in the global marketplace. We also see uncertainty surrounding GILD's ability to sustain its HIV franchise after patent expiration of its core combination therapy components.

## Quantitative Evaluations

**S&P Quality Ranking**                                    B

| D | C | B- | B | B+ | A- | A | A+ |
| --- | --- | --- | --- | --- | --- | --- | --- |

**Relative Strength Rank**                        MODERATE

69

LOWEST = 1                                    HIGHEST = 99

## Revenue/Earnings Data

### Revenue (Million $)

| | 1Q | 2Q | 3Q | 4Q | Year |
| --- | --- | --- | --- | --- | --- |
| 2011 | 1,926 | 2,137 | 2,122 | -- | -- |
| 2010 | 2,086 | 1,927 | 1,938 | 1,999 | 7,949 |
| 2009 | 1,530 | 1,647 | 1,801 | 2,032 | 7,011 |
| 2008 | 1,258 | 1,278 | 1,371 | 1,428 | 5,336 |
| 2007 | 1,028 | 1,048 | 1,059 | 1,095 | 4,230 |
| 2006 | 692.9 | 685.3 | 748.7 | 899.2 | 3,026 |

### Earnings Per Share ($)

| | | | | | |
| --- | --- | --- | --- | --- | --- |
| 2011 | 0.80 | 0.93 | 0.95 | E0.99 | E3.73 |
| 2010 | 0.92 | 0.79 | 0.83 | 0.76 | 3.32 |
| 2009 | 0.63 | 0.61 | 0.72 | 0.86 | 2.82 |
| 2008 | 0.51 | 0.46 | 0.53 | 0.60 | 2.10 |
| 2007 | 0.43 | 0.42 | 0.42 | 0.41 | 1.68 |
| 2006 | 0.28 | 0.28 | -0.06 | -1.81 | -1.30 |

Fiscal year ended Dec. 31. Next earnings report expected: NA. EPS Estimates based on S&P Operating Earnings; historical GAAP earnings are as reported.

## Dividend Data

No cash dividends have been paid.

## Highlights

► We estimate 2011 product revenues of $8.06 billion, which would be up 9% from 2010. We expect 9% growth in 2012, to $8.8 billion. While we see near-term revenue growth pressured by higher Medicaid rebates and other U.S. health care reform impacts, we view favorably GILD's dominant U.S. HIV drug market share, with an over 80% share of all new HIV patients, and positive trends for earlier HIV patient diagnosis and start of anti-viral treatment.

► We expect operating margins, including stock option expense, of 48.4% in 2011 and 50% in 2012, below 2010 levels, due to lower Tamiflu royalties and higher sales of lower-margin Atripla. However, we see long-term margin expansion should GILD secure key approvals for its wholly owned HIV "Quad Pill," which was filed for FDA approval in October 2011, and other Truvada-based combination drugs.

► We project adjusted EPS of $3.73 for 2011 and $4.32 for 2012, excluding acquisition costs. As of September 30, 2011, GILD had 779 million shares outstanding (diluted) and $5.5 billion in cash. We expect GILD to continue aggressively repurchasing shares in the coming years.

## Investment Rationale/Risk

► Despite near-term headwinds to GILD's core HIV franchise due to U.S. health care reform, variability in state HIV program purchases and concerns over HIV patent expirations late in the decade, we view GILD as a core long-term biotech holding with an attractive valuation. We are encouraged by prospects for next-generation combination HIV drugs to extend its market-leading HIV franchise, with enhanced economic terms. We see GILD as well funded to aggressively repurchase shares and to finance acquisitions of early-stage growth assets. However, we believe recent diversification efforts in building a cardiovascular unit have fallen short of expectations.

► Risks to our recommendation and target price include a slowdown in GILD's HIV product sales from competition or patent challenges, and failure to advance next-generation HIV therapies or complementary business units.

► Our 12-month target price of $52 is 12X our 2012 EPS estimate, roughly in line with our long-term growth rate for GILD, and a discount to our large-cap profitable biotech group target average, given long-term patent overhangs.

---

**Please read the Required Disclosures and Analyst Certification on the last page of this report.**

**The McGraw·Hill** Companies

# Gilead Sciences Inc

**STANDARD &POOR'S**

## Business Summary November 02, 2011

CORPORATE OVERVIEW. Gilead Sciences (GILD) focuses on the research, development and marketing of anti-infective medications, with a primary focus on treatments for HIV.

Truvada is among GILD's sales leaders, with 2010 sales of $2.65 billion, 6% above 2009. Truvada, approved in 2004, is a once-daily combination tablet formulated with previous-generation drugs Viread and Emtriva. Emtriva was the lead product of Triangle Pharmaceuticals, acquired in 2003. Viread was approved in 2001 to treat HIV patients who had become resistant to other reverse transcriptase inhibitors, as well as naive patients in front-line treatment settings. Viread sales rose 10% to $732 million in 2010, with most of its current use in treating hepatitis B.

In late 2004, GILD and Bristol-Myers Squibb (BMY) partnered on a combination tablet with Truvada and BMY's Sustiva. The formulation, marketed as Atripla, was launched in July 2006. GILD books Atripla sales and then pays BMY its 37% share for the Sustiva portion of the drug, which GILD counts as cost of goods on its financial statements. Atripla generated 2010 sales of $2.93 billion, up 23% from 2009, and surpassed Truvada in sales during the fourth quarter of 2009. Atripla received EU approval in December 2007 and began to

be launched in 2008. Atripla was available in all five of the largest European markets, after a mid-2009 launch in France.

Hepsera, approved for treatment of chronic hepatitis B in the U.S. and EU, saw sales decline by 26% in 2010 to $201 million, due to increased use of Viread in this indication. AmBisome is a liposomal formulation of amphotericin B, an antifungal agent that is approved for life-threatening fungal infections including cryptococcal meningitis in AIDS patients, generated sales of $306 million in 2010, 2% higher than in 2009. Tamiflu, an orally administered treatment for influenza A and B, was approved by the FDA for adults in October 1999 and for children aged 1-12 in December 2005. Roche markets the drug, paying GILD a 21%-22% royalty. During 2009, Roche increased production of Tamiflu in response to rising demand following the spring 2009 outbreak of swine flu. For 2010, Tamiflu-related royalties rose by 21% to $475 million, but have slowed considerably after the first quarter and throughout 2011.

## Company Financials Fiscal Year Ended Dec. 31

| Per Share Data ($) | 2010 | 2009 | 2008 | 2007 | 2006 | 2005 | 2004 | 2003 | 2002 | 2001 |
|---|---|---|---|---|---|---|---|---|---|---|
| Tangible Book Value | 5.53 | 5.38 | 4.56 | 3.71 | 1.97 | 3.30 | 2.09 | 1.17 | 0.72 | 0.58 |
| Cash Flow | 3.61 | 3.05 | 2.15 | 1.71 | -1.24 | 0.90 | 0.51 | -0.06 | 0.10 | 0.08 |
| Earnings | 3.32 | 2.82 | 2.10 | 1.68 | -1.30 | 0.86 | 0.50 | -0.09 | 0.09 | 0.06 |
| S&P Core Earnings | 3.31 | 2.81 | 2.10 | 1.67 | -1.29 | 0.78 | 0.39 | -0.17 | 0.01 | -0.14 |
| Dividends | Nil | Nil | Nil | Nil | Nil | Nil | Nil | Nil | Nil | Nil |
| Payout Ratio | Nil | Nil | Nil | Nil | Nil | Nil | Nil | Nil | Nil | Nil |
| Prices:High | 49.50 | 53.28 | 57.63 | 47.90 | 35.00 | 28.26 | 19.55 | 17.65 | 10.00 | 9.21 |
| Prices:Low | 31.73 | 40.62 | 35.60 | 30.96 | 26.24 | 15.20 | 12.88 | 7.81 | 6.52 | 3.11 |
| P/E Ratio:High | 15 | 19 | 27 | 29 | NM | 33 | 39 | NM | NM | NM |
| P/E Ratio:Low | 10 | 14 | 17 | 18 | NM | 18 | 26 | NM | NM | NM |

| Income Statement Analysis (Million $) | 2010 | 2009 | 2008 | 2007 | 2006 | 2005 | 2004 | 2003 | 2002 | 2001 |
|---|---|---|---|---|---|---|---|---|---|---|
| Revenue | 7,949 | 7,011 | 5,336 | 4,230 | 3,026 | 2,028 | 1,325 | 868 | 467 | 234 |
| Operating Income | 4,396 | 3,802 | 2,741 | 2,201 | 1,683 | 1,148 | 656 | 361 | 95.4 | -106 |
| Depreciation | 265 | 213 | 51.7 | 36.9 | 47.3 | 36.8 | 24.4 | 20.9 | 14.4 | 14.7 |
| Interest Expense | 109 | 69.7 | 12.1 | 13.5 | 20.4 | 0.44 | 7.35 | 21.9 | 13.9 | 14.0 |
| Pretax Income | 3,914 | 3,502 | 2,726 | 2,261 | -644 | 1,158 | 656 | -168 | 73.4 | 55.3 |
| Effective Tax Rate | NA | 25.0% | 26.5% | 29.0% | NM | 30.0% | 31.5% | NM | 1.77% | 7.48% |
| Net Income | 2,901 | 2,636 | 2,011 | 1,615 | -1,190 | 814 | 449 | -72.0 | 72.1 | 51.2 |
| S&P Core Earnings | 2,895 | 2,630 | 2,008 | 1,610 | -1,188 | 737 | 354 | -133 | 8.55 | -108 |

| Balance Sheet & Other Financial Data (Million $) | 2010 | 2009 | 2008 | 2007 | 2006 | 2005 | 2004 | 2003 | 2002 | 2001 |
|---|---|---|---|---|---|---|---|---|---|---|
| Cash | 5,318 | 3,905 | 3,240 | 1,172 | 937 | 2,324 | 1,254 | 707 | 942 | 583 |
| Current Assets | 8,144 | 4,813 | 4,300 | 3,028 | 2,429 | 3,092 | 1,850 | 1,266 | 1,184 | 708 |
| Total Assets | 11,593 | 9,699 | 7,019 | 5,835 | 4,086 | 3,765 | 2,156 | 1,555 | 1,288 | 795 |
| Current Liabilities | 2,465 | 1,872 | 1,221 | 736 | 764 | 455 | 253 | 186 | 105 | 80.1 |
| Long Term Debt | 3,006 | 1,322 | 1,300 | 1,301 | 1,300 | 241 | 0.23 | 345 | 595 | 250 |
| Common Equity | 6,122 | 6,505 | 4,152 | 3,460 | 1,816 | 3,028 | 1,871 | 1,003 | 571 | 452 |
| Total Capital | 9,128 | 7,827 | 5,672 | 4,772 | 3,169 | 3,277 | 1,871 | 1,348 | 1,166 | 703 |
| Capital Expenditures | 61.9 | 230 | 115 | 78.7 | 105 | 2,226 | 51.4 | 38.6 | 17.6 | 26.3 |
| Cash Flow | 3,155 | 2,849 | 2,063 | 1,652 | -1,143 | 851 | 474 | -51.1 | 86.5 | 65.9 |
| Current Ratio | 3.3 | 3.4 | 3.5 | 4.1 | 3.2 | 6.8 | 7.3 | 6.8 | 11.3 | 8.8 |
| % Long Term Debt of Capitalization | 32.9 | 16.9 | 22.9 | 27.2 | 41.0 | 7.3 | NM | 25.6 | 51.0 | 35.6 |
| % Net Income of Revenue | 36.5 | 37.6 | 37.7 | 38.2 | NM | 40.1 | 33.9 | NM | 15.4 | 21.9 |
| % Return on Assets | 27.3 | 31.5 | 31.3 | 32.6 | NM | 27.5 | 24.2 | NM | 6.9 | 6.9 |
| % Return on Equity | 46.5 | 49.5 | 52.8 | 61.2 | NM | 33.2 | 31.3 | NM | 14.1 | 12.7 |

Data as orig reptd.; bef. results of disc opers/spec. items. Per share data adj. for stk. divs.; EPS diluted. E-Estimated. NA-Not Available. NM-Not Meaningful. NR-Not Ranked. UR-Under Review.

**Office:** 333 Lakeside Drive, Foster City, CA 94404.
**Telephone:** 650-574-3000.
**Email:** investor_relations@gilead.com
**Website:** http://www.gilead.com

**Chrmn & CEO:** J.C. Martin
**Pres & COO:** J.F. Milligan
**EVP & CSO:** N.W. Bischofberger
**SVP, CFO & Chief Acctg Officer:** R.L. Washington

**Secy:** G.H. Alton
**Investor Contact:** S. Hubbard (650 522-5715)
**Auditor:** ERNST & YOUNG, New York, NY
**Board Members:** J. F. Cogan, V. E. Davignon, J. M. Denny, C. A. Hills, K. E. Lofton, J. W. Madigan, J. C. Martin, G. E. Moore, N. G. Moore, R. J. Whitley, G. E. Wilson, P. Wold-Olsen

**Founded:** 1987
**Domicile:** Delaware
**Employees:** 4,000

**The McGraw-Hill Companies**

# Goldman Sachs Group Inc (The)

**STANDARD &POOR'S**

| S&P Recommendation | HOLD ★ ★ ★ ★ ☆ | Price $88.75 (as of Nov 25, 2011) | 12-Mo. Target Price $115.00 | Investment Style Large-Cap Growth |
|---|---|---|---|---|

**GICS Sector** Financials
**Sub-Industry** Investment Banking & Brokerage

**Summary** Goldman Sachs is one of the world's leading investment banking and securities companies.

## Key Stock Statistics (Source S&P, Vickers, company reports)

| | | | | | | | |
|---|---|---|---|---|---|---|---|
| 52-Wk Range | $175.34–84.27 | S&P Oper. EPS 2011E | 4.92 | Market Capitalization(B) | $43.693 | Beta | 1.40 |
| Trailing 12-Month EPS | $6.57 | S&P Oper. EPS 2012E | 14.12 | Yield (%) | 1.58 | S&P 3-Yr. Proj. EPS CAGR(%) | -12 |
| Trailing 12-Month P/E | 13.5 | P/E on S&P Oper. EPS 2011E | 18.0 | Dividend Rate/Share | $1.40 | S&P Credit Rating | A |
| $10K Invested 5 Yrs Ago | $4,604 | Common Shares Outstg. (M) | 492.3 | Institutional Ownership (%) | 69 | | |

## Price Performance

30-Week Mov. Avg. · · · 10-Week Mov. Avg. – – GAAP Earnings vs. Previous Year Volume Above Avg. STARS
12-Mo. Target Price — Relative Strength — ▲ Up ▼ Down ► No Change Below Avg. ★

Options: ASE, CBOE, P, Ph

Analysis prepared by Equity Analyst **Robert McMillan** on Oct 27, 2011, when the stock traded at **$114.73**.

## Highlights

➤ Third-quarter 2011 trading revenues were weak, reflecting heightened risk aversion and volatility due to ongoing fears about sovereign risk and slowing economic growth around the world. Consequently, total net revenues fell 60%, driven by a 33% fall in the investment banking business, a 13% drop in institutional client services, a 4% decline in investment management and a loss in lending and investing versus a gain last year. We look for weak market conditions to persist for the rest of this year, causing net revenues to decrease about 23% for full-year 2011. However, we expect that GS, with its powerful franchise, will benefit from improving investor and business sentiment in 2012, and we see revenues rising 21% next year.

➤ We forecast that the compensation ratio will be about 44% in both 2011 and 2012. We expect non-compensation costs to vary with activity levels, and we see the pretax margin narrowing to 22% in 2011, from 33% in 2010, before widening to 28% in 2012.

➤ We estimate EPS of $4.92 in 2011, rising to $14.12 in 2012.

## Investment Rationale/Risk

➤ We view positively GS's capital position and global reach. However, we think results will be tempered in the near term by macroeconomic headwinds that may subdue client activity levels as well as by the potential charges stemming from lawsuits and government agency investigations. All told, however, we think GS's strong franchise and latent earnings power offsets the downside risk of further potential legal developments. Going forward, we expect GS to place more importance on client execution services, asset management and expansion in developing countries.

➤ Risks to our recommendation and target price include stock and bond market depreciation and stricter regulations.

➤ Our 12-month target price of $115 is based on a multiple of 9.5X our forward 12-month EPS estimate of $12.12; the shares recently traded at 8.8X our forward 12-month estimate. We think the valuation multiple will expand as economic uncertainty and market volatility ease and GS's businesses rebound over the course of 2012.

## Qualitative Risk Assessment

| LOW | MEDIUM | HIGH |
|---|---|---|

Our risk assessment reflects our view of the company's global footprint and strong client relationships, offset by industry cyclicality, GS's high leverage ratio, litigation, and proposed new government regulations.

## Quantitative Evaluations

**S&P Quality Ranking** A-

| D | C | B- | B | B+ | A- | A | A+ |
|---|---|---|---|---|---|---|---|

**Relative Strength Rank** WEAK

21

LOWEST = 1    HIGHEST = 99

## Revenue/Earnings Data

**Revenue (Million $)**

| | 1Q | 2Q | 3Q | 4Q | Year |
|---|---|---|---|---|---|
| 2011 | 13,643 | 7,281 | 1,998 | -- | -- |
| 2010 | 14,358 | 10,524 | 10,712 | 10,373 | 45,967 |
| 2009 | 11,880 | 15,189 | 13,682 | 10,922 | 51,673 |
| 2008 | 18,629 | 17,643 | 13,625 | 3,682 | 53,579 |
| 2007 | 22,280 | 20,351 | 23,803 | 21,534 | 87,968 |
| 2006 | 17,246 | 18,002 | 15,979 | 18,126 | 69,353 |

**Earnings Per Share ($)**

| | | | | | |
|---|---|---|---|---|---|
| 2011 | 1.56 | 1.85 | -0.84 | E2.35 | E4.92 |
| 2010 | 5.59 | 0.78 | 2.98 | 3.79 | 13.18 |
| 2009 | 3.39 | 4.93 | 5.25 | 8.20 | 22.13 |
| 2008 | 3.23 | 4.58 | 1.81 | -4.97 | 4.47 |
| 2007 | 6.67 | 4.93 | 1.81 | 7.01 | 24.73 |
| 2006 | 5.08 | 4.78 | 3.26 | 6.59 | 19.69 |

Fiscal year ended Dec. 31. Next earnings report expected: NA. EPS Estimates based on S&P Operating Earnings; historical GAAP earnings are as reported.

## Dividend Data (Dates: mm/dd Payment Date: mm/dd/yy)

| Amount ($) | Date Decl. | Ex-Div. Date | Stk. of Record | Payment Date |
|---|---|---|---|---|
| 0.350 | 01/18 | 02/28 | 03/02 | 03/30/11 |
| 0.350 | 04/19 | 05/27 | 06/01 | 06/29/11 |
| 0.350 | 07/19 | 08/30 | 09/01 | 09/29/11 |
| 0.350 | 10/18 | 11/29 | 12/01 | 12/29/11 |

Dividends have been paid since 1999. Source: Company reports.

# Goldman Sachs Group Inc (The)

**STANDARD &POOR'S**

## Business Summary October 27, 2011

CORPORATE OVERVIEW. Goldman Sachs (GS) is a global investment banking, securities and investment management firm that provides a wide range of services to corporations, financial institutions, governments and high-net-worth individuals. GS operates through three core businesses: Trading and Principal Investments, Investment Banking, and Asset Management and Securities Services. In January 2011, GS announced that going forward it would modify its financial reporting disclosures to increase transparency of its operations and improve client and investor relations.

GS breaks down its operations into four distinct segments. Investment Banking (12% of 2010 net revenues) provides a broad range of investment banking services to a diverse group of corporations, financial institutions, governments and individuals. The activities of the Investment Banking business are divided into two segments: Financial Advisory and Underwriting. The Financial Advisory segment includes advisory assignments with respect to mergers and acquisitions, divestitures, corporate defense activities, restructurings and spin-offs, while the Underwriting segment includes public offerings and private placements of equity and debt instruments.

Investment Management (12% of 2010 net revenues) offers a broad array of investment strategies, advice and planning across all major asset classes to a diverse group of institutions and individuals worldwide, and provides prime

brokerage, financing services and securities lending services to mutual funds, pension funds, hedge funds, foundations, and high net worth individuals. GS's assets under management reached $840 billion at the end of 2010.

The segment formerly classified as Trading and Principal Investments is now separated into Institutional Client Services (ICS) and Investing and Lending. ICS (56% of 2010 net revenues) contributes the majority of GS's revenues and includes the revenues that GS generates from client execution activities related to market making in a variety of products. In addition to market making and execution operations, revenues from the firm's Securities Services business, formerly included in Asset Management and Securities Services are included in ICS. Together, these operations comprise the majority of the firm's client franchise businesses.

Investing and Lending (20% of 2010 net revenues) pertains to the revenues GS derives from proprietary lending and investing. GS invests independently and alongside clients across various asset classes, both directly and indirectly through funds, and the results of these activities are included in this segment.

## Company Financials Fiscal Year Ended Dec. 31

| Per Share Data ($) | 2010 | 2009 | 2008 | 2007 | 2006 | 2005 | 2004 | 2003 | 2002 | 2001 |
|---|---|---|---|---|---|---|---|---|---|---|
| Tangible Book Value | 118.59 | 108.32 | 104.56 | 101.62 | 119.66 | 52.15 | 52.14 | 45.73 | 40.18 | 38.30 |
| Cash Flow | 15.91 | 25.66 | 7.24 | 27.68 | 20.78 | 12.22 | 9.90 | 6.97 | 5.20 | 5.39 |
| Earnings | 13.18 | 22.13 | 4.47 | 24.73 | 19.69 | 11.21 | 8.92 | 5.87 | 4.03 | 4.26 |
| S&P Core Earnings | 14.11 | 22.20 | 4.40 | 24.76 | 19.72 | 11.12 | 8.63 | 5.26 | 3.30 | 3.60 |
| Dividends | 1.40 | 1.52 | 1.40 | 1.40 | 1.30 | 1.00 | 1.00 | 0.74 | 0.48 | 0.48 |
| Payout Ratio | 11% | 7% | 31% | 6% | 7% | 9% | 11% | 13% | 12% | 11% |
| Prices:High | 186.41 | 193.60 | 215.05 | 250.70 | 206.70 | 134.99 | 110.88 | 100.78 | 97.25 | 120.00 |
| Prices:Low | 129.50 | 59.13 | 47.41 | 157.38 | 124.23 | 94.75 | 83.29 | 61.02 | 58.57 | 63.27 |
| P/E Ratio:High | 14 | 9 | 27 | 10 | 10 | 12 | 12 | 17 | 24 | 28 |
| P/E Ratio:Low | 10 | 3 | 6 | 6 | 6 | 8 | 9 | 10 | 15 | 15 |
| **Income Statement Analysis** (Million $) | | | | | | | | | | |
| Commissions | 4,810 | 4,797 | 5,179 | 12,286 | 10,140 | 6,689 | 5,941 | 4,317 | 3,273 | 3,020 |
| Interest Income | 12,309 | 13,907 | 35,633 | 45,968 | 35,186 | 21,250 | 11,914 | 10,751 | 11,269 | 16,620 |
| Total Revenue | 45,967 | 51,673 | 53,579 | 87,968 | 69,353 | 43,391 | 29,839 | 23,623 | 22,854 | 31,138 |
| Interest Expense | 6,806 | 6,500 | 31,357 | 41,981 | 31,688 | 18,153 | 8,888 | 7,600 | 8,868 | 15,327 |
| Pretax Income | 12,892 | 19,829 | 2,336 | 17,604 | 14,560 | 8,273 | 6,676 | 4,445 | 3,253 | 3,696 |
| Effective Tax Rate | 35.2% | 32.5% | 0.60% | 34.1% | 34.5% | 32.0% | 31.8% | 32.4% | 35.0% | 37.5% |
| Net Income | 8,354 | 13,385 | 2,322 | 11,599 | 9,537 | 5,626 | 4,553 | 3,005 | 2,114 | 2,310 |
| S&P Core Earnings | 8,214 | 12,196 | 2,009 | 11,419 | 9,416 | 5,560 | 4,406 | 2,693 | 1,737 | 1,949 |
| **Balance Sheet & Other Financial Data** (Million $) | | | | | | | | | | |
| Total Assets | 911,332 | 848,942 | 884,547 | 1,119,796 | 838,201 | 706,804 | 531,379 | 403,799 | 355,574 | 312,218 |
| Cash Items | 754,123 | 74,954 | 122,404 | 131,821 | 87,283 | 61,666 | 52,544 | 36,802 | 25,211 | 29,043 |
| Receivables | 244,446 | 257,839 | 271,359 | 425,596 | 312,355 | 75,381 | 52,545 | 36,377 | 28,938 | 33,463 |
| Securities Owned | 356,953 | 342,402 | 338,325 | 452,595 | 416,687 | 238,043 | 183,880 | 160,719 | 129,775 | 108,885 |
| Securities Borrowed | 11,212 | 15,207 | 17,060 | 28,624 | 22,208 | 23,331 | 19,394 | 17,528 | 12,238 | 81,579 |
| Due Brokers & Customers | 190,504 | 185,634 | 254,043 | 318,453 | 223,874 | 188,318 | 161,221 | 109,028 | 95,590 | 97,297 |
| Other Liabilities | 30,011 | 33,855 | 23,216 | 38,907 | 31,866 | 13,830 | 10,360 | 8,144 | 6,002 | 7,129 |
| Capitalization:Debt | 174,399 | 185,085 | 168,220 | 164,174 | 122,842 | 100,007 | 80,696 | 57,482 | 38,711 | 31,016 |
| Capitalization:Equity | 70,399 | 63,757 | 47,898 | 39,700 | 32,686 | 26,252 | 25,079 | 21,632 | 19,003 | 18,231 |
| Capitalization:Total | 251,755 | 255,799 | 232,589 | 206,974 | 189,521 | 128,009 | 105,775 | 79,114 | 57,714 | 49,247 |
| % Return on Revenue | 18.2 | 25.9 | 4.3 | 13.1 | 13.8 | 13.0 | 15.3 | 12.7 | 9.3 | 7.4 |
| % Return on Assets | 0.9 | 1.5 | 0.2 | 1.1 | 1.2 | 0.9 | 1.0 | 0.8 | 0.6 | 0.8 |
| % Return on Equity | 11.5 | 24.0 | 4.7 | 32.0 | 31.9 | 21.9 | 19.5 | 14.8 | 11.4 | 13.3 |

Data as orig reptd.; bef. results of disc opers/spec. items. Per share data adj. for stk. divs.; EPS diluted. Prior to 2009, fiscal year ended November 30. E-Estimated. NA-Not Available. NM-Not Meaningful. NR-Not Ranked. UR-Under Review.

**Office:** 85 Broad Street, New York, NY 10004.
**Telephone:** 212-902-1000.
**Email:** gs-investor-relations@gs.com
**Website:** http://www.gs.com

**Chrmn & CEO:** L.C. Blankfein
**Pres & COO:** G.D. Cohn
**EVP & CFO:** D.A. Viniar
**EVP & Secy:** E.E. Stecher

**EVP & Secy:** G.K. Palm
**Investor Contact:** J. Andrews (212-357-2674)
**Board Members:** L. C. Blankfein, J. H. Bryan, M. M. Burns, G. D. Cohn, C. Dahlback, S. Friedman, W. W. George, J. A. Johnson, L. D. Juliber, L. N. Mittal, J. J. Schiro, D. L. Spar

**Founded:** 1869
**Domicile:** Delaware
**Employees:** 35,700

The McGraw-Hill Companies

# Goodrich Corp

**STANDARD &POOR'S**

| S&P Recommendation HOLD ★★★☆☆ | Price $122.96 (as of Nov 28, 2011) | 12-Mo. Target Price $128.00 | Investment Style Large-Cap Value |
|---|---|---|---|

**GICS Sector** Industrials
**Sub-Industry** Aerospace & Defense

**Summary** In September 2011, Goodrich, a provider of aerospace components, systems and services, agreed to be acquired by United Technologies in an all cash transaction.

## Key Stock Statistics (Source S&P, Vickers, company reports)

| | | | | | | | |
|---|---|---|---|---|---|---|---|
| 52-Wk Range | $123.54– 79.71 | S&P Oper. EPS 2011E | 6.05 | Market Capitalization(B) | $15.395 | Beta | 1.02 |
| Trailing 12-Month EPS | $5.64 | S&P Oper. EPS 2012E | 6.50 | Yield (%) | 0.94 | S&P 3-Yr. Proj. EPS CAGR(%) | 16 |
| Trailing 12-Month P/E | 21.8 | P/E on S&P Oper. EPS 2011E | 20.3 | Dividend Rate/Share | $1.16 | S&P Credit Rating | BBB+ |
| $10K Invested 5 Yrs Ago | $29,483 | Common Shares Outstg. (M) | 125.2 | Institutional Ownership (%) | 91 | | |

## Price Performance

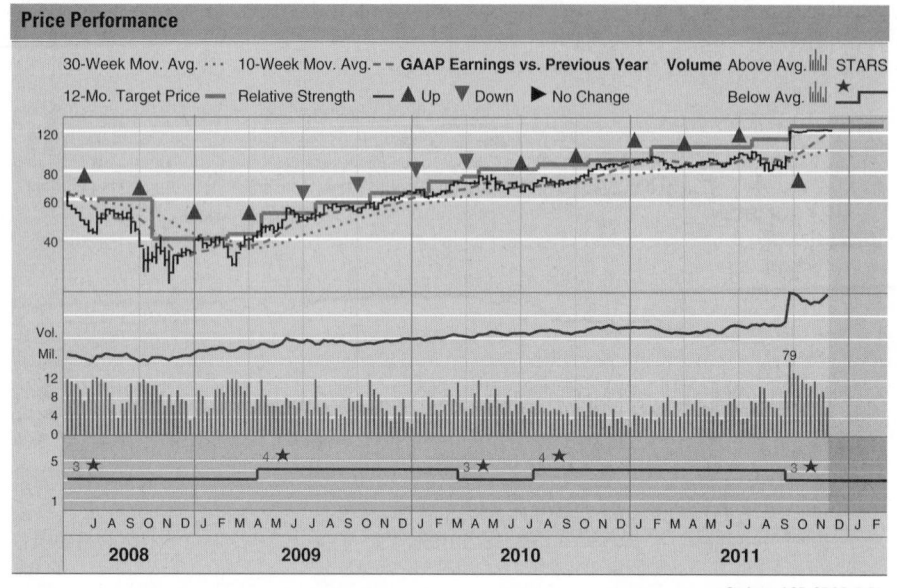

30-Week Mov. Avg. · · · 10-Week Mov. Avg. — **GAAP Earnings vs. Previous Year** Volume Above Avg. STARS
12-Mo. Target Price — Relative Strength — ▲ Up ▼ Down ► No Change Below Avg.

Options: ASE, CBOE, P, Ph

Analysis prepared by Equity Analyst **R. Tortoriello** on Nov 28, 2011, when the stock traded at **$122.82**.

## Highlights

► On September 21, United Technologies (UTX 70 Buy) agreed to purchase all common shares of GR for $127.50 per share in cash. UTX expects to finance the transaction through a combined debt and equity issuance, with equity expected to be about 25% of the total. The purchase price represents an enterprise value multiple of 11X our 2012 EBITDA estimate for GR ($1.64 billion). We view this as a fair multiple, since GR's average EV/EBITDA multiple since 2003, when Marshall Larsen became CEO, is 8.8X. We estimate sales growth of 16% in 2011 for GR, and 6% in 2012.

► We estimate segment operating margins of 17.5% in 2011, up from 16.6% in 2010. For 2012, we project a slight further increase to 17.7%.

► We estimate EPS of $6.05 in 2011, with growth to $6.50 in 2012. We expect free cash flow (cash generated from operations less capital expenditures) of about $5.35 per share in 2011, up significantly from $2.31 in 2010, due primarily to decreased cash pension contributions in 2011.

## Investment Rationale/Risk

► We expect a strong increase in commercial aftermarket demand in 2012, as we see passenger air traffic trending up and believe that maintenance schedules and low parts inventories mean airlines must increase spending. We see this demand positively affecting GR's profitability. Boeing and Airbus have announced planned production increases for their narrow-body models and for the 777 (Boeing), which began in late 2010 and stretch through 2014. In addition, the business jet market should improve in 2012, in our opinion. We also note our view of strong defense sales for GR, despite an overall weakening defense market.

► Risks to our recommendation and target price include the potential that the purchase of GR by UTX falls through due to UTX being unable to raise equity financing for the deal due to a declining U.S. equity market, or the risk that the deal could face opposition from anti-trust regulators.

► Our 12-month target price of $128 is based on United Technologies' offer price, as we view the deal as likely to go through.

## Qualitative Risk Assessment

| LOW | MEDIUM | HIGH |
|---|---|---|

Our risk assessment is based in part on GR's S&P Quality Ranking of B+ (average), which reflects its uneven earnings and dividend record of the past 10 years. We also take into account GR's long-term debt-to-capital ratio of 38% as of June 30, 2011, which is slightly above average for peers in the aerospace & defense sub-industry.

## Quantitative Evaluations

**S&P Quality Ranking** B+

| D | C | B- | B | B+ | A- | A | A+ |
|---|---|---|---|---|---|---|---|

**Relative Strength Rank** STRONG

93

LOWEST = 1          HIGHEST = 99

## Revenue/Earnings Data

**Revenue (Million $)**

| | 1Q | 2Q | 3Q | 4Q | Year |
|---|---|---|---|---|---|
| 2011 | 1,896 | 2,001 | 2,033 | -- | -- |
| 2010 | 1,695 | 1,718 | 1,748 | 1,806 | 6,967 |
| 2009 | 1,696 | 1,700 | 1,648 | 1,642 | 6,686 |
| 2008 | 1,745 | 1,849 | 1,772 | 1,695 | 7,062 |
| 2007 | 1,589 | 1,622 | 1,602 | 1,668 | 6,392 |
| 2006 | 1,424 | 1,483 | 1,436 | 1,535 | 5,878 |

**Earnings Per Share ($)**

| | | | | | |
|---|---|---|---|---|---|
| 2011 | 1.52 | 1.38 | 1.57 | E1.58 | E6.05 |
| 2010 | 0.86 | 1.24 | 1.25 | 1.15 | 4.50 |
| 2009 | 1.35 | 1.15 | 1.12 | 0.83 | 4.43 |
| 2008 | 1.21 | 1.44 | 1.33 | 1.35 | 5.33 |
| 2007 | 0.78 | 0.98 | 1.10 | 1.05 | 3.89 |
| 2006 | 1.59 | 0.64 | 0.80 | 0.78 | 3.80 |

Fiscal year ended Dec. 31. Next earnings report expected: Early February. EPS Estimates based on S&P Operating Earnings; historical GAAP earnings are as reported.

## Dividend Data (Dates: mm/dd Payment Date: mm/dd/yy)

| Amount ($) | Date Decl. | Ex-Div. Date | Stk. of Record | Payment Date |
|---|---|---|---|---|
| 0.290 | 02/15 | 02/25 | 03/01 | 04/01/11 |
| 0.290 | 04/19 | 05/27 | 06/01 | 07/01/11 |
| 0.290 | 07/22 | 08/30 | 09/01 | 10/03/11 |
| 0.290 | 10/25 | 11/29 | 12/01 | 01/03/12 |

Dividends have been paid since 1939. Source: Company reports.

---

**Please read the Required Disclosures and Analyst Certification on the last page of this report.**

**The McGraw·Hill Companies**

# Goodrich Corp

**STANDARD &POOR'S**

## Business Summary November 28, 2011

CORPORATE OVERVIEW. Goodrich Corp., a $7.8 billion in estimated 2011 revenue global aircraft components maker and services provider, is also a leading supplier of systems and products to the global defense and aerospace markets. Operations are divided into three segments.

Nacelles and Interior Systems (33% of revenues and 48% of operating profits in 2010) manufactures products and provides maintenance, repair and overhaul associated with aircraft engines, including thrust reversers, cowlings, nozzles and their components (a nacelle is the structure that surrounds an aircraft engine and includes all of the foregoing items), and aircraft interior products, including evacuation slides, aircraft crew and ejection seats, and cargo and lighting systems. N&IS's largest customers include Airbus, Boeing, Rolls-Royce and global airlines. Primary competitors in this market include Aircelle (a subsidiary of SAFRAN), GE, and Spirit Aerosystems.

Actuation and Landing Systems (36% of revenues and 24% of operating profit) provides systems, components and related services pertaining to aircraft taxi, takeoff, flight control, landing and stopping, as well as engine components, including fuel delivery systems and rotating assemblies. Key products include

primary and secondary flight controls; helicopter main and tail rotor actuation; engine and nacelle actuation; precision weapon actuation; aircraft wheels, brakes, and brake control systems; and landing gear. A&LS and Messier-Dowty (a division of France-based SAFRAN) each control about 50% of the global landing gear market. Other competitors include Honeywell (wheels and brakes), Meggitt Aircraft Braking Systems, Messier-Bugati (wheels and brakes), Parker Hannifin (actuation, fuel systems), and United Technologies (actuation).

The unit is also a major global provider of aircraft maintenance, repair and overhaul (MRO) services. A&LS's MRO customers mostly comprise the world's major airlines and aircraft leasing companies. Primary aircraft maintenance competitors include TIMCO Aviation Services, SIA Engineering Co., Singapore Technologies and Lufthansa Technik.

## Company Financials Fiscal Year Ended Dec. 31

| Per Share Data ($) | 2010 | 2009 | 2008 | 2007 | 2006 | 2005 | 2004 | 2003 | 2002 | 2001 |
|---|---|---|---|---|---|---|---|---|---|---|
| Tangible Book Value | 7.27 | 5.63 | 2.42 | 7.15 | 1.31 | NM | NM | NM | NM | 4.66 |
| Cash Flow | 6.84 | 6.49 | 7.00 | 5.48 | 5.78 | 3.79 | 3.18 | 2.18 | 3.31 | 3.28 |
| Earnings | 4.50 | 4.43 | 5.33 | 3.89 | 3.80 | 1.97 | 1.30 | 0.33 | 1.57 | 1.65 |
| S&P Core Earnings | 4.99 | 5.03 | 4.21 | 3.77 | 3.94 | 2.10 | 1.57 | 0.42 | 0.42 | 0.41 |
| Dividends | 1.10 | 1.02 | 0.93 | 0.83 | 1.00 | 0.80 | 0.80 | 0.80 | 0.88 | 1.10 |
| Payout Ratio | 24% | 23% | 17% | 21% | 26% | 41% | 62% | 242% | 56% | 67% |
| Prices:High | 88.60 | 65.93 | 71.14 | 75.74 | 47.45 | 45.82 | 33.90 | 30.30 | 34.45 | 44.50 |
| Prices:Low | 60.10 | 29.95 | 25.11 | 44.97 | 37.15 | 30.11 | 26.60 | 12.20 | 14.17 | 15.91 |
| P/E Ratio:High | 20 | 15 | 13 | 19 | 12 | 23 | 26 | 92 | 22 | 27 |
| P/E Ratio:Low | 13 | 7 | 5 | 12 | 10 | 15 | 20 | 37 | 9 | 10 |

| Income Statement Analysis (Million $) | 2010 | 2009 | 2008 | 2007 | 2006 | 2005 | 2004 | 2003 | 2002 | 2001 |
|---|---|---|---|---|---|---|---|---|---|---|
| Revenue | 6,967 | 6,686 | 7,062 | 6,392 | 5,878 | 5,397 | 4,725 | 4,383 | 3,910 | 4,185 |
| Operating Income | 1,278 | 1,200 | 1,313 | 1,086 | 886 | 759 | 636 | 515 | 586 | 666 |
| Depreciation | 280 | 249 | 212 | 205 | 240 | 226 | 223 | 219 | 184 | 174 |
| Interest Expense | 138 | 121 | 117 | 130 | 126 | 131 | 143 | 163 | 117 | 118 |
| Pretax Income | 805 | 784 | 967 | 717 | 462 | 375 | 199 | 61.3 | 259 | 271 |
| Effective Tax Rate | NA | 26.5% | 30.3% | 30.8% | NM | 31.8% | 21.7% | 37.2% | 36.0% | 34.8% |
| Net Income | 584 | 563 | 674 | 496 | 481 | 244 | 156 | 38.5 | 166 | 177 |
| S&P Core Earnings | 630 | 629 | 532 | 482 | 499 | 260 | 189 | 48.6 | 44.9 | 44.7 |

| Balance Sheet & Other Financial Data (Million $) | 2010 | 2009 | 2008 | 2007 | 2006 | 2005 | 2004 | 2003 | 2002 | 2001 |
|---|---|---|---|---|---|---|---|---|---|---|
| Cash | 799 | 811 | 370 | 406 | 201 | 251 | 298 | 378 | 150 | 85.8 |
| Current Assets | 4,671 | 4,414 | 3,668 | 3,549 | 3,008 | 2,425 | 2,357 | 2,087 | 2,008 | 1,921 |
| Total Assets | 9,272 | 8,741 | 7,483 | 7,534 | 6,901 | 6,454 | 6,218 | 5,890 | 5,990 | 4,638 |
| Current Liabilities | 1,592 | 1,613 | 1,841 | 1,743 | 1,633 | 1,615 | 1,565 | 1,401 | 1,554 | 1,159 |
| Long Term Debt | 2,353 | 2,008 | 1,410 | 1,563 | 1,722 | 1,742 | 1,899 | 2,137 | 2,254 | 1,432 |
| Common Equity | 3,347 | 2,921 | 2,091 | 2,579 | 1,977 | 1,473 | 1,343 | 1,194 | 933 | 1,361 |
| Total Capital | 5,782 | 4,976 | 3,564 | 4,313 | 3,756 | 3,215 | 3,276 | 3,330 | 3,187 | 2,808 |
| Capital Expenditures | 222 | 169 | 285 | 283 | 257 | 216 | 152 | 125 | 107 | 191 |
| Cash Flow | 864 | 812 | 885 | 701 | 721 | 470 | 379 | 258 | 349 | 351 |
| Current Ratio | 2.9 | 2.7 | 2.0 | 2.0 | 1.8 | 1.5 | 1.5 | 1.5 | 1.3 | 1.7 |
| % Long Term Debt of Capitalization | 40.7 | 40.4 | 39.6 | 36.2 | 45.8 | 54.2 | 58.0 | 64.2 | 70.7 | 51.0 |
| % Net Income of Revenue | 8.4 | 8.4 | 9.5 | 7.8 | 8.2 | 4.5 | 3.3 | 0.9 | 4.2 | 4.2 |
| % Return on Assets | 6.5 | 6.9 | 9.0 | 6.9 | 7.2 | 3.8 | 2.5 | 0.6 | 3.0 | 3.6 |
| % Return on Equity | 18.7 | 22.5 | 28.8 | 21.8 | 27.9 | 17.3 | 12.3 | 3.6 | 14.5 | 13.7 |

Data as orig reptd.; bef. results of disc opers/spec. items. Per share data adj. for stk. divs.; EPS diluted. E-Estimated. NA-Not Available. NM-Not Meaningful. NR-Not Ranked. UR-Under Review.

**Office:** Four Coliseum Centre, Charlotte, NC 28217-4578.
**Telephone:** 704-423-7000.
**Website:** http://www.goodrich.com
**Chrmn, Pres & CEO:** M.O. Larsen

**CFO:** S.E. Kuechle
**Chief Admin Officer & General Counsel:** T.G. Linnert
**CTO:** J. Witowski
**Chief Acctg Officer & Cntlr:** S. Cottrill

**Investor Contact:** P. Gifford (704-423-5517)
**Board Members:** C. Corvi, D. C. Creel, H. E. DeLoach, Jr., J. W. Griffith, W. R. Holland, J. P. Jumper, M. O. Larsen, L. W. Newton, A. M. Rankin, Jr.

**Founded:** 1912
**Domicile:** New York
**Employees:** 25,600

# Goodyear Tire & Rubber Co

**STANDARD &POOR'S**

| S&P Recommendation **BUY** ★★★★☆ | Price **$11.93** (as of Nov 25, 2011) | 12-Mo. Target Price **$19.00** | Investment Style Large-Cap Blend |
|---|---|---|---|

**GICS Sector** Consumer Discretionary
**Sub-Industry** Tires & Rubber

**Summary** GT is the largest U.S. manufacturer of tires, and one of the biggest worldwide. Operations also include rubber and plastic products and chemicals.

## Key Stock Statistics (Source S&P, Vickers, company reports)

| | | | | | | | |
|---|---|---|---|---|---|---|---|
| 52-Wk Range | $18.83– 8.53 | S&P Oper. EPS 2011E | 2.06 | Market Capitalization(B) | $2.915 | Beta | 2.74 |
| Trailing 12-Month EPS | $0.54 | S&P Oper. EPS 2012E | 2.20 | Yield (%) | Nil | S&P 3-Yr. Proj. EPS CAGR(%) | 60 |
| Trailing 12-Month P/E | 22.1 | P/E on S&P Oper. EPS 2011E | 5.8 | Dividend Rate/Share | Nil | S&P Credit Rating | BB- |
| $10K Invested 5 Yrs Ago | $6,669 | Common Shares Outstg. (M) | 244.4 | Institutional Ownership (%) | 82 | | |

## Price Performance

30-Week Mov. Avg. ··· 10-Week Mov. Avg. – – **GAAP Earnings vs. Previous Year**   Volume Above Avg. STARS
12-Mo. Target Price — Relative Strength — ▲ Up ▼ Down ▶ No Change   Below Avg. ★

Options: ASE, CBOE, P, Ph

Analysis prepared by Equity Analyst **Efraim Levy, CFA** on Nov 15, 2011, when the stock traded at **$13.86**.

## Qualitative Risk Assessment

| LOW | MEDIUM | HIGH |
|---|---|---|

Our risk assessment reflects the highly cyclical nature of the company's markets as well as the current and long-term challenges that we believe GT faces given its highly leveraged balance sheet, intensifying competition, high fixed costs, and legacy costs.

## Quantitative Evaluations

**S&P Quality Ranking**          C

| D | C | B- | B | B+ | A- | A | A+ |
|---|---|---|---|---|---|---|---|

**Relative Strength Rank**          MODERATE

44

LOWEST = 1          HIGHEST = 99

## Revenue/Earnings Data

**Revenue (Million $)**

| | 1Q | 2Q | 3Q | 4Q | Year |
|---|---|---|---|---|---|
| 2011 | 5,402 | 55,620 | 6,062 | -- | -- |
| 2010 | 4,270 | 4,528 | 4,962 | 5,072 | 18,832 |
| 2009 | 3,536 | 3,943 | 4,385 | 4,437 | 16,301 |
| 2008 | 4,942 | 5,239 | 5,172 | 4,135 | 19,488 |
| 2007 | 4,499 | 4,921 | 5,064 | 5,160 | 19,644 |
| 2006 | 4,856 | 5,142 | 5,284 | 4,976 | 20,258 |

**Earnings Per Share ($)**

| | 1Q | 2Q | 3Q | 4Q | Year |
|---|---|---|---|---|---|
| 2011 | 0.42 | 0.34 | 0.60 | E0.34 | E2.06 |
| 2010 | -0.19 | 0.11 | -0.08 | -0.73 | -0.89 |
| 2009 | -1.38 | -0.92 | 0.30 | 0.44 | -1.55 |
| 2008 | 0.60 | 0.31 | 0.13 | -1.37 | -0.32 |
| 2007 | -0.61 | 0.14 | 0.67 | 0.26 | 0.66 |
| 2006 | 0.37 | 0.01 | -0.27 | -2.02 | -1.86 |

Fiscal year ended Dec. 31. Next earnings report expected: Mid February. EPS Estimates based on S&P Operating Earnings; historical GAAP earnings are as reported.

## Dividend Data

Dividends were last paid in 2002.

## Highlights

➤ We expect global vehicle production to rise in 2011 and 2012. We foresee expanding U.S. and global demand for original equipment and after-market tires for both commercial and consumer markets. We look for higher volume, a more favorable mix and increased prices to drive sales 22% higher in 2011 and an additional 9% in 2012, as well as improve profitability for GT.

➤ Margins should be aided by higher selling prices, greater capacity utilization, plant closings, and improved mix as well as by past and present expense reductions from restructuring activities. We see reductions in higher-cost plant capacity and a shift to Asia-based production leading to savings. Still, we expect sharply higher raw material costs to limit profit growth through 2012. Interest expense should rise, and foreign exchange rates may be unfavorable. GT has projected a 25% tax rate for international profits and $250 million to $275 million in global pension expense for 2011.

➤ We expect GT to save $100 million a year now that the courts have approved the transfer of union health care benefits to union responsibility. We look for additional savings from restructuring actions to benefit 2011 and 2012 results.

## Investment Rationale/Risk

➤ GT has been extending its debt maturities. There are no funded debt maturities due until 2014, and no long-term debt due until 2016. While we have increased confidence in GT's near-term liquidity, we regard liquidity challenges from debt and employee retirement obligations as matters of concern for the long term. We see the possibility of capital market actions to enhance liquidity.

➤ Risks to our recommendation and target price include an increase in GT's need for cash, weaker-than-anticipated demand for tires, lower-than-expected cost savings, an inability to achieve expected price increases, and higher-than-projected raw material costs.

➤ Although we expect higher profits in 2011, projected higher capital spending should lead to negative free cash flow, in our view, after cash contributions to fund Goodyear's pension plan. We expect further cost savings and higher sales to result in 2012 EPS of $2.20. Applying a multiple of about 8.6X, based on historical and peer comparisons, to our 2012 EPS estimate, we derive our 12-month target price of $19.

---

**Please read the Required Disclosures and Analyst Certification on the last page of this report.**

**The McGraw-Hill Companies**

# Goodyear Tire & Rubber Co

**STANDARD  
&POOR'S**

## Business Summary November 15, 2011

CORPORATE OVERVIEW. Goodyear Tire & Rubber is the largest U.S. manufacturer of tires, and one of the largest worldwide. Operations also include rubber and plastic products and chemicals. GT holds the leading market share in North America, Latin America, China and India.

In February 2008, Goodyear formed a new strategic business unit, Europe, Middle East and Africa (EMEA). These regions collectively had about $7.2 billion in revenues in 2007, making the unit the second largest, after North America, in terms of sales. The company began reporting the new segment results in the 2008 first quarter.

CORPORATE STRATEGY. The company achieved more than $2.5 billion in aggregate cost savings from 2006 through 2009 through a four-point plan. Sources of savings included continuous improvement in processes, increased low-cost country sourcing, high-cost capacity reductions and reduced SG&A expenses, including ongoing savings from the master labor agreement with

the United Steel Workers. In February 2010, GT announced plans for an additional $1.0 billion in savings over the next three years.

The company sometimes uses joint ventures to facilitate the growth of its business. GT and Sumitomo Rubber Industries (SRI) have a global alliance. The North American and European joint ventures with SRI are 75% owned by GT with SRI owning 25%. In Japan, the ownership ratio is reversed.

GT and Pacific Dunlop Ltd. participate in equally owned joint ventures in South Pacific Tyres, an Australian partnership, and South Pacific Tyres N.Z. Ltd., a New Zealand company.

## Company Financials Fiscal Year Ended Dec. 31

| Per Share Data ($) | 2010 | 2009 | 2008 | 2007 | 2006 | 2005 | 2004 | 2003 | 2002 | 2001 |
|---|---|---|---|---|---|---|---|---|---|---|
| Tangible Book Value | NM | NM | 0.74 | 8.58 | NM | NM | NM | NM | NM | 14.06 |
| Cash Flow | 2.01 | 1.08 | 2.42 | 3.25 | 1.95 | 4.16 | 3.87 | -0.62 | -3.01 | 2.71 |
| Earnings | -0.89 | -1.55 | -0.32 | 0.66 | -1.86 | 1.21 | 0.63 | -4.58 | -6.62 | -1.27 |
| S&P Core Earnings | -0.39 | -0.60 | -1.48 | 1.15 | -0.88 | 2.61 | 0.84 | -3.32 | -8.16 | -3.09 |
| Dividends | Nil | Nil | Nil | Nil | Nil | Nil | Nil | Nil | 0.48 | 1.02 |
| Payout Ratio | Nil | Nil | Nil | Nil | Nil | Nil | Nil | Nil | NM | NM |
| Prices:High | 16.39 | 18.84 | 30.10 | 36.90 | 21.35 | 18.59 | 15.01 | 8.19 | 28.85 | 32.10 |
| Prices:Low | 9.10 | 3.17 | 3.93 | 21.40 | 9.75 | 11.24 | 7.06 | 3.35 | 6.50 | 17.37 |
| P/E Ratio:High | NM | NM | NM | 56 | NM | 15 | 24 | NM | NM | NM |
| P/E Ratio:Low | NM | NM | NM | 32 | NM | 9 | 11 | NM | NM | NM |

| Income Statement Analysis (Million $) | | | | | | | | | | |
|---|---|---|---|---|---|---|---|---|---|---|
| Revenue | 18,832 | 16,301 | 19,488 | 19,644 | 20,258 | 19,723 | 18,370 | 15,119 | 13,850 | 14,147 |
| Operating Income | 1,412 | 900 | 1,434 | 1,677 | 1,256 | 1,706 | 1,457 | -549 | 915 | 916 |
| Depreciation | 652 | 636 | 660 | 614 | 675 | 630 | 629 | 693 | 603 | 637 |
| Interest Expense | 316 | 311 | 397 | 566 | 451 | 411 | 369 | 296 | 241 | 292 |
| Pretax Income | 8.00 | -357 | 186 | 464 | -113 | 584 | 381 | -655 | 37.9 | -273 |
| Effective Tax Rate | NA | NM | 112.4% | 55.0% | NM | 42.8% | 54.6% | NM | NM | NM |
| Net Income | -164 | -375 | -77.0 | 139 | -330 | 239 | 115 | -802 | -1,106 | -204 |
| S&P Core Earnings | -94.8 | -150 | -355 | 253 | -157 | 522 | 142 | -584 | -1,362 | -495 |

| Balance Sheet & Other Financial Data (Million $) | | | | | | | | | | |
|---|---|---|---|---|---|---|---|---|---|---|
| Cash | 2,005 | 1,922 | 1,894 | 3,654 | 3,899 | 2,178 | 1,968 | 1,565 | 947 | 959 |
| Current Assets | 8,045 | 7,225 | 8,340 | 10,172 | 10,179 | 8,680 | 8,632 | 6,988 | 5,227 | 5,255 |
| Total Assets | 15,630 | 14,410 | 15,226 | 17,191 | 17,029 | 15,627 | 16,533 | 15,006 | 13,147 | 13,513 |
| Current Liabilities | 5,307 | 4,095 | 4,779 | 4,664 | 4,666 | 4,811 | 5,113 | 3,686 | 4,071 | 3,327 |
| Long Term Debt | 4,304 | 4,167 | 4,132 | 4,329 | 6,563 | 4,742 | 449 | 4,826 | 2,989 | 3,204 |
| Common Equity | 644 | 735 | 1,022 | 2,850 | -758 | 73.0 | 72.8 | -13.1 | 651 | 2,864 |
| Total Capital | 6,855 | 5,857 | 6,550 | 8,456 | 7,015 | 5,910 | 1,774 | 5,639 | 4,380 | 6,855 |
| Capital Expenditures | 944 | 746 | 1,049 | 739 | 671 | 634 | 519 | 375 | 458 | 435 |
| Cash Flow | 488 | 261 | 583 | 753 | 345 | 869 | 744 | -109 | -503 | 433 |
| Current Ratio | 1.5 | 1.8 | 1.8 | 2.2 | 2.2 | 1.8 | 1.7 | 1.9 | 1.3 | 1.6 |
| % Long Term Debt of Capitalization | 62.8 | 71.2 | 62.6 | 51.2 | 93.6 | 80.2 | 25.3 | 85.6 | 68.2 | 46.7 |
| % Net Income of Revenue | NM | NM | NM | 0.7 | NM | 1.2 | 0.6 | NM | NM | NM |
| % Return on Assets | NM | NM | NM | 0.8 | NM | 1.5 | 0.7 | NM | NM | NM |
| % Return on Equity | NM | NM | NM | 13.3 | NM | 325.2 | 565.5 | NM | NM | NM |

Data as orig reptd.; bef. results of disc opers/spec. items. Per share data adj. for stk. divs.; EPS diluted. E-Estimated. NA-Not Available. NM-Not Meaningful. NR-Not Ranked. UR-Under Review.

**Office:** 1144 East Market Street, Akron, OH, USA 44316-0001.  
**Telephone:** 330-796-2121.  
**Email:** goodyear.investor.relations@goodyear.com  
**Website:** http://www.goodyear.com

**Chrmn, Pres, CEO & COO:** R.J. Kramer  
**COO:** G.L. Smith  
**SVP & CTO:** J. Kihn  
**SVP, Secy & General Counsel:** D.L. Bialosky

**CFO:** D.R. Wells  
**Investor Contact:** G. Dooley (330-796-6704)  
**Board Members:** J. C. Boland, W. J. Conaty, J. A. Firestone, W. Geissler, P. S. Hellman, R. J. Kramer, W. A. McCollough, R. O'Neal, S. D. Peterson, S. A. Streeter, G. C. Sullivan, T. H. Weidemeyer, M. R. Wessel

**Auditor:** PRICEWATERHOUSECOOPERS  
**Founded:** 1898  
**Domicile:** Ohio  
**Employees:** 72,000

# Google Inc

**STANDARD &POOR'S**

| S&P Recommendation | HOLD ★★★★★ | Price | 12-Mo. Target Price | Investment Style |
|---|---|---|---|---|
| | | $563.00 (as of Nov 25, 2011) | $625.00 | Large-Cap Growth |

**GICS Sector** Information Technology
**Sub-Industry** Internet Software & Services

**Summary** Google is the world's largest Internet company, specializing in search and advertising. In August 2011, it announced the proposed acquisition of Motorola Mobility for $12.5 billion.

## Key Stock Statistics (Source S&P, Vickers, company reports)

| | | | | | | | | |
|---|---|---|---|---|---|---|---|---|
| 52-Wk Range | $642.96– 473.02 | S&P Oper. EPS 2011**E** | 32.30 | Market Capitalization(B) | $144.129 | Beta | 1.14 |
| Trailing 12-Month EPS | $29.34 | S&P Oper. EPS 2012**E** | 40.50 | Yield (%) | Nil | S&P 3-Yr. Proj. EPS CAGR(%) | 22 |
| Trailing 12-Month P/E | 19.2 | P/E on S&P Oper. EPS 2011**E** | 17.4 | Dividend Rate/Share | Nil | S&P Credit Rating | AA- |
| $10K Invested 5 Yrs Ago | $11,149 | Common Shares Outstg. (M) | 323.9 | Institutional Ownership (%) | 80 | | |

## Price Performance

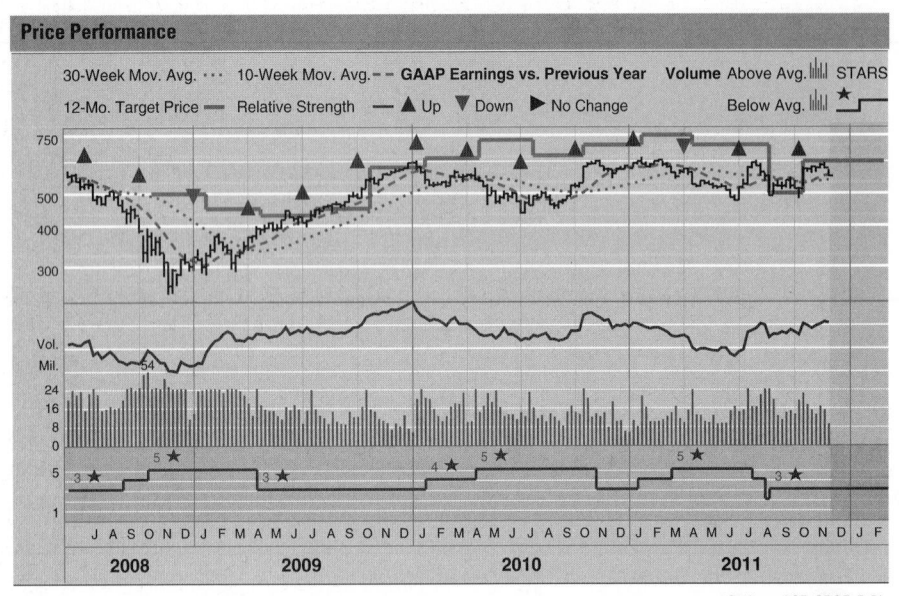

30-Week Mov. Avg. ···· 10-Week Mov. Avg. ── GAAP Earnings vs. Previous Year  Volume Above Avg. STARS
12-Mo. Target Price ── Relative Strength ▲ Up ▼ Down ► No Change  Below Avg. ★

Options: ASE, CBOE, P, Ph

Analysis prepared by Equity Analyst **Scott Kessler** on Oct 18, 2011, when the stock traded at **$589.00**.

## Highlights

➤ We believe gross revenues will rise 31% in 2011 and 26% in 2012, reflecting secular growth in online advertising, international expansion, and increasing traction for display advertising. We think uncertain economies pose difficulties.

➤ We expect pro forma operating margins to dip in 2011, reflecting aggressive spending on growth initiatives. We think the magnitude of expense growth will moderate and contribute to margin improvement in 2012. Revenues have been aided by weakness in the U.S. dollar, but we believe a hedging program has offset the impact on profits. We see continuing spending related to government inquiries/investigations.

➤ In August 2011, GOOG announced the proposed acquisition of Motorola Mobility Holdings (MMI 39, Hold) for $12.5 billion in cash. We expect this pending deal to ultimately be approved by regulators around mid-2012. We believe the pursuit of MMI was motivated by GOOG's interest in fortifying its patent portfolio, to help protect its key Android franchise. We also think GOOG will keep MMI's production operations centered on smartphones and set-top boxes.

## Investment Rationale/Risk

➤ We have been constructive on GOOG's efforts to expand, especially in display advertising, certain mobile contexts, and social media. However, we are skeptical about the proposed purchase of MMI, and believe it will not necessarily protect Android from IP-related attacks, and will weaken GOOG's growth, margins and balance sheet. Adding MMI could hurt Android, as OEM partners could pursue alternatives, with its purveyor now positioned as a competitor.

➤ Risks to our opinion and target price include possible market share losses, new offerings succeeding less than we expect, excess expenditures associated with expansion, adverse legal/regulatory developments, and questions/issues related to proposed purchase of MMI.

➤ Our DCF model assumes a WACC of 13.6%, five-year average annual FCF growth of 26%, and a perpetuity growth rate of 3%, and yields an intrinsic value of about $625, which is our 12-month target price. Our assumptions and related estimates do not fully account for the pending purchase of MMI.

## Qualitative Risk Assessment

| LOW | MEDIUM | HIGH |
|---|---|---|

Our risk assessment reflects what we see as relatively low barriers to entry in the Internet segment, significant competition, substantial and increasing investment and related new offerings, considerable ongoing legal and regulatory matters, and potential issues related to the pending purchase of Motorola Mobility.

## Quantitative Evaluations

**S&P Quality Ranking**  NR

| D | C | B- | B | B+ | A- | A | A+ |
|---|---|---|---|---|---|---|---|

**Relative Strength Rank**  STRONG

71

LOWEST = 1        HIGHEST = 99

## Revenue/Earnings Data

### Revenue (Million $)

| | 1Q | 2Q | 3Q | 4Q | Year |
|---|---|---|---|---|---|
| 2011 | 8,575 | 9,026 | 9,720 | -- | -- |
| 2010 | 6,775 | 6,820 | 7,286 | 8,440 | 29,321 |
| 2009 | 5,509 | 5,523 | 5,945 | 6,674 | 23,651 |
| 2008 | 5,186 | 5,367 | 5,541 | 5,701 | 21,796 |
| 2007 | 3,664 | 3,872 | 4,231 | 4,827 | 16,594 |
| 2006 | 2,254 | 2,456 | 2,690 | 3,206 | 10,605 |

### Earnings Per Share ($)

| | | | | | |
|---|---|---|---|---|---|
| 2011 | 5.51 | 7.68 | 8.33 | E9.23 | E32.30 |
| 2010 | 6.06 | 5.71 | 6.72 | 7.81 | 26.31 |
| 2009 | 4.49 | 4.66 | 5.13 | 6.13 | 20.41 |
| 2008 | 4.12 | 3.92 | 4.06 | 1.21 | 13.31 |
| 2007 | 3.18 | 2.93 | 3.38 | 3.79 | 13.29 |
| 2006 | 1.95 | 2.33 | 2.36 | 3.29 | 9.94 |

Fiscal year ended Dec. 31. Next earnings report expected: NA. EPS Estimates based on S&P Operating Earnings; historical GAAP earnings are as reported.

## Dividend Data

No cash dividends have been paid.

*The McGraw-Hill Companies*

# Google Inc

**STANDARD &POOR'S**

## Business Summary October 18, 2011

CORPORATE OVERVIEW. Google is a global technology company whose stated mission is to organize the world's information and make it universally accessible and useful. GOOG has amassed and maintains what we believe is the Internet's largest index of information (consisting of billions of items, including Web pages, images and videos), and makes most of it freely accessible and usable to anyone with online access. GOOG's websites are a leading Internet destination, and its brand is one of the most recognized in the world. International sources contributed 55% of revenues in the third quarter of 2011 and 52% of revenues in the prior-year period.

GOOG's advertising program, called AdWords, enables advertisers to present online ads when users are searching for related information. Advertisers employ GOOG's tools to create text-based ads, bid on keywords that trigger display of their ads, and set daily spending budgets. Ads are ranked for presentation based on the maximum cost per click set by the advertiser, click-through rates, and other factors used to determine ad relevance. This process is designed to favor the most relevant ads. GOOG's AdSense technology enables Google Network websites to provide targeted ads from AdWords advertisers.

Advertising accounted for 96% of revenues in the third quarter of 2011 and

97% of revenues in the third quarter of 2010. Google websites accounted for 69% of third-quarter revenues in 2011 and 67% in 2010, and Google Network websites contributed 27% of revenues in the 2011 period and 30% in the 2010 period.

In April 2011, co-founder Larry Page became CEO, replacing Eric Schmidt, who became executive chairman. Co-founder Sergey Brin is working on special projects. Page quickly restructured the management team to have business leaders report directly to him. We think these changes have already started to contribute to faster decision-making and more successful innovation. We expect Schmidt to largely remain the public face of the company, as he serves as GOOG's spokesperson and statesman around the world, in contexts from meetings with customers and partners, to sessions with government representatives. We think Page was a driving force behind GOOG's proposed purchase of Motorola Mobility Holdings (MMI 39, Hold) for $12.5 billion.

## Company Financials Fiscal Year Ended Dec. 31

| Per Share Data ($) | 2010 | 2009 | 2008 | 2007 | 2006 | 2005 | 2004 | 2003 | 2002 | 2001 |
|---|---|---|---|---|---|---|---|---|---|---|
| Tangible Book Value | 121.20 | 95.44 | 71.09 | 63.67 | 49.02 | 31.20 | 10.25 | 7.66 | NA | NA |
| Cash Flow | 30.63 | 25.19 | 18.01 | 16.36 | 11.79 | 5.90 | 1.93 | 0.75 | 0.53 | 0.09 |
| Earnings | 26.31 | 20.41 | 13.31 | 13.29 | 9.94 | 5.02 | 1.46 | 0.51 | 0.45 | 0.04 |
| S&P Core Earnings | 25.94 | 20.21 | 15.54 | 13.18 | 9.92 | 4.68 | 1.85 | 0.40 | 0.44 | NA |
| Dividends | Nil | Nil | Nil | Nil | Nil | Nil | Nil | NA | NA | NA |
| Payout Ratio | Nil | Nil | Nil | Nil | Nil | Nil | Nil | NA | NA | NA |
| Prices:High | 630.85 | 625.99 | 697.37 | 747.24 | 513.00 | 446.21 | 201.60 | NA | NA | NA |
| Prices:Low | 433.63 | 282.75 | 247.30 | 437.00 | 331.55 | 172.57 | 85.00 | NA | NA | NA |
| P/E Ratio:High | 24 | 31 | 52 | 56 | 52 | 89 | NM | NA | NA | NA |
| P/E Ratio:Low | 17 | 14 | 19 | 33 | 33 | 34 | NM | NA | NA | NA |

| Income Statement Analysis (Million $) | | | | | | | | | | |
|---|---|---|---|---|---|---|---|---|---|---|
| Revenue | 29,321 | 23,651 | 21,796 | 16,594 | 10,605 | 6,139 | 3,189 | 1,466 | 440 | 86.4 |
| Operating Income | 11,777 | 9,836 | 8,219 | 6,052 | 3,550 | 2,274 | 970 | 393 | 204 | 21.0 |
| Depreciation | 1,396 | 1,524 | 1,492 | 968 | 572 | 257 | 129 | 50.2 | 18.0 | 10.0 |
| Interest Expense | NA | NA | Nil | 1.30 | 0.26 | 0.78 | 0.86 | 1.93 | 2.57 | 1.76 |
| Pretax Income | 10,796 | 8,381 | 5,854 | 5,674 | 4,011 | 2,142 | 650 | 347 | 185 | 10.1 |
| Effective Tax Rate | NA | 22.2% | 27.8% | 26.0% | 23.3% | 31.6% | 38.6% | 69.5% | 46.1% | 30.6% |
| Net Income | 8,505 | 6,520 | 4,227 | 4,204 | 3,077 | 1,465 | 399 | 106 | 99.7 | 6.99 |
| S&P Core Earnings | 8,385 | 6,458 | 4,933 | 4,170 | 3,071 | 1,366 | 503 | 103 | 97.4 | NA |

| Balance Sheet & Other Financial Data (Million $) | | | | | | | | | | |
|---|---|---|---|---|---|---|---|---|---|---|
| Cash | 34,975 | 24,485 | 15,846 | 14,219 | 11,244 | 8,034 | 2,132 | 1,712 | 146 | 33.6 |
| Current Assets | 41,562 | 29,167 | 20,178 | 17,289 | 13,040 | 9,001 | 2,693 | 560 | 232 | NA |
| Total Assets | 57,851 | 40,497 | 31,768 | 25,336 | 18,473 | 10,272 | 3,313 | 2,492 | 286 | 84.5 |
| Current Liabilities | 9,996 | 2,747 | 2,302 | 2,036 | 1,305 | 745 | 340 | 235 | 89.5 | NA |
| Long Term Debt | NA | NA | Nil | Nil | Nil | Nil | Nil | NA | 6.50 | NA |
| Common Equity | 46,241 | 36,004 | 28,239 | 22,690 | 17,040 | 9,419 | 2,929 | 2,181 | 130 | NA |
| Total Capital | 46,241 | 36,004 | 28,251 | 22,690 | 17,080 | 9,454 | 2,929 | 603 | 178 | 50.2 |
| Capital Expenditures | 4,018 | 810 | 2,358 | 2,403 | 1,903 | 838 | 319 | 177 | 37.2 | 13.1 |
| Cash Flow | 9,901 | 8,045 | 5,719 | 5,172 | 3,649 | 1,722 | 528 | 156 | 118 | 17.0 |
| Current Ratio | 4.2 | 10.6 | 8.8 | 8.5 | 10.0 | 12.1 | 7.9 | 2.4 | 2.6 | NA |
| % Long Term Debt of Capitalization | Nil | Nil | Nil | Nil | Nil | Nil | Nil | Nil | 3.7 | Nil |
| % Net Income of Revenue | 29.0 | 27.6 | 19.4 | 25.3 | 29.0 | 23.9 | 12.5 | 7.2 | 22.7 | 8.1 |
| % Return on Assets | 17.3 | 18.1 | 14.8 | 19.1 | 21.4 | 21.6 | 19.1 | 18.2 | NA | NA |
| % Return on Equity | 20.7 | 20.3 | 16.6 | 21.1 | 23.3 | 23.7 | 23.0 | 31.4 | NA | NA |

Data as orig reptd.; bef. results of disc opers/spec. items. Per share data adj. for stk. divs.; EPS diluted. E-Estimated. NA-Not Available. NM-Not Meaningful. NR-Not Ranked. UR-Under Review.

**Office:** 1600 Amphitheatre Parkway, Mountain View, CA 94043.
**Telephone:** 650-253-0000.
**Email:** info@google.com
**Website:** http://www.google.com

**Chrmn:** E.E. Schmidt
**CEO:** L. Page
**COO & SVP:** U. Holzle
**SVP, CFO & Chief Acctg Officer:** P. Pichette

**CTO:** C. Silverstein
**Investor Contact:** J. Penner (650-214-1624)
**Board Members:** S. Brin, L. J. Doerr, III, J. L. Hennessy, A. Mather, P. S. Otellini, L. Page, E. E. Schmidt, K. R. Shriram, S. M. Tilghman

**Auditor:** ERNST & YOUNG
**Employees:** 24,400

# Grainger (W W) Inc.

| S&P Recommendation BUY ★★★★☆ | Price $170.31 (as of Nov 25, 2011) | 12-Mo. Target Price $205.00 | Investment Style Large-Cap Blend |
|---|---|---|---|

**GICS Sector** Industrials
**Sub-Industry** Trading Companies & Distributors

**Summary** Grainger is the largest global distributor of industrial and commercial supplies, such as hand tools, electric motors, light bulbs and janitorial items.

## Key Stock Statistics (Source S&P, Vickers, company reports)

| | | | | | | |
|---|---|---|---|---|---|---|
| 52-Wk Range | $181.72–123.62 | S&P Oper. EPS 2011**E** | 8.95 | Market Capitalization(B) | $11.879 | Beta | 0.94 |
| Trailing 12-Month EPS | $8.86 | S&P Oper. EPS 2012**E** | 10.50 | Yield (%) | 1.55 | S&P 3-Yr. Proj. EPS CAGR(%) | 18 |
| Trailing 12-Month P/E | 19.2 | P/E on S&P Oper. EPS 2011**E** | 19.0 | Dividend Rate/Share | $2.64 | S&P Credit Rating | AA+ |
| $10K Invested 5 Yrs Ago | $25,476 | Common Shares Outstg. (M) | 69.7 | Institutional Ownership (%) | 72 | | |

## Price Performance

30-Week Mov. Avg. ··· 10-Week Mov. Avg. - - GAAP Earnings vs. Previous Year Volume Above Avg. STARS
12-Mo. Target Price — Relative Strength — ▲ Up ▼ Down ▶ No Change Below Avg.

Options: ASE, CBOE, P, Ph

Analysis prepared by Equity Analyst **Stewart Scharf** on Nov 23, 2011, when the stock traded at **$171.34**.

### Highlights

➤ We project near 12% sales growth for 2011, with slightly stronger growth in 2012 (about 8% organic, driven by market share gains), reflecting strength in heavy manufacturing and commercial volume in North America, and the Fabory acquisition. We see a gradual rebound in the light manufacturing and retail markets, as well as in the contractor sector, while government volume growth remains soft. Latin America and Asia should remain strong, while Europe weakens.

➤ We look for gross margins to expand by about 130 basis points (bps) in 2011, to 43.3%, due mainly to supply chain cost savings and price hikes; 2012's should widen by 30 bps organically. Following our near 15.8% EBITDA margin forecast for 2011 (14% in 2010), we project 40 bps of expansion in 2012 (70 bps organically), reflecting tougher comparisons, while improved productivity outweighs investment ramp-up costs and a negative acquisition mix.

➤ For 2011, we forecast a slightly lower effective tax rate of about 38.5%, and project operating EPS of $8.95 (before about $0.14 of charges and a $0.19 gain), increasing 17% in 2012, to $10.50.

### Investment Rationale/Risk

➤ Our buy opinion is based on our view that GWW will continue to expand its geographic reach, and that global economic conditions will gradually improve in 2012, although the environment in Europe remains uncertain. In our view, GWW will continue to gain market share as it ramps up its sales force and targets more sales via e-commerce, while expanding its product line.

➤ Risks to our recommendation and target price include another significant downturn in industrial production and non-farm payrolls; a negative impact from entering new markets; loss of customers; and a negative foreign currency effect mainly versus the Canadian dollar.

➤ Our 12-month target price of $205 is based on a blend of our relative and DCF analyses. Based on price-to-EBITDA and P/E-to-EPS growth ratios, we believe GWW deserves an above historical P/E multiple of over 19X our 2012 operating EPS estimate, which leads to a value of $200. Our DCF-based model, assuming a 3.5% terminal growth rate and an 8.3% weighted average cost of capital, indicates intrinsic value of $210.

### Qualitative Risk Assessment

| LOW | MEDIUM | HIGH |
|---|---|---|

Our risk assessment reflects uncertain economic conditions, pricing pressures, and possible facilities disruptions or shutdowns, offset by GWW's S&P Quality Ranking of A+, which indicates the highest and most consistent level of earnings and dividend growth.

### Quantitative Evaluations

**S&P Quality Ranking** A+

| D | C | B- | B | B+ | A- | A | A+ |
|---|---|---|---|---|---|---|---|

**Relative Strength Rank** STRONG

91

LOWEST = 1 HIGHEST = 99

### Revenue/Earnings Data

**Revenue (Million $)**

| | 1Q | 2Q | 3Q | 4Q | Year |
|---|---|---|---|---|---|
| 2011 | 1,884 | 2,003 | 2,115 | -- | -- |
| 2010 | 1,672 | 1,784 | 1,899 | 1,827 | 7,182 |
| 2009 | 1,465 | 1,533 | 1,590 | 1,634 | 6,222 |
| 2008 | 1,661 | 1,757 | 1,839 | 1,593 | 6,850 |
| 2007 | 1,547 | 1,601 | 1,659 | 1,612 | 6,418 |
| 2006 | 1,419 | 1,483 | 1,520 | 1,462 | 5,884 |

**Earnings Per Share ($)**

| | | | | | |
|---|---|---|---|---|---|
| 2011 | 2.18 | 2.34 | 2.51 | E2.04 | E8.95 |
| 2010 | 1.31 | 1.73 | 2.07 | 1.83 | 6.93 |
| 2009 | 1.25 | 1.21 | 1.88 | 1.27 | 5.62 |
| 2008 | 1.43 | 1.43 | 1.79 | 1.39 | 6.04 |
| 2007 | 1.17 | 1.21 | 1.29 | 1.28 | 4.94 |
| 2006 | 0.93 | 1.02 | 1.16 | 1.13 | 4.24 |

Fiscal year ended Dec. 31. Next earnings report expected: Late January. EPS Estimates based on S&P Operating Earnings; historical GAAP earnings are as reported.

### Dividend Data (Dates: mm/dd Payment Date: mm/dd/yy)

| Amount ($) | Date Decl. | Ex-Div. Date | Stk. of Record | Payment Date |
|---|---|---|---|---|
| 0.540 | 01/26 | 02/10 | 02/14 | 03/01/11 |
| 0.660 | 04/27 | 05/05 | 05/09 | 06/01/11 |
| 0.660 | 07/27 | 08/04 | 08/08 | 09/01/11 |
| 0.660 | 10/26 | 11/09 | 11/14 | 12/01/11 |

Dividends have been paid since 1965. Source: Company reports.

# Grainger (W W) Inc.

**STANDARD
&POOR'S**

## Business Summary November 23, 2011

CORPORATE OVERVIEW. W.W. Grainger distributes facilities maintenance and other industrial and commercial supplies, including pumps, tools, motors, and electrical and safety products. The company holds a 4% share of the estimated $140 billion North American facilities maintenance market. As of September 30, 2011, it had 725 branches and multiple websites. The branch-based business segment consists mainly of 394 U.S. traditional branch stores, 170 Canadian (Acklands-Grainger) branches, and 11 Will Call Express branches, as well as 21 stores in Mexico, five stores in Colombia, three stores in Puerto Rico, and one branch each in China and Panama. In the third quarter of 2011, GWW closed five stores and opened one, and added 130 stores via the acquisition of Fabory. Express branches sell company-made -- as well as third-party -- industrial supplies via in-store catalogs and Internet services. GWW estimates China's current market for facilities maintenance supplies at $38 billion, and projects that it will exceed $70 billion by 2014.

In 2010, the U.S. branch-based unit accounted for 84% of sales and had a pretax return on invested capital (ROIC) of nearly 43%. The Acklands unit accounted for 11% of sales, with ROIC of 10.7%. Other businesses (Japan, Mexico, India, China and Panama) accounted for 5.4% of sales. In June 2010, GWW formed Grainger Colombia, an 80%-owned joint venture with an affiliate of Torhefe S.A., a distributor of maintenance, repair and operating (MRO) supplies in Colombia. In September 2009, the company increased its stake in

Japanese MRO marketer MonotaRO Co. Ltd. to 53% from 38% via a $4 million tender offer.

Sales in 2010 broke down approximately as follows: 16% heavy manufacturing, 20% commercial, 17% government, 12% contractor, 9% light manufacturing, 7% retail/wholesale, 4% reseller, 6% agriculture and mining, and 9% other.

GWW's 2011 catalog offered 354,000 facilities maintenance and other products, up 15% from 2010, with the company targeting 500,000 products eventually. Through Grainger.com, customers can access more than 700,000 products. E-commerce sales in 2010 accounted for 25% of the total, with the company planning to double that by 2015.

In the second quarter of 2011, GWW recorded a $0.12 a share tax settlement gain. It expects to record a $5 million after-tax gain (about $0.07 a share) in the fourth quarter on the sale of its minority stake in MRO Korea in October 2011. In the first quarter of 2010, GWW incurred a $0.15 per share charge related to new health care legislation.

## Company Financials Fiscal Year Ended Dec. 31

| Per Share Data ($) | 2010 | 2009 | 2008 | 2007 | 2006 | 2005 | 2004 | 2003 | 2002 | 2001 |
|---|---|---|---|---|---|---|---|---|---|---|
| Tangible Book Value | 24.11 | 25.06 | 24.35 | 23.47 | 23.40 | 23.47 | 20.89 | 18.43 | 16.92 | 15.51 |
| Cash Flow | 9.16 | 7.41 | 7.52 | 6.25 | 5.35 | 4.85 | 4.06 | 3.28 | 3.30 | 2.73 |
| Earnings | 6.93 | 5.62 | 6.04 | 4.94 | 4.24 | 3.78 | 3.13 | 2.46 | 2.50 | 1.84 |
| S&P Core Earnings | 7.00 | 5.34 | 6.13 | 4.94 | 4.26 | 3.65 | 2.96 | 2.36 | 2.29 | 1.87 |
| Dividends | 2.08 | 1.78 | 1.55 | 1.34 | 1.11 | 0.92 | 0.79 | 0.74 | 0.72 | 0.70 |
| Payout Ratio | 30% | 32% | 26% | 27% | 26% | 24% | 25% | 30% | 29% | 38% |
| Prices:High | 139.09 | 102.54 | 93.99 | 98.60 | 79.95 | 72.45 | 66.99 | 53.30 | 59.40 | 48.99 |
| Prices:Low | 96.14 | 59.95 | 58.86 | 68.77 | 60.60 | 51.65 | 45.00 | 41.40 | 39.20 | 29.51 |
| P/E Ratio:High | 20 | 18 | 16 | 20 | 19 | 19 | 21 | 22 | 24 | 27 |
| P/E Ratio:Low | 14 | 11 | 10 | 14 | 14 | 14 | 14 | 17 | 16 | 16 |

| Income Statement Analysis (Million $) | 2010 | 2009 | 2008 | 2007 | 2006 | 2005 | 2004 | 2003 | 2002 | 2001 |
|---|---|---|---|---|---|---|---|---|---|---|
| Revenue | 7,182 | 6,222 | 6,850 | 6,418 | 5,884 | 5,527 | 5,050 | 4,667 | 4,644 | 4,754 |
| Operating Income | 1,010 | 799 | 906 | 782 | 679 | 617 | 525 | 463 | 467 | 461 |
| Depreciation | 150 | 148 | 117 | 111 | 101 | 98.1 | 85.6 | 76.1 | 75.9 | 83.7 |
| Interest Expense | 8.19 | 8.77 | 15.8 | 4.37 | 1.93 | 1.86 | 4.39 | 6.02 | 6.16 | 10.7 |
| Pretax Income | 854 | 707 | 773 | 682 | 603 | 533 | 445 | 381 | 398 | 297 |
| Effective Tax Rate | NA | 39.1% | 38.5% | 38.4% | 36.4% | 35.0% | 35.5% | 40.4% | 40.8% | 41.3% |
| Net Income | 511 | 430 | 475 | 420 | 383 | 346 | 287 | 227 | 235 | 175 |
| S&P Core Earnings | 504 | 399 | 482 | 420 | 385 | 336 | 272 | 217 | 213 | 177 |

| Balance Sheet & Other Financial Data (Million $) | 2010 | 2009 | 2008 | 2007 | 2006 | 2005 | 2004 | 2003 | 2002 | 2001 |
|---|---|---|---|---|---|---|---|---|---|---|
| Cash | 313 | 460 | 396 | 134 | 361 | 545 | 429 | 403 | 209 | 169 |
| Current Assets | 2,238 | 2,132 | 2,144 | 1,801 | 1,862 | 1,998 | 1,755 | 1,633 | 1,485 | 1,393 |
| Total Assets | 3,904 | 3,726 | 3,513 | 3,094 | 3,046 | 3,108 | 2,810 | 2,625 | 2,437 | 2,331 |
| Current Liabilities | 869 | 777 | 762 | 826 | 706 | 727 | 662 | 707 | 586 | 554 |
| Long Term Debt | 426 | 438 | 488 | 4.90 | 4.90 | 4.90 | Nil | 4.90 | 120 | 118 |
| Common Equity | 2,288 | 2,227 | 2,034 | 2,098 | 2,178 | 2,289 | 2,068 | 1,845 | 1,668 | 1,603 |
| Total Capital | 2,745 | 2,718 | 2,543 | 27,720 | 2,189 | 2,301 | 2,072 | 1,850 | 1,787 | 1,723 |
| Capital Expenditures | 121 | 141 | 169 | 189 | 128 | 112 | 128 | 74.1 | 134 | 100 |
| Cash Flow | 661 | 555 | 592 | 531 | 484 | 444 | 372 | 303 | 311 | 258 |
| Current Ratio | 2.6 | 2.7 | 2.8 | 2.2 | 2.6 | 2.7 | 2.6 | 2.3 | 2.5 | 2.5 |
| % Long Term Debt of Capitalization | 15.5 | 16.1 | 19.2 | NM | 0.2 | 0.2 | Nil | 0.3 | 6.7 | 6.9 |
| % Net Income of Revenue | 7.1 | 6.9 | 6.9 | 6.6 | 6.5 | 6.3 | 5.7 | 4.9 | 5.1 | 3.7 |
| % Return on Assets | 13.4 | 11.9 | 14.4 | 13.7 | 12.5 | 11.7 | 10.6 | 9.0 | 9.9 | 7.3 |
| % Return on Equity | 23.0 | 20.2 | 23.0 | 19.7 | 17.2 | 15.9 | 14.7 | 12.9 | 14.4 | 11.1 |

Data as orig reptd.; bef. results of disc opers/spec. items. Per share data adj. for stk. divs.; EPS diluted. E-Estimated. NA-Not Available. NM-Not Meaningful. NR-Not Ranked. UR-Under Review.

**Office:** 100 Grainger Pkwy, Lake Forest, IL 60045.
**Telephone:** 847-535-1000.
**Website:** http://www.grainger.com
**Chrmn & CEO:** J.T. Ryan

**SVP & General Counsel:** J.L. Howard
**CFO:** R.L. Jadin
**Chief Acctg Officer & Cntlr:** G.S. Irving
**Secy:** C.L. Kogl

**Investor Contact:** W.D. Chapman (847-535-0881)
**Board Members:** B. P. Anderson, W. H. Gantz, V. A. Hailey, W. W. Hall, S. L. Levenick, J. W. McCarter, Jr., N. S. Novich, M. J. Roberts, G. L. Rogers, J. T. Ryan, E. S. Santi, J. D. Slavik

**Founded:** 1927
**Domicile:** Illinois
**Employees:** 18,500

# Halliburton Co

**STANDARD &POOR'S**

**S&P Recommendation** BUY ★★★★☆

| Price | 12-Mo. Target Price | Investment Style |
|---|---|---|
| $31.80 (as of Nov 25, 2011) | $48.00 | Large-Cap Growth |

**GICS Sector** Energy
**Sub-Industry** Oil & Gas Equipment & Services

**Summary** This leading oilfield services company provides products and services to the global energy industry.

## Key Stock Statistics (Source S&P, Vickers, company reports)

| | | | | | | | |
|---|---|---|---|---|---|---|---|
| 52-Wk Range | $57.77–27.21 | S&P Oper. EPS 2011E | 3.23 | Market Capitalization(B) | $29.261 | Beta | 1.57 |
| Trailing 12-Month EPS | $2.76 | S&P Oper. EPS 2012E | 4.37 | Yield (%) | 1.13 | S&P 3-Yr. Proj. EPS CAGR(%) | 50 |
| Trailing 12-Month P/E | 11.5 | P/E on S&P Oper. EPS 2011E | 9.8 | Dividend Rate/Share | $0.36 | S&P Credit Rating | A |
| $10K Invested 5 Yrs Ago | $10,642 | Common Shares Outstg. (M) | 920.2 | Institutional Ownership (%) | 81 | | |

## Price Performance

30-Week Mov. Avg. ···· 10-Week Mov. Avg. ─ ─ GAAP Earnings vs. Previous Year  Volume Above Avg. |ıl|ı STARS
12-Mo. Target Price ── Relative Strength ── ▲ Up ▼ Down ► No Change  Below Avg. ıl|ıı ★

Options: ASE, CBOE, P, Ph

Analysis prepared by Equity Analyst **S. Glickman, CFA** on Oct 25, 2011, when the stock traded at **$35.12**.

## Qualitative Risk Assessment

| LOW | MEDIUM | HIGH |
|---|---|---|

Our risk assessment reflects HAL's exposure to volatile crude oil and natural gas prices, leverage to the North American oilfield services market, and political risk associated with operating in frontier regions such as West Africa and the Middle East. A partial offset is HAL's strong number two position in oilfield services.

## Quantitative Evaluations

**S&P Quality Ranking** B

| D | C | B- | B | B+ | A- | A | A+ |
|---|---|---|---|---|---|---|---|

**Relative Strength Rank** WEAK

19

LOWEST = 1          HIGHEST = 99

## Revenue/Earnings Data

**Revenue (Million $)**

| | 1Q | 2Q | 3Q | 4Q | Year |
|---|---|---|---|---|---|
| 2011 | 5,282 | 5,935 | 6,548 | -- | -- |
| 2010 | 3,761 | 4,387 | 4,665 | 5,160 | 17,973 |
| 2009 | 113.5 | 3,494 | 3,588 | 3,686 | 14,675 |
| 2008 | 4,029 | 4,487 | 4,853 | 4,910 | 18,279 |
| 2007 | 3,422 | 3,735 | 3,928 | 4,179 | 15,264 |
| 2006 | 5,184 | 5,545 | 5,831 | 6,016 | 22,576 |

**Earnings Per Share ($)**

| | | | | | |
|---|---|---|---|---|---|
| 2011 | 0.56 | 0.80 | 0.92 | E0.95 | E3.23 |
| 2010 | 0.23 | 0.52 | 0.53 | 0.68 | 1.97 |
| 2009 | 0.42 | 0.29 | 0.29 | 0.27 | 1.28 |
| 2008 | 0.64 | 0.68 | -0.02 | 0.87 | 2.17 |
| 2007 | 0.52 | 0.63 | 0.79 | 0.74 | 2.66 |
| 2006 | 0.45 | 0.48 | 0.58 | 0.65 | 2.16 |

Fiscal year ended Dec. 31. Next earnings report expected: Late January. EPS Estimates based on S&P Operating Earnings; historical GAAP earnings are as reported.

## Highlights

► HAL's North American operating margins widened 40 basis points in the third quarter to 29.3%, approaching the low 30% levels of 2006 and 2007. Given the high service intensity of U.S. unconventional plays, and the ongoing shift toward liquids-rich fields, we think North American operating margins still have upside potential, albeit modest, as we remain concerned that activity in dry gas plays will weaken toward year end. Operating margins in the Eastern Hemisphere remained weak in the third quarter, which we attribute in part to ongoing political unrest in key operating areas such as Libya, and startup costs. We see Eastern Hemisphere margins in the low double digits in 2011, but widening in 2012.

► We think the international margin picture will improve, but patience will be required, in our view. International project delays should ultimately end, hastening fixed cost absorption, and HAL, as one of the early movers in Iraq, should benefit.

► We see revenue growth of 35% in 2011 and 14% in 2012. Our EPS estimates are $3.23 and $4.37 for the respective years, mainly driven by North America.

## Investment Rationale/Risk

► HAL appears determined to defend its North American leadership position and to close the gap on Schlumberger (SLB 69, Strong Buy) in the international arena, in our opinion. HAL's financial performance has improved in large part due to its stimulation franchise in North America. While we remain cautious on the extent to which a dry gas pullback might act as a headwind, we think the sizable increase in liquids plays should still lead to overall margin expansion. HAL believes it has taken a first-mover advantage in Iraq, which may yield benefits down the road, although near-term margins may suffer as startup costs get absorbed.

► Risks to our recommendation and target price include reduced oil and gas drilling activity; lower-than-expected oil and natural gas prices; political risk, especially in regard to hydraulic fracturing in the U.S.; and legal risk from work performed on the Deepwater Horizon.

► Our DCF model, assuming a WACC of 9.3% and terminal growth of 3%, shows intrinsic value of $57. Blending this with relative multiples of 6X estimated 2012 EBITDA and 7X projected 2012 cash flow, our 12-month target price is $48.

## Dividend Data (Dates: mm/dd Payment Date: mm/dd/yy)

| Amount ($) | Date Decl. | Ex-Div. Date | Stk. of Record | Payment Date |
|---|---|---|---|---|
| 0.090 | 11/08 | 12/01 | 12/03 | 12/23/10 |
| 0.090 | 02/14 | 02/28 | 03/02 | 03/23/11 |
| 0.090 | 07/22 | 08/30 | 09/01 | 09/22/11 |
| 0.090 | 11/07 | 11/30 | 12/02 | 12/23/11 |

Dividends have been paid since 1947. Source: Company reports.

---

**Please read the Required Disclosures and Analyst Certification on the last page of this report.**

*The McGraw-Hill Companies*

## Business Summary October 25, 2011

CORPORATE OVERVIEW. Halliburton is a leading global provider of oilfield services to the energy industry, and until April 2007, provided engineering and construction expertise to energy, industrial and governmental customers. In 2006, HAL was comprised of two main business units: the Energy Services Group (ESG), and the KBR unit. In April 2007, HAL effected the complete separation of KBR via a split-off of its 135.6 million share stake in KBR in exchange for HAL shares. Under the transaction, HAL exchanged its stake in KBR for about 85.3 million shares of HAL which were retired as treasury stock in early April. Following the separation, HAL was transformed into a pure-play oilfield services company. In the second half of 2007, the company reorganized its four ESG operating segments into two new segments: Completion & Production (56% of 2010 revenues, and 63% of 2010 operating income), and Drilling & Evaluation (44%, 37%). Results from the former KBR segment have been reclassified under discontinued operations. Geographically, HAL generated 49% of its total 2010 revenues from North America, followed by Europe/CIS/West Africa (22%), Middle East/Asia (17%) and Latin America (12%). Approximately 70% of HAL's North American revenues in 2009 were derived from C&P activity.

CORPORATE STRATEGY. Subsequent to the split-off, with HAL's financial

obligations to KBR for the Barracuda-Caratinga project and the Foreign Corrupt Practices Act (FCPA) investigations limited by terms of the Master Separation Agreement with KBR, we view HAL's exposure to such issues as reduced. While we expect HAL to defend its strong market position in North America, we believe that future capital expenditures will increasingly flow to the Eastern Hemisphere, which we see as growing faster in the long term. In 2007, HAL moved its corporate headquarters to Dubai, from Houston, which we view as symbolic of the growing importance of the Eastern Hemisphere to company operations.

UPCOMING CATALYSTS. Geographically, North America remains the dominant source of revenue for HAL, and is the primary driver for the Completion & Production segment. However, results in the Drilling & Evaluation segment are likely to be increasingly drawn from overseas, in our view, given expectations that offshore rig demand will show the strongest growth outside of North America.

## Company Financials Fiscal Year Ended Dec. 31

| Per Share Data ($) | 2010 | 2009 | 2008 | 2007 | 2006 | 2005 | 2004 | 2003 | 2002 | 2001 |
|---|---|---|---|---|---|---|---|---|---|---|
| Tangible Book Value | 9.95 | 8.46 | NA | 8.72 | 6.61 | 5.46 | 3.55 | 2.14 | 3.25 | 4.65 |
| Cash Flow | 3.20 | 2.31 | 2.99 | 3.27 | 2.66 | 2.76 | 1.01 | 0.98 | 0.18 | 1.26 |
| Earnings | 1.97 | 1.28 | 2.17 | 2.66 | 2.16 | 2.27 | 0.44 | 0.39 | -0.40 | 0.64 |
| S&P Core Earnings | 1.97 | 1.29 | 2.10 | 2.64 | 2.12 | 2.11 | 0.37 | 0.34 | -0.52 | 0.33 |
| Dividends | 0.36 | 0.36 | 0.36 | 0.35 | 0.30 | 0.25 | 0.25 | 0.25 | 0.25 | 0.25 |
| Payout Ratio | 18% | 28% | 17% | 13% | 14% | 11% | 57% | 64% | NM | 39% |
| Prices:High | 41.73 | 32.00 | 55.38 | 41.95 | 41.99 | 34.89 | 20.85 | 13.60 | 10.83 | 24.63 |
| Prices:Low | 21.10 | 14.68 | 12.80 | 27.65 | 26.33 | 18.59 | 12.90 | 8.60 | 4.30 | 5.47 |
| P/E Ratio:High | 21 | 25 | 26 | 16 | 19 | 15 | 48 | 35 | NM | 38 |
| P/E Ratio:Low | 11 | 11 | 6 | 10 | 12 | 8 | 30 | 22 | NM | 9 |
| **Income Statement Analysis** (Million $) | | | | | | | | | | |
| Revenue | 17,973 | 14,675 | 18,279 | 15,264 | 22,576 | 20,994 | 20,466 | 16,271 | 12,572 | 13,046 |
| Operating Income | NA | NA | 4,703 | 4,029 | 3,875 | 2,972 | 1,291 | 1,191 | 363 | 1,615 |
| Depreciation, Depletion and Amortization | 1,119 | 931 | 738 | 583 | 527 | 504 | 509 | 518 | 505 | 531 |
| Interest Expense | 308 | 297 | 160 | 154 | 175 | 207 | 229 | 139 | 113 | 147 |
| Pretax Income | 2,655 | 1,682 | 3,163 | 3,460 | 3,449 | 2,492 | 651 | 612 | -228 | 954 |
| Effective Tax Rate | NA | 30.8% | 38.3% | 26.2% | 33.2% | 3.17% | 37.0% | 38.2% | NM | 40.3% |
| Net Income | 1,795 | 1,154 | 1,961 | 2,524 | 2,272 | 2,357 | 385 | 339 | -346 | 551 |
| S&P Core Earnings | 1,796 | 1,161 | 1,893 | 2,505 | 2,220 | 2,181 | 320 | 299 | -445 | 287 |
| **Balance Sheet & Other Financial Data** (Million $) | | | | | | | | | | |
| Cash | 2,051 | 3,394 | 1,124 | 2,235 | 4,379 | 2,391 | 2,808 | 1,815 | 1,107 | 290 |
| Current Assets | 8,886 | 8,638 | 7,411 | 7,573 | 11,183 | 9,327 | 9,962 | 7,919 | 5,560 | 5,573 |
| Total Assets | 18,297 | 16,538 | 14,385 | 13,135 | 16,820 | 15,010 | 15,796 | 15,463 | 12,844 | 10,966 |
| Current Liabilities | 2,757 | 2,889 | 2,781 | 2,411 | 4,727 | 4,437 | 7,064 | 6,542 | 3,272 | 2,908 |
| Long Term Debt | 3,824 | 3,824 | 2,586 | 2,627 | 2,786 | 2,813 | 3,593 | 3,415 | 1,181 | 1,403 |
| Common Equity | 10,373 | 8,728 | 7,725 | 6,866 | 7,376 | 6,372 | 3,932 | 2,547 | 3,558 | 4,752 |
| Total Capital | 14,211 | 13,331 | 10,330 | 9,587 | 10,609 | 9,330 | 7,633 | 6,062 | 4,810 | 6,196 |
| Capital Expenditures | 2,069 | 1,864 | 1,824 | 1,583 | 891 | 651 | 575 | 515 | 764 | 797 |
| Cash Flow | 2,914 | 2,085 | 2,699 | 3,107 | 2,799 | 2,861 | 894 | 857 | 159 | 1,082 |
| Current Ratio | 3.2 | 3.0 | 2.7 | 3.1 | 2.4 | 2.1 | 1.4 | 1.2 | 1.7 | 1.9 |
| % Long Term Debt of Capitalization | 26.9 | 28.8 | 26.9 | 27.4 | 26.3 | 30.2 | 47.1 | 56.3 | 24.6 | 22.6 |
| % Return on Assets | 10.3 | 7.5 | 14.3 | 16.9 | 14.3 | 15.3 | 2.5 | 2.4 | NM | 5.2 |
| % Return on Equity | 18.8 | 14.0 | 26.9 | 35.4 | 33.1 | 45.7 | 14.4 | 11.1 | NM | 12.7 |

Data as orig reptd.; bef. results of disc opers/spec. items. Per share data adj. for stk. divs.; EPS diluted. E-Estimated. NA-Not Available. NM-Not Meaningful. NR-Not Ranked. UR-Under Review.

**Office:** 3000 N Sam Houston Pkwy E, Houston, TX 77072.
**Telephone:** 281-575-3000.
**Email:** investors@halliburton.com
**Website:** http://www.halliburton.com

**Chrmn, Pres & CEO:** D.J. Lesar
**EVP & General Counsel:** A.O. Cornelison, Jr.
**SVP & Secy:** S.D. Williams
**CFO:** M.A. McCollum

**Chief Admin Officer:** L. Pope
**Investor Contact:** C. Garcia (713-759-2688)
**Board Members:** A. M. Bennett, J. R. Boyd, M. Carroll, N. K. Dicciani, S. M. Gillis, A. S. Jum'ah, D. J. Lesar, R. A. Malone, J. L. Martin, D. L. Reed

**Founded:** 1919
**Domicile:** Delaware
**Employees:** 58,000

# Harley-Davidson Inc.

## STANDARD &POOR'S

| S&P Recommendation **HOG** ★★★☆☆ | Price $34.80 (as of Nov 25, 2011) | 12-Mo. Target Price $35.00 | Investment Style Large-Cap Growth |
|---|---|---|---|

**GICS Sector** Consumer Discretionary
**Sub-Industry** Motorcycle Manufacturers

**Summary** This leading maker of heavyweight motorcycles also produces a line of motorcycle parts and accessories.

## Key Stock Statistics (Source S&P, Vickers, company reports)

| | | | | | | | |
|---|---|---|---|---|---|---|---|
| 52-Wk Range | $46.88–30.89 | S&P Oper. EPS 2011E | 2.27 | Market Capitalization(B) | $8.087 | Beta | 2.23 |
| Trailing 12-Month EPS | $1.89 | S&P Oper. EPS 2012E | 2.35 | Yield (%) | 1.44 | S&P 3-Yr. Proj. EPS CAGR(%) | 20 |
| Trailing 12-Month P/E | 18.4 | P/E on S&P Oper. EPS 2011E | 15.3 | Dividend Rate/Share | $0.50 | S&P Credit Rating | BBB |
| $10K Invested 5 Yrs Ago | $5,209 | Common Shares Outstg. (M) | 232.4 | Institutional Ownership (%) | 85 | | |

## Price Performance

30-Week Mov. Avg. · · · 10-Week Mov. Avg. - - GAAP Earnings vs. Previous Year   Volume Above Avg. STARS
12-Mo. Target Price — Relative Strength — ▲ Up ▼ Down ► No Change   Below Avg.

Options: ASE, CBOE, P, Ph

Analysis prepared by Equity Analyst **Efraim Levy, CFA** on Oct 25, 2011, when the stock traded at **$39.10**.

## Highlights

► We expect sales of motorcycles and related products to rise 11% in 2011 and 4.0% in 2012. In October, HOG reiterated plans to ship about 228,000 to 235,000 new Harley-Davidson motorcycles for the full year, up 8%-12% from 2010. In addition to stronger demand amid an economic recovery, we believe part of the increased shipments was to replenish dealers' inventories. We project a 3.5% decline in financial services revenues in 2011. However, we see lower provision for credit losses for 2011, due to improvement in credit quality. For 2012, see financial services revenues advancing 5.0%.

► We forecast a mid-teens operating margin for bother 2011 and 2012, up from 12% in 2010. One main factor for the wider operating margin we see is lower restructuring expenses. We project restructuring charges of $62 million in 2011, down from $163 million in 2010, as HOG has now completed most major projects. A further decrease in restructuring costs is projected for 2012.

► We estimate EPS of $2.27 and $2.35 in 2011 and 2012, respectively, compared to $1.11 in 2010, which excludes a $0.49 loss per share from discontinued operations.

## Investment Rationale/Risk

► Our hold recommendation reflects our outlook for a sluggish economic recovery, given uncertainties about employment and sovereign debt issues. Thus, we expect demand for its motorcycles to be lackluster near term. However, we are positive on HOG's cost-cutting efforts, although we question the company's decision to keep its main manufacturing facility in York, PA, given higher wages associated with the facility's unionized workers. We think HOG has strengthened its financial service arm, Harley-Davidson Financial Services, and expect that business to contribute about $280 million of operating profits in 2011. Additionally, we think HOG has a solid balance sheet, with cash and equivalents totaling about $1.4 billion as of September 25, 2011.

► Risks to our recommendation and target price include weaker-than-expected economic growth and lower consumer spending on discretionary items, resulting in lower demand for HOG bikes.

► Our 12-month target price of $35 is based on a historical multiple of 15X our 2012 EPS estimate of $2.35.

## Qualitative Risk Assessment

| LOW | MEDIUM | HIGH |
|---|---|---|

Our risk assessment reflects our view that HOG's market leadership position and strong brand will help offset the prospect that an aging U.S. population will limit future domestic demand for motorcycles.

## Quantitative Evaluations

**S&P Quality Ranking**  A-

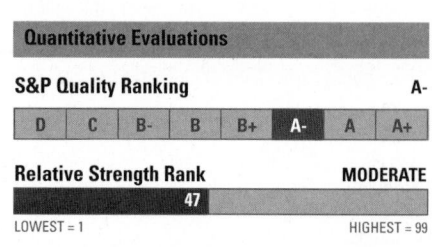

| D | C | B- | B | B+ | A- | A | A+ |
|---|---|---|---|---|---|---|---|

**Relative Strength Rank**  MODERATE

47

LOWEST = 1   HIGHEST = 99

## Revenue/Earnings Data

**Revenue (Million $)**

| | 1Q | 2Q | 3Q | 4Q | Year |
|---|---|---|---|---|---|
| 2011 | 1,225 | 1,506 | 1,397 | -- | -- |
| 2010 | 1,207 | 1,309 | 1,260 | 1,083 | 4,859 |
| 2009 | 1,383 | 1,260 | 1,246 | 893.7 | 4,782 |
| 2008 | 1,306 | 1,573 | 1,423 | 1,293 | 5,594 |
| 2007 | 1,179 | 1,620 | 1,541 | 1,386 | 5,727 |
| 2006 | 1,285 | 1,377 | 1,636 | 1,503 | 5,801 |

**Earnings Per Share ($)**

| | | | | | |
|---|---|---|---|---|---|
| 2011 | 0.51 | 0.81 | 0.78 | E0.18 | E2.27 |
| 2010 | 0.29 | 0.59 | 0.40 | -0.18 | 1.11 |
| 2009 | 0.55 | 0.14 | 0.24 | -0.63 | 0.30 |
| 2008 | 0.79 | 0.95 | 0.71 | 0.34 | 2.79 |
| 2007 | 0.74 | 1.14 | 1.07 | 0.78 | 3.74 |
| 2006 | 0.86 | 0.91 | 1.20 | 0.97 | 3.93 |

Fiscal year ended Dec. 31. Next earnings report expected: Early March. EPS Estimates based on S&P Operating Earnings; historical GAAP earnings are as reported.

## Dividend Data (Dates: mm/dd Payment Date: mm/dd/yy)

| Amount ($) | Date Decl. | Ex-Div. Date | Stk. of Record | Payment Date |
|---|---|---|---|---|
| 0.100 | 12/07 | 12/17 | 12/21 | 12/31/10 |
| 0.100 | 02/10 | 02/17 | 02/22 | 03/04/11 |
| 0.125 | 04/30 | 05/31 | 06/02 | 06/17/11 |
| 0.125 | 09/08 | 09/28 | 09/30 | 10/14/11 |

Dividends have been paid since 1993. Source: Company reports.

# Harley-Davidson Inc.

STANDARD &POOR'S

## Business Summary October 25, 2011

CORPORATE OVERVIEW. Harley-Davidson is a leading supplier of heavy-weight motorcycles (engine displacement exceeding about 651 cubic centimeters). The company also sells motorcycle parts, accessories, clothing and collectibles, and has a sizable financial services business.

HOG manufactures five families of Harley-Davidson brand motorcycles: Sportster, Dyna, Softail, Touring and VRSC. In 2011, the engines in these product lines ranged in size from 883 cc to 1800 cc.

The company's 2011 model year line-up includes 32 models of Harley-Davidson heavyweight motorcycles, with domestic manufacturer's suggested retail prices ranging from $13,225 to $53,095. In 2010, HOG shipped 210,494 Harley-Davidson brand motorcycles, down from 223,023 in 2009, 303,479 in 2008, and 330,619 in 2007. HOG shipped 5,572 Buell motorcycles in 2009 before shuttering the brand, down from 13,119 in 2008 and 11,513 in 2007.

CORPORATE STRATEGY. We expect the company to focus both on current owners of HOG motorcycles and on potential new customers. We believe that many purchasers of a new Harley-Davidson motorcycle previously owned a HOG bike. We expect HOG's marketing focus to include international markets, where we project that its opportunities for growth are stronger than they are

in the U.S. In 2010, HOG's international sales totaled about $1.36 billion (33% of total sales), higher on a percentage basis from $1.38 billion (32%) in 2009, and $1.75 billion (31%) in 2008.

HOG has in the past earned sizable profits from financial services it provides to independent dealers and to retail customers of those dealers. During 2010, Harley-Davidson Financial Services financed 47.9% of the new Harley-Davidson motorcycles retailed by independent dealers in the United States, as compared to 48.8% in 2009 and 53.5% in 2008.

In August 2008, HOG completed its acquisition of 100% of MV Agusta Group, an Italian motorcycle manufacturer, for total consideration of $109 million. In 2007, MVAG shipped 5,819 motorcycles. HOG did not disclose how many units MVAG shipped in 2008. Then, in October 2009, HOG announced it intends to divest the brand to focus on its "single-brand strategy," and MV Agusta was ultimately sold to Claudio Castiglioni in August 2010.

## Company Financials Fiscal Year Ended Dec. 31

| Per Share Data ($) | 2010 | 2009 | 2008 | 2007 | 2006 | 2005 | 2004 | 2003 | 2002 | 2001 |
|---|---|---|---|---|---|---|---|---|---|---|
| Tangible Book Value | 9.33 | 8.86 | 8.49 | 16.32 | 10.46 | 11.05 | 10.73 | 9.63 | 7.21 | 5.64 |
| Cash Flow | 2.19 | 1.36 | 3.83 | 4.55 | 4.87 | 4.25 | 3.72 | 3.18 | 2.48 | 1.93 |
| Earnings | 1.11 | 0.30 | 2.79 | 3.74 | 3.93 | 3.41 | 3.00 | 2.50 | 1.90 | 1.43 |
| S&P Core Earnings | 1.25 | 0.54 | 2.57 | 3.76 | 3.95 | 3.44 | 2.98 | 2.51 | 1.85 | 1.34 |
| Dividends | 0.40 | 0.40 | 1.29 | 1.06 | 0.81 | 0.63 | 0.41 | 0.20 | 0.14 | 0.12 |
| Payout Ratio | 36% | 133% | 46% | 28% | 21% | 18% | 13% | 8% | 7% | 8% |
| Prices:High | 36.13 | 30.00 | 48.05 | 74.03 | 75.87 | 62.49 | 63.75 | 52.51 | 57.25 | 55.99 |
| Prices:Low | 21.26 | 7.99 | 11.54 | 44.37 | 47.86 | 44.40 | 45.20 | 35.01 | 42.60 | 32.00 |
| P/E Ratio:High | 33 | NM | NA | 17 | 19 | 18 | 21 | 21 | 30 | 39 |
| P/E Ratio:Low | 19 | NM | 4 | 12 | 12 | 13 | 15 | 14 | 22 | 22 |

| Income Statement Analysis (Million $) | | | | | | | | | | |
|---|---|---|---|---|---|---|---|---|---|---|
| Revenue | 4,859 | 4,782 | 5,594 | 5,727 | 5,801 | 5,342 | 5,015 | 4,624 | 4,091 | 3,363 |
| Operating Income | 990 | 695 | 1,441 | 1,721 | 1,431 | 1,676 | 1,576 | 1,346 | 1,059 | 816 |
| Depreciation | 255 | 246 | 242 | 204 | 214 | 206 | 214 | 197 | 176 | 153 |
| Interest Expense | 90.4 | 21.7 | 141 | 81.5 | Nil | Nil | Nil | Nil | Nil | Nil |
| Pretax Income | 390 | 179 | 1,034 | 1,448 | 1,624 | 1,488 | 1,379 | 1,166 | 886 | 673 |
| Effective Tax Rate | 33.5% | 60.5% | 36.7% | 35.5% | 35.8% | 35.5% | 35.5% | 34.7% | 34.5% | 35.0% |
| Net Income | 260 | 70.6 | 655 | 934 | 1,043 | 960 | 890 | 761 | 580 | 438 |
| S&P Core Earnings | 291 | 128 | 604 | 940 | 1,048 | 969 | 881 | 763 | 564 | 411 |

| Balance Sheet & Other Financial Data (Million $) | | | | | | | | | | |
|---|---|---|---|---|---|---|---|---|---|---|
| Cash | 1,162 | 1,670 | 594 | 405 | 897 | 1,046 | 1,612 | 1,323 | 796 | 635 |
| Total Assets | 9,431 | 9,156 | 7,829 | 5,657 | 5,532 | 5,255 | 5,483 | 4,923 | 3,861 | 3,118 |
| Long Term Debt | 4,521 | 4,114 | 2,176 | 980 | 87.0 | 1,000 | 800 | 670 | 380 | 380 |
| Total Debt | 5,752 | 5,636 | 3,915 | 2,100 | 87.0 | 1,205 | 1,295 | 794 | 763 | 597 |
| Common Equity | 2,207 | 2,108 | 2,116 | 2,375 | 2,757 | 3,084 | 3,218 | 2,958 | 2,233 | 1,756 |
| Capital Expenditures | 171 | 117 | 232 | 242 | 220 | 198 | 214 | 227 | 324 | 204 |
| Cash Flow | 515 | 317 | 897 | 1,138 | 1,257 | 1,165 | 1,104 | 958 | 756 | 591 |
| % Return on Assets | 2.8 | 0.8 | 9.7 | 16.7 | 19.3 | 17.9 | 17.1 | 17.3 | 16.6 | 15.8 |
| % Return on Equity | 12.0 | 3.3 | 29.2 | 36.4 | 35.7 | 30.5 | 28.8 | 29.3 | 29.1 | 27.7 |
| % Long Term Debt of Capitalization | 67.2 | 66.1 | 50.7 | 29.2 | 3.1 | 23.6 | 19.7 | 17.8 | 14.4 | 17.6 |

Data as orig reptd.; bef. results of disc opers/spec. items. Per share data adj. for stk. divs.; EPS diluted. E-Estimated. NA-Not Available. NM-Not Meaningful. NR-Not Ranked. UR-Under Review.

Office: 3700 W Juneau Ave, Milwaukee, WI 53208.
Telephone: 414-342-4680.
Email: investor_relations@harley-davidson.com
Website: http://www.harley-davidson.com

Chrmn: B.K. Allen
Pres & CEO: K.E. Wandell
SVP & CFO: J. Olin
Chief Acctg Officer: M.R. Kornetzke

Treas: J.D. Thomas
Investor Contact: T.E. Bergmann (414-342-4680)
Board Members: B. K. Allen, R. J. Anderson, R. I. Beattie, M. F. Brooks, G. H. Conrades, D. James, S. Levinson, N. T. Linebarger, G. L. Miles, Jr., J. A. Norling, K. E. Wandell, J. Zeitz

Founded: 1903
Domicile: Wisconsin
Employees: 6,900

# Harman International Industries Inc.

**STANDARD &POOR'S**

| S&P Recommendation  HOLD ★★★☆☆ | Price $36.72 (as of Nov 25, 2011) | 12-Mo. Target Price $50.00 | Investment Style Large-Cap Growth |
|---|---|---|---|

**GICS Sector** Consumer Discretionary
**Sub-Industry** Consumer Electronics

**Summary** This company manufactures and markets high-fidelity audio products and electronic systems targeted at OEM, consumer and professional markets.

## Key Stock Statistics (Source S&P, Vickers, company reports)

| | | | | | | | |
|---|---|---|---|---|---|---|---|
| 52-Wk Range | $52.54– 25.53 | S&P Oper. EPS 2012**E** | 2.93 | Market Capitalization(B) | $2.574 | Beta | 2.14 |
| Trailing 12-Month EPS | $2.18 | S&P Oper. EPS 2013**E** | 3.81 | Yield (%) | 0.82 | S&P 3-Yr. Proj. EPS CAGR(%) | 20 |
| Trailing 12-Month P/E | 16.8 | P/E on S&P Oper. EPS 2012**E** | 12.5 | Dividend Rate/Share | $0.30 | S&P Credit Rating | BB+ |
| $10K Invested 5 Yrs Ago | $3,466 | Common Shares Outstg. (M) | 70.1 | Institutional Ownership (%) | NM | | |

## Price Performance

30-Week Mov. Avg. · · · · 10-Week Mov. Avg. – – **GAAP Earnings vs. Previous Year**  Volume Above Avg. STARS
12-Mo. Target Price — Relative Strength — ▲ Up ▼ Down ► No Change  Below Avg. ★

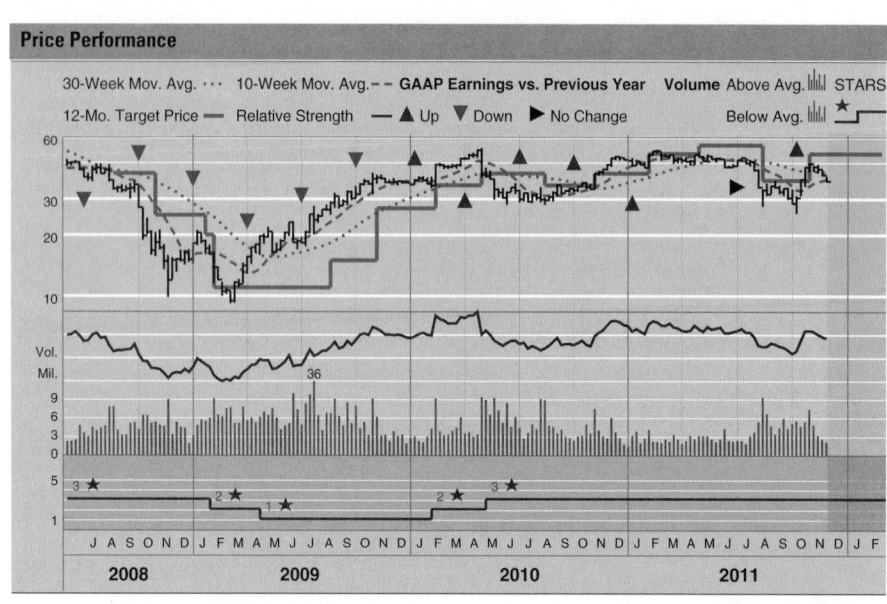

Options: ASE, CBOE, P, Ph

Analysis prepared by Equity Analyst **Michael Souers** on Nov 14, 2011, when the stock traded at **$41.23**.

### Highlights

➤ We see FY 12 (Jun.) revenues rising 16%, following a 12% advance in FY 11. We expect this increase to be driven by an uptick in automotive sales and market share gains, particularly in emerging markets. In addition, HAR has captured several audio and infotainment awards, which should lead to sales growth over the next several years, and it now has a backlog of $14.5 billion. Offsetting these positive drivers should be a weak global economy, which we expect to pressure consumer spending over the near to medium term.

➤ We expect gross margins to widen modestly on productivity improvement in Infotainment business, partially offset by raw material cost pressure. In addition, HAR has captured over $400 million of cost savings across engineering, sourcing and manufacturing, and we expect these efforts to be ongoing. In FY 12, we see continued cost controls leading to a 150 basis point widening of operating margins.

➤ We project FY 12 EPS of $2.93, a 41% increase from the $2.08 the company earned in FY 11, excluding $0.18 of net charges related to restructuring activities and goodwill impairment. We see EPS of $3.81 in FY 13.

### Investment Rationale/Risk

➤ We think HAR's plans to sharply reduce costs have paid off handsomely, and we expect much-improved operating margins as a result. In addition, we think HAR's selection by Toyota to provide infotainment systems for vehicles sold in Europe is a potentially major boon for future sales. Nevertheless, we continue to project a weak global economic recovery, with only modest improvement in automotive sales over the next couple of years. The shares recently traded at about 14X our FY 12 EPS estimate, a modest premium to the S&P 500, but we think this premium is merited by the company's potential for operating margin improvement over the medium term.

➤ Risks to our recommendation and target price include higher-than-anticipated research and development costs; a double-dip recession, which would adversely affect automotive sales and overall consumer spending; and unfavorable foreign currency translation.

➤ We derive our 12-month target price of $50 from our discounted cash flow analysis. Our model assumes a weighted average cost of capital of 10.9% and a terminal growth rate of 3.0%.

### Qualitative Risk Assessment

| LOW | MEDIUM | **HIGH** |
|---|---|---|

Our risk assessment reflects HAR's customer concentration in the automotive segment and sensitivity to the cyclical automobile industry, only partly offset by our view of its strong balance sheet.

### Quantitative Evaluations

**S&P Quality Ranking** B

| D | C | B- | **B** | B+ | A- | A | A+ |
|---|---|---|---|---|---|---|---|

**Relative Strength Rank** MODERATE

58

LOWEST = 1  HIGHEST = 99

### Revenue/Earnings Data

**Revenue (Million $)**

| | 1Q | 2Q | 3Q | 4Q | Year |
|---|---|---|---|---|---|
| 2012 | 1,051 | -- | -- | -- | -- |
| 2011 | 837.0 | 956.1 | 948.2 | 1,031 | 3,772 |
| 2010 | 748.4 | 928.3 | 837.0 | 850.7 | 3,364 |
| 2009 | 869.2 | 755.9 | 598.3 | 667.7 | 2,891 |
| 2008 | 947.0 | 1,066 | 1,033 | 1,067 | 4,113 |
| 2007 | 825.5 | 931.7 | 882.8 | 911.1 | 3,551 |

**Earnings Per Share ($)**

| | 1Q | 2Q | 3Q | 4Q | Year |
|---|---|---|---|---|---|
| 2012 | 0.67 | E0.88 | E0.71 | E0.68 | E2.93 |
| 2011 | 0.39 | 0.74 | E0.60 | 0.26 | 1.90 |
| 2010 | -0.17 | 0.19 | 0.21 | 0.26 | 0.50 |
| 2009 | 0.40 | -5.41 | -1.14 | -1.05 | -7.19 |
| 2008 | 0.55 | 0.68 | -0.06 | 0.54 | 1.73 |
| 2007 | 0.85 | 1.22 | 1.07 | 1.58 | 4.72 |

Fiscal year ended Jun. 30. Next earnings report expected: Early February. EPS Estimates based on S&P Operating Earnings; historical GAAP earnings are as reported.

### Dividend Data (Dates: mm/dd Payment Date: mm/dd/yy)

| Amount ($) | Date Decl. | Ex-Div. Date | Stk. of Record | Payment Date |
|---|---|---|---|---|
| 0.025 | 02/16 | 02/24 | 02/28 | 03/14/11 |
| 0.025 | 04/28 | 05/05 | 05/09 | 05/23/11 |
| 0.075 | 08/10 | 08/18 | 08/22 | 09/06/11 |
| 0.075 | 10/21 | 10/27 | 10/31 | 11/14/11 |

Dividends have been paid since 2011. Source: Company reports.

# Harman International Industries Inc.

STANDARD &POOR'S

## Business Summary November 14, 2011

CORPORATE OVERVIEW. Harman International Industries (HAR) has three main operating segments: Automotive (73% of FY 11 (Jun.) sales), Professional (16%) and Consumer (11%). Within Automotive, HAR designs, manufactures and markets audio, electronic and infotainment systems to be installed as original equipment by automotive manufacturers. Infotainment systems are a combination of information and entertainment components that may include or control GPS navigation, traffic information, voice-activated telephone and climate control, rear seat entertainment, wireless Internet access, hard disk recording, MP3 playback, and high-end branded audio systems. Brand names include JBL, Infinity, Mark Levinson, Harmon/Kardon, Logic 7, Lexicon and Becker. Customers include Audi/Volkswagen, BMW, Daimler AG, Chrysler, Toyota/Lexus, Hyundai, Porsche, Land Rover, PSA Peugeot Citroen and Jaguar. HAR also produces an infotainment system for Harley-Davidson motorcycles. HAR believes its competitive position is enhanced by the company's technical expertise in designing and integrating acoustics, navigation, speech recognition and human-machine interfaces into complete infotainment systems uniquely adapted to the specific requirements of each automotive model.

HAR's Professional segment designs, manufactures and markets an extensive range of loudspeakers, power amplifiers, digital signal processors, microphones, headphones and mixing consoles used by audio professionals in concert halls, stadiums, airports, houses of worship and other public spaces. HAR's products were used at such venues as the 2008 Beijing Olympics and the 2009 Presidential Inauguration. Products are marketed globally under a number of brand names including JBL Professional, AKG, Crown, Soundcraft, Lexicon, Mark Levinson, Revel, DigiTech, dbx and Studer.

In the Consumer segment, HAR makes audio, video and electronic systems for home, mobile and multimedia applications. Mobile products include an array of aftermarket systems to deliver audio entertainment and navigation in vehicles. Products for multimedia applications are primarily focused on enhancing sound for Apple's iPods and iPhones, computers, headphones and MP3 players. Brands include AKG, Harman/Kardon, Infinity, JBL, Mark Levinson and Selenium.

## Company Financials Fiscal Year Ended Jun. 30

| Per Share Data ($) | 2011 | 2010 | 2009 | 2008 | 2007 | 2006 | 2005 | 2004 | 2003 | 2002 |
|---|---|---|---|---|---|---|---|---|---|---|
| Tangible Book Value | 18.65 | 14.80 | 12.87 | 15.44 | 16.71 | 12.82 | 10.74 | 9.43 | 6.66 | 5.04 |
| Cash Flow | 3.62 | 2.31 | -4.68 | 4.18 | 6.64 | 5.66 | 4.99 | 3.80 | 2.85 | 2.00 |
| Earnings | 1.90 | 0.50 | -7.19 | 1.73 | 4.72 | 3.75 | 3.31 | 2.27 | 1.55 | 0.85 |
| S&P Core Earnings | 1.77 | 0.65 | -3.50 | 1.79 | 4.75 | 3.75 | 3.28 | 2.27 | 1.51 | 0.76 |
| Dividends | 0.05 | Nil | 0.04 | 0.05 | 0.05 | 0.05 | 0.05 | 0.05 | 0.05 | 0.05 |
| Payout Ratio | 3% | Nil | NM | 3% | 1% | 1% | 2% | 2% | 3% | 6% |
| Prices:High | 52.54 | 53.36 | 40.33 | 73.75 | 125.13 | 115.85 | 130.45 | 131.74 | 75.35 | 32.65 |
| Prices:Low | 25.53 | 28.10 | 9.17 | 9.87 | 69.48 | 74.65 | 68.54 | 66.12 | 26.15 | 19.09 |
| P/E Ratio:High | 28 | NM | NM | 43 | 27 | 31 | 39 | 58 | 49 | 38 |
| P/E Ratio:Low | 13 | NM | NM | 6 | 15 | 20 | 21 | 29 | 17 | 22 |

| Income Statement Analysis (Million $) | | | | | | | | | | |
|---|---|---|---|---|---|---|---|---|---|---|
| Revenue | 3,772 | 3,364 | 2,891 | 4,113 | 3,551 | 3,248 | 3,031 | 2,711 | 2,229 | 1,826 |
| Operating Income | 313 | 263 | -31.2 | 351 | 514 | 527 | 470 | 360 | 255 | 181 |
| Depreciation | 123 | 128 | 147 | 152 | 127 | 130 | 119 | 106 | 88.5 | 78.1 |
| Interest Expense | 32.5 | 30.2 | 15.3 | 21.2 | 1.50 | 13.0 | 10.5 | 17.2 | 22.6 | 22.4 |
| Pretax Income | 160 | 49.1 | -520 | 124 | 382 | 376 | 335 | 228 | 142 | 80.2 |
| Effective Tax Rate | NA | NA | NM | 13.8% | 18.4% | 32.4% | 30.6% | 30.6% | 26.0% | 28.2% |
| Net Income | 136 | 35.2 | -423 | 108 | 314 | 255 | 233 | 158 | 105 | 57.5 |
| S&P Core Earnings | 126 | 45.8 | -206 | 111 | 316 | 256 | 231 | 158 | 102 | 51.5 |

| Balance Sheet & Other Financial Data (Million $) | | | | | | | | | | |
|---|---|---|---|---|---|---|---|---|---|---|
| Cash | 921 | 646 | 591 | 223 | 106 | 292 | 291 | 378 | 148 | 116 |
| Current Assets | 2,108 | 1,674 | 1,511 | 1,439 | 1,233 | 1,249 | 1,183 | 1,204 | 968 | 877 |
| Total Assets | 3,059 | 2,556 | 2,492 | 2,827 | 2,509 | 2,355 | 2,187 | 1,989 | 1,704 | 1,480 |
| Current Liabilities | 1,048 | 863 | 744 | 907 | 816 | 869 | 729 | 662 | 487 | 433 |
| Long Term Debt | 379 | 364 | 629 | 427 | 57.7 | 179 | 331 | 388 | 498 | 470 |
| Common Equity | 1,424 | 1,135 | 974 | 1,340 | 1,510 | 1,228 | 1,061 | 875 | 656 | 527 |
| Total Capital | 1,803 | 1,499 | 1,603 | 1,767 | 1,568 | 1,410 | 1,392 | 1,263 | 1,154 | 999 |
| Capital Expenditures | 108 | 60.0 | 79.9 | 139 | 175 | 131 | 176 | 135 | 116 | 114 |
| Cash Flow | 259 | 163 | -275 | 260 | 441 | 385 | 352 | 264 | 194 | 136 |
| Current Ratio | 2.0 | 1.9 | 2.0 | 1.6 | 1.5 | 1.4 | 1.6 | 1.8 | 2.0 | 2.0 |
| % Long Term Debt of Capitalization | 21.0 | 24.3 | 39.2 | 24.2 | 3.7 | 12.7 | 23.8 | 30.7 | 43.2 | 47.1 |
| % Net Income of Revenue | 3.6 | 1.1 | NM | 2.6 | 8.8 | 7.9 | 7.7 | 5.8 | 4.7 | 3.1 |
| % Return on Assets | 4.8 | 1.4 | NM | 4.0 | 12.9 | 11.2 | 11.2 | 8.6 | 6.6 | 4.4 |
| % Return on Equity | 10.6 | 3.3 | NM | 7.6 | 22.8 | 22.3 | 24.1 | 20.6 | 17.8 | 12.1 |

Data as orig reptd.; bef. results of disc opers/spec. items. Per share data adj. for stk. divs.; EPS diluted. E-Estimated. NA-Not Available. NM-Not Meaningful. NR-Not Ranked. UR-Under Review.

Office: 400 Atlantic Street, Suite 1500, Stamford, CT 06901.
Telephone: 203-328-3500.
Website: http://www.harman.com
Chrmn, Pres & CEO: D.C. Paliwal

EVP & CFO: H.K. Parker
EVP & CTO: S. Lawande
EVP, Secy & General Counsel: T.A. Suko
Chief Acctg Officer: J. Peter

Investor Contact: S.B. Robinson (202-393-1101)
Board Members: B. F. Carroll, H. Einsmann, A. M. Korologos, J. Liu, E. H. Meyer, D. C. Paliwal, K. M. Reiss, H. S. Runtagh, G. G. Steel

Founded: 1980
Domicile: Delaware
Employees: 10,103

The McGraw-Hill Companies

# Harris Corp

**STANDARD &POOR'S**

| S&P Recommendation | STRONG BUY ★★★★★ | Price | 12-Mo. Target Price | Investment Style |
|---|---|---|---|---|
| | | $33.26 (as of Nov 25, 2011) | $47.00 | Large-Cap Growth |

**GICS Sector** Information Technology
**Sub-Industry** Communications Equipment

**Summary** This company focuses on communications equipment for voice, data and video applications for commercial and governmental customers.

## Key Stock Statistics (Source S&P, Vickers, company reports)

| | | | | | | | |
|---|---|---|---|---|---|---|---|
| 52-Wk Range | $53.39– 32.68 | S&P Oper. EPS 2012**E** | 5.13 | Market Capitalization(B) | $3.852 | Beta | 0.94 |
| Trailing 12-Month EPS | $4.34 | S&P Oper. EPS 2013**E** | NA | Yield (%) | 3.37 | S&P 3-Yr. Proj. EPS CAGR(%) | 7 |
| Trailing 12-Month P/E | 7.7 | P/E on S&P Oper. EPS 2012**E** | 6.5 | Dividend Rate/Share | $1.12 | S&P Credit Rating | BBB+ |
| $10K Invested 5 Yrs Ago | NA | Common Shares Outstg. (M) | 115.8 | Institutional Ownership (%) | 95 | | |

## Price Performance

30-Week Mov. Avg. ···   10-Week Mov. Avg. – – GAAP Earnings vs. Previous Year   Volume Above Avg. STARS
12-Mo. Target Price —   Relative Strength —   ▲ Up ▼ Down ▶ No Change   Below Avg.

Options: ASE, CBOE, P, Ph

Analysis prepared by Equity Analyst **Todd Rosenbluth** on Nov 02, 2011, when the stock traded at **$36.66**.

## Qualitative Risk Assessment

| LOW | MEDIUM | HIGH |
|---|---|---|

With most of the company's sales coming from the U.S. federal government and government agencies, we believe HRS is exposed to uneven sales patterns and fixed-price contract risks, which may affect profitability. However, we think HRS's balance sheet and competitive position are strong.

## Quantitative Evaluations

**S&P Quality Ranking** A-

| D | C | B- | B | B+ | A- | A | A+ |
|---|---|---|---|---|---|---|---|

**Relative Strength Rank** WEAK

29

LOWEST = 1     HIGHEST = 99

## Highlights

➤ We forecast revenues of $6.2 billion in FY 12 (Jun.), up from $5.9 billion in FY 11, supported by growth from recently acquired companies. We look for revenues in the RF Communications segment to decline slightly in FY 12 due to slower U.S. demand and international delays, but we see gains in public safety. We expect growth in the government communications segment as newer projects begin. We look for recent acquisitions in the integrated network solutions segment to drive revenues in energy and health care verticals. We expect revenue growth to improve throughout the year.

➤ We look for gross margins to widen in the second half of the year, relative to the first half and overall average of 35.5%, as lower pricing for new contracts is offset by improved sales of higher-margin products. With continued investment in R&D, we see the operating margin narrowing slightly to 16% in FY 12.

➤ We estimate operating EPS of $5.13 in FY 12, helped by share repurchase activities in the first half of FY 12.

## Investment Rationale/Risk

➤ While we think HRS will see a modestly negative impact from efforts to lower U.S. military spending, we think long-term trends favor growth in HRS's core segments. We see HRS benefiting as local and federal government agencies focus on improving the technological capabilities of their communications systems, and we see recent acquisitions supporting growth in FY 12. We believe HRS has a strong balance sheet and generates strong cash flow to support its recent dividend increase and planned share repurchases.

➤ Risks to our recommendation and target price include greater-than-expected pressure on funding for military contracts, failure to smoothly integrate recent acquisitions, and technological issues with its products.

➤ The shares recently traded at a discount P/E of about 7X our FY 12 estimate. Based on a narrower discount to communications and defense peers' P/E of about 9X, we arrive at our 12-month target price of $47. The stock's indicated 3% dividend yield adds to its appeal, in our view.

## Revenue/Earnings Data

### Revenue (Million $)

| | 1Q | 2Q | 3Q | 4Q | Year |
|---|---|---|---|---|---|
| 2012 | 1,460 | -- | -- | -- | -- |
| 2011 | 1,405 | 1,439 | 1,413 | 1,667 | 5,925 |
| 2010 | 1,203 | 1,218 | 1,330 | 1,456 | 5,206 |
| 2009 | 1,173 | 1,333 | 1,205 | 1,294 | 5,005 |
| 2008 | 1,231 | 1,318 | 1,330 | 1,433 | 5,311 |
| 2007 | 946.8 | 1,016 | 1,072 | 1,208 | 4,243 |

### Earnings Per Share ($)

| | | | | | |
|---|---|---|---|---|---|
| 2012 | 1.01 | E1.21 | E1.32 | E1.58 | E5.13 |
| 2011 | 1.27 | 1.18 | 1.09 | 1.06 | 4.60 |
| 2010 | 0.79 | 1.06 | 1.26 | 1.16 | 4.28 |
| 2009 | 0.89 | 1.06 | 1.02 | -0.64 | 2.35 |
| 2008 | 0.73 | 0.83 | 0.78 | 0.91 | 3.26 |
| 2007 | 0.60 | 0.67 | 1.52 | 0.63 | 3.43 |

Fiscal year ended Jun. 30. Next earnings report expected: Late January. EPS Estimates based on S&P Operating Earnings; historical GAAP earnings are as reported.

## Dividend Data (Dates: mm/dd Payment Date: mm/dd/yy)

| Amount ($) | Date Decl. | Ex-Div. Date | Stk. of Record | Payment Date |
|---|---|---|---|---|
| 0.250 | 04/22 | 05/26 | 05/31 | 06/10/11 |
| 0.280 | 08/02 | 09/02 | 09/07 | 09/16/11 |
| 0.280 | 10/28 | 11/16 | 11/18 | 12/02/11 |

Dividends have been paid since 1941. Source: Company reports.

---

**Please read the Required Disclosures and Analyst Certification on the last page of this report.**

**The McGraw-Hill Companies**

# Harris Corp

## Business Summary November 02, 2011

CORPORATE OVERVIEW. Harris Corp. is an international communications equipment company that focuses on providing product, system and service solutions for commercial and governmental customers, including communications networks, antennas, aviation electronics, and handheld radios. Effective March 2011, the company operated in three main business segments: government communications systems, RF Communications (which includes the tactical handheld radios) and integrated network solutions, which includes information technology (IT) services, health care services and broadcast communications.

PRIMARY BUSINESS DYNAMICS. The government communications systems (GCS) segment, which contributed 30% of revenues in FY 11 (Jun.), conducts advanced research studies and produces, integrates and supports highly reliable, net-centric communications and information technology that solve the mission-critical challenges of the company's defense, intelligence and civilian U.S. government customers. Integrated network solutions (34% of revenues), includes broadcast communications along with assets that were previously part of GCS and those that were recently acquired, such as CapRock Communications and the Global Connectivity Services business of Schlumberger. During the fourth quarter of FY 11, new business included a drilling contract for offshore satellite communications services and one to operate sea floor

communication equipment for deep-ocean observation.

The RF Communications segment (39% of revenues) supplies secure wireless voice and data communications products, systems and networks to the U.S. DoD and other federal and state agencies, and foreign government defense agencies. The segment offers a line of secure tactical radio products and systems for person-transportable, mobile, strategic fixed-site and shipboard applications used by military personnel. Ongoing political instability internationally has slowed orders for tactical radios, but HRS is confident it will benefit from demand both inside and outside of the U.S. At June 2011, total backlog amounted to $1.5 billion.

In May 2009, HRS acquired, for $675 million cash, Tyco Electronics' Wireless Systems business, which provides wireless systems for law enforcement, fire and rescue and public service organizations. In the fourth quarter of FY 11, the segment's orders rose from the prior quarter.

## Company Financials Fiscal Year Ended Jun. 30

| Per Share Data ($) | 2011 | 2010 | 2009 | 2008 | 2007 | 2006 | 2005 | 2004 | 2003 | 2002 |
|---|---|---|---|---|---|---|---|---|---|---|
| Tangible Book Value | NM | 2.48 | 0.20 | 2.69 | NM | 3.90 | 5.79 | 7.96 | 7.21 | 7.05 |
| Cash Flow | 6.33 | 5.59 | 3.68 | 4.46 | 4.75 | 2.53 | 1.94 | 1.36 | 0.87 | 1.04 |
| Earnings | 4.60 | 4.28 | 2.35 | 3.26 | 3.43 | 1.71 | 1.46 | 0.94 | 0.45 | 0.63 |
| S&P Core Earnings | 4.60 | 4.28 | 3.14 | 3.19 | 2.74 | 1.74 | 1.43 | 0.90 | 0.31 | 0.28 |
| Dividends | 1.25 | 0.88 | 0.80 | 0.60 | 0.44 | 0.32 | 0.24 | 0.20 | 0.16 | 0.10 |
| Payout Ratio | 27% | 21% | 34% | 18% | 13% | 19% | 16% | 21% | 36% | 16% |
| Prices:High | 53.39 | 54.50 | 48.25 | 66.71 | 66.94 | 49.78 | 45.78 | 34.58 | 19.74 | 19.35 |
| Prices:Low | 32.68 | 40.24 | 26.11 | 27.56 | 45.85 | 37.69 | 26.94 | 18.92 | 12.68 | 12.05 |
| P/E Ratio:High | 12 | 13 | 21 | 20 | 20 | 29 | 31 | 37 | 44 | 31 |
| P/E Ratio:Low | 7 | 9 | 11 | 8 | 13 | 22 | 18 | 20 | 28 | 19 |

### Income Statement Analysis (Million $)

| | 2011 | 2010 | 2009 | 2008 | 2007 | 2006 | 2005 | 2004 | 2003 | 2002 |
|---|---|---|---|---|---|---|---|---|---|---|
| Revenue | 5,925 | 5,206 | 5,005 | 5,311 | 4,243 | 3,475 | 3,001 | 2,519 | 2,093 | 1,876 |
| Operating Income | 1,229 | 1,105 | 972 | 958 | 676 | 505 | 393 | 264 | 142 | 153 |
| Depreciation | 212 | 166 | 178 | 164 | 135 | 98.4 | 71.4 | 55.1 | 56.4 | 55.1 |
| Interest Expense | 90.4 | 72.1 | 52.8 | 55.8 | 41.1 | 36.5 | 24.0 | 24.5 | 24.9 | 26.7 |
| Pretax Income | 881 | 840 | 485 | 638 | 661 | 381 | 298 | 180 | 90.1 | 125 |
| Effective Tax Rate | NA | 33.2% | 35.6% | 31.6% | 28.9% | 37.5% | 32.2% | 30.2% | 34.0% | 34.0% |
| Net Income | 587 | 562 | 312 | 444 | 480 | 238 | 202 | 126 | 59.5 | 82.6 |
| S&P Core Earnings | 581 | 556 | 417 | 435 | 382 | 243 | 199 | 120 | 40.8 | 36.5 |

### Balance Sheet & Other Financial Data (Million $)

| | 2011 | 2010 | 2009 | 2008 | 2007 | 2006 | 2005 | 2004 | 2003 | 2002 |
|---|---|---|---|---|---|---|---|---|---|---|
| Cash | 367 | 455 | 285 | 392 | 409 | 181 | 378 | 644 | 466 | 278 |
| Current Assets | 2,217 | 1,996 | 1,859 | 2,047 | 1,829 | 1,428 | 1,318 | 1,554 | 1,358 | 1,154 |
| Total Assets | 6,173 | 4,735 | 4,465 | 4,559 | 4,406 | 3,142 | 2,457 | 2,226 | 2,080 | 1,859 |
| Current Liabilities | 1,431 | 1,043 | 1,110 | 995 | 1,638 | 752 | 590 | 543 | 496 | 426 |
| Long Term Debt | 1,887 | 1,177 | 1,177 | 832 | 409 | 700 | 401 | 401 | 402 | 283 |
| Common Equity | 2,512 | 2,190 | 1,869 | 2,274 | 1,904 | 1,662 | 1,439 | 1,279 | 1,188 | 1,150 |
| Total Capital | 4,404 | 3,367 | 3,046 | 3,466 | 2,701 | 2,390 | 1,867 | 1,683 | 1,590 | 1,433 |
| Capital Expenditures | 311 | 190 | 98.7 | 113 | 88.8 | 102 | 75.0 | 66.4 | 73.0 | 45.9 |
| Cash Flow | 799 | 727 | 490 | 609 | 616 | 336 | 274 | 181 | 116 | 138 |
| Current Ratio | 1.6 | 1.9 | 1.7 | 2.1 | 1.1 | 1.9 | 2.2 | 2.9 | 2.7 | 2.7 |
| % Long Term Debt of Capitalization | 42.9 | 34.9 | 38.6 | 24.0 | 15.1 | 29.3 | 21.5 | 23.9 | 25.3 | 19.8 |
| % Net Income of Revenue | 9.9 | 10.8 | 6.2 | 8.4 | 11.3 | 6.8 | 6.7 | 5.0 | 2.8 | 4.4 |
| % Return on Assets | 10.8 | 12.2 | 6.9 | 9.9 | 12.7 | 8.5 | 8.6 | 5.8 | 3.0 | 4.3 |
| % Return on Equity | 25.0 | 27.7 | 15.1 | 21.3 | 26.9 | 15.3 | 14.9 | 10.2 | 5.1 | 7.3 |

Data as orig reptd.; bef. results of disc opers/spec. items. Per share data adj. for stk. divs.; EPS diluted. E-Estimated. NA-Not Available. NM-Not Meaningful. NR-Not Ranked. UR-Under Review.

Office: 1025 West NASA Boulevard, Melbourne, FL 32919-0001.
Telephone: 321-727-9100.
Website: http://www.harris.com
Chrmn, Pres & CEO: H.L. Lance

Pres & CEO: W.M. Brown
COO & EVP: D.R. Pearson
SVP & Chief Admin Officer: J.S. Shuman
CFO: G.L. McArthur

Investor Contact: P. Padgett (321-727-9383)
Board Members: T. A. Dattilo, T. D. Growcock, L. Hay, III, K. L. Katen, S. P. Kaufman, L. F. Kenne, H. L. Lance, D. B. Rickard, J. C. Stoffel, G. T. Swienton, H. E. Tookes, II

Founded: 1916
Domicile: Delaware
Employees: 16,900

# Hartford Financial Services Group Inc. (The)

STANDARD
&POOR'S

| S&P Recommendation **BUY** ★★★★☆ | Price | 12-Mo. Target Price | Investment Style |
|---|---|---|---|
| | $15.46 (as of Nov 25, 2011) | $21.00 | Large-Cap Blend |

**GICS Sector** Financials
**Sub-Industry** Multi-line Insurance

**Summary** One of the largest U.S. multi-line insurance holding companies, Hartford is a leading writer of property and casualty insurance.

## Key Stock Statistics (Source S&P, Vickers, company reports)

| | | | | | | | |
|---|---|---|---|---|---|---|---|
| 52-Wk Range | $31.08– 14.56 | S&P Oper. EPS 2011**E** | 2.13 | Market Capitalization(B) | $6.891 | Beta | 3.04 |
| Trailing 12-Month EPS | $2.31 | S&P Oper. EPS 2012**E** | 4.14 | Yield (%) | 2.59 | S&P 3-Yr. Proj. EPS CAGR(%) | 17 |
| Trailing 12-Month P/E | 6.7 | P/E on S&P Oper. EPS 2011**E** | 7.3 | Dividend Rate/Share | $0.40 | S&P Credit Rating | BBB |
| $10K Invested 5 Yrs Ago | $2,026 | Common Shares Outstg. (M) | 445.7 | Institutional Ownership (%) | 90 | | |

## Price Performance

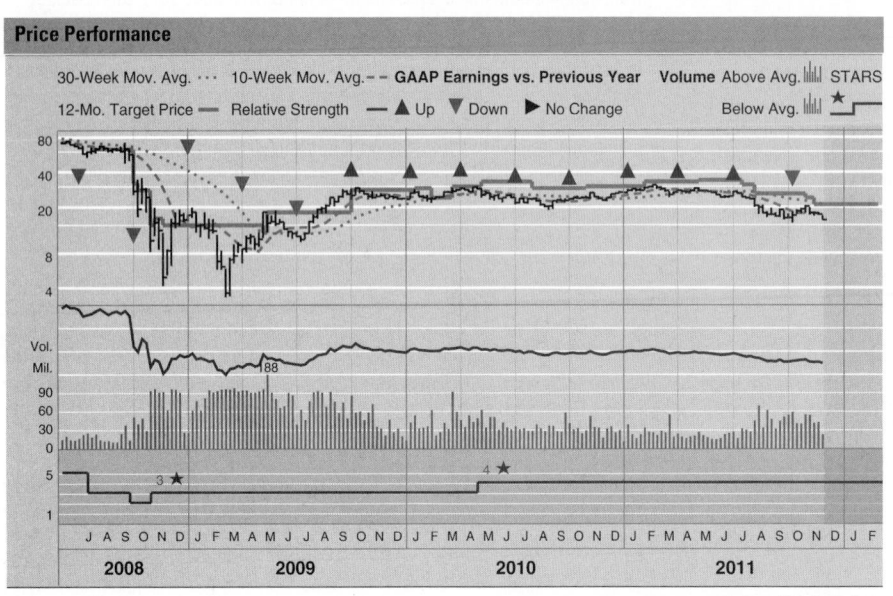

30-Week Mov. Avg. ···  10-Week Mov. Avg. --  **GAAP Earnings vs. Previous Year**  **Volume** Above Avg. STARS
12-Mo. Target Price —  Relative Strength —  ▲ Up  ▼ Down  ► No Change  Below Avg.

J A S O N D J F M A M J J A S O N D J F M A M J J A S O N D J F M A M J J A S O N D J F
2008   2009   2010   2011

Options: ASE, CBOE, P, Ph

### Qualitative Risk Assessment

| LOW | MEDIUM | **HIGH** |
|---|---|---|

Our risk assessment reflects our view of HIG's vulnerability to further credit write downs, especially considering its sizable holdings of lower quality CMBS. This is partially offset by our view of the relative earnings stability of HIG's P&C operations, increased hedging activity, and the company's overall improved capital position.

### Quantitative Evaluations

**S&P Quality Ranking**  B-

| D | C | **B-** | B | B+ | A- | A | A+ |
|---|---|---|---|---|---|---|---|

**Relative Strength Rank**  WEAK
20
LOWEST = 1   HIGHEST = 99

### Highlights

> The 12-month target price for HIG has recently been changed to $21.00 from $24.00. The Highlights section of this Stock Report will be updated accordingly.

### Investment Rationale/Risk

> The Investment Rationale/Risk section of this Stock Report will be updated shortly. For the latest News story on HIG from MarketScope, see below.

> 11/04/11 05:28 pm ET ... S&P KEEPS BUY OPINION ON SHARES OF HARTFORD FINANCIAL SERVICES GROUP (HIG 17.83****): HIG reports Q3 operating EPS of $0.05, vs. $1.42, well below our $0.22 estimate and the Capital IQ consensus operating EPS estimate of $0.25, largely due to higher than expected DAC (deferred acquisition cost) unlocking charge. This exacerbated some adverse claim trends in the property-casualty unit as well. We cut our 2011 operating EPS estimate to $2.13 from $2.30. We lower our 12-month target price by $3, to $21, assuming the shares trade at less than 1X estimated tangible book value and at 5.1X our $4.14 operating EPS estimate for 2012, a discount to peers. /C. Seifert

### Revenue/Earnings Data

**Revenue (Million $)**

| | 1Q | 2Q | 3Q | 4Q | Year |
|---|---|---|---|---|---|
| 2011 | 6,308 | 5,401 | 4,520 | -- | -- |
| 2010 | 6,319 | 3,336 | 6,673 | 6,055 | 22,383 |
| 2009 | 5,394 | 7,637 | 5,230 | 6,440 | 24,701 |
| 2008 | 1,544 | 7,503 | -393.0 | 565.0 | 9,219 |
| 2007 | 6,759 | 7,660 | 5,823 | 5,674 | 25,916 |
| 2006 | 6,543 | 4,971 | 7,407 | 7,579 | 26,500 |

**Earnings Per Share ($)**

| | 1Q | 2Q | 3Q | 4Q | Year |
|---|---|---|---|---|---|
| 2011 | 0.69 | 0.19 | -0.03 | E0.93 | E2.13 |
| 2010 | -0.42 | 0.14 | 1.34 | 1.24 | 2.49 |
| 2009 | -3.77 | -0.06 | -0.79 | 1.19 | -2.93 |
| 2008 | 0.46 | 1.73 | -8.74 | -2.71 | -8.99 |
| 2007 | 2.71 | 1.96 | 2.68 | 1.88 | 9.24 |
| 2006 | 2.34 | 1.52 | 2.39 | 2.42 | 8.69 |

Fiscal year ended Dec. 31. Next earnings report expected: NA. EPS Estimates based on S&P Operating Earnings; historical GAAP earnings are as reported.

### Dividend Data (Dates: mm/dd Payment Date: mm/dd/yy)

| Amount ($) | Date Decl. | Ex-Div. Date | Stk. of Record | Payment Date |
|---|---|---|---|---|
| 0.100 | 02/02 | 02/25 | 03/01 | 04/01/11 |
| 0.100 | 05/19 | 05/27 | 06/01 | 07/01/11 |
| 0.100 | 07/27 | 08/30 | 09/01 | 10/03/11 |
| 0.100 | 10/27 | 11/29 | 12/01 | 01/03/12 |

Dividends have been paid since 1996. Source: Company reports.

# Hartford Financial Services Group Inc. (The)

STANDARD
&POOR'S

## Business Summary October 31, 2011

CORPORATE OVERVIEW. Hartford Financial Services Group (HIG) is a multi-line insurer and one of the largest providers of investment, life insurance and property and casualty insurance products in the U.S. Operating revenues (excluding net realized capital gains) totaled $22.9 billion in 2010 (down from $26.7 billion in 2009). In 2010, HIG made changes to its reporting segments. As a result, it created three customer-oriented divisions -- Commercial Markets, Consumer Markets, and Wealth Management, conducting business in seven reporting segments. In addition, HIG includes a Corporate and Other segment.

The Commercial Markets segment (44% of total operating revenues in 2010) consists of the P&C commercial and group benefits sub-segments. P&C commercial provides a wide range of commercial and specialty coverages, while group benefits provides group life, accident and disability coverage, in addition to other lines. P&C commercial constitutes one of the largest U.S. property-casualty insurance organizations and reported earned premiums of $5.7 billion in 2010. Group benefits reported operating revenues of $4.8 billion.

The Consumer Markets segment (17%) provides automobile, homeowner, and home-based coverages to individuals in the U.S., including a special program designed exclusively for members of AARP. Business sold direct to AARP members amounted to earned premiums of $2.9 billion in 2010. Total operating

revenues generated by HIG's Consumer Markets division totaled $3.9 billion.

The Wealth Management segment (20%) consist of the global annuity, life insurance, and retirement plans and mutual fund sub-segments. The segment provides investment products for over 7 million customers and life insurance for approximately 716,000 customers. Global annuity offers individual variable, fixed market adjusted, and single premium immediate annuities in the U.S. The life insurance segment sells a variety of individual life insurance products including universal life, variable universal life, and term life. Retirement plans provides products and services to corporations, municipalities, and not-for-profit organizations. Mutual funds offers retail funds, investment-only mutual funds and college savings plans. Total operating revenues generated by HIG's Wealth Management division totaled $4.7 billion.

The Corporate and Other segment (18%) reports HIG's debt financing and related interest expense, as well as other capital raising activities; banking operations; certain fee income and commission expenses.

## Company Financials Fiscal Year Ended Dec. 31

| Per Share Data ($) | 2010 | 2009 | 2008 | 2007 | 2006 | 2005 | 2004 | 2003 | 2002 | 2001 |
|---|---|---|---|---|---|---|---|---|---|---|
| Tangible Book Value | 41.93 | 66.44 | 26.18 | 55.69 | 53.12 | 45.05 | 42.58 | 34.80 | 35.31 | 29.87 |
| Operating Earnings | NA | NA | NA | NA | NA | NA | NA | -0.93 | 4.96 | 3.00 |
| Earnings | 2.49 | -2.93 | -8.99 | 9.24 | 8.69 | 7.44 | 7.20 | -0.33 | 3.97 | 2.27 |
| S&P Core Earnings | 3.67 | 0.90 | 4.11 | 11.27 | 8.98 | 7.62 | 6.52 | -1.15 | 4.27 | 2.22 |
| Dividends | 0.20 | 0.20 | 1.91 | 2.03 | 1.70 | 1.17 | 1.13 | 1.09 | 1.05 | 1.01 |
| Relative Payout | 8% | NM | NM | 22% | 20% | 16% | 16% | NM | 26% | 44% |
| Prices:High | 30.46 | 29.59 | 87.88 | 106.23 | 94.03 | 89.49 | 69.57 | 59.27 | 70.24 | 71.15 |
| Prices:Low | 18.81 | 3.33 | 4.16 | 83.00 | 79.24 | 65.35 | 52.73 | 31.64 | 37.25 | 45.50 |
| P/E Ratio:High | 12 | NM | NM | 11 | 11 | 12 | 10 | NM | 18 | 31 |
| P/E Ratio:Low | 8 | NM | NM | 9 | 9 | 9 | 7 | NM | 9 | 20 |

| Income Statement Analysis (Million $) | | | | | | | | | | |
|---|---|---|---|---|---|---|---|---|---|---|
| Life Insurance in Force | 1,031,103 | 1,018,728 | 968,723 | 906,890 | 920,964 | 764,293 | 853,184 | 704,369 | 629,028 | 534,489 |
| Premium Income:Life A & H | 14,055 | 14,424 | 15,503 | 15,619 | 15,023 | 14,359 | 13,566 | 11,891 | 4,884 | 4,903 |
| Premium Income:Casualty/Property. | NA | NA | NA | NA | NA | NA | NA | 8,805 | 8,114 | 7,266 |
| Net Investment Income | 3,618 | 7,219 | -6,005 | 5,359 | 6,515 | 8,231 | 5,162 | 3,233 | 2,953 | 2,850 |
| Total Revenue | 22,383 | 24,701 | 9,219 | 25,916 | 26,500 | 27,083 | 22,693 | 18,733 | 15,907 | 15,147 |
| Pretax Income | 2,264 | -1,728 | -4,591 | 4,005 | 3,602 | 2,985 | 2,523 | -550 | 1,068 | 354 |
| Net Operating Income | NA | NA | NA | NA | NA | NA | NA | -253 | 1,250 | 724 |
| Net Income | 1,680 | -887 | -2,749 | 2,949 | 2,745 | 2,274 | 2,138 | -91.0 | 1,000 | 549 |
| S&P Core Earnings | 1,727 | 313 | 1,290 | 3,598 | 2,839 | 2,335 | 1,936 | -315 | 1,078 | 538 |

| Balance Sheet & Other Financial Data (Million $) | | | | | | | | | | |
|---|---|---|---|---|---|---|---|---|---|---|
| Cash & Equivalent | 2,062 | 2,142 | 1,811 | 2,011 | 1,424 | 1,273 | 1,148 | 462 | 377 | 353 |
| Premiums Due | 3,273 | 3,404 | 3,604 | 3,681 | 3,675 | 6,360 | 6,178 | 9,043 | 7,706 | 2,432 |
| Investment Assets:Bonds | 78,469 | 71,153 | 65,112 | 81,657 | 80,755 | 76,440 | 75,100 | 61,263 | 48,889 | 40,046 |
| Investment Assets:Stocks | 33,793 | 33,542 | 32,278 | 38,777 | 31,132 | 25,495 | 14,466 | 565 | 917 | 1,349 |
| Investment Assets:Loans | 6,670 | 8,112 | 8,677 | 7,471 | 5,369 | 3,747 | 2,662 | 2,512 | 2,934 | 3,317 |
| Investment Assets:Total | 130,995 | 25,556 | 118,531 | 131,086 | 119,173 | 106,935 | 94,408 | 65,847 | 54,530 | 46,689 |
| Deferred Policy Costs | 9,857 | 10,686 | 13,248 | 11,742 | 10,268 | 9,702 | 8,509 | 7,599 | 6,689 | 6,420 |
| Total Assets | 318,346 | 307,717 | 287,583 | 360,361 | 326,710 | 285,557 | 259,735 | 225,853 | 182,043 | 181,238 |
| Debt | 6,589 | 6,632 | 7,033 | 3,951 | 3,762 | 4,048 | 4,308 | 4,613 | 4,064 | 3,377 |
| Common Equity | 19,755 | 14,905 | 9,268 | 19,204 | 18,876 | 15,325 | 14,238 | 11,639 | 10,734 | 9,013 |
| Combined Loss-Expense Ratio | 89.7 | 90.4 | 90.7 | 90.8 | 89.3 | 93.2 | 95.3 | 98.0 | 99.2 | 112.4 |
| % Return on Revenue | 7.5 | NM | NM | 11.4 | 10.4 | 8.4 | 9.4 | NM | 6.3 | 3.6 |
| % Return on Equity | 9.7 | NM | NM | 15.5 | 16.1 | 15.4 | 16.5 | NM | 10.1 | 6.7 |
| % Investment Yield | 3.4 | 5.9 | NM | 4.3 | 5.8 | 8.2 | 6.4 | 5.4 | 5.8 | 6.5 |

Data as orig reptd.; bef. results of disc opers/spec. items. Per share data adj. for stk. divs.; EPS diluted. E-Estimated. NA-Not Available. NM-Not Meaningful. NR-Not Ranked. UR-Under Review.

**Office:** 1 Hartford Plz, Hartford, CT 06155-0001.
**Telephone:** 860-547-5000.
**Website:** http://www.thehartford.com
**Chrmn, Pres & CEO:** L.E. McGee

**EVP & CFO:** C.J. Swift
**SVP, Chief Acctg Officer & Cntlr:** B.A. Bombara
**SVP & Secy:** D.C. Robinson
**SVP & CIO:** B. O'Connell

**Investor Contact:** R. Costello (860-547-8480)
**Board Members:** R. B. Allardice, III, T. Fetter, P. G. Kirk, Jr., L. E. McGee, K. A. Mikells, M. G. Morris, T. A. Renyi, C. B. Strauss, H. P. Swygert

**Founded:** 1810
**Domicile:** Delaware
**Employees:** 26,800

*The McGraw-Hill Companies*

# Hasbro Inc.

| S&P Recommendation **BUY** ★★★★☆ | Price $34.15 (as of Nov 25, 2011) | 12-Mo. Target Price $45.00 |
|---|---|---|

**GICS Sector** Consumer Discretionary
**Sub-Industry** Leisure Products

**Summary** This company's broad portfolio of toys, games, and entertainment offerings includes brands such as Transformers, Playskool, Monopoly, and My Little Pony.

## Key Stock Statistics (Source S&P, Vickers, company reports)

| | | | | | | | |
|---|---|---|---|---|---|---|---|
| 52-Wk Range | $50.17– 31.36 | S&P Oper. EPS 2011E | 3.00 | Market Capitalization(B) | $4.405 | Beta | 0.95 |
| Trailing 12-Month EPS | $2.76 | S&P Oper. EPS 2012E | 3.40 | Yield (%) | 3.51 | S&P 3-Yr. Proj. EPS CAGR(%) | 12 |
| Trailing 12-Month P/E | 12.4 | P/E on S&P Oper. EPS 2011E | 11.4 | Dividend Rate/Share | $1.20 | S&P Credit Rating | BBB+ |
| $10K Invested 5 Yrs Ago | $14,256 | Common Shares Outstg. (M) | 129.0 | Institutional Ownership (%) | 85 | | |

## Price Performance

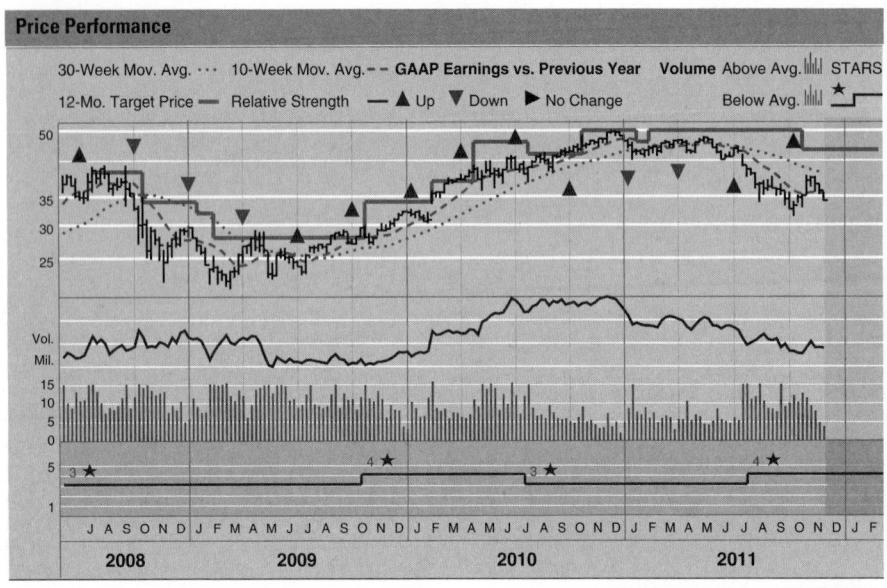

Options: ASE, CBOE, P, Ph

Analysis prepared by Equity Analyst **Michael Souers** on Oct 19, 2011, when the stock traded at **$34.59**.

## Qualitative Risk Assessment

| LOW | MEDIUM | HIGH |
|---|---|---|

Our risk assessment takes into account our view of HAS's strong market share position and healthy balance sheet, offset by intense industry rivalry and the concentrated buying power of U.S. toy retailers.

## Quantitative Evaluations

**S&P Quality Ranking**                                    A

| D | C | B- | B | B+ | A- | A | A+ |
|---|---|---|---|---|---|---|---|

**Relative Strength Rank**                        MODERATE

46

LOWEST = 1                                     HIGHEST = 99

## Revenue/Earnings Data

**Revenue (Million $)**

| | 1Q | 2Q | 3Q | 4Q | Year |
|---|---|---|---|---|---|
| 2011 | 672.0 | 908.5 | 1,376 | -- | -- |
| 2010 | 672.4 | 737.8 | 1,313 | 1,279 | 4,002 |
| 2009 | 621.3 | 792.2 | 1,279 | 1,375 | 4,068 |
| 2008 | 704.2 | 784.3 | 1,302 | 1,231 | 4,022 |
| 2007 | 625.3 | 691.4 | 1,223 | 1,298 | 3,838 |
| 2006 | 468.2 | 527.8 | 1,039 | 1,116 | 3,151 |

**Earnings Per Share ($)**

| | | | | | |
|---|---|---|---|---|---|
| 2011 | 0.12 | 0.42 | 1.27 | E1.20 | E3.00 |
| 2010 | 0.40 | 0.30 | 1.09 | 0.99 | 2.74 |
| 2009 | 0.14 | 0.26 | 0.99 | 1.09 | 2.48 |
| 2008 | 0.25 | 0.25 | 0.89 | 0.62 | 2.00 |
| 2007 | 0.19 | 0.03 | 0.95 | 0.84 | 1.97 |
| 2006 | -0.03 | 0.07 | 0.58 | 0.62 | 1.29 |

Fiscal year ended Dec. 31. Next earnings report expected: Early February. EPS Estimates based on S&P Operating Earnings; historical GAAP earnings are as reported.

## Highlights

➤ We see strong growth in the boys category being driven by global distribution of the Transformers: Dark of the Moon motion picture and the halo effect on Transformers products, including new KRE-O brand construction sets. We also see the boys category benefiting from high demand for Beyblades, Nerf and other core brands. While we think consumer demand for games, which has traditionally been a higher-margin category, will remain weak over the near term, we expect the girls and preschool categories to gain traction this fall with the introduction of new products. All told, we look for net revenues of $4.36 billion in 2011 and $4.63 billion in 2012.

➤ We expect near-term margin pressure from clearance of excess games inventory. We also forecast higher royalty expense and television program products costs, and continued investment in new products and growth in emerging markets. However, we look for improved sales leverage to offset these cost pressures.

➤ Factoring in share buybacks, we see EPS of $3.00 in 2011 (before a favorable tax adjustment of $0.15 and a restructuring charge of $0.06) and $3.40 in 2012.

## Investment Rationale/Risk

➤ We see positive momentum in the boys category, the addition of Sesame Street characters in the preschool category, and ongoing refresh of core girls product lines such as My Little Pony and Furreal Friends boding well for HAS this fall and into 2012. We think the company is effectively promoting its brands through global distribution of Hasbro Studios programming (over 30 markets targeted by year end), and we look for the recently reorganized games business to return to growth next year.

➤ Risks to our recommendation and target price include tight inventory management at toy retailers, weaker-than-expected consumer spending in light of economic uncertainty, poorly received new toy introductions, and increased competition in the consumer electronic toy category from larger consumer electronics manufacturers.

➤ Our 12-month target price of $45 is based on a blend of our historical and relative analyses. Our historical analysis suggests a value of $50, using a forward P/E multiple of 14.8X, the five-year median, applied to our 2012 EPS forecast. Our peer analysis applies the group median of 11.8X, implying a value of $40.

## Dividend Data (Dates: mm/dd Payment Date: mm/dd/yy)

| Amount ($) | Date Decl. | Ex-Div. Date | Stk. of Record | Payment Date |
|---|---|---|---|---|
| 0.300 | 02/03 | 04/28 | 05/02 | 05/16/11 |
| 0.300 | 02/03 | 04/28 | 05/02 | 05/16/11 |
| 0.300 | 05/19 | 07/28 | 08/01 | 08/15/11 |
| 0.300 | 10/06 | 10/28 | 11/01 | 11/15/11 |

Dividends have been paid since 1981. Source: Company reports.

**Please read the Required Disclosures and Analyst Certification on the last page of this report.**

# Hasbro Inc.

**STANDARD &POOR'S**

## Business Summary October 19, 2011

**CORPORATE OVERVIEW.** Hasbro is a worldwide leader in children's and family leisure time and entertainment products and services. Some of the company's widely recognized core brands are Transformers, G.I. Joe, Nerf, Monopoly, Playskool, Supersoaker, Battleship, Tonka, Play-Doh, My Little Pony, Milton Bradley, Parker Brothers, and Magic: The Gathering. HAS markets its brands under four product categories: boys' toys (34.2% of 2010 net revenues) such as action figures, sports products, and licensed products based on popular movie, television and comic book characters; games and puzzles (32.3%) including traditional board games, role-playing games, jigsaw puzzles, and electronic learning aids; girls' toys (20.8%) comprised mainly of plush products; and preschool toys (12.7%). The company's growth strategy is to build its core brands through development of a wide range of innovative toys and games, entertainment offerings, and licensed products.

HAS operates in the U.S. and internationally. International operations contributed 46% of net revenues in 2010. Over the past two years, the company expanded its operations in the emerging markets of China, Brazil, Russia, Korea, Romania, and the Czech Republic.

**CORPORATE STRATEGY.** HAS licenses certain of its trademarks, characters, and other property rights to third parties for use in connection with digital gaming, consumer promotions, and the sale of non-competing merchandise, such as apparel, publishing, home goods, and electronics. In the digital licensing category, Electronic Arts, Inc. has worldwide rights to create digital games for mobile phones, gaming consoles, and personal computers based on Monopoly, Scrabble, Yahtzee, Nerf, Tonka, G.I. Joe, and Littlest Pet Shop.

HAS also develops entertainment-based licensed products based on popular movie, television, and comic book characters. The company's primary licensing agreements are with Marvel Characters B.V. for Marvel characters including Iron Man, Thor, Captain America, and Spider-Man; Lucas Licensing, Ltd. for the Star Wars brand; and, beginning in 2011, Sesame Workshop for Sesame Street characters, including Elmo, Big Bird, and Cookie Monster. HAS incurred $248.6 million of royalty expense in 2010.

## Company Financials Fiscal Year Ended Dec. 31

| Per Share Data ($) | 2010 | 2009 | 2008 | 2007 | 2006 | 2005 | 2004 | 2003 | 2002 | 2001 |
|---|---|---|---|---|---|---|---|---|---|---|
| Tangible Book Value | 4.66 | 4.12 | 2.50 | 2.95 | 3.34 | 3.61 | 3.01 | 1.32 | 0.08 | NM |
| Cash Flow | 3.74 | 3.64 | 3.05 | 2.86 | 2.35 | 2.20 | 1.75 | 2.37 | 0.95 | 1.66 |
| Earnings | 2.74 | 2.48 | 2.00 | 1.97 | 1.29 | 1.09 | 0.96 | 0.98 | 0.43 | 0.35 |
| S&P Core Earnings | 2.74 | 2.51 | 1.91 | 1.96 | 1.29 | 1.02 | 0.90 | 0.93 | 0.44 | 0.19 |
| Dividends | 0.95 | 0.80 | 0.76 | 0.60 | 0.45 | 0.33 | 0.21 | 0.12 | 0.12 | 0.12 |
| Payout Ratio | 35% | 32% | 39% | 30% | 35% | 30% | 22% | 12% | 28% | 34% |
| Prices:High | 50.17 | 32.57 | 41.68 | 33.49 | 27.69 | 22.35 | 23.33 | 22.63 | 17.30 | 18.44 |
| Prices:Low | 30.20 | 21.14 | 21.57 | 25.25 | 17.00 | 17.75 | 16.90 | 11.23 | 9.87 | 10.31 |
| P/E Ratio:High | 18 | 13 | 21 | 17 | 21 | 21 | 24 | 23 | 40 | 53 |
| P/E Ratio:Low | 11 | 9 | 11 | 13 | 13 | 16 | 18 | 11 | 23 | 29 |

| Income Statement Analysis (Million $) | 2010 | 2009 | 2008 | 2007 | 2006 | 2005 | 2004 | 2003 | 2002 | 2001 |
|---|---|---|---|---|---|---|---|---|---|---|
| Revenue | 4,002 | 4,068 | 4,022 | 3,838 | 3,151 | 3,088 | 2,998 | 3,139 | 2,816 | 2,856 |
| Operating Income | 736 | 776 | 660 | 686 | 523 | 491 | 439 | 509 | 309 | 435 |
| Depreciation | 146 | 181 | 166 | 157 | 147 | 180 | 146 | 240 | 89.3 | 226 |
| Interest Expense | 82.1 | 61.6 | 47.1 | 34.6 | 27.5 | 30.5 | 31.7 | 52.5 | 77.5 | 104 |
| Pretax Income | 508 | 530 | 441 | 462 | 341 | 311 | 260 | 244 | 104 | 96.2 |
| Effective Tax Rate | NA | 29.2% | 30.5% | 28.0% | 32.6% | 31.8% | 24.6% | 28.3% | 27.9% | 36.8% |
| Net Income | 398 | 375 | 307 | 333 | 230 | 212 | 196 | 175 | 75.1 | 60.8 |
| S&P Core Earnings | 398 | 379 | 293 | 332 | 230 | 199 | 184 | 166 | 79.1 | 33.8 |

| Balance Sheet & Other Financial Data (Million $) | 2010 | 2009 | 2008 | 2007 | 2006 | 2005 | 2004 | 2003 | 2002 | 2001 |
|---|---|---|---|---|---|---|---|---|---|---|
| Cash | 728 | 636 | 630 | 774 | 715 | 942 | 725 | 521 | 495 | 233 |
| Current Assets | 2,221 | 2,045 | 1,714 | 1,888 | 1,718 | 1,830 | 1,718 | 1,509 | 1,432 | 1,369 |
| Total Assets | 4,093 | 3,897 | 3,169 | 3,237 | 3,097 | 3,301 | 3,241 | 3,163 | 3,143 | 3,369 |
| Current Liabilities | 719 | 816 | 800 | 888 | 906 | 911 | 1,149 | 930 | 967 | 759 |
| Long Term Debt | 1,398 | 1,132 | 710 | 710 | 495 | 496 | 303 | 687 | 857 | 1,166 |
| Common Equity | 1,615 | 1,595 | 1,391 | 1,385 | 1,538 | 1,723 | 1,640 | 1,405 | 1,191 | 1,353 |
| Total Capital | 3,013 | 2,727 | 2,107 | 2,095 | 2,033 | 2,219 | 1,942 | 2,092 | 2,049 | 2,519 |
| Capital Expenditures | 113 | 104 | 117 | 91.5 | 82.1 | 70.6 | 79.2 | 63.1 | 58.7 | 50.0 |
| Cash Flow | 544 | 556 | 473 | 490 | 377 | 392 | 342 | 415 | 164 | 287 |
| Current Ratio | 3.1 | 2.5 | 2.1 | 2.1 | 1.9 | 2.0 | 1.5 | 1.6 | 1.5 | 1.8 |
| % Long Term Debt of Capitalization | 46.4 | 41.5 | 33.7 | 33.8 | 24.3 | 22.3 | 15.6 | 32.8 | 41.8 | 46.3 |
| % Net Income of Revenue | 9.9 | 9.2 | 7.6 | 8.7 | 7.3 | 6.9 | 6.5 | 5.6 | 2.7 | 2.1 |
| % Return on Assets | 10.0 | 10.6 | 9.6 | 10.5 | 7.2 | 6.5 | 6.1 | 5.6 | 2.3 | 1.7 |
| % Return on Equity | 24.8 | 25.1 | 22.1 | 22.8 | 14.1 | 12.6 | 12.9 | 13.5 | 5.9 | 4.5 |

Data as orig reptd.; bef. results of disc opers/spec. items. Per share data adj. for stk. divs.; EPS diluted. E-Estimated. NA-Not Available. NM-Not Meaningful. NR-Not Ranked. UR-Under Review.

**Office:** 1027 Newport Avenue, PO Box 1059, Pawtucket, RI 02862-1059.
**Telephone:** 401-431-8697.
**Website:** http://www.hasbro.com
**Chrmn:** A.J. Verrecchia

**Pres & CEO:** B.D. Goldner
**COO:** D.D. Hargreaves
**SVP & Treas:** M.R. Trueb
**SVP, Secy & General Counsel:** B. Finigan

**Investor Contact:** K.A. Warren (401-727-5401)
**Board Members:** B. L. Anderson, A. R. Batkin, F. J. Biondi, Jr., K. A. Bronfin, J. M. Connors, Jr., M. W. Garrett, L. Gersh, B. D. Goldner, J. M. Greenberg, A. G. Hassenfeld, T. A. Leinbach, E. M. Philip, A. J. Verrecchia

**Founded:** 1926
**Domicile:** Rhode Island
**Employees:** 5,800

*The McGraw-Hill Companies*

# HCP Inc

STANDARD
&POOR'S

| **S&P Recommendation** BUY ★★★★☆ | Price $36.09 (as of Nov 25, 2011) | 12-Mo. Target Price $45.00 | Investment Style Large-Cap Value |

**GICS Sector** Financials
**Sub-Industry** Specialized REITS

**Summary** This equity-oriented real estate investment trust, based in California, has direct or joint venture investments in health care-related facilities across the U.S.

## Key Stock Statistics (Source S&P, Vickers, company reports)

| | | | | | |
|---|---|---|---|---|---|
| 52-Wk Range | $40.87– 28.76 | S&P FFO/Sh. 2011E | 2.58 | Market Capitalization(B) | $14.717 | Beta | 1.25 |
| Trailing 12-Month FFO/Share | $1.88 | S&P FFO/Sh. 2012E | 2.80 | Yield (%) | 5.32 | S&P 3-Yr. FFO/Sh. Proj. CAGR(%) | 16 |
| Trailing 12-Month P/FFO | NA | P/FFO on S&P FFO/Sh. 2011E | 14.0 | Dividend Rate/Share | $1.92 | S&P Credit Rating | BBB |
| $10K Invested 5 Yrs Ago | $13,363 | Common Shares Outstg. (M) | 407.8 | Institutional Ownership (%) | 100 | | |

## Price Performance

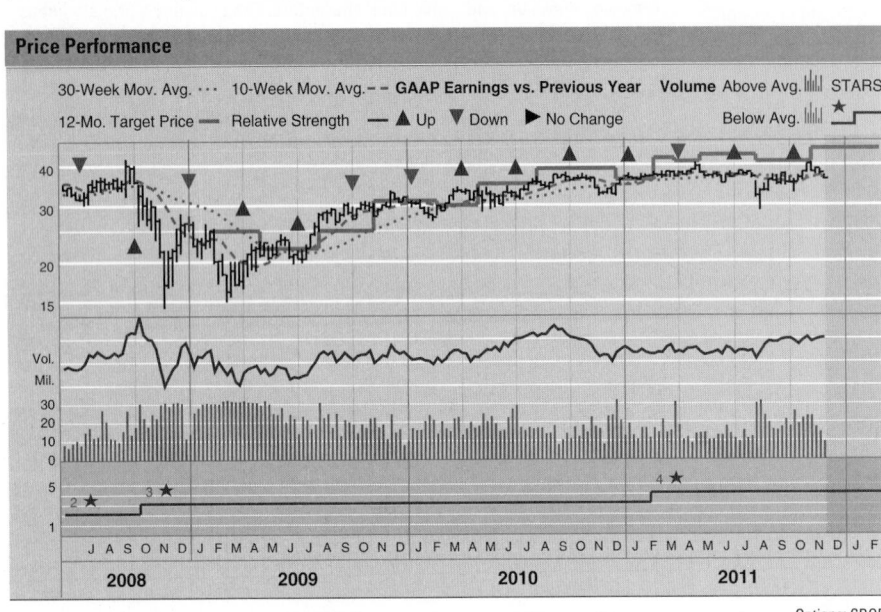

- 30-Week Mov. Avg. · · ·    10-Week Mov. Avg. - - GAAP Earnings vs. Previous Year    Volume Above Avg. STARS
- 12-Mo. Target Price —  Relative Strength — ▲ Up ▼ Down ► No Change    Below Avg.

Options: CBOE

Analysis prepared by Equity Analyst **R. Shepard, CFA** on Nov 10, 2011, when the stock traded at **$37.54**.

## Highlights

- ➤ We believe HCP has assembled a portfolio of health care properties that is well diversified in terms of asset type, geography, and tenant base. Its holdings were significantly augmented, in our view, by April's $6.1 billion purchase of skilled nursing facilities from HCR Manor-Care. In 2012, we see senior housing and skilled nursing facilities accounting for over two-thirds of segment operating income.

- ➤ Following an estimated 11% rise in 2011, we see rental revenue growth in HCP's need-based businesses advancing another 4.5% in 2012, driven largely by a full-year contribution from the HCR acquisition. The majority of HCP's facilities are under triple-net leases, in which the operator assumes the risk of changes in occupancy and revenue levels. As a result, we expect little near-term impact from expected declines in 2012 Medicare reimbursement for skilled nursing services. We expect management to focus on opportunistic acquisitions, while also attempting to reduce overall exposure to state-based Medicaid.

- ➤ We forecast FFO per share of $2.58 for 2011, expanding to $2.80 for 2012. Our estimates exclude non-recurring impairment charges.

## Investment Rationale/Risk

- ➤ We like the predictable nature of HCP's long-term, needs-oriented businesses, and believe the stock correlates less with macroeconomic trends than most other REITs. Amid a sluggish economic recovery, we favor HCP's stable revenue stream with minimal short-term lease expirations and an improving balance sheet. We believe the trust is making a successful transition toward senior housing and skilled nursing assets through acquisitions and select new development. We expect management to pursue additional acquisitions that leverage its existing operating infrastructure.

- ➤ Risks to our recommendation and target price include a faster-than-expected decline in senior housing occupancy, and a larger-than-expected decrease in government reimbursement rates.

- ➤ Our 12-month target price of $45 is 16.1X our 2012 FFO per share estimate of $2.80, a multiple that is a moderate premium to health care REIT peers. We find the valuation reasonable in view HCP's diversified portfolio, potential synergies from recent acquisitions, and relatively conservative financial structure.

## Qualitative Risk Assessment

| LOW | MEDIUM | HIGH |

Our risk assessment reflects HCP's position as a major and diversified owner of health care-related properties.

## Quantitative Evaluations

**S&P Quality Ranking**   B+

| D | C | B- | B | B+ | A- | A | A+ |

**Relative Strength Rank**   MODERATE

66

LOWEST = 1          HIGHEST = 99

## Revenue/FFO Data

**Revenue (Million $)**

| | 1Q | 2Q | 3Q | 4Q | Year |
|---|---|---|---|---|---|
| 2011 | 331.7 | 488.7 | 444.7 | -- | -- |
| 2010 | 294.8 | 301.9 | 317.1 | 341.4 | 1,255 |
| 2009 | 251.6 | 267.3 | 255.3 | 383.4 | 1,157 |
| 2008 | 252.2 | 251.4 | 269.9 | 263.3 | 1,026 |
| 2007 | 223.8 | 223.2 | 262.5 | 273.1 | 982.5 |
| 2006 | 126.5 | 127.5 | 130.2 | 234.9 | 619.1 |

**FFO Per Share ($)**

| | | | | | |
|---|---|---|---|---|---|
| 2011 | 0.40 | 0.77 | 0.64 | E0.66 | E2.58 |
| 2010 | 0.54 | 0.55 | 0.31 | 0.62 | 2.02 |
| 2009 | 0.56 | 0.55 | 0.52 | 0.36 | 1.50 |
| 2008 | 0.55 | 0.51 | 0.71 | 0.48 | 2.25 |
| 2007 | 0.50 | 0.58 | 0.52 | 0.54 | 2.14 |
| 2006 | 0.53 | 0.47 | 0.50 | 0.35 | 1.82 |

Fiscal year ended Dec. 31. Next earnings report expected: Mid February. FFO Estimates based on S&P Funds From Operations Est..

## Dividend Data (Dates: mm/dd Payment Date: mm/dd/yy)

| Amount ($) | Date Decl. | Ex-Div. Date | Stk. of Record | Payment Date |
|---|---|---|---|---|
| 0.480 | 01/27 | 02/08 | 02/10 | 02/23/11 |
| 0.480 | 04/28 | 05/05 | 05/09 | 05/24/11 |
| 0.480 | 07/28 | 08/04 | 08/08 | 08/23/11 |
| 0.480 | 10/27 | 11/03 | 11/07 | 11/22/11 |

Dividends have been paid since 1985. Source: Company reports.

# HCP Inc

**STANDARD &POOR'S**

## Business Summary November 10, 2011

HCP Inc. is a self-administered real estate investment trust (REIT) that invests exclusively in health care real estate throughout the U.S. At December 31, 2010, HCP managed $14.5 billion of investments in its owned portfolio and its investment management platform; it also owned $467 million of assets under development, including redevelopment, and land held for future development. The trust primarily generates revenue by leasing properties under long-term leases. Most of HCP's rents and other earned income from leases are received under triple-net leases or leases that provide for a substantial recovery of operating expenses.

HCP's investment strategy is based on three principles: opportunistic investing, portfolio diversification, and conservative financing. The trust completes real estate transactions when they are expected to drive profitable growth and create long-term stockholder value. HCP believes that diversification within the health care industry reduces the likelihood that a single event will materially harm its business. This allows HCP to take advantage of opportunities in different markets, based on individual market dynamics. During 2010, five companies accounted for about 38% of HCP's total revenues: Emeritus Corp. (10%), HCR ManorCare (9%), Sunrise Senior Living (8%), HCA (6%), and Brookdale Senior Living (5%). HCP strives to maintain multiple sources of liquidity, such as a revolving line of credit facility, access to capital markets and secured debt lenders, relationships with current and prospective institutional joint venture partners, and the divestment of existing assets. Debt obligations are primarily fixed rate, designed to reduce the impact of rising interest rates

on operations.

The trust's portfolio is comprised of investments in five health care segments: senior housing, life sciences, medical office, post-acute/skilled nursing, and hospital.

HCP's senior housing portfolio consists of interests in facilities including independent living facilities, assisted living facilities and continuing care retirement communities, which cater to different segments of the elderly population based on their needs. Services provided by HCP's operators or tenants in these facilities are primarily paid for by the residents directly or through private insurance and are less reliant on government reimbursement programs such as Medicaid and Medicare.

The life sciences portfolio holds properties that contain laboratory and office space primarily for biotechnology and pharmaceutical companies, scientific research institutions, government agencies and other organizations involved in the life science industry. The properties are located in well established geographical markets known for scientific research, including San Francisco, San Diego and Salt Lake City.

## Company Financials Fiscal Year Ended Dec. 31

| Per Share Data ($) | 2010 | 2009 | 2008 | 2007 | 2006 | 2005 | 2004 | 2003 | 2002 | 2001 |
|---|---|---|---|---|---|---|---|---|---|---|
| Tangible Book Value | 19.70 | 17.22 | 17.18 | 14.50 | 12.47 | 7.82 | 8.41 | 8.82 | 8.46 | 8.62 |
| Earnings | 0.93 | 0.25 | 0.77 | 0.67 | 0.57 | 1.02 | 1.03 | 0.94 | 0.97 | 0.89 |
| S&P Core Earnings | 0.93 | 0.49 | 0.65 | 0.67 | 0.57 | 1.02 | 1.02 | 0.94 | 0.96 | 0.88 |
| Dividends | 1.40 | 1.84 | 1.82 | 1.82 | 1.78 | 1.70 | 1.68 | 1.67 | 1.66 | 1.63 | 1.55 |
| Payout Ratio | 150% | NM | NM | NM | NM | 165% | 162% | 177% | 169% | 174% |
| Prices:High | 38.05 | 33.45 | 42.16 | 42.11 | 37.84 | 28.92 | 29.67 | 25.85 | 22.54 | 19.52 |
| Prices:Low | 26.70 | 14.93 | 14.26 | 25.11 | 25.12 | 23.13 | 20.00 | 16.53 | 17.90 | 14.63 |
| P/E Ratio:High | 41 | NM | 55 | 63 | 66 | 28 | 29 | 27 | 23 | 22 |
| P/E Ratio:Low | 29 | NM | 19 | 37 | 44 | 23 | 19 | 18 | 19 | 16 |

| Income Statement Analysis (Million $) | | | | | | | | | | |
|---|---|---|---|---|---|---|---|---|---|---|
| Rental Income | 952 | 886 | 962 | 836 | 557 | 452 | 389 | 349 | 332 | 311 |
| Mortgage Income | Nil | Nil | Nil | Nil | Nil | Nil | Nil | Nil | Nil | Nil |
| Total Income | 1,255 | 1,157 | 1,026 | 983 | 619 | 477 | 429 | 400 | 360 | 332 |
| General Expenses | 293 | 264 | 268 | 257 | 137 | 91.1 | 79.3 | 63.4 | 51.1 | 43.3 |
| Interest Expense | 289 | 299 | 348 | 357 | 213 | 107 | 89.1 | 90.7 | 78.0 | 78.5 |
| Provision for Losses | Nil | Nil | Nil | Nil | Nil | Nil | Nil | Nil | Nil | Nil |
| Depreciation | 312 | 320 | 315 | 274 | 144 | 107 | 87.0 | 79.1 | 75.7 | 84.1 |
| Net Income | 308 | 90.4 | 204 | 161 | 107 | 159 | 158 | 155 | 137 | 121 |
| S&P Core Earnings | 285 | 136 | 155 | 140 | 85.5 | 138 | 136 | 118 | 112 | 94.5 |

| Balance Sheet & Other Financial Data (Million $) | | | | | | | | | | |
|---|---|---|---|---|---|---|---|---|---|---|
| Cash | 1,037 | 112 | 57.6 | 133 | 764 | 69.9 | 81.1 | 228 | 41.2 | 30.2 |
| Total Assets | 13,332 | 12,210 | 11,850 | 12,522 | 10,013 | 3,597 | 3,103 | 3,036 | 2,748 | 2,431 |
| Real Estate Investment | 10,539 | 10,246 | 10,186 | 9,979 | 7,463 | 3,856 | 3,351 | 2,992 | 2,796 | 2,535 |
| Loss Reserve | Nil | Nil | Nil | Nil | Nil | Nil | Nil | Nil | Nil | Nil |
| Net Investment | 9,288 | 9,185 | 9,358 | 9,250 | 6,867 | 3,242 | 2,816 | 2,506 | 2,371 | 2,195 |
| Short Term Debt | NA | NA | NA | NA | NA | NA | NA | NA | NA | NA |
| Capitalization:Debt | 4,646 | 5,656 | 5,685 | 7,027 | 4,318 | 1,837 | 1,242 | 1,407 | 1,334 | 358 |
| Capitalization:Equity | 7,672 | 5,495 | 4,916 | 3,819 | 3,009 | 1,115 | 1,134 | 1,155 | 1,006 | 972 |
| Capitalization:Total | 12,792 | 11,615 | 10,751 | 11,954 | 7,774 | 3,386 | 2,783 | 2,965 | 2,686 | 1,674 |
| % Earnings & Depreciation/Assets | 4.9 | 3.4 | 4.3 | 3.9 | 3.6 | 7.9 | 8.0 | 8.1 | 8.2 | 8.5 |
| Price Times Book Value:High | 1.9 | 1.9 | 2.5 | 2.9 | 3.0 | 3.7 | 3.5 | 2.9 | 2.7 | 2.3 |
| Price Times Book Value:Low | 1.4 | 0.9 | 0.8 | 1.7 | 2.0 | 3.0 | 2.4 | 1.9 | 2.1 | 1.7 |

Data as orig reptd.; bef. results of disc opers/spec. items. Per share data adj. for stk. divs.; EPS diluted. E-Estimated. NA-Not Available. NM-Not Meaningful. NR-Not Ranked. UR-Under Review.

**Office:** 3760 Kilroy Airport Way Ste 300, Long Beach, CA 90806-6862.
**Telephone:** 562-733-5100.
**Email:** investorrelations@hcpi.com
**Website:** http://www.hcpi.com

**Chrmn & CEO:** J.F. Flaherty, III
**EVP & CFO:** T.M. Schoen
**EVP, Secy & General Counsel:** J.W. Mercer
**SVP & Chief Acctg Officer:** S.A. Anderson

**Investor Contact:** T.M. Herzog
**Board Members:** J. F. Flaherty, III, C. N. Garvey, D. B. Henry, L. E. Martin, M. D. McKee, P. L. Rhein, K. B. Roath, J. P. Sullivan

**Founded:** 1985
**Domicile:** Maryland
**Employees:** 148

# Health Care REIT Inc.

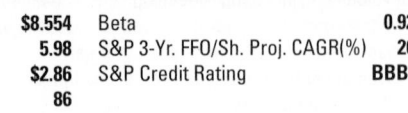

| S&P Recommendation | BUY ★★★★☆ | Price $47.81 (as of Nov 25, 2011) | 12-Mo. Target Price $58.00 | Investment Style Large-Cap Value |
|---|---|---|---|---|

**GICS Sector** Financials
**Sub-Industry** Specialized REITS

**Summary** This real estate investment trust invests in health care facilities, including senior housing and specialty care and medical office buildings.

## Key Stock Statistics (Source S&P, Vickers, company reports)

| | | | | | | |
|---|---|---|---|---|---|---|
| 52-Wk Range | $55.21– 41.03 | S&P FFO/Sh. 2011E | 3.39 | Market Capitalization(B) | $8.554 | Beta | 0.92 |
| Trailing 12-Month FFO/Share | $2.13 | S&P FFO/Sh. 2012E | 3.72 | Yield (%) | 5.98 | S&P 3-Yr. FFO/Sh. Proj. CAGR(%) | 26 |
| Trailing 12-Month P/FFO | NA | P/FFO on S&P FFO/Sh. 2011E | 14.1 | Dividend Rate/Share | $2.86 | S&P Credit Rating | BBB- |
| $10K Invested 5 Yrs Ago | $15,807 | Common Shares Outstg. (M) | 178.9 | Institutional Ownership (%) | 86 | | |

## Price Performance

30-Week Mov. Avg. · · · 10-Week Mov. Avg. – – GAAP Earnings vs. Previous Year   Volume Above Avg. STARS
12-Mo. Target Price — Relative Strength — ▲ Up ▼ Down ► No Change   Below Avg. ★

Options: CBOE, Ph

Analysis prepared by Equity Analyst **R. Shepard, CFA** on Nov 11, 2011, when the stock traded at **$49.55**.

## Qualitative Risk Assessment

| LOW | MEDIUM | HIGH |
|---|---|---|

Our risk assessment reflects HCN's position as an owner of a large and diversified portfolio of health care-related properties that are leased under long-term contracts and provide what we see as a steady and predictable stream of income.

## Quantitative Evaluations

**S&P Quality Ranking**   A-

| D | C | B- | B | B+ | A- | A | A+ |
|---|---|---|---|---|---|---|---|

**Relative Strength Rank**   MODERATE

63

LOWEST = 1   HIGHEST = 99

## Revenue/FFO Data

**Revenue (Million $)**

| | 1Q | 2Q | 3Q | 4Q | Year |
|---|---|---|---|---|---|
| 2011 | 255.5 | 381.1 | 384.8 | -- | -- |
| 2010 | 147.4 | 157.7 | 173.0 | 202.5 | 680.5 |
| 2009 | 139.3 | 139.5 | 142.9 | 147.3 | 569.0 |
| 2008 | 127.8 | 133.1 | 143.2 | 147.1 | 551.0 |
| 2007 | 110.4 | 117.7 | 124.4 | 133.5 | 486.0 |
| 2006 | 76.01 | 78.64 | 80.39 | 87.79 | 322.8 |

**FFO Per Share ($)**

| | | | | | |
|---|---|---|---|---|---|
| 2011 | 0.46 | 0.84 | 0.85 | E0.90 | E3.39 |
| 2010 | 0.51 | 0.74 | 0.33 | 0.60 | 2.18 |
| 2009 | 0.81 | 0.80 | 0.77 | 0.44 | 2.53 |
| 2008 | 0.81 | 0.87 | 0.86 | 0.83 | 3.38 |
| 2007 | 0.76 | 0.78 | 0.79 | 0.80 | 3.16 |
| 2006 | 0.71 | 0.74 | 0.73 | 0.77 | 2.86 |

Fiscal year ended Dec. 31. Next earnings report expected: Mid February. FFO Estimates based on S&P Funds From Operations Est..

## Highlights

➤ We forecast 2012 revenues will expand 15% due primarily to recent acquisitions, including the April purchase of Genesis HealthCare for $2.4 billion. In addition, we expect revenues to expand on a same property basis on price hikes at existing facilities. Overall, as of September 30, 2011, HCN facilities derive about 68.6% of revenues from private pay sources, which should minimize any impact from potential cuts in 2012 government reimbursement rates.

➤ Through September, HCN had completed a total of $4.5 billion in 2011 acquisitions and concentrated largely in the senior housing and skill nursing sectors. In our view, an aging U.S. population will help drive demand for these facilities in 2012 and beyond. We expect new development activity to be concentrated on medical office buildings adjacent to healthcare facilities. As of September 30, HCN had over 1 million square feet of new space under construction.

➤ We forecast per share funds from operations (FFO) of $3.41 for 2011, expanding to $3.72 for 2012.

## Investment Rationale/Risk

➤ We like the predictable nature of HCN's long-term triple net lease revenue stream, and we believe the stock correlates less with macro-economic trends than most other REITs in our coverage. In addition, the trust has assembled a portfolio of properties likely to benefit from increased demand from an aging U.S. population. We view positively management's strategy to make accretive acquisitions, such as the Genesis transaction, while also attempting to reduce leverage through select dispositions and newly raised capital. We also note what we view as HCN's minimal exposure to short-term lease expirations, solid balance sheet, and relatively secure dividend payout.

➤ Risks to our opinion and target price include a slower-than-expected economic recovery, higher interest rates, a lack of suitable acquisition candidates, and decreased government reimbursement rates.

➤ Our 12-month target price of $58 is equal to 15.6X our 2012 FFO estimate of $3.72, a moderate premium to less diversified peers with greater financial leverage.

## Dividend Data (Dates: mm/dd Payment Date: mm/dd/yy)

| Amount ($) | Date Decl. | Ex-Div. Date | Stk. of Record | Payment Date |
|---|---|---|---|---|
| 0.690 | 01/27 | 02/04 | 02/08 | 02/22/11 |
| 0.715 | 04/28 | 05/06 | 05/10 | 05/20/11 |
| 0.715 | 07/28 | 08/05 | 08/09 | 08/19/11 |
| 0.715 | 10/27 | 11/04 | 11/08 | 11/21/11 |

Dividends have been paid since 1971. Source: Company reports.

---

**Please read the Required Disclosures and Analyst Certification on the last page of this report.**

# Health Care REIT Inc.

STANDARD
&POOR'S

## Business Summary November 11, 2011

Health Care REIT is a self-administered equity real estate investment trust that invests in health care facilities offering skilled nursing, assisted living, independent living and specialty care services, and medical office buildings. HCN's investments are primarily real estate properties leased to operators under long-term operating leases or financed with operators under long-term mortgages.

As of December 31, 2010, HCN had real estate investments totaling nearly $9 billion, consisting of 683 properties in 41 states. Its portfolio included 303 senior housing facilities, 180 skilled nursing facilities, 31 hospitals, 162 medical office buildings, and seven life science buildings.

An assisted living facility is a combination of housing, personalized supportive services and health care designed to meet the needs of those who require help with the activities of daily living. Skilled nursing facilities provide inpatient skilled nursing and personal care services as well as rehabilitative, restorative and transitional medical services. Specialty care facilities include acute care hospitals, long-term acute care hospitals and other specialty care hospitals. Medical office buildings are office and clinical facilities designed for the use of physicians and other health care professionals.

HCN invests mainly in long-term care facilities managed by experienced operators, and diversifies its investment portfolio by operator and by geographic location. Each facility, which includes the land, building, improvements and related rights owned by HCN, is leased to an operator pursuant to a long-term operating lease. To better diversify the risk from any one facility, a large percentage of HCN's leased properties is subject to master leases. The leases generally cover multiple facilities under one lease and have a fixed term of 12 to 15 years and contain one or more five- to 15-year renewal options. The tenants are required to repair, rebuild and maintain the leased properties. The leases for HCN's medical office buildings are generally structured as long-term gross leases, where HCN is responsible for all or a portion of the property operating expenses.

One of the key variables in operating health care facility operations industry is the changing government reimbursement rates for Medicare and Medicaid programs. These government programs tend to account for the majority of revenue for health care facility operators, and have come under pressure in recent years as the government attempts to deal with rising health care costs. Health care facilities are also subject to state licensing and registration laws. Certificates of need (CON) may be required to demonstrate the need for constructing a new facility, adding beds or expanding an existing facility, investing in major capital equipment or adding new services, changing the ownership or control of an existing licensed facility, or terminating services that have been previously approved through the CON process.

## Company Financials Fiscal Year Ended Dec. 31

| Per Share Data ($) | 2010 | 2009 | 2008 | 2007 | 2006 | 2005 | 2004 | 2003 | 2002 | 2001 |
|---|---|---|---|---|---|---|---|---|---|---|
| Tangible Book Value | 27.54 | 27.64 | 27.07 | 24.26 | 27.04 | 19.85 | 24.23 | 20.43 | 19.20 | 18.57 |
| Earnings | 0.49 | 1.22 | 1.35 | 1.26 | 1.32 | 1.06 | 1.38 | 1.44 | 1.47 | 1.52 |
| S&P Core Earnings | 0.49 | 1.22 | 1.35 | 1.26 | 1.32 | 1.06 | 1.38 | 1.41 | 1.46 | 1.51 |
| Dividends | 2.74 | 2.72 | 2.70 | 2.28 | 2.88 | 2.46 | 2.39 | 2.34 | 2.34 | 2.34 |
| Payout Ratio | NM | NM | NM | 182% | NM | NM | 173% | 163% | 159% | 154% |
| Prices:High | 52.06 | 46.74 | 53.98 | 48.55 | 43.02 | 39.20 | 40.88 | 36.10 | 31.82 | 26.40 |
| Prices:Low | 38.42 | 25.86 | 30.14 | 35.08 | 32.80 | 31.15 | 27.70 | 24.84 | 24.02 | 16.06 |
| P/E Ratio:High | NM | 38 | 40 | 39 | 33 | 37 | 30 | 25 | 22 | 17 |
| P/E Ratio:Low | NM | 21 | 22 | 28 | 25 | 29 | 20 | 17 | 16 | 11 |

| Income Statement Analysis (Million $) | | | | | | | | | | |
|---|---|---|---|---|---|---|---|---|---|---|
| Rental Income | 581 | 520 | 501 | 450 | 300 | 253 | 226 | 177 | 134 | 99.0 |
| Mortgage Income | 40.9 | 40.9 | 40.1 | 25.8 | 18.8 | 24.0 | 22.8 | 20.8 | 26.5 | 31.3 |
| Total Income | 681 | 569 | 551 | 486 | 323 | 282 | 251 | 201 | 163 | 135 |
| General Expenses | 138 | 95.6 | 91.2 | 75.1 | 27.1 | 17.2 | 16.6 | 11.5 | 9.67 | 8.08 |
| Interest Expense | 157 | 106 | 131 | 135 | 94.8 | 80.1 | 72.0 | 54.1 | 41.1 | 32.0 |
| Provision for Losses | 29.7 | 23.3 | 0.01 | Nil | 1.00 | 1.20 | 1.20 | 2.87 | 1.00 | 1.00 |
| Depreciation | 211 | 157 | 156 | 146 | 93.1 | 80.0 | 73.0 | 51.1 | 39.3 | 30.2 |
| Net Income | 84.0 | 162 | 150 | 125 | 104 | 79.2 | 84.9 | 75.7 | 67.4 | 60.8 |
| S&P Core Earnings | 62.4 | 140 | 127 | 100 | 82.0 | 57.4 | 71.9 | 62.4 | 54.4 | 46.8 |

| Balance Sheet & Other Financial Data (Million $) | | | | | | | | | | |
|---|---|---|---|---|---|---|---|---|---|---|
| Cash | 132 | 35.5 | 23.4 | 30.3 | 36.2 | 36.2 | 19.8 | 125 | 9.55 | 9.83 |
| Total Assets | 9,452 | 6,367 | 6,193 | 5,214 | 4,281 | 2,972 | 2,550 | 2,183 | 1,594 | 1,270 |
| Real Estate Investment | 9,429 | 6,764 | 6,463 | 5,498 | 4,477 | 3,131 | 2,667 | 2,153 | 1,643 | 1,301 |
| Loss Reserve | 1.28 | 5.18 | 7.50 | 7.41 | 7.41 | 6.46 | 5.26 | 7.83 | 4.96 | 6.86 |
| Net Investment | 8,591 | 6,081 | 5,854 | 5,013 | 4,123 | 2,850 | 2,442 | 1,992 | 1,524 | 1,214 |
| Short Term Debt | 24.0 | 12.2 | 39.7 | 70.3 | 71.7 | 2.60 | 6.28 | 45.8 | 0.40 | 12.6 |
| Capitalization:Debt | 4,446 | 2,402 | 2,824 | 2,634 | 2,126 | 1,498 | 1,180 | 967 | 676 | 479 |
| Capitalization:Equity | 4,311 | 3,508 | 2,922 | 2,074 | 1,640 | 1,154 | 1,052 | 1,029 | 770 | 608 |
| Capitalization:Total | 9,179 | 6,210 | 6,046 | 5,048 | 4,107 | 2,929 | 2,515 | 2,117 | 1,574 | 1,236 |
| % Earnings & Depreciation/Assets | 3.7 | 5.1 | 5.4 | 6.1 | 5.4 | 5.7 | 6.6 | 6.7 | 7.5 | 7.5 |
| Price Times Book Value:High | 1.9 | 1.7 | 2.0 | 2.0 | 1.6 | 2.0 | 1.7 | 1.7 | 1.7 | 1.4 |
| Price Times Book Value:Low | 1.4 | 0.9 | 1.1 | 1.4 | 1.2 | 1.6 | 1.1 | 1.2 | 1.3 | 0.9 |

Data as orig reptd.; bef. results of disc opers/spec. items. Per share data adj. for stk. divs.; EPS diluted. E-Estimated. NA-Not Available. NM-Not Meaningful. NR-Not Ranked. UR-Under Review.

**Office:** One Seagate Ste 1500, Toledo, OH 43604-1541.
**Telephone:** 419-247-2800.
**Website:** http://www.hcreit.com
**Chrmn, Pres & CEO:** G.L. Chapman

**COO & General Counsel:** J.H. Miller
**Investor Contact:** S.A. Estes (419-247-2800)
**EVP & CFO:** S.A. Estes
**SVP & Treas:** M.A. Crabtree

**Board Members:** W. C. Ballard, Jr., P. C. Borra, G. L. Chapman, T. J. DeRosa, D. A. Decker, J. H. Donahue, P. J. Grua, F. S. Klipsch, S. M. Oster, J. R. Otten, R. S. Trumbull

**Founded:** 1970
**Domicile:** Delaware
**Employees:** 263

The McGraw-Hill Companies

# Heinz (H J) Co

**STANDARD &POOR'S**

| S&P Recommendation | STRONG BUY ★★★★★ | Price $49.99 (as of Nov 25, 2011) | 12-Mo. Target Price $60.00 | Investment Style Large-Cap Blend |
| --- | --- | --- | --- | --- |

**GICS Sector** Consumer Staples
**Sub-Industry** Packaged Foods & Meats

**Summary** This company produces a wide variety of food products worldwide, primarily condiments, convenience meals and snacks.

## Key Stock Statistics (Source S&P, Vickers, company reports)

| | | | | | |
| --- | --- | --- | --- | --- | --- |
| 52-Wk Range | $55.00–46.99 | S&P Oper. EPS 2012**E** | 3.30 | Market Capitalization(B) | $16.009 | Beta | 0.57 |
| Trailing 12-Month EPS | $2.96 | S&P Oper. EPS 2013**E** | 3.59 | Yield (%) | 3.84 | S&P 3-Yr. Proj. EPS CAGR(%) | 8 |
| Trailing 12-Month P/E | 16.9 | P/E on S&P Oper. EPS 2012**E** | 15.1 | Dividend Rate/Share | $1.92 | S&P Credit Rating | BBB+ |
| $10K Invested 5 Yrs Ago | $13,558 | Common Shares Outstg. (M) | 320.2 | Institutional Ownership (%) | 66 | | |

## Price Performance

30-Week Mov. Avg. · · · · 10-Week Mov. Avg. - - GAAP Earnings vs. Previous Year   Volume Above Avg. STARS
12-Mo. Target Price — Relative Strength — ▲ Up ▼ Down ► No Change   Below Avg.

Options: ASE, CBOE, P

Analysis prepared by Equity Analyst **Tom Graves, CFA** on Sep 30, 2011, when the stock traded at **$50.48**.

## Highlights

► Including a recently acquired 80% ownership interest in a Brazilian food company, we look for HNZ's FY 12 (Apr.) net sales to rise about 11% from the $10.7 billion reported for FY 11, with the majority of HNZ's net external sales expected to come from outside the U.S. We look for what HNZ calls emerging markets to be a growth driver. These markets produced 16% of total sales in FY 11, and, including the Brazilian company and a Chinese acquisition, we expect an emerging markets contribution of at least 22% in FY 12.

► We look for HNZ's market share to be bolstered by marketing activity and product innovation. We anticipate some commodity cost pressure in the year ahead, but look for this to be at least partly offset by pricing and productivity gains. Currency fluctuation helped FY 12 first-quarter results, but we think a stronger U.S. dollar could limit or be unfavorable to future results.

► Before some special items, we project FY 12 EPS of $3.34, up from the $3.06 reported for FY 11. We look for FY 13 EPS of $3.65. In FY 12's first quarter, HNZ's EPS had a negative impact of about $0.08 a share from what we are calling special charges.

## Investment Rationale/Risk

► We expect HNZ's strategy to include a focus on innovation investments in its core brands, growth in emerging markets, reducing or controlling costs, and leveraging the company's global scale. Also, we look for HNZ to be a strong free cash flow generator in FY 12, with cash flow from operations, net of capital expenditures and PP&E disposals, of at least $1.0 billion.

► Risks to our recommendation and target price include competitive product and pricing pressures, adverse currency fluctuations, raw material cost inflation, unfavorable consumer acceptance of new products, and disappointing results from acquisition activity.

► Our 12-month target price of $60 reflects our view that the shares should trade at a 13%-to-17% P/E premium (based on estimated CY 2011 and 2012 EPS) to the recent averages for a group of other food stocks. We think this is merited by our favorable view of HNZ's overall growth prospects and what we expect will be an increasing presence in emerging markets. HNZ shares recently had an indicated dividend yield of 3.8%.

## Qualitative Risk Assessment

| LOW | MEDIUM | HIGH |
| --- | --- | --- |

Our risk assessment for H. J. Heinz reflects the relatively stable nature of the company's end markets, our view of its strong cash flow, and corporate governance practices that we believe are favorable relative to peers.

## Quantitative Evaluations

**S&P Quality Ranking**   B+

| D | C | B- | B | B+ | A- | A | A+ |
| --- | --- | --- | --- | --- | --- | --- | --- |

**Relative Strength Rank**   MODERATE

60

LOWEST = 1      HIGHEST = 99

## Revenue/Earnings Data

**Revenue (Million $)**

| | 1Q | 2Q | 3Q | 4Q | Year |
| --- | --- | --- | --- | --- | --- |
| 2012 | 2,850 | 2,832 | -- | -- | -- |
| 2011 | 2,481 | 2,615 | 2,722 | 2,889 | 10,707 |
| 2010 | 2,442 | 2,647 | 2,682 | 2,725 | 10,495 |
| 2009 | 2,583 | 2,613 | 2,415 | 2,538 | 10,148 |
| 2008 | 2,248 | 2,523 | 2,611 | 2,688 | 10,071 |
| 2007 | 2,060 | 2,232 | 2,295 | 2,414 | 9,002 |

**Earnings Per Share ($)**

| | | | | | |
| --- | --- | --- | --- | --- | --- |
| 2012 | 0.70 | 0.73 | E0.84 | E0.87 | E3.30 |
| 2011 | 0.75 | 0.80 | 0.84 | 0.69 | 3.06 |
| 2010 | 0.68 | 0.76 | 0.83 | 0.60 | 2.87 |
| 2009 | 0.72 | 0.87 | 0.76 | 0.76 | 2.90 |
| 2008 | 0.72 | 0.71 | 0.68 | 0.61 | 2.63 |
| 2007 | 0.58 | 0.59 | 0.66 | 0.55 | 2.38 |

Fiscal year ended Apr. 30. Next earnings report expected: Early March. EPS Estimates based on S&P Operating Earnings; historical GAAP earnings are as reported.

## Dividend Data (Dates: mm/dd Payment Date: mm/dd/yy)

| Amount ($) | Date Decl. | Ex-Div. Date | Stk. of Record | Payment Date |
| --- | --- | --- | --- | --- |
| 0.450 | 03/09 | 03/22 | 03/24 | 04/10/11 |
| 0.480 | 05/26 | 06/22 | 06/24 | 07/10/11 |
| 0.480 | 08/30 | 09/20 | 09/22 | 10/10/11 |
| 0.480 | 11/09 | 12/20 | 12/22 | 01/10/12 |

Dividends have been paid since 1911. Source: Company reports.

Please read the **Required Disclosures and Analyst Certification on the last page of this report.**

**The McGraw·Hill Companies**

# Heinz (H J) Co

## Business Summary September 30, 2011

CORPORATE OVERVIEW. Although largely known for its familiar ketchup, H.J. Heinz boasts many other branded food products, ranging from Ore-Ida frozen potatoes to Weight Watchers frozen dinners. In FY 11 (Apr.), the North American Consumer Products segment represented 31% of sales from continuing operations, while Europe accounted for 30%, Asia/Pacific for 22%, U.S. Foodservice for 13%, and the rest of the world for 4%. In FY 11, one customer, Wal-Mart Stores Inc., accounted for 11% of sales.

The company's revenues are generated via the manufacture and sale of products in the following categories: ketchup and sauces (43% of FY 11 sales); meals and snacks (40%); infant/nutrition (11%); and other products (6%). Brands or trademarks utilized by HNZ include Heinz, Classico, Weight Watchers (licensed), Smart Ones, and Ore-Ida.

CORPORATE STRATEGY. We see acquisition activity being utilized to accelerate growth in what HNZ calls emerging markets. In FY 11, emerging markets accounted for 16% of HNZ's total sales from continuing operations.

In April 2011, HNZ said it had completed the acquisition of an 80% stake in Coniexpress S.A. Industrias Alimenticias, a Brazilian manufacturer of the

Quero brand of tomato-based sauces, tomato paste, ketchup, condiments and vegetables. HNZ said that the Quero business has annual sales of about $325 million, and gives HNZ its first major business in Brazil. HNZ said it expects the Quero business to approximately double its sales in Latin America in the first full year of ownership. Terms of the acquisition were not disclosed. Also, HNZ said it expects the acquisition to be modestly dilutive to earnings in FY 11 and FY 12, but accretive starting in FY 13.

In November 2010, HNZ said it had completed the acquisition of Foodstar, a manufacturer of branded soy sauces and fermented bean curd in China, from Transpac Industrial Holdings Ltd., a private equity holding company, and various Transpac Funds. The purchase price consisted of a cash payment of $165 million and a potential earn-out payment in 2014 based on the performance of the business.

## Company Financials Fiscal Year Ended Apr. 30

| Per Share Data ($) | 2011 | 2010 | 2009 | 2008 | 2007 | 2006 | 2005 | 2004 | 2003 | 2002 |
|---|---|---|---|---|---|---|---|---|---|---|
| Tangible Book Value | NM | NM | NM | NM | NM | NM | NM | NM | NM | NM |
| Cash Flow | 4.04 | 3.83 | 3.76 | 3.49 | 3.88 | 2.07 | 2.82 | 2.86 | 2.17 | 3.22 |
| Earnings | 3.06 | 2.88 | 2.90 | 2.63 | 2.38 | 1.29 | 2.08 | 2.20 | 1.57 | 2.36 |
| S&P Core Earnings | 3.04 | 2.82 | 2.55 | 2.26 | 2.36 | 1.72 | 2.29 | 2.11 | 1.43 | 1.99 |
| Dividends | NA | 1.68 | 1.66 | 1.52 | 1.20 | 1.14 | 1.10 | 1.08 | 1.61 | 1.55 |
| Payout Ratio | NA | 58% | 57% | 58% | 50% | 88% | 53% | 49% | 88% | 65% |
| Calendar Year | 2010 | 2009 | 2008 | 2007 | 2006 | 2005 | 2004 | 2003 | 2002 | 2001 |
| Prices:High | 50.77 | 43.75 | 53.00 | 53.00 | 46.75 | 39.13 | 40.61 | 36.82 | 43.48 | 47.94 |
| Prices:Low | 40.00 | 30.51 | 35.26 | 35.26 | 33.42 | 33.64 | 34.53 | 28.90 | 29.60 | 36.90 |
| P/E Ratio:High | 17 | 15 | 18 | 20 | 20 | 30 | 20 | 17 | 24 | 20 |
| P/E Ratio:Low | 13 | 11 | 12 | 13 | 14 | 26 | 17 | 13 | 16 | 16 |

| Income Statement Analysis (Million $) | | | | | | | | | | |
|---|---|---|---|---|---|---|---|---|---|---|
| Revenue | 10,707 | 10,495 | 10,148 | 10,071 | 9,002 | 8,643 | 8,912 | 8,415 | 8,237 | 9,431 |
| Operating Income | 1,931 | 1,852 | 1,765 | 1,847 | 1,946 | 1,377 | 1,607 | 1,613 | 1,389 | 1,892 |
| Depreciation | 299 | 303 | 272 | 279 | 500 | 264 | 252 | 234 | 215 | 302 |
| Interest Expense | 275 | 296 | 340 | 333 | 333 | 316 | 232 | 212 | 224 | 294 |
| Pretax Income | 1,374 | 1,290 | 1,296 | 1,218 | 1,124 | 693 | 1,059 | 1,169 | 869 | 1,279 |
| Effective Tax Rate | NA | NA | 28.8% | 30.6% | 29.6% | 36.2% | 30.5% | 33.3% | 36.1% | 34.8% |
| Net Income | 1,006 | 914 | 923 | 845 | 792 | 443 | 736 | 779 | 555 | 834 |
| S&P Core Earnings | 982 | 897 | 812 | 725 | 784 | 587 | 809 | 747 | 500 | 702 |

| Balance Sheet & Other Financial Data (Million $) | | | | | | | | | | |
|---|---|---|---|---|---|---|---|---|---|---|
| Cash | 763 | 554 | 373 | 618 | 653 | 445 | 1,084 | 1,180 | 802 | 207 |
| Current Assets | 3,754 | 3,051 | 2,945 | 3,326 | 3,019 | 2,704 | 3,646 | 3,611 | 3,284 | 3,374 |
| Total Assets | 12,231 | 10,076 | 9,664 | 10,565 | 10,033 | 9,738 | 10,578 | 9,877 | 9,225 | 10,278 |
| Current Liabilities | 4,161 | 2,175 | 2,063 | 2,670 | 2,505 | 2,018 | 2,587 | 2,469 | 1,926 | 2,509 |
| Long Term Debt | 3,078 | 4,568 | 5,076 | 4,406 | 4,414 | 4,357 | 4,122 | 4,538 | 4,776 | 4,643 |
| Common Equity | 3,109 | 1,891 | 1,220 | 1,888 | 2,280 | 2,049 | 2,614 | 8,841 | 2,876 | 1,719 |
| Total Capital | 8,031 | 6,531 | 6,701 | 7,013 | 7,256 | 7,045 | 7,359 | 13,797 | 8,252 | 7,197 |
| Capital Expenditures | 336 | 278 | 292 | 302 | 245 | 231 | 241 | 232 | 154 | 213 |
| Cash Flow | 1,305 | 1,217 | 1,195 | 1,123 | 1,291 | 707 | 988 | 1,013 | 770 | 1,136 |
| Current Ratio | 0.9 | 1.4 | 1.4 | 1.3 | 1.2 | 1.3 | 1.4 | 1.5 | 1.7 | 1.3 |
| % Long Term Debt of Capitalization | 38.3 | 69.9 | 75.8 | 62.8 | 60.8 | 61.8 | 56.0 | 32.9 | 57.9 | 64.5 |
| % Net Income of Revenue | 9.4 | 8.7 | 9.1 | 8.4 | 8.8 | 5.1 | 8.3 | 9.3 | 6.7 | 8.8 |
| % Return on Assets | NA | NA | 9.1 | 8.2 | 8.0 | 4.4 | 7.2 | 8.2 | 5.7 | 8.6 |
| % Return on Equity | NA | NA | 59.4 | 45.3 | 34.0 | 19.0 | 26.3 | 8.9 | 17.9 | 53.9 |

Data as orig reptd.; bef. results of disc opers/spec. items. Per share data adj. for stk. divs.; EPS diluted. E-Estimated. NA-Not Available. NM-Not Meaningful. NR-Not Ranked. UR-Under Review.

**Office:** One PPG Place, Suite 3100, Pittsburgh, PA 15222.
**Telephone:** 412-456-5700.
**Website:** http://www.heinz.com
**Chrmn, Pres & CEO:** W.R. Johnson

**EVP & CFO:** A.B. Winkleblack
**CTO:** W. Eismont
**Treas:** L.A. Cullo, Jr.
**Secy:** R.D. Biedzinski

**Investor Contact:** M.R. Nollen (412-456-1048)
**Board Members:** C. E. Bunch, L. S. Coleman, Jr., J. G. Drosdick, E. E. Holiday, W. R. Johnson, C. Kendle, D. R. O'Hare, N. Peltz, D. H. Reilley, L. C. Swann, T. J. Usher, M. F. Weinstein

**Founded:** 1869
**Domicile:** Pennsylvania
**Employees:** 34,800

# Helmerich & Payne Inc.

**STANDARD &POOR'S**

| S&P Recommendation **BUY** ★★★★☆ | Price $50.70 (as of Nov 25, 2011) | 12-Mo. Target Price $64.00 | Investment Style Large-Cap Blend |
|---|---|---|---|

**GICS Sector** Energy
**Sub-Industry** Oil & Gas Drilling

**Summary** Helmerich & Payne, Inc. is the holding company for Helmerich & Payne International Drilling Company, an international drilling contractor.

## Key Stock Statistics (Source S&P, Vickers, company reports)

| | | | | | | | |
|---|---|---|---|---|---|---|---|
| 52-Wk Range | $73.40– 35.58 | S&P Oper. EPS 2012**E** | 4.58 | Market Capitalization(B) | $5.429 | Beta | 1.25 |
| Trailing 12-Month EPS | $3.99 | S&P Oper. EPS 2013**E** | NA | Yield (%) | 0.55 | S&P 3-Yr. Proj. EPS CAGR(%) | 7 |
| Trailing 12-Month P/E | 12.7 | P/E on S&P Oper. EPS 2012**E** | 11.1 | Dividend Rate/Share | $0.28 | S&P Credit Rating | NA |
| $10K Invested 5 Yrs Ago | $20,320 | Common Shares Outstg. (M) | 107.1 | Institutional Ownership (%) | 93 | | |

## Price Performance

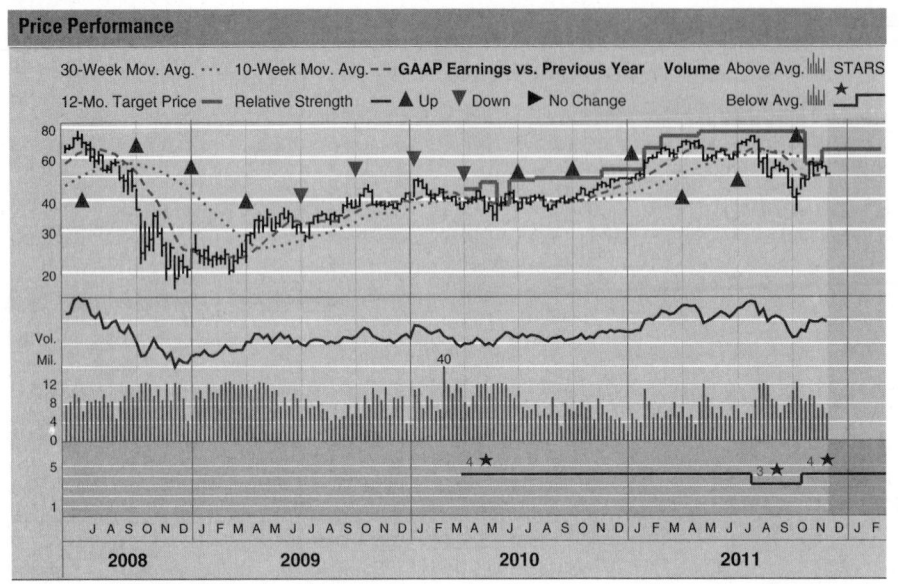

- 30-Week Mov. Avg. · · · 10-Week Mov. Avg. - - GAAP Earnings vs. Previous Year   Volume Above Avg. ⊪⊪ STARS
- 12-Mo. Target Price — Relative Strength — ▲ Up ▼ Down ▶ No Change   Below Avg. ⊪⊪ ★

2008   2009   2010   2011

Options: ASE, CBOE, P, Ph

Analysis prepared by Equity Analyst **Tanjila Shafi** on Nov 21, 2011, when the stock traded at **$52.99**.

## Highlights

- ➤ We believe HP, with the best utilization (86%) in the land drilling segment, has gained pricing power despite rig oversupply. On rising operator spending, specifically in U.S. shale plays, HP's FlexRigs saw a pickup in activity in FY 10 (Sep.), while older rigs became idle or were retired. With the overhaul of its U.S. fleet near completion, we think HP will market its FlexRigs more aggressively globally. HP has 224 rigs under contract in the U.S. with 149 rigs on term contracts, versus 110 rigs in FY 10. HP sees an average of 144 rigs on term contracts in FY 12. Since January 2011, HP has announced 71 newbuilds; 24 have been completed and 47 are under construction.

- ➤ HP estimates that its capital expenditure for FY 12 will total $1.1 billion, versus $694 million in FY 11. We believe that HP will benefit from increasing demand for high-spec drilling.

- ➤ We estimate a single-digit increase in revenues for FY 12. We believe that the company will see continued growth at its U.S. land segment, due to increasing demand for drilling more complex horizontal and directional wells. We estimate EPS of $4.58 in FY 12.

## Investment Rationale/Risk

- ➤ Our buy recommendation is based on our positive outlook for the company as we believe HP will benefit from the continued development of shale plays in the U.S., its high-spec rigs, and potential upside from its international operations. In addition, HP's rig utilization has held up better than many peers who have older, less efficient conventional rigs. The company has done well gaining market share, in our view, as customers prefer the efficiency of its rigs capable of horizontal drilling and faster drilling times versus conventional rigs.

- ➤ Risks to our recommendation and target price include lower-than-expected dayrates or utilization; political risk; and cost inflation.

- ➤ Our 12-month target price of $64 is based on a blend of 6.2X projected FY 12 EBITDA and 14X estimated FY 12 EPS, higher than peer averages. We apply a premium valuation on our view of HP's top-tier rig fleet and balance sheet, EPS and cash flow growth projections.

## Qualitative Risk Assessment

| LOW | MEDIUM | **HIGH** |
|---|---|---|

Our risk assessment reflects HP's sensitivity to volatile crude oil and natural gas prices, capital spending decisions made by its oil and gas producing customers, and project management risk associated with a large newbuild program. Partially offsetting these risks is HP's high percentage of rigs committed to long-term contracts.

## Quantitative Evaluations

**S&P Quality Ranking**   B

| D | C | B- | **B** | B+ | A- | A | A+ |
|---|---|---|---|---|---|---|---|

**Relative Strength Rank**   MODERATE

62

LOWEST = 1   HIGHEST = 99

## Revenue/Earnings Data

**Revenue (Million $)**

| | 1Q | 2Q | 3Q | 4Q | Year |
|---|---|---|---|---|---|
| 2011 | 594.6 | 604.4 | 644.1 | 700.8 | 2,544 |
| 2010 | 396.2 | 436.6 | 483.4 | 559.0 | 1,875 |
| 2009 | 623.8 | 520.3 | 387.8 | 362.2 | 1,894 |
| 2008 | 456.7 | 473.6 | 522.5 | 583.7 | 2,037 |
| 2007 | 386.4 | 372.5 | 421.3 | 449.5 | 1,630 |
| 2006 | 255.4 | 290.8 | 319.8 | 358.8 | 1,225 |

**Earnings Per Share ($)**

| | | | | | |
|---|---|---|---|---|---|
| 2011 | 0.96 | 0.91 | 1.01 | 1.11 | 3.99 |
| 2010 | 0.60 | 0.68 | 0.61 | 0.77 | 2.66 |
| 2009 | 1.36 | 0.99 | 0.50 | 0.48 | 3.32 |
| 2008 | 1.02 | 0.96 | 1.18 | 1.18 | 4.34 |
| 2007 | 1.06 | 1.02 | 1.09 | 1.10 | 4.27 |
| 2006 | 0.48 | 0.61 | 0.75 | 0.93 | 2.77 |

Fiscal year ended Sep. 30. Next earnings report expected: NA. EPS Estimates based on S&P Operating Earnings; historical GAAP earnings are as reported.

## Dividend Data (Dates: mm/dd Payment Date: mm/dd/yy)

| Amount ($) | Date Decl. | Ex-Div. Date | Stk. of Record | Payment Date |
|---|---|---|---|---|
| 0.060 | 12/07 | 02/11 | 02/15 | 03/01/11 |
| 0.060 | 03/02 | 05/11 | 05/13 | 06/01/11 |
| 0.070 | 06/01 | 08/11 | 08/15 | 09/01/11 |
| 0.070 | 09/07 | 11/10 | 11/15 | 12/01/11 |

Dividends have been paid since 1959. Source: Company reports.

# Helmerich & Payne Inc.

**STANDARD &POOR'S**

## Business Summary November 21, 2011

CORPORATE OVERVIEW. Helmerich & Payne, Inc. is the holding company for Helmerich & Payne International Drilling Company, an international drilling contactor with land and offshore operations in the United States, South America, Mexico, Trinidad and Africa. It specializes in deep drilling in major gas producing basins of the U.S., and in drilling for oil and gas in remote international areas. Contract drilling operations comprised nearly all of the company's revenue base (99% of FY 10 (Sep.) revenues). The remaining 1% of FY 10 total revenues was derived mainly from its real estate operations. HP generated about 57% of FY 10 consolidated revenues from its 10 largest customers, including Occidental Oil and Gas Corp., Devon Energy and ExxonMobil.

The company's contract drilling operations are principally comprised of three operating segments. The U.S. Land Drilling segment (83% of total FY 11 external sales, 91% of segment operating income) operated 224 land rigs at the end of September 2011, the same as a year earlier. As of September 2010, 201 rigs were of FlexRig design, while the remainder were highly mobile or conventional rigs. Average rig utilization in this segment in FY 11 was 86%, up from 73% in FY 10. Average rig revenue per day was $25,809 in FY 11, up 8% from FY 10, while the average rig margin per day rose 13%, to $13,271.

The U.S. Offshore Platform segment (8% of total FY 11 revenues and 6% of segment operating income) operated nine platform rigs in FY 11. Average utilization was 77% in FY 11, versus 81% in FY 10, while the average dayrates increased 9%, to $51,794. The average rig margin per day fell 2%, to $22,415.

The International Drilling segment (9% of total FY 11 revenues, 3% of segment operating income) operated 25 land rigs. HP has rigs in Ecuador, Colombia, Argentina and other areas. Average rig utilization was 70% in FY 11, up from 63% in FY 10. Average rig revenue per day fell 5%, to $31,633, while the average margin per day declined 26%, to $8,217.

## Company Financials Fiscal Year Ended Sep. 30

| Per Share Data ($) | 2011 | 2010 | 2009 | 2008 | 2007 | 2006 | 2005 | 2004 | 2003 | 2002 |
|---|---|---|---|---|---|---|---|---|---|---|
| Tangible Book Value | NA | 26.60 | 25.48 | NA | 17.54 | 13.30 | 10.39 | 9.06 | 9.15 | 8.95 |
| Cash Flow | 6.91 | 5.11 | 5.53 | 6.32 | 5.66 | 3.73 | 2.15 | 0.97 | 0.99 | 1.14 |
| Earnings | 3.99 | 2.66 | 3.32 | 4.34 | 4.27 | 2.77 | 1.23 | 0.05 | 0.18 | 0.54 |
| S&P Core Earnings | 3.89 | 2.65 | 3.25 | 4.02 | 3.54 | 2.60 | 0.93 | -0.19 | 0.12 | 0.33 |
| Dividends | 0.25 | 0.21 | 0.20 | NA | 0.18 | 0.17 | 0.17 | 0.16 | 0.16 | 0.15 |
| Payout Ratio | 6% | 8% | 6% | NA | 4% | 6% | 13% | NM | 91% | 29% |
| Prices:High | 73.40 | 49.46 | 46.24 | NA | 46.25 | 40.24 | 32.81 | 17.13 | 16.40 | 21.62 |
| Prices:Low | 35.58 | 32.34 | 19.50 | NA | 22.72 | 21.26 | 15.68 | 11.97 | 11.30 | 11.73 |
| P/E Ratio:High | 18 | 19 | 14 | NA | 11 | 15 | 27 | NM | 94 | 40 |
| P/E Ratio:Low | 9 | 12 | 6 | NA | 5 | 8 | 13 | NM | 65 | 22 |

| Income Statement Analysis (Million $) | | | | | | | | | | |
|---|---|---|---|---|---|---|---|---|---|---|
| Revenue | 2,544 | 1,875 | 1,894 | 2,037 | 1,630 | 1,225 | 801 | 621 | 515 | 482 |
| Operating Income | NA | NA | 813 | 891 | 720 | 511 | 275 | 167 | 129 | 154 |
| Depreciation, Depletion and Amortization | 315 | 263 | 236 | 211 | 146 | 102 | 96.3 | 94.4 | 82.5 | 61.4 |
| Interest Expense | 17.4 | 17.2 | 13.5 | 18.7 | 10.1 | 6.64 | 12.6 | 12.7 | 12.3 | 0.98 |
| Pretax Income | 687 | 438 | 586 | 717 | 690 | 448 | 215 | 8.72 | 32.5 | 94.3 |
| Effective Tax Rate | NA | NA | 39.7% | 35.6% | 36.4% | 34.4% | 40.7% | 50.0% | 45.0% | 43.0% |
| Net Income | 435 | 286 | 354 | 462 | 449 | 294 | 128 | 4.36 | 17.9 | 53.7 |
| S&P Core Earnings | 422 | 284 | 347 | 428 | 372 | 277 | 98.5 | -19.2 | 11.9 | 32.7 |

| Balance Sheet & Other Financial Data (Million $) | | | | | | | | | | |
|---|---|---|---|---|---|---|---|---|---|---|
| Cash | 364 | 63.0 | 141 | 122 | 89.2 | 82.5 | 289 | 65.3 | 38.2 | 46.9 |
| Current Assets | 956 | 653 | 523 | 691 | 499 | 429 | 500 | 246 | 198 | 179 |
| Total Assets | 5,004 | 4,265 | 4,161 | 3,588 | 2,885 | 2,135 | 1,663 | 1,407 | 1,416 | 1,227 |
| Current Liabilities | 417 | 233 | 302 | 309 | 227 | 265 | 89.5 | 59.9 | 88.6 | 72.9 |
| Long Term Debt | 235 | 360 | 420 | 475 | 445 | 175 | 200 | 200 | 200 | 100 |
| Common Equity | 3,270 | 2,807 | 2,683 | 2,265 | 1,816 | 1,480 | 1,130 | 914 | 917 | 879 |
| Total Capital | 3,505 | 3,167 | 3,785 | 3,220 | 2,624 | 1,925 | 1,577 | 1,309 | 1,299 | 1,110 |
| Capital Expenditures | 694 | 330 | 881 | 706 | 894 | 529 | 86.8 | 89.0 | 246 | 312 |
| Cash Flow | 750 | 549 | 590 | 672 | 595 | 395 | 224 | 98.8 | 100 | 115 |
| Current Ratio | 2.3 | 2.8 | 1.7 | 2.2 | 2.2 | 1.6 | 5.6 | 4.1 | 2.2 | 2.5 |
| % Long Term Debt of Capitalization | 6.7 | 11.4 | 11.1 | 14.8 | 17.0 | 9.1 | 12.7 | 15.3 | 15.4 | 9.0 |
| % Return on Assets | 9.4 | 6.8 | 9.1 | 14.3 | 17.9 | 15.5 | 8.3 | 0.3 | 1.4 | 4.2 |
| % Return on Equity | 14.3 | 10.4 | 14.3 | 22.6 | 27.3 | 22.5 | 12.0 | 0.5 | 2.0 | 5.8 |

Data as orig reptd.; bef. results of disc opers/spec. items. Per share data adj. for stk. divs.; EPS diluted. E-Estimated. NA-Not Available. NM-Not Meaningful. NR-Not Ranked. UR-Under Review.

**Office:** 1437 South Boulder Avenue, Suite 1400, Tulsa, OK 74119.
**Telephone:** 918-742-5531.
**Website:** http://www.hpinc.com
**Chrmn:** W.H. Helmerich, III

**Pres & CEO:** H. Helmerich
**COO:** J. Lindsay
**CFO:** J.P. Tardio
**Chief Admin Officer, Secy & General Counsel:** S.R. Mackey

**Board Members:** W. Armstrong, III, R. A. Foutch, H. Helmerich, W. H. Helmerich, III, P. Marshall, E. B. Rust, Jr., J. D. Zeglis,

**Founded:** 1920
**Domicile:** Delaware
**Employees:** 8,724

The **McGraw·Hill** Companies

# Hershey Co (The)

STANDARD
&POOR'S

| S&P Recommendation | HOLD ★★★☆☆ | Price $55.36 (as of Nov 25, 2011) | 12-Mo. Target Price $58.00 | Investment Style Large-Cap Growth |
|---|---|---|---|---|

**GICS Sector** Consumer Staples
**Sub-Industry** Packaged Foods & Meats

**Summary** Hershey is a major producer of chocolate and confectionery products.

## Key Stock Statistics (Source S&P, Vickers, company reports)

| | | | | | | | |
|---|---|---|---|---|---|---|---|
| 52-Wk Range | $60.96– 45.67 | S&P Oper. EPS 2011E | 2.81 | Market Capitalization(B) | $9.106 | Beta | 0.27 |
| Trailing 12-Month EPS | $2.70 | S&P Oper. EPS 2012E | 3.03 | Yield (%) | 2.49 | S&P 3-Yr. Proj. EPS CAGR(%) | 8 |
| Trailing 12-Month P/E | 20.5 | P/E on S&P Oper. EPS 2011E | 19.7 | Dividend Rate/Share | $1.38 | S&P Credit Rating | A |
| $10K Invested 5 Yrs Ago | $12,031 | Common Shares Outstg. (M) | 225.1 | Institutional Ownership (%) | 77 | | |

## Price Performance

30-Week Mov. Avg. ···  10-Week Mov. Avg. - - GAAP Earnings vs. Previous Year   Volume Above Avg. ▦ STARS
12-Mo. Target Price — Relative Strength  — ▲ Up  ▼ Down  ► No Change   Below Avg. ▦  ★

[price chart covering years 2008, 2009, 2010, 2011]

Options: ASE, CBOE, P, Ph

Analysis prepared by Equity Analyst **Tom Graves, CFA** on Oct 31, 2011, when the stock traded at **$57.38**.

### Highlights

▶ In 2012, we expect HSY's sales to rise about 5% from the $6.07 billion that we project for 2011, with the increase largely coming from higher prices.

▶ We expect that higher product prices, improved productivity and cost savings will offset at least a portion of an expected impact from higher input costs in 2012. Before special items, we estimate 2012 EPS of $3.03, up from the $2.81 that we project for 2011. This would be up from $2.55 in 2010, which excludes $0.34 of business realignment and impairment charges (net). In 2011, we expect special items to include $0.11 to $0.12 a share of costs related to a multi-year improvement and modernization program called Project Next Century, and a $0.05 gain on the sale of trademark licensing rights.

▶ In June 2011, HSY named John P. Bilbrey as President and Chief Executive Officer, effective immediately. Mr. Bilbrey had been named interim President and CEO in May 2011, replacing David J. West, who became CEO of privately owned Del Monte Foods in August.

### Investment Rationale/Risk

▶ Over the long term, we have some concern that Kraft Foods' (KFT 35, Hold) acquisition of British company Cadbury plc will weaken HSY's competitive position in the candy industry and limit HSY's international expansion opportunities. However, we have been impressed by recent HSY sales growth, and we think that its efforts to create an improved supply chain have bolstered its longer-term profit growth prospects.

▶ Risks to our recommendation and target price include the possibility that sales will be weaker than we anticipate; that profit margins will be less favorable; and that new products or cost-saving efforts will be less beneficial than expected. We have an unfavorable view of Hershey's dual class capital structure with unequal voting rights.

▶ Our 12-month target price of $58 reflects a P/E premium of about 25% to the recent average valuation (on estimated 2011 EPS) for a group of other packaged food stocks, which we think is merited by the strength of the candy market and HSY's growth prospects. HSY shares recently had an indicated dividend yield of 2.4%.

### Qualitative Risk Assessment

| LOW | MEDIUM | HIGH |
|---|---|---|

Our risk assessment reflects what we see as the relative stability of Hershey's primary end markets, the strength of its U.S. business, and the strength of its balance sheet and cash flow.

### Quantitative Evaluations

**S&P Quality Ranking** B+

| D | C | B- | B | B+ | A- | A | A+ |
|---|---|---|---|---|---|---|---|

**Relative Strength Rank** MODERATE

60

LOWEST = 1          HIGHEST = 99

### Revenue/Earnings Data

**Revenue (Million $)**

| | 1Q | 2Q | 3Q | 4Q | Year |
|---|---|---|---|---|---|
| 2011 | 1,564 | 1,325 | 1,624 | -- | -- |
| 2010 | 1,408 | 1,233 | 1,547 | 1,483 | 5,671 |
| 2009 | 1,236 | 1,171 | 1,484 | 1,407 | 5,299 |
| 2008 | 1,160 | 1,105 | 1,490 | 1,377 | 5,133 |
| 2007 | 1,153 | 1,052 | 1,399 | 1,342 | 4,947 |
| 2006 | 1,140 | 1,052 | 1,416 | 1,337 | 4,944 |

**Earnings Per Share ($)**

| | 1Q | 2Q | 3Q | 4Q | Year |
|---|---|---|---|---|---|
| 2011 | 0.70 | 0.56 | 0.86 | E0.71 | E2.81 |
| 2010 | 0.64 | 0.20 | 0.78 | 0.59 | 2.21 |
| 2009 | 0.33 | 0.31 | 0.71 | 0.55 | 1.90 |
| 2008 | 0.28 | 0.18 | 0.54 | 0.36 | 1.36 |
| 2007 | 0.40 | 0.01 | 0.27 | 0.24 | 0.93 |
| 2006 | 0.50 | 0.41 | 0.78 | 0.65 | 2.34 |

Fiscal year ended Dec. 31. Next earnings report expected: NA. EPS Estimates based on S&P Operating Earnings; historical GAAP earnings are as reported.

### Dividend Data (Dates: mm/dd Payment Date: mm/dd/yy)

| Amount ($) | Date Decl. | Ex-Div. Date | Stk. of Record | Payment Date |
|---|---|---|---|---|
| 0.345 | 02/02 | 02/23 | 02/25 | 03/15/11 |
| 0.345 | 04/28 | 05/23 | 05/25 | 06/15/11 |
| 0.345 | 08/02 | 08/23 | 08/25 | 09/15/11 |
| 0.345 | 10/03 | 11/22 | 11/25 | 12/15/11 |

Dividends have been paid since 1930. Source: Company reports.

# Hershey Co (The)

## Business Summary October 31, 2011

CORPORATE OVERVIEW. The Hershey Co. produces and distributes a variety of chocolate, confectionery and grocery products. The company's brands include Hershey's, Kisses and Reese's.

CORPORATE STRATEGY. In June 2010, HSY announced a project called Next Century as part of its efforts to create an enhanced supply chain and cost structure. The project is expected to include a plant expansion in West Hershey, PA, and investment in distribution and administrative facilities located in Hershey. In October 2011, HSY indicated that the Next Century program would incur pretax charges and non-recurring project implementation costs of $140 million to $160 million from 2010 to 2013. We expect total capital expenditures related to the program to be $280 million to $300 million. At the conclusion of the program in 2014, we look for ongoing annual savings to have reached about $60 million to $80 million.

In February 2007, HSY announced a supply chain transformation program that was completed in 2009's fourth quarter. In 2009, HSY took $0.27 a share of charges related to the program. Since inception, total charges for the pro-

gram amounted to $620.1 million (pretax), including $85 million of non-cash pension settlement charges. In July 2010, HSY said that except for possible non-cash pension settlement charges, it did not expect any significant charges related to the program in 2010. HSY estimated total program savings through 2009 at $160 million, with total ongoing annual savings from the program of $175 million to $185 million expected to be achieved by the end of 2010. Under the program, HSY expected to significantly increase manufacturing capacity utilization by reducing the number of its production lines; outsource the production of low-value-added items; and construct a production facility in Mexico. HSY planned to invest a portion of these savings in strategic growth initiatives.

In 2010, 15.2% of HSY's net sales were from businesses outside the U.S.

## Company Financials Fiscal Year Ended Dec. 31

| Per Share Data ($) | 2010 | 2009 | 2008 | 2007 | 2006 | 2005 | 2004 | 2003 | 2002 | 2001 |
|---|---|---|---|---|---|---|---|---|---|---|
| Tangible Book Value | 1.12 | 0.10 | NM | NM | 0.18 | 1.63 | 2.03 | 3.29 | 3.55 | 2.65 |
| Cash Flow | 3.02 | 2.68 | 2.11 | 2.27 | 3.17 | 2.96 | 3.17 | 2.44 | 2.17 | 1.44 |
| Earnings | 2.21 | 1.90 | 1.36 | 0.93 | 2.34 | 1.99 | 2.30 | 1.76 | 1.46 | 0.75 |
| S&P Core Earnings | 2.45 | 2.13 | 1.22 | 1.14 | 2.26 | 1.94 | 2.23 | 1.73 | 1.37 | 0.94 |
| Dividends | 1.28 | 1.19 | 1.19 | 1.14 | 1.03 | 0.93 | 0.84 | 0.72 | 0.63 | 0.58 |
| Payout Ratio | 58% | 63% | 87% | 122% | 44% | 47% | 36% | 41% | 43% | 78% |
| Prices:High | 52.10 | 42.25 | 44.32 | 56.75 | 57.65 | 67.37 | 56.75 | 39.33 | 39.75 | 35.08 |
| Prices:Low | 35.76 | 30.27 | 32.10 | 38.21 | 48.20 | 52.49 | 37.28 | 30.35 | 28.23 | 27.56 |
| P/E Ratio:High | 24 | 22 | 33 | 61 | 25 | 34 | 25 | 22 | 27 | 47 |
| P/E Ratio:Low | 16 | 16 | 24 | 41 | 21 | 26 | 16 | 17 | 19 | 37 |

| Income Statement Analysis (Million $) | | | | | | | | | | |
|---|---|---|---|---|---|---|---|---|---|---|
| Revenue | 5,671 | 5,299 | 5,133 | 4,947 | 4,944 | 4,836 | 4,429 | 4,173 | 4,120 | 4,557 |
| Operating Income | 1,198 | 1,039 | 941 | 1,047 | 1,207 | 1,175 | 1,092 | 992 | 904 | 812 |
| Depreciation | 185 | 178 | 171 | 311 | 200 | 218 | 190 | 181 | 178 | 190 |
| Interest Expense | 96.4 | 91.3 | 105 | 119 | 116 | 89.5 | 66.5 | 63.5 | 60.7 | 71.5 |
| Pretax Income | 809 | 671 | 492 | 340 | 877 | 773 | 836 | 733 | 638 | 344 |
| Effective Tax Rate | NA | 35.0% | 36.7% | 37.1% | 36.2% | 36.2% | 29.3% | 36.6% | 36.7% | 39.7% |
| Net Income | 510 | 436 | 311 | 214 | 559 | 493 | 591 | 465 | 404 | 207 |
| S&P Core Earnings | 563 | 488 | 279 | 264 | 540 | 482 | 573 | 455 | 377 | 258 |

| Balance Sheet & Other Financial Data (Million $) | | | | | | | | | | |
|---|---|---|---|---|---|---|---|---|---|---|
| Cash | 885 | 254 | 37.1 | 129 | 97.1 | 67.2 | 54.8 | 115 | 298 | 134 |
| Current Assets | 2,005 | 1,385 | 1,345 | 1,427 | 1,418 | 1,409 | 1,182 | 1,132 | 1,264 | 1,168 |
| Total Assets | 4,273 | 3,675 | 3,635 | 4,247 | 4,158 | 4,295 | 3,798 | 3,583 | 3,481 | 3,247 |
| Current Liabilities | 1,299 | 911 | 1,270 | 1,619 | 1,454 | 1,518 | 1,285 | 586 | 547 | 606 |
| Long Term Debt | 1,542 | 1,503 | 1,506 | 1,280 | 1,248 | 943 | 691 | 968 | 852 | 877 |
| Common Equity | 938 | 760 | 318 | 593 | 683 | 1,021 | 1,089 | 1,280 | 1,372 | 1,147 |
| Total Capital | 2,479 | 2,263 | 1,860 | 2,084 | 2,218 | 2,364 | 2,109 | 2,626 | 2,572 | 2,280 |
| Capital Expenditures | 180 | 126 | 263 | 190 | 183 | 181 | 182 | 219 | 133 | 160 |
| Cash Flow | 695 | 614 | 482 | 525 | 759 | 711 | 781 | 646 | 581 | 398 |
| Current Ratio | 1.5 | 1.5 | 1.1 | 0.9 | 1.0 | 0.9 | 0.9 | 1.9 | 2.3 | 1.9 |
| % Long Term Debt of Capitalization | 62.2 | 66.4 | 81.0 | 61.4 | 56.3 | 39.9 | 32.7 | 36.9 | 33.1 | 38.5 |
| % Net Income of Revenue | 9.0 | 8.2 | 6.1 | 4.3 | 11.3 | 10.2 | 13.3 | 11.1 | 9.8 | 4.5 |
| % Return on Assets | 12.8 | 11.9 | 7.9 | 5.1 | 13.3 | 12.2 | 16.0 | 13.2 | 12.0 | 6.2 |
| % Return on Equity | 61.5 | 80.9 | 68.4 | 33.6 | 65.8 | 45.7 | 46.4 | 35.1 | 32.0 | 17.8 |

Data as orig reptd.; bef. results of disc opers/spec. items. Per share data adj. for stk. divs.; EPS diluted. E-Estimated. NA-Not Available. NM-Not Meaningful. NR-Not Ranked. UR-Under Review.

**Office:** 100 Crystal A Drive, Hershey, PA 17033-9790.
**Telephone:** 717-534-4200.
**Website:** http://www.thehersheycompany.com
**Chrmn:** J.E. Nevels

**Pres & CEO:** J.P. Bilbrey
**EVP, CFO & Chief Admin Officer:** H.P. Alfonso
**Chief Acctg Officer:** D.W. Tacka
**Secy & General Counsel:** B.H. Snyder

**Investor Contact:** M.K. Pogharian (800-539-0261)
**Board Members:** P. M. Arway, R. F. Cavanaugh, C. A. Davis, J. M. Mead, J. E. Nevels, A. J. Palmer, T. J. Ridge, D. L. Shedlarz

**Founded:** 1894
**Domicile:** Delaware
**Employees:** 13,500

# Hess Corp

STANDARD &POOR'S

| S&P Recommendation | **BUY** ★★★★☆ | Price $54.33 (as of Nov 25, 2011) | 12-Mo. Target Price $76.00 | Investment Style Large-Cap Blend |
|---|---|---|---|---|

**GICS Sector** Energy
**Sub-Industry** Integrated Oil & Gas

**Summary** This integrated oil and natural gas company has exploration and production activities worldwide, and markets refined petroleum products on the U.S. East Coast.

## Key Stock Statistics (Source S&P, Vickers, company reports)

| | | | | | | | |
|---|---|---|---|---|---|---|---|
| 52-Wk Range | $87.40–46.66 | S&P Oper. EPS 2011**E** | 6.67 | Market Capitalization(B) | $18.467 | Beta | 1.15 |
| Trailing 12-Month EPS | $5.56 | S&P Oper. EPS 2012**E** | 6.81 | Yield (%) | 0.74 | S&P 3-Yr. Proj. EPS CAGR(%) | 44 |
| Trailing 12-Month P/E | 9.8 | P/E on S&P Oper. EPS 2011**E** | 8.1 | Dividend Rate/Share | $0.40 | S&P Credit Rating | BBB |
| $10K Invested 5 Yrs Ago | $12,364 | Common Shares Outstg. (M) | 339.9 | Institutional Ownership (%) | 76 | | |

## Price Performance

30-Week Mov. Avg. ···· 10-Week Mov. Avg. - - GAAP Earnings vs. Previous Year   Volume Above Avg. ▌▎▌ STARS
12-Mo. Target Price — Relative Strength — ▲ Up ▼ Down ▶ No Change   Below Avg. ▌▎▌ ★

Options: ASE, CBOE, Ph

## Qualitative Risk Assessment

| LOW | **MEDIUM** | HIGH |
|---|---|---|

Our risk assessment reflects HES's diversified business profile in volatile, cyclical, and capital-intensive segments of the energy industry. While we see risk from its investments in politically troubled locales, we think offsets include its improved, relatively low cost structure in exploration and production.

## Quantitative Evaluations

**S&P Quality Ranking**     A-

| D | C | B- | B | B+ | **A-** | A | A+ |
|---|---|---|---|---|---|---|---|

**Relative Strength Rank**     MODERATE

33

LOWEST = 1           HIGHEST = 99

## Revenue/Earnings Data

**Revenue (Million $)**

| | 1Q | 2Q | 3Q | 4Q | Year |
|---|---|---|---|---|---|
| 2011 | 10,201 | 9,855 | 8,726 | -- | -- |
| 2010 | 9,305 | 7,756 | 8,953 | 9,038 | 35,135 |
| 2009 | 6,915 | 6,751 | 7,270 | 8,678 | 29,614 |
| 2008 | 10,667 | 11,717 | 11,398 | 7,383 | 41,165 |
| 2007 | 7,319 | 7,421 | 7,451 | 9,456 | 31,647 |
| 2006 | 7,159 | 6,718 | 7,035 | 7,155 | 28,067 |

**Earnings Per Share ($)**

| | 1Q | 2Q | 3Q | 4Q | Year |
|---|---|---|---|---|---|
| 2011 | 2.74 | 1.78 | 0.88 | E1.95 | E6.67 |
| 2010 | 1.65 | 1.15 | 3.52 | 0.18 | 6.47 |
| 2009 | -0.18 | 0.31 | 1.05 | 1.10 | 2.27 |
| 2008 | 2.34 | 2.76 | 2.37 | -0.23 | 7.24 |
| 2007 | 1.17 | 1.75 | 1.23 | 1.59 | 5.74 |
| 2006 | 2.21 | 1.79 | 0.94 | 1.13 | 6.07 |

Fiscal year ended Dec. 31. Next earnings report expected: Late January. EPS Estimates based on S&P Operating Earnings; historical GAAP earnings are as reported.

## Highlights

- The 12-month target price for HES has recently been changed to $76.00 from $86.00. The Highlights section of this Stock Report will be updated accordingly.

## Investment Rationale/Risk

- The Investment Rationale/Risk section of this Stock Report will be updated shortly. For the latest News story on HES from MarketScope, see below.

- 10/27/11 02:15 pm ET ... S&P MAINTAINS BUY OPINION ON SHARES OF HESS CORPORATION (HES 64.89****): Q3 EPS of $1.11 before $0.27 of net 1X charges, vs. $1.26 before 1X gains of $2.26, is $0.73 below our estimate. Results were hurt by unrest in Libya and downtime in Europe. Despite the miss, we still expect solid growth opportunities in '12. HES's entry into the Utica Shale should bear fruit, as should its ongoing expansion in the Bakken play. However, refining continues to lag. We cut our '11 EPS forecast $0.58 to $6.67, and '12's by $1.39 to $6.81. On our DCF model and relative metrics, we trim our 12-month target price by $10 to $76. / Stewart Glickman, CFA

## Dividend Data (Dates: mm/dd Payment Date: mm/dd/yy)

| Amount ($) | Date Decl. | Ex-Div. Date | Stk. of Record | Payment Date |
|---|---|---|---|---|
| 0.100 | 12/01 | 12/16 | 12/20 | 01/03/11 |
| 0.100 | 03/02 | 03/10 | 03/14 | 03/31/11 |
| 0.100 | 06/01 | 06/14 | 06/16 | 06/30/11 |
| 0.100 | 09/08 | 09/15 | 09/19 | 09/30/11 |

Dividends have been paid since 1922. Source: Company reports.

---

**Please read the Required Disclosures and Analyst Certification on the last page of this report.**

The **McGraw·Hill** Companies

# Hess Corp

**STANDARD &POOR'S**

## Business Summary September 14, 2011

CORPORATE OVERVIEW. Hess Corp. (HES; formerly Amerada Hess Corp.) has two operating segments: Exploration and Production (2010 revenues of $9.0 billion; 2010 net income of $2.74 billion), and Marketing and Refining ($24.9 billion, a loss of $231 million). Business is conducted in the U.S. (83% of 2010 revenues; 23% of proved reserves), Europe (6%; 38%), Africa (7%; 18%), and Asia and elsewhere (4%; 21%). As of March 2011, the Hess family owned about 11% of the common shares.

Oil and gas production rose 2.5% in 2010, to 418,000 barrels of oil equivalent (boe) per day (73% crude oil and natural gas liquids (NGLs)). Net proved oil and gas reserves rose 6.9%, to 1.54 billion boe (55% developed; 72% crude oil and NGLs). Using data from John S. Herold, an oil industry consultant, we estimate HES's three-year (2007-09) average proved acquisition costs at $21.29 per boe, above the peer average; its three-year finding and development costs at $18.85 per boe, above the peer average; its three-year reserve replacement costs at $18.94 per boe, above the peer average; and its three-year reserve replacement at 146%, slightly above the peer average.

In 2010, about 29% of the company's oil and NGL production and 16% of its natural gas production were from U.S. operations: onshore in the Williston Basin of North Dakota and in the Permian Basin in Texas, and offshore in the Gulf of Mexico, which included Shenzi (HES 28%), Llano (50%), Conger (38%), Baldpate (50%), Hack Wilson (25%), and Penn State (50%) fields.

HES's refining earnings are mainly derived from its 50% ownership in the refining joint venture HOVENSA, formed in October 1998 with a subsidiary of Petroleos de Venezuela S.A. (PdVSA) in the U.S. Virgin Islands. Refining operations at HOVENSA consist of crude units (500,000 b/d), a fluid catalytic cracker (150,000 b/d), and a delayed coker (58,000 b/d). In addition, HES owns and operates a 70,000 b/d fluid catalytic cracking facility in Port Reading, NJ, to produce gasoline and heating oil. In January 2011, HOVENSA announced plans to shut down certain older and smaller processing units, which would reduce distillation capacity by 30% to 350,000 barrels per day.

As of year-end 2010, HOVENSA had a long-term supply contract with PdVSA to purchase 115,000 b/d of Venezuelan Merey heavy crude oil. PdVSA also supplies 155,000 b/d of Venezuelan Masa medium gravity crude oil to HOVENSA under a long-term supply contract.

## Company Financials Fiscal Year Ended Dec. 31

| Per Share Data ($) | 2010 | 2009 | 2008 | 2007 | 2006 | 2005 | 2004 | 2003 | 2002 | 2001 |
|---|---|---|---|---|---|---|---|---|---|---|
| Tangible Book Value | 42.65 | 37.50 | 34.31 | 26.67 | 21.77 | 16.61 | 14.34 | 13.62 | 12.17 | 14.70 |
| Cash Flow | 15.19 | 9.19 | 13.86 | 10.99 | 9.80 | 7.11 | 6.18 | 5.61 | 4.17 | 7.04 |
| Earnings | 6.47 | 2.27 | 7.24 | 5.74 | 6.07 | 3.98 | 3.17 | 1.72 | -0.83 | 3.42 |
| S&P Core Earnings | 4.19 | 2.21 | 7.12 | 5.83 | 5.38 | 3.78 | 3.06 | 1.75 | -1.28 | 3.25 |
| Dividends | 0.40 | 0.40 | 0.30 | 0.40 | 0.40 | 0.40 | 0.40 | 0.40 | 0.40 | 0.40 |
| Payout Ratio | 6% | 18% | 4% | 7% | 7% | 10% | 13% | 23% | NM | 12% |
| Prices:High | 76.98 | 69.74 | 137.00 | 105.85 | 56.45 | 47.50 | 31.30 | 19.07 | 28.23 | 30.13 |
| Prices:Low | 48.70 | 46.33 | 35.50 | 45.96 | 37.62 | 25.94 | 17.75 | 13.71 | 16.47 | 17.92 |
| P/E Ratio:High | 12 | 31 | 19 | 18 | 9 | 12 | 10 | 11 | NM | 9 |
| P/E Ratio:Low | 8 | 20 | 5 | 8 | 6 | 7 | 6 | 8 | NM | 5 |

| Income Statement Analysis (Million $) | | | | | | | | | | |
|---|---|---|---|---|---|---|---|---|---|---|
| Revenue | 35,135 | 29,614 | 41,165 | 31,647 | 28,067 | 22,747 | 16,733 | 14,480 | 12,093 | 13,413 |
| Operating Income | NA | NA | 7,207 | 5,259 | 4,812 | 2,967 | 2,769 | 2,127 | 2,382 | 2,399 |
| Depreciation, Depletion and Amortization | 2,849 | 2,254 | 2,154 | 1,678 | 1,224 | 1,025 | 970 | 1,053 | 1,320 | 967 |
| Interest Expense | 361 | 360 | 267 | 306 | 201 | 224 | 241 | 293 | 269 | 194 |
| Pretax Income | 3,311 | 1,522 | 4,700 | 3,704 | 4,040 | 2,226 | 1,558 | 781 | -51.0 | 1,438 |
| Effective Tax Rate | NA | 47.0% | 49.8% | 50.5% | 52.6% | 44.2% | 37.7% | 40.2% | NM | 36.4% |
| Net Income | 2,125 | 740 | 2,360 | 1,832 | 1,916 | 1,242 | 970 | 467 | -218 | 914 |
| S&P Core Earnings | 1,377 | 720 | 2,320 | 1,865 | 1,657 | 1,131 | 888 | 468 | -339 | 870 |

| Balance Sheet & Other Financial Data (Million $) | | | | | | | | | | |
|---|---|---|---|---|---|---|---|---|---|---|
| Cash | 1,608 | 1,362 | 908 | 607 | 383 | 315 | 877 | 518 | 197 | 37.0 |
| Current Assets | 8,746 | 7,987 | 7,332 | 6,926 | 5,848 | 5,290 | 4,335 | 3,186 | 2,756 | 3,946 |
| Total Assets | 35,281 | 29,419 | 28,908 | 26,131 | 22,404 | 19,115 | 16,312 | 13,983 | 13,262 | 15,369 |
| Current Liabilities | 7,579 | 6,850 | 7,730 | 8,024 | 6,739 | 6,447 | 4,697 | 2,669 | 2,553 | 3,718 |
| Long Term Debt | 5,537 | 4,319 | 3,812 | 3,918 | 3,745 | 3,759 | 3,785 | 3,868 | 4,976 | 5,283 |
| Common Equity | 16,809 | 13,528 | 12,307 | 9,774 | 8,111 | 6,272 | 5,583 | 5,326 | 8,498 | 4,907 |
| Total Capital | 22,346 | 17,995 | 18,360 | 16,054 | 13,955 | 11,446 | 10,566 | 10,352 | 14,518 | 11,301 |
| Capital Expenditures | 5,492 | 2,918 | 4,438 | 3,578 | 3,844 | 2,341 | 1,521 | 1,358 | 1,404 | 2,501 |
| Cash Flow | 4,987 | 2,994 | 4,514 | 3,510 | 3,096 | 2,219 | 1,892 | 1,515 | 1,102 | 1,881 |
| Current Ratio | 1.2 | 1.2 | 1.0 | 0.9 | 0.9 | 0.8 | 0.9 | 1.2 | 1.1 | 1.1 |
| % Long Term Debt of Capitalization | 24.8 | 24.0 | 20.8 | 24.4 | 26.8 | 32.8 | 35.8 | 37.4 | 34.3 | 46.7 |
| % Return on Assets | 6.6 | 2.6 | 8.6 | 7.5 | 9.2 | 7.0 | 6.4 | 3.4 | NM | 7.1 |
| % Return on Equity | 14.1 | 5.7 | 21.4 | 20.5 | 26.0 | 20.1 | 16.9 | 9.7 | NM | 20.8 |

Data as orig reptd.; bef. results of disc opers/spec. items. Per share data adj. for stk. divs.; EPS diluted. E-Estimated. NA-Not Available. NM-Not Meaningful. NR-Not Ranked. UR-Under Review.

Office: 1185 Avenue Of The Americas, New York, NY 10036.
Telephone: 212-997-8500.
Email: investorrelations@hess.com
Website: http://www.hess.com

Chrmn & CEO: J.B. Hess
SVP, CFO & Chief Acctg Officer: J.P. Rielly
SVP & General Counsel: T.B. Goodell
Treas: R.M. Biglin

Secy: G.C. Barry
Investor Contact: J.R. Wilson (212-536-8940)
Board Members: S. W. Bodman, III, N. F. Brady, J. B. Hess, G. P. Hill, E. E. Holiday, T. H. Kean, R. J. Lavizzo-Mourey, C. G. Matthews, J. H. Mullin, III, F. A. Olson, F. B. Walker, R. N. Wilson, E. H. von Metzsch

Founded: 1920
Domicile: Delaware
Employees: 13,800

The McGraw-Hill Companies

# Hewlett-Packard Co

**STANDARD &POOR'S**

| S&P Recommendation **HOLD** ★★★☆☆ | Price $26.53 (as of Nov 28, 2011) | 12-Mo. Target Price $29.00 | Investment Style Large-Cap Blend |
|---|---|---|---|

**GICS Sector** Information Technology
**Sub-Industry** Computer Hardware

**Summary** This leading maker of computer products, including printers, servers and PCs, has a large service and support network.

## Key Stock Statistics (Source S&P, Vickers, company reports)

| | | | | | | | |
|---|---|---|---|---|---|---|---|
| 52-Wk Range | $49.39– 21.50 | S&P Oper. EPS 2012**E** | 4.02 | Market Capitalization(B) | $52.714 | Beta | 1.11 |
| Trailing 12-Month EPS | $3.32 | S&P Oper. EPS 2013**E** | 4.53 | Yield (%) | 1.81 | S&P 3-Yr. Proj. EPS CAGR(%) | 3 |
| Trailing 12-Month P/E | 8.0 | P/E on S&P Oper. EPS 2012**E** | 6.6 | Dividend Rate/Share | $0.48 | S&P Credit Rating | A |
| $10K Invested 5 Yrs Ago | $6,699 | Common Shares Outstg. (M) | 1,987.0 | Institutional Ownership (%) | 76 | | |

## Price Performance

30-Week Mov. Avg. ··· 10-Week Mov. Avg. -- **GAAP Earnings vs. Previous Year**    Volume Above Avg. |||| STARS
12-Mo. Target Price — Relative Strength — ▲ Up ▼ Down ▶ No Change    Below Avg. |||| ★

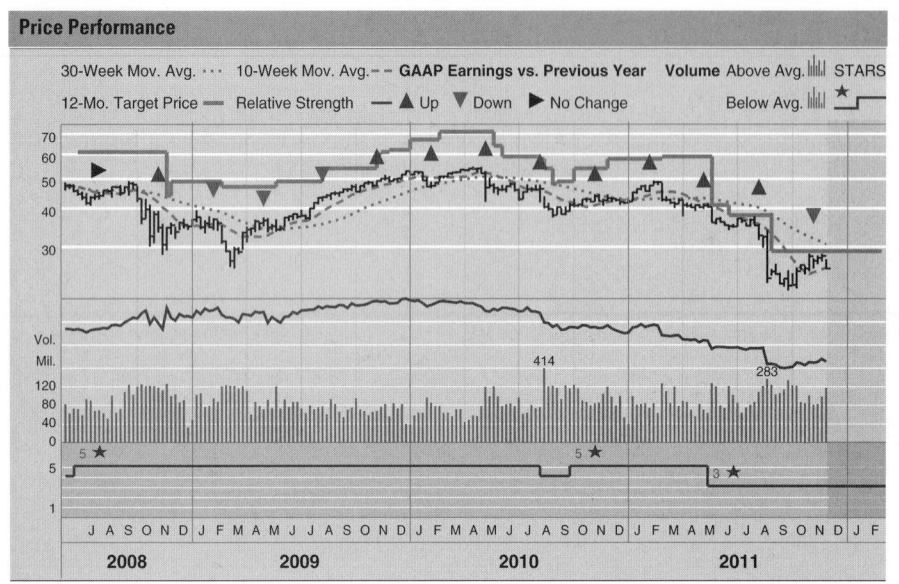

Options: ASE, CBOE, P, Ph

Analysis prepared by Equity Analyst **Dylan Cathers** on Nov 28, 2011, when the stock traded at **$26.11**.

## Highlights

➤ We expect a revenue decline of 2.5% in FY 12 (Oct.), as HPQ is facing a number of both internal and external headwinds. Internally, the company has work to do reshaping its Services business, and it has printing supplies inventory to work through. Externally, it is dealing with weakness in demand from consumers, particularly in Europe; uncertain levels of demand from the enterprise segment; and hard disk drive inventory disruptions from the flooding in Thailand, which could last into the spring. We expect revenue growth of 2.0% in FY 13.

➤ Non-GAAP operating margins narrowed in FY 11, and we expect further narrowing this fiscal year. Margin pressures are coming from several sources, including lower leverage from falling revenues. Additionally, we expect the company to affected by investments in the business, an unfavorable sales mix, and competitive pricing. Lastly, the company simply needs better execution, which has been lacking over the past year, in our view.

➤ Operating EPS, excluding restructuring charges, was $4.87 in FY 11. We see $4.02 and $4.53 for FY 12 and FY 13, respectively, aided by share buybacks.

## Investment Rationale/Risk

➤ HPQ is in a period of strategic self-exploration, which is being led by Meg Whitman. We believe her strength lies in operations, where HPQ needs increased attention. In the long run, we think aiming at higher margin enterprise markets will help the company, but we see rising near-term uncertainties, and the company needs to prove to investors it is on the right track after a series of management missteps. We are waiting for a final decision on the webOS operating system for mobile phones and tablets; future webOS products were canceled by the former CEO.

➤ Risks to our recommendation and target price include potential problems integrating acquisitions, transition challenges since the arrival of new top leadership in September, and potential weakening of demand for computer hardware generally, or for PCs in particular, as new tablet computers offer a substitute.

➤ We apply a target multiple near 6.6X, toward the low end of the seven-year historical range for HPQ to reflect near-term pressure we project for revenues and margins, to our calendar 2012 EPS estimate of $4.42 to arrive at our 12-month target price of $29.

## Qualitative Risk Assessment

| LOW | MEDIUM | HIGH |
|---|---|---|

Our risk assessment reflects the intensely price competitive environment in the computer hardware industry and potential integration risk surrounding planned and completed acquisitions, balanced by our view of the company's broad worldwide customer base and its successful efforts in reducing its cost structure.

## Quantitative Evaluations

**S&P Quality Ranking** A-

| D | C | B- | B | B+ | A- | A | A+ |
|---|---|---|---|---|---|---|---|

**Relative Strength Rank** MODERATE

66

LOWEST = 1                           HIGHEST = 99

## Revenue/Earnings Data

**Revenue (Million $)**

| | 1Q | 2Q | 3Q | 4Q | Year |
|---|---|---|---|---|---|
| 2011 | 32,302 | 31,632 | 31,189 | 32,122 | 127,245 |
| 2010 | 31,177 | 30,849 | 30,729 | 33,278 | 126,033 |
| 2009 | 28,807 | 27,383 | 27,585 | 30,777 | 114,552 |
| 2008 | 28,467 | 28,262 | 28,032 | 33,603 | 118,364 |
| 2007 | 25,082 | 25,534 | 25,377 | 28,293 | 104,286 |
| 2006 | 22,659 | 22,554 | 21,890 | 24,555 | 91,658 |

**Earnings Per Share ($)**

| | 1Q | 2Q | 3Q | 4Q | Year |
|---|---|---|---|---|---|
| 2011 | 1.17 | 1.05 | 0.93 | 0.12 | 3.32 |
| 2010 | 0.95 | 0.91 | 0.75 | 1.10 | 3.69 |
| 2009 | 0.75 | 0.71 | 0.69 | 0.99 | 3.14 |
| 2008 | 0.80 | 0.81 | 0.80 | 0.84 | 3.25 |
| 2007 | 0.55 | 0.65 | 0.80 | 0.81 | 2.68 |
| 2006 | 0.42 | 0.66 | 0.48 | 0.60 | 2.18 |

Fiscal year ended Oct. 31. Next earnings report expected: Late February. EPS Estimates based on S&P Operating Earnings; historical GAAP earnings are as reported.

## Dividend Data (Dates: mm/dd Payment Date: mm/dd/yy)

| Amount ($) | Date Decl. | Ex-Div. Date | Stk. of Record | Payment Date |
|---|---|---|---|---|
| 0.080 | 01/20 | 03/14 | 03/16 | 04/06/11 |
| 0.120 | 05/26 | 06/13 | 06/15 | 07/06/11 |
| 0.120 | 07/21 | 09/12 | 09/14 | 10/05/11 |
| 0.120 | 11/17 | 12/12 | 12/14 | 01/04/12 |

Dividends have been paid since 1965. Source: Company reports.

---

**Please read the Required Disclosures and Analyst Certification on the last page of this report.**

The **McGraw·Hill** Companies

# Hewlett-Packard Co

STANDARD
&POOR'S

## Business Summary November 28, 2011

CORPORATE OVERVIEW. Hewlett-Packard provides personal computers, printers, enterprise server and storage technology, software, and a wide range of related products and services to individual and enterprise customers worldwide. Revenues in FY 11 (Oct.) came approximately 70% from products and 30% from services, including financing services.

Workforce restructurings have enabled HPQ to develop a global delivery structure that has improved margins by taking advantage of low-cost technical expertise. The cost and efficiency campaign was led by former NCR Corp. CEO Mark Hurd, who was named CEO and president of HPQ effective April 1, 2005. Mr. Hurd resigned from the company on August 6, 2010, following an internal investigation that found violations of HPQ's standards of business conduct. On November 1, 2010, Leo Apoteker, a former CEO of software rival SAP AG (SAP 58, Buy), became CEO and president. He was replaced less than a year later by Meg Whitman, who had been on the board for eight months.

The breadth of the company's customer base is illustrated by the 66% of FY 11 revenues that came from outside the U.S., up from 65% in FY 10. Further, no single customer, nor any single country other than the U.S., accounted for more than 10% of sales in FY 10 (latest available).

The company reports in seven segments. Three segments accounting for about 47% of sales are often grouped together as HP Enterprise Business. These include Enterprise Storage and Servers, representing approximately 17.0% of FY 11 sales, Services 27.5%, and HP Software 2.5%. Other segments include the Personal Systems Group, representing about 30.5% of FY 11 sales, the Imaging and Printing Group 19.5%, HP Financial Services 2.5%, and Corporate Investments 0.5%.

## Company Financials Fiscal Year Ended Oct. 31

| Per Share Data ($) | 2011 | 2010 | 2009 | 2008 | 2007 | 2006 | 2005 | 2004 | 2003 | 2002 |
|---|---|---|---|---|---|---|---|---|---|---|
| Tangible Book Value | NA | NM | 0.34 | NM | 4.91 | 6.57 | 6.04 | 6.06 | 6.08 | 5.35 |
| Cash Flow | 5.67 | 5.73 | 5.10 | 4.56 | 3.67 | 3.00 | 1.63 | 1.93 | 1.65 | 0.48 |
| Earnings | 3.32 | 3.69 | 3.14 | 3.25 | 2.68 | 2.18 | 0.82 | 1.15 | 0.83 | -0.37 |
| S&P Core Earnings | NA | 3.69 | 3.14 | 2.97 | 2.56 | 2.10 | 0.74 | 0.94 | 0.65 | -0.65 |
| Dividends | 0.40 | 0.32 | 0.32 | 0.32 | 0.32 | 0.32 | 0.32 | 0.32 | 0.32 | 0.32 |
| Payout Ratio | 12% | 9% | 10% | 10% | 12% | 15% | 39% | 28% | 39% | NM |
| Prices:High | 49.39 | 54.75 | 52.95 | 50.98 | 53.48 | 41.70 | 30.25 | 26.28 | 23.90 | 24.12 |
| Prices:Low | 21.50 | 37.32 | 25.39 | 28.23 | 38.15 | 28.37 | 18.89 | 16.08 | 14.18 | 10.75 |
| P/E Ratio:High | 15 | 15 | 17 | 16 | 20 | 19 | 37 | 23 | 29 | NM |
| P/E Ratio:Low | 6 | 10 | 8 | 9 | 14 | 13 | 23 | 14 | 17 | NM |

| Income Statement Analysis (Million $) | | | | | | | | | | |
|---|---|---|---|---|---|---|---|---|---|---|
| Revenue | 127,245 | 126,033 | 114,552 | 118,364 | 104,286 | 91,658 | 86,696 | 79,905 | 73,061 | 56,588 |
| Operating Income | 16,373 | 17,736 | 15,798 | 14,196 | 11,773 | 9,372 | 7,520 | 7,017 | 6,713 | 4,570 |
| Depreciation | 4,984 | 4,820 | 4,773 | 3,367 | 2,705 | 2,353 | 2,344 | 2,395 | 2,527 | 2,119 |
| Interest Expense | 419 | 505 | 259 | 467 | 289 | 249 | 334 | 247 | 277 | 212 |
| Pretax Income | 8,982 | 10,974 | 9,415 | 10,473 | 9,177 | 7,191 | 3,543 | 4,196 | 2,888 | -1,052 |
| Effective Tax Rate | NA | NA | 18.6% | 20.5% | 20.9% | 13.8% | 32.3% | 16.7% | 12.1% | NM |
| Net Income | 7,074 | 8,761 | 7,660 | 8,329 | 7,264 | 6,198 | 2,398 | 3,497 | 2,539 | -923 |
| S&P Core Earnings | NA | 8,773 | 7,659 | 7,598 | 6,913 | 5,992 | 2,150 | 2,886 | 1,983 | -1,635 |

| Balance Sheet & Other Financial Data (Million $) | | | | | | | | | | |
|---|---|---|---|---|---|---|---|---|---|---|
| Cash | 8,043 | 10,934 | 13,334 | 10,246 | 11,293 | 16,400 | 13,911 | 12,663 | 14,188 | 11,192 |
| Current Assets | 51,021 | 54,184 | 52,539 | 51,728 | 47,402 | 48,264 | 43,334 | 42,901 | 40,996 | 36,075 |
| Total Assets | 129,517 | 124,503 | 114,799 | 113,331 | 88,699 | 81,981 | 77,317 | 76,138 | 74,708 | 70,710 |
| Current Liabilities | 50,442 | 49,403 | 43,003 | 52,939 | 39,260 | 2,490 | 31,460 | 28,588 | 26,630 | 24,310 |
| Long Term Debt | 22,551 | 15,258 | 13,980 | 7,676 | 4,997 | 2,490 | 3,392 | 4,623 | 6,494 | 6,035 |
| Common Equity | 38,625 | 40,449 | 40,517 | 38,942 | 38,526 | 38,144 | 37,176 | 37,564 | 37,746 | 36,262 |
| Total Capital | 61,934 | 56,039 | 54,497 | 49,292 | 43,523 | 40,634 | 40,568 | 42,187 | 44,240 | 42,297 |
| Capital Expenditures | 4,539 | 4,133 | 3,695 | 2,990 | 3,040 | 2,536 | 1,995 | 2,126 | 1,995 | 1,710 |
| Cash Flow | 12,058 | 13,581 | 12,433 | 11,696 | 9,969 | 8,551 | 4,742 | 5,892 | 5,066 | 1,196 |
| Current Ratio | 1.0 | 1.1 | 1.2 | 1.0 | 1.2 | 1.3 | 1.4 | 1.5 | 1.5 | 1.5 |
| % Long Term Debt of Capitalization | 36.4 | 27.2 | 25.7 | 15.4 | 11.5 | 6.1 | 8.4 | 11.0 | 14.7 | 14.3 |
| % Net Income of Revenue | 5.6 | 7.0 | 6.7 | 7.0 | 7.0 | 6.8 | 2.8 | 4.4 | 3.5 | NM |
| % Return on Assets | 5.6 | 7.3 | 6.7 | 8.3 | 8.5 | 7.8 | 3.1 | 4.6 | 3.5 | NM |
| % Return on Equity | 17.9 | 21.6 | 19.3 | 21.5 | 19.0 | 16.5 | 6.4 | 9.3 | 6.9 | NM |

Data as orig reptd.; bef. results of disc opers/spec. items. Per share data adj. for stk. divs.; EPS diluted. E-Estimated. NA-Not Available. NM-Not Meaningful. NR-Not Ranked. UR-Under Review.

**Office:** 3000 Hanover Street, Palo Alto, CA 94304-1112.
**Telephone:** 650-857-1501.
**Website:** http://www.hp.com
**Chrmn:** R.J. Lane

**Pres & CEO:** M.C. Whitman
**EVP & CTO:** S.V. Robison
**EVP, Secy & General Counsel:** M.J. Holston
**SVP, Chief Acctg Officer & Cntlr:** J.T. Murrin

**Investor Contact:** B. Humphries (650-857-3342)
**Board Members:** M. L. Andreessen, L. T. Babbio, Jr., S. Baldauf, S. Banerji, R. L. Gupta, J. H. Hammergren, R. J. Lane, A. M. Livermore, G. M. Reiner, P. A. Russo, D. Senequier, G. K. Thompson, M. C. Whitman, R. V. Whitworth

**Founded:** 1939
**Domicile:** Delaware
**Employees:** 324,600

# Home Depot Inc. (The)

**STANDARD &POOR'S**

**S&P Recommendation** HOLD ★★★☆☆

| | | |
|---|---|---|
| **Price** $36.47 (as of Nov 25, 2011) | **12-Mo. Target Price** $40.00 | **Investment Style** Large-Cap Blend |

**GICS Sector** Consumer Discretionary
**Sub-Industry** Home Improvement Retail

**Summary** HD operates a chain of over 2,200 retail warehouse-type stores, selling a wide variety of home improvement products for the do-it-yourself and home remodeling markets.

## Key Stock Statistics (Source S&P, Vickers, company reports)

| | | | | | | | |
|---|---|---|---|---|---|---|---|
| 52-Wk Range | $39.38– 28.13 | S&P Oper. EPS 2012E | 2.39 | Market Capitalization(B) | $57.050 | Beta | 0.77 |
| Trailing 12-Month EPS | $2.32 | S&P Oper. EPS 2013E | 2.74 | Yield (%) | 3.18 | S&P 3-Yr. Proj. EPS CAGR(%) | 13 |
| Trailing 12-Month P/E | 15.7 | P/E on S&P Oper. EPS 2012E | 15.3 | Dividend Rate/Share | $1.16 | S&P Credit Rating | A- |
| $10K Invested 5 Yrs Ago | $11,306 | Common Shares Outstg. (M) | 1,564.3 | Institutional Ownership (%) | 72 | | |

## Price Performance

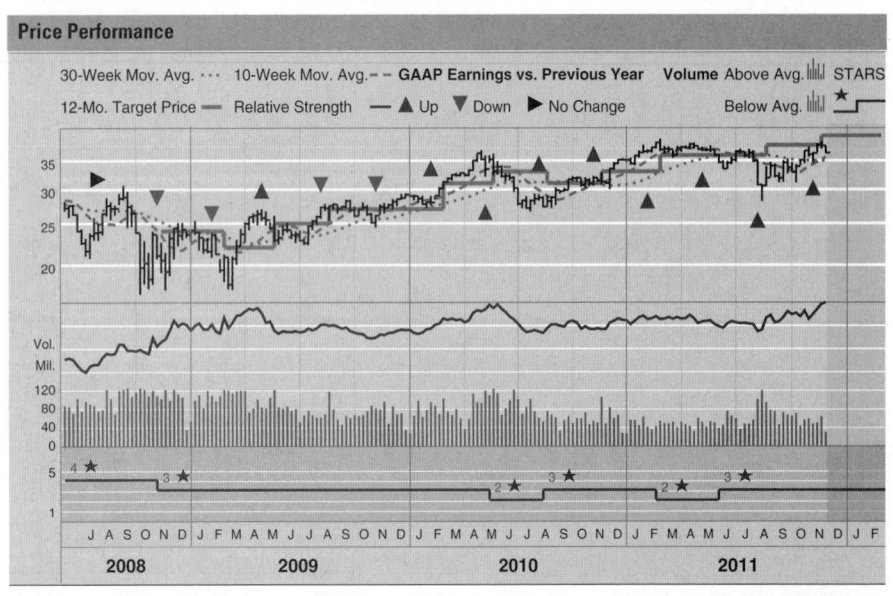

30-Week Mov. Avg. · · · 10-Week Mov. Avg. – – GAAP Earnings vs. Previous Year  Volume Above Avg. STARS
12-Mo. Target Price — Relative Strength — ▲ Up ▼ Down ► No Change  Below Avg.
★

Options: ASE, CBOE, P, Ph

Analysis prepared by Equity Analyst **Michael Souers** on Nov 16, 2011, when the stock traded at **$38.64**.

## Qualitative Risk Assessment

| LOW | MEDIUM | HIGH |
|---|---|---|

Our risk assessment for Home Depot reflects our view of ample opportunities for growth in the professional market domestically and the retail business overseas, and an S&P Quality Ranking of A. This is partially offset by the cyclical nature of the home improvement retail industry, which is reliant on economic growth.

## Quantitative Evaluations

**S&P Quality Ranking** A

| D | C | B- | B | B+ | A- | A | A+ |
|---|---|---|---|---|---|---|---|

**Relative Strength Rank** STRONG

88

LOWEST = 1    HIGHEST = 99

## Highlights

➤ We expect retail sales to increase 3.4% in FY 13 (Jan.), following our projection of a 2.9% advance in FY 12. We see this rise reflecting a handful of net new retail store additions, including international store openings, and a 3% to 4% increase in same-store sales. We project a continued slow recovery in the housing market in calendar 2012, and expect tight consumer credit to also adversely affect near-term sales for home improvement retailers, particularly on big-ticket remodeling projects.

➤ We see FY 13 operating margins widening 40 basis points, driven by a rational pricing environment, continued tight expense control, supply chain benefits from the recent investment in rapid deployment centers, and an improving mix. We also expect the projected increase in same-store sales to leverage fixed expenses slightly, given HD's stringent cost controls.

➤ After taxes at an effective rate of 36.5%, and a 4% reduction in the diluted share count, we see FY 13 EPS of $2.74. This would be a 15% improvement from the $2.39 we project the company to earn in FY 12.

## Investment Rationale/Risk

➤ We expect the housing market to recover gradually over the coming year and believe HD will reap rewards from an accelerated focus on customer service. Favorable demographic trends, such as the aging of houses and low interest rates, should help support home remodeling efforts over the long term. However, although we view HD's balance sheet and free cash flow generation as strong, we remain concerned that the recovery in housing will take much longer than widely anticipated. We think the shares are fairly valued, trading at about 14X our FY 13 EPS estimate, a slight premium to both the S&P 500 and to key peer Lowe's (LOW 23, Hold).

➤ Risks to our recommendation and target price include a renewed slowdown in consumer spending; a slower-than-expected improvement or weakening of the housing market; and unfavorable currency movements.

➤ Our 12-month target price of $40, which is equal to 14.6X our FY 13 EPS estimate, is derived from our DCF model, which assumes a weighted average cost of capital of 9.5% and a terminal growth rate of 3.0%.

## Revenue/Earnings Data

### Revenue (Million $)

| | 1Q | 2Q | 3Q | 4Q | Year |
|---|---|---|---|---|---|
| 2012 | 16,823 | 20,232 | 177,326 | -- | -- |
| 2011 | 16,863 | 19,410 | 16,598 | 15,126 | 67,997 |
| 2010 | 16,175 | 19,071 | 16,361 | 14,569 | 66,176 |
| 2009 | 17,907 | 20,990 | 17,784 | 14,607 | 71,288 |
| 2008 | 21,585 | 22,184 | 18,961 | 17,659 | 77,349 |
| 2007 | 21,461 | 26,026 | 23,085 | 20,265 | 90,837 |

### Earnings Per Share ($)

| | | | | | |
|---|---|---|---|---|---|
| 2012 | 0.50 | 0.86 | 0.60 | E0.42 | E2.39 |
| 2011 | 0.43 | 0.72 | 0.51 | 0.36 | 2.01 |
| 2010 | 0.30 | 0.66 | 0.41 | 0.18 | 1.55 |
| 2009 | 0.21 | 0.71 | 0.45 | -0.03 | 1.37 |
| 2008 | 0.53 | 0.71 | 0.59 | 0.40 | 2.27 |
| 2007 | 0.70 | 0.90 | 0.73 | 0.46 | 2.79 |

Fiscal year ended Jan. 31. Next earnings report expected: NA. EPS Estimates based on S&P Operating Earnings; historical GAAP earnings are as reported.

## Dividend Data (Dates: mm/dd Payment Date: mm/dd/yy)

| Amount ($) | Date Decl. | Ex-Div. Date | Stk. of Record | Payment Date |
|---|---|---|---|---|
| 0.250 | 02/22 | 03/08 | 03/10 | 03/24/11 |
| 0.250 | 06/01 | 06/14 | 06/16 | 06/30/11 |
| 0.250 | 08/18 | 08/30 | 09/01 | 09/15/11 |
| 0.290 | 11/15 | 11/29 | 12/01 | 12/15/11 |

Dividends have been paid since 1987. Source: Company reports.

---

**Please read the Required Disclosures and Analyst Certification on the last page of this report.**

The **McGraw-Hill** Companies

# Home Depot Inc. (The)

**STANDARD &POOR'S**

## Business Summary November 16, 2011

**CORPORATE OVERVIEW.** Home Depot is the world's largest home improvement retailer, with nearly $68 billion in revenues in FY 11 (Jan.). At January 31, 2011, HD operated 2,248 Home Depot stores (including 179 in Canada, 85 in Mexico and eight in China). Stores average approximately 105,000 sq. ft., plus 24,000 sq. ft. of garden center and storage space, and stock 30,000 to 40,000 items, including brand name and proprietary items.

Home Depot stores serve three primary customer groups: Do-It-Yourself (DIY) customers, typically homeowners who complete their own projects and installations; Do-It-For-Me (DIFM) customers, usually homeowners who purchase materials and hire third parties to complete the project and/or installation; and Professional customers, consisting of professional remodelers, general contractors, repairpeople and tradespeople. By product group, plumbing, electrical and kitchen (30% of FY 11 revenues) represented HD's largest source of revenue, followed by hardware and seasonal (29%), building materials, lumber and millwork (22%), and paint and flooring (19%).

**CORPORATE STRATEGY.** We believe HD is in a period of transition after years of expanding rapidly. We expect Home Depot to confront a rapidly saturating domestic market by accelerating its expansion efforts abroad, particularly in Mexico. Domestically, HD is increasing its focus on service and customer retention as a means to gain market share.

At the end of 2006, Home Depot acquired The Home Way, a Chinese home improvement retailer, including 12 stores in six cities. After closing four of those stores over the past two years, it appears as though HD is looking to exit the Chinese market rather than to aggressively expand there.

In August 2007, Home Depot closed the sale of HD Supply for $8.3 billion, recognizing a $4 million loss, net of tax. In connection with the sale, it purchased a 12.5% equity interest in newly formed HD Supply for $325 million, but completely wrote down this investment in FY 10 due to asset impairment.

## Company Financials Fiscal Year Ended Jan. 31

| Per Share Data ($) | 2011 | 2010 | 2009 | 2008 | 2007 | 2006 | 2005 | 2004 | 2003 | 2002 |
|---|---|---|---|---|---|---|---|---|---|---|
| Tangible Book Value | 10.91 | 10.73 | 9.81 | 9.75 | 11.81 | 11.12 | 9.54 | 9.56 | 8.39 | 7.53 |
| Cash Flow | 3.05 | 2.62 | 2.43 | 3.19 | 3.65 | 3.45 | 2.85 | 2.35 | 1.95 | 1.62 |
| Earnings | 2.01 | 1.55 | 1.37 | 2.27 | 2.79 | 2.72 | 2.26 | 1.88 | 1.56 | 1.29 |
| S&P Core Earnings | 2.01 | 1.61 | 1.43 | 2.27 | 2.79 | 2.68 | 2.19 | 1.78 | 1.46 | 1.18 |
| Dividends | NA | 0.90 | 0.90 | 0.68 | 0.68 | 0.40 | 0.33 | 0.26 | 0.21 | 0.17 |
| Payout Ratio | NA | 58% | 58% | 30% | 24% | 15% | 15% | 14% | 13% | 13% |
| Calendar Year | 2010 | 2009 | 2008 | 2007 | 2006 | 2005 | 2004 | 2003 | 2002 | 2001 |
| Prices:High | 37.03 | 29.44 | 31.08 | 42.01 | 43.95 | 43.98 | 44.30 | 37.89 | 52.60 | 53.73 |
| Prices:Low | 26.62 | 17.49 | 17.05 | 25.57 | 32.85 | 34.56 | 32.34 | 20.10 | 23.01 | 30.30 |
| P/E Ratio:High | 18 | 19 | 23 | 19 | 16 | 16 | 20 | 20 | 41 | 43 |
| P/E Ratio:Low | 13 | 11 | 12 | 11 | 12 | 13 | 14 | 11 | 18 | 24 |

| Income Statement Analysis (Million $) | | | | | | | | | | |
|---|---|---|---|---|---|---|---|---|---|---|
| Revenue | 67,997 | 66,176 | 71,288 | 77,349 | 90,837 | 81,511 | 73,094 | 64,816 | 58,247 | 53,553 |
| Operating Income | 7,557 | 6,755 | 7,093 | 9,032 | 11,435 | 10,942 | 9,245 | 7,922 | 6,733 | 5,696 |
| Depreciation | 1,718 | 1,806 | 1,783 | 1,702 | 1,762 | 1,579 | 1,319 | 1,076 | 903 | 764 |
| Interest Expense | 530 | 676 | 644 | 742 | 427 | 143 | 70.0 | 62.0 | 37.0 | 28.0 |
| Pretax Income | 5,273 | 3,982 | 3,590 | 6,620 | 9,308 | 9,282 | 7,912 | 6,843 | 5,872 | 4,957 |
| Effective Tax Rate | NA | 34.2% | 35.6% | 36.4% | 38.1% | 37.1% | 36.8% | 37.1% | 37.6% | 38.6% |
| Net Income | 3,338 | 2,620 | 2,312 | 4,210 | 5,761 | 5,838 | 5,001 | 4,304 | 3,664 | 3,044 |
| S&P Core Earnings | 3,338 | 2,721 | 2,418 | 4,210 | 5,761 | 5,751 | 4,843 | 4,067 | 3,414 | 2,780 |

| Balance Sheet & Other Financial Data (Million $) | | | | | | | | | | |
|---|---|---|---|---|---|---|---|---|---|---|
| Cash | 545 | 1,427 | 525 | 457 | 614 | 793 | 506 | 2,826 | 2,188 | 2,477 |
| Current Assets | 13,479 | 13,900 | 13,362 | 14,674 | 18,000 | 15,346 | 14,190 | 13,328 | 11,917 | 10,361 |
| Total Assets | 40,125 | 40,877 | 41,164 | 44,324 | 52,263 | 44,482 | 38,907 | 34,437 | 30,011 | 26,394 |
| Current Liabilities | 10,122 | 10,363 | 11,153 | 12,706 | 12,931 | 12,901 | 10,529 | 9,554 | 8,035 | 6,501 |
| Long Term Debt | 8,707 | 8,662 | 9,667 | 10,983 | 11,237 | 2,302 | 1,807 | 545 | 1,049 | 1,022 |
| Common Equity | 18,889 | 19,393 | 17,777 | 17,714 | 25,030 | 26,909 | 24,158 | 22,407 | 19,802 | 18,082 |
| Total Capital | 28,638 | 29,075 | 28,794 | 28,982 | 36,272 | 29,713 | 25,976 | 23,461 | 20,853 | 19,105 |
| Capital Expenditures | 1,096 | 966 | 1,847 | 3,558 | 3,542 | 3,881 | 3,948 | 3,508 | 2,749 | 3,393 |
| Cash Flow | 5,056 | 4,426 | 4,095 | 5,912 | 7,523 | 7,417 | 6,320 | 5,380 | 4,567 | 3,808 |
| Current Ratio | 1.3 | 1.3 | 1.2 | 1.2 | 1.4 | 1.2 | 1.3 | 1.4 | 1.5 | 1.6 |
| % Long Term Debt of Capitalization | 30.4 | 29.8 | 33.1 | 38.2 | 31.8 | 8.7 | 7.8 | 3.5 | 6.1 | 6.4 |
| % Net Income of Revenue | 4.9 | 4.0 | 3.2 | 5.4 | 6.3 | 7.2 | 6.8 | 6.6 | 6.3 | 5.7 |
| % Return on Assets | 8.2 | 6.4 | 5.4 | 8.7 | 11.9 | 14.0 | 13.6 | 13.4 | 13.0 | 12.7 |
| % Return on Equity | 17.4 | 14.1 | 13.0 | 19.7 | 22.2 | 22.9 | 21.5 | 20.4 | 19.3 | 18.4 |

Data as orig reptd.; bef. results of disc opers/spec. items. Per share data adj. for stk. divs.; EPS diluted. E-Estimated. NA-Not Available. NM-Not Meaningful. NR-Not Ranked. UR-Under Review.

**Office:** 2455 Paces Ferry Road NW, Atlanta, GA 30339.
**Telephone:** 770-433-8211.
**Website:** http://www.homedepot.com
**Chrmn & CEO:** F.S. Blake

**COO:** M.D. Powers
**EVP, Secy & General Counsel:** T.W. Roseborough
**EVP & CIO:** M.A. Carey
**CFO & Chief Acctg Officer:** C.B. Tome

**Investor Contact:** D. Dayhoff (770-384-2666)
**Board Members:** F. D. Ackerman, F. S. Blake, A. Bousbib, G. D. Brenneman, J. F. Brown, A. P. Carey, A. M. Codina, B. Hill, K. L. Katen, R. L. Sargent

**Founded:** 1978
**Domicile:** Delaware
**Employees:** 321,000

**The McGraw-Hill Companies**

# Honeywell International Inc.

**STANDARD &POOR'S**

| S&P Recommendation **BUY** ★★★★☆ | Price $49.14 (as of Nov 25, 2011) | 12-Mo. Target Price $65.00 | Investment Style Large-Cap Value |
|---|---|---|---|

**GICS Sector** Industrials
**Sub-Industry** Aerospace & Defense

**Summary** Honeywell is the world's largest maker of avionics, small jet engines, and climate and process control equipment, and also makes industrial materials and automotive products.

## Key Stock Statistics (Source S&P, Vickers, company reports)

| | | | | | | |
|---|---|---|---|---|---|---|
| 52-Wk Range | $62.28– 41.22 | S&P Oper. EPS 2011**E** | 3.83 | Market Capitalization(B) | $38.010 | Beta | 1.39 |
| Trailing 12-Month EPS | $3.46 | S&P Oper. EPS 2012**E** | 4.20 | Yield (%) | 3.03 | S&P 3-Yr. Proj. EPS CAGR(%) | 10 |
| Trailing 12-Month P/E | 14.2 | P/E on S&P Oper. EPS 2011**E** | 12.8 | Dividend Rate/Share | $1.49 | S&P Credit Rating | A |
| $10K Invested 5 Yrs Ago | $13,117 | Common Shares Outstg. (M) | 773.5 | Institutional Ownership (%) | 82 | | |

## Price Performance

30-Week Mov. Avg.  ···· 10-Week Mov. Avg. -- **GAAP Earnings vs. Previous Year**   **Volume** Above Avg. ▮▮▮ STARS
12-Mo. Target Price — Relative Strength — ▲ Up ▼ Down ► No Change   Below Avg. ▮▮▮ ★

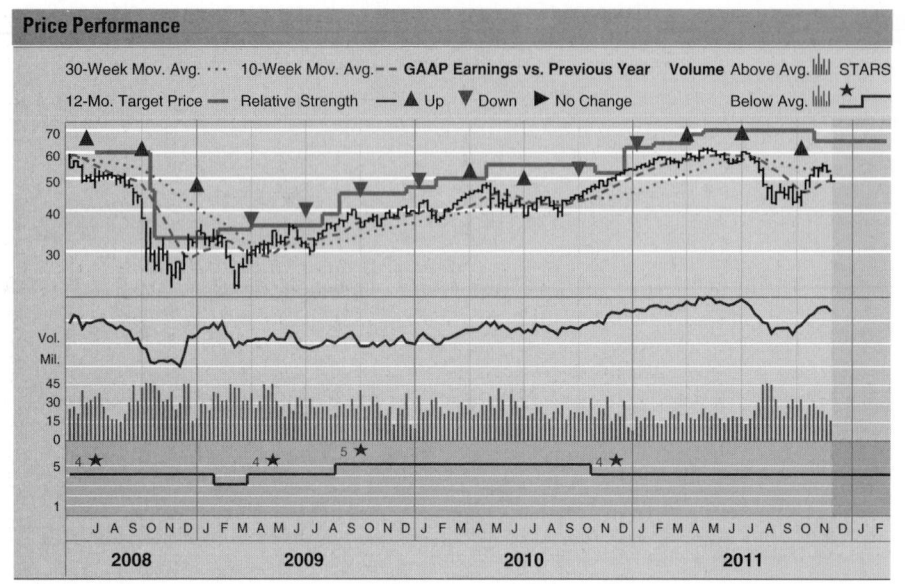

Options: ASE, CBOE, P, Ph

Analysis prepared by Equity Analyst **R. Tortoriello** on Oct 31, 2011, when the stock traded at **$52.40**.

### Highlights

➤ HON sold its car-care products business (CPG) to a private equity group for $950 million in the third quarter, and used the resulting gain ($0.23 per share) to fund restructuring activities. We estimate sales growth of 12% in 2011. For 2012, we project a sharp slowing in growth, to 3.5%, on our view that moderate growth in Aerospace (6%), Automation & Control Systems (4%), and Specialty Materials (5%), will be offset by a decline in the Transportation segment, as a result of the CPG divestiture.

➤ We estimate operating margins of 14.6% in 2011, up from 13.9% in 2010, on improvement in every segment, due to increased volume and efficiency programs. For 2012, we see flat operating margins, due to our view of increased pension expense.

➤ We expect EPS of $3.83 for 2011, and project growth to $4.20 for 2012. We estimate free cash flow (cash from operations minus capital expenditures) per share of about $1.90 in 2011, below EPS due to significant cash pension contributions.

### Investment Rationale/Risk

➤ We view HON's emphasis on building environmental and combustion controls and its turbocharger products as benefiting from a strong global trend toward energy efficiency. We see Aerospace benefiting from rising global fleet sizes, demand for better fuel economy, and aftermarket demand. We also expect specialty chemical volume to reflect global demand for petroleum products and overall global economic growth. At the same time, we view HON's valuation as near historical averages on a variety of measures.

➤ Risks to our recommendation and target price include a weakening of the global economy, operational difficulties, and less-than-expected restructuring benefits.

➤ Our 12-month target price of $65 is based on an enterprise value-to-EBITDA multiple of 9.5X, using our 2012 EBITDA estimate of $6.3 billion. This multiple is slightly above the 20-year average EV-to-EBITDA multiple for HON (9X), reflecting our view of the company's prospects for good earnings growth.

## Qualitative Risk Assessment

| LOW | MEDIUM | HIGH |
|---|---|---|

Our risk assessment reflects what we believe is HON's above-average exposure to market movements, economic cycles, currency fluctuations and raw material costs, offset by our view of its strong balance sheet and its ability to generate significant amounts of cash.

## Quantitative Evaluations

**S&P Quality Ranking**  **A-**

| D | C | B- | B | B+ | A- | A | A+ |
|---|---|---|---|---|---|---|---|

**Relative Strength Rank**  **MODERATE**

66

LOWEST = 1   HIGHEST = 99

## Revenue/Earnings Data

**Revenue (Million $)**

| | 1Q | 2Q | 3Q | 4Q | Year |
|---|---|---|---|---|---|
| 2011 | 8,909 | 9,086 | 9,298 | -- | -- |
| 2010 | 7,776 | 8,161 | 8,392 | 9,041 | 33,370 |
| 2009 | 7,570 | 7,566 | 7,700 | 8,072 | 30,908 |
| 2008 | 8,895 | 9,674 | 9,275 | 8,712 | 36,556 |
| 2007 | 8,041 | 8,538 | 8,735 | 9,275 | 34,589 |
| 2006 | 7,241 | 7,898 | 7,952 | 8,276 | 31,367 |

**Earnings Per Share ($)**

| | 1Q | 2Q | 3Q | 4Q | Year |
|---|---|---|---|---|---|
| 2011 | 0.88 | 1.00 | 0.87 | E1.07 | E3.83 |
| 2010 | 0.63 | 0.73 | 0.76 | 0.47 | 2.59 |
| 2009 | 0.54 | 0.60 | 0.80 | 0.91 | 2.85 |
| 2008 | 0.85 | 0.96 | 0.97 | 0.97 | 3.76 |
| 2007 | 0.66 | 0.78 | 0.81 | 0.91 | 3.16 |
| 2006 | 0.51 | 0.63 | 0.66 | 0.72 | 2.51 |

Fiscal year ended Dec. 31. Next earnings report expected: Late January. EPS Estimates based on S&P Operating Earnings; historical GAAP earnings are as reported.

## Dividend Data (Dates: mm/dd Payment Date: mm/dd/yy)

| Amount ($) | Date Decl. | Ex-Div. Date | Stk. of Record | Payment Date |
|---|---|---|---|---|
| 0.333 | 02/10 | 02/16 | 02/18 | 03/10/11 |
| 0.333 | 04/25 | 05/18 | 05/20 | 06/10/11 |
| 0.333 | 07/29 | 08/17 | 08/19 | 09/09/11 |
| 0.373 | 10/28 | 11/16 | 11/18 | 12/09/11 |

Dividends have been paid since 1887. Source: Company reports.

**The McGraw-Hill Companies**

# Honeywell International Inc.

STANDARD
&POOR'S

## Business Summary October 31, 2011

CORPORATE OVERVIEW. Honeywell International Inc., an aerospace and industrial conglomerate with $37 billion in estimated 2011 revenues, conducts business through four operating segments. HON generated about 52% of sales from products sold outside of the U.S. in 2010, primarily in Europe, Canada, Asia, and Latin America. Sales to the U.S. government accounted for 13% of the total in 2010, while sales to the U.S. Defense Department were 10% of the total.

The Aerospace segment (32% of 2010 revenues and 38% of operating profits) makes a variety of products for commercial and military aircraft, including cockpit controls and other avionics, flight safety systems, auxiliary power units, environmental controls, electric power systems, inertial sensors, aircraft lighting, and wheels and brakes. It is also a leading maker of jet engines for regional and business jet manufacturers, and makes space and military products and subsystems. The Aerospace segment is also a major player in the estimated $103 billion global aircraft maintenance, repair, and overhaul (MRO) industry, and distributes aircraft hardware. It also produces space products and substems, including guidance and control systems and gyroscopes.

HON's Automation and Control Solutions segment (41% of revenues and 37% of operating profits) is a leading global producer of environmental and combustion controls, sensing controls, security and life safety products and services, scanning and mobility products (e.g., bar code scanners), process automation products and solutions, and building solutions and services for homes, buildings, and industrial facilities. Building solutions and services include energy management, security and asset management, building information services, and HVAC and building control. In September 2010, HON purchased Sperian Protection for about $1.4 billion, including assumed net debt. Sperian makes personal protection gear, including respiratory equipment, fall protection equipment, gloves, clothing, and hearing, eye & face protection.

The Specialty Materials segment (14% and 15%) makes specialty chemicals and fibers. Products include resins and chemicals, hydrofluoric acid, fluorocarbons and fluorine products, specialty films and additives, advanced fibers and composites, intermediates, specialty chemicals, electronic materials and chemicals, and catalysts, absorbents, and equipment and technologies for the petrochemical and oil refining industries. HON sells its industrial materials primarily to the petrochemical, food, pharmaceutical, and electronic packaging industries.

## Company Financials Fiscal Year Ended Dec. 31

| Per Share Data ($) | 2010 | 2009 | 2008 | 2007 | 2006 | 2005 | 2004 | 2003 | 2002 | 2001 |
|---|---|---|---|---|---|---|---|---|---|---|
| Tangible Book Value | NM | NM | NM | NM | 0.09 | 1.95 | 4.70 | 4.46 | 2.52 | 3.45 |
| Cash Flow | 3.85 | 4.12 | 4.97 | 4.24 | 3.59 | 2.74 | 2.24 | 2.25 | 0.53 | 1.02 |
| Earnings | 2.59 | 2.85 | 3.76 | 3.16 | 2.51 | 1.86 | 1.49 | 1.56 | -0.27 | -0.12 |
| S&P Core Earnings | 2.96 | 2.68 | 2.14 | 3.15 | 2.62 | 1.83 | 1.42 | 1.57 | 0.15 | -0.26 |
| Dividends | 1.21 | 1.21 | 1.10 | 1.00 | 0.91 | 1.03 | 0.75 | 0.75 | 0.75 | 0.75 |
| Payout Ratio | 47% | 42% | 29% | 32% | 36% | 55% | 50% | 48% | NM | NM |
| Prices:High | 53.74 | 41.55 | 62.99 | 62.29 | 45.77 | 39.50 | 38.46 | 33.50 | 40.95 | 53.90 |
| Prices:Low | 36.68 | 23.06 | 23.24 | 43.14 | 35.24 | 32.68 | 31.23 | 20.20 | 18.77 | 22.15 |
| P/E Ratio:High | 21 | 15 | 17 | 20 | 18 | 21 | 26 | 21 | NM | NM |
| P/E Ratio:Low | 14 | 8 | 6 | 14 | 14 | 18 | 21 | 13 | NM | NM |

| Income Statement Analysis (Million $) | 2010 | 2009 | 2008 | 2007 | 2006 | 2005 | 2004 | 2003 | 2002 | 2001 |
|---|---|---|---|---|---|---|---|---|---|---|
| Revenue | 33,370 | 30,908 | 36,556 | 34,589 | 31,367 | 27,653 | 25,601 | 23,103 | 22,274 | 23,652 |
| Operating Income | 4,121 | 4,339 | 5,444 | 4,561 | 3,855 | 3,178 | 2,350 | 2,513 | 2,573 | 1,085 |
| Depreciation | 987 | 957 | 903 | 837 | 794 | 697 | 650 | 595 | 671 | 926 |
| Interest Expense | 386 | 459 | 482 | 456 | 374 | 356 | 331 | 335 | 344 | 405 |
| Pretax Income | 2,843 | 2,978 | 3,801 | 3,321 | 2,798 | 2,323 | 1,680 | 1,647 | -945 | -422 |
| Effective Tax Rate | NA | 26.5% | 26.6% | 26.4% | 25.7% | 31.9% | 23.8% | 18.0% | NM | NM |
| Net Income | 2,022 | 2,153 | 2,792 | 2,444 | 2,078 | 1,581 | 1,281 | 1,344 | -220 | NA |
| S&P Core Earnings | 2,309 | 2,027 | 1,590 | 2,445 | 2,168 | 1,554 | 1,225 | 1,363 | 119 | -207 |

| Balance Sheet & Other Financial Data (Million $) | 2010 | 2009 | 2008 | 2007 | 2006 | 2005 | 2004 | 2003 | 2002 | 2001 |
|---|---|---|---|---|---|---|---|---|---|---|
| Cash | 3,108 | 2,801 | 2,065 | 1,829 | 1,224 | 1,234 | 3,586 | 2,950 | 2,021 | 1,393 |
| Current Assets | 15,011 | 13,936 | 13,263 | 13,685 | 12,304 | 11,962 | 12,820 | 11,523 | 10,195 | 9,894 |
| Total Assets | 37,962 | 36,004 | 35,490 | 33,805 | 30,941 | 32,294 | 31,062 | 29,344 | 27,559 | 24,226 |
| Current Liabilities | 11,717 | 11,147 | 12,289 | 11,941 | 10,135 | 10,430 | 8,739 | 6,783 | 6,574 | 6,220 |
| Long Term Debt | 5,755 | 6,246 | 5,865 | 5,419 | 3,909 | 3,082 | 4,069 | 4,961 | 4,719 | 4,731 |
| Common Equity | 10,915 | 8,954 | 7,187 | 9,222 | 9,720 | 11,254 | 11,252 | 7,243 | 8,925 | 9,170 |
| Total Capital | 17,193 | 16,218 | 13,750 | 15,375 | 13,981 | 14,839 | 15,718 | 12,520 | 14,063 | 14,776 |
| Capital Expenditures | 651 | 609 | 884 | 767 | 733 | 684 | 629 | 655 | 671 | 876 |
| Cash Flow | 3,009 | 3,110 | 3,695 | 3,281 | 2,872 | 2,278 | 1,931 | 1,939 | 451 | 827 |
| Current Ratio | 1.3 | 1.3 | 1.1 | 1.2 | 1.2 | 1.1 | 1.5 | 1.7 | 1.6 | 1.6 |
| % Long Term Debt of Capitalization | 33.5 | 38.5 | 42.7 | 35.2 | 28.0 | 20.8 | 25.9 | 39.6 | 33.6 | 32.0 |
| % Net Income of Revenue | 6.1 | 7.0 | 7.6 | 7.0 | 6.6 | 5.7 | 5.0 | 5.8 | NM | NM |
| % Return on Assets | 5.5 | 6.0 | 8.1 | 7.5 | 6.5 | 5.0 | 4.2 | 4.7 | NM | NM |
| % Return on Equity | 20.5 | 26.7 | 34.0 | 25.8 | 20.3 | 14.0 | 11.7 | 21.1 | NM | NM |

Data as orig reptd.; bef. results of disc opers/spec. items. Per share data adj. for stk. divs.; EPS diluted. E-Estimated. NA-Not Available. NM-Not Meaningful. NR-Not Ranked. UR-Under Review.

**Office:** 101 Columbia Rd, Morristown, NJ 07960-4640.
**Telephone:** 973-455-2000.
**Website:** http://www.honeywell.com
**Chrmn & CEO:** D.M. Cote

**COO:** K. Mikkilineni
**SVP & CFO:** D.J. Anderson
**SVP & General Counsel:** K. Adams
**Chief Acctg Officer & Cntlr:** K.A. Winters

**Investor Contact:** M. Grainger (973-455-2222)
**Board Members:** G. M. Bethune, K. Burke, J. Chico
Pardo, D. M. Cote, D. S. Davis, L. F. Deily, J. A. Gregg, C.
R. Hollick, G. Paz, B. T. Sheares

**Auditor:** PRICEWATERHOUSECOOPERS
**Founded:** 1920
**Domicile:** Delaware
**Employees:** 130,000

The McGraw-Hill Companies

# Hormel Foods Corp

STANDARD &POOR'S

| S&P Recommendation | SELL ★ ★ ★ ★ ★ | Price $28.69 (as of Nov 25, 2011) | 12-Mo. Target Price $27.00 | Investment Style Large-Cap Blend |
|---|---|---|---|---|

**GICS Sector** Consumer Staples
**Sub-Industry** Packaged Foods & Meats

**Summary** This company is a leading processor of branded, convenience meat products (primarily pork) for the consumer market.

## Key Stock Statistics (Source S&P, Vickers, company reports)

| | | | | | | | |
|---|---|---|---|---|---|---|---|
| 52-Wk Range | $30.50– 24.20 | S&P Oper. EPS 2011E | 1.73 | Market Capitalization(B) | $7.609 | Beta | 0.48 |
| Trailing 12-Month EPS | $1.76 | S&P Oper. EPS 2012E | 1.83 | Yield (%) | 2.09 | S&P 3-Yr. Proj. EPS CAGR(%) | 9 |
| Trailing 12-Month P/E | 16.3 | P/E on S&P Oper. EPS 2011E | 16.6 | Dividend Rate/Share | $0.60 | S&P Credit Rating | A |
| $10K Invested 5 Yrs Ago | $16,652 | Common Shares Outstg. (M) | 265.2 | Institutional Ownership (%) | 33 | | |

## Price Performance

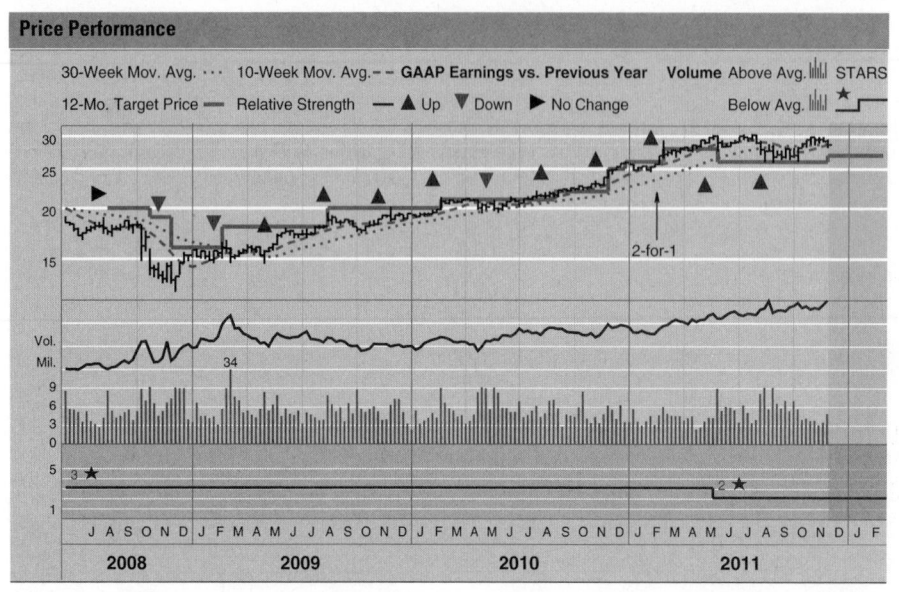

30-Week Mov. Avg. ···  10-Week Mov. Avg.--  **GAAP Earnings vs. Previous Year**  Volume Above Avg. STARS
12-Mo. Target Price —  Relative Strength —  ▲ Up  ▼ Down  ▶ No Change  Below Avg.  ★

2-for-1

Options: Ph

## Qualitative Risk Assessment

| LOW | **MEDIUM** | HIGH |
|---|---|---|

Our risk assessment reflects our view of HRL's relatively strong balance sheet, offset by the company's sensitivity to changes in commodity costs.

## Quantitative Evaluations

**S&P Quality Ranking**  A+

| D | C | B- | B | B+ | A- | A | **A+** |
|---|---|---|---|---|---|---|---|

**Relative Strength Rank**  STRONG

77

LOWEST = 1      HIGHEST = 99

## Revenue/Earnings Data

**Revenue (Million $)**

| | 1Q | 2Q | 3Q | 4Q | Year |
|---|---|---|---|---|---|
| 2011 | 1,922 | 1,959 | 1,911 | -- | -- |
| 2010 | 1,727 | 1,700 | 1,730 | 2,063 | 7,221 |
| 2009 | 1,689 | 1,595 | 1,574 | 1,675 | 6,534 |
| 2008 | 1,621 | 1,594 | 1,678 | 1,862 | 6,755 |
| 2007 | 1,504 | 1,505 | 1,520 | 1,664 | 6,193 |
| 2006 | 1,416 | 1,365 | 1,407 | 1,557 | 5,745 |

**Earnings Per Share ($)**

| | | | | | |
|---|---|---|---|---|---|
| 2011 | 0.55 | 0.40 | 0.36 | E0.42 | E1.73 |
| 2010 | 0.41 | 0.29 | 0.32 | 0.45 | 1.46 |
| 2009 | 0.30 | 0.29 | 0.29 | 0.39 | 1.27 |
| 2008 | 0.32 | 0.28 | 0.19 | 0.25 | 1.04 |
| 2007 | 0.27 | 0.25 | 0.19 | 0.37 | 1.09 |
| 2006 | 0.25 | 0.24 | -- | 0.32 | 1.03 |

Fiscal year ended Oct. 31. Next earnings report expected: NA. EPS Estimates based on S&P Operating Earnings; historical GAAP earnings are as reported.

## Highlights

➤ The 12-month target price for HRL has recently been changed to $27.00 from $26.00. The Highlights section of this Stock Report will be updated accordingly.

## Investment Rationale/Risk

➤ The Investment Rationale/Risk section of this Stock Report will be updated shortly. For the latest News story on HRL from MarketScope, see below.

➤ 11/22/11 01:20 pm ET ... S&P REITERATES SELL OPINION ON SHARES OF HORMEL FOODS (HRL 29.12**): Oct-Q EPS of $0.43, vs. $0.45, is $0.01 above our estimate and the Capital IQ consensus forecast. Year earlier quarter had an additional week. In FY 12 (Oct), we look for EPS growth to resume in the Apr-Q, and we keep our full-year FY 12 EPS estimate at $1.83. We think the company is well positioned for long-term growth, including an expected benefit from higher-margin products becoming a larger part of its business. We are raising our 12-month target price to $27 from $26, which brings our target P/E closer to a recent average P/E for a group of packaged foods & meats stocks. /Tom Graves, CFA

## Dividend Data (Dates: mm/dd Payment Date: mm/dd/yy)

| Amount ($) | Date Decl. | Ex-Div. Date | Stk. of Record | Payment Date |
|---|---|---|---|---|
| 0.128 | 03/28 | 04/19 | 04/23 | 05/15/11 |
| 0.128 | 05/23 | 07/20 | 07/23 | 08/15/11 |
| 0.128 | 09/26 | 10/19 | 10/22 | 11/15/11 |
| 0.150 | 11/21 | 01/20 | 01/23 | 02/15/12 |

Dividends have been paid since 1928. Source: Company reports.

# Hormel Foods Corp

STANDARD
&POOR'S

## Business Summary September 19, 2011

Hormel Foods Corporation engages in the production of various meat and food products and the marketing of those products throughout the United States and Internationally.

The company operates under the grocery products, refrigerated foods, Jennie-O Turkey Store, specialty foods, and other business segments. The grocery product segment (14% of FY 10 (Oct.) revenues and 23% of segment operating income) primarily processes, markets and sells shelf-stable food products predominately in the retail market. The refrigerated foods segment (53%; 40%) primarily processes, markets and sells branded and unbranded pork and beef products for the retail, food service, and fresh product customer markets. Jennie-O Turkey Store (18%; 21%) primarily processes, markets and sells branded and unbranded turkey products for the retail, food service and fresh product customer markets. The specialty foods segment (11%; 12%) packages and sells various sugar and sugar substitute products, salt and pepper products, liquid portion products, and other products. The "other" segment (4%; 4%) manufactures, markets and sells company products internationally.

The company's meat products are sold fresh, frozen, cured, smoked, cooked, and canned. Its products include perishable meat, poultry, shelf-stable, and other. Excluding poultry, the perishable meat category (54% of FY 10 sales) includes fresh meats, sausages, hams, wieners, and bacon. Poultry (19% of

sales) is composed primarily of Jennie-O Turkey Store products, while the shelf-stable category (about 18% of sales) includes canned luncheon meats, shelf-stable microwaveable entrees, stews, chilies, hash, meat spreads, flour and corn tortillas, salsas, and tortilla chips. The other category (about 10%) primarily consists of nutritional food products and supplements, sugar and sugar substitutes, creamers, salt and pepper products, sauces and salad dressings, dessert and drink mixes, and industrial gelatin products.

Internationally, the company markets its products through Hormel Foods International Corporation (HFIC), a wholly owned subsidiary. Markets for HFIC include Australia, Canada, China, England, Japan, Mexico, Micronesia, the Philippines, and South Korea. Through HFIC, Hormel has licensed companies to manufacture various company products internationally on a royalty basis, with the primary licensees being Tulip International of Denmark and CJ Cheil-Jedang Corporation of South Korea. The HFIC business includes joint ventures, placement of personnel in strategic foreign locations, and minority positions in some food-related companies.

## Company Financials Fiscal Year Ended Oct. 31

| Per Share Data ($) | 2010 | 2009 | 2008 | 2007 | 2006 | 2005 | 2004 | 2003 | 2002 | 2001 |
|---|---|---|---|---|---|---|---|---|---|---|
| Tangible Book Value | 6.13 | 5.10 | 4.60 | 4.16 | 4.02 | 3.39 | 3.22 | 2.68 | 2.71 | 2.22 |
| Cash Flow | 1.93 | 1.74 | 1.46 | 1.54 | 1.46 | 1.32 | 1.16 | 0.98 | 0.97 | 0.97 |
| Earnings | 1.46 | 1.27 | 1.04 | 1.09 | 1.03 | 0.91 | 0.83 | 0.67 | 0.68 | 0.65 |
| S&P Core Earnings | 1.49 | 1.13 | 0.94 | 1.08 | 1.05 | 0.94 | 0.81 | 0.61 | 0.55 | 0.62 |
| Dividends | 0.42 | 0.38 | 0.37 | 0.30 | 0.28 | 0.26 | 0.23 | 0.21 | 0.20 | 0.19 |
| Payout Ratio | 29% | 30% | 36% | 28% | 27% | 29% | 27% | 32% | 29% | 28% |
| Prices:High | 26.14 | 20.23 | 21.39 | 20.91 | 19.55 | 17.72 | 16.06 | 13.75 | 14.10 | 13.68 |
| Prices:Low | 18.89 | 14.58 | 12.41 | 15.02 | 15.94 | 14.58 | 12.45 | 9.97 | 10.01 | 8.50 |
| P/E Ratio:High | 18 | 16 | 21 | 19 | 19 | 19 | 19 | 21 | 21 | 21 |
| P/E Ratio:Low | 13 | 12 | 12 | 14 | 16 | 16 | 15 | 15 | 15 | 13 |

| Income Statement Analysis (Million $) | | | | | | | | | | |
|---|---|---|---|---|---|---|---|---|---|---|
| Revenue | 7,221 | 6,534 | 6,755 | 6,193 | 5,745 | 5,414 | 4,780 | 4,200 | 3,910 | 4,124 |
| Operating Income | 759 | 659 | 624 | 611 | 567 | 534 | 448 | 393 | 394 | 390 |
| Depreciation | 126 | 127 | 115 | 127 | 121 | 115 | 94.8 | 88.0 | 83.2 | 90.2 |
| Interest Expense | 26.6 | 28.0 | 28.0 | 27.7 | 25.6 | 27.7 | 27.1 | 31.9 | 31.4 | 28.0 |
| Pretax Income | 625 | 525 | 458 | 470 | 431 | 405 | 365 | 289 | 294 | 285 |
| Effective Tax Rate | NA | 34.7% | 37.6% | 35.7% | 33.5% | 37.4% | 36.5% | 35.8% | 35.6% | 36.0% |
| Net Income | 396 | 343 | 286 | 302 | 286 | 253 | 232 | 186 | 189 | 182 |
| S&P Core Earnings | 403 | 307 | 258 | 300 | 294 | 263 | 225 | 171 | 155 | 173 |

| Balance Sheet & Other Financial Data (Million $) | | | | | | | | | | |
|---|---|---|---|---|---|---|---|---|---|---|
| Cash | 518 | 385 | 155 | 150 | 172 | 170 | 289 | 98.0 | 310 | 186 |
| Current Assets | 1,858 | 1,575 | 1,438 | 1,232 | 1,142 | 1,041 | 1,029 | 824 | 962 | 883 |
| Total Assets | 4,054 | 3,692 | 3,616 | 3,394 | 3,060 | 2,822 | 2,534 | 2,393 | 2,220 | 2,163 |
| Current Liabilities | 1,101 | 685 | 781 | 665 | 585 | 583 | 464 | 442 | 410 | 420 |
| Long Term Debt | NA | 350 | 350 | 350 | 350 | 350 | 362 | 395 | 410 | 462 |
| Common Equity | 2,407 | 2,123 | 2,008 | 1,885 | 1,803 | 1,575 | 1,399 | 1,253 | 1,115 | 993 |
| Total Capital | 2,407 | 2,473 | 2,358 | 2,235 | 2,153 | 1,925 | 1,765 | 1,659 | 1,525 | 1,455 |
| Capital Expenditures | 84.9 | 92.0 | 126 | 126 | 142 | 107 | 80.4 | 67.1 | 64.5 | 77.1 |
| Cash Flow | 521 | 470 | 400 | 429 | 407 | 369 | 326 | 274 | 273 | 273 |
| Current Ratio | 1.7 | 2.3 | 1.8 | 1.9 | 2.0 | 1.8 | 2.2 | 1.9 | 2.3 | 2.1 |
| % Long Term Debt of Capitalization | Nil | 14.2 | 14.9 | 15.6 | 16.3 | 18.2 | 20.5 | 23.8 | 26.9 | 31.8 |
| % Net Income of Revenue | 5.5 | 5.3 | 4.2 | 4.8 | 5.0 | 4.7 | 4.8 | 4.4 | 4.8 | 4.4 |
| % Return on Assets | 10.2 | 9.4 | 8.2 | 9.3 | 9.7 | 9.5 | 9.4 | 8.1 | 8.6 | 9.6 |
| % Return on Equity | 17.5 | 16.6 | 14.7 | 16.3 | 16.8 | 17.0 | 17.5 | 15.7 | 18.0 | 19.5 |

Data as orig reptd.; bef. results of disc opers/spec. items. Per share data adj. for stk. divs.; EPS diluted. E-Estimated. NA-Not Available. NM-Not Meaningful. NR-Not Ranked. UR-Under Review.

**Office:** 1 Hormel Place, Austin, MN 55912-3680.
**Telephone:** 507-437-5611.
**Website:** http://www.hormel.com
**Chrmn, Pres & CEO:** J.M. Ettinger

**EVP & CFO:** J.H. Feragen
**Chief Acctg Officer & Cntlr:** J.N. Sheehan
**Treas:** R.G. Gentzler
**Secy:** B.D. Johnson

**Investor Contact:** K.C. Jones (507-437-5248)
**Board Members:** T. K. Crews, J. M. Ettinger, J. H. Feragen, G. S. Forbes, S. M. Lacy, S. I. Marvin, M. J. Mendes, J. L. Morrison, E. A. Murano, R. C. Nakasone, S. K. Nestegard, D. A. Pippins

**Founded:** 1891
**Domicile:** Delaware
**Employees:** 19,300

The McGraw-Hill Companies

# Hospira Inc

## STANDARD &POOR'S

| S&P Recommendation **BUY** ★★★★☆ | Price $30.07 (as of Nov 25, 2011) | 12-Mo. Target Price $39.00 | Investment Style Large-Cap Growth |
|---|---|---|---|

**GICS Sector** Health Care
**Sub-Industry** Pharmaceuticals

**Summary** Hospira, spun off from Abbott Laboratories in May 2004, provides a variety of hospital products, including injectable generic drugs, pumps, and syringes.

### Key Stock Statistics (Source S&P, Vickers, company reports)

| | | | | | | |
|---|---|---|---|---|---|---|
| 52-Wk Range | $59.20–28.04 | S&P Oper. EPS 2011**E** | 3.00 | Market Capitalization(B) | $4.953 | Beta | 0.82 |
| Trailing 12-Month EPS | $1.57 | S&P Oper. EPS 2012**E** | 3.10 | Yield (%) | Nil | S&P 3-Yr. Proj. EPS CAGR(%) | 11 |
| Trailing 12-Month P/E | 19.2 | P/E on S&P Oper. EPS 2011**E** | 10.0 | Dividend Rate/Share | Nil | S&P Credit Rating | BBB+ |
| $10K Invested 5 Yrs Ago | $9,267 | Common Shares Outstg. (M) | 164.7 | Institutional Ownership (%) | 85 | | |

### Price Performance

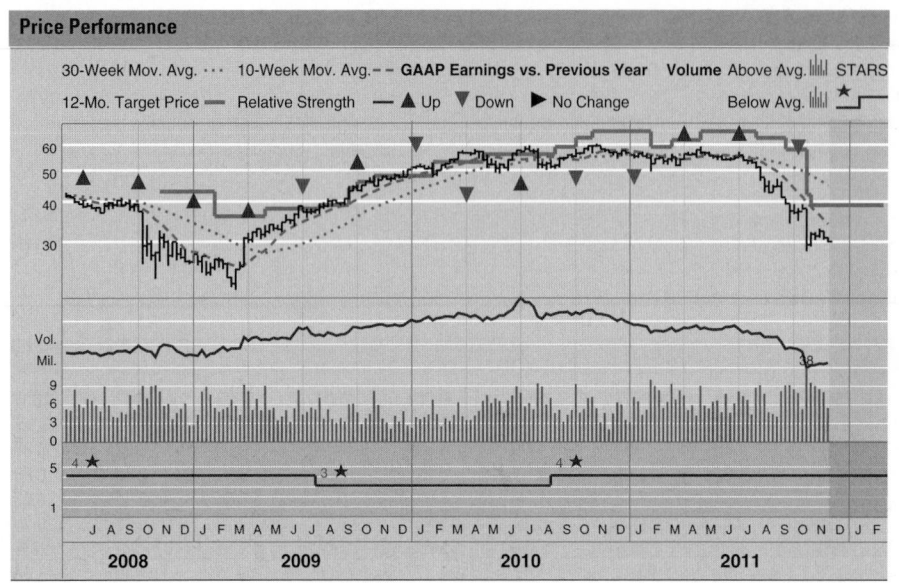

30-Week Mov. Avg. · · · 10-Week Mov. Avg. - - GAAP Earnings vs. Previous Year   Volume Above Avg. STARS
12-Mo. Target Price — Relative Strength ▲ Up ▼ Down ► No Change   Below Avg.

Options: ASE, CBOE, P, Ph

Analysis prepared by Equity Analyst **Steven Silver** on Oct 27, 2011, when the stock traded at **$29.97**.

### Highlights

▸ We expect revenues to increase 2% in 2011, to $4.0 billion, with drug supply constraints due to facility quality initiatives and a hold on Symbiq pump device shipments due to alarm issues mitigating the positive impact of the March 2011 approval of generic cancer drug taxotere and favorable foreign exchange. We look for sales to rise 5%, to $4.2 billion, in 2012, on new product growth and more normalized sales from the medical management unit and production at key plants.

▸ We project gross margins around 38% and 37% in 2011 and 2012, respectively, compared with 43% in 2010, as HSP invests in long-term global expansion initiatives and incurs costs to remediate issues at several key production facilities following FDA warning letters. Over the long-term, we expect margins to benefit from higher-margin products, particularly in HSP's medication management business, and lower Plum field servicing costs.

▸ We see adjusted EPS of $3.00 in 2011 and $3.10 for 2012, excluding restructuring charges and other non-recurring items. We expect HSP to average low-double digit annual adjusted EPS growth through 2016.

### Investment Rationale/Risk

▸ Our buy recommendation reflects a belief that HSP's long-term results will benefit from its strategy of global expansion of its generic specialty injectable pharmaceutical pipeline and its medication management systems business, despite recent issues that have significantly impacted near-term results and earnings visibility. While we are wary of production declines and lost sales stemming from quality improvement initiatives at HSP's key Rocky Mount facility, we see unappreciated potential in its biosimilars portfolio, where HSP has launched two drugs in Europe and is advancing in the U.S.

▸ Risks to our recommendation and target price include failure to gain regulatory approval for its generic injectable drugs and biosimilars, failure to satisfy regulatory concerns over its production facilities, and a decrease in medication delivery product demand.

▸ Our 12-month target price of $39 applies a 12.5X multiple to our 2012 adjusted EPS estimate of $3.10, a discount to its long-term historical forward multiple, given overhangs from facility remediation efforts, impacting near-term sales and gross margins.

### Qualitative Risk Assessment

| LOW | MEDIUM | HIGH |
|---|---|---|

Our risk assessment reflects HSP's broad product portfolio, which reduces dependence on any one product. While we expect stable demand for hospital products and services, we see cost pressures limiting growth for that industry.

### Quantitative Evaluations

**S&P Quality Ranking** NR

| D | C | B- | B | B+ | A- | A | A+ |
|---|---|---|---|---|---|---|---|

**Relative Strength Rank** WEAK

19

LOWEST = 1    HIGHEST = 99

### Revenue/Earnings Data

**Revenue (Million $)**

| | 1Q | 2Q | 3Q | 4Q | Year |
|---|---|---|---|---|---|
| 2011 | 1,002 | 1,064 | 976.7 | -- | -- |
| 2010 | 1,008 | 968.2 | 949.3 | 992.1 | 3,917 |
| 2009 | 859.7 | 956.9 | 1,008 | 1,055 | 3,879 |
| 2008 | 888.7 | 901.6 | 925.5 | 913.7 | 3,630 |
| 2007 | 782.8 | 869.4 | 838.0 | 946.1 | 3,436 |
| 2006 | 664.3 | 629.9 | 646.6 | 706.5 | 2,689 |

**Earnings Per Share ($)**

| | 1Q | 2Q | 3Q | 4Q | Year |
|---|---|---|---|---|---|
| 2011 | 0.88 | 0.85 | -0.54 | E0.48 | E3.00 |
| 2010 | 0.84 | 0.49 | 0.42 | 0.36 | 2.11 |
| 2009 | 1.03 | 0.16 | 0.71 | 0.58 | 2.48 |
| 2008 | 0.41 | 0.43 | 0.51 | 0.65 | 1.99 |
| 2007 | -0.19 | 0.20 | 0.37 | 0.47 | 0.85 |
| 2006 | 0.49 | 0.34 | 0.35 | 0.30 | 1.48 |

Fiscal year ended Dec. 31. Next earnings report expected: Early February. EPS Estimates based on S&P Operating Earnings; historical GAAP earnings are as reported.

### Dividend Data

No cash dividends have been paid.

# Hospira Inc

STANDARD
&POOR'S

## Business Summary October 27, 2011

CORPORATE OVERVIEW. Hospira (HSP) was created on May 3, 2004, as a spinoff from Abbott Laboratories. HSP provides medication delivery systems and specialty pharmaceuticals to hospitals, clinics, and physicians. The legal separation to become a standalone company was completed in the second quarter of 2006.

Hospira has operations in the Americas (80% of 2010 revenues); Europe, the Middle East, and Africa (12.5%); and Asia-Pacific (7.5%), and operates manufacturing facilities both domestically and internationally.

Operating segments include specialty injectable pharmaceuticals -- including specialty injectables and biogenerics (2010 sales of $2.35 billion, 60% of sales); medication management systems -- principally infusion pumps as well as related software and services ($999 million, 25.5%); and other pharmaceuticals -- encompassing large volume I.V. solutions, nutritionals and contract

manufacturing services ($569 million, 14.5%). Major competitors include Baxter International, Bedford Laboratories (a divisions of Boehringer Ingelheim), Fresenius Medical Care AG, Sandoz, Teva Pharmaceuticals, and CareFusion.

The specialty injectable pharmaceuticals division provides over 200 generic injectable drugs available in a wide array of dosages and formulations. Therapeutic areas of focus include oncology, anti-infectives, cardiovascular, and others. In March 2011, HSP secured FDA approval of a generic, single vial formulation version of cancer drug Taxotere, which generated $1.2 billion in 2010 U.S. sales.

## Company Financials Fiscal Year Ended Dec. 31

| Per Share Data ($) | 2010 | 2009 | 2008 | 2007 | 2006 | 2005 | 2004 | 2003 | 2002 | 2001 |
|---|---|---|---|---|---|---|---|---|---|---|
| Tangible Book Value | 7.52 | 5.96 | 1.28 | NM | 8.03 | 7.57 | 5.74 | NM | NA | NA |
| Cash Flow | 3.56 | 3.77 | 3.55 | 2.32 | 2.45 | 2.42 | 2.84 | NA | NA | NA |
| Earnings | 2.11 | 2.48 | 1.99 | 0.85 | 1.48 | 1.46 | 1.92 | 1.65 | NA | NA |
| S&P Core Earnings | 2.16 | 2.58 | 1.89 | 0.79 | 1.45 | 1.35 | 1.31 | 1.46 | NA | NA |
| Dividends | Nil | Nil | Nil | Nil | Nil | Nil | Nil | NA | NA | NA |
| Payout Ratio | Nil | Nil | Nil | Nil | Nil | Nil | Nil | NA | NA | NA |
| Prices:High | 60.49 | 51.40 | 44.00 | 44.64 | 47.99 | 45.10 | 34.86 | NA | NA | NA |
| Prices:Low | 47.48 | 21.21 | 23.00 | 33.60 | 31.15 | 28.35 | 24.02 | NA | NA | NA |
| P/E Ratio:High | 29 | 21 | 22 | 53 | 32 | 31 | 18 | NA | NA | NA |
| P/E Ratio:Low | 23 | 9 | 12 | 40 | 21 | 19 | 13 | NA | NA | NA |

### Income Statement Analysis (Million $)

| | 2010 | 2009 | 2008 | 2007 | 2006 | 2005 | 2004 | 2003 | 2002 | 2001 |
|---|---|---|---|---|---|---|---|---|---|---|
| Revenue | 3,917 | 3,879 | 3,630 | 3,436 | 2,689 | 2,627 | 2,645 | 2,624 | 2,603 | 2,514 |
| Operating Income | 851 | 878 | 836 | 763 | 506 | 493 | 509 | 506 | 512 | 555 |
| Depreciation | 246 | 230 | 252 | 235 | 157 | 156 | 146 | 146 | 134 | 123 |
| Interest Expense | 101 | 106 | 124 | 145 | 31.0 | 28.3 | 18.8 | Nil | NA | NA |
| Pretax Income | 392 | 385 | 408 | 188 | 324 | 322 | 412 | 359 | 352 | 390 |
| Effective Tax Rate | NA | NM | 21.3% | 27.2% | 26.9% | 26.8% | 26.7% | 27.5% | 30.0% | 30.0% |
| Net Income | 357 | 404 | 321 | 137 | 237 | 236 | 302 | 260 | 247 | 273 |
| S&P Core Earnings | 367 | 422 | 304 | 128 | 233 | 217 | 206 | 231 | 187 | NA |

### Balance Sheet & Other Financial Data (Million $)

| | 2010 | 2009 | 2008 | 2007 | 2006 | 2005 | 2004 | 2003 | 2002 | 2001 |
|---|---|---|---|---|---|---|---|---|---|---|
| Cash | 604 | 946 | 484 | 241 | 322 | 521 | 200 | Nil | NA | NA |
| Current Assets | 2,478 | 2,526 | 2,149 | 1,841 | 1,523 | 1,561 | 1,198 | 1,075 | 982 | 1,029 |
| Total Assets | 6,046 | 5,503 | 5,074 | 5,085 | 2,848 | 2,789 | 2,343 | 2,250 | 2,154 | 2,133 |
| Current Liabilities | 932 | 882 | 1,048 | 794 | 606 | 596 | 536 | 360 | 411 | 373 |
| Long Term Debt | 1,714 | 1,707 | 1,834 | 2,243 | 702 | 695 | 699 | Nil | NA | NA |
| Common Equity | 3,184 | 2,624 | 1,776 | 1,745 | 1,361 | 1,328 | 984 | 1,453 | 1,334 | 1,461 |
| Total Capital | 4,931 | 4,355 | 3,636 | 3,980 | 2,066 | 2,027 | 1,687 | 1,453 | 1,334 | 1,461 |
| Capital Expenditures | 209 | 159 | 164 | 211 | 235 | 256 | 229 | 197 | 191 | 200 |
| Cash Flow | 603 | 615 | 573 | 372 | 393 | 392 | 447 | 406 | 380 | 396 |
| Current Ratio | 2.7 | 2.9 | 2.1 | 2.3 | 2.5 | 2.6 | 2.2 | 3.0 | 2.4 | 2.8 |
| % Long Term Debt of Capitalization | 34.8 | 39.2 | 50.5 | 55.6 | 34.0 | 34.3 | 41.4 | Nil | Nil | Nil |
| % Net Income of Revenue | 9.1 | 10.4 | 8.8 | 4.0 | 8.8 | 9.0 | 11.4 | 9.9 | 9.5 | 10.9 |
| % Return on Assets | 6.2 | 7.6 | 6.3 | 3.5 | 8.4 | 9.2 | 13.1 | 11.8 | 11.5 | NA |
| % Return on Equity | 12.3 | 18.4 | 18.2 | 8.8 | 17.6 | 20.4 | 24.7 | 18.7 | 17.7 | NA |

Data as orig reptd.; bef. results of disc opers/spec. items. Per share data adj. for stk. divs.; EPS diluted. E-Estimated. NA-Not Available. NM-Not Meaningful. NR-Not Ranked. UR-Under Review.

**Office:** 275 North Field Drive, Lake Forest, IL 60045.
**Telephone:** 224-212-2000.
**Website:** http://www.hospira.com
**CEO:** M.M. Ball

**COO:** J.H. Hardy, Jr.
**SVP & CFO:** T.E. Werner
**SVP & CSO:** S. Ramachandra
**SVP, Secy & General Counsel:** B.J. Smith

**Investor Contact:** K. King (224-212-2711)
**Board Members:** I. W. Bailey, II, M. M. Ball, C. B. Begley, B. L. Bowles, C. R. Curran, W. G. Dempsey, R. W. Hale, J. J. Sokolov, J. C. Staley, M. F. Wheeler, H. von Prondzynski

**Founded:** 2003
**Domicile:** Delaware
**Employees:** 14,000

The **McGraw·Hill** Companies

# Host Hotels & Resorts Inc

**STANDARD &POOR'S**

| S&P Recommendation | HOLD ★★★☆☆ | Price $12.81 (as of Nov 25, 2011) | 12-Mo. Target Price $13.00 | Investment Style Large-Cap Value |
|---|---|---|---|---|

**GICS Sector** Financials
**Sub-Industry** Specialized REITS

**Summary** This real estate investment trust owns a portfolio of luxury and upper-upscale full-service hotels.

## Key Stock Statistics (Source S&P, Vickers, company reports)

| | | | | | | | |
|---|---|---|---|---|---|---|---|
| 52-Wk Range | $19.88– 9.78 | S&P FFO/Sh. 2011E | 0.90 | Market Capitalization(B) | $9.047 | Beta | 2.28 |
| Trailing 12-Month FFO/Share | $0.72 | S&P FFO/Sh. 2012E | 1.00 | Yield (%) | 1.25 | S&P 3-Yr. FFO/Sh. Proj. CAGR(%) | 12 |
| Trailing 12-Month P/FFO | NA | P/FFO on S&P FFO/Sh. 2011E | 14.2 | Dividend Rate/Share | $0.16 | S&P Credit Rating | BB- |
| $10K Invested 5 Yrs Ago | $5,763 | Common Shares Outstg. (M) | 706.2 | Institutional Ownership (%) | 100 | | |

## Price Performance

30-Week Mov. Avg. ··· 10-Week Mov. Avg. – – GAAP Earnings vs. Previous Year    Volume Above Avg. STARS
12-Mo. Target Price — Relative Strength — ▲ Up ▼ Down ▶ No Change    Below Avg.

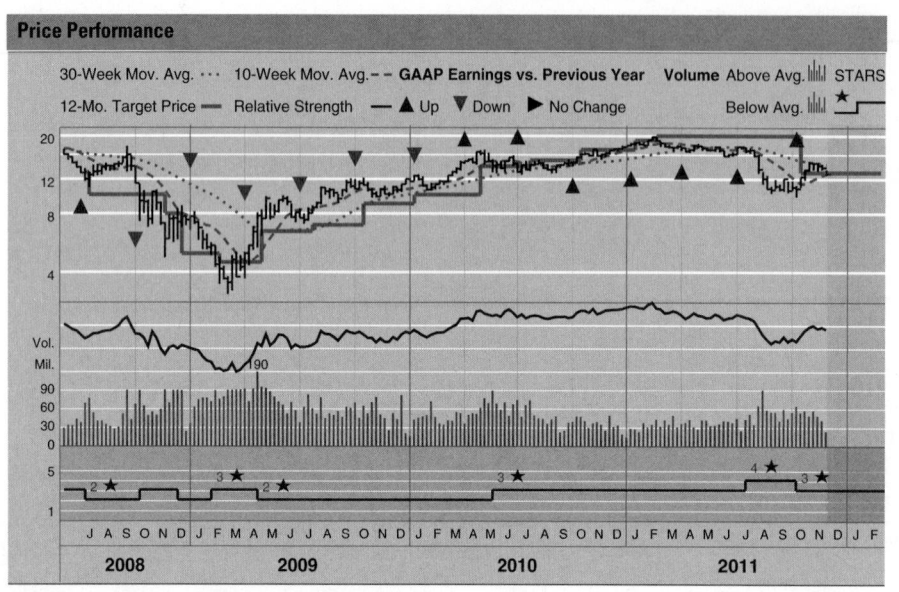

Options: ASE, CBOE, P, Ph

Analysis prepared by Equity Analyst **R. Shepard, CFA** on Oct 17, 2011, when the stock traded at **$11.99**.

## Qualitative Risk Assessment

| LOW | **MEDIUM** | HIGH |
|---|---|---|

Our risk assessment reflects the highly cyclical nature of the lodging industry, offset by what we view as the advantages of HST's large and well-diversified portfolio.

## Quantitative Evaluations

**S&P Quality Ranking**   B-

| D | C | **B-** | B | B+ | A- | A | A+ |
|---|---|---|---|---|---|---|---|

**Relative Strength Rank**   MODERATE

66

LOWEST = 1    HIGHEST = 99

## Revenue/FFO Data

### Revenue (Million $)

| | 1Q | 2Q | 3Q | 4Q | Year |
|---|---|---|---|---|---|
| 2011 | 903.0 | 1,296 | 1,142 | -- | -- |
| 2010 | 823.0 | 1,114 | 1,006 | 1,494 | 4,437 |
| 2009 | 882.0 | 1,064 | 912.0 | 1,336 | 4,158 |
| 2008 | 1,058 | 1,417 | 1,168 | 1,634 | 5,278 |
| 2007 | 1,031 | 1,385 | 1,201 | 1,809 | 5,426 |
| 2006 | 840.0 | 1,195 | 1,119 | 1,734 | 4,888 |

### FFO Per Share ($)

| | 1Q | 2Q | 3Q | 4Q | Year |
|---|---|---|---|---|---|
| 2011 | 0.11 | 0.31 | 0.16 | E0.32 | E0.90 |
| 2010 | 0.08 | 0.23 | 0.11 | 0.27 | 0.69 |
| 2009 | 0.10 | 0.12 | 0.11 | 0.18 | 0.52 |
| 2008 | 0.33 | 0.56 | 0.31 | 0.53 | 1.74 |
| 2007 | 0.30 | 0.48 | 0.38 | 0.75 | 1.91 |
| 2006 | 0.27 | 0.39 | 0.28 | 0.44 | 1.53 |

Fiscal year ended Dec. 31. Next earnings report expected: Mid February. FFO Estimates based on S&P Funds From Operations Est..

## Dividend Data (Dates: mm/dd Payment Date: mm/dd/yy)

| Amount ($) | Date Decl. | Ex-Div. Date | Stk. of Record | Payment Date |
|---|---|---|---|---|
| 0.010 | 12/17 | 12/29 | 12/31 | 01/18/11 |
| 0.020 | 03/17 | 03/29 | 03/31 | 04/15/11 |
| 0.030 | 06/15 | 06/28 | 06/30 | 07/15/11 |
| 0.040 | 09/19 | 09/28 | 09/30 | 10/17/11 |

Dividends have been paid since 2005. Source: Company reports.

## Highlights

➤ We expect room demand for the hotel industry to improve about 2.5% in 2011 and another 1.5% in 2012. Due to a lack of new supply, we also expect higher occupancy levels and improved pricing flexibility for hotel owners. For HST, we forecast that revenues per available room (RevPAR) will expand 6.9% in 2011 followed by a 5.3% increase in 2012.

➤ As we approach 2012, we think HST may slow down the pace of new U.S. acquisitions. The trust recently postponed the planned $442 million purchase of the Grand Hyatt in Washington DC while it assesses macro economic trends. HST, in our view, will continue to pursue acquisitions through a European joint venture, in which it owns a 33.4% interest. The Euro Fund currently owns two hotels and has remaining equity investment capacity of about $500 million.

➤ We forecast per-share FFO of $0.90 in 2011 and $1.00 in 2012, reflecting our outlook for a gradual slowing in demand due to uncertain global economic conditions. We expect improved room pricing to widen profit margins in 2012, and see an operating margin of 9.4%, up from our 7.7% forecast for 2011.

## Investment Rationale/Risk

➤ For the hotel industry, we think a cyclical recovery in demand and room rates will continue in 2012, albeit at a moderate pace due to slow U.S. economic growth. We believe HST is well positioned to maintain a steady improvement in profits, given what we view as its high-quality portfolio and strong capital-raising efforts. We think the trust will pursue acquisition opportunities on a global basis contingent on local economic conditions. We also expect a significant upturn in operating margins, as room rates rebound toward more historical levels. Over the next 12 months, we look for HST to perform in line with industry trends and hotel REIT peers.

➤ Risks to our recommendation and target price include a slower-than-expected recovery in demand for business and leisure travel caused by any slowing momentum in the economic recovery.

➤ Our 12-month target price of $13 is based on a multiple of 13.0X our 2012 FFO estimate of $1.00 a share, a moderate premium to hotel REIT peers, based on our view of HST's strong financial position.

---

**Please read the Required Disclosures and Analyst Certification on the last page of this report.**

The McGraw·Hill Companies

# Host Hotels & Resorts Inc

**STANDARD &POOR'S**

## Business Summary October 17, 2011

CORPORATE OVERVIEW. Host Hotels & Resorts operates as a self-managed and self-administered real estate investment trust (REIT). At December 31, 2010, HST owned a portfolio consisting of 104 luxury and upper-upscale hotels containing approximately 62,000 rooms. HST's hotels operate under a number of well known brands, including Marriott, Ritz-Carlton, Hyatt, Sheraton, Swissotel, Four Seasons, Hilton, Fairmont and Westin. Seventy-five of the company's properties were operated under the Marriott brand name. HST also holds a minority interest in a joint venture that owns 11 hotels in Europe with approximately 3,500 rooms. HST is geographically diversified, with hotels in most of the major metropolitan areas. The company's locations primarily include central business districts of major cities, airport areas, and resort/conference destinations.

HST's hotel revenue has traditionally experienced moderate seasonality, with a greater percentage of revenue falling in the second and fourth quarters. In addition, the fourth quarter reflects 16 or 17 weeks of results, versus 12 weeks in each of the first three fiscal quarters.

MARKET PROFILE. In 2010, hotel room demand is rebounded 7.7% after declining 6.0% in 2009, according to estimates by Smith Travel Research. We estimate business demand, including both transient and group travel, picked up 7% to 9% after falling about 12% in 2009. Domestic leisure travel did not decline nearly as much in 2009, but we believe high unemployment continued to crimp demand in 2010. Overseas tourist arrivals in the U.S. in 2009 were down about 9%, but for 2010, we believe there was a pickup in demand in the high single-digits. We forecast a further rise in overall demand of about 2.5% in 2011.

The number of available room nights in 2009 increased 3.0%, reflecting construction and redevelopment projects already financed before the financial crisis. For 2010, room night supply increased a lesser 2.0%. The room occupancy rate fell 8.8% in 2009, with occupancy of 54.5% indicative of severe, near depressionary levels, in our view. In 2010, the smaller increase in supply and higher demand led to a rise in occupancy to 57.6%, from 54.5%, according to data from Smith Travel Research. In 2011, we forecast a further deceleration in growth of room supply to less than 1%.

Room rates, which tend to lag changes in occupancy, declined 8.8% in 2009 and 0.1% in 2010. RevPAR, which fell 16.7% in 2009, rose 5.5% in 2010, according to Smith Travel Research, and we forecast growth at a slightly higher rate in 2011.

## Company Financials Fiscal Year Ended Dec. 31

| Per Share Data ($) | 2010 | 2009 | 2008 | 2007 | 2006 | 2005 | 2004 | 2003 | 2002 | 2001 |
|---|---|---|---|---|---|---|---|---|---|---|
| Tangible Book Value | 9.33 | 9.43 | 10.32 | 10.22 | 9.83 | NM | 5.64 | 5.57 | 4.87 | 4.77 |
| Earnings | -0.20 | -0.43 | 0.71 | 1.01 | 0.60 | 0.30 | -0.31 | -0.92 | -0.24 | 0.09 |
| S&P Core Earnings | -0.20 | -0.38 | 0.70 | 0.92 | 0.57 | 0.27 | -0.31 | -0.95 | -0.25 | 0.09 |
| Dividends | 0.04 | 0.25 | 0.65 | 0.80 | 0.71 | 0.41 | 0.10 | Nil | Nil | 0.78 |
| Payout Ratio | NM | NM | 92% | 79% | 118% | 137% | NM | Nil | Nil | NM |
| Prices:High | 17.97 | 12.20 | 18.81 | 28.98 | 25.79 | 19.24 | 17.40 | 12.33 | 12.25 | 13.95 |
| Prices:Low | 10.46 | 3.08 | 4.77 | 16.55 | 18.77 | 15.46 | 11.16 | 6.07 | 7.50 | 6.22 |
| P/E Ratio:High | NM | NM | 26 | 29 | 43 | 64 | NM | NM | NM | NM |
| P/E Ratio:Low | NM | NM | 7 | 16 | 31 | 52 | NM | NM | NM | NM |

| Income Statement Analysis (Million $) | 2010 | 2009 | 2008 | 2007 | 2006 | 2005 | 2004 | 2003 | 2002 | 2001 |
|---|---|---|---|---|---|---|---|---|---|---|
| Rental Income | 199 | 107 | 120 | 120 | 119 | 111 | 106 | 100 | 101 | 126 |
| Mortgage Income | Nil | Nil | Nil | Nil | Nil | Nil | Nil | Nil | Nil | Nil |
| Total Income | 4,437 | 4,158 | 5,278 | 5,426 | 4,888 | 3,881 | 3,640 | 3,448 | 3,680 | 3,754 |
| General Expenses | 3,625 | 3,398 | 3,955 | 4,007 | 3,665 | 2,936 | 2,812 | 2,765 | 2,823 | 2,821 |
| Interest Expense | 384 | 379 | 341 | 422 | 450 | 443 | 483 | 523 | 498 | 492 |
| Provision for Losses | Nil | Nil | Nil | Nil | Nil | Nil | Nil | Nil | Nil | Nil |
| Depreciation | 592 | 662 | 582 | 517 | 459 | 368 | 354 | 367 | 372 | 378 |
| Net Income | -126 | -242 | 402 | 550 | 309 | 138 | -64.0 | -225 | -29.0 | 53.0 |
| S&P Core Earnings | -137 | -224 | 386 | 490 | 276 | 98.0 | -106 | -267 | -65.0 | 20.0 |

| Balance Sheet & Other Financial Data (Million $) | 2010 | 2009 | 2008 | 2007 | 2006 | 2005 | 2004 | 2003 | 2002 | 2001 |
|---|---|---|---|---|---|---|---|---|---|---|
| Cash | 1,113 | 1,642 | 508 | 553 | 524 | 225 | 416 | 838 | 627 | 608 |
| Total Assets | 12,411 | 12,555 | 11,951 | 11,812 | 11,808 | 8,245 | 8,421 | 8,592 | 8,316 | 8,338 |
| Real Estate Investment | 15,812 | 14,974 | 15,038 | 14,288 | 13,897 | 10,382 | 9,924 | 9,511 | 9,193 | 8,828 |
| Loss Reserve | Nil | Nil | Nil | Nil | Nil | Nil | Nil | Nil | Nil | Nil |
| Net Investment | 10,514 | 10,231 | 10,739 | 10,588 | 10,584 | 7,434 | 7,274 | 7,085 | 7,031 | 6,999 |
| Short Term Debt | 192 | Nil | 410 | 261 | 268 | NA | NA | NA | NA | 148 |
| Capitalization:Debt | 5,285 | 5,837 | 5,542 | 5,364 | 5,610 | 5,370 | 5,523 | 3,976 | 5,638 | 5,929 |
| Capitalization:Equity | 6,303 | 6,092 | 5,420 | 5,344 | 5,125 | 2,176 | 2,058 | 1,797 | 1,271 | 1,270 |
| Capitalization:Total | 11,808 | 12,187 | 11,239 | 11,021 | 11,045 | 7,932 | 8,126 | 6,112 | 7,471 | 7,748 |
| % Earnings & Depreciation/Assets | 3.7 | 3.4 | 8.3 | 9.0 | 7.6 | 6.0 | 3.4 | 1.7 | 4.1 | 5.2 |
| Price Times Book Value:High | 1.9 | 1.3 | 1.8 | 2.8 | 2.6 | NM | 3.1 | 2.2 | 2.5 | 2.9 |
| Price Times Book Value:Low | 1.1 | 0.3 | 0.5 | 1.6 | 1.9 | NM | 2.0 | 1.1 | 1.5 | 1.3 |

Data as orig reptd.; bef. results of disc opers/spec. items. Per share data adj. for stk. divs.; EPS diluted. E-Estimated. NA-Not Available. NM-Not Meaningful. NR-Not Ranked. UR-Under Review.

**Office:** 6903 Rockledge Drive, Bethesda, MD 20817.
**Telephone:** 240-744-5121.
**Website:** http://www.hosthotels.com
**Chrmn:** R.E. Marriott

**Pres & CEO:** W.E. Walter
**EVP, Secy & General Counsel:** E.A. Abdoo
**SVP, Chief Acctg Officer & Cntlr:** B.G. MacNamara
**CFO:** L.K. Harvey

**Investor Contact:** G.J. Larson (1-240-744-5120)
**Board Members:** R. M. Baylis, W. W. Brittain, Jr., T. C. Golden, A. M. Korologos, R. E. Marriott, J. B. Morse, Jr., G. H. Smith, W. E. Walter

**Founded:** 1927
**Domicile:** Maryland
**Employees:** 203

The McGraw-Hill Companies

# Block (H&R) Inc.

**STANDARD &POOR'S**

| S&P Recommendation BUY ★★★★☆ | Price $14.41 (as of Nov 25, 2011) | 12-Mo. Target Price $18.00 | Investment Style Large-Cap Blend |
|---|---|---|---|

**GICS Sector** Consumer Discretionary
**Sub-Industry** Specialized Consumer Services

**Summary** H&R Block is one of the world's largest providers of tax services. The company plans to sell its business services division by the end of 2011.

## Key Stock Statistics (Source S&P, Vickers, company reports)

| | | | | | | | |
|---|---|---|---|---|---|---|---|
| 52-Wk Range | $18.00–11.43 | S&P Oper. EPS 2012E | 1.51 | Market Capitalization(B) | $4.406 | Beta | 0.61 |
| Trailing 12-Month EPS | $1.18 | S&P Oper. EPS 2013E | 1.56 | Yield (%) | 4.16 | S&P 3-Yr. Proj. EPS CAGR(%) | 8 |
| Trailing 12-Month P/E | 12.2 | P/E on S&P Oper. EPS 2012E | 9.5 | Dividend Rate/Share | $0.60 | S&P Credit Rating | BBB |
| $10K Invested 5 Yrs Ago | $7,123 | Common Shares Outstg. (M) | 305.8 | Institutional Ownership (%) | 91 | | |

## Price Performance

Options: ASE, CBOE, P, Ph

Analysis prepared by Equity Analyst **Jim Yin, CFA** on Sep 13, 2011, when the stock traded at **$13.19**.

## Qualitative Risk Assessment

| LOW | MEDIUM | HIGH |
|---|---|---|

Despite HRB's leading tax preparer position in its market, our risk assessment reflects uncertainty following the loss of HRB's ability to offer refund anticipation loan products. We are also concerned about internal accounting control issues, which caused HRB to restate almost three years of results in years past.

## Quantitative Evaluations

**S&P Quality Ranking** B

| D | C | B- | B | B+ | A- | A | A+ |
|---|---|---|---|---|---|---|---|

**Relative Strength Rank** MODERATE

66

LOWEST = 1    HIGHEST = 99

## Revenue/Earnings Data

**Revenue (Million $)**

| | 1Q | 2Q | 3Q | 4Q | Year |
|---|---|---|---|---|---|
| 2012 | 267.6 | -- | -- | -- | -- |
| 2011 | 274.5 | 322.9 | 851.5 | 2,325 | 3,776 |
| 2010 | 275.5 | 326.1 | 934.9 | 2,338 | 3,874 |
| 2009 | 271.9 | 351.5 | 993.5 | 2,467 | 4,084 |
| 2008 | 381.2 | 434.8 | 972.6 | 2,615 | 4,404 |
| 2007 | 342.8 | 396.1 | 931.2 | 2,351 | 4,021 |

**Earnings Per Share ($)**

| | 1Q | 2Q | 3Q | 4Q | Year |
|---|---|---|---|---|---|
| 2012 | -0.57 | E-0.36 | E0.17 | E2.07 | E1.51 |
| 2011 | -0.40 | -0.35 | -0.01 | 2.14 | 1.34 |
| 2010 | -0.39 | -0.38 | 0.16 | 2.10 | 1.46 |
| 2009 | -0.39 | -0.40 | 0.20 | 2.09 | 1.53 |
| 2008 | -0.39 | -0.42 | 0.03 | 2.11 | 1.39 |
| 2007 | -0.36 | -0.38 | 0.07 | 1.81 | 1.15 |

Fiscal year ended Apr. 30. Next earnings report expected: Early December. EPS Estimates based on S&P Operating Earnings; historical GAAP earnings are as reported.

## Highlights

▶ We see total revenues rising 1.7% in FY 12 (Apr.), after a 2.6% decline in FY 11. Our forecast includes full-year contributions from HRB's business services division, RSM McGladrey, which the company plans to sell by the end of calendar 2011 for $610 million. Although we believe more people may prefer to do their own taxes or choose e-filing options out of necessity in a difficult economy, we are encouraged to hear HRB's goals of reducing early season customer losses and increasing digital competitiveness. We also think advertising has been relatively effective in attracting new customers.

▶ After a 230 basis points (bps) contraction in the operating margin in FY 11, largely due to the inability to offer refund anticipation loans (RALs), we see 260 bps of improvement to 20.5% in FY 12. This reflects a growing digital business, as well as increased migration of customers to non-RAL products.

▶ We project EPS from continuing operations of $1.51 in FY 12, following FY 10's $1.34, on 1.3% fewer shares outstanding. In 2009, HRB authorized $2 billion of share repurchases through FY 12.

## Investment Rationale/Risk

▶ We recently raised our recommendation to buy, from hold, on valuation, as HRB shares declined significantly along with the overall market. Although we believe the U.S. economy is slowing and the odds of another recession are increasing, we think HRB will be less affected than most companies. While some people will choose to do their own tax filings due to economic necessity, we think HRB has been effective in attracting new customers with its advertising. We note that 2011 tax-season filings rose 6.5%, on both strong retail and digital filings. We also believe the current dividend yield of 4.5% will lend support to the share price.

▶ Risks to our recommendation and target price include a slowdown in the U.S. economy causing more people to do their own tax filings, increased competition, adverse litigation, and problems with the transition to new senior management.

▶ We derive our 12-month target price of $18 by applying a 12X multiple to our FY 12 operating EPS estimate of $1.51, slightly below peers and HRB's historical five-year range, given the near-term risks that could affect our EPS estimate.

## Dividend Data (Dates: mm/dd Payment Date: mm/dd/yy)

| Amount ($) | Date Decl. | Ex-Div. Date | Stk. of Record | Payment Date |
|---|---|---|---|---|
| 0.150 | 11/30 | 12/09 | 12/13 | 01/03/11 |
| 0.150 | 02/22 | 03/08 | 03/10 | 04/01/11 |
| 0.150 | 05/25 | 06/08 | 06/10 | 07/01/11 |
| 0.150 | 08/15 | 09/13 | 09/15 | 10/03/11 |

Dividends have been paid since 1962. Source: Company reports.

# Block (H&R) Inc.

**STANDARD &POOR'S**

## Business Summary September 13, 2011

**CORPORATE OVERVIEW.** H&R Block (HRB) provides various financial products and services, which the company believes are complementary. In FY 11 (Apr.), Tax Services accounted for 77.2% of revenues and 113.4% of profits, Business Services 22.0% and 7.2% (being sold), and the corporate division accounted for 0.9% and -20.6%.

The Tax Services division served about 23.2 million clients in FY 10 vs. 24.0 million in FY 09 and 24.6 million in FY 08. HRB's revenues related directly to the RAL program totaled $146.2 million in FY 10 or 3.8% of consolidated revenues. There were 11,506 company-owned and franchised U.S. H&R Block offices at April 30, 2010. In addition, HRB offers tax preparation services at hundreds of H&R Block Premium offices for more complex returns. International operations are located primarily in Australia and Canada, with combined company-owned and franchise offices numbering 1,643 at April 30, 2010. Tax Services also offers online tax preparation, tax preparation software, and guarantee programs.

The company is also one of the leading providers of business services through RSM McGladrey (to be sold for $610 million by the end of 2011).

**MARKET PROFILE.** HRB's largest segment, Tax Services, competes with other tax service chains, professional CPA/accounting firms, "mom and pop" local tax service providers and do-it-yourselfers (DIYers). In addition, HRB and some other online tax service product providers participate in the Free Filing Alliance, which offers free online federal return preparation with no income limitations. We believe HRB competes successfully by offering many services at what customers believe is an acceptable price-to-value relationship. These services include: the convenience of the largest retail tax office network in the U.S.; a "Peace of Mind" Guarantee" (POM) whereby HRB commits to representing its clients if they are audited by the IRS, and assuming the cost of additional taxes resulting from errors attributable to an HRB tax professional; "Refund Anticipation Loans" and "Refund Anticipation Checks" and a service whereby DIYers using HRB's online service can have an HRB tax professional check their returns and receive the POM guarantee. By offering increased value, HRB has been able to raise its rates 5%-7% annually since 2002.

## Company Financials Fiscal Year Ended Apr. 30

| Per Share Data ($) | 2011 | 2010 | 2009 | 2008 | 2007 | 2006 | 2005 | 2004 | 2003 | 2002 |
|---|---|---|---|---|---|---|---|---|---|---|
| Tangible Book Value | 0.77 | 0.72 | 0.51 | NM | 0.74 | 1.90 | 1.64 | 1.41 | 1.69 | 0.73 |
| Cash Flow | 1.69 | 1.78 | 1.90 | 1.83 | 1.62 | 2.05 | 2.43 | 2.42 | 2.02 | 1.57 |
| Earnings | 1.34 | 1.46 | 1.53 | 1.39 | 1.15 | 1.47 | 1.88 | 1.95 | 1.58 | 1.16 |
| S&P Core Earnings | 1.31 | 1.52 | 1.53 | 1.40 | 1.15 | 1.53 | 1.76 | 1.85 | 1.44 | 1.07 |
| Dividends | NA | 0.60 | 0.56 | 0.53 | 0.49 | 0.54 | 0.39 | 0.39 | 0.35 | 0.29 |
| Payout Ratio | NA | 41% | 37% | 38% | 42% | 37% | 21% | 20% | 22% | 25% |
| Calendar Year | 2010 | 2009 | 2008 | 2007 | 2006 | 2005 | 2004 | 2003 | 2002 | 2001 |
| Prices:High | 23.23 | 23.27 | 27.97 | 24.95 | 25.75 | 30.00 | 30.50 | 27.89 | 26.75 | 23.19 |
| Prices:Low | 10.13 | 13.73 | 15.00 | 17.57 | 19.80 | 22.99 | 22.08 | 17.64 | 14.50 | 9.16 |
| P/E Ratio:High | 17 | 16 | 18 | 18 | 22 | 20 | 16 | 14 | 17 | 20 |
| P/E Ratio:Low | 8 | 9 | 10 | 13 | 17 | 16 | 12 | 9 | 9 | 8 |

| Income Statement Analysis (Million $) | | | | | | | | | | |
|---|---|---|---|---|---|---|---|---|---|---|
| Revenue | 3,640 | 3,874 | 4,084 | 4,404 | 4,021 | 4,873 | 4,420 | 4,206 | 3,780 | 3,318 |
| Operating Income | 752 | 865 | 963 | 871 | 810 | 128 | 215 | 1,411 | 240 | 987 |
| Depreciation | 103 | 105 | 122 | 146 | 150 | 192 | 184 | 172 | 162 | 155 |
| Interest Expense | 95.4 | 90.6 | 1.65 | 243 | 46.9 | 49.1 | 62.4 | 84.6 | 92.6 | 116 |
| Pretax Income | 677 | 784 | 839 | 745 | 636 | 827 | 1,018 | 1,164 | 987 | 717 |
| Effective Tax Rate | NA | NA | 38.9% | 39.0% | 41.1% | 40.7% | 37.5% | 39.5% | 41.2% | 39.4% |
| Net Income | 419 | 489 | 513 | 454 | 374 | 490 | 636 | 704 | 580 | 434 |
| S&P Core Earnings | 405 | 506 | 514 | 458 | 374 | 509 | 593 | 665 | 527 | 400 |

| Balance Sheet & Other Financial Data (Million $) | | | | | | | | | | |
|---|---|---|---|---|---|---|---|---|---|---|
| Cash | 1,678 | 1,804 | 1,655 | 729 | 1,254 | 1,088 | 1,617 | 1,617 | 1,337 | 617 |
| Current Assets | 2,478 | 2,649 | 2,571 | 2,382 | 3,454 | 2,824 | 3,071 | 2,961 | 2,747 | 2,245 |
| Total Assets | 5,208 | 5,234 | 5,360 | 5,623 | 7,499 | 5,989 | 5,539 | 5,380 | 4,604 | 4,231 |
| Current Liabilities | 2,215 | 2,321 | 2,398 | 3,096 | 5,176 | 2,893 | 2,209 | 2,472 | 1,897 | 1,880 |
| Long Term Debt | 1,039 | 1,060 | 1,107 | 1,032 | 520 | 418 | 923 | 546 | 822 | 868 |
| Common Equity | 1,450 | 1,441 | 1,406 | 988 | 1,414 | 2,148 | 1,976 | 1,897 | 1,664 | 1,369 |
| Total Capital | 2,517 | 2,554 | 2,546 | 2,131 | 1,934 | 2,565 | 2,899 | 2,443 | 2,486 | 2,238 |
| Capital Expenditures | 63.0 | 90.5 | 97.9 | 106 | 161 | 251 | 209 | 128 | 151 | 112 |
| Cash Flow | 522 | 594 | 635 | 600 | 525 | 682 | 820 | 876 | 742 | 590 |
| Current Ratio | 1.1 | 1.1 | 1.1 | 0.8 | 0.7 | 1.0 | 1.4 | 1.2 | 1.4 | 1.2 |
| % Long Term Debt of Capitalization | 41.3 | 41.5 | 43.5 | 48.4 | 26.9 | 16.3 | 31.8 | 22.3 | 33.1 | 38.8 |
| % Net Income of Revenue | 11.5 | 12.6 | 12.6 | 10.3 | 9.3 | 12.4 | 14.3 | 16.7 | 21.4 | 13.1 |
| % Return on Assets | 8.0 | 9.2 | 9.3 | 6.9 | 5.6 | 8.5 | 11.8 | 13.9 | 13.1 | 10.4 |
| % Return on Equity | 29.0 | 34.4 | 42.9 | 37.8 | 21.0 | 23.9 | 33.5 | 39.6 | 38.2 | 34.2 |

Data as orig reptd.; bef. results of disc opers/spec. items. Per share data adj. for stk. divs.; EPS diluted. E-Estimated. NA-Not Available. NM-Not Meaningful. NR-Not Ranked. UR-Under Review.

**Office:** One H&R Block Way, Kansas City, MO 64105.
**Telephone:** 816-854-3000.
**Email:** investorrelations@hrblock.com
**Website:** http://www.hrblock.com

**Chrmn:** R.A. Gerard
**Pres & CEO:** W.C. Cobb
**SVP & CFO:** J.T. Brown
**SVP & CIO:** R. Agar

**Chief Acctg Officer & Cntlr:** C.R. Brown
**Investor Contact:** S. Dudley (816-854-4505)
**Board Members:** P. J. Brown, W. C. Cobb, M. R. Ellison, R. A. Gerard, D. B. Lewis, V. J. Reich, B. C. Rohde, T. D. Seip, C. Wood, J. F. Wright

**Founded:** 1946
**Domicile:** Missouri
**Employees:** 115,100

# Hudson City Bancorp Inc

STANDARD &POOR'S

| S&P Recommendation HOLD ★★★★★ | Price $5.13 (as of Nov 25, 2011) | 12-Mo. Target Price $6.50 | Investment Style Large-Cap Blend |
| --- | --- | --- | --- |

**GICS Sector** Financials
**Sub-Industry** Thrifts & Mortgage Finance

**Summary** Hudson City Bancorp, through Hudson City Savings Bank, operates 135 branches in the New York metropolitan area. It caters to high median household income counties and focuses on jumbo mortgage loan funding, largely through time deposits.

## Key Stock Statistics (Source S&P, Vickers, company reports)

| | | | | | | | |
| --- | --- | --- | --- | --- | --- | --- | --- |
| 52-Wk Range | $13.26– 5.09 | S&P Oper. EPS 2011**E** | -0.60 | Market Capitalization(B) | $2.706 | Beta | 0.74 |
| Trailing 12-Month EPS | $-0.51 | S&P Oper. EPS 2012**E** | 0.65 | Yield (%) | 6.24 | S&P 3-Yr. Proj. EPS CAGR(%) | -16 |
| Trailing 12-Month P/E | NM | P/E on S&P Oper. EPS 2011**E** | NM | Dividend Rate/Share | $0.32 | S&P Credit Rating | NA |
| $10K Invested 5 Yrs Ago | $4,629 | Common Shares Outstg. (M) | 527.5 | Institutional Ownership (%) | 64 | | |

## Price Performance

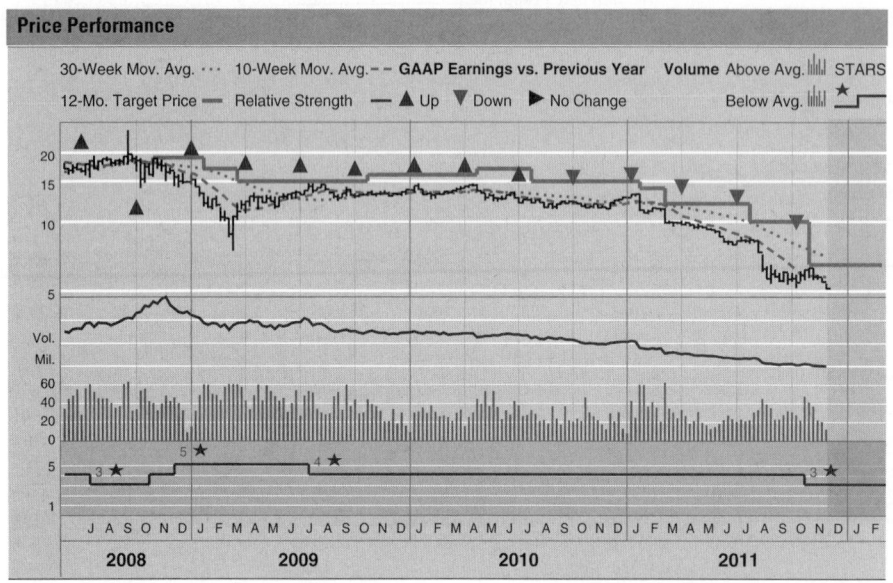

30-Week Mov. Avg. ··· 10-Week Mov. Avg. - - **GAAP Earnings vs. Previous Year** Volume Above Avg. STARS
12-Mo. Target Price — Relative Strength ▲ Up ▼ Down ▶ No Change Below Avg. ★

Options: ASE, CBOE, Ph

Analysis prepared by Equity Analyst **Erik Oja** on Nov 10, 2011, when the stock traded at **$5.75**.

## Highlights

▸ We expect quarterly net revenue declines to continue through the third quarter of 2012. We expect 2011 net revenues of $1.05 billion, down nearly 12%, and we see 2012 net revenues of $1.01 billion, down 3.8%. However, for 2013, we expect 1.0% revenue growth. We see a 16% decrease in interest-earning assets in 2011, and 1.0% shrinkage in 2012, followed by slow growth in 2013. We forecast a 1.70% net interest margin by the end of 2011, and a 1.55% net interest margin by the end of 2012. We also expect balance sheet shrinkage to end in the third quarter of 2012.

▸ We expect a 2011 loan loss provision of $114.2 million, down from $133.8 million in 2010. For 2012 and 2013, we expect provisions of $97 million per year. These provision forecasts are based on our net chargeoff estimates of $81 million in 2011 and $80 million in each of 2012 and 2013. The $269 million September 30 allowance for loan losses covered 0.90% of total loans and 28.3% of impaired loans. We do not expect reserve releases in 2011 or 2012.

▸ We see a loss per share of $0.60 in 2011 and EPS of $0.65 in 2012.

## Investment Rationale/Risk

▸ Earlier this year, HCBK restructured its balance sheet to reduce high-cost borrowings, thus bringing the company back into compliance with the interest rate risk limits set by its board of directors. We think the company's lower quarterly dividend of $0.08, down from $0.15, will help preserve capital and will be maintained in 2011 and 2012. We also think HCBK's avoidance of subprime and option adjustable rate mortgages and high loan-to-value products will enable the company to weather the difficult housing market better than competitors. We expect balance sheet shrinkage to end in mid-2012, and steady EPS of $0.16 to $0.17 per quarter through 2012.

▸ Risks to our opinion and target price include greater-than-expected job losses in the New York City metropolitan area, significantly increased competition in the jumbo loan market, and deterioration in prime loans.

▸ Our 12-month target price of $6.50 is based on a discount to peers 0.65X our year-end 2011 estimate of tangible book value per share of $9.85, a peer equivalent 9.8X our forward four quarters EPS estimate of $0.66.

## Qualitative Risk Assessment

| LOW | MEDIUM | HIGH |
| --- | --- | --- |

Our risk assessment reflects the solid credit quality of HCBK's loan portfolio, offset by our view of HCBK's relatively narrow range of products and lack of geographical diversification.

## Quantitative Evaluations

**S&P Quality Ranking** A

| D | C | B- | B | B+ | A- | A | A+ |
| --- | --- | --- | --- | --- | --- | --- | --- |

**Relative Strength Rank** WEAK

22

LOWEST = 1    HIGHEST = 99

## Revenue/Earnings Data

**Revenue (Million $)**

| | 1Q | 2Q | 3Q | 4Q | Year |
| --- | --- | --- | --- | --- | --- |
| 2011 | 722.7 | 555.5 | 527.6 | -- | -- |
| 2010 | 767.9 | 750.8 | 722.7 | 706.2 | 2,947 |
| 2009 | 725.6 | 754.4 | 746.7 | 748.7 | 2,975 |
| 2008 | 615.5 | 648.8 | 683.5 | 714.0 | 2,662 |
| 2007 | 481.2 | 513.3 | 550.3 | 590.0 | 2,135 |
| 2006 | 361.0 | 385.6 | 423.7 | 449.0 | 1,621 |

**Earnings Per Share ($)**

| | 1Q | 2Q | 3Q | 4Q | Year |
| --- | --- | --- | --- | --- | --- |
| 2011 | -1.13 | 0.19 | 0.17 | E0.17 | E-0.60 |
| 2010 | 0.30 | 0.29 | 0.25 | 0.25 | 1.09 |
| 2009 | 0.26 | 0.26 | 0.27 | 0.28 | 1.07 |
| 2008 | 0.18 | 0.22 | 0.25 | 0.25 | 0.90 |
| 2007 | 0.13 | 0.14 | 0.15 | 0.16 | 0.58 |
| 2006 | 0.13 | 0.13 | 0.13 | 0.13 | 0.53 |

Fiscal year ended Dec. 31. Next earnings report expected: NA. EPS Estimates based on S&P Operating Earnings; historical GAAP earnings are as reported.

## Dividend Data (Dates: mm/dd Payment Date: mm/dd/yy)

| Amount ($) | Date Decl. | Ex-Div. Date | Stk. of Record | Payment Date |
| --- | --- | --- | --- | --- |
| 0.150 | 01/18 | 02/02 | 02/04 | 02/25/11 |
| 0.080 | 04/20 | 05/03 | 05/05 | 05/27/11 |
| 0.080 | 07/20 | 08/03 | 08/05 | 08/30/11 |
| 0.080 | 10/26 | 11/02 | 11/04 | 11/30/11 |

Dividends have been paid since 1999. Source: Company reports.

**Please read the Required Disclosures and Analyst Certification on the last page of this report.**

# Hudson City Bancorp Inc

**STANDARD &POOR'S**

## Business Summary November 10, 2011

CORPORATE OVERVIEW. New Jersey-based Hudson City Bancorp, Inc. (HCBK), a community- and consumer-oriented retail savings bank holding company, offers traditional deposit products, residential real estate mortgage loans and consumer loans. In addition, HCBK purchases mortgages, mortgage-backed securities, securities issued by the U.S. government and government-sponsored agencies and other investments permitted by applicable laws and regulations. HCBK is the holding company of its only subsidiary, Hudson City Savings Bank. The company's revenues are derived principally from interest on mortgage loans & mortgage-backed securities and interest & dividends on investment securities. The bank's primary sources of funds are customer deposits, borrowings, scheduled amortization and prepayments of mortgage loans and mortgage-backed securities, maturities and calls of investment securities and funds provided by operations.

PRIMARY BUSINESS DYNAMICS. As of September 30, 2011, HCBK had total loans of $30.0 billion. Hudson's loan portfolio primarily consists of one-to-four family residential first mortgage loans. HCBK's first mortgage loans totaled $29.8 billion, representing 99% of the total loan portfolio. HCBK's loan portfolio also includes multi-family and commercial mortgage loans, construction loans and consumer and other loans, which primarily consist of fixed-rate second mortgage loans and home equity credit lines. The company does not originate or purchase subprime loans, negative amortization loans or option adjustable rate mortgage loans.

CORPORATE STRATEGY. HCBK seeks to continue its growth by focusing on the origination and purchase of mortgage loans, while purchasing mortgage-backed securities and investment securities as a supplement. It intends to fund its growth with customer deposits and borrowed funds. The company aims to increase customer deposits by continuing to offer desirable products at competitive rates and by opening new branch offices. HCBK continues to focus on high median household income counties, in line with its jumbo mortgage loan and consumer deposit business model.

## Company Financials Fiscal Year Ended Dec. 31

| Per Share Data ($) | 2010 | 2009 | 2008 | 2007 | 2006 | 2005 | 2004 | 2003 | 2002 | 2001 |
|---|---|---|---|---|---|---|---|---|---|---|
| Tangible Book Value | 10.86 | 10.55 | 9.77 | 9.22 | 8.54 | 8.83 | 2.35 | 2.18 | 2.14 | 2.03 |
| Earnings | 1.09 | 1.07 | 0.90 | 0.58 | 0.53 | 0.48 | 0.40 | 0.35 | 0.32 | 0.21 |
| S&P Core Earnings | 1.09 | 1.07 | 0.89 | 0.58 | 0.53 | 0.47 | 0.39 | 0.34 | 0.31 | 0.20 |
| Dividends | 0.60 | 0.59 | 0.60 | 0.33 | 0.30 | 0.27 | 0.22 | 0.16 | 0.11 | 0.07 |
| Payout Ratio | 55% | 55% | 67% | 57% | 57% | 56% | 54% | 47% | 34% | 35% |
| Prices:High | 14.75 | 15.89 | 25.05 | 16.08 | 14.09 | 12.61 | 12.79 | 12.00 | 6.71 | 4.14 |
| Prices:Low | 11.34 | 7.46 | 13.28 | 11.45 | 11.90 | 10.09 | 9.79 | 5.79 | 4.04 | 2.72 |
| P/E Ratio:High | 14 | 15 | 28 | 28 | 27 | 26 | 32 | 35 | 21 | 20 |
| P/E Ratio:Low | 10 | 7 | 15 | 20 | 22 | 21 | 24 | 17 | 13 | 13 |

| Income Statement Analysis (Million $) | 2010 | 2009 | 2008 | 2007 | 2006 | 2005 | 2004 | 2003 | 2002 | 2001 |
|---|---|---|---|---|---|---|---|---|---|---|
| Net Interest Income | 1,191 | 1,243 | 942 | 647 | 613 | 562 | 485 | 401 | 388 | 287 |
| Loan Loss Provision | 195 | 138 | 19.5 | 4.80 | Nil | 0.07 | 0.79 | 0.90 | 1.50 | 1.88 |
| Non Interest Income | 163 | 33.6 | 8.50 | 7.27 | 6.29 | 5.27 | 16.6 | 5.34 | 5.95 | 4.69 |
| Non Interest Expenses | 266 | 266 | 198 | 168 | 159 | 128 | 118 | 103 | 93.5 | 81.8 |
| Pretax Income | 892 | 874 | 733 | 482 | 461 | 442 | 382 | 327 | 301 | 208 |
| Effective Tax Rate | 39.8% | 39.7% | 39.2% | 38.6% | 37.3% | 37.6% | 37.4% | 36.6% | 36.3% | 35.3% |
| Net Income | 537 | 527 | 446 | 296 | 289 | 276 | 239 | 207 | 192 | 135 |
| % Net Interest Margin | 2.01 | 2.21 | 1.96 | 1.64 | 1.96 | 2.35 | 3.66 | 2.65 | 3.10 | 2.87 |
| S&P Core Earnings | 536 | 529 | 440 | 294 | 287 | 272 | 235 | 204 | 186 | 128 |

| Balance Sheet & Other Financial Data (Million $) | 2010 | 2009 | 2008 | 2007 | 2006 | 2005 | 2004 | 2003 | 2002 | 2001 |
|---|---|---|---|---|---|---|---|---|---|---|
| Total Assets | 61,166 | 60,268 | 54,163 | 44,424 | 35,507 | 28,075 | 20,146 | 17,033 | 14,145 | 11,427 |
| Loans | 30,774 | 31,721 | 29,441 | 24,198 | 19,069 | 15,037 | 11,328 | 8,766 | 6,932 | 5,932 |
| Deposits | 25,173 | 24,578 | 18,464 | 15,153 | 13,416 | 11,383 | 11,477 | 10,454 | 9,139 | 7,913 |
| Capitalization:Debt | 29,675 | 29,975 | 30,225 | 24,141 | 16,966 | 11,350 | 7,150 | 5,150 | 3,600 | 2,150 |
| Capitalization:Equity | 5,510 | 5,339 | 4,949 | 4,611 | 4,930 | 5,201 | 1,403 | 1,329 | 1,316 | 1,289 |
| Capitalization:Total | 35,185 | 35,314 | 35,174 | 28,752 | 21,896 | 16,551 | 8,553 | 6,479 | 4,916 | 3,439 |
| % Return on Assets | 0.9 | 0.9 | 0.9 | 0.7 | 0.9 | 1.1 | 1.3 | 1.3 | 1.5 | 1.3 |
| % Return on Equity | 9.9 | 10.3 | 9.3 | 6.2 | 5.7 | 8.4 | 17.5 | 15.7 | 14.7 | 9.8 |
| % Loan Loss Reserve | 0.8 | 0.4 | 0.2 | 0.1 | 0.2 | 0.2 | 0.2 | 0.2 | 0.4 | 0.4 |
| % Risk Based Capital | 22.7 | 21.0 | 21520.0 | 24.8 | 31.0 | 41.3 | 17.5 | 7.5 | 26.8 | 32.0 |
| Price Times Book Value:High | 1.3 | 1.5 | 2.6 | 1.1 | 1.6 | 1.4 | 5.4 | 5.5 | 3.1 | 2.0 |
| Price Times Book Value:Low | 1.0 | 0.7 | 1.4 | 0.8 | 1.4 | 1.1 | 4.2 | 2.7 | 1.9 | 1.3 |

Data as orig reptd.; bef. results of disc opers/spec. items. Per share data adj. for stk. divs.; EPS diluted. E-Estimated. NA-Not Available. NM-Not Meaningful. NR-Not Ranked. UR-Under Review.

**Office:** 80 W Century Rd, Paramus, NJ, USA 07652-1405.
**Telephone:** 201-967-1900.
**Website:** http://www.hcbk.com
**Chrmn & CEO:** R.E. Hermance, Jr.

**Pres & COO:** D.J. Salamone
**SVP & CIO:** S.M. Schlesinger
**CFO:** J.C. Kranz
**Chief Acctg Officer:** A.J. Fabiano

**Investor Contact:** S. Munhall (201-967-8290)
**Board Members:** M. W. Azzara, W. G. Bardel, S. A. Belair, V. H. Bruni, C. E. Golding, R. E. Hermance, Jr., D. O. Quest, D. J. Salamone, J. G. Sponholz

**Founded:** 1868
**Domicile:** Delaware
**Employees:** 1,562

# Humana Inc.

STANDARD
&POOR'S

| S&P Recommendation **BUY** ★★★★☆ | Price<br>$88.68 (as of Nov 30, 2011) | 12-Mo. Target Price<br>$95.00 | Investment Style<br>Large-Cap Growth |
|---|---|---|---|

**GICS Sector** Health Care
**Sub-Industry** Managed Health Care

**Summary** This company provides a broad range of managed health care services to almost 11.1 million individuals.

## Key Stock Statistics (Source S&P, Vickers, company reports)

| | | | | | | | | |
|---|---|---|---|---|---|---|---|---|
| 52-Wk Range | $89.22– 54.24 | S&P Oper. EPS 2011**E** | 8.40 | Market Capitalization(B) | $14.500 | Beta | 1.06 |
| Trailing 12-Month EPS | $7.86 | S&P Oper. EPS 2012**E** | 7.80 | Yield (%) | 1.13 | S&P 3-Yr. Proj. EPS CAGR(%) | 7 |
| Trailing 12-Month P/E | 11.3 | P/E on S&P Oper. EPS 2011**E** | 10.6 | Dividend Rate/Share | $1.00 | S&P Credit Rating | BBB |
| $10K Invested 5 Yrs Ago | $16,495 | Common Shares Outstg. (M) | 163.5 | Institutional Ownership (%) | 95 | | |

## Price Performance

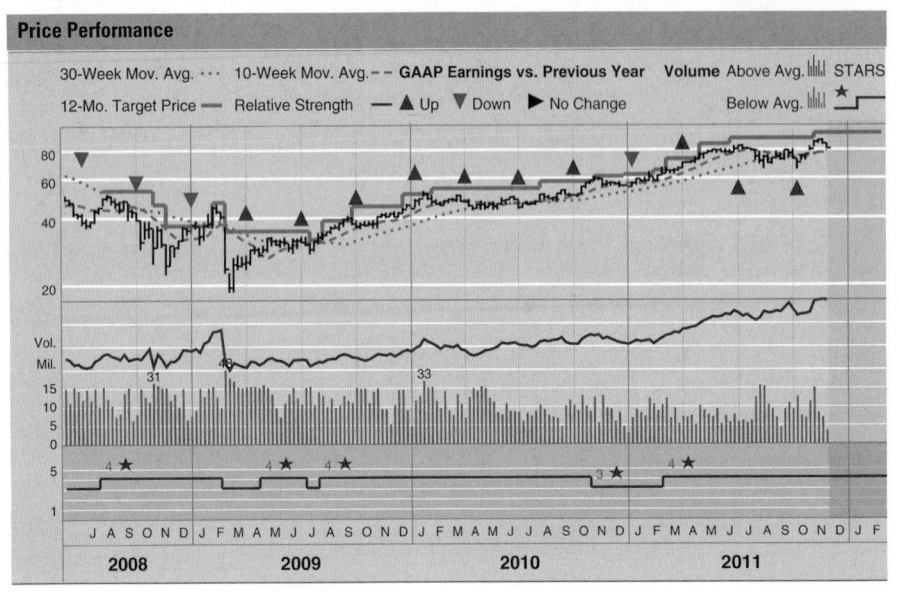

30-Week Mov. Avg. ···· 10-Week Mov. Avg. ‐ ‐ **GAAP Earnings vs. Previous Year** Volume Above Avg. STARS
12-Mo. Target Price — Relative Strength — ▲ Up ▼ Down ► No Change Below Avg. ★

Options: ASE, CBOE, Ph

Analysis prepared by Equity Analyst **Phillip Seligman** on Nov 08, 2011, when the stock traded at **$87.15**.

## Qualitative Risk Assessment

| LOW | MEDIUM | **HIGH** |
|---|---|---|

Our risk assessment reflects HUM's heavy reliance on Medicare Advantage (MA) for growth. We also believe that intense competition will continue to limit commercial enrollment growth.

## Quantitative Evaluations

**S&P Quality Ranking** B+

| D | C | B- | B | **B+** | A- | A | A+ |
|---|---|---|---|---|---|---|---|

**Relative Strength Rank** STRONG

93

LOWEST = 1    HIGHEST = 99

## Revenue/Earnings Data

**Revenue (Million $)**

| | 1Q | 2Q | 3Q | 4Q | Year |
|---|---|---|---|---|---|
| 2011 | 9,191 | 9,284 | 9,301 | -- | -- |
| 2010 | 8,441 | 8,653 | 8,425 | 8,350 | 33,868 |
| 2009 | 7,712 | 7,899 | 7,717 | 7,633 | 30,960 |
| 2008 | 6,960 | 7,351 | 7,148 | 7,488 | 28,946 |
| 2007 | 6,205 | 6,427 | 6,320 | 6,339 | 25,290 |
| 2006 | 4,704 | 5,407 | 5,650 | 5,655 | 21,417 |

**Earnings Per Share ($)**

| | 1Q | 2Q | 3Q | 4Q | Year |
|---|---|---|---|---|---|
| 2011 | 1.86 | 2.71 | 2.67 | E1.15 | E8.40 |
| 2010 | 1.52 | 2.00 | 2.32 | 0.63 | 6.47 |
| 2009 | 1.22 | 1.67 | 1.78 | 1.48 | 6.15 |
| 2008 | 0.47 | 1.24 | 1.09 | 1.03 | 3.83 |
| 2007 | 0.42 | 1.28 | 1.78 | 1.43 | 4.91 |
| 2006 | 0.50 | 0.53 | 0.95 | 0.92 | 2.90 |

Fiscal year ended Dec. 31. Next earnings report expected: Early February. EPS Estimates based on S&P Operating Earnings; historical GAAP earnings are as reported.

## Dividend Data (Dates: mm/dd Payment Date: mm/dd/yy)

| Amount ($) | Date Decl. | Ex-Div. Date | Stk. of Record | Payment Date |
|---|---|---|---|---|
| 0.250 | 04/26 | 06/28 | 06/30 | 07/28/11 |
| 0.250 | -- | 09/28 | 09/30 | 10/28/11 |
| 0.250 | 10/24 | 12/28 | 12/30 | 01/31/12 |

Dividends have been paid since 2011. Source: Company reports.

## Highlights

► We look for operating revenues to rise about 10% in 2011, to almost $36.6 billion, and by 3.7% in 2012, to $37.9 billion. Drivers we see include 170,000 additional Medicare Advantage (MA; health plan) members and 880,000 more Medicare Part D (drug plan) members by year-end 2011, and an additional 220,000 and 550,000 members, respectively, in 2012. We also expect a partial recovery in the number of fully insured commercial members, following a decline in 2011, but a continued decline in self-funded (ASO) commercial members. We assume the TRICARE contract will be accounted for on an ASO basis starting in the second quarter of 2012.

► We believe medical costs will decline in 2011 as a percentage of premium revenues (MCR; medical cost ratio), mainly on moderated medical cost trends in the first nine months. We expect the MCR to rise in 2012, assuming more-normalized medical cost trends start in late 2011. We also expect a higher SG&A cost ratio, on the December 2010 Concentra acquisition, and for it to be stable in 2012.

► We estimate operating EPS of $8.40 in 2011, versus $7.10 in 2010, and look for $7.80 in 2012.

## Investment Rationale/Risk

► We think HUM has the scale, diversity and flexibility to adjust to the health care reform law. We are encouraged by HUM's ability to achieve healthy enrollment gains in its MA and Part D programs. Looking ahead, we believe HUM has a good opportunity to gain additional MA members, assuming a health insurance industry shake-out occurs amid health care reform and the potential decline in MA reimbursement that might arise amid federal deficit reduction initiatives. We view HUM's cash flows from operations as healthy, providing financial flexibility. Separately, we do not see any major change in HUM's long-term strategy under Bruce D. Broussard, a seasoned outside health care executive, who becomes president in December 2011 and CEO in 12 to 18 months, when chairman and CEO Mike McAllister plans to retire as CEO.

► Risks to our recommendation and target price include intensified competition, a medical cost spike, and MA rate cuts.

► Our 12-month target price of $95 assumes an above-peers multiple of 12.2X applied to our 2012 EPS estimate.

# Humana Inc.

## Business Summary November 08, 2011

CORPORATE OVERVIEW. Humana is one of the largest managed care organizations, with medical membership of 11,082,200 (8,599,900 excluding stand-alone Medicare Prescription Drug Program (PDP) enrollment) as of September 30, 2011, versus 10,238,300 (8,479,500) at December 31, 2010. On April 26, 2011, HUM realigned its business segments to more closely reflect its evolving business model. It has begun managing and reporting its operating results using the following segments:

Retail is comprised of products sold on a retail basis to individuals. Products include Medicare Advantage and stand-alone Prescription Drug Plans (PDPs), and a portfolio of individual health plans marketed under the HumanaOne brand. Medical membership includes fully insured individual (424,000, versus 372,300), Medicare Advantage (1,613,400, versus 1,460,700), Medicare PDP (2,478,100, versus 1,670,300) and Medicare Supplement (56,700, versus 38,900) plans.

Employer Group includes a broad spectrum of major medical benefits with multiple in-network coinsurance levels and annual deductible choices that employers of all sizes can offer to their employees on either a fully insured or self-funded (ASO, or administrative services only) basis. The segment also offers group Medicare Advantage and PDPs for employers that provide post-retirement health care benefits. Medical membership includes Medicare Advantage (287,900, versus 273,100), Medicare Advantage ASO (27,600, versus

28,200), Medicare PDP (4,200, versus 2,400), fully insured medical (1,181,300, versus 1,252,200), and ASO (1,287,000, versus 1,453,600) plans.

Health and Well-Being Services provides services to other Humana businesses, external health plan members and other employers or individuals. Humana Pharmacy Solutions manages prescription drug coverage. Primary Care Services consists of CAC Medical Centers in South Florida and Concentra, which delivers occupational medicine, urgent care, physical therapy and wellness services to employees and the general public through its operation of medical centers and worksite medical facilities. Humana Cares provides home care services for individuals living with multiple chronic conditions, individuals with disabilities, and fragile and aging-in-place patients and their caregivers. Integrated Wellness Services consists of LifeSynch, which provides programs that integrate behavioral health services with wellness programs, employee assistance programs and work-life services, and HumanaVitality. HumanaVitality, a new (2011) joint venture with Discovery Holdings Ltd., provides offerings encouraging healthy behaviors that reduce long-term health care costs by rewarding members for improving their health.

## Company Financials Fiscal Year Ended Dec. 31

| Per Share Data ($) | 2010 | 2009 | 2008 | 2007 | 2006 | 2005 | 2004 | 2003 | 2002 | 2001 |
|---|---|---|---|---|---|---|---|---|---|---|
| Tangible Book Value | 23.49 | 20.80 | 12.99 | 13.91 | 10.46 | 7.41 | 7.52 | 6.54 | 5.09 | 4.33 |
| Cash Flow | NA | NA | 5.13 | 6.00 | 3.79 | 2.68 | 2.45 | 2.20 | 1.57 | 1.67 |
| Earnings | 6.47 | 6.15 | 3.83 | 4.91 | 2.90 | 1.87 | 1.72 | 1.41 | 0.85 | 0.70 |
| S&P Core Earnings | 6.45 | 6.08 | 4.14 | 4.87 | 2.64 | 1.99 | 1.55 | 1.23 | 0.87 | 0.63 |
| Dividends | Nil | Nil | Nil | Nil | Nil | Nil | Nil | Nil | Nil | Nil |
| Payout Ratio | Nil | Nil | Nil | Nil | Nil | Nil | Nil | Nil | Nil | Nil |
| Prices:High | 61.33 | 46.20 | 88.10 | 81.50 | 68.24 | 55.70 | 31.02 | 23.39 | 17.45 | 15.63 |
| Prices:Low | 43.05 | 18.57 | 22.33 | 51.00 | 41.08 | 28.92 | 15.20 | 8.68 | 9.78 | 8.38 |
| P/E Ratio:High | 10 | 8 | 23 | 17 | 24 | 30 | 18 | 17 | 21 | 22 |
| P/E Ratio:Low | 7 | 3 | 6 | 10 | 14 | 15 | 9 | 6 | 12 | 12 |

### Income Statement Analysis (Million $)

| | 2010 | 2009 | 2008 | 2007 | 2006 | 2005 | 2004 | 2003 | 2002 | 2001 |
|---|---|---|---|---|---|---|---|---|---|---|
| Revenue | 33,868 | 30,960 | 28,946 | 25,290 | 21,417 | 14,418 | 13,104 | 12,226 | 11,261 | 10,195 |
| Operating Income | NA | NA | 1,293 | 1,543 | 974 | 590 | 415 | 489 | 384 | 114 |
| Depreciation | NA | NA | 220 | 185 | 149 | 129 | 118 | 127 | 121 | 162 |
| Interest Expense | 105 | 106 | 80.3 | 68.9 | 63.1 | 39.3 | 23.2 | 17.4 | 17.0 | 25.0 |
| Pretax Income | 1,750 | 1,602 | 993 | 1,289 | 762 | 422 | 416 | 345 | 210 | 183 |
| Effective Tax Rate | NA | 35.1% | 34.8% | 35.3% | 36.0% | 26.9% | 32.7% | 33.6% | 32.0% | 36.1% |
| Net Income | 1,099 | 1,040 | 647 | 834 | 487 | 308 | 280 | 229 | 143 | 117 |
| S&P Core Earnings | 1,096 | 1,027 | 699 | 826 | 443 | 330 | 252 | 200 | 145 | 104 |

### Balance Sheet & Other Financial Data (Million $)

| | 2010 | 2009 | 2008 | 2007 | 2006 | 2005 | 2004 | 2003 | 2002 | 2001 |
|---|---|---|---|---|---|---|---|---|---|---|
| Cash | 1,673 | 1,614 | 1,970 | 5,676 | 1,740 | 732 | 580 | 931 | 721 | 651 |
| Current Assets | NA | NA | 8,396 | 8,733 | 7,333 | 4,206 | 3,596 | 3,321 | 2,795 | 2,623 |
| Total Assets | 16,103 | 14,153 | 13,042 | 12,879 | 10,127 | 6,870 | 5,658 | 5,293 | 4,600 | 4,404 |
| Current Liabilities | NA | NA | 5,184 | 5,792 | 5,192 | 3,220 | 2,327 | 2,265 | 2,390 | 2,307 |
| Long Term Debt | 1,669 | 1,678 | 1,937 | 1,688 | 1,269 | 514 | 637 | 643 | 340 | 315 |
| Common Equity | 6,924 | 5,776 | 4,457 | 4,029 | 3,054 | 2,474 | 2,090 | 1,836 | 1,606 | 1,508 |
| Total Capital | NA | NA | 6,394 | 5,717 | 4,323 | 2,988 | 2,727 | 2,479 | 1,946 | 1,823 |
| Capital Expenditures | NA | NA | 262 | 239 | 193 | 166 | 114 | 101 | 112 | 115 |
| Cash Flow | NA | NA | 868 | 1,018 | 636 | 437 | 398 | 356 | 264 | 279 |
| Current Ratio | 1.8 | 1.8 | 1.6 | 1.5 | 1.4 | 1.3 | 1.5 | 1.5 | 1.2 | 1.1 |
| % Long Term Debt of Capitalization | 19.4 | 22.5 | 30.3 | 29.5 | 29.4 | 17.2 | 23.3 | 25.9 | 17.5 | 17.3 |
| % Net Income of Revenue | 3.3 | 3.4 | 2.2 | 3.3 | 2.3 | 2.1 | 102.6 | 1.9 | 1.3 | 1.2 |
| % Return on Assets | 7.3 | 7.7 | 5.0 | 7.3 | 5.7 | 4.9 | 5.1 | 4.5 | 3.2 | 2.7 |
| % Return on Equity | 17.3 | 20.3 | 15.3 | 23.5 | 17.5 | 13.5 | 14.3 | 13.3 | 9.2 | 8.2 |

Data as orig reptd.; bef. results of disc opers/spec. items. Per share data adj. for stk. divs.; EPS diluted. E-Estimated. NA-Not Available. NM-Not Meaningful. NR-Not Ranked. UR-Under Review.

**Office:** 500 West Main Street, Louisville, KY 40202.
**Telephone:** 502-580-1000.
**Website:** http://www.humana.com
**Chrmn & CEO:** M.B. McCallister

**COO:** J.E. Murray
**SVP, CFO & Treas:** J.H. Bloem
**SVP & General Counsel:** C.M. Todoroff
**SVP & CIO:** B.J. Goodman

**Investor Contact:** R.C. Nethery (502-580-3644)
**Board Members:** F. A. D'Amelio, W. R. Dunbar, K. J. Hilzinger, D. A. Jones, Jr., M. B. McCallister, W. J. McDonald, W. E. Mitchell, D. B. Nash, J. J. O'Brien, M. T. Peterson

**Founded:** 1964
**Domicile:** Delaware
**Employees:** 35,200

# Huntington Bancshares Inc

**STANDARD &POOR'S**

| S&P Recommendation **BUY** ★★★★☆ | Price $4.86 (as of Nov 29, 2011) | 12-Mo. Target Price $8.00 | Investment Style Large-Cap Blend |
|---|---|---|---|

**GICS Sector** Financials
**Sub-Industry** Regional Banks

**Summary** This regional bank holding company has 671 banking offices in Ohio, Michigan, Pennsylvania, Indiana, West Virginia, Kentucky, Florida.

## Key Stock Statistics (Source S&P, Vickers, company reports)

| | | | | | | |
|---|---|---|---|---|---|---|
| 52-Wk Range | $7.70– 4.46 | S&P Oper. EPS 2011**E** | 0.62 | Market Capitalization(B) | $4.199 | Beta | 1.70 |
| Trailing 12-Month EPS | $0.51 | S&P Oper. EPS 2012**E** | 0.63 | Yield (%) | 3.29 | S&P 3-Yr. Proj. EPS CAGR(%) | 51 |
| Trailing 12-Month P/E | 9.5 | P/E on S&P Oper. EPS 2011**E** | 7.8 | Dividend Rate/Share | $0.16 | S&P Credit Rating | BBB |
| $10K Invested 5 Yrs Ago | $2,281 | Common Shares Outstg. (M) | 864.1 | Institutional Ownership (%) | 68 | | |

## Price Performance

30-Week Mov. Avg. ···· 10-Week Mov. Avg. --- **GAAP Earnings vs. Previous Year** Volume Above Avg.▥ STARS
12-Mo. Target Price — Relative Strength — ▲ Up ▼ Down ▶ No Change Below Avg.▥ ★

Options: CBOE, Ph

Analysis prepared by Equity Analyst **Erik Oja** on Nov 29, 2011, when the stock traded at **$4.86**.

## Highlights

➤ We expect HBAN to earn $1.63 billion of net interest income in 2011, up 0.6% from 2010. In 2011, we expect loan growth of 3.7%, and we see a stable net interest margin. However, for 2012, we expect net interest income to fall 2.1%, on a lower net interest margin. We expect core net revenues, including noninterest income, to fall 4.5% in 2011 and to rise 1.1% in 2012, on a rebound in fee income.

➤ We expect 2011 earnings growth to be driven by declining loan loss provisions. HBAN's September 30 allowance for loan losses, at 180.5% of nonperforming loans and 2.61% of total loans, was well above peers, while nonperforming loans were only 1.45% of total loans, below peers. We think these will give HBAN some leeway for additional reserve releases if credit quality continues to improve as we expect. For 2011, we forecast $445 million of net chargeoffs, below the $868 million recorded in 2010. For 2012, we expect net chargeoffs of $275 million. We expect 2011 loan loss provisions of $175 million, down from $635 million in 2010. For 2012, we expect provisions of $200 million, due to expected loan growth.

➤ We see EPS of $0.62 in 2011 and $0.63 in 2012.

## Investment Rationale/Risk

➤ We think HBAN is in a better position than peers to grow loans in 2011. Most of HBAN's lending portfolio is not in "run-off" mode, unlike at several peers that are still winding down lending. HBAN's commercial construction loans, which are in run-off mode, are only 1.5% of HBAN's loans. However, we expect growth to continue in HBAN's Commercial and Industrial lending (36% of HBAN's loans), which have grown strongly in the past four quarters, up 12.2% from a year earlier. We also see strength in HBAN's home equity lending (21% of lending, up 5.1% from a year ago), and in other consumer loans (16% of lending, up 1.4%). We think HBAN is competitive in loan pricing while maintaining credit quality.

➤ Risks to our recommendation and target price include worsening economic conditions, greater-than-expected loan losses, additional common stock offerings, and lower than expected noninterest income.

➤ Our 12-month target price of $8.00 equals 1.4X our $5.70 estimate of year-end 2011 tangible book value per share. This multiple is above peers, on our positive view of HBAN's growth initiatives.

## Qualitative Risk Assessment

| LOW | MEDIUM | HIGH |
|---|---|---|

Our risk assessment reflects HBAN's Midwestern lending exposure, offset by our view of its recently strengthened capital position, and prospects for improving credit metrics.

## Quantitative Evaluations

**S&P Quality Ranking**   B-

| D | C | B- | B | B+ | A- | A | A+ |
|---|---|---|---|---|---|---|---|

**Relative Strength Rank**   MODERATE

**41**

LOWEST = 1          HIGHEST = 99

## Revenue/Earnings Data

**Revenue (Million $)**

| | 1Q | 2Q | 3Q | 4Q | Year |
|---|---|---|---|---|---|
| 2011 | 738.1 | 747.9 | 749.6 | -- | -- |
| 2010 | 787.6 | 805.3 | 801.8 | 761.2 | 3,200 |
| 2009 | 809.1 | 829.0 | 809.9 | 795.9 | 3,244 |
| 2008 | 971.2 | 933.1 | 853.6 | 729.6 | 3,505 |
| 2007 | 689.1 | 698.7 | 1,056 | 985.0 | 3,420 |
| 2006 | 624.3 | 684.9 | 636.9 | 685.5 | 2,632 |

**Earnings Per Share ($)**

| | | | | | |
|---|---|---|---|---|---|
| 2011 | 0.14 | 0.16 | 0.16 | E0.16 | E0.62 |
| 2010 | 0.01 | 0.03 | 0.10 | 0.05 | 0.19 |
| 2009 | -6.79 | -0.40 | -0.33 | -0.56 | -6.14 |
| 2008 | 0.35 | 0.25 | 0.17 | -1.20 | -0.44 |
| 2007 | 0.40 | 0.34 | 0.38 | -0.65 | 0.25 |
| 2006 | 0.45 | 0.46 | 0.65 | 0.37 | 1.92 |

Fiscal year ended Dec. 31. Next earnings report expected: NA. EPS Estimates based on S&P Operating Earnings; historical GAAP earnings are as reported.

## Dividend Data (Dates: mm/dd Payment Date: mm/dd/yy)

| Amount ($) | Date Decl. | Ex-Div. Date | Stk. of Record | Payment Date |
|---|---|---|---|---|
| 0.010 | 01/19 | 03/16 | 03/18 | 04/01/11 |
| 0.010 | 04/18 | 06/15 | 06/17 | 07/01/11 |
| 0.040 | 07/21 | 09/15 | 09/19 | 10/03/11 |
| 0.040 | 10/20 | 12/16 | 12/20 | 01/03/12 |

Dividends have been paid since 1912. Source: Company reports.

---

**Please read the Required Disclosures and Analyst Certification on the last page of this report.**

*The McGraw·Hill Companies*

# Huntington Bancshares Inc

**STANDARD &POOR'S**

## Business Summary November 29, 2011

CORPORATE OVERVIEW. Huntington Bancshares Inc. (HBAN) is a multi-state diversified regional bank holding company headquartered in Columbus, Ohio. HBAN provides full-service commercial, small business, consumer banking services, mortgage banking services, automobile financing, equipment leasing, investment management, trust services, brokerage services, customized insurance programs, and other financial products and services.

As of June 30, 2011, which is the latest available FDIC branch level data, HBAN had 671 branches and $41.4 billion in deposits, with nearly 65% of deposits and 59% of branches concentrated in Ohio. In Ohio, HBAN had 388 branches, $26.7 billion in deposits, and a 10.6% deposit market share, ranking second. In Michigan, HBAN had 124 branches, $7.1 billion in deposits, and a deposit market share of 3.7%, ranking sixth. In Pennsylvania, HBAN had 62 branches, $2.9 billion in deposits, and a deposit market share of 0.9%, ranking 20th. In Indiana, HBAN had 51 branches, $2.3 billion in deposits, and a deposit market share of slightly under 2.0%, ranking 11th. In West Virginia, HBAN had 30 offices, $1.85 billion in deposits, and a deposit market share of 5.9%, ranking fifth. In Kentucky, HBAN had 14 offices, $470 million in deposits, and a deposit market share of 0.6%, ranking 31st. In addition, HBAN had two offices in

Florida.

HBAN's Retail and Business Banking segment provides financial products and services to consumer and small business customers located within Ohio, Michigan, Pennsylvania, Indiana, West Virginia and Kentucky. Its products include individual and small business checking accounts, savings accounts, money market accounts, certificates of deposit, consumer loans, and small business loans and leases.

The Commercial Banking segment provides a wide array of products and services to the middle market and large corporate client base located primarily within HBAN's core geographic banking markets. Products and services include commercial lending, depository and liquidity management products, treasury management solutions, equipment and technology leasing, international services, and capital markets services.

## Company Financials Fiscal Year Ended Dec. 31

| Per Share Data ($) | 2010 | 2009 | 2008 | 2007 | 2006 | 2005 | 2004 | 2003 | 2002 | 2001 |
|---|---|---|---|---|---|---|---|---|---|---|
| Tangible Book Value | 4.57 | 4.07 | 6.27 | 7.14 | 10.12 | 11.41 | 10.02 | 8.99 | 8.95 | 6.77 |
| Earnings | 0.19 | -6.14 | -0.44 | 0.25 | 1.92 | 1.77 | 1.71 | 1.67 | 1.49 | 0.71 |
| S&P Core Earnings | 0.20 | -1.25 | -0.52 | 0.32 | 1.95 | 1.73 | 1.66 | 1.56 | 0.67 | 0.60 |
| Dividends | 0.04 | 0.04 | 0.04 | 1.06 | 1.00 | 0.85 | 0.75 | 0.67 | 0.64 | 0.72 |
| Payout Ratio | 21% | NM | NM | NM | 52% | 48% | 44% | 40% | 43% | 101% |
| Prices:High | 7.40 | 8.00 | 14.87 | 24.14 | 24.97 | 25.41 | 25.38 | 22.55 | 21.77 | 19.28 |
| Prices:Low | 3.65 | 1.00 | 4.37 | 13.50 | 22.56 | 20.97 | 20.89 | 17.78 | 16.00 | 12.63 |
| P/E Ratio:High | 39 | NM | NM | 97 | 13 | 14 | 15 | 14 | 15 | 27 |
| P/E Ratio:Low | 19 | NM | NM | 54 | 12 | 12 | 12 | 11 | 11 | 18 |

| Income Statement Analysis (Million $) | 2010 | 2009 | 2008 | 2007 | 2006 | 2005 | 2004 | 2003 | 2002 | 2001 |
|---|---|---|---|---|---|---|---|---|---|---|
| Net Interest Income | 1,619 | 1,424 | 1,532 | 1,302 | 1,019 | 962 | 911 | 849 | 984 | 996 |
| Tax Equivalent Adjustment | 11.1 | 11.5 | 20.2 | 19.3 | 16.0 | 13.4 | NA | 9.68 | 5.21 | 6.35 |
| Non Interest Income | 1,042 | 1,006 | 707 | 706 | 634 | 640 | 803 | 1,064 | 680 | 509 |
| Loan Loss Provision | 635 | 2,075 | 1,057 | 644 | 65.2 | 81.3 | 55.1 | 164 | 227 | 309 |
| % Expense/Operating Revenue | 62.9% | 166.0% | 57.0% | 62.5% | 60.0% | 60.5% | 65.5% | 64.3% | 50.6% | 67.4% |
| Pretax Income | 352 | -3,678 | -296 | 22.6 | 514 | 544 | 553 | 524 | 589 | 173 |
| Effective Tax Rate | 11.3% | NM | NM | NM | 10.3% | 24.2% | 27.8% | 26.4% | 38.4% | NM |
| Net Income | 312 | -3,094 | -114 | 75.2 | 461 | 412 | 399 | 386 | 363 | 179 |
| % Net Interest Margin | 3.44 | 3.11 | 3.25 | 3.36 | 3.29 | 3.33 | 3.33 | 3.49 | 4.19 | 4.02 |
| S&P Core Earnings | 144 | -662 | -190 | 96.8 | 467 | 405 | 388 | 360 | 165 | 152 |

| Balance Sheet & Other Financial Data (Million $) | 2010 | 2009 | 2008 | 2007 | 2006 | 2005 | 2004 | 2003 | 2002 | 2001 |
|---|---|---|---|---|---|---|---|---|---|---|
| Money Market Assets | 320 | 403 | 419 | 1,965 | 551 | 105 | 960 | 138 | 86.6 | 118 |
| Investment Securities | 9,895 | 8,588 | 4,384 | 4,500 | 4,363 | 4,527 | 4,239 | 4,929 | 3,411 | 2,862 |
| Commercial Loans | 19,715 | 20,577 | 23,639 | 22,308 | 12,354 | 10,845 | 10,303 | 9,486 | 9,336 | 10,415 |
| Other Loans | 17,142 | 14,731 | 16,553 | 17,746 | 13,799 | 13,627 | 13,257 | 11,590 | 11,619 | 11,187 |
| Total Assets | 53,820 | 51,555 | 54,312 | 54,697 | 35,329 | 32,765 | 32,565 | 30,484 | 27,579 | 28,500 |
| Demand Deposits | 12,686 | 12,797 | 9,560 | 5,372 | 3,616 | 3,390 | 3,392 | 2,987 | 3,074 | 3,741 |
| Time Deposits | 29,168 | 27,697 | 32,466 | 32,371 | 21,432 | 19,020 | 17,376 | 15,500 | 14,425 | 16,446 |
| Long Term Debt | 3,814 | 3,803 | 6,871 | 6,955 | 4,513 | 4,597 | 6,227 | 6,808 | 3,304 | 3,039 |
| Common Equity | 4,618 | 3,648 | 5,349 | 5,949 | 3,014 | 2,594 | 2,538 | 2,275 | 2,304 | 2,416 |
| % Return on Assets | 0.6 | NM | NM | 0.2 | 1.4 | 1.3 | 1.3 | 1.3 | 1.3 | 0.6 |
| % Return on Equity | 7.6 | NM | NM | 1.7 | 16.6 | 16.0 | 16.6 | 17.3 | 15.4 | 7.5 |
| % Loan Loss Reserve | 3.3 | 4.0 | 2.2 | 1.4 | 1.0 | -0.7 | 1.1 | 1.6 | 1.7 | 1.8 |
| % Loans/Deposits | 91.1 | 90.9 | 108.3 | 105.4 | 105.5 | 171.3 | 114.5 | 115.2 | 122.8 | 110.1 |
| % Equity to Assets | 7.8 | 8.5 | 10.4 | 10.0 | 8.2 | 7.8 | 7.6 | 7.7 | 8.4 | 8.4 |

Data as orig reptd.; bef. results of disc opers/spec. items. Per share data adj. for stk. divs.; EPS diluted. E-Estimated. NA-Not Available. NM-Not Meaningful. NR-Not Ranked. UR-Under Review.

**Office:** 41 S High St, Columbus, OH 43287.
**Telephone:** 614-480-8300.
**Website:** http://www.huntington.com
**Chrmn, Pres & CEO:** S.D. Steinour

**COO, EVP, CTO & CIO:** Z. Afzal
**EVP, Chief Acctg Officer & Cntlr:** D.S. Anderson
**CFO & Treas:** D.R. Kimble
**Secy & General Counsel:** R.A. Cheap

**Investor Contact:** D.R. Kimble (614-480-5676)
**Board Members:** D. M. Casto, III, A. B. Crane, S. G. Elliott, M. J. Endres, J. B. Gerlach, Jr., D. J. Hilliker, D. P. Lauer, J. A. Levy, W. J. Lhota, G. P. Mastroianni, R. W. Neu, D. L. Porteous, K. H. Ransier, W. R. Robertson, S. D. Steinour

**Founded:** 1966
**Domicile:** Maryland
**Employees:** 11,341

*The McGraw-Hill Companies*

# Illinois Tool Works Inc.

STANDARD &POOR'S

| S&P Recommendation HOLD ★★★☆☆ | Price $42.58 (as of Nov 25, 2011) | 12-Mo. Target Price $52.00 | Investment Style Large-Cap Growth |
|---|---|---|---|

**GICS Sector** Industrials
**Sub-Industry** Industrial Machinery

**Summary** This diversified manufacturer operates a portfolio of 60 business units that serve the industrial and consumer markets globally.

## Key Stock Statistics (Source S&P, Vickers, company reports)

| | | | | | | | | |
|---|---|---|---|---|---|---|---|---|
| 52-Wk Range | $59.27– 39.12 | S&P Oper. EPS 2011**E** | 3.78 | Market Capitalization(B) | $20.574 | Beta | | 1.12 |
| Trailing 12-Month EPS | $3.98 | S&P Oper. EPS 2012**E** | 4.15 | Yield (%) | 3.38 | S&P 3-Yr. Proj. EPS CAGR(%) | | 9 |
| Trailing 12-Month P/E | 10.7 | P/E on S&P Oper. EPS 2011**E** | 11.3 | Dividend Rate/Share | $1.44 | S&P Credit Rating | | A+ |
| $10K Invested 5 Yrs Ago | $10,228 | Common Shares Outstg. (M) | 483.2 | Institutional Ownership (%) | 81 | | | |

## Price Performance

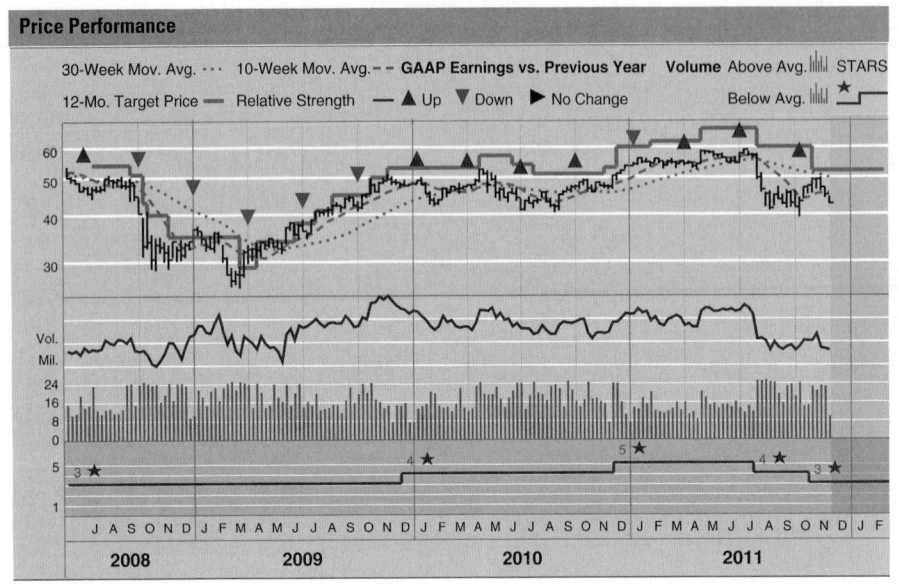

30-Week Mov. Avg. ··· 10-Week Mov. Avg. -- **GAAP Earnings vs. Previous Year** Volume Above Avg. STARS
12-Mo. Target Price — Relative Strength ▲ Up ▼ Down ► No Change Below Avg.

Options: ASE, CBOE, Ph

Analysis prepared by Equity Analyst **R. Tortoriello** on Nov 18, 2011, when the stock traded at **$44.77**.

## Highlights

➤ Following a 14% sales increase in 2010, we estimate that sales will rise 14% in 2011, with growth across all ITW's operating segments. For 2012, we see a deceleration in growth to about 3%, as comparisons become more difficult and we expect slowing economic growth, particularly in Europe. Our outlook is based on our belief that ITW sales will grow on increased global industrial and manufacturing activity, along with the company's focus on increasing its international exposure, especially in countries like China and India.

➤ We estimate that operating margins will rise to 15.3% in 2011, from 14.8% in 2010, on higher volume and efficiency programs. For 2012, we project margins of 15.5%, on further efficiency improvements.

➤ We estimate EPS of $3.78 for 2011, which excludes a tax gain of $0.33 realized in the first quarter, and project EPS of $4.15 for 2012.

## Investment Rationale/Risk

➤ We recently downgraded our recommendation on the shares to hold, from buy, on our expectation of flat growth or outright declines in European markets. However, we see ITW benefiting from continued growth in its end markets; its growth strategy, which focuses on product innovation; a shift to more centralized operations in a number of operational activities versus a decentralized model practiced historically; a focus on penetrating emerging markets and tapping their growth potential; and the build-out of new sales/product platforms.

➤ Risks to our recommendation and target price include lower-than-expected industrial activity and/or capital spending; acquisition execution risk; and a slowing of construction activity and/or automotive markets.

➤ Our 12-month target price of $52 is based on an enterprise value multiple of 8X our 2012 EBITDA estimate of $3.5 billion, below ITW's 10-year historical average EV-EBITDA multiple of approximately 11X, on our view of slowing economic growth.

## Qualitative Risk Assessment

| LOW | MEDIUM | HIGH |
|---|---|---|

Our risk assessment reflects an S&P Quality Ranking of A, indicating a strong long-term record or earnings and dividend growth, and a balance sheet that we see as strong, with total debt of 32% of capital as of September 2011.

## Quantitative Evaluations

**S&P Quality Ranking** A

| D | C | B- | B | B+ | A- | A | A+ |
|---|---|---|---|---|---|---|---|

**Relative Strength Rank** MODERATE

40

LOWEST = 1 HIGHEST = 99

## Revenue/Earnings Data

**Revenue (Million $)**

| | 1Q | 2Q | 3Q | 4Q | Year |
|---|---|---|---|---|---|
| 2011 | 4,388 | 4,615 | 4,581 | -- | -- |
| 2010 | 3,606 | 4,076 | 4,018 | 4,169 | 15,870 |
| 2009 | 2,914 | 3,393 | 3,580 | 3,757 | 13,877 |
| 2008 | 4,139 | 4,570 | 4,148 | 3,678 | 15,869 |
| 2007 | 3,759 | 4,160 | 4,094 | 4,244 | 16,171 |
| 2006 | 3,297 | 3,579 | 3,538 | 3,641 | 14,055 |

**Earnings Per Share ($)**

| | | | | | |
|---|---|---|---|---|---|
| 2011 | 1.24 | 0.96 | 1.00 | E0.90 | E3.78 |
| 2010 | 0.58 | 0.83 | 0.83 | 0.79 | 3.03 |
| 2009 | -0.06 | 0.36 | 0.60 | 0.98 | 1.93 |
| 2008 | 0.57 | 1.01 | 0.85 | 0.54 | 3.04 |
| 2007 | 0.71 | 0.90 | 0.89 | 0.87 | 3.28 |
| 2006 | 0.65 | 0.81 | 0.78 | 0.77 | 3.01 |

Fiscal year ended Dec. 31. Next earnings report expected: Early February. EPS Estimates based on S&P Operating Earnings; historical GAAP earnings are as reported.

## Dividend Data (Dates: mm/dd Payment Date: mm/dd/yy)

| Amount ($) | Date Decl. | Ex-Div. Date | Stk. of Record | Payment Date |
|---|---|---|---|---|
| 0.340 | 02/11 | 03/29 | 03/31 | 04/12/11 |
| 0.340 | 05/06 | 06/28 | 06/30 | 07/12/11 |
| 0.360 | 08/05 | 09/28 | 09/30 | 10/12/11 |
| 0.360 | 10/28 | 12/28 | 12/30 | 01/10/12 |

Dividends have been paid since 1933. Source: Company reports.

---

**Please read the Required Disclosures and Analyst Certification on the last page of this report.**

# Illinois Tool Works Inc.

## Business Summary November 18, 2011

CORPORATE OVERVIEW. Illinois Tool Works (ITW) operates through 60 business units operating in 57 countries in a highly decentralized structure that places responsibility on managers at the lowest level possible, in an attempt to focus each business unit on the needs of particular customers. Each business unit manager is held strictly accountable for the results of his or her individual business. These 60 operating units are aggregated into eight reporting segments, which we detail below:

The Industrial Packaging segment (14.3% of revenues and 10% of operating income in 2010; with 10.3% operating profit margin) produces steel, plastic and paper products used for bundling, shipping and protecting transported goods. In 2010, major markets served were general industrial (24%), primary metals (22%), food and beverage (13%), and construction (9%).

The Power Systems & Electronics segment (12.2% and 17.4%; 21.1%) produces equipment and consumables associated with specialty power conversion, metallurgy, welding, and electronics. In 2010, this segment primarily served the general industrial (46%), electronics (17%) and construction (6%) markets.

The Transportation segment (15.9% and 15.9%; 14.8%) produces components, fasteners, fluids, fillers and putties, truck parts services, and polymers for transportation-related applications. In 2010, this segment primarily served the automotive original equipment manufacturers (61%) and auto aftermarket (25%).

The Construction Products segment (11% and 8.5%; 11.4%) produces fasteners and related fastening tools for wood applications; anchors, fasteners and related tools for concrete and wood applications; metal plate truss components and related equipment and software; and packaged hardware fasteners, anchors and other products for retail. In 2010, this segment primarily served the residential (45%), renovation (28%), and commercial (23%) construction markets.

## Company Financials Fiscal Year Ended Dec. 31

| Per Share Data ($) | 2010 | 2009 | 2008 | 2007 | 2006 | 2005 | 2004 | 2003 | 2002 | 2001 |
|---|---|---|---|---|---|---|---|---|---|---|
| Tangible Book Value | 5.62 | 4.43 | 2.78 | 7.37 | 6.94 | 6.89 | 7.59 | 8.22 | 6.90 | 5.42 |
| Cash Flow | 4.12 | 3.06 | 3.71 | 4.22 | 3.79 | 3.26 | 2.78 | 2.18 | 2.01 | 1.94 |
| Earnings | 3.03 | 1.93 | 3.04 | 3.28 | 3.01 | 2.60 | 2.20 | 1.69 | 1.51 | 1.31 |
| S&P Core Earnings | 3.01 | 2.12 | 2.84 | 3.27 | 3.03 | 2.60 | 2.13 | 1.63 | 1.38 | 1.13 |
| Dividends | 1.30 | 1.24 | 1.18 | 0.98 | 0.92 | 0.61 | 0.52 | 0.47 | 0.45 | 0.42 |
| Payout Ratio | 43% | 64% | 39% | 30% | 30% | 23% | 24% | 28% | 30% | 32% |
| Prices:High | 53.89 | 51.16 | 55.59 | 60.00 | 53.54 | 47.32 | 48.35 | 42.35 | 38.90 | 36.00 |
| Prices:Low | 40.33 | 25.60 | 28.50 | 45.60 | 41.54 | 39.25 | 36.46 | 27.28 | 27.52 | 24.58 |
| P/E Ratio:High | 18 | 27 | 18 | 18 | 18 | 18 | 22 | 25 | 26 | 27 |
| P/E Ratio:Low | 13 | 13 | 9 | 14 | 14 | 15 | 17 | 16 | 18 | 19 |
| **Income Statement Analysis** (Million $) | | | | | | | | | | |
| Revenue | 15,870 | 13,877 | 15,869 | 16,171 | 14,055 | 12,922 | 11,731 | 10,036 | 9,468 | 9,293 |
| Operating Income | 2,901 | 2,060 | 2,690 | 3,147 | 2,865 | 2,558 | 2,410 | 1,940 | 1,812 | 1,692 |
| Depreciation | 547 | 569 | 351 | 523 | 444 | 383 | 353 | 307 | 306 | 386 |
| Interest Expense | 175 | 165 | 152 | 102 | 85.6 | 87.0 | 69.2 | 70.7 | 68.5 | 68.1 |
| Pretax Income | 2,212 | 1,214 | 2,191 | 2,581 | 2,445 | 2,182 | 1,999 | 1,576 | 1,434 | 1,231 |
| Effective Tax Rate | NA | 20.1% | 27.8% | 29.3% | 29.8% | 31.5% | 33.0% | 34.0% | 35.0% | 34.8% |
| Net Income | 1,527 | 969 | 1,583 | 1,826 | 1,718 | 1,495 | 1,340 | 1,040 | 932 | 802 |
| S&P Core Earnings | 1,524 | 1,064 | 1,476 | 1,818 | 1,729 | 1,493 | 1,299 | 1,009 | 851 | 691 |
| **Balance Sheet & Other Financial Data** (Million $) | | | | | | | | | | |
| Cash | 1,190 | 1,319 | 743 | 828 | 590 | 370 | 667 | 1,684 | 1,058 | 282 |
| Current Assets | 5,968 | 5,675 | 5,924 | 6,166 | 5,206 | 4,112 | 4,322 | 4,783 | 3,879 | 3,163 |
| Total Assets | 16,250 | 16,082 | 15,213 | 15,526 | 13,880 | 11,446 | 11,352 | 11,193 | 10,623 | 9,822 |
| Current Liabilities | 3,094 | 2,836 | 4,876 | 2,960 | 2,637 | 2,001 | 1,851 | 1,489 | 1,567 | 1,518 |
| Long Term Debt | 2,512 | 2,915 | 1,244 | 2,299 | 956 | 958 | 921 | 920 | 1,460 | 1,267 |
| Common Equity | 9,370 | 8,808 | 7,663 | 9,351 | 9,018 | 7,547 | 7,628 | 7,874 | 6,649 | 6,041 |
| Total Capital | 11,893 | 11,733 | 9,022 | 11,501 | 9,973 | 8,505 | 8,549 | 8,795 | 8,109 | 7,308 |
| Capital Expenditures | 286 | 247 | 355 | 353 | 301 | 293 | 283 | 258 | 271 | 257 |
| Cash Flow | 2,074 | 1,538 | 1,935 | 2,349 | 2,162 | 1,878 | 1,693 | 1,347 | 1,238 | 1,189 |
| Current Ratio | 1.9 | 2.0 | 1.2 | 2.1 | 2.0 | 2.1 | 2.3 | 3.2 | 2.5 | 2.1 |
| % Long Term Debt of Capitalization | 21.1 | 24.8 | 13.8 | 16.8 | 9.6 | 11.3 | 10.8 | 10.5 | 18.0 | 17.3 |
| % Net Income of Revenue | 9.6 | 7.0 | 10.0 | 11.3 | 12.2 | 11.6 | 11.4 | 10.4 | 9.8 | 8.6 |
| % Return on Assets | 9.5 | 6.2 | 10.3 | 12.4 | 13.6 | 13.1 | 11.9 | 9.5 | 9.1 | 8.3 |
| % Return on Equity | 16.8 | 11.8 | 18.6 | 19.9 | 20.7 | 19.7 | 17.3 | 14.3 | 14.7 | 14.0 |

Data as orig reptd.; bef. results of disc opers/spec. items. Per share data adj. for stk. divs.; EPS diluted. E-Estimated. NA-Not Available. NM-Not Meaningful. NR-Not Ranked. UR-Under Review.

Office: 3600 W. Lake Avenue, Glenview, IL 60026-5811.
Telephone: 847-724-7500.
Website: http://www.itw.com
Chrmn & CEO: D.B. Speer

SVP & CFO: R.D. Kropp
SVP, Secy & General Counsel: J.H. Wooten, Jr.
Chief Acctg Officer: R.J. Scheuneman
Secy & General Counsel: M.C. Green

Investor Contact: J. Brooklier (847-657-4104)
Board Members: S. M. Crown, D. H. Davis, Jr., R. C. McCormack, R. S. Morrison, J. A. Skinner, D. H. Smith, Jr., D. B. Speer, P. B. Strobel, K. M. Warren, A. D. Williams

Founded: 1912
Domicile: Delaware
Employees: 61,000

# Ingersoll-Rand Plc

**STANDARD &POOR'S**

| S&P Recommendation HOLD ★★★☆☆ | Price $30.82 (as of Nov 28, 2011) | 12-Mo. Target Price $30.00 | Investment Style Large-Cap Blend |
|---|---|---|---|

**GICS Sector** Industrials
**Sub-Industry** Industrial Machinery

**Summary** This company manufactures a wide range of industrial and commercial products for uses such as climate control, industrial technology and security.

## Key Stock Statistics (Source S&P, Vickers, company reports)

| | | | | | | | |
|---|---|---|---|---|---|---|---|
| 52-Wk Range | $52.33–25.86 | S&P Oper. EPS 2011E | 2.75 | Market Capitalization(B) | $9.621 | Beta | 1.81 |
| Trailing 12-Month EPS | $0.90 | S&P Oper. EPS 2012E | 2.90 | Yield (%) | 1.56 | S&P 3-Yr. Proj. EPS CAGR(%) | 8 |
| Trailing 12-Month P/E | 34.2 | P/E on S&P Oper. EPS 2011E | 11.2 | Dividend Rate/Share | $0.48 | S&P Credit Rating | NA |
| $10K Invested 5 Yrs Ago | $8,048 | Common Shares Outstg. (M) | 312.2 | Institutional Ownership (%) | 89 | | |

## Price Performance

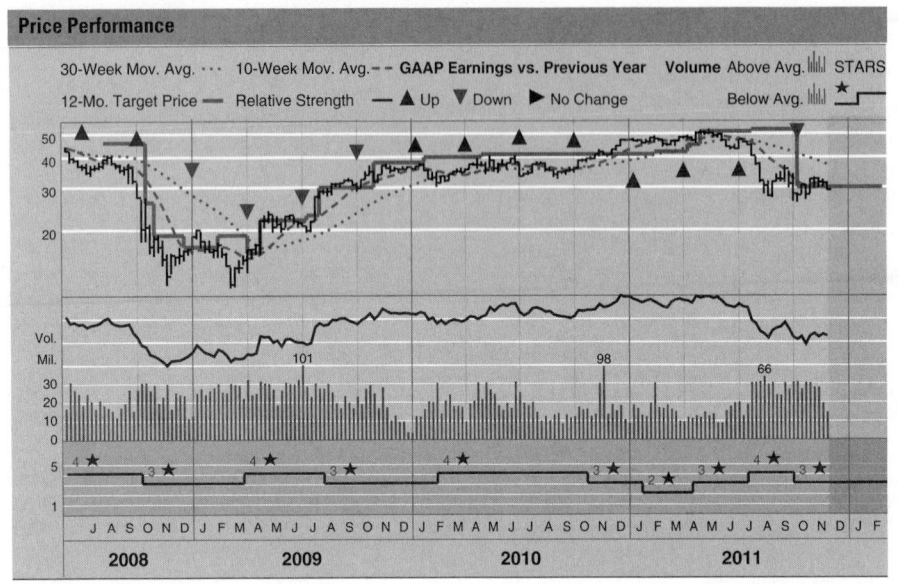

30-Week Mov. Avg. · · · 10-Week Mov. Avg. – – GAAP Earnings vs. Previous Year Volume Above Avg. STARS
12-Mo. Target Price — Relative Strength ▲ Up ▼ Down ▶ No Change Below Avg.

Options: ASE, CBOE, Ph

Analysis prepared by Equity Analyst **R. Tortoriello** on Nov 28, 2011, when the stock traded at **$29.17**.

## Highlights

➤ Following a 6.7% advance in revenues in 2010, we estimate revenues will rise 5% in 2011. This forecast is based on our expectation for continued growth in the global economy leading to improved results at units such as Climate Solutions and Industrial. For 2012, we project a slower revenue increase of about 2%, on gains in all segments except Residential. We expect 2012 results to be held back by a slowing in the rate of growth in the global economy, with particularly weak results projected for Europe.

➤ We estimate operating margins will expand to 10.3% in 2011, from 8.9% in 2010. This projection is based mainly on our expectation for increased operating leverage and cost rationalizations. For 2012, we forecast that IR's operating margins remain flat, on weak demand, particularly in the Residential business.

➤ We estimate EPS of $2.75 in 2011, which excludes a $0.53 charge for impairment/loss on the Hussman sale, rising to $2.90 in 2012.

## Investment Rationale/Risk

➤ In October, IR said that it was "recalibrating" its previous long-term EPS target of $5.00-$5.75 in 2013, due to lack of a residential / non-residential construction recovery in the U.S. and Europe, commodity-price inflation, and a variety of other factors. IR also cited a loophole in the HVAC regulations, which we believe the company was slow to exploit. While we see these factors weighing on results, we also have a more positive view than IR of the global economy, and believe that low historical valuations on IR shares, along with projected economic growth, mean that shares are fairly valued at present.

➤ Risks to our recommendation and target price include a downturn (recession) in the global economy; deceleration in industrial and HVAC market demand growth; and acceleration in commodity costs.

➤ Our 12-month target price of $30 is based on an approximate 10X multiple of our 2012 EPS estimate. This is below IR's 10-year historical average forward P/E of 12.5X, due to our view of slowing economic growth.

## Qualitative Risk Assessment

| LOW | MEDIUM | HIGH |
|---|---|---|

Our risk assessment reflects the cyclical nature of several of IR's major end markets, and an active acquisition strategy, offset by an expanding recurring revenue base and a strong history of cash flow generation.

## Quantitative Evaluations

**S&P Quality Ranking**   NR

| D | C | B- | B | B+ | A- | A | A+ |
|---|---|---|---|---|---|---|---|

**Relative Strength Rank**   MODERATE

58

LOWEST = 1   HIGHEST = 99

## Revenue/Earnings Data

**Revenue (Million $)**

| | 1Q | 2Q | 3Q | 4Q | Year |
|---|---|---|---|---|---|
| 2011 | 31,388 | 3,892 | 3,929 | -- | -- |
| 2010 | 2,953 | 3,703 | 3,730 | 3,712 | 14,079 |
| 2009 | 2,933 | 3,474 | 3,483 | 3,306 | 13,195 |
| 2008 | 2,163 | 3,081 | 4,313 | 3,670 | 13,227 |
| 2007 | 2,668 | 2,225 | 2,239 | 2,323 | 8,763 |
| 2006 | 2,711 | 3,042 | 2,766 | 2,891 | 11,409 |

**Earnings Per Share ($)**

| | | | | | |
|---|---|---|---|---|---|
| 2011 | 0.35 | 0.88 | 0.28 | E0.70 | E2.75 |
| 2010 | 0.04 | 0.76 | 0.80 | 0.62 | 2.23 |
| 2009 | -0.08 | 0.41 | 0.68 | 0.37 | 1.41 |
| 2008 | 0.77 | 0.90 | 0.72 | -10.22 | -8.54 |
| 2007 | 0.70 | 0.68 | 0.68 | 0.62 | 2.48 |
| 2006 | 0.79 | 0.97 | 0.79 | 0.74 | 3.31 |

Fiscal year ended Dec. 31. Next earnings report expected: Early February. EPS Estimates based on S&P Operating Earnings; historical GAAP earnings are as reported.

## Dividend Data (Dates: mm/dd Payment Date: mm/dd/yy)

| Amount ($) | Date Decl. | Ex-Div. Date | Stk. of Record | Payment Date |
|---|---|---|---|---|
| 0.070 | 02/02 | 03/09 | 03/11 | 03/30/11 |
| 0.120 | 04/07 | 06/15 | 06/17 | 06/30/11 |
| 0.120 | 08/05 | 09/09 | 09/13 | 09/30/11 |
| 0.120 | 10/05 | 12/12 | 12/14 | 12/29/11 |

Dividends have been paid since 1910. Source: Company reports.

---

**Please read the Required Disclosures and Analyst Certification on the last page of this report.**

The McGraw·Hill Companies

# Ingersoll-Rand Plc

## Business Summary November 28, 2011

CORPORATE OVERVIEW. Ingersoll-Rand is a diversified global provider of equipment, products and services. The company's offerings include climate control, air conditioning and heating systems used in industrial, commercial and residential markets; tools, pumps, fluid control equipment, air compressors systems, and golf and other utility vehicles used in industrial and commercial applications; and security and safety products used in residential and commercial construction markets. The company reports its results in four segments: Climate Solutions, Residential Solutions, Industrial Technologies, and Security Technologies.

The Climate Solutions segment (55% of 2010 sales; 42.1% of operating profits, with operating profit margins of 7.6%) produces heating, ventilation and air conditioning (HVAC) products and also provides services predominantly for commercial and industrial customers globally. Segment brands include Hussman (being divested; 2010 sales of $800 million), Thermo King and Trane. This segment had 2010 sales of $7.8 billion, an increase of 7.2% versus 2009.

The Residential Solutions unit (15%; 12.9%: 8.6%) contains brands such as American Standard, Schlage and Trane. The segment markets products and services used in residential HVAC and security solutions, mainly in North and South America. Segment sales gained 6% in 2010 and totaled more than $2.1 billion

The Industrial Technologies segment (18%; 21.9%; 12.4%) provides equipment and services to enhance customer industrial efficiency and has offerings in areas such as air solutions, productivity solutions, compressed air systems, power tools, pumps, fluid handling equipment, and golf and utility vehicles. The segment markets to customers globally and contains brands such as Club Car and Ingersoll-Rand. Sales in this segment totaled nearly $2.5 billion in 2010, representing an increase of 14% over 2009 results.

The Security Technologies unit (12%; 23.1%; 19.4%) includes brands such as CISA, LCN, Schlage and Von Duprin. The unit makes locks, door closers, biometric access control systems, exit devices, steel doors and frames, access control systems, and other security devices for the commercial and do-it-yourself markets, electronic security products, exit devices, time and scheduling recording devices, and other security equipment used by a wide range of customers and industries. Segment sales totaled nearly $1.7 billion in 2010, down 2.8% as compared to 2009 sales.

## Company Financials Fiscal Year Ended Dec. 31

| Per Share Data ($) | 2010 | 2009 | 2008 | 2007 | 2006 | 2005 | 2004 | 2003 | 2002 | 2001 |
|---|---|---|---|---|---|---|---|---|---|---|
| Tangible Book Value | NM | NM | NM | 11.70 | 0.21 | 1.60 | 2.54 | NM | NM | NM |
| Cash Flow | 3.59 | 2.55 | -6.96 | 2.95 | 4.10 | 3.66 | 2.81 | 2.28 | 1.68 | 1.83 |
| Earnings | 2.23 | 1.41 | -8.54 | 2.48 | 3.31 | 3.09 | 2.37 | 1.72 | 1.08 | 0.74 |
| Dividends | NA | 0.50 | Nil | 0.18 | 0.68 | 0.57 | 0.44 | 0.36 | 0.34 | 0.34 |
| Payout Ratio | NA | 35% | Nil | 7% | 21% | 18% | 19% | 21% | 31% | 46% |
| Prices:High | 47.50 | 37.60 | 46.84 | 56.66 | 49.00 | 43.96 | 41.45 | 34.10 | 27.20 | 25.14 |
| Prices:Low | 30.12 | 11.46 | 11.75 | 38.25 | 34.95 | 35.13 | 29.52 | 17.26 | 14.85 | 15.20 |
| P/E Ratio:High | 21 | 27 | NM | 23 | 15 | 14 | 18 | 20 | 25 | 34 |
| P/E Ratio:Low | 14 | 8 | NM | 15 | 11 | 11 | 12 | 10 | 14 | 21 |

| Income Statement Analysis (Million $) | 2010 | 2009 | 2008 | 2007 | 2006 | 2005 | 2004 | 2003 | 2002 | 2001 |
|---|---|---|---|---|---|---|---|---|---|---|
| Revenue | 14,079 | 13,195 | 13,227 | 8,763 | 11,409 | 10,547 | 9,394 | 9,876 | 8,951 | 9,682 |
| Operating Income | 1,687 | 1,331 | 1,589 | 1,224 | 1,632 | 1,558 | 1,295 | 1,061 | 891 | 979 |
| Depreciation | 437 | 378 | 453 | 138 | 191 | 196 | 174 | 194 | 206 | 363 |
| Interest Expense | NA | NA | 245 | 136 | 132 | 144 | 153 | 177 | 230 | 253 |
| Pretax Income | 1,007 | 559 | -2,776 | 952 | 1,315 | 1,270 | 984 | 703 | 402 | 263 |
| Effective Tax Rate | NA | 12.8% | NM | 21.5% | 17.6% | 16.1% | 14.1% | 13.4% | 5.05% | NM |
| Net Income | 782 | 463 | -2,567 | 733 | 1,068 | 1,053 | 830 | 594 | 367 | 246 |

| Balance Sheet & Other Financial Data (Million $) | 2010 | 2009 | 2008 | 2007 | 2006 | 2005 | 2004 | 2003 | 2002 | 2001 |
|---|---|---|---|---|---|---|---|---|---|---|
| Cash | 1,014 | 877 | 550 | 4,735 | 363 | 1,037 | 1,704 | 460 | 342 | 121 |
| Current Assets | NA | NA | 5,400 | 7,701 | 4,096 | 4,248 | 4,610 | 3,539 | 4,112 | 3,188 |
| Total Assets | 19,991 | 19,991 | 20,925 | 14,376 | 12,146 | 11,756 | 11,415 | 10,665 | 10,810 | 11,064 |
| Current Liabilities | NA | NA | 5,511 | 3,236 | 3,614 | 3,200 | 2,877 | 3,053 | 3,798 | 2,851 |
| Long Term Debt | 2,922 | 3,220 | 2,774 | 713 | 905 | 1,184 | 1,268 | 1,519 | 2,092 | 2,901 |
| Common Equity | 7,964 | 7,102 | 6,661 | 7,908 | 5,405 | 5,762 | 5,734 | 4,493 | 3,478 | 3,917 |
| Total Capital | 11,797 | 11,296 | 10,084 | 8,718 | 6,310 | 6,946 | 7,001 | 6,133 | 5,685 | 7,098 |
| Capital Expenditures | 180 | 204 | 306 | 120 | 212 | 112 | 109 | 108 | 123 | 201 |
| Cash Flow | 1,219 | 840 | -2,114 | 871 | 1,259 | 1,249 | 1,004 | 788 | 573 | 609 |
| Current Ratio | 1.3 | 1.2 | 1.0 | 2.4 | 1.1 | 1.3 | 1.6 | 1.2 | 1.1 | 1.1 |
| % Long Term Debt of Capitalization | 24.8 | Nil | 27.5 | 8.2 | 14.3 | 17.0 | 18.1 | 24.8 | 36.8 | 40.9 |
| % Net Income of Revenue | 5.6 | 3.5 | NM | 8.4 | 9.4 | 10.0 | 8.8 | 6.0 | 4.1 | 2.5 |
| % Return on Assets | NA | NA | NM | 5.5 | 8.9 | 9.1 | 7.5 | 5.5 | 3.3 | 2.2 |
| % Return on Equity | NA | NA | NM | 11.0 | 19.1 | 18.3 | 16.2 | 14.9 | 9.9 | 6.7 |

Data as orig reptd.; bef. results of disc opers/spec. items. Per share data adj. for stk. divs.; EPS diluted. E-Estimated. NA-Not Available. NM-Not Meaningful. NR-Not Ranked. UR-Under Review.

**Office:** 170/175 Lakeview Drive, Dublin, Ireland HM 11.
**Telephone:** 353 1 870 7400.
**Email:** seekinfo@irco.com
**Website:** http://www.ingersollrand.com

**Chrmn, Pres & CEO:** M.W. Lamach
**SVP & CFO:** S.R. Shawley
**SVP & CTO:** P.A. Camuti
**SVP & General Counsel:** R.L. Katz

**Chief Acctg Officer & Cntlr:** R.J. Weller
**Investor Contact:** B. Brasier
**Board Members:** A. C. Berzin, J. Bruton, J. L. Cohon, G. D. Forsee, P. C. Godsoe, E. E. Hagenlocker, C. J. Horner, M. W. Lamach, T. E. Martin, R. J. Swift, T. L. White

**Founded:** 1905
**Domicile:** Ireland
**Employees:** 59,000

# Integrys Energy Group Inc

**STANDARD &POOR'S**

| S&P Recommendation HOLD ★★★★☆ | Price $49.09 (as of Nov 25, 2011) | 12-Mo. Target Price $49.00 | Investment Style Large-Cap Blend |
|---|---|---|---|

**GICS Sector** Utilities
**Sub-Industry** Multi-Utilities

**Summary** This utility holding company serves about 491,000 regulated electric and 1.7 million regulated gas customers. It also operates an unregulated retail marketing business.

## Key Stock Statistics (Source S&P, Vickers, company reports)

| | | | | | | | |
|---|---|---|---|---|---|---|---|
| 52-Wk Range | $54.02–42.76 | S&P Oper. EPS 2011**E** | 3.37 | Market Capitalization(B) | $3.825 | Beta | 0.88 |
| Trailing 12-Month EPS | $3.30 | S&P Oper. EPS 2012**E** | 3.55 | Yield (%) | 5.54 | S&P 3-Yr. Proj. EPS CAGR(%) | 5 |
| Trailing 12-Month P/E | 14.9 | P/E on S&P Oper. EPS 2011**E** | 14.6 | Dividend Rate/Share | $2.72 | S&P Credit Rating | BBB+ |
| $10K Invested 5 Yrs Ago | $12,470 | Common Shares Outstg. (M) | 77.9 | Institutional Ownership (%) | 51 | | |

## Price Performance

30-Week Mov. Avg. ···· 10-Week Mov. Avg. ‑‑ GAAP Earnings vs. Previous Year    Volume Above Avg. STARS
12-Mo. Target Price — Relative Strength ▲ Up ▼ Down ► No Change    Below Avg. ★

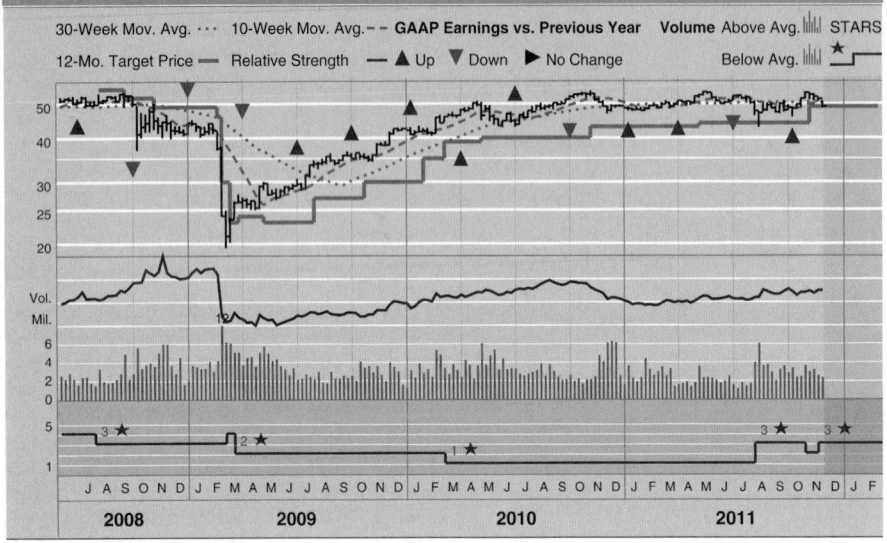

Options: P, Ph

Analysis prepared by Equity Analyst **C. Muir** on Nov 23, 2011, when the stock traded at **$48.72**.

## Highlights

➤ We see 2011 revenues falling 6.4%. We project flat utility revenues, reflecting customer growth and higher rates, offset by lower prices. We estimate an 18% decline in unregulated revenues, reflecting the scaling back of the company's unregulated operations. In 2012, we see revenues rising 2.6% due to 3.5% higher utility revenues and 0.6% higher unregulated revenues.

➤ We forecast operating margins of 9.8% for 2011 and 10.3% for 2012, versus 2010's 8.8%, as we see lower per-revenue fuel costs partly offset by higher per-revenue operations and maintenance expenses this year. Margins are being helped as TEG scales back lower margin unregulated operations. Our pretax profit margin estimates are 8.7% for 2011 and 9.1% for 2012, versus 2010's 7.6%. We see lower interest expense in 2011, partly offset by lower non-operating income.

➤ Our 2011 EPS estimate is $3.37, up 8.0% from 2010's $3.12, which excluded $0.30 of net mark-to-market and nonrecurring charges. We see EPS of $3.55 in 2012, up 5.3%, and $3.65 in 2013, up 2.8%.

## Investment Rationale/Risk

➤ TEG recently completed the scaling back of its unregulated businesses. As a result, it has substantially higher cash balances due to the return of capital, which we think will be used to maintain its dividend as well as to lower debt. TEG also said it would consider stock repurchases with any excess cash. However, we think it will take TEG until 2018 to lower its 96% 2010 payout ratio to about 58%, a level that is more in line with the multi-utility peer average, assuming 5% EPS growth from a 2011 base and no dividend growth.

➤ Risks to our recommendation and target price include lower-than-expected economic activity, merger savings and share repurchases, and higher-than-expected interest rates.

➤ TEG recently traded at 14.0X our 2012 EPS estimate, a 2% premium to multi-utility peers. Our 12-month target price of $49 is 13.8X our 2012 EPS estimate, a slight discount to peers valuation. We think a discounted valuation is warranted by the anticipated absence of dividend growth and the near peer average earnings growth we see.

## Qualitative Risk Assessment

| LOW | MEDIUM | HIGH |
|---|---|---|

Our risk assessment reflects what we see as a balanced portfolio of operations, which includes lower risk gas and electric utility businesses as well as higher risk unregulated retail energy marketing services.

## Quantitative Evaluations

**S&P Quality Ranking**    B

| D | C | B- | B | B+ | A- | A | A+ |
|---|---|---|---|---|---|---|---|

**Relative Strength Rank**    MODERATE

65

LOWEST = 1    HIGHEST = 99

## Revenue/Earnings Data

**Revenue (Million $)**

| | 1Q | 2Q | 3Q | 4Q | Year |
|---|---|---|---|---|---|
| 2011 | 1,627 | 1,011 | 938.7 | -- | -- |
| 2010 | 1,903 | 1,015 | 997.9 | 1,287 | 5,203 |
| 2009 | 3,201 | 1,428 | 1,298 | 1,574 | 7,500 |
| 2008 | 3,989 | 3,417 | 3,223 | 3,418 | 14,048 |
| 2007 | 2,747 | 2,362 | 2,123 | 3,062 | 10,292 |
| 2006 | 1,996 | 1,475 | 1,555 | 1,865 | 6,891 |

**Earnings Per Share ($)**

| | 1Q | 2Q | 3Q | 4Q | Year |
|---|---|---|---|---|---|
| 2011 | 1.56 | 0.38 | 0.47 | E1.00 | E3.37 |
| 2010 | 0.64 | 1.01 | 0.26 | 0.91 | 2.83 |
| 2009 | -2.35 | 0.45 | 0.63 | 0.30 | -0.96 |
| 2008 | 1.77 | -0.31 | -0.77 | 0.27 | 1.58 |
| 2007 | 2.01 | -0.53 | 0.14 | 1.19 | 2.48 |
| 2006 | 1.44 | 0.97 | 0.63 | 0.50 | 3.50 |

Fiscal year ended Dec. 31. Next earnings report expected: Late February. EPS Estimates based on S&P Operating Earnings; historical GAAP earnings are as reported.

## Dividend Data (Dates: mm/dd Payment Date: mm/dd/yy)

| Amount ($) | Date Decl. | Ex-Div. Date | Stk. of Record | Payment Date |
|---|---|---|---|---|
| 0.680 | 02/10 | 02/24 | 02/28 | 03/19/11 |
| 0.680 | 05/11 | 05/26 | 05/31 | 06/20/11 |
| 0.680 | 07/12 | 08/29 | 08/31 | 09/20/11 |
| 0.680 | 11/11 | 11/28 | 11/30 | 12/20/11 |

Dividends have been paid since 1940. Source: Company reports.

# Integrys Energy Group Inc

STANDARD &POOR'S

## Business Summary November 23, 2011

CORPORATE OVERVIEW. Integrys Energy Group (TEG) is a holding company with regulated and unregulated business units. As of December 31, 2010, the company's subsidiaries were organized in three operating segments: electric utility, gas utility, and Integrys Energy Services, Inc. (ESI). A holding company and other segment includes operations that do not fit into the other segments, including nonutility operations of the regulated utilities. In 2010, ESI was the second largest contributor to TEG's revenues, at 35%, although we expect this contribution to continue to decline in 2011 as a result of the sale of part of the business in 2010. The electric utility segment contributed 25%, while the gas utility segment contributed 40%.

The electric utility segment includes the electric operations of Wisconsin Public Service Corporation (WPSC) and Upper Peninsula Power Company (UPPCO). The gas utility segment includes the gas operations of WPSC, Michigan Gas Utilities Corporation (MGUC), Minnesota Energy Resources Corporation (MERC), The Peoples Gas Light and Coke Company (PGL); and North Shore Gas Company (NSG). Integrys Energy Services is an unregulated subsidiary that operates electric generation facilities and energy marketing operations and provides energy generation and management services.

IMPACT OF MAJOR DEVELOPMENTS. On February 25, 2009, TEG announced that it intended to either fully or partially divest its ESI segment, or reduce its size, risk and financial requirements in response to increased collateral requirements. On January 20, 2010, TEG said it had achieved the objectives of its reorganization and decided to retain its retail marketing business. TEG reduced the invested capital at ESI from approximately $1 billion to $300 million as of April 30, 2010. TEG reduced collateral support to its target of $500 million for the retail energy marketing business by the end of 2010 .TEG said it expects the remaining retail business to contribute about 16% of its 2011 EPS and for that segment to increase its earnings at a rate of 6% to 8%, faster than the 3% to 4% growth that we expect at the utility. As a result, TEG has forecast a long-term EPS growth rate of 4% to 6%. The retail segment is also planning to reduce its scope to focus on the northeastern quadrant of the U.S. Longer term, ESI will be a smaller segment that requires significantly less capital, parental guarantees and overall financial liquidity.

## Company Financials Fiscal Year Ended Dec. 31

| Per Share Data ($) | 2010 | 2009 | 2008 | 2007 | 2006 | 2005 | 2004 | 2003 | 2002 | 2001 |
|---|---|---|---|---|---|---|---|---|---|---|
| Tangible Book Value | 29.18 | 29.10 | 28.22 | 29.97 | 28.36 | 31.69 | 29.12 | 27.25 | 24.48 | 22.91 |
| Earnings | 2.83 | -0.96 | 1.58 | 2.48 | 3.50 | 4.11 | 4.07 | 3.24 | 3.42 | 2.74 |
| S&P Core Earnings | 2.90 | 2.43 | 0.73 | 2.49 | 3.58 | 2.86 | 3.82 | 3.12 | 1.48 | 0.99 |
| Dividends | 2.72 | 2.72 | 2.68 | 2.50 | 2.28 | 2.24 | 2.20 | 2.16 | 2.12 | 2.08 |
| Payout Ratio | 96% | NM | 170% | 101% | 62% | 55% | 54% | 67% | 62% | 76% |
| Prices:High | 54.45 | 45.10 | 53.92 | 60.63 | 57.75 | 60.00 | 50.53 | 46.80 | 42.68 | 36.80 |
| Prices:Low | 40.53 | 19.44 | 36.91 | 48.10 | 47.39 | 47.67 | 43.50 | 36.80 | 30.47 | 31.00 |
| P/E Ratio:High | 19 | NM | 34 | 24 | 16 | 15 | 12 | 14 | 12 | 13 |
| P/E Ratio:Low | 14 | NM | 23 | 19 | 13 | 12 | 11 | 11 | 9 | 11 |
| **Income Statement Analysis** (Million $) | | | | | | | | | | |
| Revenue | 5,203 | 7,500 | 14,048 | 10,292 | 6,891 | 6,826 | 4,891 | 4,321 | 2,675 | 2,676 |
| Depreciation | 266 | 231 | 235 | 195 | 106 | 142 | 107 | 138 | 98.0 | 86.6 |
| Maintenance | NA | NA | NA | NA | NA | NA | NA | NA | NA | NA |
| Fixed Charges Coverage | 3.44 | 1.05 | 2.07 | 2.57 | 2.85 | 3.80 | 4.31 | 3.55 | 3.97 | 2.32 |
| Construction Credits | NA | NA | NA | NA | NA | NA | NA | NA | NA | NA |
| Effective Tax Rate | 40.2% | NM | 29.6% | 32.2% | 23.3% | 20.7% | 16.1% | 22.0% | 18.5% | 5.83% |
| Net Income | 220 | -73.7 | 122 | 181 | 152 | 148 | 153 | 114 | 109 | 77.6 |
| S&P Core Earnings | 226 | 186 | 56.4 | 179 | 152 | 111 | 144 | 103 | 47.1 | 28.2 |
| **Balance Sheet & Other Financial Data** (Million $) | | | | | | | | | | |
| Gross Property | 7,914 | 7,792 | 7,483 | 7,066 | 3,961 | 3,099 | 3,308 | 3,065 | 3,186 | 2,979 |
| Capital Expenditures | 259 | 444 | 533 | 393 | 342 | 414 | 290 | 176 | 229 | 249 |
| Net Property | 5,013 | 4,945 | 4,773 | 4,464 | 2,535 | 2,044 | 2,003 | 1,829 | 1,610 | 1,464 |
| Capitalization:Long Term Debt | 2,213 | 2,446 | 2,339 | 2,316 | 1,338 | 918 | 866 | 923 | 926 | 829 |
| Capitalization:% Long Term Debt | 43.2 | 46.1 | 43.0 | 41.7 | 46.6 | 41.3 | 42.0 | 47.9 | 53.7 | 53.7 |
| Capitalization:Preferred | Nil | Nil | Nil | Nil | Nil | Nil | Nil | Nil | Nil | Nil |
| Capitalization:% Preferred | Nil | Nil | Nil | Nil | Nil | Nil | Nil | Nil | Nil | Nil |
| Capitalization:Common | 2,906 | 2,859 | 3,100 | 3,236 | 1,534 | 1,304 | 1,114 | 1,003 | 798 | 716 |
| Capitalization:% Common | 56.8 | 53.9 | 57.0 | 58.3 | 53.4 | 58.7 | 58.0 | 52.1 | 46.3 | 46.3 |
| Total Capital | 5,596 | 5,420 | 5,911 | 6,085 | 2,970 | 2,317 | 2,062 | 2,024 | 1,816 | 1,635 |
| % Operating Ratio | 93.4 | 95.1 | 98.6 | 97.3 | 97.0 | 98.2 | 96.7 | 97.8 | 95.3 | 96.2 |
| % Earned on Net Property | 9.9 | 9.3 | 5.5 | 10.5 | 10.9 | 9.2 | 9.9 | 7.4 | 9.8 | 7.6 |
| % Return on Revenue | 4.2 | NM | 0.9 | 1.8 | 2.2 | 2.2 | 3.1 | 2.6 | 4.1 | 2.9 |
| % Return on Invested Capital | 6.7 | 1.7 | 4.7 | 7.7 | 9.4 | 25.0 | 18.6 | 9.3 | 10.1 | 9.1 |
| % Return on Common Equity | 7.7 | NM | 3.8 | 7.5 | 10.5 | 13.3 | 14.5 | 12.8 | 14.5 | 12.3 |

Data as orig reptd.; bef. results of disc opers/spec. items. Per share data adj. for stk. divs.; EPS diluted. E-Estimated. NA-Not Available. NM-Not Meaningful. NR-Not Ranked. UR-Under Review.

**Office:** 130 East Randolph Drive, Chicago, IL 60601.
**Telephone:** 312-228-5400.
**Email:** investor@integrysgroup.com
**Website:** http://www.integrysgroup.com

**Chrmn, Pres & CEO:** C.A. Schrock
**SVP & CFO:** J.P. O'Leary
**Chief Acctg Officer & Cntlr:** D.L. Ford
**Treas:** W.J. Guc

**Secy & General Counsel:** B.J. Wolf
**Investor Contact:** S.P. Eschbach (312-228-5408)
**Board Members:** K. E. Bailey, W. J. Brodsky, A. J. Budney, Jr., P. S. Cafferty, E. Carnahan, M. L. Collins, K. M. Hasselblad-Pascale, J. W. Higgins, J. L. Kemerling, M. E. Lavin, W. F. Protz, Jr., C. A. Schrock

**Founded:** 1883
**Domicile:** Wisconsin
**Employees:** 4,612

# Intel Corp

STANDARD &POOR'S

| S&P Recommendation HOLD ★★★★★ | Price $22.73 (as of Nov 25, 2011) | 12-Mo. Target Price $27.00 | Investment Style Large-Cap Growth |
|---|---|---|---|

**GICS Sector** Information Technology
**Sub-Industry** Semiconductors

**Summary** This company is the world's largest manufacturer of microprocessors, the central processing units of PCs, and also produces other semiconductor products.

## Key Stock Statistics (Source S&P, Vickers, company reports)

| | | | | | | | |
|---|---|---|---|---|---|---|---|
| 52-Wk Range | $25.50– 19.16 | S&P Oper. EPS 2011E | 2.46 | Market Capitalization(B) | $115.741 | Beta | 1.09 |
| Trailing 12-Month EPS | $2.31 | S&P Oper. EPS 2012E | 2.50 | Yield (%) | 3.70 | S&P 3-Yr. Proj. EPS CAGR(%) | 17 |
| Trailing 12-Month P/E | 9.8 | P/E on S&P Oper. EPS 2011E | 9.2 | Dividend Rate/Share | $0.84 | S&P Credit Rating | A+ |
| $10K Invested 5 Yrs Ago | $12,171 | Common Shares Outstg. (M) | 5,092.0 | Institutional Ownership (%) | 64 | | |

## Price Performance

Options: ASE, CBOE, P, Ph

Analysis prepared by Equity Analyst **Angelo Zino, CFA** on Oct 20, 2011, when the stock traded at **$23.77**.

### Highlights

► We think sales will rise 4.2% in 2012, after a projected 26% increase in 2011, including revenues from its recently acquired wireless and security businesses. We believe IT spending, driven by Microsoft Windows 7, aging computers and bandwidth-consuming applications for PCs and servers, will provide healthy demand for microprocessors. Laptop sales growth should help balance desktop weakness and tablet cannibalization to support top-line advances, in our view. We expect Intel's 32 nanometer (nm) and 22 nm chips to outperform competitors' offerings, which should lead to share gains in higher-end computing segments, helping preserve average selling prices.

► We forecast a gross margin of 63% in 2012, matching our outlook for 2011. We see higher volume and lower start-up costs related to ramp new process technologies, but foresee increasing competition. We see modestly higher expenses for compensation and headcount additions resulting in an operating margin of 32% in 2012, versus an estimated 33% in 2011.

► Our EPS projections assumes an effective tax rates of 28% going forward and modestly decreasing share counts.

### Investment Rationale/Risk

► Our hold opinion is based our view of uninspiring organic growth and fair valuations. Intel has the best competitive position in our semiconductor coverage universe, a solid balance sheet, and strong free cash flows, while carrying lower business and financial risks than most other chipmakers, in our opinion. Although we think that the company will continue to thrive in the PC and server segments, we expect INTC's limited share in fast-growing portable markets to limit top-line advances. Despite what we see as soft consumer PC demand and our cautious stance on the potential success of Ultrabooks, enterprise orders as well as emerging markets remain strong. We believe the stock deserves a slight below-industry multiple given INTC's growth prospects.

► Risks to our recommendation and target price include lower-than-expected demand for PCs, accelerated ASP erosion, and less-than-anticipated traction for INTC's latest chips.

► Our 12-month target price of $27 is based on our P/E analysis. We apply a P/E multiple of 11X, which reflects our view of INTC's relative growth, return on equity, and risk compared to the chip industry, to our 2012 EPS estimate.

### Qualitative Risk Assessment

| LOW | MEDIUM | HIGH |
|---|---|---|

Our risk assessment reflects Intel's exposure to the sales cycles of the semiconductor industry and demand trends for personal computers, offset by its large size, long corporate history, and its low debt levels compared to peers.

### Quantitative Evaluations

**S&P Quality Ranking**      B+

| D | C | B- | B | B+ | A- | A | A+ |
|---|---|---|---|---|---|---|---|

**Relative Strength Rank**      MODERATE

70

LOWEST = 1          HIGHEST = 99

### Revenue/Earnings Data

**Revenue (Million $)**

| | 1Q | 2Q | 3Q | 4Q | Year |
|---|---|---|---|---|---|
| 2011 | 12,847 | 13,032 | 14,233 | -- | -- |
| 2010 | 10,299 | 10,765 | 11,102 | 11,457 | 43,623 |
| 2009 | 7,145 | 8,024 | 9,389 | 10,569 | 35,127 |
| 2008 | 9,673 | 9,470 | 10,217 | 8,226 | 37,586 |
| 2007 | 8,852 | 8,680 | 10,090 | 10,712 | 38,334 |
| 2006 | 8,940 | 8,009 | 8,739 | 9,694 | 35,382 |

**Earnings Per Share ($)**

| | | | | | |
|---|---|---|---|---|---|
| 2011 | 0.56 | 0.54 | 0.65 | E0.71 | E2.46 |
| 2010 | 0.43 | 0.51 | 0.52 | 0.59 | 2.05 |
| 2009 | 0.12 | -0.07 | 0.33 | 0.40 | 0.77 |
| 2008 | 0.25 | 0.28 | 0.35 | 0.04 | 0.92 |
| 2007 | 0.28 | 0.22 | 0.30 | 0.38 | 1.18 |
| 2006 | 0.23 | 0.15 | 0.22 | 0.26 | 0.86 |

Fiscal year ended Dec. 31. Next earnings report expected: NA. EPS Estimates based on S&P Operating Earnings; historical GAAP earnings are as reported.

### Dividend Data (Dates: mm/dd Payment Date: mm/dd/yy)

| Amount ($) | Date Decl. | Ex-Div. Date | Stk. of Record | Payment Date |
|---|---|---|---|---|
| 0.181 | 01/24 | 02/03 | 02/07 | 03/01/11 |
| 0.181 | 03/18 | 05/04 | 05/07 | 06/01/11 |
| 0.210 | 07/27 | 08/03 | 08/07 | 09/01/11 |
| 0.210 | 09/22 | 11/03 | 11/07 | 12/01/11 |

Dividends have been paid since 1992. Source: Company reports.

---

**Please read the Required Disclosures and Analyst Certification on the last page of this report.**

The McGraw·Hill Companies

# Intel Corp

STANDARD &POOR'S

## Business Summary October 20, 2011

CORPORATE OVERVIEW. Intel is the world's largest chipmaker based on revenue and unit shipments, and is well known for its dominant market share in microprocessors for personal computers (PCs). The microprocessor is the central processing unit of the computer system, and acts like "the brain" of the computer. The company also sells chipsets, which it refers to as "the nervous system" in a PC or computing device, sending data between the microprocessor and input, display, and storage devices.

Intel has three main operating segments: PC Client Group, Data Center Group, and Other Intel Architecture.

The PC Client Group (74% of 2010 total sales) makes microprocessors and related chipsets for the notebook, netbook, and desktop segments. This segment also includes motherboards designed for desktop and wireless connectivity products.

The Data Center Group (20%) makes products, including microprocessors, chipsets, motherboards, and wired connectivity devices, that are used in servers, storage, workstations, and other applications that are used in the data center and for cloud computing.

The Other Intel Architecture segments (4%) includes Intel's smaller businesses such as the Embedded and Communications Group, which makes scalable microprocessors and chipsets for various embedded applications, the Ultra-Mobility Group, which offers processors an chipsets for mobile Internet devices, and the Digital Home Group, which produces products for use in various consumer electronics devices.

MARKET PROFILE. The microprocessor market accounts for about 15% of the total semiconductor industry's revenues, and is dominated by two companies, Intel and Advanced Micro Devices (AMD). The two competitors have battled for preeminence in the segment for decades. Several years ago, as AMD improved its product line and cut prices, Intel lost market share and, in 2006, experienced notable earnings decreases. But later that year, Intel started to turn the tide by improving its product development, manufacturing, and cost structure. Regaining market share, Intel now ships over 80% of the world's microprocessors, and is still the clear leader in this space. It has accomplished this by extending its leadership in key technologies that have provided competitive advantages. Manufacturing technology enables it to produce chips with more transistors at a lower cost. As a result, the technology has led to improved profitability, which in 2010 was the highest in several years.

## Company Financials Fiscal Year Ended Dec. 31

| Per Share Data ($) | 2010 | 2009 | 2008 | 2007 | 2006 | 2005 | 2004 | 2003 | 2002 | 2001 |
|---|---|---|---|---|---|---|---|---|---|---|
| Tangible Book Value | 7.99 | 6.59 | 6.18 | 6.51 | 5.70 | 5.46 | 5.57 | 5.26 | 4.74 | 4.59 |
| Cash Flow | 2.83 | 1.67 | 1.72 | 1.98 | 1.65 | 2.15 | 1.91 | 1.62 | 1.25 | 1.13 |
| Earnings | 2.01 | 0.77 | 0.92 | 1.18 | 0.86 | 1.40 | 1.16 | 0.85 | 0.46 | 0.19 |
| S&P Core Earnings | 2.01 | 0.94 | 0.96 | 1.18 | 0.77 | 1.22 | 0.99 | 0.83 | 0.35 | 0.11 |
| Dividends | 0.63 | 0.56 | 0.55 | 0.45 | 0.40 | 0.32 | 0.16 | 0.08 | 0.08 | 0.08 |
| Payout Ratio | 31% | 73% | 60% | 38% | 47% | 23% | 14% | 9% | 17% | 42% |
| Prices:High | 24.37 | 21.27 | 26.34 | 27.99 | 26.63 | 28.84 | 34.60 | 34.51 | 36.78 | 38.59 |
| Prices:Low | 17.60 | 12.05 | 12.06 | 18.75 | 16.75 | 21.94 | 19.64 | 14.88 | 12.95 | 18.96 |
| P/E Ratio:High | 12 | 28 | 29 | 24 | 31 | 21 | 30 | 41 | 80 | NM |
| P/E Ratio:Low | 9 | 16 | 13 | 16 | 19 | 16 | 17 | 18 | 28 | NM |

| Income Statement Analysis (Million $) | 2010 | 2009 | 2008 | 2007 | 2006 | 2005 | 2004 | 2003 | 2002 | 2001 |
|---|---|---|---|---|---|---|---|---|---|---|
| Revenue | 43,623 | 35,127 | 37,586 | 38,334 | 35,382 | 38,826 | 34,209 | 30,141 | 26,764 | 26,539 |
| Operating Income | 20,488 | 13,691 | 14,283 | 13,643 | 10,861 | 16,685 | 15,019 | 13,225 | 9,746 | 8,923 |
| Depreciation | 4,638 | 5,052 | 4,619 | 4,798 | 4,654 | 4,595 | 4,889 | 5,070 | 5,344 | 6,469 |
| Interest Expense | NA | 1.00 | 8.00 | 15.0 | 1,202 | 19.0 | 50.0 | 62.0 | 84.0 | 56.0 |
| Pretax Income | 16,045 | 5,704 | 7,686 | 9,166 | 7,068 | 12,610 | 10,417 | 7,442 | 4,204 | 2,183 |
| Effective Tax Rate | NA | 23.4% | 31.2% | 23.9% | 28.6% | 31.3% | 27.8% | 24.2% | 25.9% | 40.9% |
| Net Income | 11,464 | 4,369 | 5,292 | 6,976 | 5,044 | 8,664 | 7,516 | 5,641 | 3,117 | 1,291 |
| S&P Core Earnings | 11,519 | 5,325 | 5,521 | 6,978 | 4,518 | 7,555 | 6,374 | 5,467 | 2,332 | 740 |

| Balance Sheet & Other Financial Data (Million $) | 2010 | 2009 | 2008 | 2007 | 2006 | 2005 | 2004 | 2003 | 2002 | 2001 |
|---|---|---|---|---|---|---|---|---|---|---|
| Cash | 21,885 | 13,920 | 11,843 | 15,363 | 6,598 | 7,324 | 8,407 | 7,971 | 7,404 | 7,970 |
| Current Assets | 31,563 | 21,157 | 19,871 | 23,885 | 18,280 | 21,194 | 24,058 | 22,882 | 18,925 | 17,633 |
| Total Assets | 63,138 | 53,095 | 50,715 | 55,651 | 48,368 | 48,314 | 48,143 | 47,143 | 44,224 | 44,395 |
| Current Liabilities | 9,070 | 7,591 | 7,818 | 8,571 | 8,514 | 9,234 | 8,006 | 6,879 | 6,595 | 6,570 |
| Long Term Debt | 2,077 | 2,049 | 1,886 | 1,980 | 1,848 | 2,106 | 703 | 936 | 929 | 1,050 |
| Common Equity | 49,638 | 41,704 | 39,088 | 42,762 | 36,752 | 36,182 | 38,579 | 37,846 | 35,468 | 35,830 |
| Total Capital | 51,715 | 43,753 | 41,020 | 45,153 | 38,865 | 38,991 | 40,137 | 40,264 | 37,629 | 37,825 |
| Capital Expenditures | 5,207 | 4,515 | 5,197 | 5,000 | 5,779 | 5,818 | 3,843 | 3,656 | 4,703 | 7,309 |
| Cash Flow | 16,102 | 9,421 | 9,911 | 11,774 | 9,698 | 13,259 | 12,405 | 10,711 | 8,461 | 7,760 |
| Current Ratio | 3.5 | 2.8 | 2.5 | 2.8 | 2.1 | 2.3 | 3.0 | 3.3 | 2.9 | 2.7 |
| % Long Term Debt of Capitalization | 4.0 | 4.7 | 4.6 | 4.4 | 4.8 | 5.4 | 1.8 | 2.3 | 2.5 | 2.8 |
| % Net Income of Revenue | 26.8 | 12.4 | 14.1 | 18.2 | 14.3 | 22.3 | 22.0 | 18.7 | 11.6 | 4.9 |
| % Return on Assets | 20.1 | 8.4 | 10.0 | 13.4 | 10.4 | 18.0 | 15.8 | 12.3 | 7.0 | 2.8 |
| % Return on Equity | 25.6 | 10.8 | 12.9 | 17.6 | 13.8 | 23.2 | 19.7 | 15.4 | 8.7 | 3.5 |

Data as orig reptd.; bef. results of disc opers/spec. items. Per share data adj. for stk. divs.; EPS diluted. E-Estimated. NA-Not Available. NM-Not Meaningful. NR-Not Ranked. UR-Under Review.

**Office:** 2200 Mission College Boulevard, Santa Clara, CA 95054-1549.
**Telephone:** 408-765-8080.
**Website:** http://www.intc.com
**Chrmn:** J.E. Shaw

**Pres & CEO:** P.S. Otellini
**Vice Chrmn, EVP & Chief Admin Officer:** A.D. Bryant
**SVP, CFO & Chief Acctg Officer:** S.J. Smith
**SVP & General Counsel:** A.D. Melamed

**Investor Contact:** R. Gallegos (408-765-5374)
**Board Members:** C. Barshefsky, A. D. Bryant, S. L. Decker, J. J. Donahoe, R. E. Hundt, P. S. Otellini, J. D. Plummer, D. S. Pottruck, J. E. Shaw, F. D. Yeary, D. B. Yoffie

**Founded:** 1968
**Domicile:** Delaware
**Employees:** 82,500

# IntercontinentalExchange Inc

**STANDARD &POOR'S**

| S&P Recommendation **BUY** ★★★★☆ | Price<br>$113.78 (as of Nov 25, 2011) | 12-Mo. Target Price<br>$154.00 | Investment Style<br>Large-Cap Growth |
|---|---|---|---|

**GICS Sector** Financials
**Sub-Industry** Specialized Finance

**Summary** ICE is a fully electronic marketplace that offers exchange-based and over-the-counter trading of a variety of energy and soft commodity products.

## Key Stock Statistics (Source S&P, Vickers, company reports)

| | | | | | | | |
|---|---|---|---|---|---|---|---|
| 52-Wk Range | $135.38– 102.57 | S&P Oper. EPS 2011**E** | 6.89 | Market Capitalization(B) | $8.266 | Beta | 1.06 |
| Trailing 12-Month EPS | $6.51 | S&P Oper. EPS 2012**E** | 7.68 | Yield (%) | Nil | S&P 3-Yr. Proj. EPS CAGR(%) | 16 |
| Trailing 12-Month P/E | 17.5 | P/E on S&P Oper. EPS 2011**E** | 16.5 | Dividend Rate/Share | Nil | S&P Credit Rating | NA |
| $10K Invested 5 Yrs Ago | $10,930 | Common Shares Outstg. (M) | 72.7 | Institutional Ownership (%) | 91 | | |

## Price Performance

30-Week Mov. Avg. ···  10-Week Mov. Avg. -- **GAAP Earnings vs. Previous Year**  Volume Above Avg. STARS
12-Mo. Target Price — Relative Strength ▲ Up ▼ Down ▶ No Change  Below Avg.

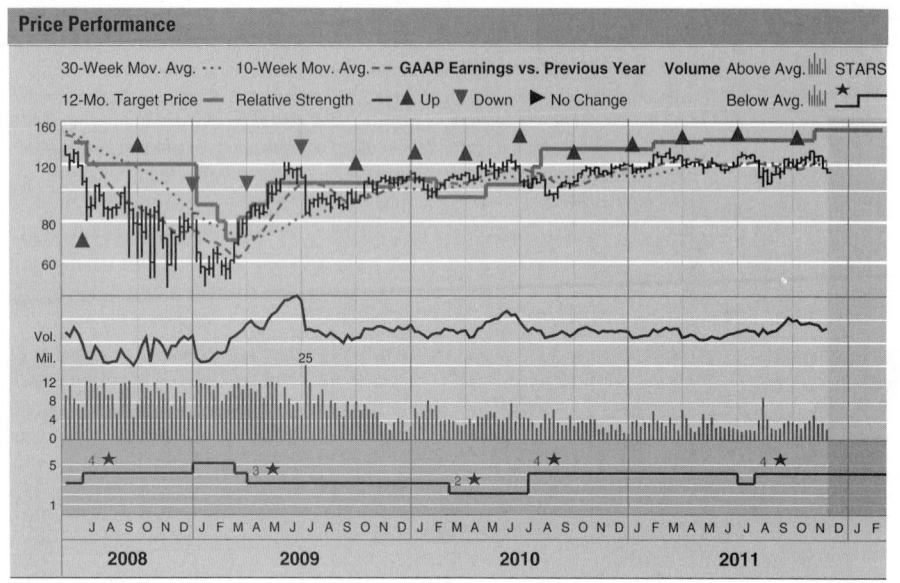

Options: ASE, CBOE, P, Ph

Analysis prepared by Equity Analyst **Robert McMillan** on Nov 03, 2011, when the stock traded at **$127.81**.

## Highlights

➤ After a 16% rise in revenue in 2010, we forecast growth of about 13% in 2011 and 16% in 2012. We expect an increase in trading volume in 2011 driven by strength in the popular U.K.-based oil futures contracts and the U.S. derivatives business as well as increased trading driven by higher volatility amid concerns about sovereign risk and global economic growth. We also see additional revenues from the new credit default swap clearing business and the recently acquired Climate Exchange Plc. During the 2011 third quarter, average daily volume for all ICE futures contracts rose 27% from a year earlier.

➤ We expect total expenses in 2011 and 2012 to increase, but we see them remaining under control, which should allow the net income margin to expand in both years. We expect management to continue to make acquisitions that should increase the heft and diversification of ICE's footprint around the world.

➤ We estimate operating EPS of $6.89 in 2011 and $7.68 in 2012, excluding one-time items.

## Investment Rationale/Risk

➤ In the short term, we believe ICE has an advantage over competitors in the credit default swap clearing business, as we see its platform generating higher trading volumes. We think the recently acquired Climate Exchange will be accretive to EPS in 2011, based on our outlook for leveraging the company's existing resources. While we see a recovery in trading volumes in 2011 and 2012, we believe they will remain below historical levels.

➤ Risks to our recommendation and target price include greater-than-expected competition in the credit default swap clearing business, a significant decline in trading volumes, regulation of position limits on derivatives contracts, and a slowdown in the macroeconomic environment.

➤ Our 12-month target price of $154 is 20.2X our forward four-quarter EPS estimate of $7.65; the shares recently traded at about 16.7X this estimate. We see the valuation multiple widening to a level in line with recent historical levels, driven by expected continued growth in trading volumes as well as expected market share gains as ICE enters new markets.

## Qualitative Risk Assessment

| LOW | MEDIUM | HIGH |
|---|---|---|

Our risk assessment reflects the volatility of energy product trading volumes, recent acquisition activity in the sector, and a changing regulatory environment.

## Quantitative Evaluations

**S&P Quality Ranking** NR

| D | C | B- | B | B+ | A- | A | A+ |
|---|---|---|---|---|---|---|---|

**Relative Strength Rank** MODERATE

46

LOWEST = 1    HIGHEST = 99

## Revenue/Earnings Data

**Revenue (Million $)**

| | 1Q | 2Q | 3Q | 4Q | Year |
|---|---|---|---|---|---|
| 2011 | 334.3 | 325.2 | 340.8 | -- | -- |
| 2010 | 281.6 | 296.2 | 287.2 | 285.0 | 1,150 |
| 2009 | 231.6 | 250.4 | 256.3 | 256.6 | 994.8 |
| 2008 | 207.2 | 197.2 | 201.4 | 207.3 | 813.1 |
| 2007 | 126.6 | 136.7 | 151.7 | 159.3 | 574.3 |
| 2006 | 73.59 | 73.59 | 94.66 | 95.26 | 313.8 |

**Earnings Per Share ($)**

| | 1Q | 2Q | 3Q | 4Q | Year |
|---|---|---|---|---|---|
| 2011 | 1.74 | 1.64 | 1.80 | E1.57 | E6.89 |
| 2010 | 1.36 | 1.36 | 1.29 | 1.34 | 5.35 |
| 2009 | 0.98 | 0.97 | 1.18 | 1.13 | 4.27 |
| 2008 | 1.29 | 1.19 | 1.04 | 0.67 | 4.17 |
| 2007 | 0.80 | 0.75 | 0.93 | 0.90 | 3.39 |
| 2006 | 0.33 | 0.52 | 0.73 | 0.81 | 2.40 |

Fiscal year ended Dec. 31. Next earnings report expected: Early February. EPS Estimates based on S&P Operating Earnings; historical GAAP earnings are as reported.

## Dividend Data

No cash dividends have been paid.

# IntercontinentalExchange Inc

**STANDARD &POOR'S**

## Business Summary November 03, 2011

CORPORATE OVERVIEW. IntercontinentalExchange, Inc. operates a fully electronic marketplace offering exchange-based and over-the-counter (OTC) trading of a variety of energy products, and is the leading global exchange for soft commodities. The company's primary products include futures contracts for Brent crude oil and West Texas Intermediate crude oil, OTC trading of Henry Hub natural gas contracts, and various soft commodity futures. ICE provides trading for financial settlement and contracts for physical delivery of the underlying commodity. In addition, the company provides clearing services for credit default swaps.

ICE was formed in May 2000 to provide a platform for OTC energy trading. In June 2001, the company acquired the International Petroleum Exchange (IPE), which was mainly a floor-based futures exchange. In early 2002, the company introduced the industry's first cleared OTC contract through its partnership with LCH.Clearnet. In April 2005, ICE closed the IPE trading floor and moved to an entirely electronic marketplace. In January 2007, ICE acquired the New York Board of Trade (NYBOT) for approximately $1.1 billion. NYBOT, which has been renamed ICE Futures U.S., is a leading soft commodity exchange for products such as sugar, coffee, cocoa, orange juice, pulp and cotton, as well as several financial products.

In 2010, ICE derived approximately 89% of its revenue from transaction fees associated with trading its products on its exchange and OTC platforms. ICE generates a majority of its trading commissions from a relatively small amount of crude, gas oil, and North American power futures and OTC contracts. The remaining 11% of 2010 revenues is dominated by the market data business. This business provides various data products covering the company's energy futures, OTC markets, agricultural commodities, equity indexes, and currencies.

COMPETITIVE LANDSCAPE. ICE's principal competitor in the energy market is the New York Mercantile Exchange (NYMEX). In August 2008, NYMEX merged with the Chicago Mercantile Exchange. ICE also faces global competition from a number of natural gas and power exchanges and OTC brokers. We believe competition is based on a number of factors, including the depth and liquidity of markets, transaction costs, reliability, and clearing and settlement support.

## Company Financials Fiscal Year Ended Dec. 31

| Per Share Data ($) | 2010 | 2009 | 2008 | 2007 | 2006 | 2005 | 2004 | 2003 | 2002 | 2001 |
|---|---|---|---|---|---|---|---|---|---|---|
| Tangible Book Value | NM | 3.15 | NM | NM | 6.42 | 2.82 | 2.56 | NA | NA | NA |
| Cash Flow | 6.77 | 5.50 | 5.03 | 3.85 | 2.63 | 1.04 | 0.73 | 0.72 | 0.89 | NA |
| Earnings | 5.35 | 4.27 | 4.17 | 3.39 | 2.40 | 0.39 | 0.41 | 0.37 | 0.37 | NA |
| S&P Core Earnings | 5.35 | 4.26 | 4.31 | 3.30 | 2.39 | 0.82 | 0.32 | 0.18 | NA | NA |
| Dividends | Nil | Nil | Nil | Nil | Nil | Nil | NA | NA | NA | NA |
| Payout Ratio | Nil | Nil | Nil | Nil | Nil | Nil | NA | NA | NA | NA |
| Prices:High | 129.53 | 121.93 | 193.87 | 194.92 | 113.85 | 44.21 | NA | NA | NA | NA |
| Prices:Low | 92.18 | 50.10 | 49.69 | 108.15 | 36.00 | 26.00 | NA | NA | NA | NA |
| P/E Ratio:High | 24 | 29 | 46 | 57 | 47 | NM | NA | NA | NA | NA |
| P/E Ratio:Low | 17 | 12 | 12 | 32 | 15 | NM | NA | NA | NA | NA |

| Income Statement Analysis (Million $) | | | | | | | | | | |
|---|---|---|---|---|---|---|---|---|---|---|
| Revenue | 1,150 | 995 | 813 | 574 | 314 | 156 | 108 | 93.7 | 125 | NA |
| Operating Income | 779 | 617 | 556 | 397 | 218 | 91.1 | 49.4 | 38.3 | 65.3 | NA |
| Depreciation | 96.6 | 91.4 | 62.3 | 32.7 | 13.7 | 15.1 | 17.0 | 19.3 | 14.4 | NA |
| Interest Expense | 29.8 | 22.9 | 19.6 | 18.6 | 0.23 | 0.61 | 0.14 | 0.08 | 0.40 | NA |
| Pretax Income | 610 | 494 | 474 | 358 | 213 | 60.0 | 33.7 | 19.9 | 25.4 | NA |
| Effective Tax Rate | NA | 36.4% | 36.4% | 32.9% | 32.6% | 32.6% | 34.7% | 32.7% | 33.8% | NA |
| Net Income | 408 | 316 | 301 | 241 | 143 | 40.4 | 21.9 | 13.4 | 34.7 | NA |
| S&P Core Earnings | 398 | 315 | 311 | 234 | 143 | 43.8 | 17.0 | 9.81 | NA | NA |

| Balance Sheet & Other Financial Data (Million $) | | | | | | | | | | |
|---|---|---|---|---|---|---|---|---|---|---|
| Cash | 624 | 554 | 287 | 280 | 204 | 32.6 | 89.2 | 56.9 | NA | NA |
| Current Assets | 23,576 | 19,460 | 12,553 | 1,142 | 341 | 164 | 100 | 106 | NA | NA |
| Total Assets | 26,642 | 21,885 | 14,960 | 2,796 | 493 | 266 | 208 | 215 | NA | NA |
| Current Liabilities | 23,127 | 18,968 | 12,312 | 911 | 37.9 | 26.4 | 34.4 | 17.9 | NA | NA |
| Long Term Debt | 326 | 209 | 336 | 184 | Nil | Nil | Nil | NA | NA | NA |
| Common Equity | 2,778 | 2,400 | 2,006 | 1,477 | 454 | 233 | 221 | 186 | NA | NA |
| Total Capital | 3,434 | 2,741 | 2,544 | 1,770 | 454 | 238 | 221 | 186 | NA | NA |
| Capital Expenditures | 21.8 | 24.4 | 30.5 | 43.3 | 12.4 | 8.61 | 1.70 | 1.61 | 14.8 | NA |
| Cash Flow | 504 | 407 | 363 | 273 | 157 | 55.5 | 38.9 | 39.3 | 49.1 | NA |
| Current Ratio | 1.0 | 1.0 | 1.0 | 1.3 | 9.0 | 6.2 | 2.9 | 5.9 | NA | NA |
| % Long Term Debt of Capitalization | 9.5 | 7.6 | 13.2 | 10.4 | Nil | Nil | Nil | Nil | Nil | NA |
| % Net Income of Revenue | 35.5 | 31.8 | 37.0 | 41.9 | 45.5 | 25.9 | 20.3 | 14.3 | 27.8 | NA |
| % Return on Assets | 1.7 | 1.7 | 3.4 | 14.6 | 37.7 | NM | 10.4 | NA | NA | NA |
| % Return on Equity | 15.8 | 14.3 | 17.3 | 24.9 | 41.6 | NM | 13.1 | NA | NA | NA |

Data as orig reptd.; bef. results of disc opers/spec. items. Per share data adj. for stk. divs.; EPS diluted. E-Estimated. NA-Not Available. NM-Not Meaningful. NR-Not Ranked. UR-Under Review.

**Office:** 2100 RiverEdge Parkway, Atlanta, GA 30328.
**Telephone:** 770-857-4700.
**Email:** ir@theice.com
**Website:** http://www.theice.com

**Chrmn & CEO:** J.C. Sprecher
**Pres & COO:** C.A. Vice
**SVP, CFO & Chief Acctg Officer:** S.A. Hill
**SVP & CTO:** E.D. Marcial

**SVP, Secy & General Counsel:** J.H. Short
**Investor Contact:** K. Loeffler (770-857-4726)
**Board Members:** C. R. Crisp, J. Forneri, J. A. Gregg, F. W. Hatfield, T. F. Martell, M. C. McCarthy Callum, R. Reid, F. V. Salerno, J. C. Sprecher, J. Sprieser, V. Tese

**Founded:** 2000
**Domicile:** Delaware
**Employees:** 933

# International Business Machines Corp

**STANDARD &POOR'S**

| S&P Recommendation **STRONG BUY** ★★★★★ | Price $177.06 (as of Nov 25, 2011) | 12-Mo. Target Price $205.00 | Investment Style Large-Cap Growth |

**GICS Sector** Information Technology
**Sub-Industry** IT Consulting & Other Services

**Summary** IBM's global capabilities include information technology services, software, computer hardware equipment, fundamental research, and related financing.

## Key Stock Statistics (Source S&P, Vickers, company reports)

| | | | | | | | |
|---|---|---|---|---|---|---|---|
| 52-Wk Range | $190.53– 141.28 | S&P Oper. EPS 2011E | 13.40 | Market Capitalization(B) | $208.686 | Beta | 0.67 |
| Trailing 12-Month EPS | $12.69 | S&P Oper. EPS 2012E | 14.91 | Yield (%) | 1.69 | S&P 3-Yr. Proj. EPS CAGR(%) | 13 |
| Trailing 12-Month P/E | 14.0 | P/E on S&P Oper. EPS 2011E | 13.2 | Dividend Rate/Share | $3.00 | S&P Credit Rating | A+ |
| $10K Invested 5 Yrs Ago | $20,694 | Common Shares Outstg. (M) | 1,178.6 | Institutional Ownership (%) | 57 | | |

## Price Performance

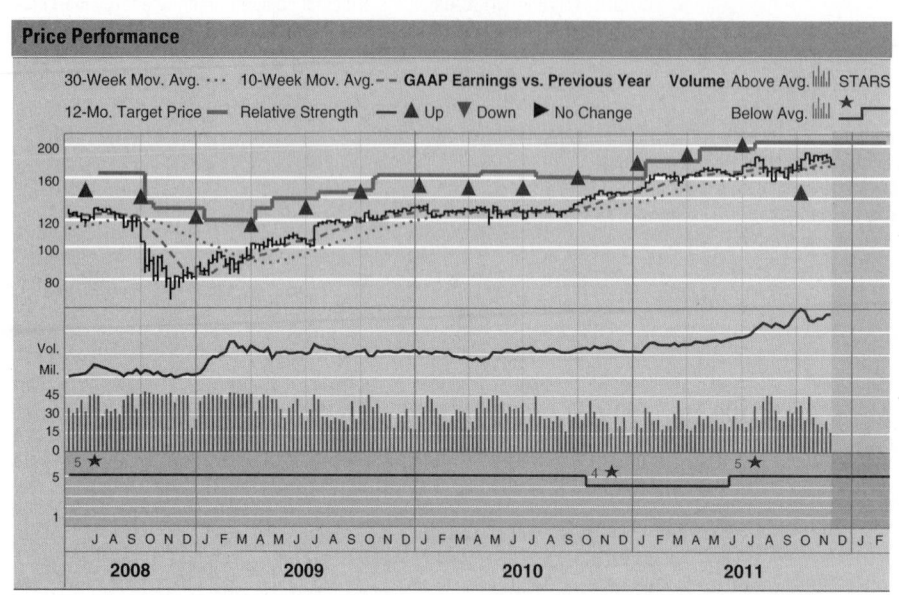

- 30-Week Mov. Avg. ··· 10-Week Mov. Avg. - - **GAAP Earnings vs. Previous Year** Volume Above Avg. STARS
- 12-Mo. Target Price — Relative Strength — ▲ Up ▼ Down ▶ No Change Below Avg. ★

Options: ASE, CBOE, P, Ph

Analysis prepared by Equity Analyst **Dylan Cathers** on Oct 18, 2011, when the stock traded at **$178.12**.

## Qualitative Risk Assessment

| LOW | **MEDIUM** | HIGH |

Our risk assessment reflects what we view as IBM's competitively positioned solutions offerings, global market presence, and significant economies of scale, offset by what we see as an intensely competitive pricing environment.

## Quantitative Evaluations

**S&P Quality Ranking**        A+

| D | C | B- | B | B+ | A- | A | **A+** |

**Relative Strength Rank**        **STRONG**

71

LOWEST = 1        HIGHEST = 99

## Revenue/Earnings Data

**Revenue (Million $)**

| | 1Q | 2Q | 3Q | 4Q | Year |
|---|---|---|---|---|---|
| 2011 | 24,607 | 26,666 | 26,157 | -- | -- |
| 2010 | 25,857 | 23,724 | 24,271 | 29,019 | 99,870 |
| 2009 | 21,711 | 23,250 | 23,566 | 27,230 | 95,758 |
| 2008 | 24,502 | 26,820 | 25,302 | 27,006 | 103,630 |
| 2007 | 22,029 | 23,772 | 24,119 | 28,866 | 98,786 |
| 2006 | 20,659 | 21,890 | 22,617 | 26,257 | 91,424 |

**Earnings Per Share ($)**

| | | | | | |
|---|---|---|---|---|---|
| 2011 | 2.31 | 3.00 | 3.19 | E4.62 | E13.40 |
| 2010 | 1.97 | 2.61 | 2.82 | 4.18 | 11.52 |
| 2009 | 1.70 | 2.32 | 2.40 | 3.59 | 10.01 |
| 2008 | 1.65 | 1.98 | 2.05 | 3.28 | 8.93 |
| 2007 | 1.21 | 1.55 | 1.68 | 2.80 | 7.18 |
| 2006 | 1.08 | 1.30 | 1.45 | 2.30 | 6.06 |

Fiscal year ended Dec. 31. Next earnings report expected: NA. EPS Estimates based on S&P Operating Earnings; historical GAAP earnings are as reported.

## Highlights

▶ We expect revenues to rise about 7.5% in 2011 and 3.5% in 2012. The solid gain we see this year reflects healthy performance in the first three quarters. However, we have some concerns about the global economy. We are also concerned about a lessening of the favorable currency translation rates IBM has been enjoying, as the U.S. dollar is strengthening. We think that demand for software will remain robust; this segment should also benefit from recent acquisitions. Growth in emerging markets should remain in the low double digits, in our view. The Global Business Services segment will likely continue to be hurt by softness from the public sector, and Systems and Technology has a difficult comparison.

▶ We look for gross margins to widen modestly this year and next, reflecting ongoing cost reduction efforts and an improved sales mix. Effective tax rates should benefit from more international business.

▶ We estimate operating EPS of $13.40 for 2011 and $14.91 for 2012. The company spent about $15 billion on share repurchases in the 12 months ended September, and we expect share buybacks to bolster EPS going forward.

## Investment Rationale/Risk

▶ Despite our near-term concerns about IBM's revenue growth, we have a strong buy recommendation on the shares as we believe the company is well positioned to weather any economic storms that may arise, given its diversity. We think that healthy gains in the majority of the company's segments will help drive earnings per share, as will a robust share buyback program and a lower tax rate. A dividend yield recently near 1.7% adds appeal, in our view.

▶ Risks to our recommendation and target price include pricing pressure and other competitive risks, the potential for product transitions to go less smoothly than we project, and the possibility that antitrust and other lawsuits could hamper results.

▶ Our 12-month target price of $205 reflects a target multiple of 13.7X, which is in the upper half of the five-year historical range for IBM, applied to our 2012 EPS estimate of $14.91. Our target P/E is above a recent P/E of 11.9X for Information Technology Sector companies in the S&P 500 Index based on 2012 earnings estimates. We view the stock's valuation as compelling, given IBM's economies of scale and relatively steady earnings performance.

## Dividend Data (Dates: mm/dd Payment Date: mm/dd/yy)

| Amount ($) | Date Decl. | Ex-Div. Date | Stk. of Record | Payment Date |
|---|---|---|---|---|
| 0.650 | 01/25 | 02/08 | 02/10 | 03/10/11 |
| 0.750 | 04/26 | 05/06 | 05/10 | 06/10/11 |
| 0.750 | 07/26 | 08/08 | 08/10 | 09/10/11 |
| 0.750 | 10/25 | 11/08 | 11/10 | 12/10/11 |

Dividends have been paid since 1916. Source: Company reports.

---

**Please read the Required Disclosures and Analyst Certification on the last page of this report.**

*The McGraw-Hill Companies*

# International Business Machines Corp

**STANDARD &POOR'S**

## Business Summary October 18, 2011

CORPORATE OVERVIEW. With a corporate history dating back to 1911, International Business Machines has grown to be a major contributor to each major category that comprises the total information technology market: hardware, software, and services. The company is a leading server vendor, among the largest software vendors (behind Microsoft Corp.), and has the largest global services organization.

The company strives for innovation as a means of product differentiation, and had a research and development budget of $6.0 billion in 2010, up from $5.8 billion in 2009, which is approximately 6% of revenue for each year. IBM reports being awarded 5,896 patents in 2010, more than any other company.

The company operates in over 170 countries. The global scope of operations is reflected in the mix of revenue sources in 2010, with the Americas representing about 43%, EMEA (Europe, Middle East and Africa) 33%, and Asia Pacific 24%. Regional revenue performance was strongest in Asia Pacific in 2010. The company's revenue from the so-called BRIC countries (Brazil, Russia, India and China) grew 23% in 2010.

CORPORATE STRATEGY. IBM has evolved from being a computer hardware vendor to a systems, services and software company that focuses on integrated solutions. While computer hardware (included in the Systems and Technology segment) accounted for about 18% of sales in 2010 (17% of sales in 2009), IBM has emphasized -- through acquisitions and investments -- services and software. These areas serving adjacent markets to hardware have gained momentum as IBM leverages its ability to offer total solutions to customers. IBM's focus on higher value added segments such as services, at almost 57% of 2010 sales (58% of 2009 sales), and software 23% (23%) resulted in these areas together representing about 80% of revenue in 2010 (81%). Global financing represented approximately 2% (2%) of 2010 revenues, and is primarily used to leverage IBM's financial structuring and portfolio management, and to expand the customer base.

## Company Financials Fiscal Year Ended Dec. 31

| Per Share Data ($) | 2010 | 2009 | 2008 | 2007 | 2006 | 2005 | 2004 | 2003 | 2002 | 2001 |
|---|---|---|---|---|---|---|---|---|---|---|
| Tangible Book Value | NM | NM | NM | 8.72 | 8.93 | 13.97 | 11.86 | 12.36 | 10.84 | 12.96 |
| Cash Flow | 15.27 | 13.73 | 12.49 | 10.22 | 9.39 | 8.10 | 7.82 | 7.01 | 5.61 | 7.08 |
| Earnings | 11.52 | 10.01 | 8.93 | 7.18 | 6.06 | 4.91 | 4.94 | 4.34 | 3.07 | 4.35 |
| S&P Core Earnings | 10.78 | 9.43 | 6.04 | 6.94 | 5.88 | 3.93 | 4.06 | 3.00 | 0.08 | 1.33 |
| Dividends | 2.50 | 2.15 | 1.90 | 1.50 | 1.10 | 0.78 | 0.70 | 0.63 | 0.59 | 0.55 |
| Payout Ratio | 22% | 21% | 21% | 21% | 18% | 16% | 14% | 15% | 19% | 13% |
| Prices:High | 147.53 | 132.85 | 130.93 | 121.46 | 97.88 | 99.10 | 100.43 | 94.54 | 126.39 | 124.70 |
| Prices:Low | 116.00 | 81.76 | 69.50 | 88.77 | 72.73 | 71.85 | 90.82 | 73.17 | 54.01 | 83.75 |
| P/E Ratio:High | 13 | 13 | 15 | 17 | 16 | 20 | 20 | 22 | 41 | 29 |
| P/E Ratio:Low | 10 | 8 | 8 | 12 | 12 | 15 | 18 | 17 | 18 | 19 |

| Income Statement Analysis (Million $) | | | | | | | | | | |
|---|---|---|---|---|---|---|---|---|---|---|
| Revenue | 99,870 | 95,757 | 103,630 | 98,786 | 91,424 | 91,134 | 96,293 | 89,131 | 81,186 | 85,866 |
| Operating Income | 24,100 | 23,660 | 21,680 | 18,765 | 16,912 | 14,564 | 15,890 | 14,790 | 11,175 | 14,115 |
| Depreciation | 4,831 | 4,994 | 4,930 | 4,405 | 4,983 | 5,188 | 4,915 | 4,701 | 4,379 | 4,820 |
| Interest Expense | 368 | 402 | 1,477 | 1,431 | 278 | 220 | 139 | 145 | 145 | 238 |
| Pretax Income | 19,723 | 18,138 | 16,715 | 14,489 | 13,317 | 12,226 | 12,028 | 10,874 | 7,524 | 10,953 |
| Effective Tax Rate | NA | 26.0% | 26.2% | 28.1% | 29.3% | 34.6% | 29.8% | 30.0% | 29.1% | 29.5% |
| Net Income | 14,833 | 13,425 | 12,334 | 10,418 | 9,416 | 7,994 | 8,448 | 7,613 | 5,334 | 7,723 |
| S&P Core Earnings | 13,883 | 12,648 | 8,340 | 10,072 | 9,116 | 6,395 | 6,923 | 5,270 | 111 | 2,302 |

| Balance Sheet & Other Financial Data (Million $) | | | | | | | | | | |
|---|---|---|---|---|---|---|---|---|---|---|
| Cash | 11,651 | 13,974 | 12,907 | 16,146 | 10,656 | 13,686 | 10,570 | 7,647 | 5,975 | 6,393 |
| Current Assets | 48,116 | 48,935 | 49,004 | 53,177 | 44,660 | 45,661 | 46,970 | 44,998 | 41,652 | 42,461 |
| Total Assets | 113,452 | 109,022 | 109,524 | 120,431 | 103,234 | 105,748 | 109,183 | 104,457 | 96,484 | 88,313 |
| Current Liabilities | 40,562 | 36,002 | 42,435 | 44,310 | 40,091 | 35,152 | 39,798 | 37,900 | 34,550 | 35,119 |
| Long Term Debt | 21,846 | 21,932 | 22,689 | 23,039 | 13,780 | 15,425 | 14,828 | 16,986 | 19,986 | 15,963 |
| Common Equity | 23,046 | 22,637 | 13,465 | 28,470 | 28,506 | 33,098 | 29,747 | 27,864 | 22,782 | 23,614 |
| Total Capital | 45,018 | 44,687 | 45,096 | 51,509 | 42,286 | 48,523 | 44,575 | 44,850 | 42,768 | 39,577 |
| Capital Expenditures | 4,185 | 3,447 | 4,171 | 4,630 | 4,362 | 3,842 | 4,368 | 4,393 | 4,753 | 5,660 |
| Cash Flow | 19,664 | 18,419 | 17,264 | 14,823 | 14,399 | 13,182 | 13,363 | 12,314 | 9,713 | 12,533 |
| Current Ratio | 1.2 | 1.4 | 1.2 | 1.2 | 1.1 | 1.3 | 1.2 | 1.2 | 1.2 | 1.2 |
| % Long Term Debt of Capitalization | 48.5 | 49.1 | 71.6 | 44.7 | 32.6 | 31.7 | 33.3 | 37.9 | 46.7 | 40.3 |
| % Net Income of Revenue | 14.9 | 14.0 | 11.9 | 10.6 | 10.3 | 8.8 | 8.8 | 8.5 | 6.6 | 9.0 |
| % Return on Assets | 13.3 | 12.3 | 10.7 | 9.3 | 9.0 | 7.4 | 7.9 | 7.6 | 5.7 | 8.7 |
| % Return on Equity | 64.9 | 74.4 | 58.8 | 36.6 | 30.6 | 24.7 | 29.3 | 30.1 | 23.1 | 35.1 |

Data as orig reptd.; bef. results of disc opers/spec. items. Per share data adj. for stk. divs.; EPS diluted. E-Estimated. NA-Not Available. NM-Not Meaningful. NR-Not Ranked. UR-Under Review.

**Office:** 1 New Orchard Road, Armonk, NY 10504-1722.
**Telephone:** 914-499-1900.
**Website:** http://www.ibm.com
**Chrmn, Pres & CEO:** S.J. Palmisano

**SVP & CFO:** M. Loughridge
**SVP & General Counsel:** R.C. Weber
**CTO:** R.C. Adkins
**Treas:** R. DelBene

**Investor Contact:** T.S. Shaughnessy (914-499-1900)
**Board Members:** A. J. Belda, W. R. Brody, K. I. Chenault, M. L. Eskew, S. A. Jackson, A. N. Liveris, W. J. McNerney, Jr., J. W. Owens, S. J. Palmisano, J. E. Spero, S. Taurel, L. H. Zambrano

**Founded:** 1910
**Domicile:** New York
**Employees:** 426,751

*The McGraw-Hill Companies*

# International Flavors & Fragrances Inc.

STANDARD &POOR'S

| S&P Recommendation HOLD ★★★☆☆ | Price $51.62 (as of Nov 25, 2011) | 12-Mo. Target Price $60.00 | Investment Style Large-Cap Growth |
|---|---|---|---|

**GICS Sector** Materials
**Sub-Industry** Specialty Chemicals

**Summary** This leading producer of flavors and fragrances used in a wide variety of consumer goods derives over 75% of sales from operations outside the U.S.

## Key Stock Statistics (Source S&P, Vickers, company reports)

| | | | | | |
|---|---|---|---|---|---|
| 52-Wk Range | $66.29– 51.45 | S&P Oper. EPS 2011**E** | 3.85 | Market Capitalization(B) | $4.176 | Beta | 0.91 |
| Trailing 12-Month EPS | $3.64 | S&P Oper. EPS 2012**E** | 4.25 | Yield (%) | 2.40 | S&P 3-Yr. Proj. EPS CAGR(%) | 10 |
| Trailing 12-Month P/E | 14.2 | P/E on S&P Oper. EPS 2011**E** | 13.4 | Dividend Rate/Share | $1.24 | S&P Credit Rating | BBB |
| $10K Invested 5 Yrs Ago | $12,103 | Common Shares Outstg. (M) | 80.9 | Institutional Ownership (%) | 85 | | |

## Price Performance

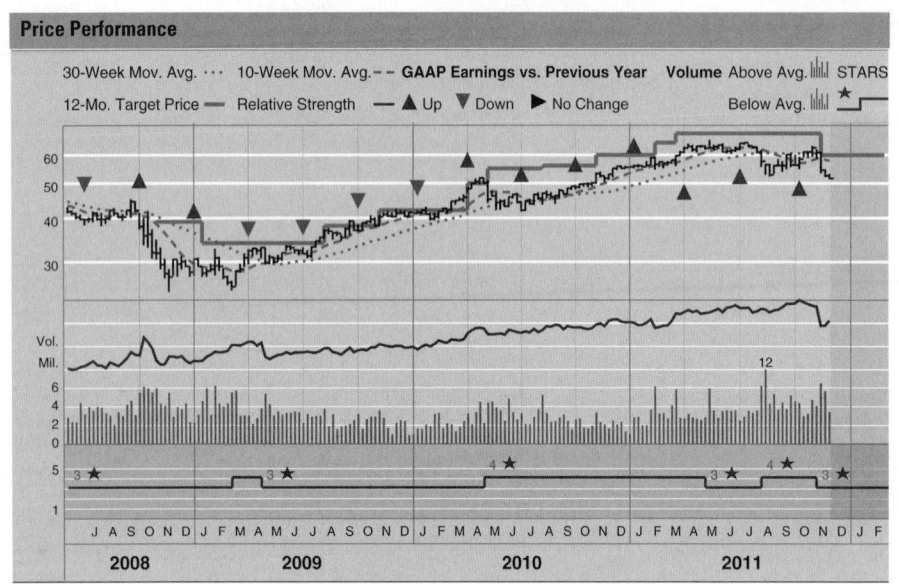

30-Week Mov. Avg. ··· 10-Week Mov. Avg. – – GAAP Earnings vs. Previous Year  Volume Above Avg. STARS
12-Mo. Target Price — Relative Strength — ▲ Up ▼ Down ► No Change  Below Avg.

Options: CBOE

## Highlights

► The STARS recommendation for IFF has recently been changed to 3 (hold) from 4 (buy) and the 12-month target price has recently been changed to $60.00 from $69.00. The Highlights section of this Stock Report will be updated accordingly.

## Investment Rationale/Risk

► The Investment Rationale/Risk section of this Stock Report will be updated shortly. For the latest News story on IFF from MarketScope, see below.

► 11/08/11 02:41 pm ET ... S&P LOWERS VIEW ON SHARES OF INTERNATIONAL FLAVORS & FRAGRANCES TO HOLD FROM BUY (IFF 55.01***): Q3 EPS of $1.00, vs. $0.98 before $0.03 of 1X charges, is $0.03 above our estimate, but $0.04 below Capital IQ consensus. Efforts to protect margins from higher raw material costs in the Ingredients business through price hikes led to volume losses greater than IFF expected, perhaps in part to more price aggressiveness than employed by peers. While such aggressiveness may generate above-peer margins in the long term, we are concerned that volume loss headwinds will continue near term. Applying average historical forward multiples, we cut our 12-month target price by $9 to $60. /Stewart Glickman, CFA

## Qualitative Risk Assessment

| LOW | MEDIUM | HIGH |
|---|---|---|

Our risk assessment reflects our view of the stable nature of the company's businesses and end markets, and its leadership product positions, offset by a somewhat concentrated customer base.

## Quantitative Evaluations

**S&P Quality Ranking**  A

| D | C | B- | B | B+ | A- | A | A+ |
|---|---|---|---|---|---|---|---|

**Relative Strength Rank**  MODERATE

33

LOWEST = 1    HIGHEST = 99

## Revenue/Earnings Data

**Revenue (Million $)**

| | 1Q | 2Q | 3Q | 4Q | Year |
|---|---|---|---|---|---|
| 2011 | 714.3 | 715.6 | 713.8 | -- | -- |
| 2010 | 653.9 | 665.8 | 673.3 | 629.9 | 2,623 |
| 2009 | 599.6 | 568.3 | 612.6 | 585.6 | 2,326 |
| 2008 | 596.6 | 636.1 | 617.5 | 539.1 | 2,389 |
| 2007 | 566.1 | 573.7 | 583.3 | 553.5 | 2,277 |
| 2006 | 511.4 | 530.5 | 539.1 | 514.3 | 2,095 |

**Earnings Per Share ($)**

| | 1Q | 2Q | 3Q | 4Q | Year |
|---|---|---|---|---|---|
| 2011 | 1.03 | 0.93 | 1.00 | E0.87 | E3.85 |
| 2010 | 0.80 | 0.83 | 0.95 | 0.68 | 3.26 |
| 2009 | 0.60 | 0.60 | 0.66 | 0.59 | 2.46 |
| 2008 | 0.69 | 0.83 | 0.73 | 0.62 | 2.87 |
| 2007 | 0.69 | 0.87 | 0.67 | 0.58 | 2.82 |
| 2006 | 0.58 | 0.67 | 0.70 | 0.53 | 2.48 |

Fiscal year ended Dec. 31. Next earnings report expected: Mid February. EPS Estimates based on S&P Operating Earnings; historical GAAP earnings are as reported.

## Dividend Data (Dates: mm/dd Payment Date: mm/dd/yy)

| Amount ($) | Date Decl. | Ex-Div. Date | Stk. of Record | Payment Date |
|---|---|---|---|---|
| 0.270 | 05/03 | 06/20 | 06/22 | 07/06/11 |
| 0.310 | 07/26 | 09/19 | 09/21 | 10/05/11 |
| 0.310 | 07/26 | 09/19 | 09/21 | 10/05/11 |
| 0.310 | 10/25 | 12/23 | 12/28 | 01/10/12 |

Dividends have been paid since 1956. Source: Company reports.

The McGraw-Hill Companies

# International Flavors & Fragrances Inc.

## Business Summary August 10, 2011

CORPORATE OVERVIEW. International Flavors & Fragrances, founded in 1909, is a leading global maker of products used by other manufacturers to enhance the aromas and tastes of consumer products.

IFF receives more than 75% of its sales outside the U.S. In 2010, North America contributed 25% of sales; Europe 34%; Latin America 15%; and Asia-Pacific 26%. About 56% of sales in 2010 occurred in the developed markets of North America, Western Europe and Australasia.

Fragrance products accounted for 54% of sales and 49% of operating profits in 2010. Fragrances are used in the manufacture of soaps, detergents, cosmetic creams, lotions and powders, lipsticks, after shave lotions, deodorants, hair preparations, air fresheners, perfumes and colognes and other consumer products. Most major global and regional companies in these industries are IFF customers. Cosmetics (including perfumes and toiletries) and household products (soaps and detergents) are the two largest customer groups.

Flavor products account for IFF's remaining sales and profits. Flavors are sold principally to the food, beverage and other industries for use in consumer products such as soft drinks, candies, baked goods, desserts, prepared foods,

dietary foods, dairy products, drink powders, pharmaceuticals, oral care products, and alcoholic beverages. Two of the largest customers for flavor products are major U.S. producers of prepared foods and beverages.

By category, 46% of sales in 2010 were from flavor compounds, 23% functional fragrances (for personal care and household products, including soaps, detergents, and fabric care), 19% fine fragrances and beauty care (perfumes, colognes, hair care and toiletries), and 12% ingredients.

The company uses both synthetic and natural ingredients in its compounds. IFF manufactures most of the synthetic ingredients, of which a substantial portion (45%) is sold to others. It has had a consistent commitment to R&D spending, spending 8.0% to 8.5% of annual revenues on research and development activities for each of the three years through 2010. R&D is conducted in 33 laboratories in 26 countries.

## Company Financials Fiscal Year Ended Dec. 31

| Per Share Data ($) | 2010 | 2009 | 2008 | 2007 | 2006 | 2005 | 2004 | 2003 | 2002 | 2001 |
|---|---|---|---|---|---|---|---|---|---|---|
| Tangible Book Value | 3.55 | 0.21 | NM | NM | 1.78 | 1.54 | 1.28 | NM | NM | NM |
| Cash Flow | 4.26 | 3.46 | 3.82 | 3.77 | 3.46 | 3.07 | 3.01 | 2.77 | 2.72 | 2.47 |
| Earnings | 3.26 | 2.46 | 2.87 | 2.82 | 2.48 | 2.04 | 2.05 | 1.83 | 1.84 | 1.20 |
| S&P Core Earnings | 3.30 | 2.45 | 2.29 | 2.75 | 2.35 | 2.04 | 1.82 | 1.70 | 1.37 | 0.70 |
| Dividends | 1.04 | 1.00 | 0.96 | 0.88 | 0.77 | 0.73 | 0.69 | 0.63 | 0.60 | 0.60 |
| Payout Ratio | 32% | 41% | 33% | 31% | 31% | 36% | 33% | 34% | 33% | 50% |
| Prices:High | 56.10 | 42.58 | 48.01 | 54.75 | 49.88 | 42.90 | 43.20 | 36.61 | 37.45 | 31.69 |
| Prices:Low | 39.28 | 24.96 | 24.72 | 45.71 | 32.53 | 31.19 | 32.77 | 29.18 | 26.05 | 19.75 |
| P/E Ratio:High | 17 | 17 | 17 | 19 | 20 | 21 | 21 | 20 | 20 | 26 |
| P/E Ratio:Low | 12 | 10 | 9 | 16 | 13 | 15 | 16 | 16 | 14 | 16 |

| Income Statement Analysis (Million $) | | | | | | | | | | |
|---|---|---|---|---|---|---|---|---|---|---|
| Revenue | 2,623 | 2,326 | 2,389 | 2,277 | 2,095 | 1,993 | 2,034 | 1,902 | 1,809 | 1,844 |
| Operating Income | 506 | 443 | 452 | 452 | 421 | 382 | 433 | 415 | 396 | 409 |
| Depreciation | 79.2 | 78.5 | 76.0 | 82.8 | 89.7 | 91.9 | 91.0 | 86.7 | 84.5 | 123 |
| Interest Expense | 48.7 | 61.8 | 74.0 | 41.5 | 25.5 | 24.0 | 24.0 | 28.5 | 37.0 | 70.4 |
| Pretax Income | 360 | 277 | 281 | 329 | 313 | 246 | 281 | 252 | 266 | 188 |
| Effective Tax Rate | NA | 29.3% | 18.1% | 24.8% | 27.7% | 21.6% | 30.2% | 31.5% | 34.0% | 38.2% |
| Net Income | 264 | 196 | 230 | 247 | 227 | 193 | 196 | 173 | 176 | 116 |
| S&P Core Earnings | 265 | 195 | 183 | 241 | 214 | 193 | 174 | 161 | 131 | 68.5 |

| Balance Sheet & Other Financial Data (Million $) | | | | | | | | | | |
|---|---|---|---|---|---|---|---|---|---|---|
| Cash | 131 | 80.1 | 179 | 152 | 115 | 273 | 32.6 | 12.1 | 14.9 | 48.5 |
| Current Assets | 1,325 | 1,128 | 1,161 | 1,190 | 1,080 | 1,191 | 961 | 903 | 867 | 896 |
| Total Assets | 2,872 | 2,645 | 2,762 | 2,727 | 2,479 | 2,638 | 2,363 | 2,307 | 2,233 | 2,268 |
| Current Liabilities | 661 | 484 | 451 | 539 | 447 | 1,203 | 400 | 526 | 359 | 560 |
| Long Term Debt | 788 | 935 | 1,154 | 1,060 | 791 | 131 | 669 | 690 | 1,007 | 939 |
| Common Equity | 1,003 | 772 | 573 | 617 | 873 | 915 | 910 | 743 | 575 | 524 |
| Total Capital | 1,791 | 1,707 | 1,727 | 1,677 | 1,665 | 1,047 | 1,579 | 1,433 | 1,582 | 1,508 |
| Capital Expenditures | 106 | 66.8 | 85.4 | 65.6 | 58.3 | 93.4 | 70.6 | 6.40 | 81.8 | 52.0 |
| Cash Flow | 343 | 274 | 306 | 330 | 316 | 285 | 287 | 259 | 260 | 239 |
| Current Ratio | 2.0 | 2.3 | 2.6 | 2.2 | 2.4 | 1.0 | 2.4 | 1.7 | 2.4 | 1.6 |
| % Long Term Debt of Capitalization | 44.0 | 54.8 | 66.8 | 63.2 | 47.5 | 12.5 | 42.4 | 48.2 | 63.7 | 62.3 |
| % Net Income of Revenue | 10.1 | 8.4 | 9.6 | 10.9 | 10.8 | 9.7 | 9.6 | 9.1 | 9.7 | 6.3 |
| % Return on Assets | 9.6 | 7.3 | 8.4 | 9.1 | 8.9 | 7.7 | 8.4 | 7.6 | 7.8 | 4.9 |
| % Return on Equity | 29.7 | 29.1 | 38.6 | 33.2 | 26.0 | 21.1 | 23.7 | 26.2 | 32.0 | 20.1 |

Data as orig reptd.; bef. results of disc opers/spec. items. Per share data adj. for stk. divs.; EPS diluted. E-Estimated. NA-Not Available. NM-Not Meaningful. NR-Not Ranked. UR-Under Review.

**Office:** 521 West 57th Street, New York, NY 10019-2960.
**Telephone:** 212-765-5500.
**Email:** investor.relations@iff.com
**Website:** http://www.iff.com

**Pres:** B.M. Tansky
**CEO:** D.D. Tough
**SVP, Secy & General Counsel:** A. Chwat
**CFO:** K.C. Berryman

**Investor Contact:** M. DeVeau (212-708-7164)
**Board Members:** M. H. Adame, M. V. Bottoli, L. B. Buck, J. M. Cook, R. W. Ferguson, Jr., A. Fibig, A. A. Herzan, H. W. Howell, Jr., K. M. Hudson, A. C. Martinez, D. F. Morrison, D. D. Tough

**Founded:** 1909
**Domicile:** New York
**Employees:** 5,514

# International Game Technology

STANDARD &POOR'S

| S&P Recommendation | HOLD ★★★★★ | Price $16.31 (as of Nov 25, 2011) | 12-Mo. Target Price $19.00 | Investment Style Large-Cap Growth |
|---|---|---|---|---|

**GICS Sector** Consumer Discretionary
**Sub-Industry** Casinos & Gaming

**Summary** This company is a leading maker of gaming machines and proprietary software systems for gaming machine networks.

## Key Stock Statistics (Source S&P, Vickers, company reports)

| | | | | | |
|---|---|---|---|---|---|
| 52-Wk Range | $19.15–13.38 | S&P Oper. EPS 2012E | 1.01 | Market Capitalization(B) | $4.869 | Beta | 1.55 |
| Trailing 12-Month EPS | $0.94 | S&P Oper. EPS 2013E | NA | Yield (%) | 1.47 | S&P 3-Yr. Proj. EPS CAGR(%) | 6 |
| Trailing 12-Month P/E | 17.4 | P/E on S&P Oper. EPS 2012E | 16.1 | Dividend Rate/Share | $0.24 | S&P Credit Rating | BBB |
| $10K Invested 5 Yrs Ago | $3,972 | Common Shares Outstg. (M) | 298.5 | Institutional Ownership (%) | 85 | | |

## Price Performance

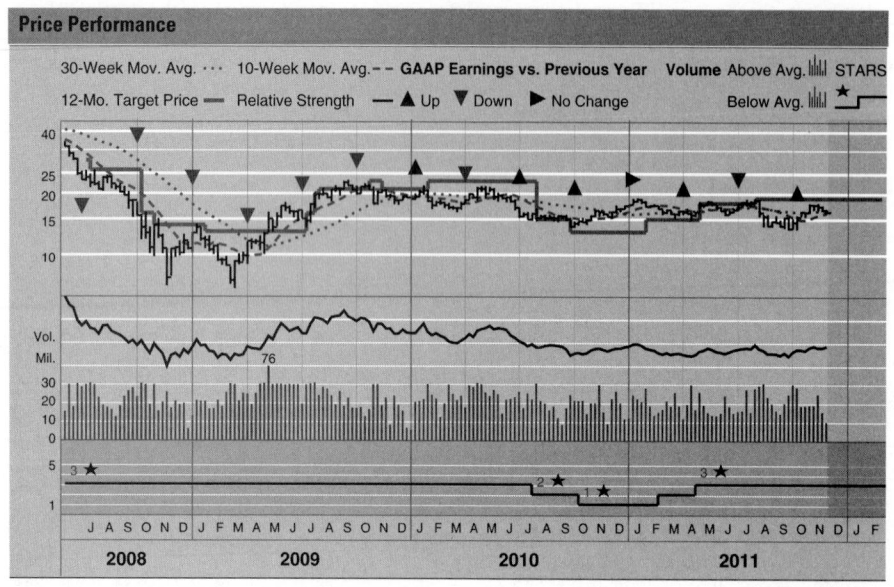

30-Week Mov. Avg. ··· 10-Week Mov. Avg. -- GAAP Earnings vs. Previous Year   Volume Above Avg. STARS
12-Mo. Target Price — Relative Strength  ▲ Up  ▼ Down  ▶ No Change   Below Avg.

Options: ASE, CBOE

Analysis prepared by Equity Analyst **Esther Kwon, CFA** on Nov 10, 2011, when the stock traded at **$16.93**.

## Qualitative Risk Assessment

| LOW | MEDIUM | HIGH |
|---|---|---|

Our risk assessment reflects the company's industry-leading position as a supplier of gaming machines. We expect the company to generate free cash flow, with at least some of it used for stock repurchases. This is offset by our projection that IGT will continue to spend heavily on research and development and our view that growth prospects depend on regulatory factors and technology changes, including the legalization of gaming markets.

## Quantitative Evaluations

**S&P Quality Ranking**   B+

| D | C | B- | B | B+ | A- | A | A+ |
|---|---|---|---|---|---|---|---|

**Relative Strength Rank**   STRONG

LOWEST = 1    76    HIGHEST = 99

## Highlights

► In FY 11 (Sep.), revenue slipped about 1%, after a 5.4% drop in FY 10, on a decline in gaming operations but a slight increase in product sales. In FY 12, we forecast revenues to rise over 7% on increases in both gaming operations and product sales as IGT recovers lost market share. We expect overall replacement market sales to remain lackluster with product sales largely being driven by openings in new markets and expansion of existing markets while we see growth in international.

► Although gross margins expanded in FY 11, primarily on a significant improvement in product margin, we see overall company gross margins being largely stable in FY 12, with gaming gross margins at approximately 61.5%. Total SG&A and R&D expenses in dollars should be up somewhat. We project operating margin expansion and EPS of $1.01 in FY 12, versus operating EPS of $0.94 in FY 11, and see $1.09 in FY 13.

► In May 2009, IGT issued $850 million of convertible notes due May 2014 and entered into hedging transactions on its common stock and separate warrant transactions with hedge counterparties. These actions may affect share count, depending on the stock price.

## Investment Rationale/Risk

► Our hold recommendation is based on valuation. While new management appears to have stabilized operations, we think the shares already incorporate significant prospective improvement, and we remain cautious on the consumer spending environment and the spending intentions of IGT's casino customers. We see a recovery in replacement sales less likely in the near term and forecast gaming operations revenue growth to struggle given high gas prices, an elevated unemployment rate, and negative real consumer wage growth. Additionally, we think pricing competition has become more acute over the past two quarters.

► Risks to our opinion and target price include prospects for growth from new or expanded gaming markets becoming less favorable, and a re-acceleration of market share losses.

► Our 12-month target price of $19 reflects a P/E multiple at a significant premium to the peer average of approximately 11X.

## Revenue/Earnings Data

**Revenue (Million $)**

| | 1Q | 2Q | 3Q | 4Q | Year |
|---|---|---|---|---|---|
| 2011 | 464.8 | 492.3 | 489.0 | 539.8 | 1,957 |
| 2010 | 515.1 | 486.8 | 489.3 | 496.0 | 1,987 |
| 2009 | 601.6 | 475.7 | 522.1 | 514.6 | 2,114 |
| 2008 | 645.8 | 573.2 | 677.4 | 632.2 | 2,529 |
| 2007 | 642.3 | 609.7 | 706.5 | 662.9 | 2,621 |
| 2006 | 616.2 | 644.4 | 612.4 | 638.7 | 2,512 |

**Earnings Per Share ($)**

| | | | | | |
|---|---|---|---|---|---|
| 2011 | 0.25 | 0.23 | 0.30 | 0.20 | 0.97 |
| 2010 | 0.25 | Nil | 0.32 | 0.09 | 0.75 |
| 2009 | 0.22 | 0.13 | 0.22 | -0.07 | 0.51 |
| 2008 | 0.36 | 0.22 | 0.35 | 0.18 | 1.10 |
| 2007 | 0.35 | 0.38 | 0.41 | 0.38 | 1.51 |
| 2006 | 0.34 | 0.35 | 0.33 | 0.33 | 1.34 |

Fiscal year ended Sep. 30. Next earnings report expected: NA. EPS Estimates based on S&P Operating Earnings; historical GAAP earnings are as reported.

## Dividend Data (Dates: mm/dd Payment Date: mm/dd/yy)

| Amount ($) | Date Decl. | Ex-Div. Date | Stk. of Record | Payment Date |
|---|---|---|---|---|
| 0.060 | 02/28 | 03/17 | 03/21 | 04/08/11 |
| 0.060 | 06/07 | 06/16 | 06/20 | 07/08/11 |
| 0.060 | 08/23 | 09/20 | 09/22 | 10/07/11 |
| 0.060 | 11/15 | 12/20 | 12/22 | 01/06/12 |

Dividends have been paid since 2003. Source: Company reports.

# International Game Technology

**STANDARD &POOR'S**

## Business Summary November 10, 2011

International Game Technology engages in the design, manufacture and marketing of electronic gaming equipment and systems products.

The company provides electronic gaming equipment and systems, as well as licensing, services, and component parts. The company offers video and physical reel slot machines. Its advanced video platform (AVP) machines are designed to support server-based gaming networks. The machine configurations include stand-alone casino-style slot machines that determine the game play outcome at the machine, known as Class III in tribal jurisdictions; wide area progressive jackpot systems with linked machines across various casinos; and central determination system machines connected to a central server that determines the game outcome, encompassing video lottery terminals used in government-sponsored applications and electronic or video bingo machines known as Class II in tribal jurisdictions.

The company also offers multi-player community-style configurations with a common display. Its electronic table games include live dealer hosted configurations with digital cards and live chips or virtual chips/electronic credits, as well as a virtual platform that can be approved as a slot game, providing table-like gaming for slot only or limited table jurisdictions. Its international gaming machines include AWP (amusement with prizes) games.

The company's systems products include applications for casino management, customer relationship marketing (CRM), server-based games, and player management. Its casino management solutions include integrated modules for machine accounting, patron management, cage and table accounting, ticket-in/ticket-out, bonusing, and table game automation. Its CRM solution features integrated marketing and business intelligence modules that provide analytical, predictive and management tools. Its server-based solutions enable game delivery to slot machines, computers, mobile phones, tablets, and other networked devices. In 2010, the company installed the first floor-wide version of its sbX Experience Management system at the Las Vegas ARIA Resort and Casino at City Center.

The company develops video-reel and poker games, as well as improvements for its classic spinning-reel games, such as multi-line, and multi-coin configurations. It builds on its traditional game development with customization for video lottery, CDS, Class II and international markets.

## Company Financials Fiscal Year Ended Sep. 30

| Per Share Data ($) | 2011 | 2010 | 2009 | 2008 | 2007 | 2006 | 2005 | 2004 | 2003 | 2002 |
|---|---|---|---|---|---|---|---|---|---|---|
| Tangible Book Value | NA | NM | NM | NM | 0.29 | 2.06 | 1.56 | 1.98 | 1.42 | 0.55 |
| Cash Flow | 1.73 | 1.55 | 1.45 | 2.03 | 2.30 | 1.99 | 1.78 | 1.56 | 1.45 | 1.23 |
| Earnings | 0.97 | 0.75 | 0.51 | 1.10 | 1.51 | 1.34 | 1.20 | 1.18 | 1.07 | 0.80 |
| S&P Core Earnings | NA | 0.82 | 0.54 | 1.20 | 1.47 | 1.33 | 1.15 | 1.11 | 1.02 | 0.79 |
| Dividends | 0.24 | 0.24 | 0.33 | 0.57 | 0.52 | 0.50 | 0.48 | 0.30 | 0.18 | Nil |
| Payout Ratio | 25% | 32% | 64% | 51% | 34% | 37% | 40% | 25% | 16% | Nil |
| Prices:High | 19.15 | 21.94 | 23.30 | 49.41 | 48.79 | 46.76 | 34.63 | 47.12 | 37.00 | 20.03 |
| Prices:Low | 13.38 | 13.65 | 6.81 | 7.03 | 33.57 | 30.12 | 24.20 | 28.22 | 18.05 | 11.94 |
| P/E Ratio:High | 20 | 29 | 46 | 45 | 32 | 35 | 29 | 40 | 35 | 25 |
| P/E Ratio:Low | 14 | 18 | 13 | 6 | 22 | 22 | 20 | 24 | 17 | 15 |
| **Income Statement Analysis** (Million $) | | | | | | | | | | |
| Revenue | 1,957 | 1,987 | 2,114 | 2,529 | 2,621 | 2,512 | 2,379 | 2,485 | 2,128 | 1,848 |
| Operating Income | 747 | 738 | 713 | 947 | 1,066 | 960 | 886 | 964 | 800 | 646 |
| Depreciation | 226 | 237 | 277 | 286 | 266 | 235 | 222 | 150 | 134 | 146 |
| Interest Expense | 131 | 162 | 125 | 102 | 77.6 | 50.8 | 58.1 | 90.5 | 117 | 117 |
| Pretax Income | 428 | 313 | 238 | 591 | 805 | 747 | 681 | 653 | 599 | 110 |
| Effective Tax Rate | NA | NA | 37.4% | 42.0% | 36.9% | 36.6% | 35.9% | 34.2% | 37.3% | NM |
| Net Income | 292 | 224 | 149 | 343 | 508 | 474 | 437 | 430 | 375 | 277 |
| S&P Core Earnings | NA | 244 | 159 | 371 | 493 | 470 | 415 | 405 | 357 | 273 |
| **Balance Sheet & Other Financial Data** (Million $) | | | | | | | | | | |
| Cash | 460 | 158 | 168 | 266 | 261 | 295 | 289 | 765 | 1,316 | 424 |
| Current Assets | 1,410 | 1,202 | 1,234 | 1,470 | 1,287 | 1,376 | 1,437 | 1,510 | 2,078 | 1,195 |
| Total Assets | 4,154 | 4,007 | 4,388 | 4,557 | 4,168 | 3,903 | 3,864 | 3,873 | 4,185 | 3,316 |
| Current Liabilities | 535 | 582 | 624 | 737 | 692 | 1,247 | 1,218 | 560 | 945 | 511 |
| Long Term Debt | 1,646 | 1,674 | 2,170 | 2,247 | 1,503 | 200 | 200 | 792 | 1,146 | 971 |
| Common Equity | 1,445 | 1,234 | 967 | 909 | 1,453 | 2,042 | 1,906 | 1,977 | 1,687 | 1,433 |
| Total Capital | 3,091 | 2,909 | 3,142 | 3,156 | 2,956 | 2,242 | 2,106 | 2,768 | 2,833 | 2,413 |
| Capital Expenditures | 205 | 240 | 257 | 298 | 344 | 311 | 239 | 211 | 30.8 | 33.8 |
| Cash Flow | 519 | 461 | 426 | 628 | 774 | 709 | 659 | 580 | 509 | 423 |
| Current Ratio | 2.6 | 2.1 | 2.0 | 2.0 | 1.9 | 1.1 | 1.2 | 2.7 | 2.2 | 2.3 |
| % Long Term Debt of Capitalization | 53.3 | 57.6 | 69.2 | 71.2 | 50.9 | 8.9 | 9.5 | 28.6 | 40.4 | 40.3 |
| % Net Income of Revenue | 14.9 | 11.3 | 7.1 | 13.6 | 19.4 | 18.9 | 18.3 | 17.3 | 17.6 | 15.0 |
| % Return on Assets | 7.2 | 5.3 | 3.3 | 7.9 | 12.6 | 12.2 | 11.3 | 10.7 | 10.0 | 10.6 |
| % Return on Equity | 21.8 | 20.4 | 15.9 | 29.0 | 29.1 | 24.0 | 22.5 | 23.5 | 24.1 | 32.0 |

Data as orig reptd.; bef. results of disc opers/spec. items. Per share data adj. for stk. divs.; EPS diluted. E-Estimated. NA-Not Available. NM-Not Meaningful. NR-Not Ranked. UR-Under Review.

**Office:** 9295 Prototype Drive, Reno, NV 89521.
**Telephone:** 775-448-7777.
**Website:** http://www.igt.com
**Chrmn:** P.G. Satre

**Pres:** E.A. Berg
**CEO:** P.S. Hart
**EVP, CFO, Chief Acctg Officer & Treas:** P.W. Cavanaugh
**EVP & CTO:** C.J. Satchell

**Board Members:** P. L. Alves, J. D. Chaffin, G. Creed, P. S. Hart, R. A. Mathewson, T. J. Matthews, R. J. Miller, D. E. Roberson, V. L. Sadusky, P. G. Satre

**Founded:** 1980
**Domicile:** Nevada
**Employees:** 4,900

# International Paper Co

STANDARD
&POOR'S

| S&P Recommendation | HOLD ★★★☆☆ | Price | 12-Mo. Target Price | Investment Style |
|---|---|---|---|---|
| | | $25.89 (as of Nov 25, 2011) | $30.00 | Large-Cap Value |

**GICS Sector** Materials
**Sub-Industry** Paper Products

**Summary** This company is a leading worldwide producer and distributor of printing papers and packaging products.

## Key Stock Statistics (Source S&P, Vickers, company reports)

| | | | | | | | |
|---|---|---|---|---|---|---|---|
| 52-Wk Range | $33.01 – 21.55 | S&P Oper. EPS 2011E | 3.00 | Market Capitalization(B) | $11.316 | Beta | 2.19 |
| Trailing 12-Month EPS | $3.20 | S&P Oper. EPS 2012E | 3.10 | Yield (%) | 4.06 | S&P 3-Yr. Proj. EPS CAGR(%) | 15 |
| Trailing 12-Month P/E | 8.1 | P/E on S&P Oper. EPS 2011E | 8.6 | Dividend Rate/Share | $1.05 | S&P Credit Rating | BBB |
| $10K Invested 5 Yrs Ago | $9,251 | Common Shares Outstg. (M) | 437.1 | Institutional Ownership (%) | 85 | | |

## Price Performance

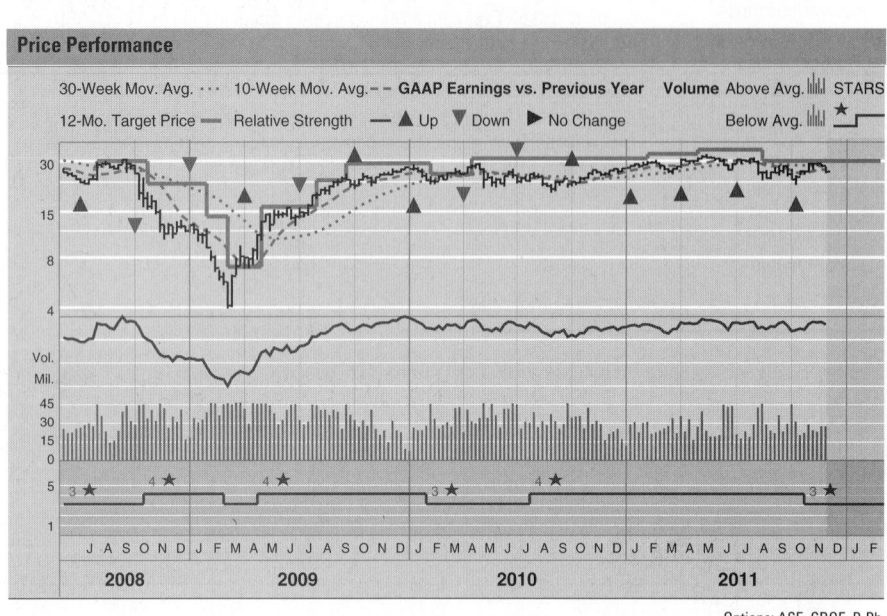

30-Week Mov. Avg. · · · ·    10-Week Mov. Avg. - -  **GAAP Earnings vs. Previous Year**    **Volume** Above Avg. Ⅰⅼⅼⅼ STARS
12-Mo. Target Price —  Relative Strength —  ▲ Up  ▼ Down  ▶ No Change    Below Avg. Ⅰⅼⅼⅼ ★

Options: ASE, CBOE, P, Ph

Analysis prepared by Equity Analyst **S. Benway, CFA** on Nov 08, 2011, when the stock traded at **$29.07**.

## Highlights

▶ We forecast that sales will increase 4% in 2011 followed by a 5% advance in 2012. Volume in the industrial and consumer packaging businesses should improve along with renewed growth in the economy. We expect prices, on average, to be up modestly, but we see little contribution from the forest products business with most lands having been divested.

▶ We project operating margins to widen this year to 9.2%, from 8.1% in 2010. IP is continuing to find opportunities for cost reduction, especially in its packaging business, and capacity is likely to be better utilized. Profits in 2011 are also expected to be helped by a growing contribution from international joint ventures. High recycled fiber and energy costs could offset some off this improvement, however. We look for similar trends to lead to further margin expansion in 2012 to 9.1%.

▶ We see operating EPS of $3.00 in 2011, excluding unusual items. In our view, IP will continue to benefit from its restructuring and its presence in faster-growing emerging markets. For 2012, we forecast EPS of $3.10.

## Investment Rationale/Risk

▶ IP has made many moves in recent years aimed at focusing on faster-growing regions and higher-return businesses. The company has investments and joint ventures in Brazil, China, and Russia that we believe will add to earnings growth. In September, IP agreed to acquire Temple-Inland (TIN 32, Hold) for total consideration of $4.3 billion, subject to certain approvals. We expect this planned deal to provide additional cost savings opportunities.

▶ Risks to our recommendation and target price include a lack of further economic recovery, lower demand and pricing trends for uncoated paper and packaging, and the failure of new ventures to achieve targeted returns.

▶ Our discounted cash flow model, which assumes a 10.6% blended weighted average cost of capital, modest capital expenditures over the next several years, and a 2.5% terminal growth rate, calculates intrinsic value of $28. A peer group of paper stocks was recently trading at 11.1X our 2012 EPS estimates. Applying this valuation to our 2012 EPS forecast for IP, we derive a value of $34. Our 12-month target price of $30 is a blend of these two metrics.

## Qualitative Risk Assessment

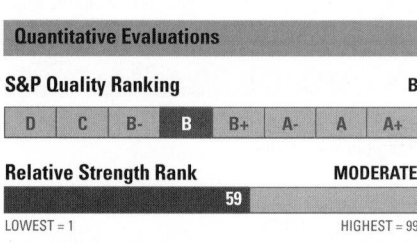

| LOW | MEDIUM | HIGH |
|---|---|---|

IP operates in a cyclical and capital-intensive industry and is affected by changes in industrial production, interest rates, and economic growth. However, it is one of the largest companies in the sector, and has greater economies of scale than many of its competitors.

## Quantitative Evaluations

**S&P Quality Ranking**    B

| D | C | B- | B | B+ | A- | A | A+ |
|---|---|---|---|---|---|---|---|

**Relative Strength Rank**    MODERATE

59

LOWEST = 1    HIGHEST = 99

## Revenue/Earnings Data

**Revenue (Million $)**

| | 1Q | 2Q | 3Q | 4Q | Year |
|---|---|---|---|---|---|
| 2011 | 6,387 | 6,648 | 6,632 | -- | -- |
| 2010 | 5,807 | 6,121 | 6,720 | 6,531 | 25,179 |
| 2009 | 5,668 | 5,802 | 5,919 | 5,977 | 23,366 |
| 2008 | 5,668 | 5,807 | 6,808 | 6,546 | 24,829 |
| 2007 | 5,217 | 5,291 | 5,541 | 5,841 | 21,890 |
| 2006 | 5,668 | 6,270 | 5,867 | 5,324 | 21,995 |

**Earnings Per Share ($)**

| | | | | | |
|---|---|---|---|---|---|
| 2011 | 0.67 | 0.52 | 1.19 | E0.54 | E3.00 |
| 2010 | -0.38 | 0.22 | 0.92 | 0.73 | 1.48 |
| 2009 | 0.61 | 0.32 | 0.87 | -0.24 | 1.55 |
| 2008 | 0.35 | 0.54 | 0.35 | -1.08 | 0.17 |
| 2007 | 1.02 | 0.46 | 0.52 | 0.80 | 2.81 |
| 2006 | 0.14 | 0.24 | 0.23 | 4.53 | 2.65 |

Fiscal year ended Dec. 31. Next earnings report expected: Early February. EPS Estimates based on S&P Operating Earnings; historical GAAP earnings are as reported.

## Dividend Data (Dates: mm/dd Payment Date: mm/dd/yy)

| Amount ($) | Date Decl. | Ex-Div. Date | Stk. of Record | Payment Date |
|---|---|---|---|---|
| 0.188 | 01/11 | 02/11 | 02/15 | 03/15/11 |
| 0.263 | 03/29 | 05/13 | 05/17 | 06/15/11 |
| 0.263 | 07/12 | 08/11 | 08/15 | 09/15/11 |
| 0.263 | 10/11 | 11/14 | 11/16 | 12/15/11 |

Dividends have been paid since 1946. Source: Company reports.

---

**Please read the Required Disclosures and Analyst Certification on the last page of this report.**

The **McGraw·Hill** Companies

# International Paper Co

STANDARD &POOR'S

## Business Summary November 08, 2011

CORPORATE OVERVIEW. International Paper is the world's largest paper and forest products company. It has the leading share in the manufacturing of containerboard in the U.S. with annual production capacity of about 10 million tons and an estimated share of 30%. Its products include linerboard, medium, whitetop, recycled linerboard, recycled medium, and saturating kraft. IP has containerboard operations in the U.S., Europe, Asia, and the Middle East. The company is a major producer of printing and writing papers, and we believe its market share is about 25% in uncoated free sheet (UFS). These papers are used in copiers, desktop and laser printers, and digital imaging. End uses include brochures, pamphlets, books, direct mail, envelopes, forms, and tablets. IP's distribution business provides products and services to customers such as commercial printers, building services, and manufacturers. It is the largest wholesale distributor of printing papers and supplies in North America with 120 warehouse locations. The company has smaller businesses that make cups, lids, plates, and packaging for tobacco, cosmetics, and pharmaceuticals.

IMPACT OF MAJOR DEVELOPMENTS. On September 6, 2011, International Paper agreed to acquire Temple-Inland for $32.00 per share in cash or total consideration of $4.3 billion, subject to certain approvals. Temple-Inland is a major manufacturer of linerboard and building products for residential construction. The planned deal would make IP the largest producer of linerboard in the U.S. with a share of about 35%. The company expects the acquisition to be accretive in the first year after closing, and also plans to generate $300 million of synergies within the first 24 months following closing. This planned acquisition follows IP's purchase in 2008 of Weyerhaeuser's corrugated packaging business, which proved to be very successful. The Temple-Inland deal is expected to close in the first quarter of 2012.

## Company Financials Fiscal Year Ended Dec. 31

| Per Share Data ($) | 2010 | 2009 | 2008 | 2007 | 2006 | 2005 | 2004 | 2003 | 2002 | 2001 |
|---|---|---|---|---|---|---|---|---|---|---|
| Tangible Book Value | 10.34 | 8.62 | 5.01 | 14.08 | 11.10 | 6.75 | 6.69 | 6.01 | 4.31 | 7.78 |
| Cash Flow | 4.88 | 4.99 | 0.19 | 5.31 | 4.99 | 4.38 | 4.19 | 4.07 | 3.90 | 1.51 |
| Earnings | 1.48 | 1.55 | 0.17 | 2.81 | 2.65 | 1.74 | 0.98 | 0.66 | 0.61 | -2.37 |
| S&P Core Earnings | 1.59 | 1.68 | 0.12 | 2.45 | 1.13 | 1.67 | 0.84 | 0.51 | 0.92 | -2.25 |
| Dividends | 0.40 | 0.32 | 1.00 | 1.00 | 1.00 | 1.00 | 1.00 | 1.00 | 1.00 | 1.00 |
| Payout Ratio | 27% | 21% | 588% | 36% | 38% | 57% | 102% | 152% | 164% | NM |
| Prices:High | 29.25 | 27.79 | 33.77 | 41.57 | 37.98 | 42.59 | 45.01 | 43.32 | 46.20 | 43.31 |
| Prices:Low | 19.33 | 3.93 | 10.20 | 31.05 | 30.69 | 26.97 | 37.12 | 33.09 | 31.35 | 30.70 |
| P/E Ratio:High | 20 | 18 | NM | 15 | 14 | 24 | 46 | 66 | 76 | NM |
| P/E Ratio:Low | 13 | 3 | NM | 11 | 12 | 15 | 38 | 50 | 51 | NM |

| Income Statement Analysis (Million $) | | | | | | | | | | |
|---|---|---|---|---|---|---|---|---|---|---|
| Revenue | 25,179 | 23,366 | 24,829 | 21,890 | 21,995 | 24,097 | 25,548 | 25,179 | 24,976 | 26,363 |
| Operating Income | 3,275 | 3,139 | 2,717 | 2,796 | 2,609 | 3,228 | 3,251 | 3,293 | 3,576 | 3,305 |
| Depreciation | 1,456 | 1,472 | 1,347 | 1,086 | 1,158 | 1,376 | 1,565 | 1,644 | 1,587 | 1,870 |
| Interest Expense | 608 | 702 | 572 | 483 | 651 | 593 | 743 | 766 | 783 | 929 |
| Pretax Income | 886 | 1,150 | 235 | 1,654 | 3,188 | 586 | 746 | 346 | 371 | -1,265 |
| Effective Tax Rate | NA | 40.8% | 68.9% | 25.1% | 59.3% | NM | 27.6% | NM | NM | NM |
| Net Income | 665 | 663 | 70.0 | 1,215 | 1,282 | 859 | 478 | 315 | 295 | -1,142 |
| S&P Core Earnings | 689 | 719 | 55.0 | 1,058 | 539 | 819 | 402 | 242 | 444 | -1,091 |

| Balance Sheet & Other Financial Data (Million $) | | | | | | | | | | |
|---|---|---|---|---|---|---|---|---|---|---|
| Cash | 2,073 | 1,892 | 1,144 | 905 | 1,624 | 1,641 | 2,596 | 2,363 | 1,074 | 1,224 |
| Current Assets | 8,028 | 7,551 | 7,360 | 6,735 | 8,637 | 7,409 | 9,319 | 9,337 | 7,738 | 8,312 |
| Total Assets | 25,368 | 25,548 | 28,252 | 24,159 | 24,034 | 28,771 | 34,217 | 35,525 | 33,792 | 37,158 |
| Current Liabilities | 4,503 | 4,012 | 4,755 | 3,842 | 4,641 | 4,844 | 4,872 | 6,803 | 4,579 | 5,374 |
| Long Term Debt | 8,358 | 8,729 | 11,246 | 6,620 | 6,531 | 11,023 | 14,132 | 13,450 | 13,042 | 14,262 |
| Common Equity | 6,834 | 6,023 | 5,508 | 8,672 | 10,839 | 8,351 | 8,254 | 8,237 | 7,374 | 10,291 |
| Total Capital | 15,692 | 14,984 | 16,215 | 18,172 | 19,816 | 20,311 | 25,631 | 25,085 | 25,435 | 29,804 |
| Capital Expenditures | 775 | 534 | 1,002 | 1,288 | 1,009 | 1,155 | 1,262 | 1,166 | 1,009 | 1,049 |
| Cash Flow | 2,121 | 2,135 | 78.0 | 2,301 | 2,440 | 2,235 | 2,043 | 1,959 | 1,882 | 728 |
| Current Ratio | 1.8 | 1.9 | 1.6 | 1.8 | 1.9 | 1.5 | 1.9 | 1.4 | 1.7 | 1.5 |
| % Long Term Debt of Capitalization | 53.3 | 58.3 | 69.3 | 41.7 | 33.0 | 54.3 | 55.1 | 53.6 | 51.3 | 47.9 |
| % Net Income of Revenue | 2.6 | 2.8 | 0.3 | 5.6 | 5.8 | 3.6 | 1.9 | 1.3 | 1.2 | NM |
| % Return on Assets | 2.6 | 2.5 | 0.3 | 5.0 | 4.9 | 2.7 | 1.4 | 0.9 | 0.8 | NM |
| % Return on Equity | 10.3 | 13.0 | 1.0 | 14.6 | 13.4 | 10.3 | 5.8 | 4.0 | 3.3 | NM |

Data as orig reptd.; bef. results of disc opers/spec. items. Per share data adj. for stk. divs.; EPS diluted. E-Estimated. NA-Not Available. NM-Not Meaningful. NR-Not Ranked. UR-Under Review.

Office: 6400 Poplar Ave, Memphis, TN 38197-0198.
Telephone: 901-419-7000.
Email: comm@ipaper.com
Website: http://www.internationalpaper.com

Chrmn & CEO: J.V. Faraci
SVP & CFO: C.L. Roberts
SVP, Secy & General Counsel: S.R. Ryan
Investor Contact: T.A. Cleves (901-419-7566)

Cntlr: T.L. Herrington
Board Members: D. J. Bronczek, A. C. Dorduncu, L. L. Elsenhans, J. V. Faraci, S. G. Gibara, S. J. Mobley, J. E. Spero, J. L. Townsend, III, J. F. Turner, W. G. Walter, A. Weisser, J. S. Whisler

Founded: 1898
Domicile: New York
Employees: 59,500

# Interpublic Group of Companies Inc. (The)

**STANDARD &POOR'S**

| | | | |
|---|---|---|---|
| **S&P Recommendation** BUY ★★★★☆ | **Price** $8.41 (as of Nov 25, 2011) | **12-Mo. Target Price** $12.00 | **Investment Style** Large-Cap Blend |

**GICS Sector** Consumer Discretionary
**Sub-Industry** Advertising

**Summary** Interpublic is one of the world's largest organizations of advertising agencies and marketing communications companies.

## Key Stock Statistics (Source S&P, Vickers, company reports)

| | | | | | | | |
|---|---|---|---|---|---|---|---|
| 52-Wk Range | $13.35– 6.73 | S&P Oper. EPS 2011**E** | 0.72 | Market Capitalization(B) | $3.878 | Beta | 1.70 |
| Trailing 12-Month EPS | $0.86 | S&P Oper. EPS 2012**E** | 0.86 | Yield (%) | 2.85 | S&P 3-Yr. Proj. EPS CAGR(%) | 15 |
| Trailing 12-Month P/E | 9.8 | P/E on S&P Oper. EPS 2011**E** | 11.7 | Dividend Rate/Share | $0.24 | S&P Credit Rating | BB+ |
| $10K Invested 5 Yrs Ago | $7,185 | Common Shares Outstg. (M) | 461.2 | Institutional Ownership (%) | 95 | | |

## Price Performance

30-Week Mov. Avg. · · · 10-Week Mov. Avg. – – GAAP Earnings vs. Previous Year Volume Above Avg. STARS
12-Mo. Target Price — Relative Strength — ▲ Up ▼ Down ► No Change Below Avg.

Options: ASE, CBOE, Ph

Analysis prepared by Equity Analyst **Joseph Agnese** on Nov 04, 2011, when the stock traded at **$9.72**.

## Highlights

➤ The global rebound in advertising spending showed signs of continuing in the first nine months of 2011, with IPG's U.S. organic revenues climbing 7.6% and overall organic revenues rising 7.5%, despite deteriorating sales in continental Europe, with organic sales down 1.8% in the third quarter and up only 1.5% in the first nine months. In 2012, we expect benefits from increased advertising demand associated with the Summer Olympics and U.S. presidential elections, despite more difficult macroeconomic comparisons, resulting in overall 2012 revenues growing 3.7% to $7.399 billion, from our estimate of $7.134 billion in 2011.

➤ We see margin expansion in 2011 and 2012 due to improved sales leverage, despite organic sales growth slowing. While we see headcount rising in 2011, we think year-to-year comparisons will become more difficult in 2012, as the company overlaps benefits from significant reductions taken during the global economic recession through 2009. Additionally, we see savings from reduced rent costs and severance expenses.

➤ We project EPS of $0.86 for 2012, up significantly from our estimate of $0.72 in 2011.

## Investment Rationale/Risk

➤ Advertising industry fundamentals softened in the third quarter of 2011, which we believe reflects clients increased macroeconomic environment concerns. With a more stable macroeconomic environment expected in the U.S. going forward, and increased marketing demand associated with the Summer Olympics and U.S. Presidential elections, we look for increased client marketing budgets to benefit earnings growth in 2012. However, we believe visibility regarding a recovery in demand in continental Europe remains poor and could offset some of the benefits we are expecting in the U.S.

➤ Risks to our recommendation and target price include unexpected business losses, unfavorable forex impacts, a slower-than-expected global economic recovery, and higher-than-expected severance expenses or professional fees.

➤ Our 12-month target price of $12 is derived by applying an enterprise value/EBITDA multiple of 5.5X to our 2012 EBITDA estimate of $1.06 billion. This is near the midpoint of the historical 2.5X-9.4X range, reflecting potential EPS benefits we see from a more favorable economic environment and poor macroeconomic visibility.

## Qualitative Risk Assessment

| LOW | MEDIUM | HIGH |
|---|---|---|

Our risk assessment reflects our view of a highly competitive advertising industry, and economic cyclicality associated with advertising spending, offset by what we see as a moderately conservative balance sheet structure and structural improvements in profitability for IPG.

## Quantitative Evaluations

**S&P Quality Ranking** B-

| D | C | B- | B | B+ | A- | A | A+ |
|---|---|---|---|---|---|---|---|

**Relative Strength Rank** MODERATE

54

LOWEST = 1 HIGHEST = 99

## Revenue/Earnings Data

**Revenue (Million $)**

| | 1Q | 2Q | 3Q | 4Q | Year |
|---|---|---|---|---|---|
| 2011 | 1,475 | 1,741 | 1,727 | -- | -- |
| 2010 | 1,341 | 1,618 | 1,561 | 2,012 | 6,532 |
| 2009 | 1,325 | 1,474 | 1,427 | 1,801 | 6,028 |
| 2008 | 1,485 | 1,836 | 1,740 | 1,902 | 6,963 |
| 2007 | 1,359 | 1,653 | 1,560 | 1,983 | 6,554 |
| 2006 | 1,327 | 1,533 | 1,454 | 1,877 | 6,191 |

**Earnings Per Share ($)**

| | | | | | |
|---|---|---|---|---|---|
| 2011 | E-0.09 | 0.19 | 0.40 | E0.44 | E0.72 |
| 2010 | -0.15 | 0.15 | 0.08 | 0.36 | 0.47 |
| 2009 | -0.16 | 0.04 | 0.03 | 0.24 | 0.18 |
| 2008 | -0.15 | 0.17 | 0.08 | 0.39 | 0.52 |
| 2007 | -0.29 | 0.24 | -0.06 | 0.31 | 0.26 |
| 2006 | -0.43 | 0.09 | -0.03 | 0.11 | -0.20 |

Fiscal year ended Dec. 31. Next earnings report expected: NA. EPS Estimates based on S&P Operating Earnings; historical GAAP earnings are as reported.

## Dividend Data (Dates: mm/dd Payment Date: mm/dd/yy)

| Amount ($) | Date Decl. | Ex-Div. Date | Stk. of Record | Payment Date |
|---|---|---|---|---|
| 0.060 | 02/25 | 03/09 | 03/11 | 03/25/11 |
| 0.060 | 05/26 | 06/08 | 06/10 | 06/24/11 |
| 0.060 | 08/17 | 09/07 | 09/09 | 09/23/11 |
| 0.060 | 11/16 | 11/29 | 12/01 | 12/15/11 |

Dividends have been paid since 2011. Source: Company reports.

---

**Please read the Required Disclosures and Analyst Certification on the last page of this report.**

**The McGraw-Hill Companies**

# Interpublic Group of Companies Inc. (The)

**STANDARD &POOR'S**

## Business Summary November 04, 2011

CORPORATE OVERVIEW. The Interpublic Group of Companies, along with its subsidiaries, is one of the world's largest advertising and marketing services companies, made up of communication agencies around the world that deliver custom marketing solutions to clients. These agencies cover the spectrum of marketing disciplines and specialties, from traditional services such as consumer advertising and direct marketing, to emerging services such as mobile and search engine marketing.

The company generates revenue from planning, creating and placing advertising in various media and from planning and executing other communications or marketing programs. IPG also receives commissions from clients for planning and supervising work done by outside contractors in the physical preparation of finished print advertisements and the production of TV and radio commercials and other forms of advertising. In addition, IPG derives revenue in a number of other ways, including the planning and placement in media of advertising produced by unrelated advertising agencies, the creation and publication of brochures, billboards, point of sale materials and direct marketing pieces for clients, the planning and carrying out of specialized marketing research, public relations campaigns, and creating and managing special events at which client products are featured.

IPG has two reportable segments: the McCann Worldgroup unit, comprised of Draftfcb, Lowe, Momentum, McCann Healthcare, media agencies and other standalone agencies, and the Constituent Management Group (CMG), which is made up of the bulk of IPG's specialist marketing service offerings. Draftfcb was formed from the merger of two IPG companies in 2006, and is focused on consumer advertising and behavioral, data-driven direct marketing. Lowe is a creative advertising agency operating in the world's largest advertising markets. McCann Worldgroup is a marketing communications company that consists of McCann Erickson Advertising, MRM Worldwide for relationship marketing and digital expertise, Momentum for experiential marketing, and McCann Healthcare for health care communications, as well as various other brands.

Mediabrands was installed in recent years to oversee all media operations in order to align the company's media networks with its global brand agencies. Also, in recent years the company has focused on making strategic investments, including a number of acquisitions in Brazil, India, Russia, and China, or "BRIC" countries.

## Company Financials Fiscal Year Ended Dec. 31

| Per Share Data ($) | 2010 | 2009 | 2008 | 2007 | 2006 | 2005 | 2004 | 2003 | 2002 | 2001 |
|---|---|---|---|---|---|---|---|---|---|---|
| Tangible Book Value | NM | NM | NM | NM | NM | NM | NM | NM | NM | NM |
| Cash Flow | 0.76 | 0.52 | 0.85 | 0.63 | 0.21 | -0.30 | -0.91 | -0.90 | 0.83 | -0.36 |
| Earnings | 0.47 | 0.18 | 0.52 | 0.26 | -0.20 | -0.70 | -1.36 | -1.43 | 0.26 | -1.37 |
| S&P Core Earnings | 0.48 | 0.21 | 0.51 | 0.29 | -0.18 | -0.62 | -0.82 | -0.84 | 0.36 | -0.60 |
| Dividends | Nil | Nil | Nil | Nil | Nil | Nil | Nil | Nil | 0.38 | 0.38 |
| Payout Ratio | Nil | Nil | Nil | Nil | Nil | Nil | Nil | Nil | 146% | NM |
| Prices:High | 12.25 | 7.77 | 10.47 | 13.94 | 12.83 | 13.80 | 17.31 | 16.50 | 34.98 | 47.44 |
| Prices:Low | 6.86 | 3.08 | 2.57 | 7.91 | 7.79 | 9.08 | 10.47 | 7.20 | 9.85 | 18.25 |
| P/E Ratio:High | 26 | 43 | 20 | 54 | NM | NM | NM | NM | NM | NM |
| P/E Ratio:Low | 15 | 17 | 5 | 30 | NM | NM | NM | NM | NM | NM |

| Income Statement Analysis (Million $) | | | | | | | | | | |
|---|---|---|---|---|---|---|---|---|---|---|
| Revenue | 6,532 | 6,028 | 6,963 | 6,554 | 6,191 | 6,274 | 6,387 | 5,863 | 6,204 | 6,727 |
| Operating Income | 799 | 681 | 780 | 547 | 341 | 156 | 589 | 719 | 762 | 1,113 |
| Depreciation | 148 | 170 | 173 | 177 | 174 | 169 | 185 | 204 | 218 | 372 |
| Interest Expense | 140 | 156 | 212 | 237 | 219 | 182 | 172 | 173 | 146 | 165 |
| Pretax Income | 453 | 234 | 475 | 243 | 2.00 | -173 | -261 | -330 | 271 | -519 |
| Effective Tax Rate | NA | 38.6% | 33.0% | 24.2% | NM | NM | NM | NM | 51.8% | NM |
| Net Income | 281 | 121 | 295 | 168 | -36.7 | -272 | -545 | -553 | 99.5 | -505 |
| S&P Core Earnings | 280 | 104 | 265 | 150 | -75.8 | -265 | -363 | -325 | 136 | -217 |

| Balance Sheet & Other Financial Data (Million $) | | | | | | | | | | |
|---|---|---|---|---|---|---|---|---|---|---|
| Cash | 2,689 | 2,506 | 2,275 | 2,083 | 1,957 | 2,192 | 1,970 | 2,006 | 933 | 935 |
| Current Assets | 8,454 | 7,638 | 7,488 | 7,686 | 7,209 | 7,497 | 7,637 | 7,350 | 6,322 | 6,467 |
| Total Assets | 13,071 | 12,263 | 12,125 | 12,458 | 11,864 | 11,945 | 12,272 | 12,235 | 11,794 | 11,515 |
| Current Liabilities | 7,741 | 6,906 | 6,877 | 7,121 | 6,663 | 6,857 | 7,563 | 6,625 | 7,090 | 6,434 |
| Long Term Debt | 1,583 | 1,638 | 1,787 | 2,044 | 2,249 | 2,183 | Nil | 2,192 | 1,818 | 2,481 |
| Common Equity | 2,308 | 1,973 | 1,951 | 1,807 | 1,416 | 1,047 | 1,345 | 2,721 | 2,100 | 2,384 |
| Total Capital | 4,809 | 4,667 | 4,517 | 4,376 | 4,236 | 4,178 | 1,773 | 5,356 | 3,988 | 4,953 |
| Capital Expenditures | 96.3 | 67.1 | 138 | 148 | 128 | 141 | 194 | 160 | 183 | 268 |
| Cash Flow | 414 | 264 | 441 | 317 | 89.3 | -129 | -380 | -349 | 317 | -133 |
| Current Ratio | 1.1 | 1.1 | 1.1 | 1.1 | 1.1 | 1.1 | 1.0 | 1.1 | 0.9 | 1.0 |
| % Long Term Debt of Capitalization | 32.9 | Nil | 39.5 | 46.7 | 53.1 | 52.3 | Nil | 40.9 | 45.6 | 50.1 |
| % Net Income of Revenue | 4.3 | 2.0 | 4.2 | 2.6 | NM | NM | NM | NM | 1.6 | NM |
| % Return on Assets | NA | NA | 2.4 | 1.4 | NM | NM | NM | NM | 0.9 | NM |
| % Return on Equity | NA | NA | 14.2 | 10.4 | NM | NM | NM | NM | 5.1 | NM |

Data as orig reptd.; bef. results of disc opers/spec. items. Per share data adj. for stk. divs.; EPS diluted. E-Estimated. NA-Not Available. NM-Not Meaningful. NR-Not Ranked. UR-Under Review.

**Office:** 1114 Avenue of the Americas, New York, NY 10036.
**Telephone:** 212-704-1200.
**Website:** http://www.interpublic.com
**Chrmn & CEO:** M.I. Roth

**EVP & CFO:** F. Mergenthaler
**SVP, Chief Acctg Officer & Cntlr:** C.F. Carroll
**SVP & Treas:** E.T. Johnson
**SVP, Secy & General Counsel:** N.J. Camera

**Investor Contact:** J. Leshne (212-704-1439)
**Board Members:** R. K. Brack, Jr., J. E. Carter-Miller, J. M. Considine, R. A. Goldstein, H. J. Greeniaus, M. J. Guilfoile, D. Hudson, W. T. Kerr, M. I. Roth, D. M. Thomas

**Founded:** 1902
**Domicile:** Delaware
**Employees:** 41,000

*The McGraw·Hill Companies*

# Intuitive Surgical Inc

**STANDARD &POOR'S**

| **S&P Recommendation** HOLD ★★★★★ | **Price** $413.26 (as of Nov 25, 2011) | **12-Mo. Target Price** $430.00 | **Investment Style** Large-Cap Blend |
|---|---|---|---|

**GICS Sector** Health Care
**Sub-Industry** Health Care Equipment

**Summary** This company has developed the da Vinci Surgical System, which uses advanced robotics and computerized visualization technology for minimally invasive surgeries.

## Key Stock Statistics (Source S&P, Vickers, company reports)

| | | | | | |
|---|---|---|---|---|---|
| 52-Wk Range | $449.06– 250.40 | S&P Oper. EPS 2011**E** | 11.90 | Market Capitalization(B) | $16.115 |
| Trailing 12-Month EPS | $11.58 | S&P Oper. EPS 2012**E** | 14.00 | Yield (%) | Nil |
| Trailing 12-Month P/E | 35.7 | P/E on S&P Oper. EPS 2011**E** | 34.7 | Dividend Rate/Share | Nil |
| $10K Invested 5 Yrs Ago | $41,718 | Common Shares Outstg. (M) | 39.0 | Institutional Ownership (%) | 89 |
| | | | | Beta | 1.50 |
| | | | | S&P 3-Yr. Proj. EPS CAGR(%) | 19 |
| | | | | S&P Credit Rating | NA |

## Price Performance

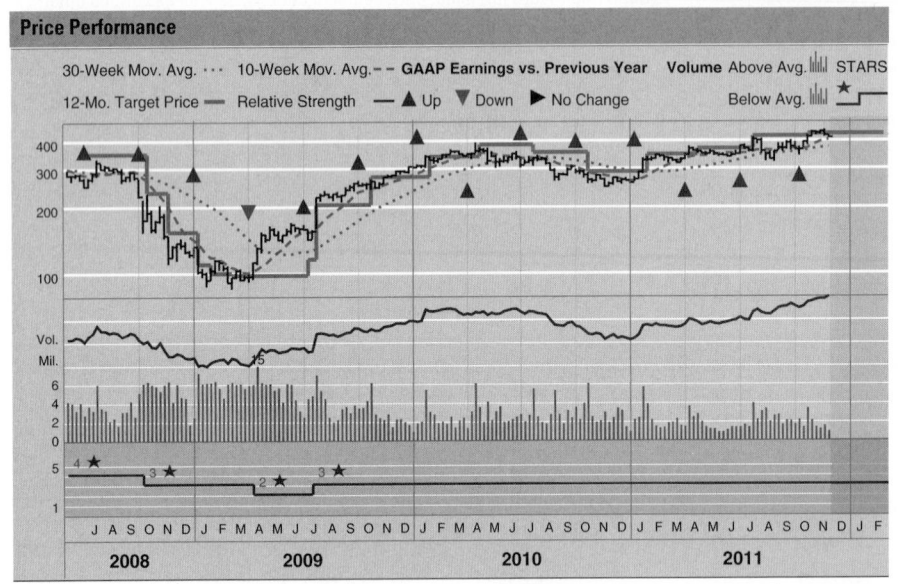

Options: ASE, CBOE, Ph

Analysis prepared by Equity Analyst **Phillip Seligman** on Oct 20, 2011, when the stock traded at **$420.92**.

### Highlights

➤ We look for sales to rise more than 23% in 2011 and in the mid-teens in 2012, driven by increasing sales of the new da Vinci Si system, other new products, higher procedure volumes, and a higher recurring service revenue stream. The number of da Vinci system-based procedures is expected to climb 29%-30%, compared to 2010's 35% growth, and we see further deceleration in 2012. We attribute the deceleration in sales and procedures to slowing growth from an expanding base, despite a greater variety of da Vinci-based procedures. While we still see most sales in the U.S., we see increasing international penetration, partly reflecting an expanded sales force and the increasing attraction of robotics-based procedures.

➤ We look for gross margins to narrow slightly this year, partly on lower average selling prices and trade-ins from the older daVinci model, and to be stable in 2012. We expect the operating cost ratio to decline on revenue leverage, but expand slightly in 2012.

➤ We forecast adjusted EPS of $11.90 in 2011, versus $9.47 in 2010, and look for $14.00 in 2012.

### Investment Rationale/Risk

➤ We think ISRG's technology represents the leading edge in minimally invasive surgery and will continue to gain validity over time through use in a growing number and variety of surgical procedures, and published studies noting their safety. While ISRG has seen slower growth of prostatectomies in the U.S., other procedures using its products, particularly hysterectomies, and newer procedures are ramping. While we expect the capital equipment market in Europe to remain challenging in the near term, ISRG continues to sell systems, and the number of da Vinci-based procedures, including prostatectomies, is growing strongly there.

➤ Risks to our recommendation and target price include increased pricing pressures, lower system sales than we project, and tighter hospital capital budgets.

➤ Our 12-month target price of $430 assumes a P/E-to-growth ratio of 1.9X, using our 2011 EPS estimate, a steep premium to the medical device group to reflect the faster growth we see long term, and our three-year EPS compound annual growth rate forecast of 19%. The shares' run-up limits the price appreciation potential we see over the next 12 months.

### Qualitative Risk Assessment

| LOW | MEDIUM | HIGH |
|---|---|---|

Our risk assessment reflects risks that we see as specific to a maker of medical devices such as ISRG, including those associated with protecting its intellectual property rights, compliance with regulations of U.S. and foreign health agencies, and legal liability for injury that may result from use of the company's products, such as inappropriate or "off-label" use.

### Quantitative Evaluations

**S&P Quality Ranking** B-

| D | C | B- | B | B+ | A- | A | A+ |
|---|---|---|---|---|---|---|---|

**Relative Strength Rank** STRONG
87
LOWEST = 1    HIGHEST = 99

### Revenue/Earnings Data

**Revenue (Million $)**

| | 1Q | 2Q | 3Q | 4Q | Year |
|---|---|---|---|---|---|
| 2011 | 388.1 | 425.7 | 446.7 | -- | -- |
| 2010 | 328.6 | 350.7 | 344.4 | 389.3 | 1,413 |
| 2009 | 188.4 | 260.6 | 280.1 | 323.0 | 1,052 |
| 2008 | 118.2 | 219.2 | 236.0 | 231.6 | 874.9 |
| 2007 | 114.2 | 140.3 | 156.9 | 189.5 | 600.8 |
| 2006 | 77.26 | 87.03 | 95.83 | 112.6 | 372.7 |

**Earnings Per Share ($)**

| | | | | | |
|---|---|---|---|---|---|
| 2011 | 2.59 | 2.91 | 3.05 | E3.35 | E11.90 |
| 2010 | 2.12 | 2.19 | 2.14 | 3.02 | 9.47 |
| 2009 | 0.72 | 1.62 | 1.64 | 1.95 | 5.93 |
| 2008 | 1.12 | 1.28 | 1.44 | 1.27 | 5.12 |
| 2007 | 0.62 | 0.79 | 1.04 | 1.24 | 3.70 |
| 2006 | 0.38 | 0.44 | 0.45 | 0.62 | 1.89 |

Fiscal year ended Dec. 31. Next earnings report expected: NA. EPS Estimates based on S&P Operating Earnings; historical GAAP earnings are as reported.

### Dividend Data

No cash dividends have been paid.

# Intuitive Surgical Inc

**STANDARD
&POOR'S**

## Business Summary October 20, 2011

Intuitive Surgical (ISRG) has designed the da Vinci Surgical System, a product that incorporates advanced robotics and computerized visualization technologies to improve the ability of surgeons to perform complex, minimally invasive procedures. As of 2010 year end, the company had an installed base of 1,752 da Vinci Surgical Systems; during 2010, surgeons using the company's technology had successfully completed about 278,000 surgical procedures of various types, including urologic, gynecologic, cardiothoracic and general surgery, up 35% from the 2009 level.

The da Vinci Surgical System consists of a surgeon's console, a patient-side cart, a high performance vision system, and proprietary wristed instruments. By placing computer-enhanced technology between the surgeon and patient, ISRG believes da Vinci lets surgeons perform better surgery in a manner never before experienced. The system translates a surgeon's natural hand movements on instrument controls on a console into corresponding micro-movements of instruments positioned inside the patient through small puncture incisions (ports). It gives a surgeon the intuitive control, range of motion, fine tissue manipulation capability, and 3-D visualization characteristics of open surgery, while simultaneously allowing use of the small ports of minimal-

ly invasive surgery. During 2010, surgeons using ISRG products performed about 98,000 prostatectomy procedures and 100,000 hysterectomy procedures worldwide.

Intuitive's strategy is targeted at establishing Intuitive surgery as the standard for complex surgical procedures and many other procedures. Over time, the company hopes to broaden the number of procedures performed using the da Vinci Surgical System and to educate surgeons and hospitals about the benefits of Intuitive surgery.

The da Vinci System is covered by over 290 U.S. patents and 300 foreign patents that are licensed or owned by the company. The manufacture, marketing, and use of Class II medical devices such as the da Vinci System is governed by extensive regulations administered by the FDA, which we think act as significant barriers to entry by competitors.

## Company Financials Fiscal Year Ended Dec. 31

| Per Share Data ($) | 2010 | 2009 | 2008 | 2007 | 2006 | 2005 | 2004 | 2003 | 2002 | 2001 |
|---|---|---|---|---|---|---|---|---|---|---|
| Tangible Book Value | 47.67 | 35.59 | 28.07 | 19.61 | 12.55 | 8.64 | 4.83 | 3.87 | 3.46 | 4.14 |
| Cash Flow | 10.48 | 6.82 | 5.74 | 4.04 | 2.15 | 2.64 | 0.82 | -0.23 | -0.80 | -0.76 |
| Earnings | 9.47 | 5.93 | 5.12 | 3.70 | 1.89 | 2.51 | 0.67 | -0.41 | -1.02 | -0.94 |
| S&P Core Earnings | 9.47 | 5.93 | 5.31 | 3.70 | 1.89 | 2.14 | 0.39 | -0.57 | -1.10 | -1.14 |
| Dividends | Nil | Nil | Nil | Nil | Nil | Nil | Nil | Nil | Nil | Nil |
| Payout Ratio | Nil | Nil | Nil | Nil | Nil | Nil | Nil | Nil | Nil | Nil |
| Prices:High | 393.92 | 309.09 | 357.98 | 359.59 | 139.50 | 124.79 | 40.60 | 18.61 | 22.50 | 29.56 |
| Prices:Low | 246.05 | 84.86 | 110.35 | 86.20 | 85.63 | 35.69 | 15.08 | 7.34 | 11.20 | 6.00 |
| P/E Ratio:High | 42 | 52 | 70 | 97 | 74 | 50 | 61 | NM | NM | NM |
| P/E Ratio:Low | 26 | 14 | 22 | 23 | 45 | 14 | 23 | NM | NM | NM |

| Income Statement Analysis (Million $) | | | | | | | | | | |
|---|---|---|---|---|---|---|---|---|---|---|
| Revenue | 1,413 | 1,052 | 875 | 601 | 373 | 227 | 139 | 91.7 | 72.0 | 51.7 |
| Operating Income | 595 | 412 | 336 | 220 | 117 | 73.6 | 26.3 | -7.73 | -16.3 | -17.3 |
| Depreciation | 40.4 | 34.6 | 25.1 | 13.0 | 10.0 | 4.86 | 5.10 | 4.15 | 3.89 | 3.12 |
| Interest Expense | NA | NA | Nil | Nil | Nil | 0.02 | 0.09 | 0.20 | 0.20 | 0.27 |
| Pretax Income | 572 | 396 | 335 | 237 | 120 | 73.8 | 24.2 | -9.62 | -18.4 | -16.7 |
| Effective Tax Rate | NA | 41.3% | 39.1% | 39.1% | 40.0% | NM | 3.00% | NM | NM | NM |
| Net Income | 382 | 233 | 204 | 145 | 72.0 | 94.1 | 23.5 | -9.62 | -18.4 | -16.7 |
| S&P Core Earnings | 382 | 233 | 212 | 145 | 72.0 | 80.1 | 13.6 | -13.6 | -20.0 | -20.3 |

| Balance Sheet & Other Financial Data (Million $) | | | | | | | | | | |
|---|---|---|---|---|---|---|---|---|---|---|
| Cash | 1,609 | 1,172 | 902 | 427 | 34.4 | 5.51 | 5.77 | 11.3 | 17.6 | 10.5 |
| Current Assets | 1,943 | 847 | 704 | 610 | 374 | 209 | 177 | 152 | 78.6 | 89.2 |
| Total Assets | 2,390 | 1,810 | 1,475 | 1,040 | 672 | 502 | 354 | 315 | 91.6 | 100 |
| Current Liabilities | 226 | 203 | 165 | 132 | 80.7 | 58.0 | 38.4 | 34.2 | 26.1 | 21.3 |
| Long Term Debt | NA | NA | Nil | Nil | Nil | Nil | Nil | 0.70 | 1.84 | 0.77 |
| Common Equity | 2,037 | 1,537 | 1,267 | 889 | 590 | 443 | 315 | 279 | 63.7 | 78.3 |
| Total Capital | 2,037 | 1,537 | 1,267 | 889 | 590 | 443 | 315 | 280 | 65.5 | 79.1 |
| Capital Expenditures | 96.0 | 53.4 | 62.5 | 20.3 | 15.9 | 30.1 | 22.4 | 2.53 | 5.79 | 5.53 |
| Cash Flow | 422 | 267 | 229 | 158 | 82.1 | 99.0 | 28.6 | -5.47 | -14.5 | -13.6 |
| Current Ratio | 8.6 | 8.4 | 4.3 | 4.6 | 4.6 | 3.6 | 4.6 | 4.4 | 3.0 | 4.2 |
| % Long Term Debt of Capitalization | Nil | Nil | Nil | Nil | Nil | Nil | Nil | 0.2 | 2.8 | 1.0 |
| % Net Income of Revenue | 27.0 | 22.1 | 23.4 | 24.1 | 19.3 | 41.4 | 16.9 | NM | NM | NM |
| % Return on Assets | 18.2 | 14.2 | 16.3 | 16.9 | 12.3 | 22.0 | 7.0 | NM | NM | NM |
| % Return on Equity | 21.4 | 16.6 | 19.0 | 19.6 | 14.0 | 24.9 | 7.9 | NM | NM | NM |

Data as orig reptd.; bef. results of disc opers/spec. items. Per share data adj. for stk. divs.; EPS diluted. E-Estimated. NA-Not Available. NM-Not Meaningful. NR-Not Ranked. UR-Under Review.

**Office:** 1266 Kifer Rd, Sunnyvale, CA, USA 94086-5304.
**Telephone:** 408-523-2100 .
**Email:** ir@intusurg.com
**Website:** http://www.intuitivesurgical.com

**Chrmn:** L.M. Smith
**Pres & CEO:** G.S. Guthart
**SVP, CFO & Chief Acctg Officer:** M.L. Mohr
**SVP & General Counsel:** M.J. Meltzer

**Cntlr:** J.J. Skoglund
**Board Members:** C. H. Barratt, G. S. Guthart, E. H. Halvorson, A. M. Johnson, A. J. Levy, F. D. Loop, H. E. Rubash, L. M. Smith, G. J. Stalk, Jr.

**Founded:** 1995
**Domicile:** Delaware
**Employees:** 1,660

# Intuit Inc

**STANDARD &POOR'S**

| | |
|---|---|
| **S&P Recommendation** HOLD ★★★☆☆ | |

| Price | 12-Mo. Target Price | Investment Style |
|---|---|---|
| $49.27 (as of Nov 25, 2011) | $58.00 | Large-Cap Growth |

**GICS Sector** Information Technology
**Sub-Industry** Application Software

**Summary** This company develops and markets small business accounting and management, tax preparation and personal finance software.

## Key Stock Statistics (Source S&P, Vickers, company reports)

| | | | | | | | | |
|---|---|---|---|---|---|---|---|---|
| 52-Wk Range | $56.46–39.87 | S&P Oper. EPS 2012E | 2.62 | Market Capitalization(B) | $14.821 | Beta | | 0.75 |
| Trailing 12-Month EPS | $2.05 | S&P Oper. EPS 2013E | 2.79 | Yield (%) | 1.22 | S&P 3-Yr. Proj. EPS CAGR(%) | | 10 |
| Trailing 12-Month P/E | 24.0 | P/E on S&P Oper. EPS 2012E | 18.8 | Dividend Rate/Share | $0.60 | S&P Credit Rating | | BBB |
| $10K Invested 5 Yrs Ago | $15,548 | Common Shares Outstg. (M) | 300.8 | Institutional Ownership (%) | 89 | | | |

## Price Performance

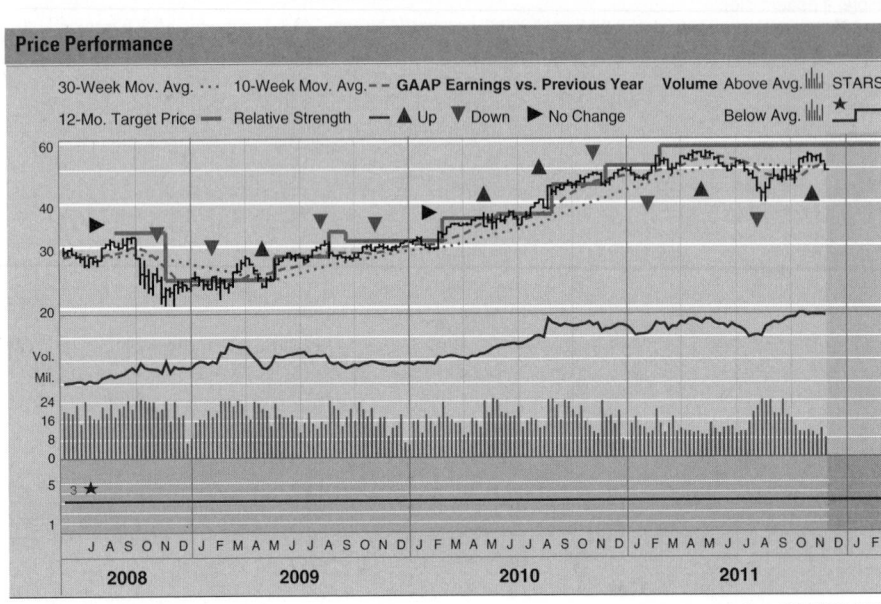

30-Week Mov. Avg. · · · 10-Week Mov. Avg. – – GAAP Earnings vs. Previous Year Volume Above Avg. STARS
12-Mo. Target Price — Relative Strength — ▲ Up ▼ Down ► No Change Below Avg. ★

Options: ASE, CBOE, P, Ph

Analysis prepared by Equity Analyst **Jim Yin, CFA** on Nov 21, 2011, when the stock traded at **$50.76**.

## Highlights

➤ We estimate that sales will rise 10% in FY 12 (Jul.), to $4.3 billion, following an 11% rise in FY 11, driven mainly by organic growth in all of IN-TU's business segments. We forecast 10% sales growth for INTU's consumer tax business, supported by rising usage of online consumer tax preparation offerings. We expect small business segment sales to increase nearly 10%, with QuickBooks sales projected to rise at a healthy clip, supported by growth in INTU's online offering even as the economic backdrop limits new business formation.

➤ We expect INTU to continue to exercise cost discipline, and we see FY 12 non-GAAP operating margins widening as the company benefits from higher sales and a favorable mix. Organically, we believe the company will benefit from selective hiring and data center consolidation, but we see ongoing investment in R&D, marketing and infrastructure.

➤ We forecast operating EPS of $2.62 for FY 12, compared to $2.23 in FY 11, excluding amortization and acquisition-related charges but including projected stock-based compensation expense.

## Investment Rationale/Risk

➤ We expect INTU's small business segment to see improving growth as economic conditions continue to stabilize. While there are modest signs of new business formation, we see INTU having success through cross-sales and from its online channel. INTU's tax franchise is less sensitive to the economy, and we see the company continuing to outpace the market with projected growth of 10%. We expect previously completed acquisitions to help drive growth, and we are encouraged by recent gains in the user base for its online financial offerings.

➤ Risks to our recommendation and target price include increased competition in the consumer tax market and a material worsening of the economic environment, leading to elevated losses in INTU's small business segments. We are also concerned about potential acquisition-integration issues.

➤ Our 12-month target price of $58 is derived using our valuation of discounted cash flows. We expect near-term revenue growth in the low double digits, moderating over time. We also assume a terminal growth rate of 2% and a weighted average cost of capital of 7.7% in our DCF model.

## Qualitative Risk Assessment

| LOW | MEDIUM | HIGH |
|---|---|---|

Our risk assessment reflects our view of the company's strong market position within the consumer and professional tax segments and its solid balance sheet. However, this is tempered by our concern about the potential for a slowdown in the company's small business segment (excluding acquisitions) if the economy weakens considerably.

## Quantitative Evaluations

**S&P Quality Ranking**      B+

| D | C | B- | B | B+ | A- | A | A+ |
|---|---|---|---|---|---|---|---|

**Relative Strength Rank**      MODERATE

64

LOWEST = 1      HIGHEST = 99

## Revenue/Earnings Data

### Revenue (Million $)

| | 1Q | 2Q | 3Q | 4Q | Year |
|---|---|---|---|---|---|
| 2012 | 594.0 | -- | -- | -- | -- |
| 2011 | 532.0 | 878.0 | 1,848 | 593.0 | 3,851 |
| 2010 | 474.0 | 837.0 | 1,607 | 537.0 | 3,455 |
| 2009 | 481.4 | 791.0 | 1,434 | 475.8 | 3,183 |
| 2008 | 444.9 | 834.9 | 1,313 | 478.2 | 3,071 |
| 2007 | 350.5 | 750.6 | 1,139 | 432.7 | 2,673 |

### Earnings Per Share ($)

| | | | | | |
|---|---|---|---|---|---|
| 2012 | -0.21 | E0.40 | E2.35 | E0.06 | E2.62 |
| 2011 | -0.22 | 0.23 | 2.20 | -0.19 | 2.00 |
| 2010 | -0.21 | 0.26 | 1.78 | -0.15 | 1.66 |
| 2009 | -0.16 | 0.26 | 1.47 | -0.22 | 1.35 |
| 2008 | -0.14 | 0.34 | 1.33 | -0.19 | 1.33 |
| 2007 | -0.17 | 0.40 | 1.04 | -0.19 | 1.25 |

Fiscal year ended Jul. 31. Next earnings report expected: Mid February. EPS Estimates based on S&P Operating Earnings; historical GAAP earnings are as reported.

## Dividend Data (Dates: mm/dd Payment Date: mm/dd/yy)

| Amount ($) | Date Decl. | Ex-Div. Date | Stk. of Record | Payment Date |
|---|---|---|---|---|
| 0.150 | 08/18 | 10/05 | 10/10 | 10/18/11 |
| 0.150 | 11/17 | 01/06 | 01/10 | 01/18/12 |

Dividends have been paid since 2011. Source: Company reports.

---

# Intuit Inc

STANDARD
&POOR'S

## Business Summary November 21, 2011

CORPORATE OVERVIEW. Intuit is a leading provider of accounting, financial management, personal finance and tax software for consumers and small businesses. The company's flagship products include QuickBooks, TurboTax, Lacerte and Quicken. In FY 10 (Jul.), the company had four main product categories, which contained seven segments. The company's Small Business Group includes the Financial Management Solutions (formerly QuickBooks), Employee Management Solutions (formerly Payroll) and Payment Solutions (formerly Payments) segments. Its Tax Products group includes the Consumer Tax and Accounting Professional segments; other segments include Financial Services and Other Businesses.

Financial Management Solutions (which accounted for 18% of total net revenues in FY 10) includes products and services that provide bookkeeping capabilities and business management tools. INTU offers QuickBooks Simple Start for very small, less complex businesses; QuickBooks Pro for slightly larger businesses and QuickBooks Pro for Mac; QuickBooks Premier, to support businesses that need advanced accounting capabilities and business planning tools; and QuickBooks Enterprise Solutions, designed for mid-sized companies. INTU also offers an online version of QuickBooks and Premier and Enterprise versions that cater to specific industries, including Manufacturing, Wholesale, Retail, Non-Profit, Contractor, and Professional Services.

Employee Management Solutions (12%) consists of solutions including outsourced payroll services QuickBooks Payroll in different varieties and QuickBooks Online Payroll, for use with QuickBooks Online Edition. Direct deposit and electronic tax payment and filing services are available with some of these offerings for additional fees. The Payment Solutions (9%) segment includes credit card, debit card, electronic benefits, check guarantee and gift card processing, Web-based transaction processing services for online merchants as well as customer service, charge-back retrieval and support, and fraud and loss prevention screening.

The Consumer Tax (33%) segment is centered on TurboTax. TurboTax software enables individuals and small businesses to prepare and file income tax returns using computers. TurboTax for the Web allows individuals to prepare tax returns online. Versions of TurboTax Premier software are designed to address the special income tax needs of different types of users, including investors, those planning for retirement, and rental property owners. Electronic tax filing services are also provided.

## Company Financials Fiscal Year Ended Jul. 31

| Per Share Data ($) | 2011 | 2010 | 2009 | 2008 | 2007 | 2006 | 2005 | 2004 | 2003 | 2002 |
|---|---|---|---|---|---|---|---|---|---|---|
| Tangible Book Value | 1.83 | 2.07 | 1.35 | 0.32 | 0.66 | 3.41 | 3.61 | 2.75 | 3.44 | 4.02 |
| Cash Flow | 2.76 | 2.45 | 2.19 | 1.97 | 1.51 | 1.34 | 1.31 | 1.03 | 0.81 | 0.30 |
| Earnings | 2.00 | 1.66 | 1.35 | 1.33 | 1.25 | 1.05 | 1.00 | 0.79 | 0.82 | 0.16 |
| S&P Core Earnings | 2.05 | 1.66 | 1.35 | 1.22 | 1.19 | 1.04 | 0.86 | 0.61 | 0.41 | NA |
| Dividends | NA | Nil | Nil | Nil | Nil | Nil | Nil | Nil | Nil | Nil |
| Payout Ratio | Nil | Nil | Nil | Nil | Nil | Nil | Nil | Nil | Nil | Nil |
| Prices:High | 56.46 | 50.33 | 31.29 | 32.00 | 33.10 | 35.98 | 27.97 | 26.63 | 26.95 | 27.52 |
| Prices:Low | 39.87 | 29.00 | 21.07 | 20.18 | 26.14 | 23.99 | 18.62 | 17.92 | 16.65 | 17.26 |
| P/E Ratio:High | 28 | 30 | 23 | 24 | 26 | 34 | 28 | 34 | 33 | NM |
| P/E Ratio:Low | 20 | 17 | 16 | 15 | 21 | 23 | 19 | 23 | 20 | NM |

| Income Statement Analysis (Million $) | | | | | | | | | | |
|---|---|---|---|---|---|---|---|---|---|---|
| Revenue | 3,851 | 3,455 | 3,183 | 3,071 | 2,673 | 2,342 | 2,038 | 1,868 | 1,651 | 1,358 |
| Operating Income | 1,278 | 1,119 | 957 | 891 | 773 | 677 | 659 | 561 | 461 | 343 |
| Depreciation | 241 | 256 | 275 | 216 | 135 | 104 | 118 | 97.0 | 76.5 | 59.9 |
| Interest Expense | 60.0 | 61.0 | 51.2 | 52.3 | 27.1 | Nil | Nil | Nil | Nil | Nil |
| Pretax Income | 966 | 815 | 653 | 698 | 696 | 610 | 556 | 453 | 393 | 84.9 |
| Effective Tax Rate | NA | NA | 31.4% | 35.2% | 36.1% | 38.0% | 32.6% | 30.0% | 33.0% | 17.9% |
| Net Income | 634 | 539 | 447 | 451 | 443 | 377 | 375 | 317 | 263 | 69.8 |
| S&P Core Earnings | 648 | 538 | 446 | 414 | 422 | 372 | 323 | 245 | 172 | -0.77 |

| Balance Sheet & Other Financial Data (Million $) | | | | | | | | | | |
|---|---|---|---|---|---|---|---|---|---|---|
| Cash | 1,421 | 1,622 | 1,347 | 828 | 255 | 180 | 83.8 | 27.2 | 1,207 | 452 |
| Current Assets | 2,254 | 2,295 | 1,968 | 1,774 | 1,952 | 1,817 | 1,614 | 1,517 | 1,669 | 1,995 |
| Total Assets | 5,110 | 5,198 | 4,826 | 4,667 | 4,252 | 2,770 | 2,716 | 2,696 | 2,790 | 2,963 |
| Current Liabilities | 1,805 | 1,221 | 1,084 | 1,467 | 1,160 | 1,016 | 1,003 | 857 | 796 | 733 |
| Long Term Debt | 499 | 998 | 998 | 1,000 | 998 | 15.4 | 17.5 | 5.77 | 29.3 | 14.6 |
| Common Equity | 2,616 | 2,821 | 2,556 | 2,073 | 2,035 | 1,738 | 1,695 | 1,822 | 1,965 | 2,216 |
| Total Capital | 3,615 | 3,819 | 3,556 | 3,079 | 3,034 | 1,754 | 1,713 | 1,828 | 1,994 | 2,230 |
| Capital Expenditures | 114 | 130 | 182 | 306 | 105 | 44.6 | 38.2 | 52.3 | 50.4 | 42.6 |
| Cash Flow | 875 | 795 | 722 | 667 | 538 | 482 | 493 | 414 | 340 | 130 |
| Current Ratio | 1.3 | 1.9 | 1.8 | 1.2 | 1.7 | 1.8 | 1.6 | 1.8 | 2.1 | 2.7 |
| % Long Term Debt of Capitalization | 13.8 | 26.1 | 28.1 | 32.5 | 32.9 | 0.9 | 1.0 | 0.3 | 1.5 | 0.7 |
| % Net Income of Revenue | 16.5 | 15.6 | 14.1 | 14.7 | 16.6 | 16.1 | 18.4 | 17.0 | 15.9 | 5.1 |
| % Return on Assets | 12.3 | 10.8 | 9.4 | 10.1 | 24.1 | 13.8 | 13.8 | 11.6 | 9.2 | 2.4 |
| % Return on Equity | 23.3 | 20.1 | 19.3 | 22.0 | 23.5 | 22.0 | 21.3 | 16.7 | 12.6 | 3.2 |

Data as orig reptd.; bef. results of disc opers/spec. items. Per share data adj. for stk. divs.; EPS diluted. E-Estimated. NA-Not Available. NM-Not Meaningful. NR-Not Ranked. UR-Under Review.

**Office:** 2700 Coast Ave, Mountain View, CA 94043-1140.
**Telephone:** 650-944-6000.
**Email:** investor_relations@intuit.com
**Website:** http://www.intuit.com

**Chrmn:** W.V. Campbell
**Pres & CEO:** B.D. Smith
**SVP & CFO:** R.N. Williams
**SVP & CTO:** T. Stansbury

**SVP, Secy & General Counsel:** L.A. Fennell
**Investor Contact:** K. Patel (650-944-3560)
**Board Members:** D. H. Batchelder, C. W. Brody, W. V. Campbell, S. D. Cook, D. B. Greene, M. R. Hallman, S. N. Johnson, E. A. Kangas, D. D. Powell, B. D. Smith

**Founded:** 1984
**Domicile:** Delaware
**Employees:** 8,000

The McGraw-Hill Companies

# Invesco Ltd

STANDARD
&POOR'S

| S&P Recommendation **BUY** ★★★★☆ | Price<br>$17.91 (as of Nov 25, 2011) | 12-Mo. Target Price<br>$23.00 | Investment Style<br>Large-Cap Blend |
|---|---|---|---|

**GICS Sector** Financials
**Sub-Industry** Asset Management & Custody Banks

**Summary** This diversified investment manager offers an array of investment options to individuals and institutions through offices around the world. As of September 30, 2011, Invesco had $598 billion in assets under management.

## Key Stock Statistics (Source S&P, Vickers, company reports)

| | | | | | |
|---|---|---|---|---|---|
| 52-Wk Range | $29.94– 14.52 | S&P Oper. EPS 2011E | 1.68 | Market Capitalization(B) | $8.077 |
| Trailing 12-Month EPS | $1.51 | S&P Oper. EPS 2012E | 1.72 | Yield (%) | 2.74 |
| Trailing 12-Month P/E | 11.9 | P/E on S&P Oper. EPS 2011E | 10.7 | Dividend Rate/Share | $0.49 |
| $10K Invested 5 Yrs Ago | $9,188 | Common Shares Outstg. (M) | 451.0 | Institutional Ownership (%) | 89 |

| | |
|---|---|
| Beta | 1.80 |
| S&P 3-Yr. Proj. EPS CAGR(%) | 24 |
| S&P Credit Rating | BBB+ |

## Price Performance

30-Week Mov. Avg. · · · · 10-Week Mov. Avg. – – GAAP Earnings vs. Previous Year Volume Above Avg. STARS
12-Mo. Target Price — Relative Strength — ▲ Up ▼ Down ▶ No Change Below Avg. ★

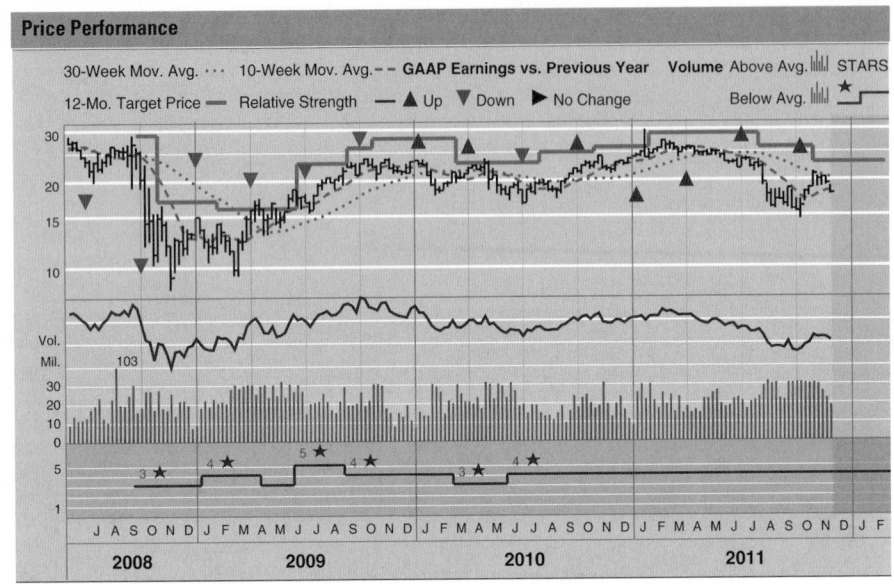

## Qualitative Risk Assessment

| LOW | MEDIUM | HIGH |
|---|---|---|

Our risk assessment reflects our view of the company's strong market share, broad product base and improving investment performance, offset by economic and industry cyclicality, the firm's bias toward equity products, and recent relative fund underperformance.

## Quantitative Evaluations

**S&P Quality Ranking** NR

| D | C | B- | B | B+ | A- | A | A+ |
|---|---|---|---|---|---|---|---|

**Relative Strength Rank** MODERATE

53

LOWEST = 1 HIGHEST = 99

## Revenue/Earnings Data

**Revenue (Million $)**

| | 1Q | 2Q | 3Q | 4Q | Year |
|---|---|---|---|---|---|
| 2011 | 1,027 | 1,070 | 997.8 | -- | -- |
| 2010 | 719.1 | 787.0 | 953.1 | 1,029 | 3,488 |
| 2009 | 548.6 | 625.1 | 705.8 | 747.8 | 2,627 |
| 2008 | 910.4 | 935.6 | 827.2 | 634.4 | 3,308 |
| 2007 | 900.2 | 979.0 | 976.6 | 1,023 | 3,879 |
| 2006 | 584.1 | 588.1 | 587.1 | 655.3 | 2,415 |

**Earnings Per Share ($)**

| | | | | | |
|---|---|---|---|---|---|
| 2011 | 0.38 | 0.39 | 0.36 | E0.41 | E1.68 |
| 2010 | 0.21 | 0.09 | 0.32 | 0.37 | 1.01 |
| 2009 | 0.08 | 0.18 | 0.24 | 0.25 | 0.76 |
| 2008 | 0.39 | 0.41 | 0.33 | 0.08 | 1.21 |
| 2007 | 0.38 | 0.43 | 0.41 | 0.43 | 1.64 |
| 2006 | 0.26 | 0.30 | 0.26 | 0.40 | 1.20 |

Fiscal year ended Dec. 31. Next earnings report expected: NA. EPS Estimates based on S&P Operating Earnings; historical GAAP earnings are as reported.

Analysis prepared by Equity Analyst **Erik Oja** on Nov 02, 2011, when the stock traded at **$19.70**.

### Highlights

➤ Although third-quarter results showed a decline in assets under management (AUM), particularly in fixed income and money market funds, we think strong overall fund performance will provide support for average AUM. We also believe IVZ's purchase of Morgan Stanley's (MS 17 Hold) retail asset management business, including the Van Kampen funds, will give the company an improved distribution platform. We think inflows into long-term funds are likely to continue, particularly for international equity and alternative investment products. We view the management fee rate as stable, but we think revenues will be boosted by strong performance fee and service/distribution fee growth. We forecast operating revenue growth of 17% in 2011.

➤ We look for improved operating margins in the next two years, given IVZ's move for cost savings via lower relative compensation and general & administrative costs despite steady distribution costs.

➤ We estimate EPS of $1.68 in 2011 and $1.72 in 2012.

### Investment Rationale/Risk

➤ We think that Invesco, with its broad product offerings and global reach, is in a position to attract and retain client assets. Although the firm's asset base is weighted toward equities, IVZ has achieved international diversification, and its customer base is composed of both retail and institutional clients. We expect IVZ's assets under management growth to outpace peers, and we think the shares do not adequately reflect the value of the Van Kampen acquisition from Morgan Stanley. We also have a positive view of IVZ's corporate governance policies, including the independence of a majority of directors and the separation of the chairman and chief executive roles. All told, we believe the shares are undervalued at recent levels.

➤ Risks to our recommendation and target price include equity and bond market depreciation, poor relative investment performance, and increased government regulation within the industry.

➤ Our 12-month target price of $23 is equal to 13.7X our forward earnings forecast of $1.68, in line with peers.

## Dividend Data (Dates: mm/dd Payment Date: mm/dd/yy)

| Amount<br>($) | Date<br>Decl. | Ex-Div.<br>Date | Stk. of<br>Record | Payment<br>Date |
|---|---|---|---|---|
| 0.110 | 01/27 | 02/18 | 02/23 | 03/09/11 |
| 0.123 | 04/27 | 05/18 | 05/20 | 06/08/11 |
| 0.123 | 07/26 | 08/18 | 08/22 | 09/08/11 |
| 0.123 | 10/24 | 11/16 | 11/18 | 12/07/11 |

Dividends have been paid since 1995. Source: Company reports.

**Please read the Required Disclosures and Analyst Certification on the last page of this report.**

The McGraw·Hill Companies

# Invesco Ltd

## Business Summary November 02, 2011

CORPORATE OVERVIEW. Invesco Ltd. is an independent global investment management company that provides an array of investment choices for retail, institutional and high-net-worth clients around the globe. It is incorporated under the laws of Bermuda and headquartered in Atlanta, GA. Prior to May 2007, the company was called AMVESCAP PLC, formed through the 1997 merger of Invesco and AIM. Through its subsidiaries, it offers equity, fixed income and alternative strategies to investors domiciled throughout the world. Assets under management (AUM) totaled $598.4 billion at September 30, 2011, down from $616.5 billion at year-end 2010.

The company distributes its products utilizing a number of brands through various distribution channels. Its retail products are distributed through Invesco AIM in the U.S., Invesco Trimark in Canada, Invesco Perpetual in the U.K., Invesco in Europe and Asia, and PowerShares for exchange-traded funds (ETFs). Retail products are primarily distributed through third parties, including broker-dealers, retirement platforms, financial advisers and insurance companies. Its assets in China are managed through its joint venture Invesco Great Wall. It offers a full array of investment options, including money market, fixed income, balanced, equity and alternative fund choices. As of September 30, 2011, IVZ's retail channel had AUM of $354.4 billion.

Institutional clients are served throughout the world through Invesco and Invesco AIM, with a range of products, including equities, fixed income, real estate, financial structures and absolute return strategies. Private equity options are offered through W.L. Ross & Co. A global sales force distributes products and provides service to clients around the world, including public entities, corporations, unions, non-profits, endowments, foundations, and financial institutions. As of September 30, 2011, IVZ's institutional channel had AUM of $227.2 billion.

Invesco's private wealth management services are offered through Atlantic Trust, providing high-net-worth individuals with personalized service, including financial counseling, estate planning, asset allocation, investment management, private equity, trust, custody and other services. Atlantic Trust had offices in 11 U.S. cities, and managed $16.8 billion as of September 30, 2011.

## Company Financials Fiscal Year Ended Dec. 31

| Per Share Data ($) | 2010 | 2009 | 2008 | 2007 | 2006 | 2005 | 2004 | 2003 | 2002 | 2001 |
|---|---|---|---|---|---|---|---|---|---|---|
| Tangible Book Value | NA | NA | NM | NM | NM | NM | NM | NM | NM | NM |
| Cash Flow | NA | NA | 1.33 | 1.85 | 1.37 | 0.76 | -0.60 | 0.80 | 0.89 | 1.27 |
| Earnings | 1.01 | 0.76 | 1.21 | 1.64 | 1.20 | 0.52 | -0.84 | -0.08 | 0.06 | 0.54 |
| Dividends | 0.43 | 0.31 | 0.52 | 0.37 | 0.36 | 0.33 | 0.32 | 0.37 | 0.36 | 0.30 |
| Payout Ratio | 43% | 40% | 43% | 23% | 30% | 63% | NM | NM | NM | 56% |
| Prices:High | 24.38 | 24.07 | 31.40 | 32.25 | 25.04 | 15.92 | 17.33 | 18.16 | 31.80 | 48.00 |
| Prices:Low | 16.37 | 9.33 | 8.35 | 26.10 | 15.46 | 11.15 | 9.62 | 7.65 | 7.62 | 16.20 |
| P/E Ratio:High | 24 | 32 | 3 | 20 | 21 | 31 | NM | NM | NM | 89 |
| P/E Ratio:Low | 16 | 12 | 1 | 16 | 13 | 21 | NM | NM | NM | 30 |

| Income Statement Analysis (Million $) | | | | | | | | | | |
|---|---|---|---|---|---|---|---|---|---|---|
| Revenue | 3,488 | 2,627 | 3,308 | 3,879 | 2,415 | 2,173 | 1,158 | 1,158 | 1,345 | 1,620 |
| Operating Income | NA | NA | 795 | 1,058 | 853 | 595 | -63.3 | 362 | 427 | 591 |
| Depreciation | NA | NA | 47.6 | 64.1 | 67.6 | 94.5 | 45.6 | 200 | 210 | 206 |
| Interest Expense | NA | NA | 76.9 | 71.3 | 81.3 | 85.1 | 44.1 | 48.3 | 52.6 | 55.9 |
| Pretax Income | 834 | 358 | 657 | 1,244 | 755 | 360 | -138 | 36.4 | 102 | 280 |
| Effective Tax Rate | NA | 41.5% | 35.9% | 28.7% | 35.0% | 40.7% | NM | NM | 83.5% | 44.8% |
| Net Income | 466 | 323 | 482 | 674 | 490 | 212 | -173 | -17.3 | 16.9 | 155 |

| Balance Sheet & Other Financial Data (Million $) | | | | | | | | | | |
|---|---|---|---|---|---|---|---|---|---|---|
| Cash | 1,686 | 972 | 658 | 1,130 | 924 | 1,957 | 369 | 393 | 424 | 209 |
| Current Assets | NA | NA | 2,379 | 4,194 | 3,497 | 2,706 | 1,385 | 1,297 | 1,150 | 785 |
| Total Assets | 20,444 | 10,910 | 9,757 | 12,925 | 9,292 | 7,578 | 3,907 | 4,110 | 4,138 | 4,432 |
| Current Liabilities | NA | NA | 2,103 | 3,641 | 3,582 | 2,523 | 1,253 | 1,070 | 1,139 | 641 |
| Long Term Debt | 7,181 | 746 | 862 | 1,276 | 973 | 1,212 | 683 | 730 | 596 | 844 |
| Common Equity | 8,265 | 6,913 | 5,690 | 6,591 | 4,270 | 3,613 | 1,863 | 2,232 | 2,283 | 2,282 |
| Total Capital | NA | NA | 7,458 | 8,988 | 5,248 | 4,872 | 2,590 | 2,993 | 2,918 | 3,126 |
| Capital Expenditures | NA | NA | 84.1 | 36.7 | 37.7 | 38.2 | 27.6 | 36.6 | 54.6 | 68.0 |
| Cash Flow | NA | NA | 529 | 738 | 558 | 307 | -128 | 183 | 227 | 361 |
| Current Ratio | 1.3 | 1.4 | 1.1 | 1.2 | 1.0 | 1.1 | 1.1 | 1.2 | 1.0 | 1.2 |
| % Long Term Debt of Capitalization | 43.4 | Nil | 11.6 | 14.2 | 18.5 | 24.9 | 26.4 | 24.4 | 20.4 | 27.0 |
| % Net Income of Revenue | 13.4 | 12.3 | 14.6 | 17.4 | 20.3 | 9.8 | NM | NM | 1.3 | 9.6 |
| % Return on Assets | NA | NA | 5.9 | 5.3 | 5.8 | 2.8 | NM | NM | 0.4 | 3.6 |
| % Return on Equity | NA | NA | 7.8 | 10.6 | 12.4 | 5.9 | NM | NM | 0.7 | 7.1 |

Data as orig reptd.; bef. results of disc opers/spec. items. Per share data adj. for stk. divs.; EPS diluted. Prior to 2005, balance sheet and income statement data in U.K. pounds. E-Estimated. NA-Not Available. NM-Not Meaningful. NR-Not Ranked. UR-Under Review.

**Office:** 1555 Peachtree St, NE Ste 1800, Atlanta, GA 30309.
**Telephone:** 404-479-1095.
**Email:** jordan.krugman@invesco.com
**Website:** http://www.invesco.com

**Chrmn:** R.D. Adams
**Pres & CEO:** M.L. Flanagan
**CFO:** L.M. Starr
**Chief Admin Officer:** C.D. Meadows

**Chief Acctg Officer & Cntlr:** R.G. Ellis
**Investor Contact:** J. Krugman (404-439-4605)
**Board Members:** R. D. Adams, J. Banham, J. R. Canion, M. L. Flanagan, B. F. Johnson, III, D. Kessler, E. P. Lawrence, J. T. Presby, J. I. Robertson, P. A. Wood

**Founded:** 1935
**Domicile:** Bermuda
**Employees:** 5,617

# Iron Mountain Inc

## STANDARD &POOR'S

| S&P Recommendation **HOLD** ★★★☆☆ | Price $28.57 (as of Nov 25, 2011) | 12-Mo. Target Price $34.00 | Investment Style Large-Cap Growth |
|---|---|---|---|

**GICS Sector** Industrials
**Sub-Industry** Diversified Support Services

**Summary** This company provides information protection and storage services.

### Key Stock Statistics (Source S&P, Vickers, company reports)

| | | | | | | | |
|---|---|---|---|---|---|---|---|
| 52-Wk Range | $35.79–22.08 | S&P Oper. EPS 2011**E** | 1.19 | Market Capitalization(B) | $5.303 | Beta | 0.95 |
| Trailing 12-Month EPS | $1.98 | S&P Oper. EPS 2012**E** | 1.25 | Yield (%) | 3.50 | S&P 3-Yr. Proj. EPS CAGR(%) | 9 |
| Trailing 12-Month P/E | 14.4 | P/E on S&P Oper. EPS 2011**E** | 24.0 | Dividend Rate/Share | $1.00 | S&P Credit Rating | BB- |
| $10K Invested 5 Yrs Ago | $10,273 | Common Shares Outstg. (M) | 185.6 | Institutional Ownership (%) | NM | | |

## Price Performance

30-Week Mov. Avg. · · · 10-Week Mov. Avg. - - GAAP Earnings vs. Previous Year   Volume Above Avg. ▊▊▊ STARS
12-Mo. Target Price — Relative Strength ▲ Up ▼ Down ► No Change   Below Avg. ▊▊▊

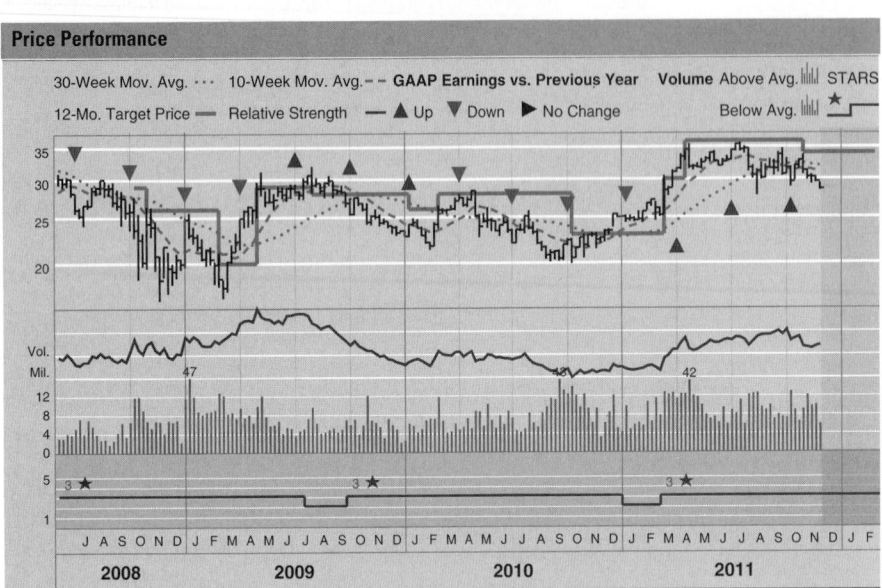

Options: CBOE, P, Ph

Analysis prepared by Equity Analyst **Dylan Cathers** on Nov 11, 2011, when the stock traded at **$30.09**.

### Highlights

➤ We expect total revenues to decline about 3% in 2011, reflecting the sale of the company's on-line backup and recovery, digital archiving, and eDiscovery businesses. In 2012, we expect a 1% revenue drop. We think internal growth will be weak, reflecting low recycled paper prices, and anticipate a currency headwind, given current exchange rates. We also look for weakness in the IRM's services segment to continue for the next couple of quarters, and the overall pace of economic activity is likely to be a negative as well. Still, we look for some growth in the storage business internationally.

➤ We expect incremental improvements in operating margins this year and next. The company is seeing gains from increased productivity in North America and ongoing cost-cutting measures, although more normal compensation levels this year. Rising costs from investments in North America sales and marketing, and expenses related to the proxy contest with Elliott Management Corp should be a headwind. We expect a larger improvement in 2012.

➤ In 2010, operating EPS was $1.16 before various one-time charges. We see EPS of $1.19 in 2011 and $1.25 in 2012.

### Investment Rationale/Risk

➤ Our hold recommendation is based on our concerns about the company's focus as it goes through its shift in management's strategy. Specifically, a special committee is looking at strategic alternatives for the company, including the possibility of restructuring into a REIT. Either way, the company will be managed more with an eye toward higher ROIC and cash flows to support higher levels of share buybacks and dividends.

➤ Risks to our recommendation and target price include slower growth in corporate storage spending than we project, lower-than-expected recycled paper prices, further deterioration in overseas markets, and less favorable foreign currency rates. Our corporate governance concerns center around a "poison pill" put in place in March 2011 and the combination of the roles of CEO and chairman of the board.

➤ Our 12-month target price of $34 is based on our P/E analysis. We use a peer-premium multiple of 27.2X our 2012 EPS estimate, given the potential we see for further positive board action and a higher dividend yield.

### Qualitative Risk Assessment

| LOW | **MEDIUM** | HIGH |
|---|---|---|

Our risk assessment reflects our view of IRM's diversified and significant recurring revenue base, offset by notable and increasing competition and a substantial amount of debt.

### Quantitative Evaluations

**S&P Quality Ranking**  B

| D | C | B- | **B** | B+ | A- | A | A+ |
|---|---|---|---|---|---|---|---|

**Relative Strength Rank**  MODERATE

**42**

LOWEST = 1     HIGHEST = 99

### Revenue/Earnings Data

**Revenue (Million $)**

| | 1Q | 2Q | 3Q | 4Q | Year |
|---|---|---|---|---|---|
| 2011 | 799.0 | 762.9 | 772.1 | -- | -- |
| 2010 | 776.5 | 779.8 | 782.6 | 788.7 | 3,128 |
| 2009 | 723.4 | 746.0 | 764.9 | 779.3 | 3,014 |
| 2008 | 749.4 | 768.9 | 784.3 | 752.6 | 3,055 |
| 2007 | 632.5 | 668.7 | 701.8 | 727.0 | 2,730 |
| 2006 | 563.7 | 581.6 | 595.6 | 609.5 | 2,350 |

**Earnings Per Share ($)**

| | | | | | |
|---|---|---|---|---|---|
| 2011 | 0.37 | 0.32 | 0.17 | E0.29 | E1.19 |
| 2010 | 0.13 | 0.20 | -0.76 | 0.16 | -0.27 |
| 2009 | 0.14 | 0.43 | 0.21 | 0.30 | 1.08 |
| 2008 | 0.17 | 0.18 | 0.06 | 0.01 | 0.40 |
| 2007 | 0.17 | 0.19 | 0.25 | 0.14 | 0.76 |
| 2006 | 0.13 | 0.19 | 0.13 | 0.18 | 0.64 |

Fiscal year ended Dec. 31. Next earnings report expected: Late February. EPS Estimates based on S&P Operating Earnings; historical GAAP earnings are as reported.

### Dividend Data (Dates: mm/dd Payment Date: mm/dd/yy)

| Amount ($) | Date Decl. | Ex-Div. Date | Stk. of Record | Payment Date |
|---|---|---|---|---|
| 0.188 | 12/13 | 12/22 | 12/27 | 01/14/11 |
| 0.188 | 03/11 | 03/23 | 03/25 | 04/15/11 |
| 0.250 | 06/13 | 06/22 | 06/24 | 07/15/11 |
| 0.250 | 09/08 | 09/21 | 09/23 | 10/14/11 |

Dividends have been paid since 2010. Source: Company reports.

Stock Report | November 26, 2011 | NYS Symbol: **IRM**

# Iron Mountain Inc

## Business Summary November 11, 2011

CORPORATE OVERVIEW. We view Iron Mountain as the global leader in information protection and storage services. IRM helps organizations reduce related costs and risks. Specifically, the company offers records-management and data protection solutions, and helps address information challenges including rising storage costs, litigation, regulatory compliance, and disaster recovery.

Revenues are generated by providing storage for a variety of information media formats, core records management services, data and recovery offerings, information destruction services, and an expanding menu of complementary products and services to a diverse customer base. Core services, which are highly recurring, primarily consist of the collection, handling and transportation of stored records and information. In 2010, IRM's storage and core service revenues represented about 87% of total revenues.

As of year-end 2010, IRM had more than 150,000 corporate clients around the world, including more than 95% of the Fortune 1000. The company provides services in more than 35 countries and operates over 1,000 records management facilities. The share of international contributions to IRM's revenue in 2010 was 31%, up from 28% in 2005.

The customer base is diversified by industry, with commercial, legal, banking, health care, accounting, financial, entertainment and government organizations all represented. Further, no single customer represented more than 2% of revenue in 2010 or any of the four prior years.

CORPORATE STRATEGY. Primary growth drivers include increasing revenues from existing customers, adding new clients, introducing new products and services (such as secure shredding, electronic vaulting and digital archiving), and acquisitions.

## Company Financials Fiscal Year Ended Dec. 31

| Per Share Data ($) | 2010 | 2009 | 2008 | 2007 | 2006 | 2005 | 2004 | 2003 | 2002 | 2001 |
|---|---|---|---|---|---|---|---|---|---|---|
| Tangible Book Value | NM | NM | NM | NM | NM | NM | NM | NM | NM | NM |
| Cash Flow | 1.46 | 2.64 | 1.83 | 1.99 | 1.71 | 1.54 | 1.31 | 1.12 | 0.91 | 0.64 |
| Earnings | -0.27 | 1.08 | 0.40 | 0.76 | 0.64 | 0.57 | 0.48 | 0.43 | 0.35 | -0.17 |
| S&P Core Earnings | 1.06 | 1.08 | 0.40 | 0.69 | 0.61 | 0.55 | 0.46 | 0.43 | 0.33 | -0.17 |
| Dividends | 0.37 | Nil | Nil | Nil | Nil | Nil | Nil | Nil | Nil | Nil |
| Payout Ratio | NM | Nil | Nil | Nil | Nil | Nil | Nil | Nil | Nil | Nil |
| Prices:High | 28.49 | 32.04 | 37.13 | 38.85 | 29.91 | 30.06 | 23.39 | 18.06 | 15.20 | 13.54 |
| Prices:Low | 19.93 | 16.91 | 16.71 | 25.05 | 22.64 | 17.77 | 17.22 | 13.44 | 8.95 | 9.37 |
| P/E Ratio:High | NM | 30 | 93 | 51 | 47 | 52 | 49 | 41 | 44 | NM |
| P/E Ratio:Low | NM | 16 | 42 | 33 | 35 | 31 | 36 | 31 | 26 | NM |

| Income Statement Analysis (Million $) | | | | | | | | | | |
|---|---|---|---|---|---|---|---|---|---|---|
| Revenue | 3,128 | 3,014 | 3,055 | 2,730 | 2,350 | 2,078 | 1,818 | 1,501 | 1,319 | 1,171 |
| Operating Income | 946 | 868 | 791 | 699 | 611 | 575 | 507 | 441 | 364 | 302 |
| Depreciation | 344 | 319 | 291 | 249 | 214 | 192 | 164 | 135 | 110 | 154 |
| Interest Expense | 221 | 230 | 237 | 229 | 195 | 184 | 186 | 150 | 137 | 135 |
| Pretax Income | 101 | 333 | 225 | 223 | 224 | 197 | 167 | 157 | 120 | -8.13 |
| Effective Tax Rate | NA | 33.2% | 63.6% | 30.9% | 41.8% | 41.4% | 41.7% | 42.5% | 41.1% | NM |
| Net Income | -49.0 | 221 | 82.0 | 153 | 129 | 114 | 94.2 | 84.6 | 67.0 | -32.2 |
| S&P Core Earnings | 213 | 221 | 82.4 | 139 | 122 | 110 | 91.9 | 83.4 | 63.5 | -31.7 |

| Balance Sheet & Other Financial Data (Million $) | | | | | | | | | | |
|---|---|---|---|---|---|---|---|---|---|---|
| Cash | 259 | 447 | 278 | 133 | 45.4 | 53.4 | 31.9 | 74.7 | 56.3 | 21.4 |
| Current Assets | 1,055 | 1,211 | 976 | 822 | 680 | 554 | 501 | 472 | 367 | 309 |
| Total Assets | 6,396 | 6,847 | 6,357 | 6,308 | 5,210 | 4,766 | 4,442 | 3,892 | 3,231 | 2,860 |
| Current Liabilities | 855 | 815 | 730 | 766 | 639 | 592 | 515 | 585 | 428 | 359 |
| Long Term Debt | 2,912 | 3,211 | 3,207 | 3,213 | 2,606 | 2,504 | 2,439 | 1,974 | 1,662 | 1,461 |
| Common Equity | 1,956 | 2,141 | 1,803 | 1,795 | 1,553 | 1,370 | 1,219 | 1,066 | 945 | 886 |
| Total Capital | 4,980 | 5,397 | 5,050 | 5,389 | 4,444 | 4,105 | 3,877 | 3,262 | 2,748 | 2,459 |
| Capital Expenditures | 278 | 313 | 387 | 386 | 382 | 272 | 232 | 204 | 197 | 197 |
| Cash Flow | 295 | 540 | 373 | 402 | 343 | 306 | 258 | 219 | 177 | 121 |
| Current Ratio | 1.2 | 1.5 | 1.3 | 1.1 | 1.1 | 0.9 | 1.0 | 0.8 | 0.9 | 0.9 |
| % Long Term Debt of Capitalization | 58.5 | 59.5 | 63.5 | 64.2 | 58.6 | 61.0 | 62.9 | 60.5 | 60.5 | 59.4 |
| % Net Income of Revenue | NM | 7.3 | 2.7 | 5.6 | 5.5 | 5.5 | 5.2 | 5.6 | 5.1 | NM |
| % Return on Assets | NM | 3.4 | 1.3 | 2.7 | 2.6 | 2.5 | 2.3 | 2.4 | 2.2 | NM |
| % Return on Equity | NM | 11.2 | 4.6 | 9.1 | 8.8 | 8.8 | 8.2 | 8.4 | 7.3 | NM |

Data as orig reptd.; bef. results of disc opers/spec. items. Per share data adj. for stk. divs.; EPS diluted. E-Estimated. NA-Not Available. NM-Not Meaningful. NR-Not Ranked. UR-Under Review.

Office: 745 Atlantic Ave, Boston, MA 02111-2717.
Telephone: 617-535-4766.
Website: http://www.ironmountain.com
EVP, CFO & Chief Acctg Officer: B.P. McKeon

EVP & CIO: T. Tsolakis
SVP, Secy & General Counsel: E.W. Cloutier
Investor Contact: S.P. Golden (617-535-4766)

Board Members: T. R. Antenucci, C. H. Bailey, K. P. Dauten, P. F. Deninger, P. Halvorsen, M. W. Lamach, A. D. Little, A. Z. Loren, C. R. Reese, V. J. Ryan, L. A. Tucker, A. J. Verrecchia

Founded: 1951
Domicile: Delaware
Employees: 19,400

Redistribution or reproduction is prohibited without written permission. Copyright ©2011 The McGraw-Hill Companies, Inc.

The McGraw·Hill Companies

# Jabil Circuit Inc

**STANDARD &POOR'S**

| S&P Recommendation | HOLD ★★★☆☆ | Price $18.34 (as of Nov 25, 2011) | 12-Mo. Target Price $19.00 | Investment Style Large-Cap Growth |
|---|---|---|---|---|

**GICS Sector** Information Technology
**Sub-Industry** Electronic Manufacturing Services

**Summary** This company manufactures circuit board assemblies for international OEMs in the computing, peripheral, storage, communications, networking and industrial markets.

## Key Stock Statistics (Source S&P, Vickers, company reports)

| | | | | | | | |
|---|---|---|---|---|---|---|---|
| 52-Wk Range | $23.09–13.94 | S&P Oper. EPS 2012**E** | 2.15 | Market Capitalization(B) | $3.818 | Beta | 1.99 |
| Trailing 12-Month EPS | $1.73 | S&P Oper. EPS 2013**E** | 2.35 | Yield (%) | 1.74 | S&P 3-Yr. Proj. EPS CAGR(%) | 30 |
| Trailing 12-Month P/E | 10.6 | P/E on S&P Oper. EPS 2012**E** | 8.5 | Dividend Rate/Share | $0.32 | S&P Credit Rating | BB+ |
| $10K Invested 5 Yrs Ago | $6,984 | Common Shares Outstg. (M) | 208.2 | Institutional Ownership (%) | 92 | | |

## Price Performance

30-Week Mov. Avg. ···· 10-Week Mov. Avg. - - **GAAP Earnings vs. Previous Year** Volume Above Avg. STARS
12-Mo. Target Price — Relative Strength — ▲ Up ▼ Down ► No Change Below Avg.

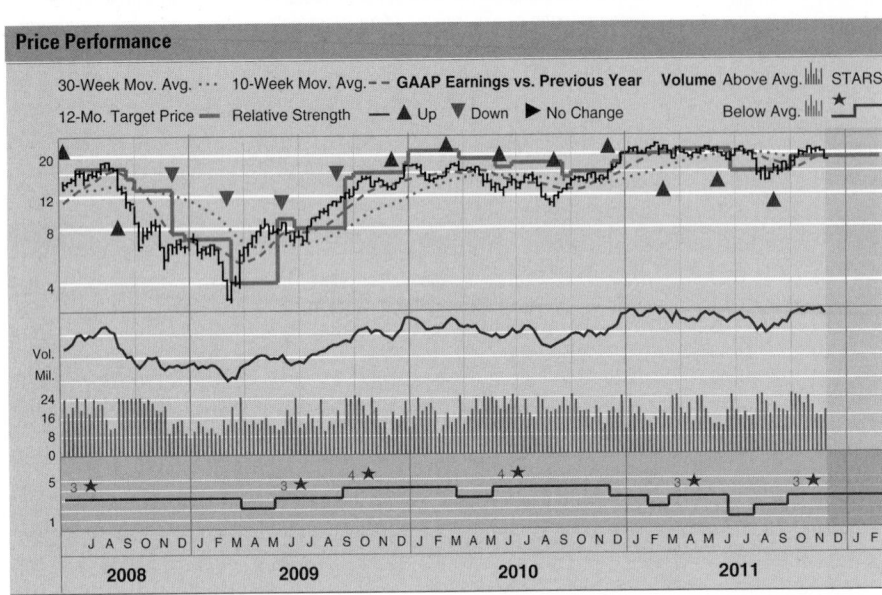

Options: ASE, CBOE, P, Ph

Analysis prepared by Equity Analyst **Dylan Cathers** on Oct 21, 2011, when the stock traded at **$19.58**.

## Qualitative Risk Assessment

| LOW | MEDIUM | HIGH |
|---|---|---|

Our risk assessment reflects our view of the historically volatile nature of the cyclical electronic manufacturing services industry as well as what we see as relatively high share price volatility as indicated by a beta score above 2.

## Quantitative Evaluations

**S&P Quality Ranking** B-

| D | C | B- | B | B+ | A- | A | A+ |
|---|---|---|---|---|---|---|---|

**Relative Strength Rank** MODERATE

54

LOWEST = 1 HIGHEST = 99

## Revenue/Earnings Data

**Revenue (Million $)**

| | 1Q | 2Q | 3Q | 4Q | Year |
|---|---|---|---|---|---|
| 2011 | 4,082 | 3,929 | 4,228 | 4,280 | 16,519 |
| 2010 | 3,088 | 3,005 | 3,456 | 3,861 | 13,409 |
| 2009 | 3,383 | 2,887 | 2,615 | 2,800 | 11,685 |
| 2008 | 3,368 | 3,059 | 3,088 | 3,265 | 12,780 |
| 2007 | 3,224 | 2,935 | 3,002 | 3,130 | 12,291 |
| 2006 | 2,404 | 2,315 | 2,592 | 2,954 | 10,265 |

**Earnings Per Share ($)**

| | | | | | |
|---|---|---|---|---|---|
| 2011 | 0.49 | 0.25 | 0.47 | 0.52 | 1.73 |
| 2010 | 0.13 | 0.14 | 0.24 | 0.27 | 0.78 |
| 2009 | -1.34 | -4.19 | -0.14 | 0.03 | -5.63 |
| 2008 | 0.30 | -0.12 | 0.19 | 0.28 | 0.65 |
| 2007 | 0.20 | 0.07 | 0.03 | 0.06 | 0.35 |
| 2006 | 0.37 | 0.32 | 0.30 | -0.22 | 0.77 |

Fiscal year ended Aug. 31. Next earnings report expected: Late December. EPS Estimates based on S&P Operating Earnings; historical GAAP earnings as reported.

## Highlights

➤ We forecast revenues to increase 6.6% in FY 12 (Aug.), following a 23% advance in FY 11. Our projected growth deceleration reflects our view of uncertain macroeconomic conditions, soft demand from end-markets, and the deteriorating competitiveness of a few of JBL's large customers. However, we believe that the company is effectively countering this by increasing penetration in a broader range of end-markets, such as healthcare and industrial, and through market share gains.

➤ Although we are concerned about wage increases in China and places of JBL's operations, we still expect operating margins to widen modestly to 4.0% for FY 12 from 3.9% in FY 11, largely reflecting an increasing mix of its higher-margin Diversified Manufacturing segment. We also expect higher volumes and continued cost management in its supply chain to support profitability.

➤ Assuming an effective tax rate of 19%, we estimate EPS of $2.15 for FY 12, above FY 11's $2.00.

## Investment Rationale/Risk

➤ Although our optimism for fast growth among Electronic Manufacturing Services firms has dimmed after cautious statements from key customers, lower projections for various consumer electronics sales, and a spate of weak indicators for the global economy, we believe that the company's success in new and less-cyclical markets and customers will help to support sales and margins. We view positively JBL's relative profitability, and think that earnings growth, though not as fast as those of smaller competitors, will be more stable.

➤ Risks to our recommendation and target price include smaller market share gains than we project, slower and more costly implementation of new contracts than we expect, and financial risk due to its debt load.

➤ Our 12-month target price of $19 is based on a price-to-earnings multiple of 9X, near the peer average to account for our view of company growth, risk, and return metrics, to our FY 12 EPS estimate of $2.15.

## Dividend Data (Dates: mm/dd Payment Date: mm/dd/yy)

| Amount ($) | Date Decl. | Ex-Div. Date | Stk. of Record | Payment Date |
|---|---|---|---|---|
| 0.070 | 01/19 | 02/11 | 02/15 | 03/01/11 |
| 0.070 | 04/13 | 05/12 | 05/16 | 06/01/11 |
| 0.070 | 07/21 | 08/11 | 08/15 | 09/01/11 |
| 0.080 | 10/20 | 11/10 | 11/15 | 12/01/11 |

Dividends have been paid since 2006. Source: Company reports.

# Jabil Circuit Inc

**STANDARD &POOR'S**

## Business Summary October 21, 2011

CORPORATE OVERVIEW. Jabil Circuit provides electronic manufacturing services (EMS), working with customers in a variety of industries at facilities around the world. Among the many services the company offers are design and engineering, component selection and procurement, automated assembly, product testing, parallel global production, systems assembly, direct order fulfillment, and aftermarket services.

The company reported in the following three operating segments in FY 10 (Aug.): Electronic Manufacturing Services (EMS) represented 59% of sales (58% in FY 09), Consumer represented 35% (36%), and Aftermarket Services (AMS) represented 6% (6%). Within the EMS segment, industry sectors served include Instrumentation and Medical at 23% of FY 10 total sales (19% in FY 09), Networking 17% (17%), Computing and Storage 10% (11%), Telecommunications 5% (6%), and Other 4% (5%). Within the Consumer segment, Digital Home Office represented 20% of FY 10 total sales (16% in FY 09), and Mobility 15% (20%). Notable trends include an increase in activity in the Instrumentation and Medical area, which can have more complex products with higher margins, and the absence of an automotive category following a divestiture in October 2009.

Following a reorganization, the company plans to report in different main segments beginning in FY 11: Diversified Manufacturing Services (DMS), Enterprise & Infrastructure (E&I), and High Velocity Systems (HVS). DMS will focus on more complex products and regulated industries; E&I will target cost effective solutions mainly for the computing and storage, networking and telecommunications industries; and HVS will aim at consumer lines such as mobility, set-top boxes, printers, and point of sale terminals.

In FY 10, Cisco Systems and Research in Motion were the only customers accounting for more than 10% of sales, with Cisco at 15% (13% of FY 09 sales) and Research in Motion also at 15% (12%). Among other large customers are Hewlett-Packard, which accounted for 11% of FY 08 sales, Apple, EchoStar, General Electric, IBM, NetApp, Nokia, and Pace PLC.

## Company Financials Fiscal Year Ended Aug. 31

| Per Share Data ($) | 2011 | 2010 | 2009 | 2008 | 2007 | 2006 | 2005 | 2004 | 2003 | 2002 |
|---|---|---|---|---|---|---|---|---|---|---|
| Tangible Book Value | 8.56 | 6.87 | 6.15 | 6.90 | 5.97 | 8.26 | 8.22 | 7.29 | 6.06 | 6.63 |
| Cash Flow | 3.18 | 2.08 | -4.22 | 1.99 | 1.51 | 1.71 | 2.18 | 1.89 | 1.32 | 1.11 |
| Earnings | 1.73 | 0.78 | -5.63 | 0.65 | 0.35 | 0.77 | 1.12 | 0.81 | 0.21 | 0.17 |
| S&P Core Earnings | 1.81 | 0.87 | -0.73 | 0.64 | 0.35 | 0.77 | 0.64 | 0.59 | 0.04 | NA |
| Dividends | 0.28 | 0.28 | 0.28 | 0.28 | 0.28 | 0.14 | Nil | Nil | Nil | Nil |
| Payout Ratio | 16% | 36% | NM | 43% | 80% | 18% | Nil | Nil | Nil | Nil |
| Prices:High | 23.09 | 20.38 | 17.91 | 18.78 | 27.86 | 43.70 | 39.00 | 32.40 | 31.66 | 26.79 |
| Prices:Low | 13.94 | 10.17 | 3.10 | 4.77 | 14.27 | 22.01 | 21.80 | 19.18 | 21.20 | 11.13 |
| P/E Ratio:High | 13 | 26 | NM | 29 | 80 | 57 | 35 | 40 | NM | NM |
| P/E Ratio:Low | 8 | 13 | NM | 7 | 41 | 29 | 19 | 24 | NM | 65 |

| Income Statement Analysis (Million $) | | | | | | | | | | |
|---|---|---|---|---|---|---|---|---|---|---|
| Revenue | 16,519 | 13,409 | 11,685 | 12,780 | 12,291 | 10,265 | 7,524 | 6,253 | 4,729 | 3,545 |
| Operating Income | 936 | 643 | 457 | 582 | 494 | 522 | 507 | 439 | 369 | 296 |
| Depreciation | 319 | 283 | 292 | 276 | 240 | 199 | 220 | 222 | 224 | 188 |
| Interest Expense | 97.6 | 80.3 | 82.3 | 94.3 | 86.1 | 23.5 | 24.8 | 19.4 | 17.0 | 13.1 |
| Pretax Income | 481 | 247 | -1,005 | 157 | 94.5 | 225 | 276 | 198 | 37.0 | 44.8 |
| Effective Tax Rate | 20.4% | 30.9% | NM | 16.0% | 22.6% | 26.9% | 16.1% | 15.5% | NM | 22.4% |
| Net Income | 381 | 169 | -1,165 | 134 | 73.2 | 165 | 232 | 167 | 43.0 | 34.7 |
| S&P Core Earnings | 399 | 189 | -152 | 131 | 73.9 | 165 | 134 | 122 | 8.12 | -0.11 |

| Balance Sheet & Other Financial Data (Million $) | | | | | | | | | | |
|---|---|---|---|---|---|---|---|---|---|---|
| Cash | 889 | 744 | 876 | 773 | 664 | 774 | 796 | 621 | 700 | 641 |
| Current Assets | 5,135 | 4,503 | 3,677 | 4,139 | 3,666 | 3,679 | 2,686 | 2,183 | 2,094 | 1,588 |
| Total Assets | 7,058 | 6,217 | 5,318 | 7,032 | 6,295 | 5,412 | 4,077 | 3,329 | 3,245 | 2,548 |
| Current Liabilities | 3,890 | 3,455 | 2,686 | 3,048 | 2,991 | 2,701 | 1,568 | 1,159 | 1,263 | 593 |
| Long Term Debt | 1,113 | 1,019 | 1,037 | 1,100 | 760 | 330 | 327 | 305 | 297 | 355 |
| Common Equity | 1,867 | 1,578 | 1,435 | 2,716 | 2,443 | 2,294 | 2,135 | 1,819 | 1,588 | 1,507 |
| Total Capital | 3,087 | 2,779 | 2,677 | 3,832 | 3,226 | 2,632 | 2,462 | 2,125 | 1,905 | 1,903 |
| Capital Expenditures | 459 | 398 | 292 | 338 | 302 | 280 | 257 | 218 | 117 | 85.5 |
| Cash Flow | 702 | 452 | -873 | 410 | 313 | 363 | 452 | 389 | 267 | 223 |
| Current Ratio | 1.3 | 1.3 | 1.4 | 1.4 | 1.2 | 1.4 | 1.7 | 1.9 | 1.7 | 2.7 |
| % Long Term Debt of Capitalization | 36.0 | 36.7 | 38.7 | 28.7 | 23.6 | 12.5 | 13.3 | 14.4 | 15.6 | 18.6 |
| % Net Income of Revenue | 2.3 | 1.3 | NM | 1.1 | 0.6 | 1.6 | 3.1 | 2.7 | 0.9 | 1.0 |
| % Return on Assets | 5.7 | 2.9 | NM | 2.0 | 1.3 | 3.5 | 6.3 | 5.1 | 1.5 | 1.4 |
| % Return on Equity | 22.1 | 11.2 | NM | 5.2 | 3.1 | 7.4 | 11.7 | 9.8 | 2.8 | 2.4 |

Data as orig reptd.; bef. results of disc opers/spec. items. Per share data adj. for stk. divs.; EPS diluted. E-Estimated. NA-Not Available. NM-Not Meaningful. NR-Not Ranked. UR-Under Review.

**Office:** 10560 Dr. Martin Luther King Jr. Street North, St. Petersburg, FL 33716.
**Telephone:** 727-577-9749.
**Email:** investor_relations@jabil.com
**Website:** http://www.jabil.com

**Chrmn:** W.D. Morean
**Pres & CEO:** T.L. Main
**Vice Chrmn:** T.A. Sansone
**COO:** M.T. Mondello

**SVP & Cntlr:** M.K. Dastoor
**Investor Contact:** B. Walters (727-803-3349)
**Board Members:** M. F. Brooks, M. S. Lavitt, T. L. Main, W. D. Morean, L. J. Murphy, F. A. Newman, S. A. Raymund, T. A. Sansone, D. M. Stout

**Founded:** 1969
**Domicile:** Delaware
**Employees:** 121,000

*The McGraw-Hill Companies*

# Jacobs Engineering Group Inc.

**STANDARD &POOR'S**

| S&P Recommendation | STRONG BUY ★★★★★ | Price | 12-Mo. Target Price | Investment Style |
|---|---|---|---|---|
| | | $38.51 (as of Nov 25, 2011) | $50.00 | Large-Cap Growth |

**GICS Sector** Industrials
**Sub-Industry** Construction & Engineering

**Summary** This company provides engineering, construction and maintenance services to private industry and federal government agencies on a worldwide basis.

## Key Stock Statistics (Source S&P, Vickers, company reports)

| | | | | | | | |
|---|---|---|---|---|---|---|---|
| 52-Wk Range | $55.73– 30.74 | S&P Oper. EPS 2012E | 3.15 | Market Capitalization(B) | $4.934 | Beta | 1.39 |
| Trailing 12-Month EPS | $2.60 | S&P Oper. EPS 2013E | 3.80 | Yield (%) | Nil | S&P 3-Yr. Proj. EPS CAGR(%) | 19 |
| Trailing 12-Month P/E | 14.8 | P/E on S&P Oper. EPS 2012E | 12.2 | Dividend Rate/Share | Nil | S&P Credit Rating | NA |
| $10K Invested 5 Yrs Ago | $9,280 | Common Shares Outstg. (M) | 128.1 | Institutional Ownership (%) | 83 | | |

## Price Performance

30-Week Mov. Avg. · · · 10-Week Mov. Avg. - - GAAP Earnings vs. Previous Year  Volume Above Avg. ⃒⃒⃒⃒ STARS
12-Mo. Target Price — Relative Strength — ▲ Up ▼ Down ► No Change  Below Avg. ⃒⃒⃒⃒ ★

Options: ASE, CBOE, Ph

Analysis prepared by Equity Analyst **Stewart Scharf** on Nov 21, 2011.

## Highlights

➤ We project at least 10% revenue growth for FY 12 (Sep.), based on more favorable trends and a sequentially improving backlog, driven by strength in the upstream oil & gas and chemicals (shale gas and gas liquids), buildings and mining & minerals markets, while refining and other private sector projects gradually recover. Although public sector projects will grow less rapidly, in our view, we see growth in certain infrastructure and national government projects, and an improving biopharm segment. Additionally, we look for JEC to continue to supplement organic growth with strategic acquisitions in emerging regions.

➤ We think gross margins in FY 12 will narrow somewhat from 15.2% in FY 11, due to mix issues as more projects in backlog shift into the traditionally lower-margin field services (construction) stage. However, operating margins (EBITDA) should widen to above 6%, on well controlled SG&A expenses.

➤ We forecast an unchanged effective tax rate of about 35% in FY 12, and operating EPS of $3.15, advancing 21% to $3.80, in FY 13.

## Investment Rationale/Risk

➤ We base our strong buy opinion on our valuation metrics, along with JEC's diversified customer and geographic base, and relationship-based business model, which focuses on relatively small, lower-risk projects. We also see favorable global trends in most of the company's sectors, and attractive acquisition candidates.

➤ Risks to our recommendation and target price include a worsening of global economic conditions; major U.S. federal government budget issues; project delays or cancellations based on customer liquidity issues or sharply lower oil prices; an inability to outsource skilled labor overseas; and a lack of acquisition opportunities.

➤ Our discounted cash flow (DCF) model suggests an intrinsic value of $55, assuming a perpetuity growth rate of 4% and a weighted average cost of capital (WACC) of about 13%. Based on relative metrics and JEC's risk-averse business model, we apply an above-peer but below-historical P/E of near 14.5X to our FY 12 EPS estimate, resulting in a value of $45. Blending these metrics, we arrive at our 12-month target price of $50.

## Qualitative Risk Assessment

| LOW | MEDIUM | HIGH |
|---|---|---|

Our risk assessment reflects the cyclical nature of the company's various markets, its growth-by-acquisition strategy, changes in global political conditions, timing issues related to new awards, and fluctuations in interest rates and foreign currencies. These factors are offset by what we see as JEC's strong cash position and virtually no debt.

## Quantitative Evaluations

**S&P Quality Ranking**      **B+**

| D | C | B- | B | B+ | A- | A | A+ |
|---|---|---|---|---|---|---|---|

**Relative Strength Rank**      **STRONG**

83

LOWEST = 1          HIGHEST = 99

## Revenue/Earnings Data

**Revenue (Million $)**

| | 1Q | 2Q | 3Q | 4Q | Year |
|---|---|---|---|---|---|
| 2011 | 2,356 | 2,558 | 2,744 | 2,723 | 10,382 |
| 2010 | 2,478 | 2,587 | 2,508 | 2,343 | 9,916 |
| 2009 | 3,233 | 2,975 | 2,707 | 2,553 | 11,467 |
| 2008 | 2,472 | 2,665 | 2,919 | 3,197 | 11,252 |
| 2007 | 2,019 | 2,092 | 2,084 | 2,280 | 8,474 |
| 2006 | 1,683 | 1,832 | 1,926 | 1,979 | 7,421 |

**Earnings Per Share ($)**

| | | | | | |
|---|---|---|---|---|---|
| 2011 | 0.52 | 0.63 | 0.71 | 0.74 | 2.60 |
| 2010 | 0.58 | 0.62 | 0.15 | 0.61 | 1.96 |
| 2009 | 0.94 | 0.88 | 0.76 | 0.63 | 3.21 |
| 2008 | 0.79 | 0.80 | 0.87 | 0.92 | 3.38 |
| 2007 | 0.51 | 0.55 | 0.61 | 0.68 | 2.35 |
| 2006 | 0.36 | 0.37 | 0.42 | 0.49 | 1.64 |

Fiscal year ended Sep. 30. Next earnings report expected: Late January. EPS Estimates based on S&P Operating Earnings; historical GAAP earnings are as reported.

## Dividend Data

No cash dividends have been paid since 1984.

---

**Please read the Required Disclosures and Analyst Certification on the last page of this report.**

**The McGraw-Hill Companies**

# Jacobs Engineering Group Inc.

**STANDARD &POOR'S**

## Business Summary November 21, 2011

CORPORATE OVERVIEW. Jacobs Engineering focuses on providing a broad range of technical, professional and construction services to a large number of industrial, commercial and governmental clients worldwide. The company offers project services; consulting services; operations and maintenance services; and construction services via offices primarily in North America, Europe, Asia and Australia. In November 2007, the company was moved into the S&P 500 Index from S&P's MidCap 400 Index.

In FY 11 (Sep.), revenues by sector were: refining (downstream), 22%; national government (environmental, defense and NASA), 22%; chemicals, 14%; pharmaBio (pharmaceutical and biotech), 4%; oil and gas (upstream), 7%; infrastructure, 12%; buildings, 9%; mining and minerals, 4%; and other (power, pulp and paper, high tech, food & consumer products), 6%. The higher-margin technical professional services component accounted for 57% of revenues and 64% of backlog in FY 11, with the balance derived from field services (construction). The company generally realizes about 60% to 65% of its backlog as revenues during any 12-month period. As of September 30, 2011, backlog was $14.3 billion ($9.1 billion technical professional), up 2% sequentially, but up 8% from a year earlier. About 30% of revenues was generated from operations outside of the U.S in FY 10 (latest available), including 17% in Europe,

10% in Canada, and 2.4% in Asia.

Project services include the engineering and design of process plants and high-technology facilities. Construction services offers traditional field services to private and public sector clients. Operations and maintenance services include all tasks required to keep a process plant in day-to-day operation.

In FY 10, revenues derived from agencies of the U.S. government accounted for over 25% of the total, up from 20% in FY 09. Cost-reimbursable projects accounted for 86% of the FY 10 total, up slightly from 85% in FY 09. Fixed-price contracts accounted for 13%, while guaranteed maximum price contracts accounted for the remaining 1%.

At the end of FY 10, the company's pension plans were underfunded by $398 million, up from $312 million a year earlier.

## Company Financials Fiscal Year Ended Sep. 30

| Per Share Data ($) | 2011 | 2010 | 2009 | 2008 | 2007 | 2006 | 2005 | 2004 | 2003 | 2002 |
|---|---|---|---|---|---|---|---|---|---|---|
| Tangible Book Value | 10.24 | 13.03 | 13.19 | 10.28 | 8.42 | 7.36 | 5.10 | 4.04 | 4.00 | 2.73 |
| Cash Flow | 3.38 | 2.66 | 3.90 | 3.97 | 2.85 | 2.04 | 1.70 | 1.44 | 1.45 | 1.31 |
| Earnings | 2.60 | 1.96 | 3.21 | 3.38 | 2.35 | 1.64 | 1.29 | 1.13 | 1.14 | 0.99 |
| S&P Core Earnings | 2.36 | 2.55 | 3.01 | 3.08 | 2.38 | 1.68 | 1.16 | 1.02 | 0.91 | 0.75 |
| Dividends | NA | Nil | Nil | Nil | Nil | Nil | Nil | Nil | Nil | Nil |
| Payout Ratio | Nil | Nil | Nil | Nil | Nil | Nil | Nil | Nil | Nil | Nil |
| Prices:High | 55.73 | 50.68 | 54.71 | 103.29 | 99.62 | 46.64 | 34.71 | 24.11 | 24.97 | 21.45 |
| Prices:Low | 30.74 | 34.39 | 30.16 | 26.00 | 38.25 | 33.90 | 22.33 | 18.43 | 17.48 | 13.05 |
| P/E Ratio:High | 21 | 26 | 17 | 31 | 42 | 29 | 27 | 21 | 22 | 22 |
| P/E Ratio:Low | 12 | 18 | 9 | 8 | 16 | 21 | 17 | 16 | 15 | 13 |

| Income Statement Analysis (Million $) | | | | | | | | | | |
|---|---|---|---|---|---|---|---|---|---|---|
| Revenue | 10,382 | 9,916 | 11,467 | 11,252 | 8,474 | 7,421 | 5,635 | 4,594 | 4,616 | 4,556 |
| Operating Income | 611 | 488 | 707 | 716 | 498 | 350 | 288 | 232 | 232 | 207 |
| Depreciation | 95.4 | 88.5 | 86.3 | 73.1 | 55.7 | 48.3 | 46.4 | 34.2 | 35.4 | 35.1 |
| Interest Expense | 8.80 | 9.87 | 2.92 | 4.41 | 8.00 | 7.50 | 6.47 | 3.57 | 3.25 | 7.50 |
| Pretax Income | 517 | 392 | 625 | 657 | 449 | 305 | 236 | 198 | 197 | 169 |
| Effective Tax Rate | NA | NA | 36.0% | 36.0% | 36.0% | 35.5% | 36.0% | 35.0% | 35.0% | 35.0% |
| Net Income | 335 | 246 | 400 | 421 | 287 | 197 | 151 | 129 | 128 | 110 |
| S&P Core Earnings | 301 | 320 | 374 | 383 | 290 | 202 | 136 | 118 | 102 | 82.3 |

| Balance Sheet & Other Financial Data (Million $) | | | | | | | | | | |
|---|---|---|---|---|---|---|---|---|---|---|
| Cash | 906 | 939 | 1,034 | 604 | 613 | 434 | 240 | 100 | 126 | 48.5 |
| Current Assets | 3,157 | 2,767 | 2,818 | 2,750 | 2,278 | 1,818 | 1,337 | 1,084 | 970 | 975 |
| Total Assets | 6,049 | 4,684 | 4,429 | 4,278 | 3,389 | 2,854 | 2,354 | 2,071 | 1,671 | 1,674 |
| Current Liabilities | 2,058 | 1,239 | 1,296 | 1,577 | 1,276 | 1,041 | 785 | 686 | 611 | 740 |
| Long Term Debt | 2.04 | 0.51 | 0.74 | 55.7 | 40.0 | 77.7 | 89.6 | 78.8 | 17.8 | 85.7 |
| Common Equity | 3,313 | 2,859 | 2,626 | 2,245 | 1,844 | 1,423 | 1,141 | 1,005 | 842 | 690 |
| Total Capital | 3,336 | 2,865 | 2,650 | 2,386 | 1,884 | 1,508 | 1,237 | 1,089 | 865 | 781 |
| Capital Expenditures | 98.8 | 49.1 | 55.5 | 115 | 64.6 | 54.0 | 43.9 | 37.1 | 25.8 | 37.2 |
| Cash Flow | 431 | 334 | 486 | 494 | 343 | 245 | 197 | 163 | 163 | 145 |
| Current Ratio | 1.5 | 2.2 | 2.2 | 1.7 | 1.8 | 1.7 | 1.7 | 1.6 | 1.6 | 1.3 |
| % Long Term Debt of Capitalization | 0.1 | 0.0 | NM | 2.3 | 2.1 | 5.2 | 7.2 | 7.2 | 2.1 | 11.0 |
| % Net Income of Revenue | 3.2 | 2.5 | 3.5 | 3.7 | 3.3 | 2.7 | 2.7 | 2.8 | 2.8 | 2.4 |
| % Return on Assets | NA | NA | 9.2 | 11.0 | 9.1 | 7.5 | 6.8 | 6.9 | 7.7 | 6.8 |
| % Return on Equity | NA | NA | 16.4 | 20.6 | 17.5 | 15.2 | 14.1 | 14.0 | 16.7 | 17.1 |

Data as orig reptd.; bef. results of disc opers/spec. items. Per share data adj. for stk. divs.; EPS diluted. E-Estimated. NA-Not Available. NM-Not Meaningful. NR-Not Ranked. UR-Under Review.

**Office:** 1111 South Arroyo Parkway, Pasadena, CA 91105.
**Telephone:** 626-578-3500.
**Website:** http://www.jacobs.com
**Pres & CEO:** C.L. Martin

**EVP, Chief Admin Officer & Treas:** J. Prosser, Jr.
**SVP, Chief Acctg Officer & Cntlr:** N.G. Thawerbhoy
**SVP & General Counsel:** W.C. Markley, III
**Secy:** M.S. Udovic

**Investor Contact:** J.W. Prosser, Jr. (626-578-6803)
**Board Members:** J. R. Bronson, J. F. Coyne, R. C. Davidson, Jr., E. V. Fritzky, J. P. Jumper, C. L. Martin, B. Montoya, T. M. Niles, P. Robertson, N. G. Watson, L. F. levinson

**Founded:** 1957
**Domicile:** Delaware
**Employees:** 60,200

**The McGraw·Hill Companies**

**STANDARD &POOR'S**

# JDS Uniphase Corp

| S&P Recommendation | HOLD ★★★☆☆ | Price $9.56 (as of Nov 25, 2011) | 12-Mo. Target Price $14.00 | Investment Style Large-Cap Blend |
|---|---|---|---|---|

**GICS Sector** Information Technology
**Sub-Industry** Communications Equipment

**Summary** This company manufactures fiber optic products and communications test and measurement solutions.

## Key Stock Statistics (Source S&P, Vickers, company reports)

| | | | | | | | |
|---|---|---|---|---|---|---|---|
| 52-Wk Range | $29.12– 8.59 | S&P Oper. EPS 2012**E** | 0.63 | Market Capitalization(B) | $2.191 | Beta | 2.36 |
| Trailing 12-Month EPS | $0.28 | S&P Oper. EPS 2013**E** | 0.80 | Yield (%) | Nil | S&P 3-Yr. Proj. EPS CAGR(%) | 15 |
| Trailing 12-Month P/E | 34.1 | P/E on S&P Oper. EPS 2012**E** | 15.2 | Dividend Rate/Share | Nil | S&P Credit Rating | NA |
| $10K Invested 5 Yrs Ago | $4,997 | Common Shares Outstg. (M) | 229.1 | Institutional Ownership (%) | 71 | | |

## Price Performance

30-Week Mov. Avg. · · · 10-Week Mov. Avg. - - - GAAP Earnings vs. Previous Year   Volume Above Avg. |||| STARS
12-Mo. Target Price — Relative Strength — ▲ Up ▼ Down ► No Change   Below Avg. |||| ★

Options: ASE, CBOE, P, Ph

Analysis prepared by Equity Analyst **J. Moorman, CFA** on Aug 24, 2011, when the stock traded at **$10.57**.

## Highlights

➤ Following a 32% sales increase in FY 11 (Jun.), aided by roughly $200 million of additional revenue from the May 2010 Network Solutions Division (NSD) acquisition, we forecast flat performance for FY 12, to $1.8 billion, before increasing 15% in FY 13, reflecting higher demand for optical communication and test measurement products. We also see JDSU materially benefiting from its first-mover advantage in the attractive XFP transceiver and integrated transport blade segments.

➤ We expect FY 12 gross margins to widen about 40 basis points from the prior year, to 48%, on product mix and lean manufacturing initiatives, partly offset by higher component expediting fees. Despite aggressive R&D investment, we believe JDSU will manage costs prudently, but we see FY 12 operating expenses rising at about the same rate as sales.

➤ We project FY 12 operating margins of 13.2%, up from 12.7% in FY 11. After modest interest expense and a low effective tax rate of 10%, we foresee FY 12 EPS of $0.67, and we expect $0.82 for FY 13. Estimates for both periods include $0.20 of projected stock option expense.

## Investment Rationale/Risk

➤ While we expect a temporary pullback in optical equipment demand due to customer inventory adjustments, we think JDSU's broad product portfolio and large customer base will enable the company to navigate industry demand fluctuations. Industry fundamentals remain strong, in our view, for both the optical and test measurement markets as carriers deploy high-speed transport to handle a continued rapid increase in bandwidth usage and implement several emerging technologies, such as LTE and DOCSIS3.0.

➤ Risks to our recommendation and target price include a downturn in telecom spending, market share losses, and slower-than-expected margin improvement.

➤ Our 12-month target price of $14 equals a P/E of 17X our FY 13 EPS estimate, slightly below the peer mean and JDSU's five-year historical multiple average, reflecting our view of uncertain sales visibility amid widespread industry inventory adjustments. Our target price also represents 1.6X our FY 13 revenue forecast. Cash and investments stood at roughly $3 per share as of July 2, 2011.

## Qualitative Risk Assessment

| LOW | MEDIUM | HIGH |
|---|---|---|

Our risk assessment reflects the highly competitive nature of the communications equipment industry, and the company's dependence on telecom carrier spending, which tends to be uneven due to uncertain timing of network projects and upgrades.

## Quantitative Evaluations

**S&P Quality Ranking**     C

| D | C | B- | B | B+ | A- | A | A+ |
|---|---|---|---|---|---|---|---|

**Relative Strength Rank**     WEAK

15

LOWEST = 1     HIGHEST = 99

## Revenue/Earnings Data

**Revenue (Million $)**

| | 1Q | 2Q | 3Q | 4Q | Year |
|---|---|---|---|---|---|
| 2012 | 420.8 | -- | -- | -- | -- |
| 2011 | 405.2 | 473.5 | 454.0 | 471.8 | 1,805 |
| 2010 | 297.8 | 342.9 | 332.3 | 390.9 | 1,364 |
| 2009 | 380.7 | 357.0 | 280.6 | 276.1 | 1,294 |
| 2008 | 356.7 | 399.2 | 383.9 | 390.3 | 1,530 |
| 2007 | 318.1 | 366.3 | 361.7 | 350.7 | 1,397 |

**Earnings Per Share ($)**

| | | | | | |
|---|---|---|---|---|---|
| 2012 | -0.03 | E0.16 | E0.16 | E0.18 | E0.63 |
| 2011 | E0.16 | 0.10 | 0.16 | 0.04 | 0.31 |
| 2010 | -0.14 | -0.09 | -0.05 | 0.01 | -0.27 |
| 2009 | -0.08 | -3.28 | -0.39 | -0.27 | -4.02 |
| 2008 | -0.03 | 0.09 | -0.03 | -0.13 | -0.10 |
| 2007 | -0.08 | 0.10 | -0.07 | -0.08 | -0.12 |

Fiscal year ended Jun. 30. Next earnings report expected: Early February. EPS Estimates based on S&P Operating Earnings; historical GAAP earnings are as reported.

## Dividend Data

No cash dividends have been paid.

# JDS Uniphase Corp

STANDARD
&POOR'S

## Business Summary August 24, 2011

CORPORATE OVERVIEW. JDS Uniphase supplies optical components, as well as communications test and measurement solutions for the communications market. The company also leverages its optical science capabilities on non-communications applications, offering products for display, security, medical environmental instrumentation, decorative, aerospace and defense applications.

The company operates in three principal segments: communications test and measurement (47% of FY 10 (Jun.) revenue); communications and commercial optical products (37%); and advanced optical technologies (16%).

PRIMARY BUSINESS DYNAMICS. The communications test and measurement segment provides instruments, software, systems and services that help communications equipment manufacturers and service providers accelerate the deployment of broadband networks and services from the core of the network to the home, including deployment over fiber to the curb, node or premise and digital networks. Solutions focus primarily on lab and production test platforms, field test instrumentation and software, and network and service as-

surance systems.

The communications and commercial optical product group supplies the basic building blocks for fiber optic networks, which enable the rapid transmission of large amounts of data over long distances via light waves through fiber optic components, modules and subsystems. Transmission products include optical transceivers, optical transponders, and their supporting components such as modulators and source lasers. Transport products primarily consist of amplifiers and reconfigurable optical add/drop multiplexers (ROADMs) and their supporting components such as pump lasers, passive devices, and array waveguides. The segment also offers a broad portfolio of lasers used by customers in markets and applications such as biotechnology and graphics imaging, remote sensing, and materials processing and precision machining.

## Company Financials Fiscal Year Ended Jun. 30

| Per Share Data ($) | 2011 | 2010 | 2009 | 2008 | 2007 | 2006 | 2005 | 2004 | 2003 | 2002 |
|---|---|---|---|---|---|---|---|---|---|---|
| Tangible Book Value | 3.17 | 2.19 | 2.44 | 2.73 | 2.80 | 2.72 | 5.76 | 7.12 | 7.92 | 11.44 |
| Cash Flow | 0.97 | 0.35 | -3.35 | 0.55 | 0.48 | -0.46 | -1.11 | -0.32 | -4.82 | -42.21 |
| Earnings | 0.31 | -0.27 | -4.02 | -0.10 | -0.12 | -0.72 | -1.44 | -0.64 | -5.28 | -52.00 |
| S&P Core Earnings | 0.29 | -0.32 | -0.52 | -0.12 | -0.21 | -0.88 | -2.24 | -2.56 | -7.84 | -32.88 |
| Dividends | NA | Nil | Nil | Nil | Nil | Nil | Nil | Nil | Nil | Nil |
| Payout Ratio | Nil | Nil | Nil | Nil | Nil | Nil | Nil | Nil | Nil | Nil |
| Prices:High | 29.12 | 14.70 | 8.75 | 15.33 | 17.99 | 34.40 | 26.08 | 47.08 | 37.68 | 82.72 |
| Prices:Low | 8.59 | 7.66 | 2.21 | 2.01 | 12.41 | 13.93 | 10.56 | 22.72 | 19.84 | 12.64 |
| P/E Ratio:High | 94 | NM | NM | NM | NM | NM | NM | NM | NM | NM |
| P/E Ratio:Low | 28 | NM | NM | NM | NM | NM | NM | NM | NM | NM |

| Income Statement Analysis (Million $) | | | | | | | | | | |
|---|---|---|---|---|---|---|---|---|---|---|
| Revenue | 1,805 | 1,364 | 1,294 | 1,530 | 1,397 | 1,204 | 712 | 636 | 676 | 1,098 |
| Operating Income | 235 | 93.7 | 39.8 | 87.6 | 36.8 | -107 | -83.9 | -58.5 | -306 | -374 |
| Depreciation | 154 | 137 | 145 | 145 | 128 | 57.4 | 61.3 | 55.9 | 79.2 | 1,645 |
| Interest Expense | 25.4 | 24.3 | 7.70 | 8.80 | 7.10 | 27.7 | Nil | Nil | Nil | Nil |
| Pretax Income | 45.6 | -57.2 | -869 | -19.3 | -24.3 | -152 | -255 | -128 | -920 | -8,501 |
| Effective Tax Rate | NA | NM | NM | NM | NM | NM | NM | NM | NM | NM |
| Net Income | 71.6 | -59.7 | -866 | -21.7 | -26.3 | -151 | -261 | -113 | -934 | -8,738 |
| S&P Core Earnings | 68.8 | -69.4 | -111 | -27.5 | -45.7 | -181 | -394 | -446 | -1,399 | -5,534 |

| Balance Sheet & Other Financial Data (Million $) | | | | | | | | | | |
|---|---|---|---|---|---|---|---|---|---|---|
| Cash | 693 | 568 | 685 | 874 | 363 | 365 | 511 | 328 | 242 | 412 |
| Current Assets | 1,304 | 1,075 | 1,108 | 1,429 | 1,661 | 1,805 | 1,588 | 1,866 | 1,515 | 1,857 |
| Total Assets | 1,951 | 1,704 | 1,670 | 2,906 | 3,025 | 3,065 | 2,080 | 2,422 | 2,138 | 3,005 |
| Current Liabilities | 419 | 351 | 310 | 445 | 348 | 422 | 240 | 350 | 423 | 483 |
| Long Term Debt | 286 | 267 | 325 | 427 | 808 | 900 | 467 | 465 | Nil | 5.50 |
| Common Equity | 1,065 | 909 | 861 | 1,817 | 1,736 | 1,584 | 1,335 | 1,571 | 1,671 | 2,471 |
| Total Capital | 1,351 | 1,176 | 1,186 | 2,267 | 2,544 | 2,484 | 1,802 | 2,063 | 1,699 | 2,519 |
| Capital Expenditures | 117 | 41.4 | 54.7 | 51.7 | 75.7 | 67.2 | 35.8 | 66.4 | 47.2 | 133 |
| Cash Flow | 225 | 77.5 | -722 | 123 | 102 | -93.8 | -200 | -56.7 | -855 | -7,093 |
| Current Ratio | 3.1 | 3.1 | 3.6 | 3.2 | 4.8 | 4.3 | 6.6 | 5.3 | 3.6 | 3.8 |
| % Long Term Debt of Capitalization | 21.2 | 22.7 | 27.4 | 18.8 | 31.8 | 36.2 | 25.9 | 22.5 | Nil | 0.2 |
| % Net Income of Revenue | 4.0 | NM | NM | NM | NM | NM | NM | NM | NM | NM |
| % Return on Assets | 3.9 | NM | NM | NM | NM | NM | NM | NM | NM | NM |
| % Return on Equity | 7.3 | NM | NM | NM | NM | NM | NM | NM | NM | NM |

Data as orig reptd.; bef. results of disc opers/spec. items. Per share data adj. for stk. divs.; EPS diluted. E-Estimated. NA-Not Available. NM-Not Meaningful. NR-Not Ranked. UR-Under Review.

**Office:** 430 North McCarthy Boulevard, Milpitas, CA 95035.
**Telephone:** 408-546-5000.
**Email:** investor.relations@jdsu.com
**Website:** http://www.jdsu.com

**Chrmn:** M.A. Kaplan
**Pres & CEO:** T.H. Waechter
**Vice Chrmn:** K.J. Kennedy
**Investor Contact:** D. Vellequette (408-546-4445)

**EVP & CFO:** D. Vellequette
**Board Members:** K. L. Barnes, R. E. Belluzzo, H. L. Covert, Jr., P. A. Herscher, M. Jabbar, M. A. Kaplan, K. J. Kennedy, T. H. Waechter

**Founded:** 1979
**Domicile:** Delaware
**Employees:** 5,000

The McGraw·Hill Companies

**STANDARD &POOR'S**

# Johnson Controls Inc.

| S&P Recommendation | STRONG BUY ★★★★★ | Price | 12-Mo. Target Price | Investment Style |
|---|---|---|---|---|
| | | $27.59 (as of Nov 25, 2011) | $45.00 | Large-Cap Blend |

**GICS Sector** Consumer Discretionary
**Sub-Industry** Auto Parts & Equipment

**Summary** This company supplies building controls and energy management systems, automotive seating, and batteries.

## Key Stock Statistics (Source S&P, Vickers, company reports)

| | | | | | | | | |
|---|---|---|---|---|---|---|---|---|
| 52-Wk Range | $42.92– 24.29 | S&P Oper. EPS 2012**E** | 3.03 | Market Capitalization(B) | $18.772 | Beta | | 1.88 |
| Trailing 12-Month EPS | $2.36 | S&P Oper. EPS 2013**E** | NA | Yield (%) | 2.61 | S&P 3-Yr. Proj. EPS CAGR(%) | | 24 |
| Trailing 12-Month P/E | 11.7 | P/E on S&P Oper. EPS 2012**E** | 9.1 | Dividend Rate/Share | $0.72 | S&P Credit Rating | | BBB+ |
| $10K Invested 5 Yrs Ago | $10,937 | Common Shares Outstg. (M) | 680.4 | Institutional Ownership (%) | 80 | | | |

## Price Performance

30-Week Mov. Avg. · · · 10-Week Mov. Avg. – – GAAP Earnings vs. Previous Year  Volume Above Avg. STARS
12-Mo. Target Price — Relative Strength — ▲ Up ▼ Down ▶ No Change  Below Avg.

Options: ASE, CBOE, Ph

Analysis prepared by Equity Analyst **Efraim Levy, CFA** on Nov 02, 2011, when the stock traded at **$31.75**.

### Highlights

➤ In 2012, we see increasing vehicle sales and production in most regions. We see JCI's total revenues rising 9.3% in FY 12 (Sep.), above company guidance for an 8% increase. Over the longer term, we see the building efficiency unit benefiting from new customers, as outsourcing trends persist and the backlog of orders for installed systems grows. Auto interior sales should benefit from increased business with non-U.S. manufacturers and emerging market demand. Battery demand should rise on higher global demand.

➤ We see operating margins improving in FY 12 on stronger domestic and foreign demand, benefits from restructuring activities, and a reduction in restructuring costs. Partly offsetting factors are likely to be pricing pressures from customers, and increases in some raw material costs.

➤ From depressed levels in FY 09, JCI's adjusted EPS rebounded to $1.99 in FY 10 and $2.38 in FY 11. Post-crisis, we estimate compensatory higher volume will help FY 12 EPS reach $3.03.

### Investment Rationale/Risk

➤ We expect JCI's long-term sales and earnings growth to exceed that of peers, and for the company to show greater earnings stability, aided by its diversification in geography, products and customers. The stock's P/E multiple was recently above that of the S&P 500, based on our calendar 2012 estimates. We view the balance sheet as strong, with long-term debt generally at 20% to 36% of capitalization over the past decade.

➤ Risks to our recommendation and target price include lower-than-expected demand, especially for automotive parts, higher-than-anticipated raw material costs, and less-than-expected acquisition synergies and restructuring savings.

➤ Applying a multiple of 15X, within the historical range, to our FY 12 EPS estimate of $3.03 results in a value of approximately $45. Our DCF model, which assumes a weighted average cost of capital of 9.0%, a compound annual growth rate of 6.9% over the next 15 years, and a terminal growth rate of 3.0%, leads to intrinsic value of about $45. Our 12-month target price of $45 is based on a weighted blend of these two metrics.

### Qualitative Risk Assessment

| LOW | MEDIUM | HIGH |
|---|---|---|

Our risk assessment reflects our view of favorable growth prospects in the building controls markets that JCI serves and what we see as a strong management team and healthy balance sheet, offset by the challenges faced by its automotive operations.

### Quantitative Evaluations

**S&P Quality Ranking**   A

| D | C | B- | B | B+ | A- | A | A+ |
|---|---|---|---|---|---|---|---|

**Relative Strength Rank**   WEAK

28

LOWEST = 1   HIGHEST = 99

### Revenue/Earnings Data

**Revenue (Million $)**

| | 1Q | 2Q | 3Q | 4Q | Year |
|---|---|---|---|---|---|
| 2011 | 9,537 | 10,144 | 10,364 | 10,788 | 40,833 |
| 2010 | 8,408 | 8,317 | 8,540 | 9,040 | 34,305 |
| 2009 | 7,336 | 6,315 | 6,979 | 7,867 | 28,497 |
| 2008 | 9,484 | 9,406 | 9,865 | 9,307 | 38,062 |
| 2007 | 8,210 | 8,492 | 8,911 | 9,011 | 34,624 |
| 2006 | 7,528 | 8,167 | 8,390 | 8,150 | 32,235 |

**Earnings Per Share ($)**

| | | | | | |
|---|---|---|---|---|---|
| 2011 | 0.55 | 0.51 | 0.52 | 0.78 | 2.36 |
| 2010 | 0.52 | 0.40 | 0.61 | 0.66 | 2.19 |
| 2009 | -1.02 | -0.32 | 0.26 | 0.47 | -0.57 |
| 2008 | 0.39 | 0.48 | 0.73 | 0.03 | 1.63 |
| 2007 | 0.28 | 0.44 | 0.66 | 0.77 | 2.16 |
| 2006 | 0.29 | 0.28 | 0.57 | 0.62 | 1.75 |

Fiscal year ended Sep. 30. Next earnings report expected: Late January. EPS Estimates based on S&P Operating Earnings; historical GAAP earnings are as reported.

### Dividend Data (Dates: mm/dd Payment Date: mm/dd/yy)

| Amount ($) | Date Decl. | Ex-Div. Date | Stk. of Record | Payment Date |
|---|---|---|---|---|
| 0.160 | 01/26 | 03/09 | 03/11 | 04/04/11 |
| 0.160 | 05/25 | 06/08 | 06/10 | 07/05/11 |
| 0.160 | 07/27 | 09/07 | 09/09 | 10/04/11 |
| 0.180 | 11/16 | 12/07 | 12/09 | 01/03/12 |

Dividends have been paid since 1887. Source: Company reports.

---

**Please read the Required Disclosures and Analyst Certification on the last page of this report.**

*The McGraw-Hill Companies*

# Johnson Controls Inc.

STANDARD
&POOR'S

## Business Summary November 02, 2011

CORPORATE OVERVIEW. Johnson Controls, founded in 1885, is a leading manufacturer of automotive interior systems, automotive batteries and automated building control systems. It also provides facility management services for commercial buildings.

The automotive interior segment manufactures interior products and systems, including complete seats and seating components for North American and European car and light-truck manufacturers. The segment has grown rapidly in recent years, gaining contracts to produce seats formerly manufactured in-house by automakers, and expanding in Europe. Automotive interiors accounted for 49% of sales in FY 11 (Sep.).

The power solutions unit, the largest automotive battery operation in North America, makes lead-acid batteries primarily for the automotive replacement market and for OEMs. Batteries accounted for about 14% of FY 11 sales, and the unit is expanding operations in Europe and Asia

The building efficiency (formerly called controls) segment manufactures, installs and services controls and control systems, principally for nonresidential

buildings, which are used for temperature and energy management, and fire safety and security maintenance. The segment also includes custom engineering, installation and servicing of process control systems and a growing facilities management business. Building efficiency sales accounted for 36% of FY 11 revenues. As of September 30, 2011, JCI had an unearned backlog of building systems and services contracts totaling $5.1 billion.

Government building trends promoting facility management outsourcing and energy efficiency programs are creating additional opportunities, in our view.

Ford, GM and Daimler were the company's three largest customers in FY 10 (latest available). We expect the share of revenues from the three U.S.-based customers (Ford, GM and Chrysler) to shrink as the company grows its sales outside the U.S. and with non-domestic customers expanding in the U.S.

## Company Financials Fiscal Year Ended Sep. 30

| Per Share Data ($) | 2011 | 2010 | 2009 | 2008 | 2007 | 2006 | 2005 | 2004 | 2003 | 2002 |
|---|---|---|---|---|---|---|---|---|---|---|
| Tangible Book Value | NA | 4.20 | 2.77 | 3.63 | 3.38 | 1.10 | 3.52 | 1.93 | 1.27 | 0.74 |
| Cash Flow | 3.58 | 3.20 | 0.68 | 2.93 | 3.38 | 2.95 | 2.41 | 2.48 | 2.17 | 1.97 |
| Earnings | 2.36 | 2.19 | -0.57 | 1.63 | 2.16 | 1.75 | 1.30 | 1.41 | 1.20 | 1.06 |
| S&P Core Earnings | NA | 2.11 | -0.50 | 1.39 | 2.16 | 1.74 | 1.31 | 1.42 | 1.16 | 0.89 |
| Dividends | 0.64 | 0.52 | 0.52 | 0.63 | 0.33 | 0.37 | 0.33 | 0.30 | 0.24 | 0.22 |
| Payout Ratio | 27% | 24% | NM | 39% | 15% | 21% | 26% | 21% | 20% | 21% |
| Prices:High | 42.92 | 40.15 | 28.34 | 36.52 | 44.46 | 30.00 | 25.07 | 21.33 | 19.37 | 15.53 |
| Prices:Low | 24.29 | 25.56 | 8.35 | 13.65 | 28.09 | 22.12 | 17.52 | 16.52 | 11.96 | 11.52 |
| P/E Ratio:High | 18 | 18 | NM | 22 | 21 | 17 | 19 | 15 | 16 | 15 |
| P/E Ratio:Low | 10 | 12 | NM | 8 | 13 | 13 | 13 | 12 | 10 | 11 |

| Income Statement Analysis (Million $) | 2011 | 2010 | 2009 | 2008 | 2007 | 2006 | 2005 | 2004 | 2003 | 2002 |
|---|---|---|---|---|---|---|---|---|---|---|
| Revenue | 40,833 | 34,305 | 28,497 | 38,062 | 34,624 | 32,235 | 27,479 | 26,553 | 22,646 | 20,103 |
| Operating Income | 2,718 | 2,392 | 1,214 | 2,744 | 2,527 | 2,184 | 1,913 | 1,918 | 1,720 | 1,639 |
| Depreciation | 731 | 691 | 745 | 783 | 732 | 705 | 636 | 617 | 558 | 517 |
| Interest Expense | 174 | 170 | 255 | 270 | 277 | 248 | 121 | 111 | 114 | 122 |
| Pretax Income | 2,111 | 1,763 | -318 | 1,324 | 1,607 | 1,138 | 1,003 | 1,212 | 1,058 | 1,006 |
| Effective Tax Rate | NA | NA | NM | 24.2% | 18.7% | 5.54% | 20.4% | 26.0% | 31.0% | 34.6% |
| Net Income | 1,741 | 1,491 | -338 | 979 | 1,295 | 1,033 | 757 | 818 | 683 | 600 |
| S&P Core Earnings | NA | 1,444 | -293 | 833 | 1,292 | 1,025 | 764 | 818 | 650 | 497 |

| Balance Sheet & Other Financial Data (Million $) | 2011 | 2010 | 2009 | 2008 | 2007 | 2006 | 2005 | 2004 | 2003 | 2002 |
|---|---|---|---|---|---|---|---|---|---|---|
| Cash | 257 | 560 | 761 | 384 | 674 | 293 | 171 | 170 | 136 | 262 |
| Current Assets | 12,095 | 10,538 | 9,826 | 10,676 | 10,872 | 9,264 | 7,139 | 6,377 | 5,620 | 4,946 |
| Total Assets | 29,722 | 25,616 | 23,983 | 25,318 | 24,105 | 21,921 | 16,144 | 15,091 | 13,127 | 11,165 |
| Current Liabilities | 10,797 | 9,779 | 8,716 | 9,810 | 9,920 | 8,146 | 6,841 | 6,602 | 5,584 | 4,806 |
| Long Term Debt | 4,536 | 2,652 | 3,168 | 3,201 | 3,255 | 4,166 | 1,578 | 1,631 | 1,777 | 1,827 |
| Common Equity | 11,066 | 10,089 | 9,121 | 9,411 | 8,907 | 7,355 | 6,058 | 5,206 | 4,164 | 3,396 |
| Total Capital | 16,398 | 13,043 | 12,490 | 12,890 | 11,290 | 11,650 | 7,831 | 7,106 | 6,260 | 5,515 |
| Capital Expenditures | 1,325 | 777 | 647 | 807 | 828 | 711 | 664 | 862 | 664 | 496 |
| Cash Flow | 2,472 | 2,182 | 407 | 1,762 | 2,027 | 1,738 | 1,394 | 1,434 | 1,234 | 1,110 |
| Current Ratio | 1.1 | 1.1 | 1.1 | 1.1 | 1.1 | 1.1 | 1.0 | 1.0 | 1.0 | 1.0 |
| % Long Term Debt of Capitalization | 27.7 | 20.3 | 25.2 | 24.8 | 28.8 | 35.8 | 20.1 | 22.9 | 28.4 | 33.1 |
| % Net Income of Revenue | 4.3 | 4.4 | NM | 2.6 | 3.7 | 3.2 | 2.8 | 3.1 | 3.0 | 3.0 |
| % Return on Assets | 6.3 | 6.0 | NM | 4.0 | 5.6 | 5.4 | 4.9 | 5.8 | 5.6 | 5.7 |
| % Return on Equity | 16.5 | 15.5 | NM | 10.7 | 15.9 | 15.4 | 13.4 | 17.4 | 17.9 | 18.9 |

Data as orig reptd.; bef. results of disc opers/spec. items. Per share data adj. for stk. divs.; EPS diluted. E-Estimated. NA-Not Available. NM-Not Meaningful. NR-Not Ranked. UR-Under Review.

Office: 5757 North Green Bay Avenue, P O Box 591, Milwaukee, WI 53209.
Telephone: 414-524-1200.
Website: http://www.johnsoncontrols.com
Chrmn, Pres & CEO: S.A. Roell

COO: W.C. Jackson
EVP & CFO: R.B. McDonald
Chief Acctg Officer & Cntlr: B.J. Stief
Treas: F.A. Voltolina

Investor Contact: G.Z. Ponczak (414-524-1200)
Board Members: D. P. Abney, D. W. Archer, R. L. Barnett, N. A. Black, R. A. Cornog, R. A. Goodman, J. A. Joerres, W. H. Lacy, E. Reyes-Retana, S. A. Roell, M. P. Vergnano

Founded: 1900
Domicile: Wisconsin
Employees: 162,000

The McGraw·Hill Companies

# Johnson & Johnson

**STANDARD &POOR'S**

| S&P Recommendation | BUY ★★★★☆ | Price | 12-Mo. Target Price | Investment Style |
|---|---|---|---|---|
| | | $61.27 (as of Nov 25, 2011) | $73.00 | Large-Cap Growth |

**GICS Sector** Health Care
**Sub-Industry** Pharmaceuticals

**Summary** This company is a leader in the pharmaceutical, medical device and consumer products industries.

## Key Stock Statistics (Source S&P, Vickers, company reports)

| | | | | | | | | |
|---|---|---|---|---|---|---|---|---|
| 52-Wk Range | $68.05– 57.50 | S&P Oper. EPS 2011**E** | 4.95 | Market Capitalization(B) | $167.319 | Beta | | 0.59 |
| Trailing 12-Month EPS | $4.10 | S&P Oper. EPS 2012**E** | 5.25 | Yield (%) | 3.72 | S&P 3-Yr. Proj. EPS CAGR(%) | | 6 |
| Trailing 12-Month P/E | 14.9 | P/E on S&P Oper. EPS 2011**E** | 12.4 | Dividend Rate/Share | $2.28 | S&P Credit Rating | | AAA |
| $10K Invested 5 Yrs Ago | $10,882 | Common Shares Outstg. (M) | 2,730.8 | Institutional Ownership (%) | 65 | | | |

## Price Performance

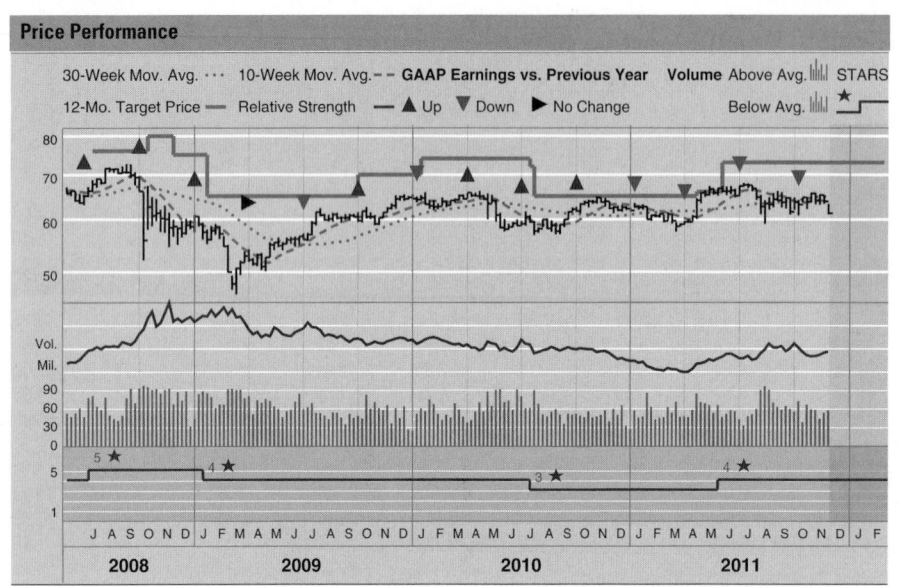

Options: ASE, CBOE, P, Ph

Analysis prepared by Equity Analyst **Herman Saftlas** on Oct 20, 2011, when the stock traded at **$62.62**.

## Qualitative Risk Assessment

| LOW | MEDIUM | HIGH |
|---|---|---|

Our risk assessment reflects our belief that JNJ has products that are largely immune from economic cycles, has modest reliance on any single product category or customer for sustained growth, and enjoys competitive advantages owing to its substantial financial resources, business scale and global sales capabilities.

## Quantitative Evaluations

**S&P Quality Ranking** — A+

| D | C | B- | B | B+ | A- | A | A+ |
|---|---|---|---|---|---|---|---|

**Relative Strength Rank** — MODERATE

58

LOWEST = 1   HIGHEST = 99

## Highlights

➤ We expect revenues in 2012 to advance about 5% from the $65 billion that we estimate for 2011, driven by projected gains in drugs, devices and consumer products. Pharmaceutical sales growth should reflect gains in Simponi and other immunology therapies, as well as contributions from new products such as Zytiga, Incivek and Xarelto. Medical device sales should benefit from gains in diabetes care, Ethicon and diagnostics lines. The planned acquisition of Synthes should augment the orthopedics business. We also project higher consumer products sales, bolstered by plant remediation measures, and the acquisition of Merck's interest in a OTC products joint venture.

➤ Despite pricing pressures associated with U.S. health care reform, and remediation costs related to quality control issues and an FDA Consent Decree at the McNeil OTC division, we expect operating margins to benefit from accretion from the Crucell acquisition and cost streamlining measures.

➤ After a projected tax rate similar to the 21.5% that we estimate for 2011, we forecast operating EPS of $5.25 for 2012 and $4.95 for 2011.

## Investment Rationale/Risk

➤ We believe JNJ's diversified sales base across drugs, medical devices and consumer products, along with its decentralized business model, has served it well in the past and should continue to do so in the years ahead. In our view, JNJ's pharma segment should benefit from a number of key new products, including Xarelto blood thinner, Incivek treatment for hepatitis C, Zytiga for prostate cancer, and Edurant for HIV. In late April 2011, JNJ agreed to acquire Synthes for $21.3 billion in cash and stock. We see significant operating synergies accruing from the proposed Synthes combination, which is expected to be completed in the first half of 2012.

➤ Risks to our recommendation and target price include worse-than-expected product pricing pressures, extended delays in OTC plant remediations, possible pipeline disappointments, and adverse foreign exchange.

➤ Our 12-month target price of $73 applies a multiple of 13.9X to our 2012 EPS estimate, a valuation that is near JNJ's average multiple of recent years. Our DCF analysis also shows intrinsic value of $73, assuming a 9.6% WACC and 1% terminal growth.

## Revenue/Earnings Data

**Revenue (Million $)**

| | 1Q | 2Q | 3Q | 4Q | Year |
|---|---|---|---|---|---|
| 2011 | 16,173 | 16,597 | 16,005 | -- | -- |
| 2010 | 15,631 | 15,330 | 14,982 | 15,644 | 61,587 |
| 2009 | 15,026 | 15,239 | 15,081 | 16,551 | 61,897 |
| 2008 | 16,194 | 16,450 | 15,921 | 15,182 | 63,747 |
| 2007 | 15,037 | 15,131 | 14,970 | 15,957 | 61,095 |
| 2006 | 12,992 | 13,363 | 13,287 | 13,682 | 53,324 |

**Earnings Per Share ($)**

| | | | | | |
|---|---|---|---|---|---|
| 2011 | 1.25 | 1.00 | 1.15 | E1.08 | E4.95 |
| 2010 | 1.62 | 1.23 | 1.23 | 0.70 | 4.78 |
| 2009 | 1.26 | 1.15 | 1.20 | 0.79 | 4.40 |
| 2008 | 1.26 | 1.17 | 1.17 | 0.97 | 4.57 |
| 2007 | 0.88 | 1.05 | 0.88 | 0.82 | 3.63 |
| 2006 | 1.10 | 0.95 | 0.94 | 0.74 | 3.73 |

Fiscal year ended Dec. 31. Next earnings report expected: NA. EPS Estimates based on S&P Operating Earnings; historical GAAP earnings are as reported.

## Dividend Data (Dates: mm/dd Payment Date: mm/dd/yy)

| Amount ($) | Date Decl. | Ex-Div. Date | Stk. of Record | Payment Date |
|---|---|---|---|---|
| 0.540 | 01/03 | 02/25 | 03/01 | 03/15/11 |
| 0.570 | 04/28 | 05/26 | 05/31 | 06/14/11 |
| 0.570 | 07/18 | 08/26 | 08/30 | 09/13/11 |
| 0.570 | 10/21 | 11/25 | 11/29 | 12/13/11 |

Dividends have been paid since 1944. Source: Company reports.

---

**Please read the Required Disclosures and Analyst Certification on the last page of this report.**

*The McGraw-Hill Companies*

# Johnson & Johnson

STANDARD
&POOR'S

## Business Summary October 20, 2011

CORPORATE OVERVIEW. Johnson & Johnson ranks as one of the largest and most diversified health care firms, with products spanning across the pharmaceutical and medical device industries. The company is also a major participant in the global consumer products business, and, in December 2006, purchased the consumer products unit of Pfizer for $16.6 billion. International sales accounted for about 52% of 2010 sales.

The pharmaceutical segment (36% of 2010 sales) includes products in therapeutic areas including anti-infective, anti-psychotic, cardiovascular, contraceptive, dermatology, gastrointestinal, hematology, immunology, neurology, oncology, pain management, urology and virology. Principal pharmaceutical products include Procrit/Eprex (sales of $1.9 billion in 2010), Remicade ($4.6 billion), Risperdal Consta ($1.5 billion), Floxin/Levaquin ($1.4 billion), Aciphex/Pariet ($1.1 billion), and Concerta ($1.3 billion). Patents on Concerta and Levaquin expired during the first half of 2011.

The medical devices and diagnostics segment (40%) sells a wide range of

products, including Ethicon's wound care, surgical sports medicine and women's health care products; Cordis's circulatory disease management products; Lifescan's blood glucose monitoring products; Ortho-Clinical Diagnostic's professional diagnostic products; Depuy's orthopaedic joint reconstruction and spinal products; and Vistakon's disposable contact lenses.

The consumer segment (24%) primarily sells personal care products, including nonprescription drugs, adult skin and hair care products, baby care products, oral care products, first aid products, women's health products, and nutritional products. Major brands include Band-Aid Brand Adhesive Bandages, Imodium A-D antidiarrheal, Johnson's Baby line of products, Neutrogena skin and hair care products, and Tylenol pain reliever.

## Company Financials Fiscal Year Ended Dec. 31

| Per Share Data ($) | 2010 | 2009 | 2008 | 2007 | 2006 | 2005 | 2004 | 2003 | 2002 | 2001 |
|---|---|---|---|---|---|---|---|---|---|---|
| Tangible Book Value | 8.97 | 7.04 | 5.35 | 5.13 | 3.67 | 8.64 | 6.72 | 5.17 | 4.53 | 4.97 |
| Cash Flow | 5.84 | 5.39 | 5.57 | 4.59 | 4.57 | 4.20 | 3.58 | 3.01 | 2.67 | 2.35 |
| Earnings | 4.78 | 4.40 | 4.57 | 3.63 | 3.73 | 3.46 | 2.84 | 2.40 | 2.16 | 1.84 |
| S&P Core Earnings | 4.55 | 4.22 | 4.17 | 3.61 | 3.65 | 3.38 | 2.77 | 2.26 | 1.99 | 1.66 |
| Dividends | 2.11 | 1.93 | 1.80 | 1.62 | 1.46 | 1.28 | 1.10 | 0.93 | 0.80 | 0.70 |
| Payout Ratio | 44% | 44% | 39% | 45% | 39% | 37% | 39% | 39% | 37% | 38% |
| Prices:High | 66.20 | 65.41 | 72.76 | 68.75 | 69.41 | 69.99 | 64.25 | 59.08 | 65.89 | 60.97 |
| Prices:Low | 56.86 | 46.25 | 52.06 | 59.72 | 56.65 | 59.76 | 49.25 | 48.05 | 41.40 | 40.25 |
| P/E Ratio:High | 14 | 15 | 16 | 19 | 19 | 20 | 23 | 25 | 31 | 33 |
| P/E Ratio:Low | 12 | 11 | 11 | 16 | 15 | 17 | 17 | 20 | 19 | 22 |

| Income Statement Analysis (Million $) | | | | | | | | | | |
|---|---|---|---|---|---|---|---|---|---|---|
| Revenue | 61,587 | 61,897 | 63,747 | 61,095 | 53,324 | 50,514 | 47,348 | 41,862 | 36,298 | 33,004 |
| Operating Income | 19,420 | 19,550 | 19,001 | 17,990 | 15,886 | 15,464 | 14,987 | 12,740 | 11,340 | 9,490 |
| Depreciation | 2,939 | 2,774 | 2,832 | 2,777 | 2,177 | 2,093 | 2,124 | 1,869 | 1,662 | 1,605 |
| Interest Expense | 348 | 451 | 582 | 426 | 63.0 | 54.0 | 187 | 207 | 160 | 153 |
| Pretax Income | 16,947 | 15,755 | 16,929 | 13,283 | 14,587 | 13,656 | 12,838 | 10,308 | 9,291 | 7,898 |
| Effective Tax Rate | NA | 22.2% | 23.5% | 20.4% | 24.2% | 23.8% | 33.7% | 30.2% | 29.0% | 28.2% |
| Net Income | 13,334 | 12,266 | 12,949 | 10,576 | 11,053 | 10,411 | 8,509 | 7,197 | 6,597 | 5,668 |
| S&P Core Earnings | 12,687 | 11,779 | 11,832 | 10,534 | 10,814 | 10,161 | 8,263 | 6,785 | 6,052 | 5,090 |

| Balance Sheet & Other Financial Data (Million $) | | | | | | | | | | |
|---|---|---|---|---|---|---|---|---|---|---|
| Cash | 27,658 | 19,425 | 12,809 | 9,315 | 4,084 | 16,138 | 12,884 | 9,523 | 7,596 | 8,941 |
| Current Assets | 47,307 | 39,541 | 34,377 | 29,945 | 22,975 | 31,394 | 27,320 | 22,995 | 19,266 | 18,473 |
| Total Assets | 102,908 | 94,682 | 84,912 | 80,954 | 70,556 | 58,025 | 53,317 | 48,263 | 40,556 | 38,488 |
| Current Liabilities | 23,072 | 21,731 | 20,852 | 19,837 | 19,161 | 12,635 | 13,927 | 13,448 | 11,449 | 8,044 |
| Long Term Debt | 9,156 | 8,223 | 8,120 | 7,074 | 2,014 | 2,017 | 2,565 | 2,955 | 2,022 | 2,217 |
| Common Equity | 56,579 | 50,588 | 42,511 | 43,319 | 61,266 | 37,871 | 31,813 | 26,869 | 22,697 | 24,233 |
| Total Capital | 65,748 | 60,235 | 52,063 | 51,886 | 42,651 | 40,099 | 34,781 | 30,604 | 25,362 | 26,943 |
| Capital Expenditures | 2,384 | 2,365 | 3,066 | 2,942 | 2,666 | 2,632 | 2,175 | 2,262 | 2,099 | 1,731 |
| Cash Flow | 16,273 | 15,040 | 15,781 | 13,353 | 13,230 | 12,504 | 10,633 | 9,066 | 8,259 | 7,273 |
| Current Ratio | 2.1 | 1.8 | 1.7 | 1.5 | 1.2 | 2.5 | 2.0 | 1.7 | 1.7 | 2.3 |
| % Long Term Debt of Capitalization | 13.9 | 13.7 | 15.6 | 13.6 | 4.7 | 5.0 | 7.4 | 9.7 | 8.0 | 8.2 |
| % Net Income of Revenue | 21.7 | 19.8 | 20.3 | 17.3 | 20.7 | 20.6 | 18.0 | 17.2 | 18.2 | 17.2 |
| % Return on Assets | NA | 13.7 | 15.6 | 14.9 | 17.1 | 18.7 | 16.8 | 16.2 | 16.7 | 15.6 |
| % Return on Equity | NA | 26.4 | 30.2 | 20.2 | 19.8 | 29.9 | 29.0 | 29.0 | 28.1 | 25.4 |

Data as orig reptd.; bef. results of disc opers/spec. items. Per share data adj. for stk. divs.; EPS diluted. E-Estimated. NA-Not Available. NM-Not Meaningful. NR-Not Ranked. UR-Under Review.

**Office:** One Johnson & Johnson Plaza, New Brunswick, NJ 08933.
**Telephone:** 732-524-0400.
**Website:** http://www.jnj.com
**Chrmn & CEO:** W.C. Weldon

**COO:** A. Shetty
**CFO:** D.J. Caruso
**CSO:** T.J. Torphy
**Chief Acctg Officer & Cntlr:** S.J. Cosgrove

**Investor Contact:** L. Mehrotra (732-524-6491)
**Board Members:** M. S. Coleman, J. G. Cullen, I. E. Davis, M. M. Johns, A. J. Khoury, S. L. Lindquist, A. M. Mulcahy, L. F. Mullin, W. D. Perez, C. Prince, III, D. Satcher, W. C. Weldon, R. A. Williams

**Founded:** 1887
**Domicile:** New Jersey
**Employees:** 114,000

The McGraw·Hill Companies

# Joy Global Inc

| S&P Recommendation | BUY ★★★★☆ | Price<br>$78.78 (as of Nov 25, 2011) | 12-Mo. Target Price<br>$90.00 | Investment Style<br>Large-Cap Blend |
|---|---|---|---|---|

**GICS Sector** Industrials
**Sub-Industry** Construction & Farm Machinery & Heavy Trucks

**Summary** This global manufacturer of surface and underground mining equipment also markets original equipment and aftermarket parts and services.

## Key Stock Statistics (Source S&P, Vickers, company reports)

| | | | | | | | |
|---|---|---|---|---|---|---|---|
| 52-Wk Range | $103.44–57.48 | S&P Oper. EPS 2011**E** | 6.05 | Market Capitalization(B) | $8.280 | Beta | 2.11 |
| Trailing 12-Month EPS | $5.49 | S&P Oper. EPS 2012**E** | 7.45 | Yield (%) | 0.89 | S&P 3-Yr. Proj. EPS CAGR(%) | 25 |
| Trailing 12-Month P/E | 14.4 | P/E on S&P Oper. EPS 2011**E** | 13.0 | Dividend Rate/Share | $0.70 | S&P Credit Rating | BBB |
| $10K Invested 5 Yrs Ago | $18,947 | Common Shares Outstg. (M) | 105.1 | Institutional Ownership (%) | 89 | | |

## Price Performance

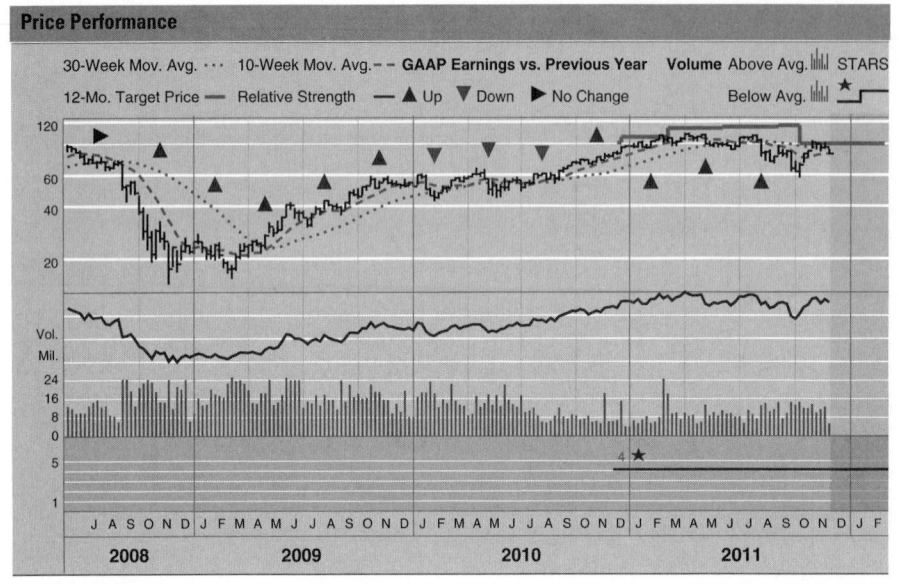

30-Week Mov. Avg. · · · 10-Week Mov. Avg. - - GAAP Earnings vs. Previous Year   Volume Above Avg. STARS
12-Mo. Target Price — Relative Strength — ▲ Up ▼ Down ► No Change   Below Avg.

Options: ASE, CBOE, P, Ph

Analysis prepared by Equity Analyst **Michael Jaffe** on Oct 06, 2011, when the stock traded at **$66.06**.

## Highlights

➤ We expect net sales to rise 17% in FY 12 (Oct.), on projected growth of 27% in surface mining equipment sales and 10% in underground mining machinery sales. Although recent sluggishness in a number of global economies will provide a challenge to JOYG's client markets, we expect still strong commodities markets, large infrastructure projects in China and limited available mining capacity to continue to drive demand for the company's products. We also see JOYG aided by the fulfillment of its large order backlog ($3.2 billion at July 29, 2011, a 78% rise from a year earlier) and the full-year inclusion of LeTourneau Technologies, which was acquired from the Rowan Companies in June 2011.

➤ We think that operating margins will widen in FY 12, when we see stronger demand for JOYG's products leading to favorable price realization and improved manufacturing overhead absorption.

➤ In light of economic challenges, JOYG planned to increase the scrutiny of all costs, but it expected to maintain its focus and funding on key strategic programs, such as the next step of capacity addition and major R&D programs.

## Investment Rationale/Risk

➤ Although challenging economic trends have reduced the visibility for ongoing gains in JOYG's business, we think demand will remain strong, as we expect conditions to remain favorable in commodities markets (despite the downturn in recent periods). We also believe the recent acquisitions announced by JOYG will strengthen its position in what we view as an increasingly competitive market. Based on these factors and our valuation model, we believe that JOYG shares are undervalued.

➤ Risks to our recommendation and target price include slower-than-expected demand for mining equipment; a slowdown in developing market demand for commodities; increased competition following recent industry mergers; and acquisition integration risk.

➤ The shares recently traded at about 9X our calendar 2012 forecast, or the low end of its range over the past decade. Based on our outlook for ongoing earnings gains at JOYG, we believe its shares are undervalued. However, in light of growing economic uncertainties, our 12-month target price of $90, or 11.8X our calendar 2012 estimate, falls into the bottom half of the company's range over the past decade.

## Qualitative Risk Assessment

| LOW | MEDIUM | HIGH |
|---|---|---|

Our risk assessment reflects the highly cyclical nature of the company's original equipment and aftermarket businesses, long lead times for original equipment manufacturing, and commodity price exposure, offset by our outlook for favorable end-market conditions over the next several years.

## Quantitative Evaluations

**S&P Quality Ranking**   B

| D | C | B- | B | B+ | A- | A | A+ |
|---|---|---|---|---|---|---|---|

**Relative Strength Rank**   MODERATE

61

LOWEST = 1         HIGHEST = 99

## Revenue/Earnings Data

**Revenue (Million $)**

| | 1Q | 2Q | 3Q | 4Q | Year |
|---|---|---|---|---|---|
| 2011 | 869.5 | 1,063 | 1,136 | -- | -- |
| 2010 | 729.2 | 896.2 | 850.0 | 1,049 | 3,524 |
| 2009 | 754.9 | 923.5 | 956.4 | 963.5 | 3,598 |
| 2008 | 640.3 | 843.1 | 903.8 | 1,032 | 3,419 |
| 2007 | 560.5 | 629.2 | 621.8 | 735.9 | 2,547 |
| 2006 | 553.3 | 560.4 | 598.7 | 689.3 | 2,402 |

**Earnings Per Share ($)**

| | | | | | |
|---|---|---|---|---|---|
| 2011 | 0.96 | 1.52 | 1.61 | E1.99 | E6.05 |
| 2010 | 0.73 | 1.15 | 1.13 | 1.39 | 4.40 |
| 2009 | 0.83 | 1.17 | 1.21 | 1.20 | 4.41 |
| 2008 | 0.64 | 0.66 | 1.03 | 1.11 | 3.44 |
| 2007 | 0.51 | 0.70 | 1.03 | 0.64 | 2.51 |
| 2006 | 0.47 | 0.66 | 1.53 | 0.71 | 3.37 |

Fiscal year ended Oct. 31. Next earnings report expected: Mid December. EPS Estimates based on S&P Operating Earnings; historical GAAP earnings are as reported.

## Dividend Data (Dates: mm/dd Payment Date: mm/dd/yy)

| Amount<br>($) | Date<br>Decl. | Ex-Div.<br>Date | Stk. of<br>Record | Payment<br>Date |
|---|---|---|---|---|
| 0.175 | 02/16 | 03/02 | 03/04 | 03/18/11 |
| 0.175 | 05/19 | 06/02 | 06/06 | 06/20/11 |
| 0.175 | 08/23 | 08/31 | 09/05 | 09/19/11 |
| 0.175 | 11/22 | 12/01 | 12/05 | 12/19/11 |

Dividends have been paid since 2004. Source: Company reports.

---

**Please read the Required Disclosures and Analyst Certification on the last page of this report.**

# Joy Global Inc

## Business Summary October 06, 2011

CORPORATE OVERVIEW. Joy Global is a leading global manufacturer of mining equipment and a provider of aftermarket parts and services used in the extraction of coal, iron ore, copper, oil sands and other minerals. The company breaks down its operations into two segments -- underground (Joy Global Machinery) and surface (P&H Mining). JOYG has taken recent actions to expand its operations, including the June 2011, acquisition of LeTourneau Technologies, a maker of surface mining equipment, and its calendar 2011 third-quarter agreement to acquire China-based International Mining Machinery Holdings, which makes underground longwall coal mining equipment.

Joy Global's underground mining division (about 58% of FY 10 sales and 58.5% of operating profit, with an operating profit margin of 16.9%) provides equipment used in the extraction of minerals from underground mines. Segment products include continuous miners, shuttle cars, flexible conveyor trains, longwall mining systems and equipment, continuous haulage systems, battery haulers, roof bolters, and completed conveyor & crushing systems. Continuous miners are large, electric, self-propelled mining machinery with carbide-tipped bits on a horizontal cutting surface, while shuttle cars are a type of haulage vehicle, with some able to haul up to 22 metric tons of coal. Flexible conveyor trains are able to carry mined materials from continuous mining equipment to a main belt line. The segment maintains operating facilities and sales offices in some of the major mining centers of the world, including Australia, South Africa, the United Kingdom, China, India, Russia, and the United States.

The company believes its surface segment (42% and 41.5%, 16.8%) is the world's largest manufacturer of electric mining shovels, and it also produces other surface mining equipment such as rotary blasthole drills and walking draglines. Electric mining shovels are used primarily to load mined materials, overburden (the rock and soil that lie above the coal being mined) and rocks onto trucks. Rotary blasthole drills are used to bore holes in the ground area to be mined into which explosives are placed to remove rock, overburden or ore. Draglines are large machines used primarily in the surface mining of coal to remove overburden. Draglines are the largest and most expensive type of surface mining equipment. This segment also provides services and aftermarket parts for surface mining equipment. Surface equipment facilities are global in scope, and the company has operations for this segment in Australia, Brazil, Canada, Chile, China, South Africa and the United States. Equipment sold in this segment is used to mine various minerals, including copper, coal, iron ore, oil sands, silver, gold, diamonds, phosphate, and other minerals.

## Company Financials Fiscal Year Ended Oct. 31

| Per Share Data ($) | 2010 | 2009 | 2008 | 2007 | 2006 | 2005 | 2004 | 2003 | 2002 | 2001 |
|---|---|---|---|---|---|---|---|---|---|---|
| Tangible Book Value | 10.15 | 4.84 | 2.07 | 5.98 | 7.18 | 5.43 | 3.44 | 2.58 | 1.42 | NA |
| Cash Flow | 4.97 | 4.98 | 4.10 | 2.94 | 3.70 | 1.53 | 0.84 | 0.62 | 0.32 | 0.28 |
| Earnings | 4.40 | 4.41 | 3.44 | 2.51 | 3.37 | 1.19 | 0.46 | 0.16 | -0.20 | -0.68 |
| S&P Core Earnings | 4.58 | 4.40 | 2.92 | 2.60 | 3.39 | 1.20 | 0.45 | 0.10 | -0.74 | 0.31 |
| Dividends | 0.70 | 0.70 | NA | 0.60 | 0.34 | 0.28 | 0.12 | Nil | Nil | NA |
| Payout Ratio | 16% | 16% | NA | 24% | 10% | 23% | 27% | Nil | Nil | NA |
| Prices:High | 88.21 | 59.30 | NA | 67.61 | 72.23 | 41.94 | 19.86 | 11.97 | 7.97 | NA |
| Prices:Low | 42.45 | 15.38 | NA | 40.36 | 31.32 | 17.18 | 10.43 | 4.41 | 3.40 | NA |
| P/E Ratio:High | 20 | 13 | NA | 27 | 21 | 35 | 43 | 73 | NM | NA |
| P/E Ratio:Low | 10 | 3 | NA | 16 | 9 | 14 | 23 | 27 | NM | NA |

| Income Statement Analysis (Million $) | | | | | | | | | | |
|---|---|---|---|---|---|---|---|---|---|---|
| Revenue | 3,524 | 3,598 | 3,419 | 2,547 | 2,402 | 1,927 | 1,432 | 1,216 | 1,151 | 1,148 |
| Operating Income | 757 | 775 | 668 | 522 | 475 | 306 | 151 | 104 | 42.9 | 48.1 |
| Depreciation | 59.8 | 58.6 | 71.4 | 48.8 | 41.3 | 41.9 | 46.2 | 52.5 | 59.1 | 56.4 |
| Interest Expense | 16.8 | 32.2 | 34.2 | 31.9 | 5.67 | 15.2 | 24.3 | 27.0 | 31.0 | 40.3 |
| Pretax Income | 679 | 683 | 527 | 449 | 450 | 227 | 94.6 | 27.9 | -35.7 | -37.1 |
| Effective Tax Rate | NA | 33.4% | 29.2% | 37.7% | 7.88% | 35.4% | 41.5% | 33.6% | NM | 36.5% |
| Net Income | 462 | 455 | 373 | 280 | 415 | 147 | 55.3 | 18.5 | -23.2 | -25.9 |
| S&P Core Earnings | 481 | 454 | 317 | 290 | 418 | 148 | 54.3 | 11.5 | -83.9 | 34.7 |

| Balance Sheet & Other Financial Data (Million $) | | | | | | | | | | |
|---|---|---|---|---|---|---|---|---|---|---|
| Cash | 816 | 472 | 202 | 173 | 101 | 144 | 232 | 149 | 71.2 | 39.7 |
| Current Assets | 2,362 | 1,950 | 1,738 | 1,538 | 1,228 | 1,117 | 992 | 777 | 700 | 799 |
| Total Assets | 3,284 | 3,008 | 2,644 | 2,135 | 1,954 | 1,649 | 1,440 | 1,287 | 1,257 | 1,372 |
| Current Liabilities | 1,023 | 927 | 1,140 | 754 | 600 | 600 | 432 | 326 | 317 | 355 |
| Long Term Debt | 396 | 524 | 541 | 396 | 98.1 | Nil | 203 | 203 | 215 | 288 |
| Common Equity | 1,355 | 814 | 532 | 724 | 920 | 668 | 452 | 370 | 351 | 484 |
| Total Capital | 1,752 | 1,338 | 1,092 | 1,120 | 1,018 | 668 | 655 | 573 | 577 | 782 |
| Capital Expenditures | 73.5 | 94.1 | 84.2 | 51.2 | 49.1 | 38.8 | 18.7 | 27.5 | 19.1 | 22.3 |
| Cash Flow | 521 | 513 | 445 | 329 | 456 | 189 | 101 | 71.1 | 36.0 | 30.6 |
| Current Ratio | 2.3 | 2.1 | 1.5 | 2.0 | 2.0 | 1.9 | 2.3 | 2.4 | 2.2 | 2.3 |
| % Long Term Debt of Capitalization | 22.6 | 39.2 | 47.1 | 35.3 | 9.6 | Nil | 31.0 | 35.4 | 37.3 | 36.9 |
| % Net Income of Revenue | 13.1 | 12.6 | 10.9 | 11.0 | 17.3 | 7.6 | 3.9 | 1.5 | NM | NM |
| % Return on Assets | 14.7 | 16.1 | 15.6 | 13.7 | 23.0 | 9.5 | 4.1 | 1.5 | NM | NM |
| % Return on Equity | 42.6 | 67.6 | 59.4 | 34.0 | 52.3 | 26.2 | 13.5 | 5.1 | NM | NM |

Data as orig reptd.; bef. results of disc opers/spec. items. Per share data adj. for stk. divs.; EPS diluted. E-Estimated. NA-Not Available. NM-Not Meaningful. NR-Not Ranked. UR-Under Review.

**Office:** 100 East Wisconsin Avenue, Milwaukee, WI, USA 53202.
**Telephone:** 414-319-8500.
**Website:** http://www.joyglobal.com
**Chrmn:** J.N. Hanson

**Pres & CEO:** M.W. Sutherlin
**EVP, CFO & Treas:** M.S. Olsen
**EVP, Secy & General Counsel:** S.D. Major
**Chief Admin Officer:** D.R. Winkleman

**Board Members:** S. L. Gerard, J. N. Hanson, G. E. Klappa, R. B. Loynd, P. E. Siegert, M. W. Sutherlin, J. H. Tate

**Founded:** 1884
**Domicile:** Delaware
**Employees:** 11,900

# JPMorgan Chase & Co

STANDARD &POOR'S

| S&P Recommendation | HOLD ★★★★★ | Price $30.97 (as of Nov 30, 2011) | 12-Mo. Target Price $40.00 | Investment Style Large-Cap Value |
|---|---|---|---|---|

**GICS Sector** Financials
**Sub-Industry** Other Diversified Financial Services

**Summary** This leading global financial services company has assets of $2.3 trillion and operations in more than 50 countries.

## Key Stock Statistics (Source S&P, Vickers, company reports)

| | | | | | | | |
|---|---|---|---|---|---|---|---|
| 52-Wk Range | $48.36– 27.85 | S&P Oper. EPS 2011**E** | 4.67 | Market Capitalization(B) | $117.614 | Beta | 1.20 |
| Trailing 12-Month EPS | $4.69 | S&P Oper. EPS 2012**E** | 5.37 | Yield (%) | 3.23 | S&P 3-Yr. Proj. EPS CAGR(%) | 12 |
| Trailing 12-Month P/E | 6.6 | P/E on S&P Oper. EPS 2011**E** | 6.6 | Dividend Rate/Share | $1.00 | S&P Credit Rating | A |
| $10K Invested 5 Yrs Ago | $7,453 | Common Shares Outstg. (M) | 3,797.7 | Institutional Ownership (%) | 75 | | |

## Price Performance

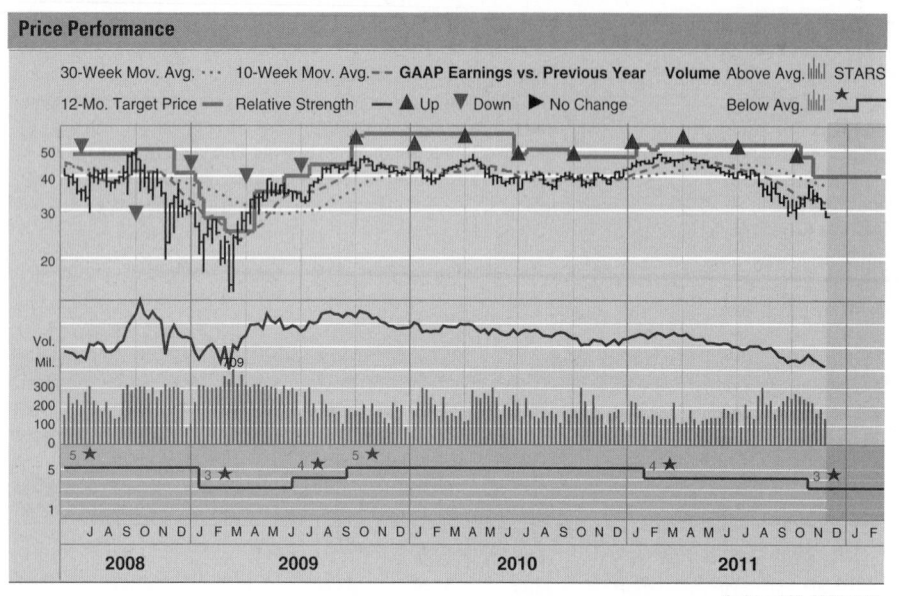

Options: ASE, CBOE, P, Ph

Analysis prepared by Equity Analyst **Erik Oja** on Nov 02, 2011, when the stock traded at **$33.64**.

## Highlights

▶ Challenging third-quarter results reflected the mid-August turmoil in Europe, U.S. economic softness attributable to Japan, and low consumer confidence driven by the downgrade of U.S. federal debt. Investment banking fees were $1.05 billion, including $1.9 billion of valuation adjustments. Trading revenue fell to $1.37 billion, from $3.14 billion in the second quarter and $4.75 billion in the first quarter. We expect both to be down about 1.5% for 2011. We also expect net interest income to fall 7.1% in 2011, on a decline in the net interest margin. We forecast a 3.4% net revenue decline in 2011, with 1.0% growth expected in 2012, on a rebound in net interest income.

▶ In our view, declining loan loss provisions will be the major driver of earnings growth for JPM in 2011. We expect net chargeoffs of $11.6 billion in 2011, down from 2010's $23.7 billion and 2009's $22.4 billion. On our view that JPM's allowance for loan losses is adequate and will continue to decline, our loan loss provisioning estimate for 2011 is $7.7 billion, down sharply from 2010's $16.6 billion.

▶ We see EPS of $4.67 in 2011 and $5.37 in 2012.

## Investment Rationale/Risk

▶ JPM's fundamentals are near the top of the U.S. banking industry, in our view. JPM's $0.25 quarterly dividend, yielding 2.7%, is only 19.5% of our $5.12 estimate of forward four quarters EPS, and we think JPM could be in a position to again raise it next spring. Should the U.S. economy continue to improve, JPM's capital levels should rise from retained earnings and be sufficient to meet upcoming Basel III requirements. Also, JPM has ample reserve coverage, at 2.6X nonperforming loans and 4.4% of total loans, above most peers. The biggest blemish on third quarter results, in our view, was investment banking, which reported negative results, excluding the impact of valuation adjustments to debt investment securities, and we think results will improve once the European debt crisis is contained.

▶ Risks to our recommendation and target price include the European crisis, the Dodd-Frank bill, Basel III requirements, and foreclosure issues.

▶ Our 12-month target price of $40 is based on peer equivalent multiples of 7.8X our forward four quarters EPS estimate of $5.12 and 1.2X our $33.25 estimate of year-end tangible book value per share.

## Qualitative Risk Assessment

| LOW | MEDIUM | HIGH |
|---|---|---|

Our risk assessment reflects our view of the company's well-reserved balance sheet, diversified lines of business and strong capital ratios. We believe JPM's diversity in its geographic presence and product offerings provides significant protection from a local or regional downturn.

## Quantitative Evaluations

**S&P Quality Ranking** B+

| D | C | B- | B | B+ | A- | A | A+ |
|---|---|---|---|---|---|---|---|

**Relative Strength Rank** MODERATE
30
LOWEST = 1          HIGHEST = 99

## Revenue/Earnings Data

**Revenue (Million $)**

| | 1Q | 2Q | 3Q | 4Q | Year |
|---|---|---|---|---|---|
| 2011 | 28,959 | 30,575 | 27,106 | -- | -- |
| 2010 | 30,806 | 28,133 | 26,928 | 29,608 | 115,475 |
| 2009 | 29,584 | 29,502 | 30,145 | 26,401 | 115,632 |
| 2008 | 26,763 | 26,634 | 23,069 | 25,025 | 101,491 |
| 2007 | 29,486 | 30,082 | 16,112 | 28,104 | 116,353 |
| 2006 | 23,477 | 24,175 | 24,957 | 26,693 | 99,302 |

**Earnings Per Share ($)**

| | 1Q | 2Q | 3Q | 4Q | Year |
|---|---|---|---|---|---|
| 2011 | 1.28 | 1.27 | 1.02 | E1.10 | E4.67 |
| 2010 | 0.74 | 1.09 | 1.01 | 1.12 | 3.96 |
| 2009 | 0.40 | 0.28 | 0.80 | 0.74 | 2.24 |
| 2008 | 0.68 | 0.54 | -0.06 | -0.28 | 0.84 |
| 2007 | 1.34 | 1.20 | 0.97 | 0.86 | 4.38 |
| 2006 | 0.86 | 0.98 | 0.90 | 1.26 | 3.82 |

Fiscal year ended Dec. 31. Next earnings report expected: Mid January. EPS Estimates based on S&P Operating Earnings; historical GAAP earnings are as reported.

## Dividend Data (Dates: mm/dd Payment Date: mm/dd/yy)

| Amount ($) | Date Decl. | Ex-Div. Date | Stk. of Record | Payment Date |
|---|---|---|---|---|
| 0.050 | 12/14 | 01/04 | 01/06 | 01/31/11 |
| 0.250 | 03/18 | 04/04 | 04/06 | 04/30/11 |
| 0.250 | 05/17 | 07/01 | 07/06 | 07/31/11 |
| 0.250 | 09/20 | 10/04 | 10/06 | 10/31/11 |

Dividends have been paid since 1827. Source: Company reports.

**Please read the Required Disclosures and Analyst Certification on the last page of this report.**

The McGraw-Hill Companies

# JPMorgan Chase & Co

**STANDARD &POOR'S**

## Business Summary November 02, 2011

CORPORATE OVERVIEW. JPMorgan Chase's operations are divided into six major business lines: Investment Banking, Retail Financial Services (RFS), Card Services (CS), Commercial Banking (CB), Treasury & Securities Services (TSS), and Asset Management (AM), as well as a Corporate/Private Equity segment.

JPM is one of the world's leading investment banks, with clients consisting of corporations, financial institutions, governments, and institutional investors worldwide. Its products and services include advising on corporate strategy and structure, equity and debt capital raising, sophisticated risk management, research, market making in cash securities and derivative instruments, and prime brokerage and research.

RFS includes Home Finance, Consumer & Small Business Banking, Auto & Education Finance and Insurance. At year-end 2010, RFS had 5,268 branches and 16,145 ATMs.

CS offers a wide variety of products to satisfy the needs of its card members, including cards issued on behalf of many well-known partners, such as major

airlines, hotels, universities, retailers, and other financial institutions. CS had 90.7 million cards in circulation, on a managed basis, and $137.7 billion in managed loans as of December 31, 2010.

CB provides lending, treasury services, investment banking and investment management services to corporations, municipalities, financial institutions and not-for-profit entities.

TSS offers transaction, investment and information services to support the needs of corporations, issuers and institutional investors worldwide. TSS reported assets under custody of $16.1 trillion in 2010, up 8.3% from 2009.

AM provides investment management to retail and institutional investors, financial intermediaries and high-net-worth families and individuals globally. Assets under management rose by 3.9% in 2010 to $1.3 trillion.

## Company Financials Fiscal Year Ended Dec. 31

| Per Share Data ($) | 2010 | 2009 | 2008 | 2007 | 2006 | 2005 | 2004 | 2003 | 2002 | 2001 |
|---|---|---|---|---|---|---|---|---|---|---|
| Tangible Book Value | 29.52 | 26.45 | 19.27 | 18.77 | 16.11 | 15.88 | 14.77 | 14.77 | 15.82 | 12.54 |
| Earnings | 3.96 | 2.24 | 0.84 | 4.38 | 3.82 | 2.38 | 1.55 | 3.24 | 0.80 | 0.81 |
| S&P Core Earnings | 3.94 | 2.28 | 0.67 | 4.44 | 3.88 | 2.76 | 2.25 | 3.12 | 0.65 | 0.34 |
| Dividends | 0.20 | 0.53 | 1.52 | 1.44 | 1.36 | 1.36 | 1.36 | 1.36 | 1.36 | 1.34 |
| Payout Ratio | 5% | 24% | NM | 33% | 34% | 57% | 88% | 42% | 170% | 165% |
| Prices:High | 48.20 | 47.47 | 50.63 | 53.25 | 49.00 | 40.56 | 43.84 | 38.26 | 39.68 | 57.33 |
| Prices:Low | 35.16 | 14.96 | 19.69 | 40.15 | 37.88 | 32.92 | 34.62 | 20.13 | 15.26 | 29.04 |
| P/E Ratio:High | 12 | 21 | 60 | 12 | 12 | 17 | 28 | 12 | 50 | 71 |
| P/E Ratio:Low | 9 | 7 | 23 | 9 | 9 | 14 | 22 | 6 | 19 | 36 |

| Income Statement Analysis (Million $) | | | | | | | | | | |
|---|---|---|---|---|---|---|---|---|---|---|
| Net Interest Income | 51,001 | 51,152 | 38,779 | 26,406 | 21,242 | 19,831 | 16,761 | 12,337 | 11,526 | 10,802 |
| Tax Equivalent Adjustment | 403 | 330 | 579 | 377 | NA | 269 | NA | NA | NA | NA |
| Non Interest Income | 51,693 | 49,282 | 28,937 | 44,802 | 17,959 | 34,702 | 26,336 | 19,473 | 16,525 | 17,382 |
| Loan Loss Provision | 16,639 | 32,015 | 20,979 | 6,864 | 3,270 | 3,483 | NA | NA | 4,331 | 3,185 |
| % Expense/Operating Revenue | 59.6% | 52.1% | 60.0% | 58.6% | 97.7% | 66.5% | 85.6% | 73.0% | 81.2% | 82.7% |
| Pretax Income | 24,859 | 16,067 | 2,773 | 22,805 | 19,886 | 12,215 | 6,194 | 10,028 | 2,519 | 2,566 |
| Effective Tax Rate | 30.1% | 27.5% | NM | 32.6% | 31.4% | 30.6% | 27.9% | 33.0% | 34.0% | 33.0% |
| Net Income | 17,370 | 11,652 | 3,699 | 15,365 | 13,649 | 8,483 | 4,466 | 6,719 | 1,663 | 1,719 |
| % Net Interest Margin | 3.06 | 3.12 | 2.87 | 2.39 | 2.16 | 2.19 | 2.27 | 2.10 | 2.09 | 1.99 |
| S&P Core Earnings | 15,707 | 8,861 | 2,409 | 15,563 | 13,852 | 9,802 | 6,456 | 6,439 | 1,290 | 698 |

| Balance Sheet & Other Financial Data (Million $) | | | | | | | | | | |
|---|---|---|---|---|---|---|---|---|---|---|
| Money Market Assets | 712,446 | 606,532 | 713,098 | 662,306 | 506,262 | 432,358 | 390,168 | 329,739 | 314,110 | 265,875 |
| Investment Securities | 439,923 | 480,020 | 329,943 | 169,634 | 172,022 | 128,578 | 149,675 | 109,328 | 126,834 | 105,537 |
| Commercial Loans | 222,510 | 204,175 | 111,654 | 238,210 | 188,372 | 150,111 | 135,067 | 83,097 | 91,548 | 104,864 |
| Other Loans | 470,417 | 429,283 | 610,080 | 281,164 | 294,755 | 269,037 | 267,047 | 136,421 | 124,816 | 112,580 |
| Total Assets | 2,117,605 | 2,031,989 | 2,175,052 | 1,562,147 | 1,351,520 | 1,198,942 | 1,157,248 | 770,912 | 758,800 | 693,575 |
| Demand Deposits | 242,260 | 204,003 | 210,899 | 135,748 | 140,443 | 143,075 | 136,188 | 79,465 | 82,029 | 76,974 |
| Time Deposits | 688,109 | 734,364 | 790,681 | 604,980 | 498,345 | 411,916 | 385,268 | 247,027 | 222,724 | 216,676 |
| Long Term Debt | 247,669 | 266,318 | 270,683 | 197,878 | 117,358 | 119,886 | 105,718 | 54,782 | 45,190 | 44,172 |
| Common Equity | 168,306 | 157,213 | 134,945 | 123,221 | 115,790 | 107,072 | 105,314 | 45,145 | 41,297 | 40,090 |
| % Return on Assets | 0.8 | 0.6 | 0.2 | 1.1 | 1.1 | 0.7 | 0.5 | 0.9 | 0.2 | 0.2 |
| % Return on Equity | 10.7 | 8.0 | 2.9 | 12.9 | 12.2 | 8.0 | 5.9 | 15.4 | 4.0 | 4.1 |
| % Loan Loss Reserve | 4.7 | 5.0 | 3.1 | 1.8 | 1.5 | 1.7 | 1.8 | 2.1 | 2.5 | 2.1 |
| % Loans/Deposits | 73.7 | 67.5 | 73.8 | 72.6 | 75.6 | 75.5 | 77.1 | 67.2 | 71.0 | 74.0 |
| % Equity to Assets | 7.8 | 6.9 | 6.9 | 8.2 | 8.7 | 9.0 | 7.8 | 5.7 | 5.6 | 5.7 |

Data as orig reptd.; bef. results of disc opers/spec. items. Per share data adj. for stk. divs.; EPS diluted. E-Estimated. NA-Not Available. NM-Not Meaningful. NR-Not Ranked. UR-Under Review.

**Office:** 270 Park Ave, New York, NY 10017-2070.
**Telephone:** 212-270-6000.
**Website:** http://www.jpmorganchase.com
**Chrmn & CEO:** J. Dimon

**Pres:** C. Berquo
**COO & CTO:** P. Cherasia
**CFO:** D.L. Braunstein
**Chief Admin Officer:** F. Bisignano

**Investor Contact:** J. Bates (212-270-7318)
**Board Members:** J. A. Bell, C. C. Bowles, S. B. Burke, D. M. Cote, J. S. Crown, J. Dimon, E. Futter, W. H. Gray, III, L. P. Jackson, Jr., D. C. Novak, L. R. Raymond, W. C. Weldon

**Founded:** 1823
**Domicile:** Delaware
**Employees:** 239,831

The **McGraw·Hill** Companies

# Juniper Networks Inc

**STANDARD &POOR'S**

| S&P Recommendation | HOLD ★★★★☆ | Price $20.85 (as of Nov 29, 2011) | 12-Mo. Target Price $26.00 | Investment Style Large-Cap Blend |
| --- | --- | --- | --- | --- |

**GICS Sector** Information Technology
**Sub-Industry** Communications Equipment

**Summary** This company provides Internet Protocol networking products and services, with an emphasis on telecom routing solutions.

## Key Stock Statistics (Source S&P, Vickers, company reports)

| | | | | | | |
| --- | --- | --- | --- | --- | --- | --- |
| 52-Wk Range | $45.01– 16.67 | S&P Oper. EPS 2011**E** | 0.93 | Market Capitalization(B) | $10.967 | Beta | 1.57 |
| Trailing 12-Month EPS | $0.95 | S&P Oper. EPS 2012**E** | 1.21 | Yield (%) | Nil | S&P 3-Yr. Proj. EPS CAGR(%) | 15 |
| Trailing 12-Month P/E | 22.0 | P/E on S&P Oper. EPS 2011**E** | 22.4 | Dividend Rate/Share | Nil | S&P Credit Rating | BBB |
| $10K Invested 5 Yrs Ago | $9,483 | Common Shares Outstg. (M) | 526.0 | Institutional Ownership (%) | 87 | | |

## Price Performance

30-Week Mov. Avg. ···· 10-Week Mov. Avg. -- GAAP Earnings vs. Previous Year Volume Above Avg. STARS
12-Mo. Target Price — Relative Strength — ▲ Up ▼ Down ► No Change Below Avg.

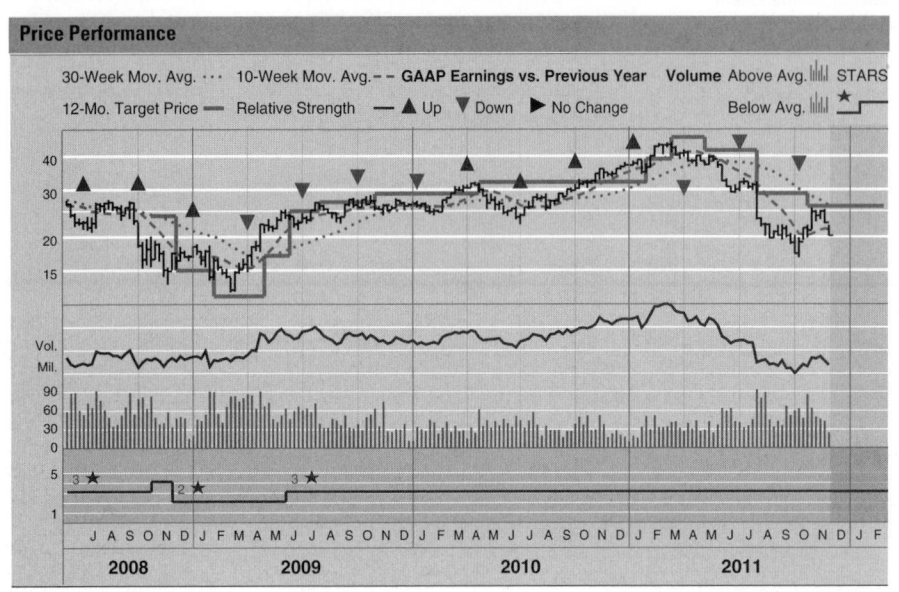

Options: ASE, CBOE, P, Ph

Analysis prepared by Equity Analyst **J. Moorman, CFA** on Oct 20, 2011, when the stock traded at **$20.52**.

## Highlights

► Following a 23% increase in 2010, we see sales growth decelerating to 10.5% in 2011, largely reflecting a weak macroeconomic climate in Europe and disruptions related to the March earthquake in Japan. We also believe customers are delaying purchases as they await the release of the company's new T-4000, Q-Fabric and PTX products. While competition remains intense, we see an opportunity for JNPR to leverage its leading position in the carrier market toward the enterprise networking sector.

► Owing to an unfavorable product mix shift and higher overhead costs, we look for 2011 gross margins to narrow modestly, to 66.3%. We expect 2011 operating margins to be pressured by aggressive investment to drive growth, particularly in R&D, in part to support new data center and wireless packet transport projects.

► After an effective tax rate of 28%, we look for 2011 operating EPS of $0.93, down from the $1.15 posted in 2010. We see 2012 operating EPS of $1.21. Estimates for 2012 include projected stock option expense of $0.34.

## Investment Rationale/Risk

► While we see the continued rapid increase in IP traffic acting as a strong underlying growth driver for JNPR, we expect sales growth trends to remain muted for the next several quarters due to a more cautious customer spending environment amid the uncertain economy. Despite a temporary slowdown in product demand, we remain optimistic about recent portfolio enhancements and product introductions, specifically the new MX3D edge router, and about a concerted push into the attractive mobile Internet and data center markets.

► Risks to our recommendation and target price include lower carrier spending, routing market share losses, and slower-than-expected sales traction in the enterprise sector.

► Our 12-month target price of $26 represents multiples of 21X our 2012 EPS estimate of $1.21 and 2.75X our 2012 sales per share forecast, valuation metrics that are above peers, warranted, we believe, by JNPR's strong position in the fast-growing IP networking sector. Using our three-year earnings growth estimate of 15%, our target price represents a forward P/E-to-growth (PEG) ratio of 1.4X, in line with the industry average.

## Qualitative Risk Assessment

| LOW | MEDIUM | HIGH |
| --- | --- | --- |

Our risk assessment reflects the highly competitive nature of the telecommunications equipment industry and execution risks related to the company's expansion into the enterprise market.

## Quantitative Evaluations

**S&P Quality Ranking** B

| D | C | B- | B | B+ | A- | A | A+ |
| --- | --- | --- | --- | --- | --- | --- | --- |

**Relative Strength Rank** MODERATE

32

LOWEST = 1    HIGHEST = 99

## Revenue/Earnings Data

**Revenue (Million $)**

| | 1Q | 2Q | 3Q | 4Q | Year |
| --- | --- | --- | --- | --- | --- |
| 2011 | 1,102 | 1,121 | 1,106 | -- | -- |
| 2010 | 912.6 | 978.3 | 1,012 | 1,190 | 4,093 |
| 2009 | 764.2 | 786.4 | 823.9 | 941.5 | 3,316 |
| 2008 | 822.9 | 879.0 | 947.0 | 923.5 | 3,572 |
| 2007 | 626.9 | 664.9 | 735.1 | 809.2 | 2,836 |
| 2006 | 566.7 | 567.5 | 573.6 | 595.8 | 2,304 |

**Earnings Per Share ($)**

| | | | | | |
| --- | --- | --- | --- | --- | --- |
| 2011 | 0.24 | 0.21 | 0.16 | E0.28 | E0.93 |
| 2010 | 0.30 | 0.24 | 0.25 | 0.35 | 1.15 |
| 2009 | -0.01 | 0.03 | 0.16 | 0.24 | 0.42 |
| 2008 | 0.20 | 0.22 | 0.27 | 0.25 | 0.93 |
| 2007 | 0.11 | 0.15 | 0.15 | 0.22 | 0.62 |
| 2006 | 0.13 | -2.13 | 0.10 | 0.12 | -1.76 |

Fiscal year ended Dec. 31. Next earnings report expected: NA. EPS Estimates based on S&P Operating Earnings; historical GAAP earnings are as reported.

## Dividend Data

No cash dividends have been paid.

---

**Please read the Required Disclosures and Analyst Certification on the last page of this report.**

*The McGraw-Hill Companies*

# Juniper Networks Inc

**STANDARD &POOR'S**

## Business Summary October 20, 2011

CORPORATE OVERVIEW. Juniper Networks, founded in 1996, makes secure Internet Protocol (IP) networking solutions that are designed to address the needs at the core and at the edge of the network, and for wireless access. The company's core product is IP backbone routers for service providers. The acquisition of NetScreen in 2004 added a broad family of network security solutions aimed at enterprises, service providers, and government entities.

The service provider sector remains the core market for JNPR, accounting for 64% of total revenue in 2010, versus 66% in the prior year. However, the enterprise market is becoming an increasingly important growth market for the company, representing 36% of 2010 sales, up from 34% and 28% in 2009 and 2008, respectively. JNPR enjoys good customer diversification, having sold its products to all of the 100 largest service providers in the world.

During 2010, international revenue represented 51% of total sales, up from 49% in 2009. Operations are organized into three operating segments: infrastructure, service layer technologies (SLT), and service.

PRIMARY BUSINESS DYNAMICS. The infrastructure segment (80% of total sales in 2010) primarily offers scalable router products that are used to control and direct network traffic from the core, through the edge, aggregation and

the customer premise equipment level. The company has experienced an increased demand for infrastructure products due to the adoption and expansion of IP networks as a result of peer-to-peer interaction, increased broadband usage, video, and IP television.

Infrastructure products include the M-series and T-series routers, geared to service providers, offering carrier class reliability and scalability. The M-series can be deployed at the edge of operator networks, in small and medium core networks. The MX-Series addresses the Carrier Ethernet market. The T-series and TX Matrix are primarily designed for core IP infrastructures. Other product platforms include E-series and J-series (wireless routers, developed through JNPR's joint venture with Ericsson). The EX-series, introduced in early 2008, extends JNPR's product portfolio for routers to the Ethernet switches. Products run on JNPR's JUNOS Internet software, and are differentiated from their competition in that they also feature the company's high-performance, ASIC-based packet forwarding technology.

## Company Financials Fiscal Year Ended Dec. 31

| Per Share Data ($) | 2010 | 2009 | 2008 | 2007 | 2006 | 2005 | 2004 | 2003 | 2002 | 2001 |
|---|---|---|---|---|---|---|---|---|---|---|
| Tangible Book Value | 4.87 | 4.14 | 4.26 | 3.09 | 4.08 | 3.04 | 2.89 | 1.48 | 1.18 | 2.36 |
| Cash Flow | 1.44 | 0.50 | 1.23 | 0.96 | -1.46 | 0.82 | 0.52 | 0.27 | -0.16 | 0.42 |
| Earnings | 1.15 | 0.42 | 0.93 | 0.62 | -1.76 | 0.59 | 0.25 | 0.10 | -0.34 | -0.04 |
| S&P Core Earnings | 1.14 | 0.45 | 0.96 | 0.60 | -0.27 | 0.26 | 0.12 | -0.06 | -0.51 | -0.38 |
| Dividends | Nil | Nil | Nil | Nil | Nil | Nil | Nil | Nil | Nil | Nil |
| Payout Ratio | Nil | Nil | Nil | Nil | Nil | Nil | Nil | Nil | Nil | Nil |
| Prices:High | 37.95 | 28.74 | 33.30 | 37.95 | 22.63 | 27.65 | 31.25 | 19.38 | 23.01 | 145.00 |
| Prices:Low | 22.25 | 12.43 | 3.29 | 17.21 | 12.09 | 19.65 | 18.75 | 6.88 | 4.15 | 8.90 |
| P/E Ratio:High | 33 | 68 | 36 | 61 | NM | 47 | NM | NM | NM | NM |
| P/E Ratio:Low | 19 | 30 | 14 | 28 | NM | 33 | NM | NM | NM | NM |

| Income Statement Analysis (Million $) | 2010 | 2009 | 2008 | 2007 | 2006 | 2005 | 2004 | 2003 | 2002 | 2001 |
|---|---|---|---|---|---|---|---|---|---|---|
| Revenue | 4,093 | 3,316 | 3,572 | 2,836 | 2,304 | 2,064 | 1,336 | 701 | 547 | 887 |
| Operating Income | 940 | 661 | 876 | 610 | 496 | 595 | 376 | 141 | 42.2 | 205 |
| Depreciation | 155 | 148 | 167 | 193 | 173 | 139 | 145 | 70.0 | 63.0 | 148 |
| Interest Expense | NA | NA | 2.90 | 1.70 | 3.59 | 3.93 | 5.38 | 39.1 | 55.6 | 61.4 |
| Pretax Income | 778 | 481 | 729 | 511 | -897 | 502 | 219 | 59.0 | -115 | 16.5 |
| Effective Tax Rate | NA | 53.6% | 29.8% | 29.3% | NM | 29.5% | 38.0% | 33.6% | NM | NM |
| Net Income | 618 | 225 | 512 | 361 | -1,001 | 354 | 136 | 39.2 | -120 | -13.4 |
| S&P Core Earnings | 613 | 239 | 527 | 353 | -156 | 156 | 65.9 | -25.6 | -180 | -122 |

| Balance Sheet & Other Financial Data (Million $) | 2010 | 2009 | 2008 | 2007 | 2006 | 2005 | 2004 | 2003 | 2002 | 2001 |
|---|---|---|---|---|---|---|---|---|---|---|
| Cash | 2,286 | 2,175 | 2,192 | 1,956 | 1,596 | 918 | 713 | 396 | 194 | 607 |
| Current Assets | 3,214 | 2,879 | 2,816 | 2,555 | 2,522 | 1,818 | 1,414 | 691 | 681 | 1,126 |
| Total Assets | 8,468 | 7,530 | 7,187 | 6,885 | 7,368 | 8,027 | 7,000 | 2,411 | 2,615 | 2,390 |
| Current Liabilities | 1,472 | 1,376 | 1,057 | 1,380 | 763 | 627 | 503 | 291 | 242 | 242 |
| Long Term Debt | NA | NA | Nil | Nil | 400 | 400 | Nil | 558 | 942 | 1,150 |
| Common Equity | 6,609 | 5,930 | 5,901 | 5,354 | 6,115 | 6,900 | 5,993 | 1,562 | 1,431 | 997 |
| Total Capital | 6,609 | 5,933 | 5,901 | 5,354 | 6,515 | 7,300 | 5,993 | 2,120 | 2,373 | 2,147 |
| Capital Expenditures | 185 | 153 | 165 | 147 | 102 | 98.2 | 63.2 | 19.4 | 36.1 | 241 |
| Cash Flow | 774 | 265 | 679 | 554 | -828 | 493 | 281 | 109 | -56.6 | 134 |
| Current Ratio | 2.2 | 2.3 | 2.7 | 1.9 | 3.3 | 2.9 | 2.8 | 2.4 | 2.8 | 4.6 |
| % Long Term Debt of Capitalization | Nil | Nil | Nil | Nil | 6.1 | 5.5 | Nil | 26.3 | 39.7 | 53.6 |
| % Net Income of Revenue | 15.1 | 6.8 | 14.3 | 12.7 | NM | 17.2 | 10.2 | 5.6 | NM | NM |
| % Return on Assets | 7.7 | 3.1 | 7.3 | 5.1 | NM | 4.7 | 2.9 | 1.6 | NM | NM |
| % Return on Equity | 10.0 | 3.8 | 9.1 | 6.3 | NM | 5.5 | 3.6 | 2.6 | NM | NM |

Data as orig reptd.; bef. results of disc opers/spec. items. Per share data adj. for stk. divs.; EPS diluted. E-Estimated. NA-Not Available. NM-Not Meaningful. NR-Not Ranked. UR-Under Review.

**Office:** 1194 North Mathilda Avenue, Sunnyvale, CA 94089.
**Telephone:** 408-745-2000.
**Email:** investor-relations@juniper.net
**Website:** http://www.juniper.net

**Chrmn & Pres:** S.G. Kriens
**Vice Chrmn & CTO:** P. Sindhu
**CEO:** K.R. Johnson
**EVP & CFO:** R.M. Denholm

**EVP, Secy & General Counsel:** M.L. Gaynor
**Board Members:** R. M. Calderoni, M. B. Cranston, K. R. Johnson, M. Johnson, S. G. Kriens, J. M. Lawrie, W. F. Meehan, III, D. Schlotterbeck, S. D. Sclavos, P. Sindhu, B. Stensrud

**Founded:** 1996
**Domicile:** Delaware
**Employees:** 8,772

# Kellogg Co

## STANDARD &POOR'S

| S&P Recommendation | HOLD ★★★★★ | Price $48.75 (as of Nov 25, 2011) | 12-Mo. Target Price $52.00 | Investment Style Large-Cap Growth |
|---|---|---|---|---|

**GICS Sector** Consumer Staples
**Sub-Industry** Packaged Foods & Meats

**Summary** This leading producer of ready-to-eat cereal also sells convenience foods such as cookies, crackers, cereal bars, fruit snacks and frozen waffles.

## Key Stock Statistics (Source S&P, Vickers, company reports)

| | | | | | | | |
|---|---|---|---|---|---|---|---|
| 52-Wk Range | $57.70– 48.11 | S&P Oper. EPS 2011E | 3.39 | Market Capitalization(B) | $17.509 | Beta | 0.47 |
| Trailing 12-Month EPS | $3.24 | S&P Oper. EPS 2012E | 3.45 | Yield (%) | 3.53 | S&P 3-Yr. Proj. EPS CAGR(%) | 4 |
| Trailing 12-Month P/E | 15.1 | P/E on S&P Oper. EPS 2011E | 14.4 | Dividend Rate/Share | $1.72 | S&P Credit Rating | BBB+ |
| $10K Invested 5 Yrs Ago | $11,192 | Common Shares Outstg. (M) | 359.2 | Institutional Ownership (%) | 81 | | |

## Price Performance

30-Week Mov. Avg. ··· 10-Week Mov. Avg. – – GAAP Earnings vs. Previous Year   Volume Above Avg. STARS
12-Mo. Target Price — Relative Strength — ▲ Up ▼ Down ► No Change   Below Avg. ★

Options: CBOE, Ph

Analysis prepared by Equity Analyst **Tom Graves, CFA** on Nov 11, 2011, when the stock traded at **$49.72**.

### Highlights

➤ In 2012, we look for sales to increase about 4% from the $13.2 billion that we estimate for 2011, with less benefit from currency translation. In both years, we expect that more than 50% of sales will come from North America.

➤ For 2012, we estimate EPS of $3.45, up from the $3.39 that we project for 2011. We expect investments in the company's supply chain to limit profit gains more than we had previously anticipated. Also, 2011's third quarter EPS comparison was hurt by a reinstatement of incentive compensation costs. In 2012, we anticipate some additional costs related to technology implementation. In 2011's first nine months, Kellogg spent $693 million on repurchase of its common stock.

➤ In January 2011, John A. Bryant became president and CEO of Kellogg. Mr. Bryant, who succeeded David Mackay in those positions, joined Kellogg in 1998, and had recently served as chief operating officer.

### Investment Rationale/Risk

➤ Looking ahead, we expect sales of Kellogg products to benefit from marketing support and product innovation. We think this will lessen the risk of consumers trading down to less expensive private label products.

➤ Risks to our recommendation and target price include competitive pressures in Kellogg's businesses, poor consumer acceptance of new product introductions, and commodity cost inflation.

➤ In our view, the prospect of strong free cash flow (after capital expenditures) should help bolster the stock price. For 2011, we anticipate cash flow of about $1.1 billion, compared to approximately $534 million in 2010, which was after a pension contribution of $467 million net of tax. However, we view the profit outlook for 2012 as lackluster. Our 12-month target price of $52 reflects our view that the stock should receive a P/E valuation (15.1X estimated 2012 EPS) that is similar to the recent average P/E (on estimated 2012 EPS) for a group of other packaged foods stocks. Also, Kellogg shares recently had an indicated dividend yield of 3.5%.

### Qualitative Risk Assessment

| LOW | MEDIUM | HIGH |
|---|---|---|

Our risk assessment for Kellogg reflects the relatively stable nature of the company's end markets, what we consider its strong balance sheet and cash flow, and corporate governance practices that we think are favorable versus peers.

### Quantitative Evaluations

**S&P Quality Ranking**                    A+

| D | C | B- | B | B+ | A- | A | A+ |
|---|---|---|---|---|---|---|---|

**Relative Strength Rank**          MODERATE

47

LOWEST = 1                    HIGHEST = 99

### Revenue/Earnings Data

**Revenue (Million $)**

| | 1Q | 2Q | 3Q | 4Q | Year |
|---|---|---|---|---|---|
| 2011 | 3,485 | 3,386 | 3,312 | -- | -- |
| 2010 | 3,318 | 3,062 | 3,157 | 2,860 | 12,397 |
| 2009 | 3,169 | 3,229 | 3,277 | 2,900 | 12,575 |
| 2008 | 3,258 | 3,343 | 3,288 | 2,933 | 12,822 |
| 2007 | 2,963 | 3,015 | 3,004 | 2,794 | 11,776 |
| 2006 | 2,727 | 2,774 | 2,822 | 2,584 | 10,907 |

**Earnings Per Share ($)**

| | | | | | |
|---|---|---|---|---|---|
| 2011 | 1.00 | 0.94 | 0.80 | E0.66 | E3.39 |
| 2010 | 1.09 | 0.79 | 0.90 | 0.51 | 3.30 |
| 2009 | 0.84 | 0.92 | 0.94 | 0.46 | 3.16 |
| 2008 | 0.81 | 0.82 | 0.89 | 0.47 | 2.98 |
| 2007 | 0.80 | 0.75 | 0.76 | 0.44 | 2.76 |
| 2006 | 0.68 | 0.67 | 0.70 | 0.45 | 2.51 |

Fiscal year ended Dec. 31. Next earnings report expected: Early February. EPS Estimates based on S&P Operating Earnings; historical GAAP earnings are as reported.

### Dividend Data (Dates: mm/dd Payment Date: mm/dd/yy)

| Amount ($) | Date Decl. | Ex-Div. Date | Stk. of Record | Payment Date |
|---|---|---|---|---|
| 0.405 | 02/18 | 02/25 | 03/01 | 03/15/11 |
| 0.405 | 04/29 | 05/27 | 06/01 | 06/15/11 |
| 0.430 | 07/22 | 08/30 | 09/01 | 09/15/11 |
| 0.430 | 10/28 | 11/29 | 12/01 | 12/15/11 |

Dividends have been paid since 1923. Source: Company reports.

---

**Please read the Required Disclosures and Analyst Certification on the last page of this report.**

The McGraw·Hill Companies

# Kellogg Co

**STANDARD &POOR'S**

## Business Summary November 11, 2011

CORPORATE OVERVIEW. Kellogg Co., incorporated in 1922, is a leading producer of ready-to-eat cereal. The company has expanded its operations to include convenience food products such as Pop-Tarts toaster pastries, Eggo frozen waffles, Nutri-Grain cereal bars, and Rice Krispies Treats squares.

With the 2001 acquisition of Keebler Foods Co., the company also markets cookies, crackers and other convenience food products under brand names such as Keebler, Cheez-It, Murray and Famous Amos, and manufactures private label cookies, crackers and other products.

Sales contributions by geographic region in 2010 were: North America 68%, Europe 18%, Latin America 7%, and Asia Pacific 7%.

In 2010, cereal sold through North American retail channels represented 24% of total net sales, while international cereal sales represented 27%. Other

sales categories included North American retail snacks (33%), North American frozen and specialty channels (11%), and international convenience foods (6%).

In 2010, Kellogg's top five customers accounted for about 34% of net sales collectively, and about 46% of U.S. net sales. Kellogg's largest customer, Wal-Mart Stores, Inc., and its affiliates, accounted for about 21% of consolidated net sales during 2010.

Kellogg's expenditures for research and development were about $187 million in 2010, and about $181 million in 2009.

## Company Financials Fiscal Year Ended Dec. 31

| Per Share Data ($) | 2010 | 2009 | 2008 | 2007 | 2006 | 2005 | 2004 | 2003 | 2002 | 2001 |
|---|---|---|---|---|---|---|---|---|---|---|
| Tangible Book Value | NM | NM | NM | NM | NM | NM | NM | NM | NM | NM |
| Cash Flow | 4.32 | 4.16 | 3.96 | 3.69 | 3.39 | 3.30 | 3.15 | 2.83 | 2.60 | 2.26 |
| Earnings | 3.30 | 3.16 | 2.98 | 2.76 | 2.51 | 2.36 | 2.14 | 1.92 | 1.75 | 1.18 |
| S&P Core Earnings | 3.31 | 3.08 | 2.48 | 2.74 | 2.62 | 2.29 | 2.10 | 1.86 | 1.24 | 0.77 |
| Dividends | 1.94 | 1.43 | 1.30 | 1.49 | 1.14 | 1.06 | 1.01 | 1.01 | 1.01 | 1.01 |
| Payout Ratio | 59% | 45% | 44% | 54% | 45% | 45% | 47% | 53% | 58% | 86% |
| Prices:High | 56.00 | 54.10 | 58.51 | 56.89 | 50.95 | 46.99 | 45.32 | 38.57 | 37.00 | 34.00 |
| Prices:Low | 47.28 | 35.64 | 40.32 | 48.68 | 42.41 | 42.35 | 37.00 | 27.85 | 29.02 | 24.25 |
| P/E Ratio:High | 17 | 17 | 20 | 21 | 20 | 20 | 21 | 20 | 21 | 29 |
| P/E Ratio:Low | 14 | 11 | 14 | 18 | 17 | 18 | 17 | 15 | 17 | 21 |
| **Income Statement Analysis** (Million $) | | | | | | | | | | |
| Revenue | 12,397 | 12,575 | 12,822 | 11,776 | 10,907 | 10,177 | 9,614 | 8,812 | 8,304 | 8,853 |
| Operating Income | 2,477 | 2,542 | 2,431 | 2,347 | 2,119 | 2,142 | 2,091 | 1,917 | 1,857 | 1,640 |
| Depreciation | 392 | 384 | 375 | 372 | 353 | 392 | 410 | 373 | 348 | 439 |
| Interest Expense | 248 | 295 | 314 | 324 | 307 | 300 | 309 | 371 | 391 | 352 |
| Pretax Income | 1,742 | 1,684 | 1,633 | 1,547 | 1,471 | 1,425 | 1,366 | 1,170 | 1,144 | 804 |
| Effective Tax Rate | NA | 28.3% | 29.7% | 28.7% | 31.7% | 31.2% | 34.8% | 32.7% | 37.0% | 40.1% |
| Net Income | 1,240 | 1,212 | 1,148 | 1,103 | 1,004 | 980 | 891 | 787 | 721 | 482 |
| S&P Core Earnings | 1,255 | 1,182 | 955 | 1,093 | 1,047 | 953 | 875 | 763 | 510 | 312 |
| **Balance Sheet & Other Financial Data** (Million $) | | | | | | | | | | |
| Cash | 444 | 334 | 255 | 524 | 411 | 219 | 417 | 141 | 101 | 2,318 |
| Current Assets | 2,915 | 2,558 | 2,521 | 2,717 | 2,427 | 2,197 | 2,122 | 1,797 | 1,763 | 1,902 |
| Total Assets | 11,847 | 11,200 | 10,946 | 11,397 | 10,714 | 10,575 | 10,790 | 10,231 | 10,219 | 10,369 |
| Current Liabilities | 3,184 | 2,288 | 3,552 | 4,044 | 4,020 | 3,163 | 2,846 | 2,766 | 3,015 | 2,208 |
| Long Term Debt | 4,908 | 4,835 | 4,068 | 3,276 | 3,053 | 3,703 | 3,893 | 4,265 | 4,519 | 5,619 |
| Common Equity | 2,158 | 2,272 | 1,448 | 2,526 | 2,069 | 2,284 | 2,257 | 1,443 | 895 | 871 |
| Total Capital | 8,010 | 7,111 | 5,816 | 6,443 | 5,122 | 5,986 | 6,150 | 5,709 | 5,415 | 6,491 |
| Capital Expenditures | 474 | 377 | 461 | 472 | 453 | 374 | 279 | 247 | 254 | 277 |
| Cash Flow | 1,632 | 1,596 | 1,523 | 1,475 | 1,357 | 1,372 | 1,301 | 1,160 | 1,069 | 921 |
| Current Ratio | 0.9 | 1.1 | 0.7 | 0.7 | 0.6 | 0.7 | 0.7 | 0.6 | 0.6 | 0.9 |
| % Long Term Debt of Capitalization | 61.3 | 68.0 | 69.9 | 50.9 | 59.6 | 61.9 | 63.3 | 74.7 | 83.5 | 86.6 |
| % Net Income of Revenue | 10.0 | 9.6 | 9.0 | 9.4 | 9.2 | 9.6 | 9.3 | 8.9 | 8.7 | 5.4 |
| % Return on Assets | 10.8 | 11.0 | 10.3 | 10.0 | 9.4 | 9.3 | 8.5 | 7.7 | 7.0 | 6.3 |
| % Return on Equity | 56.0 | 65.2 | 57.8 | 48.0 | 46.1 | 43.2 | 48.1 | 67.3 | 81.6 | 54.5 |

Data as orig reptd.; bef. results of disc opers/spec. items. Per share data adj. for stk. divs.; EPS diluted. E-Estimated. NA-Not Available. NM-Not Meaningful. NR-Not Ranked. UR-Under Review.

**Office:** One Kellogg Square, PO Box 3599, Battle Creek, MI 49016-3599.
**Telephone:** 269-961-2000.
**Website:** http://www.kelloggcompany.com
**Chrmn:** J.M. Jenness

**Pres & CEO:** J.A. Bryant
**SVP & CFO:** R.L. Dissinger
**SVP & CIO:** B.S. Rice
**Chief Acctg Officer & Cntlr:** A.R. Andrews

**Investor Contact:** K. Koessel (269-961-9089)
**Board Members:** J. A. Bryant, B. S. Carson, J. T. Dillon, G. Gund, J. M. Jenness, D. A. Johnson, D. R. Knauss, A. M. Korologos, R. M. Rebolledo, S. K. Speirn, R. A. Steele, J. L. Zabriskie

**Founded:** 1906
**Domicile:** Delaware
**Employees:** 30,645

# KeyCorp

STANDARD
&POOR'S

| S&P Recommendation BUY ★★★★☆ | Price $6.67 (as of Nov 25, 2011) | 12-Mo. Target Price $11.00 | Investment Style Large-Cap Value |
|---|---|---|---|

**GICS Sector** Financials
**Sub-Industry** Regional Banks

**Summary** Cleveland-based KeyCorp is one of the largest bank-based financial services companies in the U.S., with assets of $89 billion at September 30, 2011.

## Key Stock Statistics (Source S&P, Vickers, company reports)

| | | | | | | | |
|---|---|---|---|---|---|---|---|
| 52-Wk Range | $9.77– 5.59 | S&P Oper. EPS 2011E | 0.90 | Market Capitalization(B) | $6.356 | Beta | 0.76 |
| Trailing 12-Month EPS | $0.98 | S&P Oper. EPS 2012E | 0.89 | Yield (%) | 1.80 | S&P 3-Yr. Proj. EPS CAGR(%) | 24 |
| Trailing 12-Month P/E | 6.8 | P/E on S&P Oper. EPS 2011E | 7.4 | Dividend Rate/Share | $0.12 | S&P Credit Rating | BBB+ |
| $10K Invested 5 Yrs Ago | $2,094 | Common Shares Outstg. (M) | 952.9 | Institutional Ownership (%) | 82 | | |

## Price Performance

30-Week Mov. Avg. · · ·   10-Week Mov. Avg. – –   GAAP Earnings vs. Previous Year   Volume Above Avg. STARS
12-Mo. Target Price —   Relative Strength —   ▲ Up  ▼ Down  ► No Change   Below Avg. ★

Options: ASE, CBOE, P, Ph

Analysis prepared by Equity Analyst **Erik Oja** on Nov 22, 2011, when the stock traded at **$6.69**.

## Highlights

➤ We expect net interest income to fall 8.5% in 2011 and 1.0% in 2012, before rebounding in 2013. We see revenues falling 7.3% in 2011, on declines in insurance income and leasing income. However, we expect 1.4% revenue growth in 2012, on a rebound in fee income.

➤ Only $788 million of loans were nonperforming at September 30, or a better-than-peers 1.64% of total loans. Net chargeoffs ($109 million in the third quarter) were down significantly in each of the past seven quarters, after peaking in late 2009. We forecast net chargeoffs of $515 million in 2011 and $290 million in 2012, down from $1.57 billion in 2010. We think KEY can continue reducing its allowance for loan losses, which totaled $1.131 billion at September 30, equal to a higher than-peers 143.5% of year-end nonperforming loans. We think the allowance can come down to $995 million by the end of 2012, which would be a relatively high 167% of our $595 million year-end 2012 estimate of non-performing loans. Our 2011 loan loss provisioning estimate is -$12 million, as compared to $638 million in 2010. For 2012, we expect $212 million in provisions.

➤ We see EPS of $0.90 in 2011 and $0.89 in 2012.

## Investment Rationale/Risk

➤ After years of paring down its loan portfolios, KEY should be in a good position for revenue growth in 2012, as U.S. employment regains its footing and the Midwest manufacturing sector rebounds. KEY did well on the second round of stress tests, announced in March. Following on what peers have done, KEY then announced a $625 million equity capital raise and a payback of its $2.5 billion TARP preferred obligation, which will save it at least $125 million a year in preferred dividend payments. KEY also raised its quarterly dividend to $0.03, from $0.01, for a yield of about 1.7%. We do not see KEY as a near-term takeover target, partly due to recent management changes. However, we view the stock, currently trading at 8.0X our forward four quarters EPS estimate of $0.91, as attractively valued relative to historical levels and to peers.

➤ Risks to our recommendation and target price include a weakening of the economic recovery.

➤ Our 12-month target price of $11 is based on slightly-above-peers multiples of 1.20X our year-end 2011 tangible book value per share estimate of $9.30 and 12.1X our forward four quarters EPS estimate of $0.91.

## Qualitative Risk Assessment

| LOW | MEDIUM | HIGH |
|---|---|---|

Our risk assessment reflects KEY's large cap valuation and history of profitability, offset by exposure to possible declines in residential and commercial lending credit quality.

## Quantitative Evaluations

**S&P Quality Ranking**                    B-

| D | C | B- | B | B+ | A- | A | A+ |
|---|---|---|---|---|---|---|---|

**Relative Strength Rank**          MODERATE

61

LOWEST = 1                                          HIGHEST = 99

## Revenue/Earnings Data

**Revenue (Million $)**

| | 1Q | 2Q | 3Q | 4Q | Year |
|---|---|---|---|---|---|
| 2011 | 1,217 | 1,180 | 1,188 | -- | -- |
| 2010 | 1,342 | 1,353 | 1,330 | 1,337 | 5,362 |
| 2009 | 1,524 | 1,709 | 1,322 | 1,402 | 5,798 |
| 2008 | 1,882 | 1,435 | 1,620 | 1,562 | 6,434 |
| 2007 | 2,022 | 2,044 | 1,872 | 1,935 | 7,621 |
| 2006 | 1,732 | 1,872 | 1,932 | 1,971 | 7,507 |

**Earnings Per Share ($)**

| | | | | | |
|---|---|---|---|---|---|
| 2011 | 0.21 | 0.26 | 0.24 | E0.24 | E0.90 |
| 2010 | -0.11 | 0.06 | 0.19 | 0.33 | 0.47 |
| 2009 | -1.09 | -0.69 | -0.50 | -0.29 | -2.27 |
| 2008 | 0.55 | -2.70 | -0.07 | -1.12 | -3.35 |
| 2007 | 0.89 | 0.85 | 0.57 | 0.06 | 2.38 |
| 2006 | 0.66 | 0.75 | 0.74 | 0.76 | 2.91 |

Fiscal year ended Dec. 31. Next earnings report expected: NA. EPS Estimates based on S&P Operating Earnings; historical GAAP earnings are as reported.

## Dividend Data (Dates: mm/dd Payment Date: mm/dd/yy)

| Amount ($) | Date Decl. | Ex-Div. Date | Stk. of Record | Payment Date |
|---|---|---|---|---|
| 0.010 | 01/20 | 02/25 | 03/01 | 03/15/11 |
| 0.030 | 05/19 | 05/26 | 05/31 | 06/15/11 |
| 0.030 | 07/22 | 08/26 | 08/30 | 09/15/11 |
| 0.030 | 11/17 | 11/25 | 11/29 | 12/15/11 |

Dividends have been paid since 1963. Source: Company reports.

---

**Please read the Required Disclosures and Analyst Certification on the last page of this report.**

The McGraw-Hill Companies

# KeyCorp

## Business Summary November 22, 2011

CORPORATE OVERVIEW. KEY owns KeyBank, with operations in Ohio, New York, Washington, Oregon, Maine, Colorado, Indiana, Utah, Idaho, Vermont, Alaska, Michigan, Florida and Kentucky. The company has two business groups: Community Banking and National Banking.

The Community Banking segment houses Regional Banking and Commercial Banking. National Banking contains Real Estate Capital and Corporate Banking Services, Equipment Finance, Institutional and Capital Markets, and Consumer Finance. In 2008, KEY's Consumer Finance unit discontinued retail and floor-plan financing of marine and recreational vehicles. In September 2009, the Consumer Finance unit discontinued education lending, which had accounted for about 5% of loans outstanding.

MARKET PROFILE. As of June 30, 2011 (latest available FDIC data), KEY had 1,051 branches and $59.8 billion in deposits, with about 58% of its deposits and 44% of its branches concentrated in Ohio and New York. In Ohio, KEY had 239 branches, $18.9 billion of deposits, and a deposit market share of about 7.5%, ranking sixth. In New York, KEY had 228 branches, $15.9 billion of deposits,

and a deposit market share of about 1.5%, ranking 11th. In Washington State, KEY had 162 branches, $8.1 billion of deposits, and a deposit market share of about 5.8%, ranking sixth. In Oregon, KEY had 78 branches, $3.3 billion of deposits, and a deposit market share of about 4.5%, ranking sixth. In Indiana, KEY had 74 branches, $2.6 billion of deposits, and a deposit market share of about 2.3%, ranking eighth. In Maine, KEY had 61 branches, $2.5 billion of deposits, and a deposit market share of 6.9%, ranking second. In Colorado, KEY had 67 branches, $2.1 billion of deposits, and a deposit market share of about 1.8%, ranking seventh. In addition, KEY had a number five ranking in Idaho, a number five market ranking in Vermont, and a number four ranking in Alaska. Finally, KEY had offices in Utah and Michigan, with a small presence in Kentucky, Florida and Connecticut.

## Company Financials Fiscal Year Ended Dec. 31

| Per Share Data ($) | 2010 | 2009 | 2008 | 2007 | 2006 | 2005 | 2004 | 2003 | 2002 | 2001 |
|---|---|---|---|---|---|---|---|---|---|---|
| Tangible Book Value | 8.39 | 7.84 | 11.87 | 16.39 | 15.99 | 15.05 | 13.91 | 13.87 | 13.34 | 11.85 |
| Earnings | 0.47 | -2.27 | -3.35 | 2.38 | 2.91 | 2.73 | 2.30 | 2.12 | 2.27 | 0.37 |
| S&P Core Earnings | 0.46 | -2.14 | -2.54 | 2.12 | 2.93 | 2.72 | 2.41 | 2.12 | 2.10 | 0.43 |
| Dividends | 0.04 | 0.09 | 1.00 | 1.46 | 1.38 | 1.30 | 1.24 | 1.22 | 1.20 | 1.18 |
| Payout Ratio | 9% | NM | NM | 61% | 47% | 48% | 54% | 58% | 53% | NM |
| Prices:High | 9.84 | 9.82 | 27.23 | 39.90 | 38.63 | 35.00 | 34.50 | 29.41 | 29.40 | 29.25 |
| Prices:Low | 5.65 | 4.40 | 4.99 | 21.04 | 32.90 | 30.10 | 28.23 | 22.31 | 20.98 | 20.49 |
| P/E Ratio:High | 21 | NM | NM | 17 | 13 | 13 | 15 | 14 | 13 | 79 |
| P/E Ratio:Low | 12 | NM | NM | 9 | 11 | 11 | 12 | 11 | 9 | 55 |

| Income Statement Analysis (Million $) | | | | | | | | | | |
|---|---|---|---|---|---|---|---|---|---|---|
| Net Interest Income | 2,511 | 2,380 | 2,409 | 2,769 | 2,815 | 2,790 | 2,637 | 2,725 | 2,749 | 2,825 |
| Tax Equivalent Adjustment | 26.0 | 26.0 | 436 | 99.0 | 103 | 121 | 94.0 | 71.0 | 120 | 45.0 |
| Non Interest Income | 1,954 | 2,003 | 1,805 | 2,264 | 2,126 | 2,077 | 1,742 | 1,749 | 1,763 | 1,690 |
| Loan Loss Provision | 638 | 3,159 | 1,835 | 529 | 150 | 143 | 185 | 501 | 553 | 1,350 |
| % Expense/Operating Revenue | 68.0% | 81.1% | 68.2% | 64.5% | 62.4% | 64.5% | 62.8% | 60.3% | 57.3% | 64.5% |
| Pretax Income | 793 | -2,298 | -1,134 | 1,221 | 1,643 | 1,588 | 1,388 | 1,242 | 1,312 | 259 |
| Effective Tax Rate | 23.5% | NM | NM | 22.9% | 27.4% | 28.9% | 31.3% | 27.3% | 25.6% | 39.4% |
| Net Income | 577 | -1,287 | -1,468 | 941 | 1,193 | 1,129 | 954 | 903 | 976 | 157 |
| % Net Interest Margin | 3.26 | 2.83 | 2.16 | 3.46 | 3.67 | 3.69 | 3.64 | 3.80 | 3.97 | 3.81 |
| S&P Core Earnings | 399 | -1,497 | -1,143 | 840 | 1,198 | 1,125 | 1,006 | 898 | 896 | 179 |

| Balance Sheet & Other Financial Data (Million $) | | | | | | | | | | |
|---|---|---|---|---|---|---|---|---|---|---|
| Money Market Assets | 985 | 1,209 | 1,280 | 1,056 | Nil | Nil | NA | NA | NA | NA |
| Investment Securities | 23,308 | 18,153 | 9,988 | 7,860 | NA | NA | NA | NA | NA | NA |
| Commercial Loans | 34,520 | 41,904 | 54,835 | 52,705 | 48,306 | 39,291 | 43,276 | 36,189 | 36,612 | 38,063 |
| Other Loans | 15,587 | 17,361 | 21,669 | 18,118 | 17,520 | 20,078 | 25,188 | 26,522 | 25,845 | 25,246 |
| Total Assets | 91,843 | 93,287 | 104,531 | 99,983 | 92,337 | 93,126 | 90,739 | 84,487 | 85,202 | 80,938 |
| Demand Deposits | 43,719 | 38,756 | 35,676 | 38,663 | 13,553 | 13,335 | 11,581 | 11,175 | 10,630 | 23,128 |
| Time Deposits | 16,891 | 26,815 | 29,584 | 24,436 | 45,563 | 45,430 | 39,683 | 39,683 | 38,716 | 21,667 |
| Long Term Debt | 10,592 | 11,558 | 14,995 | 11,957 | 14,533 | 13,939 | 14,846 | 15,294 | 16,865 | 15,842 |
| Common Equity | 8,380 | 7,942 | 7,408 | 7,746 | 7,703 | 7,598 | 7,117 | 6,969 | 6,835 | 6,155 |
| % Return on Assets | 0.6 | NM | NM | 1.0 | 1.3 | 1.2 | 1.1 | 1.1 | 1.2 | 0.2 |
| % Return on Equity | 7.1 | NM | NM | 12.2 | 15.6 | 15.3 | 13.5 | 13.1 | 15.0 | 2.5 |
| % Loan Loss Reserve | 3.2 | 4.3 | 2.5 | 1.7 | 1.4 | 1.4 | 1.7 | 2.2 | 2.3 | 2.7 |
| % Loans/Deposits | 82.7 | 89.6 | 112.2 | 111.8 | 117.5 | 118.9 | 118.4 | 123.3 | 126.6 | 138.0 |
| % Equity to Assets | 8.8 | 7.8 | 7.4 | 8.0 | 8.3 | 8.0 | 8.0 | 8.1 | 7.8 | 7.6 |

Data as orig reptd.; bef. results of disc opers/spec. items. Per share data adj. for stk. divs.; EPS diluted. E-Estimated. NA-Not Available. NM-Not Meaningful. NR-Not Ranked. UR-Under Review.

**Office:** 127 Public Square, Cleveland, OH 44114-1306.
**Telephone:** 216-689-6300.
**Website:** http://www.key.com
**Chrmn, Pres, CEO & COO:** B.E. Mooney

**Vice Chrmn & Chief Admin Officer:** T.C. Stevens
**EVP & CFO:** J.B. Weeden
**EVP & Chief Acctg Officer:** R.L. Morris
**EVP & Treas:** J.M. Vayda

**Board Members:** W. G. Bares, E. P. Campbell, J. A. Carrabba, C. A. Cartwright, C. P. Cooley, A. M. Cutler, H. J. Dallas, B. R. Gile, R. A. Gillis, W. G. Gisel, Jr., K. L. Manos, E. R. Menasce, B. E. Mooney, B. R. Sanford, B. R. Snyder, T. C. Stevens

**Founded:** 1849
**Domicile:** Ohio

# Kimberly-Clark Corp

**STANDARD &POOR'S**

| S&P Recommendation **HOLD** ★★★☆☆ | Price<br>$68.69 (as of Nov 25, 2011) | 12-Mo. Target Price<br>$71.00 | Investment Style<br>Large-Cap Blend |
|---|---|---|---|

**GICS Sector** Consumer Staples
**Sub-Industry** Household Products

**Summary** This leading consumer products company's global tissue, personal care and health care brands include Huggies, Pull-Ups, Kotex, Depend, Kleenex and Scott.

## Key Stock Statistics (Source S&P, Vickers, company reports)

| | | | | | |
|---|---|---|---|---|---|
| 52-Wk Range | $73.23–61.00 | S&P Oper. EPS 2011**E** | 4.81 | Market Capitalization(B) | $27.071 |
| Trailing 12-Month EPS | $4.19 | S&P Oper. EPS 2012**E** | 5.17 | Yield (%) | 4.08 |
| Trailing 12-Month P/E | 16.4 | P/E on S&P Oper. EPS 2011**E** | 14.3 | Dividend Rate/Share | $2.80 |
| $10K Invested 5 Yrs Ago | $12,565 | Common Shares Outstg. (M) | 394.1 | Institutional Ownership (%) | 68 |

| | |
|---|---|
| Beta | 0.38 |
| S&P 3-Yr. Proj. EPS CAGR(%) | 6 |
| S&P Credit Rating | A |

## Price Performance

- 30-Week Mov. Avg. ···· 10-Week Mov. Avg. – – GAAP Earnings vs. Previous Year   Volume Above Avg.|||| STARS
- 12-Mo. Target Price — Relative Strength — ▲ Up ▼ Down ► No Change   Below Avg.|||| ★

Options: ASE, CBOE, P

Analysis prepared by Equity Analyst **Tom Graves, CFA** on Oct 27, 2011, when the stock traded at **$70.77**.

## Highlights

➤ In 2012, we look for sales to increase about 3% from the $21 billion that we project for 2011. We think that reported 2012 sales may be adversely affected by strength of the U.S. dollar relative to other currencies, following an expected benefit from currency fluctuation in 2011. In both 2011 and 2012, we expect higher sales growth from developing and emerging markets than from developed markets.

➤ In 2012, we look for less margin pressure from input cost inflation than we anticipate in 2011. In both years, we expect cost savings from KMB's FORCE program to bolster profit margins. In October 2011, KMB projected inflation in key input costs in 2011 of $575 million to $625 million, which compares to $790 million in 2010.

➤ Before special items, we estimate 2012 EPS of $5.17, up from the $4.81 that we forecast for 2011. In 2011, this excludes projected after-tax restructuring charges of $265 million to $315 million and a non tax-deductible business tax charge related to a law change in Colombia. Adjusted EPS in 2010 was $4.68.

## Investment Rationale/Risk

➤ Our near-term outlook is tempered by concern about economic conditions and competition in developed markets. We see KMB working to increase the market share of its core consumer brands through targeted investments in product innovation and marketing support. In addition, sales growth should be helped by expansion in non-traditional categories for KMB and focusing on certain developing markets. We think the company is doing a good job of managing its cost structure.

➤ Risks to our recommendation and target price include increased promotional activity in the consumer paper category, higher commodity costs, a lack of product innovation, unfavorable foreign currency shifts, and decreased consumer acceptance of KMB's products.

➤ Our 12-month target price of $71 is based on a blend of our historical and relative analyses. Our historical analysis suggests a value of $72, using a forward P/E of about 14X, a discount to a 10-year average, applied to our 2012 EPS estimate. Our peer analysis applies a discount to a peer group average of about 17X.

## Qualitative Risk Assessment

| LOW | MEDIUM | HIGH |
|---|---|---|

Our risk assessment reflects the generally static demand for household and personal care products, which is usually not affected by changes in the economy or geopolitical factors.

## Quantitative Evaluations

**S&P Quality Ranking**     A

| D | C | B- | B | B+ | A- | A | A+ |
|---|---|---|---|---|---|---|---|

**Relative Strength Rank**     STRONG

72

LOWEST = 1                    HIGHEST = 99

## Revenue/Earnings Data

**Revenue (Million $)**

| | 1Q | 2Q | 3Q | 4Q | Year |
|---|---|---|---|---|---|
| 2011 | 5,029 | 5,259 | 5,382 | -- | -- |
| 2010 | 4,835 | 4,857 | 4,979 | 5,075 | 19,746 |
| 2009 | 4,493 | 4,727 | 4,913 | 4,982 | 19,115 |
| 2008 | 4,813 | 5,006 | 4,998 | 4,598 | 19,415 |
| 2007 | 4,385 | 4,502 | 4,621 | 4,758 | 18,266 |
| 2006 | 4,068 | 4,161 | 4,210 | 4,307 | 16,747 |

**Earnings Per Share ($)**

| | | | | | |
|---|---|---|---|---|---|
| 2011 | 0.86 | 1.03 | 1.09 | E1.27 | E4.81 |
| 2010 | 0.92 | 1.20 | 1.14 | 1.20 | 4.45 |
| 2009 | 0.98 | 0.97 | 1.40 | 1.17 | 4.52 |
| 2008 | 1.04 | 1.01 | 0.99 | 1.01 | 4.06 |
| 2007 | 0.98 | 1.00 | 1.04 | 1.07 | 4.09 |
| 2006 | 0.60 | 0.82 | 0.79 | 1.05 | 3.25 |

Fiscal year ended Dec. 31. Next earnings report expected: NA. EPS Estimates based on S&P Operating Earnings; historical GAAP earnings are as reported.

## Dividend Data (Dates: mm/dd Payment Date: mm/dd/yy)

| Amount ($) | Date Decl. | Ex-Div. Date | Stk. of Record | Payment Date |
|---|---|---|---|---|
| 0.700 | 01/25 | 03/02 | 03/04 | 04/04/11 |
| 0.700 | 04/21 | 06/08 | 06/10 | 07/05/11 |
| 0.700 | 08/01 | 09/07 | 09/09 | 10/04/11 |
| 0.700 | 11/15 | 12/07 | 12/09 | 01/04/12 |

Dividends have been paid since 1935. Source: Company reports.

**Please read the Required Disclosures and Analyst Certification on the last page of this report.**

**The McGraw·Hill Companies**

# Kimberly-Clark Corp

**STANDARD &POOR'S**

## Business Summary October 27, 2011

CORPORATE OVERVIEW. Kimberly-Clark, best known for brands such as Kleenex, Scott, Huggies and Kotex, sells consumer and other products in more than 150 countries. After operating as a broadly diversified enterprise, KMB made a major transition since the early 1990s, transforming itself into a global consumer products company. The company further developed its health care business through the acquisitions of Technol Medical Products, Ballard Medical Products, and Safeskin Corp. Reflecting more than 30 strategic acquisitions and 20 strategic divestitures since 1992, KMB has become a leading global manufacturer of tissue, personal care and health care products, manufactured in 38 countries. In 2004, KMB distributed to its shareholders all of the outstanding shares of Neenah Paper, Inc., which was formed in 2004 to facilitate the spin-off of KMB's U.S. fine paper and technical paper businesses and its Canadian pulp mills.

KMB classifies its business into four reportable global segments: Personal Care; Consumer Tissue; K-C Professional & Other; and Health Care. In 2010, Personal Care contributed 44% of sales and 58% of segment operating profits; Consumer Tissue 33% and 22%; K-C Professional & Other 16% and 15%; and Health Care 7% and 5%.

In 2010, sales by geographic region were: U.S. 50%; Canada 3%; Europe 15%; and Asia, Latin America and other 32%. Wal-Mart Stores, Inc. is KMB's single largest customer, accounting for about 13% of net sales in both 2010 and 2009.

CORPORATE STRATEGY. In mid-2003, KMB introduced a new strategic plan called the Global Business Plan (GBP), which involves prioritizing growth opportunities and applying greater financial discipline to KMB's global operations. The annual goals established by the GBP are: top-line growth of 3%-5%; EPS growth in the mid- to high single digits; an operating margin improvement of 40 to 50 basis points; capital spending of 4.5%-5.5% of net sales; an ROIC improvement of 20 to 40 basis points; and dividend increases in line with EPS growth. Also, under the GBP, capital allocation is focused on more targeted expansion activity and an increased emphasis on innovation and cost reduction.

## Company Financials Fiscal Year Ended Dec. 31

| Per Share Data ($) | 2010 | 2009 | 2008 | 2007 | 2006 | 2005 | 2004 | 2003 | 2002 | 2001 |
|---|---|---|---|---|---|---|---|---|---|---|
| Tangible Book Value | 5.50 | 4.40 | 2.45 | 5.92 | 7.10 | 6.22 | 8.13 | 8.21 | 6.65 | 7.10 |
| Cash Flow | 6.65 | 6.40 | 5.91 | 5.90 | 5.34 | 5.08 | 5.32 | 4.80 | 4.60 | 1.39 |
| Earnings | 4.45 | 4.52 | 4.06 | 4.09 | 3.25 | 3.31 | 3.55 | 3.33 | 3.24 | 3.02 |
| S&P Core Earnings | 4.58 | 4.81 | 3.57 | 4.09 | 3.32 | 3.32 | 3.56 | 3.35 | 2.74 | 2.49 |
| Dividends | 2.64 | 2.40 | 2.32 | 2.12 | 1.96 | 1.80 | 1.60 | 1.36 | 1.20 | 1.12 |
| Payout Ratio | 59% | 53% | 57% | 52% | 60% | 54% | 45% | 41% | 37% | 37% |
| Prices:High | 67.24 | 67.03 | 69.69 | 72.79 | 68.58 | 68.29 | 69.00 | 59.30 | 66.79 | 72.19 |
| Prices:Low | 58.25 | 43.05 | 50.27 | 63.79 | 56.59 | 55.60 | 56.19 | 42.92 | 45.30 | 52.06 |
| P/E Ratio:High | 15 | 15 | 17 | 18 | 21 | 21 | 19 | 18 | 21 | 24 |
| P/E Ratio:Low | 13 | 10 | 12 | 16 | 17 | 17 | 16 | 13 | 14 | 17 |

**Income Statement Analysis** (Million $)

| | 2010 | 2009 | 2008 | 2007 | 2006 | 2005 | 2004 | 2003 | 2002 | 2001 |
|---|---|---|---|---|---|---|---|---|---|---|
| Revenue | 19,746 | 19,115 | 19,415 | 18,266 | 16,747 | 15,903 | 15,083 | 14,348 | 13,566 | 14,524 |
| Operating Income | 3,700 | 3,846 | 3,414 | 3,553 | 3,034 | 3,155 | 3,358 | 3,158 | 3,170 | 3,162 |
| Depreciation | 813 | 783 | 775 | 806 | 933 | 844 | 800 | 746 | 707 | 740 |
| Interest Expense | 243 | 275 | 318 | 283 | 220 | 190 | 163 | 168 | 182 | 192 |
| Pretax Income | 2,731 | 2,740 | 2,455 | 2,488 | 2,064 | 2,106 | 2,328 | 2,153 | 2,411 | 2,319 |
| Effective Tax Rate | NA | 27.2% | 25.2% | 21.6% | 22.7% | 20.8% | 20.8% | 23.9% | 27.7% | 27.8% |
| Net Income | 1,843 | 1,884 | 1,698 | 1,823 | 1,500 | 1,581 | 1,770 | 1,694 | 1,686 | 1,610 |
| S&P Core Earnings | 1,896 | 2,004 | 1,497 | 1,820 | 1,533 | 1,581 | 1,777 | 1,708 | 1,424 | 1,329 |

**Balance Sheet & Other Financial Data** (Million $)

| | 2010 | 2009 | 2008 | 2007 | 2006 | 2005 | 2004 | 2003 | 2002 | 2001 |
|---|---|---|---|---|---|---|---|---|---|---|
| Cash | 876 | 798 | 364 | 762 | 361 | 364 | 594 | 291 | 495 | 405 |
| Current Assets | 6,328 | 5,864 | 5,813 | 6,097 | 5,270 | 4,783 | 4,962 | 4,438 | 4,274 | 3,922 |
| Total Assets | 19,864 | 19,182 | 18,074 | 18,440 | 17,067 | 16,303 | 17,018 | 16,780 | 15,586 | 15,008 |
| Current Liabilities | 5,735 | 4,923 | 4,752 | 4,929 | 5,016 | 4,643 | 4,537 | 3,919 | 4,038 | 4,168 |
| Long Term Debt | 5,264 | 5,844 | 4,882 | 4,394 | 3,069 | 3,352 | 3,021 | 3,301 | 3,398 | 2,962 |
| Common Equity | 6,202 | 5,696 | 3,878 | 5,224 | 6,097 | 5,558 | 6,630 | 6,766 | 5,650 | 5,647 |
| Total Capital | 11,972 | 11,540 | 10,852 | 11,476 | 9,981 | 9,878 | 10,859 | 10,366 | 10,158 | 9,923 |
| Capital Expenditures | 964 | 848 | 906 | 989 | 972 | 710 | 535 | 878 | 871 | 1,100 |
| Cash Flow | 2,756 | 2,667 | 2,473 | 2,629 | 2,432 | 2,425 | 2,571 | 2,440 | 2,393 | 740 |
| Current Ratio | 1.1 | 1.2 | 1.2 | 1.2 | 1.1 | 1.0 | 1.1 | 1.1 | 1.1 | 0.9 |
| % Long Term Debt of Capitalization | 44.0 | 50.6 | 44.9 | 38.3 | 30.8 | 33.9 | 27.8 | 31.8 | 33.4 | 29.9 |
| % Net Income of Revenue | 9.3 | 9.9 | 8.8 | 10.0 | 9.0 | 9.9 | 11.7 | 11.8 | 12.4 | 11.1 |
| % Return on Assets | 9.4 | 10.1 | 9.3 | 10.3 | 9.0 | 9.5 | 10.5 | 10.5 | 11.0 | 10.9 |
| % Return on Equity | 31.8 | 39.4 | 37.3 | 32.2 | 25.7 | 25.9 | 26.4 | 27.3 | 29.8 | 28.2 |

Data as orig reptd.; bef. results of disc opers/spec. items. Per share data adj. for stk. divs.; EPS diluted. E-Estimated. NA-Not Available. NM-Not Meaningful. NR-Not Ranked. UR-Under Review.

Office: P.O. Box 619100, Dallas, TX 75261-9100.
Telephone: 972-281-1200.
Website: http://www.kimberly-clark.com
Chrmn, Pres & CEO: T.J. Falk

SVP & CFO: M.A. Buthman
Chief Acctg Officer & Cntlr: M.T. Azbell
Secy: J.W. Wesley
Investor Contact: M.D. Masseth (972-281-1478)

Board Members: J. R. Alm, J. F. Bergstrom, A. E. Bru, R. W. Decherd, T. J. Falk, F. T. Garcia, M. C. Jemison, J. M. Jenness, N. J. Karch, I. C. Read, L. J. Rice, M. J. Shapiro, G. C. Sullivan

Founded: 1872
Domicile: Delaware
Employees: 57,000

**The McGraw·Hill** Companies

**STANDARD &POOR'S**

# Kimco Realty Corp

| S&P Recommendation | HOLD ★★★☆☆ | Price $14.72 (as of Nov 25, 2011) | 12-Mo. Target Price $20.00 | Investment Style Large-Cap Blend |
|---|---|---|---|---|

**GICS Sector** Financials
**Sub-Industry** Retail REITS

**Summary** This real estate investment trust is one of the largest U.S. owners and operators of neighborhood and community shopping centers.

## Key Stock Statistics (Source S&P, Vickers, company reports)

| | | | | | | | | |
|---|---|---|---|---|---|---|---|---|
| 52-Wk Range | $20.31–13.55 | S&P FFO/Sh. 2011E | 1.20 | Market Capitalization(B) | $5.990 | Beta | | 1.79 |
| Trailing 12-Month FFO/Share | $1.10 | S&P FFO/Sh. 2012E | 1.24 | Yield (%) | 5.16 | S&P 3-Yr. FFO/Sh. Proj. CAGR(%) | | 5 |
| Trailing 12-Month P/FFO | NA | P/FFO on S&P FFO/Sh. 2011E | 12.3 | Dividend Rate/Share | $0.76 | S&P Credit Rating | | BBB+ |
| $10K Invested 5 Yrs Ago | $4,100 | Common Shares Outstg. (M) | 406.9 | Institutional Ownership (%) | 99 | | | |

## Price Performance

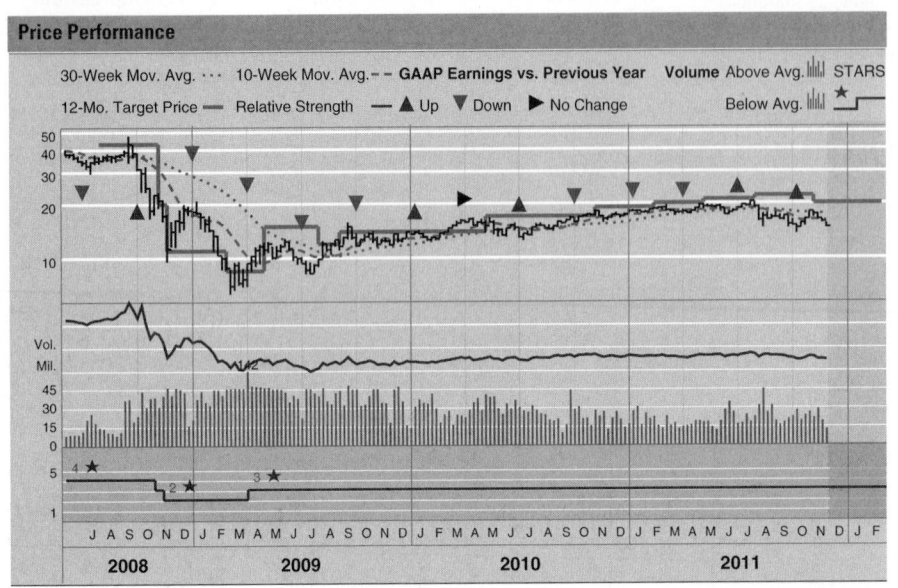

30-Week Mov. Avg. ···· 10-Week Mov. Avg. – – **GAAP Earnings vs. Previous Year** Volume Above Avg. STARS
12-Mo. Target Price — Relative Strength ▲ Up ▼ Down ► No Change Below Avg. ★

Options: ASE, CBOE, P, Ph

Analysis prepared by Equity Analyst **Robert McMillan** on Nov 04, 2011, when the stock traded at **$17.44**.

## Highlights

➤ We expect the trust to continue to benefit from what we view as a successful strategy of operating neighborhood and community shopping centers in North America and expanding further in high-growth international markets via joint ventures. After total revenues rose 9.8% in 2010, we forecast gains of 3.9% and 4.9% for 2011 and 2012, largely on higher rents and occupancy levels .

➤ We see improving retailer sentiment boosting demand for KIM's space, which, on top of limited new construction, should help results in 2011 and 2012. KIM's U.S. portfolio occupancy rose to 92.9% at the end of the 2011 third quarter, from 92.4% a year earlier. Rents on new and renewal leases in the U.S. rose 2.7% during the third quarter. We also look for growth in Canadian and Latin American properties to benefit KIM's portfolio long term; the Canadian portfolio was 97% occupied at the end of the third quarter. We expect management to continue pruning the portfolio of non-strategic assets while acquiring other properties at prudent prices.

➤ We project FFO per share of $1.20 for 2011 and $1.24 for 2012.

## Investment Rationale/Risk

➤ As one of the largest owners and operators of neighborhood and community shopping centers in the U.S., with a broad array of established relationships, KIM should generate above-average rent growth over the long term, in our view. Near term, though, we think an expected drop in development, stemming from the weak economy and tight credit, will limit the shares.

➤ Risks to our recommendation and target price include slower-than-expected growth in retailer expansion and rental rates, higher-than-expected retailer bankruptcies, and a sharp drop in development activity.

➤ Our 12-month target price of $20 is equal to 16.5X our forward four-quarter FFO estimate of $1.20; the shares recently traded at about 14.2X this estimate. We think the multiple will expand over time as KIM shows that its core portfolio, anchored by long-term leases, continues to grow. We also see the trust's expansion in Canada and Latin America contributing to long-term portfolio growth.

## Qualitative Risk Assessment

| LOW | MEDIUM | HIGH |
|---|---|---|

Our risk assessment reflects our view of KIM's strong fundamentals, healthy credit quality and diversified customer base. We also believe KIM's geographic diversity helps provide significant protection from a local or regional downturn.

## Quantitative Evaluations

**S&P Quality Ranking** A-

| D | C | B- | B | B+ | A- | A | A+ |
|---|---|---|---|---|---|---|---|

**Relative Strength Rank** MODERATE

34

LOWEST = 1 HIGHEST = 99

## Revenue/FFO Data

**Revenue (Million $)**

| | 1Q | 2Q | 3Q | 4Q | Year |
|---|---|---|---|---|---|
| 2011 | 235.5 | 230.1 | 226.8 | -- | -- |
| 2010 | 239.5 | 227.7 | 222.1 | 226.7 | 849.5 |
| 2009 | 208.0 | 203.3 | 205.5 | 227.3 | 844.3 |
| 2008 | 190.5 | 199.9 | 208.6 | 213.6 | 824.7 |
| 2007 | 158.3 | 170.8 | 210.3 | 179.7 | 750.6 |
| 2006 | 138.1 | 147.9 | 150.7 | 157.3 | 653.0 |

**FFO Per Share ($)**

| | | | | | |
|---|---|---|---|---|---|
| 2011 | 0.28 | 0.29 | 0.31 | E0.30 | E1.20 |
| 2010 | 0.31 | 0.26 | 0.27 | 0.29 | 1.13 |
| 2009 | 0.43 | 0.31 | 0.30 | 0.75 | 0.82 |
| 2008 | 0.64 | 0.66 | 0.37 | 0.04 | 2.02 |
| 2007 | 0.78 | 0.71 | 0.57 | 0.53 | 2.59 |
| 2006 | 0.53 | 0.54 | 0.56 | 0.58 | 2.21 |

Fiscal year ended Dec. 31. Next earnings report expected: Early February. FFO Estimates based on S&P Funds From Operations Est..

## Dividend Data (Dates: mm/dd Payment Date: mm/dd/yy)

| Amount ($) | Date Decl. | Ex-Div. Date | Stk. of Record | Payment Date |
|---|---|---|---|---|
| 0.180 | 02/09 | 04/01 | 04/05 | 04/15/11 |
| 0.180 | 05/04 | 07/01 | 07/06 | 07/15/11 |
| 0.180 | 07/26 | 10/03 | 10/05 | 10/17/11 |
| 0.190 | 11/02 | 12/30 | 01/04 | 01/17/12 |

Dividends have been paid since 1992. Source: Company reports.

---

**Please read the Required Disclosures and Analyst Certification on the last page of this report.**

**The McGraw·Hill Companies**

# Kimco Realty Corp

**STANDARD &POOR'S**

## Business Summary November 04, 2011

Kimco Realty specializes in the acquisition, development and management of shopping centers that it believes are well located and have good growth potential. At the end of 2010, KIM had interests in 1,857 properties, totaling approximately 172.4 million square feet of gross leasable area (GLA) in 44 states, Canada, Mexico, Puerto Rico, Brazil, Chile and Peru. The trust's ownership interests in real estate consist of its consolidated portfolio and portfolios in which it owns an economic interest, such as properties in its investment management programs, where it partners with institutional investors and also retains management.

The trust's investment objective has been to increase cash flow, current income, and, consequently, the value of its existing portfolio of properties, and to seek continued growth through the strategic re-tenanting, renovation and expansion of its existing centers, and through the selective acquisition of established income-producing real estate properties and properties requiring significant re-tenanting and redevelopment. These properties are mainly located in neighborhood and community shopping centers in geographic regions in which KIM currently operates.

For KIM as well as other retail-oriented REITs, we believe that location and

the financial health and growth of their retail tenants are among the most important factors affecting the success of their portfolios. KIM's neighborhood and community shopping center properties are designed to attract local area customers and typically are anchored by a discount department store, a supermarket or a drugstore tenant offering day-to-day necessities rather than high-priced luxury items. The trust seeks to reduce operating and leasing risks through diversification achieved by the geographic distribution of its properties and a large tenant base. As of December 31, 2010, no single neighborhood and community shopping center accounted for more than 0.8% of the trust's annualized base rental revenues or more than 1.0% of its total shopping center GLA. The trust's five largest customers were: The Home Depot (3.0% of KIM's 2010 annualized base rental revenues, including the proportionate share of base rental revenues from properties in which KIM has less than a 100% economic interest), TJX Companies (2.8%), Wal-Mart (2.4%), Sears Holdings (2.3%), and Best Buy (1.6%).

## Company Financials Fiscal Year Ended Dec. 31

| Per Share Data ($) | 2010 | 2009 | 2008 | 2007 | 2006 | 2005 | 2004 | 2003 | 2002 | 2001 |
|---|---|---|---|---|---|---|---|---|---|---|
| Tangible Book Value | 12.14 | 11.96 | 14.66 | 15.40 | 13.24 | 9.70 | 9.17 | 8.87 | 8.04 | 7.95 |
| Earnings | 0.19 | -0.15 | 0.69 | 1.33 | 1.36 | 1.40 | 1.19 | 1.04 | 1.10 | 1.08 |
| S&P Core Earnings | 0.19 | -0.15 | 0.69 | 1.33 | 1.36 | 1.40 | 1.18 | 1.03 | 1.08 | 1.07 |
| Dividends | 0.66 | 0.72 | 0.24 | 1.52 | 1.38 | 1.27 | 1.16 | 1.10 | 1.05 | 0.98 |
| Payout Ratio | NM | NM | 35% | 114% | 101% | 91% | 97% | 105% | 96% | 91% |
| Prices:High | 18.41 | 20.90 | 47.80 | 53.60 | 47.13 | 33.35 | 29.64 | 22.93 | 16.94 | 17.03 |
| Prices:Low | 12.40 | 6.33 | 9.56 | 33.74 | 32.02 | 25.90 | 19.77 | 15.13 | 12.98 | 13.58 |
| P/E Ratio:High | 97 | NM | 69 | 40 | 35 | 24 | 25 | 22 | 15 | 16 |
| P/E Ratio:Low | 65 | NM | 14 | 25 | 24 | 18 | 17 | 14 | 12 | 13 |

| Income Statement Analysis (Million $) | | | | | | | | | | |
|---|---|---|---|---|---|---|---|---|---|---|
| Rental Income | 850 | 787 | 759 | 682 | 594 | 523 | 517 | 480 | 451 | 469 |
| Mortgage Income | Nil | Nil | Nil | 14.2 | 18.8 | NA | NA | NA | NA | NA |
| Total Income | 850 | 787 | 825 | 751 | 653 | 581 | 517 | 480 | 451 | 469 |
| General Expenses | 253 | 111 | 118 | 104 | 164 | 128 | 111 | 104 | 9.15 | 89.7 |
| Interest Expense | 226 | 210 | 213 | 214 | 173 | 128 | 108 | 103 | 86.9 | 89.4 |
| Provision for Losses | Nil | Nil | Nil | Nil | Nil | Nil | Nil | Nil | Nil | Nil |
| Depreciation | 238 | 228 | 204 | 190 | 141 | 106 | 102 | 86.2 | 76.7 | 74.2 |
| Net Income | 126 | -4.05 | 225 | 362 | 343 | 334 | 282 | 247 | 249 | 237 |
| S&P Core Earnings | 73.8 | -51.3 | 178 | 342 | 333 | 322 | 268 | 222 | 227 | 209 |

| Balance Sheet & Other Financial Data (Million $) | | | | | | | | | | |
|---|---|---|---|---|---|---|---|---|---|---|
| Cash | 125 | 122 | 136 | 87.5 | 1,616 | 1,018 | 757 | 581 | 36.0 | 93.8 |
| Total Assets | 9,834 | 10,162 | 9,397 | 9,098 | 7,869 | 5,535 | 4,747 | 4,604 | 3,757 | 3,385 |
| Real Estate Investment | 8,593 | 8,882 | 7,819 | 7,325 | 6,002 | 4,560 | 4,877 | 4,137 | 3,399 | 3,201 |
| Loss Reserve | Nil | Nil | Nil | Nil | Nil | Nil | Nil | Nil | Nil | Nil |
| Net Investment | 7,043 | 7,539 | 6,659 | 6,348 | 5,195 | 3,820 | 4,242 | 3,569 | 2,882 | 2,748 |
| Short Term Debt | NA | 380 | 186 | 281 | 209 | NA | NA | 570 | 147 | 123 |
| Capitalization:Debt | 4,059 | 4,054 | 4,371 | 3,936 | 3,378 | 2,397 | 1,860 | 1,585 | 1,430 | 1,205 |
| Capitalization:Equity | 4,935 | 4,852 | 3,974 | 3,894 | 3,366 | 2,387 | 2,236 | 2,135 | 1,906 | 1,889 |
| Capitalization:Total | 5,256 | 9,172 | 8,691 | 8,279 | 7,170 | 4,907 | 4,203 | 3,820 | 3,431 | 3,103 |
| % Earnings & Depreciation/Assets | 3.6 | 2.3 | 4.6 | 6.5 | 7.2 | 8.5 | 8.2 | 8.0 | 9.1 | 9.5 |
| Price Times Book Value:High | 1.5 | 1.7 | 3.3 | 3.5 | 3.6 | 3.4 | 3.2 | 2.6 | 2.1 | 2.1 |
| Price Times Book Value:Low | 1.0 | 0.5 | 0.7 | 2.2 | 2.4 | 2.7 | 2.2 | 1.7 | 1.6 | 1.7 |

Data as orig reptd.; bef. results of disc opers/spec. items. Per share data adj. for stk. divs.; EPS diluted. E-Estimated. NA-Not Available. NM-Not Meaningful. NR-Not Ranked. UR-Under Review.

**Office:** 3333 New Hyde Park Road, Suite 100, New Hyde Park, NY 11042.
**Telephone:** 516-869-9000.
**Email:** ir@kimcorealty.com
**Website:** http://www.kimcorealty.com

**Chrmn:** M. Cooper
**Pres, Vice Chrmn & CEO:** D.B. Henry
**COO & EVP:** M.V. Pappagallo
**EVP, CFO & Treas:** G.G. Cohen

**EVP & Chief Admin Officer:** B.M. Pooley
**Investor Contact:** D. Bujnicki (866-831-4297)
**Board Members:** M. Cooper, P. E. Coviello, R. G. Dooley, J. Grills, D. B. Henry, F. P. Hughes, F. Lourenso, C. M. Nicholas, R. B. Saltzman

**Founded:** 1966
**Domicile:** Maryland
**Employees:** 687

# KLA Tencor Corp

**STANDARD &POOR'S**

| S&P Recommendation **BUY** ★★★★★ | Price $42.08 (as of Nov 25, 2011) | 12-Mo. Target Price $54.00 | Investment Style Large-Cap Growth |
|---|---|---|---|

**GICS Sector** Information Technology
**Sub-Industry** Semiconductor Equipment

**Summary** This company is the world's leading manufacturer of yield monitoring and process control systems for the semiconductor industry.

## Key Stock Statistics (Source S&P, Vickers, company reports)

| | | | | | | |
|---|---|---|---|---|---|---|
| 52-Wk Range | $51.83– 33.20 | S&P Oper. EPS 2012**E** | 3.78 | Market Capitalization(B) | $7.013 | Beta | 1.72 |
| Trailing 12-Month EPS | $4.88 | S&P Oper. EPS 2013**E** | 4.28 | Yield (%) | 3.33 | S&P 3-Yr. Proj. EPS CAGR(%) | -3 |
| Trailing 12-Month P/E | 8.6 | P/E on S&P Oper. EPS 2012**E** | 11.1 | Dividend Rate/Share | $1.40 | S&P Credit Rating | BBB |
| $10K Invested 5 Yrs Ago | $9,057 | Common Shares Outstg. (M) | 166.7 | Institutional Ownership (%) | 90 | | |

## Price Performance

30-Week Mov. Avg. · · · 10-Week Mov. Avg. - - **GAAP Earnings vs. Previous Year**   Volume Above Avg. STARS
12-Mo. Target Price — Relative Strength  ▲ Up  ▼ Down  ► No Change   Below Avg. ★

Options: ASE, CBOE, P, Ph

Analysis prepared by Equity Analyst **Angelo Zino, CFA** on Nov 01, 2011, when the stock traded at **$45.66**.

## Highlights

➤ We estimate sales will decline 9.6% in FY 12 (Jun.) and rise 4.7% in FY 13, after a 74% increase in FY 11. We expect sequential orders to trend upwards in the intermediate term, driven by foundries, KLAC's largest customer segment, as yield challenges at more advanced technology nodes are likely to result in the need to invest in equipment. We think prospects for flash memory spending remain bright, as unit demand remains robust, and we view Dynamic Random Access Memory (DRAM) spending at depressed levels. In addition, we expect yield monitoring and process control systems products to fare better than other types of semiconductor equipment over the next few years.

➤ We see the annual gross margin widening to 60% in FY 13 versus our 58% margin forecast for FY 12. We view KLAC's yield management and process control systems as only moderately susceptible to pricing pressure due to the critical value they add to semiconductor customers. We forecast an operating margin of 30% in FY 12 and 32% in FY 13.

➤ We see operating EPS of $3.78 for FY 12 and $4.28 for FY 13. We view positively KLAC's lead market share position in respective markets.

## Investment Rationale/Risk

➤ Our buy recommendation reflects valuation as well as our belief that orders are likely to sequentially rebound over the next several quarters. We view KLAC's competitive position in both inspection and metrology as strong, and we see long-term growth in yield management and process control. We think the transition to lower nanometer nodes will cause yield and defectivity challenges, which we believe will stimulate customers to increase spending. Longer term, we believe growth in KLAC's core semiconductor business continues to outpace the industry, and we see opportunities in areas such as alternative energy. In the most recent September quarter, the distribution in new orders by customer was 57% from foundries, logic customers 22%, and memory orders 21%.

➤ Risks to our recommendation and target price include weaker-than-projected industry sales, greater competition pressuring KLAC's market share position, and a faltering global economic recovery.

➤ Our 12-month target price of $54 is based on a P/E of 13.5X to our 2012 calendar year operating EPS estimate, near comparable front-end semiconductor equipment manufacturers.

## Qualitative Risk Assessment

| LOW | MEDIUM | **HIGH** |
|---|---|---|

Our risk assessment reflects the company's exposure to the cyclicality of the semiconductor equipment industry and changes in relevant technologies, only partially offset by limited pricing pressure and our view of KLAC's strong market position, size, and financial condition.

## Quantitative Evaluations

**S&P Quality Ranking**  B

| D | C | B- | **B** | B+ | A- | A | A+ |
|---|---|---|---|---|---|---|---|

**Relative Strength Rank**  MODERATE

67

LOWEST = 1   HIGHEST = 99

## Revenue/Earnings Data

**Revenue (Million $)**

| | 1Q | 2Q | 3Q | 4Q | Year |
|---|---|---|---|---|---|
| 2012 | 796.5 | -- | -- | -- | -- |
| 2011 | 682.3 | 766.3 | 834.1 | 892.4 | 3,175 |
| 2010 | 342.7 | 440.4 | 478.3 | 559.4 | 1,821 |
| 2009 | 532.5 | 396.6 | 309.6 | 281.5 | 1,520 |
| 2008 | 693.0 | 635.8 | 602.2 | 590.7 | 2,522 |
| 2007 | 629.4 | 649.3 | 716.2 | 736.4 | 2,731 |

**Earnings Per Share ($)**

| | 1Q | 2Q | 3Q | 4Q | Year |
|---|---|---|---|---|---|
| 2012 | 1.13 | E0.65 | E0.92 | E1.05 | E3.78 |
| 2011 | 0.91 | 1.09 | 1.22 | 1.43 | 4.66 |
| 2010 | 0.12 | 0.13 | 0.33 | 0.66 | 1.23 |
| 2009 | 0.11 | -2.57 | -0.49 | -0.15 | -3.07 |
| 2008 | 0.46 | 0.45 | 0.61 | 0.43 | 1.95 |
| 2007 | 0.67 | 0.44 | 0.76 | 0.75 | 2.61 |

Fiscal year ended Jun. 30. Next earnings report expected: Late January. EPS Estimates based on S&P Operating Earnings; historical GAAP earnings are as reported.

## Dividend Data (Dates: mm/dd Payment Date: mm/dd/yy)

| Amount ($) | Date Decl. | Ex-Div. Date | Stk. of Record | Payment Date |
|---|---|---|---|---|
| 0.250 | 02/11 | 02/17 | 02/22 | 03/01/11 |
| 0.250 | 05/05 | 05/12 | 05/16 | 06/01/11 |
| 0.350 | 08/04 | 08/11 | 08/15 | 09/01/11 |
| 0.350 | 11/03 | 11/09 | 11/14 | 12/01/11 |

Dividends have been paid since 2005. Source: Company reports.

---

**Please read the Required Disclosures and Analyst Certification on the last page of this report.**

*The McGraw-Hill Companies*

# KLA Tencor Corp

**STANDARD &POOR'S**

## Business Summary November 01, 2011

CORPORATE OVERVIEW. KLA-Tencor (KLAC) is the world's leading manufacturer of yield management and process monitoring systems for the semiconductor industry. Its products are also used in other industries, including the high brightness light emitting diode, data storage and photovoltaic industries.

Maximizing yields, or the number of good die (chips) per wafer, is a key goal in manufacturing integrated circuits (ICs). Higher yields increase revenues obtained for each semiconductor wafer processed. As IC line widths decrease, yields become more sensitive to microscopic-sized defects. KLAC's systems are used to improve yields by identifying defects, analyzing them to determine process problems and patterns, and facilitate corrective actions. These systems monitor subsequent results to ensure that problems have been contained. With in-line systems, corrections can be made while the wafer is still in the production line, rather than waiting for end-of-process testing and feedback.

KLAC offers a broad range of inspection and yield management. The company's wafer inspection systems include unpatterned and patterned wafer inspection tools used to find, count and characterize particles and pattern defects on wafers both in engineering applications and in-line at various stages during the semiconductor manufacturing process. KLAC's brightfield inspection systems are extremely sensitive to small defects and capture a large

range of defect types, which is critical as customers move to 32nm and smaller production.

Reticle inspection systems look for defects on the quartz plates used in copying circuit designs onto an IC during the photolithography process. Film measurement products measure a variety of optical and electrical properties of thin films. Scanning electron beam microscopes (SEMs) can measure the critical dimensions (CDs) of tiny semiconductor features. For chip manufacturing below 90nm, e-beam inspection is becoming increasingly important, not only during the research and development phase, where the highest levels of sensitivity are needed to highlight and eradicate potential design problems, but also in production, where dedicated high-speed e-beam inspection systems.

At the end of FY 10 (Jun.), KLAC's revenues by geographic region were divided as follows: United States 19% (24% in FY 10), Europe & Israel 6% (11%), Japan 13% (29%), Taiwan 38% (12%), Korea 8% (12%), and Rest of Asia 16% (12%). In FY 10, Taiwan Semiconductor Manufacturing and Intel both accounted for more than 10% of total sales.

## Company Financials Fiscal Year Ended Jun. 30

| Per Share Data ($) | 2011 | 2010 | 2009 | 2008 | 2007 | 2006 | 2005 | 2004 | 2003 | 2002 |
|---|---|---|---|---|---|---|---|---|---|---|
| Tangible Book Value | 14.64 | 10.72 | 10.00 | 11.96 | 16.00 | 17.56 | 15.49 | 13.34 | 11.56 | 10.70 |
| Cash Flow | 5.17 | 1.73 | 2.34 | 2.58 | 3.15 | 2.20 | 2.67 | 1.62 | 1.07 | 1.45 |
| Earnings | 4.66 | 1.23 | -3.07 | 1.95 | 2.61 | 1.86 | 2.32 | 1.21 | 0.70 | 1.10 |
| S&P Core Earnings | 4.68 | 1.22 | -1.48 | 2.05 | 2.64 | 1.89 | 1.88 | 0.77 | 0.12 | 0.49 |
| Dividends | 1.00 | 0.60 | 0.60 | 0.60 | 0.48 | 0.48 | 0.12 | Nil | Nil | Nil |
| Payout Ratio | 21% | 49% | NM | 31% | 18% | 26% | 5% | Nil | Nil | Nil |
| Prices:High | 51.83 | 40.44 | 37.71 | 48.35 | 62.67 | 55.03 | 55.00 | 62.82 | 61.25 | 70.58 |
| Prices:Low | 33.20 | 26.69 | 15.28 | 14.81 | 46.59 | 38.38 | 37.39 | 35.02 | 31.20 | 25.16 |
| P/E Ratio:High | 11 | 33 | NM | 25 | 24 | 30 | 24 | 52 | 88 | 64 |
| P/E Ratio:Low | 7 | 22 | NM | 8 | 18 | 21 | 16 | 29 | 45 | 23 |

| Income Statement Analysis (Million $) | 2011 | 2010 | 2009 | 2008 | 2007 | 2006 | 2005 | 2004 | 2003 | 2002 |
|---|---|---|---|---|---|---|---|---|---|---|
| Revenue | 3,175 | 1,821 | 1,520 | 2,522 | 2,731 | 2,071 | 2,085 | 1,497 | 1,323 | 1,637 |
| Operating Income | 1,245 | 423 | -7.00 | 708 | 699 | 379 | 653 | 380 | 201 | 314 |
| Depreciation | 86.0 | 87.4 | 124 | 116 | 109 | 69.4 | 70.9 | 82.9 | 71.4 | 69.6 |
| Interest Expense | 50.3 | 54.5 | 55.3 | 10.8 | Nil | Nil | Nil | Nil | 0.39 | Nil |
| Pretax Income | 1,110 | 291 | -603 | 560 | 680 | 378 | 627 | 325 | 181 | 287 |
| Effective Tax Rate | NA | NA | NM | 35.9% | 22.1% | NM | 25.0% | 24.9% | 24.0% | 24.8% |
| Net Income | 794 | 212 | -523 | 359 | 528 | 380 | 467 | 244 | 137 | 216 |
| S&P Core Earnings | 798 | 212 | -251 | 379 | 535 | 386 | 377 | 156 | 22.4 | 96.5 |

| Balance Sheet & Other Financial Data (Million $) | 2011 | 2010 | 2009 | 2008 | 2007 | 2006 | 2005 | 2004 | 2003 | 2002 |
|---|---|---|---|---|---|---|---|---|---|---|
| Cash | 2,039 | 1,534 | 1,330 | 1,579 | 1,711 | 2,326 | 2,195 | 1,876 | 1,488 | 1,334 |
| Current Assets | 3,676 | 2,835 | 2,399 | 3,036 | 3,253 | 3,543 | 3,203 | 2,192 | 1,806 | 1,619 |
| Total Assets | 4,676 | 3,907 | 3,610 | 4,848 | 4,623 | 4,576 | 3,986 | 3,539 | 2,867 | 2,718 |
| Current Liabilities | 882 | 772 | 564 | 950 | 1,073 | 1,002 | 932 | 912 | 651 | 687 |
| Long Term Debt | 746 | 746 | 745 | 745 | Nil | Nil | Nil | Nil | Nil | Nil |
| Common Equity | 2,861 | 2,247 | 2,184 | 2,982 | 3,550 | 3,568 | 3,045 | 2,628 | 2,216 | 2,030 |
| Total Capital | 3,607 | 2,992 | 2,930 | 3,726 | 3,550 | 3,573 | 3,055 | 2,628 | 2,216 | 2,030 |
| Capital Expenditures | 51.2 | 30.2 | 22.2 | 57.3 | 83.8 | 73.8 | 59.7 | 55.5 | 134 | 68.7 |
| Cash Flow | 881 | 300 | -399 | 475 | 637 | 450 | 538 | 327 | 209 | 286 |
| Current Ratio | 4.2 | 3.7 | 4.3 | 3.2 | 3.0 | 3.5 | 3.4 | 2.4 | 2.8 | 2.4 |
| % Long Term Debt of Capitalization | 20.7 | 24.9 | 25.4 | 20.0 | Nil | Nil | Nil | Nil | Nil | Nil |
| % Net Income of Revenue | 25.0 | 11.7 | NM | 14.2 | 19.3 | 18.4 | 22.4 | 16.3 | 10.4 | 13.2 |
| % Return on Assets | 18.5 | 5.7 | NM | 7.6 | 11.5 | 8.8 | 12.4 | 7.6 | 4.9 | 7.9 |
| % Return on Equity | 31.1 | 9.6 | NM | 11.0 | 14.8 | 11.4 | 16.5 | 10.1 | 6.5 | 11.4 |

Data as orig reptd.; bef. results of disc opers/spec. items. Per share data adj. for stk. divs.; EPS diluted. E-Estimated. NA-Not Available. NM-Not Meaningful. NR-Not Ranked. UR-Under Review.

**Office:** 1 Technology Dr, Milpitas, CA 95035-7916.
**Telephone:** 408-875-3000.
**Website:** http://www.tencor.com
**Chrmn:** E.W. Barnholt

**Pres & CEO:** R.P. Wallace
**EVP & CFO:** M.P. Dentinger
**SVP & Chief Acctg Officer:** V.A. Kirloskar
**SVP, Secy & General Counsel:** B.M. Martin

**Investor Contact:** W. Lin (408-875-3000)
**Board Members:** R. P. Akins, E. W. Barnholt, R. T. Bond, R. M. Calderoni, J. T. Dickson, E. Higashi, S. P. Kaufman, K. J. Kennedy, K. M. Patel, R. P. Wallace, D. C. Wang

**Founded:** 1975
**Domicile:** Delaware
**Employees:** 5,500

# Kohl's Corp

**STANDARD
&POOR'S**

| S&P Recommendation **BUY** ★★★★☆ | Price $51.81 (as of Nov 25, 2011) | 12-Mo. Target Price $63.00 | Investment Style Large-Cap Growth |
|---|---|---|---|

**GICS Sector** Consumer Discretionary
**Sub-Industry** Department Stores

**Summary** This company operates over 1,100 specialty department stores in 49 states, featuring moderately priced apparel, shoes, accessories, and products for the home.

## Key Stock Statistics (Source S&P, Vickers, company reports)

| | | | | | | | |
|---|---|---|---|---|---|---|---|
| 52-Wk Range | $57.39–42.14 | S&P Oper. EPS 2012**E** | 4.53 | Market Capitalization(B) | $13.960 | Beta | 0.88 |
| Trailing 12-Month EPS | $4.26 | S&P Oper. EPS 2013**E** | 5.10 | Yield (%) | 1.93 | S&P 3-Yr. Proj. EPS CAGR(%) | 15 |
| Trailing 12-Month P/E | 12.2 | P/E on S&P Oper. EPS 2012**E** | 11.4 | Dividend Rate/Share | $1.00 | S&P Credit Rating | BBB+ |
| $10K Invested 5 Yrs Ago | $7,404 | Common Shares Outstg. (M) | 269.4 | Institutional Ownership (%) | 87 | | |

## Price Performance

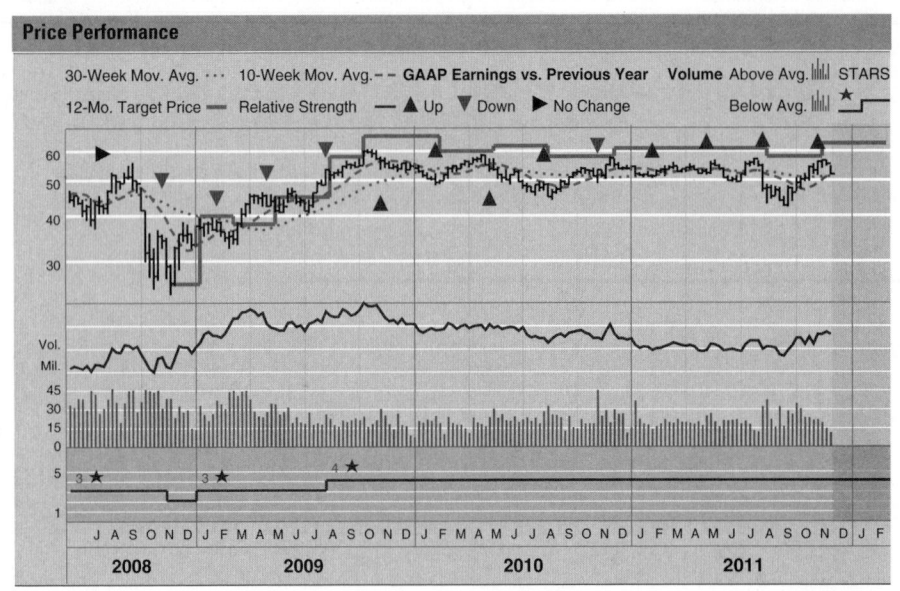

30-Week Mov. Avg. ··· 10-Week Mov. Avg. – – **GAAP Earnings vs. Previous Year** Volume Above Avg. STARS
12-Mo. Target Price — Relative Strength — ▲ Up ▼ Down ▶ No Change Below Avg. ★

Options: ASE, CBOE, P, Ph

Analysis prepared by Equity Analyst **Jason N. Asaeda** on Nov 11, 2011, when the stock traded at **$56.35**.

## Highlights

➤ In our view, middle-income consumers, KSS's core demographic, are spending cautiously due to macroeconomic concerns. We look for the company to drive low single digit same-store sales growth annually through investments in new brands (including the Jennifer Lopez and Marc Anthony brands this fall), store remodels, and size optimization, which improves apparel in-stock positions by ensuring that individual stores have inventory in the correct sizes, colors and styles. We also expect online sales to positively impact same-store sales by 1.5 percentage points. Coupled with planned new store openings, we see net sales reaching $19.1 billion in FY 12 (Jan.) and $19.9 billion in FY 13.

➤ While we expect KSS to increase promotional activity to offset apparel inflation, to incur incremental expenses in support of new stores, and to increase investment in brand marketing, we see operating margins widening on increased penetration of private and exclusive brands, as well as inventory and cost controls.

➤ Factoring in planned share repurchases, we estimate EPS of $4.53 in FY 12 and $5.10 in FY 13.

## Investment Rationale/Risk

➤ Our buy recommendation on the shares is based on valuation and our positive outlook for the company. We view KSS's value pricing, lifestyle merchandising, and off-mall expansion strategies as underlying strengths in a challenging retail environment. We look for the company's focus on more exclusive, higher-quality brands and products, efforts to better tailor assortments to reflect regional market preferences (KSS is focusing on the South Central region in FY 12), and a rapidly growing e-commerce business to support positive sales momentum and margin improvement in FY 12. We also expect the company to generate ample operating cash flow to fund share repurchases and its newly initiated dividend program.

➤ Risks to our recommendation and target price include sales shortfalls due to unforeseen shifts in fashion trends, significant weakening in consumer confidence, and negative customer reaction to expected apparel price increases.

➤ We arrive at our 12-month target price of $63 by applying a peer-average forward P/E multiple of 12.4X to our FY 13 EPS estimate.

## Qualitative Risk Assessment

| LOW | MEDIUM | HIGH |
|---|---|---|

Our risk assessment reflects our view of KSS's improving sales, increasing market share in the moderate department store sector, and healthy balance sheet and cash flow, offset by uncertainty over consumer discretionary spending in light of economic conditions and debt levels.

## Quantitative Evaluations

**S&P Quality Ranking** B+

| D | C | B- | B | B+ | A- | A | A+ |
|---|---|---|---|---|---|---|---|

**Relative Strength Rank** STRONG

75

LOWEST = 1     HIGHEST = 99

## Revenue/Earnings Data

**Revenue (Million $)**

| | 1Q | 2Q | 3Q | 4Q | Year |
|---|---|---|---|---|---|
| 2012 | 4,162 | 4,248 | 4,376 | -- | -- |
| 2011 | 4,035 | 4,100 | 4,218 | 6,038 | 18,391 |
| 2010 | 3,638 | 3,806 | 4,051 | 5,682 | 17,178 |
| 2009 | 3,624 | 3,725 | 3,804 | 5,235 | 16,389 |
| 2008 | 3,572 | 3,589 | 3,825 | 5,487 | 16,474 |
| 2007 | 3,185 | 3,291 | 3,637 | 5,431 | 15,544 |

**Earnings Per Share ($)**

| | | | | | |
|---|---|---|---|---|---|
| 2012 | 0.73 | 1.08 | 0.80 | E2.04 | E4.53 |
| 2011 | 0.64 | 0.84 | 0.53 | 1.66 | 3.65 |
| 2010 | 0.45 | 0.75 | 0.63 | 1.40 | 3.23 |
| 2009 | 0.49 | 0.77 | 0.52 | 1.10 | 2.88 |
| 2008 | 0.64 | 0.77 | 0.61 | 1.31 | 3.39 |
| 2007 | 0.48 | 0.69 | 0.68 | 1.48 | 3.31 |

Fiscal year ended Jan. 31. Next earnings report expected: NA. EPS Estimates based on S&P Operating Earnings; historical GAAP earnings are as reported.

## Dividend Data (Dates: mm/dd Payment Date: mm/dd/yy)

| Amount ($) | Date Decl. | Ex-Div. Date | Stk. of Record | Payment Date |
|---|---|---|---|---|
| 0.250 | 02/23 | 03/07 | 03/09 | 03/30/11 |
| 0.250 | 05/12 | 06/06 | 06/08 | 06/29/11 |
| 0.250 | 08/11 | 09/02 | 09/07 | 09/28/11 |
| 0.250 | 11/10 | 12/05 | 12/07 | 12/28/11 |

Dividends have been paid since 2011. Source: Company reports.

# Kohl's Corp

**STANDARD &POOR'S**

## Business Summary November 11, 2011

CORPORATE OVERVIEW. Kohl's (KSS), with its "Expect Great Things" line, has positioned itself as a preferred shopping destination for busy women. Its traditional customers are married women aged 25 to 54. The company's stores feature easy-to-shop layouts and emphasize moderately priced exclusive and national brand family apparel and shoes, accessories, cosmetics, home furnishings, and housewares. KSS uses a "nine-box grid" merchandising strategy. Product assortments fall into three categories, "good," "better," and "best," differentiated by price and quality, and also reflect three distinct customer styles: the "classic" customer who wants a coordinated look without bending the rules; the "updated" customer who likes classic styles with a twist; and the more fashion-forward "contemporary" customer. Private and exclusive brands accounted for 48% of sales in FY 11.

PRIMARY BUSINESS DYNAMICS. KSS is one of the fastest-growing retail chains in the U.S. From FY 06 through FY 11, the company increased its selling square footage at a compound annual growth rate (CAGR) of 7.2% as it expanded its store count from 732 to 1,089. In FY 12, KSS opened nine stores in the spring and an additional 31 stores in the fall, for a total of 40 new stores, as well as 100 store remodels. The company plans to open 30 new stores (8 in the spring and 22 in the fall) and to remodel an additional 100 stores in FY 13.

From a merchandising standpoint, we believe KSS fell behind competitors such as J.C. Penney and Macy's in delivering newness and better quality merchandise sought by its customers in FY 04. Since then, however, we have seen the company prove itself capable of creating a more compelling sales mix by investing in new contemporary brands such as Candie's in juniors and young girls, and by entering the beauty business. KSS also responded successfully, in our view, to dress clothing trends in FY 06 with the launch of Chaps (by Ralph Lauren) in men's career casual sportswear.

In FY 07, the company filled out its contemporary apparel offerings, and expanded its most popular brands into additional product categories (e.g., Chaps into women's and boys), creating true lifestyle brands. We think these rollouts complemented KSS's ongoing efforts to capture more share of wallet among empty nesters aged 45 to 54 and single women aged 25 to 34.

## Company Financials Fiscal Year Ended Jan. 31

| Per Share Data ($) | 2011 | 2010 | 2009 | 2008 | 2007 | 2006 | 2005 | 2004 | 2003 | 2002 |
|---|---|---|---|---|---|---|---|---|---|---|
| Tangible Book Value | 27.18 | 24.92 | 21.41 | 21.77 | 18.32 | 16.62 | 13.78 | 11.60 | 9.85 | 7.78 |
| Cash Flow | 5.78 | 5.17 | 4.65 | 4.80 | 4.47 | 3.42 | 2.95 | 2.43 | 2.41 | 1.93 |
| Earnings | 3.65 | 3.23 | 2.88 | 3.39 | 3.31 | 2.43 | 2.12 | 1.72 | 1.87 | 1.35 |
| S&P Core Earnings | 3.66 | 3.23 | 2.89 | 3.39 | 3.31 | 2.43 | 2.04 | 1.62 | 1.78 | 1.38 |
| Dividends | NA | Nil | Nil | Nil | Nil | Nil | Nil | Nil | Nil | Nil |
| Payout Ratio | NA | Nil | Nil | Nil | Nil | Nil | Nil | Nil | Nil | Nil |
| Calendar Year | 2010 | 2009 | 2008 | 2007 | 2006 | 2005 | 2004 | 2003 | 2002 | 2001 |
| Prices:High | 58.99 | 60.89 | 56.00 | 79.55 | 75.54 | 58.90 | 54.10 | 65.44 | 78.83 | 72.24 |
| Prices:Low | 44.07 | 32.50 | 24.28 | 44.16 | 42.78 | 43.63 | 39.59 | 42.40 | 44.00 | 41.95 |
| P/E Ratio:High | 16 | 19 | 19 | 23 | 23 | 24 | 26 | 38 | 42 | 54 |
| P/E Ratio:Low | 12 | 10 | 8 | 13 | 13 | 18 | 19 | 25 | 24 | 31 |

| Income Statement Analysis (Million $) | | | | | | | | | | |
|---|---|---|---|---|---|---|---|---|---|---|
| Revenue | 18,391 | 17,178 | 16,389 | 16,474 | 15,544 | 13,402 | 11,701 | 10,282 | 9,120 | 7,489 |
| Operating Income | 2,570 | 2,302 | 2,077 | 2,257 | 2,202 | 1,755 | 1,525 | 1,260 | 1,282 | 1,002 |
| Depreciation | 656 | 590 | 541 | 452 | 388 | 339 | 288 | 237 | 191 | 152 |
| Interest Expense | 132 | 134 | 140 | 98.7 | 74.4 | 72.1 | 64.1 | 75.2 | 59.4 | 57.4 |
| Pretax Income | 1,782 | 1,588 | 1,425 | 1,742 | 1,774 | 1,346 | 1,174 | 950 | 1,034 | 800 |
| Effective Tax Rate | NA | 37.6% | 37.9% | 37.8% | 37.5% | 37.4% | 37.8% | 37.8% | 37.8% | 38.0% |
| Net Income | 1,114 | 991 | 885 | 1,084 | 1,109 | 842 | 730 | 591 | 643 | 496 |
| S&P Core Earnings | 1,120 | 991 | 885 | 1,084 | 1,109 | 842 | 703 | 557 | 608 | 471 |

| Balance Sheet & Other Financial Data (Million $) | | | | | | | | | | |
|---|---|---|---|---|---|---|---|---|---|---|
| Cash | 2,277 | 2,267 | 676 | 664 | 620 | 127 | 117 | 113 | 90.1 | 107 |
| Current Assets | 5,645 | 5,485 | 3,700 | 3,724 | 3,401 | 4,266 | 3,643 | 3,025 | 3,284 | 2,464 |
| Total Assets | 13,564 | 13,160 | 11,334 | 10,560 | 9,041 | 9,153 | 7,979 | 6,698 | 6,316 | 4,930 |
| Current Liabilities | 2,710 | 2,390 | 1,815 | 1,771 | 1,919 | 1,746 | 1,456 | 1,122 | 1,508 | 880 |
| Long Term Debt | 1,678 | 2,052 | 2,053 | 2,052 | 1,040 | 1,046 | 1,103 | 1,076 | 1,059 | 1,095 |
| Common Equity | 8,102 | 7,853 | 6,739 | 6,102 | 5,603 | 5,957 | 4,967 | 4,191 | 3,512 | 2,791 |
| Total Capital | 10,198 | 9,905 | 9,112 | 8,416 | 6,887 | 7,221 | 6,367 | 5,504 | 4,743 | 4,001 |
| Capital Expenditures | 761 | 666 | 1,014 | 1,542 | 1,142 | 799 | 890 | 832 | 716 | 662 |
| Cash Flow | 1,770 | 1,581 | 1,426 | 1,536 | 1,496 | 1,181 | 1,019 | 828 | 835 | 648 |
| Current Ratio | 2.1 | 2.3 | 2.0 | 2.1 | 1.8 | 2.4 | 2.5 | 2.7 | 2.2 | 2.8 |
| % Long Term Debt of Capitalization | 16.5 | 20.7 | 22.5 | 24.4 | 15.7 | 14.5 | 17.3 | 19.5 | 22.3 | 27.4 |
| % Net Income of Revenue | 6.1 | 5.8 | 5.4 | 6.6 | 7.1 | 6.3 | 6.2 | 5.7 | 7.1 | 6.6 |
| % Return on Assets | 8.3 | 8.1 | 8.1 | 11.1 | 12.2 | 9.8 | 10.0 | 9.1 | 11.4 | 11.3 |
| % Return on Equity | 14.0 | 13.6 | 13.8 | 18.5 | 19.2 | 15.3 | 16.0 | 15.3 | 20.4 | 19.9 |

Data as orig reptd.; bef. results of disc opers/spec. items. Per share data adj. for stk. divs.; EPS diluted. E-Estimated. NA-Not Available. NM-Not Meaningful. NR-Not Ranked. UR-Under Review.

**Office:** N56W17000 Ridgewood Dr, Menomonee Falls, WI 53051-5660.
**Telephone:** 262-703-7000.
**Website:** http://www.kohls.com
**Chrmn, Pres & CEO:** K. Mansell

**EVP, Secy & General Counsel:** R.D. Schepp
**Chief Admin Officer:** J.M. Worthington
**Investor Contact:** W.S. McDonald (262-703-1893)

**Board Members:** P. Boneparth, S. A. Burd, J. F. Herma, D. E. Jones, W. S. Kellogg, K. Mansell, J. E. Schlifske, P. M. Sommerhauser, S. A. Streeter, N. G. VacaHumrichouse, S. E. Watson

**Founded:** 1986
**Domicile:** Wisconsin
**Employees:** 136,000

**The McGraw·Hill** Companies

# Kraft Foods Inc.

**STANDARD &POOR'S**

| S&P Recommendation HOLD ★★★☆☆ | Price $34.32 (as of Nov 25, 2011) | 12-Mo. Target Price $38.00 | Investment Style Large-Cap Blend |
|---|---|---|---|

**GICS Sector** Consumer Staples
**Sub-Industry** Packaged Foods & Meats

**Summary** Kraft Foods is one of the world's largest branded food and beverage companies.

## Key Stock Statistics (Source S&P, Vickers, company reports)

| | | | | | | | |
|---|---|---|---|---|---|---|---|
| 52-Wk Range | $36.30–29.80 | S&P Oper. EPS 2011**E** | 2.29 | Market Capitalization(B) | $60.635 | Beta | 0.55 |
| Trailing 12-Month EPS | $1.83 | S&P Oper. EPS 2012**E** | 2.47 | Yield (%) | 3.38 | S&P 3-Yr. Proj. EPS CAGR(%) | 9 |
| Trailing 12-Month P/E | 18.8 | P/E on S&P Oper. EPS 2011**E** | 15.0 | Dividend Rate/Share | $1.16 | S&P Credit Rating | BBB |
| $10K Invested 5 Yrs Ago | $11,737 | Common Shares Outstg. (M) | 1,766.7 | Institutional Ownership (%) | 76 | | |

## Price Performance

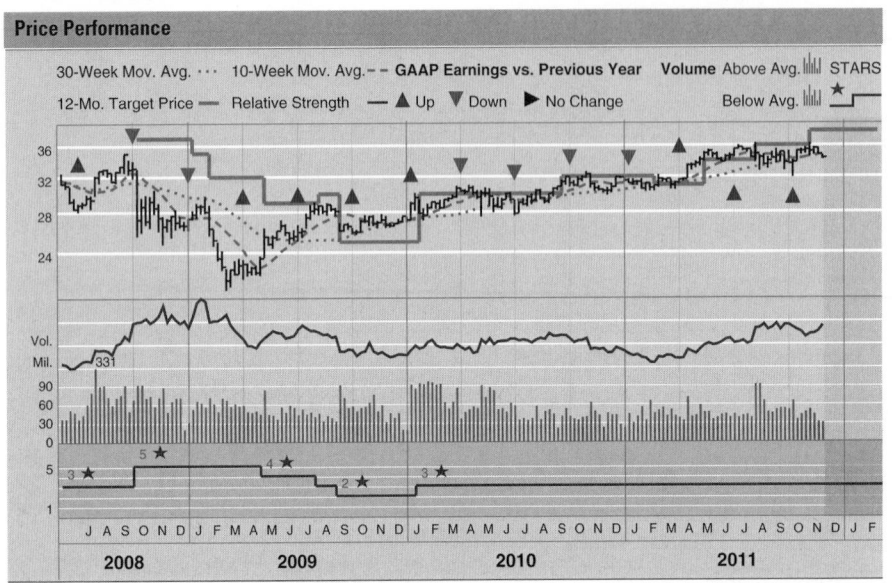

30-Week Mov. Avg. ··· 10-Week Mov. Avg. – – GAAP Earnings vs. Previous Year Volume Above Avg. STARS
12-Mo. Target Price — Relative Strength ▲ Up ▼ Down ► No Change Below Avg. ★

2008 2009 2010 2011

Options: ASE, CBOE, P, Ph

Analysis prepared by Equity Analyst **Tom Graves, CFA** on Nov 04, 2011, when the stock traded at **$35.19**.

## Qualitative Risk Assessment

| LOW | MEDIUM | HIGH |
|---|---|---|

Our risk assessment reflects the risks that we see KFT facing from competitive conditions, and other factors such as commodity costs and currency exchange rates. This is offset by the relatively stable nature of the company's end markets, by our expectation of relatively good company cash flow, and by KFT's leading market share positions.

## Quantitative Evaluations

**S&P Quality Ranking** A-

| D | C | B- | B | B+ | A- | A | A+ |
|---|---|---|---|---|---|---|---|

**Relative Strength Rank** STRONG

73

LOWEST = 1    HIGHEST = 99

## Revenue/Earnings Data

**Revenue (Million $)**

| | 1Q | 2Q | 3Q | 4Q | Year |
|---|---|---|---|---|---|
| 2011 | 12,573 | 13,878 | 13,226 | -- | -- |
| 2010 | 11,318 | 12,253 | 11,863 | 13,773 | 49,207 |
| 2009 | 9,396 | 10,162 | 9,803 | 11,025 | 40,386 |
| 2008 | 10,372 | 11,176 | 10,462 | 10,767 | 42,201 |
| 2007 | 8,586 | 9,205 | 9,054 | 10,396 | 37,241 |
| 2006 | 8,123 | 8,619 | 8,243 | 9,371 | 34,356 |

**Earnings Per Share ($)**

| | | | | | |
|---|---|---|---|---|---|
| 2011 | 0.45 | 0.55 | 0.52 | E0.57 | E2.29 |
| 2010 | 0.15 | 0.53 | 0.43 | 0.31 | 1.44 |
| 2009 | 0.45 | 0.56 | 0.55 | 0.48 | 2.03 |
| 2008 | 0.42 | 0.48 | 0.36 | 0.06 | 1.23 |
| 2007 | 0.43 | 0.44 | 0.38 | 0.38 | 1.63 |
| 2006 | 0.61 | 0.41 | 0.45 | 0.38 | 1.85 |

Fiscal year ended Dec. 31. Next earnings report expected: Mid February. EPS Estimates based on S&P Operating Earnings; historical GAAP earnings are as reported.

## Dividend Data (Dates: mm/dd Payment Date: mm/dd/yy)

| Amount ($) | Date Decl. | Ex-Div. Date | Stk. of Record | Payment Date |
|---|---|---|---|---|
| 0.290 | 12/20 | 12/29 | 12/31 | 01/14/11 |
| 0.290 | 02/25 | 03/29 | 03/31 | 04/14/11 |
| 0.290 | 05/24 | 06/28 | 06/30 | 07/14/11 |
| 0.290 | 08/17 | 09/28 | 09/30 | 10/14/11 |

Dividends have been paid since 2001. Source: Company reports.

## Highlights

➤ In August 2011, KFT said it expects to separate into two independent public companies -- a global snacks business and a North American grocery business. Ownership of the grocery business would be spun off to KFT shareholders, and KFT was targeting the split to occur before year-end 2012.

➤ In 2012, for the company as currently constituted, we look for revenue to increase about 3% from the $55 billion that we project for 2011, with the increase coming largely from higher prices. In 2011, we expect a sales increase of about 12%, benefiting from a full-year's inclusion of the Cadbury acquisition, favorable currency fluctuation, and a 53rd week in the fiscal year.

➤ In 2012, we expect KFT to be facing less margin pressure from rising commodity costs than we anticipate for 2011. We look for profit margins to be bolstered by price increases. In both 2011 and 2012, we expect the combination with Cadbury to provide incremental cost synergies. Before special items, we estimate 2012 EPS from continuing operations of $2.47, up from the $2.29 that we project for 2011.

## Investment Rationale/Risk

➤ We see KFT's valuation benefiting from a planned split into two public companies. We think the snacks business, which would also include powdered drinks and coffee, has better long-term growth prospects, and that the North American grocery business would be more of a dividend payer. Also, we see the 2010 cash-and-stock acquisition of British confectionery company Cadbury plc offering strategic value for KFT, including the opportunity to boost its presence in developing international markets and to accelerate overall growth prospects somewhat.

➤ Risks to our recommendation and target price include less optimistic expectations related to the planned business separation by KFT, a worse than anticipated outcome to KFT's acquisition of Cadbury, more unfavorable than expected commodity costs and currency exchange rates, and market share declines.

➤ Our 12-month target price of $38 reflects our view that the stock should trade at a P/E similar to an average P/E of a group of other packaged food companies.

# Kraft Foods Inc.

STANDARD
&POOR'S

## Business Summary November 04, 2011

CORPORATE OVERVIEW. Kraft Foods is one of the world's largest branded food and beverage companies. In August 2011, KFT said it expects to separate into two independent public companies -- a global snacks business, which would also include powdered drinks and coffee, and a North American grocery business. Ownership of the grocery business would be spun off to KFT shareholders, and KFT was targeting the split to occur before year-end 2012.

In 2010, KFT's North American business segments accounted for $24.0 billion, or approximately 49%, of total company net revenues from continuing operations. In comparison, revised North America revenue from continuing operations in 2009, prior to the Cadbury acquisition, and excluding a divested frozen pizza business, represented 57% of total net revenue. Kraft International had net revenues of $25.2 billion (51%) in 2010.

Business segments include U.S. Beverages (6.5% of 2010 net revenues), U.S. Cheese (7.2%), U.S. Convenient Meals (6.4%), U.S. Grocery (6.9%), U.S. Snacks (12%), Canada and North America Foodservice (9.5%), Kraft Foods Europe (24%), and Kraft Foods Developing Markets (28%). Wal-Mart Stores, Inc., and affiliates accounted for about 14% of KFT's net revenues in 2010. Kraft recently said it had 11 brands with annual revenue of at least about $1 billion each. These included Oreo, Nabisco and LU biscuits; Milka and Cadbury chocolates; Trident gum; Jacobs and Maxwell House coffees; Philadelphia cream

cheeses; Kraft cheeses, dinners and dressings; and Oscar Mayer meats.

IMPACT OF MAJOR DEVELOPMENTS. In the first quarter of 2010, KFT acquired control of British confectionery company Cadbury plc for cash and stock that we value at roughly $18.5 billion. In the transaction, KFT paid about $11 billion (based on a February 2010 currency exchange rate) and issued about 262 common shares, increasing the number of shares outstanding by about 18%. KFT has announced agreements to divest Cadbury-related businesses in Poland and Romania. In 2009, under IFRS accounting, Cadbury had net revenues of 5.975 billion pounds (about $9.7 billion at a February 2011 exchange rate), most of which we believe was from outside of North America.

We look for the combination with Cadbury to provide incremental cost synergies in 2011 and 2012. KFT says that in 2010 it achieved about $250 million of such synergies. In February 2011, KFT indicated it was looking for the acquisition to enable about $1 billion of revenue synergies by 2013. We expect additional costs related to the integration program.

## Company Financials Fiscal Year Ended Dec. 31

| Per Share Data ($) | 2010 | 2009 | 2008 | 2007 | 2006 | 2005 | 2004 | 2003 | 2002 | 2001 |
|---|---|---|---|---|---|---|---|---|---|---|
| Tangible Book Value | NM | NM | NM | NM | NM | NM | NM | NM | NM | NM |
| Cash Flow | 2.28 | 2.66 | 1.88 | 2.18 | 2.39 | 2.27 | 2.07 | 2.48 | 2.37 | 2.19 |
| Earnings | 1.44 | 2.03 | 1.23 | 1.63 | 1.85 | 1.72 | 1.55 | 2.01 | 1.96 | 1.17 |
| S&P Core Earnings | 1.53 | 2.08 | 1.04 | 1.65 | 1.80 | 1.74 | 1.53 | 1.93 | 1.65 | 0.81 |
| Dividends | 1.16 | 1.16 | 1.12 | 1.04 | 0.96 | 0.87 | 0.77 | 0.66 | 0.56 | 0.26 |
| Payout Ratio | 81% | 57% | 91% | 64% | 52% | 51% | 50% | 33% | 29% | 22% |
| Prices:High | 32.67 | 29.84 | 34.97 | 37.20 | 36.67 | 35.65 | 36.06 | 39.40 | 43.95 | 35.57 |
| Prices:Low | 27.09 | 20.81 | 24.75 | 29.95 | 27.44 | 27.88 | 29.45 | 26.35 | 32.50 | 29.50 |
| P/E Ratio:High | 23 | 15 | 28 | 23 | 20 | 21 | 23 | 20 | 22 | 30 |
| P/E Ratio:Low | 19 | 10 | 20 | 18 | 15 | 16 | 19 | 13 | 17 | 25 |

| Income Statement Analysis (Million $) | | | | | | | | | | |
|---|---|---|---|---|---|---|---|---|---|---|
| Revenue | 49,207 | 40,386 | 42,201 | 37,241 | 34,356 | 34,113 | 32,168 | 31,010 | 29,723 | 33,875 |
| Operating Income | 7,422 | 6,503 | 6,116 | 5,794 | 6,065 | 6,002 | 6,108 | 6,786 | 6,892 | 6,526 |
| Depreciation | 1,424 | 931 | 986 | 886 | 898 | 879 | 879 | 813 | 716 | 1,642 |
| Interest Expense | 2,024 | 1,260 | 1,272 | 701 | 510 | 636 | 666 | 678 | 854 | 1,437 |
| Pretax Income | 3,642 | 4,287 | 2,577 | 3,730 | 4,016 | 4,116 | 3,946 | 5,346 | 5,267 | 3,447 |
| Effective Tax Rate | NA | 29.4% | 28.3% | 30.5% | 23.7% | 29.4% | 32.3% | 34.9% | 35.5% | 45.4% |
| Net Income | 2,495 | 3,021 | 1,849 | 2,590 | 3,060 | 2,904 | 2,669 | 3,476 | 3,394 | 1,882 |
| S&P Core Earnings | 2,620 | 3,103 | 1,580 | 2,640 | 2,963 | 2,930 | 2,632 | 3,337 | 2,861 | 1,308 |

| Balance Sheet & Other Financial Data (Million $) | | | | | | | | | | |
|---|---|---|---|---|---|---|---|---|---|---|
| Cash | 2,481 | 2,254 | 1,244 | 567 | 239 | 316 | 282 | 514 | 215 | 162 |
| Current Assets | 16,221 | 12,454 | 11,366 | 10,737 | 8,254 | 8,153 | 9,722 | 8,124 | 7,456 | 7,006 |
| Total Assets | 95,289 | 66,714 | 63,078 | 67,993 | 55,574 | 57,628 | 59,928 | 59,285 | 57,100 | 55,798 |
| Current Liabilities | 15,660 | 11,491 | 11,044 | 17,086 | 10,473 | 8,724 | 9,078 | 7,861 | 7,169 | 8,875 |
| Long Term Debt | 26,859 | 18,024 | 18,589 | 12,902 | 7,081 | 8,475 | 9,723 | 11,591 | 10,416 | 13,134 |
| Common Equity | 35,942 | 25,876 | 22,200 | 27,295 | 28,555 | 29,593 | 29,911 | 28,530 | 25,832 | 23,478 |
| Total Capital | 63,916 | 44,509 | 41,554 | 45,073 | 39,566 | 44,135 | 45,484 | 45,977 | 41,676 | 41,643 |
| Capital Expenditures | 1,661 | 1,330 | 1,367 | 1,241 | 1,169 | 1,171 | 1,006 | 1,085 | 1,184 | 1,101 |
| Cash Flow | 3,919 | 3,952 | 2,835 | 3,476 | 3,958 | 3,783 | 3,548 | 4,289 | 4,110 | 3,524 |
| Current Ratio | 1.0 | 1.1 | 1.0 | 0.6 | 0.8 | 0.9 | 1.1 | 1.0 | 1.0 | 0.8 |
| % Long Term Debt of Capitalization | 42.0 | 40.5 | 44.7 | 28.6 | 17.9 | 19.2 | 21.4 | 25.2 | 25.0 | 31.5 |
| % Net Income of Revenue | 5.1 | 7.5 | 4.4 | 7.0 | 8.9 | 8.5 | 8.3 | 11.2 | 11.4 | 5.6 |
| % Return on Assets | 3.1 | 4.7 | 2.8 | 4.2 | 5.4 | 4.9 | 4.5 | 6.0 | 6.0 | 3.5 |
| % Return on Equity | 8.1 | 12.6 | 7.5 | 9.3 | 10.5 | 9.8 | 9.1 | 12.8 | 13.8 | 10.0 |

Data as orig reptd.; bef. results of disc opers/spec. items. Per share data adj. for stk. divs.; EPS diluted. E-Estimated. NA-Not Available. NM-Not Meaningful. NR-Not Ranked. UR-Under Review.

**Office:** Three Lakes Drive, Northfield, IL 60093-2753.
**Telephone:** 847-646-2000.
**Website:** http://www.kraft.com
**Chrmn & CEO:** I. Rosenfeld

**COO & CFO:** D.A. Brearton
**EVP & General Counsel:** M.S. Firestone
**SVP & Treas:** B. Brasier
**SVP & Cntlr:** K.H. Jones

**Board Members:** A. Banga, M. M. Hart, P. B. Henry, L. D. Juliber, M. D. Ketchum, R. A. Lerner, M. J. McDonald, J. C. Pope, F. G. Reynolds, I. Rosenfeld, J. van Boxmeer

**Founded:** 2000
**Domicile:** Virginia
**Employees:** 127,000

The McGraw-Hill Companies

# Kroger Co. (The)

**STANDARD &POOR'S**

| S&P Recommendation | HOLD ★★★★★ | Price $22.16 (as of Nov 25, 2011) | 12-Mo. Target Price $23.00 | Investment Style Large-Cap Blend |

**GICS Sector** Consumer Staples
**Sub-Industry** Food Retail

**Summary** This supermarket operator, with about 2,500 stores in 31 states, also operates convenience stores, jewelry stores, supermarket fuel centers, and food processing plants.

## Key Stock Statistics (Source S&P, Vickers, company reports)

| | | | | | | | | |
|---|---|---|---|---|---|---|---|---|
| 52-Wk Range | $25.85– 20.53 | S&P Oper. EPS 2012**E** | 1.89 | Market Capitalization(B) | $13.233 | Beta | 0.42 |
| Trailing 12-Month EPS | $1.92 | S&P Oper. EPS 2013**E** | 2.03 | Yield (%) | 2.08 | S&P 3-Yr. Proj. EPS CAGR(%) | 10 |
| Trailing 12-Month P/E | 11.5 | P/E on S&P Oper. EPS 2012**E** | 11.7 | Dividend Rate/Share | $0.46 | S&P Credit Rating | BBB |
| $10K Invested 5 Yrs Ago | $10,985 | Common Shares Outstg. (M) | 597.1 | Institutional Ownership (%) | 81 | | |

## Price Performance

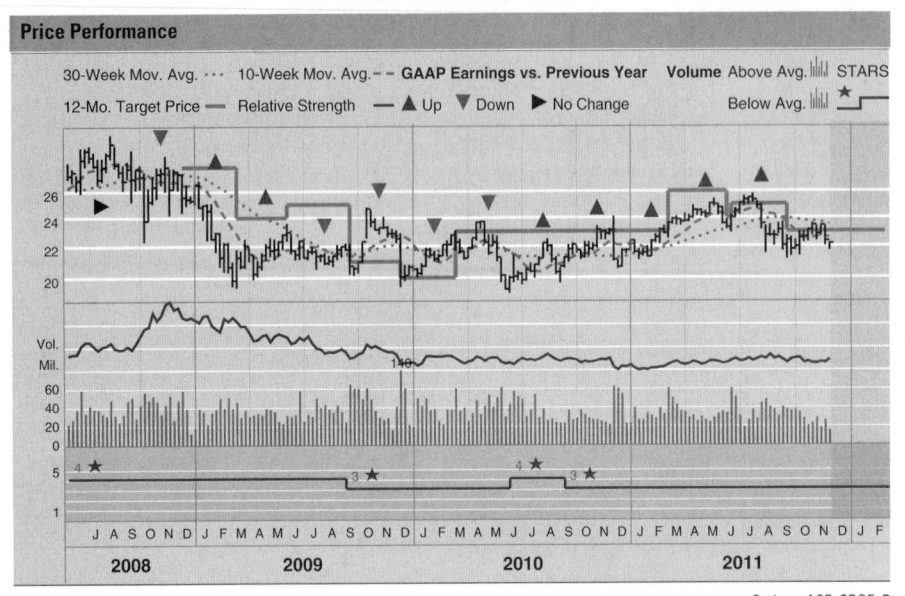

30-Week Mov. Avg. ···· 10-Week Mov. Avg. ─ ─ GAAP Earnings vs. Previous Year   Volume Above Avg. STARS
12-Mo. Target Price ── Relative Strength   ▲ Up ▼ Down ► No Change   Below Avg.

Options: ASE, CBOE, P

Analysis prepared by Equity Analyst **Joseph Agnese** on Sep 14, 2011, when the stock traded at **$21.98**.

## Highlights

➤ We see sales of $91.2 billion in FY 12 (Jan.), up 11% from $82.2 billion in FY 11, reflecting 1.0% square footage growth, 5.0% identical-store sales gains (excluding fuel), and much higher gas sales. While we continue to see the company remaining competitive on pricing, we expect price increases to accelerate through the year due to rising food cost inflation.

➤ We believe EBITDA margins will narrow in FY 12 as accelerating gross margin pressure from rising food prices offsets efforts to reduce costs. We see margin pressure from a change in product mix as consumers trade down to lower priced goods and reduce discretionary purchases as food inflation accelerates toward the mid-single digits by year end. We see margin benefits from a more stable promotional spending environment, increased sales of wider margin private label goods and cost-saving opportunities in areas such as administration, labor, shrinkage, and transportation.

➤ After benefits from fewer shares outstanding due to an active repurchase program, we expect FY 12 EPS to increase 6.8% to $1.89, from operating EPS of $1.77 in FY 11, excluding $0.02 of goodwill amortization charges.

## Investment Rationale/Risk

➤ We believe the company is better positioned than many peers to benefit from market share gains achieved during the recent recessionary economic environment. We think a low-price strategy will help the company compete as consumers look to get the most value for their dollars in a rising food cost environment. Additionally, we see the company willing and able to pass along commodity cost increases to consumers in the form of higher product prices.

➤ Risks to our recommendation and target price include greater than expected margin pressures from rising food cost inflation and potential weakness in the economy that would cause consumers to become more price conscious.

➤ Our 12-month target price of $23 is based on our P/E analysis and is supported by our EV/EBITDA valuation. Reflecting risks we see from an accelerating food price environment, we think the shares should trade at about 11.2X our FY 13 EPS estimate of $2.03, at a 10% discount to the P/E multiple of the S&P 500, leading to a projected value of $23. This valuation is supported by a 5.2X EV/EBITDA multiple, in line with KR's closest peers' average, applied to our FY 13 EBITDA estimate of $3.8 billion.

## Qualitative Risk Assessment

| LOW | MEDIUM | HIGH |

Our risk assessment reflects our view of the company's diversification through multiple format offerings, strong market share positions, and potential opportunities from industry consolidation.

## Quantitative Evaluations

**S&P Quality Ranking** B

| D | C | B- | **B** | B+ | A- | A | A+ |

**Relative Strength Rank** MODERATE

66

LOWEST = 1     HIGHEST = 99

## Revenue/Earnings Data

**Revenue (Million $)**

| | 1Q | 2Q | 3Q | 4Q | Year |
|---|---|---|---|---|---|
| 2012 | 24,761 | 20,913 | -- | -- | -- |
| 2011 | 24,779 | 18,788 | 18,694 | 19,928 | 82,189 |
| 2010 | 22,789 | 17,728 | 17,662 | 18,554 | 76,733 |
| 2009 | 23,107 | 18,053 | 17,580 | 17,260 | 76,000 |
| 2008 | 20,726 | 16,139 | 16,135 | 17,235 | 70,235 |
| 2007 | 19,415 | 15,138 | 14,999 | 16,859 | 66,111 |

**Earnings Per Share ($)**

| | | | | | |
|---|---|---|---|---|---|
| 2012 | 0.70 | 0.46 | E0.27 | E0.44 | E1.89 |
| 2011 | 0.58 | 0.41 | 0.32 | 0.44 | 1.74 |
| 2010 | 0.66 | 0.39 | -1.35 | 0.39 | 0.11 |
| 2009 | 0.58 | 0.42 | 0.36 | 0.53 | 1.90 |
| 2008 | 0.47 | 0.42 | 0.37 | 0.48 | 1.69 |
| 2007 | 0.42 | 0.29 | 0.30 | 0.54 | 1.54 |

Fiscal year ended Jan. 31. Next earnings report expected: NA. EPS Estimates based on S&P Operating Earnings; historical GAAP earnings are as reported.

## Dividend Data (Dates: mm/dd Payment Date: mm/dd/yy)

| Amount ($) | Date Decl. | Ex-Div. Date | Stk. of Record | Payment Date |
|---|---|---|---|---|
| 0.105 | 01/21 | 02/11 | 02/15 | 03/01/11 |
| 0.105 | 03/10 | 05/12 | 05/16 | 06/01/11 |
| 0.105 | 06/23 | 08/11 | 08/15 | 09/01/11 |
| 0.115 | 09/15 | 11/10 | 11/15 | 12/01/11 |

Dividends have been paid since 2006. Source: Company reports.

---

**Please read the Required Disclosures and Analyst Certification on the last page of this report.**

**The McGraw-Hill Companies**

# Kroger Co. (The)

**STANDARD &POOR'S**

## Business Summary September 14, 2011

CORPORATE OVERVIEW. Kroger is one of the largest U.S. supermarket chains, with 2,458 supermarkets as of March 2011. The company's principal operating format is combination food and drug stores (combo stores). In addition to combo stores, KR also operates multi-department stores, marketplace stores, price-impact warehouses, convenience stores, fuel centers, jewelry stores, and food processing plants. Total food store square footage was approximately 149 million as of January 29, 2011.

Retail food stores are operated under three formats: combo stores, multi-department stores, and price-impact warehouse stores. Combo stores are considered neighborhood stores, and include many specialty departments, such as whole health sections, pharmacies, general merchandise, pet centers, and perishables, such as fresh seafood and organic produce. Combo banners include Kroger, Ralphs, King Soopers, City Market, Dillons, Smith's, Fry's, QFC, Hilander, Owen's, Jay C, Baker's, Pay Less and Gerbes.

Multi-department stores offer one-stop shopping, are significantly larger in size than combo stores, and sell a wider selection of general merchandise items, including apparel, home fashion and furnishings, electronics, automotive, toys, and fine jewelry. Multi-department formats include Fred Meyer, Fry's Marketplace, Smith's Marketplace and Kroger Marketplace. Many combination and multi-department stores include a fuel center.

Price-impact warehouse stores offer everyday low prices, plus promotions for a wide selection of grocery and health and beauty care items. Price-impact warehouse stores include Food 4 Less and Foods Co.

## Company Financials Fiscal Year Ended Jan. 31

| Per Share Data ($) | 2011 | 2010 | 2009 | 2008 | 2007 | 2006 | 2005 | 2004 | 2003 | 2002 |
|---|---|---|---|---|---|---|---|---|---|---|
| Tangible Book Value | 6.70 | 5.72 | 4.48 | 7.07 | 5.61 | 3.04 | 1.85 | 1.18 | 0.36 | NM |
| Cash Flow | 4.28 | 2.45 | 4.08 | 3.64 | 3.30 | 3.04 | 1.57 | 2.02 | 2.93 | 2.44 |
| Earnings | 1.74 | 0.11 | 1.90 | 1.69 | 1.54 | 1.31 | -0.14 | 0.42 | 1.56 | 1.26 |
| S&P Core Earnings | 1.77 | 1.67 | 1.74 | 1.70 | 1.59 | 1.27 | 0.99 | 0.98 | 1.40 | 1.12 |
| Dividends | NA | 0.37 | 0.35 | 0.20 | Nil | Nil | Nil | Nil | Nil | Nil |
| Payout Ratio | NA | NM | 18% | 12% | Nil | Nil | Nil | Nil | Nil | Nil |
| Calendar Year | 2010 | 2009 | 2008 | 2007 | 2006 | 2005 | 2004 | 2003 | 2002 | 2001 |
| Prices:High | 24.14 | 26.94 | 30.99 | 31.94 | 24.48 | 20.88 | 19.67 | 19.70 | 23.81 | 27.66 |
| Prices:Low | 19.08 | 19.39 | 22.30 | 22.94 | 18.05 | 15.15 | 14.65 | 12.05 | 11.00 | 19.60 |
| P/E Ratio:High | 14 | NM | 16 | 19 | 16 | 16 | NM | 47 | 15 | 22 |
| P/E Ratio:Low | 11 | NM | 12 | 14 | 12 | 12 | NM | 29 | 7 | 16 |

| Income Statement Analysis (Million $) | | | | | | | | | | |
|---|---|---|---|---|---|---|---|---|---|---|
| Revenue | 82,189 | 76,733 | 76,000 | 70,235 | 66,111 | 60,553 | 56,434 | 53,791 | 51,760 | 50,098 |
| Operating Income | 3,800 | 3,777 | 3,918 | 3,657 | 3,508 | 3,300 | 3,003 | 3,147 | 3,676 | 3,567 |
| Depreciation | 1,600 | 1,525 | 1,442 | 1,356 | 1,272 | 1,265 | 1,256 | 1,209 | 1,087 | 973 |
| Interest Expense | 448 | 502 | 485 | 474 | 488 | 510 | 557 | 604 | 600 | 648 |
| Pretax Income | 1,734 | 589 | 1,966 | 1,827 | 1,748 | 1,525 | 290 | 770 | 1,973 | 1,711 |
| Effective Tax Rate | NA | 90.4% | 36.5% | 35.4% | 36.2% | 37.2% | NM | 59.1% | 37.5% | 39.0% |
| Net Income | 1,133 | 70.0 | 1,249 | 1,181 | 1,115 | 958 | -100 | 315 | 1,233 | 1,043 |
| S&P Core Earnings | 1,131 | 1,093 | 1,140 | 1,193 | 1,155 | 928 | 720 | 745 | 1,105 | 914 |

| Balance Sheet & Other Financial Data (Million $) | | | | | | | | | | |
|---|---|---|---|---|---|---|---|---|---|---|
| Cash | 825 | 424 | 263 | 918 | 803 | 210 | 144 | 159 | 171 | 161 |
| Current Assets | 7,621 | 7,450 | 7,206 | 7,114 | 6,755 | 6,466 | 6,406 | 5,619 | 5,566 | 5,512 |
| Total Assets | 23,505 | 23,093 | 23,211 | 22,299 | 21,215 | 20,482 | 20,491 | 20,184 | 20,102 | 19,087 |
| Current Liabilities | 8,036 | 7,714 | 7,629 | 8,689 | 7,581 | 6,715 | 6,316 | 5,586 | 5,608 | 5,485 |
| Long Term Debt | 7,338 | 7,477 | 7,505 | 6,529 | 6,154 | 6,678 | 7,900 | 8,116 | 8,222 | 8,412 |
| Common Equity | 5,298 | 4,906 | 5,176 | 4,914 | 4,923 | 4,390 | 3,540 | 4,011 | 3,850 | 3,502 |
| Total Capital | 13,189 | 12,963 | 12,913 | 11,810 | 11,799 | 11,911 | 12,379 | 13,117 | 12,072 | 11,914 |
| Capital Expenditures | 1,919 | 2,297 | 2,149 | 2,126 | 1,683 | 1,306 | 1,634 | 2,000 | 1,891 | 2,139 |
| Cash Flow | 2,733 | 1,595 | 2,691 | 2,537 | 2,387 | 2,223 | 1,156 | 1,524 | 2,320 | 2,016 |
| Current Ratio | 1.0 | 1.0 | 1.0 | 0.8 | 0.9 | 1.0 | 1.0 | 1.0 | 1.0 | 1.0 |
| % Long Term Debt of Capitalization | 55.6 | 57.7 | 58.1 | 55.3 | 55.6 | 56.1 | 63.8 | 61.9 | 68.1 | 70.6 |
| % Net Income of Revenue | 1.4 | 0.1 | 1.6 | 1.7 | 1.7 | 1.6 | NM | 0.6 | 2.4 | 2.1 |
| % Return on Assets | 4.9 | 0.3 | 5.5 | 5.4 | 5.4 | 4.7 | NM | 1.6 | 6.3 | 5.6 |
| % Return on Equity | 22.4 | 1.4 | 24.8 | 24.0 | 24.0 | 23.9 | NM | 8.0 | 33.5 | 31.6 |

Data as orig reptd.; bef. results of disc opers/spec. items. Per share data adj. for stk. divs.; EPS diluted. E-Estimated. NA-Not Available. NM-Not Meaningful. NR-Not Ranked. UR-Under Review.

**Office:** 1014 Vine Street, Cincinnati, OH 45202-1100.
**Telephone:** 513-762-4000.
**Email:** investors@kroger.com
**Website:** http://www.kroger.com

**Chrmn & CEO:** D.B. Dillon
**Pres & COO:** W.R. McMullen
**SVP & CIO:** C. Hjelm
**CFO:** J.M. Schlotman

**Chief Acctg Officer & Cntlr:** M.E. Van Oflen
**Investor Contact:** C. Fike (513-762-4969)
**Auditor:** PRICEWATERHOUSECOOPERS
**Board Members:** R. V. Anderson, R. D. Beyer, D. B. Dillon, S. J. Kropf, J. T. Lamacchia, D. B. Lewis, W. R. McMullen, J. P. Montoya, C. R. Moore, S. M. Phillips, S. Rogel, J. A. Runde, R. L. Sargent, B. S. Shackouls

**Founded:** 1883
**Domicile:** Ohio
**Employees:** 338,000

# Laboratory Corporation of America Holdings

**STANDARD &POOR'S**

| S&P Recommendation **BUY** ★★★★☆ | Price $80.70 (as of Nov 25, 2011) | 12-Mo. Target Price $110.00 | Investment Style Large-Cap Growth |
|---|---|---|---|

**GICS Sector** Health Care
**Sub-Industry** Health Care Services

**Summary** This clinical laboratory organization offers a broad range of clinical tests through a national network of laboratories.

## Key Stock Statistics (Source S&P, Vickers, company reports)

| | | | | | | | |
|---|---|---|---|---|---|---|---|
| 52-Wk Range | $100.94– 74.57 | S&P Oper. EPS 2011**E** | 6.30 | Market Capitalization(B) | $7.997 | Beta | 0.55 |
| Trailing 12-Month EPS | $5.00 | S&P Oper. EPS 2012**E** | 7.14 | Yield (%) | Nil | S&P 3-Yr. Proj. EPS CAGR(%) | 13 |
| Trailing 12-Month P/E | 16.1 | P/E on S&P Oper. EPS 2011**E** | 12.8 | Dividend Rate/Share | Nil | S&P Credit Rating | BBB+ |
| $10K Invested 5 Yrs Ago | $11,662 | Common Shares Outstg. (M) | 99.1 | Institutional Ownership (%) | 99 | | |

## Price Performance

30-Week Mov. Avg. · · · 10-Week Mov. Avg. – – GAAP Earnings vs. Previous Year   Volume Above Avg. STARS
12-Mo. Target Price — Relative Strength   ▲ Up  ▼ Down  ► No Change   Below Avg.

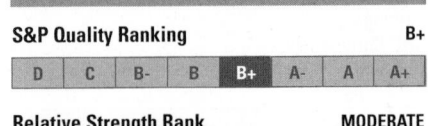

Options: ASE, CBOE, P, Ph

Analysis prepared by Equity Analyst **Jeffrey Loo, CFA** on Nov 14, 2011, when the stock traded at **$84.04**.

### Highlights

➤ We expect 2011 and 2012 sales, including recently acquired Genzyme Genetics, to rise 11.1% and 4.9%, to $5.56 billion and $5.83 billion, respectively on solid growth in esoteric testing. Although we see some client attrition from the Genzyme deal, LH reported limited client attrition as of October 2011. We expect esoteric testing to account for about 41% of sales, which should increase revenue per requisition. We see 2011 gross margins improving 10 basis points (bps), following a 40 bps decline in 2010, but we look for operating margins to decline 140 bps due to increased operating expenses related to Genzyme and Westcliff Labs.

➤ LH remains acquisitive, having recently announced deals that diversify its operations. In April, LH agreed to acquire Orchid Cellmark (ORCH 2.79, NR), for $2.80 a share, or $85.4 million, subject to approvals. Orchid provides DNA testing services for forensics. In June, LH acquired Clearstone Central Laboratories, a global provider of central laboratory services for late-stage clinical trials.

➤ We estimate 2011 and 2012 operating EPS, excluding amortization of intangible assets, of $6.30 and $7.14.

### Investment Rationale/Risk

➤ We view the shares, recently trading below historical levels at 12X our forward 12-month EPS forecast, as undervalued. We believe LH, through internal growth and recent acquisitions, will grow faster than the industry over the next several years. We also think the economic environment is stabilizing, but the anticipated rebound in physician office visits in 2011 has been slower than we expected following the estimated 5%-7% decline in 2010. In our view, LH should also be able to maintain industry-leading margins by cutting costs and through leverage, despite higher expenses associated with the Genzyme Genetics and Westcliff Medical Labs acquisitions. We are also encouraged by LH's efforts to diversify beyond its core clinical lab operations.

➤ Risks to our recommendation and target price include increased competition from potential physician in-sourcing of certain tests, and a significant slowdown in doctor visits.

➤ Our 12-month target price of $110 is based on a P/E-to-growth (PEG) ratio of about 1.2X, in line with peers, applied to our forward 12-month EPS estimate and a three-year EPS growth rate of 13%.

## Qualitative Risk Assessment

| LOW | MEDIUM | HIGH |
|---|---|---|

Our risk assessment reflects LH's leadership position in a large, mature industry, its broad geographic service area with clients in all 50 states, and our view of its diverse and balanced payor mix.

## Quantitative Evaluations

**S&P Quality Ranking**  B+

| D | C | B- | B | B+ | A- | A | A+ |
|---|---|---|---|---|---|---|---|

**Relative Strength Rank**  MODERATE

67

LOWEST = 1     HIGHEST = 99

## Revenue/Earnings Data

### Revenue (Million $)

| | 1Q | 2Q | 3Q | 4Q | Year |
|---|---|---|---|---|---|
| 2011 | 1,368 | 1,403 | 1,405 | -- | -- |
| 2010 | 1,194 | 1,238 | 1,277 | 1,295 | 5,004 |
| 2009 | 1,156 | 1,189 | 1,185 | 1,165 | 4,695 |
| 2008 | 1,103 | 1,148 | 1,135 | 1,119 | 4,505 |
| 2007 | 998.7 | 1,043 | 1,021 | 1,006 | 4,068 |
| 2006 | 878.6 | 903.7 | 909.9 | 898.6 | 3,591 |

### Earnings Per Share ($)

| | 1Q | 2Q | 3Q | 4Q | Year |
|---|---|---|---|---|---|
| 2011 | 1.23 | 1.20 | 1.31 | E1.53 | E6.30 |
| 2010 | 1.25 | 1.46 | 1.34 | 1.26 | 5.29 |
| 2009 | 1.22 | 1.24 | 1.21 | 1.33 | 4.98 |
| 2008 | 1.14 | 0.92 | 1.00 | 1.08 | 4.16 |
| 2007 | 0.98 | 1.05 | 0.92 | 0.98 | 3.93 |
| 2006 | 0.76 | 0.87 | 0.81 | 0.81 | 3.24 |

Fiscal year ended Dec. 31. Next earnings report expected: Mid February. EPS Estimates based on S&P Operating Earnings; historical GAAP earnings are as reported.

## Dividend Data

No cash dividends have been paid.

---

**Please read the Required Disclosures and Analyst Certification on the last page of this report.**

**The McGraw·Hill Companies**

# Laboratory Corporation of America Holdings

STANDARD
&POOR'S

## Business Summary November 14, 2011

CORPORATE OVERVIEW. Laboratory Corporation of America Holdings is the second largest independent U.S. clinical laboratory. Clinical laboratory tests are used by medical professionals in routine testing, patient diagnosis, and in the monitoring and treatment of disease. As of December 2010, LH had 51 primary testing facilities and more than 1,700 service sites consisting of branches, patient service centers, and STAT laboratories that have the ability to perform certain routine tests quickly and report results to the physician immediately. The company's laboratory services involve the testing of both bodily fluids and human tissues. LH offers more than 4,400 different tests, consisting of routine tests and specialty and niche testing (esoteric). The most frequently administered routine tests include blood chemistry analyses, urinalysis, blood cell counts, pap tests, HIV tests, microbiology cultures and procedures, and alcohol and other substance abuse tests. The company's esoteric tests include testing for infectious diseases, allergies, diagnostic genetics, identity, and oncology. An average of 440,000 specimens were being processed daily as of December 2010, with routine testing results generally available within 24 hours.

The company provides testing services to a broad range of health care providers, including independent physicians, hospitals, HMOs and other managed care groups, and governmental and other institutions. During 2010, no client accounted for over 9% of net sales. Most testing services are billed to a party other than the physician or other authorized person who ordered the test. Payors other than the direct patient include insurance companies, managed care organizations, Medicare and Medicaid. Client-billed accounted for 31.1% of revenue in 2010 (27% in 2009), and generated an average of $37.68 ($34.69 in 2009) in revenue per requisition; patients-billed 1.9% (8% in 2009) and $166.92 ($161.76 in 2009); managed care clients 48.9% (45% in 2009) and $39.06 ($37.23 in 2009); and Medicare and Medicaid 18.1% (20% in 2009) and $48.46 ($45.63 in 2008). In December 2010, LH acquired Genzyme Genetics, a unit of Genzyme Corporation, for $925 million. In August 2009, LH acquired Monogram Biosciences, a provider of molecular diagnostic tests. In February 2008, LH acquired NWT, Inc., a provider of drug of abuse testing. In July 2007, LH acquired DSI Labs, expanding its operations in southwest Florida. In May 2005, the company acquired Esoterix, Inc., a provider of specialty reference testing. In February 2005, LH bought US Labs, located in Irvine, CA. In March 2004, LH purchased laboratory operations in Poughkeepsie, NY, and Atlanta, GA, from MDS Diagnostic Services.

## Company Financials Fiscal Year Ended Dec. 31

| Per Share Data ($) | 2010 | 2009 | 2008 | 2007 | 2006 | 2005 | 2004 | 2003 | 2002 | 2001 |
|---|---|---|---|---|---|---|---|---|---|---|
| Tangible Book Value | NM | NM | NM | NM | NM | NM | 1.04 | 0.27 | 2.67 | 0.83 |
| Cash Flow | 6.11 | 6.45 | 5.75 | 5.26 | 4.80 | 4.24 | 3.33 | 3.18 | 2.47 | 2.03 |
| Earnings | 5.29 | 4.98 | 4.16 | 3.93 | 3.24 | 2.71 | 2.45 | 2.22 | 1.77 | 1.29 |
| S&P Core Earnings | 5.29 | 5.00 | 4.04 | 3.89 | 3.21 | 2.53 | 2.25 | 2.04 | 1.56 | 1.15 |
| Dividends | Nil | Nil | Nil | Nil | Nil | Nil | Nil | Nil | Nil | Nil |
| Payout Ratio | Nil | Nil | Nil | Nil | Nil | Nil | Nil | Nil | Nil | Nil |
| Prices:High | 89.48 | 76.74 | 80.77 | 82.32 | 74.30 | 55.00 | 50.03 | 37.72 | 52.38 | 45.68 |
| Prices:Low | 69.49 | 53.25 | 52.93 | 65.13 | 52.58 | 44.63 | 36.70 | 22.21 | 18.51 | 24.88 |
| P/E Ratio:High | 17 | 15 | 19 | 21 | 23 | 20 | 20 | 17 | 30 | 35 |
| P/E Ratio:Low | 13 | 11 | 13 | 17 | 16 | 16 | 15 | 10 | 10 | 19 |

| Income Statement Analysis (Million $) | | | | | | | | | | |
|---|---|---|---|---|---|---|---|---|---|---|
| Revenue | 5,004 | 4,695 | 4,505 | 4,068 | 3,591 | 3,328 | 3,085 | 2,939 | 2,508 | 2,200 |
| Operating Income | 1,078 | 1,118 | 1,070 | 989 | 853 | 785 | 736 | 671 | 554 | 472 |
| Depreciation | 72.7 | 62.6 | 178 | 161 | 155 | 150 | 139 | 136 | 102 | 104 |
| Interest Expense | 70.0 | 62.9 | 72.0 | 56.6 | 47.8 | 34.4 | 36.1 | 40.9 | 19.2 | 27.0 |
| Pretax Income | 916 | 885 | 786 | 802 | 721 | 641 | 615 | 540 | 432 | 332 |
| Effective Tax Rate | NA | 37.2% | 39.2% | 40.6% | 40.1% | 39.7% | 41.0% | 40.6% | 41.1% | 45.0% |
| Net Income | 572 | 543 | 465 | 477 | 432 | 386 | 363 | 321 | 255 | 183 |
| S&P Core Earnings | 559 | 546 | 451 | 472 | 428 | 368 | 339 | 295 | 226 | 162 |

| Balance Sheet & Other Financial Data (Million $) | | | | | | | | | | |
|---|---|---|---|---|---|---|---|---|---|---|
| Cash | 231 | 149 | 220 | 166 | 51.5 | 45.4 | 187 | 123 | 56.4 | 149 |
| Current Assets | 886 | 936 | 1,033 | 938 | 887 | 702 | 740 | 658 | 597 | 624 |
| Total Assets | 6,188 | 4,860 | 4,670 | 4,368 | 4,001 | 3,876 | 3,601 | 3,415 | 2,612 | 1,930 |
| Current Liabilities | 1,121 | 1,018 | 547 | 968 | 931 | 888 | 301 | 758 | 229 | 201 |
| Long Term Debt | 2,188 | 1,394 | 1,601 | 1,078 | 603 | 604 | 892 | 361 | 522 | 509 |
| Common Equity | 2,466 | 2,106 | 1,688 | 1,725 | 1,977 | 1,886 | 1,999 | 1,896 | 1,612 | 1,085 |
| Total Capital | 4,991 | 3,642 | 3,460 | 3,310 | 2,989 | 2,899 | 3,213 | 2,530 | 2,133 | 1,594 |
| Capital Expenditures | 126 | 115 | 157 | 143 | 116 | 93.6 | 95.0 | 83.6 | 74.3 | 88.1 |
| Cash Flow | 644 | 704 | 642 | 638 | 587 | 536 | 502 | 457 | 356 | 287 |
| Current Ratio | 1.0 | 0.9 | 1.9 | 1.0 | 1.0 | 0.8 | 2.5 | 0.9 | 2.6 | 3.1 |
| % Long Term Debt of Capitalization | 43.8 | 38.3 | 46.2 | 32.6 | 20.2 | 20.9 | 27.8 | 14.3 | 24.4 | 31.9 |
| % Net Income of Revenue | 11.4 | 11.6 | 10.3 | 11.7 | 12.0 | 11.6 | 11.8 | 10.9 | 10.2 | 8.3 |
| % Return on Assets | 10.4 | 11.4 | 10.3 | 11.4 | 11.0 | 10.3 | 10.3 | 10.7 | 11.2 | 10.2 |
| % Return on Equity | 25.0 | 28.6 | 27.2 | 25.8 | 22.3 | 19.9 | 18.6 | 18.3 | 18.9 | 18.6 |

Data as orig reptd.; bef. results of disc opers/spec. items. Per share data adj. for stk. divs.; EPS diluted. E-Estimated. NA-Not Available. NM-Not Meaningful. NR-Not Ranked. UR-Under Review.

**Office:** 358 South Main Street, Burlington, NC 27215.
**Telephone:** 336-229-1127.
**Website:** http://www.labcorp.com
**Chrmn, Pres & CEO:** D.P. King

**COO:** J.T. Boyle, Jr.
**EVP, CFO, Chief Acctg Officer & Treas:** W.B. Hayes
**EVP & CSO:** A. Conrad
**SVP, Secy & General Counsel:** F.S. Eberts, III

**Investor Contact:** S. Fleming (336-436-4879)
**Board Members:** K. B. Anderson, J. Belingard, N. A. Coles, D. P. King, W. E. Lane, T. P. Mac Mahon, R. E. Mittelstaedt, Jr., A. H. Rubenstein, M. K. Weikel, R. S. Williams

**Founded:** 1971
**Domicile:** Delaware
**Employees:** 31,000

The **McGraw·Hill** Companies

# Estee Lauder Companies Inc. (The)

**STANDARD &POOR'S**

| S&P Recommendation | HOLD ★★★☆☆ | Price | 12-Mo. Target Price | Investment Style |
|---|---|---|---|---|
| | | $107.23 (as of Nov 25, 2011) | $121.00 | Large-Cap Growth |

**GICS Sector** Consumer Staples
**Sub-Industry** Personal Products

**Summary** This company is one of the world's leading manufacturers and marketers of skin care, makeup and fragrance products.

## Key Stock Statistics (Source S&P, Vickers, company reports)

| | | | | | | | |
|---|---|---|---|---|---|---|---|
| 52-Wk Range | $120.73–74.00 | S&P Oper. EPS 2012**E** | 4.50 | Market Capitalization(B) | $12.503 | Beta | 1.29 |
| Trailing 12-Month EPS | $3.93 | S&P Oper. EPS 2013**E** | 5.00 | Yield (%) | 0.98 | S&P 3-Yr. Proj. EPS CAGR(%) | 15 |
| Trailing 12-Month P/E | 27.3 | P/E on S&P Oper. EPS 2012**E** | 23.8 | Dividend Rate/Share | $1.05 | S&P Credit Rating | A |
| $10K Invested 5 Yrs Ago | $27,642 | Common Shares Outstg. (M) | 192.6 | Institutional Ownership (%) | 95 | | |

## Price Performance

30-Week Mov. Avg. ···· 10-Week Mov. Avg. --- GAAP Earnings vs. Previous Year   Volume Above Avg. ▮▮▮ STARS
12-Mo. Target Price — Relative Strength — ▲ Up ▼ Down ► No Change   Below Avg. ▮▮▮ ★

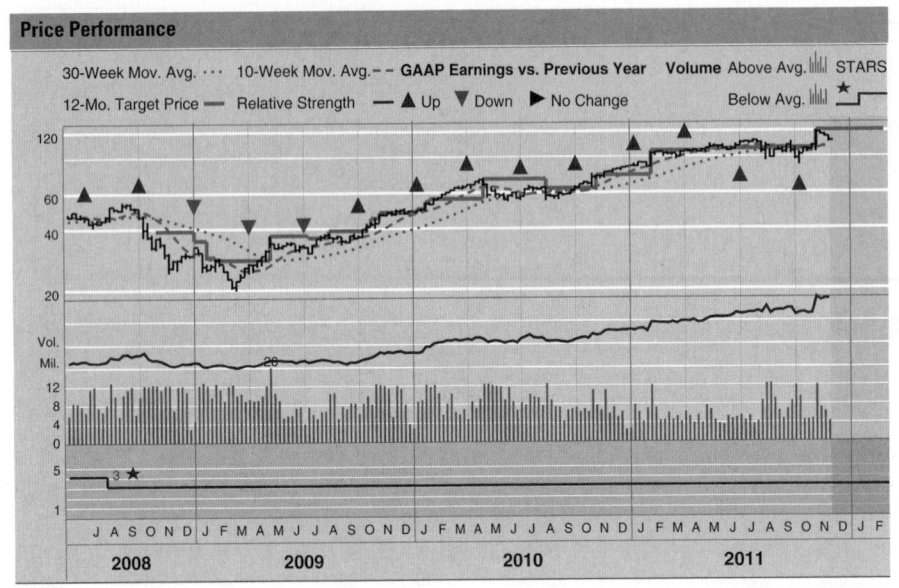

Options: ASE, CBOE, Ph

Analysis prepared by Equity Analyst **Esther Kwon, CFA** on Nov 07, 2011, when the stock traded at **$117.68**.

### Highlights

➤ In February 2009, EL outlined a four-year strategy that builds on its strengths as a brand builder and innovator and more sharply focuses on its execution capabilities and lowering its cost bases. Elements of the plan include expanding market share; increasing non-U.S. sales; improving operating margins; cutting costs; and writing off restructuring and other one-time costs.

➤ We look for sales to rise about 10% in FY 12 (Jun.). We are cautious as the year progresses about consumer spending, increased competition, and more difficult foreign exchange translation comparisons. We look for the highest growth in the Asia Pacific region and skin care category. Sales grew 13% in FY 11. We also see a continued recovery in the segmental operating margin, despite an increase in marketing and advertising expense and investment spending. We forecast that most of the margin improvement will come from restructuring and right-sizing efforts and a sales mix shift (e.g., toward skin care).

➤ For FY 12, we forecast EPS of $4.50. Excluding restructuring and return charges, FY 11 EPS was $3.69, versus FY 10's $2.76.

### Investment Rationale/Risk

➤ We think EL has been executing well on its four-year strategy, and we think its brands' prestige positioning will serve it well in international markets as well as in the U.S., where spending by higher income consumers appears to be rebounding strongly. Our hold recommendation reflects our view that EL's long-term growth prospects are appropriately reflected in the stock, which we calculate is trading at a premium to peers and its historical average. Also, EL has historically exhibited much more quarterly earnings volatility than many of the companies in our universe.

➤ Risks to our recommendation and target price include a prolonged decline in the economies of EL's major country markets, slow consumer acceptance of new products, and unfavorable foreign exchange translation. We also have concerns about corporate governance practices given the majority voting power of insiders.

➤ Over the past 10 years, EL's average trailing P/E was 22.7X. Using a 10% premium to its average P/E and our calendar 2012 EPS estimate as a base, we value the shares at $121, which is our 12-month target price.

### Qualitative Risk Assessment

| LOW | MEDIUM | HIGH |
|---|---|---|

Our risk assessment reflects our view of EL's market share advantage, leading brands, scale leverage, and strong balance sheet. This is partly offset by its exposure to short-term factors such as changes in the retail industry, geopolitical events, and consumer spending.

### Quantitative Evaluations

**S&P Quality Ranking** A-

| D | C | B- | B | B+ | A- | A | A+ |
|---|---|---|---|---|---|---|---|

**Relative Strength Rank** STRONG

**91**

LOWEST = 1    HIGHEST = 99

### Revenue/Earnings Data

**Revenue (Million $)**

| | 1Q | 2Q | 3Q | 4Q | Year |
|---|---|---|---|---|---|
| 2012 | 2,477 | -- | -- | -- | -- |
| 2011 | 2,092 | 2,492 | 2,166 | 2,061 | 8,810 |
| 2010 | 1,833 | 2,262 | 1,860 | 1,840 | 7,796 |
| 2009 | 1,904 | 2,041 | 1,697 | 1,683 | 7,324 |
| 2008 | 1,710 | 2,309 | 1,880 | 2,012 | 7,911 |
| 2007 | 1,594 | 1,991 | 1,691 | 1,762 | 7,038 |

**Earnings Per Share ($)**

| | | | | | |
|---|---|---|---|---|---|
| 2012 | 1.40 | E2.00 | E0.82 | E0.31 | E4.50 |
| 2011 | 0.95 | 1.71 | 0.62 | 0.20 | 3.48 |
| 2010 | 0.71 | 1.28 | 0.28 | 0.12 | 2.38 |
| 2009 | 0.26 | 0.80 | 0.14 | -0.09 | 1.10 |
| 2008 | 0.20 | 1.14 | 0.46 | 0.61 | 2.40 |
| 2007 | 0.27 | 0.99 | 0.45 | 0.45 | 2.16 |

Fiscal year ended Jun. 30. Next earnings report expected: Early February. EPS Estimates based on S&P Operating Earnings; historical GAAP earnings are as reported.

### Dividend Data (Dates: mm/dd Payment Date: mm/dd/yy)

| Amount ($) | Date Decl. | Ex-Div. Date | Stk. of Record | Payment Date |
|---|---|---|---|---|
| 0.750 | 11/09 | 11/24 | 11/29 | 12/15/10 |
| 1.050 | 11/03 | 11/23 | 11/29 | 12/14/11 |
| 1.050 | 11/03 | 11/23 | 11/28 | 12/14/11 |
| 2-for-1 | 11/03 | 01/23 | 01/04 | 01/20/12 |

Dividends have been paid since 1996. Source: Company reports.

---

**Please read the Required Disclosures and Analyst Certification on the last page of this report.**

**The McGraw·Hill Companies**

# Estee Lauder Companies Inc. (The)

STANDARD &POOR'S

## Business Summary November 07, 2011

CORPORATE OVERVIEW. The Estee Lauder Companies was founded in 1946 by Estee and Joseph Lauder. EL has grown into one of the world's largest manufacturers and marketers of skin care, makeup and fragrance products, sold in more than 150 countries and territories worldwide. EL has historically been a dominant player in the high-end fragrance and cosmetic categories, with brand names such as Estee Lauder, Clinique, Aramis, Prescriptives, Origins, M.A.C, Bobbi Brown, La Mer, Aveda, Stila, Jo Malone, and Bumble and Bumble. EL is also the global licensee for fragrances and cosmetics sold under the Tommy Hilfiger, Donna Karan, Michael Kors, Sean Jean and Coach brands.

EL reports sales and operating income by three regions. The Americas accounted for 43% of sales and 22% of profits in FY 11 (Jun.); Europe, the Middle East and Africa (37% and 55%); and Asia/Pacific (20% and 23%).

The skin care division (42% of FY 11 net sales) addresses various skin care needs of women and men. Products include moisturizers, creams, lotions, cleansers, sun screens and self-tanning products. The makeup division (38%) manufactures, markets and sells a full array of makeup products, including lipsticks, mascaras, foundations, eye shadows, nail polishes and powders.

The fragrance division (14%) offers a variety of fragrance products, including eau de parfum sprays and colognes, as well as lotions, powders, creams and soaps that are based on a particular fragrance. The products of the hair care division (5%) are offered mainly in salons and in freestanding retail stores and include styling products, shampoos, conditioners and finishing sprays.

As is customary in the cosmetics industry, EL accepts returns of its products from retailers under certain conditions. In recognition of this practice and in according with generally accepted accounting principals, EL reports sales on a net basis, which is computed by deducting the amount of actual returns received and an amount established for anticipated returns from gross sales. As a percentage of gross sales, returns were 3.5% in FY 11, 4.3% in FY 10, and 4.4% in FY 09.

In FY 11, Macy's, Inc. accounted for 10% of EL's accounts receivable and 11% of consolidated net sales.

## Company Financials Fiscal Year Ended Jun. 30

| Per Share Data ($) | 2011 | 2010 | 2009 | 2008 | 2007 | 2006 | 2005 | 2004 | 2003 | 2002 |
|---|---|---|---|---|---|---|---|---|---|---|
| Tangible Book Value | 7.73 | 5.49 | 3.71 | 3.86 | 2.23 | 4.29 | 6.79 | 4.35 | 2.92 | 3.20 |
| Cash Flow | 4.96 | 3.70 | 2.39 | 3.66 | 3.16 | 2.41 | 2.64 | 2.45 | 2.01 | 1.46 |
| Earnings | 3.48 | 2.38 | 1.10 | 2.40 | 2.16 | 1.49 | 1.78 | 1.62 | 1.26 | 0.78 |
| S&P Core Earnings | 3.67 | 2.57 | 1.01 | 2.28 | 2.18 | 1.52 | 1.69 | 1.51 | 1.17 | 0.70 |
| Dividends | 0.75 | 0.55 | 0.55 | 0.55 | 0.50 | 0.40 | 0.40 | 0.30 | 0.20 | 0.20 |
| Payout Ratio | 22% | 23% | 50% | 23% | 23% | 27% | 22% | 19% | 16% | 26% |
| Prices:High | 120.73 | 81.44 | 50.57 | 54.75 | 52.31 | 43.60 | 47.50 | 49.34 | 40.20 | 38.80 |
| Prices:Low | 79.67 | 47.65 | 19.81 | 24.24 | 38.41 | 32.79 | 29.98 | 37.55 | 25.73 | 25.20 |
| P/E Ratio:High | 35 | 34 | 46 | 23 | 24 | 29 | 27 | 30 | 32 | 50 |
| P/E Ratio:Low | 23 | 20 | 18 | 10 | 18 | 22 | 17 | 23 | 20 | 32 |

| Income Statement Analysis (Million $) | 2011 | 2010 | 2009 | 2008 | 2007 | 2006 | 2005 | 2004 | 2003 | 2002 |
|---|---|---|---|---|---|---|---|---|---|---|
| Revenue | 8,810 | 7,796 | 7,324 | 7,911 | 7,038 | 6,464 | 6,336 | 5,790 | 5,118 | 4,744 |
| Operating Income | 1,466 | 1,170 | 812 | 1,059 | 958 | 910 | 917 | 836 | 712 | 614 |
| Depreciation | 294 | 264 | 254 | 248 | 207 | 198 | 197 | 192 | 175 | 162 |
| Interest Expense | 63.9 | 102 | 75.7 | 66.8 | 38.9 | 23.8 | 13.9 | 27.1 | 8.10 | 9.80 |
| Pretax Income | 1,026 | 688 | 343 | 744 | 711 | 596 | 707 | 617 | 474 | 332 |
| Effective Tax Rate | NA | NA | 33.8% | 34.9% | 35.9% | 43.6% | 41.2% | 37.7% | 33.9% | 34.5% |
| Net Income | 704 | 478 | 218 | 474 | 449 | 325 | 406 | 375 | 320 | 213 |
| S&P Core Earnings | 739 | 516 | 200 | 450 | 453 | 332 | 390 | 351 | 274 | 171 |

| Balance Sheet & Other Financial Data (Million $) | 2011 | 2010 | 2009 | 2008 | 2007 | 2006 | 2005 | 2004 | 2003 | 2002 |
|---|---|---|---|---|---|---|---|---|---|---|
| Cash | 1,253 | 1,121 | 864 | 402 | 254 | 369 | 553 | 612 | 364 | 547 |
| Current Assets | 3,687 | 3,121 | 2,913 | 2,787 | 2,239 | 2,177 | 2,303 | 2,199 | 1,845 | 1,928 |
| Total Assets | 6,274 | 5,336 | 5,177 | 5,011 | 4,126 | 3,784 | 3,886 | 3,708 | 3,350 | 3,417 |
| Current Liabilities | 1,943 | 1,572 | 1,459 | 1,699 | 1,501 | 1,438 | 1,498 | 1,322 | 1,054 | 960 |
| Long Term Debt | 1,080 | 1,205 | 1,388 | 1,078 | 1,028 | 432 | 451 | 462 | 284 | 404 |
| Common Equity | 2,647 | 1,965 | 1,640 | 1,653 | 1,199 | 1,622 | 1,693 | 1,733 | 1,424 | 1,462 |
| Total Capital | 3,865 | 3,170 | 3,052 | 2,758 | 2,248 | 2,079 | 2,160 | 2,211 | 2,080 | 2,226 |
| Capital Expenditures | 351 | 271 | 280 | 358 | 312 | 261 | 230 | 207 | 163 | 203 |
| Cash Flow | 998 | 742 | 472 | 722 | 656 | 523 | 603 | 567 | 471 | 351 |
| Current Ratio | 1.9 | 2.0 | 2.0 | 1.6 | 1.5 | 1.5 | 1.5 | 1.7 | 1.8 | 2.0 |
| % Long Term Debt of Capitalization | 27.9 | 38.0 | 45.5 | 39.1 | 45.7 | 20.8 | 20.9 | 20.9 | 13.6 | 18.1 |
| % Net Income of Revenue | 8.0 | 6.1 | 3.0 | 6.0 | 6.4 | 5.0 | 6.4 | 6.5 | 6.2 | 4.5 |
| % Return on Assets | 12.1 | 9.1 | 4.3 | 10.4 | 11.3 | 8.5 | 10.7 | 10.6 | 9.5 | 6.4 |
| % Return on Equity | 30.6 | 26.5 | 13.3 | 33.2 | 31.8 | 19.6 | 23.7 | 23.8 | 20.5 | 13.4 |

Data as orig reptd.; bef. results of disc opers/spec. items. Per share data adj. for stk. divs.; EPS diluted. E-Estimated. NA-Not Available. NM-Not Meaningful. NR-Not Ranked. UR-Under Review.

**Office:** 767 Fifth Avenue, New York, NY 10153.
**Telephone:** 212-572-4200.
**Email:** irdept@estee.com
**Website:** http://www.elcompanies.com

**Chrmn:** W.P. Lauder
**Pres & CEO:** F. Freda
**EVP, CFO & Chief Acctg Officer:** R.W. Kunes
**EVP & General Counsel:** S.E. Moss

**Chief Admin Officer:** D. Krulewitch
**Investor Contact:** D. D'Andrea (212-572-4384)
**Board Members:** C. Barshefsky, R. M. Bravo, W. S. Christianson, F. Freda, P. J. Fribourg, M. L. Hobson, I. O. Hockaday, Jr., A. Lauder, J. Lauder, L. A. Lauder, W. P. Lauder, R. D. Parsons, B. S. Sternlicht, R. F. Zannino, L. F. de Rothschild

**Founded:** 1946
**Domicile:** Delaware
**Employees:** 32,300

# Leggett & Platt Inc

**STANDARD &POOR'S**

| S&P Recommendation | SELL ★★☆☆☆ | Price<br>$20.48 (as of Nov 25, 2011) | 12-Mo. Target Price<br>$21.00 | Investment Style<br>Large-Cap Blend |
|---|---|---|---|---|

**GICS Sector** Consumer Discretionary
**Sub-Industry** Home Furnishings

**Summary** This company makes a broad line of bedding and furniture components and other home, office and commercial furnishings, as well as diversified products for non-furnishings markets.

## Key Stock Statistics (Source S&P, Vickers, company reports)

| | | | | | | | | |
|---|---|---|---|---|---|---|---|---|
| 52-Wk Range | $26.95– 17.80 | S&P Oper. EPS 2011**E** | 1.19 | Market Capitalization(B) | $2.849 | Beta | 1.17 |
| Trailing 12-Month EPS | $1.19 | S&P Oper. EPS 2012**E** | 1.23 | Yield (%) | 5.47 | S&P 3-Yr. Proj. EPS CAGR(%) | 9 |
| Trailing 12-Month P/E | 17.2 | P/E on S&P Oper. EPS 2011**E** | 17.2 | Dividend Rate/Share | $1.12 | S&P Credit Rating | BBB+ |
| $10K Invested 5 Yrs Ago | $11,029 | Common Shares Outstg. (M) | 139.1 | Institutional Ownership (%) | 67 | | |

## Price Performance

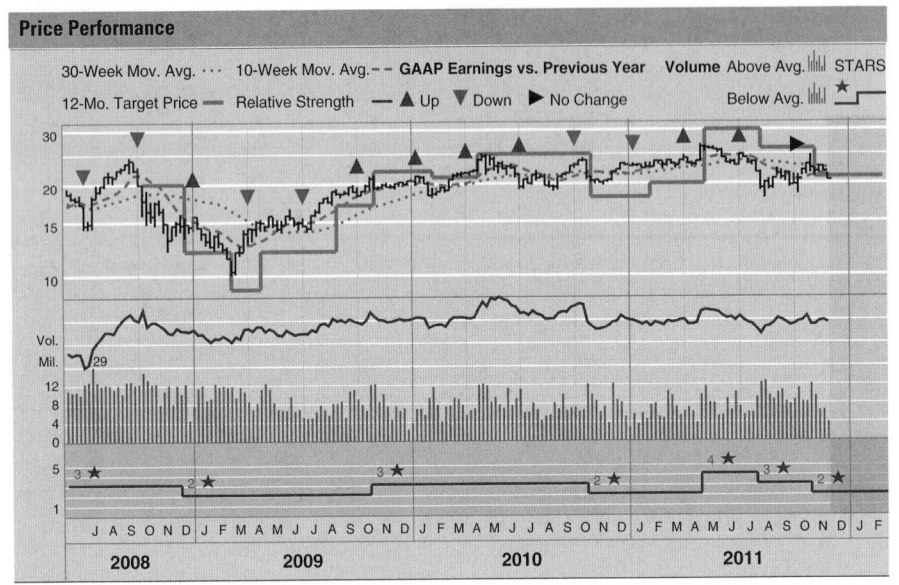

- 30-Week Mov. Avg. ···· 10-Week Mov. Avg. ─ ─ GAAP Earnings vs. Previous Year   Volume Above Avg. ▮▮ STARS
- 12-Mo. Target Price ── Relative Strength ─ ▲ Up ▼ Down ▶ No Change   Below Avg. ▮▮ ★

Options: ASE, Ph

Analysis prepared by Equity Analyst **Jim Yin, CFA** on Nov 01, 2011, when the stock traded at **$21.35**.

### Highlights

➤ We expect revenues to increase 7.4% and 5.0% in 2011 and 2012, respectively, following a 10% increase in 2010. However, we believe most of the growth in 2011 will come from higher prices, and not from higher unit shipments. We project flat sales in the residential furnishings segment and a slight decline in the commercial fixturing & components business, reflecting weakness in both the residential and commercial real estate markets. We see sales of industrial materials and specialized products rising about 17% in 2011.

➤ We project gross margins of 18% in both 2011 and 2012, down from 20% in 2010, due to rising raw material costs. Also, customers are asking for price concessions after LEG raised its prices in the second quarter of 2011. We project operating margins of 7.7% and 7.2% in 2011 and 2012, respectively, compared to 8.6% in 2010.

➤ We estimate EPS of $1.19 and $1.23 in 2011 and 2012, respectively, compared to $1.16 in 2010. The slight increases for 2011 and 2012 reflect our forecast for higher revenues and fewer shares outstanding.

### Investment Rationale/Risk

➤ We recently lowered our recommendation to sell on the view that the recovery in the housing market will take longer to materialize than we had previously thought. We believe economic growth has slowed, given the recent data which show weak job creation and lower home prices. Thus, we think demand for bedding and furniture components will remain subdued near term. We also believe price concessions and higher raw material prices will hurt operating margins in 2011 and 2012.

➤ Risks to our recommendation and target price include a stronger than expected economic recovery leading to higher sales of home furnishings and commercial fixtures, and a significant decline in raw material costs, especially for stainless steel, resulting in higher operating margins than we forecast.

➤ We arrive at our 12-month target price of $21 by applying a multiple of 17X to our 2012 EPS estimate of $1.23, in line with its peers, reflecting our concerns of continued weakness in the commercial real estate market, but our favorable view of LEG's cost management.

## Qualitative Risk Assessment

| LOW | MEDIUM | HIGH |
|---|---|---|

Our risk assessment reflects our view of LEG's long history of profitability and strong free cash flow, offset by the steep cyclicality of its addressable markets.

## Quantitative Evaluations

**S&P Quality Ranking**     **B**

| D | C | B- | B | B+ | A- | A | A+ |
|---|---|---|---|---|---|---|---|

**Relative Strength Rank**     **MODERATE**

**50**

LOWEST = 1     HIGHEST = 99

## Revenue/Earnings Data

**Revenue (Million $)**

| | 1Q | 2Q | 3Q | 4Q | Year |
|---|---|---|---|---|---|
| 2011 | 895.8 | 945.2 | 940.9 | -- | -- |
| 2010 | 816.4 | 874.3 | 866.5 | 801.9 | 3,359 |
| 2009 | 718.1 | 757.4 | 809.9 | 769.7 | 3,055 |
| 2008 | 998.3 | 1,063 | 1,132 | 882.5 | 4,076 |
| 2007 | 1,064 | 1,316 | 1,325 | 1,054 | 4,306 |
| 2006 | 1,378 | 1,403 | 1,415 | 1,311 | 5,505 |

**Earnings Per Share ($)**

| | | | | | |
|---|---|---|---|---|---|
| 2011 | 0.30 | 0.37 | 0.31 | E0.21 | E1.19 |
| 2010 | 0.29 | 0.34 | 0.31 | 0.21 | 1.16 |
| 2009 | 0.02 | 0.12 | 0.34 | 0.26 | 0.74 |
| 2008 | 0.23 | 0.25 | 0.29 | -0.05 | 0.73 |
| 2007 | 0.31 | 0.30 | 0.36 | -0.71 | 0.28 |
| 2006 | 0.33 | 0.45 | 0.45 | 0.38 | 1.61 |

Fiscal year ended Dec. 31. Next earnings report expected: Early February. EPS Estimates based on S&P Operating Earnings; historical GAAP earnings are as reported.

## Dividend Data (Dates: mm/dd Payment Date: mm/dd/yy)

| Amount ($) | Date Decl. | Ex-Div. Date | Stk. of Record | Payment Date |
|---|---|---|---|---|
| 0.270 | 05/12 | 06/13 | 06/15 | 07/15/11 |
| 0.280 | 08/02 | 09/13 | 09/15 | 10/14/11 |
| 0.280 | 11/10 | 12/13 | 12/15 | 01/13/12 |

Dividends have been paid since 1939. Source: Company reports.

---

**Please read the Required Disclosures and Analyst Certification on the last page of this report.**

**The McGraw-Hill Companies**

# Leggett & Platt Inc

STANDARD &POOR'S

## Business Summary November 01, 2011

CORPORATE OVERVIEW. Leggett & Platt, founded in 1883, is a diversified manufacturer that conceives, designs and produces a wide range of engineered components and products that can be found in most homes, offices, retail stores and automobiles.

LEG's business is organized into five business segments. Residential Furnishings (52% of 2010 sales; 54% in 2009) consists of Bedding, Home Furniture & Consumer Products, and Fabric and Carpet Underlay. The Commercial Fixturing & Components segment (16%; 16%) consists of Fixture & Display and Office Furniture Components. Industrial Materials (15%; 15%) consists of Wire and Tubing, while Specialized Products (18%; 15%) consists of Automotive, Machinery and Commercial Vehicles.

PRIMARY BUSINESS DYNAMICS. In the past 20 years, about two-thirds of LEG's sales growth has come from acquisitions. Over the past 10 years, the average acquisition target had revenues of $15 million to $20 million, which the company believes serves to minimize the risk of any single acquisition. In 2010, LEG generated $363 million in cash from operations, down from 2009's $565 million and 2007's $614 million but up from $436 million in 2008.

In 2007, LEG acquired three businesses in the Commercial Fixturing & Components ($20 million annual sales), Industrial Materials ($50 million) and Specialized Products ($30 million) segments. In Industrial Materials, LEG bought a maker of coated wire products, including racks for dishwashers. In Specialized Products, LEG bought a company that designs and assembles docking stations that secure computer and other electronic equipment in vehicles. In Commercial Fixturing & Components, LEG bought a company located in China that makes office furniture components.

In 2006, LEG acquired five businesses representing $75 million in annualized sales, all within the Residential Furnishings segment. The largest acquisition was a maker of rubber carpet underlay, a product type that accounts for 6% of LEG's overall revenue. In addition, the company divested five businesses in 2006 with annualized sales of about $45 million.

## Company Financials Fiscal Year Ended Dec. 31

| Per Share Data ($) | 2010 | 2009 | 2008 | 2007 | 2006 | 2005 | 2004 | 2003 | 2002 | 2001 |
|---|---|---|---|---|---|---|---|---|---|---|
| Tangible Book Value | 2.90 | 3.06 | 3.72 | 5.73 | 5.72 | 5.55 | 6.38 | 5.62 | 5.36 | 4.81 |
| Cash Flow | 2.00 | 1.55 | 1.42 | 1.16 | 2.67 | 2.18 | 2.35 | 1.89 | 1.99 | 1.92 |
| Earnings | 1.16 | 0.74 | 0.73 | 0.28 | 1.61 | 1.30 | 1.45 | 1.05 | 1.17 | 0.94 |
| S&P Core Earnings | 1.13 | 0.75 | 0.60 | 0.90 | 1.57 | 1.27 | 1.38 | 1.02 | 1.11 | 0.85 |
| Dividends | 1.06 | 1.02 | 1.00 | 0.78 | 0.84 | 0.63 | 0.58 | 0.54 | 0.50 | 0.48 |
| Payout Ratio | 91% | 138% | 137% | NM | 52% | 48% | 40% | 51% | 43% | 51% |
| Prices:High | 25.15 | 21.44 | 24.60 | 24.73 | 27.04 | 29.61 | 30.68 | 23.69 | 27.40 | 24.45 |
| Prices:Low | 17.89 | 10.03 | 12.03 | 17.14 | 21.93 | 18.19 | 21.19 | 17.16 | 18.60 | 16.85 |
| P/E Ratio:High | 22 | 29 | 34 | 88 | 17 | 23 | 21 | 23 | 23 | 26 |
| P/E Ratio:Low | 15 | 14 | 16 | 61 | 14 | 14 | 15 | 16 | 16 | 18 |

| Income Statement Analysis (Million $) | | | | | | | | | | |
|---|---|---|---|---|---|---|---|---|---|---|
| Revenue | 3,359 | 3,055 | 4,076 | 4,306 | 5,505 | 5,299 | 5,086 | 4,388 | 4,272 | 4,114 |
| Operating Income | 404 | 377 | 371 | 492 | 666 | 605 | 622 | 520 | 582 | 558 |
| Depreciation | 123 | 130 | 116 | 157 | 175 | 171 | 177 | 167 | 165 | 197 |
| Interest Expense | 32.5 | 37.4 | 48.4 | 58.6 | 56.2 | 46.7 | 45.9 | 46.9 | 42.1 | 58.8 |
| Pretax Income | 256 | 198 | 188 | 128 | 435 | 356 | 423 | 315 | 364 | 297 |
| Effective Tax Rate | NA | 39.0% | 34.6% | 60.3% | 30.9% | 29.4% | 32.5% | 34.7% | 35.9% | 36.9% |
| Net Income | 184 | 118 | 123 | 51.0 | 300 | 251 | 285 | 206 | 233 | 188 |
| S&P Core Earnings | 172 | 118 | 102 | 161 | 291 | 245 | 272 | 202 | 221 | 169 |

| Balance Sheet & Other Financial Data (Million $) | | | | | | | | | | |
|---|---|---|---|---|---|---|---|---|---|---|
| Cash | 245 | 261 | 165 | 205 | 132 | 64.9 | 491 | 444 | 225 | 187 |
| Current Assets | 1,219 | 1,214 | 1,307 | 1,834 | 1,894 | 1,763 | 2,065 | 1,819 | 1,488 | 1,422 |
| Total Assets | 3,001 | 3,061 | 3,162 | 4,073 | 4,265 | 4,053 | 4,197 | 3,890 | 3,501 | 3,413 |
| Current Liabilities | 523 | 535 | 524 | 800 | 691 | 738 | 960 | 626 | 598 | 457 |
| Long Term Debt | 762 | 789 | 851 | 1,001 | 1,060 | 922 | 779 | 1,012 | 809 | 978 |
| Common Equity | 1,524 | 1,576 | 1,653 | 2,133 | 2,351 | 2,249 | 2,313 | 2,114 | 1,977 | 1,867 |
| Total Capital | 2,289 | 2,375 | 2,539 | 3,176 | 3,478 | 3,230 | 3,178 | 3,221 | 2,865 | 2,909 |
| Capital Expenditures | 67.7 | 83.0 | 118 | 149 | 166 | 164 | 157 | 137 | 124 | 128 |
| Cash Flow | 306 | 248 | 239 | 208 | 476 | 422 | 463 | 373 | 398 | 384 |
| Current Ratio | 2.3 | 2.3 | 2.5 | 2.3 | 2.7 | 2.4 | 2.2 | 2.9 | 2.5 | 3.1 |
| % Long Term Debt of Capitalization | 33.3 | 33.2 | 33.5 | 31.5 | 30.5 | 28.5 | 24.5 | 31.4 | 28.2 | 33.6 |
| % Net Income of Revenue | 5.5 | 3.9 | 3.0 | 1.2 | 5.5 | 4.7 | 5.6 | 4.7 | 5.5 | 4.6 |
| % Return on Assets | 6.1 | 3.8 | 3.4 | 1.2 | 7.2 | 6.1 | 7.1 | 5.6 | 6.7 | 5.5 |
| % Return on Equity | 11.9 | 7.3 | 6.5 | 2.3 | 13.1 | 11.0 | 12.9 | 10.1 | 12.1 | 10.3 |

Data as orig reptd.; bef. results of disc opers/spec. items. Per share data adj. for stk. divs.; EPS diluted. E-Estimated. NA-Not Available. NM-Not Meaningful. NR-Not Ranked. UR-Under Review.

**Office:** No 1 Leggett Road, Carthage, MO 64836.
**Telephone:** 417-358-8131.
**Email:** invest@leggett.com
**Website:** http://www.leggett.com

**Chrmn:** R.T. Fisher
**Pres & CEO:** D.S. Haffner
**COO & EVP:** K.G. Glassman
**SVP & CFO:** M.C. Flanigan

**Chief Acctg Officer & Cntlr:** W.S. Weil
**Investor Contact:** D.M. DeSonier (417-358-8131)
**Board Members:** R. E. Brunner, R. Clark, R. T. Enloe, III, R. T. Fisher, M. C. Flanigan, K. G. Glassman, R. A. Griffith, D. S. Haffner, J. W. McClanathan, J. C. Odom, M. E. Purnell, Jr., P. A. Wood

**Founded:** 1883
**Domicile:** Missouri
**Employees:** 19,000

# Legg Mason Inc

**STANDARD &POOR'S**

| S&P Recommendation **HOLD** ★★★☆☆ | Price<br>$23.31 (as of Nov 25, 2011) | 12-Mo. Target Price<br>$29.00 | Investment Style<br>Large-Cap Growth |
|---|---|---|---|

**GICS Sector** Financials
**Sub-Industry** Asset Management & Custody Banks

**Summary** This diversified investment manager serves individual and institutional investors through offices around the United States.

## Key Stock Statistics (Source S&P, Vickers, company reports)

| | | | | | | | | | |
|---|---|---|---|---|---|---|---|---|---|
| 52-Wk Range | $37.82–22.61 | S&P Oper. EPS 2012**E** | 1.66 | Market Capitalization(B) | $3.258 | Beta | 1.84 |
| Trailing 12-Month EPS | $1.64 | S&P Oper. EPS 2013**E** | 2.08 | Yield (%) | 1.37 | S&P 3-Yr. Proj. EPS CAGR(%) | 8 |
| Trailing 12-Month P/E | 14.2 | P/E on S&P Oper. EPS 2012**E** | 14.0 | Dividend Rate/Share | $0.32 | S&P Credit Rating | BBB |
| $10K Invested 5 Yrs Ago | $2,586 | Common Shares Outstg. (M) | 139.8 | Institutional Ownership (%) | 88 | | |

## Price Performance

- 30-Week Mov. Avg. · · · ·  10-Week Mov. Avg. – – GAAP Earnings vs. Previous Year   Volume  Above Avg.|||  STARS
- 12-Mo. Target Price —  Relative Strength  ▲ Up  ▼ Down  ▶ No Change   Below Avg.|||

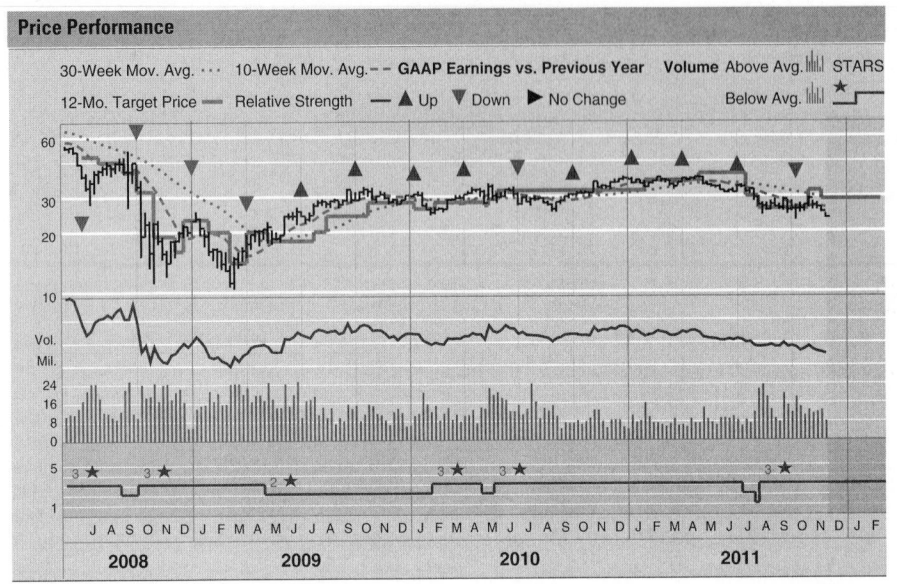

Options: ASE, CBOE, P, Ph

Analysis prepared by Equity Analyst **Cathy Seifert** on Nov 21, 2011, when the stock traded at **$24.09**.

## Highlights

- ➤ LM's year-to-date results reflected continued declines and volatility in equity and liquidity assets. We think assets under management (AUM) will continue to decline through the next couple of quarters, specifically within equity funds, as difficult flow trends and fund performance issues remain as headwinds. LM has suffered outflows for several quarters, with $17.6 billion of outflows in the second quarter of FY 12 (Mar.). We see some positives stemming from LM's restructuring efforts, but we expect below-average equity fund performance and persistent outflows to present significant challenges to top-line growth. Due to these headwinds, we look for LM's revenue growth to lag peers, and we estimate operating revenues for FY 12 will rise 7.7%.

- ➤ LM began streamlining its core business in July 2010 to increase operational efficiencies. We expect moderately lower distribution expenses to improve pretax margins by the end of FY 12.

- ➤ We estimate EPS of $1.66 in FY 12 and $2.08 in FY 13.

## Investment Rationale/Risk

- ➤ In our view, LM's longer-term track record compares unfavorably with peers and benchmarks, which we think has kept LM's quarterly net client cash flows from turning positive over the past several quarters. Despite our view of LM's strong fixed income fund performance, we think the increased volatility in the markets may further subdue any potential reversal of fund outflows. We look for improvement in LM's equity fund performance and expect successful execution from LM's streamlining efforts. June AUM levels reflect further losses in equity and liquidity assets, and as a result we see LM achieving only peer-average earnings growth. We think LM should be valued at a discount to its historical multiple, and we think the shares are appropriately valued at recent levels.

- ➤ Risks to our recommendation and target price include stock market depreciation, a decline in relative investment performance, and an increase in customer redemptions.

- ➤ Our 12-month target price of $29 is equal to 13.9X our FY 13 EPS forecast, a discount to LM's historical multiple given poor organic growth trends we see.

## Qualitative Risk Assessment

| LOW | **MEDIUM** | HIGH |
|---|---|---|

Our risk assessment reflects our view of the company's strong market share and restructured balance sheet, offset by weak relative long-term investment performance and industry cyclicality.

## Quantitative Evaluations

**S&P Quality Ranking**  B+

| D | C | B- | B | **B+** | A- | A | A+ |
|---|---|---|---|---|---|---|---|

**Relative Strength Rank**  WEAK

26

LOWEST = 1                    HIGHEST = 99

## Revenue/Earnings Data

**Revenue (Million $)**

| | 1Q | 2Q | 3Q | 4Q | Year |
|---|---|---|---|---|---|
| 2012 | 717.1 | 669.9 | -- | -- | -- |
| 2011 | 674.2 | 674.8 | 721.9 | 713.4 | 2,784 |
| 2010 | 613.1 | 659.9 | 690.5 | 671.4 | 2,635 |
| 2009 | 1,054 | 966.1 | 720.0 | 617.2 | 3,357 |
| 2008 | 1,206 | 1,172 | 1,187 | 1,069 | 4,634 |
| 2007 | 1,038 | 1,031 | 1,133 | 1,142 | 4,344 |

**Earnings Per Share ($)**

| | 1Q | 2Q | 3Q | 4Q | Year |
|---|---|---|---|---|---|
| 2012 | 0.40 | 0.39 | E0.39 | E0.45 | E1.66 |
| 2011 | 0.30 | 0.50 | 0.41 | 0.45 | 1.63 |
| 2010 | 0.35 | 0.30 | 0.28 | 0.39 | 1.32 |
| 2009 | -0.22 | -0.74 | -10.55 | -2.29 | -13.85 |
| 2008 | 1.32 | 1.23 | 1.07 | -1.81 | 1.86 |
| 2007 | 1.08 | 1.00 | 1.21 | 1.19 | 4.48 |

Fiscal year ended Mar. 31. Next earnings report expected: NA.
EPS Estimates based on S&P Operating Earnings; historical GAAP earnings are as reported.

## Dividend Data (Dates: mm/dd Payment Date: mm/dd/yy)

| Amount<br>($) | Date<br>Decl. | Ex-Div.<br>Date | Stk. of<br>Record | Payment<br>Date |
|---|---|---|---|---|
| 0.060 | 01/26 | 03/08 | 03/10 | 04/11/11 |
| 0.080 | 05/03 | 06/10 | 06/14 | 07/11/11 |
| 0.080 | 07/28 | 10/04 | 10/06 | 10/24/11 |
| 0.080 | 10/27 | 12/12 | 12/14 | 01/09/12 |

Dividends have been paid since 1983. Source: Company reports.

---

**Please read the Required Disclosures and Analyst Certification on the last page of this report.**

**The McGraw-Hill Companies**

# Legg Mason Inc

**STANDARD &POOR'S**

## Business Summary November 21, 2011

CORPORATE OVERVIEW. Legg Mason is a holding company which, through subsidiaries, is principally engaged in providing asset management and other related financial services to individuals, institutions, corporations, governments, and government agencies. At the end of FY 11 (Mar.), total assets under management were $677.6 billion, down from about $685 billion a year earlier. The company operates out of offices in the U.S., the U.K. and a number of other countries worldwide. At the end of FY 11, fixed income assets represented 53% of total assets under management, equity assets 28%, and liquidity assets 20%.

Legg Mason operates through two divisions: Americas and International. Within each division, the firm provides services through individual asset managers. They each generally market their own products and services under their own brand names, and in many cases distribute retail products and services through a centralized retail distribution network. Each subsidiary primarily earns revenues by charging fees for the management of assets for clients. Fees are typically calculated as a percentage of average assets under management, and can vary with the type of account, the asset manager, and the type of client. They may also earn performance fees from certain accounts if benchmarks are met or exceeded for the particular measurement

period. Increases in assets under management can result from inflows of new assets from new and existing clients, and from appreciation of asset values. Decreases can also occur due to client redemptions and declines in the value of client assets.

The firm does business primarily through its 16 asset managers. We think LM has a diverse collection of asset management subsidiaries, which include Western Asset, Legg Mason Capital Management, Brandywine, and Permal, among others. LM's Asset Management business provides asset management services to institutional and individual clients and investment advisory services to company-sponsored investment funds. Investment products include proprietary mutual funds ranging from money market and fixed income funds to equity funds managed in a wide variety of investing styles, non-U.S. funds, and a number of unregistered, alternative investment products. LM's mutual funds group sponsors domestic and international equity, fixed income and money market mutual funds, closed-end funds, and other proprietary funds

## Company Financials Fiscal Year Ended Mar. 31

| Per Share Data ($) | 2011 | 2010 | 2009 | 2008 | 2007 | 2006 | 2005 | 2004 | 2003 | 2002 |
|---|---|---|---|---|---|---|---|---|---|---|
| Tangible Book Value | 3.87 | 3.84 | NM | NM | NM | NM | 11.66 | 6.50 | 3.32 | 1.52 |
| Cash Flow | 2.24 | 2.05 | -12.86 | 2.84 | 5.95 | 3.90 | 3.83 | 2.62 | 1.85 | 1.49 |
| Earnings | 1.63 | 1.32 | -13.85 | 1.86 | 4.48 | 3.30 | 3.53 | 2.64 | 1.85 | 1.49 |
| S&P Core Earnings | 1.63 | 1.32 | -8.12 | 1.86 | 4.48 | 3.25 | 3.41 | 2.57 | 1.63 | 1.35 |
| Dividends | 0.20 | 0.12 | 0.96 | 0.81 | 0.69 | 0.40 | 0.37 | 0.29 | 0.29 | 0.23 |
| Payout Ratio | 12% | 9% | NM | 44% | 15% | 12% | 11% | 11% | 15% | 16% |
| Calendar Year | 2010 | 2009 | 2008 | 2007 | 2006 | 2005 | 2004 | 2003 | 2002 | 2001 |
| Prices:High | 37.72 | 33.70 | 75.33 | 110.17 | 140.00 | 129.00 | 73.70 | 56.77 | 38.10 | 37.99 |
| Prices:Low | 24.00 | 10.35 | 11.09 | 68.35 | 81.01 | 68.10 | 48.95 | 29.47 | 24.74 | 22.83 |
| P/E Ratio:High | 23 | 26 | NM | 59 | 31 | 39 | 21 | 22 | 21 | 25 |
| P/E Ratio:Low | 15 | 8 | NM | 37 | 18 | 21 | 14 | 11 | 13 | 15 |
| **Income Statement Analysis** (Million $) | | | | | | | | | | |
| Commissions | Nil | Nil | Nil | Nil | Nil | Nil | 358 | 344 | 317 | 331 |
| Interest Income | 9.25 | 7.37 | 56.3 | 77.0 | 58.9 | 48.0 | 119 | 84.3 | 109 | 168 |
| Total Revenue | 2,784 | 2,635 | 3,357 | 4,634 | 4,344 | 2,645 | 2,490 | 2,004 | 1,615 | 1,579 |
| Interest Expense | 92.2 | 126 | 150 | 83.0 | 71.5 | 52.6 | 80.8 | 63.2 | 87.1 | 127 |
| Pretax Income | 365 | 330 | -3,156 | 444 | 1,044 | 703 | 659 | 472 | 308 | 253 |
| Effective Tax Rate | 32.6% | 36.0% | NM | 39.7% | 38.1% | 39.2% | 38.0% | 38.5% | 38.1% | 39.6% |
| Net Income | 254 | 204 | -1,948 | 268 | 646 | 434 | 408 | 291 | 191 | 153 |
| S&P Core Earnings | 254 | 204 | -1,142 | 268 | 646 | 421 | 394 | 283 | 168 | 138 |
| **Balance Sheet & Other Financial Data** (Million $) | | | | | | | | | | |
| Total Assets | 8,708 | 8,614 | 9,321 | 11,830 | 9,604 | 9,302 | 8,219 | 7,263 | 6,067 | 5,940 |
| Cash Items | 1,413 | 1,508 | NA | NA | NA | NA | NA | NA | NA | NA |
| Receivables | 396 | 561 | 1,204 | 764 | 852 | 850 | 1,564 | 1,458 | 1,155 | 1,230 |
| Securities Owned | 483 | 372 | 336 | 489 | 273 | 142 | 1,298 | 870 | 419 | 458 |
| Securities Borrowed | Nil | Nil | Nil | Nil | Nil | Nil | 588 | 488 | 220 | 280 |
| Due Brokers & Customers | Nil | Nil | Nil | Nil | Nil | Nil | 3,419 | 3,657 | 75.0 | 35.0 |
| Other Liabilities | 1,421 | 1,577 | NA | 1,216 | 1,079 | 1,633 | 1,108 | 764 | 462 | 410 |
| Capitalization:Debt | 1,479 | 1,165 | 2,965 | 1,826 | 1,108 | 1,166 | 811 | 794 | 787 | 877 |
| Capitalization:Equity | 5,770 | 5,842 | 4,454 | 6,621 | 6,678 | 5,850 | 2,293 | 1,560 | 1,248 | 1,075 |
| Capitalization:Total | 7,286 | 7,037 | 7,679 | 8,802 | 8,229 | 7,016 | 3,104 | 2,354 | 2,035 | 1,952 |
| % Return on Revenue | 9.1 | 7.8 | NM | 5.8 | 14.9 | 16.4 | 19.2 | 17.5 | 14.7 | 12.3 |
| % Return on Assets | 2.9 | 2.3 | NM | 2.5 | 6.8 | 5.0 | 5.3 | 4.4 | 3.2 | 2.9 |
| % Return on Equity | 8.0 | 3.9 | NM | 4.1 | 10.2 | 10.7 | 21.2 | 20.7 | 16.4 | 15.4 |

Data as orig reptd.; bef. results of disc opers/spec. items. Per share data adj. for stk. divs.; EPS diluted. E-Estimated. NA-Not Available. NM-Not Meaningful. NR-Not Ranked. UR-Under Review.

**Office:** 100 International Drive, Baltimore, MD 21202-1099.
**Telephone:** 410-539-0000.
**Website:** http://www.leggmason.com
**Chrmn, Pres & CEO:** M.R. Fetting

**EVP, CFO & Chief Acctg Officer:** P.H. Nachtwey
**SVP & Treas:** T.L. Souders
**SVP & General Counsel:** T.P. Lemke
**Secy & General Counsel:** T.C. Merchant

**Investor Contact:** A. Magleby (410-454-5246)
**Board Members:** H. L. Adams, R. E. Angelica, D. Beresford, J. T. Cahill, E. J. Cashman, Jr., M. R. Fetting, R. P. Hearn, B. Huff, J. Koerner, III, C. G. Krongard, S. C. Nuttall, N. Peltz, W. A. Reed, M. M. Richardson, K. L. Schmoke, N. J. St. George

**Founded:** 1899
**Domicile:** Maryland
**Employees:** 3,395

# Lennar Corp

**STANDARD &POOR'S**

| S&P Recommendation **BUY** ★★★★☆ | Price $16.44 (as of Nov 25, 2011) | 12-Mo. Target Price $21.00 | Investment Style Large-Cap Blend |
|---|---|---|---|

**GICS Sector** Consumer Discretionary
**Sub-Industry** Homebuilding

**Summary** Lennar, one of the largest, most geographically diversified U.S. home builders, concentrates on moderately priced homes.

## Key Stock Statistics (Source S&P, Vickers, company reports)

| | | | | | | | |
|---|---|---|---|---|---|---|---|
| 52-Wk Range | $21.54–12.14 | S&P Oper. EPS 2011**E** | 0.55 | Market Capitalization(B) | $2.560 | Beta | 1.72 |
| Trailing 12-Month EPS | $0.50 | S&P Oper. EPS 2012**E** | 1.00 | Yield (%) | 0.97 | S&P 3-Yr. Proj. EPS CAGR(%) | 17 |
| Trailing 12-Month P/E | 32.9 | P/E on S&P Oper. EPS 2011**E** | 29.9 | Dividend Rate/Share | $0.16 | S&P Credit Rating | B+ |
| $10K Invested 5 Yrs Ago | $3,528 | Common Shares Outstg. (M) | 187.0 | Institutional Ownership (%) | NM | | |

## Price Performance

- 30-Week Mov. Avg. · · · 10-Week Mov. Avg. - - 12-Mo. Target Price — Relative Strength — GAAP Earnings vs. Previous Year ▲ Up ▼ Down ▶ No Change
- Volume Above Avg. Below Avg. STARS

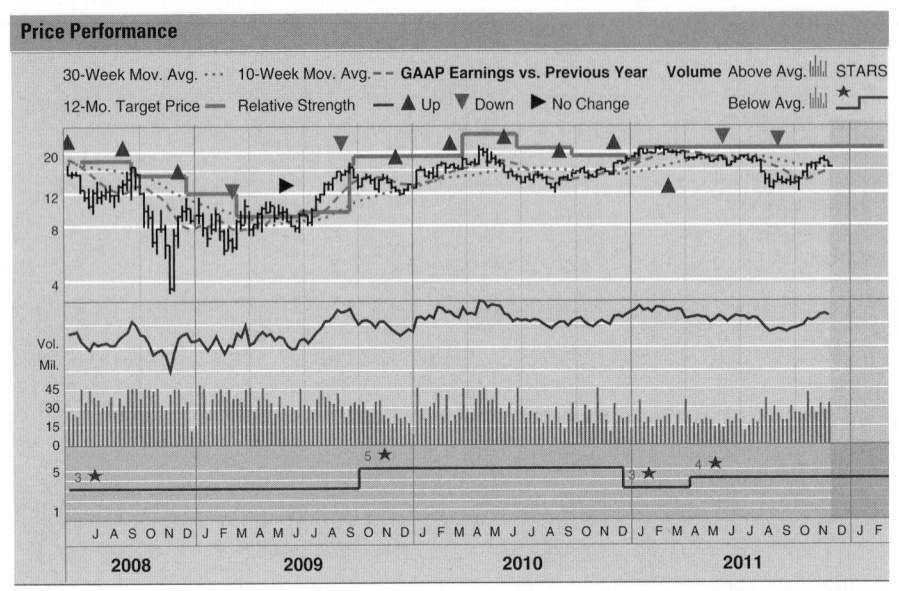

Options: ASE, CBOE, P, Ph

Analysis prepared by Equity Analyst **Kenneth Leon, CPA** on Sep 20, 2011, when the stock traded at **$14.36**.

### Highlights

➤ Following a decline of 5% in FY 10 (Nov.), we project that revenues will be flat in FY 11, reflecting an extended downturn for the U.S. housing market where LEN is seeking to gain market share. We see the company benefiting from its size relative to many of its homebuilder peers, and we forecast 12% revenue growth in FY 12 in the housing recovery we expect.

➤ We also see a benefit to gross margins from a greater mix of newer communities where land was bought at lower costs. LEN's Rialto Investments segment generated $71 million of operating income in the first nine months of FY 11, or 32% of total operating profit, but its results are difficult to forecast as evident by an $11 million asset write-off in the third quarter.

➤ Although we expect weak demand in the housing market for the rest of 2011, we see LEN as well positioned to grow profitably with continued cost controls and earnings contributions from Rialto. With flat to modest margin improvements, we estimate EPS of $0.55 in FY 11 and $1.00 in FY 12.

### Investment Rationale/Risk

➤ Despite headwinds in the housing market, we believe Lennar can sustain profitability with reduced construction and operating costs on new scaled-down homes coming to market. In our opinion, the company can also be opportunistic in new land purchases or option land contracts with abundant land coming to market from banks that took possession of distressed or bankrupt private homebuilders.

➤ Risks to our recommendation and target price include prolonged housing weakness that further restricts new home purchases, higher mortgage rates, and weaker than expected demand from first-time homebuyers after expiration of the 2010 federal tax credit. We think Rialto Investments represents a business risk with respect to market conditions, credit trends and predictability for operating income forecasts.

➤ As of August 31, 2011, the company had $800 million of cash to support its working capital and debt obligations and new land acquisitions. Our estimate of LEN's book value is $14.45 per share. Applying a forward price-to-book value multiple of just under 1.5X, near most other large homebuilders, our 12-month target price remains $21.

### Qualitative Risk Assessment

| LOW | MEDIUM | HIGH |
|---|---|---|

Our risk assessment reflects Lennar's exposure to the uncertainties of the housing market, where the confidence and job security of buyers is still weak and credit guidelines have tightened, partly offset by record low mortgage rates.

### Quantitative Evaluations

**S&P Quality Ranking** B-

| D | C | B- | B | B+ | A- | A | A+ |
|---|---|---|---|---|---|---|---|

**Relative Strength Rank** STRONG

85

LOWEST = 1    HIGHEST = 99

### Revenue/Earnings Data

**Revenue (Million $)**

| | 1Q | 2Q | 3Q | 4Q | Year |
|---|---|---|---|---|---|
| 2011 | 558.0 | 764.5 | 820.2 | -- | -- |
| 2010 | 574.4 | 814.5 | 825.0 | 860.1 | 3,074 |
| 2009 | 593.1 | 891.9 | 720.7 | 913.7 | 3,119 |
| 2008 | 1,063 | 1,128 | 1,107 | 1,278 | 4,575 |
| 2007 | 2,792 | 2,876 | 2,342 | 2,177 | 10,187 |
| 2006 | 3,241 | 4,578 | 4,182 | 4,266 | 16,267 |

**Earnings Per Share ($)**

| | | | | | |
|---|---|---|---|---|---|
| 2011 | 0.14 | 0.07 | 0.11 | E0.23 | E0.55 |
| 2010 | -0.04 | 0.21 | 0.16 | 0.17 | 0.51 |
| 2009 | -0.98 | -0.76 | -0.97 | -0.19 | -2.45 |
| 2008 | -0.56 | -0.76 | -0.56 | -5.12 | -7.00 |
| 2007 | 0.43 | -1.55 | -3.25 | -7.92 | -12.31 |
| 2006 | 1.58 | 2.00 | 1.30 | -1.24 | 3.69 |

Fiscal year ended Nov. 30. Next earnings report expected: Mid January. EPS Estimates based on S&P Operating Earnings; historical GAAP earnings are as reported.

### Dividend Data (Dates: mm/dd Payment Date: mm/dd/yy)

| Amount ($) | Date Decl. | Ex-Div. Date | Stk. of Record | Payment Date |
|---|---|---|---|---|
| 0.040 | 01/12 | 01/21 | 01/25 | 02/08/11 |
| 0.040 | 04/13 | 04/25 | 04/27 | 05/11/11 |
| 0.040 | 06/22 | 07/05 | 07/07 | 07/21/11 |
| 0.040 | 10/05 | 10/17 | 10/19 | 11/02/11 |

Dividends have been paid since 1978. Source: Company reports.

---

**Please read the Required Disclosures and Analyst Certification on the last page of this report.**

Stock Report | November 26, 2011 | NYS Symbol: **LEN**

# Lennar Corp

**STANDARD &POOR'S**

## Business Summary September 20, 2011

CORPORATE OVERVIEW. Lennar Corp., one of the largest homebuilders in the U.S., constructs homes for first-time, move-up and active adult buyers, and also provides various financial services. It takes part in all phases of planning and building, and subcontracts nearly all development and construction work. LEN sells homes primarily from models it has designed and constructed. In FY 09 (Nov.) and FY 10, these homes had an average sales price (ASP) of $234,000, compared to $270,000 in FY 08. The ASP for the fourth quarter of FY 10 was $238,000, and in FY 11's third quarter it was $247,000.

The financial services division provides mortgage financing, title insurance, closing services and insurance agency services for LEN homebuyers and others, and sells the loans it originates in the secondary mortgage market.

CORPORATE STRATEGY. Lennar greatly expanded its operations through the May 2000 purchase of U.S. Home Corp. (UH), and maintained an active acquisition program for several years. The company entered the North Carolina and South Carolina markets, and extended its positions in Colorado and Arizona through the acquisition of various operations of Fortress Group in two separate transactions in late 2001 and mid-2002. It expanded its California business by acquiring Pacific Century Homes and Cambridge Homes (combined annual

deliveries of about 2,000 homes) in 2002.

In 2005, the company entered the metropolitan New York City and Boston markets by acquiring rights to develop a portfolio of properties in New Jersey facing mid-town Manhattan and waterfront properties near Boston. It also entered the Reno, NV, market through the acquisition of Barker Coleman. In addition, LEN expanded its presence in Jacksonville through the acquisition of Admiral Homes that same year.

The company had an order backlog value of $1.4 billion at the end of FY 07, which was 65% lower than the $3.98 billion a year earlier. Its backlog value was $456 million as of November 30, 2008, but rose to $545 million at May 31, 2009, and $647 million at August 31, 2009. The company ended FY 09 with a contract backlog value of $479 million, which rose to $656 million at May 31, 2010, and fell to $407 million at November 30, 2010, reflecting expiration of the federal housing tax credit. Backlog rose to $643 million at August 31, 2011.

## Company Financials Fiscal Year Ended Nov. 30

| Per Share Data ($) | 2010 | 2009 | 2008 | 2007 | 2006 | 2005 | 2004 | 2003 | 2002 | 2001 |
|---|---|---|---|---|---|---|---|---|---|---|
| Tangible Book Value | 13.80 | 13.03 | 16.12 | 25.67 | 34.42 | 32.09 | 24.05 | 20.68 | 15.71 | 12.14 |
| Cash Flow | 0.58 | -2.33 | -6.69 | -11.95 | 4.03 | 8.60 | 5.98 | 5.11 | 4.32 | 3.45 |
| Earnings | 0.51 | -2.45 | -7.00 | -12.31 | 3.69 | 8.17 | 5.70 | 4.65 | 3.86 | 3.01 |
| S&P Core Earnings | 0.51 | -2.45 | -7.44 | -12.36 | 3.62 | 8.10 | 5.63 | 4.61 | 3.83 | 2.90 |
| Dividends | 0.16 | 0.16 | 0.52 | 0.64 | 0.64 | 0.57 | 0.39 | 0.14 | 0.03 | 0.03 |
| Payout Ratio | 31% | NM | NM | NM | 17% | 7% | 7% | 3% | 1% | 1% |
| Prices:High | 21.79 | 17.66 | 22.73 | 56.54 | 66.44 | 68.86 | 57.20 | 50.90 | 31.99 | 24.94 |
| Prices:Low | 11.93 | 5.54 | 3.42 | 14.00 | 38.66 | 50.30 | 40.30 | 24.10 | 21.60 | 15.52 |
| P/E Ratio:High | 43 | NM | NM | NM | 18 | 8 | 10 | 11 | 8 | 8 |
| P/E Ratio:Low | 23 | NM | NM | NM | 10 | 6 | 7 | 5 | 6 | 5 |

| Income Statement Analysis (Million $) | | | | | | | | | | |
|---|---|---|---|---|---|---|---|---|---|---|
| Revenue | 3,074 | 3,119 | 4,575 | 10,187 | 16,267 | 13,867 | 10,505 | 8,908 | 7,320 | 6,029 |
| Operating Income | 189 | -66.8 | -353 | -2,626 | 941 | 2,124 | 1,426 | 1,158 | 1,094 | 868 |
| Depreciation | 13.5 | 19.9 | 49.8 | 57.0 | 56.5 | 79.6 | 55.6 | 54.5 | 72.4 | 68.7 |
| Interest Expense | 70.4 | 70.9 | 148 | Nil | Nil | Nil | Nil | 141 | 146 | 120 |
| Pretax Income | 94.7 | -760 | -566 | -3,081 | 956 | 2,205 | 1,519 | 1,207 | 876 | 679 |
| Effective Tax Rate | NA | 41.3% | NM | NM | 36.5% | 37.0% | 37.8% | 37.8% | 37.8% | 38.5% |
| Net Income | 95.3 | -417 | -1,109 | -1,942 | 594 | 1,344 | 946 | 751 | 545 | 418 |
| S&P Core Earnings | 94.2 | -417 | -1,178 | -1,948 | 582 | 1,331 | 934 | 744 | 541 | 404 |

| Balance Sheet & Other Financial Data (Million $) | | | | | | | | | | |
|---|---|---|---|---|---|---|---|---|---|---|
| Cash | 1,284 | 1,331 | 1,091 | 642 | 778 | 910 | 1,322 | 1,201 | 731 | 824 |
| Current Assets | 7,404 | 6,373 | 6,471 | 7,132 | 10,108 | 10,483 | 7,713 | 5,799 | 4,996 | 4,055 |
| Total Assets | 8,788 | 7,315 | 7,425 | 9,103 | 12,408 | 12,541 | 9,165 | 6,775 | 5,756 | 4,714 |
| Current Liabilities | 647 | 852 | 900 | 1,300 | 2,330 | 1,765 | 2,554 | 1,787 | 1,722 | 1,117 |
| Long Term Debt | 3,692 | 2,297 | 2,117 | 2,295 | 2,614 | 2,565 | 2,918 | 1,552 | 1,521 | 1,488 |
| Common Equity | 2,609 | 2,443 | 2,623 | 3,822 | 5,702 | 5,251 | 4,053 | 3,264 | 2,229 | 1,659 |
| Total Capital | 7,093 | 5,349 | 4,906 | 6,146 | 8,283 | 7,895 | 6,971 | 4,816 | 3,751 | 3,147 |
| Capital Expenditures | 5.06 | NA | 1.40 | Nil | 26.8 | 21.7 | 27.4 | 29.6 | 4.09 | 13.1 |
| Cash Flow | 109 | -397 | -1,059 | -1,885 | 650 | 1,424 | 1,001 | 806 | 618 | 487 |
| Current Ratio | 11.5 | 7.5 | 7.2 | 5.5 | 4.3 | 5.9 | 3.0 | 3.3 | 2.9 | 3.6 |
| % Long Term Debt of Capitalization | 52.1 | Nil | 43.2 | 37.3 | 31.2 | 32.5 | 41.9 | 32.2 | 40.6 | 47.3 |
| % Net Income of Revenue | 3.1 | NM | NM | NM | 3.7 | 9.7 | 9.0 | 8.4 | 7.4 | 6.9 |
| % Return on Assets | NA | NA | NM | NM | 4.8 | 12.4 | 11.9 | 12.0 | 10.4 | 9.8 |
| % Return on Equity | NA | NA | NM | NM | 10.8 | 28.9 | 25.8 | 27.4 | 28.0 | 28.9 |

Data as orig reptd.; bef. results of disc opers/spec. items. Per share data adj. for stk. divs.; EPS diluted. E-Estimated. NA-Not Available. NM-Not Meaningful. NR-Not Ranked. UR-Under Review.

**Office:** 700 NW 107th Ave, Miami, FL 33172.
**Telephone:** 305-559-4000.
**Website:** http://www.lennar.com
**Pres:** R. Beckwitt

**CEO:** S. Miller
**COO:** J.M. Jaffe
**CFO:** B.E. Gross
**Chief Acctg Officer & Cntlr:** D.M. Collins

**Investor Contact:** M.H. Ames (800-741-4663)
**Auditor:** DELOITTE & TOUCHE
**Board Members:** I. Bolotin, S. L. Gerard, T. I. Gilliam, Jr., S. W. Hudson, D. J. Kaiserman, R. K. Landon, S. Lapidus, S. Miller, D. E. Shalala, J. Sonnenfeld

**Founded:** 1954
**Domicile:** Delaware
**Employees:** 4,087

# Leucadia National Corp

**STANDARD &POOR'S**

| S&P Recommendation **HOLD** ★★★★★ | Price $20.54 (as of Nov 25, 2011) | 12-Mo. Target Price $29.00 | Investment Style Large-Cap Growth |
|---|---|---|---|

**GICS Sector** Financials
**Sub-Industry** Multi-Sector Holdings

**Summary** This diversified holding company has subsidiaries engaged in manufacturing, real estate, medical product development, gaming entertainment, mining, and energy.

## Key Stock Statistics (Source S&P, Vickers, company reports)

| | | | | | | | |
|---|---|---|---|---|---|---|---|
| 52-Wk Range | $39.14– 20.19 | S&P Oper. EPS 2011E | 0.06 | Market Capitalization(B) | $5.024 | Beta | 1.78 |
| Trailing 12-Month EPS | $6.46 | S&P Oper. EPS 2012E | 1.99 | Yield (%) | NA | S&P 3-Yr. Proj. EPS CAGR(%) | 2 |
| Trailing 12-Month P/E | 3.2 | P/E on S&P Oper. EPS 2011E | NM | Dividend Rate/Share | NA | S&P Credit Rating | BB+ |
| $10K Invested 5 Yrs Ago | $7,773 | Common Shares Outstg. (M) | 244.6 | Institutional Ownership (%) | 64 | | |

## Price Performance

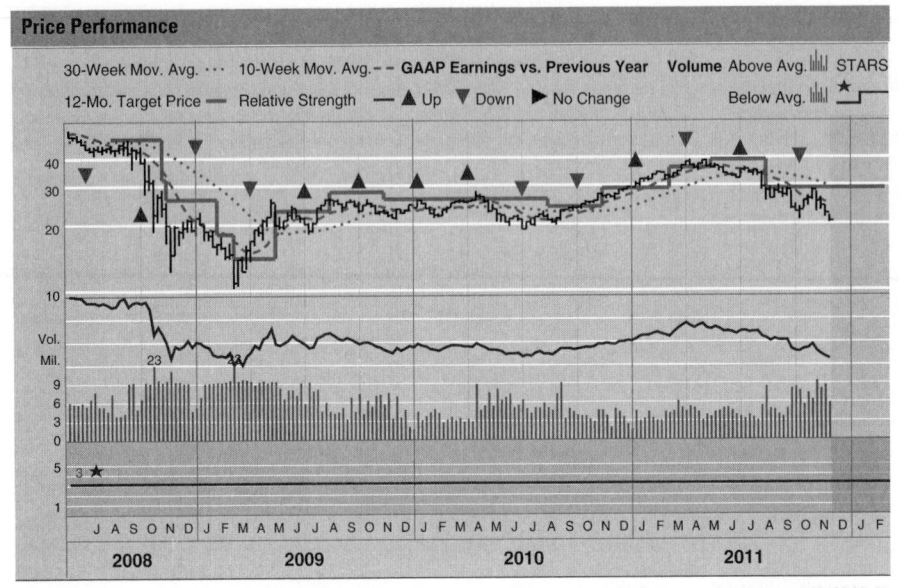

30-Week Mov. Avg. ··· 10-Week Mov. Avg. – – GAAP Earnings vs. Previous Year    Volume Above Avg. ▥ STARS
12-Mo. Target Price — Relative Strength — ▲ Up ▼ Down ▶ No Change    Below Avg. ▥ ★

Options: ASE, CBOE, Ph

Analysis prepared by Equity Analyst **Robert McMillan** on Nov 15, 2011, when the stock traded at **$23.69**.

## Highlights

➤ We look for high energy prices to help Leucadia's oil and gas drilling services in 2011 and 2012. However, a weak housing market is likely to prevent significant improvement in the timber, plastics and real estate development businesses. Higher promotional spending should boost revenue at the gaming business. An eventual recovery in housing should help several of LUK's markets longer term.

➤ Leucadia has scaled back its investments in financial entities, sold its telecom and resort management businesses, and is looking to increase its investments in the energy sector. We believe its public holdings in mining and investment banking will appreciate long term as economic growth re-accelerates. Spending on medical product and energy project development will likely increase again in 2011 and 2012, in our view.

➤ Our forecast is for operating earnings of $0.06 a share in 2011. We expect LUK to have a very uneven earnings pattern due to frequent changes in the number and types of businesses it operates, as well as changes in the value of its investments. For 2012, we project EPS of $1.99.

## Investment Rationale/Risk

➤ Leucadia has a strong long-term record of increasing its book value, aided by its success in finding assets that are out of favor or are troubled, and therefore selling at a discount to their inherent value. However, this trend was disrupted in recent years due to the broad-based decline in equity markets. We expect increased earnings from a major investment in an Australian iron ore company, and LUK could accelerate acquisition activity given the pullback in the market.

➤ Risks to our recommendation and target price include reliance on the company's two top executives for most of its investment decisions, and the potential for further volatility in the value of its holdings due to the impact of economic uncertainty.

➤ Book value per share at Leucadia rose at a compound annual rate of 14.7% from 2000 through 2010, despite a sharp drop in 2008 due to the decline in the stock market. Our 12-month target price of $29 is calculated by applying a 0.95X multiple, below historical levels due to lower equity valuations, to our 2012 book value per share estimate of $30.61.

## Qualitative Risk Assessment

| LOW | MEDIUM | HIGH |
|---|---|---|

Our risk assessment reflects the broad diversity of the company's investments and what we view as a strong management team, offset by exposure to certain development-stage businesses.

## Quantitative Evaluations

**S&P Quality Ranking**    B-

| D | C | B- | B | B+ | A- | A | A+ |
|---|---|---|---|---|---|---|---|

**Relative Strength Rank**    WEAK

14

LOWEST = 1    HIGHEST = 99

## Revenue/Earnings Data

**Revenue (Million $)**

| | 1Q | 2Q | 3Q | 4Q | Year |
|---|---|---|---|---|---|
| 2011 | 202.2 | 753.4 | 236.1 | -- | -- |
| 2010 | 259.3 | 289.2 | 185.9 | 585.6 | 1,320 |
| 2009 | 250.3 | 284.3 | 280.8 | 303.5 | 1,098 |
| 2008 | 324.9 | 337.6 | 251.6 | 166.6 | 1,081 |
| 2007 | 197.2 | 344.0 | 331.2 | 282.6 | 1,155 |
| 2006 | 291.6 | 224.4 | 170.2 | 176.4 | 862.7 |

**Earnings Per Share ($)**

| | 1Q | 2Q | 3Q | 4Q | Year |
|---|---|---|---|---|---|
| 2011 | 0.05 | 0.74 | -1.19 | E0.46 | E0.06 |
| 2010 | 0.80 | -1.01 | 1.07 | 6.77 | 7.66 |
| 2009 | -0.59 | 1.67 | 1.40 | -0.38 | 2.14 |
| 2008 | -0.43 | -0.76 | 0.37 | -11.72 | -11.19 |
| 2007 | 0.04 | 0.12 | 0.01 | 1.87 | 2.09 |
| 2006 | 0.37 | 0.17 | 0.02 | 0.03 | 0.60 |

Fiscal year ended Dec. 31. Next earnings report expected: Late February. EPS Estimates based on S&P Operating Earnings; historical GAAP earnings are as reported.

## Dividend Data (Dates: mm/dd Payment Date: mm/dd/yy)

| Amount ($) | Date Decl. | Ex-Div. Date | Stk. of Record | Payment Date |
|---|---|---|---|---|
| 0.250 | 12/06 | 12/15 | 12/17 | 12/30/10 |

Dividends have been paid since 2010. Source: Company reports.

# Leucadia National Corp

**STANDARD
&POOR'S**

## Business Summary November 15, 2011

CORPORATE OVERVIEW. Leucadia is a diversified holding company engaged in a variety of businesses, including manufacturing, land-based contract oil and gas drilling, gaming entertainment, real estate activities, medical product development, and winery operations. It also has significant investments in the common stock of several public companies including a full service investment bank and mining concerns in Australia and Canada. Additionally, Leucadia owns equity interests in operating businesses and investment partnerships, which are accounted for under the equity method of accounting, including a broker-dealer engaged in making markets and trading high-yield and special situation securities, and a commercial mortgage origination and servicing business. Revenues by major business segment in 2010 were as follows: Idaho Timber 34%; oil and gas drilling services 23%; gaming entertainment 23%; and Conwed Plastics 17%.

CORPORATE STRATEGY. Leucadia's approach to its investments is to focus on return on investment and cash flow to build long-term shareholder value. Additionally, the company continuously evaluates the retention and disposition

of its existing operations and investigates possible acquisitions of new businesses. In identifying possible acquisitions, Leucadia tends to seek assets and companies that are out of favor or troubled and, as a result, are selling substantially below the values it believes to be present. The company's principal sources of funds are its available cash resources, liquid investments, public and private capital market transactions, borrowings and dividends from its subsidiaries, as well as dispositions of existing businesses and investments. Leucadia also considers investments classified as current and non-current assets on its balance sheet to be generally available to meet its liquidity needs. As of December 31, 2010, the sum of these amounts without restrictions equaled $3 billion. We expect the composition of Leucadia's assets to change continuously as certain businesses are divested and others are acquired.

## Company Financials Fiscal Year Ended Dec. 31

| Per Share Data ($) | 2010 | 2009 | 2008 | 2007 | 2006 | 2005 | 2004 | 2003 | 2002 | 2001 |
|---|---|---|---|---|---|---|---|---|---|---|
| Tangible Book Value | 28.36 | 17.62 | 10.87 | 24.66 | 17.72 | 16.87 | 17.32 | 10.04 | 8.78 | 7.05 |
| Cash Flow | 8.05 | 2.46 | -10.91 | 2.26 | 0.75 | 6.11 | 1.71 | 0.81 | 1.02 | 0.49 |
| Earnings | 7.64 | 2.14 | -11.19 | 2.09 | 0.60 | 5.36 | 0.70 | 0.46 | 0.91 | 0.39 |
| S&P Core Earnings | 6.67 | 2.07 | -11.27 | 2.06 | NA | 4.69 | 0.05 | 0.42 | 1.05 | 0.27 |
| Dividends | 0.25 | Nil | Nil | 0.25 | 0.25 | 0.13 | 0.13 | 0.08 | 0.08 | 0.08 |
| Payout Ratio | 3% | Nil | Nil | 12% | 42% | 2% | 18% | 18% | 9% | 21% |
| Prices:High | 29.64 | 26.47 | 56.90 | 52.67 | 32.62 | 24.64 | 23.50 | 15.40 | 13.42 | 11.90 |
| Prices:Low | 18.80 | 10.26 | 12.19 | 26.52 | 23.26 | 16.20 | 15.02 | 10.86 | 9.21 | 8.77 |
| P/E Ratio:High | 4 | 12 | NM | 25 | 54 | 5 | 34 | 34 | 15 | 31 |
| P/E Ratio:Low | 3 | 5 | NM | 13 | 39 | 3 | 21 | 24 | 10 | 22 |

| Income Statement Analysis (Million $) | | | | | | | | | | |
|---|---|---|---|---|---|---|---|---|---|---|
| Revenue | 1,290 | 1,098 | 1,081 | 1,155 | 863 | 1,041 | 2,262 | 556 | 242 | 375 |
| Operating Income | 643 | -46.3 | -156 | 58.1 | 222 | 396 | 366 | 75.2 | 10.7 | 151 |
| Depreciation | 105 | 86.4 | 65.4 | 49.8 | 43.6 | 190 | 233 | 65.7 | 18.7 | 17.5 |
| Interest Expense | 125 | 129 | 145 | 112 | 79.4 | 68.4 | 96.8 | 43.6 | 33.5 | 55.2 |
| Pretax Income | 750 | 529 | -906 | -79.0 | 172 | 93.0 | 132 | 42.9 | 13.2 | 53.7 |
| Effective Tax Rate | NA | 1.35% | NM | 708.9% | 24.4% | NM | NM | NM | NM | NM |
| Net Income | 1,889 | 524 | -2,579 | 481 | 130 | 1,224 | 152 | 84.4 | 153 | 64.8 |
| S&P Core Earnings | 1,647 | 504 | -2,598 | 473 | -9.43 | 1,071 | 5.47 | 77.7 | 177 | 45.7 |

| Balance Sheet & Other Financial Data (Million $) | | | | | | | | | | |
|---|---|---|---|---|---|---|---|---|---|---|
| Cash | 706 | 239 | 604 | 1,440 | 3,430 | 3,063 | 2,781 | 2,033 | 1,044 | 1,183 |
| Current Assets | 986 | 551 | 867 | 1,720 | 1,366 | 2,229 | 2,060 | 1,350 | 1,002 | 1,263 |
| Total Assets | 9,350 | 6,762 | 5,198 | 8,127 | 5,304 | 5,261 | 4,800 | 4,397 | 2,542 | 2,577 |
| Current Liabilities | 748 | 625 | 563 | 460 | 327 | 474 | 659 | 657 | 119 | 227 |
| Long Term Debt | 1,548 | 1,660 | 1,833 | 2,004 | 975 | 987 | 1,484 | 1,155 | 328 | 424 |
| Common Equity | 6,957 | 4,362 | 2,677 | 5,570 | 3,893 | 3,662 | 2,259 | 2,134 | 1,487 | 1,195 |
| Total Capital | 8,661 | 6,347 | 4,777 | 7,596 | 4,887 | 4,665 | 3,760 | 3,307 | 1,893 | 1,666 |
| Capital Expenditures | 44.3 | 23.6 | 76.1 | 135 | 111 | 136 | 97.4 | 84.7 | NA | NA |
| Cash Flow | 1,994 | 610 | -2,514 | 531 | 173 | 1,414 | 385 | 150 | 171 | 82.3 |
| Current Ratio | 1.3 | 0.9 | 1.5 | 3.7 | 4.2 | 4.7 | 3.1 | 2.1 | 8.4 | 5.6 |
| % Long Term Debt of Capitalization | 17.9 | Nil | 38.4 | 26.4 | 19.9 | 20.8 | 38.8 | 34.7 | 17.5 | 25.7 |
| % Net Income of Revenue | 146.4 | 47.7 | NM | 41.6 | 15.7 | 117.6 | 6.8 | 15.2 | 63.1 | 16.2 |
| % Return on Assets | 23.5 | NA | NM | 77.2 | 2.5 | 24.3 | 3.3 | 2.4 | 6.0 | 2.3 |
| % Return on Equity | 33.4 | NA | NM | 10.2 | 3.4 | 41.4 | 6.9 | 4.7 | 11.4 | 5.4 |

Data as orig reptd.; bef. results of disc opers/spec. items. Per share data adj. for stk. divs.; EPS diluted. E-Estimated. NA-Not Available. NM-Not Meaningful. NR-Not Ranked. UR-Under Review.

**Office:** 315 Park Ave S, New York, NY 10010.
**Telephone:** 212-460-1900.
**Chrmn:** I.M. Cumming
**Pres & CEO:** J.S. Steinberg

**CFO:** J.A. Orlando
**Chief Acctg Officer & Cntlr:** B.L. Lowenthal
**Treas:** R.J. Nittoli
**Investor Contact:** L.E. Ulbrandt (212-460-1900)

**Auditor:** PRICEWATERHOUSECOOPERS
**Board Members:** I. M. Cumming, P. M. Dougan, A. J. Hirschfield, J. E. Jordan, J. C. Keil, J. C. Nichols, III, M. Sorkin, J. S. Steinberg

**Founded:** 1854
**Domicile:** New York
**Employees:** 2,414

*The McGraw-Hill Companies*

# Lexmark International Inc.

STANDARD &POOR'S

| S&P Recommendation | HOLD ★★★☆☆ | Price $31.17 (as of Nov 25, 2011) | 12-Mo. Target Price $34.00 | Investment Style Large-Cap Growth |
|---|---|---|---|---|

**GICS Sector** Information Technology
**Sub-Industry** Computer Storage & Peripherals

**Summary** Lexmark develops, manufactures and supplies laser and inkjet printers and associated consumable supplies for the office and home markets.

## Key Stock Statistics (Source S&P, Vickers, company reports)

| | | | | | | | | |
|---|---|---|---|---|---|---|---|---|
| 52-Wk Range | $40.54– 25.87 | S&P Oper. EPS 2011**E** | 4.65 | Market Capitalization(B) | $2.344 | Beta | | 1.10 |
| Trailing 12-Month EPS | $4.27 | S&P Oper. EPS 2012**E** | 4.63 | Yield (%) | 3.21 | S&P 3-Yr. Proj. EPS CAGR(%) | | 1 |
| Trailing 12-Month P/E | 7.3 | P/E on S&P Oper. EPS 2011**E** | 6.7 | Dividend Rate/Share | $1.00 | S&P Credit Rating | | NA |
| $10K Invested 5 Yrs Ago | $4,574 | Common Shares Outstg. (M) | 75.2 | Institutional Ownership (%) | NM | | | |

## Price Performance

30-Week Mov. Avg. · · · 10-Week Mov. Avg. - - GAAP Earnings vs. Previous Year   Volume Above Avg. STARS
12-Mo. Target Price — Relative Strength   ▲ Up ▼ Down ► No Change   Below Avg.

Options: ASE, CBOE, P, Ph

Analysis prepared by Equity Analyst **Dylan Cathers** on Oct 31, 2011, when the stock traded at **$31.70**.

### Highlights

► We expect revenues to decline 1.0% in 2011 and 0.5% in 2012. We continue to look for a difficult operating environment, given the overall macroeconomic uncertainty. Also affecting revenues in the next few quarters will likely be the continued decline of the legacy consumer inkjet business as well as less-favorable currency shifts. Color laser multi-function printers and enterprise management software should support better results over the longer term. We also believe that the company's move into new verticals will prove fruitful.

► We look for operating margins to widen in both 2011 and 2012. We think higher volumes, new products, a richer product mix, and the benefits of ongoing restructuring plans will drive gains. In general, we see potential for better margin performance over the longer term, as newer product lines start to eclipse legacy lines more decisively.

► We estimate operating EPS, excluding restructuring charges, of $4.65 for 2011 and $4.63 for 2012, assuming a tax rate of about 23% and a modest level of share buybacks.

### Investment Rationale/Risk

► We view LXK as fairly valued given our outlook for moderate recovery in demand for printers with a questionable economic global backdrop. Recent product introductions and potential cost reductions should help buoy earnings despite a drag from legacy lines. We think LXK owns some important intellectual property, and should be able to expand its branded products and laser printer businesses as the economy picks up. We view positively the recent initiation of a $0.25 per share quarterly dividend.

► Risks to our recommendation and target price include the possibility that a recent leadership succession is not as smooth as we expect, that competition in the printer industry will be tougher than we anticipate, and that savings from restructuring will come in below our estimates.

► Our 12-month target price of $34 is based mainly on our P/E analysis. We apply a target multiple of 7.3X, which is near printer industry peers and toward the low end of LXK's historical range to reflect the moderate revenue environment we foresee, to our 2012 EPS estimate.

## Qualitative Risk Assessment

| LOW | MEDIUM | HIGH |
|---|---|---|

Our risk assessment reflects what we see as a difficult competitive pricing environment in the printer market, offset by our view of LXK's strides in improving its product portfolio and cost position.

## Quantitative Evaluations

**S&P Quality Ranking**   B

| D | C | B- | B | B+ | A- | A | A+ |
|---|---|---|---|---|---|---|---|

**Relative Strength Rank**   STRONG

75

LOWEST = 1                                    HIGHEST = 99

## Revenue/Earnings Data

**Revenue (Million $)**

| | 1Q | 2Q | 3Q | 4Q | Year |
|---|---|---|---|---|---|
| 2011 | 1,034 | 1,044 | 1,035 | -- | -- |
| 2010 | 1,043 | 1,033 | 1,020 | 1,104 | 4,200 |
| 2009 | 944.1 | 904.6 | 958.0 | 1,073 | 3,880 |
| 2008 | 1,175 | 1,139 | 1,131 | 1,084 | 4,528 |
| 2007 | 1,261 | 1,208 | 1,195 | 1,310 | 4,974 |
| 2006 | 1,275 | 1,229 | 1,235 | 1,369 | 5,108 |

**Earnings Per Share ($)**

| | | | | | |
|---|---|---|---|---|---|
| 2011 | 1.04 | 1.27 | 0.86 | E1.20 | E4.65 |
| 2010 | 1.21 | 1.07 | 0.90 | 1.10 | 4.28 |
| 2009 | 0.75 | 0.22 | 0.13 | 0.76 | 1.86 |
| 2008 | 1.07 | 0.89 | 0.42 | 0.23 | 2.69 |
| 2007 | 0.95 | 0.67 | 0.48 | 1.04 | 3.14 |
| 2006 | 0.78 | 0.74 | 0.85 | 0.91 | 3.27 |

Fiscal year ended Dec. 31. Next earnings report expected: Early February. EPS Estimates based on S&P Operating Earnings; historical GAAP earnings are as reported.

## Dividend Data (Dates: mm/dd Payment Date: mm/dd/yy)

| Amount ($) | Date Decl. | Ex-Div. Date | Stk. of Record | Payment Date |
|---|---|---|---|---|
| 0.250 | 10/27 | 11/10 | 11/15 | 11/30/11 |

Dividends have been paid since 2011. Source: Company reports.

---

**Please read the Required Disclosures and Analyst Certification on the last page of this report.**

The McGraw-Hill Companies

# Lexmark International Inc.

STANDARD
&POOR'S

## Business Summary October 31, 2011

CORPORATE OVERVIEW. Lexmark shook up the printer industry with the introduction of the first desktop color printer priced under $100 with its November 1997 launch of the $99 color inkjet printer, aimed at building brand awareness and an installed base. We think LXK's competitive advantage in the past was its low cost structure and its ability to price aggressively. However, in recent years, it has been on the defensive, in our view, as peers have undercut its prices and LXK's product mix was not focused on some of the more compelling printer areas. Going forward, LXK management believes that its commitment to R&D should bear fruit and help revive unit growth and subsequently high-margin supplies sales, but we view this as a multi-year process. In autumn 2008, the company began to introduce an extensive series of new laser products. Following through in 2009, some 33 new product models were introduced. In 2010, LXK announced 13 new printers and multi-function printers (MFPs) that featured intuitive color touch screens.

By product category, revenue for 2010 came 25% from laser and inkjet printers (24% in 2009), 69% (71%) from laser and inkjet supplies, and 5% (5%) from software and other lines. Revenue grew at a 13% pace in 2010 for printers, at

6% for supplies, and at 18% for software.

In June 2010, the company acquired Perceptive Software in an effort to accelerate the development of enterprise content management (ECM) software and document workflow solutions. Although software is at present a relatively small segment for LXK, it has been growing faster than the company's other segments, and we believe it offers superior growth opportunities compared to traditional printer and supply markets.

Lexmark distributes to business customers via many channels, including its network of authorized distributors. The company distributes to consumers through retail outlets worldwide, and also sells through alliances and OEM arrangements. One customer, Dell, accounted for 11% of revenues in 2010, down from 13% in 2009.

## Company Financials Fiscal Year Ended Dec. 31

| Per Share Data ($) | 2010 | 2009 | 2008 | 2007 | 2006 | 2005 | 2004 | 2003 | 2002 | 2001 |
|---|---|---|---|---|---|---|---|---|---|---|
| Tangible Book Value | 13.41 | 12.98 | 10.45 | 15.76 | 10.67 | 12.77 | NM | 17.46 | NM | 8.25 |
| Cash Flow | 6.74 | 4.58 | 4.97 | 5.13 | 5.21 | 4.21 | 5.29 | 4.48 | 3.84 | 2.98 |
| Earnings | 4.28 | 1.86 | 2.69 | 3.14 | 3.27 | 2.91 | 4.28 | 3.34 | 2.79 | 2.05 |
| S&P Core Earnings | 4.25 | 2.00 | 2.44 | 3.10 | 3.28 | 2.52 | 3.94 | 3.04 | 2.27 | 1.57 |
| Dividends | Nil | Nil | Nil | Nil | Nil | Nil | Nil | Nil | Nil | Nil |
| Payout Ratio | Nil | Nil | Nil | Nil | Nil | Nil | Nil | Nil | Nil | Nil |
| Prices:High | 48.07 | 29.16 | 37.88 | 73.20 | 74.68 | 86.62 | 97.50 | 79.65 | 69.50 | 70.75 |
| Prices:Low | 25.10 | 14.23 | 22.13 | 32.35 | 44.09 | 39.33 | 76.00 | 56.57 | 41.94 | 40.81 |
| P/E Ratio:High | 11 | 16 | 14 | 23 | 23 | 30 | 23 | 24 | 25 | 35 |
| P/E Ratio:Low | 6 | 8 | 8 | 10 | 13 | 14 | 18 | 17 | 15 | 20 |

| Income Statement Analysis (Million $) | | | | | | | | | | |
|---|---|---|---|---|---|---|---|---|---|---|
| Revenue | 4,200 | 3,880 | 4,528 | 4,974 | 5,108 | 5,222 | 5,314 | 4,755 | 4,356 | 4,143 |
| Operating Income | 687 | 573 | 573 | 564 | 715 | 692 | 867 | 743 | 643 | 525 |
| Depreciation | 196 | 214 | 203 | 191 | 201 | 159 | 135 | 149 | 138 | 126 |
| Interest Expense | 26.3 | 39.3 | 28.9 | 13.0 | 12.1 | 11.2 | 12.3 | 12.5 | 9.00 | 14.8 |
| Pretax Income | 422 | 187 | 276 | 350 | 459 | 554 | 746 | 594 | 496 | 318 |
| Effective Tax Rate | NA | 22.0% | 12.9% | 13.9% | 26.3% | 35.7% | 23.8% | 26.0% | 26.0% | 13.9% |
| Net Income | 340 | 146 | 240 | 301 | 338 | 356 | 569 | 439 | 367 | 274 |
| S&P Core Earnings | 338 | 157 | 218 | 297 | 340 | 308 | 524 | 399 | 298 | 210 |

| Balance Sheet & Other Financial Data (Million $) | | | | | | | | | | |
|---|---|---|---|---|---|---|---|---|---|---|
| Cash | 1,217 | 1,133 | 973 | 796 | 551 | 889 | 1,567 | 1,196 | 498 | 90.7 |
| Current Assets | 2,270 | 2,141 | 2,063 | 2,067 | 1,830 | 2,170 | 3,001 | 2,444 | 1,799 | 1,493 |
| Total Assets | 3,705 | 3,354 | 3,265 | 3,121 | 2,849 | 3,330 | 4,124 | 3,450 | 2,808 | 2,450 |
| Current Liabilities | 1,246 | 1,192 | 1,258 | 1,497 | 1,324 | 1,234 | 1,468 | 1,183 | 1,099 | 931 |
| Long Term Debt | 649 | 649 | 649 | Nil | 150 | 150 | 150 | 149 | 149 | 149 |
| Common Equity | 1,394 | 1,014 | 812 | 1,278 | 1,035 | 1,429 | 2,083 | 1,643 | 1,082 | 1,076 |
| Total Capital | 2,043 | 1,663 | 1,461 | 1,278 | 1,185 | 1,578 | 2,232 | 1,792 | 1,231 | 1,225 |
| Capital Expenditures | 161 | 242 | 218 | 183 | 200 | 201 | 198 | 93.8 | 112 | 214 |
| Cash Flow | 536 | 360 | 443 | 492 | 539 | 515 | 704 | 588 | 505 | 399 |
| Current Ratio | 1.8 | 1.8 | 1.6 | 1.4 | 1.4 | 1.8 | 2.0 | 2.1 | 1.6 | 1.6 |
| % Long Term Debt of Capitalization | 31.8 | 39.0 | 44.4 | Nil | 12.6 | 9.5 | 6.7 | 8.3 | 12.1 | 12.2 |
| % Net Income of Revenue | 8.1 | 3.8 | 5.3 | 6.1 | 6.6 | 6.8 | 10.7 | 9.2 | 8.4 | 6.6 |
| % Return on Assets | 9.6 | 4.4 | 7.5 | 10.1 | 11.0 | 9.6 | 15.0 | 14.0 | 13.9 | 12.1 |
| % Return on Equity | 28.2 | 16.0 | 23.0 | 26.0 | 27.5 | 20.3 | 30.5 | 32.2 | 34.0 | 29.5 |

Data as orig reptd.; bef. results of disc opers/spec. items. Per share data adj. for stk. divs.; EPS diluted. E-Estimated. NA-Not Available. NM-Not Meaningful. NR-Not Ranked. UR-Under Review.

**Office:** 740 West New Circle Rd, Lexington, KY 40550.
**Telephone:** 859-232-2000.
**Website:** http://www.lexmark.com
**Chrmn, Pres & CEO:** P.A. Rooke

**EVP, CFO & Chief Acctg Officer:** J.W. Gamble, Jr.
**Treas:** B. Frost
**Secy:** R.J. Patton
**Investor Contact:** J. Morgan (859-232-5568)

**Board Members:** J. L. Cohon, J. E. Coleman, W. R. Dunbar, W. R. Fields, R. E. Gomory, S. R. Hardis, S. L. Helton, R. Holland, Jr., M. J. Maples, J. L. Montupet, P. A. Rooke, K. P. Seifert

**Founded:** 1990
**Domicile:** Delaware
**Employees:** 13,200

# Life Technologies Corp

**STANDARD &POOR'S**

| S&P Recommendation | STRONG BUY ★ ★ ★ ★ ★ | Price | 12-Mo. Target Price | Investment Style |
|---|---|---|---|---|
| | | $36.08 (as of Nov 25, 2011) | $58.00 | Large-Cap Growth |

**GICS Sector** Health Care
**Sub-Industry** Life Sciences Tools & Services

**Summary** This company develops and manufactures research products and instruments for biotechnology and biopharmaceutical researchers.

## Key Stock Statistics (Source S&P, Vickers, company reports)

| | | | | | | | | |
|---|---|---|---|---|---|---|---|---|
| 52-Wk Range | $57.25–35.30 | S&P Oper. EPS 2011E | 3.77 | Market Capitalization(B) | $6.430 | Beta | 0.83 |
| Trailing 12-Month EPS | $1.91 | S&P Oper. EPS 2012E | 4.18 | Yield (%) | Nil | S&P 3-Yr. Proj. EPS CAGR(%) | 14 |
| Trailing 12-Month P/E | 18.9 | P/E on S&P Oper. EPS 2011E | 9.6 | Dividend Rate/Share | Nil | S&P Credit Rating | BBB |
| $10K Invested 5 Yrs Ago | $12,803 | Common Shares Outstg. (M) | 178.2 | Institutional Ownership (%) | 97 | | |

## Price Performance

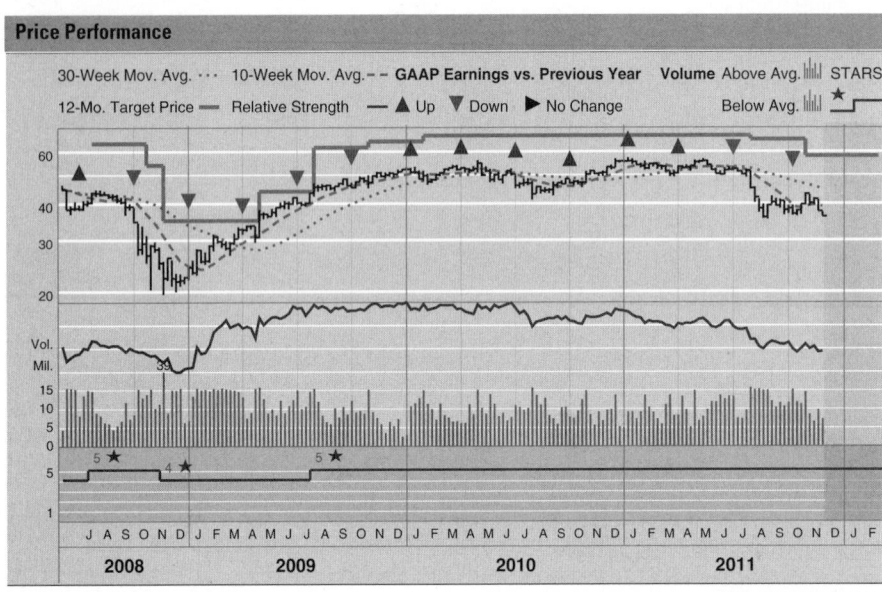

30-Week Mov. Avg. · · · 10-Week Mov. Avg. – – GAAP Earnings vs. Previous Year   Volume Above Avg. ▍▍▍ STARS
12-Mo. Target Price — Relative Strength — ▲ Up ▼ Down ► No Change   Below Avg. ▍▍▍ ★

Analysis prepared by Equity Analyst **Jeffrey Loo, CFA** on Nov 14, 2011, when the stock traded at **$41.09**.

## Highlights

➤ We expect sales to rise 4.9% in 2011 and 5.5% in 2012 to $3.76 billion and $3.97 billion, respectively. We look for sales in molecular biology, driven by robust demand for genomic assays and real-time PCR consumables, but partially offset by slower growth in government funded accounts, to rise in the low single-digits. Genetic systems, aided by strong sales from the introduction of its Ion Torrent Personal Genome Machine and from the new SOLiD 5500xl, and Cell System sales, on robust primary stem cell sales, should rise in the high single-digits. Due to higher sales of the 5500 Genetic Analyzer upgrades, we see 2011 gross margins declining 90 basis points, but we forecast operating margins will increase 50 basis points on leverage and cost saving synergies. Increased usage of the eCommerce platform, which currently processes 55% of transactions, should also boost margins.

➤ LIFE has made numerous acquisitions over the past several years to build and develop its product portfolio. However, we believe it will make only limited acquisitions over the next two years and seek to lower its debt levels.

➤ We see EPS of $3.77 and $4.18 in 2011 and 2012.

## Investment Rationale/Risk

➤ With the shares recently trading at about 10.2X our forward 12-months EPS forecast and at a 0.7X P/E-to-growth ratio, below peers and well below historical levels, we think the shares are undervalued. We believe LIFE is well positioned within its end-markets with a solid platform for expansion in high-growth markets within genomics, proteomics, and cell biology. We see continued robust growth for its next-generation sequencer, the SOLiD system, and expect it to help drive consumable sales. We think the recently introduced SOLiD 5500xl with a higher throughput and its Ion Torrent Personal Genome Machine will gain market share in an expanding marketplace. However, we see continued soft sales to government funded facilities in the U.S. and Europe, while the transition to a direct sales force in China is expected to adversely affect sales growth in 2011.

➤ Risks to our recommendation and target price include a slowdown in pharmaceutical and biotech R&D spending.

➤ Our 12-month target price of $58 reflects a 1.0X P/E-to-growth ratio, slightly below peers, based on our forward 12-months EPS forecast and a projected growth rate of 14%.

## Qualitative Risk Assessment

| LOW | MEDIUM | HIGH |
|---|---|---|

Our risk assessment reflects LIFE's diverse product portfolio and broad geographic client base. The life sciences industry is highly competitive, and companies need to develop new innovative products to remain viable, as technology is rapidly changing. Although life sciences is LIFE's main market, the company also sells products to the environmental, food safety and industrial markets.

## Quantitative Evaluations

**S&P Quality Ranking**   **B**

| D | C | B- | **B** | B+ | A- | A | A+ |
|---|---|---|---|---|---|---|---|

**Relative Strength Rank**   **MODERATE**

33

LOWEST = 1   HIGHEST = 99

## Revenue/Earnings Data

**Revenue (Million $)**

| | 1Q | 2Q | 3Q | 4Q | Year |
|---|---|---|---|---|---|
| 2011 | 895.9 | 941.1 | 928.2 | -- | -- |
| 2010 | 884.9 | 903.7 | 867.1 | 932.3 | 3,588 |
| 2009 | 775.7 | 832.8 | 800.7 | 871.1 | 3,280 |
| 2008 | 350.2 | 367.8 | 361.4 | 540.6 | 1,620 |
| 2007 | 308.7 | 321.7 | 315.0 | 336.5 | 1,282 |
| 2006 | 309.0 | 313.6 | 311.0 | 329.8 | 1,263 |

**Earnings Per Share ($)**

| | 1Q | 2Q | 3Q | 4Q | Year |
|---|---|---|---|---|---|
| 2011 | 0.50 | 0.52 | 0.52 | E1.07 | E3.77 |
| 2010 | 0.48 | 0.58 | 0.56 | 0.37 | 1.99 |
| 2009 | 0.09 | 0.22 | 0.22 | 0.26 | 0.80 |
| 2008 | 0.60 | 0.55 | 0.26 | -0.89 | 0.29 |
| 2007 | 0.31 | 0.31 | 0.32 | 0.41 | 1.35 |
| 2006 | 0.18 | 0.18 | -1.27 | -1.04 | -1.86 |

Fiscal year ended Dec. 31. Next earnings report expected: Early February. EPS Estimates based on S&P Operating Earnings; historical GAAP earnings are as reported.

## Dividend Data

No cash dividends have been paid.

---

# Life Technologies Corp

**STANDARD &POOR'S**

## Business Summary November 14, 2011

CORPORATE OVERVIEW. Life Technologies Inc. (LIFE) was formed through Invitrogen Corporation's (IVGN) $5.1 billion acquisition of Applied Biosystems Inc. (ABI) in November 2008. Prior to the transaction, IVGN had annual sales of about $1.3 billion and ABI had annual sales of about $2.2 billion. IVGN develops, manufactures and markets a broad line of tool kits and reagents, and provides other products and services, including informatics software and contract research services, used in life sciences research and the commercial manufacture of biopharmaceutical products. IVGN's revenue consisted of about 99% consumables and services and 1% instrument reagent systems. ABI develops and manufactures instrument-based systems, consumables and reagents, and software and related services for the life sciences industry, as well as for the food safety, environmental and other industrial end-markets. ABI's revenue consisted of 19% Mass Spectrometry instrument sales, 21% Instrument Reagent Systems, and 60% Consumable and Services. LIFE is now one of the largest companies within the life sciences industry based on annual revenue. LIFE's 2010 revenue breakdown was 48% (48% in 2009) molecular biology systems, 25% (24% in 2009) genetic systems, and 26% (28%in 2009) cell systems. In February 2010, LIFE sold its ownership stake in its mass spectrometry unit, to Danaher Corporation for $450 million. This unit was a joint venture with MDS Inc., with sales and income accounted for under the equity method, and provided $46 million in income in 2009.

LIFE has an extensive product portfolio offering end-to-end workflow solutions. Products primarily from IVGN's portfolio are used for sample preparation and sample processing, while ABI's instrumentation is used for detection and analysis and data interpretation. IVGN has two main units -- BioDiscovery and Cell Culture Systems. The BioDiscovery segment serves governmental and academic laboratories as well as biotechnology and pharmaceutical firms engaged in research of biological and genetic substances. The Cell Culture Systems segment primarily serves companies that are engaged in the commercialization of such substances; these concerns typically require large amounts of biologic or genetic materials or the growth media used in their manufacture. The company produces cell culture products under the GIBCO brand. These products include a variety of sera, culture media and reagents. Some of these substances are used in the manufacture of genetically engineered products, and are produced in large-scale commercial production facilities.

## Company Financials Fiscal Year Ended Dec. 31

| Per Share Data ($) | 2010 | 2009 | 2008 | 2007 | 2006 | 2005 | 2004 | 2003 | 2002 | 2001 |
|---|---|---|---|---|---|---|---|---|---|---|
| Tangible Book Value | NM | NM | NM | NM | NM | NM | 0.47 | 3.49 | 5.31 | 4.62 |
| Cash Flow | 4.17 | 3.07 | 1.57 | 2.74 | -0.28 | 2.44 | 1.95 | 1.66 | 1.28 | 1.33 |
| Earnings | 1.99 | 0.80 | 0.29 | 1.35 | -1.86 | 1.17 | 0.82 | 0.58 | 0.45 | -1.41 |
| S&P Core Earnings | 1.83 | 0.83 | 0.26 | 1.35 | 0.70 | 0.86 | 0.49 | 0.27 | 0.15 | -1.75 |
| Dividends | Nil | Nil | Nil | Nil | Nil | Nil | Nil | Nil | Nil | Nil |
| Payout Ratio | Nil | Nil | Nil | Nil | Nil | Nil | Nil | Nil | Nil | Nil |
| Prices:High | 56.78 | 52.97 | 49.00 | 49.58 | 38.33 | 44.25 | 41.00 | 35.47 | 31.35 | 42.97 |
| Prices:Low | 41.10 | 22.76 | 19.56 | 27.96 | 27.35 | 30.07 | 23.10 | 14.02 | 12.62 | 19.25 |
| P/E Ratio:High | 29 | 66 | NM | 37 | NM | 38 | 50 | 61 | 70 | NM |
| P/E Ratio:Low | 21 | 28 | NM | 21 | NM | 26 | 28 | 24 | 28 | NM |

### Income Statement Analysis (Million $)

| | 2010 | 2009 | 2008 | 2007 | 2006 | 2005 | 2004 | 2003 | 2002 | 2001 |
|---|---|---|---|---|---|---|---|---|---|---|
| Revenue | 3,588 | 3,280 | 1,620 | 1,282 | 1,263 | 1,198 | 1,024 | 778 | 649 | 629 |
| Operating Income | 1,144 | 975 | 431 | 320 | 286 | 305 | 284 | 203 | 172 | 148 |
| Depreciation | 417 | 398 | 133 | 136 | 162 | 160 | 147 | 111 | 87.7 | 287 |
| Interest Expense | 152 | 193 | 43.0 | 28.0 | 32.4 | 34.2 | 32.2 | 28.6 | 24.1 | 11.3 |
| Pretax Income | 442 | 195 | 154 | 179 | -163 | 174 | 121 | 85.1 | 71.2 | -137 |
| Effective Tax Rate | NA | 25.7% | 80.6% | 27.1% | NM | 24.0% | 26.8% | 28.6% | 31.2% | NM |
| Net Income | 378 | 145 | 30.0 | 130 | -191 | 132 | 88.8 | 60.1 | 47.7 | -148 |
| S&P Core Earnings | 349 | 151 | 27.0 | 131 | 71.4 | 94.7 | 52.8 | 28.1 | 15.4 | -183 |

### Balance Sheet & Other Financial Data (Million $)

| | 2010 | 2009 | 2008 | 2007 | 2006 | 2005 | 2004 | 2003 | 2002 | 2001 |
|---|---|---|---|---|---|---|---|---|---|---|
| Cash | 837 | 607 | 336 | 671 | 367 | 435 | 198 | 589 | 547 | 995 |
| Current Assets | 2,047 | 1,796 | 1,612 | 1,090 | 798 | 1,151 | 1,332 | 1,287 | 968 | 1,204 |
| Total Assets | 9,486 | 9,116 | 8,914 | 3,330 | 3,183 | 3,877 | 3,614 | 3,166 | 2,615 | 2,667 |
| Current Liabilities | 1,146 | 1,386 | 1,007 | 234 | 248 | 512 | 196 | 126 | 141 | 127 |
| Long Term Debt | 2,728 | 2,620 | 3,504 | 1,151 | 1,152 | 1,152 | 1,300 | 1,055 | 672 | 676 |
| Common Equity | 4,438 | 4,027 | 3,400 | 1,765 | 1,630 | 2,042 | 1,913 | 1,807 | 1,643 | 1,683 |
| Total Capital | 7,513 | 7,128 | 7,542 | 3,019 | 2,883 | 3,335 | 3,367 | 3,023 | 2,427 | 2,525 |
| Capital Expenditures | 125 | 181 | 81.9 | 78.3 | 61.1 | 71.8 | 39.1 | 32.2 | 51.5 | 44.2 |
| Cash Flow | 795 | 556 | 163 | 266 | -29.3 | 292 | 236 | 171 | 135 | 139 |
| Current Ratio | 1.8 | 1.3 | 1.6 | 4.7 | 3.2 | 2.3 | 6.8 | 10.2 | 6.9 | 9.5 |
| % Long Term Debt of Capitalization | 36.3 | 36.8 | 46.5 | 38.1 | 40.0 | 34.5 | 38.6 | 34.9 | 27.7 | 26.8 |
| % Net Income of Revenue | 10.5 | 4.4 | 1.9 | 10.2 | NM | 11.0 | 8.7 | 7.7 | 7.3 | NM |
| % Return on Assets | 4.1 | 1.6 | 0.5 | 4.0 | NM | 3.5 | 2.6 | 2.1 | 1.8 | NM |
| % Return on Equity | 8.9 | 3.9 | 1.2 | 7.7 | NM | 6.7 | 4.8 | 3.5 | 2.9 | NM |

Data as orig reptd.; bef. results of disc opers/spec. items. Per share data adj. for stk. divs.; EPS diluted. E-Estimated. NA-Not Available. NM-Not Meaningful. NR-Not Ranked. UR-Under Review.

**Office:** 5791 Van Allen Way, Carlsbad, CA 92008-7321.
**Telephone:** 760-603-7200.
**Website:** http://www.lifetechnologies.com
**Chrmn & CEO:** G.T. Lucier

**Pres & COO:** M.P. Stevenson
**SVP & CFO:** D.F. Hoffmeister
**Chief Acctg Officer:** K.A. Richard
**Secy & General Counsel:** J.A. Cottingham

**Investor Contact:** A. Clardy (760-603-7200)
**Board Members:** G. F. Adam, Jr., R. V. Dittamore, D. W. Grimm, B. S. Iyer, A. J. Levine, W. H. Longfield, B. G. Lorimier, G. T. Lucier, R. A. Matricaria, O. H. Pescovitz, P. A. Peterson, D. C. U'Prichard

**Founded:** 1987
**Domicile:** Delaware
**Employees:** 11,000

# Eli Lilly and Co

**STANDARD &POOR'S**

| S&P Recommendation **HOLD** ★★★★☆ | Price $35.58 (as of Nov 25, 2011) | 12-Mo. Target Price $40.00 | Investment Style Large-Cap Blend |
|---|---|---|---|

**GICS Sector** Health Care
**Sub-Industry** Pharmaceuticals

**Summary** This leading producer of prescription drugs offers a wide range of treatments for neurological disorders, diabetes, cancer and other conditions, and also sells animal health products.

## Key Stock Statistics (Source S&P, Vickers, company reports)

| | | | | | | | |
|---|---|---|---|---|---|---|---|
| 52-Wk Range | $39.78–33.46 | S&P Oper. EPS 2011**E** | 4.35 | Market Capitalization(B) | $41.193 | Beta | 0.71 |
| Trailing 12-Month EPS | $4.18 | S&P Oper. EPS 2012**E** | 3.63 | Yield (%) | 5.51 | S&P 3-Yr. Proj. EPS CAGR(%) | -5 |
| Trailing 12-Month P/E | 8.5 | P/E on S&P Oper. EPS 2011**E** | 8.2 | Dividend Rate/Share | $1.96 | S&P Credit Rating | AA- |
| $10K Invested 5 Yrs Ago | $8,380 | Common Shares Outstg. (M) | 1,157.8 | Institutional Ownership (%) | 75 | | |

## Price Performance

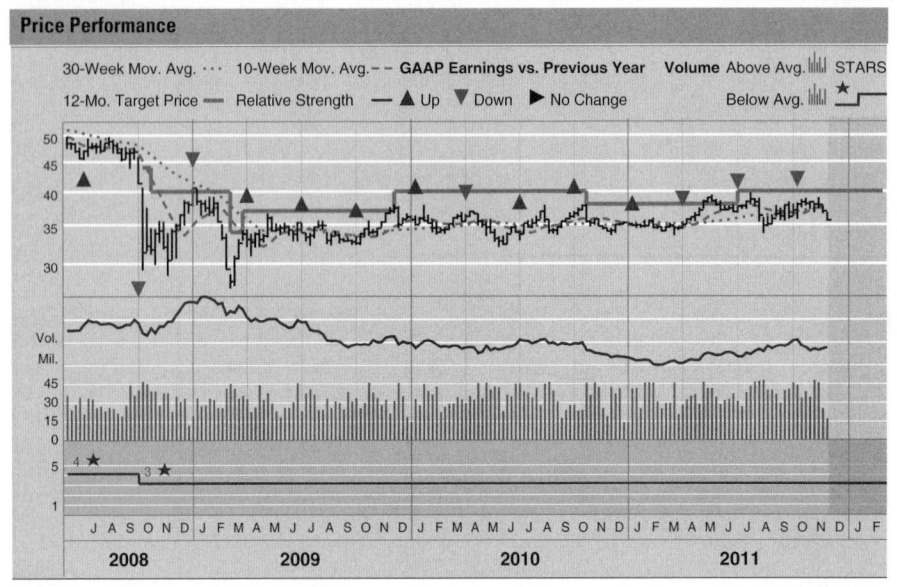

30-Week Mov. Avg. ···  10-Week Mov. Avg. – –  GAAP Earnings vs. Previous Year  Volume Above Avg. STARS
12-Mo. Target Price —  Relative Strength —  ▲ Up ▼ Down ► No Change  Below Avg.

Options: ASE, CBOE, P, Ph

Analysis prepared by Equity Analyst **Herman Saftlas** on Nov 15, 2011, when the stock traded at **$37.58**.

## Highlights

➤ We expect 2012 revenues to decline about 5% from the $24 billion that we forecast for 2011. The shortfall should primarily reflect an estimated 55% drop in sales of Zyprexa antipsychotic, which lost U.S. patent protection in October 2011. We also expect lower sales of other off-patent drugs such as Gemzar. On the plus side, we project further growth in other lines such as Cymbalta antidepressant and Alimta oncology agent. Sales of animal health products should also rise, helped by acquisitions. We also see continued strength in sales in Japan and emerging markets.

➤ We see 2012 gross margins narrowing modestly from the 78.5% indicated for 2011, largely reflecting sales mix pressure from a sharp drop in high-profit Zyprexa sales. Austerity pricing in Europe is another negative, in our opinion. On the plus side, we think the SG&A cost ratio is likely to decline, and interest costs should be lower.

➤ After a projected effective tax rate of about 22%, versus the 20% indicated for 2011, we estimate operating EPS of $3.63 in 2012, down from $4.35 that we forecast for 2011.

## Investment Rationale/Risk

➤ We believe LLY is executing well on its strategy to counter the recent patent expiration on Zyprexa and impending expirations on other drugs that in the aggregate are expected to reduce annual sales by about $7 billion from 2010 through 2014. To rejuvenate sales, LLY plans to bolster growth engines in Japan, emerging markets, animal health, and drug franchises in oncology and diabetes. As of October 2011, LLY had 13 compounds in Phase 3 trials or under regulatory review. Key promising new products, in our opinion, include Effient blood thinning agent, Axiron testosterone treatment and Tradjenta for Type 2 diabetes.

➤ Risks to our recommendation and target price include greater-than-expected competitive pressures, as well as failure to develop and commercialize new drugs.

➤ Our 12-month target price of $40 applies a peer multiple of 11X to our 2012 EPS estimate. Our DCF model, which assumes decelerating cash flow growth over the next 10 years, a WACC of 9.7%, and perpetuity growth of 2%, also indicates intrinsic value of $40. The dividend recently yielded 5.2%.

## Qualitative Risk Assessment

| LOW | **MEDIUM** | HIGH |
|---|---|---|

Our risk assessment reflects generic challenges to the company's branded patents, and drug development and regulatory risks. However, this is largely offset by our view of LLY's diverse drug portfolio, strong growth trends in Japan and emerging markets, and a robust pipeline.

## Quantitative Evaluations

**S&P Quality Ranking**  B

| D | C | B- | **B** | B+ | A- | A | A+ |
|---|---|---|---|---|---|---|---|

**Relative Strength Rank**  MODERATE

57

LOWEST = 1  HIGHEST = 99

## Revenue/Earnings Data

**Revenue (Million $)**

| | 1Q | 2Q | 3Q | 4Q | Year |
|---|---|---|---|---|---|
| 2011 | 5,839 | 6,253 | 6,148 | -- | -- |
| 2010 | 5,486 | 5,749 | 5,655 | 6,187 | 23,076 |
| 2009 | 5,047 | 5,293 | 5,562 | 5,934 | 21,836 |
| 2008 | 4,808 | 5,150 | 5,210 | 5,211 | 20,378 |
| 2007 | 4,226 | 4,631 | 4,587 | 5,190 | 18,634 |
| 2006 | 3,715 | 3,867 | 3,864 | 4,245 | 15,691 |

**Earnings Per Share ($)**

| | | | | | |
|---|---|---|---|---|---|
| 2011 | 0.95 | 1.07 | 1.11 | E0.80 | E4.35 |
| 2010 | 1.13 | 1.22 | 1.18 | 1.05 | 4.58 |
| 2009 | 1.20 | 1.06 | 0.86 | 0.83 | 3.94 |
| 2008 | 0.97 | 0.88 | -0.43 | -3.31 | -1.89 |
| 2007 | 0.47 | 0.61 | 0.85 | 0.78 | 2.71 |
| 2006 | 0.77 | 0.76 | 0.80 | 0.12 | 2.45 |

Fiscal year ended Dec. 31. Next earnings report expected: Late January. EPS Estimates based on S&P Operating Earnings; historical GAAP earnings are as reported.

## Dividend Data (Dates: mm/dd Payment Date: mm/dd/yy)

| Amount ($) | Date Decl. | Ex-Div. Date | Stk. of Record | Payment Date |
|---|---|---|---|---|
| 0.490 | 12/13 | 02/11 | 02/15 | 03/10/11 |
| 0.490 | 04/18 | 05/11 | 05/13 | 06/10/11 |
| 0.490 | 06/20 | 08/11 | 08/15 | 09/09/11 |
| 0.490 | 10/17 | 11/10 | 11/15 | 12/09/11 |

Dividends have been paid since 1885. Source: Company reports.

**Please read the Required Disclosures and Analyst Certification on the last page of this report.**

The **McGraw-Hill** Companies

# Eli Lilly and Co

STANDARD
&POOR'S

## Business Summary November 15, 2011

CORPORATE OVERVIEW. Eli Lilly and Co. is a leading maker of prescription drugs, offering a wide range of treatments for neurological disorders, diabetes, cancer and other conditions. Animal health products are also sold. Foreign drug sales accounted for about 41% of total revenues in 2010.

LLY's largest selling drug is Zyprexa, a treatment for schizophrenia and bipolar disorder that offers clinical advantages over older antipsychotic drugs. Sales of Zyprexa totaled $5.0 billion in 2010, up from $4.9 billion in 2009. However, Zyprexa lost U.S. patent protection in October 2011. LLY also offers Symbyax, a combination of Zyprexa and Prozac, to treat bipolar depression.

In August 2004, the company launched Cymbalta, a potent antidepressant. Cymbalta works on two body chemicals involved in depression -- serotonin and norepinephrine -- while most conventional antidepressants affect only serotonin. Sales of Cymbalta climbed to $3.5 billion in 2010, from $3.1 billion in 2009, reflecting greater market penetration and expanded indications.

Endocrinology products (sales of $5.9 billion in 2010) include Humulin, a hu-

man insulin produced through recombinant DNA technology; Humalog, a rapid-acting injectable human insulin analog; Iletin, an animal-source insulin; Actos, an oral agent for Type 2 diabetes that is manufactured by Takeda Chemical Industries of Japan and co-marketed by Lilly and Takeda; and Byetta, a treatment for Type 2 diabetes. Lilly shares in the profits from Byetta with Amylin Pharmaceuticals, co-developer of the drug. This group also includes Evista ($1.0 billion) and Forteo ($830 million) treatments for osteoporosis; and Humatrope, a recombinant human growth hormone.

Other important drugs are Alimta, a treatment for lung cancer (sales of $2.2 billion); Gemzar, another oncology drug now off-patent ($1.1 billion); Cialis, a treatment for erectile dysfunction ($1.7 billion); and animal health products ($1.4 billion) that include cattle feed additives, antibiotics and related items.

## Company Financials Fiscal Year Ended Dec. 31

| Per Share Data ($) | 2010 | 2009 | 2008 | 2007 | 2006 | 2005 | 2004 | 2003 | 2002 | 2001 |
|---|---|---|---|---|---|---|---|---|---|---|
| Tangible Book Value | 7.44 | 5.30 | 2.45 | 10.64 | 9.70 | 9.55 | 9.51 | 8.69 | 7.37 | 6.32 |
| Cash Flow | 5.79 | 5.12 | -1.05 | 3.49 | 3.06 | 2.41 | 2.21 | 2.87 | 2.85 | 2.91 |
| Earnings | 4.58 | 3.94 | -1.89 | 2.71 | 2.45 | 1.83 | 1.66 | 2.37 | 2.50 | 2.58 |
| S&P Core Earnings | 4.53 | 4.03 | -1.38 | 2.78 | 2.90 | 1.85 | 1.42 | 2.09 | 1.96 | 2.17 |
| Dividends | 1.96 | 1.96 | 1.88 | 1.70 | 1.60 | 1.52 | 1.42 | 1.34 | 1.24 | 1.12 |
| Payout Ratio | 43% | 50% | NM | 63% | 65% | 83% | 86% | 57% | 50% | 43% |
| Prices:High | 38.08 | 40.78 | 57.52 | 61.00 | 59.24 | 60.98 | 76.95 | 73.89 | 81.09 | 95.00 |
| Prices:Low | 32.02 | 27.21 | 28.62 | 49.09 | 50.19 | 49.47 | 50.34 | 52.77 | 43.75 | 70.01 |
| P/E Ratio:High | 8 | 10 | NM | 23 | 24 | 33 | 46 | 31 | 32 | 37 |
| P/E Ratio:Low | 7 | 7 | NM | 18 | 20 | 27 | 30 | 22 | 17 | 27 |

| Income Statement Analysis (Million $) | | | | | | | | | | |
|---|---|---|---|---|---|---|---|---|---|---|
| Revenue | 23,076 | 21,836 | 20,378 | 18,634 | 15,691 | 14,645 | 13,858 | 12,583 | 11,078 | 11,543 |
| Operating Income | 8,092 | 7,668 | 6,525 | 5,658 | 4,927 | 4,375 | 4,256 | 4,050 | 3,821 | 4,185 |
| Depreciation | 1,328 | 1,298 | 925 | 855 | 802 | 726 | 598 | 548 | 493 | 455 |
| Interest Expense | 134 | 261 | 277 | 324 | Nil | 105 | 274 | 61.0 | 79.7 | 147 |
| Pretax Income | 6,525 | 5,358 | -1,308 | 3,877 | 3,418 | 2,718 | 2,942 | 3,262 | 3,458 | 3,552 |
| Effective Tax Rate | NA | 19.2% | NM | 23.8% | 22.1% | 26.3% | 38.5% | 21.5% | 21.7% | 20.9% |
| Net Income | 5,070 | 4,329 | -2,072 | 2,953 | 2,663 | 2,002 | 1,810 | 2,561 | 2,708 | 2,809 |
| S&P Core Earnings | 5,016 | 4,421 | -1,523 | 3,028 | 3,153 | 2,016 | 1,558 | 2,261 | 2,128 | 2,359 |

| Balance Sheet & Other Financial Data (Million $) | | | | | | | | | | |
|---|---|---|---|---|---|---|---|---|---|---|
| Cash | 6,727 | 4,498 | 5,926 | 4,831 | 3,109 | 3,007 | 5,365 | 2,756 | 1,946 | 2,702 |
| Current Assets | 14,840 | 12,487 | 12,453 | 12,257 | 9,694 | 10,796 | 12,836 | 8,759 | 7,804 | 6,939 |
| Total Assets | 31,001 | 27,461 | 29,213 | 26,788 | 21,955 | 24,581 | 24,867 | 21,678 | 19,042 | 16,434 |
| Current Liabilities | 7,101 | 6,568 | 13,110 | 5,268 | 5,086 | 5,716 | 7,594 | 5,551 | 5,064 | 5,203 |
| Long Term Debt | 6,746 | 6,609 | 4,616 | 4,594 | 3,494 | 5,764 | 4,492 | 4,688 | 4,358 | 3,132 |
| Common Equity | 12,420 | 9,524 | 6,735 | 13,664 | 11,081 | 11,000 | 10,920 | 9,765 | 8,274 | 7,104 |
| Total Capital | 19,155 | 16,141 | 11,771 | 18,545 | 14,638 | 17,459 | 16,032 | 14,453 | 12,632 | 10,236 |
| Capital Expenditures | 694 | 765 | 947 | 1,082 | 1,078 | 1,298 | 1,898 | 1,707 | 1,131 | 884 |
| Cash Flow | 6,398 | 5,627 | -1,147 | 3,808 | 3,465 | 2,728 | 2,408 | 3,109 | 3,201 | 3,264 |
| Current Ratio | 2.1 | 1.9 | 1.0 | 2.3 | 1.9 | 1.9 | 1.7 | 1.6 | 1.5 | 1.3 |
| % Long Term Debt of Capitalization | 35.2 | Nil | 39.2 | 24.8 | 23.9 | 33.0 | 28.0 | 32.4 | 34.5 | 30.6 |
| % Net Income of Revenue | 22.0 | 19.8 | NM | 15.9 | 17.0 | 13.7 | 13.1 | 20.4 | 24.4 | 24.3 |
| % Return on Assets | NA | NA | NM | 12.1 | 11.4 | 8.1 | 7.8 | 12.6 | 15.3 | 18.1 |
| % Return on Equity | NA | NA | NM | 24.0 | 24.2 | 18.1 | 17.5 | 28.4 | 35.2 | 42.7 |

Data as orig reptd.; bef. results of disc opers/spec. items. Per share data adj. for stk. divs.; EPS diluted. E-Estimated. NA-Not Available. NM-Not Meaningful. NR-Not Ranked. UR-Under Review.

**Office:** Lilly Corporate Center, Indianapolis, IN 46285.
**Telephone:** 317-276-2000.
**Website:** http://www.lilly.com
**Chrmn, Pres & CEO:** J.C. Lechleiter

**EVP & CFO:** D.W. Rice
**SVP & Treas:** T.W. Grein
**SVP & General Counsel:** R.A. Armitage
**SVP & Cntlr:** E. O'Farrell

**Investor Contact:** P. Johnson (317-277-0001)
**Board Members:** R. Alvarez, W. Bischoff, M. L. Eskew, M. Feldstein, J. E. Fyrwald, A. G. Gilman, R. D. Hoover, K. N. Horn, J. C. Lechleiter, E. R. Marram, D. R. Oberhelman, F. G. Prendergast, K. P. Seifert

**Auditor:** ERNST & YOUNG
**Founded:** 1876
**Domicile:** Indiana
**Employees:** 38,350

# Limited Brands Inc.

**STANDARD &POOR'S**

| S&P Recommendation **BUY** ★★★★☆ | Price $38.33 (as of Nov 25, 2011) | 12-Mo. Target Price $50.00 | Investment Style Large-Cap Blend |
|---|---|---|---|

**GICS Sector** Consumer Discretionary
**Sub-Industry** Apparel Retail

**Summary** This specialty retailer of women's apparel, lingerie, and personal care and beauty products operates about 3,000 specialty stores.

## Key Stock Statistics (Source S&P, Vickers, company reports)

| | | | | | | | | |
|---|---|---|---|---|---|---|---|---|
| 52-Wk Range | $45.45– 28.05 | S&P Oper. EPS 2012**E** | 2.56 | Market Capitalization(B) | $11.435 | Beta | 1.52 |
| Trailing 12-Month EPS | $2.94 | S&P Oper. EPS 2013**E** | 2.85 | Yield (%) | 2.09 | S&P 3-Yr. Proj. EPS CAGR(%) | 16 |
| Trailing 12-Month P/E | 13.0 | P/E on S&P Oper. EPS 2012**E** | 15.0 | Dividend Rate/Share | $0.80 | S&P Credit Rating | BB+ |
| $10K Invested 5 Yrs Ago | $16,873 | Common Shares Outstg. (M) | 298.3 | Institutional Ownership (%) | 83 | | |

## Price Performance

30-Week Mov. Avg. · · · 10-Week Mov. Avg. – – **GAAP Earnings vs. Previous Year** Volume Above Avg. ▥ STARS
12-Mo. Target Price — Relative Strength — ▲ Up ▼ Down ► No Change Below Avg. ▥ ★

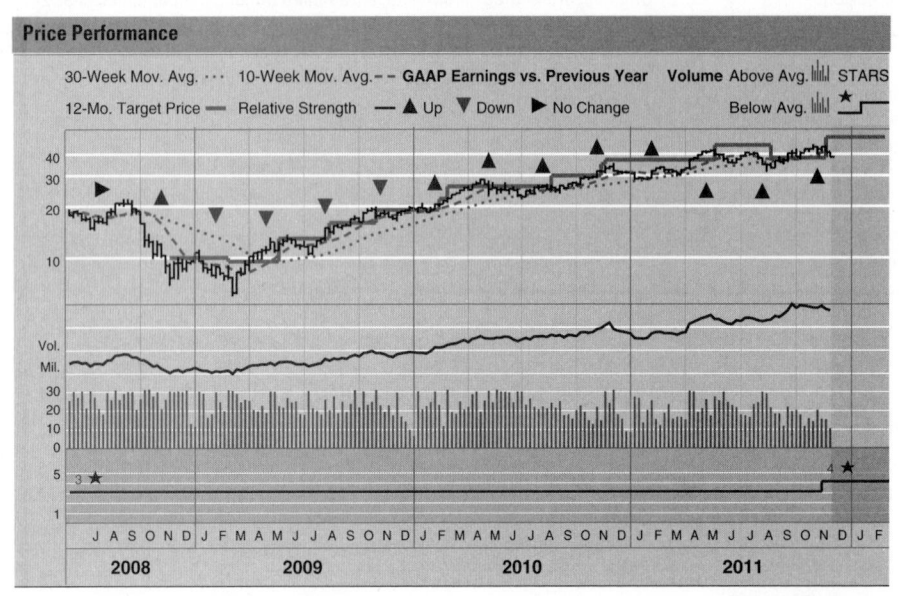

Options: ASE, CBOE, P, Ph

Analysis prepared by Equity Analyst **Jason N. Asaeda** on Nov 21, 2011, when the stock traded at **$40.14**.

## Qualitative Risk Assessment

| LOW | **MEDIUM** | HIGH |
|---|---|---|

Our risk assessment reflects LTD's strong cash flow, offset by execution risk in an increasingly competitive marketplace.

## Quantitative Evaluations

**S&P Quality Ranking**      B+

| D | C | B- | B | **B+** | A- | A | A+ |
|---|---|---|---|---|---|---|---|

**Relative Strength Rank**      MODERATE

**49**

LOWEST = 1      HIGHEST = 99

## Revenue/Earnings Data

**Revenue (Million $)**

| | 1Q | 2Q | 3Q | 4Q | Year |
|---|---|---|---|---|---|
| 2012 | 2,217 | 2,458 | 2,173 | -- | -- |
| 2011 | 1,932 | 2,242 | 1,983 | 3,456 | 9,613 |
| 2010 | 1,725 | 2,067 | 1,777 | 3,063 | 8,632 |
| 2009 | 1,925 | 2,284 | 1,843 | 2,991 | 9,043 |
| 2008 | 2,311 | 2,624 | 1,923 | 3,276 | 10,134 |
| 2007 | 2,077 | 2,454 | 2,115 | 4,025 | 10,671 |

**Earnings Per Share ($)**

| | | | | | |
|---|---|---|---|---|---|
| 2012 | 0.50 | 0.73 | 0.31 | E1.43 | E2.56 |
| 2011 | 0.34 | 0.54 | 0.18 | 1.36 | 2.42 |
| 2010 | -0.01 | 0.23 | -0.05 | 1.08 | 1.37 |
| 2009 | 0.28 | 0.30 | 0.01 | 0.05 | 0.65 |
| 2008 | 0.13 | 0.30 | -0.03 | 1.10 | 1.89 |
| 2007 | 0.25 | 0.28 | 0.06 | 1.08 | 1.68 |

Fiscal year ended Jan. 31. Next earnings report expected: Late February. EPS Estimates based on S&P Operating Earnings; historical GAAP earnings are as reported.

## Dividend Data (Dates: mm/dd Payment Date: mm/dd/yy)

| Amount ($) | Date Decl. | Ex-Div. Date | Stk. of Record | Payment Date |
|---|---|---|---|---|
| 0.200 | 05/31 | 06/03 | 06/07 | 06/17/11 |
| 1.0 Spl. | 05/31 | 06/15 | 06/17 | 07/01/11 |
| 0.200 | 08/05 | 08/24 | 08/26 | 09/11/11 |
| 0.200 | 11/05 | 11/22 | 11/25 | 12/09/11 |

Dividends have been paid since 1970. Source: Company reports.

## Highlights

➤ We see LTD's ability to execute the retail fundamentals of 'read and react' to consumer demand, disciplined inventory and expense management, along with its leading intimate apparel and personal care brands, driving sales and profit gains. These strategies support improved full-price selling and help sustain merchandise margins, in our view. Long-term growth opportunities include potential line extensions, sub-brands, and global expansion via flagships, franchise models and e-commerce.

➤ We see net sales rising 8% in FY 12 (Jan.), followed by a 6% gain in FY 13, supported annually by mid- to high-single digit same-store sales growth and international expansion. We expect retail selling square footage to be flat in FY 12, reflecting the company's plan to open 38 new stores and to close 57.

➤ Despite near-term product cost pressures and planned promotions (mostly gift with purchase and purchase with purchase offers rather than promotional pricing), we expect operating margins to expand annually on projected expense leverage off of higher sales. Factoring in share buybacks, we estimate EPS of $2.56 in FY 12 and $2.85 in FY 13.

## Investment Rationale/Risk

➤ We recently raised our recommendation on the shares to buy, from hold, based on valuation. With same-store sales up 14% at Victoria's Secret and 8% at Bath & Body Works through the third quarter in FY 12, we expect a strong holiday season for LTD. We see the company benefiting from owning the intimate apparel and personal care/beauty categories in U.S. specialty retail. We also note momentum in LTD's international business and think the company has an opportunity to expand more rapidly to take advantage of global demand, notably for Victoria's Secret. A dedicated team is executing the international agenda (thus zero distraction for domestic business).

➤ Risks to our recommendation and target price include fashion and inventory risk, consumer spending trends, and weak same-store sales trends. With an estimated 60%+ of LTD's profits earned in the fiscal fourth quarter, we think earnings risk is heightened.

➤ Given our positive company outlook, we believe the stock should trade at a premium to the 10-year historical average multiple of 14.7X. Our 12-month target price of $50 is based on a 17.5X multiple applied to our FY 13 EPS estimate.

# Limited Brands Inc.

**STANDARD &POOR'S**

## Business Summary November 21, 2011

CORPORATE OVERVIEW. Limited Brands (formerly The Limited) is a specialty retailer that conducts its business in two primary segments: Victoria's Secret (VS), a women's intimate apparel, personal care products and accessories retail brand; and Bath & Body Works (BBW), a personal care and home fragrance products retail brand. At October 29, 2011, the store base consisted of 1,017 Victoria's Secret, 249 La Senza, 1,595 Bath & Body Works, 16 Henri Bendel, 65 BBW Canada, and 17 VS Canada locations.

Victoria's Secret is the leading specialty retailer of women's intimate apparel and beauty products, with FY 11 (Jan.) sales of $5.9 billion, which includes $1.5 billion at Victoria's Secret Direct, a catalog and e-commerce retailer of women's intimate and other apparel and beauty products. Bath & Body Works is a specialty retailer of personal care and home fragrance products. FY 11 sales were $2.5 billion, including White Barn Candle Company.

MARKET PROFILE. The mature and fragmented U.S. women's apparel market generated about $108 billion at retail in 2010, according to NPD Fashionworld consumer estimated data. S&P forecasts that apparel sales will increase about 3% in 2011 following the 2% gain in 2010, a 5% drop in 2009, a 4% decline in 2008 and 4% gains in 2006 and 2007, based on NPD data. For 2011, we see demand picking up, reflecting a stable and improving economy with modest price inflation in the second half due to higher input costs (raw material and labor). The domestic personal care market is mature as well, with the demand function reflecting population trends in addition to the development of new categories.

## Company Financials Fiscal Year Ended Jan. 31

| Per Share Data ($) | 2011 | 2010 | 2009 | 2008 | 2007 | 2006 | 2005 | 2004 | 2003 | 2002 |
|---|---|---|---|---|---|---|---|---|---|---|
| Tangible Book Value | NM | 0.46 | NM | NM | 2.34 | 1.69 | 1.31 | 6.78 | 5.93 | 6.40 |
| Cash Flow | 3.60 | 2.57 | 1.77 | 2.82 | 2.46 | 2.45 | 2.17 | 1.90 | 1.48 | 1.83 |
| Earnings | 2.42 | 1.37 | 0.65 | 1.89 | 1.68 | 1.62 | 1.47 | 1.36 | 0.95 | 0.94 |
| S&P Core Earnings | 2.34 | 1.34 | 0.86 | 1.47 | 1.68 | 1.57 | 1.27 | 1.03 | 0.94 | 0.80 |
| Dividends | NA | 0.60 | 0.60 | 0.79 | 0.60 | 0.48 | 0.40 | 0.40 | 0.30 | 0.30 |
| Payout Ratio | NA | 49% | 44% | 42% | 36% | 30% | 27% | 29% | 32% | 32% |
| Calendar Year | 2010 | 2009 | 2008 | 2007 | 2006 | 2005 | 2004 | 2003 | 2002 | 2001 |
| Prices:High | 35.48 | 20.08 | 22.16 | 30.03 | 32.60 | 25.50 | 27.89 | 18.46 | 22.34 | 21.29 |
| Prices:Low | 18.34 | 5.98 | 6.90 | 16.50 | 21.62 | 18.81 | 17.35 | 10.88 | 12.53 | 9.00 |
| P/E Ratio:High | 15 | 15 | 34 | 16 | 19 | 16 | 19 | 14 | 24 | 23 |
| P/E Ratio:Low | 8 | 4 | 11 | 9 | 13 | 12 | 12 | 8 | 13 | 10 |

| Income Statement Analysis (Million $) | 2011 | 2010 | 2009 | 2008 | 2007 | 2006 | 2005 | 2004 | 2003 | 2002 |
|---|---|---|---|---|---|---|---|---|---|---|
| Revenue | 9,613 | 8,632 | 9,043 | 10,134 | 10,671 | 9,699 | 9,408 | 8,934 | 8,445 | 9,363 |
| Operating Income | 1,672 | 1,255 | 1,095 | 1,232 | 1,492 | 1,285 | 1,360 | 1,246 | 1,148 | 1,025 |
| Depreciation | 394 | 393 | 377 | 352 | 316 | 299 | 333 | 28.3 | 276 | 277 |
| Interest Expense | 208 | 237 | 181 | 149 | 102 | 94.0 | 58.0 | 62.0 | 30.0 | 34.0 |
| Pretax Income | 1,250 | 641 | 450 | 1,107 | 1,097 | 960 | 1,116 | 1,166 | 843 | 968 |
| Effective Tax Rate | NA | 37.3% | 51.9% | 37.1% | 38.5% | 30.3% | 36.8% | 38.5% | 40.5% | 39.8% |
| Net Income | 805 | 402 | 220 | 718 | 675 | 669 | 705 | 717 | 496 | 519 |
| S&P Core Earnings | 779 | 436 | 291 | 561 | 675 | 638 | 609 | 540 | 492 | 352 |

| Balance Sheet & Other Financial Data (Million $) | 2011 | 2010 | 2009 | 2008 | 2007 | 2006 | 2005 | 2004 | 2003 | 2002 |
|---|---|---|---|---|---|---|---|---|---|---|
| Cash | 1,130 | 1,804 | 1,173 | 1,018 | 500 | 1,208 | 1,161 | 3,129 | 2,262 | 1,375 |
| Current Assets | 2,592 | 3,250 | 2,867 | 2,919 | 2,771 | 2,784 | 2,684 | 4,433 | 3,606 | 2,682 |
| Total Assets | 6,451 | 7,173 | 6,972 | 7,437 | 7,093 | 6,346 | 6,089 | 7,873 | 7,246 | 4,719 |
| Current Liabilities | 1,504 | 1,322 | 1,255 | 1,374 | 1,709 | 1,575 | 1,451 | 1,392 | 1,259 | 1,319 |
| Long Term Debt | 2,564 | 2,772 | 2,897 | 2,905 | 1,665 | 1,669 | 1,646 | 648 | 547 | 250 |
| Common Equity | 1,476 | 2,183 | 1,874 | 2,219 | 2,955 | 2,471 | 2,335 | 5,266 | 4,860 | 2,744 |
| Total Capital | 4,042 | 4,958 | 4,985 | 5,354 | 4,864 | 4,319 | 4,191 | 6,048 | 5,532 | 3,171 |
| Capital Expenditures | 274 | 202 | 479 | 749 | 548 | 480 | 431 | 293 | 306 | 337 |
| Cash Flow | 1,199 | 841 | 597 | 1,070 | 991 | 968 | 1,038 | 1,000 | 772 | 796 |
| Current Ratio | 1.7 | 2.5 | 2.3 | 2.1 | 1.6 | 1.8 | 1.8 | 3.2 | 2.9 | 2.0 |
| % Long Term Debt of Capitalization | 63.4 | Nil | 58.1 | 54.3 | 35.5 | 38.6 | 39.3 | 10.7 | 9.9 | 7.9 |
| % Net Income of Revenue | 8.4 | 4.7 | 2.4 | 7.1 | 6.3 | 6.9 | 7.5 | 8.0 | 5.9 | 5.5 |
| % Return on Assets | NA | NA | 3.1 | 9.9 | 10.1 | 10.8 | 10.1 | 9.5 | 8.0 | 11.8 |
| % Return on Equity | NA | NA | 10.8 | 27.8 | 24.9 | 27.9 | 18.6 | 14.2 | 13.0 | 20.5 |

Data as orig reptd.; bef. results of disc opers/spec. items. Per share data adj. for stk. divs.; EPS diluted. E-Estimated. NA-Not Available. NM-Not Meaningful. NR-Not Ranked. UR-Under Review.

**Office:** Three Limited Parkway, PO Box 16000, Columbus, OH 43216.
**Telephone:** 614-415-7000.
**Website:** http://www.limitedbrands.com
**Chrmn & CEO:** L.H. Wexner

**EVP, CFO & Chief Acctg Officer:** S.B. Burgdoerfer
**EVP & Chief Admin Officer:** M.R. Redgrave
**SVP & Secy:** S.P. Fried
**SVP & General Counsel:** D.L. Williams

**Investor Contact:** T.J. Faber ()
**Auditor:** ERNST & YOUNG
**Board Members:** D. S. Hersch, J. L. Heskett, D. A. James, D. T. Kollat, W. R. Loomis, Jr., J. H. Miro, A. R. Tessler, A. S. Wexner, L. H. Wexner, R. Zimmerman

**Founded:** 1967
**Domicile:** Delaware
**Employees:** 96,500

*The McGraw·Hill Companies*

# Lincoln National Corp

**STANDARD &POOR'S**

| S&P Recommendation **BUY** ★★★★☆ | Price $17.58 (as of Nov 25, 2011) | 12-Mo. Target Price $23.00 | Investment Style Large-Cap Value |
|---|---|---|---|

**GICS Sector** Financials
**Sub-Industry** Life & Health Insurance

**Summary** This company offers annuities, life insurance, defined contribution plans and related advisory services to affluent individuals.

## Key Stock Statistics (Source S&P, Vickers, company reports)

| | | | | | | | |
|---|---|---|---|---|---|---|---|
| 52-Wk Range | $32.68– 13.75 | S&P Oper. EPS 2011**E** | 4.17 | Market Capitalization(B) | $5.303 | Beta | 2.58 |
| Trailing 12-Month EPS | $3.13 | S&P Oper. EPS 2012**E** | 4.36 | Yield (%) | 1.82 | S&P 3-Yr. Proj. EPS CAGR(%) | 15 |
| Trailing 12-Month P/E | 5.6 | P/E on S&P Oper. EPS 2011**E** | 4.2 | Dividend Rate/Share | $0.32 | S&P Credit Rating | A- |
| $10K Invested 5 Yrs Ago | $2,957 | Common Shares Outstg. (M) | 301.7 | Institutional Ownership (%) | 86 | | |

## Price Performance

30-Week Mov. Avg. · · · 10-Week Mov. Avg. - - GAAP Earnings vs. Previous Year Volume Above Avg. STARS
12-Mo. Target Price — Relative Strength ▲ Up ▼ Down ▶ No Change Below Avg. ★

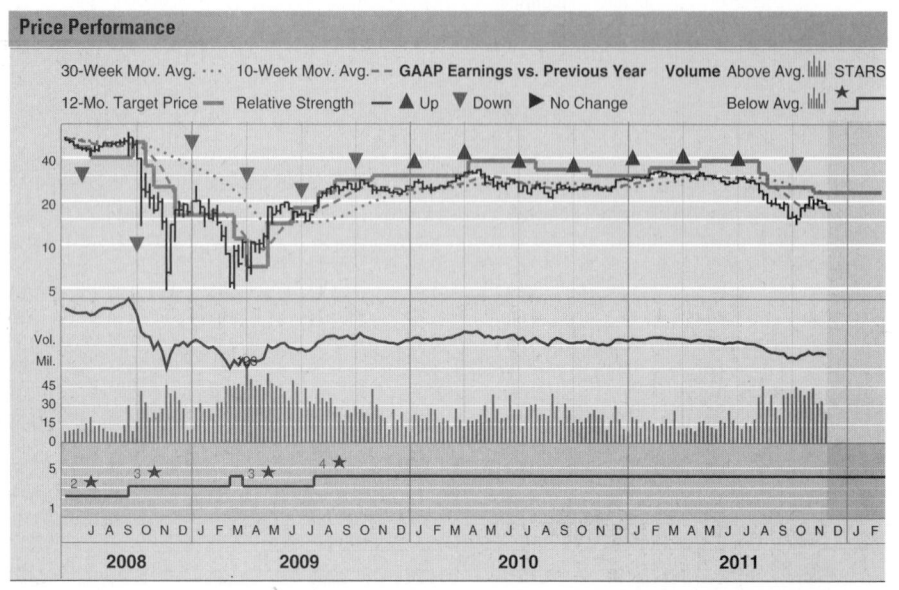

Options: ASE, CBOE, P, Ph

Analysis prepared by Equity Analyst **Cathy Seifert** on Nov 22, 2011, when the stock traded at **$18.52**.

## Highlights

▶ We see earnings in Life Insurance increasing in the mid-single digits in coming periods, led by modest sales of traditional life insurance, robust Moneyguard sales, and higher alternative investment income. We expect earnings in Annuities to benefit from strong variable annuities sales. However, we forecast weak fixed annuity sales due to low interest rates. We believe product and distribution enhancements should drive earnings growth in Defined Contribution (DC). We also see flows picking up in DC due to growth in deposits, and lower withdrawals.

▶ We remain cautious in our earnings outlook for the Group Protection business, as high unemployment should pressure enrollment levels and increase product loss ratios. However, we think LNC will look to build on its Group Protection franchise through acquisitions, to reduce its market sensitivity. About half of LNC's businesses are interest-sensitive, and we believe the rise in interest rates will benefit spreads. We expect higher financing solutions costs to remain an earnings headwind.

▶ We forecast operating EPS of $4.17 for 2011 and $4.36 for 2012, excluding realized investment gains or losses.

## Investment Rationale/Risk

▶ Our buy recommendation is based on our belief that LNC's valuation is attractive, with the stock recently trading at a discount to its peer group. We believe LNC has made strides in improving its balance sheet strength and financial position in recent periods. However, with nearly half of LNC's earnings derived from the equity markets (via the sale of equity-linked products), we expect LNC's shares to mirror much of the recent stock market volatility. We expect LNC's top-line trends to improve, driven by the strength of its distribution capabilities and product enhancements, although low interest rates could be a headwind.

▶ Risks to our opinion and target price include a significant decline in equity markets, a prolonged period of low interest rates, deterioration in sales, narrower product spreads, and instability in credit markets.

▶ Our 12-month target price of $23 assumes the shares trade at 5.3X our 2012 operating EPS estimate and less than 2X tangible book value. Both of these valuation metrics represent a discount to LNC's peers.

## Qualitative Risk Assessment

| LOW | MEDIUM | **HIGH** |
|---|---|---|

Our risk assessment reflects LNC's significant exposure to the equity markets and interest rates. This is only partly offset by LNC's capital position, which has improved following equity and debt issuances.

## Quantitative Evaluations

**S&P Quality Ranking**      B

| D | C | B- | **B** | B+ | A- | A | A+ |
|---|---|---|---|---|---|---|---|

**Relative Strength Rank**      MODERATE

36

LOWEST = 1      HIGHEST = 99

## Revenue/Earnings Data

**Revenue (Million $)**

| | 1Q | 2Q | 3Q | 4Q | Year |
|---|---|---|---|---|---|
| 2011 | 2,714 | 2,804 | 2,548 | -- | -- |
| 2010 | 2,527 | 2,605 | 2,613 | 2,662 | 10,407 |
| 2009 | 2,132 | 1,882 | 2,081 | 2,403 | 8,499 |
| 2008 | 2,592 | 2,582 | 2,436 | 2,273 | 9,883 |
| 2007 | 2,670 | 2,740 | 2,681 | 2,606 | 10,594 |
| 2006 | 1,417 | 2,496 | 2,487 | 2,658 | 9,063 |

**Earnings Per Share ($)**

| | | | | | |
|---|---|---|---|---|---|
| 2011 | 1.05 | 1.01 | 0.47 | E1.00 | E4.17 |
| 2010 | 0.76 | 0.32 | 0.76 | 0.60 | 2.45 |
| 2009 | -2.30 | -0.03 | 0.21 | 0.26 | -1.60 |
| 2008 | 1.12 | 0.48 | 0.58 | -1.98 | 0.24 |
| 2007 | 1.42 | 1.37 | 1.21 | 0.89 | 4.82 |
| 2006 | 1.24 | 1.23 | 1.29 | 1.36 | 5.13 |

Fiscal year ended Dec. 31. Next earnings report expected: Early February. EPS Estimates based on S&P Operating Earnings; historical GAAP earnings are as reported.

## Dividend Data (Dates: mm/dd Payment Date: mm/dd/yy)

| Amount ($) | Date Decl. | Ex-Div. Date | Stk. of Record | Payment Date |
|---|---|---|---|---|
| 0.050 | 02/24 | 04/07 | 04/11 | 05/01/11 |
| 0.050 | 05/26 | 07/07 | 07/11 | 08/01/11 |
| 0.050 | 08/11 | 10/06 | 10/11 | 11/01/11 |
| 0.080 | 11/10 | 01/06 | 01/10 | 02/01/12 |

Dividends have been paid since 1920. Source: Company reports.

---

**Please read the Required Disclosures and Analyst Certification on the last page of this report.**

*The McGraw·Hill Companies*

# Lincoln National Corp

STANDARD
&POOR'S

## Business Summary November 22, 2011

CORPORATE OVERVIEW. Lincoln National is a holding company with subsidiaries that operate multiple insurance and investment management businesses. Primary operating subsidiaries include Lincoln National Life Insurance Co., First Penn-Pacific Life Insurance Co., Lincoln Life & Annuity Co. of New York, Lincoln Financial Advisors (LFA), a retail distribution unit, and Lincoln Financial Distributors (LFD), a wholesale distribution unit.

Following the acquisition of Jefferson-Pilot in April 2006, LNC's segments were restructured. In 2008, LNC's businesses were realigned again, and operations were divided into five business segments. However, following the sale of Lincoln U.K. and Delaware Management in 2009, LNC now has three operating segments: Retirement Solutions (35% of 2010 operating revenue), Insurance Solutions (61%), and Other Operations (4.6%).

The Retirement Solutions segment offers products through two segments: Annuities (which accounted for 25% of operating revenues in 2010) and Defined Contribution (9.4%). LNC offers guaranteed benefit riders on some of its variable annuity products including the guaranteed death benefit (GDB), a guaranteed withdrawal benefit (GWB), and a guaranteed income benefit (GIB). The Defined Contribution segment provides employers with tax-deferred retirement savings plans for their employees mainly through 403 (b) and 401 (k)

plans. LNC offers a number of savings products including individual and group variable annuities, group fixed annuities and mutual funds. In addition, the company provides a variety of plan services including record keeping, compliance testing and participant education.

The Insurance Solutions segment provides products through its Life Insurance (44%) and Group Protection (17%) businesses. The life insurance business targets the affluent market, and underwrites and sells universal life, variable universal life, interest-sensitive whole life, corporate-owned life insurance (COLI), term life insurance, and linked products such as universal life linked with long-term care benefits (Moneyguard). The Group Protection business offers group non-medical insurance products to the employer marketplace.

The Other Operations (4.6%) segment includes investments related to the excess capital in LNC's insurance subsidiaries; investments in media properties; and other corporate investments.

## Company Financials Fiscal Year Ended Dec. 31

| Per Share Data ($) | 2010 | 2009 | 2008 | 2007 | 2006 | 2005 | 2004 | 2003 | 2002 | 2001 |
|---|---|---|---|---|---|---|---|---|---|---|
| Tangible Book Value | 30.36 | 25.40 | 15.13 | 15.20 | 27.92 | 22.47 | 22.25 | 18.74 | 15.62 | 14.10 |
| Operating Earnings | NA | NA | NA | NA | NA | NA | NA | NA | 2.56 | 3.56 |
| Earnings | 2.45 | -1.60 | 0.24 | 4.82 | 5.13 | 4.72 | 4.09 | 2.85 | 0.49 | 3.13 |
| S&P Core Earnings | 2.60 | 3.85 | 1.83 | 4.78 | 5.05 | 4.71 | 3.78 | 4.36 | 1.16 | 3.10 |
| Dividends | 0.04 | 0.24 | 1.66 | 1.58 | 1.52 | 1.46 | 1.40 | 1.34 | 1.28 | 1.22 |
| Payout Ratio | 2% | NM | NM | 31% | 30% | 31% | 34% | 47% | NM | 39% |
| Prices:High | 33.55 | 28.10 | 59.99 | 74.72 | 66.72 | 54.41 | 50.38 | 41.32 | 53.65 | 52.75 |
| Prices:Low | 20.65 | 4.90 | 4.76 | 54.40 | 52.00 | 41.59 | 39.98 | 24.73 | 25.11 | 38.00 |
| P/E Ratio:High | 14 | NM | NM | 15 | 13 | 12 | 12 | 14 | NM | 17 |
| P/E Ratio:Low | 8 | NM | NM | 11 | 10 | 9 | 10 | 9 | NM | 12 |

| Income Statement Analysis (Million $) | | | | | | | | | | |
|---|---|---|---|---|---|---|---|---|---|---|
| Life Insurance in Force | 845,300 | 802,900 | 781,400 | 748,200 | 702,600 | 339,100 | 325,700 | 307,800 | 873,595 | 651,900 |
| Premium Income:Life | 4,301 | 3,909 | 4,271 | 4,258 | 3,354 | 2,069 | 1,882 | 1,694 | 1,730 | 2,907 |
| Premium Income:A & H | 1,109 | 1,077 | 1,054 | 941 | 656 | 1.30 | 3.52 | 3.98 | 20.3 | 341 |
| Net Investment Income | 4,541 | 4,178 | 4,208 | 4,384 | 3,981 | 2,702 | 2,704 | 2,639 | 2,608 | 2,680 |
| Total Revenue | 10,407 | 8,499 | 9,883 | 10,594 | 9,063 | 5,488 | 5,371 | 5,284 | 4,635 | 6,381 |
| Pretax Income | 1,234 | -521 | -25.6 | 1,874 | 1,811 | 1,075 | 1,036 | 1,048 | 1.62 | 764 |
| Net Operating Income | NA | NA | NA | NA | NA | NA | NA | NA | 474 | 689 |
| Net Income | 951 | -415 | 61.8 | 1,321 | 1,316 | 831 | 732 | 767 | 91.6 | 606 |
| S&P Core Earnings | 832 | 1,074 | 475 | 1,311 | 1,298 | 831 | 675 | 782 | 215 | 600 |

| Balance Sheet & Other Financial Data (Million $) | | | | | | | | | | |
|---|---|---|---|---|---|---|---|---|---|---|
| Cash & Equivalent | 3,674 | 4,914 | 6,758 | 2,508 | 2,487 | 2,838 | 2,187 | 2,234 | 2,227 | 3,659 |
| Premiums Due | 335 | 321 | 481 | 401 | 356 | 343 | 233 | 352 | 213 | 400 |
| Investment Assets:Bonds | 68,614 | 60,818 | 48,935 | 56,276 | 55,853 | 33,443 | 34,701 | 32,769 | 32,767 | 28,346 |
| Investment Assets:Stocks | 197 | 278 | 288 | 518 | 701 | 3,391 | 3,399 | 3,319 | 337 | 471 |
| Investment Assets:Loans | 9,617 | 10,250 | 10,639 | 10,258 | 10,144 | 5,525 | 5,728 | 6,119 | 6,151 | 6,475 |
| Investment Assets:Total | 83,340 | 75,918 | 67,341 | 71,922 | 71,488 | 43,168 | 44,507 | 42,778 | 40,000 | 36,113 |
| Deferred Policy Costs | 8,930 | 9,510 | 11,936 | 9,580 | 8,420 | 4,092 | 3,445 | 3,192 | 2,971 | 2,885 |
| Total Assets | 193,824 | 177,433 | 163,136 | 191,435 | 178,494 | 124,788 | 116,219 | 106,745 | 93,133 | 98,001 |
| Debt | 5,399 | 5,050 | 6,758 | 5,168 | 4,116 | 1,333 | 1,083 | 1,459 | 1,512 | 1,336 |
| Common Equity | 12,805 | 10,894 | 7,976 | 11,718 | 71,017 | 6,384 | 6,175 | 5,811 | 5,296 | 5,263 |
| % Return on Revenue | 9.1 | NM | 0.6 | 12.5 | 14.5 | 15.1 | 13.6 | 14.5 | 2.0 | 9.5 |
| % Return on Assets | 0.5 | NM | 0.0 | 0.7 | 0.1 | 0.1 | 0.1 | 0.1 | 0.1 | 0.6 |
| % Return on Equity | 8.0 | NM | 0.6 | 11.1 | 2.3 | 13.2 | 12.2 | 13.8 | 1.7 | 11.9 |
| % Investment Yield | 5.8 | 5.9 | 6.2 | 6.1 | 6.8 | 6.1 | 6.8 | 7.1 | 6.9 | 7.5 |

Data as orig reptd.; bef. results of disc opers/spec. items. Per share data adj. for stk. divs.; EPS diluted. E-Estimated. NA-Not Available. NM-Not Meaningful. NR-Not Ranked. UR-Under Review.

**Office:** 150 North Radnor Chester Road, Suite A305, Radnor, PA 19087.
**Telephone:** 484-583-1400.
**Email:** investorrelations@lnc.com
**Website:** http://www.lfg.com

**Chrmn:** W.H. Cunningham
**Pres & CEO:** D.R. Glass
**EVP & CFO:** R.J. Freitag
**SVP & General Counsel:** N.S. Jones

**Chief Acctg Officer & Cntlr:** D.N. Miller
**Auditor:** ERNST & YOUNG
**Board Members:** W. J. Avery, W. H. Cunningham, D. R. Glass, G. W. Henderson, III, E. G. Johnson, G. C. Kelly, M. L. Lachman, M. F. Mee, W. P. Payne, P. S. Pittard, I. Tidwell

**Founded:** 1905
**Domicile:** Indiana
**Employees:** 8,270

# Linear Technology Corp

| S&P Recommendation | HOLD ★★★☆☆ | Price $28.39 (as of Nov 25, 2011) | 12-Mo. Target Price $32.00 | Investment Style Large-Cap Growth |
|---|---|---|---|---|

**GICS Sector** Information Technology
**Sub-Industry** Semiconductors

**Summary** This company manufactures high-performance linear integrated circuits.

## Key Stock Statistics (Source S&P, Vickers, company reports)

| | | | | | |
|---|---|---|---|---|---|
| 52-Wk Range | $36.14–25.41 | S&P Oper. EPS 2012**E** 1.72 | Market Capitalization(B) $6.466 | Beta | 1.06 |
| Trailing 12-Month EPS | $2.38 | S&P Oper. EPS 2013**E** 2.09 | Yield (%) 3.38 | S&P 3-Yr. Proj. EPS CAGR(%) | 2 |
| Trailing 12-Month P/E | 11.9 | P/E on S&P Oper. EPS 2012**E** 16.5 | Dividend Rate/Share $0.96 | S&P Credit Rating | NA |
| $10K Invested 5 Yrs Ago | $9,879 | Common Shares Outstg. (M) 227.8 | Institutional Ownership (%) 93 | | |

## Price Performance

Legend: 30-Week Mov. Avg. · · · 10-Week Mov. Avg. – – GAAP Earnings vs. Previous Year  Volume Above Avg. STARS
12-Mo. Target Price — Relative Strength — ▲ Up ▼ Down ► No Change  Below Avg.

Options: ASE, CBOE, P, Ph

Analysis prepared by Equity Analyst **Angelo Zino, CFA** on Oct 20, 2011, when the stock traded at **$29.75**.

### Highlights

➤ We think revenues will decline 16% in FY 12 (Jun.), reflecting a tough annual growth comparison and inventory correction, but anticipate an 11% rebound in FY 13. Given the cautious economic state, we believe customers are slowing orders in an effort to reduce inventories to better manage end-demand with supply. Specifically, the industrial and communications end-markets have shown recent weakness. Over the longer term, we think that the proliferation of semiconductors in electronic devices throughout all end-markets, market share gains, and new product cycles, such as tablet computers, will aid revenue advances.

➤ We project the annual gross margin to widen to 77% in FY 13 following our forecast for 75% in FY 12, as we see volume returning and expect LLTC to focus on manufacturing efficiencies. Despite near-term uncertainty, we expect LLTC to maintain high levels of profitability across every phase of the semiconductor cycle. We estimate an operating margin of 45% in FY 12 and 48% in FY 13.

➤ Our EPS projections assume $0.19 and $0.20 per share of stock-based compensation for FY 12 and FY 13, respectively.

### Investment Rationale/Risk

➤ Our hold opinion reflects our view of the company's solid and profitable business model, balanced by fair valuations. One of the better-run semiconductor companies, in our view, with relatively high margins, LLTC has been able to grow sales at an above industry pace through penetrating a broader range of markets, all while maintaining above-peer profitability. We believe LLTC generally offers less business risk than peers, and has more than enough cash and healthy free cash flows to reduce financial risks related to its leverage. Although we think LLTC should navigate through the anticipated period of demand weakness better than its peers, we still see lower earnings limiting the stock. However, we continue to believe that growth will resume on a sequential basis in the first half of calendar-year 2012.

➤ Risks to our recommendation and target price include increasing competition, higher-than-anticipated operating expenses, and worse-than-expected economic conditions.

➤ Our 12-month target price of $32 is based on a price-to-earnings multiple of 16.5X, below its historical average yet above the industry average, applied to our calendar 2012 EPS estimate.

### Qualitative Risk Assessment

| LOW | MEDIUM | HIGH |
|---|---|---|

Our risk assessment reflects the company's exposure to the sales cycles of the semiconductor industry. This is offset by stabilizing factors such as a high level of proprietary circuit design content, a varied customer base, diverse end-markets, and wider margins than most competitors.

### Quantitative Evaluations

**S&P Quality Ranking** A

| D | C | B- | B | B+ | A- | A | A+ |
|---|---|---|---|---|---|---|---|

**Relative Strength Rank** MODERATE
45
LOWEST = 1   HIGHEST = 99

### Revenue/Earnings Data

**Revenue (Million $)**

| | 1Q | 2Q | 3Q | 4Q | Year |
|---|---|---|---|---|---|
| 2012 | 329.9 | -- | -- | -- | -- |
| 2011 | 388.6 | 383.6 | 353.2 | 358.6 | 1,484 |
| 2010 | 236.1 | 256.4 | 311.3 | 366.2 | 1,170 |
| 2009 | 310.4 | 249.2 | 200.9 | 208.0 | 968.5 |
| 2008 | 281.5 | 288.7 | 297.9 | 307.1 | 1,175 |
| 2007 | 292.1 | 267.9 | 255.0 | 268.1 | 1,083 |

**Earnings Per Share ($)**

| | | | | | |
|---|---|---|---|---|---|
| 2012 | 0.47 | E0.35 | E0.39 | E0.48 | E1.72 |
| 2011 | 0.59 | 0.62 | 0.61 | 0.68 | 2.50 |
| 2010 | 0.27 | 0.33 | 0.44 | 0.54 | 1.58 |
| 2009 | 0.48 | 0.43 | 0.25 | 0.25 | 1.41 |
| 2008 | 0.40 | 0.41 | 0.44 | 0.46 | 1.71 |
| 2007 | 0.37 | 0.34 | 0.32 | 0.36 | 1.39 |

Fiscal year ended Jun. 30. Next earnings report expected: NA. EPS Estimates based on S&P Operating Earnings; historical GAAP earnings are as reported.

### Dividend Data (Dates: mm/dd Payment Date: mm/dd/yy)

| Amount ($) | Date Decl. | Ex-Div. Date | Stk. of Record | Payment Date |
|---|---|---|---|---|
| 0.240 | 01/18 | 02/16 | 02/18 | 03/02/11 |
| 0.240 | 04/19 | 05/18 | 05/20 | 06/01/11 |
| 0.240 | 07/26 | 08/17 | 08/19 | 08/31/11 |
| 0.240 | 10/18 | 11/16 | 11/18 | 11/30/11 |

Dividends have been paid since 1992. Source: Company reports.

**Please read the Required Disclosures and Analyst Certification on the last page of this report.**

# Linear Technology Corp

STANDARD &POOR'S

## Business Summary October 20, 2011

CORPORATE OVERVIEW. Linear Technology Corp. (LLTC) designs, makes and markets a broad line of high-performance standard linear integrated circuits (ICs) that address a wide range of real-world signal processing applications. Its principal product lines include operational and high-speed amplifiers, voltage regulators, voltage references, data converters, radio frequency circuits, power over ethernet controllers, power systems, signal chain modules, interface circuits, and other linear circuits, including buffers, battery monitors, comparators, drivers and filters.

The company has consistently expanded its customer base throughout its history. LLTC initially served primarily an industrial customer base, with a high percentage of revenues from the military market. Since the late 1980s, new products led to growth in the PC and hand-held device markets, and communication and networking markets contributed to growth significantly in recent years. The company now sells its products to more than 15,000 original equipment manufacturers directly or through a sales distributor channel.

Over the past few years LLTC has reduced its exposure to the consumer and cell-phone end-markets in favor of the industrial, automotive, communication infrastructure and military end-markets because these latter end-markets tend to demand more complex technology products, which have higher and more stable prices. Consolidated bookings in these markets were 82% of total bookings for FY 11 (Jun.) versus 76% in FY 10, 74% in FY 09 and 64% in FY 05.

MARKET PROFILE. As more information is digitized, more and more analog chips are required to assist the digital chips that process, transmit, and store information. Analog or "linear" semiconductors are used to handle continuous signals found in the real world, such as sound, light, heat, and pressure. In a common example, a mobile phone utilizes a baseband system for communication, and it relies on a cluster of analog chips to convert the voice signals to digital format for manipulation by the processor, then translate them back to analog format for listening. Analog chips also are needed to manage power usage, which is particularly important for portable electronics, where battery life is a key product feature. The strong push toward wireless capabilities for laptop PCs and smartphones, has helped analog sales grow faster than the broader industry's over the last few years.

## Company Financials Fiscal Year Ended Jun. 30

| Per Share Data ($) | 2011 | 2010 | 2009 | 2008 | 2007 | 2006 | 2005 | 2004 | 2003 | 2002 |
|---|---|---|---|---|---|---|---|---|---|---|
| Tangible Book Value | 2.18 | 0.11 | NM | NM | NM | 6.94 | 6.55 | 5.87 | 5.80 | 5.63 |
| Cash Flow | 2.71 | 1.78 | 1.63 | 1.93 | 1.56 | 1.53 | 1.53 | 1.17 | 0.88 | 0.74 |
| Earnings | 2.50 | 1.58 | 1.41 | 1.71 | 1.39 | 1.37 | 1.38 | 1.02 | 0.74 | 0.60 |
| S&P Core Earnings | 2.50 | 1.58 | 1.41 | 1.71 | 1.39 | 1.37 | 0.99 | 0.79 | 0.50 | 0.40 |
| Dividends | 0.94 | 0.90 | 0.86 | 0.78 | 0.66 | 0.50 | 0.36 | 0.28 | 0.21 | 0.17 |
| Payout Ratio | 38% | 57% | 61% | 46% | 47% | 36% | 26% | 27% | 28% | 28% |
| Prices:High | 36.14 | 35.07 | 31.07 | 37.77 | 38.84 | 39.35 | 41.67 | 45.09 | 44.80 | 47.50 |
| Prices:Low | 25.41 | 25.87 | 20.26 | 17.69 | 29.62 | 27.80 | 32.83 | 34.01 | 24.76 | 18.92 |
| P/E Ratio:High | 14 | 22 | 22 | 22 | 28 | 29 | 30 | 44 | 61 | 79 |
| P/E Ratio:Low | 10 | 16 | 14 | 10 | 21 | 20 | 24 | 33 | 33 | 32 |

| Income Statement Analysis (Million $) | | | | | | | | | | |
|---|---|---|---|---|---|---|---|---|---|---|
| Revenue | 1,484 | 1,170 | 968 | 1,175 | 1,083 | 1,093 | 1,050 | 807 | 607 | 512 |
| Operating Income | 816 | 609 | 464 | 617 | 575 | 613 | 638 | 485 | 340 | 271 |
| Depreciation | 50.1 | 45.5 | 48.0 | 48.1 | 50.7 | 49.3 | 48.8 | 48.7 | 45.9 | 46.3 |
| Interest Expense | 54.2 | 75.4 | 52.3 | 57.8 | 12.1 | Nil | Nil | Nil | Nil | Nil |
| Pretax Income | 724 | 490 | 407 | 541 | 570 | 617 | 620 | 462 | 333 | 278 |
| Effective Tax Rate | NA | NA | 23.0% | 28.4% | 27.8% | 30.5% | 30.0% | 29.0% | 29.0% | 29.0% |
| Net Income | 581 | 361 | 314 | 388 | 412 | 429 | 434 | 328 | 237 | 198 |
| S&P Core Earnings | 581 | 361 | 314 | 388 | 412 | 429 | 311 | 253 | 161 | 132 |

| Balance Sheet & Other Financial Data (Million $) | | | | | | | | | | |
|---|---|---|---|---|---|---|---|---|---|---|
| Cash | 923 | 958 | 869 | 967 | 156 | 541 | 323 | 204 | 136 | 212 |
| Current Assets | 1,246 | 1,264 | 1,089 | 1,246 | 861 | 2,077 | 2,007 | 1,832 | 1,776 | 1,728 |
| Total Assets | 1,631 | 1,591 | 1,422 | 1,584 | 1,219 | 2,391 | 2,286 | 2,088 | 2,057 | 1,988 |
| Current Liabilities | 183 | 583 | 125 | 175 | 180 | 237 | 208 | 203 | 162 | 169 |
| Long Term Debt | 786 | 767 | 1,406 | 1,700 | 1,700 | Nil | Nil | Nil | Nil | Nil |
| Common Equity | 506 | 39.8 | -267 | -434 | -708 | 2,104 | 2,007 | 1,811 | 1,815 | 1,781 |
| Total Capital | 1,291 | 1,200 | 1,202 | 1,308 | 1,005 | 2,104 | 2,007 | 1,811 | 1,815 | 1,819 |
| Capital Expenditures | 120 | 38.3 | 39.1 | 35.3 | 62.0 | 69.4 | 62.1 | 20.7 | 6.61 | 17.9 |
| Cash Flow | 631 | 407 | 362 | 436 | 462 | 478 | 483 | 377 | 282 | 244 |
| Current Ratio | 6.8 | 2.2 | 8.7 | 7.1 | 4.8 | 8.8 | 9.7 | 9.0 | 11.0 | 10.2 |
| % Long Term Debt of Capitalization | 60.9 | 63.9 | 116.9 | 130.0 | 169.2 | Nil | Nil | Nil | Nil | Nil |
| % Net Income of Revenue | 39.1 | 30.9 | 32.4 | 33.0 | 38.0 | 39.2 | 41.3 | 40.7 | 39.0 | 38.6 |
| % Return on Assets | 36.1 | 24.0 | 20.9 | 27.7 | 22.8 | 18.3 | 19.8 | 15.8 | 11.7 | 9.9 |
| % Return on Equity | 213.0 | NM | NM | NM | 59.0 | 20.9 | 22.7 | 18.1 | 13.2 | 11.1 |

Data as orig reptd.; bef. results of disc opers/spec. items. Per share data adj. for stk. divs.; EPS diluted. E-Estimated. NA-Not Available. NM-Not Meaningful. NR-Not Ranked. UR-Under Review.

**Office:** 1630 McCarthy Boulevard, Milpitas, CA 95035-7487.
**Telephone:** 408-432-1900.
**Website:** http://www.linear.com
**Chrmn:** R.H. Swanson, Jr.

**CEO:** L. Maier
**COO:** A.R. McCann
**Investor Contact:** P. Coghlan (408-432-1900)
**CFO, Chief Acctg Officer & Secy:** P. Coghlan

**Board Members:** A. C. Agnos, J. J. Gordon, D. S. Lee, L. Maier, R. M. Moley, R. H. Swanson, Jr., T. S. Volpe
**Founded:** 1981
**Domicile:** Delaware
**Employees:** 4,505

The McGraw-Hill Companies

# Lockheed Martin Corp

STANDARD
&POOR'S

| S&P Recommendation HOLD ★★★★★ | Price $75.39 (as of Nov 25, 2011) | 12-Mo. Target Price $84.00 | Investment Style Large-Cap Growth |
|---|---|---|---|

**GICS Sector** Industrials
**Sub-Industry** Aerospace & Defense

**Summary** This company, the world's largest military weapons manufacturer, is also a significant supplier to NASA and other non-defense government agencies. LMT receives about 93% of its revenues from global defense sales.

## Key Stock Statistics (Source S&P, Vickers, company reports)

| | | | | | |
|---|---|---|---|---|---|
| 52-Wk Range | $82.43– 66.36 | S&P Oper. EPS 2011**E** | 7.72 | Market Capitalization(B) | $24.394 |
| Trailing 12-Month EPS | $8.55 | S&P Oper. EPS 2012**E** | 8.20 | Yield (%) | 5.31 |
| Trailing 12-Month P/E | 8.8 | P/E on S&P Oper. EPS 2011**E** | 9.8 | Dividend Rate/Share | $4.00 |
| $10K Invested 5 Yrs Ago | $9,640 | Common Shares Outstg. (M) | 323.6 | Institutional Ownership (%) | 94 |

| | |
|---|---|
| Beta | 0.94 |
| S&P 3-Yr. Proj. EPS CAGR(%) | 6 |
| S&P Credit Rating | A- |

## Price Performance

30-Week Mov. Avg. · · · 10-Week Mov. Avg. - - GAAP Earnings vs. Previous Year   Volume Above Avg. STARS
12-Mo. Target Price — Relative Strength — ▲ Up ▼ Down ► No Change   Below Avg. ★

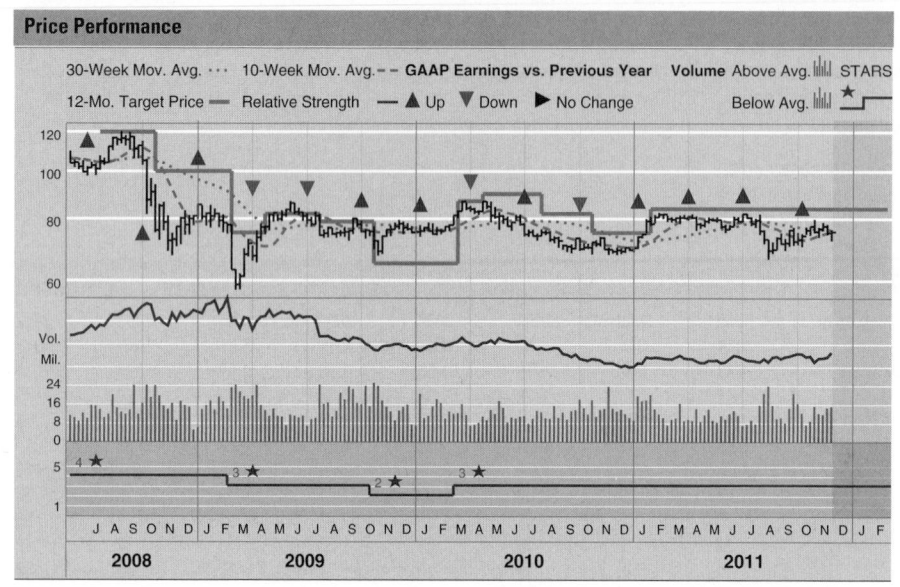

Options: ASE, CBOE, P, Ph

Analysis prepared by Equity Analyst **R. Tortoriello** on Nov 17, 2011, when the stock traded at **$75.52**.

## Highlights

▸ We estimate revenues will rise 3% in 2011, driven by aeronautics gains on the F-35, C-130J, and C-5M programs. However, we see growth of just 1% in 2012, as we project much slower growth in aeronautics, as LMT is negotiating Lot 5 of the F-35 initial production program with the Department of Defense, and we believe this funding gap will slow production in 2012. We expect slow growth in Electronics Systems in 2012, on our expectation of continued ISR demand. But we expect a significant decline in the IS&GS segment, on reduced demand for government IT projects due to budgetary pressure. We also project a slight decline in Space Systems.

▸ We estimate operating margins of 8.3% in 2011, versus 8.9% in 2010. For 2012, we project that operating margins will remain flat, as we expect increased pension expense to offset efficiency improvements.

▸ We see EPS of $7.72 in 2011, with growth to $8.20 in 2012, driven entirely by our expectation of continued large share repurchases. Through the first nine months of 2011, LMT repurchased over $2 billion of shares.

## Investment Rationale/Risk

▸ We expect significant opportunities for Lockheed in Aeronautics (LMT expects nearly $20 billion in annual revenue from Aeronautics by 2015), driven by the production ramp of the F-35 program and by international sales, but we see the outlook for U.S. defense spending growth, the main driver of LMT's earnings, as weak, given our view that the budgetary environment will worsen as the U.S. begins a withdrawal of troops from Afghanistan. We see pressure from targeted cuts in defense programs as well as cost pressure on new contracts as U.S. and European governments lean on defense contractors to help trim budget deficits.

▸ Risks to our recommendation and target price include the potential for greater-than-expected declines in defense spending and development or manufacturing issues on the F-35.

▸ Our 12-month target price of $84 is based on an enterprise value multiple of just below 6X our 2012 EBITDA estimate. This multiple is below the 20-year average EV-to-EBITDA multiple for LMT of 8X, on our view that defense spending will remain under pressure going forward.

## Qualitative Risk Assessment

| LOW | MEDIUM | HIGH |
|---|---|---|

Our risk assessment reflects the company's leading position in military markets and our view of a relatively health balance sheet, with $6.5 billion of long-term debt as of June 2011, but $4.5 billion of cash and equivalents. However, our risk evaluation also factors Lockheed's dependence on government funding, which can change with political and economic priorities.

## Quantitative Evaluations

**S&P Quality Ranking**  B+

| D | C | B- | B | B+ | A- | A | A+ |
|---|---|---|---|---|---|---|---|

**Relative Strength Rank**  STRONG

78

LOWEST = 1          HIGHEST = 99

## Revenue/Earnings Data

**Revenue (Million $)**

| | 1Q | 2Q | 3Q | 4Q | Year |
|---|---|---|---|---|---|
| 2011 | 10,633 | 11,551 | 12,119 | -- | -- |
| 2010 | 10,637 | 11,442 | 11,375 | 12,794 | 45,803 |
| 2009 | 10,373 | 11,236 | 11,056 | 12,524 | 45,189 |
| 2008 | 9,983 | 11,039 | 10,577 | 11,132 | 42,731 |
| 2007 | 9,275 | 10,651 | 11,095 | 10,841 | 41,862 |
| 2006 | 9,214 | 9,961 | 9,605 | 10,840 | 39,620 |

**Earnings Per Share ($)**

| | | | | | |
|---|---|---|---|---|---|
| 2011 | 1.55 | 2.14 | 1.99 | E2.01 | E7.72 |
| 2010 | 1.45 | 1.96 | 1.55 | 2.30 | 7.18 |
| 2009 | 1.68 | 1.88 | 2.07 | 2.17 | 7.78 |
| 2008 | 1.75 | 2.15 | 1.92 | 2.05 | 7.86 |
| 2007 | 1.60 | 1.82 | 1.80 | 1.89 | 7.10 |
| 2006 | 1.34 | 1.34 | 1.46 | 1.68 | 5.80 |

Fiscal year ended Dec. 31. Next earnings report expected: Late January. EPS Estimates based on S&P Operating Earnings; historical GAAP earnings are as reported.

## Dividend Data (Dates: mm/dd Payment Date: mm/dd/yy)

| Amount ($) | Date Decl. | Ex-Div. Date | Stk. of Record | Payment Date |
|---|---|---|---|---|
| 0.750 | 01/27 | 02/25 | 03/01 | 03/25/11 |
| 0.750 | 04/28 | 05/27 | 06/01 | 06/24/11 |
| 0.750 | 06/23 | 08/30 | 09/01 | 09/23/11 |
| 1.000 | 09/22 | 11/29 | 12/01 | 12/30/11 |

Dividends have been paid since 1995. Source: Company reports.

Please read the Required Disclosures and Analyst Certification on the last page of this report.

The McGraw·Hill Companies

# Lockheed Martin Corp

**STANDARD &POOR'S**

## Business Summary November 17, 2011

CORPORATE OVERVIEW. With estimated 2011 sales of $47 billion, Lockheed Martin is the world's largest military weapons maker. In 2010, the company derived 84% of its net sales from the U.S. government, including the Department of Defense (DoD) as well as non-DoD agencies. Sales to foreign governments contributed 15% of net sales (up from 13% in 2009), with 1% of net sales to commercial and other customers. Lockheed Martin conducts business through four operating segments: Aeronautics; Electronic Systems; Space Systems; and Information Systems & Global Services.

The Aeronautics segment (29% of revenues and 30% of operating profits in 2010) primarily makes fighter jets (68% of segment sales) and military transport planes (20%). Major development and production programs include the F-35 Lightning II, the F-22 Raptor, the F-16 Fighting Falcon, and the C-130J Super Hercules transport. F-22 production will be completed in 2012. Sales to the U.S. government under the F-35 program accounted for 12% of total LMT net sales in 2010. LMT is currently working on the System Development and Demonstration phase of the F-35, which it expects to continue into 2016. In addition, LMT's "Skunk Works" research & development laboratory is well known for its advanced R&D efforts. It is currently focused on unmanned military aircraft and long-range bombers, among other initiatives.

Electronic Systems (31% and 34%) includes three business lines. Mission Systems & Sensors (44% of segment sales) primarily provides ship system integration (C4ISR); surface ship and submarine combat systems; sea-based missile defense systems; sensors; etc. Core programs include the Aegis Weapon System, a fleet defense and sea-based U.S. missile defense system, and the Littoral Combat Ship. Missiles and Fire Control (36%) makes land-based, air, and theater missile-defense systems; electro-optical systems; fire-control and sensor systems; and precision-guided weapons. Major programs include the Terminal High Altitude Area Defense (THAAD) system (a transportable missile defense system) and the PAC-3 missile. Global Training & Logistics (20%) provides logistics support, engineering support, and integration services for fixed and rotary-wing aircraft and provides simulation and training services. The unit also operates the Sandia National Laboratories for the U.S. Department of Energy.

## Company Financials Fiscal Year Ended Dec. 31

**Per Share Data ($)**

| | 2010 | 2009 | 2008 | 2007 | 2006 | 2005 | 2004 | 2003 | 2002 | 2001 |
|---|---|---|---|---|---|---|---|---|---|---|
| Tangible Book Value | NM | NM | NM | NM | NM | NM | NM | NM | NM | NM |
| Cash Flow | 9.22 | 9.97 | 9.92 | 9.02 | 7.55 | 5.68 | 4.39 | 3.69 | 2.40 | 2.08 |
| Earnings | 7.18 | 7.78 | 7.86 | 7.10 | 5.80 | 4.10 | 2.83 | 2.34 | 1.18 | 0.18 |
| S&P Core Earnings | 7.97 | 8.23 | 4.07 | 6.65 | 5.70 | 4.11 | 3.23 | 2.20 | -0.78 | -2.29 |
| Dividends | 2.64 | 2.34 | 1.83 | 1.47 | 1.25 | 1.05 | 0.91 | 0.58 | 0.44 | 0.44 |
| Payout Ratio | 37% | 30% | 23% | 21% | 22% | 26% | 32% | 25% | 37% | NM |
| Prices:High | 87.19 | 87.06 | 120.30 | 113.74 | 93.24 | 65.46 | 61.77 | 58.95 | 71.52 | 52.98 |
| Prices:Low | 67.68 | 57.41 | 67.38 | 88.86 | 62.52 | 52.54 | 43.10 | 40.64 | 45.85 | 31.00 |
| P/E Ratio:High | 12 | 11 | 15 | 16 | 16 | 16 | 22 | 25 | 61 | NM |
| P/E Ratio:Low | 9 | 7 | 9 | 13 | 11 | 13 | 15 | 17 | 39 | NM |

**Income Statement Analysis** (Million $)

| | 2010 | 2009 | 2008 | 2007 | 2006 | 2005 | 2004 | 2003 | 2002 | 2001 |
|---|---|---|---|---|---|---|---|---|---|---|
| Revenue | 45,803 | 45,189 | 42,731 | 41,862 | 39,620 | 37,213 | 35,526 | 31,824 | 26,578 | 23,990 |
| Operating Income | 4,846 | 5,062 | 5,494 | 5,032 | 4,198 | 3,242 | 2,624 | 2,585 | 2,507 | 2,366 |
| Depreciation | 749 | 859 | 845 | 819 | 764 | 705 | 656 | 609 | 558 | 823 |
| Interest Expense | 345 | 305 | 341 | 352 | 361 | 370 | 425 | 487 | 581 | 700 |
| Pretax Income | 3,826 | 4,284 | 4,702 | 4,368 | 3,592 | 2,616 | 1,664 | 1,532 | 577 | 188 |
| Effective Tax Rate | NA | 29.4% | 31.6% | 30.6% | 29.6% | 30.2% | 23.9% | 31.3% | 7.63% | 58.0% |
| Net Income | 2,645 | 3,024 | 3,217 | 3,033 | 2,529 | 1,825 | 1,266 | 1,053 | 533 | 79.0 |
| S&P Core Earnings | 2,937 | 3,198 | 1,666 | 2,844 | 2,486 | 1,830 | 1,448 | 994 | -353 | -989 |

**Balance Sheet & Other Financial Data** (Million $)

| | 2010 | 2009 | 2008 | 2007 | 2006 | 2005 | 2004 | 2003 | 2002 | 2001 |
|---|---|---|---|---|---|---|---|---|---|---|
| Cash | 2,777 | 2,391 | 2,229 | 2,981 | 1,912 | 2,244 | 1,060 | 1,010 | 2,738 | 912 |
| Current Assets | 12,851 | 12,477 | 10,683 | 10,940 | 10,164 | 10,529 | 8,953 | 9,401 | 10,626 | 10,778 |
| Total Assets | 35,067 | 35,105 | 33,434 | 28,926 | 28,231 | 27,744 | 25,554 | 26,175 | 25,758 | 27,654 |
| Current Liabilities | 11,160 | 10,703 | 10,542 | 9,871 | 9,553 | 9,428 | 8,566 | 8,893 | 9,821 | 9,689 |
| Long Term Debt | 5,019 | 5,052 | 3,563 | 4,303 | 4,405 | 4,784 | 5,104 | 6,072 | 6,217 | 7,422 |
| Common Equity | 3,708 | 4,129 | 2,865 | 9,805 | 6,884 | 7,867 | 7,021 | 6,756 | 5,865 | 6,443 |
| Total Capital | 8,727 | 9,181 | 6,428 | 14,108 | 11,289 | 12,651 | 12,125 | 12,828 | 12,082 | 14,857 |
| Capital Expenditures | 820 | 852 | 926 | 940 | 893 | 865 | 769 | 687 | 662 | 619 |
| Cash Flow | 3,394 | 3,878 | 4,062 | 3,852 | 3,293 | 2,530 | 1,922 | 1,662 | 1,091 | 902 |
| Current Ratio | 1.2 | 1.2 | 1.0 | 1.1 | 1.1 | 1.1 | 1.0 | 1.1 | 1.1 | 1.1 |
| % Long Term Debt of Capitalization | 57.5 | 55.0 | 55.4 | 30.5 | 39.0 | 37.8 | 42.1 | 47.3 | 51.5 | 50.0 |
| % Net Income of Revenue | 5.8 | 6.7 | 7.5 | 7.3 | 6.4 | 4.9 | 3.6 | 3.3 | 2.0 | 0.3 |
| % Return on Assets | 7.5 | 8.8 | 10.3 | 10.6 | 9.0 | 6.8 | 4.9 | 4.0 | 2.0 | 0.3 |
| % Return on Equity | 67.5 | 86.5 | 50.8 | 36.4 | 34.3 | 24.5 | 18.4 | 16.7 | 8.7 | 1.2 |

Data as orig reptd.; bef. results of disc opers/spec. items. Per share data adj. for stk. divs.; EPS diluted. E-Estimated. NA-Not Available. NM-Not Meaningful. NR-Not Ranked. UR-Under Review.

**Office:** 6801 Rockledge Drive, Bethesda, MD 20817.
**Telephone:** 301-897-6000.
**Website:** http://www.lockheedmartin.com
**Chrmn & CEO:** B. Stevens

**Pres & COO:** C.E. Kubasik
**EVP & CFO:** B.L. Tanner
**SVP & CTO:** R.O. Johnson
**SVP, Secy & General Counsel:** M.R. Lavan

**Auditor:** ERNST & YOUNG
**Board Members:** N. D. Archibald, R. G. Brewer, D. B. Burritt, J. O. Ellis, Jr., T. J. Falk, G. S. King, J. M. Loy, D. H. McCorkindale, J. W. Ralston, A. L. Stevens, B. Stevens

**Founded:** 1909
**Domicile:** Maryland
**Employees:** 132,000

# Loews Corp

**STANDARD &POOR'S**

| S&P Recommendation | BUY ★★★★☆ | Price | 12-Mo. Target Price | Investment Style |
|---|---|---|---|---|
| | | $35.85 (as of Nov 25, 2011) | $47.00 | Large-Cap Value |

**GICS Sector** Financials
**Sub-Industry** Multi-line Insurance

**Summary** This conglomerate includes holdings in property/casualty insurance, offshore drilling, hotels, and natural gas pipelines.

## Key Stock Statistics (Source S&P, Vickers, company reports)

| | | | | | | |
|---|---|---|---|---|---|---|
| 52-Wk Range | $45.31– 32.90 | S&P Oper. EPS 2011**E** | 2.81 | Market Capitalization(B) | $14.217 | Beta | 1.21 |
| Trailing 12-Month EPS | $3.07 | S&P Oper. EPS 2012**E** | 3.50 | Yield (%) | 0.70 | S&P 3-Yr. Proj. EPS CAGR(%) | 7 |
| Trailing 12-Month P/E | 11.7 | P/E on S&P Oper. EPS 2011**E** | 12.8 | Dividend Rate/Share | $0.25 | S&P Credit Rating | A+ |
| $10K Invested 5 Yrs Ago | $9,275 | Common Shares Outstg. (M) | 396.6 | Institutional Ownership (%) | 61 | | |

## Price Performance

- 30-Week Mov. Avg.
- 10-Week Mov. Avg.
- 12-Mo. Target Price
- Relative Strength
- GAAP Earnings vs. Previous Year
- ▲ Up ▼ Down ► No Change
- Volume Above Avg. / Below Avg.
- STARS

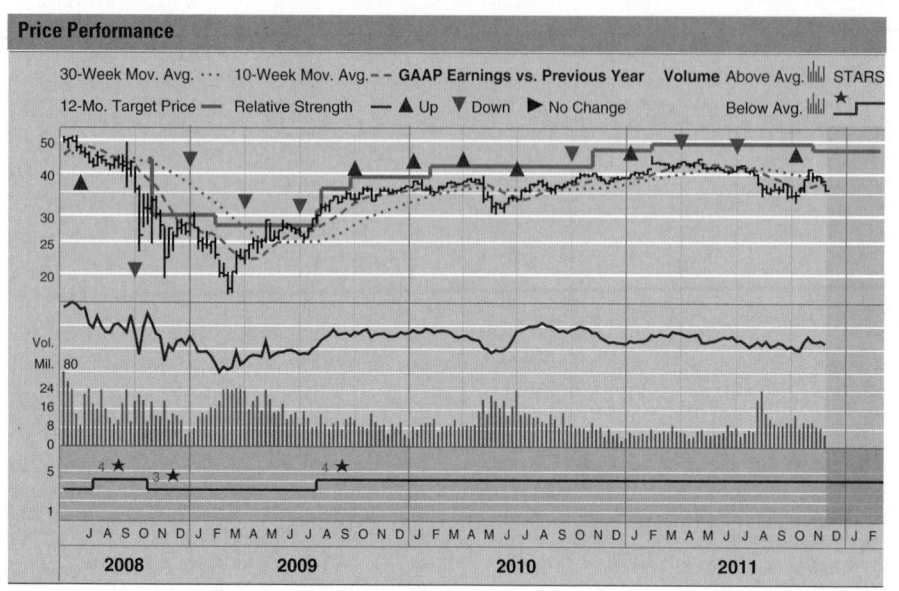

Options: ASE, CBOE, P, Ph

Analysis prepared by Equity Analyst **Cathy Seifert** on Nov 14, 2011, when the stock traded at **$39.13**.

### Highlights

➤ We see revenue growth in coming periods at L's principal subsidiary, CNA Financial (CNA 27 Hold), being aided by new business production growth, modestly higher commercial P&C rates, and a slight increase in limited partnership income. Persistently low interest rates will likely keep investment income under pressure though. We see higher day rates for midwater rigs aiding 2011 earnings at Diamond Offshore (DO 65 Hold), though year-to-year comparisons could be more difficult in 2012.

➤ The increase in operating earnings forecasted for 2012 largely reflects an expected improvement in property-casualty insurance claim trends amid an assumption of "normal" levels of catastrophe and weather-related claims, versus the elevated levels incurred by the industry so far in 2011.

➤ We forecast EPS of $2.81 for 2011 and $3.50 for 2012.

### Investment Rationale/Risk

➤ We forecast improved fundamentals at most of the company's subsidiaries and believe L is undervalued based on our calculation of the net asset values of its public and private holdings. We think a strengthening in the credit markets has considerably reduced risks related to L's investment portfolio and CNA's capital position, and we expect L to deploy excess cash by repurchasing its shares, undertaking new business ventures, and investing in the debt markets. We see the operating environment improving for CNA, and believe the P&C underwriting pricing cycle should stabilize, and improve in some businesses.

➤ Risks to our recommendation and target price include a decline in the level of production at Diamond Offshore; higher-than-projected catastrophe losses; and greater-than-expected losses in the investment portfolio.

➤ Our 12-month target price of $47 is 13.4X our 2012 EPS estimate. This represents the approximate midpoint of the stock's historical range.

## Qualitative Risk Assessment

| LOW | MEDIUM | HIGH |
|---|---|---|

Our risk assessment for Loews reflects exposure to investment and catastrophe losses from its CNA Financial subsidiary, regulatory risks, litigation risk, volatility in energy prices, and catastrophe losses. This is offset by its diversified group of holdings, substantial free cash flow, and what we consider a solid financial position.

## Quantitative Evaluations

**S&P Quality Ranking**      **B**

| D | C | B- | B | B+ | A- | A | A+ |
|---|---|---|---|---|---|---|---|

**Relative Strength Rank**      **MODERATE**

54

LOWEST = 1      HIGHEST = 99

## Revenue/Earnings Data

**Revenue (Million $)**

| | 1Q | 2Q | 3Q | 4Q | Year |
|---|---|---|---|---|---|
| 2011 | 3,668 | 3,542 | 3,438 | -- | -- |
| 2010 | 3,713 | 3,486 | 3,701 | 3,715 | 14,615 |
| 2009 | 3,023 | 3,534 | 3,738 | 3,822 | 14,117 |
| 2008 | 3,612 | 3,922 | 2,970 | 2,743 | 13,247 |
| 2007 | 4,660 | 4,637 | 4,653 | 4,567 | 18,380 |
| 2006 | 4,245 | 4,277 | 4,507 | 4,882 | 17,911 |

**Earnings Per Share ($)**

| | | | | | |
|---|---|---|---|---|---|
| 2011 | 0.92 | 0.62 | 0.40 | E0.89 | E2.81 |
| 2010 | 0.99 | 0.87 | 0.13 | 1.12 | 3.11 |
| 2009 | -1.49 | 0.78 | 1.08 | 0.94 | 1.31 |
| 2008 | 0.77 | 1.00 | -0.33 | -2.20 | -0.82 |
| 2007 | 1.19 | 0.96 | 0.76 | 0.71 | 3.64 |
| 2006 | 0.86 | 0.85 | 0.93 | 1.15 | 3.80 |

Fiscal year ended Dec. 31. Next earnings report expected: Early February. EPS Estimates based on S&P Operating Earnings; historical GAAP earnings are as reported.

## Dividend Data (Dates: mm/dd Payment Date: mm/dd/yy)

| Amount ($) | Date Decl. | Ex-Div. Date | Stk. of Record | Payment Date |
|---|---|---|---|---|
| 0.063 | 02/08 | 02/25 | 03/01 | 03/14/11 |
| 0.063 | 05/10 | 05/27 | 06/01 | 06/14/11 |
| 0.063 | 08/09 | 08/30 | 09/01 | 09/14/11 |
| 0.063 | 11/08 | 11/25 | 11/29 | 12/12/11 |

Dividends have been paid since 1967. Source: Company reports.

---

**Please read the Required Disclosures and Analyst Certification on the last page of this report.**

# Loews Corp

STANDARD &POOR'S

## Business Summary November 14, 2011

CORPORATE OVERVIEW. Loews Corp. is a holding company with interests in property/casualty insurance (CNA Financial Corp., 90% stake), hotels (Loews Hotels Holding Corp.), offshore oil and gas drilling (Diamond Offshore Drilling, Inc., 50%), exploration, production and marketing of natural gas and natural gas liquids (HighMount Exploration & Production LLC), and interstate natural gas pipelines (Boardwalk Pipeline Partners, LP, 66%).

CNA Financial Corp. (CNA 27 Hold) (63% of consolidated total revenues in 2010) is an insurance holding company with subsidiaries that primarily consist of property and casualty insurance companies. The company serves small, medium and large businesses as well as associations, professionals and groups. The Loews Hotels division (2.1%) owns and/or operates 18 hotels in the U.S. and Canada. Diamond Offshore (DO 65 Hold) (23%) operates 46 off-

shore drilling rigs that are chartered on a contract basis for fixed terms by energy exploration companies. Boardwalk Pipeline Partners (BWP 29 NR) (7.7%) owns and operates three interstate natural gas pipeline systems, Gulf Crossing Pipeline Company, Gulf South Pipeline and Texas Gas Transmission. High-Mount Exploration & Production LLC (2.9%) is involved in the exploration, production and marketing of natural gas, NGLs (predominantly ethane and propane) and oil. Coporate and other reported consolidated revenues of $154 million in 2010.

## Company Financials Fiscal Year Ended Dec. 31

| Per Share Data ($) | 2010 | 2009 | 2008 | 2007 | 2006 | 2005 | 2004 | 2003 | 2002 | 2001 |
|---|---|---|---|---|---|---|---|---|---|---|
| Tangible Book Value | 42.13 | 40.30 | 27.93 | 25.44 | NM | NM | 21.35 | NM | 19.88 | 16.23 |
| Operating Earnings | NA | NA | NA | NA | NA | NA | NA | NA | 1.71 | -2.27 |
| Earnings | 3.11 | 1.31 | -0.82 | 3.64 | 3.80 | 1.69 | 1.88 | -1.30 | 1.50 | -0.92 |
| S&P Core Earnings | 3.02 | 2.39 | 1.57 | 3.76 | 3.65 | 1.49 | 2.17 | -2.00 | 2.63 | -2.47 |
| Dividends | 0.25 | 0.25 | 0.25 | 0.25 | 0.18 | 0.20 | 0.20 | 0.20 | 0.20 | 0.19 |
| Relative Payout | 8% | 19% | NM | 7% | 5% | 12% | 11% | NM | 13% | NM |
| Prices:High | 40.34 | 36.84 | 51.51 | 53.46 | 42.18 | 32.90 | 23.67 | 16.49 | 20.77 | 24.17 |
| Prices:Low | 30.22 | 17.40 | 19.39 | 40.21 | 30.42 | 22.35 | 16.36 | 12.75 | 12.50 | 13.68 |
| P/E Ratio:High | 13 | 28 | NM | 15 | 11 | 19 | 13 | NM | 14 | NM |
| P/E Ratio:Low | 10 | 13 | NM | 11 | 8 | 13 | 9 | NM | 8 | NM |

| Income Statement Analysis (Million $) | 2010 | 2009 | 2008 | 2007 | 2006 | 2005 | 2004 | 2003 | 2002 | 2001 |
|---|---|---|---|---|---|---|---|---|---|---|
| Life Insurance in Force | NA | NA | NA | 14,090 | 15,652 | 20,548 | 56,645 | 388,968 | 437,751 | 497,732 |
| Premium Income:Life A & H | NA | 594 | 611 | 618 | 641 | 704 | 901 | 2,275 | 3,382 | 4,351 |
| Premium Income:Casualty/Property. | NA | 6,127 | 6,539 | 6,866 | 6,962 | 6,865 | 7,304 | 6,935 | 6,828 | 5,010 |
| Net Investment Income | 2,508 | 2,499 | 1,581 | 2,891 | 2,915 | 2,099 | 1,869 | 1,732 | 1,867 | 2,145 |
| Total Revenue | 14,615 | 14,117 | 13,247 | 18,380 | 17,911 | 16,018 | 15,242 | 16,461 | 17,495 | 19,417 |
| Pretax Income | 2,902 | 1,730 | 587 | 4,575 | 1,237 | 1,016 | 1,822 | -751 | 1,647 | -813 |
| Net Operating Income | NA | NA | NA | NA | NA | NA | NA | NA | 1,099 | -1,328 |
| Net Income | 1,308 | 566 | -182 | 2,481 | 760 | 623 | 1,231 | -468 | 983 | -536 |
| S&P Core Earnings | 1,272 | 1,035 | 749 | 2,014 | 2,024 | 831 | 1,205 | -1,112 | 1,594 | -1,447 |

| Balance Sheet & Other Financial Data (Million $) | 2010 | 2009 | 2008 | 2007 | 2006 | 2005 | 2004 | 2003 | 2002 | 2001 |
|---|---|---|---|---|---|---|---|---|---|---|
| Cash & Equivalent | 120 | 190 | 131 | 141 | 132 | 151 | 220 | 181 | 185 | 181 |
| Premiums Due | 10,142 | 10,212 | 11,672 | 11,677 | 12,423 | 15,314 | 18,807 | 20,468 | 16,601 | 19,453 |
| Investment Assets:Bonds | 37,814 | 35,816 | 29,451 | 34,663 | 37,570 | 33,381 | 33,502 | 28,781 | 27,434 | 31,191 |
| Investment Assets:Stocks | 1,086 | 1,007 | 1,185 | 1,347 | 1,309 | 1,107 | 664 | 888 | 1,121 | 1,646 |
| Investment Assets:Loans | Nil | Nil | Nil | Nil | Nil | Nil | Nil | Nil | NA | NA |
| Investment Assets:Total | 48,907 | 46,034 | 38,450 | 47,923 | 52,020 | 43,547 | 44,299 | 42,515 | 40,137 | 41,159 |
| Deferred Policy Costs | 1,079 | 1,108 | 1,125 | 1,161 | 1,190 | 1,197 | 1,268 | 2,533 | 2,551 | 2,424 |
| Total Assets | 76,277 | 74,070 | 69,857 | 76,079 | 75,325 | 69,548 | 73,750 | 77,881 | 70,520 | 75,251 |
| Debt | 8,830 | 9,475 | 8,187 | 6,900 | 1,230 | 1,627 | 5,980 | 2,032 | 5,652 | 5,920 |
| Common Equity | 18,450 | 16,899 | 13,126 | 17,591 | 15,580 | -201 | 45,428 | -729 | 11,235 | 9,649 |
| Combined Loss-Expense Ratio | 102.9 | 105.1 | 109.0 | 110.1 | 109.1 | 120.3 | 105.9 | 146.6 | 110.3 | 158.6 |
| % Return on Revenue | 8.9 | 4.0 | NM | 13.5 | 4.2 | 3.9 | 8.1 | 14.2 | 5.6 | NM |
| % Return on Equity | 7.4 | 3.8 | NM | 15.0 | 14.2 | 2.6 | 2.8 | NM | 8.1 | NM |
| % Investment Yield | 4.4 | 5.2 | 3.7 | 5.8 | 6.1 | 2.6 | 4.3 | 4.2 | 4.6 | 5.2 |

Data as orig reptd.; bef. results of disc opers/spec. items. Per share data adj. for stk. divs.; EPS diluted. E-Estimated. NA-Not Available. NM-Not Meaningful. NR-Not Ranked. UR-Under Review.

**Office:** 667 Madison Ave, New York, NY 10065-8087.
**Telephone:** 212-521-2000.
**Website:** http://www.loews.com
**Co-Chrmn:** J.M. Tisch

**Co-Chrmn:** A.H. Tisch
**Pres & CEO:** J.S. Tisch
**SVP & CFO:** P.W. Keegan
**SVP, Secy & General Counsel:** G.W. Garson

**Investor Contact:** D. Daugherty (212-521-2788)
**Board Members:** L. S. Bacow, A. E. Berman, J. L. Bower, C. M. Diker, J. A. Frenkel, P. J. Fribourg, W. L. Harris, P. A. Laskawy, K. Miller, G. R. Scott, A. H. Tisch, J. S. Tisch, J. M. Tisch

**Founded:** 1954
**Domicile:** Delaware
**Employees:** 18,400

# Lorillard Inc

## STANDARD &POOR'S

| S&P Recommendation BUY ★★★★☆ | Price $108.63 (as of Nov 25, 2011) | 12-Mo. Target Price $119.00 | Investment Style Large-Cap Blend |
|---|---|---|---|

**GICS Sector** Consumer Staples
**Sub-Industry** Tobacco

**Summary** Lorillard is the third largest U.S. tobacco company and the leading manufacturer and marketer of menthol cigarettes.

## Key Stock Statistics (Source S&P, Vickers, company reports)

| | | | | | | | |
|---|---|---|---|---|---|---|---|
| 52-Wk Range | $120.00– 72.40 | S&P Oper. EPS 2011E | 7.57 | Market Capitalization(B) | $14.666 | Beta | 0.45 |
| Trailing 12-Month EPS | $7.43 | S&P Oper. EPS 2012E | 8.33 | Yield (%) | 4.79 | S&P 3-Yr. Proj. EPS CAGR(%) | 9 |
| Trailing 12-Month P/E | 14.6 | P/E on S&P Oper. EPS 2011E | 14.4 | Dividend Rate/Share | $5.20 | S&P Credit Rating | BBB- |
| $10K Invested 5 Yrs Ago | $20,575 | Common Shares Outstg. (M) | 135.0 | Institutional Ownership (%) | NM | | |

## Price Performance

30-Week Mov. Avg. ···  10-Week Mov. Avg. - - GAAP Earnings vs. Previous Year  Volume Above Avg. STARS
12-Mo. Target Price — Relative Strength  ▲ Up  ▼ Down  ▶ No Change  Below Avg.

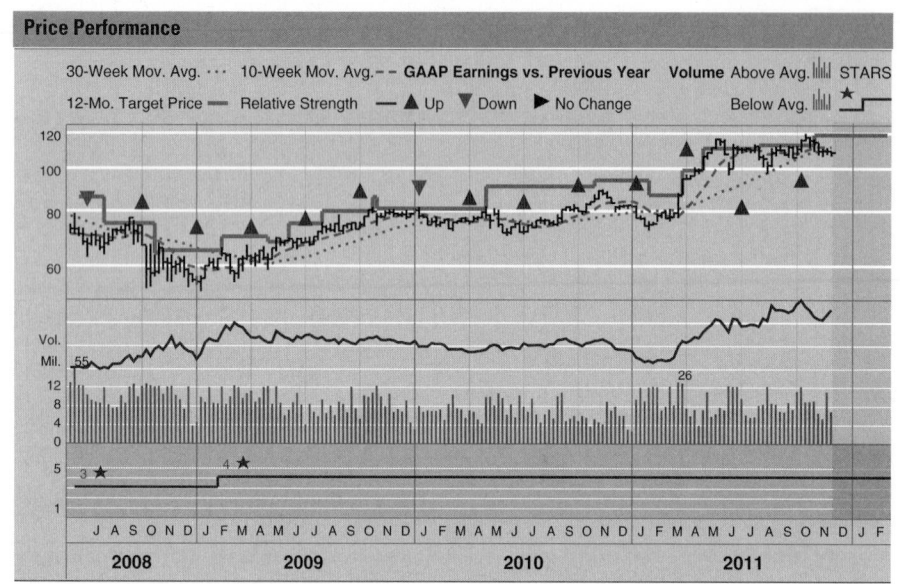

Analysis prepared by Equity Analyst **Esther Kwon, CFA** on Oct 25, 2011, when the stock traded at **$113.45**.

## Qualitative Risk Assessment

| LOW | MEDIUM | HIGH |
|---|---|---|

Our risk assessment reflects the relatively stable revenue and income streams enjoyed by the tobacco industry, offset by significant ongoing litigation.

## Quantitative Evaluations

**S&P Quality Ranking**  NR

| D | C | B- | B | B+ | A- | A | A+ |
|---|---|---|---|---|---|---|---|

**Relative Strength Rank**  STRONG

71

LOWEST = 1    HIGHEST = 99

## Revenue/Earnings Data

**Revenue (Million $)**

| | 1Q | 2Q | 3Q | 4Q | Year |
|---|---|---|---|---|---|
| 2011 | 1,056 | 1,159 | 1,113 | -- | -- |
| 2010 | 923.0 | 1,038 | 1,073 | 1,020 | 4,053 |
| 2009 | 767.0 | 1,033 | 953.0 | 932.0 | 3,686 |
| 2008 | 932.0 | 886.0 | 936.0 | 912.0 | 3,492 |
| 2007 | 947.3 | 1,055 | 1,044 | 957.0 | 3,281 |
| 2006 | 880.8 | 998.6 | 1,016 | 936.7 | 3,866 |

**Earnings Per Share ($)**

| | 1Q | 2Q | 3Q | 4Q | Year |
|---|---|---|---|---|---|
| 2011 | 1.71 | 2.05 | 1.94 | E1.87 | E7.57 |
| 2010 | 1.50 | 1.73 | 1.81 | 1.74 | 6.78 |
| 2009 | 1.09 | 1.71 | 1.44 | 1.52 | 5.76 |
| 2008 | 1.00 | 1.25 | 1.38 | 1.53 | 5.15 |
| 2007 | 1.08 | 1.30 | 1.34 | 1.18 | 5.16 |
| 2006 | 0.86 | 1.09 | 1.17 | 1.26 | 4.46 |

Fiscal year ended Dec. 31. Next earnings report expected: Early February. EPS Estimates based on S&P Operating Earnings; historical GAAP earnings are as reported.

## Highlights

▶ For 2011, we estimate a high single digit percentage increase in sales from the $4.1 billion reported for 2010, on higher volumes and pricing. We think discount brand volumes, which rose 30% in 2010, and Newport non-menthol will post strong growth through 2011, countering some of the expansion we forecast in gross margins. We expect cigarette industry pricing power to remain strong. In July 2011, Lorillard raised prices on most of its cigarette brands. For 2012, we see a mid-single digit increase in sales.

▶ On rising marketing and legal outlays, we look for an increase in selling, general and administrative expenses, but this should be offset somewhat by disciplined cost control.

▶ On higher interest expense, about a 7% reduction in the number of shares outstanding and an effective tax rate similar to 2010, we estimate 2011 EPS of $7.57, up from 2010 operating EPS of $6.77. For 2012, we forecast EPS of $8.33. In August 2010, LO's directors approved an additional share repurchase program for up to $1 billion of its common stock. As of September 30, 2011, the program had approximately $553 million remaining.

## Investment Rationale/Risk

▶ We view positively LO's continued market share gains for its leading brand, Newport, in both the menthol and premium categories. We believe efforts to increase its investment in this brand will result in long-term volume growth ahead of peers, less promotional activity, and higher average prices. Although we think a potential FDA ban of menthol would be detrimental to the shares, we do not know of any conclusive evidence that menthol cigarettes are more harmful than non-menthol ones. Furthermore, we think unintended consequences, such as the rise of illegal trade, make a ban unlikely.

▶ Risks to our recommendation and target price include a menthol ban, a slowdown in industry volume trends, and a worsening of the litigation environment.

▶ Applying a multiple of 14.3X to our 2012 EPS estimate, we arrive at our 12-month target price of $119. Our target P/E multiple is about in line with the average of cigarette manufacturing peers. While we are concerned about geographic concentration and what we see as more limited margin expansion potential, we think LO is attractive given its leadership position in the higher-growth menthol market.

## Dividend Data (Dates: mm/dd Payment Date: mm/dd/yy)

| Amount ($) | Date Decl. | Ex-Div. Date | Stk. of Record | Payment Date |
|---|---|---|---|---|
| 1.300 | 02/17 | 02/25 | 03/01 | 03/11/11 |
| 1.300 | 05/19 | 05/27 | 06/01 | 06/10/11 |
| 1.300 | 08/12 | 08/30 | 09/01 | 09/12/11 |
| 1.300 | 11/09 | 11/29 | 12/01 | 12/12/11 |

Dividends have been paid since 2002. Source: Company reports.

---

**Please read the Required Disclosures and Analyst Certification on the last page of this report.**

The McGraw·Hill Companies

# Lorillard Inc

## Business Summary October 25, 2011

CORPORATE OVERVIEW. The company produces and markets cigarettes primarily in the U.S. The tobacco used in Lorillard cigarettes includes burley leaf, flue-cured tobacco grown in the U.S. and abroad, and aromatic tobacco grown primarily in Turkey and other Near Eastern countries. Through Alliance One International, Inc., Lorillard directs the purchase of more than 66% of its U.S. leaf tobacco needs. The company stores the various types and grades of its tobacco in 29 warehouses at its Danville, VA, facility. Its sole manufacturing plant, located in Greensboro, NC, has an annual production capacity of about 50 billion cigarettes, or approximately 200 million cigarettes per day. Lorillard, formerly a division of Loews Corp., was spun off in June 2008.

The company primarily sells its cigarettes to distributors that resell them to chain store organizations and government agencies. As of December 31, 2010, Lorillard had approximately 500 direct buying customers servicing more than 400,000 retail accounts. Lorillard does not sell cigarettes directly to consumers. During 2010, 2009 and 2008, sales to McLane Company, Inc. comprised 27%, 26% and 26%, respectively, of Lorillard's revenues. No other customer accounted for more than 10% of sales in any of those years.

LEGAL/REGULATORY ISSUES. Lorillard's business operations are subject to a variety of federal, state and local laws and regulations governing, among oth-

er things, the publication of health warnings on cigarette packaging, advertising and sales of tobacco products, restrictions on smoking in public places, and fire safety standards. The U.S. cigarette industry faces a number of issues that have affected and may continue to affect its operations, including substantial litigation that seeks billions of dollars of damages. As of February 9, 2011, Lorillard was a defendant in about 9,758 cases facing the industry, including 7,082 Engle progeny cases.

MARKET PROFILE. According to Lorillard, industrywide cigarette shipments declined at a compound annual rate of approximately 3.5% from 2000 to 2010, with shipments dropping an estimated 3.8% in 2010, 8.6% in 2009, 3.3% in 2008, and 3.3% in 2007. Standard & Poor's attributes 2009's above trend decline to the significant hike in the federal excise tax on cigarettes to $1.0066 per pack from $0.6166 per pack effective April 1, 2009, to finance health insurance for children. On price increases, rising excise taxes and regulations, health concerns and proliferation of smoking bans, we expect shipments to decline at a mid-single digit rate over the next several years.

## Company Financials Fiscal Year Ended Dec. 31

| Per Share Data ($) | 2010 | 2009 | 2008 | 2007 | 2006 | 2005 | 2004 | 2003 | 2002 | 2001 |
|---|---|---|---|---|---|---|---|---|---|---|
| Tangible Book Value | NM | 0.56 | 3.76 | 6.34 | NM | NM | NM | NM | NM | NA |
| Cash Flow | 7.01 | 5.95 | 5.34 | NA | NA | NA | NA | 8.08 | NA | NA |
| Earnings | 6.78 | 5.76 | 5.15 | 5.16 | 4.46 | 3.62 | 3.15 | 2.76 | 3.50 | NA |
| S&P Core Earnings | 6.77 | 5.81 | 4.91 | 5.31 | 4.46 | 3.63 | 3.13 | 3.31 | 2.92 | NA |
| Dividends | 4.25 | 3.84 | 2.75 | 1.82 | 1.82 | 1.82 | 1.82 | 1.81 | 1.34 | NA |
| Payout Ratio | 63% | 67% | 53% | 35% | 41% | 50% | 58% | 66% | 38% | NA |
| Prices:High | 89.71 | 81.76 | 89.21 | 92.79 | 64.83 | 46.06 | 30.00 | 28.10 | 34.05 | NA |
| Prices:Low | 70.24 | 52.50 | 53.30 | 64.00 | 43.83 | 28.47 | 22.49 | 17.18 | 16.80 | NA |
| P/E Ratio:High | 13 | 14 | 17 | 18 | 15 | 13 | 10 | 10 | 10 | NA |
| P/E Ratio:Low | 10 | 9 | 10 | 12 | 10 | 8 | 7 | 6 | 5 | NA |

| Income Statement Analysis (Million $) | | | | | | | | | | |
|---|---|---|---|---|---|---|---|---|---|---|
| Revenue | 4,053 | 3,686 | 3,492 | 3,281 | 3,866 | 3,640 | 3,388 | 3,288 | 3,798 | 3,868 |
| Operating Income | 1,761 | 1,671 | 1,465 | 1,392 | 1,352 | 1,156 | 1,041 | 934 | NA | NA |
| Depreciation | 35.0 | 32.0 | 32.0 | 40.0 | 47.0 | 48.0 | 40.0 | NA | NA | NA |
| Interest Expense | 94.0 | 27.0 | NA | 74.0 | 116 | 141 | 158 | 183 | 178 | 0.70 |
| Pretax Income | 1,635 | 1,519 | 1,434 | 1,318 | 1,237 | 1,016 | 884 | 751 | 1,121 | 1,105 |
| Effective Tax Rate | NA | 37.6% | 38.2% | 35.1% | 38.5% | 38.6% | 38.2% | 37.7% | 39.2% | 39.0% |
| Net Income | 1,029 | 948 | 887 | 855 | 760 | 623 | 546 | 468 | 682 | 673 |
| S&P Core Earnings | 1,028 | 956 | 845 | 577 | 417 | 252 | 184 | 138 | 117 | 672 |

| Balance Sheet & Other Financial Data (Million $) | | | | | | | | | | |
|---|---|---|---|---|---|---|---|---|---|---|
| Cash | 2,063 | 1,384 | 1,191 | 2.00 | 1.50 | 2.50 | 36.0 | 1.90 | 2.20 | 1.70 |
| Current Assets | 2,935 | 2,181 | 1,962 | 2,103 | 2,115 | 2,069 | NA | NA | NA | NA |
| Total Assets | 3,296 | 2,575 | 2,322 | 2,702 | 2,861 | 2,897 | 2,278 | 2,725 | 2,927 | 2,769 |
| Current Liabilities | 1,426 | 1,337 | 1,273 | 1,188 | 1,151 | 1,240 | NA | NA | NA | NA |
| Long Term Debt | 1,769 | 722 | Nil | 424 | 1,230 | 1,627 | 1,871 | 2,032 | 2,438 | Nil |
| Common Equity | -225 | 87.0 | 635 | 685 | 0.16 | -201 | -502 | -729 | -884 | 1,275 |
| Total Capital | 1,544 | 809 | 631 | 1,109 | 1,230 | 1,426 | 1,369 | 1,303 | 1,555 | 1,275 |
| Capital Expenditures | 40.0 | 51.0 | 44.0 | 51.0 | 29.7 | 31.2 | 50.8 | 56.4 | 51.7 | 41.2 |
| Cash Flow | 1,064 | 980 | 919 | NA | NA | NA | NA | NA | NA | NA |
| Current Ratio | 2.1 | 1.6 | 1.5 | 1.8 | 1.8 | 1.7 | NA | NA | NA | NA |
| % Long Term Debt of Capitalization | 114.6 | 89.3 | Nil | 38.2 | 100.0 | 114.1 | 136.7 | 156.0 | 156.8 | Nil |
| % Net Income of Revenue | 25.4 | 25.7 | 25.4 | 26.1 | 19.7 | 17.1 | 16.1 | 14.2 | 17.9 | 17.4 |
| % Return on Assets | 35.1 | 38.7 | 36.0 | 30.7 | 26.4 | 22.0 | 19.8 | 16.6 | 23.9 | NA |
| % Return on Equity | NM | 264.1 | 107.7 | 203.4 | 5.4 | NM | NM | NM | 348.6 | NA |

Data as orig reptd.; bef. results of disc opers/spec. items. Per share data adj. for stk. divs.; EPS diluted. Prior to June 11, 2008, data and historical prices reflect the former Loews Corp-Carolina Group. E-Estimated. NA-Not Available. NM-Not Meaningful. NR-Not Ranked. UR-Under Review.

**Office:** 714 Green Valley Rd, Greensboro, NC 27408-7018.
**Telephone:** 339-335-7000.
**Email:** ir@loews.com
**Website:** http://www.lorillard.com

**Chrmn, Pres & CEO:** M.S. Kessler
**EVP & CFO:** D.H. Taylor
**SVP, Secy & General Counsel:** R.S. Milstein
**Chief Acctg Officer & Cntlr:** A.B. Petitt

**Investor Contact:** P.W. Keegan (212-521-2000)
**Board Members:** R. C. Almon, D. N. Blixt, A. H. Card, Jr., V. W. Colbert, D. E. Dangoor, K. D. Dietz, M. S. Kessler, R. W. Roedel, N. Travis

**Founded:** 1969
**Domicile:** Delaware
**Employees:** 2,700

# Lowe's Companies Inc.

**STANDARD &POOR'S**

| S&P Recommendation | HOLD ★★★★★ | Price $22.68 (as of Nov 25, 2011) | 12-Mo. Target Price $25.00 | Investment Style Large-Cap Growth |
|---|---|---|---|---|

**GICS Sector** Consumer Discretionary
**Sub-Industry** Home Improvement Retail

**Summary** This company retails building materials and supplies, lumber, hardware and appliances through more than 1,700 stores in the U.S. and Canada.

## Key Stock Statistics (Source S&P, Vickers, company reports)

| | | | | | | | |
|---|---|---|---|---|---|---|---|
| 52-Wk Range | $27.45– 18.07 | S&P Oper. EPS 2012E | 1.62 | Market Capitalization(B) | $28.589 | Beta | 0.99 |
| Trailing 12-Month EPS | $1.37 | S&P Oper. EPS 2013E | 1.81 | Yield (%) | 2.47 | S&P 3-Yr. Proj. EPS CAGR(%) | 12 |
| Trailing 12-Month P/E | 16.6 | P/E on S&P Oper. EPS 2012E | 14.0 | Dividend Rate/Share | $0.56 | S&P Credit Rating | A- |
| $10K Invested 5 Yrs Ago | $8,202 | Common Shares Outstg. (M) | 1,260.5 | Institutional Ownership (%) | 74 | | |

## Price Performance

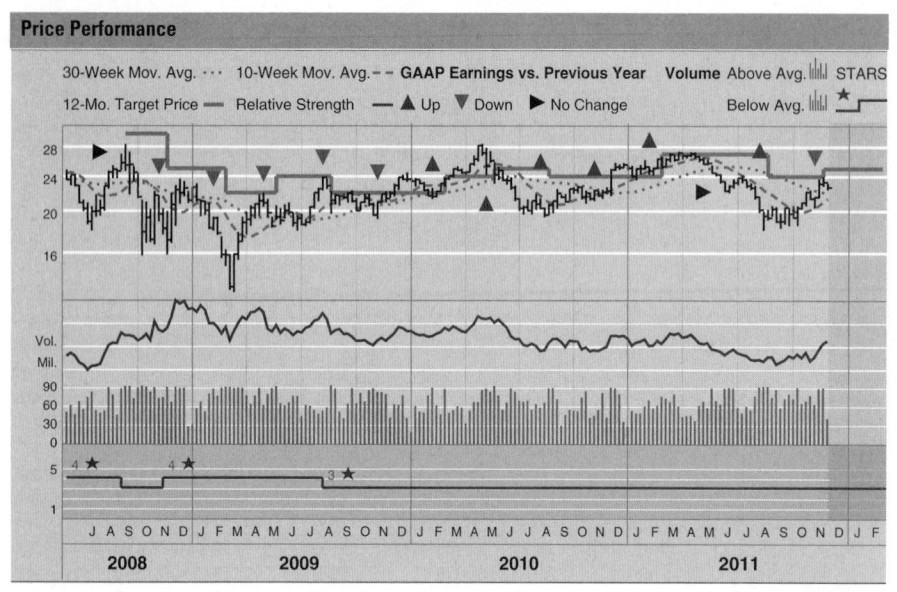

30-Week Mov. Avg. · · · 10-Week Mov. Avg. — **GAAP Earnings vs. Previous Year** Volume Above Avg. ▮▮▮ STARS
12-Mo. Target Price — Relative Strength — ▲ Up ▼ Down ► No Change Below Avg. ▮▮▮ ★

Options: ASE, CBOE, P, Ph

Analysis prepared by Equity Analyst **Michael Souers** on Nov 17, 2011, when the stock traded at **$23.38**.

## Highlights

➤ We forecast a sales increase of 2.8% in FY 13 (Jan.), following our projection of a 2.2% advance in FY 12. We expect this gain to be driven by an estimated 10-15 net new store openings, representing less than a 1.0% increase in total square footage, and a same-store-sales increase of 2%-3% after a projected 0.6% comp-store sales decline in FY 12. We believe the housing market will remain under pressure throughout much of the year, and we continue to project weak consumer spending, particularly on big-ticket home remodeling projects.

➤ We see FY 13 operating margins widening modestly on a product mix shift, a reduction in promotional activity and continued strong expense control, which we think will result in expense leverage from our projected modest same-store sales gain.

➤ We forecast a 4% decline in the diluted share count following a 9% reduction in FY 12, reflecting share repurchases. We project FY 13 EPS of $1.81, a 12% increase from the $1.62 we expect the company to earn in FY 12, excluding $0.21 of charges related to store closures.

## Investment Rationale/Risk

➤ We think the aging of homes and relatively high home ownership rates are powerful long-term demographic drivers that will help mitigate the continued weakness in housing turnover. However, with home refinancings and home equity loans likely to be somewhat sparse in the near to medium term, we expect home remodeling activity, particularly on big projects, to remain weak. While housing turnover appears to have bottomed, we do not anticipate a significant recovery over the next 12 months. With our view of LOW's strong balance sheet and impressive free cash flow generation, we think the shares are fairly valued despite trading at a slight premium to the S&P 500.

➤ Risks to our recommendation and target price include a slowdown in the economy, a spurt in long-term interest rates, and failure by LOW to execute its metro market expansion strategy.

➤ At about 13X our FY 13 EPS estimate, LOW shares recently traded at a slight discount to key peer Home Depot (HD 38, Hold). Our 12-month target price of $25 is derived from our discounted cash flow analysis, which assumes a weighted average cost of capital of 9.7% and a terminal growth rate of 3.0%.

## Qualitative Risk Assessment

| LOW | MEDIUM | HIGH |
|---|---|---|

Our risk assessment reflects the cyclical nature of the home improvement retail industry, which is reliant on economic growth, offset by our view of ample opportunities for retail growth both domestically and abroad, and an S&P Quality Ranking of A- (above average), reflecting LOW's long-term record of earnings and dividends.

## Quantitative Evaluations

**S&P Quality Ranking** A-

| D | C | B- | B | B+ | A- | A | A+ |
|---|---|---|---|---|---|---|---|

**Relative Strength Rank** STRONG

93

LOWEST = 1 HIGHEST = 99

## Revenue/Earnings Data

**Revenue (Million $)**

| | 1Q | 2Q | 3Q | 4Q | Year |
|---|---|---|---|---|---|
| 2012 | 12,185 | 14,543 | 11,852 | -- | -- |
| 2011 | 12,388 | 14,361 | 11,587 | 10,480 | 48,815 |
| 2010 | 11,832 | 13,844 | 11,375 | 10,168 | 47,220 |
| 2009 | 12,009 | 14,509 | 11,728 | 9,984 | 48,230 |
| 2008 | 12,172 | 14,167 | 11,565 | 10,379 | 48,283 |
| 2007 | 11,921 | 13,389 | 11,211 | 10,406 | 46,927 |

**Earnings Per Share ($)**

| | | | | | |
|---|---|---|---|---|---|
| 2012 | 0.34 | 0.64 | 0.18 | E0.23 | E1.62 |
| 2011 | 0.34 | 0.58 | 0.29 | 0.21 | 1.42 |
| 2010 | 0.32 | 0.51 | 0.23 | 0.14 | 1.21 |
| 2009 | 0.41 | 0.64 | 0.33 | 0.11 | 1.49 |
| 2008 | 0.48 | 0.64 | 0.43 | 0.28 | 1.86 |
| 2007 | 0.53 | 0.60 | 0.46 | 0.40 | 1.99 |

Fiscal year ended Jan. 31. Next earnings report expected: NA. EPS Estimates based on S&P Operating Earnings; historical GAAP earnings are as reported.

## Dividend Data (Dates: mm/dd Payment Date: mm/dd/yy)

| Amount ($) | Date Decl. | Ex-Div. Date | Stk. of Record | Payment Date |
|---|---|---|---|---|
| 0.110 | 03/21 | 04/18 | 04/20 | 05/04/11 |
| 0.140 | 05/27 | 07/18 | 07/20 | 08/03/11 |
| 0.140 | 08/22 | 10/17 | 10/19 | 11/02/11 |
| 0.140 | 11/14 | 01/23 | 01/25 | 02/08/12 |

Dividends have been paid since 1961. Source: Company reports.

---

**Please read the Required Disclosures and Analyst Certification on the last page of this report.**

The **McGraw·Hill** Companies

# Lowe's Companies Inc.

**STANDARD &POOR'S**

## Business Summary November 17, 2011

**CORPORATE OVERVIEW.** Lowe's Companies is the world's second largest home improvement retailer, with nearly $49 billion in revenues generated in FY 11 (Jan.). It focuses on retail do-it-yourself (DIY) customers, do-it-for-me (DIFM) customers who utilize LOW's installation services, and commercial business customers. Lowe's offers a complete line of products and services for home decorating, maintenance, repair, remodeling, and the maintenance of commercial buildings.

As of January 28, 2011, LOW operated 1,723 stores in 50 U.S. states, 24 stores in Canada and two stores in Mexico, representing approximately 197 million sq. ft. of selling space. The company has three primary prototype stores- -117,000-square-foot and 103,000-square-foot stores for larger markets and a 94,000-square-foot store format used primarily to serve smaller markets. Both prototypes include a lawn and garden center, averaging an additional 32,000 square feet. Of the total stores operating at January 28, 2011, approximately 89% were owned, including stores on leased land, while the remaining 11% were leased from unaffiliated third parties. Typical LOW stores stock more than 40,000 items, with hundreds of thousands of items available through the company's special order system.

**CORPORATE STRATEGY.** LOW is focusing much of its future expansion on metropolitan markets with populations of 500,000 or more. The company expected that the majority of its FY 12 expansion would be comprised of the 103,000 square-foot stores in larger markets, but it also planned to open 94,000 square-foot stores in smaller to mid-sized markets.

Lowe's opened eight new stores in Canada in 2010, bringing its Canadian store count to 24, and planned to continue its expansion in FY 12. Additionally, LOW expanded into Mexico in FY 11, with two stores opened in Monterrey in 2010.

During 2009, LOW entered into a joint venture with Australian retailer Woolworths Limited, to develop a chain of home improvement stores in Australia. LOW is a one-third owner in the venture, and expects to open its first stores in the second half of 2011.

## Company Financials Fiscal Year Ended Jan. 31

| Per Share Data ($) | 2011 | 2010 | 2009 | 2008 | 2007 | 2006 | 2005 | 2004 | 2003 | 2002 |
|---|---|---|---|---|---|---|---|---|---|---|
| Tangible Book Value | 13.38 | 13.07 | 12.28 | 11.04 | 10.31 | 9.15 | 7.45 | 6.55 | 5.31 | 4.30 |
| Cash Flow | 2.63 | 2.40 | 2.54 | 2.77 | 2.73 | 2.44 | 1.92 | 1.68 | 1.32 | 0.98 |
| Earnings | 1.42 | 1.21 | 1.49 | 1.86 | 1.99 | 1.73 | 1.36 | 1.16 | 0.93 | 0.65 |
| S&P Core Earnings | 1.42 | 1.21 | 1.50 | 1.86 | 1.99 | 1.73 | 1.33 | 1.13 | 0.87 | 0.61 |
| Dividends | NA | 0.36 | 0.34 | 0.18 | 0.11 | 0.08 | 0.06 | 0.06 | 0.04 | 0.04 |
| Payout Ratio | NA | 30% | 22% | 10% | 6% | 4% | 4% | 5% | 5% | 0% |
| Calendar Year | 2010 | 2009 | 2008 | 2007 | 2006 | 2005 | 2004 | 2003 | 2002 | 2001 |
| Prices:High | 28.54 | 24.50 | 28.49 | 35.74 | 34.83 | 34.85 | 30.27 | 30.21 | 25.00 | 24.44 |
| Prices:Low | 19.35 | 13.00 | 15.76 | 21.01 | 26.15 | 25.36 | 22.95 | 16.69 | 16.25 | 10.94 |
| P/E Ratio:High | 20 | 20 | 19 | 19 | 17 | 20 | 22 | 26 | 27 | 38 |
| P/E Ratio:Low | 14 | 11 | 11 | 11 | 13 | 15 | 17 | 14 | 18 | 17 |

| Income Statement Analysis (Million $) | | | | | | | | | | |
|---|---|---|---|---|---|---|---|---|---|---|
| Revenue | 48,815 | 47,220 | 48,230 | 48,283 | 46,927 | 43,243 | 36,464 | 30,838 | 26,491 | 22,111 |
| Operating Income | 5,244 | 4,959 | 5,333 | 6,071 | 6,314 | 5,715 | 4,878 | 3,959 | 3,186 | 2,332 |
| Depreciation | 1,684 | 1,733 | 1,539 | 1,366 | 1,162 | 1,051 | 920 | 781 | 645 | 534 |
| Interest Expense | 332 | 287 | 356 | 304 | 238 | 158 | 176 | 180 | 203 | 199 |
| Pretax Income | 3,228 | 2,825 | 3,506 | 4,511 | 4,998 | 4,506 | 3,536 | 2,998 | 2,359 | 1,624 |
| Effective Tax Rate | NA | 36.9% | 37.4% | 37.7% | 37.9% | 38.5% | 38.5% | 37.9% | 37.6% | 37.0% |
| Net Income | 2,010 | 1,783 | 2,195 | 2,809 | 3,105 | 2,771 | 2,176 | 1,862 | 1,471 | 1,023 |
| S&P Core Earnings | 1,989 | 1,765 | 2,204 | 2,809 | 3,105 | 2,763 | 2,134 | 1,801 | 1,386 | 968 |

| Balance Sheet & Other Financial Data (Million $) | | | | | | | | | | |
|---|---|---|---|---|---|---|---|---|---|---|
| Cash | 1,123 | 1,057 | 661 | 530 | 796 | 423 | 813 | 1,624 | 1,126 | 799 |
| Current Assets | 9,967 | 9,732 | 9,251 | 8,686 | 8,314 | 7,831 | 6,974 | 6,687 | 5,568 | 4,920 |
| Total Assets | 33,699 | 33,005 | 32,686 | 30,869 | 27,767 | 24,682 | 21,209 | 19,042 | 16,109 | 13,736 |
| Current Liabilities | 7,119 | 7,355 | 8,022 | 7,751 | 6,539 | 5,832 | 5,719 | 4,368 | 3,578 | 3,017 |
| Long Term Debt | 6,537 | 4,528 | 5,039 | 5,576 | 4,325 | 3,499 | 3,060 | 3,678 | 3,736 | 3,734 |
| Common Equity | 18,112 | 19,069 | 18,055 | 16,098 | 15,725 | 14,339 | 11,535 | 10,309 | 8,302 | 6,675 |
| Total Capital | 24,685 | 24,149 | 23,754 | 22,344 | 20,785 | 18,573 | 15,331 | 14,644 | 12,516 | 10,713 |
| Capital Expenditures | 1,329 | 1,799 | 3,322 | 4,010 | 3,916 | 3,379 | 2,927 | 2,444 | 2,362 | 2,199 |
| Cash Flow | 3,694 | 3,516 | 3,734 | 4,175 | 4,267 | 3,822 | 3,096 | 2,643 | 2,116 | 1,557 |
| Current Ratio | 1.4 | 1.3 | 1.2 | 1.1 | 1.3 | 1.3 | 1.2 | 1.5 | 1.6 | 1.6 |
| % Long Term Debt of Capitalization | 26.5 | 18.8 | 21.2 | 25.0 | 21.6 | 18.8 | 20.0 | 25.1 | 29.8 | 34.9 |
| % Net Income of Revenue | 4.1 | 3.8 | 4.6 | 5.8 | 6.6 | 6.4 | 6.0 | 6.0 | 5.6 | 4.6 |
| % Return on Assets | 6.0 | 5.4 | 6.9 | 9.6 | 11.9 | 12.1 | 10.9 | 10.6 | 9.9 | 8.2 |
| % Return on Equity | 10.8 | 9.6 | 12.9 | 17.7 | 20.7 | 21.4 | 20.0 | 20.0 | 19.6 | 16.8 |

Data as orig reptd.; bef. results of disc opers/spec. items. Per share data adj. for stk. divs.; EPS diluted. E-Estimated. NA-Not Available. NM-Not Meaningful. NR-Not Ranked. UR-Under Review.

**Office:** 1000 Lowes Boulevard, Mooresville, NC 28117.
**Telephone:** 704-758-1000.
**Website:** http://www.lowes.com
**Chrmn, Pres & CEO:** R.A. Niblock

**COO:** P.D. Ramsay
**SVP & Chief Acctg Officer:** M.V. Hollifield
**CFO:** R.F. Hull, Jr.
**Secy & General Counsel:** G.M. Keener, Jr.

**Investor Contact:** P. Taaffe (704-758-2033)
**Auditor:** DELOITTE & TOUCHE
**Board Members:** R. Alvarez, D. W. Bernauer, L. L. Berry, P. C. Browning, D. Hudson, R. L. Johnson, M. O. Larsen, R. K. Lochridge, R. A. Niblock, S. F. Page, E. C. Wiseman

**Founded:** 1952
**Domicile:** North Carolina
**Employees:** 234,000

*The McGraw-Hill Companies*

# L-3 Communications Holdings Inc

STANDARD
&POOR'S

| S&P Recommendation | HOLD ★★★☆☆ | Price $63.29 (as of Nov 25, 2011) | 12-Mo. Target Price $78.00 | Investment Style Large-Cap Blend |
|---|---|---|---|---|

**GICS Sector** Industrials
**Sub-Industry** Aerospace & Defense

**Summary** This company is a provider of defense intelligence, surveillance and reconnaissance systems; secure communications systems; aircraft modernization, training and government services; and other defense, intelligence and security products.

## Key Stock Statistics (Source S&P, Vickers, company reports)

| | | | | | | | |
|---|---|---|---|---|---|---|---|
| 52-Wk Range | $88.55–58.30 | S&P Oper. EPS 2011E | 8.78 | Market Capitalization(B) | $6.320 | Beta | 0.95 |
| Trailing 12-Month EPS | $8.72 | S&P Oper. EPS 2012E | 8.60 | Yield (%) | 2.84 | S&P 3-Yr. Proj. EPS CAGR(%) | 0 |
| Trailing 12-Month P/E | 7.3 | P/E on S&P Oper. EPS 2011E | 7.2 | Dividend Rate/Share | $1.80 | S&P Credit Rating | BBB- |
| $10K Invested 5 Yrs Ago | $8,486 | Common Shares Outstg. (M) | 99.9 | Institutional Ownership (%) | 90 | | |

## Price Performance

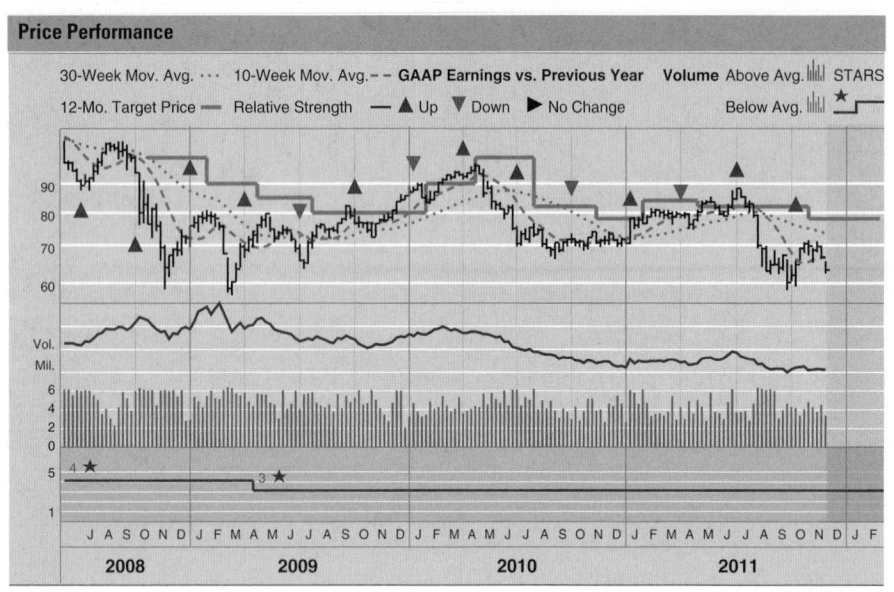

30-Week Mov. Avg. · · · 10-Week Mov. Avg. - - GAAP Earnings vs. Previous Year   Volume Above Avg. STARS
12-Mo. Target Price — Relative Strength — ▲ Up ▼ Down ► No Change   Below Avg. ★

Options: ASE, CBOE, P

Analysis prepared by Equity Analyst **R. Tortoriello** on Nov 21, 2011, when the stock traded at **$64.24**.

## Qualitative Risk Assessment

| LOW | MEDIUM | HIGH |
|---|---|---|

Our risk assessment reflects our view of LLL's strong historical record of earnings growth, offset by our view of moderately high financial leverage, and risks inherent in its dependence on government spending.

## Quantitative Evaluations

**S&P Quality Ranking** A

| D | C | B- | B | B+ | A- | A | A+ |
|---|---|---|---|---|---|---|---|

**Relative Strength Rank** MODERATE

46

LOWEST = 1    HIGHEST = 99

## Revenue/Earnings Data

**Revenue (Million $)**

| | 1Q | 2Q | 3Q | 4Q | Year |
|---|---|---|---|---|---|
| 2011 | 3,601 | 3,766 | 3,787 | -- | -- |
| 2010 | 3,624 | 3,966 | 3,835 | 4,255 | 15,680 |
| 2009 | 3,636 | 3,929 | 3,842 | 4,208 | 15,615 |
| 2008 | 3,506 | 3,722 | 3,662 | 4,011 | 14,901 |
| 2007 | 3,300 | 3,408 | 3,448 | 3,806 | 13,961 |
| 2006 | 2,904 | 3,083 | 3,105 | 3,385 | 12,477 |

**Earnings Per Share ($)**

| | 1Q | 2Q | 3Q | 4Q | Year |
|---|---|---|---|---|---|
| 2011 | 1.85 | 2.26 | 2.24 | E2.44 | E8.78 |
| 2010 | 1.87 | 1.95 | 2.07 | 2.37 | 8.25 |
| 2009 | 1.66 | 1.90 | 2.12 | 1.93 | 7.61 |
| 2008 | 1.54 | 2.24 | 1.73 | 2.21 | 7.72 |
| 2007 | 1.29 | 1.49 | 1.56 | 1.63 | 5.98 |
| 2006 | 1.13 | 0.40 | 1.31 | 1.37 | 4.22 |

Fiscal year ended Dec. 31. Next earnings report expected: Late January. EPS Estimates based on S&P Operating Earnings; historical GAAP earnings are as reported.

## Highlights

➤ We estimate revenues will decline 2% in 2011, reflecting the June 2010 loss of the Special Operations Forces Support contract, which we see resulting in a 13% decline in the Aircraft Modernization & Maintenance segment. For 2012, we project that revenue will remain about flat, as we expect Government Services, which we estimate will show a decline of 6.5% in 2011, to fall further as the U.S. government trims defense spending. We also expect weakness in Aircraft Modernization & Maintenance, but we see potential growth in C3ISR, on continued demand for intelligence, surveillance and reconnaisance systems.

➤ We estimate operating margins of 10.7% in 2011, down from 11.2% in 2010, on product mix and our view of contract cost pressure. We expect cost pressures to continue into 2012, and we estimate operating margins of 10.5%.

➤ We estimate EPS of $8.78 in 2011, and project a decline to $8.60 in 2012, despite our expectation of a significantly lower share count on share repurchases.

## Investment Rationale/Risk

➤ Although we think L-3's mix of defense electronics and specialized military products and government services is well matched with military priorities, we see an anticipated complete pullout of U.S. troops from Iraq and the beginning of a troop drawdown in Afghanistan, along with expected declines in the U.S. defense budget going forward, as preventing the shares from outperforming. We see L-3's ISR and Electronics businesses holding up well, but we expect continued pressure in the services areas of the business, due to tight government budgets.

➤ Risks to our recommendation and target price include the potential for delays and/or cuts in military budgets, and failure to perform well on existing contracts or to win new business.

➤ Our 12-month target price of $78 is based on an enterprise value to estimated 2012 EBITDA multiple of about 6.5X, below the average historical multiple of 11X, but in line with multiples we are using to value other defense contractors. We believe the likelihood of declining defense budgets and much slower-than-historical growth at LLL warrant this multiple.

## Dividend Data (Dates: mm/dd Payment Date: mm/dd/yy)

| Amount ($) | Date Decl. | Ex-Div. Date | Stk. of Record | Payment Date |
|---|---|---|---|---|
| 0.450 | 02/08 | 02/25 | 03/01 | 03/15/11 |
| 0.450 | 04/26 | 05/13 | 05/17 | 06/15/11 |
| 0.450 | 07/12 | 08/15 | 08/17 | 09/15/11 |
| 0.450 | 10/11 | 11/15 | 11/17 | 12/15/11 |

Dividends have been paid since 2004. Source: Company reports.

---

**Please read the Required Disclosures and Analyst Certification on the last page of this report.**

The McGraw-Hill Companies

# L-3 Communications Holdings Inc

## Business Summary November 21, 2011

CORPORATE OVERVIEW. L-3 Communications (LLL), with $15.5 billion in estimated 2011 revenues, is an historically acquisitive maker of military and homeland security electronics, and conducts business through four operating segments.

The Command, Control, Communications, Intelligence, Surveillance and Reconnaissance (C3ISR) business segment (23% of sales and 24% of operating income in 2010) specializes in signals intelligence (SIGINT) and communications intelligence (COMINT) products. These products provide troops the ability to collect and analyze unknown electronic signals from command centers, communications nodes and air defense systems for real-time situation awareness and response. C3ISR also provides C3 systems, networked communications systems, and secure communications products for military and other U.S. government agencies and foreign governments.

The Government Services segment (24% of sales and 17% of operating profits) provides a wide range of engineering, technical, analytical, information technology, advisory, training, logistics and support services to the Department of Defense (DoD), Dept. of State, Dept. of Justice, U.S. government intelligence agencies, and allied foreign governments. Major services include communication software support; high-end engineering and information systems support for command, control, communications and ISR architectures; developing

and managing programs in the U.S. and internationally that focus on teaching, training and education, logistics, strategic planning, leadership development, etc.; human intelligence support; command and control systems for maritime and expeditionary warfare; intelligence, analysis and solutions support for the DoD and U.S. government intelligence agencies; and conventional high-end enterprise IT support, systems and services to the DoD and U.S. federal agencies.

The Aircraft Modernization & Maintenance segment (16% of sales and 14% of operating profits) provides modernization, upgrades and sustainment, maintenance and logistics support services for military and various government aircraft and other platforms. Services are sold primarily to the U.S. DoD, the Canadian Department of National Defense, and other allied foreign governments. Major products and services include aircraft and vehicle modernization, including engineering, modification, maintenance, logistics and upgrades; aviation life-cycle management services for various military fixed and rotary wing aircraft; and aerospace and other technical services related to large fleet support.

## Company Financials Fiscal Year Ended Dec. 31

| Per Share Data ($) | 2010 | 2009 | 2008 | 2007 | 2006 | 2005 | 2004 | 2003 | 2002 | 2001 |
|---|---|---|---|---|---|---|---|---|---|---|
| Tangible Book Value | NM | NM | NM | NM | NM | NM | NM | NM | NM | NM |
| Cash Flow | 10.30 | 9.46 | 9.16 | 7.53 | 5.30 | 5.46 | 4.27 | 3.52 | 2.96 | 2.37 |
| Earnings | 8.25 | 7.61 | 7.72 | 5.98 | 4.22 | 4.20 | 3.33 | 2.71 | 2.29 | 1.48 |
| S&P Core Earnings | 8.54 | 8.04 | 6.24 | 5.68 | 4.93 | 4.07 | 3.22 | 2.66 | 1.87 | 1.08 |
| Dividends | 1.60 | 1.40 | 1.20 | 1.00 | 0.75 | 0.50 | 0.40 | Nil | Nil | Nil |
| Payout Ratio | 19% | 18% | 16% | 17% | 18% | 12% | 12% | Nil | Nil | Nil |
| Prices:High | 97.81 | 89.23 | 115.33 | 115.29 | 88.50 | 84.84 | 77.26 | 51.83 | 66.78 | 49.04 |
| Prices:Low | 66.11 | 57.12 | 58.49 | 79.26 | 66.50 | 64.66 | 49.31 | 34.22 | 40.60 | 30.35 |
| P/E Ratio:High | 12 | 12 | 15 | 19 | 21 | 20 | 23 | 19 | 29 | 33 |
| P/E Ratio:Low | 8 | 8 | 8 | 13 | 16 | 15 | 15 | 13 | 18 | 21 |

**Income Statement Analysis** (Million $)

| | 2010 | 2009 | 2008 | 2007 | 2006 | 2005 | 2004 | 2003 | 2002 | 2001 |
|---|---|---|---|---|---|---|---|---|---|---|
| Revenue | 15,680 | 15,615 | 14,901 | 13,961 | 12,477 | 9,445 | 6,897 | 5,062 | 4,011 | 2,347 |
| Operating Income | 1,998 | 1,866 | 1,771 | 1,645 | 1,376 | 1,150 | 868 | 676 | 530 | 362 |
| Depreciation | 231 | 218 | 197 | 196 | 136 | 153 | 119 | 95.4 | 75.9 | 87.0 |
| Interest Expense | 269 | 279 | 271 | 296 | 296 | 204 | 145 | 133 | 122 | 86.4 |
| Pretax Income | 1,484 | 1,386 | 1,462 | 1,183 | 835 | 798 | 606 | 437 | 336 | 191 |
| Effective Tax Rate | NA | 34.3% | 34.3% | 35.3% | 35.7% | 35.1% | 35.5% | 35.7% | 35.0% | 37.1% |
| Net Income | 955 | 901 | 949 | 756 | 526 | 509 | 382 | 278 | 212 | 115 |
| S&P Core Earnings | 984 | 944 | 768 | 719 | 615 | 493 | 370 | 274 | 171 | 82.0 |

**Balance Sheet & Other Financial Data** (Million $)

| | 2010 | 2009 | 2008 | 2007 | 2006 | 2005 | 2004 | 2003 | 2002 | 2001 |
|---|---|---|---|---|---|---|---|---|---|---|
| Cash | 607 | 1,016 | 867 | 780 | 348 | 394 | 653 | 135 | 135 | 361 |
| Current Assets | 5,044 | 5,151 | 4,961 | 4,763 | 3,930 | 3,644 | 2,808 | 1,938 | 1,639 | 1,239 |
| Total Assets | 15,418 | 14,763 | 14,630 | 14,391 | 13,287 | 11,909 | 7,781 | 6,493 | 5,242 | 3,335 |
| Current Liabilities | 3,398 | 2,482 | 2,707 | 2,582 | 2,376 | 1,854 | 1,176 | 924 | 697 | 524 |
| Long Term Debt | 3,439 | 4,112 | 4,548 | 4,547 | 4,535 | 4,634 | 2,190 | 2,457 | 1,848 | 1,315 |
| Common Equity | 6,764 | 6,565 | 5,836 | 5,989 | 5,306 | 4,491 | 3,800 | 2,574 | 2,202 | 1,214 |
| Total Capital | 10,992 | 10,770 | 10,462 | 10,857 | 10,069 | 9,325 | 6,067 | 5,108 | 4,123 | 2,599 |
| Capital Expenditures | 181 | 186 | 218 | 157 | 156 | 120 | 80.5 | 82.9 | 62.1 | 48.1 |
| Cash Flow | 1,186 | 1,111 | 1,126 | 952 | 662 | 661 | 501 | 373 | 288 | 202 |
| Current Ratio | 1.5 | 2.1 | 1.8 | 1.9 | 1.7 | 2.0 | 2.4 | 2.1 | 2.4 | 2.4 |
| % Long Term Debt of Capitalization | 31.3 | 38.2 | 43.4 | 41.8 | 45.0 | 49.7 | 36.1 | 48.1 | 44.8 | 50.6 |
| % Net Income of Revenue | 6.1 | 5.8 | 6.4 | 5.4 | 4.2 | 5.4 | 5.5 | 5.5 | 5.3 | 4.9 |
| % Return on Assets | 6.3 | 6.2 | 6.5 | 5.5 | 4.2 | 5.2 | 5.3 | 4.7 | 5.0 | 4.0 |
| % Return on Equity | 14.3 | 14.5 | 16.1 | 13.4 | 10.7 | 12.3 | 12.0 | 11.6 | 12.4 | 12.1 |

Data as orig reptd.; bef. results of disc opers/spec. items. Per share data adj. for stk. divs.; EPS diluted. E-Estimated. NA-Not Available. NM-Not Meaningful. NR-Not Ranked. UR-Under Review.

**Office:** 600 Third Avenue, 34th Floor, New York, NY 10016.
**Telephone:** 212-697-1111.
**Website:** http://www.l-3com.com
**Chrmn & Pres:** M.T. Strianese

**SVP, Secy & General Counsel:** S. Post
**CFO:** R.G. D'Ambrosio
**Chief Admin Officer:** S.M. Sheridan
**CTO:** A.M. Andrews, II

**Investor Contact:** E. Boyriven (212-850-5600)
**Board Members:** C. R. Canizares, T. A. Corcoran, L. Kramer, R. B. Millard, H. H. Shelton, A. L. Simon, M. T. Strianese, A. H. Washkowitz, J. P. White

**Founded:** 1997
**Domicile:** Delaware
**Employees:** 63,000

# LSI Corp

**STANDARD &POOR'S**

| S&P Recommendation **HOLD** ★★★★★ | Price $5.10 (as of Nov 25, 2011) | 12-Mo. Target Price $7.00 | Investment Style Large-Cap Blend |
|---|---|---|---|

**GICS Sector** Information Technology
**Sub-Industry** Semiconductors

**Summary** This company is a leading provider of silicon, systems and software technologies for the storage and networking markets.

## Key Stock Statistics (Source S&P, Vickers, company reports)

| | | | | | | | |
|---|---|---|---|---|---|---|---|
| 52-Wk Range | $7.74– 4.75 | S&P Oper. EPS 2011E | 0.33 | Market Capitalization(B) | $2.874 | Beta | 1.60 |
| Trailing 12-Month EPS | $0.53 | S&P Oper. EPS 2012E | 0.42 | Yield (%) | Nil | S&P 3-Yr. Proj. EPS CAGR(%) | 10 |
| Trailing 12-Month P/E | 9.6 | P/E on S&P Oper. EPS 2011E | 15.5 | Dividend Rate/Share | Nil | S&P Credit Rating | NR |
| $10K Invested 5 Yrs Ago | $4,705 | Common Shares Outstg. (M) | 563.5 | Institutional Ownership (%) | 83 | | |

## Price Performance

30-Week Mov. Avg. · · · 10-Week Mov. Avg. - - **GAAP Earnings vs. Previous Year** Volume Above Avg. ▫▫▫ STARS
12-Mo. Target Price — Relative Strength — ▲ Up ▼ Down ► No Change Below Avg. ▫▫▫ ★

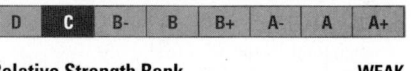

Options: ASE, CBOE, P, Ph

Analysis prepared by Equity Analyst **Angelo Zino, CFA** on Oct 28, 2011, when the stock traded at **$6.29**.

## Highlights

➤ We estimate that revenues will advance 10% in 2012, compared to a projected 20% decline in 2011, which reflects the sale of its storage systems business. For the core chip business, we believe end-market demand, which has been slow over the last couple of quarters, for computers and storage devices will pick up as excessive inventory digests. Also, LSI is winning more designs with top-tier customers, which we see leading to market share gains as customers launch new products. We think IT spending and the wireless infrastructure buildout will support longer-term growth.

➤ We anticipate non-GAAP gross margins of around 47%-50% over the next several quarters, with only modest variability due to changes in product mix. We see engineering-related costs and expenses growing at a slower pace than sales, and anticipate the adjusted operating margin expanding to 10% in 2012, from an expected 9% in 2011.

➤ Our 2012 earnings forecast includes around $0.08 per share in stock-based compensation, and a 5% decrease in the diluted share count as we see modest share repurchases for the company.

## Investment Rationale/Risk

➤ Our hold recommendation reflects our view of improving fundamentals and fair valuations. We believe that LSI will manage expenses tightly as improving demand, new product cycles, and market share gains support sales growth. Assuming above-industry sales growth and increasing margins, LSI's free cash flow generation should improve as well, in our opinion, and add to what we see as the company's healthy balance sheet. We view positively LSI's intent to acquire SandForce, a chipmaker in the flash memory space, given the long-term growth prospects in this arena. However, we see some elevated business risks as the company becomes a pure-play semiconductor company heavily tied to the storage markets.

➤ Risks to our recommendation and target price include a slower ramp of new product sales, disruptions and overproduction in the supply chain, and higher-than-expected operating expenses.

➤ Our 12-month target price of $7.00 is based on a multiple of around 17X our 2012 EPS estimate, within LSI's five-year historical average but above peers to reflect our view of relative earnings growth, return metrics, and business risk.

## Qualitative Risk Assessment

| LOW | MEDIUM | **HIGH** |
|---|---|---|

LSI is subject to the sales cycles of the semiconductor industry and consumer electronics and data storage end markets. The company faces competition from makers of programmable logic devices as well as from many custom logic chipmakers.

## Quantitative Evaluations

**S&P Quality Ranking**      C

| D | **C** | B- | B | B+ | A- | A | A+ |
|---|---|---|---|---|---|---|---|

**Relative Strength Rank**     **WEAK**

20

LOWEST = 1      HIGHEST = 99

## Revenue/Earnings Data

**Revenue (Million $)**

| | 1Q | 2Q | 3Q | 4Q | Year |
|---|---|---|---|---|---|
| 2011 | 473.3 | 500.6 | 546.9 | -- | -- |
| 2010 | 637.2 | 639.4 | 629.0 | 664.5 | 2,570 |
| 2009 | 482.3 | 520.7 | 578.4 | 637.8 | 2,219 |
| 2008 | 660.8 | 692.1 | 714.3 | 610.0 | 2,677 |
| 2007 | 465.4 | 669.9 | 727.4 | 740.9 | 2,604 |
| 2006 | 475.9 | 489.6 | 493.0 | 523.7 | 1,982 |

**Earnings Per Share ($)**

| | 1Q | 2Q | 3Q | 4Q | Year |
|---|---|---|---|---|---|
| 2011 | 0.03 | 0.05 | 0.05 | E0.07 | E0.33 |
| 2010 | 0.03 | 0.01 | 0.04 | -0.02 | 0.06 |
| 2009 | -0.16 | -0.09 | 0.08 | -- | -0.07 |
| 2008 | -0.02 | -0.02 | 0.02 | -0.94 | -0.96 |
| 2007 | 0.07 | -0.50 | -0.20 | -2.88 | -3.87 |
| 2006 | 0.03 | 0.13 | 0.11 | 0.14 | 0.42 |

Fiscal year ended Dec. 31. Next earnings report expected: Late January. EPS Estimates based on S&P Operating Earnings; historical GAAP earnings are as reported.

## Dividend Data

No cash dividends have been paid.

# LSI Corp

**STANDARD &POOR'S**

## Business Summary October 28, 2011

CORPORATE OVERVIEW. LSI Corporation makes high-performance storage and networking semiconductors and storage systems that are used in end-products that create, store, consume and transport digital information. Such products include hard disk drives, solid state drives, high-speed communications systems, computer servers, storage systems and personal computers. The company operates in two segments -- semiconductors and storage systems.

LSI's semiconductor segment is focused on providing integrated circuits (ICs) for storage and networking applications, and it also generates revenues by licensing intellectual property to other entities. LSI has taken several major actions to maintain this focus, including merging with Agere Systems in 2007 to strengthen its position in storage and networking markets, divesting in businesses in which it did not benefit from scale advantages, acquiring small companies focused on its target end-markets, and selling its manufacturing operations to preserve capital and focus on product development.

The company's storage system segment sells enterprise storage systems and storage software applications that enable storage area networks. Its products are geared toward leading original equipment manufacturers (OEMs) and storage companies rather than end-users.

In 2010, the storage system segment accounted for approximately 37% of revenues, and semiconductors 63%. By market, external storage comprised around 28% of 2010's total revenues, server and storage connectivity 27%, hard disk drive and solid state drive 23%, networking 18%, and intellectual property 4%. The company believes that the served available market sizes for each can grow at compound average growth rates in the low to mid-teens.

## Company Financials Fiscal Year Ended Dec. 31

| Per Share Data ($) | 2010 | 2009 | 2008 | 2007 | 2006 | 2005 | 2004 | 2003 | 2002 | 2001 |
|---|---|---|---|---|---|---|---|---|---|---|
| Tangible Book Value | 0.92 | 0.82 | 0.44 | 1.12 | 2.24 | 1.66 | 1.38 | 2.39 | 2.80 | 3.15 |
| Cash Flow | 0.47 | 0.34 | -0.50 | -3.48 | 0.62 | 0.36 | -0.75 | -0.12 | 0.15 | -1.32 |
| Earnings | 0.06 | -0.07 | -0.96 | -3.87 | 0.42 | -0.01 | -1.21 | -0.82 | -0.79 | -2.84 |
| S&P Core Earnings | 0.05 | -0.06 | -0.68 | -1.80 | 0.35 | -0.20 | -1.51 | -1.33 | -1.36 | -3.47 |
| Dividends | Nil | Nil | Nil | Nil | Nil | Nil | Nil | Nil | Nil | Nil |
| Payout Ratio | Nil | Nil | Nil | Nil | Nil | Nil | Nil | Nil | Nil | Nil |
| Prices:High | 6.73 | 6.14 | 7.97 | 10.68 | 11.81 | 10.75 | 11.50 | 12.90 | 18.60 | 26.10 |
| Prices:Low | 3.89 | 2.39 | 2.36 | 5.06 | 7.41 | 4.92 | 4.01 | 3.78 | 3.97 | 9.70 |
| P/E Ratio:High | NM | NM | NM | NM | 28 | NM | NM | NM | NM | NM |
| P/E Ratio:Low | NM | NM | NM | NM | 18 | NM | NM | NM | NM | NM |

| Income Statement Analysis (Million $) | | | | | | | | | | |
|---|---|---|---|---|---|---|---|---|---|---|
| Revenue | 2,570 | 2,219 | 2,677 | 2,604 | 1,982 | 1,919 | 1,700 | 1,693 | 1,817 | 1,785 |
| Operating Income | 524 | 181 | 287 | 168 | 236 | 283 | 172 | 171 | 155 | -157 |
| Depreciation | 267 | 268 | 298 | 253 | 82.3 | 146 | 177 | 263 | 349 | 533 |
| Interest Expense | 5.60 | 21.9 | 34.9 | 31.0 | 24.3 | 25.3 | 25.3 | 30.7 | 52.0 | 44.6 |
| Pretax Income | 45.4 | -131 | -595 | -2,475 | 185 | 20.9 | -439 | -284 | -291 | -1,030 |
| Effective Tax Rate | NA | 63.5% | NM | NM | 8.46% | NM | NM | NM | NM | NM |
| Net Income | 40.0 | -47.7 | -622 | -2,487 | 170 | -5.62 | -464 | -309 | -292 | -992 |
| S&P Core Earnings | 32.6 | -45.9 | -449 | -1,157 | 140 | -80.0 | -582 | -505 | -507 | -1,214 |

| Balance Sheet & Other Financial Data (Million $) | | | | | | | | | | |
|---|---|---|---|---|---|---|---|---|---|---|
| Cash | 677 | 962 | 1,119 | 1,398 | 328 | 265 | 219 | 270 | 449 | 757 |
| Current Assets | 1,264 | 1,585 | 1,799 | 2,193 | 1,636 | 1,620 | 1,365 | 1,390 | 1,626 | 1,769 |
| Total Assets | 2,425 | 2,968 | 3,344 | 4,396 | 2,852 | 2,796 | 2,874 | 3,448 | 4,143 | 4,626 |
| Current Liabilities | 485 | 854 | 798 | 762 | 527 | 743 | 396 | 391 | 398 | 510 |
| Long Term Debt | NA | NA | 350 | 718 | 350 | 350 | 782 | 866 | 1,241 | 1,336 |
| Common Equity | 1,318 | 1,461 | 1,441 | 2,485 | 1,896 | 1,628 | 1,618 | 2,042 | 2,300 | 2,480 |
| Total Capital | 1,318 | 1,811 | 2,036 | 3,388 | 2,246 | 1,978 | 2,400 | 2,916 | 3,665 | 3,995 |
| Capital Expenditures | 92.3 | 90.0 | 135 | 103 | 58.7 | 48.1 | 52.8 | 78.2 | 39.0 | 224 |
| Cash Flow | 307 | 220 | -324 | -2,234 | 252 | 141 | -287 | -45.8 | 57.0 | -459 |
| Current Ratio | 2.6 | 1.9 | 2.3 | 2.9 | 3.1 | 2.2 | 3.4 | 3.6 | 4.1 | 3.5 |
| % Long Term Debt of Capitalization | Nil | Nil | 17.2 | 21.2 | 15.6 | 17.7 | 32.6 | 29.7 | 33.8 | 33.4 |
| % Net Income of Revenue | 1.6 | NM | NM | NM | 8.6 | NM | NM | NM | NM | NM |
| % Return on Assets | 1.5 | NM | NM | NM | 6.0 | NM | NM | NM | NM | NM |
| % Return on Equity | 2.9 | NM | NM | NM | 9.6 | NM | NM | NM | NM | NM |

Data as orig reptd.; bef. results of disc opers/spec. items. Per share data adj. for stk. divs.; EPS diluted. E-Estimated. NA-Not Available. NM-Not Meaningful. NR-Not Ranked. UR-Under Review.

**Office:** 1621 Barber Lane, Milpitas, CA 95035.
**Telephone:** 408-433-8000.
**Email:** investorrelations@lsi.com
**Website:** http://www.lsi.com

**Chrmn:** G. Reyes
**Pres & CEO:** A.Y. Talwalkar
**COO:** D.J. Richardson
**EVP, CFO, Chief Admin Officer & Chief Acctg Officer:** B. Look

**EVP, Secy & General Counsel:** J.F. Rankin
**Investor Contact:** S. Shah (610-712-5471)
**Board Members:** C. A. Haggerty, R. Hill, J. H. Miner, A. Netravali, C. Pope, G. Reyes, M. G. Strachan, A. Y. Talwalkar, S. M. Whitney

**Founded:** 1980
**Domicile:** Delaware
**Employees:** 5,718

**The McGraw·Hill Companies**

# Macy's Inc

STANDARD &POOR'S

**S&P Recommendation** HOLD ★★★☆☆

| Price | 12-Mo. Target Price | Investment Style |
|---|---|---|
| $29.45 (as of Nov 25, 2011) | $35.00 | Large-Cap Blend |

**GICS Sector** Consumer Discretionary
**Sub-Industry** Department Stores

**Summary** This company operates about 850 department stores under the Macy's and Bloomingdale's names.

## Key Stock Statistics (Source S&P, Vickers, company reports)

| | | | | | | | |
|---|---|---|---|---|---|---|---|
| 52-Wk Range | $32.67–21.69 | S&P Oper. EPS 2012E | 2.78 | Market Capitalization(B) | $12.579 | Beta | 1.62 |
| Trailing 12-Month EPS | $2.73 | S&P Oper. EPS 2013E | 2.91 | Yield (%) | 1.36 | S&P 3-Yr. Proj. EPS CAGR(%) | 13 |
| Trailing 12-Month P/E | 10.8 | P/E on S&P Oper. EPS 2012E | 10.6 | Dividend Rate/Share | $0.40 | S&P Credit Rating | BB |
| $10K Invested 5 Yrs Ago | $7,413 | Common Shares Outstg. (M) | 427.1 | Institutional Ownership (%) | 93 | | |

## Price Performance

- 30-Week Mov. Avg. · · · 10-Week Mov. Avg. – – GAAP Earnings vs. Previous Year    Volume Above Avg. STARS
- 12-Mo. Target Price — Relative Strength — ▲ Up ▼ Down ▶ No Change    Below Avg.

Options: ASE, CBOE, P, Ph

Analysis prepared by Equity Analyst **Esther Kwon, CFA** on Nov 10, 2011, when the stock traded at **$30.45**.

## Highlights

➤ We see net sales reaching $26.3 billion in FY 12 (Jan.) and $27.2 billion in FY 13. Through its "My Macy's" localization initiative, M is custom-tailoring merchandise assortments, size ranges, marketing programs and shopping experiences to the specific needs of core customers surrounding each Macy's store. On expected payoff of My Macy's and momentum we see in the Bloomingdale's business, we project 5% same-store sales growth in FY 12, followed by a 3% gain in FY 13.

➤ Despite added costs related to free shipping both for online purchases over $99 and for growing use of "Search and Send" online fulfillment in stores, we anticipate operating margin expansion annually, supported by sales growth in private label merchandise and disciplined inventory and expense management. We also look for M to selectively raise its prices and to leverage its strong vendor/manufacturer relationships to offset cost inflation.

➤ We see EPS of $2.78 in FY 12 and $2.91 in FY 13, versus $2.11 in FY 11, before $15 million of store closing costs and $66 million of expenses related to M's early retirement of $1 billion of outstanding debt.

## Investment Rationale/Risk

➤ While we view the shares as appropriately valued at current levels, our outlook for the company is positive. We believe M is benefiting from successful execution of My Macy's, as well as improved confidence among its higher-income customer base at Bloomingdale's. We see these positive factors, coupled with increased investments in its omnichannel strategy (M expects online sales to boost same-store sales by about one percentage point in FY 12) and associate training enabling the company to drive top line growth in a challenging economy. However, it remains to be seen how higher prices will impact M's sales trends this fall and into the all-important holiday shopping season.

➤ Risks to our recommendation and target price include a loss of business due to unforeseen shifts in fashion trends, customers trading down to lower-priced competitors, and loss of confidence in an economy recovery among high-end shoppers.

➤ Our 12-month target price of $35 is based on a forward P/E multiple of 12X applied to our FY 13 EPS estimate, which is a discount to the department store average.

## Qualitative Risk Assessment

| LOW | MEDIUM | HIGH |
|---|---|---|

Our risk assessment reflects merchandise localization challenges and an uncertain outlook for consumer discretionary spending, offset by our view of M's strong brand and geographical presence in a consolidating industry.

## Quantitative Evaluations

**S&P Quality Ranking** B-

| D | C | B- | B | B+ | A- | A | A+ |
|---|---|---|---|---|---|---|---|

**Relative Strength Rank** STRONG

84

LOWEST = 1     HIGHEST = 99

## Revenue/Earnings Data

**Revenue (Million $)**

| | 1Q | 2Q | 3Q | 4Q | Year |
|---|---|---|---|---|---|
| 2012 | 5,889 | 5,939 | 5,853 | -- | -- |
| 2011 | 5,574 | 5,537 | 5,623 | 8,269 | 25,003 |
| 2010 | 5,199 | 5,164 | 5,277 | 7,849 | 23,489 |
| 2009 | 5,747 | 5,718 | 5,493 | 7,934 | 24,892 |
| 2008 | 5,921 | 5,892 | 5,906 | 8,594 | 26,313 |
| 2007 | 5,930 | 5,995 | 5,886 | 9,159 | 26,970 |

**Earnings Per Share ($)**

| | | | | | |
|---|---|---|---|---|---|
| 2012 | 0.30 | 0.55 | 0.32 | E1.59 | E2.78 |
| 2011 | 0.05 | 0.35 | 0.02 | 1.55 | 1.98 |
| 2010 | -0.21 | 0.02 | -0.08 | 1.10 | 0.83 |
| 2009 | -0.14 | 0.17 | -0.10 | -11.33 | -11.40 |
| 2008 | 0.11 | 0.17 | 0.08 | 1.73 | 2.01 |
| 2007 | -0.13 | 0.51 | 0.03 | 1.45 | 1.80 |

Fiscal year ended Jan. 31. Next earnings report expected: Late February. EPS Estimates based on S&P Operating Earnings; historical GAAP earnings are as reported.

## Dividend Data (Dates: mm/dd Payment Date: mm/dd/yy)

| Amount ($) | Date Decl. | Ex-Div. Date | Stk. of Record | Payment Date |
|---|---|---|---|---|
| 0.050 | 02/25 | 03/11 | 03/15 | 04/01/11 |
| 0.100 | 05/11 | 06/13 | 06/15 | 07/01/11 |
| 0.100 | 08/26 | 09/13 | 09/15 | 10/03/11 |
| 0.100 | 10/28 | 12/13 | 12/15 | 01/03/12 |

Dividends have been paid since 2003. Source: Company reports.

---

**Please read the Required Disclosures and Analyst Certification on the last page of this report.**

The McGraw-Hill Companies

# Macy's Inc

**STANDARD**
**&POOR'S**

## Business Summary November 10, 2011

CORPORATE OVERVIEW. On August 30, 2005, Federated Department Stores, Inc. completed a $17 billion merger with The May Department Stores Co. Most of the acquired May department stores were converted to the Macy's nameplate in September 2006. On June 1, 2007, the company changed its corporate name to Macy's, Inc. from Federated Department Stores, Inc. On that date, the company's shares began trading under the ticker symbol "M" (replacing "FD") on the New York Stock Exchange. Based on 2010 revenues, M is now the largest U.S. department store operator, under the Macy's and Bloomingdale's names.

MARKET PROFILE. Apparel generated $192.7 billion at retail in the U.S. in 2010, up 1.9% from 2009, according to The NPD Group, Inc. consumer estimated data. By category, sales of women's apparel accounted for 55.8% of all apparel sales last year, followed by men's at 27.4%, and children's at 16.8%. We believe M holds meaningful market share in the department stores retail channel, which captured an estimated 13.3% of U.S. apparel sales in 2010. While deflationary pressure has been an industry constant for decades, higher raw material and labor costs are likely to drive price increases in 2011.

CORPORATE STRATEGY. M is focused on four key growth initiatives: tailoring

merchandise assortments by store to improve sales productivity; offering distinctive and exclusive merchandise; improving customer engagement; and multi-channel expansion.

In February 2008, M announced "My Macy's," a new initiative aimed at accelerating same-store sales growth through custom-tailoring of merchandise assortments, size ranges, marketing programs and shopping experiences to the needs of core customers surrounding each Macy's store. In February 2009, after piloting My Macy's in 20 markets, the company announced plans to roll out the initiative nationally. All Macy's stores have since been clustered into 69 geographic districts that average 10 to 12 stores each. M has also created a unified operating structure for Macy's to support the business nationwide. Thinking local has paid off for the company, as same-store sales increased 4.6% in FY 11 (Jan.), representing a significant improvement over FY 10's 5.3% decline.

## Company Financials Fiscal Year Ended Jan. 31

| Per Share Data ($) | 2011 | 2010 | 2009 | 2008 | 2007 | 2006 | 2005 | 2004 | 2003 | 2002 |
|---|---|---|---|---|---|---|---|---|---|---|
| Tangible Book Value | 2.72 | 0.67 | 0.44 | NM | 5.56 | 5.34 | 16.55 | NM | 13.47 | 12.16 |
| Cash Flow | 4.67 | 3.69 | -8.37 | 4.90 | 4.11 | 4.29 | 4.09 | 3.92 | 3.31 | 2.94 |
| Earnings | 1.98 | 0.83 | -11.40 | 2.01 | 1.80 | 3.16 | 1.93 | 1.86 | 1.61 | 1.30 |
| S&P Core Earnings | 2.03 | 0.86 | -3.23 | 1.90 | 1.62 | 2.21 | 1.83 | 1.69 | 1.24 | 0.91 |
| Dividends | NA | 0.20 | 0.53 | 0.51 | 0.45 | 0.26 | 0.19 | Nil | Nil | Nil |
| Payout Ratio | NA | 24% | NM | 25% | 25% | 8% | 10% | Nil | Nil | Nil |
| Calendar Year | 2010 | 2009 | 2008 | 2007 | 2006 | 2005 | 2004 | 2003 | 2002 | 2001 |
| Prices:High | 26.32 | 20.84 | 28.47 | 46.70 | 45.01 | 39.03 | 29.08 | 25.30 | 22.13 | 24.95 |
| Prices:Low | 15.34 | 6.27 | 5.07 | 24.70 | 32.38 | 27.10 | 21.40 | 11.76 | 11.80 | 13.03 |
| P/E Ratio:High | 13 | 25 | NM | 23 | 25 | 12 | 15 | 14 | 14 | 19 |
| P/E Ratio:Low | 8 | 8 | NM | 12 | 18 | 9 | 11 | 6 | 7 | 10 |

### Income Statement Analysis (Million $)

| | | | | | | | | | | |
|---|---|---|---|---|---|---|---|---|---|---|
| Revenue | 25,003 | 23,489 | 24,892 | 26,313 | 26,970 | 22,390 | 15,630 | 15,264 | 15,435 | 15,651 |
| Operating Income | 3,069 | 2,664 | 2,680 | 3,167 | 2,910 | 3,087 | 2,143 | 2,047 | 2,019 | 1,923 |
| Depreciation | 1,150 | 1,210 | 1,278 | 1,304 | 1,265 | 974 | 743 | 706 | 676 | 657 |
| Interest Expense | 574 | 562 | 599 | 588 | 520 | 422 | 299 | 266 | 311 | 331 |
| Pretax Income | 1,320 | 507 | -4,938 | 1,320 | 1,446 | 2,044 | 1,116 | 1,084 | 1,048 | 780 |
| Effective Tax Rate | NA | 31.0% | NM | 31.1% | 31.7% | 32.8% | 38.3% | 36.1% | 39.1% | 33.6% |
| Net Income | 847 | 350 | -48,003 | 909 | 988 | 1,373 | 689 | 693 | 638 | 518 |
| S&P Core Earnings | 869 | 362 | -1,366 | 860 | 888 | 967 | 655 | 628 | 490 | 364 |

### Balance Sheet & Other Financial Data (Million $)

| | | | | | | | | | | |
|---|---|---|---|---|---|---|---|---|---|---|
| Cash | 1,464 | 1,686 | 1,306 | 583 | 1,211 | 248 | 868 | 925 | 716 | 636 |
| Current Assets | 6,899 | 6,882 | 6,740 | 6,324 | 7,422 | 10,145 | 7,510 | 7,452 | 7,154 | 7,280 |
| Total Assets | 20,631 | 21,300 | 22,145 | 27,789 | 29,550 | 33,168 | 14,885 | 14,550 | 14,441 | 15,044 |
| Current Liabilities | 5,065 | 4,454 | 5,126 | 5,360 | 6,359 | 7,590 | 4,301 | 3,883 | 3,601 | 3,714 |
| Long Term Debt | 6,971 | 8,456 | 8,733 | 9,087 | 7,847 | 8,860 | 2,637 | 3,151 | 3,408 | 3,859 |
| Common Equity | 5,530 | 4,701 | 4,646 | 9,907 | 12,254 | 13,519 | 6,167 | 5,940 | 5,762 | 5,564 |
| Total Capital | 12,955 | 13,399 | 14,498 | 20,440 | 21,829 | 24,083 | 10,003 | 10,089 | 10,168 | 10,768 |
| Capital Expenditures | 339 | 355 | 761 | 994 | 1,317 | 568 | 467 | 508 | 568 | 615 |
| Cash Flow | 1,997 | 1,560 | -3,525 | 2,213 | 2,253 | 2,347 | 1,432 | 1,399 | 1,314 | 1,175 |
| Current Ratio | 1.4 | 1.6 | 1.3 | 1.2 | 1.2 | 1.3 | 1.7 | 1.9 | 2.0 | 2.0 |
| % Long Term Debt of Capitalization | 53.8 | 63.1 | 60.2 | 44.5 | 39.0 | 36.8 | 26.4 | 31.2 | 33.5 | 35.8 |
| % Net Income of Revenue | 3.4 | 1.5 | NM | 3.5 | 3.7 | 6.1 | 4.4 | 4.5 | 4.1 | 3.3 |
| % Return on Assets | 4.0 | 1.6 | NM | 3.2 | 3.2 | 5.7 | 4.7 | 4.8 | 4.2 | 3.4 |
| % Return on Equity | 16.6 | 7.5 | NM | 8.2 | 7.7 | 13.9 | 11.4 | 11.8 | 11.3 | 9.1 |

Data as orig reptd.; bef. results of disc opers/spec. items. Per share data adj. for stk. divs.; EPS diluted. E-Estimated. NA-Not Available. NM-Not Meaningful. NR-Not Ranked. UR-Under Review.

**Office:** 7 W Seventh St, Cincinnati, OH 45202.
**Telephone:** 513-579-7000.
**Website:** http://www.fds.com
**Chrmn, Pres & CEO:** T.J. Lundgren

**EVP, Chief Acctg Officer & Cntlr:** J.A. Belsky
**EVP, Secy & General Counsel:** D.J. Broderick
**CFO:** K.M. Hoguet
**Chief Admin Officer:** T. Cole

**Investor Contact:** S.R. Robinson
**Board Members:** S. F. Bollenbach, D. P. Connelly, M. Feldberg, S. Levinson, T. J. Lundgren, J. Neubauer, J. A. Pichler, J. M. Roche, C. E. Weatherup, M. C. Whittington

**Founded:** 1858
**Domicile:** Delaware
**Employees:** 166,000

*The McGraw-Hill Companies*

# Marathon Oil Corp

**STANDARD &POOR'S**

| S&P Recommendation **BUY** ★★★★☆ | Price $27.96 (as of Nov 30, 2011) | 12-Mo. Target Price $35.00 | Investment Style Large-Cap Blend |
|---|---|---|---|

**GICS Sector** Energy
**Sub-Industry** Oil & Gas Exploration & Production

**Summary** Having spun of its downstream business in mid-2011, MRO is now an independent upstream company with international operations.

## Key Stock Statistics (Source S&P, Vickers, company reports)

| | | | | | | | |
|---|---|---|---|---|---|---|---|
| 52-Wk Range | $54.33– 19.13 | S&P Oper. EPS 2011E | 3.50 | Market Capitalization(B) | $19.676 | Beta | 1.35 |
| Trailing 12-Month EPS | $4.34 | S&P Oper. EPS 2012E | 3.50 | Yield (%) | 2.15 | S&P 3-Yr. Proj. EPS CAGR(%) | 29 |
| Trailing 12-Month P/E | 6.4 | P/E on S&P Oper. EPS 2011E | 8.0 | Dividend Rate/Share | $0.60 | S&P Credit Rating | BBB |
| $10K Invested 5 Yrs Ago | NA | Common Shares Outstg. (M) | 703.7 | Institutional Ownership (%) | 81 | | |

## Price Performance

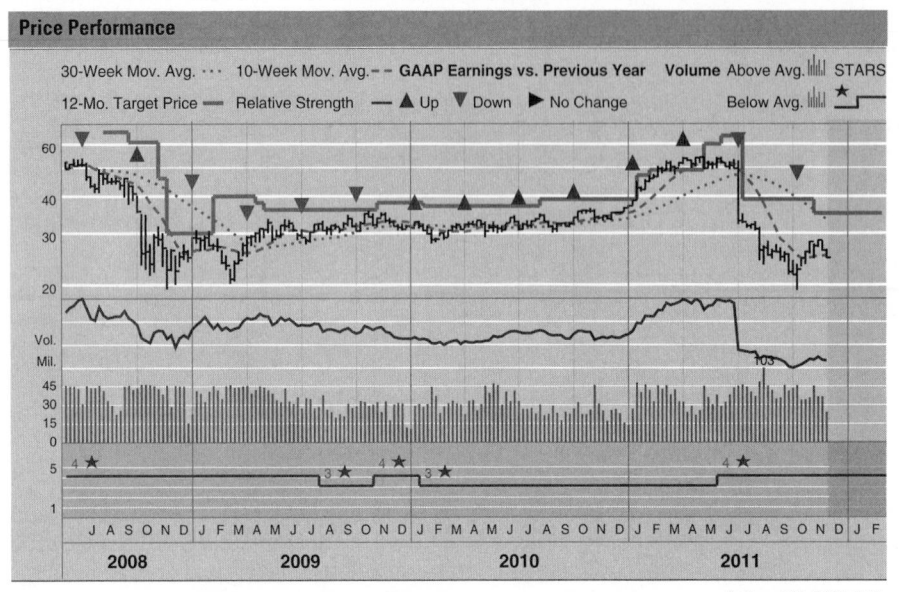

30-Week Mov. Avg. ···· 10-Week Mov. Avg. -- **GAAP Earnings vs. Previous Year** Volume Above Avg. STARS
12-Mo. Target Price — Relative Strength — ▲ Up ▼ Down ► No Change Below Avg.

Options: ASE, CBOE, P, Ph

Analysis prepared by Equity Analyst **Michael Kay** on Nov 29, 2011, when the stock traded at **$25.98**.

## Highlights

➤ Aside from sharpening its E&P focus, where we see exploration upside, we think the downstream spinoff will improve future growth, returns and capital efficiency, and offer acquisition opportunities. MRO's production fell 2% in 2010, to 391 MBOE/d, as project expansions nearly offset asset sales and declines. On MRO guidance, we see production in 2011 of 360-365 MBOE/d, down 7%-8%, on shut-ins in Libya, where MRO had targeted 48 MBOE/d, and 360-380 MBOE/d in 2012 (ex-Libya). With the expected close of the $3.5 billion Eagle Ford Shale acquisition in 2011, MRO now sees a 2010-2016 production CAGR of 5%-7%, before dispositions, and a ramp to over 40 rigs.

➤ We view MRO's execution in North American onshore (Bakken, Eagle Ford, Niobrara, Canadian oil sands) as a potential near-term cash flow driver, given the higher-margin liquids production. MRO's streamlined asset base (77% oil, based on reserves) is one of the more diversified portfolios among domestic E&P companies.

➤ Adjusted for the spinoff of Marathon Petroleum (MPC 33, Buy), we see EPS of $3.50 in 2011 and 2012. MRO expects capex of $4.5-$5 billion per year through 2016.

## Investment Rationale/Risk

➤ MRO spun off its downstream business into a new publicly traded entity, Marathon Petroleum Corp. (MPC), to shareholders (0.5 MPC share for each MRO share) in a tax-free transaction effective June 30, 2011. We had been looking for reduced refining contributions over the next five years and believe lifted exposure to upstream projects in new international and U.S. onshore basins will drive upstream growth. Production is globally diversified (32% U.S., 40% Africa, 28% Europe). We expect 65% of capex going forward to be allocated toward growth projects, notably Eagle Ford and Bakken, 24% to base assets, and 8% to exploration.

➤ Risks to our recommendation and target price include adverse economic, industry, operating, geopolitical, regulatory and environmental conditions, and difficulty replacing reserves.

➤ On DCF ($38; WACC 7.6%, terminal growth 3%), our proved-NAV ($37), a target EV multiple of 3.5X our 2012 EBITDA forecast, and other relative valuations, our 12-month target price is $35. MRO is currently trading at 7.4X our 2012 EPS estimate and 2.4X EV-to-2012 estimated EBITDA, versus large cap diversified E&Ps at 7.3X and 3.9X. We think valuations are attractive.

## Qualitative Risk Assessment

| LOW | MEDIUM | HIGH |
|---|---|---|

Our risk assessment reflects our view of the company's diversified and solid business profile in volatile and cyclical segments of the energy industry. We consider MRO's earnings stability to be good, and its corporate governance practices sound.

## Quantitative Evaluations

**S&P Quality Ranking** B+

| D | C | B- | B | B+ | A- | A | A+ |
|---|---|---|---|---|---|---|---|

**Relative Strength Rank** STRONG

82

LOWEST = 1      HIGHEST = 99

## Revenue/Earnings Data

**Revenue (Million $)**

| | 1Q | 2Q | 3Q | 4Q | Year |
|---|---|---|---|---|---|
| 2011 | 21,071 | 3,700 | 3,799 | -- | -- |
| 2010 | 14,657 | 18,574 | 17,092 | 18,787 | 67,113 |
| 2009 | 10,176 | 13,039 | 14,362 | 15,893 | 48,546 |
| 2008 | 18,100 | 20,617 | 21,841 | 13,064 | 72,128 |
| 2007 | 12,869 | 16,736 | 16,762 | 18,185 | 64,552 |
| 2006 | 16,418 | 18,179 | 16,492 | 13,807 | 64,896 |

**Earnings Per Share ($)**

| | | | | | |
|---|---|---|---|---|---|
| 2011 | 1.39 | 0.42 | 0.57 | E0.77 | E3.50 |
| 2010 | 0.64 | 1.00 | 0.98 | 0.99 | 3.61 |
| 2009 | 0.40 | 0.48 | 0.55 | 0.28 | 1.67 |
| 2008 | 1.02 | 1.08 | 2.90 | -0.06 | 4.95 |
| 2007 | 1.04 | 2.24 | 1.49 | 0.94 | 5.68 |
| 2006 | 1.07 | 2.04 | 2.26 | 1.53 | 6.87 |

Fiscal year ended Dec. 31. Next earnings report expected: Early February. EPS Estimates based on S&P Operating Earnings; historical GAAP earnings are as reported.

## Dividend Data (Dates: mm/dd Payment Date: mm/dd/yy)

| Amount ($) | Date Decl. | Ex-Div. Date | Stk. of Record | Payment Date |
|---|---|---|---|---|
| 0.250 | 04/27 | 05/16 | 05/18 | 06/10/11 |
| Stk. | 05/25 | 07/01 | 06/27 | 06/30/11 |
| 0.150 | 07/27 | 08/15 | 08/17 | 09/12/11 |
| 0.150 | 10/26 | 11/14 | 11/16 | 12/12/11 |

Dividends have been paid since 1991. Source: Company reports.

---

**Please read the Required Disclosures and Analyst Certification on the last page of this report.**

The **McGraw·Hill** Companies

# Marathon Oil Corp

STANDARD
&POOR'S

## Business Summary November 29, 2011

CORPORATE OVERVIEW. Until mid-2011, Marathon Oil (MRO; formerly USX-Marathon Group, a part of USX Corp.) was engaged in four operating segments: Exploration and Production (E&P; 15% of 2010 revenues; 71% of 2010 segment income); Oil Sands Mining (OSM; 1%; -2%), Refining, Marketing and Transportation (RM&T; 86%; 25%); and Integrated Gas (IG; less than 1%; 5%). In June 2011, MRO spun off its downstream RM&T business into a new publicly traded entity, Marathon Petroleum Corp. (MPC).

Including synthetic crude oil (SCO), proved oil and gas reserves fell 2% to 1.64 billion barrel oil equivalent (boe; 75% developed; 73% liquids and SCO) in 2010. Conventional oil and gas net sales rose 2% to 412,000 boe per day (boe/d; 65% liquids; 32% U.S., 37% Africa, and 26% Europe, 5% Canada) in 2010. Net sales of SCO production fell 25% to 24,000 barrels per day (b/d) in 2010. Using John S. Herold data, we estimate MRO's three-year (2006-08) finding and development costs at $35.37 per boe, above the peer average; its three-year proved acquisition costs at $13.72 per boe, above the peer average; its three-year reserve replacement costs at $22.96 per boe, above the peer average; and its three-year reserve replacement rate at 183%, in line with the peer average. Excluding oil sands, we estimate MRO's 2010 organic reserve replacement at

95% (overall 95%).

The RM&T segment (spun off in June 2011) owned and operated six refineries (464,000 b/d Garyville, LA; 212,000 b/d Catlettsburg, KY; 206,000 b/d Robinson, IL; 106,000 b/d Detroit, MI; 78,000 b/d Canton, OH; 76,000 b/d Texas City, TX) for a total throughput capacity of 1,142,000 b/d of crude oil, as of year-end 2010. MRO sourced about 71% of its refinery crude feedstock from North America, 21% from the Middle East and Africa, and 8% from other regions in 2010.

MRO terminals supplied petroleum products to private-brand marketers, as well as about 5,100 Marathon-branded retail outlets in 2010. Retail sales of gasoline and convenience store merchandise are also made through its wholly-owned subsidiary, Speedway SuperAmerica LLC (SSA), which had 1,358 retail outlets at the end of 2010 (primarily under the Speedway and SuperAmerica brand names).

## Company Financials Fiscal Year Ended Dec. 31

| Per Share Data ($) | 2010 | 2009 | 2008 | 2007 | 2006 | 2005 | 2004 | 2003 | 2002 | 2001 |
|---|---|---|---|---|---|---|---|---|---|---|
| Tangible Book Value | 31.54 | 28.89 | 28.16 | 22.59 | 18.72 | 13.90 | 11.17 | 9.20 | 7.57 | 7.99 |
| Cash Flow | 8.44 | 5.35 | 8.00 | 7.91 | 9.30 | 6.14 | 3.57 | 3.53 | 2.80 | 4.12 |
| Earnings | 3.61 | 1.67 | 4.95 | 5.68 | 6.87 | 4.25 | 1.86 | 1.63 | 0.86 | 2.13 |
| S&P Core Earnings | 3.07 | 1.54 | 5.77 | 5.69 | 6.85 | 4.20 | 1.91 | 1.63 | 0.69 | 2.21 |
| Dividends | 0.99 | 0.96 | 0.96 | 0.92 | 0.77 | 0.61 | 0.52 | 0.48 | 0.46 | 0.46 |
| Payout Ratio | 27% | 57% | 19% | 16% | 11% | 14% | 28% | 29% | 53% | 75% |
| Prices:High | 37.21 | 35.71 | 63.22 | 67.04 | 49.37 | 36.34 | 21.30 | 16.81 | 15.15 | 16.87 |
| Prices:Low | 27.64 | 20.18 | 19.34 | 41.50 | 31.01 | 17.76 | 15.15 | 9.93 | 9.41 | 12.48 |
| P/E Ratio:High | 10 | 21 | 13 | 12 | 7 | 9 | 11 | 10 | 18 | 28 |
| P/E Ratio:Low | 8 | 12 | 4 | 7 | 5 | 4 | 8 | 6 | 11 | 20 |

| Income Statement Analysis (Million $) | | | | | | | | | | |
|---|---|---|---|---|---|---|---|---|---|---|
| Revenue | 67,113 | 48,546 | 72,128 | 64,552 | 64,896 | 63,673 | 49,598 | 40,963 | 31,464 | 33,019 |
| Operating Income | NA | NA | 9,237 | 7,598 | 9,932 | 6,660 | 8,379 | 2,988 | 2,253 | 4,215 |
| Depreciation, Depletion and Amortization | 3,444 | 2,623 | 2,178 | 1,613 | 1,518 | 1,358 | 1,217 | 1,175 | 1,201 | 1,236 |
| Interest Expense | 103 | 149 | 50.0 | 290 | 108 | 145 | 161 | 238 | 288 | 196 |
| Pretax Income | 5,122 | 3,441 | 6,973 | 6,846 | 8,969 | 5,157 | 2,509 | 1,898 | 1,098 | 2,781 |
| Effective Tax Rate | NA | 65.6% | 49.4% | 42.4% | 44.8% | 33.5% | 29.0% | 30.8% | 35.4% | 27.3% |
| Net Income | 2,568 | 1,184 | 3,528 | 3,948 | 4,957 | 3,051 | 1,257 | 1,012 | 536 | 1,318 |
| S&P Core Earnings | 2,188 | 1,092 | 4,112 | 3,953 | 4,949 | 3,013 | 1,290 | 1,014 | 428 | 1,367 |

| Balance Sheet & Other Financial Data (Million $) | | | | | | | | | | |
|---|---|---|---|---|---|---|---|---|---|---|
| Cash | 4,177 | 2,057 | 1,285 | 1,199 | 2,585 | 2,617 | 3,369 | 1,396 | 488 | 657 |
| Current Assets | 13,829 | 10,637 | 8,403 | 10,587 | 10,096 | 9,383 | 8,867 | 6,040 | 4,479 | 4,411 |
| Total Assets | 50,014 | 47,052 | 42,686 | 42,746 | 30,831 | 28,498 | 23,423 | 19,482 | 17,812 | 16,129 |
| Current Liabilities | 11,113 | 9,057 | 7,753 | 11,260 | 8,061 | 8,154 | 5,253 | 4,207 | 3,659 | 3,468 |
| Long Term Debt | 7,601 | 8,436 | 7,087 | 6,084 | 3,061 | 3,698 | 4,057 | 4,085 | 4,410 | 3,432 |
| Common Equity | 23,771 | 21,910 | 21,409 | 19,223 | 14,607 | 11,705 | 8,111 | 6,075 | 5,082 | 4,940 |
| Total Capital | 31,667 | 30,442 | 31,826 | 28,696 | 20,083 | 17,868 | 16,411 | 12,171 | 12,908 | 11,632 |
| Capital Expenditures | 4,762 | 6,231 | 7,146 | 4,466 | 3,433 | 2,890 | 2,237 | 1,892 | 1,574 | 1,639 |
| Cash Flow | 6,012 | 3,807 | 5,706 | 5,500 | 6,475 | 4,409 | 2,474 | 2,187 | 1,737 | 2,546 |
| Current Ratio | 1.2 | 1.2 | 1.1 | 0.9 | 1.3 | 1.2 | 1.7 | 1.4 | 1.2 | 1.3 |
| % Long Term Debt of Capitalization | 24.0 | Nil | 22.3 | 21.2 | 15.2 | 20.7 | 24.7 | 33.6 | 34.2 | 29.5 |
| % Return on Assets | NA | 2.6 | 8.3 | 10.7 | 16.7 | 11.8 | 5.9 | 5.4 | 3.2 | 7.9 |
| % Return on Equity | NA | NA | 17.4 | 23.3 | 37.7 | 30.8 | 17.7 | 18.1 | 10.7 | 22.4 |

Data as orig reptd.; bef. results of disc opers/spec. items. Per share data adj. for stk. divs.; EPS diluted. E-Estimated. NA-Not Available. NM-Not Meaningful. NR-Not Ranked. UR-Under Review.

**Office:** 5555 San Felipe Road, Houston, TX 77056-2723.
**Telephone:** 713-629-6600.
**Website:** http://www.marathonoil.com
**Chrmn, Pres & CEO:** C.P. Cazalot, Jr.

**COO & EVP:** D.E. Roberts, Jr.
**EVP, CFO & Treas:** J.F. Clark
**CTO:** L.A. Capuano
**Chief Acctg Officer & Cntlr:** M.K. Stewart

**Investor Contact:** H. Thill (713-296-4140)
**Board Members:** G. H. Boyce, P. R. Brondeau, C. P. Cazalot, Jr., L. Z. Cook, S. A. Jackson, P. Lader, M. E. Phelps, D. H. Reilley

**Founded:** 1901
**Domicile:** Delaware
**Employees:** 29,677

# Marathon Petroleum Corp

**STANDARD &POOR'S**

| S&P Recommendation BUY ★★★★☆ | Price<br>$32.27 (as of Nov 25, 2011) | 12-Mo. Target Price<br>$39.00 | Investment Style<br>Large-Cap Value |
|---|---|---|---|

**GICS Sector** Energy
**Sub-Industry** Oil & Gas Refining & Marketing

**Summary** One of the largest independent refiners and marketers of petroleum products in the U.S., this mid-2011 spinoff from Marathon Oil has operations focused on the Midwest and Gulf Coast regions.

## Key Stock Statistics (Source S&P, Vickers, company reports)

| | | | | | | | |
|---|---|---|---|---|---|---|---|
| 52-Wk Range | $47.43– 26.35 | S&P Oper. EPS 2011**E** | 8.48 | Market Capitalization(B) | $11.505 | Beta | **NA** |
| Trailing 12-Month EPS | $7.54 | S&P Oper. EPS 2012**E** | 5.35 | Yield (%) | 3.10 | S&P 3-Yr. Proj. EPS CAGR(%) | **NM** |
| Trailing 12-Month P/E | 4.3 | P/E on S&P Oper. EPS 2011**E** | 3.8 | Dividend Rate/Share | $1.00 | S&P Credit Rating | **BBB** |
| $10K Invested 5 Yrs Ago | **NA** | Common Shares Outstg. (M) | 356.5 | Institutional Ownership (%) | 45 | | |

## Price Performance

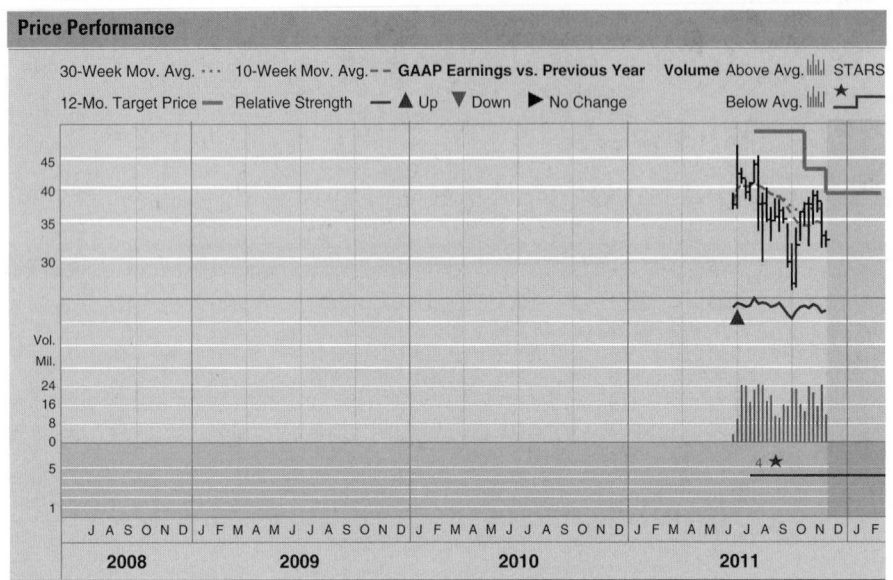

- 30-Week Mov. Avg. ···
- 10-Week Mov. Avg. - -
- GAAP Earnings vs. Previous Year
- Volume Above Avg. ⅡⅡⅡ
- STARS
- 12-Mo. Target Price —
- Relative Strength —
- ▲ Up ▼ Down ► No Change
- Below Avg. ⅠⅠⅠ ★

Analysis prepared by Equity Analyst **Tanjila Shafi** on Nov 23, 2011, when the stock traded at **$33.52**.

## Highlights

➤ We see a single digit increase in total throughputs to 1,358,000 b/d in 2011, based on higher fuel demand. We forecast that operating income from the Speedway segment will decrease to $240 million in 2011, from $293 million in 2010, due to lower retail margins. We expect operating income from the pipeline transportation segment to grow 16% to 17%, to more than $213 million, in 2011, reflecting a modest increase in volumes and higher rates. In 2012, we expect operating income for its refining business to decline to $2.7 billion from an expected $4.6 billion in 2011, due to lower margins, resulting from the narrowing of the spread between WTI and water-borne crudes.

➤ Capital expenditures for 2010 were $1.24 billion. For 2011, MPC has earmarked $1.38 billion for total capital expenditures, with $600 million budgeted for the Detroit project and $145 million for the Speedway segment.

➤ We expect continued improvement through 2012 on a better economic outlook and strategic actions. Our EPS estimates are $8.48 for 2011 and $5.35 for 2012.

## Investment Rationale/Risk

➤ We believe that the acceleration of projects intended to alleviate the crude bottleneck at Cushing, OK will narrow the spread between WTI and water-borne crudes. Therefore, we do not expect MPC to experience the same high refining margins in 2012 as it did in 2011. We are still positive on the strategic location and operational flexibility of the company's refineries. We believe that MPC's operational flexibility enables it to process a range of feedstocks and to adjust efficiently to supply disruptions, thereby maximizing refining capacity.

➤ Risks to our recommendation and target price include worse than expected economic, industry and operating conditions that lead to narrower refining margins or decreased sales.

➤ A blend of our discounted cash flow ($39 per share, assuming a WACC of 8.8% and terminal growth of 3%) and relative market valuations leads to our 12-month target price of $39. This represents an expected enterprise value multiple of about 3.6X our 2012 EBITDA estimate, in line with the peer average.

## Qualitative Risk Assessment

| LOW | MEDIUM | HIGH |
|---|---|---|

Our risk assessment reflects our view of MPC's solid business profile in the volatile and competitive oil refining industry. The company possesses above-average refining complexity, which allows it to process a large amount of lower-cost heavy and sour crudes.

## Quantitative Evaluations

**S&P Quality Ranking**  NR

| D | C | B- | B | B+ | A- | A | A+ |
|---|---|---|---|---|---|---|---|

**Relative Strength Rank**  MODERATE

39

LOWEST = 1                    HIGHEST = 99

## Revenue/Earnings Data

**Revenue (Million $)**

| | 1Q | 2Q | 3Q | 4Q | Year |
|---|---|---|---|---|---|
| 2011 | 16,652 | 19,504 | 19,304 | -- | -- |
| 2010 | 12,158 | 14,497 | 14,554 | 16,107 | 57,316 |
| 2009 | -- | -- | 11,163 | 12,141 | 40,681 |
| 2008 | -- | -- | -- | -- | 59,920 |
| 2007 | -- | -- | -- | -- | 49,888 |
| 2006 | -- | -- | -- | -- | -- |

**Earnings Per Share ($)**

| | 1Q | 2Q | 3Q | 4Q | Year |
|---|---|---|---|---|---|
| 2011 | 1.43 | 2.24 | 3.16 | E1.59 | E8.48 |
| 2010 | -- | 1.13 | -- | -- | NA |
| 2009 | -- | -- | -- | -- | -- |
| 2008 | -- | -- | -- | -- | -- |
| 2007 | -- | -- | -- | -- | -- |
| 2006 | -- | -- | -- | -- | -- |

Fiscal year ended Dec. 31. Next earnings report expected: NA. EPS Estimates based on S&P Operating Earnings; historical GAAP earnings are as reported.

## Dividend Data (Dates: mm/dd Payment Date: mm/dd/yy)

| Amount ($) | Date Decl. | Ex-Div. Date | Stk. of Record | Payment Date |
|---|---|---|---|---|
| 0.200 | 07/27 | 08/15 | 08/17 | 09/12/11 |
| 0.250 | 10/26 | 11/14 | 11/16 | 12/12/11 |
| 0.250 | 10/26 | 11/14 | 11/16 | 12/12/11 |

Dividends have been paid since 2011. Source: Company reports.

---

**Please read the Required Disclosures and Analyst Certification on the last page of this report.**

**The McGraw-Hill Companies**

# Marathon Petroleum Corp

**STANDARD &POOR'S**

## Business Summary November 23, 2011

CORPORATE OVERVIEW. Marathon Petroleum Corporation is one of the largest independent petroleum product refiners, transporters and marketers in the United States. On June 30, 2011, Marathon Oil Corporation (MRO 26, Buy) separated its downstream business to create a new publicly traded, independent refining company, Marathon Petroleum Corporation, via a tax-free spin-off (MRO shareholders received 1 MPC share for every 2 MRO shares). MPC owns and operates six refineries in the U.S., with an aggregate crude oil refining capacity in excess of 1.1 million barrels per day. MPC's marketing areas include the Midwest, Gulf Coast and Southeast. MPC conducts its business through three operating segments: Refining and Marketing (63% of segment income in 2010); Speedway (23%); and Pipeline Transportation (14%).

The Refining and Marketing segment includes operations of MPC's six refineries (total refining capacity 1,142,000 b/d as of December 31, 2010) in the Midwest, Gulf Coast and Southeast: Garyville, LA (464,000 b/d); Catlettsburg, KY (212,000 b/d); Robinson, IL (206,000 b/d); Detroit, MI (106,000 b/d); Canton, OH (78,000 b/d); and Texas City, TX (76,000 b/d). MPC purchases crude oil for its refineries from various domestic (about 61% in the first nine months of 2010) and foreign (39%) sources through negotiated contracts and the spot market. The refineries have the ability to process a wide range of crude feedstocks

and produce numerous refined products. Refined product yields rose 16%, to 1,356,000 b/d in 2010, and included gasoline (54%), distillates (30%), propane (2%), feedstocks & special products (7%), heavy fuel oil (2%) and asphalt (5%).

The company's six refineries are connected to each other through pipelines, terminals and barges. We believe that these transportation links integrate its refineries and permit the movement of intermediate products between refineries, thereby allowing MPC to utilize its processing capacity efficiently. The integration limits MPC's risk from possible supply interruptions, which we believe creates operational flexibility and gives the company a competitive advantage in comparison to other refiners.

The Speedway segment sells gasoline and merchandise through retail outlets that it owns and operates, primarily under the Speedway brand, in seven Midwestern states. As of December 31, 2010, the company owned 1,358 retail stores.

## Company Financials Fiscal Year Ended Dec. 31

| Per Share Data ($) | 2010 | 2009 | 2008 | 2007 | 2006 | 2005 | 2004 | 2003 | 2002 | 2001 |
|---|---|---|---|---|---|---|---|---|---|---|
| Tangible Book Value | NA | NA | NA | NA | NA | NA | NA | NA | NA | NA |
| Cash Flow | NA | NA | NA | NA | NA | NA | NA | NA | NA | NA |
| Earnings | NA | NA | NA | NA | NA | NA | NA | NA | NA | NA |
| S&P Core Earnings | 1.87 | 1.29 | NA | NA | NA | NA | NA | NA | NA | NA |
| Dividends | NA | NA | NA | NA | NA | NA | NA | NA | NA | NA |
| Payout Ratio | Nil | NA | NA | NA | NA | NA | NA | NA | NA | NA |
| Prices:High | NA | NA | NA | NA | NA | NA | NA | NA | NA | NA |
| Prices:Low | NA | NA | NA | NA | NA | NA | NA | NA | NA | NA |
| P/E Ratio:High | NA | NA | NA | NA | NA | NA | NA | NA | NA | NA |
| P/E Ratio:Low | NA | NA | NA | NA | NA | NA | NA | NA | NA | NA |

| Income Statement Analysis (Million $) | 2010 | 2009 | 2008 | 2007 | 2006 | 2005 | 2004 | 2003 | 2002 | 2001 |
|---|---|---|---|---|---|---|---|---|---|---|
| Revenue | 57,316 | 40,681 | 59,920 | 49,888 | NA | NA | NA | NA | NA | NA |
| Operating Income | NA | NA | NA | NA | NA | NA | NA | NA | NA | NA |
| Depreciation | 941 | 670 | 606 | 587 | NA | NA | NA | NA | NA | NA |
| Interest Expense | 7.00 | 8.00 | 8.00 | 7.00 | NA | NA | NA | NA | NA | NA |
| Pretax Income | 1,023 | 685 | 1,885 | 3,426 | NA | NA | NA | NA | NA | NA |
| Effective Tax Rate | NA | NA | NA | NA | NA | NA | NA | NA | NA | NA |
| Net Income | 623 | 449 | 1,215 | 2,262 | NA | NA | NA | NA | NA | NA |
| S&P Core Earnings | 668 | 465 | NA | NA | NA | NA | NA | NA | NA | NA |

| Balance Sheet & Other Financial Data (Million $) | 2010 | 2009 | 2008 | 2007 | 2006 | 2005 | 2004 | 2003 | 2002 | 2001 |
|---|---|---|---|---|---|---|---|---|---|---|
| Cash | 2,522 | 992 | 1,132 | NA | NA | NA | NA | NA | NA | NA |
| Current Assets | 10,056 | 7,900 | 6,734 | NA | NA | NA | NA | NA | NA | NA |
| Total Assets | 23,232 | 21,254 | 18,177 | NA | NA | NA | NA | NA | NA | NA |
| Current Liabilities | 8,620 | 6,637 | 4,767 | NA | NA | NA | NA | NA | NA | NA |
| Long Term Debt | 2,963 | 2,358 | 2,343 | NA | NA | NA | NA | NA | NA | NA |
| Common Equity | 8,244 | 9,172 | 8,936 | NA | NA | NA | NA | NA | NA | NA |
| Total Capital | 11,862 | 11,530 | 11,279 | NA | NA | NA | NA | NA | NA | NA |
| Capital Expenditures | 1,217 | 2,891 | 2,787 | 1,403 | NA | NA | NA | NA | NA | NA |
| Cash Flow | 1,564 | 1,119 | 1,821 | 2,849 | NA | NA | NA | NA | NA | NA |
| Current Ratio | 1.2 | 1.2 | 1.4 | NA | NA | NA | NA | NA | NA | NA |
| % Long Term Debt of Capitalization | 25.0 | 20.5 | 20.8 | NA | NA | NA | NA | NA | NA | NA |
| % Net Income of Revenue | 1.1 | 1.1 | 2.0 | 4.5 | NA | NA | NA | NA | NA | NA |
| % Return on Assets | 2.8 | 2.3 | NA | NA | NA | NA | NA | NA | NA | NA |
| % Return on Equity | 7.2 | 5.0 | NA | NA | NA | NA | NA | NA | NA | NA |

Data as orig reptd.; bef. results of disc opers/spec. items. Per share data adj. for stk. divs.; EPS diluted. E-Estimated. NA-Not Available. NM-Not Meaningful. NR-Not Ranked. UR-Under Review.

# Marriott International Inc.

**STANDARD &POOR'S**

| S&P Recommendation | HOLD ★★★★☆ | Price<br>$27.92 (as of Nov 25, 2011) | 12-Mo. Target Price<br>$31.00 | Investment Style<br>Large-Cap Growth |
|---|---|---|---|---|

**GICS Sector** Consumer Discretionary
**Sub-Industry** Hotels, Resorts & Cruise Lines

**Summary** Marriott's lodging brands include nearly 3,500 properties, most of which are managed by the company or are operated by others through franchise relationships.

## Key Stock Statistics (Source S&P, Vickers, company reports)

| | | | | | | | | |
|---|---|---|---|---|---|---|---|---|
| 52-Wk Range | $42.78– 25.49 | S&P Oper. EPS 2011E | 1.40 | Market Capitalization(B) | $9.357 | Beta | | 1.46 |
| Trailing 12-Month EPS | $0.61 | S&P Oper. EPS 2012E | 1.68 | Yield (%) | 1.43 | S&P 3-Yr. Proj. EPS CAGR(%) | | 15 |
| Trailing 12-Month P/E | 45.8 | P/E on S&P Oper. EPS 2011E | 19.9 | Dividend Rate/Share | $0.40 | S&P Credit Rating | | BBB |
| $10K Invested 5 Yrs Ago | NA | Common Shares Outstg. (M) | 335.1 | Institutional Ownership (%) | 61 | | | |

## Price Performance

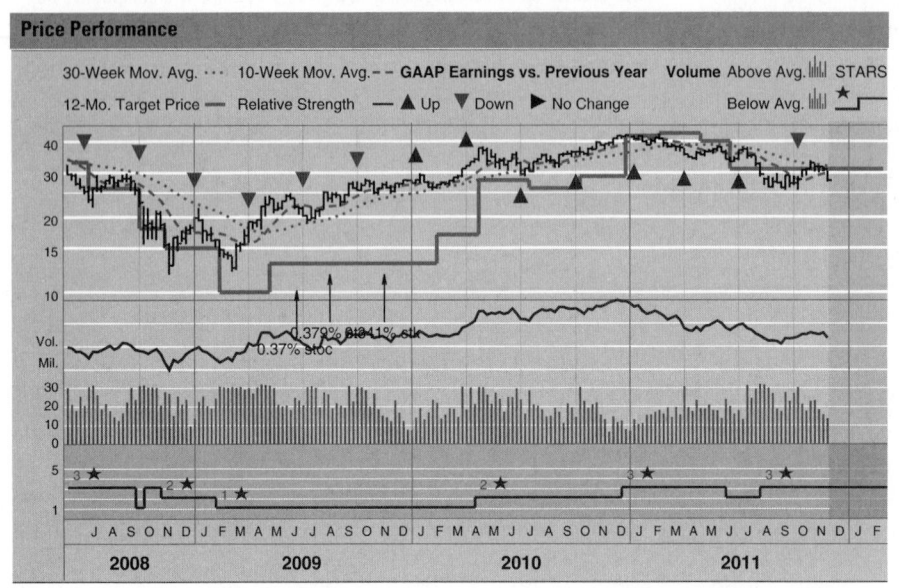

30-Week Mov. Avg. · · · 10-Week Mov. Avg. - - GAAP Earnings vs. Previous Year   Volume Above Avg. STARS
12-Mo. Target Price — Relative Strength — ▲ Up ▼ Down ► No Change   Below Avg. ★

Options: ASE, CBOE, P, Ph

Analysis prepared by Equity Analyst **Esther Kwon, CFA** on Oct 11, 2011, when the stock traded at **$29.43**.

## Qualitative Risk Assessment

| LOW | MEDIUM | HIGH |
|---|---|---|

Our risk assessment reflects our view that MAR is subject not only to improving cyclical economic factors, but also to lagging weakness in industry fundamentals, with the latter outweighing the former, so that a material increase in earnings to pre-recession levels is unlikely for some time. We expect internal cash flow to be sufficient to finance future minimum capital needs.

## Quantitative Evaluations

**S&P Quality Ranking**     A-

| D | C | B- | B | B+ | A- | A | A+ |
|---|---|---|---|---|---|---|---|

**Relative Strength Rank**     MODERATE

41

LOWEST = 1      HIGHEST = 99

## Revenue/Earnings Data

**Revenue (Million $)**

| | 1Q | 2Q | 3Q | 4Q | Year |
|---|---|---|---|---|---|
| 2011 | 2,778 | 2,972 | 2,874 | -- | -- |
| 2010 | 2,630 | 2,771 | 2,648 | 3,642 | 11,691 |
| 2009 | 2,495 | 2,562 | 2,471 | 3,380 | 10,908 |
| 2008 | 2,947 | 3,185 | 2,963 | 3,784 | 12,879 |
| 2007 | 2,836 | 3,122 | 2,943 | 4,089 | 12,990 |
| 2006 | 2,705 | 2,891 | 2,703 | 3,861 | 12,160 |

**Earnings Per Share ($)**

| | | | | | |
|---|---|---|---|---|---|
| 2011 | 0.26 | 0.37 | -0.52 | E0.48 | E1.40 |
| 2010 | 0.22 | 0.31 | 0.22 | 0.45 | 1.21 |
| 2009 | -0.06 | 0.10 | -1.31 | 0.28 | -0.97 |
| 2008 | 0.33 | 0.41 | 0.26 | -0.03 | 0.97 |
| 2007 | 0.40 | 0.43 | 0.31 | 0.61 | 1.73 |
| 2006 | 0.38 | 0.43 | 0.33 | 0.51 | 1.65 |

Fiscal year ended Dec. 31. Next earnings report expected: NA. EPS Estimates based on S&P Operating Earnings; historical GAAP earnings are as reported.

## Dividend Data (Dates: mm/dd Payment Date: mm/dd/yy)

| Amount ($) | Date Decl. | Ex-Div. Date | Stk. of Record | Payment Date |
|---|---|---|---|---|
| 0.100 | 05/06 | 05/18 | 05/20 | 06/24/11 |
| 0.100 | 08/04 | 08/16 | 08/18 | 09/16/11 |
| Stk. | 10/26 | 11/22 | 11/10 | 11/21/11 |
| 0.100 | 11/10 | 11/25 | 11/29 | 01/06/12 |

Dividends have been paid since 1998. Source: Company reports.

## Highlights

➤ In 2010, worldwide systemwide comparable RevPAR rose 5.8% (5.9% in actual dollars), paced by a 9.2% advance in international results, including a 5.9% increase in occupancy and a 0.2% decline in average daily rate. Comparable North American company-operated RevPAR rose 4.9%. As expected, full-service and luxury hotels outperformed, with comparable systemwide RevPAR advancing 5.5%, with a 3.7% increase in occupancy and a 0.3% decline in average daily rate.

➤ In 2011, we expect systemwide RevPAR in constant currency to rise at a mid-single digit pace and North American RevPAR to rise at a similar rate. For 2011, we project that base management fees, franchise fees and incentive management fees combined will increase over 10%, on system expansion, particularly in Asia, with time share contract sales down. We estimate operating profit will increase about 13%, after climbing nearly 60% in 2010.

➤ On a lower effective tax rate of 32.9%, compared to 33.4% in 2010, we forecast EPS of $1.40 for 2011, up from operating EPS of $1.15 in 2010. We estimate 2011 EBITDA of $1.08 billion. In 2012, we project EPS of $1.68.

## Investment Rationale/Risk

➤ Although we are concerned about weakening economic data in the United States and sovereign debt turmoil in Europe, we expect new North American room supply to be up less than 1% in 2011 and 2012, which we see driving higher room rates, and think the recent stock price decline has incorporated this slowdown. Additionally, while we view MAR's greater exposure to North America less positively than some peers, we expect this exposure to decline with a higher proportion of its development pipeline aimed at international markets. In February, MAR announced plans to spin off its time share business, which we view as a positive if completed.

➤ Risks to our recommendation and target price include a further weakening of the economic environment in North America as well as in international markets, and a tightening of capital markets.

➤ Our 12-month target price of $31 is based on an enterprise value of between 10X and 11X our forecast of 2012 EBITDA -- a discount to the large lodging group forward average of 12.4X.

---

# Marriott International Inc.

STANDARD
&POOR'S

## Business Summary October 11, 2011

CORPORATE OVERVIEW. Marriott International's lodging and timeshare businesses included 3,545 properties with 618,104 rooms or suites as of year-end 2010. This compared with 3,420 properties with 595,461 rooms or suites a year earlier. Of the 3,545 properties, approximately 3,074 were located in the U.S.

At year-end 2010, there were 1,104 properties (284,868 rooms or suites) that MAR operated under long-term management agreements; 45 properties (10,957 rooms) that were leased and managed by MAR; and five properties (986) that the company owned. With its management agreements, the company typically earns a base fee, and may receive an incentive management fee that is based on hotel profits. MAR also had 2,391 franchised properties, with 321,293 rooms, that were franchised and operated by other parties.

By brand (including franchises) as of year-end 2010, MAR's business included 622 Marriott Hotels & Resorts, Marriott Conference Centers or JW Marriott Hotels & Resorts properties; 74 Ritz-Carlton hotels; 144 Renaissance hotels; 892 Courtyard hotels; 658 Fairfield Inn properties; 274 SpringHill Suites properties; 613 Residence Inn hotels; 193 TownPlace Suites properties; two Bulgari Hotel & Resorts properties; 71 timeshare properties; and 28 residential and apartment units. Under a partnership with hotelier Ian Schrager, MAR operates two EDITION hotels, designed by Schrager, in Waikiki, Hawaii, and Istanbul, Turkey.

In 2010, MAR's North American full-service lodging segment, which included Marriott full-service and Renaissance businesses, accounted for approximately 44% of total revenues, while North American limited service accounted for 18%. In addition, international accounted for 11%, luxury 13%, and timeshare and other 14%.

The company's international presence as of year-end 2010 included: 120 properties (29,197 rooms or suites) in continental Europe, 60 in the British Isles (11,882), 125 properties (42,151) in Asia, 30 (8,904) in the Middle East or Africa, 130 (30,180) in the Americas ex-U.S., and six (1,768) in Australia.

CORPORATE STRATEGY. In the third quarter of 2009, MAR determined that in response to difficult business conditions and a lack of consumer confidence, it would alter its timeshare strategy to stimulate sales, accelerate cash flow, and minimize future investment spending. These changes included price reductions and a cessation of most future development, and resulted in pretax charges of $752 million during the quarter. In February 2011, the company announced plans to spin off its timeshare business.

## Company Financials Fiscal Year Ended Dec. 31

| Per Share Data ($) | 2010 | 2009 | 2008 | 2007 | 2006 | 2005 | 2004 | 2003 | 2002 | 2001 |
|---|---|---|---|---|---|---|---|---|---|---|
| Tangible Book Value | NM | NM | NM | 1.40 | 2.85 | 4.47 | 5.79 | 5.11 | 4.52 | 3.52 |
| Cash Flow | 1.68 | -0.45 | 1.48 | 2.23 | 2.30 | 1.82 | 1.66 | 1.28 | 1.21 | 0.88 |
| Earnings | 1.21 | -0.97 | 0.97 | 1.73 | 1.65 | 1.43 | 1.22 | 0.96 | 0.86 | 0.46 |
| S&P Core Earnings | 1.15 | -0.92 | 0.98 | 1.76 | 1.55 | 1.24 | 0.99 | 0.67 | 0.76 | 0.35 |
| Dividends | 0.21 | 0.08 | 0.33 | 0.28 | 0.24 | 0.20 | 0.16 | 0.15 | 0.14 | 0.13 |
| Payout Ratio | 17% | NM | 34% | 16% | 14% | 14% | 13% | 15% | 16% | 28% |
| Prices:High | 42.68 | 28.40 | 37.48 | 51.44 | 47.79 | 35.01 | 31.65 | 23.34 | 22.97 | 24.98 |
| Prices:Low | 25.63 | 12.09 | 11.75 | 31.00 | 31.97 | 28.69 | 20.10 | 14.12 | 12.98 | 13.50 |
| P/E Ratio:High | 35 | NM | 39 | 30 | 29 | 24 | 26 | 24 | 27 | 55 |
| P/E Ratio:Low | 21 | NM | 12 | 18 | 19 | 20 | 16 | 15 | 15 | 30 |

| Income Statement Analysis (Million $) | | | | | | | | | | |
|---|---|---|---|---|---|---|---|---|---|---|
| Revenue | 11,691 | 10,908 | 12,879 | 12,990 | 12,160 | 11,550 | 10,099 | 9,014 | 8,441 | 10,152 |
| Operating Income | 967 | 155 | 1,120 | 1,385 | 1,199 | 739 | 643 | 537 | 634 | 779 |
| Depreciation | 178 | 185 | 190 | 197 | 188 | 184 | 166 | 160 | 187 | 222 |
| Interest Expense | 180 | 118 | 218 | 184 | 124 | 106 | 99.0 | 110 | 86.0 | 109 |
| Pretax Income | 551 | -418 | 694 | 1,137 | 997 | 717 | 654 | 488 | 471 | 370 |
| Effective Tax Rate | NA | 15.6% | 50.4% | 39.0% | 28.7% | 13.1% | 15.3% | NM | 6.79% | 36.2% |
| Net Income | 458 | -346 | 359 | 697 | 717 | 668 | 594 | 476 | 439 | 236 |
| S&P Core Earnings | 435 | -327 | 364 | 711 | 680 | 579 | 484 | 330 | 381 | 180 |

| Balance Sheet & Other Financial Data (Million $) | | | | | | | | | | |
|---|---|---|---|---|---|---|---|---|---|---|
| Cash | 505 | 115 | 134 | 332 | 193 | 203 | 770 | 229 | 198 | 817 |
| Current Assets | 3,382 | 2,851 | 3,368 | 3,572 | 3,314 | 2,010 | 1,946 | 1,235 | 1,744 | 2,130 |
| Total Assets | 8,983 | 7,933 | 8,903 | 8,942 | 8,588 | 8,530 | 8,668 | 8,177 | 8,296 | 9,107 |
| Current Liabilities | 2,501 | 2,287 | 2,533 | 2,876 | 2,522 | 1,992 | 2,356 | 1,770 | 2,207 | 1,802 |
| Long Term Debt | 2,691 | 2,234 | 2,975 | 2,790 | 1,818 | 1,681 | 836 | 1,391 | 1,553 | 2,815 |
| Common Equity | 1,585 | 1,142 | 1,380 | 1,429 | 2,618 | 3,252 | 4,081 | 3,838 | 3,573 | 3,478 |
| Total Capital | 4,414 | 3,440 | 4,366 | 4,219 | 4,436 | 4,944 | 4,929 | 5,398 | 5,232 | 6,293 |
| Capital Expenditures | 307 | 147 | 357 | 671 | 529 | 780 | 181 | 210 | 292 | 560 |
| Cash Flow | 636 | -161 | 549 | 894 | 905 | 852 | 760 | 636 | 626 | 458 |
| Current Ratio | 1.4 | 1.3 | 1.3 | 1.2 | 1.3 | 1.0 | 0.8 | 0.7 | 0.8 | 1.2 |
| % Long Term Debt of Capitalization | 61.0 | 64.9 | 68.1 | 66.1 | 41.0 | 34.0 | 16.9 | 25.7 | 29.7 | 44.7 |
| % Net Income of Revenue | 3.9 | NM | 2.8 | 5.3 | 5.9 | 5.8 | 5.9 | 5.3 | 5.2 | 2.3 |
| % Return on Assets | NA | NM | 4.0 | 7.9 | 8.4 | 7.8 | 7.1 | 5.8 | 5.0 | 2.7 |
| % Return on Equity | NA | NM | 25.6 | 34.4 | 24.4 | 18.2 | 15.0 | 12.8 | 12.5 | 7.0 |

Data as orig reptd.; bef. results of disc opers/spec. items. Per share data adj. for stk. divs.; EPS diluted. E-Estimated. NA-Not Available. NM-Not Meaningful. NR-Not Ranked. UR-Under Review.

**Office:** 10400 Fernwood Road, Bethesda, MD 20817.
**Telephone:** 301-380-3000.
**Website:** http://www.marriott.com
**Chrmn & CEO:** J.W. Marriott, Jr.

**Pres & COO:** A.M. Sorenson
**Vice Chrmn:** J.W. Marriott, III
**EVP & Treas:** C.B. Handlon
**EVP & General Counsel:** E.A. Ryan

**Investor Contact:** T. Marder (301-380-2553)
**Board Members:** M. K. Bush, L. W. Kellner, D. L. Lee, J. W. Marriott, III, J. W. Marriott, Jr., G. Munoz, H. J. Pearce, S. S. Reinemund, L. M. Small, A. M. Sorenson

**Founded:** 1971
**Domicile:** Delaware
**Employees:** 129,000

# Marsh & McLennan Companies Inc.

STANDARD
&POOR'S

| S&P Recommendation HOLD ★★★☆☆ | Price<br>$28.47 (as of Nov 25, 2011) | 12-Mo. Target Price<br>$35.00 | Investment Style<br>Large-Cap Blend |
|---|---|---|---|

**GICS Sector** Financials
**Sub-Industry** Insurance Brokers

**Summary** This global professional services concern provides risk and insurance, investment management and consulting services through its operating companies.

## Key Stock Statistics (Source S&P, Vickers, company reports)

| | | | | | | | |
|---|---|---|---|---|---|---|---|
| 52-Wk Range | $31.93– 24.71 | S&P Oper. EPS 2011E | 1.81 | Market Capitalization(B) | $15.316 | Beta | 0.76 |
| Trailing 12-Month EPS | $1.70 | S&P Oper. EPS 2012E | 2.14 | Yield (%) | 3.09 | S&P 3-Yr. Proj. EPS CAGR(%) | 12 |
| Trailing 12-Month P/E | 16.8 | P/E on S&P Oper. EPS 2011E | 15.7 | Dividend Rate/Share | $0.88 | S&P Credit Rating | BBB- |
| $10K Invested 5 Yrs Ago | $10,476 | Common Shares Outstg. (M) | 538.0 | Institutional Ownership (%) | 83 | | |

## Price Performance

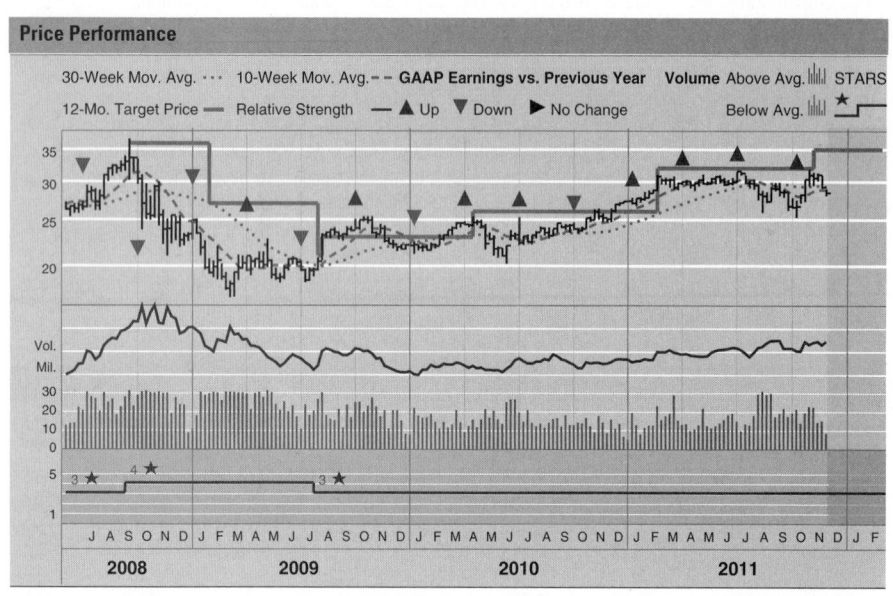

30-Week Mov. Avg. · · · 10-Week Mov. Avg. - - GAAP Earnings vs. Previous Year   Volume Above Avg. STARS
12-Mo. Target Price — Relative Strength   — ▲ Up  ▼ Down  ► No Change   Below Avg.

Options: ASE, CBOE, P, Ph

Analysis prepared by Equity Analyst **Robert McMillan** on Nov 08, 2011, when the stock traded at **$31.00**.

## Qualitative Risk Assessment

| LOW | MEDIUM | HIGH |
|---|---|---|

Our risk assessment reflects the company's leading market share position, diversified businesses and global scale, offset by regulatory scrutiny and business model changes as a result of contingent commissions, and potential impairment charges related to goodwill. We believe MMC is more exposed to the weak economy than peers due to its sizable consulting businesses.

## Quantitative Evaluations

**S&P Quality Ranking**                                    B

| D | C | B- | B | B+ | A- | A | A+ |
|---|---|---|---|---|---|---|---|

**Relative Strength Rank**                        MODERATE

66

LOWEST = 1                                      HIGHEST = 99

## Revenue/Earnings Data

**Revenue (Million $)**

| | 1Q | 2Q | 3Q | 4Q | Year |
|---|---|---|---|---|---|
| 2011 | 2,884 | 2,928 | 2,806 | -- | -- |
| 2010 | 2,795 | 2,606 | 2,524 | 2,785 | 10,550 |
| 2009 | 2,609 | 2,629 | 2,523 | 2,732 | 10,493 |
| 2008 | 3,047 | 3,048 | 2,838 | 2,662 | 11,587 |
| 2007 | 2,812 | 2,819 | 2,794 | 2,925 | 11,350 |
| 2006 | 3,016 | 2,970 | 2,872 | 3,063 | 11,921 |

**Earnings Per Share ($)**

| | 1Q | 2Q | 3Q | 4Q | Year |
|---|---|---|---|---|---|
| 2011 | 0.56 | 0.50 | 0.23 | E0.48 | E1.81 |
| 2010 | 0.50 | -0.06 | 0.22 | 0.34 | 1.00 |
| 2009 | 0.35 | -0.32 | 0.40 | 0.01 | 0.43 |
| 2008 | -0.41 | 0.11 | 0.03 | 0.14 | -0.13 |
| 2007 | 0.41 | 0.25 | 0.15 | 0.17 | 0.98 |
| 2006 | 0.43 | 0.31 | 0.32 | 0.39 | 1.45 |

Fiscal year ended Dec. 31. Next earnings report expected: Mid February. EPS Estimates based on S&P Operating Earnings; historical GAAP earnings are as reported.

## Dividend Data (Dates: mm/dd Payment Date: mm/dd/yy)

| Amount<br>($) | Date<br>Decl. | Ex-Div.<br>Date | Stk. of<br>Record | Payment<br>Date |
|---|---|---|---|---|
| 0.210 | 01/20 | 01/26 | 01/28 | 02/15/11 |
| 0.210 | 03/16 | 04/06 | 04/08 | 05/16/11 |
| 0.220 | 05/19 | 07/07 | 07/11 | 08/15/11 |
| 0.220 | 09/21 | 10/06 | 10/11 | 11/15/11 |

Dividends have been paid since 1923. Source: Company reports.

## Highlights

► After rising 7.3% in 2010 (adjusting for MMC's exit from the risk consulting and technology business), revenues should rise about 11% in both 2011 and 2012, in our view. We anticipate that stronger growth in risk management and broking on new business production, growth in key markets oversees and better pricing in some businesses will augment slower growth in the reinsurance broking business, where strong retention and new business wins will likely be partially offset by lower reinsurance rates. We think a gradual economic recovery will eventually benefit MMC's consulting business.

► We think expense reductions and capital management will lead to expanded margins in consulting and risk and insurance. We view MMC's financial position as strong, characterized by what we see as a solid cash position. We think MMC is well positioned to capitalize on M&A opportunities, and we expect investment income to improve substantially on higher interest rates and solid private equity returns.

► We forecast operating EPS of $1.81 in 2011 and $2.14 in 2012.

## Investment Rationale/Risk

► We believe shareholders will benefit from owning this globally diversified provider of advice and solutions in risk, strategy and human capital. While insurance pricing remains competitive, an eventual firming of rates should help revenues; we expect that an eventual economic pickup will benefit the consulting businesses. We also view favorably recent M&A activity, new business production, improving customer retention rates, and a share buyback program. We see considerable room for margin expansion given cost-cutting efforts, restructured operations and top-line growth.

► Risks to our recommendation and target price include lower-than-expected revenue from rate increases; deteriorating client retention; lower-than-projected cost savings from restructurings and layoffs; and unfavorable legal and regulatory developments.

► Our 12-month target price of $35 is 17.0X our four-quarter EPS estimate of $2.05; the stock recently traded at 15X this estimate. As operating results continue to improve, notwithstanding the sluggish economic recovery, we see the valuation multiple widening to levels that are still well below recent historical levels.

---

**Please read the Required Disclosures and Analyst Certification on the last page of this report.**

The McGraw-Hill Companies

# Marsh & McLennan Companies Inc.

**STANDARD &POOR'S**

## Business Summary November 08, 2011

CORPORATE OVERVIEW. Marsh & McLennan, one of the world's largest insurance brokers, also provides advice and solutions in areas of risk, strategy and human capital. In 2010, total revenues exceeded $10.0 billion, with MMC providing its services in more than 100 countries.

MMC conducts business through two operating segments: Risk and Insurance Services and Consulting. Risk and Insurance services (55% of operating segment revenues in 2010) includes insurance services, reinsurance services, risk capital holdings, risk management, insurance broking, and insurance program management. MMC conducts business in this segment through Marsh and Guy Carpenter. Marsh delivers risk and insurance services and solutions to its clients by providing risk management and risk consulting, as well as other services. Marsh generated roughly 45% of MMC's total operating revenue in 2010. Reinsurance broking and catastrophe and financial modeling services are provided under the Guy Carpenter name (9%).

Consulting and human resource outsourcing (46% in 2010 ) is offered under the Mercer and Oliver Wyman Group names. Mercer (33%) is a leading provider of human resource consulting and related outsourcing and invest-

ment services. Oliver Wyman Group (13%) delivers advisory services to clients through three operating units: Oliver Wyman; Lippincott; and NERA Economic Consulting.

LEGAL/REGULATORY ISSUES. In June 2010, MMC announced that its Mercer consulting subsidiary had reached a settlement of litigation brought by the Alaska Retirement Management Board (ARMB). Mercer will pay $400 million (excluding the $100 million covered by insurance), while denying any liability. We believe the $400 million settlement is a positive for MMC since it is significantly below the $2.8 billion that was sought by ARMB, and removes the uncertainty surrounding a jury trial in Alaska.

In the fourth quarter of 2009, MMC recorded a $205 million charge related to the securities and ERISA class action lawsuits filed in 2004. MMC did not admit to any liability or wrongdoing in connection with the settlement.

## Company Financials Fiscal Year Ended Dec. 31

| Per Share Data ($) | 2010 | 2009 | 2008 | 2007 | 2006 | 2005 | 2004 | 2003 | 2002 | 2001 |
|---|---|---|---|---|---|---|---|---|---|---|
| Tangible Book Value | NM | NM | NM | 0.13 | NM | NM | NM | NM | NM | NM |
| Cash Flow | 1.69 | 1.13 | 0.61 | 1.80 | 2.34 | 1.58 | 1.18 | 3.52 | 3.10 | 2.61 |
| Earnings | 1.00 | 0.43 | -0.13 | 0.98 | 1.45 | 0.67 | 0.33 | 2.81 | 2.45 | 1.70 |
| S&P Core Earnings | 1.28 | 0.79 | -0.12 | 0.86 | 1.30 | 0.38 | 1.11 | 2.29 | 1.60 | 0.91 |
| Dividends | 0.81 | 0.80 | 0.80 | 0.76 | 0.68 | 0.68 | 0.99 | 1.18 | 1.09 | 1.03 |
| Payout Ratio | 81% | 186% | NM | 71% | 47% | 101% | NM | 42% | 44% | 61% |
| Prices:High | 27.50 | 25.46 | 36.82 | 33.90 | 32.73 | 34.25 | 49.69 | 54.97 | 57.30 | 59.03 |
| Prices:Low | 20.21 | 17.18 | 20.96 | 23.12 | 24.00 | 26.67 | 22.75 | 38.27 | 34.61 | 39.50 |
| P/E Ratio:High | 28 | 59 | NM | 35 | 23 | 51 | NM | 19 | 23 | 35 |
| P/E Ratio:Low | 20 | 40 | NM | 24 | 17 | 40 | NM | 14 | 14 | 23 |
| **Income Statement Analysis** (Million $) | | | | | | | | | | |
| Revenue | 10,550 | 10,493 | 11,587 | 11,350 | 11,921 | 11,652 | 12,159 | 11,588 | 10,440 | 9,943 |
| Operating Income | 1,304 | 1,394 | 1,561 | 1,586 | 1,946 | 1,386 | 2,073 | 2,887 | 2,633 | 2,283 |
| Depreciation | 357 | 365 | 382 | 442 | 488 | 490 | 456 | 391 | 359 | 520 |
| Interest Expense | 233 | 241 | 220 | 267 | 303 | 332 | 219 | 185 | 160 | 196 |
| Pretax Income | 769 | 308 | 79.0 | 847 | 1,219 | 571 | 450 | 2,335 | 2,133 | 1,590 |
| Effective Tax Rate | NA | 16.6% | 173.4% | 34.8% | 31.8% | 33.6% | 57.6% | 33.0% | 35.0% | 37.7% |
| Net Income | 565 | 242 | -69.0 | 538 | 818 | 369 | 176 | 1,540 | 1,365 | 974 |
| S&P Core Earnings | 695 | 410 | -57.9 | 462 | 732 | 211 | 590 | 1,254 | 890 | 525 |
| **Balance Sheet & Other Financial Data** (Million $) | | | | | | | | | | |
| Cash | 1,894 | 1,777 | 1,685 | 2,133 | 2,089 | 2,020 | 1,396 | 665 | 546 | 537 |
| Current Assets | 5,276 | 4,931 | 4,784 | 5,454 | 5,834 | 5,262 | 4,887 | 3,901 | 3,664 | 3,792 |
| Total Assets | 15,310 | 15,322 | 15,221 | 17,359 | 18,137 | 17,892 | 18,337 | 15,053 | 13,855 | 13,293 |
| Current Liabilities | 3,105 | 3,703 | 3,386 | 3,493 | 5,549 | 4,351 | 4,735 | 4,089 | 3,863 | 3,938 |
| Long Term Debt | 3,026 | 3,034 | 3,194 | 3,604 | 3,860 | 5,044 | 4,691 | 2,910 | 2,891 | 2,334 |
| Common Equity | 6,415 | 5,878 | 5,722 | 7,822 | 5,819 | 5,360 | 5,056 | 5,451 | 5,018 | 5,173 |
| Total Capital | 9,449 | 9,470 | 8,916 | 11,426 | 9,679 | 10,404 | 9,747 | 8,361 | 7,909 | 7,507 |
| Capital Expenditures | 271 | 305 | 386 | 378 | 307 | 345 | 376 | 436 | 423 | 433 |
| Cash Flow | 922 | 592 | 313 | 980 | 1,306 | 859 | 632 | 1,931 | 1,724 | 1,494 |
| Current Ratio | 1.7 | 1.3 | 1.4 | 1.6 | 1.1 | 1.2 | 1.0 | 1.0 | 0.9 | 1.0 |
| % Long Term Debt of Capitalization | 32.0 | 32.0 | 35.8 | 31.5 | 39.9 | 48.5 | 48.1 | 34.8 | 36.6 | 31.1 |
| % Net Income of Revenue | 5.4 | 2.3 | NM | 4.7 | 6.9 | 3.2 | 1.4 | 13.3 | 13.1 | 9.8 |
| % Return on Assets | 3.7 | 1.6 | NM | 3.0 | 4.5 | 2.0 | 1.1 | 10.7 | 10.1 | 7.2 |
| % Return on Equity | 9.2 | 4.2 | NM | 7.9 | 14.6 | 7.1 | 3.4 | 29.4 | 26.8 | 18.7 |

Data as orig reptd.; bef. results of disc opers/spec. items. Per share data adj. for stk. divs.; EPS diluted. E-Estimated. NA-Not Available. NM-Not Meaningful. NR-Not Ranked. UR-Under Review.

**Office:** 1166 Avenue of the Americas, New York, NY 10036-2774.
**Telephone:** 212-345-5000.
**Email:** shareowner-svcs@email.bankofny.com
**Website:** http://www.mmc.com

**Chrmn:** I.B. Lang
**Pres & CEO:** B. Duperreault
**Pres & COO:** D.S. Glaser
**EVP & CFO:** V.A. Wittman

**EVP & General Counsel:** P.J. Beshar
**Investor Contact:** M.B. Bartley (212-345-5000)
**Board Members:** Z. W. Carter, B. Duperreault, O. Fanjul, Martin, H. E. Hanway, I. B. Lang, S. A. Mills, B. P. Nolop, M. D. Oken, M. O. Schapiro, A. Simmons, L. M. Yates

**Founded:** 1923
**Domicile:** Delaware
**Employees:** 51,000

**The McGraw·Hill Companies**

# Masco Corp

**STANDARD &POOR'S**

| S&P Recommendation | BUY ★★★★☆ | Price $8.42 (as of Nov 25, 2011) | 12-Mo. Target Price $12.00 | Investment Style Large-Cap Blend |
|---|---|---|---|---|

**GICS Sector** Industrials
**Sub-Industry** Building Products

**Summary** This company is one of the world's leading makers of faucets, cabinets, coatings, and other consumer brand-name home improvement and building products.

## Key Stock Statistics (Source S&P, Vickers, company reports)

| | | | | | |
|---|---|---|---|---|---|
| 52-Wk Range | $15.03–6.60 | S&P Oper. EPS 2011E | 0.20 | Market Capitalization(B) | $3.013 | Beta | 2.19 |
| Trailing 12-Month EPS | $-2.99 | S&P Oper. EPS 2012E | 0.55 | Yield (%) | 3.56 | S&P 3-Yr. Proj. EPS CAGR(%) | 74 |
| Trailing 12-Month P/E | NM | P/E on S&P Oper. EPS 2011E | 42.1 | Dividend Rate/Share | $0.30 | S&P Credit Rating | BBB- |
| $10K Invested 5 Yrs Ago | $3,521 | Common Shares Outstg. (M) | 357.8 | Institutional Ownership (%) | 94 | | |

## Price Performance

30-Week Mov. Avg. · · · · 10-Week Mov. Avg. - - - GAAP Earnings vs. Previous Year    Volume Above Avg. STARS
12-Mo. Target Price — Relative Strength — ▲ Up ▼ Down ► No Change    Below Avg.

Options: ASE, CBOE, P, Ph

Analysis prepared by Equity Analyst **Michael Jaffe** on Nov 09, 2011, when the stock traded at **$9.15**.

## Qualitative Risk Assessment

| LOW | MEDIUM | HIGH |
|---|---|---|

Our risk assessment for Masco reflects its generation of strong levels of free cash flow during most business cycles, and what we view as a good business model. However, it also operates in a very cyclical area, and is highly dependent on one customer, Home Depot, which accounted for 26% of sales in each of the past two years.

## Quantitative Evaluations

**S&P Quality Ranking**    B-

| D | C | B- | B | B+ | A- | A | A+ |
|---|---|---|---|---|---|---|---|

**Relative Strength Rank**    MODERATE

49

LOWEST = 1     HIGHEST = 99

## Revenue/Earnings Data

### Revenue (Million $)

| | 1Q | 2Q | 3Q | 4Q | Year |
|---|---|---|---|---|---|
| 2011 | 1,772 | 2,022 | 2,006 | -- | -- |
| 2010 | 1,852 | 2,048 | 1,957 | 1,735 | 7,592 |
| 2009 | 1,797 | 2,013 | 2,084 | 1,869 | 7,792 |
| 2008 | 2,446 | 2,640 | 2,528 | 1,979 | 9,600 |
| 2007 | 2,865 | 3,148 | 3,059 | 2,698 | 11,770 |
| 2006 | 3,167 | 3,370 | 3,295 | 2,946 | 12,778 |

### Earnings Per Share ($)

| | | | | | |
|---|---|---|---|---|---|
| 2011 | -0.13 | 0.02 | 0.10 | E0.05 | E0.20 |
| 2010 | -0.02 | 0.01 | -0.02 | -2.96 | -3.00 |
| 2009 | -0.24 | 0.19 | 0.14 | -0.49 | -0.41 |
| 2008 | 0.07 | 0.20 | 0.10 | -1.45 | -1.08 |
| 2007 | 0.37 | 0.50 | 0.57 | -0.39 | 1.06 |
| 2006 | 0.50 | 0.53 | 0.57 | -0.48 | 1.15 |

Fiscal year ended Dec. 31. Next earnings report expected: Mid February. EPS Estimates based on S&P Operating Earnings; historical GAAP earnings are as reported.

## Highlights

➤ We see 7% sales growth in 2012, following our outlook for flat sales in 2011 (but a small gain in the second half). Sales were very weak over the past four plus years, on U.S. housing market woes, much slower big-ticket consumer spending, and economic concerns in Europe. Yet, on what now seems to be a stabilization of housing, we see a small sales revival in coming periods. We expect the strongest sales in plumbing, as we see home repair and improvement spending picking up before new home markets. MAS's plan to exit from certain cabinet lines will likely have a small negative impact.

➤ We look for margins to improve in 2011 and 2012, on our better sales outlook, incremental benefits from cost cuts, and savings from MAS's early 2010 plans to integrate its cabinet businesses into one organization. Masco saw its cabinet initiatives lowering fixed costs by $180 million (with $140 million taken out as of early 2011). MAS estimates that it has cut $500 million of fixed costs out of its operations since the start of the business downturn.

➤ Our 2011 EPS estimate of $0.20 excludes $0.16 of one-time charges, and compares with operating EPS of $0.16 in 2010.

## Investment Rationale/Risk

➤ MAS has been hurt for an extended period by very soft U.S. housing and home improvement markets. Yet, we see its business starting to revive over the next year on global economic growth, and its likely positive impact on home improvement and housing markets. We also think MAS's recent amendment of debt covenants puts it in a better financial position. We view the shares as undervalued.

➤ Risks to our recommendation and target price include a further extension of the U.S. housing downturn, and weaker than expected performance in foreign markets served by MAS.

➤ MAS recently traded at about 17X our 2012 EPS forecast, which we see as the first year of a true business revival for Masco. That valuation is in the bottom half of MAS's range in the early part of its last business upturn. We think a higher valuation is merited, as we believe that aggressive streamlining actions undertaken by MAS have it poised for a strong earnings recovery once demand picks up (which we see starting in 2012). Our 12-month target price of $12 is 21.8X our 2012 EPS forecast, which is near the top part of its range during periods of revival.

## Dividend Data (Dates: mm/dd Payment Date: mm/dd/yy)

| Amount ($) | Date Decl. | Ex-Div. Date | Stk. of Record | Payment Date |
|---|---|---|---|---|
| 0.075 | 12/15 | 01/05 | 01/07 | 02/07/11 |
| 0.075 | 03/25 | 04/06 | 04/08 | 05/09/11 |
| 0.075 | 06/24 | 07/06 | 07/08 | 08/08/11 |
| 0.075 | 09/09 | 10/05 | 10/07 | 11/07/11 |

Dividends have been paid since 1944. Source: Company reports.

**Please read the Required Disclosures and Analyst Certification on the last page of this report.**

**The McGraw·Hill Companies**

# Masco Corp

STANDARD
&POOR'S

## Business Summary November 09, 2011

CORPORATE OVERVIEW. Masco is one of the largest U.S. makers of brand name consumer products for home improvement and new construction markets; it derives most of its revenues from the sale of faucets, kitchen and bath cabinets, plumbing supplies and architectural coatings. Operations are focused on North America (78% of 2010 sales) and Europe (most of the rest). Home Depot contributed 26% of sales in both 2010 and 2009.

The plumbing products division (35% of 2010 sales) is a major global producer of faucets and showering devices. Masco revolutionized faucets in 1954 with the Delta line, and also offers the Peerless, Brizo and Newport Brass brands, among others. In addition, the division offers other bath products, including plumbing fittings and valves, bathtubs and shower enclosures, and spa items; brand names include Aqua Glass and HotSpring. The cabinets and related products division (19%) makes cabinetry for kitchen, bath, storage, home office and home entertainment applications, featuring the Kraftmaid, Tvilum-Scanbirk and Merillat brands.

Masco sells decorative architectural items (22%), including paints and stains,

and decorative bath and shower accessories. Trade names include Behr in paints and stains and Franklin Brass in bath and shower. It also supplies and installs insulation products and other building products (15%) such as gutters, fireplaces, garage doors and framing components, and sells other specialty products (8%), such as windows, patio doors and electric staple guns.

MANAGEMENT. In July 2007, Richard Manoogian, Masco's chairman and CEO, gave up his CEO duties and moved into a new post as executive chairman. Based on Mr. Manoogian's recommendation, Timothy Wadhams, Masco's senior vice president and CFO since 2001, was appointed to the CEO role. In addition, Alan Barry, Masco's president, stepped down from his post at the end of 2007, when he reached normal retirement age, with Mr. Wadhams also assuming that title.

## Company Financials Fiscal Year Ended Dec. 31

| Per Share Data ($) | 2010 | 2009 | 2008 | 2007 | 2006 | 2005 | 2004 | 2003 | 2002 | 2001 |
|---|---|---|---|---|---|---|---|---|---|---|
| Tangible Book Value | NM | NM | NM | NM | 0.54 | 0.88 | 1.54 | 1.36 | 1.31 | 1.30 |
| Cash Flow | -2.07 | 0.32 | -0.41 | 1.71 | 1.76 | 2.66 | 2.56 | 2.00 | 1.85 | 1.02 |
| Earnings | -3.00 | -0.41 | -1.08 | 1.06 | 1.15 | 2.03 | 2.04 | 1.51 | 1.33 | 0.42 |
| S&P Core Earnings | -1.20 | 0.21 | 0.23 | 1.56 | 2.17 | 2.17 | 2.25 | 1.67 | 1.52 | 1.12 |
| Dividends | 0.30 | 0.46 | 0.93 | 0.91 | 0.86 | 0.78 | 0.66 | 0.58 | 0.55 | 0.52 |
| Payout Ratio | NM | NM | NM | 86% | 75% | 38% | 32% | 38% | 41% | 125% |
| Prices:High | 18.78 | 15.50 | 23.50 | 34.72 | 33.70 | 38.43 | 37.02 | 28.44 | 29.43 | 26.94 |
| Prices:Low | 9.94 | 3.64 | 6.82 | 20.89 | 25.85 | 27.15 | 25.88 | 16.59 | 17.25 | 17.76 |
| P/E Ratio:High | NM | NM | NM | 33 | 29 | 19 | 18 | 19 | 22 | 64 |
| P/E Ratio:Low | NM | NM | NM | 20 | 22 | 13 | 13 | 11 | 13 | 42 |

| Income Statement Analysis (Million $) | | | | | | | | | | |
|---|---|---|---|---|---|---|---|---|---|---|
| Revenue | 7,592 | 7,792 | 9,600 | 11,770 | 12,778 | 12,642 | 12,074 | 10,936 | 9,419 | 8,358 |
| Operating Income | 667 | 571 | 780 | 1,419 | 1,700 | 1,881 | 1,944 | 1,738 | 1,683 | 1,309 |
| Depreciation | 279 | 254 | 236 | 241 | 244 | 241 | 237 | 244 | 220 | 269 |
| Interest Expense | 251 | 225 | 228 | 258 | 240 | 247 | 217 | 262 | 237 | 239 |
| Pretax Income | -777 | -151 | -211 | 770 | 900 | 1,412 | 1,518 | 1,216 | 1,031 | 301 |
| Effective Tax Rate | NA | 32.5% | NM | 43.6% | 45.8% | 36.7% | 37.5% | 38.1% | 33.8% | 34.0% |
| Net Income | -1,002 | -140 | -382 | 397 | 461 | 872 | 930 | 740 | 682 | 199 |
| S&P Core Earnings | -419 | 78.1 | 80.1 | 582 | 866 | 936 | 1,027 | 816 | 779 | 528 |

| Balance Sheet & Other Financial Data (Million $) | | | | | | | | | | |
|---|---|---|---|---|---|---|---|---|---|---|
| Cash | 1,715 | 1,413 | 1,028 | 922 | 1,958 | 1,964 | 1,256 | 795 | 1,067 | 312 |
| Current Assets | 3,464 | 3,451 | 3,300 | 3,808 | 5,115 | 5,123 | 4,402 | 3,804 | 3,950 | 2,627 |
| Total Assets | 8,140 | 9,175 | 9,483 | 10,907 | 12,325 | 12,559 | 12,541 | 12,149 | 12,050 | 9,183 |
| Current Liabilities | 1,487 | 1,781 | 1,547 | 1,908 | 3,389 | 2,894 | 2,147 | 2,099 | 1,932 | 1,237 |
| Long Term Debt | 4,032 | 3,604 | 3,915 | 3,966 | 3,533 | 3,915 | 4,187 | 3,848 | 4,316 | 3,628 |
| Common Equity | 1,582 | 2,817 | 2,846 | 4,025 | 4,471 | 4,848 | 5,596 | 5,456 | 5,294 | 4,120 |
| Total Capital | 5,680 | 6,785 | 7,323 | 7,991 | 8,004 | 9,665 | 9,783 | 9,304 | 9,610 | 7,747 |
| Capital Expenditures | 137 | 125 | 200 | 248 | 388 | 282 | 310 | 271 | 285 | 274 |
| Cash Flow | -723 | 114 | -146 | 638 | 705 | 1,113 | 1,167 | 984 | 902 | 468 |
| Current Ratio | 2.3 | 1.9 | 2.1 | 2.0 | 1.5 | 1.8 | 2.1 | 1.8 | 2.0 | 2.1 |
| % Long Term Debt of Capitalization | 71.0 | 53.1 | 53.5 | 49.6 | 44.1 | 40.5 | 42.8 | 41.4 | 44.9 | 46.8 |
| % Net Income of Revenue | NM | NM | NM | 3.4 | 3.6 | 6.9 | 7.7 | 6.8 | 7.2 | 2.4 |
| % Return on Assets | NM | NM | NM | 3.4 | 3.7 | 6.9 | 7.5 | 6.1 | 6.5 | 2.3 |
| % Return on Equity | NM | NM | NM | 9.4 | 9.9 | 17.0 | 16.6 | 13.8 | 14.7 | 5.3 |

Data as orig reptd.; bef. results of disc opers/spec. items. Per share data adj. for stk. divs.; EPS diluted. E-Estimated. NA-Not Available. NM-Not Meaningful. NR-Not Ranked. UR-Under Review.

**Office:** 21001 Van Born Road, Taylor, MI 48180.
**Telephone:** 313-274-7400.
**Website:** http://www.masco.com
**Chrmn:** R.A. Manoogian

**Pres:** K. Allman
**CEO:** T. Wadhams
**CFO & Treas:** J.G. Sznewajs
**Chief Acctg Officer & Cntlr:** J.P. Lindow

**Investor Contact:** M.C. Duey (313-274-7400)
**Board Members:** D. W. Archer, T. G. Denomme, V. G. Istock, J. M. Losh, R. A. Manoogian, L. A. Payne, M. A. Van Lokeren, T. Wadhams

**Founded:** 1929
**Domicile:** Delaware
**Employees:** 32,500

# MasterCard Inc

**STANDARD &POOR'S**

| S&P Recommendation HOLD ★★★☆☆ | Price $346.20 (as of Nov 25, 2011) | 12-Mo. Target Price $400.00 | Investment Style Large-Cap Growth |
|---|---|---|---|

**GICS Sector** Information Technology
**Sub-Industry** Data Processing & Outsourced Services

**Summary** MasterCard is a global leader in transaction processing and brand licensing, providing its services globally. The company has nearly 30 million acceptance locations.

## Key Stock Statistics (Source S&P, Vickers, company reports)

| | | | | | | |
|---|---|---|---|---|---|---|
| 52-Wk Range | $373.55– 215.00 | S&P Oper. EPS 2011**E** | 19.00 | Market Capitalization(B) | $42.005 | Beta | 0.98 |
| Trailing 12-Month EPS | $17.80 | S&P Oper. EPS 2012**E** | 22.00 | Yield (%) | 0.17 | S&P 3-Yr. Proj. EPS CAGR(%) | 18 |
| Trailing 12-Month P/E | 19.5 | P/E on S&P Oper. EPS 2011**E** | 18.2 | Dividend Rate/Share | $0.60 | S&P Credit Rating | NA |
| $10K Invested 5 Yrs Ago | $33,329 | Common Shares Outstg. (M) | 126.9 | Institutional Ownership (%) | 81 | | |

## Price Performance

30-Week Mov. Avg. ··· 10-Week Mov. Avg. -- **GAAP Earnings vs. Previous Year**   Volume Above Avg. STARS
12-Mo. Target Price — Relative Strength — ▲ Up ▼ Down ▶ No Change   Below Avg.

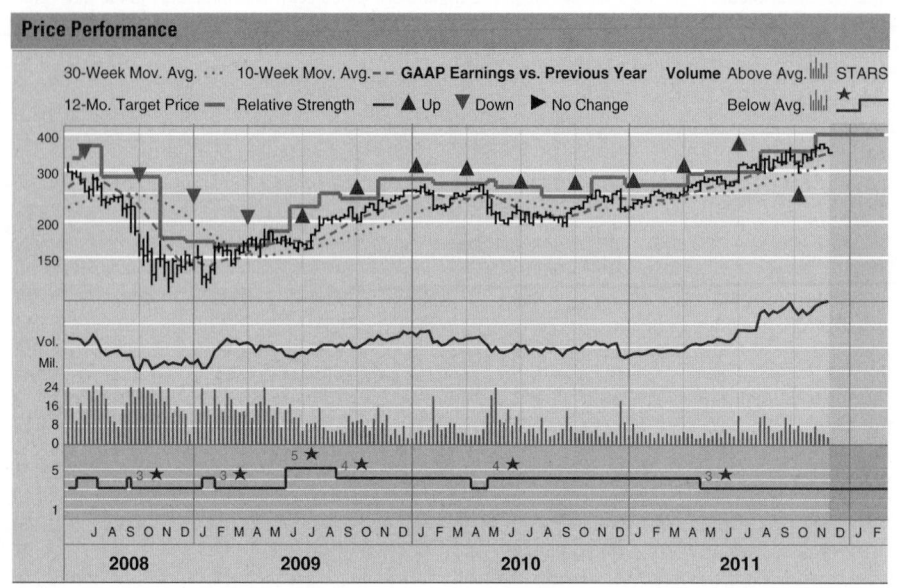

Options: ASE, CBOE, P, Ph

## Qualitative Risk Assessment

| LOW | MEDIUM | HIGH |
|---|---|---|

Our risk assessment reflects what we view as a dynamic market environment, offset by pending litigation risks and an evolving competitive and regulatory environment.

## Quantitative Evaluations

**S&P Quality Ranking**   NR

| D | C | B- | B | B+ | A- | A | A+ |
|---|---|---|---|---|---|---|---|

**Relative Strength Rank**   STRONG

86

LOWEST = 1   HIGHEST = 99

## Highlights

▶ The 12-month target price for MA has recently been changed to $400.00 from $350.00. The Highlights section of this Stock Report will be updated accordingly.

## Investment Rationale/Risk

▶ The Investment Rationale/Risk section of this Stock Report will be updated shortly. For the latest News story on MA from MarketScope, see below.

▶ 11/15/11 02:50 pm ET ... S&P COMMENTS ON PROMINENT INVESTOR'S INTEREST IN IT STOCKS (IBM 189.24*****): Warren Buffet's Berkshire Hathaway (BRK.B 76, Hold) made notable investments in IT bellwethers IBM, Intel (INTC 25, Hold), and Visa (V 96, Hold) in Q3. BRK.B also had a stake in in MasterCard (MA 372, Hold), and thus BRK.B holds interests in 4 of the 12 largest U.S. tech companies by market cap. Interestingly, 3 of these companies are categorized within the GICS IT Services industry. All of them have global franchises and pay dividends, and the 3 IT Services companies have what we view as strong earnings visibility. Equity Strategy has an Overweight opinion on the sector. /S. Kessler

## Revenue/Earnings Data

**Revenue (Million $)**

| | 1Q | 2Q | 3Q | 4Q | Year |
|---|---|---|---|---|---|
| 2011 | 1,501 | 1,667 | 1,818 | -- | -- |
| 2010 | 1,308 | 1,365 | 1,428 | 1,438 | 5,539 |
| 2009 | 1,156 | 1,280 | 1,364 | 1,298 | 5,099 |
| 2008 | 1,182 | 1,247 | 1,338 | 1,225 | 4,992 |
| 2007 | 915.1 | 997.0 | 1,083 | 1,073 | 4,068 |
| 2006 | 738.5 | 846.5 | 902.0 | 839.2 | 3,326 |

**Earnings Per Share ($)**

| | | | | | |
|---|---|---|---|---|---|
| 2011 | 4.29 | 4.76 | 5.63 | E4.32 | E19.00 |
| 2010 | 3.46 | 3.49 | 3.94 | 3.16 | 14.05 |
| 2009 | 2.80 | 2.67 | 3.45 | 2.24 | 11.16 |
| 2008 | 3.38 | -5.74 | -1.49 | 1.84 | -1.95 |
| 2007 | 1.57 | 1.85 | 2.31 | 2.26 | 8.00 |
| 2006 | 0.94 | -2.30 | 1.42 | 0.30 | 0.37 |

Fiscal year ended Dec. 31. Next earnings report expected: Early February. EPS Estimates based on S&P Operating Earnings; historical GAAP earnings are as reported.

## Dividend Data (Dates: mm/dd Payment Date: mm/dd/yy)

| Amount ($) | Date Decl. | Ex-Div. Date | Stk. of Record | Payment Date |
|---|---|---|---|---|
| 0.150 | 12/07 | 01/06 | 01/10 | 02/09/11 |
| 0.150 | 02/08 | 04/06 | 04/08 | 05/09/11 |
| 0.150 | 06/07 | 07/06 | 07/08 | 08/09/11 |
| 0.150 | 09/21 | 10/05 | 10/10 | 11/09/11 |

Dividends have been paid since 2006. Source: Company reports.

# MasterCard Inc

**STANDARD &POOR'S**

## Business Summary August 26, 2011

CORPORATE OVERVIEW. MasterCard Incorporated (MA), a leading global payment solutions company, provides a variety of services in support of the credit, debit and related payment programs of about 22,000 financial institutions and other types of entities. MA follows a three-tiered business model as a franchisor, processor and advisor. The company, through its businesses, develops and markets payment solutions, processes payment transactions, and provides consulting services to its customers and merchants. MA manages a family of payment card brands, including MasterCard, Maestro, and Cirrus, which it licenses to its customers.

MasterCard generates revenues from fees (domestic assessments, cross-border volume fees, transaction processing fees, and other service fees). The company follows a "four-party" payment system, which typically involves four parties in addition to the company: the cardholder, the merchant, the issuer (the cardholder's bank) and the acquirer (the merchant's bank). Issuers typically pay operations fees and assessments, while acquirers principally pay assessments on gross dollar volume (GDV) or cards and, to a lesser extent, certain operations fees. MA charges operations fees to its customers for providing transaction processing and other payment-related services. Operations fees include core authorization, clearing and settlement fees, cross-border and currency conversion fees, switch fees, connectivity fees and other operations fees, such as acceptance development fees, warning bulletins, holo-

grams, fees for compliance programs, and user-pay fees for a variety of transaction enhancement services. The company charges assessments based on customers' GDV of activity on the cards that carry its brands, and rates vary by region. GDV includes the aggregated dollar amount of usage (purchases, cash disbursements, balance transfers and convenience checks) on MasterCard-branded cards.

On an aggregate basis, the company processed 23.1 billion transactions (including PIN-based online transactions) during 2010, a 2.9% increase over the number of transactions processed in 2009. GDV on cards carrying the MasterCard brand, as reported by MA's customers, grew 10.7% (in U.S. dollar terms), to approximately $2.7 trillion, in 2010. In 2010, MA's five largest customers accounted for 28% of total revenue, but no single customer exceeded 10% of total revenues. MA's revenue by geographic market is based on the location of the customer who issued the cards that are generating the revenue. Revenue generated in the U.S. contributed approximately 41.6%, 42.4% and 44.1% to net revenues in 2010, 2009, and 2008, respectively. No other country generated more than 10% of total revenues in those periods.

## Company Financials Fiscal Year Ended Dec. 31

| Per Share Data ($) | 2010 | 2009 | 2008 | 2007 | 2006 | 2005 | 2004 | 2003 | 2002 | 2001 |
|---|---|---|---|---|---|---|---|---|---|---|
| Tangible Book Value | 30.54 | 21.42 | 9.56 | 18.79 | 13.90 | 6.99 | NA | NA | NA | NA |
| Cash Flow | 15.23 | 12.32 | -1.50 | 8.37 | 1.10 | 3.77 | 3.61 | -2.71 | 2.40 | 2.96 |
| Earnings | 14.05 | 11.16 | -1.95 | 8.00 | 0.37 | 2.67 | 2.38 | -3.91 | 1.35 | 1.98 |
| S&P Core Earnings | 13.98 | 11.29 | 9.37 | 5.77 | 0.53 | 2.97 | 2.56 | 1.06 | NA | NA |
| Dividends | 0.60 | 0.60 | 0.60 | 0.54 | 0.09 | Nil | NA | NA | NA | NA |
| Payout Ratio | 4% | 5% | NM | 7% | 24% | Nil | NA | NA | NA | NA |
| Prices:High | 269.88 | 259.00 | 320.30 | 227.18 | 108.60 | NA | NA | NA | NA | NA |
| Prices:Low | 191.00 | 117.06 | 113.05 | 95.30 | 39.00 | NA | NA | NA | NA | NA |
| P/E Ratio:High | 19 | 23 | NM | 28 | NM | NA | NA | NA | NA | NA |
| P/E Ratio:Low | 14 | 10 | NM | 12 | NM | NA | NA | NA | NA | NA |

| Income Statement Analysis (Million $) | 2010 | 2009 | 2008 | 2007 | 2006 | 2005 | 2004 | 2003 | 2002 | 2001 |
|---|---|---|---|---|---|---|---|---|---|---|
| Revenue | 5,539 | 5,099 | 4,992 | 4,068 | 3,326 | 2,938 | 2,593 | 2,231 | 1,892 | 1,611 |
| Operating Income | 2,905 | 2,560 | 2,007 | 1,161 | 713 | 580 | 494 | 285 | 239 | 299 |
| Depreciation | 148 | 141 | 59.1 | 49.3 | 43.5 | 110 | 123 | 120 | 90.5 | 70.0 |
| Interest Expense | 52.0 | 115 | 104 | 57.3 | 61.2 | 70.2 | 69.7 | 62.9 | 9.89 | 9.55 |
| Pretax Income | 2,757 | 2,218 | -383 | 1,671 | 294 | 407 | 324 | -612 | 158 | 229 |
| Effective Tax Rate | NA | 34.1% | NM | 35.0% | 82.9% | 34.5% | 26.5% | 36.1% | 26.5% | 39.7% |
| Net Income | 1,847 | 1,463 | -254 | 1,086 | 50.2 | 267 | 238 | -391 | 116 | 142 |
| S&P Core Earnings | 1,833 | 1,471 | 1,230 | 782 | 72.8 | 297 | 257 | 107 | NA | NA |

| Balance Sheet & Other Financial Data (Million $) | 2010 | 2009 | 2008 | 2007 | 2006 | 2005 | 2004 | 2003 | 2002 | 2001 |
|---|---|---|---|---|---|---|---|---|---|---|
| Cash | 4,198 | 2,880 | 2,247 | 2,970 | 2,484 | 1,282 | 1,138 | 911 | 872 | 670 |
| Current Assets | 6,454 | 5,003 | 4,312 | 4,592 | 3,577 | 2,228 | 1,903 | 1,610 | 1,456 | 1,118 |
| Total Assets | 8,837 | 7,470 | 6,476 | 6,260 | 5,082 | 3,701 | 3,265 | 2,901 | 2,261 | 1,486 |
| Current Liabilities | 3,143 | 3,167 | 2,990 | 2,363 | 1,812 | 1,557 | 1,301 | 1,189 | 930 | 650 |
| Long Term Debt | NA | 21.6 | 19.4 | 150 | 230 | 229 | 230 | 230 | 80.1 | 80.1 |
| Common Equity | 5,205 | 3,504 | 1,927 | 3,027 | 2,364 | 1,169 | 975 | 699 | 1,023 | 607 |
| Total Capital | 5,227 | 3,533 | 2,026 | 3,253 | 2,665 | 1,403 | 1,209 | 933 | 1,104 | 687 |
| Capital Expenditures | 61.0 | 56.6 | 75.6 | 81.6 | 61.2 | 43.9 | 30.5 | 76.3 | 54.2 | 57.9 |
| Cash Flow | 1,995 | 1,604 | -195 | 1,135 | 150 | 377 | 361 | -271 | 207 | 212 |
| Current Ratio | 2.1 | 1.6 | 1.4 | 1.9 | 2.0 | 1.4 | 1.5 | 1.4 | 1.6 | 1.7 |
| % Long Term Debt of Capitalization | Nil | 0.6 | 1.0 | 4.6 | 8.8 | 16.4 | 19.0 | 24.6 | 7.3 | 11.7 |
| % Net Income of Revenue | 33.4 | 28.7 | NM | 26.7 | 1.5 | 9.1 | 9.2 | NM | 6.2 | 8.8 |
| % Return on Assets | 22.7 | 21.0 | NM | 19.2 | 1.1 | 7.7 | 7.7 | NM | 6.2 | NA |
| % Return on Equity | 42.4 | 53.9 | NM | 40.3 | 2.8 | 24.9 | 28.5 | NM | 14.3 | NA |

Data as orig reptd.; bef. results of disc opers/spec. items. Per share data adj. for stk. divs.; EPS diluted. E-Estimated. NA-Not Available. NM-Not Meaningful. NR-Not Ranked. UR-Under Review.

**Office:** 2000 Purchase Street, Purchase, NY 10577.
**Telephone:** 914-249-2000.
**Website:** http://www.mastercard.com
**Chrmn:** R.N. Haythornthwaite

**Pres & CEO:** A. Banga
**Vice Chrmn:** W.M. MacNee
**CFO:** M. Hund-Mejean
**CTO:** M. Manchisi

**Investor Contact:** B. Gasper (914-249-4565)
**Board Members:** A. Banga, S. Barzi, D. R. Carlucci, S. T. Edward, S. J. Freiberg, R. N. Haythornthwaite, N. J. Karch, W. M. MacNee, M. R. Olivie, R. Qureshi, J. O. Reyes, M. Schwartz, J. P. Tai

**Founded:** 1966
**Domicile:** Delaware
**Employees:** 5,600

**The McGraw-Hill Companies**

# Mattel Inc.

**STANDARD &POOR'S**

| **S&P Recommendation** HOLD ★★★☆☆ | **Price** $27.55 (as of Nov 25, 2011) | **12-Mo. Target Price** $30.00 | **Investment Style** Large-Cap Blend |
|---|---|---|---|

**GICS Sector** Consumer Discretionary
**Sub-Industry** Leisure Products

**Summary** This large toy company's brands and products include Barbie dolls, Fisher-Price toys, American Girl dolls and books, and Hot Wheels.

## Key Stock Statistics (Source S&P, Vickers, company reports)

| | | | | | | | |
|---|---|---|---|---|---|---|---|
| 52-Wk Range | $29.40– 22.70 | S&P Oper. EPS 2011**E** | 2.14 | Market Capitalization(B) | $9.330 | Beta | 0.93 |
| Trailing 12-Month EPS | $2.03 | S&P Oper. EPS 2012**E** | 2.35 | Yield (%) | 3.34 | S&P 3-Yr. Proj. EPS CAGR(%) | 12 |
| Trailing 12-Month P/E | 13.6 | P/E on S&P Oper. EPS 2011**E** | 12.9 | Dividend Rate/Share | $0.92 | S&P Credit Rating | BBB+ |
| $10K Invested 5 Yrs Ago | $14,940 | Common Shares Outstg. (M) | 338.6 | Institutional Ownership (%) | 93 | | |

## Price Performance

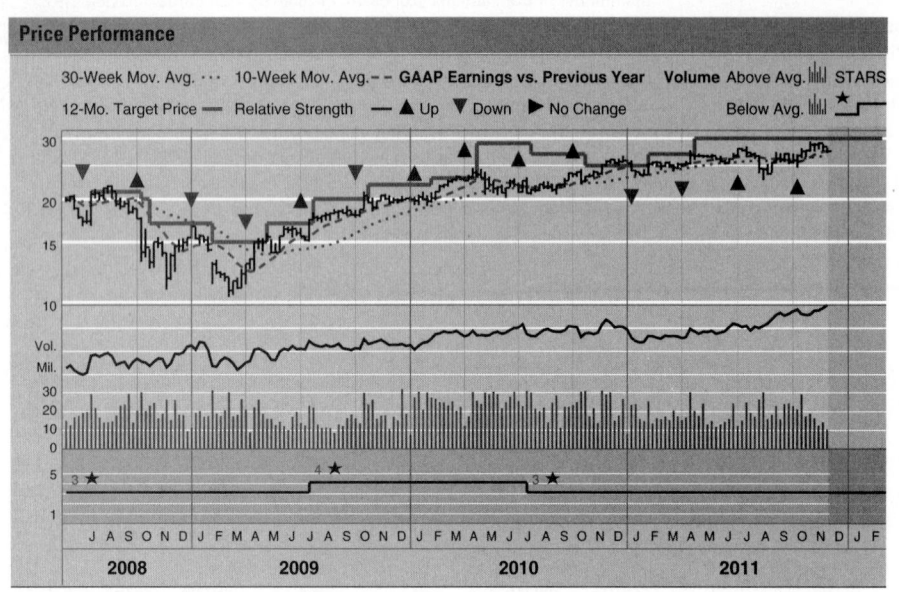

30-Week Mov. Avg. ···   10-Week Mov. Avg.– –   GAAP Earnings vs. Previous Year   Volume Above Avg. STARS
12-Mo. Target Price —   Relative Strength —   ▲ Up   ▼ Down   ► No Change   Below Avg.

Options: CBOE, P, Ph

Analysis prepared by Equity Analyst **Michael Souers** on Oct 18, 2011, when the stock traded at **$26.82**.

## Highlights

► Although we believe U.S. consumer spending will remain skittish due to high unemployment and economic uncertainty, we see global growth opportunities for MAT's portfolio of leading toy brands. We look for net sales to reach $6.35 billion in 2011 and $6.50 billion in 2012, with growth driven by momentum we see in core brands including Barbie, Fisher-Price, Hot Wheels and American Girl. We also expect top-line benefit from an improving price-value offering in Fisher-Price toys, growing popularity of Monster High, Thomas and Friends, Sing-a-ma-jigs!, and WWE Wrestling, and the introduction of new entertainment properties such as Green Lantern and Cars 2.

► We look for operating margin pressure from higher input costs and royalty expense and unfavorable foreign currency translation to ease as 2011 progresses as a result of recently taken price increases, supply chain efficiencies, and cost savings initiatives, including a projected decline in legal expenses.

► Factoring in planned share buybacks, we see EPS of $2.14 in 2011 and $2.35 in 2012, versus $1.86 in 2010 before a one-time tax benefit of $0.05.

## Investment Rationale/Risk

► In a still challenging selling environment, we see the company working to gain incremental market share through targeted investments in new products and marketing support. We also believe MAT is doing a good job of closely managing its cost structure. We note that cost-cutting efforts have been helping the bottom line, with the company realizing net savings of $48 million in 2010. MAT is targeting $150 million in incremental cost savings over the next two years. While our outlook for MAT is positive, we view the shares as appropriately valued at recent levels.

► Risks to our recommendation and target price include an uncertain toy retailing environment, an inability to reinvigorate the top line, continued cost pressures, and a material impact from toy recalls.

► Our 12-month target price of $30 is based on a blend of our historical and relative analyses. Our historical analysis suggests a value of $34, using a forward P/E of 14.5X, the five-year median, applied to our 2012 EPS estimate. Our peer analysis applies the group median of 11X, implying a value of $26.

## Qualitative Risk Assessment

| LOW | **MEDIUM** | HIGH |
|---|---|---|

Our risk assessment reflects our favorable view of MAT's leading market share position and strong balance sheet, offset by our negative view of intense industry rivalry and concentrated buying power of U.S. toy retailers.

## Quantitative Evaluations

**S&P Quality Ranking**                A-

| D | C | B- | B | B+ | **A-** | A | A+ |
|---|---|---|---|---|---|---|---|

**Relative Strength Rank**          **STRONG**

80

LOWEST = 1                          HIGHEST = 99

## Revenue/Earnings Data

**Revenue (Million $)**

| | 1Q | 2Q | 3Q | 4Q | Year |
|---|---|---|---|---|---|
| 2011 | 951.9 | 1,162 | 1,999 | -- | -- |
| 2010 | 880.1 | 1,019 | 1,833 | 2,125 | 5,856 |
| 2009 | 785.7 | 898.2 | 1,792 | 1,955 | 5,431 |
| 2008 | 919.3 | 1,112 | 1,946 | 1,940 | 5,918 |
| 2007 | 940.3 | 1,003 | 1,839 | 2,189 | 5,970 |
| 2006 | 793.3 | 957.7 | 1,790 | 2,109 | 5,650 |

**Earnings Per Share ($)**

| | | | | | |
|---|---|---|---|---|---|
| 2011 | 0.05 | 0.23 | 0.86 | E1.01 | E2.14 |
| 2010 | 0.07 | 0.14 | 0.77 | 0.89 | 1.86 |
| 2009 | -0.14 | 0.06 | 0.63 | 0.90 | 1.45 |
| 2008 | -0.13 | 0.03 | 0.66 | 0.49 | 1.05 |
| 2007 | 0.03 | 0.06 | 0.61 | 0.89 | 1.54 |
| 2006 | 0.08 | 0.10 | 0.62 | 0.75 | 1.53 |

Fiscal year ended Dec. 31. Next earnings report expected: NA. EPS Estimates based on S&P Operating Earnings; historical GAAP earnings are as reported.

## Dividend Data (Dates: mm/dd Payment Date: mm/dd/yy)

| Amount ($) | Date Decl. | Ex-Div. Date | Stk. of Record | Payment Date |
|---|---|---|---|---|
| 0.230 | 02/02 | 02/22 | 02/24 | 03/11/11 |
| 0.230 | 04/15 | 05/23 | 05/25 | 06/17/11 |
| 0.230 | 07/15 | 08/29 | 08/31 | 09/23/11 |
| 0.230 | 10/14 | 11/28 | 11/30 | 12/16/11 |

Dividends have been paid since 1990. Source: Company reports.

---

**Please read the Required Disclosures and Analyst Certification on the last page of this report.**

*The McGraw·Hill Companies*

# Mattel Inc.

STANDARD
&POOR'S

## Business Summary October 18, 2011

CORPORATE OVERVIEW. Mattel markets a wide variety of toy products on a worldwide basis. Brands are grouped in the following categories: Mattel Girls & Boys Brands, Fisher-Price Brands and American Girl Brands. Mattel brands include Barbie, Polly Pocket, Disney Classics, Monster High, Hot Wheels, Matchbox and Tyco R/C vehicles and playsets, CARS, Radica, Toy Story, WWE Wrestling, and Batman, among others. Fisher-Price brands include Fisher-Price, Power Wheels, Little People, Sing-a-ma-jigs, See 'N Say, Dora the Explorer, Thomas and Friends, and View-Master. American Girl is a direct marketer and retailer of dolls, accessories, and publications in the U.S. and Canada. Brand names include My American Girl and Bitty Baby.

MAT operates in the U.S. and internationally. Revenues from the international segment provided 46% of consolidated gross sales in 2010. In the international segment, the geographic breakdown was as follows: Europe, 52% of 2010 sales; Latin America, 30%; Asia Pacific, 11%; and Other, 7%.

CORPORATE STRATEGY. We believe a key element of MAT's growth strategy is to build its core brands through development of popular toys that are innovative and responsive to current play patterns and other trends. To further

leverage its brands, the company also pursues licensing arrangements and strategic partnerships, which we think helps to extend its portfolio of brands into areas outside of traditional toys. Royalty expense for 2010 was $245.9 million. Through its Global Cost Leadership program, which was launched during the second quarter of 2008, MAT has additionally been focused on realizing operating efficiencies and leveraging its global scale to improve profitability and cash flows.

MAT depends on a relatively small retail customer base to sell the majority of its products. In 2010, the company's three largest customers, Wal-Mart at $1.1 billion, Toys "R" Us at $800 million, and Target at $500 million, accounted for approximately 41% of MAT's gross sales of $6.4 billion. In our view, such buyer concentration reduces the bargaining power of MAT with regard to negotiating sales prices for its products, and raises the risk to the company if its customers have difficulty meeting financial obligations or selling products.

## Company Financials Fiscal Year Ended Dec. 31

| Per Share Data ($) | 2010 | 2009 | 2008 | 2007 | 2006 | 2005 | 2004 | 2003 | 2002 | 2001 |
|---|---|---|---|---|---|---|---|---|---|---|
| Tangible Book Value | 4.56 | 4.11 | 2.97 | 4.04 | 4.13 | 3.51 | 3.97 | 3.49 | 2.92 | 1.46 |
| Cash Flow | 2.33 | 1.93 | 1.51 | 1.97 | 1.98 | 1.44 | 1.79 | 1.63 | 1.47 | 1.31 |
| Earnings | 1.86 | 1.45 | 1.05 | 1.54 | 1.53 | 1.01 | 1.35 | 1.22 | 1.03 | 0.71 |
| S&P Core Earnings | 1.86 | 1.54 | 1.06 | 1.54 | 1.55 | 0.88 | 1.25 | 1.14 | 1.00 | 0.66 |
| Dividends | 0.83 | 0.75 | 0.75 | 0.75 | 0.65 | 0.50 | 0.45 | 0.40 | 0.05 | 0.05 |
| Payout Ratio | 45% | 52% | 71% | 49% | 42% | 50% | 33% | 33% | 5% | 7% |
| Prices:High | 26.70 | 21.05 | 21.99 | 29.71 | 23.98 | 21.64 | 19.79 | 23.20 | 22.36 | 19.92 |
| Prices:Low | 19.07 | 10.36 | 10.89 | 18.83 | 14.75 | 14.52 | 15.94 | 18.57 | 15.05 | 13.52 |
| P/E Ratio:High | 14 | 15 | 21 | 19 | 16 | 21 | 15 | 19 | 22 | 28 |
| P/E Ratio:Low | 10 | 7 | 10 | 12 | 10 | 14 | 12 | 15 | 15 | 19 |

| Income Statement Analysis (Million $) | | | | | | | | | | |
|---|---|---|---|---|---|---|---|---|---|---|
| Revenue | 5,856 | 5,431 | 5,918 | 5,970 | 5,650 | 5,179 | 5,103 | 4,960 | 4,885 | 4,804 |
| Operating Income | 1,068 | 964 | 761 | 1,011 | 901 | 840 | 913 | 974 | 934 | 881 |
| Depreciation | 166 | 170 | 170 | 170 | 172 | 175 | 182 | 184 | 192 | 263 |
| Interest Expense | 64.8 | 71.8 | 81.9 | 71.0 | 79.9 | 76.5 | 77.8 | 80.6 | 114 | 155 |
| Pretax Income | 847 | 660 | 488 | 703 | 684 | 652 | 696 | 741 | 621 | 430 |
| Effective Tax Rate | NA | 19.9% | 22.2% | 14.7% | 13.3% | 36.0% | 17.7% | 27.4% | 26.8% | 27.7% |
| Net Income | 685 | 529 | 380 | 600 | 593 | 417 | 573 | 538 | 455 | 311 |
| S&P Core Earnings | 679 | 555 | 380 | 601 | 600 | 359 | 531 | 502 | 439 | 288 |

| Balance Sheet & Other Financial Data (Million $) | | | | | | | | | | |
|---|---|---|---|---|---|---|---|---|---|---|
| Cash | 1,281 | 1,117 | 618 | 901 | 1,206 | 998 | 1,157 | 1,153 | 1,267 | 617 |
| Current Assets | 3,227 | 2,555 | 2,387 | 2,593 | 2,850 | 2,413 | 2,637 | 2,395 | 2,389 | 2,093 |
| Total Assets | 5,418 | 4,781 | 4,675 | 4,805 | 4,956 | 4,372 | 4,756 | 4,511 | 4,460 | 4,541 |
| Current Liabilities | 1,350 | 1,061 | 1,260 | 1,570 | 1,583 | 1,463 | 1,727 | 1,468 | 1,649 | 1,597 |
| Long Term Debt | 950 | 700 | 750 | 550 | 636 | 525 | 400 | 589 | 640 | 1,021 |
| Common Equity | 2,629 | 2,531 | 2,117 | 2,307 | 2,433 | 2,102 | 2,386 | 2,216 | 1,979 | 1,738 |
| Total Capital | 3,829 | 3,281 | 2,915 | 2,857 | 3,069 | 2,627 | 2,786 | 2,805 | 2,619 | 2,759 |
| Capital Expenditures | 137 | 120 | 199 | 147 | 64.1 | 137 | 144 | 101 | 167 | 101 |
| Cash Flow | 851 | 699 | 550 | 770 | 765 | 592 | 755 | 721 | 647 | 573 |
| Current Ratio | 2.4 | 2.4 | 1.9 | 1.7 | 1.8 | 1.6 | 1.5 | 1.6 | 1.4 | 1.3 |
| % Long Term Debt of Capitalization | 24.8 | 21.3 | 25.7 | 19.3 | 20.7 | 20.0 | 14.4 | 21.0 | 24.4 | 37.0 |
| % Net Income of Revenue | 11.7 | 9.7 | 6.4 | 10.0 | 10.5 | 8.1 | 11.2 | 10.8 | 9.3 | 6.5 |
| % Return on Assets | 13.4 | 11.2 | 8.0 | 12.3 | 12.7 | 9.1 | 12.4 | 12.0 | 10.1 | 7.0 |
| % Return on Equity | 26.6 | 22.8 | 17.2 | 25.3 | 26.2 | 18.6 | 24.9 | 25.6 | 24.5 | 19.8 |

Data as orig reptd.; bef. results of disc opers/spec. items. Per share data adj. for stk. divs.; EPS diluted. E-Estimated. NA-Not Available. NM-Not Meaningful. NR-Not Ranked. UR-Under Review.

**Office:** 333 Continental Boulevard, El Segundo, CA 90245-5012.
**Telephone:** 310-252-2000.
**Website:** http://www.mattel.com
**Chrmn & CEO:** R.A. Eckert

**COO:** B.G. Stockton
**EVP, Secy & General Counsel:** R. Normile
**SVP, Chief Acctg Officer & Cntlr:** H.S. Topham
**SVP & Treas:** M. Sadigh

**Board Members:** M. J. Dolan, R. A. Eckert, F. D. Fergusson, T. M. Friedman, D. Ng, V. M. Prabhu, A. L. Rich, D. A. Scarborough, C. A. Sinclair, G. C. Sullivan, K. B. White

**Founded:** 1945
**Domicile:** Delaware
**Employees:** 31,000

# McCormick & Co Inc

**STANDARD &POOR'S**

| S&P Recommendation | HOLD ★★★★☆ | Price $47.44 (as of Nov 25, 2011) | 12-Mo. Target Price $53.00 | Investment Style Large-Cap Growth |
| --- | --- | --- | --- | --- |

**GICS Sector** Consumer Staples
**Sub-Industry** Packaged Foods & Meats

**Summary** This company primarily produces spices, seasonings, and flavorings for the retail food, food service, and industrial markets. Trademarks include McCormick and Lawry's.

## Key Stock Statistics (Source S&P, Vickers, company reports)

| | | | | | | | |
| --- | --- | --- | --- | --- | --- | --- | --- |
| 52-Wk Range | $51.26–43.36 | S&P Oper. EPS 2011**E** | 2.79 | Market Capitalization(B) | $5.703 | Beta | 0.41 |
| Trailing 12-Month EPS | $2.80 | S&P Oper. EPS 2012**E** | 3.10 | Yield (%) | 2.61 | S&P 3-Yr. Proj. EPS CAGR(%) | 8 |
| Trailing 12-Month P/E | 16.9 | P/E on S&P Oper. EPS 2011**E** | 17.0 | Dividend Rate/Share | $1.24 | S&P Credit Rating | A- |
| $10K Invested 5 Yrs Ago | $13,927 | Common Shares Outstg. (M) | 132.7 | Institutional Ownership (%) | 78 | | |

## Price Performance

30-Week Mov. Avg. ···· 10-Week Mov. Avg. -- **GAAP Earnings vs. Previous Year**   **Volume** Above Avg. ▮▮▮ STARS
12-Mo. Target Price — Relative Strength   ▲ Up ▼ Down ► No Change   Below Avg. ▮▮▮ ★

Options: Ph

Analysis prepared by Equity Analyst **Tom Graves, CFA** on Oct 13, 2011, when the stock traded at **$46.99**.

## Highlights

➤ For FY 12 (Nov.), we look for sales to advance about 8% from the $3.7 billion projected for FY 11. We expect sales to be bolstered by recent acquisitions, price increases, sales of ethnic-related and new products, and expanded distribution. In both years, we estimate that MKC's consumer business segment will represent between 55% and 65% of total sales.

➤ In FY 11's fourth quarter, MKC acquired of ownership of Kamis, which was based in Poland and is a provider of spices, seasonings and mustards. Also, MKC entered into a joint venture with Kohinoor Foods Ltd. in India. MKC says that "Kohinoor" is a leading Indian national brand of basmati rice as well as other convenience food products.

➤ We estimate FY 12 EPS at $3.10, up from the $2.79 projected for FY 11, which includes $0.07 of transaction costs. We expect EPS accretion in FY 12 from some recent acquisitions. Also, FY 10's reported EPS of $2.75 includes a $0.10 third quarter benefit from the reversal of a tax accrual.

## Investment Rationale/Risk

➤ We expect additional cost savings in FY 11 and FY 12 from MKC's Comprehensive Continuous Improvement program. We look for incremental savings of at least $50 million related to this program in FY 11.

➤ Risks to our recommendation and target price include competitive pressures in MKC's businesses, consumer acceptance of new product introductions, consumer shifts to private label, and commodity cost inflation. In terms of corporate governance, the company has a dual class capital structure with unequal voting rights, which we view unfavorably.

➤ Our 12-month target price of $53 is based on a blend of our historical and relative analyses. Our historical analysis suggests a P/E of 19.4X, a moderate discount to a 10-year average, which, applied to our FY 11 EPS estimate, produces a value of about $54. Our peer analysis applies a P/E of 18.4X our estimate of calendar 2011 EPS, which is a premium to the average multiple of a small group of peers. This produces about a $52 prospective value for MKC.

## Qualitative Risk Assessment

| LOW | MEDIUM | HIGH |
| --- | --- | --- |

Our risk assessment reflects the relatively stable nature of the company's end markets, our view of its strong balance sheet and cash flow, and an S&P Quality Ranking of A+, which reflects historical growth of earnings and dividends.

## Quantitative Evaluations

**S&P Quality Ranking**  A+

| D | C | B- | B | B+ | A- | A | A+ |
| --- | --- | --- | --- | --- | --- | --- | --- |

**Relative Strength Rank**  STRONG

73

LOWEST = 1     HIGHEST = 99

## Revenue/Earnings Data

**Revenue (Million $)**

| | 1Q | 2Q | 3Q | 4Q | Year |
| --- | --- | --- | --- | --- | --- |
| 2011 | 782.8 | 883.7 | 920.4 | -- | -- |
| 2010 | 764.5 | 798.3 | 794.6 | 979.5 | 3,337 |
| 2009 | 718.5 | 757.3 | 791.7 | 924.5 | 3,192 |
| 2008 | 724.0 | 764.1 | 781.6 | 906.9 | 3,177 |
| 2007 | 652.6 | 687.2 | 716.2 | 860.1 | 2,916 |
| 2006 | 609.7 | 639.9 | 663.1 | 803.7 | 2,716 |

**Earnings Per Share ($)**

| | 1Q | 2Q | 3Q | 4Q | Year |
| --- | --- | --- | --- | --- | --- |
| 2011 | 0.57 | 0.55 | 0.69 | E0.98 | E2.79 |
| 2010 | 0.51 | 0.49 | 0.76 | 0.99 | 2.75 |
| 2009 | 0.44 | 0.38 | 0.57 | 0.88 | 2.27 |
| 2008 | 0.39 | 0.41 | 0.52 | 0.62 | 1.94 |
| 2007 | 0.33 | 0.31 | 0.43 | 0.67 | 1.73 |
| 2006 | 0.11 | 0.46 | 0.32 | 0.62 | 1.50 |

Fiscal year ended Nov. 30. Next earnings report expected: Late January. EPS Estimates based on S&P Operating Earnings; historical GAAP earnings are as reported.

## Dividend Data (Dates: mm/dd Payment Date: mm/dd/yy)

| Amount ($) | Date Decl. | Ex-Div. Date | Stk. of Record | Payment Date |
| --- | --- | --- | --- | --- |
| 0.280 | 03/30 | 04/07 | 04/11 | 04/25/11 |
| 0.280 | 06/28 | 07/07 | 07/11 | 07/25/11 |
| 0.280 | 09/27 | 10/05 | 10/10 | 10/24/11 |
| 0.310 | 11/22 | 12/28 | 12/30 | 01/13/12 |

Dividends have been paid since 1925. Source: Company reports.

---

**Please read the Required Disclosures and Analyst Certification on the last page of this report.**

**The McGraw-Hill Companies**

# McCormick & Co Inc

**STANDARD &POOR'S**

## Business Summary October 13, 2011

CORPORATE OVERVIEW. Founded by Willoughby M. McCormick in 1889, McCormick & Co. is a global leader in the manufacture, marketing and distribution of spices, herbs, seasonings, specialty foods and flavors to the entire food industry. The company markets its products to retail food, foodservice and industrial markets under a number of brands, including McCormick, Lawry's, Zatarain's, Thai Kitchen, Ducros, Schwartz and Vahine.

McCormick's Consumer segment, which accounted for 60% of sales and 79% of operating profits in FY 10 (Nov.), sells spices, herbs, extracts, seasoning blends, sauces, marinades and specialty foods to the consumer food market. The Industrial segment (40%, 21%) sells seasoning blends, natural spices and herbs, wet flavors, coating systems and compound flavors to multi-national food manufacturers and the food service industry, both directly and through distributors.

Sales to MKC's five largest customers in FY 10 accounted for about 34% of total sales, with the two largest customers - PepsiCo, Inc. and Wal-Mart Stores, Inc. - accounting for 10% and 11% of total sales, respectively.

In FY 10, the United States accounted for 61% of total sales (62% in FY 09) , Europe 21% (21%) and Other countries 18% (17%).

MARKET PROFILE. Although we think MKC has impressive leading market shares in the relevant spices and seasonings categories of MKC's four major geographic markets (U.S., Canada, U.K. and France), there is a constant threat from private label products. While MKC itself accounts for about half of the private label business in the U.S., this business carries lower margins than MKC's branded business.

## Company Financials Fiscal Year Ended Nov. 30

| Per Share Data ($) | 2010 | 2009 | 2008 | 2007 | 2006 | 2005 | 2004 | 2003 | 2002 | 2001 |
|---|---|---|---|---|---|---|---|---|---|---|
| Tangible Book Value | NM | NM | NM | NM | NM | NM | 0.45 | 0.28 | 0.62 | NM |
| Cash Flow | 3.45 | 2.98 | 2.50 | 2.36 | 2.14 | 2.10 | 2.11 | 1.85 | 1.73 | 1.57 |
| Earnings | 2.75 | 2.27 | 1.94 | 1.73 | 1.50 | 1.56 | 1.52 | 1.40 | 1.26 | 1.05 |
| S&P Core Earnings | 2.77 | 2.20 | 1.70 | 1.81 | 1.40 | 1.51 | 1.43 | 1.28 | 1.12 | 0.90 |
| Dividends | 1.04 | 0.96 | 0.88 | 0.80 | 0.72 | 0.64 | 0.56 | 0.46 | 0.37 | 0.40 |
| Payout Ratio | 38% | 42% | 45% | 46% | 48% | 41% | 37% | 33% | 29% | 38% |
| Prices:High | 47.83 | 36.80 | 42.06 | 39.73 | 39.82 | 39.14 | 38.94 | 30.21 | 27.25 | 23.27 |
| Prices:Low | 35.40 | 28.08 | 28.21 | 33.89 | 30.09 | 28.95 | 28.60 | 21.71 | 20.70 | 17.00 |
| P/E Ratio:High | 17 | 16 | 22 | 23 | 27 | 25 | 26 | 22 | 22 | 22 |
| P/E Ratio:Low | 13 | 12 | 15 | 20 | 20 | 19 | 19 | 16 | 16 | 16 |

| Income Statement Analysis (Million $) | | | | | | | | | | |
|---|---|---|---|---|---|---|---|---|---|---|
| Revenue | 3,337 | 3,192 | 3,177 | 2,916 | 2,716 | 2,592 | 2,526 | 2,270 | 2,320 | 2,372 |
| Operating Income | 607 | 577 | 496 | 468 | 429 | 429 | 402 | 366 | 353 | 324 |
| Depreciation | 95.1 | 94.3 | 73.5 | 83.0 | 86.8 | 74.6 | 72.0 | 65.3 | 66.8 | 73.0 |
| Interest Expense | 49.3 | 52.8 | 57.6 | 61.0 | 53.7 | 48.2 | 41.0 | 38.6 | 43.6 | 52.9 |
| Pretax Income | 488 | 433 | 356 | 302 | 270 | 316 | 308 | 286 | 257 | 212 |
| Effective Tax Rate | NA | 30.7% | 28.2% | 30.4% | 24.0% | 30.6% | 28.9% | 29.1% | 28.9% | 29.7% |
| Net Income | 370 | 300 | 256 | 230 | 202 | 215 | 215 | 199 | 180 | 147 |
| S&P Core Earnings | 373 | 291 | 224 | 240 | 189 | 208 | 202 | 182 | 158 | 126 |

| Balance Sheet & Other Financial Data (Million $) | | | | | | | | | | |
|---|---|---|---|---|---|---|---|---|---|---|
| Cash | 50.8 | 56.5 | 38.9 | 46.0 | 49.0 | 30.3 | 70.3 | 25.1 | 47.3 | 31.3 |
| Current Assets | 1,016 | 970 | 968 | 983 | 899 | 800 | 864 | 762 | 725 | 636 |
| Total Assets | 3,420 | 3,388 | 3,220 | 2,788 | 2,568 | 2,273 | 2,370 | 2,148 | 1,931 | 1,772 |
| Current Liabilities | 835 | 818 | 1,034 | 861 | 780 | 699 | 773 | 713 | 673 | 714 |
| Long Term Debt | 780 | 875 | 885 | 574 | 570 | 464 | 465 | 449 | 454 | 454 |
| Common Equity | 1,454 | 1,335 | 1,055 | 1,085 | 933 | 800 | 890 | 755 | 592 | 463 |
| Total Capital | 2,243 | 2,225 | 1,988 | 1,669 | 1,575 | 1,293 | 1,386 | 1,226 | 1,046 | 943 |
| Capital Expenditures | 89.0 | 82.4 | 85.8 | 79.0 | 84.8 | 73.8 | 69.8 | 91.6 | 111 | 112 |
| Cash Flow | 465 | 394 | 329 | 313 | 289 | 290 | 287 | 265 | 247 | 220 |
| Current Ratio | 1.2 | 1.2 | 0.9 | 1.1 | 1.2 | 1.1 | 1.1 | 1.1 | 1.1 | 0.9 |
| % Long Term Debt of Capitalization | 34.8 | 39.3 | 44.5 | 34.3 | 37.8 | 35.9 | 33.6 | 36.6 | 43.4 | 48.2 |
| % Net Income of Revenue | 11.1 | 9.4 | 8.1 | 7.8 | 7.4 | 8.3 | 8.5 | 8.8 | 7.8 | 6.2 |
| % Return on Assets | 10.9 | 9.1 | 8.5 | 8.5 | 8.4 | 9.3 | 9.5 | 9.8 | 9.7 | 8.5 |
| % Return on Equity | 26.6 | 25.1 | 23.9 | 22.7 | 23.3 | 25.4 | 26.1 | 29.6 | 34.1 | 35.7 |

Data as orig reptd.; bef. results of disc opers/spec. items. Per share data adj. for stk. divs.; EPS diluted. E-Estimated. NA-Not Available. NM-Not Meaningful. NR-Not Ranked. UR-Under Review.

**Office:** 18 Loveton Circle, PO Box 6000, Sparks, MD 21152-6000.
**Telephone:** 410-771-7301.
**Website:** http://www.mccormickcorporation.com
**Chrmn, Pres & CEO:** A.D. Wilson

**EVP & CFO:** G.M. Stetz, Jr.
**SVP, Chief Acctg Officer & Cntlr:** K.A. Kelly, Jr.
**SVP & Treas:** P.C. Beard
**CSO:** H. Faridi

**Investor Contact:** J. Brooks (410-771-7244)
**Board Members:** J. P. Bilbrey, J. T. Brady, J. Fitzpatrick, F. A. Hrabowski, III, P. Little, M. D. Mangan, M. M. Preston, G. A. Roche, G. M. Stetz, Jr., W. E. Stevens, A. D. Wilson

**Founded:** 1889
**Domicile:** Maryland
**Employees:** 7,500

The McGraw-Hill Companies

# McDonald's Corp

**STANDARD &POOR'S**

| S&P Recommendation | **STRONG BUY** ★★★★★ | Price<br>$92.10 (as of Nov 25, 2011) | 12-Mo. Target Price<br>$109.00 | Investment Style<br>Large-Cap Growth |
|---|---|---|---|---|

**GICS Sector** Consumer Discretionary
**Sub-Industry** Restaurants

**Summary** McDonald's is the largest fast-food restaurant company in the world, with about 33,144 restaurants in 119 countries.

## Key Stock Statistics (Source S&P, Vickers, company reports)

| | | | | | | | |
|---|---|---|---|---|---|---|---|
| 52-Wk Range | $95.45– 72.14 | S&P Oper. EPS 2011**E** | 5.23 | Market Capitalization(B) | $94.238 | Beta | 0.47 |
| Trailing 12-Month EPS | $5.10 | S&P Oper. EPS 2012**E** | 5.78 | Yield (%) | 3.04 | S&P 3-Yr. Proj. EPS CAGR(%) | 10 |
| Trailing 12-Month P/E | 18.1 | P/E on S&P Oper. EPS 2011**E** | 17.6 | Dividend Rate/Share | $2.80 | S&P Credit Rating | A |
| $10K Invested 5 Yrs Ago | $25,380 | Common Shares Outstg. (M) | 1,023.2 | Institutional Ownership (%) | 69 | | |

## Price Performance

30-Week Mov. Avg. · · · 10-Week Mov. Avg. - - GAAP Earnings vs. Previous Year   Volume Above Avg. STARS
12-Mo. Target Price — Relative Strength — ▲ Up ▼ Down ► No Change   Below Avg.

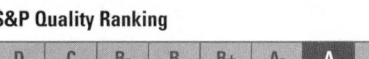

Options: ASE, CBOE, P, Ph

Analysis prepared by Equity Analyst **Jim Yin, CFA** on Nov 04, 2011, when the stock traded at **$93.81**.

## Qualitative Risk Assessment

| LOW | **MEDIUM** | HIGH |
|---|---|---|

McDonald's competes in the global fast food industry, where it arguably has the most dominant brand name presence. However, results can vary widely due to fluctuations in food costs, competitive discounting, and exchange rate volatility. Our risk assessment reflects our view that global economic weakness has started to subside, although recovery prospects remain uncertain.

## Quantitative Evaluations

**S&P Quality Ranking**   A

| D | C | B- | B | B+ | A- | **A** | A+ |
|---|---|---|---|---|---|---|---|

**Relative Strength Rank**   **STRONG**

86

LOWEST = 1          HIGHEST = 99

## Highlights

➤ We expect total revenues to rise 6.7% in 2012, following a 12% advance seen for 2011. We see global comparable sales rising 3.7% and the number of restaurants up 3.0% in 2012. While we project low- to mid- single digit growth in systemwide sales in the U.S. and Europe, we think they are likely to climb about 10% in Asia Pacific/Middle East/Africa. In a slower global economy, we believe MCD will benefit from its value offerings. We also see sales helped by its ongoing restaurant modernization efforts.

➤ We look for company-operated restaurant margins in 2012 of 19.4%, up from 18.8% seen for 2011. We think food and other commodity inflation will moderate in 2012, following a steep rise in 2011. We also think labor costs will be restrained and that selling, general and administrative expenses will decline as a percentage of revenues due to economies of scale. We see operating margins at 32% in 2011 and 2012.

➤ We project EPS of $5.23 and $5.78 for 2011 and 2012, respectively, compared to $4.58 in 2010. Besides higher revenues, we see EPS growth coming from fewer shares outstanding as a result of MCD's share repurchase program.

## Investment Rationale/Risk

➤ Although we are concerned about a slowdown in the global economy, we believe consumers are still willing to make small discretionary purchases. We also think MCD can gain market share with its wide menu offerings, as some customers trade down. We are positive on the company's new menu items, including frappes and smoothies. We see significant growth opportunities in international markets, in particular in Asia Pacific, the Middle East and Africa. Although food input costs have been rising, we expect food inflation to decelerate in 2012.

➤ Risks to our recommendation and target price include a significant slowdown in the global economy, higher-than-expected food costs, poor customer acceptance of MCD's new menu offerings, and exchange rate risk in light of MCD's substantial international business.

➤ Our 12-month target price of $109 is based on a multiple of 19X our 2012 EPS estimate of $5.78, in line with the peer group average. The 2011 fourth-quarter increase in the annual dividend rate to $2.80 provides a 3.0% dividend yield at the recent stock price.

## Revenue/Earnings Data

### Revenue (Million $)

| | 1Q | 2Q | 3Q | 4Q | Year |
|---|---|---|---|---|---|
| 2011 | 6,112 | 6,905 | 7,166 | -- | -- |
| 2010 | 5,610 | 5,946 | 6,305 | 6,214 | 24,075 |
| 2009 | 5,077 | 5,647 | 6,047 | 5,973 | 22,745 |
| 2008 | 5,615 | 6,075 | 6,267 | 5,565 | 23,522 |
| 2007 | 5,293 | 5,839 | 5,901 | 5,754 | 22,787 |
| 2006 | 4,914 | 5,367 | 5,671 | 5,634 | 21,586 |

### Earnings Per Share ($)

| | 1Q | 2Q | 3Q | 4Q | Year |
|---|---|---|---|---|---|
| 2011 | 1.15 | 1.35 | 1.45 | E1.30 | E5.23 |
| 2010 | 1.00 | 1.13 | 1.29 | 1.16 | 4.58 |
| 2009 | 0.87 | 0.98 | 1.15 | 1.11 | 4.11 |
| 2008 | 0.81 | 1.04 | 1.05 | 0.87 | 3.76 |
| 2007 | 0.63 | -0.59 | 0.83 | 1.06 | 1.93 |
| 2006 | 0.46 | 0.56 | 0.67 | 0.61 | 2.30 |

Fiscal year ended Dec. 31. Next earnings report expected: NA. EPS Estimates based on S&P Operating Earnings; historical GAAP earnings are as reported.

## Dividend Data (Dates: mm/dd Payment Date: mm/dd/yy)

| Amount ($) | Date Decl. | Ex-Div. Date | Stk. of Record | Payment Date |
|---|---|---|---|---|
| 0.610 | 01/27 | 02/25 | 03/01 | 03/15/11 |
| 0.610 | 05/19 | 05/27 | 06/01 | 06/15/11 |
| 0.610 | 07/22 | 08/30 | 09/01 | 09/16/11 |
| 0.700 | 09/22 | 11/29 | 12/01 | 12/15/11 |

Dividends have been paid since 1976. Source: Company reports.

---

**Please read the Required Disclosures and Analyst Certification on the last page of this report.**

The **McGraw·Hill** Companies

# McDonald's Corp

**STANDARD &POOR'S**

## Business Summary November 04, 2011

CORPORATE OVERVIEW. With one of the world's most widely known brand names, McDonald's operated and franchised 33,144 restaurants around the world at the end of September 2011. Systemwide sales totaled $76.7 billion in 2010, up from $72.4 billion in 2009 and $70.7 billion in 2008.

In the U.S., the McDonald's chain leads the $162 billion quick-service restaurant industry. With U.S. systemwide sales of $32 billion, its domestic business is several times larger than its closest competitors, Burger King and Wendy's Old Fashioned Hamburgers. MCD's international segment has supplied much of its earnings growth over the past two decades, and, in 2010, contributed 54% of operating income (before corporate expenses and one-time charges). All restaurants are operated by MCD, franchisees, or affiliates under joint venture agreements.

In August 2007, the company completed the sale of its existing businesses in Brazil, Argentina, Mexico, Puerto Rico, Venezuela and 13 other countries in Latin America and the Caribbean to a developmental licensee (the Latam transaction). The company recorded impairment charges totaling approximately $1.7 billion, substantially all of which was non-cash. The charges included approximately $892 million for the difference between the net book value of the Latam business and the approximately $680 million in cash proceeds,

and $773 million in foreign currency translation losses previously included in comprehensive income.

CORPORATE STRATEGY. In 2011, the company will continue its "Plan to Win" corporate strategy that it commenced in 2003. MCD's stated operating priorities include fixing operating inadequacies in existing restaurants; taking a more integrated and focused approach to growth, with an emphasis on increasing sales, margins and returns in existing restaurants; and ensuring the correct operating structure and resources, aligned behind focusing priorities that create benefits for its customers and restaurants.

A significant part of the new corporate strategy was to de-emphasize Partner Brands concepts in order to focus on the McDonald's brand. In 2006 and 2007, MCD disposed of interests in the Chipotle Mexican Grill restaurant concept as well as the Boston Market chain, and it sold its minority interest in Pret a Manger in 2008.

## Company Financials Fiscal Year Ended Dec. 31

| Per Share Data ($) | 2010 | 2009 | 2008 | 2007 | 2006 | 2005 | 2004 | 2003 | 2002 | 2001 |
|---|---|---|---|---|---|---|---|---|---|---|
| Tangible Book Value | 11.43 | 10.78 | 10.00 | 11.14 | 11.01 | 10.45 | 9.74 | 8.18 | 6.88 | 6.30 |
| Cash Flow | 5.76 | 5.21 | 4.78 | 2.87 | 3.29 | 3.05 | 2.73 | 2.08 | 1.59 | 2.08 |
| Earnings | 4.58 | 4.11 | 3.76 | 1.93 | 2.30 | 2.04 | 1.79 | 1.18 | 0.77 | 1.25 |
| S&P Core Earnings | 4.53 | 3.99 | 3.60 | 1.88 | 2.28 | 2.00 | 1.66 | 0.96 | 0.51 | 1.01 |
| Dividends | 2.26 | 2.05 | 1.63 | 1.50 | 1.00 | 0.67 | 0.55 | 0.40 | 0.24 | 0.23 |
| Payout Ratio | 49% | 50% | 43% | 78% | 43% | 33% | 31% | 34% | 31% | 18% |
| Prices:High | 80.94 | 64.75 | 67.00 | 63.69 | 44.68 | 35.69 | 32.96 | 27.01 | 30.72 | 35.06 |
| Prices:Low | 61.06 | 50.44 | 45.79 | 42.31 | 31.73 | 27.36 | 24.54 | 12.12 | 15.17 | 24.75 |
| P/E Ratio:High | 18 | 16 | 18 | 33 | 19 | 17 | 18 | 23 | 40 | 28 |
| P/E Ratio:Low | 13 | 12 | 12 | 22 | 14 | 13 | 14 | 10 | 20 | 20 |
| **Income Statement Analysis** (Million $) | | | | | | | | | | |
| Revenue | 24,075 | 22,745 | 23,522 | 22,787 | 21,586 | 20,460 | 19,065 | 17,141 | 15,406 | 14,870 |
| Operating Income | 8,560 | 7,774 | 7,445 | 6,683 | 5,829 | 5,243 | 4,742 | 3,980 | 3,164 | 3,983 |
| Depreciation | 1,276 | 1,216 | 1,162 | 1,145 | 1,250 | 1,250 | 1,201 | 1,148 | 1,051 | 1,086 |
| Interest Expense | 451 | 473 | 535 | 417 | 402 | 356 | 358 | 388 | 360 | 452 |
| Pretax Income | 7,000 | 6,487 | 6,158 | 3,572 | 4,166 | 3,702 | 3,202 | 2,346 | 1,662 | 2,330 |
| Effective Tax Rate | NA | 29.8% | 30.0% | 34.6% | 31.0% | 29.7% | 28.9% | 35.7% | 40.3% | 29.8% |
| Net Income | 4,946 | 4,551 | 4,313 | 2,335 | 2,873 | 2,602 | 2,279 | 1,508 | 992 | 1,637 |
| S&P Core Earnings | 4,895 | 4,416 | 4,127 | 2,277 | 2,848 | 2,540 | 2,100 | 1,226 | 667 | 1,328 |
| **Balance Sheet & Other Financial Data** (Million $) | | | | | | | | | | |
| Cash | 2,388 | 1,796 | 2,063 | 1,981 | 2,136 | 4,260 | 1,380 | 493 | 330 | 418 |
| Current Assets | 4,369 | 3,416 | 3,518 | 3,582 | 3,625 | 5,850 | 2,858 | 1,885 | 1,715 | 1,819 |
| Total Assets | 31,975 | 30,225 | 28,462 | 29,392 | 29,024 | 29,989 | 27,838 | 25,525 | 23,971 | 22,535 |
| Current Liabilities | 2,925 | 2,989 | 2,538 | 4,499 | 3,008 | 4,036 | 3,521 | 2,486 | 2,422 | 2,248 |
| Long Term Debt | 11,497 | 10,564 | 10,186 | 7,310 | 8,417 | 8,937 | 8,357 | 9,343 | 9,704 | 8,556 |
| Common Equity | 14,634 | 14,034 | 13,383 | 15,280 | 15,458 | 15,146 | 14,202 | 11,982 | 10,281 | 9,488 |
| Total Capital | 26,140 | 24,616 | 24,514 | 23,551 | 24,941 | 25,060 | 23,340 | 22,340 | 20,988 | 19,156 |
| Capital Expenditures | 2,136 | 1,952 | 2,136 | 1,947 | 1,742 | 1,607 | 1,419 | 1,307 | 2,004 | 1,906 |
| Cash Flow | 6,223 | 5,767 | 5,475 | 3,480 | 4,123 | 3,852 | 3,480 | 2,656 | 2,043 | 2,723 |
| Current Ratio | 1.5 | 1.1 | 1.4 | 0.8 | 1.2 | 1.4 | 0.8 | 0.8 | 0.7 | 0.8 |
| % Long Term Debt of Capitalization | 44.0 | Nil | 41.6 | 31.0 | 33.7 | 35.7 | 35.8 | 41.8 | 46.2 | 44.7 |
| % Net Income of Revenue | 20.6 | 20.0 | 18.3 | 10.3 | 13.3 | 12.7 | 12.0 | 8.8 | 6.4 | 11.0 |
| % Return on Assets | NA | NA | NA | 8.9 | 9.7 | 9.0 | 8.5 | 6.1 | 4.3 | 7.4 |
| % Return on Equity | NA | NA | NA | 15.2 | 18.8 | 17.7 | 17.4 | 13.5 | 10.0 | 17.5 |

Data as orig reptd.; bef. results of disc opers/spec. items. Per share data adj. for stk. divs.; EPS diluted. E-Estimated. NA-Not Available. NM-Not Meaningful. NR-Not Ranked. UR-Under Review.

**Office:** one Mcdonald's Plaza, Oak Brook, IL 60523.
**Telephone:** 630-623-3000.
**Website:** http://www.mcdonalds.com
**Chrmn:** A.J. McKenna

**Pres & COO:** D. Thompson
**Vice Chrmn & CEO:** J.A. Skinner
**EVP, Secy & General Counsel:** G. Santona
**SVP & Cntlr:** K.M. Ozan

**Investor Contact:** M.K. Shaw (630-623-7559)
**Board Members:** S. E. Arnold, R. A. Eckert, E. Hernandez, Jr., J. P. Jackson, R. H. Lenny, W. E. Massey, A. J. McKenna, C. D. McMillan, S. A. Penrose, J. W. Rogers, Jr., J. A. Skinner, R. W. Stone, D. Thompson, M. D. White

**Founded:** 1948
**Domicile:** Delaware
**Employees:** 400,000

*The McGraw·Hill Companies*

# McGraw-Hill Companies Inc. (The)

STANDARD
&POOR'S

| S&P Recommendation | NOT RANKED | Price $40.54 (as of Nov 25, 2011) | Investment Style Large-Cap Growth |
|---|---|---|---|

**GICS Sector** Consumer Discretionary
**Sub-Industry** Publishing

**Summary** This leading global financial information and education company plans to spin off its education business to shareholders.

## Key Stock Statistics (Source S&P, Vickers, company reports)

| | | | | | | | | |
|---|---|---|---|---|---|---|---|---|
| 52-Wk Range | $46.99– 33.80 | S&P Oper. EPS 2011**E** | NA | Market Capitalization(B) | $12.215 | Beta | | 1.07 |
| Trailing 12-Month EPS | $2.76 | S&P Oper. EPS 2012**E** | NA | Yield (%) | 2.47 | S&P 3-Yr. Proj. EPS CAGR(%) | | |
| Trailing 12-Month P/E | 14.7 | P/E on S&P Oper. EPS 2011**E** | NA | Dividend Rate/Share | $1.00 | S&P Credit Rating | | NR |
| $10K Invested 5 Yrs Ago | $7,037 | Common Shares Outstg. (M) | 301.3 | Institutional Ownership (%) | 87 | | | |

## Price Performance

30-Week Mov. Avg. · · · 10-Week Mov. Avg. - - **GAAP Earnings vs. Previous Year**  Volume Above Avg. STARS
12-Mo. Target Price — Relative Strength — ▲ Up ▼ Down ► No Change  Below Avg.

Options: ASE, CBOE, P, Ph

Analysis prepared by Equity Analyst **Tom Graves, CFA** on Nov 09, 2011, when the stock traded at **$42.21**.

## Highlights

► In September 2011, in an attempt to increase shareholder value, MHP proposed, subject to approvals, a tax-free spin-off of its education business to MHP shareholders by the end of 2012. Following the spin-off, the remaining Mc-Graw-Hill business would include such capital and commodities markets brands as Standard & Poor's, S&P Indices, the newly launched S&P Capital IQ, and Platts. MHP also said it is focusing on reducing costs to ensure efficient operating structures for the new companies, and accelerating share repurchases.

► In the 2011 third quarter, MHP's overall seg-ment profit was down 4.0%, including declines of 12% at McGraw-Hill Education and 9.7% at Standard & Poor's, and a 31% rise at McGraw-Hill Financial. In October 2011, MHP said it ex-pects 2011 EPS from continuing operations of $2.81 to $2.86.

► In November 2011, MHP and CME Group an-nounced an agreement to establish a new joint venture. MHP would contribute its S&P Indices business, and the CME Group/Dow Jones joint venture would contribute the Dow Jones Index-es business, to create S&P/Dow Jones Indices, of which MHP would own 73%.

## Investment Rationale/Risk

► In 2011's first nine months, MHP spent about $199 million on acquisitions, including BENTEK Energy, which is now part of Platts. In July 2011, MHP acquired Steel Business Briefing Group, a privately held U.K. provider of news, pricing and analytics to the global steel market. In October 2011, MHP projected 2011 free cash flow, after dividends, of about $750 million. At September 30, 2011, MHP had cash and equiva-lents of about $1.5 billion, and gross debt of about $1.2 billion.

► MHP noted in its 2010 10-K report filed with the SEC in February 2011 that possible risk factors for the company include exposure to litigation, changes in the volume of debt securities issued in capital markets, possible loss of market share or revenue due to competition or regula-tion, and changes in educational funding.

► S&P Capital IQ is a part of McGraw-Hill Finan-cial, and provides no EPS estimates, target price or recommendation for MHP.

## Qualitative Risk Assessment

A Qualitative Risk Assessment is not available for this company.

## Quantitative Evaluations

**S&P Quality Ranking**                        NR

| D | C | B- | B | B+ | A- | A | A+ |
|---|---|---|---|---|---|---|---|

**Relative Strength Rank**          MODERATE

56

LOWEST = 1                              HIGHEST = 99

## Revenue/Earnings Data

### Revenue (Million $)

| | 1Q | 2Q | 3Q | 4Q | Year |
|---|---|---|---|---|---|
| 2011 | 1,282 | 1,581 | 1,908 | -- | -- |
| 2010 | 1,190 | 1,500 | 1,980 | 1,530 | 6,200 |
| 2009 | 1,148 | 1,465 | 1,876 | 1,462 | 5,952 |
| 2008 | 1,218 | 1,673 | 2,049 | 1,415 | 6,355 |
| 2007 | 1,296 | 1,718 | 2,188 | 1,570 | 6,772 |
| 2006 | 1,141 | 1,528 | 1,993 | 1,594 | 6,255 |

### Earnings Per Share ($)

| | | | | | |
|---|---|---|---|---|---|
| 2011 | 0.39 | 1.23 | 1.23 | -- | -- |
| 2010 | 0.33 | 0.61 | 1.23 | 0.50 | 2.65 |
| 2009 | 0.20 | 0.52 | 1.07 | 0.53 | 2.33 |
| 2008 | 0.25 | 0.66 | 1.23 | 0.37 | 2.51 |
| 2007 | 0.40 | 0.79 | 1.34 | 0.43 | 2.94 |
| 2006 | 0.20 | 0.60 | 1.06 | 0.56 | 2.40 |

Fiscal year ended Dec. 31. Next earnings report expected: Early February. EPS Estimates based on S&P Operating Earnings; historical GAAP earnings are as reported.

## Dividend Data (Dates: mm/dd Payment Date: mm/dd/yy)

| Amount ($) | Date Decl. | Ex-Div. Date | Stk. of Record | Payment Date |
|---|---|---|---|---|
| 0.250 | 01/19 | 02/22 | 02/24 | 03/10/11 |
| 0.250 | 04/27 | 05/24 | 05/26 | 06/10/11 |
| 0.250 | 07/29 | 08/24 | 08/26 | 09/12/11 |
| 0.250 | 10/31 | 11/23 | 11/28 | 12/12/11 |

Dividends have been paid since 1937. Source: Company reports.

---

**Please read the Required Disclosures and Analyst Certification on the last page of this report.**

The McGraw-Hill Companies

# McGraw-Hill Companies Inc. (The)

**STANDARD &POOR'S**

## Business Summary November 09, 2011

CORPORATE OVERVIEW. The McGraw-Hill Companies, Inc. is a leading provider of information products and services to business, professional and education markets worldwide. The company believes that through acquisitions, new product and service development, and a strong commitment to customer service, many of its business units have grown to be leaders in their respective fields. Well known brands include Standard & Poor's and Platts. In 2010, 71% of MHP's total revenue came from the U.S..

The Standard & Poor's segment (27% of revenues, before intersegment elimination, and 48% of segment operating profit in 2010) is a leading provider of credit ratings. S&P provides services primarily to investors, corporations, governments, banks, insurance companies, asset managers, and other debt issuers.

In September 2011, MHP's new McGraw-Hill Financial reporting segment (19%, 20%) announced that it will market its combination of multi-asset-class data, benchmarks and analytics products under two master brands, S&P Capital IQ and S&P Indices. S&P Capital IQ is expected to be the new master brand name for integrated desktop solutions, enterprise services and proprietary market, company and fund research.

In November 2011, MHP and CME Group announced an agreement to establish a new joint venture in the index business. MHP would contribute its S&P Indices business, and the CME Group/Dow Jones joint venture would contribute the Dow Jones Indexes business, to create S&P/Dow Jones Indices, of which MHP would own 73%, CME Group would own 24.4% through its affiliates, and Dow Jones would own 2.6%. S&P/Dow Jones Indices was expected to be operational in the first half of 2012, subject to regulatory approval and customary closing conditions.

McGraw-Hill Education (39%, 23%) operates in the elementary and high school, college and university, professional, international and adult education markets. In the el-hi market, MHP sells textbooks (print and digital versions) and supplementary material, and provides assessment and reporting services. In the college and university and international markets, MHP sells eLearning platforms, textbooks and other resources to higher education institutions.

## Company Financials Fiscal Year Ended Dec. 31

| Per Share Data ($) | 2010 | 2009 | 2008 | 2007 | 2006 | 2005 | 2004 | 2003 | 2002 | 2001 |
|---|---|---|---|---|---|---|---|---|---|---|
| Tangible Book Value | NM | NM | NM | NM | 1.00 | 2.04 | 2.72 | 2.24 | 0.94 | 0.09 |
| Cash Flow | 3.20 | 2.86 | 3.07 | 3.41 | 2.85 | 3.21 | 2.98 | 2.84 | 1.71 | 2.04 |
| Earnings | 2.65 | 2.33 | 2.51 | 2.94 | 2.40 | 2.21 | 1.96 | 1.79 | 1.48 | 0.96 |
| S&P Core Earnings | 2.62 | 2.29 | 2.29 | 2.89 | 2.38 | 2.05 | 1.80 | 1.44 | 1.15 | 0.60 |
| Dividends | 0.94 | 0.90 | 0.88 | 0.82 | 0.73 | 0.66 | 0.60 | 0.54 | 0.51 | 0.49 |
| Payout Ratio | 36% | 39% | 35% | 28% | 30% | 30% | 31% | 30% | 34% | 51% |
| Prices:High | 39.45 | 35.24 | 47.13 | 72.50 | 69.25 | 53.97 | 46.06 | 35.00 | 34.85 | 35.44 |
| Prices:Low | 26.95 | 17.22 | 17.15 | 43.46 | 46.37 | 40.51 | 34.55 | 25.87 | 25.36 | 24.35 |
| P/E Ratio:High | 15 | 15 | 19 | 25 | 29 | 24 | 23 | 20 | 24 | 37 |
| P/E Ratio:Low | 10 | 7 | 7 | 15 | 19 | 18 | 18 | 14 | 17 | 25 |

| Income Statement Analysis (Million $) | 2010 | 2009 | 2008 | 2007 | 2006 | 2005 | 2004 | 2003 | 2002 | 2001 |
|---|---|---|---|---|---|---|---|---|---|---|
| Revenue | 6,168 | 5,952 | 6,355 | 6,772 | 6,255 | 6,004 | 5,251 | 4,828 | 4,788 | 4,646 |
| Operating Income | 1,607 | 1,440 | 1,607 | 1,846 | 1,580 | 1,749 | 1,467 | 1,369 | 1,037 | 1,044 |
| Depreciation | 171 | 165 | 178 | 161 | 162 | 385 | 393 | 403 | 89.6 | 421 |
| Interest Expense | 81.6 | 76.9 | 75.6 | 40.6 | 13.6 | 5.20 | 5.79 | 7.10 | 22.5 | 55.1 |
| Pretax Income | 1,339 | 1,179 | 1,279 | 1,623 | 1,405 | 1,360 | 1,169 | 1,130 | 905 | 615 |
| Effective Tax Rate | NA | 36.4% | 37.5% | 37.5% | 37.2% | 37.9% | 35.3% | 39.1% | 36.3% | 38.7% |
| Net Income | 828 | 730 | 799 | 1,014 | 882 | 844 | 756 | 688 | 577 | 377 |
| S&P Core Earnings | 818 | 717 | 729 | 995 | 874 | 786 | 694 | 552 | 446 | 233 |

| Balance Sheet & Other Financial Data (Million $) | 2010 | 2009 | 2008 | 2007 | 2006 | 2005 | 2004 | 2003 | 2002 | 2001 |
|---|---|---|---|---|---|---|---|---|---|---|
| Cash | 1,526 | 1,235 | 472 | 396 | 353 | 749 | 681 | 696 | 58.2 | 53.5 |
| Current Assets | 3,295 | 2,936 | 2,303 | 2,333 | 2,258 | 2,591 | 2,448 | 2,256 | 1,674 | 1,813 |
| Total Assets | 7,047 | 6,475 | 6,080 | 6,357 | 6,043 | 6,396 | 5,863 | 5,394 | 5,032 | 5,161 |
| Current Liabilities | 2,681 | 2,452 | 2,531 | 2,657 | 2,468 | 2,225 | 1,969 | 1,994 | 1,775 | 1,876 |
| Long Term Debt | 1,198 | 1,198 | 1,198 | 1,197 | 0.31 | 0.34 | 0.51 | 0.39 | 459 | 834 |
| Common Equity | 2,291 | 1,847 | 1,282 | 1,607 | 7,785 | 3,113 | 4,952 | 2,557 | 2,202 | 1,884 |
| Total Capital | 3,489 | 3,127 | 2,480 | 2,943 | 7,936 | 3,432 | 5,185 | 2,758 | 2,861 | 2,908 |
| Capital Expenditures | 115 | 68.5 | 106 | 230 | 127 | 120 | 139 | 115 | 70.0 | 117 |
| Cash Flow | 999 | 896 | 978 | 1,175 | 1,044 | 1,230 | 1,149 | 1,091 | 666 | 798 |
| Current Ratio | 1.2 | 1.2 | 0.9 | 0.9 | 0.9 | 1.2 | 1.2 | 1.1 | 0.9 | 1.0 |
| % Long Term Debt of Capitalization | 34.3 | Nil | 48.2 | 40.7 | NM | 0.0 | 0.0 | 0.0 | 16.0 | 28.7 |
| % Net Income of Revenue | 13.4 | 12.3 | 12.6 | 15.0 | 14.1 | 14.1 | 14.4 | 14.2 | 12.0 | 8.1 |
| % Return on Assets | 12.3 | NA | 12.8 | 16.3 | 14.2 | 13.8 | 13.5 | 13.2 | 11.3 | 7.5 |
| % Return on Equity | 40.0 | NA | 55.3 | 47.3 | 12.8 | 27.7 | 16.5 | 29.1 | 28.2 | 20.5 |

Data as orig reptd.; bef. results of disc opers/spec. items. Per share data adj. for stk. divs.; EPS diluted. E-Estimated. NA-Not Available. NM-Not Meaningful. NR-Not Ranked. UR-Under Review.

**Chrmn, Pres & CEO:** H. McGraw, III
**EVP & CFO:** J.F. Callahan, Jr.
**EVP & General Counsel:** K.M. Vittor
**SVP, Chief Acctg Officer & Cntlr:** E.K. Korakis

**SVP & Secy:** S.L. Bennett
**Investor Contact:** D.S. Rubin (212-512-4321)

**Board Members:** P. C. Armella, W. Bischoff, D. N. Daft, W. D. Green, L. K. Lorimer, R. P. McGraw, H. McGraw, III, H. M. Ochoa-Brillembourg, M. Rake, E. B. Rust, Jr., K. L. Schmoke, S. Taurel

**Founded:** 1899
**Domicile:** New York
**Employees:** 21,000

*The McGraw·Hill Companies*

# McKesson Corp

| S&P Recommendation | STRONG BUY ★★★★★ | Price $76.34 (as of Nov 25, 2011) | 12-Mo. Target Price $100.00 | Investment Style Large-Cap Blend |
|---|---|---|---|---|

**GICS Sector** Health Care
**Sub-Industry** Health Care Distributors

**Summary** This company (formerly McKesson HBOC) provides pharmaceutical supply management and information technologies to a broad range of health care customers.

## Key Stock Statistics (Source S&P, Vickers, company reports)

| | | | | | |
|---|---|---|---|---|---|
| 52-Wk Range | $87.32– 63.32 | S&P Oper. EPS 2012E | 6.35 | Market Capitalization(B) | $18.746 |
| Trailing 12-Month EPS | $4.53 | S&P Oper. EPS 2013E | 7.00 | Yield (%) | 1.05 |
| Trailing 12-Month P/E | 16.9 | P/E on S&P Oper. EPS 2012E | 12.0 | Dividend Rate/Share | $0.80 |
| $10K Invested 5 Yrs Ago | $16,513 | Common Shares Outstg. (M) | 245.6 | Institutional Ownership (%) | 85 |

| | |
|---|---|
| Beta | 0.78 |
| S&P 3-Yr. Proj. EPS CAGR(%) | 13 |
| S&P Credit Rating | A- |

## Price Performance

30-Week Mov. Avg. ···  10-Week Mov. Avg.- -  GAAP Earnings vs. Previous Year   Volume Above Avg. ▏▍▋ STARS
12-Mo. Target Price —  Relative Strength —   ▲ Up  ▼ Down  ► No Change    Below Avg. ▏▍▋ ★

Options: ASE, CBOE, P, Ph

Analysis prepared by Equity Analyst **Herman Saftlas** on Aug 23, 2011, when the stock traded at **$74.61**.

## Highlights

➤ We forecast FY 12 (Mar.) revenues to advance 7%, from $112 billion reported for FY 11, paced by higher revenues from branded and generic drugs (Distribution Solutions). Sales of generics should be driven by a projected sharp rise in branded drug patent expirations. We also see gains for medical-surgical, reflecting higher private label sales. Revenues in the Technology Solutions segment should also increase, and sales will be bolstered by the late 2010 acquisition of US Oncology. Technology sales should increase as consultations with hospitals on electronic health record systems translate into bookings.

➤ We expect gross and operating margins to widen in FY 12. Key drivers, in our opinion, should be an improved revenue mix, with a greater proportion of revenues comprised of higher-margin generic drugs; accretion from US Oncology; and cost streamlining measures.

➤ After a projected adjusted tax rate of 32%, versus 31% in FY 11, we forecast cash EPS of $6.25 for FY 12, excluding $0.47 in goodwill amortization, and other acquisition-related expenses of $0.07. We see cash EPS of $6.90 in FY 13.

## Investment Rationale/Risk

➤ We believe MCK's large footprints in drugs, medical supplies and information technology provide important cross-selling opportunities. We also think its leading positions in drug and medical products distribution, and pharmacy systems reinforce its cost-competitiveness, while distribution margins should continue to benefit from generic drug penetration. We also view the high-margin Technology Solutions segment as poised to gain greatly from stimulus-related spending, and we are encouraged that bookings have begun. We see EPS accretion of about $0.10 in FY 12 from the December 2010 acquisition of US Oncology, a leading provider of products and services to oncologists. We also view MCK as being in healthy financial shape, with some $3.1 billion in cash, and strong cash flow.

➤ Risks to our recommendation and target price include the loss of major accounts and unfavorable regulatory changes. Recent moves to cut drug spending in Canada are another risk.

➤ Our 12-month target price of $100 is derived by applying an approximate peer-level 16X multiple to our FY 12 cash EPS estimate of $6.25.

## Qualitative Risk Assessment

| LOW | MEDIUM | HIGH |
|---|---|---|

Our risk assessment reflects our view of MCK's improving profitability and the rising demand for its highly profitable IT products and services, offset by our belief the company is more price competitive than peers and that future drugmaker-distributor contract negotiations might be less favorable for distributors.

## Quantitative Evaluations

**S&P Quality Ranking**      A-

| D | C | B- | B | B+ | A- | A | A+ |
|---|---|---|---|---|---|---|---|

**Relative Strength Rank**      MODERATE

67

LOWEST = 1      HIGHEST = 99

## Revenue/Earnings Data

**Revenue (Million $)**

| | 1Q | 2Q | 3Q | 4Q | Year |
|---|---|---|---|---|---|
| 2012 | 29,980 | 30,216 | -- | -- | -- |
| 2011 | 27,450 | 27,534 | 28,247 | 28,853 | 112,084 |
| 2010 | 26,657 | 27,130 | 28,272 | 26,643 | 108,702 |
| 2009 | 26,704 | 26,574 | 27,130 | 26,224 | 106,632 |
| 2008 | 24,528 | 24,450 | 26,494 | 26,231 | 101,703 |
| 2007 | 23,315 | 22,386 | 23,111 | 24,165 | 92,977 |

**Earnings Per Share ($)**

| | 1Q | 2Q | 3Q | 4Q | Year |
|---|---|---|---|---|---|
| 2012 | 1.13 | 1.20 | E1.52 | E2.07 | E6.35 |
| 2011 | 1.10 | 0.97 | 0.60 | 1.62 | 4.29 |
| 2010 | 1.06 | 1.11 | 1.19 | 1.26 | 4.62 |
| 2009 | 0.83 | 1.17 | -0.07 | 1.01 | 2.99 |
| 2008 | 0.77 | 0.83 | 0.68 | 1.05 | 3.32 |
| 2007 | 0.60 | 0.94 | 0.79 | 0.85 | 3.17 |

Fiscal year ended Mar. 31. Next earnings report expected: Early February. EPS Estimates based on S&P Operating Earnings; historical GAAP earnings are as reported.

## Dividend Data (Dates: mm/dd Payment Date: mm/dd/yy)

| Amount ($) | Date Decl. | Ex-Div. Date | Stk. of Record | Payment Date |
|---|---|---|---|---|
| 0.180 | 01/26 | 02/25 | 03/01 | 04/01/11 |
| 0.200 | 05/25 | 06/08 | 06/10 | 07/01/11 |
| 0.200 | 07/27 | 08/30 | 09/01 | 10/03/11 |
| 0.200 | 10/28 | 11/29 | 12/01 | 01/03/12 |

Dividends have been paid since 1995. Source: Company reports.

---

**Please read the Required Disclosures and Analyst Certification on the last page of this report.**

The **McGraw·Hill** Companies

# McKesson Corp

## Business Summary August 23, 2011

CORPORATE OVERVIEW. McKesson Corp. is a leading distributor of medical products and supplies and health care information technology products and services. In December 2010, MCK acquired US Oncology, a leading provider of products and services to oncologists, for $2.1 billion in cash.

McKesson Distribution Solutions (97% of FY 11 (Mar.) revenues) distributes ethical and proprietary drugs and health and beauty care, and focuses on three customer segments: retail independent pharmacies, retail chains, and institutions, in all 50 states and Canada. The medical-surgical distribution unit provides medical-surgical supplies, equipment, logistics and related services to alternate-site health care providers, including physicians' offices, long-term care and home care. This segment includes a 49% interest in Nadro, S.A., a leading drug distributor in Mexico; and a 39% interest in Parata Systems, which markets automated pharmacy systems to hospitals and retail pharmacies.

McKesson Technology Solutions (3%) delivers enterprise-wide patient care, clinical, financial, supply chain and strategic management software solutions,

pharmacy automation for hospitals, as well as connectivity, outsourcing and other services, to health care organizations throughout North America, the United Kingdom and other European countries. This segment also includes MCK's Payer businesses, which provide medical management tools, claims payment solutions and care management programs. Customers include hospitals, physicians, home care providers, retail pharmacies and payors.

CORPORATE STRATEGY. Distribution agreements between distributors and most drugmakers have transitioned toward a more fee-based approach, with the distributors appropriately and predictably compensated for distribution and related logistic and administrative services and data, in our opinion. MCK and its peers see over 80% of their drugmaker compensation as fixed and not dependent upon drug price inflation.

## Company Financials Fiscal Year Ended Mar. 31

| Per Share Data ($) | 2011 | 2010 | 2009 | 2008 | 2007 | 2006 | 2005 | 2004 | 2003 | 2002 |
|---|---|---|---|---|---|---|---|---|---|---|
| Tangible Book Value | 3.18 | 9.95 | 4.83 | 10.42 | 9.10 | 13.36 | 12.47 | 12.66 | 10.57 | 9.81 |
| Cash Flow | 6.18 | 6.12 | 3.89 | 4.09 | 4.14 | 3.28 | 0.32 | 2.94 | 2.65 | 2.20 |
| Earnings | 4.29 | 4.62 | 2.99 | 3.32 | 3.17 | 2.34 | -0.53 | 2.19 | 1.90 | 1.43 |
| S&P Core Earnings | 4.76 | 4.62 | 4.16 | 3.33 | 3.16 | 2.07 | 1.93 | 1.29 | 1.24 | 0.87 |
| Dividends | NA | 0.48 | 0.48 | 0.24 | 0.24 | 0.24 | 0.24 | 0.24 | 0.24 | 0.24 |
| Payout Ratio | NA | 10% | 16% | 7% | 8% | 10% | NM | 11% | 13% | 17% |
| Calendar Year | 2010 | 2009 | 2008 | 2007 | 2006 | 2005 | 2004 | 2003 | 2002 | 2001 |
| Prices:High | 71.49 | 64.98 | 68.40 | 68.43 | 55.10 | 52.89 | 35.90 | 37.14 | 42.09 | 41.50 |
| Prices:Low | 57.23 | 33.13 | 28.27 | 50.80 | 44.60 | 30.13 | 22.61 | 22.61 | 24.99 | 23.40 |
| P/E Ratio:High | 17 | 14 | 23 | 21 | 17 | 23 | NM | 17 | 22 | 29 |
| P/E Ratio:Low | 13 | 7 | 9 | 15 | 14 | 13 | NM | 10 | 13 | 16 |

| Income Statement Analysis (Million $) | | | | | | | | | | |
|---|---|---|---|---|---|---|---|---|---|---|
| Revenue | 112,084 | 108,702 | 106,632 | 101,703 | 92,977 | 88,050 | 80,515 | 69,506 | 57,121 | 50,006 |
| Operating Income | 2,551 | 2,400 | 1,951 | 1,736 | 1,553 | 1,425 | 1,260 | 1,216 | 1,134 | 923 |
| Depreciation | 496 | 474 | 261 | 231 | 295 | 266 | 251 | 232 | 204 | 208 |
| Interest Expense | 222 | 187 | 144 | 142 | 99.0 | 94.0 | 118 | 120 | 121 | 119 |
| Pretax Income | 1,635 | 1,864 | 1,064 | 1,457 | 1,297 | 1,158 | -240 | 911 | 855 | 601 |
| Effective Tax Rate | NA | 32.2% | 22.7% | 32.1% | 25.4% | 36.4% | NM | 29.1% | 34.3% | 30.4% |
| Net Income | 1,130 | 1,263 | 823 | 989 | 968 | 737 | -157 | 646 | 562 | 419 |
| S&P Core Earnings | 1,255 | 1,260 | 1,159 | 991 | 964 | 650 | 565 | 380 | 364 | 255 |

| Balance Sheet & Other Financial Data (Million $) | | | | | | | | | | |
|---|---|---|---|---|---|---|---|---|---|---|
| Cash | 3,612 | 3,731 | 2,109 | 1,362 | 1,954 | 2,142 | 1,809 | 718 | 534 | 563 |
| Current Assets | 22,357 | 21,504 | 18,671 | 17,786 | 17,856 | 16,919 | 15,332 | 13,004 | 11,254 | 10,699 |
| Total Assets | 30,886 | 28,189 | 25,267 | 24,603 | 23,943 | 20,975 | 18,775 | 16,240 | 14,353 | 13,324 |
| Current Liabilities | 18,726 | 17,012 | 15,606 | 15,348 | 15,126 | 13,515 | 11,793 | 9,456 | 7,974 | 7,588 |
| Long Term Debt | 3,587 | 2,293 | 2,290 | 1,795 | 1,803 | 965 | 1,202 | 1,210 | 1,487 | 1,485 |
| Common Equity | 7,220 | 7,532 | 6,193 | 6,121 | 6,273 | 5,907 | 5,275 | 5,165 | 4,529 | 3,940 |
| Total Capital | 11,224 | 9,828 | 8,483 | 7,916 | 8,076 | 6,872 | 6,477 | 6,375 | 6,016 | 5,425 |
| Capital Expenditures | 233 | 199 | 195 | 195 | 126 | 167 | 140 | 115 | 116 | 132 |
| Cash Flow | 1,626 | 1,670 | 1,084 | 1,220 | 1,263 | 1,003 | 94.2 | 879 | 766 | 626 |
| Current Ratio | 1.2 | 1.3 | 1.2 | 1.2 | 1.2 | 1.3 | 1.3 | 1.4 | 1.4 | 1.4 |
| % Long Term Debt of Capitalization | 32.0 | 23.3 | 27.0 | 22.7 | 22.3 | 14.0 | 18.6 | 19.0 | 24.7 | 27.4 |
| % Net Income of Revenue | 1.0 | 1.2 | 0.8 | 1.0 | 1.0 | 0.8 | NM | 0.9 | 1.0 | 0.8 |
| % Return on Assets | 3.8 | 4.7 | 3.3 | 4.1 | 4.3 | 3.7 | NM | 4.2 | 4.1 | 3.4 |
| % Return on Equity | 15.3 | 18.4 | 13.4 | 16.0 | 15.9 | 13.2 | NM | 13.3 | 13.3 | 11.3 |

Data as orig reptd.; bef. results of disc opers/spec. items. Per share data adj. for stk. divs.; EPS diluted. E-Estimated. NA-Not Available. NM-Not Meaningful. NR-Not Ranked. UR-Under Review.

**Office:** McKesson Plaza, One Post Street, San Francisco, CA 94104.
**Telephone:** 415-983-8300.
**Email:** investors@mckesson.com
**Website:** http://www.mckesson.com

**Chrmn, Pres & CEO:** J.H. Hammergren
**EVP & CFO:** J.C. Campbell
**EVP, CTO & CIO:** R. Spratt
**EVP & General Counsel:** L.E. Seeger

**Chief Acctg Officer & Cntlr:** N.A. Rees
**Investor Contact:** J.C. Campbell (800-826-9360)
**Board Members:** A. D. Bryant, W. A. Budd, J. H. Hammergren, A. F. Irby, III, M. C. Jacobs, M. L. Knowles, D. M. Lawrence, E. A. Mueller, J. E. Shaw

**Founded:** 1994
**Domicile:** Delaware
**Employees:** 36,400

# Mead Johnson Nutrition Co

**STANDARD &POOR'S**

| S&P Recommendation | HOLD ★★★★☆ | Price $70.99 (as of Nov 25, 2011) | 12-Mo. Target Price $73.00 | Investment Style Large-Cap Blend |
|---|---|---|---|---|

**GICS Sector** Consumer Staples
**Sub-Industry** Packaged Foods & Meats

**Summary** Mead Johnson Nutrition, split off from Bristol-Myers Squibb in 2009, is a global leader in pediatric nutrition.

## Key Stock Statistics (Source S&P, Vickers, company reports)

| | | | | | | | |
|---|---|---|---|---|---|---|---|
| 52-Wk Range | $76.91–55.12 | S&P Oper. EPS 2011 **E** | 2.78 | Market Capitalization(B) | $14.451 | Beta | 0.64 |
| Trailing 12-Month EPS | $2.54 | S&P Oper. EPS 2012 **E** | 3.15 | Yield (%) | 1.46 | S&P 3-Yr. Proj. EPS CAGR(%) | 15 |
| Trailing 12-Month P/E | 28.0 | P/E on S&P Oper. EPS 2011 **E** | 25.5 | Dividend Rate/Share | $1.04 | S&P Credit Rating | BBB |
| $10K Invested 5 Yrs Ago | NA | Common Shares Outstg. (M) | 203.6 | Institutional Ownership (%) | 93 | | |

## Price Performance

30-Week Mov. Avg. ···  10-Week Mov. Avg. --  **GAAP Earnings vs. Previous Year**  Volume Above Avg. STARS
12-Mo. Target Price —  Relative Strength —  ▲ Up  ▼ Down  ► No Change  Below Avg. ★

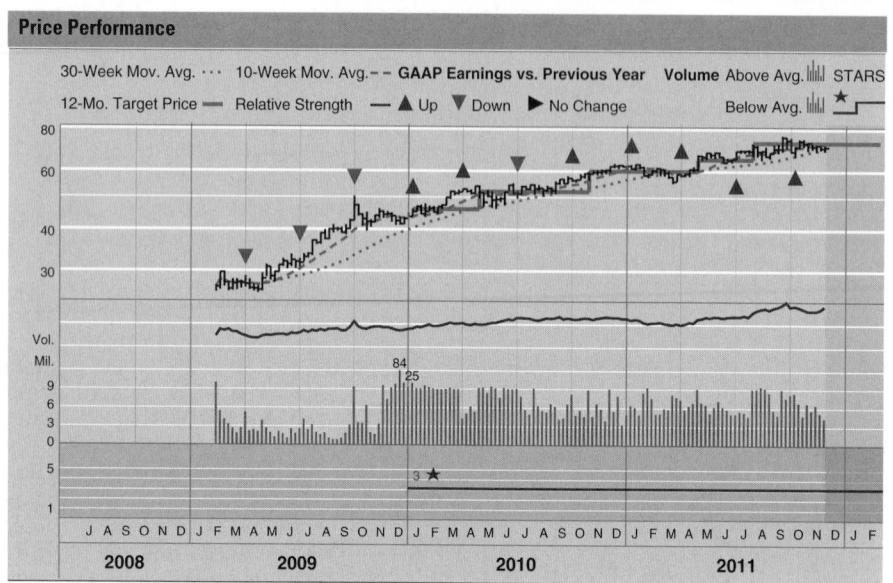

Analysis prepared by Equity Analyst **Tom Graves, CFA** on Nov 10, 2011, when the stock traded at **$69.70**.

## Highlights

➤ In 2012, we look for revenue to increase about 10% from the $3.7 billion that we estimate for 2011, with most of the growth in both years coming from the Asia/Latin America segment. In both years, we anticipate that the Asia/Latin America segment will account for more than 60% of MJN's total revenue.

➤ For 2012, we look for operating margins to be bolstered by sales leverage and productivity improvements. Also, we expect less margin pressure from rising input costs. Our 2012 operating EPS estimate is $3.15, up from the $2.78 that we project for 2011, and from $2.42 in 2010. In 2011's first nine months, MJN's reported EPS of $2.06 included a negative impact of about $0.21 from special items, which are excluded from our EPS estimate. Also, in 2011, we look for MJN's capital expenditures to total about $120 million.

➤ In December 2009, Bristol-Myers Squibb (BMY 31 Buy) completed an exchange offer that resulted in the split-off of MJN. This followed MJN's February 2009 initial public offering.

## Investment Rationale/Risk

➤ We think the current stock price largely reflects what we see as MJN's good, long-term growth prospects, especially from Asia. However, we have some concern about relatively low fertility rates in certain countries, and we think that higher-cost MJN brands may not be as attractive in a weak spending environment.

➤ Risks to our recommendation and target price include consolidation of retail customers, rising dairy costs, changes in government programs, product quality and safety issues, high financial leverage, and unfavorable foreign exchange.

➤ Our 12-month target price of $73 is a blend of our peer analysis and DCF model. We believe the shares should trade at a premium to a peer group of food and beverage companies. Applying a P/E multiple of 23X to our 2012 EPS estimate of $3.15 results in a value of about $72 per share. Our DCF model values MJN at about $73, using a terminal growth rate of 3% and a terminal weighted average cost of capital of 9.0%.

## Qualitative Risk Assessment

| LOW | MEDIUM | HIGH |
|---|---|---|

Our risk assessment reflects our view that demand for Mead Johnson's infant formula and children's nutritional products is comparatively predictable in developed economies and growing in emerging markets. Demand in these categories has a relatively low sensitivity to changes in general economic and geopolitical conditions. This is partly offset by volatility in dairy prices.

## Quantitative Evaluations

**S&P Quality Ranking** NR

| D | C | B- | B | B+ | A- | A | A+ |
|---|---|---|---|---|---|---|---|

**Relative Strength Rank** STRONG

77

LOWEST = 1    HIGHEST = 99

## Revenue/Earnings Data

**Revenue (Million $)**

| | 1Q | 2Q | 3Q | 4Q | Year |
|---|---|---|---|---|---|
| 2011 | 899.8 | 932.0 | 933.9 | -- | -- |
| 2010 | 763.5 | 764.2 | 810.2 | 803.7 | 3,142 |
| 2009 | 693.0 | 719.3 | 699.8 | 714.4 | 2,827 |
| 2008 | 716.0 | 716.0 | 742.8 | 707.7 | 2,882 |
| 2007 | 615.1 | 615.1 | 673.1 | 673.1 | 2,576 |
| 2006 | -- | -- | -- | -- | 2,345 |

**Earnings Per Share ($)**

| | | | | | |
|---|---|---|---|---|---|
| 2011 | 0.71 | 0.64 | 0.70 | E0.51 | E2.78 |
| 2010 | 0.61 | 0.59 | 0.52 | 0.48 | 2.20 |
| 2009 | 0.55 | 0.66 | 0.48 | 0.31 | 1.99 |
| 2008 | 0.77 | 0.67 | 0.60 | 0.23 | 2.32 |
| 2007 | -- | -- | -- | -- | -- |
| 2006 | -- | -- | -- | -- | -- |

Fiscal year ended Dec. 31. Next earnings report expected: Late January. EPS Estimates based on S&P Operating Earnings; historical GAAP earnings are as reported.

## Dividend Data (Dates: mm/dd Payment Date: mm/dd/yy)

| Amount ($) | Date Decl. | Ex-Div. Date | Stk. of Record | Payment Date |
|---|---|---|---|---|
| 0.225 | 12/01 | 12/15 | 12/17 | 01/03/11 |
| 0.260 | 03/02 | 03/16 | 03/18 | 04/01/11 |
| 0.260 | 06/09 | 06/15 | 06/17 | 07/01/11 |
| 0.260 | 09/13 | 09/21 | 09/23 | 10/03/11 |

Dividends have been paid since 2009. Source: Company reports.

---

**Please read the Required Disclosures and Analyst Certification on the last page of this report.**

The **McGraw·Hill** Companies

# Mead Johnson Nutrition Co

**STANDARD &POOR'S**

## Business Summary November 10, 2011

CORPORATE OVERVIEW. Mead Johnson Nutrition Company is a global leader in pediatric nutrition with about $3.1 billion in net sales in 2010. Its Enfa family of brands, including Enfamil infant formula, addresses a broad range of nutritional needs for infants, children and expectant and nursing mothers. MJN also markets some other brands on a local, regional or global basis. MJN's principal product categories are infant formula (62% of 2010 sales) and children's nutrition and other (38%).

MJN markets its portfolio of more than 70 products to mothers, health care professionals and retailers in more than 50 countries in Asia, North America, Latin America and Europe. MJN has two reportable segments -- Asia/Latin America (61% of sales and 64% of segment operating profits in 2010) and North America/Europe (39% and 36%). The U.S. represented 32% of revenues in 2010. Wal-Mart Stores, Inc. and DKSH International Ltd. were MJN's largest customers, each accounting for 12% of sales in 2010.

Mead Johnson was founded in 1905 and introduced its first infant formula product in 1911. Over the years, MJN expanded to more countries and added more products. In 1967, it became a wholly owned subsidiary of Bristol-Myers Squibb Company. In February 2009, MJN completed an initial public offering of 34.5 million shares of its Class A common stock, with Bristol-Myers owning 100% of MJN's Class B common stock and over 42 million shares (55%) of its Class A common stock. Each Class B share had 10 votes per share and Class

A one vote. Bristol-Myers retained 83.1% of the outstanding shares.

In December 2009, Bristol-Myers completed an exchange offer, resulting in the split-off of MJN. This also involved the conversion of Class B shares into Class A shares, with Bristol-Myers distributing 170 million shares of Class A stock, or 83% of the outstanding shares of MJN. Subsequently, Bristol-Myers retained no share ownership in MJN.

MARKET PROFILE. There are five general stages of child development: Stage 0 (Pre-natal); Stage 1 (0-6 months old); Stage 2 (6-12 months old); Stage 3 (12 months to 3 years old); Stage 4 (3-5 years old); and Stage 5 (beyond 5 years old).

MJN produces different products for each stage. In the U.S., its business has been focused on the infant formula category (Stages 1 and 2), while outside the U.S., it sells infant formula products (Stages 1 and 2) and children's nutritional products (Stages 3, 4 and 5). In August 2009, MJN first shipped Enfagrow, nutrition tailored for toddlers, in the U.S.

## Company Financials Fiscal Year Ended Dec. 31

| Per Share Data ($) | 2010 | 2009 | 2008 | 2007 | 2006 | 2005 | 2004 | 2003 | 2002 | 2001 |
|---|---|---|---|---|---|---|---|---|---|---|
| Tangible Book Value | NM | NM | NM | NA | NA | NA | NA | NA | NA | NA |
| Cash Flow | 2.51 | 2.28 | 2.58 | NA | NA | NA | NA | NA | NA | NA |
| Earnings | 2.20 | 1.99 | 2.32 | NA | NA | NA | NA | NA | NA | NA |
| S&P Core Earnings | 2.28 | 2.02 | 1.97 | 2.11 | 1.99 | NA | NA | NA | NA | NA |
| Dividends | 0.90 | 0.40 | Nil | NA | NA | NA | NA | NA | NA | NA |
| Payout Ratio | 41% | 20% | Nil | NA | NA | NA | NA | NA | NA | NA |
| Prices:High | 63.38 | 50.35 | NA | NA | NA | NA | NA | NA | NA | NA |
| Prices:Low | 43.50 | 25.72 | NA | NA | NA | NA | NA | NA | NA | NA |
| P/E Ratio:High | 29 | 25 | NA | NA | NA | NA | NA | NA | NA | NA |
| P/E Ratio:Low | 20 | 13 | NA | NA | NA | NA | NA | NA | NA | NA |

| Income Statement Analysis (Million $) | | | | | | | | | | |
|---|---|---|---|---|---|---|---|---|---|---|
| Revenue | 3,142 | 2,827 | 2,882 | 2,576 | 2,345 | 2,202 | NA | NA | NA | NA |
| Operating Income | 834 | 822 | 753 | 710 | 696 | 667 | NA | NA | NA | NA |
| Depreciation | 64.7 | 58.9 | 44.1 | 51.0 | 49.5 | 53.8 | NA | NA | NA | NA |
| Interest Expense | 48.6 | 95.9 | 43.3 | NA | NA | NA | NA | NA | NA | NA |
| Pretax Income | 634 | 587 | 652 | 663 | 635 | 618 | NA | NA | NA | NA |
| Effective Tax Rate | NA | 30.1% | 38.5% | 35.2% | 36.3% | 36.0% | NA | NA | NA | NA |
| Net Income | 453 | 400 | 394 | 423 | 398 | 390 | NA | NA | NA | NA |
| S&P Core Earnings | 468 | 411 | 394 | 423 | 398 | NA | NA | NA | NA | NA |

| Balance Sheet & Other Financial Data (Million $) | | | | | | | | | | |
|---|---|---|---|---|---|---|---|---|---|---|
| Cash | 596 | 561 | NA | NA | NA | NA | NA | NA | NA | NA |
| Current Assets | 1,449 | 1,336 | 717 | 688 | 624 | NA | NA | NA | NA | NA |
| Total Assets | 2,293 | 2,070 | 1,361 | 1,302 | 1,204 | NA | NA | NA | NA | NA |
| Current Liabilities | 976 | 1,100 | 653 | 563 | 530 | NA | NA | NA | NA | NA |
| Long Term Debt | 1,533 | 1,485 | 2,000 | NA | NA | NA | NA | NA | NA | NA |
| Common Equity | -367 | -675 | -1,401 | 631 | 586 | NA | NA | NA | NA | NA |
| Total Capital | 1,174 | 821 | 604 | 638 | 592 | NA | NA | NA | NA | NA |
| Capital Expenditures | 172 | 95.8 | 81.1 | 78.4 | 68.9 | 56.4 | NA | NA | NA | NA |
| Cash Flow | 517 | 459 | 438 | 466 | 441 | 436 | NA | NA | NA | NA |
| Current Ratio | 1.5 | 1.2 | 1.1 | 1.2 | 1.2 | NA | NA | NA | NA | NA |
| % Long Term Debt of Capitalization | 130.5 | Nil | 330.9 | Nil | Nil | Nil | NA | NA | NA | NA |
| % Net Income of Revenue | 14.4 | 14.1 | 13.7 | 16.4 | 17.0 | 17.7 | NA | NA | NA | NA |
| % Return on Assets | 20.8 | NA | 29.6 | 33.7 | NA | NA | NA | NA | NA | NA |
| % Return on Equity | NM | NA | NM | 69.5 | NA | NA | NA | NA | NA | NA |

Data as orig reptd.; bef. results of disc opers/spec. items. Per share data adj. for stk. divs.; EPS diluted. E-Estimated. NA-Not Available. NM-Not Meaningful. NR-Not Ranked. UR-Under Review.

**Office:** 2701 Patriot Blvd, Glenview, IL 60026.
**Telephone:** 847-832-2420.
**Website:** http://www.meadjohnson.com
**Chrmn:** J.M. Cornelius

**CEO:** S.W. Golsby
**SVP & CFO:** P.G. Leemputte
**SVP, Secy & General Counsel:** W.C. P'Pool
**Chief Acctg Officer & Cntlr:** S.D. Burhans

**Investor Contact:** K. Chieger (847-804-9896)
**Board Members:** S. M. Altschuler, H. B. Bernick, K. A. Casiano, A. C. Catalano, C. A. Clark, J. M. Cornelius, S. W. Golsby, P. G. Ratcliffe, E. Sigal, R. S. Singer

**Founded:** 1905
**Domicile:** Delaware
**Employees:** 6,500

The **McGraw-Hill** Companies

# MeadWestvaco Corp

**STANDARD &POOR'S**

| | | | |
|---|---|---|---|
| **S&P Recommendation** HOLD ★★★★★ | **Price**<br>$27.22 (as of Nov 25, 2011) | **12-Mo. Target Price**<br>$31.00 | **Investment Style**<br>Large-Cap Value |

**GICS Sector** Materials
**Sub-Industry** Paper Products

**Summary** This company is primarily a major producer of paperboard packaging used in a variety of consumer markets.

## Key Stock Statistics (Source S&P, Vickers, company reports)

| | | | | | | | |
|---|---|---|---|---|---|---|---|
| 52-Wk Range | $34.51– 22.75 | S&P Oper. EPS 2011**E** | 2.05 | Market Capitalization(B) | $4.648 | Beta | 1.73 |
| Trailing 12-Month EPS | $1.84 | S&P Oper. EPS 2012**E** | 2.15 | Yield (%) | 3.67 | S&P 3-Yr. Proj. EPS CAGR(%) | 16 |
| Trailing 12-Month P/E | 14.8 | P/E on S&P Oper. EPS 2011**E** | 13.3 | Dividend Rate/Share | $1.00 | S&P Credit Rating | BBB |
| $10K Invested 5 Yrs Ago | $11,374 | Common Shares Outstg. (M) | 170.7 | Institutional Ownership (%) | 84 | | |

## Price Performance

30-Week Mov. Avg. ···  10-Week Mov. Avg. --  **GAAP Earnings vs. Previous Year**  Volume Above Avg. STARS
12-Mo. Target Price —  Relative Strength —  ▲ Up  ▼ Down  ► No Change  Below Avg.  ★

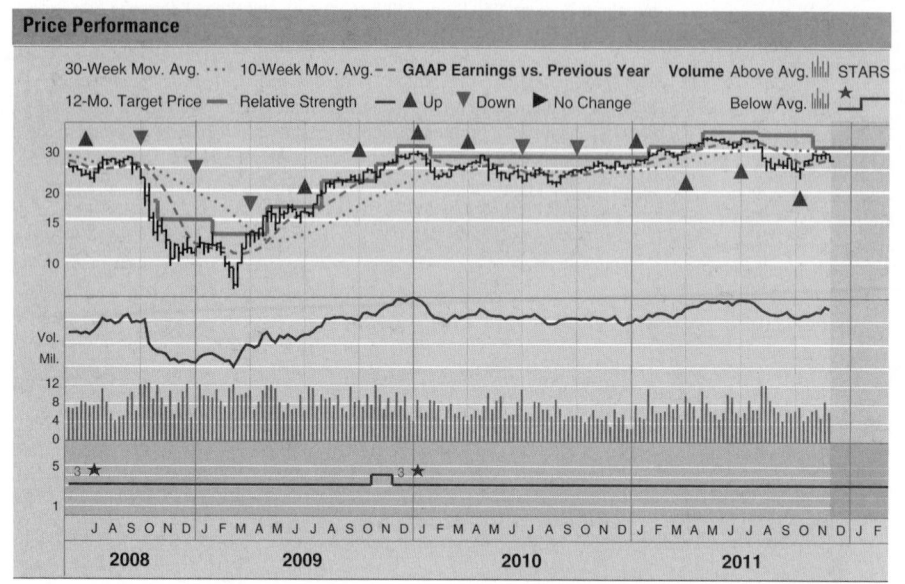

Options: ASE, CBOE, P

Analysis prepared by Equity Analyst **S. Benway, CFA** on Nov 14, 2011, when the stock traded at **$28.84**.

## Highlights

➤ We expect sales to increase 3%-5% from continuing operations (after some divestitures) in 2011, and for 2012, we see growth of about 5%. MWV has shut several facilities and eliminated product lines, but it is also actively developing new products across its businesses. We look for economic activity to improve moderately in coming quarters, which should boost demand for paperboard packaging and specialty chemicals, and growth in emerging markets should continue.

➤ We anticipate margin expansion in 2011, before modest contraction in 2012. Management has focused its product lineup on higher-margin, faster-growing categories, and we expect lower costs from reduced overhead and improved manufacturing efficiencies to help margins this year. We expect some price pressure in 2012. Our forecast is for operating margins of 11.1% in 2011 and 10.6% in 2012, versus 8.1% in 2010.

➤ Our operating EPS estimate for 2011 is $2.05, up 35% from $1.52 in 2010. Our estimate includes modest land sales gains, which could be significant in certain quarters. For 2012, we estimate EPS of $2.15.

## Investment Rationale/Risk

➤ We believe that volume will expand in 2011 and 2012 as economic activity improves and new products gain market share. MWV's strong position in emerging markets and its moves to eliminate low-margin product lines should fuel long-term growth. Additionally, we think that MWV has valuable land that it will sell gradually over the long term. However, we believe the shares appropriately reflect the improved results that we project.

➤ Risks to our recommendation and target price include a weaker-than-expected global economy, softer-than-projected demand and pricing trends for MWV's packaging grades, and a renewed rise in energy and raw material costs.

➤ Our discounted cash flow model, which assumes a weighted average cost of capital of 10.0%, solid cash flow generation in 2011 and 2012, and growth in perpetuity of 3%, values the shares at $30. A peer group of packaging stocks is trading at 15.1X our 2012 estimates. Applying this forward P/E to our 2012 forecast for MWV values the shares at $33. Our 12-month target price of $31 is a blend of these metrics.

## Qualitative Risk Assessment

| LOW | MEDIUM | HIGH |
|---|---|---|

MWV operates in a moderately cyclical and seasonal sector and is subject to swings in certain commodity prices. However, it has some pricing power due to its high market share, and its debt levels are low relative to many of its peers.

## Quantitative Evaluations

**S&P Quality Ranking**  B

| D | C | B- | B | B+ | A- | A | A+ |
|---|---|---|---|---|---|---|---|

**Relative Strength Rank**  MODERATE

68

LOWEST = 1    HIGHEST = 99

## Revenue/Earnings Data

**Revenue (Million $)**

| | 1Q | 2Q | 3Q | 4Q | Year |
|---|---|---|---|---|---|
| 2011 | 1,365 | 1,557 | 1,639 | -- | -- |
| 2010 | 1,402 | 1,552 | 1,560 | 1,498 | 5,693 |
| 2009 | 1,354 | 1,432 | 1,627 | 1,636 | 6,049 |
| 2008 | 1,518 | 1,709 | 1,811 | 1,599 | 6,637 |
| 2007 | 1,552 | 1,706 | 1,796 | 1,852 | 6,906 |
| 2006 | 1,434 | 1,570 | 1,751 | 1,775 | 6,530 |

**Earnings Per Share ($)**

| | | | | | |
|---|---|---|---|---|---|
| 2011 | 0.41 | 0.51 | 0.67 | E0.37 | E2.05 |
| 2010 | 0.14 | 0.29 | 0.64 | 0.40 | 1.52 |
| 2009 | -0.46 | 0.72 | 0.74 | 0.29 | 1.30 |
| 2008 | -0.05 | 0.33 | 0.26 | -0.09 | 0.46 |
| 2007 | -0.09 | 0.17 | 0.66 | 0.82 | 1.56 |
| 2006 | 0.02 | -0.04 | 0.31 | 0.23 | 0.52 |

Fiscal year ended Dec. 31. Next earnings report expected: Late January. EPS Estimates based on S&P Operating Earnings; historical GAAP earnings are as reported.

## Dividend Data (Dates: mm/dd Payment Date: mm/dd/yy)

| Amount ($) | Date Decl. | Ex-Div. Date | Stk. of Record | Payment Date |
|---|---|---|---|---|
| 0.250 | 01/24 | 02/01 | 02/03 | 03/01/11 |
| 0.250 | 04/18 | 04/28 | 05/02 | 06/01/11 |
| 0.250 | 06/28 | 07/28 | 08/01 | 09/01/11 |
| 0.250 | 11/15 | 11/22 | 11/25 | 12/01/11 |

Dividends have been paid since 1892. Source: Company reports.

# MeadWestvaco Corp

**STANDARD
&POOR'S**

## Business Summary November 14, 2011

MeadWestvaco Corporation (MWV) is a packaging company that provides solutions in the health care, personal care and beauty, food, beverage, media and entertainment, home and garden, tobacco, and commercial print industries. The company's business segments include Packaging Resources; Consumer Solutions; Consumer & Office Products; Specialty Chemicals; and Community Development and Land Management.

The Packaging Resources segment produces bleached paperboard (SBS), Coated Natural Kraft paperboard (CNK), and linerboard. This segment's paperboard products are manufactured at three mills located in the U.S. and two mills located in Brazil. SBS is used for packaging high-value consumer products in markets, such as pharmaceuticals, personal care, beauty, tobacco, and beverage and food service. CNK is used for a range of packaging applications, the largest of which for MWV is multi-pack beverage packaging and food packaging. Linerboard is used in the manufacture of corrugated boxes and other containers.

The Consumer Solutions segment designs and produces multi-pack cartons and packaging systems primarily for the global beverage take-home market and packaging for the global tobacco market. In addition, this segment offers a range of converting and consumer packaging solutions, including printed plastic packaging and injection-molded products used for personal care, beauty, and pharmaceutical products; and dispensing and sprayer systems for personal care, beauty, health care, fragrance and home and garden markets. Paperboard and plastic are converted into packaging products at plants located in North America, South America, Europe, and Asia. Also, this segment has a pharmaceutical packaging contract with a mass-merchant, and manufactures equipment that is leased or sold to its beverage and dairy customers to package their products.

## Company Financials Fiscal Year Ended Dec. 31

| Per Share Data ($) | 2010 | 2009 | 2008 | 2007 | 2006 | 2005 | 2004 | 2003 | 2002 | 2001 |
|---|---|---|---|---|---|---|---|---|---|---|
| Tangible Book Value | 11.93 | 12.02 | 9.37 | 13.52 | 14.74 | 14.58 | 18.44 | 19.89 | 20.44 | 17.34 |
| Cash Flow | 3.79 | 3.86 | 2.91 | 4.13 | 3.37 | 3.17 | 1.87 | 3.60 | 3.49 | 4.29 |
| Earnings | 1.52 | 1.30 | 0.46 | 1.56 | 0.52 | 0.62 | -1.73 | -0.01 | -0.01 | 0.87 |
| S&P Core Earnings | 1.05 | 0.82 | -0.68 | 0.21 | -0.11 | 0.27 | -2.67 | -0.81 | -1.37 | -1.04 |
| Dividends | 0.94 | 0.92 | 0.92 | Nil | 0.92 | 0.92 | 0.92 | 0.92 | 0.92 | 0.88 |
| Payout Ratio | 62% | 71% | NM | Nil | 177% | 148% | NM | NM | NM | 101% |
| Prices:High | 29.74 | 29.33 | 31.44 | 36.50 | 30.85 | 34.33 | 34.34 | 29.83 | 36.50 | 32.10 |
| Prices:Low | 20.81 | 7.53 | 9.44 | 28.39 | 24.76 | 25.06 | 25.16 | 21.37 | 15.57 | 22.68 |
| P/E Ratio:High | 20 | 23 | 68 | 23 | 59 | 55 | NM | NM | NM | 37 |
| P/E Ratio:Low | 14 | 6 | 21 | 18 | 48 | 40 | NM | NM | NM | 26 |

| Income Statement Analysis (Million $) | 2010 | 2009 | 2008 | 2007 | 2006 | 2005 | 2004 | 2003 | 2002 | 2001 |
|---|---|---|---|---|---|---|---|---|---|---|
| Revenue | 5,693 | 6,049 | 6,637 | 6,906 | 6,530 | 6,170 | 8,227 | 7,553 | 7,242 | 3,935 |
| Operating Income | 887 | 828 | 734 | 893 | 743 | 818 | 1,042 | 855 | 859 | 677 |
| Depreciation | 389 | 443 | 423 | 473 | 517 | 491 | 726 | 724 | 674 | 347 |
| Interest Expense | 186 | 204 | 210 | 219 | 211 | 208 | 278 | 291 | 309 | 208 |
| Pretax Income | 316 | 375 | 79.0 | 400 | 98.0 | 135 | -454 | -29.0 | -15.0 | 119 |
| Effective Tax Rate | NA | 40.0% | NM | 28.8% | 5.10% | 11.9% | NM | NM | NM | 25.6% |
| Net Income | 262 | 225 | 80.0 | 285 | 93.0 | 119 | -349 | -2.00 | -3.00 | 88.2 |
| S&P Core Earnings | 181 | 141 | -118 | 36.7 | -22.1 | 50.6 | -539 | -164 | -264 | -104 |

| Balance Sheet & Other Financial Data (Million $) | 2010 | 2009 | 2008 | 2007 | 2006 | 2005 | 2004 | 2003 | 2002 | 2001 |
|---|---|---|---|---|---|---|---|---|---|---|
| Cash | 790 | 850 | 549 | 245 | 156 | 297 | 270 | 225 | 372 | 81.2 |
| Current Assets | 2,446 | 2,530 | 2,161 | 2,167 | 2,015 | 2,030 | 2,562 | 2,426 | 2,431 | 1,016 |
| Total Assets | 8,814 | 9,021 | 8,455 | 9,837 | 9,285 | 8,908 | 11,681 | 12,487 | 12,921 | 6,787 |
| Current Liabilities | 1,226 | 1,245 | 1,274 | 1,455 | 1,465 | 1,042 | 1,751 | 1,501 | 1,620 | 701 |
| Long Term Debt | 2,042 | 2,153 | 2,309 | 2,375 | 2,372 | 2,417 | 3,427 | 3,969 | 4,233 | 2,660 |
| Common Equity | 3,286 | 3,406 | 2,967 | 3,708 | 3,533 | 3,483 | 4,317 | 4,768 | 4,831 | 2,341 |
| Total Capital | 5,348 | 5,576 | 6,195 | 7,311 | 7,082 | 7,052 | 9,249 | 10,415 | 10,821 | 6,009 |
| Capital Expenditures | 242 | 224 | 288 | 347 | 302 | 305 | 407 | 393 | 377 | 290 |
| Cash Flow | 655 | 668 | 503 | 758 | 610 | 610 | 377 | 722 | 671 | 436 |
| Current Ratio | 2.0 | 2.0 | 1.7 | 1.5 | 1.4 | 1.9 | 1.5 | 1.6 | 1.5 | 1.4 |
| % Long Term Debt of Capitalization | 38.2 | 38.6 | 37.3 | 32.5 | 33.5 | 34.3 | 37.1 | 38.1 | 39.1 | 44.3 |
| % Net Income of Revenue | 4.6 | 3.7 | 1.2 | 4.1 | 1.4 | 1.9 | NM | NM | NM | 2.2 |
| % Return on Assets | 2.9 | 2.6 | 0.9 | 3.0 | 1.0 | 1.2 | NM | NM | NM | 1.3 |
| % Return on Equity | 7.8 | 7.1 | 2.4 | 7.9 | 2.7 | 3.1 | NM | NM | NM | 3.8 |

Data as orig reptd.; bef. results of disc opers/spec. items. Per share data adj. for stk. divs.; EPS diluted. E-Estimated. NA-Not Available. NM-Not Meaningful. NR-Not Ranked. UR-Under Review.

**Office:** 501 South 5th Street, Richmond, VA 23219-0501.
**Telephone:** 804-444-1000.
**Website:** http://www.meadwestvaco.com
**Chrmn & CEO:** J.A. Luke, Jr.

**Pres:** J.A. Buzzard
**SVP & CFO:** E.M. Rajkowski
**SVP, Secy & General Counsel:** W.L. Willkie, II
**CTO:** M.T. Watkins

**Investor Contact:** E.M. Rajkowski (804-327-5200)
**Board Members:** M. E. Campbell, T. W. Cole, Jr., J. G. Kaiser, R. B. Kelson, J. M. Kilts, S. J. Kropf, D. S. Luke, J. A. Luke, Jr., R. C. McCormack, T. H. Powers, J. L. Warner, A. D. Wilson

**Founded:** 1846
**Domicile:** Delaware
**Employees:** 17,500

*The McGraw-Hill Companies*

# Medco Health Solutions Inc.

**STANDARD &POOR'S**

| S&P Recommendation | HOLD ★★★☆☆ | Price<br>$53.74 (as of Nov 25, 2011) | 12-Mo. Target Price<br>$64.00 | Investment Style<br>Large-Cap Blend |
| --- | --- | --- | --- | --- |

**GICS Sector** Health Care
**Sub-Industry** Health Care Services

**Summary** Medco is the largest U.S. pharmacy benefit manager (PBM) in terms of revenues and script count.

## Key Stock Statistics (Source S&P, Vickers, company reports)

| | | | | | | | | |
| --- | --- | --- | --- | --- | --- | --- | --- | --- |
| 52-Wk Range | $66.38– 44.60 | S&P Oper. EPS 2011**E** | 4.10 | Market Capitalization(B) | $20.801 | Beta | 0.63 |
| Trailing 12-Month EPS | $3.44 | S&P Oper. EPS 2012**E** | 4.50 | Yield (%) | Nil | S&P 3-Yr. Proj. EPS CAGR(%) | 21 |
| Trailing 12-Month P/E | 15.6 | P/E on S&P Oper. EPS 2011**E** | 13.1 | Dividend Rate/Share | Nil | S&P Credit Rating | BBB+ |
| $10K Invested 5 Yrs Ago | $22,429 | Common Shares Outstg. (M) | 387.1 | Institutional Ownership (%) | 80 | | |

## Price Performance

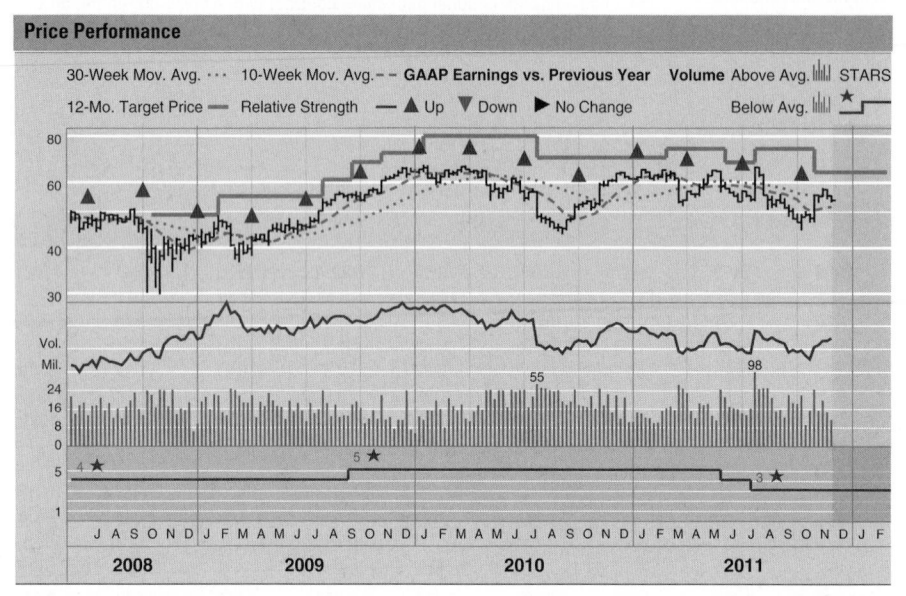

30-Week Mov. Avg. · · · · 10-Week Mov. Avg. - - **GAAP Earnings vs. Previous Year** Volume Above Avg. STARS
12-Mo. Target Price — Relative Strength — ▲ Up ▼ Down ► No Change Below Avg.

Options: ASE, CBOE, P, Ph

Analysis prepared by Equity Analyst **Herman Saftlas** on Nov 04, 2011, when the stock traded at **$53.45**.

## Highlights

▶ Based on Medco as an independent company, we forecast revenues to fall about 14.5% from the $69 billion that we estimate for 2011. Unfavorable revenue comparisons, in our opinion, should reflect the loss of large retail clients transitioning from MHS because of acquisitions and other reasons, and a greater proportion of inexpensive generics in the mix. Medco has estimated that the generic wave will reduce 2012 sales by about $6.5 billion. However, the rise in generics should have a favorable impact on profits, since PBMs typically derive higher margins from generics than from branded drug sales.

▶ We expect EBITDA to rise about 9.5% in 2012 from a projected $3.1 billion for 2011, benefiting from the generic wave and business efficiencies. MHS projected EBITDA as a percentage of revenues to rise to 5.8% in 2012, from an estimated 4.5% in 2011, reflecting higher EBITDA, and the fact that business that will be lost in 2012 carries very low margins.

▶ We estimate cash operating EPS before intangible amortization charges of $4.50 for 2012, up from the $4.10 that we forecast for 2011.

## Investment Rationale/Risk

▶ In mid-July 2011, Medco agreed to be acquired by rival PBM Express Scripts (ESRX 44 Strong Buy) for a combination of cash and stock presently valued at about $31 billion. Terms of the deal call for each share of MHS to be exchanged for $28.80 in cash, plus 0.81 shares of ESRX common. We believe Medco's loss of an $11 billion contract with UnitedHealthcare in 2013 provided a key catalyst for the deal. We see a combined ESRX/MHS emerging as a much stronger competitor, accounting for an estimated two-fifths of total U.S. adjusted prescriptions in 2010. Despite antitrust concerns, we think the FTC is likely to approve this merger, given its ability to reduce costs for healthcare consumers. Subject to customary approvals, we expect the deal to be completed during the first half of 2012.

▶ Risks to our recommendation and target price include failure to complete the merger with Express Scripts, and possible client losses.

▶ Our 12-month target price of $64 roughly approximates the current per share value of the cash/stock package that ESRX is offering for Medco common shares.

## Qualitative Risk Assessment

| LOW | MEDIUM | HIGH |
| --- | --- | --- |

Our risk assessment reflects rising drug demand and our view of MHS's improving financial performance and declining debt leverage. However, we believe intense competition and increased government regulation of pharmacy benefit managers, which we view as likely, could slow long-term progress in profits.

## Quantitative Evaluations

**S&P Quality Ranking** NR

| D | C | B- | B | B+ | A- | A | A+ |
| --- | --- | --- | --- | --- | --- | --- | --- |

**Relative Strength Rank** STRONG

83

LOWEST = 1 HIGHEST = 99

## Revenue/Earnings Data

**Revenue (Million $)**

| | 1Q | 2Q | 3Q | 4Q | Year |
| --- | --- | --- | --- | --- | --- |
| 2011 | 17,020 | 17,074 | 16,982 | -- | -- |
| 2010 | 16,311 | 16,408 | 16,320 | 16,930 | 65,968 |
| 2009 | 14,834 | 14,930 | 14,795 | 15,245 | 59,804 |
| 2008 | 12,963 | 12,775 | 12,559 | 12,961 | 51,258 |
| 2007 | 11,160 | 11,050 | 10,919 | 11,379 | 44,506 |
| 2006 | 10,564 | 10,589 | 10,461 | 10,930 | 42,544 |

**Earnings Per Share ($)**

| | | | | | |
| --- | --- | --- | --- | --- | --- |
| 2011 | 0.80 | 0.85 | 0.90 | E1.16 | E4.10 |
| 2010 | 0.67 | 0.77 | 0.85 | 0.88 | 3.16 |
| 2009 | 0.58 | 0.64 | 0.69 | 0.70 | 2.61 |
| 2008 | 0.50 | 0.51 | 0.58 | 0.54 | 2.13 |
| 2007 | 0.47 | 0.38 | 0.39 | 0.38 | 1.63 |
| 2006 | 0.08 | 0.28 | 0.31 | 0.39 | 1.05 |

Fiscal year ended Dec. 31. Next earnings report expected: Late February. EPS Estimates based on S&P Operating Earnings; historical GAAP earnings are as reported.

## Dividend Data

No cash dividends have been paid.

---

**Please read the Required Disclosures and Analyst Certification on the last page of this report.**

The **McGraw·Hill** Companies

# Medco Health Solutions Inc.

STANDARD
&POOR'S

## Business Summary November 04, 2011

CORPORATE OVERVIEW. Medco Health Solutions was spun off to Merck & Co. (MRK) shareholders in a tax-free transaction in August 2003. The company is one of the largest U.S. pharmacy benefit managers (PBMs), servicing over 65 million members. It provides programs and services to clients and members of PBMs, and to physicians and pharmacies that they use.

Revenues and net income are derived from: rebates and discounts on prescription drugs from pharmaceutical manufacturers; competitive discounts from retail pharmacies; the negotiation of favorable client pricing, including rebate sharing terms; the shift in dispensing volumes from retail to home delivery; and, the provision of services in a cost-efficient manner.

Medco's generic dispensing rate rose 3.5% to a record 71% in 2010. The mail-order generic dispensing rate increased 3.7% to 61.5%, and the retail generic dispensing rate increased 3.5% to 72.7%. Total prescription volume in 2010, adjusting for the difference in days supply between mail-order and retail, was a record 957 million, a 6.5% increase over 2009. Mail-order prescription volume increased to a record 110 million, also up 6.5%. Mail-order generic prescription volume advanced 13.4% to 67.6 million, while brand-name prescription volumes declined 3.0% to 42.2 million prescriptions.

Retail volumes in 2010 reached a record 630.3 million prescriptions, a 6.6% increase over 2009, a result of significant new client wins. The full-year 2010 adjusted mail-order penetration rate of 34.1% was relatively consistent with 34.2% in 2009.

CORPORATE STRATEGY. MHS seeks to reduce the rate of increase of client drug expenditures (drug trends). It also continues to expand its home drug delivery business, reducing drug costs. The company has been making progress in transitioning members of its large retail-heavy accounts from retail to mail service. MHS also seeks to contain costs for clients and their members by encouraging the prescription of drugs on a plan's approved list of drugs (formulary) and the use of generics. In this regard, MHS's generic dispensing rate has climbed steadily in recent years, reaching 71% in 2010. We believe that its service, technology, and cost containment initiatives have enabled Medco to help its customers save money on prescription drug spending.

## Company Financials Fiscal Year Ended Dec. 31

| Per Share Data ($) | 2010 | 2009 | 2008 | 2007 | 2006 | 2005 | 2004 | 2003 | 2002 | 2001 |
|---|---|---|---|---|---|---|---|---|---|---|
| Tangible Book Value | NM | NM | NM | NM | NM | NM | 0.49 | NM | NM | 0.85 |
| Cash Flow | 4.21 | 3.60 | 2.98 | 2.33 | 1.69 | 1.63 | 1.56 | 1.31 | 1.07 | 1.08 |
| Earnings | 3.16 | 2.61 | 2.13 | 1.63 | 1.05 | 1.03 | 0.88 | 0.79 | 0.59 | 0.48 |
| S&P Core Earnings | 3.13 | 2.62 | 2.11 | 1.62 | 1.21 | 0.93 | 0.74 | 0.52 | 0.54 | 0.36 |
| Dividends | Nil | Nil | Nil | Nil | Nil | Nil | Nil | Nil | Nil | NA |
| Payout Ratio | Nil | Nil | Nil | Nil | Nil | Nil | Nil | Nil | Nil | NA |
| Prices:High | 66.94 | 66.00 | 54.63 | 51.67 | 32.06 | 28.98 | 20.95 | 19.00 | NA | NA |
| Prices:Low | 43.45 | 36.46 | 29.80 | 26.26 | 23.54 | 20.28 | 14.70 | 10.10 | NA | NA |
| P/E Ratio:High | 21 | 25 | 26 | 32 | 31 | 28 | 24 | 24 | NA | NA |
| P/E Ratio:Low | 14 | 14 | 14 | 16 | 22 | 20 | 17 | 13 | NA | NA |

| Income Statement Analysis (Million $) | 2010 | 2009 | 2008 | 2007 | 2006 | 2005 | 2004 | 2003 | 2002 | 2001 |
|---|---|---|---|---|---|---|---|---|---|---|
| Revenue | 65,968 | 59,804 | 51,258 | 44,506 | 42,544 | 37,871 | 35,352 | 34,265 | 32,959 | 29,071 |
| Operating Income | 2,974 | 2,751 | 2,461 | 2,000 | 1,470 | 1,350 | 1,244 | 1,025 | 886 | 837 |
| Depreciation | 477 | 485 | 443 | 397 | 392 | 358 | 378 | 283 | 257 | 323 |
| Interest Expense | 173 | 173 | 234 | 134 | 65.9 | 73.9 | Nil | Nil | 73.5 | Nil |
| Pretax Income | 2,334 | 2,103 | 1,791 | 1,503 | 1,012 | 953 | 806 | 729 | 547 | 518 |
| Effective Tax Rate | NA | 39.1% | 38.4% | 39.3% | 37.7% | 36.8% | 40.3% | 41.6% | 41.7% | 50.5% |
| Net Income | 1,427 | 1,280 | 1,103 | 912 | 630 | 602 | 482 | 426 | 319 | 257 |
| S&P Core Earnings | 1,414 | 1,284 | 1,092 | 908 | 726 | 544 | 404 | 279 | 287 | 188 |

| Balance Sheet & Other Financial Data (Million $) | 2010 | 2009 | 2008 | 2007 | 2006 | 2005 | 2004 | 2003 | 2002 | 2001 |
|---|---|---|---|---|---|---|---|---|---|---|
| Cash | 910 | 2,548 | 1,002 | 844 | 818 | 888 | 1,146 | 638 | 203 | 16.3 |
| Current Assets | 6,686 | 8,159 | 7,098 | 6,303 | 5,855 | 5,061 | 4,320 | 3,760 | 3,044 | 2,534 |
| Total Assets | 17,097 | 17,916 | 17,011 | 16,218 | 14,388 | 13,703 | 10,542 | 10,263 | 9,714 | 9,252 |
| Current Liabilities | 6,882 | 6,348 | 5,798 | 5,129 | 4,827 | 3,761 | 2,645 | 2,605 | 2,370 | 1,809 |
| Long Term Debt | 5,004 | 4,000 | 4,003 | 2,894 | 866 | 944 | 1,093 | 1,346 | 1,385 | Nil |
| Common Equity | 3,987 | 6,387 | 5,958 | 6,875 | 7,504 | 7,724 | 5,719 | 5,080 | 4,738 | 6,268 |
| Total Capital | 8,990 | 10,387 | 11,026 | 10,937 | 9,531 | 9,882 | 6,812 | 7,604 | 7,305 | 7,423 |
| Capital Expenditures | 250 | 239 | 287 | 178 | 151 | 132 | 98.1 | 125 | 235 | 322 |
| Cash Flow | 1,904 | 1,765 | 1,546 | 1,309 | 1,022 | 960 | 859 | 709 | 576 | 580 |
| Current Ratio | 1.0 | 1.3 | 1.2 | 1.2 | 1.2 | 1.3 | 1.6 | 1.4 | 1.3 | 1.4 |
| % Long Term Debt of Capitalization | 55.7 | 38.5 | 36.3 | 26.5 | 9.1 | 9.6 | 16.0 | 17.7 | 19.0 | Nil |
| % Net Income of Revenue | 2.2 | 2.1 | 2.2 | 2.1 | 1.5 | 1.6 | 1.4 | 1.2 | 1.0 | 0.9 |
| % Return on Assets | 8.2 | 7.3 | 6.6 | 6.0 | 4.4 | 5.0 | 4.6 | 4.2 | NA | 2.8 |
| % Return on Equity | 27.5 | 20.7 | 17.2 | 12.7 | 8.3 | 9.0 | 8.9 | 7.3 | NA | 4.1 |

Data as orig reptd.; bef. results of disc opers/spec. items. Per share data adj. for stk. divs.; EPS diluted. E-Estimated. NA-Not Available. NM-Not Meaningful. NR-Not Ranked. UR-Under Review.

**Office:** 100 Parsons Pond Drive, Franklin Lakes, NJ 07417-2603.
**Telephone:** 201-269-3400.
**Website:** http://www.medcohealth.com
**Chrmn & CEO:** D.B. Snow, Jr.

**Pres & COO:** K.O. Klepper
**SVP, Chief Acctg Officer & Cntlr:** G.R. Cappucci
**CFO:** R.J. Rubino
**Secy & General Counsel:** T.M. Moriarty

**Board Members:** H. W. Barker, Jr., J. L. Cassis, M. Goldstein, C. M. Lillis, M. Potter, W. L. Roper, D. B. Snow, Jr., D. D. Stevens, B. J. Wilson

**Founded:** 1983
**Domicile:** Delaware
**Employees:** 24,625

# Medtronic Inc.

**STANDARD &POOR'S**

| S&P Recommendation HOLD ★★★☆☆ | Price $34.91 (as of Nov 29, 2011) | 12-Mo. Target Price $39.00 | Investment Style Large-Cap Growth |
|---|---|---|---|

**GICS Sector** Health Care
**Sub-Industry** Health Care Equipment

**Summary** This global medical device manufacturer has leadership positions in the pacemaker, defibrillator, orthopedic, diabetes management, and other medical markets.

## Key Stock Statistics (Source S&P, Vickers, company reports)

| | | | | | | | |
|---|---|---|---|---|---|---|---|
| 52-Wk Range | $43.33–30.18 | S&P Oper. EPS 2012E | 3.45 | Market Capitalization(B) | $36.864 | Beta | 0.91 |
| Trailing 12-Month EPS | $3.17 | S&P Oper. EPS 2013E | 3.75 | Yield (%) | 2.78 | S&P 3-Yr. Proj. EPS CAGR(%) | 6 |
| Trailing 12-Month P/E | 11.0 | P/E on S&P Oper. EPS 2012E | 10.1 | Dividend Rate/Share | $0.97 | S&P Credit Rating | AA- |
| $10K Invested 5 Yrs Ago | $6,915 | Common Shares Outstg. (M) | 1,056.0 | Institutional Ownership (%) | 83 | | |

## Price Performance

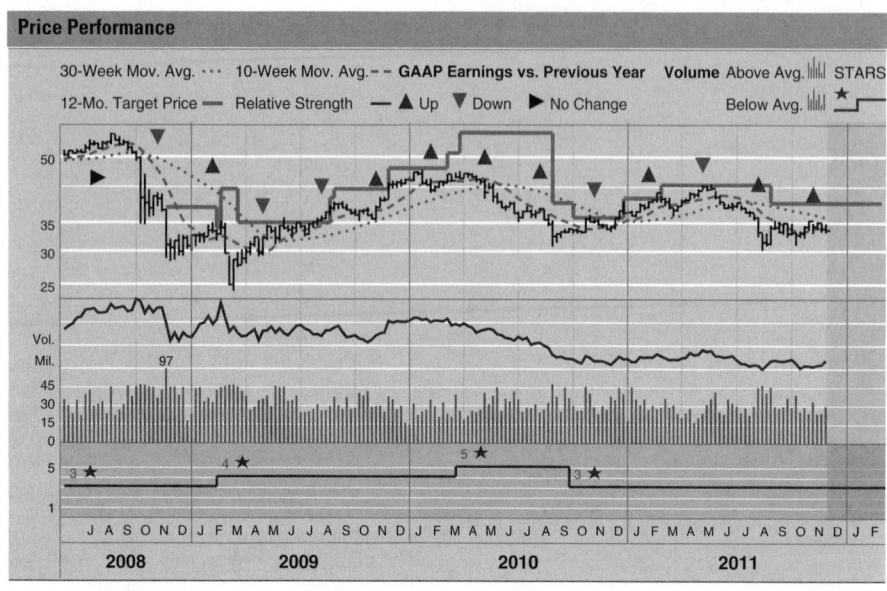

30-Week Mov. Avg. · · · · 10-Week Mov. Avg. – – **GAAP Earnings vs. Previous Year** Volume Above Avg. STARS
12-Mo. Target Price — Relative Strength — ▲ Up ▼ Down ▶ No Change Below Avg.

Options: ASE, CBOE, P, Ph

Analysis prepared by Equity Analyst **Phillip Seligman** on Nov 29, 2011, when the stock traded at **$34.84**.

## Qualitative Risk Assessment

| LOW | **MEDIUM** | HIGH |
|---|---|---|

Our risk assessment reflects MDT's exposure to intensely competitive areas of the medical equipment markets, which are typically characterized by relatively short product life cycles, pricing pressures, and threat of new market entrants. However, we believe this is offset by MDT's many competitive advantages from the scale of its operations and sales force, product breadth, and what we see as its financial strength.

## Quantitative Evaluations

**S&P Quality Ranking** A

| D | C | B- | B | B+ | A- | **A** | A+ |
|---|---|---|---|---|---|---|---|

**Relative Strength Rank** STRONG

83

LOWEST = 1 HIGHEST = 99

## Highlights

▶ For FY 12 (Apr.), we expect total reported sales to rise a little more than 4%. Drivers we look for include low-double-digit growth in cardiovascular (CV) and diabetes, mid-single digit growth in neuromodulation, high-teens growth in surgical technologies product sales, and favorable foreign exchange. We also see essentially flat sales in cardiac rhythm disease management (CRDM), on continued weak U.S. ICD markets, and a mid-single digit decline in spine, reflecting soft U.S. spinal surgery markets and controversy surrounding the Infuse Bone Graft.

▶ We look for gross margins to narrow modestly, as new products carrying slightly lower gross margins. We forecast that R&D costs will decline 40 basis points (bps) as a percentage of sales, on revenue leverage. We expect the SG&A cost ratio to contract 70 bps, as the benefits of cost reduction and revenue leverage outweigh sales force additions and the investment in new product launches.

▶ We see FY 12 non-GAAP EPS of $3.45, aided by share buybacks, versus $3.37 in FY 11. Our FY 12 estimate assumes $0.05 dilution from the January 2011 Ardian acquisition. We forecast $3.75 for FY 13.

## Investment Rationale/Risk

▶ We see MDT's new CEO moving forward on his strategy to enhance growth, which entails better execution, improving R&D productivity and accelerating globalization. In this regard, we expect to see more investment in R&D, manufacturing and possibly M&A in emerging markets. We also expect MDT to seek to improve the marketing of existing product lines, and to prioritize the development of products that allow broad utilization and have a promising return on investment. Still, we think any policy shifts will take time to implement and realize favorable returns. Meanwhile, MDT faces soft U.S. procedure volumes, particularly in its key CRDM and spine segments. We also see more pricing pressures ahead. While MDT gained market share in many product areas, we do not see its rivals standing still.

▶ Risks to our opinion and target price include loss of share in key markets, adverse reimbursement rate changes, and further weakness in the U.S. CRDM and spinal surgery markets.

▶ Our 12-month target price of $39 is 10.5X our calendar 2012 EPS estimate of $3.69, a discount to peers given difficult business conditions and intensifying competition we see.

## Revenue/Earnings Data

**Revenue (Million $)**

| | 1Q | 2Q | 3Q | 4Q | Year |
|---|---|---|---|---|---|
| 2012 | 4,049 | 4,132 | -- | -- | -- |
| 2011 | 3,773 | 3,903 | 3,961 | 4,295 | 15,933 |
| 2010 | 3,933 | 3,838 | 3,851 | 4,196 | 15,817 |
| 2009 | 3,706 | 3,570 | 3,494 | 3,829 | 14,599 |
| 2008 | 3,127 | 3,124 | 3,405 | 3,860 | 13,515 |
| 2007 | 2,897 | 3,075 | 3,048 | 3,280 | 12,299 |

**Earnings Per Share ($)**

| | 1Q | 2Q | 3Q | 4Q | Year |
|---|---|---|---|---|---|
| 2012 | 0.77 | 0.82 | E0.86 | E0.97 | E3.45 |
| 2011 | 0.76 | 0.52 | 0.86 | 0.72 | 2.86 |
| 2010 | 0.40 | 0.78 | 0.75 | 0.86 | 2.79 |
| 2009 | 0.66 | 0.51 | 0.65 | 0.11 | 1.93 |
| 2008 | 0.66 | 0.58 | 0.07 | 0.72 | 1.95 |
| 2007 | 0.51 | 0.59 | 0.61 | 0.70 | 2.41 |

Fiscal year ended Apr. 30. Next earnings report expected: Late February. EPS Estimates based on S&P Operating Earnings; historical GAAP earnings are as reported.

## Dividend Data (Dates: mm/dd Payment Date: mm/dd/yy)

| Amount ($) | Date Decl. | Ex-Div. Date | Stk. of Record | Payment Date |
|---|---|---|---|---|
| 0.225 | 12/09 | 01/05 | 01/07 | 01/28/11 |
| 0.225 | 02/17 | 04/06 | 04/08 | 04/29/11 |
| 0.243 | 06/23 | 07/06 | 07/08 | 07/29/11 |
| 0.243 | 08/25 | 10/05 | 10/07 | 10/28/11 |

Dividends have been paid since 1977. Source: Company reports.

**Please read the Required Disclosures and Analyst Certification on the last page of this report.**

*The McGraw-Hill Companies*

# Medtronic Inc.

STANDARD
&POOR'S

## Business Summary November 29, 2011

CORPORATE OVERVIEW. Medtronic has leading positions in medical device categories, including cardiac rhythm management, spinal, vascular, neurology and cardiac surgery.

Cardiac rhythm disease management products (CRDM; 31.4% of FY 11 (Apr.) revenues) include implantable pacemakers to treat bradycardia, a condition of slow or irregular heartbeats. Some models are non-invasively programmed by a physician to adjust sensing, electrical pulse intensity, duration, rate and other factors, as well as pacers that can sense in both upper and lower heart chambers and produce appropriate impulses. In May 2005, FDA approval was received for EnRhythm, a dual-chamber pacemaker and the first pacemaker to offer an exclusive pacing mode, called Managed Ventricular Pacing, which enables the device to be programmed to minimize pacing pulses to the right ventricle.

Implantable cardioverter defibrillators (ICDs) treat abnormally fast heart beats

by monitoring the heart; when a rapid rhythm is detected, electrical impulses or shocks are delivered. Cardiac resynchronization therapy (CRT) devices synchronize contractions of multiple heart chambers. The company's InSynch ICD offers CRT for heart failure, as well as advanced defibrillation capabilities for patients also at risk for potentially lethal tachyarrhythmias that may lead to cardiac arrest. The CDRM segment also includes diagnostics and monitoring devices to record the heart's electrical activity and patient management tools, including CareLink, which enables patients to transmit data from their pacemaker, ICD or CRT-D using a portable monitor that is connected to a standard telephone line.

## Company Financials Fiscal Year Ended Apr. 30

| Per Share Data ($) | 2011 | 2010 | 2009 | 2008 | 2007 | 2006 | 2005 | 2004 | 2003 | 2002 |
|---|---|---|---|---|---|---|---|---|---|---|
| Tangible Book Value | 3.41 | 3.35 | 1.95 | 1.62 | 4.56 | 2.98 | 4.26 | 3.18 | 2.21 | 1.10 |
| Cash Flow | 3.61 | 3.49 | 2.55 | 2.51 | 2.91 | 2.54 | 1.86 | 1.96 | 1.64 | 1.07 |
| Earnings | 2.86 | 2.79 | 1.93 | 1.95 | 2.41 | 2.09 | 1.48 | 1.60 | 1.30 | 0.80 |
| S&P Core Earnings | 3.01 | 3.06 | 2.12 | 2.12 | 2.44 | 2.00 | 1.65 | 1.46 | 1.10 | 0.76 |
| Dividends | NA | 0.82 | 0.50 | 0.44 | 0.39 | 0.34 | 0.29 | 0.25 | 0.25 | 0.20 |
| Payout Ratio | NA | 29% | 26% | 23% | 16% | 16% | 20% | 16% | 19% | 25% |
| Calendar Year | 2010 | 2009 | 2008 | 2007 | 2006 | 2005 | 2004 | 2003 | 2002 | 2001 |
| Prices:High | 46.66 | 44.94 | 56.97 | 57.99 | 59.87 | 58.91 | 53.70 | 52.92 | 50.69 | 60.81 |
| Prices:Low | 30.80 | 24.06 | 28.33 | 44.87 | 42.37 | 48.70 | 43.99 | 42.90 | 32.50 | 36.64 |
| P/E Ratio:High | 16 | 16 | 30 | 30 | 25 | 28 | 36 | 33 | 39 | 72 |
| P/E Ratio:Low | 11 | 9 | 15 | 23 | 18 | 23 | 30 | 27 | 25 | 43 |

| Income Statement Analysis (Million $) | 2011 | 2010 | 2009 | 2008 | 2007 | 2006 | 2005 | 2004 | 2003 | 2002 |
|---|---|---|---|---|---|---|---|---|---|---|
| Revenue | 15,933 | 15,817 | 14,599 | 13,515 | 12,299 | 11,292 | 10,055 | 9,087 | 7,665 | 6,411 |
| Operating Income | 5,345 | 5,909 | 5,276 | 4,728 | 4,322 | 4,248 | 3,907 | 3,583 | 3,062 | 2,479 |
| Depreciation | 804 | 772 | 699 | 637 | 583 | 544 | 463 | 443 | 408 | 330 |
| Interest Expense | 278 | 246 | 217 | 255 | 228 | Nil | 55.1 | 56.5 | 7.20 | Nil |
| Pretax Income | 3,723 | 3,969 | 2,772 | 2,885 | 3,515 | 3,161 | 2,544 | 2,797 | 2,341 | 1,524 |
| Effective Tax Rate | NA | NA | 17.4% | 22.7% | 20.3% | 19.4% | 29.1% | 29.9% | 31.7% | 35.4% |
| Net Income | 3,096 | 3,099 | 2,291 | 2,231 | 2,802 | 2,547 | 1,804 | 1,959 | 1,600 | 984 |
| S&P Core Earnings | 3,259 | 3,395 | 2,392 | 2,423 | 2,841 | 2,450 | 2,006 | 1,790 | 1,347 | 936 |

| Balance Sheet & Other Financial Data (Million $) | 2011 | 2010 | 2009 | 2008 | 2007 | 2006 | 2005 | 2004 | 2003 | 2002 |
|---|---|---|---|---|---|---|---|---|---|---|
| Cash | 2,428 | 3,775 | 1,676 | 1,613 | 1,256 | 2,994 | 2,232 | 1,594 | 1,470 | 411 |
| Current Assets | 9,117 | 9,839 | 7,460 | 7,322 | 7,918 | 10,377 | 7,422 | 5,313 | 4,606 | 3,488 |
| Total Assets | 30,424 | 28,090 | 23,605 | 22,198 | 19,512 | 19,665 | 16,617 | 14,111 | 12,321 | 10,905 |
| Current Liabilities | 4,714 | 5,121 | 3,147 | 3,535 | 2,563 | 4,406 | 3,380 | 4,241 | 1,813 | 3,985 |
| Long Term Debt | 8,112 | 6,944 | 6,772 | 5,700 | 5,578 | 5,486 | 1,973 | 1.10 | 1,980 | 9.50 |
| Common Equity | 15,968 | 14,629 | 12,973 | 11,536 | 10,977 | 9,383 | 10,450 | 9,077 | 7,906 | 6,431 |
| Total Capital | 24,080 | 21,573 | 19,570 | 17,330 | 16,555 | 14,891 | 12,901 | 9,486 | 10,191 | 6,674 |
| Capital Expenditures | 501 | 573 | 498 | 513 | 573 | 407 | 452 | 425 | 380 | 386 |
| Cash Flow | 3,900 | 3,871 | 2,868 | 2,868 | 3,385 | 3,090 | 2,267 | 2,402 | 2,008 | 1,314 |
| Current Ratio | 1.9 | 1.9 | 2.4 | 2.1 | 3.1 | 2.4 | 2.2 | 1.3 | 2.5 | 0.9 |
| % Long Term Debt of Capitalization | 33.7 | 32.2 | 34.6 | 33.3 | 33.7 | 36.8 | 15.3 | 0.0 | 19.4 | 0.1 |
| % Net Income of Revenue | 19.4 | 19.6 | 15.7 | 16.5 | 22.8 | 22.6 | 17.9 | 21.6 | 20.9 | 15.3 |
| % Return on Assets | 10.6 | 12.0 | 10.0 | 10.7 | 14.3 | 14.0 | 11.7 | 14.8 | 13.8 | 11.0 |
| % Return on Equity | 20.2 | 22.6 | 18.7 | 19.8 | 27.5 | 25.7 | 18.5 | 23.1 | 22.3 | 16.5 |

Data as orig reptd.; bef. results of disc opers/spec. items. Per share data adj. for stk. divs.; EPS diluted. E-Estimated. NA-Not Available. NM-Not Meaningful. NR-Not Ranked. UR-Under Review.

**Office:** 710 Medtronic Parkway, Minneapolis, MN 55432-5604.
**Telephone:** 763-514-4000.
**Website:** http://www.medtronic.com
**Chrmn & CEO:** O. Ishrak

**COO:** H.J. Dallas
**SVP, CFO & Chief Acctg Officer:** G.L. Ellis
**SVP & CSO:** R. Kuntz
**SVP, Secy & General Counsel:** D.C. Findlay

**Investor Contact:** J. Warren (763-505-2696)
**Board Members:** R. H. Anderson, D. L. Calhoun, V. J. Dzau, O. Ishrak, S. A. Jackson, M. O. Leavitt, J. T. Lenehan, D. M. O'Leary, K. J. Powell, R. C. Pozen, J. Rosso, J. W. Schuler

**Founded:** 1957
**Domicile:** Minnesota
**Employees:** 43,321

# MEMC Electronic Materials Inc

STANDARD
&POOR'S

| S&P Recommendation | SELL ★ ★ ☆ ☆ ☆ | Price $3.92 (as of Nov 25, 2011) | 12-Mo. Target Price $5.00 | Investment Style Large-Cap Growth |
|---|---|---|---|---|

**GICS Sector** Information Technology
**Sub-Industry** Semiconductor Equipment

**Summary** This company is a worldwide producer of silicon wafers used in semiconductors for microelectronic applications. It also provides silicon materials to the solar industry.

## Key Stock Statistics (Source S&P, Vickers, company reports)

| | | | | | | | | |
|---|---|---|---|---|---|---|---|---|
| 52-Wk Range | $15.04–3.92 | S&P Oper. EPS 2011E | 0.26 | Market Capitalization(B) | $0.903 | Beta | | 1.33 |
| Trailing 12-Month EPS | $-0.17 | S&P Oper. EPS 2012E | 0.25 | Yield (%) | Nil | S&P 3-Yr. Proj. EPS CAGR(%) | | 20 |
| Trailing 12-Month P/E | NM | P/E on S&P Oper. EPS 2011E | 15.1 | Dividend Rate/Share | Nil | S&P Credit Rating | | NR |
| $10K Invested 5 Yrs Ago | $1,036 | Common Shares Outstg. (M) | 230.5 | Institutional Ownership (%) | 88 | | | |

## Price Performance

30-Week Mov. Avg. · · · 10-Week Mov. Avg. – – GAAP Earnings vs. Previous Year    Volume Above Avg. ‖‖‖ STARS
12-Mo. Target Price — Relative Strength — ▲ Up ▼ Down ► No Change    Below Avg. ‖‖‖ ★

Analysis prepared by Equity Analyst **Angelo Zino, CFA** on Nov 04, 2011, when the stock traded at **$5.25**.

Options: ASE, CBOE, P, Ph

## Highlights

➤ We see sales rising 2.8% in 2012, following our forecast for a 33% increase in 2011. We project that sales from WFR's semiconductor materials segment will experience modest growth of 6.6% in 2011 and 3.1% in 2012. Within WFR's solar materials segment, we expect sales to increase 25% this year, partly due to a solar contract resolution, and fall 19% in 2012, due to steep pricing declines. Finally, we forecast sales for the SunEdison business to more than double in 2011 and rise 23% in 2012.

➤ We project an annual gross margin of 17% in 2012 versus our 18% margin view for this year. Although we see higher volume and internal wafer manufacturing benefiting margins, we anticipate pricing pressure to persist for the solar industry. We forecast more stable pricing trends within WFR's semiconductor business. We project operating expenses, excluding restructuring costs, to be 15% of sales in 2011 and 13% in 2012.

➤ We forecast operating EPS of $0.26 for 2011 and $0.25 for 2012. Our estimates account for revenues recognized in WFR's SunEdison segment using the percentage of completion accounting method, benefiting 2011 operating EPS by $0.38.

## Investment Rationale/Risk

➤ Our sell opinion reflects our belief that silicon wafer supply will exceed demand through at least the middle of 2012, as China-based solar manufacturers ramp up production. We have a cautious view of the earnings potential of WFR's solar business given the existing cost structure, competitive pressures and pricing environment. In addition, WFR continues to operate with a highly leveraged balance sheet, with high levels of interest expense. We think demand for semiconductor wafers is likely to remain below seasonal trends near term. However, we see a growing SunEdison pipeline offering some stability in a volatile solar industry. SunEdison's backlog is concentrated in the high growth potential U.S. market.

➤ Risks to our recommendation and target price include slower expansion of industry capacity than we expect, more favorable government policies related to alternative energy, and faster semiconductor growth than projected.

➤ Our 12-month target price of $5.00 is based on a price-to-book (P/B) multiple of 0.59X WFR's tangible book value per share, above solar peers but below semiconductor peers. This is well below WFR's longer-term historical averages.

## Qualitative Risk Assessment

| LOW | MEDIUM | HIGH |
|---|---|---|

Our risk assessment reflects WFR's exposure to the historical cyclicality of the semiconductor equipment industry and intense competition, partly offset by what we view as WFR's strong market position and size.

## Quantitative Evaluations

**S&P Quality Ranking**    B-

| D | C | B- | B | B+ | A- | A | A+ |
|---|---|---|---|---|---|---|---|

**Relative Strength Rank**    WEAK

6

LOWEST = 1    HIGHEST = 99

## Revenue/Earnings Data

**Revenue (Million $)**

| | 1Q | 2Q | 3Q | 4Q | Year |
|---|---|---|---|---|---|
| 2011 | 735.9 | 745.6 | 516.2 | -- | -- |
| 2010 | 437.7 | 448.3 | 503.1 | 850.1 | 2,239 |
| 2009 | 214.0 | 282.9 | 310.0 | 356.7 | 1,164 |
| 2008 | 501.4 | 531.4 | 546.0 | 425.7 | 2,005 |
| 2007 | 440.4 | 472.7 | 472.8 | 535.9 | 1,922 |
| 2006 | 341.6 | 370.5 | 408.0 | 420.6 | 1,541 |

**Earnings Per Share ($)**

| | | | | | |
|---|---|---|---|---|---|
| 2011 | -0.02 | 0.21 | -0.41 | E0.10 | E0.26 |
| 2010 | -0.04 | 0.06 | 0.08 | 0.05 | 0.15 |
| 2009 | 0.01 | 0.01 | -0.29 | -0.03 | -0.30 |
| 2008 | -0.18 | 0.76 | 0.80 | 0.33 | 1.71 |
| 2007 | 0.58 | 0.70 | 0.65 | 1.62 | 3.56 |
| 2006 | 0.29 | 0.36 | 0.40 | 0.56 | 1.61 |

Fiscal year ended Dec. 31. Next earnings report expected: Early February. EPS Estimates based on S&P Operating Earnings; historical GAAP earnings are as reported.

## Dividend Data

No cash dividends have been paid.

---

**Please read the Required Disclosures and Analyst Certification on the last page of this report.**

The McGraw-Hill Companies

# MEMC Electronic Materials Inc

STANDARD
&POOR'S

## Business Summary November 04, 2011

CORPORATE OVERVIEW. MEMC Electronic Materials, Inc. (WFR) is a global leader in the manufacture of silicon wafers. The company designs, manufactures and provides wafers and intermediate products for use in the semiconductor, solar and related industries. Its customers include virtually all of the world's major semiconductor device manufacturers, such as the major memory, microprocessor, and applications specific integrated circuit (ASIC) manufacturers, as well as the world's largest foundries.

WFR's products include prime polish wafers, epitaxial wafers, test and monitor wafers, and silicon-on-insulator (SOI) wafers. WFR's prime wafer is a polished, highly refined, pure wafer with an ultraflat and ultraclean surface. The majority of these wafers are manufactured with a sophisticated chemical-mechanical polishing process that removes defects and leaves an extremely smooth surface. WFR's epitaxial, or epi, wafers consist of a thin silicon layer grown on the polished surface of the wafer. The epitaxial layer usually has different electrical properties from the underlying wafer, which provides customers with better isolation between circuit elements than a polished wafer, and the ability to tailor the wafer to the specific demands of the device.

WFR supplies test/monitor wafers to customers for their use in testing semiconductor manufacturing lines and processes. Although test/monitor wafers

are essentially the same as prime wafers with respect to cleanliness, it has some less rigorous requirements, allowing WFR to produce some of the test/monitor wafers from the portion of the silicon ingot that does not meet customer specifications. A SOI wafer is a new type of starting material for the chip making process. SOI wafers have three layers: a thin surface layer of silicon where the transistors are formed, an underlying layer of insulating material, and a support bulk silicon wafer. Transistors built within the top silicon layer typically switch signals faster, run at lower voltages, and are much less vulnerable to signal noise from background cosmic ray particles.

Through WFR's SunEdison business, the company is a leading solar energy installer in North America, and also provides financing services under long-term power purchase arrangements and feed-in tariff arrangements. Customers pay only for the electricity output generated by the solar system installed, avoiding the significant capital outlays usually associated with solar projects.

## Company Financials Fiscal Year Ended Dec. 31

| Per Share Data ($) | 2010 | 2009 | 2008 | 2007 | 2006 | 2005 | 2004 | 2003 | 2002 | 2001 |
|---|---|---|---|---|---|---|---|---|---|---|
| Tangible Book Value | 8.15 | 8.08 | 9.27 | 8.98 | 5.23 | 3.21 | 2.13 | 0.94 | NM | NM |
| Cash Flow | 0.93 | 0.25 | 2.15 | 3.90 | 1.91 | 1.35 | 1.22 | 0.68 | 0.09 | -4.65 |
| Earnings | 0.15 | -0.30 | 1.71 | 3.56 | 1.61 | 1.10 | 1.02 | 0.53 | -0.17 | -7.51 |
| S&P Core Earnings | 0.10 | -0.28 | 1.68 | 3.57 | 1.62 | 1.06 | 0.96 | 0.49 | -0.33 | -7.60 |
| Dividends | Nil | Nil | Nil | Nil | Nil | Nil | Nil | Nil | Nil | Nil |
| Payout Ratio | Nil | Nil | Nil | Nil | Nil | Nil | Nil | Nil | Nil | Nil |
| Prices:High | 16.99 | 21.36 | 91.45 | 96.08 | 48.90 | 24.68 | 13.28 | 14.51 | 11.50 | 11.90 |
| Prices:Low | 9.19 | 11.32 | 10.00 | 39.51 | 22.60 | 10.70 | 7.33 | 7.00 | 2.25 | 1.05 |
| P/E Ratio:High | NM | NM | 53 | 27 | 30 | 17 | 13 | 27 | NM | NM |
| P/E Ratio:Low | NM | NM | 6 | 11 | 14 | 7 | 7 | 13 | NM | NM |

| Income Statement Analysis (Million $) | | | | | | | | | | |
|---|---|---|---|---|---|---|---|---|---|---|
| Revenue | 2,239 | 1,164 | 2,005 | 1,922 | 1,541 | 1,107 | 1,028 | 781 | 687 | 618 |
| Operating Income | 177 | 61.1 | 969 | 929 | 629 | 314 | 304 | 174 | 114 | -9.69 |
| Depreciation | 165 | 124 | 103 | 79.3 | 70.3 | 57.2 | 44.1 | 31.0 | 34.2 | 169 |
| Interest Expense | 28.7 | 4.00 | 2.60 | 2.40 | 2.43 | 7.26 | 13.5 | 12.9 | 73.4 | 78.4 |
| Pretax Income | -7.30 | -112 | 590 | 1,112 | 590 | 252 | 175 | 162 | 20.8 | -259 |
| Effective Tax Rate | NA | 37.7% | 33.4% | 25.4% | 36.4% | NM | NM | 22.7% | NM | NM |
| Net Income | 46.8 | -68.3 | 390 | 826 | 369 | 249 | 226 | 117 | -5.07 | -489 |
| S&P Core Earnings | 23.6 | -61.8 | 385 | 827 | 370 | 240 | 212 | 108 | -41.9 | -529 |

| Balance Sheet & Other Financial Data (Million $) | | | | | | | | | | |
|---|---|---|---|---|---|---|---|---|---|---|
| Cash | 707 | 719 | 1,137 | 1,316 | 528 | 126 | 92.3 | 96.9 | 166 | 107 |
| Current Assets | 1,746 | 1,250 | 1,454 | 1,590 | 900 | 436 | 390 | 365 | 364 | 264 |
| Total Assets | 4,619 | 3,558 | 2,940 | 2,887 | 1,766 | 1,148 | 1,010 | 727 | 632 | 549 |
| Current Liabilities | 1,292 | 509 | 473 | 444 | 258 | 225 | 216 | 244 | 286 | 222 |
| Long Term Debt | 611 | 379 | 26.1 | 25.6 | 29.4 | 34.8 | 116 | 59.3 | 161 | 145 |
| Common Equity | 2,251 | 2,169 | 2,085 | 2,035 | 1,167 | 711 | 443 | 194 | -24.7 | -9.74 |
| Total Capital | 3,021 | 2,620 | 2,146 | 2,096 | 1,235 | 791 | 605 | 317 | 194 | 186 |
| Capital Expenditures | 632 | 253 | 303 | 276 | 148 | 163 | 150 | 85.2 | 22.0 | 7.00 |
| Cash Flow | 212 | 55.7 | 490 | 906 | 440 | 307 | 270 | 148 | 12.1 | -324 |
| Current Ratio | 1.4 | 2.5 | 3.1 | 3.6 | 3.5 | 1.9 | 1.8 | 1.5 | 1.3 | 1.2 |
| % Long Term Debt of Capitalization | 20.2 | 14.5 | 1.2 | 1.2 | 2.4 | 4.4 | 19.2 | 18.7 | 82.9 | 77.8 |
| % Net Income of Revenue | 2.1 | NM | 19.5 | 43.0 | 24.0 | 22.5 | 22.0 | 14.9 | NM | NM |
| % Return on Assets | 1.1 | NM | 13.4 | 35.5 | 25.3 | 22.9 | 26.0 | 17.2 | NM | NM |
| % Return on Equity | 2.1 | NM | 19.0 | 51.6 | 39.3 | 43.2 | 71.1 | 138.1 | NM | NM |

Data as orig reptd.; bef. results of disc opers/spec. items. Per share data adj. for stk. divs.; EPS diluted. E-Estimated. NA-Not Available. NM-Not Meaningful. NR-Not Ranked. UR-Under Review.

**Office:** 501 Pearl Drive, St. Peters, MO 63376.
**Telephone:** 636-474-5000.
**Email:** invest@memc.com
**Website:** http://www.memc.com

**Chrmn:** J.W. Marren
**Pres & CEO:** A.R. Chatila
**SVP, CFO & Chief Acctg Officer:** M.J. Murphy
**SVP, Secy & General Counsel:** B.D. Kohn

**Investor Contact:** B. Michalek (636-474-5443)
**Board Members:** P. Blackmore, R. J. Boehlke, A. R. Chatila, E. Hernandez, J. W. Marren, M. McNamara, W. E. Stevens, M. C. Turner, Jr., J. B. Williams

**Founded:** 1984
**Domicile:** Delaware
**Employees:** 6,480

# Merck & Co Inc.

## STANDARD &POOR'S

| | | | |
|---|---|---|---|
| **S&P Recommendation** BUY ★★★★☆ | **Price** $33.16 (as of Nov 25, 2011) | **12-Mo. Target Price** $42.00 | **Investment Style** Large-Cap Blend |

**GICS Sector** Health Care
**Sub-Industry** Pharmaceuticals

**Summary** This company, one of the world's largest drugmakers, acquired Schering-Plough in November 2009 for about $41 billion in cash and stock.

## Key Stock Statistics (Source S&P, Vickers, company reports)

| | | | | | | | | |
|---|---|---|---|---|---|---|---|---|
| 52-Wk Range | $37.65–29.47 | S&P Oper. EPS 2011**E** | 3.76 | Market Capitalization(B) | $101.069 | Beta | | 0.68 |
| Trailing 12-Month EPS | $1.37 | S&P Oper. EPS 2012**E** | 4.00 | Yield (%) | 5.07 | S&P 3-Yr. Proj. EPS CAGR(%) | | 6 |
| Trailing 12-Month P/E | 24.2 | P/E on S&P Oper. EPS 2011**E** | 8.8 | Dividend Rate/Share | $1.68 | S&P Credit Rating | | AA |
| $10K Invested 5 Yrs Ago | $9,273 | Common Shares Outstg. (M) | 3,047.9 | Institutional Ownership (%) | 74 | | | |

## Price Performance

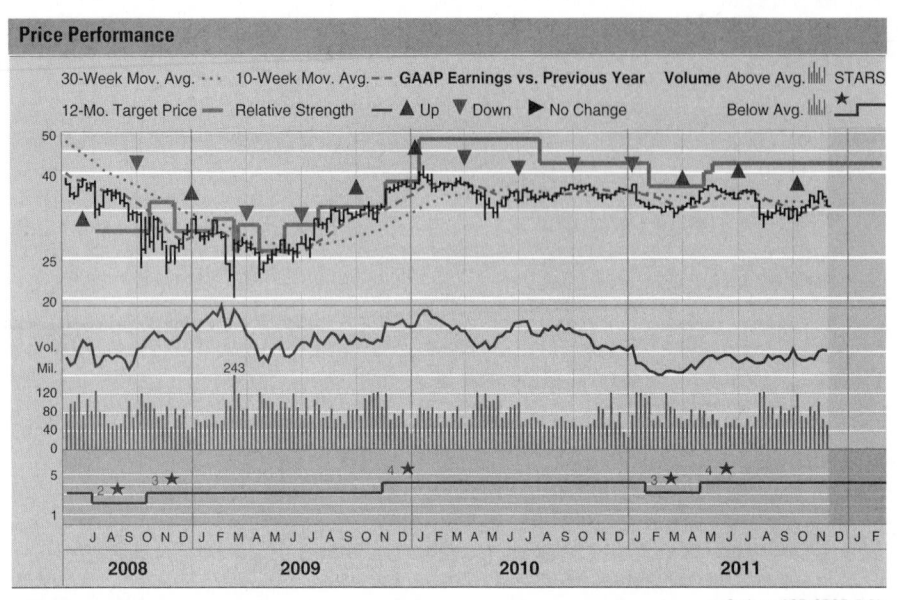

30-Week Mov. Avg. ···· 10-Week Mov. Avg. - - GAAP Earnings vs. Previous Year   Volume Above Avg. STARS
12-Mo. Target Price — Relative Strength — ▲ Up ▼ Down ▶ No Change   Below Avg. ★

Options: ASE, CBOE, P, Ph

Analysis prepared by Equity Analyst **Herman Saftlas** on Nov 15, 2011, when the stock traded at **$35.73**.

## Qualitative Risk Assessment

| LOW | MEDIUM | HIGH |
|---|---|---|

Our risk assessment reflects challenges to branded patents, new drug development, and regulatory risks. In addition, MRK's Vytorin/Zetia franchise has been affected by disappointing clinical trial results. However, we see significant synergies accruing from the recent acquisition of Schering-Plough. We also think MRK has a relatively robust R&D pipeline.

## Quantitative Evaluations

**S&P Quality Ranking**   B

| D | C | B- | B | B+ | A- | A | A+ |
|---|---|---|---|---|---|---|---|

**Relative Strength Rank**   STRONG

72

LOWEST = 1   HIGHEST = 99

## Highlights

➤ We project 2012 revenues to approximate the $48 billion that we estimate for 2011, with strength in newer drugs and expansion in emerging markets offsetting expiration losses. Key growth drivers, in our opinion, include Januvia/Janumet anti-diabetic drugs, Isentress HIV therapy and Victrelis for hepatitis C. We also see gains in animal health sales, lifted by new products. On the negative side, sales of Singulair and Cozaar/Hyzaar are expected to fall on generic erosion, while lower sales of Remicade should reflect the transitioning of marketing rights to Johnson & Johnson.

➤ We expect gross margins in 2012 to improve modestly from the 75.2% that we estimate for 2011. Despite headwinds from U.S. health care reform and European austerity pricing, we expect pretax margins to show modest improvement, helped by ongoing merger synergies, cost streamlining measures, and projected increased other income.

➤ After a projected adjusted tax rate of about 23%, versus 24% indicated for 2011, we forecast non-GAAP EPS of $4.00 for 2012, up from $3.76 that we estimate for 2011.

## Investment Rationale/Risk

➤ In mid-November 2011, MRK showcased what we consider to be an impressive 37-project R&D pipeline, with 19 compounds in late stage Phase 3 development, and another five under regulatory review. Four new drugs were approved to date in 2011, with eight new filings planned for 2012 and 2013. Key new product opportunities, in our opinion, include Victrelis for hepatitis C, Tredaptive and anacetrapib for atherosclerosis, suvorexant for insomnia, odanacatib for osteoporosis, and Bridion anesthesia reversal agent. We also see results benefiting from cost restructuring measures, which are expected to yield annual synergies of $2.8 billion, and from an ongoing $5 billion share buyback program.

➤ Risks to our opinion and target price include failure to achieve planned cost savings and synergies, worse-than-expected global drug pricing conditions, and possible pipeline setbacks.

➤ Our 12-month target price of $42 applies a peer parity P/E of 10.5X to our operating EPS estimate for 2012. The dividend, recently increased by 11%, to $0.42 quarterly, yields 4.7%.

## Revenue/Earnings Data

### Revenue (Million $)

| | 1Q | 2Q | 3Q | 4Q | Year |
|---|---|---|---|---|---|
| 2011 | 11,580 | 12,151 | 12,022 | -- | -- |
| 2010 | 11,422 | 11,346 | 11,125 | 12,094 | 45,987 |
| 2009 | 5,385 | 5,900 | 6,050 | 10,094 | 27,428 |
| 2008 | 5,822 | 6,052 | 5,944 | 6,032 | 23,850 |
| 2007 | 5,769 | 6,111 | 6,074 | 6,243 | 24,198 |
| 2006 | 5,410 | 5,772 | 5,410 | 6,044 | 22,636 |

### Earnings Per Share ($)

| | 1Q | 2Q | 3Q | 4Q | Year |
|---|---|---|---|---|---|
| 2011 | 0.34 | 0.65 | 0.55 | E0.95 | E3.76 |
| 2010 | 0.10 | 0.24 | 0.11 | -0.17 | 0.28 |
| 2009 | 0.67 | 0.74 | 1.61 | 2.35 | 5.65 |
| 2008 | 1.52 | 0.82 | 0.51 | 0.78 | 3.64 |
| 2007 | 0.78 | 0.77 | 0.70 | -0.74 | 1.49 |
| 2006 | 0.69 | 0.69 | 0.43 | 0.22 | 2.03 |

Fiscal year ended Dec. 31. Next earnings report expected: Early February. EPS Estimates based on S&P Operating Earnings; historical GAAP earnings are as reported.

### Dividend Data (Dates: mm/dd Payment Date: mm/dd/yy)

| Amount ($) | Date Decl. | Ex-Div. Date | Stk. of Record | Payment Date |
|---|---|---|---|---|
| 0.380 | 05/24 | 06/13 | 06/15 | 07/08/11 |
| 0.380 | 07/26 | 09/13 | 09/15 | 10/07/11 |
| 0.420 | 11/10 | 12/13 | 12/15 | 01/09/12 |
| 0.420 | 11/10 | 12/13 | 12/15 | 01/09/12 |

Dividends have been paid since 1935. Source: Company reports.

---

**Please read the Required Disclosures and Analyst Certification on the last page of this report.**

The McGraw·Hill Companies

# Merck & Co Inc.

STANDARD
&POOR'S

## Business Summary November 15, 2011

CORPORATE OVERVIEW. Merck & Co. is a leading global drugmaker, producing a wide range of prescription drugs in many therapeutic classes in the U.S. and abroad. Foreign operations accounted for 55% of total sales in 2010. In early November 2009, MRK acquired rival drugmaker Schering-Plough for about $41 billion in cash and stock.

MRK's largest-selling products include Singulair (sales of $5.0 billion in 2010), a treatment for asthma and seasonal allergic rhinitis; Januvia/Janumet ($3.3 billion), treatments for type 2 diabetes; Cozaar/Hyzaar ($2.1 billion), treatments for high blood pressure and congestive heart failure; Fosamax ($926 million), a drug for osteoporosis (a bone-thinning disease that affects postmenopausal women); and Isentress ($1.1 billion) treatment for HIV/AIDS.

Merck is also a leading maker of vaccines, which accounted for 8.9% of human health sales in 2010. Key vaccines include ProQuad ($1.4 billion) for measles, mumps, rubella and chicken pox; Gardasil ($988 million) for human papillomavirus, the main cause of cervical cancer; and RotaTeq for rotavirus.

With the purchase of Schering-Plough, Merck gained total rights to Zetia -- a cholesterol therapy that works by blocking cholesterol absorption in the intestines -- as well as Vytorin, a combination pill containing both Zocor and Ze-

tia. In 2010, Vytorin had sales of $2.0 billion, and Zetia had sales of $2.2 billion. Animal health products (sales of $2.9 billion) comprise anti-infective and antiparasitic drugs and related items; and consumer care products ($1.7 billion) include OTC brands such as Claritin for allergies, Dr. Scholl's foot care products, and Coppertone suntan lotion. Through a venture with AstraZeneca, Merck books sales of Nexium and other drugs.

MARKET PROFILE. The dollar value of the global drug market is projected to grow 5%-7% in 2011, to $880 billion, versus the indicated gain of 4%-5% in 2010, according to IMS Health. The key driver should be emerging markets, whose aggregate sales (17 countries) should advance 15%-17% in 2011. Growth in developing markets is being spurred by rising standards of living and rising government spending on health care. However, IMS forecasts much slower growth for developed nations, with combined growth for five major European markets projected at 1%-3% for 2011, while pharmaceutical sales in the U.S. are estimated to increase 3%-5%.

## Company Financials Fiscal Year Ended Dec. 31

| Per Share Data ($) | 2010 | 2009 | 2008 | 2007 | 2006 | 2005 | 2004 | 2003 | 2002 | 2001 |
|---|---|---|---|---|---|---|---|---|---|---|
| Tangible Book Value | 2.09 | 1.97 | 7.97 | 11.76 | 7.00 | 7.48 | 7.03 | 6.13 | 4.88 | 3.77 |
| Cash Flow | 2.41 | 6.65 | 4.30 | 2.19 | 3.06 | 2.88 | 3.29 | 3.51 | 3.79 | 3.77 |
| Earnings | 0.28 | 5.65 | 3.64 | 1.49 | 2.03 | 2.10 | 2.61 | 2.92 | 3.14 | 3.14 |
| S&P Core Earnings | 0.36 | 2.61 | 2.78 | 2.85 | 2.28 | 2.09 | 2.56 | 2.71 | 2.81 | 2.87 |
| Dividends | 1.52 | 1.52 | 1.52 | 1.52 | 1.52 | 1.52 | 1.49 | 1.45 | 1.41 | 1.37 |
| Payout Ratio | NM | 27% | 42% | 102% | 75% | 72% | 57% | 50% | 45% | 44% |
| Prices:High | 41.56 | 38.42 | 61.18 | 61.62 | 46.37 | 35.36 | 49.33 | 63.50 | 64.50 | 95.25 |
| Prices:Low | 30.70 | 20.05 | 22.82 | 42.35 | 31.81 | 25.50 | 25.60 | 40.57 | 38.50 | 56.80 |
| P/E Ratio:High | NM | 7 | 17 | 41 | 23 | 17 | 19 | 22 | 21 | 30 |
| P/E Ratio:Low | NM | 4 | 6 | 28 | 16 | 12 | 10 | 14 | 12 | 18 |

| Income Statement Analysis (Million $) | | | | | | | | | | |
|---|---|---|---|---|---|---|---|---|---|---|
| Revenue | 45,987 | 27,428 | 23,850 | 24,198 | 22,636 | 22,012 | 22,939 | 22,486 | 51,790 | 47,716 |
| Operating Income | 12,088 | 7,081 | 7,854 | 7,779 | 5,955 | 7,567 | 8,074 | 9,912 | 11,361 | 11,192 |
| Depreciation | 6,532 | 2,227 | 1,415 | 1,528 | 2,268 | 1,708 | 1,451 | 1,314 | 1,488 | 1,464 |
| Interest Expense | 715 | 458 | 251 | 384 | 375 | 386 | 294 | 351 | 391 | 465 |
| Pretax Income | 1,653 | 15,292 | 9,808 | 3,492 | 6,342 | 7,486 | 8,129 | 9,220 | 10,428 | 10,693 |
| Effective Tax Rate | NA | 14.8% | 20.4% | 2.73% | 28.2% | 36.5% | 26.6% | 26.7% | 29.3% | 29.2% |
| Net Income | 861 | 12,901 | 7,808 | 3,275 | 4,434 | 4,631 | 5,813 | 6,590 | 7,150 | 7,282 |
| S&P Core Earnings | 1,093 | 5,936 | 5,958 | 6,255 | 4,973 | 4,582 | 5,699 | 6,089 | 6,395 | 6,649 |

| Balance Sheet & Other Financial Data (Million $) | | | | | | | | | | |
|---|---|---|---|---|---|---|---|---|---|---|
| Cash | 12,201 | 9,605 | 5,486 | 8,231 | 5,915 | 9,585 | 2,879 | 1,201 | 2,243 | 2,144 |
| Current Assets | 29,064 | 28,429 | 19,305 | 15,045 | 15,230 | 21,049 | 13,475 | 11,527 | 14,834 | 12,962 |
| Total Assets | 105,781 | 112,090 | 47,196 | 48,351 | 44,570 | 44,846 | 42,573 | 40,588 | 47,561 | 44,007 |
| Current Liabilities | 15,641 | 15,751 | 14,319 | 12,258 | 12,723 | 13,304 | 11,744 | 9,570 | 12,375 | 11,544 |
| Long Term Debt | 15,489 | 16,075 | 3,943 | 3,916 | 5,551 | 5,126 | 4,692 | 5,096 | 4,879 | 4,799 |
| Common Equity | 54,376 | 59,058 | 18,758 | 18,185 | 17,560 | 17,917 | 17,288 | 15,576 | 18,200 | 16,050 |
| Total Capital | 76,223 | 78,316 | 25,118 | 24,903 | 25,517 | 25,449 | 24,387 | 24,588 | 28,008 | 25,686 |
| Capital Expenditures | 1,678 | 1,461 | 1,298 | 1,011 | 980 | 1,403 | 1,726 | 1,916 | 2,370 | 2,725 |
| Cash Flow | 7,514 | 15,127 | 9,223 | 4,803 | 6,702 | 6,339 | 7,264 | 7,904 | 8,638 | 8,746 |
| Current Ratio | 1.9 | 1.8 | 1.4 | 1.2 | 1.2 | 1.6 | 1.1 | 1.2 | 1.2 | 1.1 |
| % Long Term Debt of Capitalization | 20.3 | Nil | 15.5 | 15.7 | 21.8 | 20.1 | 19.2 | 20.7 | 17.4 | 18.7 |
| % Net Income of Revenue | 1.9 | 47.0 | 32.7 | 13.5 | 19.6 | 21.0 | 25.3 | 29.3 | 13.8 | 15.3 |
| % Return on Assets | NA | NA | 16.3 | 7.1 | 9.9 | 10.6 | 14.0 | 15.0 | 15.6 | 17.3 |
| % Return on Equity | NA | NA | 42.3 | 18.3 | 25.0 | 26.3 | 35.4 | 39.0 | 41.7 | 47.2 |

Data as orig reptd.; bef. results of disc opers/spec. items. Per share data adj. for stk. divs.; EPS diluted. E-Estimated. NA-Not Available. NM-Not Meaningful. NR-Not Ranked. UR-Under Review.

**Office:** One Merck Drive, PO Box 100, Whitehouse Station, NJ 08889-0100.
**Telephone:** 908-423-1000.
**Website:** http://www.merck.com
**Chrmn:** R.T. Clark

**Pres & CEO:** K.C. Frazier
**EVP & CFO:** P.N. Kellogg
**Chief Acctg Officer & Cntlr:** J. Canan
**Treas:** M.E. McDonough

**Investor Contact:** G. Bell (908-423-5185)
**Board Members:** L. A. Brun, T. R. Cech, R. T. Clark, K. C. Frazier, T. H. Glocer, S. F. Goldstone, W. B. Harrison, Jr., H. R. Jacobson, W. N. Kelley, C. R. Kidder, R. B. Lazarus, C. E. Represas, P. A. Russo, T. Shenk, A. M. Tatlock, C. B. Thompson, W. P. Weeks, P. C. Wendell

**Founded:** 1891
**Domicile:** New Jersey
**Employees:** 94,000

# Metlife Inc.

**STANDARD &POOR'S**

| **S&P Recommendation** BUY ★★★★☆ | **Price** $29.14 (as of Nov 28, 2011) | **12-Mo. Target Price** $35.00 | **Investment Style** Large-Cap Blend |
|---|---|---|---|

**GICS Sector** Financials
**Sub-Industry** Life & Health Insurance

**Summary** This company is a leading publicly traded diversified U.S. life insurance and financial services concern.

## Key Stock Statistics (Source S&P, Vickers, company reports)

| | | | | | | | |
|---|---|---|---|---|---|---|---|
| 52-Wk Range | $48.72–25.61 | S&P Oper. EPS 2011**E** | 4.96 | Market Capitalization(B) | $30.819 | Beta | 1.91 |
| Trailing 12-Month EPS | $5.34 | S&P Oper. EPS 2012**E** | 5.95 | Yield (%) | 2.54 | S&P 3-Yr. Proj. EPS CAGR(%) | 16 |
| Trailing 12-Month P/E | 5.5 | P/E on S&P Oper. EPS 2011**E** | 5.9 | Dividend Rate/Share | $0.74 | S&P Credit Rating | A- |
| $10K Invested 5 Yrs Ago | $5,282 | Common Shares Outstg. (M) | 1,057.6 | Institutional Ownership (%) | 73 | | |

## Price Performance

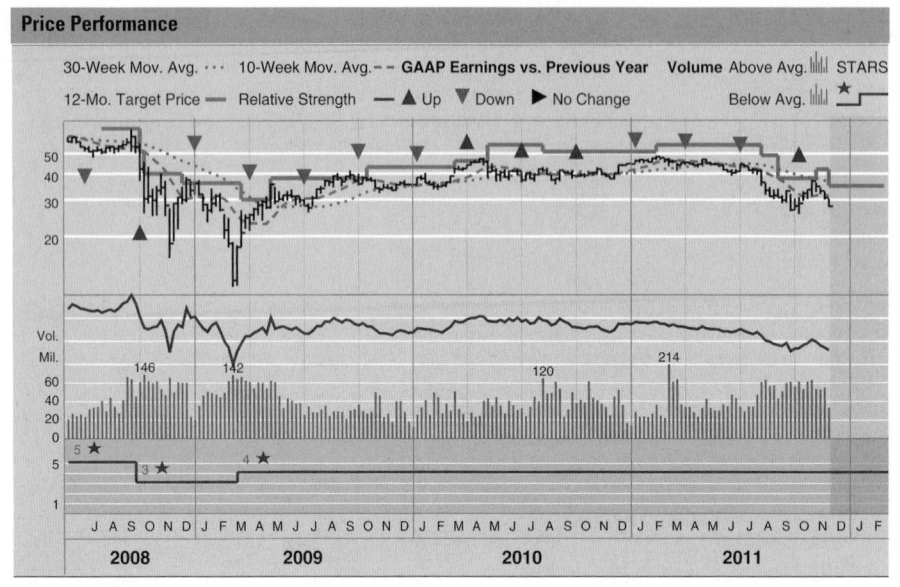

30-Week Mov. Avg. · · · · 10-Week Mov. Avg. - - **GAAP Earnings vs. Previous Year**  **Volume** Above Avg. STARS
12-Mo. Target Price — Relative Strength — ▲ Up ▼ Down ► No Change  Below Avg. ★

Options: ASE, CBOE, P

Analysis prepared by Equity Analyst **Cathy Seifert** on Nov 28, 2011, when the stock traded at **$27.91**.

## Qualitative Risk Assessment

| LOW | **MEDIUM** | HIGH |
|---|---|---|

Our risk assessment reflects our view of the company's consistent earnings growth, strong brand identity, diversified product offerings, and geographic footprint, offset by the potential for further losses in its investment portfolio, vulnerability to declines in the equity markets, and a prolonged period of low interest rates.

## Quantitative Evaluations

**S&P Quality Ranking**                                      B+

| D | C | B- | B | **B+** | A- | A | A+ |
|---|---|---|---|---|---|---|---|

**Relative Strength Rank**                                   WEAK

27

LOWEST = 1                                          HIGHEST = 99

## Revenue/Earnings Data

**Revenue (Million $)**

| | 1Q | 2Q | 3Q | 4Q | Year |
|---|---|---|---|---|---|
| 2011 | 15,912 | 17,150 | 20,458 | -- | -- |
| 2010 | 13,190 | 14,245 | 12,444 | 12,838 | 52,717 |
| 2009 | 10,216 | 8,266 | 10,238 | 12,341 | 41,058 |
| 2008 | 13,027 | 13,715 | 13,715 | 13,962 | 50,989 |
| 2007 | 12,908 | 13,216 | 13,053 | 13,830 | 53,007 |
| 2006 | 11,565 | 11,387 | 12,551 | 12,893 | 48,396 |

**Earnings Per Share ($)**

| | 1Q | 2Q | 3Q | 4Q | Year |
|---|---|---|---|---|---|
| 2011 | 0.82 | 1.10 | 3.33 | E1.28 | E4.96 |
| 2010 | 0.98 | 1.83 | 0.33 | 0.05 | 2.99 |
| 2009 | -0.75 | -1.74 | -0.79 | 0.35 | -2.94 |
| 2008 | 0.84 | 1.26 | 1.42 | 1.15 | 4.55 |
| 2007 | 1.29 | 1.47 | 1.25 | 1.44 | 5.44 |
| 2006 | 0.92 | 0.74 | 1.19 | 1.00 | 3.85 |

Fiscal year ended Dec. 31. Next earnings report expected: Early February. EPS Estimates based on S&P Operating Earnings; historical GAAP earnings are as reported.

## Highlights

➤ We see relatively favorable top-line trends in the U.S. in coming periods, with robust variable annuity sales and improved dental and individual life sales, offset by weak group life sales. We expect double-digit earnings growth in Retirement Products on positive flows and increased account values. The weak economy should be a headwind for Insurance Products although higher investment income, lower expense growth and favorable accounting adjustments should boost earnings. We anticipate volatile results in Corporate Benefit Funding due to uneven pension closeouts, although structured settlements sales should be healthy. We believe variable income should be strong as income from hedge funds and real estate joint ventures increases.

➤ We believe the International Business segment is MET's growth engine, and we forecast 20% to 25% earnings growth on strong results in Latin America and the addition of Alico. We believe International Business premium growth will be driven by strong growth in accident and health products.

➤ We forecast operating EPS of $4.96 for 2011 and $5.95 for 2012.

## Investment Rationale/Risk

➤ We believe MET is well positioned to capture market share given its strong capital position, scale, diverse businesses, distribution capabilities, and global reach. We see the acquisition of Alico significantly boosting MET's International earnings and increasing the company's exposure to faster growing and more profitable markets. We think MET will use its capital for share repurchases and to boost its dividend. We believe MET is poised to produce a double-digit ROE in coming periods, reflecting higher new business returns, investment income growth, and a greater earnings contribution from its International segment. We expect earnings growth to be fueled by strong net flows in many businesses, and better investment spreads.

➤ Risks to our recommendation and target price include credit and interest rate risk; a decline in the equity markets; deterioration in asset values; regulatory reform resulting in higher capital standards; and foreign currency risk.

➤ Our 12-month target price of $35 assumes the shares will trade at 5.9X our 2012 operating EPS estimate. This still represents a discount to peer and historical averages.

## Dividend Data (Dates: mm/dd Payment Date: mm/dd/yy)

| Amount ($) | Date Decl. | Ex-Div. Date | Stk. of Record | Payment Date |
|---|---|---|---|---|
| 0.740 | 10/26 | 11/05 | 11/09 | 12/14/10 |
| 0.740 | 10/25 | 11/07 | 11/09 | 12/14/11 |

Dividends have been paid since 2000. Source: Company reports.

---

**Please read the Required Disclosures and Analyst Certification on the last page of this report.**

**The McGraw·Hill Companies**

# Metlife Inc.

**STANDARD &POOR'S**

## Business Summary November 28, 2011

CORPORATE OVERVIEW. MetLife (MET) is one of the largest insurance and financial services companies in the U.S. The company benefits, in our view, from a strong brand, a solid financial position, international presence, and a large distribution network. At the end of 2010, the MetLife distribution channel had 5,053 agents under contract in 54 agencies, and served 90 million customers in over 60 countries. According to the American Council of Life Insurers, MetLife was the largest life insurer based on total assets and total net life insurance premiums in 2009 (latest data available). Formerly a mutual insurance company, MetLife demutualized and issued publicly traded stock in April 2000.

In the fourth quarter of 2009, MET realigned its U.S. Business segment, which now consists of Insurance Products, Retirement Products, Corporate Benefit Funding, and Auto & Home. Other segments include International Business, and Banking, Corporate & Other. MET's U.S. Business accounted for 80.6% of operating earnings in 2010, and the International Business segment acounted for 19.4% Following the acquisition of American Life Insurance Company (ALICO) from American International Group (AIG), we expect the International Business segment to contribute close to 40% of MET's operating earnings in 2011. Corporate and other activities, including MetLife Bank operations, incurred a loss of $180 million in 2010.

CORPORATE STRATEGY. We believe MET is well positioned to capture a larger share of the growing retirement and savings market in the U.S. MET's U.S. strategy is to focus on targeted, disciplined growth of its businesses, while continuing to build on its widely recognized brand name and optimize its distribution channels. In addition, MET believes it can capitalize on its large base of institutional and individual clients to drive margin improvement and return on equity expansion.

MET's international strategy is to establish meaningful positions in growing markets that can provide attractive margins. We see MET focusing on building relationships and investing in growth and upgrading systems. Following the acquisition of ALICO in 2010, MET now has a sizable presence in Japan, the second biggest insurance market in the world. MET International currently operates in 64 countries within Latin America, Asia Pacific, Europe and the Middle East. We expect investments in Japan, Brazil, China, Hong Kong and India to add to EPS significantly over the next several years.

## Company Financials Fiscal Year Ended Dec. 31

| Per Share Data ($) | 2010 | 2009 | 2008 | 2007 | 2006 | 2005 | 2004 | 2003 | 2002 | 2001 |
|---|---|---|---|---|---|---|---|---|---|---|
| Tangible Book Value | 35.65 | 52.73 | 19.54 | 34.79 | 35.64 | 32.06 | 31.16 | 27.94 | 24.83 | 22.43 |
| Operating Earnings | NA | NA | NA | NA | NA | NA | NA | NA | NA | NA |
| Earnings | 2.99 | -2.94 | 4.55 | 5.44 | 3.85 | 4.16 | 3.59 | 2.57 | 1.58 | 0.62 |
| S&P Core Earnings | 3.57 | 3.44 | 2.42 | 5.91 | 5.01 | 4.12 | 3.41 | 2.87 | 2.06 | 0.91 |
| Dividends | 0.74 | 0.74 | 0.74 | 0.74 | 0.59 | 0.52 | 0.46 | 0.23 | 0.21 | 0.20 |
| Payout Ratio | 25% | NM | 16% | 14% | 15% | 13% | 13% | 9% | 13% | 32% |
| Prices:High | 47.75 | 41.45 | 65.50 | 71.23 | 60.00 | 52.57 | 41.27 | 34.14 | 34.85 | 36.63 |
| Prices:Low | 33.40 | 11.37 | 15.72 | 58.48 | 48.00 | 37.29 | 32.30 | 23.51 | 20.60 | 24.70 |
| P/E Ratio:High | 16 | NM | 14 | 13 | 16 | 13 | 11 | 13 | 22 | 59 |
| P/E Ratio:Low | 11 | NM | 3 | 11 | 12 | 9 | 9 | 9 | 13 | 40 |

| Income Statement Analysis (Million $) | | | | | | | | | | |
|---|---|---|---|---|---|---|---|---|---|---|
| Life Insurance in Force | 4,837,571 | 4,540,576 | 4,382,280 | 6,135,797 | 5,707,215 | 5,125,427 | 4,346,898 | 3,875,110 | 2,679,870 | 2,419,341 |
| Premium Income:Life | 17,287 | 17,001 | 16,410 | 19,254 | 18,368 | 17,399 | 15,341 | 14,065 | 13,070 | 11,611 |
| Premium Income:A & H | 7,173 | 6,546 | 6,523 | 5,666 | 4,991 | 4,489 | 4,016 | 3,537 | 3,052 | 2,744 |
| Net Investment Income | 17,615 | 14,838 | NA | 19,006 | 17,192 | 14,910 | 12,418 | 11,636 | 11,329 | 11,923 |
| Total Revenue | 52,717 | 41,058 | 50,989 | 53,007 | 49,746 | 44,869 | 39,014 | 36,147 | 33,147 | 31,928 |
| Pretax Income | 3,958 | -4,333 | 5,090 | 6,279 | 4,221 | 4,399 | 3,779 | 2,630 | 1,671 | 739 |
| Net Operating Income | NA | NA | NA | NA | NA | NA | NA | NA | NA | NA |
| Net Income | 2,777 | -2,286 | 3,510 | 4,280 | 3,105 | 3,139 | 2,708 | 1,943 | 1,155 | 473 |
| S&P Core Earnings | 3,176 | 2,813 | 1,811 | 4,495 | 3,867 | 3,123 | 2,574 | 2,144 | 1,512 | 697 |

| Balance Sheet & Other Financial Data (Million $) | | | | | | | | | | |
|---|---|---|---|---|---|---|---|---|---|---|
| Cash & Equivalent | 17,427 | 13,285 | 27,268 | 13,998 | 10,454 | 7,054 | 6,389 | 5,919 | 4,411 | 9,535 |
| Premiums Due | 19,830 | 16,752 | 16,973 | 14,607 | 14,490 | 12,186 | 6,696 | 7,047 | 7,669 | 6,437 |
| Investment Assets:Bonds | 327,284 | 227,642 | 188,251 | 242,242 | 243,428 | 230,050 | 176,763 | 167,752 | 140,553 | 115,398 |
| Investment Assets:Stocks | 3,606 | 3,084 | 3,197 | 6,829 | 5,890 | 4,163 | 2,188 | 1,598 | 1,348 | 3,063 |
| Investment Assets:Loans | 74,290 | 60,970 | 61,166 | 57,449 | 52,467 | 47,170 | 41,305 | 34,998 | 33,666 | 31,893 |
| Investment Assets:Total | 463,032 | 327,567 | 298,311 | 334,734 | 324,689 | 301,709 | 234,985 | 218,099 | 188,335 | 162,222 |
| Deferred Policy Costs | 27,307 | 19,256 | 20,144 | 21,521 | 20,851 | 19,641 | 14,336 | 12,943 | 11,727 | 11,167 |
| Total Assets | 730,906 | 539,314 | 501,678 | 558,562 | 527,715 | 481,645 | 356,808 | 326,841 | 277,385 | 256,898 |
| Debt | 36,074 | 21,708 | 18,617 | 19,834 | 13,759 | 12,022 | 5,944 | 5,703 | 5,690 | 4,884 |
| Common Equity | 48,624 | 33,120 | 23,733 | 35,178 | 33,797 | 29,100 | 22,824 | 21,149 | 17,385 | 16,062 |
| % Return on Revenue | 5.3 | NM | 6.9 | 8.1 | 6.2 | 7.0 | 6.9 | 5.4 | 3.5 | 1.5 |
| % Return on Assets | 0.5 | NM | 0.7 | 0.8 | 0.6 | 0.7 | 0.8 | 0.6 | 0.4 | 0.2 |
| % Return on Equity | 6.5 | NM | 11.9 | 12.0 | 9.4 | 11.8 | 12.3 | 10.1 | 6.9 | 2.9 |
| % Investment Yield | 4.5 | 4.7 | 5.3 | 5.8 | 5.5 | 5.6 | 6.8 | 5.7 | 6.5 | 7.5 |

Data as orig reptd.; bef. results of disc opers/spec. items. Per share data adj. for stk. divs.; EPS diluted. E-Estimated. NA-Not Available. NM-Not Meaningful. NR-Not Ranked. UR-Under Review.

**Office:** 200 Park Avenue, New York, NY 10166-0188.
**Telephone:** 212-578-2211.
**Website:** http://www.metlife.com
**Chrmn:** C.R. Henrikson

**Pres & CEO:** S.A. Kandarian
**COO & CTO:** M.R. Morris
**EVP & Chief Admin Officer:** R.A. Fattori
**EVP & Chief Acctg Officer:** P.M. Carlson

**Board Members:** S. M. Burwell, E. Castro-Wright, C. W. Grise, C. R. Henrikson, R. G. Hubbard, S. A. Kandarian, J. M. Keane, A. F. Kelly, Jr., J. M. Kilts, C. R. Kinney, H. B. Price, D. Satcher, K. J. Sicchitano, L. C. Wang

**Founded:** 1999
**Domicile:** Delaware
**Employees:** 66,000

**The McGraw·Hill Companies**

# MetroPCS Communications Inc

**STANDARD &POOR'S**

| S&P Recommendation **BUY** ★★★★☆ | Price $7.51 (as of Nov 25, 2011) | 12-Mo. Target Price $11.00 | Investment Style Large-Cap Blend |
|---|---|---|---|

**GICS Sector** Telecommunication Services
**Sub-Industry** Wireless Telecommunication Services

**Summary** This company provides wireless services primarily to the youth and minority markets under the brand name MetroPCS.

## Key Stock Statistics (Source S&P, Vickers, company reports)

| | | | | | | | |
|---|---|---|---|---|---|---|---|
| 52-Wk Range | $18.79– 7.51 | S&P Oper. EPS 2011E | 0.77 | Market Capitalization(B) | $2.721 | Beta | 0.88 |
| Trailing 12-Month EPS | $0.61 | S&P Oper. EPS 2012E | 0.81 | Yield (%) | Nil | S&P 3-Yr. Proj. EPS CAGR(%) | 10 |
| Trailing 12-Month P/E | 12.3 | P/E on S&P Oper. EPS 2011E | 9.8 | Dividend Rate/Share | Nil | S&P Credit Rating | NA |
| $10K Invested 5 Yrs Ago | NA | Common Shares Outstg. (M) | 362.3 | Institutional Ownership (%) | 78 | | |

## Price Performance

30-Week Mov. Avg. ···  10-Week Mov. Avg. -- GAAP Earnings vs. Previous Year  Volume Above Avg. STARS
12-Mo. Target Price — Relative Strength — ▲ Up ▼ Down ▶ No Change  Below Avg. ★

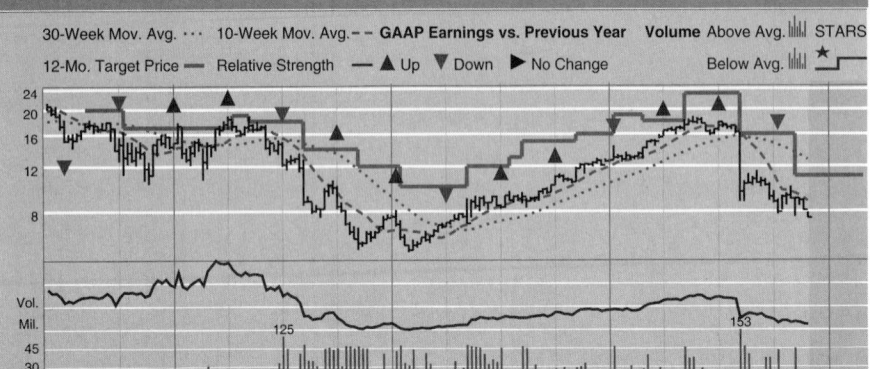

## Qualitative Risk Assessment

| LOW | MEDIUM | **HIGH** |
|---|---|---|

Our risk assessment reflects the competitive nature of the wireless market and the company's focus on the prepaid market, partly offset by our view of its relatively strong balance sheet.

## Quantitative Evaluations

**S&P Quality Ranking** — NR

| D | C | B- | B | B+ | A- | A | A+ |
|---|---|---|---|---|---|---|---|

**Relative Strength Rank** — WEAK

12

LOWEST = 1 — HIGHEST = 99

## Revenue/Earnings Data

### Revenue (Million $)

| | 1Q | 2Q | 3Q | 4Q | Year |
|---|---|---|---|---|---|
| 2011 | 1,194 | 1,209 | 1,205 | -- | -- |
| 2010 | 970.5 | 1,013 | 1,021 | 1,066 | 4,069 |
| 2009 | 795.3 | 859.6 | 895.6 | 930.0 | 3,481 |
| 2008 | 662.4 | 678.8 | 686.7 | 723.6 | 2,752 |
| 2007 | 536.7 | 551.2 | 556.7 | 591.1 | 2,236 |
| 2006 | 329.5 | 368.2 | 396.1 | 453.1 | 1,547 |

### Earnings Per Share ($)

| | | | | | |
|---|---|---|---|---|---|
| 2011 | 0.15 | 0.23 | 0.19 | E0.18 | E0.77 |
| 2010 | 0.06 | 0.22 | 0.22 | 0.04 | 0.54 |
| 2009 | 0.12 | 0.07 | 0.21 | 0.09 | 0.50 |
| 2008 | 0.11 | 0.14 | 0.13 | 0.04 | 0.42 |
| 2007 | 0.11 | 0.17 | 0.15 | -0.10 | 0.28 |
| 2006 | 0.04 | 0.06 | 0.08 | -0.08 | 0.18 |

Fiscal year ended Dec. 31. Next earnings report expected: Early January. EPS Estimates based on S&P Operating Earnings; historical GAAP earnings are as reported.

## Highlights

► The STARS recommendation for PCS has recently been changed to 4 (buy) from 5 (strong buy) and the 12-month target price has recently been changed to $11.00 from $16.00. The Highlights section of this Stock Report will be updated accordingly.

## Investment Rationale/Risk

► The Investment Rationale/Risk section of this Stock Report will be updated shortly. For the latest News story on PCS from MarketScope, see below.

► 11/01/11 01:51 pm ET ... S&P LOWERS OPINION ON SHARES OF METROPCS TO BUY FROM STRONG BUY (PCS 7.80****): PCS reports Q3 EPS, before one-time items, of $0.19, vs. $0.21, $0.02 below our estimate. We were most concerned with the rise in churn which we believe was due in part to congestion of its CDMA network. We believe network performance will improve as more subscribers migrate to the LTE network, but this could take time. We are reducing our 2011 EPS estimate $0.07 to $0.77 and 12's by $0.25 to $0.81. We are cutting our 12-month target price by $5 to $11, based on revised enterprise value/EBITDA peer analysis / James Moorman, CFA

## Dividend Data

No cash dividends have been paid.

---

**Please read the Required Disclosures and Analyst Certification on the last page of this report.**

**The McGraw·Hill Companies**

# MetroPCS Communications Inc

**STANDARD &POOR'S**

## Business Summary August 12, 2011

CORPORATE OVERVIEW. Metro PCS offers digital wireless services in the U.S. under the MetroPCS brand. The company's services are based on the Code Division Multiple Access (CDMA 1xRTT) technology. PCS offers unlimited service for a flat rate to customer segments that we believe are underserved by traditional wireless carriers. The company sells handsets that are equipped with color screens, camera phones and other features to facilitate digital data transmission. In the second quarter of 2011, equipment sales accounted for 8% of total revenues, while service revenues contributed 92%. PCS was providing services to roughly 9.1 million subscribers at the end of the second quarter of 2011, up from 7.6 million a year earlier.

In the second half of 2006, the company won eight licenses costing a total of $1.4 billion in Auction 66, the Advanced Wireless Services auction, covering roughly 126 million potential customers, including areas where PCS already provides service. The company expanded its coverage with launches in New York, Philadelphia, Boston and Las Vegas, and plans to continue to build out these markets. In March 2008, PCS participated in the 700 MHz spectrum auction and won a license covering the Boston market for roughly $360 million.

In September 2007, PCS announced a stock-based offer to merge with Leap Wireless (LEAP 7, Hold), a regional prepaid wireless carrier. The terms of the

deal, equal to 2.75 shares of PCS for every LEAP share, originally valued LEAP at $5.5 billion, or $75 a share. In November 2007, PCS withdrew its offer. In September 2008, PCS and LEAP announced a national roaming agreement and spectrum swap. As part of the agreement, both companies also settled all outstanding litigation. We believe that consolidation in the competitive prepaid market will continue in 2011.

PRIMARY BUSINESS DYNAMICS. In the second quarter of 2011, PCS added 198,810 net subscribers, and had a monthly churn rate of 3.9% and average revenue per user (ARPU) of $40.49, up 1.6% from a year earlier. In the second and third quarters of any given year, PCS's churn rate tends to increase and customer growth slows, but this is likely to be more pronounced in 2011 due to economic issues, including less disposable income. The company's customer profile is skewed toward first-time users, with roughly 55% of its customers fitting into that category. About 90% of its subscribers use their wireless phone as their primary phone service.

## Company Financials Fiscal Year Ended Dec. 31

| Per Share Data ($) | 2010 | 2009 | 2008 | 2007 | 2006 | 2005 | 2004 | 2003 | 2002 | 2001 |
|---|---|---|---|---|---|---|---|---|---|---|
| Tangible Book Value | 0.05 | NM | NM | NM | NM | NA | NA | NA | NA | NA |
| Cash Flow | 1.81 | 1.57 | 1.14 | 0.91 | 0.54 | 1.72 | 0.82 | 0.30 | 1.37 | -0.46 |
| Earnings | 0.54 | 0.50 | 0.42 | 0.28 | 0.18 | 0.62 | 0.33 | 0.01 | 0.57 | -0.48 |
| S&P Core Earnings | 0.47 | 0.49 | 0.51 | 0.47 | 0.18 | 0.17 | NA | NA | NA | NA |
| Dividends | Nil | Nil | Nil | Nil | NA | NA | NA | NA | NA | NA |
| Payout Ratio | Nil | Nil | Nil | Nil | NA | NA | NA | NA | NA | NA |
| Prices:High | 12.93 | 18.98 | 21.86 | 40.87 | NA | NA | NA | NA | NA | NA |
| Prices:Low | 5.52 | 5.65 | 10.23 | 13.77 | NA | NA | NA | NA | NA | NA |
| P/E Ratio:High | 24 | 38 | 52 | NM | NA | NA | NA | NA | NA | NA |
| P/E Ratio:Low | 10 | 11 | 24 | NM | NA | NA | NA | NA | NA | NA |

| Income Statement Analysis (Million $) | | | | | | | | | | |
|---|---|---|---|---|---|---|---|---|---|---|
| Revenue | 4,069 | 3,481 | 2,752 | 2,236 | 1,547 | 1,038 | 748 | 451 | 129 | NA |
| Operating Income | NA | NA | 742 | 639 | 381 | 292 | 193 | 84.0 | -95.9 | NA |
| Depreciation | 453 | 383 | 255 | 178 | 135 | 87.9 | 62.2 | 42.4 | 21.5 | 0.21 |
| Interest Expense | 263 | 270 | 179 | 202 | 116 | 58.0 | 19.0 | 11.1 | 6.72 | 10.5 |
| Pretax Income | 312 | 264 | 279 | 224 | 90.5 | 326 | 112 | 31.7 | 156 | -45.2 |
| Effective Tax Rate | NA | 32.9% | 46.5% | 55.1% | 40.6% | 39.1% | 42.0% | 51.1% | 16.4% | NA |
| Net Income | 193 | 177 | 149 | 100 | 53.8 | 199 | 64.9 | 15.5 | 130 | -45.2 |
| S&P Core Earnings | 168 | 175 | 182 | 164 | 59.5 | 55.2 | NA | NA | NA | NA |

| Balance Sheet & Other Financial Data (Million $) | | | | | | | | | | |
|---|---|---|---|---|---|---|---|---|---|---|
| Cash | 1,171 | 1,154 | 698 | 1,470 | 1,375 | 503 | 59.4 | 236 | 61.7 | 42.7 |
| Current Assets | 1,594 | 1,491 | 1,044 | 1,733 | NA | 612 | 157 | 293 | 110 | 51.3 |
| Total Assets | 7,919 | 7,386 | 6,422 | 5,806 | NA | 2,159 | 965 | 902 | 563 | 324 |
| Current Liabilities | 802 | 797 | 742 | 580 | NA | 236 | 163 | 200 | 119 | 204 |
| Long Term Debt | 3,757 | 3,626 | 3,058 | 2,986 | 2,596 | 903 | 171 | 182 | 41.4 | 48.6 |
| Common Equity | 2,542 | 2,288 | 2,034 | 1,849 | 1,730 | 368 | 125 | 84.9 | 76.1 | -52.9 |
| Total Capital | 6,321 | 5,761 | 5,116 | 5,130 | 4,326 | 1,744 | 712 | 660 | 422 | 119 |
| Capital Expenditures | 831 | 865 | 955 | 768 | 551 | 278 | 251 | 117 | 212 | 134 |
| Cash Flow | 646 | 560 | 405 | 271 | 164 | 265 | 106 | 43.8 | 150 | -49.9 |
| Current Ratio | 2.0 | 1.9 | 1.4 | 3.0 | NA | 2.6 | 1.0 | 1.5 | 0.9 | 0.3 |
| % Long Term Debt of Capitalization | 59.4 | 61.1 | 59.8 | 58.2 | NA | 51.8 | 24.0 | 27.6 | 9.8 | 40.8 |
| % Net Income of Revenue | 4.8 | 5.1 | 5.4 | 4.5 | NA | 19.1 | 8.7 | 4.5 | 110.7 | NA |
| % Return on Assets | 2.5 | 2.6 | 2.4 | 2.0 | NA | 12.7 | 7.0 | 2.8 | 31.4 | NA |
| % Return on Equity | 8.0 | 8.2 | 7.7 | 8.2 | NA | 80.5 | 61.7 | 25.6 | NA | NA |

Data as orig reptd.; bef. results of disc opers/spec. items. Per share data adj. for stk. divs.; EPS diluted. E-Estimated. NA-Not Available. NM-Not Meaningful. NR-Not Ranked. UR-Under Review.

**Office:** 2250 Lakeside Boulevard, Richardson, TX 75082.
**Telephone:** 214-570-5800.
**Website:** http://www.metropcs.com
**Chrmn & CEO:** R.D. Linquist

**Pres & COO:** T.C. Keys
**CFO:** J.B. Carter, II
**CTO:** M.M. Lorang
**Chief Acctg Officer & Cntlr:** C.B. Kornegay

**Investor Contact:** J. Mathias (214-570-4641)
**Board Members:** W. M. Barnes, J. F. Callahan, Jr., C. Landry, R. D. Linquist, A. C. Patterson, J. N. Perry, Jr.

**Founded:** 2004
**Domicile:** Delaware
**Employees:** 3,600

The **McGraw·Hill** Companies

# Microchip Technology Inc

| S&P Recommendation | HOLD ★★★☆☆ | Price $32.30 (as of Nov 25, 2011) | 12-Mo. Target Price $37.00 | Investment Style Large-Cap Growth |
|---|---|---|---|---|

**GICS Sector** Information Technology
**Sub-Industry** Semiconductors

**Summary** This company supplies microcontrollers and analog and other semiconductor products for a wide variety of high-volume embedded control applications.

## Key Stock Statistics (Source S&P, Vickers, company reports)

| | | | | | | | |
|---|---|---|---|---|---|---|---|
| 52-Wk Range | $41.50–29.30 | S&P Oper. EPS 2012E | 1.78 | Market Capitalization(B) | $6.174 | Beta | 1.11 |
| Trailing 12-Month EPS | $2.01 | S&P Oper. EPS 2013E | 1.99 | Yield (%) | 4.31 | S&P 3-Yr. Proj. EPS CAGR(%) | 4 |
| Trailing 12-Month P/E | 16.1 | P/E on S&P Oper. EPS 2012E | 18.1 | Dividend Rate/Share | $1.39 | S&P Credit Rating | NA |
| $10K Invested 5 Yrs Ago | $11,659 | Common Shares Outstg. (M) | 191.1 | Institutional Ownership (%) | NM | | |

## Price Performance

30-Week Mov. Avg. · · · 10-Week Mov. Avg. – – GAAP Earnings vs. Previous Year   Volume Above Avg. ▏▎▍ STARS
12-Mo. Target Price — Relative Strength   ▲ Up  ▼ Down  ► No Change   Below Avg. ▏▎▍ ★

Options: ASE, CBOE, Ph

Analysis prepared by Equity Analyst **Angelo Zino, CFA** on Nov 07, 2011, when the stock traded at **$36.08**.

## Highlights

➤ We expect sales to decline 4.0% in FY 12 (Mar.), as customers digest inventories, followed by a rebound of 6.1% in FY 13. Assuming challenging economic conditions, we believe sales growth will be below seasonal near term as demand from the computing and consumer markets remain soft. Nonetheless, we see share gains in the 8-bit, 16-bit, and 32-bit microcontroller (MCU) markets, as MCHP expands its served available market and focuses on further penetrating a wider range of end-products. We also expect MCHP's relatively small but budding analog business to outpace peers.

➤ We look for MCHP's annual non-GAAP gross margin to widen to 60% in FY 13, following our outlook for a 58% margin in FY 12. We expect a gradual ramp in MCHP's factories as inventories are burned off and cost reductions result in margin expansion. We believe that expenses will grow along with sales, and we think that non-GAAP operating margins will widen to 33% in FY 13, from our 31% view in FY 12.

➤ Our FY 12 and FY 13 operating EPS estimates include stock-based compensation of around $0.18 and $0.15 per share, respectively.

## Investment Rationale/Risk

➤ Our hold recommendation reflects valuation, uncertain end-demand environment, and our view that MCHP will outperform the semiconductor industry. We believe that soft demand and excessive inventory will hurt MCHP and the broader chip industry over the near term. However, we think MCHP, through its ability to reduce volatility in margins by effectively managing costs and expenses, has less business risk and can preserve profitability better than peers. Considering what we view as MCHP's profitable business model and attractive dividend yield, we believe its multiples should be above the industry average.

➤ Risks to our recommendation and target price include weaker than expected economic conditions, a less favorable sales mix, and slower than anticipated share gains in the 8-bit and 16-bit MCU markets.

➤ Our 12-month target price of $37 is based on a multiple of 19.0X our calendar 2012 EPS estimate, above the peer average to account for MCHP's relative growth, return metrics and risk. However, this ratio is well below historical averages.

## Qualitative Risk Assessment

| LOW | MEDIUM | HIGH |
|---|---|---|

Our risk assessment reflects the cyclicality of the semiconductor industry, offset by the company's very broad customer base and end-markets and its low cost structure.

## Quantitative Evaluations

**S&P Quality Ranking** B+

| D | C | B- | B | B+ | A- | A | A+ |
|---|---|---|---|---|---|---|---|

**Relative Strength Rank** MODERATE

49

LOWEST = 1          HIGHEST = 99

## Revenue/Earnings Data

### Revenue (Million $)

| | 1Q | 2Q | 3Q | 4Q | Year |
|---|---|---|---|---|---|
| 2012 | 374.5 | 340.6 | -- | -- | -- |
| 2011 | 357.1 | 382.3 | 367.8 | 380.0 | 1,487 |
| 2010 | 193.0 | 226.7 | 250.1 | 278.0 | 947.7 |
| 2009 | 268.2 | 269.7 | 192.2 | 173.3 | 903.3 |
| 2008 | 264.1 | 258.7 | 252.6 | 260.4 | 1,036 |
| 2007 | 262.6 | 267.9 | 251.0 | 258.2 | 1,040 |

### Earnings Per Share ($)

| | | | | | |
|---|---|---|---|---|---|
| 2012 | 0.49 | 0.40 | E0.40 | E0.47 | E1.78 |
| 2011 | 0.47 | 0.55 | 0.52 | 0.65 | 2.20 |
| 2010 | 0.15 | 0.24 | 0.37 | 0.40 | 1.16 |
| 2009 | 0.40 | 0.41 | 0.40 | 0.12 | 1.33 |
| 2008 | 0.36 | 0.27 | 0.38 | 0.40 | 1.40 |
| 2007 | 0.35 | 0.36 | 0.33 | 0.57 | 1.62 |

Fiscal year ended Mar. 31. Next earnings report expected: Late January. EPS Estimates based on S&P Operating Earnings; historical GAAP earnings are as reported.

## Dividend Data (Dates: mm/dd Payment Date: mm/dd/yy)

| Amount ($) | Date Decl. | Ex-Div. Date | Stk. of Record | Payment Date |
|---|---|---|---|---|
| 0.345 | 11/04 | 12/09 | 12/13 | 12/27/10 |
| 0.346 | 05/05 | 05/17 | 05/19 | 06/02/11 |
| 0.347 | 08/04 | 08/16 | 08/18 | 09/01/11 |
| 0.348 | 11/03 | 11/17 | 11/21 | 12/05/11 |

Dividends have been paid since 2002. Source: Company reports.

# Microchip Technology Inc

STANDARD
&POOR'S

## Business Summary November 07, 2011

CORPORATE OVERVIEW. Microchip Technology Inc. (MCHP) develops and manufactures specialized chips used in a wide variety of embedded control applications. MCHP is a leading microcontroller (MCU) company, having shipped over 7 billion PIC microcontrollers since 1990. MCHP also offers a broad range of high-performance linear, mixed-signal, power management, thermal management, battery management, and interface devices, and serial EEPROMs.

Microcontrollers are low-cost components that form the brains of the vast majority of electronic devices, except for PCs. MCHP's signature products include a broad family of proprietary 8- and 16-bit field programmable microcontrollers under the PIC name, designed for applications requiring high performance, fast time-to-market, and user programmability. The company offers a comprehensive set of low-cost and easy-to-learn application development tools that let system designers program a PIC microcontroller for specific applications.

By main product line, microcontrollers provided 81.0% of sales in FY 10 (Mar.) (81.0% in FY 09), memory products 8.5% (9.9%), and analog and interface products 10.5% (9.1%). Average selling prices are relatively stable for the microcontrollers and for analog products with significant proprietary content, which is about half the analog segment. Pricing for some commodity-type products, such as EEPROMs, tend to fluctuate.

Foreign sales accounted for 77% of FY 10 net sales, above the FY 09 result. By major region, FY 10 sales came from Asia (50.5%), Europe (25.1%) and the Americas (24.4%). Approximately 25% of sales were sourced from China, including Hong Kong, and Taiwan accounted for about 10%. About 61% of net sales were made through distributors.

## Company Financials Fiscal Year Ended Mar. 31

| Per Share Data ($) | 2011 | 2010 | 2009 | 2008 | 2007 | 2006 | 2005 | 2004 | 2003 | 2002 |
|---|---|---|---|---|---|---|---|---|---|---|
| Tangible Book Value | 8.75 | 7.86 | 5.18 | 5.39 | 9.03 | 7.89 | 6.95 | 6.19 | 5.58 | 5.36 |
| Cash Flow | 2.75 | 1.64 | 1.85 | 1.87 | 2.14 | 1.64 | 1.58 | 1.32 | 1.00 | 0.98 |
| Earnings | 2.20 | 1.16 | 1.33 | 1.40 | 1.62 | 1.13 | 1.01 | 0.65 | 0.47 | 0.45 |
| S&P Core Earnings | 2.21 | 1.16 | 1.35 | 1.48 | 1.62 | 1.05 | 0.89 | 0.47 | 0.30 | 0.28 |
| Dividends | NA | 1.36 | 1.35 | 0.97 | 0.57 | 0.21 | 0.11 | 0.04 | 0.04 | Nil |
| Payout Ratio | NA | 117% | 102% | 69% | 35% | 18% | 11% | 6% | 9% | Nil |
| Calendar Year | 2010 | 2009 | 2008 | 2007 | 2006 | 2005 | 2004 | 2003 | 2002 | 2001 |
| Prices:High | 36.41 | 29.56 | 38.37 | 42.46 | 38.56 | 34.98 | 34.88 | 36.50 | 33.99 | 28.29 |
| Prices:Low | 25.54 | 16.23 | 16.28 | 27.50 | 30.63 | 24.06 | 25.12 | 17.85 | 15.02 | 14.00 |
| P/E Ratio:High | 17 | 25 | 29 | 30 | 24 | 31 | 35 | 56 | 72 | 62 |
| P/E Ratio:Low | 12 | 14 | 12 | 20 | 19 | 21 | 25 | 27 | 32 | 31 |

### Income Statement Analysis (Million $)

| | 2011 | 2010 | 2009 | 2008 | 2007 | 2006 | 2005 | 2004 | 2003 | 2002 |
|---|---|---|---|---|---|---|---|---|---|---|
| Revenue | 1,487 | 948 | 903 | 1,036 | 1,040 | 928 | 847 | 699 | 651 | 571 |
| Operating Income | 596 | 336 | 336 | 427 | 464 | 567 | 400 | 314 | 286 | 232 |
| Depreciation | 107 | 90.1 | 96.1 | 98.2 | 116 | 111 | 120 | 142 | 111 | 109 |
| Interest Expense | 31.5 | 31.2 | 24.3 | 0.75 | 5.42 | 1.97 | 0.94 | 0.25 | 0.49 | 0.57 |
| Pretax Income | 461 | 238 | 237 | 351 | 401 | 359 | 277 | 178 | 128 | 127 |
| Effective Tax Rate | NA | 8.75% | NM | 15.2% | 11.0% | 32.5% | 22.9% | 22.8% | 22.3% | 25.5% |
| Net Income | 429 | 217 | 249 | 298 | 357 | 242 | 214 | 137 | 99.7 | 94.8 |
| S&P Core Earnings | 430 | 216 | 253 | 314 | 357 | 226 | 190 | 100 | 63.5 | 58.2 |

### Balance Sheet & Other Financial Data (Million $)

| | 2011 | 2010 | 2009 | 2008 | 2007 | 2006 | 2005 | 2004 | 2003 | 2002 |
|---|---|---|---|---|---|---|---|---|---|---|
| Cash | 1,244 | 1,214 | 1,390 | 1,325 | 167 | 565 | 68.7 | 105 | 53.9 | 281 |
| Current Assets | 1,794 | 1,611 | 1,743 | 1,718 | 1,085 | 1,119 | 1,075 | 884 | 609 | 549 |
| Total Assets | 2,987 | 2,516 | 2,421 | 2,512 | 2,270 | 2,351 | 1,818 | 1,622 | 1,428 | 1,276 |
| Current Liabilities | 340 | 203 | 156 | 191 | 256 | 609 | 307 | 270 | 215 | 168 |
| Long Term Debt | 347 | 341 | 1,149 | 1,150 | Nil | Nil | Nil | Nil | Nil | Nil |
| Common Equity | 1,812 | 1,533 | 991 | 1,036 | 2,004 | 1,726 | 1,486 | 1,321 | 1,179 | 1,076 |
| Total Capital | 2,160 | 1,874 | 2,192 | 2,208 | 2,013 | 1,741 | 1,510 | 1,351 | 1,212 | 1,107 |
| Capital Expenditures | 124 | 47.6 | 102 | 69.8 | 60.0 | 76.3 | 63.2 | 63.5 | 80.4 | 44.7 |
| Cash Flow | 536 | 307 | 345 | 396 | 473 | 353 | 334 | 279 | 211 | 204 |
| Current Ratio | 5.3 | 7.9 | 11.2 | 9.0 | 4.2 | 1.8 | 3.5 | 3.3 | 2.8 | 3.3 |
| % Long Term Debt of Capitalization | 16.1 | 18.2 | 52.4 | 52.1 | Nil | Nil | Nil | Nil | Nil | Nil |
| % Net Income of Revenue | 28.9 | 22.9 | 27.6 | 28.8 | 34.3 | 26.1 | 25.2 | 19.6 | 15.3 | 16.6 |
| % Return on Assets | 15.6 | 8.8 | 10.1 | 12.5 | 15.5 | 11.6 | 12.4 | 9.0 | 7.4 | 7.8 |
| % Return on Equity | 25.7 | 17.2 | 24.6 | 19.6 | 19.1 | 15.1 | 15.2 | 11.0 | 8.8 | 9.4 |

Data as orig reptd.; bef. results of disc opers/spec. items. Per share data adj. for stk. divs.; EPS diluted. E-Estimated. NA-Not Available. NM-Not Meaningful. NR-Not Ranked. UR-Under Review.

Office: 2355 West Chandler Boulevard, Chandler, AZ 85224-6199.
Telephone: 480-792-7200.
Email: ir@mail.microchip.com
Website: http://www.microchip.com

Chrmn, Pres & CEO: S. Sanghi
COO: G. Moorthy
CFO & Chief Acctg Officer: J.E. Bjornholt
CTO: S.V. Drehobl

Secy & General Counsel: K. Van Herk
Investor Contact: G. Parnell (480-792-7374)
Board Members: M. W. Chapman, L. B. Day, IV, A. J. Hugo-Martinez, W. F. Meyercord, S. Sanghi

Founded: 1989
Domicile: Delaware
Employees: 6,970

# Micron Technology Inc.

**STANDARD &POOR'S**

| S&P Recommendation | HOLD ★ ★ ★ ★ ★ | Price | 12-Mo. Target Price | Investment Style |
|---|---|---|---|---|
| | | $5.50 (as of Nov 25, 2011) | $7.00 | Large-Cap Value |

**GICS Sector** Information Technology
**Sub-Industry** Semiconductors

**Summary** This company is a manufacturer of semiconductor memory products, including DRAM and NAND flash memory, as well as image sensors.

## Key Stock Statistics (Source S&P, Vickers, company reports)

| | | | | | | | | |
|---|---|---|---|---|---|---|---|---|
| 52-Wk Range | $11.95– 3.97 | S&P Oper. EPS 2012**E** | 0.22 | Market Capitalization(B) | $5.432 | Beta | 1.16 |
| Trailing 12-Month EPS | $0.17 | S&P Oper. EPS 2013**E** | 1.00 | Yield (%) | Nil | S&P 3-Yr. Proj. EPS CAGR(%) | -13 |
| Trailing 12-Month P/E | 32.4 | P/E on S&P Oper. EPS 2012**E** | 25.0 | Dividend Rate/Share | Nil | S&P Credit Rating | BB- |
| $10K Invested 5 Yrs Ago | $3,719 | Common Shares Outstg. (M) | 987.6 | Institutional Ownership (%) | 83 | | |

## Price Performance

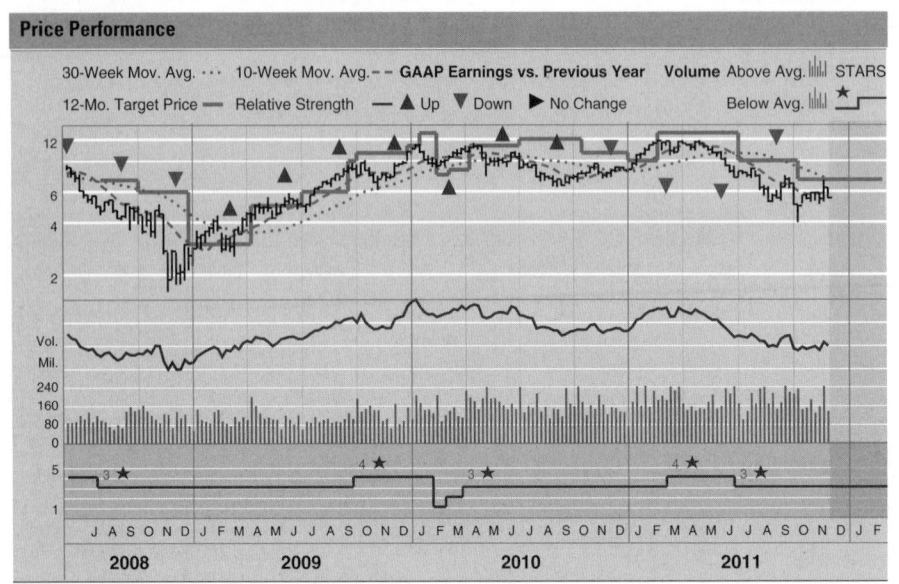

30-Week Mov. Avg. · · · 10-Week Mov. Avg. - - GAAP Earnings vs. Previous Year Volume Above Avg. STARS
12-Mo. Target Price — Relative Strength — ▲ Up ▼ Down ▶ No Change Below Avg. ★

Options: ASE, CBOE, P, Ph

Analysis prepared by Equity Analyst **C. Montevirgen** on Sep 30, 2011, when the stock traded at **$5.05**.

## Highlights

➤ We forecast that revenues will fall 4.8% in FY 12 (Aug.), after a 3.6% increase in FY 11. We expect a more favorable PC demand environment to contribute to faster bit growth and more modest DRAM average selling price (ASP) deterioration next year. However, with our view that memory makers will focus more on NAND capacity and that tier-two hardware makers will exit the tablet space, we see a NAND inventory glut leading to steeper NAND ASP declines in mid-2012, offsetting healthy NAND bit growth. Our model also assumes healthy ASPs and shipments for NOR flash memory.

➤ We expect a gross margin of 24% in FY 12, versus 20% in FY 11, largely reflecting the expected benefits from cost per bit reductions, and an improving sales mix of specialty DRAM and higher-end NAND chips. However, we believe R&D expenses will increase for new product and process development, and we see operating margins narrowing to 4.6% from 8.6% during the same period as sales contract.

➤ We note that FY 11 results have been helped by gains, which we are not projecting for FY 12.

## Investment Rationale/Risk

➤ With our opinion that Micron has the right technology to compete favorably in the memory market and to reduce cost per bit at a fast rate, we think its growth will beat that of most memory competitors. However, we see all memory makers struggling over the near-term due to soft PC demand and generally uninspiring consumer electronic sales. We expect below-semiconductor industry earnings growth for MU over the next couple of quarters, and with the company's relatively high business risk, we believe that valuation multiples should be below the industry's.

➤ Risks to our opinion and target price include lower-than-expected sales of computers and consumer electronic products, faster-than-expected capacity expansion in the memory industry, and less-than-anticipated unit cost reductions.

➤ Our 12-month target price of $7 is based on a price-to-earnings multiple of 10X, below the industry average to account for our view of business risk and relative profitability, applied to our four-quarter EPS estimate ending November 2012.

## Qualitative Risk Assessment

| LOW | MEDIUM | HIGH |
|---|---|---|

Micron is subject to semiconductor industry cyclicality and to sudden changes in pricing for commodity memory products. It is a relatively large semiconductor company and is the lone American survivor in the global DRAM industry, which has been consolidating in recent years.

## Quantitative Evaluations

**S&P Quality Ranking**   C

| D | C | B- | B | B+ | A- | A | A+ |
|---|---|---|---|---|---|---|---|

**Relative Strength Rank**   MODERATE

41

LOWEST = 1   HIGHEST = 99

## Revenue/Earnings Data

**Revenue (Million $)**

| | 1Q | 2Q | 3Q | 4Q | Year |
|---|---|---|---|---|---|
| 2011 | 2,252 | 2,257 | 2,139 | 2,140 | 8,788 |
| 2010 | 1,740 | 1,961 | 2,288 | 2,493 | 8,482 |
| 2009 | 1,402 | 993.0 | 1,106 | 1,302 | 4,803 |
| 2008 | 1,535 | 1,359 | 1,498 | 1,449 | 5,841 |
| 2007 | 1,530 | 1,427 | 1,294 | 1,437 | 5,688 |
| 2006 | 1,362 | 1,225 | 1,312 | 1,373 | 5,272 |

**Earnings Per Share ($)**

| | | | | | |
|---|---|---|---|---|---|
| 2011 | 0.15 | 0.07 | 0.07 | -0.14 | 0.17 |
| 2010 | 0.23 | 0.39 | 0.92 | 0.32 | 1.85 |
| 2009 | -0.91 | -0.97 | 0.23 | -0.10 | -2.29 |
| 2008 | -0.34 | -1.01 | -0.30 | -0.45 | -2.10 |
| 2007 | 0.15 | -0.07 | -0.29 | -0.21 | -0.42 |
| 2006 | 0.09 | 0.27 | 0.12 | 0.08 | 0.57 |

Fiscal year ended Aug. 31. Next earnings report expected: Late December. EPS Estimates based on S&P Operating Earnings; historical GAAP earnings are as reported.

## Dividend Data

No cash dividends have been paid since 1996.

# Micron Technology Inc.

STANDARD
&POOR'S

## Business Summary September 30, 2011

CORPORATE OVERVIEW. Micron Technology is a manufacturer and marketer of dynamic random access memory (DRAM) and NAND flash and NOR flash memory. The company's products are used in an increasingly broad range of electronic devices, including personal computers, network servers, mobile phones, digital still cameras, MP3 players and other consumer electronics products. Micron is one of the largest memory makers, ranking among the top five suppliers in the world, based on 2010 revenues.

Micron has two segments -- memory, which includes both DRAM and NAND flash memory, and Numonyx, which includes NOR flash memory. Other businesses, such as imaging products, are reflected in an All Other non-reportable segment. By memory type, DRAM sales accounted for 60% of the total in FY 10 (Aug.); NAND flash sales comprised 28%; and NOR flash made up 7%.

MARKET PROFILE. The memory market has been on a virtual roller coaster of highs and lows, affected by capricious end-market demand, inventory levels, price wars, and advances in technology and manufacturing. Sales tend to

have very large swings, and because of the high-fixed cost nature of the memory industry, earnings are even more volatile.

Commodity memory chips, especially DRAM, represent one of the largest and most volatile segments of the semiconductor industry. Memory sales have risen annually, as higher bit shipments have offset deteriorating prices. DRAM prices tend to decline 20%-30% annually, on average. However, DRAM prices have a vary wide range, and prices have plunged as much as 75% or increased as much as 200% in a matter of months. Although the NAND chip was invented more than 20 years ago, the NAND market has grown explosively only in recent years with the introduction of consumer electronics such as hand-held devices, MP3 players and digital cameras. NAND prices have also experienced wild swings in prices over the past several years, but have recently trended lower.

## Company Financials Fiscal Year Ended Aug. 31

| Per Share Data ($) | 2011 | 2010 | 2009 | 2008 | 2007 | 2006 | 2005 | 2004 | 2003 | 2002 |
|---|---|---|---|---|---|---|---|---|---|---|
| Tangible Book Value | 8.18 | 7.74 | 5.08 | 7.56 | 9.00 | 9.64 | 9.07 | 8.73 | 7.68 | 9.93 |
| Cash Flow | 2.28 | 3.67 | 0.35 | 0.57 | 1.81 | 2.33 | 2.07 | 2.13 | -0.10 | 0.45 |
| Earnings | 0.17 | 1.85 | -2.29 | -2.10 | -0.42 | 0.57 | 0.29 | 0.24 | -2.11 | -1.51 |
| S&P Core Earnings | 0.10 | 1.84 | -2.27 | -1.54 | -0.38 | 0.40 | -0.12 | -0.09 | -2.60 | -2.14 |
| Dividends | NA | Nil | Nil | Nil | Nil | Nil | Nil | Nil | Nil | Nil |
| Payout Ratio | Nil | Nil | Nil | Nil | Nil | Nil | Nil | Nil | Nil | Nil |
| Prices:High | 11.95 | 11.40 | 10.87 | 8.97 | 14.31 | 18.65 | 14.82 | 18.25 | 15.66 | 39.50 |
| Prices:Low | 3.97 | 6.36 | 2.55 | 1.59 | 7.11 | 13.12 | 9.32 | 10.89 | 6.60 | 9.50 |
| P/E Ratio:High | 70 | 6 | NM | NM | NM | 33 | 51 | 76 | NM | NM |
| P/E Ratio:Low | 23 | 3 | NM | NM | NM | 23 | 32 | 45 | NM | NM |

| Income Statement Analysis (Million $) | | | | | | | | | | |
|---|---|---|---|---|---|---|---|---|---|---|
| Revenue | 8,788 | 8,482 | 4,803 | 5,841 | 5,688 | 5,272 | 4,880 | 4,404 | 3,091 | 2,589 |
| Operating Income | 2,736 | 3,566 | 673 | 887 | 1,381 | 1,631 | 1,458 | 1,445 | 133 | 152 |
| Depreciation | 2,105 | 2,005 | 2,113 | 2,056 | 1,718 | 1,281 | 1,265 | 1,218 | 1,210 | 1,177 |
| Interest Expense | 101 | 160 | 138 | 95.0 | 40.0 | 25.0 | 46.9 | 36.0 | 36.5 | 17.1 |
| Pretax Income | 393 | 1,881 | -1,944 | -1,611 | -168 | 433 | 199 | 232 | -1,200 | -998 |
| Effective Tax Rate | NA | NA | NM | NM | NM | 4.16% | 5.34% | 32.2% | NM | NM |
| Net Income | 167 | 1,850 | -1,835 | -1,619 | -320 | 408 | 188 | 157 | -1,273 | -907 |
| S&P Core Earnings | 105 | 1,846 | -1,819 | -1,190 | -290 | 288 | -75.8 | -62.2 | -1,578 | -1,288 |

| Balance Sheet & Other Financial Data (Million $) | | | | | | | | | | |
|---|---|---|---|---|---|---|---|---|---|---|
| Cash | 2,160 | 2,913 | 1,485 | 1,362 | 2,192 | 1,431 | 525 | 486 | 570 | 398 |
| Current Assets | 5,832 | 6,333 | 3,344 | 3,779 | 5,234 | 5,101 | 2,926 | 2,639 | 2,037 | 2,119 |
| Total Assets | 14,752 | 14,693 | 11,455 | 13,430 | 14,818 | 12,221 | 8,006 | 7,760 | 7,158 | 7,555 |
| Current Liabilities | 2,480 | 2,702 | 1,892 | 1,598 | 2,026 | 1,661 | 979 | 972 | 993 | 753 |
| Long Term Debt | 1,861 | 1,648 | 2,674 | 2,451 | 1,987 | 405 | 1,020 | 1,028 | 997 | 361 |
| Common Equity | 8,470 | 8,020 | 4,654 | 6,178 | 7,752 | 8,114 | 5,847 | 5,615 | 5,038 | 6,367 |
| Total Capital | 13,235 | 12,176 | 9,738 | 11,503 | 12,371 | 10,115 | 6,902 | 6,685 | 6,035 | 6,727 |
| Capital Expenditures | 2,550 | 616 | 488 | 2,529 | 3,603 | 1,365 | 1,065 | 1,081 | 822 | 760 |
| Cash Flow | 2,295 | 3,855 | 278 | 437 | 1,398 | 1,689 | 1,453 | 1,375 | -63.3 | 270 |
| Current Ratio | 2.4 | 2.3 | 1.8 | 2.4 | 2.6 | 3.1 | 3.0 | 2.7 | 2.1 | 2.8 |
| % Long Term Debt of Capitalization | 14.1 | 13.5 | 27.5 | 21.3 | 16.1 | 4.0 | 14.8 | 15.4 | 16.5 | 5.4 |
| % Net Income of Revenue | 1.9 | 21.8 | NM | NM | NM | 7.7 | 3.9 | 3.6 | NM | NM |
| % Return on Assets | 1.1 | 14.2 | NM | NM | NM | 4.0 | 2.4 | 2.1 | NM | NM |
| % Return on Equity | 2.0 | 29.2 | NM | NM | NM | 5.8 | 3.3 | 3.0 | NM | NM |

Data as orig reptd.; bef. results of disc opers/spec. items. Per share data adj. for stk. divs.; EPS diluted. E-Estimated. NA-Not Available. NM-Not Meaningful. NR-Not Ranked. UR-Under Review.

**Office:** 8000 South Federal Way, Boise, ID 83707-0006.
**Telephone:** 208-368-4000.
**Email:** invrel@micron.com
**Website:** http://www.micron.com

**Chrmn & CEO:** S.R. Appleton
**Pres & COO:** D.M. Durcan
**CFO & Chief Acctg Officer:** R.C. Foster
**Treas:** P. Morali

**Secy & General Counsel:** R.W. Lewis
**Investor Contact:** K.A. Bedard (208-368-4400)
**Board Members:** T. Aoki, S. R. Appleton, J. W. Bagley, R. L. Bailey, P. J. Byrne, M. Johnson, L. N. Mondry, R. E. Switz

**Founded:** 1978
**Domicile:** Delaware
**Employees:** 26,100

# Microsoft Corp

**STANDARD &POOR'S**

| S&P Recommendation | BUY ★★★★☆ | Price $24.30 (as of Nov 25, 2011) | 12-Mo. Target Price $33.00 | Investment Style Large-Cap Growth |
|---|---|---|---|---|

**GICS Sector** Information Technology
**Sub-Industry** Systems Software

**Summary** Microsoft, the world's largest software company, develops PC software, including the Windows operating system and the Office application suite.

## Key Stock Statistics (Source S&P, Vickers, company reports)

| | | | | | | | |
|---|---|---|---|---|---|---|---|
| 52-Wk Range | $29.46– 23.65 | S&P Oper. EPS 2012**E** | 2.86 | Market Capitalization(B) | $204.416 | Beta | 0.99 |
| Trailing 12-Month EPS | $2.75 | S&P Oper. EPS 2013**E** | 3.21 | Yield (%) | 3.29 | S&P 3-Yr. Proj. EPS CAGR(%) | 6 |
| Trailing 12-Month P/E | 8.8 | P/E on S&P Oper. EPS 2012**E** | 8.5 | Dividend Rate/Share | $0.80 | S&P Credit Rating | AAA |
| $10K Invested 5 Yrs Ago | $9,039 | Common Shares Outstg. (M) | 8,412.2 | Institutional Ownership (%) | 64 | | |

## Price Performance

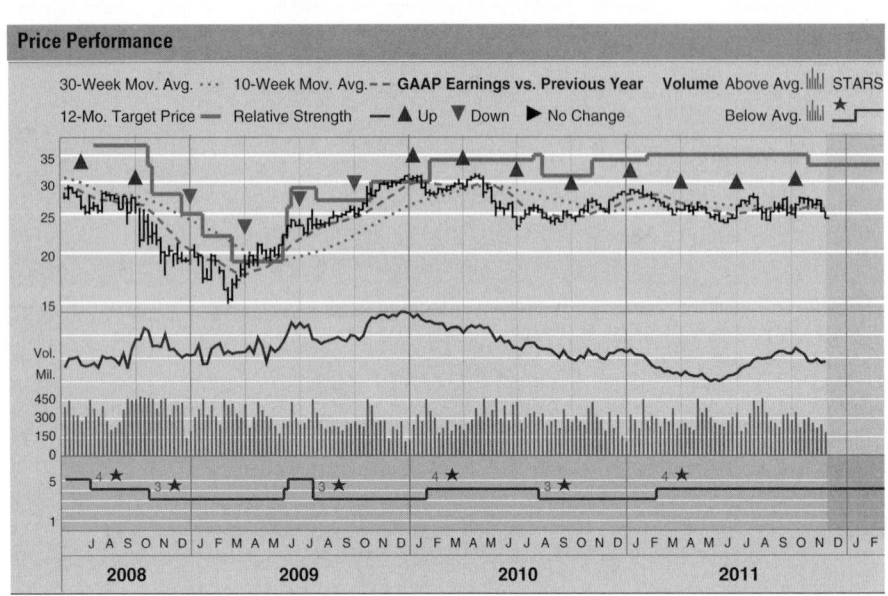

30-Week Mov. Avg. · · · 10-Week Mov. Avg. - - **GAAP Earnings vs. Previous Year**   Volume Above Avg. STARS
12-Mo. Target Price — Relative Strength — ▲ Up ▼ Down ► No Change   Below Avg. ★

Options: ASE, CBOE, P, Ph

Analysis prepared by Equity Analyst **Angelo Zino, CFA** on Oct 24, 2011, when the stock traded at **$27.34**.

## Qualitative Risk Assessment

| LOW | MEDIUM | HIGH |
|---|---|---|

Our risk assessment reflects our concerns about a sluggish recovery in enterprise IT spending, market share losses in smartphones and mobile devices, and difficulties inherent in releasing new products in a timely manner, mitigated by the company's current leading market positions and financial strength.

## Quantitative Evaluations

**S&P Quality Ranking**   A-

| D | C | B- | B | B+ | A- | A | A+ |
|---|---|---|---|---|---|---|---|

**Relative Strength Rank**   MODERATE

45

LOWEST = 1   HIGHEST = 99

## Revenue/Earnings Data

**Revenue (Million $)**

| | 1Q | 2Q | 3Q | 4Q | Year |
|---|---|---|---|---|---|
| 2012 | 17,372 | -- | -- | -- | -- |
| 2011 | 16,195 | 19,953 | 16,428 | 17,367 | 69,943 |
| 2010 | 12,920 | 19,022 | 14,503 | 16,039 | 62,484 |
| 2009 | 15,061 | 16,629 | 13,648 | 13,099 | 58,437 |
| 2008 | 13,762 | 16,367 | 14,454 | 15,837 | 60,420 |
| 2007 | 10,811 | 12,542 | 14,398 | 13,371 | 51,122 |

**Earnings Per Share ($)**

| | 1Q | 2Q | 3Q | 4Q | Year |
|---|---|---|---|---|---|
| 2012 | 0.68 | E0.85 | E0.63 | E0.71 | E2.86 |
| 2011 | 0.62 | 0.77 | 0.61 | 0.69 | 2.69 |
| 2010 | 0.40 | 0.74 | 0.45 | 0.51 | 2.10 |
| 2009 | 0.48 | 0.47 | 0.33 | 0.34 | 1.62 |
| 2008 | 0.45 | 0.50 | 0.47 | 0.46 | 1.87 |
| 2007 | 0.35 | 0.26 | 0.50 | 0.31 | 1.42 |

Fiscal year ended Jun. 30. Next earnings report expected: Late January. EPS Estimates based on S&P Operating Earnings; historical GAAP earnings are as reported.

## Highlights

► We expect revenues to rise 6.3% in FY 12 (Jun.) and 6.7% in FY 13, following 12% growth in FY 11. We see Windows and Windows Live advancing by low single digits in FY 12 and FY 13, driven by higher PC sales but tempered by lower selling prices in emerging markets. We project 6% to 7% growth in Server and Tools revenue in both FY 12 and FY 13. We estimate 5% to 6% growth in Microsoft Business in FY 12 and FY 13, on stronger enterprise spending. We see Entertainment and Devices revenue increasing 18% in FY 12 and 20% in FY 13, which includes the acquisition of Skype. For MSFT's Online Service division in FY 12 and FY 13, we forecast 12% and 7% growth.

► We look for an annual gross margin of 78% in FY 12 and FY 13. Despite higher volume, we expect a less favorable revenue mix given more robust growth in lower-margin businesses. We see an operating margin of 39% in FY 12, widening to 40% in FY 13.

► We forecast EPS of $2.86 in FY 12 and $3.21 in FY 13. We see good traction within MSFT's Entertainment and Device division, and we are encouraged by recent improved operating results in its Online Service division.

## Investment Rationale/Risk

► Our buy recommendation is based mostly on valuation. The shares are trading at 8.6X our FY 13 EPS estimate, a significant discount to the market and peers. We believe MSFT's core businesses remain solid, on healthy enterprise spending and our view that the transition to Windows 7 from older versions is in the middle innings. However, we see a potential catalyst being the eventual launch of Windows 8, which could finally help MSFT penetrate the mobile device category. We also see continued sales momentum for the Xbox, and we think its TV platform will help transform the product from a gaming console to a full entertainment suite.

► Risks to our recommendation and target price include lower-than-projected PC sales, a slowdown in the global economy, and further losses in the mobile device market.

► Our 12-month target price of $33 is based on a blend of our discounted cash flow (DCF) and P/E analyses. Our DCF model assumes a 10.6% weighted average cost of capital and 1.5% terminal growth, yielding an intrinsic value of $36. Our P/E analysis derives a value of $31, based on an industry P/E-to-growth ratio of about 1.8X, or 10.8X our FY 12 EPS estimate of $2.86.

## Dividend Data (Dates: mm/dd Payment Date: mm/dd/yy)

| Amount ($) | Date Decl. | Ex-Div. Date | Stk. of Record | Payment Date |
|---|---|---|---|---|
| 0.160 | 12/15 | 02/15 | 02/17 | 03/10/11 |
| 0.160 | 03/14 | 05/17 | 05/19 | 06/09/11 |
| 0.160 | 06/15 | 08/16 | 08/18 | 09/08/11 |
| 0.200 | 09/21 | 11/15 | 11/17 | 12/08/11 |

Dividends have been paid since 2003. Source: Company reports.

---

**Please read the Required Disclosures and Analyst Certification on the last page of this report.**

The **McGraw·Hill** Companies

# Microsoft Corp

STANDARD
&POOR'S

## Business Summary October 24, 2011

CORPORATE OVERVIEW. Microsoft is the world's largest software maker, primarily as a result of its near-monopoly position in desktop operating systems and its Office productivity suite. The combination of these two strongholds poses a formidable barrier to entry for competitors, in our opinion. MSFT has used the strong cash flows from these businesses to fund research and development of other markets, including home entertainment consoles and Internet online advertising.

The company has five operating business divisions: Windows and Windows Live, Server and Tools, Online Services Business, Microsoft Business, and Entertainment and Devices.

Windows and Windows Live is responsible for the development of the Windows product family. The division generated over 75% of its revenue from OEMs pre-installing versions of Windows operating systems. Despite some market share loss to Apple and the Linux operating system in recent years, Microsoft Windows operating systems still run more than 90% of all PCs currently in use.

Server and Tools develops and markets software server products, software developer tools, services, and solutions. Windows Server-based products are integrated server infrastructure and middleware software designed to support software applications built on the Windows Server operating system. Server

and Tools product and service offerings include Windows Server, Microsoft SQL Server, Windows Azure, Visual Studio, System Center products, Windows Embedded device platforms, and Enterprise Services. Enterprise Services comprise Premier product support services and Microsoft Consulting Services.

Online Services Business is comprised of various Internet websites that offer content and personal communications services. It also includes an online advertising platform that links publishers and advertisers to their targeted audiences. Online Service Business offerings primarily include Bing, MSN, adCenter, and advertiser tools. Bing and MSN generate revenue through the sale of search and display advertising. Search and display advertising generally accounts for nearly all of this segment's revenue.

Microsoft Business is comprised of the Microsoft Office system and Microsoft Dynamics business solutions. Despite the growing popularity of online software application suites such as Google Apps, Microsoft Office suite is the prevailing productivity application used in major enterprises.

## Company Financials  Fiscal Year Ended Jun. 30

| Per Share Data ($) | 2011 | 2010 | 2009 | 2008 | 2007 | 2006 | 2005 | 2004 | 2003 | 2002 |
|---|---|---|---|---|---|---|---|---|---|---|
| Tangible Book Value | 5.22 | 3.76 | 2.84 | 2.43 | 2.71 | 3.55 | 4.14 | 6.55 | 5.34 | 2.05 |
| Cash Flow | 3.02 | 2.40 | 1.90 | 2.07 | 1.57 | 1.28 | 1.20 | 0.86 | 1.05 | 0.80 |
| Earnings | 2.69 | 2.10 | 1.62 | 1.87 | 1.42 | 1.20 | 1.12 | 0.75 | 0.92 | 0.71 |
| S&P Core Earnings | 2.66 | 2.07 | 1.63 | 1.99 | 1.38 | 1.27 | 1.20 | 0.83 | 0.75 | 0.65 |
| Dividends | 0.61 | 0.52 | 0.50 | 0.43 | 0.39 | 0.34 | 3.32 | 0.16 | 0.08 | Nil |
| Payout Ratio | 23% | 25% | 31% | 23% | 27% | 28% | NM | 21% | 9% | Nil |
| Prices:High | 29.46 | 31.58 | 31.50 | 35.96 | 37.50 | 30.26 | 28.25 | 30.20 | 30.00 | 35.31 |
| Prices:Low | 23.65 | 22.73 | 14.87 | 17.50 | 26.60 | 21.46 | 23.82 | 24.86 | 22.55 | 20.71 |
| P/E Ratio:High | 11 | 15 | 19 | 19 | 26 | 25 | 25 | 40 | 33 | 50 |
| P/E Ratio:Low | 9 | 11 | 9 | 9 | 19 | 18 | 21 | 33 | 25 | 29 |

| Income Statement Analysis (Million $) | | | | | | | | | | |
|---|---|---|---|---|---|---|---|---|---|---|
| Revenue | 69,943 | 62,484 | 58,437 | 60,420 | 51,122 | 44,282 | 39,788 | 36,835 | 32,187 | 28,365 |
| Operating Income | 29,927 | 27,363 | 23,255 | 25,877 | 19,964 | 17,375 | 15,416 | 10,220 | 14,656 | 12,994 |
| Depreciation | 2,766 | 2,673 | 2,562 | 1,872 | 1,440 | 903 | 855 | 1,186 | 1,439 | 1,084 |
| Interest Expense | 295 | 151 | 58.0 | NA | Nil | Nil | Nil | Nil | Nil | Nil |
| Pretax Income | 28,071 | 25,013 | 19,821 | 23,814 | 20,101 | 18,262 | 16,628 | 12,196 | 14,726 | 11,513 |
| Effective Tax Rate | NA | NA | 26.5% | 25.8% | 30.0% | 31.0% | 26.3% | 33.0% | 32.1% | 32.0% |
| Net Income | 23,150 | 18,760 | 14,569 | 17,681 | 14,065 | 12,599 | 12,254 | 8,168 | 9,993 | 7,829 |
| S&P Core Earnings | 22,865 | 18,534 | 14,650 | 18,873 | 13,643 | 13,329 | 13,107 | 9,042 | 8,155 | 7,051 |

| Balance Sheet & Other Financial Data (Million $) | | | | | | | | | | |
|---|---|---|---|---|---|---|---|---|---|---|
| Cash | 51,591 | 36,726 | 29,907 | 21,171 | 6,111 | 6,714 | 4,851 | 15,982 | 6,438 | 3,016 |
| Current Assets | 74,918 | 55,676 | 49,280 | 43,242 | 40,168 | 49,010 | 48,737 | 70,566 | 58,973 | 48,576 |
| Total Assets | 108,704 | 86,113 | 77,888 | 72,793 | 63,171 | 69,597 | 70,815 | 92,389 | 79,571 | 67,646 |
| Current Liabilities | 28,774 | 26,147 | 27,034 | 29,886 | 23,754 | 22,442 | 16,877 | 14,969 | 13,974 | 12,744 |
| Long Term Debt | 11,921 | 4,939 | 3,746 | 1.00 | Nil | Nil | Nil | Nil | Nil | Nil |
| Common Equity | 57,083 | 46,175 | 39,558 | 36,286 | 31,097 | 40,104 | 48,115 | 74,825 | 61,020 | 52,180 |
| Total Capital | 69,004 | 51,114 | 43,304 | 36,287 | 31,097 | 40,104 | 48,115 | 74,825 | 62,751 | 52,578 |
| Capital Expenditures | 2,355 | 1,977 | 3,119 | 3,182 | 2,264 | 1,578 | 812 | 1,109 | 891 | 770 |
| Cash Flow | 25,916 | 21,433 | 17,131 | 19,553 | 15,505 | 13,502 | 13,109 | 9,354 | 11,432 | 8,913 |
| Current Ratio | 2.6 | 2.1 | 1.8 | 1.5 | 1.7 | 2.2 | 2.9 | 4.7 | 4.2 | 3.8 |
| % Long Term Debt of Capitalization | 17.3 | 9.7 | 8.7 | NM | Nil | Nil | Nil | Nil | Nil | Nil |
| % Net Income of Revenue | 33.1 | 30.0 | 24.9 | 29.3 | 27.5 | 28.5 | 30.8 | 22.2 | 31.0 | 27.6 |
| % Return on Assets | 23.8 | 22.9 | 19.3 | 26.0 | 21.2 | 17.9 | 14.8 | 9.4 | 13.6 | 12.4 |
| % Return on Equity | 44.8 | 43.8 | 38.4 | 52.5 | 39.5 | 28.6 | 19.9 | 11.7 | 17.7 | 15.7 |

Data as orig reptd.; bef. results of disc opers/spec. items. Per share data adj. for stk. divs.; EPS diluted. E-Estimated. NA-Not Available. NM-Not Meaningful. NR-Not Ranked. UR-Under Review.

**Office:** One Microsoft Way, Redmond, WA 98052-6399.
**Telephone:** 425-882-8080.
**Email:** msft@microsoft.com
**Website:** http://www.microsoft.com

**Chrmn:** W.H. Gates, III
**CEO:** S.A. Ballmer
**COO:** B.K. Turner
**CFO:** P.S. Klein

**Chief Admin Officer & Chief Acctg Officer:** F.H. Brod
**Investor Contact:** F. Brod (800-285-7772)
**Board Members:** S. A. Ballmer, D. Dublon, W. H. Gates, III, R. V. Gilmartin, R. Hastings, M. M. Klawe, D. F. Marquardt, C. H. Noski, H. G. Panke

**Founded:** 1975
**Domicile:** Washington
**Employees:** 90,000

# Molex Inc

## STANDARD &POOR'S

**S&P Recommendation** SELL ★ ★ ☆ ☆ ☆

| Price | 12-Mo. Target Price | Investment Style |
|---|---|---|
| $22.16 (as of Nov 25, 2011) | $17.00 | Large-Cap Growth |

**GICS Sector** Information Technology
**Sub-Industry** Electronic Manufacturing Services

**Summary** This company makes electrical and electronic devices primarily for OEMs in the computer, telecommunications, home appliance and home entertainment industries.

### Key Stock Statistics (Source S&P, Vickers, company reports)

| | | | | | | | |
|---|---|---|---|---|---|---|---|
| 52-Wk Range | $28.51–18.50 | S&P Oper. EPS 2012**E** | 1.60 | Market Capitalization(B) | $2.118 | Beta | 1.50 |
| Trailing 12-Month EPS | $1.73 | S&P Oper. EPS 2013**E** | 1.95 | Yield (%) | 3.61 | S&P 3-Yr. Proj. EPS CAGR(%) | 9 |
| Trailing 12-Month P/E | 12.8 | P/E on S&P Oper. EPS 2012**E** | 13.9 | Dividend Rate/Share | $0.80 | S&P Credit Rating | NA |
| $10K Invested 5 Yrs Ago | $7,670 | Common Shares Outstg. (M) | 175.8 | Institutional Ownership (%) | 72 | | |

### Price Performance

30-Week Mov. Avg. · · · · 10-Week Mov. Avg. - - **GAAP Earnings vs. Previous Year** Volume Above Avg. ▮▮▮ STARS
12-Mo. Target Price — Relative Strength — ▲ Up ▼ Down ▶ No Change Below Avg. ▮▮▮ ★

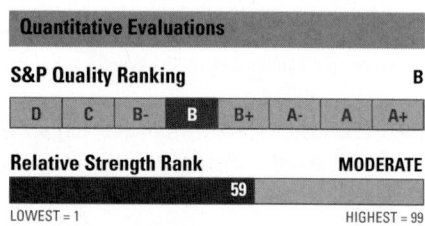

Options: CBOE, P, Ph

Analysis prepared by Equity Analyst **Stewart Scharf** on Oct 26, 2011, when the stock traded at **$24.49**.

### Highlights

➤ We project low single digit sales growth for FY 12 (Jun.), based on tougher comparisons and softening demand for telecom, infotech products and industrial products, especially in the U.S. and Europe, as well as for certain consumer electronics products globally, while automotive demand should continue to grow. We expect sales from Japan to recover as production returns to near normal levels following the earthquake in March 2011.

➤ In our view, FY 12 gross margins should widen modestly from 30.3% in FY 11, based on a better product mix and operating leverage, and supply-chain cost savings, while stabilizing copper and gold prices limit price erosion. We believe EBITDA margins will be virtually unchanged at about 19%, based on higher R&D and other operating expenses, which should outweigh cost control efforts and improved manufacturing efficiencies.

➤ For FY 12, we estimate an effective tax rate of 30.5% and operating EPS of $1.60 (before ongoing legal costs involving a former employee who obtained unauthorized loans in Molex Japan's name). We see a 22% increase to $1.95 in FY 13.

### Investment Rationale/Risk

➤ We maintain our sell opinion, based on softening demand trends recently in several segments, along with our valuation metrics. Corporate governance practices are also a concern to us, as MOLX has two classes of stock, and the board of directors consists mostly of insiders. We still think the balance sheet is solid, with a low cost structure and a strong presence in growing Asian markets.

➤ Risks to our recommendation and target price include a significant and sustained decline in copper, gold and plastics prices; positive foreign exchange rates; and a rapid global economic rebound.

➤ Based on a blend of our relative and DCF valuation metrics, our 12-month target price is $17. Our relative metrics, including historical average price-to-sales and three-year PEG ratios, lead us to a P/E multiple of near 9X our FY 12 EPS estimate, a modest discount to peers and below MOLX's five-year average historical forward P/E, valuing the shares at $14. Our DCF analysis, which assumes a 10.3% cost of capital (WACC) and a 3% terminal growth rate, suggests an intrinsic value of $20.

### Qualitative Risk Assessment

| LOW | MEDIUM | HIGH |
|---|---|---|

Our risk assessment reflects the cyclicality in MOLX's global markets, price and product competition, volatile raw material costs, and fluctuating foreign currency exchange rates. However, we view the balance sheet as strong.

### Quantitative Evaluations

**S&P Quality Ranking** B

| D | C | B- | B | B+ | A- | A | A+ |
|---|---|---|---|---|---|---|---|

**Relative Strength Rank** MODERATE

59

LOWEST = 1     HIGHEST = 99

### Revenue/Earnings Data

**Revenue (Million $)**

| | 1Q | 2Q | 3Q | 4Q | Year |
|---|---|---|---|---|---|
| 2012 | 936.0 | -- | -- | -- | -- |
| 2011 | 897.7 | 901.5 | 874.5 | 913.7 | 3,587 |
| 2010 | 674.0 | 729.6 | 756.3 | 847.3 | 3,007 |
| 2009 | 839.0 | 666.7 | 505.5 | 570.6 | 2,582 |
| 2008 | 792.6 | 841.6 | 822.3 | 871.9 | 3,328 |
| 2007 | 829.6 | 837.5 | 807.0 | 791.9 | 3,266 |

**Earnings Per Share ($)**

| | | | | | |
|---|---|---|---|---|---|
| 2012 | 0.46 | E0.37 | E0.35 | E0.41 | E1.60 |
| 2011 | 0.43 | 0.45 | 0.39 | 0.44 | 1.70 |
| 2010 | -0.09 | 0.08 | 0.22 | 0.23 | 0.44 |
| 2009 | 0.25 | -0.50 | -0.34 | -1.27 | -1.84 |
| 2008 | 0.29 | 0.33 | 0.28 | 0.29 | 1.19 |
| 2007 | 0.41 | 0.36 | 0.35 | 0.18 | 1.30 |

Fiscal year ended Jun. 30. Next earnings report expected: NA. EPS Estimates based on S&P Operating Earnings; historical GAAP earnings are as reported.

### Dividend Data (Dates: mm/dd Payment Date: mm/dd/yy)

| Amount ($) | Date Decl. | Ex-Div. Date | Stk. of Record | Payment Date |
|---|---|---|---|---|
| 0.175 | 10/26 | 12/29 | 12/31 | 01/25/11 |
| 0.175 | 10/26 | 03/29 | 03/31 | 04/25/11 |
| 0.200 | 05/03 | 06/28 | 06/30 | 07/25/11 |
| 0.200 | 09/16 | 09/28 | 09/30 | 10/25/11 |

Dividends have been paid since 1976. Source: Company reports.

---

**Please read the Required Disclosures and Analyst Certification on the last page of this report.**

The *McGraw-Hill* Companies

# Molex Inc

STANDARD
&POOR'S

## Business Summary October 26, 2011

Molex Incorporated (MOLX) engages in the design, manufacture, and sale of electronic components worldwide. The company sells approximately 100,000 products, including terminals, connectors, planar cables, cable assemblies, interconnection systems, backplanes, integrated products, and mechanical and electronic switches. It also provides manufacturing services to integrate specific components into a customer's product. The company has 39 plants in 16 countries. MOLX believes the connector industry has grown at a compound annual rate of 5.2% over the past 20 years.

In the telecommunications market, the company offers high speed optical signal product lines, backplane connector systems, power distribution product, micro-miniature connectors, global coordination, and complementary products, such as keyboards and antennas. For mobile phones, MOLX provides micro-miniature connectors, SIM card sockets, keypads, electromechanical subassemblies, and internal antennas and subsystems.

The company's products include EdgeLine Connectors, which are low-profile, 12.5 Gbps connectors for use in high-signal transmissions and high-density

signal applications; Impact 6-Pair Right-Angle Cable Assemblies, which extend the range of backplane applications to connect with next-generation telecom and data networking equipment; and VHDM H-Series Backplane Connector Systems, which achieve data rates approximately 6.25 Gbps. In the data market, the company offers its high-speed signal product line and storage input/output (I/O) products. It manufactures power, optical and signal connectors, and cables for data transfer, linking disk drives, controllers, servers, switches, and storage enclosures. MOLX offers various products for power distribution, signal integrity, processor, and memory applications. The company is also a designer in the industry for storage devices. In the consumer market, it designs and manufactures various connectors for home and portable audio, digital still and video cameras, DVD players and recorders, as well as devices that combine multiple functions.

## Company Financials Fiscal Year Ended Jun. 30

| Per Share Data ($) | 2011 | 2010 | 2009 | 2008 | 2007 | 2006 | 2005 | 2004 | 2003 | 2002 |
|---|---|---|---|---|---|---|---|---|---|---|
| Tangible Book Value | 12.41 | 10.39 | 10.89 | 12.66 | 10.64 | 11.60 | 10.78 | 10.05 | 9.10 | 8.64 |
| Cash Flow | 3.07 | 1.81 | -0.40 | 2.58 | 2.58 | 2.41 | 2.02 | 2.10 | 1.62 | 1.53 |
| Earnings | 1.70 | 0.44 | -1.84 | 1.19 | 1.30 | 1.26 | 0.81 | 0.92 | 0.44 | 0.39 |
| S&P Core Earnings | 1.71 | 0.45 | -0.36 | 1.13 | 1.30 | 1.27 | 0.76 | 0.85 | 0.39 | 0.39 |
| Dividends | 0.70 | 0.61 | 0.61 | 0.45 | 0.30 | 0.30 | 0.15 | 0.10 | 0.10 | 0.10 |
| Payout Ratio | 41% | 139% | NM | 38% | 23% | 18% | 19% | 11% | 23% | 26% |
| Prices:High | 28.51 | 23.66 | 22.41 | 30.61 | 32.34 | 40.10 | 30.00 | 36.10 | 35.12 | 39.61 |
| Prices:Low | 18.50 | 17.50 | 9.68 | 10.29 | 23.50 | 25.63 | 23.75 | 27.07 | 19.98 | 19.43 |
| P/E Ratio:High | 17 | 54 | NM | 26 | 25 | 32 | 37 | 39 | 80 | NM |
| P/E Ratio:Low | 11 | 40 | NM | 22 | 18 | 20 | 29 | 29 | 45 | 50 |

| Income Statement Analysis (Million $) | | | | | | | | | | |
|---|---|---|---|---|---|---|---|---|---|---|
| Revenue | 3,587 | 3,007 | 2,582 | 3,328 | 3,266 | 2,861 | 2,549 | 2,247 | 1,843 | 1,712 |
| Operating Income | 687 | 521 | 321 | 599 | 596 | 552 | 481 | 450 | -120 | 324 |
| Depreciation | 242 | 239 | 252 | 252 | 238 | 215 | 231 | 228 | 229 | 224 |
| Interest Expense | 5.71 | 5.42 | Nil | Nil | Nil | Nil | Nil | Nil | Nil | Nil |
| Pretax Income | 430 | 131 | -319 | 339 | 338 | 329 | 217 | 240 | 110 | 93.2 |
| Effective Tax Rate | NA | NA | NM | 36.4% | 28.8% | 28.0% | 28.8% | 26.5% | 22.5% | 17.9% |
| Net Income | 299 | 76.9 | -321 | 215 | 241 | 237 | 154 | 176 | 84.9 | 76.5 |
| S&P Core Earnings | 301 | 77.3 | -62.1 | 205 | 241 | 238 | 143 | 164 | 76.1 | 76.7 |

| Balance Sheet & Other Financial Data (Million $) | | | | | | | | | | |
|---|---|---|---|---|---|---|---|---|---|---|
| Cash | 547 | 395 | 468 | 510 | 461 | 486 | 498 | 339 | 350 | 313 |
| Current Assets | 2,055 | 1,776 | 1,448 | 1,783 | 1,591 | 1,548 | 1,374 | 1,169 | 962 | 915 |
| Total Assets | 3,598 | 3,237 | 2,942 | 3,600 | 3,316 | 2,973 | 2,728 | 2,572 | 2,335 | 2,254 |
| Current Liabilities | 882 | 913 | 714 | 649 | 531 | 595 | 470 | 428 | 356 | 360 |
| Long Term Debt | 223 | 183 | 30.3 | 146 | 128 | 8.81 | 9.98 | 14.0 | 16.9 | 17.8 |
| Common Equity | 2,368 | 1,985 | 2,063 | 2,677 | 2,523 | 2,281 | 2,168 | 2,066 | 1,897 | 1,828 |
| Total Capital | 2,711 | 2,273 | 2,093 | 2,823 | 2,651 | 2,290 | 2,180 | 2,081 | 1,914 | 1,846 |
| Capital Expenditures | 262 | 229 | 178 | 235 | 297 | 277 | 231 | 190 | 171 | 172 |
| Cash Flow | 541 | 316 | -69.4 | 468 | 479 | 452 | 385 | 404 | 314 | 300 |
| Current Ratio | 2.3 | 2.0 | 2.0 | 2.8 | 3.0 | 2.6 | 2.9 | 2.7 | 2.7 | 2.5 |
| % Long Term Debt of Capitalization | 8.2 | 8.1 | 1.5 | 5.2 | 4.8 | 0.4 | 0.5 | 0.7 | 0.9 | 1.0 |
| % Net Income of Revenue | 8.3 | 2.6 | NM | 6.5 | 7.4 | 8.3 | 6.1 | 7.8 | 4.6 | 4.5 |
| % Return on Assets | 8.7 | 2.5 | NM | 6.2 | 7.7 | 8.3 | 5.8 | 7.2 | 3.7 | 3.4 |
| % Return on Equity | 13.7 | 3.8 | NM | 8.3 | 10.0 | 10.7 | 7.3 | 8.9 | 4.6 | 4.3 |

Data as orig reptd.; bef. results of disc opers/spec. items. Per share data adj. for stk. divs.; EPS diluted. E-Estimated. NA-Not Available. NM-Not Meaningful. NR-Not Ranked. UR-Under Review.

Office: 2222 Wellington Court, Lisle, IL 60532.
Telephone: 630-969-4550.
Website: http://www.molex.com
Co-Chrmn: F.A. Krehbiel

Co-Chrmn: J.H. Krehbiel, Jr.
Pres & COO: L.G. McCarthy
Vice Chrmn & CEO: M.P. Slark
SVP & CIO: G.J. Matula

Investor Contact: S. Martens (630-527-4344)
Board Members: M. J. Birck, M. L. Collins, A. Dhebar, E. D. Jannotta, F. L. Krehbiel, F. A. Krehbiel, J. H. Krehbiel Jr., D. L. Landsittel, J. W. Laymon, D. G. Lubin, J. S. Metcalf, R. J. Potter, M. P. Slark

Founded: 1938
Domicile: Delaware
Employees: 33,613

# Molson Coors Brewing Co

STANDARD &POOR'S

| S&P Recommendation SELL ★ ★ ☆ ☆ ☆ | Price | 12-Mo. Target Price | Investment Style |
|---|---|---|---|
| | $38.00 (as of Nov 25, 2011) | $37.00 | Large-Cap Blend |

**GICS Sector** Consumer Staples
**Sub-Industry** Brewers

**Summary** TAP, the fifth largest brewer in the world, was formed in early 2005 via the combination of Adolph Coors Co. and Molson, Inc.

## Key Stock Statistics (Source S&P, Vickers, company reports)

| | | | | | | | |
|---|---|---|---|---|---|---|---|
| 52-Wk Range | $51.11–37.99 | S&P Oper. EPS 2011E | 3.50 | Market Capitalization(B) | $5.939 | Beta | 0.76 |
| Trailing 12-Month EPS | $3.26 | S&P Oper. EPS 2012E | 3.54 | Yield (%) | 3.37 | S&P 3-Yr. Proj. EPS CAGR(%) | 7 |
| Trailing 12-Month P/E | 11.7 | P/E on S&P Oper. EPS 2011E | 10.9 | Dividend Rate/Share | $1.28 | S&P Credit Rating | BBB- |
| $10K Invested 5 Yrs Ago | $11,886 | Common Shares Outstg. (M) | 181.1 | Institutional Ownership (%) | 91 | | |

## Price Performance

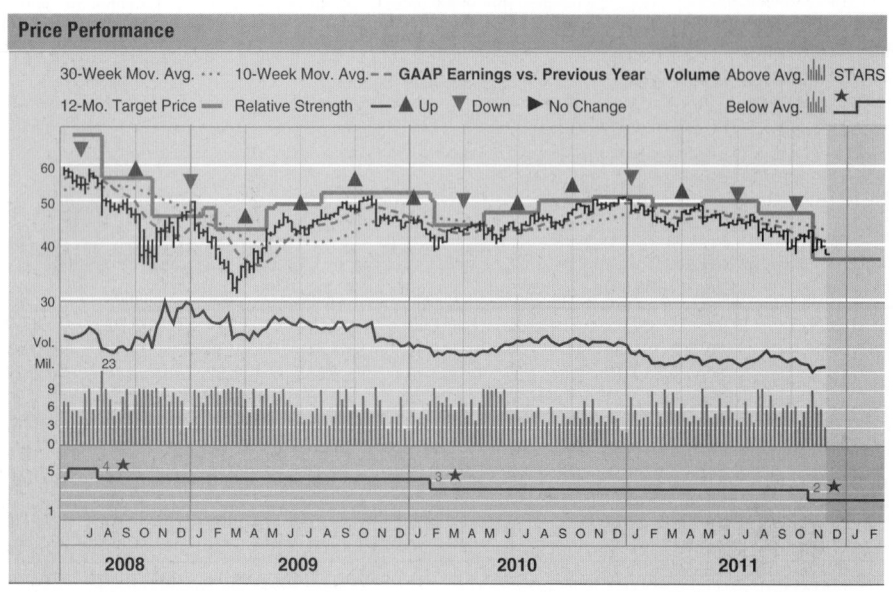

- 30-Week Mov. Avg. ···  10-Week Mov. Avg. – –  GAAP Earnings vs. Previous Year  Volume Above Avg. STARS
- 12-Mo. Target Price —  Relative Strength —  ▲ Up  ▼ Down  ► No Change  Below Avg.

Options: CBOE, P, Ph

Analysis prepared by Equity Analyst **Esther Kwon, CFA** on Nov 04, 2011, when the stock traded at **$38.92**.

## Qualitative Risk Assessment

| LOW | MEDIUM | HIGH |
|---|---|---|

Our risk assessment reflects the stable revenue streams of the brewing industry, in which TAP is a major player, offset by our corporate governance concerns with respect to TAP's multi-class stock structure and its more than 50% controlling family interest.

## Quantitative Evaluations

**S&P Quality Ranking**                                 B+

| D | C | B- | B | B+ | A- | A | A+ |
|---|---|---|---|---|---|---|---|

**Relative Strength Rank**                         MODERATE

43

LOWEST = 1                                       HIGHEST = 99

## Revenue/Earnings Data

**Revenue (Million $)**

| | 1Q | 2Q | 3Q | 4Q | Year |
|---|---|---|---|---|---|
| 2011 | 690.4 | 933.6 | 954.4 | -- | -- |
| 2010 | 661.0 | 883.3 | 875.0 | 835.1 | 3,254 |
| 2009 | 559.0 | 798.9 | 853.7 | 820.8 | 3,032 |
| 2008 | 1,357 | 1,757 | 921.1 | 739.2 | 4,774 |
| 2007 | 1,229 | 1,676 | 1,685 | 1,600 | 6,191 |
| 2006 | 1,154 | 1,583 | 1,577 | 1,531 | 5,845 |

**Earnings Per Share ($)**

| | | | | | |
|---|---|---|---|---|---|
| 2011 | 0.44 | 1.19 | 1.05 | E0.69 | E3.50 |
| 2010 | 0.33 | 1.27 | 1.37 | 0.59 | 3.57 |
| 2009 | 0.43 | 1.01 | 1.31 | 1.17 | 3.92 |
| 2008 | 0.25 | 0.50 | 0.92 | 0.49 | 2.16 |
| 2007 | 0.11 | 1.02 | 0.74 | 0.96 | 2.84 |
| 2006 | -0.11 | 0.91 | 0.71 | 0.65 | 2.16 |

Fiscal year ended Dec. 31. Next earnings report expected: Mid February. EPS Estimates based on S&P Operating Earnings; historical GAAP earnings are as reported.

## Highlights

➤ In 2011, we see sales rising at a high single digit rate, after climbing 7.3% in 2010. For 2012, we forecast a 4% increase on higher pricing. We expect Coors Light and Blue Moon to outperform the beer category in the U.S., partially offsetting underperformance by the Miller brands. We look for continued pressures in the U.K. and Canadian markets.

➤ On a new $200 million cost savings plan, we look for some operating margin improvement, but we expect it will be more than offset by higher commodity costs. We forecast Miller-Coors equity income to remain about flat as improved productivity is offset by higher expenses. In 2012, we expect a similar trend of input cost pressure offset by operating efficiency improvements and a moderate improvement in MillerCoors equity income.

➤ On an effective tax rate of 15%, compared to nearly 16% in 2010, we estimate 2011 EPS of $3.50. For 2012, we forecast EPS of $3.54 on a higher effective tax rate of 22%. On August 20, directors authorized a $1.2 billion repurchase program for the company's Class A and Class B common shares.

## Investment Rationale/Risk

➤ In light of elevated commodity prices, we remain concerned about raw material inflation, particularly in Canada and the U.K., where TAP has limited ability to hedge. While volumes improved in Canada on narrowing price gaps and new product introductions, those trends appeared to have reversed, and we look for weakness in U.S. operations as Miller brand volumes remain soft and Coors Light volumes have been lackluster. We expect U.K. results to be under pressure as sales shift to lower-margin, off-premise channels.

➤ Risks to our opinion and target price include a strengthening of Coors Light volumes in the U.S. and Canada, an ability to successfully raise prices, and lower competitive pressures, particularly in Canada. Commodity cost decreases could pose additional risks.

➤ Our 12-month target price of $37 is based on our P/E analysis. We apply a multiple of 10.5X, below both TAP's recent average and the beverage group multiple, to our 2012 EPS estimate of $3.54. We believe a discount is warranted given weak trends in the overall beer category, and we see few near-term catalysts to reverse this weakness.

## Dividend Data (Dates: mm/dd Payment Date: mm/dd/yy)

| Amount ($) | Date Decl. | Ex-Div. Date | Stk. of Record | Payment Date |
|---|---|---|---|---|
| 0.280 | 02/17 | 02/24 | 02/28 | 03/15/11 |
| 0.320 | 05/26 | 06/02 | 06/06 | 06/15/11 |
| 0.320 | 07/14 | 08/29 | 08/31 | 09/15/11 |
| 0.320 | 11/17 | 11/28 | 11/30 | 12/15/11 |

Dividends have been paid since 1970. Source: Company reports.

# Molson Coors Brewing Co

**STANDARD
&POOR'S**

## Business Summary November 04, 2011

CORPORATE OVERVIEW. Molson Coors Brewing Company was formed in February 2005 by the combination of Adolph Coors Co. and Canadian brewer Molson, Inc. The transaction resulted in each Molson Class B voting share being converted to shares with 0.126 voting rights and 0.234 non-voting rights of Molson Coors stock, and each Molson Class A converted to shares with a 0.360 non-voting share of Molson Coors. In June 2008, Molson Coors and SABMiller formed a joint venture of each company's United States and Puerto Rican operations. The deal gave TAP a 50% voting and 42% economic interest.

Molson Inc. was the world's 14th largest brewer in 2004, pre-merger, with operations in Canada, Brazil and the United States. A global brewer with C$3.5 billion in gross annual sales, Molson traces its roots back to 1786, making it North America's oldest beer brand. Adolph Coors Co. was the third largest U.S. brewer, with a 10.3% share of the U.S. beer market in 2004, selling 32.7 million barrels of beer and other malt beverage products, up 3% from the level of 2003. The company was founded in 1873.

TAP has a portfolio of over 65 strategic brands, including core brands Coors Light, Molson Canadian and Carling. In Canada, brands sold include Coors Light, Canadian, Export, Molson Canadian 67, Molson Dry , Molson M,

Creemore, Rickard's Red and other Rickard's brands, Carling, and Pilsner. In the U.S., key brands sold through MillerCoors include Coors Light and Miller Lite. Premium segment brands include Coors Banquet, Miller Genuine Draft and MGD 64, while super premium brands include Miller Chill and Sparks. Below premium brands include Miller High Life, Keystone Light and Milwaukee's Best, while craft and import brands include Blue Moon, Henry Weinhard's, George Killian's Irish Red, Leinenkugel's brands, Molson brands, Foster's, Peroni Nastro Azzurro, Pilsner Urquell and Grolsch. U.K. brands include Carling, C2, Coors Light, Worthington's, While Shield, Caffrey's, Kasteel Cru and Blue Moon.

CORPORATE STRATEGY. We look favorably on TAP's strategy to gain market share in each area by cross marketing its products. We are particularly pleased with the gains we see for Coors Light in Canada, where it now has a 14% market share according to TAP, making it among the best-selling beer brands in that country.

## Company Financials Fiscal Year Ended Dec. 31

| Per Share Data ($) | 2010 | 2009 | 2008 | 2007 | 2006 | 2005 | 2004 | 2003 | 2002 | 2001 |
|---|---|---|---|---|---|---|---|---|---|---|
| Tangible Book Value | 8.86 | 5.77 | 4.13 | NM | NM | NM | 1.72 | NM | NM | 12.03 |
| Cash Flow | 4.66 | 4.93 | 3.63 | 4.74 | 4.68 | 3.89 | 6.13 | 5.71 | 5.36 | 3.28 |
| Earnings | 3.57 | 3.92 | 2.16 | 2.84 | 2.16 | 1.44 | 2.60 | 2.39 | 2.21 | 1.66 |
| S&P Core Earnings | 3.65 | 3.74 | 1.03 | 2.53 | 1.87 | 1.07 | 2.13 | 2.10 | 0.77 | 0.68 |
| Dividends | 1.08 | 0.92 | 0.76 | 0.64 | 0.64 | 0.64 | 0.41 | 0.41 | 0.41 | 0.40 |
| Payout Ratio | 30% | 23% | 35% | 23% | 31% | 44% | 16% | 17% | 19% | 24% |
| Prices:High | 51.11 | 51.33 | 59.51 | 57.70 | 38.50 | 40.00 | 40.06 | 32.41 | 35.08 | 40.59 |
| Prices:Low | 38.44 | 30.76 | 35.00 | 37.56 | 30.38 | 28.69 | 26.87 | 22.93 | 25.25 | 21.33 |
| P/E Ratio:High | 14 | 13 | 28 | 20 | 18 | 28 | 15 | 14 | 16 | 25 |
| P/E Ratio:Low | 11 | 8 | 16 | 13 | 15 | 20 | 10 | 10 | 11 | 13 |

| Income Statement Analysis (Million $) | 2010 | 2009 | 2008 | 2007 | 2006 | 2005 | 2004 | 2003 | 2002 | 2001 |
|---|---|---|---|---|---|---|---|---|---|---|
| Revenue | 3,254 | 3,032 | 4,774 | 6,191 | 5,845 | 5,507 | 4,306 | 4,000 | 3,776 | 2,429 |
| Operating Income | 632 | 592 | 874 | 1,099 | 1,097 | 960 | 609 | 551 | 535 | 296 |
| Depreciation | 202 | 187 | 273 | 346 | 438 | 393 | 268 | 244 | 230 | 121 |
| Interest Expense | 99.4 | 96.6 | 104 | 136 | 143 | 131 | 72.4 | 81.2 | 70.9 | 2.01 |
| Pretax Income | 809 | 718 | 515 | 534 | 472 | 295 | 308 | 254 | 257 | 198 |
| Effective Tax Rate | NA | NM | 20.0% | 0.78% | 17.5% | 17.0% | 30.9% | 31.2% | 37.0% | 37.9% |
| Net Income | 670 | 729 | 400 | 515 | 374 | 230 | 197 | 175 | 162 | 123 |
| S&P Core Earnings | 682 | 695 | 190 | 459 | 324 | 172 | 161 | 154 | 56.1 | 50.7 |

| Balance Sheet & Other Financial Data (Million $) | 2010 | 2009 | 2008 | 2007 | 2006 | 2005 | 2004 | 2003 | 2002 | 2001 |
|---|---|---|---|---|---|---|---|---|---|---|
| Cash | 1,218 | 734 | 216 | 377 | 182 | 39.4 | 123 | 19.4 | 59.2 | 310 |
| Current Assets | 2,221 | 1,763 | 1,107 | 1,777 | 1,458 | 1,468 | 1,268 | 1,079 | 1,054 | 607 |
| Total Assets | 12,698 | 12,021 | 10,417 | 13,452 | 11,603 | 11,799 | 4,658 | 4,486 | 4,297 | 1,740 |
| Current Liabilities | 1,334 | 1,581 | 986 | 1,736 | 1,800 | 2,237 | 1,177 | 1,134 | 1,148 | 518 |
| Long Term Debt | 1,960 | 1,413 | 1,832 | 2,261 | 2,130 | 2,137 | 894 | 1,160 | 1,383 | 20.0 |
| Common Equity | 7,799 | 7,080 | 5,980 | 7,149 | 5,817 | 5,325 | 1,601 | 1,267 | 982 | 951 |
| Total Capital | 9,847 | 8,806 | 7,822 | 10,059 | 8,601 | 8,151 | 2,682 | 2,623 | 2,522 | 1,033 |
| Capital Expenditures | 178 | 125 | 231 | 428 | 446 | 406 | 212 | 240 | 240 | 245 |
| Cash Flow | 873 | 917 | 674 | 861 | 812 | 623 | 465 | 418 | 392 | 244 |
| Current Ratio | 1.7 | 1.1 | 1.1 | 1.0 | 0.8 | 0.7 | 1.1 | 1.0 | 0.9 | 1.2 |
| % Long Term Debt of Capitalization | 19.9 | 16.0 | 23.4 | 22.5 | 24.8 | 26.2 | 33.3 | 44.2 | 54.9 | 1.9 |
| % Net Income of Revenue | 20.6 | 24.1 | 8.4 | 8.3 | 6.4 | 4.2 | 4.6 | 4.4 | 4.3 | 5.1 |
| % Return on Assets | 5.4 | 6.5 | 3.4 | 4.1 | 3.2 | 2.8 | 4.3 | 4.0 | 5.4 | 7.3 |
| % Return on Equity | 9.0 | 11.2 | 6.1 | 7.9 | 6.7 | 6.7 | 13.7 | 15.5 | 16.7 | 13.1 |

Data as orig reptd.; bef. results of disc opers/spec. items. Per share data adj. for stk. divs.; EPS diluted. E-Estimated. NA-Not Available. NM-Not Meaningful. NR-Not Ranked. UR-Under Review.

**Office:** 1225 17th St, Denver, CO 80202-5534.
**Telephone:** 303-279-6565.
**Website:** http://www.molsoncoors.com
**Chrmn:** A.T. Molson

**Pres & CEO:** P.S. Swinburn
**Vice Chrmn:** P.H. Coors
**CFO:** S.F. Glendinning
**Chief Acctg Officer:** W.G. Waters

**Investor Contact:** D. Dunnewald (303-279-6565)
**Board Members:** F. Bellini, J. E. Cleghorn, P. H. Coors, C. C. Ficeli, B. D. Goldner, C. M. Herington, F. W. Hobbs, A. T. Molson, E. H. Molson, G. E. Molson, I. J. Napier, D. P. O'Brien, H. S. Riley, P. S. Swinburn

**Founded:** 1873
**Domicile:** Delaware
**Employees:** 14,660

# Monsanto Co

**STANDARD &POOR'S**

| S&P Recommendation | HOLD ★★★☆☆ | Price | 12-Mo. Target Price | Investment Style |
|---|---|---|---|---|
| | | $69.49 (as of Nov 28, 2011) | $74.00 | Large-Cap Blend |

**GICS Sector** Materials
**Sub-Industry** Fertilizers & Agricultural Chemicals

**Summary** This company is a global provider of agricultural products and integrated solutions for farmers.

## Key Stock Statistics (Source S&P, Vickers, company reports)

| | | | | | | | |
|---|---|---|---|---|---|---|---|
| 52-Wk Range | $78.71– 58.50 | S&P Oper. EPS 2012**E** | 3.47 | Market Capitalization(B) | $37.206 | Beta | 0.86 |
| Trailing 12-Month EPS | $2.96 | S&P Oper. EPS 2013**E** | NA | Yield (%) | 1.73 | S&P 3-Yr. Proj. EPS CAGR(%) | 14 |
| Trailing 12-Month P/E | 23.5 | P/E on S&P Oper. EPS 2012**E** | 20.0 | Dividend Rate/Share | $1.20 | S&P Credit Rating | A+ |
| $10K Invested 5 Yrs Ago | $14,820 | Common Shares Outstg. (M) | 535.4 | Institutional Ownership (%) | 82 | | |

## Price Performance

30-Week Mov. Avg. · · · 10-Week Mov. Avg. - - GAAP Earnings vs. Previous Year  Volume Above Avg. STARS
12-Mo. Target Price — Relative Strength — ▲ Up ▼ Down ► No Change  Below Avg. ★

Options: ASE, CBOE, P

Analysis prepared by Equity Analyst **Kevin Kirkeby** on Oct 06, 2011, when the stock traded at **$70.32**.

## Highlights

► We look for MON to achieve a 10% increase in revenues during FY 12 (Aug.), driven largely by farmers switching more acres over to MON's newest corn and soybean seeds. We continue to believe the strategic shift in FY 10 toward offering greater seed/trait variety and a larger number of price points will limit overall pricing, but contribute to volume gains during the coming year. For its Roundup business, we expect volumes to improve modestly in FY 12 as a result of MON's efforts to recapture market share.

► With the restructuring of its Roundup unit largely completed, and a shift in the sales mix toward more value-added seeds, we see margins widening in FY 12. However, we expect higher spending over the next year as MON expands production of its newest seeds and builds scale in its Latin American operations.

► Based on our revenue and margin outlook, and a 31% effective tax rate, our EPS estimate for FY 12 is $3.47.

## Investment Rationale/Risk

► MON shares trade at a valuation premium to the S&P 500, reflecting what we see as above-average earnings growth prospects. We forecast primary contributors being the introduction of next-generation seeds, and development of its smaller product segments. Even so, we believe the combination of increased regulatory scrutiny and reduced cash flows in its glyphosate unit due to structural market changes will partially offset growth in its seeds/traits segment, and warrants a valuation near the historical average.

► Risks to our recommendation and target price include expansion of antitrust investigations, a decline in grain prices that reduces the incentive to stretch for yield, and below peer-average yield performance from its latest seeds.

► Our DCF model, which assumes a 10.3% cost of equity and annual free cash flow growth averaging 15% for five years, slowing to 4% terminal growth thereafter, calculates intrinsic value of about $70. Our relative valuation model targets a four-quarter forward P/E multiple of 22.5X, which is the 10-year average, and produces a value near $78. Blending these two metrics yields our 12-month target price of $74.

## Qualitative Risk Assessment

| LOW | MEDIUM | HIGH |
|---|---|---|

Our risk assessment reflects MON's exposure to global agricultural markets and currencies, adverse weather, unfavorable legal and regulatory developments, and risks relating to enforcement of intellectual property rights. This is offset by relatively low exposure to economic cycles and our view of consistent cash flow generation.

## Quantitative Evaluations

**S&P Quality Ranking**  A-

| D | C | B- | B | B+ | A- | A | A+ |
|---|---|---|---|---|---|---|---|

**Relative Strength Rank**  MODERATE

62

LOWEST = 1    HIGHEST = 99

## Revenue/Earnings Data

**Revenue (Million $)**

| | 1Q | 2Q | 3Q | 4Q | Year |
|---|---|---|---|---|---|
| 2011 | 1,836 | 4,131 | 3,608 | 2,247 | 11,822 |
| 2010 | 1,697 | 3,890 | 2,962 | 1,953 | 10,502 |
| 2009 | 2,649 | 4,035 | 3,161 | 1,879 | 11,724 |
| 2008 | 2,049 | 3,727 | 3,538 | 2,051 | 11,365 |
| 2007 | 1,539 | 2,609 | 2,842 | 1,573 | 8,563 |
| 2006 | 1,405 | 2,200 | 2,348 | 1,391 | 7,344 |

**Earnings Per Share ($)**

| | | | | | |
|---|---|---|---|---|---|
| 2011 | 0.02 | 1.87 | 1.29 | -0.21 | 2.96 |
| 2010 | -0.04 | 1.60 | 0.70 | -0.27 | 2.01 |
| 2009 | 0.98 | 1.97 | 1.25 | -0.43 | 3.78 |
| 2008 | 0.45 | 2.00 | 1.46 | -0.32 | 3.59 |
| 2007 | 0.17 | 0.99 | 1.02 | -0.52 | 1.66 |
| 2006 | 0.11 | 0.80 | 0.61 | -0.25 | 1.27 |

Fiscal year ended Aug. 31. Next earnings report expected: Early January. EPS Estimates based on S&P Operating Earnings; historical GAAP earnings are as reported.

## Dividend Data (Dates: mm/dd Payment Date: mm/dd/yy)

| Amount ($) | Date Decl. | Ex-Div. Date | Stk. of Record | Payment Date |
|---|---|---|---|---|
| 0.280 | 12/06 | 01/05 | 01/07 | 01/28/11 |
| 0.280 | 01/25 | 04/06 | 04/08 | 04/29/11 |
| 0.280 | 06/08 | 07/06 | 07/08 | 07/29/11 |
| 0.300 | 08/03 | 10/05 | 10/07 | 10/28/11 |

Dividends have been paid since 2001. Source: Company reports.

---

**Please read the Required Disclosures and Analyst Certification on the last page of this report.**

The **McGraw-Hill** Companies

# Monsanto Co

**STANDARD &POOR'S**

## Business Summary October 06, 2011

CORPORATE OVERVIEW. Monsanto (MON) produces leading seed brands and develops biotechnology traits that assist farmers in controlling insects and weeds, and provides other seed companies with genetic material and biotech traits. MON's Roundup herbicides are used for agricultural, industrial and residential weed control, and are sold in more than 80 countries.

MARKET PROFILE. The company operates in two segments: agricultural productivity, and seeds and genomics. Seeds and genomics (73% of sales and 88% of gross profits in FY 11 (Aug.)) consists of the global seeds and related traits businesses, and technology platforms based on plant genomics, which increases the speed and power of genetic research. MON's seeds and genomics segment focuses on corn, soybeans and other oilseeds, cotton and wheat. We believe MON has focused on capturing value and profitability in its patent-protected seeds and traits business, as well as expanding its product line through its large acquisitions like Seminis in 2005 and De Ruiter in 2008, and smaller purchases like biotechnology research firm Divergence in Febru-

ary 2011. De Ruiter is a leader in the protected-culture segment of the vegetable seeds market, where MON had little presence. Given this trend, we think that the growth and margin outlook for MON's seeds and genomics segment is favorable.

Agricultural productivity (27%; 12%) consists of MON's crop protection products (Roundup herbicide and other glyphosate products) and its lawn and garden products. In FY 10 (latest available), Roundup and other glyphosate-based herbicides accounted for 19% of total sales, down from 37% in FY 04. Following the expiration of its patent protection for the active ingredient in Roundup herbicides in 2000, MON repositioned itself as one of the lowest cost producers.

## Company Financials Fiscal Year Ended Aug. 31

| Per Share Data ($) | 2011 | 2010 | 2009 | 2008 | 2007 | 2006 | 2005 | 2004 | 2003 | 2002 |
|---|---|---|---|---|---|---|---|---|---|---|
| Tangible Book Value | 12.84 | 10.42 | 10.02 | 8.59 | 6.35 | 6.95 | 5.99 | 7.71 | 7.26 | 7.24 |
| Cash Flow | 4.19 | 3.10 | 4.77 | 4.61 | 2.61 | 2.25 | 1.21 | 1.37 | 0.56 | 1.12 |
| Earnings | 2.96 | 2.01 | 3.78 | 3.59 | 1.66 | 1.27 | 0.29 | 0.51 | -0.02 | 0.25 |
| S&P Core Earnings | 2.98 | 2.01 | 3.60 | 3.27 | 1.72 | 1.36 | 0.67 | 0.68 | 0.61 | 0.01 |
| Dividends | 1.12 | 1.06 | 1.01 | 0.77 | 0.48 | 0.39 | 0.33 | 0.27 | 0.25 | 0.24 |
| Payout Ratio | 38% | 53% | 27% | 21% | 29% | 30% | 113% | 53% | NM | 98% |
| Prices:High | 78.71 | 87.06 | 93.35 | 145.80 | 116.25 | 53.49 | 39.93 | 28.22 | 14.45 | 17.00 |
| Prices:Low | 58.89 | 44.61 | 66.57 | 63.47 | 49.10 | 37.91 | 25.00 | 14.04 | 6.78 | 6.60 |
| P/E Ratio:High | 27 | 43 | 25 | 41 | 70 | 42 | NM | 55 | NM | 69 |
| P/E Ratio:Low | 20 | 22 | 18 | 18 | 30 | 30 | 86 | 28 | NM | 27 |

| Income Statement Analysis (Million $) | 2011 | 2010 | 2009 | 2008 | 2007 | 2006 | 2005 | 2004 | 2003 | 2002 |
|---|---|---|---|---|---|---|---|---|---|---|
| Revenue | 11,822 | 10,502 | 11,724 | 11,365 | 8,563 | 7,344 | 6,294 | 5,457 | 3,373 | 4,673 |
| Operating Income | 3,116 | 2,533 | 4,161 | 3,458 | 2,138 | 1,694 | 1,503 | 1,254 | 768 | 882 |
| Depreciation | 613 | 602 | 548 | 573 | 527 | 519 | 488 | 452 | 302 | 460 |
| Interest Expense | 162 | 162 | 163 | 132 | 139 | 134 | 115 | 91.0 | 57.0 | 59.0 |
| Pretax Income | 2,374 | 1,494 | 2,967 | 2,926 | 1,336 | 1,055 | 261 | 402 | -38.0 | 202 |
| Effective Tax Rate | NA | NA | 28.5% | 30.7% | 30.1% | 32.2% | 39.8% | 32.6% | NM | 36.1% |
| Net Income | 1,605 | 1,105 | 2,098 | 2,007 | 922 | 698 | 157 | 271 | -11.0 | 129 |
| S&P Core Earnings | 1,616 | 1,104 | 1,997 | 1,830 | 951 | 745 | 363 | 362 | 317 | 5.45 |

| Balance Sheet & Other Financial Data (Million $) | 2011 | 2010 | 2009 | 2008 | 2007 | 2006 | 2005 | 2004 | 2003 | 2002 |
|---|---|---|---|---|---|---|---|---|---|---|
| Cash | 2,778 | 1,485 | 1,956 | 1,613 | 866 | 1,460 | 525 | 1,037 | 511 | 428 |
| Current Assets | 8,841 | 7,172 | 7,883 | 7,609 | 5,084 | 5,461 | 4,644 | 4,931 | 4,962 | 4,424 |
| Total Assets | 19,876 | 17,917 | 17,874 | 17,993 | 12,983 | 11,728 | 10,579 | 9,164 | 9,461 | 8,890 |
| Current Liabilities | 4,761 | 3,587 | 3,756 | 4,439 | 3,075 | 2,279 | 2,159 | 1,894 | 1,944 | 1,810 |
| Long Term Debt | 1,543 | 1,862 | 1,724 | 1,792 | 1,150 | 1,639 | 1,458 | 1,075 | 1,258 | 851 |
| Common Equity | 11,545 | 10,099 | 10,056 | 9,374 | 7,503 | 6,680 | 5,613 | 5,258 | 5,156 | 5,180 |
| Total Capital | 13,430 | 12,005 | 11,780 | 11,370 | 8,653 | 8,319 | 7,071 | 6,333 | 6,414 | 6,031 |
| Capital Expenditures | 540 | 755 | 916 | 918 | 509 | 370 | 281 | 210 | 114 | 224 |
| Cash Flow | 2,270 | 1,707 | 2,646 | 2,580 | 1,449 | 1,217 | 645 | 723 | 291 | 589 |
| Current Ratio | 1.9 | 2.0 | 2.1 | 1.7 | 1.7 | 2.4 | 2.2 | 2.6 | 2.6 | 2.4 |
| % Long Term Debt of Capitalization | 11.5 | 15.5 | 14.6 | 15.8 | 13.3 | 19.7 | 20.6 | 17.0 | 19.6 | 14.1 |
| % Net Income of Revenue | 13.6 | 10.5 | 17.9 | 17.7 | 10.8 | 9.5 | 2.5 | 5.0 | NM | 2.8 |
| % Return on Assets | 8.5 | 6.2 | 11.7 | 13.0 | 7.5 | 6.3 | 1.6 | 2.9 | NM | 1.3 |
| % Return on Equity | 14.8 | 11.0 | 21.6 | 23.8 | 13.0 | 11.2 | 2.9 | 5.2 | NM | 2.0 |

Data as orig reptd.; bef. results of disc opers/spec. items. Per share data adj. for stk. divs.; EPS diluted. E-Estimated. NA-Not Available. NM-Not Meaningful. NR-Not Ranked. UR-Under Review.

**Office:** 800 North Lindbergh Boulevard, St. Louis, MO 63167-0001.
**Telephone:** 314-694-1000.
**Email:** info@monsanto.com
**Website:** http://www.monsanto.com

**Chrmn, Pres & CEO:** H. Grant
**EVP & CTO:** R.T. Fraley
**EVP, Secy & General Counsel:** D.F. Snively
**SVP & CFO:** P. Courduroux

**Chief Acctg Officer & Cntlr:** N.M. Ringenberg
**Investor Contact:** S.L. Foster (314-694-8148)
**Board Members:** D. L. Chicoine, J. L. Fields, H. Grant, A. H. Harper, L. K. Ipsen, G. S. King, C. S. McMillan, J. R. Moeller, W. U. Parfet, G. H. Poste, B. Stevens

**Founded:** 2000
**Domicile:** Delaware
**Employees:** 26,100

**The McGraw·Hill Companies**

# Monster Worldwide Inc

**STANDARD &POOR'S**

| S&P Recommendation | **BUY** ★★★★☆ | Price | 12-Mo. Target Price | Investment Style |
|---|---|---|---|---|
| | | $6.59 (as of Nov 25, 2011) | $12.00 | Large-Cap Blend |

**GICS Sector** Information Technology
**Sub-Industry** Internet Software & Services

**Summary** Monster Worldwide operates a multinational online career network. It also provides offerings to help consumers develop and direct their careers.

## Key Stock Statistics (Source S&P, Vickers, company reports)

| | | | | | | | | |
|---|---|---|---|---|---|---|---|---|
| 52-Wk Range | $25.90– 6.34 | S&P Oper. EPS 2011**E** | 0.42 | Market Capitalization(B) | $0.849 | Beta | 2.20 |
| Trailing 12-Month EPS | $0.34 | S&P Oper. EPS 2012**E** | 0.75 | Yield (%) | Nil | S&P 3-Yr. Proj. EPS CAGR(%) | NM |
| Trailing 12-Month P/E | 19.4 | P/E on S&P Oper. EPS 2011**E** | 15.7 | Dividend Rate/Share | Nil | S&P Credit Rating | NA |
| $10K Invested 5 Yrs Ago | $1,476 | Common Shares Outstg. (M) | 128.8 | Institutional Ownership (%) | 97 | | |

## Price Performance

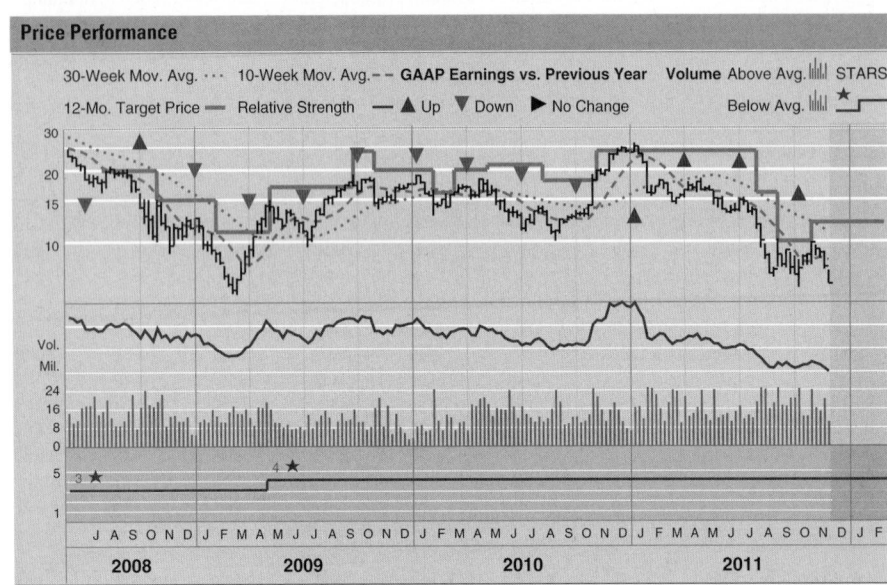

30-Week Mov. Avg. · · · · 10-Week Mov. Avg. — **GAAP Earnings vs. Previous Year** Volume Above Avg. ▌▌▌ STARS
12-Mo. Target Price — Relative Strength — ▲ Up ▼ Down ► No Change Below Avg. ▌▌▌ ★

Options: ASE, CBOE, P

Analysis prepared by Equity Analyst **Michael Jaffe** on Nov 10, 2011, when the stock traded at **$8.56**.

## Highlights

➤ We expect a 15% rise in revenues in 2012, following our projection of a 17% gain in 2011. Revenues were much lower for two-plus years, as both U.S. and foreign labor markets served by MWW were depressed. However, with global economies now recovering, we see a healthy rise in demand for MWW's services through 2012. We also see MWW's top line being boosted to an extent by the inclusion of Yahoo! HotJobs, which Monster acquired in August 2010. Our revenue forecast reflects our belief that MWW's recent guidance about a likely flat year to year level of fourth quarter order bookings will turn out to be an anomaly related to what we view as a soft patch in the economy.

➤ We see much wider margins in both 2011 and 2012, on our outlook for better revenue trends. We also see margins aided by what we view as considerable cost control discipline at Monster. Moreover, we see profitability aided somewhat by the integration of Yahoo! HotJobs.

➤ Our 2011 forecast excludes $0.08 a share of net credits in the first nine months of the year, and compares with an operating loss of $0.07 a share in 2010.

## Investment Rationale/Risk

➤ We think that a likely ongoing recovery of global economies (despite what we view as a current soft patch) will allow Monster's business to rebound in coming periods. We also have a positive view of its August 2010 acquisition of Yahoo! HotJobs, as we think Monster will derive a substantial benefit from having access to Yahoo's vast traffic network. Moreover, we have been impressed by MWW's aggressive actions to operate more efficiently and rein in costs. Based on these factors and our valuation model, we find the shares undervalued.

➤ Risks to our recommendation and target price include weaker-than-projected global labor markets, and less-than-expected success in MWW's restructuring initiatives.

➤ MWW's business is highly cyclical, but it usually records growth above that of peers. On that view, we find MWW to be undervalued. Our 12-month target price is $12, or 16X our 2012 EPS estimate, which is at the lower end of MWW's historical range. This valuation reflects our belief that MWW is poised for a solid business rebound, but it also accounts for economic uncertainties and the higher level of competition that it now faces.

## Qualitative Risk Assessment

| LOW | MEDIUM | **HIGH** |
|---|---|---|

Our risk assessment reflects the cyclicality of the help wanted industry, as it strongly correlates with the economy. In addition, foreign operations carry operating and exchange rate risks.

## Quantitative Evaluations

**S&P Quality Ranking** B-

| D | C | **B-** | B | B+ | A- | A | A+ |
|---|---|---|---|---|---|---|---|

**Relative Strength Rank** WEAK

9

LOWEST = 1 HIGHEST = 99

## Revenue/Earnings Data

**Revenue (Million $)**

| | 1Q | 2Q | 3Q | 4Q | Year |
|---|---|---|---|---|---|
| 2011 | 261.4 | 269.7 | 259.1 | -- | -- |
| 2010 | 215.3 | 214.9 | 228.8 | 255.1 | 914.1 |
| 2009 | 254.4 | 223.1 | 214.5 | 213.2 | 905.1 |
| 2008 | 366.5 | 354.3 | 332.2 | 290.7 | 1,344 |
| 2007 | 329.0 | 331.2 | 337.1 | 354.0 | 1,351 |
| 2006 | 257.0 | 275.2 | 285.9 | 298.6 | 1,117 |

**Earnings Per Share ($)**

| | | | | | |
|---|---|---|---|---|---|
| 2011 | Nil | 0.09 | 0.26 | E0.16 | E0.42 |
| 2010 | -0.20 | -0.02 | -0.05 | Nil | -0.27 |
| 2009 | -0.09 | -0.01 | 0.27 | -0.02 | 0.16 |
| 2008 | 0.19 | 0.15 | 0.36 | 0.24 | 0.94 |
| 2007 | 0.30 | 0.21 | 0.25 | 0.36 | 1.13 |
| 2006 | 0.26 | 0.29 | 0.31 | 0.31 | 1.17 |

Fiscal year ended Dec. 31. Next earnings report expected: Late January. EPS Estimates based on S&P Operating Earnings; historical GAAP earnings are as reported.

## Dividend Data

No cash dividends have been paid.

The **McGraw-Hill** Companies

# Monster Worldwide Inc

STANDARD &POOR'S

## Business Summary November 10, 2011

Monster Worldwide offers online employment solutions primarily in North America, Europe, Asia, and Latin America. The company operates in three segments: Careers - North America; Careers - International; and Internet Advertising and Fees. Through Careers - North America and Careers - International, Monster Worldwide provides online employment solutions in numerous countries worldwide. It works by connecting employers with job seekers at various levels and by providing searchable jobs and career management resources online. During 2010, the company derived 46% of its revenues from its Monster Careers - North America segment, 39% from Monster Careers - International, and 14% from Advertising & Fees. No client accounts for more than 5% of MWW's revenues.

MWW's services and solutions include searchable job postings, a resume database, recruitment media solutions throughout its network and other career-related content. Job seekers can search its job postings and post their resumes on each of Monster's career websites. The company primarily focuses on the enterprise market, with some of its focus targeting small-to-medium sized businesses. Employers and human resources companies pay to post jobs, search Monster's resume database, and utilize career site hosting and other services.

The Internet Advertising and Fees segment provides consumers with content, services, and offerings that help them manage the development and direction of their careers, while providing employers, educators, and marketers with media-driven solutions to reach out to these consumers. This segment offers three types of services: lead generation, display advertising, and products sold to consumers for a fee. Lead generation is a direct response business through which marketers pay for connections to consumers whose demographics and interests match the requirements of specific business offerings. Monster Worldwide's database of users and ongoing collection of data enables the company to provide its clients with these leads. Display advertising opportunities are integrated across the company's network of websites.

MWW also offers career services and content at a fee to job seekers, such as resume writing and a resume distribution service.

## Company Financials Fiscal Year Ended Dec. 31

| Per Share Data ($) | 2010 | 2009 | 2008 | 2007 | 2006 | 2005 | 2004 | 2003 | 2002 | 2001 |
|---|---|---|---|---|---|---|---|---|---|---|
| Tangible Book Value | NM | 1.37 | 0.85 | 3.97 | 3.65 | 1.47 | 0.27 | 0.18 | 2.02 | 2.61 |
| Cash Flow | 0.29 | 0.72 | 1.42 | 1.49 | 1.47 | 1.22 | 0.92 | 0.31 | -0.46 | 1.28 |
| Earnings | -0.27 | 0.16 | 0.94 | 1.13 | 1.17 | 0.92 | 0.62 | 0.06 | -0.96 | 0.61 |
| S&P Core Earnings | -0.28 | 0.12 | 1.16 | 1.13 | 1.17 | 0.47 | 0.37 | -0.08 | -1.48 | 0.10 |
| Dividends | Nil | Nil | Nil | Nil | Nil | Nil | Nil | Nil | Nil | Nil |
| Payout Ratio | Nil | Nil | Nil | Nil | Nil | Nil | Nil | Nil | Nil | Nil |
| Prices:High | 25.01 | 19.28 | 32.66 | 54.79 | 59.99 | 42.03 | 34.25 | 29.65 | 48.13 | 68.73 |
| Prices:Low | 10.01 | 5.95 | 8.91 | 31.07 | 34.75 | 22.44 | 17.60 | 7.63 | 7.94 | 25.21 |
| P/E Ratio:High | NM | NM | 35 | 48 | 51 | 46 | 55 | NM | NM | NM |
| P/E Ratio:Low | NM | NM | 9 | 27 | 30 | 24 | 28 | NM | NM | NM |

| Income Statement Analysis (Million $) | 2010 | 2009 | 2008 | 2007 | 2006 | 2005 | 2004 | 2003 | 2002 | 2001 |
|---|---|---|---|---|---|---|---|---|---|---|
| Revenue | 914 | 905 | 1,344 | 1,351 | 1,117 | 987 | 846 | 680 | 1,115 | 1,448 |
| Operating Income | 57.2 | 72.6 | 284 | 303 | 270 | 214 | 152 | 101 | 112 | 262 |
| Depreciation | 67.1 | 68.5 | 58.0 | 47.0 | 39.8 | 38.0 | 37.6 | 28.0 | 55.5 | 76.0 |
| Interest Expense | 4.29 | 1.43 | NA | Nil | Nil | Nil | Nil | Nil | 4.90 | 10.6 |
| Pretax Income | -46.8 | -19.0 | 179 | 232 | 241 | 179 | 112 | 23.6 | -130 | 125 |
| Effective Tax Rate | NA | 199.9% | 36.2% | 36.5% | 36.3% | 35.8% | 34.6% | 69.0% | NM | 46.1% |
| Net Income | -32.4 | 18.9 | 114 | 147 | 154 | 115 | 73.1 | 7.32 | -107 | 69.0 |
| S&P Core Earnings | -33.9 | 14.5 | 141 | 147 | 154 | 59.2 | 44.0 | -8.08 | -165 | 11.4 |

| Balance Sheet & Other Financial Data (Million $) | 2010 | 2009 | 2008 | 2007 | 2006 | 2005 | 2004 | 2003 | 2002 | 2001 |
|---|---|---|---|---|---|---|---|---|---|---|
| Cash | 163 | 285 | 224 | 578 | 58.7 | 320 | 198 | 142 | 192 | 341 |
| Current Assets | 585 | 645 | 683 | 1,185 | 1,124 | 773 | 704 | 567 | 809 | 1,006 |
| Total Assets | 1,978 | 1,827 | 1,917 | 2,078 | 1,970 | 1,679 | 1,544 | 1,122 | 1,631 | 2,206 |
| Current Liabilities | 687 | 507 | 724 | 829 | 826 | 697 | 731 | 640 | 799 | 930 |
| Long Term Debt | 40.0 | 45.0 | 0.01 | 0.23 | 0.42 | 15.7 | 34.0 | 2.09 | 3.93 | 9.13 |
| Common Equity | 1,129 | 1,133 | 1,047 | 1,117 | 1,110 | 920 | 756 | 468 | 813 | 1,229 |
| Total Capital | 1,174 | 1,183 | 1,072 | 1,136 | 1,143 | 981 | 789 | 470 | 817 | 1,238 |
| Capital Expenditures | 57.1 | 48.7 | 93.6 | 64.1 | 55.6 | 39.8 | 24.3 | 21.6 | 46.7 | 73.6 |
| Cash Flow | 34.7 | 87.5 | 173 | 194 | 193 | 153 | 111 | 35.4 | -51.0 | 145 |
| Current Ratio | 0.9 | 1.3 | 0.9 | 1.4 | 1.4 | 1.1 | 1.0 | 0.9 | 1.0 | 1.1 |
| % Long Term Debt of Capitalization | 3.4 | 3.8 | Nil | 0.0 | 0.0 | 1.6 | 4.3 | 0.4 | 0.5 | 0.7 |
| % Net Income of Revenue | NM | 2.1 | 8.5 | 10.9 | 13.8 | 11.7 | 8.6 | 1.1 | NM | 4.8 |
| % Return on Assets | NM | 1.0 | 5.7 | 7.3 | 8.4 | 7.1 | 5.5 | 0.5 | NM | 3.2 |
| % Return on Equity | NM | 1.7 | 10.6 | 13.2 | 15.0 | 13.7 | 11.9 | 1.1 | NM | 6.0 |

Data as orig reptd.; bef. results of disc opers/spec. items. Per share data adj. for stk. divs.; EPS diluted. E-Estimated. NA-Not Available. NM-Not Meaningful. NR-Not Ranked. UR-Under Review.

**Office:** 622 Third Avenue, 39th Floor, New York, NY 10017.
**Telephone:** 212-351-7000.
**Email:** corporate.communications@monsterworldwide.com
**Website:** http://www.about-monster.com

**Chrmn, Pres & CEO:** S. Iannuzzi
**EVP & Chief Admin Officer:** L. Poulos
**EVP, Secy & General Counsel:** M.C. Miller
**CFO & Chief Acctg Officer:** J.M. Langrock

**Investor Contact:** T.T. Yates
**Board Members:** J. R. Gaulding, E. P. Giambastiani, Jr., S. Iannuzzi, C. P. McCague, J. F. Rayport, R. Tunioli, T. T. Yates

**Founded:** 1967
**Domicile:** Delaware
**Employees:** 5,850

# Moody's Corp.

**STANDARD &POOR'S**

| | | | |
|---|---|---|---|
| **S&P Recommendation** HOLD ★★★☆☆ | **Price** $31.63 (as of Nov 25, 2011) | **12-Mo. Target Price** $40.00 | **Investment Style** Large-Cap Growth |

**GICS Sector** Financials
**Sub-Industry** Specialized Finance

**Summary** Moody's is a leading global credit rating, research and risk analysis concern.

## Key Stock Statistics (Source S&P, Vickers, company reports)

| | | | | | | | |
|---|---|---|---|---|---|---|---|
| 52-Wk Range | $41.93–26.10 | S&P Oper. EPS 2011**E** | 2.47 | Market Capitalization(B) | $7.022 | Beta | 1.33 |
| Trailing 12-Month EPS | $2.65 | S&P Oper. EPS 2012**E** | 2.58 | Yield (%) | 1.77 | S&P 3-Yr. Proj. EPS CAGR(%) | 10 |
| Trailing 12-Month P/E | 11.9 | P/E on S&P Oper. EPS 2011**E** | 12.8 | Dividend Rate/Share | $0.56 | S&P Credit Rating | BBB+ |
| $10K Invested 5 Yrs Ago | $4,857 | Common Shares Outstg. (M) | 222.0 | Institutional Ownership (%) | 100 | | |

## Price Performance

- 30-Week Mov. Avg. ··· 10-Week Mov. Avg. -- GAAP Earnings vs. Previous Year  Volume Above Avg. STARS
- 12-Mo. Target Price — Relative Strength — ▲ Up ▼ Down ▶ No Change  Below Avg.

Options: ASE, CBOE, P, Ph

Analysis prepared by Equity Analyst **Robert McMillan** on Oct 31, 2011, when the stock traded at **$35.81**.

## Highlights

- After their 13% advance in 2010, we look for revenues to climb more than 12% in 2011 and 8.8% in 2012. We expect a resurgence in debt issuance by U.S. corporations and financial institutions to drive revenue growth through 2011 and in 2012 as concerns about sovereign risk abate and capital markets normalize; this should help the corporate finance, financial institutions and public, project and infrastructure finance areas. Nevertheless, we view the Analytics and structured finance businesses as stronger contributors to near-term growth.

- We think MCO is experiencing renewed demand for analytical and consulting services. We also expect incremental revenues from the November 2010 acquisition of CSI Global Education, a leading provider of financial education services. We like the diversified nature of MCO's operations across the globe, which should help cushion the effect of turbulent business conditions in any one country or region; in the 2011 third quarter, MCO derived about 48% of its revenues from overseas.

- We project EPS of $2.47 in 2011 and $2.58 in 2012.

## Investment Rationale/Risk

- We believe MCO's credit ratings business has significant barriers to entry, which should help it maintain steady cash flow despite increased spending for regulatory compliance. In 2011, we think a steady flow of corporate debt refinancings will contribute to positive revenue comparisons. We also expect growth to come from capital markets development overseas, acquisitions, and analytical services. We expect the regulatory environment to also gain clarity as the SEC publishes new rules required by the Dodd-Frank Act.

- Risks to our opinion and target price include a greater-than-anticipated decline in the volume of debt issued in domestic and global capital markets, regulatory changes that increase competition, and persistently high long-term interest rates.

- Our 12-month target price of $40 is based on applying a 16.3X multiple to our forward 12-month EPS estimate of $2.47. This multiple is above MCO's recent historical average, which we think is warranted by what we view as dissipating regulatory concerns as well as our expectations for continued earnings improvement.

## Qualitative Risk Assessment

| LOW | MEDIUM | HIGH |
|---|---|---|

Our risk assessment reflects Moody's significant market share in the high barrier-to-entry ratings industry, and what we consider the company's net positive balance sheet cash position, offset by ratings business sensitivity to higher interest rates, and the possibility of regulatory reform designed to increase competition.

## Quantitative Evaluations

**S&P Quality Ranking** B+

| D | C | B- | B | B+ | A- | A | A+ |
|---|---|---|---|---|---|---|---|

**Relative Strength Rank** MODERATE

59

LOWEST = 1    HIGHEST = 99

## Revenue/Earnings Data

**Revenue (Million $)**

| | 1Q | 2Q | 3Q | 4Q | Year |
|---|---|---|---|---|---|
| 2011 | 577.1 | 605.2 | 531.3 | -- | -- |
| 2010 | 476.6 | 477.8 | 513.3 | 564.3 | 2,032 |
| 2009 | 408.9 | 450.7 | 451.8 | 485.8 | 1,797 |
| 2008 | 430.7 | 487.6 | 433.4 | 403.7 | 1,755 |
| 2007 | 583.0 | 646.1 | 525.0 | 504.9 | 2,259 |
| 2006 | 440.2 | 511.4 | 495.5 | 590.0 | 2,037 |

**Earnings Per Share ($)**

| | | | | | |
|---|---|---|---|---|---|
| 2011 | 0.67 | 0.82 | 0.57 | E0.47 | E2.47 |
| 2010 | 0.47 | 0.51 | 0.58 | 0.58 | 2.15 |
| 2009 | 0.38 | 0.46 | 0.42 | 0.43 | 1.69 |
| 2008 | 0.48 | 0.55 | 0.46 | 0.37 | 1.87 |
| 2007 | 0.62 | 0.95 | 0.51 | 0.49 | 2.58 |
| 2006 | 0.49 | 0.59 | 0.55 | 0.97 | 2.58 |

Fiscal year ended Dec. 31. Next earnings report expected: Early February. EPS Estimates based on S&P Operating Earnings; historical GAAP earnings are as reported.

## Dividend Data (Dates: mm/dd Payment Date: mm/dd/yy)

| Amount ($) | Date Decl. | Ex-Div. Date | Stk. of Record | Payment Date |
|---|---|---|---|---|
| 0.115 | 12/14 | 02/16 | 02/20 | 03/10/11 |
| 0.140 | 04/27 | 05/18 | 05/20 | 06/10/11 |
| 0.140 | 07/27 | 08/17 | 08/20 | 09/10/11 |
| 0.140 | 10/27 | 11/16 | 11/20 | 12/10/11 |

Dividends have been paid since 1934. Source: Company reports.

---

**Please read the Required Disclosures and Analyst Certification on the last page of this report.**

The McGraw·Hill Companies

# Moody's Corp.

STANDARD
&POOR'S

## Business Summary October 31, 2011

CORPORATE PROFILE. Moody's Investors Service and the Dun & Bradstreet (D&B) operating company were separated into stand-alone entities on September 30, 2000. Old D&B changed its name to Moody's Corp. (MCO), and new D&B assumed the name Dun & Bradstreet Corp. (DNB).

Moody's is a provider of credit ratings, research and analysis covering debt instruments and securities in the global capital markets, and a provider of quantitative credit assessment services, credit training services and credit process software to banks and other financial institutions. Moody's credit ratings and research help investors analyze the credit risks associated with fixed-income securities. Beyond credit rating services for issuers, Moody's provides research services, data, and analytic tools that are utilized by institutional investors and other credit and capital markets professionals.

Moody's provides ratings and credit research on governmental and commercial entities in more than 110 countries, and its customers include a wide range of corporate and governmental issuers of securities as well as institutional investors, depositors, creditors, investment banks, commercial banks, and other financial intermediaries. In 2010, 46% of total revenues were derived from non-U.S. markets.

Moody's operates in two reportable segments: Moody's Investors Service (MIS), and Moody's Analytics. Moody's Investors Service consists of core credit ratings services, including four ratings groups: corporate finance (40% of 2010 segment revenues), structured finance (21%), financial institutions and sovereign risk (20%), and public finance (19%). MIS revenues are derived from the originators and issuers of such transaction, typically known as an Issuer-Fee Model. The ratings groups generate revenue mainly from the assignment of credit ratings on fixed-income instruments in the debt markets.

Moody's Analytics (MA), formerly Moody's KMV, provides a variety of credit risk processing and credit risk management products for banks and investors in credit-sensitive assets in about 120 countries. In addition, MA distributes investor-oriented research and data developed by MIS as part of its credit rating business. MA estimates that more than 30,000 clients access its data and research, primarily through the Moody's research web site.

## Company Financials Fiscal Year Ended Dec. 31

| Per Share Data ($) | 2010 | 2009 | 2008 | 2007 | 2006 | 2005 | 2004 | 2003 | 2002 | 2001 |
|---|---|---|---|---|---|---|---|---|---|---|
| Tangible Book Value | NM | NM | NM | NM | NM | 0.30 | 0.39 | NM | NM | NM |
| Cash Flow | 2.45 | 1.96 | 2.06 | 2.73 | 2.72 | 1.95 | 1.51 | 1.30 | 1.00 | 0.72 |
| Earnings | 2.15 | 1.69 | 1.87 | 2.58 | 2.58 | 1.84 | 1.40 | 1.20 | 0.92 | 0.66 |
| S&P Core Earnings | 2.17 | 1.69 | 1.85 | 2.61 | 2.26 | 1.83 | 1.35 | 1.12 | 0.85 | 0.64 |
| Dividends | 0.42 | 0.40 | 0.38 | 0.32 | 0.28 | 0.20 | 0.15 | 0.09 | 0.07 | 0.11 |
| Payout Ratio | 20% | 24% | 20% | 12% | 11% | 11% | 11% | 8% | 7% | 17% |
| Prices:High | 31.04 | 31.79 | 46.36 | 76.09 | 73.29 | 62.50 | 43.86 | 30.43 | 26.20 | 20.55 |
| Prices:Low | 18.50 | 15.57 | 15.41 | 35.05 | 49.76 | 39.55 | 29.85 | 19.75 | 17.90 | 12.78 |
| P/E Ratio:High | 14 | 19 | 25 | 29 | 28 | 34 | 31 | 25 | 29 | 31 |
| P/E Ratio:Low | 9 | 9 | 8 | 14 | 19 | 21 | 21 | 17 | 20 | 19 |

| Income Statement Analysis (Million $) | | | | | | | | | | |
|---|---|---|---|---|---|---|---|---|---|---|
| Revenue | 2,032 | 1,797 | 1,755 | 2,259 | 2,037 | 1,732 | 1,438 | 1,247 | 1,023 | 797 |
| Operating Income | 838 | 769 | 818 | 1,222 | 1,138 | 975 | 820 | 696 | 563 | 416 |
| Depreciation | 66.3 | 64.1 | 46.7 | 41.2 | 39.5 | 35.2 | 34.1 | 32.6 | 25.0 | 17.0 |
| Interest Expense | 50.4 | 44.0 | 73.7 | 62.2 | 15.2 | 21.0 | 16.2 | 21.8 | 21.0 | 16.5 |
| Pretax Income | 714 | 646 | 726 | 1,117 | 1,261 | 935 | 771 | 656 | 517 | 382 |
| Effective Tax Rate | NA | 37.0% | 37.0% | 37.2% | 40.2% | 40.0% | 44.9% | 44.6% | 44.1% | 44.4% |
| Net Income | 513 | 402 | 458 | 702 | 754 | 561 | 425 | 364 | 289 | 212 |
| S&P Core Earnings | 512 | 402 | 452 | 710 | 662 | 558 | 413 | 340 | 269 | 203 |

| Balance Sheet & Other Financial Data (Million $) | | | | | | | | | | |
|---|---|---|---|---|---|---|---|---|---|---|
| Cash | 672 | 484 | 253 | 441 | 408 | 486 | 606 | 269 | 40.0 | 163 |
| Current Assets | 1,343 | 1,013 | 809 | 989 | 1,002 | 1,052 | 1,023 | 569 | 272 | 371 |
| Total Assets | 2,540 | 2,004 | 1,772 | 1,715 | 1,498 | 1,457 | 1,376 | 941 | 631 | 505 |
| Current Liabilities | 934 | 1,236 | 1,393 | 1,349 | 700 | 579 | 837 | 432 | 462 | 359 |
| Long Term Debt | 1,228 | 746 | 750 | 600 | 300 | 300 | Nil | 300 | 300 | 300 |
| Common Equity | -298 | -596 | -996 | -784 | 167 | 309 | 318 | -32.1 | -327 | -304 |
| Total Capital | 941 | 154 | -244 | -184 | 467 | 609 | 318 | 268 | -27.0 | -4.10 |
| Capital Expenditures | 79.0 | 90.7 | 84.4 | 182 | 31.1 | 31.3 | 21.3 | 17.9 | 18.0 | 14.8 |
| Cash Flow | 580 | 466 | 504 | 743 | 793 | 596 | 459 | 397 | 314 | 229 |
| Current Ratio | 1.4 | 0.8 | 0.6 | 0.7 | 1.4 | 1.8 | 1.2 | 1.3 | 0.6 | 1.0 |
| % Long Term Debt of Capitalization | 130.5 | 484.9 | NM | -326.8 | 64.2 | 49.2 | Nil | 112.0 | NM | NM |
| % Net Income of Revenue | 25.3 | 22.4 | 26.1 | 31.1 | 37.0 | 32.4 | 29.6 | 29.2 | 28.2 | 26.6 |
| % Return on Assets | 22.6 | 21.3 | 26.3 | 43.7 | 51.0 | 39.4 | 36.5 | 46.3 | 50.9 | 47.0 |
| % Return on Equity | NM | NM | NM | NM | 316.2 | 178.9 | 297.9 | NM | NM | NM |

Data as orig reptd.; bef. results of disc opers/spec. items. Per share data adj. for stk. divs.; EPS diluted. E-Estimated. NA-Not Available. NM-Not Meaningful. NR-Not Ranked. UR-Under Review.

**Office:** 7 World Trade Center, at 250 Greenwich Street, New York, NY 10007.
**Telephone:** 212-553-0300.
**Website:** http://www.moodys.com
**Chrmn & CEO:** R.W. McDaniel, Jr.

**COO, SVP & Treas:** C.J. Charles
**EVP & CFO:** L.S. Huber
**SVP, Chief Acctg Officer & Cntlr:** J. McCabe
**SVP & General Counsel:** J.J. Goggins

**Investor Contact:** L. Westlake (212-553-7179)
**Auditor:** KPMG
**Board Members:** B. L. Anderson, J. A. Bermudez, J. D. Duffie, R. R. Glauber, K. E. Hill, E. Kist, R. W. McDaniel, Jr., C. McGillicuddy, III, H. A. McKinnell, Jr., J. K. Wulff

**Founded:** 1998
**Domicile:** Delaware
**Employees:** 4,500

# Morgan Stanley

**STANDARD &POOR'S**

| S&P Recommendation | HOLD ★★★★☆ | Price $13.26 (as of Nov 25, 2011) | 12-Mo. Target Price $22.00 | Investment Style Large-Cap Blend |
|---|---|---|---|---|

**GICS Sector** Financials
**Sub-Industry** Investment Banking & Brokerage

**Summary** Morgan Stanley is among the largest financial services firms in the U.S., with operations in investment banking, securities, and investment and wealth management.

## Key Stock Statistics (Source S&P, Vickers, company reports)

| | | | | | | |
|---|---|---|---|---|---|---|
| 52-Wk Range | $31.04– 11.58 | S&P Oper. EPS 2011E | 1.71 | Market Capitalization(B) | $25.557 | Beta | 1.53 |
| Trailing 12-Month EPS | $1.53 | S&P Oper. EPS 2012E | 2.16 | Yield (%) | 1.51 | S&P 3-Yr. Proj. EPS CAGR(%) | NM |
| Trailing 12-Month P/E | 8.7 | P/E on S&P Oper. EPS 2011E | 7.8 | Dividend Rate/Share | $0.20 | S&P Credit Rating | A |
| $10K Invested 5 Yrs Ago | NA | Common Shares Outstg. (M) | 1,927.4 | Institutional Ownership (%) | 75 | | |

## Price Performance

30-Week Mov. Avg. ···· 10-Week Mov. Avg. – – GAAP Earnings vs. Previous Year Volume Above Avg. STARS
12-Mo. Target Price — Relative Strength — ▲ Up ▼ Down ▶ No Change Below Avg.

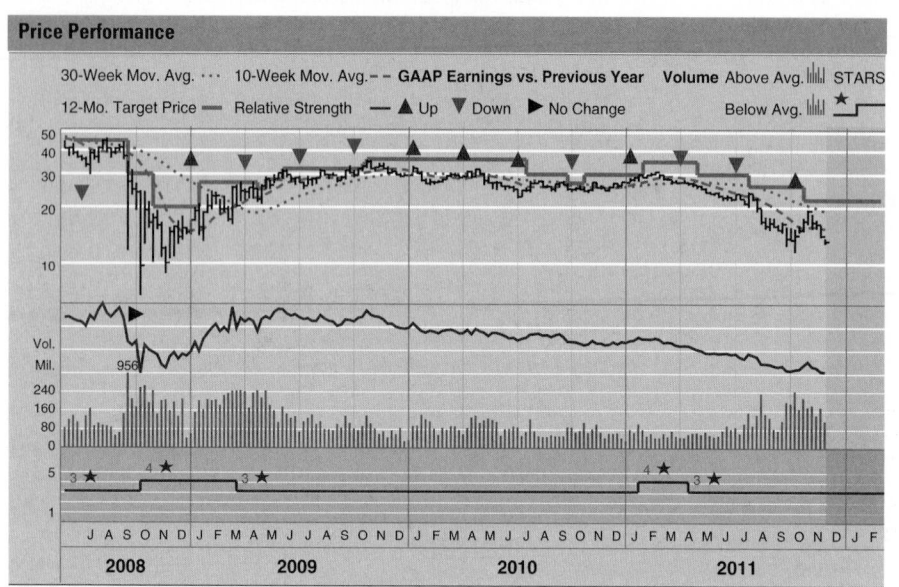

Options: ASE, CBOE, P, Ph

Analysis prepared by Equity Analyst **Robert McMillan** on Oct 20, 2011, when the stock traded at **$16.45**.

### Highlights

➤ Concerns about sovereign risk and the global economy restricted results at Morgan Stanley during the 2011 third quarter. Investment banking revenues fell 16%, year to year, while trading and investments posted a 44% drop after excluding the $3.4 billion debt valuation adjustment (DVA). Results in the consumer-oriented businesses were more resilient, with commissions and fees rising 38%, year to year, and asset management increasing 13%. After advancing 32% in 2010, we see net revenues up about 11% in 2011 (including the DVA). For 2012, we expect a nearly 10% gain in net revenues driven by increasing business and investor confidence.

➤ The third-quarter compensation ratio was about 37% of net revenues and was impacted by the DVA. For 2011, we expect compensation costs to be near 48% of net revenues, and see the pretax margin rising to about 23%. In 2012, we project a more normal compensation ratio of about 50% and look for the compensation ratio to be around 21%.

➤ We estimate EPS of $1.71 (which includes a $1.12 debt valuation adjustment) in 2011 and $2.16 in 2012.

### Investment Rationale/Risk

➤ We are encouraged that management is taking steps to further de-risk MS business, especially given ongoing changes in the regulatory environment. Value at Risk decreased about 10% sequentially to $130 million in the third quarter. We believe the integration of the Smith Barney joint venture and its sizable brokerage force will provide long-term revenue stability, especially once interest rates rise. However, in the medium term, we think that MS's costs will remain elevated relative to revenues, and make it difficult to maintain high operating margins.

➤ Risks to our recommendation and target price include stock market depreciation and additional industry regulation.

➤ Our 12-month target price of $22 is 11.2X our forward 12-month EPS estimate of $1.96; the shares recently traded at 7.6X our 2012 estimate. We expect economic uncertainty and volatility in the capital markets to ease over the next 12 months, which should allow MS's businesses and the stock's valuation multiple to expand.

### Qualitative Risk Assessment

| LOW | MEDIUM | HIGH |
|---|---|---|

Our risk assessment reflects our favorable view of the company's diversification by product and by region, offset by our concerns about corporate governance and our view that certain segments lack competitive advantages.

### Quantitative Evaluations

**S&P Quality Ranking** B-

| D | C | B- | B | B+ | A- | A | A+ |
|---|---|---|---|---|---|---|---|

**Relative Strength Rank** WEAK

15

LOWEST = 1 HIGHEST = 99

### Revenue/Earnings Data

**Revenue (Million $)**

| | 1Q | 2Q | 3Q | 4Q | Year |
|---|---|---|---|---|---|
| 2011 | 7,635 | 2,029 | 1,609 | -- | -- |
| 2010 | 10,439 | 9,566 | 8,534 | 9,499 | 38,036 |
| 2009 | -- | -- | -- | -- | 30,070 |
| 2008 | -- | -- | -- | -- | 62,264 |
| 2007 | 23,192 | 26,195 | 21,230 | 14,711 | 85,328 |
| 2006 | 18,119 | 19,062 | 20,055 | 19,473 | 76,551 |

**Earnings Per Share ($)**

| | | | | | |
|---|---|---|---|---|---|
| 2011 | 0.50 | -0.38 | 1.14 | E0.45 | E1.71 |
| 2010 | 1.03 | 0.60 | 0.05 | 0.43 | 2.46 |
| 2009 | -0.57 | -1.37 | 0.38 | 0.13 | -0.94 |
| 2008 | 1.45 | 0.95 | 1.32 | -2.24 | 1.54 |
| 2007 | 2.17 | 2.24 | 1.32 | -3.61 | 2.37 |
| 2006 | 1.50 | 1.85 | 1.75 | 2.08 | 7.09 |

Fiscal year ended Dec. 31. Next earnings report expected: NA. EPS Estimates based on S&P Operating Earnings; historical GAAP earnings are as reported.

### Dividend Data (Dates: mm/dd Payment Date: mm/dd/yy)

| Amount ($) | Date Decl. | Ex-Div. Date | Stk. of Record | Payment Date |
|---|---|---|---|---|
| 0.050 | 01/20 | 01/27 | 01/31 | 02/15/11 |
| 0.050 | 04/21 | 04/27 | 04/29 | 05/13/11 |
| 0.050 | 07/19 | 07/27 | 07/29 | 08/15/11 |
| 0.050 | 10/19 | 10/27 | 10/31 | 11/15/11 |

Dividends have been paid since 1993. Source: Company reports.

---

**Please read the Required Disclosures and Analyst Certification on the last page of this report.**

The McGraw-Hill Companies

# Morgan Stanley

STANDARD &POOR'S

## Business Summary October 20, 2011

CORPORATE OVERVIEW. Morgan Stanley is a global financial services firm that provides a comprehensive suite of products to a diverse group of clients and customers, including corporations, governments, financial institutions and individuals. MS currently has three operating segments: Institutional Securities, Global Wealth Management Group and Asset Management.

The Institutional Securities segment includes capital raising; financial advisory services; corporate lending; sales, trading, financing and market-making activities for equity and fixed-income securities and related products such as foreign exchange and commodities; benchmark indices and risk management analytics; research; and investment activities. The investment banking business is included in this segment, and includes capital raising activities, financial advisory services and corporate lending. This business is one of the largest in the world, ranking second globally during its fiscal year in announced mergers and acquisitions, third in initial public offerings, and 10th in global debt issuance. This segment accounted for approximately 52% of net revenues in 2010.

The Global Wealth Management Group provides brokerage and investment advisory services; financial and wealth planning services; annuity and insur-

ance products; credit and other lending products; banking and cash management services; retirement services; and trust and fiduciary services through the 51%-owned Morgan Stanley Smith Barney joint venture with Citigroup (C 40, Buy). It provides these services to clients through a network of more than 18,000 global representatives. The segment accounted for about 40% of net revenues in 2010.

The Asset Management segment provides global asset management products and services in equity, fixed income, alternative investments and private equity to institutional clients. It had $253 billion of assets under management or supervision at the end of 2009. These totals exclude its retail asset management unit, which the company has sold to Invesco (IVZ 17 Buy). In the deal, completed in June 2010, MS gained about a 6.5% stake in Invesco. MS hopes to renew its focus on institutional asset management customers. The segment accounted for 8% of net revenues in 2010.

## Company Financials Fiscal Year Ended Dec. 31

| Per Share Data ($) | 2010 | 2009 | 2008 | 2007 | 2006 | 2005 | 2004 | 2003 | 2002 | 2001 |
|---|---|---|---|---|---|---|---|---|---|---|
| Tangible Book Value | 24.05 | 18.38 | 27.24 | 25.75 | 34.89 | 25.23 | 23.93 | 21.52 | 19.43 | 17.36 |
| Earnings | 2.46 | -0.94 | 1.54 | 2.37 | 7.09 | 4.81 | 4.08 | 3.45 | 2.69 | 3.19 |
| S&P Core Earnings | 2.05 | -1.15 | 1.07 | 2.17 | 7.12 | 5.00 | 4.18 | 3.48 | 2.38 | 2.84 |
| Dividends | 0.20 | 0.40 | 1.08 | 1.08 | 1.08 | 1.08 | 1.00 | 0.92 | 0.92 | 0.92 |
| Payout Ratio | 8% | NM | 70% | 46% | 15% | 22% | 25% | 27% | 34% | 29% |
| Prices:High | 33.27 | 35.78 | 53.40 | 90.95 | 83.40 | 60.51 | 62.83 | 58.78 | 60.02 | 90.49 |
| Prices:Low | 22.40 | 13.10 | 6.71 | 47.25 | 54.52 | 47.66 | 46.54 | 32.46 | 28.80 | 35.75 |
| P/E Ratio:High | 14 | NM | 8 | 38 | 12 | 13 | 15 | 17 | 22 | 28 |
| P/E Ratio:Low | 9 | NM | 1 | 20 | 8 | 10 | 11 | 9 | 11 | 11 |

| Income Statement Analysis (Million $) | 2010 | 2009 | 2008 | 2007 | 2006 | 2005 | 2004 | 2003 | 2002 | 2001 |
|---|---|---|---|---|---|---|---|---|---|---|
| Net Interest Income | 864 | 990 | 3,202 | 2,781 | 3,279 | 3,750 | 3,731 | 2,935 | 3,896 | 3,348 |
| Non Interest Income | 30,758 | 22,368 | 21,537 | 25,245 | 45,558 | 23,906 | 20,959 | 19,189 | 16,549 | 19,600 |
| Loan Loss Provision | Nil | Nil | Nil | 831 | 756 | 878 | 925 | 1,267 | 1,336 | 1,052 |
| Non Interest Expenses | 25,420 | 22,501 | 22,452 | 24,858 | 23,614 | 20,857 | 18,333 | 16,636 | 15,725 | 17,264 |
| % Expense/Operating Revenue | 83.7% | 61.8% | 49.9% | 96.0% | 84.6% | 84.2% | 80.8% | 79.9% | 81.3% | 84.6% |
| Pretax Income | 6,202 | 857 | 2,287 | 3,394 | 10,772 | 7,050 | 6,312 | 5,334 | 4,633 | 5,684 |
| Effective Tax Rate | 11.9% | NM | 21.0% | 24.5% | 30.4% | 26.4% | 28.6% | 29.0% | 35.5% | 36.5% |
| Net Income | 4,464 | 1,133 | 1,807 | 2,563 | 7,497 | 5,192 | 4,509 | 3,787 | 2,988 | 3,610 |
| % Net Interest Margin | NA | NA | NA | NA | NA | NA | NA | 5.40 | 5.50 | 5.57 |
| S&P Core Earnings | 2,809 | -1,371 | 1,163 | 2,284 | 7,511 | 5,401 | 4,624 | 3,830 | 2,658 | 3,203 |

| Balance Sheet & Other Financial Data (Million $) | 2010 | 2009 | 2008 | 2007 | 2006 | 2005 | 2004 | 2003 | 2002 | 2001 |
|---|---|---|---|---|---|---|---|---|---|---|
| Money Market Assets | 188,527 | 168,211 | 140,155 | 126,887 | 174,866 | 174,330 | 123,041 | 78,205 | 76,910 | 54,618 |
| Investment Securities | 323,283 | 313,434 | 233,542 | 457,192 | 680,484 | 304,172 | 260,640 | 228,904 | 185,588 | 164,011 |
| Earning Assets:Total Loans | 10,576 | 7,259 | 6,528 | 11,629 | 24,173 | 23,754 | 21,169 | 20,384 | 24,322 | 20,955 |
| Total Assets | 807,698 | 771,462 | 658,812 | 1,045,409 | 1,120,645 | 898,523 | 775,410 | 602,843 | 529,499 | 482,628 |
| Demand Deposits | 59,856 | 57,114 | 36,673 | 27,186 | 14,872 | 2,629 | 1,117 | 1,264 | 1,441 | 1,741 |
| Time Deposits | 3,956 | 5,101 | 6,082 | 3,993 | 13,471 | 16,034 | 12,660 | 11,575 | 12,316 | 10,535 |
| Long Term Debt | 172,236 | 167,286 | 141,466 | 190,624 | 144,978 | 110,465 | 95,286 | 68,410 | 43,985 | 40,851 |
| Common Equity | 47,614 | 37,091 | 31,676 | 30,169 | 34,264 | 29,248 | 28,272 | 24,933 | 21,951 | 20,437 |
| % Return on Assets | 0.6 | 0.2 | 0.2 | 0.2 | 0.7 | 0.6 | 0.7 | 0.7 | 0.6 | 0.8 |
| % Return on Equity | 10.5 | 3.4 | 5.8 | 7.7 | 23.5 | 18.9 | 16.9 | 16.2 | 14.1 | 18.2 |
| % Loan Loss Reserve | 0.8 | Nil | Nil | Nil | 3.3 | 3.5 | 4.5 | 4.9 | 3.8 | 4.0 |
| % Loans/Deposits | 14.2 | 12.2 | 24.5 | 78.0 | 85.2 | 127.3 | 153.7 | 158.8 | 176.8 | 170.7 |
| % Loans/Assets | 1.1 | 1.0 | 1.1 | 2.1 | 2.3 | 2.7 | 3.0 | 3.9 | 4.5 | 4.7 |
| % Equity to Assets | 5.4 | 4.7 | 3.6 | 3.0 | 3.1 | 3.3 | 3.9 | 4.1 | 4.2 | 4.3 |

Data as orig reptd.; bef. results of disc opers/spec. items. Per share data adj. for stk. divs.; EPS diluted. Prior to 2009, fiscal year ended November 30. E-Estimated. NA-Not Available. NM-Not Meaningful. NR-Not Ranked. UR-Under Review.

**Office:** 1585 Broadway, New York, NY 10036.
**Telephone:** 212-761-4000.
**Website:** http://www.morganstanley.com
**Chrmn:** J.J. Mack

**Pres & CEO:** J.P. Gorman
**COO:** J.A. Rosenthal
**EVP & CFO:** R. Porat
**Chief Admin Officer:** S. Barney

**Investor Contact:** W. Pike (212-761-0008)
**Board Members:** R. J. Bostock, E. B. Bowles, H. J. Davies, J. P. Gorman, J. H. Hance, Jr., C. R. Kidder, J. J. Mack, D. T. Nicolaisen, H. S. Olayan, J. W. Owens, O. G. Sexton, R. Tamakoshi, M. Tanaka, L. D. Tyson

**Founded:** 1981
**Domicile:** Delaware
**Employees:** 62,542

# Mosaic Company (The)

**STANDARD &POOR'S**

| | | | |
|---|---|---|---|
| **S&P Recommendation** BUY ★★★★☆ | **Price**<br>$49.30 (as of Nov 25, 2011) | **12-Mo. Target Price**<br>$80.00 | **Investment Style**<br>Large-Cap Growth |

**GICS Sector** Materials
**Sub-Industry** Fertilizers & Agricultural Chemicals

**Summary** This company is one of the world's largest producers and marketers of concentrated phosphate and potash crop nutrients for the global agriculture industry.

## Key Stock Statistics (Source S&P, Vickers, company reports)

| | | | | | | | | |
|---|---|---|---|---|---|---|---|---|
| 52-Wk Range | $89.24– 44.86 | S&P Oper. EPS 2012**E** | 5.52 | Market Capitalization(B) | $22.020 | Beta | | 1.32 |
| Trailing 12-Month EPS | $6.12 | S&P Oper. EPS 2013**E** | 5.94 | Yield (%) | 0.41 | S&P 3-Yr. Proj. EPS CAGR(%) | | 16 |
| Trailing 12-Month P/E | 8.1 | P/E on S&P Oper. EPS 2012**E** | 8.9 | Dividend Rate/Share | $0.20 | S&P Credit Rating | | BBB |
| $10K Invested 5 Yrs Ago | $23,870 | Common Shares Outstg. (M) | 446.6 | Institutional Ownership (%) | 50 | | | |

## Price Performance

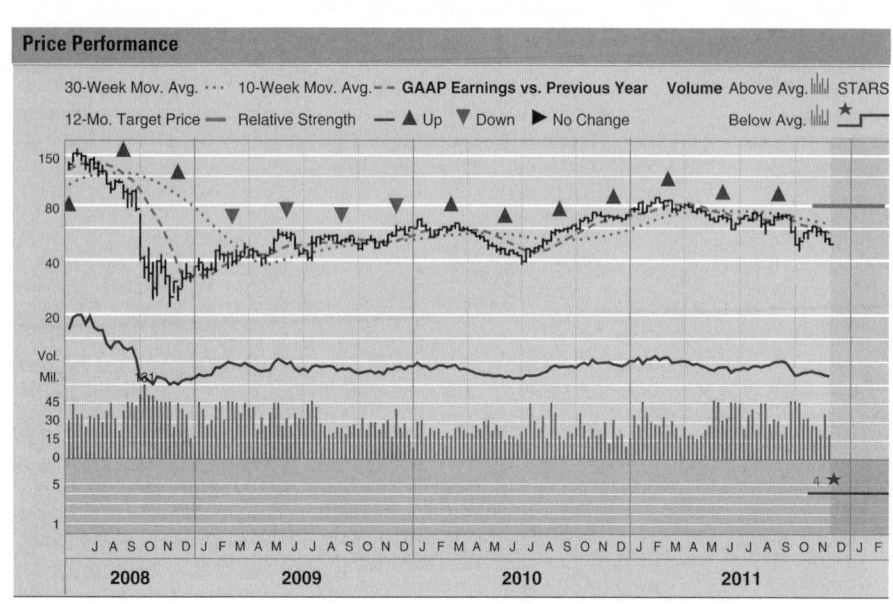

30-Week Mov. Avg. ··· 10-Week Mov. Avg. – – **GAAP Earnings vs. Previous Year** Volume Above Avg. STARS
12-Mo. Target Price — Relative Strength — ▲ Up ▼ Down ▶ No Change Below Avg.

2008  2009  2010  2011

Analysis prepared by Equity Analyst **Leo J. Larkin** on Oct 25, 2011, when the stock traded at **$58.67**.

## Highlights

➤ Following a sales rebound of 47% in FY 11 (May), we anticipate a 25% advance in FY 12, based on our expectation for a further increase in volume and average realized prices for both phosphates and potash. Our forecast rests on several assumptions. First, we expect that net farm income in the U.S. will stay at record levels. Second, we look for continued tight supply of grains as global inventories remain at low levels. Finally, we expect that planted acreage will rise.

➤ We look for a sizable increase in operating profit in FY 12 on a greater volume of shipments and higher revenue per ton. After interest expense and taxes, we project EPS of $5.52 in FY 12, versus operating EPS of $4.37 in FY 11, which excludes an unusual gain of $1.25.

➤ We think the company's long-term sales and earnings will rise on a secular increase in the demand for fertilizers, driven by a combination of population growth and rising living standards worldwide.

## Investment Rationale/Risk

➤ Following a cyclical trough in sales and earnings in FY 10, we look for the rebound to continue in FY 12 and FY 13 as prices for phosphates and potash continue to increase in response to greater global demand for fertilizers. We see volumes and prices for both products extending the gains of FY 11, albeit at a less rapid rate. Longer term, we think earnings will benefit from a secular increase in demand for fertilizers, driven by a combination of population growth and rising living standards worldwide. At the same, the company's strong free cash flow generation will enable it to expand capacity in both products with a minimum of external financing, in our view. We think the shares are attractively valued, recently trading at about 10.7X our EPS estimate for FY 12.

➤ Risks to our recommendation and target price include a decline in global demand for fertilizers in FY 12, instead of the increase we project.

➤ Our 12-month target price of $80 is based on our view that the stock will trade at 14.5X our EPS estimate for FY 12, toward the low end of its historical average P/E multiple range, reflecting concerns over global growth.

## Qualitative Risk Assessment

| LOW | MEDIUM | HIGH |
|---|---|---|

Our risk assessment reflects the company's broad product mix, its large market share in its main product lines, and its comparatively low debt levels. This is only partially offset by the cyclical and seasonal nature of the fertilizer industry and the volatility of MOS's raw material costs.

## Quantitative Evaluations

**S&P Quality Ranking**                                  NR

| D | C | B- | B | B+ | A- | A | A+ |
|---|---|---|---|---|---|---|---|

**Relative Strength Rank**                              WEAK

19

LOWEST = 1                                    HIGHEST = 99

## Revenue/Earnings Data

**Revenue (Million $)**

| | 1Q | 2Q | 3Q | 4Q | Year |
|---|---|---|---|---|---|
| 2012 | 3,083 | -- | -- | -- | -- |
| 2011 | 2,188 | 2,675 | 2,214 | 2,860 | 9,938 |
| 2010 | 1,457 | 1,710 | 1,732 | 1,860 | 6,759 |
| 2009 | 4,323 | 3,007 | 1,376 | 1,594 | 10,298 |
| 2008 | 2,003 | 2,195 | 2,147 | 3,467 | 9,813 |
| 2007 | 1,289 | 1,522 | 1,279 | 1,684 | 5,774 |

**Earnings Per Share ($)**

| | | | | | |
|---|---|---|---|---|---|
| 2012 | 1.17 | E1.37 | E1.36 | E1.62 | E5.52 |
| 2011 | 0.67 | 2.29 | 1.21 | 1.45 | 5.62 |
| 2010 | 0.23 | 0.24 | 0.50 | 0.89 | 1.85 |
| 2009 | 2.65 | 2.15 | 0.13 | 0.33 | 5.27 |
| 2008 | 0.69 | 0.89 | 1.17 | 1.93 | 4.67 |
| 2007 | 0.25 | 0.15 | 0.10 | 0.46 | 0.95 |

Fiscal year ended May 31. Next earnings report expected: Early January. EPS Estimates based on S&P Operating Earnings; historical GAAP earnings are as reported.

## Dividend Data (Dates: mm/dd Payment Date: mm/dd/yy)

| Amount ($) | Date Decl. | Ex-Div. Date | Stk. of Record | Payment Date |
|---|---|---|---|---|
| 0.050 | 12/09 | 02/01 | 02/03 | 02/17/11 |
| 0.050 | 04/14 | 04/20 | 04/25 | 05/02/11 |
| 0.050 | 07/22 | 11/01 | 11/03 | 11/17/11 |

Dividends have been paid since 2008. Source: Company reports.

---

**Please read the Required Disclosures and Analyst Certification on the last page of this report.**

The **McGraw·Hill** Companies

# Mosaic Company (The)

**STANDARD &POOR'S**

## Business Summary October 25, 2011

CORPORATE OVERVIEW. The Mosaic Co. is one of the world's largest producers and marketers of concentrated phosphate and potash crop nutrients for the global agriculture industry. The company was formed through the October 2004 combination of IMC Global Inc. and the fertilizer businesses of Cargill, Incorporated. Sales outside Canada and the U.S. were 58% of the total in FY 11 (May).

The phosphates segment (69% of sales, 49% of operating profits in FY 11) owns and operates mines and production facilities in Florida that produce concentrated phosphate crop nutrients and phosphate-based animal feed ingredients, and processing plants in Louisiana that produce concentrated phosphate crop nutrients. The segment's results include the North American distribution activities and the consolidated results of Phosphate Chemicals Export Association, Inc., a U.S. Webb-Pomerene Act association of phosphate producers that exports concentrated phosphate crop nutrient products around the world for the company and PhosChem's other member. Mosaic is the largest producer of concentrated phosphate crop nutrients and animal feed ingredients in the world. The U.S. phosphates operations have capacity

to produce some 4.4 million tons of phosphoric acid per year, or about 9% of world capacity and about 45% of North American capacity. Mosaic's U.S. phosphoric acid production totaled about 3.9 million tons during FY 11 and accounted for some 10% of estimated global production and 46% of estimated North American output during FY 11.

The potash segment (31% of sales, 51% of operating profit) mines and processes potash in Canada and the United States and sells potash in North America and internationally. Potash products are marketed worldwide to crop nutrient manufacturers, distributors and retailers and are also used in the manufacture of mixed crop nutrients and, to a lesser extent, in animal feed ingredients. Potash is also sold for industrial use and is used for de-icing and as a water softener regenerant. Mosaic operates three potash mines in Canada and two potash mines in the U.S.

## Company Financials Fiscal Year Ended May 31

| Per Share Data ($) | 2011 | 2010 | 2009 | 2008 | 2007 | 2006 | 2005 | 2004 | 2003 | 2002 |
|---|---|---|---|---|---|---|---|---|---|---|
| Tangible Book Value | 21.97 | 15.62 | 15.21 | 10.94 | 4.31 | 2.68 | 2.74 | NM | NA | NA |
| Cash Flow | 6.69 | 2.83 | 6.15 | 5.48 | 1.86 | 0.50 | 1.06 | 0.72 | NA | NA |
| Earnings | 5.62 | 1.85 | 5.27 | 4.67 | 0.95 | -0.35 | 0.47 | 0.15 | NA | NA |
| S&P Core Earnings | 4.30 | 1.82 | 4.18 | 4.60 | 0.91 | -0.33 | 0.47 | NA | NA | NA |
| Dividends | 0.20 | 0.20 | Nil | Nil | Nil | Nil | Nil | Nil | NA | NA |
| Payout Ratio | 4% | 4% | Nil | Nil | Nil | Nil | Nil | Nil | NA | NA |
| Calendar Year | 2010 | 2009 | 2008 | 2007 | 2006 | 2005 | 2004 | 2003 | 2002 | 2001 |
| Prices:High | 76.80 | 62.46 | 163.25 | 97.60 | 23.54 | 17.99 | 18.58 | NA | NA | NA |
| Prices:Low | 37.68 | 31.17 | 21.94 | 19.49 | 13.31 | 12.36 | 14.80 | NA | NA | NA |
| P/E Ratio:High | 14 | 34 | 31 | 21 | 25 | NM | 40 | NA | NA | NA |
| P/E Ratio:Low | 7 | 17 | 4 | 4 | 14 | NM | 31 | NA | NA | NA |

| Income Statement Analysis (Million $) | | | | | | | | | | |
|---|---|---|---|---|---|---|---|---|---|---|
| Revenue | 9,938 | 6,759 | 10,298 | 9,813 | 5,774 | 5,306 | 4,397 | 4,521 | 1,663 | 1,509 |
| Operating Income | 3,142 | 1,706 | 3,180 | 3,183 | 1,013 | 718 | 538 | 187 | 137 | 157 |
| Depreciation | 479 | 435 | 395 | 358 | 398 | 324 | 219 | 105 | 87.9 | 77.9 |
| Interest Expense | 27.6 | 49.6 | 105 | 124 | 172 | 167 | 121 | 29.2 | 41.2 | 42.9 |
| Pretax Income | 3,266 | 1,179 | 3,006 | 2,806 | 547 | -112 | 271 | 80.5 | 32.7 | 31.6 |
| Effective Tax Rate | 23.0% | 29.2% | 21.6% | 25.5% | 22.6% | NM | 36.3% | 4.74% | NM | NM |
| Net Income | 2,514 | 827 | 2,350 | 2,083 | 420 | -121 | 168 | 75.2 | 39.1 | 33.2 |
| S&P Core Earnings | 1,920 | 814 | 1,862 | 2,053 | 404 | -127 | 162 | NA | NA | NA |

| Balance Sheet & Other Financial Data (Million $) | | | | | | | | | | |
|---|---|---|---|---|---|---|---|---|---|---|
| Cash | 3,906 | 2,523 | 2,703 | 1,961 | 421 | 173 | 245 | 10.1 | 8.93 | 8.97 |
| Current Assets | 6,685 | 4,975 | 5,308 | 4,810 | 1,956 | 1,580 | 1,732 | 654 | 534 | 482 |
| Total Assets | 15,787 | 12,708 | 12,676 | 11,820 | 9,164 | 8,721 | 8,444 | 1,856 | 1,599 | 1,404 |
| Current Liabilities | 1,929 | 1,304 | 1,622 | 2,186 | 1,630 | 1,126 | 1,107 | 453 | 400 | 327 |
| Long Term Debt | 761 | 1,246 | 1,257 | 1,375 | 1,818 | 2,388 | 2,455 | 32.6 | 364 | 407 |
| Common Equity | 11,642 | 8,722 | 8,493 | 6,731 | 4,184 | 3,531 | 3,214 | 833 | 649 | 524 |
| Total Capital | 12,492 | 10,009 | 9,815 | 8,173 | 6,428 | 6,614 | 6,415 | 958 | 1,244 | 1,049 |
| Capital Expenditures | 1,263 | 911 | 781 | 372 | 292 | 390 | 255 | 162 | 119 | 89.4 |
| Cash Flow | 2,993 | 1,262 | 2,745 | 2,441 | 818 | 192 | 381 | 180 | 127 | 111 |
| Current Ratio | 3.5 | 3.8 | 3.3 | 2.2 | 1.2 | 1.4 | 1.6 | 1.4 | 1.3 | 1.5 |
| % Long Term Debt of Capitalization | 6.1 | 12.4 | 12.8 | 15.9 | 28.3 | 36.1 | 38.3 | 3.4 | 29.3 | 38.8 |
| % Net Income of Revenue | 25.3 | 12.2 | 22.8 | 21.2 | 7.3 | NM | 3.8 | 3.2 | 2.4 | 2.2 |
| % Return on Assets | 17.6 | 6.5 | 19.2 | 19.9 | 4.7 | NM | 3.2 | 4.4 | 2.6 | NA |
| % Return on Equity | 24.7 | 9.6 | 30.9 | 38.2 | 10.9 | NM | 8.0 | 10.1 | 6.7 | NA |

Data as orig reptd.; bef. results of disc opers/spec. items. Per share data adj. for stk. divs.; EPS diluted. E-Estimated. NA-Not Available. NM-Not Meaningful. NR-Not Ranked. UR-Under Review.

**Office:** 3033 Campus Drive, Plymouth, MN 55441.
**Telephone:** 763-577-2700.
**Website:** http://www.mosaicco.com
**Chrmn:** R.L. Lumpkins

**Pres & CEO:** J.T. Prokopanko
**COO:** J.C. O'Rourke
**EVP & CFO:** L.W. Stranghoener
**EVP, Secy & General Counsel:** R.L. Mack

**Investor Contact:** C. Battist (763-577-2828)
**Board Members:** P. E. Cochran, W. R. Graber, E. N. Koenig, R. L. Lumpkins, H. H. MacKay, D. B. Mathis, W. T. Monahan, J. L. Popowich, J. T. Prokopanko, S. A. Rial, D. T. Seaton, S. M. Seibert

**Founded:** 2004
**Domicile:** Delaware
**Employees:** 7,700

*The McGraw·Hill Companies*

# Motorola Mobility Holdings Inc

**STANDARD &POOR'S**

| S&P Recommendation **HOLD** ★★★☆☆ | Price $38.60 (as of Nov 25, 2011) | 12-Mo. Target Price $40.00 | Investment Style Large-Cap Value |
|---|---|---|---|

**GICS Sector** Information Technology
**Sub-Industry** Communications Equipment

**Summary** This manufacturer provides products and services that enable a broad range of wireless, wireline, digital communication, information and entertainment experiences. It has agreed to be purchased by Google for $40 per share in cash.

## Key Stock Statistics (Source S&P, Vickers, company reports)

| | | | | | | | |
|---|---|---|---|---|---|---|---|
| 52-Wk Range | $39.20– 20.77 | S&P Oper. EPS 2011**E** | 0.50 | Market Capitalization(B) | $11.560 | Beta | NA |
| Trailing 12-Month EPS | $-0.30 | S&P Oper. EPS 2012**E** | 1.12 | Yield (%) | Nil | S&P 3-Yr. Proj. EPS CAGR(%) | 15 |
| Trailing 12-Month P/E | NM | P/E on S&P Oper. EPS 2011**E** | 77.2 | Dividend Rate/Share | Nil | S&P Credit Rating | NA |
| $10K Invested 5 Yrs Ago | NA | Common Shares Outstg. (M) | 299.5 | Institutional Ownership (%) | 74 | | |

## Price Performance

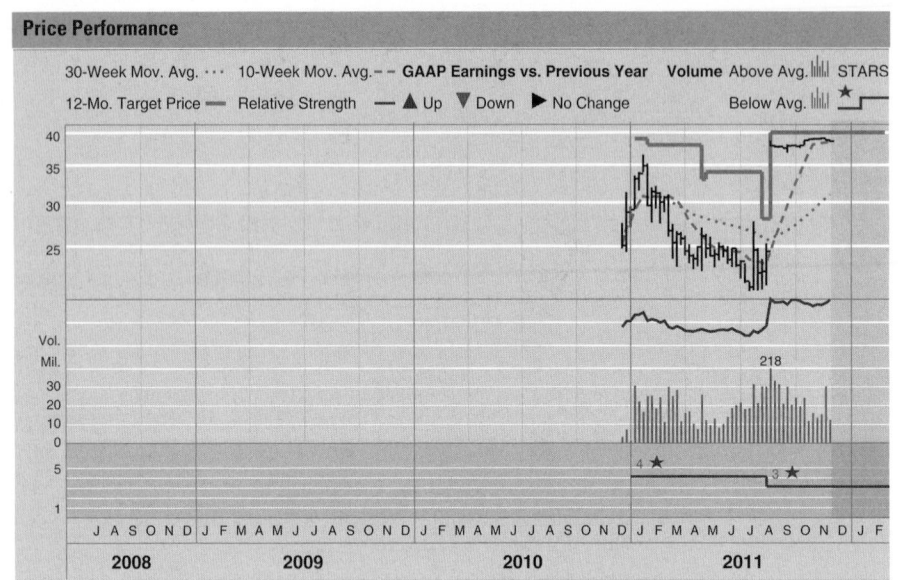

- 30-Week Mov. Avg. ···  10-Week Mov. Avg. ---  GAAP Earnings vs. Previous Year  Volume Above Avg. STARS
- 12-Mo. Target Price —  Relative Strength  —▲ Up ▼ Down ► No Change  Below Avg.

Analysis prepared by Equity Analyst **J. Moorman, CFA** on Aug 24, 2011, when the stock traded at **$37.98**.

## Highlights

➤ Following a revenue increase of 3.7% in 2010, we expect further advances of 25% in 2011 and 12% in 2012. We think the Mobile Devices business will continue to see strong growth on its further penetration into the smartphone market, and we expect the company to see growth in the tablet market as well. In the Home segment, we anticipate low single-digit revenue growth in 2011 and 2012.

➤ We believe gross margins will be roughly flat at 26.1% in 2011, versus 26.2% in 2010, before widening to 26.9% in 2012. Margins should reflect improvements in MMI's handset manufacturing process and a focus on higher-margin smartphones, slightly offset by lower margins on tablets. We believe the Home segment's profitability will improve in 2011 and 2012.

➤ After a loss per share of $0.28 in 2010, we expect EPS of $0.50 in 2011 and $1.12 in 2012. We believe the improvement will come from enhanced profitability in both segments. The company has a cash balance of over $3.0 billion and no debt other than capital lease obligations.

## Investment Rationale/Risk

➤ The company has agreed to be purchased by Google (GOOG 518, Hold) for $40 per share in cash. Separately, we are encouraged by MMI's penetration into the smartphone market, with its launch of 23 new smartphones in 2010 incorporating the Android operating system. We expect continued strong growth for Mobile Devices as MMI focuses on high-end smartphones, mass-market smartphones and media tablets. However, we believe price reductions on tablets are weighing on margins. For the Home segment, we anticipate solid video growth that could be hampered slightly by the economy and a slow housing market.

➤ Risks to our recommendation and target price include failure of the planned acquisition by Google to be completed, execution risks involving the handset unit, failure to successfully introduce and ship new handset products, increasing competition in the handset and smartphone markets, and continued malaise in the housing market that slows demand in the Home segment.

➤ Our 12-month target price of $40 is based on the agreed-upon cash purchase price from Google.

## Qualitative Risk Assessment

| LOW | **MEDIUM** | HIGH |
|---|---|---|

Our risk assessment reflects the company's exposure to the economic health of the telecom and broadband industries and risks related to high-volume manufacturing and distribution to service providers. This is offset by our view of MMI's strong cash balance.

## Quantitative Evaluations

**S&P Quality Ranking**  NR

| D | C | B- | B | B+ | A- | A | A+ |
|---|---|---|---|---|---|---|---|

**Relative Strength Rank**  STRONG

92

LOWEST = 1     HIGHEST = 99

## Revenue/Earnings Data

**Revenue (Million $)**

| | 1Q | 2Q | 3Q | 4Q | Year |
|---|---|---|---|---|---|
| 2011 | 3,032 | 3,337 | 3,259 | -- | -- |
| 2010 | -- | -- | -- | 3,425 | 11,460 |
| 2009 | -- | -- | -- | -- | 11,050 |
| 2008 | -- | -- | -- | -- | 17,099 |
| 2007 | -- | -- | -- | -- | 23,373 |
| 2006 | -- | -- | -- | -- | -- |

**Earnings Per Share ($)**

| | 1Q | 2Q | 3Q | 4Q | Year |
|---|---|---|---|---|---|
| 2011 | -0.27 | -0.19 | -0.11 | E0.38 | E0.50 |
| 2010 | -- | -- | -- | 0.27 | -0.29 |
| 2009 | -- | -- | -- | -- | -4.35 |
| 2008 | -- | -- | -- | -- | NA |
| 2007 | -- | -- | -- | -- | NA |
| 2006 | -- | -- | -- | -- | -- |

Fiscal year ended Dec. 31. Next earnings report expected: Late January. EPS Estimates based on S&P Operating Earnings; historical GAAP earnings are as reported.

## Dividend Data

No cash dividends have been paid.

---

**Please read the Required Disclosures and Analyst Certification on the last page of this report.**

*The McGraw-Hill Companies*

# Motorola Mobility Holdings Inc

**STANDARD &POOR'S**

## Business Summary August 24, 2011

CORPORATE OVERVIEW. In February 2010, Motorola Inc. announced a plan to split itself into two publicly traded entities -- the Enterprise and Government businesses, following the sale of Networks, which became Motorola Solutions, and the Mobile Devices and Home businesses, which became Motorola Mobility Holdings.

Motorola Mobility Holdings, spun off from Motorola Inc. at the beginning of 2011, offers mobile devices, wireless accessories, set-top boxes and wireline broadband infrastructure products for cable and telecom service providers. The Mobile Devices segment (72.8% of revenues in the second quarter of 2011, up from 66.0% a year earlier) manufactures wireless handsets for GSM and CDMA standards. Following the sale of 100 million units in 2008, 56 million in 2009 and 37 million in 2010, we expect MMI to ship 46 million units in 2011 and 56 million in 2012. We think smartphones' proportion of the product mix will expand from 2010's 36%.

The remainder of MMI's revenues come from the Home segment (27.2% of revenues in the second quarter of 2011, down from 34.0% a year earlier). This segment provides products to cable and wireline operators that facilitate video, voice and data services to consumers. It had an operating margin of

7.5% in 2010, which we expect to increase in 2011 and 2012.

CORPORATE STRATEGY. We believe the company has been increasing its focus on higher-end smartphones. While this has caused a reduction in units sold, it has resulted in a significant increase in average selling price. We believe that going forward, MMI will focus on higher-end smartphones with price points of $300 to $500, mass-market smartphones with price points under $300, and media tablets that we believe sell for in excess of $400 per unit.

COMPETITIVE LANDSCAPE. Within the handset market, we see ongoing pressure from diversified manufacturers such as Nokia, LG, HTC and Samsung, and smartphone specialists such as Apple and Research in Motion, which control a significant share of the smartphone market as consumers look to use their phones for data services. In the Home segment, MMI competes in producing set-top boxes and cable and wireline infrastructure products primarily with Cisco, Pace and Arris.

## Company Financials Fiscal Year Ended Dec. 31

| Per Share Data ($) | 2010 | 2009 | 2008 | 2007 | 2006 | 2005 | 2004 | 2003 | 2002 | 2001 |
|---|---|---|---|---|---|---|---|---|---|---|
| Tangible Book Value | NM | 12.30 | NA | NA | NA | NA | NA | NA | NA | NA |
| Cash Flow | 0.49 | NA | NA | NA | NA | NA | NA | NA | NA | NA |
| Earnings | -0.29 | -4.35 | NA | NA | NA | NA | NA | NA | NA | NA |
| S&P Core Earnings | -0.94 | -4.30 | -10.00 | NA | NA | NA | NA | NA | NA | NA |
| Dividends | Nil | NA | NA | NA | NA | NA | NA | NA | NA | NA |
| Payout Ratio | Nil | NA | NA | NA | NA | NA | NA | NA | NA | NA |
| Prices:High | 31.30 | NA | NA | NA | NA | NA | NA | NA | NA | NA |
| Prices:Low | 24.40 | NA | NA | NA | NA | NA | NA | NA | NA | NA |
| P/E Ratio:High | NM | NA | NA | NA | NA | NA | NA | NA | NA | NA |
| P/E Ratio:Low | NM | NA | NA | NA | NA | NA | NA | NA | NA | NA |

| Income Statement Analysis (Million $) | 2010 | 2009 | 2008 | 2007 | 2006 | 2005 | 2004 | 2003 | 2002 | 2001 |
|---|---|---|---|---|---|---|---|---|---|---|
| Revenue | 11,460 | 11,050 | 17,099 | 23,373 | NA | NA | NA | NA | NA | NA |
| Operating Income | 86.0 | NA | -1,530 | -546 | NA | NA | NA | NA | NA | NA |
| Depreciation | 230 | NA | 227 | 274 | NA | NA | NA | NA | NA | NA |
| Interest Expense | 52.0 | Nil | 71.0 | 150 | NA | NA | NA | NA | NA | NA |
| Pretax Income | -4.00 | -1,270 | -1,937 | -1,079 | NA | NA | NA | NA | NA | NA |
| Effective Tax Rate | NA | NM | NM | NM | NA | NA | NA | NA | NA | NA |
| Net Income | -86.0 | -1,277 | -2,969 | -656 | NA | NA | NA | NA | NA | NA |
| S&P Core Earnings | -275 | -1,266 | -2,939 | NA | NA | NA | NA | NA | NA | NA |

| Balance Sheet & Other Financial Data (Million $) | 2010 | 2009 | 2008 | 2007 | 2006 | 2005 | 2004 | 2003 | 2002 | 2001 |
|---|---|---|---|---|---|---|---|---|---|---|
| Cash | NA | 3,200 | 29.0 | NA | NA | NA | NA | NA | NA | NA |
| Current Assets | 3,119 | 6,425 | 3,942 | NA | NA | NA | NA | NA | NA | NA |
| Total Assets | 6,228 | 9,358 | 7,167 | NA | NA | NA | NA | NA | NA | NA |
| Current Liabilities | 3,846 | 3,810 | 4,900 | NA | NA | NA | NA | NA | NA | NA |
| Long Term Debt | NA | 55.0 | 57.0 | NA | NA | NA | NA | NA | NA | NA |
| Common Equity | 1,756 | 4,938 | 1,624 | NA | NA | NA | NA | NA | NA | NA |
| Total Capital | 1,779 | 5,017 | 1,703 | NA | NA | NA | NA | NA | NA | NA |
| Capital Expenditures | 143 | NA | 151 | 195 | NA | NA | NA | NA | NA | NA |
| Cash Flow | 144 | NA | -2,745 | -374 | NA | NA | NA | NA | NA | NA |
| Current Ratio | 0.8 | 1.7 | 0.8 | NA | NA | NA | NA | NA | NA | NA |
| % Long Term Debt of Capitalization | Nil | 1.1 | 3.3 | NA | NA | NA | NA | NA | NA | NA |
| % Net Income of Revenue | NM | NM | NM | NM | NA | NA | NA | NA | NA | NA |
| % Return on Assets | NM | NM | NM | NA | NA | NA | NA | NA | NA | NA |
| % Return on Equity | NM | NM | NM | NA | NA | NA | NA | NA | NA | NA |

Data as orig reptd.; bef. results of disc opers/spec. items. Per share data adj. for stk. divs.; EPS diluted. Pro forma data in 2009; balance sheet and book value as of October 2, 2010 E-Estimated. NA-Not Available. NM-Not Meaningful. NR-Not Ranked. UR-Under Review.

**Office:** 600 North U.S. Highway 45, Libertyville, IL 60048.
**Telephone:** 847-523-5000.
**Website:** http://www.motorola.com
**Chrmn & CEO:** S.K. Jha

**SVP & CFO:** M.E. Rothman
**SVP & CTO:** G.S. Roman
**SVP & General Counsel:** D.S. Offer
**Chief Acctg Officer & Cntlr:** M.R. Valentine

**Investor Contact:** D. Lindroth (847-523-2858)
**Board Members:** J. E. Barfield, J. P. Jackson, S. K. Jha, K. A. Meister, T. J. Meredith, D. A. Ninivaggi, J. R. Stengel, A. J. Vinciquerra, A. J. Viterbi

**Founded:** 2010
**Domicile:** Delaware
**Employees:** 19,000

**The McGraw-Hill Companies**

# Motorola Solutions Inc

**STANDARD &POOR'S**

| S&P Recommendation HOLD ★★★☆☆ | Price | 12-Mo. Target Price | Investment Style |
|---|---|---|---|
| | $43.70 (as of Nov 25, 2011) | $55.00 | Large-Cap Blend |

**GICS Sector** Information Technology
**Sub-Industry** Communications Equipment

**Summary** This company makes communication devices and systems for enterprise and government customers, including wireless networks, public safety communication systems, data capture devices, and command and control systems.

## Key Stock Statistics (Source S&P, Vickers, company reports)

| | | | | | | | |
|---|---|---|---|---|---|---|---|
| 52-Wk Range | $64.61– 36.52 | S&P Oper. EPS 2011**E** | 2.50 | Market Capitalization(B) | $14.226 | Beta | 1.56 |
| Trailing 12-Month EPS | $3.70 | S&P Oper. EPS 2012**E** | 2.77 | Yield (%) | 2.01 | S&P 3-Yr. Proj. EPS CAGR(%) | 15 |
| Trailing 12-Month P/E | 11.8 | P/E on S&P Oper. EPS 2011**E** | 17.5 | Dividend Rate/Share | $0.88 | S&P Credit Rating | BBB |
| $10K Invested 5 Yrs Ago | NA | Common Shares Outstg. (M) | 325.5 | Institutional Ownership (%) | 88 | | |

## Price Performance

30-Week Mov. Avg. ··· 10-Week Mov. Avg. -- GAAP Earnings vs. Previous Year    Volume Above Avg. ▍▍▍ STARS
12-Mo. Target Price — Relative Strength — ▲ Up ▼ Down ► No Change    Below Avg. ▍▍▍ ★

Options: ASE, CBOE, P, Ph

Analysis prepared by Equity Analyst **J. Moorman, CFA** on Nov 16, 2011, when the stock traded at **$45.59**.

### Highlights

▸ Following a revenue increase of 9.6% in 2010, we expect a 6.9% rise in 2011 and a 5.4% advance in 2012, excluding the Networks division, which was sold in April 2011. We expect revenue at the higher-growth Enterprise division to increase 10.3% in 2011, while we look for 5.1% growth in the Government division.

▸ We expect gross margins to expand to 50.8% in 2011, from 50.2% in 2010, and then increase slightly to 50.9% in 2012. Similarly, we forecast that the operating margin will widen to 16.3% in 2011 and 17.1% in 2012, from a pro forma 13.8% in 2010.

▸ After pro forma earnings per share of $1.87 in 2010, we expect EPS of $2.50 in 2011 and $2.77 in 2012. The company made an initial quarterly dividend payment of $0.22 in October 2011.

### Investment Rationale/Risk

▸ Despite the spinoff of the high-growth mobile devices division, we believe MSI offers an attractive combination of mid-single digit revenue growth and strong free cash flow growth. While the government business has lower growth potential, in our view, it carries high margins and should benefit from an analog to digital conversion for public safety networks. We view the smaller Enterprise division as having higher growth potential and significant opportunities in such areas as handheld scanners and data capture.

▸ Risks to our recommendation and target price include execution risk stemming from the weak economy, exposure to government spending in the government business, and exposure to retail in the enterprise business.

▸ Our 12-month target price of $55 is based on an average of our enterprise value-to-EBIT multiple of 9X our 2012 EBIT estimate plus $13.50 per share in cash, and 15X our 2012 EPS estimate plus $13.50 per share in cash, with both multiples slightly below peers.

## Qualitative Risk Assessment

| LOW | MEDIUM | HIGH |
|---|---|---|

Our risk assessment reflects the company's exposure to the economic health of the telecom industry and risks related to high-volume manufacturing and distribution to enterprises and governments. This is offset by our view of MSI's strong cash balance.

## Quantitative Evaluations

**S&P Quality Ranking**    C

| D | C | B- | B | B+ | A- | A | A+ |
|---|---|---|---|---|---|---|---|

**Relative Strength Rank**    MODERATE

70

LOWEST = 1    HIGHEST = 99

## Revenue/Earnings Data

**Revenue (Million $)**

| | 1Q | 2Q | 3Q | 4Q | Year |
|---|---|---|---|---|---|
| 2011 | 1,884 | 2,055 | 2,105 | -- | -- |
| 2010 | 5,044 | 5,414 | 4,890 | 5,663 | 19,282 |
| 2009 | 5,371 | 5,497 | 5,453 | 5,723 | 22,044 |
| 2008 | 7,448 | 8,082 | 7,480 | 7,136 | 30,146 |
| 2007 | 9,433 | 8,732 | 8,811 | 9,646 | 36,622 |
| 2006 | 9,608 | 10,876 | 10,603 | 11,792 | 42,879 |

**Earnings Per Share ($)**

| | 1Q | 2Q | 3Q | 4Q | Year |
|---|---|---|---|---|---|
| 2011 | 1.06 | 0.17 | 0.45 | E0.80 | E2.50 |
| 2010 | 0.21 | 0.49 | Nil | 0.61 | 0.75 |
| 2009 | -0.91 | -0.07 | 0.07 | 0.42 | -0.35 |
| 2008 | -0.63 | Nil | -1.26 | -11.27 | -13.09 |
| 2007 | -0.63 | -0.14 | 0.14 | 0.35 | -0.35 |
| 2006 | 1.82 | 3.78 | 2.03 | 1.47 | 9.10 |

Fiscal year ended Dec. 31. Next earnings report expected: Late January. EPS Estimates based on S&P Operating Earnings; historical GAAP earnings are as reported.

## Dividend Data (Dates: mm/dd Payment Date: mm/dd/yy)

| Amount ($) | Date Decl. | Ex-Div. Date | Stk. of Record | Payment Date |
|---|---|---|---|---|
| 0.220 | 07/28 | 09/13 | 09/15 | 10/14/11 |
| 0.220 | 11/09 | 12/13 | 12/15 | 01/17/12 |
| Stk. | 12/03 | -- | 12/21 | 01/04/11 |

Dividends have been paid since 2011. Source: Company reports.

---

**Please read the Required Disclosures and Analyst Certification on the last page of this report.**

*The McGraw·Hill Companies*

Stock Report | November 26, 2011 | NYS Symbol: **MSI**

# Motorola Solutions Inc

STANDARD
&POOR'S

## Business Summary November 16, 2011

CORPORATE OVERVIEW. Motorola Solutions (MSI) provides communication products and services for enterprise and government customers. The Government division (66% of sales in the third quarter of 2011, even with a year earlier) provides radio systems and devices, including public safety LTE networks, mobile broadband devices, and integrated command and control systems. We estimate that the Government division posted a revenue increase of 5.5% in 2010, and we expect revenue growth of 5.1% in 2011 and 3.4% in 2012. We believe this is typically very stable revenue; however, the impact of the weak economy on the budgets of municipal governments could have an adverse impact.

The remainder of MSI's revenues come from the Enterprise division (34%). The Enterprise division provides advanced data capture devices that include bar code scanners and RFID devices for commercial use, which mostly came from the acquisition of Symbol Technologies in 2006. This segment also provides two-way radios and wireless local area networks (WLANs) for businesses. MSI also includes Motorola's iDen infrastructure business, a proprietary wireless technology, with customers that include Sprint Nextel and Nextel International.

The Networks division was sold to Nokia Siemens Networks (NSN) on April 29, 2011. In January 2011, Huawei had filed a lawsuit to block the transfer of the Networks division to NSN, claiming that the sale would in essence transfer its intellectual property and confidential information to NSN. In April, MSI agreed to settle outstanding litigation with Huawei. MSI also altered its acquisition agreement with NSN, reducing the cash portion to $975 million from $1.2 billion.

The company's geographic breakdown is largely skewed to North America, which accounted for roughly 58% of total revenue in 2010.

COMPETITIVE LANDSCAPE. We believe the government and enterprise markets are very competitive, with competition in the government business coming from firms such as Cisco.

## Company Financials Fiscal Year Ended Dec. 31

| Per Share Data ($) | 2010 | 2009 | 2008 | 2007 | 2006 | 2005 | 2004 | 2003 | 2002 | 2001 |
|---|---|---|---|---|---|---|---|---|---|---|
| Tangible Book Value | 21.95 | 18.48 | 16.94 | 29.96 | 50.05 | 46.69 | 38.15 | 38.01 | 33.95 | 42.49 |
| Cash Flow | 2.44 | 1.96 | -10.57 | 2.45 | 10.68 | 14.44 | 8.07 | 7.62 | -1.16 | -4.38 |
| Earnings | 0.75 | -0.35 | -13.09 | -0.35 | 9.10 | 12.74 | 6.30 | 2.66 | -7.63 | -12.46 |
| S&P Core Earnings | 0.21 | -0.56 | -8.12 | 0.49 | 8.68 | 8.26 | 5.46 | 0.56 | -6.51 | -15.61 |
| Dividends | Nil | Nil | 1.40 | 1.40 | 1.33 | 1.12 | 1.12 | 1.12 | 1.12 | 1.12 |
| Payout Ratio | Nil | Nil | NM | NM | 15% | 9% | 18% | 42% | NM | NM |
| Prices:High | 64.26 | 66.15 | 113.40 | 146.37 | 184.10 | 174.93 | 146.23 | 100.80 | 119.84 | 175.88 |
| Prices:Low | 42.28 | 20.86 | 21.00 | 104.09 | 130.62 | 101.36 | 96.81 | 53.11 | 51.10 | 73.50 |
| P/E Ratio:High | 86 | NM | NM | NM | 20 | 14 | 23 | 38 | NM | NM |
| P/E Ratio:Low | 56 | NM | NM | NM | 14 | 8 | 15 | 20 | NM | NM |

| Income Statement Analysis (Million $) | | | | | | | | | | |
|---|---|---|---|---|---|---|---|---|---|---|
| Revenue | 19,282 | 22,044 | 30,146 | 36,622 | 42,879 | 36,843 | 31,323 | 27,058 | 26,679 | 30,004 |
| Operating Income | 1,350 | 1,322 | 703 | 1,349 | 4,675 | 4,851 | 3,887 | 2,694 | 2,059 | -2,595 |
| Depreciation | 572 | 751 | 829 | 906 | 558 | 613 | 659 | 1,667 | 2,108 | 2,552 |
| Interest Expense | 131 | 213 | 313 | 365 | 335 | 325 | 199 | 295 | 668 | 645 |
| Pretax Income | 677 | -165 | -2,536 | -390 | 4,610 | 6,520 | 3,252 | 1,293 | -3,446 | -5,511 |
| Effective Tax Rate | NA | 46.7% | NM | 73.1% | 29.3% | 29.5% | 32.6% | 30.9% | NM | NM |
| Net Income | 254 | -111 | -4,163 | -105 | 3,261 | 4,599 | 2,191 | 893 | -2,485 | -3,937 |
| S&P Core Earnings | 57.8 | -168 | -2,641 | 186 | 3,132 | 2,964 | 1,899 | 164 | -2,084 | -4,893 |

| Balance Sheet & Other Financial Data (Million $) | | | | | | | | | | |
|---|---|---|---|---|---|---|---|---|---|---|
| Cash | 8,863 | 7,963 | 6,979 | 8,606 | 15,416 | 14,641 | 10,556 | 7,877 | 6,507 | 6,082 |
| Current Assets | 17,154 | 16,032 | 17,363 | 22,222 | 30,975 | 27,869 | 21,082 | 17,907 | 17,134 | 17,149 |
| Total Assets | 25,577 | 25,603 | 27,887 | 34,812 | 38,593 | 35,649 | 30,889 | 32,098 | 31,152 | 33,398 |
| Current Liabilities | 8,710 | 8,261 | 10,620 | 12,500 | 15,425 | 12,488 | 10,573 | 9,433 | 9,810 | 9,698 |
| Long Term Debt | 2,194 | 3,365 | 4,092 | 3,991 | 2,704 | 3,806 | 4,578 | 7,161 | 7,674 | 8,857 |
| Common Equity | 10,885 | 9,775 | 9,525 | 15,447 | 17,142 | 16,673 | 13,331 | 12,689 | 11,239 | 13,691 |
| Total Capital | 13,181 | 13,248 | 13,602 | 20,371 | 19,846 | 20,479 | 17,909 | 19,850 | 18,913 | 22,548 |
| Capital Expenditures | 335 | 275 | 504 | 527 | 649 | 583 | 494 | 655 | 607 | 1,321 |
| Cash Flow | 826 | 640 | -3,415 | 801 | 3,819 | 5,212 | 2,850 | 2,560 | -377 | -1,385 |
| Current Ratio | 2.0 | 1.9 | 1.6 | 1.8 | 2.0 | 2.2 | 2.0 | 1.9 | 1.7 | 1.8 |
| % Long Term Debt of Capitalization | 16.7 | 25.4 | 30.1 | 19.6 | 13.6 | 18.6 | 25.6 | 36.1 | 40.6 | 39.3 |
| % Net Income of Revenue | 1.3 | NM | NM | NM | 7.6 | 12.5 | 7.0 | 3.3 | NM | NM |
| % Return on Assets | 1.0 | NM | NM | NM | 8.8 | 13.8 | 7.0 | 2.8 | NM | NM |
| % Return on Equity | 2.5 | NM | NM | NM | 19.3 | 30.7 | 16.8 | 7.5 | NM | NM |

Data as orig reptd.; bef. results of disc opers/spec. items. Per share data adj. for stk. divs.; EPS diluted. E-Estimated. NA-Not Available. NM-Not Meaningful. NR-Not Ranked. UR-Under Review.

Office: 1303 East Algonquin Road, Schaumburg, IL 60196.
Telephone: 847-576-5000.
Email: investors@motorola.com
Website: http://www.motorolasolutions.com

Chrmn, Pres & CEO: G.Q. Brown
COO: E.A. Delaney
SVP & CFO: E.J. Fitzpatrick
SVP & Treas: L.R. Raymond

SVP, Secy & General Counsel: L.A. Steverson
Investor Contact: D. Lindroth (847-576-6899)
Board Members: W. J. Bratton, G. Q. Brown, K. C. Dahlberg, D. W. Dorman, M. V. Hayden, V. J. Intrieri, J. C. Lewent, S. C. Scott, III, J. A. White

Founded: 1928
Domicile: Delaware
Employees: 51,000

The McGraw-Hill Companies

# M&T Bank Corp

**STANDARD &POOR'S**

| S&P Recommendation HOLD ★★★☆☆ | Price $72.98 (as of Nov 30, 2011) | 12-Mo. Target Price $75.00 | Investment Style Large-Cap Blend |
|---|---|---|---|

**GICS Sector** Financials
**Sub-Industry** Regional Banks

**Summary** This bank holding company, with offices in New York, Maryland and several other Eastern states, acquired Wilmington Trust Co. in 2011.

## Key Stock Statistics (Source S&P, Vickers, company reports)

| | | | | | | |
|---|---|---|---|---|---|---|
| 52-Wk Range | $91.05–66.40 | S&P Oper. EPS 2011E | 7.13 | Market Capitalization(B) | $9.168 | Beta | 0.81 |
| Trailing 12-Month EPS | $6.91 | S&P Oper. EPS 2012E | 7.39 | Yield (%) | 3.84 | S&P 3-Yr. Proj. EPS CAGR(%) | 11 |
| Trailing 12-Month P/E | 10.6 | P/E on S&P Oper. EPS 2011E | 10.2 | Dividend Rate/Share | $2.80 | S&P Credit Rating | A- |
| $10K Invested 5 Yrs Ago | $7,411 | Common Shares Outstg. (M) | 125.6 | Institutional Ownership (%) | 72 | | |

## Price Performance

30-Week Mov. Avg. · · · 10-Week Mov. Avg. - - GAAP Earnings vs. Previous Year   Volume Above Avg. ▮▮▮ STARS
12-Mo. Target Price — Relative Strength — ▲ Up ▼ Down ► No Change   Below Avg. ▮▮▮ ★

Options: ASE, CBOE, P, Ph

Analysis prepared by Equity Analyst **Erik Oja** on Nov 30, 2011, when the stock traded at **$71.52**.

## Qualitative Risk Assessment

| LOW | MEDIUM | HIGH |
|---|---|---|

Our risk assessment reflects the company's large-cap valuation, its history of profitability, its low chargeoff levels relative to peers, and its ability to build capital through income generation.

## Quantitative Evaluations

**S&P Quality Ranking** B+

| D | C | B- | B | B+ | A- | A | A+ |
|---|---|---|---|---|---|---|---|

**Relative Strength Rank** MODERATE

53

LOWEST = 1    HIGHEST = 99

## Revenue/Earnings Data

**Revenue (Million $)**

| | 1Q | 2Q | 3Q | 4Q | Year |
|---|---|---|---|---|---|
| 2011 | 981.9 | 1,190 | 1,089 | -- | -- |
| 2010 | 934.1 | 958.3 | 975.8 | 969.7 | 3,838 |
| 2009 | 891.8 | 954.3 | 984.6 | 964.5 | 3,773 |
| 2008 | 1,197 | 1,089 | 915.1 | 1,016 | 4,217 |
| 2007 | 1,098 | 1,161 | 1,146 | 1,073 | 4,478 |
| 2006 | 1,030 | 1,076 | 1,127 | 1,127 | 4,360 |

**Earnings Per Share ($)**

| | 1Q | 2Q | 3Q | 4Q | Year |
|---|---|---|---|---|---|
| 2011 | 1.59 | 2.42 | 1.32 | E1.80 | E7.13 |
| 2010 | 1.15 | 1.46 | 1.48 | 1.59 | 5.69 |
| 2009 | 0.49 | 0.36 | 0.97 | 1.04 | 2.89 |
| 2008 | 1.82 | 1.44 | 0.82 | 0.92 | 5.01 |
| 2007 | 1.57 | 1.95 | 1.83 | 0.60 | 5.95 |
| 2006 | 1.77 | 1.87 | 1.85 | 1.88 | 7.37 |

Fiscal year ended Dec. 31. Next earnings report expected: Mid January. EPS Estimates based on S&P Operating Earnings; historical GAAP earnings are as reported.

## Highlights

▶ We expect loan growth of 12.5% in 2011, due to the acquisition of Wilmington Trust, up from 0.1% growth in 2010. For 2012, we expect 2.5% growth. We forecast that net interest income will rise 5.4% in 2011 and 4.9% in 2012, based on our expectations for growth in interest-earning assets to pick up in 2011, and on our outlook for a stable net interest margin in both years. We look for non-interest income, excluding gains and losses, to increase 22.5% in 2011 and 14.5% in 2012. We expect total net revenues to grow 17.5% in 2011 and 3.5% in 2012.

▶ Although third-quarter nonperforming loans and net chargeoffs rose slightly from second-quarter levels, our view is that MTB's credit trends remain better than peers. For 2011, we expect $245 million of net chargeoffs, with provisions of $265 million. In 2012, we see net chargeoffs and provisions of $215 million. We project non-interest expenses totaling 68.5% of core revenues, excluding gains and losses, in 2011, up from 61.2% in 2010, due to the acquisition. For 2012, we expect this ratio to fall to 66.6%.

▶ We see EPS of $7.13 in 2011 and $7.39 in 2012.

## Investment Rationale/Risk

▶ MTB's May 2011 acquisition of Wilmington Trust Corp. should be accretive by 2012, by our analysis, as WL's lucrative noninterest income lines of business, such as Corporate Client Services, are expected to contribute strongly to MTB's noninterest revenues. The risk from this acquisition that we see is the possibility of additional unexpected credit losses arising from the acquired construction loan portfolios. Still, we expect MTB's internally generated capital to boost capital ratios and book value, allowing its tangible common equity to tangible assets ratio to approach peers' higher levels. We look for MTB to maintain its quarterly dividend at $0.70, which recently yielded about 3.9%.

▶ Risks to our opinion and target price include worse-than-expected credit quality in MTB's real estate construction portfolio, a dividend cut, and an equity capital raise.

▶ Our 12-month target price of $75 equals 1.9X our $39.50 estimate of year-end 2011 tangible book value per share, an above-peers multiple reflecting our view of MTB's relative earnings, capital and dividend stability versus peers.

## Dividend Data (Dates: mm/dd Payment Date: mm/dd/yy)

| Amount ($) | Date Decl. | Ex-Div. Date | Stk. of Record | Payment Date |
|---|---|---|---|---|
| 0.700 | 11/17 | 11/29 | 12/01 | 12/31/10 |
| 0.700 | 02/16 | 02/24 | 02/28 | 03/31/11 |
| 0.700 | 08/17 | 08/30 | 09/01 | 09/30/11 |
| 0.700 | 11/16 | 11/29 | 12/01 | 12/30/11 |

Dividends have been paid since 1979. Source: Company reports.

---

**Please read the Required Disclosures and Analyst Certification on the last page of this report.**

**The McGraw-Hill Companies**

# M&T Bank Corp

**STANDARD
&POOR'S**

## Business Summary November 30, 2011

CORPORATE OVERVIEW. M&T Bank Corporation is a Buffalo, NY-based bank holding company with nearly $80 billion in assets as of September 30, 2011. Its principal subsidiary is M&T Bank, a New York State chartered bank that focuses its lending on consumers and small and medium-sized businesses in the Mid-Atlantic region. It also owns M&T Bank, National Association (N.A.), a national banking association that offers selected deposit and loan products on a nationwide basis through direct mail and telephone marketing, and operates other subsidiaries that provide insurance, securities, investments, leasing, mortgage, mortgage reinsurance, real estate and other financial products and services.

MARKET PROFILE. As of June 30, 2011, which is the latest FDIC branch level data, MTB had 752 branches and $60.1 billion in deposits, with about 41% of

its deposits concentrated in New York and 29% in Maryland. In New York, MTB had 255 branches, $24.5 billion in deposits, and a deposit market share of about 2.4%, ranking seventh. In Maryland, MTB had 205 branches, $17.4 billion in deposits, and a deposit market share of 13.1%, ranking second. In Pennsylvania, MTB had 196 branches, $8.5 billion in deposits, and a deposit market share of about 2.6%, ranking seventh. In Delaware, MTB had 45 offices, $8.0 billion in deposits, and a deposit market share of 2.5%, ranking seventh. MTB also has a smaller presence in Virginia, the District of Columbia, West Virginia, New Jersey and Florida.

## Company Financials Fiscal Year Ended Dec. 31

| Per Share Data ($) | 2010 | 2009 | 2008 | 2007 | 2006 | 2005 | 2004 | 2003 | 2002 | 2001 |
|---|---|---|---|---|---|---|---|---|---|---|
| Tangible Book Value | 33.12 | 28.03 | 24.21 | 30.62 | 30.05 | 25.56 | 24.52 | 21.43 | 20.23 | 17.84 |
| Earnings | 5.69 | 2.89 | 5.01 | 5.95 | 7.37 | 6.73 | 6.00 | 4.95 | 5.07 | 3.82 |
| S&P Core Earnings | 5.71 | 2.89 | 4.63 | 5.87 | 7.36 | 6.64 | 5.97 | 4.95 | 4.60 | 3.40 |
| Dividends | 2.80 | 2.80 | 2.80 | 2.60 | 2.25 | 1.75 | 1.60 | 1.20 | 1.05 | 1.00 |
| Payout Ratio | 49% | 97% | 56% | 44% | 31% | 26% | 27% | 24% | 21% | 26% |
| Prices:High | 96.15 | 69.89 | 108.53 | 125.13 | 124.98 | 112.50 | 108.75 | 98.98 | 90.05 | 82.11 |
| Prices:Low | 66.32 | 29.11 | 52.20 | 77.39 | 105.72 | 96.71 | 82.90 | 74.71 | 67.70 | 59.80 |
| P/E Ratio:High | 17 | 24 | 22 | 21 | 17 | 17 | 18 | 20 | 18 | 21 |
| P/E Ratio:Low | 12 | 10 | 10 | 13 | 14 | 14 | 14 | 15 | 13 | 16 |

| Income Statement Analysis (Million $) | | | | | | | | | | |
|---|---|---|---|---|---|---|---|---|---|---|
| Net Interest Income | 2,268 | 2,056 | 1,940 | 1,850 | 1,818 | 1,794 | 1,735 | 1,599 | 1,248 | 1,158 |
| Tax Equivalent Adjustment | 24.0 | 22.0 | 21.9 | 20.8 | NA | 17.3 | NA | 16.3 | 14.0 | 17.5 |
| Non Interest Income | 1,108 | 1,048 | 939 | 1,059 | 1,043 | 978 | 940 | 831 | 513 | 476 |
| Loan Loss Provision | 368 | 604 | 412 | 192 | 80.0 | 88.0 | 95.0 | 131 | 122 | 104 |
| % Expense/Operating Revenue | 56.7% | 63.8% | 54.4% | 55.9% | 54.2% | 53.2% | 56.7% | 59.6% | 51.9% | 57.4% |
| Pretax Income | 1,093 | 519 | 740 | 964 | 1,232 | 1,171 | 1,067 | 851 | 716 | 584 |
| Effective Tax Rate | 32.7% | 26.8% | 24.9% | 32.1% | 31.9% | 33.2% | 32.3% | 32.5% | 32.3% | 35.2% |
| Net Income | 736 | 380 | 556 | 654 | 839 | 782 | 723 | 574 | 485 | 378 |
| % Net Interest Margin | 3.84 | 3.49 | 3.38 | 3.60 | 3.70 | 3.77 | 3.88 | 4.09 | 4.36 | 4.23 |
| S&P Core Earnings | 679 | 333 | 514 | 646 | 838 | 772 | 718 | 574 | 440 | 336 |

| Balance Sheet & Other Financial Data (Million $) | | | | | | | | | | |
|---|---|---|---|---|---|---|---|---|---|---|
| Money Market Assets | 650 | 540 | 649 | 348 | 143 | 211 | 199 | 250 | 380 | 84.4 |
| Investment Securities | 7,151 | 7,781 | 7,919 | 8,962 | 7,371 | 8,400 | 8,475 | 7,259 | 3,955 | 3,024 |
| Commercial Loans | 28,977 | 28,259 | 27,397 | 25,715 | 23,165 | 23,940 | 22,886 | 20,869 | 14,522 | 14,071 |
| Other Loans | 23,393 | 24,047 | 21,963 | 22,637 | 20,042 | 16,614 | 15,758 | 15,169 | 11,415 | 11,117 |
| Total Assets | 68,021 | 68,880 | 65,816 | 64,876 | 57,065 | 55,146 | 52,939 | 49,826 | 33,175 | 31,450 |
| Demand Deposits | 14,558 | 13,795 | 8,856 | 9,322 | 8,820 | 9,044 | 9,246 | 10,150 | 5,101 | 4,634 |
| Time Deposits | 35,347 | 33,655 | 32,584 | 31,944 | 25,660 | 28,056 | 26,183 | 20,756 | 16,564 | 16,946 |
| Long Term Debt | 7,840 | 10,240 | 12,075 | 10,318 | 6,891 | 5,586 | 6,349 | 5,535 | 4,497 | 3,462 |
| Common Equity | 7,617 | 7,023 | 6,217 | 6,485 | 6,281 | 5,876 | 5,730 | 5,717 | 3,182 | 2,939 |
| % Return on Assets | 1.1 | 0.6 | 0.9 | 1.1 | 1.5 | 1.4 | 1.4 | 1.4 | 1.5 | 1.3 |
| % Return on Equity | 10.1 | 5.7 | 8.4 | 10.3 | 13.8 | 13.5 | 12.6 | 12.9 | 15.8 | 13.4 |
| % Loan Loss Reserve | 1.7 | 1.7 | 1.6 | 1.6 | 1.5 | 1.6 | 1.6 | 1.7 | 1.7 | 1.7 |
| % Loans/Deposits | 104.4 | 109.5 | 115.1 | 112.1 | 107.6 | 108.7 | 108.4 | 108.0 | 119.7 | 116.7 |
| % Equity to Assets | 10.7 | 9.8 | 9.7 | 10.5 | 10.8 | 10.7 | 11.1 | 10.8 | 9.5 | 9.3 |

Data as orig reptd.; bef. results of disc opers/spec. items. Per share data adj. for stk. divs.; EPS diluted. E-Estimated. NA-Not Available. NM-Not Meaningful. NR-Not Ranked. UR-Under Review.

**Office:** One M & T Plaza, Buffalo, NY 14203.
**Telephone:** 716-842-5445.
**Email:** ir@mandtbank.com
**Website:** http://www.mtb.com

**Chrmn & CEO:** R.G. Wilmers
**Pres:** M.J. Czarnecki
**Vice Chrmn:** J.G. Pereira
**Vice Chrmn:** M. Pinto

**CFO:** R.F. Jones
**Investor Contact:** D.J. MacLeod (716-842-5138)
**Board Members:** B. D. Baird, R. J. Bennett, C. A. Bontempo, R. T. Brady, M. D. Buckley, T. J. Cunningham, III, M. J. Czarnecki, D. E. Foley, G. N. Geisel, P. W. Hodgson, R. G. King, J. G. Pereira, M. Pinto, M. R. Rich, R. E. Sadler, Jr., H. L. Washington, R. G. Wilmers

**Founded:** 1969
**Domicile:** New York
**Employees:** 13,365

*The McGraw·Hill Companies*

# Murphy Oil Corp

STANDARD
&POOR'S

**S&P Recommendation** HOLD ★★★★★

| | | |
|---|---|---|
| **Price** $52.49 (as of Nov 28, 2011) | **12-Mo. Target Price** $71.00 | **Investment Style** Large-Cap Blend |

**GICS Sector** Energy
**Sub-Industry** Integrated Oil & Gas

**Summary** This international integrated oil company has exploration and production interests worldwide, as well as refining and marketing operations in the U.S., which it plans to divest.

## Key Stock Statistics (Source S&P, Vickers, company reports)

| | | | | | | | |
|---|---|---|---|---|---|---|---|
| 52-Wk Range | $78.16–40.41 | S&P Oper. EPS 2011**E** | 6.14 | Market Capitalization(B) | $10.158 | Beta | 1.21 |
| Trailing 12-Month EPS | $5.97 | S&P Oper. EPS 2012**E** | 5.99 | Yield (%) | 2.10 | S&P 3-Yr. Proj. EPS CAGR(%) | 29 |
| Trailing 12-Month P/E | 8.8 | P/E on S&P Oper. EPS 2011**E** | 8.5 | Dividend Rate/Share | $1.10 | S&P Credit Rating | BBB |
| $10K Invested 5 Yrs Ago | $10,479 | Common Shares Outstg. (M) | 193.5 | Institutional Ownership (%) | 81 | | |

## Price Performance

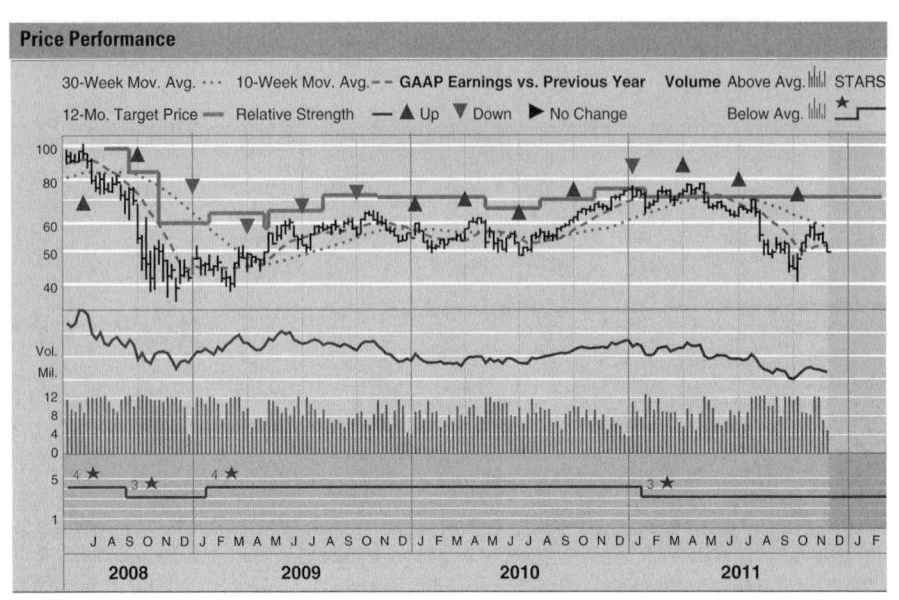

Options: ASE, CBOE, P, Ph

Analysis prepared by Equity Analyst **S. Glickman, CFA** on Nov 28, 2011, when the stock traded at **$52.49**.

### Qualitative Risk Assessment

LOW **MEDIUM** HIGH

Our risk assessment reflects our view of MUR's moderate financial policies and integrated operations in a volatile, cyclical and capital-intensive segment of the energy industry. We believe its low reserve-to-production ratio limits its operating flexibility, increasing dependence on long-term projects.

### Quantitative Evaluations

**S&P Quality Ranking** B+

| D | C | B- | B | B+ | A- | A | A+ |
|---|---|---|---|---|---|---|---|

**Relative Strength Rank** MODERATE

63

LOWEST = 1   HIGHEST = 99

## Highlights

▸ We expect MUR's oil and gas production to decline about 6% in 2011 from 2010's average of about 188,000 boe per day, due in part to workovers at Kikeh in Malaysia. For 2012, however, we see about an 8% recovery in production, led by the Eagle Ford and Seal Lake plays. Although preliminary, in November, MUR guided to capital spending of about $3.5 billion, up from a projected $3.0 billion in 2011, which we think reflects in part project build-out as well as cost inflation.

▸ In February 2011, MUR announced a production target of 300,000 boe per day by 2015, which implies a compound annual growth rate (CAGR) of about 11% from 2009 actual production. We expect Asia-Pacific to be one of the larger drivers of incremental production on a boe basis, although we also think that U.S. Lower 48 unconventional plays and Seal Lake in Canada will become increasingly important as well.

▸ We project EPS of $6.14 in 2011, an increase of 49% from 2010, as improved realized oil prices more than offset weaker volumes. For 2012, we see EPS down about 2% to $5.99, on higher expected cost inflation and slightly weaker realized prices.

## Investment Rationale/Risk

▸ MUR sold its Superior and Meraux U.S. refineries in late September/early October, with results from those businesses now classified under discontinued operations. We think a streamlined MUR, with its solid queue of upstream projects, should deliver improved EPS growth over time. We also note recent emphasis on reducing MUR's long-term debt which should enable increased flexibility with future cash flows. In terms of catalysts to achieve MUR's production goal of 300,000 boe/d by 2015, we see this goal being primarily achieved from international prospects, especially Asia-Pacific, as well as some U.S. Lower 48 unconventional oil and gas plays.

▸ Risks to our recommendation and target price include rising cost inflation, falling prices, or difficulty replacing oil and gas reserves.

▸ Blending our discounted cash flow ($69, assuming a WACC of 9.5% and terminal growth of 3%) and relative market valuations leads to our 12-month target price of $71. This represents an expected enterprise value of about 4.3X our projection of 2012 EBITDA, in line with historical forward multiples.

## Revenue/Earnings Data

### Revenue (Million $)

| | 1Q | 2Q | 3Q | 4Q | Year |
|---|---|---|---|---|---|
| 2011 | 7,346 | 8,721 | 7,240 | -- | -- |
| 2010 | 5,180 | 5,592 | 6,064 | 6,509 | 23,345 |
| 2009 | 3,416 | 4,496 | 5,202 | 5,804 | 19,012 |
| 2008 | 6,533 | 8,363 | 8,186 | 4,431 | 27,513 |
| 2007 | 3,435 | 4,614 | 4,781 | 5,610 | 18,439 |
| 2006 | 2,991 | 3,799 | 4,153 | 3,364 | 14,307 |

### Earnings Per Share ($)

| | | | | | |
|---|---|---|---|---|---|
| 2011 | 1.38 | 1.60 | 1.73 | E1.38 | E6.14 |
| 2010 | 0.77 | 1.41 | 1.05 | 0.90 | 4.13 |
| 2009 | 0.37 | 0.84 | 0.98 | 1.66 | 3.85 |
| 2008 | 2.14 | 3.22 | 3.04 | 0.83 | 9.22 |
| 2007 | 0.58 | 1.32 | 1.04 | 1.07 | 4.01 |
| 2006 | 0.60 | 1.13 | 1.18 | 0.46 | 3.37 |

Fiscal year ended Dec. 31. Next earnings report expected: Late January. EPS Estimates based on S&P Operating Earnings; historical GAAP earnings are as reported.

## Dividend Data (Dates: mm/dd Payment Date: mm/dd/yy)

| Amount ($) | Date Decl. | Ex-Div. Date | Stk. of Record | Payment Date |
|---|---|---|---|---|
| 0.275 | 02/02 | 02/11 | 02/15 | 03/01/11 |
| 0.275 | 04/06 | 05/11 | 05/13 | 06/01/11 |
| 0.275 | 08/03 | 08/11 | 08/15 | 09/01/11 |
| 0.275 | 10/05 | 11/08 | 11/10 | 12/01/11 |

Dividends have been paid since 1961. Source: Company reports.

The McGraw-Hill Companies

# Murphy Oil Corp

**STANDARD &POOR'S**

## Business Summary November 28, 2011

CORPORATE OVERVIEW. Originally incorporated in Louisiana in 1950 as Murphy Corp., the company was reincorporated in Delaware in 1964 under the name Murphy Oil Corp. (MUR). As an international integrated oil and gas company, MUR explores for oil and gas worldwide, and has refining and marketing interests in the U.S. The company operates in two business segments: Exploration and Production (13% of 2010 revenues; 84% of 2010 segment income), and Refining and Marketing (87%; 16%).

U.S. hydrocarbon production comprised about 15.5% of total 2010 production on a boe/day basis, and over 60% of MUR's U.S. hydrocarbon production was generated at two Gulf of Mexico fields - Thunder Hawk and Medusa. MUR has a 37.5% working interest in Thunder Hawk. For 2011, MUR expects Thunder Hawk to achieve lower production, due to well decline and the inability to perform drilling operations following the April 2010 Macondo incident. Medusa production is also expected to decline.

MUR's operations in Canada include limited heavy oil exploration and exploitation in Western Canada, combined with its non-operated interests in legacy properties: Terra Nova (10.475% as of January 1, 2011; previously 12.0%), Hibernia (6.5%), and Syncrude Canada Ltd. (5%). In June 2007, the company acquired the Tupper leases, a tight natural gas play in northeastern British Columbia.

In Malaysia, the company has majority interests in seven separate production-sharing contracts (PSCs) and serves as operator. In 2002, MUR made an important discovery at the Kikeh field (80%) in deepwater Block K, offshore Sabah, and added another important discovery at Kakap in 2004. In April 2010, Petronas informed MUR that offshore Blocks L and M were no longer part of Malaysia, but rather, part of Brunei; and as a result, MUR's production-sharing contracts for these blocks with Petronas were terminated in April 2010. In late 2010, MUR entered into two new PSCs for these offshore Brunei properties, with a 5% interest in Block CA-1 and a 30% interest in Block CA-2. These two blocks cover 1.45 million and 1.49 million gross acres, respectively.

The company also has interests in the U.K. sector of the North Sea, offshore Ecuador, and offshore the Republic of Congo.

## Company Financials  Fiscal Year Ended Dec. 31

| Per Share Data ($) | 2010 | 2009 | 2008 | 2007 | 2006 | 2005 | 2004 | 2003 | 2002 | 2001 |
|---|---|---|---|---|---|---|---|---|---|---|
| Tangible Book Value | 42.30 | 38.22 | 32.73 | 25.99 | 21.37 | 18.38 | 14.16 | 10.27 | 8.41 | 7.99 |
| Cash Flow | 10.89 | 9.22 | 13.48 | 6.75 | 5.40 | 6.57 | 4.38 | 3.39 | 2.16 | 3.07 |
| Earnings | 4.13 | 3.85 | 9.22 | 4.01 | 3.37 | 4.46 | 2.66 | 1.63 | 0.53 | 1.82 |
| S&P Core Earnings | 4.18 | 3.79 | 8.55 | 4.03 | 3.32 | 3.85 | 2.40 | 1.40 | 0.39 | 1.30 |
| Dividends | 1.05 | 1.00 | 0.88 | 0.68 | 0.52 | 0.45 | 0.43 | 0.40 | 0.39 | 0.38 |
| Payout Ratio | 25% | 26% | 9% | 17% | 16% | 10% | 16% | 25% | 73% | 21% |
| Prices:High | 76.00 | 65.12 | 101.47 | 85.94 | 60.18 | 57.07 | 43.69 | 34.35 | 24.86 | 21.96 |
| Prices:Low | 48.14 | 37.96 | 35.55 | 45.45 | 44.72 | 37.80 | 28.45 | 19.27 | 15.95 | 13.81 |
| P/E Ratio:High | 18 | 17 | 11 | 21 | 18 | 13 | 16 | 21 | 47 | 12 |
| P/E Ratio:Low | 12 | 10 | 4 | 11 | 13 | 8 | 11 | 12 | 30 | 8 |

| Income Statement Analysis (Million $) | | | | | | | | | | |
|---|---|---|---|---|---|---|---|---|---|---|
| Revenue | 23,345 | 19,012 | 27,513 | 18,439 | 14,307 | 11,877 | 8,360 | 5,345 | 3,967 | 4,479 |
| Operating Income | NA | NA | 3,640 | 1,845 | 1,514 | 1,854 | 1,110 | 781 | 492 | 768 |
| Depreciation, Depletion and Amortization | 1,305 | 1,028 | 850 | 523 | 384 | 397 | 321 | 328 | 300 | 229 |
| Interest Expense | 34.7 | 24.4 | 43.7 | 75.5 | 9.48 | 8.77 | 34.1 | 20.5 | 27.0 | 19.0 |
| Pretax Income | 1,414 | 1,277 | 2,850 | 1,237 | 1,028 | 1,372 | 805 | 419 | 152 | 506 |
| Effective Tax Rate | NA | 42.0% | 37.9% | 38.1% | 37.9% | 38.9% | 38.3% | 28.1% | 35.7% | 34.6% |
| Net Income | 798 | 741 | 1,771 | 767 | 638 | 838 | 496 | 301 | 97.5 | 331 |
| S&P Core Earnings | 809 | 728 | 1,643 | 772 | 630 | 725 | 448 | 259 | 71.4 | 236 |

| Balance Sheet & Other Financial Data (Million $) | | | | | | | | | | |
|---|---|---|---|---|---|---|---|---|---|---|
| Cash | 536 | 301 | 666 | 674 | 543 | 585 | 536 | 252 | 165 | 82.7 |
| Current Assets | 3,551 | 3,376 | 2,846 | 2,887 | 2,107 | 1,839 | 1,629 | 1,039 | 854 | 599 |
| Total Assets | 14,233 | 12,827 | 12,205 | 10,536 | 7,446 | 6,369 | 5,458 | 4,713 | 3,886 | 3,259 |
| Current Liabilities | 2,931 | 2,182 | 1,888 | 2,109 | 1,311 | 1,287 | 1,205 | 810 | 718 | 560 |
| Long Term Debt | 939 | 1,353 | 1,026 | 1,516 | 840 | 610 | 613 | 1,090 | 863 | 521 |
| Common Equity | 8,200 | 7,246 | 6,314 | 5,066 | 4,053 | 3,461 | 2,649 | 1,951 | 1,594 | 1,498 |
| Total Capital | 9,139 | 8,699 | 8,183 | 7,526 | 5,498 | 4,685 | 3,263 | 3,463 | 2,784 | 2,322 |
| Capital Expenditures | 2,356 | 1,989 | 2,186 | 1,949 | 1,192 | 1,246 | 938 | 938 | 834 | 814 |
| Cash Flow | 2,103 | 1,774 | 2,590 | 1,290 | 1,022 | 1,235 | 818 | 630 | 398 | 560 |
| Current Ratio | 1.2 | 1.5 | 1.5 | 1.4 | 1.6 | 1.4 | 1.4 | 1.3 | 1.2 | 1.1 |
| % Long Term Debt of Capitalization | 10.3 | 15.7 | 12.5 | 20.2 | 15.3 | 13.0 | 18.8 | 31.5 | 31.0 | 22.4 |
| % Return on Assets | 5.9 | 6.2 | 15.6 | 8.5 | 9.2 | 14.2 | 9.8 | 7.0 | 2.7 | 10.4 |
| % Return on Equity | 10.3 | 11.0 | 31.1 | 16.8 | 17.0 | 27.4 | 21.6 | 17.0 | 6.3 | 24.0 |

Data as orig reptd.; bef. results of disc opers/spec. items. Per share data adj. for stk. divs.; EPS diluted. E-Estimated. NA-Not Available. NM-Not Meaningful. NR-Not Ranked. UR-Under Review.

**Office:** 200 Peach Street, PO Box 7000, El Dorado, AR 71731-7000.
**Telephone:** 870-862-6411.
**Email:** murphyoil@murphyoilcorp.com
**Website:** http://www.murphyoilcorp.com

**Chrmn:** W.C. Nolan, Jr.
**Pres & CEO:** D.M. Wood
**SVP & CFO:** K.G. Fitzgerald
**SVP & General Counsel:** W.K. Compton

**Chief Admin Officer:** K.M. Hammock
**Investor Contact:** M. West (870-864-6315)
**Board Members:** F. W. Blue, S. A. Cosse, C. P. Deming, R. A. Hermes, J. V. Kelley, W. Mirosh, R. M. Murphy, W. C. Nolan, Jr., N. E. Schmale, D. J. Smith, C. G. Theus, D. M. Wood

**Founded:** 1950
**Domicile:** Delaware
**Employees:** 8,994

**The McGraw-Hill Companies**

# Mylan Inc

**STANDARD &POOR'S**

| S&P Recommendation | **STRONG BUY** ★★★★★ | Price<br>$17.41 (as of Nov 25, 2011) | 12-Mo. Target Price<br>$29.00 | Investment Style<br>Large-Cap Growth |
|---|---|---|---|---|

**GICS Sector** Health Care
**Sub-Industry** Pharmaceuticals

**Summary** This leading manufacturer of generic pharmaceuticals produces a broad range of generic drugs in varying strengths.

## Key Stock Statistics (Source S&P, Vickers, company reports)

| | | | | | | | |
|---|---|---|---|---|---|---|---|
| 52-Wk Range | $25.46– 15.49 | S&P Oper. EPS 2011**E** | 2.00 | Market Capitalization(B) | $7.426 | Beta | 0.82 |
| Trailing 12-Month EPS | $0.96 | S&P Oper. EPS 2012**E** | 2.35 | Yield (%) | Nil | S&P 3-Yr. Proj. EPS CAGR(%) | NA |
| Trailing 12-Month P/E | 18.1 | P/E on S&P Oper. EPS 2011**E** | 8.7 | Dividend Rate/Share | Nil | S&P Credit Rating | BB+ |
| $10K Invested 5 Yrs Ago | $8,638 | Common Shares Outstg. (M) | 426.5 | Institutional Ownership (%) | 84 | | |

## Price Performance

30-Week Mov. Avg. ···· 10-Week Mov. Avg. - - GAAP Earnings vs. Previous Year   Volume Above Avg. STARS
12-Mo. Target Price — Relative Strength   ▲ Up  ▼ Down  ▶ No Change   Below Avg.   ★

Options: ASE, CBOE, P, Ph

Analysis prepared by Equity Analyst **Herman Saftlas** on Aug 22, 2011, when the stock traded at **$17.74**.

## Qualitative Risk Assessment

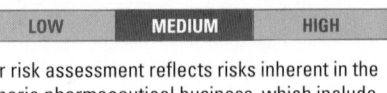

| LOW | MEDIUM | HIGH |
|---|---|---|

Our risk assessment reflects risks inherent in the generic pharmaceutical business, which include the need to successfully develop generic products, obtain regulatory approvals, and legally challenge branded patents. However, we believe these risks are offset by Mylan's wide and diverse generic portfolio and promising branded drugs business. We also think the acquisition of Merck KGaA's generics business holds long-term promise.

## Quantitative Evaluations

**S&P Quality Ranking**                                    A-

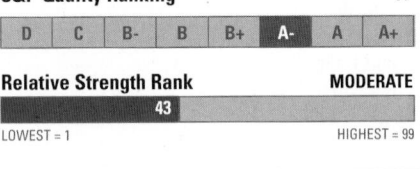

| D | C | B- | B | B+ | A- | A | A+ |
|---|---|---|---|---|---|---|---|

**Relative Strength Rank**                              MODERATE

43

LOWEST = 1                                          HIGHEST = 99

## Highlights

➤ We forecast revenue growth of about 10% in 2011, with expected strength in generics sales in North America and Asia/Pacific more than offsetting weakness in European markets. We see new products such as generic versions of Entocort, Femara, Levaquin, Effexor ER and Solodyn as key growth drivers. In total, MYL has some 162 ANDAs awaiting FDA review, of which 43 represent potential first-to-file opportunities with six months of marketing exclusivity. Volume should also be augmented by expansion into new ophthalmic and topical generics, the acquisition of Bioniche Pharma, and gains in branded drugs and Matrix units.

➤ We look for gross margins to show modest expansion from 2010's 46.5%, reflecting projected higher volume and productivity enhancements. We also see tight control of SG&A costs and R&D spending, helped by ongoing merger synergies.

➤ After an indicated adjusted tax rate slightly lower than 2010's 27.1%, we see operating EPS of $2.00 for 2011, up from $1.60 in 2010. Boosted by greater contributions from new products, we project EPS of $2.35 for 2012.

## Investment Rationale/Risk

➤ We believe MYL's efforts to expand through acquisitions hold much long-term promise. In September 2010, MYL acquired Bioniche Pharma, an Ireland-based maker of injectable drugs. Mylan expects this deal to be EPS accretive within one year after completion. Other acquisitions, such as Merck KGaA's generic business and Matrix Laboratories, have broadened MYL's geographic reach and provided access to in-house raw materials and generic biologics. We expect MYL to launch over 500 new products worldwide in 2011, including a line of generic oral contraceptives in the U.S. We see MYL as uniquely positioned to benefit from the robust growth we see for the generics market.

➤ Risks to our recommendation and target price include problems integrating acquisitions, as well as cash flow risks that could threaten MYL's ability to manage its heavy debt load.

➤ Our 12-month target price of $29 applies a modest premium to peers P/E of 12.3X to our 2012 EPS estimate. Our DCF model, which assumes a WACC of 8% and perpetuity growth of 1%, also shows intrinsic value of about $29.

## Revenue/Earnings Data

**Revenue (Million $)**

| | 1Q | 2Q | 3Q | 4Q | Year |
|---|---|---|---|---|---|
| 2011 | 1,449 | 1,574 | 1,576 | -- | -- |
| 2010 | 1,292 | 1,369 | 1,355 | 1,435 | 5,451 |
| 2009 | 1,181 | 1,267 | 1,264 | 1,352 | 5,064 |
| 2008 | 1,074 | 1,203 | 1,657 | 1,203 | 5,138 |
| 2007 | 356.1 | 366.7 | 401.8 | 487.3 | 1,612 |
| 2006 | 323.4 | 298.0 | 311.3 | 324.6 | 1,257 |

**Earnings Per Share ($)**

| | | | | | |
|---|---|---|---|---|---|
| 2011 | 0.23 | 0.33 | 0.36 | E0.52 | E2.00 |
| 2010 | 0.20 | 0.16 | 0.33 | 0.01 | 0.68 |
| 2009 | 0.23 | 0.19 | -0.13 | 0.01 | 0.30 |
| 2008 | -1.46 | -0.03 | 0.45 | -0.13 | -1.05 |
| 2007 | 0.35 | 0.36 | 0.63 | -0.31 | 0.99 |
| 2006 | 0.16 | 0.16 | 0.22 | 0.27 | 0.79 |

Fiscal year ended Dec. 31. Next earnings report expected: Late February. EPS Estimates based on S&P Operating Earnings; historical GAAP earnings are as reported.

## Dividend Data

Dividends were suspended in 2008.

---

**Please read the Required Disclosures and Analyst Certification on the last page of this report.**

*The McGraw-Hill Companies*

# Mylan Inc

## Business Summary August 22, 2011

CORPORATE PROFILE. Mylan Laboratories is a leading manufacturer of generic pharmaceutical products in finished tablet, capsule and powder dosage forms. Generic drugs are the chemical equivalents of branded drugs, and are marketed after patents on the primary products expire. Generics are typically sold at prices significantly below those of comparable branded products.

Generics accounted for some 92% of operating revenues in 2010, with specialty products representing the balance. By geographic region, generics sales in 2010 were derived as follows: North America 53%, Europe 33%, and Asia/Pacific 14%.

MYL markets more than 1,000 products throughout the world. The U.S. generic division markets about 270 generic products, primarily solid oral dose drugs encompassing a wide variety of therapeutic categories. Some 29 generics are extended-release drugs. UDL Laboratories is the largest U.S. repackager of pharmaceuticals in unit dose formats, which are used primarily in hospitals, nursing homes and similar settings. Mylan Technologies develops and markets products using transdermal drug delivery systems.

IMPACT OF MAJOR DEVELOPMENTS. In October 2007, Mylan acquired a

generic drug business from German drugmaker Merck KGaA (referred to as Merck Generics) that markets several hundred products. The operation has strong generics market exposure in France, Italy, the U.K., Japan, Canada and Australia. As part of this acquisition, MYL also acquired Dey, a producer of branded specialty respiratory and allergy drugs. Key Dey products are EpiPen, an auto-injector treatment for allergic reactions; and DuoNeb, a nebulized treatment for COPD.

In September 2010, MYL acquired Bioniche Pharma, an Ireland-based maker of injectable drugs, for some $544 million in cash. Mylan expected Bioniche to be EPS accretive within one year after the deal was completed.

Through its India-based Matrix Laboratories subsidiary, Mylan manufactures active pharmaceutical ingredients (APIs) for use in MYL products, as well as for third parties. Matrix ranks as one of the largest API producers in the world. Matrix also offers finished dose drugs and other products.

## Company Financials Fiscal Year Ended Dec. 31

| Per Share Data ($) | 2010 | 2009 | 2008 | 2007 | 2006 | 2005 | 2004 | 2003 | 2002 | 2001 |
|---|---|---|---|---|---|---|---|---|---|---|
| Tangible Book Value | NM | NM | NM | 2.75 | 2.76 | 6.03 | 5.30 | 4.39 | 3.97 | 2.97 |
| Cash Flow | 1.97 | 1.61 | 0.33 | 1.27 | 0.99 | 0.91 | 1.37 | 1.11 | 1.07 | 0.28 |
| Earnings | 0.68 | 0.30 | -1.05 | 0.99 | 0.79 | 0.74 | 1.21 | 0.97 | 0.91 | 0.13 |
| S&P Core Earnings | 0.93 | 0.75 | 0.25 | -4.50 | 0.78 | 0.64 | 1.05 | 0.89 | 0.84 | 0.40 |
| Dividends | Nil | Nil | Nil | 0.24 | 0.12 | 0.10 | 0.08 | 0.08 | 0.07 | 0.07 |
| Payout Ratio | Nil | Nil | Nil | 24% | 15% | 14% | 7% | 18% | 8% | 55% |
| Prices:High | 23.63 | 19.21 | 15.49 | 22.90 | 25.00 | 21.69 | 26.35 | 28.75 | 16.56 | 16.94 |
| Prices:Low | 16.55 | 9.65 | 5.75 | 12.93 | 18.65 | 15.21 | 14.24 | 15.56 | 11.15 | 8.96 |
| P/E Ratio:High | 35 | 64 | NM | 23 | 25 | 27 | 36 | 24 | 17 | 19 |
| P/E Ratio:Low | 24 | 32 | NM | 13 | 19 | 19 | 19 | 13 | 12 | 12 |

| Income Statement Analysis (Million $) | | | | | | | | | | |
|---|---|---|---|---|---|---|---|---|---|---|
| Revenue | 5,451 | 5,064 | 5,138 | 1,612 | 1,257 | 1,253 | 1,375 | 1,269 | 1,104 | 847 |
| Operating Income | 1,342 | 1,122 | 1,359 | 586 | 347 | 321 | 504 | 452 | 441 | 209 |
| Depreciation | 423 | 401 | 422 | 61.5 | 46.8 | 45.1 | 44.3 | 40.6 | 46.1 | 42.4 |
| Interest Expense | 331 | 319 | 357 | 52.3 | 31.3 | Nil | Nil | Nil | Nil | Nil |
| Pretax Income | 356 | 227 | -47.8 | 426 | 275 | 312 | 513 | 427 | 408 | 58.0 |
| Effective Tax Rate | NA | NM | NM | 48.9% | 32.8% | 34.8% | 34.7% | 36.1% | 36.3% | 36.0% |
| Net Income | 346 | 233 | -181 | 217 | 185 | 204 | 335 | 272 | 260 | 37.1 |
| S&P Core Earnings | 306 | 232 | 75.6 | -1,156 | 184 | 175 | 286 | 247 | 241 | 113 |

| Balance Sheet & Other Financial Data (Million $) | | | | | | | | | | |
|---|---|---|---|---|---|---|---|---|---|---|
| Cash | 691 | 408 | 599 | 1,427 | 518 | 808 | 687 | 687 | 617 | 285 |
| Current Assets | 3,559 | 3,285 | 3,175 | 2,412 | 1,192 | 1,528 | 1,318 | 1,228 | 1,062 | 879 |
| Total Assets | 11,537 | 10,802 | 10,410 | 4,254 | 1,871 | 2,136 | 1,875 | 1,745 | 1,617 | 1,466 |
| Current Liabilities | 1,810 | 1,718 | 1,545 | 701 | 265 | 246 | 174 | 266 | 175 | 291 |
| Long Term Debt | 5,263 | 4,985 | 5,165 | 1,655 | 685 | 19.3 | 19.1 | 19.9 | 21.9 | 23.3 |
| Common Equity | 3,602 | 3,131 | 2,704 | 1,649 | 4,242 | 2,786 | 2,600 | 1,446 | 1,607 | 1,133 |
| Total Capital | 8,892 | 8,130 | 8,443 | 3,390 | 4,948 | 2,830 | 2,642 | 1,479 | 1,646 | 1,175 |
| Capital Expenditures | 193 | 154 | 165 | 162 | 104 | 90.7 | 118 | 32.6 | 20.6 | 24.7 |
| Cash Flow | 647 | 495 | 101 | 279 | 231 | 249 | 379 | 313 | 306 | 79.5 |
| Current Ratio | 2.0 | 1.9 | 2.1 | 3.4 | 4.5 | 6.2 | 7.6 | 4.6 | 6.1 | 3.0 |
| % Long Term Debt of Capitalization | 59.2 | 61.3 | 61.2 | 48.8 | 13.8 | 0.7 | 0.7 | 1.3 | 1.3 | 2.0 |
| % Net Income of Revenue | 6.3 | 4.6 | NM | 13.5 | 14.7 | 16.2 | 24.3 | 21.5 | 23.6 | 4.4 |
| % Return on Assets | 3.1 | 2.2 | NM | 7.1 | 9.2 | 10.1 | 18.5 | 16.2 | 16.9 | 2.6 |
| % Return on Equity | 10.3 | 8.0 | NM | 17.8 | 5.3 | 7.6 | 14.1 | 19.1 | 17.7 | 3.2 |

Data as orig reptd.; bef. results of disc opers/spec. items. Per share data adj. for stk. divs.; EPS diluted. E-Estimated. NA-Not Available. NM-Not Meaningful. NR-Not Ranked. UR-Under Review.

**Office:** 1500 Corporate Dr, Canonsburg, PA 15317-8580.
**Telephone:** 724-514-1800.
**Email:** investor_relations@mylan.com
**Website:** http://www.mylan.com

**Chrmn & CEO:** R.J. Coury
**Pres:** H. Bresch
**Vice Chrmn:** R.L. Piatt
**COO & EVP:** R. Malik

**EVP & CFO:** J. Sheehan
**Investor Contact:** K. King (724-514-1800)
**Board Members:** H. Bresch, W. Cameron, R. J. Cindrich, R. J. Coury, N. Dimick, D. J. Leech, Jr., J. Maroon, M. W. Parrish, R. L. Piatt, C. B. Todd, R. L. Vanderveen

**Founded:** 1970
**Domicile:** Pennsylvania
**Employees:** 13,000

# Nabors Industries Ltd

| S&P Recommendation | HOLD ★★★☆☆ | Price $15.98 (as of Nov 25, 2011) | 12-Mo. Target Price $18.00 | Investment Style Large-Cap Growth |
|---|---|---|---|---|

**GICS Sector** Energy
**Sub-Industry** Oil & Gas Drilling

**Summary** This Bermuda company is the world's largest oil and gas land drilling contractor.

## Key Stock Statistics (Source S&P, Vickers, company reports)

| | | | | | | | |
|---|---|---|---|---|---|---|---|
| 52-Wk Range | $32.47–11.05 | S&P Oper. EPS 2011**E** | 1.43 | Market Capitalization(B) | $4.595 | Beta | 1.73 |
| Trailing 12-Month EPS | $1.38 | S&P Oper. EPS 2012**E** | 2.02 | Yield (%) | Nil | S&P 3-Yr. Proj. EPS CAGR(%) | 16 |
| Trailing 12-Month P/E | 11.6 | P/E on S&P Oper. EPS 2011**E** | 11.2 | Dividend Rate/Share | Nil | S&P Credit Rating | A- |
| $10K Invested 5 Yrs Ago | $4,888 | Common Shares Outstg. (M) | 287.6 | Institutional Ownership (%) | 84 | | |

## Price Performance

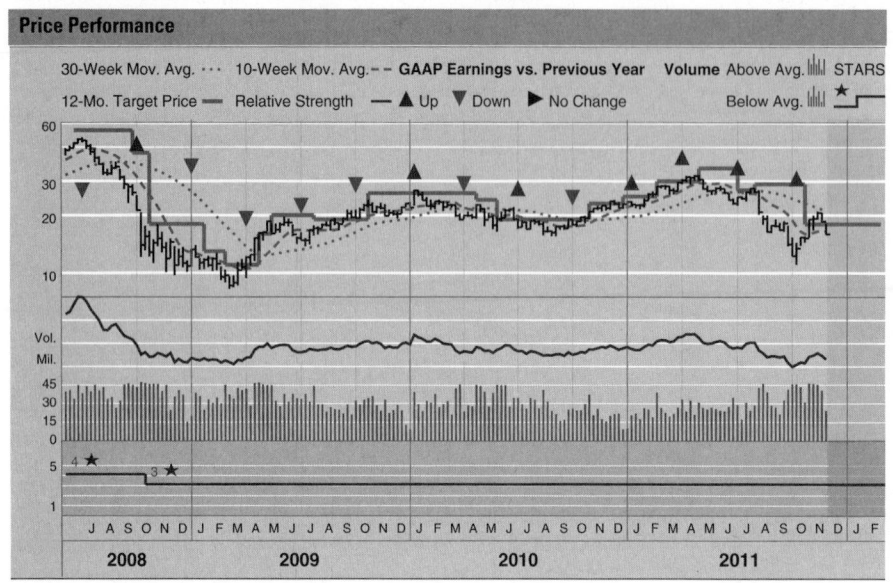

30-Week Mov. Avg. · · · 10-Week Mov. Avg. – – **GAAP Earnings vs. Previous Year**  Volume Above Avg. ▮▮▮ STARS
12-Mo. Target Price — Relative Strength — ▲ Up ▼ Down ▶ No Change   Below Avg. ▮▮▮ ★

Options: ASE, CBOE, P, Ph

Analysis prepared by Equity Analyst **Tanjila Shafi** on Oct 21, 2011, when the stock traded at **$15.21**.

## Highlights

➤ Second quarter cash margins in the U.S. Lower 48 segment rose $2,413 per day to $10,201, with an average of 194 working rigs versus 172 rigs the year before. NBR secured seven newbuild rig contracts during the quarter, bringing the newbuild backlog to 36. The company expects that 68% of its operating cash flow from its U.S. Lower 48 unit will be derived from oil and liquids-directed drilling in 2011, versus 15% in 2006. We see utilization of 56% in 2011, up from 54% in 2010.

➤ The well servicing segment is seeing a pickup in utilization and dayrates. We expect the acquired Superior Well Services pressure pumping operations will provide a lift to results this year. We have a cautious view on NBR's international segment for 2011 as it has been impacted by contract delays. However, we believe the contract delays will be resolved and revenues at its international segment will improve in 2012.

➤ We see 2011 EPS of $1.42, versus 2010's $0.37. We expect capital expenditures this year of between $1.3 billion and $1.7 billion.

## Investment Rationale/Risk

➤ North American onshore drilling has faced challenges due to capacity additions, spending cutbacks and an overall decline in natural gas drilling activity. While we view NBR as somewhat protected by long-term contracts, an emphasis on larger operators, segment diversification and a modern fleet, we expect volatility in the sector as rig counts remain below 2008 levels. In our view, NBR has strong drilling prospects in unconventional plays, given its technology advantages and newbuild program. We are positive on the outlook of acquired pressure pumping businesses.

➤ Risks to our opinion and target price include reduced oil and gas prices and dayrates, delays in rig deliveries, and cost inflation.

➤ Our 12-month target price of $18 is based on a blend 3.0X projected FY 11 EBITDA and 13X estimated FY 11 EPS, below land drilling averages, which reflects what we see as delays in contract rewards at the company's international business.

## Qualitative Risk Assessment

| LOW | MEDIUM | HIGH |
|---|---|---|

Our risk assessment reflects NBR's sensitivity to commodity prices, capital spending by oil and gas producers, and the growing U.S. rig supply. Partly offsetting these risks is NBR's diversified fleet, including overseas operations, and its leadership position in the industry.

## Quantitative Evaluations

**S&P Quality Ranking**      NR

| D | C | B- | B | B+ | A- | A | A+ |
|---|---|---|---|---|---|---|---|

**Relative Strength Rank**     WEAK

29

LOWEST = 1          HIGHEST = 99

## Revenue/Earnings Data

**Revenue (Million $)**

| | 1Q | 2Q | 3Q | 4Q | Year |
|---|---|---|---|---|---|
| 2011 | 1,381 | 1,355 | 1,625 | -- | -- |
| 2010 | 902.1 | 905.1 | 1,069 | 1,318 | 4,175 |
| 2009 | 1,143 | 867.9 | 791.9 | 834.5 | 3,692 |
| 2008 | 1,322 | 1,282 | 1,455 | 1,475 | 5,512 |
| 2007 | 1,277 | 1,128 | 1,226 | 1,309 | 4,941 |
| 2006 | 1,164 | 1,144 | 1,244 | 1,329 | 4,943 |

**Earnings Per Share ($)**

| | | | | | |
|---|---|---|---|---|---|
| 2011 | 0.29 | 0.23 | 0.28 | E0.48 | E1.43 |
| 2010 | 0.14 | 0.15 | -0.11 | 0.17 | 0.37 |
| 2009 | 0.44 | -0.68 | 0.10 | -0.17 | -0.30 |
| 2008 | 0.81 | 0.67 | 0.73 | -0.30 | 1.93 |
| 2007 | 0.92 | 0.79 | 0.68 | 0.78 | 3.13 |
| 2006 | 0.79 | 0.77 | 1.02 | 0.97 | 3.40 |

Fiscal year ended Dec. 31. Next earnings report expected: Mid February. EPS Estimates based on S&P Operating Earnings; historical GAAP earnings are as reported.

## Dividend Data

No cash dividends have been paid.

# Nabors Industries Ltd

**STANDARD &POOR'S**

## Business Summary October 21, 2011

CORPORATE OVERVIEW. The world's largest land drilling contractor, Nabors Industries Ltd. owns a fleet of about 550 land drilling rigs. Formed as a Bermuda-exempt company in December 2001, but operating continuously in the drilling sector since the early 1900s, Nabors conducts oil, gas and geothermal land drilling operations in the lower 48 U.S. states, Alaska and Canada, and internationally, mainly in South and Central America, the Middle East and Africa. NBR actively markets 550 land drilling rigs and 555 land workover and well servicing rigs in the U.S. and approximately 172 rigs in Canada. In addition, it markets 37 platform, 13 jackup and three barge rigs in the Gulf of Mexico and international markets; these rigs provide well servicing, workover and drilling services. NBR also has a 51% ownership interest in a joint venture in Saudi Arabia, which actively markets nine rigs.

The contract drilling segment (91% of 2010 revenues) provides drilling, workover, well servicing and related services in the U.S. (including the Lower 48, Alaska and offshore), Canada, and internationally. During 2010, 30% of contract drilling revenues served customers in the Lower 48, either for land drilling or land well servicing. Well servicing and workover services are provided for existing wells where some form of artificial lift is required to bring oil to the surface. To supplement its primary business, NBR offers ancillary wellsite services, such as oilfield management, engineering, transportation, construction, maintenance, and well logging.

NBR's contract drilling business is dependent on the level of capital spending by oil and gas exploration and production companies. The decline in oil and gas prices in late 2008 led to a sharp drop in drilling activity during 2009, sending rig utilization levels and dayrates plunging. We estimate NBR's U.S. onshore rig utilization averaged 46% in 2009, versus 79% in 2008, and dayrates declined about 10%, less pronounced than the industry given NBR's contract coverage. We estimate rig utilization of 54% in 2010, increasing to 64% in 2011 as drilling activity improves. Internationally, NBR's business has grown significantly in the past decade. In 2010, the company derived 25% of its revenues from its international land drilling segment, versus 30% for its U.S. land drilling segment. We see better 2011 results at U.S. land drilling, offset by a decline in international activity, most notably in Saudi Arabia and Mexico. International markets are seeing a shift in focus to natural gas, the opposite of the domestic environment, causing significant downtime and lagging results.

## Company Financials Fiscal Year Ended Dec. 31

| Per Share Data ($) | 2010 | 2009 | 2008 | 2007 | 2006 | 2005 | 2004 | 2003 | 2002 | 2001 |
|---|---|---|---|---|---|---|---|---|---|---|
| Tangible Book Value | NA | NA | 15.96 | 14.84 | 11.46 | 10.83 | 8.68 | 7.35 | 6.39 | 5.89 |
| Cash Flow | NA | NA | 4.24 | 5.01 | 4.77 | 3.04 | 1.84 | 1.36 | 1.06 | 1.59 |
| Earnings | 0.37 | -0.30 | 1.93 | 3.13 | 3.40 | 2.00 | 0.96 | 0.63 | 0.41 | 1.09 |
| Dividends | NA | Nil | Nil | Nil | Nil | Nil | Nil | Nil | Nil | Nil |
| Payout Ratio | NA | Nil | Nil | Nil | Nil | Nil | Nil | Nil | Nil | Nil |
| Prices:High | 27.05 | 24.07 | 50.58 | 36.42 | 41.35 | 39.94 | 27.13 | 22.93 | 24.99 | 31.56 |
| Prices:Low | 15.54 | 8.25 | 9.72 | 26.00 | 27.26 | 23.10 | 20.01 | 16.10 | 13.07 | 9.00 |
| P/E Ratio:High | 73 | NM | 26 | 12 | 12 | 20 | 28 | 37 | 62 | 29 |
| P/E Ratio:Low | 42 | NM | 5 | 8 | 8 | 12 | 21 | 26 | 32 | 8 |

| Income Statement Analysis (Million $) | | | | | | | | | | |
|---|---|---|---|---|---|---|---|---|---|---|
| Revenue | 4,175 | 3,692 | 5,512 | 4,941 | 4,943 | 3,551 | 2,394 | 1,880 | 1,466 | 2,121 |
| Operating Income | NA | NA | 1,264 | 1,750 | 1,952 | 1,304 | 626 | 438 | 351 | 0.69 |
| Depreciation, Depletion and Amortization | 986 | 736 | 658 | 540 | 409 | 339 | 300 | 235 | 195 | 190 |
| Interest Expense | 274 | 265 | 91.6 | 63.6 | 46.6 | 44.8 | 48.5 | 70.7 | 67.1 | 60.7 |
| Pretax Income | 81.3 | -235 | 802 | 1,135 | 1,471 | 874 | 336 | 175 | 141 | 542 |
| Effective Tax Rate | NA | 63.5% | 31.2% | 21.1% | 30.6% | 25.8% | 9.94% | NM | 13.7% | 35.9% |
| Net Income | 106 | -85.6 | 551 | 896 | 1,021 | 649 | 302 | 192 | 121 | 348 |

| Balance Sheet & Other Financial Data (Million $) | | | | | | | | | | |
|---|---|---|---|---|---|---|---|---|---|---|
| Cash | 801 | 1,091 | 584 | 767 | 701 | 565 | 1,253 | 1,532 | 1,331 | 919 |
| Current Assets | NA | NA | 2,167 | 2,205 | 2,505 | 2,617 | 1,581 | 1,516 | 1,370 | 1,031 |
| Total Assets | 11,647 | 10,664 | 10,468 | 10,103 | 9,142 | 7,230 | 5,863 | 5,603 | 5,064 | 4,152 |
| Current Liabilities | NA | NA | 1,129 | 1,494 | 854 | 1,352 | 1,199 | 598 | 751 | 330 |
| Long Term Debt | 3,064 | 3,941 | 3,888 | 3,306 | 4,004 | 1,252 | 1,202 | 1,986 | 1,615 | 1,568 |
| Common Equity | 5,328 | 5,168 | 4,692 | 4,514 | 3,537 | 3,758 | 2,929 | 2,490 | 2,158 | 1,858 |
| Total Capital | NA | NA | 9,339 | 8,363 | 8,125 | 5,727 | 4,517 | 4,849 | 4,175 | 3,711 |
| Capital Expenditures | 930 | 1,093 | 1,490 | 2,014 | 1,927 | 907 | 544 | 353 | 317 | 701 |
| Cash Flow | NA | NA | 1,209 | 1,436 | 1,430 | 987 | 603 | 427 | 317 | 538 |
| Current Ratio | 1.2 | 3.6 | 1.9 | 1.5 | 2.9 | 1.9 | 1.3 | 2.5 | 1.8 | 3.1 |
| % Long Term Debt of Capitalization | 31.1 | 43.3 | 41.6 | 39.5 | 49.3 | 21.9 | 26.6 | 41.0 | 38.7 | 42.2 |
| % Return on Assets | NA | NA | 5.4 | 9.3 | 12.5 | 9.9 | 5.3 | 3.6 | 2.6 | 9.5 |
| % Return on Equity | 2.0 | NM | 12.0 | 22.3 | 28.0 | 19.4 | 11.2 | 8.3 | 6.0 | 19.0 |

Data as orig reptd.; bef. results of disc opers/spec. items. Per share data adj. for stk. divs.; EPS diluted. E-Estimated. NA-Not Available. NM-Not Meaningful. NR-Not Ranked. UR-Under Review.

**Office:** Crown House, Second Floor, 4 Par-la-Ville Road, Hamilton, Bermuda HM 08.
**Telephone:** 441-292-1510.
**Website:** http://www.nabors.com
**Chrmn:** E.M. Isenberg

**Pres, Vice Chrmn & CEO:** A.G. Petrello
**CFO, Chief Acctg Officer & Cntlr:** R.C. Wood
**Secy:** M.D. Andrews
**Investor Contact:** D.A. Smith (281-775-8038)

**Auditor:** PRICEWATERHOUSECOOPERS
**Board Members:** W. T. Comfort, III, E. M. Isenberg, J. V. Lombardi, J. L. Payne, A. G. Petrello, M. M. Sheinfeld, J. Yearwood

**Founded:** 1968
**Domicile:** Bermuda
**Employees:** 20,520

The **McGraw-Hill** Companies

# Nasdaq OMX Group Inc (The)

**STANDARD &POOR'S**

| S&P Recommendation **HOLD** ★★★★☆ | Price $24.55 (as of Nov 25, 2011) | 12-Mo. Target Price $28.00 | Investment Style Large-Cap Blend |
|---|---|---|---|

**GICS Sector** Financials
**Sub-Industry** Specialized Finance

**Summary** This leading global exchange group delivers trading, exchange technology, securities listing and public company services across six continents.

## Key Stock Statistics (Source S&P, Vickers, company reports)

| | | | | | | | | |
|---|---|---|---|---|---|---|---|---|
| 52-Wk Range | $29.71–20.32 | S&P Oper. EPS 2011**E** | 2.54 | Market Capitalization(B) | $4.350 | Beta | | 0.95 |
| Trailing 12-Month EPS | $2.40 | S&P Oper. EPS 2012**E** | 2.85 | Yield (%) | Nil | S&P 3-Yr. Proj. EPS CAGR(%) | | 12 |
| Trailing 12-Month P/E | 10.2 | P/E on S&P Oper. EPS 2011**E** | 9.7 | Dividend Rate/Share | Nil | S&P Credit Rating | | BBB |
| $10K Invested 5 Yrs Ago | $6,042 | Common Shares Outstg. (M) | 177.2 | Institutional Ownership (%) | 77 | | | |

## Price Performance

30-Week Mov. Avg. · · · 10-Week Mov. Avg. – – **GAAP Earnings vs. Previous Year**   Volume Above Avg. ▮▮▮ STARS
12-Mo. Target Price — Relative Strength — ▲ Up ▼ Down ► No Change    Below Avg. ▮▮▮ ★

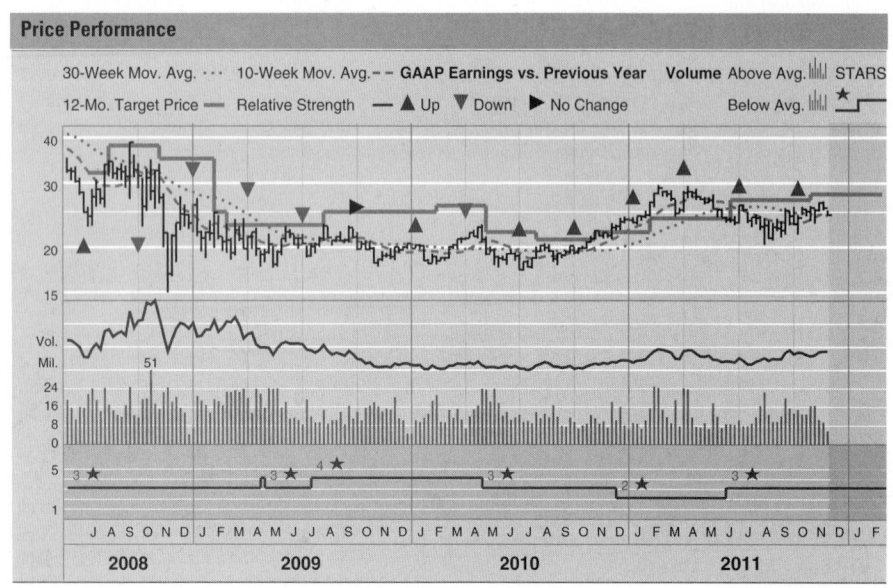

Options: ASE, CBOE, P, Ph

Analysis prepared by Equity Analyst **Robert McMillan** on Oct 28, 2011, when the stock traded at **$25.76**.

## Highlights

▶ Results for NDAQ can be particularly volatile, as its revenues are based on trading volumes of equities and derivatives. NDAQ's total matched share volume (in the U.S. cash equities segment) was 125 billion shares in the third quarter of 2011, compared with 99.7 billion shares in the second quarter of 2011 and 107.8 billion shares in the third quarter of 2010. Total average daily volume rose in its smaller European business versus last year.

▶ After a 5% increase in 2010, we expect total net revenues (excluding rebates and certain fees) to advance about 14% in 2011, reflecting our expectation for higher sales in the Market Services segment, aided principally by contributions from the U.S. derivatives businesses and the European businesses. We expect revenues to increase 9% in 2012 as market volatility subsides and trading patterns begin to normalize. While we expect trading volumes to stabilize, we look for continued pricing pressure. We believe the company's Market Technology and Issuer Services segments will experience growth.

▶ Our operating EPS estimates are $2.54 for 2011 and $2.85 for 2012.

## Investment Rationale/Risk

▶ In May 2011, following discussions with U.S. regulators, Nasdaq OMX and IntercontinentalExchange (ICE 130, Buy) withdrew their approximately $11.0 billion acquisition bid for NYSE Euronext (NYX 27, Hold). We are concerned about execution risk, given the large number of new initiatives the company began during 2011. However, we believe NDAQ has made solid progress in integrating its recent acquisitions and establishing new opportunities such as interest rate swap clearing. We also see a return to volume growth in 2011, reflecting our view of an improving economy.

▶ Risks to our recommendation and target price include a decrease in pricing, increasing government regulation, more time than expected to complete new initiatives, and a substantial drop in equity trading volumes.

▶ The shares recently traded at about 10X trailing 12-months EPS. Our 12-month target price of $28 reflects a P/E ratio of 10.5X our forward four quarter EPS forecast of $2.70. We believe this multiple, slightly above recent historical levels, is warranted, given our outlook for a gradually improving economy and improvements in NDAQ's business.

## Qualitative Risk Assessment

| LOW | **MEDIUM** | HIGH |
|---|---|---|

Our risk assessment reflects the potential volatility in results due to changes in equity trading volumes, the potential impact of future regulatory changes, and the uncertainty surrounding NDAQ's international strategy, offset by the company's strong market position.

## Quantitative Evaluations

**S&P Quality Ranking**                    NR

| D | C | B- | B | B+ | A- | A | A+ |
|---|---|---|---|---|---|---|---|

**Relative Strength Rank**                **STRONG**

LOWEST = 1            73            HIGHEST = 99

## Revenue/Earnings Data

### Revenue (Million $)

| | 1Q | 2Q | 3Q | 4Q | Year |
|---|---|---|---|---|---|
| 2011 | 817.0 | 838.0 | 946.0 | -- | -- |
| 2010 | 771.0 | 886.0 | 758.0 | 783.0 | 3,197 |
| 2009 | 895.0 | 889.0 | 810.0 | 815.0 | 3,409 |
| 2008 | 813.8 | 821.5 | 990.3 | 1,024 | 3,649 |
| 2007 | 562.0 | 558.2 | 652.0 | 664.5 | 2,437 |
| 2006 | 396.2 | 411.0 | 402.9 | 447.2 | 1,658 |

### Earnings Per Share ($)

| | | | | | |
|---|---|---|---|---|---|
| 2011 | 0.57 | 0.51 | 0.61 | E0.70 | E2.54 |
| 2010 | 0.28 | 0.46 | 0.50 | 0.69 | 1.91 |
| 2009 | 0.44 | 0.33 | 0.28 | 0.20 | 1.25 |
| 2008 | 0.69 | 0.48 | 0.28 | 0.17 | 1.56 |
| 2007 | 0.14 | 0.39 | 2.41 | 0.57 | 3.46 |
| 2006 | 0.16 | 0.13 | 0.22 | 0.43 | 0.95 |

Fiscal year ended Dec. 31. Next earnings report expected: Early February. EPS Estimates based on S&P Operating Earnings; historical GAAP earnings are as reported.

## Dividend Data

No cash dividends have been paid.

---

**Please read the Required Disclosures and Analyst Certification on the last page of this report.**

**The McGraw-Hill Companies**

# Nasdaq OMX Group Inc (The)

STANDARD
&POOR'S

## Business Summary October 28, 2011

The NASDAQ OMX Group, Inc. (NDAQ), a global exchange group, provides trading, exchange technology, securities listing and public company services. It was formerly known as The Nasdaq Stock Market, Inc. and changed its name to The NASDAQ OMX Group, Inc. in 2008. NDAQ operates in three segments: Market Services, Issuer Services, and Market Technology.

The Market Services segment includes its U.S. and European Transaction Services businesses, as well as its Market Data and Broker Services businesses. The company offers trading on multiple exchanges and facilities across various asset classes, including equities, derivatives, debt, commodities, structured products, and ETFs. The company's global offerings include trading across multiple asset classes, market data products, financial indexes, capital formation solutions, financial services, and market technology products and services. Its technology supports markets across the globe, supporting cash equity trading, derivatives trading, clearing and settlement, and various other functions. In the U.S., the company operates The NASDAQ Stock Market, a registered national securities exchange. In Europe, the company operates exchanges in Stockholm (Sweden), Copenhagen (Denmark),

Helsinki (Finland), and Iceland as NASDAQ OMX Nordic and exchanges in Tallinn (Estonia), Riga (Latvia) and Vilnius (Lithuania) as NASDAQ OMX Baltic. In addition, NDAQ operates NASDAQ OMX Europe, a marketplace for pan-European blue chip trading based in the United Kingdom, NASDAQ OMX Commodities, an offering for trading and clearing commodities based in Norway, and NASDAQ OMX Armenia. It also provides clearing, settlement and depository services. Collectively, the exchanges that comprise NASDAQ OMX Nordic and NASDAQ OMX Baltic offer trading in cash equities, bonds, structured products and exchange traded funds (ETFs), as well as trading and clearing of derivatives. The company's Nordic and Baltic operations also offer alternative marketplaces for smaller companies called NASDAQ OMX First North.

## Company Financials Fiscal Year Ended Dec. 31

| Per Share Data ($) | 2010 | 2009 | 2008 | 2007 | 2006 | 2005 | 2004 | 2003 | 2002 | 2001 |
|---|---|---|---|---|---|---|---|---|---|---|
| Tangible Book Value | NM | NM | NM | 7.54 | 2.44 | NM | NM | 2.04 | NA | NA |
| Cash Flow | 2.38 | 1.72 | 2.02 | 3.65 | 1.20 | 1.08 | 0.99 | 0.57 | 1.56 | 1.15 |
| Earnings | 1.91 | 1.25 | 1.56 | 3.46 | 0.95 | 0.57 | -0.14 | -0.68 | 0.40 | 0.35 |
| S&P Core Earnings | 1.94 | 1.55 | 1.75 | 1.62 | 0.96 | 0.53 | -0.19 | -0.69 | 0.31 | 0.21 |
| Dividends | Nil | Nil | Nil | Nil | Nil | Nil | Nil | Nil | NA | NA |
| Payout Ratio | Nil | Nil | Nil | Nil | Nil | Nil | Nil | Nil | NA | NA |
| Prices:High | 24.34 | 27.39 | 49.90 | 50.47 | 46.75 | 45.23 | NA | NA | NA | NA |
| Prices:Low | 17.18 | 17.51 | 14.96 | 26.57 | 23.91 | 8.15 | NA | NA | NA | NA |
| P/E Ratio:High | 13 | 22 | 32 | 15 | 49 | 79 | NM | NA | NA | NA |
| P/E Ratio:Low | 9 | 14 | 10 | 8 | 25 | 14 | NM | NA | NA | NA |

### Income Statement Analysis (Million $)

| | 2010 | 2009 | 2008 | 2007 | 2006 | 2005 | 2004 | 2003 | 2002 | 2001 |
|---|---|---|---|---|---|---|---|---|---|---|
| Revenue | 3,197 | 3,409 | 3,649 | 2,437 | 1,658 | 880 | 540 | 590 | 799 | 857 |
| Operating Income | 770 | 766 | 758 | 440 | 288 | 181 | 85.0 | 126 | 197 | 207 |
| Depreciation | 103 | 104 | 92.6 | 38.9 | 45.1 | 67.0 | 76.0 | 90.0 | 97.9 | 93.4 |
| Interest Expense | 102 | 102 | 86.6 | 72.9 | 91.1 | 20.0 | 11.0 | 19.0 | 19.6 | 9.65 |
| Pretax Income | 526 | 391 | 524 | 794 | 212 | 106 | 2.60 | -66.0 | 71.7 | 73.1 |
| Effective Tax Rate | NA | 32.7% | 38.6% | 34.7% | 40.2% | 41.8% | 29.3% | NM | 57.3% | 52.4% |
| Net Income | 389 | 266 | 320 | 518 | 128 | 62.0 | 1.80 | -45.0 | 43.1 | 40.5 |
| S&P Core Earnings | 401 | 330 | 355 | 238 | 129 | 50.5 | -15.2 | -54.1 | 26.4 | 24.7 |

### Balance Sheet & Other Financial Data (Million $)

| | 2010 | 2009 | 2008 | 2007 | 2006 | 2005 | 2004 | 2003 | 2002 | 2001 |
|---|---|---|---|---|---|---|---|---|---|---|
| Cash | 568 | 902 | 793 | 1,325 | 1,950 | 165 | 58.0 | 149 | 445 | 522 |
| Current Assets | 8,510 | 3,454 | 5,435 | 1,682 | 2,313 | 597 | 406 | 530 | 697 | 815 |
| Total Assets | 16,207 | 10,722 | 12,695 | 2,979 | 3,716 | 2,047 | 815 | 851 | 1,176 | 1,326 |
| Current Liabilities | 8,231 | 2,867 | 5,061 | 411 | 461 | 325 | 208 | 238 | 295 | 294 |
| Long Term Debt | 2,181 | 1,867 | 2,294 | 118 | 1,493 | 1,185 | 265 | 265 | 430 | 289 |
| Common Equity | 4,718 | 4,927 | 4,242 | 2,208 | 1,457 | 253 | 157 | 27.0 | 137 | 518 |
| Total Capital | 7,061 | 7,051 | 7,224 | 2,419 | 3,066 | 1,533 | 452 | 467 | 705 | 812 |
| Capital Expenditures | 42.0 | 59.0 | 54.7 | 18.5 | 21.0 | 25.0 | 26.0 | 32.0 | 85.4 | 123 |
| Cash Flow | 492 | 370 | 412 | 557 | 172 | 129 | 77.8 | 45.0 | 131 | 134 |
| Current Ratio | 1.0 | 1.2 | 1.1 | 4.1 | 5.0 | 1.8 | 2.0 | 2.2 | 2.4 | 2.8 |
| % Long Term Debt of Capitalization | 30.9 | 26.5 | 31.8 | 4.9 | 50.6 | 77.2 | 58.6 | 56.7 | 60.9 | 35.5 |
| % Net Income of Revenue | 12.2 | 7.8 | 8.8 | 21.3 | 7.7 | 7.0 | 0.0 | NM | 5.4 | 4.7 |
| % Return on Assets | 2.9 | 2.3 | 4.1 | 15.5 | 4.4 | 4.3 | 0.0 | NM | 3.5 | 3.4 |
| % Return on Equity | 8.1 | 5.8 | 9.9 | 28.3 | 15.8 | 30.2 | 6.7 | NM | 13.2 | 6.3 |

Data as orig reptd.; bef. results of disc opers/spec. items. Per share data adj. for stk. divs.; EPS diluted. E-Estimated. NA-Not Available. NM-Not Meaningful. NR-Not Ranked. UR-Under Review.

**Office:** One Liberty Plaza, 165 Broadway, New York, NY 10006.
**Telephone:** 212-401-8700.
**Website:** http://www.nasdaq.com
**Chrmn:** H.F. Baldwin

**Vice Chrmn:** U. Backstrom
**CEO:** R. Greifeld
**EVP & CFO:** L. Shavel
**EVP & General Counsel:** E. Knight

**Investor Contact:** V. Palmiere (212-401-8742)
**Board Members:** U. Backstrom, H. F. Baldwin, M. Casey, B. Ekholm, L. Gorman, R. Greifeld, G. H. Hutchins, B. Kantola, E. Kazim, J. D. Markese, H. M. Nielsen, T. F. O'Neill, J. S. Riepe, M. R. Splinter, L. Wedenborn, D. L. Wince-Smith

**Founded:** 1979
**Domicile:** Delaware
**Employees:** 2,395

# National Oilwell Varco Inc

**STANDARD &POOR'S**

**S&P Recommendation** BUY ★★★★☆

| | |
|---|---|
| **Price** | $64.52 (as of Nov 25, 2011) |
| **12-Mo. Target Price** | $97.00 |
| **Investment Style** | Large-Cap Growth |

**GICS Sector** Energy
**Sub-Industry** Oil & Gas Equipment & Services

**Summary** This company designs and manufactures drill rig equipment, provides downhole tools and services, and also provides supply chain integration services to the upstream oil and gas industry.

## Key Stock Statistics (Source S&P, Vickers, company reports)

| | | | | | | | |
|---|---|---|---|---|---|---|---|
| 52-Wk Range | $86.71– 47.97 | S&P Oper. EPS 2011E | 4.28 | Market Capitalization(B) | $27.346 | Beta | 1.54 |
| Trailing 12-Month EPS | $4.40 | S&P Oper. EPS 2012E | 5.62 | Yield (%) | 0.74 | S&P 3-Yr. Proj. EPS CAGR(%) | 17 |
| Trailing 12-Month P/E | 14.7 | P/E on S&P Oper. EPS 2011E | 15.1 | Dividend Rate/Share | $0.48 | S&P Credit Rating | A- |
| $10K Invested 5 Yrs Ago | $21,651 | Common Shares Outstg. (M) | 423.8 | Institutional Ownership (%) | 88 | | |

## Price Performance

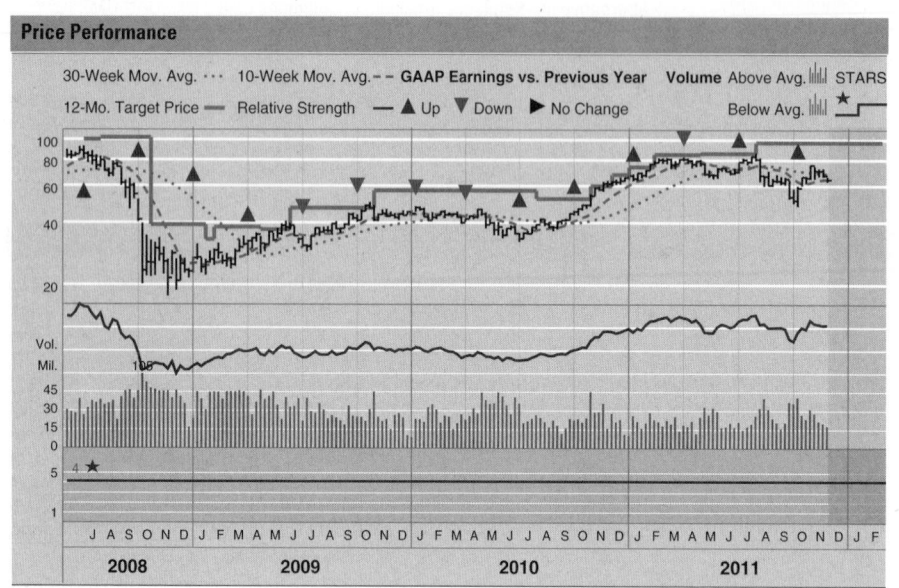

30-Week Mov. Avg. · · · 10-Week Mov. Avg. – – 12-Mo. Target Price — Relative Strength — GAAP Earnings vs. Previous Year ▲ Up ▼ Down ► No Change Volume Above Avg. Below Avg. STARS

Options: ASE, CBOE, P

Analysis prepared by Equity Analyst **S. Glickman, CFA** on Aug 15, 2011, when the stock traded at **$66.78**.

## Highlights

► At the end of June, total backlog was $7.7 billion, versus $5.0 billion at year end, after second quarter orders of $3.0 billion were well ahead of revenues out of backlog of $1.4 billion. Given the amount of work slated to be done in key markets such as Brazil, and NOV's key role in the oilfield capital equipment market, we think orders and thus backlog recovery will continue to grow, at least in the near term. We also believe that the growing bifurcation in the jackup market (between high-spec units and legacy units) will result in a revitalization of newbuild jackup demand. We project NOV to exit 2011 with a backlog of about $9.1 billion.

► With the rise of U.S. shale plays, which yield high service intensity, we see improved 2011 revenues in the Petroleum Services & Supplies segment. We expect cannibalization of oilfield equipment from idled rigs to drop off in 2011, and note that both shale plays and deepwater wells tend to require premium equipment, such as drill pipe, which NOV offers.

► We see revenues up 13% in 2011 and 20% in 2012. We expect EPS of $4.28 in 2011, rising to $5.62 in 2012.

## Investment Rationale/Risk

► We view NOV as an attractive play on the need for new rig equipment, particularly for deepwater and unconventional natural gas projects. While the current book of 149 rigs under construction implies about a 22% addition to the existing marketed fleet, we think that currently unsatisfied demand (especially for deepwater-capable equipment) will absorb most new additions. We also see potential regulatory changes to U.S. Gulf of Mexico deepwater drilling that may require new equipment.

► Risks to our opinion and target price include lower-than-expected prices for crude oil and natural gas; a slowdown in drilling activity; delays in meeting capital equipment orders; and unexpected contract cancellations.

► Our discounted cash flow (DCF) model, assuming free cash flow growth of 15% and terminal growth of 3%, yields intrinsic value of $104. Applying peer average multiples of 10X enterprise value to projected 2012 EBITDA and 12X estimated 2012 cash flow, and factoring in our DCF model, our 12-month target price is $97.

## Qualitative Risk Assessment

| LOW | MEDIUM | HIGH |
|---|---|---|

Our risk assessment reflects NOV's exposure to volatile crude oil and natural gas prices, and capital spending decisions made by its contract driller and exploration and production customers. Offsetting these risks is what we view as NOV's leading industry position as a manufacturer of rig capital equipment.

## Quantitative Evaluations

**S&P Quality Ranking**  B+

| D | C | B- | B | B+ | A- | A | A+ |
|---|---|---|---|---|---|---|---|

**Relative Strength Rank**  MODERATE

63

LOWEST = 1   HIGHEST = 99

## Revenue/Earnings Data

**Revenue (Million $)**

| | 1Q | 2Q | 3Q | 4Q | Year |
|---|---|---|---|---|---|
| 2011 | 3,146 | 3,513 | 3,740 | -- | -- |
| 2010 | 3,032 | 2,941 | 3,011 | 3,172 | 12,156 |
| 2009 | 3,481 | 3,010 | 3,087 | 3,134 | 12,712 |
| 2008 | 2,685 | 3,324 | 3,612 | 3,810 | 13,431 |
| 2007 | 2,166 | 2,385 | 2,580 | 2,659 | 9,789 |
| 2006 | 1,512 | 1,657 | 1,778 | 2,079 | 7,026 |

**Earnings Per Share ($)**

| | | | | | |
|---|---|---|---|---|---|
| 2011 | 0.96 | 1.13 | 1.25 | E1.11 | E4.28 |
| 2010 | 1.01 | 0.96 | 0.96 | 1.05 | 3.98 |
| 2009 | 1.13 | 0.53 | 0.92 | 0.94 | 3.52 |
| 2008 | 1.11 | 1.04 | 1.31 | 1.40 | 4.90 |
| 2007 | 0.78 | 0.90 | 1.02 | 1.05 | 3.76 |
| 2006 | 0.34 | 0.42 | 0.50 | 0.68 | 1.94 |

Fiscal year ended Dec. 31. Next earnings report expected: Early February. EPS Estimates based on S&P Operating Earnings; historical GAAP earnings are as reported.

## Dividend Data (Dates: mm/dd Payment Date: mm/dd/yy)

| Amount ($) | Date Decl. | Ex-Div. Date | Stk. of Record | Payment Date |
|---|---|---|---|---|
| 0.110 | 02/23 | 03/09 | 03/11 | 03/25/11 |
| 0.110 | 05/12 | 06/08 | 06/10 | 06/24/11 |
| 0.110 | 08/18 | 09/07 | 09/09 | 09/23/11 |
| 0.120 | 11/17 | 11/30 | 12/02 | 12/16/11 |

Dividends have been paid since 2009. Source: Company reports.

Stock Report | November 26, 2011 | NYS Symbol: **NOV**

# National Oilwell Varco Inc

**&POOR'S**

## Business Summary August 15, 2011

CORPORATE OVERVIEW. Formerly known as National-Oilwell, this company changed its name to National Oilwell Varco (NOV) on March 14, 2005, following the completion of the merger with Varco International. NOV, a worldwide designer, manufacturer and marketer of comprehensive systems and components used in oil and gas drilling and production, as well as a provider of downhole tools and services, also provides supply chain integration services to the upstream oil and gas industry. The company estimates that more than 90% of the mobile offshore rig fleet and the majority of the world's larger land rigs (2,000 horsepower and greater) manufactured in the past 20 years use drawworks, mud pumps and other drilling components manufactured by NOV.

The company generated 2010 revenues of about $12.2 billion and operating income of $2.4 billion, for an operating margin of approximately 20.1%, up 190 basis points from 2009. Its Rig Technology segment ($7.0 billion of revenue in 2010 and $2.1 billion of segment operating income) designs, manufactures and sells drilling systems and components for both land and offshore drilling rigs, as well as complete land drilling and well servicing rigs. The major mechanical components include drawworks, mud pumps, power swivels, SCR houses,

solids control equipment, traveling equipment and rotary tables. Many of these components are designed specifically for applications in offshore, extended reach and deep land drilling. This equipment is installed on new rigs and is often replaced during the upgrade and refurbishment of existing rigs. As of December 31, 2010, total backlog in this segment was about $5.0 billion, down $1.4 billion from a year earlier.

The Petroleum Services & Supplies segment ($4.2 billion, $585 million) provides a variety of consumable goods and services used in the drilling, completion, workover and remediation of oil and gas wells, service pipelines, flowlines, and other oilfield tubular goods. Products include transfer pumps, solids control systems, drilling motors and other downhole tools, rig instrumentation systems, and mud pump consumables. Following the April 2008 acquisition of Grant Prideco, this segment now offers drill pipe and drill bits.

## Company Financials Fiscal Year Ended Dec. 31

| Per Share Data ($) | 2010 | 2009 | 2008 | 2007 | 2006 | 2005 | 2004 | 2003 | 2002 | 2001 |
|---|---|---|---|---|---|---|---|---|---|---|
| Tangible Book Value | 13.90 | 10.93 | 7.46 | 9.65 | 5.91 | 4.20 | 3.33 | 2.49 | 2.17 | 3.19 |
| Cash Flow | 5.17 | 4.70 | 5.90 | 4.19 | 2.39 | 1.27 | 0.89 | 0.68 | 0.60 | 0.87 |
| Earnings | 3.98 | 3.52 | 4.90 | 3.76 | 1.94 | 0.91 | 0.64 | 0.45 | 0.45 | 0.64 |
| S&P Core Earnings | 3.98 | 3.75 | 4.89 | 3.76 | 1.94 | 0.90 | 0.58 | 0.41 | 0.38 | 0.57 |
| Dividends | 0.41 | 0.10 | Nil | Nil | Nil | Nil | Nil | Nil | Nil | Nil |
| Payout Ratio | 10% | 3% | Nil | Nil | Nil | Nil | Nil | Nil | Nil | Nil |
| Prices:High | 67.72 | 50.17 | 92.70 | 82.00 | 38.80 | 34.17 | 18.69 | 12.43 | 14.41 | 20.62 |
| Prices:Low | 32.18 | 22.19 | 17.60 | 26.88 | 25.81 | 16.54 | 10.83 | 8.75 | 7.60 | 6.20 |
| P/E Ratio:High | 17 | 14 | 19 | 22 | 20 | 38 | 29 | 28 | 32 | 32 |
| P/E Ratio:Low | 8 | 6 | 4 | 7 | 13 | 18 | 17 | 19 | 17 | 10 |

| Income Statement Analysis (Million $) | | | | | | | | | | |
|---|---|---|---|---|---|---|---|---|---|---|
| Revenue | 12,156 | 12,712 | 13,431 | 9,789 | 7,026 | 4,645 | 2,318 | 2,005 | 1,522 | 1,747 |
| Operating Income | NA | NA | 3,419 | 2,198 | 1,280 | 623 | 213 | 198 | 159 | 228 |
| Depreciation, Depletion and Amortization | 507 | 490 | 401 | 153 | 161 | 115 | 44.0 | 39.2 | 25.0 | 38.9 |
| Interest Expense | 50.0 | 53.0 | 67.3 | 50.3 | 48.7 | 52.9 | 38.4 | 38.9 | 27.3 | 24.9 |
| Pretax Income | 2,397 | 2,208 | 2,961 | 2,029 | 1,049 | 430 | 132 | 117 | 112 | 168 |
| Effective Tax Rate | NA | 33.3% | 33.5% | 33.3% | 33.9% | 32.3% | 14.6% | 28.9% | 35.0% | 38.1% |
| Net Income | 1,659 | 1,469 | 1,952 | 1,337 | 684 | 287 | 110 | 76.8 | 73.1 | 104 |
| S&P Core Earnings | 1,667 | 1,565 | 1,947 | 1,338 | 685 | 283 | 99.2 | 69.3 | 61.6 | 93.6 |

| Balance Sheet & Other Financial Data (Million $) | | | | | | | | | | |
|---|---|---|---|---|---|---|---|---|---|---|
| Cash | 3,333 | 2,622 | 1,543 | 1,842 | 957 | 209 | 143 | 74.2 | 118 | 43.2 |
| Current Assets | 10,535 | 9,598 | 9,657 | 7,594 | 4,966 | 2,998 | 1,537 | 1,246 | 1,115 | 909 |
| Total Assets | 23,050 | 21,532 | 21,399 | 12,115 | 9,019 | 6,679 | 2,599 | 2,243 | 1,969 | 1,472 |
| Current Liabilities | 4,085 | 4,174 | 5,624 | 4,027 | 2,665 | 1,187 | 800 | 452 | 346 | 277 |
| Long Term Debt | 514 | 876 | 870 | 738 | 835 | 836 | 350 | 594 | 595 | 300 |
| Common Equity | 15,748 | 14,113 | 12,637 | 6,661 | 5,024 | 4,194 | 1,296 | 1,090 | 933 | 868 |
| Total Capital | 16,863 | 15,111 | 15,728 | 8,026 | 6,283 | 5,428 | 1,767 | 1,753 | 1,592 | 1,188 |
| Capital Expenditures | 232 | 250 | 379 | 252 | 200 | 105 | 39.0 | 32.4 | 24.8 | 27.4 |
| Cash Flow | 2,166 | 1,959 | 2,353 | 1,490 | 845 | 402 | 154 | 116 | 98.1 | 143 |
| Current Ratio | 2.6 | 2.3 | 1.7 | 1.9 | 1.9 | 2.5 | 1.9 | 2.8 | 3.2 | 3.3 |
| % Long Term Debt of Capitalization | 3.1 | 5.8 | 5.5 | 9.2 | 13.3 | 15.4 | 19.8 | 33.9 | 37.3 | 25.3 |
| % Return on Assets | 7.4 | 6.8 | 11.6 | 12.7 | 8.7 | 6.2 | 4.6 | 3.6 | 4.2 | 7.6 |
| % Return on Equity | 11.1 | 11.0 | 20.2 | 22.9 | 14.8 | 10.5 | 9.2 | 7.6 | 8.1 | 12.7 |

Data as orig reptd.; bef. results of disc opers/spec. items. Per share data adj. for stk. divs.; EPS diluted. E-Estimated. NA-Not Available. NM-Not Meaningful. NR-Not Ranked. UR-Under Review.

**Office:** 7909 Parkwood Circle Dr, Houston, TX 77036-6565.
**Telephone:** 713-346-7500.
**Email:** investor.relations@natoil.com
**Website:** http://www.natoil.com

**Pres & CEO:** M.A. Miller, Jr.
**CFO:** C.C. Williams
**CTO:** H. Kverneland
**Chief Acctg Officer & Cntlr:** R.W. Blanchard

**Secy & General Counsel:** D.W. Rettig
**Board Members:** G. L. Armstrong, R. E. Beauchamp, B. A. Guill, D. Harrison, R. L. Jarvis, E. L. Mattson, M. A. Miller, Jr., J. A. Smisek

**Founded:** 1987
**Domicile:** Delaware
**Employees:** 41,027

The McGraw-Hill Companies

# NetApp Inc

**STANDARD &POOR'S**

| S&P Recommendation | HOLD ★★★☆☆ | Price $34.25 (as of Nov 25, 2011) | 12-Mo. Target Price $42.00 | Investment Style Large-Cap Growth |
|---|---|---|---|---|

**GICS Sector** Information Technology
**Sub-Industry** Computer Storage & Peripherals

**Summary** This company provides storage hardware, software and services to a variety of enterprise customers.

## Key Stock Statistics (Source S&P, Vickers, company reports)

| | | | | | | | |
|---|---|---|---|---|---|---|---|
| 52-Wk Range | $61.02– 33.00 | S&P Oper. EPS 2012**E** | 1.86 | Market Capitalization(B) | $12.618 | Beta | 1.43 |
| Trailing 12-Month EPS | $1.64 | S&P Oper. EPS 2013**E** | 1.96 | Yield (%) | Nil | S&P 3-Yr. Proj. EPS CAGR(%) | 10 |
| Trailing 12-Month P/E | 20.9 | P/E on S&P Oper. EPS 2012**E** | 18.4 | Dividend Rate/Share | Nil | S&P Credit Rating | NA |
| $10K Invested 5 Yrs Ago | $8,362 | Common Shares Outstg. (M) | 368.4 | Institutional Ownership (%) | 94 | | |

## Price Performance

30-Week Mov. Avg. · · · 10-Week Mov. Avg. – – GAAP Earnings vs. Previous Year   Volume Above Avg. STARS
12-Mo. Target Price — Relative Strength — ▲ Up ▼ Down ▶ No Change   Below Avg. ★

Options: ASE, CBOE, P, Ph

Analysis prepared by Equity Analyst **Jim Yin, CFA** on Nov 17, 2011, when the stock traded at **$35.56**.

## Highlights

➤ We look for revenues to rise 20% in FY 12 (Apr.), of which we estimate 13% will come from the acquisition of Engenio. Thus, we project 7% organic revenue growth in FY 12, compared to 30% growth in FY 11. Although we expect demand for data storage products to outpace the rest of the IT industry, we believe enterprise IT spending will soften due to a slower global economy. NTAP saw a sharp drop in orders from the federal government and the financial services industry in the last few weeks of July. We believe the weakness will spread to other industries.

➤ We project gross margins of 61% in FY 12, down from 65% in FY 11. We believe NTAP will increase spending for research and development to remain competitive in cloud computing. We also project higher operating expenses due to the acquisition of Engenio and recent hires. As a result, we see operating margins narrowing to 12.5% in FY 12, from 16.1% in FY 11.

➤ We estimate operating EPS of $1.86 in FY 12, compared to $1.83 in FY 11. These figures exclude acquisition-related and other one-time charges of $0.12 and $0.24 in FY 11 and FY 12, respectively.

## Investment Rationale/Risk

➤ Our hold recommendation reflects NTAP's slowing sales growth, in particular from enterprises. The company saw drops in orders from the federal government and several other large accounts in the past two quarters. Although the debate about raising the U.S. debt ceiling was a contributing factor, we think the shortfall was caused by other factors, including weak job growth and a decline in consumer confidence. We think enterprises are becoming more cautious in their outlook and are delaying new IT purchases, including data storage systems. While we continue to believe in the company's long-term growth potential, we see significant near-term risks due to a slower growing global economy.

➤ Risks to our recommendation and target price include a weaker-than-expected economic recovery, lower IT spending, increased competition, and significant loss of market share.

➤ Our 12-month target price of $42 is based on our discounted cash flow (DCF) analysis. Our DCF model assumes a 12% WACC, operating margins of 14% and revenue growth of 8% a year from 2014-2020, and 3% growth thereafter.

## Qualitative Risk Assessment

| LOW | MEDIUM | **HIGH** |
|---|---|---|

Our risk assessment takes into account the historical volatility of the data storage industry and the rapid pace of technological change that typifies the industry.

## Quantitative Evaluations

**S&P Quality Ranking**  B

| D | C | B- | **B** | B+ | A- | A | A+ |
|---|---|---|---|---|---|---|---|

**Relative Strength Rank**  WEAK

24

LOWEST = 1     HIGHEST = 99

## Revenue/Earnings Data

**Revenue (Million $)**

| | 1Q | 2Q | 3Q | 4Q | Year |
|---|---|---|---|---|---|
| 2012 | 1,458 | 1,507 | -- | -- | -- |
| 2011 | 1,154 | 1,251 | 1,290 | 1,428 | 5,123 |
| 2010 | 838.0 | 910.0 | 1,012 | 1,172 | 3,931 |
| 2009 | 868.8 | 911.6 | 746.3 | 879.6 | 3,406 |
| 2008 | 689.2 | 792.2 | 884.0 | 937.7 | 3,303 |
| 2007 | 621.3 | 652.5 | 729.3 | 801.2 | 2,804 |

**Earnings Per Share ($)**

| | | | | | |
|---|---|---|---|---|---|
| 2012 | 0.34 | 0.44 | E0.46 | E0.48 | E1.86 |
| 2011 | 0.40 | 0.45 | 0.56 | 0.40 | 1.71 |
| 2010 | 0.15 | 0.27 | 0.30 | 0.40 | 1.13 |
| 2009 | 0.11 | 0.15 | -0.23 | 0.23 | 0.26 |
| 2008 | 0.11 | 0.23 | 0.29 | 0.26 | 0.86 |
| 2007 | 0.14 | 0.22 | 0.17 | 0.23 | 0.77 |

Fiscal year ended Apr. 30. Next earnings report expected: Mid February. EPS Estimates based on S&P Operating Earnings; historical GAAP earnings are as reported.

## Dividend Data

No cash dividends have been paid.

# NetApp Inc

## Business Summary November 17, 2011

CORPORATE OVERVIEW. NetApp Inc. (formerly known as Network Appliance) is a provider of enterprise-level storage hardware and data-management software products and services. NTAP's solutions help global enterprises meet major information technology challenges such as managing the continuing growth in the volume of data, scaling existing infrastructure, complying with regulatory regimes, and security corporate networks and information.

The NTAP family of modular and scalable networked systems provides seamless access to a full range of enterprise data for users working with a variety of platforms, including Fibre Channel (FC), network-attached storage (NAS), storage area network (SAN), and iSCSI environments, as well as online data residing in central locations. NTAP refers to this as fabric-attached storage (FAS). Products include the 200, 900, 3000 and 6000 series.

NTAP's V-Series is a network-based solution that consolidates storage arrays from different suppliers, enabling unified SAN and file access to data stored in heterogeneous FC SAN storage arrays. The V-Series family supports products from Hewlett-Packard, Hitachi and IBM.

CORPORATE STRATEGY. NearStore products focus on optimizing data protection and retention applications. This system offers an alternative to customers by providing faster data access than off-line storage at a significantly lower cost than primary storage. Offerings in this category include the Virtual Tape Library (VTL), a disk-to-disk backup appliance that appears as a tape library to a back-up software application.

The NetCache suite of solutions is designed to manage, control and improve access to Web-based information. Working with a range of software partners, NetCache provides large enterprises with the ability to manage Internet access and security. It essentially enables IT managers to control user access to information, based on profiles, actions, timing, etc.

## Company Financials Fiscal Year Ended Apr. 30

| Per Share Data ($) | 2011 | 2010 | 2009 | 2008 | 2007 | 2006 | 2005 | 2004 | 2003 | 2002 |
|---|---|---|---|---|---|---|---|---|---|---|
| Tangible Book Value | 7.90 | 5.25 | 2.82 | 2.72 | 3.56 | 3.62 | 3.67 | 2.91 | 2.75 | 2.39 |
| Cash Flow | 2.13 | 1.60 | 0.77 | 1.26 | 1.05 | 0.90 | 0.77 | 0.58 | 0.38 | 0.14 |
| Earnings | 1.71 | 1.13 | 0.26 | 0.86 | 0.77 | 0.69 | 0.59 | 0.42 | 0.22 | 0.01 |
| S&P Core Earnings | 1.70 | 1.12 | 0.71 | 0.84 | 0.73 | 0.45 | 0.39 | 0.16 | -0.28 | -0.77 |
| Dividends | NA | NA | Nil | Nil | Nil | Nil | Nil | Nil | Nil | Nil |
| Payout Ratio | NA | Nil | Nil | Nil | Nil | Nil | Nil | Nil | Nil | Nil |
| Calendar Year | 2010 | 2009 | 2008 | 2007 | 2006 | 2005 | 2004 | 2003 | 2002 | 2001 |
| Prices:High | 57.96 | 34.99 | 27.49 | 40.89 | 41.56 | 34.98 | 34.99 | 26.69 | 27.95 | 74.98 |
| Prices:Low | 28.92 | 12.39 | 10.39 | 22.51 | 25.85 | 22.50 | 15.92 | 9.26 | 5.18 | 6.00 |
| P/E Ratio:High | 34 | 31 | NM | 48 | 54 | 51 | 59 | 64 | NM | NM |
| P/E Ratio:Low | 17 | 11 | NM | 26 | 34 | 33 | 27 | 22 | NM | NM |

| Income Statement Analysis (Million $) | | | | | | | | | | |
|---|---|---|---|---|---|---|---|---|---|---|
| Revenue | 5,123 | 3,931 | 3,406 | 3,303 | 2,804 | 2,066 | 1,598 | 1,170 | 892 | 798 |
| Operating Income | 997 | 617 | 410 | 464 | 387 | 395 | 319 | 228 | 146 | 76.5 |
| Depreciation | 166 | 166 | 171 | 144 | 111 | 81.8 | 65.6 | 59.5 | 57.4 | 65.3 |
| Interest Expense | 75.9 | 74.1 | 26.9 | Nil | 11.6 | 1.28 | Nil | Nil | Nil | Nil |
| Pretax Income | 794 | 447 | 44.8 | 383 | 360 | 350 | 276 | 170 | 97.8 | 2.53 |
| Effective Tax Rate | NA | NA | NM | 19.1% | 17.2% | 23.9% | 18.3% | 10.8% | 21.8% | NM |
| Net Income | 673 | 400 | 86.5 | 310 | 298 | 266 | 226 | 152 | 76.5 | 3.03 |
| S&P Core Earnings | 670 | 398 | 235 | 303 | 282 | 175 | 148 | 59.5 | -98.0 | -256 |

| Balance Sheet & Other Financial Data (Million $) | | | | | | | | | | |
|---|---|---|---|---|---|---|---|---|---|---|
| Cash | 5,175 | 3,724 | 2,604 | 1,164 | 489 | 461 | 194 | 241 | 284 | 211 |
| Current Assets | 6,394 | 4,537 | 3,439 | 2,067 | 2,241 | 2,033 | 1,576 | 1,089 | 853 | 679 |
| Total Assets | 8,499 | 6,494 | 5,453 | 4,071 | 3,658 | 3,261 | 2,373 | 1,877 | 1,319 | 1,109 |
| Current Liabilities | 3,373 | 1,911 | 1,679 | 1,414 | 1,188 | 917 | 520 | 344 | 265 | 216 |
| Long Term Debt | 115 | 1,273 | 1,430 | 173 | Nil | 138 | 4.47 | 4.86 | 3.10 | 3.73 |
| Common Equity | 3,845 | 2,531 | 1,662 | 1,700 | 1,989 | 1,923 | 1,661 | 1,416 | 987 | 858 |
| Total Capital | 4,995 | 3,804 | 3,092 | 1,873 | 1,989 | 2,061 | 1,665 | 1,421 | 990 | 862 |
| Capital Expenditures | 223 | 136 | 290 | 188 | 166 | 133 | 93.6 | 48.6 | 61.3 | 284 |
| Cash Flow | 839 | 566 | 257 | 454 | 409 | 348 | 291 | 212 | 134 | 47.4 |
| Current Ratio | 1.9 | 2.4 | 2.1 | 1.5 | 1.9 | 2.2 | 3.0 | 3.2 | 3.2 | 3.2 |
| % Long Term Debt of Capitalization | Nil | 33.5 | 46.2 | 9.2 | Nil | 6.7 | 0.3 | 0.3 | 0.3 | 0.4 |
| % Net Income of Revenue | 13.1 | 10.2 | 2.5 | 9.4 | 10.6 | 12.9 | 14.1 | 13.0 | 8.6 | 0.4 |
| % Return on Assets | 9.0 | 6.7 | 1.8 | 8.0 | 8.6 | 9.5 | 10.6 | 9.5 | 6.3 | 0.3 |
| % Return on Equity | 21.1 | 19.1 | 5.2 | 16.8 | 15.2 | 14.9 | 14.7 | 12.7 | 8.3 | 0.4 |

Data as orig reptd.; bef. results of disc opers/spec. items. Per share data adj. for stk. divs.; EPS diluted. E-Estimated. NA-Not Available. NM-Not Meaningful. NR-Not Ranked. UR-Under Review.

**Office:** 495 East Java Drive, Sunnyvale, CA 94089.
**Telephone:** 408-822-6000.
**Email:** investor_relations@netapp.com
**Website:** http://www.netapp.com

**Chrmn:** D.J. Warmenhoven
**Pres, CEO & COO:** T. Georgens
**Investor Contact:** S.J. Gomo ()
**EVP, CFO & Chief Acctg Officer:** S.J. Gomo

**SVP & CSO:** S. Kleiman
**Board Members:** J. R. Allen, A. L. Earhart, T. Georgens, J. Held, N. G. Moore, T. M. Nevens, G. T. Shaheen, R. T. Wall, R. P. Wallace, D. J. Warmenhoven

**Founded:** 1992
**Domicile:** Delaware
**Employees:** 10,212

# Netflix Inc

STANDARD
&POOR'S

| S&P Recommendation | HOLD ★★★☆☆ | Price $69.95 (as of Nov 28, 2011) | 12-Mo. Target Price $80.00 | Investment Style Large-Cap Blend |
|---|---|---|---|---|

**GICS Sector** Consumer Discretionary
**Sub-Industry** Internet Retail

**Summary** This company provides a subscription service, streaming movies and TV episodes over the Internet, and also distributes DVDs by mail.

## Key Stock Statistics (Source S&P, Vickers, company reports)

| | | | | | | | |
|---|---|---|---|---|---|---|---|
| 52-Wk Range | $304.79– 62.90 | S&P Oper. EPS 2011**E** | 4.10 | Market Capitalization(B) | $3.673 | Beta | 0.73 |
| Trailing 12-Month EPS | $4.40 | S&P Oper. EPS 2012**E** | -0.20 | Yield (%) | Nil | S&P 3-Yr. Proj. EPS CAGR(%) | 20 |
| Trailing 12-Month P/E | 15.9 | P/E on S&P Oper. EPS 2011**E** | 17.1 | Dividend Rate/Share | Nil | S&P Credit Rating | BB |
| $10K Invested 5 Yrs Ago | $21,750 | Common Shares Outstg. (M) | 52.5 | Institutional Ownership (%) | 90 | | |

## Price Performance

30-Week Mov. Avg. · · · · 10-Week Mov. Avg. - - **GAAP Earnings vs. Previous Year** Volume Above Avg. STARS

12-Mo. Target Price — Relative Strength — ▲ Up ▼ Down ▶ No Change Below Avg. ★

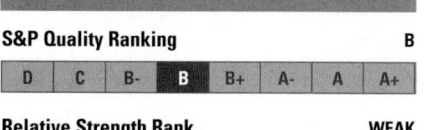

Options: ASE, CBOE, P, Ph

Analysis prepared by Equity Analyst **Michael Souers** on Nov 28, 2011, when the stock traded at **$63.86**.

## Highlights

➤ We see revenues rising 13% in 2012, following our projection of a 46% advance in 2011. We expect unique subscribers (DVDs and streaming) to grow modestly in 2012 after rising to over 25 million in 2011. This growth is benefiting from Netflix's recent launches in Canada and Latin America, along with launches expected in the U.K. and Ireland in the first quarter of 2012. We expect recent price hikes to cause increased subscriber churn and dissatisfaction in the near term, but to have a relatively limited impact on long-term growth.

➤ We project a significant narrowing of operating margins in 2012, as we anticipate substantial increases in both marketing and technology and development expenses accompanying NFLX's launch in Europe. We also see rising subscription costs, due to adding streaming content, only partially offset by growing economies of scale and diminished DVD-by-mail expenses.

➤ After a slight increase in interest expense and a flat diluted share count, we project a net loss of $0.20 in 2012, a significant decrease from the $4.10 we project the company to earn in 2011.

## Investment Rationale/Risk

➤ We think NFLX has greater flexibility, relative to peers, due to economies of scale, and that it should be able to grow its subscriber base profitably. Regarding our long-term outlook, we expect continued transformations in the home entertainment industry and rising content costs to limit margin expansion. In addition, we are concerned that Amazon.com's (AMZN 182, Hold) recent entry into the streaming business, along with other competitive pressures, will adversely impact NFLX's long-term growth trajectory. However, following a greater than 75% decline over the last five months, we view the shares as fairly valued, and we expect 2012 to be the company's trough earnings year.

➤ Risks to our opinion and target price include weaker-than-expected subscriber growth, unsuccessful expansion into multiple foreign markets, and changes in the competitive landscape that could decrease demand for NFLX's service.

➤ Our 12-month target price of $80 is derived from our discounted cash flow analysis, which assumes a weighted average cost of capital of 10.4% and a terminal growth rate of 4.0%.

## Qualitative Risk Assessment

| LOW | MEDIUM | HIGH |
|---|---|---|

With our view of evolving trends in the home entertainment industry, we see a risk that NFLX's DVD subscription business could eventually face obsolescence. We think this is partially offset by NFLX's efforts to adapt to industry trends and leverage its growing subscriber base via the Internet.

## Quantitative Evaluations

**S&P Quality Ranking** B

| D | C | B- | B | B+ | A- | A | A+ |
|---|---|---|---|---|---|---|---|

**Relative Strength Rank** WEAK

3

LOWEST = 1 HIGHEST = 99

## Revenue/Earnings Data

**Revenue (Million $)**

| | 1Q | 2Q | 3Q | 4Q | Year |
|---|---|---|---|---|---|
| 2011 | 718.6 | 788.6 | 821.8 | -- | -- |
| 2010 | 493.7 | 519.8 | 553.2 | 595.9 | 2,163 |
| 2009 | 394.1 | 408.5 | 423.1 | 444.5 | 1,670 |
| 2008 | 326.2 | 337.6 | 341.3 | 359.6 | 1,365 |
| 2007 | 305.3 | 196.7 | 226.0 | 302.4 | 1,205 |
| 2006 | 224.2 | 239.4 | 256.0 | 277.2 | 996.7 |

**Earnings Per Share ($)**

| | 1Q | 2Q | 3Q | 4Q | Year |
|---|---|---|---|---|---|
| 2011 | 1.11 | 1.26 | 1.16 | E0.58 | E4.10 |
| 2010 | 0.59 | 0.80 | 0.70 | 0.87 | 2.96 |
| 2009 | 0.37 | 0.54 | 0.52 | 0.56 | 1.98 |
| 2008 | 0.21 | 0.42 | 0.33 | 0.38 | 1.32 |
| 2007 | 0.14 | 0.37 | 0.18 | 0.24 | 0.97 |
| 2006 | 0.07 | 0.25 | 0.18 | 0.21 | 0.71 |

Fiscal year ended Dec. 31. Next earnings report expected: Late January. EPS Estimates based on S&P Operating Earnings; historical GAAP earnings are as reported.

## Dividend Data

No cash dividends have been paid.

---

**Please read the Required Disclosures and Analyst Certification on the last page of this report.**

The **McGraw·Hill** Companies

# Netflix Inc

## Business Summary November 28, 2011

CORPORATE OVERVIEW. Netflix is the world's largest subscription service, streaming movies and TV episodes over the Internet and sending DVDs by mail to 20 million subscribers as of December 31, 2010. Subscribers can instantly watch unlimited movies and TV episodes streamed to their TVs and computers, and can receive DVDs delivered quickly to their homes. NFLX offers a variety of subscription plans, with no due dates, no late fees, no shipping fees and no pay-per-view fees.

In 2010, a significant milestone was reached as a majority of NFLX subscribers viewed more of their TV shows and movies via streaming than by DVD. Streaming content can be watched on computers or TVs. The viewing experience is enabled by Netflix controlled software, which can run on a variety of consumer electronics devices, including Blu-Ray disc players, Internet-connected TVs, digital video players and game consoles.

NFLX uses its proprietary recommendation and merchandising technology to determine which titles are presented to subscribers. In doing so, Netflix believes it provides subscribers with a quick and personalized way to find titles they are more likely to enjoy, while simultaneously effectively managing its inventory utilization. NFLX's ability to generate demand for these older titles while maintaining high levels of customer satisfaction helps the company manage and maintain gross margins, subscriber acquisition costs, churn rate

and lifetime subscriber profit.

Content is obtained through direct purchases, revenue sharing agreements and licensing agreements with studios, distributors and other suppliers. DVD content is typically obtained through direct purchases or revenue sharing agreements. Streaming content is generally licensed for a fixed fee for the term of the license agreement.

CORPORATE STRATEGY. Netflix's core strategy is to grow a large streaming subscription business within the United States and globally. NFLX is continuously improving the customer experience, with a focus on expanding its streaming content, enhancing its user interfaces and extending its streaming service to even more Internet-connected devices, while staying within the parameters of its operating margin targets. With the growing popularity of Internet-delivered content, NFLX believes that the majority of subscribers will view content streamed from Netflix rather than delivered by DVD in the very near term.

## Company Financials Fiscal Year Ended Dec. 31

| Per Share Data ($) | 2010 | 2009 | 2008 | 2007 | 2006 | 2005 | 2004 | 2003 | 2002 | 2001 |
|---|---|---|---|---|---|---|---|---|---|---|
| Tangible Book Value | 2.04 | 1.66 | 4.19 | 4.57 | 6.02 | 4.12 | 2.95 | 2.16 | 1.86 | 1.62 |
| Cash Flow | 3.66 | 2.63 | 5.18 | 1.28 | 2.99 | 2.27 | 1.70 | 0.91 | 0.16 | -8.47 |
| Earnings | 2.96 | 1.98 | 1.32 | 0.97 | 0.71 | 0.64 | 0.33 | 0.10 | -0.78 | -1.30 |
| S&P Core Earnings | 2.87 | 1.91 | 1.22 | 0.84 | 0.70 | 0.72 | 0.33 | 0.11 | -0.78 | NA |
| Dividends | Nil | Nil | Nil | Nil | Nil | Nil | Nil | Nil | Nil | NA |
| Payout Ratio | Nil | Nil | Nil | Nil | Nil | Nil | Nil | Nil | Nil | NA |
| Prices:High | 209.24 | 61.65 | 40.90 | 29.14 | 33.12 | 30.25 | 39.77 | 30.50 | 9.10 | NA |
| Prices:Low | 48.52 | 28.78 | 17.90 | 15.62 | 18.12 | 8.91 | 9.25 | 5.34 | 2.43 | NA |
| P/E Ratio:High | 71 | 31 | 31 | 30 | 47 | 47 | NM | NM | NM | NA |
| P/E Ratio:Low | 16 | 15 | 14 | 16 | 26 | 14 | NM | NM | NM | NA |

| Income Statement Analysis (Million $) | | | | | | | | | | |
|---|---|---|---|---|---|---|---|---|---|---|
| Revenue | 2,163 | 1,670 | 1,365 | 1,205 | 997 | 682 | 506 | 272 | 153 | 75.9 |
| Operating Income | 322 | 228 | 364 | 106 | 217 | 108 | 108 | 55.5 | 14.8 | -6.76 |
| Depreciation | 38.1 | 38.0 | 242 | 21.6 | 157 | 107 | 88.2 | 51.0 | 26.5 | 29.8 |
| Interest Expense | 19.6 | 6.47 | 2.46 | NA | Nil | 0.41 | 0.17 | 0.42 | 12.0 | 1.85 |
| Pretax Income | 268 | 192 | 132 | 112 | 80.3 | 8.34 | 21.8 | 6.51 | -21.9 | -38.6 |
| Effective Tax Rate | NA | 39.7% | 36.9% | 40.0% | 38.9% | NM | 0.83% | Nil | Nil | Nil |
| Net Income | 161 | 116 | 83.0 | 67.0 | 49.1 | 42.0 | 21.6 | 6.51 | -21.9 | -38.6 |
| S&P Core Earnings | 156 | 112 | 76.9 | 57.7 | 48.1 | 47.3 | 21.3 | 6.51 | -21.9 | NA |

| Balance Sheet & Other Financial Data (Million $) | | | | | | | | | | |
|---|---|---|---|---|---|---|---|---|---|---|
| Cash | 350 | 320 | 297 | 385 | 400 | 212 | 174 | 89.9 | 59.8 | 76.5 |
| Current Assets | 641 | 411 | 361 | 417 | 428 | 244 | 187 | 139 | 107 | 19.6 |
| Total Assets | 982 | 680 | 618 | 647 | 609 | 365 | 252 | 176 | 131 | 105 |
| Current Liabilities | 389 | 226 | 216 | 213 | 193 | 138 | 94.9 | 63.0 | 40.4 | 26.2 |
| Long Term Debt | 200 | 200 | 38.0 | NA | Nil | Nil | Nil | 0.04 | 0.46 | 1.00 |
| Common Equity | 290 | 199 | 347 | 431 | 414 | 226 | 156 | 113 | 89.4 | 74.9 |
| Total Capital | 490 | 399 | 347 | 431 | 414 | 226 | 156 | 113 | 89.8 | 75.8 |
| Capital Expenditures | 33.8 | 45.9 | 43.8 | 44.3 | 27.3 | 30.6 | 15.0 | 8.87 | 2.75 | 3.23 |
| Cash Flow | 199 | 154 | 325 | 88.5 | 206 | 149 | 110 | 57.5 | 4.53 | -8.82 |
| Current Ratio | 1.7 | 1.8 | 1.7 | 2.0 | 2.2 | 1.8 | 2.0 | 2.2 | 2.6 | 0.8 |
| % Long Term Debt of Capitalization | 40.8 | 50.1 | 9.9 | Nil | Nil | Nil | Nil | 0.0 | Nil | 1.3 |
| % Net Income of Revenue | 7.4 | 6.9 | 6.1 | 5.6 | 4.9 | 6.2 | 4.3 | 2.4 | 0.1 | NM |
| % Return on Assets | 19.4 | 17.9 | 13.1 | 10.7 | 10.1 | 13.6 | 10.1 | 4.2 | NA | NA |
| % Return on Equity | 65.8 | 42.4 | 21.4 | 15.9 | 15.3 | 22.0 | 16.1 | 6.4 | NA | NA |

Data as orig reptd.; bef. results of disc opers/spec. items. Per share data adj. for stk. divs.; EPS diluted. E-Estimated. NA-Not Available. NM-Not Meaningful. NR-Not Ranked. UR-Under Review.

**Office:** 100 Winchester Cir, Los Gatos, CA 95032-1815.
**Telephone:** 408-540-3700.
**Website:** http://www.netflix.com
**Chrmn, Pres & CEO:** R. Hastings

**COO:** A. Rendich
**CFO:** D. Wells
**Secy & General Counsel:** D. Hyman
**Investor Contact:** D. Crawford (408-540-3712)

**Board Members:** R. N. Barton, A. G. Battle, C. H. Giancarlo, T. M. Haley, R. Hastings, J. C. Hoag, A. Mather

**Founded:** 1997
**Domicile:** Delaware
**Employees:** 4,329

# Newell Rubbermaid Inc.

**STANDARD &POOR'S**

| S&P Recommendation **HOLD** ★★★★★ | Price $14.25 (as of Nov 25, 2011) | 12-Mo. Target Price $17.00 | Investment Style Large-Cap Value |
|---|---|---|---|

**GICS Sector** Consumer Discretionary
**Sub-Industry** Housewares & Specialties

**Summary** Major product lines of this high-volume brand name consumer products concern include housewares, home furnishings, office products and hardware.

## Key Stock Statistics (Source S&P, Vickers, company reports)

| | | | | | | | |
|---|---|---|---|---|---|---|---|
| 52-Wk Range | $20.38– 10.87 | S&P Oper. EPS 2011E | 1.58 | Market Capitalization(B) | $4.125 | Beta | 1.74 |
| Trailing 12-Month EPS | $0.41 | S&P Oper. EPS 2012E | 1.78 | Yield (%) | 2.25 | S&P 3-Yr. Proj. EPS CAGR(%) | 8 |
| Trailing 12-Month P/E | 34.8 | P/E on S&P Oper. EPS 2011E | 9.0 | Dividend Rate/Share | $0.32 | S&P Credit Rating | BBB- |
| $10K Invested 5 Yrs Ago | $5,731 | Common Shares Outstg. (M) | 289.5 | Institutional Ownership (%) | 84 | | |

## Price Performance

30-Week Mov. Avg. ··· 10-Week Mov. Avg. -- GAAP Earnings vs. Previous Year  Volume Above Avg. |||| STARS
12-Mo. Target Price — Relative Strength  — ▲ Up  ▼ Down  ▶ No Change   Below Avg. |||| ★

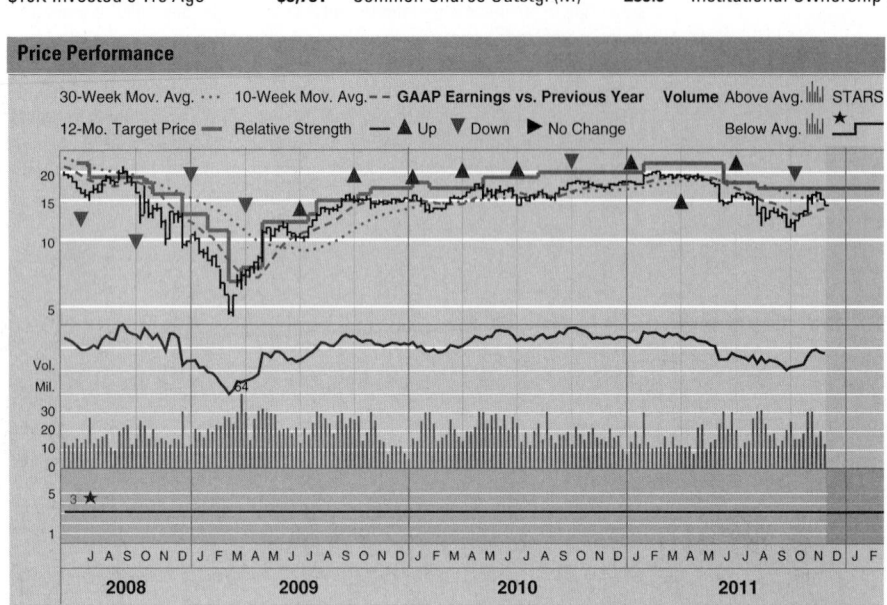

Options: ASE, CBOE, P

Analysis prepared by Equity Analyst **T. Amobi, CFA CPA** on Nov 01, 2011, when the stock traded at **$14.85**.

## Highlights

➤ We project total sales growth of 3.5% in 2011 (assuming 2% foreign exchange benefit), to $5.96 billion, and 3.9% in 2012, to $6.19 billion, with contributions across the core businesses, namely, Office Products, Tools, Hardware & Commercial Products, and Home & Family. We expect new product introductions, distribution improvements and geographic expansion to continue driving results. Further, we think inter-national gains will continue to offset more modest North American improvements.

➤ Following a multi-year program designed to streamline manufacturing and supply chain op-erations in 2010, NWL's latest restructuring ini-tiative aims to deliver $90 million to $100 million in targeted cost savings over the next 12 to 18 months, likely driving further margin expansion in 2012, for which we project operating margins of 15.2% (up from 13.9% in 2011), before re-structuring charges.

➤ After interest expense and taxes, we estimate operating EPS of $1.58 and $1.78 in 2011 and 2012, respectively, assuming some share buy-backs under a $300 million plan. As of late Octo-ber 2011, revised management guidance for 2011 normalized EPS is $1.55 to $1.62.

## Investment Rationale/Risk

➤ After what we saw as encouraging third-quarter 2011 results, we think the stock price adequately reflects NWL's improved longer-term growth prospects but a still very difficult near-term selling environment. We believe it is poised for better innovation and efficiency. In our view, NWL should be able to gain market share through better consumer research and greater product innovation. We are cautiously optimistic on the latest restructuring drive ("Project Renewal"), aimed at redirecting efforts to the most significant growth platforms.

➤ Risks to our recommendation and target price include poor consumer acceptance of new products, a prolonged weak consumer spend-ing environment, a low level of cost savings from the company's reorganization program, negative currency translation, and material in-creases in prices of key raw materials.

➤ Our 12-month target price of $17 is based on a blend of our historical and relative analyses. Our historical model uses a P/E multiple of 8.9X our 2012 EPS estimate, a discount to the 10-year median, and arrives at a $16 value. Our relative analysis uses a small discount to the peer-average multiple for a price of $19.

## Qualitative Risk Assessment

| LOW | MEDIUM | HIGH |
|---|---|---|

Our risk assessment reflects that housewares companies' products are generally affordable, low-priced goods that are only moderately affected by swings in the economy. However, there is a greater level of import competition for remaining commodity-type goods.

## Quantitative Evaluations

**S&P Quality Ranking** — **B-**

| D | C | B- | B | B+ | A- | A | A+ |
|---|---|---|---|---|---|---|---|

**Relative Strength Rank** — **STRONG**

77

LOWEST = 1          HIGHEST = 99

## Revenue/Earnings Data

### Revenue (Million $)

| | 1Q | 2Q | 3Q | 4Q | Year |
|---|---|---|---|---|---|
| 2011 | 1,303 | 1,573 | 1,550 | -- | -- |
| 2010 | 1,306 | 1,496 | 1,487 | 1,469 | 5,759 |
| 2009 | 1,204 | 1,504 | 1,449 | 1,420 | 5,578 |
| 2008 | 1,434 | 1,825 | 1,760 | 1,452 | 6,471 |
| 2007 | 1,384 | 1,693 | 1,687 | 1,643 | 6,407 |
| 2006 | 1,343 | 1,634 | 1,586 | 1,638 | 6,201 |

### Earnings Per Share ($)

| | | | | | |
|---|---|---|---|---|---|
| 2011 | 0.25 | 0.49 | -0.57 | E0.37 | E1.58 |
| 2010 | 0.19 | 0.41 | 0.09 | 0.25 | 0.96 |
| 2009 | 0.12 | 0.37 | 0.28 | 0.20 | 0.97 |
| 2008 | 0.21 | 0.33 | 0.20 | -0.93 | -0.19 |
| 2007 | 0.23 | 0.51 | 0.61 | 0.36 | 1.72 |
| 2006 | 0.47 | 0.49 | 0.41 | 0.33 | 1.71 |

Fiscal year ended Dec. 31. Next earnings report expected: Late January. EPS Estimates based on S&P Operating Earnings; historical GAAP earnings are as reported.

## Dividend Data (Dates: mm/dd Payment Date: mm/dd/yy)

| Amount ($) | Date Decl. | Ex-Div. Date | Stk. of Record | Payment Date |
|---|---|---|---|---|
| 0.050 | 02/10 | 02/24 | 02/28 | 03/15/11 |
| 0.080 | 05/12 | 05/26 | 05/31 | 06/15/11 |
| 0.080 | 08/11 | 08/29 | 08/31 | 09/15/11 |
| 0.080 | 11/10 | 11/28 | 11/30 | 12/15/11 |

Dividends have been paid since 1946. Source: Company reports.

---

**Please read the Required Disclosures and Analyst Certification on the last page of this report.**

The McGraw-Hill Companies

# Newell Rubbermaid Inc.

STANDARD
&POOR'S

## Business Summary November 01, 2011

CORPORATE OVERVIEW. Newell Rubbermaid is a global manufacturer and marketer of name brand consumer products and their commercial extensions, serving a wide array of retail channels including department stores, warehouse clubs, home centers, hardware stores, commercial distributors, office superstores, contract stationers, automotive stores and small superstores. As of April 2009, NWL recategorized its four business segments into three: Office Products (30% of 2010 sales, 37% of segment operating profits), Tools, Hardware & Commercial Products (29%, 35%), and Home & Family (41%, 39%). About 31% of 2010 sales were made outside the U.S. Sales to Wal-Mart Stores, Inc. and its subsidiaries amounted to about 12% of sales in 2010.

The global business units (GBUs) that formerly comprised the Cleaning, Organization & Decor segment (i.e., Home Products, Foodservice Products, Commercial Products and Decor) have been integrated into two of the three remaining segments. Brands include Rubbermaid, Brute, Roughneck, TakeAlongs, Levolor and Kirsch. The Rubbermaid Food & Home Products and Decor GBUs are now included in the Home & Family segment. Also, the Amerock brand, which was previously part of the Tools & Hardware segment, has been integrated into the Decor GBU.

The office products segment is comprised of the following GBUs: Markers, Highlighters, Art & Office Organization, Everyday Writing & Coloring, Technology, and Fine Writing & Luxury Accessories. Brands include Sharpie, PaperMate, Waterman, Parker, and DYMO.

The tools & hardware business is composed of the following GBUs: Commercial Products, Construction Tools & Accessories, Industrial Products & Services, and Hardware. It sells hand tools, power tool accessories, propane torches, manual paint applicator products, cabinet hardware, and window hardware under brand names such as Irwin, Lenox, Rubbermaid Commercial Products, Technical Concepts, and BernzOmatic.

The home & family segment includes the following GBUs: Rubbermaid Consumer Products, Baby & Parenting Essentials, Decor, Culinary Lifestyles and Beauty & Style. Brand names include Rubbermaid, Graco, Aprica, Levelor, Calphalon and Goody.

## Company Financials Fiscal Year Ended Dec. 31

| Per Share Data ($) | 2010 | 2009 | 2008 | 2007 | 2006 | 2005 | 2004 | 2003 | 2002 | 2001 |
|---|---|---|---|---|---|---|---|---|---|---|
| Tangible Book Value | NM | NM | NM | NM | NM | NM | NM | NM | NM | 0.44 |
| Cash Flow | 1.52 | 1.56 | 0.29 | 2.18 | 2.41 | 2.07 | 0.84 | 0.84 | 2.21 | 2.22 |
| Earnings | 0.96 | 0.97 | -0.19 | 1.72 | 1.71 | 1.29 | -0.07 | -0.17 | 1.16 | 0.99 |
| S&P Core Earnings | 0.99 | 0.98 | 0.71 | 1.73 | 1.73 | 1.22 | 0.56 | 0.39 | 0.86 | 0.71 |
| Dividends | 0.20 | 0.25 | 0.84 | 0.84 | 0.84 | 0.84 | 0.84 | 0.84 | 0.84 | 0.84 |
| Payout Ratio | 21% | 26% | NM | 49% | 49% | 65% | NM | NM | 72% | 85% |
| Prices:High | 18.48 | 16.10 | 25.94 | 32.19 | 29.98 | 25.69 | 26.41 | 32.00 | 36.70 | 29.50 |
| Prices:Low | 13.11 | 4.51 | 9.13 | 24.22 | 23.25 | 20.50 | 19.05 | 20.27 | 26.11 | 20.50 |
| P/E Ratio:High | 19 | 17 | NM | 19 | 18 | 20 | NM | NM | 32 | 30 |
| P/E Ratio:Low | 14 | 5 | NM | 14 | 14 | 16 | NM | NM | 23 | 21 |

| Income Statement Analysis (Million $) | | | | | | | | | | |
|---|---|---|---|---|---|---|---|---|---|---|
| Revenue | 5,759 | 5,578 | 6,471 | 6,407 | 6,201 | 6,343 | 6,748 | 7,750 | 7,454 | 6,909 |
| Operating Income | 880 | 850 | 752 | 970 | 916 | 843 | 870 | 992 | 1,033 | 966 |
| Depreciation | 172 | 175 | 131 | 143 | 193 | 214 | 249 | 278 | 281 | 329 |
| Interest Expense | 118 | 149 | 147 | 132 | 155 | 142 | 130 | 140 | 111 | 137 |
| Pretax Income | 300 | 428 | 1.80 | 632 | 515 | 418 | 86.3 | 20.1 | 495 | 443 |
| Effective Tax Rate | NA | 33.3% | NM | 23.7% | 8.58% | 14.8% | NM | NM | 31.7% | 34.2% |
| Net Income | 293 | 286 | -51.8 | 479 | 471 | 356 | -19.1 | -46.6 | 312 | 265 |
| S&P Core Earnings | 301 | 288 | 196 | 481 | 476 | 333 | 153 | 108 | 232 | 190 |

| Balance Sheet & Other Financial Data (Million $) | | | | | | | | | | |
|---|---|---|---|---|---|---|---|---|---|---|
| Cash | 140 | 278 | 275 | 329 | 201 | 116 | 506 | 144 | 55.1 | 6.80 |
| Current Assets | 2,132 | 2,182 | 2,394 | 2,652 | 2,477 | 2,473 | 3,012 | 3,000 | 3,080 | 2,851 |
| Total Assets | 6,405 | 6,424 | 6,793 | 6,683 | 6,311 | 6,446 | 6,666 | 7,481 | 7,389 | 7,266 |
| Current Liabilities | 1,666 | 1,760 | 2,206 | 2,564 | 1,897 | 1,798 | 1,871 | 2,022 | 2,614 | 2,534 |
| Long Term Debt | 2,064 | 2,015 | 2,118 | 1,197 | 1,972 | 2,430 | 2,424 | 2,869 | 2,357 | 1,865 |
| Common Equity | 1,902 | 1,779 | 1,614 | 2,247 | 1,890 | 1,643 | 1,764 | 2,016 | 2,064 | 2,433 |
| Total Capital | 4,139 | 4,290 | 4,485 | 3,445 | 3,863 | 4,073 | 4,189 | 4,887 | 4,426 | 4,373 |
| Capital Expenditures | 165 | 153 | 158 | 157 | 138 | 92.2 | 122 | 300 | 252 | 250 |
| Cash Flow | 465 | 461 | 79.3 | 622 | 664 | 570 | 230 | 232 | 592 | 593 |
| Current Ratio | 1.3 | 1.2 | 1.1 | 1.0 | 1.3 | 1.4 | 1.6 | 1.5 | 1.2 | 1.1 |
| % Long Term Debt of Capitalization | 49.9 | 47.0 | 47.2 | 34.8 | 51.1 | 59.7 | 57.9 | 58.7 | 53.2 | 42.7 |
| % Net Income of Revenue | 5.1 | 5.1 | NM | 7.5 | 7.6 | 5.6 | NM | NM | 4.2 | 3.8 |
| % Return on Assets | 4.6 | 4.3 | NM | 7.4 | 7.4 | 5.4 | NM | NM | 4.3 | 3.6 |
| % Return on Equity | 15.9 | 16.8 | NM | 23.2 | 26.6 | 20.9 | NM | NM | 13.9 | 10.8 |

Data as orig reptd.; bef. results of disc opers/spec. items. Per share data adj. for stk. divs.; EPS diluted. E-Estimated. NA-Not Available. NM-Not Meaningful. NR-Not Ranked. UR-Under Review.

**Office:** Three Glenlake Parkway, Atlanta, GA 30328.
**Telephone:** 770-418-7000.
**Email:** investor.relations@newellco.com
**Website:** http://www.newellrubbermaid.com

**Chrmn:** M.T. Cowhig
**Pres & CEO:** M.B. Polk
**EVP & CFO:** J.R. Figuereo
**SVP, Secy & General Counsel:** J.K. Stipancich

**Chief Acctg Officer & Cntlr:** J.B. Ellis
**Investor Contact:** N. O'Donnell (770-418-7723)
**Board Members:** T. E. Clarke, K. C. Conroy, S. S. Cowen, M. T. Cowhig, E. Cuthbert-Millett, D. De Sole, M. D. Ketchum, C. A. Montgomery, M. B. Polk, S. J. Strobel, M. A. Todman, R. Viault

**Founded:** 1903
**Domicile:** Delaware
**Employees:** 19,400

# Newfield Exploration Co

**STANDARD &POOR'S**

| S&P Recommendation | BUY ★★★★☆ | Price | 12-Mo. Target Price | Investment Style |
|---|---|---|---|---|
| | | $38.54 (as of Nov 25, 2011) | $53.00 | Large-Cap Blend |

**GICS Sector** Energy
**Sub-Industry** Oil & Gas Exploration & Production

**Summary** This independent oil and natural gas exploration and production company has a diversified asset base, with domestic as well as international offshore operations.

## Key Stock Statistics (Source S&P, Vickers, company reports)

| | | | | | | | |
|---|---|---|---|---|---|---|---|
| 52-Wk Range | $77.93– 34.42 | S&P Oper. EPS 2011E | 3.96 | Market Capitalization(B) | $5.187 | Beta | 1.56 |
| Trailing 12-Month EPS | $3.66 | S&P Oper. EPS 2012E | 5.22 | Yield (%) | Nil | S&P 3-Yr. Proj. EPS CAGR(%) | 10 |
| Trailing 12-Month P/E | 10.5 | P/E on S&P Oper. EPS 2011E | 9.7 | Dividend Rate/Share | Nil | S&P Credit Rating | BBB- |
| $10K Invested 5 Yrs Ago | $8,226 | Common Shares Outstg. (M) | 134.6 | Institutional Ownership (%) | 95 | | |

## Price Performance

30-Week Mov. Avg. · · · ·   10-Week Mov. Avg. - -   GAAP Earnings vs. Previous Year   Volume Above Avg. ▮▮▮ STARS
12-Mo. Target Price —   Relative Strength —   ▲ Up   ▼ Down   ► No Change   Below Avg. ▮▮▮  ★

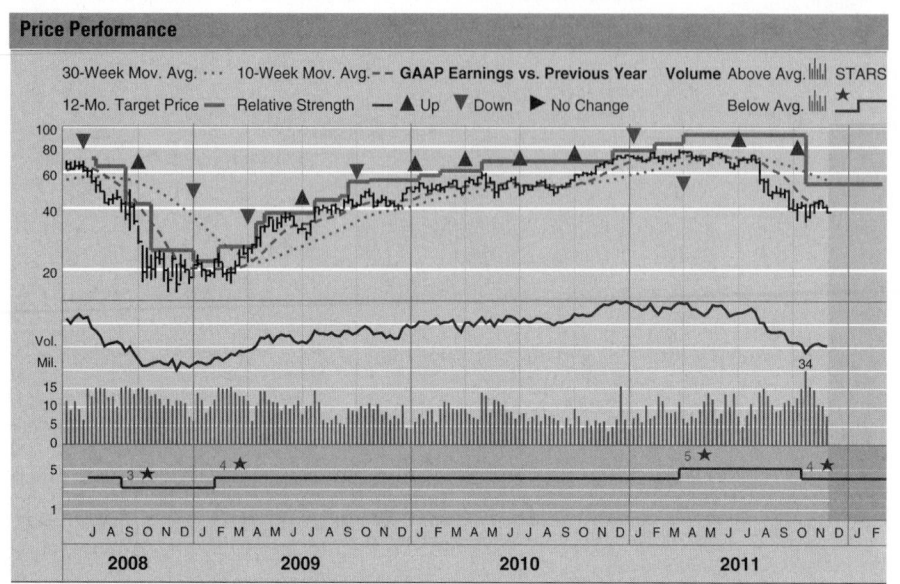

Options: ASE, CBOE, Ph

Analysis prepared by Equity Analyst **Michael Kay** on Nov 09, 2011, when the stock traded at **$42.83**.

## Highlights

► NFX will focus 100% of 2011 capex on oil and liquids-rich plays. It recently cut 2011 production guidance to 300-304 Bcfe (previously 312-323 Bcfe), up 4%-5%, as higher costs in the Williston Basin are impacting activity levels. Production is being driven by start-ups in deep-water GOM, Monument Butte in the Uinta Basin (5 rigs and rising to 8 in 2012), the Williston Basin (5 rigs, but reducing activity in 2012), Granite Wash (3 rigs), oily Woodford (2-3 rigs) and a growing position at Eagle Ford Shale (1-2 rigs). These developments are expected to drive domestic oil growth over 50% this year. First production from its Piatu project in Malaysia is likely to begin in November.

► NFX's 2011 capex budget is $1.9 billion, versus $1.6 billion in 2010 (ex-acquisitions). It expects to spend about 65% of capex in the Rockies and Midcontinent. It has remained active in the Granite Wash, the oily Woodford, Eagle Ford and the Williston Basin, but is deferring some completions in that region.

► We see EPS of $3.96 in 2011 and $5.22 in 2012, versus $4.51 in 2010, reflecting growing higher-margin liquids production. NFX has hedged over 70% of 2011 gas volumes at over $6/Mcf.

## Investment Rationale/Risk

► We expect NFX to benefit in the near term from high-impact development projects at onshore liquids-rich plays and long term from a diversified portfolio, including low-cost natural gas assets. NFX has been the most active player in the Woodford Shale for years, but has cut its rig count there to focus on several high-growth, high-impact onshore oil assets, which also include an oily part of the Woodford. We believe an asset realignment is largely complete, and NFX will see organic growth through its drilling inventory. NFX expects to raise its liquids weighting from 30% of production to 45% by year-end 2011. It has a joint venture with Hess Corp. (HES 62, Buy) in the Marcellus Shale, in which NFX operates with a 50% interest.

► Risks to our recommendation and target price include a sustained decline in oil and gas prices, an inability to replace reserves, and production declines.

► Our 12-month target price of $53 reflects our proved NAV estimate of $54 along with relative metrics, including a target enterprise value to 2012 EBITDA forecast of 4.5X ($49), in line with E&P peers.

## Qualitative Risk Assessment

| LOW | MEDIUM | HIGH |
|---|---|---|

Our risk assessment reflects the company's operations in a capital-intensive industry that derives value from producing commodities whose prices are very volatile.

## Quantitative Evaluations

**S&P Quality Ranking**   B-

| D | C | B- | B | B+ | A- | A | A+ |
|---|---|---|---|---|---|---|---|

**Relative Strength Rank**   WEAK

24

LOWEST = 1      HIGHEST = 99

## Revenue/Earnings Data

**Revenue (Million $)**

| | 1Q | 2Q | 3Q | 4Q | Year |
|---|---|---|---|---|---|
| 2011 | 545.0 | 621.0 | 628.0 | -- | -- |
| 2010 | 458.0 | 448.0 | 449.0 | 528.0 | 1,883 |
| 2009 | 262.0 | 287.0 | 375.0 | 414.0 | 1,338 |
| 2008 | 515.0 | 691.0 | 680.0 | 338.0 | 2,225 |
| 2007 | 440.0 | 528.0 | 419.0 | 398.0 | 1,783 |
| 2006 | 431.0 | 390.0 | 425.0 | 427.0 | 1,673 |

**Earnings Per Share ($)**

| | 1Q | 2Q | 3Q | 4Q | Year |
|---|---|---|---|---|---|
| 2011 | -0.13 | 1.62 | 1.99 | E0.90 | E3.96 |
| 2010 | 1.84 | 0.72 | 1.20 | 0.17 | 3.91 |
| 2009 | -5.35 | -0.30 | 0.58 | 0.85 | -4.18 |
| 2008 | -0.50 | -1.89 | 5.48 | -6.07 | -2.89 |
| 2007 | -0.37 | 1.17 | 0.70 | -0.19 | 1.32 |
| 2006 | 1.17 | 0.73 | 2.06 | 0.64 | 4.58 |

Fiscal year ended Dec. 31. Next earnings report expected: Early February. EPS Estimates based on S&P Operating Earnings; historical GAAP earnings are as reported.

## Dividend Data

No cash dividends have been paid.

---

**Please read the Required Disclosures and Analyst Certification on the last page of this report.**

The McGraw-Hill Companies

# Newfield Exploration Co

STANDARD &POOR'S

## Business Summary November 09, 2011

CORPORATE OVERVIEW. Founded in 1989 and taken public in 1993, Newfield Exploration Co. is an oil and gas exploration and production company. Its domestic operations include the onshore U.S. Gulf Coast and Gulf of Mexico, the Anadarko and Arkoma Basins of the Mid-Continent, the Appalachian Basin and the Uinta Basin of the Rocky Mountains. Internationally, the company has operations in offshore Malaysia and China.

As of year-end 2010, NFX had estimated proved reserves of 3.7 Tcfe, of which 67% was natural gas and 58% was proved developed. This compares with estimated proved reserves of 3.6 Tcfe, 72% natural gas and 53% proved developed, at the end of 2009, a 3% increase. We forecast NFX's reserve life to be 13 years. Reserve growth in 2010 was slower than anticipated, reflecting, in our view, NFX's strategic shift toward higher-margin liquids prospects throughout the year.

NFX invested about $2 billion in 2010, including $329 million in acquisitions, in developing its asset base. Finding and development (F&D) costs in 2010 averaged $5.26 per Mcfe, up from its three-year F&D cost of $2.52/Mcfe. We estimate that NFX organically replaced 126% of production in 2010 with the addition of new proved reserves.

CORPORATE STRATEGY. NFX seeks to diversify its asset base geographically, growing reserves through the drilling of a balanced portfolio and select acquisitions, controlling operations and costs, and using advanced technologies. From its founding in 1989 to 1995, NFX primarily focused on the shallow waters of the Gulf of Mexico. In 1995, it established its onshore Gulf Coast operations. From 2000 to 2005, NFX made several large acquisitions in the continental U.S. and internationally to expand its asset base. The Mid-Continent has been the company's fastest-growing region over the past several years. NFX has been active in the Mid-Continent since 2001 and has tripled proved reserves and production from this area. The current geographic distribution of reserves contrasts greatly with the distribution a decade ago, when the majority of the company's reserves were located in the Gulf of Mexico. In 2011, we expect NFX to focus on its liquids-rich prospects in the oily part of the Woodford Shale, the Bakken Shale in North Dakota and Alberta, the Granite Wash in the Texas Panhandle, the Eagle Ford Shale onshore Texas, and its growing acreage at Monument Butte. NFX looks to boost its oil weighting to 45% of its production base in 2011.

## Company Financials Fiscal Year Ended Dec. 31

| Per Share Data ($) | 2010 | 2009 | 2008 | 2007 | 2006 | 2005 | 2004 | 2003 | 2002 | 2001 |
|---|---|---|---|---|---|---|---|---|---|---|
| Tangible Book Value | 25.32 | 21.20 | 24.66 | 26.79 | 23.24 | 18.24 | 15.64 | 12.02 | 9.76 | 8.02 |
| Cash Flow | 8.76 | 10.68 | 2.51 | 6.52 | 9.42 | 6.79 | 6.61 | 5.34 | 3.80 | 4.16 |
| Earnings | 3.91 | -4.18 | -2.89 | 1.32 | 4.58 | 2.73 | 2.63 | 1.89 | 0.81 | 1.33 |
| S&P Core Earnings | 3.91 | -4.18 | -2.40 | 1.38 | 4.39 | 2.43 | 2.58 | 1.89 | 0.76 | 1.28 |
| Dividends | Nil | Nil | Nil | Nil | Nil | Nil | Nil | Nil | Nil | Nil |
| Payout Ratio | Nil | Nil | Nil | Nil | Nil | Nil | Nil | Nil | Nil | Nil |
| Prices:High | 73.58 | 51.27 | 69.77 | 58.08 | 54.50 | 53.52 | 32.92 | 22.76 | 19.62 | 23.88 |
| Prices:Low | 44.81 | 17.09 | 15.45 | 39.30 | 34.90 | 27.44 | 22.08 | 15.68 | 13.58 | 13.13 |
| P/E Ratio:High | 19 | NM | NM | 44 | 12 | 20 | 13 | 12 | 24 | 18 |
| P/E Ratio:Low | 12 | NM | NM | 30 | 8 | 10 | 8 | 8 | 17 | 10 |

| Income Statement Analysis (Million $) | | | | | | | | | | |
|---|---|---|---|---|---|---|---|---|---|---|
| Revenue | 1,883 | 1,338 | 2,225 | 1,783 | 1,673 | 1,762 | 1,353 | 1,017 | 662 | 749 |
| Operating Income | NA | NA | -143 | 1,213 | 1,216 | 1,418 | 1,074 | 798 | 477 | 579 |
| Depreciation, Depletion and Amortization | 651 | 1,931 | 697 | 682 | 624 | 521 | 471 | 395 | 303 | 283 |
| Interest Expense | 98.0 | 75.0 | 52.0 | 55.0 | 43.0 | 26.0 | 31.9 | 46.4 | 35.1 | 28.3 |
| Pretax Income | 829 | -885 | -535 | 294 | 949 | 543 | 499 | 332 | 111 | 191 |
| Effective Tax Rate | NA | 38.8% | NM | 41.4% | 37.7% | 35.9% | 37.4% | 36.4% | 33.4% | 35.3% |
| Net Income | 523 | -542 | -373 | 172 | 591 | 348 | 312 | 211 | 73.8 | 124 |
| S&P Core Earnings | 523 | -542 | -311 | 180 | 567 | 312 | 306 | 211 | 68.5 | 119 |

| Balance Sheet & Other Financial Data (Million $) | | | | | | | | | | |
|---|---|---|---|---|---|---|---|---|---|---|
| Cash | 39.0 | 78.0 | 24.0 | 250 | 80.0 | 39.0 | 58.3 | 15.3 | 48.9 | 26.6 |
| Current Assets | 731 | 893 | 1,206 | 927 | 851 | 540 | 392 | 239 | 239 | 231 |
| Total Assets | 7,494 | 6,254 | 7,305 | 6,986 | 6,635 | 5,081 | 4,328 | 2,733 | 2,316 | 1,663 |
| Current Liabilities | 928 | 873 | 1,085 | 929 | 1,123 | 670 | 474 | 300 | 296 | 165 |
| Long Term Debt | 2,304 | 2,037 | 2,211 | 1,050 | 1,048 | 870 | 992 | 643 | 853 | 572 |
| Common Equity | 3,343 | 2,768 | 3,257 | 3,581 | 3,062 | 2,418 | 2,017 | 1,369 | 1,009 | 710 |
| Total Capital | 5,647 | 4,805 | 6,126 | 5,735 | 5,073 | 4,008 | 3,560 | 2,255 | 1,992 | 1,490 |
| Capital Expenditures | 1,971 | 1,376 | 2,310 | 1,943 | 1,693 | 1,047 | 860 | 534 | 314 | 502 |
| Cash Flow | 1,174 | 1,389 | 324 | 854 | 1,215 | 869 | 784 | 606 | 377 | 406 |
| Current Ratio | 0.8 | 1.0 | 1.1 | 1.0 | 0.8 | 0.8 | 0.8 | 0.8 | 0.8 | 1.4 |
| % Long Term Debt of Capitalization | 40.8 | 42.4 | 36.1 | 18.3 | 20.7 | 21.7 | 27.9 | 28.5 | 42.8 | 38.4 |
| % Return on Assets | 7.6 | NM | NM | 2.5 | 10.1 | 7.4 | 8.8 | 8.4 | 3.7 | 9.2 |
| % Return on Equity | 17.1 | NM | NM | 5.1 | 21.7 | 15.7 | 18.4 | 17.7 | 8.6 | 20.1 |

Data as orig reptd.; bef. results of disc opers/spec. items. Per share data adj. for stk. divs.; EPS diluted. E-Estimated. NA-Not Available. NM-Not Meaningful. NR-Not Ranked. UR-Under Review.

**Office:** 4 Waterway Square Place, Suite 100, The Woodlands, TX 77380.
**Telephone:** 281-210-5100.
**Email:** info@newfld.com
**Website:** http://www.newfld.com

**Chrmn, Pres & CEO:** L.K. Boothby
**COO:** G.D. Packer
**CFO & Chief Acctg Officer:** T.W. Rathert
**Treas:** S.G. Riggs

**Secy & General Counsel:** J.D. Marziotti
**Investor Contact:** P. McKnight (281-405-4284)
**Investor Contact:** S.C. Campbell (281-847-6081)
**Board Members:** L. K. Boothby, P. J. Burguieres, P. J. Gardner, J. R. Kemp, III, J. M. Lacey, J. H. Netherland, Jr., H. H. Newman, T. G. Ricks, J. Romans, C. Shultz, J. T. Strange

**Founded:** 1988
**Domicile:** Delaware
**Employees:** 1,352

# Newmont Mining Corp

**STANDARD &POOR'S**

| S&P Recommendation BUY ★★★★☆ | Price $63.77 (as of Nov 25, 2011) | 12-Mo. Target Price $85.00 | Investment Style Large-Cap Growth |
|---|---|---|---|

**GICS Sector** Materials
**Sub-Industry** Gold

**Summary** Newmont is one of the world's largest gold producers, and is also engaged in the production of copper.

## Key Stock Statistics (Source S&P, Vickers, company reports)

| | | | | | | |
|---|---|---|---|---|---|---|
| 52-Wk Range | $72.42– 50.05 | S&P Oper. EPS 2011E | 4.58 | Market Capitalization(B) | $31.133 | Beta | 0.32 |
| Trailing 12-Month EPS | $4.39 | S&P Oper. EPS 2012E | 5.87 | Yield (%) | 2.20 | S&P 3-Yr. Proj. EPS CAGR(%) | 12 |
| Trailing 12-Month P/E | 14.5 | P/E on S&P Oper. EPS 2011E | 13.9 | Dividend Rate/Share | $1.40 | S&P Credit Rating | BBB+ |
| $10K Invested 5 Yrs Ago | $14,716 | Common Shares Outstg. (M) | 488.2 | Institutional Ownership (%) | 82 | | |

## Price Performance

30-Week Mov. Avg. · · · 10-Week Mov. Avg. - - GAAP Earnings vs. Previous Year   Volume Above Avg. STARS
12-Mo. Target Price — Relative Strength   ▲ Up ▼ Down ► No Change   Below Avg.

Options: ASE, CBOE, P, Ph

Analysis prepared by Equity Analyst **Leo J. Larkin** on Nov 08, 2011, when the stock traded at **$71.61**.

### Highlights

➤ Following an estimated rise in sales of 11% in 2011, we look for a 13% advance in 2012 on another increase in the average price for both gold and copper. We expect that production of both metals will approximate 2011's projected levels of 6.0 million oz. of gold and 381 million lbs. of copper. With respect to pricing, we think that volatility in the world's major currencies, lingering concerns over sovereign debt, quantitative easing by governments and continued low short-term interest rates worldwide will lead to another rise in the gold price. We look for the copper price to increase on continued global economic growth, tight mine supply and a gradual decline in metal exchange inventories.

➤ We see higher operating profits in 2012 on a projected gain in the average price of gold and copper. After interest expense and taxes, we estimate EPS of $5.87 for 2012, versus operating EPS of $4.58 estimated for 2011.

➤ Longer term, we see earnings and reserves being aided by a projected rise in the price of gold, further consolidation of the industry, acquisitions, and development of new and existing mines.

### Investment Rationale/Risk

➤ We see NEM's growth prospects as more secure after a series of acquisitions in recent years. Also, with its output exposed to the spot gold price, NEM appears well positioned to us for a continued bull market in gold. We believe that gold will remain in a bull market for several reasons: We expect the gap between consumption and production to persist as production worldwide stagnates; we think gold and gold shares will be seen as attractive alternative investments, given our view that financial asset returns will continue to trail the high levels from the late 1990s; and we believe that currency instability will increase gold's role as a monetary reserve asset. We view NEM as attractively valued, recently trading at 12.2X our 2012 EPS estimate with a dividend yield of just under 2%.

➤ Risks to our recommendation and target price include declines in the prices of gold and copper in 2012 instead of the gains that we project.

➤ Applying a 14.5X multiple to our 2012 EPS estimate, the low end of the historical range and about in line with the P/E we apply to NEM's major peer, we arrive at our 12-month target price of $85.

## Qualitative Risk Assessment

| LOW | MEDIUM | HIGH |
|---|---|---|

Our risk assessment reflects Newmont's exposure to the cyclical markets for copper and gold. This is offset by our view of its moderate balance sheet leverage and our expectation that the company will generate positive free cash flow on a more consistent basis.

## Quantitative Evaluations

**S&P Quality Ranking**   **B**

| D | C | B- | B | B+ | A- | A | A+ |
|---|---|---|---|---|---|---|---|

**Relative Strength Rank**   **MODERATE**

70

LOWEST = 1   HIGHEST = 99

## Revenue/Earnings Data

### Revenue (Million $)

| | 1Q | 2Q | 3Q | 4Q | Year |
|---|---|---|---|---|---|
| 2011 | 2,465 | 2,384 | 2,744 | -- | -- |
| 2010 | 2,242 | 2,153 | 2,597 | 2,548 | 9,540 |
| 2009 | 1,552 | 1,602 | 2,049 | 2,518 | 7,705 |
| 2008 | 1,943 | 1,522 | 1,392 | 1,342 | 6,199 |
| 2007 | 1,256 | 1,302 | 1,646 | 1,410 | 5,526 |
| 2006 | 1,132 | 1,293 | 1,102 | 1,460 | 4,987 |

### Earnings Per Share ($)

| | | | | | |
|---|---|---|---|---|---|
| 2011 | 1.03 | 1.04 | 0.98 | E1.36 | E4.58 |
| 2010 | 1.11 | 0.77 | 1.07 | 1.67 | 4.61 |
| 2009 | 0.40 | 0.35 | 0.79 | 1.14 | 2.68 |
| 2008 | 0.80 | 0.61 | 0.39 | 0.02 | 1.82 |
| 2007 | 0.15 | -0.90 | 0.72 | -2.03 | -2.13 |
| 2006 | 0.46 | 0.34 | 0.59 | 0.47 | 1.86 |

Fiscal year ended Dec. 31. Next earnings report expected: Late February. EPS Estimates based on S&P Operating Earnings; historical GAAP earnings are as reported.

## Dividend Data (Dates: mm/dd Payment Date: mm/dd/yy)

| Amount ($) | Date Decl. | Ex-Div. Date | Stk. of Record | Payment Date |
|---|---|---|---|---|
| 0.150 | 02/23 | 03/11 | 03/15 | 03/30/11 |
| 0.200 | 04/07 | 06/14 | 06/16 | 06/29/11 |
| 0.300 | 07/27 | 09/06 | 09/08 | 09/29/11 |
| 0.350 | 09/19 | 12/06 | 12/08 | 12/30/11 |

Dividends have been paid since 1934. Source: Company reports.

# Newmont Mining Corp

STANDARD
&POOR'S

## Business Summary November 08, 2011

CORPORATE OVERVIEW. Newmont Mining Corp. is one of the world's largest gold producers. It has significant assets and operations in the United States, Australia, Peru, Indonesia, Ghana, Canada, Bolivia, New Zealand and Mexico. The company has two large development projects in Ghana, West Africa. Newmont is also engaged in the production of copper, principally through its Batu Hijau operation in Indonesia.

As of December 31, 2010, proven and probable gold reserves totaled 93.5 million oz. using a gold price of $950/oz., versus 91.8 million oz. at the end of 2009 using a gold price of $800/oz.

At December 31, 2010 NEM's proven and probable gold reserves in North America were 33.5 million equity ounces. Outside of North America, year-end proven and probable gold reserves were 60 million equity ounces, including 31.4 million equity ounces in Asia Pacific, 17.2 million equity ounces in Africa and 11.4 million equity ounces in South America.

Copper reserves totaled 9.4 billion lbs. at the end of 2010, using a copper price of $2.50 per lb., versus 9.1 billion lbs. at the end of 2009, using a copper price of $2.00 per lb. Equity copper sales totaled 292 million lbs. in 2010, versus 226 million lbs. in 2009.

In 2010, 22% of Newmont's total sales came from the United States, 19% from Peru, 24% from Australia/New Zealand, 26% from Indonesia and 7% from Ghana and 1% from Mexico. Equity gold sales totaled 5.27 million oz. in 2010, versus 5.22 million oz. in 2009.

As of December 31, 2010, 20% of the company's total long-lived assets were located in the U.S., 13% in Canada, 11% in Peru, 33% in Australia/New Zealand, 14% in Indonesia and 8% in Ghana and 1% in Mexico.

In 2010, gold accounted for 80.6% of sales and copper comprised 19.4%.

CORPORATE STRATEGY. NEM's main strategy is to increase its portfolio of low-cost, long-life mines. On April 7, 2011, NEM announced a comprehensive plan for the development of its current global portfolio of assets that would increase annual gold production to approximately 7 million ounces and 400 million pounds of attributable annual copper production by 2017.

## Company Financials Fiscal Year Ended Dec. 31

| Per Share Data ($) | 2010 | 2009 | 2008 | 2007 | 2006 | 2005 | 2004 | 2003 | 2002 | 2001 |
|---|---|---|---|---|---|---|---|---|---|---|
| Tangible Book Value | 26.52 | 21.37 | 15.20 | 16.27 | 14.98 | 12.27 | 11.02 | 8.39 | 2.77 | 7.49 |
| Cash Flow | 8.31 | 4.45 | 3.56 | -0.59 | 3.27 | 2.27 | 2.66 | 2.60 | 1.75 | 1.38 |
| Earnings | 4.61 | 2.68 | 1.82 | -2.13 | 1.86 | 0.83 | 1.10 | 1.23 | 0.39 | -0.16 |
| S&P Core Earnings | 4.56 | 2.69 | 1.86 | 0.42 | 1.45 | 0.79 | 1.22 | 1.05 | 0.25 | -0.26 |
| Dividends | 0.50 | 0.40 | 0.40 | 0.40 | 0.40 | 0.40 | 0.30 | 0.17 | 0.12 | 0.12 |
| Payout Ratio | 11% | 15% | 22% | NM | 22% | 48% | 28% | 14% | 31% | NM |
| Prices:High | 65.50 | 56.45 | 57.55 | 56.35 | 62.72 | 53.93 | 50.20 | 50.28 | 32.75 | 25.23 |
| Prices:Low | 42.80 | 34.40 | 21.17 | 38.01 | 39.84 | 34.90 | 34.70 | 24.08 | 18.52 | 14.00 |
| P/E Ratio:High | 14 | 21 | 32 | NM | 34 | 65 | 46 | 41 | 84 | NM |
| P/E Ratio:Low | 9 | 13 | 12 | NM | 21 | 42 | 32 | 20 | 47 | NM |

| Income Statement Analysis (Million $) | | | | | | | | | | |
|---|---|---|---|---|---|---|---|---|---|---|
| Revenue | 9,540 | 7,705 | 6,199 | 5,526 | 4,987 | 4,406 | 4,524 | 3,214 | 2,658 | 1,656 |
| Operating Income | 5,177 | 3,910 | 2,057 | 2,041 | 2,059 | 1,621 | 1,878 | 1,219 | 852 | 435 |
| Depreciation | 1,010 | 852 | 789 | 695 | 636 | 644 | 697 | 564 | 506 | 300 |
| Interest Expense | 279 | 120 | 149 | 155 | 97.0 | 98.0 | 97.6 | 88.6 | 130 | 86.4 |
| Pretax Income | 4,000 | 2,897 | 1,271 | -353 | 1,627 | 1,068 | 1,102 | 890 | 268 | -10.2 |
| Effective Tax Rate | NA | 27.2% | 8.89% | NM | 26.1% | 29.4% | 25.0% | 23.2% | 7.43% | NM |
| Net Income | 2,305 | 1,308 | 829 | -963 | 840 | 374 | 490 | 510 | 150 | -23.3 |
| S&P Core Earnings | 2,277 | 1,308 | 847 | 192 | 657 | 356 | 540 | 435 | 96.7 | -52.8 |

| Balance Sheet & Other Financial Data (Million $) | | | | | | | | | | |
|---|---|---|---|---|---|---|---|---|---|---|
| Cash | 4,169 | 3,271 | 447 | 1,292 | 1,275 | 1,899 | 1,726 | 1,459 | 402 | 149 |
| Current Assets | 7,253 | 5,822 | 2,361 | 2,672 | 2,642 | 3,036 | 2,721 | 2,360 | 1,113 | 709 |
| Total Assets | 25,663 | 22,299 | 15,839 | 15,598 | 15,601 | 13,992 | 12,771 | 11,050 | 10,155 | 4,062 |
| Current Liabilities | 2,747 | 2,320 | 1,596 | 1,500 | 1,739 | 1,350 | 1,101 | 834 | 693 | 486 |
| Long Term Debt | 4,182 | 4,652 | 3,373 | 2,683 | Nil | 1,733 | 1,311 | 887 | 1,701 | 1,090 |
| Common Equity | 13,345 | 10,703 | 7,102 | 7,548 | 9,865 | 8,376 | 7,938 | 7,385 | 5,419 | 1,469 |
| Total Capital | 22,528 | 17,422 | 12,896 | 12,705 | 10,963 | 11,489 | 10,500 | 9,251 | 8,132 | 2,955 |
| Capital Expenditures | 1,402 | 1,769 | 1,881 | 1,670 | 1,551 | 1,226 | 718 | 501 | 300 | 402 |
| Cash Flow | 4,154 | 2,165 | 1,618 | -268 | 1,476 | 1,018 | 1,187 | 1,075 | 652 | 269 |
| Current Ratio | 2.6 | 2.5 | 1.5 | 1.8 | 1.5 | 2.2 | 2.5 | 2.8 | 1.6 | 1.5 |
| % Long Term Debt of Capitalization | 18.6 | 26.7 | 26.2 | 21.1 | Nil | 15.1 | 12.5 | 9.6 | 20.9 | 40.3 |
| % Net Income of Revenue | 24.2 | 17.0 | 13.4 | NM | 16.8 | 8.5 | 10.8 | 15.9 | 5.7 | NM |
| % Return on Assets | 9.6 | 6.9 | 5.3 | NM | 5.7 | 2.8 | 4.2 | 4.8 | 2.1 | NM |
| % Return on Equity | 16.3 | 14.8 | 11.3 | NM | 9.0 | 4.5 | 6.4 | 8.0 | 4.4 | NM |

Data as orig reptd.; bef. results of disc opers/spec. items. Per share data adj. for stk. divs.; EPS diluted. E-Estimated. NA-Not Available. NM-Not Meaningful. NR-Not Ranked. UR-Under Review.

**Office:** 6363 South Fiddlers Green Circle, Suite 800, Greenwood Village, CO 80111.
**Telephone:** 303-863-7414.
**Website:** http://www.newmont.com
**Chrmn:** V.A. Calarco

**Pres & CEO:** R.T. O'Brien
**COO & EVP:** B.A. Hill
**CFO:** R.D. Ball
**Chief Acctg Officer & Cntlr:** D. Ottewell

**Investor Contact:** J. Seaberg (303-837-5743)
**Board Members:** G. A. Barton, B. R. Brook, V. A. Calarco, N. Doyle, V. M. Hagen, M. S. Hamson, J. Nelson, R. T. O'Brien, J. B. Prescott, D. C. Roth

**Founded:** 1916
**Domicile:** Delaware
**Employees:** 15,500

The McGraw-Hill Companies

# News Corp

**STANDARD &POOR'S**

| S&P Recommendation | **BUY** ★★★★☆ | Price | 12-Mo. Target Price | Investment Style |
|---|---|---|---|---|
| | | $15.97 (as of Nov 25, 2011) | $20.00 | Large-Cap Blend |

**GICS Sector** Consumer Discretionary
**Sub-Industry** Movies & Entertainment

**Summary** This media conglomerate owns controlling interests in some of the world's leading media and entertainment brands, including Fox (film/TV), The Wall Street Journal, SKY Italia, BSkyB and STAR TV, as well as other newspapers and publishing businesses.

## Key Stock Statistics (Source S&P, Vickers, company reports)

| | | | | | | | |
|---|---|---|---|---|---|---|---|
| 52-Wk Range | $18.35–13.38 | S&P Oper. EPS 2012E | 1.49 | Market Capitalization(B) | $27.502 | Beta | 1.49 |
| Trailing 12-Month EPS | $1.02 | S&P Oper. EPS 2013E | 1.79 | Yield (%) | 1.19 | S&P 3-Yr. Proj. EPS CAGR(%) | 14 |
| Trailing 12-Month P/E | 15.7 | P/E on S&P Oper. EPS 2012E | 10.7 | Dividend Rate/Share | $0.19 | S&P Credit Rating | BBB+ |
| $10K Invested 5 Yrs Ago | $8,034 | Common Shares Outstg. (M) | 2,520.6 | Institutional Ownership (%) | 88 | | |

## Price Performance

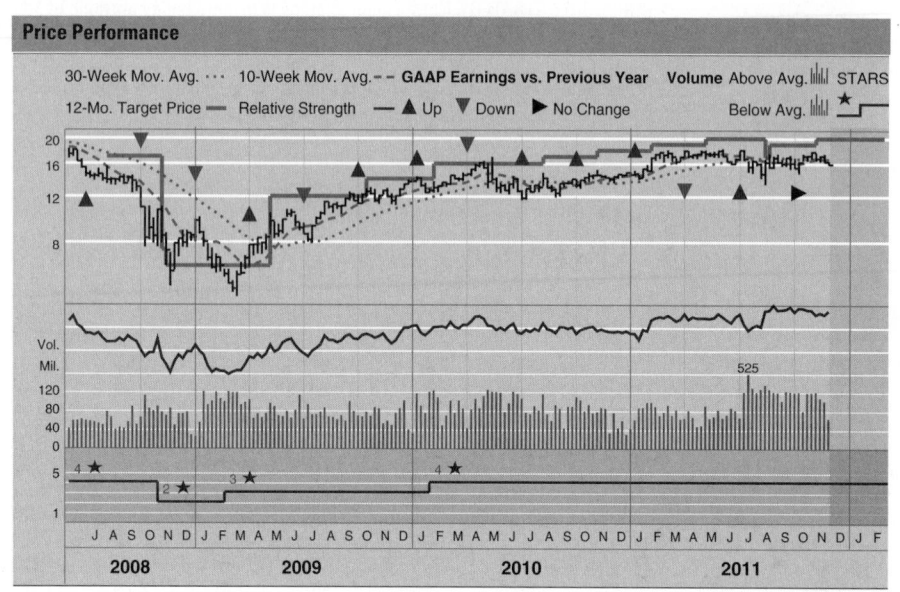

Analysis prepared by Equity Analyst **T. Amobi, CFA CPA** on Nov 08, 2011, when the stock traded at **$16.99**.

Options: ASE, CBOE, P, Ph

## Highlights

► We estimate 6.6% and 4.1% consolidated revenue growth in FY 12 (Jun.) and FY 13, respectively, to $35.6 billion and $37.1 billion, fueled by continued strong growth in cable networks' affiliate fees and advertising revenues (domestic and international). A healthy ad rebound should also benefit the TV broadcast network and stations, with the latter also poised for a ramp-up of retransmission revenues. We see easier film comparisons (Avatar) and moderately improved growth for Sky Italia (satellite TV), versus relatively stagnant publishing businesses (newspapers, inserts, book publishing).

► With further margin expansion across several key divisions (on increased operating leverage), we project FY 12 and FY 13 consolidated EBIT of about $5.9 billion and $6.7 billion, respectively -- more than half of which is expected to be derived from the cable networks segment.

► After equity affiliate earnings (mainly BSkyB), interest and taxes, we estimate operating EPS of $1.49 in FY 12 -- with the likely completion of the current $5 billion share buyback program by the end of the year -- and $1.79 in FY 13.

## Investment Rationale/Risk

► We saw continued broad-based strong gains across several core businesses in the company's FY 12 first quarter results, putting it on track for its full-year financial target of low to mid-teens EBIT growth. We see management actively cultivating incremental revenue opportunities (e.g. digital streaming, retransmission, e-books) that should increasingly affect its results in the years ahead. With investors gradually refocusing on improving fundamentals, recent price action suggests that concerns about a phone-hacking scandal may be receding.

► Risks to our recommendation and target price include a sharp macroeconomic and/or consumer spending slowdown; further negative developments on scandal-related investigations; and governance issues related to CEO succession and the Murdoch family's voting control via dual class shares.

► Our 12-month target price is $20, blending 7.0X FY 12E EV/EBITDA and P/E-to-growth analyses (on 14% long-term growth) -- applying a non-voting discount -- noting ample liquidity with cash and equivalents of about $4.40 a share, and the stock's recent dividend yield of 1.1%.

## Qualitative Risk Assessment

| LOW | **MEDIUM** | HIGH |
|---|---|---|

Our risk assessment for News Corp. reflects a relatively diversified asset portfolio with potential scale economies and a strong balance sheet that we think offers ample financial flexibility, offset by uncertainty surrounding government investigations related to a phone-hacking scandal, and some corporate governance issues.

## Quantitative Evaluations

**S&P Quality Ranking**    A-

| D | C | B- | B | B+ | **A-** | A | A+ |
|---|---|---|---|---|---|---|---|

**Relative Strength Rank**    MODERATE

59

LOWEST = 1    HIGHEST = 99

## Revenue/Earnings Data

**Revenue (Million $)**

| | 1Q | 2Q | 3Q | 4Q | Year |
|---|---|---|---|---|---|
| 2012 | 7,959 | -- | -- | -- | -- |
| 2011 | 7,426 | 8,761 | 8,256 | 8,962 | 33,405 |
| 2010 | 7,199 | 8,684 | 8,785 | 8,110 | 32,778 |
| 2009 | 7,509 | 7,871 | 7,373 | 7,670 | 30,423 |
| 2008 | 7,067 | 8,590 | 8,750 | 8,589 | 32,996 |
| 2007 | 5,914 | 7,844 | 7,530 | 7,367 | 28,655 |

**Earnings Per Share ($)**

| | 1Q | 2Q | 3Q | 4Q | Year |
|---|---|---|---|---|---|
| 2012 | 0.30 | E0.35 | E0.39 | E0.43 | E1.49 |
| 2011 | 0.30 | 0.24 | 0.24 | 0.35 | 1.14 |
| 2010 | 0.22 | 0.10 | 0.32 | 0.33 | 0.97 |
| 2009 | 0.20 | -2.45 | 1.04 | -0.08 | -1.29 |
| 2008 | 0.23 | 0.27 | 0.91 | 0.43 | 1.81 |
| 2007 | 0.28 | 0.27 | 0.29 | 0.30 | 1.14 |

Fiscal year ended Jun. 30. Next earnings report expected: Early February. EPS Estimates based on S&P Operating Earnings; historical GAAP earnings are as reported.

## Dividend Data (Dates: mm/dd Payment Date: mm/dd/yy)

| Amount ($) | Date Decl. | Ex-Div. Date | Stk. of Record | Payment Date |
|---|---|---|---|---|
| 0.075 | 02/02 | 03/14 | 03/16 | 04/20/11 |
| 0.095 | 08/10 | 09/12 | 09/14 | 10/19/11 |

Dividends have been paid since 1995. Source: Company reports.

---

**Please read the Required Disclosures and Analyst Certification on the last page of this report.**

The McGraw-Hill Companies

# News Corp

STANDARD
&POOR'S

## Business Summary November 08, 2011

CORPORATE OVERVIEW. News Corp., once a small publisher of Australian newspapers, has grown into one of the world's premier media conglomerates.

Its key U.S. assets include Fox film studio and 20th Century Fox TV; Fox broadcast network and TV stations; Fox News, FX and regional sports networks (including FSN Ohio, FSN Florida and 40% of FSN Bay Area); HarperCollins (book publishers); the Wall Street Journal and New York Post newspapers; and an inserts business.

International assets include several newspaper businesses in the U.K. and Australia (including The Times, The Sun, and The Australian); the wholly owned satellite TV provider SKY Italia; a 39% controlling stake in U.K. satellite TV provider BSkyB; a 40% stake in Sky Deutschland; and other associated entities in Asia, Australia and Latin America. About 54% of FY 10 (Jun.) revenues were derived from the U.S. and Canada, 30% from Europe, and 16% from Australasia/other.

CORPORATE STRATEGY. Increasingly, the company also seeks to exploit its content through various digital outlets (e.g., iTunes, WSJ digital subscriptions,

e-books), as well as the iPad daily (which launched in February 2011). It remains a JV partner in online video site Hulu (along with Disney and Comcast's NBC). A generational categorization of its cable channels includes networks that are fully distributed (e.g., Fox News and FX); near-fully distributed (e.g., Speed and National Geographic), and newer start-ups (e.g., Fuel, Fox College Sports, Fox Reality Channel, Fox Business Network, Big Ten Network).

In recent years, the company has completed a number of key acquisitions and divestitures. In June 2011, it sold social networking site MySpace (purchased in 2005 for about $650 million), and transferred a controlling stake in three TV channels in China, as well as its Chinese movie library, to a local firm (for undisclosed terms). In 2007, it acquired Dow Jones for $5.7 billion. In 2009, it offered a 38.4% stake in DIRECTV, plus three regional sports networks and $550 million of cash, for Liberty Media's 16.3% voting stake.

## Company Financials Fiscal Year Ended Jun. 30

| Per Share Data ($) | 2011 | 2010 | 2009 | 2008 | 2007 | 2006 | 2005 | 2004 | 2003 | 2002 |
|---|---|---|---|---|---|---|---|---|---|---|
| Tangible Book Value | NA | 0.96 | NM | NM | 2.37 | 1.86 | 1.81 | 1.85 | NM | 0.68 |
| Cash Flow | NA | 1.42 | -0.86 | 2.22 | 1.38 | 1.62 | 1.40 | 0.79 | 0.65 | -2.39 |
| Earnings | 1.14 | 0.97 | -1.29 | 1.81 | 1.14 | 0.92 | 0.73 | 0.58 | 0.46 | -2.75 |
| S&P Core Earnings | 1.21 | 1.06 | 0.53 | 1.39 | 1.00 | 0.83 | 0.66 | 0.52 | 0.51 | -1.10 |
| Dividends | 0.15 | 0.14 | 0.12 | 0.12 | 0.12 | 0.13 | 0.11 | 0.10 | 0.08 | 0.07 |
| Payout Ratio | 13% | 14% | NM | 7% | 11% | 14% | 14% | 17% | 17% | NM |
| Prices:High | 18.35 | 17.00 | 14.00 | 20.55 | 25.40 | 21.94 | 18.88 | 18.77 | 15.54 | 13.60 |
| Prices:Low | 13.38 | 11.61 | 4.95 | 5.43 | 19.00 | 15.17 | 13.94 | 14.57 | 9.33 | 7.54 |
| P/E Ratio:High | 16 | 18 | NM | 11 | 22 | 24 | 26 | 32 | 34 | NM |
| P/E Ratio:Low | 12 | 12 | NM | 3 | 17 | 16 | 19 | 25 | 20 | NM |

| Income Statement Analysis (Million $) | | | | | | | | | | |
|---|---|---|---|---|---|---|---|---|---|---|
| Revenue | NA | 32,778 | 30,423 | 32,996 | 28,655 | 25,327 | 23,859 | 29,428 | 29,913 | 29,014 |
| Operating Income | NA | 5,644 | 4,696 | 6,482 | 5,331 | 4,643 | 4,329 | 5,146 | 4,372 | 4,291 |
| Depreciation | NA | 1,185 | 1,138 | 1,207 | 879 | 775 | 765 | 844 | 776 | 749 |
| Interest Expense | NA | 991 | 927 | 970 | 843 | 791 | 736 | 958 | 1,094 | 1,384 |
| Pretax Income | NA | 3,323 | -5,539 | 7,321 | 5,306 | 4,405 | 3,561 | 3,855 | 3,000 | -10,959 |
| Effective Tax Rate | NA | 20.4% | NM | 24.6% | 34.2% | 34.6% | 34.3% | 32.3% | 25.8% | NM |
| Net Income | NA | 2,539 | -3,378 | 5,387 | 3,426 | 2,812 | 2,128 | 2,312 | 1,808 | -11,962 |
| S&P Core Earnings | 3,170 | 2,771 | 1,379 | 4,142 | 3,171 | 2,663 | 2,017 | 1,563 | 1,303 | -2,718 |

| Balance Sheet & Other Financial Data (Million $) | | | | | | | | | | |
|---|---|---|---|---|---|---|---|---|---|---|
| Cash | NA | 8,709 | 6,540 | 4,662 | 7,654 | 5,783 | 6,470 | 6,217 | 6,746 | 6,337 |
| Current Assets | NA | 18,024 | 15,836 | 14,362 | 15,906 | 13,123 | 12,779 | 15,012 | 14,861 | 14,647 |
| Total Assets | NA | 54,384 | 53,121 | 62,308 | 62,343 | 56,649 | 54,692 | 73,738 | 67,747 | 71,441 |
| Current Liabilities | NA | 8,862 | 10,639 | 9,182 | 7,494 | 6,373 | 6,649 | 10,437 | 9,303 | 11,005 |
| Long Term Debt | NA | 13,191 | 12,204 | 13,230 | 12,147 | 11,385 | 10,087 | 12,972 | 14,480 | 15,275 |
| Common Equity | NA | 25,113 | 23,224 | 28,623 | 32,922 | 29,874 | 29,377 | 39,387 | 31,834 | 34,101 |
| Total Capital | NA | 39,186 | 39,455 | 48,303 | 51,530 | 46,740 | 44,500 | 59,473 | 53,867 | 54,743 |
| Capital Expenditures | NA | 914 | 1,101 | 1,443 | 1,308 | 976 | 901 | 517 | 551 | 505 |
| Cash Flow | NA | 3,724 | -2,240 | 6,594 | 4,305 | 3,587 | 2,883 | 3,156 | 2,584 | -11,213 |
| Current Ratio | NA | 2.0 | 1.5 | 1.6 | 2.1 | 2.1 | 1.9 | 1.4 | 1.6 | 1.3 |
| % Long Term Debt of Capitalization | NA | 33.7 | 30.9 | 27.4 | 23.6 | 24.4 | 22.7 | 21.8 | 26.9 | 27.9 |
| % Net Income of Revenue | NA | 7.8 | NM | 16.3 | 12.0 | 11.1 | 8.9 | 7.9 | 6.0 | NM |
| % Return on Assets | NA | 4.7 | NM | 8.6 | 5.8 | 5.1 | 4.1 | 3.3 | 2.6 | NM |
| % Return on Equity | NA | 10.5 | NM | 17.5 | 10.9 | 9.5 | 8.4 | 6.5 | 5.5 | NM |

Data as orig reptd.; bef. results of disc opers/spec. items. Per share data adj. for stk. divs.; EPS diluted. Income and balance sheet data in Australian $ prior to 2005. E-Estimated. NA-Not Available. NM-Not Meaningful. NR-Not Ranked. UR-Under Review.

**Office:** 1211 Avenue of the Americas, New York, NY 10036.
**Telephone:** 212-852-7000.
**Website:** http://www.newscorp.com
**Chrmn & CEO:** K.R. Murdoch

**Pres, Vice Chrmn & COO:** C. Carey
**EVP, CFO & Chief Acctg Officer:** D.F. DeVoe
**SVP & General Counsel:** J.L. Nova
**SVP & Cntlr:** R. Gannon

**Investor Contact:** R. Nolte (212-852-7017)
**Board Members:** J. M. Aznar, N. Bancroft, P. L. Barnes, J. W. Breyer, C. Carey, K. E. Cowley, D. F. DeVoe, V. Dinh, R. I. Eddington, J. I. Klein, A. S. Knight, J. R. Murdoch, K. R. Murdoch, L. K. Murdoch, T. J. Perkins, A. M. Siskind, J. L. Thornton

**Founded:** 1922
**Domicile:** Delaware
**Employees:** 51,000

# NextEra Energy Inc

**STANDARD &POOR'S**

| S&P Recommendation | BUY ★★★★☆ | Price $52.57 (as of Nov 25, 2011) | 12-Mo. Target Price $62.00 | Investment Style Large-Cap Blend |
|---|---|---|---|---|

**GICS Sector** Utilities
**Sub-Industry** Electric Utilities

**Summary** NextEra Energy, Inc. (formerly FPL Group) is the holding company for Florida Power & Light and NextEra Energy Resources.

## Key Stock Statistics (Source S&P, Vickers, company reports)

| | | | | | |
|---|---|---|---|---|---|
| 52-Wk Range | $58.98– 49.00 | S&P Oper. EPS 2011**E** 4.46 | Market Capitalization(B) $22.213 | Beta | 0.57 |
| Trailing 12-Month EPS | $3.64 | S&P Oper. EPS 2012**E** 4.64 | Yield (%) 4.18 | S&P 3-Yr. Proj. EPS CAGR(%) | 5 |
| Trailing 12-Month P/E | 14.4 | P/E on S&P Oper. EPS 2011**E** 11.8 | Dividend Rate/Share $2.20 | S&P Credit Rating | A- |
| $10K Invested 5 Yrs Ago | $11,823 | Common Shares Outstg. (M) 422.5 | Institutional Ownership (%) 66 | | |

## Price Performance

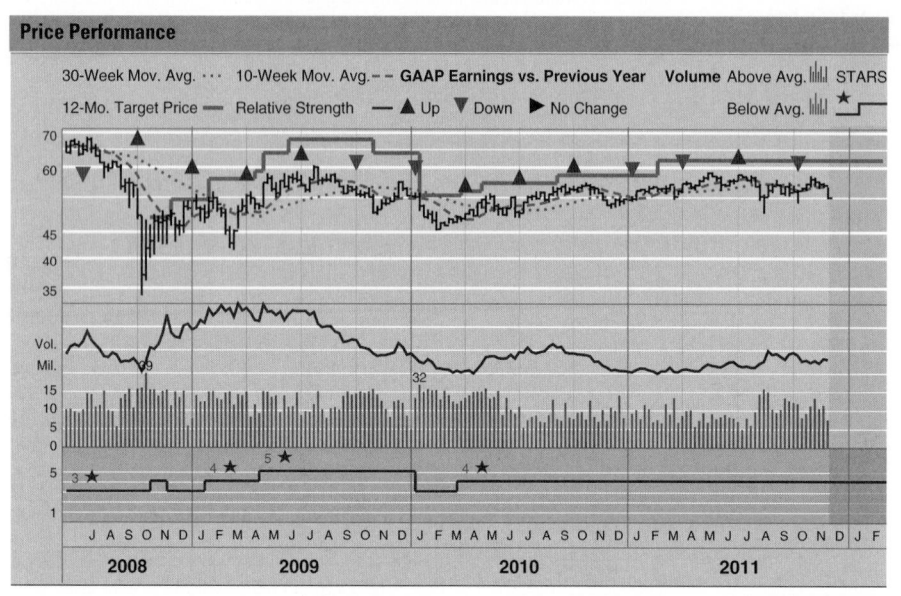

30-Week Mov. Avg. ···  10-Week Mov. Avg. - - GAAP Earnings vs. Previous Year  Volume Above Avg. STARS
12-Mo. Target Price — Relative Strength  ▲ Up ▼ Down ► No Change  Below Avg. ★

Options: ASE, CBOE, P, Ph

Analysis prepared by Equity Analyst **Justin McCann** on Nov 17, 2011, when the stock traded at **$55.60**.

## Qualitative Risk Assessment

| LOW | MEDIUM | HIGH |
|---|---|---|

Our risk assessment reflects our view of steady cash flows from Florida Power & Light, despite the weak economy and housing market and fewer customer accounts. It also reflects the recent return to a more stable political and regulatory environment for FP&L and the longer-term growth potential of NextEra Energy Resources, the independent power subsidiary, despite its higher-risk cash flows.

## Quantitative Evaluations

**S&P Quality Ranking** A

| D | C | B- | B | B+ | A- | A | A+ |
|---|---|---|---|---|---|---|---|

**Relative Strength Rank** MODERATE

56

LOWEST = 1    HIGHEST = 99

## Highlights

➤ We expect operating EPS in 2011 to increase more than 3% from 2010's $4.30. In the first nine months of 2011, operating EPS of $3.44 was $0.06 below the year-earlier period. In addition to 1.7% more shares, operating EPS was hurt by a decline at the Energy Resources subsidiary, which was hurt by extended nuclear refueling outages and lower tax credits. This was partially offset by higher earnings at Florida Power & Light due to an expanded rate base.

➤ For 2012, we expect earnings to be driven by an approximate 14% increase in FP&L's rate base. We think the utility's growth prospects will also reflect the timing and extent of a recovery in Florida's economy and housing market, but we believe that once it has recovered, FP&L should be able to realize growth rates above the national average. While we expect earnings to improve at Energy Resources due to new assets and fewer nuclear outage days, we expect the improvement to be restricted by lower margin power contracts and lower tax incentives.

➤ Longer term, we expect FP&L's rate base to increase by about 7% in 2013 and 3% in 2014, and for Energy Resources to benefit from new wind and solar assets, and improved power prices.

## Investment Rationale/Risk

➤ While the stock has benefited, in our view, from the investor shift into electric utilities due to the extraordinary volatility and often sharp declines in the broader market, we think this benefit was partially restricted by the weakened earnings outlook for both 2011 and 2012. However, we remain positive about the shares due to the longer term benefit to earnings we expect to result from FP&L' ambitious investment plans, as well as the long-term growth prospects we see for the Energy Resources subsidiary, once the environment for the development of new wind and solar power projects has improved.

➤ Risks to our opinion and target price include lower-than-expected results from NextEra Energy Resources, prolonged weakness in the Florida economy and housing market, and a reduction in the average P/E multiple for the electric utilities sub-industry as a whole.

➤ Over the long term, we believe the stock will benefit from NEE being the national leader in wind and solar power development. We expect annual dividend growth of about 5% over the next few years. Our 12-month target price is $62, a modest discount-to-peers P/E multiple of 13.4X our operating EPS estimate for 2012.

## Revenue/Earnings Data

**Revenue (Million $)**

| | 1Q | 2Q | 3Q | 4Q | Year |
|---|---|---|---|---|---|
| 2011 | 3,134 | 3,961 | 4,382 | -- | -- |
| 2010 | 3,622 | 3,591 | 4,691 | 3,413 | 15,317 |
| 2009 | 3,705 | 3,811 | 4,473 | 3,655 | 15,643 |
| 2008 | 3,434 | 3,585 | 5,387 | 4,003 | 16,410 |
| 2007 | 3,075 | 3,929 | 4,575 | 3,683 | 15,263 |
| 2006 | 3,584 | 3,809 | 4,694 | 3,623 | 15,710 |

**Earnings Per Share ($)**

| | | | | | |
|---|---|---|---|---|---|
| 2011 | 0.64 | 1.38 | 0.97 | E1.03 | E4.46 |
| 2010 | 1.36 | 1.02 | 1.74 | 0.63 | 4.74 |
| 2009 | 0.90 | 0.91 | 1.31 | 0.85 | 3.97 |
| 2008 | 0.62 | 0.52 | 1.92 | 1.01 | 4.07 |
| 2007 | 0.38 | 1.01 | 1.33 | 0.56 | 3.27 |
| 2006 | 0.64 | 0.60 | 1.32 | 0.67 | 3.23 |

Fiscal year ended Dec. 31. Next earnings report expected: NA. EPS Estimates based on S&P Operating Earnings; historical GAAP earnings are as reported.

## Dividend Data (Dates: mm/dd Payment Date: mm/dd/yy)

| Amount ($) | Date Decl. | Ex-Div. Date | Stk. of Record | Payment Date |
|---|---|---|---|---|
| 0.550 | 02/18 | 03/02 | 03/04 | 03/15/11 |
| 0.550 | 05/20 | 06/01 | 06/03 | 06/15/11 |
| 0.550 | 07/29 | 08/24 | 08/26 | 09/15/11 |
| 0.550 | 10/14 | 11/22 | 11/25 | 12/15/11 |

Dividends have been paid since 1944. Source: Company reports.

**Please read the Required Disclosures and Analyst Certification on the last page of this report.**

The McGraw-Hill Companies

# NextEra Energy Inc

**STANDARD &POOR'S**

## Business Summary November 17, 2011

CORPORATE OVERVIEW. NextEra Energy, Inc. (formerly FPL Group), one of the largest providers of electricity-related services in the U.S., is the holding company for Florida Power & Light Co. (FP&L), a regulated and vertically integrated utility, and NextEra Energy Resources (Energy Resources), a wholesale generator of electricity with operations in 28 states and Canada.

IMPACT OF MAJOR DEVELOPMENTS. On May 21, 2010, the company changed its name from FPL Group, Inc. to NextEra Energy, Inc. Management believes that the new name, which reflects the name of the company's subsidiary, NextEra Energy Resources, will better reflect the company's scale as one of the largest and cleanest energy providers in North America, and is well positioned for the ongoing transition to a low-carbon economy. The ticker symbol was subsequently changed from FPL to NEE.

MARKET PROFILE. Florida Power & Light provides electricity to about 4.5 mil-

lion customers in an area covering nearly all of Florida's eastern seaboard, as well as the southern part of the state. Electric revenues by customer class in 2010 were: residential 54%; commercial 37%; industrial 2%; wholesale, 1%; and other (including deferred, and the net change in unbilled revenues), 6%. Retail customer growth in 2010 was 0.5%, after a 0.2% decline in 2009. Positive customer growth is expected to continue in 2011, although the rate of growth is projected to be below the utility's average rate of growth of 1.6% over the past 10 years. We do not expect to see a significant recovery in the utility's retail customer growth until there is a broader recovery in the state's economy and housing market.

## Company Financials Fiscal Year Ended Dec. 31

| Per Share Data ($) | 2010 | 2009 | 2008 | 2007 | 2006 | 2005 | 2004 | 2003 | 2002 | 2001 |
|---|---|---|---|---|---|---|---|---|---|---|
| Tangible Book Value | 34.36 | 31.35 | 28.57 | 26.35 | 24.52 | 21.52 | 20.24 | 18.93 | 17.46 | 17.09 |
| Earnings | 4.74 | 3.97 | 4.07 | 3.27 | 3.23 | 2.29 | 2.46 | 2.51 | 2.01 | 2.31 |
| S&P Core Earnings | 4.46 | 3.73 | 3.84 | 3.04 | 3.00 | 2.06 | 2.17 | 2.21 | 1.52 | 1.83 |
| Dividends | 2.00 | 1.89 | 1.78 | 1.64 | 1.50 | 1.42 | 1.30 | 1.20 | 1.16 | 1.12 |
| Payout Ratio | 42% | 48% | 44% | 50% | 46% | 62% | 53% | 48% | 58% | 48% |
| Prices:High | 56.26 | 60.61 | 73.75 | 72.77 | 55.57 | 48.11 | 38.05 | 34.04 | 32.66 | 35.81 |
| Prices:Low | 45.29 | 41.48 | 33.81 | 53.72 | 37.81 | 35.90 | 30.10 | 26.78 | 22.50 | 25.61 |
| P/E Ratio:High | 12 | 15 | 18 | 22 | 17 | 21 | 15 | 14 | 16 | 16 |
| P/E Ratio:Low | 10 | 10 | 8 | 16 | 12 | 16 | 12 | 11 | 11 | 11 |
| **Income Statement Analysis** (Million $) | | | | | | | | | | |
| Revenue | 15,317 | 15,643 | 16,410 | 15,263 | 15,710 | 11,846 | 10,522 | 9,630 | 8,311 | 8,475 |
| Depreciation | 2,092 | 1,947 | 1,579 | 1,261 | 1,185 | 1,285 | 1,198 | 1,105 | 952 | 983 |
| Maintenance | NA | NA | NA | NA | NA | NA | NA | NA | NA | NA |
| Fixed Charges Coverage | 3.41 | 3.16 | 3.43 | 3.18 | 3.30 | 2.87 | 3.26 | 3.95 | 4.52 | 4.51 |
| Construction Credits | 37.0 | 53.0 | 35.0 | 23.0 | 21.0 | 28.0 | 37.0 | NA | NA | NA |
| Effective Tax Rate | 21.4% | 16.8% | 21.5% | 21.9% | 23.7% | 23.5% | 23.1% | 29.2% | 26.0% | 32.7% |
| Net Income | 1,957 | 1,615 | 1,639 | 1,312 | 1,281 | 885 | 887 | 893 | 695 | 781 |
| S&P Core Earnings | 1,843 | 1,516 | 1,547 | 1,218 | 1,187 | 797 | 782 | 786 | 527 | 616 |
| **Balance Sheet & Other Financial Data** (Million $) | | | | | | | | | | |
| Gross Property | 54,221 | 50,169 | 45,528 | 41,040 | 36,152 | 33,351 | 31,720 | 30,272 | 26,505 | 23,388 |
| Capital Expenditures | 5,572 | 5,645 | 4,989 | 1,826 | 1,763 | 1,616 | 1,394 | 1,383 | 1,277 | 1,544 |
| Net Property | 39,075 | 36,078 | 32,411 | 28,652 | 24,499 | 22,463 | 21,226 | 20,297 | 14,304 | 11,662 |
| Capitalization:Long Term Debt | 18,013 | 16,300 | 13,833 | 11,280 | 9,591 | 8,039 | 8,027 | 8,728 | 6,016 | 5,084 |
| Capitalization:% Long Term Debt | 55.5 | 55.7 | 54.2 | 51.2 | 49.1 | 48.6 | 51.6 | 55.6 | 47.4 | 45.8 |
| Capitalization:Preferred | Nil | Nil | Nil | Nil | Nil | Nil | Nil | Nil | Nil | Nil |
| Capitalization:% Preferred | Nil | Nil | Nil | Nil | Nil | Nil | Nil | Nil | Nil | Nil |
| Capitalization:Common | 14,461 | 12,967 | 11,681 | 10,735 | 9,930 | 8,499 | 7,537 | 6,967 | 6,688 | 6,015 |
| Capitalization:% Common | 44.5 | 44.3 | 45.8 | 48.8 | 50.9 | 51.4 | 48.4 | 44.4 | 52.6 | 54.2 |
| Total Capital | 34,394 | 29,836 | 29,745 | 25,836 | 22,953 | 19,615 | 15,645 | 17,850 | 14,444 | 12,629 |
| % Operating Ratio | 82.3 | 85.5 | 85.5 | 87.5 | 87.1 | 88.6 | 87.8 | 87.9 | 85.7 | 87.6 |
| % Earned on Net Property | 8.6 | 7.6 | 9.3 | 8.6 | 8.9 | 6.7 | 7.1 | 8.1 | 9.5 | 10.3 |
| % Return on Revenue | 12.8 | 10.3 | 10.0 | 8.6 | 8.2 | 7.5 | 8.4 | 9.3 | 8.4 | 9.2 |
| % Return on Invested Capital | 8.8 | 8.3 | 8.4 | 8.2 | 10.9 | 8.6 | 9.2 | 8.1 | 9.0 | 9.6 |
| % Return on Common Equity | 14.3 | 13.1 | 14.6 | 12.7 | 13.9 | 11.0 | 12.0 | 13.4 | 10.7 | 13.5 |

Data as orig reptd.; bef. results of disc opers/spec. items. Per share data adj. for stk. divs.; EPS diluted. E-Estimated. NA-Not Available. NM-Not Meaningful. NR-Not Ranked. UR-Under Review.

**Office:** 700 Universe Boulevard, Juno Beach, FL 33408.
**Telephone:** 561-694-4000.
**Website:** http://www.nexteraenergy.com
**Chrmn & CEO:** L. Hay, III

**Pres & COO:** J.L. Robo
**Vice Chrmn, EVP & CFO:** M.P. Dewhurst
**EVP & General Counsel:** C.E. Sieving
**Chief Acctg Officer & Cntlr:** C.N. Froggatt

**Investor Contact:** P. Cutler (800-222-4511)
**Board Members:** S. S. Barrat, R. Beall, II, J. H. Brown, J. L. Camaren, M. P. Dewhurst, K. B. Dunn, J. B. Ferguson, L. Hay, III, T. Jennings, O. D. Kingsley, Jr., R. E. Schupp, W. H. Swanson, M. H. Thaman, H. E. Tookes, II

**Founded:** 1984
**Domicile:** Florida
**Employees:** 14,690

**The McGraw-Hill Companies**

# Nicor Inc.

**STANDARD &POOR'S**

| S&P Recommendation **HOLD** ★★★☆☆ | Price $53.57 (as of Nov 25, 2011) | 12-Mo. Target Price $54.00 | Investment Style Large-Cap Blend |
| --- | --- | --- | --- |

**GICS Sector** Utilities
**Sub-Industry** Gas Utilities

**Summary** This holding company's Nicor Gas subsidiary is one of the largest U.S. distributors of natural gas.

## Key Stock Statistics (Source S&P, Vickers, company reports)

| | | | | | | | |
| --- | --- | --- | --- | --- | --- | --- | --- |
| 52-Wk Range | $57.76– 42.98 | S&P Oper. EPS 2011**E** | 2.40 | Market Capitalization(B) | $2.440 | Beta | 0.46 |
| Trailing 12-Month EPS | $2.38 | S&P Oper. EPS 2012**E** | 2.60 | Yield (%) | 3.47 | S&P 3-Yr. Proj. EPS CAGR(%) | -4 |
| Trailing 12-Month P/E | 22.5 | P/E on S&P Oper. EPS 2011**E** | 22.3 | Dividend Rate/Share | $1.86 | S&P Credit Rating | AA |
| $10K Invested 5 Yrs Ago | $13,550 | Common Shares Outstg. (M) | 45.5 | Institutional Ownership (%) | 67 | | |

## Price Performance

Legend: 30-Week Mov. Avg. · · · 10-Week Mov. Avg. – – GAAP Earnings vs. Previous Year · Volume Above Avg. · STARS · 12-Mo. Target Price — Relative Strength · ▲ Up ▼ Down ▶ No Change · Below Avg.

Options: P

## Qualitative Risk Assessment

| LOW | MEDIUM | HIGH |
| --- | --- | --- |

Our risk assessment reflects the low-risk nature of the company's main subsidiary, a regulated natural gas distribution company, slightly offset by the higher-risk nature of its much smaller competitive operations. The company benefits from being the lone delivery agent of natural gas to customers within its service territory.

## Quantitative Evaluations

**S&P Quality Ranking** B+

| D | C | B- | B | B+ | A- | A | A+ |
| --- | --- | --- | --- | --- | --- | --- | --- |

**Relative Strength Rank** MODERATE

65

LOWEST = 1    HIGHEST = 99

## Revenue/Earnings Data

### Revenue (Million $)

| | 1Q | 2Q | 3Q | 4Q | Year |
| --- | --- | --- | --- | --- | --- |
| 2011 | 1,037 | 477.0 | 348.4 | -- | -- |
| 2010 | 1,193 | 425.6 | 352.5 | 738.8 | 2,710 |
| 2009 | 1,111 | 447.6 | 325.6 | 768.1 | 2,652 |
| 2008 | 1,596 | 699.8 | 440.3 | 1,041 | 3,777 |
| 2007 | 1,335 | 556.9 | 365.2 | 919.5 | 3,176 |
| 2006 | 1,319 | 451.3 | 351.1 | 838.2 | 2,960 |

### Earnings Per Share ($)

| | 1Q | 2Q | 3Q | 4Q | Year |
| --- | --- | --- | --- | --- | --- |
| 2011 | 0.98 | 0.42 | 0.12 | E0.88 | E2.40 |
| 2010 | 1.33 | 0.53 | 0.30 | 0.87 | 3.02 |
| 2009 | 0.96 | 0.50 | 0.30 | 1.21 | 2.98 |
| 2008 | 0.91 | 0.64 | 0.03 | 1.05 | 2.63 |
| 2007 | 1.04 | 0.40 | 0.32 | 1.23 | 2.99 |
| 2006 | 0.99 | 0.19 | 0.39 | 1.29 | 2.87 |

Fiscal year ended Dec. 31. Next earnings report expected: Late February. EPS Estimates based on S&P Operating Earnings; historical GAAP earnings are as reported.

## Highlights

➤ The 12-month target price for GAS has recently been changed to $54.00 from $53.00. The Highlights section of this Stock Report will be updated accordingly.

## Investment Rationale/Risk

➤ The Investment Rationale/Risk section of this Stock Report will be updated shortly. For the latest News story on GAS from MarketScope, see below.

➤ 11/01/11 11:37 am ET ... S&P MAINTAINS HOLD OPINION ON SHARES OF NICOR INC. (GAS 55.32***): Q3 recurring EPS of $0.12, vs. $0.28, misses our $0.26 estimate and the Capital IQ $0.28 consensus estimate. Revenues were slightly weaker and per-revenue cost of gas and unregulated business expenses were higher than we forecast, but were partly offset by per-revenue operations & maintenance cost that was lower. With shareholder approval given, the state of Illinois has until Dec. 16 to issue a ruling on the pending merger. We are trimming our '11 EPS forecast $0.10 to $2.40 and '12's by $0.05 to $2.60. We lift our target price by $1 to $54, matching the deal's terms. /CBMuir

## Dividend Data (Dates: mm/dd Payment Date: mm/dd/yy)

| Amount ($) | Date Decl. | Ex-Div. Date | Stk. of Record | Payment Date |
| --- | --- | --- | --- | --- |
| 0.465 | 11/19 | 12/29 | 12/31 | 02/01/11 |
| 0.465 | 02/17 | 03/29 | 03/31 | 05/01/11 |
| 0.465 | 06/14 | 06/28 | 06/30 | 08/01/11 |
| 0.465 | 07/28 | 09/28 | 09/30 | 11/01/11 |

Dividends have been paid since 1954. Source: Company reports.

# Nicor Inc.

## Business Summary September 26, 2011

CORPORATE OVERVIEW. Nicor Inc. is a holding company, whose principal subsidiaries are Northern Illinois Gas Company (doing business as Nicor Gas Company), one of the nation's largest distributors of natural gas, and Tropical Shipping, a transporter of containerized freight in the Bahamas and the Caribbean region. Nicor also owns several energy-related ventures, including Nicor Services and Nicor Solutions, which provide energy-related products and services to retail markets, and Nicor Enerchange, a wholesale natural gas marketing company.

PRIMARY BUSINESS DYNAMICS. Nicor seeks earnings growth through investment in unregulated operations, including its Tropical Shipping and Other Energy Ventures segments. However, the company's main operating segment remains its regulated gas utility operations.

As of the end of 2010, Nicor Gas (80% of 2010 segment operating income) served 2.2 million customers in a service area that covers most of northern Illinois, excluding Chicago. In 2010, gas deliveries fell to 454 billion cubic feet (Bcf), from 476 Bcf in 2009. The company has an extensive storage and transmission system that is directly connected to eight interstate pipelines, and includes eight owned underground gas storage facilities, with about 150 Bcf of annual storage capacity. In addition, Nicor Gas has about 40 Bcf of purchased storage from an affiliated party under contracts that expire between 2012 and

2013.

GAS's Tropical Shipping unit (6%) is one of the largest containerized cargo carriers in the Caribbean, with a fleet of 11 owned and three chartered vessels, with total container capacity of about 4,970 20-foot equivalent units (TEU), serving 25 ports. Total volumes shipped in 2010 were 170,700 TEU, down from 176,600 TEU in 2009 and 197,100 TEU in 2008. However, revenues per TEU remained relatively steady at $2,022 in 2010, versus $1,997 in 2009, and $2,158 in 2008.

GAS's Other Energy Ventures segment (14%) includes Nicor Services and Solutions, Nicor Enerchange and the Horizon Pipeline. Corporate items make up the remainder of segment operating profits. Nicor's Services and Solutions businesses offer service contracts covering the maintenance or repair of gas piping and major appliances and provide utility-bill management and price protection plans. Nicor Enerchange engages in wholesale natural gas marketing and trading in the Midwest, and administers the Chicago Hub.

## Company Financials Fiscal Year Ended Dec. 31

| Per Share Data ($) | 2010 | 2009 | 2008 | 2007 | 2006 | 2005 | 2004 | 2003 | 2002 | 2001 |
|---|---|---|---|---|---|---|---|---|---|---|
| Tangible Book Value | 23.54 | 22.38 | 21.02 | 20.51 | 19.43 | 18.36 | 16.99 | 17.15 | 16.55 | 16.39 |
| Cash Flow | 7.46 | 7.28 | 6.40 | 6.64 | 6.44 | 6.55 | 5.05 | 5.73 | 6.00 | 6.46 |
| Earnings | 3.02 | 2.98 | 2.63 | 2.99 | 2.87 | 3.07 | 1.70 | 2.48 | 2.88 | 3.17 |
| S&P Core Earnings | 3.07 | 3.14 | 2.11 | 2.74 | 2.83 | 2.47 | 1.97 | 2.45 | 2.30 | 1.99 |
| Dividends | 1.86 | 1.86 | 1.86 | 1.86 | 1.86 | 1.86 | 1.86 | 1.86 | 1.84 | 1.76 |
| Payout Ratio | 62% | 62% | 71% | 62% | 65% | 61% | 109% | 75% | 64% | 56% |
| Prices:High | 50.81 | 43.39 | 51.99 | 53.66 | 49.92 | 42.97 | 39.65 | 39.30 | 49.00 | 42.38 |
| Prices:Low | 37.99 | 27.50 | 32.35 | 37.80 | 38.72 | 35.50 | 32.04 | 23.70 | 18.09 | 34.00 |
| P/E Ratio:High | 17 | 15 | 20 | 18 | 17 | 14 | 23 | 16 | 17 | 13 |
| P/E Ratio:Low | 13 | 9 | 12 | 13 | 13 | 12 | 19 | 10 | 6 | 11 |
| **Income Statement Analysis** (Million $) | | | | | | | | | | |
| Revenue | 2,710 | 2,652 | 3,777 | 3,176 | 2,960 | 3,358 | 2,740 | 2,663 | 1,897 | 2,544 |
| Operating Income | NA | NA | 356 | 372 | 366 | 202 | 138 | 189 | 227 | 244 |
| Depreciation | 203 | 196 | 171 | 166 | 160 | 155 | 149 | 144 | 138 | 149 |
| Interest Expense | 38.1 | 38.7 | 40.1 | 38.2 | 49.8 | 48.0 | 41.6 | 37.3 | 38.5 | 44.9 |
| Pretax Income | 208 | 201 | 164 | 184 | 174 | 171 | 105 | 169 | 186 | 217 |
| Effective Tax Rate | NA | 32.5% | 27.1% | 26.6% | 26.3% | 20.3% | 28.7% | 35.2% | 31.0% | 33.8% |
| Net Income | 138 | 136 | 120 | 135 | 128 | 136 | 75.1 | 110 | 128 | 144 |
| S&P Core Earnings | 141 | 143 | 96.2 | 124 | 127 | 110 | 87.7 | 108 | 102 | 90.4 |
| **Balance Sheet & Other Financial Data** (Million $) | | | | | | | | | | |
| Cash | 102 | 134 | 95.5 | 91.9 | 41.1 | 119 | 12.9 | 50.3 | 75.2 | 10.7 |
| Current Assets | 954 | 1,003 | 1,339 | 1,024 | 911 | 1,346 | 1,021 | 916 | 708 | 518 |
| Total Assets | 4,497 | 4,436 | 4,784 | 4,252 | 4,090 | 4,391 | 3,975 | 3,797 | 2,899 | 2,575 |
| Current Liabilities | 1,074 | 1,168 | 1,668 | 1,276 | 1,142 | 1,623 | 1,174 | 1,069 | 1,099 | 826 |
| Long Term Debt | 498 | 498 | 449 | 423 | 498 | 486 | 495 | 497 | 396 | 446 |
| Common Equity | 1,104 | 1,038 | 973 | 945 | 873 | 811 | 749 | 755 | 728 | 728 |
| Total Capital | 1,602 | 1,536 | 1,822 | 1,769 | 1,787 | 1,751 | 1,873 | 1,813 | 1,514 | 1,548 |
| Capital Expenditures | 227 | 220 | 250 | 173 | 592 | 202 | 190 | 181 | 193 | 186 |
| Cash Flow | 341 | 331 | 290 | 301 | 288 | 291 | 224 | 253 | 266 | 292 |
| Current Ratio | 0.9 | 0.9 | 0.8 | 0.8 | 0.8 | 0.8 | 0.9 | 0.9 | 0.6 | 0.6 |
| % Long Term Debt of Capitalization | 31.1 | Nil | 24.6 | 23.9 | 27.9 | 27.7 | 26.4 | 27.4 | 26.1 | 28.8 |
| % Net Income of Revenue | 5.1 | 5.1 | 3.2 | 4.3 | 4.3 | 4.5 | 2.7 | 4.1 | 6.7 | 5.6 |
| % Return on Assets | NA | 2.9 | 2.1 | 3.2 | 3.0 | 11.4 | 7.8 | 3.3 | 4.7 | 5.3 |
| % Return on Equity | NA | NA | 12.5 | 14.9 | 15.2 | 17.4 | 9.9 | 14.8 | 12.3 | 20.0 |

Data as orig reptd.; bef. results of disc opers/spec. items. Per share data adj. for stk. divs.; EPS diluted. E-Estimated. NA-Not Available. NM-Not Meaningful. NR-Not Ranked. UR-Under Review.

**Office:** 1844 Ferry Road, Naperville, IL 60563-9600.
**Telephone:** 630-305-9500.
**Website:** http://www.nicor.com
**Chrmn, Pres & CEO:** R.M. Strobel

**CFO:** R.L. Hawley
**Chief Acctg Officer & Cntlr:** K.K. Pepping
**Treas:** D.M. Ruschau
**Secy & General Counsel:** P.C. Gracey, Jr.

**Investor Contact:** K.D. Brunner (630-388-2529)
**Board Members:** R. M. Beavers, Jr., B. P. Bickner, J. H. Birdsall, III, N. R. Bobins, B. J. Gaines, R. A. Jean, D. J. Keller, R. E. Martin, G. R. Nelson, A. J. Olivera, J. E. Rau, J. C. Staley, R. M. Strobel

**Founded:** 1953
**Domicile:** Illinois
**Employees:** 3,800

# NIKE Inc

**STANDARD &POOR'S**

| S&P Recommendation **BUY** ★★★★☆ | Price $90.28 (as of Nov 25, 2011) | 12-Mo. Target Price $100.00 | Investment Style Large-Cap Growth |
|---|---|---|---|

**GICS Sector** Consumer Discretionary
**Sub-Industry** Footwear

**Summary** NIKE is the world's leading designer and marketer of high-quality athletic footwear, athletic apparel and accessories.

## Key Stock Statistics (Source S&P, Vickers, company reports)

| | | | | | | | |
|---|---|---|---|---|---|---|---|
| 52-Wk Range | $97.68–69.43 | S&P Oper. EPS 2012**E** | 5.02 | Market Capitalization(B) | $33.738 | Beta | 0.89 |
| Trailing 12-Month EPS | $4.61 | S&P Oper. EPS 2013**E** | 5.70 | Yield (%) | 1.60 | S&P 3-Yr. Proj. EPS CAGR(%) | 14 |
| Trailing 12-Month P/E | 19.6 | P/E on S&P Oper. EPS 2012**E** | 18.0 | Dividend Rate/Share | $1.44 | S&P Credit Rating | A+ |
| $10K Invested 5 Yrs Ago | $20,188 | Common Shares Outstg. (M) | 463.7 | Institutional Ownership (%) | 86 | | |

## Price Performance

30-Week Mov. Avg. ···· 10-Week Mov. Avg. --- GAAP Earnings vs. Previous Year Volume Above Avg. STARS
12-Mo. Target Price — Relative Strength — ▲ Up ▼ Down ► No Change Below Avg. ★

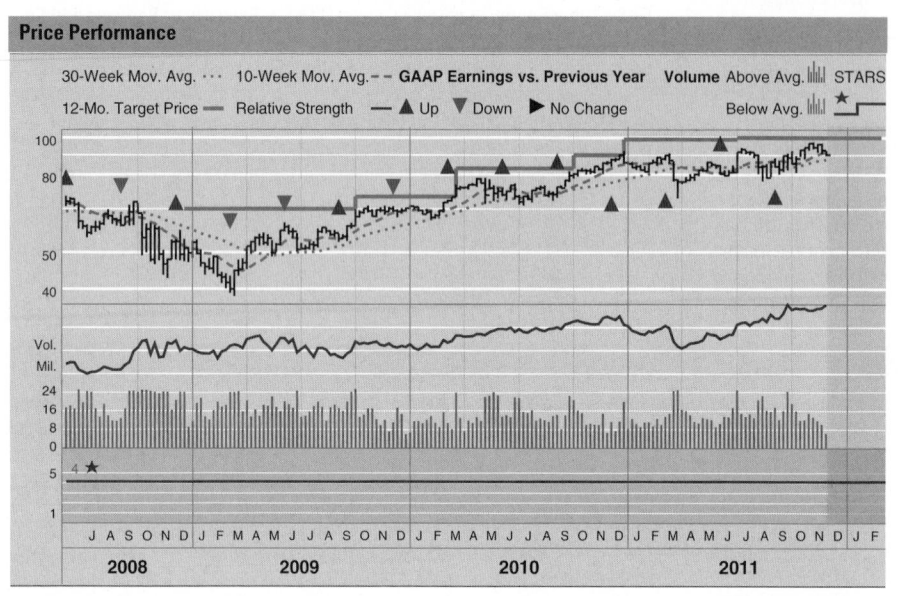

Options: ASE, CBOE, P, Ph

Analysis prepared by Equity Analyst **Jason N. Asaeda** on Sep 27, 2011, when the stock traded at **$91.00**.

### Highlights

➤ We project 16.5% revenue growth in FY 12 (May), supported by product innovation, category penetration, and geographic expansion. Globally, we think NKE is positioned to capture market share in a tough macroeconomic environment as consumers are drawn to the quality and value we believe the Nike brand provides. Future orders for Nike brand footwear and apparel are up 16% (13% on a currency-neutral basis) for scheduled deliveries for the September 2011 through January 2012 period, boding well for the second quarter.

➤ We anticipate gross margin pressure continuing through the first half of FY 12 as input costs mitigate supply chain efficiencies and other cost reduction initiatives. By the second half, we see some easing of input costs, growth in the higher-margin direct-to-consumer channels, and price increases stabilizing gross margin. We project about 60 bps of SG&A expense leverage despite expected increases in brand event spending and ongoing investments in direct-to-consumer operations.

➤ Factoring in share buybacks, we see EPS of $5.02 in FY 12.

### Investment Rationale/Risk

➤ We see strong fundamentals and a dominant global brand with exceptional international growth opportunities supporting the share price. Moreover, NKE has launched new retailing and marketing strategies designed to more closely align the company's operations with key markets. We expect NKE to pick up market share in most product categories as consumers tend to opt for established brands in uncertain environments. We also look for advertising and promotions during the European Football Championships and the 2012 London Olympic Games to build brand momentum.

➤ Risks to our recommendation and target price include a severe economic slowdown domestically and a greater-than-expected moderation in consumer spending. International risks include economic weakness, supply disruptions, and unfavorable currency fluctuations.

➤ Given our positive company outlook, we believe the stock should trade at a premium to its 10-year historical average forward P/E multiple of 17.6X. Our 12-month target price of $100 is based on a peer-average forward P/E multiple of 18.9X applied to our calendar 2012 EPS estimate of $5.30.

### Qualitative Risk Assessment

| LOW | MEDIUM | HIGH |
|---|---|---|

Our risk assessment reflects what we see as NKE's strong financial and operating metrics, offset by an increasingly competitive global marketplace and weak consumer spending in the U.S.

## Quantitative Evaluations

**S&P Quality Ranking** A+

| D | C | B- | B | B+ | A- | A | A+ |
|---|---|---|---|---|---|---|---|

**Relative Strength Rank** STRONG

74

LOWEST = 1                HIGHEST = 99

## Revenue/Earnings Data

**Revenue (Million $)**

| | 1Q | 2Q | 3Q | 4Q | Year |
|---|---|---|---|---|---|
| 2012 | 6,081 | -- | -- | -- | -- |
| 2011 | 5,175 | 4,842 | 5,079 | 5,766 | 20,862 |
| 2010 | 4,799 | 4,406 | 4,733 | 5,077 | 19,014 |
| 2009 | 5,432 | 4,590 | 4,441 | 4,713 | 19,176 |
| 2008 | 4,655 | 4,340 | 4,544 | 5,088 | 18,627 |
| 2007 | 4,194 | 3,822 | 3,927 | 4,383 | 16,326 |

**Earnings Per Share ($)**

| | | | | | |
|---|---|---|---|---|---|
| 2012 | 1.36 | E0.96 | E1.23 | E1.47 | E5.02 |
| 2011 | 1.14 | 0.94 | 1.08 | 1.24 | 4.39 |
| 2010 | 1.04 | 0.76 | 1.01 | 1.06 | 3.86 |
| 2009 | 1.03 | 0.80 | 0.50 | 0.70 | 3.03 |
| 2008 | 1.12 | 0.71 | 0.92 | 0.98 | 3.74 |
| 2007 | 0.74 | 0.64 | 0.68 | 0.86 | 2.93 |

Fiscal year ended May 31. Next earnings report expected: Late December. EPS Estimates based on S&P Operating Earnings; historical GAAP earnings are as reported.

## Dividend Data (Dates: mm/dd Payment Date: mm/dd/yy)

| Amount ($) | Date Decl. | Ex-Div. Date | Stk. of Record | Payment Date |
|---|---|---|---|---|
| 0.310 | 02/17 | 03/03 | 03/07 | 04/01/11 |
| 0.310 | 05/16 | 06/02 | 06/06 | 07/01/11 |
| 0.310 | 08/15 | 09/01 | 09/06 | 10/03/11 |
| 0.360 | 11/17 | 12/01 | 12/05 | 01/03/12 |

Dividends have been paid since 1984. Source: Company reports.

# NIKE Inc

STANDARD &POOR'S

## Business Summary September 27, 2011

CORPORATE OVERVIEW. Nike Inc. is the world's largest supplier of athletic footwear, with an estimated 50% of this $20 billion market (at wholesale). Sports apparel and equipment are also sold under the Nike banner, and the company's Other segment (13% of sales) houses its affiliated brands including Cole Haan, Converse, Hurley, Nike Golf and Umbro.

MARKET PROFILE. Innovation, marketing and the sports cycle drive the global footwear and athletic apparel markets, in our view. Technologically superior performance products, we think, convey the idea of extraordinary ability to the wearer and are the root of the marketing campaigns aimed at lifestyle consumers (individuals attracted to a brand's attributes of an active lifestyle regardless of sports participation) while providing a basis for pricing. The global market for athletic apparel is several times as large as the footwear market, and totals over $100 billion, according to industry sources. An estimated 30% of this market consists of active sports apparel (purchased with the intent to be used in an active sport), and the remainder is lifestyle or casual wear. We see apparel representing a significant opportunity for NKE via its brand extensions and market penetration. According to NPD Fashionworld

consumer estimated data, U.S. performance athletic footwear sales increased 8.6% in 2010 to $11 billion, accelerating to a 25% rate of growth in the final quarter. S&P projects a low single digit sales gain in 2011 for athletic footwear and apparel.

COMPETITIVE LANDSCAPE. The athletic apparel market is fragmented, providing opportunities for growing market share, in our view. Significant domestic footwear retail channels in 2010 included athletic footwear specialty shops (8% market share), sporting goods stores (9%), discounters or mass merchants (12%), and department stores (11%). We see NKE's prowess in athletic footwear and strong brand attributes as competitive advantages that should serve the company well as it aims to capture share of the underserved women's athletic apparel market.

## Company Financials  Fiscal Year Ended May 31

| Per Share Data ($) | 2011 | 2010 | 2009 | 2008 | 2007 | 2006 | 2005 | 2004 | 2003 | 2002 |
|---|---|---|---|---|---|---|---|---|---|---|
| Tangible Book Value | 19.55 | 18.80 | 16.54 | 13.51 | 12.93 | 11.23 | 9.77 | 8.14 | 7.22 | 6.39 |
| Cash Flow | 5.13 | 4.66 | 3.74 | 4.36 | 3.51 | 3.17 | 2.72 | 2.22 | 1.83 | 3.51 |
| Earnings | 4.39 | 3.86 | 3.03 | 3.74 | 2.93 | 2.64 | 2.24 | 1.76 | 1.39 | 1.23 |
| S&P Core Earnings | 4.39 | 3.86 | 3.56 | 3.67 | 2.89 | 2.56 | 2.14 | 1.68 | 1.31 | 1.16 |
| Dividends | 1.20 | 1.04 | 0.83 | 0.68 | 0.56 | 0.45 | 0.45 | 0.34 | 0.26 | 0.24 |
| Payout Ratio | 27% | 24% | 27% | 18% | 19% | 17% | 20% | 19% | 19% | 20% |
| Calendar Year | 2010 | 2009 | 2008 | 2007 | 2006 | 2005 | 2004 | 2003 | 2002 | 2001 |
| Prices:High | 92.49 | 66.62 | 70.60 | 67.93 | 50.60 | 45.77 | 46.22 | 34.27 | 32.14 | 30.03 |
| Prices:Low | 60.89 | 38.24 | 42.68 | 47.46 | 37.76 | 37.55 | 32.91 | 21.19 | 19.27 | 17.75 |
| P/E Ratio:High | 21 | 17 | 23 | 18 | 17 | 17 | 21 | 20 | 26 | 24 |
| P/E Ratio:Low | 14 | 10 | 14 | 13 | 13 | 14 | 15 | 12 | 16 | 14 |

### Income Statement Analysis (Million $)

| | 2011 | 2010 | 2009 | 2008 | 2007 | 2006 | 2005 | 2004 | 2003 | 2002 |
|---|---|---|---|---|---|---|---|---|---|---|
| Revenue | 20,862 | 19,014 | 19,176 | 18,627 | 16,326 | 14,955 | 13,740 | 12,253 | 10,697 | 9,893 |
| Operating Income | 3,162 | 2,824 | 2,802 | 2,747 | 2,402 | 23,912 | 2,151 | 1,802 | 1,485 | 1,291 |
| Depreciation | 358 | 396 | 347 | 313 | 270 | 282 | 257 | 252 | 239 | 224 |
| Interest Expense | 4.00 | 6.30 | 40.2 | 67.1 | Nil | Nil | 39.7 | 40.3 | 42.9 | 47.6 |
| Pretax Income | 2,844 | 2,517 | 1,957 | 2,503 | 2,200 | 2,142 | 1,860 | 1,450 | 1,123 | 2,035 |
| Effective Tax Rate | 33.3% | 24.2% | 24.0% | 24.8% | 32.2% | 35.0% | 34.9% | 34.8% | 34.1% | 17.2% |
| Net Income | 2,133 | 1,907 | 1,487 | 1,883 | 1,492 | 1,392 | 1,212 | 946 | 740 | 1,686 |
| S&P Core Earnings | 2,133 | 1,907 | 1,748 | 1,848 | 1,472 | 1,346 | 1,148 | 897 | 698 | 632 |

### Balance Sheet & Other Financial Data (Million $)

| | 2011 | 2010 | 2009 | 2008 | 2007 | 2006 | 2005 | 2004 | 2003 | 2002 |
|---|---|---|---|---|---|---|---|---|---|---|
| Cash | 4,538 | 5,146 | 3,455 | 2,776 | 1,857 | 954 | 1,388 | 828 | 634 | 576 |
| Current Assets | 11,297 | 10,959 | 9,734 | 8,839 | 8,077 | 7,359 | 6,351 | 5,512 | 4,680 | 4,158 |
| Total Assets | 14,998 | 14,419 | 13,250 | 12,443 | 10,688 | 9,870 | 8,794 | 7,892 | 6,714 | 6,443 |
| Current Liabilities | 3,958 | 3,364 | 3,277 | 3,322 | 2,584 | 2,623 | 1,999 | 2,009 | 2,015 | 1,836 |
| Long Term Debt | 276 | 446 | 437 | 441 | Nil | Nil | 687 | 682 | 552 | 626 |
| Common Equity | 9,843 | 9,754 | 8,693 | 7,825 | 7,025 | 6,285 | 5,644 | 4,782 | 3,991 | 3,839 |
| Total Capital | 10,319 | 10,207 | 9,130 | 8,267 | 7,026 | 6,286 | 6,332 | 5,464 | 4,543 | 4,465 |
| Capital Expenditures | 432 | 335 | 456 | 449 | 314 | 334 | 257 | 214 | 186 | 283 |
| Cash Flow | 2,491 | 2,302 | 1,834 | 2,196 | 1,761 | 1,674 | 1,469 | 1,198 | 979 | 1,909 |
| Current Ratio | 2.9 | 3.3 | 3.0 | 2.7 | 3.1 | 2.8 | 3.2 | 2.7 | 2.3 | 2.3 |
| % Long Term Debt of Capitalization | 2.7 | 4.4 | 4.8 | 5.3 | Nil | Nil | 10.9 | 12.5 | 12.1 | 14.0 |
| % Net Income of Revenue | 10.2 | 10.0 | 7.8 | 10.1 | 9.1 | 9.3 | 8.8 | 7.7 | 6.9 | 17.0 |
| % Return on Assets | 14.5 | 13.8 | 11.6 | 16.3 | 14.5 | 14.9 | 14.5 | 12.9 | 11.3 | 27.5 |
| % Return on Equity | 21.8 | 20.7 | 18.0 | 25.4 | 22.4 | 23.3 | 23.2 | 21.6 | 18.9 | 46.0 |

Data as orig reptd.; bef. results of disc opers/spec. items. Per share data adj. for stk. divs.; EPS diluted. E-Estimated. NA-Not Available. NM-Not Meaningful. NR-Not Ranked. UR-Under Review.

**Office:** One Bowerman Drive, Beaverton, OR 97005-6453.
**Telephone:** 503-671-6453.
**Website:** http://www.nike.com
**Chrmn:** P.H. Knight

**Pres & CEO:** M.G. Parker
**COO:** G.M. DeStefano
**CFO:** D.W. Blair
**CTO:** H. Van Alebeek

**Investor Contact:** K. Hall (800-640-8007)
**Board Members:** E. J. Comstock, J. G. Connors, T. D. Cook, A. B. Graf, Jr., D. G. Houser, P. H. Knight, J. C. Lechleiter, M. G. Parker, J. A. Rodgers, O. C. Smith, J. R. Thompson, Jr., P. M. Wise

**Founded:** 1964
**Domicile:** Oregon
**Employees:** 38,000

The McGraw-Hill Companies

# NiSource Inc.

**STANDARD &POOR'S**

| S&P Recommendation | **SELL** ★★☆☆☆ | Price $21.35 (as of Nov 25, 2011) | 12-Mo. Target Price $19.00 | Investment Style Large-Cap Value |
| --- | --- | --- | --- | --- |

**GICS Sector** Utilities
**Sub-Industry** Multi-Utilities

**Summary** NI, the third largest U.S. gas distribution utility and the fourth largest gas pipeline company, also provides electric utility services.

## Key Stock Statistics (Source S&P, Vickers, company reports)

| | | | | | | | |
| --- | --- | --- | --- | --- | --- | --- | --- |
| 52-Wk Range | $23.00– 16.65 | S&P Oper. EPS 2011**E** | 1.33 | Market Capitalization(B) | $6.002 | Beta | 0.78 |
| Trailing 12-Month EPS | $1.09 | S&P Oper. EPS 2012**E** | 1.38 | Yield (%) | 4.31 | S&P 3-Yr. Proj. EPS CAGR(%) | 5 |
| Trailing 12-Month P/E | 19.6 | P/E on S&P Oper. EPS 2011**E** | 16.1 | Dividend Rate/Share | $0.92 | S&P Credit Rating | BBB- |
| $10K Invested 5 Yrs Ago | $11,808 | Common Shares Outstg. (M) | 281.1 | Institutional Ownership (%) | 83 | | |

## Price Performance

30-Week Mov. Avg. ···· 10-Week Mov. Avg. --- **GAAP Earnings vs. Previous Year**   Volume Above Avg. ⊪⊪ STARS
12-Mo. Target Price — Relative Strength  ▲ Up  ▼ Down  ► No Change      Below Avg. ⊪⊪ ★

Options: ASE, CBOE, Ph

Analysis prepared by Equity Analyst **C. Muir** on Nov 17, 2011, when the stock traded at **$21.84**.

## Highlights

➤ We see 2011 revenues falling 2.7%. For the regulated utilities, we expect revenue expansion of 3.1% as lower gas prices are more than offset by beneficial weather, rate increases and customer growth. We see non-regulated revenues falling 52% on lower realized prices and volumes as NI winds down non-utility operations. We look for revenues to advance 3.5% in 2012, helped by customer growth and higher industrial demand.

➤ We expect NI to report operating margins of 15.3% for 2011 and 15.7% for 2012, versus 2010's 14.2%. This year, we expect lower per-revenue energy and depreciation charges, partly offset by higher per-revenue operations & maintenance expenses and operating taxes. We see pretax margins of 9.6% in 2011 and 9.8% in 2012. We project lower interest expenses in 2011, partly offset by lower non-operating income in both years.

➤ Assuming an effective tax rate of 36.1% and a slight increase in shares outstanding, our 2011 recurring EPS estimate is $1.33, up 7.3% from 2010's $1.24, which excludes $0.18 of nonrecurring charges. Our 2012 forecast is $1.38, an increase of 3.8%.

## Investment Rationale/Risk

➤ We view NI's utility service territory as having relatively slow, but stable, customer growth, and we see no near-term impetus for base revenue growth outside of rate increases. NI has several rate cases filed. Depreciation charges are rising as a result of capital spending programs now in place, and operations and maintenance costs have increased as a result of electric plant maintenance activities.

➤ Risks to our recommendation and target price include wider power margins, unusually cold winter weather, lower natural gas prices, and lower interest rates.

➤ The stock recently traded at 15.9X our 2012 EPS estimate, a 12% premium to multi-utility peers. Our 12-month target price of $19 is 13.7X our 2012 EPS estimate, close to peer valuations. We believe this is warranted by NI's lack of dividend growth and slightly below average long-term EPS growth. We do not think NI will increase its dividend until 2016, when we believe its payout ratio will be more in line with peers. The dividend yield was recently 4.2%.

## Qualitative Risk Assessment

| LOW | MEDIUM | HIGH |
| --- | --- | --- |

Our risk assessment reflects the company's reliance on fairly stable regulated sources of earnings, including gas distribution, gas transmission and electric utility services.

## Quantitative Evaluations

**S&P Quality Ranking**    B

| D | C | B- | B | B+ | A- | A | A+ |
| --- | --- | --- | --- | --- | --- | --- | --- |

**Relative Strength Rank**    **STRONG**

72

LOWEST = 1      HIGHEST = 99

## Revenue/Earnings Data

**Revenue (Million $)**

| | 1Q | 2Q | 3Q | 4Q | Year |
| --- | --- | --- | --- | --- | --- |
| 2011 | 1,061 | 1,228 | 1,069 | -- | -- |
| 2010 | 1,072 | 1,171 | 1,138 | 1,754 | 6,422 |
| 2009 | 1,685 | 1,268 | 974.7 | 1,685 | 6,649 |
| 2008 | 3,290 | 1,792 | 1,409 | 2,386 | 8,874 |
| 2007 | 2,894 | 1,577 | 1,241 | 2,245 | 7,940 |
| 2006 | 2,972 | 1,312 | 1,156 | 2,050 | 7,490 |

**Earnings Per Share ($)**

| | | | | | |
| --- | --- | --- | --- | --- | --- |
| 2011 | 0.72 | 0.16 | 0.13 | E0.35 | E1.33 |
| 2010 | 0.71 | 0.10 | 0.12 | 0.13 | 1.05 |
| 2009 | 0.58 | -0.01 | -0.05 | 0.32 | 0.84 |
| 2008 | 0.69 | 0.08 | 0.12 | 0.46 | 1.34 |
| 2007 | 0.76 | 0.11 | 0.03 | 0.24 | 1.14 |
| 2006 | 0.63 | 0.08 | 0.10 | 0.33 | 1.14 |

Fiscal year ended Dec. 31. Next earnings report expected: Early February. EPS Estimates based on S&P Operating Earnings; historical GAAP earnings are as reported.

## Dividend Data (Dates: mm/dd Payment Date: mm/dd/yy)

| Amount ($) | Date Decl. | Ex-Div. Date | Stk. of Record | Payment Date |
| --- | --- | --- | --- | --- |
| 0.230 | 01/19 | 01/27 | 01/31 | 02/18/11 |
| 0.230 | 03/22 | 04/27 | 04/29 | 05/20/11 |
| 0.230 | 05/10 | 07/27 | 07/29 | 08/19/11 |
| 0.230 | 08/23 | 10/27 | 10/31 | 11/18/11 |

Dividends have been paid since 1987. Source: Company reports.

# NiSource Inc.

**STANDARD &POOR'S**

## Business Summary November 17, 2011

CORPORATE OVERVIEW. NiSource is one of the largest U.S. natural gas distributors (measured by customers served), one of the largest owners of U.S. natural gas interstate pipelines (by route miles), and one of the largest owners of underground natural gas storage. It also provides electric utility services in northern Indiana. The company's operating divisions include Gas Distribution (36% of 2010 segment operating income), Gas Transmission and Storage (41%), Electric Operations (26%), and Other Operations and Corporate (-3%).

Gas Distribution operations provide gas utility service to 3.3 million customers in seven states. The division owns and operates 58,608 miles of pipeline, 28,479 acres of underground storage, 90 underground storage wells and 75.8 million gallons of liquefied natural gas storage facilities. In 2010, total volumes were 884 MMDth, up from 831 MMDth in 2009. Deliveries were 29% to residential customers, 19% to commercial customers, 44% to industrial customers, and 8% off-system sales and to other customers.

Gas Transmission and Storage operates 25,965 miles of interstate natural gas pipelines and 775,000 acres of underground storage systems with a capacity of about 639 billion cubic feet (Bcf). In 2010, total throughput was 1,398 MMDth, up 0.4% from 2009, helped by increased Columbia Transmission throughput, partly offset by lower Columbia Gulf throughput. The division re-

cently completed Millennium Pipeline and Hardy Storage projects and is engaged in other projects. The Millennium project is a 182-mile, 0.53 MMDth/day pipeline across southern New York State. NI said it is in the process of a potential separation of Columbia Gas, one of this segment's transmission subsidiaries, into a master limited partnership structure, but we do not expect any action until the economy and financial markets improve.

NI's Northern Indiana subsidiary, NIPSCO, is the largest natural gas distribution company and second largest electric distribution company in Indiana, serving over 795,000 natural gas customers and 458,000 electric customers through a network of four coal-fired stations, two hydroelectric plants, four gas-fired combustion turbine units, and an underground gas storage field. NI has said it was considering a possible sale of the electric portion of this business.

Other Operations participates in energy-related services including gas marketing, power and gas risk management and other ventures.

## Company Financials Fiscal Year Ended Dec. 31

| Per Share Data ($) | 2010 | 2009 | 2008 | 2007 | 2006 | 2005 | 2004 | 2003 | 2002 | 2001 |
|---|---|---|---|---|---|---|---|---|---|---|
| Tangible Book Value | 3.36 | 3.10 | 2.63 | 3.58 | 3.29 | 2.79 | 2.14 | 0.70 | NM | NM |
| Cash Flow | 3.18 | 2.87 | 3.40 | 3.17 | 3.16 | 3.04 | 3.54 | 3.53 | 4.70 | 4.07 |
| Earnings | 1.05 | 0.84 | 1.34 | 1.14 | 1.14 | 1.04 | 1.62 | 1.63 | 2.00 | 1.01 |
| S&P Core Earnings | 1.21 | 1.18 | 0.83 | 1.09 | 1.13 | 1.20 | 1.62 | 1.67 | 1.43 | 0.32 |
| Dividends | 0.92 | 0.92 | 0.92 | 0.92 | 0.92 | 0.92 | 0.92 | 1.10 | 1.16 | 1.16 |
| Payout Ratio | 88% | 110% | 69% | 78% | 81% | 88% | 57% | 67% | 58% | 115% |
| Prices:High | 17.96 | 15.82 | 19.82 | 25.43 | 24.80 | 25.50 | 22.82 | 21.97 | 24.99 | 32.55 |
| Prices:Low | 14.13 | 7.79 | 10.35 | 17.49 | 19.51 | 20.44 | 19.65 | 16.39 | 14.51 | 18.25 |
| P/E Ratio:High | 17 | 19 | 15 | 22 | 22 | 25 | 14 | 13 | 12 | 32 |
| P/E Ratio:Low | 14 | 9 | 8 | 15 | 17 | 20 | 12 | 10 | 7 | 18 |

| Income Statement Analysis (Million $) | 2010 | 2009 | 2008 | 2007 | 2006 | 2005 | 2004 | 2003 | 2002 | 2001 |
|---|---|---|---|---|---|---|---|---|---|---|
| Revenue | 6,422 | 6,649 | 8,874 | 7,940 | 7,490 | 7,899 | 6,666 | 6,247 | 6,492 | 9,459 |
| Operating Income | NA | NA | 1,468 | 1,493 | 880 | 1,520 | 1,072 | 1,116 | 1,203 | 1,009 |
| Depreciation | 596 | 589 | 567 | 559 | 549 | 545 | 510 | 497 | 574 | 642 |
| Interest Expense | 392 | 399 | 380 | 418 | 7,304 | 425 | 408 | 469 | 533 | 605 |
| Pretax Income | 436 | 397 | 555 | 484 | 484 | 433 | 671 | 662 | 680 | 416 |
| Effective Tax Rate | NA | 41.8% | 33.4% | 35.6% | 35.3% | 34.5% | 35.9% | 35.4% | 34.4% | 44.1% |
| Net Income | 295 | 231 | 370 | 312 | 314 | 284 | 430 | 426 | 426 | 212 |
| S&P Core Earnings | 338 | 328 | 229 | 298 | 310 | 324 | 429 | 437 | 305 | 67.9 |

| Balance Sheet & Other Financial Data (Million $) | 2010 | 2009 | 2008 | 2007 | 2006 | 2005 | 2004 | 2003 | 2002 | 2001 |
|---|---|---|---|---|---|---|---|---|---|---|
| Cash | 9.20 | 16.4 | 20.6 | 95.4 | 33.1 | 69.4 | 30.1 | 27.3 | 56.2 | 128 |
| Current Assets | 2,449 | 2,224 | 3,411 | 2,455 | 2,783 | 3,061 | 2,286 | 2,063 | 1,869 | 2,567 |
| Total Assets | 19,939 | 19,272 | 20,032 | 18,005 | 18,157 | 17,959 | 16,988 | 16,624 | 16,897 | 17,374 |
| Current Liabilities | 3,649 | 3,150 | 4,583 | 3,393 | 3,821 | 3,843 | 3,602 | 2,609 | 4,177 | 4,729 |
| Long Term Debt | 5,936 | 5,988 | 5,944 | 5,594 | 5,146 | 5,271 | 4,917 | 6,075 | 5,448 | 6,214 |
| Common Equity | 4,923 | 4,854 | 4,729 | 5,077 | 5,014 | 4,933 | 4,787 | 4,416 | 4,175 | 3,469 |
| Total Capital | 10,894 | 11,504 | 12,223 | 12,234 | 11,775 | 11,866 | 11,448 | 10,490 | 11,581 | 11,515 |
| Capital Expenditures | 804 | 777 | 970 | 788 | 637 | 590 | 517 | 575 | 622 | 668 |
| Cash Flow | 891 | 792 | 937 | 871 | 863 | 829 | 940 | 923 | 1,000 | 854 |
| Current Ratio | 0.7 | 0.7 | 0.7 | 0.7 | 0.7 | 0.8 | 0.6 | 0.8 | 0.4 | 0.5 |
| % Long Term Debt of Capitalization | 54.5 | 51.9 | 48.6 | 45.7 | 43.7 | 44.4 | 42.9 | 57.9 | 47.0 | 54.0 |
| % Net Income of Revenue | 4.6 | 3.5 | 4.2 | 3.9 | 4.2 | 3.6 | 6.5 | 6.8 | 6.6 | 2.2 |
| % Return on Assets | 1.5 | 1.2 | 1.9 | 1.7 | 1.7 | 1.6 | 2.6 | 2.5 | 2.5 | 1.1 |
| % Return on Equity | 6.0 | 4.8 | 7.5 | 6.2 | 6.3 | 5.8 | 9.3 | 9.9 | 11.1 | 6.2 |

Data as orig reptd.; bef. results of disc opers/spec. items. Per share data adj. for stk. divs.; EPS diluted. E-Estimated. NA-Not Available. NM-Not Meaningful. NR-Not Ranked. UR-Under Review.

**Office:** 801 East 86th Avenue, Merrillville, IN 46410.
**Telephone:** 877-647-5990.
**Email:** questions@nisource.com
**Website:** http://www.nisource.com

**Chrmn:** I.M. Rolland
**Pres & CEO:** R.C. Skaggs, Jr.
**EVP & CFO:** S.P. Smith
**EVP & General Counsel:** C.J. Hightman

**Chief Admin Officer & CIO:** V.G. Sistovaris
**Investor Contact:** D.J. Vajda (877-647-5990)
**Board Members:** R. A. Abdoo, S. C. Beering, S. L. Cornelius, M. E. Jesanis, M. R. Kittrell, W. L. Nutter, D. S. Parker, I. M. Rolland, R. C. Skaggs, Jr., R. L. Thompson, C. Y. Woo

**Founded:** 1912
**Domicile:** Delaware
**Employees:** 7,604

**The McGraw-Hill Companies**

# Noble Corp

**STANDARD &POOR'S**

| S&P Recommendation **BUY** ★★★★☆ | Price $32.46 (as of Nov 25, 2011) | 12-Mo. Target Price $47.00 | Investment Style Large-Cap Blend |
|---|---|---|---|

**GICS Sector** Energy
**Sub-Industry** Oil & Gas Drilling

**Summary** This company principally provides contract drilling services for the oil and gas industry worldwide.

## Key Stock Statistics (Source S&P, Vickers, company reports)

| | | | | | | |
|---|---|---|---|---|---|---|
| 52-Wk Range | $46.72– 27.33 | S&P Oper. EPS 2011**E** | 1.85 | Market Capitalization(B) | $8.194 | Beta | 1.15 |
| Trailing 12-Month EPS | $1.35 | S&P Oper. EPS 2012**E** | 4.43 | Yield (%) | 1.85 | S&P 3-Yr. Proj. EPS CAGR(%) | -12 |
| Trailing 12-Month P/E | 24.0 | P/E on S&P Oper. EPS 2011**E** | 17.5 | Dividend Rate/Share | $0.60 | S&P Credit Rating | A- |
| $10K Invested 5 Yrs Ago | $9,221 | Common Shares Outstg. (M) | 252.4 | Institutional Ownership (%) | 83 | | |

## Price Performance

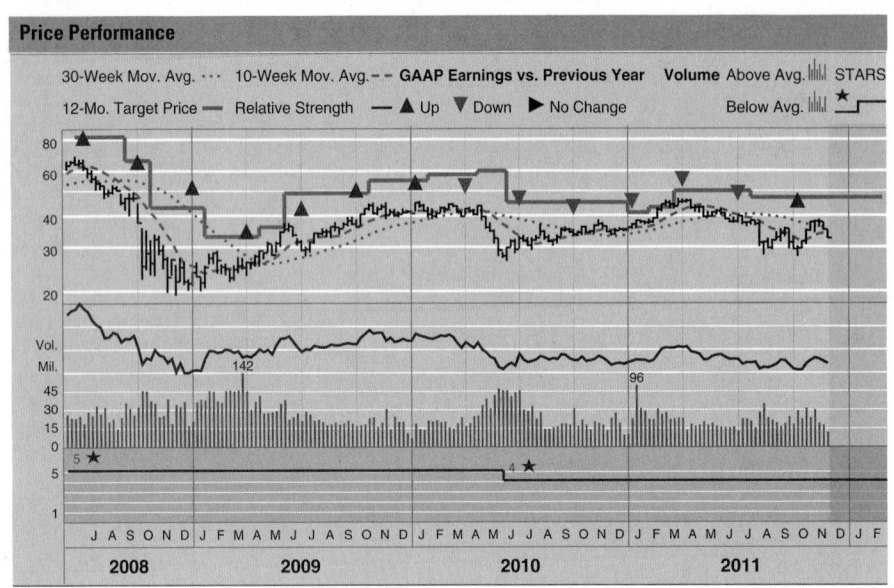

30-Week Mov. Avg. ···· 10-Week Mov. Avg. --- GAAP Earnings vs. Previous Year Volume Above Avg. STARS
12-Mo. Target Price — Relative Strength — ▲ Up ▼ Down ► No Change Below Avg. ★

Options: ASE, CBOE, Ph

Analysis prepared by Equity Analyst **S. Glickman, CFA** on Sep 15, 2011, when the stock traded at **$34.75**.

## Qualitative Risk Assessment

| LOW | MEDIUM | HIGH |
|---|---|---|

Our risk assessment reflects NE's exposure to volatile crude oil and natural gas prices, capital spending decisions made by its oil and gas producing customers, political risk associated with operating in frontier regions, an uncertain U.S. regulatory regime, and potential contract risk in the event of further force majeure declarations by operators.

## Quantitative Evaluations

**S&P Quality Ranking** B

| D | C | B- | B | B+ | A- | A | A+ |
|---|---|---|---|---|---|---|---|

**Relative Strength Rank** MODERATE

49

LOWEST = 1          HIGHEST = 99

## Revenue/Earnings Data

**Revenue (Million $)**

| | 1Q | 2Q | 3Q | 4Q | Year |
|---|---|---|---|---|---|
| 2011 | 578.9 | 628.0 | 737.9 | -- | -- |
| 2010 | 840.9 | 709.9 | 612.6 | 643.8 | 2,807 |
| 2009 | 896.2 | 898.9 | 905.6 | 940.1 | 3,641 |
| 2008 | 861.4 | 812.9 | 862.0 | 910.2 | 3,447 |
| 2007 | 646.4 | 726.0 | 791.3 | 831.6 | 2,995 |
| 2006 | 461.9 | 517.5 | 562.0 | 558.8 | 2,100 |

**Earnings Per Share ($)**

| | | | | | |
|---|---|---|---|---|---|
| 2011 | 0.21 | 0.21 | 0.53 | E0.90 | E1.85 |
| 2010 | 1.43 | 0.85 | 0.34 | 0.39 | 3.02 |
| 2009 | 1.58 | 1.49 | 1.63 | 1.72 | 6.42 |
| 2008 | 1.43 | 1.40 | 1.43 | 1.60 | 5.85 |
| 2007 | 0.93 | 1.08 | 1.18 | 1.29 | 4.48 |
| 2006 | 0.52 | 0.65 | 0.76 | 0.74 | 2.66 |

Fiscal year ended Dec. 31. Next earnings report expected: Late January. EPS Estimates based on S&P Operating Earnings; historical GAAP earnings are as reported.

## Highlights

➤ In the third quarter, NE added to its slate of newbuilds, and now has eight drillships and six jackups on order. This is a significant expansion given a total fleet size of 79 units, and implies sizable demands on cash flow; we project capital spending of about $2.5 billion in 2011, versus estimated 2011 operating cash flow of roughly $950 million. However, we see capex needs declining in 2012, and NE also has substantial contract backlog with which to fund construction. We see floaters generating about 62% of NE's projected 2012 revenues.

➤ In May, NE announced that the operator contracting the Danny Adkins semisubmersible finally obtained a permit, and thus the unit went back on full dayrate in the low $460,000 per day area (versus a prior standby rate in the mid-$150,000 per day area). We believe that the permit process in the U.S. Gulf of Mexico will improve, but timing remains uncertain, and the pace of issuance slipped in the second quarter.

➤ We see EPS of $2.00 in 2011, rising to $4.43 in 2012, led by newbuild drillship arrivals.

## Investment Rationale/Risk

➤ Notwithstanding near-term turmoil in the Gulf of Mexico, we think NE offers long-term appeal. NE has added significant contract backlog and has expanded its deepwater profile via the Frontier deal. We now view 2011 as somewhat of a transition year for the company in light of the weak Gulf visibility, but we expect that NE will respond by relocating more of its newbuild deepwater units to other regions, ultimately yielding less region-specific risk. Looking at just regular dividends, we estimate a yield of about 1.7% and a payout ratio of about 30%, and we think NE has the ability to offer another special dividend as it did in 2010.

➤ Risks to our recommendation and target price include reduced dayrates; lower oil and natural gas prices; unexpected contract cancellations, including force majeure declarations; and an uncertain domestic regulatory regime.

➤ Applying peer average multiples of 7X EV to our 2011 EBITDA estimate and 8X to projected 2011 operating cash flows (reflecting projected 2011 ROIC in line with peers), and blending with our NAV model, our 12-month target price is $47.

## Dividend Data (Dates: mm/dd Payment Date: mm/dd/yy)

| Amount ($) | Date Decl. | Ex-Div. Date | Stk. of Record | Payment Date |
|---|---|---|---|---|
| 0.137 | 02/04 | 02/10 | 02/14 | 02/24/11 |
| 0.147 | 04/29 | 05/05 | 05/09 | 05/19/11 |
| 0.166 | 07/29 | 08/04 | 08/08 | 08/18/11 |
| 0.150 | 10/28 | 11/03 | 11/07 | 11/17/11 |

Dividends have been paid since 2005. Source: Company reports.

**Please read the Required Disclosures and Analyst Certification on the last page of this report.**

The **McGraw·Hill** Companies

# Noble Corp

**STANDARD &POOR'S**

## Business Summary September 15, 2011

CORPORATE OVERVIEW. NE is one of the world's leading offshore drilling contractors, domiciled in Switzerland since July 2009 (formerly the Cayman Islands). We view the move as improving company logistics, as well as a defensive maneuver against potential changes to the U.S. tax code that might threaten its currently low effective tax rate (16% in 2010). We believe that the existence of an official tax treaty between the U.S. and Switzerland would preclude any such changes to the U.S. tax code, whereas no official treaty exists between the U.S. and the Cayman Islands.

NE provides contract drilling services in offshore markets worldwide. As of September 2010, the company had a fleet of 69 offshore drilling rigs, which included five units under construction. The company-owned active rig fleet includes 14 semisubmersibles, seven drillships, and 43 independent leg, cantilever jackup rigs. The company also recently acquired the Frontier Seillean,

a FPSO (floating production, storage & offloading) unit.

IMPACT OF MAJOR DEVELOPMENTS. The June 2010 deal for Frontier Drilling (completed in July 2010) was the linchpin of follow-on agreements with Royal Dutch Shell (RDS.A 66, Strong Buy). The combination of both events enabled NE to add $6.0 billion in backlog, which as of early 2011 stood at approximately $14.0 billion. RDS thus represents 57% of NE's total backlog, which on the one hand creates counterparty risk for NE, but on the other hand represents a vote of confidence, in our view, by RDS in NE's strong track record, including a best-in-class safety performance.

## Company Financials Fiscal Year Ended Dec. 31

| Per Share Data ($) | 2010 | 2009 | 2008 | 2007 | 2006 | 2005 | 2004 | 2003 | 2002 | 2001 |
|---|---|---|---|---|---|---|---|---|---|---|
| Tangible Book Value | NA | 26.29 | 20.31 | 16.06 | 11.96 | 9.97 | 8.87 | 8.16 | 7.45 | 6.72 |
| Cash Flow | NA | 8.06 | 6.85 | 5.28 | 3.66 | 1.97 | 1.32 | 1.18 | 1.25 | 1.43 |
| Earnings | 3.02 | 6.42 | 5.85 | 4.48 | 2.66 | 1.08 | 0.55 | 0.63 | 0.79 | 0.99 |
| Dividends | 0.18 | 0.18 | 0.91 | 0.08 | 0.08 | 0.05 | Nil | Nil | Nil | Nil |
| Payout Ratio | 6% | 3% | 16% | 2% | 3% | 5% | Nil | Nil | Nil | Nil |
| Prices:High | 45.60 | 45.18 | 68.99 | 57.64 | 43.08 | 37.81 | 25.27 | 19.20 | 22.98 | 27.00 |
| Prices:Low | 26.23 | 20.03 | 19.23 | 33.81 | 29.26 | 23.52 | 16.77 | 15.23 | 13.50 | 10.40 |
| P/E Ratio:High | 15 | 7 | 12 | 13 | 16 | 35 | 46 | 31 | 29 | 27 |
| P/E Ratio:Low | 9 | 3 | 3 | 8 | 11 | 22 | 31 | 24 | 17 | 11 |

**Income Statement Analysis** (Million $)

| | 2010 | 2009 | 2008 | 2007 | 2006 | 2005 | 2004 | 2003 | 2002 | 2001 |
|---|---|---|---|---|---|---|---|---|---|---|
| Revenue | 2,807 | 3,641 | 3,447 | 2,995 | 2,100 | 1,382 | 1,066 | 987 | 986 | 1,002 |
| Operating Income | NA | 2,450 | 2,161 | 1,751 | 1,170 | 585 | 396 | 366 | 400 | 503 |
| Depreciation, Depletion and Amortization | 540 | 408 | 266 | 217 | 253 | 242 | 209 | 148 | 125 | 119 |
| Interest Expense | 9.46 | 1.69 | 4.39 | 63.5 | 16.2 | 19.8 | 34.4 | 40.3 | 42.6 | 47.8 |
| Pretax Income | 917 | 2,016 | 1,912 | 1,489 | 921 | 364 | 162 | 187 | 243 | 350 |
| Effective Tax Rate | NA | 16.7% | 18.4% | 19.0% | 20.6% | 18.5% | 9.72% | 11.0% | 13.9% | 24.6% |
| Net Income | 773 | 1,679 | 1,561 | 1,206 | 732 | 297 | 146 | 166 | 210 | 264 |

**Balance Sheet & Other Financial Data** (Million $)

| | 2010 | 2009 | 2008 | 2007 | 2006 | 2005 | 2004 | 2003 | 2002 | 2001 |
|---|---|---|---|---|---|---|---|---|---|---|
| Cash | 338 | 735 | 513 | 161 | 61.7 | 166 | 58.8 | 139 | 274 | 288 |
| Current Assets | NA | 1,483 | 1,240 | 860 | 570 | 522 | 425 | 422 | 466 | 494 |
| Total Assets | 11,221 | 8,397 | 7,102 | 5,876 | 4,586 | 4,346 | 3,308 | 3,190 | 3,066 | 2,751 |
| Current Liabilities | NA | 434 | 679 | 493 | 426 | 259 | 214 | 244 | 281 | 208 |
| Long Term Debt | 2,686 | 751 | 751 | 774 | 684 | 1,129 | 503 | 542 | 590 | 550 |
| Common Equity | 7,163 | 6,788 | 5,290 | 4,308 | 3,229 | 2,732 | 2,384 | 2,178 | 1,989 | 1,778 |
| Total Capital | NA | 7,539 | 6,302 | 5,318 | 4,126 | 4,097 | 3,086 | 2,927 | 2,779 | 2,526 |
| Capital Expenditures | 1,320 | 1,431 | 1,231 | 1,179 | 1,053 | 434 | 261 | 307 | 268 | 134 |
| Cash Flow | NA | 2,087 | 1,827 | 1,423 | 985 | 538 | 355 | 315 | 335 | 382 |
| Current Ratio | 1.2 | 3.4 | 1.8 | 1.8 | 1.3 | 2.0 | 2.0 | 1.7 | 1.7 | 2.4 |
| % Long Term Debt of Capitalization | 27.1 | 10.0 | 11.9 | 14.6 | 16.6 | 27.6 | 16.3 | 18.5 | 21.2 | 21.8 |
| % Return on Assets | NA | 21.7 | 24.1 | 23.1 | 16.4 | 7.8 | 4.5 | 5.3 | 7.2 | 9.9 |
| % Return on Equity | 11.1 | 27.8 | 32.5 | 32.0 | 24.6 | 11.6 | 6.4 | 8.0 | 11.1 | 15.7 |

Data as orig reptd.; bef. results of disc opers/spec. items. Per share data adj. for stk. divs.; EPS diluted. E-Estimated. NA-Not Available. NM-Not Meaningful. NR-Not Ranked. UR-Under Review.

**Office:** Dorfstrasse 19A., Baar, Switzerland 6340.
**Telephone:** 41 41 761 65 55.
**Website:** www.noblecorp.com
**Chrmn, Pres & CEO:** D.W. Williams

**COO:** D.E. Jacobsen
**EVP & Secy:** J.J. Robertson
**SVP & General Counsel:** W.E. Turcotte
**CFO & Chief Acctg Officer:** D.J. Lubojacky

**Investor Contact:** L.M. Ahlstrom (281-276-6100)
**Board Members:** M. A. Cawley, L. J. Chazen, J. H. Edwards, G. T. Hall, M. E. Leland, J. E. Little, J. A. Marshall, M. P. Ricciardello, D. W. Williams

**Founded:** 1921
**Domicile:** Switzerland
**Employees:** 5,900

# Noble Energy Inc

**STANDARD &POOR'S**

| S&P Recommendation **HOLD** ★★★★★ | Price<br>$86.20 (as of Nov 25, 2011) | 12-Mo. Target Price<br>$100.00 | Investment Style<br>Large-Cap Growth |
|---|---|---|---|

**GICS Sector** Energy
**Sub-Industry** Oil & Gas Exploration & Production

**Summary** This independent exploration and production company is engaged in the exploration, development and production of oil and natural gas worldwide.

## Key Stock Statistics (Source S&P, Vickers, company reports)

| | | | | | | | |
|---|---|---|---|---|---|---|---|
| 52-Wk Range | $101.27– 65.91 | S&P Oper. EPS 2011E | 5.19 | Market Capitalization(B) | $15.227 | Beta | 1.02 |
| Trailing 12-Month EPS | $4.44 | S&P Oper. EPS 2012E | 6.34 | Yield (%) | 1.02 | S&P 3-Yr. Proj. EPS CAGR(%) | 24 |
| Trailing 12-Month P/E | 19.4 | P/E on S&P Oper. EPS 2011E | 16.6 | Dividend Rate/Share | $0.88 | S&P Credit Rating | BBB |
| $10K Invested 5 Yrs Ago | $18,216 | Common Shares Outstg. (M) | 176.6 | Institutional Ownership (%) | 95 | | |

## Price Performance

30-Week Mov. Avg. · · · 10-Week Mov. Avg. - - GAAP Earnings vs. Previous Year   Volume Above Avg. ▖▚▌ STARS
12-Mo. Target Price — Relative Strength — ▲ Up ▼ Down ► No Change   Below Avg. ▖▚▌ ★

Options: ASE, CBOE, P, Ph

Analysis prepared by Equity Analyst **Michael Kay** on Nov 10, 2011, when the stock traded at **$88.67**.

### Highlights

➤ NBL saw a 3% production increase in 2010, driven by a 5% boost in oil as onshore U.S. properties were developed and delivery improved at Dumbarton in the North Sea. Reflecting the end of production sharing in Ecuador and asset sales, we see 6% organic growth in 2011 and 7% in 2012. NBL has expanded its Wattenberg acreage in the DJ Basin, running 13 rigs, with five drilling for Niobrara oil shale. NBL recently raised 2011 production guidance to 220-222 MBOE/d on better than expected results at Marcellus Shale and the DJ Basin. Gas production in Israel grew 31% sequentially in the third quarter. NBL has closed on a $3.5 billion Marcellus Shale joint venture with CONSOL Energy (CNX 42, Hold), buying a 50% stake in 663,000 acres.

➤ NBL plans 2011 capex of $3 billion, with over 30% slated for 75 Wattenberg wells and 10% for the Gulf of Mexico (GOM). After drilling two wells in the GOM, the Gunflint appraisal is next, while South Raton is slated to begin production before year end and Galapagos in early 2012.

➤ EPS before items was up 24% in 2010, to $4.16. On higher crude prices, we see adjusted EPS of $5.19 in 2011 and $6.34 in 2012.

### Investment Rationale/Risk

➤ Solid exploration success with an attractive inventory of prospects and large development projects characterizes NBL's portfolio of assets, in our view. We view NBL as geographically balanced with financial flexibility, holding $1.5 billion in cash with low relative debt levels. NBL appears poised to translate exploration success into development in core areas. We see U.S. gas drilling projects, mainly in the Rockies, and excluding new high-return Marcellus acreage, shelved in favor of high impact international targets and domestic onshore oil. We see catalysts in horizontal drilling targeting Niobrara and production boosts in Israel and Equatorial Guinea. NBL's discoveries at Gunflint and Galapagos in the GOM, Tamar and Leviathan in Israel, and Aseng in EG are expected to add over 80,000 BOE/d by 2013.

➤ Risks to our recommendation and target price include declines in oil and gas prices and production, and exploration and geographic risks.

➤ Our 12-month target price of $100 is based on our proved NAV estimate ($108), our DCF ($121; WACC 10.8%; terminal growth 3%) and above-peer relative metrics, including a target enterprise value to 2012 EBITDA forecast of 6.5X.

## Qualitative Risk Assessment

| LOW | MEDIUM | **HIGH** |
|---|---|---|

Our risk assessment reflects our view of NBL's participation in the cyclical, competitive and capital-intensive exploration and production sector of the oil and gas industry, and its international operations, which carry heightened political and operational risk.

## Quantitative Evaluations

**S&P Quality Ranking**   B+

| D | C | B- | B | **B+** | A- | A | A+ |
|---|---|---|---|---|---|---|---|

**Relative Strength Rank**   STRONG

| 73 |
|---|

LOWEST = 1    HIGHEST = 99

## Revenue/Earnings Data

**Revenue (Million $)**

| | 1Q | 2Q | 3Q | 4Q | Year |
|---|---|---|---|---|---|
| 2011 | 899.0 | 954.0 | 924.0 | -- | -- |
| 2010 | 733.0 | 751.0 | 755.0 | 783.0 | 3,022 |
| 2009 | 441.0 | 491.0 | 621.0 | 760.0 | 2,313 |
| 2008 | 1,025 | 1,205 | 1,098 | 573.0 | 3,901 |
| 2007 | 742.6 | 794.2 | 813.8 | 921.5 | 3,272 |
| 2006 | 712.0 | 772.6 | 741.3 | 714.2 | 2,940 |

**Earnings Per Share ($)**

| | 1Q | 2Q | 3Q | 4Q | Year |
|---|---|---|---|---|---|
| 2011 | 0.08 | 1.61 | 2.39 | E1.16 | E5.19 |
| 2010 | 1.34 | 1.10 | 1.31 | 0.29 | 4.10 |
| 2009 | -1.09 | -0.33 | 0.61 | 0.05 | -0.75 |
| 2008 | 1.20 | -0.84 | 5.37 | 1.72 | 7.58 |
| 2007 | 1.22 | 1.21 | 1.28 | 1.73 | 5.45 |
| 2006 | 1.26 | -0.17 | 1.75 | 0.94 | 3.79 |

Fiscal year ended Dec. 31. Next earnings report expected: Mid February. EPS Estimates based on S&P Operating Earnings; historical GAAP earnings are as reported.

## Dividend Data (Dates: mm/dd Payment Date: mm/dd/yy)

| Amount<br>($) | Date<br>Decl. | Ex-Div.<br>Date | Stk. of<br>Record | Payment<br>Date |
|---|---|---|---|---|
| 0.180 | 04/25 | 05/05 | 05/09 | 05/23/11 |
| 0.220 | 07/26 | 08/04 | 08/08 | 08/22/11 |
| 0.220 | 07/26 | 08/04 | 08/08 | 08/22/11 |
| 0.220 | 10/25 | 11/03 | 11/07 | 11/21/11 |

Dividends have been paid since 1975. Source: Company reports.

# Noble Energy Inc

## Business Summary November 10, 2011

CORPORATE OVERVIEW. Noble Energy is a large independent exploration and production concern, engaged in exploration, development, production and marketing of oil and natural gas. In the U.S., NBL operates primarily in the Rocky Mountains, Mid-Continent region and deepwater Gulf of Mexico. International operations are focused on offshore Israel and West Africa.

As of December 31, 2010, NBL had estimated proved reserves of 6.55 Bcfe, of which 67% was natural gas and 46% proved developed. This compares with estimated proved reserves of 4.92 Bcfe, 64% natural gas and 69% proved developed, at the end of 2009, a 33% rise, mostly reflecting bookings at Tamar. The U.S. accounted for 45% of proved reserves. NBL believes substantial multi-year growth in reserves began in 2010 as it books reserves from discoveries at Tamar (Israel), Belinda (EG), Gunflint (GOM), Galapagos (GOM), Aseng (EG) and Diega/Carmen (EG).

CORPORATE STRATEGY. We believe NBL's geographical diversification has reduced dependence on any one operating region and that NBL has successfully executed a niche strategy by agreeing to undertake nontraditional construction projects with various host countries to obtain leases in potentially lucrative hydrocarbon fields. NBL aims to achieve growth in earnings and cash flow through exploration success and the development of a high-quality portfolio of assets that is balanced between U.S. and international projects. Exploration success, along with additional capex, in U.S. and international locations such as Equatorial Guinea and Israel, have resulted in solid growth in

the past several years. In addition, occasional strategic acquisitions such as Patina in 2005, combined with the sale of non-core assets, have allowed NBL to enhance its asset portfolio. The result is a company with assets and capabilities in major U.S. basins coupled with a significant portfolio of international properties.

NBL's 2010 drilling capex totaled $2 billion, within its $2.1 billion budget, and up from $1.3 billion in 2009, and excluded about $764 million in non-drilling capex. About 55% was to be spent in the U.S. Major project development capex was expected at $1 billion, with the majority directed toward development of Galapagos in the deepwater GOM, Aseng offshore Equatorial Guinea, and Tamar offshore Israel. About $500 million was allocated to exploration, targeting an estimated 700 MMBOE of resource potential with plans to drill seven high-impact offshore wells in the deepwater GOM, Equatorial Guinea and the Mediterranean Sea. The remainder of the budget was focused on liquid-rich and emerging opportunities onshore in the U.S., as well as development projects in Israel, the North Sea and China. For 2011, NBL has set capex at $3 billion, with 32% slated for 70 Niobrara wells and 10% for the Gulf of Mexico, where it expects three deepwater exploration wells to resume drilling.

## Company Financials Fiscal Year Ended Dec. 31

| Per Share Data ($) | 2010 | 2009 | 2008 | 2007 | 2006 | 2005 | 2004 | 2003 | 2002 | 2001 |
|---|---|---|---|---|---|---|---|---|---|---|
| Tangible Book Value | 35.04 | 31.11 | 31.95 | 23.51 | 19.35 | 12.68 | 12.37 | 9.38 | 8.80 | 8.86 |
| Cash Flow | 9.90 | 7.45 | 12.17 | 9.65 | 7.27 | 6.61 | 5.26 | 3.47 | 2.62 | 3.64 |
| Earnings | 4.10 | -0.75 | 7.58 | 5.45 | 3.79 | 4.12 | 2.70 | 0.78 | 0.16 | 1.17 |
| S&P Core Earnings | 3.70 | -0.84 | 7.52 | 5.42 | 3.05 | 4.08 | 2.58 | 0.70 | 0.08 | 1.08 |
| Dividends | 0.72 | 0.72 | 0.66 | 0.44 | 0.28 | 0.15 | 0.10 | 0.09 | 0.08 | 0.08 |
| Payout Ratio | 18% | NM | 9% | 8% | 7% | 4% | 4% | 11% | 52% | 7% |
| Prices:High | 89.00 | 74.09 | 105.11 | 81.71 | 54.64 | 48.75 | 32.30 | 23.00 | 20.38 | 25.55 |
| Prices:Low | 56.23 | 40.33 | 30.89 | 46.04 | 36.14 | 27.78 | 21.33 | 16.19 | 13.33 | 13.75 |
| P/E Ratio:High | 22 | NM | 14 | 15 | 14 | 12 | 12 | 29 | NM | 22 |
| P/E Ratio:Low | 14 | NM | 4 | 8 | 9 | 7 | 8 | 21 | NM | 12 |

| Income Statement Analysis (Million $) | | | | | | | | | | |
|---|---|---|---|---|---|---|---|---|---|---|
| Revenue | 2,904 | 2,229 | 3,901 | 3,272 | 2,940 | 2,187 | 1,351 | 1,011 | 1,444 | 1,572 |
| Operating Income | NA | NA | 2,295 | 2,029 | 2,019 | 1,423 | 884 | 539 | 376 | 535 |
| Depreciation, Depletion and Amortization | 1,027 | 1,420 | 791 | 728 | 623 | 391 | 309 | 309 | 285 | 284 |
| Interest Expense | 72.0 | 84.0 | 69.0 | 130 | 117 | 87.5 | 48.2 | 47.0 | 47.7 | 26.0 |
| Pretax Income | 1,031 | -264 | 2,061 | 1,368 | 1,096 | 969 | 516 | 142 | 42.6 | 225 |
| Effective Tax Rate | NA | 50.4% | 34.5% | 31.0% | 38.1% | 33.3% | 39.2% | 36.5% | 58.6% | 40.5% |
| Net Income | 725 | -131 | 1,350 | 944 | 678 | 646 | 314 | 89.9 | 17.7 | 134 |
| S&P Core Earnings | 654 | -147 | 1,340 | 938 | 548 | 640 | 305 | 81.0 | 8.88 | 123 |

| Balance Sheet & Other Financial Data (Million $) | | | | | | | | | | |
|---|---|---|---|---|---|---|---|---|---|---|
| Cash | 1,081 | 1,014 | 1,140 | 660 | 153 | 110 | 180 | 62.4 | 15.4 | 73.2 |
| Current Assets | 1,838 | 1,678 | 2,158 | 1,569 | 1,069 | 1,176 | 734 | 478 | 310 | 352 |
| Total Assets | 13,282 | 11,807 | 12,384 | 10,831 | 9,589 | 8,878 | 3,443 | 2,843 | 2,730 | 2,480 |
| Current Liabilities | 1,422 | 990 | 1,174 | 1,636 | 1,184 | 1,240 | 665 | 655 | 472 | 381 |
| Long Term Debt | 1,977 | 2,008 | 2,241 | 1,851 | 1,801 | 2,031 | 880 | 776 | 977 | 837 |
| Common Equity | 6,848 | 6,157 | 6,309 | 4,809 | 4,114 | 3,231 | 1,460 | 1,074 | 1,009 | 1,010 |
| Total Capital | 8,825 | 8,165 | 10,724 | 8,644 | 7,673 | 5,262 | 2,524 | 2,013 | 2,188 | 2,024 |
| Capital Expenditures | 1,885 | 1,268 | 1,971 | 1,415 | 1,357 | 786 | 661 | 527 | 596 | 739 |
| Cash Flow | 1,752 | 1,289 | 2,141 | 1,672 | 1,301 | 1,036 | 623 | 399 | 303 | 418 |
| Current Ratio | 1.3 | 1.7 | 1.8 | 1.0 | 0.9 | 0.9 | 1.1 | 0.7 | 0.7 | 0.9 |
| % Long Term Debt of Capitalization | 22.4 | 24.6 | 20.9 | 21.4 | 23.5 | 38.6 | 34.9 | 38.6 | 44.6 | 41.4 |
| % Return on Assets | 5.8 | NM | 11.6 | 9.2 | 7.3 | 10.5 | 10.0 | 3.2 | 0.7 | 6.1 |
| % Return on Equity | 11.2 | NM | 24.3 | 51.7 | 18.8 | 27.5 | 24.8 | 8.6 | 1.7 | 14.4 |

Data as orig reptd.; bef. results of disc opers/spec. items. Per share data adj. for stk. divs.; EPS diluted. E-Estimated. NA-Not Available. NM-Not Meaningful. NR-Not Ranked. UR-Under Review.

**Office:** 100 Glenborough Drive, Houston, TX 77067.
**Telephone:** 281-872-3100.
**Email:** info@nobleenergyinc.com
**Website:** http://www.nobleenergyinc.com

**Chrmn & CEO:** C.D. Davidson
**Pres & COO:** D.L. Stover
**SVP & CFO:** K.M. Fisher
**Chief Acctg Officer:** F. Bruning

**Secy & General Counsel:** A.J. Johnson
**Investor Contact:** D. Larson (281-872-3100)
**Board Members:** J. L. Berenson, M. A. Cawley, E. F. Cox, C. D. Davidson, T. J. Edelman, E. P. Grubman, K. L. Hedrick, S. D. Urban, W. T. Van Kleef

**Founded:** 1969
**Domicile:** Delaware
**Employees:** 1,772

The McGraw-Hill Companies

# Nordstrom Inc.

**STANDARD &POOR'S**

| S&P Recommendation **BUY** ★★★★☆ | Price $44.29 (as of Nov 25, 2011) | 12-Mo. Target Price $55.00 | Investment Style Large-Cap Growth |
|---|---|---|---|

**GICS Sector** Consumer Discretionary
**Sub-Industry** Department Stores

**Summary** This specialty retailer of apparel and accessories, widely known for its emphasis on service, operates some 210 stores in 29 states.

## Key Stock Statistics (Source S&P, Vickers, company reports)

| | | | | | | | |
|---|---|---|---|---|---|---|---|
| 52-Wk Range | $53.35– 37.28 | S&P Oper. EPS 2012**E** | 3.18 | Market Capitalization(B) | $9.416 | Beta | 1.66 |
| Trailing 12-Month EPS | $3.08 | S&P Oper. EPS 2013**E** | 3.53 | Yield (%) | 2.08 | S&P 3-Yr. Proj. EPS CAGR(%) | 13 |
| Trailing 12-Month P/E | 14.4 | P/E on S&P Oper. EPS 2012**E** | 13.9 | Dividend Rate/Share | $0.92 | S&P Credit Rating | A- |
| $10K Invested 5 Yrs Ago | $9,886 | Common Shares Outstg. (M) | 212.6 | Institutional Ownership (%) | 61 | | |

## Price Performance

30-Week Mov. Avg.   ···· 10-Week Mov. Avg.  - - GAAP Earnings vs. Previous Year   Volume Above Avg. ▥ STARS
12-Mo. Target Price — Relative Strength  — ▲ Up ▼ Down ▶ No Change   Below Avg. ▥ ★

Options: ASE, CBOE, P, Ph

Analysis prepared by Equity Analyst **Esther Kwon, CFA** on Nov 14, 2011, when the stock traded at **$49.48**.

## Highlights

➤ We see retail sales reaching $10.4 billion in FY 12 (Jan.) and $11.1 billion in FY 13, supported annually by 5% growth in total same-store sales, new store openings, and sales contribution from the recently acquired HauteLook business. JWN plans to add three new Nordstrom stores and 17 new Rack stores in FY 12 and forecasts first year sales contribution from HauteLook of between $150 million and $160 million. We expect moderate credit card revenue growth as improving economic conditions should support a recovery in customer payment rates.

➤ While we see the company's expenses increasing with higher sales, new stores, planned technology and marketing investments to enhance the customer shopping experience, and the HauteLook acquisition, we expect operating margins to expand annually, supported by effective inventory management, expense leverage off projected same-store sales growth, and improvement in credit trends.

➤ Assuming share buybacks under JWN's $750 million authorization, we see EPS of $3.18 (excluding charges) in FY 12 and $3.53 in FY 13.

## Investment Rationale/Risk

➤ Our buy recommendation is based on valuation and our positive company outlook. We perceive improved confidence among JWN's core higher-income customer base and believe the company is successfully reaching new customer segments through expansion in the online and off-price channels. We also believe that JWN's variable cost structure and disciplined inventory management will enable the company to maintain its high margins should sales trends weaken this fall. The shares recently had an indicated dividend yield of 1.8%.

➤ Risks to our recommendation and target price include a loss of business due to lackluster merchandising, uncompetitive pricing, delays in new store openings, and a weakening of confidence among core affluent shoppers due to financial market declines.

➤ While the outlook for economic growth and employment trends remains lackluster, we think JWN's customer base is less affected and believe the shares deserve to trade about in line with the recent average multiple of approximately 15X. Applying a multiple of 15.5X our FY 13 EPS estimate of $3.53, we arrive at our 12-month target price of $55.

## Qualitative Risk Assessment

| LOW | MEDIUM | HIGH |
|---|---|---|

Our risk assessment reflects our view of JWN's improving sales and profit margins, increasing market share in the better department store sector, and healthy balance sheet and cash flow. This is offset by potential for the U.S. economy to decelerate or enter into a double-dip recession.

## Quantitative Evaluations

**S&P Quality Ranking** A-

| D | C | B- | B | B+ | A- | A | A+ |
|---|---|---|---|---|---|---|---|

**Relative Strength Rank** MODERATE

41

LOWEST = 1 HIGHEST = 99

## Revenue/Earnings Data

**Revenue (Million $)**

| | 1Q | 2Q | 3Q | 4Q | Year |
|---|---|---|---|---|---|
| 2012 | 2,323 | 2,810 | 2,478 | -- | -- |
| 2011 | 2,087 | 2,515 | 2,182 | 2,916 | 9,700 |
| 2010 | 1,792 | 2,232 | 1,963 | 2,640 | 8,627 |
| 2009 | 1,949 | 2,359 | 1,879 | 2,386 | 8,573 |
| 2008 | 1,954 | 2,390 | 1,970 | 2,514 | 8,828 |
| 2007 | 1,787 | 2,270 | 1,872 | 2,631 | 8,561 |

**Earnings Per Share ($)**

| | | | | | |
|---|---|---|---|---|---|
| 2012 | 0.65 | 0.80 | 0.59 | E1.07 | E3.18 |
| 2011 | 0.52 | 0.66 | 0.53 | 1.04 | 2.75 |
| 2010 | 0.37 | 0.48 | 0.38 | 0.77 | 2.01 |
| 2009 | 0.54 | 0.65 | 0.33 | 0.31 | 1.83 |
| 2008 | 0.60 | 0.65 | 0.68 | 0.92 | 2.88 |
| 2007 | 0.48 | 0.67 | 0.52 | 0.89 | 2.55 |

Fiscal year ended Jan. 31. Next earnings report expected: NA. EPS Estimates based on S&P Operating Earnings; historical GAAP earnings are as reported.

## Dividend Data (Dates: mm/dd Payment Date: mm/dd/yy)

| Amount ($) | Date Decl. | Ex-Div. Date | Stk. of Record | Payment Date |
|---|---|---|---|---|
| 0.230 | 02/23 | 03/02 | 03/04 | 03/15/11 |
| 0.230 | 05/12 | 05/26 | 05/31 | 06/15/11 |
| 0.230 | 08/25 | 09/01 | 09/06 | 09/15/11 |
| 0.230 | 11/18 | 11/28 | 11/30 | 12/15/11 |

Dividends have been paid since 1971. Source: Company reports.

# Nordstrom Inc.

STANDARD
&POOR'S

## Business Summary November 14, 2011

CORPORATE OVERVIEW. Nordstrom, Inc. (JWN) was founded in 1901 as a retail shoe business in Seattle, Washington. Today, the company is leading retailer of national and exclusive/private branded apparel, shoes, accessories and cosmetics in the better department store and off-price channels. In FY 11 (Jan.), women's apparel accounted for 34% of the company's net sales; shoes 23%; men's apparel 15%; women's accessories 12%; cosmetics 10%; children's apparel 3%; and other 3%. JWN provides a private label credit card, two Nordstrom VISA credit cards, and a debit card for customer purchases through its wholly-owned federal savings bank, Nordstrom fsb. The company earns revenues from these cards in the form of finance charges and other fees. Both credit and debit cardholders receive loyalty program points for qualifying purchases that can be redeemed for products and services.

CORPORATE STRATEGY. JWN is pursuing a multi-channel retail strategy that included 116 Nordstrom full-line stores, Nordstrom direct (the online store at www.nordstrom.com), and 91 off-price Nordstrom Rack stores as of April 8, 2011. The Nordstrom full-line and online stores are largely integrated, providing customers with a consistent merchandise assortment across channels. A singular view of inventory enables the Nordstrom business to fulfill online orders from any store and to offer customers the option of buying items online but picking them up in a store, subject to availability. Nordstrom's shared inventory platform has also led to improvements in regular-price selling and inventory turnover rates.

We consider Nordstrom's promotional cadence to be low relative to other better department stores. As opposed to holding sales around major holidays and calendar gift giving occasions such as Valentine's Day and Mother's Day, Nordstrom holds only five major sales events annually. These are the Half-Yearly Sales for Women and Kids in May and November, the Half-Yearly Sales for Men in mid-June and late December, and the Nordstrom Anniversary Sale in July. The Anniversary Sale, which offers savings on new fall merchandise before the selling season begins in August, is unique in the department store sector.

## Company Financials Fiscal Year Ended Jan. 31

| Per Share Data ($) | 2011 | 2010 | 2009 | 2008 | 2007 | 2006 | 2005 | 2004 | 2003 | 2002 |
|---|---|---|---|---|---|---|---|---|---|---|
| Tangible Book Value | 9.03 | 6.98 | 5.37 | 4.81 | 7.90 | 7.26 | 6.10 | 5.40 | 4.55 | 4.38 |
| Cash Flow | 4.22 | 3.43 | 3.21 | 3.95 | 3.62 | 2.98 | 2.31 | 1.78 | 1.24 | 1.27 |
| Earnings | 2.75 | 2.01 | 1.83 | 2.88 | 2.55 | 1.98 | 1.39 | 0.88 | 0.38 | 0.46 |
| S&P Core Earnings | 2.76 | 2.01 | 1.84 | 2.80 | 2.55 | 1.93 | 1.31 | 0.84 | 0.31 | 0.40 |
| Dividends | NA | 0.64 | 0.64 | 0.42 | 0.32 | 0.24 | 0.21 | 0.21 | 0.19 | 0.18 |
| Payout Ratio | NA | 32% | 35% | 15% | 13% | 12% | 15% | 23% | 50% | 38% |
| Calendar Year | 2010 | 2009 | 2008 | 2007 | 2006 | 2005 | 2004 | 2003 | 2002 | 2001 |
| Prices:High | 46.22 | 38.71 | 40.59 | 59.70 | 51.40 | 39.00 | 23.68 | 17.75 | 13.44 | 11.49 |
| Prices:Low | 28.44 | 11.19 | 6.61 | 30.46 | 31.77 | 22.71 | 16.55 | 7.50 | 7.80 | 6.90 |
| P/E Ratio:High | 17 | 19 | 22 | 21 | 20 | 20 | 17 | 20 | 35 | 25 |
| P/E Ratio:Low | 10 | 6 | 4 | 11 | 12 | 11 | 12 | 9 | 20 | 15 |

| Income Statement Analysis (Million $) | | | | | | | | | | |
|---|---|---|---|---|---|---|---|---|---|---|
| Revenue | 9,700 | 8,627 | 8,573 | 8,828 | 8,561 | 7,723 | 7,131 | 6,492 | 5,975 | 5,634 |
| Operating Income | 1,445 | 1,147 | 1,072 | 1,503 | 1,195 | 1,010 | 817 | 585 | 424 | 363 |
| Depreciation | 327 | 313 | 302 | 269 | 285 | 276 | 265 | 251 | 234 | 218 |
| Interest Expense | 127 | 141 | 145 | 71.7 | 62.4 | 45.3 | 85.4 | 91.0 | 86.2 | 73.5 |
| Pretax Income | 991 | 696 | 648 | 1,173 | 1,106 | 885 | 647 | 398 | 196 | 204 |
| Effective Tax Rate | NA | 36.6% | 38.1% | 39.1% | 38.7% | 37.7% | 39.2% | 39.0% | 47.1% | 39.0% |
| Net Income | 613 | 441 | 401 | 715 | 678 | 551 | 393 | 243 | 104 | 125 |
| S&P Core Earnings | 614 | 441 | 403 | 697 | 677 | 536 | 373 | 229 | 83.9 | 107 |

| Balance Sheet & Other Financial Data (Million $) | | | | | | | | | | |
|---|---|---|---|---|---|---|---|---|---|---|
| Cash | 1,506 | 795 | 72.0 | 358 | 403 | 463 | 361 | 476 | 208 | 331 |
| Current Assets | 4,824 | 4,054 | 3,217 | 3,361 | 2,742 | 2,874 | 2,572 | 2,455 | 2,073 | 2,055 |
| Total Assets | 7,462 | 6,579 | 5,661 | 5,600 | 4,822 | 4,921 | 4,605 | 4,466 | 4,096 | 4,049 |
| Current Liabilities | 1,879 | 2,014 | 1,601 | 1,635 | 1,433 | 1,623 | 1,341 | 1,050 | 870 | 948 |
| Long Term Debt | 2,775 | 2,257 | 2,214 | 2,236 | 624 | 628 | 929 | 1,605 | 1,342 | 1,351 |
| Common Equity | 2,021 | 1,572 | 1,210 | 1,115 | 2,169 | 2,093 | 1,789 | 1,634 | 1,372 | 1,314 |
| Total Capital | 4,802 | 4,185 | 3,435 | 3,612 | 2,792 | 2,720 | 2,718 | 3,239 | 2,714 | 2,666 |
| Capital Expenditures | 399 | 360 | 563 | 501 | 264 | 272 | 247 | 258 | 328 | 390 |
| Cash Flow | 940 | 754 | 703 | 984 | 963 | 828 | 658 | 494 | 338 | 342 |
| Current Ratio | 2.6 | 2.0 | 2.0 | 2.1 | 1.9 | 1.8 | 1.9 | 2.3 | 2.4 | 2.2 |
| % Long Term Debt of Capitalization | 57.8 | 53.9 | 64.5 | 61.9 | 22.3 | 23.1 | 34.2 | 49.5 | 49.4 | 50.7 |
| % Net Income of Revenue | 6.3 | 5.1 | 4.7 | 8.1 | 7.9 | 7.1 | 5.5 | 3.7 | 1.7 | 2.2 |
| % Return on Assets | 8.7 | 7.2 | 7.1 | 13.7 | 13.9 | 11.6 | 8.6 | 5.7 | 2.5 | 3.3 |
| % Return on Equity | 34.1 | 31.7 | 34.5 | 43.6 | 31.8 | 28.4 | 23.0 | 16.2 | 7.7 | 9.8 |

Data as orig reptd.; bef. results of disc opers/spec. items. Per share data adj. for stk. divs.; EPS diluted. E-Estimated. NA-Not Available. NM-Not Meaningful. NR-Not Ranked. UR-Under Review.

**Office:** 1617 6th Ave, Seattle, WA 98101-1707.
**Telephone:** 206-628-2111.
**Email:** invrelations@nordstrom.com
**Website:** http://www.nordstrom.com

**Chrmn:** E. Hernandez, Jr.
**Pres & CEO:** B.W. Nordstrom
**EVP & CFO:** M. Koppel
**EVP & Chief Admin Officer:** D.F. Little

**EVP, Secy & General Counsel:** R.B. Sari
**Investor Contact:** C. Holloway (206-303-3200)
**Board Members:** P. J. Campbell, M. M. Ebanks, E. Hernandez, Jr., R. G. Miller, B. W. Nordstrom, E. B. Nordstrom, P. E. Nordstrom, P. G. Satre, F. D. Thornton, B. K. Turner, R. D. Walter, A. A. Winter

**Founded:** 1901
**Domicile:** Washington
**Employees:** 54,000

The McGraw-Hill Companies

# Norfolk Southern Corp

STANDARD
&POOR'S

| S&P Recommendation **BUY** ★★★★☆ | Price<br>$73.04 (as of Nov 28, 2011) | 12-Mo. Target Price<br>$85.00 | Investment Style<br>Large-Cap Blend |
|---|---|---|---|

**GICS Sector** Industrials
**Sub-Industry** Railroads

**Summary** This railroad operates 20,000 route miles serving 22 eastern states, the District of Columbia, and Ontario, Canada.

## Key Stock Statistics (Source S&P, Vickers, company reports)

| | | | | | |
|---|---|---|---|---|---|
| 52-Wk Range | $78.40– 57.57 | S&P Oper. EPS 2011E | 5.27 | Market Capitalization(B) | $24.549 | Beta | 1.10 |
| Trailing 12-Month EPS | $5.12 | S&P Oper. EPS 2012E | 5.75 | Yield (%) | 2.35 | S&P 3-Yr. Proj. EPS CAGR(%) | 16 |
| Trailing 12-Month P/E | 14.3 | P/E on S&P Oper. EPS 2011E | 13.9 | Dividend Rate/Share | $1.72 | S&P Credit Rating | BBB+ |
| $10K Invested 5 Yrs Ago | $15,964 | Common Shares Outstg. (M) | 336.1 | Institutional Ownership (%) | 69 | | |

## Price Performance

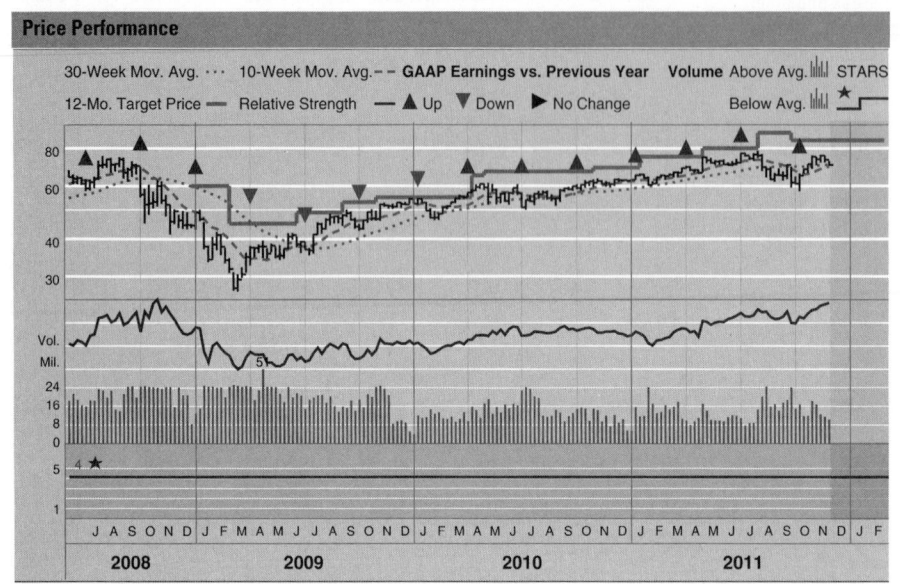

30-Week Mov. Avg. ···· 10-Week Mov. Avg. - - GAAP Earnings vs. Previous Year   Volume Above Avg. ▫▫▫ STARS
12-Mo. Target Price — Relative Strength — ▲ Up ▼ Down ► No Change   Below Avg. ▫▫▫ ★

Options: ASE, CBOE, P, Ph

Analysis prepared by Equity Analyst **Kevin Kirkeby** on Nov 28, 2011, when the stock traded at **$70.44**.

## Qualitative Risk Assessment

| LOW | MEDIUM | HIGH |
|---|---|---|

Our risk assessment reflects what we see as NSC's exposure to economic cycles, regulations, labor costs, significant capital expenditure requirements, and challenges in maintaining system fluidity, offset by our view of a diverse customer base, historically positive free cash flow, and moderate financial leverage.

## Quantitative Evaluations

**S&P Quality Ranking**      A-

| D | C | B- | B | B+ | A- | A | A+ |
|---|---|---|---|---|---|---|---|

**Relative Strength Rank**      STRONG

89

LOWEST = 1       HIGHEST = 99

## Revenue/Earnings Data

**Revenue (Million $)**

| | 1Q | 2Q | 3Q | 4Q | Year |
|---|---|---|---|---|---|
| 2011 | 2,620 | 2,866 | 2,889 | -- | -- |
| 2010 | 2,238 | 2,430 | 2,456 | 2,392 | 9,516 |
| 2009 | 1,943 | 1,857 | 2,063 | 2,106 | 7,969 |
| 2008 | 2,500 | 2,765 | 2,894 | 2,502 | 10,661 |
| 2007 | 2,247 | 2,378 | 2,353 | 2,454 | 9,432 |
| 2006 | 2,303 | 2,392 | 2,393 | 2,319 | 9,407 |

**Earnings Per Share ($)**

| | 1Q | 2Q | 3Q | 4Q | Year |
|---|---|---|---|---|---|
| 2011 | 0.90 | 1.56 | 1.59 | E1.36 | E5.27 |
| 2010 | 0.68 | 1.04 | 1.19 | 1.09 | 4.00 |
| 2009 | 0.47 | 0.66 | 0.81 | 0.82 | 2.76 |
| 2008 | 0.76 | 1.18 | 1.37 | 1.21 | 4.52 |
| 2007 | 0.71 | 0.98 | 1.02 | 1.02 | 3.68 |
| 2006 | 0.72 | 0.89 | 1.02 | 0.95 | 3.57 |

Fiscal year ended Dec. 31. Next earnings report expected: NA. EPS Estimates based on S&P Operating Earnings; historical GAAP earnings are as reported.

## Highlights

➤ We forecast revenues will increase 5.3% in 2012, with volumes up 2.7%, price and mix contributing 2.5%, and fuel surcharges relatively unchanged. We see volumes benefiting from new production at two auto plants, as well as shipments to and from the shale gas regions. We think NSC will continue to take freight away from trucking companies along the Heartland and Crescent Corridors. Our forecast anticipates further growth in export coal shipments, but looks for domestic thermal coal moves to remain muted.

➤ We expect the operating margin to widen in 2012, on improved fixed cost coverage as volumes are forecast to rise. However, we anticipate generally higher health care costs and a contractual wage hike during the coming year, but we think these will be outweighed by other cost control measures, including the deployment of new locomotives and railcars.

➤ Our EPS forecast of $5.27 for 2011 incorporates an effective tax rate of 37% and an average fully diluted share count of 352.3 million, which is 5.2% lower than in 2010.

## Investment Rationale/Risk

➤ Medium-term trends in NSC's primary markets remain favorable and support rising traffic, in our opinion. We see investments in its network improving capacity on heavily trafficked lanes like the Heartland and Crescent corridors, and leading to greater conversion of truck traffic over to rail, particularly as the economy recovers and truck capacity tightens. With global economic uncertainty rising, we believe a valuation only modestly ahead of the historical average, and in line with peers, is warranted.

➤ Risks to our recommendation and target price include a slowdown in manufacturing, unfavorable changes in the regulatory framework, a slowing in European coal demand that reduces export shipments, and government initiatives that encourage utilities to use less coal in their overall fuel mix.

➤ Blending a P/E of 14.5X our four-quarter forward EPS estimate, which is a premium to the 10-year average, with our DCF model, which assumes a 10.8% cost of equity, 13% average free cash flow growth over the next five years, and a 3.5% terminal growth rate (yielding an intrinsic value of $87), we arrive at our 12-month target price of $85.

## Dividend Data (Dates: mm/dd Payment Date: mm/dd/yy)

| Amount<br>($) | Date<br>Decl. | Ex-Div.<br>Date | Stk. of<br>Record | Payment<br>Date |
|---|---|---|---|---|
| 0.400 | 04/26 | 05/04 | 05/06 | 06/10/11 |
| 0.430 | 07/26 | 08/03 | 08/05 | 09/10/11 |
| 0.430 | 07/26 | 08/03 | 08/05 | 09/10/11 |
| 0.430 | 10/25 | 11/02 | 11/04 | 12/10/11 |

Dividends have been paid since 1901. Source: Company reports.

# Norfolk Southern Corp

**STANDARD
&POOR'S**

## Business Summary November 28, 2011

CORPORATE OVERVIEW. Norfolk Southern provides rail transportation service in the eastern U.S., operating over 20,000 miles of road, with an extensive intermodal and coal service network and a significant general freight business, including an automotive business that is the largest in North America. NSC owns 58% of Conrail's shares, with CSX holding the remainder, and holds 50% voting rights. NSC and CSX operate separate portions of Conrail's rail routes and assets. NSC's non-rail activities include real estate and natural resources.

NSC's intermodal business represented 19% of 2010 freight revenues. Although it was the second largest contributor to revenues, intermodal was the largest category by volume at 43% of total carloads. Coal, which we believe is NSC's most profitable segment due to its unit train structure, accounted for 28% of 2010 freight revenues, and 23% of carloads. Most of this traffic, which is delivered primarily to power utilities, originates from the Appalachian coal fields. However, the company has been increasing the number of carloads it carries with origins in the Illinois Basin and the Powder River Basin. General merchandise, sensitive to U.S. GDP trends, provided 53% of freight revenues in 2010. This includes the chemicals and automotive categories, representing 14% and 7% of 2010 freight revenues, respectively. We consider NSC to have

considerable exposure to the auto market since it serves 24 assembly plants, 14 of which belong to the domestic manufacturers Ford, Chrysler and General Motors.

COMPETITIVE LANDSCAPE. The U.S. rail industry has an oligopoly-like structure, with over 80% of revenues generated by the four largest railroads: NSC and CSX Corp. operating on the East Coast, and Union Pacific Corp. and Burlington Northern Santa Fe Corp. operating on the West Coast. Railroads simultaneously compete for customers while cooperating by sharing assets, interfacing systems, and completing customer movements. NSC, for example, is a net payer of equipment rents as it takes on more freight originated by other carriers than it hands off to them at its major gateways. Likewise, NSC has formed separate joint ventures with Kansas City Southern and Pan Am Railways that enhance its access along certain corridors in exchange for much needed capital investments.

## Company Financials Fiscal Year Ended Dec. 31

| Per Share Data ($) | 2010 | 2009 | 2008 | 2007 | 2006 | 2005 | 2004 | 2003 | 2002 | 2001 |
|---|---|---|---|---|---|---|---|---|---|---|
| Tangible Book Value | 29.85 | 28.06 | 26.23 | 27.12 | 24.19 | 22.66 | 19.98 | 17.83 | 16.71 | 15.78 |
| Cash Flow | 6.25 | 5.05 | 6.63 | 5.63 | 5.50 | 5.02 | 3.83 | 2.40 | 2.50 | 2.27 |
| Earnings | 4.00 | 2.76 | 4.52 | 3.68 | 3.57 | 3.11 | 2.31 | 1.05 | 1.18 | 0.94 |
| S&P Core Earnings | 4.03 | 2.72 | 4.21 | 3.48 | 3.43 | 2.97 | 2.13 | 0.95 | 0.70 | 0.41 |
| Dividends | 1.40 | 1.36 | 1.22 | 0.96 | 0.68 | 0.48 | 0.46 | 0.30 | 0.26 | 0.24 |
| Payout Ratio | 35% | 49% | 27% | 26% | 19% | 15% | 20% | 29% | 22% | 26% |
| Prices:High | 63.67 | 54.55 | 75.53 | 59.77 | 57.71 | 45.81 | 36.69 | 24.62 | 26.98 | 24.11 |
| Prices:Low | 46.18 | 26.69 | 41.36 | 45.38 | 39.10 | 29.60 | 20.38 | 17.35 | 17.20 | 13.41 |
| P/E Ratio:High | 16 | 20 | 17 | 16 | 16 | 15 | 16 | 23 | 23 | 26 |
| P/E Ratio:Low | 12 | 10 | 9 | 12 | 11 | 10 | 9 | 17 | 15 | 14 |

| Income Statement Analysis (Million $) | 2010 | 2009 | 2008 | 2007 | 2006 | 2005 | 2004 | 2003 | 2002 | 2001 |
|---|---|---|---|---|---|---|---|---|---|---|
| Revenue | 9,516 | 7,969 | 10,661 | 9,432 | 9,407 | 8,527 | 7,312 | 6,468 | 6,270 | 6,170 |
| Operating Income | 3,502 | 2,807 | 3,901 | 3,360 | 3,307 | 2,904 | 2,311 | 1,592 | 1,158 | 1,521 |
| Depreciation | 826 | 845 | 804 | 775 | 750 | 787 | 609 | 528 | 515 | 514 |
| Interest Expense | 462 | 467 | 457 | 482 | 493 | 500 | 506 | 497 | 518 | 553 |
| Pretax Income | 2,367 | 1,622 | 2,750 | 2,237 | 2,230 | 1,697 | 1,302 | 586 | 706 | 553 |
| Effective Tax Rate | NA | 36.3% | 37.6% | 34.6% | 33.6% | 24.5% | 29.1% | 29.9% | 34.8% | 34.5% |
| Net Income | 1,496 | 1,034 | 1,716 | 1,464 | 1,481 | 1,281 | 923 | 411 | 460 | 362 |
| S&P Core Earnings | 1,500 | 1,011 | 1,595 | 1,377 | 1,417 | 1,224 | 849 | 365 | 270 | 155 |

| Balance Sheet & Other Financial Data (Million $) | 2010 | 2009 | 2008 | 2007 | 2006 | 2005 | 2004 | 2003 | 2002 | 2001 |
|---|---|---|---|---|---|---|---|---|---|---|
| Cash | 1,110 | 1,086 | 618 | 206 | 527 | 289 | 579 | 284 | 184 | 204 |
| Current Assets | 2,471 | 2,246 | 1,999 | 1,675 | 2,400 | 2,650 | 1,967 | 1,425 | 1,299 | 1,047 |
| Total Assets | 28,199 | 27,369 | 26,297 | 26,144 | 26,028 | 25,861 | 24,750 | 20,596 | 19,956 | 19,418 |
| Current Liabilities | 2,082 | 1,789 | 2,105 | 1,948 | 2,093 | 1,921 | 2,201 | 1,801 | 1,853 | 2,386 |
| Long Term Debt | 6,567 | 6,679 | 6,316 | 6,132 | 6,109 | 6,616 | 6,863 | 6,800 | 7,006 | 7,027 |
| Common Equity | 10,669 | 10,353 | 9,597 | 9,727 | 9,615 | 9,289 | 7,990 | 6,976 | 6,500 | 6,090 |
| Total Capital | 17,594 | 17,406 | 22,295 | 22,290 | 22,168 | 22,525 | 21,403 | 17,008 | 16,561 | 15,943 |
| Capital Expenditures | 1,470 | 1,299 | 1,558 | 1,341 | 1,178 | 1,025 | 1,041 | 720 | 689 | 746 |
| Cash Flow | 2,322 | 1,879 | 2,520 | 2,239 | 2,231 | 2,068 | 1,532 | 939 | 975 | 876 |
| Current Ratio | 1.2 | 1.3 | 1.0 | 0.9 | 1.1 | 1.4 | 0.9 | 0.8 | 0.7 | 0.4 |
| % Long Term Debt of Capitalization | 37.3 | 38.4 | 28.3 | 27.5 | 27.6 | 29.4 | 32.1 | 40.0 | 42.3 | 44.1 |
| % Net Income of Revenue | 15.7 | 13.0 | 16.1 | 15.5 | 15.7 | 15.0 | 12.6 | 6.4 | 7.3 | 5.9 |
| % Return on Assets | 5.4 | 3.9 | 6.5 | 5.6 | 5.7 | 5.1 | 4.1 | 2.0 | 2.3 | 1.9 |
| % Return on Equity | 14.2 | 10.4 | 17.8 | 15.1 | 15.7 | 14.8 | 12.3 | 6.1 | 7.3 | 6.1 |

Data as orig reptd.; bef. results of disc opers/spec. items. Per share data adj. for stk. divs.; EPS diluted. E-Estimated. NA-Not Available. NM-Not Meaningful. NR-Not Ranked. UR-Under Review.

**Office:** 3 Commercial Pl, Norfolk, VA 23510-2191.
**Telephone:** 757-629-2680.
**Website:** http://www.nscorp.com
**Chrmn, Pres & CEO:** C.W. Moorman, IV

**COO:** M.D. Manion
**EVP & CIO:** D.H. Butler
**CFO:** J.A. Squires
**Chief Acctg Officer & Cntlr:** C.H. Allison, Jr.

**Investor Contact:** L. Marilley (757-629-2861)
**Board Members:** G. L. Baliles, T. D. Bell, Jr., E. B. Bowles, R. A. Bradway, D. A. Carp, A. D. Correll, K. N. Horn, B. M. Joyce, S. F. Leer, M. D. Lockhart, C. W. Moorman, IV, J. P. Reason

**Founded:** 1980
**Domicile:** Virginia
**Employees:** 28,559

*The McGraw-Hill Companies*

# Northeast Utilities

**STANDARD &POOR'S**

| S&P Recommendation | HOLD ★★★★★ | Price $33.18 (as of Nov 25, 2011) | 12-Mo. Target Price $34.00 | Investment Style Large-Cap Blend |
|---|---|---|---|---|

**GICS Sector** Utilities
**Sub-Industry** Electric Utilities

**Summary** This utility holding company, which serves Connecticut, western Massachusetts and New Hampshire, has agreed to buy NSTAR, a Boston-based utility.

## Key Stock Statistics (Source S&P, Vickers, company reports)

| | | | | | | | |
|---|---|---|---|---|---|---|---|
| 52-Wk Range | $36.47–30.02 | S&P Oper. EPS 2011**E** | 2.33 | Market Capitalization(B) | $5.874 | Beta | 0.48 |
| Trailing 12-Month EPS | $2.31 | S&P Oper. EPS 2012**E** | 2.45 | Yield (%) | 3.32 | S&P 3-Yr. Proj. EPS CAGR(%) | 8 |
| Trailing 12-Month P/E | 14.4 | P/E on S&P Oper. EPS 2011**E** | 14.2 | Dividend Rate/Share | $1.10 | S&P Credit Rating | BBB+ |
| $10K Invested 5 Yrs Ago | $14,162 | Common Shares Outstg. (M) | 177.0 | Institutional Ownership (%) | 78 | | |

## Price Performance

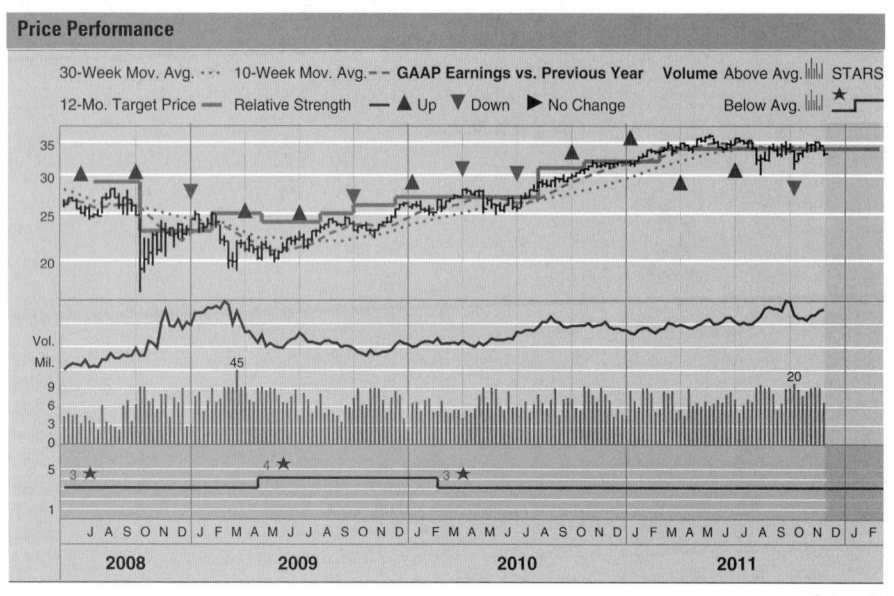

30-Week Mov. Avg. · · · 10-Week Mov. Avg. - - GAAP Earnings vs. Previous Year   Volume Above Avg. ▥ STARS
12-Mo. Target Price — Relative Strength — ▲ Up ▼ Down ▶ No Change   Below Avg. ▥ ★

Options: Ph

Analysis prepared by Equity Analyst **Justin McCann** on Sep 13, 2011, when the stock traded at **$33.58**.

## Highlights

➤ Subject to required approvals, the proposed merger with NSTAR (NST 44, Hold) is expected to close in the second half of 2011 and to result in one of the largest utility companies in the U.S. We believe the transaction would be accretive to combined earnings in the first year and that NST's balance sheet would help provide significant investment opportunities for the new company's transmission business.

➤ We expect EPS in 2011 to grow nearly 8% from 2010's $2.19. In the first half of 2011, results were up at the transmission business and all of the utilities, particularly at Connecticut Power & Light, which benefited from higher electric rates, lower uncollectible expense, and an increase in the weather-aided power demand.

➤ For full-year 2011, we expect NU's stand-alone EPS growth to be driven by higher transmission earnings and new rate hikes. We believe the distribution and generating companies will earn about $1.33 a share, the transmission business will earn about $1.08, and the parent company and the competitive businesses will combine for a recorded loss of about $0.05. For 2012, on a stand-alone basis, we expect EPS to increase nearly 4% from anticipated results for 2011.

## Investment Rationale/Risk

➤ Given the solid performance of the stock since the announcement of the agreed-to merger with NSTAR, we think it has become fairly valued for the near term. In addition to the expected benefits from the merger, we believe the shares have benefited from NU's improved earnings outlook on a stand-alone basis. If completed, the merger with NST is expected to result in a nearly 20% increase in the dividend, and to eliminate the need for the previously planned 2012 equity issuance. Over the longer term, we expect the shares to benefit from NU's investments in its transmission system.

➤ Risks to our recommendation and target price include the possibility of the planned merger with NSTAR being delayed or terminated, a slower-than-expected recovery in the company's service territory economy, and a sharp decrease in the average peer group P/E multiple.

➤ The recent yield from the dividend was about 3.3%, well below the recent peer average of around 4.5%. However, the planned merger with NST, if approved, is expected to raise the dividend by nearly 20%. Our 12-month target price is $34, a premium-to-peers P/E of 14.4X our EPS estimate for 2011.

## Qualitative Risk Assessment

| LOW | MEDIUM | HIGH |
|---|---|---|

Our risk assessment reflects the steady cash flow we expect from regulated electric and gas utility operations, a generally healthy economy in most of NU's service territories, and a relatively supportive regulatory environment. It also reflects the company's exit from its nonregulated and high-risk wholesale energy marketing and energy services businesses.

## Quantitative Evaluations

**S&P Quality Ranking**    **B**

| D | C | B- | B | B+ | A- | A | A+ |
|---|---|---|---|---|---|---|---|

**Relative Strength Rank**    **MODERATE**

69

LOWEST = 1    HIGHEST = 99

## Revenue/Earnings Data

**Revenue (Million $)**

| | 1Q | 2Q | 3Q | 4Q | Year |
|---|---|---|---|---|---|
| 2011 | 1,235 | 1,047 | 1,115 | -- | -- |
| 2010 | 1,339 | 1,111 | 1,243 | 1,204 | 4,898 |
| 2009 | 1,593 | 1,224 | 1,306 | 1,315 | 5,439 |
| 2008 | 1,520 | 1,325 | 1,507 | 1,448 | 5,800 |
| 2007 | 1,704 | 1,392 | 1,451 | 1,276 | 5,822 |
| 2006 | 2,147 | 1,671 | 1,594 | 1,483 | 6,884 |

**Earnings Per Share ($)**

| | 1Q | 2Q | 3Q | 4Q | Year |
|---|---|---|---|---|---|
| 2011 | 0.64 | 0.44 | 0.51 | E0.69 | E2.33 |
| 2010 | 0.49 | 0.41 | 0.57 | 0.73 | 2.19 |
| 2009 | 0.60 | 0.47 | 0.37 | 0.48 | 1.91 |
| 2008 | 0.38 | 0.37 | 0.47 | 0.46 | 1.67 |
| 2007 | 0.50 | 0.30 | 0.32 | 0.47 | 1.58 |
| 2006 | -0.13 | 0.09 | 0.67 | 0.19 | 0.82 |

Fiscal year ended Dec. 31. Next earnings report expected: Late February. EPS Estimates based on S&P Operating Earnings; historical GAAP earnings are as reported.

## Dividend Data (Dates: mm/dd Payment Date: mm/dd/yy)

| Amount ($) | Date Decl. | Ex-Div. Date | Stk. of Record | Payment Date |
|---|---|---|---|---|
| 0.275 | 02/08 | 02/25 | 03/01 | 03/31/11 |
| 0.275 | 04/12 | 05/27 | 06/01 | 06/30/11 |
| 0.275 | 07/12 | 08/30 | 09/01 | 09/30/11 |
| 0.278 | 10/11 | -- | 11/10 | 12/30/11 |

Dividends have been paid since 1999. Source: Company reports.

**Please read the Required Disclosures and Analyst Certification on the last page of this report.**

**The McGraw·Hill Companies**

# Northeast Utilities

STANDARD
&POOR'S

## Business Summary September 13, 2011

CORPORATE OVERVIEW. Northeast Utilities (NU) is a holding company that provides electricity and gas services through its utility subsidiaries. The company's electric subsidiaries include The Connecticut Light & Power Company, Public Service Company of New Hampshire, and Western Massachusetts Electric Company. NU distributes natural gas through its Yankee Gas Services Company subsidiary. Yankee Gas operates the largest natural gas distribution system in Connecticut. NU Enterprises Inc., the nonregulated subsidiary of NU, owns a number of competitive energy and related businesses. In 2010, the electric distribution segment accounted for 76.9% of consolidated revenues (79.7% in 2009), the transmission segment 12.7% (10.6%), the gas distribution segment 8.8% (8.2%), and the competitive businesses 1.6% (1.5%).

IMPACT OF MAJOR DEVELOPMENTS. On October 18, 2010, NU announced a definitive merger agreement with NSTAR (NST 45, Hold), a Boston-headquartered energy delivery company serving 1.1 million electric distribution customers and about 300,000 natural gas customers in Massachusetts. Under the terms of the stock-for-stock agreement, NSTAR shareholders would receive 1.312 NU shares for each NST share. Upon completion of the transaction, it is expected that NU shareholders would have a 56% interest in the combined company, which will maintain the Northeast Utilities name, with NST holders 44%. NU's chairman, president and CEO, Charles Shivery, would

become the non-executive chairman of the new company, while NST's chairman, president and CEO, Thomas May, would become president and CEO. After a period of 18 months, Mr. May would replace Mr. Shivery as chairman.

MARKET PROFILE. NU provides retail electric services in all major cities and towns in Connecticut, New Hampshire and Massachusetts. The company's electric utilities serve around 1.9 million customers in 419 cities and towns in Connecticut, New Hampshire and western Massachusetts. In 2010, residential customers contributed about 59% of NU's electric distribution revenues (58% in 2009); commercial customers 33% (34%); industrial customers 7% (7%); and others 1% (1%).

NU also distributes natural gas to approximately 206,000 customers in 71 cities and towns in Connecticut. Residential customers, the largest user segment, contributed 51% of natural gas revenues in 2010 (48% in 2009), followed by the commercial and industrial segments, which contributed 30% (31%) and 16% (18%), respectively, while others accounted for 3% (3%).

## Company Financials Fiscal Year Ended Dec. 31

| Per Share Data ($) | 2010 | 2009 | 2008 | 2007 | 2006 | 2005 | 2004 | 2003 | 2002 | 2001 |
|---|---|---|---|---|---|---|---|---|---|---|
| Tangible Book Value | 19.97 | 18.74 | 17.54 | 16.81 | 16.28 | 13.98 | 14.87 | 14.68 | 14.20 | 13.79 |
| Earnings | 2.19 | 1.91 | 1.67 | 1.58 | 0.82 | -1.74 | 0.91 | 0.95 | 1.18 | 1.96 |
| S&P Core Earnings | 2.43 | 2.01 | 1.11 | 1.55 | 0.93 | -1.59 | 0.96 | 1.13 | -0.77 | -3.68 |
| Dividends | 1.02 | 0.95 | 0.83 | 0.78 | 0.72 | 0.68 | 0.63 | 0.58 | 0.52 | 0.45 |
| Payout Ratio | 47% | 50% | 49% | 49% | 88% | NM | 69% | 61% | 44% | 23% |
| Prices:High | 32.21 | 26.48 | 31.62 | 33.62 | 28.90 | 21.95 | 20.27 | 20.32 | 20.70 | 24.35 |
| Prices:Low | 24.68 | 19.01 | 17.16 | 26.21 | 19.07 | 17.30 | 17.17 | 13.13 | 12.66 | 16.59 |
| P/E Ratio:High | 15 | 14 | 19 | 21 | 35 | NM | 22 | 21 | 18 | 12 |
| P/E Ratio:Low | 11 | 10 | 10 | 17 | 23 | NM | 19 | 14 | 11 | 8 |

| Income Statement Analysis (Million $) | 2010 | 2009 | 2008 | 2007 | 2006 | 2005 | 2004 | 2003 | 2002 | 2001 |
|---|---|---|---|---|---|---|---|---|---|---|
| Revenue | 4,898 | 5,439 | 5,800 | 5,822 | 6,884 | 7,397 | 6,687 | 6,069 | 5,216 | 6,874 |
| Depreciation | 301 | 310 | 279 | 265 | 445 | 614 | 528 | 540 | 667 | 983 |
| Maintenance | NA | 234 | 254 | 212 | 194 | 200 | 188 | 232 | 263 | 259 |
| Fixed Charges Coverage | 3.55 | 2.83 | 2.33 | 2.25 | 1.23 | -0.26 | 1.63 | 1.72 | 1.10 | -0.24 |
| Construction Credits | NA | NA | NA | NA | NA | NA | NA | NA | NA | Nil |
| Effective Tax Rate | 34.8% | 35.3% | 28.8% | 30.3% | NM | NM | 30.7% | 33.1% | 35.1% | 39.5% |
| Net Income | 388 | 330 | 261 | 251 | 126 | -229 | 117 | 121 | 152 | 266 |
| S&P Core Earnings | 431 | 348 | 173 | 240 | 144 | -209 | 122 | 143 | -99.7 | -500 |

| Balance Sheet & Other Financial Data (Million $) | 2010 | 2009 | 2008 | 2007 | 2006 | 2005 | 2004 | 2003 | 2002 | 2001 |
|---|---|---|---|---|---|---|---|---|---|---|
| Gross Property | 12,550 | 11,682 | 10,978 | 9,892 | 8,857 | 8,969 | 8,247 | 7,674 | 7,213 | 7,241 |
| Capital Expenditures | 954 | 908 | 1,255 | 1,115 | 872 | 752 | 644 | 532 | 492 | 443 |
| Net Property | 9,568 | 8,840 | 8,208 | 7,230 | 6,242 | 6,417 | 5,864 | 5,430 | 4,728 | 3,822 |
| Capitalization:Long Term Debt | 4,931 | 5,052 | 4,906 | 4,517 | 4,254 | 4,494 | 4,453 | 4,387 | 4,186 | 4,311 |
| Capitalization:% Long Term Debt | 56.4 | 58.5 | 61.9 | 60.8 | 60.3 | 64.9 | 66.0 | 66.0 | 64.3 | 65.9 |
| Capitalization:Preferred | Nil | Nil | Nil | Nil | Nil | Nil | Nil | Nil | Nil | 116 |
| Capitalization:% Preferred | Nil | Nil | Nil | Nil | Nil | Nil | Nil | Nil | Nil | 1.78 |
| Capitalization:Common | 3,811 | 3,578 | 3,020 | 2,914 | 2,798 | 2,429 | 2,297 | 2,264 | 2,211 | 2,118 |
| Capitalization:% Common | 43.6 | 41.5 | 38.1 | 39.2 | 39.7 | 35.1 | 34.0 | 34.0 | 33.9 | 32.4 |
| Total Capital | 8,810 | 8,696 | 9,175 | 8,527 | 8,184 | 8,325 | 8,283 | 8,042 | 8,056 | 8,156 |
| % Operating Ratio | 88.0 | 89.5 | 91.6 | 92.6 | 95.4 | 99.3 | 96.1 | 93.8 | 96.2 | 104.0 |
| % Earned on Net Property | 8.7 | 8.8 | 7.7 | 8.0 | 3.5 | NM | 7.3 | 8.3 | 6.1 | NM |
| % Return on Revenue | 7.9 | 6.1 | 4.5 | 4.3 | 1.8 | NM | 1.7 | 2.0 | 2.9 | 3.9 |
| % Return on Invested Capital | 7.2 | 7.3 | 6.1 | 8.6 | 4.6 | 1.1 | 4.8 | 4.7 | 5.5 | 8.2 |
| % Return on Common Equity | 10.5 | 10.0 | 8.8 | 8.6 | 4.8 | NM | 5.1 | 5.4 | 7.0 | 11.9 |

Data as orig reptd.; bef. results of disc opers/spec. items. Per share data adj. for stk. divs.; EPS diluted. E-Estimated. NA-Not Available. NM-Not Meaningful. NR-Not Ranked. UR-Under Review.

# Northern Trust Corp

## STANDARD &POOR'S

| S&P Recommendation HOLD ★★★☆☆ | Price $35.08 (as of Nov 25, 2011) | 12-Mo. Target Price $40.00 | Investment Style Large-Cap Growth |
|---|---|---|---|

**GICS Sector** Financials
**Sub-Industry** Asset Management & Custody Banks

**Summary** Northern Trust is a leading provider of fiduciary, asset management and private banking services.

## Key Stock Statistics (Source S&P, Vickers, company reports)

| | | | | | | |
|---|---|---|---|---|---|---|
| 52-Wk Range | $56.86– 33.20 | S&P Oper. EPS 2011E | 2.65 | Market Capitalization(B) | $8.454 | Beta | 0.82 |
| Trailing 12-Month EPS | $2.57 | S&P Oper. EPS 2012E | 2.85 | Yield (%) | 3.19 | S&P 3-Yr. Proj. EPS CAGR(%) | 4 |
| Trailing 12-Month P/E | 13.7 | P/E on S&P Oper. EPS 2011E | 13.2 | Dividend Rate/Share | $1.12 | S&P Credit Rating | AA- |
| $10K Invested 5 Yrs Ago | $6,768 | Common Shares Outstg. (M) | 241.0 | Institutional Ownership (%) | 80 | | |

## Price Performance

30-Week Mov. Avg. · · · 10-Week Mov. Avg. – – GAAP Earnings vs. Previous Year   Volume Above Avg. STARS
12-Mo. Target Price — Relative Strength — ▲ Up ▼ Down ► No Change   Below Avg.

Options: ASE, CBOE, P, Ph

Analysis prepared by Equity Analyst **Erik Oja** on Nov 03, 2011, when the stock traded at **$39.97**.

## Qualitative Risk Assessment

| LOW | MEDIUM | HIGH |
|---|---|---|

Our risk assessment reflects what we see as solid business fundamentals and a strong customer base. We view NTRS as well diversified geographically and able to withstand an economic downturn.

## Quantitative Evaluations

**S&P Quality Ranking**  B+

| D | C | B- | B | B+ | A- | A | A+ |
|---|---|---|---|---|---|---|---|

**Relative Strength Rank**  MODERATE

37

LOWEST = 1   HIGHEST = 99

## Revenue/Earnings Data

**Revenue (Million $)**

| | 1Q | 2Q | 3Q | 4Q | Year |
|---|---|---|---|---|---|
| 2011 | 1,011 | 1,058 | 1,062 | -- | -- |
| 2010 | 981.8 | 1,049 | 986.2 | 1,008 | 4,026 |
| 2009 | 1,010 | 1,140 | 1,013 | -- | 3,216 |
| 2008 | 1,204 | 1,434 | 1,314 | 1,373 | 5,678 |
| 2007 | 1,250 | 1,338 | 1,385 | 1,699 | 5,395 |
| 2006 | 1,030 | 1,134 | 1,117 | 1,192 | 4,473 |

**Earnings Per Share ($)**

| | | | | | |
|---|---|---|---|---|---|
| 2011 | 0.61 | 0.62 | 0.70 | E0.72 | E2.65 |
| 2010 | 0.64 | 0.82 | 0.64 | 0.64 | 2.74 |
| 2009 | 0.61 | 0.95 | 0.77 | 0.83 | 3.19 |
| 2008 | 1.71 | 0.96 | -0.67 | 1.47 | 3.47 |
| 2007 | 0.84 | 0.92 | 0.93 | 0.55 | 3.24 |
| 2006 | 0.74 | 0.76 | 0.74 | 0.77 | 3.00 |

Fiscal year ended Dec. 31. Next earnings report expected: Late January. EPS Estimates based on S&P Operating Earnings; historical GAAP earnings are as reported.

## Highlights

► Third-quarter results showed sequential losses in assets under custody and assets under management. During that period, net interest margin rose sequentially by two basis points, to 1.25%, largely on a decline in funding costs, in our view. We expect low short-term interest rates to limit NTRS's earnings growth in the near term, but we think NTRS's long-term prospects will improve with growth in interest-earning assets. We see moderate growth in asset management and servicing fees, but we do not expect growth in net interest income until interest rates begin to increase. We expect revenues to rise 3.3% in 2011.

► Given a difficult interest rate environment, we expect NTRS to attempt to cut costs in an effort to boost margins. We view NTRS as having little flexibility to materially lower expenses, but we think the company will continue to invest in its core business to encourage further net asset inflows. We forecast a pretax margin of 25.6% in 2011, down from 26.8% in 2010.

► We look for EPS of $2.65 in 2011 and $2.85 in 2012.

## Investment Rationale/Risk

► During the third quarter of 2011, non-interest income, the majority of which comes from trust, investment, and servicing fees, comprised 73% of NTRS's total revenues. Although total assets under custody increased 6.8% over the last year, non-interest income increased by 5.1% during that time. We view the inability of NTRS to leverage assets under custody growth into top line growth as a negative, but we believe the company's stellar credit quality and modest net interest income growth as positives. NTRS's leading position in the affluent market should provide further revenue stability, and NTRS's capital levels are above those required to be classified as a "well-capitalized" institution. All said, we think the shares are appropriately valued at current levels.

► Risks to our opinion and target price include failure to generate new business, a significant decline in economic activity, and adverse litigation or regulation.

► Our 12-month target price of $40 is equal to 14.0X our forward four quarters EPS estimate of $2.85, and a premium to peers, reflecting NTRS's above-average credit quality.

## Dividend Data (Dates: mm/dd Payment Date: mm/dd/yy)

| Amount ($) | Date Decl. | Ex-Div. Date | Stk. of Record | Payment Date |
|---|---|---|---|---|
| 0.280 | 01/18 | 03/08 | 03/10 | 04/01/11 |
| 0.280 | 04/19 | 06/08 | 06/10 | 07/01/11 |
| 0.280 | 07/19 | 09/07 | 09/09 | 10/03/11 |
| 0.280 | 11/15 | 12/07 | 12/09 | 01/03/12 |

Dividends have been paid since 1896. Source: Company reports.

# Northern Trust Corp

STANDARD &POOR'S

## Business Summary November 03, 2011

CORPORATE OVERVIEW. Northern Trust Corp. (NTRS) organizes its services globally around its two principal business units: Corporate and Institutional Services (C&IS) and Personal Financial Services (PFS). C&IS is a leading worldwide provider of asset servicing, asset management and related services to corporate and public entity retirement funds, foundation and endowment clients, fund managers, insurance companies and government funds. C&IS also offers a full range of commercial banking services through the bank, placing special emphasis on developing and supporting institutional relationships in two target markets: large and mid-sized corporations and financial institutions (both U.S. and non-U.S.). Asset servicing, asset management and related services encompass a full range of capabilities including: global master trust and custody, trade, settlement, and reporting; fund administration; cash management; and investment risk and performance analytical services.

In 2005, NTRS completed its acquisition of the Financial Services Group Limited (FSG) from Baring Asset Management Holdings Limited. The purchase of

FSG brought to C&IS expanded capabilities in institutional fund administration, custody, trust and related services as well as new capabilities in hedge fund and private equity administration, in our view.

PFS provides personal trust, investment management, custody and philanthropic services; financial consulting; guardianship and estate administration; qualified retirement plans; brokerage services; and private and business banking. PFS focuses on high net worth individuals and families, business owners, executives, professionals, retirees and established privately held businesses in its target markets. PFS also includes the Wealth Management Group, which provides customized products and services to meet the complex financial needs of families and individuals in the U.S. and throughout the world, with assets typically exceeding $200 million.

## Company Financials Fiscal Year Ended Dec. 31

| Per Share Data ($) | 2010 | 2009 | 2008 | 2007 | 2006 | 2005 | 2004 | 2003 | 2002 | 2001 |
|---|---|---|---|---|---|---|---|---|---|---|
| Tangible Book Value | 26.32 | 24.20 | NA | 18.04 | 15.53 | 14.72 | 14.14 | 13.88 | 13.04 | 11.97 |
| Earnings | 2.74 | 3.19 | 3.47 | 3.24 | 3.00 | 2.64 | 2.26 | 1.89 | 1.97 | 2.11 |
| S&P Core Earnings | 2.72 | 3.15 | 3.31 | 3.69 | 3.04 | 2.51 | 2.19 | 1.63 | 1.64 | 1.82 |
| Dividends | 1.12 | 1.12 | 1.12 | 1.03 | 0.94 | 0.86 | 0.78 | 0.70 | 0.68 | 0.64 |
| Payout Ratio | 41% | 35% | 32% | 32% | 31% | 33% | 35% | 37% | 35% | 30% |
| Prices:High | 59.36 | 66.08 | 88.92 | 83.17 | 61.40 | 55.00 | 51.35 | 48.75 | 62.67 | 82.25 |
| Prices:Low | 45.30 | 43.32 | 33.88 | 56.52 | 49.12 | 41.60 | 38.40 | 27.64 | 30.41 | 41.40 |
| P/E Ratio:High | 22 | 21 | 26 | 26 | 20 | 21 | 23 | 26 | 32 | 39 |
| P/E Ratio:Low | 17 | 14 | 10 | 17 | 16 | 16 | 17 | 15 | 15 | 20 |

### Income Statement Analysis (Million $)

| | 2010 | 2009 | 2008 | 2007 | 2006 | 2005 | 2004 | 2003 | 2002 | 2001 |
|---|---|---|---|---|---|---|---|---|---|---|
| Net Interest Income | 919 | NA | NA | 832 | 730 | 661 | 561 | 548 | 602 | 595 |
| Tax Equivalent Adjustment | 39.1 | 40.2 | 49.8 | 62.5 | 64.8 | 60.9 | 54.4 | 52.4 | 48.7 | 52.6 |
| Non Interest Income | 2,729 | NA | 3,032 | 2,326 | 2,018 | 1,783 | 1,711 | 1,542 | 1,537 | 1,580 |
| Loan Loss Provision | 160 | 215 | 115 | 18.0 | 15.0 | 2.50 | -15.0 | 2.50 | 37.5 | 66.5 |
| % Expense/Operating Revenue | 68.5% | NA | NA | 77.0% | 69.6% | 69.2% | 65.9% | 68.1% | 67.2% | 61.8% |
| Pretax Income | 990 | 1,255 | 1,276 | 1,061 | 1,024 | 888 | 754 | 631 | 669 | 732 |
| Effective Tax Rate | 32.4% | 31.2% | 37.7% | 31.5% | 35.0% | 34.2% | 33.1% | 32.9% | 33.2% | 33.4% |
| Net Income | 670 | 864 | 795 | 727 | 665 | 584 | 505 | 423 | 447 | 488 |
| % Net Interest Margin | 1.41 | 1.56 | 1.76 | 1.67 | 1.73 | 1.79 | 1.66 | 1.73 | 1.93 | 2.02 |
| S&P Core Earnings | 659 | 744 | 747 | 828 | 674 | 561 | 491 | 365 | 369 | 418 |

### Balance Sheet & Other Financial Data (Million $)

| | 2010 | 2009 | 2008 | 2007 | 2006 | 2005 | 2004 | 2003 | 2002 | 2001 |
|---|---|---|---|---|---|---|---|---|---|---|
| Money Market Assets | 15,511 | 13,147 | 16,890 | 25,051 | 16,790 | 16,036 | 13,168 | 9,565 | 9,332 | 10,546 |
| Investment Securities | 21,282 | 18,346 | 15,571 | 8,888 | 12,365 | 11,109 | 9,042 | 9,471 | 6,594 | 6,331 |
| Commercial Loans | 5,915 | 6,312 | 8,254 | 7,907 | 6,515 | 5,064 | 4,498 | 4,702 | 5,137 | 5,767 |
| Other Loans | 22,217 | 21,494 | 22,501 | 17,433 | 16,094 | 14,905 | 13,445 | 13,111 | 12,927 | 12,213 |
| Total Assets | 83,844 | 82,142 | 82,054 | 67,611 | 60,712 | 53,414 | 45,277 | 41,450 | 39,478 | 39,665 |
| Demand Deposits | 7,659 | 9,178 | 11,824 | 10,118 | 9,315 | 7,427 | 6,377 | 5,767 | 6,602 | 7,110 |
| Time Deposits | 56,537 | 49,103 | 50,582 | 41,095 | 34,505 | 31,093 | 24,681 | 20,503 | 19,460 | 17,909 |
| Long Term Debt | 4,902 | 4,666 | 5,359 | 5,721 | 2,421 | 2,791 | 1,340 | 1,341 | 1,284 | 1,485 |
| Common Equity | 6,830 | 6,312 | 6,389 | 4,509 | 3,944 | 3,601 | 3,296 | 3,055 | 2,880 | 2,653 |
| % Return on Assets | 0.8 | 1.1 | 1.1 | 1.1 | 1.2 | 3.0 | 1.2 | 1.0 | 1.1 | 1.3 |
| % Return on Equity | 10.2 | 15.4 | 14.6 | 17.2 | 17.6 | 42.7 | 15.9 | 14.2 | 16.1 | 19.4 |
| % Loan Loss Reserve | 1.1 | 1.1 | 0.7 | 0.6 | 0.6 | 0.6 | 0.7 | 0.8 | 0.9 | 0.9 |
| % Loans/Deposits | 45.7 | 48.5 | 50.9 | 50.5 | 51.6 | 51.8 | 57.8 | 67.8 | 69.3 | 71.9 |
| % Equity to Assets | 7.9 | 7.7 | 6.3 | 6.6 | 6.6 | 7.0 | 7.3 | 7.3 | 7.0 | 6.6 |

Data as orig reptd.; bef. results of disc opers/spec. items. Per share data adj. for stk. divs.; EPS diluted. E-Estimated. NA-Not Available. NM-Not Meaningful. NR-Not Ranked. UR-Under Review.

**Office:** 50 S La Salle St, Chicago, IL 60603-1003.
**Telephone:** 312-630-6000.
**Website:** http://www.northerntrust.com
**Chrmn & CEO:** F.H. Waddell

**Pres & COO:** W.L. Morrison
**Vice Chrmn:** S.S. Barrat
**EVP & CFO:** M.G. O'grady
**EVP & General Counsel:** K.R. Welsh

**Investor Contact:** S.L. Fradkin
**Board Members:** S. S. Barrat, L. W. Bynoe, N. D. Chabraja, S. M. Crown, D. Jain, R. W. Lane, R. C. McCormack, E. J. Mooney, J. W. Rowe, M. P. Slark, D. H. Smith, Jr., E. J. Sosa, C. A. Tribbett, III, F. H. Waddell

**Founded:** 1889
**Domicile:** Delaware
**Employees:** 12,800

# Northrop Grumman Corp

**STANDARD &POOR'S**

| S&P Recommendation | HOLD ★★★☆☆ | Price $53.42 (as of Nov 25, 2011) | 12-Mo. Target Price $62.00 | Investment Style Large-Cap Blend |
|---|---|---|---|---|

**GICS Sector** Industrials
**Sub-Industry** Aerospace & Defense

**Summary** This company is the world's fourth largest producer of military arms and equipment, and also has a large government IT services business.

## Key Stock Statistics (Source S&P, Vickers, company reports)

| | | | | | | | |
|---|---|---|---|---|---|---|---|
| 52-Wk Range | $72.50–49.20 | S&P Oper. EPS 2011**E** | 7.21 | Market Capitalization(B) | $13.958 | Beta | 1.09 |
| Trailing 12-Month EPS | $6.72 | S&P Oper. EPS 2012**E** | 7.20 | Yield (%) | 3.74 | S&P 3-Yr. Proj. EPS CAGR(%) | 3 |
| Trailing 12-Month P/E | 8.0 | P/E on S&P Oper. EPS 2011**E** | 7.4 | Dividend Rate/Share | $2.00 | S&P Credit Rating | BBB+ |
| $10K Invested 5 Yrs Ago | NA | Common Shares Outstg. (M) | 261.3 | Institutional Ownership (%) | 100 | | |

## Price Performance

30-Week Mov. Avg. · · · 10-Week Mov. Avg. - - GAAP Earnings vs. Previous Year    Volume Above Avg. STARS
12-Mo. Target Price — Relative Strength — ▲ Up ▼ Down ▶ No Change    Below Avg. ★

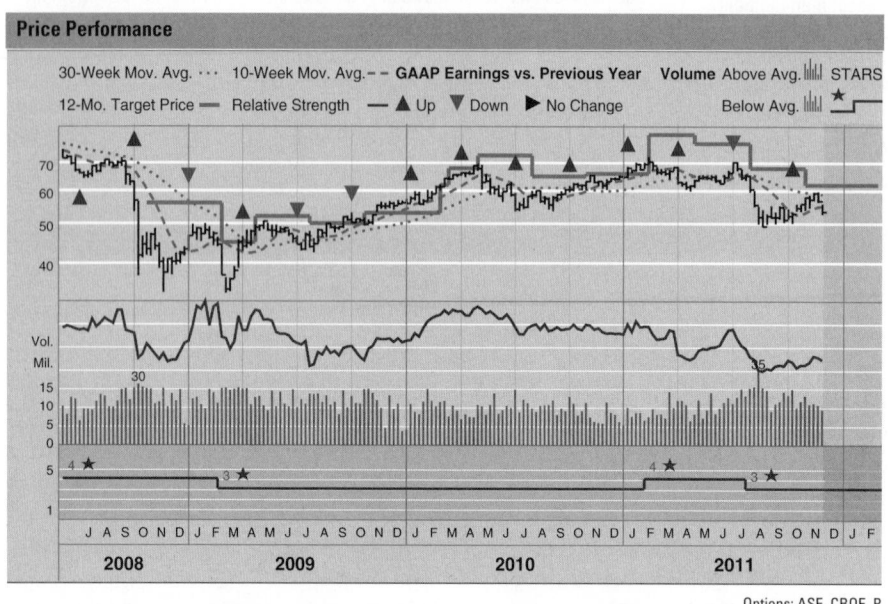

Options: ASE, CBOE, P

Analysis prepared by Equity Analyst **R. Tortoriello** on Nov 14, 2011, when the stock traded at **$59.30**.

## Highlights

➤ We estimate revenues will decline of 6% in 2011, with declines in all four business segments. For 2012, we project revenues will fall a further 2%. We project slight growth in Technical Services, and modest declines in Information Systems, Aerospace Systems, and Electronic Systems.

➤ We estimate operating margins of 12.3% in 2011, up from 10.0% in 2010, on better business segment performance, lower corporate expense, and significant pension income. For 2012 we project a decline to 11.3%, driven by our view of the absence of pension income.

➤ We project EPS of $7.21 in 2011 and $7.20 in 2012. We expect free cash flow (cash flow from operating activities less capital expenditures) of about 80% of net income in 2011, including expected voluntary cash pension contributions.

## Investment Rationale/Risk

➤ We recently downgraded NOC to hold, from buy. Although we see the company taking actions that we believe will benefit shareholders over the long term, we believe that defense and government IT budget pressure, as well as NOC's stated policy of foregoing lower-margin business, will significantly constrain revenues over the next two years. Specifically, NOC cited delays in new contract awards and continuing contract business, due to budgetary uncertainty, and the initial impact of troop withdrawals from Iraq and Afghanistan. However, we expect shareholders to benefit as strong cash flows should promote share repurchases and dividend increases.

➤ Risks to our recommendation and target price include the potential for large cuts in military budgets, and failure to perform well on existing contracts or to win new contracts.

➤ Our 12-month target price of $62 is based on an enterprise value multiple of about 5X our 2012 EBITDA estimate of $3.5 billion. This multiple is below NOC's 20-year average of 7.7X to reflect our view of a declining U.S. defense budget.

## Qualitative Risk Assessment

| LOW | MEDIUM | HIGH |
|---|---|---|

Our risk assessment reflects our view of NOC's typically strong levels of cash flow and a solid balance sheet with a relatively low level of debt. This is offset by NOC's dependence on government spending on defense and IT services, which is subject to political and budgetary considerations. .

## Quantitative Evaluations

**S&P Quality Ranking**    A-

| D | C | B- | B | B+ | A- | A | A+ |
|---|---|---|---|---|---|---|---|

**Relative Strength Rank**    MODERATE

56

LOWEST = 1    HIGHEST = 99

## Revenue/Earnings Data

**Revenue (Million $)**

| | 1Q | 2Q | 3Q | 4Q | Year |
|---|---|---|---|---|---|
| 2011 | 6,734 | 6,560 | 6,612 | -- | -- |
| 2010 | 8,610 | 8,826 | 8,714 | 8,607 | 34,757 |
| 2009 | 7,935 | 8,545 | 8,350 | 8,925 | 33,755 |
| 2008 | 7,724 | 8,628 | 8,381 | 9,154 | 33,887 |
| 2007 | 7,340 | 7,926 | 7,928 | 8,824 | 32,018 |
| 2006 | 7,093 | 7,601 | 7,433 | 8,021 | 30,148 |

**Earnings Per Share ($)**

| | | | | | |
|---|---|---|---|---|---|
| 2011 | 1.67 | 1.81 | 1.86 | E1.88 | E7.21 |
| 2010 | 1.51 | 2.34 | 1.64 | 1.27 | 6.77 |
| 2009 | 1.10 | 1.13 | 1.45 | 1.19 | 4.87 |
| 2008 | 0.76 | 1.40 | 1.50 | -7.76 | -3.83 |
| 2007 | 1.11 | 1.33 | 1.41 | 1.32 | 5.16 |
| 2006 | 1.03 | 1.26 | 0.87 | 1.29 | 4.44 |

Fiscal year ended Dec. 31. Next earnings report expected: Early February. EPS Estimates based on S&P Operating Earnings; historical GAAP earnings are as reported.

## Dividend Data (Dates: mm/dd Payment Date: mm/dd/yy)

| Amount ($) | Date Decl. | Ex-Div. Date | Stk. of Record | Payment Date |
|---|---|---|---|---|
| Stk. | 03/15 | 03/31 | 03/30 | 03/31/11 |
| 0.500 | 04/27 | 05/26 | 05/31 | 06/11/11 |
| 0.500 | 07/21 | 08/25 | 08/29 | 09/10/11 |
| 0.500 | 11/17 | 11/23 | 11/28 | 12/10/11 |

Dividends have been paid since 1951. Source: Company reports.

# Northrop Grumman Corp

**STANDARD &POOR'S**

## Business Summary November 14, 2011

CORPORATE OVERVIEW. This defense electronics and aerospace giant conducts most of its business with the U.S. government, principally the Department of Defense. NOC also transacts with foreign governments and makes commercial sales both domestically and overseas. In January 2009, the company reorganized its reported business segments into five, from seven. Its shipbuilding operations were spun off to shareholders in March 2011.

The Information & Services segment (23% of 2010 revenue and 21% of segment operating income) provides products and services in the areas of command, control, communications, computers and intelligence (C4I); air and missile defense; airborne reconnaissance; intelligence processing; decision support systems; cybersecurity; information technology (IT); and systems engineering and integration. It consists of three business areas: Defense Systems, Intelligence Systems, and Civil Systems.

The Technical Services segment (9% of revenue and 6% of segment operating

profit) is a leading provider of logistics, infrastructure and sustainment support, while also providing a wide array of technical services including training and simulation. It consists of three business areas: Defense and Government Services, Training Solutions, and Integrated Logistics and Modernization.

The Aerospace Systems segment (30% and 35%) is a developer, integrator, producer and supporter of manned and unmanned aircraft, spacecraft, high-energy laser systems, microelectronics and other systems and subsystems critical to maintaining U.S. security and leadership in technology. It consists of four business areas: Strike & Surveillance Systems, Space Systems, Battle Management & Engagement Systems, and Advanced Programs & Technology.

## Company Financials Fiscal Year Ended Dec. 31

| Per Share Data ($) | 2010 | 2009 | 2008 | 2007 | 2006 | 2005 | 2004 | 2003 | 2002 | 2001 |
|---|---|---|---|---|---|---|---|---|---|---|
| Tangible Book Value | NM | NM | NM | NM | NM | NM | NM | NM | NM | NM |
| Cash Flow | 9.22 | 7.14 | -1.71 | 7.09 | 6.34 | 5.94 | 5.01 | 4.05 | 5.29 | 6.31 |
| Earnings | 6.77 | 4.87 | -3.83 | 5.16 | 4.44 | 3.81 | 2.99 | 2.16 | 2.86 | 2.40 |
| S&P Core Earnings | 6.61 | 5.29 | 1.44 | 4.09 | 3.67 | 2.84 | 2.63 | 2.42 | -0.95 | -2.85 |
| Dividends | 1.84 | 1.69 | 1.57 | 1.48 | 1.16 | 1.01 | 0.89 | 0.80 | 0.80 | 0.80 |
| Payout Ratio | 27% | 35% | NM | 29% | 26% | 27% | 30% | 37% | 28% | 33% |
| Prices:High | 69.80 | 57.32 | 83.40 | 85.21 | 71.37 | 60.26 | 58.15 | 50.55 | 67.50 | 55.28 |
| Prices:Low | 53.50 | 33.81 | 33.96 | 66.23 | 59.10 | 51.10 | 46.91 | 41.50 | 43.60 | 38.20 |
| P/E Ratio:High | 10 | 12 | NM | 17 | 16 | 16 | 19 | 23 | 24 | 23 |
| P/E Ratio:Low | 8 | 7 | NM | 13 | 13 | 13 | 16 | 19 | 15 | 16 |

| Income Statement Analysis (Million $) | 2010 | 2009 | 2008 | 2007 | 2006 | 2005 | 2004 | 2003 | 2002 | 2001 |
|---|---|---|---|---|---|---|---|---|---|---|
| Revenue | 34,757 | 33,755 | 33,887 | 32,018 | 30,148 | 30,721 | 29,853 | 26,206 | 17,206 | 13,558 |
| Operating Income | 3,808 | 3,219 | 3,920 | 3,716 | 3,159 | 2,951 | 2,740 | 1,538 | 1,391 | 1,649 |
| Depreciation | 738 | 736 | 708 | 710 | 705 | 773 | 734 | 682 | 525 | 645 |
| Interest Expense | 281 | 281 | 295 | 336 | 347 | 388 | 431 | 497 | 422 | 373 |
| Pretax Income | 2,595 | 2,266 | -368 | 2,686 | 2,276 | 2,044 | 1,615 | 1,131 | 1,009 | 699 |
| Effective Tax Rate | NA | 30.6% | NM | 32.9% | 31.2% | 32.3% | 32.3% | 28.6% | 30.9% | 38.9% |
| Net Income | 2,038 | 1,573 | -1,281 | 1,803 | 1,567 | 1,383 | 1,093 | 808 | 697 | 427 |
| S&P Core Earnings | 1,992 | 1,712 | 481 | 1,426 | 1,288 | 1,026 | 961 | 892 | -223 | -487 |

| Balance Sheet & Other Financial Data (Million $) | 2010 | 2009 | 2008 | 2007 | 2006 | 2005 | 2004 | 2003 | 2002 | 2001 |
|---|---|---|---|---|---|---|---|---|---|---|
| Cash | 3,769 | 3,275 | 1,504 | 963 | 1,015 | 1,605 | 1,230 | 342 | 1,412 | 464 |
| Current Assets | 9,904 | 8,635 | 7,189 | 6,772 | 6,719 | 7,549 | 6,907 | 5,745 | 15,835 | 4,589 |
| Total Assets | 31,421 | 30,252 | 30,197 | 33,373 | 32,009 | 34,214 | 33,361 | 33,009 | 42,266 | 20,886 |
| Current Liabilities | 8,386 | 6,985 | 7,424 | 6,432 | 6,753 | 7,974 | 6,223 | 6,361 | 11,373 | 5,132 |
| Long Term Debt | 4,045 | 4,191 | 3,443 | 4,268 | 3,992 | 3,881 | 5,116 | 5,410 | 9,398 | 5,033 |
| Common Equity | 13,557 | 12,687 | 11,920 | 17,687 | 16,615 | 16,825 | 16,970 | 15,785 | 14,322 | 7,391 |
| Total Capital | 18,376 | 16,969 | 15,363 | 22,285 | 20,957 | 21,651 | 22,942 | 22,067 | 24,209 | 13,443 |
| Capital Expenditures | 770 | 654 | 681 | 685 | 737 | 824 | 672 | 635 | 538 | 393 |
| Cash Flow | 2,776 | 2,309 | -573 | 2,513 | 2,272 | 2,156 | 1,827 | 1,490 | 1,222 | 1,072 |
| Current Ratio | 1.2 | 1.2 | 1.0 | 1.1 | 1.0 | 0.9 | 1.1 | 0.9 | 1.4 | 0.9 |
| % Long Term Debt of Capitalization | 22.0 | 24.7 | 22.4 | 19.2 | 19.0 | 17.9 | 22.3 | 24.5 | 38.8 | 37.4 |
| % Net Income of Revenue | 5.9 | 4.7 | NM | 5.6 | 5.2 | 4.5 | 3.7 | 3.1 | 4.1 | 3.1 |
| % Return on Assets | 6.6 | 5.2 | NM | 5.5 | 4.7 | 4.1 | 3.3 | 2.1 | 2.2 | 2.8 |
| % Return on Equity | 15.5 | 12.8 | NM | 10.5 | 9.4 | 8.2 | 6.6 | 5.4 | 6.4 | 7.6 |

Data as orig reptd.; bef. results of disc opers/spec. items. Per share data adj. for stk. divs.; EPS diluted. E-Estimated. NA-Not Available. NM-Not Meaningful. NR-Not Ranked. UR-Under Review.

**Office:** 1840 Century Park E, Los Angeles, CA 90067-2199.
**Telephone:** 310-553-6262.
**Email:** investor_relations@mail.northgrum.com
**Website:** http://www.northropgrumman.com

**Chrmn, Pres & CEO:** W.G. Bush
**CFO:** J.F. Palmer
**Chief Admin Officer:** I.V. Ziskin
**CTO:** A.C. Livanos

**Chief Acctg Officer & Cntlr:** K.N. Heintz
**Investor Contact:** P. Gregory (310-201-1634)
**Board Members:** W. G. Bush, L. W. Coleman, T. B. Fargo, V. Fazio, D. E. Felsinger, S. E. Frank, B. S. Gordon, M. A. Kleiner, K. J. Krapek, R. B. Myers, A. L. Peters, T. M. Schoewe, K. W. Sharer

**Founded:** 1939
**Domicile:** Delaware
**Employees:** 117,100

# Novellus Systems Inc

STANDARD
&POOR'S

| S&P Recommendation **BUY** ★★★★☆ | Price<br>$31.57 (as of Nov 25, 2011) | 12-Mo. Target Price<br>$38.00 | Investment Style<br>Large-Cap Growth |
|---|---|---|---|

**GICS Sector** Information Technology
**Sub-Industry** Semiconductor Equipment

**Summary** This company manufactures, markets and services automated wafer fabrication systems for the deposition of thin films.

## Key Stock Statistics (Source S&P, Vickers, company reports)

| | | | | | | | | |
|---|---|---|---|---|---|---|---|---|
| 52-Wk Range | $41.82– 25.95 | S&P Oper. EPS 2011**E** | 3.07 | Market Capitalization(B) | $2.102 | Beta | | 1.20 |
| Trailing 12-Month EPS | $3.49 | S&P Oper. EPS 2012**E** | 2.84 | Yield (%) | Nil | S&P 3-Yr. Proj. EPS CAGR(%) | | 3 |
| Trailing 12-Month P/E | 9.1 | P/E on S&P Oper. EPS 2011**E** | 10.3 | Dividend Rate/Share | Nil | S&P Credit Rating | | NA |
| $10K Invested 5 Yrs Ago | $9,619 | Common Shares Outstg. (M) | 66.6 | Institutional Ownership (%) | NM | | | |

## Price Performance

30-Week Mov. Avg. · · ·  10-Week Mov. Avg. - - **GAAP Earnings vs. Previous Year**  Volume Above Avg. ⅃⅃⅃⅃ STARS
12-Mo. Target Price — Relative Strength — ▲ Up ▼ Down ▶ No Change  Below Avg. ⅃⅃⅃⅃ ★

Options: ASE, CBOE, P, Ph

Analysis prepared by Equity Analyst **Angelo Zino, CFA** on Oct 28, 2011, when the stock traded at **$35.26**.

## Highlights

➤ We forecast sales to decline 9% in 2012 following our outlook for flat revenues in 2011. Despite some uncertainty surrounding customer capital spending plans, we think industry conditions are likely to improve in early 2012, on a sequential basis, as end-demand for electronic devices remains healthy. We believe utilization rates for most chipmakers are running below seasonal levels, but see a rebound once inventory levels are depleted. In addition, we see flash memory orders improving due to healthy demand for mobile devices and tablets. However, we anticipate that foundry and logic spending will modestly decline in 2012.

➤ We look for an annual gross margin of 48% in 2012, below our 49% forecast we have for 2011. Going forward, we expect margins to remain elevated, on good execution and product mix. We look for NVLS to maintain tight cost control and refrain from significantly increasing operating costs. We see operating expenses at 29% to 30% of sales in 2012.

➤ In May 2011, NVLS recapitalized the company with a $700 million convertible debt financing, with most of the proceeds used to repurchase shares.

## Investment Rationale/Risk

➤ We think NVLS will benefit from the transition to copper processes, and we see potential for share gains. We see customers transitioning to 32nm and below technology nodes aiding orders. We also expect existing inventory levels across the supply chain to come down and foresee greater spending by NAND flash memory customers in 2012. We think DRAM and flash memory markets are poised to grow considerably over the long term, driven by tablets and robust demand for hand-held devices such as cell phones and MP3 players. We see NVLS's industrial segment witnessing gradually increasing sales as the economy improves.

➤ Risks to our recommendation and target price include a longer-than-expected semiconductor equipment downturn, weaker-than-projected global economic growth, and higher-than-expected R&D expense growth.

➤ We derive our 12-month target price of $38 based on a blend of our peer-average P/E and price-to-sales (P/S) analyses. We use a multiple of 13X our 2012 EPS estimate to obtain a $37 price. We generate a $39 price by applying a P/S ratio of 2.15X to our 2012 sales per share estimate.

## Qualitative Risk Assessment

| LOW | MEDIUM | HIGH |
|---|---|---|

Our risk assessment reflects the historical cyclicality of the semiconductor equipment industry, the lack of visibility in the medium term, the dynamic nature of semiconductor technology, and intense competition. We believe these risks are partially offset by our view of the company's strong market position, size and financial condition.

## Quantitative Evaluations

**S&P Quality Ranking**   C

| D | C | B- | B | B+ | A- | A | A+ |
|---|---|---|---|---|---|---|---|

**Relative Strength Rank**   MODERATE

67

LOWEST = 1            HIGHEST = 99

## Revenue/Earnings Data

**Revenue (Million $)**

| | 1Q | 2Q | 3Q | 4Q | Year |
|---|---|---|---|---|---|
| 2011 | 413.2 | 350.2 | 306.7 | -- | -- |
| 2010 | 276.2 | 321.4 | 367.2 | 384.4 | 1,349 |
| 2009 | 98.91 | 119.2 | 176.9 | 244.2 | 639.2 |
| 2008 | 314.7 | 257.7 | 250.1 | 188.5 | 1,011 |
| 2007 | 397.0 | 416.3 | 393.3 | 363.5 | 1,570 |
| 2006 | 365.9 | 410.1 | 444.0 | 438.5 | 1,659 |

**Earnings Per Share ($)**

| | | | | | |
|---|---|---|---|---|---|
| 2011 | 1.04 | 0.79 | 0.73 | E0.52 | E3.07 |
| 2010 | 0.43 | 0.66 | 0.82 | 0.89 | 2.79 |
| 2009 | -0.69 | -0.52 | -0.04 | 0.36 | -0.88 |
| 2008 | 0.15 | -0.02 | 0.01 | -1.36 | -1.18 |
| 2007 | 0.42 | 0.45 | 0.41 | 0.47 | 1.75 |
| 2006 | 0.18 | 0.42 | 0.57 | 0.34 | 1.49 |

Fiscal year ended Dec. 31. Next earnings report expected: Early February. EPS Estimates based on S&P Operating Earnings; historical GAAP earnings are as reported.

## Dividend Data

No cash dividends have been paid.

---

**Please read the Required Disclosures and Analyst Certification on the last page of this report.**

The **McGraw·Hill** Companies

# Novellus Systems Inc

**STANDARD &POOR'S**

## Business Summary October 28, 2011

CORPORATE OVERVIEW. Novellus is the second largest maker of deposition equipment used to deposit conductive and insulating layers on semiconductor wafers to form integrated circuits (ICs). Novellus operates in two segments, the Semiconductor Group and the Industrial Applications Group. The Semiconductor Group comprised 95% and 89% of total sales in 2010 and 2009.

NVLS's product line of deposition equipment includes chemical vapor deposition (CVD), physical vapor deposition (PVD) and electrochemical deposition (ECD), all of which are used to form the layers of wiring and insulation, known as the interconnect, of ICs. High-density plasma CVD (HDP) and plasma-enhanced CVD (PECVD) systems employ chemical plasma to deposit all of the insulating layers and some of the conductive layers on the surface of a wafer. PVD systems deposit conductive layers through a process known as sputtering, where ions of an inert gas such as argon are electrically accelerated in a high vacuum toward a target of pure metal, such as tantalum or copper. ECD systems are used to build the copper conductive layers on wafers.

Although NVLS's original tool sets established it as a leader in CVD, the company has centered its product strategy on the emergence of the copper interconnect market. Copper has lower resistance and capacitance values than

aluminum, the conductive metal generally used in ICs, offering increased speed and decreased chip size. The company's SABRE tool offers a complete solution for the deposition of copper interconnects and holds the leading market share in copper.

Surface preparation products, including photoresist strip and clean, are becoming more important with the industry's migration to copper interconnects. Surface preparation systems remove photoresist and other potential contaminants from a wafer before proceeding with the next deposition step. CMP systems polish the surface of a wafer after a deposition step to create a flat topography before moving on to subsequent manufacturing steps. Since copper is more difficult to polish and smooth than previous generation aluminum interconnects, and low-k dielectrics are much more porous than predecessors, NVLS's products in this category have become very important, in our view.

## Company Financials Fiscal Year Ended Dec. 31

| Per Share Data ($) | 2010 | 2009 | 2008 | 2007 | 2006 | 2005 | 2004 | 2003 | 2002 | 2001 |
|---|---|---|---|---|---|---|---|---|---|---|
| Tangible Book Value | 13.22 | 10.67 | 11.73 | 11.98 | 12.54 | 11.29 | 11.06 | 12.42 | 12.69 | 13.04 |
| Cash Flow | 3.21 | -0.40 | -0.53 | 2.30 | 2.05 | 1.39 | 1.66 | 0.43 | 0.45 | 1.32 |
| Earnings | 2.79 | -0.88 | -1.18 | 1.75 | 1.49 | 0.80 | 1.06 | -0.03 | 0.15 | 0.97 |
| S&P Core Earnings | 2.81 | -0.89 | -0.11 | 1.71 | 1.47 | 0.43 | 0.74 | -0.42 | -0.33 | 0.52 |
| Dividends | Nil | Nil | Nil | Nil | Nil | Nil | Nil | Nil | Nil | Nil |
| Payout Ratio | Nil | Nil | Nil | Nil | Nil | Nil | Nil | Nil | Nil | Nil |
| Prices:High | 33.24 | 26.00 | 27.66 | 34.97 | 35.00 | 30.77 | 44.52 | 45.50 | 54.48 | 58.70 |
| Prices:Low | 20.57 | 11.43 | 10.26 | 25.40 | 22.28 | 20.83 | 22.89 | 24.93 | 19.40 | 25.37 |
| P/E Ratio:High | 12 | NM | NM | 20 | 23 | 38 | 42 | NM | NM | 61 |
| P/E Ratio:Low | 7 | NM | NM | 15 | 15 | 26 | 22 | NM | NM | 26 |

| Income Statement Analysis (Million $) | | | | | | | | | | |
|---|---|---|---|---|---|---|---|---|---|---|
| Revenue | 1,349 | 639 | 1,011 | 1,570 | 1,659 | 1,340 | 1,357 | 925 | 840 | 1,339 |
| Operating Income | 347 | -4.57 | 81.1 | 329 | 388 | 228 | 308 | 56.5 | 46.3 | 273 |
| Depreciation | 40.0 | 46.9 | 63.3 | 66.9 | 69.7 | 82.8 | 89.3 | 69.6 | 44.3 | 51.9 |
| Interest Expense | 1.52 | 2.07 | 7.02 | 6.38 | 4.29 | 3.51 | 2.13 | 0.91 | 1.02 | 1.15 |
| Pretax Income | 305 | -69.4 | -107 | 315 | 339 | 159 | 223 | -15.3 | 22.9 | 209 |
| Effective Tax Rate | NA | NM | NM | 32.1% | 44.2% | 30.6% | 29.8% | NM | NM | 31.0% |
| Net Income | 262 | -85.2 | -116 | 214 | 189 | 110 | 157 | -5.03 | 22.9 | 144 |
| S&P Core Earnings | 264 | -86.7 | -10.0 | 209 | 186 | 59.8 | 108 | -67.2 | -50.7 | 81.6 |

| Balance Sheet & Other Financial Data (Million $) | | | | | | | | | | |
|---|---|---|---|---|---|---|---|---|---|---|
| Cash | 671 | 501 | 471 | 593 | 58.5 | 649 | 106 | 497 | 616 | 551 |
| Current Assets | 1,202 | 898 | 1,043 | 1,224 | 1,505 | 1,364 | 1,369 | 1,572 | 1,634 | 2,517 |
| Total Assets | 1,832 | 1,559 | 1,638 | 2,077 | 2,362 | 2,290 | 2,402 | 2,339 | 2,494 | 3,010 |
| Current Liabilities | 291 | 171 | 305 | 329 | 361 | 344 | 324 | 221 | 382 | 1,138 |
| Long Term Debt | 106 | 114 | Nil | 143 | 128 | 125 | 161 | Nil | Nil | Nil |
| Common Equity | 1,328 | 1,180 | 1,247 | 1,529 | 1,835 | 1,779 | 1,862 | 2,072 | 2,056 | 1,872 |
| Total Capital | 1,434 | 1,294 | 1,248 | 1,700 | 1,963 | 1,904 | 2,023 | 2,072 | 2,075 | 1,872 |
| Capital Expenditures | 19.9 | 11.9 | 17.9 | 33.2 | 39.4 | 44.7 | 31.7 | 31.1 | 26.8 | 80.0 |
| Cash Flow | 302 | -38.4 | -52.4 | 281 | 259 | 193 | 246 | 64.5 | 67.2 | 196 |
| Current Ratio | 4.1 | 5.4 | 3.4 | 3.7 | 4.2 | 4.0 | 4.2 | 7.1 | 4.3 | 2.2 |
| % Long Term Debt of Capitalization | 7.4 | 8.8 | Nil | 8.4 | 6.5 | 6.6 | 8.0 | Nil | Nil | Nil |
| % Net Income of Revenue | 19.4 | NM | NM | 13.6 | 11.4 | 8.2 | 11.5 | NM | 2.7 | 10.8 |
| % Return on Assets | 15.5 | NM | NM | 9.6 | 8.1 | 4.7 | 6.6 | NM | 0.8 | 5.5 |
| % Return on Equity | 20.9 | NM | NM | 12.7 | 10.5 | 6.0 | 8.0 | NM | 1.2 | 8.2 |

Data as orig reptd.; bef. results of disc opers/spec. items. Per share data adj. for stk. divs.; EPS diluted. E-Estimated. NA-Not Available. NM-Not Meaningful. NR-Not Ranked. UR-Under Review.

**Office:** 4000 North First Street, San Jose, CA 95134-1568.
**Telephone:** 408-943-9700.
**Email:** info@novellus.com
**Website:** http://www.novellus.com

**Chrmn & CEO:** R. Hill
**COO:** T.M. Archer
**CFO, Chief Acctg Officer & Cntlr:** J.D. Hertz
**Treas & Secy:** K. Rammohan

**Secy & General Counsel:** A.J. Gottlieb
**Investor Contact:** R. Yim (408-943-9700)
**Board Members:** N. R. Bonke, Y. A. El-Mansy, R. Hill, Y. Nishi, G. G. Possley, A. D. Rhoads, K. Saraswat, W. R. Spivey, D. A. Whitaker

**Founded:** 1984
**Domicile:** California
**Employees:** 2,700

# NRG Energy Inc

**STANDARD &POOR'S**

| S&P Recommendation **BUY** ★★★★☆ | Price $18.71 (as of Nov 25, 2011) | 12-Mo. Target Price $24.00 | Investment Style Large-Cap Blend |
|---|---|---|---|

**GICS Sector** Utilities
**Sub-Industry** Independent Power Producers & Energy Traders

**Summary** This wholesale power generation company owns and operates power generation facilities and sells energy, capacity, and related products internationally.

## Key Stock Statistics (Source S&P, Vickers, company reports)

| | | | | | | | |
|---|---|---|---|---|---|---|---|
| 52-Wk Range | $25.66–18.22 | S&P Oper. EPS 2011**E** | 1.08 | Market Capitalization(B) | $4.303 | Beta | 0.86 |
| Trailing 12-Month EPS | $1.15 | S&P Oper. EPS 2012**E** | 1.39 | Yield (%) | Nil | S&P 3-Yr. Proj. EPS CAGR(%) | -15 |
| Trailing 12-Month P/E | 16.3 | P/E on S&P Oper. EPS 2011**E** | 17.3 | Dividend Rate/Share | Nil | S&P Credit Rating | BB- |
| $10K Invested 5 Yrs Ago | $6,718 | Common Shares Outstg. (M) | 230.0 | Institutional Ownership (%) | NM | | |

## Price Performance

30-Week Mov. Avg. · · · 10-Week Mov. Avg. - - GAAP Earnings vs. Previous Year   Volume Above Avg. ⅢⅢⅢ STARS
12-Mo. Target Price — Relative Strength — ▲ Up ▼ Down ▶ No Change   Below Avg. ⅢⅢⅢ ★

Options: ASE, CBOE, P, Ph

Analysis prepared by Equity Analyst **C. Muir** on Nov 17, 2011, when the stock traded at **$20.81**.

## Highlights

➤ We estimate a 0.3% decline in revenues for 2011, helped by higher volumes, but offset by continued pressure on power prices. We believe the continued development of the Marcellus shale will keep downward pressure on natural gas prices, which in turn hurts peak power prices. We see 2012 revenues rising 1.8%.

➤ We forecast operating profit margins of 10.5% in 2011 and 11.9% in 2012, vs. 2010's 17.7%. We see higher per-revenue cost of operations and depreciation charges in 2011. We see pretax margins narrowing to 3.5% in 2011 and 5.8% in 2012, from 11.7% in 2010, hurt by lower nonoperating income and higher interest expense in 2011, with these trends partly reversing in 2012.

➤ Assuming an effective tax rate of 12.6%, and share repurchases reducing average shares outstanding, we estimate recurring 2011 EPS, excluding non-recurring losses of $0.36 and net gains from mark-to-market and contract amortization of $0.54, of $1.08, down 57% from 2010's $2.51, which excludes net losses from one-time items, mark-to-market and contract amortization of $0.67. Our 2012 EPS forecast is $1.39, up 29%.

## Investment Rationale/Risk

➤ We continue to like NRG's focus on strong operational performance and cost control, as well as its proposed repowering and greenfield development efforts, including a focus on solar generation with 733 MW under construction and 84 MW in development. Solar grants and some government financing help reduce the risk of solar development. We see the share repurchase program and debt repayments in 2011 as beneficial to EPS, but we see lower, albeit still substantial, cash levels at the end of 2011 as a result. We like NRG's plan to restructure the debt portion of its balance sheet, which includes refinancing $3.5 billion of debt and restructuring its revolving credit facilities.

➤ Risks to our recommendation and target price include less favorable energy market conditions, difficulty refinancing maturing debt, and inability to sell certain assets.

➤ The stock recently traded at 15.1X our 2012 EPS estimate, an 8% premium to independent power producer peers. Our 12-month target price is $24, or 17.3X our 2012 EPS, a premium to peers valuation reflecting debt restructuring, which should increase NRG's flexibility to continue its capital investment program.

## Qualitative Risk Assessment

| LOW | MEDIUM | HIGH |
|---|---|---|

Our risk assessment is based on our view that the geographic and fuel diversity benefits of NRG's power plants offset the company's exposure to volatile natural gas and power commodity markets.

## Quantitative Evaluations

**S&P Quality Ranking** NR

| D | C | B- | B | B+ | A- | A | A+ |
|---|---|---|---|---|---|---|---|

**Relative Strength Rank** WEAK

25

LOWEST = 1                HIGHEST = 99

## Revenue/Earnings Data

**Revenue (Million $)**

| | 1Q | 2Q | 3Q | 4Q | Year |
|---|---|---|---|---|---|
| 2011 | 1,995 | 2,278 | 2,674 | -- | -- |
| 2010 | 2,215 | 2,133 | 2,685 | 1,816 | 8,849 |
| 2009 | 1,658 | 2,237 | 2,916 | 2,141 | 8,952 |
| 2008 | 1,302 | 1,316 | 2,612 | 1,655 | 6,885 |
| 2007 | 1,310 | 1,548 | 1,786 | 1,382 | 5,989 |
| 2006 | 1,075 | 1,404 | 2,000 | 1,144 | 5,623 |

**Earnings Per Share ($)**

| | | | | | |
|---|---|---|---|---|---|
| 2011 | -1.06 | 2.53 | -0.24 | E0.19 | E1.08 |
| 2010 | 0.22 | 0.81 | 0.87 | -0.07 | 1.84 |
| 2009 | 0.70 | 1.56 | 1.02 | 0.11 | 3.44 |
| 2008 | 0.14 | -0.22 | 2.65 | 0.98 | 3.66 |
| 2007 | 0.21 | 0.51 | 0.93 | 0.34 | 1.95 |
| 2006 | 0.02 | 0.62 | 1.17 | -0.19 | 1.82 |

Fiscal year ended Dec. 31. Next earnings report expected: Late February. EPS Estimates based on S&P Operating Earnings; historical GAAP earnings are as reported.

## Dividend Data

No cash dividends have been paid.

# NRG Energy Inc

**STANDARD &POOR'S**

## Business Summary November 17, 2011

CORPORATE OVERVIEW. NRG Energy is a competitive wholesale power generation company that owns, operates, develops and builds generating facilities. As of December 2010, the company owned interests in 45 power plants, mostly in North America, with net generating capacity of 24,925 MW. In the U.S., NRG operates plants in Texas (10,745 MW), the Northeast (6,900 MW), South Central (4,125 MW) and the West (2,150 MW). Internationally, NRG owns 1,005 net MW of generation in Australia and Germany. NRG also owns another 1,021 MW in seven steam and chilled water facilities in the U.S., and 115 MW of co-generation thermal capacity in Delaware and Pennsylvania. The sale of capacity and power from baseload power plants accounts for the majority of NRG's revenues and provides a stable source of cash flow. As of December 2010, the company's U.S. generating capacity was fueled 46% by natural gas, 31% by coal, 16% by oil, 5% by nuclear, 2% by wind, and less than 0.1% by solar. By dispatch type, 35% of capacity was baseload, 38% intermediate, 24% peaking, and 2% intermittent. In 2010, 87% of NRG's MW hours produced were from baseload plants.

CORPORATE STRATEGY. NRG is pursuing opportunities to repower existing facilities and develop new generation capacity in markets in which it currently owns assets in an initiative referred to as Repowering NRG. The program consists of the development, construction and operation of new and enhanced power generation facilities at its existing sites, with an emphasis on new baseload capacity that is supported by long-term power sales agreements and financed with limited or non-recourse project financing. The company expects to achieve improved heat rates at existing facilities, lower delivered costs of electricity, increased overall capacity, an improvement in the firm's dispatch curve, better fuel diversity, and environmental enhancements.

In September 2007, NRG filed an application with the Nuclear Regulatory Commission (NRC) to build two new advanced boiling water reactors (ABWR) at its South Texas Project nuclear plant. In April 2011, NRG announced that it had canceled its nuclear development plans and recognized a $481 million asset impairment charge.

## Company Financials Fiscal Year Ended Dec. 31

| Per Share Data ($) | 2010 | 2009 | 2008 | 2007 | 2006 | 2005 | 2004 | 2003 | 2002 | 2001 |
|---|---|---|---|---|---|---|---|---|---|---|
| Tangible Book Value | 17.84 | 15.91 | 15.89 | 9.14 | 8.05 | 9.60 | 11.74 | 9.59 | NA | NA |
| Cash Flow | 5.31 | 7.06 | 5.86 | 4.08 | 3.66 | 1.48 | 2.34 | 0.13 | NA | 1.22 |
| Earnings | 1.84 | 3.44 | 3.66 | 1.95 | 1.82 | 0.33 | 0.81 | 0.05 | NA | 0.68 |
| S&P Core Earnings | 1.78 | 3.14 | 3.67 | 1.92 | 1.67 | 0.45 | 0.86 | NA | NA | NA |
| Dividends | Nil | Nil | Nil | Nil | Nil | Nil | Nil | NA | NA | NA |
| Payout Ratio | Nil | Nil | Nil | Nil | Nil | Nil | Nil | NA | NA | NA |
| Prices:High | 25.70 | 29.26 | 45.78 | 47.19 | 29.74 | 24.72 | 18.09 | NA | NA | NA |
| Prices:Low | 18.22 | 15.19 | 14.39 | 23.03 | 20.90 | 15.15 | 9.59 | NA | NA | NA |
| P/E Ratio:High | 14 | 9 | 13 | 24 | 16 | 75 | 22 | NA | NA | NA |
| P/E Ratio:Low | 10 | 4 | 4 | 12 | 12 | 46 | 12 | NA | NA | NA |

| Income Statement Analysis (Million $) | 2010 | 2009 | 2008 | 2007 | 2006 | 2005 | 2004 | 2003 | 2002 | 2001 |
|---|---|---|---|---|---|---|---|---|---|---|
| Revenue | 8,849 | 8,952 | 6,885 | 5,989 | 5,623 | 2,708 | 2,361 | 152 | 2,212 | 2,799 |
| Operating Income | NA | NA | 2,922 | 2,201 | 1,438 | 445 | 754 | 33.7 | NA | NA |
| Depreciation | 882 | 1,007 | 649 | 658 | 593 | 195 | 308 | 14.8 | 287 | 212 |
| Interest Expense | 632 | 634 | 620 | 689 | 786 | 253 | 341 | 21.6 | 494 | 444 |
| Pretax Income | 753 | 1,669 | 1,729 | 946 | 880 | 120 | 228 | 10.0 | -3,078 | 305 |
| Effective Tax Rate | NA | 43.6% | 41.2% | 39.9% | 36.9% | 35.8% | 28.5% | NM | 5.37% | 11.0% |
| Net Income | 476 | 942 | 1,016 | 569 | 555 | 77.0 | 162 | 10.5 | -2,908 | 265 |
| S&P Core Earnings | 454 | 829 | 967 | 507 | 460 | 77.2 | 172 | 3,357 | -2,781 | NA |

| Balance Sheet & Other Financial Data (Million $) | 2010 | 2009 | 2008 | 2007 | 2006 | 2005 | 2004 | 2003 | 2002 | 2001 |
|---|---|---|---|---|---|---|---|---|---|---|
| Cash | 2,951 | 2,304 | 1,494 | 1,161 | 795 | 506 | 1,223 | 738 | 385 | 186 |
| Current Assets | 7,137 | 6,208 | 8,492 | 3,562 | 3,083 | 2,197 | 2,118 | 2,114 | 1,486 | 1,187 |
| Total Assets | 26,896 | 23,378 | 24,808 | 19,274 | 19,435 | 7,431 | 7,830 | 9,261 | 10,884 | 12,895 |
| Current Liabilities | 4,220 | 3,762 | 6,581 | 2,277 | 2,032 | 1,356 | 1,088 | 2,026 | 9,797 | 1,951 |
| Long Term Debt | 10,048 | 7,746 | 7,704 | 7,895 | 8,647 | 2,581 | 3,254 | 1,213 | 1,193 | 7,844 |
| Common Equity | 8,055 | 7,536 | 6,256 | 4,612 | 5,055 | 1,825 | 2,286 | 2,437 | -696 | 2,237 |
| Total Capital | 18,848 | 16,239 | 16,257 | 14,489 | 15,396 | 5,194 | 6,086 | 3,801 | 7,720 | 10,649 |
| Capital Expenditures | 706 | 734 | 899 | 481 | 221 | 106 | 114 | 10.6 | 1,504 | 1,472 |
| Cash Flow | 1,349 | 1,916 | 1,610 | 1,172 | 1,098 | 252 | 470 | 25.2 | -2,621 | 478 |
| Current Ratio | 1.7 | 1.7 | 1.3 | 1.6 | 1.5 | 1.6 | 1.9 | 1.0 | 0.2 | 0.6 |
| % Long Term Debt of Capitalization | 53.3 | 47.7 | 47.4 | 54.5 | 56.2 | 49.7 | 53.5 | 31.9 | NM | 74.1 |
| % Net Income of Revenue | 5.4 | 10.5 | 14.8 | 9.5 | 9.9 | 2.8 | 6.9 | 6.9 | NM | 9.5 |
| % Return on Assets | 1.9 | 3.9 | 4.6 | 2.7 | 4.1 | 1.0 | 1.9 | NA | NM | 2.8 |
| % Return on Equity | 6.1 | 13.7 | 18.7 | 11.0 | 14.7 | 2.8 | 6.9 | NA | NM | 14.3 |

Data as orig reptd.; bef. results of disc opers/spec. items. Per share data adj. for stk. divs.; EPS diluted. E-Estimated. NA-Not Available. NM-Not Meaningful. NR-Not Ranked. UR-Under Review.

**Office:** 211 Carnegie Ctr, Princeton, NJ 08540-6213.
**Telephone:** 609-524-4500.
**Website:** http://www.nrgenergy.com
**Chrmn:** H.E. Cosgrove

**Pres & CEO:** D. Crane
**COO:** M. Gutierrez
**EVP & CFO:** K.B. Andrews
**EVP & Chief Admin Officer:** D.M. Wilson

**Investor Contact:** K. Sullivan (612-373-8875)
**Board Members:** K. H. Caldwell, J. F. Chlebowski, Jr., L. S. Coben, H. E. Cosgrove, D. Crane, S. L. Cropper, W. E. Hantke, P. W. Hobby, G. Luterman, K. A. McGinty, A. Schaumburg, H. H. Tate, Jr., T. H. Weidemeyer, W. R. Young

**Founded:** 1992
**Domicile:** Delaware
**Employees:** 4,964

The **McGraw·Hill** Companies

# Nucor Corp

**STANDARD &POOR'S**

| S&P Recommendation BUY ★★★★☆ | Price $35.57 (as of Nov 25, 2011) | 12-Mo. Target Price $45.00 | Investment Style Large-Cap Blend |
|---|---|---|---|

**GICS Sector** Materials
**Sub-Industry** Steel

**Summary** The largest minimill steelmaker in the U.S., Nucor has one of the most diverse product lines of any steelmaker in the Americas.

## Key Stock Statistics (Source S&P, Vickers, company reports)

| | | | | | | | |
|---|---|---|---|---|---|---|---|
| 52-Wk Range | $49.24–29.82 | S&P Oper. EPS 2011**E** | 2.51 | Market Capitalization(B) | $11.265 | Beta | 1.10 |
| Trailing 12-Month EPS | $1.98 | S&P Oper. EPS 2012**E** | 3.32 | Yield (%) | 4.08 | S&P 3-Yr. Proj. EPS CAGR(%) | NM |
| Trailing 12-Month P/E | 18.0 | P/E on S&P Oper. EPS 2011**E** | 14.2 | Dividend Rate/Share | $1.45 | S&P Credit Rating | A |
| $10K Invested 5 Yrs Ago | $7,228 | Common Shares Outstg. (M) | 316.7 | Institutional Ownership (%) | 76 | | |

## Price Performance

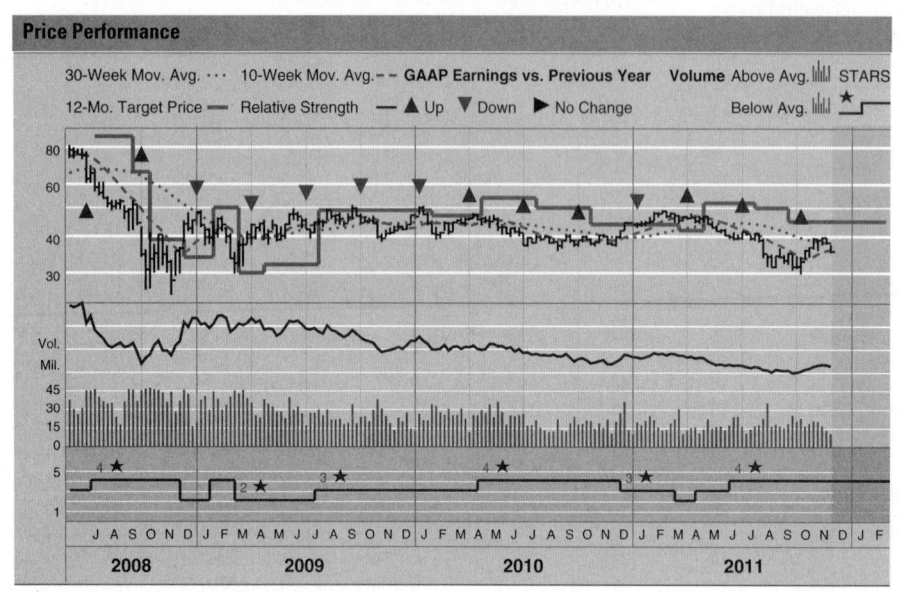

30-Week Mov. Avg. · · · 10-Week Mov. Avg. - - GAAP Earnings vs. Previous Year Volume Above Avg. STARS
12-Mo. Target Price — Relative Strength — ▲ Up ▼ Down ► No Change Below Avg.

Options: ASE, CBOE, P, Ph

Analysis prepared by Equity Analyst **Leo J. Larkin** on Sep 16, 2011, when the stock traded at **$34.98**.

### Highlights

➤ Following a 42% increase in revenues in 2010, we look for a 22% advance in 2011 on another rise in shipment volume and prices. Our projections rest on several assumptions. First, S&P forecasts U.S. GDP growth of 1.6% in 2011, versus 3.0% in 2010. Second, S&P expects non-residential construction spending to increase 3.2% in 2011, versus 2010's drop of 15.8%. We see this boosting sales of structural steel for construction as well as sales of fabricated building products. Third, we believe that distributors will continue to rebuild inventories in 2011, leading to better demand for most steel products. Lastly, another projected rise in domestic steel production should lift sales of scrap products.

➤ We expect another increase in operating profit in 2011 on further gains in pricing and shipment volume and a much smaller loss in the steel products unit. After interest expense and taxes, we estimate EPS of $2.53 for 2011, versus 2010's EPS of $0.42.

➤ For the longer term, we see earnings rising on industry consolidation, acquisitions, and better control of raw material costs.

### Investment Rationale/Risk

➤ We think sales and operating results for NUE troughed in 2009 and will rise in 2011 and 2012 on a continued upturn in durable goods demand. Beyond 2012, we see generally rising earnings on the ongoing consolidation of the global steel industry. Consolidation should result in a greater concentration of production among fewer companies. We see this leading to greater pricing power and more production discipline. Also, we believe that NUE's decision to become more vertically integrated should result in generally less volatile sales and earnings over the business cycle. Following a sharp drop, we think that the stock is attractively valued at a recent 10.5X our 2012 estimate, with a dividend yield of 4.1%.

➤ Risks to our opinion and target price include declines in steel and scrap prices in 2012 instead of the increases we currently project.

➤ Our 12-month target price of $45 is based on our view that the shares will trade at a multiple of 13.6X our 2012 EPS estimate. On this projected multiple, NUE would trade at a premium to the peer average P/E of 10.6X and at the low end of its historical range of the past 10 years.

### Qualitative Risk Assessment

| LOW | MEDIUM | HIGH |
|---|---|---|

Our risk assessment reflects Nucor's solid share of the markets in which it competes, a low ratio of total debt to assets, and a very diverse product mix. This is partly offset by the company's exposure to cyclical markets, such as non-residential construction.

### Quantitative Evaluations

**S&P Quality Ranking**     **B**

| D | C | B- | B | B+ | A- | A | A+ |
|---|---|---|---|---|---|---|---|

**Relative Strength Rank**     **MODERATE**

64

LOWEST = 1          HIGHEST = 99

### Revenue/Earnings Data

**Revenue (Million $)**

| | 1Q | 2Q | 3Q | 4Q | Year |
|---|---|---|---|---|---|
| 2011 | 4,834 | 5,108 | 5,252 | -- | -- |
| 2010 | 3,655 | 4,196 | 4,140 | 3,854 | 15,845 |
| 2009 | 2,654 | 2,478 | 3,120 | 2,938 | 11,190 |
| 2008 | 4,974 | 7,091 | 7,448 | 4,151 | 23,663 |
| 2007 | 3,769 | 4,168 | 4,259 | 4,397 | 16,593 |
| 2006 | 3,545 | 3,806 | 3,931 | 3,469 | 14,751 |

**Earnings Per Share ($)**

| | | | | | |
|---|---|---|---|---|---|
| 2011 | 0.50 | 0.94 | 0.57 | E0.58 | E2.51 |
| 2010 | 0.10 | 0.29 | 0.07 | -0.04 | 0.42 |
| 2009 | -0.60 | -0.43 | -0.10 | 0.18 | -0.94 |
| 2008 | 1.41 | 1.94 | 2.31 | 0.34 | 5.98 |
| 2007 | 1.26 | 1.14 | 1.29 | 1.26 | 4.94 |
| 2006 | 1.21 | 1.45 | 1.68 | 1.35 | 5.68 |

Fiscal year ended Dec. 31. Next earnings report expected: NA. EPS Estimates based on S&P Operating Earnings; historical GAAP earnings are as reported.

### Dividend Data (Dates: mm/dd Payment Date: mm/dd/yy)

| Amount ($) | Date Decl. | Ex-Div. Date | Stk. of Record | Payment Date |
|---|---|---|---|---|
| 0.363 | 12/08 | 12/29 | 12/31 | 02/11/11 |
| 0.363 | 02/16 | 03/29 | 03/31 | 05/11/11 |
| 0.363 | 06/07 | 06/28 | 06/30 | 08/11/11 |
| 0.363 | 09/07 | 09/28 | 09/30 | 11/11/11 |

Dividends have been paid since 1973. Source: Company reports.

---

**Please read the Required Disclosures and Analyst Certification on the last page of this report.**

The **McGraw·Hill** Companies

# Nucor Corp

STANDARD
&POOR'S

## Business Summary September 16, 2011

CORPORATE OVERVIEW. Nucor is the largest U.S. minimill steelmaker. In 2010, steel production was 18.3 million tons, and outside steel shipments were 15.8 million tons.

CORPORATE STRATEGY. Nucor's growth strategy involves four initiatives. The first is to optimize existing operations. The second is to make strategic acquisitions. The third involves construction of new plants and development of new technologies for markets where the company believes it has a major cost advantage. The fourth initiative is to expand globally through joint ventures that leverage new technologies.

MARKET PROFILE. The primary factors affecting demand for steel products are economic growth in general and growth in demand for durable goods in particular. The two largest end markets for steel products in the U.S. are autos and construction. In 2010, these two markets accounted for 32% of shipments in the U.S. market, according to preliminary statistics compiled the American Iron and Steel Institute. Other end markets include appliances, con-

tainers, machinery, and oil and gas. Distributors, also known as service centers, accounted for 26% of industry shipments in the U.S. market in 2010. Distributors are the largest single market for the steel industry in the U.S. Because distributors sell to a wide variety of OEMs, it is extremely difficult to trace the final destination of much of the industry's shipments. Consequently, demand for steel from the auto, construction and other industries may be higher than the shipment data would suggest. In terms of production, the size of the U.S. market was 88.7 million tons in 2010, and Nucor's market share was 20.6%. In the U.S. market, consumption decreased at a compound annual rate of 2.8% from 2001 through 2010. Global steel production was 1.41 billion metric tons in 2010, versus 1.23 billion metric tons in 2009.

## Company Financials Fiscal Year Ended Dec. 31

| Per Share Data ($) | 2010 | 2009 | 2008 | 2007 | 2006 | 2005 | 2004 | 2003 | 2002 | 2001 |
|---|---|---|---|---|---|---|---|---|---|---|
| Tangible Book Value | 14.02 | 14.88 | 16.72 | 13.18 | 15.56 | 13.80 | 10.84 | 7.45 | 7.43 | 7.07 |
| Cash Flow | 2.26 | 0.87 | 7.78 | 6.38 | 7.05 | 5.43 | 4.72 | 1.36 | 1.50 | 1.29 |
| Earnings | 0.42 | -0.94 | 5.98 | 4.94 | 5.68 | 4.13 | 3.51 | 0.20 | 0.52 | 0.36 |
| S&P Core Earnings | 0.42 | -0.94 | 6.19 | 4.94 | 5.68 | 4.09 | 3.49 | 0.15 | 0.46 | 0.33 |
| Dividends | 1.44 | 1.41 | 1.59 | 0.63 | 0.40 | 0.30 | 0.24 | 0.20 | 0.19 | 0.17 |
| Payout Ratio | NM | NM | 27% | 13% | 7% | 7% | 7% | 100% | 37% | 47% |
| Prices:High | 50.72 | 51.08 | 83.56 | 69.93 | 67.55 | 35.11 | 27.74 | 14.70 | 17.54 | 14.13 |
| Prices:Low | 35.71 | 29.84 | 25.25 | 41.62 | 33.63 | 22.78 | 13.04 | 8.76 | 9.00 | 8.36 |
| P/E Ratio:High | NM | NM | 14 | 14 | 12 | 9 | 8 | 73 | 34 | 39 |
| P/E Ratio:Low | NM | NM | 4 | 8 | 6 | 6 | 4 | 44 | 17 | 23 |

| Income Statement Analysis (Million $) | | | | | | | | | | |
|---|---|---|---|---|---|---|---|---|---|---|
| Revenue | 15,845 | 11,190 | 23,663 | 16,593 | 14,751 | 12,701 | 11,377 | 6,266 | 4,802 | 4,139 |
| Operating Income | 1,035 | 372 | 3,849 | 2,980 | 3,240 | 2,497 | 2,216 | 468 | 601 | 469 |
| Depreciation | 583 | 566 | 549 | 428 | 364 | 375 | 383 | 364 | 307 | 289 |
| Interest Expense | 153 | 150 | 135 | 51.1 | Nil | 4.20 | 22.4 | 24.6 | 22.9 | 22.0 |
| Pretax Income | 267 | -414 | 3,104 | 2,547 | 2,913 | 2,127 | 1,812 | 90.8 | 310 | 174 |
| Effective Tax Rate | NA | 42.7% | 30.9% | 30.7% | 32.1% | 33.2% | 33.6% | 4.51% | 22.0% | 35.0% |
| Net Income | 134 | -294 | 1,831 | 1,472 | 1,758 | 1,310 | 1,121 | 62.8 | 162 | 113 |
| S&P Core Earnings | 132 | -296 | 1,895 | 1,472 | 1,758 | 1,296 | 1,114 | 47.9 | 143 | 101 |

| Balance Sheet & Other Financial Data (Million $) | | | | | | | | | | |
|---|---|---|---|---|---|---|---|---|---|---|
| Cash | 2,479 | 2,242 | 2,355 | 1,576 | 786 | 1,838 | 779 | 350 | 219 | 462 |
| Current Assets | 5,861 | 5,182 | 6,397 | 5,073 | 4,675 | 4,072 | 3,175 | 1,621 | 1,424 | 1,374 |
| Total Assets | 13,922 | 12,572 | 13,874 | 9,826 | 7,885 | 7,139 | 6,133 | 4,492 | 4,381 | 3,759 |
| Current Liabilities | 1,504 | 1,227 | 1,854 | 1,582 | 1,450 | 1,256 | 1,066 | 630 | 592 | 484 |
| Long Term Debt | 4,280 | 3,080 | 3,086 | 2,250 | 922 | 922 | 924 | 904 | 879 | 460 |
| Common Equity | 7,120 | 7,391 | 7,929 | 5,113 | 4,826 | 4,280 | 3,456 | 2,342 | 2,323 | 2,201 |
| Total Capital | 11,611 | 10,670 | 11,523 | 7,651 | 5,987 | 5,396 | 4,553 | 3,423 | 3,419 | 2,946 |
| Capital Expenditures | 345 | 391 | 1,019 | 520 | 338 | 331 | 286 | 215 | 244 | 261 |
| Cash Flow | 717 | 273 | 2,380 | 1,900 | 2,122 | 1,685 | 1,505 | 427 | 469 | 402 |
| Current Ratio | 3.9 | 4.2 | 3.5 | 3.2 | 3.2 | 3.2 | 3.0 | 2.6 | 2.4 | 2.8 |
| % Long Term Debt of Capitalization | 36.9 | 28.9 | 26.8 | 29.4 | 15.4 | 17.1 | 20.3 | 26.4 | 25.7 | 15.6 |
| % Net Income of Revenue | 0.9 | NM | 7.7 | 8.9 | 11.9 | 10.3 | 9.9 | 1.0 | 3.4 | 2.7 |
| % Return on Assets | 1.0 | NM | 15.5 | 16.6 | 23.4 | 19.7 | 21.1 | 1.4 | 4.0 | 3.0 |
| % Return on Equity | 1.9 | NM | 28.1 | 29.6 | 38.6 | 33.9 | 38.7 | 2.7 | 5.1 | 5.2 |

Data as orig reptd.; bef. results of disc opers/spec. items. Per share data adj. for stk. divs.; EPS diluted. E-Estimated. NA-Not Available. NM-Not Meaningful. NR-Not Ranked. UR-Under Review.

**Office:** 1915 Rexford Rd, Charlotte, NC 28211-3441.
**Telephone:** 704-366-7000.
**Email:** info@nucor.com
**Website:** http://www.nucor.com

**Chrmn & CEO:** D.R. DiMicco
**Pres & COO:** J.J. Ferriola
**CFO & Treas:** J.D. Frias
**Chief Acctg Officer & Cntlr:** M.D. Keller

**Secy:** A.R. Eagle
**Board Members:** P. C. Browning, C. C. Daley, Jr., D. R. DiMicco, J. J. Ferriola, H. B. Gantt, V. F. Haynes, J. D. Hlavacek, B. L. Kasriel, C. J. Kearney, J. H. Walker

**Founded:** 1940
**Domicile:** Delaware
**Employees:** 20,500

STANDARD &POOR'S

# NVIDIA Corp

**S&P Recommendation** HOLD ★★★★★

**Price** $14.04 (as of Nov 25, 2011)

**12-Mo. Target Price** $19.00

**Investment Style** Large-Cap Growth

**GICS Sector** Information Technology
**Sub-Industry** Semiconductors

**Summary** This company develops and markets graphics processors for personal computers, workstations and mobile devices.

## Key Stock Statistics (Source S&P, Vickers, company reports)

| | | | | | | | |
|---|---|---|---|---|---|---|---|
| 52-Wk Range | $26.17– 11.47 | S&P Oper. EPS 2012E | 1.03 | Market Capitalization(B) | $8.574 | Beta | 1.60 |
| Trailing 12-Month EPS | $1.04 | S&P Oper. EPS 2013E | 1.10 | Yield (%) | Nil | S&P 3-Yr. Proj. EPS CAGR(%) | 47 |
| Trailing 12-Month P/E | 13.5 | P/E on S&P Oper. EPS 2012E | 13.6 | Dividend Rate/Share | Nil | S&P Credit Rating | NR |
| $10K Invested 5 Yrs Ago | $5,695 | Common Shares Outstg. (M) | 610.7 | Institutional Ownership (%) | 75 | | |

## Price Performance

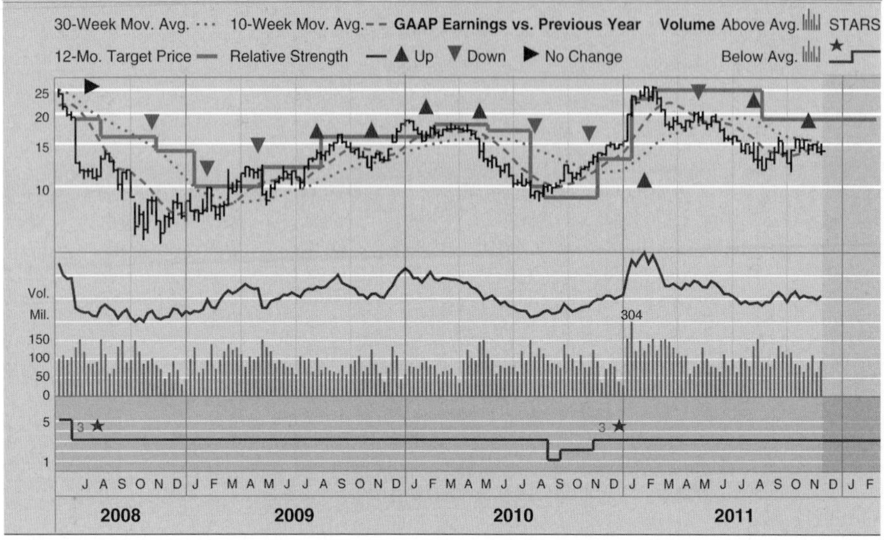
30-Week Mov. Avg. ··· 10-Week Mov. Avg. - - GAAP Earnings vs. Previous Year Volume Above Avg. STARS
12-Mo. Target Price — Relative Strength — ▲ Up ▼ Down ▶ No Change Below Avg.
Vol. Mil.
304
2008
2009
2010
2011

Options: ASE, CBOE, P, Ph

Analysis prepared by Equity Analyst **Angelo Zino, CFA** on Nov 14, 2011, when the stock traded at **$14.98**.

## Highlights

- We see sales advancing 14% in FY 13 (Jan.), after a projected 16% rise in FY 12. We think long-term drivers, such as the growth of graphics-intensive applications, healthy computer demand, and fast-growing mobile markets, remain intact. Although we view hybrid microprocessor and graphics offerings as formidable competition to graphics processing units (GPUs), we believe growth will come from share gains in the discrete graphics and high-end computing markets, and penetration in the handset and tablet spaces.
- We think that gross margins will be around the 51% to 53% area over the next several quarters, reflecting benefits from licensing revenues and sales of higher-margin non-GPU products. Although we are encouraged by Tegra design wins, we are forecasting higher operating expenses related to new products entering production. For FY 13, we estimate that R&D and SG&A expenses will absorb 25% and 11% of sales, respectively. All told, we see operating margins at 17% in FY 12 and FY 13.
- Our FY 12 and FY 13 EPS estimates of $1.03 and $1.10, respectively, both include stock compensation expense of over $0.20 per share.

## Investment Rationale/Risk

- Our hold recommendation reflects our view of improving fundamentals balanced by fair valuations. Although we expect increasing competition in the low-and-mid end PC graphics markets, we believe that NVDA's increasing exposure to tablets, handsets, and servers raises the company's long-term growth potential. Furthermore, with licensing revenues supporting gross margins, we see profitability remaining at elevated levels over the foreseeable future. Also considering our expectations for above-industry profit growth, we think NVDA's multiples should be higher than the industry average.
- Risks to our opinion and target price include weaker-than-anticipated desktop sales, slower-than-expected traction for Tegra and Tesla-based products, and competition from hybrid microprocessor and graphics chips.
- Our 12-month target price of $19 is based on our price-to-earnings (P/E) analysis. We apply a multiple of 17X, above the industry average to account for its relative profitability, growth, and returns, to our FY 13 EPS estimate. We note that without the inclusion of stock-based compensation, the P/E multiple would be closer to the industry.

## Qualitative Risk Assessment

LOW | MEDIUM | **HIGH**

Our risk assessment reflects the cyclicality of the semiconductor industry and of demand trends for electronics goods that benefit from advanced visual displays, and revenue volatility resulting from wins and losses of deals with big accounts.

## Quantitative Evaluations

**S&P Quality Ranking** B-

D | C | **B-** | B | B+ | A- | A | A+

**Relative Strength Rank** MODERATE

64

LOWEST = 1 HIGHEST = 99

## Revenue/Earnings Data

**Revenue (Million $)**

| | 1Q | 2Q | 3Q | 4Q | Year |
|---|---|---|---|---|---|
| 2012 | 962.0 | 1,017 | 1,066 | -- | -- |
| 2011 | 1,002 | 811.2 | 843.9 | 886.4 | 3,543 |
| 2010 | 664.2 | 776.5 | 903.2 | 982.5 | 3,326 |
| 2009 | 1,153 | 892.7 | 897.7 | 481.1 | 3,425 |
| 2008 | 844.3 | 935.3 | 1,116 | 1,203 | 4,098 |
| 2007 | 681.8 | 687.5 | 820.6 | 878.9 | 3,069 |

**Earnings Per Share ($)**

| | 1Q | 2Q | 3Q | 4Q | Year |
|---|---|---|---|---|---|
| 2012 | 0.22 | 0.25 | 0.29 | **E**0.27 | **E**1.03 |
| 2011 | 0.23 | -0.25 | 0.15 | 0.29 | 0.43 |
| 2010 | -0.37 | -0.19 | 0.19 | 0.23 | -0.12 |
| 2009 | 0.30 | -0.22 | 0.11 | -0.27 | -0.05 |
| 2008 | 0.22 | -0.22 | 0.38 | 0.42 | 1.32 |
| 2007 | 0.15 | 0.15 | 0.18 | 0.27 | 0.77 |

Fiscal year ended Jan. 31. Next earnings report expected: Mid February. EPS Estimates based on S&P Operating Earnings; historical GAAP earnings are as reported.

## Dividend Data

No cash dividends have been paid.

**Please read the Required Disclosures and Analyst Certification on the last page of this report.**
Redistribution or reproduction is prohibited without written permission. Copyright ©2011 The McGraw-Hill Companies, Inc.

The McGraw·Hill Companies

# NVIDIA Corp

**STANDARD &POOR'S**

## Business Summary November 14, 2011

CORPORATE OVERVIEW. NVIDIA Corporation, which invented the graphics processing unit (GPU), makes products for "visual computing, " high-performance computing, and mobile computing markets. NVDA has three major reporting segments: Graphics Processing Unit (GPU), Professional Solutions Business (PSB), and Consumer Products Business (CPB).

The GPU business includes GeForce discrete and chipset products used primarily in desktop and laptop computers to enhance the user experience for playing video games, editing photos, and watching movies. PSB is comprised of the Quadro and Tesla products. Quadro is used in workstations to improve graphics performance for applications such as computer aided design and video editing. Tesla is used in some of the world's largest supercomputers for high-performance computation and processing. CPB is based on Tegra, which is a line of application processors that manage various processing and graphics functions for smartphones, tablets, and other mobile devices.

CORPORATE STRATEGY. The company's stated objective is to be the leading supplier of programmable, high-performance GPUs and ultra-low power mobile system-on-a-chip products. In the core discrete graphics market, NVDA is developing multiple generations of GPUs for high-performance computing, and mobile and consumer products that enhance the quality and performance of 3D graphics, image processing, and computational graphics. In the higher-end computing markets, NVDA is promoting CUDA, an architecture that it states can accelerate compute-intensive applications by significant multiples over that of a CPU alone, by working closely with related developers. In mobile computing markets, Nvidia is leveraging its expertise in HD graphics and system architecture to create superior performance processors.

The company runs on a fabless model, relying on contract manufacturers that include Taiwan Semiconductor and United Microelectronics for wafer fabrication.

## Company Financials Fiscal Year Ended Jan. 31

| Per Share Data ($) | 2011 | 2010 | 2009 | 2008 | 2007 | 2006 | 2005 | 2004 | 2003 | 2002 |
|---|---|---|---|---|---|---|---|---|---|---|
| Tangible Book Value | 4.29 | 3.87 | 3.49 | 4.35 | 3.32 | 2.52 | 2.08 | 1.83 | 1.81 | 1.52 |
| Cash Flow | 0.75 | 0.23 | 0.28 | 1.54 | 0.95 | 0.73 | 0.38 | 0.30 | 0.29 | 0.43 |
| Earnings | 0.43 | -0.12 | -0.05 | 1.32 | 0.77 | 0.55 | 0.19 | 0.14 | 0.18 | 0.34 |
| S&P Core Earnings | 0.37 | -0.25 | -0.05 | 1.31 | 0.79 | 0.42 | 0.03 | -0.00 | -0.22 | 0.10 |
| Dividends | NA | Nil | Nil | Nil | Nil | Nil | Nil | Nil | Nil | Nil |
| Payout Ratio | NA | Nil | Nil | Nil | Nil | Nil | Nil | Nil | Nil | Nil |
| Calendar Year | 2010 | 2009 | 2008 | 2007 | 2006 | 2005 | 2004 | 2003 | 2002 | 2001 |
| Prices:High | 18.96 | 18.95 | 34.25 | 39.67 | 25.97 | 12.83 | 9.12 | 9.25 | 24.22 | 23.42 |
| Prices:Low | 8.65 | 7.08 | 5.75 | 18.69 | 11.45 | 6.82 | 3.10 | 3.11 | 2.40 | 4.71 |
| P/E Ratio:High | 44 | NM | NM | 30 | 34 | 23 | 48 | 65 | NM | 68 |
| P/E Ratio:Low | 20 | NM | NM | 14 | 15 | 12 | 16 | 22 | NM | 14 |

| Income Statement Analysis (Million $) | | | | | | | | | | |
|---|---|---|---|---|---|---|---|---|---|---|
| Revenue | 3,543 | 3,326 | 3,425 | 4,098 | 3,069 | 2,376 | 2,010 | 1,823 | 1,909 | 1,369 |
| Operating Income | 386 | 29.1 | 334 | 976 | 593 | 452 | 216 | 172 | 202 | 299 |
| Depreciation | 187 | 197 | 185 | 136 | 108 | 98.0 | 103 | 82.0 | 58.2 | 43.5 |
| Interest Expense | 3.13 | 3.32 | 0.41 | 0.05 | 0.02 | 0.07 | 0.16 | 12.0 | Nil | 16.2 |
| Pretax Income | 271 | -82.3 | -43.0 | 901 | 494 | 360 | 125 | 86.7 | 151 | 253 |
| Effective Tax Rate | NA | 17.4% | NM | 11.5% | 9.37% | 16.0% | 20.0% | 14.1% | 39.7% | 30.0% |
| Net Income | 253 | -68.0 | -30.0 | 798 | 448 | 303 | 100 | 74.4 | 90.8 | 177 |
| S&P Core Earnings | 215 | -140 | -30.4 | 798 | 460 | 230 | 14.6 | -1.44 | -104 | 49.4 |

| Balance Sheet & Other Financial Data (Million $) | | | | | | | | | | |
|---|---|---|---|---|---|---|---|---|---|---|
| Cash | 2,491 | 1,728 | 1,255 | 1,809 | 1,118 | 950 | 670 | 604 | 1,028 | 791 |
| Current Assets | 3,227 | 2,481 | 2,168 | 2,889 | 2,032 | 1,549 | 1,305 | 1,053 | 1,352 | 1,234 |
| Total Assets | 4,495 | 3,586 | 3,351 | 3,748 | 2,675 | 1,915 | 1,629 | 1,399 | 1,617 | 1,503 |
| Current Liabilities | 943 | 784 | 779 | 967 | 639 | 439 | 421 | 334 | 379 | 433 |
| Long Term Debt | NA | NA | 25.6 | Nil | Nil | Nil | Nil | 0.86 | 305 | 306 |
| Common Equity | 3,181 | 2,665 | 2,395 | 2,618 | 2,007 | 1,458 | 1,178 | 1,051 | 933 | 764 |
| Total Capital | 3,181 | 2,665 | 2,420 | 2,705 | 2,007 | 1,466 | 1,199 | 1,061 | 1,238 | 1,070 |
| Capital Expenditures | 97.9 | 77.6 | 408 | 188 | 145 | 79.6 | 67.3 | 128 | 63.1 | 97.0 |
| Cash Flow | 440 | 129 | 155 | 933 | 556 | 401 | 203 | 156 | 149 | 220 |
| Current Ratio | 3.4 | 3.2 | 2.8 | 3.0 | 3.2 | 3.5 | 3.1 | 3.2 | 3.6 | 2.8 |
| % Long Term Debt of Capitalization | Nil | Nil | 1.1 | Nil | Nil | Nil | Nil | 0.1 | 24.6 | 28.6 |
| % Net Income of Revenue | 7.1 | NM | NM | 19.5 | 14.6 | 12.7 | 5.0 | 4.1 | 4.8 | 12.9 |
| % Return on Assets | 6.3 | NM | NM | 24.8 | 19.4 | 17.1 | 6.6 | 4.9 | 5.8 | 14.0 |
| % Return on Equity | 8.7 | NM | NM | 34.5 | 25.6 | 23.0 | 9.0 | 7.5 | 10.7 | 30.2 |

Data as orig reptd.; bef. results of disc opers/spec. items. Per share data adj. for stk. divs.; EPS diluted. E-Estimated. NA-Not Available. NM-Not Meaningful. NR-Not Ranked. UR-Under Review.

**Office:** 2701 San Tomas Expressway, Santa Clara, CA 95050.
**Telephone:** 408-486-2000.
**Email:** ir@nvidia.com
**Website:** http://www.nvidia.com

**Pres & CEO:** J. Huang
**COO:** D. Shoquist
**SVP & CIO:** B. Worrall
**CFO:** K. Burns

**CSO:** B. Dally
**Investor Contact:** M. Hara (408-486-2511)
**Board Members:** T. Coxe, J. C. Gaither, J. Huang, H. C. Jones, Jr., W. J. Miller, M. L. Perry, B. Seawell

**Founded:** 1993
**Domicile:** Delaware
**Employees:** 6,029

# NYSE Euronext

STANDARD &POOR'S

**S&P Recommendation** BUY ★★★★☆

| Price | 12-Mo. Target Price | Investment Style |
|---|---|---|
| $25.76 (as of Nov 25, 2011) | $39.00 | Large-Cap Growth |

**GICS Sector** Financials
**Sub-Industry** Specialized Finance

**Summary** This holding company operates six cash equities exchanges and six derivatives exchanges in six countries.

## Key Stock Statistics (Source S&P, Vickers, company reports)

| | | | | | | | |
|---|---|---|---|---|---|---|---|
| 52-Wk Range | $41.60–21.80 | S&P Oper. EPS 2011E | 2.61 | Market Capitalization(B) | $6.749 | Beta | 1.67 |
| Trailing 12-Month EPS | $2.44 | S&P Oper. EPS 2012E | 2.90 | Yield (%) | 4.66 | S&P 3-Yr. Proj. EPS CAGR(%) | 14 |
| Trailing 12-Month P/E | 10.6 | P/E on S&P Oper. EPS 2011E | 9.9 | Dividend Rate/Share | $1.20 | S&P Credit Rating | A+ |
| $10K Invested 5 Yrs Ago | $2,784 | Common Shares Outstg. (M) | 262.0 | Institutional Ownership (%) | 74 | | |

## Price Performance

- 30-Week Mov. Avg. · · ·
- 10-Week Mov. Avg. – –
- 12-Mo. Target Price —
- Relative Strength —
- GAAP Earnings vs. Previous Year
- ▲ Up ▼ Down ► No Change
- Volume Above Avg. STARS
- Below Avg.

Analysis prepared by Equity Analyst **Robert McMillan** on Nov 08, 2011, when the stock traded at **$27.41**.

### Highlights

➤ We expect revenues, after falling 4.4% in 2010, to rise about 4.9% in 2011 (driven in large part by extreme market volatility), before a slight moderation in 2012 to 4.6% growth. We think the heightened volatility in stock markets in both the U.S. and Europe will pressure transaction and clearing fees as well as the listing business. Our outlook reflects our expectation for market share stabilization in the cash equities business, as the company is making significant progress reducing order execution times. In addition, we believe NYX's new initiatives, technology services, and listing business units will help long-term growth.

➤ We foresee the company's cost-cutting program helping to reduce expenses, including selling, general, and administrative costs, liquidity payments, routing fees, and professional services. This should be partially offset by what we expect to be an increase in other expenses such as compensation costs and systems and communications expenses related to the new data center and other initiatives.

➤ Our operating EPS estimates are $2.61 for 2011 and $2.90 for 2012.

### Investment Rationale/Risk

➤ The company is in the process of attempting to complete a merger with Deutsche Boerse, which, after receiving shareholder approvals, is now awaiting regulatory approvals. We are concerned about regulatory issues related to the proposed transaction, reflecting our view of the potential combination's market power. However, we believe NYX is taking the right steps to position itself for what we view as a globally competitive exchange environment, including initiatives such as its move to UTP-Direct, a universal trading platform, and block trading in the U.S. and Europe.

➤ Risks to our recommendation and target price include execution risk related to growth initiatives, lower-than-expected trading volumes, an economic slowdown, and the merger with Deutsche Boerse not being completed.

➤ Our 12-month target price of $39 represents 0.47X our 12-month target price of $84 (EUR61) for Deutsche Boerse (Buy EUR41), reflecting terms of the proposed merger. NYX and Deutsche Boerse are in discussions with the European Union Competition Commission about the Commission's concerns regarding the planned merger.

### Qualitative Risk Assessment

| LOW | MEDIUM | HIGH |
|---|---|---|

Our risk assessment reflects the potential volatility in results due to changes in equity and equity options trading volumes, the impact of current and future regulatory changes, and the integration of a number of recent acquisitions.

### Quantitative Evaluations

**S&P Quality Ranking** NR

| D | C | B- | B | B+ | A- | A | A+ |
|---|---|---|---|---|---|---|---|

**Relative Strength Rank** MODERATE

55

LOWEST = 1    HIGHEST = 99

### Revenue/Earnings Data

**Revenue (Million $)**

| | 1Q | 2Q | 3Q | 4Q | Year |
|---|---|---|---|---|---|
| 2011 | 1,059 | 661.0 | 1,149 | -- | -- |
| 2010 | 1,020 | 1,148 | 973.0 | 969.0 | 4,110 |
| 2009 | 1,112 | 1,125 | 1,048 | 1,014 | 4,299 |
| 2008 | 1,191 | 1,112 | 1,159 | 1,177 | 4,474 |
| 2007 | 702.0 | 1,078 | 1,198 | 1,180 | 4,158 |
| 2006 | 478.9 | 659.5 | 602.9 | 658.5 | 2,376 |

**Earnings Per Share ($)**

| | | | | | |
|---|---|---|---|---|---|
| 2011 | 0.59 | 0.59 | 0.76 | E0.61 | E2.61 |
| 2010 | 0.50 | 0.71 | 0.49 | 0.51 | 2.20 |
| 2009 | 0.40 | -0.70 | 0.48 | 0.66 | 0.84 |
| 2008 | 0.87 | 0.73 | 0.64 | -5.08 | -2.81 |
| 2007 | 0.43 | 0.62 | 0.97 | 0.59 | 2.70 |
| 2006 | 0.24 | 0.39 | 0.43 | 0.29 | 1.36 |

Fiscal year ended Dec. 31. Next earnings report expected: NA. EPS Estimates based on S&P Operating Earnings; historical GAAP earnings are as reported.

### Dividend Data (Dates: mm/dd Payment Date: mm/dd/yy)

| Amount ($) | Date Decl. | Ex-Div. Date | Stk. of Record | Payment Date |
|---|---|---|---|---|
| 0.300 | 02/08 | 03/14 | 03/16 | 03/31/11 |
| 0.300 | 04/28 | 06/14 | 06/16 | 06/30/11 |
| 0.300 | 08/02 | 09/13 | 09/15 | 09/30/11 |
| 0.300 | 11/03 | 12/13 | 12/15 | 12/30/11 |

Dividends have been paid since 2007. Source: Company reports.

---

**Please read the Required Disclosures and Analyst Certification on the last page of this report.**

The McGraw-Hill Companies

# NYSE Euronext

## Business Summary November 08, 2011

**CORPORATE OVERVIEW.** NYSE Euronext (NYX) is a holding company created by the combination of NYSE Group and Euronext on April 4, 2007. NYX operates the world's largest and most liquid exchange group and offers a diverse array of financial products and services. The company, which brings together six cash equities exchanges in five countries and six derivatives exchanges in six countries, offers listings, trading in cash equities, equity and interest rate derivatives, bonds and the distribution of market data.

NYX generates revenue primarily from transactions and clearing fees, market data company listing fees, technology services, and other. The company also records activity assessment revenue, which is a pass through netted against section 31 fee expense. Following the combination of the NYSE with Archipelago (now NYSE Arca), transaction and clearing fees have become the largest revenue driver for NYX (71% of total revenue in 2010). Transaction revenue is generated from fees paid for trading on NYX's exchanges, and benefits from higher trading volumes. Listing fees (10%) include initial fees charged for companies listing on one of NYX's exchanges and an ongoing annual listing fee. Market data is NYX's third largest revenue contributor (8%)

and includes real time information related to price, transaction or order data of all instruments traded on the cash and derivatives markets on NYX's exchanges. The technology services business (7%) provides transaction, data and infrastructure products and services to internal and external customers. The remaining revenue (4%) represent other minimal items.

**CORPORATE STRATEGY.** We believe NYX is in the middle of a transformational phase as it fully integrates the NYSE Arca assets with the NYSE, transitions the NYSE from a floor-based trading system to a hybrid floor/electronic model, completes its merger with Euronext, and readies for significant regulatory and structural changes in U.S. and European equity and equity options trading. We expect the number and scope of ongoing projects and regulatory changes to likely make for uneven financial performance and difficult historical and peer comparisons over the coming quarters.

## Company Financials Fiscal Year Ended Dec. 31

| Per Share Data ($) | 2010 | 2009 | 2008 | 2007 | 2006 | 2005 | 2004 | 2003 | 2002 | 2001 |
|---|---|---|---|---|---|---|---|---|---|---|
| Tangible Book Value | NM | NM | NM | NM | 3.51 | NA | NA | NA | NA | NA |
| Cash Flow | 3.00 | 1.99 | -1.86 | 3.76 | 2.27 | 1.50 | NA | NA | NA | NA |
| Earnings | 2.20 | 0.84 | -2.81 | 2.70 | 1.36 | 0.58 | NA | NA | NA | NA |
| S&P Core Earnings | 2.04 | 0.83 | 0.92 | 2.55 | 1.28 | 0.35 | 0.31 | NA | NA | NA |
| Dividends | 1.20 | 1.20 | 1.15 | 0.75 | Nil | NA | NA | NA | NA | NA |
| Payout Ratio | 55% | 143% | NM | 28% | Nil | NA | NA | NA | NA | NA |
| Prices:High | 34.82 | 31.93 | 87.70 | 109.50 | 112.00 | NA | NA | NA | NA | NA |
| Prices:Low | 22.30 | 14.52 | 16.33 | 64.26 | 48.62 | NA | NA | NA | NA | NA |
| P/E Ratio:High | 16 | 38 | NM | 41 | 82 | NA | NA | NA | NA | NA |
| P/E Ratio:Low | 10 | 17 | NM | 24 | 36 | NA | NA | NA | NA | NA |

| Income Statement Analysis (Million $) | 2010 | 2009 | 2008 | 2007 | 2006 | 2005 | 2004 | 2003 | 2002 | 2001 |
|---|---|---|---|---|---|---|---|---|---|---|
| Revenue | 4,110 | 4,299 | 4,474 | 4,158 | 2,376 | 1,667 | 1,044 | 1,034 | 1,018 | 1,035 |
| Operating Income | 1,125 | 1,104 | 1,403 | 1,228 | 424 | 3.18 | 130 | 115 | 56.6 | 53.3 |
| Depreciation | 228 | 301 | 253 | 252 | 136 | 143 | 95.7 | 67.6 | 61.9 | 60.6 |
| Interest Expense | 108 | 122 | 150 | 129 | Nil | Nil | NA | NA | NA | NA |
| Pretax Income | 686 | 205 | -645 | 921 | 328 | 176 | NA | 87.3 | 42.1 | 52.8 |
| Effective Tax Rate | NA | NM | NM | 27.5% | 36.7% | 47.6% | NA | 41.7% | 27.8% | 33.6% |
| Net Income | 558 | 219 | -745 | 643 | 205 | 90.0 | NA | 49.6 | 28.1 | 31.8 |
| S&P Core Earnings | 536 | 215 | 244 | 609 | 193 | 54.1 | 42.3 | NA | NA | NA |

| Balance Sheet & Other Financial Data (Million $) | 2010 | 2009 | 2008 | 2007 | 2006 | 2005 | 2004 | 2003 | 2002 | 2001 |
|---|---|---|---|---|---|---|---|---|---|---|
| Cash | 379 | 490 | 1,013 | 973 | 298 | 328 | 930 | 880 | 963 | 963 |
| Current Assets | 1,135 | 1,520 | 2,026 | 2,278 | 1,443 | 1,204 | 1,245 | 1,223 | 1,156 | 1,168 |
| Total Assets | 13,299 | 14,358 | 13,948 | 16,618 | 3,466 | 3,154 | NA | 1,777 | 1,757 | 1,730 |
| Current Liabilities | 1,375 | 2,149 | 2,582 | 3,462 | 832 | 823 | 487 | 416 | 340 | 390 |
| Long Term Debt | 2,074 | 2,166 | 1,787 | 522 | Nil | Nil | NA | NA | NA | NA |
| Common Equity | 6,844 | 6,935 | 6,556 | 9,384 | 1,669 | 1,366 | NA | 952 | 896 | 882 |
| Total Capital | 8,918 | 9,101 | 8,770 | 12,469 | 1,934 | 1,646 | 801 | 983 | 921 | 910 |
| Capital Expenditures | 305 | 497 | 376 | 182 | 97.8 | NA | 84.6 | 68.5 | 113 | 89.0 |
| Cash Flow | 786 | 520 | -492 | 895 | 341 | 233 | 126 | 117 | 89.9 | 92.4 |
| Current Ratio | 0.8 | 0.7 | 0.8 | 0.7 | 1.7 | 1.5 | 2.6 | 2.9 | 3.4 | 3.0 |
| % Long Term Debt of Capitalization | 23.3 | 23.8 | 21.4 | 4.2 | Nil | Nil | Nil | Nil | Nil | Nil |
| % Net Income of Revenue | 13.6 | 5.1 | NM | 15.5 | 8.6 | 5.4 | 2.9 | 4.8 | 2.8 | 3.1 |
| % Return on Assets | 4.0 | 1.6 | NM | 6.4 | 7.2 | NA | 1.6 | 2.8 | 1.6 | NA |
| % Return on Equity | 8.1 | 3.3 | NM | 11.6 | 16.6 | NA | 3.5 | 5.4 | 3.2 | NA |

Data as orig reptd.; bef. results of disc opers/spec. items. Per share data adj. for stk. divs.; EPS diluted. E-Estimated. NA-Not Available. NM-Not Meaningful. NR-Not Ranked. UR-Under Review.

**Office:** 11 Wall Street, New York, NY 10005.
**Telephone:** 212-656-3000.
**Website:** http://www.nyse.com
**Chrmn:** J.M. Hessels

**Pres & CTO:** D. Cerutti
**Vice Chrmn:** M.N. Carter
**CEO:** D.L. Niederauer
**COO:** L. Leibowitz

**Investor Contact:** S.C. Davidson (212-656-2183)
**Board Members:** A. Bergen, E. L. Brown, M. N. Carter, D. Cerutti, P. M. Cloherty, G. Cox, S. M. Hefes, J. M. Hessels, D. M. McFarland, J. J. McNulty, D. L. Niederauer, R. G. Scott, R. E. Silva Salgado, J. P. Tai, R. W. Van Tets, B. Williamson

**Founded:** 2006
**Domicile:** Delaware
**Employees:** 2,968

# Occidental Petroleum Corp

STANDARD
&POOR'S

**S&P Recommendation** HOLD ★ ★ ★ ☆ ☆

| Price | 12-Mo. Target Price | Investment Style |
|---|---|---|
| $98.90 (as of Nov 30, 2011) | $105.00 | Large-Cap Blend |

**GICS Sector** Energy
**Sub-Industry** Integrated Oil & Gas

**Summary** One of the largest oil and gas companies in the U.S., OXY has global exploration and production operations. Its subsidiary, OxyChem, is one of the largest U.S. merchant marketers of chlorine and caustic soda.

## Key Stock Statistics (Source S&P, Vickers, company reports)

| | | | | | | | | |
|---|---|---|---|---|---|---|---|---|
| 52-Wk Range | $117.89– 66.36 | S&P Oper. EPS 2011**E** | 8.20 | Market Capitalization(B) | $80.286 | Beta | | 1.06 |
| Trailing 12-Month EPS | $7.80 | S&P Oper. EPS 2012**E** | 8.05 | Yield (%) | 1.86 | S&P 3-Yr. Proj. EPS CAGR(%) | | 29 |
| Trailing 12-Month P/E | 12.7 | P/E on S&P Oper. EPS 2011**E** | 12.1 | Dividend Rate/Share | $1.84 | S&P Credit Rating | | A |
| $10K Invested 5 Yrs Ago | $21,499 | Common Shares Outstg. (M) | 811.8 | Institutional Ownership (%) | 82 | | | |

## Price Performance

30-Week Mov. Avg. · · · 10-Week Mov. Avg. - - GAAP Earnings vs. Previous Year    Volume Above Avg. STARS
12-Mo. Target Price — Relative Strength — ▲ Up ▼ Down ► No Change    Below Avg. ★

Options: ASE, CBOE, P, Ph

Analysis prepared by Equity Analyst **Michael Kay** on Nov 30, 2011, when the stock traded at **$92.19**.

## Highlights

▶ After 14% production growth in 2010, the impact of higher oil prices on production-sharing contracts and suspended Libyan operations has led to disappointing production in 2011 and lower guidance. We see 4% growth in 2011, accelerating in 2012, on a rampup in Permian and Bakken drilling, a resolution to California permitting issues, new gas processing in California, and higher volumes from Oman, Iraq and Bahrain. De-risking efforts in California have added drilling locations, and OXY sees potential at the play of 8 billion BOE. OXY is running 68 rigs, 30 in California and 20 in the Permian, and plans to exit 2011 with 73 rigs, with additional rigs added to Permian.

▶ OXY's 2011 capex budget is $7 billion, reflecting faster California (21% of capex) well permitting and entry into the Shah project in Abu Dhabi. About 32% of capex is slated for the MENA region. Under this plan, up from $3.9 billion in 2010, we see strong 2012 free cash flow and possible dividend growth.

▶ We see 2011 EPS of $8.20, up 57% on oil prices and better chemicals, and $8.05 in 2012, on more modest price assumptions.

## Investment Rationale/Risk

▶ With its oil focus and no refining, a pipeline of development projects, and strong balance sheet, we expect OXY to benefit from higher production and oil prices. We expect growth to be driven by strong prospects in long-lived reserves in California (limited royalties), the Permian Basin, and the Bakken Shale, with potential contributions from international developments in Bahrain, Oman, Libya and Iraq. We project U.S. production growth of about 11% per annum between 2010 and 2014, and international growth of 4% over the same period, and OXY sees 5%-8% total production growth per annum. We think liquid projects will drive growth, and we see OXY financing projects away from U.S. gas through at least 2012.

▶ Risks to our recommendation and target price include negative changes in economic, industry and operating conditions, including geopolitical risk and difficulty replacing reserves.

▶ On DCF ($107: WACC 9%, terminal growth 3%) and relative metrics, including an EV multiple of 5.5X our 2012 EBITDA forecast, a premium to integrated oils but in line with standalone E&P peers, our 12-month target price is $105.

## Qualitative Risk Assessment

| LOW | MEDIUM | HIGH |
|---|---|---|

Our risk assessment reflects our view of OXY's strong business profile, its modest financial risk profile, its large, geographically diverse reserve base, and substantial liquidity. This is offset by its participation in a volatile, competitive and capital-intensive business.

## Quantitative Evaluations

**S&P Quality Ranking**    A-

| D | C | B- | B | B+ | A- | A | A+ |
|---|---|---|---|---|---|---|---|

**Relative Strength Rank**    **STRONG**

93

LOWEST = 1    HIGHEST = 99

## Revenue/Earnings Data

**Revenue (Million $)**

| | 1Q | 2Q | 3Q | 4Q | Year |
|---|---|---|---|---|---|
| 2011 | 5,726 | 6,208 | 6,006 | -- | -- |
| 2010 | 4,616 | 4,603 | 4,763 | 5,063 | 19,157 |
| 2009 | 3,073 | 3,687 | 4,104 | 4,539 | 15,403 |
| 2008 | 6,020 | 7,116 | 7,060 | 4,021 | 24,217 |
| 2007 | 4,015 | 4,411 | 4,841 | 5,517 | 18,784 |
| 2006 | 4,396 | 4,599 | 4,522 | 4,144 | 17,661 |

**Earnings Per Share ($)**

| | | | | | |
|---|---|---|---|---|---|
| 2011 | 1.72 | 2.23 | 2.18 | E1.83 | E8.20 |
| 2010 | 1.35 | 1.32 | 1.48 | 1.47 | 5.61 |
| 2009 | 0.45 | 0.84 | 1.14 | 1.16 | 3.59 |
| 2008 | 2.20 | 2.79 | 2.78 | 0.55 | 8.33 |
| 2007 | 1.38 | 1.36 | 1.57 | 1.74 | 6.05 |
| 2006 | 1.34 | 1.39 | 1.35 | 1.08 | 5.15 |

Fiscal year ended Dec. 31. Next earnings report expected: NA. EPS Estimates based on S&P Operating Earnings; historical GAAP earnings are as reported.

## Dividend Data (Dates: mm/dd Payment Date: mm/dd/yy)

| Amount ($) | Date Decl. | Ex-Div. Date | Stk. of Record | Payment Date |
|---|---|---|---|---|
| 0.460 | 02/10 | 03/08 | 03/10 | 04/15/11 |
| 0.460 | 05/05 | 06/08 | 06/10 | 07/15/11 |
| 0.460 | 07/14 | 09/07 | 09/09 | 10/15/11 |
| 0.460 | 10/13 | 12/07 | 12/09 | 01/15/12 |

Dividends have been paid since 1975. Source: Company reports.

---

**Please read the Required Disclosures and Analyst Certification on the last page of this report.**

The McGraw-Hill Companies

# Occidental Petroleum Corp

STANDARD
&POOR'S

## Business Summary November 30, 2011

CORPORATE OVERVIEW. One of the largest oil and gas companies in the U.S., Occidental Petroleum Corp. (OXY) engages in oil and gas exploration and production in three main regions: the U.S. (64% of 2010 net sales), the Middle East/North Africa (28%), and Latin America (7%). OxyChem, a wholly owned subsidiary, manufactures and markets chlor-alkali products and vinyls, and is one of the largest merchant marketers of chlorine and caustic soda in the U.S.

OXY's businesses operate in three segments: Oil and Gas (75% of 2010 net sales; 89% of 2010 earnings), Chemicals (21%; 5%), and Midstream, Marketing and Other (8%; 6%).

The Oil and Gas segment explores for, develops, produces and markets crude oil and natural gas. Oil and gas sales volumes rose 5%, to 748,000 boe per day (65% liquids, 51% U.S., 38% Middle East/North Africa, 5% Latin America, 6% discontinued), in 2010, compared with 712,000 boe/d in 2009. Volume increases in the Middle East/North Africa, resulting from new production in Bahrain and higher production in the Mukhaizna field in Oman, and gas production from domestic assets, were partially offset by a decline in Colombia. Production was hurt in the Middle East/North Africa, California and Colombia by higher year-over-year average oil prices affecting production-sharing and similar

contracts by 16,000 boe/d.

Proved oil and gas reserves rose 4.1% in 2010, to 3.36 billion boe (77% developed, 74% liquids). Using data from John S. Herold, an industry research firm, we estimate OXY's three-year (2007-09) proved acquisition costs at $8.32 per boe, above the peer average; three-year finding and development costs at $20.40 per boe, above peers; three-year reserve replacement costs at $15.46, above peers; and three-year reserve replacement at 159%, above the peer average. We estimate OXY's 2010 overall reserve replacement at 150%.

OxyChem manufactures and markets basic chemicals, vinyls, and performance chemicals, focused on the chlorovinyls chain beginning with chlorine. As of year-end 2010, the company owned and operated chemical plants at 22 domestic sites in the U.S., and at three international sites in Brazil, Canada and Chile. In 2009, OxyChem acquired Dow Chemical Co.'s calcium chloride operations, the world's largest.

## Company Financials Fiscal Year Ended Dec. 31

| Per Share Data ($) | 2010 | 2009 | 2008 | 2007 | 2006 | 2005 | 2004 | 2003 | 2002 | 2001 |
|---|---|---|---|---|---|---|---|---|---|---|
| Tangible Book Value | 39.97 | 35.82 | 33.69 | 27.63 | 22.84 | 18.69 | 13.30 | 10.25 | 8.35 | 7.53 |
| Cash Flow | 9.49 | 7.43 | 12.31 | 8.86 | 7.71 | 8.26 | 4.93 | 3.56 | 2.87 | 2.88 |
| Earnings | 5.61 | 3.59 | 8.33 | 6.05 | 5.15 | 6.45 | 3.25 | 2.06 | 1.54 | 1.59 |
| S&P Core Earnings | 5.65 | 3.63 | 8.28 | 5.19 | 4.97 | 5.78 | 3.26 | 2.03 | 1.28 | 1.70 |
| Dividends | 1.47 | 1.31 | 1.21 | 0.94 | NA | 0.65 | 0.41 | 0.52 | 0.50 | 0.50 |
| Payout Ratio | 26% | 36% | 15% | 16% | NA | 10% | 13% | 25% | 33% | 32% |
| Prices:High | 99.57 | 85.20 | 100.04 | 79.25 | NA | 44.90 | 30.38 | 21.49 | 15.38 | 15.55 |
| Prices:Low | 72.13 | 47.50 | 39.93 | 42.06 | NA | 27.09 | 20.98 | 13.59 | 11.49 | 10.94 |
| P/E Ratio:High | 18 | 24 | 12 | 13 | NA | 7 | 9 | 10 | 10 | 10 |
| P/E Ratio:Low | 13 | 13 | 5 | 7 | NA | 4 | 6 | 7 | 7 | 7 |

| Income Statement Analysis (Million $) | 2010 | 2009 | 2008 | 2007 | 2006 | 2005 | 2004 | 2003 | 2002 | 2001 |
|---|---|---|---|---|---|---|---|---|---|---|
| Revenue | 19,045 | 15,403 | 24,217 | 18,784 | 17,661 | 15,208 | 11,368 | 9,326 | 7,338 | 13,985 |
| Operating Income | NA | NA | 14,652 | 10,044 | 9,664 | 7,860 | 5,573 | 4,281 | 3,119 | 3,638 |
| Depreciation, Depletion and Amortization | 3,153 | 3,117 | 3,267 | 2,356 | 2,042 | 1,485 | 1,303 | 1,177 | 1,012 | 971 |
| Interest Expense | 93.0 | 109 | 26.0 | 396 | 291 | 293 | 260 | 332 | 295 | 392 |
| Pretax Income | 7,564 | 4,845 | 11,468 | 8,660 | 8,012 | 7,365 | 4,389 | 2,884 | 1,662 | 1,892 |
| Effective Tax Rate | NA | 39.6% | 40.4% | 40.5% | 43.3% | 27.4% | 38.9% | 42.5% | 25.4% | 29.8% |
| Net Income | 4,569 | 2,927 | 6,839 | 5,078 | 4,435 | 5,272 | 2,606 | 1,595 | 1,163 | 1,186 |
| S&P Core Earnings | 4,596 | 2,954 | 6,803 | 4,360 | 4,280 | 4,729 | 2,607 | 1,568 | 963 | 1,273 |

| Balance Sheet & Other Financial Data (Million $) | 2010 | 2009 | 2008 | 2007 | 2006 | 2005 | 2004 | 2003 | 2002 | 2001 |
|---|---|---|---|---|---|---|---|---|---|---|
| Cash | 2,578 | 1,230 | 1,777 | 1,964 | 1,339 | 2,189 | 1,449 | 683 | 146 | 199 |
| Current Assets | 13,059 | 8,086 | 7,172 | 8,595 | 6,006 | 6,574 | 4,431 | 2,474 | 1,873 | 1,483 |
| Total Assets | 52,432 | 44,229 | 41,537 | 36,519 | 32,355 | 26,108 | 21,391 | 18,168 | 16,548 | 17,850 |
| Current Liabilities | 7,825 | 6,092 | 6,134 | 6,266 | 4,724 | 4,280 | 3,423 | 2,526 | 2,235 | 1,890 |
| Long Term Debt | 5,111 | 2,557 | 2,073 | 1,742 | 2,619 | 2,873 | 3,345 | 3,993 | 4,452 | 4,528 |
| Common Equity | 32,484 | 29,081 | 27,300 | 22,823 | 19,184 | 15,032 | 10,550 | 7,929 | 6,318 | 5,634 |
| Total Capital | 37,595 | 31,955 | 32,058 | 26,923 | 24,470 | 19,207 | 15,470 | 13,235 | 12,085 | 13,489 |
| Capital Expenditures | 3,940 | 5,363 | 9,365 | 3,497 | 3,005 | 2,423 | 1,843 | 1,601 | 1,236 | 1,401 |
| Cash Flow | 7,722 | 6,044 | 10,106 | 7,434 | 6,477 | 6,757 | 3,909 | 2,772 | 2,175 | 2,157 |
| Current Ratio | 1.7 | 1.3 | 1.2 | 1.4 | 1.3 | 1.5 | 1.3 | 1.0 | 0.8 | 0.8 |
| % Long Term Debt of Capitalization | 13.6 | Nil | 6.5 | 6.5 | 10.7 | 15.0 | 21.6 | 30.2 | 36.8 | 33.6 |
| % Return on Assets | NA | 6.8 | 17.5 | 14.7 | 15.2 | 22.2 | 13.2 | 9.2 | 6.8 | 6.4 |
| % Return on Equity | NA | NA | 27.3 | 24.2 | 25.9 | 41.2 | 28.2 | 22.4 | 19.5 | 22.8 |

Data as orig reptd.; bef. results of disc opers/spec. items. Per share data adj. for stk. divs.; EPS diluted. E-Estimated. NA-Not Available. NM-Not Meaningful. NR-Not Ranked. UR-Under Review.

Office: 10889 Wilshire Boulevard, Los Angeles, CA 90024-4201.
Telephone: 310-208-8800.
Email: investorrelations_newyork@oxy.com
Website: http://www.oxy.com

Chrmn: R.R. Irani
Pres & CEO: S.I. Chazen
EVP, Secy & General Counsel: D.P. de Brier
CFO: J.M. Lienert

Chief Acctg Officer & Cntlr: R. Pineci
Investor Contact: C.G. Stavros (212-603-8184)
Investor Contact: C.M. Degner (212-603-8185)
Board Members: S. Abraham, H. I. Atkins, S. I. Chazen, E. P. Djerejian, J. E. Feick, M. M. Foran, C. M. Gutierrez, R. R. Irani, A. B. Poladian, R. Segovia, A. R. Syriani, R. Tomich, W. L. Weisman

Founded: 1920
Domicile: Delaware
Employees: 11,000

The McGraw-Hill Companies

# Omnicom Group Inc.

STANDARD &POOR'S

| S&P Recommendation | BUY ★★★★☆ | Price | 12-Mo. Target Price | Investment Style |
|---|---|---|---|---|
| | | $40.02 (as of Nov 25, 2011) | $48.00 | Large-Cap Growth |

**GICS Sector** Consumer Discretionary
**Sub-Industry** Advertising

**Summary** This company owns the DDB Worldwide, BBDO Worldwide and TBWA Worldwide advertising agency networks; and more than 100 marketing and specialty services firms.

## Key Stock Statistics (Source S&P, Vickers, company reports)

| | | | | | | | |
|---|---|---|---|---|---|---|---|
| 52-Wk Range | $51.25–35.27 | S&P Oper. EPS 2011**E** | 3.28 | Market Capitalization(B) | $11.040 | Beta | 1.17 |
| Trailing 12-Month EPS | $3.20 | S&P Oper. EPS 2012**E** | 3.65 | Yield (%) | 2.50 | S&P 3-Yr. Proj. EPS CAGR(%) | 11 |
| Trailing 12-Month P/E | 12.5 | P/E on S&P Oper. EPS 2011**E** | 12.2 | Dividend Rate/Share | $1.00 | S&P Credit Rating | BBB+ |
| $10K Invested 5 Yrs Ago | $8,473 | Common Shares Outstg. (M) | 275.9 | Institutional Ownership (%) | 93 | | |

## Price Performance

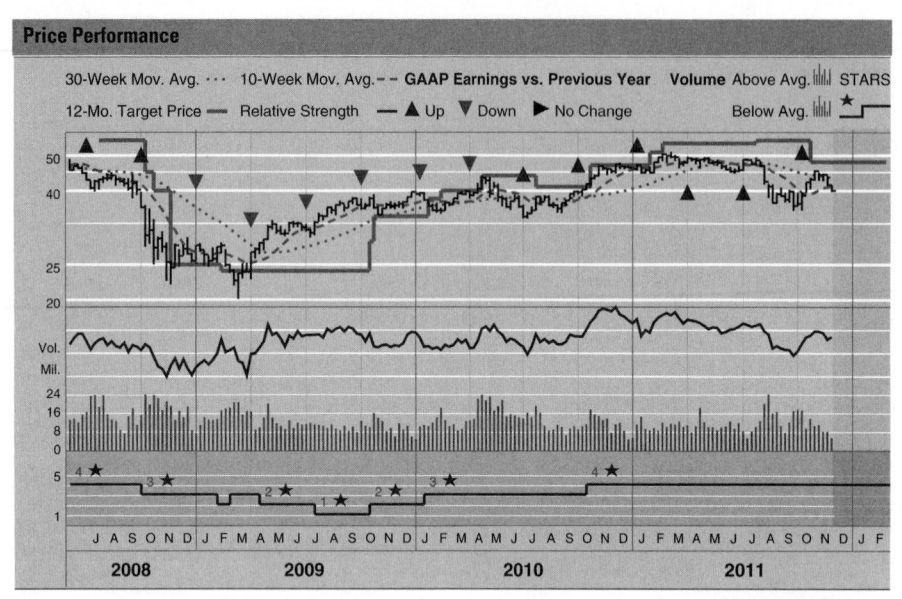

30-Week Mov. Avg. ··· · 10-Week Mov. Avg. – – GAAP Earnings vs. Previous Year   Volume Above Avg. STARS
12-Mo. Target Price — Relative Strength   ▲ Up ▼ Down ► No Change   Below Avg.

Options: ASE, CBOE, P, Ph

Analysis prepared by Equity Analyst **Joseph Agnese** on Oct 21, 2011, when the stock traded at **$42.19**.

## Qualitative Risk Assessment

| LOW | MEDIUM | HIGH |
|---|---|---|

Our risk assessment reflects OMC's diversified geographic and product revenue sources coupled with its position as the world's largest advertising agency by revenue, and our view of its strong track record of EPS and free cash flow growth, partly offset by a highly competitive advertising industry.

## Quantitative Evaluations

**S&P Quality Ranking**   A+

| D | C | B- | B | B+ | A- | A | A+ |
|---|---|---|---|---|---|---|---|

**Relative Strength Rank**   MODERATE

56

LOWEST = 1   HIGHEST = 99

## Revenue/Earnings Data

**Revenue (Million $)**

| | 1Q | 2Q | 3Q | 4Q | Year |
|---|---|---|---|---|---|
| 2011 | 3,151 | 3,487 | 3,381 | -- | -- |
| 2010 | 2,920 | 3,041 | 2,995 | 3,587 | 12,543 |
| 2009 | 2,747 | 2,871 | 2,838 | 3,266 | 11,721 |
| 2008 | 3,195 | 3,477 | 3,316 | 3,371 | 13,360 |
| 2007 | 2,841 | 3,126 | 3,101 | 3,626 | 12,694 |
| 2006 | 2,563 | 2,823 | 2,774 | 3,216 | 11,377 |

**Earnings Per Share ($)**

| | | | | | |
|---|---|---|---|---|---|
| 2011 | 0.69 | 0.96 | 0.72 | E0.99 | E3.28 |
| 2010 | 0.52 | 0.79 | 0.57 | 0.83 | 2.70 |
| 2009 | 0.53 | 0.75 | 0.53 | 0.73 | 2.53 |
| 2008 | 0.65 | 0.96 | 0.69 | 0.88 | 3.17 |
| 2007 | 0.55 | 0.84 | 0.62 | 0.96 | 2.95 |
| 2006 | 0.47 | 0.71 | 0.52 | 0.81 | 2.50 |

Fiscal year ended Dec. 31. Next earnings report expected: Mid February. EPS Estimates based on S&P Operating Earnings; historical GAAP earnings are as reported.

## Highlights

➤ We expect organic revenue growth trends to remain positive through 2011 before stabilizing in 2012, as growth of 7.2% in the third quarter of 2011 was in line with our expectations. We see the U.S. and UK markets continuing to experience positive organic revenue trends driven by new business wins and easing comparisons. However, European market visibility remains poor despite experiencing an improving trend through the first half of 2011.

➤ Business spending continued to increase through the first nine months of 2011 from the lows reached during recessionary levels in 2008 and 2009. In addition to benefits we see from increased client spending in 2011 and in 2012, we believe an increased ability to support new technologies will lead to new client wins. We estimate foreign currency exchange rates will contribute a 3.0% benefit to overall sales growth in 2011 and negatively impact 2012 sales by 1.5%. Overall, we project a revenue increase of 11% in 2011 slowing to 7.2% in 2012 on more difficult comparisons.

➤ For 2012, we see operating EPS of $3.65, up 11% from our estimate of $3.28 (excluding $0.07 in one-time items) in 2011.

## Investment Rationale/Risk

➤ We believe the shares will benefit from easing comparisons, new business wins and increased capabilities in 2011 and 2012. Our valuation incorporates our view that the global economic recovery will continue slowly through 2012. We look for international and U.S. organic sales to continue to be the main driver of growth, with European growth positive but lagging the U.S. Due to OMC's efforts to cut costs, we expect significant margin expansion to be generated as more stable revenue growth returns in 2011.

➤ Risks to our recommendation and target price include weaker-than-expected global GDP, an unexpected loss of a significant number of clients, and a tightening of credit markets.

➤ We derive our 12-month target price of $48 by applying an EV/EBITDA multiple of 7.0X to our 2012 EBITDA estimate of $2.11 billion. This multiple is slightly below the company's 10-year historical average and below peers' 10-year average multiple of 8.5X, which we believe is appropriate given a still-elevated level of risk we see in the global economic environment and our expectation for long term growth to moderate.

## Dividend Data (Dates: mm/dd Payment Date: mm/dd/yy)

| Amount ($) | Date Decl. | Ex-Div. Date | Stk. of Record | Payment Date |
|---|---|---|---|---|
| 0.200 | 12/10 | 12/20 | 12/22 | 01/10/11 |
| 0.250 | 02/15 | 03/02 | 03/04 | 04/01/11 |
| 0.250 | 05/24 | 06/10 | 06/14 | 07/11/11 |
| 0.250 | 07/21 | 09/21 | 09/23 | 10/07/11 |

Dividends have been paid since 1986. Source: Company reports.

# Omnicom Group Inc.

STANDARD
&POOR'S

## Business Summary October 21, 2011

CORPORATE OVERVIEW. Omnicom Group, a global advertising and marketing services company, is one of the world's largest corporate communications companies. OMC is comprised of more than 1,500 subsidiary agencies, operating in over 100 countries. It operates as three independent global agency networks: the BBDO Worldwide Network, the DDB Worldwide Network, and the TBWA Worldwide Network. Each agency network has its own clients, and the networks compete with each other in the same markets.

OMC's companies provide an extensive range of services, which it groups into four disciplines: traditional media advertising (45.3% of 2010 revenues), customer relationship management (36.3%), public relations (9.1%), and specialty communications (9.3%). In 2010, the company's 100 largest clients accounted for approximately 50.6% of consolidated revenue. The largest client accounted for about 3.0% of 2010 revenues; no other single client accounted for more than 2.5% of revenues. Operations cover the major regions of North America, the U.K., Europe, the Middle East, Africa, Latin America, the Far East and Australia. In 2010, 53.3% of revenues were derived from the U.S., 19.6% from euro-denominated markets, 8.7% from the U.K., and 18.4% from other international markets.

The services in these categories include but are not limited to: advertising, brand consultancy, crisis communications, database management, digital and interactive marketing, direct marketing, directory advertising, experiential marketing, field marketing, health care communications, in-store design, investor relations, marketing research, media planning and buying, organizational communications, product placement, promotional marketing, public relations, recruitment communications, reputation consulting, retail marketing, and sports and event marketing.

In our opinion, the breadth, depth and diversity of OMC's business reduces exposure to any single industry, and to an economic reversal in any world region. It also provides the company with significant opportunities to benefit from growth in non-advertising services, such as public relations and event marketing, expenditures for which are growing faster than those for traditional advertising.

## Company Financials Fiscal Year Ended Dec. 31

| Per Share Data ($) | 2010 | 2009 | 2008 | 2007 | 2006 | 2005 | 2004 | 2003 | 2002 | 2001 |
|---|---|---|---|---|---|---|---|---|---|---|
| Tangible Book Value | NM | NM | NM | NM | NM | NM | NM | NM | NM | NM |
| Cash Flow | 3.88 | 3.34 | 3.75 | 3.45 | 3.13 | 2.71 | 2.40 | 2.10 | 2.03 | 1.88 |
| Earnings | 2.70 | 2.53 | 3.17 | 2.95 | 2.50 | 2.18 | 1.94 | 1.80 | 1.72 | 1.35 |
| S&P Core Earnings | 2.65 | 2.57 | 3.17 | 2.95 | 2.50 | 2.18 | 1.92 | 1.69 | 1.56 | 1.24 |
| Dividends | 0.80 | 0.60 | 0.60 | 0.50 | 0.50 | 0.46 | 0.45 | 0.40 | 0.40 | 0.39 |
| Payout Ratio | 30% | 24% | 19% | 17% | 20% | 21% | 23% | 22% | 23% | 29% |
| Prices:High | 47.88 | 39.99 | 50.16 | 55.45 | 53.03 | 45.74 | 44.41 | 43.80 | 48.68 | 49.10 |
| Prices:Low | 33.50 | 20.09 | 22.02 | 45.82 | 39.38 | 37.88 | 33.22 | 23.25 | 18.25 | 29.55 |
| P/E Ratio:High | 18 | 16 | 16 | 19 | 21 | 21 | 23 | 24 | 28 | 36 |
| P/E Ratio:Low | 12 | 8 | 7 | 16 | 16 | 17 | 17 | 13 | 11 | 22 |

| Income Statement Analysis (Million $) | | | | | | | | | | |
|---|---|---|---|---|---|---|---|---|---|---|
| Revenue | 12,543 | 11,721 | 13,360 | 12,694 | 11,377 | 10,481 | 9,747 | 8,621 | 7,536 | 6,889 |
| Operating Income | 1,708 | 1,669 | 1,872 | 1,823 | 1,674 | 1,515 | 1,388 | 1,289 | 1,224 | 1,179 |
| Depreciation | 253 | 243 | 183 | 164 | 190 | 175 | 172 | 124 | 120 | 211 |
| Interest Expense | 110 | 122 | 125 | 107 | 125 | 78.0 | 51.1 | 57.9 | 45.5 | 72.8 |
| Pretax Income | 1,384 | 1,305 | 1,657 | 1,624 | 1,422 | 1,308 | 1,196 | 1,137 | 1,087 | 908 |
| Effective Tax Rate | NA | 33.2% | 32.8% | 33.1% | 32.8% | 33.3% | 33.1% | 33.5% | 34.5% | 38.8% |
| Net Income | 924 | 793 | 1,000 | 976 | 864 | 791 | 724 | 676 | 643 | 503 |
| S&P Core Earnings | 807 | 796 | 1,000 | 976 | 866 | 790 | 715 | 631 | 584 | 456 |

| Balance Sheet & Other Financial Data (Million $) | | | | | | | | | | |
|---|---|---|---|---|---|---|---|---|---|---|
| Cash | 2,300 | 1,595 | 1,112 | 1,841 | 1,740 | 836 | 1,166 | 1,529 | 667 | 472 |
| Current Assets | 10,194 | 8,789 | 8,565 | 10,504 | 9,647 | 7,967 | 8,095 | 7,286 | 5,637 | 5,234 |
| Total Assets | 19,566 | 17,921 | 17,318 | 19,272 | 18,164 | 15,920 | 16,002 | 14,499 | 11,820 | 10,617 |
| Current Liabilities | 11,023 | 10,083 | 9,754 | 11,227 | 10,296 | 8,700 | 8,744 | 7,762 | 6,840 | 6,644 |
| Long Term Debt | 3,149 | 2,221 | 3,054 | 3,055 | 3,055 | 2,357 | 2,358 | 2,537 | 1,945 | 1,340 |
| Common Equity | 3,581 | 4,195 | 3,523 | 4,092 | 3,871 | 3,948 | 4,079 | 3,466 | 2,569 | 2,178 |
| Total Capital | 7,758 | 6,906 | 6,810 | 7,563 | 7,562 | 6,921 | 6,949 | 6,394 | 4,687 | 3,677 |
| Capital Expenditures | 154 | 131 | 212 | 223 | 178 | 163 | 160 | 141 | 117 | 149 |
| Cash Flow | 1,177 | 1,036 | 1,183 | 1,140 | 1,054 | 966 | 896 | 800 | 763 | 714 |
| Current Ratio | 0.9 | 0.9 | 0.9 | 0.9 | 0.9 | 0.9 | 0.9 | 0.9 | 0.8 | 0.8 |
| % Long Term Debt of Capitalization | 40.6 | Nil | 42.9 | 40.4 | 40.4 | 34.1 | 33.9 | 39.7 | 41.5 | 36.4 |
| % Net Income of Revenue | 7.4 | 6.8 | 7.5 | 7.7 | 7.6 | 7.5 | 7.4 | 7.8 | 8.5 | 7.3 |
| % Return on Assets | NA | NA | 5.5 | 5.2 | 5.1 | 5.0 | 4.7 | 5.1 | 5.7 | 4.9 |
| % Return on Equity | NA | NA | 26.3 | 24.5 | 22.1 | 19.7 | 18.8 | 22.4 | 27.1 | 27.0 |

Data as orig reptd.; bef. results of disc opers/spec. items. Per share data adj. for stk. divs.; EPS diluted. E-Estimated. NA-Not Available. NM-Not Meaningful. NR-Not Ranked. UR-Under Review.

**Office:** 437 Madison Ave Bsmt, New York, NY 10022-7000.
**Telephone:** 212-415-3600.
**Email:** IR@OmnicomGroup.com
**Website:** http://www.omnicomgroup.com

**Chrmn:** B.A. Crawford
**Pres & CEO:** J. Wren
**Vice Chrmn:** S. Dumont
**Vice Chrmn:** W.T. Love

**Investor Contact:** R.J. Weisenburger
**Board Members:** A. R. Batkin, M. C. Choksi, R. C. Clark, L. S. Coleman, Jr., E. M. Cook, B. A. Crawford, S. Denison, S. Dumont, M. A. Henning, W. T. Love, J. R. Murphy, J. R. Purcell, L. J. Rice, G. L. Roubos, J. Wren

**Founded:** 1944
**Domicile:** New York
**Employees:** 65,500

The McGraw-Hill Companies

# ONEOK Inc.

STANDARD
&POOR'S

| S&P Recommendation BUY ★★★★☆ | Price<br>$77.73 (as of Nov 25, 2011) | 12-Mo. Target Price<br>$83.00 | Investment Style<br>Large-Cap Value |
|---|---|---|---|

**GICS Sector** Utilities
**Sub-Industry** Gas Utilities

**Summary** This Oklahoma-based integrated natural gas company also has an energy marketing and trading business.

## Key Stock Statistics (Source S&P, Vickers, company reports)

| | | | | | |
|---|---|---|---|---|---|
| 52-Wk Range | $80.39–50.39 | S&P Oper. EPS 2011E | 3.30 | Market Capitalization(B) | $8.005 | Beta | 1.08 |
| Trailing 12-Month EPS | $3.04 | S&P Oper. EPS 2012E | 3.75 | Yield (%) | 2.88 | S&P 3-Yr. Proj. EPS CAGR(%) | 11 |
| Trailing 12-Month P/E | 25.6 | P/E on S&P Oper. EPS 2011E | 23.6 | Dividend Rate/Share | $2.24 | S&P Credit Rating | BBB |
| $10K Invested 5 Yrs Ago | $22,397 | Common Shares Outstg. (M) | 103.0 | Institutional Ownership (%) | 73 | | |

## Price Performance

30-Week Mov. Avg. · · · 10-Week Mov. Avg. – – **GAAP Earnings vs. Previous Year** Volume Above Avg. STARS
12-Mo. Target Price — Relative Strength ▲ Up ▼ Down ▶ No Change Below Avg.

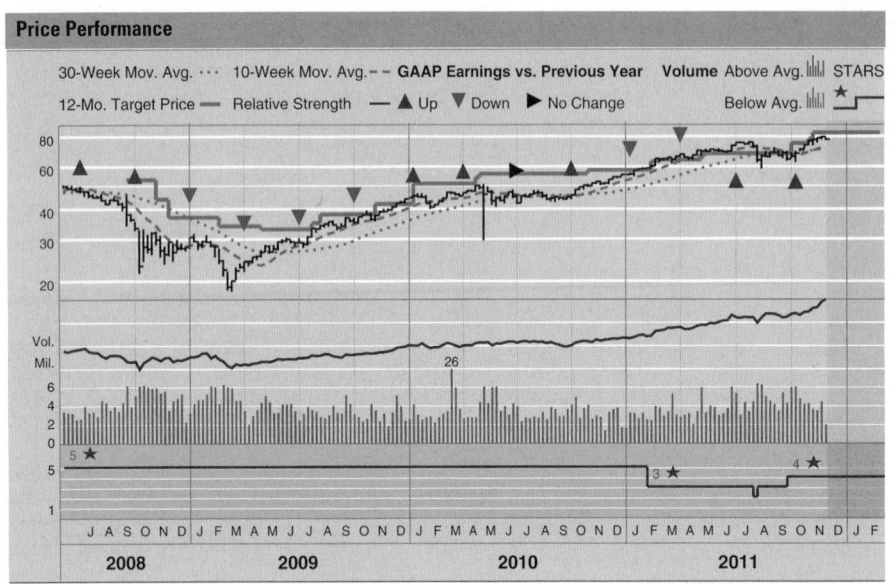

Options: CBOE, Ph

## Qualitative Risk Assessment

| LOW | MEDIUM | HIGH |
|---|---|---|

Our risk assessment reflects our view of steady cash flow from the company's regulated utility and pipeline operations, offset by unregulated trading and gathering and processing operations.

## Quantitative Evaluations

**S&P Quality Ranking** A-

| D | C | B- | B | B+ | A- | A | A+ |
|---|---|---|---|---|---|---|---|

**Relative Strength Rank** STRONG

94

LOWEST = 1 HIGHEST = 99

## Revenue/Earnings Data

**Revenue (Million $)**

| | 1Q | 2Q | 3Q | 4Q | Year |
|---|---|---|---|---|---|
| 2011 | 3,867 | 3,514 | 3,595 | -- | -- |
| 2010 | 3,924 | 2,807 | 2,943 | 3,356 | 13,030 |
| 2009 | 2,790 | 2,228 | 2,365 | 3,729 | 11,112 |
| 2008 | 4,902 | 4,173 | 4,239 | 2,843 | 16,157 |
| 2007 | 3,806 | 2,876 | 2,810 | 3,985 | 13,477 |
| 2006 | 3,756 | 2,432 | 2,641 | 3,068 | 11,896 |

**Earnings Per Share ($)**

| | | | | | |
|---|---|---|---|---|---|
| 2011 | 1.19 | 0.51 | 0.57 | E1.02 | E3.30 |
| 2010 | 1.44 | 0.39 | 0.51 | 0.76 | 3.10 |
| 2009 | 1.16 | 0.39 | 0.45 | 0.87 | 2.87 |
| 2008 | 1.36 | 0.40 | 0.55 | 0.65 | 2.95 |
| 2007 | 1.36 | 0.31 | 0.13 | 0.98 | 2.79 |
| 2006 | 1.17 | 0.65 | 0.21 | 0.66 | 2.68 |

Fiscal year ended Dec. 31. Next earnings report expected: NA. EPS Estimates based on S&P Operating Earnings; historical GAAP earnings are as reported.

## Highlights

➤ The 12-month target price for OKE has recently been changed to $83.00 from $78.00. The Highlights section of this Stock Report will be updated accordingly.

## Investment Rationale/Risk

➤ The Investment Rationale/Risk section of this Stock Report will be updated shortly. For the latest News story on OKE from MarketScope, see below.

➤ 11/02/11 09:41 am ET ... S&P MAINTAINS BUY OPINION ON SHARES OF ONEOK INC. (OKE 75.66****): Q3 recurring EPS of $0.57, vs. $0.42, beats our $0.50 estimate and the $0.56 Capital IQ consensus forecast. Revenues were higher and per-revenue operations & maintenance expenses and depreciation charges were lower than we expected, but were partly offset by per-revenue cost of gas that was higher. We expect the gas transportation segment to continue driving earnings growth with several growth projects in the works. We are raising our '11 EPS projection $0.16 to $3.30, 12's by $0.07 to 3.75 and initiating '13's at 4.05. We are boosting our target price by $5 to $83. /CBMuir

## Dividend Data (Dates: mm/dd Payment Date: mm/dd/yy)

| Amount ($) | Date Decl. | Ex-Div. Date | Stk. of Record | Payment Date |
|---|---|---|---|---|
| 0.520 | 01/19 | 01/27 | 01/31 | 02/14/11 |
| 0.520 | 04/19 | 04/27 | 04/29 | 05/13/11 |
| 0.560 | 07/20 | 07/28 | 08/01 | 08/12/11 |
| 0.560 | 10/26 | 11/03 | 11/07 | 11/14/11 |

Dividends have been paid since 1939. Source: Company reports.

# ONEOK Inc.

STANDARD
&POOR'S

## Business Summary October 24, 2011

CORPORATE OVERVIEW. ONEOK is an integrated energy company engaged in gas marketing and trading, transportation and storage, gathering and processing, natural gas liquids and gas utility distribution. The distribution segment is the largest gas utility in Kansas and Oklahoma and the third largest in Texas.

PRIMARY BUSINESS DYNAMICS. OKE derives earnings from geographically diverse operations in various segments of the energy and utility sectors. Utility operations include the Distribution segment (24% of total 2010 operating income, or $226 million). Non-utility reporting segments include Energy Services (14%, $131 million) and ONEOK Partners, L.P. (OKS) (62%, $586 million).

The Distribution segment serves nearly 2.1 million natural gas utility customers in Oklahoma, Kansas and Texas. We think the regulatory environment appears productive in all the states in which the company operates. In June 2009, Oklahoma Natural Gas (ONG) filed for a base rate increase of $66.1 million, which includes existing riders that would effectively reduce the requested rate increase to a net amount of $37.6 million. In December 2009, the company received approval to raise rates by $25.7 million including riders. Performance-based rates and a more streamlined regulatory process were approved in May 2009.

In November 2006, Kansas Gas Service (KGS) received approval for a settlement that included a $52.0 million increase. Since then, KGS has received an authorization to recover costs related to system reliability, including a $3.4 million increase authorized in December 2009 and a $1.7 million increase in December 2010.

Texas Gas Service (TGS) files rate cases with individual municipalities in Texas and has received approvals for rate increases totaling $14.8 million since the beginning of 2006. In February 2009, TGS filed for a $3.6 million rate increase in central Texas. In June 2009, regulators approved a $1.1 million rate increase. In August 2009, the cities of the Rio Grande Valley service area approved an increase in base rates of $1.3 million. In December 2009, TGS submitted its intent to file for a $7.3 million rate increase in El Paso. In April 2010, El Paso rejected the increase and OKE appealed. Regulators granted a $0.8 million increase in annual rates and a reduction of depreciation of $0.8 million.

## Company Financials Fiscal Year Ended Dec. 31

| Per Share Data ($) | 2010 | 2009 | 2008 | 2007 | 2006 | 2005 | 2004 | 2003 | 2002 | 2001 |
|---|---|---|---|---|---|---|---|---|---|---|
| Tangible Book Value | 13.35 | 11.11 | 10.01 | 8.90 | 10.52 | 11.38 | 13.26 | 10.67 | 20.60 | 19.19 |
| Earnings | 3.10 | 2.87 | 2.95 | 2.79 | 2.68 | 3.73 | 2.30 | 2.13 | 1.30 | 0.85 |
| S&P Core Earnings | 3.15 | 2.97 | 2.66 | 2.89 | 2.07 | 2.11 | 2.19 | 2.12 | 1.08 | 0.45 |
| Dividends | 1.82 | 1.64 | 1.56 | 1.40 | 1.22 | 1.09 | 0.88 | 0.69 | 0.62 | 0.62 |
| Payout Ratio | 59% | 57% | 53% | 50% | 46% | 29% | 38% | 32% | 48% | 73% |
| Prices:High | 56.09 | 44.97 | 51.33 | 55.27 | 44.48 | 35.85 | 28.99 | 22.44 | 23.14 | 24.34 |
| Prices:Low | 29.56 | 18.10 | 21.56 | 39.26 | 26.35 | 26.30 | 19.69 | 16.00 | 14.62 | 14.17 |
| P/E Ratio:High | 18 | 16 | 17 | 20 | 17 | 10 | 13 | 11 | 18 | 29 |
| P/E Ratio:Low | 10 | 6 | 7 | 14 | 10 | 7 | 9 | 8 | 11 | 17 |

| Income Statement Analysis (Million $) | 2010 | 2009 | 2008 | 2007 | 2006 | 2005 | 2004 | 2003 | 2002 | 2001 |
|---|---|---|---|---|---|---|---|---|---|---|
| Revenue | 13,030 | 11,112 | 16,157 | 13,477 | 11,896 | 12,676 | 5,988 | 2,999 | 2,104 | 6,803 |
| Depreciation | 307 | 289 | 244 | 228 | 236 | 183 | 189 | 161 | 148 | 157 |
| Maintenance | NA | NA | NA | NA | NA | NA | NA | NA | NA | NA |
| Fixed Charges Coverage | 3.17 | 3.06 | 3.61 | 3.31 | 3.53 | 7.16 | 4.79 | 3.50 | 2.54 | 1.67 |
| Construction Credits | NA | NA | NA | NA | NA | NA | NA | NA | NA | NA |
| Effective Tax Rate | 28.3% | 29.7% | 24.4% | 27.0% | 26.8% | 37.6% | 38.2% | 37.9% | 39.7% | 33.3% |
| Net Income | 335 | 305 | 312 | 305 | 307 | 403 | 242 | 214 | 156 | 104 |
| S&P Core Earnings | 340 | 316 | 281 | 315 | 237 | 229 | 231 | 181 | 71.8 | 8.23 |

| Balance Sheet & Other Financial Data (Million $) | 2010 | 2009 | 2008 | 2007 | 2006 | 2005 | 2004 | 2003 | 2002 | 2001 |
|---|---|---|---|---|---|---|---|---|---|---|
| Gross Property | 9,854 | 10,146 | 9,477 | 7,893 | 6,725 | 5,575 | 5,406 | 5,180 | 4,216 | 4,508 |
| Capital Expenditures | 583 | 791 | 1,473 | 884 | 376 | 250 | 264 | 215 | 0.21 | 342 |
| Net Property | 7,313 | 7,794 | 7,264 | 5,845 | 4,845 | 3,994 | 3,787 | 3,692 | 3,015 | 3,273 |
| Capitalization:Long Term Debt | 3,687 | 4,334 | 4,113 | 4,215 | 4,031 | 2,024 | 1,543 | 1,979 | 1,620 | 1,620 |
| Capitalization:% Long Term Debt | 60.1 | 66.3 | 66.3 | 68.2 | 64.5 | 53.0 | 49.0 | 61.4 | 54.3 | 56.1 |
| Capitalization:Preferred | Nil | Nil | Nil | Nil | Nil | Nil | Nil | Nil | 0.20 | Nil |
| Capitalization:% Preferred | Nil | Nil | Nil | Nil | Nil | Nil | Nil | Nil | 0.01 | Nil |
| Capitalization:Common | 2,449 | 2,207 | 2,088 | 1,969 | 2,216 | 1,795 | 1,606 | 1,241 | 1,365 | 1,266 |
| Capitalization:% Common | 39.9 | 33.7 | 33.7 | 31.8 | 35.5 | 47.0 | 51.0 | 38.6 | 45.7 | 43.9 |
| Total Capital | 8,251 | 8,048 | 8,171 | 7,667 | 7,755 | 4,423 | 3,793 | 3,635 | 3,461 | 3,385 |
| % Operating Ratio | 94.5 | 93.9 | 95.5 | 95.3 | 95.4 | 97.7 | 94.3 | 89.5 | 87.2 | 96.4 |
| % Earned on Net Property | 12.3 | 11.8 | 14.0 | 15.4 | 24.0 | 19.7 | 13.1 | 13.3 | 12.3 | 9.3 |
| % Return on Revenue | 2.6 | 2.8 | 1.9 | 2.3 | 2.6 | 3.2 | 4.0 | 7.1 | 7.4 | 1.5 |
| % Return on Invested Capital | 8.8 | 9.3 | 9.6 | 8.6 | 13.0 | 14.0 | 9.6 | 9.1 | 7.7 | 7.5 |
| % Return on Common Equity | 14.4 | 14.2 | 15.4 | 14.6 | 15.3 | 23.7 | 17.0 | 14.6 | 9.0 | 5.4 |

Data as orig reptd.; bef. results of disc opers/spec. items. Per share data adj. for stk. divs.; EPS diluted. E-Estimated. NA-Not Available. NM-Not Meaningful. NR-Not Ranked. UR-Under Review.

**Office:** 100 West Fifth Street, Tulsa, OK 74103.
**Telephone:** 918-588-7000.
**Website:** http://www.oneok.com
**Chrmn, Pres & CEO:** J.W. Gibson

**COO:** P.H. Norton, II
**SVP & Chief Acctg Officer:** D.S. Reiners
**CFO & Treas:** R.F. Martinovich
**Chief Admin Officer:** D.E. Roth

**Investor Contact:** D. Harrison (918-588-7950)
**Board Members:** J. C. Day, J. H. Edwards, W. L. Ford, J. W. Gibson, B. H. Mackie, J. W. Mogg, P. L. Moore, G. D. Parker, E. Rodriguez, G. B. Smith, D. J. Tippeconnic

**Founded:** 1906
**Domicile:** Oklahoma
**Employees:** 4,839

The McGraw-Hill Companies

# Oracle Corp

**STANDARD & POOR'S**

| S&P Recommendation | STRONG BUY ★★★★★ | Price | 12-Mo. Target Price | Investment Style |
|---|---|---|---|---|
| | | $28.74 (as of Nov 25, 2011) | $40.00 | Large-Cap Growth |

**GICS Sector** Information Technology
**Sub-Industry** Systems Software

**Summary** This leading supplier of enterprise database management systems and business applications added hardware with the January 2010 acquisition of Sun Microsystems.

## Key Stock Statistics (Source S&P, Vickers, company reports)

| | | | | | | | |
|---|---|---|---|---|---|---|---|
| 52-Wk Range | $36.50– 24.72 | S&P Oper. EPS 2012**E** | 2.35 | Market Capitalization(B) | $144.982 | Beta | 1.09 |
| Trailing 12-Month EPS | $1.76 | S&P Oper. EPS 2013**E** | 2.60 | Yield (%) | 0.84 | S&P 3-Yr. Proj. EPS CAGR(%) | 15 |
| Trailing 12-Month P/E | 16.3 | P/E on S&P Oper. EPS 2012**E** | 12.2 | Dividend Rate/Share | $0.24 | S&P Credit Rating | A |
| $10K Invested 5 Yrs Ago | $14,997 | Common Shares Outstg. (M) | 5,044.6 | Institutional Ownership (%) | 67 | | |

## Price Performance

- 30-Week Mov. Avg. ····
- 10-Week Mov. Avg. -- -
- GAAP Earnings vs. Previous Year
- Volume Above Avg. ▮▮▮ STARS
- 12-Mo. Target Price —
- Relative Strength —
- ▲ Up ▼ Down ▶ No Change
- Below Avg. ▮▮▮

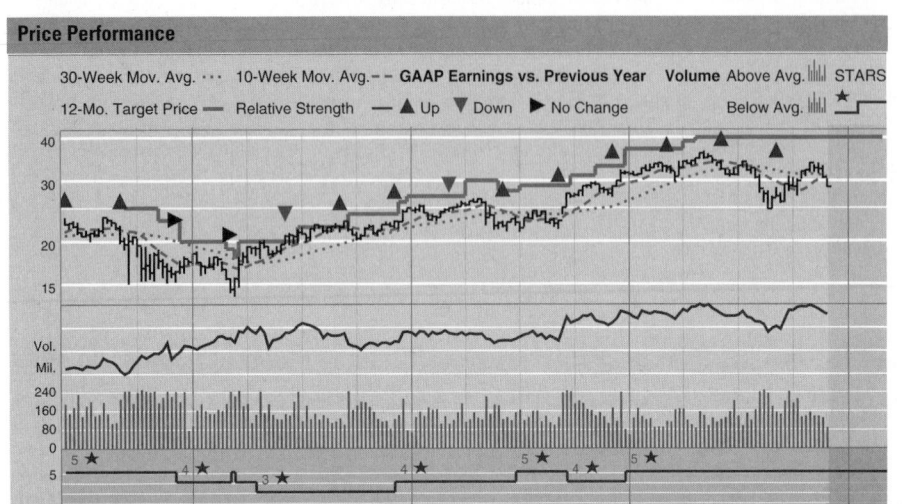

Options: ASE, CBOE, P, Ph

Analysis prepared by Equity Analyst **Zaineb Bokhari** on Sep 23, 2011, when the stock traded at **$28.11**.

## Highlights

➤ We expect non-GAAP sales to rise 9.5% in FY 12 (May), to $39 billion. We think ORCL is well positioned due to its product breadth. We see growth in new software licenses of 13% for FY 12, reflecting ongoing strength in databases and middleware, and healthy applications growth amid an uncertain global economic environment. We look for 11% growth for software license updates and support, which we consider to be more stable than licenses. In FY 13, we see sales rising 7%, to $42 billion.

➤ In view of ORCL's past success in integrating acquisitions and strong progress in integrating Sun Microsystems thus far, we expect the company to achieve targeted synergies in its hardware business. In FY 11, non-GAAP operating margins narrowed to 44%, from 46% in FY 10, reflecting a full year's impact of Sun, stepped-up R&D investment, and variable compensation rising with sales. We see higher margins in FY 12 and FY 13 as ORCL emphasizes its wide margin hardware systems.

➤ We estimate non-GAAP EPS of $2.35 in FY 12 and $2.60 in FY 13, excluding amortization and other items.

## Investment Rationale/Risk

➤ The Sun acquisition transformed ORCL into a software and systems vendor. While this is not without risk, we see earnings accretion as ORCL streamlines Sun's supply chain and refines its sales approach. For customers, we see benefits in the form of integrated and optimized hardware and software offerings and lower implementation risk. Execution remains key, in our view, but we give ORCL the benefit of the doubt based on its acquisition track record. We think successes with the company's Exa-line of hardware systems point to long-term success with an integrated offering.

➤ Risks to our recommendation and target price include acquisition integration risk, pricing pressure, and adverse currency movement.

➤ We blend relative and intrinsic valuation metrics to derive our 12-month target price of $40. For our DCF model, we assume a WACC of 7.9% over a five-year horizon, rising to 9.3% in the subsequent five years, and 3% terminal growth, which yields a value of $45. We apply a 13.8X multiple, a little higher than the average over the past eight years or so, to our FY 13 EPS estimate, resulting in a value of $36.

## Qualitative Risk Assessment

| LOW | MEDIUM | HIGH |
|---|---|---|

Our risk assessment reflects acquisition integration risks following a series of large deals over the past few years. This is offset by our favorable view of ORCL's balance sheet, free cash flow, and talent and depth of management.

## Quantitative Evaluations

**S&P Quality Ranking**          A-

| D | C | B- | B | B+ | A- | A | A+ |
|---|---|---|---|---|---|---|---|

**Relative Strength Rank**          MODERATE

46

LOWEST = 1          HIGHEST = 99

## Revenue/Earnings Data

**Revenue (Million $)**

| | 1Q | 2Q | 3Q | 4Q | Year |
|---|---|---|---|---|---|
| 2012 | 8,374 | -- | -- | -- | -- |
| 2011 | 7,502 | 8,582 | 8,764 | 10,775 | 35,622 |
| 2010 | 5,054 | 5,858 | 6,404 | 9,505 | 26,820 |
| 2009 | 5,331 | 5,607 | 5,453 | 6,861 | 23,252 |
| 2008 | 4,529 | 5,313 | 5,349 | 7,239 | 22,430 |
| 2007 | 3,591 | 4,163 | 4,414 | 5,828 | 17,996 |

**Earnings Per Share ($)**

| | 1Q | 2Q | 3Q | 4Q | Year |
|---|---|---|---|---|---|
| 2012 | 0.36 | E0.55 | E0.57 | E0.77 | E2.35 |
| 2011 | 0.27 | 0.37 | 0.41 | 0.62 | 1.67 |
| 2010 | 0.22 | 0.29 | 0.23 | 0.46 | 1.21 |
| 2009 | 0.21 | 0.25 | 0.26 | 0.38 | 1.09 |
| 2008 | 0.16 | 0.26 | 0.26 | 0.39 | 1.06 |
| 2007 | 0.13 | 0.18 | 0.20 | 0.31 | 0.81 |

Fiscal year ended May 31. Next earnings report expected: NA. EPS Estimates based on S&P Operating Earnings; historical GAAP earnings are as reported.

## Dividend Data (Dates: mm/dd Payment Date: mm/dd/yy)

| Amount ($) | Date Decl. | Ex-Div. Date | Stk. of Record | Payment Date |
|---|---|---|---|---|
| 0.060 | 03/24 | 04/11 | 04/13 | 05/04/11 |
| 0.050 | 03/24 | 04/11 | 04/13 | 05/04/11 |
| 0.060 | 06/23 | 07/11 | 07/13 | 08/03/11 |
| 0.060 | 09/20 | 10/07 | 10/12 | 11/02/11 |

Dividends have been paid since 2009. Source: Company reports.

# Oracle Corp

## Business Summary September 23, 2011

CORPORATE OVERVIEW. Oracle Corp., a leading provider of enterprise software, added hardware to its product portfolio via the acquisition of Sun Microsystems in January 2010. The company's major businesses are database and middleware software (46% of non-GAAP revenues in FY 11 (May)), application software (21%), hardware (20%), and services (13%).

MARKET PROFILE. Enterprises scaled back spending on information technology in 2009, exercising caution as the global economy began to stabilize. There was a spending recovery in 2010, particularly at the end of the year with a budget flush reported by several vendors, which saw growth in demand for license and professional services and improving maintenance attach and renewal rates. We believe growth in 2011 and 2012 will be consistent with economic conditions.

While we think the economic climate has improved from the depths of the

economic crisis seen in late 2008/early 2009, we think the specter of increased regulation and economic weakness in certain markets, coupled with weak job growth, will keep buyers cautious. We see this accruing to the benefit of technology vendors that provide solutions that support and maintain mission critical systems, including database and storage-related technology assets. While growth in applications is tied more closely to an economic recovery, we see a recovery in spending after a period of under-investment. We think cloud computing in its various iterations will see above-average growth. We still expect visibility on large deals to be limited, and we think software vendors face intense competition and pricing pressure as they close deals.

## Company Financials Fiscal Year Ended May 31

| Per Share Data ($) | 2011 | 2010 | 2009 | 2008 | 2007 | 2006 | 2005 | 2004 | 2003 | 2002 |
|---|---|---|---|---|---|---|---|---|---|---|
| Tangible Book Value | 2.04 | 0.29 | NM | NM | NM | 0.13 | 0.09 | 1.55 | 1.21 | 1.13 |
| Cash Flow | 2.21 | 1.66 | 1.48 | 1.34 | 1.03 | 0.79 | 0.63 | 0.55 | 0.49 | 0.45 |
| Earnings | 1.67 | 1.21 | 1.09 | 1.06 | 0.81 | 0.64 | 0.55 | 0.50 | 0.43 | 0.39 |
| S&P Core Earnings | 1.65 | 1.21 | 1.09 | 1.05 | 0.80 | 0.62 | 0.52 | 0.46 | 0.37 | 0.34 |
| Dividends | 0.21 | 0.20 | 0.05 | Nil | Nil | Nil | Nil | Nil | Nil | Nil |
| Payout Ratio | 13% | 12% | 5% | Nil | Nil | Nil | Nil | Nil | Nil | Nil |
| Calendar Year | 2010 | 2009 | 2008 | 2007 | 2006 | 2005 | 2004 | 2003 | 2002 | 2001 |
| Prices:High | 32.27 | 25.11 | 23.62 | 23.31 | 19.75 | 14.51 | 15.51 | 14.03 | 17.50 | 35.00 |
| Prices:Low | 21.24 | 13.80 | 15.00 | 15.97 | 12.06 | 11.25 | 9.78 | 10.64 | 7.25 | 10.16 |
| P/E Ratio:High | 19 | 21 | 22 | 22 | 24 | 23 | 28 | 28 | 41 | 90 |
| P/E Ratio:Low | 13 | 11 | 14 | 15 | 15 | 18 | 18 | 21 | 17 | 26 |
| **Income Statement Analysis** (Million $) | | | | | | | | | | |
| Revenue | 35,622 | 26,820 | 23,252 | 22,430 | 17,996 | 14,380 | 11,799 | 10,156 | 9,475 | 9,673 |
| Operating Income | 15,524 | 12,109 | 10,531 | 9,489 | 726 | 5,764 | 4,802 | 4,098 | 3,767 | 3,934 |
| Depreciation | 2,796 | 2,271 | 1,976 | 1,480 | 1,127 | 806 | 425 | 234 | 327 | 363 |
| Interest Expense | 808 | 754 | 630 | 24.0 | 343 | 169 | 135 | 21.0 | 16.0 | 20.0 |
| Pretax Income | 11,411 | 8,243 | 7,834 | 7,834 | 5,986 | 4,810 | 4,051 | 3,945 | 3,425 | 3,408 |
| Effective Tax Rate | NA | NA | 28.6% | 29.5% | 28.6% | 29.7% | 28.8% | 32.0% | 32.6% | 34.7% |
| Net Income | 8,547 | 6,135 | 5,593 | 5,521 | 4,274 | 3,381 | 2,886 | 2,681 | 2,307 | 2,224 |
| S&P Core Earnings | 8,469 | 6,135 | 5,593 | 5,481 | 4,224 | 3,237 | 2,750 | 2,459 | 2,049 | 1,923 |
| **Balance Sheet & Other Financial Data** (Million $) | | | | | | | | | | |
| Cash | 28,848 | 18,469 | 12,624 | 11,043 | 7,020 | 7,605 | 4,802 | 4,138 | 4,737 | 3,095 |
| Current Assets | 39,174 | 27,004 | 18,581 | 18,103 | 12,883 | 11,974 | 8,479 | 11,336 | 9,227 | 8,728 |
| Total Assets | 73,535 | 61,578 | 47,416 | 47,268 | 34,572 | 29,029 | 20,687 | 12,763 | 11,064 | 10,800 |
| Current Liabilities | 14,192 | 14,691 | 9,149 | 10,029 | 9,387 | 6,930 | 8,063 | 4,272 | 4,158 | 3,960 |
| Long Term Debt | 14,772 | 11,510 | 9,237 | 10,234 | 6,235 | 5,735 | 159 | 163 | 175 | 298 |
| Common Equity | 40,245 | 31,199 | 25,090 | 23,025 | 16,919 | 15,012 | 10,837 | 7,995 | 6,320 | 6,117 |
| Total Capital | 56,167 | 45,854 | 35,682 | 34,628 | 24,275 | 21,311 | 12,006 | 8,217 | 6,681 | 6,619 |
| Capital Expenditures | 450 | 230 | 529 | 243 | 319 | 236 | 188 | 189 | 291 | 278 |
| Cash Flow | 11,343 | 8,406 | 7,569 | 7,001 | 5,401 | 4,187 | 3,311 | 2,915 | 2,634 | 2,587 |
| Current Ratio | 2.8 | 1.8 | 2.0 | 1.8 | 1.4 | 1.7 | 1.1 | 2.7 | 2.2 | 2.2 |
| % Long Term Debt of Capitalization | 26.3 | 25.1 | 25.9 | 29.7 | 25.7 | 26.9 | 1.3 | 2.0 | 2.6 | 4.5 |
| % Net Income of Revenue | 24.0 | 22.9 | 24.1 | 24.6 | 22.7 | 23.5 | 24.4 | 26.4 | 24.3 | 23.0 |
| % Return on Assets | 12.7 | 11.3 | 11.8 | 13.5 | 13.4 | 13.6 | 17.3 | 22.6 | 21.1 | 20.4 |
| % Return on Equity | 24.1 | 21.8 | 23.3 | 27.6 | 26.8 | 26.2 | 30.7 | 37.5 | 37.1 | 35.9 |

Data as orig reptd.; bef. results of disc opers/spec. items. Per share data adj. for stk. divs.; EPS diluted. E-Estimated. NA-Not Available. NM-Not Meaningful. NR-Not Ranked. UR-Under Review.

**Office:** 500 Oracle Parkway, Redwood City, CA 94065.
**Telephone:** 650-506-7000.
**Email:** investor_us@oracle.com
**Website:** http://www.oracle.com

**Chrmn:** J.O. Henley
**CEO:** L.J. Ellison
**SVP, Secy & General Counsel:** D. Daley
**SVP & CIO:** M.E. Sunday

**CFO & Co-Pres:** S.A. Catz
**Investor Contact:** K. Bond (650-607-0349)
**Board Members:** J. S. Berg, H. R. Bingham, M. J. Boskin, S. A. Catz, B. R. Chizen, G. H. Conrades, L. J. Ellison, H. Garcia-Molina, J. O. Henley, M. V. Hurd, D. L. Lucas, N. O. Seligman

**Founded:** 1977
**Domicile:** Delaware
**Employees:** 108,000

# O'Reilly Automotive Inc

**STANDARD &POOR'S**

| S&P Recommendation | HOLD ★★★☆☆ | Price | 12-Mo. Target Price | Investment Style |
|---|---|---|---|---|
| | | $75.51 (as of Nov 25, 2011) | $80.00 | Large-Cap Growth |

**GICS Sector** Consumer Discretionary
**Sub-Industry** Automotive Retail

**Summary** This company is one of the largest U.S. retailers of car parts and accessories.

## Key Stock Statistics (Source S&P, Vickers, company reports)

| | | | | | | | |
|---|---|---|---|---|---|---|---|
| 52-Wk Range | $78.99–53.33 | S&P Oper. EPS 2011**E** | 3.72 | Market Capitalization(B) | $9.690 | Beta | 0.36 |
| Trailing 12-Month EPS | $3.47 | S&P Oper. EPS 2012**E** | 4.30 | Yield (%) | Nil | S&P 3-Yr. Proj. EPS CAGR(%) | 15 |
| Trailing 12-Month P/E | 21.8 | P/E on S&P Oper. EPS 2011**E** | 20.3 | Dividend Rate/Share | Nil | S&P Credit Rating | NR |
| $10K Invested 5 Yrs Ago | $23,198 | Common Shares Outstg. (M) | 128.3 | Institutional Ownership (%) | 99 | | |

## Price Performance

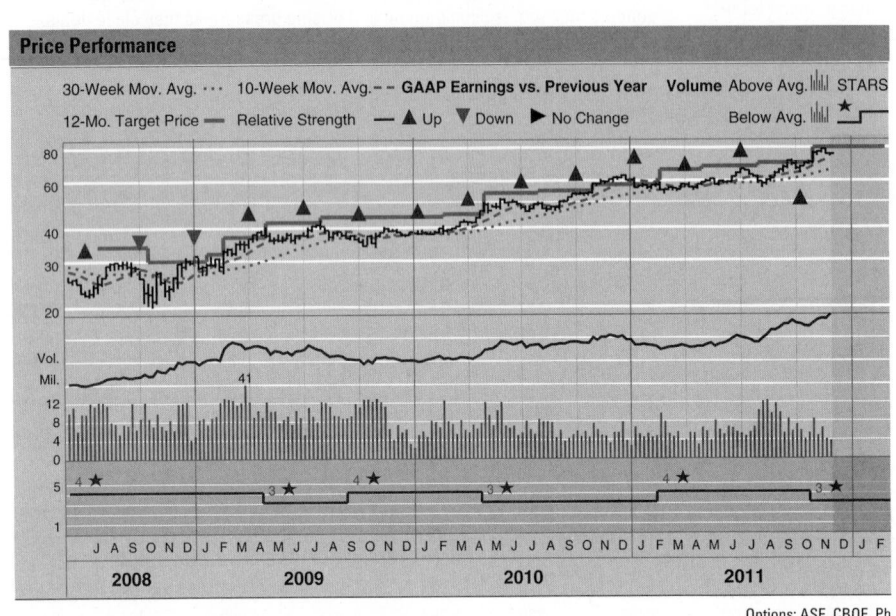

30-Week Mov. Avg. · · ·   10-Week Mov. Avg. – –   GAAP Earnings vs. Previous Year   Volume Above Avg. STARS
12-Mo. Target Price —   Relative Strength —   ▲ Up   ▼ Down   ▶ No Change   Below Avg.

Options: ASE, CBOE, Ph

Analysis prepared by Equity Analyst **Michael Souers** on Nov 09, 2011, when the stock traded at **$77.74**.

## Highlights

➤ We look for sales to increase 7.0% in 2012, following our projection of a 7.7% rise in 2011. We expect 2012 sales to be bolstered by the opening of about 170 net new stores and a 4% same-store sales increase. This forecast follows our projection of a 5.0% same-store sales rise in 2011. We believe challenging macro conditions will lead consumers to defer vehicle maintenance when possible, but that industry tailwinds such as the increasing age of vehicles and a recent uptick in miles driven should support continued growth.

➤ We think operating margins will widen modestly in 2012, as the continued conversion of CSK Auto stores should drive additional cost synergies. Also, we see continued efficiency improvements from current distribution centers and increased buying power with vendors. Lastly, we expect strong comp-store growth to modestly leverage SG&A expenses.

➤ After slightly higher interest expense and taxes at 38.5%, we see 2012 EPS of $4.30. This represents a 16% increase from the $3.72 we expect the company to earn in 2011, excluding an $0.11 charge related to debt issuance costs.

## Investment Rationale/Risk

➤ We expect ORLY to outpace the industry in terms of square footage, sales and EPS growth over the next few years, and we like its dual sales strategy focused on commercial as well as retail customers. In addition, we think strong recent execution bodes well for continued market share gains in a fragmented industry. We also favor the company's 2008 acquisition of CSK Auto, and expect continued revenue and cost benefits to accrue over the medium term. However, following a greater than 35% increase in price over the past four months, we think the shares are fairly valued at about 18X our 2012 EPS estimate, a modest premium to slower-growing peers.

➤ Risks to our recommendation and target price include an increase in new car sales and a decline in miles driven. Corporate governance concerns include ORLY's board of directors being controlled by a large percentage of insiders as well as a non-shareholder-approved "poison pill" anti-takeover plan.

➤ Our 12-month target price of $80 is based on our DCF model, which assumes a weighted average cost of capital of 9.8% and a terminal growth rate of 3.5%.

## Qualitative Risk Assessment

| LOW | MEDIUM | HIGH |
|---|---|---|

Our risk assessment reflects the cyclical nature of the auto parts retailing industry. However, what we see as the company's stronger-than-average balance sheet and its large opportunity for continued domestic expansion offset the industry risk, in our opinion.

## Quantitative Evaluations

**S&P Quality Ranking**  B+

| D | C | B- | B | B+ | A- | A | A+ |
|---|---|---|---|---|---|---|---|

**Relative Strength Rank**  STRONG

93

LOWEST = 1    HIGHEST = 99

## Revenue/Earnings Data

**Revenue (Million $)**

| | 1Q | 2Q | 3Q | 4Q | Year |
|---|---|---|---|---|---|
| 2011 | 1,383 | 1,479 | 1,535 | -- | -- |
| 2010 | 1,280 | 1,381 | 1,426 | 1,310 | 5,398 |
| 2009 | 1,164 | 1,251 | 1,258 | 1,174 | 4,847 |
| 2008 | 646.2 | 704.4 | 1,111 | 1,115 | 3,577 |
| 2007 | 613.2 | 643.1 | 661.8 | 604.3 | 2,522 |
| 2006 | 536.6 | 591.2 | 597.1 | 558.3 | 2,283 |

**Earnings Per Share ($)**

| | 1Q | 2Q | 3Q | 4Q | Year |
|---|---|---|---|---|---|
| 2011 | 0.72 | 0.96 | 1.10 | E0.86 | E3.72 |
| 2010 | 0.70 | 0.71 | 0.82 | 0.74 | 2.95 |
| 2009 | 0.46 | 0.62 | 0.63 | 0.52 | 2.23 |
| 2008 | 0.40 | 0.48 | 0.31 | 0.32 | 1.49 |
| 2007 | 0.42 | 0.45 | 0.46 | 0.35 | 1.67 |
| 2006 | 0.35 | 0.43 | 0.42 | 0.35 | 1.55 |

Fiscal year ended Dec. 31. Next earnings report expected: Mid February. EPS Estimates based on S&P Operating Earnings; historical GAAP earnings are as reported.

## Dividend Data

No cash dividends have been paid.

The McGraw·Hill Companies

# O'Reilly Automotive Inc

**STANDARD &POOR'S**

## Business Summary November 09, 2011

CORPORATE OVERVIEW. O'Reilly Automotive is one of the largest specialty retailers of automotive aftermarket parts, tools, supplies, equipment and accessories in the United States, with 3,570 stores in 38 states as of December 31, 2010. This includes the July 2008 acquisition of CSK Auto, one of the largest specialty retailers of auto parts in the Western U.S. At the time of acquisition, CSK was comprised of 1,342 stores operating under four brand names: Checker Auto Parts, Schuck's Auto Supply, Kragen Auto Parts, and Murray's Discount Auto Parts. As of December 31, 2010, ORLY had converted all of the CSK stores to O'Reilly systems, merged 41 CSK stores with existing O'Reilly locations, closed 17 stores, and opened five new stores in CSK historical markets.

ORLY stores carry, on average, about 22,000 SKUs, and average approximately 7,100 total square feet in size. The company's stores carry an extensive product line of new and remanufactured automotive hard parts (alternators, starters, fuel pumps, water pumps, brake shoes and pads), maintenance items (oil, antifreeze, fluids, filters, lighting, engine additives, appearance products), accessories (floor mats, seat covers), and a complete line of autobody paint,

automotive tools, and professional service equipment. Merchandise consists of nationally recognized brands and a wide variety of private label products. ORLY offers engine machining services through its stores, but does not sell tires or perform automotive repairs or installations.

ORLY currently operates 23 distribution centers, in Alabama, Arizona, Arkansas, California, Colorado, Georgia, Indiana, Iowa, Michigan, Minnesota, Missouri, Montana, North Carolina, Oklahoma, Tennessee,Texas, Utah and Washington. Inventory management and distribution systems electronically link each of ORLY's stores to a distribution center, providing for efficient inventory control and management. The distribution system provides each of the stores with same day or overnight access to over 118,000 SKUs, many of which are hard-to-find items.

## Company Financials Fiscal Year Ended Dec. 31

| Per Share Data ($) | 2010 | 2009 | 2008 | 2007 | 2006 | 2005 | 2004 | 2003 | 2002 | 2001 |
|---|---|---|---|---|---|---|---|---|---|---|
| Tangible Book Value | 17.24 | 13.82 | 11.16 | 13.38 | 11.97 | 10.19 | 8.56 | 7.18 | 6.10 | 5.27 |
| Cash Flow | 4.09 | 3.30 | 2.41 | 2.35 | 2.11 | 1.95 | 1.54 | 1.31 | 1.11 | 0.92 |
| Earnings | 2.95 | 2.23 | 1.49 | 1.67 | 1.55 | 1.45 | 1.05 | 0.92 | 0.77 | 0.63 |
| S&P Core Earnings | 2.95 | 2.23 | 1.48 | 1.67 | 1.55 | 1.27 | 1.97 | 1.67 | 1.39 | 1.15 |
| Dividends | Nil | Nil | Nil | Nil | Nil | Nil | Nil | Nil | Nil | Nil |
| Payout Ratio | Nil | Nil | Nil | Nil | Nil | Nil | Nil | Nil | Nil | Nil |
| Prices:High | 63.05 | 42.93 | 32.68 | 38.84 | 38.30 | 32.53 | 23.54 | 22.45 | 18.63 | 19.22 |
| Prices:Low | 37.47 | 26.47 | 20.00 | 30.43 | 27.49 | 21.98 | 18.03 | 11.46 | 12.05 | 7.75 |
| P/E Ratio:High | 21 | 19 | 22 | 23 | 25 | 22 | 22 | 24 | 24 | 31 |
| P/E Ratio:Low | 13 | 12 | 13 | 18 | 18 | 15 | 17 | 12 | 16 | 12 |

| Income Statement Analysis (Million $) | 2010 | 2009 | 2008 | 2007 | 2006 | 2005 | 2004 | 2003 | 2002 | 2001 |
|---|---|---|---|---|---|---|---|---|---|---|
| Revenue | 5,398 | 4,847 | 3,577 | 2,522 | 2,283 | 2,045 | 1,721 | 1,512 | 1,312 | 1,092 |
| Operating Income | 895 | 686 | 462 | 384 | 347 | 310 | 245 | 208 | 175 | 144 |
| Depreciation | 161 | 148 | 117 | 78.9 | 64.9 | 57.2 | 54.3 | 42.4 | 36.9 | 30.5 |
| Interest Expense | 39.3 | 45.2 | 28.5 | 6.28 | 4.32 | 5.06 | 4.70 | 6.86 | 9.25 | 9.09 |
| Pretax Income | 689 | 497 | 303 | 307 | 282 | 251 | 188 | 160 | 131 | 107 |
| Effective Tax Rate | NA | 38.1% | 38.4% | 36.9% | 36.9% | 34.6% | 37.3% | 37.5% | 37.4% | 37.8% |
| Net Income | 419 | 308 | 186 | 194 | 178 | 164 | 118 | 100 | 82.0 | 66.4 |
| S&P Core Earnings | 419 | 307 | 186 | 194 | 178 | 143 | 110 | 90.9 | 74.8 | 60.9 |

| Balance Sheet & Other Financial Data (Million $) | 2010 | 2009 | 2008 | 2007 | 2006 | 2005 | 2004 | 2003 | 2002 | 2001 |
|---|---|---|---|---|---|---|---|---|---|---|
| Cash | 29.7 | 26.9 | 31.3 | 58.4 | 29.9 | 31.4 | 69.0 | 21.1 | 29.3 | 15.0 |
| Current Assets | 2,301 | 2,227 | 1,875 | 1,102 | 1,001 | 911 | 813 | 687 | 631 | 551 |
| Total Assets | 5,048 | 4,781 | 4,193 | 2,280 | 1,977 | 1,714 | 1,432 | 1,188 | 1,009 | 857 |
| Current Liabilities | 1,229 | 1,231 | 1,054 | 529 | 434 | 486 | 334 | 246 | 147 | 121 |
| Long Term Debt | 357 | 684 | 718 | 75.2 | 110 | 25.5 | 100 | 121 | 190 | 166 |
| Common Equity | 3,210 | 2,686 | 2,282 | 1,592 | 1,364 | 1,181 | 973 | 784 | 651 | 556 |
| Total Capital | 3,568 | 3,370 | 3,000 | 1,695 | 1,512 | 1,249 | 1,112 | 935 | 857 | 731 |
| Capital Expenditures | 365 | 415 | 342 | 283 | 229 | 205 | 173 | 136 | 102 | 68.5 |
| Cash Flow | 581 | 456 | 303 | 273 | 243 | 221 | 172 | 142 | 119 | 96.9 |
| Current Ratio | 1.9 | 1.8 | 1.8 | 2.1 | 2.3 | 1.9 | 2.4 | 2.8 | 4.3 | 4.5 |
| % Long Term Debt of Capitalization | 10.0 | 20.3 | 24.1 | 4.4 | 7.3 | 2.0 | 9.0 | 12.9 | 22.2 | 22.7 |
| % Net Income of Revenue | 7.8 | 6.3 | 5.2 | 7.7 | 7.8 | 8.0 | 6.8 | 6.6 | 6.2 | 6.1 |
| % Return on Assets | 8.5 | 6.9 | 5.8 | 9.1 | 9.6 | 10.4 | 9.1 | 9.1 | 8.8 | 8.4 |
| % Return on Equity | 14.2 | 12.4 | 9.6 | 13.1 | 14.2 | 15.3 | 13.3 | 14.0 | 13.6 | 13.0 |

Data as orig reptd.; bef. results of disc opers/spec. items. Per share data adj. for stk. divs.; EPS diluted. E-Estimated. NA-Not Available. NM-Not Meaningful. NR-Not Ranked. UR-Under Review.

**Office:** 233 S Patterson Ave, Springfield, MO 65802.
**Telephone:** 417-862-6708.
**Website:** http://www.oreillyauto.com
**Chrmn:** D. O'Reilly

**Vice Chrmn:** C.H. O'Reilly, Jr.
**Vice Chrmn:** L.P. O'Reilly
**CEO & Co-Pres:** G.L. Henslee
**COO & Co-Pres:** T.F. Wise

**Investor Contact:** T.G. McFall
**Board Members:** J. D. Burchfield, T. T. Hendrickson, P. R. Lederer, J. R. Murphy, D. O'Reilly, L. P. O'Reilly, C. H. O'Reilly, Jr., R. O'Reilly-Wooten, R. Rashkow

**Founded:** 1957
**Domicile:** Missouri
**Employees:** 46,858

**The McGraw-Hill Companies**

# Owens-Illinois Inc.

**STANDARD & POOR'S**

| S&P Recommendation HOLD ★★★☆☆ | Price $17.43 (as of Nov 25, 2011) | 12-Mo. Target Price $22.00 | Investment Style Large-Cap Blend |
|---|---|---|---|

**GICS Sector** Materials
**Sub-Industry** Metal & Glass Containers

**Summary** This company is a large global maker of glass bottles and containers.

## Key Stock Statistics (Source S&P, Vickers, company reports)

| | | | | | | | |
|---|---|---|---|---|---|---|---|
| 52-Wk Range | $33.32– 13.43 | S&P Oper. EPS 2011**E** | 2.30 | Market Capitalization(B) | $2.863 | Beta | 2.09 |
| Trailing 12-Month EPS | $-0.93 | S&P Oper. EPS 2012**E** | 2.75 | Yield (%) | Nil | S&P 3-Yr. Proj. EPS CAGR(%) | 7 |
| Trailing 12-Month P/E | NM | P/E on S&P Oper. EPS 2011**E** | 7.6 | Dividend Rate/Share | Nil | S&P Credit Rating | BB+ |
| $10K Invested 5 Yrs Ago | $9,689 | Common Shares Outstg. (M) | 164.2 | Institutional Ownership (%) | 90 | | |

## Price Performance

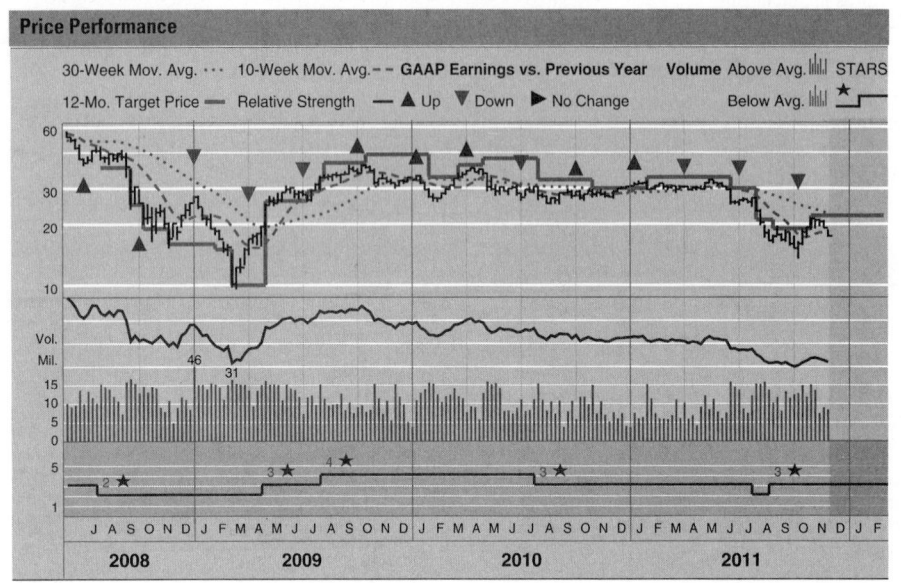

30-Week Mov. Avg. · · · · 10-Week Mov. Avg. - - GAAP Earnings vs. Previous Year    Volume Above Avg.▐▌▐ STARS
12-Mo. Target Price — Relative Strength — ▲ Up ▼ Down ▶ No Change    Below Avg.▐▌▐ ★

Options: ASE, CBOE, P, Ph

Analysis prepared by Equity Analyst **Stewart Scharf** on Nov 08, 2011, when the stock traded at **$20.54**.

## Highlights

➤ We expect net sales to rise about 10% in 2011, driven by contributions from acquisitions in South America and China. However, we project low single digit growth for 2012, as soft global markets restrict shipments, and stronger currencies in Australia and New Zealand continue to affect exports of wine and beer from that region, in our view, while beer consumption there remains soft.

➤ We believe gross margins will narrow to about 18.5% in 2011, from 20.4% in 2010, as cost inflation in Europe and North America outweighs price hikes and energy surcharges, while supply chain and production inefficiencies in North America lead to unabsorbed manufacturing costs. We expect contractual and other pass-through initiatives (8% to 12%) to offset inflationary cost pressures in 2012, aiding margins. Operating (EBITDA) margins should expand to near 18% in 2012, due to price actions, improved supply chain efficiencies and plant closures.

➤ We forecast a lower effective tax rate of 21.5% for 2011, and estimate operating EPS of $2.30, rising close to 20%, to $2.75, in 2012.

## Investment Rationale/Risk

➤ Our hold opinion is based on uncertain global market conditions, along with our valuation metrics. We expect OI to align production with customer demand, while it closes two plants in Australia to reduce costs and improve margins, as part of its value over volume strategy. Longer term, we expect new strategic initiatives abroad to help improve OI's footprint.

➤ Risks to our recommendation and target price include softening global markets, a stronger U.S. dollar mainly versus the euro, a rise in inflationary input costs based on higher commodity prices, more inventory de-stocking, and fewer long-term contract extensions.

➤ Based on our relative valuation, we apply a multiple of 6.5X to our 2012 EPS estimate, a discount to other companies in S&P's Metal & Glass group as well as to our projected P/E for the S&P 500, which values the shares at $18. Our DCF model, assuming a 9.5% weighted average cost of capital and a 4% terminal growth rate, derives intrinsic value of $26. Blending these metrics, we arrive at our 12-month target price of $22.

## Qualitative Risk Assessment

| LOW | MEDIUM | HIGH |
|---|---|---|

Our risk assessment reflects ongoing asbestos claims and volatile commodity costs, offset by our view of sound corporate governance practices and an improving balance sheet.

## Quantitative Evaluations

**S&P Quality Ranking**    B-

| D | C | B- | B | B+ | A- | A | A+ |
|---|---|---|---|---|---|---|---|

**Relative Strength Rank**    MODERATE

34

LOWEST = 1    HIGHEST = 99

## Revenue/Earnings Data

**Revenue (Million $)**

| | 1Q | 2Q | 3Q | 4Q | Year |
|---|---|---|---|---|---|
| 2011 | 1,719 | 1,959 | 1,862 | -- | -- |
| 2010 | 1,546 | 1,670 | 1,689 | 1,728 | 6,633 |
| 2009 | 1,519 | 1,807 | 1,875 | 1,866 | 7,067 |
| 2008 | 1,961 | 2,211 | 2,009 | 1,705 | 7,885 |
| 2007 | 1,684 | 1,997 | 1,928 | 1,957 | 7,567 |
| 2006 | 1,688 | 1,946 | 1,912 | 1,877 | 7,422 |

**Earnings Per Share ($)**

| | | | | | |
|---|---|---|---|---|---|
| 2011 | 0.44 | 0.42 | 0.72 | E0.40 | E2.30 |
| 2010 | 0.48 | 0.79 | 0.77 | -0.51 | 1.51 |
| 2009 | 0.27 | 0.88 | 0.74 | -0.95 | 0.95 |
| 2008 | 1.02 | 1.33 | 0.46 | -1.38 | 1.48 |
| 2007 | 0.31 | 0.92 | 0.45 | 0.06 | 1.78 |
| 2006 | 0.12 | 0.24 | 0.02 | -0.71 | -0.32 |

Fiscal year ended Dec. 31. Next earnings report expected: Late January. EPS Estimates based on S&P Operating Earnings; historical GAAP earnings are as reported.

## Dividend Data

No cash dividends have been paid.

# Owens-Illinois Inc.

**STANDARD &POOR'S**

## Business Summary November 08, 2011

Owens-Illinois, Inc. (OI), through its subsidiaries, manufactures and sells glass containers primarily in Europe, North America, Asia-Pacific and South America. The company produces glass containers for beer, ready-to-drink low alcohol refreshers, spirits, wine, food, tea, juice and pharmaceuticals. It also produces glass containers for soft drinks and other non-alcoholic beverages, principally outside the U.S.

The company's customers include manufacturers and marketers of glass packaged products. In the U.S., the majority of customers for glass containers are brewers, wine vintners, distillers and food producers. OI also produces glass containers for soft drinks and other non-alcoholic beverages, principally outside the U.S. Principal markets for glass container products are in Europe, North and South America and Asia-Pacific. The company sees itself as a low-cost producer in the glass container segment of the rigid packaging market in many of the countries in which it competes. U.S. glass container customers include Anheuser-Busch InBev, Brown Forman, Diageo, H.J. Heinz, Miller/Coors, PepsiCo and Saxco-Demptos, Inc. Glass container customers outside the U.S. include Anheuser-Busch InBev, Carlsberg, Diageo, Foster's, Heineken, Lion Nathan, Molson/Coors, Pernod Ricard and SABMiller.

Principal glass container competitors in the U.S. are Saint-Gobain Containers, Inc., a wholly owned subsidiary of Compagnie de Saint-Gobain, and Anchor Glass Container Corporation. In supplying glass containers outside of the U.S., the company competes directly with Compagnie de Saint-Gobain in Europe and Brazil, Ardagh plc in the U.K., Germany and Poland, Vetropak in the Czech Republic, and Amcor Limited in Australia. In other locations in Europe, OI competes indirectly with various glass container firms, including Compagnie de Saint-Gobain, Vetropak, and Ardagh plc.

Principal competitors producing metal containers are Amcor, Ball Corporation, Crown Holdings, Inc., Rexam plc and Silgan Holdings Inc. The principal competitors producing plastic containers are Consolidated Container Holdings, LLC, Graham Packaging Company, Plastipak Packaging Inc. and Silgan Holdings Inc.

## Company Financials Fiscal Year Ended Dec. 31

| Per Share Data ($) | 2010 | 2009 | 2008 | 2007 | 2006 | 2005 | 2004 | 2003 | 2002 | 2001 |
|---|---|---|---|---|---|---|---|---|---|---|
| Tangible Book Value | NM | NM | NM | NM | NM | NM | NM | NM | NM | NM |
| Cash Flow | 3.85 | 3.27 | 3.99 | 4.18 | 2.53 | -0.99 | 3.91 | -3.67 | 2.84 | 5.08 |
| Earnings | 1.51 | 0.95 | 1.48 | 1.78 | -0.32 | -4.26 | 1.00 | -6.89 | -0.08 | 2.33 |
| S&P Core Earnings | 1.66 | 0.95 | 0.39 | 1.47 | 0.36 | -0.89 | 1.22 | 0.04 | -1.45 | -0.92 |
| Dividends | Nil | Nil | Nil | Nil | Nil | Nil | Nil | Nil | Nil | Nil |
| Payout Ratio | Nil | Nil | Nil | Nil | Nil | Nil | Nil | Nil | Nil | Nil |
| Prices:High | 37.97 | 39.56 | 60.60 | 50.97 | 22.60 | 27.50 | 23.89 | 15.50 | 19.19 | 10.08 |
| Prices:Low | 24.92 | 9.53 | 15.20 | 18.48 | 13.10 | 17.50 | 10.80 | 7.51 | 9.55 | 3.62 |
| P/E Ratio:High | 25 | 42 | 8 | 29 | NM | NM | 24 | NM | NM | 4 |
| P/E Ratio:Low | 17 | 10 | 2 | 10 | NM | NM | 11 | NM | NM | 2 |

| Income Statement Analysis (Million $) | | | | | | | | | | |
|---|---|---|---|---|---|---|---|---|---|---|
| Revenue | 6,633 | 7,067 | 7,885 | 7,567 | 7,422 | 7,090 | 6,128 | 6,059 | 5,640 | 5,403 |
| Operating Income | 1,199 | 1,315 | 1,529 | 1,432 | -1,100 | 1,297 | 1,185 | 1,175 | 1,281 | 1,173 |
| Depreciation | 391 | 396 | 431 | 423 | 469 | 480 | 436 | 473 | 428 | 403 |
| Interest Expense | 249 | 222 | 253 | 339 | 488 | 467 | 475 | 491 | 422 | 434 |
| Pretax Income | 424 | 325 | 558 | 507 | 143 | -219 | 210 | -1,091 | 16.6 | 667 |
| Effective Tax Rate | NA | 39.2% | 42.4% | 29.2% | NM | NM | 2.81% | NM | NM | 42.9% |
| Net Income | 253 | 162 | 252 | 299 | -27.5 | -622 | 172 | -991 | 9.40 | 361 |
| S&P Core Earnings | 276 | 161 | 60.3 | 226 | 55.4 | -134 | 185 | 5.85 | -213 | -135 |

| Balance Sheet & Other Financial Data (Million $) | | | | | | | | | | |
|---|---|---|---|---|---|---|---|---|---|---|
| Cash | 640 | 813 | 405 | 448 | 223 | 247 | 278 | 163 | 126 | 156 |
| Current Assets | 2,738 | 2,797 | 2,445 | 2,695 | 2,433 | 2,282 | 2,401 | 2,122 | 1,887 | 1,987 |
| Total Assets | 9,754 | 8,727 | 7,977 | 9,325 | 9,321 | 9,522 | 10,737 | 9,531 | 9,869 | 10,107 |
| Current Liabilities | 2,079 | 2,034 | 2,003 | 2,530 | 2,366 | 1,822 | 1,907 | 1,363 | 1,297 | 1,232 |
| Long Term Debt | 3,924 | 3,258 | 2,940 | 3,014 | 4,719 | 5,019 | 5,168 | 5,333 | 5,268 | 5,330 |
| Common Equity | 1,815 | 1,538 | 1,041 | 1,735 | -83.9 | 271 | 1,092 | 551 | 1,218 | 1,699 |
| Total Capital | 5,950 | 4,994 | 4,311 | 5,562 | 5,407 | 6,110 | 7,065 | 6,617 | 7,359 | 8,106 |
| Capital Expenditures | 500 | 428 | 362 | 293 | 320 | 404 | 437 | 432 | 496 | 365 |
| Cash Flow | 644 | 558 | 677 | 701 | 420 | -163 | 586 | -539 | 416 | 742 |
| Current Ratio | 1.3 | 1.4 | 1.2 | 1.1 | 1.0 | 1.3 | 1.3 | 1.6 | 1.5 | 1.6 |
| % Long Term Debt of Capitalization | 66.0 | 65.2 | 68.2 | 54.2 | 87.3 | 82.1 | 73.1 | 80.6 | 71.6 | 65.8 |
| % Net Income of Revenue | 3.8 | 2.3 | 3.2 | 4.0 | NM | NM | 2.8 | NM | 0.2 | 6.7 |
| % Return on Assets | 2.7 | 1.9 | 2.9 | 3.0 | NM | NM | 1.7 | NM | 0.1 | 3.5 |
| % Return on Equity | 15.1 | 12.6 | 18.1 | 33.9 | NM | NM | 18.3 | NM | 0.6 | 21.7 |

Data as orig reptd.; bef. results of disc opers/spec. items. Per share data adj. for stk. divs.; EPS diluted. E-Estimated. NA-Not Available. NM-Not Meaningful. NR-Not Ranked. UR-Under Review.

**Office:** One Michael Owens Way, Perrysburg, OH 43551-2999.
**Telephone:** 567-336-5000.
**Website:** http://www.o-i.com
**Chrmn, Pres & CEO:** A.P. Stroucken

**COO & CTO:** L.R. Crawford
**SVP, CFO & Chief Acctg Officer:** E.C. White
**SVP & General Counsel:** J.W. Baehren
**Treas:** C. Neel

**Investor Contact:** S. Sekpeh (567-336-2355)
**Board Members:** G. F. Colter, J. L. Geldmacher, P. S. Hellman, D. H. Ho, A. D. Kelly, J. J. McMackin, Jr., C. A. McNeill, Jr., H. H. Roberts, A. P. Stroucken, H. H. Wehmeier, D. K. Williams, T. L. Young

**Founded:** 1903
**Domicile:** Delaware
**Employees:** 24,000

The McGraw-Hill Companies

# PACCAR Inc

STANDARD &POOR'S

| S&P Recommendation BUY ★★★★☆ | Price $37.28 (as of Nov 25, 2011) | 12-Mo. Target Price $66.00 | Investment Style Large-Cap Blend |
|---|---|---|---|

**GICS Sector** Industrials
**Sub-Industry** Construction & Farm Machinery & Heavy Trucks

**Summary** This heavy-duty truck manufacturer produces the well-known Peterbilt and Kenworth brand heavy-duty highway trucks.

## Key Stock Statistics (Source S&P, Vickers, company reports)

| | | | | | | | |
|---|---|---|---|---|---|---|---|
| 52-Wk Range | $58.75– 31.57 | S&P Oper. EPS 2011E | 2.73 | Market Capitalization(B) | $13.354 | Beta | 1.46 |
| Trailing 12-Month EPS | $2.41 | S&P Oper. EPS 2012E | 3.70 | Yield (%) | 1.93 | S&P 3-Yr. Proj. EPS CAGR(%) | 10 |
| Trailing 12-Month P/E | 15.5 | P/E on S&P Oper. EPS 2011E | 13.7 | Dividend Rate/Share | $0.72 | S&P Credit Rating | A+ |
| $10K Invested 5 Yrs Ago | $9,788 | Common Shares Outstg. (M) | 358.2 | Institutional Ownership (%) | 57 | | |

## Price Performance

30-Week Mov. Avg. ···· 10-Week Mov. Avg. - - GAAP Earnings vs. Previous Year   Volume Above Avg. STARS
12-Mo. Target Price — Relative Strength — ▲ Up ▼ Down ► No Change   Below Avg.

Options: ASE, CBOE, P, Ph

Analysis prepared by Equity Analyst **Jim Corridore** on Nov 01, 2011, when the stock traded at **$42.51**.

## Qualitative Risk Assessment

| LOW | MEDIUM | HIGH |
|---|---|---|

Our risk assessment for Paccar reflects the highly cyclical nature of the heavy-duty (Class 8) truck market, offset by our view of a strong balance sheet with a relatively low amount of manufacturing debt and a geographical sales mix that is increasingly diversified.

## Quantitative Evaluations

**S&P Quality Ranking**                                B+

| D | C | B- | B | B+ | A- | A | A+ |
|---|---|---|---|---|---|---|---|

**Relative Strength Rank**                         MODERATE

44

LOWEST = 1                                          HIGHEST = 99

## Revenue/Earnings Data

**Revenue (Million $)**

| | 1Q | 2Q | 3Q | 4Q | Year |
|---|---|---|---|---|---|
| 2011 | 3,284 | 3,961 | 4,257 | -- | -- |
| 2010 | 2,231 | 2,464 | 2,543 | 3,056 | 10,293 |
| 2009 | 1,985 | 1,846 | 2,000 | 2,240 | 8,087 |
| 2008 | 3,938 | 4,113 | 4,005 | 2,917 | 14,973 |
| 2007 | 3,985 | 3,716 | 3,762 | 3,759 | 15,222 |
| 2006 | 3,852 | 3,937 | 3,959 | 3,968 | 16,454 |

**Earnings Per Share ($)**

| | 1Q | 2Q | 3Q | 4Q | Year |
|---|---|---|---|---|---|
| 2011 | 0.53 | 0.65 | 0.77 | E0.78 | E2.73 |
| 2010 | 0.19 | 0.27 | 0.33 | 0.46 | 1.25 |
| 2009 | 0.07 | 0.07 | 0.04 | 0.13 | 0.31 |
| 2008 | 0.79 | 0.86 | 0.82 | 0.31 | 2.78 |
| 2007 | 0.97 | 0.79 | 0.81 | 0.71 | 3.29 |
| 2006 | 0.90 | 0.98 | 1.07 | 1.01 | 3.97 |

Fiscal year ended Dec. 31. Next earnings report expected: Early February. EPS Estimates based on S&P Operating Earnings; historical GAAP earnings are as reported.

## Highlights

► We project truck revenues will rise about 60% in 2011, after a 32% increase in 2010 and a 48% decline in 2009. We see truck revenue rising a further 37% in 2012. We look for the North American market for heavy trucks to start showing strong improvement in 2011, driven by fleet owners replacing older vehicles and positioning their fleets ahead of more stringent emission standards, as well as strengthening transportation demand. We expect a recovery in Europe in mid-2011, lagging the North American economy by about six months.

► We forecast that margins within the truck division will benefit from the leverage of fixed costs over an improving revenue base as well as more efficient capacity utilization and ongoing benefits from recent cost-cutting actions. Within the financial services segment, we believe operating margins will continue to be pressured by rising provisions for credit losses and reduced finance margins.

► We estimate EPS of $2.73 in 2011, compared to 2010 EPS of $1.25. For 2012, we see EPS rising a further 36%, to $3.70.

## Investment Rationale/Risk

► We believe demand in the North American and international truck markets has likely bottomed and should begin to show improvement. We think earnings have also troughed and should show improvement during the next economic upcycle, which we believe is under way and in its early stages. We view favorably the company's ability to remain profitable in 2009 on a 48% decline in truck sales. Given our view that PCAR is likely to see strong revenue and earnings improvement over the next 2-3 years, we find the shares attractive at recent levels.

► Risks to our recommendation and target price include a slower economic recovery than we expect, a delayed improvement in North American truck demand, along with potential supply disruptions, foreign exchange volatility, and increases in raw material costs.

► Our 12-month target price of $66 values the shares at 18X our 2012 EPS estimate of $3.70, in the middle of PCAR's historical P/E range, reflecting our view that earnings are at a trough and should improve over the next several years.

## Dividend Data (Dates: mm/dd Payment Date: mm/dd/yy)

| Amount ($) | Date Decl. | Ex-Div. Date | Stk. of Record | Payment Date |
|---|---|---|---|---|
| 0.120 | 12/07 | 02/15 | 02/17 | 03/07/11 |
| 0.120 | 04/19 | 05/17 | 05/19 | 06/06/11 |
| 0.180 | 07/11 | 08/16 | 08/18 | 09/06/11 |
| 0.180 | 09/13 | 11/16 | 11/18 | 12/05/11 |

Dividends have been paid since 1943. Source: Company reports.

---

**Please read the Required Disclosures and Analyst Certification on the last page of this report.**

The McGraw-Hill Companies

# PACCAR Inc

STANDARD
&POOR'S

## Business Summary November 01, 2011

CORPORATE OVERVIEW. Originally incorporated in 1924 as the Pacific Car and Foundry Company, and tracing its roots back to the Seattle Car Manufacturing Company, PACCAR has grown into a multinational company with principal businesses that include the design, manufacture and distribution of high-quality light, medium and heavy-duty commercial trucks and related aftermarket parts. The company's heavy-duty (Class 8) diesel trucks are marketed under the Peterbilt, Kenworth, DAF and Foden names. In addition, through its Peterbilt and Kenworth divisions, PCAR competes in the North American medium-duty (Class 6/7) markets and the European light/medium (6 to 15 metric ton) commercial vehicle market with DAF cab-over-engine trucks.

In 2010, the company's truck production and related aftermarket parts distribution businesses accounted for 89.7% of revenues. Segment profit margins in 2010, 2009 and 2008 were 5.4%, 0.96%, and 8.5%, respectively; in the previous

cycle, during the boom years of 2000, 1999 and 1998, segment profit margins were 6.9%, 9.0% and 7.4%, respectively.

Like other big truck makers, the company aims to capitalize on a growing trend toward truck leasing and financing. The Finance Services segment accounted for 9.4% of 2010 revenues, but generated 23% of pretax income; it posted operating margins of 15.8%, 8.4%, 17% in 2010, 2009, and 2008, respectively. In 2010, 2009 and 2008, provisions for losses on receivables were $61 million, $90.8 million and $99.2 million, respectively.

## Company Financials Fiscal Year Ended Dec. 31

| Per Share Data ($) | 2010 | 2009 | 2008 | 2007 | 2006 | 2005 | 2004 | 2003 | 2002 | 2001 |
|---|---|---|---|---|---|---|---|---|---|---|
| Tangible Book Value | 14.67 | 14.02 | 13.36 | 13.66 | 11.98 | 10.27 | 9.61 | 7.36 | 6.08 | 5.64 |
| Cash Flow | 2.93 | 2.06 | 4.56 | 4.70 | 5.12 | 3.87 | 3.09 | 2.00 | 1.50 | 0.91 |
| Earnings | 1.25 | 0.31 | 2.78 | 3.29 | 3.97 | 2.92 | 2.29 | 1.33 | 0.95 | 0.45 |
| S&P Core Earnings | 1.23 | 0.18 | 2.63 | 3.24 | 3.97 | 2.92 | 2.25 | 1.32 | 0.89 | 0.37 |
| Dividends | 0.69 | 0.54 | 0.82 | 0.83 | 0.64 | 0.39 | 0.33 | 0.46 | 0.29 | 0.24 |
| Payout Ratio | 55% | 174% | 29% | 25% | 16% | 13% | 15% | 35% | 30% | 53% |
| Prices:High | 57.83 | 40.26 | 55.54 | 65.75 | 46.17 | 36.17 | 36.19 | 25.95 | 15.70 | 13.68 |
| Prices:Low | 33.45 | 20.38 | 21.96 | 42.15 | 30.12 | 28.13 | 22.05 | 12.37 | 9.09 | 8.44 |
| P/E Ratio:High | 46 | NM | 20 | 20 | 12 | 12 | 16 | 20 | 17 | 31 |
| P/E Ratio:Low | 27 | NM | 8 | 13 | 8 | 10 | 10 | 9 | 10 | 19 |

### Income Statement Analysis (Million $)

| | 2010 | 2009 | 2008 | 2007 | 2006 | 2005 | 2004 | 2003 | 2002 | 2001 |
|---|---|---|---|---|---|---|---|---|---|---|
| Revenue | 10,293 | 8,087 | 14,973 | 15,222 | 16,454 | 14,057 | 11,396 | 8,195 | 7,219 | 6,089 |
| Operating Income | 1,265 | 812 | 2,859 | 2,932 | 3,136 | 2,572 | 1,972 | 1,313 | 1,012 | 672 |
| Depreciation | 616 | 638 | 649 | 526 | 435 | 370 | 315 | 268 | 218 | 180 |
| Interest Expense | 14.4 | 12.8 | NA | 737 | 573 | 445 | 331 | 3.50 | 249 | 275 |
| Pretax Income | 660 | 175 | 1,464 | 1,764 | 2,175 | 1,774 | 1,368 | 806 | 574 | 255 |
| Effective Tax Rate | NA | 36.1% | 30.5% | 30.4% | 31.2% | 36.1% | 33.7% | 34.6% | 35.2% | 32.0% |
| Net Income | 458 | 112 | 1,018 | 1,227 | 1,496 | 1,133 | 907 | 527 | 372 | 174 |
| S&P Core Earnings | 451 | 64.5 | 962 | 1,208 | 1,496 | 1,134 | 889 | 523 | 349 | 145 |

### Balance Sheet & Other Financial Data (Million $)

| | 2010 | 2009 | 2008 | 2007 | 2006 | 2005 | 2004 | 2003 | 2002 | 2001 |
|---|---|---|---|---|---|---|---|---|---|---|
| Cash | 2,433 | 2,056 | 2,075 | 1,948 | 2,628 | 2,290 | 2,220 | 1,724 | 1,308 | 1,062 |
| Current Assets | 11,455 | 10,040 | 3,643 | 3,919 | 4,200 | 3,508 | 3,332 | 2,599 | 2,102 | 1,834 |
| Total Assets | 14,234 | 14,569 | 16,250 | 17,228 | 16,107 | 13,715 | 12,228 | 9,940 | 8,703 | 7,914 |
| Current Liabilities | 2,634 | 5,286 | 1,829 | 2,503 | 2,738 | 2,182 | 2,151 | 1,482 | 1,258 | 1,134 |
| Long Term Debt | 150 | 172 | 19.3 | 3,039 | 498 | 936 | 2,314 | 1,557 | 1,552 | 1,547 |
| Common Equity | 5,358 | 5,104 | 4,847 | 5,013 | 4,456 | 3,901 | 3,762 | 3,246 | 2,601 | 2,253 |
| Total Capital | 5,508 | 5,276 | 4,866 | 8,052 | 4,954 | 4,837 | 6,077 | 4,803 | 4,152 | 3,800 |
| Capital Expenditures | 884 | 971 | 1,550 | 1,267 | 312 | 300 | 232 | 111 | 78.8 | 83.9 |
| Cash Flow | 1,074 | 750 | 1,667 | 1,754 | 1,931 | 1,503 | 1,222 | 794 | 590 | 354 |
| Current Ratio | 4.4 | 1.3 | 2.0 | 1.6 | 1.5 | 1.6 | 1.5 | 1.8 | 1.7 | 1.6 |
| % Long Term Debt of Capitalization | 2.7 | 3.3 | 0.3 | 37.7 | 10.1 | 19.3 | 38.1 | 32.4 | 37.4 | 40.7 |
| % Net Income of Revenue | 4.5 | 1.4 | 6.8 | 8.1 | 9.1 | 8.1 | 8.0 | 6.4 | 5.2 | 2.9 |
| % Return on Assets | 3.2 | 0.7 | 6.1 | 7.4 | 10.0 | 8.7 | 8.2 | 5.6 | 4.5 | 2.1 |
| % Return on Equity | 8.8 | 2.3 | 20.7 | 25.9 | 35.8 | 29.6 | 25.9 | 18.0 | 15.3 | 7.7 |

Data as orig reptd.; bef. results of disc opers/spec. items. Per share data adj. for stk. divs.; EPS diluted. E-Estimated. NA-Not Available. NM-Not Meaningful. NR-Not Ranked. UR-Under Review.

**Office:** 777 106th Avenue NE, Bellevue, WA 98004-5027.
**Telephone:** 425-468-7400.
**Website:** http://www.paccar.com
**Chrmn & CEO:** M.C. Pigott

**Pres & CFO:** R.E. Armstrong
**Chief Acctg Officer & Cntlr:** M.T. Barkley
**Treas:** R.E. Easton
**Secy:** J.M. D'Amato

**Investor Contact:** R. Easton
**Board Members:** A. J. Carnwath, J. M. Fluke, Jr., K. S. Hachigian, S. F. Page, R. T. Parry, J. M. Pigott, M. C. Pigott, G. M. Spierkel, W. R. Staley, C. R. Williamson

**Founded:** 1905
**Domicile:** Delaware
**Employees:** 17,700

# Pall Corp

**STANDARD &POOR'S**

| S&P Recommendation | HOLD ★★★★☆ | Price<br>$49.92 (as of Nov 25, 2011) | 12-Mo. Target Price<br>$50.00 |
|---|---|---|---|

**GICS Sector** Industrials
**Sub-Industry** Industrial Machinery

**Summary** This company is a leading producer of filters for the health care, aerospace, microelectronics and other industries.

## Key Stock Statistics (Source S&P, Vickers, company reports)

| | | | | | | | |
|---|---|---|---|---|---|---|---|
| 52-Wk Range | $59.50–39.81 | S&P Oper. EPS 2012**E** | 3.10 | Market Capitalization(B) | $5.743 | Beta | 1.20 |
| Trailing 12-Month EPS | $2.67 | S&P Oper. EPS 2013**E** | 3.55 | Yield (%) | 1.40 | S&P 3-Yr. Proj. EPS CAGR(%) | 12 |
| Trailing 12-Month P/E | 18.7 | P/E on S&P Oper. EPS 2012**E** | 16.1 | Dividend Rate/Share | $0.70 | S&P Credit Rating | BBB |
| $10K Invested 5 Yrs Ago | $16,928 | Common Shares Outstg. (M) | 115.0 | Institutional Ownership (%) | 94 | | |

## Price Performance

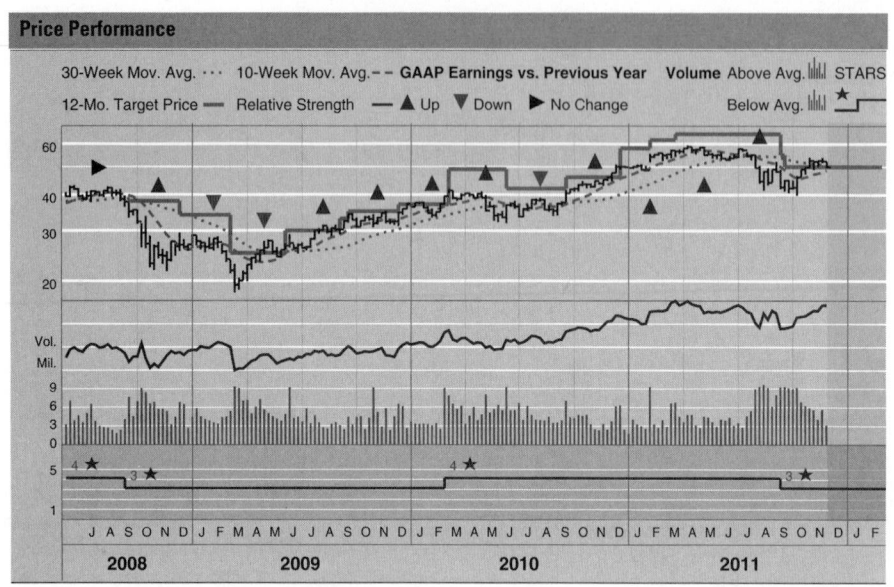

30-Week Mov. Avg. ···· 10-Week Mov. Avg.– – **GAAP Earnings vs. Previous Year**   **Volume** Above Avg. ▮▮▮ STARS
12-Mo. Target Price — Relative Strength  — ▲ Up ▼ Down ▶ No Change   Below Avg. ▮▮▮ ★

Options: CBOE, Ph

Analysis prepared by Equity Analyst **Stewart Scharf** on Sep 16, 2011, when the stock traded at **$44.51**.

## Highlights

➤ Following 14% higher sales in FY 11 (Jul.), we project mid-single digit growth for FY 12, driven by increased global demand for biopharmaceutical and military aerospace products. We also see growth in the energy & water and food & beverage segments, while microelectronics sales decline somewhat. Although some markets remain challenging, we expect favorable trends in all geographic regions, especially Asia as Japan rebounds.

➤ We see gross margins widening to about 50.5% in FY 12, from 50.1% in FY 11, based on pricing initiatives and better cost absorption, along with a better mix as PLL improves margins for systems and capital goods products, which generally carry lower margins. We think operating margins (EBITDA) will expand by close to 75 basis points, to 22.2%, in FY 12, as PLL implements restructuring efforts, including staff reductions and plant closures.

➤ We forecast a lower underlying tax rate of 24.5% in FY 12, with operating EPS of $3.10, up from $2.77 in FY 11 (before $0.10 of net charges, but including $0.13 positive foreign exchange). We project EPS of $3.55 for FY 13.

## Investment Rationale/Risk

➤ We recently downgraded our opinion to hold, from buy, as we believe uncertain markets and margin pressures will lead to PLL revisiting its long-term EBIT margin goals. Our valuation metrics suggest the shares are fairly valued, and we still think the company could eventually be a takeover target, given recent industry consolidation, although market volatility will likely delay any potential deal.

➤ Risks to our recommendation and target price include a weaker economy, negative foreign currency effect, and a significant rise in raw material costs. We have some corporate governance concerns based on past financial reporting errors, but we think internal controls have improved.

➤ Our relative valuation results in a value of $48, using a multiple of 15.5X our FY 12 EPS estimate, a premium to our projected P/E (adjusted for FY end) for S&P's Industrial Machinery sub-industry group. Our intrinsic value estimate of $52 is based on our DCF model, which assumes a terminal growth rate of 3.5% and a weighted average cost of capital of 8.5%. Blending these metrics, our 12-month target price is $50.

## Qualitative Risk Assessment

| LOW | MEDIUM | HIGH |
|---|---|---|

Our risk assessment reflects the historically cyclical semiconductor industry and PLL's exposure to foreign markets, while civil lawsuits and an SEC and U.S. Attorney inquiry related to understating tax payments are still pending since 2007. This is offset by our view of PLL's reduced debt levels and positive cash generation.

## Quantitative Evaluations

**S&P Quality Ranking**  B+

| D | C | B- | B | B+ | A- | A | A+ |
|---|---|---|---|---|---|---|---|

**Relative Strength Rank**  STRONG

82

LOWEST = 1                 HIGHEST = 99

## Revenue/Earnings Data

**Revenue (Million $)**

| | 1Q | 2Q | 3Q | 4Q | Year |
|---|---|---|---|---|---|
| 2011 | 605.5 | 645.2 | 709.8 | 780.4 | 2,741 |
| 2010 | 546.9 | 560.4 | 616.0 | 678.6 | 2,402 |
| 2009 | 578.0 | 543.3 | 555.9 | 652.0 | 2,329 |
| 2008 | 561.0 | 625.8 | 661.7 | 723.2 | 2,572 |
| 2007 | 499.3 | 544.9 | 559.4 | 646.3 | 2,250 |
| 2006 | 431.2 | 478.4 | 510.0 | 597.3 | 2,017 |

**Earnings Per Share ($)**

| | | | | | |
|---|---|---|---|---|---|
| 2011 | 0.61 | 0.64 | 0.60 | 0.82 | 2.67 |
| 2010 | 0.56 | 0.42 | 0.58 | 0.46 | 2.03 |
| 2009 | 0.36 | 0.33 | 0.37 | 0.58 | 1.64 |
| 2008 | 0.29 | 0.39 | 0.51 | 0.57 | 1.76 |
| 2007 | 0.13 | 0.36 | 0.40 | 0.57 | 1.03 |
| 2006 | 0.20 | 0.26 | 0.20 | 0.50 | 1.16 |

Fiscal year ended Jul. 31. Next earnings report expected: Early December. EPS Estimates based on S&P Operating Earnings; historical GAAP earnings are as reported.

## Dividend Data (Dates: mm/dd Payment Date: mm/dd/yy)

| Amount<br>($) | Date<br>Decl. | Ex-Div.<br>Date | Stk. of<br>Record | Payment<br>Date |
|---|---|---|---|---|
| 0.175 | 01/20 | 02/04 | 02/08 | 02/23/11 |
| 0.175 | 04/21 | 05/06 | 05/10 | 05/24/11 |
| 0.175 | 07/14 | 08/03 | 08/05 | 08/19/11 |
| 0.175 | 09/26 | 10/11 | 10/13 | 11/03/11 |

Dividends have been paid since 1974. Source: Company reports.

# Pall Corp

**STANDARD &POOR'S**

## Business Summary September 16, 2011

CORPORATE OVERVIEW. Pall Corp. is a global producer of filters for health care, aerospace and industrial markets. Pall divides these markets into the following subsegments: Medical, BioPharmaceuticals and Food & Beverage (the Life Sciences segment), Energy & Water, Aeropower and Microelectronics (the Industrial segment). The Industrial segment includes machinery and equipment, aerospace, fuels & chemicals, power generation and municipal water. System sales accounted for 18% of total sales in the fourth quarter of FY 11 (Jul.)., up from over 12% in the third quarter.

The Life Sciences segment contributed 51% of total revenues and $338 million of operating profits in FY 11. The BioPharmaceuticals division makes filter products used in the development of drugs and vaccines, while food and beverage filters help produce yeast- and bacteria-free water. The rapidly expanding blood division offers hospitals and blood centers blood filters that reduce leukocyte (white cells) and other bloodborne viral contaminants, such as bacteria. Biopharmaceutical sales accounted for 52% of the segment's total sales in FY 11, while medical products (blood and cardiovascular filtration) accounted for 30%, and food & beverage 18%. PLL projects the potential size of the medical market at $6.8 billion by FY 13.

The Industrial segment (49% and $196 million) makes filters and separation products for three markets. Aeropower (36% of segment sales) includes commercial and military markets. Energy & Water (40%) produces filters for the aluminum, paper, automobile, oil, gas, chemical, petrochemical and power industries. Microelectronics (24%) makes products for the semiconductor, data storage and photographic film industries. Main competitors in the Energy & Water group include 3M's CUNO, General Electric's GE Infrastructure unit, Siemens's U.S. Filter, Rohm & Haas (acquired by Dow Chemical in 2009), and Parker-Hannifin. More than 90% of systems sales are in this segment. PLL sees a potential market for this group of $39 billion.

In FY 11, the Western Hemisphere accounted for 33% of sales, Europe for 39%, and Asia for 28%. In FY 11, pro forma EPS was $2.77, excluding $0.10 of restructuring and other charges. Foreign currency added $0.13 to EPS.

## Company Financials Fiscal Year Ended Jul. 31

| Per Share Data ($) | 2011 | 2010 | 2009 | 2008 | 2007 | 2006 | 2005 | 2004 | 2003 | 2002 |
|---|---|---|---|---|---|---|---|---|---|---|
| Tangible Book Value | 9.89 | 7.19 | 6.57 | 6.94 | 6.14 | 7.21 | 6.73 | 6.21 | 5.16 | NM |
| Cash Flow | 3.50 | 2.82 | 2.38 | 2.51 | 1.78 | 1.92 | 1.85 | 1.90 | 1.51 | 1.19 |
| Earnings | 2.67 | 2.03 | 1.64 | 1.76 | 1.03 | 1.16 | 1.12 | 1.20 | 0.83 | 0.59 |
| S&P Core Earnings | 2.82 | 2.11 | 1.55 | 1.67 | 1.05 | 1.22 | 1.13 | 1.16 | 0.70 | 0.42 |
| Dividends | 0.67 | 0.61 | 0.42 | 0.50 | 0.35 | 0.53 | 0.38 | 0.27 | 0.36 | 0.52 |
| Payout Ratio | 25% | 30% | 26% | 28% | 34% | 46% | 34% | 23% | 43% | 88% |
| Prices:High | 59.50 | 51.01 | 37.25 | 43.19 | 49.00 | 35.57 | 31.52 | 29.80 | 27.00 | 24.48 |
| Prices:Low | 39.81 | 31.84 | 18.20 | 21.61 | 33.23 | 25.26 | 25.21 | 22.00 | 15.01 | 14.68 |
| P/E Ratio:High | 22 | 25 | 23 | 25 | 48 | 31 | 28 | 25 | 33 | 41 |
| P/E Ratio:Low | 15 | 16 | 11 | 12 | 32 | 22 | 23 | 18 | 18 | 25 |

| Income Statement Analysis (Million $) | | | | | | | | | | |
|---|---|---|---|---|---|---|---|---|---|---|
| Revenue | 2,741 | 2,402 | 2,329 | 2,572 | 2,250 | 2,017 | 1,902 | 1,771 | 1,614 | 1,291 |
| Operating Income | 570 | 484 | 419 | 483 | 419 | 341 | 337 | 320 | 299 | 215 |
| Depreciation | 98.1 | 93.6 | 89.2 | 93.2 | 94.0 | 95.7 | 90.9 | 88.9 | 83.9 | 74.0 |
| Interest Expense | 26.1 | 14.3 | 36.9 | 50.9 | 56.8 | 23.0 | 26.0 | 20.5 | 24.4 | 14.3 |
| Pretax Income | 420 | 328 | 271 | 326 | 261 | 210 | 181 | 198 | 143 | 100.0 |
| Effective Tax Rate | NA | NA | 27.8% | 33.3% | 51.1% | 30.8% | 22.2% | 23.4% | 27.9% | 26.7% |
| Net Income | 316 | 241 | 196 | 217 | 128 | 145 | 141 | 152 | 103 | 73.2 |
| S&P Core Earnings | 334 | 250 | 185 | 205 | 131 | 153 | 142 | 148 | 87.4 | 52.1 |

| Balance Sheet & Other Financial Data (Million $) | | | | | | | | | | |
|---|---|---|---|---|---|---|---|---|---|---|
| Cash | 558 | 499 | 414 | 454 | 443 | 318 | 165 | 199 | 127 | 105 |
| Current Assets | 1,809 | 1,703 | 1,570 | 1,660 | 1,606 | 1,377 | 1,160 | 1,070 | 938 | 916 |
| Total Assets | 3,232 | 2,999 | 2,841 | 2,957 | 2,709 | 2,553 | 2,265 | 2,140 | 2,017 | 2,027 |
| Current Liabilities | 790 | 637 | 717 | 574 | 832 | 531 | 457 | 419 | 421 | 438 |
| Long Term Debt | 492 | 741 | 578 | 747 | 592 | 640 | 510 | 489 | 490 | 620 |
| Common Equity | 1,490 | 1,182 | 1,115 | 1,139 | 1,061 | 1,179 | 1,140 | 1,054 | 935 | 820 |
| Total Capital | 1,982 | 1,924 | 1,692 | 1,890 | 1,654 | 1,826 | 1,660 | 1,559 | 1,439 | 1,478 |
| Capital Expenditures | 161 | 136 | 133 | 124 | 97.8 | 96.0 | 86.2 | 61.3 | 62.2 | 69.9 |
| Cash Flow | 414 | 335 | 285 | 310 | 221 | 241 | 232 | 241 | 187 | 147 |
| Current Ratio | 2.3 | 2.7 | 2.2 | 2.9 | 1.9 | 2.6 | 2.5 | 2.6 | 2.2 | 2.1 |
| % Long Term Debt of Capitalization | 24.8 | 38.5 | 34.1 | 39.4 | 35.8 | 35.0 | 30.7 | 31.3 | 34.0 | 41.9 |
| % Net Income of Revenue | 11.5 | 10.0 | 8.4 | 8.5 | 5.7 | 7.2 | 7.4 | 8.6 | 6.4 | 5.7 |
| % Return on Assets | 10.1 | 8.3 | 6.8 | 7.7 | 4.9 | 6.0 | 6.3 | 7.3 | 5.1 | 4.1 |
| % Return on Equity | 23.6 | 21.0 | 17.4 | 19.8 | 11.4 | 12.5 | 12.8 | 15.2 | 11.8 | 9.2 |

Data as orig reptd.; bef. results of disc opers/spec. items. Per share data adj. for stk. divs.; EPS diluted. E-Estimated. NA-Not Available. NM-Not Meaningful. NR-Not Ranked. UR-Under Review.

**Office:** 25 Harbor Park Dr, Port Washington, NY 11050.
**Telephone:** 516-484-5400.
**Email:** investor_relations@pall.com
**Website:** http://www.pall.com

**Chrmn:** R.L. Hoffman
**Pres & CEO:** L.D. Kingsley
**COO:** R. Perez
**SVP, Secy & General Counsel:** R.G. Kuhbach

**CFO & Treas:** L. McDermott
**Investor Contact:** P. Iannucci (516-801-9848)
**Board Members:** A. E. Alving, D. J. Carroll, Jr., R. B. Coutts, C. W. Grise, R. L. Hoffman, L. D. Kingsley, D. N. Longstreet, E. W. Martin, Jr., K. L. Plourde, E. L. Snyder, E. Travaglianti

**Founded:** 1946
**Domicile:** New York
**Employees:** 10,900

*The McGraw-Hill Companies*

# Parker-Hannifin Corp



**S&P Recommendation** STRONG BUY ★★★★★

**Price** $78.26 (as of Nov 29, 2011)

**12-Mo. Target Price** $110.00

**Investment Style** Large-Cap Blend

**GICS Sector** Industrials
**Sub-Industry** Industrial Machinery

**Summary** This company is a global maker of industrial pneumatic, hydraulic and vacuum motion/control systems, including related pumps, valves, filters, hoses, etc. Its products are used in everything from jet engines to trucks and autos and utility turbines.

## Key Stock Statistics (Source S&P, Vickers, company reports)

| | | | | | | | |
|---|---|---|---|---|---|---|---|
| 52-Wk Range | **$99.40– 59.26** | S&P Oper. EPS 2012**E** | **7.55** | Market Capitalization(B) | **$11.824** | Beta | **1.50** |
| Trailing 12-Month EPS | **$6.76** | S&P Oper. EPS 2013**E** | **8.10** | Yield (%) | **1.89** | S&P 3-Yr. Proj. EPS CAGR(%) | **10** |
| Trailing 12-Month P/E | **11.6** | P/E on S&P Oper. EPS 2012**E** | **10.4** | Dividend Rate/Share | **$1.48** | S&P Credit Rating | **A** |
| $10K Invested 5 Yrs Ago | **$14,468** | Common Shares Outstg. (M) | **151.1** | Institutional Ownership (%) | **80** | | |

## Price Performance

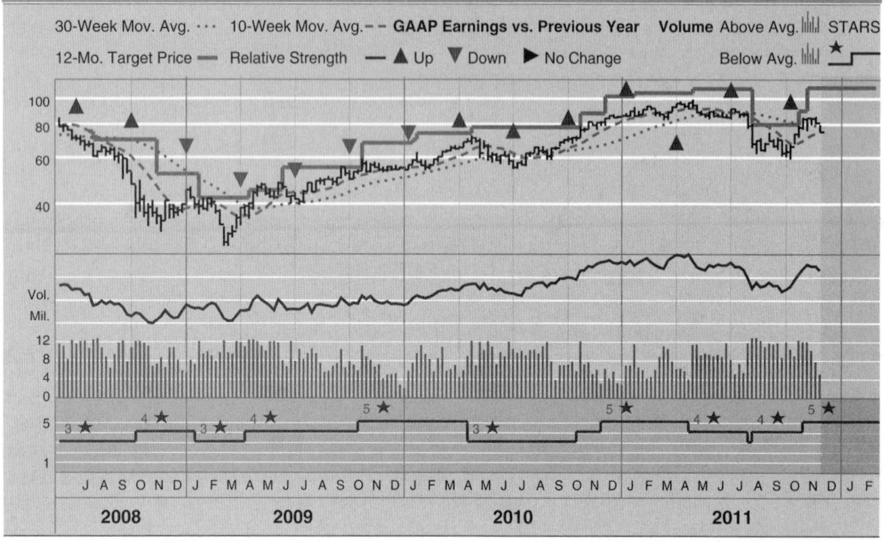
30-Week Mov. Avg. ··· 10-Week Mov. Avg. – – GAAP Earnings vs. Previous Year Volume Above Avg. STARS
12-Mo. Target Price — Relative Strength — ▲ Up ▼ Down ▶ No Change Below Avg.
100
80
60
40
Vol.
Mil.
12
8
4
0
5
1
J A S O N D J F M A M J J A S O N D J F M A M J J A S O N D J F M A M J J A S O N D J F
2008
2009
2010
2011

Options: ASE, CBOE, Ph

Analysis prepared by Equity Analyst **R. Tortoriello** on Nov 29, 2011, when the stock traded at **$78.68**.

## Highlights

- We project revenues will increase 8% in FY 12 (Jun.), to an all-time high for PH of over $13 billion. Our revenue projection is supported by recent order trends, with order growth of 24% in the third quarter of FY 11, 15% in the fourth quarter, and 9% in the first quarter of FY 12. The Industrial North America segment showed particularly strong order growth of 16% in the FY 12 first quarter. Although we see slowing international economic activity, particularly in Europe, we note that emerging markets still continue to grow strongly.
- We believe PH has put in place excellent productivity enhancement programs, and note that operating margins reached an all-time record (along with sales) of 13.4% in FY 11. Although compensation expenses are rising, we see further operating margin gains to 13.8% in FY 12, on increased volume.
- We estimate EPS of $7.55 in FY 12 and $8.10 in FY 13. We see free cash flow (cash flow from operations minus capital expenditures) about even with income in FY 13.

## Investment Rationale/Risk

- We believe that trends in all four of Parker's business segments remain positive, despite expectations of weakening in Europe and evidence of some slowing growth in China. In commercial aerospace, we see plans by Boeing and Airbus to increase production through 2014 as aiding growth at PH. In Industrial, we expect rising aftermarket demand in the U.S. to support growth, and project international growth will continue, but at a slower pace than in FY 11. We see current valuations as compelling, due to our belief that a cyclical economic recovery is continuing.
- Risks to our recommendation and target price include the potential for an economic recession in the Europe, difficulties in the aerospace market, and operational or other missteps at the company.
- Our 12-month target price of $110 is based on an enterprise value-to-EBITDA multiple of about 8.5X our FY 12 EBITDA estimate, versus PH's historical average of 8X. We view this valuation as appropriate given what we view that profits will continue to grow significantly over the next two years.

## Qualitative Risk Assessment

LOW | **MEDIUM** | HIGH

Our risk assessment reflects the highly cyclical nature of the company's industrial and aviation markets, volatile energy and materials costs, and a competitive environment. This is offset by our view of PH's favorable earnings and dividend track record, as exemplified by an S&P Quality Ranking of A (High).

## Quantitative Evaluations

**S&P Quality Ranking** **A**

D | C | B- | B | B+ | A- | **A** | A+

**Relative Strength Rank** **STRONG**

82

LOWEST = 1 HIGHEST = 99

## Revenue/Earnings Data

**Revenue (Million $)**

| | 1Q | 2Q | 3Q | 4Q | Year |
|---|---|---|---|---|---|
| 2012 | 3,234 | -- | -- | -- | -- |
| 2011 | 2,829 | 2,867 | 3,240 | 3,410 | 12,346 |
| 2010 | 2,237 | 2,355 | 2,615 | 2,786 | 9,993 |
| 2009 | 3,065 | 2,689 | 2,345 | 2,211 | 10,309 |
| 2008 | 2,787 | 2,829 | 3,183 | 3,347 | 12,146 |
| 2007 | 2,552 | 2,511 | 2,781 | 2,874 | 10,718 |

**Earnings Per Share ($)**

| | | | | | |
|---|---|---|---|---|---|
| 2012 | 1.91 | **E**1.66 | **E**2.00 | **E**1.99 | **E**7.55 |
| 2011 | 1.51 | 1.39 | 1.68 | 1.79 | 6.37 |
| 2010 | 0.45 | 0.64 | 0.94 | 1.35 | 3.40 |
| 2009 | 1.50 | 0.96 | 0.33 | 0.31 | 3.13 |
| 2008 | 1.33 | 1.23 | 1.49 | 1.47 | 5.53 |
| 2007 | 1.17 | 1.09 | 1.19 | 1.23 | 4.67 |

Fiscal year ended Jun. 30. Next earnings report expected: Late January. EPS Estimates based on S&P Operating Earnings; historical GAAP earnings are as reported.

## Dividend Data (Dates: mm/dd Payment Date: mm/dd/yy)

| Amount ($) | Date Decl. | Ex-Div. Date | Stk. of Record | Payment Date |
|---|---|---|---|---|
| 0.320 | 01/27 | 02/08 | 02/10 | 03/04/11 |
| 0.370 | 04/27 | 05/06 | 05/10 | 06/03/11 |
| 0.370 | 08/18 | 08/25 | 08/29 | 09/09/11 |
| 0.370 | 10/26 | 11/08 | 11/10 | 12/02/11 |

Dividends have been paid since 1949. Source: Company reports.



Redistribution or reproduction is prohibited without written permission. Copyright ©2011 The McGraw-Hill Companies, Inc.

The McGraw·Hill Companies

# Parker-Hannifin Corp

**STANDARD &POOR'S**

## Business Summary November 29, 2011

CORPORATE OVERVIEW. Parker-Hannifin is one of the world's largest makers of components that control the flow of industrial fluids. It is also a major global maker of components that move and/or control the operation of a variety of machinery and equipment. In addition to motion control products, PH also produces fluid purification, fluid and fuel control, process instrumentation, air conditioning, refrigeration, electromagnetic shielding, and thermal management products and systems. PH's offerings include a wide range of valves, pumps, hydraulics, filters and related products. The company's components are used in everything from jet engines to medical devices, farm tractors and utility turbines.

PH has been expanding its overseas presence in recent years. International sales accounted for 42% of total revenue in FY 11 (Jun.) and 41% in FY 10.

PH's Industrial business (77% of FY 12 sales and 82% of segment operating earnings) makes valves, pumps, filters, seals and hydraulic components for a broad range of industries, as well as pneumatic and electromechanical components and systems. The company's industrial components are sold to manufacturers (as part of original equipment) and to end-users (as replacement parts). Replacement part sales are generally more profitable than original

equipment sales, and are primarily sold through distributors. PH's industrial components are designed for both standard and custom specifications. Custom-made components are typically more profitable than standard components. The industrial business is reported as two segments: Industrial North America (37% of sales and 41% of operating profits) and Industrial International (40% and 41%). Sales through distributors account for about half of PH's total industrial business.

Aerospace (15% of sales and 14% of segment operating profits) primarily makes hydraulic, pneumatic and fuel equipment used in civilian and military airframes and jet engines. It also makes aircraft wheels and brakes for small planes and military aircraft. PH sells aircraft components to aircraft manufacturers as new equipment, and to end-users (such as airlines) as replacement parts. As with industrial components, aircraft-related replacement parts sales are generally more profitable than are original equipment sales.

## Company Financials Fiscal Year Ended Jun. 30

| Per Share Data ($) | 2011 | 2010 | 2009 | 2008 | 2007 | 2006 | 2005 | 2004 | 2003 | 2002 |
|---|---|---|---|---|---|---|---|---|---|---|
| Tangible Book Value | 7.72 | 2.68 | 0.07 | 8.59 | 10.69 | 9.75 | 9.23 | 9.39 | 7.63 | 8.18 |
| Cash Flow | 8.48 | 5.63 | 5.32 | 7.43 | 6.45 | 5.07 | 4.50 | 3.34 | 2.57 | 2.37 |
| Earnings | 6.37 | 3.40 | 3.13 | 5.53 | 4.67 | 3.52 | 3.03 | 1.94 | 1.12 | 0.75 |
| S&P Core Earnings | 6.65 | 3.76 | 2.71 | 5.10 | 4.77 | 3.83 | 3.08 | 2.00 | 0.61 | 0.37 |
| Dividends | 1.25 | 1.01 | 1.00 | 0.84 | 0.69 | 0.61 | 0.52 | 0.51 | 0.49 | 0.48 |
| Payout Ratio | 20% | 30% | 32% | 15% | 15% | 17% | 17% | 26% | 44% | 64% |
| Prices:High | 99.40 | 87.36 | 59.36 | 86.91 | 86.56 | 58.67 | 50.82 | 52.28 | 39.87 | 36.59 |
| Prices:Low | 59.26 | 53.50 | 27.69 | 31.29 | 50.41 | 43.44 | 37.87 | 34.49 | 23.88 | 23.01 |
| P/E Ratio:High | 16 | 26 | 19 | 16 | 19 | 17 | 17 | 27 | 36 | 49 |
| P/E Ratio:Low | 9 | 16 | 9 | 6 | 11 | 12 | 12 | 18 | 21 | 31 |

| Income Statement Analysis (Million $) | | | | | | | | | | |
|---|---|---|---|---|---|---|---|---|---|---|
| Revenue | 12,346 | 9,993 | 10,309 | 12,146 | 10,718 | 9,386 | 8,215 | 7,107 | 6,411 | 6,149 |
| Operating Income | 1,830 | 1,232 | 1,196 | 1,773 | 1,513 | 1,263 | 1,100 | 817 | 639 | 628 |
| Depreciation | 340 | 363 | 358 | 325 | 295 | 281 | 265 | 253 | 259 | 282 |
| Interest Expense | 99.7 | 104 | 112 | 99.0 | 83.4 | 75.8 | 67.0 | 73.4 | 81.6 | 82.0 |
| Pretax Income | 1,414 | 755 | 681 | 1,327 | 1,159 | 900 | 756 | 494 | 297 | 218 |
| Effective Tax Rate | NA | NA | 25.4% | 28.4% | 28.4% | NM | 27.6% | 30.0% | 34.0% | 40.3% |
| Net Income | 1,057 | 554 | 509 | 949 | 830 | 638 | 548 | 346 | 196 | 130 |
| S&P Core Earnings | 1,095 | 613 | 441 | 876 | 846 | 694 | 557 | 357 | 107 | 65.0 |

| Balance Sheet & Other Financial Data (Million $) | | | | | | | | | | |
|---|---|---|---|---|---|---|---|---|---|---|
| Cash | 657 | 576 | 188 | 326 | 173 | 172 | 336 | 184 | 246 | 46.0 |
| Current Assets | 4,305 | 3,589 | 3,124 | 4,096 | 3,386 | 3,139 | 2,786 | 2,537 | 2,397 | 2,236 |
| Total Assets | 10,887 | 9,910 | 9,856 | 10,387 | 8,441 | 8,173 | 6,899 | 6,257 | 5,986 | 5,733 |
| Current Liabilities | 2,391 | 2,205 | 2,006 | 2,183 | 1,925 | 1,681 | 1,336 | 1,260 | 1,424 | 1,360 |
| Long Term Debt | 1,691 | 1,414 | 1,840 | 1,952 | 1,087 | 1,059 | 938 | 954 | 966 | 1,089 |
| Common Equity | 5,384 | 4,368 | 4,280 | 5,259 | 4,712 | 4,241 | 3,340 | 2,982 | 2,521 | 2,584 |
| Total Capital | 7,284 | 5,873 | 6,393 | 7,374 | 5,913 | 5,419 | 4,314 | 4,015 | 3,508 | 3,750 |
| Capital Expenditures | 207 | 129 | 271 | 280 | 238 | 198 | 157 | 142 | 158 | 207 |
| Cash Flow | 1,397 | 917 | 866 | 1,274 | 1,125 | 919 | 813 | 599 | 455 | 412 |
| Current Ratio | 1.8 | 1.6 | 1.6 | 1.9 | 1.8 | 1.9 | 2.1 | 2.0 | 1.7 | 1.6 |
| % Long Term Debt of Capitalization | 23.2 | 24.1 | 28.8 | 26.5 | 18.4 | 19.6 | 21.8 | 23.8 | 27.5 | 29.0 |
| % Net Income of Revenue | 8.6 | 5.5 | 4.9 | 7.8 | 7.7 | 6.8 | 6.7 | 4.9 | 3.1 | 2.1 |
| % Return on Assets | 10.2 | 5.6 | 5.0 | 10.1 | 10.0 | 8.5 | 8.3 | 5.6 | 3.3 | 2.3 |
| % Return on Equity | 21.7 | 12.8 | 10.7 | 19.1 | 18.5 | 16.8 | 17.3 | 12.6 | 7.7 | 5.1 |

Data as orig reptd.; bef. results of disc opers/spec. items. Per share data adj. for stk. divs.; EPS diluted. E-Estimated. NA-Not Available. NM-Not Meaningful. NR-Not Ranked. UR-Under Review.

**Office:** 6035 Parkland Boulevard, Cleveland, OH 44124-4141.
**Telephone:** 216-896-3000.
**Website:** http://www.parker.com
**Chrmn, Pres & CEO:** D.E. Washkewicz

**CFO, Chief Admin Officer & Chief Acctg Officer:** J.P. Marten
**CTO:** M.C. Maxwell
**Investor Contact:** P.J. Huggins (216-896-2240)
**Secy & General Counsel:** T.A. Piraino, Jr.

**Board Members:** R. G. Bohn, L. S. Harty, W. E. Kassling, R. J. Kohlhepp, K. Muller, C. M. Obourn, J. M. Scaminace, W. R. Schmitt, A. Svensson, J. L. Wainscott, D. E. Washkewicz

**Founded:** 1924
**Domicile:** Ohio
**Employees:** 58,409

# Patterson Companies Inc

**STANDARD &POOR'S**

| | | | |
|---|---|---|---|
| **S&P Recommendation** HOLD ★★★★★ | **Price**<br>$28.73 (as of Nov 29, 2011) | **12-Mo. Target Price**<br>$31.00 | **Investment Style**<br>Large-Cap Growth |

**GICS Sector** Health Care
**Sub-Industry** Health Care Distributors

**Summary** One of the largest distributors of dental supplies in North America, this company also sells veterinary supplies and rehabilitative equipment.

## Key Stock Statistics (Source S&P, Vickers, company reports)

| | | | | | | | |
|---|---|---|---|---|---|---|---|
| 52-Wk Range | $36.93– 26.19 | S&P Oper. EPS 2012E | 1.96 | Market Capitalization(B) | $3.403 | Beta | 0.89 |
| Trailing 12-Month EPS | $1.84 | S&P Oper. EPS 2013E | 2.17 | Yield (%) | 1.67 | S&P 3-Yr. Proj. EPS CAGR(%) | 8 |
| Trailing 12-Month P/E | 15.6 | P/E on S&P Oper. EPS 2012E | 14.7 | Dividend Rate/Share | $0.48 | S&P Credit Rating | NA |
| $10K Invested 5 Yrs Ago | $7,813 | Common Shares Outstg. (M) | 118.5 | Institutional Ownership (%) | 73 | | |

## Price Performance

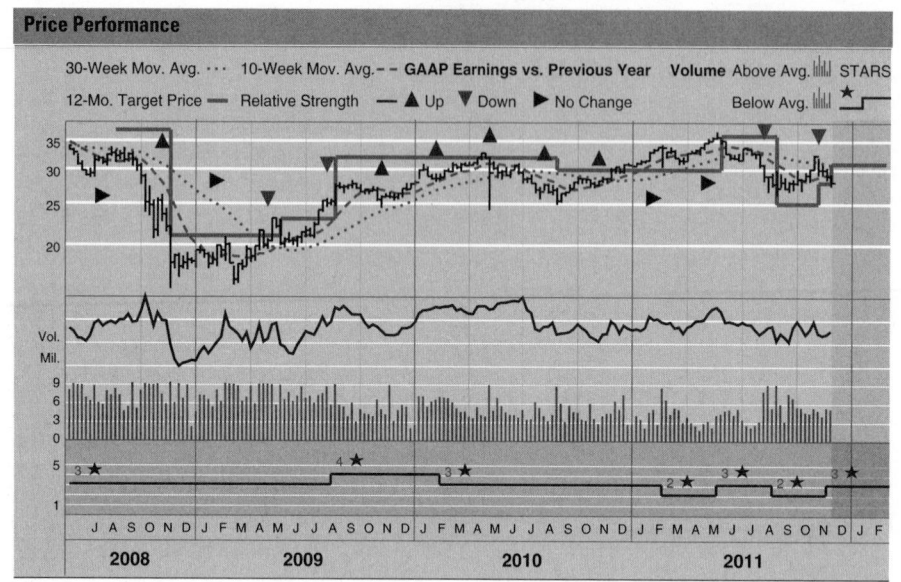

30-Week Mov. Avg. · · · 10-Week Mov. Avg. - - GAAP Earnings vs. Previous Year Volume Above Avg. STARS
12-Mo. Target Price — Relative Strength — ▲ Up ▼ Down ▶ No Change Below Avg.

Options: CBOE, Ph

Analysis prepared by Equity Analyst **Herman Saftlas** on Nov 29, 2011, when the stock traded at **$29.01**.

## Qualitative Risk Assessment

| LOW | MEDIUM | HIGH |
|---|---|---|

Our risk assessment is based on our view of PDCO's strong long-term record of earnings growth, offset by the impact that the economy and consumer confidence can have on consumer demand for the services of the company's dental, medical and veterinary clients. Another risk relates to the company's ability to make accretive acquisitions.

## Quantitative Evaluations

**S&P Quality Ranking** B+

| D | C | B- | B | B+ | A- | A | A+ |
|---|---|---|---|---|---|---|---|

**Relative Strength Rank** MODERATE

55

LOWEST = 1          HIGHEST = 99

## Highlights

▶ Revenues are expected to increase about 3% in FY 12 (Apr.), based on the consensus forecast from Capital IQ. We look for modest growth in sales of dental consumables, largely reflecting higher prices. However, sales of the company's Cerec dental restorative systems and digital radiography products are expected to decline, based on more constrained dental budgets, especially for high-priced technology equipment. We also project higher sales of rehabilitation supplies, and veterinary products should show modest growth, helped by contributions from new products and acquisitions.

▶ We expect FY 12 gross margins to slip somewhat from FY 11's 33.5%, reflecting a less profitable sales mix. Also, FY 12 will have 52 weeks, versus 53 weeks in FY 11, and FY 12 will include a non-cash charge of $0.12 a share resulting from a change in accounting for an employee stock ownership plan. We expect the FY 12 effective tax rate to be in the 36.5% to 37% range.

▶ The consensus EPS estimates from Capital IQ are $1.96 for FY 12 and $2.17 for FY 13, versus $1.89 in FY 11. EPS should benefit from share buybacks.

## Investment Rationale/Risk

▶ Well positioned as one of the two largest distributors of dental products and equipment in North America, Patterson has diversified its business through acquisitions in veterinary products and patient rehabilitation products. We expect PDCO's key business segments to exhibit growth over the coming years, helped by expanded production capacity, acquisitions and new products. We also see long-term potential from Cerec dental restorative systems and digital radiography products. However, we think near-term prospects are likely to be challenged by slowing trends in consumer spending and government measures aimed at curtailing growth in health care spending.

▶ Risks to our recommendation and target price include weaker than expected demand for dental equipment and supplies in the U.S., greater than expected pricing pressures in Europe, and lack of success in completing new accretive acquisitions.

▶ Our 12-month target price of $31 applies a multiple of 15.8X to the consensus FY 12 EPS estimate of $1.96, which is near the upper end of PDCO's recent P/E range.

## Revenue/Earnings Data

**Revenue (Million $)**

| | 1Q | 2Q | 3Q | 4Q | Year |
|---|---|---|---|---|---|
| 2012 | 847.4 | 856.9 | -- | -- | -- |
| 2011 | 849.8 | 857.4 | 824.7 | 883.8 | 3,416 |
| 2010 | 789.6 | 815.0 | 820.1 | 812.8 | 3,237 |
| 2009 | 743.9 | 759.5 | 811.0 | 779.9 | 3,094 |
| 2008 | 701.4 | 742.0 | 777.0 | 778.4 | 2,999 |
| 2007 | 655.5 | 694.3 | 709.5 | 739.1 | 2,798 |

**Earnings Per Share ($)**

| | | | | | |
|---|---|---|---|---|---|
| 2012 | 0.42 | 0.43 | E0.50 | E0.56 | E1.96 |
| 2011 | 0.45 | 0.45 | 0.47 | 0.52 | 1.89 |
| 2010 | 0.38 | 0.41 | 0.47 | 0.52 | 1.78 |
| 2009 | 0.39 | 0.40 | 0.45 | 0.46 | 1.69 |
| 2008 | 0.39 | 0.39 | 0.45 | 0.51 | 1.69 |
| 2007 | 0.30 | 0.35 | 0.43 | 0.44 | 1.51 |

Fiscal year ended Apr. 30. Next earnings report expected: Late February. EPS Estimates based on S&P Operating Earnings; historical GAAP earnings are as reported.

## Dividend Data (Dates: mm/dd Payment Date: mm/dd/yy)

| Amount ($) | Date Decl. | Ex-Div. Date | Stk. of Record | Payment Date |
|---|---|---|---|---|
| 0.100 | 12/08 | 01/07 | 01/11 | 01/28/11 |
| 0.120 | 03/16 | 04/07 | 04/11 | 04/28/11 |
| 0.120 | 06/14 | 07/07 | 07/11 | 07/28/11 |
| 0.120 | 09/14 | 10/06 | 10/11 | 10/28/11 |

Dividends have been paid since 2010. Source: Company reports.

# Patterson Companies Inc

**STANDARD &POOR'S**

## Business Summary November 29, 2011

Patterson Companies, Inc. (PDCO) operates as a distributor serving the dental, companion-pet veterinarian and rehabilitation supply markets. Dental Supply accounted for 65% of revenues and 72% of operating profits in FY 11 (Apr.); Veterinary Supply for 20% and 10%; and Rehabilitation Supply for 15% and 18%. Foreign operations represented 12% of sales and 11% of pretax income in FY 11.

The Dental Supply segment distributes dental products in North America. Patterson Dental, a supplier to dentists, dental laboratories, institutions, and other health care professionals, provides consumable products (including X-ray film, restorative materials, hand instruments and sterilization products); basic and advanced technology dental equipment; practice management and clinical software; patient education systems; and office forms and stationery.

Consumable dental supplies comprise a broad portfolio of products such as X-ray film and solutions; impression materials; restorative materials (composites and alloys); hand instruments; sterilization products; anesthetics; infection control products such as gloves, facemasks and other protective clothing; paper, cotton, and other disposable products; and toothbrushes and a full line of dental accessories, including instruments, burs and diamonds. The company provides various printed office products, office filing supplies and practice

management systems to office-based health care providers.

The Veterinary Supply segment includes Webster Veterinary, a distributor of veterinary supplies to companion-pet (dogs, cats and other common household pets) veterinary clinics in the eastern United States. Webster distributes various consumable supplies, equipment, diagnostic supplies, biologicals, and pharmaceuticals. Webster's product offering totals approximately 11,000 items.

Webster also offers its customers a selection of veterinary supply products, including consumable supplies, pharmaceuticals, diagnostics, and biologicals. Consumable supplies distributed by Webster include lab supplies, various types and sizes of paper goods, needles and syringes, gauze and wound dressings, sutures, latex gloves, and orthopedic and casting products. Webster's pharmaceutical products include anesthetics, antibiotics, injectibles, ointments and nutraceuticals.

## Company Financials Fiscal Year Ended Apr. 30

| Per Share Data ($) | 2011 | 2010 | 2009 | 2008 | 2007 | 2006 | 2005 | 2004 | 2003 | 2002 |
|---|---|---|---|---|---|---|---|---|---|---|
| Tangible Book Value | 4.44 | 3.53 | 1.79 | 1.01 | 3.70 | 2.73 | 1.95 | 0.76 | 3.66 | 2.85 |
| Cash Flow | 2.24 | 2.11 | 1.88 | 1.84 | 1.70 | 1.60 | 1.52 | 1.27 | 0.94 | 0.80 |
| Earnings | 1.89 | 1.78 | 1.69 | 1.69 | 1.51 | 1.43 | 1.32 | 1.09 | 0.85 | 0.70 |
| S&P Core Earnings | 1.89 | 1.78 | 1.69 | 1.69 | 1.51 | 1.39 | 1.30 | 1.08 | 0.84 | 0.70 |
| Dividends | NA | Nil | Nil | Nil | Nil | Nil | Nil | Nil | Nil | Nil |
| Payout Ratio | NA | Nil | Nil | Nil | Nil | Nil | Nil | Nil | Nil | Nil |
| Calendar Year | 2010 | 2009 | 2008 | 2007 | 2006 | 2005 | 2004 | 2003 | 2002 | 2001 |
| Prices:High | 32.84 | 28.34 | 37.78 | 40.08 | 38.28 | 53.85 | 44.20 | 35.75 | 27.56 | 21.03 |
| Prices:Low | 24.13 | 16.08 | 15.75 | 28.32 | 29.61 | 33.21 | 29.70 | 17.71 | 19.00 | 13.75 |
| P/E Ratio:High | 17 | 16 | 22 | 24 | 25 | 38 | 33 | 33 | 32 | 30 |
| P/E Ratio:Low | 13 | 9 | 9 | 17 | 20 | 23 | 22 | 16 | 22 | 20 |

| Income Statement Analysis (Million $) | | | | | | | | | | |
|---|---|---|---|---|---|---|---|---|---|---|
| Revenue | 3,416 | 3,237 | 3,094 | 2,999 | 2,798 | 2,615 | 2,421 | 1,969 | 1,657 | 1,416 |
| Operating Income | 417 | 395 | 369 | 379 | 361 | 347 | 329 | 262 | 192 | 161 |
| Depreciation | 41.3 | 39.5 | 22.9 | 19.5 | 25.5 | 23.7 | 26.9 | 19.4 | 12.8 | 14.3 |
| Interest Expense | 25.8 | 25.7 | 30.2 | 0.12 | 14.2 | 13.4 | 15.1 | 9.60 | 0.07 | 0.11 |
| Pretax Income | 356 | 339 | 320 | 357 | 330 | 317 | 293 | 240 | 186 | 152 |
| Effective Tax Rate | NA | NA | 37.6% | 37.1% | 36.8% | 37.4% | 37.4% | 37.6% | 37.6% | 37.4% |
| Net Income | 225 | 212 | 200 | 225 | 208 | 198 | 184 | 150 | 116 | 95.3 |
| S&P Core Earnings | 225 | 212 | 200 | 225 | 208 | 194 | 180 | 147 | 115 | 95.3 |

| Balance Sheet & Other Financial Data (Million $) | | | | | | | | | | |
|---|---|---|---|---|---|---|---|---|---|---|
| Cash | 389 | 341 | 158 | 308 | 242 | 224 | 233 | 287 | 195 | 126 |
| Current Assets | 1,231 | 1,134 | 938 | 985 | 886 | 847 | 800 | 778 | 606 | 529 |
| Total Assets | 2,565 | 2,423 | 2,129 | 2,076 | 1,940 | 1,912 | 1,685 | 1,589 | 824 | 718 |
| Current Liabilities | 367 | 348 | 334 | 466 | 377 | 410 | 322 | 264 | 184 | 198 |
| Long Term Debt | 525 | 525 | 525 | 525 | 130 | 210 | 302 | 480 | 0.13 | Nil |
| Common Equity | 1,561 | 1,442 | 1,186 | 1,005 | 1,379 | 1,243 | 1,015 | 802 | 634 | 514 |
| Total Capital | 2,086 | 1,967 | 1,250 | 1,660 | 1,563 | 1,502 | 1,363 | 1,325 | 634 | 514 |
| Capital Expenditures | 36.8 | 29.8 | 32.3 | 36.0 | 19.5 | 49.2 | 31.5 | 19.6 | 11.4 | 11.1 |
| Cash Flow | 267 | 252 | 223 | 244 | 234 | 222 | 211 | 169 | 129 | 110 |
| Current Ratio | 3.4 | 3.3 | 2.8 | 2.1 | 2.3 | 2.1 | 2.5 | 2.9 | 3.3 | 2.7 |
| % Long Term Debt of Capitalization | 25.2 | 26.7 | 42.0 | 33.1 | 8.3 | 14.0 | 22.1 | 36.2 | Nil | Nil |
| % Net Income of Revenue | 6.6 | 6.6 | 6.5 | 7.5 | 7.4 | 7.6 | 7.6 | 7.6 | 7.0 | 6.7 |
| % Return on Assets | 9.0 | 9.3 | 9.5 | 11.2 | 10.8 | 11.0 | 11.2 | 12.4 | 15.1 | 15.0 |
| % Return on Equity | 15.0 | 16.2 | 18.2 | 18.9 | 15.9 | 17.6 | 20.2 | 20.8 | 20.3 | 20.7 |

Data as orig reptd.; bef. results of disc opers/spec. items. Per share data adj. for stk. divs.; EPS diluted. E-Estimated. NA-Not Available. NM-Not Meaningful. NR-Not Ranked. UR-Under Review.

**Office:** 1031 Mendota Heights Road, St Paul, MN 55120.
**Telephone:** 651-686-1600.
**Email:** investors@pattersondental.com
**Website:** http://www.pattersoncompanies.com

**Chrmn:** P.L. Frechette
**Pres & CEO:** S.P. Anderson
**EVP, CFO, Chief Acctg Officer & Treas:** R.S. Armstrong
**Secy & General Counsel:** M.L. Levitt

**CIO:** R.M. Hamm
**Board Members:** S. P. Anderson, J. D. Buck, J. H. Feragen, P. L. Frechette, A. B. Lacy, C. Reich, E. A. Rudnick, H. C. Slavkin, B. S. Tyler, L. C. Vinney, J. W. Wiltz

**Founded:** 1877
**Domicile:** Minnesota
**Employees:** 7,100

# Paychex Inc

**STANDARD & POOR'S**

**S&P Recommendation** BUY ★★★★☆

| Price | 12-Mo. Target Price | Investment Style |
|---|---|---|
| $27.33 (as of Nov 25, 2011) | $33.00 | Large-Cap Growth |

**GICS Sector** Information Technology
**Sub-Industry** Data Processing & Outsourced Services

**Summary** Paychex provides payroll accounting services to small- and medium-sized concerns throughout the U.S.

## Key Stock Statistics (Source S&P, Vickers, company reports)

| | | | | | |
|---|---|---|---|---|---|
| 52-Wk Range | $33.91–25.12 | S&P Oper. EPS 2012E | 1.52 | Market Capitalization(B) | $9.904 |
| Trailing 12-Month EPS | $1.47 | S&P Oper. EPS 2013E | 1.62 | Yield (%) | 4.68 |
| Trailing 12-Month P/E | 18.6 | P/E on S&P Oper. EPS 2012E | 18.0 | Dividend Rate/Share | $1.28 |
| $10K Invested 5 Yrs Ago | $8,373 | Common Shares Outstg. (M) | 362.4 | Institutional Ownership (%) | 67 |

| | |
|---|---|
| Beta | 0.84 |
| S&P 3-Yr. Proj. EPS CAGR(%) | 4 |
| S&P Credit Rating | NA |

## Price Performance

Options: ASE, CBOE, Ph

Analysis prepared by Equity Analyst **Dylan Cathers** on Sep 30, 2011, when the stock traded at **$26.60**.

## Highlights

➤ We look for total revenue growth of 6.0% in FY 12 (May), and expect an improvement to 7.0% in FY 13. We see company benefiting from an improving pricing environment, slowly rising levels of checks per client, and additional clients from two recent acquisitions. Nonetheless, we believe that new client growth will remain lackluster in the near term, as the company reports weak new business formation. We estimate a gain in the company's core payroll services business of 4.0% for the full fiscal year, versus 2.4% last year, but we think HR services growth will be in the low double digits. Interest on funds held for clients should remain weak due to low short-term interest rates.

➤ We expect higher expenses this fiscal year relating to the additional workforce from recent acquisitions, from PAYX's own sales force increases, an updated compensation plan, training programs, and other investments in the business. We believe these extra expenses will mostly offset solid cost controls, reduced attrition levels, improving customer retention rates, and increased checks per client.

➤ We look for EPS of $1.52 in FY 12, with an increase to $1.62 in FY 13.

## Investment Rationale/Risk

➤ Given the current economic weakness and accompanying stagnant employment market, we believe growth in the small and mid-sized business segment that PAYX caters to will be slow to materialize. There have been some improvements in PAYX's fundamentals, and we expect some traction on efforts to revitalize the sales force. We view the balance sheet as strong, with no debt and over $485 million in cash and corporate investments. We also point to the shares' recent 4.5%-plus dividend yield.

➤ Risks to our recommendation and target price stem from volatility in the small- to medium-sized business environment, and the impact of competition on pricing and margins. Automatic Data Processing (ADP 47, Buy) is the leader in the payroll processing space, and is promoting a payroll processing and tax filing software solution coupled with Microsoft's small business software. Separately, the employment environment could remain weak for an extended period of time.

➤ We arrive at our 12-month target price of $33 by applying a roughly peer-average P/E of 21.2X to our calendar 2012 EPS estimate of $1.56.

## Qualitative Risk Assessment

| LOW | MEDIUM | HIGH |
|---|---|---|

Our risk assessment reflects what we see as the company's strong balance sheet and regular cash inflows, offset by the highly competitive nature of the outsourcing industry as well as the threat of new entrants into the human resources segment.

## Quantitative Evaluations

**S&P Quality Ranking**  A

| D | C | B- | B | B+ | A- | A | A+ |
|---|---|---|---|---|---|---|---|

**Relative Strength Rank**  MODERATE

64

LOWEST = 1    HIGHEST = 99

## Revenue/Earnings Data

**Revenue (Million $)**

| | 1Q | 2Q | 3Q | 4Q | Year |
|---|---|---|---|---|---|
| 2012 | 563.1 | -- | -- | -- | -- |
| 2011 | 518.3 | 512.0 | 531.3 | 522.7 | 2,084 |
| 2010 | 500.2 | 496.6 | 507.8 | 496.2 | 2,001 |
| 2009 | 534.1 | 524.2 | 528.6 | 495.9 | 2,083 |
| 2008 | 507.1 | 307.8 | 532.2 | 519.2 | 2,066 |
| 2007 | 459.4 | 455.0 | 485.3 | 487.4 | 1,887 |

**Earnings Per Share ($)**

| | | | | | |
|---|---|---|---|---|---|
| 2012 | 0.41 | E0.38 | E0.38 | E0.35 | E1.52 |
| 2011 | 0.36 | 0.37 | 0.36 | 0.33 | 1.42 |
| 2010 | 0.34 | 0.35 | 0.31 | 0.32 | 1.32 |
| 2009 | 0.41 | 0.39 | 0.36 | 0.32 | 1.48 |
| 2008 | 0.40 | 0.40 | 0.39 | 0.38 | 1.56 |
| 2007 | 0.35 | 0.35 | 0.33 | 0.32 | 1.39 |

Fiscal year ended May 31. Next earnings report expected: Late December. EPS Estimates based on S&P Operating Earnings; historical GAAP earnings are as reported.

## Dividend Data (Dates: mm/dd Payment Date: mm/dd/yy)

| Amount ($) | Date Decl. | Ex-Div. Date | Stk. of Record | Payment Date |
|---|---|---|---|---|
| 0.310 | 01/07 | 01/28 | 02/01 | 02/15/11 |
| 0.310 | 04/07 | 04/28 | 05/02 | 05/16/11 |
| 0.310 | 07/07 | 07/28 | 08/01 | 08/15/11 |
| 0.320 | 10/11 | 10/28 | 11/01 | 11/15/11 |

Dividends have been paid since 1988. Source: Company reports.

**Please read the Required Disclosures and Analyst Certification on the last page of this report.**

The McGraw-Hill Companies

# Paychex Inc

STANDARD
&POOR'S

## Business Summary September 30, 2011

CORPORATE OVERVIEW. Paychex is a leading provider of payroll processing, human resources and benefits services. The company was founded in 1971, and began by serving the payroll accounting services of businesses with fewer than 200 employees. It currently has more than 100 locations and serves over 536,000 clients throughout the U.S.

The company's payroll segment prepares payroll checks, earnings statements, internal accounting records, all federal, state and local payroll tax returns, and provides collection and remittance of payroll obligations. PAYX's tax filing and payment services provide automatic tax filing and payment, preparation and submission of tax returns, plus deposit of funds with tax authorities. Employee Payment Services provides a variety of ways for businesses to pay employees.

In our opinion, PAYX has shown an ability to expand its client base and increase the use of ancillary services, which we believe will lead to consistent growth for its mainstay payroll segment.

The Human Resources/Professional Employer Organization (HRS/PEO) segment provides employee benefits, management and human resources ser-

vices. The Paychex Administrative Services (PAS) product offers businesses a bundled package that includes payroll, employer compliance, and human resource and employee benefit administration. PAYX also offers 401(k) plan services.

MARKET PROFILE. The worldwide market for HR services totaled $101.6 billion in calendar 2010, according to market researcher IDC. Between 2010 and 2015, IDC expects this area to post a compound annual growth rate (CAGR) of 4.4%, with the market in the U.S. increasing at a CAGR of 3.5% from $50.9 billion in 2010. For the more narrow U.S. payroll processing services market, where we believe Automatic Data Processing is the market leader, IDC sees a CAGR of 2.5% between 2010 and 2015. In contrast, in the U.S. market for business process outsourcing (BPO) services, IDC expects a CAGR of 3.4% over the same time frame.

## Company Financials Fiscal Year Ended May 31

| Per Share Data ($) | 2011 | 2010 | 2009 | 2008 | 2007 | 2006 | 2005 | 2004 | 2003 | 2002 |
|---|---|---|---|---|---|---|---|---|---|---|
| Tangible Book Value | 2.50 | 2.54 | 2.30 | 1.91 | 3.87 | 3.12 | 2.40 | 1.88 | 1.55 | 2.43 |
| Cash Flow | 1.67 | 1.56 | 1.72 | 1.78 | 1.54 | 1.39 | 1.13 | 1.02 | 0.89 | 0.80 |
| Earnings | 1.42 | 1.32 | 1.48 | 1.56 | 1.39 | 1.22 | 0.97 | 0.80 | 0.78 | 0.73 |
| S&P Core Earnings | 1.42 | 1.34 | 1.48 | 1.55 | 1.41 | 1.17 | 0.93 | 0.80 | 0.72 | 0.66 |
| Dividends | NA | 1.24 | 1.20 | 0.79 | 0.61 | 0.51 | 0.47 | 0.44 | 0.33 | 0.33 |
| Payout Ratio | NA | 87% | 81% | 51% | 44% | 42% | 48% | 55% | 56% | 45% |
| Calendar Year | 2010 | 2009 | 2008 | 2007 | 2006 | 2005 | 2004 | 2003 | 2002 | 2001 |
| Prices:High | 32.82 | 32.88 | 37.47 | 47.14 | 42.37 | 43.37 | 39.12 | 40.54 | 42.15 | 51.00 |
| Prices:Low | 24.65 | 20.31 | 23.22 | 35.96 | 32.98 | 28.60 | 28.83 | 23.76 | 20.39 | 28.27 |
| P/E Ratio:High | 23 | 25 | 25 | 30 | 30 | 36 | 40 | 51 | 54 | 70 |
| P/E Ratio:Low | 17 | 15 | 16 | 23 | 24 | 23 | 30 | 30 | 26 | 39 |

### Income Statement Analysis (Million $)

| | 2011 | 2010 | 2009 | 2008 | 2007 | 2006 | 2005 | 2004 | 2003 | 2002 |
|---|---|---|---|---|---|---|---|---|---|---|
| Revenue | 2,084 | 2,001 | 2,083 | 2,066 | 1,887 | 1,675 | 1,445 | 1,294 | 1,099 | 955 |
| Operating Income | 875 | 811 | 891 | 909 | 775 | 716 | 596 | 516 | 444 | 393 |
| Depreciation | 88.7 | 86.4 | 85.8 | 80.6 | 73.4 | 66.5 | 62.0 | 82.8 | 43.4 | 29.5 |
| Interest Expense | NA | NA | Nil | Nil | Nil | Nil | Nil | Nil | Nil | Nil |
| Pretax Income | 792 | 729 | 812 | 855 | 743 | 675 | 546 | 450 | 432 | 395 |
| Effective Tax Rate | NA | NA | 34.3% | 32.6% | 30.7% | 31.1% | 32.5% | 32.6% | 32.0% | 30.5% |
| Net Income | 515 | 477 | 534 | 576 | 515 | 465 | 369 | 303 | 293 | 275 |
| S&P Core Earnings | 514 | 486 | 533 | 572 | 537 | 445 | 353 | 304 | 272 | 252 |

### Balance Sheet & Other Financial Data (Million $)

| | 2011 | 2010 | 2009 | 2008 | 2007 | 2006 | 2005 | 2004 | 2003 | 2002 |
|---|---|---|---|---|---|---|---|---|---|---|
| Cash | 464 | 367 | 492 | 393 | 79.4 | 137 | 281 | 219 | 79.9 | 61.9 |
| Current Assets | 4,258 | 4,159 | 4,240 | 4,466 | 4,861 | 4,444 | 3,689 | 3,280 | 3,033 | 2,815 |
| Total Assets | 5,394 | 5,226 | 5,127 | 5,310 | 6,247 | 5,549 | 4,379 | 3,950 | 3,691 | 2,953 |
| Current Liabilities | 3,788 | 3,742 | 3,702 | 4,037 | 4,237 | 3,838 | 2,942 | 2,722 | 2,588 | 2,023 |
| Long Term Debt | NA | NA | Nil | Nil | Nil | Nil | Nil | Nil | Nil | Nil |
| Common Equity | 1,496 | 1,402 | 1,341 | 1,197 | 1,985 | 1,670 | 1,411 | 1,235 | 1,077 | 924 |
| Total Capital | 1,496 | 1,402 | 1,341 | 1,197 | 1,994 | 1,686 | 1,429 | 1,249 | 1,084 | 924 |
| Capital Expenditures | 101 | 61.3 | 64.7 | 82.3 | 79.0 | 81.1 | 70.7 | 50.6 | 60.2 | 54.4 |
| Cash Flow | 604 | 563 | 619 | 657 | 589 | 531 | 431 | 386 | 337 | 304 |
| Current Ratio | 1.1 | 1.1 | 1.2 | 1.1 | 1.1 | 1.2 | 1.3 | 1.2 | 1.2 | 1.4 |
| % Long Term Debt of Capitalization | Nil | Nil | Nil | Nil | Nil | Nil | Nil | Nil | Nil | Nil |
| % Net Income of Revenue | 24.7 | 23.8 | 25.6 | 27.9 | 27.3 | 27.8 | 25.5 | 23.4 | 26.7 | 28.7 |
| % Return on Assets | 9.7 | 9.2 | 10.2 | 10.0 | 8.7 | 9.1 | 8.9 | 7.9 | 8.8 | 9.4 |
| % Return on Equity | 35.6 | 34.8 | 42.0 | 36.6 | 28.2 | 30.2 | 27.9 | 26.2 | 29.3 | 32.6 |

Data as orig reptd.; bef. results of disc opers/spec. items. Per share data adj. for stk. divs.; EPS diluted. E-Estimated. NA-Not Available. NM-Not Meaningful. NR-Not Ranked. UR-Under Review.

**Office:** 911 Panorama Trail South, Rochester, NY 14625-2396.
**Telephone:** 585-385-6666.
**Website:** http://www.paychex.com
**Chrmn:** B.T. Golisano

**Pres & CEO:** M. Mucci
**SVP, CFO & Treas:** E. Rivera
**Secy & General Counsel:** S.L. Schaeffer
**Investor Contact:** T.J. Allen (585-383-3406)

**Board Members:** J. G. Doody, D. J. Flaschen, B. T. Golisano, P. Horsley, G. M. Inman, P. A. Joseph, M. Mucci, J. M. Tucci, J. M. Velli

**Founded:** 1979
**Domicile:** Delaware
**Employees:** 12,400

# Peabody Energy Corp

**STANDARD &POOR'S**

| S&P Recommendation **BUY** ★★★★☆ | Price<br>$32.78 (as of Nov 25, 2011) | 12-Mo. Target Price<br>$68.00 | Investment Style<br>Large-Cap Blend |
|---|---|---|---|

**GICS Sector** Energy
**Sub-Industry** Coal & Consumable Fuels

**Summary** BTU is the world's largest publicly traded coal company, with 9 billion tons of coal reserves. Its coal fuels about 10% of the electricity generated in the U.S. and 2% worldwide.

## Key Stock Statistics (Source S&P, Vickers, company reports)

| | | | | | | | |
|---|---|---|---|---|---|---|---|
| 52-Wk Range | $73.95–30.60 | S&P Oper. EPS 2011**E** | 4.08 | Market Capitalization(B) | $8.879 | Beta | 1.55 |
| Trailing 12-Month EPS | $3.47 | S&P Oper. EPS 2012**E** | 5.70 | Yield (%) | 1.04 | S&P 3-Yr. Proj. EPS CAGR(%) | 30 |
| Trailing 12-Month P/E | 9.5 | P/E on S&P Oper. EPS 2011**E** | 8.0 | Dividend Rate/Share | $0.34 | S&P Credit Rating | BB+ |
| $10K Invested 5 Yrs Ago | NA | Common Shares Outstg. (M) | 270.9 | Institutional Ownership (%) | 81 | | |

## Price Performance

30-Week Mov. Avg. ···  10-Week Mov. Avg.- -  **GAAP Earnings vs. Previous Year**   Volume Above Avg. ▯▮▯ STARS
12-Mo. Target Price —  Relative Strength —  ▲ Up ▼ Down ► No Change      Below Avg. ▯▮▯ ★

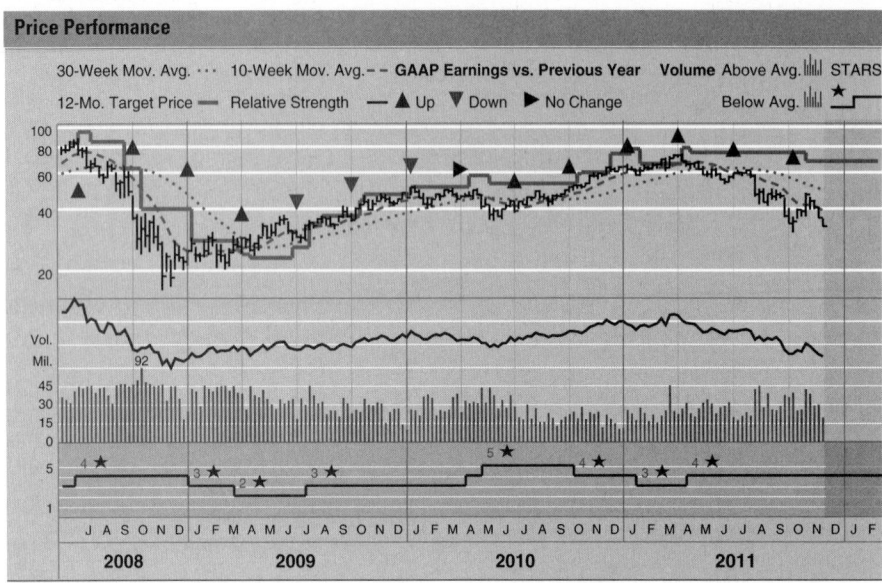

Analysis prepared by Equity Analyst **Jim Corridore** on Oct 31, 2011, when the stock traded at **$44.49**.

## Qualitative Risk Assessment

| LOW | **MEDIUM** | HIGH |
|---|---|---|

Our risk assessment reflects the industry's cyclicality and extensive regulation, the potential for geological difficulties with mines, transportation problems, volatility in the prices of competing fuels, and a narrow customer focus. This is offset by the company's leading market position and geographically well diversified coal holdings.

## Quantitative Evaluations

**S&P Quality Ranking**   B+

| D | C | B- | B | **B+** | A- | A | A+ |
|---|---|---|---|---|---|---|---|

**Relative Strength Rank**   **WEAK**

▮ 12

LOWEST = 1     HIGHEST = 99

## Highlights

▸ We expect revenues to rise about 20% in 2011, after a 14% increase in revenue in 2010 on somewhat higher volumes and stronger pricing. Our forecast is based partly on a projected 1% rise in coal volume in 2011. In addition, we think BTU will benefit from higher industry pricing for thermal and metallurgical coal following supply disruptions earlier in 2011, and we expect a roughly 17% increase in pricing in 2011. For 2012, we project that revenue will advance more than 7%, on higher expected volume and coal pricing.

▸ Following a five percentage point increase in 2010's EBITDA margin, we think that higher coal volumes and pricing will lead to improved operating leverage and better overall EBITDA margins again in 2011. Our estimate assumes that production costs per ton will increase 15%. For 2012, we project a further increase in BTU's EBITDA margin, mainly due to continued improvement in operating leverage.

▸ On a projected effective tax rate of about 25% in both years, we estimate EPS of $4.08 for 2011 and $5.70 in 2012.

## Investment Rationale/Risk

▸ Despite our negative fundamental outlook on the coal & consumable fuels sub-industry, we have a buy recommendation on BTU, reflecting our belief that the shares will outperform the peer group. Our opinion is based, in part, on the company's significant operating scale, which we view as a competitive advantage. In addition, we see BTU's direct exposure to international coal demand as an avenue of growth not afforded to BTU's competitors. We also view positively the recent announcement that the company was selected as part of a consortium to develop coking coal assets in Mongolia.

▸ Risks to our recommendation and target price include declines in commodity coal and natural gas prices, lower productivity and production, unfavorable inflation leading to higher production costs, and higher coal market inventories.

▸ Our 12-month target price of $68 values the shares at 12X our 2012 EPS estimate of $5.70, and is derived by pushing forward the peer average P/E of 2011 earnings estimates ahead to our 2012 EPS estimate, since we are near the end of 2011.

## Revenue/Earnings Data

### Revenue (Million $)

| | 1Q | 2Q | 3Q | 4Q | Year |
|---|---|---|---|---|---|
| 2011 | 1,745 | 2,008 | 2,036 | -- | -- |
| 2010 | 1,516 | 1,661 | 1,865 | 1,818 | 6,860 |
| 2009 | 1,453 | 1,338 | 1,667 | 1,554 | 6,012 |
| 2008 | 1,276 | 1,531 | 1,906 | 1,881 | 6,593 |
| 2007 | 1,365 | 1,322 | 1,494 | 1,212 | 4,575 |
| 2006 | 1,312 | 1,316 | 1,265 | 1,363 | 5,256 |

### Earnings Per Share ($)

| | | | | | |
|---|---|---|---|---|---|
| 2011 | 0.65 | 1.05 | 1.01 | E1.40 | E4.08 |
| 2010 | 0.50 | 0.77 | 0.84 | 0.78 | 2.87 |
| 2009 | 0.50 | 0.32 | 0.41 | 0.41 | 1.68 |
| 2008 | 0.26 | 0.89 | 1.38 | 1.11 | 3.63 |
| 2007 | 0.33 | 0.40 | 0.12 | 0.71 | 1.56 |
| 2006 | 0.48 | 0.57 | 0.53 | 0.65 | 2.23 |

Fiscal year ended Dec. 31. Next earnings report expected: Early March. EPS Estimates based on S&P Operating Earnings; historical GAAP earnings are as reported.

## Dividend Data (Dates: mm/dd Payment Date: mm/dd/yy)

| Amount ($) | Date Decl. | Ex-Div. Date | Stk. of Record | Payment Date |
|---|---|---|---|---|
| 0.085 | 01/27 | 02/08 | 02/10 | 03/03/11 |
| 0.085 | 05/03 | 05/13 | 05/17 | 06/07/11 |
| 0.085 | 07/22 | 08/02 | 08/04 | 08/25/11 |
| 0.085 | 10/20 | 11/01 | 11/03 | 11/25/11 |

Dividends have been paid since 2001. Source: Company reports.

Options: ASE, CBOE, P, Ph

---

**Please read the Required Disclosures and Analyst Certification on the last page of this report.**

**The McGraw-Hill Companies**

# Peabody Energy Corp

STANDARD &POOR'S

## Business Summary October 31, 2011

CORPORATE OVERVIEW. Peabody Energy Corp. (BTU) was founded in 1883 as Peabody, Daniels and Co., a retail coal supplier. BTU is currently the world's largest private sector coal company. In 2010, it produced nearly 218.4 million tons of coal, up from 210.8 million tons in 2009 but down from 225.2 million tons produced in 2008. The company's U.S. operations produced more than 191 million tons, or about a 17.6% share of U.S. production, by our calculation, and 26.7 million tons produced in Australia. Including the company's trading operations, BTU sold nearly 246 million tons of coal to electricity generating and industrial plants globally. At December 31, 2010, BTU had 9 billion tons of proven and probable coal reserves. BTU owns majority interests in 28 coal operations located in the Western and Midwestern U.S. coal producing regions and in Australia. In addition, the company owns a 50% interest in Mongolian coal and mineral interests and owns purchase rights for up to 15% of its Mongolian joint venture partner, Winsway Coking Coal. It also owns a minority interest in one Venezuelan mine through a joint venture agreement. In 2010, 85% of the U.S. mining operation's coal sales were shipped from the U.S. West, and the remaining 15% from the Midwest. Most production in the West is low sulfur coal from the Powder River Basin, which has seen the fastest growth of all U.S. coal regions, according to the Energy Information Administration (EIA). In the West, the company owns and operates mines in Arizona, Colorado,

New Mexico and Wyoming. In the Midwest, BTU owns and operates mines in Illinois and Indiana.

In 2010, 84% of sales were to U.S. electricity generators, 2% to the U.S. industrial sector, and 14% to foreign customers. About 91% of 2010 coal sales were under long-term contracts. As of April 2011, the company had 9 million to 11 million tons of thermal and metallurgical coal left to price in 2011. More importantly, we estimate that BTU has about 90% of its Australian production unpriced, which we think will allow the company to book production at favorable pricing. In the company's U.S. operations, essentially all of the planned production in 2011 is priced, while more than 30% of planned production in 2012 is unpriced. In addition to its mining operations, BTU markets and trades coal and emission allowances. Total tons traded amounted to 25.4 million in 2010 as compared to 29.4 million tons in 2009. Other energy-related businesses include coalbed methane production, transportation services, and the development of coal-fueled generation plants.

## Company Financials Fiscal Year Ended Dec. 31

| Per Share Data ($) | 2010 | 2009 | 2008 | 2007 | 2006 | 2005 | 2004 | 2003 | 2002 | 2001 |
|---|---|---|---|---|---|---|---|---|---|---|
| Tangible Book Value | 17.25 | 13.98 | 10.96 | 9.33 | 7.95 | 8.27 | 3.33 | 5.18 | 5.16 | 4.98 |
| Cash Flow | 4.62 | 3.17 | 5.31 | 2.91 | 3.63 | 2.76 | 0.88 | 1.26 | 1.57 | 0.96 |
| Earnings | 2.87 | 1.68 | 3.63 | 1.56 | 2.23 | 1.58 | 0.70 | 0.19 | 0.49 | 0.10 |
| S&P Core Earnings | 2.90 | 1.60 | 3.36 | 1.42 | 2.00 | 1.43 | 0.63 | 0.11 | 0.27 | -0.03 |
| Dividends | 0.29 | 0.25 | 0.24 | 0.24 | 0.24 | 0.17 | 0.13 | 0.11 | 0.10 | 0.05 |
| Payout Ratio | 10% | 15% | 7% | 15% | 11% | 11% | 19% | 59% | 20% | 53% |
| Prices:High | 64.59 | 48.21 | 88.69 | 62.55 | 76.29 | 43.48 | 21.70 | 10.75 | 7.69 | 9.51 |
| Prices:Low | 34.89 | 20.17 | 16.00 | 36.20 | 32.94 | 18.37 | 9.10 | 6.13 | 4.38 | 5.55 |
| P/E Ratio:High | 23 | 29 | 24 | 40 | 34 | 28 | 31 | 57 | 16 | NM |
| P/E Ratio:Low | 12 | 12 | 4 | 23 | 15 | 12 | 13 | 32 | 9 | NM |

| Income Statement Analysis (Million $) | | | | | | | | | | |
|---|---|---|---|---|---|---|---|---|---|---|
| Revenue | 6,860 | 6,012 | 6,593 | 4,575 | 5,256 | 4,644 | 3,632 | 2,829 | 2,717 | 2,027 |
| Operating Income | NA | NA | 1,774 | 827 | 884 | 703 | 519 | 385 | 390 | 276 |
| Depreciation | 441 | 405 | 454 | 362 | 377 | 316 | 270 | 234 | 232 | 175 |
| Interest Expense | 204 | 201 | 226 | 237 | 143 | 103 | 96.8 | 98.5 | 102 | 89.0 |
| Pretax Income | 1,113 | 652 | 1,177 | 341 | 531 | 426 | 153 | -3.18 | 78.8 | 29.0 |
| Effective Tax Rate | NA | 29.7% | 15.8% | NM | NM | 0.23% | NM | NM | NM | 12.9% |
| Net Income | 777 | 443 | 985 | 421 | 601 | 423 | 178 | 41.5 | 106 | 19.0 |
| S&P Core Earnings | 780 | 431 | 910 | 383 | 541 | 382 | 160 | 23.9 | 58.5 | -5.74 |

| Balance Sheet & Other Financial Data (Million $) | | | | | | | | | | |
|---|---|---|---|---|---|---|---|---|---|---|
| Cash | 1,295 | 989 | 450 | 45.3 | 327 | 503 | 390 | 118 | 71.2 | 39.0 |
| Current Assets | 2,958 | 2,189 | 1,971 | 1,927 | 1,274 | 1,325 | 1,055 | 683 | 550 | 527 |
| Total Assets | 11,363 | 9,955 | 9,822 | 9,668 | 9,514 | 6,852 | 6,179 | 5,280 | 5,140 | 5,151 |
| Current Liabilities | 1,623 | 1,312 | 1,856 | 2,187 | 1,368 | 1,023 | 774 | 632 | 632 | 684 |
| Long Term Debt | 2,707 | 2,738 | 3,139 | 3,139 | 3,168 | 1,383 | 1,406 | 1,173 | 982 | 985 |
| Common Equity | 4,689 | 3,756 | 2,904 | 2,520 | 2,339 | 2,178 | 1,725 | 1,132 | 1,081 | 1,040 |
| Total Capital | 7,439 | 6,508 | 6,061 | 5,975 | 5,735 | 3,902 | 3,526 | 2,742 | 2,599 | 2,590 |
| Capital Expenditures | 633 | 441 | 486 | 649 | 478 | 384 | 267 | 156 | 209 | 194 |
| Cash Flow | 1,246 | 848 | 1,439 | 783 | 978 | 739 | 448 | 276 | 338 | 194 |
| Current Ratio | 1.8 | 1.7 | 1.1 | 0.9 | 0.9 | 1.3 | 1.4 | 1.1 | 0.9 | 0.8 |
| % Long Term Debt of Capitalization | 36.4 | 42.1 | 51.9 | 52.5 | 55.2 | 35.4 | 39.9 | 42.8 | 37.8 | 38.0 |
| % Net Income of Revenue | 11.3 | 7.4 | 14.9 | 9.2 | 11.4 | 9.1 | 4.9 | NM | 3.9 | 0.1 |
| % Return on Assets | 7.3 | 4.5 | 10.1 | 4.4 | 7.3 | 6.5 | 3.1 | NM | 2.1 | 0.3 |
| % Return on Equity | 18.4 | 13.3 | 36.3 | 17.3 | 26.6 | 21.7 | 12.5 | NM | 10.0 | 2.3 |

Data as orig reptd.; bef. results of disc opers/spec. items. Per share data adj. for stk. divs.; EPS diluted. E-Estimated. NA-Not Available. NM-Not Meaningful. NR-Not Ranked. UR-Under Review.

Office: 701 Market St, St. Louis, MO 63101-1826.
Telephone: 314-342-3400.
Email: publicrelations@peabodyenergy.com
Website: http://www.peabodyenergy.com

Chrmn & CEO: G.H. Boyce
Pres: R.A. Navarre
COO & EVP: E. Ford
EVP & CFO: M.C. Crews

EVP & Chief Admin Officer: S.D. Fiehler
Investor Contact: C. Morrow (314-342-7900)
Board Members: G. H. Boyce, W. A. Coley, W. E. James, R. B. Karn, III, M. F. Keeth, H. E. Lentz, Jr., R. A. Malone, W. C. Rusnack, J. F. Turner, S. A. Van Trease, A. H. Washkowitz

Founded: 1883
Domicile: Delaware
Employees: 7,200

The McGraw-Hill Companies

# J. C. Penney Company Inc.

**STANDARD & POOR'S**

**S&P Recommendation** HOLD ★★★☆☆

| **Price** | **12-Mo. Target Price** | **Investment Style** |
|---|---|---|
| $29.61 (as of Nov 25, 2011) | $36.00 | Large-Cap Blend |

**GICS Sector** Consumer Discretionary
**Sub-Industry** Department Stores

**Summary** This company is the leading mall-based family department store operator in the U.S., with over 1,100 retail locations and catalog/Internet operations.

## Key Stock Statistics (Source S&P, Vickers, company reports)

| | | | | | | | |
|---|---|---|---|---|---|---|---|
| 52-Wk Range | $41.00–23.44 | S&P Oper. EPS 2012**E** | 1.62 | Market Capitalization(B) | $6.316 | Beta | 1.78 |
| Trailing 12-Month EPS | $0.92 | S&P Oper. EPS 2013**E** | 2.10 | Yield (%) | 2.70 | S&P 3-Yr. Proj. EPS CAGR(%) | 14 |
| Trailing 12-Month P/E | 32.2 | P/E on S&P Oper. EPS 2012**E** | 18.3 | Dividend Rate/Share | $0.80 | S&P Credit Rating | BB+ |
| $10K Invested 5 Yrs Ago | $4,128 | Common Shares Outstg. (M) | 213.3 | Institutional Ownership (%) | NM | | |

## Price Performance

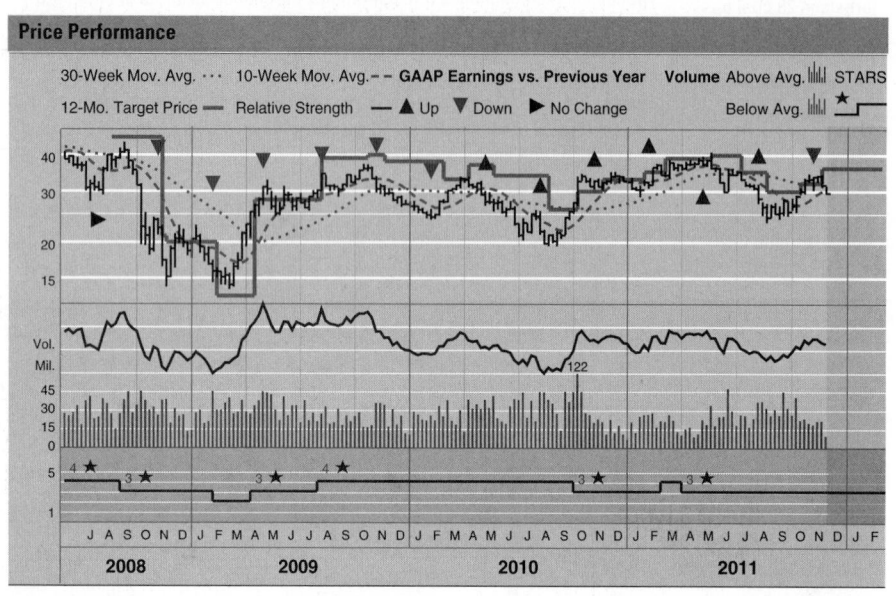

30-Week Mov. Avg. · · · 10-Week Mov. Avg. – – GAAP Earnings vs. Previous Year  Volume Above Avg. STARS
12-Mo. Target Price — Relative Strength — ▲ Up ▼ Down ▶ No Change  Below Avg. ★

Options: ASE, CBOE, P

Analysis prepared by Equity Analyst **Jason N. Asaeda** on Nov 15, 2011, when the stock traded at **$32.98**.

## Highlights

➤ We project net sales of $17.4 billion in FY 12 (Jan.) and $17.7 billion in FY 13. In our view, middle-income consumers are increasingly making mostly need-based purchases in response to macroeconomic concerns. We also think a weak U.S. housing market has dampened demand for home furnishings. We see these factors limiting same-store sales growth over the near term. However, we look for JCP to continue to invest prudently in its center core business, which includes cosmetics, jewelry, shoes, and accessories, and in exclusive apparel brands in support of growth.

➤ Despite the elimination of higher-margin "big book" catalog sales in FY 11 and our expectation of aggressive promotions and cost inflation, we see the company maintaining a 4.7% EBIT margin in FY 12, supported by disciplined inventory management, selective price increases, expense savings, and lower projected non-cash pension expense. We see a 5.5% EBIT margin for FY 13.

➤ Factoring in JCP's completion of its $900 million share repurchase program in May, we see EPS of $1.62 (before $1.14 in estimated restructuring charges) in FY 12 and $2.10 in FY 13.

## Investment Rationale/Risk

➤ We view the shares as appropriately valued at recent levels. On November 1, 2011, Ronald Johnson succeeded Myron Ullman, III as CEO. Mr. Johnson has brought to JCP over 25 years of retail experience, including 11 years as senior vice president of retail at Apple Inc. and 15 years at Target Corp., where he last served as vice president of merchandising. We credit Mr. Ullman for elevating JCPenney's image with sharper merchandising and marketing. It remains to be seen how product assortments or pricing will evolve under Mr. Johnson's leadership, but we see potential for him to create a more engaging multi-channel shopping experience. We look for Mr. Johnson to communicate his growth strategies for the company at an investor meeting in New York City on January 25, 2012.

➤ Risk to our recommendation and target price include sales shortfalls due to uncompetitive pricing or lackluster merchandising.

➤ Our 12-month target price of $36 is based on a forward P/E multiple of 17.3X, JCP's 10-year historical average, applied to our FY 13 EPS estimate.

## Qualitative Risk Assessment

| LOW | MEDIUM | HIGH |
|---|---|---|

Our risk assessment reflects our view of JCP's strong brand and increasing market share in the moderate department store sector, offset by a challenging macroeconomic environment that has led to weakening sales and profit trends in recent quarters.

## Quantitative Evaluations

**S&P Quality Ranking**     B

| D | C | B- | **B** | B+ | A- | A | A+ |
|---|---|---|---|---|---|---|---|

**Relative Strength Rank**     MODERATE

61

LOWEST = 1      HIGHEST = 99

## Revenue/Earnings Data

**Revenue (Million $)**

| | 1Q | 2Q | 3Q | 4Q | Year |
|---|---|---|---|---|---|
| 2012 | 3,943 | 3,906 | 3,986 | -- | -- |
| 2011 | 3,929 | 3,938 | 4,189 | 5,703 | 17,759 |
| 2010 | 3,884 | 3,943 | 4,179 | 5,550 | 17,556 |
| 2009 | 4,127 | 4,282 | 4,318 | 5,759 | 18,486 |
| 2008 | 4,350 | 4,391 | 4,729 | 6,390 | 19,860 |
| 2007 | 4,220 | 4,238 | 4,781 | 6,664 | 19,903 |

**Earnings Per Share ($)**

| | | | | | |
|---|---|---|---|---|---|
| 2012 | 0.28 | 0.07 | -0.67 | E1.10 | E1.62 |
| 2011 | 0.25 | 0.06 | 0.19 | 1.09 | 1.59 |
| 2010 | -0.11 | Nil | 0.11 | 0.83 | 1.07 |
| 2009 | 0.54 | 0.52 | 0.55 | 0.93 | 2.54 |
| 2008 | 1.04 | 0.52 | 1.17 | 1.93 | 4.91 |
| 2007 | 0.90 | 0.75 | 1.26 | 2.00 | 4.88 |

Fiscal year ended Jan. 31. Next earnings report expected: NA. EPS Estimates based on S&P Operating Earnings; historical GAAP earnings are as reported.

## Dividend Data (Dates: mm/dd Payment Date: mm/dd/yy)

| Amount ($) | Date Decl. | Ex-Div. Date | Stk. of Record | Payment Date |
|---|---|---|---|---|
| 0.200 | 12/08 | 01/06 | 01/10 | 02/01/11 |
| 0.200 | 03/24 | 04/06 | 04/08 | 05/02/11 |
| 0.200 | 05/20 | 07/06 | 07/08 | 08/01/11 |
| 0.200 | 09/16 | 10/05 | 10/10 | 11/01/11 |

Dividends have been paid since 1922. Source: Company reports.

# J. C. Penney Company Inc.

STANDARD &POOR'S

## Business Summary November 15, 2011

CORPORATE OVERVIEW. In our view, JCP is the leading mall-based family department store operator, with over 1,100 JCPenney stores in 49 states and Puerto Rico. We think the company is also adeptly addressing the needs of time-strapped shoppers with the shopping convenience afforded by its direct business, comprised of JCPenney specialty catalogs and the jcpenney.com web site, as well as its growing off-mall retail presence. JCP discontinued publishing its twice-yearly "big book" catalogs in FY 11 (Jan.).

CORPORATE STRATEGY. From FY 01 to FY 06, JCP executed a turnaround plan to improve the profitability of its JCPenney stores. The company focused on delivering competitive, fashionable merchandise assortments; developing a compelling and appealing marketing program; improving store environments; reducing its expense structure; and attracting and retaining an experienced and professional work force. In support of these objectives, JCP moved from decentralized to centralized merchandising, marketing and operating functions, and invested in a new store distribution network and in new merchandise planning, allocation and replenishment systems.

With what we view as the success of its turnaround, JCP has mapped out a new long-range plan for making JCPenney the preferred shopping choice for

"Middle America," which it defines as customers aged 35 to 54 with annual household incomes of $35,000 to $85,000. Key strategies include offering styles that make an emotional connection with the customer; making it easier for the customer to shop seamlessly across store/catalog/Internet channels; creating and sustaining a customer-focused culture; and using the off-mall store format to expand the company's presence in high-potential markets.

Since 2005, consistent with its long-range plan, JCP has pursued lifestyle merchandising by aligning its assortments with four distinct customer profiles: the "conservative" customer who seeks mainly comfort and ease of care; the "traditional" customer who wants timeless, classic styles; the "modern" customer who likes classic looks with a twist; and the fashion-forward "trendy" customer. The company launched its new "Every Day Matters" marketing campaign aimed at better conveying its lifestyle merchandise focus in late February 2007.

## Company Financials Fiscal Year Ended Jan. 31

| Per Share Data ($) | 2011 | 2010 | 2009 | 2008 | 2007 | 2006 | 2005 | 2004 | 2003 | 2002 |
|---|---|---|---|---|---|---|---|---|---|---|
| Tangible Book Value | 22.05 | 19.49 | 18.09 | 23.93 | 18.97 | 17.20 | 17.92 | 18.54 | 12.04 | 11.46 |
| Cash Flow | 3.74 | 3.19 | 4.65 | 6.80 | 6.57 | 5.79 | 3.33 | 2.68 | 3.45 | 3.00 |
| Earnings | 1.59 | 1.07 | 2.54 | 4.91 | 4.88 | 3.83 | 2.23 | 1.21 | 1.25 | 0.32 |
| S&P Core Earnings | 1.95 | 1.70 | 1.15 | 4.37 | 4.66 | 3.77 | 2.26 | 1.24 | 0.66 | 0.15 |
| Dividends | NA | 0.80 | 0.80 | 0.72 | 0.50 | 0.50 | 0.50 | 0.50 | 0.50 | 0.50 |
| Payout Ratio | NA | 75% | 75% | 15% | 10% | 13% | 22% | 41% | 40% | 156% |
| Calendar Year | 2010 | 2009 | 2008 | 2007 | 2006 | 2005 | 2004 | 2003 | 2002 | 2001 |
| Prices:High | 35.12 | 37.21 | 51.42 | 87.18 | 82.49 | 57.99 | 41.82 | 26.42 | 27.75 | 29.50 |
| Prices:Low | 19.42 | 13.71 | 13.95 | 39.98 | 54.18 | 40.26 | 25.29 | 15.57 | 14.07 | 10.50 |
| P/E Ratio:High | 22 | 35 | 20 | 18 | 17 | 15 | 19 | 22 | 22 | 92 |
| P/E Ratio:Low | 12 | 13 | 5 | 8 | 11 | 11 | 11 | 13 | 11 | 33 |

### Income Statement Analysis (Million $)

| | 2011 | 2010 | 2009 | 2008 | 2007 | 2006 | 2005 | 2004 | 2003 | 2002 |
|---|---|---|---|---|---|---|---|---|---|---|
| Revenue | 17,759 | 17,556 | 18,486 | 19,860 | 19,903 | 18,781 | 18,424 | 17,786 | 32,347 | 32,004 |
| Operating Income | 1,343 | 1,187 | 1,579 | 2,268 | 2,277 | 1,949 | 1,680 | 1,184 | 1,681 | 1,473 |
| Depreciation | 511 | 495 | 469 | 426 | 389 | 372 | 368 | 394 | 667 | 717 |
| Interest Expense | 231 | 255 | 268 | 278 | 270 | 169 | 233 | 261 | 388 | 386 |
| Pretax Income | 581 | 403 | 910 | 1,723 | 1,792 | 1,444 | 1,020 | 546 | 584 | 203 |
| Effective Tax Rate | NA | 38.2% | 37.7% | 35.9% | 36.7% | 32.3% | 34.6% | 33.3% | 36.5% | 43.8% |
| Net Income | 378 | 249 | 567 | 1,105 | 1,134 | 977 | 667 | 345 | 371 | 114 |
| S&P Core Earnings | 464 | 396 | 258 | 986 | 1,081 | 960 | 662 | 345 | 171 | 41.0 |

### Balance Sheet & Other Financial Data (Million $)

| | 2011 | 2010 | 2009 | 2008 | 2007 | 2006 | 2005 | 2004 | 2003 | 2002 |
|---|---|---|---|---|---|---|---|---|---|---|
| Cash | 2,622 | 3,011 | 2,352 | 2,471 | 2,747 | 3,016 | 4,687 | 2,994 | 2,474 | 2,840 |
| Current Assets | 6,370 | 6,652 | 6,220 | 6,751 | 6,648 | 6,702 | 8,427 | 6,515 | 8,353 | 8,677 |
| Total Assets | 13,042 | 12,581 | 12,011 | 14,309 | 12,673 | 12,461 | 14,127 | 18,300 | 17,867 | 18,048 |
| Current Liabilities | 2,647 | 3,249 | 2,794 | 3,338 | 3,492 | 2,762 | 3,447 | 3,754 | 4,159 | 4,499 |
| Long Term Debt | 3,099 | 2,999 | 3,505 | 3,505 | 3,010 | 3,444 | 3,464 | 5,114 | 4,940 | 5,179 |
| Common Equity | 5,460 | 4,778 | 4,155 | 5,312 | 4,288 | 4,007 | 4,856 | 5,121 | 6,037 | 5,766 |
| Total Capital | 8,559 | 8,170 | 7,659 | 10,280 | 8,504 | 8,738 | 9,638 | 11,756 | 12,701 | 12,539 |
| Capital Expenditures | 499 | 600 | 969 | 1,243 | 772 | 535 | 412 | 373 | 658 | 631 |
| Cash Flow | 889 | 744 | 1,036 | 1,531 | 1,523 | 1,349 | 1,023 | 733 | 1,011 | 802 |
| Current Ratio | 2.4 | 2.1 | 2.2 | 2.0 | 1.9 | 2.4 | 2.4 | 1.7 | 2.0 | 1.9 |
| % Long Term Debt of Capitalization | 36.2 | 36.7 | 45.8 | 34.1 | 41.2 | 39.4 | 35.9 | 43.5 | 38.9 | 41.3 |
| % Net Income of Revenue | 2.1 | 1.4 | 3.1 | 5.6 | 5.7 | 5.2 | 3.6 | 2.0 | 1.1 | 0.4 |
| % Return on Assets | 3.0 | 2.0 | 4.3 | 8.2 | 9.0 | 7.3 | 4.1 | 2.0 | 2.1 | 0.1 |
| % Return on Equity | 7.4 | 5.6 | 12.0 | 23.0 | 27.3 | 22.0 | 13.1 | 6.1 | 5.8 | 1.9 |

Data as orig reptd.; bef. results of disc opers/spec. items. Per share data adj. for stk. divs.; EPS diluted. E-Estimated. NA-Not Available. NM-Not Meaningful. NR-Not Ranked. UR-Under Review.

**Office:** 6501 Legacy Drive, Plano, TX 75024-3698.
**Telephone:** 972-431-1000.
**Website:** http://www.jcpenney.net
**Chrmn:** M.E. Ullman, III

**Pres:** M.R. Francis
**EVP & CFO:** M.P. Dastugue
**EVP, Secy & General Counsel:** J.L. Dhillon
**SVP, Chief Acctg Officer & Cntlr:** D.P. Miller

**Investor Contact:** P. Sanchez (972-431-5575)
**Board Members:** W. A. Ackman, C. C. Barrett, T. J. Engibous, K. B. Foster, G. B. Laybourne, B. Osborne, L. H. Roberts, S. Roth, J. G. Teruel, R. G. Turner, M. E. Ullman, III, M. B. West

**Founded:** 1902
**Domicile:** Delaware
**Employees:** 156,000

# People's United Financial Inc

**STANDARD &POOR'S**

| S&P Recommendation | HOLD ★★★☆☆ | Price $11.82 (as of Nov 25, 2011) | 12-Mo. Target Price $15.00 | Investment Style Large-Cap Blend |
|---|---|---|---|---|

**GICS Sector** Financials
**Sub-Industry** Thrifts & Mortgage Finance

**Summary** This company provides a full range of banking and financial service products to individuals, corporations and municipal customers in the U.S. Northeast.

## Key Stock Statistics (Source S&P, Vickers, company reports)

| | | | | | | |
|---|---|---|---|---|---|---|
| 52-Wk Range | $14.49– 10.50 | S&P Oper. EPS 2011**E** | 0.61 | Market Capitalization(B) | $4.120 | Beta 0.33 |
| Trailing 12-Month EPS | $0.54 | S&P Oper. EPS 2012**E** | 0.74 | Yield (%) | 5.33 | S&P 3-Yr. Proj. EPS CAGR(%) 49 |
| Trailing 12-Month P/E | 21.9 | P/E on S&P Oper. EPS 2011**E** | 19.4 | Dividend Rate/Share | $0.63 | S&P Credit Rating A- |
| $10K Invested 5 Yrs Ago | $6,854 | Common Shares Outstg. (M) | 348.6 | Institutional Ownership (%) | 74 | |

## Price Performance

30-Week Mov. Avg. · · · 10-Week Mov. Avg. - - GAAP Earnings vs. Previous Year   Volume Above Avg.ıllıl   STARS

12-Mo. Target Price — Relative Strength — ▲ Up ▼ Down ► No Change    Below Avg.ıllıl ★

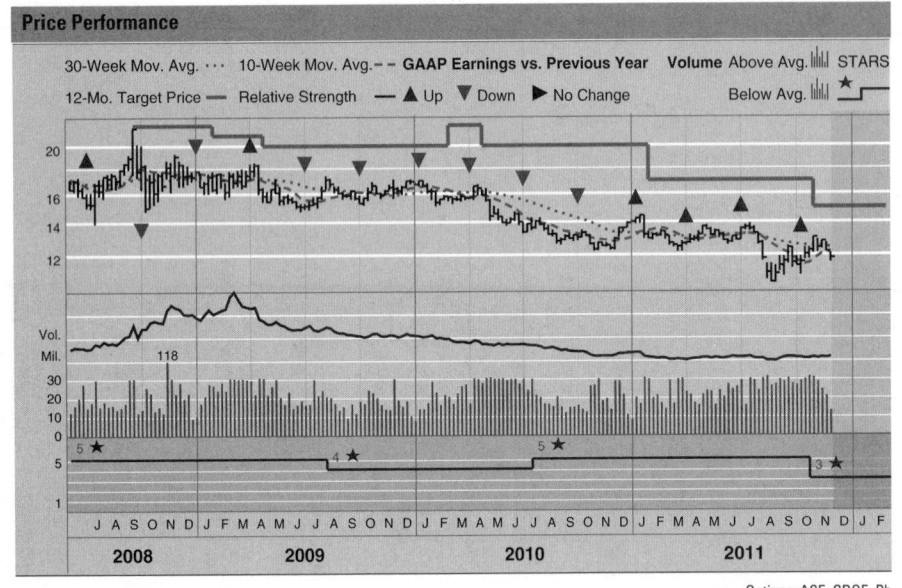

Options: ASE, CBOE, Ph

Analysis prepared by Equity Analyst **Erik Oja** on Nov 02, 2011, when the stock traded at **$12.44**.

## Highlights

➤ We forecast total net revenue growth of 28% in 2011 and 5.7% in 2012, reflecting recent acquisitions and our expectations for a stable net interest margin. Our estimates assume a net interest margin of 4.10% in 2011, up from 3.69% in 2010. We expect net interest income growth of 32% in 2011 and 6% in 2012. Our non-interest income growth estimates for 2011 and 2012 are 18% and 5.5%, respectively. Net interest income accounts for about 75% of PBCT's revenues, a well above peers level.

➤ We expect expenses as a percentage of total net revenues to decrease to 75.4% in 2011 and 73.4% in 2012, from 84.9% in 2010. We also see loan loss provisions declining, to $55 million in 2011, from $60 million in 2010, covering our $51 million net chargeoff forecast for 2011. For 2012, we expect provisions and net chargeoffs of $49 million. PBCT's $177 million allowance for loan losses at September 30 was 0.88% of total loans, in line with peers, and 68.5% of non-performing loans, below peers. However, PBCT's loan credit quality was better than peers at September 30, with only 1.28% of loans non-performing.

➤ We see EPS of $0.61 in 2011 and $0.74 in 2012.

## Investment Rationale/Risk

➤ We expect PBCT's recently completed acquisitions to raise its Northeast market share, and boost PBCT's revenue and EPS growth rates in 2011 and 2012. We expect further deals to follow, as PBCT will likely continue to put its excess liquidity to work. We also expect PBCT to maintain well above peers credit quality and capital levels. However, we see non-interest expenses as far higher than at peers, which will likely be a drag on earnings growth. Also, allowance levels are relatively low, which will likely mean little or no reserve releases, thus low growth, and high quality earnings. We think the current valuation, on earnings and book value, is ample.

➤ Risks to our recommendation and target price include a further decline in interest rates, credit quality deterioration, and a drop-off of insurance revenue and brokerage commissions.

➤ Our 12-month target price of $15 is an above-peers 1.63X September 30 tangible book value per share, which in our view is in line with peers having similar revenue growth outlooks and high credit quality. This equates to an above-peers 21.7X our forward four quarter EPS estimate of $0.69.

## Qualitative Risk Assessment

| LOW | MEDIUM | HIGH |
|---|---|---|

Our risk assessment reflects our view of the good credit quality of PBCT's loan portfolio and its history of profitability, offset by acquisition risk.

## Quantitative Evaluations

**S&P Quality Ranking** B

| D | C | B- | B | B+ | A- | A | A+ |
|---|---|---|---|---|---|---|---|

**Relative Strength Rank** MODERATE

**64**

LOWEST = 1            HIGHEST = 99

## Revenue/Earnings Data

**Revenue (Million $)**

| | 1Q | 2Q | 3Q | 4Q | Year |
|---|---|---|---|---|---|
| 2011 | 327.4 | 329.4 | 358.7 | -- | -- |
| 2010 | 264.2 | 283.7 | 283.4 | 296.7 | 1,128 |
| 2009 | 267.4 | 277.2 | 272.1 | 259.2 | 1,076 |
| 2008 | 337.2 | 300.9 | 296.6 | 286.1 | 1,221 |
| 2007 | 193.0 | 233.0 | 239.6 | 226.8 | 892.4 |
| 2006 | 179.5 | 183.5 | 161.4 | 195.9 | 729.5 |

**Earnings Per Share ($)**

| | | | | | |
|---|---|---|---|---|---|
| 2011 | 0.15 | 0.15 | 0.15 | E0.15 | E0.61 |
| 2010 | 0.04 | 0.05 | 0.07 | 0.09 | 0.24 |
| 2009 | 0.08 | 0.08 | 0.08 | 0.08 | 0.30 |
| 2008 | 0.05 | 0.13 | 0.14 | 0.11 | 0.42 |
| 2007 | 0.11 | 0.15 | 0.20 | 0.16 | 0.51 |
| 2006 | 0.11 | 0.11 | 0.05 | 0.13 | 0.40 |

Fiscal year ended Dec. 31. Next earnings report expected: NA. EPS Estimates based on S&P Operating Earnings; historical GAAP earnings are as reported.

## Dividend Data (Dates: mm/dd Payment Date: mm/dd/yy)

| Amount ($) | Date Decl. | Ex-Div. Date | Stk. of Record | Payment Date |
|---|---|---|---|---|
| 0.155 | 01/20 | 01/28 | 02/01 | 02/15/11 |
| 0.158 | 04/20 | 04/27 | 05/01 | 05/15/11 |
| 0.158 | 07/21 | 07/28 | 08/01 | 08/15/11 |
| 0.158 | 10/20 | 10/28 | 11/01 | 11/15/11 |

Dividends have been paid since 1993. Source: Company reports.

# People's United Financial Inc

**STANDARD &POOR'S**

## Business Summary November 02, 2011

CORPORATE OVERVIEW. People's United Financial (formerly People's Bank of Connecticut), formed in 1842, is a state-chartered stock savings bank headquartered in Bridgeport, CT. PBCT offers a range of financial services to individual, corporations, and municipal customers. In addition to traditional banking activities, PBCT provides specialized services tailored to specific markets, including personal, institutional and employee benefits; cash management; and municipal banking and finance. PBCT offers brokerage, financial advisory services and life insurance through its People's Securities subsidiary and Chittenden Securities; equipment financing through People's Capital and Leasing (PCLC) and People's United Equity Financing; and other insurance services through R.C. Knox and Company, Inc. and Chittenden Insurance Group, LLC. Services are delivered through a network of branches in Connecticut, Massachusetts, New Hampshire, Vermont, Maine and New York.

PBCT has increased its residential mortgage and home equity lending activities in New York and Massachusetts. In addition, PBCT maintains a loan production office in Massachusetts, and PCLC maintains a sales presence in six states to support its equipment financing operations outside of New England. Within the Commercial Banking division, PBCT maintains a national credits group, which has participated in commercial loans and real estate loans to borrowers in various industries on a national scale.

IMPACT OF MAJOR DEVELOPMENTS. In January 2011, PBCT announced an agreement to acquire Danvers Bancorp for $480 million (45% cash and 55% stock), and this deal closed July 1, 2011, for a final value of $481 million. At March 31, 2011, Danvers reported total assets of $2.77 billion and total deposits of $2.13 billion and operated 28 branches in the greater Boston area. The price paid was 0.17X Danvers's total assets, in line with current acquisition multiples.

In July 2010, PBCT agreed to acquire LSB Corp. for $97 million in cash; the deal closed in December. The acquisition price was 0.12X LSB's total assets. Also in July 2010, PBCT agreed to acquire Smithtown Bancorp for $60 million in cash and stock ($56.5 million closing price); this deal also closed in December. The acquisition price was 0.03X Smithtown's total assets.

## Company Financials Fiscal Year Ended Dec. 31

| Per Share Data ($) | 2010 | 2009 | 2008 | 2007 | 2006 | 2005 | 2004 | 2003 | 2002 | 2001 |
|---|---|---|---|---|---|---|---|---|---|---|
| Tangible Book Value | 9.30 | 10.68 | 10.87 | 15.06 | 8.68 | 3.98 | 5.53 | 4.55 | 2.83 | 2.82 |
| Earnings | 0.24 | 0.30 | 0.42 | 0.51 | 0.40 | 0.42 | -0.02 | 0.22 | 0.19 | 0.30 |
| S&P Core Earnings | 0.24 | 0.29 | 0.37 | 0.51 | 0.41 | 0.41 | -0.01 | 0.22 | 0.16 | 0.09 |
| Dividends | 0.46 | 0.61 | 0.58 | 0.52 | 0.46 | 0.41 | 0.45 | 0.32 | 0.30 | 0.28 |
| Payout Ratio | 193% | NM | 138% | 102% | 115% | 96% | NM | 148% | 158% | 96% |
| Prices:High | 17.08 | 18.54 | 21.76 | 22.81 | 21.62 | 16.07 | 14.12 | 7.20 | 5.94 | 6.01 |
| Prices:Low | 12.20 | 14.72 | 13.92 | 14.78 | 14.29 | 11.43 | 6.88 | 5.13 | 4.37 | 4.37 |
| P/E Ratio:High | 71 | 62 | 52 | 45 | 54 | 38 | NM | 33 | 31 | 20 |
| P/E Ratio:Low | 51 | 49 | 33 | 29 | 36 | 27 | NM | 23 | 23 | 15 |

| Income Statement Analysis (Million $) | | | | | | | | | | |
|---|---|---|---|---|---|---|---|---|---|---|
| Net Interest Income | 699 | 577 | 636 | 487 | 382 | 370 | 327 | 320 | 351 | 354 |
| Loan Loss Provision | 60.0 | 57.0 | 26.2 | 8.00 | 3.40 | 8.60 | 13.3 | 48.6 | 77.7 | 101 |
| Non Interest Income | 299 | 309 | 303 | 180 | 175 | 172 | 155 | 252 | 251 | 339 |
| Non Interest Expenses | 811 | 685 | 654 | 439 | 347 | 343 | 479 | 436 | 441 | 441 |
| Pretax Income | 127 | 144 | 208 | 225 | 180 | 190 | -14.2 | 86.9 | 80.4 | 133 |
| Effective Tax Rate | 32.5% | 29.9% | 32.8% | 33.6% | 32.2% | 33.7% | NM | 26.6% | 31.1% | 34.8% |
| Net Income | 85.7 | 101 | 140 | 149 | 122 | 126 | -5.60 | 63.8 | 55.4 | 86.7 |
| % Net Interest Margin | 3.69 | 3.19 | 3.62 | 4.12 | 3.87 | 3.68 | 3.33 | 2.95 | 3.40 | 4.33 |
| S&P Core Earnings | 86.5 | 98.4 | 124 | 147 | 124 | 124 | -4.16 | 63.9 | 46.6 | 27.2 |

| Balance Sheet & Other Financial Data (Million $) | | | | | | | | | | |
|---|---|---|---|---|---|---|---|---|---|---|
| Total Assets | 25,037 | 21,256 | 20,168 | 13,555 | 10,687 | 10,933 | 10,718 | 11,672 | 12,261 | 11,891 |
| Loans | 17,346 | 14,061 | 14,408 | 8,877 | 9,298 | 8,498 | 7,861 | 8,122 | 7,336 | 6,931 |
| Deposits | 17,933 | 15,446 | 14,269 | 8,881 | 9,083 | 9,083 | 8,862 | 8,714 | 8,426 | 7,983 |
| Capitalization:Debt | 1,193 | 341 | 368 | 65.4 | 65.3 | 109 | 122 | 1,162 | 1,165 | 1,478 |
| Capitalization:Equity | 5,219 | 5,101 | 5,176 | 4,445 | 1,340 | 1,289 | 1,200 | 1,002 | 940 | 935 |
| Capitalization:Total | 6,412 | 5,442 | 5,544 | 4,511 | 1,405 | 1,398 | 1,322 | 2,164 | 2,104 | 2,413 |
| % Return on Assets | 0.4 | 0.5 | 0.8 | 1.2 | 1.1 | 1.2 | NM | 0.5 | 0.5 | 0.7 |
| % Return on Equity | 1.7 | 2.0 | 2.9 | 5.2 | 9.3 | 10.1 | NM | 6.6 | 5.9 | 9.5 |
| % Loan Loss Reserve | 1.0 | 1.2 | 1.1 | 0.8 | 0.8 | 0.9 | 0.9 | 1.4 | 1.5 | 1.6 |
| % Risk Based Capital | 14.5 | 14.1 | 13.4 | 33.4 | 16.1 | 16.4 | 16.7 | 13.1 | 12.5 | 12.3 |
| Price Times Book Value:High | 1.8 | 1.7 | 2.0 | 1.5 | 2.5 | 4.0 | 2.6 | 1.6 | 2.1 | 2.1 |
| Price Times Book Value:Low | 1.3 | 1.4 | 1.3 | 1.0 | 1.6 | 2.9 | 1.2 | 1.1 | 1.5 | 1.6 |

Data as orig reptd.; bef. results of disc opers/spec. items. Per share data adj. for stk. divs.; EPS diluted. E-Estimated. NA-Not Available. NM-Not Meaningful. NR-Not Ranked. UR-Under Review.

**Office:** 850 Main Street, Bridgeport, CT 06604.
**Telephone:** 203-338-7171.
**Website:** http://www.peoples.com
**Chrmn:** G.P. Carter

**Pres & CEO:** J.P. Barnes
**COO:** M.K. Vitelli
**EVP & CIO:** J.A. Coleman
**SVP, CFO, Chief Acctg Officer & Cntlr:** J.A. Hoyt

**Investor Contact:** J. Shaw
**Board Members:** J. P. Barnes, C. P. Baron, K. T. Bottomley, G. P. Carter, J. K. Dwight, J. Franklin, E. S. Groark, J. M. Hansen, R. M. Hoyt, M. W. Richards, J. A. Thomas, K. W. Walters

**Founded:** 1842
**Domicile:** Connecticut
**Employees:** 5,198

The *McGraw-Hill* Companies

# Pepco Holdings Inc.

**STANDARD
&POOR'S**

| S&P Recommendation | HOLD ★★★★★ | Price $18.71 (as of Nov 25, 2011) | 12-Mo. Target Price $19.00 | Investment Style Large-Cap Blend |
|---|---|---|---|---|

**GICS Sector** Utilities
**Sub-Industry** Electric Utilities

**Summary** This energy holding company for three regulated utilities and an unregulated energy services business recently sold its Conectiv Energy power generation business.

## Key Stock Statistics (Source S&P, Vickers, company reports)

| | | | | | | |
|---|---|---|---|---|---|---|
| 52-Wk Range | $20.36–16.57 | S&P Oper. EPS 2011**E** | 1.19 | Market Capitalization(B) | $4.246 | Beta | 0.52 |
| Trailing 12-Month EPS | $1.20 | S&P Oper. EPS 2012**E** | 1.28 | Yield (%) | 5.77 | S&P 3-Yr. Proj. EPS CAGR(%) | 15 |
| Trailing 12-Month P/E | 15.6 | P/E on S&P Oper. EPS 2011**E** | 15.7 | Dividend Rate/Share | $1.08 | S&P Credit Rating | BBB+ |
| $10K Invested 5 Yrs Ago | $9,633 | Common Shares Outstg. (M) | 227.0 | Institutional Ownership (%) | 55 | | |

## Price Performance

30-Week Mov. Avg. · · · 10-Week Mov. Avg. – – **GAAP Earnings vs. Previous Year**   Volume Above Avg. STARS

12-Mo. Target Price — Relative Strength — ▲ Up ▼ Down ► No Change   Below Avg. ★

Options: Ph

Analysis prepared by Equity Analyst **Justin McCann** on Sep 15, 2011, when the stock traded at **$19.06**.

## Highlights

► We expect EPS from continuing operations in 2011 to remain essentially flat with 2010's $1.24. In the first half of 2011, operating EPS was up nearly 47% from the year-earlier period. This primarily reflected a sharp decline in interest expense and fuel and purchased power costs, as well as higher transmission revenues due to increased investments in new assets, and higher distribution revenues due to rate increases.

► For full-year 2011, operating EPS should benefit from rate increases and a sharp decline in interest expense, as proceeds from the Conectiv Energy sale were used to reduce debt. However, this could be largely offset by the return to less favorable summer weather, the absence of tax benefits realized in 2010, and the potentially adverse impact of other pending tax issues. We see EPS growth for 2012 and the next few years thereafter being driven by the expansion of the rate base through infrastructure investments.

► Following the sale of Conectiv Energy and the liquidation of its remaining assets, we believe the previous volatility of POM's earnings should be greatly reduced as the company's regulated utility operations now account for at least 90% of its consolidated earnings.

## Investment Rationale/Risk

► With POM trading at a significant P/E premium to peers, we see minimal near-term price appreciation potential. The shares were up about 3% year to date through mid-September 2011. This followed an 8.3% rise in 2010, reflecting, we believe, the sale of Conectiv Energy and an above-peers dividend yield. We believe the sale of Conectiv greatly reduced POM's exposure to the energy commodity market and its earnings volatility. We think that with the proceeds from the transaction used for debt reduction, POM's balance sheet and credit profile has been strengthened, and the need to issue new equity eliminated through at least 2012.

► Risks to our investment recommendation and target price include much weaker than expected earnings from the unregulated Pepco Energy Services unit, unfavorable regulatory rulings, and the potential for a sharp decline in the average P/E of the group as a whole.

► Despite an 87% payout ratio on its operating EPS for 2010, we believe POM remains committed to the current dividend, which was recently yielding a well above peers 5.7%. Our target price is $19, reflecting a premium-to-peers multiple of 14.7X our EPS estimate for 2012.

## Qualitative Risk Assessment

| LOW | MEDIUM | HIGH |
|---|---|---|

Our risk assessment reflects our view that with the completion of the sale of Conectiv Energy, whose earnings and cash flows were highly volatile, there will be much greater financial stability, with the regulated electric transmission and distribution businesses accounting for at least 90% of earnings and cash flows.

## Quantitative Evaluations

**S&P Quality Ranking**   B

| D | C | B- | B | B+ | A- | A | A+ |
|---|---|---|---|---|---|---|---|

**Relative Strength Rank**   MODERATE

66

LOWEST = 1   HIGHEST = 99

## Revenue/Earnings Data

**Revenue (Million $)**

| | 1Q | 2Q | 3Q | 4Q | Year |
|---|---|---|---|---|---|
| 2011 | 1,634 | 1,409 | 1,643 | -- | -- |
| 2010 | 1,819 | 1,636 | 2,067 | 1,517 | 7,039 |
| 2009 | 2,520 | 2,065 | 2,539 | 2,135 | 9,259 |
| 2008 | 2,641 | 2,518 | 3,060 | 2,481 | 10,700 |
| 2007 | 2,179 | 2,084 | 2,770 | 2,333 | 9,366 |
| 2006 | 1,952 | 1,917 | 2,590 | 1,905 | 8,363 |

**Earnings Per Share ($)**

| | 1Q | 2Q | 3Q | 4Q | Year |
|---|---|---|---|---|---|
| 2011 | 0.27 | 0.42 | 0.35 | E0.15 | E1.19 |
| 2010 | 0.13 | 0.34 | 0.09 | 0.06 | 0.62 |
| 2009 | 0.21 | 0.11 | 0.56 | 0.19 | 1.06 |
| 2008 | 0.49 | 0.07 | 0.59 | 0.32 | 1.47 |
| 2007 | 0.27 | 0.30 | 0.87 | 0.29 | 1.72 |
| 2006 | 0.29 | 0.27 | 0.54 | 0.19 | 1.30 |

Fiscal year ended Dec. 31. Next earnings report expected: Late February. EPS Estimates based on S&P Operating Earnings; historical GAAP earnings are as reported.

## Dividend Data (Dates: mm/dd Payment Date: mm/dd/yy)

| Amount ($) | Date Decl. | Ex-Div. Date | Stk. of Record | Payment Date |
|---|---|---|---|---|
| 0.270 | 01/27 | 03/08 | 03/10 | 03/31/11 |
| 0.270 | 04/28 | 06/08 | 06/10 | 06/30/11 |
| 0.270 | 07/28 | 09/08 | 09/12 | 09/30/11 |
| 0.270 | 10/27 | 12/08 | 12/12 | 12/30/11 |

Dividends have been paid since 1904. Source: Company reports.

---

**Please read the Required Disclosures and Analyst Certification on the last page of this report.**

The **McGraw·Hill** Companies

# Pepco Holdings Inc.

STANDARD
&POOR'S

## Business Summary September 15, 2011

CORPORATE OVERVIEW. Pepco Holdings (POM) is an energy holding company involved in the power delivery business, providing transmission and distribution of electricity and distribution of natural gas. These operations are conducted through POM's three regulated utility subsidiaries: Potomac Electric Power Company (Pepco), Delmarva Power & Light Company (DPL), and Atlantic City Electric Company (ACE). POM is also involved in the competitive energy business, but with the July 2010 sale of the bulk of Conectiv Energy, which provided non-regulated generation and the marketing and supply of electricity and natural gas, this segment of POM's operations was reduced to the energy management services provided by its Pepco Energy Services (PES) subsidiary. In 2010, the power delivery business contributed 73% of POM's consolidated operating revenues, and PES 27%.

IMPACT OF MAJOR DEVELOPMENTS. On July 1, 2010, the company completed the sale (announced on April 21, 2010) of its Conectiv Energy power gener-

ation business to Calpine Corporation (CPN) for $1.63 billion, after adjustments. The sale did not include Conectiv's power supply contracts, its energy hedging portfolio, and other non-core assets, the subsequent disposition of which POM has substantially completed. The estimated $2 billion in proceeds from the sales (which includes the return of related collateral, working capital and the liquidation of the supply contracts) were earmarked for the payment of $300 million of projected taxes, and the reduction of $1.75 billion of POM debt. With the completion of the transaction, the regulated operations are now expected to account for 90% to 95% of POM's consolidated operating income, compared to 71% in 2009.

## Company Financials  Fiscal Year Ended Dec. 31

| Per Share Data ($) | 2010 | 2009 | 2008 | 2007 | 2006 | 2005 | 2004 | 2003 | 2002 | 2001 |
|---|---|---|---|---|---|---|---|---|---|---|
| Tangible Book Value | 12.54 | 12.82 | 12.69 | 13.01 | 11.48 | 11.34 | 10.28 | 9.12 | 9.20 | 17.01 |
| Earnings | 0.62 | 1.06 | 1.47 | 1.72 | 1.30 | 1.91 | 1.47 | 0.63 | 1.61 | 1.50 |
| S&P Core Earnings | 0.83 | 1.25 | 1.08 | 1.60 | 1.28 | 1.37 | 1.38 | 0.87 | 1.31 | 1.20 |
| Dividends | 1.08 | 0.54 | 0.54 | 1.04 | 1.04 | 1.00 | 1.00 | 1.00 | 0.92 | 1.17 |
| Payout Ratio | 174% | 51% | 37% | 60% | 80% | 52% | 68% | 159% | 57% | 78% |
| Prices:High | 19.80 | 18.71 | 29.64 | 30.71 | 26.99 | 24.46 | 21.71 | 20.56 | 23.83 | 24.90 |
| Prices:Low | 15.13 | 10.07 | 15.27 | 24.20 | 21.79 | 20.26 | 16.94 | 16.10 | 15.37 | 20.08 |
| P/E Ratio:High | 32 | 18 | 20 | 18 | 21 | 13 | 15 | 33 | 15 | 17 |
| P/E Ratio:Low | 24 | 9 | 10 | 14 | 17 | 11 | 12 | 26 | 10 | 13 |

| Income Statement Analysis (Million $) | 2010 | 2009 | 2008 | 2007 | 2006 | 2005 | 2004 | 2003 | 2002 | 2001 |
|---|---|---|---|---|---|---|---|---|---|---|
| Revenue | 7,039 | 9,259 | 10,700 | 9,366 | 8,363 | 8,066 | 7,222 | 7,271 | 4,325 | 2,503 |
| Depreciation | 393 | 391 | 377 | 366 | 413 | 423 | 441 | 422 | 240 | 171 |
| Maintenance | NA | NA | NA | NA | NA | NA | NA | NA | NA | NA |
| Fixed Charges Coverage | NA | 1.82 | 2.42 | 2.41 | 2.25 | 2.37 | 2.06 | 1.43 | 2.47 | 3.06 |
| Construction Credits | NA | NA | NA | NA | NA | NA | NA | NA | NA | NA |
| Effective Tax Rate | 7.30% | 31.9% | 35.9% | 36.0% | 39.4% | 41.3% | 40.1% | 38.0% | 37.1% | 33.1% |
| Net Income | 139 | 235 | 300 | 334 | 248 | 362 | 259 | 108 | 211 | 168 |
| S&P Core Earnings | 187 | 279 | 219 | 311 | 246 | 259 | 241 | 147 | 171 | 130 |

| Balance Sheet & Other Financial Data (Million $) | 2010 | 2009 | 2008 | 2007 | 2006 | 2005 | 2004 | 2003 | 2002 | 2001 |
|---|---|---|---|---|---|---|---|---|---|---|
| Gross Property | 12,120 | 13,717 | 12,926 | 12,307 | 11,820 | 11,384 | 11,045 | 10,747 | 10,625 | 4,367 |
| Capital Expenditures | 940 | 864 | 781 | 623 | 475 | 467 | 517 | 564 | 504 | 245 |
| Net Property | 7,673 | 8,863 | 8,314 | 7,877 | 7,577 | 7,312 | 7,088 | 6,965 | 6,798 | 2,758 |
| Capitalization:Long Term Debt | 4,062 | 4,947 | 5,378 | 4,735 | 4,367 | 4,885 | 5,128 | 5,373 | 5,122 | 1,722 |
| Capitalization:% Long Term Debt | 49.0 | 53.8 | 56.2 | 54.1 | 54.7 | 57.7 | 60.4 | 63.7 | 62.2 | 45.9 |
| Capitalization:Preferred | Nil | Nil | Nil | Nil | Nil | Nil | Nil | 63.2 | 111 | 210 |
| Capitalization:% Preferred | Nil | Nil | Nil | Nil | Nil | Nil | Nil | 0.75 | 1.35 | 5.59 |
| Capitalization:Common | 4,230 | 4,256 | 4,190 | 4,018 | 3,612 | 3,584 | 3,366 | 3,003 | 2,996 | 1,823 |
| Capitalization:% Common | 51.0 | 46.2 | 43.8 | 45.9 | 45.3 | 42.3 | 39.6 | 35.6 | 36.4 | 48.5 |
| Total Capital | 8,381 | 9,752 | 11,883 | 10,903 | 10,134 | 10,455 | 10,532 | 8,439 | 9,833 | 4,282 |
| % Operating Ratio | 92.2 | 95.8 | 94.4 | 93.7 | 93.2 | 92.4 | 91.6 | 92.6 | 90.3 | 87.1 |
| % Earned on Net Property | 6.7 | 5.8 | 9.5 | 10.0 | 9.3 | 12.6 | 11.0 | 18.6 | 16.4 | 27.5 |
| % Return on Revenue | 2.0 | 2.5 | 2.8 | 3.6 | 3.0 | 4.5 | 3.6 | 1.5 | 4.9 | 6.7 |
| % Return on Invested Capital | NA | 5.8 | 5.5 | 6.0 | 6.2 | 8.0 | 6.7 | 8.3 | 6.4 | 9.6 |
| % Return on Common Equity | 3.3 | 5.6 | 7.3 | 8.8 | 6.9 | 10.5 | 8.1 | 3.4 | 8.7 | 8.9 |

Data as orig reptd.; bef. results of disc opers/spec. items. Per share data adj. for stk. divs.; EPS diluted. E-Estimated. NA-Not Available. NM-Not Meaningful. NR-Not Ranked. UR-Under Review.

**Office:** 701 Ninth Street N.W., Washington, DC 20068.
**Telephone:** 202-872-2000.
**Email:** shareholder@pepco.com
**Website:** http://www.pepcoholdings.com

**Chrmn, Pres & CEO:** J.M. Rigby
**CFO:** A.J. Kamerick
**Chief Acctg Officer & Cntlr:** R. Clark
**Treas:** K.M. McGowan

**Secy:** J. Storero
**Investor Contact:** E.J. Bourscheid (202-872-2797)
**Board Members:** J. B. Dunn, IV, T. C. Golden, P. T. Harker, F. O. Heintz, B. J. Krumsiek, G. F. MacCormack, L. C. Nussdorf, P. A. Oelrich, J. M. Rigby, F. K. Ross, P. A. Schneider, L. P. Silverman

**Founded:** 1896
**Domicile:** Delaware
**Employees:** 5,014

The McGraw-Hill Companies

# PepsiCo Inc

**STANDARD & POOR'S**

| S&P Recommendation | BUY ★★★★☆ | Price $62.49 (as of Nov 25, 2011) | 12-Mo. Target Price $70.00 | Investment Style Large-Cap Growth |
|---|---|---|---|---|

**GICS Sector** Consumer Staples
**Sub-Industry** Soft Drinks

**Summary** This company is a major international producer of branded beverage and snack food products.

## Key Stock Statistics (Source S&P, Vickers, company reports)

| | | | | | | |
|---|---|---|---|---|---|---|
| 52-Wk Range | $71.89–58.50 | S&P Oper. EPS 2011E | 4.41 | Market Capitalization(B) | $97.697 | Beta 0.54 |
| Trailing 12-Month EPS | $3.99 | S&P Oper. EPS 2012E | 4.81 | Yield (%) | 3.30 | S&P 3-Yr. Proj. EPS CAGR(%) 8 |
| Trailing 12-Month P/E | 15.7 | P/E on S&P Oper. EPS 2011E | 14.2 | Dividend Rate/Share | $2.06 | S&P Credit Rating A |
| $10K Invested 5 Yrs Ago | $11,476 | Common Shares Outstg. (M) | 1,563.4 | Institutional Ownership (%) | 69 | |

## Price Performance

30-Week Mov. Avg. · · · 10-Week Mov. Avg. - - GAAP Earnings vs. Previous Year   Volume Above Avg. STARS
12-Mo. Target Price — Relative Strength — ▲ Up ▼ Down ▶ No Change   Below Avg.

Options: ASE, CBOE, P, Ph

Analysis prepared by Equity Analyst **Esther Kwon, CFA** on Oct 14, 2011, when the stock traded at **$62.01**.

## Qualitative Risk Assessment

| LOW | MEDIUM | HIGH |
|---|---|---|

Our risk assessment reflects the relatively stable nature of the company's end markets, its strong cash flow, leading global market positions, corporate governance practices that we view as favorable versus peers, and an S&P Quality Ranking of A+, reflecting superior long-term earnings and dividend growth.

## Quantitative Evaluations

**S&P Quality Ranking**   A+

| D | C | B- | B | B+ | A- | A | A+ |
|---|---|---|---|---|---|---|---|

**Relative Strength Rank**   STRONG

74

LOWEST = 1   HIGHEST = 99

## Revenue/Earnings Data

**Revenue (Million $)**

| | 1Q | 2Q | 3Q | 4Q | Year |
|---|---|---|---|---|---|
| 2011 | 11,937 | 16,827 | 17,582 | -- | -- |
| 2010 | 9,368 | 14,801 | 15,514 | 18,155 | 57,838 |
| 2009 | 8,263 | 10,592 | 11,080 | 13,297 | 43,232 |
| 2008 | 8,333 | 10,945 | 11,244 | 12,729 | 43,251 |
| 2007 | 7,350 | 9,607 | 10,171 | 12,346 | 39,474 |
| 2006 | 7,205 | 8,599 | 8,950 | 10,383 | 35,137 |

**Earnings Per Share ($)**

| | 1Q | 2Q | 3Q | 4Q | Year |
|---|---|---|---|---|---|
| 2011 | 0.71 | 1.17 | 1.25 | E1.15 | E4.41 |
| 2010 | 0.89 | 0.98 | 1.19 | 0.85 | 3.91 |
| 2009 | 0.72 | 1.06 | 1.09 | 0.91 | 3.77 |
| 2008 | 0.70 | 1.05 | 0.99 | 0.46 | 3.21 |
| 2007 | 0.65 | 0.94 | 1.06 | 0.77 | 3.41 |
| 2006 | 0.60 | 0.80 | 0.88 | 1.06 | 3.34 |

Fiscal year ended Dec. 31. Next earnings report expected: Mid February. EPS Estimates based on S&P Operating Earnings; historical GAAP earnings are as reported.

## Dividend Data (Dates: mm/dd Payment Date: mm/dd/yy)

| Amount ($) | Date Decl. | Ex-Div. Date | Stk. of Record | Payment Date |
|---|---|---|---|---|
| 0.480 | 02/04 | 03/02 | 03/04 | 03/31/11 |
| 0.515 | 05/04 | 06/01 | 06/03 | 06/30/11 |
| 0.515 | 07/15 | 08/31 | 09/02 | 09/30/11 |
| 0.515 | 11/17 | 11/30 | 12/02 | 01/03/12 |

Dividends have been paid since 1952. Source: Company reports.

## Highlights

▶ For 2011, we forecast sales growth of approximately 15% from 2010's $57.8 billion, after about 34% growth in the prior year due to the acquisitions of anchor bottlers Pepsi Bottling Co. and PepsiAmericas, completed in February 2010. We see beverage volumes in the Americas continuing to struggle, but we expect better performance from Gatorade as the brand is refreshed. We also think PEP will improve sales in the convenience and gas and food service channels. In 2012, we look for approximately 6% revenue growth.

▶ We see operating margins down from the prior year on higher commodity costs, continuing investments in infrastructure and product and packaging innovation, offset somewhat by acquisition synergies. We expect a positive impact from foreign exchange.

▶ On higher interest expense, we estimate 2011 EPS of $4.41, up from 2010's $4.13. In March 2010, PEP's directors reinstated the company's share repurchase program upon the close of the bottler acquisitions, and PEP said it planned to repurchase about $2.5 billion of stock in 2011 after repurchasing $5 billion in 2010. For 2012, we forecast EPS of $4.81.

## Investment Rationale/Risk

▶ Although we remain cautious about sluggish Americas beverage trends, we see exposure to stronger international markets as a potential offset. In February 2011, PEP acquired a majority interest in leading Russian food and beverage company Wimm-Bill-Dann Foods OJSC for $3.8 billion and launched a tender offer for the remaining interest in March. In addition to the company's leading market positions, we view PEP's product innovation strategy as trendsetting for the industry. Its focus on health and wellness should continue to drive the top line, and we look for strong returns to shareholders in the form of dividends and share repurchases.

▶ Risks to our recommendation and target price include unfavorable weather conditions in the company's markets and increased competitive activity. As PEP boosts its exposure to foreign markets, political and currency risks also increase.

▶ Our relative valuation model, which is derived from analysis of peer and historical P/E multiples, indicates a value of $70, which is our 12-month target price. This reflects a multiple of projected 2012 EPS below the recent historical range of 19X to 27X.

---

**Please read the Required Disclosures and Analyst Certification on the last page of this report.**

**The McGraw-Hill Companies**

# PepsiCo Inc

## Business Summary October 14, 2011

CORPORATE OVERVIEW. Originally incorporated in 1919, PepsiCo is a leader in the global snack and beverage industry. The company manufactures, markets and sells a variety of salty, convenient, sweet and grain-based snacks, carbonated and non-carbonated beverages, and foods. PepsiCo is organized into three business units with six reportable segments: PepsiCo Americas Foods (PAF), which includes Frito-Lay North America (FLNA), Quaker Foods North America (QFNA), and Latin America Foods (LAF); PepsiCo Beverages America (PAB), which includes PepsiCo Beverages North America and all of its Latin American beverage businesses; and PepsiCo International, which includes all of PepsiCo businesses in Europe and Asia, the Middle East and Africa (AMEA).

FLNA (23% of 2010 net revenue, 37% of operating profits before corporate overhead) produces the best-selling line of snack foods in the U.S., including Fritos brand corn chips, Lay's and Ruffles potato chips, Doritos and Tostitos tortilla chips, Cheetos cheese-flavored snacks, SunChips multigrain snacks, and Quaker Chewy granola bars. FLNA branded products are sold to independent distributors and retailers. Products are transported from Frito-Lay's manufacturing plants to major distribution centers, principally in company-owned trucks.

QFNA (3%, 6%) manufactures, markets and sells Cap'n Crunch and Life ready-to-eat cereals, Quaker hot cereals, Rice-A-Roni, Near East and Pasta Roni side dishes, Aunt Jemima mixes and syrups and Quaker grits.

LAF (11%, 10%) manufactures, markets and sells snack foods under the brands Gamesa, Doritos, Cheetos, Ruffles, Lay's and Sabritas, as well as many Quaker branded products.

PAB (35%, 29%) manufactures or uses contract manufacturers, markets and sells beverage concentrates, fountain syrups and finished goods, under the brands Pepsi, Mountain Dew, Gatorade, 7UP (outside the U.S.), Tropicana Pure Premium, Sierra Mist, SoBe Lifewater, Tropicana juice drinks, Amp Energy, Naked juice and Izze. PBNA also manufactures, markets and sells ready-to-drink tea and coffee products through joint ventures with Lipton and Starbucks. In addition, it markets the Aquafina water brand and licenses it to its bottlers.

## Company Financials Fiscal Year Ended Dec. 31

| Per Share Data ($) | 2010 | 2009 | 2008 | 2007 | 2006 | 2005 | 2004 | 2003 | 2002 | 2001 |
|---|---|---|---|---|---|---|---|---|---|---|
| Tangible Book Value | NM | 4.95 | 3.36 | 6.80 | 1.93 | 2.17 | 1.96 | 3.82 | 2.37 | 1.90 |
| Cash Flow | 5.37 | 4.73 | 4.14 | 4.27 | 4.30 | 3.25 | 2.45 | 2.75 | 2.47 | 2.07 |
| Earnings | 3.91 | 3.77 | 3.21 | 3.41 | 3.34 | 2.39 | 2.41 | 2.05 | 1.85 | 1.47 |
| S&P Core Earnings | 3.44 | 3.77 | 2.99 | 3.38 | 3.30 | 2.37 | 2.44 | 2.03 | 1.54 | 1.20 |
| Dividends | 1.89 | 1.77 | 1.65 | 1.43 | 1.16 | 1.01 | 0.85 | 0.63 | 0.60 | 0.58 |
| Payout Ratio | 48% | 47% | 51% | 42% | 35% | 42% | 35% | 31% | 32% | 39% |
| Prices:High | 68.11 | 64.48 | 79.79 | 79.00 | 65.99 | 60.34 | 55.71 | 48.88 | 53.50 | 50.46 |
| Prices:Low | 58.75 | 43.78 | 49.74 | 61.89 | 56.00 | 51.34 | 45.30 | 36.24 | 34.00 | 40.25 |
| P/E Ratio:High | 17 | 17 | 25 | 23 | 20 | 25 | 23 | 24 | 29 | 34 |
| P/E Ratio:Low | 15 | 12 | 15 | 18 | 17 | 21 | 19 | 18 | 18 | 27 |

| Income Statement Analysis (Million $) | | | | | | | | | | |
|---|---|---|---|---|---|---|---|---|---|---|
| Revenue | 57,838 | 43,232 | 43,251 | 39,474 | 35,137 | 32,562 | 29,261 | 26,971 | 25,112 | 26,935 |
| Operating Income | 11,971 | 9,596 | 8,964 | 8,596 | 7,845 | 7,230 | 6,673 | 6,208 | 6,066 | 5,490 |
| Depreciation | 2,327 | 1,635 | 1,486 | 1,426 | 1,406 | 1,308 | 1,264 | 1,221 | 1,112 | 1,082 |
| Interest Expense | 903 | 397 | 329 | 224 | 239 | 256 | 167 | 163 | 178 | 219 |
| Pretax Income | 8,232 | 8,079 | 7,021 | 7,631 | 6,989 | 6,382 | 5,546 | 4,992 | 4,868 | 4,029 |
| Effective Tax Rate | NA | 26.0% | 26.8% | 25.8% | 19.3% | 36.1% | 24.7% | 28.5% | 31.9% | 33.9% |
| Net Income | 6,338 | 5,946 | 5,142 | 5,658 | 5,642 | 4,078 | 4,174 | 3,568 | 3,313 | 2,662 |
| S&P Core Earnings | 5,569 | 5,945 | 4,781 | 5,602 | 5,565 | 4,028 | 4,191 | 3,543 | 2,749 | 2,164 |

| Balance Sheet & Other Financial Data (Million $) | | | | | | | | | | |
|---|---|---|---|---|---|---|---|---|---|---|
| Cash | 6,369 | 4,135 | 2,277 | 910 | 1,651 | 1,716 | 1,280 | 820 | 1,638 | 683 |
| Current Assets | 17,569 | 12,571 | 10,806 | 10,151 | 9,130 | 10,454 | 8,639 | 6,930 | 6,413 | 5,853 |
| Total Assets | 68,153 | 39,848 | 35,994 | 34,628 | 29,930 | 31,727 | 27,987 | 25,327 | 23,474 | 21,695 |
| Current Liabilities | 15,892 | 8,756 | 8,787 | 7,753 | 6,860 | 9,406 | 6,752 | 6,415 | 6,052 | 4,998 |
| Long Term Debt | 19,999 | 7,400 | 7,858 | 4,203 | 2,550 | 2,313 | 2,397 | 1,702 | 2,187 | 2,651 |
| Common Equity | 21,273 | 16,908 | 12,203 | 17,325 | 15,327 | 14,210 | 13,572 | 11,896 | 9,250 | 8,648 |
| Total Capital | 41,787 | 24,842 | 20,190 | 22,174 | 18,446 | 17,998 | 17,226 | 14,837 | 13,196 | 12,821 |
| Capital Expenditures | 3,253 | 2,128 | 2,446 | 2,430 | 2,068 | 1,736 | 1,387 | 1,345 | 1,437 | 1,324 |
| Cash Flow | 8,665 | 7,461 | 6,626 | 7,084 | 7,047 | 5,384 | 4,109 | 4,786 | 4,421 | 3,744 |
| Current Ratio | 1.1 | 1.4 | 1.2 | 1.3 | 1.3 | 1.1 | 1.3 | 1.1 | 1.1 | 1.2 |
| % Long Term Debt of Capitalization | 47.9 | 29.8 | 38.9 | 18.9 | 13.8 | 12.9 | 13.9 | 11.5 | 16.6 | 20.7 |
| % Net Income of Revenue | 11.0 | 13.8 | 11.9 | 14.3 | 16.1 | 12.5 | 14.3 | 13.2 | 13.2 | 9.9 |
| % Return on Assets | 11.7 | 15.7 | 14.6 | 17.5 | 18.3 | 13.7 | 15.7 | 14.6 | 14.7 | 12.5 |
| % Return on Equity | 33.2 | 40.9 | 34.8 | 34.6 | 38.2 | 29.4 | 22.3 | 33.3 | 37.0 | 32.8 |

Data as orig reptd.; bef. results of disc opers/spec. items. Per share data adj. for stk. divs.; EPS diluted. E-Estimated. NA-Not Available. NM-Not Meaningful. NR-Not Ranked. UR-Under Review.

**Office:** 700 Anderson Hill Road, Purchase, NY 10577.
**Telephone:** 914-253-2000.
**Website:** http://www.pepsico.com
**Chrmn & CEO:** I.K. Nooyi

**COO:** E. Guimaraes
**EVP, Secy & General Counsel:** M.A. Smith
**SVP & CSO:** M. Khan
**SVP, Chief Acctg Officer & Cntlr:** M.T. Gallagher

**Board Members:** S. L. Brown, I. M. Cook, D. Dublon, V. J. Dzau, R. L. Hunt, A. Ibarguen, A. C. Martinez, I. K. Nooyi, S. P. Rockefeller, J. J. Schiro, L. G. Trotter, D. L. Vasella, A. Weisser

**Founded:** 1916
**Domicile:** North Carolina
**Employees:** 294,000

# PerkinElmer Inc.

**S&P Recommendation** BUY ★★★★☆

| Price | 12-Mo. Target Price | Investment Style |
|---|---|---|
| $17.49 (as of Nov 25, 2011) | $26.00 | Large-Cap Value |

**GICS Sector** Health Care
**Sub-Industry** Life Sciences Tools & Services

**Summary** This diversified technology company provides advanced scientific and technical products and services worldwide to pharmaceutical and industrial markets.

## Key Stock Statistics (Source S&P, Vickers, company reports)

| | | | | | | | |
|---|---|---|---|---|---|---|---|
| 52-Wk Range | $28.75–17.45 | S&P Oper. EPS 2011**E** | 1.68 | Market Capitalization(B) | $1.978 | Beta | 0.92 |
| Trailing 12-Month EPS | $3.27 | S&P Oper. EPS 2012**E** | 1.92 | Yield (%) | 1.60 | S&P 3-Yr. Proj. EPS CAGR(%) | 14 |
| Trailing 12-Month P/E | 5.4 | P/E on S&P Oper. EPS 2011**E** | 10.4 | Dividend Rate/Share | $0.28 | S&P Credit Rating | BBB |
| $10K Invested 5 Yrs Ago | $8,612 | Common Shares Outstg. (M) | 113.1 | Institutional Ownership (%) | 97 | | |

## Price Performance

30-Week Mov. Avg. ···   10-Week Mov. Avg. - - -   GAAP Earnings vs. Previous Year   Volume Above Avg. STARS
12-Mo. Target Price —   Relative Strength —   ▲ Up   ▼ Down   ► No Change   Below Avg. ★

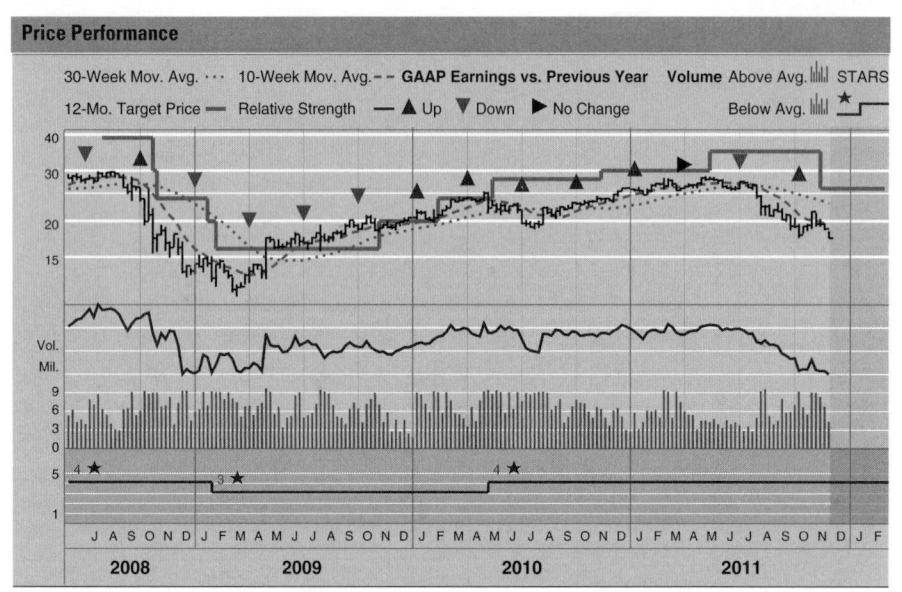

Options: ASE, CBOE, Ph

Analysis prepared by Equity Analyst **Jeffrey Loo, CFA** on Nov 21, 2011, when the stock traded at **$18.22**.

## Qualitative Risk Assessment

| LOW | **MEDIUM** | HIGH |
|---|---|---|

Our risk assessment reflects PKI's broad product mix and diverse global client base. However, the company has been actively restructuring its business units and product portfolio and pursuing acquisitions, which we believe could increase operating risks.

## Quantitative Evaluations

**S&P Quality Ranking**     B+

| D | C | B- | B | **B+** | A- | A | A+ |
|---|---|---|---|---|---|---|---|

**Relative Strength Rank**     WEAK

24

LOWEST = 1       HIGHEST = 99

## Revenue/Earnings Data

**Revenue (Million $)**

| | 1Q | 2Q | 3Q | 4Q | Year |
|---|---|---|---|---|---|
| 2011 | 447.9 | 479.5 | 453.7 | -- | -- |
| 2010 | 465.1 | 497.8 | 419.1 | 470.0 | 1,704 |
| 2009 | 435.2 | 438.3 | 440.5 | 498.3 | 1,812 |
| 2008 | 482.3 | 528.6 | 505.1 | 495.0 | 1,937 |
| 2007 | 402.9 | 437.3 | 435.7 | 511.5 | 1,787 |
| 2006 | 355.5 | 377.0 | 386.9 | 427.0 | 1,546 |

**Earnings Per Share ($)**

| | | | | | |
|---|---|---|---|---|---|
| 2011 | 0.22 | 0.25 | 0.24 | E0.51 | E1.68 |
| 2010 | 0.22 | 0.46 | 0.23 | 0.36 | 1.15 |
| 2009 | 0.13 | 0.20 | 0.14 | 0.33 | 0.80 |
| 2008 | 0.20 | 0.27 | 0.37 | 0.29 | 1.06 |
| 2007 | 0.12 | 0.28 | 0.26 | 0.46 | 1.11 |
| 2006 | 0.17 | 0.21 | 0.23 | 0.33 | 0.94 |

Fiscal year ended Dec. 31. Next earnings report expected: Early February. EPS Estimates based on S&P Operating Earnings; historical GAAP earnings are as reported.

## Highlights

➤ We expect sales to grow 13% to $1.92 billion in 2011, accounting for the divestiture of PKI's Illumination and Detection Solutions (IDS) unit in late 2010. In 2012, we see sales growing 11.5% to $2.14 billion, including the acquisition of Caliper Life Sciences. Within the Human Health segment, we see continued solid growth in the screening business with strong neonatal sales growth, aided by expansion into emerging markets with robust growth of over 20% in China and India on increased adoption of prenatal and neonatal genetic tests. Within Environmental Health, we expect strong demand for inorganic analysis solutions for both food and environmental applications, aided by tighter food safety regulations in China. We look for flat gross margins on higher instrument sales, but forecast an 60 basis point improvement in operating margins from leverage.

➤ In November 2011, PKI acquired Caliper Life Sciences, a provider of imaging and detection solutions, for $600 million.

➤ Excluding intangible amortization, we estimate operating EPS of $1.68 and $1.92 in 2011 and 2012, respectively.

## Investment Rationale/Risk

➤ We believe the shares, recently trading at 10.5X our forward 12 months EPS forecast and at a P/E-to-growth ratio of 0.75X, both below peers and historical levels, are undervalued. We see signs that PKI's end-markets are stabilizing, and we believe growth, particularly within its Environmental Health unit, will be more robust than we initially anticipated. We also think PKI is benefiting from its years-long portfolio re-structuring and strategic efforts of international expansion, significant R&D investments, and strategic acquisitions, focused on supplementing organic growth. We believe PKI's expanding geographic presence in developing countries, particularly India and China, where it has made acquisitions will benefit both its Human Health and Environmental Health units.

➤ Risks to our recommendation and target price include a greater-than-anticipated decline in instrument sales, and slowing growth in industrial end-markets.

➤ Our 12-month target price of $26 is based on our relative valuation analysis, which uses a 14% projected three-year EPS growth rate, our 2011 EPS estimate and a P/E-to-growth ratio of 1.05X, in line with peers.

## Dividend Data (Dates: mm/dd Payment Date: mm/dd/yy)

| Amount ($) | Date Decl. | Ex-Div. Date | Stk. of Record | Payment Date |
|---|---|---|---|---|
| 0.070 | 10/27 | 01/19 | 01/21 | 02/11/11 |
| 0.070 | 01/24 | 04/19 | 04/22 | 05/13/11 |
| 0.070 | 06/14 | 07/20 | 07/22 | 08/12/11 |
| 0.070 | 07/25 | 10/19 | 10/21 | 11/11/11 |

Dividends have been paid since 1965. Source: Company reports.

**Please read the Required Disclosures and Analyst Certification on the last page of this report.**

The McGraw-Hill Companies

# PerkinElmer Inc.

**STANDARD &POOR'S**

## Business Summary November 21, 2011

PerkinElmer, Inc. (PKI) provides technology, services and solutions to the di-agnostics, research, environmental, safety and security, industrial, and labo-ratory services markets. The company operates through two segments, Hu-man Health and Environmental Health.

The Human Health segment focuses on developing diagnostics, tools and ap-plications to help detect disease earlier and to accelerate the discovery and development of critical new therapies. Within the Human Health segment, the company serves both the diagnostics and research markets. The Human Health segment includes its products and services that address the genetic screening and bio-discovery markets. In the diagnostics market, the company provides early detection for genetic disorders from pre-conception to early childhood, as well as medical imaging for the diagnostics market. Its products are designed to provide insights into the health of expectant mothers during pregnancy and their newborns. The company's instruments, reagents and software test and screen for disorders and diseases, including Down syn-drome, infertility, anemia, and diabetes. The company's medical imaging de-tectors are used to enable doctors to make diagnoses of conditions ranging

from broken bones to reduced blood flow in vascular systems. In addition, its detectors improve oncology treatments by focusing radiation directly at tu-mors. In the research market, PKI provides a suite of solutions, including reagents, liquid handling and detection technologies that enable researchers to improve the drug discovery process. These applications, solutions and ser-vices enable pharmaceutical companies to create therapeutics. The portfolio of liquid handling and detection technologies includes a range of systems consisting of instrumentation for automation and detection solutions, cellular imaging and analysis hardware and software.

In addition, the company has a portfolio of consumables products, including drug discovery and research reagents. It sells its research solutions to phar-maceutical, biotechnology and academic research customers globally.

## Company Financials Fiscal Year Ended Dec. 31

| Per Share Data ($) | 2010 | 2009 | 2008 | 2007 | 2006 | 2005 | 2004 | 2003 | 2002 | 2001 |
|---|---|---|---|---|---|---|---|---|---|---|
| Tangible Book Value | NM | NM | NM | NM | 0.45 | 1.91 | NM | NM | NM | NM |
| Cash Flow | 1.91 | 1.58 | 1.81 | 1.76 | 1.52 | 1.03 | 1.35 | 1.07 | 0.58 | 0.77 |
| Earnings | 1.15 | 0.80 | 1.06 | 1.11 | 0.94 | 0.51 | 0.75 | 0.43 | -0.03 | -0.01 |
| S&P Core Earnings | 1.03 | 0.84 | 0.91 | 1.03 | 0.91 | 0.40 | 0.63 | 0.25 | -0.34 | -0.68 |
| Dividends | 0.28 | 0.28 | 0.28 | 0.28 | 0.28 | 0.28 | 0.28 | 0.28 | 0.28 | 0.28 |
| Payout Ratio | 24% | 35% | 26% | 25% | 30% | 55% | 37% | 65% | NM | NM |
| Prices:High | 26.24 | 21.09 | 29.95 | 30.00 | 24.17 | 24.02 | 23.28 | 18.71 | 36.30 | 52.31 |
| Prices:Low | 18.69 | 10.88 | 12.70 | 21.28 | 16.31 | 17.92 | 15.05 | 7.22 | 4.28 | 21.28 |
| P/E Ratio:High | 23 | 26 | 28 | 27 | 26 | 47 | 31 | 44 | NM | NM |
| P/E Ratio:Low | 16 | 14 | 12 | 19 | 17 | 35 | 20 | 17 | NM | NM |
| **Income Statement Analysis** (Million $) | | | | | | | | | | |
| Revenue | 1,704 | 1,812 | 1,937 | 1,787 | 1,546 | 1,474 | 1,687 | 1,535 | 1,505 | 1,330 |
| Operating Income | 262 | 261 | 287 | 249 | 221 | 229 | 253 | 211 | 131 | 196 |
| Depreciation | 89.2 | 91.8 | 88.3 | 78.0 | 69.2 | 67.0 | 76.2 | 80.2 | 76.6 | 80.5 |
| Interest Expense | 15.9 | 17.2 | 25.2 | 15.3 | 9.16 | 74.3 | 38.0 | Nil | Nil | Nil |
| Pretax Income | 162 | 131 | 147 | 151 | 151 | 66.7 | 137 | 80.9 | -8.55 | 34.2 |
| Effective Tax Rate | NA | 29.0% | 14.4% | 11.5% | 21.5% | 0.19% | 28.2% | 32.0% | NM | NM |
| Net Income | 136 | 92.7 | 126 | 134 | 118 | 66.5 | 98.3 | 55.0 | -4.14 | -0.62 |
| S&P Core Earnings | 122 | 96.7 | 109 | 124 | 114 | 53.8 | 81.3 | 31.2 | -43.1 | -71.3 |
| **Balance Sheet & Other Financial Data** (Million $) | | | | | | | | | | |
| Cash | 420 | 180 | 179 | 203 | 199 | 502 | 208 | 202 | 317 | 138 |
| Current Assets | 1,085 | 884 | 831 | 843 | 745 | 999 | 748 | 766 | 991 | 997 |
| Total Assets | 3,209 | 3,064 | 2,935 | 2,949 | 2,510 | 2,693 | 2,576 | 2,608 | 2,836 | 2,919 |
| Current Liabilities | 515 | 496 | 516 | 548 | 477 | 495 | 446 | 452 | 698 | 708 |
| Long Term Debt | 424 | 558 | 509 | 516 | 152 | 243 | 365 | 544 | 614 | 598 |
| Common Equity | 1,926 | 1,629 | 1,568 | 1,575 | 1,578 | 1,651 | 1,460 | 1,349 | 1,252 | 1,364 |
| Total Capital | 2,350 | 2,187 | 2,077 | 2,159 | 1,730 | 1,894 | 1,825 | 1,893 | 1,866 | 1,962 |
| Capital Expenditures | 33.7 | 31.7 | 43.3 | 47.0 | 44.5 | 25.1 | 19.0 | 16.6 | 37.8 | 88.7 |
| Cash Flow | 225 | 185 | 214 | 212 | 188 | 134 | 174 | 135 | 72.4 | 79.9 |
| Current Ratio | 2.1 | 1.8 | 1.6 | 1.5 | 1.6 | 2.0 | 1.7 | 1.7 | 1.4 | 1.4 |
| % Long Term Debt of Capitalization | 18.0 | 25.5 | 24.5 | 23.9 | 8.8 | 12.8 | 20.0 | 28.7 | 32.9 | 30.5 |
| % Net Income of Revenue | 8.0 | 5.1 | 6.5 | 7.5 | 7.7 | 4.5 | 5.8 | 3.6 | NM | NM |
| % Return on Assets | 4.3 | 3.1 | 4.3 | 4.9 | 4.5 | 2.5 | 3.8 | 2.0 | NM | NM |
| % Return on Equity | 7.7 | 5.8 | 8.0 | 8.5 | 7.3 | 4.3 | 7.0 | 4.2 | NM | NM |

Data as orig reptd.; bef. results of disc opers/spec. items. Per share data adj. for stk. divs.; EPS diluted. E-Estimated. NA-Not Available. NM-Not Meaningful. NR-Not Ranked. UR-Under Review.

**Office:** 940 Winter St, Waltham, MA 02451-1457.
**Telephone:** 781-663-6900.
**Website:** http://www.perkinelmer.com
**Chrmn, Pres & CEO:** R.F. Friel

**SVP & CFO:** F.A. Wilson
**SVP, Secy & General Counsel:** J.S. Goldberg
**CSO:** D.R. Marshak
**Chief Acctg Officer:** A. Okun

**Board Members:** R. F. Friel, N. A. Lopardo, A. P. Michas, J. C. Mullen, V. L. Sato, G. Schmergel, K. J. Sicchitano, P. J. Sullivan, G. R. Tod

**Founded:** 1947
**Domicile:** Massachusetts
**Employees:** 6,200

# Pfizer Inc

 STANDARD &POOR'S

| S&P Recommendation **BUY** ★★★★☆ | Price<br>$19.40 (as of Nov 29, 2011) | 12-Mo. Target Price<br>$24.00 | Investment Style<br>Large-Cap Blend |
| --- | --- | --- | --- |

**GICS Sector** Health Care
**Sub-Industry** Pharmaceuticals

**Summary** The world's largest pharmaceutical company, Pfizer produces a wide range of drugs across a broad therapeutic spectrum. In October 2009, PFE acquired rival drugmaker Wyeth for some $68 billion in cash and stock.

## Key Stock Statistics (Source S&P, Vickers, company reports)

| | | | | | | |
| --- | --- | --- | --- | --- | --- | --- |
| 52-Wk Range | $21.45– 16.42 | S&P Oper. EPS 2011**E** | 2.29 | Market Capitalization(B) | $149.127 | Beta | 0.73 |
| Trailing 12-Month EPS | $1.44 | S&P Oper. EPS 2012**E** | 2.35 | Yield (%) | 4.12 | S&P 3-Yr. Proj. EPS CAGR(%) | 2 |
| Trailing 12-Month P/E | 13.5 | P/E on S&P Oper. EPS 2011**E** | 8.5 | Dividend Rate/Share | $0.80 | S&P Credit Rating | AA |
| $10K Invested 5 Yrs Ago | $8,770 | Common Shares Outstg. (M) | 7,687.0 | Institutional Ownership (%) | 73 | | |

## Price Performance

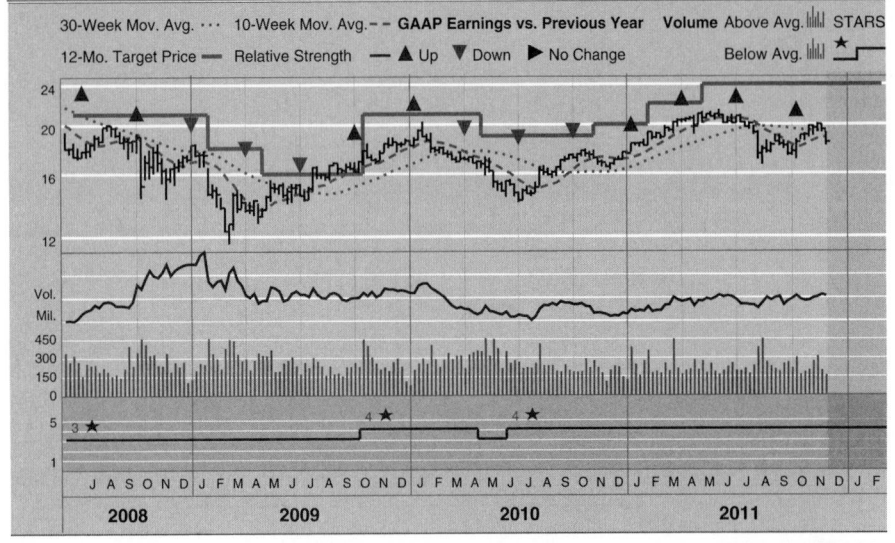

30-Week Mov. Avg. · · · 10-Week Mov. Avg. - - GAAP Earnings vs. Previous Year   Volume Above Avg. ▐▐▌▌ STARS
12-Mo. Target Price — Relative Strength — ▲ Up ▼ Down ▶ No Change          Below Avg. ▐▐▌▌ ★

Options: ASE, CBOE, P, Ph

Analysis prepared by Equity Analyst **Herman Saftlas** on Nov 16, 2011, when the stock traded at **$19.57**.

## Highlights

➤ We project 2012 sales to fall 6% from the $67 billion that we forecast for 2011, largely reflecting heavy generic erosion in the Lipitor cholesterol franchise (estimated sales of $9.3 billion in 2011) whose U.S. marketing exclusivity ended in November 2011. We also see lower sales of other off-patent drugs such as Xalatan and Effexor. On the plus side, we project solid gains in the Enbrel, Lyrica and Prevnar lines. We also see higher sales of animal health products, consumer products and infant nutritionals. Sales in emerging markets should also remain robust.

➤ We estimate adjusted gross margins will decline to about 79% in 2012 from an expected 80.3% in 2011, largely reflecting a less profitable sales mix with Lipitor off patent, and ongoing pricing headwinds in the U.S. and Europe. However, we expect pretax margins to benefit from cost streamlining measures, including a planned $1.5 billion reduction in R&D spending.

➤ After a projected tax rate comparable with the 29% that we forecast for 2011, we see adjusted operating EPS increasing to $2.35 in 2012, from an expected $2.29 in 2011.

## Investment Rationale/Risk

➤ PFE recently lost patent protection on Lipitor, its largest-selling drug estimated to account for about 14% of total sales in 2011. Despite this loss, we still expect PFE to post higher share profits in 2012, driven by new products, growth in emerging markets, cost restructurings and common share buybacks. Key pipeline opportunities, in our opinion, include Eliquis for stroke prevention, and tofacitinib for rheumatoid arthritis. We are also encouraged by PFE's recent increase in its stock buyback program to $9 billion from $7 billion, and the planned spinoff to shareholders of non-core businesses.

➤ Risks to our recommendation and target price include an inability to achieve planned synergies from Wyeth and King, and possible pipeline setbacks.

➤ Our 12-month target price of $24 applies a peer multiple of 10.2X to our 2012 EPS estimate. Our target price is also close to our calculation of intrinsic value, derived from our DCF model, which assumes slowing cash flow growth over the next few years, a WACC of 9.3%, and terminal growth of 1%. The dividend yields about 4%.

## Qualitative Risk Assessment

| LOW | MEDIUM | HIGH |
| --- | --- | --- |

Our risk assessment reflects PFE's leading position in the global pharmaceutical market, which we believe affords important competitive operating and financial advantages. While we believe PFE's 2009 acquisition of Wyeth has bolstered sales and margins ahead of major patent expirations in 2011, we remain uncertain whether PFE will be able to realize all of its key strategic objectives from the deal.

## Quantitative Evaluations

**S&P Quality Ranking**                     B

| D | C | B- | B | B+ | A- | A | A+ |
| --- | --- | --- | --- | --- | --- | --- | --- |

**Relative Strength Rank**          STRONG

83

LOWEST = 1                          HIGHEST = 99

## Revenue/Earnings Data

### Revenue (Million $)

| | 1Q | 2Q | 3Q | 4Q | Year |
| --- | --- | --- | --- | --- | --- |
| 2011 | 16,502 | 16,984 | 17,193 | -- | -- |
| 2010 | 16,750 | 17,327 | 16,171 | 17,561 | 67,809 |
| 2009 | 10,867 | 10,984 | 11,621 | 16,537 | 50,009 |
| 2008 | 11,848 | 12,129 | 11,973 | 12,346 | 48,296 |
| 2007 | 12,474 | 11,084 | 11,990 | 12,870 | 48,418 |
| 2006 | 11,747 | 11,741 | 12,280 | 12,603 | 48,371 |

### Earnings Per Share ($)

| | | | | |
| --- | --- | --- | --- | --- |
| 2011 | 0.28 | 0.33 | 0.31 | E0.47 | E2.29 |
| 2010 | 0.25 | 0.31 | 0.11 | 0.36 | 1.02 |
| 2009 | 0.40 | 0.33 | 0.43 | 0.10 | 1.23 |
| 2008 | 0.41 | 0.41 | 0.33 | 0.03 | 1.19 |
| 2007 | 0.48 | 0.19 | 0.12 | 0.40 | 1.18 |
| 2006 | 0.55 | 0.31 | 0.44 | 0.21 | 1.52 |

Fiscal year ended Dec. 31. Next earnings report expected: Early February. EPS Estimates based on S&P Operating Earnings; historical GAAP earnings are as reported.

## Dividend Data (Dates: mm/dd Payment Date: mm/dd/yy)

| Amount ($) | Date Decl. | Ex-Div. Date | Stk. of Record | Payment Date |
| --- | --- | --- | --- | --- |
| 0.200 | 12/13 | 02/02 | 02/04 | 03/01/11 |
| 0.200 | 04/28 | 05/11 | 05/13 | 06/07/11 |
| 0.200 | 06/23 | 08/03 | 08/05 | 09/06/11 |
| 0.200 | 10/27 | 11/08 | 11/11 | 12/06/11 |

Dividends have been paid since 1901. Source: Company reports.

**Please read the Required Disclosures and Analyst Certification on the last page of this report.**

# Pfizer Inc

## Business Summary November 16, 2011

CORPORATE OVERVIEW. Pfizer stands out above its peers in the $780 billion global pharmaceutical sector, in our opinion. Growth over the past 10 years was largely augmented by two major acquisitions -- Warner-Lambert Co. in 2000 and Pharmacia Corp. in 2003 -- as well as by in-licensed products. The business was significantly further expanded with the acquisition of Wyeth in October 2009.

Pfizer's drug portfolio is unmatched in terms of breadth and depth in the global drug market, by our analysis. Lipitor cholesterol-lowering agent has been PFE's largest-selling drug (sales of $10.7 billion in 2010). However, we see Lipitor sales dropping sharply in 2012, with the expiration of U.S. marketing exclusivity in November 2011. Other cardiovasculars include Norvasc ($1.5 billion), and Caduet ($527 million), a combination of Lipitor and Norvasc. Key central nervous system medicines include Lyrica, a treatment for nerve pain and epileptic seizures ($3.1 billion); Geodon, an antipsychotic ($1.0 billion); and Zyvox, an anti-infective ($1.2 billion). Foreign sales accounted for 57% of total revenues in 2010.

Other key drugs sold include Celebrex COX-2 inhibitor for arthritis and pain (sales of $2.4 billion); Viagra for male erectile dysfunction ($1.9 billion); Xalatan/Xalcom, for glaucoma ($1.7 billion); Detrol and LA/Detrol, treatments for incontinence ($1.0 billion); Sutent ($1.1 billion) for kidney and other cancers; Genotropin ($885 million), a human growth hormone; and Chantix ($755 million) for smoking cessation.

The animal health division ($3.6 billion) offers one of the largest-selling and broadest product lines in the field. Principal products include feed additives, vaccines, antibiotics, antihelmintics, and other veterinary products. Consumer healthcare products ($2.8 billion) include OTC medicines, dietary supplements and other items. Nutrition products ($1.9 billion) consist of infant formulas and gelatin capsules.

## Company Financials Fiscal Year Ended Dec. 31

| Per Share Data ($) | 2010 | 2009 | 2008 | 2007 | 2006 | 2005 | 2004 | 2003 | 2002 | 2001 |
|---|---|---|---|---|---|---|---|---|---|---|
| Tangible Book Value | NM | NM | 2.71 | 4.93 | 3.65 | 1.91 | 1.48 | 0.85 | 3.04 | 2.64 |
| Cash Flow | 1.98 | 1.90 | 1.94 | 1.93 | 2.24 | 1.84 | 2.16 | 0.78 | 1.64 | 1.39 |
| Earnings | 1.02 | 1.23 | 1.19 | 1.18 | 1.52 | 1.09 | 1.49 | 0.22 | 1.47 | 1.22 |
| S&P Core Earnings | 1.18 | 1.35 | 1.42 | 1.14 | 1.53 | 1.02 | 1.45 | 0.29 | 1.35 | 1.09 |
| Dividends | 0.72 | 0.80 | 1.28 | 1.16 | 0.96 | 0.76 | 0.68 | 0.60 | 0.52 | 0.44 |
| Payout Ratio | 71% | 65% | 108% | 98% | 63% | 70% | 46% | 273% | 35% | 36% |
| Prices:High | 20.36 | 18.99 | 24.24 | 27.73 | 28.60 | 29.21 | 38.89 | 36.92 | 42.46 | 46.75 |
| Prices:Low | 14.00 | 11.62 | 14.26 | 22.24 | 22.16 | 20.27 | 21.99 | 27.90 | 25.13 | 34.00 |
| P/E Ratio:High | 20 | 15 | 20 | 23 | 19 | 27 | 26 | NM | 29 | 38 |
| P/E Ratio:Low | 14 | 9 | 12 | 19 | 15 | 19 | 15 | NM | 17 | 28 |

| Income Statement Analysis (Million $) | | | | | | | | | | |
|---|---|---|---|---|---|---|---|---|---|---|
| Revenue | 67,809 | 50,009 | 48,296 | 48,418 | 48,371 | 51,298 | 52,516 | 45,188 | 32,373 | 32,259 |
| Operating Income | 26,742 | 21,268 | 21,925 | 19,983 | 19,575 | 20,501 | 22,117 | 17,061 | 13,436 | 12,147 |
| Depreciation | 7,700 | 4,757 | 5,090 | 5,200 | 5,293 | 5,576 | 5,093 | 4,078 | 1,036 | 1,068 |
| Interest Expense | 1,799 | 1,233 | 562 | 440 | 488 | 488 | 359 | 290 | 279 | 432 |
| Pretax Income | 9,422 | 10,827 | 9,694 | 9,278 | 13,028 | 11,534 | 14,007 | 3,263 | 11,796 | 10,329 |
| Effective Tax Rate | NA | 20.3% | 17.0% | 11.0% | 15.3% | 29.7% | 19.0% | 49.7% | 22.1% | 24.8% |
| Net Income | 8,266 | 8,621 | 8,026 | 8,213 | 11,024 | 8,094 | 11,332 | 1,639 | 9,181 | 7,752 |
| S&P Core Earnings | 9,501 | 9,377 | 9,538 | 7,963 | 11,048 | 7,588 | 11,030 | 2,147 | 8,441 | 6,862 |

| Balance Sheet & Other Financial Data (Million $) | | | | | | | | | | |
|---|---|---|---|---|---|---|---|---|---|---|
| Cash | 28,012 | 25,969 | 23,731 | 25,475 | 1,827 | 2,247 | 1,808 | 1,520 | 1,878 | 1,036 |
| Current Assets | 60,468 | 61,670 | 43,076 | 46,849 | 46,949 | 41,896 | 39,694 | 29,741 | 24,781 | 18,450 |
| Total Assets | 195,014 | 212,949 | 111,148 | 115,268 | 114,837 | 117,565 | 123,684 | 116,775 | 46,356 | 39,153 |
| Current Liabilities | 28,609 | 37,225 | 27,009 | 21,835 | 21,389 | 28,448 | 26,458 | 23,657 | 18,555 | 13,640 |
| Long Term Debt | 38,411 | 43,218 | 7,963 | 7,314 | 5,546 | 6,347 | 7,279 | 5,755 | 3,140 | 2,609 |
| Common Equity | 87,761 | 89,953 | 57,483 | 64,917 | 71,217 | 65,458 | 68,085 | 65,158 | 19,950 | 18,293 |
| Total Capital | 130,630 | 133,691 | 66,640 | 80,134 | 84,919 | 82,214 | 88,189 | 84,370 | 23,454 | 21,354 |
| Capital Expenditures | 1,513 | 1,205 | 1,701 | 1,880 | 2,050 | 2,106 | 2,601 | 2,641 | 1,758 | 2,203 |
| Cash Flow | 15,996 | 13,376 | 13,113 | 13,409 | 16,317 | 13,661 | 16,417 | 5,710 | 10,217 | 8,820 |
| Current Ratio | 2.1 | 1.7 | 1.6 | 2.2 | 2.2 | 1.5 | 1.5 | 1.3 | 1.3 | 1.4 |
| % Long Term Debt of Capitalization | 29.4 | Nil | 11.6 | 9.1 | 6.5 | 7.7 | 8.3 | 6.8 | 13.4 | 12.2 |
| % Net Income of Revenue | 12.2 | 17.2 | 16.6 | 17.0 | 22.8 | 15.8 | 21.6 | 3.6 | 28.4 | 24.0 |
| % Return on Assets | NA | NA | 7.1 | 7.1 | 9.5 | 6.7 | 9.4 | 2.0 | 21.5 | 21.3 |
| % Return on Equity | NA | NA | 13.1 | 12.1 | 16.1 | 12.1 | 17.0 | 3.8 | 48.0 | 45.1 |

Data as orig reptd.; bef. results of disc opers/spec. items. Per share data adj. for stk. divs.; EPS diluted. E-Estimated. NA-Not Available. NM-Not Meaningful. NR-Not Ranked. UR-Under Review.

Office: 235 East 42nd Street, New York, NY 10017-5703.
Telephone: 212-733-2323.
Website: http://www.pfizer.com
Chrmn: G.A. Lorch

Pres & CEO: I.C. Read
CFO: F.A. D'Amelio
CSO: M. Ehlers
Chief Acctg Officer & Cntlr: L.V. Cangialosi

Investor Contact: J. Davis (212-733-0717)
Board Members: D. A. Ausiello, M. S. Brown, M. A. Burns, W. D. Cornwell, F. D. Fergusson, W. H. Gray, III, C. J. Horner, S. N. Johnson, J. M. Kilts, G. A. Lorch, J. P. Mascotte, I. C. Read, S. W. Sanger

Founded: 1849
Domicile: Delaware
Employees: 110,600

# PG&E Corp

## STANDARD &POOR'S

**S&P Recommendation** HOLD ★★★☆☆

| Price | 12-Mo. Target Price | Investment Style |
|---|---|---|
| $37.21 (as of Nov 25, 2011) | $43.00 | Large-Cap Blend |

**GICS Sector** Utilities
**Sub-Industry** Multi-Utilities

**Summary** This energy holding company is the parent of Pacific Gas & Electric Co., which serves northern and central California.

### Key Stock Statistics (Source S&P, Vickers, company reports)

| | | | | | | | |
|---|---|---|---|---|---|---|---|
| 52-Wk Range | $48.63– 36.84 | S&P Oper. EPS 2011E | 3.53 | Market Capitalization(B) | $14.996 | Beta | 0.31 |
| Trailing 12-Month EPS | $2.53 | S&P Oper. EPS 2012E | 3.21 | Yield (%) | 4.89 | S&P 3-Yr. Proj. EPS CAGR(%) | 3 |
| Trailing 12-Month P/E | 14.7 | P/E on S&P Oper. EPS 2011E | 10.5 | Dividend Rate/Share | $1.82 | S&P Credit Rating | BBB+ |
| $10K Invested 5 Yrs Ago | $9,919 | Common Shares Outstg. (M) | 403.0 | Institutional Ownership (%) | 71 | | |

### Price Performance

30-Week Mov. Avg. ··· 10-Week Mov. Avg. – – S&P Earnings vs. Previous Year  Volume Above Avg. STARS
12-Mo. Target Price — Relative Strength — ▲ Up ▼ Down ▶ No Change  Below Avg.

Options: ASE, CBOE, P

Analysis prepared by Equity Analyst **Justin McCann** on Nov 17, 2011, when the stock traded at **$38.68**.

### Highlights

➤ We expect operating EPS in 2011 to grow about 3% from 2010's $3.42, reflecting the benefit of the general rate case (GRC), and more than offsetting the impact of first-quarter storm costs and more common shares. For 2012, however, we look for operating EPS to decline about 9% from projected results for 2011, due to sharply higher O&M costs as PCG accelerates its work to improve its gas and electric system in the aftermath of the deadly San Bruno gas explosion.

➤ On May 5, 2011, the CPUC issued its 2011-2013 GRC ruling, in which it authorized Pacific Gas & Electric (retroactive to January 1) electric rate increases of $403 million for 2011, $145 million for 2012, and $150 million for 2013; and gas rate increases of $47.4 million for 2011, and $35 million for both 2012 and 2013. The increases were based on a return on equity (ROE) of 11.35%. It also authorized an increase of an additional $55 million in 2011 for the recovery of the financing costs associated with the conventional meters that have been replaced by "SmartMeters".

➤ On September 13, 2011, Anthony F. Earley, Jr., became the new Chairman, CEO, and President of PCG. He had retired from the same positions at DTE Energy (DTE 51 Hold) on September 12.

### Investment Rationale/Risk

➤ The stock was down about 19% year to date through mid-November, hurt, in our view, by the judgement made of PG&E management in the independent investigation of the San Bruno gas pipeline explosion, in which the utility could not provide key safety records. We believe the stock was also hurt by the sharply reduced earnings outlook for 2012, as PG&E plans to accelerate the upgrading of its infrastructure, as well as by the nuclear crisis in Japan, given that the utility's Diablo Canyon nuclear facility is located in an earthquake prone area.

➤ Risks to our recommendation and target price include a much worse-than-expected earnings performance, and/or a major decline in the average P/E multiple of the peer group.

➤ The recent yield from the dividend was 4.7%, well above the average peer yield (about 4.3%) for combined electric and gas utilities. However, despite an approximate peers dividend payout ratio of 57% of our operating EPS estimate for 2012, PCG will not increase its dividend in 2012, as it works to put the costs related to the San Bruno explosion behind it. Our 12-month target price is $43, a discount-to-peers P/E of 13.4X our operating EPS estimate for 2012.

### Qualitative Risk Assessment

| LOW | MEDIUM | HIGH |
|---|---|---|

Our risk assessment reflects our view of the company's strong and steady cash flow from the regulated Pacific Gas & Electric subsidiary, its much improved balance sheet and credit profile, a healthy economy in its service territory, and a greatly improved regulatory environment.

### Quantitative Evaluations

**S&P Quality Ranking**    B

| D | C | B- | B | B+ | A- | A | A+ |
|---|---|---|---|---|---|---|---|

**Relative Strength Rank**    MODERATE

35

LOWEST = 1    HIGHEST = 99

### Revenue/Earnings Data

**Revenue (Million $)**

| | 1Q | 2Q | 3Q | 4Q | Year |
|---|---|---|---|---|---|
| 2011 | 3,597 | 3,684 | 3,860 | -- | -- |
| 2010 | 3,475 | 3,232 | 3,513 | 3,621 | 13,841 |
| 2009 | 3,431 | 3,194 | 3,235 | 3,539 | 13,399 |
| 2008 | 3,733 | 3,578 | 3,674 | 3,643 | 14,628 |
| 2007 | 3,356 | 3,187 | 3,279 | 3,415 | 13,237 |
| 2006 | 3,148 | 3,017 | 3,168 | 3,206 | 12,539 |

**Earnings Per Share ($)**

| | | | | | |
|---|---|---|---|---|---|
| 2011 | 0.50 | 0.91 | 0.50 | E0.84 | E3.53 |
| 2010 | 0.67 | 0.86 | 0.66 | 0.63 | 2.82 |
| 2009 | 0.65 | 1.02 | 0.83 | 0.71 | 3.20 |
| 2008 | 0.62 | 0.80 | 0.83 | 0.97 | 3.22 |
| 2007 | 0.71 | 0.74 | 0.77 | 0.56 | 2.78 |
| 2006 | 0.60 | 0.65 | 1.09 | 0.43 | 2.76 |

Fiscal year ended Dec. 31. Next earnings report expected: Mid February. EPS Estimates based on S&P Operating Earnings; historical GAAP earnings are as reported.

### Dividend Data (Dates: mm/dd Payment Date: mm/dd/yy)

| Amount ($) | Date Decl. | Ex-Div. Date | Stk. of Record | Payment Date |
|---|---|---|---|---|
| 0.455 | 12/15 | 12/29 | 12/31 | 01/15/11 |
| 0.455 | 02/17 | 03/29 | 03/31 | 04/15/11 |
| 0.455 | 06/15 | 06/28 | 06/30 | 07/15/11 |

Dividends have been paid since 2005. Source: Company reports.

---

**Please read the Required Disclosures and Analyst Certification on the last page of this report.**

The McGraw-Hill Companies

# PG&E Corp

**STANDARD &POOR'S**

## Business Summary November 17, 2011

CORPORATE OVERVIEW. PG&E Corporation (PCG) is an energy-based holding company that conducts its business through Pacific Gas and Electric Company (PG&E), a public utility operating in northern and central California. The utility's business consists of four main operational units: electricity and natural gas distribution, electricity generation, gas transmission, and electricity transmission. The utility is primarily regulated by the California Public Utilities Commission (CPUC) and the Federal Energy Regulatory Commission (FERC).

CORPORATE STRATEGY. To support anticipated customer growth and the improvement of its existing services, Pacific Gas & Electric plans to make major capital additions to its infrastructure. The utility is also devoting substantial resources to the building and expansion of its transmission lines, which has become the fastest-growing part of its business. It has proposed constructing additional gas and electric transmission arteries so as to create access to new supplies of renewable energy and new sources of natural gas. California law requires its electric utilities to purchase 30% of their power from renewable resources by 2017. In addition to maintaining its ongoing investment in its existing hydroelectric and nuclear facilities, the company has brought into service three new state-of-the-art power plants during the past couple of years that are capable of generating enough power for approximately 950,000 average-size homes.

IMPACT OF IMPORTANT DEVELOPMENTS. On June 9, 2011, the independent review panel that had been appointed by the CPUC issued its report on the natural gas pipeline explosion that occurred in San Bruno, California on September 9, 2010, which resulted in the death of eight people, numerous individual injuries and extensive property damage. The report, which stated that "multiple weaknesses in PG&E's management ... had contributed to a dysfunctional company culture", recommended many changes including the establishment of a multi-year capital program that would lead to ... "either the retrofitting of existing pipelines to accommodate in-line inspection technology or to pipeline segment replacement." PG&E estimated that its costs to perform these tasks in 2011 would range between $350 million to $500 million. The utility, which maintains liability insurance of about $992 million (in excess of a $10 million deductible), has also estimated that it may incur up to $400 million in third-party claims.

## Company Financials Fiscal Year Ended Dec. 31

| Per Share Data ($) | 2010 | 2009 | 2008 | 2007 | 2006 | 2005 | 2004 | 2003 | 2002 | 2001 |
|---|---|---|---|---|---|---|---|---|---|---|
| Tangible Book Value | 28.41 | 27.69 | 25.97 | 25.80 | 20.89 | 19.67 | 20.60 | 10.11 | 8.92 | 11.87 |
| Earnings | 2.82 | 3.20 | 3.22 | 2.78 | 2.76 | 2.34 | 8.97 | 1.96 | -0.15 | 2.99 |
| S&P Core Earnings | 3.13 | 3.65 | 1.91 | 2.53 | 2.64 | 2.45 | 9.00 | 2.05 | -1.08 | 1.59 |
| Dividends | 1.82 | 1.68 | 1.56 | 1.44 | 1.32 | 1.23 | Nil | Nil | Nil | Nil |
| Payout Ratio | 65% | 52% | 48% | 52% | 48% | 53% | Nil | Nil | Nil | Nil |
| Prices:High | 48.63 | 45.80 | 45.68 | 52.17 | 48.17 | 40.10 | 34.46 | 27.98 | 23.75 | 20.94 |
| Prices:Low | 34.95 | 34.50 | 26.67 | 42.58 | 36.25 | 31.83 | 25.90 | 11.69 | 8.00 | 6.50 |
| P/E Ratio:High | 17 | 14 | 14 | 19 | 17 | 17 | 4 | 14 | NM | 7 |
| P/E Ratio:Low | 12 | 11 | 8 | 15 | 13 | 14 | 3 | 6 | NM | 2 |

| Income Statement Analysis (Million $) | | | | | | | | | | |
|---|---|---|---|---|---|---|---|---|---|---|
| Revenue | 13,841 | 13,399 | 14,628 | 13,237 | 12,539 | 11,703 | 11,080 | 10,435 | 12,495 | 22,959 |
| Depreciation | 2,057 | 1,947 | 1,863 | 1,770 | 1,709 | 1,735 | 1,497 | 1,222 | 1,309 | 1,068 |
| Maintenance | NA | NA | NA | NA | NA | NA | NA | NA | NA | NA |
| Fixed Charges Coverage | 3.36 | 3.34 | 3.21 | 3.03 | 3.09 | 3.48 | 2.75 | 2.23 | 2.94 | 2.48 |
| Construction Credits | NA | NA | NA | NA | NA | NA | NA | NA | NA | NA |
| Effective Tax Rate | 33.2% | 27.4% | 26.4% | 34.9% | 35.9% | 37.6% | 39.2% | 36.7% | NM | 35.8% |
| Net Income | 1,099 | 1,220 | 1,184 | 1,006 | 991 | 904 | 3,820 | 791 | -57.0 | 1,090 |
| S&P Core Earnings | 1,220 | 1,391 | 720 | 940 | 972 | 974 | 3,828 | 830 | -404 | 580 |

| Balance Sheet & Other Financial Data (Million $) | | | | | | | | | | |
|---|---|---|---|---|---|---|---|---|---|---|
| Gross Property | 46,289 | 43,080 | 39,833 | 36,584 | 34,214 | 32,030 | 30,509 | 29,222 | 31,179 | 33,012 |
| Capital Expenditures | 3,802 | 3,958 | 3,628 | 2,769 | 2,402 | 1,804 | 1,559 | 1,698 | 3,032 | 2,665 |
| Net Property | 31,449 | 28,892 | 26,261 | 23,656 | 21,785 | 19,955 | 18,989 | 18,107 | 16,928 | 19,167 |
| Capitalization:Long Term Debt | 11,581 | 11,460 | 10,786 | 10,005 | 8,885 | 9,794 | 8,311 | 9,924 | 11,590 | 9,527 |
| Capitalization:% Long Term Debt | 50.7 | 52.6 | 53.5 | 53.9 | 53.2 | 57.5 | 49.0 | 70.2 | 76.2 | 68.8 |
| Capitalization:Preferred | Nil | Nil | Nil | Nil | Nil | Nil | Nil | Nil | Nil | Nil |
| Capitalization:% Preferred | Nil | Nil | Nil | Nil | Nil | Nil | Nil | Nil | Nil | Nil |
| Capitalization:Common | 11,282 | 10,333 | 9,377 | 8,553 | 7,811 | 7,240 | 8,633 | 4,215 | 3,613 | 4,322 |
| Capitalization:% Common | 49.3 | 47.4 | 46.5 | 46.1 | 46.8 | 42.5 | 51.0 | 29.8 | 23.8 | 31.2 |
| Total Capital | 23,672 | 22,521 | 23,654 | 21,710 | 19,642 | 20,238 | 20,596 | 15,122 | 16,786 | 15,668 |
| % Operating Ratio | 87.3 | 86.3 | 87.4 | 88.1 | 87.6 | 87.8 | 102.2 | 80.4 | 67.2 | 90.3 |
| % Earned on Net Property | 7.6 | 8.3 | 9.1 | 9.3 | 10.1 | 10.1 | 38.4 | 14.6 | 31.2 | 15.0 |
| % Return on Revenue | 7.9 | 9.1 | 8.1 | 7.6 | 7.9 | 7.7 | 34.5 | 7.6 | NM | 4.7 |
| % Return on Invested Capital | 7.8 | 8.9 | 8.4 | 8.6 | 8.7 | 7.3 | 15.6 | 13.9 | 22.8 | 16.7 |
| % Return on Common Equity | 10.2 | 12.4 | 13.2 | 12.3 | 11.4 | 59.5 | 20.2 | NM | 29.1 | |

Data as orig reptd.; bef. results of disc opers/spec. items. Per share data adj. for stk. divs.; EPS diluted. E-Estimated. NA-Not Available. NM-Not Meaningful. NR-Not Ranked. UR-Under Review.

**Office:** One Market Spear Tower, Suite 2400, San Francisco, CA 94105-1126.
**Telephone:** 415-267-7000.
**Email:** invrel@pg-corp.com
**Website:** http://www.pgecorp.com

**Chrmn, Pres & CEO:** A.F. Earley, Jr.
**SVP & General Counsel:** H. Park
**CFO & Treas:** K.M. Harvey
**Chief Acctg Officer & Cntlr:** D.B. Mistry

**Secy:** L.Y. Cheng
**Investor Contact:** L.Y. Cheng (415-267-7070)
**Board Members:** D. R. Andrews, L. Chew, C. L. Cox, A. F. Earley, Jr., M. C. Herringer, R. H. Kimmel, R. Meserve, F. E. Miller, R. G. Parra, B. L. Rambo, B. L. Williams

**Founded:** 1995
**Domicile:** California
**Employees:** 19,424

*The McGraw·Hill Companies*

# Philip Morris International Inc

**STANDARD & POOR'S**

| S&P Recommendation | STRONG BUY ★★★★★ | Price $71.31 (as of Nov 25, 2011) | 12-Mo. Target Price $81.00 | Investment Style Large-Cap Blend |
|---|---|---|---|---|

**GICS Sector** Consumer Staples
**Sub-Industry** Tobacco

**Summary** This company, comprising the international operations spun off by Altria in early 2008, is the largest publicly traded manufacturer and marketer of tobacco products.

## Key Stock Statistics (Source S&P, Vickers, company reports)

| | | | | | | | |
|---|---|---|---|---|---|---|---|
| 52-Wk Range | $73.46–55.85 | S&P Oper. EPS 2011**E** | 4.89 | Market Capitalization(B) | $123.864 | Beta | 0.85 |
| Trailing 12-Month EPS | $4.71 | S&P Oper. EPS 2012**E** | 5.18 | Yield (%) | 4.32 | S&P 3-Yr. Proj. EPS CAGR(%) | 12 |
| Trailing 12-Month P/E | 15.1 | P/E on S&P Oper. EPS 2011**E** | 14.6 | Dividend Rate/Share | $3.08 | S&P Credit Rating | A |
| $10K Invested 5 Yrs Ago | NA | Common Shares Outstg. (M) | 1,737.0 | Institutional Ownership (%) | 71 | | |

## Price Performance

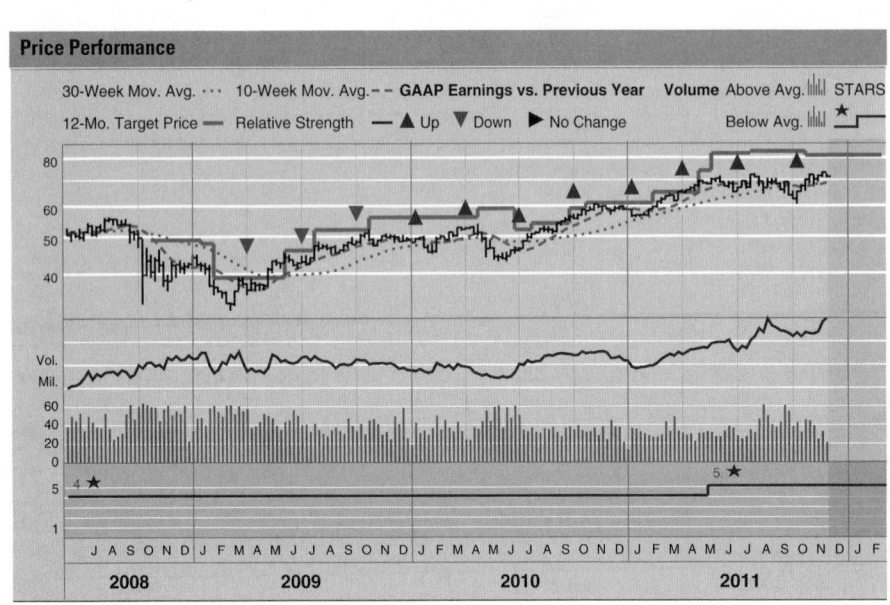

30-Week Mov. Avg. · · · 10-Week Mov. Avg. - - **GAAP Earnings vs. Previous Year** Volume Above Avg. ▮▮▮ STARS
12-Mo. Target Price — Relative Strength — ▲ Up ▼ Down ▶ No Change  Below Avg. ▮▮▮ ★

Options: ASE, CBOE, Ph

Analysis prepared by Equity Analyst **Esther Kwon, CFA** on Oct 21, 2011, when the stock traded at **$68.19**.

## Highlights

▶ For 2011, we expect revenues to climb 14% on higher pricing and foreign exchange, after a nearly 9% rise in 2010. With growing health concerns, smoking bans and higher taxes, we look for a mid-single digit percentage decline in consumption in Western Europe, partially offset by low single digit or faster growth in emerging markets. While we still see downtrading persisting in Greece and Spain, we believe these negative trends will moderate and be offset by growth in other countries, such as Indonesia and Korea. For 2012, we see about 4% growth.

▶ After embarking on an extensive three-year cost reduction program that we calculate will widen operating margins on net savings of about $1 billion, PM should see further savings on continued rationalization of less dynamic brands, offset by investments in new and existing markets in 2011. We see synergies from PM's venture in the Philippines with Fortune Tobacco, which we forecast will be accretive to earnings in 2011 after being neutral in 2010.

▶ On a slightly higher effective tax rate, we estimate 2011 EPS of $4.89, up over 25% from 2010 operating EPS of $3.87. For 2012, we forecast EPS of $5.18.

## Investment Rationale/Risk

▶ Separated from operations in the U.S. and the regulatory and litigation risk of that market, PM will, in our view, be better positioned to innovate, tailor offerings to higher-growth emerging markets, achieve cost savings, and incentivize managers. We think PM's low penetration of markets with potentially high cigarette consumption, such as China, India and Vietnam, also provides attractive opportunities. Also, the spinoff provided PM with currency for acquisitions. We believe its high cash flow generation is supportive of regular stock repurchases and its dividend, which recently yielded 4.6%.

▶ Risks to our recommendation and target price include execution risk, higher-than-expected excise taxes or regulatory constraints, greater-than-expected price competition, and commodity cost inflation.

▶ Our 12-month target price of $81 is based on a blend of comparative and historical forward P/E multiples. Considering PM's scale, growth prospects and brand equity, we believe a premium to its domestic tobacco comparables is appropriate. We assign a multiple of over 15X to our 2012 EPS estimate of $5.18, which is above the historical average.

## Qualitative Risk Assessment

| LOW | MEDIUM | HIGH |
|---|---|---|

Our risk assessment reflects the geographic diversity of the company's operations and end-markets and its participation in a generally stable industry, producing ample free cash flow. Health concerns, excise tax increases, extensive regulation and, to some extent, litigation have limited the growth prospects for the industry, but have also kept barriers to entry high.

## Quantitative Evaluations

**S&P Quality Ranking** NR

| D | C | B- | B | B+ | A- | A | A+ |
|---|---|---|---|---|---|---|---|

**Relative Strength Rank** STRONG

90

LOWEST = 1    HIGHEST = 99

## Revenue/Earnings Data

**Revenue (Million $)**

| | 1Q | 2Q | 3Q | 4Q | Year |
|---|---|---|---|---|---|
| 2011 | 6,791 | 8,273 | 8,362 | -- | -- |
| 2010 | 6,496 | 7,061 | 6,614 | 7,037 | 27,208 |
| 2009 | 5,597 | 6,134 | 6,587 | 6,717 | 25,035 |
| 2008 | 6,330 | 6,709 | 6,953 | 6,122 | 25,705 |
| 2007 | 5,549 | 5,835 | 5,916 | 5,498 | 55,096 |
| 2006 | 5,228 | 5,346 | 5,412 | 4,926 | 20,794 |

**Earnings Per Share ($)**

| | | | | | |
|---|---|---|---|---|---|
| 2011 | 1.06 | 1.35 | 1.35 | E1.11 | E4.89 |
| 2010 | 0.90 | 1.07 | 0.99 | 0.96 | 3.92 |
| 2009 | 0.74 | 0.79 | 0.93 | 0.80 | 3.24 |
| 2008 | 0.89 | 0.80 | 1.01 | 0.71 | 3.32 |
| 2007 | 0.69 | -- | -- | -- | 2.75 |
| 2006 | -- | -- | -- | -- | -- |

Fiscal year ended Dec. 31. Next earnings report expected: Mid February. EPS Estimates based on S&P Operating Earnings; historical GAAP earnings are as reported.

## Dividend Data (Dates: mm/dd Payment Date: mm/dd/yy)

| Amount ($) | Date Decl. | Ex-Div. Date | Stk. of Record | Payment Date |
|---|---|---|---|---|
| 0.640 | 12/08 | 12/21 | 12/23 | 01/10/11 |
| 0.640 | 03/09 | 03/22 | 03/24 | 04/11/11 |
| 0.640 | 06/08 | 06/21 | 06/23 | 07/11/11 |
| 0.770 | 09/14 | 09/23 | 09/27 | 10/11/11 |

Dividends have been paid since 2008. Source: Company reports.

**Please read the Required Disclosures and Analyst Certification on the last page of this report.**

The **McGraw-Hill** Companies

# Philip Morris International Inc

## Business Summary October 21, 2011

CORPORATE OVERVIEW. Philip Morris International is the world's largest publicly traded manufacturer and marketer of tobacco products, with a 16% share of 2010 international market volumes, up from 15.4% in 2009 and 15.7% in 2008, according to Philip Morris estimates. Excluding China, PM's estimated market share was 27.6%, 25.9%, and 25.8% in 2010, 2009 and 2008, respectively. PM sold 899.9 billion cigarettes in 2010, with the Marlboro brand contributing about 33% of total PM volume. Other brands include Merit, Parliament and Virginia Slims in the premium category; L&M and Chesterfield in the mid-price category; Bond Street, Lark, Muratti, Next, Philip Morris, and Red & White in the value category; and local brands such as A Mild, Diana, Optima, f6, Assos and Delicados.

The geographic breakdown of 2010 revenue was as follows: European Union 41%; Eastern Europe, Middle East & Africa 24%; Asia 22%; and Latin America and Canada 13%. Adjusted operating income (on revenues minus excise taxes) from the European Union was 38% of the company total, followed by Eastern Europe, Middle East & Africa (27%), Asia (27%), and Latin America and Canada (8%).

CORPORATE STRATEGY. Philip Morris International seeks to grow organically

as well as through acquisitions. Using its existing brands, PM plans to introduce new packaging, new blends and other line extensions across its portfolio and in existing and new markets. It sees four major markets -- China, India, Bangladesh and Vietnam -- where it has little or no presence and which account for approximately 40% of total international cigarette consumption as opportunities. We estimate China alone accounts for about one-third of the total market. In addition, PM plans to spend about half of its R&D budget to develop next-generation products that meet consumer preferences and that could cause less harm than traditional tobacco products.

PM also plans to evaluate potential acquisitions and other business development opportunities. In February 2010, a PM affiliate and Fortune Tobacco Corporation combined their businesses in the Philippines to form a new company called PMFTC Inc. While both entities hold an equal economic interest in the company, PM manages the daily operations and has a majority of its board of directors.

## Company Financials Fiscal Year Ended Dec. 31

| Per Share Data ($) | 2010 | 2009 | 2008 | 2007 | 2006 | 2005 | 2004 | 2003 | 2002 | 2001 |
|---|---|---|---|---|---|---|---|---|---|---|
| Tangible Book Value | NM | NM | NM | 2.31 | NA | NA | NA | NA | NA | NA |
| Cash Flow | 4.58 | 3.69 | 3.72 | 3.10 | NA | NA | NA | NA | NA | NA |
| Earnings | 3.92 | 3.24 | 3.32 | 2.75 | NA | NA | NA | NA | NA | NA |
| S&P Core Earnings | 3.88 | 3.27 | 3.30 | 2.91 | 2.81 | NA | NA | NA | NA | NA |
| Dividends | 2.44 | 2.24 | 1.54 | Nil | NA | NA | NA | NA | NA | NA |
| Payout Ratio | 62% | 69% | 46% | Nil | NA | NA | NA | NA | NA | NA |
| Prices:High | 60.87 | 52.35 | 56.26 | NA | NA | NA | NA | NA | NA | NA |
| Prices:Low | 42.94 | 32.04 | 33.30 | NA | NA | NA | NA | NA | NA | NA |
| P/E Ratio:High | 16 | 16 | 17 | NA | NA | NA | NA | NA | NA | NA |
| P/E Ratio:Low | 11 | 10 | 10 | NA | NA | NA | NA | NA | NA | NA |

| Income Statement Analysis (Million $) | | | | | | | | | | |
|---|---|---|---|---|---|---|---|---|---|---|
| Revenue | 27,208 | 25,035 | 25,705 | 55,096 | 20,794 | 20,013 | 17,583 | NA | NA | NA |
| Operating Income | 12,179 | 10,922 | 11,174 | 9,685 | 8,664 | 8,352 | 7,235 | NA | NA | NA |
| Depreciation | 932 | 853 | 842 | 748 | 658 | 527 | 459 | NA | NA | NA |
| Interest Expense | 974 | 905 | 528 | 209 | 371 | 325 | 191 | NA | NA | NA |
| Pretax Income | 10,324 | 9,243 | 9,937 | 8,572 | 8,226 | 7,641 | 6,478 | NA | NA | NA |
| Effective Tax Rate | NA | 29.1% | 28.1% | 28.9% | 22.2% | 24.0% | 27.2% | NA | NA | NA |
| Net Income | 7,498 | 6,342 | 6,890 | 5,821 | 6,146 | 5,620 | 4,570 | NA | NA | NA |
| S&P Core Earnings | 7,158 | 6,368 | 6,852 | 6,153 | 5,904 | NA | NA | NA | NA | NA |

| Balance Sheet & Other Financial Data (Million $) | | | | | | | | | | |
|---|---|---|---|---|---|---|---|---|---|---|
| Cash | 1,703 | 1,540 | 1,531 | 1,284 | 1,676 | 1,209 | NA | NA | NA | NA |
| Current Assets | 13,756 | 14,682 | 14,939 | 14,423 | 11,925 | 10,025 | NA | NA | NA | NA |
| Total Assets | 35,050 | 34,552 | 32,972 | 31,414 | 26,120 | 23,135 | NA | NA | NA | NA |
| Current Liabilities | 12,804 | 11,178 | 10,144 | 8,465 | 6,989 | 6,334 | NA | NA | NA | NA |
| Long Term Debt | 13,370 | 13,672 | 11,377 | 5,578 | 2,222 | 4,141 | NA | NA | NA | NA |
| Common Equity | 3,506 | 5,716 | 7,500 | 14,700 | 14,267 | 10,307 | NA | NA | NA | NA |
| Total Capital | 21,491 | 19,899 | 19,086 | 21,481 | 16,634 | 14,593 | NA | NA | NA | NA |
| Capital Expenditures | 713 | 715 | 1,099 | 1,072 | 886 | 736 | 711 | NA | NA | NA |
| Cash Flow | 8,430 | 7,195 | 7,732 | 6,569 | 6,804 | 6,147 | 5,029 | NA | NA | NA |
| Current Ratio | 1.1 | 1.3 | 1.5 | 1.7 | 1.7 | 1.6 | NA | NA | NA | NA |
| % Long Term Debt of Capitalization | 62.2 | 68.7 | 59.6 | 26.0 | 13.4 | 28.4 | Nil | NA | NA | NA |
| % Net Income of Revenue | 27.6 | 25.3 | 26.8 | 10.6 | 29.6 | 28.1 | 26.0 | NA | NA | NA |
| % Return on Assets | 21.6 | 18.8 | 21.2 | NA | 25.0 | NA | NA | NA | NA | NA |
| % Return on Equity | 162.6 | 96.0 | 60.2 | NA | 50.0 | NA | NA | NA | NA | NA |

Data as orig reptd.; bef. results of disc opers/spec. items. Per share data adj. for stk. divs.; EPS diluted. Data prior to 2008 are pro forma. E-Estimated. NA-Not Available. NM-Not Meaningful. NR-Not Ranked. UR-Under Review.

**Office:** 120 Park Avenue, New York, NY 10017-5592.
**Telephone:** 917-663-2000.
**Website:** http://www.pmi.com
**Chrmn & CEO:** L.C. Camilleri

**Vice Chrmn:** M. Cabiallavetta
**COO:** A. Calantzopoulos
**EVP & CFO:** H.G. Waldemer
**SVP & General Counsel:** D.M. Bernick

**Board Members:** H. Brown, M. Cabiallavetta, L. C. Camilleri, J. D. Fishburn, C. S. Helu, J. Li, G. Mackay, S. Marchionne, L. Noto, R. B. Polet, S. M. Wolf

**Founded:** 1987
**Domicile:** Virginia
**Employees:** 78,300

# Pinnacle West Capital Corp

**STANDARD &POOR'S**

| S&P Recommendation **HOLD** ★★★★☆ | Price $44.57 (as of Nov 25, 2011) | 12-Mo. Target Price $46.00 | Investment Style Large-Cap Value |
|---|---|---|---|

**GICS Sector** Utilities
**Sub-Industry** Electric Utilities

**Summary** This utility holding company is the parent of Arizona Public Service (APS), Arizona's largest electric utility.

## Key Stock Statistics (Source S&P, Vickers, company reports)

| | | | | | | | |
|---|---|---|---|---|---|---|---|
| 52-Wk Range | $47.36–37.28 | S&P Oper. EPS 2011E | 2.95 | Market Capitalization(B) | $4.866 | Beta | 0.54 |
| Trailing 12-Month EPS | $3.02 | S&P Oper. EPS 2012E | 3.33 | Yield (%) | 4.71 | S&P 3-Yr. Proj. EPS CAGR(%) | 1 |
| Trailing 12-Month P/E | 14.8 | P/E on S&P Oper. EPS 2011E | 15.1 | Dividend Rate/Share | $2.10 | S&P Credit Rating | BBB |
| $10K Invested 5 Yrs Ago | $12,289 | Common Shares Outstg. (M) | 109.2 | Institutional Ownership (%) | 75 | | |

## Price Performance

30-Week Mov. Avg. · · · 10-Week Mov. Avg. — GAAP Earnings vs. Previous Year   Volume Above Avg. STARS
12-Mo. Target Price — Relative Strength — ▲ Up ▼ Down ► No Change   Below Avg.

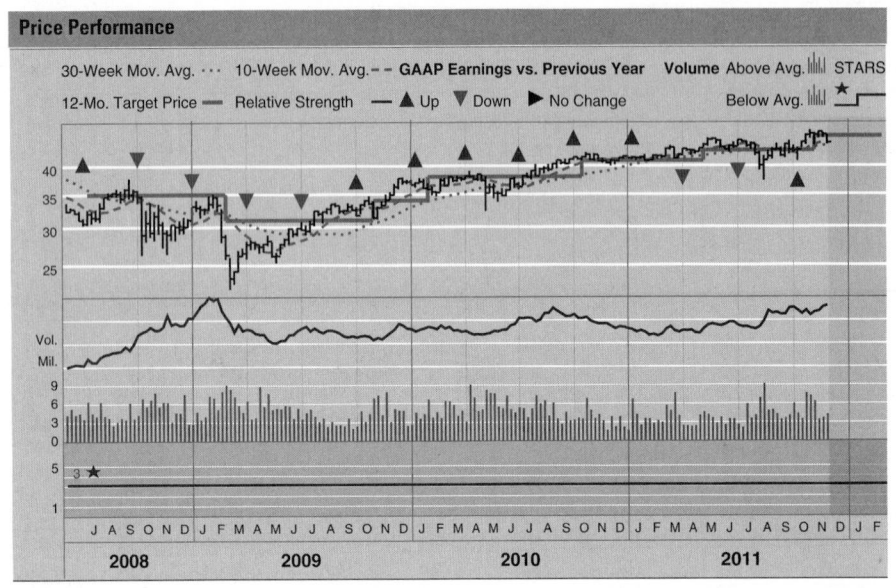

Options: P

Analysis prepared by Equity Analyst **Justin McCann** on Nov 03, 2011, when the stock traded at **$45.76**.

## Qualitative Risk Assessment

| LOW | MEDIUM | HIGH |
|---|---|---|

Our risk assessment reflects the steady cash flow that we project from the electric utility operations of Arizona Public Service, which has one of the fastest-growing service territories in the U.S. While the regulatory environment has often been difficult, we do not expect to see the general strength of the utility significantly impeded by regulatory rulings. This should help offset the less-predictable earnings stream from the real estate business and the power marketing and trading operations.

## Quantitative Evaluations

**S&P Quality Ranking**      B

| D | C | B- | **B** | B+ | A- | A | A+ |
|---|---|---|---|---|---|---|---|

**Relative Strength Rank**     STRONG

75

LOWEST = 1      HIGHEST = 99

## Highlights

► We expect operating EPS in 2011 to decline about 4% from 2010's $3.08. In the first nine months of 2011, operating EPS was $0.13 below the year-earlier level, as lower O&M costs and the extremely hot weather in the third quarter (with August recording average temperatures of 98.3 degrees) was more than offset by the very mild weather in the second quarter and the higher O&M in the first quarter due to the level of maintenance at two of its power plants.

► For 2012, we expect operating EPS to grow about 13% from anticipated results in 2011, reflecting an expected rate increase and effectively managed O&M costs. Assuming a gradual recovery in the Arizona economy and housing situation, we project annual customer growth at APS to accelerate from 0.6% in 2010 to an average of around 1.7% for the 2011 through 2013 period. However, for the same period, we expect average weather-normalized electricity demand to remain fairly flat.

► On June 1, 2011, APS filed an application with the Arizona Corporation Commission (ACC) for a net base rate increase of $95.5 million, effective July 1, 2012. The ACC is expected to schedule a hearing for early 2012.

## Investment Rationale/Risk

► The shares were up 10% in the first 10 months of 2011, reflecting, in our view, the shift to the electric utility subsector due to the volatility and often sharp declines in the broader market. The strong performance of the stock had also reflected, we believe, the authorization of a favorable regulatory ruling on APS's base rate case, and the well-above-peers yield from the dividend. We believe the stock had earlier been hurt by the weak local economy and real estate market and the uncertainty as to whether regulators would authorize a rate increase that would enable APS to recover the costs of its infrastructure expansion.

► Risks to our recommendation and target price include extended weakness in the local economy, unfavorable regulatory rulings, and/or a sharp decline in the average P/E multiple of the group as a whole.

► Following the recent increase in the shares, the yield from the dividend (recently at 4.6%) was still above peers (4.4%). However, we do not expect the company to declare an increase in the dividend in 2011. Our 12-month target price of $46 reflects an approximate peers P/E multiple of 13.8X our EPS estimate for 2012.

## Revenue/Earnings Data

**Revenue (Million $)**

| | 1Q | 2Q | 3Q | 4Q | Year |
|---|---|---|---|---|---|
| 2011 | 659.6 | 803.1 | 1,125 | -- | -- |
| 2010 | 633.6 | 820.6 | 1,139 | 683.6 | 3,264 |
| 2009 | 625.9 | 836.0 | 1,142 | 693.1 | 3,297 |
| 2008 | 736.7 | 926.2 | 1,080 | 624.2 | 3,367 |
| 2007 | 695.1 | 863.4 | 1,206 | 759.1 | 3,524 |
| 2006 | 670.2 | 925.0 | 1,076 | 730.1 | 3,402 |

**Earnings Per Share ($)**

| | | | | | |
|---|---|---|---|---|---|
| 2011 | -0.14 | 0.78 | 2.24 | E0.06 | E2.95 |
| 2010 | -0.06 | 0.83 | 2.08 | -0.06 | 3.08 |
| 2009 | -1.50 | 0.70 | 1.85 | -0.29 | 0.81 |
| 2008 | -0.05 | 1.13 | 1.49 | -0.46 | 2.12 |
| 2007 | 0.16 | 0.78 | 1.99 | -0.03 | 2.96 |
| 2006 | 0.12 | 1.11 | 1.84 | 0.10 | 3.17 |

Fiscal year ended Dec. 31. Next earnings report expected: Late February. EPS Estimates based on S&P Operating Earnings; historical GAAP earnings are as reported.

## Dividend Data (Dates: mm/dd Payment Date: mm/dd/yy)

| Amount ($) | Date Decl. | Ex-Div. Date | Stk. of Record | Payment Date |
|---|---|---|---|---|
| 0.525 | 01/19 | 01/28 | 02/01 | 03/01/11 |
| 0.525 | 04/20 | 04/28 | 05/02 | 06/01/11 |
| 0.525 | 06/24 | 07/28 | 08/01 | 09/01/11 |
| 0.525 | 10/19 | 10/28 | 11/01 | 12/01/11 |

Dividends have been paid since 1993. Source: Company reports.

**Please read the Required Disclosures and Analyst Certification on the last page of this report.**

*The McGraw-Hill Companies*

# Pinnacle West Capital Corp

**STANDARD &POOR'S**

## Business Summary November 03, 2011

CORPORATE OVERVIEW. Pinnacle West Capital, formed in 1985, is the holding company for Arizona Public Service (APS), which, with about 1.1 million customers, is Arizona's largest electric utility. PNW's other major subsidiaries are APS Energy Services (APSES), which provides energy-related services; SunCor, whose real estate business is reflected as discontinued operations; and El Dorado, which is involved in investment activities. In 2010, the regulated electricity segment accounted for 97.5% of PNW's consolidated revenues from continuing operations (compared to 99.2% in 2009).

MARKET PROFILE. APS provides vertically integrated retail and wholesale electric service to the entire state of Arizona, with the exception of Tucson and about 50% of the Phoenix area. In 2010, residential customers accounted for 47.5% of total electric revenues (47.5% in 2009); retail business customers 45.3% (46.6%); off-system sales 2.7% (1.9%); traditional contracts 2.1% (1.9%); transmission for others 1.1% (1.0%); and other 1.5% (1.1%). Consolidated fuel sources for APS in 2010 were: coal, 36.6% (36.3% in 2009); nuclear, 26.8% (25.9%); purchased power, 24.3% (20.6%); and gas, oil and other, 12.3% (17.2%). With APS dependent on purchased power for so much of its fuel sources, its earnings can be significantly affected by the price of natural gas and by the time lags involved in being authorized to recover the difference between its actual fuel costs and the rates it is allowed to charge its customers.

As of December 31, 2010, APS had a 29.1% owned or leased interest in the Pa-

lo Verde Nuclear Generating Station's Units 1 and 3, and about 17% in Unit 2. It has a 100% interest in Units 1, 2 and 3 (which APS has proposed to close by 2014) and a 15% interest in Units 4 and 5 of the coal-fueled Four Corners Steam Generating Station; and a 14.0% interest in Units 1, 2 and 3 of the coal-fueled Navajo Steam Generating Station (NGS). On November 8, 2010, APS agreed to acquire Southern California Edison's 48% interest in Units 4 and 5 of the coal-fired Four Corners Power Plant for $294 million. The acquisition, which would increase APS's interest in the units to 63%, is expected to close, pending approvals, in the second half of 2012.

SunCor develops residential, commercial and industrial real estate projects in Arizona, Idaho, New Mexico and Utah. The company, which had total assets of $16 million at the end of 2010, has been hurt by the impact of the housing crisis in Arizona. The decline in 2010 from total assets of $166 million at the end of 2009 was primarily due to asset sales. In 2010, SunCor had revenues of $102 million, compared to $158 million in 2009 and $242 million in 2008, and a net loss of $9 million, compared to net losses of $279 million in 2009 and $26 million in 2008. All of SunCor's real estate sales activities are now reported as discontinued operations.

## Company Financials Fiscal Year Ended Dec. 31

| Per Share Data ($) | 2010 | 2009 | 2008 | 2007 | 2006 | 2005 | 2004 | 2003 | 2002 | 2001 |
|---|---|---|---|---|---|---|---|---|---|---|
| Tangible Book Value | 32.16 | 31.07 | 32.85 | 34.11 | 34.48 | 34.58 | 30.99 | 29.81 | 28.23 | 29.46 |
| Earnings | 3.08 | 0.81 | 2.12 | 2.96 | 3.17 | 2.31 | 2.57 | 2.52 | 2.53 | 3.85 |
| S&P Core Earnings | 2.91 | 0.54 | 1.76 | 2.71 | 3.00 | 2.00 | 2.15 | 2.43 | 1.65 | 3.00 |
| Dividends | 2.10 | 2.10 | 2.10 | 2.10 | 2.03 | 1.93 | 1.83 | 1.73 | 1.63 | 1.53 |
| Payout Ratio | 68% | NM | 99% | 71% | 64% | 83% | 71% | 68% | 64% | 40% |
| Prices:High | 42.68 | 37.96 | 42.92 | 51.67 | 51.00 | 46.68 | 45.84 | 40.48 | 46.68 | 50.70 |
| Prices:Low | 32.31 | 22.32 | 26.27 | 36.79 | 38.31 | 39.81 | 36.30 | 28.34 | 21.70 | 37.65 |
| P/E Ratio:High | 14 | 47 | 20 | 17 | 16 | 20 | 18 | 16 | 18 | 13 |
| P/E Ratio:Low | 11 | 28 | 12 | 12 | 12 | 17 | 14 | 11 | 9 | 10 |

| Income Statement Analysis (Million $) | | | | | | | | | | |
|---|---|---|---|---|---|---|---|---|---|---|
| Revenue | 3,264 | 3,297 | 3,367 | 3,524 | 3,402 | 2,988 | 2,900 | 2,818 | 2,637 | 4,551 |
| Depreciation | 473 | 443 | 424 | 373 | 359 | 348 | 401 | 438 | 425 | 428 |
| Maintenance | NA | NA | NA | NA | NA | NA | NA | NA | NA | NA |
| Fixed Charges Coverage | 3.26 | 1.47 | 2.68 | 3.37 | 3.23 | 2.77 | 2.75 | 2.43 | 2.64 | 3.80 |
| Construction Credits | 38.6 | 15.0 | 18.6 | 21.2 | 14.3 | 11.2 | 4.89 | 14.2 | NA | NA |
| Effective Tax Rate | 31.9% | 36.0% | 23.5% | 33.6% | 33.0% | 36.2% | 35.4% | 31.4% | 39.1% | 39.5% |
| Net Income | 351 | 82.0 | 214 | 299 | 317 | 223 | 235 | 231 | 215 | 327 |
| S&P Core Earnings | 313 | 54.6 | 178 | 273 | 300 | 193 | 197 | 223 | 140 | 255 |

| Balance Sheet & Other Financial Data (Million $) | | | | | | | | | | |
|---|---|---|---|---|---|---|---|---|---|---|
| Gross Property | 14,094 | 13,599 | 13,059 | 12,442 | 11,679 | 11,200 | 18,280 | 10,470 | 16,316 | 9,285 |
| Capital Expenditures | 765 | 775 | 954 | 919 | 738 | 634 | 538 | 693 | 896 | 1,041 |
| Net Property | 9,579 | 9,258 | 8,917 | 8,437 | 7,882 | 7,577 | 14,914 | 7,310 | 12,842 | 5,907 |
| Capitalization:Long Term Debt | 3,046 | 3,371 | 3,032 | 3,127 | 3,233 | 2,608 | 2,585 | 2,898 | 2,882 | 2,673 |
| Capitalization:% Long Term Debt | 45.3 | 50.4 | 46.8 | 47.0 | 48.4 | 43.2 | 46.7 | 50.6 | 51.8 | 51.7 |
| Capitalization:Preferred | Nil | Nil | Nil | Nil | Nil | Nil | Nil | Nil | Nil | Nil |
| Capitalization:% Preferred | Nil | Nil | Nil | Nil | Nil | Nil | Nil | Nil | Nil | Nil |
| Capitalization:Common | 3,683 | 3,316 | 3,446 | 3,532 | 3,446 | 3,425 | 2,950 | 2,830 | 2,686 | 2,499 |
| Capitalization:% Common | 54.7 | 49.6 | 53.2 | 53.0 | 51.6 | 56.8 | 53.3 | 49.4 | 48.2 | 48.3 |
| Total Capital | 7,453 | 6,994 | 7,881 | 7,902 | 7,905 | 7,259 | 6,763 | 7,057 | 6,777 | 6,237 |
| % Operating Ratio | 82.9 | 83.5 | 86.2 | 86.7 | 85.6 | 82.4 | 85.8 | 86.6 | 81.7 | 89.9 |
| % Earned on Net Property | 7.6 | 6.4 | 6.1 | 7.6 | 8.0 | 6.8 | 3.4 | 6.8 | 4.2 | 24.6 |
| % Return on Revenue | 10.7 | 2.5 | 6.3 | 8.5 | 9.3 | 7.5 | 8.1 | 8.2 | 8.2 | 7.2 |
| % Return on Invested Capital | 7.9 | 4.1 | 5.9 | 6.2 | 7.2 | 8.0 | 6.9 | 6.2 | 7.7 | 7.9 |
| % Return on Common Equity | 10.0 | 2.4 | 6.1 | 8.6 | 9.2 | 7.0 | 8.1 | 8.4 | 8.3 | 13.4 |

Data as orig reptd.; bef. results of disc opers/spec. items. Per share data adj. for stk. divs.; EPS diluted. E-Estimated. NA-Not Available. NM-Not Meaningful. NR-Not Ranked. UR-Under Review.

**Office:** 400 North Fifth Street, Phoenix, AZ 85004.
**Telephone:** 602-250-1000.
**Website:** http://www.pinnaclewest.com
**Chrmn, Pres & CEO:** D.E. Brandt

**CFO:** J.R. Hatfield
**Chief Acctg Officer & Cntlr:** D.R. Danner
**Treas:** L.R. Nickloy
**Secy & General Counsel:** D.P. Falck

**Investor Contact:** R. Hickman (602-250-5668)
**Board Members:** E. N. Basha, Jr., D. E. Brandt, S. Clark-Johnson, D. A. Cortese, M. L. Gallagher, P. Grant, R. A. Herberger, D. E. Klein, H. S. Lopez, K. L. Munro, B. J. Nordstrom, W. D. Parker

**Founded:** 1920
**Domicile:** Arizona
**Employees:** 6,740

*The McGraw-Hill Companies*

# Pioneer Natural Resources Co

**STANDARD &POOR'S**

| S&P Recommendation BUY ★★★★☆ | Price $83.44 (as of Nov 25, 2011) | 12-Mo. Target Price $106.00 | Investment Style Large-Cap Blend |
|---|---|---|---|

**GICS Sector** Energy
**Sub-Industry** Oil & Gas Exploration & Production

**Summary** This company explores for and produces oil and natural gas in the U.S. and Canada.

## Key Stock Statistics (Source S&P, Vickers, company reports)

| | | | | | | | |
|---|---|---|---|---|---|---|---|
| 52-Wk Range | $106.07– 58.63 | S&P Oper. EPS 2011**E** | 3.54 | Market Capitalization(B) | $9.753 | Beta | 1.85 |
| Trailing 12-Month EPS | $8.52 | S&P Oper. EPS 2012**E** | 3.87 | Yield (%) | 0.10 | S&P 3-Yr. Proj. EPS CAGR(%) | NM |
| Trailing 12-Month P/E | 9.8 | P/E on S&P Oper. EPS 2011**E** | 23.6 | Dividend Rate/Share | $0.08 | S&P Credit Rating | BBB- |
| $10K Invested 5 Yrs Ago | $20,438 | Common Shares Outstg. (M) | 116.9 | Institutional Ownership (%) | 97 | | |

## Price Performance

30-Week Mov. Avg. ···· 10-Week Mov. Avg. -- GAAP Earnings vs. Previous Year  Volume Above Avg. STARS
12-Mo. Target Price — Relative Strength — ▲ Up ▼ Down ► No Change  Below Avg. ★

Options: ASE, CBOE, P, Ph

Analysis prepared by Equity Analyst **Michael Kay** on Nov 22, 2011, when the stock traded at **$87.51**.

## Qualitative Risk Assessment

| LOW | MEDIUM | HIGH |
|---|---|---|

Our risk assessment reflects our view of the company's participation in a volatile and capital-intensive segment of the energy industry.

## Quantitative Evaluations

**S&P Quality Ranking**    B

| D | C | B- | B | B+ | A- | A | A+ |
|---|---|---|---|---|---|---|---|

**Relative Strength Rank**    STRONG

80

LOWEST = 1    HIGHEST = 99

## Revenue/Earnings Data

**Revenue (Million $)**

| | 1Q | 2Q | 3Q | 4Q | Year |
|---|---|---|---|---|---|
| 2011 | 527.6 | 602.1 | 1,032 | -- | -- |
| 2010 | 817.4 | 662.4 | 616.7 | 471.8 | 1,803 |
| 2009 | 373.8 | 370.7 | 410.0 | 461.5 | 1,610 |
| 2008 | 584.2 | 653.3 | 612.2 | 453.4 | 2,277 |
| 2007 | 367.3 | 444.7 | 490.4 | 530.9 | 1,833 |
| 2006 | 396.5 | 413.9 | 432.6 | 389.8 | 1,633 |

**Earnings Per Share ($)**

| | | | | | |
|---|---|---|---|---|---|
| 2011 | -0.57 | 2.05 | 2.95 | E0.78 | E3.54 |
| 2010 | 2.08 | 1.19 | 0.93 | 0.11 | 3.97 |
| 2009 | -0.13 | -0.82 | -0.17 | -0.17 | -1.24 |
| 2008 | 1.07 | 1.32 | -0.02 | -0.54 | 1.86 |
| 2007 | 0.25 | 0.29 | 0.77 | 0.71 | 1.99 |
| 2006 | -0.01 | 0.52 | 0.64 | 0.22 | 1.36 |

Fiscal year ended Dec. 31. Next earnings report expected: Early February. EPS Estimates based on S&P Operating Earnings; historical GAAP earnings are as reported.

## Dividend Data (Dates: mm/dd Payment Date: mm/dd/yy)

| Amount ($) | Date Decl. | Ex-Div. Date | Stk. of Record | Payment Date |
|---|---|---|---|---|
| 0.040 | 02/17 | 03/29 | 03/31 | 04/14/11 |
| 0.040 | 08/26 | 09/28 | 09/30 | 10/14/11 |

Dividends have been paid since 2004. Source: Company reports.

## Highlights

➤ Production fell 2% in 2010, to 109 MBOE/day, reflecting asset sales. However, on accelerated drilling at the Spraberry field in the Permian Basin and the Eagle Ford Shale in South Texas, PXD sees 2011 production of 125 MBOE/d, up 15%, with an 18% CAGR through 2014. PXD expects Spraberry production, up 35% in the third quarter, to rise at a 25% CAGR through 2014. It plans to ramp to 45 rigs at Spraberry by year end, ahead of schedule as it targets deeper intervals. PXD has ramped to 12 rigs at Eagle Ford (14 MBOE/d of production), and plans to increase to 19 rigs by 2014. PXD is adding a second rig in Alaska for the winter drilling season. PXD and Reliance recently approved an accelerated 2011 Eagle Ford program.

➤ PXD recently lifted its 2011 capex plan to $2.1 billion for drilling activities, on accelerated drilling at Spraberry, with 68% allocated to Spraberry and Eagle Ford, compared to $1 billion in 2010. Total capex is expected to be funded via cash flow and the Tunisia asset sale.

➤ We see production growth at Spraberry and Eagle Ford and a higher mix of liquids-to-gas production boosting EPS to $3.54 in 2011 and $3.87 in 2012, from $1.76 (before items) in 2010.

## Investment Rationale/Risk

➤ PXD is now an onshore producer with strong liquids production prospects and impending growth. We see PXD focusing on core Spraberry properties and the Eagle Ford Shale, which should drive overall production growth; the oil focus of these assets is helping returns. We expect more near-term asset sales such as the $866 million sale of Tunisia assets. Over the past two years, PXD has cut natural gas production 4% and upped exposure to oil and natural gas liquids (NGLs). We think investors will focus on PXD's accelerated activity at Eagle Ford, where the $1.2 billion JV with Reliance involved selling a 45% stake in 212,000 net acres, cutting drilling costs. PXD's recent 5.5 million share equity sale allows it to drill acreage in the Spraberry that has Wolfcamp Shale potential.

➤ Risks to our recommendation and target price include negative changes to economic, industry and operating conditions, such as rising costs or increased geopolitical risk.

➤ We expect Spraberry growth and Eagle Ford success to act as catalysts for PXD shares. We blend our proved reserve NAV estimate of $120 with premium relative metrics to arrive at our 12-month target price of $106.

---

**Please read the Required Disclosures and Analyst Certification on the last page of this report.**

The McGraw-Hill Companies

# Pioneer Natural Resources Co

STANDARD
&POOR'S

## Business Summary November 22, 2011

CORPORATE OVERVIEW. This independent oil and gas exploration and production company has an asset base anchored by the Spraberry oil field in West Texas, the Hugoton gas field in Kansas, the West Panhandle gas field in the Texas Panhandle, and the Raton gas field in southern Colorado. Complementing these areas, PXD has oil and gas exploration, development and production activities in the onshore Gulf Coast area, and Alaska.

As of December 31, 2010, PXD had estimated proved reserves of 1,011 MM-BOE, of which 56% consisted of crude oil and natural gas liquids, and 44% natural gas. This compares to estimated proved reserves of 898.6 MMBOE, of which 54% was crude oil and natural gas liquids, and 46% was natural gas, at year-end 2009. We estimate PXD's year-end 2010 reserve life to be 22 years, compared to 19.9 years at the end of 2009. About 54% of reserves consisted of Spraberry assets.

CORPORATE STRATEGY. PXD believes it offers significant upside potential from its exposure to oil with a large drilling inventory, an aggressive Spraberry program, and early Eagle Ford Shale success. Over the next five years, PXD expects liquids production to go from 45% to 60% of its production portfolio.

On development of Eagle Ford and Spraberry, PXD is forecasting a production CAGR between 2011 and 2013 of 18%. In 2010, capex totaled $1.2 billion, with $999 million for drilling, and 100% allocated to oil activity.

Like many operators, PXD drastically curtailed drilling activity early in 2009 due to plummeting oil and gas prices, high costs and a global economic recession. As costs have realigned with prices, PXD appeared poised to boost rig counts, capex and activity levels in 2010, as oil prices have risen nearly 80% since early 2009. In October 2009, PXD initiated production from its most prolific well at the South Coast Gas Project in Africa and drilled its first two wells in the Pierre Shale in the Rocky Mountains. At Ooguruk in Alaska's North Slope, drilling results have been better than expected. In 2009, PXD curtailed activity at the Raton field in the Rockies, given weakening returns, and we expect weak activity in the Edwards Trend, where drilling is dependent on natural gas prices.

## Company Financials Fiscal Year Ended Dec. 31

| Per Share Data ($) | 2010 | 2009 | 2008 | 2007 | 2006 | 2005 | 2004 | 2003 | 2002 | 2001 |
|---|---|---|---|---|---|---|---|---|---|---|
| Tangible Book Value | 33.15 | 28.21 | 28.56 | 24.38 | 22.01 | 14.82 | 19.55 | 14.75 | 11.73 | 12.37 |
| Cash Flow | 9.46 | 4.74 | 6.66 | 5.40 | 4.17 | 7.01 | 6.96 | 6.63 | 2.32 | 3.27 |
| Earnings | 3.97 | -1.24 | 1.86 | 1.99 | 1.36 | 3.02 | 2.46 | 3.33 | 0.43 | 1.04 |
| S&P Core Earnings | 3.09 | -1.25 | 1.82 | 1.57 | 1.34 | 2.00 | 2.41 | 3.26 | 0.32 | 0.93 |
| Dividends | 0.08 | 0.08 | 0.30 | 0.27 | 0.25 | 0.22 | 0.20 | Nil | Nil | Nil |
| Payout Ratio | 2% | NM | 16% | 14% | 18% | 7% | 8% | Nil | Nil | Nil |
| Prices:High | 88.00 | 50.00 | 82.21 | 54.87 | 54.46 | 56.35 | 37.50 | 32.90 | 27.50 | 23.05 |
| Prices:Low | 41.88 | 11.88 | 14.03 | 35.51 | 36.43 | 32.91 | 29.27 | 22.76 | 16.10 | 12.62 |
| P/E Ratio:High | 22 | NM | 44 | 28 | 40 | 19 | 15 | 10 | 64 | 22 |
| P/E Ratio:Low | 11 | NM | 8 | 18 | 27 | 11 | 12 | 7 | 37 | 12 |

| Income Statement Analysis (Million $) | | | | | | | | | | |
|---|---|---|---|---|---|---|---|---|---|---|
| Revenue | 1,803 | 1,610 | 2,277 | 1,833 | 1,633 | 2,216 | 1,833 | 1,299 | 702 | 847 |
| Operating Income | NA | NA | 1,256 | 1,019 | 757 | 1,262 | 1,191 | 804 | 351 | 433 |
| Depreciation, Depletion and Amortization | 585 | 684 | 569 | 415 | 360 | 568 | 575 | 391 | 216 | 223 |
| Interest Expense | 183 | 173 | 154 | 168 | 107 | 128 | 103 | 91.4 | 95.8 | 132 |
| Pretax Income | 788 | -180 | 448 | 355 | 309 | 715 | 479 | 331 | 54.1 | 108 |
| Effective Tax Rate | NA | 26.7% | 45.9% | 31.7% | 44.2% | 40.8% | 34.7% | NM | 9.35% | 3.73% |
| Net Income | 516 | -142 | 221 | 242 | 172 | 424 | 313 | 395 | 49.1 | 104 |
| S&P Core Earnings | 358 | -142 | 217 | 192 | 170 | 280 | 307 | 386 | 36.4 | 92.2 |

| Balance Sheet & Other Financial Data (Million $) | | | | | | | | | | |
|---|---|---|---|---|---|---|---|---|---|---|
| Cash | 111 | 27.4 | 48.3 | 12.2 | 7.03 | 18.8 | 7.26 | 19.3 | 8.49 | 14.3 |
| Current Assets | 1,197 | 616 | 487 | 765 | 537 | 624 | 312 | 205 | 147 | 256 |
| Total Assets | 9,679 | 8,867 | 9,163 | 8,617 | 7,355 | 7,329 | 6,647 | 3,952 | 3,455 | 3,271 |
| Current Liabilities | 769 | 571 | 695 | 994 | 887 | 1,033 | 544 | 430 | 275 | 228 |
| Long Term Debt | 2,602 | 2,761 | 2,964 | 2,755 | 1,497 | 2,058 | 2,569 | 1,604 | 1,669 | 1,577 |
| Common Equity | 4,226 | 3,643 | 3,582 | 3,043 | 2,985 | 2,217 | 2,832 | 1,760 | 1,375 | 1,285 |
| Total Capital | 6,828 | 6,404 | 8,083 | 7,028 | 5,654 | 4,276 | 5,927 | 3,376 | 3,052 | 2,876 |
| Capital Expenditures | 1,011 | 437 | 1,403 | 2,204 | 1,499 | 1,123 | 616 | 688 | 615 | 530 |
| Cash Flow | 1,101 | 541 | 790 | 657 | 532 | 992 | 888 | 786 | 265 | 326 |
| Current Ratio | 1.6 | 1.1 | 0.7 | 0.8 | 0.6 | 0.6 | 0.6 | 0.5 | 0.5 | 1.1 |
| % Long Term Debt of Capitalization | 38.1 | 43.1 | 36.7 | 39.2 | 26.5 | 48.1 | 43.3 | 47.5 | 54.7 | 54.8 |
| % Return on Assets | 5.6 | NM | 2.5 | 3.0 | 2.3 | 6.0 | 5.9 | 10.7 | 1.5 | 3.3 |
| % Return on Equity | 13.3 | NM | 6.7 | 8.0 | 6.6 | 16.8 | 13.6 | 25.2 | 3.7 | 9.5 |

Data as orig reptd.; bef. results of disc opers/spec. items. Per share data adj. for stk. divs.; EPS diluted. E-Estimated. NA-Not Available. NM-Not Meaningful. NR-Not Ranked. UR-Under Review.

**Office:** 5205 North O Connor Boulevard, Suite 200, Irving, TX 75039.
**Telephone:** 972-444-9001.
**Email:** ir@pxd.com
**Website:** http://www.pxd.com

**Chrmn & CEO:** S.D. Sheffield
**Pres & COO:** T.L. Dove
**EVP & CFO:** R.P. Dealy
**EVP & General Counsel:** M.S. Berg

**Chief Admin Officer:** L.N. Paulsen
**Investor Contact:** F.E. Hopkins (972-969-4065)
**Board Members:** T. D. Arthur, E. Buchanan, A. F. Cates, R. H. Gardner, A. Lundquist, C. E. Ramsey, Jr., S. J. Reiman, F. A. Risch, S. D. Sheffield, J. K. Thompson, J. A. Watson

**Founded:** 1997
**Domicile:** Delaware
**Employees:** 2,248

The McGraw-Hill Companies

# Pitney Bowes Inc.

STANDARD &POOR'S

| **S&P Recommendation** HOLD ★★★☆☆ | Price<br>$17.35 (as of Nov 25, 2011) | 12-Mo. Target Price<br>$21.00 | Investment Style<br>Large-Cap Growth |
| --- | --- | --- | --- |

**GICS Sector** Industrials
**Sub-Industry** Office Services & Supplies

**Summary** PBI, the world's largest maker of mailing systems, also provides production and document management equipment and facilities management services.

## Key Stock Statistics (Source S&P, Vickers, company reports)

| | | | | | | | |
| --- | --- | --- | --- | --- | --- | --- | --- |
| 52-Wk Range | $26.36– 17.33 | S&P Oper. EPS 2011E | 2.31 | Market Capitalization(B) | $3.464 | Beta | 1.03 |
| Trailing 12-Month EPS | $2.07 | S&P Oper. EPS 2012E | 2.12 | Yield (%) | 8.53 | S&P 3-Yr. Proj. EPS CAGR(%) | 1 |
| Trailing 12-Month P/E | 8.4 | P/E on S&P Oper. EPS 2011E | 7.5 | Dividend Rate/Share | $1.48 | S&P Credit Rating | BBB+ |
| $10K Invested 5 Yrs Ago | $4,867 | Common Shares Outstg. (M) | 199.6 | Institutional Ownership (%) | 90 | | |

## Price Performance

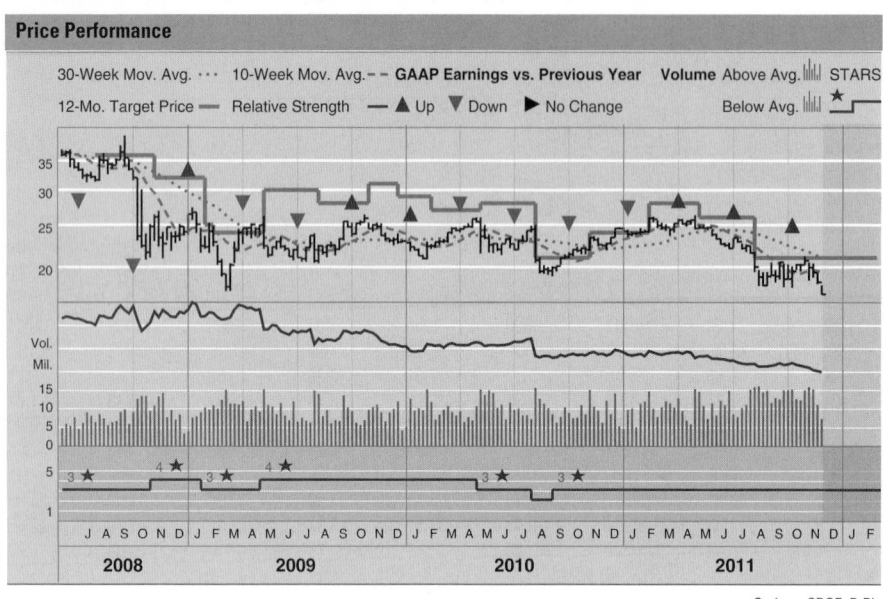

30-Week Mov. Avg. · · · 10-Week Mov. Avg. – – GAAP Earnings vs. Previous Year   Volume Above Avg. STARS
12-Mo. Target Price — Relative Strength — ▲ Up ▼ Down ► No Change   Below Avg.

Options: CBOE, P, Ph

Analysis prepared by Equity Analyst **Dylan Cathers** on Nov 08, 2011, when the stock traded at **$20.21**.

## Highlights

➤ We believe total revenues will decrease 2.0% in 2011 and 1.0% in 2012, following declines in 2009 and 2010. In general, the soft economic climate is hampering sales. We think customers are hesitant to make decisions on capital spending, and visibility into 2012 spending budgets is poor. Further, we anticipate additional spending declines in PBI's core equipment business. We do see some positives within software, which appears to be doing well in both the Americas and in Asia/Pacific. We believe that office products and services related to mail processing face a protracted recovery after a global economic slowdown in 2009.

➤ The company has been working on a set of transformation initiatives including workforce reductions, enterprise-wide systems and common platforms, enhanced procurement processes, and more outsourcing relationships. These efforts should help operating margins in 2012 as cost savings from restructurings are more fully realized.

➤ We estimate operating EPS, excluding restructuring charges, at $2.31 for 2011 and $2.12 for 2012. Share buybacks should aid per-share results slightly.

## Investment Rationale/Risk

➤ PBI has a large recurring revenue stream and a leadership position within its market, in our view. We project modest demand for office equipment to limit near-term sales potential, although we expect new product introductions focusing on digital technology to aid long-term growth. The cash dividend yield is over 7%, approximately three times the yield for Industrials sector peers, but we think the high payout ratio may limit financial flexibility.

➤ Risks to our recommendation and target price include a slower economic recovery and more competition in the document management outsourcing market than we project. Cash flows might weaken more than we expect in a period of slow demand.

➤ Our 12-month target price of $21 is based mainly on our P/E analysis. We apply a target P/E multiple of 9.9X, a discount to Industrials sector peers in the S&P 500 Index and a little below the mid-point of a recent historical range for PBI to reflect sluggish revenue growth that we foresee, to our 12-month forward operating EPS estimate of $2.12.

## Qualitative Risk Assessment

| LOW | MEDIUM | HIGH |
| --- | --- | --- |

Our risk assessment reflects our view of PBI's steady cash flow, recurring revenue streams, consistent dividend increases and share buybacks. However, we think these factors are offset by a lackluster rate of revenue growth and integration risk associated with recent acquisitions.

## Quantitative Evaluations

**S&P Quality Ranking**   B+

| D | C | B- | B | B+ | A- | A | A+ |
| --- | --- | --- | --- | --- | --- | --- | --- |

**Relative Strength Rank**   WEAK

28

LOWEST = 1                               HIGHEST = 99

## Revenue/Earnings Data

**Revenue (Million $)**

| | 1Q | 2Q | 3Q | 4Q | Year |
| --- | --- | --- | --- | --- | --- |
| 2011 | 1,323 | 1,314 | 1,300 | -- | -- |
| 2010 | 1,348 | 1,297 | 1,346 | 1,434 | 5,425 |
| 2009 | 1,380 | 1,378 | 1,357 | 1,454 | 5,569 |
| 2008 | 1,574 | 1,588 | 1,548 | 1,553 | 6,262 |
| 2007 | 1,414 | 1,543 | 1,508 | 1,664 | 6,130 |
| 2006 | 1,362 | 1,389 | 1,433 | 1,546 | 5,730 |

**Earnings Per Share ($)**

| | | | | | |
| --- | --- | --- | --- | --- | --- |
| 2011 | 0.43 | 0.50 | 0.56 | E0.57 | E2.31 |
| 2010 | 0.40 | 0.31 | 0.44 | 0.36 | 1.50 |
| 2009 | 0.49 | 0.54 | 0.51 | 0.54 | 2.08 |
| 2008 | 0.58 | 0.63 | 0.48 | 0.45 | 2.13 |
| 2007 | 0.66 | 0.69 | 0.59 | -0.32 | 1.63 |
| 2006 | 0.60 | 0.54 | 0.64 | 0.73 | 2.51 |

Fiscal year ended Dec. 31. Next earnings report expected: NA. EPS Estimates based on S&P Operating Earnings; historical GAAP earnings are as reported.

## Dividend Data (Dates: mm/dd Payment Date: mm/dd/yy)

| Amount ($) | Date Decl. | Ex-Div. Date | Stk. of Record | Payment Date |
| --- | --- | --- | --- | --- |
| 0.370 | 02/08 | 02/16 | 02/18 | 03/12/11 |
| 0.370 | 04/11 | 05/11 | 05/13 | 06/12/11 |
| 0.370 | 07/11 | 08/10 | 08/12 | 09/12/11 |
| 0.370 | 11/04 | 11/16 | 11/18 | 12/12/11 |

Dividends have been paid since 1934. Source: Company reports.

---

**Please read the Required Disclosures and Analyst Certification on the last page of this report.**

The McGraw-Hill Companies

# Pitney Bowes Inc.

STANDARD
&POOR'S

## Business Summary November 08, 2011

CORPORATE OVERVIEW. In business since 1920, Pitney Bowes is a major global provider of mail processing equipment and integrated mail solutions. The company's postage meters and other offerings help business customers optimize the flow of physical and electronic mail, documents and packages. The company operates seven business units within two business groups known as Small & Medium Business Solutions (SMB Solutions) and Enterprise Business Solutions (EB Solutions).

The SMB Solutions segment, which accounted for 52% of 2010 revenue (53% in 2009), is comprised of two units. The first, U.S. Mailing, includes U.S. revenue and related expenses from the sale, rental and financing of mail finishing, mail creation, shipping equipment and software, services, and payment solutions. The second, International Mailing, includes non-U.S. revenue and related expenses from activities similar to those of the first unit.

The EB Solutions segment (48%, 47%) is made up of five units. The first unit, Production Mail, includes the worldwide sales and service of high-speed production mail systems and sorting and print production equipment. The second

unit, Software, includes the worldwide sales and support services of non-equipment-based mailing and customer relationship and communication and location intelligence software. The third, Management Services, includes worldwide facilities management services, secure mail services, reprographic, document management, litigation support, eDiscovery and other services. The fourth, Mail Services, offers presort mail services and cross-border mail services. The fifth, Marketing Services, focuses on direct marketing services for targeted customers.

Business services contributed the most to revenues in 2010, representing 32% of revenues (32% in 2009), followed by equipment sales 19% (18%), support services 13% (13%), financing 12% (12%), rentals 11% (12%), software 7% (7%) and supplies 6% (6%).

## Company Financials Fiscal Year Ended Dec. 31

| Per Share Data ($) | 2010 | 2009 | 2008 | 2007 | 2006 | 2005 | 2004 | 2003 | 2002 | 2001 |
|---|---|---|---|---|---|---|---|---|---|---|
| Tangible Book Value | NM | NM | NM | NM | NM | NM | NM | NM | 0.10 | 1.05 |
| Cash Flow | 3.06 | 3.72 | 3.60 | 3.37 | 4.21 | 3.70 | 3.36 | 3.32 | 2.98 | 3.44 |
| Earnings | 1.50 | 2.08 | 2.13 | 1.63 | 2.51 | 2.27 | 2.05 | 2.10 | 1.81 | 2.08 |
| S&P Core Earnings | 1.62 | 2.10 | 1.67 | 1.61 | 2.50 | 2.09 | 1.94 | 1.87 | 1.34 | 0.81 |
| Dividends | 1.46 | 1.44 | 1.40 | 1.32 | 1.28 | 1.24 | 1.22 | 1.20 | 1.18 | 1.16 |
| Payout Ratio | 97% | 69% | 66% | 81% | 51% | 55% | 60% | 57% | 65% | 56% |
| Prices:High | 26.00 | 27.46 | 39.98 | 49.70 | 47.97 | 47.50 | 46.97 | 42.75 | 44.41 | 44.70 |
| Prices:Low | 19.06 | 17.62 | 20.83 | 36.40 | 40.18 | 40.34 | 38.88 | 29.45 | 28.55 | 32.00 |
| P/E Ratio:High | 17 | 13 | 19 | 30 | 19 | 21 | 23 | 20 | 25 | 21 |
| P/E Ratio:Low | 13 | 8 | 10 | 22 | 16 | 18 | 19 | 14 | 16 | 15 |

| Income Statement Analysis (Million $) | | | | | | | | | | |
|---|---|---|---|---|---|---|---|---|---|---|
| Revenue | 5,425 | 5,569 | 6,262 | 6,130 | 5,730 | 5,492 | 4,957 | 4,577 | 4,410 | 4,122 |
| Operating Income | 1,139 | 1,187 | 1,437 | 1,549 | 1,487 | 1,435 | 1,352 | 1,291 | 1,276 | 1,046 |
| Depreciation | 304 | 339 | 307 | 383 | 363 | 332 | 307 | 289 | 264 | 317 |
| Interest Expense | 116 | 111 | 229 | 251 | 228 | 214 | 172 | 168 | 185 | 193 |
| Pretax Income | 535 | 693 | 713 | 661 | 914 | 867 | 699 | 721 | 619 | 766 |
| Effective Tax Rate | NA | 34.7% | 34.3% | 42.4% | 36.6% | 39.3% | 31.3% | 31.4% | 29.3% | 32.9% |
| Net Income | 329 | 432 | 447 | 361 | 566 | 527 | 481 | 495 | 438 | 514 |
| S&P Core Earnings | 335 | 435 | 352 | 357 | 564 | 485 | 456 | 440 | 324 | 199 |

| Balance Sheet & Other Financial Data (Million $) | | | | | | | | | | |
|---|---|---|---|---|---|---|---|---|---|---|
| Cash | 515 | 427 | 398 | 440 | 239 | 244 | 316 | 294 | 315 | 232 |
| Current Assets | 2,998 | 2,971 | 3,033 | 3,320 | 2,919 | 2,742 | 2,693 | 2,513 | 2,553 | 2,557 |
| Total Assets | 8,430 | 8,551 | 8,827 | 9,550 | 8,480 | 10,621 | 9,821 | 8,891 | 8,732 | 8,318 |
| Current Liabilities | 2,579 | 2,566 | 3,243 | 3,556 | 2,747 | 2,911 | 3,294 | 2,647 | 3,350 | 3,083 |
| Long Term Debt | 4,239 | 4,214 | 3,935 | 3,802 | 4,232 | 3,850 | 3,109 | 3,151 | 2,317 | 2,419 |
| Common Equity | -97.3 | 12.8 | -189 | 642 | 698 | 1,301 | 1,289 | 1,086 | 852 | 890 |
| Total Capital | 4,735 | 4,524 | 4,405 | 5,302 | 5,287 | 7,074 | 4,399 | 5,898 | 4,706 | 4,584 |
| Capital Expenditures | 120 | 167 | 237 | 265 | 328 | 292 | 317 | 286 | 225 | 256 |
| Cash Flow | 632 | 770 | 754 | 744 | 929 | 858 | 787 | 784 | 702 | 832 |
| Current Ratio | 1.2 | 1.2 | 0.9 | 0.9 | 1.1 | 0.9 | 0.8 | 0.9 | 0.8 | 0.8 |
| % Long Term Debt of Capitalization | 89.5 | 93.2 | 89.3 | 71.7 | 80.0 | 54.4 | 70.7 | 53.4 | 49.2 | 52.8 |
| % Net Income of Revenue | 6.1 | 7.8 | 7.2 | 5.9 | 9.9 | 11.2 | 9.7 | 10.8 | 9.9 | 12.5 |
| % Return on Assets | 3.9 | 5.0 | 4.9 | 4.0 | 5.9 | 5.1 | 5.1 | 5.6 | 5.1 | 6.3 |
| % Return on Equity | NM | NM | NM | 53.9 | 54.9 | 40.7 | 40.5 | 51.1 | 50.3 | 47.3 |

Data as orig reptd.; bef. results of disc opers/spec. items. Per share data adj. for stk. divs.; EPS diluted. E-Estimated. NA-Not Available. NM-Not Meaningful. NR-Not Ranked. UR-Under Review.

**Office:** 1 Elmcroft Rd, Stamford, CT 06926-0700.
**Telephone:** 203-351-6858.
**Email:** investorrelations@pb.com
**Website:** http://www.pb.com

**Chrmn, Pres & CEO:** M. Martin
**EVP & CFO:** M. Monahan
**EVP & General Counsel:** D.J. Goldstein
**EVP & CIO:** G.E. Buoncontri

**SVP & CTO:** J.E. Wall
**Investor Contact:** C.F. McBride (203-351-6349)
**Board Members:** R. C. Adkins, L. G. Alvarado, A. M. Busquet, A. S. Fuchs, E. Green, J. H. Keyes, M. Martin, E. R. Menasce, M. I. Roth, D. L. Shedlarz, D. B. Snow, Jr., R. E. Weissman

**Founded:** 1920
**Domicile:** Delaware
**Employees:** 30,700

The **McGraw-Hill** Companies

# Plum Creek Timber Co Inc.

**STANDARD &POOR'S**

**S&P Recommendation** HOLD ★★★☆☆

| Price | 12-Mo. Target Price | Investment Style |
|---|---|---|
| $34.64 (as of Nov 25, 2011) | $40.00 | Large-Cap Blend |

**GICS Sector** Financials
**Sub-Industry** Specialized REITS

**Summary** Plum Creek Timber Co., a real estate investment trust (REIT), is the largest private timberland owner in the United States, with 6.7 million acres of timberland in 19 states.

## Key Stock Statistics (Source S&P, Vickers, company reports)

| | | | | | | | |
|---|---|---|---|---|---|---|---|
| 52-Wk Range | $44.28–33.02 | S&P Oper. EPS 2011E | 1.20 | Market Capitalization(B) | $5.587 | Beta | 1.02 |
| Trailing 12-Month EPS | $1.18 | S&P Oper. EPS 2012E | 1.45 | Yield (%) | 4.85 | S&P 3-Yr. Proj. EPS CAGR(%) | 6 |
| Trailing 12-Month P/E | 29.4 | P/E on S&P Oper. EPS 2011E | 28.9 | Dividend Rate/Share | $1.68 | S&P Credit Rating | BBB |
| $10K Invested 5 Yrs Ago | $11,804 | Common Shares Outstg. (M) | 161.3 | Institutional Ownership (%) | 67 | | |

## Price Performance

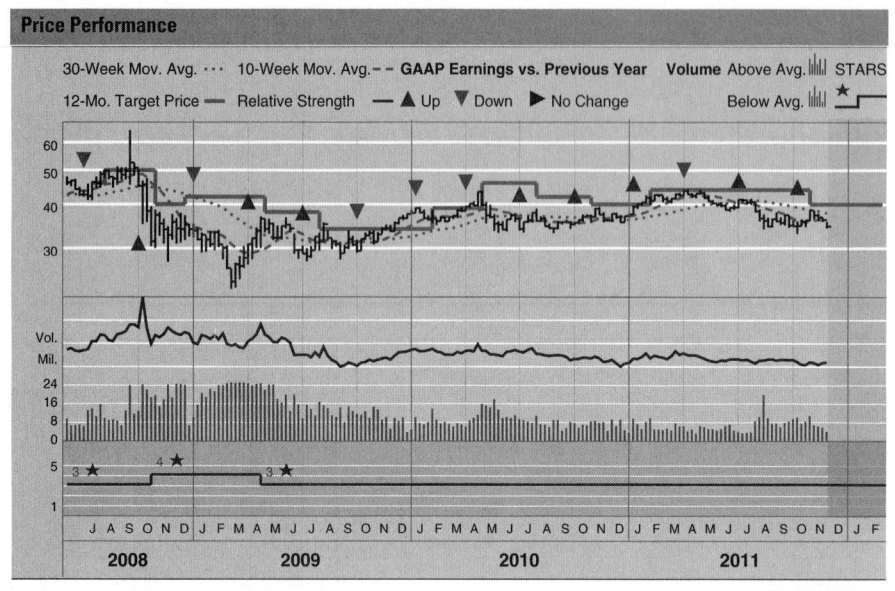

Options: CBOE, P, Ph

Analysis prepared by Equity Analyst **S. Benway, CFA** on Oct 27, 2011, when the stock traded at **$38.04**.

## Highlights

➤ S&P projects that housing starts will rise less than 1% in 2011. We expect this to keep lumber and sawlog prices at relatively low levels. Additionally, unusually dry weather in the south is leading to higher pulpwood harvests and lower prices in that category. Moreover, rural land sales are expected to decline due to lower sales of large tracts in Montana. All told, we expect revenues to decline about 3% in 2011. In 2012, we forecast sales growth of about 10% due mostly to a stronger housing market.

➤ We think average wood product prices in 2011 will be about the same as those of 2010, as weak demand from the housing market is offset by rising exports to Asia. This should make margin improvement difficult, despite more profitable land sales. Higher volume should help margins in 2012 due to increased demand for timber both domestically and in Asia.

➤ Our 2011 operating EPS estimate is $1.20, down from the $1.33 recorded in 2010. The timing of real estate transactions will likely create quarterly volatility. For 2012, we project EPS of $1.45.

## Investment Rationale/Risk

➤ We believe PCL has significant value in its land holdings, and we expect real estate to become a rising source of earnings in coming years. It plans to develop 100,000 acres of land over the next 15 years, and we estimate that these properties can be sold at high margin levels. However, near-term demand and prices for timber are likely to remain below historical averages due to an expected weak housing market. A sustained level of higher earnings will be needed for a dividend increase, in our opinion.

➤ Risks to our recommendation and target price include renewed declines in log demand and prices due to weakness in the U.S. housing market, and lower-than-projected profits on sales of higher and better use land.

➤ Using a sum-of-the-parts analysis, which recognizes the value of PCL's land holdings, we value the shares at $39. Our dividend discount model, which assumes a $1.68 payout in 2011, a required rate of return of 8.0%, and constant dividend growth of 4.0%, indicates that PCL has an intrinsic value of $42. Our 12-month target price of $40 is based on a blend of these two measures.

## Qualitative Risk Assessment

| LOW | MEDIUM | HIGH |
|---|---|---|

Our risk assessment reflects that Plum Creek operates in a cyclical industry, with demand for its products tied to residential construction and paper manufacturing. It is subject to movements in interest rates, economic conditions and currency, and prices for its products have historically been volatile. However, it is a major landowner, and its debt levels are relatively low.

## Quantitative Evaluations

**S&P Quality Ranking** B

| D | C | B- | B | B+ | A- | A | A+ |
|---|---|---|---|---|---|---|---|

**Relative Strength Rank** MODERATE

55

LOWEST = 1    HIGHEST = 99

## Revenue/Earnings Data

**Revenue (Million $)**

| | 1Q | 2Q | 3Q | 4Q | Year |
|---|---|---|---|---|---|
| 2011 | 275.0 | 284.0 | 293.0 | -- | -- |
| 2010 | 317.0 | 258.0 | 259.0 | 356.0 | 1,190 |
| 2009 | 470.0 | 272.0 | 294.0 | 258.0 | 1,294 |
| 2008 | 363.0 | 376.0 | 414.0 | 461.0 | 1,614 |
| 2007 | 369.0 | 395.0 | 407.0 | 504.0 | 1,675 |
| 2006 | 414.0 | 380.0 | 454.0 | 379.0 | 1,627 |

**Earnings Per Share ($)**

| | 1Q | 2Q | 3Q | 4Q | Year |
|---|---|---|---|---|---|
| 2011 | 0.23 | 0.27 | 0.31 | E0.39 | E1.20 |
| 2010 | 0.47 | 0.22 | 0.20 | 0.37 | 1.24 |
| 2009 | 0.95 | 0.19 | 0.12 | 0.17 | 1.44 |
| 2008 | 0.22 | 0.18 | 0.40 | 0.57 | 1.37 |
| 2007 | 0.25 | 0.33 | 0.34 | 0.68 | 1.60 |
| 2006 | 0.50 | 0.34 | 0.51 | 0.39 | 1.74 |

Fiscal year ended Dec. 31. Next earnings report expected: Early February. EPS Estimates based on S&P Operating Earnings; historical GAAP earnings are as reported.

## Dividend Data (Dates: mm/dd Payment Date: mm/dd/yy)

| Amount ($) | Date Decl. | Ex-Div. Date | Stk. of Record | Payment Date |
|---|---|---|---|---|
| 0.420 | 02/08 | 02/16 | 02/18 | 03/04/11 |
| 0.420 | 05/03 | 05/12 | 05/16 | 05/31/11 |
| 0.420 | 08/02 | 08/12 | 08/16 | 08/31/11 |
| 0.420 | 11/01 | 11/10 | 11/15 | 11/30/11 |

Dividends have been paid since 1989. Source: Company reports.

---

**Please read the Required Disclosures and Analyst Certification on the last page of this report.**

The **McGraw·Hill** Companies

# Plum Creek Timber Co Inc.

## Business Summary October 27, 2011

CORPORATE OVERVIEW. Plum Creek Timber Co., a real estate investment trust (REIT), is the largest private timberland owner in the United States, with 6.8 million acres of timberlands in 19 states. In addition, the trust operates several wood products manufacturing facilities and is actively involved in land purchases and sales. The company conducts operations through four business segments: the timber operation accounted for 48% of 2010 revenues, real estate (28%), manufacturing (22%), and other (2%). The Northern Resources portion of the timber segment encompasses 3.3 million acres of timberlands, in Maine, Michigan, Montana, New Hampshire, Oregon, Vermont, Washington, West Virginia and Wisconsin. The Southern Resources portion of the timber segment consists of 3.5 million acres of timberlands in Alabama, Arkansas, Florida, Georgia, Louisiana, Mississippi, North Carolina, Oklahoma, South Carolina and Texas.

MARKET PROFILE. The timber industry, which consists primarily of timberland owners, provides raw material and conducts resource management activities for the paper and forest products industry, including the planting, fertilizing, thinning and harvesting of trees and the marketing of logs. Harvested logs are marketed either as sawlogs to lumber and other wood products manufacturers or as pulplogs to pulp and paper manufacturers or producers of oriented strand board. Over time, timberlands may become more valuable for purposes other than growing timber. In these circumstances, timberlands may be sold to realize these values. There are six primary end markets for most of the

timber harvested in the United States: new housing construction, home repair and remodeling, products for industrial uses, raw material for the manufacture of pulp and paper, wood fiber for energy production, and logs for export.

The demand for timber is directly related to the underlying demand for pulp and paper products, lumber, panels, and other wood products. The demand for pulp and paper is largely driven by population growth, per-capita income levels, and industry capacity. The demand for lumber and manufactured wood products is primarily affected by the level of new residential construction activity and repair and remodeling activity, which, in turn, is affected by changes in general economic and demographic factors, including population growth and interest rates for home mortgages and construction loans. The demand for U.S. timber is also affected by the amounts of pulp and paper products, lumber, panel, and other wood products that are imported into the United States. In addition to these historically significant factors, the demand for timber could also be affected by emerging markets for wood-based biofuel and bioenergy. We believe that Plum Creek has only limited control over the prices that it can charge for timber and wood products.

## Company Financials Fiscal Year Ended Dec. 31

| Per Share Data ($) | 2010 | 2009 | 2008 | 2007 | 2006 | 2005 | 2004 | 2003 | 2002 | 2001 |
|---|---|---|---|---|---|---|---|---|---|---|
| Tangible Book Value | NA | NA | 9.47 | 12.06 | 11.80 | 12.62 | 12.19 | 11.57 | 12.04 | 12.21 |
| Cash Flow | NA | NA | 2.10 | 2.37 | 2.45 | 1.92 | 2.46 | 1.63 | 1.82 | 3.00 |
| Earnings | 1.24 | 1.44 | 1.37 | 1.60 | 1.74 | 1.79 | 1.84 | 1.04 | 1.26 | 2.58 |
| S&P Core Earnings | 1.25 | 1.47 | 1.35 | 1.61 | 1.67 | 1.78 | 1.82 | 1.04 | 1.24 | 2.57 |
| Dividends | 1.68 | 1.68 | 1.26 | 1.68 | 1.60 | 1.52 | 1.42 | 1.40 | 1.49 | 2.85 |
| Payout Ratio | 136% | 117% | 2% | 105% | 92% | 85% | 77% | 135% | 118% | 110% |
| Prices:High | 43.75 | 38.69 | 65.00 | 48.45 | 40.00 | 39.63 | 39.45 | 30.75 | 31.98 | 30.00 |
| Prices:Low | 33.11 | 22.88 | 27.33 | 37.13 | 31.21 | 33.40 | 27.30 | 20.88 | 18.92 | 23.30 |
| P/E Ratio:High | 35 | 27 | 47 | 30 | 23 | 22 | 21 | 30 | 25 | 12 |
| P/E Ratio:Low | 27 | 16 | 20 | 23 | 18 | 19 | 15 | 20 | 15 | 9 |

| Income Statement Analysis (Million $) | | | | | | | | | | |
|---|---|---|---|---|---|---|---|---|---|---|
| Revenue | 1,190 | 1,294 | 1,614 | 1,675 | 1,627 | 1,576 | 1,528 | 1,196 | 1,137 | 598 |
| Operating Income | NA | NA | 453 | 558 | 571 | 561 | 586 | 410 | 443 | 305 |
| Depreciation | 96.0 | 99.0 | 125 | 134 | 128 | 113 | 114 | 107 | 105 | 55.0 |
| Interest Expense | 138 | 147 | 148 | 147 | 133 | 109 | 111 | 117 | 103 | 54.0 |
| Pretax Income | 203 | 205 | 206 | 277 | 328 | 339 | 366 | 186 | 235 | 196 |
| Effective Tax Rate | NA | NM | NM | NM | 3.90% | 2.30% | 7.40% | NM | 0.85% | NM |
| Net Income | 202 | 236 | 233 | 280 | 315 | 331 | 339 | 192 | 233 | 338 |
| S&P Core Earnings | 203 | 241 | 229 | 281 | 301 | 329 | 336 | 193 | 229 | 336 |

| Balance Sheet & Other Financial Data (Million $) | | | | | | | | | | |
|---|---|---|---|---|---|---|---|---|---|---|
| Cash | 252 | 299 | 369 | 240 | 301 | 395 | 376 | 260 | 246 | 193 |
| Current Assets | NA | NA | 699 | 456 | 513 | 574 | 499 | 405 | 378 | 306 |
| Total Assets | 4,251 | 4,448 | 4,780 | 4,664 | 4,661 | 4,812 | 4,378 | 4,387 | 4,289 | 4,122 |
| Current Liabilities | NA | NA | 307 | 303 | 281 | 375 | 184 | 168 | 155 | 149 |
| Long Term Debt | 2,426 | 2,728 | 2,807 | 2,376 | 1,617 | 1,524 | 1,853 | 2,031 | 1,839 | 1,667 |
| Common Equity | 1,374 | 1,466 | 1,572 | 1,901 | 2,089 | 2,325 | 2,240 | 2,119 | 2,222 | 2,247 |
| Total Capital | NA | NA | 4,383 | 4,297 | 3,731 | 3,888 | 4,138 | 4,187 | 4,105 | 3,952 |
| Capital Expenditures | NA | NA | 189 | Nil | 86.0 | 89.0 | 70.0 | 246 | 231 | 59.0 |
| Cash Flow | NA | NA | 358 | 414 | 443 | 444 | 453 | 299 | 338 | 393 |
| Current Ratio | 1.1 | 2.8 | 2.3 | 1.5 | 1.8 | 1.5 | 2.7 | 2.4 | 2.4 | 2.1 |
| % Long Term Debt of Capitalization | 59.8 | 64.2 | 64.0 | 55.3 | 43.3 | 39.1 | 44.8 | 48.5 | 44.8 | 42.2 |
| % Net Income of Revenue | 17.0 | 18.2 | 14.4 | 16.7 | 19.3 | 21.0 | 22.2 | 16.1 | 20.5 | 56.5 |
| % Return on Assets | 4.6 | 5.1 | 4.9 | 6.0 | 6.6 | 7.2 | 7.7 | 4.4 | 5.5 | 11.8 |
| % Return on Equity | 14.2 | 15.5 | 13.4 | 14.0 | 14.2 | 14.5 | 15.6 | 8.8 | 10.4 | 28.3 |

Data as orig reptd.; bef. results of disc opers/spec. items. Per share data adj. for stk. divs.; EPS diluted. E-Estimated. NA-Not Available. NM-Not Meaningful. NR-Not Ranked. UR-Under Review.

**Office:** 999 3rd Ave Ste 4300, Seattle, WA 98104-4096.
**Telephone:** 206-467-3600.
**Email:** info@plumcreek.com
**Website:** http://www.plumcreek.com

**Chrmn:** J.F. Morgan
**Pres & CEO:** R.R. Holley
**COO:** T.M. Lindquist
**SVP & CFO:** D.W. Lambert

**SVP, Secy & General Counsel:** J.A. Kraft
**Investor Contact:** J. Hobbs (800-858-5347)
**Board Members:** R. R. Holley, R. Josephs, J. G. McDonald, R. B. McLeod, J. F. Morgan, M. F. Racicot, J. H. Scully, S. C. Tobias, M. A. White

**Founded:** 1989
**Domicile:** Delaware
**Employees:** 1,202

# PNC Financial Services Group Inc.

STANDARD
&POOR'S

| S&P Recommendation **BUY** ★★★★☆ | Price $49.07 (as of Nov 25, 2011) | 12-Mo. Target Price $65.00 | Investment Style Large-Cap Value |
|---|---|---|---|

**GICS Sector** Financials
**Sub-Industry** Regional Banks

**Summary** This large bank holding company conducts regional banking, wholesale banking and asset management in 15 eastern states, plus DC, with a concentration in Pennsylvania and Ohio.

## Key Stock Statistics (Source S&P, Vickers, company reports)

| | | | | | | | | |
|---|---|---|---|---|---|---|---|---|
| 52-Wk Range | $65.19–42.70 | S&P Oper. EPS 2011**E** | 6.33 | Market Capitalization(B) | $25.816 | Beta | 1.22 |
| Trailing 12-Month EPS | $6.29 | S&P Oper. EPS 2012**E** | 6.53 | Yield (%) | 2.85 | S&P 3-Yr. Proj. EPS CAGR(%) | 11 |
| Trailing 12-Month P/E | 7.8 | P/E on S&P Oper. EPS 2011**E** | 7.8 | Dividend Rate/Share | $1.40 | S&P Credit Rating | A |
| $10K Invested 5 Yrs Ago | $7,997 | Common Shares Outstg. (M) | 526.1 | Institutional Ownership (%) | 81 | | |

## Price Performance

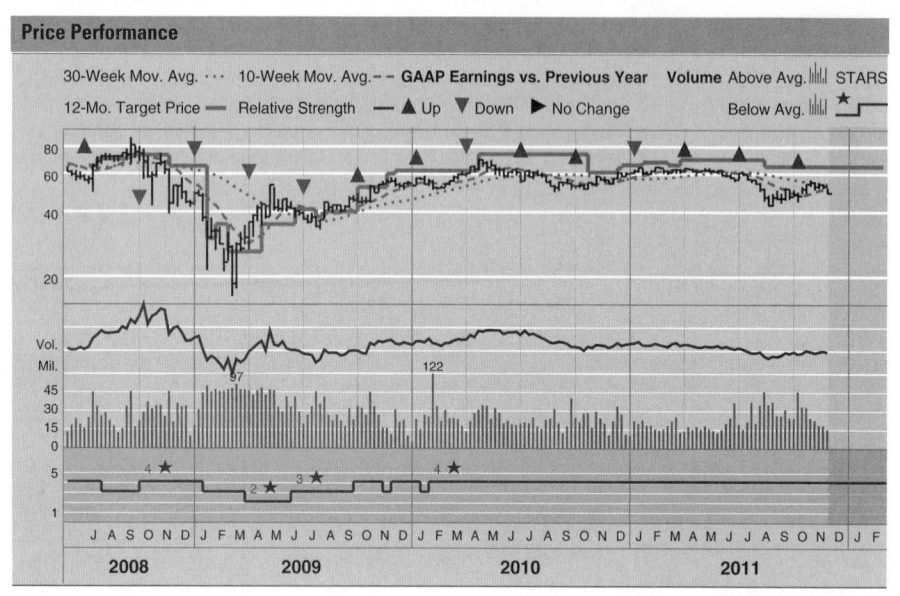

30-Week Mov. Avg. · · · 10-Week Mov. Avg. — **GAAP Earnings vs. Previous Year** Volume Above Avg. STARS
12-Mo. Target Price — Relative Strength — ▲ Up ▼ Down ▶ No Change Below Avg.

Options: ASE, CBOE, Ph

Analysis prepared by Equity Analyst **Erik Oja** on Nov 18, 2011, when the stock traded at **$52.69**.

## Highlights

➤ We expect loans to grow 3.1% in 2011 and 2.7% in 2012, accompanied by a slight narrowing of the net interest margin. Thus, we forecast net interest income of $8.653 billion in 2011, down 6.4% from 2010, and $8.475 billion in 2012, down 2.0% from our 2011 estimate. We see core fee income, ex-gains and losses and fund servicing, declining 6.4% in 2011, to $4.49 billion, before rising 0.2% in 2012. We expect total revenues to fall 5.1% in 2011, and 2.6% in 2012.

➤ Nonperforming loans fell 4.4% sequentially in the third quarter, to $3.69 billion, or 2.39% of total loans, a ratio we see as better than peers. As of quarter end, nonperforming loans were covered by a $4.507 billion loan loss allowance, with a better-than-peers 122% coverage ratio. We forecast 2011 loan loss provisions of $1.24 billion, based on our forecast of $1.68 billion of net chargeoffs and reserve releases of $440 million. We see 2012 loan loss provisions of $905 million, based on our forecast of $1.05 billion of net chargeoffs and reserve releases of $145 million.

➤ Our 2011 and 2012 EPS estimates are $6.33 and $6.53, respectively.

## Investment Rationale/Risk

➤ Third-quarter earnings demonstrated better-than-peers improvement in credit quality. We believe quality of earnings was high in the third quarter, with only 12% coming from reserve releases, better than most peers. We expect this trend to continue in 2012. Also, with the acquisition of National City Corp., PNC is more oriented than many peers in our coverage to consumer lending. At this stage in the credit cycle, we see this as an advantage over other regional banks, many of which have a greater commercial lending focus. In April, PNC raised its quarterly dividend to $0.35, from $0.10. The stock recently yielded 2.7%, above peers, and the payout is only about 21% of our forward four quarters EPS estimate of $6.39, below peers.

➤ Risks to our opinion and target price include a relapse into recession, or a slower-than-expected economic recovery, plus higher regulatory burdens.

➤ Our 12-month target price of $65 equates to above-peers multiples of 1.25X our year-end 2011 tangible book value per share estimate of $52.00, and 10.2X our forward four quarters EPS estimate.

## Qualitative Risk Assessment

| LOW | MEDIUM | HIGH |
|---|---|---|

Our risk assessment reflects PNC's large-cap valuation and history of profitability, offset by exposure to possible declines in residential and commercial lending credit quality.

## Quantitative Evaluations

**S&P Quality Ranking** B+

| D | C | B- | B | B+ | A- | A | A+ |
|---|---|---|---|---|---|---|---|

**Relative Strength Rank** MODERATE

54

LOWEST = 1 HIGHEST = 99

## Revenue/Earnings Data

**Revenue (Million $)**

| | 1Q | 2Q | 3Q | 4Q | Year |
|---|---|---|---|---|---|
| 2011 | 4,038 | 3,999 | 3,899 | -- | -- |
| 2010 | 4,289 | 4,350 | 4,084 | 4,373 | 17,096 |
| 2009 | 4,625 | 4,610 | 4,517 | 5,479 | 19,231 |
| 2008 | 2,586 | 2,639 | 2,228 | 2,227 | 9,680 |
| 2007 | 2,306 | 1,721 | 1,757 | 1,634 | 10,083 |
| 2006 | 2,251 | 2,356 | 4,146 | 2,186 | 10,939 |

**Earnings Per Share ($)**

| | | | | | |
|---|---|---|---|---|---|
| 2011 | 1.57 | 1.67 | 1.55 | E1.52 | E6.33 |
| 2010 | 0.61 | 1.43 | 1.45 | 1.50 | 5.02 |
| 2009 | 1.01 | 0.11 | 0.96 | 2.16 | 4.36 |
| 2008 | 1.09 | 1.45 | 0.71 | -0.77 | 2.46 |
| 2007 | 1.46 | 1.22 | 1.19 | 0.51 | 4.35 |
| 2006 | 1.19 | 1.28 | 5.01 | 1.27 | 8.73 |

Fiscal year ended Dec. 31. Next earnings report expected: Late January. EPS Estimates based on S&P Operating Earnings; historical GAAP earnings are as reported.

## Dividend Data (Dates: mm/dd Payment Date: mm/dd/yy)

| Amount ($) | Date Decl. | Ex-Div. Date | Stk. of Record | Payment Date |
|---|---|---|---|---|
| 0.100 | 01/06 | 01/12 | 01/14 | 01/24/11 |
| 0.350 | 04/07 | 04/14 | 04/18 | 05/05/11 |
| 0.350 | 07/07 | 07/14 | 07/18 | 08/05/11 |
| 0.350 | 10/06 | 10/17 | 10/19 | 11/05/11 |

Dividends have been paid since 1865. Source: Company reports.

---

**Please read the Required Disclosures and Analyst Certification on the last page of this report.**

The **McGraw·Hill** Companies

# PNC Financial Services Group Inc.

**STANDARD &POOR'S**

## Business Summary November 18, 2011

CORPORATE OVERVIEW. PNC Financial Services Group has six primary reportable business segments: Retail Banking, Corporate and Institutional Banking, Asset Management, Residential Mortgage Banking, the Distressed Assets Portfolio (largely from NCC), and Other. Effective July 2010, PNC's Global Investment Servicing unit, which until then had been PNC's seventh business segment, was sold to Bank of New York Mellon Corp (BK 19, Hold) for $2.3 billion cash.

MARKET PROFILE. As of June 30, 2011, which is the latest available FDIC data, PNC had 2,485 branches and $180.8 billion in deposits. In Pennsylvania, PNC had 481 branches, $62.3 billion in deposits, and a deposit market share of 18.8%, ranking first. In Ohio, PNC had 394 branches, $24.8 billion in deposits, and a deposit market share of 9.8%, ranking fourth. In New Jersey, PNC had 324 branches, $19.5 billion in deposits, and a deposit market share of about 7.3%, ranking fifth. In Michigan, PNC had 231 branches, $15.1 billion in deposits, and a deposit market share of about 7.8%, ranking third. In Illinois, PNC had 181 branches, $14.5 billion in deposits, and a deposit market share of about 3.7%, ranking fifth. In Maryland, PNC had 222 branches, $10.6 billion in deposits, and a deposit market share of about 8.0%, ranking third. In Indiana,

PNC had 157 branches, $10.5 billion in deposits, and a deposit market share of about 9.1%, ranking second. PNC also had a total of 495 offices and $23.7 billion in deposits in the District of Columbia, Kentucky, Alabama, North Carolina, Florida, Georgia, Missouri, Virginia, Delaware, Wisconsin, South Carolina, West Virginia, and New York.

IMPACT OF MAJOR DEVELOPMENTS. On June 20, 2011, PNC agreed to acquire select U.S. assets from RBC (Royal Bank of Canada, (RY 43, Buy)) for $3.45 billion. This deal is subject to regulatory and shareholder approvals, and is expected to close in the first quarter of 2012.

In March 2011, PNC's capital plan, submitted in January, was accepted by the Federal Reserve. PNC proposed a dividend increase and the continuation of its share buyback program. On April 7, PNC raised its quarterly dividend to $0.35, from $0.10.

## Company Financials Fiscal Year Ended Dec. 31

| Per Share Data ($) | 2010 | 2009 | 2008 | 2007 | 2006 | 2005 | 2004 | 2003 | 2002 | 2001 |
|---|---|---|---|---|---|---|---|---|---|---|
| Tangible Book Value | 39.06 | 24.50 | 13.13 | 15.55 | 23.02 | 13.98 | 14.55 | 14.22 | 14.78 | 12.19 |
| Earnings | 5.02 | 4.36 | 2.46 | 4.35 | 8.73 | 4.55 | 4.21 | 3.65 | 4.20 | 1.26 |
| S&P Core Earnings | 4.77 | 2.79 | 1.83 | 4.47 | 8.63 | 4.43 | 4.00 | 3.53 | 3.83 | 0.92 |
| Dividends | 0.40 | 0.96 | 2.61 | 2.44 | 2.15 | 2.00 | 2.00 | 1.94 | 1.92 | 1.92 |
| Payout Ratio | 8% | 22% | 106% | 56% | 25% | 44% | 48% | 53% | 46% | 152% |
| Prices:High | 70.45 | 57.86 | 87.99 | 76.41 | 75.15 | 65.66 | 59.79 | 55.55 | 62.80 | 75.81 |
| Prices:Low | 49.43 | 16.20 | 39.09 | 63.54 | 61.78 | 49.35 | 48.90 | 41.63 | 32.70 | 51.14 |
| P/E Ratio:High | 14 | 13 | 36 | 18 | 9 | 14 | 14 | 15 | 15 | 60 |
| P/E Ratio:Low | 10 | 4 | 16 | 15 | 7 | 11 | 12 | 11 | 8 | 41 |
| **Income Statement Analysis** (Million $) | | | | | | | | | | |
| Net Interest Income | 9,230 | 9,083 | 3,823 | 2,915 | 2,245 | 2,154 | 1,969 | 1,996 | 2,197 | 2,262 |
| Tax Equivalent Adjustment | 81.0 | 65.0 | 36.0 | 27.0 | 25.0 | 33.0 | NA | NA | NA | NA |
| Non Interest Income | 5,946 | 7,934 | 3,306 | 3,795 | 6,534 | 4,203 | 3,508 | 3,141 | 3,108 | 2,412 |
| Loan Loss Provision | 2,502 | 3,930 | 1,517 | 315 | 124 | 21.0 | 52.0 | 177 | 309 | 903 |
| % Expense/Operating Revenue | 56.8% | 53.3% | 62.0% | 64.0% | 50.5% | 48.6% | 68.2% | 67.7% | 60.8% | 71.4% |
| Pretax Income | 4,061 | 3,324 | 1,243 | 2,094 | 4,005 | 1,962 | 1,745 | 1,600 | 1,858 | 564 |
| Effective Tax Rate | 25.5% | 27.7% | 29.0% | 29.9% | 34.0% | 30.8% | 30.8% | 33.7% | 33.4% | 33.2% |
| Net Income | 3,039 | 2,447 | 882 | 1,467 | 2,595 | 1,325 | 1,197 | 1,029 | 1,200 | 377 |
| % Net Interest Margin | 4.14 | 3.82 | 3.37 | 3.00 | 2.92 | 3.00 | 3.22 | 3.64 | 3.99 | 3.84 |
| S&P Core Earnings | 2,496 | 1,277 | 639 | 1,503 | 2,565 | 1,294 | 1,134 | 993 | 1,093 | 270 |
| **Balance Sheet & Other Financial Data** (Million $) | | | | | | | | | | |
| Money Market Assets | 3,704 | 2,390 | 1,856 | 2,729 | 1,763 | 350 | 1,635 | 50.0 | 3,658 | 1,335 |
| Investment Securities | 64,262 | 56,027 | 43,473 | 30,225 | 31,651 | 23,253 | 18,609 | 16,409 | 17,421 | 15,243 |
| Commercial Loans | 61,570 | 61,020 | 99,516 | 39,956 | 27,672 | 26,115 | 19,418 | 15,987 | 22,335 | 23,134 |
| Other Loans | 89,025 | 96,523 | 75,973 | 28,363 | 22,433 | 23,821 | 24,077 | 18,093 | 13,115 | 14,840 |
| Total Assets | 264,284 | 269,863 | 291,081 | 138,920 | 101,820 | 91,954 | 79,723 | 68,168 | 66,377 | 69,568 |
| Demand Deposits | 50,019 | 44,384 | 43,212 | 19,440 | 16,070 | 14,988 | 12,915 | 11,505 | 9,538 | 10,124 |
| Time Deposits | 133,371 | 142,538 | 149,653 | 63,256 | 50,231 | 45,287 | 40,354 | 33,736 | 35,444 | 37,180 |
| Long Term Debt | 35,344 | 35,263 | 47,087 | 21,157 | 10,266 | 6,797 | 8,684 | 7,667 | 9,112 | 8,922 |
| Common Equity | 29,595 | 21,968 | 17,504 | 14,854 | 10,788 | 8,563 | 7,548 | 6,735 | 6,943 | 5,822 |
| % Return on Assets | 1.1 | 0.9 | 0.4 | 1.2 | 2.7 | 1.5 | 1.6 | 1.5 | 1.8 | 0.5 |
| % Return on Equity | 11.8 | 12.4 | 5.5 | 11.4 | 26.8 | 16.5 | 16.8 | 15.0 | 18.7 | 5.9 |
| % Loan Loss Reserve | 3.3 | 3.2 | 2.2 | 1.2 | 1.1 | 1.2 | 1.3 | 1.8 | 1.8 | 1.5 |
| % Loans/Deposits | 82.1 | 84.3 | 91.0 | 79.5 | 79.1 | 123.7 | 84.8 | 78.4 | 82.4 | 89.1 |
| % Equity to Assets | 11.3 | 7.0 | 7.5 | 10.7 | 10.0 | 9.3 | 9.7 | 10.2 | 9.4 | 8.9 |

Data as orig reptd.; bef. results of disc opers/spec. items. Per share data adj. for stk. divs.; EPS diluted. E-Estimated. NA-Not Available. NM-Not Meaningful. NR-Not Ranked. UR-Under Review.

**Office:** 249 5th Ave, 1 PNC Plz, Pittsburgh, PA 15222-2707.
**Telephone:** 412-762-2000.
**Email:** corporate.communiations@pncbank.com
**Website:** http://www.pnc.com

**Chrmn & CEO:** J.E. Rohr
**Pres:** J.C. Guyaux
**EVP & CFO:** R.J. Johnson
**EVP & Treas:** E.W. Parsley, III

**EVP & General Counsel:** H.P. Pudlin
**Investor Contact:** W. Callihan (800-843-2206)
**Board Members:** R. O. Berndt, C. E. Bunch, P. W. Chellgren, K. C. James, R. B. Kelson, B. C. Lindsay, A. A. Massaro, J. G. Pepper, J. E. Rohr, D. J. Shepard, L. K. Steffes, D. F. Strigl, T. J. Usher, G. H. Walls, Jr., H. H. Wehmeier

**Founded:** 1922
**Domicile:** Pennsylvania
**Employees:** 50,769

*The McGraw-Hill Companies*

# PPG Industries Inc.

**STANDARD &POOR'S**

| S&P Recommendation **STRONG BUY** ★★★★★ | Price<br>$79.45 (as of Nov 25, 2011) | 12-Mo. Target Price<br>$105.00 | Investment Style<br>Large-Cap Blend |
|---|---|---|---|

**GICS Sector** Materials
**Sub-Industry** Diversified Chemicals

**Summary** This company is a leading manufacturer of coatings and resins, flat and fiber glass, and industrial and specialty chemicals.

## Key Stock Statistics (Source S&P, Vickers, company reports)

| | | | | | | | |
|---|---|---|---|---|---|---|---|
| 52-Wk Range | $97.81– 66.43 | S&P Oper. EPS 2011**E** | 6.96 | Market Capitalization(B) | $12.269 | Beta | 1.33 |
| Trailing 12-Month EPS | $6.71 | S&P Oper. EPS 2012**E** | 7.25 | Yield (%) | 2.87 | S&P 3-Yr. Proj. EPS CAGR(%) | 10 |
| Trailing 12-Month P/E | 11.8 | P/E on S&P Oper. EPS 2011**E** | 11.4 | Dividend Rate/Share | $2.28 | S&P Credit Rating | BBB+ |
| $10K Invested 5 Yrs Ago | $14,485 | Common Shares Outstg. (M) | 154.4 | Institutional Ownership (%) | 77 | | |

## Price Performance

30-Week Mov. Avg. · · · 10-Week Mov. Avg. - - GAAP Earnings vs. Previous Year  Volume Above Avg. STARS
12-Mo. Target Price — Relative Strength — ▲ Up ▼ Down ► No Change  Below Avg. ★

Options: ASE, CBOE, Ph

Analysis prepared by Equity Analyst **Leo J. Larkin** on Nov 03, 2011, when the stock traded at **$88.66**.

## Highlights

➤ Following an estimated rise of 11.8% in 2011, we look for an 8% sales gain in 2012 on higher prices in all segments. We think volumes will be flat to up just slightly. Our forecast for higher sales assumes global GDP growth of 2.6% in 2012, versus global growth of 2.7% estimated for 2011. We see continued sales gains for all three coatings businesses, stemming from strength in global auto, industrial and electronics-related markets. Optical products sales should continue to advance in 2012, and we look for increased commodity chemical sales on higher prices. We believe the fiberglass business will be modestly better as commercial construction activity begins to recover.

➤ Aided mostly by higher prices, we see an increase in operating profit. But, due to rising raw material costs, we think the projected gain in operating profit will lag the estimated increase in sales. After interest expense and taxes, and with fewer shares outstanding, we project EPS of $7.25 for 2012, versus EPS of $6.96 estimated for 2011.

➤ We see PPG's long-term EPS rising on acquisitions, share repurchases and expansion into the more rapidly growing markets in Asia.

## Investment Rationale/Risk

➤ We think PPG is very attractively valued, recently trading at about 12X our EPS estimate for 2012, with a dividend yield above 2.5%. We think sales and EPS troughed in 2009 and will head higher through 2012. Despite a lackluster global economy in 2011, PPG managed to obtain price increases in all 13 of its businesses in 2011's first three quarters. Also, the company generated substantial free cash flow in the same period despite a 49% rise in capital spending. We think PPG will generate greater free cash flow in 2012 and continue to increase its dividend, make acquisitions and repurchase shares.

➤ Risks to our recommendation and target price include slower-than-projected industrial activity, unplanned production outages and interruptions, higher raw material costs, and unexpected weakness in selling prices for commodity chemicals.

➤ Our 12-month target price is $105, based on a multiple of 14.5X our $7.25 EPS estimate for 2012. Our projected multiple is toward the low end of the historical range to reflect a slow growth world economy.

## Qualitative Risk Assessment

| LOW | MEDIUM | HIGH |
|---|---|---|

Our risk assessment reflects the company's diversified business mix, large market shares in key products, and what we see as its healthy balance sheet, offset by the cyclical nature of the commodity chemicals business and the auto and construction-related end markets.

## Quantitative Evaluations

**S&P Quality Ranking** B+

| D | C | B- | B | B+ | A- | A | A+ |
|---|---|---|---|---|---|---|---|

**Relative Strength Rank** MODERATE

66

LOWEST = 1  HIGHEST = 99

## Revenue/Earnings Data

**Revenue (Million $)**

| | 1Q | 2Q | 3Q | 4Q | Year |
|---|---|---|---|---|---|
| 2011 | 3,533 | 3,986 | 3,849 | -- | -- |
| 2010 | 3,126 | 3,458 | 3,460 | 3,379 | 13,423 |
| 2009 | 2,783 | 3,115 | 3,225 | 3,116 | 12,239 |
| 2008 | 3,962 | 4,474 | 4,225 | 3,188 | 15,849 |
| 2007 | 2,917 | 3,173 | 2,823 | 2,874 | 11,206 |
| 2006 | 2,638 | 2,824 | 2,802 | 2,773 | 11,037 |

**Earnings Per Share ($)**

| | | | | | |
|---|---|---|---|---|---|
| 2011 | 1.40 | 2.12 | 1.96 | E1.45 | E6.96 |
| 2010 | 0.18 | 1.63 | 1.58 | 1.24 | 4.63 |
| 2009 | -0.68 | 0.89 | 0.96 | 0.85 | 2.03 |
| 2008 | 0.53 | 1.51 | 0.70 | 0.43 | 3.25 |
| 2007 | 1.17 | 1.50 | 1.29 | 1.17 | 4.91 |
| 2006 | 1.11 | 1.68 | 0.54 | 0.94 | 4.27 |

Fiscal year ended Dec. 31. Next earnings report expected: Late January. EPS Estimates based on S&P Operating Earnings; historical GAAP earnings are as reported.

## Dividend Data (Dates: mm/dd Payment Date: mm/dd/yy)

| Amount<br>($) | Date<br>Decl. | Ex-Div.<br>Date | Stk. of<br>Record | Payment<br>Date |
|---|---|---|---|---|
| 0.550 | 01/20 | 02/16 | 02/18 | 03/11/11 |
| 0.570 | 04/21 | 05/06 | 05/10 | 06/10/11 |
| 0.570 | 07/21 | 08/08 | 08/10 | 09/12/11 |
| 0.570 | 10/21 | 11/08 | 11/10 | 12/12/11 |

Dividends have been paid since 1899. Source: Company reports.

---

**Please read the Required Disclosures and Analyst Certification on the last page of this report.**

*The McGraw-Hill Companies*

# PPG Industries Inc.

**STANDARD &POOR'S**

## Business Summary November 03, 2011

CORPORATE OVERVIEW. PPG Industries is a diversified producer of coatings, chemicals and glass products. International operations contributed 58% of sales and 48% of operating profits in 2010.

PPG Industries is one of the world's leading producers of protective and decorative coatings. Industrial coatings (28% of sales in 2010 and 22% of operating profits) is comprised of original automotive, industrial (used in appliance and industrial equipment), and packaging (container) coatings. PPG also produces adhesives and sealants for the automotive industry and metal pretreatments.

Performance coatings (32%, 38%) consists of automotive and industrial refinish coatings, aerospace coatings, specialty marine and protective coatings, and a major North American supplier of architectural coatings (Pittsburgh, Olympic, Porter and Lucite brands). The architectural finishes business at the end of 2010 operated 400 company-owned stores in North America and 50 stores in Australia. The company is a global supplier of aircraft coatings, sealants, and transparencies to OEM, maintenance and aftermarket customers. The European Architectural coatings (14%, 7%) segment consists of the majority of the sales of the former SigmaKalon acquired in January 2008, and includes about 600 company-owned stores. The coatings industry is high-

ly competitive and consists of a few large firms with a global presence and many smaller firms serving local or regional markets.

PPG's commodity chemicals business (11%, 11%) is the fourth largest U.S. producer of chlorine and caustic soda (used in a wide variety of industrial applications), vinyl chloride monomer (for use in polyvinyl chloride resins), calcium hypochlorite, and chlorinated solvents. These commodity chemicals are highly cyclical; PPG's volumes rebounded 15% in 2010, following a 9% decline in 2009. The company's electrochemical unit (ECU) prices averaged lower in both 2009 and 2010.

Optical and specialty materials (8%, 18%) consists of optical resins (Transitions photochromic lenses, sun lenses, and polarized film), silica compounds, and Teslin synthetic printing sheet. Sales and profits of the optical products business rebounded in 2010, reflecting increased sales of Transitions and despite higher advertising spending.

## Company Financials Fiscal Year Ended Dec. 31

| Per Share Data ($) | 2010 | 2009 | 2008 | 2007 | 2006 | 2005 | 2004 | 2003 | 2002 | 2001 |
|---|---|---|---|---|---|---|---|---|---|---|
| Tangible Book Value | NM | NM | NM | 12.59 | 7.59 | 8.46 | 10.81 | 7.36 | 3.49 | 9.10 |
| Cash Flow | 8.14 | 4.93 | 6.55 | 7.20 | 6.61 | 5.66 | 6.19 | 5.23 | 1.99 | 4.93 |
| Earnings | 4.63 | 2.03 | 3.25 | 4.91 | 4.27 | 3.49 | 3.95 | 2.92 | -0.36 | 2.29 |
| S&P Core Earnings | 5.07 | 2.61 | 2.62 | 5.28 | 4.78 | 4.57 | 4.42 | 3.48 | 1.76 | 1.17 |
| Dividends | 2.18 | 2.13 | 2.09 | 2.04 | 1.91 | 1.86 | 1.79 | 1.73 | 1.70 | 1.68 |
| Payout Ratio | 47% | 105% | 64% | 42% | 45% | 53% | 45% | 59% | NM | 73% |
| Prices:High | 84.59 | 62.31 | 71.00 | 82.42 | 69.80 | 74.73 | 68.79 | 64.42 | 62.86 | 59.75 |
| Prices:Low | 56.96 | 28.16 | 35.94 | 64.01 | 56.53 | 55.64 | 54.81 | 42.61 | 41.39 | 38.99 |
| P/E Ratio:High | 18 | 31 | 22 | 17 | 16 | 21 | 17 | 22 | NM | 26 |
| P/E Ratio:Low | 12 | 14 | 11 | 13 | 13 | 16 | 14 | 15 | NM | 17 |

| Income Statement Analysis (Million $) | | | | | | | | | | |
|---|---|---|---|---|---|---|---|---|---|---|
| Revenue | 13,423 | 12,239 | 15,849 | 11,206 | 11,037 | 10,201 | 9,513 | 8,756 | 8,067 | 8,169 |
| Operating Income | 1,835 | 1,376 | 1,924 | 1,698 | 1,703 | 1,648 | 1,496 | 1,367 | 1,309 | 1,371 |
| Depreciation | 470 | 480 | 546 | 380 | 380 | 372 | 388 | 394 | 398 | 447 |
| Interest Expense | 189 | 193 | 262 | 104 | 83.0 | 81.0 | 90.0 | 107 | 128 | 169 |
| Pretax Income | 1,295 | 617 | 908 | 1,243 | 1,060 | 947 | 1,063 | 843 | -28.0 | 666 |
| Effective Tax Rate | NA | 31.0% | 31.3% | 28.6% | 26.2% | 29.8% | 30.3% | 34.8% | NM | 37.1% |
| Net Income | 769 | 336 | 538 | 815 | 711 | 596 | 683 | 500 | -60.0 | 387 |
| S&P Core Earnings | 844 | 432 | 434 | 877 | 797 | 780 | 765 | 597 | 300 | 197 |

| Balance Sheet & Other Financial Data (Million $) | | | | | | | | | | |
|---|---|---|---|---|---|---|---|---|---|---|
| Cash | 1,978 | 1,057 | 1,021 | 2,232 | 455 | 466 | 709 | 499 | 117 | 108 |
| Current Assets | 7,058 | 5,981 | 6,348 | 7,136 | 4,592 | 4,019 | 4,054 | 3,537 | 2,945 | 2,703 |
| Total Assets | 14,975 | 14,240 | 14,698 | 12,629 | 10,021 | 8,681 | 8,932 | 8,424 | 7,863 | 8,452 |
| Current Liabilities | 3,625 | 3,577 | 4,210 | 4,661 | 2,787 | 2,349 | 2,221 | 2,139 | 1,920 | 1,955 |
| Long Term Debt | 4,011 | 3,044 | 3,009 | 1,201 | 1,155 | 1,169 | 1,184 | 1,339 | 1,699 | 1,699 |
| Common Equity | 3,638 | 3,753 | 3,333 | 4,151 | 3,234 | 3,053 | 3,572 | 2,911 | 2,150 | 3,080 |
| Total Capital | 8,041 | 6,968 | 6,923 | 5,649 | 4,673 | 4,420 | 4,997 | 4,475 | 4,044 | 5,453 |
| Capital Expenditures | 307 | 239 | 383 | 353 | 372 | 288 | 244 | 217 | 238 | 291 |
| Cash Flow | 1,350 | 816 | 1,084 | 1,195 | 1,091 | 968 | 1,071 | 894 | 338 | 834 |
| Current Ratio | 2.0 | 1.7 | 1.5 | 1.5 | 1.6 | 1.7 | 1.8 | 1.7 | 1.5 | 1.4 |
| % Long Term Debt of Capitalization | 49.9 | Nil | 43.5 | 21.3 | 24.7 | 26.4 | 23.7 | 29.9 | 42.0 | 31.2 |
| % Net Income of Revenue | 5.7 | 2.8 | 3.4 | 7.8 | 6.4 | 5.8 | 7.2 | 5.7 | NM | 4.7 |
| % Return on Assets | 5.3 | 2.3 | 3.9 | 7.2 | 7.6 | 6.8 | 7.9 | 6.1 | NM | 4.4 |
| % Return on Equity | 20.8 | 9.5 | 14.4 | 22.1 | 22.6 | 18.0 | 21.1 | 19.8 | NM | 12.5 |

Data as orig reptd.; bef. results of disc opers/spec. items. Per share data adj. for stk. divs.; EPS diluted. E-Estimated. NA-Not Available. NM-Not Meaningful. NR-Not Ranked. UR-Under Review.

**Office:** 1 PPG Pl, Pittsburgh, PA 15272.
**Telephone:** 412-434-3131.
**Website:** http://www.ppg.com
**Chrmn & CEO:** C.E. Bunch

**SVP & CFO:** D.B. Navikas
**SVP & General Counsel:** G.E. Bost, II
**CTO:** C.F. Kahle, II
**Treas:** A.S. Giga

**Investor Contact:** V. Morales (412-434-3740)
**Board Members:** S. F. Angel, J. G. Berges, C. E. Bunch, H. Grant, V. F. Haynes, M. J. Hooper, R. Mehrabian, M. H. Richenhagen, R. Ripp, T. J. Usher, D. R. Whitwam

**Founded:** 1883
**Domicile:** Pennsylvania
**Employees:** 38,300

# PPL Corp

**STANDARD &POOR'S**

| **S&P Recommendation** BUY ★★★★☆ | **Price** $28.57 (as of Nov 25, 2011) | **12-Mo. Target Price** $32.00 | **Investment Style** Large-Cap Blend |
|---|---|---|---|

**GICS Sector** Utilities
**Sub-Industry** Electric Utilities

**Summary** This holding company for electric utilities in Pennsylvania and Kentucky (acquired in late 2010) also owns a U.K. utility and has agreed to acquire another.

## Key Stock Statistics (Source S&P, Vickers, company reports)

| | | | | | | | |
|---|---|---|---|---|---|---|---|
| 52-Wk Range | $30.27–24.10 | S&P Oper. EPS 2011E | 2.67 | Market Capitalization(B) | $16.522 | Beta | 0.45 |
| Trailing 12-Month EPS | $2.64 | S&P Oper. EPS 2012E | 2.54 | Yield (%) | 4.90 | S&P 3-Yr. Proj. EPS CAGR(%) | 8 |
| Trailing 12-Month P/E | 10.8 | P/E on S&P Oper. EPS 2011E | 10.7 | Dividend Rate/Share | $1.40 | S&P Credit Rating | BBB |
| $10K Invested 5 Yrs Ago | $9,998 | Common Shares Outstg. (M) | 578.3 | Institutional Ownership (%) | 75 | | |

## Price Performance

30-Week Mov. Avg. ···   10-Week Mov. Avg. --   **GAAP Earnings vs. Previous Year**   Volume Above Avg. ▍▍▍ STARS
12-Mo. Target Price —   Relative Strength —   ▲ Up   ▼ Down   ▶ No Change   Below Avg. ▍▍▍ ★

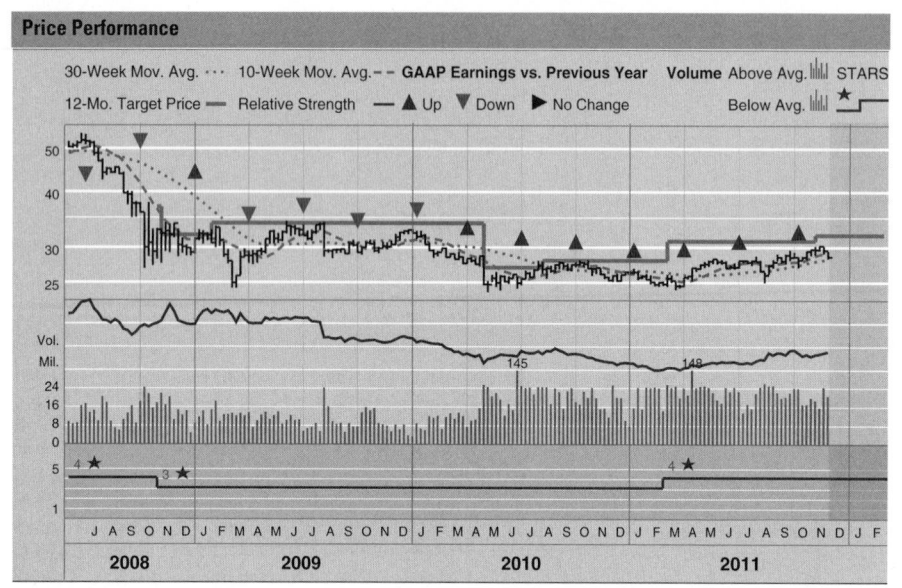

Options: CBOE, P, Ph

Analysis prepared by Equity Analyst **Justin McCann** on Nov 04, 2011, when the stock traded at **$29.60**.

## Highlights

▸ We expect operating EPS in 2011 to decline nearly 16% from 2010's $3.16. In the first nine months of 2011, operating EPS was $0.27 below the year-earlier period, as the earnings benefit from the November 1, 2010, acquisition of the Kentucky utilities and the April 1, 2011, acquisition of the Central Networks electric distribution business in the U.K. were more than offset by sharply lower margins at the power supply operations and 30.7% more shares.

▸ Given the progress made in the integration of the acquired U.K. utilities, we expect them to realize operating earnings of about $0.89 in 2011 (up from $0.54 in 2010). While the Kentucky utilities are expected to earn approximately $0.41 in 2011 (versus $0.06 for two months in 2010), we expect the Pennsylvania utility to earn around $0.28 (essentially flat with 2010's $0.27). The power supply business, however, is expected to decline sharply, from about $2.29 in 2010, to approximately $1.10 in 2011.

▸ For 2012, we expect operating EPS to decline by nearly 5% from anticipated results for 2011, as higher earnings at the U.K. utilities are more than offset by the continuing weakness at the power supply segment in the U.S.

## Investment Rationale/Risk

▸ The shares were up about 13% in the first 44 weeks of 2011, aided, in our view, by the investor shift to the electric utility sector, and the acquisition of the Midlands utilities in the U.K. In addition to being increasingly accretive to earnings over the next few years, the acquisition should greatly increase the portion of earnings realized from PPL's regulated operations and reduce its exposure to the weakness in the power markets. With PPL's highly efficient WPD management assuming control of the acquired utility, we expect it to enhance earnings in a regulatory environment that provides revenue incentives for operating efficiencies.

▸ Risks to our recommendation and target price include potentially unfavorable regulatory rulings, significantly lower results from the unregulated operations, and a major shift in the average P/E multiple of the peer group as a whole.

▸ We believe the shares could be restricted by the continuing weakness in the power supply business. However, with the dividend recently yielding 4.7%, we still view the stock as attractive for potential above-average total return. Our 12-month target price is $32, a discount-to-peers P/E of 12.6X our EPS estimate for 2012.

## Qualitative Risk Assessment

| LOW | MEDIUM | HIGH |
|---|---|---|

Our risk assessment reflects the steady cash flow we expect from the regulated Pennsylvania and U.K. distribution segments, which operate within supportive regulatory environments, offset by the highly profitable but less predictable earnings and cash flow from the power supply segment, as well as the currency risks related to the U.K. business.

## Quantitative Evaluations

**S&P Quality Ranking**   A-

| D | C | B- | B | B+ | A- | A | A+ |
|---|---|---|---|---|---|---|---|

**Relative Strength Rank**   STRONG

73

LOWEST = 1                                          HIGHEST = 99

## Revenue/Earnings Data

**Revenue (Million $)**

| | 1Q | 2Q | 3Q | 4Q | Year |
|---|---|---|---|---|---|
| 2011 | 2,910 | 2,489 | 3,120 | -- | -- |
| 2010 | 3,006 | 1,473 | 2,179 | 1,863 | 8,521 |
| 2009 | 2,359 | 1,673 | 1,805 | 1,727 | 7,556 |
| 2008 | 1,526 | 1,024 | 2,981 | 2,513 | 8,044 |
| 2007 | 1,638 | 1,613 | 1,763 | 1,606 | 6,498 |
| 2006 | 1,781 | 1,642 | 1,752 | 1,724 | 6,899 |

**Earnings Per Share ($)**

| | 1Q | 2Q | 3Q | 4Q | Year |
|---|---|---|---|---|---|
| 2011 | 0.82 | 0.35 | 0.77 | E0.65 | E2.67 |
| 2010 | 0.66 | 0.22 | 0.62 | 0.70 | 2.20 |
| 2009 | 0.64 | 0.07 | 0.12 | 0.37 | 1.18 |
| 2008 | 0.65 | 0.50 | 0.55 | 0.74 | 2.45 |
| 2007 | 0.58 | 0.63 | 0.72 | 0.57 | 2.63 |
| 2006 | 0.73 | 0.52 | 0.58 | 0.47 | 2.29 |

Fiscal year ended Dec. 31. Next earnings report expected: Early February. EPS Estimates based on S&P Operating Earnings; historical GAAP earnings are as reported.

## Dividend Data (Dates: mm/dd Payment Date: mm/dd/yy)

| Amount ($) | Date Decl. | Ex-Div. Date | Stk. of Record | Payment Date |
|---|---|---|---|---|
| 0.350 | 02/25 | 03/08 | 03/10 | 04/01/11 |
| 0.350 | 05/18 | 06/08 | 06/10 | 07/01/11 |
| 0.350 | 08/26 | 09/07 | 09/09 | 10/03/11 |
| 0.350 | 11/18 | 12/07 | 12/09 | 01/03/12 |

Dividends have been paid since 1946. Source: Company reports.

---

**Please read the Required Disclosures and Analyst Certification on the last page of this report.**

The McGraw-Hill Companies

# PPL Corp

**STANDARD &POOR'S**

## Business Summary November 04, 2011

CORPORATE OVERVIEW. PPL Corporation is an energy and utility holding company organized into three principal subsidiaries: PPL Electric, which includes the Pennsylvania electricity transmission and distribution operations; the LKE subsidiary, which includes Louisville Gas & Electric Company (LG&E) and Kentucky Utilities (KU); and the PPL Energy Supply subsidiary, which in addition to the international electricity distribution businesses in the U.K., includes PPL Generation and PPL EnergyPlus, which are respectively involved in competitive electricity generation (primarily in Pennsylvania and Montana), and the marketing and trading of electricity and other power purchases to deregulated wholesale and retail markets.

IMPACT OF MAJOR DEVELOPMENTS. On April 1, 2011, PPL completed the acquisition (announced on March 1, 2011) of Central Networks, the second largest electric distribution business in the U.K., for about 3.6 billion British pounds (approximately $5.7 billion) in cash and the assumption of 500 million British pounds (about $800 million) of existing debt. The utility serves 5 million customers in the Midlands area of England through its subsidiaries Central Networks East plc and Central Networks West plc. The service territory, which includes the cities of Birmingham and Nottingham, is adjacent to the territory of PPL's Western Power Distribution unit, whose subsidiaries WPD

South West and WPD South Wales provide electricity to 2.6 million customers in England and Wales. The acquisition, which did not require any regulatory or shareholder approvals, is expected to be immediately accretive to earnings.

On November 1, 2010, PPL completed the $7.625 billion acquisition (announced on April 28, 2010) of E.ON U.S. LLC, the parent company of Kentucky's two major utilities, Louisville Gas & Electric Company (LG&E) and Kentucky Utilities Company (KU). LG&E and KU, which have combined power generating capacity of about 8,100 megawatts (mw), provide electricity service to 939,000 customers, mostly in Kentucky, with some customers in Virginia and Tennessee. LG&E also provides natural gas delivery service to 320,000 customers in Kentucky. PPL paid for the transaction with $6.7 billion of cash and through the assumption of $925 million of tax-exempt debt. Including the projected tax benefits with a present value of about $450 million, PPL has effectively valued the transaction at $7.125 billion.

## Company Financials Fiscal Year Ended Dec. 31

| Per Share Data ($) | 2010 | 2009 | 2008 | 2007 | 2006 | 2005 | 2004 | 2003 | 2002 | 2001 |
|---|---|---|---|---|---|---|---|---|---|---|
| Tangible Book Value | 11.34 | 10.80 | 9.93 | 11.33 | 9.35 | 7.73 | 7.50 | 5.53 | 5.87 | 6.98 |
| Earnings | 2.20 | 1.18 | 2.45 | 2.63 | 2.29 | 1.92 | 1.89 | 2.08 | 1.17 | 0.58 |
| S&P Core Earnings | 2.32 | 1.23 | 1.86 | 2.61 | 2.33 | 1.87 | 1.74 | 1.95 | 0.79 | 0.90 |
| Dividends | 1.40 | 1.38 | 1.34 | 1.22 | 1.10 | 1.21 | 0.82 | 0.77 | 0.68 | 0.53 |
| Payout Ratio | 63% | 117% | 55% | 47% | 48% | 63% | 43% | 37% | 57% | 92% |
| Prices:High | 32.77 | 34.42 | 55.23 | 54.58 | 37.34 | 33.68 | 27.08 | 22.17 | 19.98 | 31.18 |
| Prices:Low | 23.75 | 24.25 | 26.84 | 34.43 | 27.83 | 25.52 | 19.92 | 15.83 | 13.00 | 15.50 |
| P/E Ratio:High | 15 | 29 | 23 | 21 | 16 | 18 | 14 | 11 | 17 | 54 |
| P/E Ratio:Low | 11 | 21 | 11 | 13 | 12 | 13 | 11 | 8 | 11 | 27 |

| Income Statement Analysis (Million $) | | | | | | | | | | |
|---|---|---|---|---|---|---|---|---|---|---|
| Revenue | 8,521 | 7,556 | 8,044 | 6,498 | 6,899 | 6,219 | 5,812 | 5,587 | 5,429 | 5,725 |
| Depreciation | 786 | 556 | 551 | 756 | 446 | 420 | 412 | 380 | 367 | 254 |
| Maintenance | NA | NA | NA | NA | NA | NA | NA | NA | 314 | 269 |
| Fixed Charges Coverage | 3.10 | 2.60 | 3.86 | 3.61 | 3.46 | 2.70 | 2.72 | 2.72 | 2.49 | 3.08 |
| Construction Credits | NA | NA | NA | NA | NA | NA | NA | NA | NA | NA |
| Effective Tax Rate | 21.2% | 21.8% | 32.3% | 20.7% | 23.5% | 14.0% | 21.6% | 18.5% | 29.5% | 54.4% |
| Net Income | 955 | 447 | 922 | 1,013 | 885 | 737 | 700 | 748 | 425 | 221 |
| S&P Core Earnings | 1,005 | 466 | 705 | 1,007 | 897 | 716 | 645 | 674 | 240 | 262 |

| Balance Sheet & Other Financial Data (Million $) | | | | | | | | | | |
|---|---|---|---|---|---|---|---|---|---|---|
| Gross Property | 29,300 | 21,385 | 20,299 | 20,377 | 20,079 | 18,615 | 18,692 | 17,775 | 16,406 | 12,477 |
| Capital Expenditures | 1,597 | 1,225 | 1,429 | 1,685 | 1,394 | 811 | 703 | 771 | 648 | 565 |
| Net Property | 20,858 | 13,174 | 12,416 | 12,605 | 12,069 | 10,916 | 11,209 | 10,446 | 9,566 | 6,135 |
| Capitalization:Long Term Debt | 12,161 | 7,143 | 7,151 | 6,890 | 6,728 | 6,044 | 6,881 | 8,145 | 6,562 | 5,906 |
| Capitalization:% Long Term Debt | 59.7 | 56.5 | 57.1 | 54.1 | 55.4 | 57.5 | 61.6 | 71.1 | 74.0 | 75.3 |
| Capitalization:Preferred | Nil | Nil | 301 | 301 | 301 | 51.0 | 51.0 | 51.0 | 82.0 | 82.0 |
| Capitalization:% Preferred | Nil | Nil | 2.40 | 2.40 | 2.50 | 0.50 | 0.46 | 0.45 | 0.92 | 1.05 |
| Capitalization:Common | 8,210 | 5,496 | 5,077 | 5,556 | 5,122 | 4,418 | 4,239 | 3,259 | 2,224 | 1,857 |
| Capitalization:% Common | 40.3 | 43.5 | 40.5 | 43.5 | 42.1 | 42.0 | 37.9 | 28.5 | 25.1 | 23.7 |
| Total Capital | 21,141 | 12,958 | 14,311 | 14,958 | 14,241 | 12,766 | 13,653 | 13,710 | 11,274 | 9,332 |
| % Operating Ratio | 81.2 | 89.0 | 82.9 | 78.3 | 80.8 | 80.3 | 79.5 | 78.9 | 76.8 | 81.1 |
| % Earned on Net Property | 11.0 | 7.5 | 14.5 | 13.6 | 13.9 | 12.2 | 12.7 | 13.4 | 17.5 | 14.2 |
| % Return on Revenue | 11.2 | 5.9 | 11.5 | 15.6 | 12.8 | 11.9 | 12.0 | 13.4 | 7.8 | 3.9 |
| % Return on Invested Capital | 9.2 | 6.9 | 9.6 | 12.1 | 10.3 | 9.5 | 9.0 | 10.0 | 12.6 | 12.4 |
| % Return on Common Equity | 13.9 | 8.5 | 17.3 | 19.0 | 18.6 | 17.0 | 18.6 | 26.2 | 17.5 | 8.7 |

Data as orig reptd.; bef. results of disc opers/spec. items. Per share data adj. for stk. divs.; EPS diluted. E-Estimated. NA-Not Available. NM-Not Meaningful. NR-Not Ranked. UR-Under Review.

**Office:** Two North Ninth Street, Allentown, PA 18101-1179.
**Telephone:** 610-774-5151.
**Email:** invrel@pplweb.com
**Website:** http://www.pplweb.com

**Chrmn & CEO:** J.H. Miller
**Pres & CEO:** W.H. Spence
**SVP, Secy & General Counsel:** R.J. Grey
**CFO:** P. Farr

**Treas:** J.E. Abel
**Investor Contact:** T.J. Paukovits (610-774-4124)
**Board Members:** F. Bernthal, J. W. Conway, S. G. Elliott, L. Goeser, S. E. Graham, S. Heydt, V. R. Madabhushi, J. H. Miller, R. Rajamannar, C. A. Rogerson, W. H. Spence, N. Von Althann, K. H. Williamson

**Founded:** 1920
**Domicile:** Pennsylvania
**Employees:** 13,809

The **McGraw·Hill** Companies

# Praxair Inc.

**STANDARD &POOR'S**

| S&P Recommendation | BUY ★★★★★ | Price<br>$93.51 (as of Nov 25, 2011) | 12-Mo. Target Price<br>$115.00 | Investment Style<br>Large-Cap Growth |
|---|---|---|---|---|

**GICS Sector** Materials
**Sub-Industry** Industrial Gases

**Summary** This company is the largest producer of industrial gases in North and South America, and the second largest worldwide. It also provides ceramic and metallic coatings.

## Key Stock Statistics (Source S&P, Vickers, company reports)

| | | | | | | | | |
|---|---|---|---|---|---|---|---|---|
| 52-Wk Range | $111.74– 88.64 | S&P Oper. EPS 2011**E** | 5.42 | Market Capitalization(B) | $28.031 | Beta | | 0.86 |
| Trailing 12-Month EPS | $4.49 | S&P Oper. EPS 2012**E** | 6.10 | Yield (%) | 2.14 | S&P 3-Yr. Proj. EPS CAGR(%) | | 12 |
| Trailing 12-Month P/E | 20.8 | P/E on S&P Oper. EPS 2011**E** | 17.3 | Dividend Rate/Share | $2.00 | S&P Credit Rating | | A |
| $10K Invested 5 Yrs Ago | $16,261 | Common Shares Outstg. (M) | 299.8 | Institutional Ownership (%) | 90 | | |

## Price Performance

- 30-Week Mov. Avg. · · ·
- 10-Week Mov. Avg. - -
- **GAAP Earnings vs. Previous Year**
- Volume Above Avg. ▮▮▮ STARS
- 12-Mo. Target Price —
- Relative Strength —
- ▲ Up ▼ Down ▶ No Change
- Below Avg. ▮▮▮ ★

Options: ASE, CBOE, Ph

Analysis prepared by Equity Analyst **R. O'Reilly, CFA** on Aug 02, 2011, when the stock traded at **$100.57**.

## Qualitative Risk Assessment

| LOW | MEDIUM | HIGH |
|---|---|---|

Our risk assessment reflects the relatively stable growth and cash flow of the industrial gases industry versus commodity chemicals, and PX's superior S&P Quality Ranking of A+, offset by the company's exposure to volatile energy costs.

## Quantitative Evaluations

**S&P Quality Ranking** A+

| D | C | B- | B | B+ | A- | A | A+ |
|---|---|---|---|---|---|---|---|

**Relative Strength Rank** MODERATE

50

LOWEST = 1 HIGHEST = 99

## Revenue/Earnings Data

**Revenue (Million $)**

| | 1Q | 2Q | 3Q | 4Q | Year |
|---|---|---|---|---|---|
| 2011 | 2,702 | 2,858 | 2,896 | -- | -- |
| 2010 | 2,428 | 2,527 | 2,538 | 2,623 | 10,116 |
| 2009 | 2,123 | 2,138 | 2,288 | 2,407 | 8,956 |
| 2008 | 2,663 | 2,878 | 2,852 | 2,403 | 10,796 |
| 2007 | 2,175 | 2,332 | 2,372 | 2,523 | 9,402 |
| 2006 | 2,026 | 2,076 | 2,099 | 2,123 | 8,324 |

**Earnings Per Share ($)**

| | | | | | |
|---|---|---|---|---|---|
| 2011 | 1.29 | 1.38 | 1.40 | E1.35 | E5.42 |
| 2010 | 1.01 | 1.19 | 1.21 | 0.43 | 3.84 |
| 2009 | 0.93 | 0.96 | 1.04 | 1.09 | 4.01 |
| 2008 | 0.96 | 1.08 | 1.11 | 0.64 | 3.80 |
| 2007 | 0.81 | 0.89 | 0.94 | 0.98 | 3.62 |
| 2006 | 0.68 | 0.75 | 0.75 | 0.82 | 3.00 |

Fiscal year ended Dec. 31. Next earnings report expected: Late January. EPS Estimates based on S&P Operating Earnings; historical GAAP earnings are as reported.

## Highlights

➤ We expect sales in 2011 to increase about 11%, to about $11.2 billion, followed by further growth in 2012, on growing global demand for industrial gases and applications, including during the second half of 2011. We also expect a modest positive trend in merchant prices in North America. In March 2011, PX sold its U.S. home health care business, which had annual sales of about $150 million.

➤ We look for Surface Technologies' sales (6% of total) to be stronger in 2011 on greater demand for coatings services for commercial jet engines and industrial uses, and an expected recovery in gas turbines.

➤ We forecast that operating margins in 2011 will be almost 22%, modestly higher than the 21.4% in 2010, on the volume leverage and continuing productivity improvements, excluding any impact from the pass-through of changes in energy costs. We expect higher interest expense in 2011, and an effective tax rate of 28%. Reported EPS for 2010 includes charges totaling $0.90, mostly in the fourth quarter.

## Investment Rationale/Risk

➤ Our buy opinion is based on valuation and our view of the company's favorable earnings outlook. The shares were recently trading at about 19X our 2011 EPS estimate of $5.45. We believe the global manufacturing sector will continue to strengthen modestly, which should result in growing demand for industrial gases, while the scheduled start-up through 2014 of a record backlog of new gases plants should also contribute to revenue growth over the next few years.

➤ Risks to our recommendation and target price include an unexpected decline in industrial activity, especially in general manufacturing and metal-related markets; higher-than-projected power and natural gas costs; and an inability to rapidly develop and successfully introduce new products and applications for industrial gases.

➤ Our 12-month target price of $115 assumes a multiple of 21X our 2011 EPS estimate, above industry peers, reflecting our view of the company's EPS growth outlook. The quarterly dividend was raised in January 2011 for the 18th consecutive year. We expect PX to continue to repurchase its common stock.

## Dividend Data (Dates: mm/dd Payment Date: mm/dd/yy)

| Amount ($) | Date Decl. | Ex-Div. Date | Stk. of Record | Payment Date |
|---|---|---|---|---|
| 0.500 | 01/26 | 03/03 | 03/07 | 03/15/11 |
| 0.500 | 04/27 | 06/03 | 06/07 | 06/15/11 |
| 0.500 | 07/27 | 09/02 | 09/07 | 09/15/11 |
| 0.500 | 10/26 | 12/05 | 12/07 | 12/15/11 |

Dividends have been paid since 1992. Source: Company reports.

---

**Please read the Required Disclosures and Analyst Certification on the last page of this report.**

The **McGraw·Hill** Companies

# Praxair Inc.

STANDARD &POOR'S

## Business Summary August 02, 2011

CORPORATE OVERVIEW. Praxair Inc. (PX), the largest producer of industrial gases in North and South America, serves about 25 diverse industries across more than 40 countries. Foreign sales accounted for 61% of the total in 2010, with Brazil alone providing 16%.

PX conducts its industrial gases business through four operating segments: North America (51% of sales and 55% of profits in 2010); South America (19%, 21%); Europe (13%,12%); and Asia (11%, 8%). The capital-intensive industrial gases business involves the production, distribution and sale of atmospheric gases (oxygen, nitrogen, argon and rare gases), carbon dioxide, hydrogen, helium, acetylene, and specialty and electronic gases. Atmospheric gases are produced through air separation processes, primarily cryogenic, while other gases are produced by various methods. PX also produces specialty products (sputtering targets, mechanical planarization slurries and polishing pads, and coatings) for use in semiconductor manufacturing. In addition, the business includes the construction and sale of equipment to produce industrial gases.

Industrial gases are supplied to customers through three basic methods: on-

site/pipeline (25% of total 2010 sales, sold under long-term contracts), merchant (30%, with three- to five-year contracts) and packaged (29%). At the end of 2010, the company had 250 major production facilities (air separation, hydrogen and carbon dioxide plants) and five major pipeline complexes in North America; more than 50 facilities and three pipeline complexes (in Spain and Germany) in Europe; more than 40 plants in South America, primarily in Brazil; and 35 plants in Asia, mainly in China, Korea, India and Thailand. The company's industrial gases operations in South America are conducted by S.A. White Martins, the largest producer of industrial gases in the region.

The Surface Technologies business (6%, 4%) applies metallic and ceramic coatings and powders to parts and equipment provided by customers, including aircraft engine, printing, power generation and other industrial markets, and manufactures electric arc, plasma and oxygen fuel spray equipment.

## Company Financials Fiscal Year Ended Dec. 31

| Per Share Data ($) | 2010 | 2009 | 2008 | 2007 | 2006 | 2005 | 2004 | 2003 | 2002 | 2001 |
|---|---|---|---|---|---|---|---|---|---|---|
| Tangible Book Value | 11.82 | 10.12 | 6.45 | 9.64 | 8.91 | 7.05 | 6.08 | 6.00 | 4.03 | 7.59 |
| Cash Flow | 6.81 | 6.72 | 6.48 | 6.01 | 5.12 | 4.23 | 3.85 | 3.33 | 3.12 | 2.84 |
| Earnings | 3.84 | 4.01 | 3.80 | 3.62 | 3.00 | 2.22 | 2.10 | 1.77 | 1.66 | 1.32 |
| S&P Core Earnings | 4.00 | 4.62 | 3.60 | 3.55 | 2.99 | 2.16 | 2.02 | 1.67 | 1.38 | 1.04 |
| Dividends | 1.80 | 1.60 | 1.50 | 1.20 | 1.00 | 0.72 | 0.60 | 0.46 | 0.38 | 0.34 |
| Payout Ratio | 47% | 40% | 39% | 33% | 33% | 32% | 29% | 26% | 23% | 26% |
| Prices:High | 96.34 | 86.07 | 99.74 | 92.12 | 63.70 | 54.31 | 46.25 | 38.26 | 30.56 | 27.96 |
| Prices:Low | 72.70 | 53.35 | 4740 | 57.97 | 50.36 | 41.06 | 34.52 | 25.02 | 22.28 | 18.25 |
| P/E Ratio:High | 25 | 21 | 26 | 25 | 21 | 24 | 22 | 22 | 18 | 21 |
| P/E Ratio:Low | 19 | 13 | 12 | 16 | 17 | 18 | 16 | 14 | 13 | 14 |

| Income Statement Analysis (Million $) | | | | | | | | | | |
|---|---|---|---|---|---|---|---|---|---|---|
| Revenue | 10,116 | 8,956 | 10,796 | 9,402 | 8,324 | 7,656 | 6,594 | 5,613 | 5,128 | 5,158 |
| Operating Income | 3,007 | 2,449 | 2,892 | 2,557 | 2,183 | 1,948 | 1,681 | 1,444 | 1,358 | 1,333 |
| Depreciation | 925 | 846 | 850 | 774 | 696 | 665 | 578 | 517 | 483 | 499 |
| Interest Expense | 118 | 138 | 247 | 208 | 155 | 163 | 155 | 151 | 206 | 224 |
| Pretax Income | 2,002 | 1,466 | 1,721 | 1,639 | 1,312 | 1,145 | 959 | 735 | 726 | 585 |
| Effective Tax Rate | NA | 11.5% | 27.0% | 25.6% | 27.1% | 32.8% | 24.2% | 23.7% | 21.8% | 23.1% |
| Net Income | 1,195 | 1,254 | 1,211 | 1,177 | 988 | 732 | 697 | 585 | 548 | 432 |
| S&P Core Earnings | 1,244 | 1,441 | 1,145 | 1,154 | 983 | 711 | 671 | 552 | 454 | 343 |

| Balance Sheet & Other Financial Data (Million $) | | | | | | | | | | |
|---|---|---|---|---|---|---|---|---|---|---|
| Cash | 39.0 | 45.0 | 32.0 | 17.0 | 36.0 | 173 | 25.0 | 50.0 | 39.0 | 39.0 |
| Current Assets | 2,378 | 2,223 | 2,301 | 2,408 | 2,059 | 2,133 | 1,744 | 1,449 | 1,286 | 1,276 |
| Total Assets | 15,274 | 14,317 | 13,054 | 13,382 | 11,102 | 10,491 | 9,878 | 8,305 | 7,401 | 7,715 |
| Current Liabilities | 2,110 | 1,813 | 2,979 | 2,650 | 1,758 | 2,001 | 1,875 | 1,117 | 1,100 | 1,194 |
| Long Term Debt | 5,155 | 4,757 | 3,709 | 3,364 | 2,981 | 2,926 | 2,876 | 2,661 | 2,510 | 2,725 |
| Common Equity | 5,792 | 5,315 | 4,009 | 5,142 | 4,554 | 3,902 | 3,608 | 3,088 | 2,340 | 2,477 |
| Total Capital | 11,332 | 10,476 | 8,551 | 8,506 | 7,757 | 6,828 | 6,709 | 5,944 | 5,014 | 5,363 |
| Capital Expenditures | 1,388 | 1,352 | 1,611 | 1,376 | 1,100 | 877 | 668 | 983 | 498 | 595 |
| Cash Flow | 2,120 | 2,100 | 2,061 | 1,951 | 1,684 | 1,397 | 1,275 | 1,102 | 1,031 | 931 |
| Current Ratio | 1.1 | 1.2 | 0.8 | 0.9 | 1.2 | 1.1 | 0.9 | 1.3 | 1.2 | 1.1 |
| % Long Term Debt of Capitalization | 45.5 | 45.4 | 43.4 | 39.5 | 38.4 | 42.9 | 42.9 | 44.8 | 50.1 | 50.8 |
| % Net Income of Revenue | 11.8 | 14.0 | 11.2 | 12.5 | 11.9 | 9.6 | 10.6 | 10.4 | 10.7 | 8.4 |
| % Return on Assets | 8.1 | 9.2 | 9.2 | 9.6 | 9.2 | 7.2 | 7.7 | 7.4 | 7.3 | 5.6 |
| % Return on Equity | 21.5 | 26.9 | 26.5 | 24.3 | 23.4 | 19.5 | 20.8 | 21.6 | 22.8 | 17.9 |

Data as orig reptd.; bef. results of disc opers/spec. items. Per share data adj. for stk. divs.; EPS diluted. E-Estimated. NA-Not Available. NM-Not Meaningful. NR-Not Ranked. UR-Under Review.

**Office:** 39 Old Ridgebury Rd, Danbury, CT 06810-5113.
**Telephone:** 203-837-2000.
**Website:** http://www.praxair.com
**Chrmn, Pres & CEO:** S.F. Angel

**EVP & CFO:** J.S. Sawyer
**SVP & CTO:** R.P. Roberge
**SVP, Secy & General Counsel:** J.T. Breedlove
**Treas:** T.S. Heenan

**Board Members:** S. F. Angel, O. D. Bernardes, N. K. Dicciani, E. G. Galante, C. W. Gargalli, I. D. Hall, R. W. Leboeuf, L. D. McVay, W. T. Smith, R. L. Wood

**Founded:** 1988
**Domicile:** Delaware
**Employees:** 26,261

Stock Report | November 26, 2011 | NYS Symbol: **PCP** | **PCP** is in the S&P 500

# Precision Castparts Corp.

**STANDARD &POOR'S**

**S&P Recommendation** BUY ★★★★☆

**Price**
$152.93 (as of Nov 25, 2011)

**12-Mo. Target Price**
$200.00

**Investment Style**
Large-Cap Growth

**GICS Sector** Industrials
**Sub-Industry** Aerospace & Defense

**Summary** This company is a provider of complex cast and forged metal components used primarily in the manufacture of jet engines and industrial gas turbines, and in the oil and gas, chemicals and automotive industries.

## Key Stock Statistics (Source S&P, Vickers, company reports)

| | | | | | | | |
|---|---|---|---|---|---|---|---|
| 52-Wk Range | $178.98– 135.23 | S&P Oper. EPS 2012E | 8.55 | Market Capitalization(B) | $22.051 | Beta | 1.42 |
| Trailing 12-Month EPS | $7.66 | S&P Oper. EPS 2013E | 10.15 | Yield (%) | 0.08 | S&P 3-Yr. Proj. EPS CAGR(%) | 18 |
| Trailing 12-Month P/E | 20.0 | P/E on S&P Oper. EPS 2012E | 17.9 | Dividend Rate/Share | $0.12 | S&P Credit Rating | A- |
| $10K Invested 5 Yrs Ago | $20,295 | Common Shares Outstg. (M) | 144.2 | Institutional Ownership (%) | 96 | | |

## Price Performance

- 30-Week Mov. Avg. ···
- 10-Week Mov. Avg. --
- GAAP Earnings vs. Previous Year
- Volume Above Avg.
- STARS
- 12-Mo. Target Price —
- Relative Strength —
- ▲ Up ▼ Down ▶ No Change
- Below Avg.

Options: ASE, CBOE, Ph

Analysis prepared by Equity Analyst **R. Tortoriello** on Nov 15, 2011, when the stock traded at **$163.84**.

## Qualitative Risk Assessment

LOW **MEDIUM** HIGH

Precision Castparts operates in a cyclical and capital-intensive industry and is subject to swings in commodity prices. However, due to PCP's large market share in most markets, we believe the company has significant pricing power for its products. We also consider its financial condition to be solid, including a relatively low debt level (total debt was 3% of capital as of September 2011).

## Quantitative Evaluations

**S&P Quality Ranking** B

| D | C | B- | **B** | B+ | A- | A | A+ |
|---|---|---|---|---|---|---|---|

**Relative Strength Rank** MODERATE

53

LOWEST = 1    HIGHEST = 99

## Highlights

► We project a sales rise of 18% in FY 12 (Mar.), as global aerospace OEM production increases. Specifically, we see rising production schedules at Boeing and Airbus, with production increases scheduled through early 2014; a production ramp on the 787 from 2.5 currently to 10 scheduled by the end of 2013; and modest production increases for business jets. We also look for a slow recovery unfolding in industrial gas turbines and seamless pipe, expect good growth in aerospace aftermarket parts demand, and see PCP's general industrial business recovering. For FY 13, we are modeling a 15% revenue increase.

► We estimate an operating margin of 25.0% for FY 12, versus FY 11's 24.2%, as we expect a rebound in margins (FY 10's operating margins were 25.9%), due to improvement in the seamless pipe market and in fasteners, as well as continued efficiency improvements at PCP. We project further improvement to 26% in FY 13.

► We project EPS of $8.55 in FY 12, with growth to $10.15 in FY 13.

## Investment Rationale/Risk

► We recently downgraded the shares to buy, from strong buy, on valuation. We see six- to seven-year order backlogs at both Boeing and Airbus, as well as increased recent order rates, supporting production increases at both planemakers. We also see opportunity for PCP with the 787, for which Boeing had about 820 aircraft on order as of the end of October. PCP estimates revenues of $5.5 million per aircraft on the 787, with about half in Fastener Products. We also expect further operating leverage at the company as sales volumes rise, aiding profit margins.

► Risks to our recommendation and target price include a slower-than-anticipated rise in aerospace demand, 787 production delays, and operational or other difficulties.

► Our 12-month target price of $200 is based on an enterprise value to estimated FY 13 EBITDA multiple of 12.5X, above PCP's 20-year average of 9.5X. We believe an unusually strong aerospace cycle and improvement in PCP's other markets warrant the above-average multiple.

## Revenue/Earnings Data

### Revenue (Million $)

| | 1Q | 2Q | 3Q | 4Q | Year |
|---|---|---|---|---|---|
| 2012 | 1,675 | 1,790 | -- | -- | -- |
| 2011 | 1,447 | 1,508 | 1,590 | 1,675 | 6,220 |
| 2010 | 1,376 | 1,298 | 1,372 | 1,441 | 5,487 |
| 2009 | 1,810 | 1,799 | 1,615 | 1,604 | 6,828 |
| 2008 | 1,660 | 1,727 | 1,697 | 1,791 | 6,852 |
| 2007 | 1,112 | 1,318 | 1,385 | 1,547 | 5,361 |

### Earnings Per Share ($)

| | | | | | |
|---|---|---|---|---|---|
| 2012 | 1.97 | 2.03 | E2.19 | E2.36 | E8.55 |
| 2011 | 1.65 | 1.70 | 1.80 | 1.87 | 7.01 |
| 2010 | 1.70 | 1.54 | 1.61 | 1.66 | 6.50 |
| 2009 | 1.94 | 1.88 | 1.69 | 1.87 | 7.38 |
| 2008 | 1.61 | 1.67 | 1.73 | 1.88 | 6.89 |
| 2007 | 0.83 | 1.03 | 1.15 | 1.44 | 4.45 |

Fiscal year ended Mar. 31. Next earnings report expected: Late January. EPS Estimates based on S&P Operating Earnings; historical GAAP earnings are as reported.

## Dividend Data (Dates: mm/dd Payment Date: mm/dd/yy)

| Amount ($) | Date Decl. | Ex-Div. Date | Stk. of Record | Payment Date |
|---|---|---|---|---|
| 0.030 | 02/18 | 03/02 | 03/04 | 04/04/11 |
| 0.030 | 05/26 | 06/08 | 06/10 | 07/05/11 |
| 0.030 | 08/17 | 09/07 | 09/09 | 10/03/11 |
| 0.030 | 11/18 | 12/07 | 12/09 | 01/03/12 |

Dividends have been paid since 1978. Source: Company reports.

**Please read the Required Disclosures and Analyst Certification on the last page of this report.**

Redistribution or reproduction is prohibited without written permission. Copyright ©2011 The McGraw-Hill Companies, Inc.

*The McGraw-Hill Companies*

# Precision Castparts Corp.

STANDARD &POOR'S

## Business Summary November 15, 2011

CORPORATE OVERVIEW. Precision Castparts, a manufacturer of jet engine and industrial gas turbine (IGT) engine components, conducts business through three operating units. The aerospace market accounted for 62% of FY 11 (Mar.) sales, power generation for 27%, and general industrial and automotive for the remaining 11%. General Electric accounted for 12.5% of FY 11 sales. Although no other customer accounted for more than 10% of sales, the Pratt & Whitney division of United Technologies, Rolls-Royce and Boeing are all key customers.

PCP's Investment Cast Products segment (34% and 41% of FY 11 revenues and operating earnings, respectively) includes Aerospace Structural Castings, Aerospace Airfoil Castings, IGT Castings, and the Specialty Materials and Alloys Group (SMAG). These operations manufacture investment castings for aircraft engines, IGT engines, and airframes. PCP also makes metal castings for medical prostheses, unmanned aerial vehicles, satellites, and armament systems (such as howitzers). Investment casting involves a technical, multi-step process that uses ceramic molds in the manufacture of metal components with more complex shapes, closer tolerances and finer surface finishes than parts manufactured using other casting methods. PCP is the world's largest maker of jet engine structural castings used to strengthen sections of a jet engine, and makes castings for every jet engine program in production or

under development. It is also the leading supplier of investment casts for industrial gas turbine (IGT) engines, used in power generation. The company emphasizes low-cost, high-quality products and timely delivery. SMAG principally provides metal alloys to the company's investment casting operations, as well as to other companies with investment casting or other foundry operations.

The Forged Products segment (45% of sales and 33% of operating income) is a large maker of forged components for the aerospace and power generation markets. Forged Products segment aerospace and IGT sales are primarily derived from the same large engine customers served by the Investment Cast segment, with additional aerospace sales to manufacturers of landing gear and airframes. In addition, Forged Products manufactures high-performance nickel-based alloys used to produce forged components for aerospace and non-aerospace markets, which includes products for oil and gas, chemical processing and pollution control applications.

## Company Financials Fiscal Year Ended Mar. 31

| Per Share Data ($) | 2011 | 2010 | 2009 | 2008 | 2007 | 2006 | 2005 | 2004 | 2003 | 2002 |
|---|---|---|---|---|---|---|---|---|---|---|
| Tangible Book Value | 26.56 | 18.13 | 16.42 | 12.28 | 5.37 | 3.56 | 1.51 | 0.62 | 0.74 | NM |
| Cash Flow | 8.16 | 7.60 | 8.37 | 7.81 | 5.27 | 3.30 | 2.53 | 1.73 | 2.28 | 1.37 |
| Earnings | 7.01 | 6.51 | 7.38 | 6.89 | 4.45 | 2.57 | 1.80 | 1.18 | 1.51 | 0.41 |
| S&P Core Earnings | 6.96 | 6.49 | 6.95 | 6.87 | 4.47 | 2.51 | 1.79 | 1.21 | 1.17 | 0.63 |
| Dividends | NA | 0.12 | 0.12 | 0.12 | 0.11 | 0.06 | 0.06 | 0.06 | 0.06 | 0.06 |
| Payout Ratio | NA | 2% | 2% | 2% | 2% | 2% | 3% | 5% | 4% | 15% |
| Calendar Year | 2010 | 2009 | 2008 | 2007 | 2006 | 2005 | 2004 | 2003 | 2002 | 2001 |
| Prices:High | 145.40 | 115.60 | 142.94 | 160.73 | 80.90 | 53.91 | 34.19 | 22.97 | 19.00 | 24.75 |
| Prices:Low | 100.99 | 47.71 | 47.08 | 77.51 | 48.80 | 31.15 | 20.68 | 10.61 | 8.43 | 9.00 |
| P/E Ratio:High | 21 | 18 | 19 | 23 | 18 | 21 | 19 | 19 | 13 | 61 |
| P/E Ratio:Low | 14 | 7 | 6 | 11 | 11 | 12 | 11 | 9 | 6 | 22 |

| Income Statement Analysis (Million $) | | | | | | | | | | |
|---|---|---|---|---|---|---|---|---|---|---|
| Revenue | 6,220 | 5,487 | 6,828 | 6,852 | 5,361 | 3,546 | 2,919 | 2,175 | 2,117 | 2,557 |
| Operating Income | 1,666 | 1,576 | 1,739 | 1,639 | 1,086 | 656 | 517 | 380 | 390 | 448 |
| Depreciation | 164 | 155 | 139 | 128 | 113 | 99.2 | 97.0 | 88.2 | 82.5 | 101 |
| Interest Expense | 13.5 | 16.2 | 18.1 | 81.0 | 52.2 | 41.4 | 56.6 | 54.1 | 56.4 | 66.2 |
| Pretax Income | 1,510 | 1,411 | 1,578 | 1,463 | 918 | 513 | 360 | 212 | 242 | 135 |
| Effective Tax Rate | NA | 34.4% | 34.2% | 33.9% | 33.2% | 31.6% | 33.7% | 35.7% | 34.5% | 68.6% |
| Net Income | 1,011 | 924 | 1,038 | 966 | 615 | 349 | 240 | 136 | 159 | 42.4 |
| S&P Core Earnings | 1,003 | 924 | 978 | 963 | 618 | 341 | 237 | 140 | 123 | 65.4 |

| Balance Sheet & Other Financial Data (Million $) | | | | | | | | | | |
|---|---|---|---|---|---|---|---|---|---|---|
| Cash | 1,159 | 112 | 554 | 221 | 150 | 59.9 | 154 | 80.3 | 28.7 | 38.1 |
| Current Assets | 3,651 | 2,522 | 2,785 | 2,372 | 2,037 | 1,234 | 1,213 | 1,188 | 786 | 878 |
| Total Assets | 8,956 | 7,661 | 6,721 | 6,050 | 5,259 | 3,751 | 3,625 | 3,756 | 2,467 | 2,565 |
| Current Liabilities | 942 | 894 | 1,061 | 1,205 | 1,658 | 768 | 780 | 913 | 625 | 727 |
| Long Term Debt | 222 | 235 | 251 | 335 | 319 | 600 | 799 | 823 | 532 | 697 |
| Common Equity | 7,162 | 5,889 | 4,860 | 4,045 | 2,836 | 2,244 | 1,780 | 1,715 | 1,062 | 952 |
| Total Capital | 7,404 | 6,142 | 5,222 | 4,400 | 3,182 | 2,844 | 2,579 | 2,538 | 1,594 | 1,649 |
| Capital Expenditures | 120 | 170 | 205 | 226 | 222 | 99.2 | 61.7 | 65.5 | 70.5 | 125 |
| Cash Flow | 1,175 | 1,080 | 1,177 | 1,094 | 727 | 448 | 337 | 224 | 242 | 143 |
| Current Ratio | 3.9 | 2.8 | 2.6 | 2.0 | 1.2 | 1.6 | 1.6 | 1.3 | 1.3 | 1.2 |
| % Long Term Debt of Capitalization | 3.0 | Nil | 4.8 | 7.6 | 10.0 | 21.1 | 31.0 | 32.4 | 33.4 | 42.3 |
| % Net Income of Revenue | 16.3 | 16.9 | 15.2 | 14.1 | 11.5 | 9.8 | 8.2 | 6.2 | 7.5 | 1.7 |
| % Return on Assets | NA | NA | 16.3 | 17.1 | 13.6 | 9.5 | 6.5 | 4.4 | 6.3 | 1.7 |
| % Return on Equity | NA | NA | 23.3 | 28.1 | 24.7 | 17.0 | 13.7 | 9.8 | 15.8 | 4.6 |

Data as orig reptd.; bef. results of disc opers/spec. items. Per share data adj. for stk. divs.; EPS diluted. E-Estimated. NA-Not Available. NM-Not Meaningful. NR-Not Ranked. UR-Under Review.

**Office:** 4650 SW Macadam Ave Ste 400, Portland, OR 97239-4262.
**Telephone:** 503-417-4850.
**Email:** info@precastcorp.com
**Website:** http://www.precast.com

**Chrmn, Pres & CEO:** M. Donegan
**SVP, CFO & Chief Acctg Officer:** S.R. Hagel
**Treas:** S.C. Blackmore
**Secy & General Counsel:** R.A. Cooke

**Investor Contact:** W.D. Larsson
**Board Members:** M. Donegan, D. R. Graber, L. L. Lyles, D. J. Murphy, Jr., V. E. Oechsle, S. G. Rothmeier, U. Schmidt, R. L. Wambold, T. A. Wicks

**Founded:** 1949
**Domicile:** Oregon
**Employees:** 18,130

# priceline.com Inc

**STANDARD &POOR'S**

| S&P Recommendation | HOLD ★★★☆☆ | Price $459.18 (as of Nov 25, 2011) | 12-Mo. Target Price $650.00 | Investment Style Large-Cap Growth |
|---|---|---|---|---|

**GICS Sector** Consumer Discretionary
**Sub-Industry** Internet Retail

**Summary** This company is a leading provider of online travel services, primarily in Europe and the U.S.

## Key Stock Statistics (Source S&P, Vickers, company reports)

| | | | | | |
|---|---|---|---|---|---|
| 52-Wk Range | $561.88–392.05 | S&P Oper. EPS 2011**E** | 20.50 | Market Capitalization(B) | $22.860 |
| Trailing 12-Month EPS | $18.88 | S&P Oper. EPS 2012**E** | 25.00 | Yield (%) | Nil |
| Trailing 12-Month P/E | 24.3 | P/E on S&P Oper. EPS 2011**E** | 22.4 | Dividend Rate/Share | Nil |
| $10K Invested 5 Yrs Ago | $118,498 | Common Shares Outstg. (M) | 49.8 | Institutional Ownership (%) | 99 |

| | |
|---|---|
| Beta | 1.15 |
| S&P 3-Yr. Proj. EPS CAGR(%) | 35 |
| S&P Credit Rating | BBB- |

## Price Performance

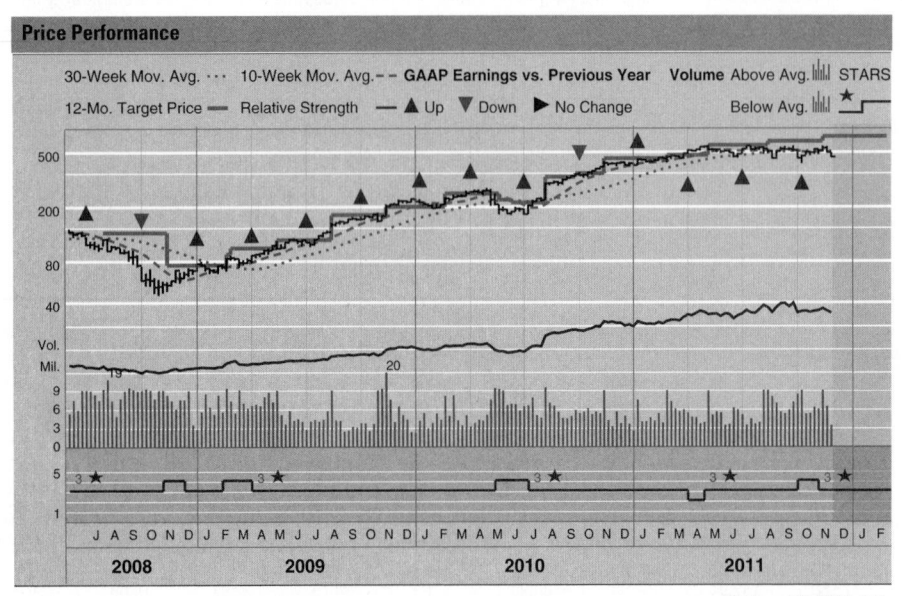

30-Week Mov. Avg.  ···· 10-Week Mov. Avg. -- GAAP Earnings vs. Previous Year   Volume Above Avg. STARS
12-Mo. Target Price — Relative Strength — ▲ Up ▼ Down ► No Change   Below Avg.

Options: ASE, CBOE, P, Ph

Analysis prepared by Equity Analyst **Scott Kessler** on Nov 09, 2011, when the stock traded at **$538.35**.

## Highlights

➤ We estimate revenues will increase 40% in 2011 and 25% in 2012, due to market share gains, healthy volumes, and stable-to-improving pricing, offset somewhat by notable European economic uncertainties. We expect international and merchant operations to drive growth, reflecting PCLN's past acquisitions of Active Hotels and Bookings B.V., providers of Internet hotel reservation services in Europe, which have enabled the company to become an overseas leader in online hotel reservations.

➤ We believe PCLN will continue to build on its user and supplier bases in Europe, largely reflecting the benefits of efficient marketing efforts and the "network effect" (where more users beget more suppliers, etc.). In particular, we see PCLN's opaque travel offerings (where some details are not disclosed until the transaction is completed), especially in the U.S., as attractive in light of relatively high retail pricing.

➤ In March 2010, PCLN issued $575 million of convertible debt. It also announced a $500 million stock buyback, and immediately repurchased $100 million of shares. We see the company's financial position as strong and flexible.

## Investment Rationale/Risk

➤ PCLN has established itself as a global leader in online travel services, and we do not think it is widely known that well over half of PCLN's gross bookings, revenues and operating profits are derived from international businesses (mostly focused on Europe). Although we have concerns about the euro and European economies, we think positive secular trends are intact, such as a growing percentage of travel purchases being effected online. PCLN hopes it can replicate its European success in Asia, with Agoda (which was acquired in 2007). We think the company is strongly positioned and well managed.

➤ Risks to our recommendation and target price include possible negative impacts from weaker leisure travel demand than we expect, and less success than we foresee with regard to new offerings and/or acquisitions.

➤ Our DCF model (which assumes a WACC of 10.9%, annual free cash flow growth averaging 26% from 2011 to 2015, and a terminal growth rate of 3%) yields an intrinsic value of around $650, which is our 12-month target price.

## Qualitative Risk Assessment

| LOW | MEDIUM | HIGH |
|---|---|---|

Our risk assessment reflects our view of a very competitive online travel segment, with relatively low barriers to entry.

## Quantitative Evaluations

**S&P Quality Ranking**   **B**

| D | C | B- | B | B+ | A- | A | A+ |
|---|---|---|---|---|---|---|---|

**Relative Strength Rank**   **MODERATE**
37
LOWEST = 1          HIGHEST = 99

## Revenue/Earnings Data

**Revenue (Million $)**

| | 1Q | 2Q | 3Q | 4Q | Year |
|---|---|---|---|---|---|
| 2011 | 809.3 | 1,103 | 1,453 | -- | -- |
| 2010 | 584.4 | 767.4 | 1,002 | 731.3 | 3,085 |
| 2009 | 462.1 | 603.7 | 730.7 | 541.8 | 2,338 |
| 2008 | 403.2 | 514.0 | 561.6 | 406.0 | 1,885 |
| 2007 | 301.4 | 355.9 | 417.3 | 334.9 | 1,409 |
| 2006 | 241.9 | 307.7 | 313.5 | 260.1 | 1,123 |

**Earnings Per Share ($)**

| | 1Q | 2Q | 3Q | 4Q | Year |
|---|---|---|---|---|---|
| 2011 | 2.05 | 5.02 | 9.17 | E4.26 | E20.50 |
| 2010 | 1.06 | 2.26 | 4.41 | 2.66 | 10.35 |
| 2009 | 0.53 | 1.38 | 6.42 | 1.55 | 9.88 |
| 2008 | 0.37 | 1.08 | 1.81 | 0.73 | 3.98 |
| 2007 | -0.44 | 0.79 | 2.27 | 0.68 | 3.42 |
| 2006 | -0.02 | 0.28 | 1.05 | 0.33 | 1.68 |

Fiscal year ended Dec. 31. Next earnings report expected: Late February. EPS Estimates based on S&P Operating Earnings; historical GAAP earnings are as reported.

## Dividend Data

No cash dividends have been paid.

**The McGraw-Hill Companies**

# priceline.com Inc

## Business Summary November 09, 2011

CORPORATE OVERVIEW. Priceline.com is an online travel company that provides a broad range of travel services, including airline tickets, hotel rooms, car rentals, vacation packages, cruises, and destination services. PCLN offers customers a choice of purchasing certain travel services in a traditional, price-disclosed manner (retail products), or of using its proprietary Name Your Own Price service, which allows users to make offers for travel services at discounted prices (opaque products). Internationally, PCLN offers hotel room reservations in over 99 countries and 41 languages.

PCLN enables customers to make hotel reservations on a worldwide basis primarily under the Booking.com and Agoda brands internationally, and the priceline.com brand in the U.S. In the U.S., PCLN also allows users to purchase many other types of travel offerings. Interestingly, even though PCLN is best known in the U.S. for its Name Your Own Price system, 69% of its gross bookings and 82% of its operating income in 2010 were derived from its international (primarily European) operations. We expects these percentages to

increase in 2011 and beyond.

The U.S. business consists of Name Your Own Price offerings (provided via a unique e-commerce pricing system intended to enable consumers to use the Internet to save money on products and services, while allowing sellers to generate incremental revenue and retail offerings) and retail services (whereby customers can choose specific suppliers and/or itineraries when making purchases of airline tickets and hotel and rental car reservations, and travel packages). The company has provided retail offerings since 2003, and believes that offering both opaque and retail products enables it to serve a broad array of value-conscious travelers, while providing diversified revenues.

## Company Financials  Fiscal Year Ended Dec. 31

| Per Share Data ($) | 2010 | 2009 | 2008 | 2007 | 2006 | 2005 | 2004 | 2003 | 2002 | 2001 |
|---|---|---|---|---|---|---|---|---|---|---|
| Tangible Book Value | 21.78 | 17.53 | 5.13 | 3.43 | NM | 0.53 | 0.79 | 3.44 | 3.12 | 3.30 |
| Cash Flow | 11.35 | 10.68 | 4.86 | 4.24 | 2.41 | 4.70 | 1.03 | 0.56 | -0.09 | 0.02 |
| Earnings | 10.35 | 9.88 | 3.98 | 3.42 | 1.68 | 4.21 | 0.96 | 0.27 | -0.54 | -0.48 |
| S&P Core Earnings | 10.37 | 9.91 | 3.99 | 4.19 | 1.70 | 4.13 | 0.53 | -0.49 | -2.94 | -4.62 |
| Dividends | Nil | Nil | Nil | Nil | Nil | Nil | Nil | Nil | Nil | Nil |
| Payout Ratio | Nil | Nil | Nil | Nil | Nil | Nil | Nil | Nil | Nil | Nil |
| Prices:High | 428.10 | 231.49 | 144.34 | 120.67 | 44.28 | 27.08 | 29.52 | 39.81 | 41.36 | 62.12 |
| Prices:Low | 173.32 | 64.95 | 45.15 | 41.80 | 21.06 | 18.20 | 17.42 | 6.78 | 6.30 | 7.88 |
| P/E Ratio:High | 41 | 23 | 36 | 35 | 26 | 6 | 31 | NM | NM | NM |
| P/E Ratio:Low | 17 | 7 | 11 | 12 | 13 | 4 | 18 | NM | NM | NM |

| Income Statement Analysis (Million $) | | | | | | | | | | |
|---|---|---|---|---|---|---|---|---|---|---|
| Revenue | 3,085 | 2,338 | 1,885 | 1,409 | 1,123 | 963 | 914 | 864 | 1,004 | 1,172 |
| Operating Income | 839 | 509 | 333 | 175 | 95.6 | 64.9 | 43.9 | 26.0 | 22.7 | 23.3 |
| Depreciation | 50.5 | 39.2 | 43.2 | 37.5 | 33.4 | 27.3 | 13.5 | 11.5 | 18.3 | 16.6 |
| Interest Expense | 29.9 | 24.1 | 9.38 | 10.4 | 7.06 | 5.07 | 3.72 | 0.91 | Nil | Nil |
| Pretax Income | 746 | 442 | 292 | 145 | 62.1 | 36.5 | 31.3 | 11.9 | -19.2 | -7.30 |
| Effective Tax Rate | NA | NM | 33.7% | NM | NM | NM | NM | NM | NM | NM |
| Net Income | 528 | 489 | 193 | 157 | 74.5 | 193 | 31.5 | 11.9 | -19.2 | -7.30 |
| S&P Core Earnings | 529 | 491 | 194 | 191 | 73.3 | 187 | 20.3 | -18.6 | -111 | -157 |

| Balance Sheet & Other Financial Data (Million $) | | | | | | | | | | |
|---|---|---|---|---|---|---|---|---|---|---|
| Cash | 1,662 | 800 | 463 | 509 | 424 | 80.3 | 101 | 93.7 | 85.4 | 115 |
| Current Assets | 1,957 | 1,023 | 624 | 613 | 503 | 224 | 273 | 284 | 170 | 185 |
| Total Assets | 2,906 | 1,834 | 1,344 | 1,351 | 1,106 | 754 | 542 | 338 | 211 | 262 |
| Current Liabilities | 471 | 409 | 547 | 695 | 101 | 71.0 | 74.4 | 49.6 | 65.3 | 87.3 |
| Long Term Debt | 476 | 36.0 | Nil | Nil | 569 | 224 | 224 | 125 | Nil | Nil |
| Common Equity | 1,813 | 1,322 | 730 | 579 | 349 | 369 | 199 | 149 | 132 | 147 |
| Total Capital | 2,381 | 1,517 | 779 | 643 | 953 | 672 | 467 | 287 | 145 | 172 |
| Capital Expenditures | 22.6 | 15.1 | 18.3 | 16.0 | 12.9 | 11.0 | 6.94 | 6.58 | 9.13 | 9.42 |
| Cash Flow | 579 | 529 | 237 | 193 | 108 | 218 | 43.5 | 22.0 | -3.26 | 0.71 |
| Current Ratio | 4.2 | 2.5 | 1.1 | 0.9 | 5.0 | 3.1 | 3.7 | 5.7 | 2.6 | 2.1 |
| % Long Term Debt of Capitalization | 20.0 | 2.4 | Nil | Nil | 59.7 | 33.3 | 48.1 | 43.4 | Nil | Nil |
| % Net Income of Revenue | 17.1 | 20.9 | 10.3 | 11.1 | 6.6 | 20.0 | 3.4 | 1.4 | NM | NM |
| % Return on Assets | 22.3 | 30.8 | 14.4 | 12.7 | 8.0 | 29.7 | 7.2 | 4.3 | NM | NM |
| % Return on Equity | 33.7 | 47.7 | 29.6 | 33.5 | 20.8 | 67.2 | 17.2 | 7.4 | NM | NM |

Data as orig reptd.; bef. results of disc opers/spec. items. Per share data adj. for stk. divs.; EPS diluted. E-Estimated. NA-Not Available. NM-Not Meaningful. NR-Not Ranked. UR-Under Review.

**Office:** 800 Connecticut Ave, Norwalk, CT 06854-1625.
**Telephone:** 203-299-8000.
**Website:** http://www.priceline.com
**Chrmn:** R.M. Bahna

**Pres & CEO:** J.H. Boyd
**EVP, Secy & General Counsel:** P.J. Millones
**Investor Contact:** D.J. Finnegan (203-299-8000)
**SVP, CFO & Chief Acctg Officer:** D.J. Finnegan

**Board Members:** R. M. Bahna, H. W. Barker, Jr., J. H. Boyd, J. L. Docter, J. E. Epstein, J. M. Guyette, N. B. Peretsman, C. W. Rydin

**Founded:** 1997
**Domicile:** Delaware
**Employees:** 3,400

# Principal Financial Group Inc.

**STANDARD &POOR'S**

| S&P Recommendation | HOLD ★★★☆☆ | Price | 12-Mo. Target Price | Investment Style |
|---|---|---|---|---|
| | | $21.43 (as of Nov 25, 2011) | $28.00 | Large-Cap Blend |

**GICS Sector** Financials
**Sub-Industry** Life & Health Insurance

**Summary** This company offers businesses, individuals and other clients various financial products and services, including insurance, retirement and investment services.

## Key Stock Statistics (Source S&P, Vickers, company reports)

| | | | | | | | |
|---|---|---|---|---|---|---|---|
| 52-Wk Range | $35.00–20.48 | S&P Oper. EPS 2011E | 2.74 | Market Capitalization(B) | $6.539 | Beta | 2.76 |
| Trailing 12-Month EPS | $2.22 | S&P Oper. EPS 2012E | 3.43 | Yield (%) | 3.27 | S&P 3-Yr. Proj. EPS CAGR(%) | 6 |
| Trailing 12-Month P/E | 9.7 | P/E on S&P Oper. EPS 2011E | 7.8 | Dividend Rate/Share | $0.70 | S&P Credit Rating | BBB |
| $10K Invested 5 Yrs Ago | $4,135 | Common Shares Outstg. (M) | 305.2 | Institutional Ownership (%) | 66 | | |

## Price Performance

30-Week Mov. Avg. · · · 10-Week Mov. Avg. – – GAAP Earnings vs. Previous Year  Volume Above Avg. STARS
12-Mo. Target Price — Relative Strength — ▲ Up ▼ Down ▶ No Change  Below Avg.

Options: CBOE

Analysis prepared by Equity Analyst **Cathy Seifert** on Nov 23, 2011, when the stock traded at **$21.86**.

## Qualitative Risk Assessment

| LOW | MEDIUM | HIGH |
|---|---|---|

Our risk assessment reflects our view of PFG's significant exposure to equity markets and potential for further investment losses, especially considering its exposure to commercial real estate. We believe PFG's capital position could come under strain if the economic environment and capital markets worsen. However, we believe PFG's financial position has improved following recent capital raises.

## Quantitative Evaluations

**S&P Quality Ranking** B+

| D | C | B- | B | B+ | A- | A | A+ |
|---|---|---|---|---|---|---|---|

**Relative Strength Rank** WEAK

26

LOWEST = 1    HIGHEST = 99

## Revenue/Earnings Data

**Revenue (Million $)**

| | 1Q | 2Q | 3Q | 4Q | Year |
|---|---|---|---|---|---|
| 2011 | 2,220 | 2,342 | 2,089 | -- | -- |
| 2010 | 2,264 | 2,234 | 2,289 | 2,373 | 9,159 |
| 2009 | 2,189 | 2,158 | 2,270 | 2,232 | 8,849 |
| 2008 | 2,501 | 2,658 | 2,498 | 2,279 | 9,936 |
| 2007 | 2,661 | 2,832 | 2,850 | 2,564 | 10,907 |
| 2006 | 2,402 | 2,460 | 2,450 | 2,559 | 9,871 |

**Earnings Per Share ($)**

| | 1Q | 2Q | 3Q | 4Q | Year |
|---|---|---|---|---|---|
| 2011 | 0.60 | 0.80 | 0.20 | E0.69 | E2.74 |
| 2010 | 0.59 | 0.42 | 0.44 | 0.62 | 2.06 |
| 2009 | 0.43 | 0.52 | 0.57 | 0.44 | 1.98 |
| 2008 | 0.67 | 0.64 | 0.35 | -0.03 | 1.63 |
| 2007 | 0.95 | 1.14 | 0.88 | 0.05 | 3.01 |
| 2006 | 1.01 | 0.76 | 0.92 | 0.93 | 3.63 |

Fiscal year ended Dec. 31. Next earnings report expected: Early February. EPS Estimates based on S&P Operating Earnings; historical GAAP earnings are as reported.

## Dividend Data (Dates: mm/dd Payment Date: mm/dd/yy)

| Amount ($) | Date Decl. | Ex-Div. Date | Stk. of Record | Payment Date |
|---|---|---|---|---|
| 0.550 | 11/01 | 11/17 | 11/19 | 12/03/10 |
| 0.700 | 10/27 | 11/08 | 11/10 | 12/02/11 |

Dividends have been paid since 2002. Source: Company reports.

## Highlights

▶ We expect results in the Retirement and Investor Services (RIS) segment to remain under pressure in coming periods. We are modeling for net flows at Full Service Accumulation (FSA) to rise modestly, driven by better sales and declining withdrawals. However, earnings at FSA should be adversely affected by limited enrollment growth, low deferral rates, and modest new plan formation. We expect ongoing equity market turmoil to hurt margins at RIS. We see sluggish earnings growth for the life unit on weak sales and lower margins, but we believe the divestiture of the health insurance unit is a positive.

▶ We expect earnings to be down modestly at International Asset Management and Accumulation (IAMA). We believe IAMA will benefit from greater assets under management and higher investment income. However, PFG reduced its stake in a joint venture in Brazil, which should adversely affect earnings.

▶ We forecast operating EPS of $2.74 for 2011 and $3.43 for 2012, excluding any investment gains or losses.

## Investment Rationale/Risk

▶ We believe PFG's economically sensitive businesses still face headwinds, although we believe PFG will benefit significantly once the macro environment improves. Although we think multiple expansion will be held back by slow revenue growth and concerns about investment losses, we believe this is reflected in PFG's shares. PFG trades at only a slight premium to the group, but we believe a premium is warranted since its businesses are less capital-intensive and generate a higher return on equity versus peers. We expect losses tied to PFG's commercial real estate portfolio to be manageable. We think PFG's financial position has improved, and we are encouraged the company has made several acquisitions.

▶ Risks to our recommendation and target price include a decline in the equity markets, outflows in the RIS segment, and deteriorating credit and economic conditions.

▶ Our 12-month target price of $28 assumes the shares trade at 8.2X our 2012 operating EPS estimate and at less than 2X estimated 2012 tangible book value. These metrics are in line with peer averages, but below historical multiples due to the challenging operating environment.

---

**Please read the Required Disclosures and Analyst Certification on the last page of this report.**

The McGraw-Hill Companies

# Principal Financial Group Inc.

## Business Summary November 23, 2011

CORPORATE OVERVIEW. The Principal Financial Group is a leading provider of retirement savings, investment and insurance products and services, with approximately $319 billion in assets under management and approximately 19.1 million customers worldwide at December 31, 2010. The focus of the company is to provide retirement and employment products and services, specifically 401(k) plans, to small and medium-sized businesses. According to PFG, the company is a leading corporate retirement plan provider in the U.S. and provides 30,000 defined contribution pension plans, of which roughly 24,500 were 401 (k) plans, covering 3.1 million plan participants, and over 2,500 defined benefit pension plans, covering over 319,000 plan participants.

PFG's businesses are organized into five operating segments. The Retirement and Investor Services (RIS) segment accounted for 51% of operating revenues excluding corporate and other in 2010. RIS is organized into six product and service categories: Full Service Accumulation (FSA), principal funds, individual annuities, bank trust services, and investment only and full service payout. RIS provides retirement savings and related investment products and services, and asset management operations, with a concentration on small and medium-sized businesses. At year-end 2010, RIS account values totaled $178 billion.

The Global Asset Management segment includes Principal Global Investors

(PGI) and its affiliates, and focuses on providing a range of asset management services. The segment accounted for 5.9% of operating revenues excluding corporate and other in 2010.

The International Asset Management and Accumulation (IAMA) segment consists of Principal International and offers retirement products and services, annuities, mutual funds and life insurance through operations in Brazil, Chile, Mexico, China, Hong Kong and India. IAMA accounted for 9.7% of operating revenues from continuing operations in 2010.

The U.S. Insurance Solutions segment, which accounted for 34% of operating revenues from continuing operations in 2010, offers individual life insurance and specialty benefits, including group dental, group vision, group life, group disability, wellness and individual disability insurance. Corporate and other includes, among other things, inter segment eliminations, income on capital not allocated to other segments, and the company's financing activities. The segment reported a loss of $119 million in 2010.

## Company Financials Fiscal Year Ended Dec. 31

| Per Share Data ($) | 2010 | 2009 | 2008 | 2007 | 2006 | 2005 | 2004 | 2003 | 2002 | 2001 |
|---|---|---|---|---|---|---|---|---|---|---|
| Tangible Book Value | 26.68 | 33.18 | 4.41 | 22.35 | 22.24 | 24.14 | 23.67 | 22.12 | 19.32 | 10.59 |
| Operating Earnings | NA | NA | NA | NA | NA | NA | NA | NA | 2.46 | 1.96 |
| Earnings | 2.06 | 1.98 | 1.63 | 3.01 | 3.63 | 3.02 | 2.23 | 2.23 | 1.77 | 1.02 |
| S&P Core Earnings | 2.63 | 3.07 | 2.77 | 3.69 | 3.45 | 3.02 | 2.36 | 2.38 | 1.85 | 1.69 |
| Dividends | 0.55 | 0.50 | 0.45 | 0.90 | 0.80 | 0.65 | 0.55 | 0.45 | 0.25 | Nil |
| Payout Ratio | 27% | 25% | 28% | 30% | 22% | 22% | 25% | 20% | 14% | Nil |
| Prices:High | 33.34 | 30.87 | 68.94 | 70.85 | 59.40 | 52.00 | 41.26 | 34.67 | 31.50 | 24.75 |
| Prices:Low | 20.89 | 5.41 | 8.78 | 51.52 | 45.91 | 36.80 | 32.00 | 25.21 | 22.00 | 18.50 |
| P/E Ratio:High | 16 | 16 | 42 | 24 | 16 | 17 | 19 | 16 | 18 | 24 |
| P/E Ratio:Low | 10 | 3 | 5 | 17 | 13 | 12 | 14 | 11 | 12 | 18 |

| Income Statement Analysis (Million $) | | | | | | | | | | |
|---|---|---|---|---|---|---|---|---|---|---|
| Life Insurance in Force | 244,048 | 239,782 | 246,329 | 243,119 | 218,947 | 197,690 | 180,344 | 136,530 | 137,794 | 62,309 |
| Premium Income:Life | 1,295 | 1,254 | 1,564 | 1,827 | 1,560 | 1,546 | 1,477 | 1,500 | 1,824 | 2,089 |
| Premium Income:A & H | 2,260 | 2,496 | 2,646 | 2,808 | 2,745 | 2,429 | 2,233 | 2,135 | 2,058 | 2,033 |
| Net Investment Income | 3,497 | 3,401 | 3,994 | 3,967 | 3,618 | 3,361 | 3,227 | 3,420 | 3,305 | 3,395 |
| Total Revenue | 9,159 | 8,849 | 9,936 | 10,907 | 9,871 | 9,008 | 8,304 | 9,404 | 9,223 | 8,818 |
| Pretax Income | 940 | 746 | 454 | 1,048 | 1,329 | 1,124 | 882 | 954 | 666 | 449 |
| Net Operating Income | NA | NA | NA | NA | NA | NA | NA | NA | 864 | 711 |
| Net Income | 706 | 623 | 458 | 840 | 1,034 | 892 | 702 | 728 | 620 | 370 |
| S&P Core Earnings | 848 | 918 | 722 | 991 | 951 | 871 | 742 | 778 | 647 | 608 |

| Balance Sheet & Other Financial Data (Million $) | | | | | | | | | | |
|---|---|---|---|---|---|---|---|---|---|---|
| Cash & Equivalent | 2,544 | 2,932 | 3,359 | 2,119 | 2,314 | 2,324 | 1,131 | 2,344 | 1,685 | 1,218 |
| Premiums Due | 1,063 | 1,065 | 988 | 951 | 1,252 | 593 | 628 | 720 | 460 | 531 |
| Investment Assets:Bonds | 49,757 | 47,253 | 40,961 | 47,268 | 44,727 | 42,117 | 40,916 | 37,553 | 34,287 | 30,030 |
| Investment Assets:Stocks | 487 | 436 | 401 | 586 | 848 | 815 | 763 | 712 | 379 | 834 |
| Investment Assets:Loans | 12,187 | 12,748 | 12,748 | 13,522 | 12,515 | 12,312 | 12,529 | 14,312 | 11,900 | 11,898 |
| Investment Assets:Total | 65,978 | 63,937 | 59,107 | 64,365 | 60,367 | 57,583 | 57,012 | 55,578 | 48,996 | 44,773 |
| Deferred Policy Costs | 3,530 | 3,681 | 4,153 | 2,810 | 2,419 | 2,174 | 1,838 | 1,572 | 1,414 | 1,373 |
| Total Assets | 145,631 | 137,759 | 128,182 | 154,520 | 143,658 | 127,035 | 113,798 | 107,754 | 89,861 | 88,351 |
| Debt | 1,584 | 1,585 | 1,291 | 1,399 | 1,554 | 899 | 844 | 2,767 | 1,333 | 1,378 |
| Common Equity | 9,728 | 7,893 | 2,473 | 7,422 | 7,861 | 7,807 | 7,544 | 7,400 | 13,314 | 6,820 |
| % Return on Revenue | 8.8 | 7.0 | 4.6 | 7.7 | 10.5 | 9.9 | 8.5 | 7.7 | 7.0 | 4.2 |
| % Return on Assets | 0.5 | 0.5 | 0.3 | 0.6 | 0.8 | 0.7 | 0.6 | 0.7 | 0.7 | 0.4 |
| % Return on Equity | 7.6 | 12.0 | 9.3 | 10.6 | 12.8 | 11.4 | 9.4 | 10.4 | 4.6 | 5.7 |
| % Investment Yield | 5.4 | 5.5 | 6.7 | 6.4 | 6.1 | 5.9 | 5.8 | 6.5 | 7.0 | 7.8 |

Data as orig reptd.; bef. results of disc opers/spec. items. Per share data adj. for stk. divs.; EPS diluted. E-Estimated. NA-Not Available. NM-Not Meaningful. NR-Not Ranked. UR-Under Review.

**Office:** 711 High Street, Des Moines, IA 50392-9992.
**Telephone:** 515-247-5111.
**Website:** http://www.principal.com
**Chrmn, Pres & CEO:** L.D. Zimpleman

**SVP, CFO & Chief Acctg Officer:** T.J. Lillis
**SVP & Secy:** J.N. Hoffman
**General Counsel:** K.E. Shaff
**Investor Contact:** T. Graf (515-235-9500)

**Board Members:** B. J. Bernard, J. E. Carter-Miller, G. E. Costley, M. T. Dan, D. H. Ferro, III, C. Gelatt, Jr., S. L. Helton, R. L. Keyser, A. K. Mathrani, E. E. Tallett, L. D. Zimpleman

**Founded:** 1998
**Domicile:** Delaware
**Employees:** 13,627

# Procter & Gamble Co (The)

**STANDARD &POOR'S**

| S&P Recommendation | HOLD ★★★☆☆ | Price $61.00 (as of Nov 25, 2011) | 12-Mo. Target Price $67.00 | Investment Style Large-Cap Growth |
|---|---|---|---|---|

**GICS Sector** Consumer Staples
**Sub-Industry** Household Products

**Summary** This leading consumer products company markets household and personal care products in more than 180 countries.

## Key Stock Statistics (Source S&P, Vickers, company reports)

| | | | | | | | |
|---|---|---|---|---|---|---|---|
| 52-Wk Range | $67.72– 57.56 | S&P Oper. EPS 2012**E** | 4.21 | Market Capitalization(B) | $167.831 | Beta | 0.45 |
| Trailing 12-Month EPS | $3.94 | S&P Oper. EPS 2013**E** | 4.60 | Yield (%) | 3.44 | S&P 3-Yr. Proj. EPS CAGR(%) | 7 |
| Trailing 12-Month P/E | 15.5 | P/E on S&P Oper. EPS 2012**E** | 14.5 | Dividend Rate/Share | $2.10 | S&P Credit Rating | AA- |
| $10K Invested 5 Yrs Ago | $11,022 | Common Shares Outstg. (M) | 2,751.3 | Institutional Ownership (%) | 58 | | |

## Price Performance

30-Week Mov. Avg. ···  10-Week Mov. Avg. - - GAAP Earnings vs. Previous Year  Volume Above Avg. STARS
12-Mo. Target Price — Relative Strength  — ▲ Up  ▼ Down  ► No Change  Below Avg. ★

Options: ASE, CBOE, P, Ph

Analysis prepared by Equity Analyst **Tom Graves, CFA** on Nov 14, 2011, when the stock traded at **$63.05**.

## Highlights

▶ We think PG has benefited from its tiered portfolio, which offers products at different price points, from new products that command higher pricing through innovation, and from its broad geographic reach. For PG as currently constituted, we estimate FY 12 (Jun.) sales will increase about 5% from the $82.6 billion reported for FY 11, largely due to higher prices.

▶ In November 2012, PG said that it planned to spend between $700 million and $800 million after tax on restructuring projects in FY 12, of which $260 million would be considered "core" spending, and the remainder (about $0.15 to $0.18 a share) would be viewed as "incremental" restructuring and not part of core earnings. For FY 12, we estimate EPS of $4.21, compared to $3.95 in FY 11. Our estimate excludes a prospective $0.55 to $0.65 gain related to the sale of the Pringles business. For FY 13, we estimate EPS of $4.60.

▶ In November 2011, PG and Teva Pharmaceutical Industries (TEVA 40 Hold) announced the creation of a new partnership and joint venture in consumer health care. Also, PG expects a proposed sale of its Pringles snack food business to close in FY 12's second half.

## Investment Rationale/Risk

▶ Looking ahead, we expect PG to benefit from innovation, acquisitions and growth in new markets and categories. In our view, PG's competitive strengths in developing markets include its broad product portfolio and sizable distribution network. However, we have seen recent gross margin pressure from commodity costs.

▶ Risks to our recommendation and target price include heightened competition, a worsening consumer spending environment, unfavorable currency translation, greater commodity cost pressures, higher promotional spending, and slow consumer acceptance of new products.

▶ Our 12-month target price of $67 is based on a blended valuation. Our historical P/E analysis uses a multiple of 14.3X our calendar 2012 EPS estimate of $4.40, which is below a 10-year average, and produces an implied value of $63. Our peer analysis uses a 15.3X multiple, similar to a peer average, and produces a value of $67. Our DCF model produces an intrinsic value of $72, assuming a terminal growth rate of 2.8% and a terminal WACC of 8.6%. The stock has an indicated dividend yield of 3.3%.

## Qualitative Risk Assessment

| LOW | MEDIUM | HIGH |
|---|---|---|

Our risk assessment reflects that demand for household and personal care products is generally stable and not affected by changes in the economy or geopolitical factors, except for select categories such as fragrances.

## Quantitative Evaluations

**S&P Quality Ranking**  A+

| D | C | B- | B | B+ | A- | A | A+ |
|---|---|---|---|---|---|---|---|

**Relative Strength Rank**  MODERATE

61

LOWEST = 1   HIGHEST = 99

## Revenue/Earnings Data

**Revenue (Million $)**

| | 1Q | 2Q | 3Q | 4Q | Year |
|---|---|---|---|---|---|
| 2012 | 21,917 | -- | | | -- |
| 2011 | 20,122 | 21,347 | 20,230 | 20,860 | 82,559 |
| 2010 | 19,807 | 21,027 | 19,178 | 18,926 | 78,938 |
| 2009 | 21,582 | 20,368 | 18,417 | 18,662 | 79,029 |
| 2008 | 20,199 | 21,575 | 20,463 | 21,266 | 83,503 |
| 2007 | 18,785 | 19,725 | 18,694 | 19,272 | 76,476 |

**Earnings Per Share ($)**

| | | | | | |
|---|---|---|---|---|---|
| 2012 | 1.03 | E1.08 | E1.09 | E1.03 | E4.21 |
| 2011 | 1.02 | 1.11 | 0.96 | 0.84 | 3.93 |
| 2010 | 0.97 | 1.01 | 0.83 | 0.71 | 3.53 |
| 2009 | 1.03 | 0.94 | 0.83 | 0.80 | 3.58 |
| 2008 | 0.92 | 0.98 | 0.82 | 0.92 | 3.64 |
| 2007 | 0.79 | 0.84 | 0.74 | 0.67 | 3.04 |

Fiscal year ended Jun. 30. Next earnings report expected: Late January. EPS Estimates based on S&P Operating Earnings; historical GAAP earnings are as reported.

## Dividend Data (Dates: mm/dd Payment Date: mm/dd/yy)

| Amount ($) | Date Decl. | Ex-Div. Date | Stk. of Record | Payment Date |
|---|---|---|---|---|
| 0.482 | 01/11 | 01/19 | 01/21 | 02/15/11 |
| 0.525 | 04/11 | 04/27 | 04/29 | 05/16/11 |
| 0.525 | 07/12 | 07/20 | 07/22 | 08/15/11 |
| 0.525 | 10/11 | 10/19 | 10/21 | 11/15/11 |

Dividends have been paid since 1891. Source: Company reports.

**Please read the Required Disclosures and Analyst Certification on the last page of this report.**

The **McGraw·Hill** Companies

# Procter & Gamble Co (The)

STANDARD &POOR'S

## Business Summary November 14, 2011

CORPORATE OVERVIEW. Procter & Gamble's business is focused on providing branded products of what it considers superior quality and value to improve the lives of the world's consumers. PG's products are sold in more than 180 countries. In FY 11 (Jun.), North America accounted for 41% of total sales, Western Europe 20%, Asia 16%, Latin America 9%, and other geographic areas 14%. PG's customers include mass merchandisers, grocery stores, membership club stores, drug stores and high-frequency stores. Sales to Wal-Mart Stores, Inc., and its affiliates represented about 15% of total FY 11 revenue. PG's top 10 customers accounted for about 32% of total unit volume.

Under U.S. accounting standards, PG has six reportable business segments: Beauty (24% of FY 11 net sales and 23% of net income from continuing operations); Grooming (10%; 14%); Health Care (15%; 15%); Snacks and Pet Care (4%; 2%); Fabric Care and Home Care (30%; 26%); and Baby Care and Family

Care (19%; 17%). (Note: Total net sales and net income also include a Corporate segment.)

IMPACT OF MAJOR DEVELOPMENTS. In October 2005, PG acquired The Gillette Company for about $54 billion. Gillette is the world leader in the male and female grooming categories and holds the number one position worldwide in alkaline batteries and toothbrushes. We expect the acquisition to add to increased shareholder value over time through cost synergies and sales growth opportunities, following the initial two years of dilution.

## Company Financials Fiscal Year Ended Jun. 30

| Per Share Data ($) | 2011 | 2010 | 2009 | 2008 | 2007 | 2006 | 2005 | 2004 | 2003 | 2002 |
|---|---|---|---|---|---|---|---|---|---|---|
| Tangible Book Value | NM | NM | NM | NM | NM | NM | NM | NM | 0.43 | NM |
| Cash Flow | 4.88 | 4.53 | 4.50 | 4.54 | 4.30 | 3.56 | 3.30 | 2.90 | 2.41 | 2.11 |
| Earnings | 3.93 | 3.53 | 3.58 | 3.64 | 3.04 | 2.64 | 2.66 | 2.32 | 1.85 | 1.54 |
| S&P Core Earnings | 3.95 | 3.53 | 3.38 | 3.24 | 2.96 | 2.60 | 2.45 | 2.17 | 1.58 | 1.28 |
| Dividends | 1.97 | 1.80 | 1.64 | 1.45 | 1.28 | 1.15 | 1.03 | 0.93 | 0.82 | 0.76 |
| Payout Ratio | 50% | 51% | 46% | 40% | 42% | 44% | 39% | 40% | 44% | 49% |
| Prices:High | 67.72 | 65.38 | 63.48 | 73.81 | 75.18 | 64.73 | 59.70 | 57.40 | 49.97 | 47.38 |
| Prices:Low | 57.56 | 39.37 | 43.93 | 54.92 | 60.42 | 52.75 | 51.16 | 48.89 | 39.79 | 37.04 |
| P/E Ratio:High | 17 | 19 | 18 | 20 | 25 | 25 | 22 | 25 | 27 | 31 |
| P/E Ratio:Low | 15 | 11 | 12 | 15 | 20 | 20 | 19 | 21 | 22 | 24 |

**Income Statement Analysis** (Million $)

| | 2011 | 2010 | 2009 | 2008 | 2007 | 2006 | 2005 | 2004 | 2003 | 2002 |
|---|---|---|---|---|---|---|---|---|---|---|
| Revenue | 82,559 | 78,938 | 79,029 | 83,503 | 76,476 | 68,222 | 56,741 | 51,407 | 43,377 | 40,238 |
| Operating Income | 18,656 | 19,129 | 19,205 | 20,249 | 18,580 | 15,876 | 12,811 | 11,560 | 9,556 | 8,371 |
| Depreciation | 2,838 | 3,108 | 3,082 | 3,166 | 3,130 | 2,627 | 1,884 | 1,733 | 1,703 | 1,693 |
| Interest Expense | 831 | 946 | 1,358 | 1,467 | 1,304 | 1,119 | 834 | 629 | 561 | 603 |
| Pretax Income | 15,189 | 15,047 | 15,325 | 16,078 | 14,710 | 12,413 | 10,439 | 9,350 | 7,530 | 6,383 |
| Effective Tax Rate | NA | NA | 26.3% | 24.9% | 29.7% | 30.0% | 30.5% | 30.7% | 31.1% | 31.8% |
| Net Income | 11,797 | 10,946 | 11,293 | 12,075 | 10,340 | 8,684 | 7,257 | 6,481 | 5,186 | 4,352 |
| S&P Core Earnings | 11,624 | 10,730 | 10,467 | 10,575 | 9,917 | 8,420 | 6,552 | 5,922 | 4,313 | 3,486 |

**Balance Sheet & Other Financial Data** (Million $)

| | 2011 | 2010 | 2009 | 2008 | 2007 | 2006 | 2005 | 2004 | 2003 | 2002 |
|---|---|---|---|---|---|---|---|---|---|---|
| Cash | 2,768 | 2,879 | 4,781 | 3,541 | 5,354 | 6,693 | 6,389 | 5,469 | 5,912 | 3,427 |
| Current Assets | 21,970 | 18,782 | 21,905 | 24,515 | 24,031 | 24,329 | 20,329 | 17,115 | 15,220 | 12,166 |
| Total Assets | 138,354 | 128,172 | 134,833 | 143,992 | 138,014 | 135,695 | 61,527 | 57,048 | 43,706 | 40,776 |
| Current Liabilities | 27,293 | 24,282 | 30,901 | 30,958 | 30,717 | 19,985 | 25,039 | 22,147 | 12,358 | 12,704 |
| Long Term Debt | 22,033 | 21,360 | 20,652 | 23,581 | 23,375 | 35,976 | 12,887 | 12,554 | 11,475 | 11,201 |
| Common Equity | 68,001 | 61,439 | 63,099 | 69,494 | 65,354 | 61,457 | 15,994 | 15,752 | 14,606 | 12,072 |
| Total Capital | 100,015 | 91,271 | 95,827 | 104,880 | 102,150 | 111,238 | 33,258 | 32,093 | 29,057 | 25,984 |
| Capital Expenditures | 3,306 | 3,067 | 3,238 | 3,046 | 2,945 | 2,667 | 2,181 | 2,024 | 1,482 | 1,679 |
| Cash Flow | 14,635 | 14,054 | 14,183 | 15,065 | 13,470 | 11,311 | 9,005 | 8,083 | 6,764 | 5,921 |
| Current Ratio | 0.8 | 0.8 | 0.7 | 0.8 | 0.8 | 1.2 | 0.8 | 0.8 | 1.2 | 1.0 |
| % Long Term Debt of Capitalization | 22.0 | 23.4 | 21.6 | 22.5 | 22.9 | 32.3 | 38.7 | 39.1 | 39.5 | 43.1 |
| % Net Income of Revenue | 14.3 | 13.9 | 14.3 | 14.5 | 13.5 | 12.7 | 12.8 | 12.6 | 12.0 | 10.8 |
| % Return on Assets | 8.9 | 8.3 | 8.1 | 8.6 | 7.6 | 8.8 | 12.2 | 12.9 | 12.3 | 11.6 |
| % Return on Equity | 18.5 | 17.8 | 17.2 | 17.9 | 16.3 | 22.1 | 45.7 | 41.8 | 37.9 | 37.8 |

Data as orig reptd.; bef. results of disc opers/spec. items. Per share data adj. for stk. divs.; EPS diluted. E-Estimated. NA-Not Available. NM-Not Meaningful. NR-Not Ranked. UR-Under Review.

**Office:** One Procter & Gamble Plaza, Cincinnati, OH 45202.
**Telephone:** 513-983-1100.
**Website:** http://www.pg.com
**Chrmn, Pres & CEO:** R.A. McDonald

**COO:** W. Geissler
**SVP, Chief Acctg Officer & Cntlr:** V.L. Sheppard
**SVP & Treas:** T.L. List-Stoll
**CFO:** J.R. Moeller

**Investor Contact:** M. Erceg (800-742-6253)
**Auditor:** DELOITTE & TOUCHE
**Board Members:** A. F. Braly, K. I. Chenault, S. D. Cook, S. D. Desmond-Hellmann, R. A. McDonald, W. J. McNerney, Jr., J. A. Rodgers, M. C. Whitman, M. A. Wilderotter, P. A. Woertz, E. Z. de Leon

**Founded:** 1837
**Domicile:** Ohio
**Employees:** 129,000

# Progressive Corp (The)

STANDARD
&POOR'S

| S&P Recommendation **HOLD** ★★★☆☆ | Price<br>$17.58 (as of Nov 25, 2011) | 12-Mo. Target Price<br>$21.00 | Investment Style<br>Large-Cap Growth |
|---|---|---|---|

**GICS Sector** Financials
**Sub-Industry** Property & Casualty Insurance

**Summary** One of the largest auto insurance groups in the U.S., Progressive is the largest seller of motorcycle policies and a market leader in commercial auto insurance.

## Key Stock Statistics (Source S&P, Vickers, company reports)

| | | | | | | | |
|---|---|---|---|---|---|---|---|
| 52-Wk Range | $22.08– 16.88 | S&P Oper. EPS 2011E | 1.50 | Market Capitalization(B) | $10.911 | Beta | 0.85 |
| Trailing 12-Month EPS | $1.63 | S&P Oper. EPS 2012E | 1.70 | Yield (%) | 2.27 | S&P 3-Yr. Proj. EPS CAGR(%) | 3 |
| Trailing 12-Month P/E | 10.8 | P/E on S&P Oper. EPS 2011E | 11.7 | Dividend Rate/Share | $0.40 | S&P Credit Rating | A+ |
| $10K Invested 5 Yrs Ago | $9,190 | Common Shares Outstg. (M) | 620.6 | Institutional Ownership (%) | 71 | | |

## Price Performance

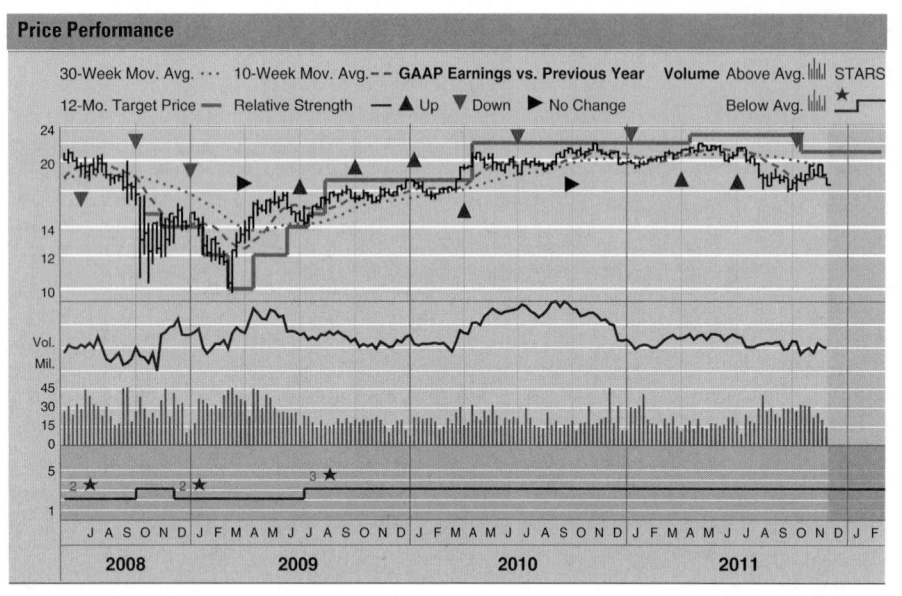

30-Week Mov. Avg. ··· 10-Week Mov. Avg. — **GAAP Earnings vs. Previous Year** Volume Above Avg. STARS
12-Mo. Target Price — Relative Strength — ▲ Up ▼ Down ▶ No Change Below Avg. ★

Options: ASE, CBOE, P, Ph

Analysis prepared by Equity Analyst **Cathy Seifert** on Nov 01, 2011, when the stock traded at **$18.63**.

## Highlights

➤ We believe earned premiums will rise by 3% to 5% in both 2011 and 2012, reflecting likely market share gains amid continued price competition. Earned premiums advanced 2.8% in 2009 and 2.2% in 2010. We expect total operating revenue growth in coming periods to reflect an anticipated rise in net investment income of between 2% and 4%.

➤ Barring a surge in catastrophe losses, we expect underwriting results to remain profitable in coming periods. Underwriting results in the first nine months of 2011 reflected a 5% rise in loss costs, 3% higher policy acquisition costs, and a 4% rise in other underwriting expenses. As a result, the combined (loss and expense) ratio deteriorated slightly to 93.0% in the 2011 interim, from 92.2% in the 2010 period.

➤ We estimate operating EPS of $1.50 for 2011 and $1.70 for 2012. Our estimates assume a flat to modestly higher earned premium base, profitable underwriting results, and modestly higher net investment income in a challenging investment environment.

## Investment Rationale/Risk

➤ We view PGR's technology and marketing capabilities as superior to many peers. However, at recent levels, the shares trade at a premium to most peers on both a forward price/earnings and price/tangible book value basis, which we view as appropriate. We note that the company is still being affected by ongoing competitive pressures that we think may force PGR to lower its underwriting standards in order to gain market share.

➤ Risks to our recommendation and target price include a greater-than-expected deterioration in premium revenues, higher-than-expected claim cost inflation and erosion in claim trends, and greater-that-expected erosion in the company's investment portfolio.

➤ Our 12-month target price of $21 assumes that the shares will trade at a premium to property-casualty insurance peers, albeit a smaller one, on a forward price-to-tangible book value basis and a forward price/earnings basis.

## Qualitative Risk Assessment

| LOW | MEDIUM | HIGH |
|---|---|---|

Our risk assessment reflects our view of PGR's position as a leading underwriter of personal lines coverage. As primarily an auto insurer, PGR is less exposed to catastrophe losses than a number of peers, but they still pose a risk.

## Quantitative Evaluations

**S&P Quality Ranking** B+

| D | C | B- | B | B+ | A- | A | A+ |
|---|---|---|---|---|---|---|---|

**Relative Strength Rank** MODERATE

51

LOWEST = 1 HIGHEST = 99

## Revenue/Earnings Data

**Revenue (Million $)**

| | 1Q | 2Q | 3Q | 4Q | Year |
|---|---|---|---|---|---|
| 2011 | 3,894 | 3,873 | 3,811 | -- | -- |
| 2010 | 3,666 | 3,686 | 3,770 | 3,842 | 14,963 |
| 2009 | 3,468 | 3,584 | 3,611 | 3,901 | 14,564 |
| 2008 | 3,586 | 3,537 | 2,210 | 3,508 | 12,840 |
| 2007 | 3,687 | 3,671 | 3,710 | 3,615 | 14,687 |
| 2006 | 3,661 | 3,708 | 3,724 | 3,694 | 14,786 |

**Earnings Per Share ($)**

| | | | | | |
|---|---|---|---|---|---|
| 2011 | 0.55 | 0.38 | 0.25 | E0.40 | E1.50 |
| 2010 | 0.44 | 0.32 | 0.40 | 0.45 | 1.61 |
| 2009 | 0.35 | 0.37 | 0.40 | 0.46 | 1.57 |
| 2008 | 0.35 | 0.32 | -1.03 | 0.24 | -0.10 |
| 2007 | 0.49 | 0.39 | 0.42 | 0.34 | 1.65 |
| 2006 | 0.55 | 0.51 | 0.53 | 0.53 | 2.10 |

Fiscal year ended Dec. 31. Next earnings report expected: Mid December. EPS Estimates based on S&P Operating Earnings; historical GAAP earnings are as reported.

## Dividend Data (Dates: mm/dd Payment Date: mm/dd/yy)

| Amount<br>($) | Date<br>Decl. | Ex-Div.<br>Date | Stk. of<br>Record | Payment<br>Date |
|---|---|---|---|---|
| 0.399 | 12/10 | 01/25 | 01/27 | 02/04/11 |

Dividends have been paid since 2010. Source: Company reports.

The McGraw-Hill Companies

# Progressive Corp (The)

STANDARD
&POOR'S

## Business Summary November 01, 2011

CORPORATE OVERVIEW. Progressive Corp. underwrites an array of personal and commercial lines insurance. Net written premiums totaled $14.5 billion in 2010, of which personal lines accounted for 90% and commercial and other lines 10%.

PGR's core business (90% of 2010's $13.0 billion in personal lines net premiums written) is underwriting private passenger automobile insurance. Based on year-end 2009 industry net written premium data (latest available), the company was the fourth largest private U.S. passenger auto insurer, a position that PGR believes it retained in 2010. PGR's other lines of business include recreational vehicle, motorcycle and small commercial vehicle insurance, and, to a lesser degree, commercial indemnity insurance.

Personal lines products are distributed through a network of more than 30,000, including independent, agents, as well as brokers in New York and California, and strategic alliance business relationships with an array of financial institu-

tions. During 2010, 58% of total personal lines net written premiums were distributed through the agency channel (59% in 2009). Distribution through direct channels, including a toll free telephone line and the Internet, accounted for 42% of net written premiums in 2010 (41% in 2009).

PGR conducts its personal lines business in 50 states and in the District of Columbia. Commercial auto policies are written in every state except Hawaii; and not in the District of Columbia.

The commercial auto business (10% of net written premiums in 2010) writes primarily liability and physical damage insurance for automobiles and trucks owned by small businesses.

## Company Financials Fiscal Year Ended Dec. 31

| Per Share Data ($) | 2010 | 2009 | 2008 | 2007 | 2006 | 2005 | 2004 | 2003 | 2002 | 2001 |
|---|---|---|---|---|---|---|---|---|---|---|
| Tangible Book Value | 9.13 | 9.15 | 6.23 | 7.26 | 9.15 | 7.74 | 6.43 | 5.85 | 4.32 | 3.69 |
| Operating Earnings | NA | NA | NA | NA | NA | NA | NA | NA | 0.81 | 0.54 |
| Earnings | 1.61 | 1.57 | -0.10 | 1.65 | 2.10 | 1.75 | 1.91 | 1.42 | 0.75 | 0.46 |
| S&P Core Earnings | 1.52 | 1.54 | 1.29 | 1.55 | 2.11 | 1.77 | 1.85 | 1.40 | 0.79 | 0.52 |
| Dividends | 0.16 | Nil | Nil | Nil | 0.06 | 0.03 | 0.04 | 0.03 | 0.02 | 0.02 |
| Payout Ratio | 10% | Nil | Nil | Nil | 3% | 2% | 2% | 2% | 3% | 5% |
| Prices:High | 22.13 | 18.22 | 21.31 | 25.16 | 30.09 | 31.23 | 24.32 | 21.17 | 15.12 | 12.65 |
| Prices:Low | 16.18 | 9.76 | 10.29 | 17.26 | 22.18 | 20.34 | 18.28 | 11.56 | 11.19 | 6.84 |
| P/E Ratio:High | 14 | 12 | NM | 15 | 14 | 18 | 13 | 15 | 20 | 28 |
| P/E Ratio:Low | 10 | 6 | NM | 10 | 11 | 12 | 10 | 8 | 15 | 15 |

| Income Statement Analysis (Million $) | | | | | | | | | | |
|---|---|---|---|---|---|---|---|---|---|---|
| Premium Income | 14,315 | 14,013 | 13,631 | 13,877 | 14,118 | 13,764 | 13,170 | 11,341 | 8,884 | 7,162 |
| Net Investment Income | 520 | 507 | 638 | 681 | 648 | 537 | 484 | 465 | 455 | 414 |
| Other Revenue | 128 | 44.0 | -1,429 | 116 | 20.7 | 539 | 612 | 54.5 | 34.3 | 24.7 |
| Total Revenue | 14,963 | 14,564 | 12,840 | 14,687 | 14,786 | 14,303 | 13,782 | 11,892 | 9,373 | 7,488 |
| Pretax Income | 1,565 | 1,557 | -222 | 1,693 | 2,433 | 2,059 | 2,451 | 1,860 | 981 | 588 |
| Net Operating Income | NA | NA | NA | NA | NA | NA | NA | NA | 718 | 486 |
| Net Income | 1,068 | 1,058 | -70.0 | 1,183 | 1,648 | 1,394 | 1,649 | 1,255 | 667 | 411 |
| S&P Core Earnings | 1,006 | 1,040 | 869 | 1,113 | 1,654 | 1,415 | 1,591 | 1,234 | 702 | 469 |

| Balance Sheet & Other Financial Data (Million $) | | | | | | | | | | |
|---|---|---|---|---|---|---|---|---|---|---|
| Cash & Equivalent | 268 | 271 | 129 | 148 | 140 | 139 | 124 | 110 | 94.8 | 86.4 |
| Premiums Due | 3,480 | 3,020 | 2,697 | 2,730 | 2,932 | 2,906 | 2,669 | 2,351 | 1,959 | 1,497 |
| Investment Assets:Bonds | 11,850 | 11,563 | 9,559 | 9,185 | 9,959 | 10,222 | 9,084 | 9,133 | 7,713 | 5,949 |
| Investment Assets:Stocks | 2,583 | 2,072 | 2,266 | 4,598 | 4,149 | 3,279 | 2,621 | 2,751 | 2,004 | 2,050 |
| Investment Assets:Loans | Nil | Nil | Nil | Nil | Nil | Nil | Nil | Nil | Nil | Nil |
| Investment Assets:Total | 15,523 | 14,713 | 12,978 | 14,165 | 14,689 | 14,275 | 13,082 | 12,532 | 10,284 | 8,226 |
| Deferred Policy Costs | 417 | 402 | 414 | 426 | 441 | 445 | 432 | 412 | 364 | 317 |
| Total Assets | 21,150 | 19,846 | 18,251 | 18,843 | 19,482 | 18,899 | 17,184 | 16,282 | 13,564 | 11,122 |
| Debt | 1,958 | 2,177 | 2,176 | 2,174 | 1,186 | 1,285 | 1,284 | 1,490 | 1,489 | 1,096 |
| Common Equity | 6,049 | 5,749 | 4,215 | 4,936 | 6,847 | 6,108 | 5,155 | 5,060 | 3,768 | 3,251 |
| Property & Casualty:Loss Ratio | 70.8 | 70.7 | 73.5 | 71.5 | 66.6 | 68.1 | 65.0 | 67.4 | 70.9 | 73.6 |
| Property & Casualty:Expense Ratio | 21.6 | 20.9 | 21.1 | 21.1 | 19.9 | 87.4 | 19.6 | 18.8 | 20.4 | 21.0 |
| Property & Casualty Combined Ratio | 92.4 | 91.6 | 94.6 | 92.6 | 86.5 | 19.3 | 84.6 | 86.2 | 91.3 | 94.7 |
| % Return on Revenue | 7.1 | 7.3 | NM | 8.1 | 11.1 | 9.7 | 12.0 | 10.6 | 7.1 | 5.4 |
| % Return on Equity | 18.1 | 21.2 | NM | 20.1 | 25.4 | 24.8 | 32.4 | 28.4 | 19.3 | 13.4 |

Data as orig reptd.; bef. results of disc opers/spec. items. Per share data adj. for stk. divs.; EPS diluted. E-Estimated. NA-Not Available. NM-Not Meaningful. NR-Not Ranked. UR-Under Review.

**Office:** 6300 Wilson Mills Road, Mayfield Village, OH 44143.
**Telephone:** 440-461-5000.
**Website:** http://www.progressive.com
**Chrmn:** P.B. Lewis

**Pres & CEO:** G.M. Renwick
**CFO:** B. Domeck
**Chief Acctg Officer:** J.W. Basch
**Treas:** T.A. King

**Investor Contact:** P. Brennan (440-395-2370)
**Board Members:** S. B. Burgdoerfer, C. A. Davis, R. N. Farah, L. W. Fitt, S. R. Hardis, P. B. Lewis, N. S. Matthews, H. G. Miller, P. H. Nettles, G. M. Renwick, B. T. Sheares

**Founded:** 1965
**Domicile:** Ohio
**Employees:** 24,638

# Progress Energy Inc.

STANDARD &POOR'S

**S&P Recommendation** HOLD ★★★★★

| | | |
|---|---|---|
| **Price** | **12-Mo. Target Price** | **Investment Style** |
| $51.54 (as of Nov 25, 2011) | $51.00 | Large-Cap Blend |

**GICS Sector** Utilities
**Sub-Industry** Electric Utilities

**Summary** This diversified energy company, with two electric utilities serving the Carolinas and Florida, has agreed to merge with Duke Energy.

## Key Stock Statistics (Source S&P, Vickers, company reports)

| | | | | | | | |
|---|---|---|---|---|---|---|---|
| 52-Wk Range | $53.82– 42.05 | S&P Oper. EPS 2011**E** | 3.16 | Market Capitalization(B) | $15.205 | Beta | 0.31 |
| Trailing 12-Month EPS | $2.62 | S&P Oper. EPS 2012**E** | 3.21 | Yield (%) | 4.81 | S&P 3-Yr. Proj. EPS CAGR(%) | 2 |
| Trailing 12-Month P/E | 19.7 | P/E on S&P Oper. EPS 2011**E** | 16.3 | Dividend Rate/Share | $2.48 | S&P Credit Rating | BBB+ |
| $10K Invested 5 Yrs Ago | $14,387 | Common Shares Outstg. (M) | 295.0 | Institutional Ownership (%) | 55 | | |

## Price Performance

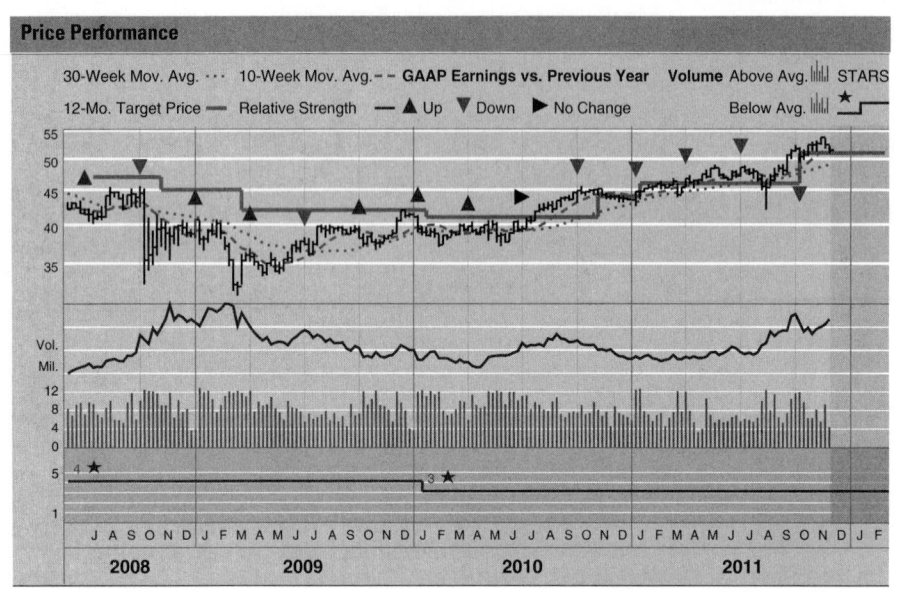

30-Week Mov. Avg. · · · 10-Week Mov. Avg. – – GAAP Earnings vs. Previous Year   Volume Above Avg. STARS
12-Mo. Target Price — Relative Strength — ▲ Up ▼ Down ► No Change   Below Avg.

Options: ASE, CBOE, Ph

Analysis prepared by Equity Analyst **Justin McCann** on Oct 05, 2011, when the stock traded at **$50.14**.

### Qualitative Risk Assessment

| LOW | MEDIUM | HIGH |
|---|---|---|

With the higher risk synthetic fuel business having been discontinued, our risk assessment reflects the strong and steady cash flow we still forecast from the regulated utilities in the Carolinas and Florida, despite the slowdown in customer growth due to the downturn in the economy and the housing market and an unfavorable regulatory environment in Florida.

### Quantitative Evaluations

**S&P Quality Ranking**     B

| D | C | B- | B | B+ | A- | A | A+ |
|---|---|---|---|---|---|---|---|

**Relative Strength Rank**     **STRONG**

83

LOWEST = 1      HIGHEST = 99

## Revenue/Earnings Data

**Revenue (Million $)**

| | 1Q | 2Q | 3Q | 4Q | Year |
|---|---|---|---|---|---|
| 2011 | 2,167 | 2,256 | 2,747 | -- | -- |
| 2010 | 2,535 | 2,372 | 2,962 | 2,321 | 10,190 |
| 2009 | 2,442 | 2,312 | 2,824 | 2,307 | 9,885 |
| 2008 | 2,066 | 2,244 | 2,696 | 2,161 | 9,167 |
| 2007 | 2,072 | 2,129 | 2,750 | 2,202 | 9,153 |
| 2006 | 2,433 | 2,499 | 2,913 | 2,273 | 9,570 |

**Earnings Per Share ($)**

| | 1Q | 2Q | 3Q | 4Q | Year |
|---|---|---|---|---|---|
| 2011 | 0.63 | 0.60 | 0.98 | E0.57 | E3.16 |
| 2010 | 0.67 | 0.62 | 1.23 | 0.43 | 2.96 |
| 2009 | 0.66 | 0.62 | 1.24 | 0.46 | 2.99 |
| 2008 | 0.58 | 0.77 | 1.18 | 0.44 | 2.96 |
| 2007 | 0.62 | 0.41 | 1.27 | 0.09 | 2.70 |
| 2006 | 0.19 | 0.06 | 0.97 | 0.51 | 2.05 |

Fiscal year ended Dec. 31. Next earnings report expected: NA. EPS Estimates based on S&P Operating Earnings; historical GAAP earnings are as reported.

## Highlights

► Subject to required approvals, the agreed-to merger with Duke Energy (DUK 19 Hold) is expected to close by the end of 2011 and result in the largest regulated utility in the U.S., with 7.1 million electricity customers in six states, and about 57,000 megawatts of generating capacity. We believe the combined company, with more than $90 billion in total assets, would have substantial financial and operational strength.

► Excluding one-time charges of $0.18, we expect stand-alone operating EPS in 2011 to rise about 3% from 2010's $3.06. Results should be aided by an expected modest economic recovery in Florida and above-average customer growth in the Carolinas, partially offset by a return to more normal weather. Operating EPS in the first half of 2011 was $0.03 above the year-earlier period, reflecting lower amortization expense and nuclear plant outage costs, partially offset by lower wholesale sales, less favorable weather, and 2.8% more shares.

► On June 27, 2011, the company announced that it plans to spend up to $1.3 billion to repair the Crystal River Nuclear Plant. It expects the plant, whose containment building was damaged in late 2009, to return to service in 2014.

## Investment Rationale/Risk

► While the regulatory approval process for the pending merger with Duke Energy could take longer than anticipated, we believe it will ultimately receive the required approvals and close by year-end or early 2012. The merger is expected to result in fuel and operational efficiencies in the Carolinas, and a stronger balance sheet that would enable rate base investments that could lead to 4%-6% long-term EPS growth. The proposed annual dividend of the combined company ($0.98 a share) would be a 3.2% increase over PGN's current dividend.

► Risks to our recommendation and target price include the possibility of the planned merger being delayed or terminated, extended weakness in the Florida economy and housing market, and a sharp reduction in the average P/E for the electric utilities group as a whole.

► Our 12-month target price of $51, a premium-to-peers multiple of 16.1X our operating EPS estimate for 2011, primarily reflects the terms of the merger agreement based on the recent share price of Duke Energy. We would expect the shares to be supported, in part, by the projected financial strength of the combined company and the above-peers dividend yield.

## Dividend Data (Dates: mm/dd Payment Date: mm/dd/yy)

| Amount ($) | Date Decl. | Ex-Div. Date | Stk. of Record | Payment Date |
|---|---|---|---|---|
| 0.620 | 12/08 | 01/06 | 01/10 | 02/01/11 |
| 0.620 | 03/16 | 04/07 | 04/11 | 05/02/11 |
| 0.620 | 05/11 | 07/07 | 07/11 | 08/01/11 |
| 0.620 | 09/16 | 10/06 | 10/11 | 11/01/11 |

Dividends have been paid since 1937. Source: Company reports.

---

**Please read the Required Disclosures and Analyst Certification on the last page of this report.**

# Progress Energy Inc.

STANDARD &POOR'S

## Business Summary October 05, 2011

CORPORATE OVERVIEW. Headquartered in Raleigh, NC, Progress Energy operates in retail utility markets in the southeastern U.S., and in competitive electricity, gas and other fuel markets in the eastern U.S. It is the holding company for the fully integrated regulated utilities Progress Energy Carolinas (PEC) and Progress Energy Florida (PEF), which together serve approximately 3.1 million retail electric customers. In 2010, PEC contributed about 57% of utility income (54% in 2009), and PEF 43% (46%).

IMPACT OF MAJOR DEVELOPMENTS. On January 10, 2011, PGN announced a definitive merger agreement with Duke Energy (DUK 18, Hold), a Charlotte-headquartered electric power holding company serving approximately 4 million customers located in five states in the Southeast and Midwest. Under the terms of the stock-for-stock agreement, which would have a total equity value

of approximately $13.7 billion, Progress Energy shareholders would receive 2.6125 DUK shares for each PGN share. Upon the close of the merger, it is expected that PGN shareholders would have a 37% interest in the combined company, which would maintain the Duke Energy name, and DUK shareholders 63%. DUK's chairman, president and CEO, James E. Rogers, would become the executive chairman of the combined company, while PGN's chairman, president and CEO, William D. Johnson, would become the president and CEO.

## Company Financials Fiscal Year Ended Dec. 31

| Per Share Data ($) | 2010 | 2009 | 2008 | 2007 | 2006 | 2005 | 2004 | 2003 | 2002 | 2001 |
|---|---|---|---|---|---|---|---|---|---|---|
| Tangible Book Value | 21.73 | 20.69 | 19.15 | 18.33 | 18.09 | 15.94 | 14.48 | 13.78 | 12.43 | 10.58 |
| Earnings | 2.96 | 2.99 | 2.96 | 2.70 | 2.05 | 2.94 | 3.10 | 3.40 | 2.53 | 2.64 |
| S&P Core Earnings | 3.07 | 3.18 | 2.59 | 2.67 | 1.95 | 2.94 | 2.93 | 3.44 | 2.04 | 2.59 |
| Dividends | 2.48 | 2.48 | 2.46 | 2.44 | 2.42 | 2.36 | 2.30 | 2.24 | 2.18 | 2.12 |
| Payout Ratio | 84% | 83% | 83% | 90% | 118% | 80% | 74% | 66% | 86% | 80% |
| Prices:High | 45.61 | 42.20 | 49.16 | 52.75 | 49.55 | 46.00 | 47.95 | 48.00 | 52.70 | 49.25 |
| Prices:Low | 37.04 | 31.35 | 32.60 | 43.12 | 40.27 | 40.19 | 40.09 | 37.45 | 32.84 | 38.78 |
| P/E Ratio:High | 15 | 14 | 17 | 20 | 24 | 16 | 15 | 14 | 21 | 19 |
| P/E Ratio:Low | 13 | 10 | 11 | 16 | 20 | 14 | 13 | 11 | 13 | 15 |

| Income Statement Analysis (Million $) | | | | | | | | | | |
|---|---|---|---|---|---|---|---|---|---|---|
| Revenue | 10,190 | 9,885 | 9,167 | 9,153 | 9,570 | 10,108 | 9,772 | 8,743 | 7,945 | 8,461 |
| Depreciation | 1,083 | 1,135 | 957 | 905 | 1,032 | 1,074 | 1,068 | 1,040 | 820 | 1,090 |
| Maintenance | NA | NA | NA | NA | NA | NA | NA | NA | NA | NA |
| Fixed Charges Coverage | 2.88 | 2.82 | 2.84 | 2.76 | 2.28 | 1.93 | 2.21 | 2.16 | 1.64 | 1.75 |
| Construction Credits | 124 | 163 | 162 | 17.0 | 7.00 | 13.0 | 6.00 | 7.00 | 8.13 | 18.0 |
| Effective Tax Rate | 38.3% | 32.2% | 33.7% | 32.2% | 28.1% | NM | 13.5% | NM | NM | NM |
| Net Income | 860 | 846 | 773 | 693 | 514 | 727 | 753 | 811 | 552 | 542 |
| S&P Core Earnings | 891 | 887 | 677 | 685 | 487 | 726 | 712 | 819 | 445 | 532 |

| Balance Sheet & Other Financial Data (Million $) | | | | | | | | | | |
|---|---|---|---|---|---|---|---|---|---|---|
| Gross Property | 32,807 | 31,309 | 29,591 | 27,500 | 25,796 | 26,401 | 25,602 | 25,172 | 23,021 | 22,541 |
| Capital Expenditures | 2,221 | 2,295 | 2,333 | 2,201 | 1,423 | 1,286 | 998 | 1,018 | 2,109 | 1,216 |
| Net Property | 21,240 | 19,733 | 18,293 | 16,605 | 15,732 | 16,799 | 16,819 | 17,056 | 12,541 | 12,445 |
| Capitalization:Long Term Debt | 12,230 | 12,365 | 10,983 | 9,069 | 8,928 | 10,539 | 9,650 | 10,027 | 9,840 | 9,577 |
| Capitalization:% Long Term Debt | 55.0 | 56.7 | 55.8 | 51.8 | 51.9 | 56.7 | 55.8 | 57.4 | 59.6 | 61.5 |
| Capitalization:Preferred | Nil | Nil | Nil | Nil | Nil | Nil | Nil | Nil | Nil | Nil |
| Capitalization:% Preferred | Nil | Nil | Nil | Nil | Nil | Nil | Nil | Nil | Nil | Nil |
| Capitalization:Common | 10,023 | 9,449 | 8,687 | 8,422 | 8,286 | 8,038 | 7,633 | 7,444 | 6,677 | 6,004 |
| Capitalization:% Common | 45.0 | 43.3 | 44.2 | 48.2 | 48.1 | 43.3 | 44.2 | 42.6 | 40.4 | 38.5 |
| Total Capital | 22,762 | 22,226 | 19,803 | 17,714 | 17,681 | 19,061 | 18,058 | 18,398 | 17,656 | 17,241 |
| % Operating Ratio | 85.1 | 86.1 | 85.9 | 86.8 | 87.5 | 87.2 | 86.7 | 66.8 | 85.4 | 83.5 |
| % Earned on Net Property | 10.0 | 9.3 | 9.6 | 9.7 | 8.5 | 7.7 | 8.8 | 8.2 | 8.3 | 10.3 |
| % Return on Revenue | 8.4 | 8.6 | 8.4 | 7.6 | 5.4 | 7.2 | 7.7 | 9.3 | 6.9 | 6.4 |
| % Return on Invested Capital | 7.2 | 7.3 | 7.6 | 7.4 | 6.8 | 7.3 | 7.6 | 8.2 | 7.2 | 9.2 |
| % Return on Common Equity | 8.8 | 9.3 | 9.0 | 8.3 | 6.3 | 9.3 | 10.0 | 11.5 | 8.7 | 9.4 |

Data as orig reptd.; bef. results of disc opers/spec. items. Per share data adj. for stk. divs.; EPS diluted. E-Estimated. NA-Not Available. NM-Not Meaningful. NR-Not Ranked. UR-Under Review.

**Office:** 410 South Wilmington Street, Raleigh, NC 27601-1748.
**Telephone:** 919-546-6111.
**Email:** shareholder.relations@progress-energy.com
**Website:** http://www.progress-energy.com

**Chrmn, Pres & CEO:** W.D. Johnson
**CFO:** M.F. Mulhern
**Chief Admin Officer, Secy & General Counsel:** J.R. McArthur
**Chief Acctg Officer & Cntlr:** J.M. Stone

**Treas:** T.R. Sullivan
**Investor Contact:** B. Drennan (919-546-7474)
**Board Members:** J. D. Baker, II, J. E. Bostic, Jr., H. E. DeLoach, Jr., J. B. Hyler, Jr., W. D. Johnson, R. W. Jones, W. S. Jones, R. Korpan, M. Martinez, E. M. McKee, J. H. Mullin, III, C. W. Pryor, Jr., C. A. Saladrigas, T. M. Stone, A. C. Tollison, Jr.

**Founded:** 1926
**Domicile:** North Carolina
**Employees:** 11,000

# ProLogis Inc

**STANDARD &POOR'S**

| S&P Recommendation | HOLD ★★★☆☆ | Price | 12-Mo. Target Price |
|---|---|---|---|
| | | $25.21 (as of Nov 25, 2011) | $32.00 |

**GICS Sector** Financials
**Sub-Industry** Industrial REITS

**Summary** This real estate investment trust, a global provider of distribution facilities, is the result of the June 2011 merger of the former ProLogis and AMB Property Corp.

## Key Stock Statistics (Source S&P, Vickers, company reports)

| | | | | | | | | |
|---|---|---|---|---|---|---|---|---|
| 52-Wk Range | $37.52–21.74 | S&P FFO/Sh. 2011E | 1.53 | Market Capitalization(B) | $11.553 | Beta | | 2.68 |
| Trailing 12-Month FFO/Share | $-5.02 | S&P FFO/Sh. 2012E | 1.75 | Yield (%) | 4.44 | S&P 3-Yr. FFO/Sh. Proj. CAGR(%) | | 5 |
| Trailing 12-Month P/FFO | NA | P/FFO on S&P FFO/Sh. 2011E | 16.5 | Dividend Rate/Share | $1.12 | S&P Credit Rating | | BBB- |
| $10K Invested 5 Yrs Ago | $2,259 | Common Shares Outstg. (M) | 458.3 | Institutional Ownership (%) | NM | | | |

## Price Performance

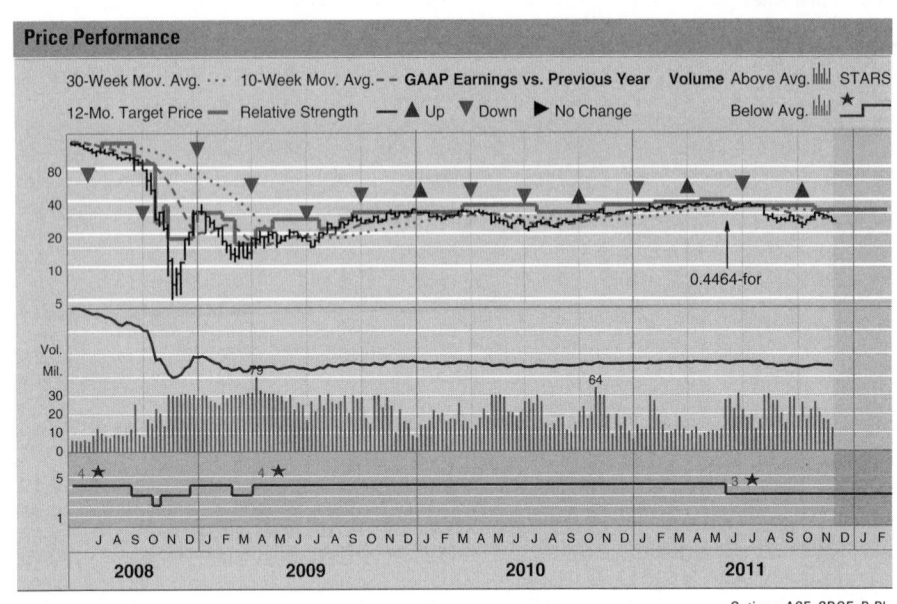

Analysis prepared by Equity Analyst **R. Shepard, CFA** on Nov 09, 2011, when the stock traded at **$27.89**.

Options: ASE, CBOE, P, Ph

## Highlights

▶ We think PLD is on track to saving about $90 million in annual administrative costs, following the June 2011 merger of the former ProLogis and AMB Property Corp. We also expect 2012 occupancy to increase about 100 basis points, to 92.0%, due to expanding demand for distribution facilities positioned to serve global distribution. In our view, higher demand may still be partially offset in 2012 by lower market rental rates as existing tenants renew leases.

▶ Developers such as PLD have sharply reduced new developments over the past two years, helping to limit supply, which we believe will allow rents to increase once demand recovers. However, we expect a gradual rebound in global trade to also act as a catalyst for investments in new development and acquisitions going forward. We expect PLD to deploy about $1.0 billion annually on construction projects, principally in joint venture funds.

▶ Our 2012 FFO per share estimate of $1.75, up from $1.53 seen in 2011, reflects a full year of operations from the combined companies and related administrative cost savings. We exclude one-time merger expenses and related impairment charges.

## Investment Rationale/Risk

▶ Longer term, we see shareholders benefiting from PLD's position as one of the largest owners of global distribution facilities. The trust estimates that 80% of its assets are located in population centers featuring major seaports, airports and other infrastructure. We see the merger with AMB Property offering significant administrative synergies and creating an organization with an unrivaled portfolio of industrial assets around the world. But the integration of two large property owners holds integration risks, in our view. We believe the shares, recently trading at about 16X our 2012 FFO per share estimate, are fairly valued at their current price.

▶ Risks to our recommendation and target price include a sharp drop in demand and rental rates for industrial space, unexpected delays in planned new development projects, and a lack of available financing for potential acquisitions.

▶ Our 12-month target price of $32 is based on a multiple of 18.3X our 2012 FFO estimate of $1.75, a premium to peers reflecting our view of PLD's potential economies of scale and well located properties.

## Qualitative Risk Assessment

| LOW | MEDIUM | HIGH |
|---|---|---|

Our risk assessment reflects our view of PLD's position as one of the largest owners of industrial space in the world, and its broad geographic and customer diversification. We consider the trust's financial position on a post-merger basis adequate to meet its debt obligations.

## Quantitative Evaluations

**S&P Quality Ranking**  B-

| D | C | B- | B | B+ | A- | A | A+ |
|---|---|---|---|---|---|---|---|

**Relative Strength Rank**  MODERATE

38

LOWEST = 1    HIGHEST = 99

## Revenue/FFO Data

**Revenue (Million $)**

| | 1Q | 2Q | 3Q | 4Q | Year |
|---|---|---|---|---|---|
| 2011 | 238.8 | 347.3 | 532.4 | -- | -- |
| 2010 | 217.8 | 219.5 | 220.1 | 242.7 | 909.1 |
| 2009 | 433.3 | 259.1 | 270.4 | 260.3 | 1,223 |
| 2008 | 1,637 | 1,515 | 1,122 | 1,388 | 5,599 |
| 2007 | 955.9 | 989.4 | 3,461 | 799.9 | 6,205 |
| 2006 | 571.1 | 687.4 | 580.5 | 624.9 | 2,464 |

**FFO Per Share ($)**

| | | | | | |
|---|---|---|---|---|---|
| 2011 | 0.11 | 0.03 | 0.45 | E0.40 | E1.53 |
| 2010 | 0.02 | 0.45 | 0.49 | -5.33 | -5.02 |
| 2009 | 1.93 | 0.76 | 0.47 | -1.43 | 0.78 |
| 2008 | 3.09 | 2.37 | 1.41 | 1.37 | 8.24 |
| 2007 | 2.80 | 2.60 | 3.16 | 1.77 | 10.33 |
| 2006 | 2.02 | 2.02 | 1.77 | 2.49 | 8.27 |

Fiscal year ended Dec. 31. Next earnings report expected: Early February. FFO Estimates based on S&P Funds From Operations Est..

## Dividend Data (Dates: mm/dd Payment Date: mm/dd/yy)

| Amount ($) | Date Decl. | Ex-Div. Date | Stk. of Record | Payment Date |
|---|---|---|---|---|
| 0.113 | 10/27 | 11/10 | 11/15 | 11/30/10 |
| 0.113 | 01/31 | 02/10 | 02/14 | 02/28/11 |
| 0.113 | 05/05 | 05/12 | 05/16 | 05/25/11 |
| 0.280 | 09/09 | 09/15 | 09/19 | 09/30/11 |

Dividends have been paid since 1994. Source: Company reports.

---

**Please read the Required Disclosures and Analyst Certification on the last page of this report.**

**The McGraw·Hill Companies**

Stock Report | November 26, 2011 | NYS Symbol: **PLD**

# ProLogis Inc

STANDARD
&POOR'S

## Business Summary November 09, 2011

ProLogis, Inc. (PLD) is a real estate investment trust that owns and operates industrial distribution facilities in North America, Europe and Asia. The trust's business strategy is to integrate international scope and expertise with a strong local presence in its markets, thereby becoming an attractive choice for its targeted customer base, the largest global users of distribution space, while achieving long-term sustainable growth in cash flow.

On January 31, 2011, the former ProLogis and AMB Property Corp. announced a definitive agreement to combine in a merger of equals. On June 3, 2011, the merger was completed, with each ProLogis common share converted into 0.4464 of a newly issued AMB common share. Upon completion of the merger, the company was named ProLogis, Inc., and trades under the ticker symbol PLD. We believe that the combined company, with estimated gross assets owned and managed square feet with a book value of $48 billion and encompassing about 598 million square feet, has a very strong portfolio of industrial properties around the world.

The trust's operating strategy includes the location of properties near key passenger and cargo airports, highway systems, and ports in major metropolitan areas. PLD targets customers with business ties to global trade. To serve the facilities needs of these customers, its invests in major distribution markets, transportation hubs and gateways in both the U.S. and internationally.

The trust estimates that 71% of assets (measured by square feet) are located in The Americas, 24% are located in Europe, and 5% are positioned in Asia.

PLD's properties are often a critical component of the operations of its major customers, such as Deutsche Post World Net/DHL (2.6% of pro forma 2010 annualized base rent), Kuehne + Nagel (1.2%), Home Depot (1.1%), and CEVA Logistics (1.0%). We believe the trust's positioning near major trade distribution infrastructure, combined with its broad array of customer relationships, should help create barriers to entry for newer and smaller competitors over the longer term and help insulate the portfolio from regional slowdowns.

We expect the trust to generate long-term internal growth through rent increases on existing space and renewals on rollover space, striving to maintain a high occupancy rate. As of December 31, 2010, on a combined basis to reflect the merger, PLD faces lease expirations of 77 million square feet in 2011, representing an estimated 12.8% of total available space and about 19.8% of annualized base rent.

## Company Financials Fiscal Year Ended Dec. 31

| Per Share Data ($) | 2010 | 2009 | 2008 | 2007 | 2006 | 2005 | 2004 | 2003 | 2002 | 2001 |
|---|---|---|---|---|---|---|---|---|---|---|
| Tangible Book Value | 27.98 | 34.21 | 47.65 | 56.99 | 51.72 | 47.22 | 33.20 | 32.15 | 31.27 | 28.99 |
| Earnings | -7.33 | -1.64 | -1.90 | 8.09 | 6.07 | 3.11 | 2.44 | 2.60 | 2.69 | 1.16 |
| S&P Core Earnings | -6.23 | -1.64 | -1.90 | 8.09 | 6.07 | 3.11 | 2.37 | 2.55 | 2.62 | 1.10 |
| Dividends | 1.26 | 1.57 | 4.64 | 4.12 | 3.58 | 3.32 | 3.27 | 3.23 | 3.18 | 3.09 |
| Payout Ratio | NM | NM | NM | 51% | 59% | 106% | 134% | 124% | 118% | NM |
| Prices:High | 33.53 | 37.37 | 149.15 | 164.31 | 151.25 | 106.68 | 97.07 | 73.07 | 58.24 | 52.20 |
| Prices:Low | 20.49 | 10.91 | 4.93 | 115.68 | 103.70 | 81.77 | 61.87 | 52.93 | 46.95 | 43.35 |
| P/E Ratio:High | NM | NM | NM | 20 | 25 | 34 | 40 | 28 | 22 | 45 |
| P/E Ratio:Low | NM | NM | NM | 14 | 17 | 26 | 25 | 20 | 17 | 37 |

| Income Statement Analysis (Million $) | | | | | | | | | | |
|---|---|---|---|---|---|---|---|---|---|---|
| Rental Income | 771 | 891 | 1,002 | 1,068 | 928 | 635 | 527 | Nil | 449 | 466 |
| Mortgage Income | Nil | Nil | Nil | Nil | Nil | Nil | Nil | Nil | Nil | Nil |
| Total Income | 909 | 1,223 | 5,599 | 6,205 | 2,464 | 1,868 | 598 | 734 | 675 | 574 |
| General Expenses | 447 | 493 | 4,692 | 4,760 | 1,403 | 1,210 | 224 | 210 | 91.0 | 83.0 |
| Interest Expense | 461 | 373 | 341 | 368 | 294 | 178 | 153 | 155 | 153 | 164 |
| Provision for Losses | Nil | Nil | Nil | Nil | Nil | Nil | Nil | Nil | Nil | Nil |
| Depreciation | 320 | 316 | 339 | 309 | 293 | 199 | 172 | 165 | 153 | 143 |
| Net Income | -1,582 | -266 | -195 | 987 | 718 | 318 | 234 | 251 | 249 | 128 |
| S&P Core Earnings | -1,368 | -292 | -221 | 962 | 692 | 292 | 199 | 208 | 210 | 86.8 |

| Balance Sheet & Other Financial Data (Million $) | | | | | | | | | | |
|---|---|---|---|---|---|---|---|---|---|---|
| Cash | 37.6 | 34.4 | 175 | 419 | 1,775 | 1,241 | 1,145 | 1,009 | 111 | 28.0 |
| Total Assets | 14,903 | 16,885 | 19,252 | 19,724 | 15,904 | 13,114 | 7,098 | 6,369 | 5,924 | 5,604 |
| Real Estate Investment | 15,781 | 15,216 | 15,706 | 16,579 | 13,954 | 11,875 | 6,334 | 5,854 | 5,396 | 4,588 |
| Loss Reserve | Nil | Nil | Nil | Nil | Nil | Nil | Nil | Nil | Nil | Nil |
| Net Investment | 14,186 | 13,545 | 14,123 | 15,210 | 12,674 | 10,757 | 5,345 | 5,007 | 4,683 | 4,013 |
| Short Term Debt | Nil | Nil | Nil | Nil | Nil | Nil | Nil | Nil | 222 | 49.3 |
| Capitalization:Debt | 6,506 | 7,977 | 11,008 | 9,650 | 7,844 | 6,678 | 3,414 | 2,991 | 2,510 | 2,529 |
| Capitalization:Equity | 7,155 | 7,637 | 6,075 | 7,086 | 6,049 | 5,138 | 2,752 | 2,586 | 2,486 | 2,276 |
| Capitalization:Total | 14,026 | 15,984 | 17,453 | 17,165 | 14,295 | 12,225 | 6,583 | 6,089 | 5,439 | 5,251 |
| % Earnings & Depreciation/Assets | NM | 0.3 | 7.4 | 7.3 | 4.7 | 5.1 | 6.0 | 6.8 | 7.0 | 4.7 |
| Price Times Book Value:High | 1.2 | 1.1 | 3.1 | 2.9 | 2.9 | 2.3 | 2.9 | 2.3 | 1.9 | 1.8 |
| Price Times Book Value:Low | 0.7 | 0.3 | 0.1 | 2.0 | 2.0 | 1.7 | 1.9 | 1.6 | 1.5 | 1.5 |

Data as orig reptd.; bef. results of disc opers/spec. items. Per share data adj. for stk. divs.; EPS diluted. E-Estimated. NA-Not Available. NM-Not Meaningful. NR-Not Ranked. UR-Under Review.

**Office:** Pier 1, Bay 1, San Francisco, CA 94111.
**Telephone:** 415-394-9000.
**Email:** info@prologis.com
**Website:** http://www.prologis.com

**Chrmn & Co-CEO:** H.R. Moghadam
**Pres:** T.R. Antenucci
**Co-CEO:** W.C. Rakowich
**CFO:** W.E. Sullivan

**Chief Admin Officer:** C.E. Sullivan
**Investor Contact:** M. Marsden (303-567-5622)
**Trustees:** G. L. Fotiades, C. N. Garvey, L. H. Kennard, J. M. Losh, I. F. Lyons, III, H. R. Moghadam, W. C. Rakowich, J. L. Skelton, D. M. Steuert, C. B. Webb, W. D. Zollars

**Founded:** 1991
**Domicile:** Maryland
**Employees:** 1,100

Redistribution or reproduction is prohibited without written permission. Copyright ©2011 The McGraw-Hill Companies, Inc.

The **McGraw·Hill** Companies

# Prudential Financial Inc

**STANDARD &POOR'S**

| | | |
|---|---|---|
| **S&P Recommendation** HOLD ★★★☆☆ | **Price**<br>$44.91 (as of Nov 25, 2011) | **12-Mo. Target Price**<br>$54.00 |

**Investment Style**
Large-Cap Value

**GICS Sector** Financials
**Sub-Industry** Life & Health Insurance

**Summary** This company provides a wide range of insurance, investment management, and other financial products and services to customers in the U.S. and overseas.

## Key Stock Statistics (Source S&P, Vickers, company reports)

| | | | | | | | |
|---|---|---|---|---|---|---|---|
| 52-Wk Range | $67.52– 42.45 | S&P Oper. EPS 2011**E** | 6.18 | Market Capitalization(B) | $21.198 | Beta | 2.32 |
| Trailing 12-Month EPS | $6.41 | S&P Oper. EPS 2012**E** | 7.70 | Yield (%) | 3.23 | S&P 3-Yr. Proj. EPS CAGR(%) | 8 |
| Trailing 12-Month P/E | 7.0 | P/E on S&P Oper. EPS 2011**E** | 7.3 | Dividend Rate/Share | $1.45 | S&P Credit Rating | A |
| $10K Invested 5 Yrs Ago | $6,488 | Common Shares Outstg. (M) | 472.0 | Institutional Ownership (%) | 65 | | |

## Price Performance

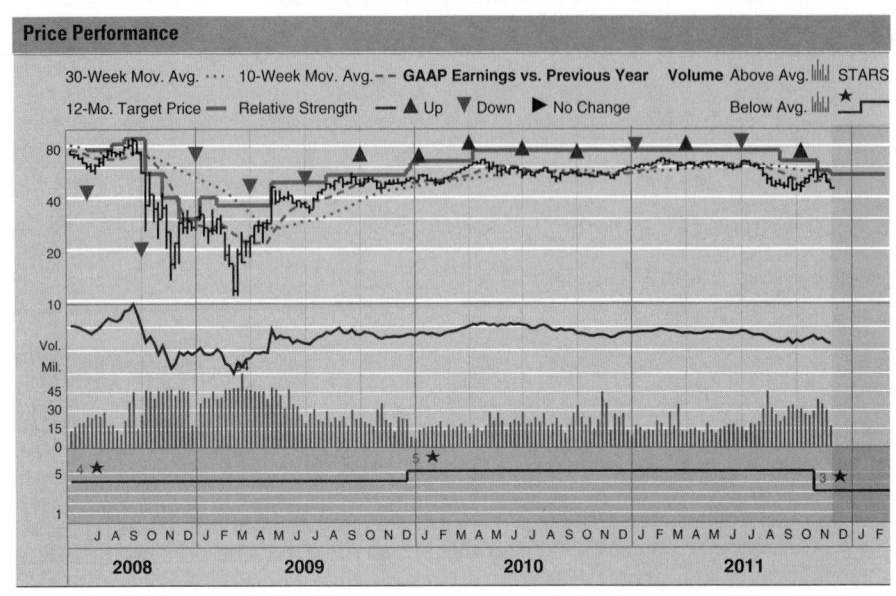

30-Week Mov. Avg. ···· 10-Week Mov. Avg. -- **GAAP Earnings vs. Previous Year** Volume Above Avg. STARS
12-Mo. Target Price — Relative Strength — ▲ Up ▼ Down ► No Change Below Avg.

Options: ASE, CBOE, Ph

Analysis prepared by Equity Analyst **Cathy Seifert** on Nov 23, 2011, when the stock traded at **$45.17**.

## Qualitative Risk Assessment

| LOW | MEDIUM | HIGH |
|---|---|---|

Our risk assessment reflects PRU's exposure to equity markets and interest rates, and the risk of further asset impairments on its balance sheet, especially considering its sizable holdings of commercial real estate loans and CMBS. However, we believe its financial flexibility and excess capital cushion will make future losses manageable. We also view favorably PRU's varied product offerings, geographic diversification, and prominent market position.

## Quantitative Evaluations

**S&P Quality Ranking** B+

| D | C | B- | B | B+ | A- | A | A+ |
|---|---|---|---|---|---|---|---|

**Relative Strength Rank** WEAK

27

LOWEST = 1          HIGHEST = 99

## Highlights

➤ We expect relatively strong sales for PRU's U.S. units in coming periods, most notably in-stitutional products and asset management. We believe PRU's variable annuity franchise is strong, given the attractiveness of its products and superior distribution capabilities. We ex-pect results in asset management to be aided by growth in assets under management, partly offset by mixed investment returns.

➤ We expect margins in coming periods to remain under pressure from a myriad of factors, includ-ing some adverse claim trends. Revenues in the nine months ended September 30, 2011, rose 29%, year to year, reflecting expanded distribu-tion initiatives, organic growth and contribu-tions from acquisitions. However, benefits and expenses surged 33%, paced by a 36% rise in annuity and insurance benefits.

➤ We forecast EPS of $6.18 in 2011 and $7.70 in 2012, before realized investment gains or loss-es. Our 2011 estimate reflects non-recurring ex-pense charges and an 18 million share is-suance associated with the Star/Edison acqui-sition.

## Investment Rationale/Risk

➤ We recently downgraded our opinion on the shares to hold, from strong buy, after PRU re-ported third quarter results that we viewed as disappointing. Our hold recommendation re-flects our view that near-term margins may re-main under pressure form some adverse claim and benefit trends in several core lines of busi-ness. Longer term, though, we view positively PRU's mix of business and its superior financial flexibility. We also believe PRU is well posi-tioned to gain market share in many product ar-eas. We expect PRU's acquisition of Star/ Edison to add meaningfully to earnings and ROE by 2012.

➤ Risks to our recommendation and target price include currency risk; reserving risks for new guaranteed minimum benefits; acquisition inte-gration risks; credit risk; equity market declines; and a prolonged period of low interest rates.

➤ Our 12-month target price of $54 assumes the shares will trade at approximately 7X our 2012 operating EPS estimate. This is still at the low end of PRU's historical range.

## Revenue/Earnings Data

**Revenue (Million $)**

| | 1Q | 2Q | 3Q | 4Q | Year |
|---|---|---|---|---|---|
| 2011 | 10,186 | 12,247 | 14,917 | -- | -- |
| 2010 | 9,292 | 11,054 | 9,962 | -8,106 | 38,414 |
| 2009 | 8,563 | 6,906 | 8,564 | 8,659 | 32,688 |
| 2008 | 7,564 | 7,709 | 7,036 | 6,966 | 29,275 |
| 2007 | 8,775 | 8,425 | 8,383 | 8,808 | 34,401 |
| 2006 | 7,850 | 7,373 | 8,408 | 8,857 | 32,488 |

**Earnings Per Share ($)**

| | | | | | |
|---|---|---|---|---|---|
| 2011 | 1.17 | 1.65 | 3.08 | E1.71 | E6.18 |
| 2010 | 1.16 | 1.70 | 2.44 | 0.45 | 5.73 |
| 2009 | 0.01 | 1.22 | 2.36 | 3.82 | 7.66 |
| 2008 | 0.20 | 1.35 | -0.24 | -3.91 | -2.49 |
| 2007 | 2.10 | 1.86 | 1.89 | 1.89 | 7.58 |
| 2006 | 1.39 | 0.92 | 2.24 | 1.85 | 6.37 |

Fiscal year ended Dec. 31. Next earnings report expected: Early February. EPS Estimates based on S&P Operating Earnings; historical GAAP earnings are as reported.

## Dividend Data (Dates: mm/dd Payment Date: mm/dd/yy)

| Amount ($) | Date Decl. | Ex-Div. Date | Stk. of Record | Payment Date |
|---|---|---|---|---|
| 1.150 | 11/09 | 11/19 | 11/23 | 12/17/10 |
| 1.450 | 11/08 | 11/18 | 11/22 | 12/16/11 |

Dividends have been paid since 2002. Source: Company reports.

# Prudential Financial Inc

STANDARD
&POOR'S

## Business Summary November 23, 2011

CORPORATE OVERVIEW. Prudential Financial is one of the largest U.S. financial services companies, with $784 billion in assets under management and approximately $3.0 trillion in life insurance in force at year-end 2010, with operations in the U.S., Asia, Europe, and Latin America.

The financial services business operates through three divisions: retirement and investments (33% of 2010 operating revenues, 33% in 2009), insurance (27%, 29%), and international insurance and investments (40%, 39%). PRU also has a corporate and other segment which reported a pre-tax loss of $871 million in 2010. The insurance division consists of the individual life unit (34% of the division's 2010 operating revenues) and the group insurance unit (66%), which distributes group life, disability and related insurance products through employee and member benefit plans.

The asset management unit (18% of the division's 2010 operating revenues), the individual annuities unit (31%) and the retirement services unit (50%) comprise the retirement and investments division. International insurance and in-

vestments consists of insurance (97% of the division's 2010 operating revenues) and investments (2.8%). PRU distributes life insurance products to the mass affluent markets mostly in Japan and Korea through its Life Planner operations (which contributed to 58% of the division's insurance operating revenues in 2010). Additionally, the company's Life Advisor agents market insurance products to the middle class in Japan through its Gibraltar Life subsidiary (39%).

The closed block businesses represent some insurance products no longer offered, including certain participating insurance and annuity policies. At December 31, 2010, general account investments totaled $66 billion for the closed block and PRU had reinsurance agreements covering about 73% of policies.

## Company Financials Fiscal Year Ended Dec. 31

### Per Share Data ($)

| | 2010 | 2009 | 2008 | 2007 | 2006 | 2005 | 2004 | 2003 | 2002 | 2001 |
|---|---|---|---|---|---|---|---|---|---|---|
| Tangible Book Value | 64.89 | 84.86 | 31.18 | 52.43 | 46.32 | 45.53 | 42.40 | 39.65 | 37.89 | 34.90 |
| Operating Earnings | NA | NA | NA | NA | NA | NA | NA | NA | NA | NA |
| Earnings | 5.73 | 7.66 | -2.49 | 7.58 | 6.37 | 6.46 | 3.45 | 2.06 | 1.36 | 0.07 |
| S&P Core Earnings | 5.49 | 10.75 | 2.77 | 6.18 | 5.41 | 4.96 | 1.91 | 1.79 | 1.13 | NA |
| Dividends | 1.15 | 0.70 | 0.58 | 1.15 | 0.95 | 0.78 | 0.63 | 0.50 | 0.40 | Nil |
| Payout Ratio | 20% | 9% | NM | 15% | 15% | 12% | 18% | 24% | 29% | Nil |
| Prices:High | 66.80 | 55.99 | 93.14 | 103.27 | 87.18 | 78.62 | 55.62 | 42.21 | 36.00 | 33.74 |
| Prices:Low | 46.33 | 10.63 | 13.10 | 81.61 | 71.28 | 52.07 | 40.14 | 27.03 | 25.25 | 27.50 |
| P/E Ratio:High | 12 | 7 | NM | 14 | 14 | 12 | 16 | 20 | 26 | NM |
| P/E Ratio:Low | 8 | 1 | NM | 11 | 11 | 8 | 12 | 13 | 19 | NM |

### Income Statement Analysis (Million $)

| | 2010 | 2009 | 2008 | 2007 | 2006 | 2005 | 2004 | 2003 | 2002 | 2001 |
|---|---|---|---|---|---|---|---|---|---|---|
| Life Insurance in Force | NA | NA | NA | NA | NA | NA | NA | 1,928,650 | 1,800,788 | 1,768,038 |
| Premium Income:Life | 18,260 | 16,545 | 15,468 | 14,351 | 13,908 | 13,685 | 12,580 | 10,972 | 10,897 | 10,078 |
| Premium Income:A & H | NA | NA | NA | NA | NA | NA | NA | 806 | 586 | 515 |
| Net Investment Income | 11,875 | 11,421 | 11,883 | 12,017 | 11,354 | 10,560 | 9,079 | 8,681 | 8,832 | 9,151 |
| Total Revenue | 38,414 | 32,688 | 29,275 | 34,401 | 32,488 | 31,708 | 28,348 | 27,907 | 26,675 | 27,177 |
| Pretax Income | 4,506 | 3,092 | -1,565 | 4,932 | 4,611 | 4,471 | 3,287 | 1,958 | 64.0 | -227 |
| Net Operating Income | NA | NA | NA | NA | NA | NA | NA | NA | NA | NA |
| Net Income | 3,185 | 3,105 | -1,104 | 3,687 | 3,363 | 3,602 | 2,332 | 1,308 | 256 | -170 |
| S&P Core Earnings | 2,588 | 4,810 | 1,189 | 2,899 | 2,675 | 2,580 | 1,022 | 981 | 650 | -403 |

### Balance Sheet & Other Financial Data (Million $)

| | 2010 | 2009 | 2008 | 2007 | 2006 | 2005 | 2004 | 2003 | 2002 | 2001 |
|---|---|---|---|---|---|---|---|---|---|---|
| Cash & Equivalent | 34,911 | 32,217 | 33,239 | 13,234 | 10,731 | 9,866 | 10,100 | 9,746 | 11,688 | 20,364 |
| Premiums Due | NA | NA | 1,558 | 2,119 | 1,958 | 3,548 | 32,790 | Nil | Nil | Nil |
| Investment Assets:Bonds | 200,209 | 180,345 | 161,864 | 165,710 | 166,285 | 158,515 | 153,715 | 132,011 | 128,075 | 110,316 |
| Investment Assets:Stocks | 29,737 | 25,948 | 24,276 | 26,216 | 24,574 | 18,792 | 4,283 | 6,703 | 2,807 | 2,272 |
| Investment Assets:Loans | 42,498 | 41,530 | 42,817 | 39,384 | 34,626 | 32,811 | 32,761 | 27,621 | 22,094 | 28,299 |
| Investment Assets:Total | 283,912 | 260,552 | 242,025 | 243,107 | 245,349 | 221,401 | 216,624 | 181,041 | 183,094 | 165,834 |
| Deferred Policy Costs | 16,435 | 14,578 | 15,126 | 12,339 | 10,863 | 9,438 | 8,847 | 7,826 | 7,031 | 6,868 |
| Total Assets | 539,854 | 480,203 | 445,011 | 485,814 | 454,266 | 417,776 | 401,058 | 321,274 | 292,746 | 293,030 |
| Debt | 23,653 | 21,037 | 20,290 | 14,101 | 11,423 | 8,270 | 7,627 | 5,610 | 4,757 | 5,304 |
| Common Equity | 32,415 | 25,195 | 13,422 | 23,457 | 22,892 | 22,763 | 22,344 | 21,292 | 21,330 | 20,453 |
| % Return on Revenue | 8.3 | 9.5 | NM | 10.7 | 10.4 | 11.4 | 8.2 | 4.7 | 1.0 | NM |
| % Return on Assets | 0.6 | 0.7 | NM | 0.8 | 0.8 | 0.9 | 0.6 | 0.4 | 0.1 | NM |
| % Return on Equity | 11.2 | 16.1 | NA | 15.9 | 14.7 | 16.0 | 10.7 | 6.1 | 1.2 | NM |
| % Investment Yield | 4.4 | 4.5 | 4.9 | 5.0 | 4.8 | 4.8 | 4.6 | 4.8 | 5.1 | 5.8 |

Data as orig reptd.; bef. results of disc opers/spec. items. Per share data adj. for stk. divs.; EPS diluted. E-Estimated. NA-Not Available. NM-Not Meaningful. NR-Not Ranked. UR-Under Review.

Office: 751 Broad St, Newark, NJ 07102.
Telephone: 973-802-6000.
Email: investor.relations@prudential.com
Website: http://www.investor.prudential.com

Chrmn, Pres & CEO: J.R. Strangfeld, Jr.
Vice Chrmn: M.B. Grier
COO & EVP: E.P. Baird
EVP & CFO: R.J. Carbone

SVP & Chief Acctg Officer: P.B. Sayre
Board Members: T. J. Baltimore, Jr., G. M. Bethune, W.
G. Caperton, III, G. F. Casellas, J. G. Cullen, W. H. Gray,
III, M. B. Grier, C. J. Horner, M. Hund-Mejean, K. J.
Krapek, C. A. Poon, J. R. Strangfeld, Jr., J. A. Unruh

Founded: 1875
Domicile: New Jersey
Employees: 41,044

# Public Storage

**STANDARD &POOR'S**

**S&P Recommendation** BUY ★★★★☆

| Price | 12-Mo. Target Price | Investment Style |
|---|---|---|
| $122.30 (as of Nov 25, 2011) | $138.00 | Large-Cap Blend |

**GICS Sector** Financials
**Sub-Industry** Specialized REITS

**Summary** This real estate investment trust primarily invests in self-service storage facilities (mini-warehouses), but also has commercial and industrial properties.

## Key Stock Statistics (Source S&P, Vickers, company reports)

| | | | | | | | |
|---|---|---|---|---|---|---|---|
| 52-Wk Range | $132.20– 96.00 | S&P FFO/Sh. 2011E | 5.86 | Market Capitalization(B) | $20.921 | Beta | 0.90 |
| Trailing 12-Month FFO/Share | $4.72 | S&P FFO/Sh. 2012E | 6.25 | Yield (%) | 3.11 | S&P 3-Yr. FFO/Sh. Proj. CAGR(%) | 14 |
| Trailing 12-Month P/FFO | NA | P/FFO on S&P FFO/Sh. 2011E | 20.9 | Dividend Rate/Share | $3.80 | S&P Credit Rating | A |
| $10K Invested 5 Yrs Ago | $14,845 | Common Shares Outstg. (M) | 171.1 | Institutional Ownership (%) | 77 | | |

## Price Performance

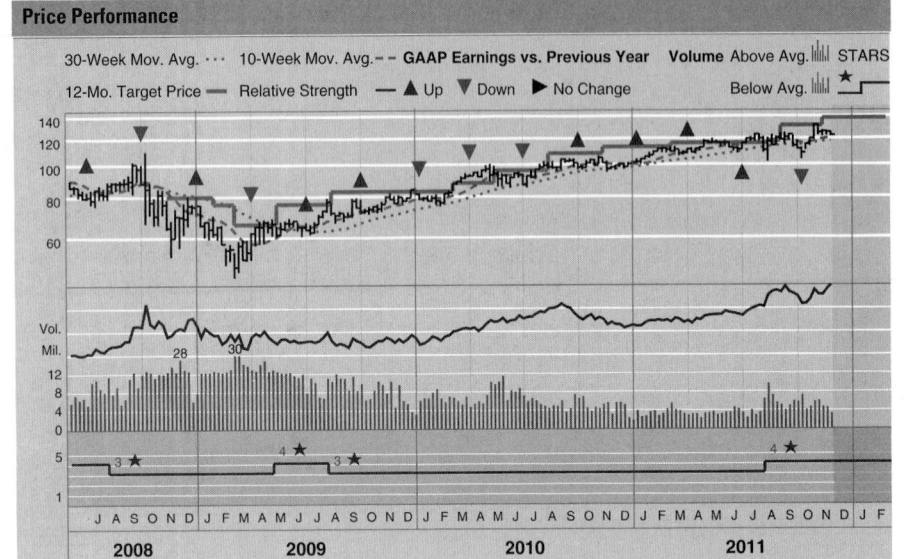

30-Week Mov. Avg. · · ·   10-Week Mov. Avg. - -  GAAP Earnings vs. Previous Year   Volume Above Avg. |ılıl STARS
12-Mo. Target Price —  Relative Strength —  ▲ Up  ▼ Down  ► No Change   Below Avg. |ılıl ★

Options: ASE, Ph

Analysis prepared by Equity Analyst **R. Shepard, CFA** on Nov 15, 2011, when the stock traded at **$123.02**.

## Qualitative Risk Assessment

| LOW | MEDIUM | HIGH |
|---|---|---|

Our risk assessment reflects PSA's position as one of the largest providers of self-storage space in a consolidating industry. In our opinion, the trust has a very strong balance sheet.

## Quantitative Evaluations

**S&P Quality Ranking**    B+

| D | C | B- | B | B+ | A- | A | A+ |
|---|---|---|---|---|---|---|---|

**Relative Strength Rank**    STRONG

85

LOWEST = 1    HIGHEST = 99

## Revenue/FFO Data

### Revenue (Million $)

| | 1Q | 2Q | 3Q | 4Q | Year |
|---|---|---|---|---|---|
| 2011 | 419.8 | 434.8 | 461.4 | -- | -- |
| 2010 | 397.8 | 408.0 | 422.8 | 418.2 | 1,647 |
| 2009 | 404.7 | 407.3 | 412.9 | 402.9 | 1,628 |
| 2008 | 462.8 | 428.8 | 443.2 | 428.5 | 1,766 |
| 2007 | 434.4 | 449.2 | 469.0 | 464.4 | 1,829 |
| 2006 | 278.5 | 297.9 | 371.4 | 433.9 | 1,382 |

### FFO Per Share ($)

| | 1Q | 2Q | 3Q | 4Q | Year |
|---|---|---|---|---|---|
| 2011 | E1.28 | 1.39 | 1.29 | E1.59 | E5.86 |
| 2010 | 0.78 | 0.92 | 1.69 | 1.33 | 4.72 |
| 2009 | 1.51 | 1.40 | 1.44 | 1.27 | 5.61 |
| 2008 | 1.39 | 1.10 | 1.09 | 1.49 | 5.07 |
| 2007 | 1.05 | 1.10 | 1.43 | 1.40 | 4.97 |
| 2006 | 0.94 | 0.99 | 0.77 | 0.89 | 3.57 |

Fiscal year ended Dec. 31. Next earnings report expected: Late February. FFO Estimates based on S&P Funds From Operations Est..

## Highlights

► We see shareholders benefiting from PSA's strategy of owning what we view as an unrivaled portfolio of self-storage facilities that have demonstrated their resiliency in tough economic environments. After an estimated revenue increase of 7.7% in 2011, we expect a 7.6% advance in 2012 on increased occupancy and rents as well as contributions from acquisitions.

► Same-store U.S. occupancy rose to 92.2% at the end of the 2011 third quarter, from 91.0% a year earlier; realized annual rent per available square foot increased 4.0%, on improved rents and reduced discounting. By the end of 2012, we expect occupancy to reach 93% with continued 2012 rent gains of 3% to 4%. We view favorably that the partially-owned European storage business also seems to be improving. Shurgard Europe's occupancy rose to 86.4%, from 86.1%, and rents per occupied square foot increased 1.9%. In view of recent financial turmoil overseas, we expect slow gains in occupancy during 2012.

► We estimate FFO of $5.86 for 2011 and $6.25 for 2012. Our forecasts exclude the impact of fluctuations in foreign current exchange rates.

## Investment Rationale/Risk

► We see PSA benefiting from its ability to continue to gain share at the expense of smaller competitors by creating customer awareness in its markets and offering an array of customer services that many small competitors cannot provide. Also, given its size versus the competition, the trust has significant market and pricing power, in our view. We also view the trust's capital structure, which is dominated by preferred and common equity, as well as its very modest debt burden and large cash balances, as positive factors in our favorable evaluation.

► Risks to our recommendation and target price include slower-than-expected growth in rental rates and occupancy levels, a sharp drop in moving activity, and higher interest rates.

► Our 12-month target price of $138 is equal to 22.1X our 2012 FFO estimate of $6.25, a premium to peers with higher financial leverage. We think the premium valuation will be maintained as FFO climbs, driven by organic growth and contributions from acquisitions.

## Dividend Data (Dates: mm/dd Payment Date: mm/dd/yy)

| Amount ($) | Date Decl. | Ex-Div. Date | Stk. of Record | Payment Date |
|---|---|---|---|---|
| 0.800 | 02/25 | 03/11 | 03/15 | 03/31/11 |
| 0.950 | 05/05 | 06/13 | 06/15 | 06/30/11 |
| 0.950 | 08/04 | 09/12 | 09/14 | 09/29/11 |
| 0.950 | 11/03 | 12/12 | 12/14 | 12/29/11 |

Dividends have been paid since 2010. Source: Company reports.

# Public Storage

**STANDARD &POOR'S**

## Business Summary November 15, 2011

Public Storage is an equity real estate investment trust that was organized as a corporation under the laws of California on July 10, 1980. At December 31, 2010, PSA operated three business segments: domestic self-storage, Europe self-storage, and commercial. In the U.S., PSA is the largest owner and operator of storage space, with direct and indirect equity investments in 2,048 self-storage facilities located in 38 states within the U.S. operating under the Public Storage name at the end of 2010. The facilities contain approximately 130 million net rentable square feet of space. The Europe self-storage business comprises PSA's 49% equity interest in Shurgard Europe, which owns 188 self-storage facilities (10 million net rentable square feet of space) located in seven countries in Europe that operate under the "Shurgard Storage Centers" brand name and manages one facility located in the United Kingdom that was wholly owned by PSA at the end of 2010. PSA also has direct and indirect equity interests in approximately 24 million net rentable square feet of commercial space located in 11 states in the U.S. operated under the PS Business Parks and Public Storage, Inc. brands. PSA has a 41% ownership interest in PS Business Parks, Inc. (PSB 58, Hold).

PSA's growth strategies consist of improving the operating performance of stabilized existing traditional self-storage properties; acquiring additional interests in entities that own properties operated by the trust; purchasing interests in properties that are owned or operated by others; developing properties in selected markets; improving the operating performance of the containerized storage operations; and participating in the growth of PS Business Parks, Inc as well as its European business.

The trust's storage facilities are designed to offer accessible storage space for personal and business use at a relatively low cost. Individuals usually obtain this space for storage of furniture, household appliances, personal belongings, motor vehicles, boats, campers, motorcycles and other household goods. Businesses normally employ this space for storage of excess inventory, business records, seasonal goods, equipment and fixtures. A user rents a fully enclosed space that is for the user's exclusive use and that only the user has access to on an unrestricted basis during business hours. Some storage facilities also include rentable uncovered parking areas for vehicle storage, as well as space for portable storage containers. Leases for storage facility space may be on a long-term or short-term basis, although typically spaces are rented on a month-to-month basis. Rental rates vary according to the location of the property, the size of the storage space and the length of stay. PSA's self-storage facilities generally consist of three to seven buildings containing an aggregate of between 350 and 750 storage spaces, most of which have between 25 and 400 square feet and an interior height of approximately eight to 12 feet.

## Company Financials Fiscal Year Ended Dec. 31

| Per Share Data ($) | 2010 | 2009 | 2008 | 2007 | 2006 | 2005 | 2004 | 2003 | 2002 | 2001 |
|---|---|---|---|---|---|---|---|---|---|---|
| Tangible Book Value | 29.92 | 30.13 | 30.21 | 28.85 | 28.16 | 16.72 | 16.69 | 17.03 | 16.16 | 28.37 |
| Earnings | 2.49 | 3.52 | 4.20 | 1.17 | 0.32 | 1.92 | 1.39 | 1.27 | 1.28 | 1.51 |
| S&P Core Earnings | 2.31 | 3.52 | 4.20 | 1.15 | 0.32 | 1.91 | 1.38 | 1.25 | 1.26 | 1.48 |
| Dividends | 3.42 | 2.20 | 2.20 | 2.00 | 2.00 | 1.85 | 1.80 | 1.80 | 1.80 | 1.69 |
| Payout Ratio | 137% | 63% | 52% | 171% | NM | 97% | 129% | 142% | 1% | 112% |
| Prices:High | 106.12 | 85.10 | 110.00 | 117.16 | 98.05 | 72.02 | 57.64 | 45.81 | 39.29 | 35.15 |
| Prices:Low | 74.74 | 45.35 | 52.52 | 68.09 | 67.72 | 51.50 | 39.50 | 28.25 | 27.98 | 24.13 |
| P/E Ratio:High | 43 | 24 | 26 | NM | NM | 38 | 41 | 36 | 33 | 23 |
| P/E Ratio:Low | 30 | 13 | 13 | NM | NM | 27 | 28 | 22 | 24 | 16 |
| **Income Statement Analysis (Million $)** | | | | | | | | | | |
| Rental Income | 1,513 | 1,490 | 1,581 | 1,663 | 1,240 | 980 | 894 | 844 | 813 | 782 |
| Mortgage Income | Nil | Nil | Nil | Nil | Nil | Nil | Nil | Nil | Nil | Nil |
| Total Income | 1,647 | 1,628 | 1,766 | 1,829 | 1,382 | 1,061 | 928 | 875 | 841 | 835 |
| General Expenses | 569 | 459 | 644 | 712 | 585 | 400 | 349 | 336 | 311 | 297 |
| Interest Expense | 30.2 | 29.9 | 44.0 | 64.0 | 33.1 | 8.22 | 0.76 | 1.12 | 3.81 | 3.23 |
| Provision for Losses | Nil | Nil | Nil | Nil | Nil | Nil | Nil | Nil | Nil | Nil |
| Depreciation | 354 | 340 | 414 | 622 | 438 | 196 | 183 | 186 | 180 | 168 |
| Net Income | 680 | 843 | 936 | 458 | 312 | 450 | 367 | 335 | 319 | 324 |
| S&P Core Earnings | 392 | 595 | 710 | 197 | 44.7 | 247 | 179 | 157 | 156 | 183 |
| **Balance Sheet & Other Financial Data (Million $)** | | | | | | | | | | |
| Cash | 456 | 764 | 681 | 245 | 857 | 329 | 708 | 205 | 103 | 49.3 |
| Total Assets | 9,495 | 9,806 | 9,936 | 10,643 | 11,198 | 5,552 | 5,205 | 4,968 | 4,844 | 4,626 |
| Real Estate Investment | 10,594 | 10,296 | 10,227 | 11,719 | 11,262 | 6,314 | 5,908 | 5,544 | 5,424 | 5,062 |
| Loss Reserve | Nil | Nil | Nil | Nil | Nil | Nil | Nil | Nil | Nil | Nil |
| Net Investment | 7,533 | 7,562 | 7,822 | 9,591 | 9,507 | 4,814 | 4,588 | 4,391 | 4,436 | 4,242 |
| Short Term Debt | 134 | 12.7 | 13.0 | 216 | Nil | Nil | Nil | Nil | 39.8 | Nil |
| Capitalization:Debt | 435 | 506 | 631 | 808 | 1,848 | 134 | 130 | 76.0 | 76.1 | 144 |
| Capitalization:Equity | 5,281 | 5,529 | 5,291 | 5,236 | 5,353 | 2,319 | 2,328 | 2,353 | 2,342 | 2,369 |
| Capitalization:Total | 9,156 | 9,581 | 9,710 | 9,270 | 8,785 | 5,205 | 4,989 | 4,722 | 4,675 | 4,508 |
| % Earnings & Depreciation/Assets | 10.7 | 12.0 | 13.1 | 9.8 | 8.9 | 12.0 | 10.8 | 10.6 | 10.5 | 7.1 |
| Price Times Book Value:High | 3.5 | 2.8 | 3.6 | 4.1 | 3.5 | 4.3 | 3.5 | 2.7 | 2.4 | 1.2 |
| Price Times Book Value:Low | 2.5 | 1.5 | 1.7 | 2.4 | 2.4 | 3.1 | 2.4 | 1.7 | 1.7 | 0.9 |

Data as orig reptd.; bef. results of disc opers/spec. items. Per share data adj. for stk. divs.; EPS diluted. E-Estimated. NA-Not Available. NM-Not Meaningful. NR-Not Ranked. UR-Under Review.

**Office:** 701 Western Ave, Glendale, CA 91201-2349.
**Telephone:** 818-244-8080.
**Email:** investor@publicstorage.com
**Website:** http://www.publicstorage.com

**Chrmn, Pres & CEO:** R.L. Havner, Jr.
**COO:** S. Weidmann
**SVP, CFO & Chief Acctg Officer:** J. Reyes
**SVP & General Counsel:** S.M. Glick

**Secy:** S.G. Heim
**Investor Contact:** C. Teng (818-244-8080)
**Board Members:** T. H. Gustavson, U. P. Harkham, R. L. Havner, Jr., B. Hughes, B. W. Hughes, Jr., A. B. Poladian, G. E. Pruitt, R. P. Spogli, D. C. Staton, II

**Auditor:** ERNST & YOUNG
**Founded:** 1980
**Domicile:** Maryland
**Employees:** 4,900

*The McGraw-Hill Companies*

# Public Service Enterprise Group Inc

**STANDARD &POOR'S**

| S&P Recommendation BUY ★★★★☆ | Price $31.21 (as of Nov 25, 2011) | 12-Mo. Target Price $36.00 | Investment Style Large-Cap Blend |
|---|---|---|---|

**GICS Sector** Utilities
**Sub-Industry** Multi-Utilities

**Summary** PEG is the holding company for Public Service Electric and Gas (PSE&G), with a service area that encompasses 70% of New Jersey.

## Key Stock Statistics (Source S&P, Vickers, company reports)

| | | | | | | | |
|---|---|---|---|---|---|---|---|
| 52-Wk Range | $35.48– 27.97 | S&P Oper. EPS 2011E | 2.77 | Market Capitalization(B) | $15.789 | Beta | 0.51 |
| Trailing 12-Month EPS | $2.80 | S&P Oper. EPS 2012E | 2.53 | Yield (%) | 4.39 | S&P 3-Yr. Proj. EPS CAGR(%) | -2 |
| Trailing 12-Month P/E | 11.2 | P/E on S&P Oper. EPS 2011E | 11.3 | Dividend Rate/Share | $1.37 | S&P Credit Rating | BBB |
| $10K Invested 5 Yrs Ago | $11,541 | Common Shares Outstg. (M) | 505.9 | Institutional Ownership (%) | 64 | | |

## Price Performance

30-Week Mov. Avg. · · · ·   10-Week Mov. Avg. – –   GAAP Earnings vs. Previous Year   Volume Above Avg. ▮▮▮   STARS
12-Mo. Target Price —   Relative Strength —   ▲ Up   ▼ Down   ▶ No Change   Below Avg. ▮▮▮   ★

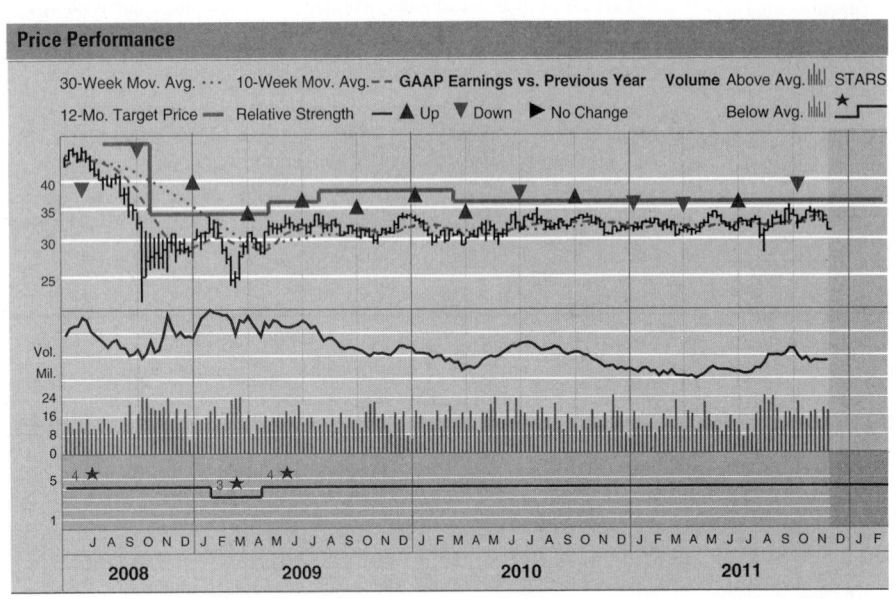

Options: ASE, CBOE, Ph

Analysis prepared by Equity Analyst **Justin McCann** on Sep 22, 2011, when the stock traded at **$32.91**.

## Highlights

- Excluding net one-time gains of $0.23, we expect EPS from continuing operations in 2011 to decline about 11% from 2010's $3.12. While operating EPS in the first half of 2011 benefited from rate increases and more favorable weather than in the year-earlier period, this was more than offset by a drop in earnings from the Power segment and the loss of customers to power supply competitors.

- For the second half of 2011, we expect the decline in earnings to reflect a return to more normal summer weather after the abnormally warm weather in the third quarter of 2010, partially offset by a full year of a rate increase at PSE&G. For 2012, we expect operating EPS to decline about 8% from anticipated results in 2011, reflecting lower-margin power contracts and the continuing weakness in the economy.

- As of mid-September 2011, PEG's Power segment had hedged all of its anticipated coal and nuclear generation for 2011 at an average price of $68 per megawatt hour (MWh), about 78% of 2012's at $64 per MWh, and about 38% of 2013's at $63 per MWh. This compared with an average hedged price of $72 per MWh in 2010.

## Investment Rationale/Risk

- Given the volatility and often sharp declines in the broader market, we believe PEG's stock provides an attractive investment opportunity, and we recommend it for above-average total return potential over the next 12 months. The shares were up more than 3% in the first 38 weeks of 2011, after being down 4.3% in 2010. While we expect near-term earnings to be pressured by the ongoing weakness in the economy and power markets, we believe PEG's cost-control efforts and effective management of its power supply operations will leave it well positioned for an economic recovery.

- Risks to our recommendation and target price include a sharp decline in PEG's wholesale power margins, as well as weakness in the broader market and/or an event that would reduce the average P/E of the group as a whole.

- The recent yield from the dividend was 4.2%. While still below the recent peer average of about 4.5%, it is roughly in line with the yields of other utility holding companies that have large wholesale power operations. Our 12-month target price is $36, reflecting a modest premium-to-peers multiple of 14.2X our EPS estimate for 2012.

## Qualitative Risk Assessment

| LOW | MEDIUM | HIGH |
|---|---|---|

Our risk assessment reflects our view of the strong and steady cash flows from the regulated electric and gas utility operations of PSE&G, as well as the strong albeit less predictable earnings and cash flows from the non-regulated power generating operations. It also reflects what we see as a lowering of PEG's risk profile through the divestiture of non-core international investments.

## Quantitative Evaluations

**S&P Quality Ranking**      B+

| D | C | B- | B | B+ | A- | A | A+ |
|---|---|---|---|---|---|---|---|

**Relative Strength Rank**      MODERATE

51

LOWEST = 1         HIGHEST = 99

## Revenue/Earnings Data

**Revenue (Million $)**

| | 1Q | 2Q | 3Q | 4Q | Year |
|---|---|---|---|---|---|
| 2011 | 3,354 | 2,469 | 2,620 | -- | -- |
| 2010 | 3,680 | 2,455 | 3,254 | 2,745 | 11,793 |
| 2009 | 3,921 | 2,561 | 3,039 | 2,886 | 12,406 |
| 2008 | 3,803 | 2,561 | 3,718 | 3,262 | 13,322 |
| 2007 | 3,508 | 2,718 | 3,356 | 3,271 | 12,853 |
| 2006 | 3,461 | 2,556 | 3,212 | 2,935 | 12,164 |

**Earnings Per Share ($)**

| | | | | | |
|---|---|---|---|---|---|
| 2011 | 0.91 | 0.63 | 0.52 | E0.58 | E2.77 |
| 2010 | 0.97 | 0.44 | 1.12 | 0.57 | 3.07 |
| 2009 | 0.88 | 0.61 | 0.96 | 0.69 | 3.14 |
| 2008 | 0.85 | -0.33 | 0.94 | 0.47 | 1.93 |
| 2007 | 0.64 | 0.56 | 0.96 | 0.44 | 2.59 |
| 2006 | 0.41 | Nil | 0.75 | 0.35 | 1.49 |

Fiscal year ended Dec. 31. Next earnings report expected: Late February. EPS Estimates based on S&P Operating Earnings; historical GAAP earnings are as reported.

## Dividend Data (Dates: mm/dd Payment Date: mm/dd/yy)

| Amount ($) | Date Decl. | Ex-Div. Date | Stk. of Record | Payment Date |
|---|---|---|---|---|
| 0.343 | 02/15 | 03/08 | 03/10 | 03/31/11 |
| 0.343 | 04/19 | 06/07 | 06/09 | 06/30/11 |
| 0.343 | 07/19 | 09/07 | 09/09 | 09/30/11 |
| 0.343 | 11/15 | 12/07 | 12/09 | 12/30/11 |

Dividends have been paid since 1907. Source: Company reports.

---

**Please read the Required Disclosures and Analyst Certification on the last page of this report.**

**The McGraw-Hill Companies**

# Public Service Enterprise Group Inc

**STANDARD &POOR'S**

## Business Summary September 22, 2011

CORPORATE OVERVIEW. Headquartered in Newark, NJ, Public Service Enterprise Group has three primary operating units: Public Service Electric and Gas Co. - PSE&G ($359 million of net income in 2010), Power ($1.136 billion), and Energy Holdings ($49 million). PEG has sought to minimize its earnings and cash flow volatility by entering into long-term contracts for most of its competitive wholesale power generation.

MARKET PROFILE. At the end of 2010, the company's New Jersey utility operations served about 2.2 million electric customers and 1.8 million natural gas customers. PSE&G earns income from the delivery of electricity and gas, with the cost of the gas passed through to ratepayers. In 2010, commercial customers accounted for 57% of total electric customers (36% of gas customers), residential 33% (61%), and industrial 10% (3%). As part of New Jersey's utility deregulation, PSE&G transferred its power generating and gas supply operations to PEG's unregulated Power division in 2000 and 2002, respectively.

Based on the proximity of its plants to PSE&G's customer base, Power has been able to win competitive bids for a significant portion of the utility's electricity supply obligations. Excluding 2,000 megawatts (MW) of aggregated owned generating capacity in Texas (which PEG agreed to sell in January 2011), Power's generating fleet had 13,538 MW of owned generating capacity as of December 31, 2010, which is concentrated in Pennsylvania and New Jersey and serves the Pennsylvania, New Jersey and Maryland Interconnection (known as PJM). Power also has plants in Connecticut and New York. In addition to its electric business, Power provides PSE&G with all of the utility's gas supply needs under a contract that was extended from March 31, 2007, to March 31, 2012, and year to year thereafter.

## Company Financials Fiscal Year Ended Dec. 31

| Per Share Data ($) | 2010 | 2009 | 2008 | 2007 | 2006 | 2005 | 2004 | 2003 | 2002 | 2001 |
|---|---|---|---|---|---|---|---|---|---|---|
| Tangible Book Value | 18.74 | 17.09 | 15.22 | 14.23 | 12.23 | 10.79 | 10.71 | 10.42 | 7.39 | 8.47 |
| Earnings | 3.07 | 3.14 | 1.93 | 2.59 | 1.49 | 1.76 | 1.52 | 1.86 | 1.00 | 1.84 |
| S&P Core Earnings | 3.30 | 3.33 | 1.85 | 2.59 | 1.92 | 1.70 | 1.49 | 2.02 | 1.53 | 1.58 |
| Dividends | 1.37 | 1.33 | 1.29 | 1.17 | 1.14 | 1.12 | 1.10 | 1.08 | 1.08 | 1.08 |
| Payout Ratio | 45% | 42% | 67% | 45% | 77% | 64% | 73% | 58% | 109% | 59% |
| Prices:High | 34.93 | 34.14 | 52.30 | 49.88 | 36.31 | 34.24 | 26.32 | 22.25 | 23.63 | 25.78 |
| Prices:Low | 29.01 | 23.65 | 22.09 | 32.16 | 29.50 | 24.66 | 19.05 | 16.05 | 10.00 | 18.44 |
| P/E Ratio:High | 11 | 11 | 27 | 19 | 24 | 20 | 17 | 12 | 24 | 14 |
| P/E Ratio:Low | 9 | 8 | 11 | 12 | 20 | 14 | 13 | 9 | 10 | 10 |

| Income Statement Analysis (Million $) | 2010 | 2009 | 2008 | 2007 | 2006 | 2005 | 2004 | 2003 | 2002 | 2001 |
|---|---|---|---|---|---|---|---|---|---|---|
| Revenue | 11,793 | 12,406 | 13,322 | 12,853 | 12,164 | 12,430 | 10,996 | 11,116 | 8,390 | 9,815 |
| Depreciation | 955 | 838 | 792 | 783 | 832 | 748 | 719 | 527 | 571 | 522 |
| Maintenance | NA | NA | NA | NA | NA | NA | NA | NA | NA | NA |
| Fixed Charges Coverage | 6.53 | 5.97 | 4.18 | 4.10 | 2.73 | 2.55 | 2.21 | 2.43 | 2.38 | 2.46 |
| Construction Credits | NA | NA | NA | NA | NA | NA | NA | NA | NA | NA |
| Effective Tax Rate | 40.5% | 39.6% | 48.5% | 44.5% | NM | 38.7% | 38.2% | 35.3% | 37.3% | NM |
| Net Income | 1,557 | 1,592 | 983 | 1,319 | 752 | 858 | 721 | 852 | 416 | 763 |
| S&P Core Earnings | 1,673 | 1,682 | 945 | 1,316 | 967 | 834 | 708 | 925 | 638 | 656 |

| Balance Sheet & Other Financial Data (Million $) | 2010 | 2009 | 2008 | 2007 | 2006 | 2005 | 2004 | 2003 | 2002 | 2001 |
|---|---|---|---|---|---|---|---|---|---|---|
| Gross Property | 23,272 | 22,069 | 20,818 | 19,310 | 18,851 | 18,896 | 19,121 | 17,406 | 16,562 | 14,886 |
| Capital Expenditures | 2,160 | 1,794 | 1,771 | 1,348 | 1,015 | 1,024 | 1,255 | 1,351 | 1,814 | 2,053 |
| Net Property | 16,390 | 15,440 | 14,433 | 13,275 | 13,002 | 13,336 | 13,750 | 12,422 | 11,449 | 10,064 |
| Capitalization:Long Term Debt | 7,819 | 7,725 | 8,085 | 8,742 | 10,450 | 11,359 | 13,005 | 13,025 | 12,391 | 11,061 |
| Capitalization:% Long Term Debt | 44.8 | 46.8 | 51.0 | 54.5 | 60.8 | 65.4 | 69.4 | 70.2 | 75.7 | 72.8 |
| Capitalization:Preferred | Nil | Nil | Nil | Nil | Nil | Nil | Nil | Nil | Nil | Nil |
| Capitalization:% Preferred | Nil | Nil | Nil | Nil | Nil | Nil | Nil | Nil | Nil | Nil |
| Capitalization:Common | 9,633 | 8,788 | 7,771 | 7,299 | 6,747 | 6,022 | 5,739 | 5,529 | 3,987 | 4,137 |
| Capitalization:% Common | 55.2 | 53.2 | 49.0 | 45.5 | 39.2 | 34.6 | 30.6 | 29.8 | 24.3 | 27.2 |
| Total Capital | 18,581 | 17,044 | 19,721 | 20,495 | 21,659 | 21,629 | 23,091 | 22,750 | 19,302 | 18,403 |
| % Operating Ratio | 84.1 | 83.3 | 87.3 | 85.0 | 78.7 | 88.6 | 87.5 | 86.5 | 78.8 | 76.9 |
| % Earned on Net Property | 18.8 | 20.9 | 18.9 | 23.3 | 15.1 | 15.9 | 14.9 | 17.3 | 14.3 | 21.3 |
| % Return on Revenue | 13.2 | 12.8 | 7.4 | 10.3 | 6.2 | 6.9 | 6.6 | 7.7 | 5.0 | 7.8 |
| % Return on Invested Capital | 11.4 | 12.4 | 7.8 | 9.3 | 9.3 | 7.6 | 6.9 | 8.1 | 9.3 | 9.6 |
| % Return on Common Equity | 16.9 | 19.2 | 13.0 | 18.8 | 11.8 | 14.6 | 12.8 | 18.1 | 10.2 | 18.8 |

Data as orig reptd.; bef. results of disc opers/spec. items. Per share data adj. for stk. divs.; EPS diluted. E-Estimated. NA-Not Available. NM-Not Meaningful. NR-Not Ranked. UR-Under Review.

Office: 80 Park Plaza, Newark, NJ 07102-4109.
Telephone: 973-430-7000.
Email: stkserv@pseg.com
Website: http://www.pseg.com

Chrmn, Pres & CEO: R. Izzo
EVP & CFO: C.D. Dorsa
Chief Acctg Officer & Cntlr: D.M. Dirisio
Treas: M.A. Plawner

Secy: M.C. McCormick
Investor Contact: K.A. Lally
Board Members: A. R. Gamper, Jr., C. K. Harper, W. V. Hickey, R. Izzo, S. A. Jackson, D. Lilley, T. A. Renyi, H. C. Shin, R. J. Swift

Founded: 1985
Domicile: New Jersey
Employees: 9,965

*The McGraw·Hill Companies*

# PulteGroup Inc

# STANDARD &POOR'S

| | | | |
|---|---|---|---|
| **S&P Recommendation** BUY ★★★★☆ | **Price**<br>$5.22 (as of Nov 25, 2011) | **12-Mo. Target Price**<br>$8.00 | **Investment Style**<br>Large-Cap Blend |

**GICS Sector** Consumer Discretionary
**Sub-Industry** Homebuilding

**Summary** This company became the largest U.S. homebuilder after the 2009 acquisition of rival Centex Corp.

## Key Stock Statistics (Source S&P, Vickers, company reports)

| | | | | | | | | |
|---|---|---|---|---|---|---|---|---|
| 52-Wk Range | $8.69– 3.29 | S&P Oper. EPS 2011**E** | -0.60 | Market Capitalization(B) | $1.998 | Beta | | 1.10 |
| Trailing 12-Month EPS | $-1.03 | S&P Oper. EPS 2012**E** | 0.10 | Yield (%) | Nil | S&P 3-Yr. Proj. EPS CAGR(%) | | NM |
| Trailing 12-Month P/E | NM | P/E on S&P Oper. EPS 2011**E** | NM | Dividend Rate/Share | Nil | S&P Credit Rating | | BB- |
| $10K Invested 5 Yrs Ago | $1,686 | Common Shares Outstg. (M) | 382.8 | Institutional Ownership (%) | 83 | | | |

## Price Performance

30-Week Mov. Avg. · · · ·   10-Week Mov. Avg. - -   **GAAP Earnings vs. Previous Year**   Volume Above Avg. ||||| STARS
12-Mo. Target Price —   Relative Strength —   ▲ Up  ▼ Down  ▶ No Change   Below Avg. ||||| ★

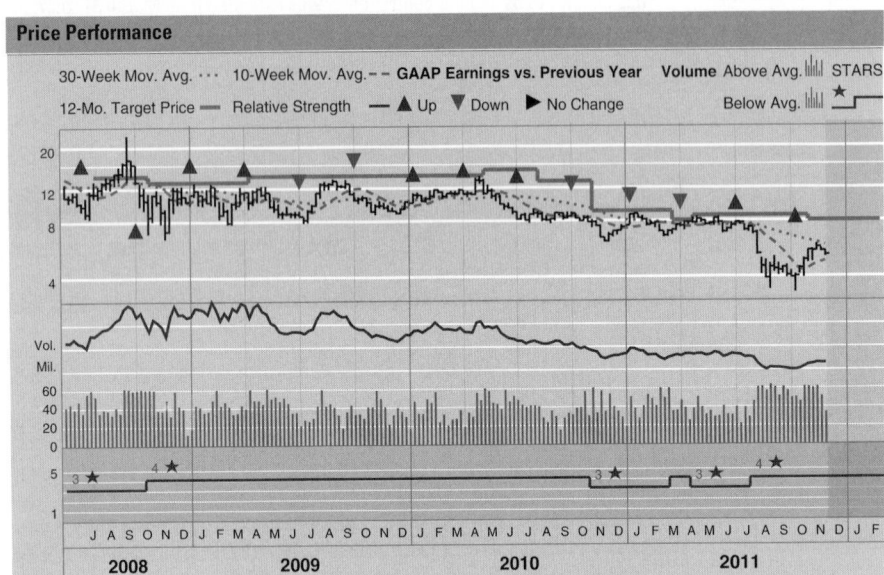

Options: ASE, CBOE, P, Ph

Analysis prepared by Equity Analyst **Kenneth Leon, CPA** on Oct 28, 2011, when the stock traded at **$5.37**.

## Highlights

➤ Following revenue growth of 12% in 2010 (aided by the mid-2009 Centex acquisition), and taking into account a contract backlog of $1.3 billion, we forecast that revenues will decline 12% in 2011 and then rebound 9% in 2012 in an expected housing market recovery. PHM reported an 8% revenue increase in 2011's third quarter, while net orders were up slightly year over year, and revenues were flat sequentially.

➤ We believe PHM will be able to gain market share as the housing market slowly recovers. While gaining Centex land inventory in attractive markets was viewed as a positive, it resulted in a writedowns of close to $1 billion in 2010's third quarter and $240 million in 2011's third quarter. Nonetheless, PHM has scale to gain market share from smaller builders.

➤ We estimate homebuilding gross margins will widen to 14% to 15% in 2012, from an estimated 13.6% in 2011. We see SG&A costs as a percentage of total revenue remaining low at 12% in 2012 until customer traffic picks up in its communities. Following a loss of $2.90 a share in 2010 including asset charges, we see a $0.60 a share loss in 2011 and EPS of $0.10 in 2012.

## Investment Rationale/Risk

➤ In August 2009, PHM finalized the purchase of rival Centex Corp. via a stock swap valued at around $1.3 billion. The combined $1.25 billion of third-quarter writeoffs in 2010 and 2011 were mostly tied to the merger, which indicates to us that the timing of this purchase was far from optimal. However, we see opportunities for improved sales and better cost control ahead following the writeoffs.

➤ Risks to our recommendation and target price include problems integrating the Centex operations, lower housing demand, a continued weak pace of the U.S. economic recovery, tighter mortgage lending, and the potential for downward revisions to PHM's land inventory.

➤ PHM has $1.1 billion in cash that can be used to build or acquire communities, and the company has one of the industry's largest land inventories. However, large writeoffs have reduced shareholders' equity. Our 12-month target price of $8 is derived by applying a target price-to-book multiple just below 1.6X -- near the middle of the historical range, and close to peers -- to our forward book value per share estimate of $5.05.

## Qualitative Risk Assessment

| LOW | MEDIUM | HIGH |
|---|---|---|

Our risk assessment reflects risks involved with integrating the Centex operations, which requires the combination of the home communities and the streamlining of sales and marketing and support services. While PHM enjoys greater scale post-merger, market risks remain given the sluggish U.S. housing market.

## Quantitative Evaluations

**S&P Quality Ranking**     B

| D | C | B- | B | B+ | A- | A | A+ |
|---|---|---|---|---|---|---|---|

**Relative Strength Rank**     STRONG

86

LOWEST = 1     HIGHEST = 99

## Revenue/Earnings Data

### Revenue (Million $)

| | 1Q | 2Q | 3Q | 4Q | Year |
|---|---|---|---|---|---|
| 2011 | 805.2 | 927.2 | 1,142 | -- | -- |
| 2010 | 1,020 | 1,306 | 1,058 | 1,185 | 4,569 |
| 2009 | 583.9 | 678.6 | 1,091 | 1,731 | 4,084 |
| 2008 | 1,442 | 1,619 | 1,565 | 1,644 | 6,263 |
| 2007 | 1,871 | 2,021 | 2,472 | 2,899 | 9,257 |
| 2006 | 2,963 | 3,359 | 3,564 | 4,389 | 14,274 |

### Earnings Per Share ($)

| | | | | | |
|---|---|---|---|---|---|
| 2011 | -0.10 | -0.15 | -0.34 | E0.01 | E-0.60 |
| 2010 | -0.03 | -0.20 | -2.63 | -0.44 | -2.90 |
| 2009 | -2.02 | -0.74 | -1.15 | -0.31 | -3.94 |
| 2008 | -2.75 | -0.62 | -1.11 | -1.33 | -5.81 |
| 2007 | -0.34 | -2.01 | -3.12 | -3.54 | -9.02 |
| 2006 | 1.01 | 0.94 | 0.74 | -0.03 | 2.67 |

Fiscal year ended Dec. 31. Next earnings report expected: Early February. EPS Estimates based on S&P Operating Earnings; historical GAAP earnings are as reported.

## Dividend Data

The most recent payment, $0.04 a share, was made in early January 2009.

---

**Please read the Required Disclosures and Analyst Certification on the last page of this report.**

The **McGraw·Hill** Companies

# PulteGroup Inc

**STANDARD &POOR'S**

## Business Summary October 28, 2011

CORPORATE OVERVIEW. As of 2010 year end, following the 2009 merger with Centex, the new Pulte had nearly 800 home communities. The average selling price for company homes in 2009 was $258,000, down from $284,000 in 2008 and a high of $337,000 in 2006. The average selling price in 2010 was $262,000, with sales in 67 markets in 29 states.

PHM targets buyers in nearly all home categories, but has recently concentrated its expansion efforts on affordable housing and on mature buyers (age 50 and over). In July 2001, it acquired Del Webb Corp., the leading U.S. builder of active adult communities, for a total of $1.9 billion in stock, cash, and the assumption of debt. Growth in this active adult segment and among first-time buyers, two groups that often prefer townhouses, condominiums or duplexes, helps to explain the decrease in single-family homes in PHM's product mix over the past five years.

CORPORATE STRATEGY. As of December 31, 2010, the company controlled 147,194 lots, of which 131,964 were owned and 15,230 were under option agreements. Land is generally purchased after it is properly zoned and developed or is ready for development. In addition, PHM will dispose of owned land not required in the business through sales to appropriate end users. Where

the company develops land, it engages directly in many phases of the development process, including land and site planning, and obtaining environmental and other regulatory approvals, as well as constructing roads, sewers, water and drainage facilities, and other amenities.

To assist its home sales effort, PHM offers mortgage banking and title insurance services through Pulte Mortgage and other units mainly for the benefit of its domestic home buyers, but it also services the general public. In addition, it engages in the sale of loans and related servicing rights. Mortgage underwriting, processing and closing functions are centralized in Denver, CO, and Charlotte, NC, using a mortgage operations center concept.

In December 2005, the company sold Pulte Mexico, sharply reducing its international presence, and realized cash proceeds of $131.5 million. In the fourth quarter of 2005, PHM reported these results as discontinued operations.

## Company Financials Fiscal Year Ended Dec. 31

| Per Share Data ($) | 2010 | 2009 | 2008 | 2007 | 2006 | 2005 | 2004 | 2003 | 2002 | 2001 |
|---|---|---|---|---|---|---|---|---|---|---|
| Tangible Book Value | 4.50 | 5.54 | 10.59 | 16.35 | 23.82 | 21.49 | 15.95 | 12.13 | 9.41 | 7.64 |
| Cash Flow | -2.78 | -3.76 | -5.52 | -8.69 | 2.99 | 5.70 | 4.01 | 2.61 | 1.92 | 1.67 |
| Earnings | -2.90 | -3.94 | -5.81 | -9.02 | 2.67 | 5.47 | 3.84 | 2.46 | 1.80 | 1.50 |
| S&P Core Earnings | -1.77 | -2.72 | -5.80 | -7.69 | 2.59 | 5.46 | 3.82 | 2.45 | 1.76 | 1.43 |
| Dividends | Nil | Nil | 0.16 | 0.16 | 0.16 | 0.09 | 0.10 | 0.04 | 0.04 | 0.04 |
| Payout Ratio | Nil | Nil | NM | NM | 6% | 2% | 3% | 2% | 2% | 3% |
| Prices:High | 13.91 | 13.59 | 23.24 | 35.56 | 44.70 | 48.23 | 32.50 | 24.71 | 14.94 | 12.56 |
| Prices:Low | 7.28 | 7.71 | 6.49 | 8.78 | 26.02 | 30.01 | 20.00 | 11.36 | 9.05 | 6.53 |
| P/E Ratio:High | NM | NM | NM | NM | 17 | 9 | 8 | 10 | 8 | 8 |
| P/E Ratio:Low | NM | NM | NM | NM | 10 | 5 | 5 | 5 | 5 | 4 |

### Income Statement Analysis (Million $)

| | 2010 | 2009 | 2008 | 2007 | 2006 | 2005 | 2004 | 2003 | 2002 | 2001 |
|---|---|---|---|---|---|---|---|---|---|---|
| Revenue | 4,569 | 4,084 | 6,263 | 9,263 | 14,274 | 14,695 | 11,711 | 9,049 | 7,472 | 5,382 |
| Operating Income | -455 | -262 | -1,496 | -1,800 | 2,678 | 244 | 1,587 | 997 | 746 | 601 |
| Depreciation | 45.7 | 54.3 | 74.0 | 83.9 | 83.7 | 62.0 | 46.3 | 40.2 | 29.8 | 32.9 |
| Interest Expense | 2.73 | 2.26 | 229 | 260 | 256 | 43.3 | 56.4 | Nil | Nil | 81.6 |
| Pretax Income | -1,235 | -1,975 | -1,683 | -2,497 | 1,083 | 2,277 | 1,601 | 996 | 729 | 492 |
| Effective Tax Rate | NA | 40.1% | NM | NM | 36.3% | 36.8% | 37.6% | 38.0% | 39.0% | 38.5% |
| Net Income | -1,097 | -1,183 | -1,473 | -2,274 | 690 | 1,437 | 998 | 617 | 445 | 302 |
| S&P Core Earnings | -670 | -817 | -1,469 | -1,939 | 670 | 1,435 | 993 | 615 | 436 | 288 |

### Balance Sheet & Other Financial Data (Million $)

| | 2010 | 2009 | 2008 | 2007 | 2006 | 2005 | 2004 | 2003 | 2002 | 2001 |
|---|---|---|---|---|---|---|---|---|---|---|
| Cash | 1,471 | 1,858 | 1,655 | 1,060 | 551 | 1,002 | 315 | 404 | 613 | 72.1 |
| Current Assets | 6,618 | 8,494 | 7,162 | 8,869 | 11,335 | 10,954 | 8,521 | 6,596 | 5,568 | 4,407 |
| Total Assets | 7,699 | 10,051 | 7,708 | 10,226 | 13,177 | 13,048 | 10,407 | 8,063 | 6,888 | 5,714 |
| Current Liabilities | 2,121 | 1,544 | 1,258 | 2,273 | 2,782 | 3,276 | 2,702 | 2,359 | 2,224 | 1,703 |
| Long Term Debt | 3,392 | 4,282 | 3,143 | 3,478 | 3,538 | 3,387 | 2,737 | 1,962 | 1,913 | 1,738 |
| Common Equity | 2,135 | 3,194 | 2,836 | 4,320 | 6,577 | 5,957 | 4,522 | 3,448 | 2,760 | 2,277 |
| Total Capital | 5,527 | 7,476 | 5,978 | 7,798 | 10,115 | 9,352 | 7,274 | 5,418 | 4,674 | 4,015 |
| Capital Expenditures | 15.2 | 39.3 | 18.9 | 70.1 | 98.6 | 88.9 | 75.2 | 39.1 | NA | NA |
| Cash Flow | -1,051 | -1,128 | -1,399 | -2,191 | 773 | 1,499 | 1,044 | 657 | 474 | 335 |
| Current Ratio | 3.1 | 3.2 | 3.9 | 3.9 | 4.1 | 3.3 | 3.2 | 2.8 | 2.5 | 2.6 |
| % Long Term Debt of Capitalization | 61.4 | 57.3 | 52.6 | 44.6 | 35.0 | 36.2 | 37.6 | 36.2 | 40.9 | 43.3 |
| % Net Income of Revenue | NM | NM | NM | NM | 4.8 | 9.7 | 8.5 | 6.8 | 6.0 | 5.6 |
| % Return on Assets | NM | NM | NM | NM | 5.3 | 12.2 | 10.8 | 8.3 | 7.1 | 7.0 |
| % Return on Equity | NM | NM | NM | NM | 11.0 | 27.4 | 25.0 | 19.9 | 17.7 | 17.2 |

Data as orig reptd.; bef. results of disc opers/spec. items. Per share data adj. for stk. divs.; EPS diluted. E-Estimated. NA-Not Available. NM-Not Meaningful. NR-Not Ranked. UR-Under Review.

**Office:** 100 Bloomfield Hills Pkwy Ste 300, Bloomfield Hills, MI 48304-2950.
**Telephone:** 248-647-2750.
**Website:** http://www.pulte.com
**Chrmn, Pres & CEO:** R.J. Dugas, Jr.

**EVP & CFO:** R. Shaughnessy
**SVP, Secy & General Counsel:** S.M. Cook
**Chief Acctg Officer & Cntlr:** M.J. Schweninger
**Treas:** B.E. Robinson

**Investor Contact:** C. Boyd (248-647-2750)
**Board Members:** B. P. Anderson, B. Blair, R. J. Dugas, Jr., C. W. Grise, D. J. Kelly-Ennis, D. N. McCammon, P. J. O'Leary, J. J. Postl, B. W. Reznicek, T. M. Schoewe

**Founded:** 1969
**Domicile:** Michigan
**Employees:** 4,363

The **McGraw-Hill** Companies

# QEP Resources Inc

STANDARD
&POOR'S

| S&P Recommendation | BUY ★★★★☆ | Price<br>$28.79 (as of Nov 25, 2011) | 12-Mo. Target Price<br>$42.00 | Investment Style<br>Large-Cap Growth |
|---|---|---|---|---|

**GICS Sector** Energy
**Sub-Industry** Oil & Gas Exploration & Production

**Summary** This Questar spinoff is an independent oil and gas exploration and production company focused on the Rocky Mountain and Midcontinent regions of the U.S.

## Key Stock Statistics (Source S&P, Vickers, company reports)

| | | | | | | | |
|---|---|---|---|---|---|---|---|
| 52-Wk Range | $45.20–23.56 | S&P Oper. EPS 2011E | 1.57 | Market Capitalization(B) | $5.094 | Beta | NA |
| Trailing 12-Month EPS | $1.87 | S&P Oper. EPS 2012E | 1.88 | Yield (%) | 0.28 | S&P 3-Yr. Proj. EPS CAGR(%) | 18 |
| Trailing 12-Month P/E | 15.4 | P/E on S&P Oper. EPS 2011E | 18.3 | Dividend Rate/Share | $0.08 | S&P Credit Rating | BB+ |
| $10K Invested 5 Yrs Ago | NA | Common Shares Outstg. (M) | 177.0 | Institutional Ownership (%) | 82 | | |

## Price Performance

30-Week Mov. Avg. ···   10-Week Mov. Avg. – –   GAAP Earnings vs. Previous Year   Volume Above Avg. ▮▮▮ STARS
12-Mo. Target Price —   Relative Strength —   ▲ Up   ▼ Down   ▶ No Change   Below Avg. ▮▮▮ ★

Analysis prepared by Equity Analyst **Michael Kay** on Nov 10, 2011, when the stock traded at **$34.61**.

## Highlights

▶ On growth from programs at Haynesville/Cotton Valley, Woodford Cana, and Granite Wash, QEP lifted production 21% in 2010 (up 11% in 2009). QEP currently has 6 rigs running at Haynesville, is ramping to six rigs (currently 4) at the Pinedale Anticline, has one rig at Granite Wash and three rigs at Woodford, and added a third rig at Bakken Shale on a ramp in 2011 activity for oil. It is seeing a higher liquid content at Woodford than anticipated and recently lifted 2011 production guidance to 270-274 Bcfe, up 18%-20%, with liquids volumes up over 45%. Lease operating cost per unit continue to decline on drilling efficiencies.

▶ QEP's 2011 capex budget is $1.35 billion (88% E&P, 12% field services). We think QEP will fund its capital program via cash flow in 2011. The company sees 2011 EBITDA of $1.315-$1.350 billion, versus $1.14 billion in 2010.

▶ QEP posted 2010 adjusted EPS of $1.23, down 31% from $1.79 in 2009, reflecting lower gas price realizations. On rising oil prices and production, partly offset by weak gas, we forecast 2011 and 2012 EPS of $1.57 and $1.88, respectively. QEP has about 62% of its forecast 2011 production hedged.

## Investment Rationale/Risk

▶ QEP's 2010 reserve mix showed a growing proportion of liquids versus natural gas, with oil at 14% of reserves, versus 8% in 2009. We see further advancement in liquids, reflecting its position in some of the top unconventional plays. On June 30, 2010, QEP was spun off from Questar Corp. (STR 19 Hold) and began trading as a standalone E&P company, focusing onshore. This has allowed for a sharper focus on core E&P assets, greater capital commitment, and the pursuit of growth, possibly by acquisition. We think minimal balance sheet leverage and a complementary midstream business in Haynesville and the Rockies will support strategic growth initiatives. QEP has three-year production and reserve compound annual growth rates (CAGRs) of 15% and 18%, respectively.

▶ Risks to our recommendation and target price include a sustained decline in natural gas prices, an inability to replace reserves at a reasonable cost, and production declines.

▶ Our 12-month target price of $42 is based on our proved reserve NAV ($47) estimate and above-peer average relative metrics of 6X EV-to-2012 EBITDA forecast and 5X our 2012 cash flow estimate of $7.87 per share.

## Qualitative Risk Assessment

| LOW | MEDIUM | HIGH |
|---|---|---|

Our risk assessment reflects QEP's operations in a capital-intensive industry that derives value from producing commodities whose prices are very volatile.

## Quantitative Evaluations

**S&P Quality Ranking**  NR

| D | C | B- | B | B+ | A- | A | A+ |
|---|---|---|---|---|---|---|---|

**Relative Strength Rank**  WEAK

22

LOWEST = 1                                    HIGHEST = 99

## Revenue/Earnings Data

**Revenue (Million $)**

| | 1Q | 2Q | 3Q | 4Q | Year |
|---|---|---|---|---|---|
| 2011 | 596.2 | 784.1 | 852.4 | -- | -- |
| 2010 | 580.2 | 529.6 | 564.6 | 572.0 | 2,246 |
| 2009 | -- | -- | -- | -- | 1,973 |
| 2008 | -- | -- | -- | -- | 2,319 |
| 2007 | -- | -- | -- | -- | 1,688 |
| 2006 | -- | -- | -- | -- | -- |

**Earnings Per Share ($)**

| | | | | | |
|---|---|---|---|---|---|
| 2011 | 0.41 | 0.52 | 0.57 | E0.38 | E1.57 |
| 2010 | 0.44 | 0.39 | 0.40 | 0.37 | 1.60 |
| 2009 | -- | -- | -- | -- | 1.21 |
| 2008 | -- | -- | -- | -- | 2.90 |
| 2007 | -- | -- | -- | -- | 2.05 |
| 2006 | -- | -- | -- | -- | -- |

Fiscal year ended Dec. 31. Next earnings report expected: Late February. EPS Estimates based on S&P Operating Earnings; historical GAAP earnings are as reported.

## Dividend Data (Dates: mm/dd Payment Date: mm/dd/yy)

| Amount<br>($) | Date<br>Decl. | Ex-Div.<br>Date | Stk. of<br>Record | Payment<br>Date |
|---|---|---|---|---|
| 0.020 | 02/25 | 03/09 | 03/11 | 03/28/11 |
| 0.020 | 05/18 | 05/25 | 05/27 | 06/13/11 |
| 0.020 | 08/03 | 08/17 | 08/19 | 09/07/11 |
| 0.020 | 11/04 | 11/16 | 11/18 | 12/07/11 |

Dividends have been paid since 2010. Source: Company reports.

**Please read the Required Disclosures and Analyst Certification on the last page of this report.**

The McGraw-Hill Companies

# QEP Resources Inc

**STANDARD &POOR'S**

## Business Summary November 10, 2011

CORPORATE OVERVIEW. QEP Resources, Inc. is a leading independent natural gas and oil exploration and production company. On June 30, 2010, Questar Corporation (STR) spun off the shares of QEP Resources, Inc., creating a new publicly traded, independent natural gas and oil exploration and production company. QEP Resources is a major Rocky Mountain and Midcontinent region producer. QEP also gathers, compresses, treats and processes natural gas in its core producing areas.

As of December 31, 2010, QEP had estimated proved reserves of 3,036 Bcfe, of which 86% consisted of natural gas and 14% crude oil and liquids. This compares to estimated proved reserves of 2,747 Bcfe (92% natural gas) at year-end 2009. We estimate QEP's year-end 2010 reserve life at 13.3 years, compared to 14.5 years at the end of 2009, reflecting production increases. We estimate QEP has grown reserves at a three-year CAGR of 18%. Production in 2010 was 229 Bcfe, up 21%, and we estimate a 2010 reserve replacement ratio of 227%, versus a three-year average of 301%. Total costs incurred for drilling in 2010 were $1.245 billion, up 18% on higher drilling activity, and we calculate a 2010 finding and development cost of $2.18 per Mcf, with a three-year F&D cost of $2.49 per Mcf.

CORPORATE STRATEGY. QEP intends to create value through strong growth, superior execution, and a low cost structure. QEP plans to allocate capital to projects that generate top returns; maintain a sustainable inventory of low-cost, high-margin resource plays; build contiguous acreage positions to drive efficiencies; own and operate midstream infrastructure in core areas to capture value; build gas processing plants to extract liquids from gas streams; gather, compress and treat its own production to drive down costs; and maintain a strong balance sheet and financial flexibility. QEP operates under three segments: Exploration & Production, Midstream and Marketing.

The E&P segment acquires, explores for, develops and produces natural gas, crude oil and natural gas liquids. QEP operates and is active in some of the most economic, high-growth domestic resources plays. As it develops acreage in these plays, QEP is forecasting 2011 production growth of 19%-20%, to 270-274 Bcfe, for 2011. QEP plans to spend about $1.35 billion on E&P capex in 2011, up from $1.05 billion in 2010.

## Company Financials Fiscal Year Ended Dec. 31

| Per Share Data ($) | 2010 | 2009 | 2008 | 2007 | 2006 | 2005 | 2004 | 2003 | 2002 | 2001 |
|---|---|---|---|---|---|---|---|---|---|---|
| Tangible Book Value | 16.77 | NA | NA | NA | NA | NA | NA | NA | NA | NA |
| Cash Flow | 5.51 | 4.39 | 5.01 | NA | NA | NA | NA | NA | NA | NA |
| Earnings | 1.60 | 1.21 | 2.90 | NA | NA | NA | NA | NA | NA | NA |
| S&P Core Earnings | 1.61 | NA | NA | NA | NA | NA | NA | NA | NA | NA |
| Dividends | 0.04 | NA | NA | NA | NA | NA | NA | NA | NA | NA |
| Payout Ratio | 3% | NA | NA | NA | NA | NA | NA | NA | NA | NA |
| Prices:High | 38.33 | NA | NA | NA | NA | NA | NA | NA | NA | NA |
| Prices:Low | 27.90 | NA | NA | NA | NA | NA | NA | NA | NA | NA |
| P/E Ratio:High | 24 | NA | NA | NA | NA | NA | NA | NA | NA | NA |
| P/E Ratio:Low | 17 | NA | NA | NA | NA | NA | NA | NA | NA | NA |

| Income Statement Analysis (Million $) | | | | | | | | | | |
|---|---|---|---|---|---|---|---|---|---|---|
| Revenue | 2,246 | 1,973 | 2,319 | 1,688 | NA | NA | NA | NA | NA | NA |
| Operating Income | NA | 1,163 | 1,280 | 860 | NA | NA | NA | NA | NA | NA |
| Depreciation | 692 | 559 | 362 | 264 | NA | NA | NA | NA | NA | NA |
| Interest Expense | 84.4 | 70.1 | 61.7 | 33.6 | NA | NA | NA | NA | NA | NA |
| Pretax Income | 453 | 333 | 804 | 573 | NA | NA | NA | NA | NA | NA |
| Effective Tax Rate | NA | 35.3% | 35.3% | 36.9% | NA | NA | NA | NA | NA | NA |
| Net Income | 286 | 215 | 521 | 362 | NA | NA | NA | NA | NA | NA |
| S&P Core Earnings | 286 | 294 | 586 | 421 | 356 | 258 | 165 | 121 | 66.2 | 92.1 |

| Balance Sheet & Other Financial Data (Million $) | | | | | | | | | | |
|---|---|---|---|---|---|---|---|---|---|---|
| Cash | NA | Nil | NA | NA | NA | NA | NA | NA | NA | NA |
| Current Assets | 654 | 685 | NA | NA | NA | NA | NA | NA | NA | NA |
| Total Assets | 6,785 | 6,190 | NA | NA | NA | NA | NA | NA | NA | NA |
| Current Liabilities | 624 | 700 | NA | NA | NA | NA | NA | NA | NA | NA |
| Long Term Debt | 1,472 | 999 | NA | NA | NA | NA | NA | NA | NA | NA |
| Common Equity | 3,010 | 2,885 | NA | NA | NA | NA | NA | NA | NA | NA |
| Total Capital | 4,647 | 4,088 | NA | NA | NA | NA | NA | NA | NA | NA |
| Capital Expenditures | 1,469 | NA | NA | NA | NA | NA | NA | NA | NA | NA |
| Cash Flow | 978 | 774 | 883 | 626 | NA | NA | NA | NA | NA | NA |
| Current Ratio | 1.1 | 1.0 | NA | NA | NA | NA | NA | NA | NA | NA |
| % Long Term Debt of Capitalization | 31.7 | 24.4 | NA | NA | NA | NA | NA | NA | NA | NA |
| % Net Income of Revenue | 12.7 | 10.9 | 22.5 | 21.4 | NA | NA | NA | NA | NA | NA |
| % Return on Assets | 4.3 | NM | NA | NA | NA | NA | NA | NA | NA | NA |
| % Return on Equity | 9.9 | NM | NA | NA | NA | NA | NA | NA | NA | NA |

Data as orig reptd.; bef. results of disc opers/spec. items. Per share data adj. for stk. divs.; EPS diluted. Pro forma data to 2009; 2009 bal. sheet as of Mar. 31, 2010. E-Estimated. NA-Not Available. NM-Not Meaningful. NR-Not Ranked. UR-Under Review.

**Office:** 1050 17th Street, Suite 500, Denver, CO 80265.
**Telephone:** 303-672-6900.
**Website:** http://www.qepres.com
**Chrmn:** K.O. Rattie

**Pres & CEO:** C.B. Stanley
**EVP, CFO & Treas:** R.J. Doleshek
**Chief Acctg Officer & Cntlr:** B.K. Watts
**Secy:** A.L. Jones

**Investor Contact:** S.S. Gutberlet (303-672-6988)
**Board Members:** P. S. Baker, Jr., L. R. Flury, R. E. McKee, III, K. O. Rattie, M. W. Scoggins, C. B. Stanley, D. A. Trice

**Founded:** 2010
**Domicile:** Delaware
**Employees:** 823

*The McGraw-Hill Companies*

# QUALCOMM Inc

STANDARD &POOR'S

**S&P Recommendation** BUY ★★★★☆

| Price | 12-Mo. Target Price | Investment Style |
|---|---|---|
| $51.86 (as of Nov 25, 2011) | $73.00 | Large-Cap Growth |

**GICS Sector** Information Technology
**Sub-Industry** Communications Equipment

**Summary** This company focuses on developing products and services based on its advanced wireless broadband technology.

## Key Stock Statistics (Source S&P, Vickers, company reports)

| | | | | | | | | |
|---|---|---|---|---|---|---|---|---|
| 52-Wk Range | $59.84– 45.98 | S&P Oper. EPS 2012**E** | 3.09 | Market Capitalization(B) | $87.176 | Beta | | 0.94 |
| Trailing 12-Month EPS | $2.52 | S&P Oper. EPS 2013**E** | 3.48 | Yield (%) | 1.66 | S&P 3-Yr. Proj. EPS CAGR(%) | | 14 |
| Trailing 12-Month P/E | 20.6 | P/E on S&P Oper. EPS 2012**E** | 16.8 | Dividend Rate/Share | $0.86 | S&P Credit Rating | | NA |
| $10K Invested 5 Yrs Ago | $14,963 | Common Shares Outstg. (M) | 1,681.0 | Institutional Ownership (%) | 82 | | | |

## Price Performance

30-Week Mov. Avg. · · · 10-Week Mov. Avg. - - **GAAP Earnings vs. Previous Year**  Volume Above Avg. ▮▮▮ STARS
12-Mo. Target Price — Relative Strength — ▲ Up ▼ Down ► No Change   Below Avg. ▮▮▮ ★

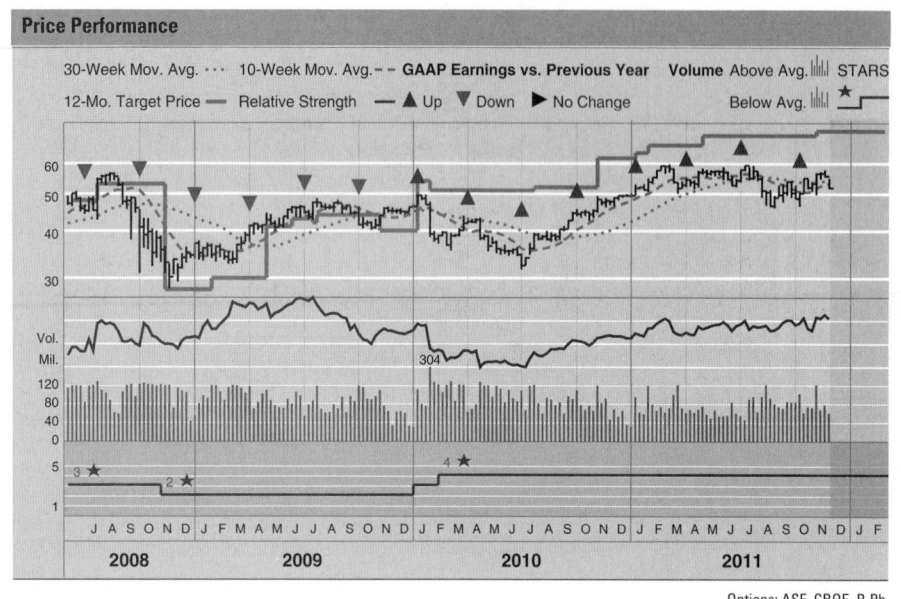

Options: ASE, CBOE, P, Ph

Analysis prepared by Equity Analyst **J. Moorman, CFA** on Nov 08, 2011, when the stock traded at **$57.03**.

## Highlights

➤ We forecast a 24.1% revenue increase for FY 12 (Sep.) and a 12.0% rise for FY 13, following a 36.1% increase in FY 11. We believe strong reception with high-end chips followed by penetration of mid-tier handsets throughout FY 12 will drive growth, in addition to revenue from the Atheros acquisition. While we see stronger growth for QCOM's royalty business, we look for this to be tempered by a slightly lower overall royalty rate.

➤ We expect growth in the WCDMA handset market, which supports QCOM's high-margin royalty business. We look for gross margins to decline to 64.5% in FY 12, from 64.8% in FY 11, as handset and chipset sales continue to accelerate with growth in the smartphone segment, but with QCOM aggressively seeking to increase chipset share. We expect a slight expansion in FY 13, to 65.1%.

➤ We estimate that operating EPS will increase to $3.09 in FY 12 and $3.48 in FY 13, from the $2.52 reported for FY 11.

## Investment Rationale/Risk

➤ We believe QCOM will see solid chipset sales throughout the coming year as the economy begins to improve and with rapid growth in the smartphone market. We also believe that the popularity of QCOM's Snapdragon chipset will give it an advantage as media-centric wireless devices continue to be popular. QCOM has a strong balance sheet, in our view, and should continue to generate sizable cash flow, but we are moderately concerned about handset and chipset pricing. With our view of upside potential in the share price, our recommendation is buy.

➤ Risks to our recommendation and target price include weaker demand in the replacement rate for more advanced CDMA handsets; lower selling prices for handsets and chipsets; and a slower recovery in orders to shore up low inventory levels.

➤ Applying a multiple of 21X to our FY 13 EPS estimate, a premium to peers reflecting QCOM's above-average margins and cash flow generation, we arrive at our 12-month target price of $73.

## Qualitative Risk Assessment

| LOW | MEDIUM | HIGH |
|---|---|---|

We believe QCOM's intellectual property rights and strong service provider relations give it a solid position in its industry. With our view of its healthy cash flow, we think the company's cash balance can support potentially weaker demand from customers and litigation risks related to its CDMA patents.

## Quantitative Evaluations

**S&P Quality Ranking** B+

| D | C | B- | B | B+ | A- | A | A+ |
|---|---|---|---|---|---|---|---|

**Relative Strength Rank** MODERATE

64

LOWEST = 1    HIGHEST = 99

## Revenue/Earnings Data

**Revenue (Million $)**

| | 1Q | 2Q | 3Q | 4Q | Year |
|---|---|---|---|---|---|
| 2011 | 3,348 | 3,870 | 3,623 | 4,117 | 14,957 |
| 2010 | 2,670 | 2,663 | 2,706 | 2,952 | 10,991 |
| 2009 | 2,517 | 2,455 | 2,753 | 2,690 | 10,416 |
| 2008 | 2,440 | 2,606 | 2,762 | 3,334 | 11,142 |
| 2007 | 2,019 | 2,221 | 2,325 | 2,306 | 8,871 |
| 2006 | 1,741 | 1,834 | 1,951 | 1,999 | 7,526 |

**Earnings Per Share ($)**

| | | | | | |
|---|---|---|---|---|---|
| 2011 | 0.76 | 0.75 | 0.58 | 0.62 | 2.70 |
| 2010 | 0.50 | 0.46 | 0.47 | 0.53 | 1.96 |
| 2009 | 0.20 | -0.18 | 0.44 | 0.49 | 0.95 |
| 2008 | 0.46 | 0.47 | 0.45 | 0.52 | 1.90 |
| 2007 | 0.38 | 0.43 | 0.47 | 0.67 | 1.95 |
| 2006 | 0.36 | 0.34 | 0.37 | 0.36 | 1.44 |

Fiscal year ended Sep. 30. Next earnings report expected: Late January. EPS Estimates based on S&P Operating Earnings; historical GAAP earnings are as reported.

## Dividend Data (Dates: mm/dd Payment Date: mm/dd/yy)

| Amount ($) | Date Decl. | Ex-Div. Date | Stk. of Record | Payment Date |
|---|---|---|---|---|
| 0.190 | 01/14 | 02/23 | 02/25 | 03/25/11 |
| 0.215 | 04/07 | 05/25 | 05/27 | 06/24/11 |
| 0.215 | 07/13 | 08/24 | 08/26 | 09/23/11 |
| 0.215 | 10/11 | 11/21 | 11/23 | 12/21/11 |

Dividends have been paid since 2003. Source: Company reports.

# QUALCOMM Inc

**STANDARD &POOR'S**

## Business Summary November 08, 2011

CORPORATE OVERVIEW. QUALCOMM Inc. is comprised of the following operating segments: CDMA technology (QCT), technology licensing (QTL), wireless and Internet (QWI), and strategic initiatives (QSI). The equipment and services unit, mostly in QCT, accounted for about 65% of total sales in the fourth quarter of FY 11 (Sep.), providing integrated circuits and system software solutions to top wireless handset and infrastructure manufacturers. QCOM uses a fabless business model, employing several independent semiconductor foundries to manufacture its semiconductor products. Approximately 127 million model station modem (MSM) integrated circuits were sold during the fourth quarter of FY 11, compared to approximately 111 million a year earlier. QCOM expects to sell between 146 million and 154 million MSM circuits in the first quarter of FY 12.

The license and royalty fee segment (QTL) accounted for about 33% of total sales, with 88% operating margins. QCOM holds a number of patents related to CDMA, and derives royalties from licensing its technology. Royalties are paid when manufacturers earn revenue from the sale of CDMA-based equipment, including CDMA and WCDMA handsets made by customers Samsung, LG Electronics, Motorola, and others. QCOM expects 16% growth in CDMA and WCDMA handsets in calendar 2012, mostly from WCDMA handsets.

LEGAL/REGULATORY ISSUES. QCOM has been involved in various legal issues involving patents on its chipsets and competitors' chipsets. QCOM resolved one dispute with a licensee in the first quarter of FY 11 and settled a dispute with Panasonic in the second quarter of FY 11. The company's multiple disputes with Nokia included litigation over Nokia's obligation to pay royalties for the use of certain of QCOM's patents. Without a license contract with QCOM, Nokia had opted to cancel its CDMA-related handset division. However, in July 2008, QCOM and Nokia signed a new 15-year agreement covering various second, third, and fourth-generation technology standards that we believe keeps QCOM's royalty pipeline active beyond supporting current handset offerings. In addition to a lump-sum cash payment that helped boost fourth-quarter FY 08 revenues by $580 million, Nokia returned to being a royalty customer of QCOM in late FY 08.

## Company Financials Fiscal Year Ended Sep. 30

| Per Share Data ($) | 2011 | 2010 | 2009 | 2008 | 2007 | 2006 | 2005 | 2004 | 2003 | 2002 |
|---|---|---|---|---|---|---|---|---|---|---|
| Tangible Book Value | 12.15 | 10.14 | 9.44 | 8.05 | 8.82 | 7.37 | 6.43 | 5.69 | 4.54 | 2.77 |
| Cash Flow | 3.31 | 2.36 | 1.33 | 2.18 | 2.18 | 1.60 | 1.38 | 1.13 | 0.62 | 0.47 |
| Earnings | 2.70 | 1.96 | 0.95 | 1.90 | 1.95 | 1.44 | 1.26 | 1.03 | 0.51 | 0.22 |
| S&P Core Earnings | 2.48 | 1.85 | 1.64 | 2.05 | 1.86 | 1.40 | 1.03 | 0.83 | 0.37 | 0.17 |
| Dividends | 0.81 | 0.72 | 0.66 | 0.60 | 0.52 | 0.42 | 0.32 | 0.19 | 0.09 | Nil |
| Payout Ratio | 30% | 37% | 69% | 32% | 27% | 29% | 25% | 18% | 17% | Nil |
| Prices:High | 59.84 | 50.31 | 48.72 | 56.88 | 47.72 | 53.01 | 46.60 | 44.99 | 27.43 | 26.67 |
| Prices:Low | 45.98 | 31.63 | 32.64 | 28.16 | 35.23 | 32.76 | 32.08 | 26.67 | 14.79 | 11.61 |
| P/E Ratio:High | 22 | 26 | 51 | 30 | 24 | 37 | 37 | 44 | 54 | NM |
| P/E Ratio:Low | 17 | 16 | 34 | 15 | 18 | 23 | 25 | 26 | 29 | NM |

| Income Statement Analysis (Million $) | | | | | | | | | | |
|---|---|---|---|---|---|---|---|---|---|---|
| Revenue | 14,957 | 10,991 | 10,416 | 11,142 | 8,871 | 7,526 | 5,673 | 4,880 | 3,971 | 3,040 |
| Operating Income | 6,361 | 3,949 | 3,880 | 4,200 | 3,266 | 2,962 | 2,586 | 2,266 | 1,684 | 1,068 |
| Depreciation | 1,061 | 666 | 635 | 456 | 383 | 272 | 200 | 163 | 180 | 394 |
| Interest Expense | 114 | 58.0 | 24.0 | 22.0 | Nil | Nil | 3.00 | 2.00 | 30.7 | 25.7 |
| Pretax Income | 5,687 | 4,034 | 2,076 | 3,826 | 3,626 | 3,156 | 2,809 | 2,313 | 1,285 | 461 |
| Effective Tax Rate | NA | NA | 23.3% | 17.4% | 8.90% | 21.7% | 23.7% | 25.4% | 35.6% | 22.0% |
| Net Income | 4,537 | 3,247 | 1,592 | 3,160 | 3,303 | 2,470 | 2,143 | 1,725 | 827 | 360 |
| S&P Core Earnings | 4,201 | 3,065 | 2,744 | 3,407 | 3,148 | 2,397 | 1,733 | 1,395 | 610 | 274 |

| Balance Sheet & Other Financial Data (Million $) | | | | | | | | | | |
|---|---|---|---|---|---|---|---|---|---|---|
| Cash | 11,652 | 10,279 | 11,069 | 6,411 | 6,581 | 5,721 | 6,548 | 5,982 | 4,561 | 2,795 |
| Current Assets | 14,293 | 12,133 | 12,570 | 11,723 | 8,821 | 7,049 | 7,791 | 7,227 | 5,949 | 3,941 |
| Total Assets | 36,422 | 30,572 | 27,445 | 24,563 | 18,495 | 15,208 | 12,479 | 10,820 | 8,822 | 6,510 |
| Current Liabilities | 5,289 | 5,468 | 2,813 | 2,291 | 2,258 | 1,422 | 1,070 | 894 | 808 | 675 |
| Long Term Debt | NA | NA | 187 | 142 | Nil | Nil | Nil | Nil | 123 | 94.3 |
| Common Equity | 26,951 | 20,858 | 20,316 | 17,944 | 15,835 | 13,406 | 11,119 | 9,664 | 7,599 | 5,392 |
| Total Capital | 26,993 | 20,858 | 20,316 | 18,087 | 15,835 | 13,406 | 11,119 | 9,664 | 7,722 | 5,530 |
| Capital Expenditures | 593 | 426 | 761 | 1,397 | 818 | 685 | 576 | 332 | 231 | 142 |
| Cash Flow | 5,598 | 3,913 | 2,227 | 3,616 | 3,686 | 2,742 | 2,343 | 1,888 | 1,007 | 754 |
| Current Ratio | 2.7 | 2.2 | 4.5 | 5.1 | 3.9 | 5.0 | 7.3 | 8.1 | 7.4 | 5.8 |
| % Long Term Debt of Capitalization | Nil | Nil | 0.9 | 0.8 | Nil | Nil | Nil | Nil | 1.6 | 1.7 |
| % Net Income of Revenue | 30.3 | 29.5 | 15.3 | 28.4 | 37.2 | 32.8 | 37.8 | 35.3 | 20.8 | 11.8 |
| % Return on Assets | 13.5 | 11.2 | 6.1 | 14.7 | 19.6 | 17.8 | 18.4 | 17.6 | 10.8 | 5.9 |
| % Return on Equity | 19.0 | 15.8 | 8.3 | 18.7 | 22.5 | 20.1 | 20.6 | 20.0 | 12.7 | 7.1 |

Data as orig reptd.; bef. results of disc opers/spec. items. Per share data adj. for stk. divs.; EPS diluted. E-Estimated. NA-Not Available. NM-Not Meaningful. NR-Not Ranked. UR-Under Review.

**Office:** 5775 Morehouse Drive, San Diego, CA 92121-1714.
**Telephone:** 858-587-1121.
**Email:** ir@qualcomm.com
**Website:** http://www.qualcomm.com

**Chrmn & CEO:** P.E. Jacobs
**Pres & COO:** S.M. Mollenkopf
**Vice Chrmn:** S.R. Altman
**EVP, CFO & Chief Acctg Officer:** W.E. Keitel

**EVP & CTO:** M.S. Grob
**Investor Contact:** J. Gilbert (858-658-4813)
**Board Members:** B. T. Alexander, S. M. Bennett, D. G. Cruickshank, R. V. Dittamore, T. Horton, I. M. Jacobs, P. E. Jacobs, R. E. Kahn, S. L. Lansing, D. A. Nelles, F. Ros, B. Scowcroft, M. I. Stern

**Founded:** 1985
**Domicile:** Delaware
**Employees:** 21,200

# Quanta Services Inc.

STANDARD
&POOR'S

| S&P Recommendation | **BUY** ★ ★ ★ ★ ☆ | Price $18.87 (as of Nov 25, 2011) | 12-Mo. Target Price $23.00 | Investment Style Large-Cap Blend |
|---|---|---|---|---|

**GICS Sector** Industrials
**Sub-Industry** Construction & Engineering

**Summary** This company provides specialized contracting services, offering end-to-end network solutions to the electric power, natural gas, telecom and cable TV industries.

## Key Stock Statistics (Source S&P, Vickers, company reports)

| | | | | | |
|---|---|---|---|---|---|
| 52-Wk Range | $24.18– 15.37 | S&P Oper. EPS 2011E | 0.83 | Market Capitalization(B) | $3.891 |
| Trailing 12-Month EPS | $0.46 | S&P Oper. EPS 2012E | 1.20 | Yield (%) | Nil |
| Trailing 12-Month P/E | 41.0 | P/E on S&P Oper. EPS 2011E | 22.7 | Dividend Rate/Share | Nil |
| $10K Invested 5 Yrs Ago | $10,425 | Common Shares Outstg. (M) | 210.1 | Institutional Ownership (%) | 90 |

| | |
|---|---|
| Beta | 1.07 |
| S&P 3-Yr. Proj. EPS CAGR(%) | 25 |
| S&P Credit Rating | NR |

## Price Performance

30-Week Mov. Avg. · · · 10-Week Mov. Avg. – – GAAP Earnings vs. Previous Year   Volume Above Avg. ▌▌▐ STARS
12-Mo. Target Price — Relative Strength — ▲ Up ▼ Down ► No Change   Below Avg. ▐▐▌ ★

Options: ASE, CBOE, P, Ph

Analysis prepared by Equity Analyst **Stewart Scharf** on Nov 08, 2011, when the stock traded at **$20.89**.

## Qualitative Risk Assessment

| LOW | MEDIUM | **HIGH** |
|---|---|---|

Our risk assessment reflects PWR's dependence on just a few industries, the erratic spending patterns of its major customers, the lack of minimum service volumes in most contracts, the ability of customers to terminate agreements on short notice, the volatility of the storm restoration service business, and the large portion of revenue derived from fixed-price agreements.

## Quantitative Evaluations

**S&P Quality Ranking**      **B-**

| D | C | **B-** | B | B+ | A- | A | A+ |
|---|---|---|---|---|---|---|---|

**Relative Strength Rank**      **MODERATE**

| | 62 | |
|---|---|---|
| LOWEST = 1 | | HIGHEST = 99 |

## Revenue/Earnings Data

**Revenue (Million $)**

| | 1Q | 2Q | 3Q | 4Q | Year |
|---|---|---|---|---|---|
| 2011 | 849.0 | 1,011 | 1,251 | -- | -- |
| 2010 | 748.3 | 870.5 | 1,206 | 1,106 | 3,931 |
| 2009 | 738.5 | 813.4 | 780.8 | 985.4 | 3,318 |
| 2008 | 844.4 | 960.9 | 1,053 | 921.5 | 3,780 |
| 2007 | 574.9 | 557.6 | 655.9 | 879.0 | 2,656 |
| 2006 | 496.5 | 514.1 | 528.5 | 592.0 | 2,131 |

**Earnings Per Share ($)**

| | | | | | |
|---|---|---|---|---|---|
| 2011 | -0.08 | 0.15 | 0.25 | E0.43 | E0.83 |
| 2010 | 0.11 | 0.16 | 0.30 | 0.16 | 0.72 |
| 2009 | 0.11 | 0.17 | 0.32 | 0.21 | 0.81 |
| 2008 | 0.14 | 0.22 | 0.29 | 0.24 | 0.88 |
| 2007 | 0.23 | 0.17 | 0.30 | 0.18 | 0.87 |
| 2006 | 0.07 | 0.14 | 0.17 | -0.26 | 0.15 |

Fiscal year ended Dec. 31. Next earnings report expected: Late February. EPS Estimates based on S&P Operating Earnings; historical GAAP earnings are as reported.

## Dividend Data

No cash dividends have been paid.

## Highlights

➤ We project revenue growth near 15% in 2011, reflecting strength in the electric power segment, driven by an increase in pipeline and renewable activity, as solar projects pick up. PWR recently won several new contracts for transmission infrastructure services, with more awards likely through 2012. We also see the Valard Construction and other acquisitions contributing to growth, along with its selection by TransCanada for the Keystone XL pipeline joint venture. We project mid-teens revenue growth again in 2012, with a rebound in natural gas and telecom projects.

➤ In our view, gross margins will narrow in 2011 to below 15%, on less fixed-cost absorption due to lower natural gas project revenues and higher prices. Margins should improve during 2012 on a better mix and stabilized input costs, and we expect cost controls and more normal weather-related comparisons to aid operating margins (EBITDA) through 2012. Interest expense should decline further.

➤ We project an effective tax rate near 40%, and estimate operating EPS of $0.83 (before $0.15 of charges) in 2011, climbing to $1.20 in 2012.

## Investment Rationale/Risk

➤ Our buy opinion is based on what we see as the benefits associated with recent acquisitions and better customer spending levels. Despite regulatory and permitting challenges for customers on near-term projects, we view positively the long-term trend toward capital investments for upgrading aging transmission and distribution networks.

➤ Risks to our recommendation and target price include lower-than-expected capital spending by utilities and gas, telecommunications and cable companies, delays in transmission pipeline projects due to permitting challenges, based on tighter government and environmental regulations, and higher commodity and energy costs.

➤ Our 12-month target price of $23 is based on a blend of valuation metrics. Our discounted cash flow model, which assumes 3% growth in perpetuity and a 10.5% discount rate, indicates a $21 value. In terms of relative valuation, we apply an EV/EBITDA multiple near 9X to our 2012 EBITDA estimate, above peers due to PWR's historical premium valuation, implying a value of $25.

---

**Please read the Required Disclosures and Analyst Certification on the last page of this report.**

The *McGraw-Hill* Companies

# Quanta Services Inc.

## Business Summary November 08, 2011

CORPORATE OVERVIEW. Quanta Services, Inc. (PWR) is a provider of special-ty contracting services that designs, installs and maintains the infrastructure and networks for four primary areas: electric power, natural gas, telecommu-nications and cable television, and fiber optic licensing and leasing. PWR had over 13,700 employees in 2010, of which approximately 39% were covered by collective bargaining agreements, primarily with the International Brother-hood of Electrical Workers (IBEW) and the Canadian Union of Skilled Workers (CUSW).

The electric power infrastructure segment (52% of PWR's 2010 revenues) in-stalls, repairs and maintains electric power distribution networks and trans-mission lines. The natural gas and pipeline segment (nearly 36%) provides de-sign, installation, repair and maintenance services for natural gas distribution and transmission networks. The telecommunications and cable network seg-ment (9.5%) designs, installs and maintains fiber optic, coaxial and copper ca-ble for video, data and voice transmission, and builds wireless communica-tions towers and installs switching systems for telecommunications carriers. The fiber optic licensing and leasing segment (nearly 3%) designs, procures, constructs, maintains and licenses fiber optic networks in select markets in the U.S.

MARKET PROFILE. During the recent economic downturn in 2009, we believe the lack of available credit dampened demand dynamics and spending levels. For instance, several large telecom customers, including Verizon and AT&T, slowed spending on their fiber optic build-out initiatives such as fiber to the premises (FTTP) and fiber to the node (FTTN) in 2009, while the utility industry reduced or deferred capital expenditures that were slated for 2009. In 2010, PWR again experienced a subdued spending environment, as demand for power remained anemic and customers remained reluctant to spend on large, capital-intensive projects. That said, we think the spending environment is im-proving as the economy improves, and that the longer-term demand for in-frastructure services in the electric, gas, telecom and cable industries is pow-ered by the need to maintain and upgrade aging networks. Due to the Energy Policy Act of 2005 and the American Recovery and Reinvestment Act of 2009, which both promote investment in aging U.S. energy infrastructure, we expect many utilities to continue spending on the upgrade of their power transmis-sion and distribution networks.

## Company Financials Fiscal Year Ended Dec. 31

| Per Share Data ($) | 2010 | 2009 | 2008 | 2007 | 2006 | 2005 | 2004 | 2003 | 2002 | 2001 |
|---|---|---|---|---|---|---|---|---|---|---|
| Tangible Book Value | 7.47 | 7.08 | 5.87 | 4.01 | 3.36 | 2.67 | 2.34 | 2.35 | 3.05 | 2.79 |
| Cash Flow | 1.42 | 1.43 | 1.39 | 1.24 | 0.63 | 0.73 | 0.45 | 0.23 | -1.41 | 2.10 |
| Earnings | 0.72 | 0.81 | 0.88 | 0.87 | 0.15 | 0.25 | -0.08 | -0.30 | -2.26 | 1.10 |
| S&P Core Earnings | 0.73 | 0.84 | 0.88 | 0.88 | 0.61 | 0.26 | -0.09 | -0.30 | -1.91 | 0.83 |
| Dividends | Nil | Nil | Nil | Nil | Nil | Nil | Nil | Nil | Nil | Nil |
| Payout Ratio | Nil | Nil | Nil | Nil | Nil | Nil | Nil | Nil | Nil | Nil |
| Prices:High | 23.23 | 25.80 | 35.39 | 33.42 | 20.05 | 14.97 | 9.52 | 9.87 | 18.90 | 37.50 |
| Prices:Low | 16.75 | 15.84 | 10.56 | 18.66 | 12.24 | 7.18 | 4.83 | 2.80 | 1.75 | 9.94 |
| P/E Ratio:High | 32 | 32 | 40 | 38 | NM | 60 | NM | NM | NM | 34 |
| P/E Ratio:Low | 23 | 20 | 12 | 21 | NM | 29 | NM | NM | NM | 9 |

| Income Statement Analysis (Million $) | 2010 | 2009 | 2008 | 2007 | 2006 | 2005 | 2004 | 2003 | 2002 | 2001 |
|---|---|---|---|---|---|---|---|---|---|---|
| Revenue | 3,931 | 3,318 | 3,780 | 2,656 | 2,131 | 1,859 | 1,627 | 1,643 | 1,751 | 2,015 |
| Operating Income | 401 | 375 | 403 | 250 | 189 | 124 | 70.2 | 83.1 | 71.6 | 273 |
| Depreciation | 146 | 126 | 114 | 74.7 | 56.2 | 55.4 | 60.4 | 60.1 | 60.6 | 79.4 |
| Interest Expense | 4.91 | 11.3 | 17.5 | 21.5 | 26.8 | 23.9 | 25.1 | 31.8 | 35.9 | 36.1 |
| Pretax Income | 246 | 234 | 282 | 167 | 65.1 | 52.2 | -12.6 | -53.1 | -194 | 157 |
| Effective Tax Rate | NA | 30.0% | 40.8% | 20.5% | 73.2% | 43.4% | NM | NM | NM | 45.4% |
| Net Income | 156 | 162 | 167 | 133 | 17.5 | 29.6 | -9.19 | -35.0 | -174 | 85.8 |
| S&P Core Earnings | 156 | 168 | 167 | 134 | 74.1 | 30.3 | -10.2 | -33.9 | -96.4 | 64.5 |

| Balance Sheet & Other Financial Data (Million $) | 2010 | 2009 | 2008 | 2007 | 2006 | 2005 | 2004 | 2003 | 2002 | 2001 |
|---|---|---|---|---|---|---|---|---|---|---|
| Cash | 539 | 700 | 438 | 407 | 384 | 304 | 266 | 180 | 27.9 | 6.29 |
| Current Assets | 1,596 | 1,583 | 1,381 | 1,305 | 991 | 831 | 700 | 676 | 529 | 577 |
| Total Assets | 4,341 | 4,117 | 3,555 | 3,388 | 1,639 | 1,555 | 1,460 | 1,466 | 1,365 | 2,043 |
| Current Liabilities | 500 | 496 | 452 | 757 | 334 | 258 | 221 | 199 | 212 | 242 |
| Long Term Debt | NA | 127 | 144 | 144 | 414 | 450 | 464 | 501 | 386 | 500 |
| Common Equity | 3,366 | 3,109 | 2,658 | 2,185 | 729 | 704 | 663 | 663 | 612 | 1,207 |
| Total Capital | 3,370 | 3,241 | 2,803 | 2,430 | 1,143 | 1,154 | 1,128 | 1,164 | 1,153 | 1,801 |
| Capital Expenditures | 150 | 165 | 186 | 128 | 48.5 | 42.6 | 39.0 | 35.9 | 49.5 | 85.0 |
| Cash Flow | 302 | 288 | 281 | 208 | 73.7 | 85.0 | 51.2 | 25.1 | -114 | 164 |
| Current Ratio | 3.2 | 3.2 | 3.1 | 1.7 | 3.0 | 3.2 | 3.2 | 3.4 | 2.5 | 2.4 |
| % Long Term Debt of Capitalization | Nil | 3.9 | 5.1 | 5.9 | 36.2 | 39.0 | 41.2 | 43.0 | 33.5 | 27.8 |
| % Net Income of Revenue | 4.0 | 4.9 | 4.4 | 5.0 | 0.8 | 1.6 | NM | NM | NM | 4.3 |
| % Return on Assets | 3.7 | 4.2 | 4.8 | 5.3 | 1.1 | 2.0 | NM | NM | NM | 4.4 |
| % Return on Equity | 4.8 | 5.6 | 6.9 | 9.1 | 2.4 | 4.3 | NM | NM | NM | 7.5 |

Data as orig reptd.; bef. results of disc opers/spec. items. Per share data adj. for stk. divs.; EPS diluted. E-Estimated. NA-Not Available. NM-Not Meaningful. NR-Not Ranked. UR-Under Review.

**Office:** 2800 Post Oak Boulevard, Suite 2600, Houston, TX 77056-6175.
**Telephone:** 713-629-7600.
**Email:** headquarters@quantaservices.com
**Website:** http://www.quantaservices.com

**Pres & CEO:** J.F. O'Neil, III
**CFO:** J. Haddox
**Chief Admin Officer & Chief Acctg Officer:** D.A. Jensen
**Treas:** N.M. Grindstaff

**Secy:** V.A. Mercaldic
**Investor Contact:** K. Dennard (713-529-6600)
**Board Members:** J. R. Ball, J. R. Colson, J. M. Conaway, R. R. DiSibio, V. D. Foster, B. Fried, L. Golm, W. F. Jackman, J. F. O'Neil, III, B. Ranck, J. R. Wilson, P. Wood, III

**Founded:** 1997
**Domicile:** Delaware
**Employees:** 13,751

# Quest Diagnostics Inc

STANDARD
&POOR'S

| S&P Recommendation | HOLD ★★★★★ | Price $54.43 (as of Nov 25, 2011) | 12-Mo. Target Price $60.00 | Investment Style Large-Cap Growth |
|---|---|---|---|---|

**GICS Sector** Health Care
**Sub-Industry** Health Care Services

**Summary** This company provides diagnostic testing, information and services to physicians, hospitals, managed care organizations, employers and government agencies.

## Key Stock Statistics (Source S&P, Vickers, company reports)

| | | | | | | | |
|---|---|---|---|---|---|---|---|
| 52-Wk Range | $61.21– 45.13 | S&P Oper. EPS 2011**E** | 4.32 | Market Capitalization(B) | $8.587 | Beta | 0.52 |
| Trailing 12-Month EPS | $2.70 | S&P Oper. EPS 2012**E** | 4.70 | Yield (%) | 1.25 | S&P 3-Yr. Proj. EPS CAGR(%) | 11 |
| Trailing 12-Month P/E | 20.2 | P/E on S&P Oper. EPS 2011**E** | 12.6 | Dividend Rate/Share | $0.68 | S&P Credit Rating | BBB+ |
| $10K Invested 5 Yrs Ago | $10,825 | Common Shares Outstg. (M) | 157.8 | Institutional Ownership (%) | 88 | | |

## Price Performance

30-Week Mov. Avg. · · ·   10-Week Mov. Avg. – –   **GAAP Earnings vs. Previous Year**   Volume Above Avg. ‖‖‖ STARS
12-Mo. Target Price —   Relative Strength —   ▲ Up  ▼ Down  ▶ No Change   Below Avg. ‖‖‖ ★

Options: ASE, CBOE, Ph

Analysis prepared by Equity Analyst **Jeffrey Loo, CFA** on Nov 02, 2011, when the stock traded at **$55.59**.

### Highlights

► We see 2011 sales, including a 2% contribution from the Athena and Celera acquisitions, growing a modest 1.5%, to $7.5 billion. In 2012, we project sales growth of 3.5% to $7.79 billion. We expect physician office visits, which fell about 5% in 2010, to remain soft the rest of 2011 and gradually improve in 2012 as the economy stabilizes and as some patients who deferred doctor visits likely return. We also expect some pressure in revenue per requisition due to the 1.75% Medicare fee decrease and some pricing changes in a few large contracts, despite more higher-margin esoteric testing. We see gross margins declining 10 basis points (bps) and operating margins falling 40 bps in 2011 as DGX has ramped up its sales force to focus on esoteric tests. But we look for cost cutting starting in 2012 to lift operating margins 20 bps.

► In October, CEO Surya Mohapatra announced a succession plan to find a new CEO. Mr. Mohapatra agreed to remain CEO for up to six months to ensure a smooth transition. We are not surprised by the resignation as we think DGX's market leadership position has been declining.

► Our 2011 and 2012 adjusted EPS estimates are $4.32 and $4.70, respectively.

### Investment Rationale/Risk

► We believe the shares, recently trading at 12.4X our forward 12 months EPS estimate, slightly below historical levels, are fairly valued. We anticipate only modest sales growth in 2011 and 2012 as external growth through acquisitions aids sluggish organic growth. However, we think its core lab testing business is fundamentally sound and that DGX has been successful in renewing managed care contracts; we do not see significant pricing pressure over the next two years. But we believe DGX may be losing some market share as competitors have reported more robust organic growth. We also expect some margin compression as DGX increases its sales force to help drive sales, but cost cutting in 2012 should aid margins. DGX has also been actively buying back its shares; it repurchased 16.4 million shares in the first nine months of 2011.

► Risks to our recommendation and target price include a greater-than-expected slowdown in physician office visits.

► Our 12-month target price of $60 is based on a P/E-to-growth ratio of 1.2X on our forward 12 months EPS estimate, and assumes a three-year EPS growth rate of 11%, in line with peers.

### Qualitative Risk Assessment

| LOW | MEDIUM | HIGH |
|---|---|---|

Our risk assessment reflects our view of DGX's leadership position in the large and mature diagnostic testing industry, the company's broad geographic service area, its diverse and balanced payor mix, and the growing recognition of the importance and significance of diagnostic testing.

### Quantitative Evaluations

**S&P Quality Ranking**                     A-

| D | C | B- | B | B+ | A- | A | A+ |
|---|---|---|---|---|---|---|---|

**Relative Strength Rank**                  STRONG

88

LOWEST = 1                               HIGHEST = 99

### Revenue/Earnings Data

**Revenue (Million $)**

| | 1Q | 2Q | 3Q | 4Q | Year |
|---|---|---|---|---|---|
| 2011 | 1,822 | 1,903 | 1,906 | -- | -- |
| 2010 | 1,806 | 1,875 | 1,865 | 1,824 | 7,369 |
| 2009 | 1,808 | 1,902 | 1,897 | 1,848 | 7,455 |
| 2008 | 1,785 | 1,838 | 1,827 | 1,800 | 7,249 |
| 2007 | 1,526 | 1,641 | 1,767 | 1,770 | 6,705 |
| 2006 | 1,553 | 1,583 | 1,583 | 1,549 | 6,269 |

**Earnings Per Share ($)**

| | | | | | |
|---|---|---|---|---|---|
| 2011 | -0.33 | 1.02 | 1.08 | E1.09 | E4.32 |
| 2010 | 0.89 | 1.07 | 1.13 | 0.97 | 4.06 |
| 2009 | 0.89 | 1.00 | 1.02 | 0.97 | 3.88 |
| 2008 | 0.72 | 0.83 | 0.81 | 0.87 | 3.23 |
| 2007 | 0.55 | 0.73 | 0.77 | 0.79 | 2.84 |
| 2006 | 0.77 | 0.78 | 0.82 | 0.77 | 3.14 |

Fiscal year ended Dec. 31. Next earnings report expected: NA. EPS Estimates based on S&P Operating Earnings; historical GAAP earnings are as reported.

### Dividend Data (Dates: mm/dd Payment Date: mm/dd/yy)

| Amount ($) | Date Decl. | Ex-Div. Date | Stk. of Record | Payment Date |
|---|---|---|---|---|
| 0.100 | 12/02 | 01/06 | 01/10 | 01/25/11 |
| 0.100 | 02/16 | 04/01 | 04/05 | 04/19/11 |
| 0.100 | 08/12 | 10/05 | 10/07 | 10/24/11 |
| 0.170 | 10/25 | 01/05 | 01/09 | 01/24/12 |

Dividends have been paid since 2004. Source: Company reports.

---

**Please read the Required Disclosures and Analyst Certification on the last page of this report.**

The McGraw·Hill Companies

# Quest Diagnostics Inc

## Business Summary November 02, 2011

CORPORATE OVERVIEW. Quest Diagnostics is the largest independent U.S. clinical lab operator. The clinical lab market is estimated to be about a $45 billion market, with hospital-based labs accounting for about 60% of the market, independent commercial labs, such as DGX, accounting for 33%, and physician-office labs the rest. DGX offers a broad range of clinical laboratory testing services used by physicians in the detection, diagnosis, and treatment of diseases and other medical conditions. Tests range from routine (such as blood cholesterol tests) to highly complex esoteric (such as gene-based testing and molecular diagnostics testing). At the end of 2010, DGX had a network of 35 principal laboratories throughout the U.S., 150 smaller "rapid response" (STAT) laboratories, and over 2,000 patient service centers, along with facilities in Mexico, Puerto Rico and England. In 2008, DGX started providing clinical lab services in India.

In 2010, DGX processed approximately 146 million requisitions (physician testing requests) annually. Routine testing and anatomic pathology generated 69% of net sales in 2010 (70% in 2009), esoteric testing 22% (20% in 2009), and clinical trials and risk assessment services from LabOne (acquired in November 2005) 9% (8%). Routine tests measure important health parameters such as the function of the kidney, heart, liver, thyroid and other organs. Esoteric tests are performed less frequently than routine tests, and/or require more sophisticated equipment and materials, professional hands-on attention, and more highly skilled personnel. As a result, they are generally priced substantially higher than routine tests.

## Company Financials Fiscal Year Ended Dec. 31

| Per Share Data ($) | 2010 | 2009 | 2008 | 2007 | 2006 | 2005 | 2004 | 2003 | 2002 | 2001 |
|---|---|---|---|---|---|---|---|---|---|---|
| Tangible Book Value | NM | NM | NM | NM | NM | NM | NM | NM | NM | NM |
| Cash Flow | 5.51 | 5.26 | 4.58 | 4.06 | 4.24 | 3.51 | 3.12 | 2.79 | 2.31 | 1.70 |
| Earnings | 4.06 | 3.88 | 3.23 | 2.84 | 3.14 | 2.66 | 2.35 | 2.06 | 1.62 | 0.94 |
| S&P Core Earnings | 4.08 | 3.83 | 3.29 | 2.85 | 3.17 | 2.57 | 2.13 | 1.80 | 1.42 | 0.83 |
| Dividends | 0.40 | 0.40 | 0.40 | 0.40 | 0.39 | 0.26 | 0.30 | Nil | Nil | Nil |
| Payout Ratio | 10% | 10% | 12% | 14% | 12% | 10% | 13% | Nil | Nil | Nil |
| Prices:High | 61.72 | 62.83 | 59.95 | 58.63 | 64.69 | 54.80 | 48.41 | 37.50 | 48.07 | 37.88 |
| Prices:Low | 40.80 | 42.36 | 38.66 | 47.98 | 48.59 | 44.32 | 35.94 | 23.68 | 24.55 | 18.30 |
| P/E Ratio:High | 15 | 16 | 19 | 21 | 21 | 21 | 21 | 18 | 30 | 40 |
| P/E Ratio:Low | 10 | 11 | 12 | 17 | 15 | 17 | 15 | 11 | 15 | 19 |

| Income Statement Analysis (Million $) | | | | | | | | | | |
|---|---|---|---|---|---|---|---|---|---|---|
| Revenue | 7,369 | 7,455 | 7,249 | 6,705 | 6,269 | 5,504 | 5,127 | 4,738 | 4,108 | 3,628 |
| Operating Income | 1,586 | 1,600 | 1,508 | 1,350 | 1,325 | 1,144 | 1,060 | 950 | 724 | 559 |
| Depreciation | 254 | 257 | 265 | 238 | 197 | 176 | 169 | 154 | 131 | 148 |
| Interest Expense | 146 | 147 | 185 | 186 | 96.5 | 61.4 | 57.9 | 59.8 | 53.7 | 70.5 |
| Pretax Income | 1,184 | 1,228 | 1,051 | 939 | 1,057 | 930 | 854 | 755 | 557 | 343 |
| Effective Tax Rate | NA | 37.5% | 36.8% | 38.2% | 38.6% | 39.2% | 39.3% | 39.9% | 39.5% | 43.4% |
| Net Income | 723 | 730 | 632 | 554 | 626 | 546 | 499 | 437 | 322 | 184 |
| S&P Core Earnings | 722 | 719 | 644 | 556 | 632 | 531 | 456 | 377 | 279 | 162 |

| Balance Sheet & Other Financial Data (Million $) | | | | | | | | | | |
|---|---|---|---|---|---|---|---|---|---|---|
| Cash | 449 | 534 | 254 | 168 | 150 | 92.1 | 73.3 | 155 | 96.8 | 122 |
| Current Assets | 1,605 | 1,679 | 1,497 | 1,374 | 1,191 | 1,069 | 931 | 996 | 824 | 877 |
| Total Assets | 8,528 | 8,564 | 8,404 | 8,566 | 5,661 | 5,306 | 4,204 | 4,301 | 3,324 | 2,931 |
| Current Liabilities | 1,214 | 1,059 | 1,225 | 1,288 | 1,151 | 1,101 | 1,044 | 724 | 636 | 659 |
| Long Term Debt | 2,641 | 2,937 | 3,078 | 3,377 | 1,239 | 1,255 | 724 | 1,029 | 797 | 820 |
| Common Equity | 4,033 | 3,990 | 3,605 | 3,324 | 3,019 | 2,763 | 2,289 | 2,397 | 1,769 | 1,336 |
| Total Capital | 7,044 | 7,119 | 6,873 | 6,911 | 4,258 | 4,018 | 3,013 | 3,426 | 2,565 | 2,156 |
| Capital Expenditures | 205 | 167 | 213 | 219 | 193 | 224 | 176 | 175 | 155 | 149 |
| Cash Flow | 977 | 987 | 897 | 792 | 823 | 722 | 668 | 591 | 454 | 332 |
| Current Ratio | 1.3 | 1.6 | 1.2 | 1.1 | 1.0 | 1.0 | 0.9 | 1.4 | 1.3 | 1.3 |
| % Long Term Debt of Capitalization | 37.5 | 41.3 | 44.8 | 48.9 | 29.1 | 31.2 | 24.0 | 30.0 | 31.0 | 38.0 |
| % Net Income of Revenue | 9.8 | 9.8 | 8.7 | 8.3 | 10.0 | 9.9 | 9.7 | 9.2 | 7.8 | 5.1 |
| % Return on Assets | 8.5 | 8.6 | 7.5 | 7.8 | 11.4 | 11.5 | 11.7 | 11.5 | 10.3 | 6.3 |
| % Return on Equity | 18.0 | 19.2 | 18.3 | 17.5 | 21.6 | 21.6 | 21.3 | 20.9 | 20.8 | 15.5 |

Data as orig reptd.; bef. results of disc opers/spec. items. Per share data adj. for stk. divs.; EPS diluted. E-Estimated. NA-Not Available. NM-Not Meaningful. NR-Not Ranked. UR-Under Review.

**Office:** Three Giralda Farms, Madison, NJ 07940.
**Telephone:** 973-520-2700.
**Email:** investor@questdiagnostics.com
**Website:** http://www.questdiagnostics.com

**Chrmn, Pres & CEO:** S.N. Mohapatra
**COO:** W.R. Simmons
**SVP & CFO:** R.A. Hagemann
**SVP & General Counsel:** M.E. Prevoznik

**Chief Acctg Officer & Cntlr:** T.F. Bongiorno
**Investor Contact:** L. Park (973-520-2900)
**Board Members:** J. C. Baldwin, J. K. Britell, W. F. Buehler, S. N. Mohapatra, G. M. Pfeiffer, D. C. Stanzione, G. R. Wilensky, J. Ziegler

**Founded:** 1967
**Domicile:** Delaware
**Employees:** 42,000

# Ralph Lauren Corp

**STANDARD &POOR'S**

**S&P Recommendation** HOLD ★★★☆☆

| Price | 12-Mo. Target Price | Investment Style |
|---|---|---|
| $138.80 (as of Nov 25, 2011) | $157.00 | Large-Cap Growth |

**GICS Sector** Consumer Discretionary
**Sub-Industry** Apparel, Accessories & Luxury Goods

**Summary** This company designs, markets and distributes men's and women's apparel, accessories, fine watches and jewelry as well as other premium lifestyle products.

## Key Stock Statistics (Source S&P, Vickers, company reports)

| | | | | | | | |
|---|---|---|---|---|---|---|---|
| 52-Wk Range | $164.55– 102.33 | S&P Oper. EPS 2012**E** | 6.81 | Market Capitalization(B) | $8.318 | Beta | 1.46 |
| Trailing 12-Month EPS | $6.77 | S&P Oper. EPS 2013**E** | 7.90 | Yield (%) | 0.58 | S&P 3-Yr. Proj. EPS CAGR(%) | 17 |
| Trailing 12-Month P/E | 20.5 | P/E on S&P Oper. EPS 2012**E** | 20.4 | Dividend Rate/Share | $0.80 | S&P Credit Rating | BBB+ |
| $10K Invested 5 Yrs Ago | $18,335 | Common Shares Outstg. (M) | 90.7 | Institutional Ownership (%) | NM | | |

## Price Performance

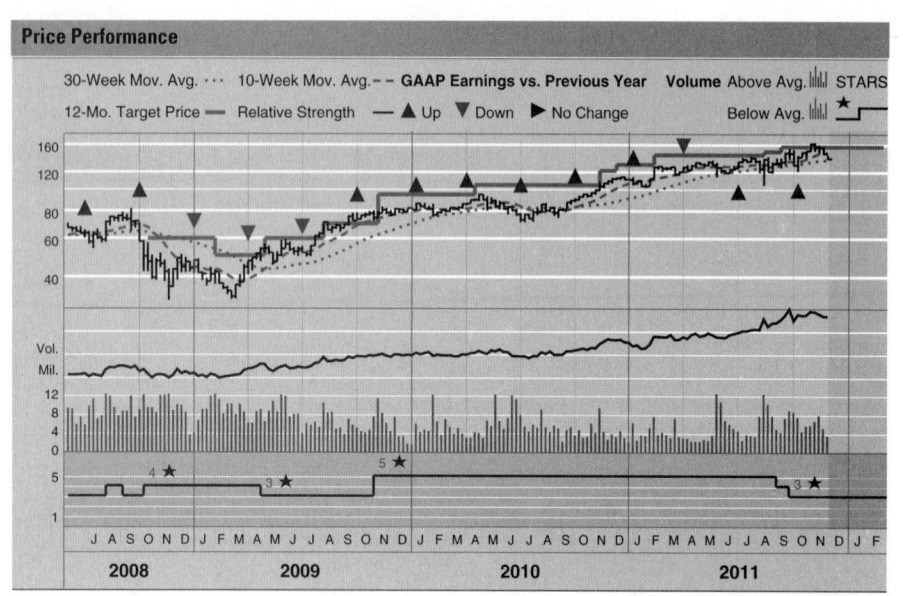

30-Week Mov. Avg. ··· 10-Week Mov. Avg. -- GAAP Earnings vs. Previous Year Volume Above Avg. STARS
12-Mo. Target Price — Relative Strength — ▲ Up ▼ Down ▶ No Change Below Avg. ★

Options: ASE, CBOE, Ph

Analysis prepared by Equity Analyst **Jason N. Asaeda** on Nov 14, 2011, when the stock traded at **$155.72**.

## Highlights

➤ We look for 21% revenue growth in FY 12 (Mar.), to $6.84 billion. We see RL benefiting from expansion of recently expanded product lines, including handbags, footwear and denim, and the assumption of direct control of its formerly licensed bedding and bath business and the Ralph Lauren apparel and accessories business in South Korea. That said, with the company seeing its retail same-store sales trends weaken in the U.S. and Europe since September, likely due to market volatility and geopolitical uncertainty, we forecast revenue growth in the second half of FY 12 at 15%, below the first half's 28% pace.

➤ We project about 50 basis points of operating margin contraction in FY 12, to 14.4%, due to significant increases in sourcing costs, inclusion of expenses related to now in-house bedding and bath and South Korea businesses, and investments to support growth, partially offset by selective price increases and increased penetration of international and retail sales.

➤ Assuming an effective tax rate of approximately 33%, versus FY 11's 31.2%, and share repurchases, we estimate FY 12 EPS of $6.81.

## Investment Rationale/Risk

➤ We view the shares as appropriately valued at recent levels. While our near-term outlook is guarded, we continue to see ample opportunities for RL to further penetrate the global premium apparel market, via geographic and product diversification, and a tiered pricing strategy that appeals to a broad range of shoppers spanning the high-end to value. We view e-commerce as a largely untapped growth driver in Europe and see substantial long-term growth opportunities in Asia, which contributed about 12% of net revenues in FY 11. We also see further development of the accessories and childrenswear businesses expanding the company's market opportunity and enhancing its accessible luxury positioning.

➤ Risks to our recommendation and target price include execution risk in Asia and a sharp decline in consumer discretionary spending. We also note that chairman, CEO and founder Ralph Lauren controls approximately 76% of the voting shares.

➤ Our 12-month target price of $157 is based on a peer-average forward P/E multiple of 20.4X applied to our calendar 2012 EPS estimate of $7.70.

## Qualitative Risk Assessment

| LOW | MEDIUM | HIGH |
|---|---|---|

Our risk assessment reflects our view of RL's strong balance sheet, offset by its exposure to the consolidating and contracting department store channel.

## Quantitative Evaluations

**S&P Quality Ranking** A-

| D | C | B- | B | B+ | A- | A | A+ |
|---|---|---|---|---|---|---|---|

**Relative Strength Rank** MODERATE

55

LOWEST = 1 HIGHEST = 99

## Revenue/Earnings Data

**Revenue (Million $)**

| | 1Q | 2Q | 3Q | 4Q | Year |
|---|---|---|---|---|---|
| 2012 | 1,526 | 1,905 | -- | -- | -- |
| 2011 | 1,153 | 1,532 | 1,548 | 1,427 | 5,660 |
| 2010 | 1,024 | 1,374 | 1,244 | 1,337 | 4,979 |
| 2009 | 1,114 | 1,429 | 1,252 | 1,224 | 5,019 |
| 2008 | 1,070 | 1,299 | 1,270 | 1,241 | 4,880 |
| 2007 | 953.6 | 1,167 | 1,144 | 1,031 | 4,295 |

**Earnings Per Share ($)**

| | | | | | |
|---|---|---|---|---|---|
| 2012 | 1.90 | 2.46 | E1.57 | E0.88 | E6.81 |
| 2011 | 1.21 | 2.09 | 1.72 | 0.74 | 5.75 |
| 2010 | 0.76 | 1.75 | 1.10 | 1.13 | 4.73 |
| 2009 | 0.93 | 1.58 | 1.05 | 0.44 | 4.01 |
| 2008 | 0.82 | 1.09 | 1.08 | 1.00 | 3.99 |
| 2007 | 0.74 | 1.28 | 1.03 | 0.68 | 3.73 |

Fiscal year ended Mar. 31. Next earnings report expected: NA. EPS Estimates based on S&P Operating Earnings; historical GAAP earnings are as reported.

## Dividend Data (Dates: mm/dd Payment Date: mm/dd/yy)

| Amount ($) | Date Decl. | Ex-Div. Date | Stk. of Record | Payment Date |
|---|---|---|---|---|
| 0.100 | 12/20 | 12/29 | 12/31 | 01/14/11 |
| 0.200 | 02/09 | 03/30 | 04/01 | 04/15/11 |
| 0.200 | 06/20 | 06/29 | 07/01 | 07/15/11 |
| 0.200 | 09/19 | 09/28 | 09/30 | 10/14/11 |

Dividends have been paid since 2003. Source: Company reports.

---

**Please read the Required Disclosures and Analyst Certification on the last page of this report.**

*The McGraw-Hill Companies*

# Ralph Lauren Corp

**STANDARD &POOR'S**

## Business Summary November 14, 2011

**CORPORATE OVERVIEW.** Since its modest beginnings in men's ties in 1967, Polo Ralph Lauren has grown into one of America's leading lifestyle brands encompassing multiple permutations targeted at specific demographics, usage occasions and price points, with merchandise available at approximately 10,000 retail locations throughout the world. Licensor relationships extend the brand to fragrance, eyewear and jewelry, and an extensive home merchandise offering. All told, we believe the Polo Ralph Lauren brand generates about $12 billion at retail worldwide.

**MARKET PROFILE.** The domestic men's, women's and children's apparel market represented an estimated $193 billion at retail in 2010, according to NPD Fashionworld consumer estimated data. S&P forecasts a 2% to 3% increase in 2011 apparel sales, which compares with a 2% gain in 2010, a 5% decline in 2009, a 3% drop in 2008, and 4% increases in 2006 and 2007. The apparel market is fragmented, with national brands marketed by 20 companies accounting for about 30% of total apparel sales, and the remaining 70% comprised of smaller and/or private label "store" brands. The market is mature, and subject to pricing pressure due to channel competition and production steadily moving offshore to low-cost producers in India, Asia and China. In the past year, we've seen increased raw material, labor and freight costs, which will likely result in inflationary pricing pressure at retail in the second half of 2011.

**COMPETITIVE LANDSCAPE.** By channel, specialty stores account for the largest share of apparel sales (32% in 2010, according to NPD). Mass merchants (Wal-Mart and Target) came in second, at 20%, and department stores, RL's primary channel, and national chains (Sears and JC Penney) each captured about 13% of 2010 apparel sales, with the department store channel losing about 700 basis points since 2003. Off-price retailers (TJX and Ross Stores) accounted for 9%, and the remaining 12% is divided among factory outlets and direct and e-mail pure plays. RL holds leading market shares in department stores, with four key department stores accounting for about 40% of its wholesale volume and Macy's (the largest wholesale account) for 19%. RL competes with Jones Apparel Group, Liz Claiborne and VF Corp., as well as private label offerings, which garner about a third of total apparel purchases and are an important differentiator for retailers. RL also sells directly to consumers through 367 specialty retail locations globally as of April 2011, spanning the luxury, mid-market and factory channels and at RalphLauren.com and Rugby.com.

## Company Financials Fiscal Year Ended Mar. 31

| Per Share Data ($) | 2011 | 2010 | 2009 | 2008 | 2007 | 2006 | 2005 | 2004 | 2003 | 2002 |
|---|---|---|---|---|---|---|---|---|---|---|
| Tangible Book Value | 20.42 | 18.33 | 14.41 | 10.71 | 11.99 | 10.35 | 10.38 | 10.56 | 8.93 | 7.38 |
| Cash Flow | 7.72 | 6.52 | 5.83 | 5.90 | 5.07 | 4.06 | 2.83 | 2.52 | 2.55 | 2.60 |
| Earnings | 5.75 | 4.73 | 4.01 | 3.99 | 3.73 | 2.87 | 1.83 | 1.69 | 1.76 | 1.75 |
| S&P Core Earnings | 5.73 | 4.75 | 4.01 | 3.99 | 3.75 | 2.80 | 2.32 | 1.53 | 1.55 | 1.54 |
| Dividends | NA | 0.30 | 0.20 | 0.20 | 0.20 | 0.20 | 0.20 | Nil | Nil | Nil |
| Payout Ratio | NA | 6% | 5% | 5% | 5% | 7% | 11% | Nil | Nil | Nil |
| Calendar Year | 2010 | 2009 | 2008 | 2007 | 2006 | 2005 | 2004 | 2003 | 2002 | 2001 |
| Prices:High | 115.45 | 83.50 | 82.02 | 102.58 | 83.15 | 56.84 | 42.83 | 31.52 | 30.82 | 31.34 |
| Prices:Low | 71.12 | 31.64 | 31.22 | 60.41 | 45.65 | 34.19 | 27.28 | 19.30 | 16.49 | 17.80 |
| P/E Ratio:High | 20 | 18 | 20 | 26 | 22 | 20 | 23 | 19 | 18 | 18 |
| P/E Ratio:Low | 12 | 7 | 8 | 15 | 12 | 12 | 15 | 11 | 9 | 10 |

### Income Statement Analysis (Million $)

| | 2011 | 2010 | 2009 | 2008 | 2007 | 2006 | 2005 | 2004 | 2003 | 2002 |
|---|---|---|---|---|---|---|---|---|---|---|
| Revenue | 5,660 | 4,979 | 5,019 | 4,880 | 4,295 | 3,746 | 3,305 | 2,650 | 2,439 | 2,364 |
| Operating Income | 1,047 | 898 | 859 | 860 | 802 | 663 | 406 | 377 | 382 | 393 |
| Depreciation | 194 | 181 | 184 | 201 | 145 | 127 | 104 | 83.2 | 78.6 | 83.9 |
| Interest Expense | 18.3 | 22.2 | 26.6 | 25.1 | 21.6 | 12.5 | 11.0 | 10.0 | 13.5 | 19.0 |
| Pretax Income | 825 | 689 | 588 | 644 | 659 | 516 | 298 | 266 | 274 | 276 |
| Effective Tax Rate | NA | NA | 30.9% | 34.5% | 36.8% | 37.7% | 36.0% | 35.7% | 36.5% | 37.5% |
| Net Income | 568 | 480 | 406 | 420 | 401 | 308 | 190 | 171 | 174 | 173 |
| S&P Core Earnings | 565 | 481 | 406 | 420 | 403 | 299 | 242 | 154 | 154 | 151 |

### Balance Sheet & Other Financial Data (Million $)

| | 2011 | 2010 | 2009 | 2008 | 2007 | 2006 | 2005 | 2004 | 2003 | 2002 |
|---|---|---|---|---|---|---|---|---|---|---|
| Cash | 1,047 | 1,147 | 820 | 626 | 564 | 286 | 350 | 343 | 344 | 239 |
| Current Assets | 2,478 | 2,276 | 2,057 | 1,894 | 1,686 | 1,379 | 1,414 | 1,271 | 1,166 | 1,008 |
| Total Assets | 4,981 | 4,649 | 4,357 | 4,366 | 3,758 | 2,089 | 2,727 | 2,270 | 2,039 | 1,749 |
| Current Liabilities | 832 | 747 | 674 | 909 | 640 | 844 | 622 | 501 | 500 | 392 |
| Long Term Debt | 292 | 282 | 406 | 546 | 399 | Nil | 291 | 277 | 248 | 285 |
| Common Equity | 3,305 | 3,117 | 2,735 | 2,390 | 2,335 | 2,050 | 1,676 | 1,422 | 1,209 | 998 |
| Total Capital | 3,597 | 3,399 | 3,142 | 2,966 | 2,734 | 2,070 | 1,967 | 1,699 | 1,457 | 1,284 |
| Capital Expenditures | 255 | 201 | 185 | 217 | 184 | 159 | 174 | 123 | 98.7 | 88.0 |
| Cash Flow | 762 | 661 | 590 | 621 | 546 | 435 | 294 | 254 | 253 | 256 |
| Current Ratio | 3.0 | 3.1 | 3.1 | 2.1 | 2.6 | 1.6 | 2.3 | 2.5 | 2.3 | 2.6 |
| % Long Term Debt of Capitalization | 8.1 | 8.3 | 12.9 | 18.4 | 14.6 | Nil | 14.8 | 16.3 | 17.1 | 22.2 |
| % Net Income of Revenue | 10.0 | 9.6 | 8.1 | 8.6 | 9.3 | 8.2 | 5.8 | 6.5 | 7.1 | 7.3 |
| % Return on Assets | 11.8 | 10.7 | 9.3 | 10.3 | 11.7 | 12.8 | 7.6 | 7.9 | 9.2 | 10.2 |
| % Return on Equity | 17.7 | 16.4 | 15.8 | 17.8 | 18.3 | 16.5 | 12.3 | 13.0 | 15.8 | 19.1 |

Data as orig reptd.; bef. results of disc opers/spec. items. Per share data adj. for stk. divs.; EPS diluted. E-Estimated. NA-Not Available. NM-Not Meaningful. NR-Not Ranked. UR-Under Review.

**Office:** 650 Madison Avenue, New York, NY 10022.
**Telephone:** 212-318-7000.
**Website:** http://www.ralphlauren.com
**Chrmn & CEO:** R. Lauren

**Pres & COO:** R.N. Farah
**SVP, CFO & Chief Acctg Officer:** T.T. Travis
**SVP, Secy & General Counsel:** A.S. Fischer
**Investor Contact:** J. Hurley (212-318-7000)

**Board Members:** J. R. Alchin, A. H. Aronson, F. A. Bennack, Jr., J. F. Brown, R. N. Farah, J. L. Fleishman, H. Joly, R. Lauren, J. A. McHale, S. P. Murphy, J. L. Nemerov, R. C. Wright

**Founded:** 1967
**Domicile:** Delaware
**Employees:** 24,000

The McGraw-Hill Companies

# Range Resources Corp.

**STANDARD &POOR'S**

| S&P Recommendation | HOLD ★★★☆☆ | Price $63.90 (as of Nov 25, 2011) | 12-Mo. Target Price $70.00 | Investment Style Large-Cap Growth |
|---|---|---|---|---|

**GICS Sector** Energy
**Sub-Industry** Oil & Gas Exploration & Production

**Summary** This company explores and develops oil and gas properties, primarily in the Appalachian, Southwest and Midcontinent regions of the U.S.

## Key Stock Statistics (Source S&P, Vickers, company reports)

| | | | | | |
|---|---|---|---|---|---|
| 52-Wk Range | $77.24–41.27 | S&P Oper. EPS 2011E | 1.04 | Market Capitalization(B) | $10.304 | Beta | 0.52 |
| Trailing 12-Month EPS | $-1.63 | S&P Oper. EPS 2012E | 1.29 | Yield (%) | 0.25 | S&P 3-Yr. Proj. EPS CAGR(%) | 8 |
| Trailing 12-Month P/E | NM | P/E on S&P Oper. EPS 2011E | 61.4 | Dividend Rate/Share | $0.16 | S&P Credit Rating | BB |
| $10K Invested 5 Yrs Ago | $23,239 | Common Shares Outstg. (M) | 161.3 | Institutional Ownership (%) | NM | | |

## Price Performance

30-Week Mov. Avg. · · · ·   10-Week Mov. Avg. - -   **GAAP Earnings vs. Previous Year**   Volume Above Avg. ▌▌▌ STARS
12-Mo. Target Price —   Relative Strength —   ▲ Up  ▼ Down  ► No Change   Below Avg. ▌▌▌ ★

Options: ASE, CBOE, P, Ph

Analysis prepared by Equity Analyst **Michael Kay** on Nov 23, 2011, when the stock traded at **$65.29**.

### Highlights

▶ RRC has ramped production at a 15% annual rate since the end of 2007, reflecting development efforts in the Marcellus Shale. On an aggressive horizontal program at Marcellus, where it believes returns rival those of oil plays, and its Nora field coal-bed methane project in Virginia, RRC sees production growth of 11% in 2011 and 25%-30% in 2012. It believes it is well on schedule to achieve its Marcellus year-end 2011 production exit rate target of 400 Mmcfe/day, up from 260 Mmcfe/d in the first quarter. RRC closed on the $900 million sale of Barnett Shale properties in May and is targeting another $200-$250 million in asset sales. It is now running four rigs at liquids-rich plays in the Texas Panhandle and Woodford Shale.

▶ RRC's industry-leading cost structure and finding and development costs provides for versatility, with Marcellus growth and drilling efficiencies providing top-tier gas industry returns, allowing it to drill through price weakness.

▶ We see adjusted EPS of $1.04 in 2011 ($0.56 in 2010) and $1.29 in 2012 on production growth and lower costs. RRC's 2011 capex budget is $1.47 billion. About 50% of forecasted 2012 volumes are hedged over $5.00/Mcf.

### Investment Rationale/Risk

▶ RRC's most recent five-year reserve compound annual growth rate was 26%, and it has a reserve life of 25 years. We believe average three-year reserve replacement of 630% (584% organic) and three-year finding and development costs of $1.20/Mcf demonstrate RRC's ability to replace reserves at attractive prices at Marcellus. Most reserves are based in Marcellus, where we think economics are attractive. RRC plans to spend 86% of its 2011 drilling capex at Marcellus; we see proceeds from Barnett sale being used to accelerate Marcellus growth. Our hold opinion is based on our view that RRC's premium valuation reflects upside potential seen from Marcellus acreage.

▶ Risks to our recommendation and target price include a sustained decline in oil and gas prices, an inability to replace reserves at reasonable costs, and production declines.

▶ Our 12-month target price of $70 reflects our proved NAV estimate ($78), an above-peer 12X enterprise value to 2012 EBITDA target, and 12X projected 2012 cash flows. Despite weak gas, RRC is up sharply in 2011 along with peer Marcellus operators, reflecting massive growth at the play and takeover speculation, in our view.

### Qualitative Risk Assessment

| LOW | MEDIUM | HIGH |
|---|---|---|

Our risk assessment reflects operations in a capital-intensive industry that is cyclical and derives value from producing a commodity whose price is very volatile.

### Quantitative Evaluations

**S&P Quality Ranking**   B

| D | C | B- | B | B+ | A- | A | A+ |
|---|---|---|---|---|---|---|---|

**Relative Strength Rank**   MODERATE
59
LOWEST = 1     HIGHEST = 99

### Revenue/Earnings Data

**Revenue (Million $)**

| | 1Q | 2Q | 3Q | 4Q | Year |
|---|---|---|---|---|---|
| 2011 | 187.6 | 306.6 | 338.2 | -- | -- |
| 2010 | 348.5 | 224.8 | 227.0 | 247.6 | 911.9 |
| 2009 | 276.4 | 180.4 | 203.6 | 246.8 | 907.3 |
| 2008 | 205.3 | 150.1 | 622.7 | 344.9 | 1,323 |
| 2007 | 152.8 | 243.5 | 242.4 | 223.4 | 862.1 |
| 2006 | 189.2 | 177.6 | 228.9 | 184.1 | 779.7 |

**Earnings Per Share ($)**

| | | | | | |
|---|---|---|---|---|---|
| 2011 | -0.21 | 0.28 | 0.20 | E0.27 | E1.04 |
| 2010 | 0.48 | 0.06 | -0.05 | -2.02 | -1.53 |
| 2009 | 0.21 | -0.26 | -0.19 | -0.11 | -0.35 |
| 2008 | 0.01 | -0.23 | 1.81 | 0.60 | 2.22 |
| 2007 | 0.06 | 0.43 | 0.39 | 0.22 | 1.11 |
| 2006 | 0.41 | 0.37 | 0.46 | 0.19 | 1.42 |

Fiscal year ended Dec. 31. Next earnings report expected: Late January. EPS Estimates based on S&P Operating Earnings; historical GAAP earnings are as reported.

### Dividend Data (Dates: mm/dd Payment Date: mm/dd/yy)

| Amount ($) | Date Decl. | Ex-Div. Date | Stk. of Record | Payment Date |
|---|---|---|---|---|
| 0.040 | 12/02 | 12/13 | 12/15 | 12/31/10 |
| 0.040 | 03/01 | 03/11 | 03/15 | 03/31/11 |
| 0.040 | 06/07 | 06/15 | 06/17 | 06/30/11 |
| 0.040 | 09/01 | 09/13 | 09/15 | 09/30/11 |

Dividends have been paid since 2004. Source: Company reports.

---

**Please read the Required Disclosures and Analyst Certification on the last page of this report.**

**The McGraw·Hill Companies**

# Range Resources Corp.

STANDARD &POOR'S

## Business Summary November 23, 2011

CORPORATE OVERVIEW. Range Resources Corp. is an independent oil and gas company primarily engaged in acquiring, developing, exploring and producing oil and gas properties. RRC has established three core operating areas in the Appalachian, Southwestern and Gulf Coast regions of the U.S. The Southwest business unit encompasses operations in East Texas, West Texas, New Mexico, and the Mid-continent region of Oklahoma and the Texas Panhandle.

As of December 31, 2010, RRC had estimated proved reserves of 4.44 Tcfe, of which 80% was natural gas and 49% was proved developed. This compares with estimated proved reserves of 3.13 Tcfe (84% natural gas and 55% proved developed) at the end of 2009, a 42% increase, reflecting Marcellus Shale development. We estimate RRC's 2010 year end reserve life at 24.6 years, compared to 19.7 years at the end of 2009.

We estimate that RRC replaced 931% (486% in 2009) of production in 2010, almost all of it from organic drilling. We estimate finding and development costs (exclude acquisitions) in 2010 were $0.70 per Mcfe, versus a three-year average of $1.20 per Mcfe (down from a previous three-year average of $1.83/Mcfe). Total reserve replacement costs (including acquisitions) in 2010 were $0.72 per Mcfe, versus a three-year average of $1.24 per Mcfe.

CORPORATE STRATEGY. RRC pursues what we consider a balanced growth strategy that targets the exploitation of its inventory of development drilling locations, higher potential exploration projects, and acquisitions. RRC focuses on acquisition opportunities within its core operating areas to capitalize on regional expertise and drive down costs.

Since 2004, RRC has sold $870 million of non-core properties, and recently entered into a definitive agreement to sell its Barnett Shale assets in the Fort Worth Basin for $900 million. Since 2007, asset sales have provided the second largest source of funding, behind cash flow. RRC has sold these lower growth properties to re-direct capital toward the Marcellus Shale and to help streamline and simplify the company.

IMPACT OF MAJOR DEVELOPMENTS. In February 2007, RRC completed the sale of its Austin Chalk assets acquired in the Stroud Energy transaction in 2006 for $82 million. RRC originally stated its intention to sell the assets In late July 2006, just as natural gas prices fell into a fairly steep decline, and RRC had difficulty selling the assets.

## Company Financials Fiscal Year Ended Dec. 31

| Per Share Data ($) | 2010 | 2009 | 2008 | 2007 | 2006 | 2005 | 2004 | 2003 | 2002 | 2001 |
|---|---|---|---|---|---|---|---|---|---|---|
| Tangible Book Value | 13.91 | 15.10 | 15.82 | 11.57 | 9.04 | 5.36 | 4.65 | 3.24 | 2.50 | 3.11 |
| Cash Flow | 4.30 | 2.74 | 4.45 | 2.59 | 2.65 | 1.84 | 1.43 | 1.34 | 1.23 | 1.05 |
| Earnings | -1.53 | -0.35 | 2.22 | 1.11 | 1.42 | 0.86 | 0.38 | 0.35 | 0.29 | 0.07 |
| S&P Core Earnings | -1.84 | -0.38 | 2.14 | 1.11 | 1.42 | 0.82 | 0.29 | 0.33 | 0.29 | 0.18 |
| Dividends | 0.16 | 0.16 | 0.16 | 0.13 | 0.09 | 0.07 | 0.03 | Nil | Nil | Nil |
| Payout Ratio | NM | NM | 7% | 12% | 6% | 8% | 9% | Nil | Nil | Nil |
| Prices:High | 54.65 | 60.13 | 76.81 | 51.88 | 31.77 | 28.37 | 14.43 | 6.57 | 3.97 | 4.75 |
| Prices:Low | 32.25 | 30.90 | 23.77 | 25.29 | 21.74 | 12.34 | 6.25 | 3.33 | 2.69 | 2.62 |
| P/E Ratio:High | NM | NM | 35 | 47 | 22 | 33 | 38 | 19 | 14 | 65 |
| P/E Ratio:Low | NM | NM | 11 | 23 | 15 | 14 | 16 | 9 | 9 | 36 |

| Income Statement Analysis (Million $) | | | | | | | | | | |
|---|---|---|---|---|---|---|---|---|---|---|
| Revenue | 912 | 907 | 1,323 | 862 | 780 | 536 | 321 | 230 | 195 | 219 |
| Operating Income | NA | NA | 965 | 564 | 549 | 344 | 193 | 140 | 119 | 152 |
| Depreciation, Depletion and Amortization | 913 | 478 | 348 | 221 | 170 | 128 | 103 | 86.5 | 76.8 | 77.8 |
| Interest Expense | 131 | 117 | 99.8 | 77.7 | 57.6 | 38.8 | 23.1 | 22.2 | 23.2 | 30.7 |
| Pretax Income | -366 | -58.7 | 543 | 266 | 321 | 177 | 66.8 | 49.4 | 19.3 | 4.99 |
| Effective Tax Rate | NA | 8.28% | 36.2% | 37.2% | 38.5% | 37.4% | 36.8% | 37.4% | NM | NM |
| Net Income | -239 | -53.9 | 346 | 167 | 198 | 111 | 42.2 | 30.9 | 23.8 | 5.05 |
| S&P Core Earnings | -288 | -57.3 | 333 | 167 | 198 | 105 | 27.9 | 27.3 | 23.5 | 14.1 |

| Balance Sheet & Other Financial Data (Million $) | | | | | | | | | | |
|---|---|---|---|---|---|---|---|---|---|---|
| Cash | 2.85 | 0.77 | 0.75 | 4.02 | 2.38 | 4.75 | 18.4 | 0.63 | 1.33 | 3.25 |
| Current Assets | 262 | 175 | 404 | 262 | 320 | 208 | 136 | 66.1 | 37.4 | 78.6 |
| Total Assets | 5,499 | 5,396 | 5,563 | 4,017 | 3,188 | 2,019 | 1,595 | 830 | 658 | 692 |
| Current Liabilities | 431 | 314 | 354 | 305 | 232 | 322 | 177 | 107 | 67.2 | 44.0 |
| Long Term Debt | 1,961 | 1,708 | 1,791 | 1,151 | 1,049 | 616 | 621 | 358 | 368 | 392 |
| Common Equity | 2,224 | 2,379 | 2,458 | 1,728 | 1,346 | 770 | 566 | 224 | 206 | 246 |
| Total Capital | 4,184 | 4,086 | 5,032 | 3,470 | 2,864 | 1,561 | 1,305 | 643 | 574 | 648 |
| Capital Expenditures | 832 | 574 | 918 | 808 | 517 | 277 | 175 | 2.62 | 2.82 | 2.33 |
| Cash Flow | 674 | 424 | 694 | 388 | 367 | 239 | 140 | 117 | 101 | 82.9 |
| Current Ratio | 0.6 | 0.6 | 1.1 | 0.9 | 1.4 | 0.6 | 0.8 | 0.6 | 0.6 | 1.8 |
| % Long Term Debt of Capitalization | 46.9 | 41.8 | 35.6 | 33.1 | 36.6 | 39.5 | 47.6 | 55.7 | 64.1 | 60.6 |
| % Return on Assets | NM | NM | 7.2 | 4.7 | 7.6 | 6.1 | 3.5 | 4.2 | 3.5 | 0.7 |
| % Return on Equity | NM | NM | 16.5 | 10.9 | 18.7 | 16.1 | 9.4 | 14.0 | 10.8 | 2.3 |

Data as orig reptd.; bef. results of disc opers/spec. items. Per share data adj. for stk. divs.; EPS diluted. E-Estimated. NA-Not Available. NM-Not Meaningful. NR-Not Ranked. UR-Under Review.

**Office:** 100 Throckmorton Street, Suite 1200, Fort Worth, TX 76102.
**Telephone:** 817-870-2601.
**Website:** http://www.rangeresources.com
**Chrmn & CEO:** J.H. Pinkerton

**Pres & COO:** J.L. Ventura
**EVP & CFO:** R.S. Manny
**SVP, Secy & General Counsel:** D.P. Poole
**Investor Contact:** R.L. Waller (817-870-2601)

**Board Members:** C. L. Blackburn, A. V. Dub, V. R. Eales, A. Finkelson, J. M. Funk, J. S. Linker, A. P. Lynch, K. S. McCarthy, J. H. Pinkerton, J. L. Ventura

**Founded:** 1976
**Domicile:** Delaware
**Employees:** 713

# Raytheon Co.

**STANDARD &POOR'S**

| **S&P Recommendation** HOLD ★★★☆☆ | **Price** $43.12 (as of Nov 25, 2011) | **12-Mo. Target Price** $48.00 | **Investment Style** Large-Cap Value |
|---|---|---|---|

**GICS Sector** Industrials
**Sub-Industry** Aerospace & Defense

**Summary** Raytheon, the world's sixth largest military contractor, specializes in making high-tech missiles, advanced radar systems and sensors, defense electronics, and missile-defense systems.

## Key Stock Statistics (Source S&P, Vickers, company reports)

| | | | | | | | |
|---|---|---|---|---|---|---|---|
| 52-Wk Range | $53.12– 38.35 | S&P Oper. EPS 2011**E** | 5.05 | Market Capitalization(B) | $14.924 | Beta | 0.68 |
| Trailing 12-Month EPS | $4.89 | S&P Oper. EPS 2012**E** | 5.40 | Yield (%) | 3.99 | S&P 3-Yr. Proj. EPS CAGR(%) | 3 |
| Trailing 12-Month P/E | 8.8 | P/E on S&P Oper. EPS 2011**E** | 8.5 | Dividend Rate/Share | $1.72 | S&P Credit Rating | A- |
| $10K Invested 5 Yrs Ago | $9,642 | Common Shares Outstg. (M) | 346.1 | Institutional Ownership (%) | 74 | | |

## Price Performance

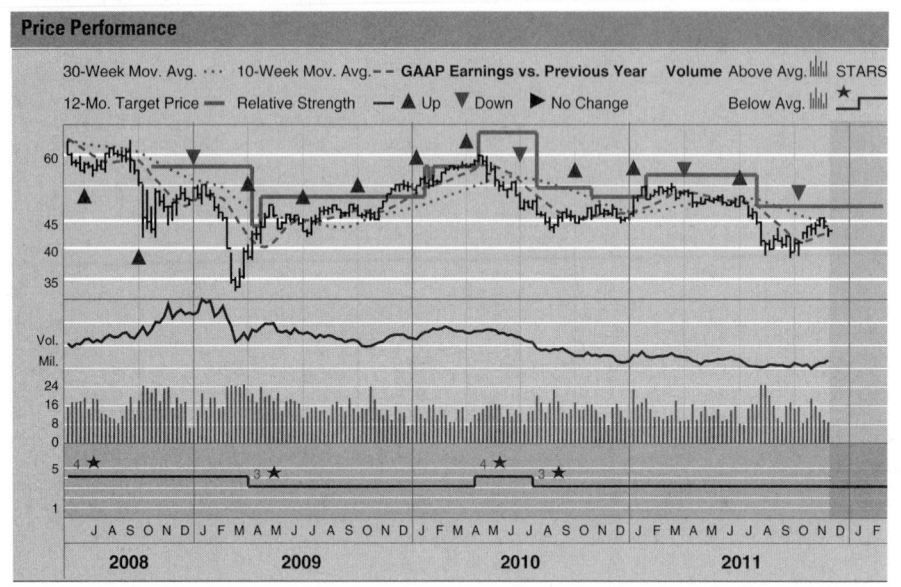

- 30-Week Mov. Avg. ···· 10-Week Mov. Avg. - - GAAP Earnings vs. Previous Year  Volume Above Avg. STARS
- 12-Mo. Target Price — Relative Strength — ▲ Up ▼ Down ► No Change  Below Avg.

Options: ASE, CBOE, P

Analysis prepared by Equity Analyst **R. Tortoriello** on Nov 15, 2011, when the stock traded at **$45.13**.

### Highlights

➤ We estimate revenue will decline 1% in 2011, on significant declines in Integrated Defense Systems (IDS), Network Centric Systems, and Technical Services. The bookings (orders) to billings ratio for 2010 was 0.97, but has improved to 1.05 for the first nine months of 2011; however, backlog has been declining slightly. As a result, we project only about 1% sales growth in 2012, with growth primarily in Intelligence & Information Systems, IDS (on easy comparisons), and Space & Airborne Systems.

➤ We estimate operating margins of 10.9% in 2011, up slightly versus 10.4% in 2010, on the absence of a $300 million pretax charge taken in 2010 on the e-Borders program. For 2012, we project that margins will remain flat or increase slightly.

➤ We estimate EPS of $5.05 in 2011, rising to $5.40 in 2012, aided by share repurchases. We look for free cash flow (cash generated from operations less capital expenditures) per share of about $4.90 in 2011, up 14% from 2010.

### Investment Rationale/Risk

➤ Although RTN's orders grew strongly from 2005 to 2008, orders fell in 2009 and 2010, and despite order improvement in 2011, backlog has continued to decline. We see good opportunities for RTN with U.S. and international customers for missile defense and defense electronics, but note European defense budgets are being cut and the U.S. budget is likely to decline going forward, which we believe will severely constrain growth at large defense contractors. We expect missile defense and electronics growth in Asia and the Middle East, where a new arms race may be emerging, but do not see this growth offsetting weakness elsewhere.

➤ Risks to our recommendation and target price include the potential for delays and/or cuts in military contracts and failure to perform well on existing contracts or win new business.

➤ Our 12-month target price of $48 is based on an enterprise value multiple of 5X our 2012 EBITDA estimate of $3.2 billion. This compares to a 20-year low EV/EBITDA multiple for RTN of 3.5X and a 20-year average of 8.8X. We believe the shares deserve a below-average valuation due to our forecast of weak defense spending.

### Qualitative Risk Assessment

| LOW | **MEDIUM** | HIGH |
|---|---|---|

Our risk assessment reflects RTN's exposure to changes in defense spending and its historical earnings stability that is about average, offset by relatively low total debt to capital ratio of 26% (as of September 2011), its leading defense contractor status and large project backlog.

### Quantitative Evaluations

**S&P Quality Ranking**  B+

| D | C | B- | B | **B+** | A- | A | A+ |
|---|---|---|---|---|---|---|---|

**Relative Strength Rank**  STRONG

75

LOWEST = 1   HIGHEST = 99

### Revenue/Earnings Data

**Revenue (Million $)**

| | 1Q | 2Q | 3Q | 4Q | Year |
|---|---|---|---|---|---|
| 2011 | 6,062 | 6,222 | 6,132 | -- | -- |
| 2010 | 6,053 | 5,973 | 6,272 | 6,885 | 25,183 |
| 2009 | 5,884 | 6,125 | 6,205 | 6,667 | 24,881 |
| 2008 | 5,354 | 5,870 | 5,864 | 6,086 | 23,174 |
| 2007 | 4,928 | 5,419 | 5,355 | 6,000 | 21,301 |
| 2006 | 4,660 | 4,973 | 4,936 | 5,722 | 20,291 |

**Earnings Per Share ($)**

| | | | | | |
|---|---|---|---|---|---|
| 2011 | 1.06 | 1.23 | 1.43 | E1.35 | E5.05 |
| 2010 | 1.18 | 0.55 | 1.71 | 1.37 | 4.79 |
| 2009 | 1.11 | 1.24 | 1.25 | 1.30 | 4.89 |
| 2008 | 0.93 | 1.00 | 1.01 | 1.02 | 3.95 |
| 2007 | 0.69 | 0.79 | 0.69 | 1.45 | 3.80 |
| 2006 | 0.61 | 0.61 | 0.59 | 0.81 | 2.46 |

Fiscal year ended Dec. 31. Next earnings report expected: Late January. EPS Estimates based on S&P Operating Earnings; historical GAAP earnings are as reported.

### Dividend Data (Dates: mm/dd Payment Date: mm/dd/yy)

| Amount ($) | Date Decl. | Ex-Div. Date | Stk. of Record | Payment Date |
|---|---|---|---|---|
| 0.430 | 03/23 | 04/04 | 04/06 | 04/28/11 |
| 0.430 | 05/27 | 07/01 | 07/06 | 08/11/11 |
| 0.430 | 09/22 | 10/03 | 10/05 | 11/03/11 |
| 0.430 | 11/16 | 12/30 | 01/04 | 02/09/12 |

Dividends have been paid since 1964. Source: Company reports.

---

**Please read the Required Disclosures and Analyst Certification on the last page of this report.**

*The McGraw-Hill Companies*

# Raytheon Co.

STANDARD
&POOR'S

## Business Summary November 15, 2011

CORPORATE OVERVIEW. Raytheon, with estimated 2010 revenues of $26 billion, is the world's sixth largest military contractor and a leading maker of missiles and radar. It does business through six segments.

Integrated Defense Systems (20% of sales and 29% of operating profits in 2010) is a leading provider of integrated naval, air and missile defense and civil security response solutions. Customers include the U.S. Missile Defense Agency (MDA), the U.S. Armed Forces, as well as key international customers. IDS leverages key domain knowledge in the areas of sensors; command, control, and communications (C3); persistent surveillance/intelligence; surveillance and reconnaissance (ISR); and effects and mission support. IDS is the prime contractor for the Patriot Air & Missile Defense System. Other programs include the X-band family of radars, the JLENS missile defense sensors, and seapower capability systems, focusing on the DDG-1000, the Navy's next-generation destroyer.

Intelligence & Information Systems (10% of sales and negative 5% of operating profits) provides intelligence and information solutions specializing in defense and civil mission solutions (ground systems, unmanned systems, etc.); ground processing (signals and geospatial intelligence); integrated mission support and engineering for civil, intelligence, and defense agencies; intelligence data management and dissemination; cybersecurity and information

assurance solutions, and advanced intelligence technologies. About half its business is classified. In 2010, IIS won an $886 million contract to develop the first two deliverables of the advanced control segment (OCX) of the Global Positioning System.

Missile Systems (21% and 21%) makes and supports a broad range of leading-edge missile and missile defense systems for the armed forces of the U.S. and other countries. Business areas include air warfare systems (including the AMRAAM air-to-air missile, the Tomahawk cruise missile, and the Small Diameter Bomb II); air and missile defense systems (including the Standard Missile 2, 3, and 6 series); naval weapon systems (including the Phalanx Close-In Weapon System and the Sea Sparrow missile), which provides defensive missiles and guided projectiles to the navies of over 30 countries; and land combat, which includes the Javelin anti-tank missile and the Stinger air defense weapon system; and other programs. In 2010, MS won a $450 contract for the Small Diameter Bomb II and $600 million in international awards for the Paveway laser and GPS-guided smart bombs.

## Company Financials Fiscal Year Ended Dec. 31

| Per Share Data ($) | 2010 | 2009 | 2008 | 2007 | 2006 | 2005 | 2004 | 2003 | 2002 | 2001 |
|---|---|---|---|---|---|---|---|---|---|---|
| Tangible Book Value | NM | NM | NM | 2.15 | NM | NM | NM | NM | NM | NM |
| Cash Flow | 5.90 | 5.69 | 4.69 | 4.63 | 3.28 | 3.19 | 1.93 | 2.22 | 2.74 | 2.03 |
| Earnings | 4.79 | 4.89 | 3.95 | 3.80 | 2.46 | 2.08 | 0.99 | 1.29 | 1.85 | 0.01 |
| S&P Core Earnings | 5.50 | 5.21 | 2.50 | 4.15 | 3.10 | 2.61 | 1.96 | 1.11 | -0.25 | -2.68 |
| Dividends | 1.13 | 1.24 | 1.12 | 1.02 | 0.96 | 0.86 | 0.80 | 0.80 | 0.80 | 0.80 |
| Payout Ratio | 24% | 25% | 28% | 27% | 34% | 41% | 81% | 62% | 43% | NM |
| Prices:High | 60.10 | 53.84 | 67.49 | 65.94 | 54.17 | 40.57 | 41.89 | 33.97 | 45.70 | 37.44 |
| Prices:Low | 42.65 | 33.20 | 41.81 | 50.96 | 39.43 | 35.96 | 29.28 | 24.31 | 26.30 | 23.95 |
| P/E Ratio:High | 13 | 11 | 17 | 17 | 19 | 21 | 42 | 26 | 25 | NM |
| P/E Ratio:Low | 9 | 7 | 11 | 13 | 14 | 19 | 30 | 19 | 14 | NM |

| Income Statement Analysis (Million $) | | | | | | | | | | |
|---|---|---|---|---|---|---|---|---|---|---|
| Revenue | 25,183 | 24,881 | 23,174 | 21,301 | 20,291 | 21,894 | 20,245 | 18,109 | 16,760 | 16,867 |
| Operating Income | 3,027 | 3,358 | 2,907 | 2,700 | 2,213 | 2,131 | 1,822 | 1,709 | 2,118 | 1,488 |
| Depreciation | 420 | 402 | 311 | 372 | 373 | 444 | 434 | 393 | 364 | 729 |
| Interest Expense | 126 | 123 | 129 | 196 | 273 | 312 | 418 | 537 | 497 | 660 |
| Pretax Income | 2,432 | 2,930 | 2,498 | 2,225 | 1,688 | 1,440 | 579 | 762 | 1,074 | 117 |
| Effective Tax Rate | NA | 32.5% | 33.0% | 23.9% | 34.4% | 34.6% | 24.2% | 29.8% | 29.7% | 95.7% |
| Net Income | 1,804 | 1,936 | 1,674 | 1,693 | 1,107 | 942 | 439 | 535 | 755 | 5.00 |
| S&P Core Earnings | 2,073 | 2,064 | 1,059 | 1,848 | 1,392 | 1,180 | 866 | 460 | -105 | -970 |

| Balance Sheet & Other Financial Data (Million $) | | | | | | | | | | |
|---|---|---|---|---|---|---|---|---|---|---|
| Cash | 3,638 | 2,642 | 2,259 | 2,655 | 2,460 | 1,202 | 556 | 661 | 544 | 1,214 |
| Current Assets | 8,822 | 7,868 | 7,417 | 7,616 | 9,517 | 7,567 | 7,124 | 6,585 | 7,190 | 8,362 |
| Total Assets | 24,422 | 23,607 | 23,296 | 23,281 | 25,491 | 24,381 | 24,153 | 23,668 | 23,946 | 26,636 |
| Current Liabilities | 5,960 | 5,523 | 5,149 | 4,788 | 6,715 | 5,900 | 5,644 | 3,849 | 5,107 | 5,753 |
| Long Term Debt | 3,610 | 2,329 | 2,309 | 2,268 | 3,278 | 3,969 | 4,637 | 7,376 | 7,138 | 6,875 |
| Common Equity | 9,754 | 9,827 | 9,087 | 12,542 | 11,101 | 10,798 | 10,611 | 9,162 | 8,870 | 11,290 |
| Total Capital | 13,500 | 12,268 | 11,659 | 15,261 | 14,544 | 15,011 | 15,345 | 16,538 | 16,008 | 18,743 |
| Capital Expenditures | 319 | 280 | 304 | 313 | 295 | 75.0 | 363 | 428 | 458 | 486 |
| Cash Flow | 2,224 | 2,252 | 1,985 | 2,065 | 1,480 | 1,386 | 873 | 928 | 1,119 | 734 |
| Current Ratio | 1.5 | 1.4 | 1.4 | 1.6 | 1.4 | 1.3 | 1.3 | 1.7 | 1.4 | 1.5 |
| % Long Term Debt of Capitalization | 26.7 | 19.0 | 19.8 | 14.9 | 22.5 | 26.4 | 30.2 | 44.6 | 44.6 | 36.7 |
| % Net Income of Revenue | 7.2 | 7.8 | 7.2 | 8.0 | 5.5 | 4.3 | 2.2 | 3.0 | 4.5 | 0.0 |
| % Return on Assets | 7.5 | 8.3 | 7.2 | 19.8 | 4.4 | 3.9 | 1.8 | 2.2 | 3.0 | 0.0 |
| % Return on Equity | 18.4 | 20.5 | 15.5 | 14.3 | 10.2 | 8.8 | 4.4 | 5.9 | 7.5 | 0.0 |

Data as orig reptd.; bef. results of disc opers/spec. items. Per share data adj. for stk. divs.; EPS diluted. E-Estimated. NA-Not Available. NM-Not Meaningful. NR-Not Ranked. UR-Under Review.

Office: 870 Winter St, Waltham, MA 02451-1449.
Telephone: 781-522-3000.
Email: invest@raytheon.com
Website: http://www.raytheon.com

Chrmn & CEO: W.H. Swanson
SVP & CFO: D.C. Wajsgras
SVP, Secy & General Counsel: J.B. Stephens
CFO: D.E. Smith

CTO: W.F. Kiczuk
Investor Contact: M. Kaplan (781-522-5141)
Board Members: V. Clark, J. M. Deutch, S. J. Hadley, F. M. Poses, M. C. Ruettgers, R. L. Skates, W. R. Spivey, L. G. Stuntz, W. H. Swanson

Founded: 1928
Domicile: Delaware
Employees: 72,400

The McGraw·Hill Companies

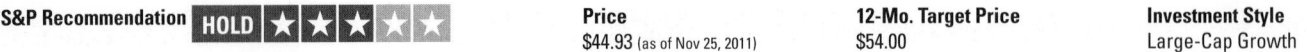

# Red Hat Inc

**STANDARD &POOR'S**

| S&P Recommendation HOLD ★★★★★ | Price $44.93 (as of Nov 25, 2011) | 12-Mo. Target Price $54.00 | Investment Style Large-Cap Growth |
|---|---|---|---|

**GICS Sector** Information Technology
**Sub-Industry** Systems Software

**Summary** This company is a leading provider of Linux operating systems for enterprises, and related middleware and virtualization software offerings.

## Key Stock Statistics (Source S&P, Vickers, company reports)

| | | | | | | | | |
|---|---|---|---|---|---|---|---|---|
| 52-Wk Range | $53.42–31.77 | S&P Oper. EPS 2012**E** | 0.84 | Market Capitalization(B) | $8.664 | Beta | 1.19 |
| Trailing 12-Month EPS | $0.67 | S&P Oper. EPS 2013**E** | 0.91 | Yield (%) | Nil | S&P 3-Yr. Proj. EPS CAGR(%) | 20 |
| Trailing 12-Month P/E | 67.1 | P/E on S&P Oper. EPS 2012**E** | 53.5 | Dividend Rate/Share | Nil | S&P Credit Rating | BB+ |
| $10K Invested 5 Yrs Ago | $25,704 | Common Shares Outstg. (M) | 192.8 | Institutional Ownership (%) | 95 | | |

## Price Performance

30-Week Mov. Avg. ··· 10-Week Mov. Avg. --- GAAP Earnings vs. Previous Year  Volume Above Avg. STARS
12-Mo. Target Price — Relative Strength ▲ Up ▼ Down ▶ No Change  Below Avg. ★

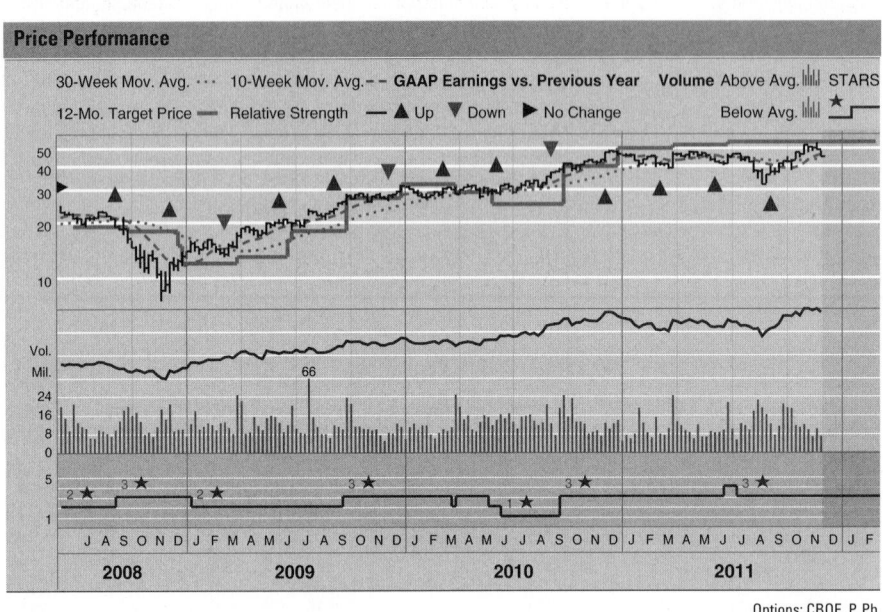

Options: CBOE, P, Ph

Analysis prepared by Equity Analyst **Zaineb Bokhari** on Sep 29, 2011, when the stock traded at **$43.93**.

## Highlights

➤ We estimate that total revenue in FY 12 (Feb.) will rise nearly 24%, following a 22% advance in FY 11. Our revenue outlook is supported by our view that growth in unit sales of servers will be above the historical average due to the severity of the decline in server unit sales during the recent downturn. We also expect the company to extend its lead in the Linux operating system market. We project total revenues to rise 14% in FY 13.

➤ We expect gross margins of nearly 84% in FY 12 and FY 13, the same level as in FY 11. We see operating expenses increasing 19%, as RHT improves product and service offerings. We project that operating margins in FY 12 will rise to 17.7%, from 16% in FY 11, reflecting economies of scale on higher demand for cloud computing solutions. We look for operating margins to remain near 18% in FY 13.

➤ Our FY 12 operating EPS forecast is $0.84, versus $0.65 in FY 11. Our estimates exclude $0.10 of acquisition-related charges in both years. The projected rise in EPS in FY 12 reflects our expectations for higher revenues. We estimate EPS of $0.91 in FY 13.

## Investment Rationale/Risk

➤ Despite concerns about a slow-growing global economy, we see continued solid demand for Linux offerings. We believe RHT is gaining traction for its middleware and virtualization products, as companies upgrade their cloud computing infrastructure. Although we see tougher competition in these segments than in Linux, given the presence of incumbent market leaders, we believe RHT will be at least modestly successful in expanding its presence in these areas.

➤ Risks to our recommendation and target price include a slowdown in the global economy, lower IT spending, and the lack of market share gains in new categories.

➤ Our 12-month target price of $54 is based on a blend of DCF and enterprise value (EV)-to-sales analyses. Our DCF model assumes an 11.2% weighted average cost of capital and 3% terminal growth, yielding intrinsic value of $54. From our EV-to-sales analysis, we also derive a value of $54, based on an EV-to-sales ratio of 8.5X, a premium to the industry average, reflecting our view of RHT's higher growth potential.

## Qualitative Risk Assessment

| LOW | MEDIUM | HIGH |
|---|---|---|

Our risk assessment reflects the volatility of the enterprise software sector due to rapid changes in technology and competition as a result of mergers and acquisitions.

## Quantitative Evaluations

**S&P Quality Ranking** B

| D | C | B- | B | B+ | A- | A | A+ |
|---|---|---|---|---|---|---|---|

**Relative Strength Rank** MODERATE

69

LOWEST = 1     HIGHEST = 99

## Revenue/Earnings Data

**Revenue (Million $)**

| | 1Q | 2Q | 3Q | 4Q | Year |
|---|---|---|---|---|---|
| 2012 | 264.8 | 281.3 | -- | -- | -- |
| 2011 | 209.1 | 219.8 | 235.6 | 244.8 | 909.3 |
| 2010 | 174.4 | 183.6 | 194.4 | 195.9 | 748.2 |
| 2009 | 156.6 | 164.4 | 165.3 | 166.2 | 652.6 |
| 2008 | 118.9 | 127.3 | 135.4 | 141.5 | 523.0 |
| 2007 | 84.00 | 99.67 | 105.8 | 111.1 | 400.6 |

**Earnings Per Share ($)**

| | | | | | |
|---|---|---|---|---|---|
| 2012 | 0.17 | 0.20 | E0.20 | E0.21 | E0.84 |
| 2011 | 0.12 | 0.12 | 0.13 | 0.17 | 0.55 |
| 2010 | 0.10 | 0.15 | 0.08 | 0.12 | 0.45 |
| 2009 | 0.08 | 0.10 | 0.12 | 0.08 | 0.39 |
| 2008 | 0.08 | 0.09 | 0.10 | 0.10 | 0.36 |
| 2007 | 0.07 | 0.05 | 0.07 | 0.10 | 0.29 |

Fiscal year ended Feb. 28. Next earnings report expected: Late December. EPS Estimates based on S&P Operating Earnings; historical GAAP earnings are as reported.

## Dividend Data

No cash dividends have been paid.

# Red Hat Inc

**STANDARD
&POOR'S**

## Business Summary September 29, 2011

CORPORATE OVERVIEW. RHT is the leading provider of Linux operating systems and sub-systems, capturing 65% of the market in terms of new license and maintenance revenues in 2009, according to IDC, a technology research firm, followed by Novell with 31%. The company introduced its core operating system, Red Hat Enterprise Linux (RHEL), in 2002. RHT also offers enterprise middleware software, called JBoss Enterprise Middleware. Both software packages utilize an open source software development model, which provides users and developers access to the source code and permits them to copy, modify and redistribute the software. RHT enhances the open source software and delivers the technologies and related services in the form of annual or multi-year subscriptions, which accounted for 85% of revenues in FY 11 (Feb.). The remaining 15% of revenues came from services, primarily customization, implementation and training.

CORPORATE STRATEGY. RHT is focused on increasing the adoption of RHEL by large enterprises and growing sales of services to its customers. To drive increased adoption, RHT has formed partnerships and strategic relationships with BMC Software, Computer Associates, Dell, Fujitsu, Fujitsu Siemens,

Hewlett-Packard, IBM, NEC, Oracle, SAP, Sybase, Symantec and VMware. These partners and others generally contribute between 50% and 60% of bookings in any given quarter, with the balance coming from direct sales. We believe this heavy reliance on the indirect channel will enable RHT to maintain higher operating margins than would be possible with an entirely in-house sales team, but we believe this will come at the cost of control over this portion of its business.

RHT will continue to expand its capabilities through strategic acquisitions. In June 2006, the company acquired JBoss, a provider of open source middleware, and the remaining minority interest in the Indian joint venture. In 2007, RHT acquired MetaMatrix, a leading provider of enterprise data management software. In September 2008, RHT acquired Qumranet for $107 million. Qumranet is a provider of virtualization software for managing Microsoft desktops.

## Company Financials Fiscal Year Ended Feb. 28

| Per Share Data ($) | 2011 | 2010 | 2009 | 2008 | 2007 | 2006 | 2005 | 2004 | 2003 | 2002 |
|---|---|---|---|---|---|---|---|---|---|---|
| Tangible Book Value | 3.71 | 3.01 | 2.87 | 2.94 | 2.06 | 2.12 | 1.54 | 1.79 | 1.73 | 1.76 |
| Cash Flow | 0.79 | 0.69 | 0.56 | 0.50 | 0.38 | 0.46 | 0.26 | 0.11 | Nil | -0.35 |
| Earnings | 0.55 | 0.45 | 0.39 | 0.36 | 0.29 | 0.41 | 0.24 | 0.08 | -0.04 | -0.71 |
| S&P Core Earnings | 0.54 | 0.48 | 0.39 | 0.35 | 0.29 | 0.28 | 0.06 | -0.37 | -0.20 | -0.75 |
| Dividends | NA | Nil | Nil | Nil | Nil | Nil | Nil | Nil | Nil | Nil |
| Payout Ratio | NA | Nil | Nil | Nil | Nil | Nil | Nil | Nil | Nil | Nil |
| Calendar Year | 2010 | 2009 | 2008 | 2007 | 2006 | 2005 | 2004 | 2003 | 2002 | 2001 |
| Prices:High | 49.00 | 31.76 | 24.84 | 25.25 | 32.48 | 28.65 | 29.06 | 19.98 | 9.50 | 10.12 |
| Prices:Low | 26.51 | 12.98 | 7.50 | 18.04 | 13.70 | 10.37 | 11.21 | 4.95 | 3.46 | 2.40 |
| P/E Ratio:High | 89 | 71 | 64 | 70 | NM | 70 | NM | NM | NM | NM |
| P/E Ratio:Low | 48 | 29 | 19 | 50 | NM | 25 | NM | NM | NM | NM |

| Income Statement Analysis (Million $) | | | | | | | | | | |
|---|---|---|---|---|---|---|---|---|---|---|
| Revenue | 909 | 748 | 653 | 523 | 401 | 278 | 196 | 126 | 90.9 | 78.9 |
| Operating Income | 194 | 155 | 123 | 103 | 76.1 | 73.5 | 39.5 | 10.1 | -8.38 | -17.7 |
| Depreciation | 48.0 | 45.9 | 40.3 | 33.0 | 23.9 | 15.4 | 10.9 | 6.87 | 6.52 | 59.7 |
| Interest Expense | NA | 0.16 | 4.80 | 6.25 | 6.02 | 6.12 | 6.44 | Nil | Nil | Nil |
| Pretax Income | 154 | 122 | 122 | 125 | 89.6 | 82.0 | 44.9 | 14.0 | -6.34 | -120 |
| Effective Tax Rate | NA | 28.2% | 35.2% | 38.4% | 33.1% | 2.84% | NM | NM | NM | NM |
| Net Income | 107 | 87.3 | 78.7 | 76.7 | 59.9 | 79.7 | 45.4 | 14.0 | -6.34 | -120 |
| S&P Core Earnings | 105 | 92.9 | 78.7 | 73.5 | 59.9 | 53.1 | 6.25 | -63.8 | -34.4 | -126 |

| Balance Sheet & Other Financial Data (Million $) | | | | | | | | | | |
|---|---|---|---|---|---|---|---|---|---|---|
| Cash | 861 | 761 | 663 | 990 | 527 | 268 | 140 | 545 | 45.3 | 55.5 |
| Current Assets | 1,185 | 1,003 | 891 | 1,192 | 1,007 | 881 | 385 | 658 | 120 | 119 |
| Total Assets | 2,199 | 1,871 | 1,754 | 2,080 | 1,786 | 1,314 | 1,134 | 1,110 | 390 | 370 |
| Current Liabilities | 680 | 566 | 447 | 970 | 300 | 201 | 139 | 83.6 | 47.1 | 37.0 |
| Long Term Debt | NA | NA | Nil | Nil | 570 | 570 | 600 | 601 | 1.39 | 1.56 |
| Common Equity | 1,291 | 1,111 | 1,106 | 951 | 821 | 477 | 361 | 409 | 336 | 327 |
| Total Capital | 1,291 | 1,111 | 1,106 | 951 | 1,391 | 1,048 | 962 | 1,010 | 338 | 329 |
| Capital Expenditures | 32.8 | 28.4 | 24.5 | 41.8 | 22.6 | 16.8 | 14.9 | 13.2 | 6.77 | 6.75 |
| Cash Flow | 155 | 133 | 119 | 110 | 83.8 | 95.1 | 56.3 | 20.9 | 0.18 | -59.8 |
| Current Ratio | 1.7 | 1.8 | 2.0 | 1.2 | 3.4 | 4.4 | 2.8 | 7.9 | 2.6 | 3.2 |
| % Long Term Debt of Capitalization | Nil | Nil | Nil | Nil | 41.0 | 54.4 | 62.4 | 59.5 | 0.4 | 0.5 |
| % Net Income of Revenue | 11.8 | 11.7 | 12.1 | 14.7 | 15.0 | 28.6 | 23.1 | 11.1 | NM | NM |
| % Return on Assets | 5.3 | 4.8 | 4.1 | 4.0 | 3.9 | 6.5 | 4.0 | 1.9 | NM | NM |
| % Return on Equity | 8.9 | 7.9 | 7.7 | 8.7 | 9.2 | 19.0 | 11.8 | 3.8 | NM | NM |

Data as orig reptd.; bef. results of disc opers/spec. items. Per share data adj. for stk. divs.; EPS diluted. E-Estimated. NA-Not Available. NM-Not Meaningful. NR-Not Ranked. UR-Under Review.

**Office:** 1801 Varsity Drive, Raleigh, NC 27606.
**Telephone:** 919-754-3700.
**Email:** investors@redhat.com
**Website:** http://www.redhat.com

**Chrmn:** H.H. Shelton
**Pres & CEO:** J.M. Whitehurst
**EVP & CFO:** C.E. Peters, Jr.
**EVP, Secy & General Counsel:** M.R. Cunningham

**CTO:** B. Stevens
**Investor Contact:** L. Brewton (919-754-4476)
**Board Members:** S. Abbasi, W. S. Albrecht, M. Chau, J. J. Clarke, M. A. Fox, N. K. Gupta, W. S. Kaiser, D. H. Livingstone, H. H. Shelton, J. M. Whitehurst

**Founded:** 1993
**Domicile:** Delaware
**Employees:** 3,700

The **McGraw·Hill** Companies

# Regions Financial Corp

**STANDARD &POOR'S**

| S&P Recommendation HOLD ★★★☆☆ | Price $3.69 (as of Nov 25, 2011) | 12-Mo. Target Price $6.00 | Investment Style Large-Cap Value |
|---|---|---|---|

**GICS Sector** Financials
**Sub-Industry** Regional Banks

**Summary** This major southeastern U.S. financial holding company has $130 billion in assets, with some 1,800 banking offices in 16 mostly Sunbelt states, plus about 325 Morgan Keegan brokerage branches.

## Key Stock Statistics (Source S&P, Vickers, company reports)

| | | | | | | | |
|---|---|---|---|---|---|---|---|
| 52-Wk Range | $8.09–2.82 | S&P Oper. EPS 2011**E** | 0.19 | Market Capitalization(B) | $4.645 | Beta | 1.38 |
| Trailing 12-Month EPS | $0.18 | S&P Oper. EPS 2012**E** | 0.49 | Yield (%) | 1.08 | S&P 3-Yr. Proj. EPS CAGR(%) | NM |
| Trailing 12-Month P/E | 20.5 | P/E on S&P Oper. EPS 2011**E** | 19.4 | Dividend Rate/Share | $0.04 | S&P Credit Rating | BB+ |
| $10K Invested 5 Yrs Ago | $1,187 | Common Shares Outstg. (M) | 1,258.9 | Institutional Ownership (%) | 71 | | |

## Price Performance

30-Week Mov. Avg. · · · ·   10-Week Mov. Avg. – –   **GAAP Earnings vs. Previous Year**   Volume Above Avg. STARS
12-Mo. Target Price —   Relative Strength —   ▲ Up   ▼ Down   ▶ No Change   Below Avg.

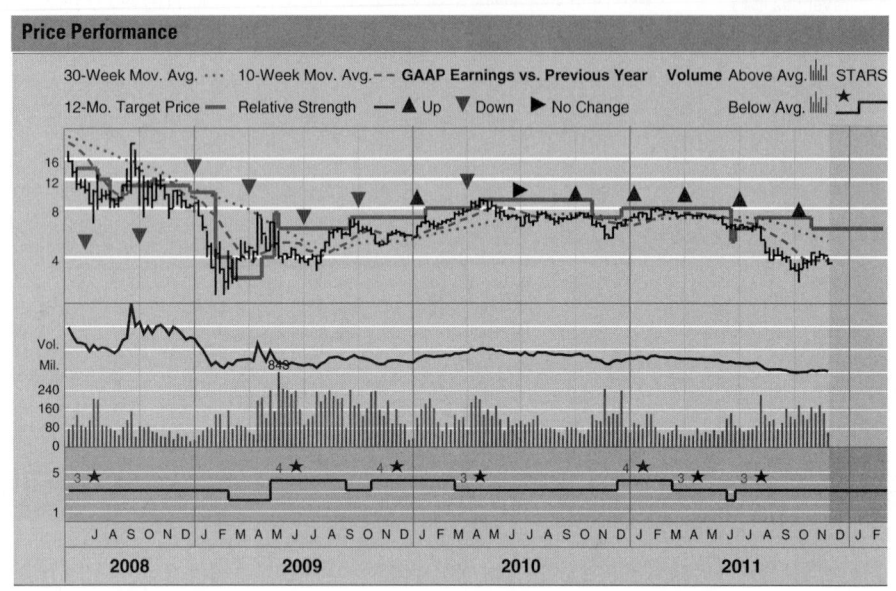

Options: C, Ph

Analysis prepared by Equity Analyst **Erik Oja** on Nov 22, 2011, when the stock traded at **$3.89**.

## Highlights

▶ We look for net interest income to decrease 0.3% in 2011, worse than peers, on our forecast for a 5.5% decline in loans outstanding. For 2012, we expect net interest income to fall 3.3%, on low loan growth and some shrinkage of the net interest margin. We project total revenues to decline 6.4% in 2011 and 4.3% in 2012. However, core revenues, which exclude gains and losses, should fall by a lesser amount, 1.8% in 2011 and 2.7% in 2012. We expect net revenue growth and core revenues to turn positive in 2013.

▶ We expect higher earnings in 2011 and 2012 on lower loan loss provisions. We project total net chargeoffs of $1.910 billion in 2011, versus $2.79 billion in 2010. Our 2011 estimate for loan loss provisions is $1.575 billion, equal to about 0.80X net chargeoffs, down sharply from 2010's $2.86 billion, which was equal to 1.03X net charge-offs. For 2012, we see a sharp drop in the loan loss provision to $1.12 billion, equal to about 0.95X our net chargeoff forecast of $1.21 billion.

▶ We see 2011 EPS of $0.19, rising to $0.49 in 2012. For 2013, we expect EPS of $0.81.

## Investment Rationale/Risk

▶ In the face of increasing capital requirements, we think RF's capital is too low, and that revenues are not strong enough to generate the level of earnings needed to build capital. This, in our view, will likely lead RF to require an equity capital raise. RF's third-quarter results were held back by a 2.1% shrinkage of the loan portfolio, worse than almost all of RF's primary regional banking competitors. We expect only two more quarters of large reductions, and we see underlying growth starting in mid-2012, at a low level. However, we think RF is losing ground to its banking competitors in the Southeast, many of which have stronger loan growth or have already conducted planned shrinkages of their residential and commercial construction portfolios.

▶ Risks to our recommendation and target price include an economic downturn, and an equity capital raise.

▶ Our 12-month target price of $6.00 equates to a below-peers 0.95X our $6.29 estimate of RF's tangible book value per share for year-end 2011, reflecting RF's lower-than-peers capital levels and revenue growth levels.

## Qualitative Risk Assessment

| LOW | MEDIUM | HIGH |
|---|---|---|

Our risk assessment reflects our positive view of the many steps RF has taken since early 2009 to rebuild capital levels and credit quality, offset by numerous remaining credit challenges in the company's loan portfolios.

## Quantitative Evaluations

**S&P Quality Ranking** B-

| D | C | B- | B | B+ | A- | A | A+ |
|---|---|---|---|---|---|---|---|

**Relative Strength Rank** MODERATE

33

LOWEST = 1     HIGHEST = 99

## Revenue/Earnings Data

**Revenue (Million $)**

| | 1Q | 2Q | 3Q | 4Q | Year |
|---|---|---|---|---|---|
| 2011 | 1,923 | 1,867 | 1,809 | -- | -- |
| 2010 | 2,027 | 1,936 | 1,908 | 2,349 | 8,220 |
| 2009 | 2,445 | 2,550 | 2,086 | 2,006 | 9,087 |
| 2008 | 1,935 | 2,360 | 2,288 | 2,283 | 9,587 |
| 2007 | 2,797 | 2,724 | 2,742 | 2,667 | 10,925 |
| 2006 | 1,666 | 1,756 | 1,806 | 2,529 | 7,756 |

**Earnings Per Share ($)**

| | | | | | |
|---|---|---|---|---|---|
| 2011 | 0.01 | 0.04 | 0.08 | E0.08 | E0.19 |
| 2010 | -0.21 | -0.28 | -0.17 | 0.03 | -0.62 |
| 2009 | 0.04 | -0.28 | -0.37 | -0.51 | -1.27 |
| 2008 | 0.48 | 0.30 | 0.13 | -8.97 | -8.03 |
| 2007 | 0.65 | 0.63 | 0.56 | 0.10 | 1.96 |
| 2006 | 0.64 | 0.75 | 0.77 | 0.56 | 2.67 |

Fiscal year ended Dec. 31. Next earnings report expected: NA. EPS Estimates based on S&P Operating Earnings; historical GAAP earnings are as reported.

## Dividend Data (Dates: mm/dd Payment Date: mm/dd/yy)

| Amount ($) | Date Decl. | Ex-Div. Date | Stk. of Record | Payment Date |
|---|---|---|---|---|
| 0.010 | 10/15 | 12/14 | 12/16 | 01/03/12 |

Dividends have been paid since 1968. Source: Company reports.

---

**Please read the Required Disclosures and Analyst Certification on the last page of this report.**

The McGraw-Hill Companies

# Regions Financial Corp

STANDARD
&POOR'S

## Business Summary November 22, 2011

CORPORATE OVERVIEW. Regions Financial is a financial holding company that operates primarily in the southeastern U.S., with operations consisting of banking, brokerage and investment services, mortgage banking, insurance brokerage, credit life insurance, commercial accounts receivable factoring and specialty financing. RF conducts its banking operations through Regions Bank, an Alabama-chartered commercial bank that is a member of the Federal Reserve System. Banking operations also include Regions Mortgage (RMI). RMI's primary business is the origination and servicing of mortgage loans for long-term investors. RMI generally provides services in the same states in which RF has banking operations. Financial services operations include Morgan Keegan, a regional full-service brokerage and investment bank, which was acquired in 2001. Other subsidiaries include Regions Insurance Group, Inc., Regions Agency Inc., Regions Life Insurance Company, Regions Interstate Billings Service Inc., and Regions Equipment Finance Corporation, providing all lines of personal and commercial insurance, credit-related insurance products, and other financial services.

MARKET PROFILE. As of June 30, 2011, which is the latest available FDIC data, RF had 1,686 branches and $98.4 billion in deposits. In Alabama, RF had 228

branches, $22.1 billion of deposits, and a deposit market share of about 22.3%, ranking first. In Florida, RF had 394 branches, $19.3 billion of deposits, and a deposit market share of about 4.3%, ranking fourth. In Tennessee, RF had 248 branches, $17.4 billion of deposits, and a deposit market share of about 13.4%, ranking first. In Mississippi, RF had 136 branches, $7.2 billion of deposits, and a deposit market share of about 14.2%, ranking first. In Georgia, RF had 139 branches, $6.1 billion of deposits, and a deposit market share of about 3.0%, ranking sixth. In Louisiana, RF had 113 branches, $7.3 billion of deposits, and a deposit market share of about 7.7%, ranking fourth. In Arkansas, RF had 87 branches, $4.2 billion of deposits, and a deposit market share of about 7.7%, ranking second. In Texas, RF had 79 branches, $4.5 billion of deposits, and a deposit market share of 0.8%, ranking 13th. RF also had a total of 262 offices and $10.3 billion of deposits in Illinois, Missouri, Indiana, South Carolina, Kentucky, Iowa, North Carolina and Virginia.

## Company Financials Fiscal Year Ended Dec. 31

| Per Share Data ($) | 2010 | 2009 | 2008 | 2007 | 2006 | 2005 | 2004 | 2003 | 2002 | 2001 |
|---|---|---|---|---|---|---|---|---|---|---|
| Tangible Book Value | 5.90 | 6.89 | 10.35 | 10.45 | 11.74 | 11.55 | 11.58 | 16.25 | 15.29 | 10.58 |
| Earnings | -0.62 | -1.27 | -8.03 | 1.96 | 2.67 | 2.15 | 2.19 | 2.35 | 2.20 | 1.81 |
| S&P Core Earnings | -0.64 | -1.23 | 0.39 | 1.97 | 2.67 | 2.11 | 2.17 | 2.32 | 2.11 | 1.63 |
| Dividends | Nil | 0.12 | 0.96 | 1.46 | 2.11 | 1.36 | 0.93 | 1.00 | 0.94 | 0.91 |
| Payout Ratio | Nil | NM | NM | 74% | 79% | 63% | 43% | 43% | 43% | 50% |
| Prices:High | 9.33 | 9.07 | 25.84 | 38.17 | 39.15 | 35.54 | 35.97 | 30.70 | 31.10 | 26.72 |
| Prices:Low | 5.97 | 2.35 | 6.41 | 22.84 | 32.37 | 29.16 | 27.26 | 24.16 | 21.95 | 20.84 |
| P/E Ratio:High | NM | NM | NM | 19 | 15 | 17 | 16 | 13 | 14 | 15 |
| P/E Ratio:Low | NM | NM | NM | 12 | 12 | 14 | 12 | 10 | 10 | 11 |

| Income Statement Analysis (Million $) | | | | | | | | | | |
|---|---|---|---|---|---|---|---|---|---|---|
| Net Interest Income | 3,432 | 3,335 | 3,843 | 4,398 | 3,353 | 2,821 | 2,113 | 1,475 | 1,498 | 1,425 |
| Tax Equivalent Adjustment | NA | 32.0 | 36.7 | 38.1 | NA | NA | NA | NA | NA | NA |
| Non Interest Income | 3,451 | 3,032 | 3,021 | 2,864 | 2,054 | 1,832 | 1,591 | 1,373 | 1,207 | 950 |
| Loan Loss Provision | 2,863 | 3,541 | 2,057 | 555 | 143 | 165 | 129 | 122 | 128 | 165 |
| % Expense/Operating Revenue | 72.4% | 74.6% | 66.4% | 64.2% | 61.3% | 65.5% | 66.5% | 64.6% | 65.1% | 64.2% |
| Pretax Income | -885 | -1,202 | -5,932 | 2,039 | 1,959 | 1,422 | 1,176 | 912 | 869 | 718 |
| Effective Tax Rate | NM | NM | NM | 31.7% | 30.9% | 29.6% | 29.9% | 28.5% | 28.7% | 29.1% |
| Net Income | -539 | -1,031 | -5,584 | 1,393 | 1,353 | 1,001 | 824 | 652 | 620 | 509 |
| % Net Interest Margin | 2.90 | 2.67 | 3.23 | 3.79 | 4.17 | 3.91 | 3.66 | 3.49 | 3.73 | 3.66 |
| S&P Core Earnings | -792 | -1,225 | 272 | 1,405 | 1,355 | 983 | 811 | 647 | 592 | 458 |

| Balance Sheet & Other Financial Data (Million $) | | | | | | | | | | |
|---|---|---|---|---|---|---|---|---|---|---|
| Money Market Assets | 6,392 | 8,998 | 9,380 | 2,116 | 2,610 | 1,794 | 1,761 | 1,491 | 1,424 | 1,502 |
| Investment Securities | 23,313 | 24,100 | 18,896 | 17,369 | 18,562 | 11,979 | 12,617 | 9,088 | 8,995 | 7,847 |
| Commercial Loans | 22,540 | 21,547 | 23,595 | 20,907 | 24,145 | 14,728 | 15,180 | 9,914 | 10,842 | 9,912 |
| Other Loans | 60,324 | 69,127 | 73,823 | 74,472 | 70,360 | 43,677 | 42,556 | 22,501 | 20,144 | 21,225 |
| Total Assets | 132,351 | 142,318 | 146,248 | 141,042 | 143,369 | 84,786 | 84,106 | 48,598 | 47,939 | 45,383 |
| Demand Deposits | 25,733 | 23,204 | 18,457 | 18,417 | 20,709 | 13,699 | 11,424 | 5,718 | 5,148 | 5,085 |
| Time Deposits | 68,881 | 75,476 | 72,447 | 76,358 | 80,519 | 46,679 | 47,243 | 27,015 | 27,779 | 26,463 |
| Long Term Debt | 13,190 | 18,464 | 19,231 | 11,325 | 8,643 | 11,938 | 7,240 | 5,712 | 5,386 | 4,748 |
| Common Equity | 13,354 | 14,279 | 13,505 | 19,823 | 20,701 | 10,614 | 10,749 | 4,452 | 4,178 | 4,036 |
| % Return on Assets | NM | NM | NM | 1.0 | 1.2 | 1.2 | 1.2 | 1.4 | 1.3 | 1.1 |
| % Return on Equity | NM | NM | NM | 6.9 | 8.6 | 9.4 | 10.8 | 15.1 | 15.1 | 13.6 |
| % Loan Loss Reserve | 3.8 | 3.4 | 1.9 | 1.4 | 1.1 | 1.3 | 1.3 | 1.4 | 1.3 | 1.3 |
| % Loans/Deposits | 87.6 | 91.9 | 107.2 | 97.0 | 98.3 | 99.3 | 101.1 | 102.1 | 98.7 | 100.7 |
| % Equity to Assets | 10.1 | 9.6 | 11.6 | 14.3 | 13.7 | 12.6 | 11.5 | 8.9 | 8.8 | 8.4 |

Data as orig reptd.; bef. results of disc opers/spec. items. Per share data adj. for stk. divs.; EPS diluted. E-Estimated. NA-Not Available. NM-Not Meaningful. NR-Not Ranked. UR-Under Review.

**Office:** 1900 Fifth Avenue North, Birmingham, AL 35203.
**Telephone:** 205-326-5807.
**Email:** askus@regionsbank.com
**Website:** http://www.regions.com

**Chrmn:** E.W. Deavenport, Jr.
**Pres, Vice Chrmn & CEO:** O.B. Hall, Jr.
**COO & CTO:** C.M. Rogers
**EVP & Chief Admin Officer:** D.B. Edmonds

**EVP, Chief Acctg Officer & Cntlr:** H.B. Kimbrough, Jr.
**Investor Contact:** L. Underwood (205-801-0265)
**Board Members:** S. W. Bartholomew, Jr., G. W. Bryan, C. H. Byrd, D. J. Cooper, D. DeFosset, Jr., E. W. Deavenport, Jr., E. C. Fast, O. B. Hall, Jr., J. D. Johns, J. R. Malone, R. A. Marshall, S. W. Matlock, J. E. Maupin, Jr., C. D. McCrary, J. R. Roberts, L. Styslinger, III

**Founded:** 1970
**Domicile:** Delaware
**Employees:** 27,829

# Republic Services Inc.

**STANDARD &POOR'S**

| S&P Recommendation HOLD ★★★☆☆ | Price $25.82 (as of Nov 25, 2011) | 12-Mo. Target Price $33.00 | Investment Style Large-Cap Growth |
|---|---|---|---|

**GICS Sector** Industrials
**Sub-Industry** Environmental & Facilities Services

**Summary** This company became the second largest U.S. provider of solid waste services in North America when it acquired Allied Waste Industries in December 2008.

## Key Stock Statistics (Source S&P, Vickers, company reports)

| | | | | | | | |
|---|---|---|---|---|---|---|---|
| 52-Wk Range | $33.10– 24.72 | S&P Oper. EPS 2011**E** | 1.85 | Market Capitalization(B) | $9.563 | Beta | 0.87 |
| Trailing 12-Month EPS | $1.44 | S&P Oper. EPS 2012**E** | 2.15 | Yield (%) | 3.41 | S&P 3-Yr. Proj. EPS CAGR(%) | 14 |
| Trailing 12-Month P/E | 17.9 | P/E on S&P Oper. EPS 2011**E** | 14.0 | Dividend Rate/Share | $0.88 | S&P Credit Rating | BBB |
| $10K Invested 5 Yrs Ago | $10,462 | Common Shares Outstg. (M) | 370.4 | Institutional Ownership (%) | 80 | | |

## Price Performance

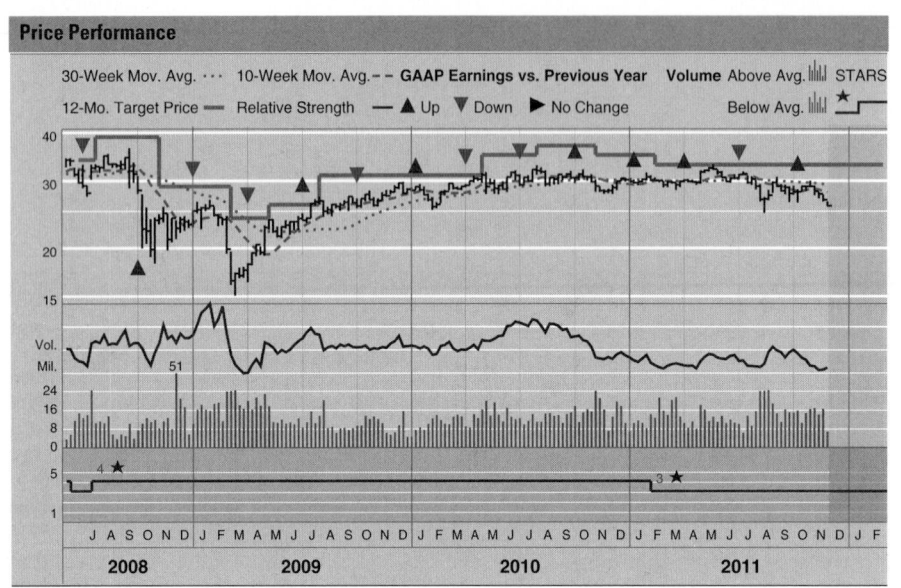

30-Week Mov. Avg. · · · 10-Week Mov. Avg. - - GAAP Earnings vs. Previous Year Volume Above Avg. STARS
12-Mo. Target Price — Relative Strength ▲ Up ▼ Down ► No Change Below Avg.

2008 2009 2010 2011

Options: CBOE, Ph

Analysis prepared by Equity Analyst **Stewart Scharf** on Nov 04, 2011, when the stock traded at **$28.18**.

## Highlights

➤ We forecast core organic revenue growth of about 2% in 2011, as higher core and commodity recycling prices outweigh lower volume. Revenues should improve modestly in 2012. In our view, collection volume should continue to recover sequentially in all lines, while a weak housing market continues to impact construction & demolition (C&D) waste, and commercial volume remains soft.

➤ Gross margins should narrow modestly in 2011, from 41% in 2010, as pricing initiatives are offset by higher -- albeit stabilizing -- fuel and other input costs, and lower-margin C&D and special waste work. We look for margins to rebound during 2012, with adjusted EBITDA margins expanding from our 30.8% projection for 2011 (31% in 2010), reflecting productivity improvements, and well-controlled safety, training and insurance costs.

➤ We forecast lower interest expense in 2011, and an effective tax rate of 41%, leading to operating EPS of $1.85 (before at least $0.38 of charges, mainly from the extinguishment of debt), and see a 16% advance to $2.15 in 2012.

## Investment Rationale/Risk

➤ Our hold opinion is based on our valuation metrics and our view that markets will remain relatively soft into 2012. However, we still see strong cash generation targeted mainly for share repurchases and dividends (recently raised by 10%), and we expect the balance sheet to remain solid while the company maintains its above-peers return on invested capital.

➤ Risks to our recommendation and target price include a slower-than-expected recovery in the housing market and economy, a decline in the customer retention rate due to competitive pricing, a rapid decline in commodity recycling prices, and sharply higher fuel and commodity costs. We also have corporate governance concerns related to compensation and board issues.

➤ Our DCF model, assuming a 3.5% perpetual growth rate and a weighted average cost of capital of 7%, results in an intrinsic value of $35. We apply a near-peer-average forward P/E of 14.5X to our 2012 operating EPS estimate to arrive at a value of $31. Blending these metrics, our 12-month target price is $33.

## Qualitative Risk Assessment

| LOW | MEDIUM | HIGH |
|---|---|---|

Our risk assessment reflects our view of the company's strong balance sheet and focus on cash generation mainly for debt paydowns, share buybacks and dividend payments. The company also maintains consistent return on invested capital levels above 10%.

## Quantitative Evaluations

**S&P Quality Ranking** B+

| D | C | B- | B | B+ | A- | A | A+ |
|---|---|---|---|---|---|---|---|

**Relative Strength Rank** MODERATE

41

LOWEST = 1 HIGHEST = 99

## Revenue/Earnings Data

**Revenue (Million $)**

| | 1Q | 2Q | 3Q | 4Q | Year |
|---|---|---|---|---|---|
| 2011 | 1,965 | 2,087 | 2,116 | -- | -- |
| 2010 | 1,958 | 2,066 | 2,062 | 2,021 | 8,107 |
| 2009 | 2,061 | 2,066 | 2,074 | 1,999 | 8,199 |
| 2008 | 779.2 | 827.5 | 834.0 | 1,244 | 3,685 |
| 2007 | 765.6 | 808.4 | 806.2 | 796.0 | 3,176 |
| 2006 | 737.5 | 779.8 | 787.1 | 766.2 | 3,071 |

**Earnings Per Share ($)**

| | | | | | |
|---|---|---|---|---|---|
| 2011 | 0.41 | 0.12 | 0.52 | E0.41 | E1.85 |
| 2010 | 0.17 | 0.42 | 0.35 | 0.38 | 1.32 |
| 2009 | 0.30 | 0.59 | 0.32 | 0.09 | 1.30 |
| 2008 | 0.41 | 0.34 | 0.48 | -0.55 | 0.37 |
| 2007 | 0.28 | 0.45 | 0.35 | 0.44 | 1.51 |
| 2006 | 0.31 | 0.35 | 0.39 | 0.34 | 1.38 |

Fiscal year ended Dec. 31. Next earnings report expected: NA. EPS Estimates based on S&P Operating Earnings; historical GAAP earnings are as reported.

## Dividend Data (Dates: mm/dd Payment Date: mm/dd/yy)

| Amount ($) | Date Decl. | Ex-Div. Date | Stk. of Record | Payment Date |
|---|---|---|---|---|
| 0.200 | 02/10 | 03/30 | 04/01 | 04/15/11 |
| 0.200 | 04/28 | 06/29 | 07/01 | 07/15/11 |
| 0.220 | 07/28 | 09/29 | 10/03 | 10/17/11 |
| 0.220 | 10/27 | 12/29 | 01/03 | 01/17/12 |

Dividends have been paid since 2003. Source: Company reports.

# Republic Services Inc.

STANDARD
&POOR'S

## Business Summary November 04, 2011

CORPORATE OVERVIEW. Republic Services is the third largest U.S. provider of services in the non-hazardous solid waste industry. It provides collection services to commercial, industrial, municipal and residential customers through 376 collection companies in 40 states and Puerto Rico, and operates 223 transfer stations, 192 solid waste landfills and 78 recycling facilities. RSG also operates 74 landfill gas and renewable energy projects. At the end of 2010, operations were divided into five regions: eastern, central, southern, southwestern and western. Collection revenues accounted for 76% of the total in 2010 (27% residential, 31% commercial, 18% industrial and 0.4% other), while 18% was derived from net transfer and disposal revenues, and 5.6% from other. The average estimated landfill life for all of RSG's 192 landfills is 46 years. Twelve of its landfills meet the criteria for probable expansion airspace, and have an estimated remaining site life of 39 years. RSG's internalization rate in 2010 was less than 70% (69% in 2009). The average age of the company's truck fleet is about seven years. The customer churn rate was less than 8% in 2010. The industry tends to lag economic swings by six to nine months. About 60% of volumes are protected either through a floor contract or financial hedge, while 50% of customer contracts, primarily in the residential and commercial collection business (some also in landfill MSW volumes), contain pricing restrictions, mostly tied to index-based pricing (CPI).

In the third quarter of 2011, the average wholesale price of diesel fuel per gallon was $3.87, down from $4.01 three months earlier and up 32% from $2.94 a year earlier; diesel fuel was $3.83 per gallon in late October 2011. RSG notes that a $0.10 change in the price of diesel fuel would have a less than $0.01 effect on EPS (including fuel recovery fees).

Commodity recycling prices received by the company in the first nine months of 2011 increased 36% to an average of $160 per ton from $118 per ton a year earlier ($143 average in 2010). A $10 change per ton in commodity values equals $0.02 of EPS (including rebates).

In 2010, RSG incurred charges of $0.39 per share related to extinguishment of debt, restructuring and synergy-related costs, and the disposition of assets and impairments.

Bill Gates's investment firm, Cascade Investments LLC, owns over 15% of RSG's common stock.

## Company Financials Fiscal Year Ended Dec. 31

| Per Share Data ($) | 2010 | 2009 | 2008 | 2007 | 2006 | 2005 | 2004 | 2003 | 2002 | 2001 |
|---|---|---|---|---|---|---|---|---|---|---|
| Tangible Book Value | NM | NM | NM | NM | NM | 0.07 | 1.24 | 1.36 | 1.27 | 0.80 |
| Cash Flow | 3.69 | 3.82 | 2.28 | 3.08 | 2.84 | 2.45 | 2.13 | 1.87 | 1.76 | 1.33 |
| Earnings | 1.32 | 1.30 | 0.37 | 1.51 | 1.38 | 1.17 | 1.02 | 0.89 | 0.96 | 0.49 |
| S&P Core Earnings | 1.33 | 1.05 | 0.44 | 1.47 | 1.38 | 1.10 | 0.99 | 0.85 | 0.90 | 0.45 |
| Dividends | 0.78 | 0.76 | 0.72 | 0.55 | 0.40 | 0.35 | 0.24 | 0.08 | Nil | Nil |
| Payout Ratio | 59% | 58% | 195% | 37% | 29% | 30% | 24% | 9% | Nil | Nil |
| Prices:High | 32.95 | 29.82 | 36.52 | 35.00 | 29.47 | 25.56 | 22.65 | 17.39 | 14.84 | 13.93 |
| Prices:Low | 25.15 | 15.05 | 18.25 | 26.22 | 24.47 | 20.07 | 16.33 | 12.17 | 10.84 | 9.17 |
| P/E Ratio:High | 25 | 23 | 99 | 23 | 21 | 22 | 22 | 19 | 15 | 29 |
| P/E Ratio:Low | 19 | 12 | 49 | 17 | 18 | 17 | 16 | 14 | 11 | 19 |

| Income Statement Analysis (Million $) | | | | | | | | | | |
|---|---|---|---|---|---|---|---|---|---|---|
| Revenue | 8,107 | 8,199 | 3,685 | 3,176 | 3,071 | 2,864 | 2,708 | 2,518 | 2,365 | 2,258 |
| Operating Income | 2,484 | 2,516 | 1,017 | 892 | 816 | 756 | 712 | 1,077 | 654 | 598 |
| Depreciation | 914 | 958 | 378 | 302 | 296 | 279 | 259 | 239 | 200 | 215 |
| Interest Expense | 507 | 596 | 135 | 97.8 | 95.8 | 81.0 | 76.7 | 78.0 | 77.0 | 80.1 |
| Pretax Income | 877 | 865 | 159 | 468 | 444 | 409 | 384 | 347 | 387 | 209 |
| Effective Tax Rate | NA | 42.6% | 53.6% | 38.0% | 37.0% | 38.0% | 38.0% | 38.0% | 38.0% | 40.0% |
| Net Income | 508 | 495 | 73.8 | 290 | 280 | 254 | 238 | 215 | 240 | 126 |
| S&P Core Earnings | 507 | 400 | 87.8 | 282 | 280 | 240 | 229 | 206 | 225 | 114 |

| Balance Sheet & Other Financial Data (Million $) | | | | | | | | | | |
|---|---|---|---|---|---|---|---|---|---|---|
| Cash | 88.3 | 48.0 | 68.7 | 21.8 | 29.1 | 132 | 142 | 334 | 317 | 158 |
| Current Assets | 1,246 | 1,265 | 1,326 | 414 | 393 | 482 | 497 | 556 | 452 | 325 |
| Total Assets | 19,462 | 19,540 | 19,921 | 4,468 | 4,429 | 4,551 | 4,465 | 4,554 | 4,209 | 3,856 |
| Current Liabilities | 2,677 | 2,549 | 2,566 | 629 | 602 | 667 | 447 | 672 | 392 | 386 |
| Long Term Debt | 5,865 | 6,420 | 7,199 | 1,566 | 1,545 | 1,472 | 1,352 | 1,289 | 1,439 | 1,334 |
| Common Equity | 7,847 | 7,565 | 7,281 | 1,304 | 1,422 | 1,606 | 1,873 | 3,809 | 1,881 | 1,756 |
| Total Capital | 14,595 | 14,530 | 14,985 | 2,869 | 3,386 | 3,468 | 3,631 | 5,452 | 3,515 | 3,209 |
| Capital Expenditures | 795 | 826 | 387 | 293 | 338 | 329 | 284 | 273 | 259 | 249 |
| Cash Flow | 1,422 | 1,454 | 452 | 592 | 576 | 533 | 497 | 455 | 439 | 341 |
| Current Ratio | 0.5 | 0.5 | 0.5 | 0.7 | 0.7 | 0.7 | 1.1 | 0.8 | 1.2 | 0.8 |
| % Long Term Debt of Capitalization | 40.2 | 44.2 | 48.0 | 54.6 | 45.6 | 42.4 | 37.2 | 23.6 | 40.9 | 41.6 |
| % Net Income of Revenue | 6.3 | 6.0 | 2.0 | 9.1 | 9.1 | 8.9 | 8.8 | 8.6 | 10.1 | 5.6 |
| % Return on Assets | 2.6 | 2.5 | 0.6 | 6.5 | 6.2 | 5.6 | 5.3 | 4.9 | 5.9 | 3.4 |
| % Return on Equity | 6.6 | 6.7 | 1.7 | 21.3 | 18.5 | 14.6 | 12.6 | 5.7 | 13.2 | 7.3 |

Data as orig reptd.; bef. results of disc opers/spec. items. Per share data adj. for stk. divs.; EPS diluted. E-Estimated. NA-Not Available. NM-Not Meaningful. NR-Not Ranked. UR-Under Review.

**Office:** 18500 North Allied Way, Phoenix, AZ 85054.
**Telephone:** 480-627-2700.
**Website:** http://www.republicservices.com
**Chrmn:** J.W. Crownover

**Pres & CEO:** D.W. Slager
**COO:** K.C. Walbridge
**EVP, Secy & General Counsel:** M.P. Rissman
**SVP & Chief Acctg Officer:** C.F. Serianni

**Investor Contact:** T.C. Holmes
**Board Members:** J. W. Croghan, J. W. Crownover, W. J. Flynn, M. Larson, N. Lehmann, W. L. Nutter, R. A. Rodriguez, D. W. Slager, A. Sorensen, J. M. Trani, M. W. Wickham

**Founded:** 1996
**Domicile:** Delaware
**Employees:** 30,000

The *McGraw-Hill* Companies

# Reynolds American Inc

**STANDARD &POOR'S**

| S&P Recommendation | BUY ★★★★☆ | Price $39.99 (as of Nov 25, 2011) | 12-Mo. Target Price $40.00 | Investment Style Large-Cap Value |
|---|---|---|---|---|

**GICS Sector** Consumer Staples
**Sub-Industry** Tobacco

**Summary** Reynolds American, the second largest U.S. cigarette manufacturer, was formed via the mid-2004 merger of R.J. Reynolds and Brown & Williamson.

## Key Stock Statistics (Source S&P, Vickers, company reports)

| | | | | | |
|---|---|---|---|---|---|
| 52-Wk Range | $40.80– 30.94 | S&P Oper. EPS 2011**E** | 2.63 | Market Capitalization(B) | $23.311 | Beta | 0.62 |
| Trailing 12-Month EPS | $2.27 | S&P Oper. EPS 2012**E** | 2.77 | Yield (%) | 5.60 | S&P 3-Yr. Proj. EPS CAGR(%) | 6 |
| Trailing 12-Month P/E | 17.6 | P/E on S&P Oper. EPS 2011**E** | 15.2 | Dividend Rate/Share | $2.24 | S&P Credit Rating | BBB- |
| $10K Invested 5 Yrs Ago | $16,684 | Common Shares Outstg. (M) | 582.9 | Institutional Ownership (%) | 45 | | |

## Price Performance

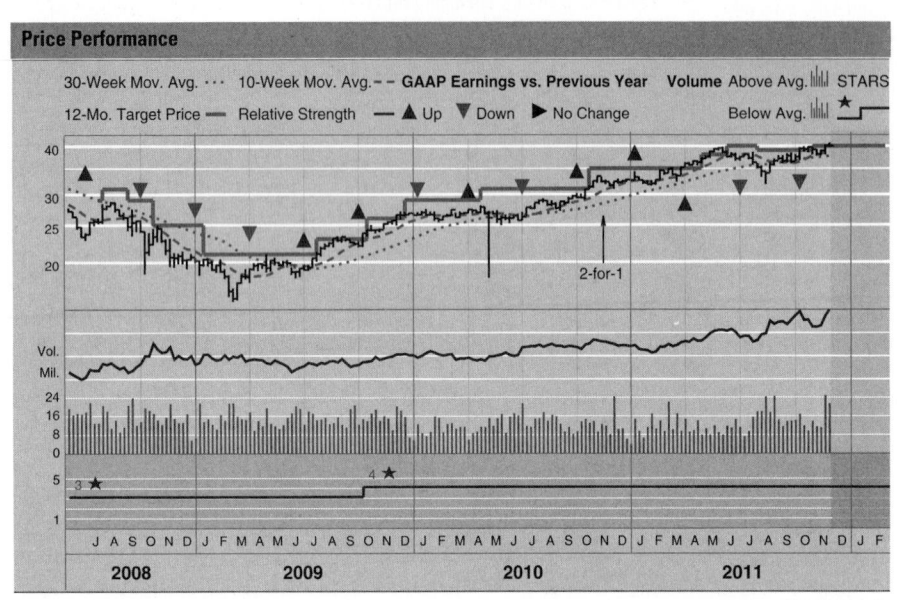

30-Week Mov. Avg. · · · 10-Week Mov. Avg. - - GAAP Earnings vs. Previous Year Volume Above Avg. STARS
12-Mo. Target Price — Relative Strength ▲ Up ▼ Down ► No Change Below Avg.

Options: ASE, CBOE, P, Ph

Analysis prepared by Equity Analyst **Esther Kwon, CFA** on Oct 26, 2011, when the stock traded at **$38.05**.

## Qualitative Risk Assessment

| LOW | **MEDIUM** | HIGH |
|---|---|---|

The domestic tobacco industry typically produces stable revenue streams and strong cash flow. While the industry is involved in significant litigation, recent rulings have led to an improvement in the litigation environment.

## Quantitative Evaluations

**S&P Quality Ranking**  B+

| D | C | B- | B | **B+** | A- | A | A+ |
|---|---|---|---|---|---|---|---|

**Relative Strength Rank**  STRONG
92
LOWEST = 1   HIGHEST = 99

## Revenue/Earnings Data

**Revenue (Million $)**

| | 1Q | 2Q | 3Q | 4Q | Year |
|---|---|---|---|---|---|
| 2011 | 1,991 | 2,267 | 2,200 | -- | -- |
| 2010 | 1,986 | 1,113 | 2,239 | 2,081 | 8,551 |
| 2009 | 1,921 | 2,250 | 2,152 | 2,096 | 8,419 |
| 2008 | 2,057 | 2,339 | 2,272 | 2,177 | 8,845 |
| 2007 | 2,148 | 2,348 | 2,297 | 2,230 | 9,023 |
| 2006 | 1,960 | 2,291 | 2,190 | 2,069 | 8,510 |

**Earnings Per Share ($)**

| | | | | | |
|---|---|---|---|---|---|
| 2011 | 0.60 | 0.52 | 0.63 | E0.67 | E2.63 |
| 2010 | 0.51 | 0.58 | 0.65 | 0.53 | 2.27 |
| 2009 | 0.02 | 0.65 | 0.62 | 0.37 | 1.65 |
| 2008 | 0.86 | 0.62 | 0.36 | 0.45 | 2.29 |
| 2007 | 0.56 | 0.55 | 0.61 | 0.51 | 2.21 |
| 2006 | 0.48 | 0.62 | 0.52 | 0.31 | 1.93 |

Fiscal year ended Dec. 31. Next earnings report expected: Early February. EPS Estimates based on S&P Operating Earnings; historical GAAP earnings are as reported.

## Highlights

► We expect RAI's revenues for 2011 to be up slightly from 2010's $8.6 billion, with a favorable product mix shift, price increases, and new product introductions offset by a mid-single digit decline in shipments. We believe growth brands Camel, Pall Mall and American Spirit, which now account for well over half the company's total cigarette volume, will see gains, with other brands, including low-margin private labels, suffering declines as marketing efforts remain minimal. For 2012, we see revenues rising at a low single digit rate.

► We believe operating margins will continue to improve in 2011 as gross margins benefit from the rationalization of non-core brands and brand styles, higher pricing, and lower promotions, while SG&A spending, excluding additional pension expense, remains well controlled as the company benefits from cost-saving actions. We expect savings of about $35 million in 2011 on rationalization of cigarette manufacturing facilities.

► For 2011, we estimate EPS of $2.63 on lower interest expense and a reduced effective tax rate, up from operating EPS of $2.49 in 2010. For 2012, we forecast EPS of $2.77.

## Investment Rationale/Risk

► We think leading smokeless tobacco company Conwood, which RAI acquired in mid-2006 for $3.5 billion, will continue to drive profits as higher-margin smokeless tobacco growth offsets declining cigarette sales and RAI continues to rationalize its operations to focus on core growth categories. To that end, in March 2011, RAI sold Lane Limited, its other tobacco products segment, for $205 million in cash. We also see continued good performance from Pall Mall as consumers trade down in a weak economic environment. We find the shares, with an indicated dividend yield of about 5.6%, attractive on a total return basis.

► Risks to our opinion and target price include additional regulation and taxation of tobacco products, in addition to near-term pressure on trading multiples due to ongoing litigation. We also think RAI's "poison pill" anti-takeover provision is not in shareholders' best interests.

► Applying a multiple of 14.3X, a slight premium to the peer average but a discount to the S&P 500 Consumer Staples P/E of 15.2X, to our 2012 EPS estimate of $2.77, we arrive at a value of $40, which is our 12-month target price.

## Dividend Data (Dates: mm/dd Payment Date: mm/dd/yy)

| Amount ($) | Date Decl. | Ex-Div. Date | Stk. of Record | Payment Date |
|---|---|---|---|---|
| 0.530 | 02/16 | 03/08 | 03/10 | 04/01/11 |
| 0.530 | 05/06 | 06/08 | 06/10 | 07/01/11 |
| 0.530 | 07/15 | 09/08 | 09/12 | 10/03/11 |
| 0.560 | 10/25 | 12/07 | 12/09 | 01/03/12 |

Dividends have been paid since 1999. Source: Company reports.

The **McGraw-Hill** Companies

# Reynolds American Inc

STANDARD &POOR'S

## Business Summary October 26, 2011

CORPORATE OVERVIEW. On July 30, 2004, R.J. Reynolds Tobacco Co. (RJRT) merged with Brown & Williamson (B&W), the U.S. operations of British American Tobacco (BTI), to form a new publicly traded company, Reynolds American, Inc. Combining RJRT and B&W, the second and third largest players, RAI is the second largest U.S. cigarette manufacturer, having a combined market share of 28.1% in 2010, down slightly from 28.3% in 2009 and 28.4% in 2008.

RAI is the parent company of RJRT, Santa Fe Natural Tobacco, which RJRT acquired in 2002, and Lane Limited, which was purchased from BTI for $400 million as part of the merger. In 2003, prior to the merger, RJRT began a significant restructuring plan, targeting cost savings of $1 billion by the end of 2005 through a significant work force reduction, asset divestitures and associated exit activities. Full integration of RJRT and B&W was expected to be completed in 2006, but realization of cost savings continued into 2007. The business combination was expected to result in approximately $600 million in annualized savings, including headcount reductions and operations consolidation, when compared with a separate entity basis.

In May 2006, RAI completed the acquisition of Conwood, the second largest manufacturer of smokeless tobacco products in the U.S., for $3.5 billion. RAI combined Conwood with its Lane, Limited subsidiary into an Other Tobacco Products division in 2007. That division has been renamed American Snuff. RAI's reportable segments are RJRT and American Snuff. Lane, Limited was sold in March 2011 to Scandanavian Tobacco Group.

The company's leading products are its Camel, Kool, Pall Mall, Doral and Winston brand cigarettes. The company's other brands include Salem, Misty and Capri. RAI also manages and contract manufactures cigarettes and tobacco products through its relationship with BAT affiliates.

American Snuff's primary brands included Grizzly and Kodiak moist snuff.

## Company Financials Fiscal Year Ended Dec. 31

| Per Share Data ($) | 2010 | 2009 | 2008 | 2007 | 2006 | 2005 | 2004 | 2003 | 2002 | 2001 |
|---|---|---|---|---|---|---|---|---|---|---|
| Tangible Book Value | NM | NM | NM | NM | NM | NM | NM | NM | NM | NM |
| Cash Flow | 2.53 | 1.85 | 2.53 | 2.46 | 2.19 | 2.00 | 1.33 | -10.41 | 1.67 | 2.36 |
| Earnings | 2.27 | 1.65 | 2.29 | 2.21 | 1.93 | 1.67 | 1.41 | -11.02 | 1.16 | 1.12 |
| S&P Core Earnings | 2.41 | 2.38 | 1.82 | 2.21 | 1.98 | 1.98 | 1.80 | 1.07 | 0.87 | 0.76 |
| Dividends | 1.84 | 1.73 | 1.70 | 1.60 | 0.69 | 1.05 | 0.48 | 0.95 | 0.93 | 0.83 |
| Payout Ratio | 81% | 105% | 74% | 72% | 36% | 63% | 34% | NM | 80% | 74% |
| Prices:High | 33.41 | 27.13 | 36.00 | 35.86 | 33.54 | 25.60 | 20.14 | 15.04 | 17.98 | 15.68 |
| Prices:Low | 18.17 | 15.78 | 18.61 | 29.28 | 23.74 | 19.12 | 13.34 | 6.88 | 8.71 | 11.05 |
| P/E Ratio:High | 15 | 16 | 16 | 16 | 17 | 15 | 14 | NM | 15 | 14 |
| P/E Ratio:Low | 8 | 10 | 8 | 13 | 12 | 11 | 9 | NM | 8 | 10 |

| Income Statement Analysis (Million $) | | | | | | | | | | |
|---|---|---|---|---|---|---|---|---|---|---|
| Revenue | 8,551 | 8,419 | 8,845 | 9,023 | 8,510 | 8,256 | 6,437 | 5,267 | 6,211 | 8,585 |
| Operating Income | 2,516 | 2,516 | 2,602 | 2,496 | 2,183 | 1,880 | 1,239 | 873 | 1,200 | 1,409 |
| Depreciation | 151 | 118 | 142 | 143 | 162 | 195 | 153 | 151 | 184 | 491 |
| Interest Expense | 232 | 251 | 275 | 338 | 270 | 113 | 85.0 | 111 | 147 | 150 |
| Pretax Income | 2,192 | 1,534 | 2,128 | 2,073 | 1,809 | 1,416 | 829 | -3,918 | 683 | 892 |
| Effective Tax Rate | NA | 37.3% | 37.1% | 37.0% | 37.2% | 30.4% | 24.4% | NM | 38.8% | 50.2% |
| Net Income | 1,329 | 962 | 1,338 | 1,307 | 1,136 | 985 | 627 | -3,689 | 418 | 444 |
| S&P Core Earnings | 1,415 | 1,388 | 1,063 | 1,302 | 1,167 | 1,167 | 800 | 357 | 313 | 301 |

| Balance Sheet & Other Financial Data (Million $) | | | | | | | | | | |
|---|---|---|---|---|---|---|---|---|---|---|
| Cash | 2,195 | 2,727 | 2,601 | 2,592 | 1,433 | 1,333 | 1,499 | 1,523 | 1,584 | 2,020 |
| Current Assets | 4,802 | 5,495 | 5,019 | 4,992 | 4,935 | 5,065 | 4,624 | 3,331 | 3,992 | 3,856 |
| Total Assets | 17,078 | 18,009 | 18,154 | 18,629 | 18,178 | 14,519 | 14,428 | 9,677 | 14,651 | 15,050 |
| Current Liabilities | 4,372 | 4,340 | 3,923 | 3,903 | 4,092 | 4,149 | 4,055 | 2,865 | 3,427 | 2,792 |
| Long Term Debt | 3,701 | 4,136 | 4,486 | 4,515 | 4,389 | 1,558 | 1,595 | 1,671 | 1,755 | 1,631 |
| Common Equity | 6,510 | 6,498 | 6,237 | 7,466 | 7,043 | 6,553 | 6,176 | 3,057 | 6,716 | 8,026 |
| Total Capital | 10,211 | 10,634 | 11,005 | 13,165 | 12,599 | 8,750 | 8,576 | 5,534 | 9,707 | 11,383 |
| Capital Expenditures | 174 | 141 | 113 | 142 | 136 | 105 | 92.0 | 70.0 | 111 | 74.0 |
| Cash Flow | 1,480 | 1,080 | 1,480 | 1,450 | 1,298 | 1,180 | 780 | -3,538 | 602 | 935 |
| Current Ratio | 1.1 | 1.3 | 1.3 | 1.3 | 1.2 | 1.2 | 1.1 | 1.2 | 1.2 | 1.4 |
| % Long Term Debt of Capitalization | 36.3 | 38.9 | 40.8 | 34.3 | 34.8 | 17.8 | 18.6 | 30.2 | 18.1 | 14.3 |
| % Net Income of Revenue | 15.5 | 11.4 | 15.1 | 14.5 | 13.3 | 11.9 | 9.7 | NM | 6.7 | 5.2 |
| % Return on Assets | 7.6 | 5.3 | 7.3 | 7.1 | 6.9 | 6.8 | 5.2 | NM | 2.8 | 2.9 |
| % Return on Equity | 20.4 | 15.1 | 19.5 | 18.0 | 16.7 | 15.5 | 13.6 | NM | 5.7 | 5.4 |

Data as orig reptd.; bef. results of disc opers/spec. items. Per share data adj. for stk. divs.; EPS diluted. E-Estimated. NA-Not Available. NM-Not Meaningful. NR-Not Ranked. UR-Under Review.

**Office:** 401 North Main Street, Winston-Salem, NC 27102-2866.
**Telephone:** 336-741-2000.
**Email:** talktorjrt@rjrt.com
**Website:** http://www.reynoldsamerican.com

**Chrmn:** T.C. Wajnert
**Pres & CEO:** D.M. Delen
**EVP & General Counsel:** M.L. Holton, III
**CFO:** T.R. Adams

**Chief Acctg Officer:** F.W. Smothers
**Board Members:** J. Daly, D. M. Delen, M. D. Feinstein, L. Jobin, H. Kahler, H. K. Koeppel, N. Mensah, L. L. Nowell, III, H. G. Powell, T. C. Wajnert, N. R. Withington, J. Zillmer

**Auditor:** KPMG, Greensboro
**Founded:** 1875
**Domicile:** Delaware
**Employees:** 5,750

The McGraw-Hill Companies

# Robert Half International Inc.

STANDARD &POOR'S

| **S&P Recommendation** BUY ★★★★☆ | **Price** $23.83 (as of Nov 25, 2011) | **12-Mo. Target Price** $36.00 | **Investment Style** Large-Cap Blend |
|---|---|---|---|

**GICS Sector** Industrials
**Sub-Industry** Human Resource & Employment Services

**Summary** This company is the world's largest specialized provider of temporary and permanent personnel in the fields of accounting and finance.

## Key Stock Statistics (Source S&P, Vickers, company reports)

| | | | | | | | |
|---|---|---|---|---|---|---|---|
| 52-Wk Range | $34.26–19.69 | S&P Oper. EPS 2011**E** | 1.08 | Market Capitalization(B) | $3.407 | Beta | 1.17 |
| Trailing 12-Month EPS | $0.91 | S&P Oper. EPS 2012**E** | 1.50 | Yield (%) | 2.35 | S&P 3-Yr. Proj. EPS CAGR(%) | 59 |
| Trailing 12-Month P/E | 26.2 | P/E on S&P Oper. EPS 2011**E** | 22.1 | Dividend Rate/Share | $0.56 | S&P Credit Rating | NA |
| $10K Invested 5 Yrs Ago | $6,722 | Common Shares Outstg. (M) | 143.0 | Institutional Ownership (%) | 91 | | |

## Price Performance

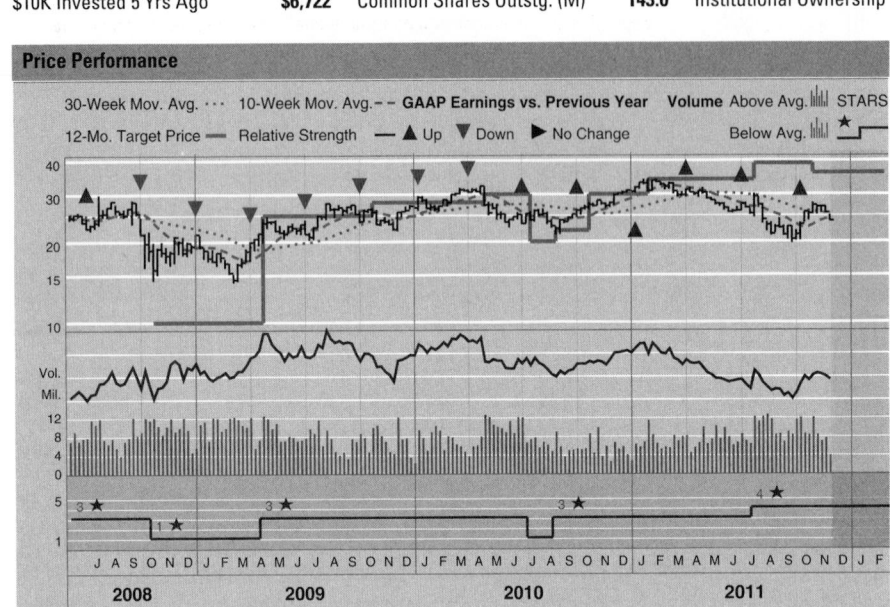

Options: ASE, CBOE, Ph

Analysis prepared by Equity Analyst **Michael Jaffe** on Nov 01, 2011, when the stock traded at **$25.73**.

## Highlights

➤ We see a 14% revenue gain in 2012, following a projected 20% rise in 2011. After a period of depressed demand that started in 2008's second half, RHI's business has been improving since the middle of 2010. We believe this has been related to the start of a recovery in global economies, after extreme economic weakness in geographies such as the U.S. and Europe were the primary factors behind RHI's business downturn. These shifts have also enabled professional and business hirings (the company's primary areas of placements) to pick up since the summer of 2009. We see these trends continuing for an extended period.

➤ We expect RHI's business to benefit in coming periods from the ongoing caution of businesses in their hiring processes, including the greater use of temporary and project professionals, which are areas dominated by placement companies. We also think major staff cuts in human resources departments have led many businesses to turn to employment services companies for assistance in their hiring activities.

➤ We also see expected stronger demand trends and cost control efforts aiding margins in both 2011 and 2012.

## Investment Rationale/Risk

➤ After a severe downturn during 2008 and 2009, we think that labor markets are in the process of recovery, with 2.0 million net workers added to nonfarm payrolls in the U.S. from the start of 2010 through September 2011. With businesses posting better operating results in recent quarters, we think they will eventually grow more confident about adding to their staffs, and that RHI will benefit from this expected recovery. Combining these factors with our valuation model, we find the shares undervalued.

➤ Risks to our recommendation and target price include a resumed downturn in U.S. and Western European economies, and a smaller-than-expected contribution from RHI's cost cuts.

➤ The shares recently traded at about 17X our 2012 EPS forecast, or the bottom of RHI's range during a similar stage of the past economic recovery. We think the shares should be valued higher, based on our belief that the global economy is in the midst of a recovery, and that Robert Half's business will continue its currently strong rebound over the next few years. We set our 12-month target price at $36, or 24X our 2012 EPS estimate.

## Qualitative Risk Assessment

| LOW | MEDIUM | HIGH |
|---|---|---|

Our risk assessment reflects what we view as RHI's strong position in accounting and finance placements and a healthy balance sheet. This is offset by the highly cyclical nature of the company's business, which is largely dependent on the U.S. economy and the health of labor markets.

## Quantitative Evaluations

**S&P Quality Ranking**      B

| D | C | B- | B | B+ | A- | A | A+ |
|---|---|---|---|---|---|---|---|

**Relative Strength Rank**      MODERATE

58

LOWEST = 1      HIGHEST = 99

## Revenue/Earnings Data

### Revenue (Million $)

| | 1Q | 2Q | 3Q | 4Q | Year |
|---|---|---|---|---|---|
| 2011 | 880.9 | 938.0 | 984.7 | -- | -- |
| 2010 | 737.2 | 769.1 | 817.3 | 851.6 | 3,175 |
| 2009 | 823.3 | 749.9 | 725.9 | 737.4 | 3,037 |
| 2008 | 1,226 | 1,225 | 1,160 | 989.8 | 4,601 |
| 2007 | 1,097 | 1,149 | 1,179 | 1,220 | 4,646 |
| 2006 | 943.9 | 981.8 | 1,028 | 1,060 | 4,014 |

### Earnings Per Share ($)

| | | | | | |
|---|---|---|---|---|---|
| 2011 | 0.18 | 0.25 | 0.31 | E0.33 | E1.08 |
| 2010 | 0.05 | 0.08 | 0.14 | 0.17 | 0.44 |
| 2009 | 0.06 | 0.03 | 0.06 | 0.09 | 0.24 |
| 2008 | 0.45 | 0.48 | 0.43 | 0.26 | 1.63 |
| 2007 | 0.42 | 0.44 | 0.46 | 0.50 | 1.81 |
| 2006 | 0.38 | 0.39 | 0.43 | 0.45 | 1.65 |

Fiscal year ended Dec. 31. Next earnings report expected: Late January. EPS Estimates based on S&P Operating Earnings; historical GAAP earnings are as reported.

## Dividend Data (Dates: mm/dd Payment Date: mm/dd/yy)

| Amount ($) | Date Decl. | Ex-Div. Date | Stk. of Record | Payment Date |
|---|---|---|---|---|
| 0.140 | 02/09 | 02/23 | 02/25 | 03/15/11 |
| 0.140 | 05/04 | 05/23 | 05/25 | 06/15/11 |
| 0.140 | 07/27 | 08/23 | 08/25 | 09/15/11 |
| 0.140 | 11/02 | 11/21 | 11/23 | 12/15/11 |

Dividends have been paid since 2004. Source: Company reports.

---

**Please read the Required Disclosures and Analyst Certification on the last page of this report.**

The *McGraw-Hill* Companies

# Robert Half International Inc.

**STANDARD &POOR'S**

## Business Summary November 01, 2011

CORPORATE OVERVIEW. Robert Half International is the world's largest specialized staffing service in the fields of accounting and finance. In May 2002, RHI expanded its offerings to include risk consulting and internal audit services through its Protiviti unit. In 2010, the company derived 81% of its revenues from activities in temporary and consultant staffing, 7% from permanent placement staffing, and 12% from risk consulting and internal audit services. Foreign operations accounted for 29% of RHI's revenues in 2010 (same percentage in 2009). As of 2010 year-end, the company's staffing businesses had more than 350 offices in 42 states, the District of Columbia and 18 foreign countries, while Protiviti had 60 offices in 23 states and 15 foreign countries.

RHI's Accountemps temporary services division offers customers an economical means of dealing with uneven or peak work loads for accounting, tax and finance personnel. The temporary workers are employees of Accountemps, and are paid by Accountemps only when working on customer assignments. The customer pays a fixed rate for hours worked. If the client converts the temporary hire to a permanent worker, it typically pays a one-time fee for the conversion.

RHI offers permanent placement services through Robert Half Finance & Accounting, which specializes in accounting, financial, tax and banking personnel. Fees for successful permanent placements are paid only by the employer and are usually a percentage of the new employee's annual salary.

Since the early 1990s, the company has expanded into additional specialty fields. OfficeTeam, formed in 1991, provides skilled temporary and full-time administrative and office personnel. In 1992, RHI acquired Robert Half Legal (formerly The Affiliates), which places temporary and regular employees in attorney, paralegal, legal administrative and other legal support positions. In 1994, Robert Half Technology (formerly RHI Consulting) was created to concentrate on the placement of contract and full-time information technology consultants. In 1997, the company established Robert Half Management Resources (formerly RHI Management Resources) to provide senior level project professionals specializing in the accounting and finance fields. The Creative Group, which started up in 1999, provides project staffing in the advertising, marketing and Web design fields. In 2010, Accountemps provided 38% of revenues, OfficeTeam 20%, other placement businesses 30%, and Protiviti 12%.

## Company Financials Fiscal Year Ended Dec. 31

| Per Share Data ($) | 2010 | 2009 | 2008 | 2007 | 2006 | 2005 | 2004 | 2003 | 2002 | 2001 |
|---|---|---|---|---|---|---|---|---|---|---|
| Tangible Book Value | 4.41 | 4.78 | 5.26 | 4.99 | 5.15 | 4.72 | 4.30 | 3.65 | 3.41 | 3.69 |
| Cash Flow | 0.85 | 0.70 | 2.11 | 2.25 | 2.00 | 1.66 | 1.07 | 0.42 | 0.42 | 1.07 |
| Earnings | 0.44 | 0.24 | 1.63 | 1.81 | 1.65 | 1.36 | 0.79 | 0.04 | 0.01 | 0.67 |
| S&P Core Earnings | 0.44 | 0.24 | 1.63 | 1.81 | 1.65 | 1.29 | 0.71 | -0.11 | -0.17 | 0.51 |
| Dividends | 0.52 | 0.48 | 0.44 | 0.40 | 0.32 | 0.28 | 0.18 | Nil | Nil | Nil |
| Payout Ratio | 118% | NM | 27% | 22% | 19% | 21% | 23% | Nil | Nil | Nil |
| Prices:High | 32.25 | 28.06 | 29.99 | 42.21 | 43.94 | 39.86 | 30.98 | 25.18 | 30.90 | 30.90 |
| Prices:Low | 21.16 | 14.06 | 14.31 | 24.41 | 29.91 | 23.95 | 20.69 | 11.44 | 11.94 | 18.50 |
| P/E Ratio:High | 73 | NM | 18 | 23 | 27 | 29 | 39 | NM | NM | 46 |
| P/E Ratio:Low | 48 | NM | 9 | 13 | 18 | 18 | 26 | NM | NM | 28 |

| Income Statement Analysis (Million $) | 2010 | 2009 | 2008 | 2007 | 2006 | 2005 | 2004 | 2003 | 2002 | 2001 |
|---|---|---|---|---|---|---|---|---|---|---|
| Revenue | 3,175 | 3,037 | 4,601 | 4,646 | 4,014 | 3,338 | 2,676 | 1,975 | 1,905 | 2,453 |
| Operating Income | 172 | 131 | 487 | 549 | 511 | 433 | 280 | 75.0 | 71.2 | 261 |
| Depreciation | 56.0 | 65.3 | 73.2 | 71.4 | 61.1 | 51.3 | 49.1 | 65.9 | 72.3 | 73.1 |
| Interest Expense | 0.60 | 0.50 | 5.30 | 4.10 | Nil | Nil | Nil | Nil | Nil | Nil |
| Pretax Income | 115 | 66.8 | 419 | 490 | 466 | 392 | 235 | 11.7 | 3.50 | 196 |
| Effective Tax Rate | NA | 44.2% | 40.3% | 39.6% | 39.3% | 39.3% | 40.1% | 45.5% | 38.0% | 38.3% |
| Net Income | 66.1 | 37.3 | 250 | 296 | 283 | 238 | 141 | 6.39 | 2.17 | 121 |
| S&P Core Earnings | 63.7 | 35.1 | 250 | 296 | 283 | 224 | 125 | -18.4 | -30.2 | 91.1 |

| Balance Sheet & Other Financial Data (Million $) | 2010 | 2009 | 2008 | 2007 | 2006 | 2005 | 2004 | 2003 | 2002 | 2001 |
|---|---|---|---|---|---|---|---|---|---|---|
| Cash | 315 | 366 | 355 | 310 | 447 | 458 | 437 | 377 | 317 | 347 |
| Current Assets | 972 | 923 | 1,033 | 1,060 | 1,112 | 1,017 | 916 | 699 | 643 | 686 |
| Total Assets | 1,274 | 1,284 | 1,412 | 1,450 | 1,459 | 1,319 | 1,199 | 980 | 936 | 994 |
| Current Liabilities | 408 | 367 | 413 | 448 | 403 | 337 | 280 | 189 | 184 | 177 |
| Long Term Debt | 1.66 | 1.78 | 1.89 | 3.75 | 3.83 | 2.70 | 2.27 | 2.34 | 2.40 | 2.48 |
| Common Equity | 834 | 900 | 984 | 984 | 1,043 | 971 | 912 | 789 | 745 | 806 |
| Total Capital | 836 | 902 | 986 | 988 | 1,047 | 974 | 914 | 791 | 747 | 808 |
| Capital Expenditures | 35.1 | 41.3 | 73.4 | 83.8 | 80.4 | 61.8 | 32.9 | 36.5 | 48.3 | 84.7 |
| Cash Flow | 122 | 103 | 323 | 368 | 344 | 289 | 190 | 72.3 | 74.5 | 194 |
| Current Ratio | 2.4 | 2.5 | 2.5 | 2.4 | 2.8 | 3.0 | 3.3 | 3.7 | 3.5 | 3.9 |
| % Long Term Debt of Capitalization | 0.2 | Nil | 0.2 | 0.4 | 0.4 | 0.3 | 0.2 | 0.3 | 0.3 | 0.3 |
| % Net Income of Revenue | 2.1 | 1.2 | 5.4 | 6.4 | 7.1 | 7.1 | 5.3 | 0.3 | 0.1 | 4.9 |
| % Return on Assets | NA | NA | 17.5 | 20.4 | 20.4 | 18.9 | 12.9 | 0.7 | 0.2 | 12.3 |
| % Return on Equity | NA | NA | 25.4 | 29.2 | 28.1 | 25.3 | 16.5 | 0.8 | 0.3 | 15.9 |

Data as orig reptd.; bef. results of disc opers/spec. items. Per share data adj. for stk. divs.; EPS diluted. E-Estimated. NA-Not Available. NM-Not Meaningful. NR-Not Ranked. UR-Under Review.

**Office:** 2884 Sand Hill Rd, Menlo Park, CA 94025-7072.
**Telephone:** 650-234-6000.
**Website:** http://www.rhi.com
**Chrmn & CEO:** H.M. Messmer, Jr.

**Pres, Vice Chrmn & CFO:** M.K. Waddell
**EVP, Chief Admin Officer, Chief Acctg Officer & Treas:** M.C. Buckley
**EVP, Secy & General Counsel:** S. Karel
**CIO:** K. White

**Board Members:** A. S. Berwick, Jr., H. M. Messmer, Jr., B. J. Novogradac, R. J. Pace, F. A. Richman, M. K. Waddell

**Founded:** 1967
**Domicile:** Delaware
**Employees:** 186,400

**The McGraw-Hill Companies**

# Rockwell Automation Inc.

**STANDARD &POOR'S**

| S&P Recommendation | STRONG BUY ★★★★★ | Price $75.03 (as of Nov 30, 2011) | 12-Mo. Target Price $90.00 | Investment Style Large-Cap Blend |
| --- | --- | --- | --- | --- |

**GICS Sector** Industrials
**Sub-Industry** Electrical Components & Equipment

**Summary** This company manufactures and develops automated industrial equipment and power generators for applications in many different manufacturing processes.

## Key Stock Statistics (Source S&P, Vickers, company reports)

| | | | | | | | |
| --- | --- | --- | --- | --- | --- | --- | --- |
| 52-Wk Range | $98.19–50.36 | S&P Oper. EPS 2012**E** | 5.38 | Market Capitalization(B) | $10.648 | Beta | 1.73 |
| Trailing 12-Month EPS | $4.80 | S&P Oper. EPS 2013**E** | 5.80 | Yield (%) | 2.27 | S&P 3-Yr. Proj. EPS CAGR(%) | 10 |
| Trailing 12-Month P/E | 15.6 | P/E on S&P Oper. EPS 2012**E** | 13.9 | Dividend Rate/Share | $1.70 | S&P Credit Rating | A |
| $10K Invested 5 Yrs Ago | $11,576 | Common Shares Outstg. (M) | 141.9 | Institutional Ownership (%) | 76 | | |

## Price Performance

30-Week Mov. Avg. · · · · 10-Week Mov. Avg. – – **GAAP Earnings vs. Previous Year** Volume Above Avg. ▮▮▮ STARS
12-Mo. Target Price — Relative Strength — ▲ Up ▼ Down ▶ No Change Below Avg. ▮▮▮ ★

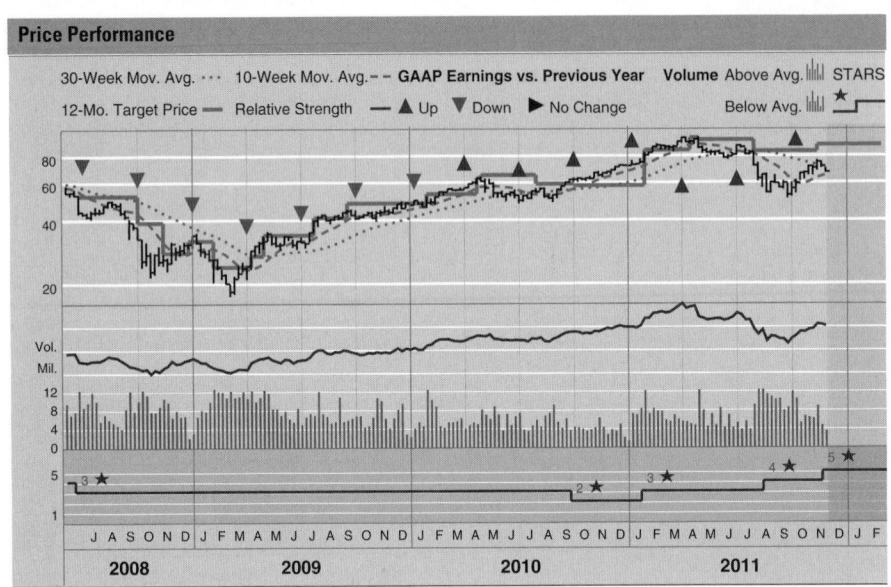

Options: ASE, CBOE, Ph

Analysis prepared by Equity Analyst **R. Tortoriello** on Nov 29, 2011, when the stock traded at **$70.93**.

## Highlights

➤ After a 24% decline in FY 09 (Sep.), revenue rebounded 38% over the next two years, and FY 11 revenue of $6 billion surpassed FY 08 peak levels of $5.7 billion. Given this strong recovery, as well as some slowing we see in global economic growth, we expect revenue growth in FY 12 to moderate to about 8% (versus 24% in FY 11). We project similar growth in the Architecture & Software and Control Products & Solutions segments, driven by emerging market demand and continued manufacturing efficiency demand in the U.S., with much slower growth in Europe.

➤ We project operating margins of 16.5% in FY 12, up from 15.5% in FY 11, primarily on efficiency improvements in both operating segments due to past restructuring efforts.

➤ We project 12% EPS growth in FY 12, to $5.38, and further growth of 8% in FY 13, to $5.80. Rockwell expects free cash flow (cash from operating minus capital expenditures) of about 75% of net income in FY 12.

## Investment Rationale/Risk

➤ Our strong buy recommendation is based on continued strong organic revenue growth (20% in FY 11), amid what we view as a compelling valuation. Although we see growth slowing in FY 12, primarily in Europe, we expect demand for automation products and services to remain strong. We see automation demand being driven by two factors: a continued build-out of automation systems in emerging markets, due to plant expansion and the need for modernization of existing plants, and a focus on efficiency and productivity in the U.S. and other developed markets in order to further boost profit margins.

➤ Risks to our recommendation and target price include lower-than-expected global economic growth, reduced project spending, a slowing in global manufacturing capacity utilization, and higher input costs.

➤ Our 12-month target price of $90 reflects an enterprise value multiple of 10X our FY 13 EBITDA estimate of $1.3 billion. This is slightly below ROK's 10-year historical average EV/EBITDA multiple of 10.5X. We believe a historical average ratio appropriately values ROK at this stage of a cyclical recovery.

## Qualitative Risk Assessment

| LOW | MEDIUM | HIGH |
| --- | --- | --- |

Our risk assessment reflects the highly cyclical end-market demand for the company's products, offset by corporate governance practices that we view favorably. We also note the company has an S&P Quality Ranking of B+, which reflects average growth and stability in earnings and dividends, and low capital requirements.

## Quantitative Evaluations

**S&P Quality Ranking** **B+**

| D | C | B- | B | B+ | A- | A | A+ |
| --- | --- | --- | --- | --- | --- | --- | --- |

**Relative Strength Rank** **STRONG**

94

LOWEST = 1 HIGHEST = 99

## Revenue/Earnings Data

**Revenue (Million $)**

| | 1Q | 2Q | 3Q | 4Q | Year |
| --- | --- | --- | --- | --- | --- |
| 2011 | 1,366 | 1,464 | 1,516 | 1,654 | 6,000 |
| 2010 | 1,068 | 1,165 | 1,268 | 1,357 | 4,857 |
| 2009 | 1,189 | 1,058 | 1,011 | 1,074 | 4,333 |
| 2008 | 1,332 | 1,407 | 1,475 | 1,484 | 5,698 |
| 2007 | 1,146 | 1,207 | 1,281 | 1,371 | 5,004 |
| 2006 | 1,301 | 1,378 | 1,428 | 1,454 | 5,561 |

**Earnings Per Share ($)**

| | | | | | |
| --- | --- | --- | --- | --- | --- |
| 2011 | 1.04 | 1.14 | 1.22 | 1.39 | 4.88 |
| 2010 | 0.54 | 0.77 | 0.83 | 0.91 | 3.05 |
| 2009 | 0.81 | 0.29 | 0.23 | 0.20 | 1.53 |
| 2008 | 1.04 | 0.96 | 1.03 | 0.87 | 3.90 |
| 2007 | 0.76 | 0.65 | 1.07 | 1.07 | 3.53 |
| 2006 | 0.80 | 0.83 | 0.83 | 1.04 | 3.49 |

Fiscal year ended Sep. 30. Next earnings report expected: Late January. EPS Estimates based on S&P Operating Earnings; historical GAAP earnings are as reported.

## Dividend Data (Dates: mm/dd Payment Date: mm/dd/yy)

| Amount ($) | Date Decl. | Ex-Div. Date | Stk. of Record | Payment Date |
| --- | --- | --- | --- | --- |
| 0.350 | 02/02 | 02/10 | 02/14 | 03/10/11 |
| 0.350 | 04/06 | 05/12 | 05/16 | 06/10/11 |
| 0.425 | 06/02 | 08/11 | 08/15 | 09/12/11 |
| 0.425 | 11/02 | 11/09 | 11/14 | 12/12/11 |

Dividends have been paid since 1948. Source: Company reports.

---

**Please read the Required Disclosures and Analyst Certification on the last page of this report.**

*The McGraw-Hill Companies*

# Rockwell Automation Inc.

**STANDARD &POOR'S**

## Business Summary November 29, 2011

CORPORATE OVERVIEW. In the early 1990s, Rockwell Automation (formerly Rockwell International) operated a broad range of manufacturing businesses. Following a series of divestitures that included the 2001 spin-off of Rockwell Collins, the 2006 divestiture of ElectroCraft Engineered Solutions, the sale of a 50% interest in Rockwell Scientific, and the 2007 divestiture of Dodge Mechanical and Reliance Electric Motors, ROK now operates two business segments: Control Products and Solutions and Architecture and Software. Both these segments primarily serve global manufacturers and provide a host of automation equipment and services.

The Control Products and Solutions (CS) segment accounted for 57% of FY 11 (Sep.) total revenues and 36% of total operating profits, with 10.8% segment profit margins. CS provides products, solutions and services focused on helping customers control, monitor and improve manufacturing processes. Products include industrial controls, variable frequency drives, smart motor controls, electronic overload controls, power control and motor control centers, drive systems, custom OEM panels, information systems and systems integration. Competitors include Emerson Electric, General Electric, and Schneider Electric.

The Architecture and Software (A&S) segment generated 43% of FY 11 sales and 36% of operating profits, with 25.4% segment operating margins. The segment offers products, including control platforms and software, as well as bundled automation products for enterprise business systems, distribution and supply chains. Control offerings include controllers, electronic interface devices, communications and network products, motor control sensors, programmable logic controllers (PLCs), input/output devices, sensors, safety components, and other products used in the automation of manufacturing operations. Software product offerings include configuration and visualization software, control platforms, and other manufacturing control software. Major competitors include Siemens AG, Mitsubishi Corp, ABB Ltd., Schneider Electric, Honeywell International, and Emerson Electric.

## Company Financials Fiscal Year Ended Sep. 30

| Per Share Data ($) | 2011 | 2010 | 2009 | 2008 | 2007 | 2006 | 2005 | 2004 | 2003 | 2002 |
|---|---|---|---|---|---|---|---|---|---|---|
| Tangible Book Value | 4.07 | 2.33 | 1.21 | 3.65 | 4.29 | 4.40 | 2.95 | 3.95 | 2.41 | 2.61 |
| Cash Flow | 5.71 | 3.94 | 2.36 | 4.72 | 4.26 | 4.35 | 3.68 | 2.83 | 2.53 | 2.29 |
| Earnings | 4.79 | 3.05 | 1.53 | 3.90 | 3.53 | 3.49 | 2.77 | 1.85 | 1.49 | 1.20 |
| S&P Core Earnings | 4.34 | 3.05 | 0.71 | 3.03 | 3.45 | 3.48 | 2.68 | 1.88 | 1.16 | 0.75 |
| Dividends | 1.48 | 1.22 | 1.16 | 1.16 | 1.16 | 0.90 | 0.78 | 0.66 | 0.66 | 0.66 |
| Payout Ratio | 31% | 40% | 76% | 30% | 33% | 26% | 28% | 36% | 44% | 55% |
| Prices:High | 98.19 | 72.75 | 49.25 | 69.72 | 75.60 | 799.47 | 63.30 | 49.97 | 36.10 | 22.79 |
| Prices:Low | 50.36 | 45.72 | 17.50 | 21.51 | 56.73 | 53.49 | 45.40 | 28.45 | 18.75 | 14.71 |
| P/E Ratio:High | 20 | 24 | 32 | 18 | 21 | 23 | 23 | 27 | 24 | 19 |
| P/E Ratio:Low | 11 | 15 | 11 | 6 | 16 | 15 | 16 | 15 | 13 | 12 |

| Income Statement Analysis (Million $) | 2011 | 2010 | 2009 | 2008 | 2007 | 2006 | 2005 | 2004 | 2003 | 2002 |
|---|---|---|---|---|---|---|---|---|---|---|
| Revenue | 6,000 | 4,857 | 4,333 | 5,698 | 5,004 | 5,561 | 5,003 | 4,411 | 4,104 | 3,909 |
| Operating Income | 1,061 | 740 | 520 | 1,021 | 937 | 1,073 | 944 | 691 | 543 | 488 |
| Depreciation | 131 | 127 | 118 | 122 | 118 | 154 | 171 | 187 | 198 | 206 |
| Interest Expense | 59.5 | 60.5 | 60.9 | 68.2 | 63.4 | 58.4 | 45.8 | 41.7 | 52.0 | 66.0 |
| Pretax Income | 868 | 544 | 274 | 809 | 789 | 365 | 737 | 438 | 299 | 233 |
| Effective Tax Rate | NA | NA | 20.5% | 28.6% | 27.8% | NM | 29.7% | 19.2% | 5.69% | 3.00% |
| Net Income | 697 | 440 | 218 | 578 | 569 | 628 | 518 | 354 | 282 | 226 |
| S&P Core Earnings | 630 | 440 | 102 | 449 | 556 | 628 | 498 | 361 | 221 | 142 |

| Balance Sheet & Other Financial Data (Million $) | 2011 | 2010 | 2009 | 2008 | 2007 | 2006 | 2005 | 2004 | 2003 | 2002 |
|---|---|---|---|---|---|---|---|---|---|---|
| Cash | 989 | 813 | 644 | 582 | 624 | 415 | 464 | 474 | 226 | 289 |
| Current Assets | 2,694 | 2,276 | 2,135 | 2,437 | 2,382 | 2,188 | 2,187 | 2,026 | 1,736 | 1,775 |
| Total Assets | 5,285 | 4,748 | 4,306 | 4,594 | 4,546 | 4,735 | 4,525 | 4,201 | 3,986 | 4,024 |
| Current Liabilities | 455 | 436 | 947 | 1,303 | 1,745 | 1,293 | 941 | 864 | 820 | 966 |
| Long Term Debt | 905 | 905 | 905 | 904 | 406 | 748 | 748 | 758 | 764 | 767 |
| Common Equity | 1,748 | 1,460 | 1,316 | 1,689 | 1,743 | 1,918 | 1,649 | 1,861 | 1,587 | 1,609 |
| Total Capital | 2,653 | 2,365 | 2,221 | 2,593 | 2,149 | 2,822 | 2,397 | 2,708 | 2,388 | 2,534 |
| Capital Expenditures | 120 | 99.4 | 98.0 | 151 | 131 | 150 | 124 | 98.0 | 109 | 104 |
| Cash Flow | 828 | 568 | 336 | 700 | 687 | 782 | 690 | 541 | 480 | 432 |
| Current Ratio | 5.9 | 5.2 | 2.3 | 1.9 | 1.4 | 1.7 | 2.3 | 2.3 | 2.1 | 1.8 |
| % Long Term Debt of Capitalization | 34.1 | 38.3 | 40.7 | 34.9 | 18.9 | 26.5 | 31.2 | 28.0 | 32.0 | 30.3 |
| % Net Income of Revenue | 11.6 | 9.1 | 5.0 | 10.1 | 11.4 | 11.3 | 10.4 | 8.0 | 6.9 | 5.8 |
| % Return on Assets | 13.9 | 9.7 | 4.9 | 12.6 | 12.3 | 13.6 | 11.9 | 8.7 | 7.1 | 5.6 |
| % Return on Equity | 43.5 | 31.7 | 14.5 | 33.7 | 31.1 | 35.2 | 29.5 | 20.5 | 17.6 | 14.1 |

Data as orig reptd.; bef. results of disc opers/spec. items. Per share data adj. for stk. divs.; EPS diluted. E-Estimated. NA-Not Available. NM-Not Meaningful. NR-Not Ranked. UR-Under Review.

**Office:** 1201 South Second Street, Milwaukee, WI 53204.
**Telephone:** 414-382-2000.
**Website:** http://www.rockwell.com
**Chrmn, Pres & CEO:** K.D. Nosbusch

**COO:** M. Thomas
**SVP & CFO:** T.D. Crandall
**SVP & CTO:** S. Chand
**SVP, Secy & General Counsel:** D.M. Hagerman

**Board Members:** B. C. Alewine, V. G. Istock, B. C. Johnson, S. R. Kalmanson, J. P. Keane, W. T. McCormick, Jr., K. D. Nosbusch, D. R. Parfet, D. B. Speer

**Founded:** 1928
**Domicile:** Delaware
**Employees:** 21,000

The **McGraw-Hill** Companies

# Rockwell Collins Inc.

**STANDARD & POOR'S**

| S&P Recommendation HOLD ★★★★★ | Price $54.90 (as of Nov 30, 2011) | 12-Mo. Target Price $60.00 | Investment Style Large-Cap Growth |
| --- | --- | --- | --- |

**GICS Sector** Industrials
**Sub-Industry** Aerospace & Defense

**Summary** This company is one of the world's largest makers of military and commercial avionics and electronics, including cockpit controls, communications and navigation systems, and in-flight entertainment systems.

## Key Stock Statistics (Source S&P, Vickers, company reports)

| | | | | | | | |
| --- | --- | --- | --- | --- | --- | --- | --- |
| 52-Wk Range | $67.30– 43.82 | S&P Oper. EPS 2012**E** | 4.50 | Market Capitalization(B) | $8.308 | Beta | 1.20 |
| Trailing 12-Month EPS | $4.06 | S&P Oper. EPS 2013**E** | 4.90 | Yield (%) | 1.75 | S&P 3-Yr. Proj. EPS CAGR(%) | 8 |
| Trailing 12-Month P/E | 13.5 | P/E on S&P Oper. EPS 2012**E** | 12.2 | Dividend Rate/Share | $0.96 | S&P Credit Rating | A |
| $10K Invested 5 Yrs Ago | $9,276 | Common Shares Outstg. (M) | 151.3 | Institutional Ownership (%) | 69 | | |

## Price Performance

30-Week Mov. Avg. · · · 10-Week Mov. Avg. – – **GAAP Earnings vs. Previous Year**   Volume Above Avg. STARS

12-Mo. Target Price — Relative Strength — ▲ Up ▼ Down ► No Change   Below Avg. ★

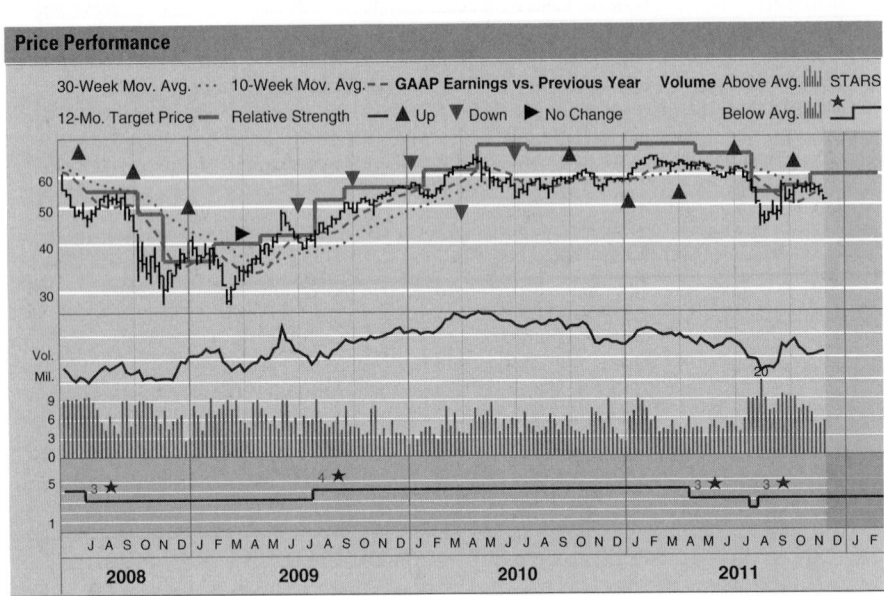

Options: ASE, CBOE, Ph

Analysis prepared by Equity Analyst **R. Tortoriello** on Nov 30, 2011, when the stock traded at **$55.14**.

### Highlights

➤ We project a 3.4% sales gain in FY 12 (Sep.), as we expect strong growth in Commercial Systems (about 12%), partially offset by a modest decline in Government Systems (3%). We see Commercial growth being driven by rising demand from large commercial aircraft OEMs and improving aftermarket demand for both large commercial and business jets, as air traffic continues to rise amid a slow global economic recovery. We see Government being negatively affected by a decrease in spending and tightening of contract terms by the U.S. Department of Defense, due to large U.S. federal budget deficits.

➤ We project segment operating margins of 21.4% in FY 12, up from 20.3% in FY 11, on volume increases and productivity improvement. We are modeling flat operating margins for FY 13.

➤ We estimate EPS of $4.50 for FY 12, and project growth to $4.90 for FY 13, driven in large part by our expectation of a falling share count, on share repurchases.

### Investment Rationale/Risk

➤ Due to our expectation of continued declines in U.S. government spending over the next few years, we see results at COL's Government Systems segment being constrained, although we believe COL has done an admirable job of maintaining what we view as high operating margins in the segment despite budgetary pressure. We see good growth in the Commercial segment, primarily driven, on the OEM side, by rising deliveries at Boeing, as well as service entry of the 787. We see business jet demand improving modestly in FY 12 and more so in FY 13. Given offsetting trends in COL's business, we view the shares as fairly valued.

➤ Risks to our recommendation and target price include worse-than-expected Commercial Systems growth and greater-than-expected U.S. defense budget pressure on COL.

➤ Our 12-month target price of $60 is based on an enterprise value to FY 12 estimated EBITDA multiple of 8X. Over its nine-year operating history, COL has recorded an average EV-to-EBITDA multiple of about 10.5X. Given our view of defense market pressure, we view a lower-than average multiple as appropriate.

## Qualitative Risk Assessment

| LOW | **MEDIUM** | HIGH |
| --- | --- | --- |

Our risk assessment reflects the company's exposure to the commercial airline industry, dependence on U.S. military procurement and R&D budgets, and high fixed-cost structure, offset by what we view as a solid balance sheet and strong returns.

## Quantitative Evaluations

**S&P Quality Ranking** A

| D | C | B- | B | B+ | A- | **A** | A+ |
| --- | --- | --- | --- | --- | --- | --- | --- |

**Relative Strength Rank** STRONG

72

LOWEST = 1   HIGHEST = 99

## Revenue/Earnings Data

**Revenue (Million $)**

| | 1Q | 2Q | 3Q | 4Q | Year |
| --- | --- | --- | --- | --- | --- |
| 2011 | 1,104 | 1,216 | 1,190 | 1,296 | 4,806 |
| 2010 | 1,027 | 1,142 | 1,214 | 1,282 | 4,665 |
| 2009 | 1,058 | 1,138 | 1,084 | 1,190 | 4,470 |
| 2008 | 1,112 | 1,186 | 1,194 | 1,277 | 4,769 |
| 2007 | 993.0 | 1,083 | 1,113 | 1,226 | 4,415 |
| 2006 | 881.0 | 957.0 | 964.0 | 1,061 | 3,863 |

**Earnings Per Share ($)**

| | | | | | |
| --- | --- | --- | --- | --- | --- |
| 2011 | 0.95 | 0.96 | 1.01 | 1.02 | 3.94 |
| 2010 | 0.76 | 0.93 | 0.89 | 0.94 | 3.52 |
| 2009 | 0.95 | 1.03 | 0.91 | 0.84 | 3.73 |
| 2008 | 0.93 | 1.03 | 1.07 | 1.13 | 4.16 |
| 2007 | 0.84 | 0.82 | 0.86 | 0.93 | 3.45 |
| 2006 | 0.59 | 0.65 | 0.70 | 0.79 | 2.73 |

Fiscal year ended Sep. 30. Next earnings report expected: NA. EPS Estimates based on S&P Operating Earnings; historical GAAP earnings are as reported.

## Dividend Data (Dates: mm/dd Payment Date: mm/dd/yy)

| Amount ($) | Date Decl. | Ex-Div. Date | Stk. of Record | Payment Date |
| --- | --- | --- | --- | --- |
| 0.240 | 01/17 | 02/10 | 02/14 | 03/07/11 |
| 0.240 | 04/20 | 05/12 | 05/16 | 06/06/11 |
| 0.240 | 07/25 | 08/11 | 08/15 | 09/06/11 |
| 0.240 | 10/25 | 11/09 | 11/14 | 12/05/11 |

Dividends have been paid since 2001. Source: Company reports.

# Rockwell Collins Inc.

STANDARD &POOR'S

## Business Summary November 30, 2011

CORPORATE OVERVIEW. This global $5 billion revenue aircraft electronics (avionics) maker conducts its business through two segments: Commercial Systems (CS) and Government Systems (GS). CS (42% of revenues and 39% of segment operating earnings, and segment operating margins of 19.2% in FY 11 (Sep.)) primarily makes flight deck electronic systems. CS also provides a range of repair and overhaul services. GS (58%; 61%; 21.0%) primarily makes communication systems, navigation systems, and avionics and cockpit displays for military jets and rotorcraft. GS also makes navigation equipment embedded in guided missiles.

Commercial Systems products include integrated avionics systems (such as COL's Pro Line Fusion system); integrated cabin electronics systems (cabin management, passenger entertainment and connectivity); communication systems (datalink and satellite communications systems); navigation systems and products (landing sensors, flight management systems); situational awareness and surveillance systems (enhanced vision, head-up/head-down/helmet mounted displays, weather radar, collision avoidance); integrated information management solutions (on-board information management and connectivity); electro-mechanical systems (cockpit controls and actuation); simulation and training systems (including full flight simulators); and maintenance, repair, parts, and service. About 53% of segment sales in FY 11

were to the air transport market (large commercial jets), with the remaining 47% to the business and regional jet markets. Aftermarket parts and service represented 41% of sales.

Government Systems products include communications systems and products (including satellite communications); navigation systems and products (radio navigation systems, GPS systems, handheld and multi-mode systems); subsystems for the flight deck that combine flight operations with navigation and guidance functions; cockpit display systems (flat panel, wide field of view head-up and helmet-mounted displays); simulation and training systems (visual system products, training systems and services); maintenance, repair, parts, and support services. Customers include the U.S. Department of Defense, other government agencies, civil agencies, defense contractors, and foreign ministries of defense. Products are used for airborne, ground and shipboard applications. Segment sales by business line in FY 11 were avionics 51%, communication products 25%, surface solutions 13%, and navigation products 11%.

## Company Financials Fiscal Year Ended Sep. 30

| Per Share Data ($) | 2011 | 2010 | 2009 | 2008 | 2007 | 2006 | 2005 | 2004 | 2003 | 2002 |
|---|---|---|---|---|---|---|---|---|---|---|
| Tangible Book Value | 2.84 | 2.61 | 2.09 | 3.79 | 5.97 | 3.30 | 2.13 | 3.29 | 2.21 | 2.93 |
| Cash Flow | 4.84 | 4.46 | 4.63 | 4.95 | 4.14 | 3.34 | 2.86 | 2.28 | 2.02 | 1.85 |
| Earnings | 3.94 | 3.52 | 3.73 | 4.16 | 3.45 | 2.73 | 2.20 | 1.67 | 1.43 | 1.28 |
| S&P Core Earnings | 3.16 | 3.56 | 3.08 | 3.39 | 3.35 | 2.66 | 2.04 | 1.47 | 0.82 | 0.46 |
| Dividends | 0.96 | 0.96 | 0.96 | 0.88 | 0.64 | 0.56 | 0.48 | 0.39 | 0.36 | 0.36 |
| Payout Ratio | 24% | 27% | 26% | 21% | 19% | 21% | 22% | 23% | 25% | 28% |
| Prices:High | 67.30 | 68.04 | 56.88 | 72.41 | 76.00 | 64.31 | 49.80 | 40.94 | 30.10 | 28.00 |
| Prices:Low | 43.82 | 51.85 | 27.67 | 27.76 | 61.25 | 43.49 | 37.22 | 29.16 | 17.20 | 18.50 |
| P/E Ratio:High | 17 | 19 | 15 | 17 | 22 | 24 | 23 | 25 | 21 | 22 |
| P/E Ratio:Low | 11 | 15 | 7 | 7 | 18 | 16 | 17 | 17 | 12 | 14 |

| Income Statement Analysis (Million $) | 2011 | 2010 | 2009 | 2008 | 2007 | 2006 | 2005 | 2004 | 2003 | 2002 |
|---|---|---|---|---|---|---|---|---|---|---|
| Revenue | 4,806 | 4,665 | 4,470 | 4,769 | 4,415 | 3,863 | 3,445 | 2,930 | 2,542 | 2,492 |
| Operating Income | 1,042 | 970 | 1,029 | 1,090 | 959 | 776 | 660 | 539 | 440 | 427 |
| Depreciation | 141 | 149 | 144 | 129 | 118 | 106 | 119 | 109 | 105 | 105 |
| Interest Expense | 19.0 | 20.0 | 18.0 | 21.0 | 13.0 | 13.0 | 11.0 | 8.00 | 3.00 | 6.00 |
| Pretax Income | 855 | 802 | 867 | 953 | 843 | 689 | 547 | 430 | 368 | 341 |
| Effective Tax Rate | NA | NA | 31.5% | 28.9% | 30.6% | 30.8% | 27.6% | 30.0% | 29.9% | 30.8% |
| Net Income | 615 | 561 | 594 | 678 | 585 | 477 | 396 | 301 | 258 | 236 |
| S&P Core Earnings | 493 | 568 | 491 | 552 | 568 | 465 | 367 | 264 | 148 | 86.8 |

| Balance Sheet & Other Financial Data (Million $) | 2011 | 2010 | 2009 | 2008 | 2007 | 2006 | 2005 | 2004 | 2003 | 2002 |
|---|---|---|---|---|---|---|---|---|---|---|
| Cash | 530 | 435 | 235 | 175 | 231 | 144 | 145 | 196 | 66.0 | 49.0 |
| Current Assets | 2,889 | 2,689 | 2,362 | 2,338 | 2,169 | 1,927 | 1,775 | 1,663 | 1,427 | 1,438 |
| Total Assets | 5,389 | 5,064 | 4,645 | 4,144 | 3,750 | 3,278 | 3,140 | 2,874 | 2,591 | 2,560 |
| Current Liabilities | 1,495 | 1,452 | 1,359 | 1,740 | 1,459 | 1,324 | 1,177 | 964 | 901 | 1,043 |
| Long Term Debt | 528 | 525 | 532 | 228 | 223 | 245 | 200 | 201 | Nil | Nil |
| Common Equity | 1,528 | 1,486 | 1,292 | 1,408 | 1,573 | 1,206 | 939 | 1,133 | 833 | 987 |
| Total Capital | 2,056 | 2,011 | 1,824 | 1,646 | 1,840 | 1,451 | 1,139 | 1,334 | 833 | 987 |
| Capital Expenditures | 152 | 109 | 153 | 171 | 125 | 144 | 111 | 94.0 | 72.0 | 62.0 |
| Cash Flow | 756 | 710 | 738 | 807 | 703 | 583 | 515 | 410 | 363 | 341 |
| Current Ratio | 1.9 | 1.9 | 1.7 | 1.3 | 1.5 | 1.5 | 1.5 | 1.7 | 1.6 | 1.4 |
| % Long Term Debt of Capitalization | 25.7 | 26.1 | 29.2 | 13.9 | 12.1 | 16.9 | 17.6 | 15.1 | Nil | Nil |
| % Net Income of Revenue | 12.8 | 12.0 | 13.3 | 14.2 | 13.3 | 12.3 | 11.5 | 10.3 | 10.1 | 9.5 |
| % Return on Assets | 11.8 | 11.6 | 13.5 | 17.2 | 16.7 | 14.8 | 13.2 | 11.0 | 10.0 | 9.1 |
| % Return on Equity | 40.9 | 40.4 | 44.0 | 45.5 | 42.1 | 44.5 | 38.2 | 30.6 | 28.4 | 22.5 |

Data as orig reptd.; bef. results of disc opers/spec. items. Per share data adj. for stk. divs.; EPS diluted. E-Estimated. NA-Not Available. NM-Not Meaningful. NR-Not Ranked. UR-Under Review.

Office: 400 Collins Rd NE, Cedar Rapids, IA 52498-0503.
Telephone: 319-295-1000.
Email: investorrelations@rockwellcollins.com
Website: http://www.rockwellcollins.com

Chrmn, Pres & CEO: C. Jones
SVP & CTO: N. Mattai
SVP, Secy & General Counsel: G.R. Chadick
CFO: P.E. Allen

Chief Acctg Officer & Cntlr: M.A. Schulte
Investor Contact: D. Crookshank (319-295-7575)
Board Members: D. R. Beall, A. J. Carbone, C. A. Davis, R. E. Eberhart, C. Jones, D. Lilley, A. J. Policano, C. L. Shavers, J. L. Turner

Founded: 2001
Domicile: Delaware
Employees: 20,500

# Roper Industries Inc.

**STANDARD &POOR'S**

| S&P Recommendation HOLD ★★★★★ | Price $79.43 (as of Nov 25, 2011) | 12-Mo. Target Price $87.00 | Investment Style Large-Cap Growth |
| --- | --- | --- | --- |

**GICS Sector** Industrials
**Sub-Industry** Electrical Components & Equipment

**Summary** This company makes high-tech industrial equipment and analytical instruments for oil and gas producers, semiconductor equipment makers, and industrial companies.

## Key Stock Statistics (Source S&P, Vickers, company reports)

| | | | | | | | |
| --- | --- | --- | --- | --- | --- | --- | --- |
| 52-Wk Range | $88.76–64.90 | S&P Oper. EPS 2011**E** | 4.28 | Market Capitalization(B) | $7.663 | Beta | 0.80 |
| Trailing 12-Month EPS | $4.22 | S&P Oper. EPS 2012**E** | 4.62 | Yield (%) | 0.55 | S&P 3-Yr. Proj. EPS CAGR(%) | 14 |
| Trailing 12-Month P/E | 18.8 | P/E on S&P Oper. EPS 2011**E** | 18.6 | Dividend Rate/Share | $0.44 | S&P Credit Rating | BBB- |
| $10K Invested 5 Yrs Ago | $15,963 | Common Shares Outstg. (M) | 96.5 | Institutional Ownership (%) | 96 | | |

## Price Performance

30-Week Mov. Avg. ···· 10-Week Mov. Avg. -- **GAAP Earnings vs. Previous Year**   Volume Above Avg. ▏▍▍ STARS
12-Mo. Target Price — Relative Strength — ▲ Up ▼ Down ► No Change   Below Avg. ▏▍▍ ★

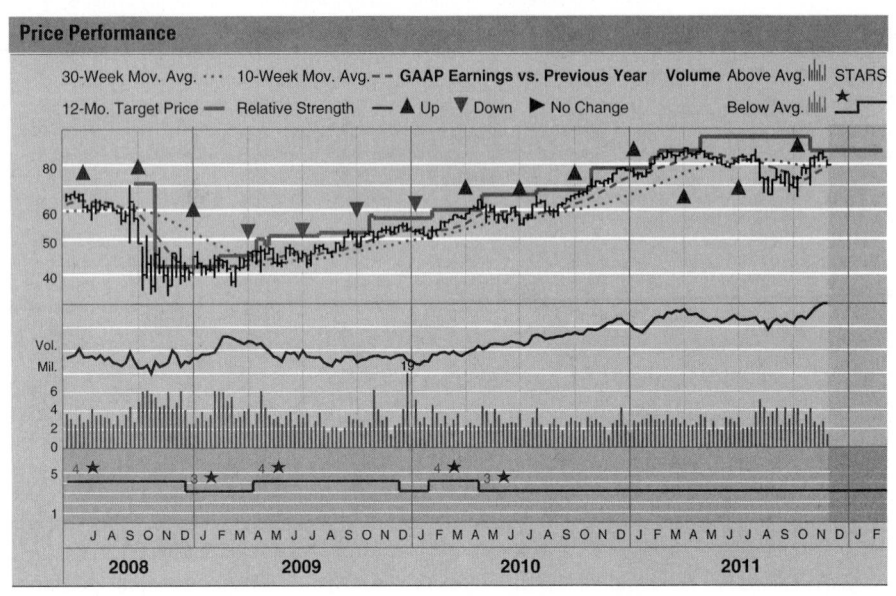

Analysis prepared by Equity Analyst **Kevin Kirkeby** on Nov 03, 2011, when the stock traded at **$83.77**.

## Qualitative Risk Assessment

| LOW | MEDIUM | HIGH |
| --- | --- | --- |

Our risk assessment reflects the company's significant proportion of rapidly growing international sales and ROP's proprietary product portfolio, offset by its acquisition strategy and corporate governance practices that we view unfavorably versus peers.

## Quantitative Evaluations

**S&P Quality Ranking**                                A

| D | C | B- | B | B+ | A- | A | A+ |
| --- | --- | --- | --- | --- | --- | --- | --- |

**Relative Strength Rank**                          STRONG

82

LOWEST = 1                                         HIGHEST = 99

## Revenue/Earnings Data

**Revenue (Million $)**

| | 1Q | 2Q | 3Q | 4Q | Year |
| --- | --- | --- | --- | --- | --- |
| 2011 | 645.3 | 699.9 | 712.7 | -- | -- |
| 2010 | 534.4 | 567.1 | 605.1 | 679.5 | 2,386 |
| 2009 | 505.4 | 504.9 | 485.7 | 553.6 | 2,050 |
| 2008 | 543.0 | 594.4 | 593.1 | 575.9 | 2,306 |
| 2007 | 478.4 | 530.6 | 530.9 | 560.1 | 2,102 |
| 2006 | 382.7 | 425.3 | 427.2 | 465.5 | 1,701 |

**Earnings Per Share ($)**

| | | | | | |
| --- | --- | --- | --- | --- | --- |
| 2011 | 0.91 | 1.08 | 1.12 | E1.21 | E4.28 |
| 2010 | 0.62 | 0.74 | 0.87 | 1.10 | 3.34 |
| 2009 | 0.56 | 0.64 | 0.61 | 0.77 | 2.58 |
| 2008 | 0.68 | 0.80 | 0.80 | 0.78 | 3.06 |
| 2007 | 0.56 | 0.66 | 0.70 | 0.77 | 2.68 |
| 2006 | 0.42 | 0.53 | 0.56 | 0.62 | 2.13 |

Fiscal year ended Dec. 31. Next earnings report expected: Early February. EPS Estimates based on S&P Operating Earnings; historical GAAP earnings are as reported.

### Highlights

➤ Following an expected 18% increase in 2011, we forecast revenue growth to slow to 8% in 2012. This reflects the ongoing rollout of new product and applications in nearly all business segments. We note that order rates reached a record high at the end of the 2011 third quarter, but, at 9.9%, the rate of growth has slowed from 14% growth in the second quarter and 24% in the first. We do expect ROP to benefit from its exposure to the oil and gas markets, where capital investment trends continue to appear favorable.

➤ We see margins improving during 2012 due to improved operating leverage, since we forecast further improvements in volumes, and to cost control efforts. We also think ROP will continue to recover any rise in raw material costs through price actions, aided in part by its focus on niche markets. Our earnings model uses a 30% tax rate, similar to the level expected for 2011.

➤ Our EPS estimate for 2011 of $4.28 excludes a $0.04 gain related to a currency remeasurement booked in the second quarter.

### Investment Rationale/Risk

➤ We view ROP's asset-light business model, which we believe leads to above average operating margins and cash flow generation, favorably, and see the company benefiting from a gradually improving economy. In addition, we think ROP is has positioned itself in markets with above-average secular growth potential, where it has competitive advantages through development of proprietary products and customer-centric services. We think the shares are appropriately valued at recent levels.

➤ Risks to our recommendation and target price include weaker-than-expected global economic growth, along with value-diminishing acquisitions and execution risks.

➤ Our 12-month target price of $87 represents a blend of two valuation metrics. Our DCF model, which assumes a 3% perpetuity growth rate and a discount rate of 8.9%, indicates an intrinsic value approaching $86. As for our relative valuation analysis, we apply an above-peer-average multiple of 19.3X to our four-quarter forward EPS estimate, suggesting an $88 value.

## Dividend Data (Dates: mm/dd Payment Date: mm/dd/yy)

| Amount ($) | Date Decl. | Ex-Div. Date | Stk. of Record | Payment Date |
| --- | --- | --- | --- | --- |
| 0.110 | 12/08 | 01/05 | 01/07 | 01/28/11 |
| 0.110 | 03/21 | 04/06 | 04/08 | 04/22/11 |
| 0.110 | 06/20 | 07/06 | 07/08 | 07/29/11 |
| 0.110 | 08/12 | 10/05 | 10/07 | 10/28/11 |

Dividends have been paid since 1992. Source: Company reports.

**The McGraw-Hill Companies**

# Roper Industries Inc.

**STANDARD &POOR'S**

## Business Summary November 03, 2011

CORPORATE OVERVIEW. Roper Industries is a high-tech industrial components and equipment maker that designs, manufactures and distributes energy systems and controls, scientific and industrial imaging products and software, specialty industrial technology products, and instrumentation products and services. ROP's target end markets include radio frequency (RF) applications, water and wastewater, oil and gas, research, power generation, and general industry.

The Industrial Technology segment (25% of 2010 sales; 28.7% of segment operating profits; 26.7% operating margins) provides products and solutions for improving customer productivity. Offerings include industrial pumps, flow measurement and metering equipment, industrial valves and controls, and water meter and automatic meter reading products and systems. ROP's strategy for this segment includes global sourcing, geographic expansion, asset velocity improvements, and the capture of market-based synergies among business units. Orders rates in this segment gained nearly 27% in 2010 while the book-to-bill ratio was 1.1X.

The Energy Systems and Controls segment (21%; 21.4%; 23.9%) provides service and solutions to improve quality, safety and efficiency for customer equipment and processes, primarily in energy markets. Customers benefit from application expertise, coupled with advanced vibration-monitoring components, turbo-machinery control systems and non-destructive testing solutions, often incorporating significant software content. ROP's strategy for the segment includes focusing on expanding into new applications and increasing aftermarket revenue. A large percentage of this segment's revenues come from the oil and gas industry. New orders in the Energy Systems units gained 265 and the book-to-bill ratio was nearly 1.1X.

The Scientific and Industrial Imaging segment (23%; 23.2%; 23.8%) provides solutions that enable global research in life and physical sciences. Key products are digital imaging cameras, spectrographic systems, electron microscope accessories, high-speed digital video equipment and image processing software. In addition, through ROP's Imaging Alliance, these businesses are working closely with internal and external sources. This segment's book-to-bill ratio was less than 1.1X in 2010 as new order rates rose over 65%.

The RF Technology segment (30%; 26.7%; 20.8%) provides radio frequency identification and satellite-based communications technologies that are used in toll and traffic systems and processing, security and access control, and mobile asset tracking. Segment orders increased by 4% while the book-to-bill ration was about 1X in 2010.

## Company Financials Fiscal Year Ended Dec. 31

| Per Share Data ($) | 2010 | 2009 | 2008 | 2007 | 2006 | 2005 | 2004 | 2003 | 2002 | 2001 |
|---|---|---|---|---|---|---|---|---|---|---|
| Tangible Book Value | NM | NM | NM | NM | NM | NM | NM | NM | NM | NM |
| Cash Flow | 4.61 | 3.69 | 3.42 | 3.02 | 3.03 | 2.55 | 1.79 | 1.01 | 1.28 | 1.32 |
| Earnings | 3.34 | 2.58 | 3.06 | 2.68 | 2.13 | 1.74 | 1.24 | 0.75 | 1.04 | 0.89 |
| S&P Core Earnings | 3.34 | 2.55 | 3.06 | 2.68 | 2.13 | 1.63 | 1.11 | 0.66 | 0.93 | 0.81 |
| Dividends | 0.38 | 0.33 | 0.29 | 0.26 | 0.24 | 0.27 | 0.19 | 0.18 | 0.17 | 0.15 |
| Payout Ratio | 11% | 13% | 9% | 10% | 11% | 15% | 16% | 23% | 16% | 17% |
| Prices:High | 78.62 | 55.50 | 70.48 | 71.01 | 51.75 | 41.10 | 31.84 | 25.98 | 26.46 | 26.13 |
| Prices:Low | 49.84 | 36.82 | 34.85 | 48.40 | 38.32 | 28.28 | 22.33 | 13.18 | 13.63 | 15.50 |
| P/E Ratio:High | 24 | 22 | 23 | 26 | 24 | 24 | 26 | 35 | 25 | 30 |
| P/E Ratio:Low | 15 | 14 | 11 | 18 | 18 | 16 | 18 | 18 | 13 | 18 |

| Income Statement Analysis (Million $) | | | | | | | | | | |
|---|---|---|---|---|---|---|---|---|---|---|
| Revenue | 2,386 | 2,050 | 2,306 | 2,102 | 1,701 | 1,454 | 970 | 657 | 627 | 587 |
| Operating Income | 637 | 511 | 524 | 470 | 420 | 336 | 213 | 124 | 130 | 126 |
| Depreciation | 123 | 103 | 33.9 | 31.8 | 82.0 | 71.3 | 41.4 | 16.4 | 15.2 | 27.5 |
| Interest Expense | 66.5 | 58.5 | 53.7 | 52.2 | 44.8 | 43.4 | 28.8 | 16.4 | 18.5 | 15.9 |
| Pretax Income | 448 | 340 | 436 | 384 | 293 | 221 | 134 | 66.3 | 95.7 | 86.4 |
| Effective Tax Rate | NA | 29.5% | 34.3% | 34.8% | 34.0% | 30.6% | 29.8% | 27.5% | 31.0% | 35.4% |
| Net Income | 323 | 239 | 287 | 250 | 193 | 153 | 93.9 | 48.1 | 66.0 | 55.8 |
| S&P Core Earnings | 323 | 237 | 287 | 250 | 193 | 144 | 83.8 | 42.1 | 59.0 | 50.9 |

| Balance Sheet & Other Financial Data (Million $) | | | | | | | | | | |
|---|---|---|---|---|---|---|---|---|---|---|
| Cash | 270 | 168 | 178 | 309 | 69.5 | 53.1 | 129 | 70.2 | 12.4 | 16.2 |
| Current Assets | 998 | 871 | 858 | 951 | 627 | 498 | 556 | 381 | 248 | 233 |
| Total Assets | 5,070 | 4,328 | 3,972 | 3,453 | 2,995 | 2,522 | 2,366 | 1,515 | 829 | 762 |
| Current Liabilities | 540 | 478 | 619 | 668 | 588 | 506 | 254 | 161 | 130 | 104 |
| Long Term Debt | 1,248 | 1,041 | 1,034 | 727 | 727 | 621 | 855 | 630 | 312 | 324 |
| Common Equity | 2,751 | 2,421 | 2,004 | 1,790 | 1,487 | 1,250 | 1,114 | 656 | 376 | 324 |
| Total Capital | 4,092 | 3,575 | 3,271 | 2,739 | 2,384 | 1,995 | 2,095 | 1,336 | 688 | 647 |
| Capital Expenditures | 28.6 | 25.9 | 30.1 | 30.1 | 32.2 | 24.8 | 12.1 | 10.4 | 7.78 | 7.46 |
| Cash Flow | 446 | 343 | 320 | 282 | 275 | 224 | 135 | 64.4 | 81.2 | 83.3 |
| Current Ratio | 1.9 | 1.8 | 1.4 | 1.4 | 1.1 | 1.0 | 2.2 | 2.4 | 1.9 | 2.2 |
| % Long Term Debt of Capitalization | 30.5 | 29.1 | 31.6 | 26.6 | 30.5 | 31.1 | 40.8 | 47.2 | 45.3 | 50.0 |
| % Net Income of Revenue | 13.5 | 11.7 | 12.4 | 11.9 | 11.4 | 10.5 | 9.7 | 7.3 | 10.5 | 9.5 |
| % Return on Assets | 6.9 | 5.8 | 7.7 | 7.8 | 7.0 | 6.3 | 4.8 | 4.1 | 8.3 | 8.2 |
| % Return on Equity | 12.5 | 10.8 | 15.1 | 15.3 | 14.1 | 13.0 | 10.6 | 9.3 | 18.9 | 18.8 |

Data as orig reptd.; bef. results of disc opers/spec. items. Per share data adj. for stk. divs.; EPS diluted. E-Estimated. NA-Not Available. NM-Not Meaningful. NR-Not Ranked. UR-Under Review.

**Office:** 6901 Professional Pkwy E Ste 200, Sarasota, FL 34240-8473.
**Telephone:** 941-556-2601.
**Email:** investor_relations@roperind.com
**Website:** http://www.roperind.com

**Chrmn, Pres & CEO:** B.D. Jellison
**CFO:** J. Humphrey
**Chief Acctg Officer & Cntlr:** P.J. Soni
**Secy & General Counsel:** D.B. Liner

**Board Members:** D. W. Devonshire, J. F. Fort, III, B. D. Jellison, R. D. Johnson, R. E. Knowling, Jr., J. Prezzano, Jr., R. F. Wallman, C. Wright
**Founded:** 1981
**Domicile:** Delaware
**Employees:** 8,050

# Ross Stores Inc

## STANDARD &POOR'S

| S&P Recommendation HOLD ★★★★★ | Price $85.43 (as of Nov 25, 2011) | 12-Mo. Target Price $90.00 | Investment Style Large-Cap Growth |
|---|---|---|---|

**GICS Sector** Consumer Discretionary
**Sub-Industry** Apparel Retail

**Summary** This off-price retailer offers in-season branded apparel and other merchandise through over 1,100 stores in 29 states, the District of Columbia and Guam.

## Key Stock Statistics (Source S&P, Vickers, company reports)

| | | | | | | | |
|---|---|---|---|---|---|---|---|
| 52-Wk Range | $90.69–60.15 | S&P Oper. EPS 2012**E** | 5.60 | Market Capitalization(B) | $9.876 | Beta | 0.70 |
| Trailing 12-Month EPS | $5.41 | S&P Oper. EPS 2013**E** | 6.35 | Yield (%) | 1.03 | S&P 3-Yr. Proj. EPS CAGR(%) | 16 |
| Trailing 12-Month P/E | 15.8 | P/E on S&P Oper. EPS 2012**E** | 15.3 | Dividend Rate/Share | $0.88 | S&P Credit Rating | BBB+ |
| $10K Invested 5 Yrs Ago | $30,176 | Common Shares Outstg. (M) | 115.6 | Institutional Ownership (%) | 95 | | |

## Price Performance

30-Week Mov. Avg. ···· 10-Week Mov. Avg. ‑‑ **GAAP Earnings vs. Previous Year** Volume Above Avg. STARS
12-Mo. Target Price — Relative Strength — ▲ Up ▼ Down ▶ No Change Below Avg.

Options: ASE, CBOE, Ph

Analysis prepared by Equity Analyst **Jason N. Asaeda** on Nov 21, 2011, when the stock traded at **$86.72**.

## Qualitative Risk Assessment

| LOW | MEDIUM | HIGH |
|---|---|---|

Our risk assessment reflects our view of favorable growth prospects for both the Ross Stores and dd's DISCOUNTS chains, offset by our concerns over how expected apparel inflation will impact consumer spending.

## Quantitative Evaluations

**S&P Quality Ranking** A+

| D | C | B- | B | B+ | A- | A | A+ |
|---|---|---|---|---|---|---|---|

**Relative Strength Rank** STRONG

87

LOWEST = 1          HIGHEST = 99

## Revenue/Earnings Data

**Revenue (Million $)**

| | 1Q | 2Q | 3Q | 4Q | Year |
|---|---|---|---|---|---|
| 2012 | 2,075 | 2,089 | 2,046 | -- | -- |
| 2011 | 1,935 | 1,912 | 1,874 | 2,145 | 7,866 |
| 2010 | 1,692 | 1,769 | 1,744 | 1,980 | 7,184 |
| 2009 | 1,556 | 1,640 | 1,555 | 1,734 | 6,486 |
| 2008 | 1,411 | 1,445 | 1,468 | 1,652 | 5,975 |
| 2007 | 1,292 | 1,308 | 1,362 | 1,608 | 5,570 |

**Earnings Per Share ($)**

| | | | | | |
|---|---|---|---|---|---|
| 2012 | 1.48 | 1.28 | 1.26 | E1.58 | E5.60 |
| 2011 | 1.16 | 1.07 | 1.02 | 1.37 | 4.63 |
| 2010 | 0.72 | 0.82 | 0.84 | 1.16 | 3.54 |
| 2009 | 0.60 | 0.54 | 0.44 | 0.76 | 2.33 |
| 2008 | 0.48 | 0.54 | 0.36 | 0.70 | 1.90 |
| 2007 | 0.41 | 0.32 | 0.31 | 0.66 | 1.70 |

Fiscal year ended Jan. 31. Next earnings report expected: Mid March. EPS Estimates based on S&P Operating Earnings; historical GAAP earnings are as reported.

## Highlights

➤ Weighing a challenging retail environment against continuing benefits we see for ROST from cost-conscious consumers seeking out the best values on brand-name apparel and home fashions, we forecast annual same-store sales growth of 3% to 4% in FY 12 (Jan.) and FY 13. We look for the company's Ross Stores and dd's DISCOUNTS chains to drive higher store traffic through continuous in-flow of new merchandise. Coupled with projected 6% to 7% annual growth in number of stores, we expect net sales to reach $8.52 billion in FY 12 and $9.81 billion in FY 13.

➤ We see opportunity for margin expansion in FY 12 and FY 13, supported by effective inventory and expense management. We also expect a higher level of packaway inventory (43% of total inventories at the end of the third quarter of FY 12, up from 37% a year ago) to help offset expected apparel cost inflation. However, the company should also incur higher storage-related distribution costs.

➤ Factoring in planned share buybacks under ROST's new two-year $900 million repurchase authorization, we see EPS of $5.60 in FY 12 and $6.35 in FY 13.

## Investment Rationale/Risk

➤ While our outlook for the company is positive, we view the shares as fully valued at recent levels. We believe ROST's recent expansion of Ross Stores into the Midwest (12 stores in Chicago opened in early October), along with improved execution of off-price buying (making purchases opportunistically and closer to need during a season) and better assortment planning and allocation at the store level, bode well for company fundamentals. Coupled with fine-tuning of merchandise offerings driving profit improvement, we view dd's DISCOUNTS as an attractive long-term growth vehicle.

➤ Risks to our recommendation and target price include sales shortfalls due to changes in consumer confidence, spending habits and buying preferences; availability of brand-name merchandise; and increased promotional activity by department stores and other competitors.

➤ Our 12-month target price of $90 is based on a forward P/E multiple of 14.1X, ROST's 10-year historical average, applied to our FY 13 EPS estimate.

## Dividend Data (Dates: mm/dd Payment Date: mm/dd/yy)

| Amount ($) | Date Decl. | Ex-Div. Date | Stk. of Record | Payment Date |
|---|---|---|---|---|
| 0.220 | 05/18 | 06/03 | 06/07 | 06/30/11 |
| 0.220 | 08/17 | 08/31 | 09/02 | 09/30/11 |
| 0.110 | 11/17 | 11/25 | 11/29 | 12/30/11 |
| 2-for-1 | 11/17 | 12/16 | 11/29 | 12/15/11 |

Dividends have been paid since 1994. Source: Company reports.

# Ross Stores Inc

## Business Summary November 21, 2011

CORPORATE OVERVIEW. Ross Stores operated 1,126 (as of November 17, 2011) off-price retail stores that feature first-quality, in-season apparel, shoes, fragrances, and apparel-related accessories, as well as home furnishings and jewelry under the Ross (1,038) and dd's DISCOUNTS (88) names. Both chains target value-conscious 25 to 54 year-old men and women, with Ross targeting mainly middle-income households and dd's DISCOUNTS more moderate income households. Ross stores average 29,800 sq. ft. of selling space, and are located in 27 states (mainly warm weather) and Guam. dd's DISCOUNTS stores average 24,900 sq. ft of selling space, and are located in California, Florida, Texas and Arizona. Nearly all stores occupy leased facilities and are situated in neighborhood or strip shopping centers in heavily populated urban and suburban areas.

The company believes it derives a competitive advantage by offering a wide assortment of quality brand-name and fashion merchandise in an easy-to-shop environment at prices generally 20% to 60% below those charged by most department and specialty stores at Ross, and 20% to 70% below moderate department and discount store regular prices at dd's DISCOUNTS. Working with more than 7,700 vendors and manufacturers, ROST purchases later in the buying cycle than department and specialty stores, and can take advan-

tage of supply/demand imbalances. The vast majority of merchandise is acquired through opportunistic purchases of cancellations and overruns. Most orders have one delivery, and generally exclude promotional and markdown allowances and return privileges, enabling buyers to obtain significant discounts on in-season purchases.

MARKET PROFILE. Apparel generated $192.7 billion at retail in the U.S. in 2010, up 1.9% from 2009, according to The NPD Group, Inc. consumer estimated data. Sales of women's apparel accounted for 56% of all apparel sales, followed by men's at 27%, and children's at 17%. In 2010, specialty stores accounted for approximately 32% of U.S. apparel sales, followed by mass merchants, such as Target and Kmart at 20%, department stores, including Nordstrom and Macy's at 13%, and national chains like Kohl's and JCPenney at 13%. ROST participates in the off-price retail channel, which captured an estimated 9% of U.S. apparel sales in both 2009 and 2010.

## Company Financials Fiscal Year Ended Jan. 31

| Per Share Data ($) | 2011 | 2010 | 2009 | 2008 | 2007 | 2006 | 2005 | 2004 | 2003 | 2002 |
|---|---|---|---|---|---|---|---|---|---|---|
| Tangible Book Value | 11.26 | 9.39 | 7.74 | 7.23 | 6.53 | 5.80 | 5.22 | 4.99 | 4.15 | 3.45 |
| Cash Flow | 5.97 | 4.81 | 3.41 | 2.78 | 2.47 | 2.12 | 1.76 | 1.96 | 1.68 | 1.26 |
| Earnings | 4.63 | 3.54 | 2.33 | 1.90 | 1.70 | 1.36 | 1.13 | 1.47 | 1.26 | 0.96 |
| S&P Core Earnings | 4.63 | 3.54 | 2.33 | 1.90 | 1.70 | 1.30 | 1.07 | 1.41 | 1.22 | 0.92 |
| Dividends | NA | 0.44 | 0.38 | 0.24 | 0.21 | 0.17 | 0.12 | 0.10 | 0.10 | 0.09 |
| Payout Ratio | NA | 10% | 11% | 13% | 12% | 12% | 10% | 6% | 8% | 9% |
| Calendar Year | 2010 | 2009 | 2008 | 2007 | 2006 | 2005 | 2004 | 2003 | 2002 | 2001 |
| Prices:High | 66.58 | 50.50 | 41.56 | 35.17 | 31.80 | 31.37 | 32.86 | 28.08 | 23.62 | 17.07 |
| Prices:Low | 42.30 | 28.08 | 21.23 | 24.42 | 22.12 | 22.34 | 20.95 | 16.29 | 15.85 | 8.28 |
| P/E Ratio:High | 14 | 14 | 18 | 19 | 19 | 23 | 29 | 19 | 19 | 18 |
| P/E Ratio:Low | 9 | 8 | 9 | 13 | 13 | 16 | 19 | 11 | 13 | 9 |

| Income Statement Analysis (Million $) | | | | | | | | | | |
|---|---|---|---|---|---|---|---|---|---|---|
| Revenue | 7,866 | 7,184 | 6,486 | 5,975 | 5,570 | 4,944 | 4,240 | 3,921 | 3,531 | 2,987 |
| Operating Income | 1,067 | 885 | 637 | 542 | 498 | 436 | 390 | 451 | 397 | 308 |
| Depreciation | 161 | 159 | 142 | 121 | 108 | 111 | 94.6 | 76.7 | 66.2 | 49.9 |
| Interest Expense | 9.57 | 9.40 | 11.5 | 10.7 | 8.63 | Nil | 0.92 | Nil | 0.28 | 3.17 |
| Pretax Income | 897 | 719 | 495 | 425 | 398 | 328 | 279 | 375 | 330 | 255 |
| Effective Tax Rate | NA | 38.4% | 38.3% | 38.6% | 39.3% | 39.2% | 39.1% | 39.1% | 39.1% | 39.1% |
| Net Income | 555 | 443 | 305 | 261 | 242 | 200 | 170 | 228 | 201 | 155 |
| S&P Core Earnings | 555 | 443 | 305 | 261 | 242 | 190 | 160 | 218 | 193 | 149 |

| Balance Sheet & Other Financial Data (Million $) | | | | | | | | | | |
|---|---|---|---|---|---|---|---|---|---|---|
| Cash | 837 | 770 | 322 | 264 | 367 | 192 | 115 | 202 | 151 | 40.4 |
| Current Assets | 2,043 | 1,745 | 1,314 | 1,398 | 1,515 | 1,229 | 1,123 | 1,121 | 922 | 715 |
| Total Assets | 3,116 | 2,769 | 2,356 | 2,371 | 2,359 | 1,939 | 1,736 | 1,657 | 1,361 | 1,083 |
| Current Liabilities | 1,352 | 1,191 | 955 | 1,011 | 1,083 | 879 | 712 | 712 | 627 | 490 |
| Long Term Debt | 150 | 150 | 150 | 150 | 150 | Nil | 50.0 | 50.0 | 25.0 | Nil |
| Common Equity | 1,333 | 1,157 | 996 | 971 | 910 | 836 | 766 | 755 | 643 | 544 |
| Total Capital | 1,483 | 1,307 | 1,244 | 1,200 | 1,146 | 937 | 908 | 885 | 668 | 544 |
| Capital Expenditures | 199 | 158 | 224 | 236 | 137 | 176 | 150 | 147 | 133 | 86.0 |
| Cash Flow | 715 | 602 | 447 | 382 | 350 | 310 | 264 | 305 | 267 | 205 |
| Current Ratio | 1.5 | 1.5 | 1.4 | 1.4 | 1.4 | 1.4 | 1.6 | 1.6 | 1.5 | 1.5 |
| % Long Term Debt of Capitalization | 10.1 | 11.5 | 12.1 | 12.5 | 13.1 | Nil | 5.5 | 5.6 | 3.7 | Nil |
| % Net Income of Revenue | 7.1 | 6.2 | 4.7 | 4.4 | 4.3 | 4.0 | 4.0 | 5.8 | 5.7 | 5.2 |
| % Return on Assets | 18.9 | 17.3 | 12.9 | 11.0 | 11.2 | 10.8 | 9.9 | 15.0 | 16.5 | 15.1 |
| % Return on Equity | 44.6 | 41.1 | 31.1 | 27.8 | 27.7 | 24.9 | 22.4 | 32.6 | 33.9 | 30.6 |

Data as orig reptd.; bef. results of disc opers/spec. items. Per share data adj. for stk. divs.; EPS diluted. E-Estimated. NA-Not Available. NM-Not Meaningful. NR-Not Ranked. UR-Under Review.

Office: 4440 Rosewood Drive, Pleasanton, CA 94588-3050.
Telephone: 925-965-4400.
Email: investor.relations@ros.com
Website: http://www.rossstores.com

Chrmn: N.A. Ferber
Vice Chrmn & CEO: M. Balmuth
COO & Co-Pres: M.B. O'Sullivan
SVP, CFO & Chief Acctg Officer: J.G. Call

SVP, Secy & General Counsel: M. LeHocky
Investor Contact: B. Chaville (925-965-4289)
Board Members: M. Balmuth, K. Bjorklund, M. J. Bush, N. A. Ferber, S. D. Garrett, G. Orban, G. L. Quesnel, D. H. Seiler

Founded: 1957
Domicile: Delaware
Employees: 49,500

# Rowan Companies Inc.

**STANDARD &POOR'S**

| S&P Recommendation | BUY ★★★★☆ | Price $31.29 (as of Nov 25, 2011) | 12-Mo. Target Price $40.00 | Investment Style Large-Cap Value |
| --- | --- | --- | --- | --- |

**GICS Sector** Energy
**Sub-Industry** Oil & Gas Drilling

**Summary** This company performs contract oil and natural gas drilling, and builds heavy equipment and offshore drilling rigs.

## Key Stock Statistics (Source S&P, Vickers, company reports)

| | | | | | | | |
| --- | --- | --- | --- | --- | --- | --- | --- |
| 52-Wk Range | $44.83–28.13 | S&P Oper. EPS 2011E | 1.64 | Market Capitalization(B) | $3.911 | Beta | 1.65 |
| Trailing 12-Month EPS | $5.91 | S&P Oper. EPS 2012E | 3.48 | Yield (%) | Nil | S&P 3-Yr. Proj. EPS CAGR(%) | 2 |
| Trailing 12-Month P/E | 5.3 | P/E on S&P Oper. EPS 2011E | 19.1 | Dividend Rate/Share | Nil | S&P Credit Rating | BBB- |
| $10K Invested 5 Yrs Ago | $9,218 | Common Shares Outstg. (M) | 125.0 | Institutional Ownership (%) | 81 | | |

## Price Performance

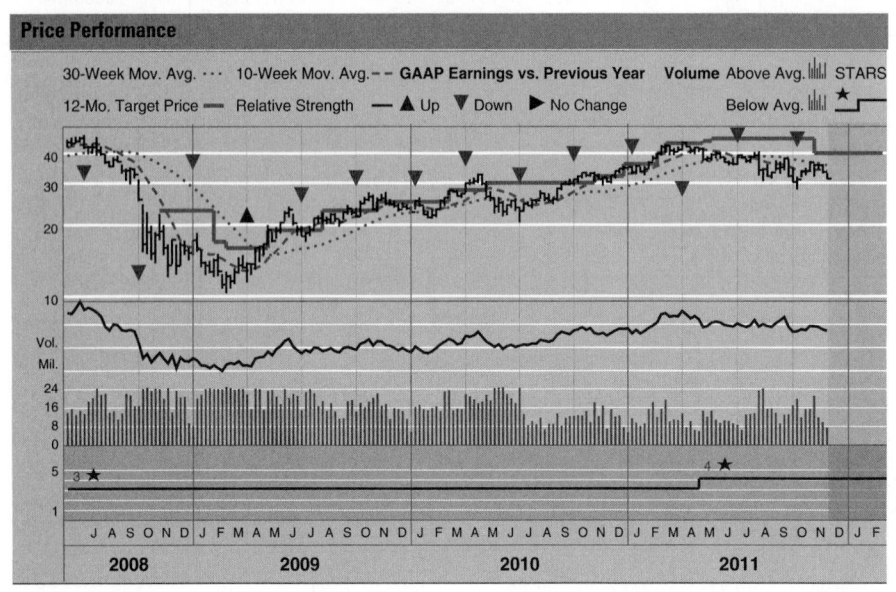

30-Week Mov. Avg. · · · 10-Week Mov. Avg. - - GAAP Earnings vs. Previous Year Volume Above Avg. STARS
12-Mo. Target Price — Relative Strength — ▲ Up ▼ Down ▶ No Change Below Avg. ★

Options: ASE, CBOE, P

## Qualitative Risk Assessment

| LOW | MEDIUM | HIGH |
| --- | --- | --- |

Our risk assessment reflects RDC's exposure to volatile crude oil and natural gas prices and capital spending decisions made by its oil and gas producing customers. Offsetting these risks is the company's relatively higher specification jackup rig fleet than peers.

## Quantitative Evaluations

**S&P Quality Ranking**  B-

| D | C | B- | B | B+ | A- | A | A+ |
| --- | --- | --- | --- | --- | --- | --- | --- |

**Relative Strength Rank**  MODERATE

39

LOWEST = 1          HIGHEST = 99

## Revenue/Earnings Data

**Revenue (Million $)**

| | 1Q | 2Q | 3Q | 4Q | Year |
| --- | --- | --- | --- | --- | --- |
| 2011 | 364.3 | 223.5 | 234.7 | -- | -- |
| 2010 | 432.4 | 490.1 | 437.9 | 458.8 | 1,819 |
| 2009 | 494.8 | 482.2 | 393.4 | 399.8 | 1,770 |
| 2008 | 485.5 | 587.1 | 527.1 | 613.0 | 2,213 |
| 2007 | 465.3 | 507.0 | 502.2 | 623.6 | 2,095 |
| 2006 | 299.8 | 382.9 | 417.1 | 411.0 | 1,511 |

**Earnings Per Share ($)**

| | 1Q | 2Q | 3Q | 4Q | Year |
| --- | --- | --- | --- | --- | --- |
| 2011 | 0.25 | 0.35 | 0.25 | E0.79 | E1.64 |
| 2010 | 0.56 | 0.79 | 0.57 | 0.45 | 2.36 |
| 2009 | 1.16 | 0.85 | 0.69 | 0.53 | 3.24 |
| 2008 | 0.88 | 1.06 | 1.00 | 0.81 | 3.77 |
| 2007 | 0.77 | 1.14 | 1.16 | 1.23 | 4.31 |
| 2006 | 0.53 | 0.98 | 0.77 | 0.56 | 2.84 |

Fiscal year ended Dec. 31. Next earnings report expected: Late February. EPS Estimates based on S&P Operating Earnings; historical GAAP earnings are as reported.

## Dividend Data

Quarterly dividends were eliminated in January 2009.

## Highlights

➤ The 12-month target price for RDC has recently been changed to $40.00 from $46.00. The Highlights section of this Stock Report will be updated accordingly.

## Investment Rationale/Risk

➤ The Investment Rationale/Risk section of this Stock Report will be updated shortly. For the latest News story on RDC from MarketScope, see below.

➤ 11/02/11 03:24 pm ET ... S&P MAINTAINS BUY OPINION ON SHARES OF ROWAN COMPANIES (RDC 33.18****): RDC posts Q3 EPS of $0.25, vs. $0.57, $0.21 below our estimate. Results were hurt by a high level of rig mobilizations during Q3, most of which are related to shipyard prep work in advance of new contracts that begin in late '11 or early '12. Consequently, we view the miss as largely a Q3 anomaly (with some spillover to Q4) but unlikely to continue into '12. Pending additions to the deepwater fleet look promising as well. We cut our '11 EPS forecast $0.33 to $1.64 and '12's by $0.44 to $3.48. On our NAV model and relative metrics, we cut our 12-month target price by $6 to $40. /Stewart Glickman, CFA

# Rowan Companies Inc.

**STANDARD &POOR'S**

## Business Summary September 12, 2011

CORPORATE OVERVIEW. Rowan Companies is a major provider of international and domestic contract drilling services, and also has manufacturing operations. As of February 2011, RDC operated 28 jackup rigs (comprised of 25 cantilever jackups and three conventional jackups), and a fleet of 30 land rigs. The company is also in the process of constructing three more newbuild jackup rigs, the last of which is due for delivery in late 2011. Of the 28 active jackups in the fleet, 10 were in the Gulf of Mexico (GOM), 10 were in the Middle East and five were in the North Sea, with one each in Mexico, Egypt and Trinidad. RDC's jackup rigs perform both exploratory and development drilling and, in certain areas, well workover operations. Its larger jackups can drill to depths of 20,000 ft. to 30,000 ft. in maximum water depths of 250 ft. to 490 ft.

RDC conducts business via two main operations. In 2010, Drilling Services operations, which includes the offshore rigs and land rigs, contributed $1.21 billion in revenues (flat with 2009) and accounted for 66% of RDC's total 2010 revenues (84% offshore, 16% land). Manufacturing operations via its LeTourneau Technologies Inc. (LTI) subsidiary contributed $610 million in net revenues in 2009 (up 10% from 2009), accounting for the remaining 34% of total revenues. Manufacturing operations are further subdivided into two business segments. The Drilling Products and Services segment (DPS) provides equipment, parts and services for the drilling industry, including jack-up rigs, rig kits and component packages. DPS generated $310 million in revenues to external customers in 2009 (after eliminations), down 16% from 2009. The Mining, Forestry and Steel Products segment (MFS), which produces large-wheeled mining and timber equipment and related parts and carbon and alloy steel, generated $300 million in revenues from external customers in 2010, up 61% from 2009.

IMPACT OF MAJOR DEVELOPMENTS. In May 2011, RDC reached an agreement to sell its LTI subsidiary to Joy Global Inc. (JOYG 88, Buy) for $1.1 billion in cash. We estimate that the deal value represents approximately a 10X multiple of LTI's 2010 EBITDA adjusted for impairment charges, which we think is a fairly attractive price for RDC. Subject to regulatory approval, we think the deal, if completed, renders RDC as an attractive takeover target with a much greater focus on premium offshore assets. As a stand-alone business, we expect RDC to use proceeds from the deal, if completed, to construct ultradeepwater newbuild assets to complement its high-specification shallow water jackup units. RDC said in May that it is in discussions with Korean shipyards to potentially construct one or two newbuild units capable of deepwater drilling, although RDC also said it would ultimately want greater deepwater scale than a mere two units. RDC had stated previously that its fleet of 30 onshore land rigs are candidates for separation, either via sale or spinoff.

## Company Financials Fiscal Year Ended Dec. 31

| Per Share Data ($) | 2010 | 2009 | 2008 | 2007 | 2006 | 2005 | 2004 | 2003 | 2002 | 2001 |
|---|---|---|---|---|---|---|---|---|---|---|
| Tangible Book Value | 29.71 | 27.32 | 23.52 | 20.99 | 16.97 | 14.75 | 12.97 | 11.95 | 12.09 | 11.84 |
| Cash Flow | 3.93 | 4.74 | 5.02 | 5.37 | 3.64 | 2.71 | 1.14 | 0.84 | 1.72 | 1.52 |
| Earnings | 2.36 | 3.24 | 3.77 | 4.31 | 2.84 | 1.97 | 0.25 | -0.08 | 0.90 | 0.80 |
| S&P Core Earnings | 2.43 | 3.30 | 3.22 | 4.10 | 2.76 | 1.63 | 0.28 | -0.05 | -0.31 | 0.65 |
| Dividends | Nil | Nil | 0.40 | 0.40 | 0.30 | Nil | Nil | Nil | Nil | Nil |
| Payout Ratio | Nil | Nil | 11% | 9% | 11% | Nil | Nil | Nil | Nil | Nil |
| Prices:High | 35.39 | 27.54 | 47.94 | 46.16 | 48.15 | 39.50 | 27.26 | 26.72 | 27.03 | 33.89 |
| Prices:Low | 20.44 | 10.28 | 12.00 | 29.48 | 29.03 | 24.53 | 20.44 | 17.70 | 16.04 | 11.10 |
| P/E Ratio:High | 15 | 8 | 13 | 11 | 17 | 20 | NM | NM | 30 | 42 |
| P/E Ratio:Low | 9 | 3 | 3 | 7 | 10 | 12 | NM | NM | 18 | 14 |

| Income Statement Analysis (Million $) | 2010 | 2009 | 2008 | 2007 | 2006 | 2005 | 2004 | 2003 | 2002 | 2001 |
|---|---|---|---|---|---|---|---|---|---|---|
| Revenue | 1,819 | 1,770 | 2,213 | 2,095 | 1,511 | 1,069 | 709 | 679 | 617 | 731 |
| Operating Income | NA | NA | 843 | 812 | 555 | 355 | 152 | 89.0 | 65.1 | 193 |
| Depreciation, Depletion and Amortization | 187 | 171 | 141 | 119 | 90.0 | 81.3 | 95.7 | 86.9 | 78.1 | 68.5 |
| Interest Expense | 24.9 | 8.03 | 4.00 | 25.9 | 20.6 | 22.0 | 18.7 | 15.9 | 15.9 | 13.1 |
| Pretax Income | 379 | 501 | 654 | 739 | 493 | 345 | 42.8 | -12.0 | 133 | 120 |
| Effective Tax Rate | NA | 26.7% | 34.6% | 34.5% | 35.8% | 36.9% | 38.4% | NM | 35.0% | 35.9% |
| Net Income | 280 | 368 | 428 | 484 | 317 | 218 | 26.4 | -7.77 | 86.3 | 77.0 |
| S&P Core Earnings | 289 | 375 | 366 | 460 | 308 | 181 | 28.9 | -4.74 | -30.2 | 62.8 |

| Balance Sheet & Other Financial Data (Million $) | 2010 | 2009 | 2008 | 2007 | 2006 | 2005 | 2004 | 2003 | 2002 | 2001 |
|---|---|---|---|---|---|---|---|---|---|---|
| Cash | 437 | 640 | 222 | 284 | 258 | 676 | 466 | 58.2 | 179 | 237 |
| Current Assets | 1,325 | 1,550 | 1,369 | 1,303 | 1,103 | 1,208 | 815 | 444 | 470 | 507 |
| Total Assets | 6,217 | 5,211 | 4,549 | 3,875 | 3,435 | 2,975 | 2,492 | 2,191 | 2,055 | 1,939 |
| Current Liabilities | 529 | 568 | 745 | 496 | 517 | 341 | 235 | 150 | 116 | 201 |
| Long Term Debt | 1,134 | 788 | 356 | 420 | 485 | 550 | 574 | 569 | 513 | 438 |
| Common Equity | 3,752 | 3,110 | 2,660 | 2,348 | 1,874 | 1,620 | 1,409 | 1,137 | 1,132 | 1,108 |
| Total Capital | 4,938 | 3,963 | 3,442 | 3,182 | 2,707 | 2,485 | 2,147 | 1,924 | 1,811 | 1,674 |
| Capital Expenditures | 491 | 566 | 829 | 463 | 479 | 200 | 137 | 250 | 243 | 305 |
| Cash Flow | 467 | 539 | 569 | 603 | 407 | 299 | 122 | 79.1 | 164 | 145 |
| Current Ratio | 2.5 | 2.7 | 1.8 | 2.6 | 2.1 | 3.5 | 3.5 | 3.0 | 4.1 | 2.5 |
| % Long Term Debt of Capitalization | 23.0 | 19.9 | 10.3 | 13.2 | 17.9 | 22.1 | 26.8 | 29.6 | 28.3 | 26.2 |
| % Return on Assets | 4.9 | 7.5 | 10.2 | 13.2 | 9.9 | 8.0 | 1.1 | NM | 4.3 | 4.3 |
| % Return on Equity | 8.2 | 12.7 | 17.1 | 22.9 | 18.1 | 14.4 | 2.1 | NM | 7.7 | 7.1 |

Data as orig reptd.; bef. results of disc opers/spec. items. Per share data adj. for stk. divs.; EPS diluted. E-Estimated. NA-Not Available. NM-Not Meaningful. NR-Not Ranked. UR-Under Review.

**Office:** 2800 Post Oak Blvd Ste 5450, Houston, TX 77056-6189.
**Telephone:** 713-621-7800.
**Email:** ir@rowancompanies.com
**Website:** http://www.rowancompanies.com

**Chrmn:** H.E. Lentz, Jr.
**Pres & CEO:** W.M. Ralls
**COO:** T.P. Burke
**SVP, Chief Admin Officer & Secy:** M.M. Trent

**CFO:** W.H. Wells
**Investor Contact:** S.M. McLeod (713-960-7517)
**Board Members:** W. T. Fox, III, G. Hearne, T. R. Hix, R. E. Kramek, F. R. Lausen, H. E. Lentz, Jr., C. B. Moynihan, S. P. Nimocks, P. D. Peacock, J. J. Quicke, W. M. Ralls

**Founded:** 1923
**Domicile:** Delaware
**Employees:** 5,217

# Ryder System Inc

STANDARD &POOR'S

| | | | |
|---|---|---|---|
| **S&P Recommendation** BUY ★★★★☆ | **Price** $46.74 (as of Nov 25, 2011) | **12-Mo. Target Price** $69.00 | **Investment Style** Large-Cap Value |

**GICS Sector** Industrials
**Sub-Industry** Trucking

**Summary** This company provides truck leasing and rental, logistics and supply chain management solutions.

## Key Stock Statistics (Source S&P, Vickers, company reports)

| | | | | | | | |
|---|---|---|---|---|---|---|---|
| 52-Wk Range | $60.38–34.28 | S&P Oper. EPS 2011**E** | 3.47 | Market Capitalization(B) | $2.390 | Beta | 1.62 |
| Trailing 12-Month EPS | $3.07 | S&P Oper. EPS 2012**E** | 3.92 | Yield (%) | 2.48 | S&P 3-Yr. Proj. EPS CAGR(%) | 24 |
| Trailing 12-Month P/E | 15.2 | P/E on S&P Oper. EPS 2011**E** | 13.5 | Dividend Rate/Share | $1.16 | S&P Credit Rating | BBB+ |
| $10K Invested 5 Yrs Ago | $9,694 | Common Shares Outstg. (M) | 51.1 | Institutional Ownership (%) | 96 | | |

## Price Performance

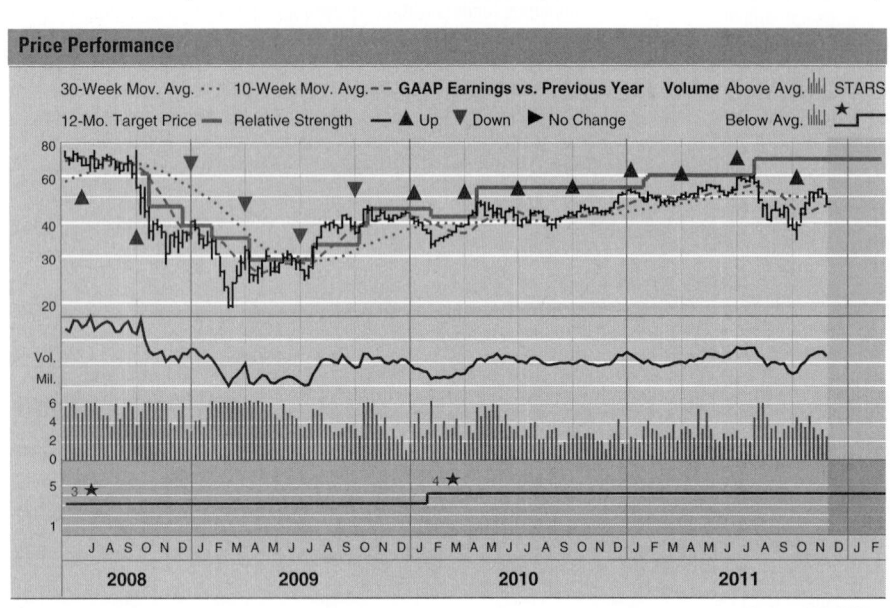

30-Week Mov. Avg. · · · 10-Week Mov. Avg. – – **GAAP Earnings vs. Previous Year** Volume Above Avg. STARS
12-Mo. Target Price — Relative Strength — ▲ Up ▼ Down ► No Change Below Avg. ★

Options: ASE, CBOE, P

Analysis prepared by Equity Analyst **Kevin Kirkeby** on Nov 08, 2011, when the stock traded at **$51.06**.

## Highlights

➤ Following an expected 16% increase during 2011, we forecast operating revenue, excluding fuel and subcontracted transportation, will improve another 6% in 2012. Commercial rentals have been growing strongly during 2011, due in part to R's customers using rental vehicles to cover capacity needs. Going into 2012, we expect more of these customers to commit to new lease contracts and take on additional vehicles. We also see momentum improving in R's supply chain and dedicated units as those customers become more comfortable with the current operating environment. We estimate that acquisitions will contribute about 10 percentage points to revenue growth in 2011.

➤ We see margins widening during 2012 due to a general improvement in pricing and revenue mix. However, we think wages will rise as business recovers and R looks to add drivers. Depreciation expense will also start to rise, in our view, on account of equipment purchases. Still, with the age of its overall tractor fleet creeping higher, maintenance expenses will remain elevated through 2012.

➤ Our EPS forecast of $3.47 for 2011 excludes $0.13 in one-time charges.

## Investment Rationale/Risk

➤ We see R's rental operations as a key near-term capacity supplier to companies reluctant to commit to new trucks due to weak economic conditions. We believe R's other segments will show sequential gains over the coming year as the economy improves. We note that leasing operations are contract-based and generally slower to respond to changes in the economy. Balancing these factors with current market uncertainties, we think valuations modestly above the 10-year average are justified.

➤ Risks to our recommendation and target price include renewed weakness in the economy and a slowing in rental activity; lower average rates on lease renewals; higher interest rates, to which R is exposed in light of its financial leverage; and, difficulties integrating recent acquisitions.

➤ Our DCF model assumes an 11.8% cost of equity and terminal growth of 3.5%, and calculates intrinsic value of $68. Using a 0.81X multiple, which is one standard deviation above the historical average, in our price-to-invested capital model, yields a $70 value. Blending these two metrics, we arrive at our 12-month target price of $69.

## Qualitative Risk Assessment

| LOW | MEDIUM | HIGH |
|---|---|---|

Our risk assessment reflects our view of the company's financial leverage, exposure to low-margin businesses, and heavy capital spending needs to maintain its rental fleet, offset by its strong market position in truck leasing and what we see as steady cash flow generated by multi-year lease contracts.

## Quantitative Evaluations

**S&P Quality Ranking** B+

| D | C | B- | B | B+ | A- | A | A+ |
|---|---|---|---|---|---|---|---|

**Relative Strength Rank** MODERATE

68

LOWEST = 1    HIGHEST = 99

## Revenue/Earnings Data

**Revenue (Million $)**

| | 1Q | 2Q | 3Q | 4Q | Year |
|---|---|---|---|---|---|
| 2011 | 1,425 | 1,513 | 1,571 | -- | -- |
| 2010 | 1,220 | 1,286 | 1,317 | 1,313 | 5,136 |
| 2009 | 1,174 | 1,212 | 1,254 | 1,247 | 4,887 |
| 2008 | 1,544 | 1,660 | 1,626 | 1,374 | 6,204 |
| 2007 | 1,594 | 1,658 | 1,648 | 1,666 | 6,566 |
| 2006 | 1,496 | 1,596 | 1,621 | 1,594 | 6,307 |

**Earnings Per Share ($)**

| | | | | | |
|---|---|---|---|---|---|
| 2011 | 0.50 | 0.79 | 1.10 | E0.95 | E3.47 |
| 2010 | 0.24 | 0.58 | 0.76 | 0.80 | 2.37 |
| 2009 | 0.20 | 0.48 | 0.51 | 0.43 | 1.62 |
| 2008 | 0.96 | 1.10 | 1.25 | 0.19 | 3.52 |
| 2007 | 0.84 | 1.07 | 1.11 | 1.24 | 4.24 |
| 2006 | 0.77 | 1.13 | 1.06 | 1.08 | 4.04 |

Fiscal year ended Dec. 31. Next earnings report expected: Early February. EPS Estimates based on S&P Operating Earnings; historical GAAP earnings are as reported.

## Dividend Data (Dates: mm/dd Payment Date: mm/dd/yy)

| Amount ($) | Date Decl. | Ex-Div. Date | Stk. of Record | Payment Date |
|---|---|---|---|---|
| 0.270 | 02/11 | 02/17 | 02/22 | 03/18/11 |
| 0.270 | 05/06 | 05/19 | 05/23 | 06/17/11 |
| 0.290 | 07/20 | 08/18 | 08/22 | 09/16/11 |
| 0.290 | 10/13 | 11/17 | 11/21 | 12/16/11 |

Dividends have been paid since 1976. Source: Company reports.

---

**Please read the Required Disclosures and Analyst Certification on the last page of this report.**

The McGraw-Hill Companies

# Ryder System Inc

STANDARD
&POOR'S

## Business Summary November 08, 2011

CORPORATE OVERVIEW. Ryder System is primarily a provider of transportation services and equipment to third parties. In 2009, the company generated over 93% of revenues in the United States and Canada, with the remainder spread across Europe, Asia and Mexico. The company serves a broad array of industries, with clients in the automotive, electronics, paper and paper products, food and beverage and retailing industries, among others. For reporting purposes, operations are divided into three segments: Fleet Management Solutions (FMS), Supply Chain Solutions (SCS), and Dedicated Contract Carriage (DCC).

FMS (66% of revenues and 69% of operating profits before eliminations in 2010) provides full-service truck leasing to customers worldwide. Under a typical full-service lease, R provides customers with vehicles, maintenance, supplies and related equipment necessary for operation, while customers furnish and supervise their own drivers, as well as dispatch and exercise control over the vehicles. R leased approximately 111,100 vehicles under full-service leases at December 31, 2010, which is down from 115,100 at the end of 2009. FMS also provides short-term truck rental to commercial customers that need to supplement their fleets during peak periods. About 14% of FMS revenue in

2010 was generated through commercial rentals. At December 31, 2010, the commercial rental fleet had about 29,700 units, up from 27,400 units in 2009, but still down from 38,400 at the end of 2005.

SCS (24%, 19%) provides logistics support and transportation along the entire supply chain for its customers. This includes managing inbound raw materials all the way through to distribution of finished goods. Services include combinations of logistics systems and information technology design, the provision of vehicles and equipment (including maintenance and drivers), warehouse and transportation management, vehicle dispatch, and just-in-time delivery. The company said that its business with auto manufacturers, as well as parts suppliers, represented about 51% of SCS operating revenue in 2010. We believe General Motors is one of the unit's largest customers (13% of SCS revenues in 2009).

## Company Financials  Fiscal Year Ended Dec. 31

| Per Share Data ($) | 2010 | 2009 | 2008 | 2007 | 2006 | 2005 | 2004 | 2003 | 2002 | 2001 |
|---|---|---|---|---|---|---|---|---|---|---|
| Tangible Book Value | 19.08 | 21.93 | 19.95 | 29.32 | 25.48 | 21.81 | 20.65 | 18.09 | 14.97 | 17.51 |
| Cash Flow | 18.02 | 16.62 | 18.38 | 17.89 | 10.57 | 15.65 | 14.03 | 11.90 | 10.65 | 9.30 |
| Earnings | 2.37 | 1.62 | 3.52 | 4.24 | 4.04 | 3.53 | 3.28 | 2.12 | 1.80 | 0.31 |
| S&P Core Earnings | 2.28 | 1.93 | 1.93 | 3.43 | 3.72 | 3.09 | 2.80 | 2.26 | 0.84 | -0.76 |
| Dividends | 1.04 | 0.96 | 0.92 | 0.84 | 0.72 | 0.64 | 0.60 | 0.60 | 0.60 | 0.60 |
| Payout Ratio | 44% | 59% | 26% | 20% | 18% | 18% | 18% | 28% | 33% | 194% |
| Prices:High | 52.80 | 46.58 | 76.64 | 57.70 | 59.93 | 47.82 | 55.55 | 34.65 | 31.09 | 23.19 |
| Prices:Low | 31.86 | 19.00 | 27.71 | 38.95 | 39.61 | 32.00 | 33.61 | 20.00 | 21.05 | 16.06 |
| P/E Ratio:High | 22 | 29 | 22 | 14 | 15 | 14 | 17 | 16 | 17 | 75 |
| P/E Ratio:Low | 13 | 12 | 8 | 9 | 10 | 9 | 10 | 9 | 12 | 52 |

| Income Statement Analysis (Million $) | 2010 | 2009 | 2008 | 2007 | 2006 | 2005 | 2004 | 2003 | 2002 | 2001 |
|---|---|---|---|---|---|---|---|---|---|---|
| Revenue | 5,136 | 4,887 | 6,204 | 6,566 | 6,307 | 5,741 | 5,150 | 4,802 | 4,776 | 5,006 |
| Operating Income | 1,129 | 1,111 | 1,384 | 1,336 | 1,218 | 1,165 | 1,076 | 905 | 854 | 798 |
| Depreciation | 811 | 826 | 844 | 817 | 743 | 740 | 706 | 625 | 552 | 545 |
| Interest Expense | 130 | 144 | 157 | 160 | 141 | 120 | 100 | 96.2 | 91.7 | 119 |
| Pretax Income | 186 | 144 | 350 | 405 | 786 | 357 | 331 | 212 | 176 | 30.7 |
| Effective Tax Rate | NA | 37.3% | 42.9% | 37.4% | 18.3% | 36.3% | 34.9% | 36.2% | 36.0% | 39.2% |
| Net Income | 125 | 90.2 | 200 | 254 | 642 | 228 | 216 | 136 | 113 | 18.7 |
| S&P Core Earnings | 118 | 107 | 110 | 206 | 229 | 200 | 184 | 145 | 53.1 | -46.3 |

| Balance Sheet & Other Financial Data (Million $) | 2010 | 2009 | 2008 | 2007 | 2006 | 2005 | 2004 | 2003 | 2002 | 2001 |
|---|---|---|---|---|---|---|---|---|---|---|
| Cash | 213 | 98.5 | 120 | 200 | 129 | 129 | 101 | 141 | 104 | 118 |
| Current Assets | 1,023 | 880 | 951 | 1,222 | 1,262 | 1,164 | 1,228 | 1,107 | 1,024 | 982 |
| Total Assets | 6,652 | 6,260 | 6,690 | 6,855 | 6,829 | 6,033 | 5,638 | 5,279 | 4,767 | 4,924 |
| Current Liabilities | 1,132 | 850 | 1,111 | 1,019 | 1,268 | 1,253 | 1,455 | 1,074 | 862 | 1,014 |
| Long Term Debt | 2,327 | 2,265 | 2,479 | 2,553 | 2,484 | 1,916 | 1,394 | 1,449 | 1,389 | 1,392 |
| Common Equity | 1,404 | 1,427 | 1,345 | 1,888 | 1,721 | 1,527 | 1,510 | 1,344 | 1,108 | 1,231 |
| Total Capital | 3,731 | 3,692 | 4,741 | 5,425 | 5,112 | 4,293 | 3,775 | 3,688 | 3,431 | 3,625 |
| Capital Expenditures | 1,070 | 652 | 1,234 | 1,317 | 1,695 | 1,399 | 1,092 | 725 | 600 | 657 |
| Cash Flow | 935 | 916 | 1,044 | 1,071 | 642 | 968 | 922 | 760 | 665 | 564 |
| Current Ratio | 0.9 | 1.0 | 0.9 | 1.2 | 1.0 | 0.9 | 0.8 | 1.0 | 1.2 | 1.0 |
| % Long Term Debt of Capitalization | 62.4 | 61.4 | 52.3 | 47.1 | 48.6 | 44.6 | 36.9 | 39.3 | 40.5 | 38.4 |
| % Net Income of Revenue | 2.4 | 1.9 | 3.2 | 3.9 | 10.2 | 4.0 | 4.2 | 2.8 | 2.4 | 0.4 |
| % Return on Assets | 1.9 | 1.4 | 3.0 | 3.7 | 10.0 | 3.9 | 3.9 | 2.7 | 2.3 | 0.4 |
| % Return on Equity | 8.8 | 6.5 | 12.4 | 14.1 | 39.5 | 15.0 | 15.1 | 11.1 | 9.6 | 1.5 |

Data as orig reptd.; bef. results of disc opers/spec. items. Per share data adj. for stk. divs.; EPS diluted. E-Estimated. NA-Not Available. NM-Not Meaningful. NR-Not Ranked. UR-Under Review.

**Office:** 11690 NW 105th Street, Miami, FL 33178.
**Telephone:** 305-500-3726.
**Email:** ryderforinvestor@ryder.com
**Website:** http://www.ryder.com

**Chrmn & CEO:** G.T. Swienton
**COO:** D.C. Cooke
**EVP & Chief Admin Officer:** G.F. Greene
**CFO:** A.A. Garcia

**Chief Acctg Officer & Cntlr:** C. Gallo-Aquino
**Investor Contact:** B. Brunn (305-500-4053)
**Board Members:** J. S. Beard, J. M. Berra, R. J. Eck, L. P. Hassey, L. M. Martin, L. P. Nieto, Jr., E. A. Renna, A. J. Smith, E. F. Smith, G. T. Swienton, H. E. Tookes, II

**Founded:** 1933
**Domicile:** Florida
**Employees:** 25,900

# Safeway Inc

**STANDARD &POOR'S**

| S&P Recommendation | HOLD ★★★☆☆ | Price | 12-Mo. Target Price | Investment Style |
|---|---|---|---|---|
| | | $18.83 (as of Nov 25, 2011) | $20.00 | Large-Cap Blend |

**GICS Sector** Consumer Staples
**Sub-Industry** Food Retail

**Summary** This major food and drug retailer operates about 1,700 stores in the U.S. and Canada.

## Key Stock Statistics (Source S&P, Vickers, company reports)

| | | | | | |
|---|---|---|---|---|---|
| 52-Wk Range | $25.43– 15.93 | S&P Oper. EPS 2011E | 1.76 | Market Capitalization(B) | $6.383 | Beta | 0.74 |
| Trailing 12-Month EPS | $1.48 | S&P Oper. EPS 2012E | 1.85 | Yield (%) | 3.08 | S&P 3-Yr. Proj. EPS CAGR(%) | 7 |
| Trailing 12-Month P/E | 12.7 | P/E on S&P Oper. EPS 2011E | 10.7 | Dividend Rate/Share | $0.58 | S&P Credit Rating | BBB |
| $10K Invested 5 Yrs Ago | $6,730 | Common Shares Outstg. (M) | 339.0 | Institutional Ownership (%) | NM | | |

## Price Performance

30-Week Mov. Avg. ···  10-Week Mov. Avg. - - GAAP Earnings vs. Previous Year   Volume Above Avg. STARS
12-Mo. Target Price —  Relative Strength  — ▲ Up ▼ Down ▶ No Change   Below Avg.

Options: ASE, CBOE, P

Analysis prepared by Equity Analyst **Joseph Agnese** on Oct 21, 2011, when the stock traded at **$18.18**.

## Highlights

➤ We expect sales to increase 2.8% in 2012, to $44.8 billion, from our estimate of $43.6 billion in 2011, as food price inflation moderates in 2012 to about 3% following inflation at an estimated 4% in 2011, and gasoline sales prices stabilize, partially offset by lower unit volumes as consumers cut back on purchases in a weak macroeconomic environment. We project that square footage will rise about 1%, reflecting new store openings and remodels, partially offset by store closings.

➤ We project that gross margins will narrow slightly in 2011 and 2012, as the company delays the pass- through of rising food prices in an effort to maintain market share in a competitive environment, and despite benefits from improved shrinkage control and a favorable shift in product mix with increased sales of wider-margin private label goods. We look for operating margins to remain flat in 2012 as an improvement in sales leverage offsets increased labor costs.

➤ Interest expense will likely be lower on a reduction in interest rates. We project 2012 EPS of $1.85, up 5.1% from our estimate of $1.76 in 2011.

## Investment Rationale/Risk

➤ Despite the implementation of a new pricing strategy completed in mid-2010, we believe margins will be pressured in the near term as intense pricing competition restricts the company's ability to pass along higher raw material costs to economically stressed consumers, particularly in the second half of 2011 and early 2012. We see additional pressure as an adverse generic drug market adds to margin strains in 2011.

➤ Risks to our recommendation and target price include a more competitive environment than we anticipate, and a longer than expected lack of pricing power due to rising food price inflation.

➤ Due to our expectation of increased margin pressures stemming from rising food cost inflation and the high risks we see from intense competition, we believe the shares should trade near the low end of their historical P/E trading range of 9.7X-25.1X. We apply a P/E multiple of 10.7X, in line with SWY's three-year average discount of 6% to the S&P 500 forward P/E multiple, to our 2012 EPS estimate of $1.85, resulting in our 12-month target price of $20.

## Qualitative Risk Assessment

| LOW | MEDIUM | HIGH |
|---|---|---|

Our risk assessment reflects our view of an improved shopping experience associated with the company's Lifestyle store remodelings. This is offset by a continued intense competitive environment as high unemployment and reduced consumer spending results in increased pricing pressure and trading down by consumers.

## Quantitative Evaluations

**S&P Quality Ranking** B

| D | C | B- | B | B+ | A- | A | A+ |
|---|---|---|---|---|---|---|---|

**Relative Strength Rank** STRONG

76

LOWEST = 1    HIGHEST = 99

## Revenue/Earnings Data

**Revenue (Million $)**

| | 1Q | 2Q | 3Q | 4Q | Year |
|---|---|---|---|---|---|
| 2011 | 9,772 | 10,196 | 10,064 | -- | -- |
| 2010 | 9,327 | 9,520 | 9,400 | 12,804 | 41,050 |
| 2009 | 9,236 | 9,462 | 9,458 | 12,694 | 40,851 |
| 2008 | 9,999 | 10,120 | 10,169 | 13,816 | 44,104 |
| 2007 | 9,322 | 9,823 | 9,785 | 13,356 | 42,286 |
| 2006 | 8,895 | 9,367 | 9,420 | 12,504 | 40,185 |

**Earnings Per Share ($)**

| | | | | | |
|---|---|---|---|---|---|
| 2011 | 0.07 | 0.41 | 0.38 | E0.70 | E1.76 |
| 2010 | 0.25 | 0.37 | 0.33 | 0.62 | 1.55 |
| 2009 | 0.34 | 0.57 | 0.31 | -4.06 | -2.66 |
| 2008 | 0.44 | 0.53 | 0.46 | 0.79 | 2.21 |
| 2007 | 0.39 | 0.49 | 0.44 | 0.68 | 1.99 |
| 2006 | 0.32 | 0.55 | 0.39 | 0.69 | 1.94 |

Fiscal year ended Dec. 31. Next earnings report expected: Late February. EPS Estimates based on S&P Operating Earnings; historical GAAP earnings are as reported.

## Dividend Data (Dates: mm/dd Payment Date: mm/dd/yy)

| Amount ($) | Date Decl. | Ex-Div. Date | Stk. of Record | Payment Date |
|---|---|---|---|---|
| 0.120 | 12/08 | 12/21 | 12/23 | 01/13/11 |
| 0.120 | 03/16 | 03/22 | 03/24 | 04/14/11 |
| 0.145 | 05/19 | 06/21 | 06/23 | 07/14/11 |
| 0.145 | 08/25 | 09/20 | 09/22 | 10/13/11 |

Dividends have been paid since 2005. Source: Company reports.

**Please read the Required Disclosures and Analyst Certification on the last page of this report.**

The McGraw-Hill Companies

# Safeway Inc

**STANDARD &POOR'S**

## Business Summary October 21, 2011

CORPORATE OVERVIEW. Safeway is one of the largest food and drug retailers in North America, operating about 1,700 stores principally in California, Oregon, Washington, Alaska, Colorado, Arizona, Texas, the Chicago metropolitan area, and the Mid-Atlantic region in the U.S., and in British Columbia, Alberta, Manitoba and Saskatchewan in Canada. To support its store network, SWY has a network of distribution, manufacturing and food processing facilities. The company seeks to provide value to customers by maintaining high store standards while differentiating its offerings with a wide selection of high-quality produce and meat at competitive prices. The company also provides third-party gift cards, prepaid cards and sports and entertainment cards to retailers for sales to customers in North America and the U.K. through its Blackhawk subsidiary.

MARKET PROFILE. The U.S. grocery industry was a $1.03 trillion business in

2010, according to Progressive Grocer. Supermarkets generated $563 billion, or 55%, of total grocery industry sales, followed by convenience stores ($331.4 billion, 32%) and warehouse clubs ($116 billion, 11%). When supermarkets are broken down by format, conventional supermarkets have the largest market share, holding 66% of the supermarket category, with $370 billion in sales. However, the natural/gourmet foods format is the fastest-growing category, with a 4.1% market share in 2010 ($23.2 billion in sales). With $31.6 billion in sales, excluding fuel ($3.2 billion), in 2010, Safeway had about a 5.6% market share within the supermarket category and 3.1% of total grocery sales.

## Company Financials  Fiscal Year Ended Dec. 31

| Per Share Data ($) | 2010 | 2009 | 2008 | 2007 | 2006 | 2005 | 2004 | 2003 | 2002 | 2001 |
|---|---|---|---|---|---|---|---|---|---|---|
| Tangible Book Value | 12.40 | 11.64 | 10.25 | 9.76 | 7.44 | 5.60 | 4.24 | 2.79 | 1.77 | 1.67 |
| Cash Flow | 4.62 | 0.18 | 4.83 | 4.40 | 4.16 | 3.32 | 3.24 | 1.57 | 2.91 | 4.29 |
| Earnings | 1.55 | -2.66 | 2.21 | 1.99 | 1.94 | 1.25 | 1.25 | -0.38 | 1.20 | 2.44 |
| S&P Core Earnings | 1.63 | 1.90 | 2.00 | 1.87 | 1.91 | 1.26 | 1.15 | 1.21 | 2.42 | 2.19 |
| Dividends | 0.46 | 0.38 | 0.32 | 0.26 | 0.22 | 0.15 | Nil | Nil | Nil | Nil |
| Payout Ratio | 30% | NM | 14% | 13% | 11% | 12% | Nil | Nil | Nil | Nil |
| Prices:High | 27.04 | 24.25 | 34.87 | 38.31 | 35.61 | 26.46 | 25.64 | 25.83 | 46.90 | 61.38 |
| Prices:Low | 18.73 | 17.19 | 17.19 | 30.10 | 22.23 | 17.85 | 17.26 | 16.20 | 18.45 | 37.44 |
| P/E Ratio:High | 17 | NM | 16 | 19 | 18 | 21 | 21 | NM | 39 | 25 |
| P/E Ratio:Low | 12 | NM | 8 | 15 | 11 | 14 | 14 | NM | 15 | 15 |

| Income Statement Analysis (Million $) | 2010 | 2009 | 2008 | 2007 | 2006 | 2005 | 2004 | 2003 | 2002 | 2001 |
|---|---|---|---|---|---|---|---|---|---|---|
| Revenue | 41,050 | 40,851 | 44,104 | 42,286 | 40,185 | 38,416 | 35,823 | 35,553 | 32,399 | 34,301 |
| Operating Income | 2,322 | 2,604 | 2,994 | 2,816 | 2,591 | 2,147 | 2,067 | 2,167 | 3,190 | 3,535 |
| Depreciation | 1,162 | 1,171 | 1,141 | 1,071 | 991 | 933 | 895 | 864 | 812 | 946 |
| Interest Expense | 299 | 332 | 371 | 405 | 396 | 403 | 411 | 442 | 369 | 447 |
| Pretax Income | 881 | -953 | 1,505 | 1,404 | 1,240 | 849 | 794 | 141 | 1,320 | 2,095 |
| Effective Tax Rate | NA | NM | 35.8% | 36.7% | 29.8% | 33.9% | 29.4% | NM | 56.9% | 40.1% |
| Net Income | 591 | -1,098 | 965 | 888 | 871 | 561 | 560 | -170 | 568 | 1,254 |
| S&P Core Earnings | 624 | 788 | 875 | 835 | 859 | 566 | 517 | 538 | 1,140 | 1,122 |

| Balance Sheet & Other Financial Data (Million $) | 2010 | 2009 | 2008 | 2007 | 2006 | 2005 | 2004 | 2003 | 2002 | 2001 |
|---|---|---|---|---|---|---|---|---|---|---|
| Cash | 779 | 472 | 383 | 278 | 217 | 373 | 267 | 175 | 73.7 | 68.5 |
| Current Assets | 4,233 | 3,825 | 3,976 | 4,008 | 3,566 | 3,702 | 3,598 | 3,508 | 4,259 | 3,312 |
| Total Assets | 15,148 | 14,964 | 17,485 | 17,651 | 16,274 | 15,757 | 15,377 | 15,097 | 16,047 | 17,463 |
| Current Liabilities | 4,314 | 4,238 | 4,499 | 5,136 | 4,601 | 4,264 | 3,792 | 3,464 | 3,936 | 3,883 |
| Long Term Debt | 3,844 | 3,874 | 4,184 | 4,658 | 5,037 | 5,605 | 6,124 | 7,072 | 7,522 | 6,712 |
| Common Equity | 4,993 | 4,946 | 6,786 | 6,702 | 5,667 | 4,920 | 4,307 | 3,644 | 3,628 | 5,890 |
| Total Capital | 9,352 | 9,330 | 11,729 | 11,614 | 10,821 | 10,748 | 10,894 | 11,139 | 11,727 | 13,100 |
| Capital Expenditures | 838 | 852 | 1,596 | 1,769 | 1,674 | 1,384 | 1,213 | 936 | 1,371 | 1,793 |
| Cash Flow | 1,753 | 73.7 | 2,106 | 1,960 | 1,862 | 1,494 | 1,455 | 694 | 1,381 | 2,200 |
| Current Ratio | 1.0 | 0.9 | 0.9 | 0.8 | 0.8 | 0.9 | 0.9 | 1.0 | 1.1 | 0.9 |
| % Long Term Debt of Capitalization | 41.1 | 41.5 | 35.7 | 40.1 | 46.5 | 52.2 | 56.2 | 63.5 | 64.1 | 51.2 |
| % Net Income of Revenue | 1.4 | NM | 2.2 | 2.1 | 2.2 | 1.5 | 1.6 | NM | 1.8 | 3.7 |
| % Return on Assets | 3.9 | NM | 5.5 | 5.2 | 5.4 | 3.6 | 3.7 | NM | 3.4 | 7.5 |
| % Return on Equity | 11.9 | NM | 14.3 | 14.4 | 16.4 | 12.2 | 14.1 | NM | 11.9 | 22.2 |

Data as orig reptd.; bef. results of disc opers/spec. items. Per share data adj. for stk. divs.; EPS diluted. E-Estimated. NA-Not Available. NM-Not Meaningful. NR-Not Ranked. UR-Under Review.

**Office:** 5918 Stoneridge Mall Road, Pleasanton, CA 94588-3229.
**Telephone:** 925-467-3000.
**Website:** http://www.safeway.com
**Chrmn, Pres & CEO:** S.A. Burd

**EVP & CFO:** R.L. Edwards
**SVP & Chief Acctg Officer:** D.F. Bond
**SVP & CIO:** D.T. Ching
**Secy & General Counsel:** R.A. Gordon

**Investor Contact:** M.C. Plaisance (925-467-3136)
**Board Members:** S. A. Burd, J. Grove, M. S. Gyani, P. M. Hazen, F. C. Herringer, K. W. Oder, T. G. Rogers, A. Sarin, M. S. Shannon, W. Y. Tauscher

**Founded:** 1915
**Domicile:** Delaware
**Employees:** 180,000

# SAIC Inc

**STANDARD &POOR'S**

| S&P Recommendation | HOLD ★★★☆☆ | Price $11.56 (as of Nov 28, 2011) | 12-Mo. Target Price $13.00 | Investment Style Large-Cap Value |
|---|---|---|---|---|

**GICS Sector** Information Technology
**Sub-Industry** IT Consulting & Other Services

**Summary** This company is a provider of scientific, engineering, systems integration and technical services and solutions primarily to the U.S. government.

## Key Stock Statistics (Source S&P, Vickers, company reports)

| | | | | | | | |
|---|---|---|---|---|---|---|---|
| 52-Wk Range | $17.65–11.06 | S&P Oper. EPS 2012**E** | 1.38 | Market Capitalization(B) | $3.942 | Beta | 0.37 |
| Trailing 12-Month EPS | $1.69 | S&P Oper. EPS 2013**E** | 1.38 | Yield (%) | Nil | S&P 3-Yr. Proj. EPS CAGR(%) | 3 |
| Trailing 12-Month P/E | 6.8 | P/E on S&P Oper. EPS 2012**E** | 8.4 | Dividend Rate/Share | Nil | S&P Credit Rating | A- |
| $10K Invested 5 Yrs Ago | $5,952 | Common Shares Outstg. (M) | 341.0 | Institutional Ownership (%) | 47 | | |

## Price Performance

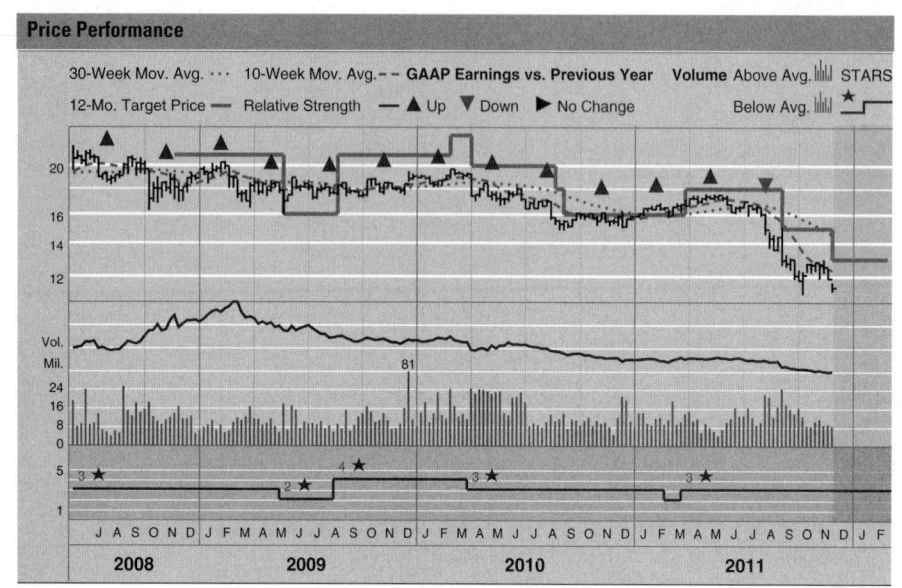

30-Week Mov. Avg. · · ·    10-Week Mov. Avg. – –    GAAP Earnings vs. Previous Year    Volume Above Avg. STARS
12-Mo. Target Price —    Relative Strength —    ▲ Up  ▼ Down  ► No Change    Below Avg.

Analysis prepared by Equity Analyst **Dylan Cathers** on Nov 28, 2011, when the stock traded at **$11.62**.

## Highlights

➤ We expect revenues to decline 1.5% in FY 12 (Jan.) and 2.5% in FY 13 due to the difficult Federal government spending environment. The situation could deteriorate further now that the Federal supercommittee has failed to reach a compromise on budget cuts. Despite signing contracts with agencies, having the funding allocated and beginning the programs is proving difficult. In our view, there is currently uncertainty surrounding the entire budgetary process, which is causing a reluctance on the parts of the agencies to spend. We see this situation playing out particularly within the Federal civilian agencies.

➤ We expect FY 12's operating margins to be in line with FY 10's level (FY 11 margins were aided by a one-time royalty payment). We think the company has made some strides with expense controls and overall operational performance, but we see headwinds in the form of increased levels of research and development, bid and proposal activity, and pricing pressure.

➤ We estimate EPS of $1.38 in FY 12, aided by share buybacks, and $1.38 in FY 13.

## Investment Rationale/Risk

➤ We believe that the company will continue to be affected by elongated procurement cycles and hesitancy of government agencies, especially civilian agencies, to spend. Longer term, we have some concerns about defense spending levels, which are expected to decline over the coming 10 years. However, we are more sanguine on the growth prospects related to cybersecurity and intelligence, as well as energy and health care IT, areas where SAI is attempting to expand. Still, recent diversification moves may be slow to pay dividends.

➤ Risks to our recommendation and target price include acquisition integration risk, pricing pressures from the outsourcing arena, changes in government procurement policies, increased contract protest activity by competitors, a slowdown in defense spending, ongoing use of the federal government's continuing resolution, and headline risk from the fraud charges surrounding the CityTime contract.

➤ We use a peer-discount multiple of 9.4X our FY 13 EPS estimate to arrive at our 12-month target price of $13.

## Qualitative Risk Assessment

| LOW | MEDIUM | HIGH |
|---|---|---|

Our risk assessment reflects the long-term nature of SAI's contracts, which typically provide steady cash flow, offset by intense industry competition and the company's high percentage of revenue from the intelligence community and the Department of Defense.

## Quantitative Evaluations

**S&P Quality Ranking** NR

| D | C | B- | B | B+ | A- | A | A+ |
|---|---|---|---|---|---|---|---|

**Relative Strength Rank** WEAK

29

LOWEST = 1    HIGHEST = 99

## Revenue/Earnings Data

**Revenue (Million $)**

| | 1Q | 2Q | 3Q | 4Q | Year |
|---|---|---|---|---|---|
| 2012 | 2,688 | 2,596 | -- | -- | -- |
| 2011 | 2,685 | 2,794 | 2,869 | 2,769 | 11,117 |
| 2010 | 2,649 | 2,749 | 2,765 | 2,683 | 10,846 |
| 2009 | 2,369 | 2,555 | 2,631 | 2,518 | 10,070 |
| 2008 | 2,011 | 2,222 | 2,365 | 2,337 | 8,935 |
| 2007 | 1,954 | 2,051 | 2,142 | 2,147 | 8,294 |

**Earnings Per Share ($)**

| | | | | | |
|---|---|---|---|---|---|
| 2012 | 0.36 | 0.32 | E0.36 | E0.34 | E1.38 |
| 2011 | 0.32 | 0.42 | 0.41 | 0.36 | 1.51 |
| 2010 | 0.30 | 0.31 | 0.34 | 0.31 | 1.24 |
| 2009 | 0.25 | 0.26 | 0.29 | 0.30 | 1.10 |
| 2008 | 0.18 | 0.24 | 0.26 | 0.24 | 0.93 |
| 2007 | 0.27 | 0.30 | 0.26 | 0.20 | 1.01 |

Fiscal year ended Jan. 31. Next earnings report expected: Early December. EPS Estimates based on S&P Operating Earnings; historical GAAP earnings are as reported.

## Dividend Data

No cash dividends have been paid.

# SAIC Inc

**STANDARD &POOR'S**

## Business Summary November 28, 2011

**CORPORATE OVERVIEW.** SAIC Inc. is the successor, through an October 2006 reorganization merger, to Science Applications International Corporation, which was formed in 1969.

The company provides scientific, engineering, systems integration and technical services and solutions primarily to the U.S. government, with specific emphasis on all branches of the U.S. military, the Department of Defense (DoD), the intelligence community, and the Department of Homeland Security (DoHS). It also provides these services to U.S. government, civil, state and local agencies, as well as to foreign governments and customers in select commercial markets.

SAI has three reportable segments: Defense Solutions; Health, Energy and Civil Solutions; and Intelligence and Cybersecurity Solutions. Defense is the largest, with sales from this segment contributing 42% of the company total in FY 11 (Jan.), in line with FY 10. It provides systems engineering and specialized technical services, as well as logistics and product support. The Health, Energy and Civil Solutions segment (25% vs. 26.5%) provides services such as design and construction, health care IT and research, and the detection of chemical, biological and other threats. The Cybersecurity Solutions business

(33% vs. 31.5%) provides various types of surveillance systems, as well as intelligence services and cybersecurity technology.

**CORPORATE STRATEGY.** Acquisitions are common in the IT services industry and are particularly prevalent among the companies that cater to the DoD and other related military, defense and intelligence communities. Acquisitions are an effective way for companies to increase their breadth of offerings and gain new skills. Equally important, acquisitions have become a method for adding employees, specifically those with high security clearances.

During the past five fiscal years, SAI has made many acquisitions. In FY 10, it acquired R.W. Beck Group, Inc. a provider of business, engineering, energy and infrastructure consulting services. In FY 09, it acquired Icon Systems, Inc., which designs, develops and produces laser-based systems and products for military testing, and SM Consulting, Inc., which provides various services to the government and private industry.

## Company Financials Fiscal Year Ended Jan. 31

| Per Share Data ($) | 2011 | 2010 | 2009 | 2008 | 2007 | 2006 | 2005 | 2004 | 2003 | 2002 |
|---|---|---|---|---|---|---|---|---|---|---|
| Tangible Book Value | 1.66 | 1.94 | 1.84 | 4.03 | 5.17 | 16.28 | NA | NA | NA | NA |
| Cash Flow | 1.86 | 1.52 | 1.25 | 1.12 | 1.21 | 0.89 | 0.87 | 1.14 | 0.84 | 0.43 |
| Earnings | 1.51 | 1.24 | 1.10 | 0.93 | 1.01 | 0.74 | 0.72 | 0.93 | 0.61 | 0.04 |
| S&P Core Earnings | 1.42 | 1.24 | 1.10 | 0.92 | 0.83 | 0.72 | NA | NA | NA | NA |
| Dividends | NA | NA | Nil | Nil | Nil | Nil | Nil | NA | NA | NA |
| Payout Ratio | NA | Nil | Nil | Nil | Nil | Nil | NA | NA | NA | NA |
| Calendar Year | 2010 | 2009 | 2008 | 2007 | 2006 | 2005 | 2004 | 2003 | 2002 | 2001 |
| Prices:High | 19.76 | 20.42 | 21.90 | 21.13 | 21.10 | NA | NA | NA | NA | NA |
| Prices:Low | 14.87 | 15.94 | 16.25 | 16.11 | 15.00 | NA | NA | NA | NA | NA |
| P/E Ratio:High | 13 | 16 | 20 | 23 | 21 | NA | NA | NA | NA | NA |
| P/E Ratio:Low | 10 | 13 | 15 | 17 | 15 | NA | NA | NA | NA | NA |

| Income Statement Analysis (Million $) | | | | | | | | | | |
|---|---|---|---|---|---|---|---|---|---|---|
| Revenue | 11,117 | 10,846 | 10,070 | 8,935 | 8,294 | 7,792 | 7,187 | 5,833 | 5,903 | 6,095 |
| Operating Income | 1,069 | 960 | 835 | 746 | 657 | 567 | 542 | 439 | 619 | 712 |
| Depreciation | 111 | 93.0 | 59.0 | 80.0 | 72.0 | 70.0 | 56.0 | 37.0 | 96.3 | 179 |
| Interest Expense | 79.0 | 76.0 | 78.0 | 90.0 | 92.0 | 89.0 | 88.0 | 80.0 | 45.0 | 18.1 |
| Pretax Income | 883 | 799 | 703 | 629 | 615 | 497 | 417 | 374 | 365 | 43.9 |
| Effective Tax Rate | NA | 37.4% | 36.4% | 38.2% | 38.0% | 28.0% | 31.4% | 37.4% | 30.4% | 20.2% |
| Net Income | 569 | 500 | 447 | 386 | 369 | 345 | 272 | 224 | 247 | 18.2 |
| S&P Core Earnings | 517 | 485 | 448 | 382 | 370 | 334 | NA | NA | NA | NA |

| Balance Sheet & Other Financial Data (Million $) | | | | | | | | | | |
|---|---|---|---|---|---|---|---|---|---|---|
| Cash | 1,367 | 861 | 936 | 1,096 | 1,113 | 3,455 | 2,350 | 2,365 | 2,189 | 1,189 |
| Current Assets | 3,849 | 3,193 | 3,217 | 3,237 | 2,945 | NA | 4,986 | 3,928 | 3,505 | 2,586 |
| Total Assets | 6,223 | 5,295 | 5,048 | 4,981 | 4,558 | 6,419 | 6,010 | 5,493 | 4,804 | 4,948 |
| Current Liabilities | 1,748 | 1,706 | 1,683 | 1,832 | 1,663 | NA | 2,299 | 1,713 | 1,552 | 1,711 |
| Long Term Debt | 1,849 | 1,103 | 1,099 | 1,098 | 1,199 | 1,192 | 1,215 | 1,232 | 897 | 123 |
| Common Equity | 2,491 | 2,291 | 2,084 | 1,901 | 1,536 | 1,221 | 2,351 | 2,190 | 2,007 | 2,524 |
| Total Capital | 4,340 | 3,397 | 3,183 | 2,999 | 2,791 | 2,413 | 3,682 | 3,510 | 2,952 | 2,695 |
| Capital Expenditures | 74.0 | 58.0 | 59.0 | 61.0 | 74.0 | 54.0 | 42.0 | 131 | 43.4 | 127 |
| Cash Flow | 680 | 593 | 506 | 466 | 441 | 415 | 328 | 432 | 343 | 197 |
| Current Ratio | 2.2 | 1.9 | 1.9 | 1.8 | 1.8 | NA | 2.2 | 2.3 | 2.3 | 1.5 |
| % Long Term Debt of Capitalization | 42.6 | 32.5 | 34.5 | 36.6 | 43.0 | 49.4 | 33.0 | 35.1 | 30.4 | 4.6 |
| % Net Income of Revenue | 5.1 | 4.6 | 4.4 | 4.3 | 4.4 | 4.4 | 3.8 | 5.2 | 4.2 | 0.3 |
| % Return on Assets | 9.9 | 9.7 | 8.9 | 8.1 | 7.2 | NA | 4.7 | 6.8 | 5.1 | 0.3 |
| % Return on Equity | 23.8 | 22.9 | 22.4 | 22.5 | 17.0 | NA | 12.0 | 16.7 | 10.9 | 0.6 |

Data as orig reptd.; bef. results of disc opers/spec. items. Per share data adj. for stk. divs.; EPS diluted. Data for 2006 pro forma as adj.; bal. sheet & book value as of July 31, 2006; per sh. data based on adj. pro forma shs. E-Estimated. NA-Not Available. NM-Not Meaningful. NR-Not Ranked. UR-Under Review.

**Office:** 1710 SAIC Drive, McLean, VA 22102.
**Telephone:** 703-676-4300.
**Website:** http://www.saic.com
**Chrmn:** A.T. Young

**Pres:** T. Baybrook
**CEO:** W.P. Havenstein
**COO:** A.J. Moraco
**EVP & CFO:** M.W. Sopp

**Investor Contact:** S. Davis (703-676-2283)
**Board Members:** F. A. Cordova, J. Drummond, T. F. Frist, III, J. J. Hamre, W. P. Havenstein, M. E. John, A. K. Jones, J. P. Jumper, H. M. Kraemer, Jr., L. C. Nussdorf, E. J. Sanderson, Jr., L. A. Simpson, A. T. Young

**Founded:** 1969
**Domicile:** Delaware
**Employees:** 43,400

*The McGraw·Hill Companies*

# St. Jude Medical Inc.

| S&P Recommendation **BUY** ★★★★☆ | Price $38.44 (as of Nov 30, 2011) | 12-Mo. Target Price $50.00 | Investment Style Large-Cap Growth |
|---|---|---|---|

**GICS Sector** Health Care
**Sub-Industry** Health Care Equipment

**Summary** This leading maker of mechanical heart valves also produces pacemakers, defibrillators, and other cardiac devices. In July 2008, it acquired EP Medsystems for $91 million in a deal that expanded its capabilities in the atrial fibrillation market.

## Key Stock Statistics (Source S&P, Vickers, company reports)

| | | | | | | | |
|---|---|---|---|---|---|---|---|
| 52-Wk Range | $54.18– 33.54 | S&P Oper. EPS 2011E | 3.27 | Market Capitalization(B) | $12.262 | Beta | 0.75 |
| Trailing 12-Month EPS | $2.75 | S&P Oper. EPS 2012E | 3.60 | Yield (%) | 2.19 | S&P 3-Yr. Proj. EPS CAGR(%) | 9 |
| Trailing 12-Month P/E | 14.0 | P/E on S&P Oper. EPS 2011E | 11.8 | Dividend Rate/Share | $0.84 | S&P Credit Rating | A |
| $10K Invested 5 Yrs Ago | $9,397 | Common Shares Outstg. (M) | 319.0 | Institutional Ownership (%) | 86 | | |

## Price Performance

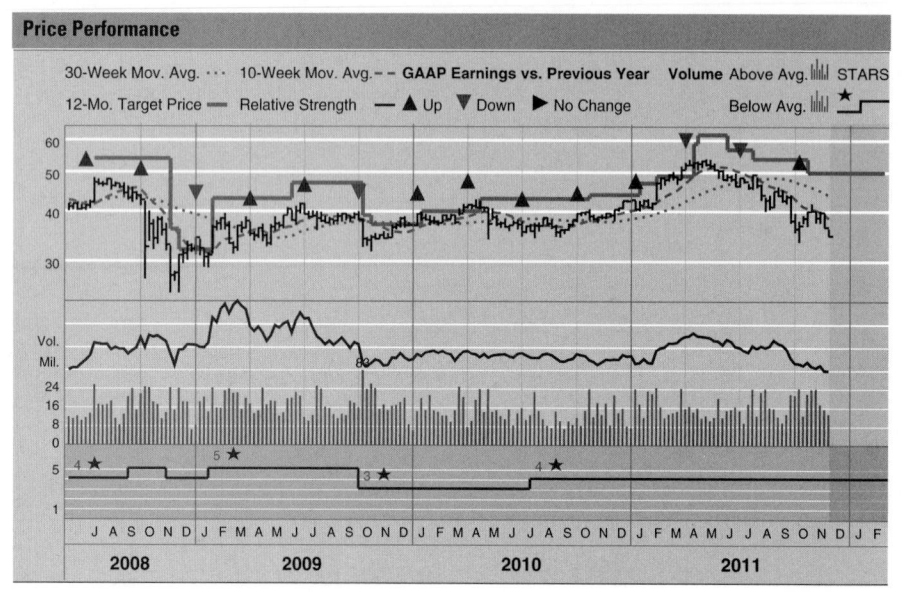

30-Week Mov. Avg. ··· 10-Week Mov. Avg. - - **GAAP Earnings vs. Previous Year** Volume Above Avg. STARS
12-Mo. Target Price — Relative Strength — ▲ Up ▼ Down ► No Change Below Avg. ★

Options: ASE, CBOE

Analysis prepared by Equity Analyst **Phillip Seligman** on Oct 24, 2011, when the stock traded at **$40.22**.

## Highlights

➤ We look for revenues to rise by 8.5% in 2011 and 10% in 2012, on new products, acquisitions, and, in the first nine months of 2011, favorable foreign exchange. In the CRM space, we believe STJ's U.S. ICD sales, like those of its peers, have been hurt by a science journal article on improper implantations. We think its U.S. pacemaker sales have been hurt by a rival's new MRI-compatible pacemaker. Both product lines are performing better overseas, and we think its new quadripolar CRT-Ds, available in Europe and awaiting FDA approval, should help it increase its global CRM market share. Meanwhile, we expect its atrial fibrillation (AF) and cardiovascular segment to grow strongly on new products, with the latter also benefiting from the November 2010 AGA Medical acquisition.

➤ We expect gross margins to expand through 2012, mainly on an improved product mix. We look for the operating cost ratio to rise in 2011 on the AGA acquisition and new initiatives, and see it stable in 2012.

➤ We estimate 2011 adjusted EPS of $3.27, versus 2010's $3.01, and $3.60 for 2012.

## Investment Rationale/Risk

➤ We are encouraged by the several initiatives STJ has to continue to grow market share in each of its major categories, with strong pipelines of what we view as innovative technologies. Promising new and pending products include wireless monitoring technology for heart failure patients, a pericardial stented tissue valve, an MRI-compatible pacemaker, and a quadripolar CRT-D. Interesting longer-term projects, in our view, include transcatheter aortic valves, renal denervation, percutaneous mitral valve repair devices, and a left atrial appendage closure system. Meanwhile, its international sales are benefiting from new technologies, and we expect domestic sales to benefit as it brings those technologies to the U.S.

➤ Risks to our recommendation and target price include failure to successfully commercialize new products, reimbursement rate cuts, and adverse foreign currency fluctuations.

➤ Our 12-month target price of $50 applies a multiple of 14X to our 2012 EPS estimate, a discount to STJ's historical levels, reflecting recent groupwide valuation compression and our view of the market's near-term challenges.

## Qualitative Risk Assessment

| LOW | **MEDIUM** | HIGH |
|---|---|---|

The company operates in a highly competitive industry characterized by relatively short product life cycles and volatile market share fluctuations. However, there are significant barriers to entry in the company's core markets, as products must obtain FDA approval prior to launch, and they require significant investments in research and development and sales efforts.

## Quantitative Evaluations

**S&P Quality Ranking** B+

| D | C | B- | B | **B+** | A- | A | A+ |
|---|---|---|---|---|---|---|---|

**Relative Strength Rank** MODERATE

44

LOWEST = 1 HIGHEST = 99

## Revenue/Earnings Data

**Revenue (Million $)**

| | 1Q | 2Q | 3Q | 4Q | Year |
|---|---|---|---|---|---|
| 2011 | 1,376 | 1,447 | 1,383 | -- | -- |
| 2010 | 1,262 | 1,313 | 1,240 | 1,350 | 5,165 |
| 2009 | 1,134 | 1,184 | 1,160 | 1,203 | 4,681 |
| 2008 | 1,011 | 1,136 | 1,084 | 1,133 | 4,363 |
| 2007 | 887.0 | 947.3 | 926.8 | 1,018 | 3,779 |
| 2006 | 784.4 | 832.9 | 821.3 | 863.8 | 3,302 |

**Earnings Per Share ($)**

| | | | | | |
|---|---|---|---|---|---|
| 2011 | 0.71 | 0.72 | 0.69 | E0.84 | E3.27 |
| 2010 | 0.73 | 0.77 | 0.63 | 0.62 | 2.75 |
| 2009 | 0.58 | 0.63 | 0.48 | 0.57 | 2.26 |
| 2008 | 0.53 | 0.58 | 0.55 | -0.56 | 1.10 |
| 2007 | 0.41 | 0.39 | 0.46 | 0.34 | 1.59 |
| 2006 | 0.36 | 0.38 | 0.32 | 0.42 | 1.47 |

Fiscal year ended Dec. 31. Next earnings report expected: Late January. EPS Estimates based on S&P Operating Earnings; historical GAAP earnings are as reported.

## Dividend Data (Dates: mm/dd Payment Date: mm/dd/yy)

| Amount ($) | Date Decl. | Ex-Div. Date | Stk. of Record | Payment Date |
|---|---|---|---|---|
| 0.210 | 02/28 | 03/29 | 03/31 | 04/29/11 |
| 0.210 | 05/12 | 06/28 | 06/30 | 07/29/11 |
| 0.210 | 08/03 | 09/28 | 09/30 | 10/31/11 |

Dividends have been paid since 2011. Source: Company reports.

**Please read the Required Disclosures and Analyst Certification on the last page of this report.**

The McGraw-Hill Companies

# St. Jude Medical Inc.

**STANDARD &POOR'S**

## Business Summary October 24, 2011

CORPORATE OVERVIEW. St. Jude Medical sells medical devices in the cardiac rhythm management (CRM), cardiac surgery, atrial fibrillation and pain management categories. Although the company has a diversified product line, the principal driver of growth in recent years has been the CRM segment, where it sells pacemakers and defibrillators.

CRM products (59% of 2010 sales) include implantable cardioverter defibrillators (ICDs) and cardiac resynchronization therapy-defibrillators (CRT-Ds), which are used to treat hearts that beat too fast (tachycardia). ICDs prevent dangerous arrhythmias by monitoring the heartbeat and delivering high energy electrical impulses to terminate ventricular tachycardia and ventricular fibrillation. CRT-Ds are a form of ICDs that protect patients with heart disease from sudden cardiac death from arrhythmia while simultaneously improving the pumping action of the heart for patients with heart damage. ICD products include the AnalyST Accel (approved in Europe in 2009) and Current Plus and Promote Plus devices (approved in 2009) with features that provide physicians more options for customizing therapy for patients with potentially lethal heart arrhythmias and heart failure. In addition, the company's products include the Current RF (radio frequency) VR/DR (single chamber/dual chamber) ICDs and Promote RF CRT-D. These devices are available in both standard and high energy versions and feature wireless telemetry.

Also within the CRM division, pacemakers and related systems are sold to

treat patients with hearts that beat too slowly (bradycardia). STJ's other pacing products include the Zephyr family of pacemakers, Victory product line as well as Team ADx pacemakers, a group comprised of the Identity ADx, Integrity ADx, and Verity ADx families of devices.

The Zephyr family of pacemakers includes automatic features to simplify device follow-up; the Victory line which includes the Victory and Victory XL family models, adding new capabilities, such as automatic P-wave and R-wave measurements with trends, lead monitoring, and automatic polarity switching. The Identity ADx family models maintain the therapeutic features of previous St. Jude Medical pacemakers, including the AF Suppression algorithm and the beat-by-beat auto capture pacing system that lets the pacemaker monitor each paced beat to verify heart stimulation. This family offers atrial tachycardia and atrial fibrillation arrhythmia diagnostics.

In 2009, STJ received both European and FDA of its Accent RF pacemaker and Anthem RF CRT-P (cardiac resynchronization therapy pacemaker). In 2010, STJ anticipated introducing an MRI compatible pacemaker in Europe, but it was delayed and it now expects it to launch there in 2011.

## Company Financials Fiscal Year Ended Dec. 31

| Per Share Data ($) | 2010 | 2009 | 2008 | 2007 | 2006 | 2005 | 2004 | 2003 | 2002 | 2001 |
|---|---|---|---|---|---|---|---|---|---|---|
| Tangible Book Value | 1.71 | 2.65 | 2.19 | 2.25 | 2.23 | 1.84 | 4.27 | 3.02 | 3.27 | 2.28 |
| Cash Flow | 3.48 | 2.88 | 1.63 | 2.08 | 1.92 | 1.38 | 1.34 | 1.12 | 0.96 | 0.74 |
| Earnings | 2.75 | 2.26 | 1.10 | 1.59 | 1.47 | 1.04 | 1.10 | 0.92 | 0.76 | 0.48 |
| S&P Core Earnings | 2.81 | 2.27 | 1.12 | 1.64 | 1.47 | 0.90 | 1.03 | 0.82 | 0.63 | 0.38 |
| Dividends | Nil | Nil | Nil | Nil | Nil | Nil | Nil | Nil | Nil | Nil |
| Payout Ratio | Nil | Nil | Nil | Nil | Nil | Nil | Nil | Nil | Nil | Nil |
| Prices:High | 42.98 | 41.96 | 48.49 | 48.10 | 54.75 | 52.80 | 42.90 | 32.00 | 21.56 | 19.52 |
| Prices:Low | 34.00 | 28.86 | 24.98 | 34.90 | 31.20 | 34.48 | 29.90 | 19.38 | 15.26 | 11.11 |
| P/E Ratio:High | 16 | 19 | 44 | 30 | 37 | 51 | 39 | 35 | 29 | 41 |
| P/E Ratio:Low | 12 | 13 | 23 | 22 | 21 | 33 | 27 | 21 | 20 | 23 |

| Income Statement Analysis (Million $) | | | | | | | | | | |
|---|---|---|---|---|---|---|---|---|---|---|
| Revenue | 5,165 | 4,681 | 4,363 | 3,779 | 3,302 | 2,915 | 2,294 | 1,933 | 1,590 | 1,347 |
| Operating Income | 1,615 | 1,440 | 1,275 | 1,093 | 945 | 911 | 672 | 533 | 445 | 347 |
| Depreciation | 244 | 213 | 186 | 176 | 167 | 130 | 85.8 | 76.7 | 74.9 | 90.3 |
| Interest Expense | 67.4 | 45.6 | 22.6 | 38.2 | 33.9 | Nil | Nil | Nil | Nil | Nil |
| Pretax Income | 1,209 | 1,057 | 631 | 744 | 721 | 621 | 537 | 459 | 373 | 228 |
| Effective Tax Rate | NA | 26.5% | 39.1% | 24.9% | 23.9% | 36.7% | 23.7% | 26.0% | 26.0% | 24.3% |
| Net Income | 907 | 777 | 384 | 559 | 548 | 393 | 410 | 339 | 276 | 173 |
| S&P Core Earnings | 925 | 782 | 393 | 576 | 548 | 341 | 377 | 302 | 231 | 136 |

| Balance Sheet & Other Financial Data (Million $) | | | | | | | | | | |
|---|---|---|---|---|---|---|---|---|---|---|
| Cash | 500 | 393 | 136 | 389 | 79.9 | 535 | 688 | 461 | 402 | 148 |
| Current Assets | 2,912 | 2,560 | 2,080 | 2,128 | 1,690 | 1,941 | 1,863 | 1,492 | 1,114 | 798 |
| Total Assets | 8,584 | 6,426 | 5,724 | 5,329 | 4,790 | 4,845 | 3,231 | 2,556 | 1,951 | 1,629 |
| Current Liabilities | 1,017 | 1,067 | 1,029 | 1,849 | 676 | 1,534 | 605 | 510 | 375 | 322 |
| Long Term Debt | 2,432 | 1,588 | 1,126 | 182 | 859 | 177 | 235 | 352 | Nil | 123 |
| Common Equity | 4,372 | 3,324 | 3,236 | 2,928 | 2,969 | 2,883 | 2,334 | 1,604 | 1,577 | 1,184 |
| Total Capital | 6,883 | 5,246 | 4,476 | 3,217 | 3,992 | 3,217 | 2,625 | 2,046 | 1,577 | 1,307 |
| Capital Expenditures | 305 | 326 | 344 | 287 | 268 | 159 | 89.5 | 49.6 | 62.2 | 63.1 |
| Cash Flow | 1,151 | 991 | 570 | 735 | 715 | 524 | 496 | 416 | 351 | 263 |
| Current Ratio | 2.9 | 2.4 | 2.0 | 1.2 | 2.5 | 1.3 | 3.1 | 2.9 | 3.0 | 2.5 |
| % Long Term Debt of Capitalization | 35.3 | 30.3 | 25.2 | 5.7 | 21.5 | 5.5 | 8.9 | 17.2 | Nil | 9.4 |
| % Net Income of Revenue | 17.6 | 16.6 | 8.8 | 14.8 | 16.6 | 13.5 | 17.9 | 17.6 | 17.4 | 12.8 |
| % Return on Assets | 12.1 | 12.8 | 7.0 | 29.3 | 11.4 | 9.7 | 14.2 | 15.1 | 15.4 | 10.9 |
| % Return on Equity | 23.6 | 23.7 | 12.5 | 19.0 | 18.7 | 15.1 | 20.8 | 21.3 | 20.0 | 16.2 |

Data as orig reptd.; bef. results of disc opers/spec. items. Per share data adj. for stk. divs.; EPS diluted. E-Estimated. NA-Not Available. NM-Not Meaningful. NR-Not Ranked. UR-Under Review.

**Office:** One St Jude Medical Drive, St Paul, MN 55117-9983.
**Telephone:** 651-756-2000.
**Website:** http://www.sjm.com
**Chrmn, Pres & CEO:** D.J. Starks

**EVP, CFO & Chief Acctg Officer:** J.C. Heinmiller
**Secy & General Counsel:** P.S. Krop
**Investor Contact:** A. Craig (651-481-7789)
**Cntlr:** D.J. Zurbay

**Board Members:** J. W. Brown, R. Devenuti, S. M. Essig, T. H. Garrett, III, B. B. Hill, M. A. Rocca, D. J. Starks, W. L. Yarno

**Founded:** 1976
**Domicile:** Minnesota
**Employees:** 15,000

**The McGraw·Hill Companies**

# salesforce.com inc

## STANDARD &POOR'S

**S&P Recommendation** HOLD ★★★☆☆

**Price**
$104.93 (as of Nov 25, 2011)

**12-Mo. Target Price**
$135.00

**Investment Style**
Large-Cap Growth

**GICS Sector** Information Technology
**Sub-Industry** Application Software

**Summary** This San Francisco-based company is a leading provider of on-demand customer relationship management applications.

### Key Stock Statistics (Source S&P, Vickers, company reports)

| | | | | | | | |
|---|---|---|---|---|---|---|---|
| 52-Wk Range | $160.12– 103.38 | S&P Oper. EPS 2012**E** | 0.30 | Market Capitalization(B) | $14.218 | Beta | 1.41 |
| Trailing 12-Month EPS | $0.02 | S&P Oper. EPS 2013**E** | 0.40 | Yield (%) | Nil | S&P 3-Yr. Proj. EPS CAGR(%) | NM |
| Trailing 12-Month P/E | NM | P/E on S&P Oper. EPS 2012**E** | NM | Dividend Rate/Share | Nil | S&P Credit Rating | NA |
| $10K Invested 5 Yrs Ago | $25,493 | Common Shares Outstg. (M) | 135.5 | Institutional Ownership (%) | 100 | | |

### Price Performance

30-Week Mov. Avg. · · · 10-Week Mov. Avg. – – GAAP Earnings vs. Previous Year Volume Above Avg. STARS
12-Mo. Target Price — Relative Strength — ▲ Up ▼ Down ► No Change Below Avg. ★

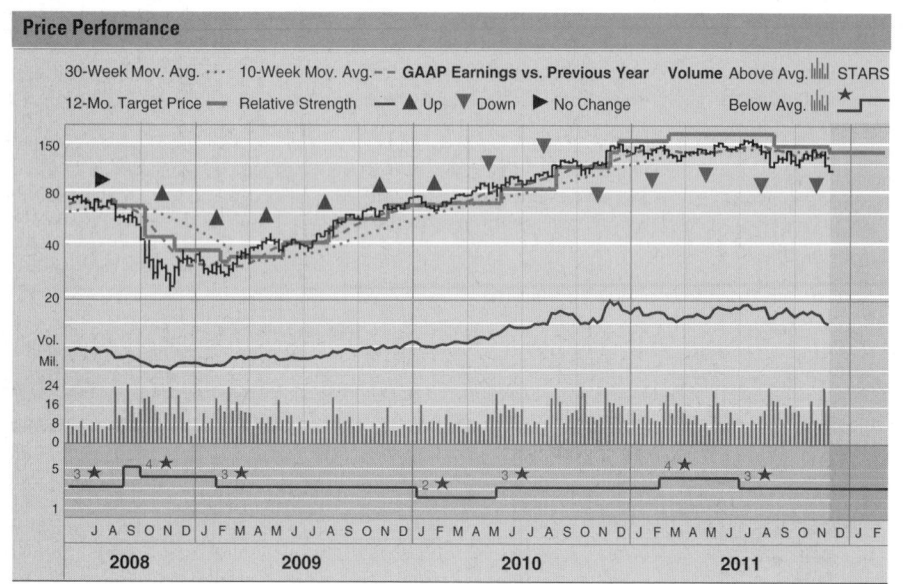

Options: CBOE, Ph

### Qualitative Risk Assessment

| LOW | MEDIUM | HIGH |
|---|---|---|

Our risk assessment reflects the company's dominance in one of the growth areas of the software market, offset by competition from traditional software vendors and increasingly difficult annual comparisons.

### Quantitative Evaluations

**S&P Quality Ranking** NR

| D | C | B- | B | B+ | A- | A | A+ |
|---|---|---|---|---|---|---|---|

**Relative Strength Rank** WEAK

16

LOWEST = 1 HIGHEST = 99

### Revenue/Earnings Data

**Revenue (Million $)**

| | 1Q | 2Q | 3Q | 4Q | Year |
|---|---|---|---|---|---|
| 2012 | 504.4 | 546.0 | 584.3 | -- | -- |
| 2011 | 376.8 | 394.4 | 429.1 | 456.9 | 1,657 |
| 2010 | 304.9 | 316.1 | 330.6 | 354.1 | 1,306 |
| 2009 | 247.6 | 263.1 | 276.5 | 289.6 | 1,077 |
| 2008 | 162.4 | 176.6 | 192.8 | 216.9 | 748.7 |
| 2007 | 104.7 | 118.1 | 130.1 | 144.2 | 497.1 |

**Earnings Per Share ($)**

| | | | | | |
|---|---|---|---|---|---|
| 2012 | Nil | -0.03 | -0.03 | E0.09 | E0.30 |
| 2011 | 0.13 | 0.11 | 0.15 | 0.08 | 0.47 |
| 2010 | 0.15 | 0.17 | 0.16 | 0.16 | 0.63 |
| 2009 | 0.08 | 0.08 | 0.08 | 0.11 | 0.35 |
| 2008 | 0.01 | 0.08 | 0.05 | 0.06 | 0.15 |
| 2007 | Nil | Nil | Nil | Nil | Nil |

Fiscal year ended Jan. 31. Next earnings report expected: Late February. EPS Estimates based on S&P Operating Earnings; historical GAAP earnings are as reported.

### Dividend Data

No cash dividends have been paid.

### Highlights

➤ The 12-month target price for CRM has recently been changed to $135.00 from $145.00. The Highlights section of this Stock Report will be updated accordingly.

### Investment Rationale/Risk

➤ The Investment Rationale/Risk section of this Stock Report will be updated shortly. For the latest News story on CRM from MarketScope, see below.

➤ 11/18/11 12:32 pm ET ... S&P REITERATES HOLD OPINION ON SHARES OF SALESFORCE.COM (CRM 114.19***): CRM posts adjusted Q3 EPS of $0.08, vs. $0.20, above our estimate of $0.03. Revenues rose 36%, with notable performance in the customer service, social and Force.com areas. We are raising our EPS forecasts for FY 12 (Jan.) to $0.30 from $0.27 and FY 13's to $0.40 from $0.38. However, we see growth in deferred revenues decelerating somewhat faster than we previously anticipated, and reflecting this and revised relative analysis, we are trimming our 12-month target price to $135 from $145. We think the company is attractively positioned, but see the stock as fairly valued. /S. Kessler

# salesforce.com inc

STANDARD &POOR'S

## Business Summary August 31, 2011

CORPORATE OVERVIEW. Salesforce.com is a leading provider of "on-demand" customer relationship management software. On-demand, used interchangeably with software-as-a-service (SaaS), refers to the delivery of application or programming or platform services over the Internet as needed. Under this delivery model, customers access a software provider's solutions via the Web, with minor implementation and customization and little to no on-premise installation or maintenance of software. Payment for this "service" is generally on a per-seat per-user basis over an agreed-upon term.

In our view, the delivery of software on demand offers several benefits to customers, including lower upfront investment, increased vendor accountability and risk sharing, greater awareness of customer needs due to the constant feedback from customers, and flexible subscription pricing, which can be tailored to customer requirements. This model also offers benefits to the software vendor, including improved visibility into customers' needs and potentially higher customer satisfaction and retention levels. Another benefit we see is lower development and support costs arising from the use of a single version of software across a vendor's installed base. Among the drawbacks to this model for the customer is that over time, depending on the number of seats contracted for or level of usage, the ultimate cost of buying software on-demand can become quite high and the level of customization may not always address a client's specific needs. A vendor typically incurs considerable upfront cost in launching and supporting an SaaS solution. Many SaaS vendors operate at losses until they cross a certain revenue threshold. We note that Salesforce.com, in particular, had 92,300 customers at the end of January 2011 (excluding Heroku and Dimdim, but achieved 5.9% GAAP operating margins (14.3% non-GAAP, before amortization and stock-based compensation expense).

CRM experienced service outages in late December 2005 and in early 2006. We believe these service issues have been largely addressed, although we note another outage took place in early January 2010. We credit the company with the transparency it provides regarding the performance, uptime, and security of its system. Since the delivery of its service over the Web is a point of differentiation, we expect the company to continue to invest in infrastructure in future quarters. The low upfront cost of CRM's products has natural appeal to small and mid-sized businesses, in our view, although the company has had considerable success in selling its services to larger institutions.

## Company Financials Fiscal Year Ended Jan. 31

| Per Share Data ($) | 2011 | 2010 | 2009 | 2008 | 2007 | 2006 | 2005 | 2004 | 2003 | 2002 |
|---|---|---|---|---|---|---|---|---|---|---|
| Tangible Book Value | 5.38 | 7.50 | 4.78 | 3.71 | 2.40 | 1.78 | 1.38 | 1.13 | NA | NA |
| Cash Flow | 1.06 | 0.97 | 0.51 | 0.29 | 0.11 | 0.29 | 0.09 | 0.06 | -0.27 | -1.25 |
| Earnings | 0.47 | 0.63 | 0.35 | 0.15 | Nil | 0.24 | 0.07 | 0.04 | -0.37 | -1.36 |
| S&P Core Earnings | 0.42 | 0.58 | 0.36 | 0.14 | NA | 0.07 | -0.04 | -0.02 | -0.43 | NA |
| Dividends | NA | Nil | Nil | Nil | Nil | Nil | Nil | NA | NA | NA |
| Payout Ratio | NA | Nil | Nil | Nil | Nil | Nil | Nil | NA | NA | NA |
| Calendar Year | 2010 | 2009 | 2008 | 2007 | 2006 | 2005 | 2004 | 2003 | 2002 | 2001 |
| Prices:High | 151.26 | 74.95 | 75.21 | 65.52 | 44.58 | 36.19 | 22.70 | NA | NA | NA |
| Prices:Low | 60.30 | 25.19 | 20.82 | 35.55 | 21.64 | 12.96 | 9.00 | NA | NA | NA |
| P/E Ratio:High | NM | NM | NM | NM | NM | NM | NM | NA | NA | NA |
| P/E Ratio:Low | NM | NM | NM | NM | NM | NM | NM | NA | NA | NA |

### Income Statement Analysis (Million $)

| | 2011 | 2010 | 2009 | 2008 | 2007 | 2006 | 2005 | 2004 | 2003 | 2002 |
|---|---|---|---|---|---|---|---|---|---|---|
| Revenue | 1,657 | 1,306 | 1,077 | 749 | 497 | 310 | 176 | 96.0 | 51.0 | 22.4 |
| Operating Income | 173 | 159 | 84.7 | 37.1 | 8.91 | 25.8 | 9.67 | 2.86 | -7.84 | -19.5 |
| Depreciation | 75.8 | 53.2 | 21.0 | 16.8 | 12.5 | 6.03 | 3.15 | 2.59 | 2.66 | 2.40 |
| Interest Expense | 24.9 | 2.00 | 0.11 | 0.05 | 0.19 | 0.07 | 0.04 | 0.02 | 0.08 | 0.27 |
| Pretax Income | 104 | 142 | 85.6 | 46.2 | 12.5 | 28.2 | 9.15 | 4.24 | -10.0 | -29.0 |
| Effective Tax Rate | NA | 40.5% | 43.9% | 50.6% | 78.4% | NM | 13.3% | 12.8% | Nil | Nil |
| Net Income | 69.7 | 80.7 | 43.4 | 18.4 | 0.48 | 28.5 | 7.35 | 3.51 | -9.72 | -28.6 |
| S&P Core Earnings | 58.3 | 74.7 | 44.4 | 17.5 | 0.48 | 8.59 | -3.26 | -0.61 | -11.4 | NA |

### Balance Sheet & Other Financial Data (Million $)

| | 2011 | 2010 | 2009 | 2008 | 2007 | 2006 | 2005 | 2004 | 2003 | 2002 |
|---|---|---|---|---|---|---|---|---|---|---|
| Cash | 497 | 1,242 | 698 | 451 | 252 | 208 | 119 | 142 | 16.0 | 11.7 |
| Current Assets | 1,075 | 1,706 | 1,069 | 741 | 419 | 303 | 179 | NA | 30.1 | 18.2 |
| Total Assets | 3,091 | 2,460 | 1,480 | 1,090 | 665 | 435 | 280 | 191 | 39.4 | 29.1 |
| Current Liabilities | 1,276 | 908 | 767 | 606 | 377 | 235 | 132 | NA | 28.8 | 12.3 |
| Long Term Debt | 473 | 450 | 4.05 | Nil | 0.01 | 0.18 | 0.72 | Nil | NA | NA |
| Common Equity | 1,276 | 1,044 | 672 | 452 | 282 | 196 | 145 | 115 | -56.1 | -52.0 |
| Total Capital | 1,749 | 1,507 | 687 | 461 | 286 | 199 | 147 | 115 | 5.42 | 9.47 |
| Capital Expenditures | 369 | 53.9 | 61.1 | 43.6 | 22.1 | 23.4 | 4.31 | NA | 2.37 | 0.71 |
| Cash Flow | 145 | 124 | 64.4 | 35.2 | 13.0 | 34.5 | 10.5 | 6.11 | -7.06 | -26.2 |
| Current Ratio | 0.8 | 1.9 | 1.4 | 1.2 | 1.1 | 1.3 | 1.4 | NA | 1.1 | 1.5 |
| % Long Term Debt of Capitalization | 27.0 | 29.9 | 0.6 | Nil | 0.0 | 0.1 | 0.5 | Nil | Nil | Nil |
| % Net Income of Revenue | 4.2 | 6.2 | 4.0 | 2.5 | 0.1 | 9.2 | 4.2 | 3.7 | NM | NM |
| % Return on Assets | 2.5 | 4.1 | 3.4 | 2.1 | 0.1 | 8.0 | 4.0 | NA | NM | NA |
| % Return on Equity | 6.0 | 9.4 | 7.7 | 5.0 | 0.2 | 16.7 | 14.9 | NA | NM | NA |

Data as orig reptd.; bef. results of disc opers/spec. items. Per share data adj. for stk. divs.; EPS diluted. E-Estimated. NA-Not Available. NM-Not Meaningful. NR-Not Ranked. UR-Under Review.

**Office:** The Landmark @ One Market, San Francisco, CA 94105.
**Telephone:** 415-901-7000.
**Website:** http://www.salesforce.com
**Chrmn & CEO:** M. Benioff

**COO:** G. Hu
**EVP, CFO & Chief Acctg Officer:** G.V. Smith
**EVP & General Counsel:** B.F. Norton
**CSO:** J.P. Rangaswami

**Board Members:** M. Benioff, C. A. Conway, A. G. Hassenfeld, C. Ramsey, S. R. Robertson, S. D. Sclavos, L. J. Tomlinson, M. G. Webb, Jr., S. Young

**Founded:** 1999
**Domicile:** Delaware
**Employees:** 5,306

# SanDisk Corp

**STANDARD &POOR'S**

| **S&P Recommendation** BUY ★★★★★ | **Price** $45.56 (as of Nov 25, 2011) | **12-Mo. Target Price** $58.00 | **Investment Style** Large-Cap Growth |
|---|---|---|---|

**GICS Sector** Information Technology
**Sub-Industry** Computer Storage & Peripherals

**Summary** This company designs, makes and markets flash memory storage products used in a wide variety of electronic systems.

## Key Stock Statistics (Source S&P, Vickers, company reports)

| | | | | | | | |
|---|---|---|---|---|---|---|---|
| 52-Wk Range | $53.61– 32.24 | S&P Oper. EPS 2011E | 3.93 | Market Capitalization(B) | $10.948 | Beta | 1.67 |
| Trailing 12-Month EPS | $4.92 | S&P Oper. EPS 2012E | 4.45 | Yield (%) | Nil | S&P 3-Yr. Proj. EPS CAGR(%) | 3 |
| Trailing 12-Month P/E | 9.3 | P/E on S&P Oper. EPS 2011E | 11.6 | Dividend Rate/Share | Nil | S&P Credit Rating | BB- |
| $10K Invested 5 Yrs Ago | $9,535 | Common Shares Outstg. (M) | 240.3 | Institutional Ownership (%) | 82 | | |

## Price Performance

30-Week Mov. Avg. · · · 10-Week Mov. Avg. - - GAAP Earnings vs. Previous Year Volume Above Avg. STARS
12-Mo. Target Price — Relative Strength — ▲ Up ▼ Down ▶ No Change Below Avg.

Options: ASE, CBOE, P, Ph

Analysis prepared by Equity Analyst **Angelo Zino, CFA** on Oct 24, 2011, when the stock traded at **$51.00**.

## Highlights

➤ We forecast that sales will increase 16% in 2012 after our projection for a 17% rise in 2011, as we see growth in megabytes partially offset by average price deflation. We see demand for SNDK's products increasing at a modest pace, with growth primarily being driven by higher demand for new mobile phones. In addition, we anticipate that the increasing adoption of devices such as tablets and smartphones will drive the need for increased NAND flash-based storage solutions.

➤ We project an annual gross margin of 37% in 2012, below our 39% margin expectation for 2011. We think SNDK will benefit from higher growth in megabytes, but we expect some pricing pressure despite a relatively healthy supply and demand picture for NAND flash memory. We see margins being aided by cost reductions as the company transitions to more advanced processes. We estimate operating margins of 27% in 2011 and 26% in 2012.

➤ We forecast EPS of $3.93 for 2011 and $4.45 for 2012. Despite higher projected unit sales, we expect profit margins to narrow going forward, given our view of a lower pricing environment in 2012.

## Investment Rationale/Risk

➤ Our buy opinion is primarily based on valuation and our belief that SNDK is poised to benefit from new applications in flash memory, such as solid state drives. We believe the balance between demand and supply for flash memory will remain healthy given the robust unit growth outlook that we anticipate, aided by end-demand growth for smartphones. We expect the mobile market to be SNDK's highest growth business and comprise more than half of the company's total sales. Also, we expect SNDK to remain the technology leader as it moves to more advanced technology nodes. We see the shares aided to some extent by net cash per share (including long term securities) of over $15 as of September 2011 end.

➤ Risks to our recommendation and target price include the potential for more aggressive price erosion than we forecast, and more weakening in end-market demand than we foresee.

➤ Our 12-month target price of $58 is based on a multiple of 13X our 2012 EPS estimate of $4.45, near comparable semiconductor manufacturers. Our target price is supported by a multiple of 2.15X our 2012 sales per share estimate, within the five-year historical range.

## Qualitative Risk Assessment

| LOW | MEDIUM | **HIGH** |
|---|---|---|

Our risk assessment reflects the volatile nature of the flash memory space, an intensifying competitive environment, and what we deem to be significant price erosion within the industry.

## Quantitative Evaluations

**S&P Quality Ranking** B-

| D | C | **B-** | B | B+ | A- | A | A+ |
|---|---|---|---|---|---|---|---|

**Relative Strength Rank** STRONG

72

LOWEST = 1　　　　　　HIGHEST = 99

## Revenue/Earnings Data

**Revenue (Million $)**

| | 1Q | 2Q | 3Q | 4Q | Year |
|---|---|---|---|---|---|
| 2011 | 1,294 | 1,375 | 1,416 | -- | -- |
| 2010 | 1,087 | 1,179 | 1,234 | 1,327 | 4,827 |
| 2009 | 659.5 | 730.6 | 935.2 | 1,242 | 3,567 |
| 2008 | 850.0 | 816.0 | 821.5 | 863.9 | 3,351 |
| 2007 | 786.1 | 827.0 | 1,037 | 1,246 | 3,896 |
| 2006 | 623.3 | 719.2 | 751.4 | 1,164 | 3,258 |

**Earnings Per Share ($)**

| | 1Q | 2Q | 3Q | 4Q | Year |
|---|---|---|---|---|---|
| 2011 | 0.92 | 1.02 | 0.96 | E1.03 | E3.93 |
| 2010 | 0.99 | 1.08 | 1.34 | 2.01 | 5.44 |
| 2009 | -0.92 | 0.23 | 0.99 | 1.45 | 1.79 |
| 2008 | 0.08 | -0.30 | -0.69 | -8.25 | -9.19 |
| 2007 | Nil | 0.12 | 0.36 | 0.45 | 0.93 |
| 2006 | 0.17 | 0.47 | 0.51 | -0.17 | 0.96 |

Fiscal year ended Dec. 31. Next earnings report expected: Late January. EPS Estimates based on S&P Operating Earnings; historical GAAP earnings are as reported.

## Dividend Data

No cash dividends have been paid.

---

**Please read the Required Disclosures and Analyst Certification on the last page of this report.**

*The McGraw·Hill Companies*

# SanDisk Corp

## Business Summary October 24, 2011

CORPORATE OVERVIEW. SanDisk Corp. (SNDK) designs, makes and markets flash storage card products used in a wide variety of consumer electronics products such as digital cameras, mobile phones, laptops, Universal Serial Bus, or USB, drives, gaming devices and MP3 players. Flash storage technology allows data to be stored in a durable, compact format that retains the digital information even after the power has been switched off. SNDK also provides high-speed and high-capacity storage solutions, known as solid-state drives, or SSDs, that can be used in lieu of hard disk drives in a variety of computing devices, including personal computers and enterprise servers.

SNDK focuses on three primary markets: mobile phones, consumer, and computing. For mobile phones, SNDK's cards are experiencing increasing demand as multimedia features such as video and Internet access become more prevalent. The company is a leading supplier of the microSD and Memory Stick Micro product lines of removable storage cards used in mobile phones.

Within the consumer market, SNDK provides flash storage products for imaging, gaming, audio/video and global positioning system (GPS). Flash storage cards are used as the film for all major brands of digital cameras. Its cards are also used to store video in solid-state digital camcorders and to store digital data in many other devices, such as maps in GPS devices.

In the computing market, SNDK sells USB flash drives that allow consumers to store computer files, pictures and music on keychain-sized devices and then transfer these files between laptops, notebooks, desktops and other devices that incorporate a USB connection. SNDK is currently developing SSDs for the mainstream notebook and desktop computer markets and it believes that SSDs will become a major application for NAND flash memory over the next several years as they are increasingly likely to replace hard disk drives.

We believe SNDK's primary competitors include: Hynix Semiconductor, Intel, Micron, Samsung, and Toshiba. Although competitive pressures are high within the industry, SNDK also holds tight relationships with many of its peers due to supply agreements that it has with some of these manufacturers. In 2010 and 2009, SNDK's top ten customers and licensees represented 46% and 42% of total revenues, respectively. However, no customer comprised more than 10% of sales the last two years.

## Company Financials Fiscal Year Ended Dec. 31

| Per Share Data ($) | 2010 | 2009 | 2008 | 2007 | 2006 | 2005 | 2004 | 2003 | 2002 | 2001 |
|---|---|---|---|---|---|---|---|---|---|---|
| Tangible Book Value | 24.29 | 16.85 | 13.76 | 16.94 | 15.31 | 13.41 | 10.78 | 9.32 | 4.54 | 4.93 |
| Cash Flow | 6.39 | 2.79 | -8.00 | 1.97 | 1.61 | 2.34 | 1.62 | 1.12 | 0.40 | -2.04 |
| Earnings | 5.44 | 1.79 | -9.19 | 0.93 | 0.96 | 2.00 | 1.44 | 1.02 | 0.26 | -2.19 |
| S&P Core Earnings | 5.34 | 1.77 | -5.06 | 0.96 | 0.94 | 1.76 | 1.29 | 0.89 | 0.18 | -1.05 |
| Dividends | Nil | Nil | Nil | Nil | Nil | Nil | Nil | Nil | Nil | Nil |
| Payout Ratio | Nil | Nil | Nil | Nil | Nil | Nil | Nil | Nil | Nil | Nil |
| Prices:High | 52.31 | 31.18 | 33.73 | 59.75 | 79.80 | 65.49 | 36.35 | 43.15 | 14.60 | 24.34 |
| Prices:Low | 24.90 | 7.53 | 5.07 | 32.74 | 37.34 | 20.25 | 19.28 | 7.39 | 4.80 | 4.30 |
| P/E Ratio:High | 10 | 17 | NM | 64 | 83 | 33 | 25 | 42 | 57 | NM |
| P/E Ratio:Low | 5 | 4 | NM | 35 | 39 | 10 | 13 | 7 | 19 | NM |

| Income Statement Analysis (Million $) | 2010 | 2009 | 2008 | 2007 | 2006 | 2005 | 2004 | 2003 | 2002 | 2001 |
|---|---|---|---|---|---|---|---|---|---|---|
| Revenue | 4,827 | 3,567 | 3,351 | 3,896 | 3,258 | 2,306 | 1,777 | 1,080 | 541 | 366 |
| Operating Income | 1,688 | 750 | -569 | 536 | 688 | 642 | 457 | 280 | 79.5 | -124 |
| Depreciation | 227 | 231 | 254 | 246 | 136 | 65.8 | 38.9 | 23.0 | 21.3 | 20.5 |
| Interest Expense | 88.1 | 68.6 | 16.5 | 16.9 | Nil | 0.57 | 5.95 | 6.75 | 6.70 | Nil |
| Pretax Income | 1,457 | 504 | -1,903 | 398 | 431 | 613 | 423 | 242 | 40.0 | -442 |
| Effective Tax Rate | NA | 17.6% | NM | 43.9% | 53.4% | 37.0% | 37.0% | 30.2% | 9.35% | NM |
| Net Income | 1,300 | 415 | -2,070 | 218 | 199 | 386 | 267 | 169 | 36.2 | -298 |
| S&P Core Earnings | 1,276 | 411 | -1,138 | 225 | 195 | 339 | 239 | 149 | 25.7 | -144 |

| Balance Sheet & Other Financial Data (Million $) | 2010 | 2009 | 2008 | 2007 | 2006 | 2005 | 2004 | 2003 | 2002 | 2001 |
|---|---|---|---|---|---|---|---|---|---|---|
| Cash | 2,848 | 1,919 | 1,439 | 1,835 | 1,581 | 762 | 464 | 734 | 267 | 254 |
| Current Assets | 4,033 | 2,915 | 2,703 | 3,300 | 4,242 | 2,576 | 1,880 | 1,725 | 757 | 542 |
| Total Assets | 8,777 | 6,002 | 5,879 | 7,235 | 6,968 | 3,120 | 2,320 | 2,024 | 976 | 932 |
| Current Liabilities | 960 | 871 | 1,263 | 914 | 896 | 571 | 353 | 347 | 173 | 127 |
| Long Term Debt | 1,711 | 935 | 1,225 | 1,225 | 1,225 | Nil | Nil | 150 | 150 | 125 |
| Common Equity | 5,783 | 3,910 | 3,162 | 4,960 | 4,768 | 2,524 | 1,940 | 1,501 | 628 | 675 |
| Total Capital | 7,490 | 4,918 | 4,400 | 6,200 | 5,999 | 2,524 | 1,940 | 1,651 | 778 | 800 |
| Capital Expenditures | 108 | 59.7 | 184 | 259 | 176 | 134 | 126 | 52.5 | 16.6 | 26.2 |
| Cash Flow | 1,527 | 646 | -1,803 | 464 | 334 | 452 | 305 | 192 | 57.6 | -277 |
| Current Ratio | 4.2 | 3.4 | 2.1 | 3.6 | 4.7 | 4.5 | 5.3 | 5.0 | 4.4 | 4.3 |
| % Long Term Debt of Capitalization | 22.8 | 19.0 | 27.9 | 19.8 | 20.4 | Nil | Nil | 9.1 | 19.3 | 15.6 |
| % Net Income of Revenue | 26.9 | 11.6 | NM | 5.6 | 6.1 | 16.8 | 15.0 | 15.6 | 6.7 | NM |
| % Return on Assets | 17.6 | 7.0 | NM | 3.1 | 3.9 | 14.2 | 12.2 | 11.3 | 3.8 | NM |
| % Return on Equity | 26.8 | 11.7 | NM | 4.5 | 5.5 | 17.3 | 15.4 | 15.9 | 5.6 | NM |

Data as orig reptd.; bef. results of disc opers/spec. items. Per share data adj. for stk. divs.; EPS diluted. E-Estimated. NA-Not Available. NM-Not Meaningful. NR-Not Ranked. UR-Under Review.

**Office:** 601 McCarthy Blvd, Milpitas, CA 95035-7932.
**Telephone:** 408-801-1000.
**Email:** investor_relations@sandisk.com
**Website:** http://www.sandisk.com

**Chrmn:** M.E. Marks
**Pres & CEO:** S. Mehrotra
**Vice Chrmn:** I.B. Federman
**Investor Contact:** J. Bruner

**CFO & Chief Admin Officer:** J. Bruner
**Board Members:** K. A. DeNuccio, I. B. Federman, S. J. Gomo, E. Hartenstein, C. C. Hu, C. P. Lego, M. E. Marks, S. Mehrotra

**Founded:** 1988
**Domicile:** Delaware
**Employees:** 3,469

# Sara Lee Corp

**STANDARD &POOR'S**

| S&P Recommendation | HOLD ★★★☆☆ | Price $17.74 (as of Nov 25, 2011) | 12-Mo. Target Price $19.00 | Investment Style Large-Cap Blend |

**GICS Sector** Consumer Staples
**Sub-Industry** Packaged Foods & Meats

**Summary** This diversified provider of branded food products such as meats, fresh and frozen baked goods and coffee is planning to split into two companies.

## Key Stock Statistics (Source S&P, Vickers, company reports)

| | | | | | | | |
|---|---|---|---|---|---|---|---|
| 52-Wk Range | $20.26– 14.94 | S&P Oper. EPS 2012**E** | 0.92 | Market Capitalization(B) | $10.480 | Beta | 0.88 |
| Trailing 12-Month EPS | $1.44 | S&P Oper. EPS 2013**E** | NA | Yield (%) | 2.59 | S&P 3-Yr. Proj. EPS CAGR(%) | 12 |
| Trailing 12-Month P/E | 12.3 | P/E on S&P Oper. EPS 2012**E** | 19.3 | Dividend Rate/Share | $0.46 | S&P Credit Rating | BBB |
| $10K Invested 5 Yrs Ago | $12,690 | Common Shares Outstg. (M) | 590.7 | Institutional Ownership (%) | 75 | | |

## Price Performance

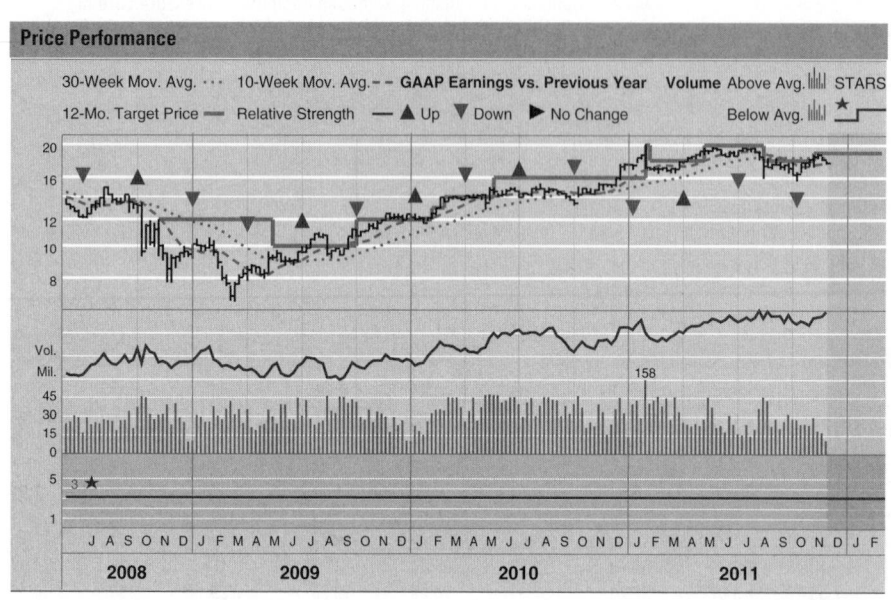

30-Week Mov. Avg. ··· 10-Week Mov. Avg. - - GAAP Earnings vs. Previous Year   Volume Above Avg. STARS
12-Mo. Target Price — Relative Strength — ▲ Up ▼ Down ▶ No Change   Below Avg.

Options: ASE, CBOE, P

Analysis prepared by Equity Analyst **Tom Graves, CFA** on Nov 10, 2011, when the stock traded at **$18.34**.

## Highlights

➤ SLE is planning to divide itself into two separate, publicly traded companies. We look for SLE to spin off ownership of its international coffee and tea business to SLE shareholders in the first half of calendar 2012. Also, directors have announced plans for a $3.00 per share special dividend on SLE's common stock.

➤ In the fourth quarter of calendar 2011, SLE completed the sale of its North American Fresh Bakery business and its North American refrigerated dough business. In addition, SLE has decided to divest its Spanish bakery and French refrigerated dough businesses, and is planning to sell or close assets of its North American coffee business. The company has already divested much of its international Household and Body Care (H&BC) segment.

➤ Before special items, for the company as currently constituted, we estimate FY 12 (Jun.) EPS from continuing operations of $0.92, up from $0.78 in FY 11, including a benefit from fewer shares outstanding.

## Investment Rationale/Risk

➤ During the next couple of years, we look for various cost reduction efforts to at least largely offset corporate expenses that the two separate companies would have after the split-up, plus some stranded costs left over after divestitures by SLE.

➤ Risks to our recommendation and target price include divestiture or transaction activity proceeding less favorably than expected, weaker-than-expected sales resulting from disappointing demand, and significantly more cost pressure than we anticipate.

➤ In our view, SLE's plan to split into two parts indicates that the company did not receive an acceptable acquisition offer. We do not rule out the possibility that a new bid may emerge for SLE before a prospective 2012 split-up, but we think this has become less likely. Our 12-month target price of $19 reflects a premium P/E, relative to peers, and also includes anticipation of divestiture proceeds, plus the prospect of a $3 per share special dividend which we expect will paid to SLE shareholders in FY 12, prior to SLE's separation into two companies.

## Qualitative Risk Assessment

| LOW | MEDIUM | HIGH |

Our risk assessment for Sara Lee reflects the relatively stable nature of the company's end markets, what we expect to be sizable cash flow from operating activities, and corporate governance practices that we view as favorable relative to peers, offset by prospective commodity cost pressure and changes related to a prospective special dividend and split-up of the company.

## Quantitative Evaluations

**S&P Quality Ranking**   B

| D | C | B- | B | B+ | A- | A | A+ |

**Relative Strength Rank**   STRONG
74
LOWEST = 1                                    HIGHEST = 99

## Revenue/Earnings Data

**Revenue (Million $)**

| | 1Q | 2Q | 3Q | 4Q | Year |
|---|---|---|---|---|---|
| 2012 | 1,943 | -- | -- | -- | -- |
| 2011 | 1,988 | 2,254 | 2,142 | 2,297 | 8,681 |
| 2010 | 2,588 | 2,858 | 2,578 | 2,769 | 10,793 |
| 2009 | 3,349 | 3,340 | 3,028 | 3,164 | 12,881 |
| 2008 | 3,054 | 3,408 | 3,243 | 3,507 | 13,212 |
| 2007 | 2,891 | 3,182 | 3,006 | 3,199 | 12,278 |

**Earnings Per Share ($)**

| | 1Q | 2Q | 3Q | 4Q | Year |
|---|---|---|---|---|---|
| 2012 | -0.06 | E0.25 | E0.27 | E0.26 | E0.92 |
| 2011 | 0.10 | 0.15 | 0.21 | 0.08 | 0.54 |
| 2010 | 0.27 | 0.43 | 0.04 | 0.17 | 0.92 |
| 2009 | 0.32 | -0.02 | 0.24 | -0.02 | 0.52 |
| 2008 | 0.28 | 0.25 | 0.33 | -0.96 | -0.06 |
| 2007 | 0.34 | -0.08 | 0.15 | 0.16 | 0.57 |

Fiscal year ended Jun. 30. Next earnings report expected: Early February. EPS Estimates based on S&P Operating Earnings; historical GAAP earnings are as reported.

## Dividend Data (Dates: mm/dd Payment Date: mm/dd/yy)

| Amount ($) | Date Decl. | Ex-Div. Date | Stk. of Record | Payment Date |
|---|---|---|---|---|
| 0.115 | 01/27 | 02/25 | 03/01 | 04/08/11 |
| 0.115 | 04/28 | 05/25 | 06/01 | 07/08/11 |
| 0.115 | 06/30 | 09/01 | 09/06 | 10/07/11 |
| 0.115 | 10/27 | 11/29 | 12/01 | 01/09/12 |

Dividends have been paid since 1946. Source: Company reports.

**The McGraw-Hill Companies**

# Sara Lee Corp

STANDARD &POOR'S

## Business Summary November 10, 2011

CORPORATE OVERVIEW. Sara Lee, best known for its baked goods, also has various other branded food and non-food businesses. In North America, this includes Jimmy Dean and Hillshire Farm meat products, while outside the U.S., it includes coffee and tea. In North America, in addition to providing products to retailers, SLE provides products to foodservice operators.

SLE is planning to divide itself into two separate, publicly traded companies, and we look for the split-up to be completed in the first half of 2012. Under the separation plan, for which an update was provided in June 2011, we expect that SLE's International Coffee and Tea business would be spun off to SLE shareholders. The remainder of SLE, not part of the spin-off, would include various North American operations, including meat products sold under the Hillshire Farm, Jimmy Dean and Ball Park brands, and sales to foodservice operators.

In conjunction with the planned separation, SLE directors intend to declare a $3.00 per share special dividend on SLE's common stock, the majority of which would be funded with proceeds from the pending sale of the company's North American Fresh Bakery business. We expect the special dividend to be paid in FY 12 (Jun.), prior to SLE's separation into two companies.

CORPORATE STRATEGY. Prior to announcing the planned separation of SLE into two companies, SLE had been selling some businesses.

In November 2011, SLE completed the sale of its North American Fresh Bakery business to Mexico's Grupo Bimbo for $709 million, including the assumption of debt. As part of the transaction, Grupo Bimbo assumed employee-related commitments, including pension obligations. Also, in October 2011, SLE said that it had agreed to sell its fresh bakery businesses in Spain and Portugal to Grupo Bombo for 115 million euros.

As of November 2011, SLE had divested much of its International Household and Body Care business. Closed transactions included the body care business for 1.21 billion euros, the air care business for 320 million euros, and its stake in an Indian insecticides business for 185 million euros.

## Company Financials Fiscal Year Ended Jun. 30

| Per Share Data ($) | 2011 | 2010 | 2009 | 2008 | 2007 | 2006 | 2005 | 2004 | 2003 | 2002 |
|---|---|---|---|---|---|---|---|---|---|---|
| Tangible Book Value | 1.38 | NM | NM | NM | NM | NM | NM | NM | NM | NM |
| Cash Flow | 1.10 | 1.58 | 1.22 | 0.51 | 1.33 | 1.46 | 1.87 | 2.53 | 2.44 | 1.94 |
| Earnings | 0.54 | 0.92 | 0.52 | -0.06 | 0.57 | 0.53 | 0.92 | 1.59 | 1.50 | 1.23 |
| S&P Core Earnings | 0.54 | 0.84 | 0.47 | 0.69 | 0.50 | 0.44 | 0.86 | 1.67 | 1.30 | 1.00 |
| Dividends | 0.46 | 0.44 | 0.44 | 0.42 | 0.50 | 0.79 | 0.78 | 0.60 | 0.62 | 0.60 |
| Payout Ratio | NA | 48% | 84% | NM | 88% | 149% | 85% | 38% | 41% | 48% |
| Prices:High | 20.26 | 17.72 | 12.61 | 16.08 | 18.15 | 19.64 | 25.00 | 24.49 | 23.13 | 23.84 |
| Prices:Low | 15.66 | 11.67 | 6.80 | 7.74 | 14.75 | 14.08 | 17.31 | 20.17 | 16.25 | 16.15 |
| P/E Ratio:High | 38 | 19 | 24 | NM | 32 | 37 | 27 | 15 | 15 | 19 |
| P/E Ratio:Low | 29 | 13 | 13 | NM | 26 | 27 | 19 | 13 | 11 | 13 |

| Income Statement Analysis (Million $) | 2011 | 2010 | 2009 | 2008 | 2007 | 2006 | 2005 | 2004 | 2003 | 2002 |
|---|---|---|---|---|---|---|---|---|---|---|
| Revenue | 8,681 | 10,793 | 12,881 | 13,212 | 12,278 | 15,944 | 19,254 | 19,566 | 18,291 | 17,628 |
| Operating Income | 1,196 | 1,418 | 1,488 | 1,484 | 1,242 | 1,779 | 2,183 | 2,386 | 2,345 | 2,138 |
| Depreciation | 351 | 455 | 497 | 403 | 539 | 701 | 737 | 734 | 674 | 582 |
| Interest Expense | 117 | 147 | 170 | 205 | 265 | 308 | 290 | 271 | 276 | 304 |
| Pretax Income | 487 | 795 | 588 | 137 | 419 | 683 | 934 | 1,542 | 1,484 | 1,185 |
| Effective Tax Rate | NA | NA | 38.1% | 146.7% | NM | 40.0% | 21.7% | 17.5% | 17.7% | 14.8% |
| Net Income | 338 | 635 | 364 | -64.0 | 426 | 410 | 731 | 1,272 | 1,221 | 1,010 |
| S&P Core Earnings | 336 | 586 | 327 | 501 | 385 | 339 | 684 | 1,336 | 1,047 | 806 |

| Balance Sheet & Other Financial Data (Million $) | 2011 | 2010 | 2009 | 2008 | 2007 | 2006 | 2005 | 2004 | 2003 | 2002 |
|---|---|---|---|---|---|---|---|---|---|---|
| Cash | 2,066 | 955 | 959 | 1,284 | 2,520 | 2,231 | 545 | 638 | 942 | 298 |
| Current Assets | 4,584 | 3,810 | 3,830 | 4,467 | 5,643 | 6,774 | 5,811 | 5,746 | 5,953 | 4,986 |
| Total Assets | 9,533 | 8,836 | 9,417 | 10,830 | 12,190 | 14,522 | 14,412 | 14,883 | 15,084 | 13,753 |
| Current Liabilities | 4,122 | 2,723 | 2,846 | 3,841 | 4,301 | 6,277 | 4,968 | 5,423 | 5,199 | 5,463 |
| Long Term Debt | 1,934 | 2,693 | 2,704 | 2,340 | 2,803 | 3,807 | 4,115 | 4,171 | 5,157 | 4,326 |
| Common Equity | 1,945 | 1,487 | 2,036 | 2,811 | 2,615 | 2,449 | 2,938 | 2,948 | 1,870 | 1,534 |
| Total Capital | 4,409 | 4,214 | 4,872 | 5,347 | 6,066 | 6,324 | 7,134 | 7,194 | 7,806 | 7,252 |
| Capital Expenditures | 337 | 373 | 357 | 454 | 529 | 625 | 538 | 530 | 746 | 669 |
| Cash Flow | 689 | 1,090 | 861 | 362 | 965 | 1,111 | 1,468 | 2,006 | 1,895 | 1,592 |
| Current Ratio | 1.1 | 1.4 | 1.4 | 1.2 | 1.3 | 1.1 | 1.2 | 1.1 | 1.1 | 0.9 |
| % Long Term Debt of Capitalization | 43.9 | 63.9 | 55.5 | 43.8 | 46.2 | 60.2 | 57.6 | 58.0 | 66.1 | 59.7 |
| % Net Income of Revenue | 3.9 | 5.9 | 2.8 | NM | 3.5 | 2.6 | 3.8 | 6.5 | 6.7 | 5.7 |
| % Return on Assets | NA | NA | 3.6 | NM | 3.2 | 2.8 | 5.0 | 8.4 | 8.5 | 8.4 |
| % Return on Equity | NA | NA | 15.0 | NM | 16.8 | 15.2 | 24.7 | 52.8 | 71.7 | 83.0 |

Data as orig reptd.; bef. results of disc opers/spec. items. Per share data adj. for stk. divs.; EPS diluted. E-Estimated. NA-Not Available. NM-Not Meaningful. NR-Not Ranked. UR-Under Review.

**Office:** 3500 Lacey Rd, Downers Grove, IL 60515-5424. **Telephone:** 630-598-6000. **Website:** http://www.saralee.com **Chrmn:** J. Bennink

**CEO:** M.H. Smits **EVP & CFO:** M.A. Garvey **SVP, Secy & General Counsel:** P.R. Dodson **Chief Acctg Officer & Cntlr:** J.P. Zyck

**Investor Contact:** L.M. de Kool **Board Members:** C. B. Begley, J. Bennink, C. C. Bowles, V. W. Colbert, J. S. Crown, L. T. Koellner, C. J. Lede, J. D. McAdam, I. Prosser, N. R. Sorensen, J. W. Ubben, J. P. Ward

**Founded:** 1941 **Domicile:** Maryland **Employees:** 21,000

# SCANA Corp

**STANDARD &POOR'S**

| | | | |
|---|---|---|---|
| **S&P Recommendation** BUY ★★★★☆ | **Price** $40.97 (as of Nov 25, 2011) | **12-Mo. Target Price** $44.00 | **Investment Style** Large-Cap Blend |

**GICS Sector** Utilities
**Sub-Industry** Multi-Utilities

**Summary** Through its subsidiaries, this energy-based holding company provides electric, natural gas, and telecommunications services.

## Key Stock Statistics (Source S&P, Vickers, company reports)

| | | | | | | | |
|---|---|---|---|---|---|---|---|
| 52-Wk Range | $43.19– 34.64 | S&P Oper. EPS 2011**E** | 3.05 | Market Capitalization(B) | $5.312 | Beta | 0.54 |
| Trailing 12-Month EPS | $2.97 | S&P Oper. EPS 2012**E** | 3.25 | Yield (%) | 4.74 | S&P 3-Yr. Proj. EPS CAGR(%) | 5 |
| Trailing 12-Month P/E | 13.8 | P/E on S&P Oper. EPS 2011**E** | 13.4 | Dividend Rate/Share | $1.94 | S&P Credit Rating | BBB+ |
| $10K Invested 5 Yrs Ago | $12,595 | Common Shares Outstg. (M) | 129.7 | Institutional Ownership (%) | 47 | | |

## Price Performance

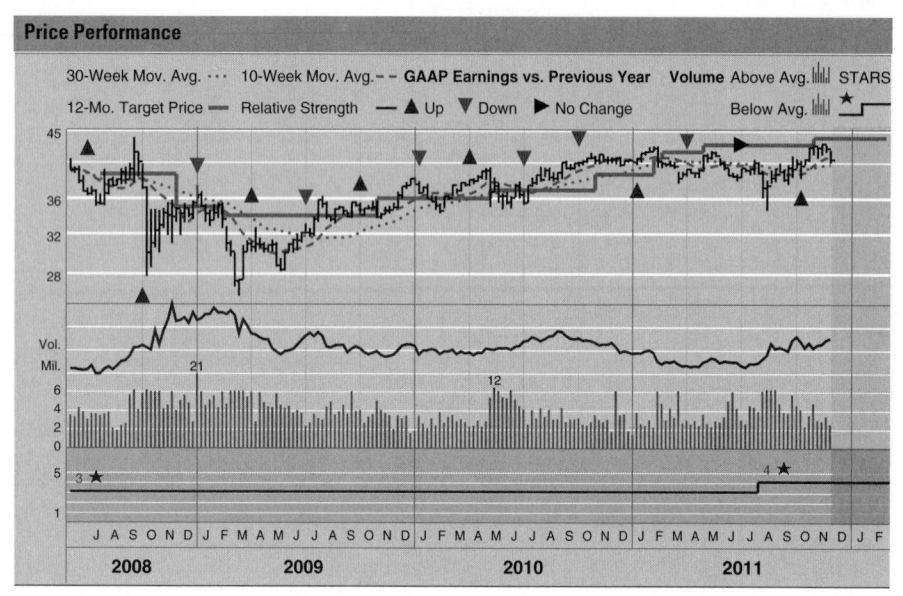

30-Week Mov. Avg. ···· 10-Week Mov. Avg. – – **GAAP Earnings vs. Previous Year** Volume Above Avg. STARS
12-Mo. Target Price — Relative Strength — ▲ Up ▼ Down ► No Change Below Avg. ★

Options: Ph

Analysis prepared by Equity Analyst **C. Muir** on Oct 26, 2011, when the stock traded at **$41.94**.

## Highlights

➤ We see 2011 revenue contraction of 1.5%, hurt by lower natural gas prices, partly offset by customer growth and an increase in usage per customer driven by a slowly improving economy. SCG's gas and electric distribution territories should provide the utility with steady annual customer growth. In 2012, we look for revenues to rise 3.1% as we expect to see continuing economic improvements and slightly rising gas prices, offset by more normal weather.

➤ We forecast operating margins of 18.3% in 2011, versus 17.0% in 2010, helped by lower per-revenue cost of sales, partly offset by higher per-revenue operations & maintenance costs and depreciation expense. For 2012, we see operating margins of 19.5%. We expect lower per-revenue operating expenses in most categories. We expect pretax margins of 12.6% in 2011 and 14.1% in 2012, up from 12.0% in 2010, affected by slightly rising interest expense and relatively flat nonoperating income.

➤ Assuming an effective tax rate of 30.7% and continued upward share drift related to compensation, we estimate 2011 EPS of $3.05, up 2.0% from 2009's $2.99. Our 2012 EPS estimate is $3.25, up 6.6%.

## Investment Rationale/Risk

➤ We think above-average population growth in SCG's service areas will provide solid opportunities for further rate and rate base increases. SCG's cash flow generation has been solid, in our view. We see the unregulated gas business in Georgia providing more growth than the regulated businesses. We also like SCG's declining leverage ratios. We expect a 4.5% EPS compound annual growth rate over the next three years, about average for multi-utilities.

➤ Risks to our recommendation and target price include a sharp increase in interest rates, prolonged mild temperatures, unfavorable regulatory actions, and weaker-than-expected economic growth in the utility's service area.

➤ The stock recently traded at 12.9X our 2012 EPS estimate, a 9% discount to its multi-utility peers. Our 12-month target price of $44 is 13.5X our 2012 estimate, a near peer valuation. We believe this valuation is warranted by what we see as a relatively strong balance sheet, offset by our expectation for EPS growth in line with its peers and little improvement in the capital structure over the next three years. The dividend recently yielded 4.5%.

## Qualitative Risk Assessment

| LOW | MEDIUM | HIGH |
|---|---|---|

We think the largely regulated nature of SCG's operations provides a stable source of cash flow and earnings. In addition, the company has a less leveraged balance sheet than peers.

## Quantitative Evaluations

**S&P Quality Ranking** B+

| D | C | B- | B | B+ | A- | A | A+ |
|---|---|---|---|---|---|---|---|

**Relative Strength Rank** STRONG

75

LOWEST = 1 HIGHEST = 99

## Revenue/Earnings Data

**Revenue (Million $)**

| | 1Q | 2Q | 3Q | 4Q | Year |
|---|---|---|---|---|---|
| 2011 | 1,281 | 1,000 | 1,092 | -- | -- |
| 2010 | 1,428 | 939.0 | 1,088 | 1,145 | 4,601 |
| 2009 | 1,343 | 878.0 | 921.0 | 1,094 | 4,237 |
| 2008 | 1,533 | 1,218 | 1,266 | 1,301 | 5,319 |
| 2007 | 1,363 | 1,007 | 1,079 | 1,172 | 4,621 |
| 2006 | 1,389 | 944.0 | 1,062 | 1,168 | 4,563 |

**Earnings Per Share ($)**

| | | | | | |
|---|---|---|---|---|---|
| 2011 | 1.00 | 0.43 | 0.81 | E0.81 | E3.05 |
| 2010 | 1.03 | 0.43 | 0.79 | 0.74 | 2.98 |
| 2009 | 0.94 | 0.45 | 0.84 | 0.62 | 2.85 |
| 2008 | 0.93 | 0.49 | 0.80 | 0.73 | 2.96 |
| 2007 | 0.73 | 0.47 | 0.79 | 0.75 | 2.74 |
| 2006 | 0.80 | 0.50 | 0.76 | 0.57 | 2.63 |

Fiscal year ended Dec. 31. Next earnings report expected: Mid February. EPS Estimates based on S&P Operating Earnings; historical GAAP earnings are as reported.

## Dividend Data (Dates: mm/dd Payment Date: mm/dd/yy)

| Amount ($) | Date Decl. | Ex-Div. Date | Stk. of Record | Payment Date |
|---|---|---|---|---|
| 0.485 | 02/11 | 03/08 | 03/10 | 04/01/11 |
| 0.485 | 04/21 | 06/08 | 06/10 | 07/01/11 |
| 0.485 | 08/11 | 09/07 | 09/09 | 10/01/11 |
| 0.485 | 10/26 | 12/07 | 12/09 | 01/01/12 |

Dividends have been paid since 1946. Source: Company reports.

# SCANA Corp

**STANDARD &POOR'S**

## Business Summary October 26, 2011

CORPORATE OVERVIEW. Scana Corp.'s (SCG) primary regulated operating businesses are South Carolina Electric & Gas (SCE&G), Public Service of North Carolina (PSNC), SCANA Energy, and an intrastate pipeline operation in South Carolina. As of December 31, 2010, SCE&G had 660,000 electric customers and 313,500 natural gas customers. PSNC had 482,000 gas utility customers. The company projects that its consolidated regulated base of more than 1.4 million electric and gas customers will grow 2.4% annually. The company's unregulated SCANA Energy served about 30% of the 1.5 million customers in Georgia's competitive natural gas supply market, with about 90,000 of its 460,000 gas customers receiving regulated services.

In 2010, 51% of SCG's external revenues were derived from electric operations (51% in 2009), 21% (22%) from natural gas distribution, 15% (14%) from energy marketing, and 12% (12%) from retail gas marketing. SCE&G owned 5,604 megawatt (MW) of generating plants as of December 2010. This capacity consisted of 45% coal, 30% oil/gas, 14% hydro and 11% nuclear. In 2010, 65% of SCE&G's power was generated by coal plants, 18% by nuclear, 13% by natural gas and oil, and 4% by hydroelectric.

CORPORATE STRATEGY. SCG sees reserve margins falling in its service territory over the next several years and believes that new baseload power will be needed. As a result, it plans to invest in nuclear generation to fill the gap. SCE&G submitted a joint application to the NRC on March 31, 2008, with Santee Cooper, a state-owned utility, for a combined construction and operating license (COL) that covers two nuclear units. SCE&G has said that the companies have elected to use a 1,117 MW design, which would be built at the existing VC Summer nuclear station, if the economic need still exists after the approximately three-year COL application process. If the companies decide to move ahead with the project, SCG said the first plant could be built by 2016. SCE&G operates the VC Summer nuclear station and would remain the operator for all units after completion. Financially, SCG aims to increase earnings at a rate of 4%-6% annually and maintain a dividend payout ratio in the 55%-60% range.

## Company Financials Fiscal Year Ended Dec. 31

| Per Share Data ($) | 2010 | 2009 | 2008 | 2007 | 2006 | 2005 | 2004 | 2003 | 2002 | 2001 |
|---|---|---|---|---|---|---|---|---|---|---|
| Tangible Book Value | 27.34 | 25.84 | 23.86 | 23.33 | 24.32 | 23.28 | 21.69 | 20.77 | 19.61 | 20.90 |
| Earnings | 2.98 | 2.85 | 2.96 | 2.74 | 2.63 | 2.81 | 2.30 | 2.54 | 0.83 | 5.15 |
| S&P Core Earnings | 3.02 | 2.99 | 2.55 | 2.52 | 2.44 | 2.60 | 2.51 | 2.40 | 1.93 | 1.59 |
| Dividends | 1.90 | 1.88 | 1.84 | 1.76 | 1.68 | 1.56 | 1.46 | 1.38 | 1.30 | 1.20 |
| Payout Ratio | 64% | 66% | 62% | 64% | 64% | 56% | 63% | 54% | 157% | 23% |
| Prices:High | 41.97 | 38.64 | 44.06 | 45.49 | 42.43 | 43.65 | 39.71 | 35.70 | 32.15 | 30.00 |
| Prices:Low | 34.23 | 26.01 | 27.75 | 32.93 | 36.92 | 36.56 | 32.82 | 28.10 | 23.50 | 24.25 |
| P/E Ratio:High | 14 | 14 | 15 | 17 | 16 | 16 | 17 | 14 | 39 | 6 |
| P/E Ratio:Low | 12 | 9 | 9 | 12 | 14 | 13 | 14 | 11 | 28 | 5 |

| Income Statement Analysis (Million $) | 2010 | 2009 | 2008 | 2007 | 2006 | 2005 | 2004 | 2003 | 2002 | 2001 |
|---|---|---|---|---|---|---|---|---|---|---|
| Revenue | 4,601 | 4,237 | 5,319 | 4,621 | 4,563 | 4,777 | 3,885 | 3,416 | 2,954 | 3,451 |
| Depreciation | 377 | 347 | 344 | 324 | 333 | 510 | 265 | 238 | 220 | 224 |
| Maintenance | NA | NA | NA | NA | NA | NA | NA | 558 | 522 | 482 |
| Fixed Charges Coverage | 3.01 | 3.12 | 3.25 | 3.18 | 3.02 | 2.18 | 2.83 | 2.81 | 2.68 | 2.49 |
| Construction Credits | NA | NA | NA | NA | NA | 3.00 | 26.0 | 11.0 | NA | NA |
| Effective Tax Rate | 29.7% | 32.4% | 35.3% | 30.0% | 28.1% | NM | 32.4% | 32.4% | 29.0% | 36.1% |
| Net Income | 376 | 348 | 346 | 320 | 304 | 320 | 257 | 282 | 88.0 | 539 |
| S&P Core Earnings | 381 | 365 | 299 | 294 | 282 | 296 | 280 | 268 | 204 | 167 |

| Balance Sheet & Other Financial Data (Million $) | 2010 | 2009 | 2008 | 2007 | 2006 | 2005 | 2004 | 2003 | 2002 | 2001 |
|---|---|---|---|---|---|---|---|---|---|---|
| Gross Property | 13,456 | 12,602 | 11,645 | 10,650 | 9,954 | 9,540 | 9,181 | 9,025 | 7,777 | 7,215 |
| Capital Expenditures | 876 | 914 | 904 | 712 | 485 | 366 | 498 | 738 | 675 | 523 |
| Net Property | 9,961 | 9,300 | 8,499 | 7,669 | 7,139 | 6,842 | 6,866 | 6,745 | 5,301 | 4,851 |
| Capitalization:Long Term Debt | 4,152 | 4,483 | 4,361 | 2,879 | 3,067 | 3,062 | 3,301 | 3,340 | 2,999 | 2,812 |
| Capitalization:% Long Term Debt | 52.9 | 56.8 | 58.0 | 48.4 | 50.9 | 53.4 | 58.3 | 59.2 | 57.9 | 56.2 |
| Capitalization:Preferred | Nil | Nil | 113 | 113 | 114 | Nil | Nil | Nil | Nil | Nil |
| Capitalization:% Preferred | Nil | Nil | 1.50 | 1.90 | 1.89 | Nil | Nil | Nil | Nil | Nil |
| Capitalization:Common | 3,702 | 3,408 | 3,045 | 2,960 | 2,846 | 2,677 | 2,357 | 2,306 | 2,177 | 2,194 |
| Capitalization:% Common | 47.1 | 43.2 | 40.5 | 49.7 | 47.2 | 46.6 | 41.7 | 40.8 | 42.1 | 43.8 |
| Total Capital | 8,191 | 7,919 | 8,631 | 7,000 | 7,094 | 6,800 | 6,658 | 6,550 | 6,041 | 5,844 |
| % Operating Ratio | 86.8 | 87.4 | 90.2 | 89.3 | 89.4 | 88.4 | 87.8 | 87.8 | 83.8 | 93.5 |
| % Earned on Net Property | 8.0 | 7.9 | 8.8 | 8.5 | 8.6 | 6.4 | 8.9 | 8.5 | 10.1 | 11.3 |
| % Return on Revenue | 8.2 | 8.2 | 6.5 | 6.9 | 6.7 | 6.7 | 6.6 | 8.3 | 3.0 | 15.6 |
| % Return on Invested Capital | 8.0 | 7.5 | 7.3 | 9.8 | 8.8 | 10.9 | 7.6 | 8.8 | 9.9 | 14.2 |
| % Return on Common Equity | 10.6 | 10.8 | 11.5 | 11.0 | 11.0 | 12.5 | 10.8 | 12.3 | 4.0 | 25.5 |

Data as orig reptd.; bef. results of disc opers/spec. items. Per share data adj. for stk. divs.; EPS diluted. E-Estimated. NA-Not Available. NM-Not Meaningful. NR-Not Ranked. UR-Under Review.

**Office:** 100 Scana Parkway, Cayce, SC 29033.
**Telephone:** 803-217-9000.
**Email:** invrel@scana.com
**Website:** http://www.scana.com

**Chrmn & CEO:** W.B. Timmerman
**Pres & COO:** K.B. Marsh
**SVP & CFO:** J. Addison
**SVP & General Counsel:** R.T. Lindsay

**Chief Acctg Officer & Cntlr:** J.E. Swan, IV
**Investor Contact:** J. Winn (803-217-9240)
**Board Members:** B. Amick, J. A. Bennett, S. A. Decker, D. M. Hagood, K. B. Marsh, J. W. Martin, III, J. M. Micali, L. M. Miller, J. W. Roquemore, M. K. Sloan, H. C. Stowe, W. B. Timmerman

**Founded:** 1924
**Domicile:** South Carolina
**Employees:** 5,877

**The McGraw-Hill Companies**

# Schlumberger Ltd

**STANDARD &POOR'S**

| S&P Recommendation **STRONG BUY** ★★★★★ | Price $66.37 (as of Nov 25, 2011) | 12-Mo. Target Price $94.00 | Investment Style Large-Cap Blend |
|---|---|---|---|

**GICS Sector** Energy
**Sub-Industry** Oil & Gas Equipment & Services

**Summary** This leading oilfield services company provides equipment and technology to the oil and gas industry worldwide.

## Key Stock Statistics (Source S&P, Vickers, company reports)

| | | | | | | | |
|---|---|---|---|---|---|---|---|
| 52-Wk Range | $95.64– 54.79 | S&P Oper. EPS 2011**E** | 3.54 | Market Capitalization(B) | $89.077 | Beta | 1.33 |
| Trailing 12-Month EPS | $3.38 | S&P Oper. EPS 2012**E** | 5.10 | Yield (%) | 1.51 | S&P 3-Yr. Proj. EPS CAGR(%) | 30 |
| Trailing 12-Month P/E | 19.6 | P/E on S&P Oper. EPS 2011**E** | 18.7 | Dividend Rate/Share | $1.00 | S&P Credit Rating | A+ |
| $10K Invested 5 Yrs Ago | $10,786 | Common Shares Outstg. (M) | 1,342.1 | Institutional Ownership (%) | 77 | | |

## Price Performance

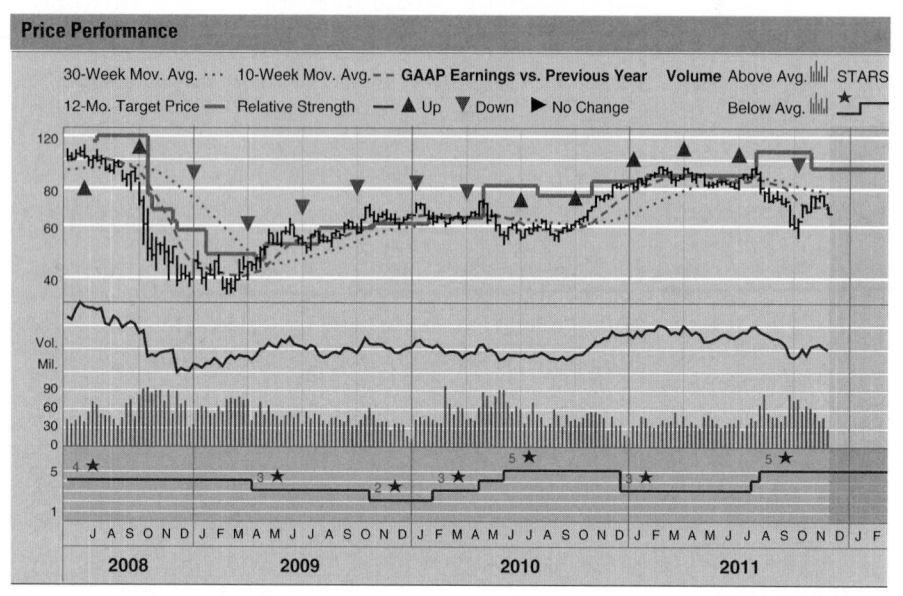

30-Week Mov. Avg. · · · 10-Week Mov. Avg. - - **GAAP Earnings vs. Previous Year** Volume Above Avg. STARS
12-Mo. Target Price — Relative Strength — ▲ Up ▼ Down ► No Change Below Avg. ★

Options: ASE, CBOE, P, Ph

Analysis prepared by Equity Analyst **S. Glickman, CFA** on Oct 25, 2011, when the stock traded at **$69.29**.

## Qualitative Risk Assessment

| LOW | MEDIUM | HIGH |
|---|---|---|

Our risk assessment reflects the company's exposure to volatile crude oil and natural gas prices; its dependence on capital spending decisions by its oil and gas producing customers; and political risk associated with operating in frontier regions around the world. This is offset by the company's leading industry position.

## Quantitative Evaluations

**S&P Quality Ranking** NR

| D | C | B- | B | B+ | A- | A | A+ |
|---|---|---|---|---|---|---|---|

**Relative Strength Rank** MODERATE

40

LOWEST = 1 HIGHEST = 99

## Highlights

► With crude oil prices still above the $80 a barrel mark, even with the recent downdraft, we think upstream producers will remain confident about exploration drilling, which we think bodes well for SLB and its portfolio of oilfield services. We also note that SLB is perhaps the most overseas-oriented of all of the major oilfield services providers, and we expect that overseas regions (particularly Brazil) will be at the forefront of incremental upstream spending on oil & gas exploration.

► SLB completed its acquisition of the former Smith International (SII) in August 2010. We think the acquisition enhances SLB's position in deepwater fluids, and helps to marry SII's fluids and drillbit engineering with SLB's drilling and completion expertise. SII had a strong position in the deepwater U.S. Gulf of Mexico, which we think yields some potential near-term choppiness, but longer term we think presents a potentially strong growth catalyst. While the pace of recovery in the U.S. Gulf is a wild card for near-term results, we believe the longer-term growth profile in this region remains intact.

► We see EPS of $3.54 in 2011, rising 44% to $5.10 in 2012, led by higher operating margins.

## Investment Rationale/Risk

► We see low integration risk from the SII acquisition, as the two companies were previously joint venture partners in the M-I Swaco fluids business. Longer term, we see SLB as a best-of-breed oilfield services company, well positioned to benefit from the trend toward new oil and gas development requiring higher levels of technology content. We also think that SII's deepwater expertise will bolster SLB's growth prospects in this area.

► Risks to our recommendation and target price include slower-than-expected recovery in drilling permit issuance in the U.S. Gulf of Mexico; lower activity volumes; reduced demand for integrated systems in oilfield services; rising political risk in emerging markets; and a major collapse in crude oil prices.

► Our DCF model, applying free cash flow growth of 11% per year and terminal growth of 3%, shows intrinsic value of about $102. For 2012, we see ROIC of 18%, slightly above peers, so we think peer-premium multiples are merited. Applying peer-premium multiples of 10X estimated 2012 EBITDA and 12X projected 2012 cash flow, and blending with our DCF model, leads to our 12-month target price of $94.

## Revenue/Earnings Data

**Revenue (Million $)**

| | 1Q | 2Q | 3Q | 4Q | Year |
|---|---|---|---|---|---|
| 2011 | 8,716 | 9,621 | 10,229 | -- | -- |
| 2010 | 5,598 | 5,937 | 6,845 | 9,067 | 27,447 |
| 2009 | 6,000 | 5,528 | 5,430 | 5,744 | 22,702 |
| 2008 | 6,290 | 6,746 | 7,259 | 6,868 | 27,163 |
| 2007 | 5,464 | 5,639 | 5,926 | 6,248 | 23,277 |
| 2006 | 4,239 | 4,687 | 4,955 | 5,350 | 19,230 |

**Earnings Per Share ($)**

| | | | | | |
|---|---|---|---|---|---|
| 2011 | 0.69 | 0.82 | 0.96 | E1.07 | E3.54 |
| 2010 | 0.56 | 0.68 | 1.38 | 0.76 | 3.38 |
| 2009 | 0.78 | 0.51 | 0.65 | 0.67 | 2.61 |
| 2008 | 1.06 | 1.16 | 1.25 | 0.95 | 4.42 |
| 2007 | 0.96 | 1.02 | 1.09 | 1.12 | 4.20 |
| 2006 | 0.59 | 0.69 | 0.81 | 0.92 | 3.01 |

Fiscal year ended Dec. 31. Next earnings report expected: NA. EPS Estimates based on S&P Operating Earnings; historical GAAP earnings are as reported.

## Dividend Data (Dates: mm/dd Payment Date: mm/dd/yy)

| Amount ($) | Date Decl. | Ex-Div. Date | Stk. of Record | Payment Date |
|---|---|---|---|---|
| 0.250 | 01/20 | 02/14 | 02/16 | 04/01/11 |
| 0.250 | 04/21 | 05/27 | 06/01 | 07/01/11 |
| 0.250 | 07/21 | 08/30 | 09/01 | 10/03/11 |
| 0.250 | 10/20 | 11/29 | 12/01 | 01/06/12 |

Dividends have been paid since 1957. Source: Company reports.

---

**Please read the Required Disclosures and Analyst Certification on the last page of this report.**

The **McGraw-Hill** Companies

# Schlumberger Ltd

**STANDARD
&POOR'S**

## Business Summary October 25, 2011

CORPORATE OVERVIEW. Schlumberger Ltd. is a global provider of oilfield services to the energy industry. SLB historically operated, until the end of 2010, in two primary business segments: Oilfield Services, which provides exploration and production services, solutions and technology to the petroleum industry; and Western Geco, its seismic division. It is managed through four geographic areas (North America, South America, Europe/CIS/West Africa, and Middle East/Asia). In the first quarter of 2011, however, SLB changed its reporting methodology. Under the new methodology, SLB will continue to report results on a geographic basis, but will also report under three new operating segments. The Reservoir Characterization Group (which will consist of technologies involved in the finding and defining of hydrocarbon deposits, and includes results from Western Geco), contributed 30% of oilfield services' revenues in 2010, and 41% of segment pretax income during this period. The Drilling segment (41%, 34%) will include the M-I Swaco fluids business, drill bits, Geoservices, drilling & measurements, drilling tools, and other drilling-related offerings. The Reservoir Production segment (29%, 25%) will focus on well services, completions, artificial lift, subsea services, water and carbon services, and production activities in IPM projects. The Distribution segment acquired in the Smith transaction will be reported as a stand-alone business.

The company is largely focused on international operations; North America

generated only 27% of Oilfield Services' total revenues in 2010, and just 24% of the segment's 2010 pretax operating income. The Middle East/Asia region generated the highest operating margins in 2010, at 25.0%, with Europe/ CIS/West Africa second, at 17.0%.

Operations within Oilfield Services has been historically organized into eight technology segments: (1) wireline services, providing information technology to evaluate the reservoir, plan and monitor wells, and evaluate and monitor production; (2) drilling and measurements, including directional drilling, measurement while drilling and logging while drilling services; (3) well testing; (4) well services, which includes pressure pumping, coiled tubing, well cementing and stimulation; (5) completions, which includes gas-lift and safety valves, and a range of intelligent well completions technology and equipment; (6) artificial lift, which offers production optimization services using electric submersible pumps and other equipment; (7) data and consulting services; and (8) Schlumberger Information Solutions.

## Company Financials Fiscal Year Ended Dec. 31

| Per Share Data ($) | 2010 | 2009 | 2008 | 2007 | 2006 | 2005 | 2004 | 2003 | 2002 | 2001 |
|---|---|---|---|---|---|---|---|---|---|---|
| Tangible Book Value | NA | NA | 8.85 | 7.23 | 3.84 | 3.63 | 2.54 | 1.87 | 0.70 | 1.14 |
| Cash Flow | NA | NA | 5.97 | 5.41 | 4.24 | 2.89 | 1.89 | 1.74 | -0.75 | 2.08 |
| Earnings | 3.38 | 2.61 | 4.42 | 4.20 | 3.01 | 1.81 | 0.85 | 0.41 | -2.09 | 0.46 |
| Dividends | NA | 0.84 | 0.84 | 0.70 | 0.50 | 0.42 | 0.38 | 0.38 | 0.38 | 0.38 |
| Payout Ratio | NA | 32% | 19% | 17% | 17% | 23% | 44% | 93% | NM | 82% |
| Prices:High | 84.11 | 71.10 | 111.95 | 114.84 | 74.75 | 51.49 | 34.95 | 28.12 | 31.22 | 41.41 |
| Prices:Low | 51.67 | 35.05 | 37.07 | 55.68 | 49.20 | 31.57 | 26.27 | 17.81 | 16.70 | 20.42 |
| P/E Ratio:High | 25 | 27 | 25 | 27 | 25 | 28 | 41 | 69 | NM | 91 |
| P/E Ratio:Low | 15 | 13 | 8 | 13 | 16 | 17 | 31 | 44 | NM | 45 |

| Income Statement Analysis (Million $) | | | | | | | | | | |
|---|---|---|---|---|---|---|---|---|---|---|
| Revenue | 27,447 | 22,702 | 27,163 | 23,277 | 19,230 | 14,309 | 11,480 | 14,059 | 13,474 | 13,746 |
| Operating Income | NA | NA | 8,602 | 7,994 | 6,458 | 4,520 | 2,895 | 2,474 | -456 | 3,165 |
| Depreciation, Depletion and Amortization | 2,759 | 2,476 | 1,904 | 1,526 | 1,561 | 1,351 | 1,308 | 1,571 | 1,545 | 1,896 |
| Interest Expense | 207 | 221 | 247 | 275 | 235 | 197 | 272 | 334 | 368 | 385 |
| Pretax Income | 5,156 | 3,934 | 6,852 | 6,624 | 4,948 | 2,972 | 1,327 | 568 | -2,230 | 1,126 |
| Effective Tax Rate | NA | 19.6% | 20.9% | 21.9% | 24.0% | 22.9% | 20.9% | 36.9% | NM | 51.1% |
| Net Income | 4,267 | 3,156 | 5,397 | 5,177 | 3,710 | 2,199 | 1,014 | 473 | -2,418 | 522 |

| Balance Sheet & Other Financial Data (Million $) | | | | | | | | | | |
|---|---|---|---|---|---|---|---|---|---|---|
| Cash | 4,990 | 4,616 | 3,692 | 3,169 | 166 | 191 | 224 | 234 | 168 | 178 |
| Current Assets | NA | NA | 12,894 | 11,055 | 9,186 | 8,554 | 7,060 | 10,369 | 7,185 | 7,705 |
| Total Assets | 51,719 | 33,465 | 31,991 | 27,853 | 22,832 | 18,077 | 16,001 | 20,041 | 19,435 | 22,326 |
| Current Liabilities | NA | NA | 8,125 | 7,505 | 6,455 | 5,515 | 4,701 | 6,795 | 6,451 | 6,218 |
| Long Term Debt | 5,517 | 4,355 | 3,694 | 3,794 | 4,664 | 3,591 | 3,944 | 6,097 | 6,029 | 6,216 |
| Common Equity | 31,444 | 19,229 | 16,862 | 14,876 | 10,420 | 7,592 | 6,117 | 5,881 | 5,606 | 8,378 |
| Total Capital | NA | NA | 20,628 | 18,732 | 15,084 | 11,688 | 10,477 | 12,376 | 12,188 | 15,231 |
| Capital Expenditures | 2,914 | 2,395 | 3,723 | 3,191 | 2,457 | 1,593 | 1,216 | 1,025 | 1,366 | 2,053 |
| Cash Flow | NA | NA | 7,301 | 6,703 | 5,271 | 3,550 | 2,322 | 2,044 | -872 | 2,418 |
| Current Ratio | 1.7 | 1.9 | 1.6 | 1.5 | 1.4 | 1.6 | 1.5 | 1.5 | 1.1 | 1.2 |
| % Long Term Debt of Capitalization | 14.9 | 18.2 | 17.9 | 20.3 | 30.9 | 30.7 | 37.6 | 49.3 | 49.5 | 40.8 |
| % Return on Assets | NA | NA | 18.0 | 20.4 | 18.1 | 12.9 | 5.6 | 2.4 | NM | 2.6 |
| % Return on Equity | 16.9 | 17.5 | 34.0 | 40.9 | 41.2 | 32.1 | 16.9 | 8.2 | NM | 6.3 |

Data as orig reptd.; bef. results of disc opers/spec. items. Per share data adj. for stk. divs.; EPS diluted. E-Estimated. NA-Not Available. NM-Not Meaningful. NR-Not Ranked. UR-Under Review.

**Office:** 5599 San Felipe, 17th Floor, Houston, TX 77056.
**Telephone:** 713-375-3400.
**Email:** irsupport@slb.com
**Website:** http://www.slb.com

**Chrmn:** A. Gould
**Pres:** A.G. Floridia
**CEO & COO:** P. Kibsgaard
**EVP & CFO:** S. Ayat

**Chief Acctg Officer:** H. Guild
**Investor Contact:** M. Theobald (713-375-3535)
**Board Members:** L. S. Al Olayan, P. Camus, P. L. Currie, A. Gould, A. E. Isaac, K. V. Kamath, P. Kibsgaard, N. Kudryavtsev, A. Lajous, M. E. Marks, E. A. Moler, L. R. Reif, T. I. Sandvold, H. Seydoux

**Founded:** 1926
**Domicile:** Netherlands Antilles
**Employees:** 108,000

*The McGraw·Hill Companies*

# Schwab (Charles) Corp

**STANDARD &POOR'S**

| **S&P Recommendation** HOLD ★★★★☆ | **Price**<br>$10.77 (as of Nov 25, 2011) | **12-Mo. Target Price**<br>$14.00 | **Investment Style**<br>Large-Cap Blend |
|---|---|---|---|

**GICS Sector** Financials
**Sub-Industry** Investment Banking & Brokerage

**Summary** This company's subsidiary, Charles Schwab & Co., is among the largest brokerage firms in the U.S., primarily serving retail clients.

## Key Stock Statistics (Source S&P, Vickers, company reports)

| | | | | | | |
|---|---|---|---|---|---|---|
| 52-Wk Range | $19.69–10.56 | S&P Oper. EPS 2011E | 0.74 | Market Capitalization(B) | $13.678 | Beta | 1.29 |
| Trailing 12-Month EPS | $0.67 | S&P Oper. EPS 2012E | 0.86 | Yield (%) | 2.23 | S&P 3-Yr. Proj. EPS CAGR(%) | NM |
| Trailing 12-Month P/E | 16.1 | P/E on S&P Oper. EPS 2011E | 14.6 | Dividend Rate/Share | $0.24 | S&P Credit Rating | A |
| $10K Invested 5 Yrs Ago | $6,361 | Common Shares Outstg. (M) | 1,270.0 | Institutional Ownership (%) | 77 | | |

## Price Performance

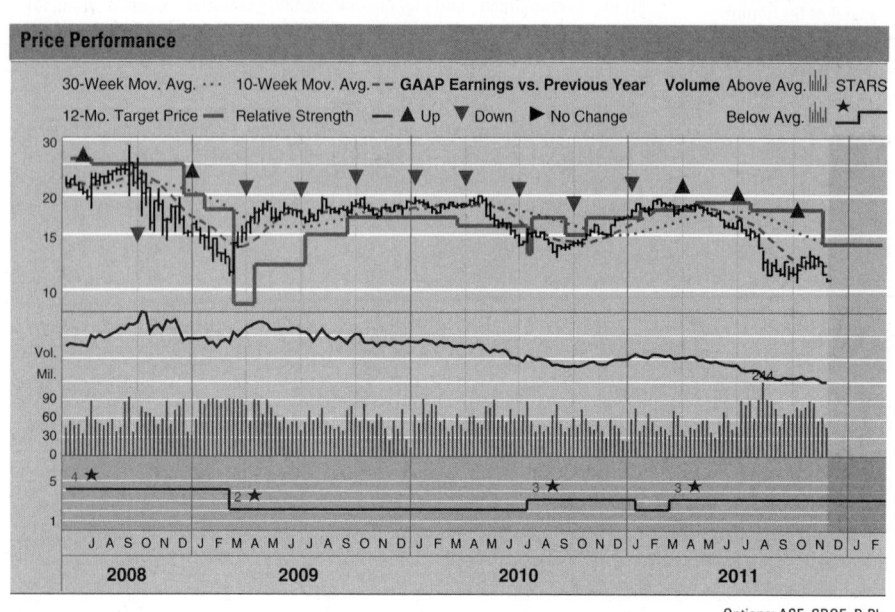

30-Week Mov. Avg. ···· 10-Week Mov. Avg. – – GAAP Earnings vs. Previous Year   Volume Above Avg. ⅃ STARS
12-Mo. Target Price — Relative Strength — ▲ Up ▼ Down ► No Change   Below Avg. ⅃ ★

Options: ASE, CBOE, P, Ph

Analysis prepared by Equity Analyst **Cathy Seifert** on Nov 15, 2011, when the stock traded at **$12.11**.

## Highlights

➤ Net revenue growth in coming periods will likely be in the low double digit range, reflecting growth in both fee income and net interest revenue. Net revenues advanced 15%, year to year, in the first nine months of 2011, reflecting 11% higher fee income and a nearly 20% rise in net interest revenue. We expect trading commissions to increase modestly going forward. We view SCHW's steady stream of asset-based revenues as a sign of earnings stability, although growth in fee income could slow if market pressures continue.

➤ We expect pretax margins to expand to 33% in 2011, from 18% in 2010, as expenses were inflated in 2010 by legal charges. We look for rising advertising expenses and increased investment spending, but for other costs to decline on a relative basis.

➤ We forecast EPS of $0.74 in 2011 and $0.86 in 2012.

## Investment Rationale/Risk

➤ In our view, SCHW is heavily geared toward short-term interest rates, given that 37% of its top line came from net interest income in the first nine months of 2011. We view favorably SCHW's stable asset-based revenues, but we think SCHW's earnings growth will remain in line with peers until the Federal Reserve raises short-term interest rates, which we do not expect to happen this year. However, we do see continued growth in SCHW's active brokerage accounts as well as its ETF business. We also expect steady growth in interest-earning assets. Although we expect SCHW to benefit from improving retail investor activity, we think that current low short-term interest rates will persist in the near term and cause SCHW to produce peer-average earnings growth. All told, we believe the shares are appropriately valued at recent levels.

➤ Risks to our recommendation and target price include a decrease in trading volume and equity market depreciation.

➤ Our 12-month target price of $14 is 16.3X our forward earnings estimate of $0.86, in line with the historical multiple but still a premium to some peers.

## Qualitative Risk Assessment

| LOW | **MEDIUM** | HIGH |
|---|---|---|

Our risk assessment reflects our view of the company's strong competitive position, brand recognition and affluent client base, offset by industry cyclically and our concerns about corporate governance.

## Quantitative Evaluations

**S&P Quality Ranking**   B

| D | C | B- | **B** | B+ | A- | A | A+ |
|---|---|---|---|---|---|---|---|

**Relative Strength Rank**   WEAK

27

LOWEST = 1                        HIGHEST = 99

## Revenue/Earnings Data

**Revenue (Million $)**

| | 1Q | 2Q | 3Q | 4Q | Year |
|---|---|---|---|---|---|
| 2011 | 45.00 | 45.00 | 44.00 | -- | -- |
| 2010 | 978.0 | 1,080 | 1,063 | 1,127 | 4,248 |
| 2009 | 1,111 | 1,085 | 1,011 | 986.0 | 4,193 |
| 2008 | 1,307 | 1,308 | 1,251 | 1,284 | 5,150 |
| 2007 | 1,153 | 1,205 | 1,291 | 1,345 | 4,994 |
| 2006 | 1,054 | 1,093 | 1,066 | 1,096 | 4,309 |

**Earnings Per Share ($)**

| | | | | | |
|---|---|---|---|---|---|
| 2011 | 0.20 | 0.20 | 0.18 | E0.16 | E0.74 |
| 2010 | Nil | 0.17 | 0.10 | 0.10 | 0.38 |
| 2009 | 0.19 | 0.18 | 0.17 | 0.14 | 0.68 |
| 2008 | 0.26 | 0.26 | 0.26 | 0.27 | 1.06 |
| 2007 | 0.19 | 0.23 | 0.27 | 0.26 | 0.92 |
| 2006 | 0.19 | 0.19 | 0.21 | 0.37 | 0.69 |

Fiscal year ended Dec. 31. Next earnings report expected: NA. EPS Estimates based on S&P Operating Earnings; historical GAAP earnings are as reported.

## Dividend Data (Dates: mm/dd Payment Date: mm/dd/yy)

| Amount ($) | Date Decl. | Ex-Div. Date | Stk. of Record | Payment Date |
|---|---|---|---|---|
| 0.060 | 01/27 | 02/09 | 02/11 | 02/25/11 |
| 0.060 | 04/26 | 05/04 | 05/06 | 05/20/11 |
| 0.060 | 07/26 | 08/10 | 08/12 | 08/26/11 |
| 0.060 | 10/27 | 11/08 | 11/10 | 11/25/11 |

Dividends have been paid since 1989. Source: Company reports.

---

**Please read the Required Disclosures and Analyst Certification on the last page of this report.**

**The McGraw·Hill Companies**

# Schwab (Charles) Corp

## Business Summary November 15, 2011

CORPORATE OVERVIEW. Charles Schwab Corp. (SCHW) is a financial holding company that provides securities brokerage and related financial services through three segments, Schwab Investor Services, Schwab Institutional and Schwab Corporate and Retirement Services. Another subsidiary, Charles Schwab Investment Management, is the investment adviser for Schwab's proprietary mutual funds. In December 2007, CyberTrader, Inc., formerly a subsidiary of SCHW, which provides electronic trading and brokerage services to highly active, online traders, was merged into Schwab.

Through the Schwab Investor Services segment (67% of 2010 net revenue), the company provides retail brokerage and banking services. Through various types of brokerage accounts, Schwab offers the purchase and sale of securities, including NASDAQ, exchange-listed and other equity securities, options, mutual funds, unit investment trusts, variable annuities and fixed-income investments. At the end of 2010, the company, through subsidiaries, served about 10 million active client accounts, and held client assets of approximately $1.6 trillion.

Through the Institutional Services segment (33%), Schwab provides custodial, trading, technology, practice management, trust asset and other support services to independent advisers (IAs). To attract and serve independent advis-

ers, this segment has a dedicated sales force and service teams assigned to meet their needs. Institutional Services offers an array of services to help advisers establish their own independent practices, which includes access to dedicated service teams and outsourcing of back-office operations, as well as third-party firms that provide assistance with real estate, errors and omissions insurance, and company benefits. SCHW also offers a variety of educational materials and events to IAs seeking to expand their knowledge of industry issues and trends, as well as sharpen their individual expertise and practice management skills.

The Institutional Services segment also provides retirement plan services, plan administrator services, stock plan services and mutual fund clearing services, and supports the availability of Schwab proprietary mutual funds on third-party platforms. The company serves a range of employer-sponsored plans: equity compensation plans, defined contribution plans, defined benefit plans and other investment-related benefits plans.

## Company Financials Fiscal Year Ended Dec. 31

| Per Share Data ($) | 2010 | 2009 | 2008 | 2007 | 2006 | 2005 | 2004 | 2003 | 2002 | 2001 |
|---|---|---|---|---|---|---|---|---|---|---|
| Tangible Book Value | 4.61 | 3.89 | 3.03 | 2.76 | 3.63 | 2.71 | 2.57 | 2.56 | 0.55 | 2.58 |
| Cash Flow | 0.50 | 0.82 | 1.19 | 1.04 | 0.81 | 0.72 | 0.47 | 0.35 | 0.30 | 0.30 |
| Earnings | 0.38 | 0.68 | 1.06 | 0.92 | 0.69 | 0.56 | 0.30 | 0.35 | 0.07 | 0.06 |
| S&P Core Earnings | 0.56 | 0.67 | 1.08 | 0.92 | 0.68 | 0.53 | 0.23 | 0.27 | -0.02 | -0.09 |
| Dividends | 0.24 | 0.24 | 0.22 | 0.20 | 0.14 | 0.09 | 0.07 | 0.05 | 0.04 | 0.04 |
| Payout Ratio | 63% | 35% | 21% | 22% | 14% | 16% | 25% | 14% | 63% | 73% |
| Prices:High | 19.95 | 19.87 | 28.75 | 25.72 | 19.49 | 16.14 | 13.92 | 14.20 | 19.00 | 33.00 |
| Prices:Low | 12.64 | 11.00 | 14.28 | 17.41 | 14.00 | 9.65 | 8.25 | 6.25 | 7.22 | 8.13 |
| P/E Ratio:High | 53 | 29 | 27 | 28 | 21 | 29 | 46 | 41 | NM | NM |
| P/E Ratio:Low | 33 | 16 | 13 | 19 | 15 | 17 | 28 | 18 | NM | NM |

| Income Statement Analysis (Million $) | 2010 | 2009 | 2008 | 2007 | 2006 | 2005 | 2004 | 2003 | 2002 | 2001 |
|---|---|---|---|---|---|---|---|---|---|---|
| Commissions | 830 | 996 | 1,080 | 860 | 785 | 779 | 936 | 1,207 | 1,206 | 1,355 |
| Interest Income | 1,723 | 1,428 | 1,908 | 2,270 | 2,113 | 1,944 | 1,213 | 970 | 1,186 | 1,857 |
| Total Revenue | 4,474 | 4,414 | 5,393 | 5,617 | 4,988 | 5,151 | 4,479 | 4,328 | 4,480 | 5,281 |
| Interest Expense | 199 | 221 | 243 | 623 | 679 | 687 | 277 | 241 | 345 | 928 |
| Pretax Income | 779 | 1,276 | 2,028 | 1,853 | 1,476 | 1,185 | 645 | 710 | 168 | 135 |
| Effective Tax Rate | 41.7% | 38.3% | 39.4% | 39.6% | 39.6% | 38.4% | 35.8% | 33.5% | 42.3% | 42.2% |
| Net Income | 454 | 787 | 1,230 | 1,120 | 891 | 730 | 414 | 472 | 97.0 | 78.0 |
| S&P Core Earnings | 673 | 779 | 1,247 | 1,117 | 875 | 678 | 314 | 357 | -31.5 | -131 |

| Balance Sheet & Other Financial Data (Million $) | 2010 | 2009 | 2008 | 2007 | 2006 | 2005 | 2004 | 2003 | 2002 | 2001 |
|---|---|---|---|---|---|---|---|---|---|---|
| Total Assets | 92,568 | 75,431 | 51,675 | 42,286 | 48,992 | 47,351 | 47,133 | 45,866 | 39,705 | 40,464 |
| Cash Items | 28,017 | 27,530 | 20,127 | 15,567 | 15,369 | 17,589 | 21,797 | 24,175 | 24,119 | 22,148 |
| Receivables | 20,375 | 16,535 | 13,932 | 16,482 | 11,577 | 11,600 | 10,323 | 9,137 | 7,067 | 10,066 |
| Securities Owned | 24,330 | 23,036 | 15,072 | 8,201 | 6,386 | 6,857 | 5,335 | 4,023 | 1,716 | 1,700 |
| Securities Borrowed | Nil | Nil | Nil | Nil | Nil | Nil | Nil | Nil | Nil | Nil |
| Due Brokers & Customers | 32,250 | 28,619 | 21,356 | 22,212 | 22,119 | 25,994 | 28,622 | 29,845 | 27,877 | 27,822 |
| Other Liabilities | 52,086 | 40,227 | 25,375 | 15,441 | 21,477 | NA | NA | NA | NA | NA |
| Capitalization:Debt | 2,006 | 1,512 | 883 | 899 | 388 | 514 | 585 | 772 | 642 | 730 |
| Capitalization:Equity | 6,226 | 5,073 | 4,061 | 3,732 | 5,008 | 4,450 | 4,386 | 4,461 | 4,011 | 4,163 |
| Capitalization:Total | 8,232 | 6,585 | 4,944 | 4,631 | 5,396 | 4,964 | 4,971 | 5,233 | 4,653 | 4,893 |
| % Return on Revenue | 10.1 | 17.8 | 22.8 | 19.9 | 17.9 | 14.2 | 9.2 | 15.1 | 3.0 | 2.0 |
| % Return on Assets | 0.5 | 1.2 | 2.6 | 2.5 | 1.8 | 1.5 | 0.9 | 1.1 | 0.2 | 0.2 |
| % Return on Equity | 8.0 | 1.2 | 31.6 | 25.6 | 18.8 | 16.5 | 9.4 | 11.1 | 2.4 | 1.9 |

Data as orig reptd.; bef. results of disc opers/spec. items. Per share data adj. for stk. divs.; EPS diluted. Quarterly revs. excl. interest expense. E-Estimated. NA-Not Available. NM-Not Meaningful. NR-Not Ranked. UR-Under Review.

Office: 211 Main Street, San Francisco, CA 94105.
Telephone: 415-667-7000.
Email: investor.relations@schwab.com
Website: http://www.schwab.com

Chrmn: C.R. Schwab, Jr.
Pres & CEO: W.W. Bettinger, II
COO & EVP: R. Carter
EVP, CFO & Chief Acctg Officer: J.R. Martinetto

EVP, Secy & General Counsel: C.E. Dwyer
Investor Contact: R.G. Fowler (415-636-9869)
Board Members: N. H. Bechtle, W. W. Bettinger, II, P. P. Butcher, F. C. Herringer, S. T. McLin, A. Sarin, C. R. Schwab, Jr., P. A. Sneed, R. O. Walther, R. N. Wilson

Founded: 1971
Domicile: Delaware
Employees: 12,800

# Scripps Networks Interactive Inc

**STANDARD &POOR'S**

| S&P Recommendation | HOLD ★★★★★ | Price $37.88 (as of Nov 25, 2011) | 12-Mo. Target Price $46.00 | Investment Style Large-Cap Value |
|---|---|---|---|---|

**GICS Sector** Consumer Discretionary
**Sub-Industry** Broadcasting & Cable TV

**Summary** SNI, spun off by E.W. Scripps in 2008, is one of the leading developers of lifestyle-oriented content for television and the Internet.

## Key Stock Statistics (Source S&P, Vickers, company reports)

| | | | | | | | |
|---|---|---|---|---|---|---|---|
| 52-Wk Range | $53.66–33.82 | S&P Oper. EPS 2011**E** | 2.88 | Market Capitalization(B) | $4.826 | Beta | 1.18 |
| Trailing 12-Month EPS | $2.43 | S&P Oper. EPS 2012**E** | 3.33 | Yield (%) | 1.06 | S&P 3-Yr. Proj. EPS CAGR(%) | 15 |
| Trailing 12-Month P/E | 15.6 | P/E on S&P Oper. EPS 2011**E** | 13.2 | Dividend Rate/Share | $0.40 | S&P Credit Rating | NA |
| $10K Invested 5 Yrs Ago | NA | Common Shares Outstg. (M) | 159.4 | Institutional Ownership (%) | 71 | | |

## Price Performance

- 30-Week Mov. Avg.
- 10-Week Mov. Avg.
- 12-Mo. Target Price
- Relative Strength
- GAAP Earnings vs. Previous Year
- ▲ Up ▼ Down ▶ No Change
- Volume Above Avg. STARS Below Avg. ★

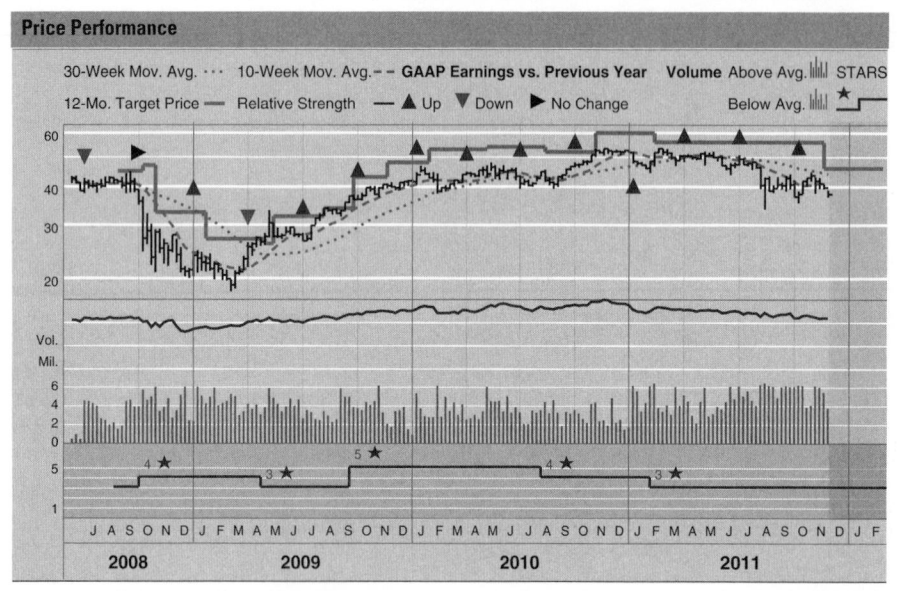

Options: Ph

Analysis prepared by Equity Analyst **T. Amobi, CFA CPA** on Nov 15, 2011, when the stock traded at **$40.31**.

## Highlights

▶ We project 2011 and 2012 revenues for the core Lifestyle Media businesses to increase approximately 11% and 8%, respectively, to $2.07 billion and $2.24 billion, mainly driven by double-digit affiliate and advertising revenue gains for the Food Network, and relatively moderate gains for the Travel Channel and HGTV. While representing a smaller base, we see stronger double-digit gains from flanker brands Cooking Channel and DIY networks, combined with continued strong growth in digital revenues.

▶ We expect some margin expansion to reflect increased contributions from significantly higher-margin digital revenues and some affiliate rate increases, outweighing continued investments in programming. Also, in May 2011, SNI divested Shopzilla, its comparison shopping site subsidiary, which has constrained its results in the past few years.

▶ Assuming additional equity earnings from newly acquired U.K.-based affiliates, versus higher interest expense, D&A and taxes, and after higher minority interest share of net income, we forecast operating EPS of $2.88 and $3.33 in 2011 and 2012, respectively, with some share buybacks under a $1 billion plan.

## Investment Rationale/Risk

▶ We see SNI further leveraging the appeal of its core Food Network and HGTV into successful flanker brands such as Cooking Channel and DIY Network, respectively, while Travel Channel perhaps offers the single largest long-term growth opportunity, in our view. Also, we see potentially significant economic upside as key affiliate contracts are renewed over the next several years. We note SNI's increased focus on international expansion, recently underscored by a new UKTV joint venture with the BBC (which management expects to be accretive to EPS in its first year), while maintaining relatively ample financial flexibility for continued share buybacks, in our opinion.

▶ Risks to our recommendation and target price include a sharp macroeconomic slowdown and/or major pullback in ad spending; sharp ratings declines for the TV networks; dilutive acquisitions; and foreign currency exposure.

▶ Our 12-month target price of $46 reflects a blend of EV/EBITDA of 8.5X and P/E-to-growth of 0.9X, using 2012 estimates, slightly below peers with more exposure to higher-growth international markets. We note more than $60 million of NOLs for certain U.K. subsidiaries.

## Qualitative Risk Assessment

| LOW | **MEDIUM** | HIGH |
|---|---|---|

Our risk assessment reflects what we view as strong ratings of popular network brands such as Food Channel and HGTV, potential upside from a successful integration of the Travel Channel, and potentially significant opportunities for international expansion, versus a relatively high cyclical exposure that could manifest from SNI's relative lack of business and geographic diversification.

## Quantitative Evaluations

**S&P Quality Ranking** NR

| D | C | B- | B | B+ | A- | A | A+ |
|---|---|---|---|---|---|---|---|

**Relative Strength Rank** MODERATE

41

LOWEST = 1    HIGHEST = 99

## Revenue/Earnings Data

**Revenue (Million $)**

| | 1Q | 2Q | 3Q | 4Q | Year |
|---|---|---|---|---|---|
| 2011 | 536.0 | 534.0 | 503.7 | -- | -- |
| 2010 | 469.4 | 516.0 | 508.7 | 573.0 | 2,067 |
| 2009 | 361.2 | 391.3 | 364.5 | 429.7 | 1,541 |
| 2008 | 388.3 | 416.1 | 374.7 | 411.5 | 1,591 |
| 2007 | 332.4 | 367.2 | 344.0 | 397.7 | 1,441 |
| 2006 | -- | -- | -- | -- | 1,323 |

**Earnings Per Share ($)**

| | 1Q | 2Q | 3Q | 4Q | Year |
|---|---|---|---|---|---|
| 2011 | 0.59 | 0.78 | 0.65 | E0.82 | E2.88 |
| 2010 | 0.43 | 0.57 | 0.61 | 0.77 | 2.39 |
| 2009 | 0.37 | 0.49 | 0.39 | 0.40 | 1.65 |
| 2008 | 0.41 | 0.33 | 0.35 | -0.94 | 0.14 |
| 2007 | -- | 0.43 | 0.35 | -1.83 | -0.72 |
| 2006 | -- | -- | -- | -- | -- |

Fiscal year ended Dec. 31. Next earnings report expected: Mid February. EPS Estimates based on S&P Operating Earnings; historical GAAP earnings are as reported.

## Dividend Data (Dates: mm/dd Payment Date: mm/dd/yy)

| Amount ($) | Date Decl. | Ex-Div. Date | Stk. of Record | Payment Date |
|---|---|---|---|---|
| 0.075 | 11/16 | 11/26 | 11/30 | 12/10/10 |
| 0.075 | 02/17 | 02/24 | 02/28 | 03/10/11 |
| 0.100 | 08/03 | 08/29 | 08/31 | 09/09/11 |
| 0.100 | 11/17 | 11/28 | 11/30 | 12/09/11 |

Dividends have been paid since 2008. Source: Company reports.

---

**Please read the Required Disclosures and Analyst Certification on the last page of this report.**

**The McGraw-Hill Companies**

# Scripps Networks Interactive Inc

**STANDARD
&POOR'S**

## Business Summary November 15, 2011

CORPORATE OVERVIEW. Scripps Networks Interactive is a lifestyle content and Internet search company with national television networks and interactive brands. SNI manages its operations mainly through its core Lifestyle Media (formerly Scripps Networks) business -- which includes HGTV, Food Network (75%-owned), Travel Channel (65%-owned), DIY, Fine Living, Great American Country, a minority interest in Fox-BRV South Sports Holdings, and Internet-based businesses, including RecipeZaar.com, HGTVPro.com, and FrontDoor.com. (In May 2011, the company sold Shopzilla, its comparison shopping site subsidiary, to certain private parties, for $165 million.)

The Lifestyle Media business derives revenues principally from advertising sales, affiliate fees, and ancillary sales, including the sale and licensing of consumer products. Revenues from the Interactive Media segment are generated primarily from referral fees and commissions paid by merchants and service providers for online leads generated by its websites. Lifestyle Media and Interactive Services accounted for 90% and 9% of 2010 revenue, respectively -- compared to 88% and 12% in 2009, 82% and 18% in 2008, 83% and 17% in 2007, 80% and 20% in 2006, and 90% and 10% in 2005.

In 2010, HGTV accounted for 36.7% of operating revenue, Food Network for 35.5%, Travel Channel for 13.3%, DIY for 4.7%, Cooking for 3.0%, GAC for 1.6%, SN Digital for 4.8%, and Other 0.4%. In 2010, the HGTV network reached 99,400 homes, according to Nielsen; Food Network 100,100; Travel Channel 95,600; DIY 53,500; Cooking Channel 57,100; and GAC 59,300.

Scripps Networks Interactive was spun off from E.W. Scripps Company (SSP) on July 1, 2008. In October 2007, the E.W. Scripps board of directors authorized management to pursue a separation of Scripps into two companies -- one focused on national and global lifestyle media and interactive services, and the other on market-leading local media franchises. Shareholders approved the split on June 13, 2008. All shareholders of E.W. Scripps received a tax-free distribution of SNI stock.

## Company Financials Fiscal Year Ended Dec. 31

| Per Share Data ($) | 2010 | 2009 | 2008 | 2007 | 2006 | 2005 | 2004 | 2003 | 2002 | 2001 |
|---|---|---|---|---|---|---|---|---|---|---|
| Tangible Book Value | 1.34 | NM | 2.26 | 2.25 | NA | NA | NA | NA | NA | NA |
| Cash Flow | 3.83 | 2.14 | 0.59 | -0.19 | NA | NA | NA | NA | NA | NA |
| Earnings | 2.39 | 1.65 | 0.14 | -0.72 | NA | NA | NA | NA | NA | NA |
| S&P Core Earnings | 2.41 | 1.68 | 1.63 | 1.11 | 1.44 | NA | NA | NA | NA | NA |
| Dividends | 0.30 | 0.30 | 0.15 | NA | NA | NA | NA | NA | NA | NA |
| Payout Ratio | 13% | 18% | 107% | NA | NA | NA | NA | NA | NA | NA |
| Prices:High | 53.34 | 42.36 | 44.98 | NA | NA | NA | NA | NA | NA | NA |
| Prices:Low | 37.94 | 18.10 | 20.00 | NA | NA | NA | NA | NA | NA | NA |
| P/E Ratio:High | 22 | 26 | NM | NA | NA | NA | NA | NA | NA | NA |
| P/E Ratio:Low | 16 | 11 | NM | NA | NA | NA | NA | NA | NA | NA |

### Income Statement Analysis (Million $)

| | 2010 | 2009 | 2008 | 2007 | 2006 | 2005 | 2004 | 2003 | 2002 | 2001 |
|---|---|---|---|---|---|---|---|---|---|---|
| Revenue | 2,067 | 1,541 | 1,591 | 1,441 | 1,323 | 1,002 | NA | NA | NA | NA |
| Operating Income | NA | NA | 651 | 591 | NA | NA | NA | NA | NA | NA |
| Depreciation | 125 | 81.5 | 73.9 | 86.7 | 101 | 67.0 | NA | NA | NA | NA |
| Interest Expense | 35.2 | 2.81 | 14.2 | 15.2 | 54.0 | 37.0 | NA | NA | NA | NA |
| Pretax Income | 740 | 520 | 309 | 98.7 | 427 | 343 | NA | NA | NA | NA |
| Effective Tax Rate | NA | 31.0% | 62.5% | NM | 28.3% | 32.8% | NA | NA | NA | NA |
| Net Income | 519 | 273 | 23.6 | -118 | 234 | 176 | NA | NA | NA | NA |
| S&P Core Earnings | 404 | 278 | 267 | 183 | 235 | NA | NA | NA | NA | NA |

### Balance Sheet & Other Financial Data (Million $)

| | 2010 | 2009 | 2008 | 2007 | 2006 | 2005 | 2004 | 2003 | 2002 | 2001 |
|---|---|---|---|---|---|---|---|---|---|---|
| Cash | 550 | 254 | 12.7 | 44.2 | 19.0 | NA | NA | NA | NA | NA |
| Current Assets | 1,446 | 982 | 638 | 658 | 604 | NA | NA | NA | NA | NA |
| Total Assets | 3,388 | 2,963 | 1,773 | 2,064 | 2,385 | NA | NA | NA | NA | NA |
| Current Liabilities | 209 | 211 | 166 | 124 | 172 | NA | NA | NA | NA | NA |
| Long Term Debt | 884 | 884 | 80.0 | 450 | 765 | NA | NA | NA | NA | NA |
| Common Equity | 1,776 | 1,384 | 1,135 | 1,157 | 1,186 | NA | NA | NA | NA | NA |
| Total Capital | 3,269 | 2,533 | 1,368 | 1,391 | 2,069 | NA | NA | NA | NA | NA |
| Capital Expenditures | 77.0 | 90.0 | 77.4 | NA | 40.4 | 29.0 | NA | NA | NA | NA |
| Cash Flow | 644 | 355 | 97.5 | -31.0 | 335 | 243 | NA | NA | NA | NA |
| Current Ratio | 6.9 | 4.7 | 3.8 | 5.3 | 3.5 | NA | NA | NA | NA | NA |
| % Long Term Debt of Capitalization | 27.1 | Nil | 5.8 | 32.3 | 39.2 | Nil | NA | NA | NA | NA |
| % Net Income of Revenue | 25.1 | 17.7 | 1.5 | NM | 17.7 | 17.5 | NA | NA | NA | NA |
| % Return on Assets | 16.3 | 11.5 | 1.2 | NM | NA | NA | NA | NA | NA | NA |
| % Return on Equity | 32.9 | NA | 2.2 | NM | NA | NA | NA | NA | NA | NA |

Data as orig reptd.; bef. results of disc opers/spec. items. Per share data adj. for stk. divs.; EPS diluted. Data for 2007 pro forma; bal. sheet & book val. as of March 31, 2008. E-Estimated. NA-Not Available. NM-Not Meaningful. NR-Not Ranked. UR-Under Review.

**Office:** 312 Walnut Street, Cincinnati, OH 45202.
**Telephone:** 513-824-3200.
**Website:**
http://www.scrippsnetworksinteractive.com
**Chrmn, Pres & CEO:** K.W. Lowe

**COO:** R. Boehne
**SVP & Treas:** M.F. Schuermann
**SVP & Cntlr:** C.M. Boydston
**CFO, Chief Admin Officer & Chief Acctg Officer:** J.G. NeCastro

**Board Members:** J. H. Burlingame, M. R. Costa, D. A. Galloway, K. W. Lowe, J. Mohn, N. B. Paumgarten, M. M. Peirce, D. Pond, J. Sagansky, N. E. Scagliotti, R. W. Tysoe
**Founded:** 2007
**Domicile:** Ohio
**Employees:** 2,000

The McGraw-Hill Companies

# Sealed Air Corp

**STANDARD &POOR'S**

| S&P Recommendation **BUY** ★★★★☆ | Price<br>$16.31 (as of Nov 25, 2011) | 12-Mo. Target Price<br>$20.00 | Investment Style<br>Large-Cap Growth |
|---|---|---|---|

**GICS Sector** Materials
**Sub-Industry** Paper Packaging

**Summary** This leading global manufacturer of a wide range of food and protective packaging materials and systems recently acquired Diversey Holdings, a leading solutions provider to the global cleaning and sanitization market, for over $4 billion.

## Key Stock Statistics (Source S&P, Vickers, company reports)

| | | | | | | | |
|---|---|---|---|---|---|---|---|
| 52-Wk Range | $28.77– 15.05 | S&P Oper. EPS 2011**E** | 1.70 | Market Capitalization(B) | $3.132 | Beta | 1.39 |
| Trailing 12-Month EPS | $1.40 | S&P Oper. EPS 2012**E** | 2.05 | Yield (%) | 3.19 | S&P 3-Yr. Proj. EPS CAGR(%) | 12 |
| Trailing 12-Month P/E | 11.7 | P/E on S&P Oper. EPS 2011**E** | 9.6 | Dividend Rate/Share | $0.52 | S&P Credit Rating | BB |
| $10K Invested 5 Yrs Ago | $6,021 | Common Shares Outstg. (M) | 192.0 | Institutional Ownership (%) | 66 | | |

## Price Performance

30-Week Mov. Avg. · · · · 10-Week Mov. Avg. – – GAAP Earnings vs. Previous Year Volume Above Avg. STARS
12-Mo. Target Price — Relative Strength ▲ Up ▼ Down ▶ No Change Below Avg. ★

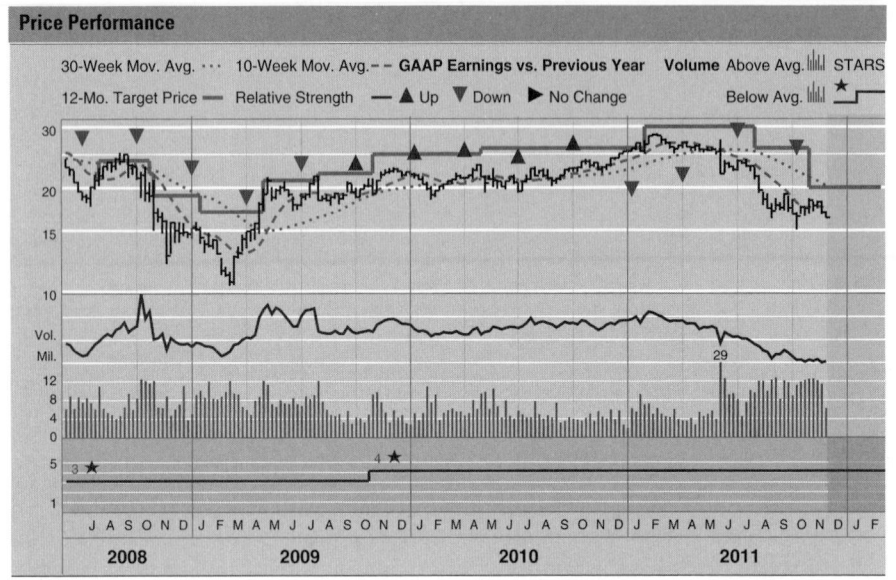

Options: CBOE, P, Ph

Analysis prepared by Equity Analyst **Stewart Scharf** on Nov 02, 2011, when the stock traded at **$17.75**.

### Highlights

▶ We project about 9% sales growth for 2011 (includes 5% positive forex), with a low-double digit advance in 2012, driven by unit volume in Asia/Pacific and Europe, and a better price/mix in the U.S. We see strength in protective packaging volume, and a better product mix and more favorable trends for new food packaging and solutions products, with contributions from Diversey Holdings (acquired in October 2011) aiding results.

▶ We look for gross margins to narrow somewhat in 2011, from 27.9% in 2010, but improve late in 2011 and during 2012, due to price hikes and stabilizing resin costs, along with contractual pricing pass-throughs. We project that adjusted EBITDA margins will narrow by about 100 bps in 2011, to 15.3%, but expand in 2012, based on operating leverage, a better price/mix, production efficiencies from supply-chain efficiencies and cost controls, while synergies from Diversey begin to kick in late in the year.

▶ We estimate a higher effective tax rate of about 27% for 2011, and operating EPS of $1.70 for 2011 (excluding Diversey), advancing 21% to $2.05 for 2012.

### Investment Rationale/Risk

▶ Our buy recommendation is based on our view that global markets will gradually recover and SEE will continue to develop innovative products. Our valuation models also suggest the shares are undervalued, and we expect the recent acquisition of food safety and hygiene provider Diversey to expand the company's reach into developing markets.

▶ Risks to our recommendation and target price include softer global economic conditions, sharply higher resin costs, geopolitical issues, adverse foreign currency effect, and any new "mad cow" type disease scare. We have some concern regarding corporate governance issues, since at least one former CEO serves on the board of directors.

▶ Applying a multiple of 9X to our 2012 EPS estimate -- a discount to historical forward levels and S&P's Paper Packaging sub-industry group -- we arrive at a value of $18. Our discounted cash flow model, which assumes a perpetual growth rate of 3.5% and a weighted average cost of capital of 9.5%, leads to an intrinsic value of $22. Our 12-month target price of $20 is a blend of these metrics.

### Qualitative Risk Assessment

| LOW | MEDIUM | HIGH |
|---|---|---|

Our risk assessment reflects challenging global markets, volatile resin costs, and food-related health issues that could lead to restrictions on imports and exports. This is offset by our view of the company's sound balance sheet and cash flow generation.

### Quantitative Evaluations

**S&P Quality Ranking** B+

| D | C | B- | B | B+ | A- | A | A+ |
|---|---|---|---|---|---|---|---|

**Relative Strength Rank** MODERATE

36

LOWEST = 1    HIGHEST = 99

### Revenue/Earnings Data

**Revenue (Million $)**

| | 1Q | 2Q | 3Q | 4Q | Year |
|---|---|---|---|---|---|
| 2011 | 1,129 | 1,213 | 1,247 | -- | -- |
| 2010 | 1,061 | 1,090 | 1,130 | 1,209 | 4,490 |
| 2009 | 988.5 | 1,028 | 1,080 | 1,146 | 4,243 |
| 2008 | 1,177 | 1,279 | 1,219 | 1,168 | 4,844 |
| 2007 | 1,095 | 1,145 | 1,161 | 1,250 | 4,651 |
| 2006 | 1,019 | 1,082 | 1,081 | 1,146 | 4,328 |

**Earnings Per Share ($)**

| | | | | | |
|---|---|---|---|---|---|
| 2011 | 0.34 | 0.37 | 0.41 | E0.48 | E1.70 |
| 2010 | 0.35 | 0.38 | 0.43 | 0.29 | 1.44 |
| 2009 | 0.32 | 0.33 | 0.34 | 0.37 | 1.35 |
| 2008 | 0.33 | 0.34 | 0.05 | 0.26 | 0.99 |
| 2007 | 0.67 | 0.40 | 0.39 | 0.43 | 1.89 |
| 2006 | 0.30 | 0.31 | 0.41 | 0.45 | 1.47 |

Fiscal year ended Dec. 31. Next earnings report expected: NA. EPS Estimates based on S&P Operating Earnings; historical GAAP earnings are as reported.

### Dividend Data (Dates: mm/dd Payment Date: mm/dd/yy)

| Amount<br>($) | Date<br>Decl. | Ex-Div.<br>Date | Stk. of<br>Record | Payment<br>Date |
|---|---|---|---|---|
| 0.130 | 02/17 | 03/02 | 03/04 | 03/18/11 |
| 0.130 | 04/07 | 06/01 | 06/03 | 06/17/11 |
| 0.130 | 07/14 | 08/31 | 09/02 | 09/16/11 |
| 0.130 | 10/13 | 11/30 | 12/02 | 12/16/11 |

Dividends have been paid since 2006. Source: Company reports.

---

**Please read the Required Disclosures and Analyst Certification on the last page of this report.**

**The McGraw·Hill Companies**

# Sealed Air Corp

## Business Summary November 02, 2011

Founded in 1996, Sealed Air Corporation (SEE), through its subsidiaries, manufactures a range of packaging and performance-based materials and equipment systems that serve an array of food, industrial, medical, and consumer applications. Company brands include Bubble Wrap cushioning, Jiffy protective mailers, Instapak foam-in-place systems, and Cryovac packaging technology. SEE operates in four segments: Food Packaging; Food Solutions; Protective Packaging, which includes Shrink Packaging; and Other, which includes Specialty Materials, Medical Applications and New Ventures. In the Food Packaging segment, the company focuses on the automated packaging of perishable foods, including shrink bags to vacuum package fresh food products. Its products are primarily focused on fresh and processed meats and cheeses that are sold primarily to food processors, distributors, supermarket retailers, and foodservice businesses. The company markets these products primarily under the Cryovac trademark. Product offerings in this segment include Oven Ease ovenable bag for bone-in or boneless meat and poultry prod-

ucts; Cryovac Roboloader system, which measures a product's width, and, using a robotic arm, selects and opens the corresponding bag for the product's size from one of up to six dispensing units; PakFormance integrated packaging solutions that give food processors control and oversight of the food packaging process; Multi-Seal package, a reclosable deli package; Freshness Plus oxygen scavenging systems and odor scavenging materials; and Cryovac Grip & Tear bags, end-seal bags for fresh meats, poultry, and smoked and processed products; Cryovac BL145 and BL175 automatic loaders for roll-serrated bags; and Cryovac CNP310 heavy bags for post-packaging pasteurization of smoked and processed products.

## Company Financials Fiscal Year Ended Dec. 31

| Per Share Data ($) | 2010 | 2009 | 2008 | 2007 | 2006 | 2005 | 2004 | 2003 | 2002 | 2001 |
|---|---|---|---|---|---|---|---|---|---|---|
| Tangible Book Value | 2.39 | 1.21 | NM | NM | NM | NM | NM | NM | NM | NM |
| Cash Flow | 2.33 | 2.18 | 1.77 | 2.62 | 2.30 | 2.64 | 1.99 | 1.95 | -1.17 | 1.92 |
| Earnings | 1.44 | 1.35 | 0.99 | 1.89 | 1.47 | 1.35 | 1.13 | 1.00 | -2.15 | 0.61 |
| S&P Core Earnings | 1.46 | 1.42 | 1.06 | 1.78 | 1.49 | 1.37 | 1.14 | 1.03 | 1.29 | 0.63 |
| Dividends | 0.50 | 0.48 | 0.48 | 0.40 | 0.30 | Nil | Nil | Nil | Nil | Nil |
| Payout Ratio | 35% | 36% | 48% | 21% | 20% | Nil | Nil | Nil | Nil | Nil |
| Prices:High | 25.70 | 22.99 | 28.32 | 33.87 | 32.88 | 28.32 | 27.45 | 27.24 | 24.20 | 23.55 |
| Prices:Low | 18.43 | 10.38 | 12.01 | 22.41 | 22.81 | 22.78 | 22.03 | 17.50 | 6.35 | 14.40 |
| P/E Ratio:High | 18 | 17 | 29 | 18 | 22 | 21 | 24 | 27 | NM | 39 |
| P/E Ratio:Low | 13 | 8 | 12 | 12 | 16 | 17 | 20 | 17 | NM | 24 |

### Income Statement Analysis (Million $)

| | 2010 | 2009 | 2008 | 2007 | 2006 | 2005 | 2004 | 2003 | 2002 | 2001 |
|---|---|---|---|---|---|---|---|---|---|---|
| Revenue | 4,490 | 4,243 | 4,844 | 4,651 | 4,328 | 4,085 | 3,798 | 3,532 | 3,204 | 3,067 |
| Operating Income | 701 | 653 | 642 | 712 | 707 | 687 | 716 | 693 | 1,766 | 641 |
| Depreciation | 156 | 155 | 155 | 149 | 168 | 175 | 180 | 154 | 166 | 221 |
| Interest Expense | 162 | 155 | 137 | 150 | 148 | 150 | 154 | 134 | 65.3 | 76.4 |
| Pretax Income | 343 | 330 | 222 | 456 | 400 | 377 | 323 | 377 | -392 | 297 |
| Effective Tax Rate | NA | 26.0% | 19.1% | 22.6% | 31.5% | 32.1% | 33.2% | 36.2% | NM | 47.3% |
| Net Income | 256 | 244 | 180 | 353 | 274 | 256 | 216 | 240 | -309 | 157 |
| S&P Core Earnings | 258 | 254 | 193 | 333 | 278 | 259 | 219 | 192 | 227 | 111 |

### Balance Sheet & Other Financial Data (Million $)

| | 2010 | 2009 | 2008 | 2007 | 2006 | 2005 | 2004 | 2003 | 2002 | 2001 |
|---|---|---|---|---|---|---|---|---|---|---|
| Cash | 676 | 694 | 129 | 430 | 407 | 456 | 412 | 365 | 127 | 13.8 |
| Current Assets | 2,038 | 2,073 | 1,673 | 1,936 | 1,757 | 1,695 | 1,611 | 1,428 | 1,056 | 776 |
| Total Assets | 5,401 | 5,416 | 4,978 | 5,438 | 5,021 | 4,864 | 4,855 | 4,704 | 4,261 | 3,908 |
| Current Liabilities | 1,448 | 1,434 | 1,622 | 1,742 | 1,406 | 1,534 | 1,304 | 1,190 | 1,153 | 627 |
| Long Term Debt | 1,399 | 1,626 | 1,290 | 1,532 | 1,827 | 1,813 | 2,088 | 2,260 | 868 | 788 |
| Common Equity | 2,380 | 2,212 | 1,942 | 2,020 | 1,530 | 1,392 | 1,334 | 1,124 | 813 | 850 |
| Total Capital | 3,783 | 3,845 | 3,220 | 3,561 | 3,364 | 3,229 | 3,448 | 3,418 | 3,039 | 3,215 |
| Capital Expenditures | 87.6 | 80.3 | 181 | 211 | 168 | 96.9 | 103 | 124 | 91.6 | 146 |
| Cash Flow | 412 | 399 | 335 | 502 | 442 | 430 | 395 | 366 | -197 | 322 |
| Current Ratio | 1.4 | 1.4 | 1.0 | 1.1 | 1.2 | 1.1 | 1.2 | 1.2 | 0.9 | 1.2 |
| % Long Term Debt of Capitalization | 37.0 | 42.3 | 40.1 | 43.0 | 54.3 | 56.1 | 60.5 | 66.1 | 28.6 | 24.5 |
| % Net Income of Revenue | 5.7 | 5.8 | 3.7 | 7.6 | 6.3 | 6.3 | 5.7 | 6.8 | NM | 5.1 |
| % Return on Assets | 4.7 | 4.7 | 3.5 | 6.8 | 5.5 | 5.3 | 4.5 | 5.4 | NM | 3.9 |
| % Return on Equity | 11.2 | 11.8 | 9.1 | 19.2 | 19.9 | 18.8 | 17.5 | 21.9 | NM | 12.7 |

Data as orig reptd.; bef. results of disc opers/spec. items. Per share data adj. for stk. divs.; EPS diluted. E-Estimated. NA-Not Available. NM-Not Meaningful. NR-Not Ranked. UR-Under Review.

**Office:** 200 Riverfront Blvd, Elmwood Park, NJ 07407-1033.
**Telephone:** 201-791-7600.
**Website:** http://www.sealedair.com
**Pres & CEO:** W.V. Hickey

**CFO & Treas:** T.S. Christie
**Chief Acctg Officer & Cntlr:** J.S. Warren
**Secy & General Counsel:** H.K. White
**Investor Contact:** A. Butler (201-703-4210)

**Board Members:** G. H. Brown, S. Chu, L. R. Codey, P. Duff, D. T. Dunphy, W. V. Hickey, J. B. Kosecoff, K. P. Manning, W. J. Marino

**Founded:** 1996
**Domicile:** Delaware
**Employees:** 16,100

# Sears Holdings Corp

STANDARD &POOR'S

| S&P Recommendation **HOLD** ★★★☆☆ | Price $58.40 (as of Nov 25, 2011) | 12-Mo. Target Price $66.00 | Investment Style Large-Cap Blend |
|---|---|---|---|

**GICS Sector** Consumer Discretionary
**Sub-Industry** Department Stores

**Summary** Through its wholly owned Sears and Kmart subsidiaries, Sears Holdings is among the largest broadline retailers in the U.S.

## Key Stock Statistics (Source S&P, Vickers, company reports)

| | | | | | | | |
|---|---|---|---|---|---|---|---|
| 52-Wk Range | $94.79–51.14 | S&P Oper. EPS 2012**E** | -4.00 | Market Capitalization(B) | $6.242 | Beta | 1.67 |
| Trailing 12-Month EPS | $-3.37 | S&P Oper. EPS 2013**E** | -3.20 | Yield (%) | Nil | S&P 3-Yr. Proj. EPS CAGR(%) | NM |
| Trailing 12-Month P/E | NM | P/E on S&P Oper. EPS 2012**E** | NM | Dividend Rate/Share | Nil | S&P Credit Rating | B |
| $10K Invested 5 Yrs Ago | $3,310 | Common Shares Outstg. (M) | 106.9 | Institutional Ownership (%) | 85 | | |

## Price Performance

30-Week Mov. Avg. · · · 10-Week Mov. Avg. - - **GAAP Earnings vs. Previous Year** Volume Above Avg. STARS
12-Mo. Target Price — Relative Strength — ▲ Up ▼ Down ▶ No Change Below Avg. ★

Options: ASE, CBOE, P, Ph

Analysis prepared by Equity Analyst **Jason N. Asaeda** on Nov 18, 2011, when the stock traded at **$63.95**.

## Highlights

➤ We project net sales of $42.7 billion in FY 12 (Jan.) and $42.2 billion in FY 13. We look for Kmart to drive sales of its higher-margin discretionary categories with value pricing and the purchasing flexibility of layaway that meets the needs of cash-strapped customers. We expect Sears Domestic to reinvigorate its apparel and center core businesses with new fashion brands and beauty products, but believe a soft U.S. housing market will hurt demand for hardlines. Finally, we see a cautious consumer and aggressive competition negatively impacting Sears Canada.

➤ We expect SHLD's consolidated operating margins to be pressured annually by promotional activity and markdowns to keep inventory levels aligned with sales trends, costs related to free appliance delivery and online shipping offers, and investments in the company's multichannel capabilities and the Shop Your Way Rewards program at Kmart and Sears Domestic, partially offset by expense controls and closure of underperforming stores.

➤ Factoring in likely share buybacks, we see losses per share of $4.00 in FY 12 and $3.20 in FY 13.

## Investment Rationale/Risk

➤ We view the shares as appropriately valued at recent levels. Under Chairman Edward Lampert's direction, we think limited investment in store upgrades hurt SHLD's ability to attract and retain talented merchants, to engage store employees, and to win new customers. We think store-level improvements are occurring gradually under new CEO Lou D'Ambrosio's stewardship, and we think an increased focus on newness and innovation in merchandising as well as online integration at Kmart and Sears Domestic is enjoying modest early success, which we expect to build in FY 13.

➤ Risks to our recommendation and target price include sales shortfalls due to changes in consumer confidence, spending habits, and buying preferences; significant apparel cost inflation; and heightened promotional activity by competitors.

➤ Given near-term company headwinds, we apply a forward price-to-sales multiple of 0.17X, below SHLD's five-year historical median of 0.22X, to our FY 13 sales per share estimate of $396 to arrive at our 12-month target price of $66.

## Qualitative Risk Assessment

| LOW | MEDIUM | HIGH |
|---|---|---|

Our risk assessment reflects what we consider Kmart's and Sears's long records of inconsistent sales and earnings. This is partially offset by our view of SHLD's opportunity to leverage the two units' best practices and brands to strengthen its competitive positioning.

## Quantitative Evaluations

**S&P Quality Ranking** NR

| D | C | B- | B | B+ | A- | A | A+ |
|---|---|---|---|---|---|---|---|

**Relative Strength Rank** WEAK

22

LOWEST = 1     HIGHEST = 99

## Revenue/Earnings Data

**Revenue (Million $)**

| | 1Q | 2Q | 3Q | 4Q | Year |
|---|---|---|---|---|---|
| 2012 | 9,705 | 10,333 | 9,565 | -- | -- |
| 2011 | 10,046 | 10,458 | 9,678 | 13,144 | 43,326 |
| 2010 | 10,055 | 10,551 | 10,190 | 13,247 | 44,043 |
| 2009 | 11,068 | 11,762 | 10,660 | 13,280 | 46,770 |
| 2008 | 11,702 | 12,239 | 11,548 | 1,507 | 50,703 |
| 2007 | 11,998 | 12,785 | 11,941 | 16,288 | 53,012 |

**Earnings Per Share ($)**

| | | | | | |
|---|---|---|---|---|---|
| 2012 | -1.58 | -1.37 | -3.95 | E2.94 | E-4.00 |
| 2011 | 0.14 | -0.35 | -1.98 | 3.43 | 1.19 |
| 2010 | -0.22 | -0.79 | -1.09 | 3.74 | 1.99 |
| 2009 | -0.42 | 0.50 | -1.16 | 1.55 | 0.42 |
| 2008 | 1.40 | 0.51 | 0.01 | 3.21 | 5.70 |
| 2007 | 1.14 | 1.88 | 1.27 | 5.33 | 9.57 |

Fiscal year ended Jan. 31. Next earnings report expected: Late January. EPS Estimates based on S&P Operating Earnings; historical GAAP earnings are as reported.

## Dividend Data

No cash dividends have been paid.

---

**Please read the Required Disclosures and Analyst Certification on the last page of this report.**

The McGraw·Hill Companies

# Sears Holdings Corp

STANDARD
&POOR'S

## Business Summary November 18, 2011

CORPORATE OVERVIEW. Through the March 2005 merger of Kmart Holding Corp. and Sears, Roebuck and Co., Sears Holdings has emerged as one of the largest broadline retailers in the U.S. based on FY 11 (Jan.) reported revenues. As of July 30, 2011, SHLD operated 884 Sears-branded full-line and 1,370 specialty stores and 1,304 Kmart-branded discount stores and supercenters across the U.S. Through Sears Canada, a 94%-owned subsidiary, the company also operated 122 Sears-branded full-line and 373 specialty stores in Canada.

CORPORATE STRATEGY. We see SHLD building customer loyalty through its Shop Your Way Rewards and layaway programs. Shoppers enrolled in the Shop Your Way Rewards program earn points on qualifying purchases at all Kmart and Sears stores and related websites that are redeemable on future purchases. With layaway, Kmart and Sears customers make a minimum down payment of $15 or 20% (whichever is more) on qualified merchandise. This is followed by biweekly payments over eight weeks until the balance is paid off. We view layaway as a competitive differentiator for the company.

SHLD has started to lease space within its owned Sears stores to raise their

productivity. Examples include leasing space to fast fashion retailer Forever 21, Inc., which is expected to open a two-level, 43,000 square foot XXI Forever concept store in Costa Mesa, California, this spring, and upscale grocery chain Whole Foods Market Inc., which plans to open a 34,000 square foot store in Greensboro, NC in spring 2012.

SHLD is also competing with Amazon.com in the online marketplace. The company offers third parties access to its sears.com customers through three options. They can advertise on sears.com on a cost-per-click fee basis; sell on sears.com, with the seller handling product shipment and Sears earning a sales commission and charging a monthly fee; and/or sell through sears.com, with Sears both selling and shipping the products in exchange for sales commissions and monthly fees. The sears.com marketplace assortment had over 17 million items in 2010.

## Company Financials  Fiscal Year Ended Jan. 31

| Per Share Data ($) | 2011 | 2010 | 2009 | 2008 | 2007 | 2006 | 2005 | 2004 | 2003 | 2002 |
|---|---|---|---|---|---|---|---|---|---|---|
| Tangible Book Value | 36.51 | 39.10 | 38.57 | 42.64 | 49.25 | 41.80 | 50.21 | 24.36 | NA | NA |
| Cash Flow | 9.40 | 9.85 | 8.14 | 12.95 | 16.90 | 12.24 | 11.59 | 2.81 | -4.02 | -3.57 |
| Earnings | 1.19 | 1.99 | 0.42 | 5.70 | 9.57 | 6.17 | 11.00 | 2.52 | -5.47 | -5.24 |
| S&P Core Earnings | 1.47 | 2.33 | -0.99 | 4.44 | 9.24 | 4.53 | 4.51 | -4.53 | -6.80 | -5.74 |
| Dividends | NA | Nil | Nil | Nil | Nil | Nil | Nil | Nil | Nil | NA |
| Payout Ratio | NA | Nil | Nil | Nil | Nil | Nil | Nil | Nil | NA | NA |
| Calendar Year | 2010 | 2009 | 2008 | 2007 | 2006 | 2005 | 2004 | 2003 | 2002 | 2001 |
| Prices:High | 125.42 | 86.53 | 114.00 | 195.18 | 182.38 | 163.50 | 119.69 | 34.55 | NA | NA |
| Prices:Low | 59.21 | 34.27 | 26.80 | 98.25 | 114.90 | 84.51 | 22.41 | 12.00 | NA | NA |
| P/E Ratio:High | NM | 43 | NM | 34 | 19 | 26 | 11 | 14 | NA | NA |
| P/E Ratio:Low | NM | 17 | NM | 17 | 12 | 14 | 2 | 5 | NA | NA |

| Income Statement Analysis (Million $) | | | | | | | | | | |
|---|---|---|---|---|---|---|---|---|---|---|
| Revenue | 43,326 | 44,043 | 46,770 | 50,703 | 53,012 | 49,124 | 19,701 | 17,072 | 30,762 | 36,151 |
| Operating Income | 1,324 | 1,834 | 1,530 | 2,542 | 3,611 | 2,901 | 944 | 442 | -1,303 | -386 |
| Depreciation | 900 | 926 | 981 | 1,049 | 1,142 | 932 | 69.0 | 31.0 | 737 | 824 |
| Interest Expense | 310 | 265 | 272 | 286 | 337 | 322 | 146 | 105 | 155 | 418 |
| Pretax Income | 186 | 420 | 184 | 1,452 | 2,464 | 1,965 | 1,775 | 400 | -3,286 | -2,702 |
| Effective Tax Rate | NA | 29.3% | 46.2% | 37.9% | 37.7% | 36.4% | 37.7% | 38.0% | NM | 4.26% |
| Net Income | 150 | 235 | 53.0 | 826 | 1,490 | 948 | 1,106 | 248 | -3,262 | -2,587 |
| S&P Core Earnings | 165 | 276 | -126 | 645 | 1,439 | 696 | 448 | -405 | -3,439 | -2,840 |

| Balance Sheet & Other Financial Data (Million $) | | | | | | | | | | |
|---|---|---|---|---|---|---|---|---|---|---|
| Cash | 1,375 | 1,689 | 1,173 | 1,622 | 3,968 | 4,440 | 3,435 | 2,088 | 613 | 1,245 |
| Current Assets | 11,535 | 11,438 | 11,416 | 12,802 | 15,406 | 15,207 | 7,541 | 5,811 | 6,102 | 7,884 |
| Total Assets | 24,268 | 24,808 | 25,342 | 27,397 | 30,066 | 30,573 | 8,651 | 6,084 | 11,238 | 14,298 |
| Current Liabilities | 8,618 | 8,786 | 8,512 | 9,562 | 10,052 | 10,350 | 2,086 | 1,776 | 2,120 | 624 |
| Long Term Debt | 2,663 | 1,698 | 1,527 | 2,606 | 2,849 | 3,268 | 661 | 819 | 623 | 4,565 |
| Common Equity | 8,614 | 9,435 | 9,380 | 10,667 | 12,714 | 11,611 | 4,469 | 2,192 | -301 | 3,459 |
| Total Capital | 11,786 | 11,615 | 14,168 | 13,586 | 15,563 | 14,879 | 5,130 | 3,011 | 322 | 8,024 |
| Capital Expenditures | 441 | 361 | 497 | 570 | 513 | 546 | 230 | 108 | 252 | 1,456 |
| Cash Flow | 1,050 | 1,161 | 1,034 | 1,875 | 2,632 | 1,880 | 1,175 | 279 | -2,525 | -1,763 |
| Current Ratio | 1.3 | 1.3 | 1.3 | 1.3 | 1.5 | 1.5 | 3.6 | 3.3 | 2.9 | 12.6 |
| % Long Term Debt of Capitalization | 22.6 | 14.6 | 10.8 | 19.2 | 18.3 | 22.0 | 12.9 | 27.2 | NM | 56.9 |
| % Net Income of Revenue | 0.4 | 0.5 | 0.1 | 1.6 | 2.8 | 1.9 | 5.6 | 1.5 | NM | NM |
| % Return on Assets | 0.6 | 0.9 | 0.2 | 2.9 | 4.9 | 4.8 | 15.0 | 3.9 | NM | NM |
| % Return on Equity | 1.7 | 2.5 | 0.5 | 7.1 | 12.3 | 11.8 | 33.1 | 12.7 | NM | NM |

Data as orig reptd.; bef. results of disc opers/spec. items. Per share data adj. for stk. divs.; EPS diluted. E-Estimated. NA-Not Available. NM-Not Meaningful. NR-Not Ranked. UR-Under Review.

**Office:** 3333 Beverly Rd, Hoffman Estates, IL 60179-0001.
**Telephone:** 847-286-2500.
**Website:** http://www.searsholdings.com
**Chrmn:** E.S. Lampert

**Pres & CEO:** L.J. D'Ambrosio
**SVP, Secy & General Counsel:** D.A. Drobny
**SVP & CIO:** T. Kasbe
**CFO, Chief Acctg Officer & Cntlr:** W.K. Phelan

**Board Members:** L. J. D'Ambrosio, W. C. Kunkler, III, E. S. Lampert, S. T. Mnuchin, A. N. Reese, E. Scott, T. J. Tisch
**Founded:** 1899
**Domicile:** Delaware
**Employees:** 312,000

# Sempra Energy

**STANDARD &POOR'S**

| S&P Recommendation **BUY** ★★★★☆ | Price $50.88 (as of Nov 25, 2011) | 12-Mo. Target Price $59.00 | Investment Style Large-Cap Blend |
|---|---|---|---|

**GICS Sector** Utilities
**Sub-Industry** Multi-Utilities

**Summary** This gas and electric utility is also engaged in unregulated power, liquefied natural gas and international energy projects.

## Key Stock Statistics (Source S&P, Vickers, company reports)

| | | | | | | | | |
|---|---|---|---|---|---|---|---|---|
| 52-Wk Range | $55.97–44.78 | S&P Oper. EPS 2011E | 4.30 | Market Capitalization(B) | $12.188 | Beta | | 0.55 |
| Trailing 12-Month EPS | $5.55 | S&P Oper. EPS 2012E | 4.60 | Yield (%) | 3.77 | S&P 3-Yr. Proj. EPS CAGR(%) | | 8 |
| Trailing 12-Month P/E | 9.2 | P/E on S&P Oper. EPS 2011E | 11.8 | Dividend Rate/Share | $1.92 | S&P Credit Rating | | BBB+ |
| $10K Invested 5 Yrs Ago | $10,773 | Common Shares Outstg. (M) | 239.5 | Institutional Ownership (%) | 69 | | | |

## Price Performance

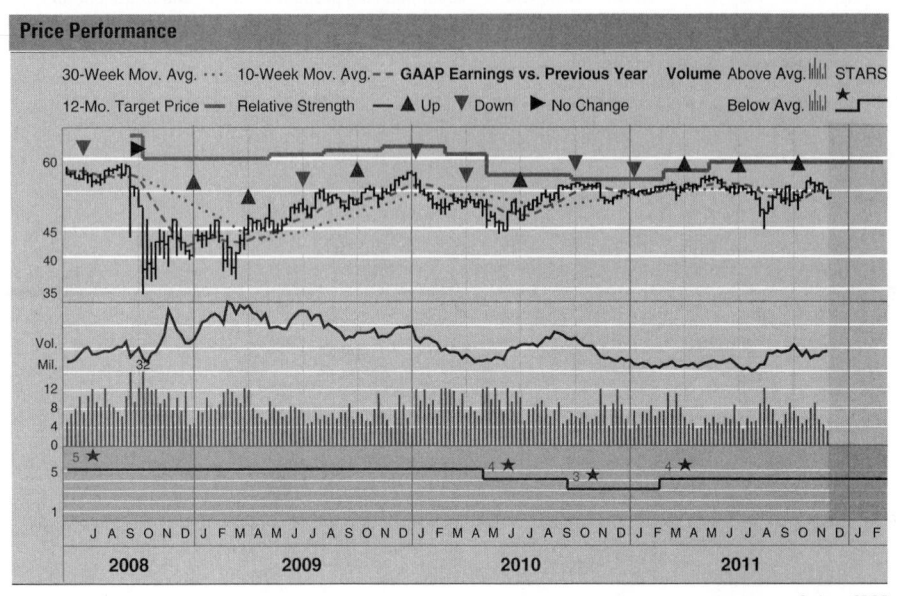

30-Week Mov. Avg. ···· 10-Week Mov. Avg. -- **GAAP Earnings vs. Previous Year** Volume Above Avg. STARS
12-Mo. Target Price — Relative Strength — ▲ Up ▼ Down ► No Change Below Avg. ★

Options: CBOE

Analysis prepared by Equity Analyst **C. Muir** on Aug 31, 2011, when the stock traded at **$52.52**.

## Highlights

➤ We estimate revenues will rise 11% in 2011 and 7.2% in 2012. We expect 2011 to benefit from higher volumes, rate increases and customer growth, partly offset by lower gas prices. We see some expansion projects being completed later in 2011. In 2012, we look for slightly higher natural gas and power prices to complement higher rates and increased volumes.

➤ We expect wider operating margins of 16.3% in 2011 and 16.7% in 2012, versus 17.1% in 2010. In 2011, we see higher per-revenue utility cost of energy and depreciation charges, partly offset by higher per-revenue operating taxes, and operations & maintenance expense. We estimate pretax margins of 14.4% in 2011 and 14.6% in 2012, up from 14.3% in 2010. We project higher non-operating income, partly offset by lower interest costs.

➤ We see debt reduction and share repurchases benefiting 2011 EPS. Assuming an effective tax rate of 29.2%, we estimate 2011 operating EPS, excluding net nonrecurring gains of $1.15, of $4.30, up 8.9% from 2010's $3.95, which excludes net nonrecurring charges of $0.97. Our 2012 EPS forecast is $4.60, a 7.0% increase.

## Investment Rationale/Risk

➤ We view favorably SRE's recent sale of its commodities trading joint venture. We see proceeds being used to reduce debt and repurchase shares. The company's utility segment has filed for rate increases at both of its utilities. In addition, this segment has several utility growth projects under way. Several non-utility projects have been completed in recent years and we look for others to be finished between 2011 and 2013. Also, we expect more projects to be announced in the next few years. We see growth opportunities in most of SRE's businesses.

➤ Risks to our recommendation and target price include declining wholesale power margins, potential losses from energy and metals trading, or a weaker-than-expected economy.

➤ The stock recently traded at a multiple of 11.3X our 2012 EPS estimate, an 18% discount to multi-utility peers. Our 12-month target price of $59 is about 12.8X our 2012 EPS estimate, a smaller discount-to-peers valuation. We believe the valuation is warranted by SRE's prospects for close-to-peers EPS and dividend growth and a constructive regulatory environment.

## Qualitative Risk Assessment

| LOW | MEDIUM | HIGH |
|---|---|---|

Our risk assessment reflects a balance between stable and steady earnings provided by SRE's regulated gas and electric utility operations and cyclical and volatile earnings from unregulated businesses, including power generation, energy marketing and trading, and international energy investments.

## Quantitative Evaluations

**S&P Quality Ranking** A-

| D | C | B- | B | B+ | A- | A | A+ |
|---|---|---|---|---|---|---|---|

**Relative Strength Rank** MODERATE

65

LOWEST = 1 HIGHEST = 99

## Revenue/Earnings Data

**Revenue (Million $)**

| | 1Q | 2Q | 3Q | 4Q | Year |
|---|---|---|---|---|---|
| 2011 | 2,434 | 2,422 | 2,576 | -- | -- |
| 2010 | 2,534 | 2,008 | 2,116 | 2,345 | 9,003 |
| 2009 | 2,108 | 1,689 | 1,853 | 2,456 | 8,106 |
| 2008 | 3,270 | 2,503 | 2,692 | 2,293 | 10,758 |
| 2007 | 3,004 | 2,661 | 2,663 | 3,110 | 11,438 |
| 2006 | 3,336 | 2,486 | 2,694 | 3,245 | 11,761 |

**Earnings Per Share ($)**

| | | | | | |
|---|---|---|---|---|---|
| 2011 | 1.07 | 2.12 | 1.22 | E1.04 | E4.30 |
| 2010 | 0.42 | 0.89 | 0.53 | 1.15 | 2.98 |
| 2009 | 1.29 | 0.80 | 1.27 | 1.16 | 4.52 |
| 2008 | 0.92 | 0.98 | 1.24 | 1.31 | 4.43 |
| 2007 | 0.86 | 1.06 | 1.24 | 1.10 | 4.26 |
| 2006 | 0.90 | 0.71 | 2.07 | 0.49 | 4.17 |

Fiscal year ended Dec. 31. Next earnings report expected: NA. EPS Estimates based on S&P Operating Earnings; historical GAAP earnings are as reported.

## Dividend Data (Dates: mm/dd Payment Date: mm/dd/yy)

| Amount ($) | Date Decl. | Ex-Div. Date | Stk. of Record | Payment Date |
|---|---|---|---|---|
| 0.390 | 12/07 | 12/21 | 12/23 | 01/15/11 |
| 0.480 | 02/22 | 03/16 | 03/18 | 04/15/11 |
| 0.480 | 06/14 | 06/22 | 06/24 | 07/15/11 |
| 0.480 | 09/13 | 09/27 | 09/29 | 10/15/11 |

Dividends have been paid since 1998. Source: Company reports.

# Sempra Energy

**STANDARD
&POOR'S**

## Business Summary August 31, 2011

CORPORATE OVERVIEW. Sempra Energy is a holding company that operates five segments in two major divisions: California Utilities (CU) and Sempra Global. The CU division includes regulated public utilities Southern California Gas (SCG -- 34% of 2010 revenue) and San Diego Gas & Electric (SDGE -- 43%), which provide electricity and natural gas services in Southern California. Sempra Global includes Sempra Generation (12%), which develops and operates power plants and energy infrastructure; Sempra LNG (7%), which operates LNG receipt terminals in North America; and Sempra Pipelines & Storage (4%), which operates in Mexico, the U.S. and South America.

CORPORATE STRATEGY. Sempra seeks to increase EPS through faster growth in its unregulated businesses through both acquisitions and organic growth. In the utility segment, the company focuses on managing regulatory risk as well as operating and capital expenditures. SRE has focused on project development at many of its segments in recent years. Currently, it is focused on developing renewable generation, building transmission lines, and the installation of smart meters. In December 2010, SDGE and SCG filed general rate case applications.

On January 19, 2011, SRE announced that it would acquire the remaining

stakes in two South American (Chile and Peru) utilities for $875 million. SRE expects the acquisitions to be accretive to 2011 EPS by $0.15 and 2012 EPS by $0.22. The deal is subject to regulatory approvals and successful resolution of tax issues.

Royal Bank of Scotland (RBS) was forced to sell its stake in the commodities trading joint venture with SRE by the European Commission. On February 16, 2010, the venture agreed to sell the European and Asian businesses for $1.7 billion. SRE's share of the proceeds was about $1.2 billion. RBS Sempra sold its retail business on September 20, 2010, for $317 million and took a charge for $150 million. There are minimal operations left in the business that we believe will be shut down over the coming year.

In October 2008, SRE purchased, for $510 million, EnergySouth, which is building several storage projects in the Southeast.

## Company Financials Fiscal Year Ended Dec. 31

| Per Share Data ($) | 2010 | 2009 | 2008 | 2007 | 2006 | 2005 | 2004 | 2003 | 2002 | 2001 |
|---|---|---|---|---|---|---|---|---|---|---|
| Tangible Book Value | 35.41 | 34.53 | 30.54 | 31.27 | 28.67 | 23.97 | 20.79 | 17.14 | 13.78 | 13.17 |
| Cash Flow | 6.41 | 7.66 | 7.17 | 6.86 | 6.70 | 6.25 | 6.59 | 6.12 | 5.68 | 5.35 |
| Earnings | 2.98 | 4.52 | 4.43 | 4.26 | 4.17 | 3.69 | 3.93 | 3.24 | 2.79 | 2.52 |
| S&P Core Earnings | 3.63 | 4.83 | 3.59 | 4.26 | 4.19 | 3.44 | 3.65 | 3.29 | 2.16 | 1.76 |
| Dividends | 1.56 | 1.56 | 1.37 | 1.24 | 1.20 | 1.16 | 1.00 | 1.00 | 1.00 | 1.00 |
| Payout Ratio | 52% | 35% | 31% | 29% | 29% | 31% | 25% | 31% | 36% | 40% |
| Prices:High | 56.61 | 57.18 | 63.00 | 66.38 | 57.35 | 47.86 | 37.93 | 30.90 | 26.25 | 28.61 |
| Prices:Low | 43.91 | 36.43 | 34.29 | 50.95 | 42.90 | 35.53 | 29.51 | 22.25 | 15.50 | 17.31 |
| P/E Ratio:High | 19 | 13 | 14 | 16 | 14 | 13 | 10 | 10 | 9 | 11 |
| P/E Ratio:Low | 15 | 8 | 8 | 12 | 10 | 10 | 8 | 7 | 6 | 7 |
| **Income Statement Analysis** (Million $) | | | | | | | | | | |
| Revenue | 9,003 | 8,106 | 10,758 | 11,438 | 11,761 | 11,737 | 9,410 | 7,887 | 6,020 | 8,029 |
| Operating Income | NA | NA | 2,027 | 2,365 | 1,785 | 1,111 | 1,272 | 939 | 987 | 993 |
| Depreciation | 867 | 775 | 687 | 686 | 657 | 646 | 621 | 615 | 596 | 579 |
| Interest Expense | 446 | 377 | 263 | 381 | 361 | 321 | 332 | 327 | 323 | 352 |
| Pretax Income | 825 | 1,534 | 1,551 | 1,659 | 1,732 | 971 | 1,113 | 742 | 721 | 731 |
| Effective Tax Rate | NA | 27.5% | 28.2% | 31.6% | 37.0% | 4.33% | 17.3% | 6.33% | 20.2% | 29.1% |
| Net Income | 723 | 1,119 | 1,113 | 1,135 | 1,091 | 929 | 920 | 695 | 575 | 518 |
| S&P Core Earnings | 901 | 1,197 | 904 | 1,124 | 1,096 | 866 | 855 | 708 | 445 | 362 |
| **Balance Sheet & Other Financial Data** (Million $) | | | | | | | | | | |
| Cash | 912 | 110 | 507 | 669 | 920 | 772 | 419 | 432 | 455 | 605 |
| Current Assets | 3,353 | 2,295 | 2,476 | 11,338 | 12,016 | 13,318 | 8,776 | 7,886 | 7,010 | 4,808 |
| Total Assets | 30,283 | 28,512 | 26,400 | 30,091 | 28,949 | 29,213 | 23,643 | 22,009 | 17,757 | 15,156 |
| Current Liabilities | 3,786 | 3,888 | 3,612 | 10,394 | 10,349 | 12,157 | 9,082 | 8,348 | 7,247 | 5,524 |
| Long Term Debt | 8,980 | 7,462 | 6,646 | 4,655 | 4,704 | 5,002 | 4,371 | 4,199 | 4,487 | 3,840 |
| Common Equity | 9,027 | 9,007 | 7,969 | 8,339 | 7,511 | 6,160 | 4,865 | 3,890 | 2,825 | 2,692 |
| Total Capital | 18,972 | 17,394 | 15,980 | 13,852 | 12,694 | 11,480 | 9,734 | 8,807 | 8,202 | 7,474 |
| Capital Expenditures | 2,062 | 1,912 | 2,061 | 2,011 | 1,907 | 1,404 | 1,083 | 1,049 | 1,214 | 1,068 |
| Cash Flow | 1,590 | 1,894 | 1,800 | 1,811 | 1,748 | 1,575 | 1,541 | 1,310 | 1,171 | 1,097 |
| Current Ratio | 0.9 | 0.6 | 0.7 | 1.1 | 1.2 | 1.1 | 1.0 | 0.9 | 1.0 | 0.9 |
| % Long Term Debt of Capitalization | 47.3 | 43.7 | 41.6 | 33.6 | 37.1 | 43.6 | 44.9 | 47.7 | 54.7 | 51.4 |
| % Net Income of Revenue | 8.0 | 13.8 | 10.4 | 9.9 | 9.3 | 7.9 | 9.8 | 8.8 | 9.6 | 6.5 |
| % Return on Assets | 2.5 | 4.1 | 3.9 | 3.8 | 3.7 | 3.5 | 4.0 | 3.3 | 3.5 | 3.4 |
| % Return on Equity | 8.0 | 13.2 | 13.7 | 14.2 | 16.0 | 16.9 | 21.0 | 20.7 | 20.8 | 20.0 |

Data as orig reptd.; bef. results of disc opers/spec. items. Per share data adj. for stk. divs.; EPS diluted. E-Estimated. NA-Not Available. NM-Not Meaningful. NR-Not Ranked. UR-Under Review.

**Office:** 101 Ash Street, San Diego, CA 92101.
**Telephone:** 619-696-2000.
**Email:** investor@sempra.com
**Website:** http://www.sempra.com

**Chrmn:** D.E. Felsinger
**Pres:** M.A. Snell
**CEO:** D.L. Reed
**EVP, CFO, Chief Acctg Officer & Cntlr:** J.A. Householder

**EVP & General Counsel:** J. Chaudhri
**Investor Contact:** S. Davis (619-696-2901)
**Board Members:** A. L. Boeckmann, J. G. Brocksmith, Jr., D. E. Felsinger, W. D. Godbold, Jr., W. D. Jones, W. G. Ouchi, D. L. Reed, C. Ruiz, W. C. Rusnack, W. Rutledge, L. Schenk

**Founded:** 1998
**Domicile:** California
**Employees:** 17,500

# Sherwin-Williams Co (The)

**STANDARD &POOR'S**

| | | | |
|---|---|---|---|
| **S&P Recommendation** SELL ★★★★★ | **Price** $83.64 (as of Nov 25, 2011) | **12-Mo. Target Price** $72.00 | **Investment Style** Large-Cap Growth |

**GICS Sector** Materials
**Sub-Industry** Specialty Chemicals

**Summary** This company, the largest U.S. producer of paints, is also a major seller of wallcoverings and related products.

## Key Stock Statistics (Source S&P, Vickers, company reports)

| | | | | | | | |
|---|---|---|---|---|---|---|---|
| 52-Wk Range | $87.87– 69.47 | S&P Oper. EPS 2011E | 4.78 | Market Capitalization(B) | $8.679 | Beta | 0.65 |
| Trailing 12-Month EPS | $4.64 | S&P Oper. EPS 2012E | 5.41 | Yield (%) | 1.75 | S&P 3-Yr. Proj. EPS CAGR(%) | 13 |
| Trailing 12-Month P/E | 18.0 | P/E on S&P Oper. EPS 2011E | 17.5 | Dividend Rate/Share | $1.46 | S&P Credit Rating | A |
| $10K Invested 5 Yrs Ago | $14,919 | Common Shares Outstg. (M) | 103.8 | Institutional Ownership (%) | 73 | | |

## Price Performance

30-Week Mov. Avg. · · · 10-Week Mov. Avg. - - GAAP Earnings vs. Previous Year   Volume Above Avg. STARS
12-Mo. Target Price — Relative Strength   ▲ Up ▼ Down ► No Change   Below Avg.   ★

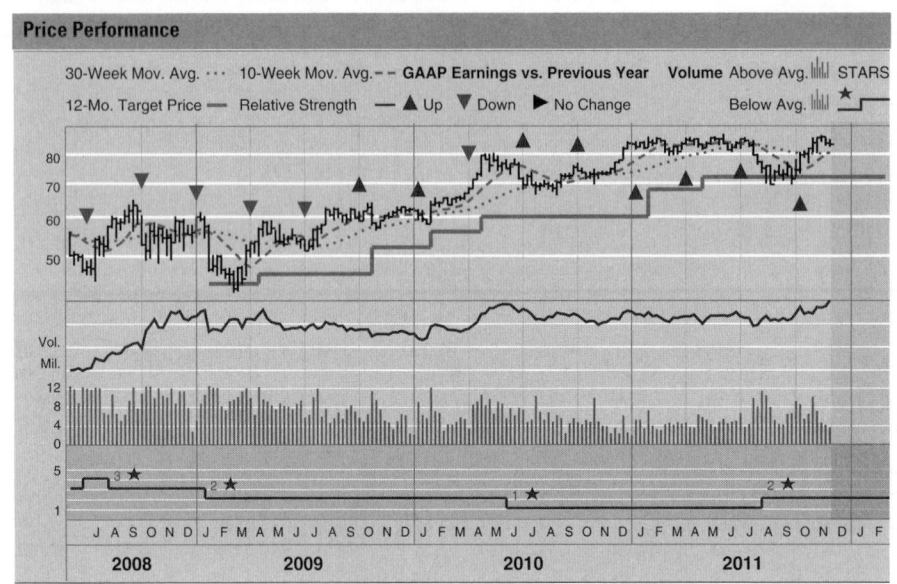

Options: CBOE

Analysis prepared by Equity Analyst **Michael Souers** on Nov 09, 2011, when the stock traded at **$86.72**.

## Highlights

➤ We expect sales to increase 5.4% in 2012, following our projections of a 12% advance in 2011. We expect this growth to be driven by acquisitions and continued slight improvement in residential construction, which should positively affect architectural and do-it-yourself (DIY) sales. In addition, we think Paint Stores segment sales will increase modestly on a projected 50-60 net new stores and a slight increase in same-store-sales. We think non-residential construction will remain challenging over the next 12 months.

➤ We project a slight improvement in gross margins in 2012, following a significant narrowing in 2011 driven by rapidly rising raw material costs. We also anticipate a slight widening of operating margins, as continued cost-cutting efforts and pricing increases are sufficient to overcome additional expected raw material cost pressure.

➤ We project a slight decline in interest expense and a 4% decrease in share count due to SHW's active share repurchase program. We see 2012 EPS of $5.41, a 13% increase from the $4.78 we project the company to earn in 2011.

## Investment Rationale/Risk

➤ We continue to have a positive outlook with regard to the company's balance sheet and generation of free cash flow. In addition, we think the ruling by the Rhode Island Supreme Court, which overturned a negative verdict against SHW over the manufacturing and selling of lead paint, continues to make future negative rulings far less likely. However, we remain concerned that the weak housing market and commercial real estate market will limit sales and earnings growth over the medium term. We think the shares lack a positive near-term catalyst and are overvalued, recently trading at about 16X our 2012 EPS estimate, a significant premium to the S&P 500.

➤ Risks to our recommendation and target price include a significant increase in economic growth; a rapid recovery in the housing market; and declines in raw material costs, which would ease pressure on gross margins.

➤ Our 12-month target price of $72, about 13X our 2012 EPS estimate, is based on our DCF analysis, which assumes a weighted average cost of capital of 9.5% and a terminal growth rate of 3.0%.

## Qualitative Risk Assessment

| LOW | **MEDIUM** | HIGH |
|---|---|---|

Our risk assessment for Sherwin-Williams reflects the cyclical nature of the company's business, which is reliant on new housing starts and remodeling, and lead pigment litigation risk, offset by an above-average S&P Quality Ranking of A.

## Quantitative Evaluations

**S&P Quality Ranking**   A

| D | C | B- | B | B+ | A- | **A** | A+ |
|---|---|---|---|---|---|---|---|

**Relative Strength Rank**   **STRONG**

**90**

LOWEST = 1   HIGHEST = 99

## Revenue/Earnings Data

**Revenue (Million $)**

| | 1Q | 2Q | 3Q | 4Q | Year |
|---|---|---|---|---|---|
| 2011 | 1,856 | 2,355 | 2,485 | -- | -- |
| 2010 | 1,565 | 2,143 | 2,172 | 1,896 | 7,776 |
| 2009 | 1,551 | 1,948 | 1,997 | 1,599 | 7,094 |
| 2008 | 1,782 | 2,230 | 2,269 | 1,700 | 7,980 |
| 2007 | 1,756 | 2,198 | 2,197 | 1,854 | 8,005 |
| 2006 | 1,769 | 2,130 | 2,117 | 1,795 | 7,810 |

**Earnings Per Share ($)**

| | | | | | |
|---|---|---|---|---|---|
| 2011 | 0.63 | 1.66 | 1.71 | E0.74 | E4.78 |
| 2010 | 0.30 | 1.64 | 1.62 | 0.67 | 4.21 |
| 2009 | 0.32 | 1.35 | 1.51 | 0.58 | 3.78 |
| 2008 | 0.64 | 1.45 | 1.50 | 0.42 | 4.00 |
| 2007 | 0.83 | 1.52 | 1.55 | 0.80 | 4.70 |
| 2006 | 0.82 | 1.33 | 1.30 | 0.73 | 4.19 |

Fiscal year ended Dec. 31. Next earnings report expected: NA. EPS Estimates based on S&P Operating Earnings; historical GAAP earnings are as reported.

## Dividend Data (Dates: mm/dd Payment Date: mm/dd/yy)

| Amount ($) | Date Decl. | Ex-Div. Date | Stk. of Record | Payment Date |
|---|---|---|---|---|
| 0.029 | -- | 05/17 | 05/19 | 06/13/11 |
| 0.365 | 04/20 | 05/18 | 05/20 | 06/03/11 |
| 0.365 | 07/20 | 08/17 | 08/19 | 09/09/11 |
| 0.365 | 10/20 | 11/16 | 11/18 | 12/02/11 |

Dividends have been paid since 1979. Source: Company reports.

---

**Please read the Required Disclosures and Analyst Certification on the last page of this report.**

*The McGraw·Hill Companies*

# Sherwin-Williams Co (The)

**STANDARD &POOR'S**

## Business Summary November 09, 2011

CORPORATE PROFILE. Sherwin-Williams develops, manufactures, distributes and sells paints, coatings and related products to professional, industrial, commercial and retail customers primarily in North and South America with additional operations in the Caribbean region, Europe and Asia. The company is structured into three reportable segments: Paint Stores, Consumer and Global Finishes.

The Paint Stores segment (56% of revenues in 2010) offers Sherwin-Williams branded architectural and industrial paints, stains and related products. Its diverse customer base includes architectural and industrial painting contractors, residential and commercial builders, property owners and managers, OEM product finishers and do-it-yourself (DIY) homeowners. In 2010, SHW opened 36 net new stores, bringing the North America Paint Stores store count to 3,390. Architects, builders, designers and consumers have embraced the "green" movement, and SHW leads the industry in the sale of environmentally favorable paints and coatings.

The Consumer segment (17%) develops, manufactures and distributes architectural paints, stains, varnishes, industrial maintenance products, wood finishing products, paint applicators, corrosion inhibitors and paint-related products. Brands include Dutch Boy, Krylon, Minwax, Thompson's Water Seal, Purdy and Pratt & Lambert, as well as private label brands. Approximately

53% of the total sales of the Consumer Group in 2010, including inter-segment transfers, represented products sold through the Paint Stores Group.

The Global Finishes segment (27%) develops, licenses, manufactures, distributes and sells paints, stains, coatings, varnishes, industrial products, wood finishing products, applicators, aerosols, high-performance interior and exterior coatings for the automotive, aviation, fleet and heavy truck markets, OEM product finishes and related products. SHW sells these products through 564 company-operated architectural, automotive, industrial and chemical coatings branches and other operations in the United States, Argentina, Belarus, Belgium, Brazil, Canada, Chile, China, Czech Republic, Denmark, Ecuador, Finland, France, Germany, India, Ireland, Italy, Lithuania, Malaysia, Mexico, Norway, Peru, Philippines, Poland, Portugal, Romania, Russia, Singapore, Sweden, Spain, Thailand, Ukraine, United Kingdom, Uruguay and Vietnam. It also distributes these products to 10 other countries through wholly owned subsidiaries, joint ventures and licensees of technology, trademarks and tradenames.

## Company Financials Fiscal Year Ended Dec. 31

| Per Share Data ($) | 2010 | 2009 | 2008 | 2007 | 2006 | 2005 | 2004 | 2003 | 2002 | 2001 |
|---|---|---|---|---|---|---|---|---|---|---|
| Tangible Book Value | 1.74 | 1.80 | 2.55 | 23.99 | 2.67 | 3.83 | 3.12 | 2.95 | 4.05 | 3.69 |
| Cash Flow | 5.86 | 5.26 | 5.20 | 5.76 | 5.41 | 4.30 | 3.59 | 3.13 | 2.86 | 2.39 |
| Earnings | 4.21 | 3.78 | 4.00 | 4.70 | 4.19 | 3.28 | 2.72 | 2.26 | 2.04 | 1.68 |
| S&P Core Earnings | 4.22 | 3.98 | 4.06 | 4.59 | 4.11 | 3.24 | 2.60 | 2.15 | 1.81 | 1.62 |
| Dividends | 1.44 | 1.42 | 1.40 | 1.58 | 1.00 | 0.82 | 0.68 | 0.62 | 0.60 | 0.58 |
| Payout Ratio | 34% | 38% | 35% | 34% | 24% | 25% | 25% | 27% | 29% | 35% |
| Prices:High | 84.99 | 64.13 | 65.00 | 73.96 | 64.76 | 48.84 | 45.61 | 34.77 | 33.24 | 28.23 |
| Prices:Low | 57.86 | 42.19 | 44.51 | 56.75 | 37.40 | 40.47 | 32.95 | 24.42 | 21.75 | 19.73 |
| P/E Ratio:High | 20 | 17 | 16 | 16 | 15 | 15 | 17 | 15 | 16 | 17 |
| P/E Ratio:Low | 14 | 11 | 11 | 12 | 9 | 12 | 12 | 11 | 11 | 12 |

| Income Statement Analysis (Million $) | | | | | | | | | | |
|---|---|---|---|---|---|---|---|---|---|---|
| Revenue | 7,776 | 7,094 | 7,980 | 8,005 | 7,810 | 7,191 | 6,114 | 5,408 | 5,185 | 5,067 |
| Operating Income | 909 | 875 | 998 | 1,145 | 1,024 | 898 | 758 | 690 | 670 | 599 |
| Depreciation | 175 | 171 | 143 | 139 | 146 | 144 | 126 | 117 | 116 | 109 |
| Interest Expense | 70.6 | 40.0 | 65.7 | 71.6 | 67.2 | 49.6 | 39.9 | 38.7 | 40.5 | 54.6 |
| Pretax Income | 678 | 623 | 714 | 913 | 834 | 656 | 580 | 523 | 497 | 424 |
| Effective Tax Rate | NA | 30.0% | 33.3% | 32.6% | 31.0% | 29.2% | 32.0% | 36.5% | 37.5% | 38.0% |
| Net Income | 462 | 436 | 477 | 616 | 576 | 463 | 393 | 332 | 311 | 263 |
| S&P Core Earnings | 459 | 459 | 483 | 602 | 564 | 458 | 376 | 317 | 276 | 254 |

| Balance Sheet & Other Financial Data (Million $) | | | | | | | | | | |
|---|---|---|---|---|---|---|---|---|---|---|
| Cash | 58.6 | 69.3 | 26.2 | 27.3 | 469 | 36.0 | 45.9 | 303 | 164 | 119 |
| Current Assets | 2,214 | 1,770 | 1,909 | 2,070 | 2,450 | 1,891 | 1,782 | 1,715 | 1,506 | 1,507 |
| Total Assets | 5,169 | 4,324 | 4,416 | 4,855 | 4,995 | 4,369 | 4,274 | 3,683 | 3,432 | 3,628 |
| Current Liabilities | 2,064 | 1,394 | 1,937 | 2,141 | 2,075 | 1,554 | 1,520 | 1,154 | 1,083 | 1,141 |
| Long Term Debt | 648 | 783 | 304 | 293 | 292 | 487 | 488 | 503 | 507 | 504 |
| Common Equity | 1,609 | 1,491 | 1,606 | 1,461 | 1,559 | 1,696 | 1,475 | 1,174 | 1,300 | 1,319 |
| Total Capital | 2,266 | 2,286 | 1,923 | 2,079 | 2,284 | 2,218 | 2,139 | 1,962 | 1,849 | 1,991 |
| Capital Expenditures | 125 | 91.3 | 117 | 166 | 210 | 143 | 107 | 117 | 127 | 82.6 |
| Cash Flow | 638 | 607 | 620 | 755 | 722 | 607 | 519 | 449 | 426 | 372 |
| Current Ratio | 1.1 | 1.3 | 1.0 | 1.0 | 1.2 | 1.2 | 1.2 | 1.5 | 1.4 | 1.3 |
| % Long Term Debt of Capitalization | 28.6 | Nil | 15.7 | 14.0 | 12.8 | 22.0 | 22.8 | 25.6 | 27.4 | 25.3 |
| % Net Income of Revenue | 6.0 | 6.1 | 6.0 | 7.7 | 7.4 | 6.4 | 6.4 | 6.1 | 6.0 | 5.2 |
| % Return on Assets | 9.7 | NA | 10.3 | 12.5 | 12.3 | 10.7 | 9.9 | 9.3 | 8.8 | 7.1 |
| % Return on Equity | 29.8 | NA | 31.1 | 32.6 | 35.4 | 29.2 | 29.7 | 26.8 | 23.7 | 18.9 |

Data as orig reptd.; bef. results of disc opers/spec. items. Per share data adj. for stk. divs.; EPS diluted. E-Estimated. NA-Not Available. NM-Not Meaningful. NR-Not Ranked. UR-Under Review.

**Office:** 101 West Prospect Avenue, Cleveland, OH 44115-1075.
**Telephone:** 216-566-2000.
**Website:** http://www.sherwin.com
**Chrmn & CEO:** C.M. Connor

**Pres & COO:** J.G. Morikis
**SVP & CFO:** S.P. Hennessy
**Chief Acctg Officer & Cntlr:** A.J. Mistysyn
**Treas:** C.D. Brogan

**Investor Contact:** R.J. Wells (216-566-2244)
**Board Members:** A. F. Anton, J. C. Boland, C. M. Connor, D. F. Hodnik, T. G. Kadien, S. J. Kropf, G. E. McCullough, A. Mixon, III, C. E. Moll, R. K. Smucker, J. M. Stropki, Jr.

**Founded:** 1866
**Domicile:** Ohio
**Employees:** 32,228

*The McGraw-Hill Companies*

# Sigma Aldrich Corporation

STANDARD
&POOR'S

**S&P Recommendation** BUY ★★★★☆

| | | |
|---|---|---|
| **Price** | **12-Mo. Target Price** | **Investment Style** |
| $58.89 (as of Nov 25, 2011) | $82.00 | Large-Cap Growth |

**GICS Sector** Materials
**Sub-Industry** Specialty Chemicals

**Summary** This company makes and sells a wide range of biochemicals, organic chemicals, and chromatography products.

## Key Stock Statistics (Source S&P, Vickers, company reports)

| | | | | | | | |
|---|---|---|---|---|---|---|---|
| 52-Wk Range | $76.16–56.18 | S&P Oper. EPS 2011**E** | 3.76 | Market Capitalization(B) | $7.093 | Beta | 0.88 |
| Trailing 12-Month EPS | $3.60 | S&P Oper. EPS 2012**E** | 4.04 | Yield (%) | 1.22 | S&P 3-Yr. Proj. EPS CAGR(%) | 12 |
| Trailing 12-Month P/E | 16.4 | P/E on S&P Oper. EPS 2011**E** | 15.7 | Dividend Rate/Share | $0.72 | S&P Credit Rating | A+ |
| $10K Invested 5 Yrs Ago | $16,155 | Common Shares Outstg. (M) | 120.4 | Institutional Ownership (%) | 83 | | |

## Price Performance

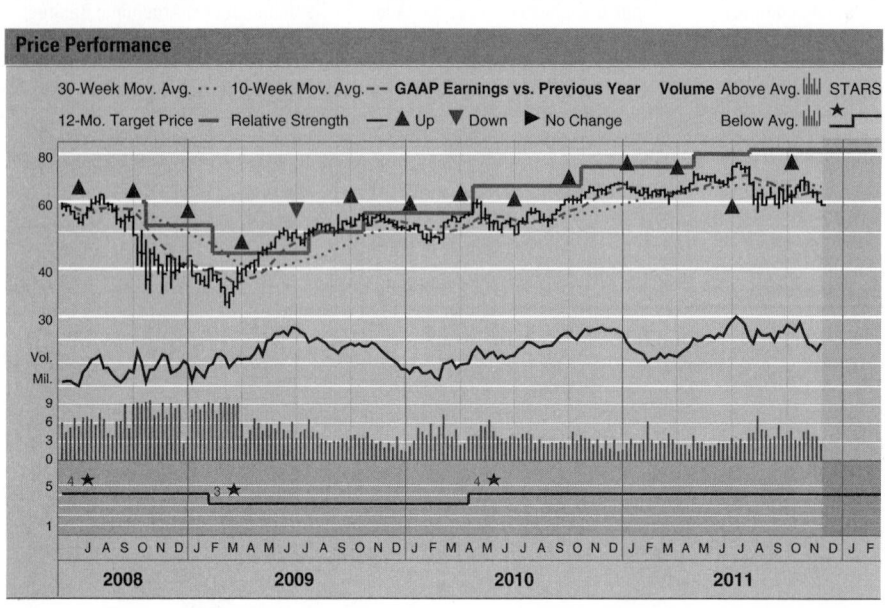

30-Week Mov. Avg. · · · 10-Week Mov. Avg. – – GAAP Earnings vs. Previous Year Volume Above Avg. STARS
12-Mo. Target Price — Relative Strength — ▲ Up ▼ Down ► No Change Below Avg.

Options: ASE, CBOE

Analysis prepared by Equity Analyst **Jeffrey Loo, CFA** on Nov 23, 2011, when the stock traded at **$59.89**.

## Qualitative Risk Assessment

| LOW | **MEDIUM** | HIGH |
|---|---|---|

Our risk assessment reflects the stable nature of the company's laboratory chemicals business, its broad geographic sales mix, and our view of its strong balance sheet. However, SIAL's business lines are highly competitive.

## Quantitative Evaluations

**S&P Quality Ranking** A+

| D | C | B- | B | B+ | A- | A | **A+** |
|---|---|---|---|---|---|---|---|

**Relative Strength Rank** MODERATE

43

LOWEST = 1 HIGHEST = 99

## Revenue/Earnings Data

**Revenue (Million $)**

| | 1Q | 2Q | 3Q | 4Q | Year |
|---|---|---|---|---|---|
| 2011 | 632.0 | 637.0 | 626.0 | -- | -- |
| 2010 | 572.0 | 554.0 | 563.0 | 582.0 | 2,271 |
| 2009 | 519.3 | 522.0 | 533.8 | 572.0 | 2,148 |
| 2008 | 569.6 | 580.7 | 540.6 | 509.8 | 2,201 |
| 2007 | 495.9 | 507.5 | 503.2 | 532.1 | 2,039 |
| 2006 | 443.1 | 448.5 | 441.4 | 464.5 | 1,798 |

**Earnings Per Share ($)**

| | | | | | |
|---|---|---|---|---|---|
| 2011 | 0.97 | 0.91 | 0.95 | E0.93 | E3.76 |
| 2010 | 0.81 | 0.79 | 0.76 | 0.76 | 3.12 |
| 2009 | 0.68 | 0.68 | 0.70 | 0.75 | 2.80 |
| 2008 | 0.64 | 0.70 | 0.64 | 0.68 | 2.65 |
| 2007 | 0.56 | 0.60 | 0.54 | 0.64 | 2.34 |
| 2006 | 0.49 | 0.52 | 0.51 | 0.53 | 2.05 |

Fiscal year ended Dec. 31. Next earnings report expected: NA. EPS Estimates based on S&P Operating Earnings; historical GAAP earnings are as reported.

## Highlights

➤ We expect 2011 sales, including a 4% foreign exchange benefit and a 2% contribution from acquisitions, to grow 11%, to $2.52 billion, with organic growth of 5% in Research Essentials, 5% in Research Specialties, 3% in Research Biotech (driven by synthetic DNA and molecular biology products), and 7% in SAFC (Fine Chemicals). We see sales rising 6% in 2012 to $2.67 billion. We think SIAL's efforts to increase international sales are paying off, and we project robust growth in the high teens in India, China, Brazil, Canada and Latin America (with Brazil, India and China growing about 25%), along with slow but improving growth in Europe. We also expect SIAL to supplement growth with strategic acquisitions. SIAL has made three small acquisitions (Resource Technology, Cerilliant and Vetec) since late 2010.

➤ We project gross margin improvement of 10 basis points (bps) in 2011, aided by SIAL's supply chain initiatives and see operating margins improving 80 bps on leverage. We also see potential for greater margin expansion with increased Internet sales. Web-based sales now account for about 50% of research sales.

➤ We see EPS of $3.76 in 2011 and $4.04 in 2012.

## Investment Rationale/Risk

➤ We believe the shares, recently trading at 15.1X our forward 12-months EPS estimate, slightly above peers, are attractively valued. We think SIAL deserves a premium valuation, as we view the company as an industry leader with a robust growth rate that we forecast to be better than the industry average. We also see improved stability in SIAL's end markets, particularly biosciences and high tech, in a challenging economic environment. SIAL's five-year supply chain initiative, which began in 2007, should improve its industry-leading margins, in our view.

➤ Risks to our recommendation and target price include greater-than-expected weakness in key markets such as pharmaceuticals, greater price competition, and an inability to successfully introduce new products.

➤ Our 12-month target price of $82 is based on a slightly above peers P/E-to-growth ratio of about 1.7X, using our forward 12-months EPS estimate and our three-year projected growth rate of 12%. We believe a slight premium is warranted based on SIAL's industry-leading margins and our expectation of above industry average sales growth.

## Dividend Data (Dates: mm/dd Payment Date: mm/dd/yy)

| Amount ($) | Date Decl. | Ex-Div. Date | Stk. of Record | Payment Date |
|---|---|---|---|---|
| 0.180 | 02/09 | 02/25 | 03/01 | 03/15/11 |
| 0.180 | 05/03 | 05/27 | 06/01 | 06/15/11 |
| 0.180 | 08/10 | 08/30 | 09/01 | 09/15/11 |
| 0.180 | 11/08 | 11/29 | 12/01 | 12/15/11 |

Dividends have been paid since 1970. Source: Company reports.

---

**Please read the Required Disclosures and Analyst Certification on the last page of this report.**

The McGraw·Hill Companies

# Sigma Aldrich Corporation

**STANDARD &POOR'S**

## Business Summary November 23, 2011

CORPORATE OVERVIEW. Sigma-Aldrich, well known for its extensive catalog business, is one of the world's largest providers of research chemicals, reagents, chromatography products, and related products.

Foreign sales accounted for over 65% of the total in 2010 (65% in 2009).

SIAL distributes more than 170,000 chemical products, under the Sigma, Aldrich, Fluka and Supelco brand names, for use primarily in research and development, diagnosis of disease, and as specialty chemicals for manufacturing. About 75% of sales are to customers in the life sciences, with the remaining 25% used in high-technology applications. Customer sectors include pharmaceutical (40% of sales), academia and government (30%), chemical industry (20%), and hospitals and commercial laboratories (10%). The company itself produces about 48,000 products, accounting for 65% of 2010 (65% in 2009) net sales of chemical products. Remaining products are purchased from outside sources. The company also supplies 40,000 equipment products.

The Research Essentials unit, 19% of sales in 2010 (20% in 2009), sells biological buffers, cell culture reagents, biochemicals, chemicals, solvents, and other reagents and kits. The Research Specialties unit, 37% of sales in 2010 (37%), sells organic chemicals, biochemicals, analytical reagents, chromatography consumables, reference materials and high-purity products. The Research Biotech unit, 15% of sales in 2010 (16%), supplies immunochemical, molecular biology, cell signaling and neuroscience biochemicals and kits used in biotechnology, genomic, proteomic and other life science research applications. Sigma-Genosys (acquired in 1998) is a major maker of custom synthetic DNA products, synthetic peptides and genes to the life science product categories. SIAL believes it is the leading supplier of products used in cell signaling and neuroscience. The SAFC (Fine Chemicals) unit, 29% of sales in 2010 (28%), is a top 10 supplier of large-scale organic chemicals and biochemicals used in development and production by pharmaceutical, biotechnology, industrial and diagnostic companies. The February 2007 purchase of Epichem Group (annual sales of $40 million) greatly expanded SAFC's high technology sales.

SIAL also offers about 80,000 esoteric chemicals (less than 1% of total sales) as a special service to customers that screen them for potential applications.

## Company Financials Fiscal Year Ended Dec. 31

| Per Share Data ($) | 2010 | 2009 | 2008 | 2007 | 2006 | 2005 | 2004 | 2003 | 2002 | 2001 |
|---|---|---|---|---|---|---|---|---|---|---|
| Tangible Book Value | 11.43 | 9.50 | 7.13 | 8.19 | 7.00 | 5.71 | 7.67 | 6.42 | 5.45 | 3.38 |
| Cash Flow | 3.88 | 3.55 | 3.42 | 3.07 | 1.37 | 2.54 | 2.19 | 1.83 | 1.72 | 1.41 |
| Earnings | 3.12 | 2.80 | 2.65 | 2.34 | 2.05 | 1.88 | 1.67 | 1.34 | 0.89 | 0.94 |
| S&P Core Earnings | 3.17 | 2.86 | 2.56 | 2.34 | 2.05 | 1.81 | 1.58 | 1.28 | 1.05 | 0.88 |
| Dividends | 0.64 | 0.58 | 0.52 | 0.46 | 0.42 | 0.38 | 0.34 | 0.25 | 0.17 | 0.17 |
| Payout Ratio | 21% | 21% | 20% | 20% | 20% | 20% | 20% | 19% | 19% | 18% |
| Prices:High | 67.76 | 56.29 | 63.04 | 56.59 | 39.68 | 33.55 | 30.81 | 28.96 | 26.40 | 25.75 |
| Prices:Low | 46.50 | 31.45 | 34.33 | 37.40 | 31.27 | 27.67 | 26.61 | 20.47 | 19.08 | 18.13 |
| P/E Ratio:High | 22 | 20 | 24 | 24 | 19 | 18 | 18 | 22 | 30 | 28 |
| P/E Ratio:Low | 15 | 11 | 13 | 16 | 15 | 15 | 16 | 15 | 21 | 19 |

| Income Statement Analysis (Million $) | 2010 | 2009 | 2008 | 2007 | 2006 | 2005 | 2004 | 2003 | 2002 | 2001 |
|---|---|---|---|---|---|---|---|---|---|---|
| Revenue | 2,271 | 2,148 | 2,201 | 2,039 | 1,798 | 1,667 | 1,409 | 1,298 | 1,207 | 1,179 |
| Operating Income | 675 | 601 | 602 | 557 | 494 | 452 | 392 | 353 | 323 | 291 |
| Depreciation | 93.0 | 92.4 | 98.6 | 97.8 | 90.9 | 90.1 | 73.4 | 69.3 | 66.3 | 71.4 |
| Interest Expense | 7.00 | 10.0 | 21.0 | 28.9 | 24.0 | 18.1 | 7.20 | 10.1 | 13.8 | 18.2 |
| Pretax Income | 544 | 490 | 490 | 438 | 379 | 343 | 312 | 273 | 272 | 202 |
| Effective Tax Rate | NA | 29.2% | 30.2% | 28.9% | 26.9% | 24.8% | 25.3% | 30.2% | 31.4% | 30.2% |
| Net Income | 384 | 347 | 342 | 311 | 277 | 258 | 233 | 190 | 187 | 141 |
| S&P Core Earnings | 391 | 354 | 331 | 310 | 276 | 249 | 221 | 180 | 155 | 133 |

| Balance Sheet & Other Financial Data (Million $) | 2010 | 2009 | 2008 | 2007 | 2006 | 2005 | 2004 | 2003 | 2002 | 2001 |
|---|---|---|---|---|---|---|---|---|---|---|
| Cash | 569 | 373 | 252 | 238 | 174 | 98.6 | 169 | 128 | 52.4 | 37.6 |
| Current Assets | 1,602 | 1,384 | 1,309 | 1,283 | 1,113 | 950 | 893 | 815 | 695 | 727 |
| Total Assets | 3,014 | 2,714 | 2,557 | 2,629 | 2,334 | 2,131 | 1,745 | 1,548 | 1,390 | 1,440 |
| Current Liabilities | 530 | 742 | 794 | 635 | 443 | 461 | 231 | 257 | 266 | 398 |
| Long Term Debt | 300 | 100 | 200 | 207 | 338 | 283 | 177 | 176 | 177 | 178 |
| Common Equity | 1,976 | 1,686 | 1,379 | 1,617 | 1,411 | 1,233 | 1,212 | 999 | 882 | 810 |
| Total Capital | 2,276 | 1,886 | 1,598 | 1,866 | 1,797 | 1,597 | 1,389 | 1,176 | 1,059 | 987 |
| Capital Expenditures | 99.0 | 120 | 89.9 | 79.7 | 74.5 | 92.2 | 70.3 | 57.7 | 60.7 | 110 |
| Cash Flow | 477 | 439 | 440 | 409 | 368 | 348 | 306 | 260 | 253 | 212 |
| Current Ratio | 3.0 | 1.9 | 1.7 | 2.0 | 2.5 | 2.1 | 3.9 | 3.2 | 2.6 | 1.8 |
| % Long Term Debt of Capitalization | 13.2 | 5.3 | 12.5 | 11.1 | 18.8 | 17.7 | 12.8 | 15.0 | 16.7 | 18.0 |
| % Net Income of Revenue | 16.9 | 16.1 | 15.5 | 15.3 | 15.4 | 15.5 | 16.5 | 14.7 | 15.5 | 11.9 |
| % Return on Assets | 13.4 | 13.2 | 13.2 | 12.5 | 12.4 | 13.3 | 14.1 | 12.7 | 13.2 | 10.1 |
| % Return on Equity | 21.0 | 22.6 | 22.8 | 20.6 | 20.9 | 21.1 | 21.1 | 20.2 | 22.1 | 16.9 |

Data as orig reptd.; bef. results of disc opers/spec. items. Per share data adj. for stk. divs.; EPS diluted. E-Estimated. NA-Not Available. NM-Not Meaningful. NR-Not Ranked. UR-Under Review.

**Office:** 3050 Spruce Street, St. Louis, MO 63103.
**Telephone:** 314-771-5765.
**Website:** http://www.sigma-aldrich.com
**Chrmn:** B. Toan

**Pres & CEO:** R. Sachdev
**SVP, Secy & General Counsel:** G.L. Miller
**Investor Contact:** K.A. Richter (314-286-8004)
**CFO & Treas:** K.A. Richter

**Board Members:** R. M. Bergman, G. Church, D. R. Harvey, W. L. McCollum, A. M. Nash, S. M. Paul, J. P. Reinhard, R. Sachdev, D. D. Spatz, B. Toan

**Founded:** 1951
**Domicile:** Delaware
**Employees:** 7,890

The McGraw-Hill Companies

**STANDARD &POOR'S**

# Simon Property Group Inc.

| S&P Recommendation | STRONG BUY ★★★★★ | Price | 12-Mo. Target Price | Investment Style |
|---|---|---|---|---|
| | | $116.33 (as of Nov 25, 2011) | $142.00 | Large-Cap Blend |

**GICS Sector** Financials
**Sub-Industry** Retail REITS

**Summary** This real estate investment trust owns, develops, and manages retail real estate, primarily regional malls, outlet centers, and community/lifestyle centers, mainly in the U.S.

## Key Stock Statistics (Source S&P, Vickers, company reports)

| | | | | | | | |
|---|---|---|---|---|---|---|---|
| 52-Wk Range | $131.21– 94.30 | S&P FFO/Sh. 2011**E** | 6.83 | Market Capitalization(B) | $34.176 | Beta | 1.53 |
| Trailing 12-Month FFO/Share | $6.85 | S&P FFO/Sh. 2012**E** | 7.18 | Yield (%) | 3.09 | S&P 3-Yr. FFO/Sh. Proj. CAGR(%) | 16 |
| Trailing 12-Month P/FFO | NA | P/FFO on S&P FFO/Sh. 2011**E** | 17.0 | Dividend Rate/Share | $3.60 | S&P Credit Rating | A- |
| $10K Invested 5 Yrs Ago | $13,776 | Common Shares Outstg. (M) | 293.8 | Institutional Ownership (%) | NM | | |

## Price Performance

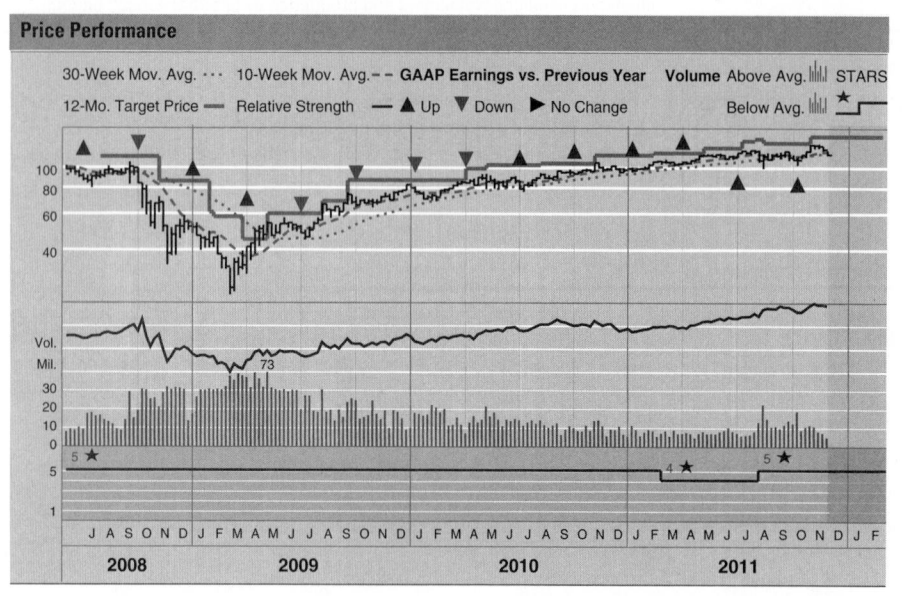

30-Week Mov. Avg. · · ·   10-Week Mov. Avg. – –   **GAAP Earnings vs. Previous Year**   Volume Above Avg. ▮▮▮ STARS
12-Mo. Target Price ——   Relative Strength —   ▲ Up  ▼ Down  ► No Change   Below Avg. ▮▮▮ ★

Options: ASE, CBOE, Ph

Analysis prepared by Equity Analyst **Robert McMillan** on Oct 25, 2011, when the stock traded at **$122.14**.

## Highlights

➤ We expect the trust to continue to benefit from what we view as a successful strategy of operating large and strategically located regional malls and shopping centers in major markets. After a fractional revenue decline in 2009 and a 4.8% gain in 2010, we look for total revenues to advance 7.4% in 2011 and 4.3% in 2012, on higher rents and tenant reimbursements and contributions from acquisitions.

➤ We believe that improving retailer demand for SPG's space, combined with a prolonged drop in new construction activity, will give SPG additional pricing leverage as demand firms. Occupancy in SPG's U.S. operational portfolio increased to 93.9% at the end of the 2011 third quarter from 93.8% a year earlier, while the releasing spread rose 9.6% for the 12-month period ended September 2011. We view planned store closures by a several retailers as an opportunity for SPG to generate higher rents for the vacated space. Occupancy levels also remained healthy in the community and lifestyle, Mills regional malls and at international properties in Europe and Japan.

➤ We see FFO per share of $6.83 in 2011 and $7.18 in 2012.

## Investment Rationale/Risk

➤ We think SPG's position as one of the largest owners and managers of shopping centers in the U.S., and its established relationships with numerous retailers, will allow it to continue to generate solid growth long term. We also view the geographic, customer, and format diversity of SPG's portfolio and management's acquisition acumen as positive factors in our valuation.

➤ Risks to our recommendation and target price include slower-than-expected retailer expansion, higher-than-normal retailer bankruptcies, and a rise in interest rates.

➤ The shares recently traded at 18.1X trailing 12-month FFO per share. Our 12-month target price of $142 is equal to 20.0X our forward four-quarter FFO estimate of $7.11. Although the shares recently traded at relatively high levels, we believe the multiple will expand further, driven by continuing improvements in SPG's operating performance and easing concerns about the impact of the economy on its retailer-dependent business, which is anchored by long-term leases. Our view of a likely near-term increase in the annual dividend is also a positive factor in our valuation.

## Qualitative Risk Assessment

| LOW | MEDIUM | HIGH |
|---|---|---|

Our risk assessment reflects SPG's position as one of the largest owners of shopping centers, with a diverse tenant and geographic mix and variety of shopping center formats. The majority of SPG's customers are under long-term leases, reducing short-term volatility. Although the trust has sizable maturing debt, we believe the company can access the capital markets to remain liquid.

## Quantitative Evaluations

**S&P Quality Ranking**                                **B**

| D | C | B- | **B** | B+ | A- | A | A+ |
|---|---|---|---|---|---|---|---|

**Relative Strength Rank**                          **MODERATE**

64

LOWEST = 1                                              HIGHEST = 99

## Revenue/FFO Data

**Revenue (Million $)**

| | 1Q | 2Q | 3Q | 4Q | Year |
|---|---|---|---|---|---|
| 2011 | 1,020 | 1,041 | 1,073 | -- | -- |
| 2010 | 925.1 | 933.6 | 979.3 | 1,120 | 3,958 |
| 2009 | 918.5 | 903.6 | 924.9 | 1,028 | 3,775 |
| 2008 | 895.3 | 913.5 | 932.2 | 1,029 | 3,783 |
| 2007 | 852.1 | 855.9 | 907.2 | 1,036 | 3,651 |
| 2006 | 787.7 | 798.7 | 818.7 | 927.0 | 3,332 |

**FFO Per Share ($)**

| | | | | | |
|---|---|---|---|---|---|
| 2011 | 1.95 | 1.99 | 2.06 | E1.86 | E6.83 |
| 2010 | 1.11 | 1.66 | 1.09 | 2.15 | 6.05 |
| 2009 | 1.61 | 0.96 | 1.38 | 1.40 | 5.33 |
| 2008 | 1.46 | 1.49 | 1.61 | 1.86 | 6.42 |
| 2007 | 1.37 | 1.31 | 1.46 | 1.76 | 5.90 |
| 2006 | 1.26 | 1.26 | 1.30 | 1.57 | 5.39 |

Fiscal year ended Dec. 31. Next earnings report expected: NA. FFO Estimates based on S&P Funds From Operations Est..

## Dividend Data (Dates: mm/dd Payment Date: mm/dd/yy)

| Amount ($) | Date Decl. | Ex-Div. Date | Stk. of Record | Payment Date |
|---|---|---|---|---|
| 0.800 | 07/26 | 08/15 | 08/17 | 08/31/11 |
| 0.900 | 10/25 | 11/14 | 11/16 | 11/30/11 |
| .2 Spl. | 10/25 | 12/14 | 12/16 | 12/30/11 |

Dividends have been paid since 1994. Source: Company reports.

---

**Please read the Required Disclosures and Analyst Certification on the last page of this report.**

**The McGraw·Hill** Companies

# Simon Property Group Inc.

STANDARD
&POOR'S

## Business Summary October 25, 2011

CORPORATE OVERVIEW. Simon Property Group is a real estate investment trust that owns, develops, manages, leases and acquires primarily regional malls and community shopping centers. It is one of the largest owners of shopping centers in the world. As of December 31, 2001, SPG owned or held an interest in 338 income-producing properties in the United States, which consisted of 161 regional malls, 58 premium outlet centers, 66 community/ lifestyle centers, 36 properties acquired in the 2007 acquisition of The Mills Corporation, and 17 other shopping centers or outlet centers in 41 states and Puerto Rico. The company also had ownership interests in 45 European shopping centers in Italy, and 10 premium outlet centers in Japan, Mexico and South Korea.

SPG's regional malls typically contain at least one traditional department store anchor or a combination of anchors and big box retailers with a wide variety of smaller stores located in enclosed malls connecting the anchors. Additional freestanding stores are usually located along the perimeter of the parking area. SPG's regional malls range in size from approximately 400,000 to 2.3 million square feet of gross leasable area (GLA) and contain more than 18,000 occupied stores, including approximately 709 anchors, which are mostly national retailers. SPG's premium outlet centers, ranging in size from

150,000 to 850,000 square feet of GLA, contain a wide variety of retailers located in open-air manufacturers' outlet centers near metropolitan areas .

SPG's community and lifestyle shopping centers are generally unenclosed and smaller than its regional malls. The community and lifestyle centers usually range in size from approximately 100,000 to 950,000 square feet of GLA and are designed to serve a larger trade area, and typically contain at least two anchors and other tenants that are usually national retailers among the leaders in their markets. These tenants generally occupy a significant portion of the GLA of the center. The trust also owns traditional community shopping centers that focus primarily on value-oriented and convenience goods and services. These centers are normally anchored by a supermarket, discount retailer or drugstore and are designed to service a neighborhood area. The trust also owns open-air centers adjacent to its regional malls designed to take advantage of the drawing power of the mall.

## Company Financials Fiscal Year Ended Dec. 31

| Per Share Data ($) | 2010 | 2009 | 2008 | 2007 | 2006 | 2005 | 2004 | 2003 | 2002 | 2001 |
|---|---|---|---|---|---|---|---|---|---|---|
| Tangible Book Value | 15.71 | 15.25 | 10.93 | 12.40 | 13.98 | 14.64 | 16.21 | 14.66 | 13.87 | 13.00 |
| Earnings | 2.10 | 1.05 | 1.77 | 2.08 | 2.19 | 1.27 | 1.44 | 1.53 | 1.93 | 0.87 |
| S&P Core Earnings | 2.10 | 1.05 | 1.87 | 2.20 | 2.19 | 1.12 | 1.44 | 1.55 | 2.07 | 0.97 |
| Dividends | 2.60 | 2.70 | 3.60 | 3.36 | 3.04 | 2.80 | 2.60 | 2.40 | 2.18 | 2.08 |
| Payout Ratio | 124% | NM | 203% | 162% | 139% | NM | 181% | 157% | 113% | NM |
| Prices:High | 106.54 | 83.82 | 106.43 | 123.96 | 104.08 | 80.97 | 65.87 | 48.59 | 36.95 | 30.97 |
| Prices:Low | 68.76 | 24.27 | 33.78 | 82.60 | 76.14 | 58.29 | 44.39 | 31.70 | 28.80 | 23.75 |
| P/E Ratio:High | 51 | 80 | 60 | 60 | 48 | 64 | 46 | 32 | 19 | 36 |
| P/E Ratio:Low | 33 | 23 | 19 | 40 | 35 | 46 | 31 | 21 | 15 | 27 |
| **Income Statement Analysis** (Million $) | | | | | | | | | | |
| Rental Income | 3,624 | 3,464 | 3,458 | 3,288 | 3,063 | 2,920 | 2,411 | 1,423 | 1,386 | 1,320 |
| Mortgage Income | Nil | Nil | Nil | Nil | Nil | Nil | Nil | Nil | Nil | Nil |
| Total Income | 3,958 | 3,775 | 3,783 | 3,651 | 3,332 | 3,167 | 2,642 | 2,314 | 2,186 | 2,045 |
| General Expenses | 1,231 | 1,174 | 1,191 | 1,210 | 856 | 820 | 675 | 611 | 788 | 712 |
| Interest Expense | 1,027 | 992 | 965 | 1,535 | 822 | 799 | 662 | 615 | 603 | 622 |
| Provision for Losses | 3.13 | 22.7 | 24.0 | 9.56 | 9.50 | 8.10 | 17.7 | Nil | 8.97 | 8.41 |
| Depreciation | 1,016 | 998 | 970 | 906 | 856 | 850 | 623 | 498 | 423 | 453 |
| Net Income | 617 | 309 | 464 | 519 | 563 | 457 | 450 | 339 | 1,109 | 201 |
| S&P Core Earnings | 610 | 283 | 423 | 491 | 486 | 247 | 301 | 288 | 371 | 169 |
| **Balance Sheet & Other Financial Data** (Million $) | | | | | | | | | | |
| Cash | 797 | 3,958 | 774 | 502 | 929 | 929 | 520 | 536 | 397 | 255 |
| Total Assets | 24,857 | 25,948 | 23,597 | 23,606 | 22,084 | 21,131 | 22,070 | 15,685 | 14,905 | 13,794 |
| Real Estate Investment | 27,509 | 25,336 | 25,206 | 24,415 | 24,390 | 23,307 | 23,175 | 14,972 | 14,250 | 13,187 |
| Loss Reserve | Nil | Nil | Nil | Nil | Nil | Nil | Nil | Nil | 20.5 | 24.7 |
| Net Investment | 19,797 | 18,332 | 19,021 | 19,103 | 19,784 | 19,499 | 20,012 | 12,415 | 12,027 | 11,311 |
| Short Term Debt | 896 | 2,312 | 1,476 | 810 | NA | NA | NA | 1,481 | 940 | 665 |
| Capitalization:Debt | 16,578 | 16,318 | 16,567 | 16,409 | 13,711 | 14,106 | 13,044 | 8,786 | 8,606 | 8,176 |
| Capitalization:Equity | 4,785 | 4,412 | 2,615 | 2,817 | 3,095 | 3,227 | 3,580 | 2,971 | 2,653 | 2,327 |
| Capitalization:Total | 22,298 | 21,501 | 19,607 | 21,821 | 18,885 | 19,681 | 19,065 | 13,241 | 12,074 | 11,381 |
| % Earnings & Depreciation/Assets | 6.4 | 5.3 | 6.1 | 6.2 | 6.7 | 6.0 | 5.7 | 5.5 | 10.7 | 4.7 |
| Price Times Book Value:High | 6.8 | 5.5 | 9.7 | 10.0 | 7.4 | 5.5 | 4.1 | 3.3 | 2.7 | 2.4 |
| Price Times Book Value:Low | 2.1 | 1.6 | 3.1 | 6.7 | 5.4 | 4.0 | 2.7 | 2.2 | 2.1 | 1.8 |

Data as orig reptd.; bef. results of disc opers/spec. items. Per share data adj. for stk. divs.; EPS diluted. E-Estimated. NA-Not Available. NM-Not Meaningful. NR-Not Ranked. UR-Under Review.

**Office:** 225 West Washington Street, Indianapolis, IN 46204.
**Telephone:** 317-636-1600.
**Website:** http://www.simon.com/about_simon/index.aspx
**Chrmn & CEO:** D.E. Simon

**Pres & COO:** R.S. Sokolov
**EVP & CFO:** S.E. Sterrett
**EVP & Treas:** A.A. Juster
**SVP & Chief Acctg Officer:** S.K. Broadwater

**Investor Contact:** S.J. Doran (317-685-7330)
**Board Members:** M. E. Bergstein, L. W. Bynoe, L. C. Glasscock, K. N. Horn, A. B. Hubbard, R. S. Leibowitz, D. E. Simon, H. Simon, D. C. Smith, J. A. Smith, Jr., R. S. Sokolov

**Founded:** 1993
**Domicile:** Delaware
**Employees:** 5,900

The McGraw-Hill Companies

# SLM Corp

**STANDARD &POOR'S**

| S&P Recommendation | HOLD ★★★★★ | Price<br>$11.99 (as of Nov 25, 2011) | 12-Mo. Target Price<br>$17.00 | Investment Style<br>Large-Cap Growth |
|---|---|---|---|---|

**GICS Sector** Financials
**Sub-Industry** Consumer Finance

**Summary** This company (formerly USA Education) is a leading U.S. provider of post-secondary educational financial services.

## Key Stock Statistics (Source S&P, Vickers, company reports)

| | | | | | | | |
|---|---|---|---|---|---|---|---|
| 52-Wk Range | $17.11– 10.91 | S&P Oper. EPS 2011**E** | 1.79 | Market Capitalization(B) | $6.100 | Beta | 1.45 |
| Trailing 12-Month EPS | $1.05 | S&P Oper. EPS 2012**E** | 1.99 | Yield (%) | 3.34 | S&P 3-Yr. Proj. EPS CAGR(%) | 13 |
| Trailing 12-Month P/E | 11.4 | P/E on S&P Oper. EPS 2011**E** | 6.7 | Dividend Rate/Share | $0.40 | S&P Credit Rating | BBB- |
| $10K Invested 5 Yrs Ago | $2,672 | Common Shares Outstg. (M) | 508.7 | Institutional Ownership (%) | 96 | | |

## Price Performance

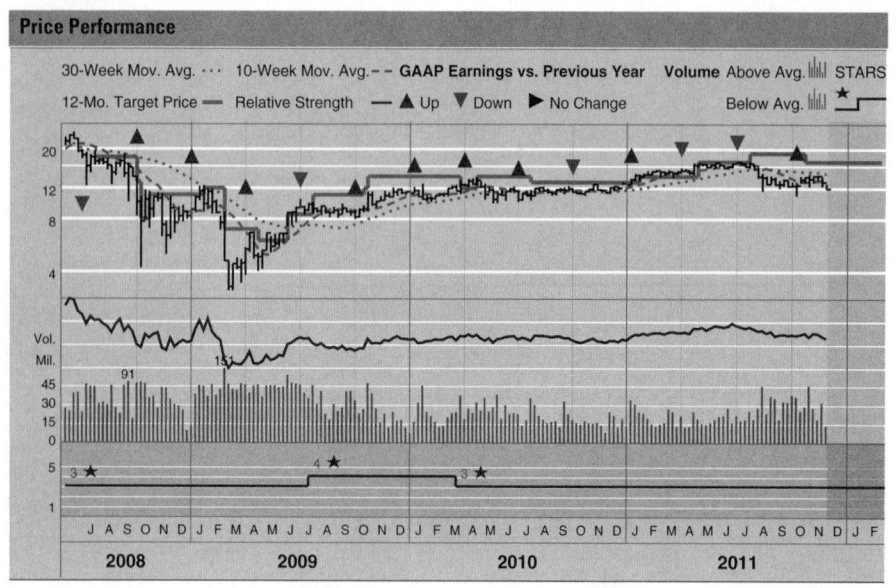

- 30-Week Mov. Avg. ····
- 10-Week Mov. Avg. - -
- 12-Mo. Target Price ——
- Relative Strength ——
- GAAP Earnings vs. Previous Year
- ▲ Up ▼ Down ► No Change
- Volume Above Avg. / Below Avg.
- STARS ★

Options: ASE, CBOE, P

Analysis prepared by Equity Analyst **Robert McMillan** on Oct 24, 2011, when the stock traded at **$13.99**.

## Highlights

► We project that the loan portfolio mix will shift toward private student loans in 2011, reflecting legislation to eliminate student loan subsidies for government-sponsored loans. In addition, we think recent legislation will negatively affect the company's origination business. Longer term, we see SLM's net interest margin declining; however, in the 2011 third quarter, the net interest margin (core earnings) rose to 4.03%, from 3.87% last year. In January 2011, SLM completed its $28 billion acquisition of securitized federal student loans and other assets from The Student Loan Corporation.

► We forecast that loan loss provisions will decline in both 2011 and 2012, given our outlook for lower charge-offs from improved forbearance policies. We believe the company's restructuring of its business from origination to servicing of loans, following the passage of the new legislation, will occur gradually during 2011 and 2012. As a result, we see other expenses declining slightly in both years.

► We estimate operating EPS of $1.79 for 2011 and $1.99 for 2012, compared to $1.92 in 2010.

## Investment Rationale/Risk

► In 2010, both houses of Congress passed legislation that eliminated student loan subsidies for government-sponsored loans. We believe the company will transition its primary business to focus on servicing loans instead of originating them. As a result, we think SLM, the largest provider of government-sponsored loans, will experience lower loan volumes and a decline in interest-earning assets. On a positive note, we expect SLM's run-off portfolio of government-sponsored loans to generate solid financial returns, and we see credit spreads continuing to improve in 2011, reflecting our outlook for ongoing economic recovery.

► Risks to our recommendation and target price include changes in government legislation that can remove subsidies for the company's loan products, loss of market share, and higher-than-expected loss provisions.

► The shares recently traded at 6.5X trailing 12-month operating EPS. Our 12-month target price of $17 is based on a multiple of 10X our 12-month operating EPS estimate of $1.95, a discount to the historical average to reflect what we think is a transition period in the company's business.

## Qualitative Risk Assessment

| LOW | MEDIUM | HIGH |
|---|---|---|

Our risk assessment reflects what we see as the negative impact from new legislation, offset by our view of lower loss provisions and a potentially higher net interest margin.

## Quantitative Evaluations

**S&P Quality Ranking**      B-

| D | C | B- | B | B+ | A- | A | A+ |
|---|---|---|---|---|---|---|---|

**Relative Strength Rank**      WEAK

29

LOWEST = 1       HIGHEST = 99

## Revenue/Earnings Data

**Revenue (Million $)**

| | 1Q | 2Q | 3Q | 4Q | Year |
|---|---|---|---|---|---|
| 2011 | 1,487 | -- | -- | -- | -- |
| 2010 | 1,641 | 1,849 | 1,371 | 1,915 | 6,776 |
| 2009 | 1,530 | 1,248 | 1,551 | 1,815 | 6,145 |
| 2008 | 1,963 | 2,331 | 1,697 | 631.2 | 7,881 |
| 2007 | 2,466 | 2,495 | 2,119 | 1,270 | 9,171 |
| 2006 | 1,766 | 2,695 | 2,252 | 2,038 | 8,751 |

**Earnings Per Share ($)**

| | 1Q | 2Q | 3Q | 4Q | Year |
|---|---|---|---|---|---|
| 2011 | 0.32 | -0.04 | -0.14 | E0.47 | E1.79 |
| 2010 | 0.45 | 0.61 | -1.07 | 0.94 | 1.08 |
| 2009 | Nil | -0.31 | 0.26 | 0.71 | 0.71 |
| 2008 | -0.28 | 0.50 | -0.40 | -0.52 | -0.39 |
| 2007 | 0.26 | 1.03 | -0.85 | -3.98 | -2.26 |
| 2006 | 0.34 | 1.52 | 0.60 | 0.02 | 2.63 |

Fiscal year ended Dec. 31. Next earnings report expected: Late January. EPS Estimates based on S&P Operating Earnings; historical GAAP earnings are as reported.

## Dividend Data (Dates: mm/dd Payment Date: mm/dd/yy)

| Amount ($) | Date Decl. | Ex-Div. Date | Stk. of Record | Payment Date |
|---|---|---|---|---|
| 0.100 | 04/20 | 06/01 | 06/03 | 06/17/11 |
| 0.100 | 07/29 | 08/31 | 09/02 | 09/16/11 |
| 0.100 | 11/17 | 11/30 | 12/02 | 12/16/11 |

Dividends have been paid since 2011. Source: Company reports.

# SLM Corp

**STANDARD &POOR'S**

## Business Summary October 24, 2011

SLM Corporation, through its subsidiaries, originates, services, and collects loans made to students and/or their parents to finance the cost of their education. The company provides funding, delivery, and servicing support for education loans in the United States through its non-federally guaranteed Private Education Loan programs and as a servicer and collector of loans for the Department of Education (ED). The company has three primary business segments- the Federal Family Education Loan Program (FFELP) Loans segment, Consumer Lending segment, and the Business Services segment.

The company's FFELP Loans business segment consists of its FFELP Loan portfolio and the underlying debt and capital funding the loans. These FFELP Loans are financed through various types of secured non-recourse financing vehicles and unsecured debt.

In the Consumer Lending Segment, the company originates, acquires, finances, and services private education loans. Private Education Loans consist of two general types - those that are designed to bridge the gap between the cost of higher education and the amount financed through either federal loans or the borrowers' resources, and those that are used to meet the needs of students in alternative learning programs, such as career training, distance learning, and lifelong learning programs. Private Education Loans bear the credit risk of the borrower. The company manages this risk by underwriting

and pricing according to credit risk based upon customized credit scoring criteria and the addition of qualified cosigners.

The Business Services segment services its FFELP Loan portfolio, as well as services FFELP and other loans for other financial institutions, guarantors, and the Department of Education. The segment also performs default aversion work and contingency collections on behalf of Guarantors and the Department of Education, Campus Payment Solutions, account asset servicing, and transaction processing activities. The company provides a complement of default aversion and default collection services on a contingency or pay for performance basis to certain guarantors, campus-based programs, and the Department of Education. The company has performed default collections work for over ten years. Through Upromise, the company provides program management services for 529 college-savings plans. The company's Campus Payment Solutions business offers a suite of solutions designed to help campus business offices increase their services to students and families. The product suite includes electronic billing, collection, payment, and refund services plus full tuition payment plan administration.

## Company Financials Fiscal Year Ended Dec. 31

| Per Share Data ($) | 2010 | 2009 | 2008 | 2007 | 2006 | 2005 | 2004 | 2003 | 2002 | 2001 |
|---|---|---|---|---|---|---|---|---|---|---|
| Tangible Book Value | 7.53 | 5.62 | 4.37 | 5.93 | 5.90 | 5.13 | 4.81 | 4.55 | 3.08 | 3.59 |
| Earnings | 1.08 | 0.71 | -0.39 | -2.26 | 2.63 | 3.05 | 4.04 | 3.01 | 1.64 | 0.76 |
| S&P Core Earnings | 1.96 | 0.70 | -0.70 | -2.24 | 2.62 | 2.98 | 3.95 | 2.75 | 1.40 | 0.53 |
| Dividends | Nil | Nil | Nil | 0.25 | 0.97 | 0.85 | 0.74 | 0.59 | 0.28 | 0.24 |
| Payout Ratio | Nil | Nil | Nil | NM | 37% | 28% | 18% | 20% | 17% | 32% |
| Prices:High | 13.96 | 12.43 | 25.05 | 58.00 | 58.35 | 56.48 | 54.44 | 42.92 | 35.65 | 29.33 |
| Prices:Low | 9.85 | 3.11 | 4.19 | 18.68 | 44.65 | 45.56 | 36.43 | 33.73 | 25.67 | 18.63 |
| P/E Ratio:High | 13 | 18 | NM | NM | 22 | 19 | 13 | 14 | 22 | 39 |
| P/E Ratio:Low | 9 | 4 | NM | NM | 17 | 15 | 9 | 11 | 16 | 25 |

| Income Statement Analysis (Million $) | 2010 | 2009 | 2008 | 2007 | 2006 | 2005 | 2004 | 2003 | 2002 | 2001 |
|---|---|---|---|---|---|---|---|---|---|---|
| Interest on:Mortgages | 5,728 | 4,732 | 6,994 | 7,966 | 6,074 | 4,233 | 2,500 | 2,197 | 2,124 | 2,625 |
| Interest on:Investment | 25.9 | 26.1 | 276 | 708 | 503 | 277 | 233 | 151 | 87.9 | 373 |
| Interest Expense | 2,275 | 3,036 | 5,905 | 7,086 | 5,123 | 3,059 | 1,434 | 1,022 | 1,203 | 2,124 |
| Guaranty Fees | Nil | Nil | Nil | Nil | Nil | Nil | Nil | Nil | Nil | Nil |
| Loan Loss Provision | 1,419 | 1,119 | 720 | 1,015 | 287 | 203 | 111 | 147 | 117 | 66.0 |
| Administration Expenses | 1,208 | 1,255 | 1,357 | 1,529 | 1,346 | 1,138 | 895 | 808 | 690 | 708 |
| Pretax Income | 1,090 | 721 | -376 | -482 | 1,995 | 2,117 | 2,557 | 2,183 | 1,223 | 617 |
| Effective Tax Rate | 45.2% | 33.1% | NM | NM | 41.8% | 34.4% | 25.1% | 35.7% | 35.3% | 36.2% |
| Net Income | 598 | 482 | -213 | -896 | 1,157 | 1,382 | 1,913 | 1,404 | 792 | 384 |
| S&P Core Earnings | 954 | 330 | -327 | -923 | 1,119 | 1,324 | 1,853 | 1,276 | 664 | 261 |

| Balance Sheet & Other Financial Data (Million $) | 2010 | 2009 | 2008 | 2007 | 2006 | 2005 | 2004 | 2003 | 2002 | 2001 |
|---|---|---|---|---|---|---|---|---|---|---|
| Mortgages | 184,305 | 144,227 | 145,532 | 125,327 | 97,228 | 83,980 | 66,161 | 51,078 | 43,541 | 42,037 |
| Investment | 7,211 | 7,183 | 4,577 | 6,008 | 5,986 | 4,775 | 3,579 | 5,268 | 4,231 | 5,072 |
| Cash & Equivalent | 4,342 | 6,070 | 4,070 | 7,582 | 2,621 | 2,499 | 3,395 | 1,652 | 758 | 715 |
| Total Assets | 205,307 | 169,985 | 168,768 | 155,565 | 116,136 | 99,339 | 84,094 | 64,611 | 53,175 | 52,874 |
| Short Term Debt | 33,616 | 30,897 | 41,933 | 35,947 | 3.50 | 3,810 | 2,208 | 18,735 | 25,619 | 31,065 |
| Long Term Debt | 163,544 | 130,546 | 118,225 | 111,098 | 104,559 | 88,119 | 75,915 | 23,211 | 22,242 | 17,285 |
| Equity | 4,447 | 3,903 | 3,284 | 3,659 | 3,795 | 3,226 | 2,937 | 3,564 | 1,833 | 1,507 |
| % Return on Assets | 0.3 | 0.3 | NM | NM | 1.1 | 1.5 | 2.6 | 2.4 | 1.5 | 0.8 |
| % Return on Equity | 14.3 | 13.4 | NM | NM | 31.9 | 44.1 | 70.4 | 25.8 | 47.4 | 27.8 |
| Equity/Assets Ratio | 2.4 | 2.1 | 2.1 | 2.7 | 3.3 | 3.4 | 4.4 | 4.6 | 3.1 | 2.7 |
| Price Times Book Value:High | 1.9 | 2.2 | 5.7 | 9.8 | 9.9 | 11.0 | 11.3 | 9.4 | 11.6 | 8.2 |
| Price Times Book Value:Low | 1.3 | 0.6 | 1.0 | 3.2 | 7.6 | 8.9 | 7.6 | 7.4 | 8.3 | 5.2 |

Data as orig reptd.; bef. results of disc opers/spec. items. Per share data adj. for stk. divs.; EPS diluted. E-Estimated. NA-Not Available. NM-Not Meaningful. NR-Not Ranked. UR-Under Review.

**Office:** 300 Continental Drive, Newark, DE 19713.
**Telephone:** 302-283-8000.
**Website:** http://www.salliemae.com
**Chrmn:** A.P. Terracciano

**Pres & COO:** J.F. Remondi
**EVP, CFO & Chief Acctg Officer:** J.C. Clark
**EVP & General Counsel:** L.C. Lutz
**SVP & Cntlr:** T. Morris

**Investor Contact:** S. McGarry (703-810-7746)
**Board Members:** A. T. Bates, W. M. Diefenderfer, III, D. S. Gilleland, E. A. Goode, R. F. Hunt, A. L. Lord, M. E. Martin, B. A. Munitz, H. H. Newman, A. A. Porter, Jr., F. C. Puleo, W. Schoellkopf, S. L. Shapiro, J. T. Strange, A. P. Terracciano, B. L. Williams

**Founded:** 1972
**Domicile:** Delaware
**Employees:** 7,600

# J.M. Smucker Co (The)

STANDARD
&POOR'S

**S&P Recommendation** BUY ★★★★☆

| Price | 12-Mo. Target Price | Investment Style |
|---|---|---|
| $73.03 (as of Nov 25, 2011) | $80.00 | Large-Cap Blend |

**GICS Sector** Consumer Staples
**Sub-Industry** Packaged Foods & Meats

**Summary** This company's products include coffee, fruit spreads, peanut butter, shortening and oils, ice cream toppings, health and natural foods, and beverages. The Folgers coffee business was acquired in November 2008.

## Key Stock Statistics (Source S&P, Vickers, company reports)

| | | | | | | | |
|---|---|---|---|---|---|---|---|
| 52-Wk Range | $80.26– 61.16 | S&P Oper. EPS 2012**E** | 4.91 | Market Capitalization(B) | $8.314 | Beta | 0.66 |
| Trailing 12-Month EPS | $4.03 | S&P Oper. EPS 2013**E** | 5.45 | Yield (%) | 2.63 | S&P 3-Yr. Proj. EPS CAGR(%) | 8 |
| Trailing 12-Month P/E | 18.1 | P/E on S&P Oper. EPS 2012**E** | 14.9 | Dividend Rate/Share | $1.92 | S&P Credit Rating | BBB+ |
| $10K Invested 5 Yrs Ago | $19,218 | Common Shares Outstg. (M) | 113.8 | Institutional Ownership (%) | 74 | | |

## Price Performance

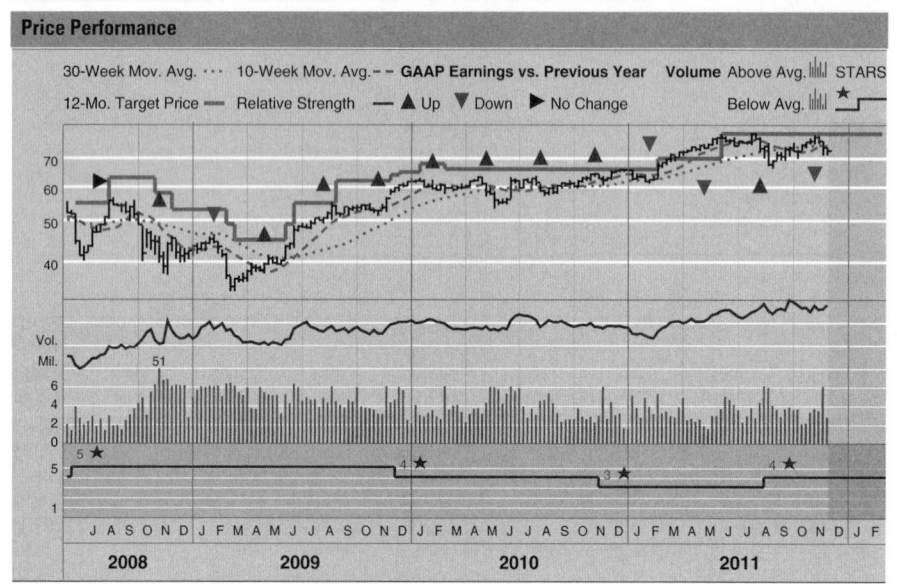

30-Week Mov. Avg. · · · 10-Week Mov. Avg. - - **GAAP Earnings vs. Previous Year** Volume Above Avg. STARS
12-Mo. Target Price — Relative Strength — ▲ Up ▼ Down ► No Change Below Avg.

Options: ASE, CBOE, Ph

Analysis prepared by Equity Analyst **Tom Graves, CFA** on Aug 29, 2011, when the stock traded at **$69.93**.

### Highlights

➤ For FY 12 (Apr.), we estimate that SJM's sales will rise about 18% from the $4.8 billion reported for FY 11, largely due to higher product prices.

➤ From FY 10 through FY 14, we anticipate about $235 million of restructuring costs related to a supply chain improvement plan, plus an initiative to address capacity underutilization at the Canadian pickle and condiments operations, and improvement to SJM's overall cost structure. We look for annual savings of about $68 million, excluding one-time costs, to be fully realized in FY 15. This excludes expected costs and savings related to the May 2011 acquisition of a coffee business.

➤ Before some special items, we estimate FY 12 EPS at $5.05, up from about $4.79 for FY 11, which excludes a negative impact of about $0.74 from special items. Our FY 12 estimate includes about $0.50 of non-cash amortization charges, up from an estimated $0.42 in FY 11. For FY 13, we estimate EPS of $5.50. In May 2011, SJM acquired the coffee brands and business operations of Rowland Coffee Roasters, Inc.

### Investment Rationale/Risk

➤ We generally like what SJM has accomplished with the Folgers coffee business, which provided diversification and economies of scale. However, we have some concern about the extent of a recent volume decline in SJM's coffee segment, and the prospect of at least near-term profit margin pressure from higher coffee costs and recently announced decreases in SJM coffee prices.

➤ Risks to our recommendation and target price include competitive pressures and commodity cost inflation. Also, the 2009 adoption by SJM directors of a shareholder rights plan seems to have been aimed at protecting SJM's independence.

➤ Our 12-month target price of $80 reflects our view that the shares should trade at a similar P/E (based on estimated calendar 2011 EPS) to a recent average for a group of other packaged food stocks. Also, based on a recent 9% boost in the quarterly dividend, SJM shares recently had an indicated dividend yield of 2.7%.

## Qualitative Risk Assessment

| LOW | MEDIUM | HIGH |
|---|---|---|

Our risk assessment reflects the relative stability of the company's end markets, our view of its relatively strong balance sheet, and an S&P Quality Ranking of A, indicating a strong long-term record of earnings and dividend growth.

## Quantitative Evaluations

**S&P Quality Ranking** A

| D | C | B- | B | B+ | A- | A | A+ |
|---|---|---|---|---|---|---|---|

**Relative Strength Rank** MODERATE

67

LOWEST = 1    HIGHEST = 99

## Revenue/Earnings Data

**Revenue (Million $)**

| | 1Q | 2Q | 3Q | 4Q | Year |
|---|---|---|---|---|---|
| 2012 | 1,189 | 1,514 | -- | -- | -- |
| 2011 | 1,047 | 1,279 | 1,312 | 1,187 | 4,826 |
| 2010 | 1,052 | 1,279 | 1,206 | 1,069 | 4,605 |
| 2009 | 663.7 | 843.1 | 1,183 | 1,069 | 3,758 |
| 2008 | 561.5 | 707.9 | 665.4 | 590.0 | 2,525 |
| 2007 | 526.5 | 605.0 | 523.1 | 493.5 | 2,148 |

**Earnings Per Share ($)**

| | | | | | |
|---|---|---|---|---|---|
| 2012 | 0.98 | 1.12 | E1.45 | E1.05 | E4.91 |
| 2011 | 0.86 | 1.25 | 1.11 | 0.82 | 4.05 |
| 2010 | 0.83 | 1.18 | 1.14 | 1.01 | 4.15 |
| 2009 | 0.77 | 0.94 | 0.68 | 0.80 | 3.12 |
| 2008 | 0.77 | 0.87 | 0.75 | 0.67 | 3.00 |
| 2007 | 0.50 | 0.80 | 0.71 | 0.75 | 2.76 |

Fiscal year ended Apr. 30. Next earnings report expected: Mid February. EPS Estimates based on S&P Operating Earnings; historical GAAP earnings are as reported.

## Dividend Data (Dates: mm/dd Payment Date: mm/dd/yy)

| Amount ($) | Date Decl. | Ex-Div. Date | Stk. of Record | Payment Date |
|---|---|---|---|---|
| 0.440 | 01/27 | 02/09 | 02/11 | 03/01/11 |
| 0.440 | 04/21 | 05/11 | 05/13 | 06/01/11 |
| 0.480 | 07/22 | 08/10 | 08/12 | 09/01/11 |
| 0.480 | 10/25 | 11/08 | 11/11 | 12/01/11 |

Dividends have been paid since 1949. Source: Company reports.

The McGraw·Hill Companies

# J.M. Smucker Co (The)

**STANDARD &POOR'S**

## Business Summary August 29, 2011

CORPORATE PROFILE. From its origins in 1897, when Jerome M. Smucker first pressed cider at a mill that he opened that year, the J. M. Smucker Co. has become a leading U.S. producer of such products as fruit spreads, peanut butter, shortening, ice cream toppings, and coffee.

SJM's U.S. Retail Consumer Foods segment (41% of FY 11 (Apr.) net sales) includes such product categories as peanut butter, fruit spreads, baking products, shortenings and oils, and canned milk. Trademarks or brands include Jif, Smucker's, Pillsbury and Crisco. The Pillsbury trademark is used by SJM under a 20-year, perpetually renewable, royalty-free license.

SJM's U.S. retail coffee market segment (40% of FY 11 (Apr.) net sales) includes the Folgers business, acquired in 2008, plus Dunkin' Donuts packaged coffee, Millstone K-Cups, and Rowland Coffee. Dunkin' Donuts is a registered trademark used by SJM under license for packaged coffee products sold in retail channels such as grocery stores, mass merchandisers, club stores and drug stores. The license does not pertain to products for sale in Dunkin' Donuts restaurants.

The International, Foodservice and Natural Foods segment (19%) includes, among others, Santa Cruz Organic beverages and Bick's pickles.

SJM's international business (largely in Canada) accounted for 9.7% of net sales in FY 11. Sales to Wal-Mart Stores, Inc. and its subsidiaries accounted for about 26% of SJM's total net sales.

SJM product categories include coffee (44% of FY 11 sales), peanut butter (12%), fruit spreads (8%), shortening and oils (7%), baking mixes and frostings (6%), canned milk (5%), flour and baking ingredients (5%), portion control (3%), juices and beverages (3%), Uncrustables frozen sandwiches (2%), toppings and syrups (2%), and other (3%).

## Company Financials Fiscal Year Ended Apr. 30

| Per Share Data ($) | 2011 | 2010 | 2009 | 2008 | 2007 | 2006 | 2005 | 2004 | 2003 | 2002 |
|---|---|---|---|---|---|---|---|---|---|---|
| Tangible Book Value | NM | NM | NM | 0.98 | 5.75 | 5.52 | 4.61 | 7.10 | 5.58 | 9.32 |
| Cash Flow | 5.63 | 5.73 | 4.50 | 4.11 | 3.81 | 3.77 | 3.19 | 3.01 | 2.81 | 2.39 |
| Earnings | 4.05 | 4.15 | 3.12 | 3.00 | 2.76 | 2.45 | 2.26 | 2.21 | 2.02 | 1.24 |
| S&P Core Earnings | 4.21 | 4.23 | 2.98 | 2.55 | 2.70 | 2.30 | 2.16 | 2.20 | 1.89 | 1.10 |
| Dividends | NA | 1.40 | 1.28 | 1.12 | 1.08 | 1.00 | 0.92 | 0.76 | 0.76 | 0.64 |
| Payout Ratio | NA | 35% | 41% | 37% | 39% | 41% | 41% | 34% | 38% | 52% |
| Calendar Year | 2010 | 2009 | 2008 | 2007 | 2006 | 2005 | 2004 | 2003 | 2002 | 2001 |
| Prices:High | 66.28 | 62.70 | 56.69 | 64.32 | 49.98 | 51.65 | 53.50 | 46.75 | 40.42 | 37.73 |
| Prices:Low | 53.27 | 34.09 | 37.22 | 46.57 | 37.15 | 43.64 | 40.80 | 33.00 | 28.71 | 22.61 |
| P/E Ratio:High | 16 | 15 | 18 | 21 | 18 | 21 | 24 | 21 | 20 | 30 |
| P/E Ratio:Low | 13 | 8 | 12 | 16 | 13 | 18 | 18 | 15 | 14 | 18 |

| Income Statement Analysis (Million $) | | | | | | | | | | |
|---|---|---|---|---|---|---|---|---|---|---|
| Revenue | 4,826 | 4,605 | 3,758 | 2,525 | 2,148 | 2,155 | 2,044 | 1,417 | 1,312 | 687 |
| Operating Income | 1,101 | 1,021 | 655 | 354 | 318 | 325 | 526 | 227 | 214 | 88.4 |
| Depreciation | 186 | 182 | 118 | 62.6 | 58.9 | 71.1 | 56.0 | 39.9 | 37.8 | 28.6 |
| Interest Expense | 69.6 | 65.2 | 62.5 | 42.1 | 23.4 | 24.0 | 22.6 | 6.37 | 8.75 | 9.21 |
| Pretax Income | 717 | 731 | 396 | 255 | 241 | 216 | 205 | 179 | 155 | 50.2 |
| Effective Tax Rate | NA | NA | 32.9% | 33.1% | 34.8% | 33.5% | 36.2% | 37.7% | 38.0% | 38.5% |
| Net Income | 479 | 494 | 266 | 170 | 157 | 143 | 130 | 111 | 96.3 | 30.9 |
| S&P Core Earnings | 493 | 500 | 254 | 144 | 154 | 134 | 126 | 111 | 90.5 | 25.9 |

| Balance Sheet & Other Financial Data (Million $) | | | | | | | | | | |
|---|---|---|---|---|---|---|---|---|---|---|
| Cash | 320 | 284 | 457 | 184 | 200 | 121 | 75.8 | 163 | 181 | 91.9 |
| Current Assets | 1,637 | 1,224 | 1,399 | 776 | 639 | 571 | 556 | 425 | 467 | 280 |
| Total Assets | 8,325 | 7,975 | 8,192 | 3,130 | 2,694 | 2,650 | 2,636 | 1,684 | 1,615 | 525 |
| Current Liabilities | 483 | 479 | 1,061 | 239 | 236 | 235 | 308 | 175 | 167 | 80.4 |
| Long Term Debt | 1,304 | 900 | 910 | 790 | 393 | 429 | 432 | 135 | 135 | 135 |
| Common Equity | 5,292 | 5,326 | 4,940 | 1,800 | 1,796 | 1,728 | 1,691 | 1,211 | 1,124 | 280 |
| Total Capital | 6,596 | 6,236 | 6,127 | 2,765 | 2,347 | 2,312 | 2,233 | 1,482 | 1,393 | 419 |
| Capital Expenditures | 180 | 137 | 109 | 76.4 | 57.0 | 63.2 | 87.6 | 100 | 49.5 | 23.5 |
| Cash Flow | 666 | 676 | 384 | 233 | 216 | 214 | 187 | 151 | 134 | 59.4 |
| Current Ratio | 3.4 | 2.6 | 1.3 | 3.2 | 2.7 | 2.4 | 1.8 | 2.4 | 2.8 | 3.5 |
| % Long Term Debt of Capitalization | 19.8 | 14.4 | 14.9 | 28.6 | 16.7 | 18.5 | 19.3 | 9.1 | 9.7 | 32.2 |
| % Net Income of Revenue | 9.9 | 10.7 | 7.1 | 6.8 | 7.3 | 6.7 | 6.4 | 7.9 | 7.3 | 4.5 |
| % Return on Assets | 5.9 | 6.1 | 4.7 | 5.9 | 5.9 | 5.4 | 6.0 | 6.7 | 9.0 | 6.1 |
| % Return on Equity | 9.0 | 9.6 | 7.9 | 9.5 | 8.9 | 8.4 | 9.0 | 9.5 | 13.7 | 11.6 |

Data as orig reptd.; bef. results of disc opers/spec. items. Per share data adj. for stk. divs.; EPS diluted. E-Estimated. NA-Not Available. NM-Not Meaningful. NR-Not Ranked. UR-Under Review.

**Office:** 1 Strawberry Ln, Orrville, OH 44667-0280.
**Telephone:** 330-682-3000.
**Email:** investor.relations@jmsmucker.com
**Website:** http://www.smuckers.com

**Chrmn:** T.P. Smucker
**Pres & COO:** V.C. Byrd
**CEO:** R.K. Smucker
**SVP & CFO:** M.R. Belgya

**SVP & Chief Admin Officer:** B.C. Dunaway
**Investor Contact:** S. Robinson (330-684-3440)
**Board Members:** V. C. Byrd, R. D. Cowan, K. W. Dindo, P. J. Dolan, N. L. Knight, E. V. Long, G. A. Oatey, A. Shumate, M. T. Smucker, R. K. Smucker, T. P. Smucker, W. H. Steinbrink, P. S. Wagstaff

**Founded:** 1897
**Domicile:** Ohio
**Employees:** 4,500

# Snap-On Inc

**STANDARD &POOR'S**

| S&P Recommendation | BUY ★★★★☆ | Price | 12-Mo. Target Price | Investment Style |
|---|---|---|---|---|
| | | $48.05 (as of Nov 25, 2011) | $65.00 | Large-Cap Value |

**GICS Sector** Industrials
**Sub-Industry** Industrial Machinery

**Summary** This company is the largest manufacturer and distributor of hand tools, storage units and diagnostic equipment for professional mechanics.

## Key Stock Statistics (Source S&P, Vickers, company reports)

| | | | | | | | |
|---|---|---|---|---|---|---|---|
| 52-Wk Range | $64.36–41.74 | S&P Oper. EPS 2011**E** | 4.45 | Market Capitalization(B) | $2.795 | Beta | 1.52 |
| Trailing 12-Month EPS | $4.43 | S&P Oper. EPS 2012**E** | 5.00 | Yield (%) | 2.83 | S&P 3-Yr. Proj. EPS CAGR(%) | 21 |
| Trailing 12-Month P/E | 10.9 | P/E on S&P Oper. EPS 2011**E** | 10.8 | Dividend Rate/Share | $1.36 | S&P Credit Rating | A- |
| $10K Invested 5 Yrs Ago | $11,521 | Common Shares Outstg. (M) | 58.2 | Institutional Ownership (%) | 92 | | |

## Price Performance

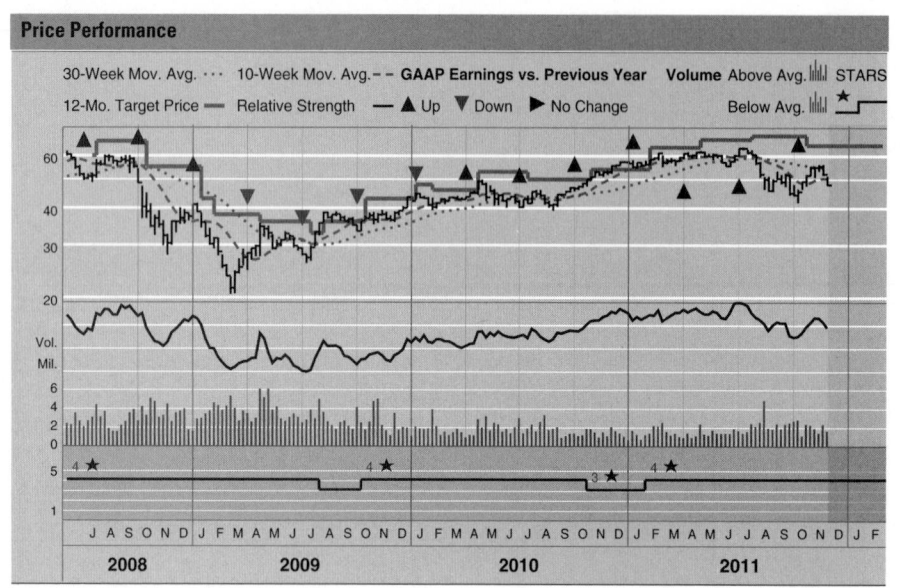

30-Week Mov. Avg. · · ·    10-Week Mov. Avg. - - -    **GAAP Earnings vs. Previous Year**    Volume Above Avg. STARS
12-Mo. Target Price —    Relative Strength —    ▲ Up    ▼ Down    ▶ No Change    Below Avg. ★

Options: ASE, Ph

Analysis prepared by Equity Analyst **Michael Jaffe** on Nov 22, 2011, when the stock traded at **$49.93**.

## Highlights

➤ We forecast an 8% increase in total revenues in 2012, following the 12% gain we project for 2011. Our forecast reflects our belief that ongoing economic growth will lead to higher order rates and sales across SNA's segments. On a geographic basis, we see the largest sales improvement taking place in emerging markets, which continue to record stronger economic gains than those being posted in developed markets. On a segment basis, we expect the biggest gains in the Snap-On Tools segment, where we believe SNA has been very successful in expanding its market share in serving the franchised dealer van channel.

➤ We expect operating margins to widen in both 2011 and 2012. We expect these forecasted gains to be driven by the benefits of the higher sales base that we see, plus SNA's ongoing attention to cost controls. We also see profitability being aided by higher financial services profits, on a larger portfolio.

➤ Our EPS forecast of $5.00 for 2012 compares with our operating estimate of $4.45 for 2011, which excludes a $0.19 a share second quarter gain from an arbitration settlement.

## Investment Rationale/Risk

➤ We believe SNA is undergoing a transformation to become a leaner organization, with a high priority on bettering customer responsiveness and top-line growth. We expect these ongoing efforts to bring incremental improvement to SNA's operating margins in coming years. We also think the company's diversified products and customer base around the globe will buffer some of its exposure to slower growing markets, such as in Europe. We believe the shares, recently trading at about 10X our 2012 EPS estimate, a 9% discount to the peer average, are attractively valued.

➤ Risks to our recommendation and target price include weaker-than-expected results in SNA's major markets, failure to successfully introduce new products, and a renewed global recession.

➤ Our 12-month target price of $65 is based on our relative peer valuation analysis. We apply a multiple of 13X, above SNA's peer group average, to our 2012 EPS estimate. We think an above average peer multiple is appropriate, given the company's historical premium valuation and our outlook for strong earnings growth.

## Qualitative Risk Assessment

| LOW | MEDIUM | HIGH |
|---|---|---|

Our risk assessment is based on our view of SNA's strong brand equity and healthy balance sheet, offset by an industry categorized by intense competition.

## Quantitative Evaluations

**S&P Quality Ranking**                          A-

| D | C | B- | B | B+ | A- | A | A+ |
|---|---|---|---|---|---|---|---|

**Relative Strength Rank**                MODERATE

| 44 |
|---|

LOWEST = 1                          HIGHEST = 99

## Revenue/Earnings Data

**Revenue (Million $)**

| | 1Q | 2Q | 3Q | 4Q | Year |
|---|---|---|---|---|---|
| 2011 | 719.5 | 757.0 | 729.9 | -- | -- |
| 2010 | 631.3 | 661.5 | 670.3 | 718.4 | 2,682 |
| 2009 | 592.6 | 615.6 | 587.8 | 624.8 | 2,421 |
| 2008 | 747.0 | 784.4 | 713.8 | 687.5 | 2,935 |
| 2007 | 705.7 | 711.9 | 680.7 | 742.9 | 2,841 |
| 2006 | 593.5 | 624.4 | 599.5 | 656.0 | 2,522 |

**Earnings Per Share ($)**

| | | | | | |
|---|---|---|---|---|---|
| 2011 | 0.96 | 1.33 | 1.16 | E1.19 | E4.45 |
| 2010 | 0.63 | 0.78 | 0.80 | 0.99 | 3.19 |
| 2009 | 0.60 | 0.65 | 0.44 | 0.63 | 2.32 |
| 2008 | 0.97 | 1.15 | 0.94 | 1.01 | 4.07 |
| 2007 | 0.66 | 0.90 | 0.70 | 0.99 | 3.23 |
| 2006 | 0.37 | 0.20 | 0.48 | 0.64 | 1.69 |

Fiscal year ended Dec. 31. Next earnings report expected: Early February. EPS Estimates based on S&P Operating Earnings; historical GAAP earnings are as reported.

## Dividend Data (Dates: mm/dd Payment Date: mm/dd/yy)

| Amount ($) | Date Decl. | Ex-Div. Date | Stk. of Record | Payment Date |
|---|---|---|---|---|
| 0.320 | 02/09 | 02/22 | 02/24 | 03/10/11 |
| 0.320 | 04/28 | 05/18 | 05/20 | 06/10/11 |
| 0.320 | 08/04 | 08/18 | 08/22 | 09/09/11 |
| 0.340 | 11/04 | 11/16 | 11/18 | 12/09/11 |

Dividends have been paid since 1939. Source: Company reports.

# Snap-On Inc

## Business Summary November 22, 2011

CORPORATE OVERVIEW. Snap-on Inc. is a major global manufacturer and marketer of high-quality tool, diagnostic, service and equipment solutions for professional tool and equipment users under various brands and trade names. Product lines include a broad range of hand and power tools, tool storage, saws and cutting tools, pruning tools, vehicle service diagnostics equipment, vehicle service equipment, including wheel service, safety testing and collision repair equipment, vehicle service information, business management systems, equipment repair services, and other tool and equipment solutions. SNA's customers include automotive technicians, vehicle service centers, manufacturers, industrial tool and equipment users, and those involved in commercial applications such as construction, electrical and agriculture. SNA services these customers through three primary channels of distribution: the mobile dealer van channel, including the company's technical representatives; company direct sales; and non-franchise, independent distributors.

SNA has four reportable business segments. The Snap-on Tools Group, formerly the Dealer Group (35% of both 2010 and 2009 revenues) consists of SNA's business operations serving the worldwide franchised dealer van

channel, which in turn sells primarily to automotive technicians. The Commercial & Industrial Group (35% of 2010 revenues and 34% of 2009's) provides tools, equipment products and equipment repair services to industrial and commercial customers worldwide through direct, distributor and other non-franchised distribution channels. The Repair Systems & Information Group (28%, 29%) provides diagnostic equipment, vehicle service information, business management systems and other solutions for customers in the vehicle service and repair marketplace. Financial Services (2%, 2%) is a relatively new business segment, originated in 2004. It consists of Snap-on Credit LLC, which, following the July 2009 acquisition of the 50% ownership controlled by The CIT Group (for $8.1 million), became a fully controlled subsidiary, and SNA's wholly owned finance subsidiaries in international markets where SNA has dealer operations. In regard to global reach, nearly 41% of total revenues in 2010 were outside the U.S. market.

## Company Financials Fiscal Year Ended Dec. 31

| Per Share Data ($) | 2010 | 2009 | 2008 | 2007 | 2006 | 2005 | 2004 | 2003 | 2002 | 2001 |
|---|---|---|---|---|---|---|---|---|---|---|
| Tangible Book Value | 6.83 | 4.67 | 2.90 | 3.94 | 0.72 | 8.17 | 9.67 | 8.29 | 6.27 | 6.01 |
| Cash Flow | 4.55 | 3.44 | 5.17 | 4.52 | 2.57 | 2.48 | 2.45 | 2.38 | 2.65 | 1.54 |
| Earnings | 3.19 | 2.32 | 4.07 | 3.23 | 1.69 | 1.59 | 1.40 | 1.35 | 1.76 | 0.37 |
| S&P Core Earnings | 3.39 | 2.35 | 3.31 | 3.15 | 2.07 | 1.56 | 1.35 | 1.31 | 0.92 | 0.09 |
| Dividends | 1.22 | 1.20 | 1.20 | 1.11 | 1.08 | 1.00 | 1.00 | 1.00 | 0.97 | 0.96 |
| Payout Ratio | 38% | 52% | 29% | 34% | 64% | 63% | 71% | 74% | 55% | NM |
| Prices:High | 57.77 | 43.88 | 62.21 | 57.81 | 48.65 | 38.71 | 34.67 | 32.38 | 35.15 | 34.40 |
| Prices:Low | 39.23 | 20.51 | 27.70 | 44.58 | 36.38 | 30.57 | 27.15 | 22.60 | 20.71 | 21.15 |
| P/E Ratio:High | 18 | 19 | 15 | 18 | 29 | 24 | 25 | 24 | 20 | 93 |
| P/E Ratio:Low | 12 | 9 | 7 | 14 | 22 | 19 | 19 | 17 | 12 | 57 |

| Income Statement Analysis (Million $) | | | | | | | | | | |
|---|---|---|---|---|---|---|---|---|---|---|
| Revenue | 2,682 | 2,421 | 2,935 | 2,841 | 2,522 | 2,362 | 2,407 | 2,233 | 2,109 | 2,096 |
| Operating Income | 404 | 338 | 467 | 401 | 217 | 220 | 203 | 167 | 217 | 168 |
| Depreciation | 72.7 | 74.6 | 63.8 | 76.0 | 51.9 | 52.2 | 61.0 | 60.3 | 51.7 | 68.0 |
| Interest Expense | 54.8 | 47.7 | 33.8 | 46.0 | 20.6 | 21.7 | 23.0 | 24.4 | 28.7 | 35.5 |
| Pretax Income | 281 | 206 | 355 | 284 | 146 | 148 | 120 | 117 | 161 | 47.6 |
| Effective Tax Rate | NA | 30.4% | 33.2% | 32.5% | 31.4% | 37.2% | 32.1% | 32.6% | 36.0% | 54.8% |
| Net Income | 193 | 134 | 237 | 189 | 100 | 92.9 | 81.7 | 78.7 | 103 | 21.5 |
| S&P Core Earnings | 198 | 136 | 193 | 184 | 123 | 91.6 | 78.3 | 76.6 | 53.9 | 5.49 |

| Balance Sheet & Other Financial Data (Million $) | | | | | | | | | | |
|---|---|---|---|---|---|---|---|---|---|---|
| Cash | 463 | 699 | 116 | 93.0 | 63.4 | 170 | 150 | 96.1 | 18.4 | 6.70 |
| Current Assets | 1,766 | 1,676 | 1,141 | 1,187 | 1,113 | 1,073 | 1,193 | 1,132 | 1,051 | 1,139 |
| Total Assets | 3,729 | 3,447 | 2,710 | 2,765 | 2,655 | 2,008 | 2,290 | 2,139 | 1,994 | 1,974 |
| Current Liabilities | 881 | 740 | 548 | 639 | 682 | 506 | 674 | 567 | 552 | 549 |
| Long Term Debt | 419 | 675 | 530 | 502 | 506 | 202 | 203 | 303 | 304 | 446 |
| Common Equity | 1,389 | 1,290 | 1,187 | 1,280 | 1,076 | 962 | 1,111 | 1,011 | 830 | 868 |
| Total Capital | 1,839 | 1,980 | 1,834 | 1,873 | 1,671 | 1,239 | 1,390 | 1,348 | 1,168 | 1,339 |
| Capital Expenditures | 51.1 | 64.4 | 73.9 | 62.0 | 50.5 | 40.1 | 38.7 | 29.4 | 45.8 | 53.6 |
| Cash Flow | 266 | 199 | 301 | 265 | 152 | 145 | 143 | 139 | 155 | 89.5 |
| Current Ratio | 2.0 | 2.3 | 2.1 | 1.9 | 1.6 | 2.1 | 1.8 | 2.0 | 1.9 | 2.1 |
| % Long Term Debt of Capitalization | 22.8 | 34.1 | 28.9 | 26.8 | 30.3 | 16.3 | 14.6 | 22.5 | 26.0 | 33.3 |
| % Net Income of Revenue | 7.2 | 5.5 | 8.1 | 6.6 | 4.0 | 3.9 | 3.4 | 3.5 | 4.9 | 1.0 |
| % Return on Assets | 5.4 | 4.4 | 8.7 | 6.9 | 4.3 | 4.3 | 3.7 | 3.8 | 5.2 | 1.1 |
| % Return on Equity | 14.4 | 10.8 | 19.2 | 16.0 | 9.8 | 9.0 | 7.7 | 8.5 | 12.9 | 2.4 |

Data as orig reptd.; bef. results of disc opers/spec. items. Per share data adj. for stk. divs.; EPS diluted. E-Estimated. NA-Not Available. NM-Not Meaningful. NR-Not Ranked. UR-Under Review.

**Office:** 2801 80th St, Kenosha, WI 53143-5656.
**Telephone:** 262-656-5200.
**Website:** http://www.snapon.com
**Chrmn, Pres & CEO:** N.T. Pinchuk

**SVP & CFO:** A.J. Pagliari
**Chief Acctg Officer & Cntlr:** C.R. Johnsen
**Secy & General Counsel:** I.M. Shur
**Investor Contact:** L. Kratcoski (262-656-6121)

**Board Members:** B. S. Chelberg, K. L. Daniel, R. Decyk, J. F. Fiedler, J. P. Holden, N. J. Jones, A. L. Kelly, H. W. Knueppel, W. D. Lehman, N. T. Pinchuk, E. H. Rensi, G. M. Sherrill

**Founded:** 1920
**Domicile:** Delaware
**Employees:** 11,300

STANDARD &POOR'S

# Southern Co (The)

**S&P Recommendation** HOLD ★★★★★ | **Price** $42.47 (as of Nov 25, 2011) | **12-Mo. Target Price** $43.00 | **Investment Style** Large-Cap Value

**GICS Sector** Utilities
**Sub-Industry** Electric Utilities

**Summary** This Atlanta-based energy holding company is one of the largest producers of electricity in the U.S.

## Key Stock Statistics (Source S&P, Vickers, company reports)

| | | | | | | | |
|---|---|---|---|---|---|---|---|
| 52-Wk Range | **$43.97– 35.73** | S&P Oper. EPS 2011**E** | **2.56** | Market Capitalization(B) | **$36.425** | Beta | **0.29** |
| Trailing 12-Month EPS | **$2.45** | S&P Oper. EPS 2012**E** | **2.72** | Yield (%) | **4.45** | S&P 3-Yr. Proj. EPS CAGR(%) | **6** |
| Trailing 12-Month P/E | **17.3** | P/E on S&P Oper. EPS 2011**E** | **16.6** | Dividend Rate/Share | **$1.89** | S&P Credit Rating | **A** |
| $10K Invested 5 Yrs Ago | **$14,980** | Common Shares Outstg. (M) | **857.7** | Institutional Ownership (%) | **45** | | |

## Price Performance

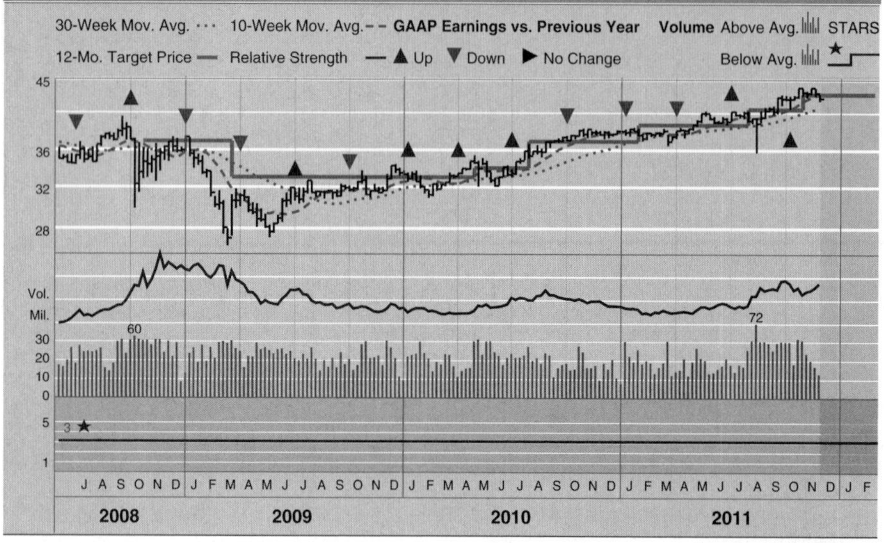
30-Week Mov. Avg. ··· 10-Week Mov. Avg. - - GAAP Earnings vs. Previous Year Volume Above Avg. STARS
12-Mo. Target Price — Relative Strength — ▲ Up ▼ Down ► No Change Below Avg.
45
36
32
28
Vol.
Mil.
60
72
30
20
10
0
5
3
1
J A S O N D J F M A M J J A S O N D J F M A M J J A S O N D J F M A M J J A S O N D J F
2008
2009
2010
2011

Options: ASE, CBOE, P, Ph

Analysis prepared by Equity Analyst **Justin McCann** on Oct 27, 2011, when the stock traded at **$43.61**.

## Highlights

- We expect operating EPS in 2011 to grow about 8% from 2010's $2.37. Earnings have benefited from higher rates at Georgia Power, increased earnings at the Southern Power subsidiary, and a gradual recovery in SO's service territory economy, driven by the continuing expansion of industrial activity. This has been partially offset, however, by the impact of several major storms and by more shares outstanding.
- Although net income was up 6.6% in the first nine months of 2011, operating EPS was up only 3.2% due to 3.0% more shares. While earnings comparisons in the first quarter were hurt by the expiration of a long-term wholesale contract and the absence of the abnormally cold weather in the year-earlier quarter, results in the second and third quarters were aided by the rate increase at Georgia Power and higher industrial sales, which reached about 95% of their pre-recession levels in the third quarter.
- For 2012, we expect operating EPS to grow about 6% from anticipated results in 2011. Longer term, we expect average annual EPS growth of 5% to 7%, with the utilities having customer growth of about 1.7% and demand growth of approximately 2%.

## Investment Rationale/Risk

- While we expect the stock to trade at a premium to SO's peers, reflecting the relative predictability of its earnings and dividend stream, we believe it has become fairly valued at recent levels. After a 14.7% gain in 2010, the stock rose about 12% in the first 43 weeks of 2011, largely driven, in our view, by an investor shift away from the volatility and often sharp declines in the broader market to the higher yielding electric utility sector, as well as by the improvement in SO's service territory economy, particularly in the industrial sector.
- Risks to our recommendation and target price include an economic downturn in SO's service territory, and a significant decline in the average P/E of the electric utility group as a whole.
- SO raised its dividend 3.8% with the June payment, and we expect similar annual increases in the future. With the current dividend payout ratio at 74% (based on our operating EPS estimate for 2011), such increases would keep payouts at the top of SO's targeted payout range of 70% to 75%. We see the stock trading at a premium-to-peers P/E of about 15.8X our operating EPS estimate for 2012. Our 12-month target price is $43.

## Qualitative Risk Assessment

**LOW** | MEDIUM | HIGH

Our risk assessment reflects our view of the company's strong and steady cash flow from its regulated electric utility operations, its solid balance sheet, and a generally supportive regulatory environment, partially offset by a slowing economy in its service territories.

## Quantitative Evaluations

**S&P Quality Ranking** **A-**

D | C | B- | B | B+ | **A-** | A | A+

**Relative Strength Rank** **STRONG**

78

LOWEST = 1 HIGHEST = 99

## Revenue/Earnings Data

**Revenue (Million $)**

| | 1Q | 2Q | 3Q | 4Q | Year |
|---|---|---|---|---|---|
| 2011 | 4,012 | 4,521 | 5,428 | -- | -- |
| 2010 | 4,157 | 4,207 | 5,320 | 3,771 | 17,456 |
| 2009 | 3,666 | 3,885 | 4,682 | 3,510 | 15,743 |
| 2008 | 3,683 | 4,215 | 5,426 | 3,802 | 17,127 |
| 2007 | 3,409 | 3,772 | 4,832 | 3,340 | 15,353 |
| 2006 | 3,063 | 3,592 | 4,549 | 3,152 | 14,356 |

**Earnings Per Share ($)**

| | 1Q | 2Q | 3Q | 4Q | Year |
|---|---|---|---|---|---|
| 2011 | 0.49 | 0.71 | 1.07 | **E**0.29 | **E**2.56 |
| 2010 | 0.60 | 0.62 | 0.98 | 0.18 | 2.37 |
| 2009 | 0.18 | 0.60 | 0.99 | 0.31 | 2.07 |
| 2008 | 0.47 | 0.55 | 1.01 | 0.24 | 2.26 |
| 2007 | 0.45 | 0.57 | 1.00 | 0.27 | 2.28 |
| 2006 | 0.35 | 0.52 | 0.99 | 0.25 | 2.10 |

Fiscal year ended Dec. 31. Next earnings report expected: Late January. EPS Estimates based on S&P Operating Earnings; historical GAAP earnings are as reported.

## Dividend Data (Dates: mm/dd Payment Date: mm/dd/yy)

| Amount ($) | Date Decl. | Ex-Div. Date | Stk. of Record | Payment Date |
|---|---|---|---|---|
| 0.455 | 01/13 | 02/03 | 02/07 | 03/05/11 |
| 0.473 | 04/18 | 04/28 | 05/02 | 06/06/11 |
| 0.473 | 07/18 | 07/28 | 08/01 | 09/06/11 |
| 0.473 | 10/17 | 11/03 | 11/07 | 12/06/11 |

Dividends have been paid since 1948. Source: Company reports.

**Please read the Required Disclosures and Analyst Certification on the last page of this report.**
Redistribution or reproduction is prohibited without written permission. Copyright ©2011 The McGraw-Hill Companies, Inc.

The McGraw-Hill Companies

# Southern Co (The)

STANDARD &POOR'S

## Business Summary October 27, 2011

CORPORATE OVERVIEW. The Southern Company is one of the largest producers of electricity in the U.S. Based in Atlanta, GA, this utility holding company has nearly 42,963 megawatts of generating capacity and provides electricity to approximately 4.4 million customers in the Southeast through the following integrated utilities: Alabama Power, Georgia Power, Gulf Power (located in the northwestern portion of Florida), and Mississippi Power. Savannah Electric & Power was merged into Georgia Power on July 1, 2006.

MARKET PROFILE. Southern Power Company (SPC) was formed by SO in January 2001 to own, manage and finance wholesale generating assets in the Southeast. It serves both the utility units and the wholesale power market. Energy from SPC's assets, which included 7,880 megawatts of generating capacity at the end of 2010, is marketed to wholesale customers through the Southern Company Generation and Energy Marketing unit. SPC and the utility units enter into contracts for power purchases, sales and exchanges among themselves, as well as with other utilities in the Southeast. Although Southern Power is not subject to state regulation, it is subject to regulation by the Federal Energy Regulatory Commission.

SO is also the parent company of SouthernLINC Wireless, which provides digital wireless communications services to SO's four utility units as well as to

non-affiliates within the Southeast. It also provides wholesale fiber optic solutions to telecommunication providers in the Southeast.

LEGAL/REGULATORY ISSUES. On December 21, 2010, the Georgia Public Service Commission (GPSC) approved, effective January 1, 2011, a $347 million increase in Georgia Power's annual base rate, a $168 million increase in its environmental compliance cost recovery tariff, a $31 million increase in its demand side management (DSM) tariff, and a $16 million increase in its municipal franchise fee tariff, for a total increase of approximately $562 million. The GPSC also approved an additional annual increase of $17 million in the DSM tariff effective as of January 1, 2012, and an additional $18 million increase in the DSM tariff effective as of January 1, 2013. SO estimates that these increases as well as projected increases in the utility's base tariffs, will result in annualized base rate increases of approximately $190 million in 2012 and $93 million in 2013. The utility is required to file a new, general rate case by July 1, 2013, in response to which the GPSC would determine if the 2010 rate plan should be continued, modified or discontinued.

## Company Financials Fiscal Year Ended Dec. 31

| Per Share Data ($) | 2010 | 2009 | 2008 | 2007 | 2006 | 2005 | 2004 | 2003 | 2002 | 2001 |
|---|---|---|---|---|---|---|---|---|---|---|
| Tangible Book Value | 19.21 | 18.15 | 17.08 | 16.23 | 15.00 | 14.19 | 13.65 | 12.92 | 11.56 | 10.87 |
| Earnings | 2.37 | 2.07 | 2.26 | 2.28 | 2.10 | 2.14 | 2.06 | 2.02 | 1.85 | 1.61 |
| S&P Core Earnings | 2.30 | 2.29 | 1.83 | 2.26 | 2.06 | 2.04 | 1.93 | 1.85 | 1.35 | 1.12 |
| Dividends | 2.26 | 1.73 | 1.66 | 1.60 | 1.54 | 1.48 | 1.77 | 1.39 | 1.36 | 1.34 |
| Payout Ratio | 95% | 84% | 74% | 70% | 72% | 69% | 86% | 69% | 74% | 83% |
| Prices:High | 38.62 | 37.62 | 40.60 | 39.35 | 37.40 | 36.47 | 33.96 | 32.00 | 31.14 | 35.72 |
| Prices:Low | 30.85 | 26.48 | 29.82 | 33.16 | 30.48 | 31.14 | 27.44 | 27.00 | 23.22 | 20.89 |
| P/E Ratio:High | 16 | 18 | 18 | 17 | 18 | 17 | 16 | 16 | 17 | 22 |
| P/E Ratio:Low | 13 | 13 | 13 | 15 | 14 | 15 | 13 | 13 | 13 | 13 |

| Income Statement Analysis (Million $) | | | | | | | | | | |
|---|---|---|---|---|---|---|---|---|---|---|
| Revenue | 17,456 | 15,743 | 17,127 | 15,353 | 14,356 | 13,554 | 11,902 | 11,251 | 10,549 | 10,155 |
| Depreciation | 1,831 | 1,788 | 1,704 | 1,245 | 1,200 | 1,176 | 955 | 1,027 | 1,047 | 1,173 |
| Maintenance | NA | NA | NA | 1,175 | 1,096 | 1,116 | 1,027 | 937 | 961 | 909 |
| Fixed Charges Coverage | 4.13 | 3.82 | 3.84 | 3.73 | 3.73 | 3.90 | 4.11 | 4.21 | 3.80 | 3.25 |
| Construction Credits | 194 | 200 | 152 | 106 | 50.0 | 51.0 | 47.0 | 25.0 | 22.0 | NA |
| Effective Tax Rate | 34.2% | 35.3% | 34.4% | 31.9% | 33.2% | 27.2% | 27.7% | 29.3% | 28.6% | 33.3% |
| Net Income | 1,975 | 1,645 | 1,742 | 1,734 | 1,574 | 1,591 | 1,532 | 1,474 | 1,318 | 1,119 |
| S&P Core Earnings | 1,924 | 1,822 | 1,412 | 1,720 | 1,551 | 1,532 | 1,436 | 1,351 | 964 | 776 |

| Balance Sheet & Other Financial Data (Million $) | | | | | | | | | | |
|---|---|---|---|---|---|---|---|---|---|---|
| Gross Property | 64,447 | 60,314 | 56,152 | 53,094 | 50,167 | 47,580 | 45,585 | 43,722 | 41,764 | 38,104 |
| Capital Expenditures | 4,086 | 4,670 | 3,961 | 3,545 | 2,994 | 2,370 | 2,110 | 2,002 | 2,717 | 2,617 |
| Net Property | 44,273 | 41,193 | 37,866 | 35,681 | 33,585 | 31,853 | 30,634 | 29,418 | 26,315 | 23,084 |
| Capitalization:Long Term Debt | 19,236 | 19,213 | 17,898 | 15,223 | 13,247 | 13,442 | 13,010 | 10,587 | 8,956 | 10,941 |
| Capitalization:% Long Term Debt | 54.3 | 56.4 | 57.4 | 55.1 | 53.8 | 55.7 | 55.9 | 52.3 | 50.7 | 57.8 |
| Capitalization:Preferred | Nil | Nil | Nil | Nil | Nil | Nil | Nil | Nil | Nil | Nil |
| Capitalization:% Preferred | Nil | Nil | Nil | Nil | Nil | Nil | Nil | Nil | Nil | Nil |
| Capitalization:Common | 16,202 | 14,878 | 13,276 | 12,385 | 11,371 | 10,689 | 10,278 | 9,648 | 8,710 | 7,984 |
| Capitalization:% Common | 45.7 | 43.6 | 42.6 | 44.9 | 46.2 | 44.3 | 44.1 | 47.7 | 49.3 | 42.2 |
| Total Capital | 36,739 | 35,204 | 37,968 | 34,198 | 31,110 | 30,394 | 29,077 | 25,809 | 22,937 | 24,147 |
| % Operating Ratio | 84.1 | 83.6 | 84.9 | 83.8 | 83.0 | 82.5 | 81.2 | 79.7 | 80.5 | 81.9 |
| % Earned on Net Property | 8.9 | 8.8 | 9.5 | 9.6 | 9.9 | 9.5 | 9.4 | 10.0 | 10.1 | 10.7 |
| % Return on Revenue | 11.3 | 10.5 | 10.2 | 11.3 | 11.0 | 11.7 | 12.9 | 13.1 | 12.5 | 11.0 |
| % Return on Invested Capital | 8.2 | 8.4 | 7.4 | 8.3 | 8.0 | 8.0 | 7.9 | 8.9 | 8.5 | 7.4 |
| % Return on Common Equity | 12.7 | 11.7 | 13.6 | 14.6 | 14.3 | 15.2 | 15.4 | 16.1 | 15.8 | 12.0 |

Data as orig reptd.; bef. results of disc opers/spec. items. Per share data adj. for stk. divs.; EPS diluted. E-Estimated. NA-Not Available. NM-Not Meaningful. NR-Not Ranked. UR-Under Review.

**Office:** 30 Ivan Allen Jr Blvd NW, Atlanta, GA 30308-3003.
**Telephone:** 404-506-5000.
**Email:** investors@southerncompany.com
**Website:** http://www.southernco.com

**Chrmn, Pres & CEO:** T.A. Fanning
**COO & EVP:** A.J. Topazi
**EVP & CFO:** A.P. Beattie
**EVP, Secy & General Counsel:** G.E. Holland, Jr.

**SVP & CIO:** B. Blalock
**Investor Contact:** G. Kundert (404-506-5135)
**Board Members:** J. P. Baranco, J. A. Boscia, H. A. Clark, III, T. A. Fanning, H. W. Habermeyer, Jr., V. M. Hagen, W. A. Hood, Jr., D. M. James, D. E. Klein, J. N. Purcell, W. G. Smith, Jr., S. R. Specker, L. D. Thompson

**Founded:** 1945
**Domicile:** Delaware
**Employees:** 25,940

**STANDARD &POOR'S**

# Southwestern Energy Co

| S&P Recommendation HOLD ★★★☆☆ | Price $36.45 (as of Nov 28, 2011) | 12-Mo. Target Price $49.00 | Investment Style Large-Cap Growth |
|---|---|---|---|

**GICS Sector** Energy
**Sub-Industry** Oil & Gas Exploration & Production

**Summary** This Houston-based company is engaged in oil and gas exploration and production, natural gas gathering and marketing.

## Key Stock Statistics (Source S&P, Vickers, company reports)

| | | | | | | | |
|---|---|---|---|---|---|---|---|
| 52-Wk Range | $49.25–30.94 | S&P Oper. EPS 2011E | 1.89 | Market Capitalization(B) | $12.662 | Beta | 0.57 |
| Trailing 12-Month EPS | $1.80 | S&P Oper. EPS 2012E | 2.25 | Yield (%) | Nil | S&P 3-Yr. Proj. EPS CAGR(%) | 14 |
| Trailing 12-Month P/E | 20.3 | P/E on S&P Oper. EPS 2011E | 19.3 | Dividend Rate/Share | Nil | S&P Credit Rating | BBB- |
| $10K Invested 5 Yrs Ago | $17,612 | Common Shares Outstg. (M) | 347.4 | Institutional Ownership (%) | 92 | | |

## Price Performance

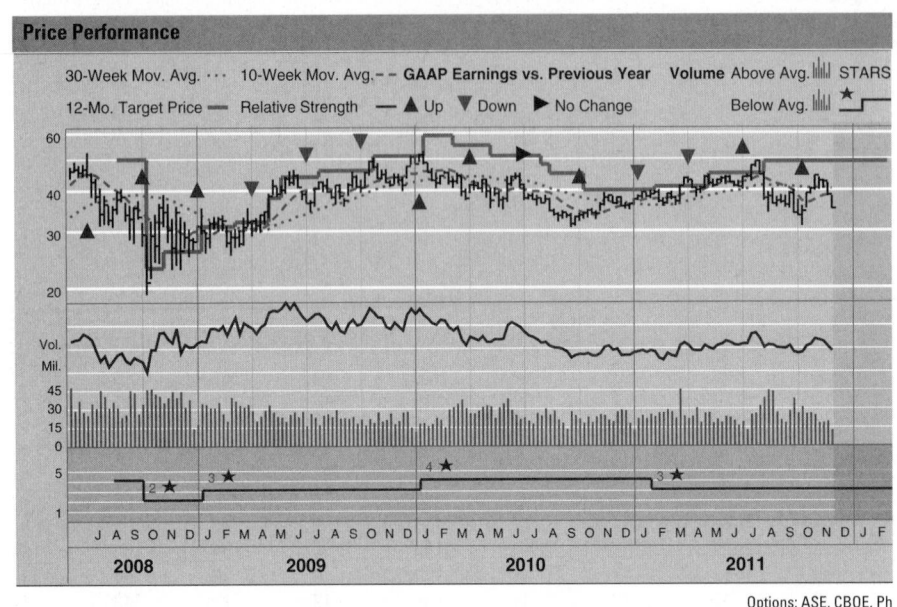

30-Week Mov. Avg. · · · 10-Week Mov. Avg. - - GAAP Earnings vs. Previous Year   Volume Above Avg. ⅢⅢ STARS
12-Mo. Target Price — Relative Strength — ▲ Up ▼ Down ► No Change   Below Avg. ⅢⅢ

Options: ASE, CBOE, Ph

Analysis prepared by Equity Analyst **Michael Kay** on Nov 28, 2011, when the stock traded at **$36.79.**

## Highlights

➤ Since SWN's discovery of the Fayetteville Shale in 2004, production there has grown at a 40% compound annual growth rate and is expected to reach 430-434 Bcfe in 2011. SWN recently raised total 2011 production guidance to 496-500 Bcfe, up 23%. On growth at Fayetteville, we see 2011 production up 22% and 2012 up 20%. On lower gas prices and to coincide with current economic returns, SWN has dropped rigs, and currently runs 19 rigs at Fayetteville. It has added a rig, and now runs two rigs at the Marcellus Shale. On an expected capex cut, SWN's well count should drop from 700 in 2010 to under 600 in 2011.

➤ As SWN is one of the lowest-cost producers in our E&P universe, we expect drilling efficiencies at Fayetteville in 2011 with improved drill times and well spacing. SWN lifted 2011 capex plans to $2 billion, down 6% from 2010, with $1.4 billion for Fayetteville, where it plans 470-480 wells. It expects to drill 40-45 Marcellus wells. We see similar capex in 2012.

➤ We see adjusted EPS of $1.89 in 2011, versus $1.73 in 2010, as higher production offsets weaker prices. On production growth and modest price gains, we see 2012 EPS of $2.25.

## Investment Rationale/Risk

➤ We believe SWN spent $1.3 billion at Fayetteville in 2010 and plans $1.4 billion (70% of budget) in 2011, providing production and reserve growth visibility. We view positively its growth prospects and low-cost operations, which we think position it well to boost earnings and cash flow when gas markets improve. SWN leasehold acreage was acquired at attractive prices due to limited attention paid to the region before 2004. We believe additional acreage at Marcellus and South Texas and growing exploration acreage in Canada should add value. We expect capex and production growth to be internally funded in 2012. We believe the shares have been hampered by aggressive spending in the past.

➤ Risks to our opinion and target price include a sustained drop in oil and gas prices and further deterioration in global economic conditions.

➤ We blend our NAV estimate of $46 with a target of 8X our 2012 EBITDA estimate, well above peers, and other relative metrics to arrive at our 12-month target price of $49. We think SWN's growth metrics warrant a premium valuation, but with currently depressed gas market conditions, our opinion is hold.

## Qualitative Risk Assessment

| LOW | MEDIUM | HIGH |
|---|---|---|

Our risk assessment reflects SWN's operations in a capital-intensive industry that is competitive and cyclical and derives value from producing a commodity whose price is very volatile.

## Quantitative Evaluations

**S&P Quality Ranking**   **B**

| D | C | B- | B | B+ | A- | A | A+ |
|---|---|---|---|---|---|---|---|

**Relative Strength Rank**   **MODERATE**

37

LOWEST = 1   HIGHEST = 99

## Revenue/Earnings Data

### Revenue (Million $)

| | 1Q | 2Q | 3Q | 4Q | Year |
|---|---|---|---|---|---|
| 2011 | 676.3 | 765.2 | 767.3 | -- | -- |
| 2010 | 668.1 | 589.9 | 682.2 | 670.4 | 2,611 |
| 2009 | 540.8 | 477.5 | 503.0 | 624.5 | 2,146 |
| 2008 | 524.1 | 604.5 | 683.0 | 500.1 | 2,312 |
| 2007 | 284.7 | 270.1 | 297.6 | 402.8 | 1,255 |
| 2006 | 226.7 | 154.0 | 168.4 | 214.0 | 763.1 |

### Earnings Per Share ($)

| | 1Q | 2Q | 3Q | 4Q | Year |
|---|---|---|---|---|---|
| 2011 | 0.39 | 0.48 | 0.50 | E0.52 | E1.89 |
| 2010 | 0.49 | 0.35 | 0.46 | 0.43 | 1.73 |
| 2009 | -1.26 | 0.35 | 0.34 | 0.45 | -0.10 |
| 2008 | 0.31 | 0.39 | 0.63 | 0.30 | 1.64 |
| 2007 | 0.15 | 0.14 | 0.15 | 0.21 | 0.64 |
| 2006 | 0.17 | 0.11 | 0.10 | 0.10 | 0.48 |

Fiscal year ended Dec. 31. Next earnings report expected: Late February. EPS Estimates based on S&P Operating Earnings; historical GAAP earnings are as reported.

## Dividend Data

Cash dividends have not been paid since 2000.

The **McGraw-Hill** Companies

# Southwestern Energy Co

**STANDARD
&POOR'S**

## Business Summary November 28, 2011

CORPORATE OVERVIEW. Southwestern Energy Company (SWN) is primarily focused on the exploration and production of natural gas. SWN is engaged in natural gas and crude oil exploration and production (E&P) in the Arkoma Basin, Oklahoma, Texas and Pennsylvania. SWN also has natural gas gathering and marketing activities located in core market areas. Current operations are being principally focused on development of the unconventional gas reservoir located on the Arkansas side of the Arkoma Basin, the Fayetteville Shale play. In 2010, SWN commenced an exploration program under 32 licenses in New Brunswick, Canada.

As of December 31, 2010, SWN had estimated proved reserves of 4.94 Tcfe, of which 100% was natural gas and 46% was proved developed. This compares with estimated proved reserves of 3.66 Tcfe, 100% natural gas and 54% proved developed, at the end of 2009, a 35% increase. We calculate SWN's reserve life was 12.2 years as of year-end 2010. We believe this is especially impressive given SWN's production growth and indicative of very strong reserve additions.

We estimate that SWN replaced 430% of production in 2010 (592% in 2009). As of the end of 2010, SWN's three-year average reserve replacement ratio was 504%. During 2010, SWN invested a total of $1.8 billion, with $1.6 billion allo-

cated to exploration and development.

CORPORATE STRATEGY. SWN is focused on promoting long-term growth in the net asset value of its business. The key elements of SWN's E&P business strategy are to exploit and develop its existing asset base, control operations and costs, hedge production to stabilize cash flow, and achieve growth through new exploration and development activities.

SWN's primary business is natural gas and oil exploration, development and production, with operations primarily located in Arkansas, Oklahoma and Texas. These operations are conducted through its wholly owned subsidiaries, SEECO, Inc., and Southwestern Energy Production Company (SEPCO). Diamond M, also wholly owned, has interests in properties in the Permian Basin of Texas. DeSoto Drilling, Inc. (DDI), a wholly owned subsidiary of SEPCO, operates drilling rigs in the Fayetteville Shale play and in East Texas.

## Company Financials Fiscal Year Ended Dec. 31

| Per Share Data ($) | 2010 | 2009 | 2008 | 2007 | 2006 | 2005 | 2004 | 2003 | 2002 | 2001 |
|---|---|---|---|---|---|---|---|---|---|---|
| Tangible Book Value | 8.55 | 6.76 | 7.30 | 4.82 | 4.25 | 3.32 | 1.54 | 1.19 | 0.86 | 0.91 |
| Cash Flow | 3.42 | 3.98 | 2.84 | 1.49 | 0.92 | 0.78 | 0.60 | 0.39 | 0.33 | 0.43 |
| Earnings | 1.73 | -0.10 | 1.64 | 0.64 | 0.48 | 0.48 | 0.35 | 0.19 | 0.07 | 0.17 |
| S&P Core Earnings | 1.73 | -0.11 | 1.54 | 0.63 | 0.46 | 0.46 | 0.33 | 0.17 | 0.05 | 0.15 |
| Dividends | Nil | Nil | Nil | Nil | Nil | Nil | Nil | Nil | Nil | Nil |
| Payout Ratio | Nil | Nil | Nil | Nil | Nil | Nil | Nil | Nil | Nil | Nil |
| Prices:High | 52.82 | 51.33 | 52.69 | 28.50 | 22.14 | 20.90 | 6.93 | 3.19 | 1.91 | 2.04 |
| Prices:Low | 30.61 | 25.26 | 19.05 | 15.57 | 11.83 | 5.51 | 2.42 | 1.36 | 1.19 | 1.10 |
| P/E Ratio:High | 31 | NM | 32 | 45 | 47 | 44 | 20 | 17 | 28 | 12 |
| P/E Ratio:Low | 18 | NM | 12 | 24 | 25 | 12 | 7 | 7 | 17 | 6 |
| **Income Statement Analysis** (Million $) | | | | | | | | | | |
| Revenue | 2,611 | 2,146 | 2,312 | 1,255 | 763 | 676 | 477 | 327 | 262 | 345 |
| Operating Income | NA | NA | 1,301 | 969 | 246 | 246 | 182 | 97.3 | 111 | 145 |
| Depreciation | 592 | 1,403 | 414 | 294 | 151 | 96.2 | 73.7 | 55.9 | 54.0 | 52.9 |
| Interest Expense | 26.2 | 18.6 | 28.9 | 37.7 | 12.4 | 21.0 | 19.8 | 19.1 | 21.5 | 24.0 |
| Pretax Income | 995 | -52.2 | 920 | 357 | 262 | 234 | 163 | 78.6 | 23.0 | 57.2 |
| Effective Tax Rate | NA | 31.4% | 38.2% | 38.1% | 38.0% | 36.7% | 36.2% | 35.8% | 35.6% | 38.3% |
| Net Income | 604 | -35.7 | 568 | 221 | 163 | 148 | 104 | 49.8 | 14.3 | 35.3 |
| S&P Core Earnings | 603 | -37.0 | 533 | 217 | 157 | 143 | 98.6 | 46.6 | 10.3 | 30.8 |
| **Balance Sheet & Other Financial Data** (Million $) | | | | | | | | | | |
| Cash | 16.1 | 13.2 | 196 | 0.73 | 43.0 | 224 | 1.20 | 1.30 | 1.69 | 3.64 |
| Current Assets | 581 | 564 | 889 | 363 | 324 | 461 | 131 | 100 | 76.1 | 93.2 |
| Total Assets | 6,017 | 4,770 | 4,760 | 3,623 | 2,379 | 1,869 | 1,146 | 891 | 740 | 743 |
| Current Liabilities | 694 | 536 | 793 | 431 | 379 | 302 | 134 | 95.1 | 74.6 | 71.5 |
| Long Term Debt | 1,093 | 998 | 674 | 978 | 136 | 100 | 325 | 279 | 342 | 350 |
| Common Equity | 2,965 | 2,331 | 2,508 | 1,647 | 1,434 | 1,110 | 448 | 342 | 177 | 183 |
| Total Capital | 4,059 | 3,340 | 3,253 | 103 | 1,953 | 1,477 | 989 | 780 | 649 | 668 |
| Capital Expenditures | 2,073 | 1,780 | 1,756 | 1,519 | 851 | 454 | 291 | 167 | 92.1 | 106 |
| Cash Flow | 1,196 | 1,367 | 982 | 515 | 314 | 244 | 177 | 106 | 68.3 | 88.2 |
| Current Ratio | 0.8 | 1.1 | 1.1 | 0.8 | 0.9 | 1.5 | 1.0 | 1.1 | 1.0 | 1.3 |
| % Long Term Debt of Capitalization | 26.9 | 30.0 | 20.7 | 31.5 | 6.9 | 6.7 | 32.9 | 35.7 | 52.8 | 52.4 |
| % Net Income of Revenue | 23.1 | NM | 24.6 | 17.6 | 21.3 | 21.8 | 21.7 | 15.2 | 5.5 | 10.2 |
| % Return on Assets | 11.2 | NM | 13.6 | 7.4 | 7.6 | 9.8 | 10.2 | 6.1 | 1.9 | 4.9 |
| % Return on Equity | 22.8 | NM | 27.3 | 14.3 | 12.7 | 18.9 | 26.2 | 19.2 | 7.9 | 21.8 |

Data as orig reptd.; bef. results of disc opers/spec. items. Per share data adj. for stk. divs.; EPS diluted. E-Estimated. NA-Not Available. NM-Not Meaningful. NR-Not Ranked. UR-Under Review.

**Office:** 2350 North Sam Houston Parkway East, Suite 125, Houston, TX 77032.
**Telephone:** 281-618-4700.
**Website:** http://www.swn.com
**Chrmn:** H.M. Korell

**Pres & CEO:** S.L. Mueller
**COO & EVP:** W.J. Way
**EVP & CFO:** G.D. Kerley
**EVP, Secy & General Counsel:** M.K. Boling

**Investor Contact:** B.D. Sylvester (281-618-4897)
**Board Members:** L. E. Epley, Jr., R. L. Howard, C. A. Kehr, G. D. Kerley, H. M. Korell, V. A. Kuuskraa, K. R. Mourton, S. L. Mueller, C. E. Scharlau, A. H. Stevens

**Founded:** 1929
**Domicile:** Delaware
**Employees:** 2,088

*The McGraw-Hill Companies*

# Southwest Airlines Co.

STANDARD &POOR'S

| S&P Recommendation | **BUY** ★★★★☆ | Price $7.93 (as of Nov 29, 2011) | 12-Mo. Target Price $13.00 |
|---|---|---|---|

**GICS Sector** Industrials
**Sub-Industry** Airlines

**Summary** The fourth largest U.S. airline, Southwest offers discounted fares, primarily on shorter-haul, point-to-point flights.

## Key Stock Statistics (Source S&P, Vickers, company reports)

| | | | | | | | |
|---|---|---|---|---|---|---|---|
| 52-Wk Range | $13.61– 7.15 | S&P Oper. EPS 2011**E** | 0.47 | Market Capitalization(B) | $6.174 | Beta | 1.12 |
| Trailing 12-Month EPS | $0.20 | S&P Oper. EPS 2012**E** | 0.95 | Yield (%) | 0.23 | S&P 3-Yr. Proj. EPS CAGR(%) | 14 |
| Trailing 12-Month P/E | 39.7 | P/E on S&P Oper. EPS 2011**E** | 16.9 | Dividend Rate/Share | $0.02 | S&P Credit Rating | BBB- |
| $10K Invested 5 Yrs Ago | $4,654 | Common Shares Outstg. (M) | 778.5 | Institutional Ownership (%) | 84 | | |

## Price Performance

30-Week Mov. Avg. ··· 10-Week Mov. Avg. -- **GAAP Earnings vs. Previous Year** Volume Above Avg. STARS
12-Mo. Target Price — Relative Strength — ▲ Up ▼ Down ► No Change Below Avg.

Options: ASE, CBOE, P, Ph

Analysis prepared by Equity Analyst **Jim Corridore** on Oct 25, 2011, when the stock traded at **$8.73**.

### Highlights

➤ LUV completed its acquisition of AirTran Holdings on May 2, 2011, for a total of $1.4 billion in cash and stock. Under terms of the deal, LUV exchanged $3.25 in cash and 0.321 of a LUV share for each AirTran share. We look for LUV's combined revenues to rise about 30% in 2011, and 12% in 2012, on improving demand, yields and the addition of the AirTran revenues. We expect incremental revenues from the sale of assigned boarding slots, a more sophisticated revenue management system, and other ancillary revenue-generating initiatives.

➤ We see margins in 2011 and 2012 being aided by revenue and mix improvements stemming from LUV's recent initiative to redeploy flights to more profitable markets, coupled with a rebound in business travel. We see a new frequent flyer program and the addition of the Atlanta market via the AirTran acquisition helping to increase LUV's presence among business travelers. We expect fuel costs to rise about 57% in 2011 and 12% in 2012.

➤ We estimate 2011 EPS of $0.47, versus 2010 operating EPS of $0.74. For 2012, we see EPS of $0.95.

### Investment Rationale/Risk

➤ While LUV is straying from its traditional business model with the acquisition of AirTran, we think the benefits are likely to outweigh the risks. LUV got about 20% larger without adding a single seat to industrywide capacity. AirTran shares a low cost culture and has a strong presence in Atlanta, a heavy business travel market. While LUV is taking on more complexity with the addition of new plane types, we think it will be able to manage this risk to keep expenses low. We believe LUV had the balance sheet strength to be able to make this acquisition without harming its financial health.

➤ Risks to our recommendation and target price include a poorly integrated acquisition, a possible price war with one or more competitors, and weakening of air travel demand. We are concerned about LUV's corporate governance relating to its use of affiliated outsiders on its board of directors' nominating and compensation committees.

➤ Our 12-month target price of $13 values the shares at an enterprise value-to-EBITDAR (EBITDA plus aircraft rent) multiple of 5X our 2012 EBITDAR estimate, a premium to peers.

### Qualitative Risk Assessment

| LOW | **MEDIUM** | HIGH |
|---|---|---|

Even though Southwest participates in the highly volatile airline industry, we think its conservative balance sheet, with low debt to total capitalization, and its track record of 38 consecutive years of profitability mitigate this risk.

### Quantitative Evaluations

**S&P Quality Ranking** B

| D | C | B- | **B** | B+ | A- | A | A+ |
|---|---|---|---|---|---|---|---|

**Relative Strength Rank** MODERATE

39

LOWEST = 1 HIGHEST = 99

### Revenue/Earnings Data

**Revenue (Million $)**

| | 1Q | 2Q | 3Q | 4Q | Year |
|---|---|---|---|---|---|
| 2011 | 3,103 | 4,136 | 4,311 | -- | -- |
| 2010 | 2,630 | 3,168 | 3,192 | 3,114 | 12,104 |
| 2009 | 2,357 | 2,616 | 2,666 | 2,712 | 10,350 |
| 2008 | 2,530 | 2,869 | 2,891 | 2,734 | 11,023 |
| 2007 | 2,198 | 2,583 | 2,588 | 2,492 | 9,861 |
| 2006 | 2,019 | 2,449 | 2,342 | 2,276 | 9,086 |

**Earnings Per Share ($)**

| | | | | | |
|---|---|---|---|---|---|
| 2011 | 0.01 | 0.21 | -0.18 | E0.10 | E0.47 |
| 2010 | 0.01 | 0.15 | 0.27 | 0.18 | 0.61 |
| 2009 | -0.12 | 0.12 | -0.02 | 0.16 | 0.13 |
| 2008 | 0.05 | 0.44 | -0.16 | -0.08 | 0.24 |
| 2007 | 0.12 | 0.36 | 0.22 | 0.15 | 0.84 |
| 2006 | 0.07 | 0.40 | 0.06 | 0.07 | 0.61 |

Fiscal year ended Dec. 31. Next earnings report expected: Early December. EPS Estimates based on S&P Operating Earnings; historical GAAP earnings are as reported.

### Dividend Data (Dates: mm/dd Payment Date: mm/dd/yy)

| Amount ($) | Date Decl. | Ex-Div. Date | Stk. of Record | Payment Date |
|---|---|---|---|---|
| 0.005 | 01/27 | 03/01 | 03/03 | 03/24/11 |
| 0.005 | 05/18 | 06/06 | 06/08 | 06/22/11 |
| 0.005 | 07/28 | 08/23 | 08/25 | 09/15/11 |
| 0.005 | 11/17 | 12/06 | 12/08 | 01/05/12 |

Dividends have been paid since 1976. Source: Company reports.

**Please read the Required Disclosures and Analyst Certification on the last page of this report.**

The **McGraw·Hill** Companies

# Southwest Airlines Co.

STANDARD
&POOR'S

## Business Summary October 25, 2011

CORPORATE OVERVIEW. Southwest Airlines was the largest provider of scheduled domestic passenger air travel in the U.S. in 2010. Overall, the airline ranks as the fourth largest in U.S., based on total revenue passenger miles (RPMs). At December 31, 2010, it served 69 cities in 35 states. LUV specializes in low-fare, point-to-point, short-haul, high-frequency service. Although 80% of its work force belongs to unions, the company believes that it has generally enjoyed harmonious labor relations. LUV began service to three new cities in March 2011: Charleston, S.C., Greenville, S.C. and Newark, N.J.

On May 2, 2011, LUV acquired AirTran Holdings, the parent company of Air-Tran Airlines (AAI), for $3.75 a share in cash plus 0.321 of a LUV share for each AAI share. Based on LUV's closing price on September 24, the deal was valued at $1.0 billion, or $3.2 billion including the assumption of debt and operating leases. AirTran is a low-cost carrier based primarily in the southeast U.S. with 2010 revenues of $2.6 billion.

MARKET PROFILE. The U.S. airline industry is a $155 billion market, according to 2009 data (latest available) from the U.S. Department of Transportation. With 2009 revenues of $10.4 billion (which rose 17%, to $12.1 billion, in 2010), LUV comprised around 6.7% of total industry revenues. Southwest also has an approximate 9.7% market share when measured by RPMs, as of December

2009 (latest available). Southwest was profitable in 2010 for the 38th consecutive year and was profitable throughout the industry downturn that took place after 9/11/01, with net income totaling $2.1 billion in 2001-2005. Over the same period, S&P believes the 10 largest U.S. airlines lost about $58.6 billion.

COMPETITIVE LANDSCAPE. The industry consists of about 50 mainline commercial passenger airlines, of which about 20 are considered major airlines, defined as airlines with annual revenues in excess of $1.0 billion. Major competitors include Delta Air Lines (24.6% market share, as measured by RPMs, as of December 2009), AMR Corp.'s American Airlines (17.0%), United Continental Holdings (23.5%) US Airways (7.5%) and JetBlue Airways (3.4%). The U.S. airline industry is fragmented and highly competitive. Barriers to entry are high, and there are strongly entrenched competitors. Pricing is extremely competitive. Fuel costs, the second largest cost category for Southwest, have risen sharply over the past three years, although Southwest is partly protected by a fuel hedging position that we think is by far the best in the industry.

## Company Financials Fiscal Year Ended Dec. 31

| Per Share Data ($) | 2010 | 2009 | 2008 | 2007 | 2006 | 2005 | 2004 | 2003 | 2002 | 2001 |
|---|---|---|---|---|---|---|---|---|---|---|
| Tangible Book Value | 8.34 | 7.36 | 6.69 | 10.49 | 8.23 | 8.38 | 7.04 | 6.40 | 5.69 | 5.23 |
| Cash Flow | 1.46 | 0.96 | 1.05 | 1.56 | 1.23 | 1.25 | 0.91 | 1.00 | 0.74 | 1.03 |
| Earnings | 0.61 | 0.13 | 0.24 | 0.84 | 0.61 | 0.67 | 0.38 | 0.54 | 0.30 | 0.63 |
| S&P Core Earnings | 0.61 | 0.12 | 0.23 | 0.83 | 0.60 | 0.62 | 0.30 | 0.48 | 0.23 | 0.61 |
| Dividends | 0.02 | 0.02 | 0.02 | 0.02 | 0.02 | 0.02 | 0.02 | 0.02 | 0.02 | 0.01 |
| Payout Ratio | 3% | 14% | 8% | 2% | 3% | 3% | 5% | 3% | 6% | 2% |
| Prices:High | 14.32 | 11.78 | 16.77 | 16.96 | 18.20 | 16.95 | 17.06 | 19.69 | 22.00 | 23.32 |
| Prices:Low | 10.42 | 4.95 | 7.05 | 12.12 | 14.61 | 13.05 | 12.88 | 11.72 | 10.90 | 11.25 |
| P/E Ratio:High | 24 | 91 | 70 | 20 | 30 | 25 | 45 | 36 | 73 | 37 |
| P/E Ratio:Low | 17 | 38 | 29 | 14 | 24 | 19 | 34 | 22 | 36 | 18 |

| Income Statement Analysis (Million $) | | | | | | | | | | |
|---|---|---|---|---|---|---|---|---|---|---|
| Revenue | 12,104 | 10,350 | 11,023 | 9,861 | 9,086 | 7,584 | 6,530 | 5,937 | 5,522 | 5,555 |
| Operating Income | 1,616 | 944 | 1,058 | 1,371 | 1,449 | 1,289 | 985 | 867 | 774 | 949 |
| Depreciation | 628 | 616 | 599 | 555 | 515 | 469 | 431 | 384 | 356 | 318 |
| Interest Expense | 149 | 165 | 130 | 119 | 77.0 | 83.0 | 49.0 | 58.0 | 89.3 | 49.3 |
| Pretax Income | 745 | 164 | 278 | 1,058 | 790 | 874 | 489 | 708 | 393 | 828 |
| Effective Tax Rate | NA | 39.6% | 36.0% | 39.0% | 36.8% | 37.3% | 36.0% | 37.6% | 38.6% | 38.2% |
| Net Income | 459 | 99.0 | 178 | 645 | 499 | 548 | 313 | 442 | 241 | 511 |
| S&P Core Earnings | 456 | 93.2 | 169 | 635 | 489 | 504 | 236 | 385 | 188 | 486 |

| Balance Sheet & Other Financial Data (Million $) | | | | | | | | | | |
|---|---|---|---|---|---|---|---|---|---|---|
| Cash | 3,538 | 2,593 | 1,803 | 2,779 | 1,390 | 2,280 | 1,305 | 1,865 | 1,815 | 2,280 |
| Current Assets | 4,279 | 3,358 | 2,893 | 4,443 | 2,601 | 3,620 | 2,172 | 2,313 | 2,232 | 2,520 |
| Total Assets | 15,463 | 14,269 | 14,308 | 16,772 | 13,460 | 14,218 | 11,337 | 9,878 | 8,954 | 8,997 |
| Current Liabilities | 3,305 | 2,676 | 2,806 | 4,838 | 2,887 | 3,848 | 2,142 | 172 | 1,434 | 2,239 |
| Long Term Debt | 2,875 | 3,325 | 3,498 | 2,050 | 1,567 | 1,394 | 1,700 | 1,332 | 1,553 | 1,327 |
| Common Equity | 6,237 | 5,466 | 4,953 | 6,941 | 6,449 | 6,675 | 5,524 | 5,052 | 4,422 | 4,014 |
| Total Capital | 9,617 | 8,981 | 10,355 | 11,526 | 10,120 | 9,965 | 8,834 | 7,804 | 7,202 | 6,399 |
| Capital Expenditures | 493 | 585 | 923 | 1,331 | 1,399 | 1,210 | 1,775 | 1,238 | 603 | 998 |
| Cash Flow | 1,087 | 715 | 777 | 1,200 | 1,014 | 1,017 | 744 | 826 | 597 | 829 |
| Current Ratio | 1.3 | 1.3 | 1.0 | 0.9 | 0.9 | 0.9 | 1.0 | 13.4 | 1.6 | 1.1 |
| % Long Term Debt of Capitalization | 29.9 | 37.0 | 33.8 | 17.8 | 15.5 | 14.0 | 19.2 | 17.1 | 21.6 | 20.7 |
| % Net Income of Revenue | 3.8 | 1.0 | 1.6 | 6.5 | 5.5 | 7.2 | 4.8 | 7.4 | 4.4 | 9.2 |
| % Return on Assets | 3.1 | 0.7 | 1.2 | 4.3 | 3.6 | 4.3 | 3.0 | 4.7 | 2.7 | 6.5 |
| % Return on Equity | 7.8 | 1.9 | 3.0 | 9.6 | 7.6 | 9.0 | 5.9 | 9.3 | 5.7 | 13.7 |

Data as orig reptd.; bef. results of disc opers/spec. items. Per share data adj. for stk. divs.; EPS diluted. E-Estimated. NA-Not Available. NM-Not Meaningful. NR-Not Ranked. UR-Under Review.

**Office:** P.O. Box 36611, Dallas, TX 75235-1611.
**Telephone:** 214-792-4000.
**Website:** http://www.southwest.com
**Chrmn, Pres & CEO:** G.C. Kelly

**CEO:** J.O. Parker, Jr.
**COO & EVP:** M.G. Van De Ven
**EVP & Chief Admin Officer:** J. Lamb
**EVP, Secy & General Counsel:** R. Ricks

**Investor Contact:** L. Wright (214-792-4415)
**Board Members:** D. W. Biegler, J. V. Biggins, D. H. Brooks, W. H. Cunningham, J. G. Denison, G. C. Kelly, N. B. Loeffler, J. Montford, T. M. Nealon, D. D. Villanueva

**Founded:** 1967
**Domicile:** Texas
**Employees:** 34,901

The McGraw·Hill Companies

# Spectra Energy Corp

STANDARD &POOR'S

| S&P Recommendation | BUY ★★★★☆ | Price $28.23 (as of Nov 25, 2011) | 12-Mo. Target Price $33.00 | Investment Style Large-Cap Blend |
|---|---|---|---|---|

**GICS Sector** Energy
**Sub-Industry** Oil & Gas Storage & Transportation

**Summary** This integrated natural gas holding company is engaged in gas gathering and processing and gas transportation and storage in the U.S. and Canada, and provides retail gas distribution to 1.3 million customers in Ontario, Canada.

## Key Stock Statistics (Source S&P, Vickers, company reports)

| | | | | | | | |
|---|---|---|---|---|---|---|---|
| 52-Wk Range | $29.75– 22.80 | S&P Oper. EPS 2011E | 1.81 | Market Capitalization(B) | $18.359 | Beta | 0.95 |
| Trailing 12-Month EPS | $1.86 | S&P Oper. EPS 2012E | 1.90 | Yield (%) | 3.97 | S&P 3-Yr. Proj. EPS CAGR(%) | 13 |
| Trailing 12-Month P/E | 15.2 | P/E on S&P Oper. EPS 2011E | 15.6 | Dividend Rate/Share | $1.12 | S&P Credit Rating | NA |
| $10K Invested 5 Yrs Ago | NA | Common Shares Outstg. (M) | 650.3 | Institutional Ownership (%) | 65 | | |

## Price Performance

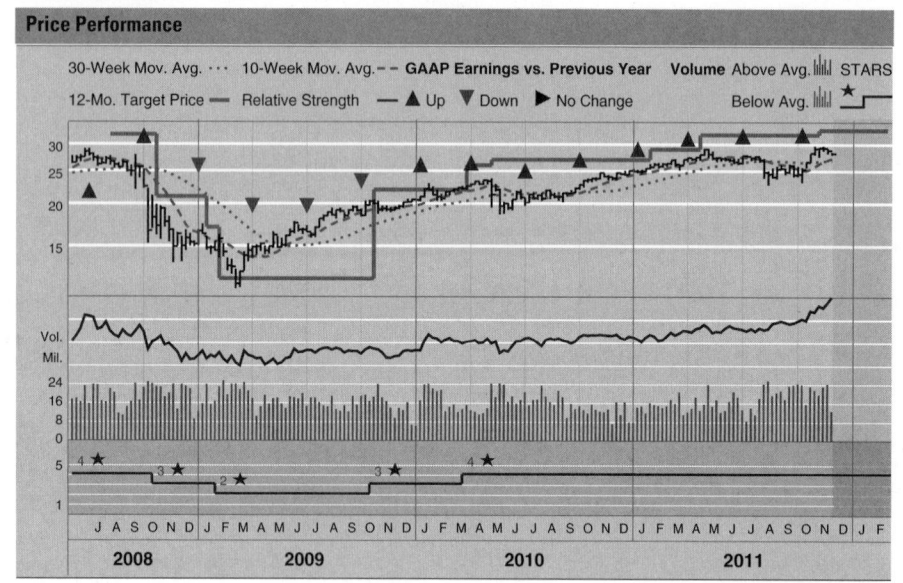

30-Week Mov. Avg. · · · 10-Week Mov. Avg. – – GAAP Earnings vs. Previous Year Volume Above Avg. STARS
12-Mo. Target Price — Relative Strength — ▲ Up ▼ Down ► No Change Below Avg.

Options: ASE, CBOE, Ph

Analysis prepared by Equity Analyst **Tanjila Shafi** on Nov 21, 2011, when the stock traded at **$28.28**.

### Highlights

➤ We believe that 2011 earnings will benefit from the company's fee-based businesses. We expect EBIT of $2.4 billion in 2011, versus 2010's EBIT of $2.1 billion. We see improving earnings at the company's Distribution segment, reflecting higher storage and transportation revenues. We look for its U.S. Transmission business to benefit from contributions from new projects placed into service. We see the company's Western Canada Transmission and Processing segment being aided by higher contracted volumes and revenues from expansions. In 2012, we forecast EBIT of $2.5 billion, reflecting continued growth at its U.S. Transmission and Distribution segments.

➤ SE has placed five projects, in which it invested about $900 million, into full or partial service. The company sees expansion opportunities of over $1 billion from 2011 through 2015.

➤ On October 25, the company declared a quarterly dividend of $0.28 per share, 12% higher than a year earlier. Our 2011 cash dividend forecast is $1.08 per share.

### Investment Rationale/Risk

➤ We are positive on SE's diverse asset base which we believe is strategically positioned for growth. SE's assets connect growing supplies to high demand markets in the Northeast and Florida. We believe SE's fee-based businesses and expansion projects will enhance earnings growth in 2012. In August 2010, SE completed the acquisition of the Bobcat Gas Storage assets and development project from privately held Haddington Energy Partners III LP and GE (GE 15, Buy) for $540 million. We expect SE to benefit from strong NGL and ethane pricing; it, along with El Paso (EP 25, Hold), is building the Marcellus Ethane Pipeline System project, which is transporting ethane from fractionation plants in the Marcellus region to pipelines and storage facilities along the Gulf Coast.

➤ Risks to our opinion and target price include slower natural gas production growth, lower natural gas prices, and a less favorable credit environment.

➤ Our 12-month target price of $33 is based on an enterprise value multiple of 10.3X our 2011 EBITDA estimate, in line with SE's historical multiples.

## Qualitative Risk Assessment

| LOW | MEDIUM | HIGH |
|---|---|---|

Our risk assessment reflects the company's large market capitalization and the lower risk inherent in its regulated gas transmission and distribution businesses, offset by its investments in higher-risk gas gathering and processing businesses.

## Quantitative Evaluations

**S&P Quality Ranking**                     NR

| D | C | B- | B | B+ | A- | A | A+ |
|---|---|---|---|---|---|---|---|

**Relative Strength Rank**              STRONG

89

LOWEST = 1                          HIGHEST = 99

## Revenue/Earnings Data

**Revenue (Million $)**

| | 1Q | 2Q | 3Q | 4Q | Year |
|---|---|---|---|---|---|
| 2011 | 1,612 | 1,188 | 1,123 | -- | -- |
| 2010 | 1,480 | 1,063 | 1,019 | 1,383 | 4,945 |
| 2009 | 1,384 | 937.0 | 933.0 | 1,298 | 4,552 |
| 2008 | 1,608 | 1,141 | 1,080 | 1,261 | 5,074 |
| 2007 | 1,401 | 985.0 | 959.0 | 1,397 | 4,742 |
| 2006 | NA | NA | NA | -- | 4,532 |

**Earnings Per Share ($)**

| | | | | | |
|---|---|---|---|---|---|
| 2011 | 0.54 | 0.42 | 0.38 | E0.45 | E1.81 |
| 2010 | 0.53 | 0.27 | 0.30 | 0.51 | 1.60 |
| 2009 | 0.47 | 0.22 | 0.29 | 0.33 | 1.31 |
| 2008 | 0.58 | 0.47 | 0.49 | 0.27 | 1.81 |
| 2007 | 0.37 | 0.29 | 0.38 | 0.45 | 1.49 |
| 2006 | NA | NA | NA | -- | NA |

Fiscal year ended Dec. 31. Next earnings report expected: Early February. EPS Estimates based on S&P Operating Earnings; historical GAAP earnings are as reported.

## Dividend Data (Dates: mm/dd Payment Date: mm/dd/yy)

| Amount ($) | Date Decl. | Ex-Div. Date | Stk. of Record | Payment Date |
|---|---|---|---|---|
| 0.260 | 01/03 | 02/09 | 02/11 | 03/14/11 |
| 0.260 | 04/19 | 05/11 | 05/13 | 06/13/11 |
| 0.260 | 07/01 | 08/10 | 08/12 | 09/12/11 |
| 0.280 | 10/25 | 11/08 | 11/11 | 12/12/11 |

Dividends have been paid since 2007. Source: Company reports.

---

**Please read the Required Disclosures and Analyst Certification on the last page of this report.**

The McGraw-Hill Companies

# Spectra Energy Corp

## Business Summary November 21, 2011

CORPORATE OVERVIEW. SE owns and operates a diversified portfolio of natural gas-related energy assets and is primarily a natural gas midstream company. The company operates in three areas of the natural gas industry: transmission and storage, distribution, and gathering and processing. SE also owns a natural gas distribution company, Union Gas, and participates in a 50%-owned joint venture, DCP Midstream.

MARKET PROFILE. The company manages its business in four segments: U.S. Transmission, Distribution, Western Canada Transmission and Processing, and Field Services.

The U.S. Transmission segment provides transportation and storage of natural gas for customers in the eastern and southeastern U.S. and the Maritime provinces of Canada. The segment had 14,400 miles of natural gas with seven primary transmission systems at year-end 2010: Texas Eastern Transmission, LP, Algonquin Gas Transmission, LLC, East Tennessee Natural Gas, LLC, Maritimes & Northeast Pipeline, L.L.C. and Maritimes & Northeast Pipeline Limited

Partnership, Ozark Gas Transmission, L.L.C., Gulfstream Natural Gas System, LLC, and Southeast Supply Header, LLC. U.S. Transmission's proportional throughput for its pipelines totaled 2,708 TBtu in 2010, up from 2,574 TBtu in 2009.

The Distribution segment provides retail natural gas distribution in Ontario, Canada, as well as natural gas transportation and storage services to other utilities and energy market participants in Ontario, Quebec and the U.S. Union Gas is the company's regulated transmission and distribution subsidiary, serving 1.3 million customers in communities throughout Ontario. Union Gas distributes its gas through 37,600 miles of distribution pipelines and owns 3,000 miles of transmission pipelines and 155 bcf of high deliverability storage.

## Company Financials Fiscal Year Ended Dec. 31

| Per Share Data ($) | 2010 | 2009 | 2008 | 2007 | 2006 | 2005 | 2004 | 2003 | 2002 | 2001 |
|---|---|---|---|---|---|---|---|---|---|---|
| Tangible Book Value | 5.40 | 4.91 | 3.53 | 4.60 | NM | NA | NA | NA | NA | NA |
| Cash Flow | 2.68 | 2.24 | 2.72 | 2.31 | NA | 2.04 | NA | NA | NA | NA |
| Earnings | 1.60 | 1.31 | 1.81 | 1.49 | NA | 1.07 | NA | NA | NA | NA |
| S&P Core Earnings | 1.64 | 1.33 | 1.71 | 1.46 | NA | NA | NA | NA | NA | NA |
| Dividends | 1.00 | 1.00 | 0.96 | 0.88 | Nil | Nil | NA | NA | NA | NA |
| Payout Ratio | 63% | 76% | 53% | 59% | Nil | Nil | NA | NA | NA | NA |
| Prices:High | 25.45 | 20.78 | 29.18 | 30.00 | 29.00 | NA | NA | NA | NA | NA |
| Prices:Low | 18.57 | 11.21 | 13.36 | 21.24 | 27.50 | NA | NA | NA | NA | NA |
| P/E Ratio:High | 16 | 16 | 16 | 20 | NA | NA | NA | NA | NA | NA |
| P/E Ratio:Low | 12 | 9 | 7 | 14 | NA | NA | NA | NA | NA | NA |

| Income Statement Analysis (Million $) | | | | | | | | | | |
|---|---|---|---|---|---|---|---|---|---|---|
| Revenue | 4,945 | 4,552 | 5,074 | 4,742 | 4,532 | 4,132 | 13,255 | 10,784 | NA | NA |
| Operating Income | NA | NA | 2,061 | 1,967 | 1,804 | 1,697 | NA | NA | NA | NA |
| Depreciation | 621 | 562 | 569 | 525 | 606 | 458 | NA | NA | NA | NA |
| Interest Expense | 630 | 610 | 636 | 651 | 605 | 607 | 744 | 806 | NA | NA |
| Pretax Income | 1,506 | 1,271 | 1,688 | 1,458 | 1,376 | 862 | 1,156 | 719 | NA | NA |
| Effective Tax Rate | NA | 27.8% | 29.4% | 30.4% | 28.7% | 41.7% | 123.8% | 29.2% | NA | NA |
| Net Income | 1,123 | 843 | 1,129 | 944 | 936 | 502 | -489 | 404 | NA | NA |
| S&P Core Earnings | 1,061 | 852 | 1,060 | 928 | 926 | NA | NA | NA | NA | NA |

| Balance Sheet & Other Financial Data (Million $) | | | | | | | | | | |
|---|---|---|---|---|---|---|---|---|---|---|
| Cash | 130 | 196 | 214 | 94.0 | 299 | NA | NA | NA | NA | NA |
| Current Assets | 1,638 | 1,429 | 1,450 | 1,379 | 1,625 | 18,601 | NA | NA | NA | NA |
| Total Assets | 26,686 | 24,079 | 21,924 | 22,970 | 20,345 | 21,442 | NA | NA | NA | NA |
| Current Liabilities | 2,523 | 2,495 | 3,044 | 2,422 | 2,358 | 2,052 | NA | NA | NA | NA |
| Long Term Debt | 10,169 | 8,947 | 8,290 | 8,345 | 7,726 | 7,957 | NA | NA | NA | NA |
| Common Equity | 8,487 | 7,665 | 5,540 | 6,857 | 5,639 | 5,225 | NA | NA | NA | NA |
| Total Capital | 20,323 | 17,663 | 15,346 | 16,008 | 16,910 | 16,100 | NA | NA | NA | NA |
| Capital Expenditures | 1,356 | 1,336 | 2,030 | 1,202 | 987 | NA | NA | NA | NA | NA |
| Cash Flow | 1,744 | 1,441 | 1,698 | 1,469 | 1,542 | 960 | NA | NA | NA | NA |
| Current Ratio | 0.7 | 0.6 | 0.5 | 0.6 | 0.7 | NA | NA | NA | NA | NA |
| % Long Term Debt of Capitalization | 50.0 | 53.9 | 54.0 | 52.1 | 45.7 | Nil | Nil | Nil | NA | NA |
| % Net Income of Revenue | 22.7 | 18.5 | 22.3 | 19.9 | 20.7 | 12.2 | NM | 3.8 | NA | NA |
| % Return on Assets | 4.4 | 3.7 | 5.0 | 4.4 | 3.4 | NA | NA | NA | NA | NA |
| % Return on Equity | 14.4 | 12.8 | 18.2 | 15.1 | 10.9 | NA | NA | NA | NA | NA |

Data as orig reptd.; bef. results of disc opers/spec. items. Per share data adj. for stk. divs.; EPS diluted. E-Estimated. NA-Not Available. NM-Not Meaningful. NR-Not Ranked. UR-Under Review.

**Office:** 5400 Westheimer Court, Houston, TX 77056-5310.
**Telephone:** 713-627-5400 .
**Website:** http://www.spectraenergy.com
**Chrmn:** W.T. Esrey

**Pres & CEO:** G.L. Ebel
**COO:** J. Alvarado
**CFO:** J.P. Reddy
**Chief Admin Officer:** D.M. Ables

**Investor Contact:** J. Arensdorf (713-627-4600)
**Board Members:** A. A. Adams, J. Alvarado, P. M. Anderson, P. L. Carter, F. A. Comper, G. L. Ebel, W. T. Esrey, P. B. Hamilton, D. Hendrix, M. McShane, J. H. Netherland, Jr., M. E. Phelps

**Founded:** 2006
**Domicile:** Delaware
**Employees:** 5,500

# Sprint Nextel Corp

**STANDARD &POOR'S**

| S&P Recommendation | **BUY** ★★★★☆ | Price $2.38 (as of Nov 25, 2011) | 12-Mo. Target Price $5.00 | Investment Style Large-Cap Value |

**GICS Sector** Telecommunication Services
**Sub-Industry** Wireless Telecommunication Services

**Summary** This leading provider of wireless and other telecommunications services was formed in August 2005 through the merger of Sprint Corp. and Nextel Communications, Inc.

## Key Stock Statistics (Source S&P, Vickers, company reports)

| | | | | | | | |
|---|---|---|---|---|---|---|---|
| 52-Wk Range | $6.45– 2.10 | S&P Oper. EPS 2011E | -0.87 | Market Capitalization(B) | $7.130 | Beta | 1.22 |
| Trailing 12-Month EPS | $-0.84 | S&P Oper. EPS 2012E | -1.04 | Yield (%) | Nil | S&P 3-Yr. Proj. EPS CAGR(%) | NA |
| Trailing 12-Month P/E | NM | P/E on S&P Oper. EPS 2011E | NM | Dividend Rate/Share | Nil | S&P Credit Rating | B+ |
| $10K Invested 5 Yrs Ago | $1,202 | Common Shares Outstg. (M) | 2,995.8 | Institutional Ownership (%) | 89 | | |

## Price Performance

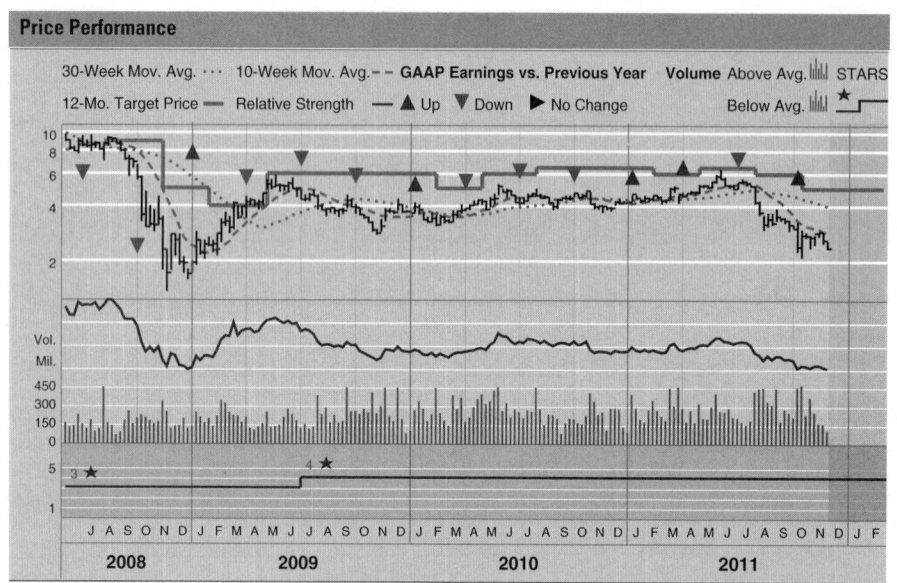

30-Week Mov. Avg. · · · · 10-Week Mov. Avg. – – **GAAP Earnings vs. Previous Year** Volume Above Avg. STARS
12-Mo. Target Price — Relative Strength — ▲ Up ▼ Down ▶ No Change Below Avg. ★

Options: ASE, CBOE, P, Ph

Analysis prepared by Equity Analyst **J. Moorman, CFA** on Nov 01, 2011, when the stock traded at **$2.49**.

## Qualitative Risk Assessment

| LOW | MEDIUM | **HIGH** |

Given our view that S is undergoing a network overhaul, we think its free cash flow could continue to be pressured in the near term. We believe this risk is partly offset by our view of the company's strong balance sheet and operating expense reductions.

## Quantitative Evaluations

**S&P Quality Ranking**      **B**

| D | C | B- | **B** | B+ | A- | A | A+ |

**Relative Strength Rank**      **WEAK**

11

LOWEST = 1        HIGHEST = 99

## Revenue/Earnings Data

**Revenue (Million $)**

| | 1Q | 2Q | 3Q | 4Q | Year |
|---|---|---|---|---|---|
| 2011 | 8,313 | 8,311 | 8,333 | -- | -- |
| 2010 | 8,085 | 8,025 | 8,152 | 8,301 | 32,563 |
| 2009 | 8,209 | 8,141 | 8,042 | 7,868 | 32,260 |
| 2008 | 9,334 | 9,055 | 8,816 | 8,430 | 35,635 |
| 2007 | 10,092 | 10,163 | 10,044 | 9,847 | 40,146 |
| 2006 | 11,548 | 10,014 | 10,496 | 10,444 | 41,028 |

**Earnings Per Share ($)**

| | | | | | |
|---|---|---|---|---|---|
| 2011 | -0.15 | -0.28 | -0.10 | E-0.34 | E-0.87 |
| 2010 | -0.29 | -0.25 | -0.30 | -0.31 | -1.16 |
| 2009 | -0.21 | -0.13 | -0.17 | -0.34 | -0.84 |
| 2008 | -0.18 | -0.12 | -0.11 | -0.57 | -0.98 |
| 2007 | -0.07 | 0.01 | 0.02 | -10.36 | -10.31 |
| 2006 | 0.14 | 0.10 | 0.08 | 0.09 | 0.34 |

Fiscal year ended Dec. 31. Next earnings report expected: Mid February. EPS Estimates based on S&P Operating Earnings; historical GAAP earnings are as reported.

## Dividend Data

No cash dividends have been paid since 2007.

## Highlights

➤ Following 0.9% higher revenues in 2010, we expect increases of 2.9% in 2011, 6.5% in 2012, 3.6% in 2013 and 3.0% in 2014, as S looks to add to its postpaid subscriber base with the addition of the iPhone. S is looking to start an accelerated buildout of LTE or 4G as part of its Network Vision overhaul to its existing network. We believe the company is making progress in improving its network quality and customer satisfaction, and we expect positive net subscriber additions for 2011. Within global markets, we see revenues declining roughly 15% in 2011 due to competitive pressures and the loss of a significant customer.

➤ We estimate total EBITDA margins of 14.8% in 2011, 12.9% in 2012, 15.5% in 2013 and 19.2% in 2014, versus 17.3% in 2010. We see higher subsidies from the new iPhones, as well as costs associated with Network Vision, negatively impacting margins. But we expect opex saving and benefits from Network Vision to help rapidly expand margins in 2013 and 2014.

➤ We estimate operating losses per share of $0.87 in 2011, $1.04 in 2012, $0.65 in 2013 and EPS of $0.10 in 2014, following an operating loss per share of $0.79 in 2010.

## Investment Rationale/Risk

➤ Our buy recommendation is largely based on valuation and our expectations for an accelerated margin recovery in 2013. In our view, the company is in a transition, trying to regain favor with customers as competitors take market share. However, we believe S is making progress, as the company added postpaid subscribers for the first time in several years in the fourth quarter of 2010. We believe the addition of the iPhone will accelerate postpaid subscriber growth, as well as a better network as Network Vision is rolled out.

➤ Risks to our recommendation and target price include higher capital spending to deploy new services, liquidity issues relating to declining cash flow and debt maturities. Also, increased competition from nationwide peers could lead to delays in subscriber additions.

➤ Our 12-month target price of $5.00 assumes an enterprise value of 5.0X our 2013 EBITDA estimate, slightly below larger-cap telecom peers, to reflect S's subscriber losses, and below smaller pure-play wireless carriers that we think have stronger growth prospects.

---

**Please read the Required Disclosures and Analyst Certification on the last page of this report.**

*The McGraw-Hill Companies*

# Sprint Nextel Corp

**STANDARD
&POOR'S**

## Business Summary November 01, 2011

CORPORATE OVERVIEW. Sprint Nextel, a leading provider of wireless and other telecommunications services, was formed in August 2005 through the merger of Sprint Corp. and Nextel Communications, Inc. The company has a balanced mix of consumer, business and government wireless customers. S spun off the local telephone business to shareholders in May 2006. As of the end of the third quarter of 2011, S provided service to roughly 53.4 million wireless subscribers, with 61% of them direct post-paid customers, while 27% were prepaid (Boost Mobile and Virgin Mobile), and 12% were wholesale customers. S also generates revenues from wireline voice and data communication services, and services to the cable multiple systems operators that use S's network and back-office capabilities.

COMPETITIVE LANDSCAPE. In most major U.S. metropolitan markets, four national carriers offer competing wireless services to customers along with some regional carriers. Wireless carriers such as S have adjusted to potential substitutes by integrating the service features into the handsets. Until recently, S had a unique service with push-to-talk service through Nextel's iDEN network, but AT&T (formerly Cingular) has launched a competing nationwide service aimed at the consumer segment, in contrast to S's dominant position

with small business and enterprise firms.

Wireless services are very price elastic. For the consumer market, service rate plans have taken on new features such as $9.99 for each family member added to the account. S realized 1.91% post-paid churn in the third quarter of 2011, up from 1.75% in the second quarter, and generated $58 in monthly average revenue per user (ARPU). Prepaid customers had a 4.07% churn rate and generated $27 in ARPU. The company has simplified its pricing with plans that include a $100 plan with unlimited voice, data, text and other features, but includes a $10 extra charge with smartphones. In our view, we believe the focus on unlimited data is a good move that will help change S's image and to better compete. S also provides a $50 unlimited prepaid plan under its Boost Mobile brand on its iDEN and CDMA networks that we believe continues to be very successful.

## Company Financials Fiscal Year Ended Dec. 31

| Per Share Data ($) | 2010 | 2009 | 2008 | 2007 | 2006 | 2005 | 2004 | 2003 | 2002 | 2001 |
|---|---|---|---|---|---|---|---|---|---|---|
| Tangible Book Value | NM | NM | NM | NM | NM | 0.88 | 3.85 | 14.40 | 11.45 | 11.41 |
| Cash Flow | 0.93 | 1.73 | 1.96 | -7.17 | 3.67 | 3.93 | 2.56 | 3.12 | 4.14 | 2.60 |
| Earnings | -1.16 | -0.84 | -0.98 | -10.31 | 0.34 | 0.87 | -0.71 | 0.33 | 1.18 | -0.16 |
| S&P Core Earnings | -1.17 | -0.91 | -0.66 | -0.05 | 0.30 | 0.86 | -0.72 | 1.20 | 1.26 | -0.12 |
| Dividends | Nil | Nil | Nil | 0.10 | 0.13 | 0.30 | 0.50 | 0.50 | 0.50 | 0.50 |
| Payout Ratio | Nil | Nil | Nil | NM | 37% | 34% | NM | 152% | 42% | NM |
| Prices:High | 5.31 | 5.94 | 13.16 | 23.42 | 26.89 | 27.20 | 25.80 | 16.76 | 20.47 | 29.31 |
| Prices:Low | 3.10 | 1.83 | 1.35 | 12.96 | 15.92 | 21.57 | 15.74 | 10.22 | 6.65 | 18.50 |
| P/E Ratio:High | NM | NM | NM | NM | 79 | 31 | NM | 51 | 17 | NM |
| P/E Ratio:Low | NM | NM | NM | NM | 47 | 25 | NM | 31 | 6 | NM |

| Income Statement Analysis (Million $) | | | | | | | | | | |
|---|---|---|---|---|---|---|---|---|---|---|
| Revenue | 32,563 | 32,260 | 35,635 | 40,146 | 41,028 | 34,680 | 27,428 | 14,185 | 15,182 | 16,924 |
| Operating Income | NA | NA | 7,664 | 10,282 | 12,283 | 10,220 | 8,148 | 4,376 | 4,488 | 4,238 |
| Depreciation | 6,248 | 7,416 | 8,396 | 9,023 | 9,592 | 6,269 | 4,720 | 2,519 | 2,645 | 2,449 |
| Interest Expense | 1,429 | 1,416 | 1,362 | 1,433 | 1,533 | 1,351 | 1,248 | 236 | 295 | 57.0 |
| Pretax Income | -3,299 | -3,494 | -4,060 | -29,945 | 1,817 | 2,906 | -1,603 | 434 | 1,453 | -129 |
| Effective Tax Rate | NA | 30.3% | NM | NM | 26.9% | 38.0% | NM | 32.3% | 28.0% | NM |
| Net Income | -3,465 | -2,436 | -2,796 | -29,580 | 1,329 | 1,801 | -1,012 | 294 | 1,046 | -146 |
| S&P Core Earnings | -3,520 | -2,632 | -1,864 | -155 | 849 | 1,772 | -1,036 | 1,096 | 1,132 | -112 |

| Balance Sheet & Other Financial Data (Million $) | | | | | | | | | | |
|---|---|---|---|---|---|---|---|---|---|---|
| Cash | 5,473 | 3,924 | 3,719 | 2,440 | 2,061 | 10,665 | 4,556 | 1,635 | 641 | 134 |
| Current Assets | 9,880 | 8,593 | 8,344 | 8,661 | 10,304 | 19,092 | 9,975 | 4,378 | 3,327 | 3,485 |
| Total Assets | 51,654 | 55,424 | 58,252 | 64,109 | 97,161 | 102,580 | 41,321 | 21,862 | 23,043 | 24,164 |
| Current Liabilities | 7,891 | 6,785 | 6,281 | 9,104 | 9,798 | 14,050 | 6,902 | 2,359 | 4,320 | 6,298 |
| Long Term Debt | 18,535 | 20,293 | 20,992 | 20,469 | 21,011 | Nil | 15,916 | 2,627 | 2,736 | 3,258 |
| Common Equity | 14,546 | 18,095 | 19,605 | 21,999 | 53,131 | 51,937 | 13,521 | 13,372 | 11,814 | 11,704 |
| Total Capital | 34,737 | 39,156 | 47,793 | 51,157 | 84,237 | 52,184 | 29,684 | 17,632 | 16,385 | 16,514 |
| Capital Expenditures | 1,935 | 1,603 | 3,882 | 6,322 | 7,556 | 5,057 | 3,980 | 1,674 | 2,181 | 5,295 |
| Cash Flow | 2,783 | 4,980 | 5,600 | -20,557 | 10,919 | 8,063 | 3,701 | 2,821 | 3,698 | 2,310 |
| Current Ratio | 1.3 | 1.3 | 1.3 | 1.0 | 1.1 | 1.4 | 1.4 | 1.9 | 0.8 | 0.6 |
| % Long Term Debt of Capitalization | 53.4 | 51.8 | 43.9 | 40.0 | 24.9 | Nil | 53.6 | 14.9 | 16.7 | 19.7 |
| % Net Income of Revenue | NM | NM | NM | NM | 3.2 | 5.2 | NM | 2.1 | 6.9 | NM |
| % Return on Assets | NM | NM | NM | NM | 1.3 | 2.5 | NM | 1.3 | 4.4 | NM |
| % Return on Equity | NM | NM | NM | NM | 2.5 | 5.5 | NM | 2.3 | 8.8 | NM |

Data as orig reptd.; bef. results of disc opers/spec. items. Per share data adj. for stk. divs.; EPS diluted. E-Estimated. NA-Not Available. NM-Not Meaningful. NR-Not Ranked. UR-Under Review.

**Office:** 6200 Sprint Pkwy, Overland Park, KS 66251-6117.
**Telephone:** 800-829-0965.
**Email:** investorrelation.sprintcom@mail.sprint.com
**Website:** http://www.sprint.com

**Chrmn:** J.H. Hance, Jr.
**Pres & CEO:** D.R. Hesse
**SVP, Secy & General Counsel:** C.R. Wunsch
**CFO:** J.J. Euteneuer

**CTO:** R.H. Johnson
**Board Members:** R. R. Bennett, G. M. Bethune, L. C. Glasscock, J. H. Hance, Jr., D. R. Hesse, V. J. Hill, F. Ianna, S. Nilsson, W. R. Nuti, R. O'Neal

**Founded:** 1925
**Domicile:** Kansas
**Employees:** 40,000

The **McGraw·Hill** Companies

# Stanley Black & Decker Inc

**STANDARD &POOR'S**

| S&P Recommendation | BUY ★★★★☆ | Price $60.23 (as of Nov 25, 2011) | 12-Mo. Target Price $83.00 | Investment Style Large-Cap Blend |
|---|---|---|---|---|

**GICS Sector** Industrials
**Sub-Industry** Industrial Machinery

**Summary** This diversified global provider of hand tools, power tools and related accessories and systems resulted from the March 2010 merger of Stanley Works and Black & Decker.

## Key Stock Statistics (Source S&P, Vickers, company reports)

| | | | | | | | |
|---|---|---|---|---|---|---|---|
| 52-Wk Range | $78.19–47.07 | S&P Oper. EPS 2011**E** | 5.20 | Market Capitalization(B) | $10.173 | Beta | 1.36 |
| Trailing 12-Month EPS | $3.80 | S&P Oper. EPS 2012**E** | 6.05 | Yield (%) | 2.72 | S&P 3-Yr. Proj. EPS CAGR(%) | 15 |
| Trailing 12-Month P/E | 15.9 | P/E on S&P Oper. EPS 2011**E** | 11.6 | Dividend Rate/Share | $1.64 | S&P Credit Rating | A |
| $10K Invested 5 Yrs Ago | $13,368 | Common Shares Outstg. (M) | 168.9 | Institutional Ownership (%) | 89 | | |

## Price Performance

30-Week Mov. Avg. · · · 10-Week Mov. Avg. – – GAAP Earnings vs. Previous Year  Volume Above Avg. STARS
12-Mo. Target Price — Relative Strength — ▲ Up ▼ Down ► No Change  Below Avg. ★

Options: P

Analysis prepared by Equity Analyst **Michael Jaffe** on Oct 27, 2011, when the stock traded at **$65.75**.

## Highlights

➤ We look for revenues to increase by 9% in 2012. This projection is based on our outlook for modest organic revenue growth, the full-year inclusion of Niscayah Group AB (acquired in September 2011), and revenue synergies following the merger of the legacy operations of Stanley Works and Black & Decker. We see the largest proportion of our organic revenue growth forecast coming from the Industrial Tools segment, on new product launches and strength in emerging markets.

➤ We see operating margins widening in 2012 on the higher sales volumes that we see and cost savings from the mergers with Black & Decker and Niscayah. The Black & Decker transaction is expected to bring $115 million in incremental cost synergies in 2012, while cost synergies from Niscayah are expected to total $45 million, for combined accretion of $0.70 a share.

➤ Our EPS forecast of $6.05 in 2012 compares with our operating EPS forecast of $5.20 in 2011, which excludes $0.90 a share of charges in the first nine months of the year, mostly from employee severance, facility closures and restructuring from acquisitions.

## Investment Rationale/Risk

➤ We are positive on SWK's ability to manage its diversified businesses. While the company is reducing manufacturing plant capacity and staffing, we believe it is well positioned to gain market share in its three customer markets as the global economy recovers and the company benefits from recent acquisitions.

➤ Risks to our recommendation and target price include a renewed downturn in global economies, and lower-than-projected revenue and expense synergies from recent acquisitions.

➤ The shares recently traded at about 10X our 2012 EPS forecast, at the low end of their range of the past decade. Despite economic uncertainties, we think the company is well positioned to continue posting gains in sales and profits. We think it will particularly benefit from what we view as its well reasoned business combinations of recent years, which we see greatly boosting earnings. Based on these factors, our 12-month target price is $83, or 13.7X our 2012 estimate, and closer to the middle of SWK's range during years of earnings growth.

## Qualitative Risk Assessment

| LOW | MEDIUM | HIGH |
|---|---|---|

Our risk assessment takes into account our positive view of SWK's strong brand names and solid competitive position, offset by our negative view of industry cyclicality.

## Quantitative Evaluations

**S&P Quality Ranking**  B+

| D | C | B- | B | B+ | A- | A | A+ |
|---|---|---|---|---|---|---|---|

**Relative Strength Rank**  MODERATE
67
LOWEST = 1    HIGHEST = 99

## Revenue/Earnings Data

**Revenue (Million $)**

| | 1Q | 2Q | 3Q | 4Q | Year |
|---|---|---|---|---|---|
| 2011 | 2,381 | 2,623 | 2,636 | -- | -- |
| 2010 | 1,262 | 2,366 | 2,369 | 2,413 | 8,410 |
| 2009 | 913.0 | 919.2 | 935.5 | 969.4 | 3,737 |
| 2008 | 1,097 | 1,154 | 1,120 | 1,086 | 4,426 |
| 2007 | 1,062 | 1,123 | 1,131 | 1,167 | 4,484 |
| 2006 | 968.7 | 1,018 | 1,013 | 1,019 | 4,019 |

**Earnings Per Share ($)**

| | | | | | |
|---|---|---|---|---|---|
| 2011 | 0.92 | 1.14 | 0.92 | E1.32 | E5.20 |
| 2010 | -1.11 | 0.28 | 0.73 | 0.81 | 1.32 |
| 2009 | 0.48 | 0.89 | 0.77 | -- | 2.82 |
| 2008 | 0.85 | 0.95 | 0.98 | 0.07 | 2.82 |
| 2007 | 0.80 | 1.01 | 1.09 | 1.11 | 4.00 |
| 2006 | 0.45 | 0.90 | 1.09 | 1.04 | 3.47 |

Fiscal year ended Dec. 31. Next earnings report expected: Late January. EPS Estimates based on S&P Operating Earnings; historical GAAP earnings are as reported.

## Dividend Data (Dates: mm/dd Payment Date: mm/dd/yy)

| Amount ($) | Date Decl. | Ex-Div. Date | Stk. of Record | Payment Date |
|---|---|---|---|---|
| 0.410 | 02/15 | 02/28 | 03/02 | 03/22/11 |
| 0.410 | 04/19 | 05/27 | 06/01 | 06/21/11 |
| 0.410 | 07/15 | 08/31 | 09/02 | 09/20/11 |
| 0.410 | 10/13 | 11/30 | 12/02 | 12/13/11 |

Dividends have been paid since 1877. Source: Company reports.

# Stanley Black & Decker Inc

**STANDARD &POOR'S**

## Business Summary October 27, 2011

CORPORATE OVERVIEW. Stanley Black & Decker, the result of the March 2010 merger of Stanley Works and Black & Decker, is a diversified global provider of hand tools, power tools and related accessories, mechanical access solutions and electronic security solutions, engineered fastening systems, and more. The company offers a broad line of hand tools and has many well-known brands. The company's operations are classified into three business segments: Construction & Do-it-Yourself (CDIY, 53% of 2010 sales); Industrial Tools (22%); and Security Solutions (25%).

MARKET PROFILE. The CDIY segment manufactures and markets hand tools, mechanical and electrical tools, lawn and garden products, portable power products, plumbing products, storage systems, and other hardware. Products are distributed directly to retailers (including home centers, mass merchants, hardware stores, and retail lumber yards) as well as third-party distributors, and include measuring instruments, hammers, knives and blades, screwdrivers, sockets and tool boxes. Among the company's brands in this segment are Stanley, Bostitch, Bailey, Powerlock, FatMax, Black & Decker, DeWalt, DustBuster, and Pfister.

The Industrial Tools segment manufactures and markets professional mechanics tools and storage systems, pneumatic tools and fasteners, hydraulic tools and accessories, assembly tools and systems, and electronic measuring tools. Sales are made primarily to industrial and automotive mechanics. Products are distributed primarily through third-party distributors. Brands include Stanley, CRC, MAC, Mac Tools, Proto, Vidmar, Facom, USAG, and Emhart Teknologies.

The Security Solutions segment is a provider of access and security solutions primarily for retailers, educational and health care institutions, government, financial institutions, and commercial and industrial customers. Products include security integration systems, software, related installation and maintenance services, automatic doors, and locking mechanisms, and are sold on a direct sales basis. Brands include Stanley, The Best, Blick, HSM, National, Sargent & Greenleaf, Xmark, Weiser and Baldwin.

## Company Financials Fiscal Year Ended Dec. 31

| Per Share Data ($) | 2010 | 2009 | 2008 | 2007 | 2006 | 2005 | 2004 | 2003 | 2002 | 2001 |
|---|---|---|---|---|---|---|---|---|---|---|
| Tangible Book Value | NM | NM | NM | NM | NM | 4.59 | 3.56 | 2.65 | 5.05 | 7.05 |
| Cash Flow | 6.35 | 5.31 | 5.11 | 5.94 | 4.92 | 4.40 | 4.07 | 2.16 | 2.90 | 2.76 |
| Earnings | 4.12 | 2.82 | 2.82 | 4.00 | 3.47 | 3.18 | 2.85 | 1.14 | 2.10 | 1.81 |
| S&P Core Earnings | 1.24 | 2.88 | 2.63 | 4.08 | 3.57 | 3.16 | 2.49 | 1.12 | 1.43 | 1.30 |
| Dividends | 1.01 | 1.30 | 1.26 | 1.22 | 1.18 | 1.14 | 1.08 | 1.03 | 0.99 | 0.94 |
| Payout Ratio | 25% | 46% | 45% | 30% | 34% | 36% | 38% | 90% | 47% | 52% |
| Prices:High | 67.70 | 53.42 | 52.18 | 64.25 | 54.59 | 51.75 | 49.33 | 37.87 | 52.00 | 46.97 |
| Prices:Low | 48.76 | 22.61 | 24.19 | 47.01 | 41.60 | 41.51 | 36.42 | 20.84 | 27.31 | 28.06 |
| P/E Ratio:High | 16 | 19 | 19 | 16 | 16 | 16 | 17 | 33 | 25 | 26 |
| P/E Ratio:Low | 12 | 8 | 9 | 12 | 12 | 13 | 13 | 18 | 13 | 16 |

### Income Statement Analysis (Million $)

| | 2010 | 2009 | 2008 | 2007 | 2006 | 2005 | 2004 | 2003 | 2002 | 2001 |
|---|---|---|---|---|---|---|---|---|---|---|
| Revenue | 8,410 | 3,737 | 4,426 | 4,484 | 4,019 | 3,285 | 3,043 | 2,678 | 2,594 | 2,624 |
| Operating Income | 1,229 | 564 | 747 | 800 | 567 | 493 | 513 | 342 | 360 | 412 |
| Depreciation | 335 | 200 | 183 | 162 | 121 | 96.5 | 95.0 | 86.5 | 71.2 | 82.9 |
| Interest Expense | 101 | 63.7 | 82.0 | 85.2 | 69.3 | 40.4 | 38.6 | 34.2 | 28.5 | 18.9 |
| Pretax Income | 776 | 283 | 301 | 451 | 367 | 358 | 329 | 133 | 273 | 237 |
| Effective Tax Rate | NA | 19.7% | 25.2% | 25.4% | 20.8% | 24.1% | 27.0% | 27.3% | 32.1% | 33.1% |
| Net Income | 619 | 226 | 225 | 337 | 291 | 272 | 240 | 96.7 | 185 | 158 |
| S&P Core Earnings | 186 | 232 | 211 | 343 | 299 | 270 | 209 | 94.7 | 127 | 113 |

### Balance Sheet & Other Financial Data (Million $)

| | 2010 | 2009 | 2008 | 2007 | 2006 | 2005 | 2004 | 2003 | 2002 | 2001 |
|---|---|---|---|---|---|---|---|---|---|---|
| Cash | 1,745 | 401 | 212 | 240 | 177 | 658 | 250 | 204 | 122 | 115 |
| Current Assets | 4,701 | 1,412 | 1,499 | 1,768 | 1,639 | 1,826 | 1,372 | 1,201 | 1,190 | 1,141 |
| Total Assets | 15,041 | 4,773 | 4,879 | 4,780 | 3,935 | 3,545 | 2,851 | 2,424 | 2,418 | 2,056 |
| Current Liabilities | 2,628 | 1,192 | 1,197 | 1,278 | 1,251 | 875 | 819 | 754 | 681 | 826 |
| Long Term Debt | 3,018 | 1,085 | 1,420 | 1,212 | 679 | 895 | 482 | 535 | 564 | 197 |
| Common Equity | 7,017 | 1,985 | 1,688 | 1,729 | 1,552 | 1,946 | 1,388 | 1,032 | 1,165 | 844 |
| Total Capital | 10,088 | 3,095 | 3,121 | 3,022 | 2,298 | 2,925 | 1,960 | 1,567 | 1,729 | 1,041 |
| Capital Expenditures | 186 | 93.4 | 141 | 65.5 | 59.6 | 53.3 | 47.6 | 31.4 | 37.2 | 55.7 |
| Cash Flow | 954 | 427 | 408 | 499 | 412 | 368 | 335 | 183 | 256 | 241 |
| Current Ratio | 1.8 | 1.2 | 1.3 | 1.4 | 1.3 | 2.1 | 1.7 | 1.6 | 1.7 | 1.4 |
| % Long Term Debt of Capitalization | 29.9 | 35.1 | 45.7 | 40.1 | 29.6 | 30.6 | 24.6 | 34.1 | 32.6 | 18.9 |
| % Net Income of Revenue | 7.4 | 6.0 | 5.1 | 7.5 | 7.2 | 8.3 | 7.9 | 3.6 | 7.1 | 6.0 |
| % Return on Assets | 6.3 | 4.7 | 4.7 | 7.7 | 7.8 | 8.5 | 9.1 | 4.0 | 8.3 | 8.0 |
| % Return on Equity | 13.8 | 12.3 | 13.2 | 20.5 | 19.4 | 14.4 | 19.8 | 8.8 | 16.9 | 20.0 |

Data as orig reptd.; bef. results of disc opers/spec. items. Per share data adj. for stk. divs.; EPS diluted. E-Estimated. NA-Not Available. NM-Not Meaningful. NR-Not Ranked. UR-Under Review.

**Office:** 1000 Stanley Drive, New Britain, CT 06053.
**Telephone:** 860-225-5111.
**Website:** http://www.stanleyblackanddecker.com/
**Chrmn:** N.D. Archibald

**Pres & CEO:** J.F. Lundgren
**COO:** J.M. Loree
**CFO:** D. Allan, Jr.
**Chief Acctg Officer:** J.S. Belisle

**Investor Contact:** K.W. Vanek (860-827-3833)
**Board Members:** N. D. Archibald, J. G. Breen, G. W. Buckley, P. D. Campbell, C. M. Cardoso, V. W. Colbert, R. B. Coutts, M. A. Fernandez, B. H. Griswold, IV, E. S. Kraus, A. Luiso, J. F. Lundgren, M. M. Parrs, R. L. Ryan, L. Zimmerman

**Founded:** 1843
**Domicile:** Connecticut
**Employees:** 36,700

**The McGraw·Hill Companies**

# Staples Inc

STANDARD
&POOR'S

| S&P Recommendation | BUY ★★★★☆ | Price | 12-Mo. Target Price | Investment Style |
|---|---|---|---|---|
| | | $13.68 (as of Nov 25, 2011) | $20.00 | Large-Cap Growth |

**GICS Sector** Consumer Discretionary
**Sub-Industry** Specialty Stores

**Summary** This leading operator of office products superstores has about 2,300 units in the U.S. and internationally.

## Key Stock Statistics (Source S&P, Vickers, company reports)

| | | | | | | | |
|---|---|---|---|---|---|---|---|
| 52-Wk Range | $23.75–11.94 | S&P Oper. EPS 2012E | 1.38 | Market Capitalization(B) | $9.568 | Beta | 0.85 |
| Trailing 12-Month EPS | $1.37 | S&P Oper. EPS 2013E | 1.54 | Yield (%) | 2.92 | S&P 3-Yr. Proj. EPS CAGR(%) | 12 |
| Trailing 12-Month P/E | 10.0 | P/E on S&P Oper. EPS 2012E | 9.9 | Dividend Rate/Share | $0.40 | S&P Credit Rating | BBB |
| $10K Invested 5 Yrs Ago | $5,765 | Common Shares Outstg. (M) | 699.4 | Institutional Ownership (%) | 91 | | |

## Price Performance

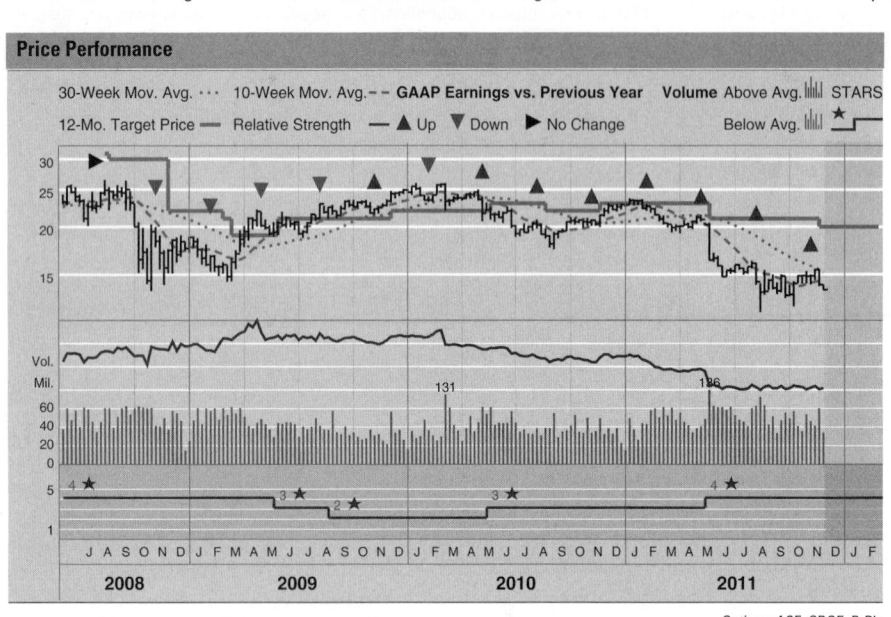

30-Week Mov. Avg. · · · 10-Week Mov. Avg. - - GAAP Earnings vs. Previous Year Volume Above Avg. STARS
12-Mo. Target Price — Relative Strength — ▲ Up ▼ Down ▶ No Change Below Avg. ★

Options: ASE, CBOE, P, Ph

Analysis prepared by Equity Analyst **Michael Souers** on Nov 21, 2011, when the stock traded at **$14.01**.

## Qualitative Risk Assessment

| LOW | MEDIUM | HIGH |
|---|---|---|

Our risk assessment reflects the cyclicality of the company's business, which relies on consumer as well as business spending and investments in emerging markets for future growth. This is offset by untapped growth areas in major domestic metro markets.

## Quantitative Evaluations

**S&P Quality Ranking** B+

| D | C | B- | B | B+ | A- | A | A+ |
|---|---|---|---|---|---|---|---|

**Relative Strength Rank** MODERATE

49

LOWEST = 1     HIGHEST = 99

## Revenue/Earnings Data

**Revenue (Million $)**

| | 1Q | 2Q | 3Q | 4Q | Year |
|---|---|---|---|---|---|
| 2012 | 6,173 | 5,820 | 6,570 | -- | -- |
| 2011 | 6,058 | 5,534 | 6,538 | 6,415 | 24,545 |
| 2010 | 5,818 | 5,534 | 6,518 | 6,406 | 24,275 |
| 2009 | 4,885 | 5,075 | 6,951 | 6,174 | 23,084 |
| 2008 | 4,589 | 4,290 | 5,168 | 5,324 | 19,373 |
| 2007 | 4,238 | 3,881 | 4,757 | 5,286 | 18,161 |

**Earnings Per Share ($)**

| | | | | | |
|---|---|---|---|---|---|
| 2012 | 0.28 | 0.25 | 0.47 | E0.42 | E1.38 |
| 2011 | 0.26 | 0.18 | 0.41 | 0.38 | 1.21 |
| 2010 | 0.20 | 0.13 | 0.37 | 0.32 | 1.02 |
| 2009 | 0.30 | 0.21 | 0.22 | 0.40 | 1.13 |
| 2008 | 0.29 | 0.21 | 0.38 | 0.47 | 1.38 |
| 2007 | 0.25 | 0.22 | 0.39 | 0.46 | 1.32 |

Fiscal year ended Jan. 31. Next earnings report expected: Early March. EPS Estimates based on S&P Operating Earnings; historical GAAP earnings are as reported.

## Highlights

➤ We see sales growth of 3.5% in FY 13 (Jan.), following our projection of a 2.3% rise in FY 12. We expect this growth to be driven by the opening of about 20 net new stores in North America, continued international penetration, and 1%-2% same-store sales growth in North American Retail. We look for customer traffic to increase slightly, along with a minor increase in average ticket. We also project marginal improvement in the contract business as customers react to a gradual economic recovery.

➤ We expect a slight widening of gross margins in FY 13, with a growing private label business, supply chain initiatives and lower sourcing costs. We see operating margins widening slightly, as continued cost synergies from the Corporate Express acquisition are only partially offset by fixed expense deleveraging from meager same-store sales growth.

➤ We project a 2%-3% reduction in the diluted share count related to share repurchases, and a tax rate of 34%. We see FY 13 EPS of $1.54, a 12% improvement from the $1.38 we expect the company to earn in FY 12, which excludes a $0.03 gain related to a tax benefit.

## Investment Rationale/Risk

➤ We continue to favor SPLS's management, strong balance sheet, significant free cash flow generation and cost synergies from the Corporate Express acquisition that should accrue over the next few years. We also anticipate strong results for SPLS's North American Delivery division over the longer term, although we have been surprised by the severity of the recent slowdown. While we think the office supply industry is extremely mature, with limited long-term growth potential, we believe SPLS will continue to capture market share from peers. We think the shares are attractively valued, trading at about 9X our FY 13 EPS estimate, a modest discount to the S&P 500.

➤ Risks to our recommendation and target price include a double-dip recession and weaker-than-expected capital spending and hiring by businesses. International risks include unfavorable currency movements and debt contagion fears.

➤ Our 12-month target price of $20, about 13X our FY 13 EPS projection, is derived from our discounted cash flow model, which assumes a weighted average cost of capital of 10.0% and a terminal growth rate of 3.0%.

## Dividend Data (Dates: mm/dd Payment Date: mm/dd/yy)

| Amount ($) | Date Decl. | Ex-Div. Date | Stk. of Record | Payment Date |
|---|---|---|---|---|
| 0.090 | 12/07 | 12/21 | 12/23 | 01/13/11 |
| 0.100 | 03/08 | 03/23 | 03/25 | 04/14/11 |
| 0.100 | 06/07 | 06/22 | 06/24 | 07/14/11 |
| 0.100 | 09/13 | 09/21 | 09/23 | 10/13/11 |

Dividends have been paid since 2004. Source: Company reports.

---

**Please read the Required Disclosures and Analyst Certification on the last page of this report.**

The McGraw-Hill Companies

# Staples Inc

STANDARD &POOR'S

## Business Summary November 21, 2011

CORPORATE OVERVIEW. Staples is the world's leading office products company, with net sales of over $24.5 billion in FY 11 (Jan.). Staples operates in three segments: North American Delivery (39% of total revenues in FY 11); North American Retail (39%); and International Operations (21%). Sales by product line: office supplies and services 49%; business machines and related products 31%; computers and related products 15%; and office furniture 5%.

At January 29, 2011, SPLS operated 2,281 superstores, mostly in the United States (1,575 stores) and Canada (325 stores), but also in a number of other countries, including: the U.K. (139), Germany (59), the Netherlands (47), Portugal (35), China (28), Norway (21), Australia (19), Sweden (18), Finland (7), Belgium (6) and Argentina (2).

SPLS has approximately 8,000 stock-keeping units (SKUs) stocked in each of its typical North American retail stores and approximately 15,000 SKUs stocked in its North American Delivery fulfillment centers. On Staples.com,

the company's Internet site, approximately 50,000 SKUs are available to customers.

CORPORATE STRATEGY. Staples seeks to maintain its leadership position in the office products industry by differentiating itself from the competition, delivering industry-best execution and expanding its market share. In FY 11, it added 41 new stores in North America, filling in existing markets along with expansion into untapped metro markets. A few of the new stores were stand-alone copy and print shops, which average 4,000 square feet with 1,800 SKUs in supplies. We believe significant growth opportunities remain in other metropolitan markets where SPLS has yet to venture, and we expect the company to establish a strong Midwest presence over the next several years.

## Company Financials Fiscal Year Ended Jan. 31

| Per Share Data ($) | 2011 | 2010 | 2009 | 2008 | 2007 | 2006 | 2005 | 2004 | 2003 | 2002 |
|---|---|---|---|---|---|---|---|---|---|---|
| Tangible Book Value | 3.26 | 2.89 | 1.51 | 5.28 | 4.64 | 3.84 | 3.45 | 3.01 | 1.74 | 2.63 |
| Cash Flow | 1.91 | 1.79 | 1.90 | 1.92 | 1.78 | 1.56 | 1.33 | 1.03 | 1.01 | 0.73 |
| Earnings | 1.21 | 1.02 | 1.13 | 1.38 | 1.32 | 1.12 | 0.93 | 0.66 | 0.63 | 0.42 |
| S&P Core Earnings | 1.19 | 1.06 | 1.20 | 1.42 | 1.32 | 1.05 | 0.88 | 0.61 | 0.58 | 0.32 |
| Dividends | NA | 0.33 | 0.33 | 0.22 | 0.17 | 0.17 | 0.13 | Nil | Nil | Nil |
| Payout Ratio | NA | 32% | 29% | 16% | 13% | 15% | 14% | Nil | Nil | Nil |
| Calendar Year | 2010 | 2009 | 2008 | 2007 | 2006 | 2005 | 2004 | 2003 | 2002 | 2001 |
| Prices:High | 26.00 | 25.10 | 26.57 | 27.66 | 28.00 | 24.14 | 22.57 | 18.58 | 14.97 | 12.97 |
| Prices:Low | 17.45 | 14.35 | 13.57 | 19.69 | 21.08 | 18.64 | 15.79 | 10.49 | 7.79 | 7.35 |
| P/E Ratio:High | 21 | 25 | 24 | 20 | 21 | 22 | 24 | 28 | 24 | 31 |
| P/E Ratio:Low | 14 | 14 | 12 | 14 | 16 | 17 | 17 | 16 | 12 | 17 |

### Income Statement Analysis (Million $)

| | 2011 | 2010 | 2009 | 2008 | 2007 | 2006 | 2005 | 2004 | 2003 | 2002 |
|---|---|---|---|---|---|---|---|---|---|---|
| Revenue | 24,545 | 24,275 | 23,084 | 19,373 | 18,161 | 16,079 | 14,448 | 13,181 | 11,596 | 10,744 |
| Operating Income | 2,130 | 2,019 | 2,094 | 1,975 | 1,802 | 1,617 | 1,405 | 1,081 | 950 | 768 |
| Depreciation | 499 | 552 | 549 | 389 | 339 | 304 | 279 | 283 | 267 | 249 |
| Interest Expense | 215 | 237 | 150 | 38.3 | 47.8 | 56.8 | 39.9 | 20.2 | 20.6 | 27.2 |
| Pretax Income | 1,357 | 1,156 | 1,243 | 1,554 | 1,471 | 1,314 | 1,116 | 778 | 662 | 431 |
| Effective Tax Rate | NA | 34.5% | 34.5% | 36.0% | 33.8% | 36.5% | 36.5% | 37.0% | 32.6% | 38.5% |
| Net Income | 889 | 739 | 805 | 996 | 974 | 834 | 708 | 490 | 446 | 265 |
| S&P Core Earnings | 869 | 766 | 857 | 1,020 | 974 | 784 | 667 | 450 | 413 | 221 |

### Balance Sheet & Other Financial Data (Million $)

| | 2011 | 2010 | 2009 | 2008 | 2007 | 2006 | 2005 | 2004 | 2003 | 2002 |
|---|---|---|---|---|---|---|---|---|---|---|
| Cash | 1,461 | 1,416 | 634 | 1,272 | 1,018 | 978 | 997 | 457 | 596 | 395 |
| Current Assets | 6,468 | 6,175 | 5,730 | 4,555 | 4,431 | 4,145 | 3,782 | 3,479 | 2,717 | 2,403 |
| Total Assets | 13,912 | 13,717 | 13,006 | 9,036 | 8,397 | 7,677 | 7,071 | 6,503 | 5,721 | 4,093 |
| Current Liabilities | 4,294 | 3,782 | 4,778 | 2,610 | 2,788 | 2,480 | 2,197 | 2,123 | 2,175 | 1,596 |
| Long Term Debt | 2,014 | 2,500 | 1,969 | 342 | 569 | 528 | 558 | 567 | 732 | 350 |
| Common Equity | 6,944 | 6,772 | 5,564 | 5,718 | 5,022 | 4,425 | 4,115 | 3,663 | 2,659 | 2,054 |
| Total Capital | 9,560 | 9,423 | 7,591 | 6,094 | 5,600 | 4,963 | 4,696 | 4,230 | 3,441 | 2,411 |
| Capital Expenditures | 409 | 313 | 378 | 470 | 528 | 456 | 335 | 278 | 265 | 340 |
| Cash Flow | 1,387 | 1,291 | 1,354 | 1,385 | 1,313 | 1,138 | 987 | 773 | 713 | 514 |
| Current Ratio | 1.5 | 1.6 | 1.2 | 1.8 | 1.6 | 1.7 | 1.7 | 1.6 | 1.2 | 1.5 |
| % Long Term Debt of Capitalization | 21.1 | 26.5 | 25.9 | 5.6 | 10.2 | 10.6 | 11.9 | 13.4 | 21.3 | 14.5 |
| % Net Income of Revenue | 3.6 | 3.0 | 3.5 | 5.1 | 5.4 | 5.2 | 4.9 | 3.7 | 3.8 | 2.5 |
| % Return on Assets | 6.4 | 5.5 | 7.3 | 11.4 | 12.1 | 11.3 | 10.4 | 8.0 | 9.1 | 6.6 |
| % Return on Equity | 13.0 | 12.0 | 14.3 | 18.5 | 20.5 | 19.5 | 18.2 | 15.5 | 18.9 | 13.9 |

Data as orig reptd.; bef. results of disc opers/spec. items. Per share data adj. for stk. divs.; EPS diluted. E-Estimated. NA-Not Available. NM-Not Meaningful. NR-Not Ranked. UR-Under Review.

**Office:** Five Hundred Staples Dr, Framingham , MA 01702.
**Telephone:** 508-253-5000.
**Email:** investor@staples.com
**Website:** http://www.staples.com

**Chrmn & CEO:** R.L. Sargent
**Pres & COO:** M.A. Miles, Jr.
**SVP, Chief Acctg Officer & Cntlr:** C.T. Komola
**CFO:** J.J. Mahoney, Jr.

**Treas:** L. Scopa
**Investor Contact:** N. Hotchkin (800-468-7751)
**Board Members:** B. L. Anderson, A. M. Blank, M. E. Burton, J. M. King, C. M. Meyrowitz, R. T. Moriarty, R. C. Nakasone, R. L. Sargent, E. A. Smith, R. E. Sulentic, V. Vishwanath, P. F. Walsh

**Founded:** 1985
**Domicile:** Delaware
**Employees:** 89,019

# Starbucks Corp

**STANDARD &POOR'S**

| S&P Recommendation | HOLD ★★★★★ | Price $40.84 (as of Nov 25, 2011) | 12-Mo. Target Price $46.00 | Investment Style Large-Cap Growth |
|---|---|---|---|---|

**GICS Sector** Consumer Discretionary
**Sub-Industry** Restaurants

**Summary** Starbucks is the world's leading coffee roaster and retailer of high-quality coffee products, which it sells through its approximately 16,850 retail stores globally, as well as increasingly through multiple retail channels.

## Key Stock Statistics (Source S&P, Vickers, company reports)

| | | | | | | | |
|---|---|---|---|---|---|---|---|
| 52-Wk Range | $44.70–30.14 | S&P Oper. EPS 2012E | 1.77 | Market Capitalization(B) | $30.430 | Beta | 1.19 |
| Trailing 12-Month EPS | $1.62 | S&P Oper. EPS 2013E | NA | Yield (%) | 1.67 | S&P 3-Yr. Proj. EPS CAGR(%) | 14 |
| Trailing 12-Month P/E | 25.2 | P/E on S&P Oper. EPS 2012E | 23.1 | Dividend Rate/Share | $0.68 | S&P Credit Rating | BBB+ |
| $10K Invested 5 Yrs Ago | $11,578 | Common Shares Outstg. (M) | 745.1 | Institutional Ownership (%) | 78 | | |

## Price Performance

30-Week Mov. Avg. · · · 10-Week Mov. Avg. – – GAAP Earnings vs. Previous Year  Volume Above Avg. STARS
12-Mo. Target Price — Relative Strength — ▲ Up ▼ Down ▶ No Change   Below Avg.

Options: ASE, CBOE, P, Ph

Analysis prepared by Equity Analyst **Jim Yin, CFA** on Nov 08, 2011, when the stock traded at **$44.36.**

## Highlights

➤ We expect total revenues to rise 11% in FY 12 (Sep.), following a 9.3% increase in FY 11, driven by same-store sales growth of 7%. We believe the company is benefiting from its initiatives to revitalize the brand. In addition, we think its customers, who are comprised of more affluent people, have been less affected by the economy. We see incremental growth from increased sales of its Consumer Products Group, due to the launch of Starbucks-branded K-Cups through multiple channels. We project 800 new store openings in FY 12.

➤ We estimate that GAAP operating margins will widen to 15.5% in FY 12, from 14.5% in FY 11, reflecting our view that food and other commodity inflation will decelerate somewhat in the second half of FY 12. Still, we see food prices rising at a mid-single digit rate in FY 12. We think higher food input costs will be partially offset by modest price hikes. We also see gains in operating margins due to economies of scale.

➤ We expect GAAP EPS of $1.77 in FY 12, up from $1.62 in FY 11.

## Investment Rationale/Risk

➤ We think the company's revitalization agenda is on the right track, and that the restructuring and cost cutting of FY 09 and FY 10 have resulted in a material improvement in fundamentals, with positive trends seen continuing through FY 12. Plans to offer Keurig K-Cup products by fall 2011 are also encouraging to us. Additionally, we think international opportunities should help drive further top-line growth, while POS upgrades and better labor management should lead to further operating margin improvements.

➤ Risks to our recommendation and target price include a weaker than anticipated impact from the company's revitalization initiatives on customer traffic, lower cost savings from restructuring initiatives, and higher than expected pricing for commodity items such as coffee.

➤ Our 12-month target price of $46 is based on our relative P/E analysis. We use an above peer average multiple of 26X applied to our FY 12 EPS estimate of $1.77, reflecting our view of SBUX's improved near-term prospects.

## Qualitative Risk Assessment

| LOW | MEDIUM | HIGH |
|---|---|---|

Our risk assessment reflects uncertainties of ongoing steps to reinvigorate the Starbucks brand. We also see a threat from specialty coffee offerings by competitors. Offsetting these concerns, we think the company has significant financial strength, affording it the potential to return to moderate growth. Recent cost cutting has further bolstered the company's finances.

## Quantitative Evaluations

**S&P Quality Ranking**                               B+

| D | C | B- | B | B+ | A- | A | A+ |
|---|---|---|---|---|---|---|---|

**Relative Strength Rank**                          STRONG

77

LOWEST = 1                                        HIGHEST = 99

## Revenue/Earnings Data

**Revenue (Million $)**

| | 1Q | 2Q | 3Q | 4Q | Year |
|---|---|---|---|---|---|
| 2011 | 2,951 | 2,786 | 2,932 | 3,032 | 11,700 |
| 2010 | 2,723 | 2,535 | 2,612 | 2,838 | 10,707 |
| 2009 | 2,615 | 2,333 | 2,404 | 2,422 | 9,775 |
| 2008 | 2,768 | 2,526 | 2,574 | 2,515 | 10,383 |
| 2007 | 2,356 | 2,256 | 2,359 | 2,441 | 9,411 |
| 2006 | 1,934 | 1,886 | 1,964 | 2,003 | 7,787 |

**Earnings Per Share ($)**

| | | | | | |
|---|---|---|---|---|---|
| 2011 | 0.45 | 0.34 | 0.36 | 0.47 | 1.62 |
| 2010 | 0.32 | 0.28 | 0.27 | 0.37 | 1.24 |
| 2009 | 0.09 | 0.03 | 0.20 | 0.20 | 0.52 |
| 2008 | 0.28 | 0.15 | -0.01 | 0.01 | 0.43 |
| 2007 | 0.26 | 0.19 | 0.21 | 0.21 | 0.87 |
| 2006 | 0.22 | 0.16 | 0.18 | 0.17 | 0.73 |

Fiscal year ended Sep. 30. Next earnings report expected: NA. EPS Estimates based on S&P Operating Earnings; historical GAAP earnings are as reported.

## Dividend Data (Dates: mm/dd Payment Date: mm/dd/yy)

| Amount ($) | Date Decl. | Ex-Div. Date | Stk. of Record | Payment Date |
|---|---|---|---|---|
| 0.130 | 01/26 | 02/07 | 02/09 | 02/25/11 |
| 0.130 | 04/27 | 05/09 | 05/11 | 05/27/11 |
| 0.130 | 07/28 | 08/08 | 08/10 | 08/26/11 |
| 0.170 | 11/03 | 11/15 | 11/17 | 12/02/11 |

Dividends have been paid since 2010. Source: Company reports.

# Starbucks Corp

**STANDARD &POOR'S**

## Business Summary November 08, 2011

CORPORATE OVERVIEW. The Starbucks brand is nearly synonymous with specialty coffee. However, a slowing economy and over-expansion under prior management led the company, beginning in FY 08 (Sep.) under returning CEO Howard Schultz, to dramatically reduce expansion and begin to evolve the brand.

At October 2, 2011, SBUX owned and operated 6,705 (6,707 as of October 3, 2010) of its stores in the U.S., and 2,326 (2,182) stores in international markets. In FY 11, it closed about 475 Seattle's Best Coffee locations due to the bankruptcy of Borders. Revenues from company-operated stores accounted for 82.3% of total revenues in FY 11 (83.7% in FY 10). Stores are typically clustered in high-traffic, high-visibility locations in each market. In FY 10, the retail store sales mix by product type was 75% beverages, 19% food items, 4% whole bean coffees, and 2% coffee-related hardware items.

There were also 4,082 (4,424 as of October 3, 2010) licensed retail stores in the U.S. and 3,890 (3,545) in international markets at October 2, 2011. Revenue

from retail licensees was approximately 9.7% of total revenues in FY 11 (10.5% in FY 10). The Global Consumer Products Group and a number of foodservice accounts contributed 8.0% of total revenues in FY 11 (5.8% in FY 10).

IMPACT OF MAJOR DEVELOPMENTS. At the time of the January 2008 reappointment of Howard Schultz as CEO, the company outlined a five-point agenda: 1) improve the U.S. business by focusing on the customer experience and other factors affecting store operations; 2) slow the pace of U.S. expansion and close underperforming U.S. locations; 3) re-energize the Starbucks brand and create an emotional connection to the brand with customers and employees; 4) realign and streamline management and back-end functions to better support customer-focused initiatives; and 5) accelerate expansion outside the U.S. and drive profit margins higher at international operations.

## Company Financials Fiscal Year Ended Sep. 30

| Per Share Data ($) | 2011 | 2010 | 2009 | 2008 | 2007 | 2006 | 2005 | 2004 | 2003 | 2002 |
|---|---|---|---|---|---|---|---|---|---|---|
| Tangible Book Value | NA | 4.50 | 3.66 | 2.93 | 2.74 | 2.68 | 2.56 | 3.00 | 2.52 | 2.20 |
| Cash Flow | 2.34 | 1.95 | 1.24 | 1.17 | 1.51 | 1.25 | 1.06 | 0.85 | 0.66 | 0.55 |
| Earnings | 1.62 | 1.24 | 0.52 | 0.43 | 0.87 | 0.73 | 0.61 | 0.48 | 0.34 | 0.27 |
| S&P Core Earnings | 1.53 | 1.24 | 0.53 | 0.44 | 0.86 | 0.73 | 0.53 | 0.42 | 0.29 | 0.23 |
| Dividends | 0.52 | 0.23 | Nil | Nil | Nil | Nil | Nil | Nil | Nil | Nil |
| Payout Ratio | 32% | 19% | Nil | Nil | Nil | Nil | Nil | Nil | Nil | Nil |
| Prices:High | 44.70 | 33.15 | 23.95 | 21.01 | 36.61 | 40.01 | 32.46 | 32.13 | 16.72 | 12.85 |
| Prices:Low | 30.75 | 21.26 | 8.12 | 7.06 | 19.89 | 28.72 | 22.29 | 16.45 | 9.81 | 9.22 |
| P/E Ratio:High | 28 | 27 | 46 | 49 | 42 | 55 | 53 | 68 | 50 | 48 |
| P/E Ratio:Low | 19 | 17 | 16 | 16 | 23 | 39 | 37 | 35 | 29 | 34 |

| Income Statement Analysis (Million $) | 2011 | 2010 | 2009 | 2008 | 2007 | 2006 | 2005 | 2004 | 2003 | 2002 |
|---|---|---|---|---|---|---|---|---|---|---|
| Revenue | 11,700 | 10,707 | 9,775 | 10,383 | 9,411 | 7,787 | 6,369 | 5,294 | 4,076 | 3,289 |
| Operating Income | 2,075 | 1,865 | 1,331 | 1,279 | 1,437 | 1,213 | 1,071 | 854 | 646 | 504 |
| Depreciation | 550 | 541 | 535 | 549 | 491 | 413 | 367 | 305 | 259 | 221 |
| Interest Expense | 33.3 | 32.7 | 42.0 | 60.6 | Nil | Nil | Nil | Nil | Nil | Nil |
| Pretax Income | 1,811 | 1,437 | 559 | 460 | 1,056 | 906 | 796 | 624 | 436 | 341 |
| Effective Tax Rate | NA | NA | 30.1% | 31.3% | 36.3% | 35.8% | 37.9% | 37.2% | 38.5% | 37.0% |
| Net Income | 1,248 | 946 | 391 | 316 | 673 | 581 | 494 | 392 | 268 | 215 |
| S&P Core Earnings | 1,176 | 944 | 399 | 325 | 668 | 579 | 437 | 346 | 231 | 181 |

| Balance Sheet & Other Financial Data (Million $) | 2011 | 2010 | 2009 | 2008 | 2007 | 2006 | 2005 | 2004 | 2003 | 2002 |
|---|---|---|---|---|---|---|---|---|---|---|
| Cash | 2,051 | 1,450 | 666 | 322 | 281 | 313 | 174 | 299 | 201 | 175 |
| Current Assets | 3,795 | 2,756 | 2,036 | 1,748 | 1,696 | 1,530 | 1,209 | 1,368 | 924 | 848 |
| Total Assets | 7,360 | 6,386 | 5,577 | 5,673 | 5,344 | 4,429 | 3,514 | 3,328 | 2,730 | 2,293 |
| Current Liabilities | 2,076 | 1,779 | 1,581 | 2,190 | 2,156 | 1,936 | 1,227 | 783 | 609 | 537 |
| Long Term Debt | 550 | 549 | 549 | 550 | 550 | 1.96 | 2.87 | 3.62 | 4.35 | 5.08 |
| Common Equity | 4,385 | 3,675 | 3,046 | 2,491 | 2,284 | 2,229 | 2,091 | 2,487 | 2,082 | 1,727 |
| Total Capital | 4,939 | 4,232 | 3,595 | 3,059 | 2,834 | 2,230 | 2,094 | 2,537 | 2,120 | 1,754 |
| Capital Expenditures | 532 | 441 | 446 | 984 | 1,080 | 771 | 644 | 386 | 357 | 375 |
| Cash Flow | 1,798 | 1,486 | 926 | 865 | 1,164 | 994 | 862 | 697 | 528 | 436 |
| Current Ratio | 1.8 | 1.6 | 1.3 | 0.8 | 0.8 | 0.8 | 1.0 | 1.7 | 1.5 | 1.6 |
| % Long Term Debt of Capitalization | 11.1 | 13.0 | 15.3 | 18.0 | 19.4 | 0.1 | 0.1 | 0.1 | 0.2 | 0.3 |
| % Net Income of Revenue | 10.7 | 8.8 | 4.0 | 3.0 | 7.1 | 7.5 | 7.8 | 7.4 | 6.6 | 6.5 |
| % Return on Assets | 18.2 | 15.8 | 7.0 | 5.7 | 13.8 | 14.6 | 14.3 | 12.9 | 10.9 | 10.4 |
| % Return on Equity | 31.0 | 28.1 | 14.1 | 13.2 | 29.8 | 26.9 | 21.7 | 17.1 | 14.1 | 13.9 |

Data as orig reptd.; bef. results of disc opers/spec. items. Per share data adj. for stk. divs.; EPS diluted. E-Estimated. NA-Not Available. NM-Not Meaningful. NR-Not Ranked. UR-Under Review.

**Office:** 2401 Utah Avenue South, Seattle, WA 98134-1436.
**Telephone:** 206-447-1575.
**Email:** investorrelations@starbucks.com
**Website:** http://www.starbucks.com

**Chrmn, Pres & CEO:** H.D. Schultz
**EVP, Secy & General Counsel:** P.E. Boggs
**EVP & CIO:** S. Gillett
**CFO, Chief Admin Officer & Chief Acctg Officer:** T. Alstead

**Board Members:** W. W. Bradley, M. L. Hobson, K. R. Johnson, O. C. Lee, J. C. Ramo, S. Sandberg, H. D. Schultz, J. G. Shennan, Jr., J. G. Teruel, M. E. Ullman, III, C. E. Weatherup

**Founded:** 1985
**Domicile:** Washington
**Employees:** 149,000

# Starwood Hotels & Resorts Worldwide Inc.

**STANDARD &POOR'S**

| S&P Recommendation | HOLD ★★★☆☆ | Price | 12-Mo. Target Price | Investment Style |
|---|---|---|---|---|
| | | $43.41 (as of Nov 25, 2011) | $55.00 | Large-Cap Blend |

**GICS Sector** Consumer Discretionary
**Sub-Industry** Hotels, Resorts & Cruise Lines

**Summary** Starwood is one of the world's largest lodging companies, with over 1,000 hotels in approximately 100 countries operating under nine brands.

## Key Stock Statistics (Source S&P, Vickers, company reports)

| | | | | | | | |
|---|---|---|---|---|---|---|---|
| 52-Wk Range | $65.51– 35.78 | S&P Oper. EPS 2011**E** | 1.81 | Market Capitalization(B) | $8.479 | Beta | 2.02 |
| Trailing 12-Month EPS | $3.40 | S&P Oper. EPS 2012**E** | 2.22 | Yield (%) | 1.15 | S&P 3-Yr. Proj. EPS CAGR(%) | 15 |
| Trailing 12-Month P/E | 12.8 | P/E on S&P Oper. EPS 2011**E** | 24.0 | Dividend Rate/Share | $0.50 | S&P Credit Rating | BB+ |
| $10K Invested 5 Yrs Ago | $7,279 | Common Shares Outstg. (M) | 195.3 | Institutional Ownership (%) | 94 | | |

## Price Performance

30-Week Mov. Avg. · · · 10-Week Mov. Avg. – – GAAP Earnings vs. Previous Year    Volume Above Avg. ⅏ STARS
12-Mo. Target Price — Relative Strength — ▲ Up ▽ Down ► No Change    Below Avg. ⅏ ★

Options: CBOE, Ph

Analysis prepared by Equity Analyst **Esther Kwon, CFA** on Oct 31, 2011, when the stock traded at **$51.98**.

## Qualitative Risk Assessment

| LOW | MEDIUM | HIGH |
|---|---|---|

Starwood's financial flexibility was substantially constrained by the industry downturn, but since then its financial condition has improved. This was due in part to its decision to use cash and increase leverage to repurchase just over a quarter of its outstanding shares from 2006 to 2008. During 2009, it sold non-core assets and substantially reduced capital expenditures, enabling it to reduce its net debt position by almost $700 million.

## Quantitative Evaluations

**S&P Quality Ranking**    NR

| D | C | B- | B | B+ | A- | A | A+ |
|---|---|---|---|---|---|---|---|

**Relative Strength Rank**    MODERATE

40

LOWEST = 1    HIGHEST = 99

## Highlights

➤ In 2010, systemwide same-store hotels worldwide RevPAR rose 9.4%, with North America RevPAR up 8.3%. In 2011, we forecast systemwide same-store hotels worldwide RevPAR will increase at a high-single digit rate. We see outsized gains in the Asia/Pacific region, mixed results in Europe, and higher RevPAR in North America. We see vacation ownership revenues rising at a high single digit rate, and management fees, franchise fees, and other income increasing over 13%. Overall, we forecast about a 9% total revenue gain for 2011 and 6% for 2012.

➤ We expect cash operating costs to rise somewhat less than revenues, owing to prior restructuring and asset writedowns, but see HOT investing in higher growth markets while keeping tight control on costs in slower growth developed markets.

➤ With an effective tax rate of approximately 26%, versus 21% in 2010, we estimate EPS will increase to $1.81 in 2011. For 2012, we expect costs to rise to support the growing worldwide portfolio, but at a lower rate than the greater than 6% revenue increase we forecast, resulting in EPS of $2.22, using a similar number of shares outstanding as in 2010 and 2011.

## Investment Rationale/Risk

➤ Although we do not expect the hotel industry to stage a full recovery to pre-2008 levels until some time in 2012, we believe HOT is positioned to disproportionately benefit from stronger international economies, and we expect major metropolitan markets, in which HOT has higher exposure, to outperform. Moreover, we see its premium positioning as a key differentiator. Still, we are cautious in light of recent weak U.S. economic data and sovereign debt turmoil in Europe, which we think will impact corporate investment and travel spending plans.

➤ Risks to our opinion and target price include the potential for industry conditions to improve at a slower rate than we foresee. Capital for some of the unfunded projects in the development pipeline may be less available under a tightening of capital market conditions.

➤ Our 12-month target price of $55 is based on an enterprise value multiple of 11X our 2012 EBITDA projection, which is a discount to Marriott (MAR 33, Hold), despite HOT's greater exposure to international and large metropolitan markets as well as the premium positioning of its properties, and a discount to the large hotel group average.

## Revenue/Earnings Data

**Revenue (Million $)**

| | 1Q | 2Q | 3Q | 4Q | Year |
|---|---|---|---|---|---|
| 2011 | 1,295 | 1,426 | 1,372 | -- | -- |
| 2010 | 1,187 | 1,289 | 1,255 | 1,340 | 5,071 |
| 2009 | 1,091 | 1,190 | 1,192 | 1,283 | 4,712 |
| 2008 | 1,466 | 1,573 | 1,535 | 1,333 | 5,907 |
| 2007 | 1,431 | 1,572 | 1,540 | 1,610 | 6,153 |
| 2006 | 1,441 | 1,505 | 1,461 | 1,572 | 5,979 |

**Earnings Per Share ($)**

| | 1Q | 2Q | 3Q | 4Q | Year |
|---|---|---|---|---|---|
| 2011 | 0.15 | 0.77 | 0.85 | E0.59 | E1.81 |
| 2010 | 0.16 | 0.42 | -0.03 | 1.08 | 1.63 |
| 2009 | 0.04 | 0.78 | 0.20 | -1.03 | Nil |
| 2008 | 0.42 | 0.57 | 0.62 | -0.25 | 1.37 |
| 2007 | 0.56 | 0.67 | 0.61 | 0.74 | 2.57 |
| 2006 | 0.34 | 3.01 | 0.71 | 0.94 | 5.01 |

Fiscal year ended Dec. 31. Next earnings report expected: Early February. EPS Estimates based on S&P Operating Earnings; historical GAAP earnings are as reported.

## Dividend Data (Dates: mm/dd Payment Date: mm/dd/yy)

| Amount ($) | Date Decl. | Ex-Div. Date | Stk. of Record | Payment Date |
|---|---|---|---|---|
| 0.500 | 11/08 | 12/13 | 12/15 | 12/30/11 |

Dividends have been paid since 1995. Source: Company reports.

# Starwood Hotels & Resorts Worldwide Inc.

STANDARD
&POOR'S

## Business Summary October 31, 2011

CORPORATE OVERVIEW. Starwood Hotels & Resorts (HOT) is one of the world's largest hotel companies, with owned, leased, managed or franchised hotels in approximately 100 countries. At December 31, 2010, the company's business included 1,027 hotels, with 302,000 rooms, vs. 992 properties with 298,522 rooms as of December 31, 2009. Of the 1,027 properties, 62 were wholly or majority owned, 463 were managed or operated as a joint venture, and 502 were franchised.

HOT's business includes owned, managed and franchised properties. Its brands include St. Regis (luxury full-service hotels and resorts), The Luxury Collection (luxury full-service hotels and resorts), Westin (luxury and upscale full-service hotels and resorts), Sheraton (full-service hotels and resorts), W (boutique full-service urban hotels) and Four Points (moderately priced full-service hotels). At December 31, 2010, the company's hotel business included 401 Sheratons (141,500 rooms), 181 Westins (71,200 rooms), 97 properties (19,400 rooms) in the St. Regis and Luxury Collection groups, 158 Four Points (27,400 rooms), 38 hotels (11,200 rooms) in the W chain, 100 Le Meridien properties (26,700 rooms), and 46 hotels with 6,800 rooms in HOT's new boutique hotel brand, aloft.

Approximately 67% of management fees in 2010 were generated outside the U.S. The top five international markets as a percentage of total owned hotel revenues were: Canada 10.8%, Italy 7.0%, Spain 5.5%, Mexico 4.1% and Australia 4.1%. Worldwide operating statistics for the 54 owned hotels operating in both 2009 and 2010 were: average daily rate of $196.62 in 2010, up 2.6% from $191.60 in 2009, occupancy of 69.3% vs. 64.0%, and RevPAR of $136.27, up 11.2% from $122.57. In North America: average daily rate was $147.99, up slightly from $147.29; occupancy was 67.4%, up from 62.6% and RevPAR of $99.81, up 8.3% from $92.17 in 2009. In International: average daily rate was $177.08, up 1.4% from $174.68; occupancy rose to 65.5% from 60.0%; and RevPAR jumped 10.6% to $115.90 from $104.75.

In addition, the company had 23 vacation ownership resorts as of December 31, 2010, including 14 stand-alone, eight mixed use and one unconsolidated joint venture.

## Company Financials Fiscal Year Ended Dec. 31

| Per Share Data ($) | 2010 | 2009 | 2008 | 2007 | 2006 | 2005 | 2004 | 2003 | 2002 | 2001 |
|---|---|---|---|---|---|---|---|---|---|---|
| Tangible Book Value | 2.19 | NM | NM | NM | 3.31 | 13.59 | 10.73 | 4.55 | 3.57 | 2.35 |
| Cash Flow | 2.93 | 1.51 | 3.12 | 4.02 | 6.37 | 3.69 | 3.72 | 2.58 | 2.28 | 3.29 |
| Earnings | 1.63 | Nil | 1.37 | 2.57 | 5.01 | 1.88 | 1.72 | 0.51 | 1.20 | 0.73 |
| S&P Core Earnings | 1.34 | 0.36 | 1.31 | 2.69 | 4.87 | 1.66 | 1.37 | 0.12 | 0.77 | 0.52 |
| Dividends | 0.30 | 0.20 | 0.90 | 0.90 | 0.84 | 0.84 | 0.84 | 0.84 | 0.84 | 0.80 |
| Payout Ratio | 18% | NM | 66% | 35% | 17% | 45% | 49% | 165% | 70% | 110% |
| Prices:High | 62.72 | 37.55 | 56.00 | 75.45 | 68.87 | 65.22 | 59.50 | 37.60 | 39.94 | 40.89 |
| Prices:Low | 33.15 | 8.99 | 10.97 | 42.78 | 49.68 | 51.50 | 34.81 | 21.68 | 19.00 | 17.10 |
| P/E Ratio:High | 39 | NM | 41 | 29 | 14 | 35 | 35 | 74 | 33 | 56 |
| P/E Ratio:Low | 20 | NM | 8 | 17 | 10 | 27 | 20 | 43 | 16 | 23 |

| Income Statement Analysis (Million $) | 2010 | 2009 | 2008 | 2007 | 2006 | 2005 | 2004 | 2003 | 2002 | 2001 |
|---|---|---|---|---|---|---|---|---|---|---|
| Revenue | 5,071 | 4,712 | 5,907 | 6,153 | 5,979 | 5,977 | 5,368 | 4,630 | 4,659 | 3,967 |
| Operating Income | 818 | 678 | 1,083 | 1,217 | 1,145 | 1,242 | 1,047 | 1,698 | 1,856 | 1,191 |
| Depreciation | 249 | 273 | 323 | 306 | 306 | 407 | 431 | 429 | 222 | 526 |
| Interest Expense | 238 | 194 | 245 | 215 | 244 | 258 | 257 | 287 | 338 | 369 |
| Pretax Income | 335 | -296 | 330 | 733 | 682 | 642 | 412 | -5.00 | 252 | 200 |
| Effective Tax Rate | NA | 99.0% | 23.0% | 25.8% | NM | 34.1% | 10.4% | NM | 1.59% | 23.0% |
| Net Income | 308 | -1.00 | 254 | 543 | 1,115 | 423 | 369 | 105 | 246 | 151 |
| S&P Core Earnings | 254 | 65.3 | 241 | 570 | 1,084 | 376 | 291 | 27.7 | 157 | 107 |

| Balance Sheet & Other Financial Data (Million $) | 2010 | 2009 | 2008 | 2007 | 2006 | 2005 | 2004 | 2003 | 2002 | 2001 |
|---|---|---|---|---|---|---|---|---|---|---|
| Cash | 753 | 87.0 | 389 | 358 | 183 | 897 | 326 | 508 | 216 | 157 |
| Current Assets | 2,306 | 1,491 | 2,166 | 1,824 | 1,810 | 2,283 | 1,683 | 1,245 | 950 | 897 |
| Total Assets | 9,785 | 8,761 | 9,703 | 9,622 | 9,280 | 12,454 | 12,298 | 11,894 | 12,259 | 12,461 |
| Current Liabilities | 2,189 | 2,027 | 2,688 | 2,101 | 2,461 | 2,879 | 2,128 | 1,644 | 2,199 | 1,587 |
| Long Term Debt | 3,215 | 2,955 | 3,502 | 3,590 | 1,827 | 2,926 | 3,823 | 4,393 | 4,449 | 5,269 |
| Common Equity | 2,471 | 1,824 | 1,621 | 2,076 | 3,008 | 5,211 | 4,788 | 4,326 | 6,357 | 3,756 |
| Total Capital | 5,852 | 4,805 | 5,652 | 5,720 | 4,891 | 8,724 | 9,518 | 9,676 | 11,882 | 10,380 |
| Capital Expenditures | 227 | 196 | 476 | 384 | 371 | 464 | 333 | 307 | 82.0 | 477 |
| Cash Flow | 557 | 272 | 577 | 849 | 1,421 | 830 | 800 | 534 | 468 | 677 |
| Current Ratio | 1.1 | 0.7 | 0.8 | 0.9 | 0.7 | 0.8 | 0.8 | 0.8 | 0.4 | 0.6 |
| % Long Term Debt of Capitalization | 54.9 | 61.5 | 61.9 | 62.8 | 37.4 | 33.5 | 40.2 | 45.4 | 37.4 | 50.8 |
| % Net Income of Revenue | 6.1 | NM | 4.3 | 8.8 | 18.6 | 7.1 | 6.9 | NM | 5.3 | 3.8 |
| % Return on Assets | 3.3 | NM | 2.6 | 5.8 | 10.2 | 3.4 | 3.1 | NM | 2.0 | 1.2 |
| % Return on Equity | 14.3 | NM | 13.7 | 21.4 | 27.1 | 8.5 | 8.1 | NM | 3.9 | 4.0 |

Data as orig reptd.; bef. results of disc opers/spec. items. Per share data adj. for stk. divs.; EPS diluted. E-Estimated. NA-Not Available. NM-Not Meaningful. NR-Not Ranked. UR-Under Review.

**Office:** 1111 Westchester Avenue, White Plains, NY 10604.
**Telephone:** 914-640-8100.
**Website:** http://www.starwoodhotels.com
**Chrmn:** B.W. Duncan

**Pres & CEO:** F. van Paasschen
**Investor Contact:** V.M. Prabhu (914-640-8100)
**Chief Admin Officer, Secy & General Counsel:** K.S. Siegel
**Chief Acctg Officer & Cntlr:** A.M. Schnaid

**Board Members:** A. M. Aron, C. Barshefsky, T. E. Clarke, C. C. Daley, Jr., B. W. Duncan, L. Galbreath, E. C. Hippeau, S. R. Quazzo, T. O. Ryder, K. C. Youngblood, F. van Paasschen

**Founded:** 1969
**Domicile:** Maryland
**Employees:** 145,000

# State Street Corp

STANDARD
&POOR'S

| S&P Recommendation | BUY ★★★★☆ | Price $36.24 (as of Nov 25, 2011) | 12-Mo. Target Price $42.00 | Investment Style Large-Cap Growth |
|---|---|---|---|---|

**GICS Sector** Financials
**Sub-Industry** Asset Management & Custody Banks

**Summary** This bank holding company, with $21.5 trillion in assets under custody, is a leading servicer of financial assets worldwide.

## Key Stock Statistics (Source S&P, Vickers, company reports)

| | | | | | | | |
|---|---|---|---|---|---|---|---|
| 52-Wk Range | $50.26–29.86 | S&P Oper. EPS 2011E | 4.08 | Market Capitalization(B) | $17.828 | Beta | 1.34 |
| Trailing 12-Month EPS | $3.19 | S&P Oper. EPS 2012E | 4.30 | Yield (%) | 1.99 | S&P 3-Yr. Proj. EPS CAGR(%) | 13 |
| Trailing 12-Month P/E | 11.4 | P/E on S&P Oper. EPS 2011E | 8.9 | Dividend Rate/Share | $0.72 | S&P Credit Rating | A+ |
| $10K Invested 5 Yrs Ago | $5,976 | Common Shares Outstg. (M) | 492.0 | Institutional Ownership (%) | 91 | | |

## Price Performance

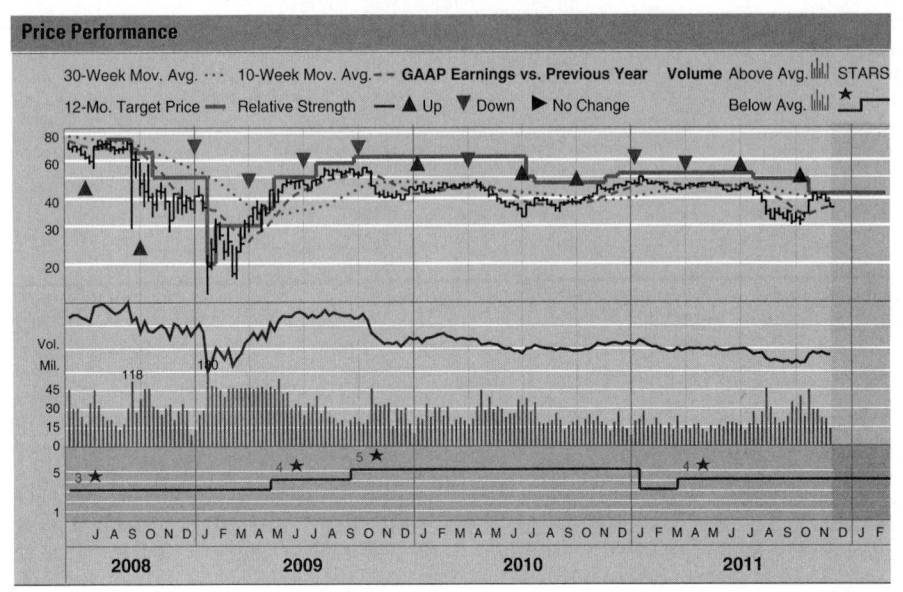

30-Week Mov. Avg. · · · 10-Week Mov. Avg. – – GAAP Earnings vs. Previous Year   Volume Above Avg. STARS
12-Mo. Target Price — Relative Strength ▲ Up ▼ Down ► No Change   Below Avg.

Options: Ph

Analysis prepared by Equity Analyst **Erik Oja** on Nov 02, 2011, when the stock traded at **$40.23**.

## Highlights

► Third-quarter 2011 results showed a revenue increase of 5.1% from the year-earlier quarter. We view positively the strength seen in management fees and securities lending revenue, but as we expected, the net interest margin decreased sequentially by 20 basis points to 1.56%; we project the net interest margin to be stagnant in the short term. We look for assets under management to benefit from a secular shift to passive investing, and we think that operating revenue should rise about 8.0% this year. We see the management fee rate increasing moderately going forward, and expect an increase in trading service revenue to offset a slight decline in net interest income on lower new money yields.

► We expect the operating margin to rise modestly in 2011. In our view, higher compensation ratios and fees associated with regulatory reform and restructuring initiatives will be offset by operating efficiencies, reduced headcount, and other streamlining initiatives.

► We forecast operating EPS of $4.08 in 2011, rising to $4.30 in 2012. Operating earnings exclude the accretion of the discount associated with conduits consolidated on STT's balance sheet.

## Investment Rationale/Risk

► We think that STT is well positioned for earnings growth as we expect strong servicing fee growth to supplement stable net interest revenues. In our view, STT's asset servicing and asset management franchises are strong, and should benefit from strong industry trends. We expect STT to aggressively manage its expenses through headcount reductions as communicated by management on the third-quarter conference call, which should result in positive operating leverage. Further, we think that STT's capital position is the strongest of the trust banks, with an estimated Tier 1 common ratio of 11.7% under Basel III capital requirements. The shares are trading at a sizable discount to their historical average, and we consider STT's valuation attractive based on our view of the firm's strong capital position, share repurchase program, and sound expense management.

► Risks to our recommendation and target price include a slowdown in capital markets, a prolonged period of low interest rates, and adverse litigation.

► Our 12-month target price of $42 is 12X our forward earnings estimate, roughly in line with its peer group.

## Qualitative Risk Assessment

| LOW | MEDIUM | HIGH |
|---|---|---|

Our risk assessment reflects our view of solid fundamentals coupled with a strong customer base, good diversification, healthy earnings growth and higher-than-peers capital ratios, offset by challenges presented by the evolving regulatory environment, and our belief that the securities book is risky.

## Quantitative Evaluations

**S&P Quality Ranking** B+

| D | C | B- | B | B+ | A- | A | A+ |
|---|---|---|---|---|---|---|---|

**Relative Strength Rank** MODERATE

61

LOWEST = 1   HIGHEST = 99

## Revenue/Earnings Data

**Revenue (Million $)**

| | 1Q | 2Q | 3Q | 4Q | Year |
|---|---|---|---|---|---|
| 2011 | 2,361 | 2,491 | 2,427 | -- | -- |
| 2010 | 2,296 | 2,304 | 2,310 | 2,043 | 8,953 |
| 2009 | 2,002 | 2,122 | 2,236 | 2,280 | 8,640 |
| 2008 | 2,577 | 2,672 | 2,771 | 2,673 | 10,693 |
| 2007 | 2,542 | 2,740 | 3,165 | 3,364 | 11,818 |
| 2006 | 2,218 | 2,409 | 2,349 | 2,531 | 9,510 |

**Earnings Per Share ($)**

| | | | | | |
|---|---|---|---|---|---|
| 2011 | 0.93 | 1.00 | 1.10 | E1.05 | E4.08 |
| 2010 | 0.99 | 0.87 | 1.08 | 0.16 | 3.09 |
| 2009 | 1.02 | 0.79 | 0.66 | 1.00 | 3.46 |
| 2008 | 1.35 | 1.35 | 1.09 | 0.54 | 4.30 |
| 2007 | 0.93 | 1.07 | 0.91 | 0.57 | 3.45 |
| 2006 | 0.84 | 0.68 | 0.83 | 0.91 | 3.26 |

Fiscal year ended Dec. 31. Next earnings report expected: Late January. EPS Estimates based on S&P Operating Earnings; historical GAAP earnings are as reported.

## Dividend Data (Dates: mm/dd Payment Date: mm/dd/yy)

| Amount ($) | Date Decl. | Ex-Div. Date | Stk. of Record | Payment Date |
|---|---|---|---|---|
| 0.010 | 12/16 | 12/30 | 01/03 | 01/18/11 |
| 0.180 | 03/18 | 03/30 | 04/01 | 04/15/11 |
| 0.180 | 06/16 | 06/29 | 07/01 | 07/18/11 |
| 0.180 | 09/15 | 09/29 | 10/03 | 10/17/11 |

Dividends have been paid since 1910. Source: Company reports.

The McGraw-Hill Companies

# State Street Corp

**STANDARD
&POOR'S**

## Business Summary November 02, 2011

CORPORATE OVERVIEW. State Street Corp. (STT) is a leading specialist in meeting the needs of institutional investors worldwide. At year-end 2010, STT reported $21.5 trillion of assets under custody and $2.0 trillion of assets under management. Its customers include mutual funds, collective investment funds and other investment pools, corporate and public retirement plans, insurance companies, foundations, endowments and investment managers. STT operates in 26 countries and more than 100 geographic markets worldwide including the U.S., Australia, Austria, Belgium, Canada, the Cayman Islands, Chile, France, Germany, India, Ireland, Italy, Japan, Luxembourg, Mauritius, the Netherlands, New Zealand, China, Singapore, South Africa, South Korea, Switzerland, Taiwan, Thailand, the United Arab Emirates and the United Kingdom.

STT reports two lines of business: Investment Servicing, which accounted for 88% of 2010 total revenues, and Investment Management (12%). Investment Servicing provides services for U.S. mutual funds, collective investment funds and other investment pools, corporate and public retirement plans, insurance companies, foundations and endowments worldwide. Products include custody, product- and participant-level accounting, daily pricing and administration; master trust and master custody; record keeping; foreign exchange, bro-

kerage and other trading services; securities finance; deposit and short-term investment facilities; loans and lease financing; investment manager and hedge fund manager operations outsourcing; and performance, risk and compliance analytics to support institutional investors.

Investment Management offers a broad array of services for managing financial assets, including investment management and investment research services, primarily for institutional investors worldwide. These services include passive and active U.S. and non-U.S. equity and fixed income strategies, and other related services, such as securities finance. Its exchange-traded fund (ETF)family holds onto a second place market share with a little under a quarter of industry assets under management at year-end 2010. We think the secular shift by investors to ETFs in lieu of mutual funds is a sustainable long-term trend, and STT is well positioned to increase assets under management faster than the industry average over the next few years.

## Company Financials Fiscal Year Ended Dec. 31

| Per Share Data ($) | 2010 | 2009 | 2008 | 2007 | 2006 | 2005 | 2004 | 2003 | 2002 | 2001 |
|---|---|---|---|---|---|---|---|---|---|---|
| Tangible Book Value | 19.13 | 16.43 | 10.46 | 12.67 | 16.37 | 13.73 | 12.49 | 11.66 | 12.92 | 11.87 |
| Earnings | 3.09 | 3.46 | 4.30 | 3.45 | 3.26 | 2.82 | 2.35 | 2.15 | 3.10 | 1.90 |
| S&P Core Earnings | 3.11 | 3.84 | 3.73 | 3.47 | 3.30 | 2.80 | 2.30 | 1.41 | 2.01 | 1.83 |
| Dividends | 0.04 | 0.04 | 0.95 | 0.88 | 0.80 | 0.72 | 0.64 | 0.56 | 0.48 | 0.41 |
| Payout Ratio | 1% | 1% | 22% | 26% | 25% | 26% | 27% | 26% | 15% | 21% |
| Prices:High | 48.80 | 55.87 | 86.55 | 82.53 | 68.56 | 59.80 | 56.90 | 53.63 | 58.36 | 63.93 |
| Prices:Low | 32.47 | 14.43 | 28.06 | 59.13 | 54.39 | 40.62 | 39.91 | 30.37 | 32.11 | 36.25 |
| P/E Ratio:High | 16 | 16 | 20 | 24 | 21 | 21 | 24 | 25 | 19 | 34 |
| P/E Ratio:Low | 11 | 4 | 7 | 17 | 17 | 14 | 17 | 14 | 10 | 19 |
| **Income Statement Analysis** (Million $) | | | | | | | | | | |
| Net Interest Income | 2,699 | 2,564 | 2,650 | 1,730 | 1,110 | 907 | 859 | 810 | 979 | 1,025 |
| Tax Equivalent Adjustment | 129 | 126 | 104 | 58.0 | NA | 42.0 | 45.0 | 51.0 | 61.0 | 67.0 |
| Non Interest Income | 6,540 | 5,935 | 7,747 | 6,599 | 5,201 | 4,566 | 4,074 | 3,925 | 3,421 | 2,782 |
| Loan Loss Provision | Nil | Nil | Nil | Nil | Nil | Nil | -18.0 | Nil | 4.00 | 10.0 |
| % Expense/Operating Revenue | 74.1% | 70.2% | 75.5% | 77.2% | 71.9% | 73.8% | 76.2% | 76.5% | 64.6% | 75.3% |
| Pretax Income | 2,086 | 2,525 | 2,564 | 1,903 | 1,771 | 1,432 | 1,192 | 1,112 | 1,555 | 930 |
| Effective Tax Rate | 25.4% | 28.6% | 36.0% | 33.7% | 38.1% | 34.0% | 33.1% | 35.1% | 34.7% | 32.5% |
| Net Income | 1,556 | 1,803 | 1,642 | 1,261 | 1,096 | 945 | 798 | 722 | 1,015 | 628 |
| % Net Interest Margin | 2.24 | 2.19 | 2.08 | 1.71 | 1.25 | 1.08 | 1.08 | 1.17 | 1.42 | 1.66 |
| S&P Core Earnings | 1,554 | 1,822 | 1,549 | 1,269 | 1,107 | 939 | 782 | 473 | 658 | 604 |
| **Balance Sheet & Other Financial Data** (Million $) | | | | | | | | | | |
| Money Market Assets | 22,713 | 26,780 | 56,548 | 29,841 | 20,699 | 12,039 | 26,829 | 31,694 | 46,342 | 37,991 |
| Investment Securities | 94,130 | 93,576 | 76,017 | 74,559 | 64,992 | 59,870 | 37,571 | 38,215 | 28,071 | 20,781 |
| Commercial Loans | 8,288 | 6,710 | 7,287 | 13,822 | 6,617 | 4,152 | 2,352 | 2,768 | 2,052 | 3,289 |
| Other Loans | 3,669 | 4,098 | 1,844 | 1,980 | 2,329 | 2,312 | 2,277 | 2,253 | 2,122 | 2,052 |
| Total Assets | 160,809 | 157,946 | 173,631 | 142,543 | 107,353 | 97,968 | 94,040 | 87,534 | 85,794 | 69,896 |
| Demand Deposits | 17,464 | 11,969 | 32,785 | 15,039 | 10,194 | 9,402 | 13,671 | 7,893 | 7,279 | 9,390 |
| Time Deposits | 80,881 | 78,093 | 79,440 | 80,750 | 55,452 | 50,244 | 41,458 | 39,623 | 38,189 | 29,169 |
| Long Term Debt | 8,553 | 8,838 | 4,419 | 3,636 | 2,616 | 2,659 | 2,458 | 2,222 | 1,270 | 1,217 |
| Common Equity | 17,787 | 14,491 | 10,721 | 11,299 | 7,252 | 6,367 | 6,159 | 5,747 | 4,787 | 3,845 |
| % Return on Assets | 1.0 | 1.1 | 1.0 | 1.0 | 1.1 | 1.0 | 0.9 | 0.8 | 1.3 | 0.9 |
| % Return on Equity | 9.6 | 14.2 | 14.9 | 13.6 | 16.1 | 15.1 | 13.4 | 13.7 | 23.5 | 17.7 |
| % Loan Loss Reserve | 0.8 | 0.7 | 0.2 | 0.1 | 0.2 | 0.3 | 0.4 | 1.2 | 1.5 | 1.1 |
| % Loans/Deposits | 12.1 | 9.9 | 9.2 | 15.3 | 13.6 | 10.9 | 8.4 | 10.6 | 9.2 | 13.9 |
| % Equity to Assets | 10.1 | 7.6 | 7.0 | 7.4 | 6.6 | 6.5 | 6.6 | 6.1 | 5.5 | 5.1 |

Data as orig reptd.; bef. results of disc opers/spec. items. Per share data adj. for stk. divs.; EPS diluted. E-Estimated. NA-Not Available. NM-Not Meaningful. NR-Not Ranked. UR-Under Review.

**Office:** 1 Lincoln St, Boston, MA 02111-2900.
**Telephone:** 617-786-3000.
**Email:** ir@statestreet.com
**Website:** http://www.statestreet.com

**Chrmn, Pres & CEO:** J.L. Hooley
**EVP & CFO:** E.J. Resch
**EVP & Chief Admin Officer:** D.C. O'Leary
**EVP, Chief Acctg Officer & Cntlr:** J.J. Malerba

**EVP & Treas:** D.J. Gutschenritter
**Investor Contact:** S.K. MacDonald (617-664-3477)
**Board Members:** K. F. Burnes, P. Coym, P. De Saint-Aignan, D. A. Fawcett, D. P. Gruber, L. A. Hill, J. L. Hooley, R. S. Kaplan, C. R. Lamantia, R. P. Sergel, R. L. Skates, G. L. Summe, R. E. Weissman

**Founded:** 1832
**Domicile:** Massachusetts
**Employees:** 28,670

*The McGraw-Hill Companies*

# Stericycle Inc

STANDARD
&POOR'S

| S&P Recommendation | HOLD ★★★★★ | Price | 12-Mo. Target Price | Investment Style |
|---|---|---|---|---|
| | | $77.07 (as of Nov 25, 2011) | $95.00 | Large-Cap Growth |

**GICS Sector** Industrials
**Sub-Industry** Environmental & Facilities Services

**Summary** SRCL provides medical waste collection, transportation, treatment and disposal services, and safety and compliance programs to health care concerns throughout the U.S.

## Key Stock Statistics (Source S&P, Vickers, company reports)

| | | | | | | | |
|---|---|---|---|---|---|---|---|
| 52-Wk Range | $95.71– 71.82 | S&P Oper. EPS 2011**E** | 2.80 | Market Capitalization(B) | $6.560 | Beta | 0.29 |
| Trailing 12-Month EPS | $2.52 | S&P Oper. EPS 2012**E** | 3.15 | Yield (%) | Nil | S&P 3-Yr. Proj. EPS CAGR(%) | 15 |
| Trailing 12-Month P/E | 30.6 | P/E on S&P Oper. EPS 2011**E** | 27.5 | Dividend Rate/Share | Nil | S&P Credit Rating | NR |
| $10K Invested 5 Yrs Ago | $21,258 | Common Shares Outstg. (M) | 85.1 | Institutional Ownership (%) | 93 | | |

## Price Performance

30-Week Mov. Avg. · · · ·  10-Week Mov. Avg. - - **GAAP Earnings vs. Previous Year**  Volume Above Avg. STARS

12-Mo. Target Price — Relative Strength  — ▲ Up  ▼ Down  ▶ No Change  Below Avg. ★

Options: CBOE, P, Ph

Analysis prepared by Equity Analyst **Stewart Scharf** on Nov 01, 2011, when the stock traded at **$80.94**.

## Highlights

➤ We project at least 15% total revenue growth through 2012 (mid-single digit organic), driven by acquisitions and increased small-quantity (SQ) volume in the Steri-Safe regulatory program and clinical services. We also see large-quantity (LQ) growth aided by the expansion of the sharps waste management service (Bio Systems) and pharmaceutical waste services, and new medical waste accounts. We see growth both domestically and abroad, as SRCL continues to expand its presence overseas.

➤ In our view, gross margins should narrow by close to 100 basis points in 2011, from 46.4% in 2010, reflecting a negative acquisition effect in the second half. We expect margins to improve somewhat during 2012, as acquisition issues subside and energy costs stabilize. We believe operating margins (EBITDA) will also narrow somewhat in 2011, from 31% in 2010, before improving in 2012, on synergies and well controlled SG&A expenses.

➤ We expect the effective tax rate to remain near 37% in 2011, with operating EPS of $2.80, followed by a 13% advance to $3.15 in 2012.

## Investment Rationale/Risk

➤ We recently downgraded our opinion to hold, from buy, based on softer market trends and mix issues related to acquisitions, along with our valuation metrics. We still view the medical waste industry as recession-resistant, and believe SRCL will continue to generate solid cash flow and target niche acquisitions.

➤ Risks to our recommendation and target price include potential new competitors, significant changes in environmental regulations for medical waste disposal, a rebound in fuel and energy costs, and problems integrating acquisitions.

➤ We attribute the stock's steep multiple of near 27X our 2012 operating EPS estimate to the company's broad medical services network and its expanding market reach. However, using historical and projected price-to-sales, P/E-to-three-year-EPS-growth (PEG) and price-to-EBITDA ratios, we derive a relative valuation of $93. Based on our DCF analysis, assuming 4% terminal growth and a 7.5% weighted average cost of capital, our intrinsic valuation estimate is $97. Blending these metrics, we arrive at our 12-month target price of $95.

## Qualitative Risk Assessment

| LOW | MEDIUM | HIGH |
|---|---|---|

Our risk assessment reflects our view that the regulated medical waste industry is relatively recession resistant, debt levels are reasonable, cash flow generation is sufficient, and ROIC is strong.

## Quantitative Evaluations

**S&P Quality Ranking**  B+

| D | C | B- | B | B+ | A- | A | A+ |
|---|---|---|---|---|---|---|---|

**Relative Strength Rank**  MODERATE

52

LOWEST = 1    HIGHEST = 99

## Revenue/Earnings Data

### Revenue (Million $)

| | 1Q | 2Q | 3Q | 4Q | Year |
|---|---|---|---|---|---|
| 2011 | 398.1 | 410.4 | 420.9 | -- | -- |
| 2010 | 335.2 | 347.7 | 363.0 | 393.5 | 1,439 |
| 2009 | 277.1 | 289.3 | 297.8 | 313.5 | 1,178 |
| 2008 | 254.8 | 277.8 | 277.1 | 274.0 | 1,084 |
| 2007 | 211.1 | 232.9 | 237.3 | 251.6 | 932.8 |
| 2006 | 179.3 | 198.4 | 203.3 | 208.7 | 789.6 |

### Earnings Per Share ($)

| | | | | | |
|---|---|---|---|---|---|
| 2011 | 0.64 | 0.63 | 0.68 | E0.72 | E2.80 |
| 2010 | 0.56 | 0.61 | 0.65 | 0.57 | 2.39 |
| 2009 | 0.47 | 0.51 | 0.54 | 0.52 | 2.03 |
| 2008 | 0.35 | 0.44 | 0.45 | 0.45 | 1.68 |
| 2007 | 0.33 | 0.36 | 0.37 | 0.27 | 1.32 |
| 2006 | 0.26 | 0.28 | 0.31 | 0.32 | 1.17 |

Fiscal year ended Dec. 31. Next earnings report expected: Early February. EPS Estimates based on S&P Operating Earnings; historical GAAP earnings are as reported.

## Dividend Data

No cash dividends have been paid.

---

**Please read the Required Disclosures and Analyst Certification on the last page of this report.**

The McGraw-Hill Companies

# Stericycle Inc

**STANDARD &POOR'S**

## Business Summary November 01, 2011

CORPORATE OVERVIEW. Stericycle, North America's largest regulated medical waste management company, serves customers throughout the U.S., Canada, Mexico, the United Kingdom, Ireland, Portugal and Romania, Argentina, Brazil, Chile and Japan. In addition to waste collection, transfer and disposal, the company provides OSHA compliance services, accreditation readiness monitoring software, hospital-acquired infection monitoring software, and expired medications return services. It entered the U.K. market through the June 2004 acquisition of White Rose Environmental Ltd., and the February 2006 purchase of Sterile Technologies Group Limited (STG).

SRCL's global network includes 136 processing or processing/collection sites and 129 additional transfer, collection or combined transfer/collection sites. The company uses its network to provide the industry's broadest service offering, including medical waste collection, transportation and treatment, and related consulting, training and education services and products.

The company's two principal groups had 517,000 customers as of September 30, 2011, including 501,600 small-quantity (SQ) medical waste generators, such as outpatient clinics, medical and dental offices, and long-term and sub-acute care facilities; and about 15,400 large-quantity (LQ) medical waste generators, such as hospitals, blood banks and pharmaceutical manufacturers. In the U.K., the mix is over 70% LQ and near 30% SQ customers. SQ customers accounted for 63% of domestic medical waste revenues in 2010, up from 33% in 1996, with a gross margin of about 47%, up from 21% in 1996. Foreign revenues accounted for 25% of the total in 2010, with Europe responsible for 56% (14% of total sales).

MARKET PROFILE. SRCL estimates that annual revenues in the U.S. regulated medical waste services market are $3 billion, and about $10.5 billion globally. The company believes its global market share increased to about 15% in early 2011, from 11.2% in 2009. Waste generators outsource medical waste handling to reduce costs. Compliance issues have historically grown more complex, which has led to a shift toward more outsourcing.

## Company Financials Fiscal Year Ended Dec. 31

| Per Share Data ($) | 2010 | 2009 | 2008 | 2007 | 2006 | 2005 | 2004 | 2003 | 2002 | 2001 |
|---|---|---|---|---|---|---|---|---|---|---|
| Tangible Book Value | NM | NM | NM | NM | NM | NM | NM | NM | NM | NM |
| Cash Flow | 3.04 | 2.49 | 2.08 | 1.66 | 1.47 | 0.98 | 1.08 | 0.90 | 0.67 | 0.56 |
| Earnings | 2.39 | 2.03 | 1.68 | 1.32 | 1.17 | 0.74 | 0.85 | 0.72 | 0.51 | 0.26 |
| S&P Core Earnings | 2.38 | 2.03 | 1.72 | 1.39 | 1.16 | 0.98 | 0.79 | 0.65 | 0.45 | 0.20 |
| Dividends | Nil | Nil | Nil | Nil | Nil | Nil | Nil | Nil | Nil | Nil |
| Payout Ratio | Nil | Nil | Nil | Nil | Nil | Nil | Nil | Nil | Nil | Nil |
| Prices:High | 82.16 | 58.34 | 66.15 | 62.56 | 38.22 | 31.80 | 26.61 | 26.01 | 20.27 | 15.71 |
| Prices:Low | 50.62 | 44.36 | 46.45 | 36.52 | 28.33 | 21.38 | 20.85 | 16.03 | 12.50 | 6.50 |
| P/E Ratio:High | 34 | 29 | 39 | 47 | 33 | 43 | 31 | 36 | 40 | 60 |
| P/E Ratio:Low | 21 | 22 | 28 | 28 | 24 | 29 | 25 | 22 | 25 | 25 |

| Income Statement Analysis (Million $) | 2010 | 2009 | 2008 | 2007 | 2006 | 2005 | 2004 | 2003 | 2002 | 2001 |
|---|---|---|---|---|---|---|---|---|---|---|
| Revenue | 1,439 | 1,178 | 1,084 | 933 | 790 | 610 | 516 | 453 | 402 | 359 |
| Operating Income | 445 | 365 | 316 | 272 | 233 | 191 | 169 | 144 | 119 | 102 |
| Depreciation | 53.9 | 40.0 | 34.2 | 31.1 | 27.0 | 21.4 | 21.8 | 17.3 | 15.0 | 25.2 |
| Interest Expense | 37.1 | 34.3 | 33.1 | 34.0 | 28.4 | 13.0 | 11.2 | 12.8 | 21.5 | 35.4 |
| Pretax Income | 332 | 278 | 239 | 191 | 173 | 112 | 129 | 109 | 75.6 | 36.7 |
| Effective Tax Rate | NA | 36.5% | 37.8% | 38.1% | 39.0% | 40.0% | 39.2% | 39.5% | 39.5% | 40.1% |
| Net Income | 210 | 176 | 149 | 118 | 105 | 67.2 | 78.2 | 65.8 | 45.7 | 22.0 |
| S&P Core Earnings | 207 | 176 | 152 | 124 | 105 | 87.6 | 71.8 | 59.0 | 39.7 | 14.0 |

| Balance Sheet & Other Financial Data (Million $) | 2010 | 2009 | 2008 | 2007 | 2006 | 2005 | 2004 | 2003 | 2002 | 2001 |
|---|---|---|---|---|---|---|---|---|---|---|
| Cash | 95.5 | 16.9 | 10.5 | 18.4 | 13.5 | 7.83 | 7.85 | 7.24 | 8.38 | 12.7 |
| Current Assets | 368 | 247 | 224 | 210 | 219 | 144 | 115 | 97.7 | 94.4 | 98.0 |
| Total Assets | 2,643 | 2,183 | 1,759 | 1,608 | 1,328 | 1,048 | 834 | 707 | 667 | 615 |
| Current Liabilities | 307 | 221 | 180 | 150 | 142 | 98.8 | 83.2 | 69.0 | 53.8 | 63.4 |
| Long Term Debt | 1,014 | 923 | 754 | 614 | 443 | 349 | 190 | 163 | 224 | 267 |
| Common Equity | 1,051 | 846 | 670 | 714 | 625 | 522 | 495 | 408 | 327 | 233 |
| Total Capital | 2,218 | 1,846 | 1,571 | 1,453 | 1,174 | 942 | 743 | 634 | 610 | 545 |
| Capital Expenditures | 48.3 | 39.9 | 47.5 | 48.4 | 36.4 | 26.3 | 33.3 | 21.0 | 14.8 | 15.4 |
| Cash Flow | 264 | 216 | 183 | 150 | 132 | 88.6 | 100.0 | 83.0 | 60.7 | 47.3 |
| Current Ratio | 1.2 | 1.1 | 1.3 | 1.4 | 1.5 | 1.5 | 1.4 | 1.4 | 1.8 | 1.5 |
| % Long Term Debt of Capitalization | 45.7 | 50.0 | 48.0 | 42.3 | 37.8 | 37.0 | 25.6 | 25.7 | 36.8 | 49.1 |
| % Net Income of Revenue | 14.6 | 14.9 | 13.7 | 12.7 | 13.3 | 11.0 | 15.1 | 14.5 | 11.4 | 6.1 |
| % Return on Assets | 8.7 | 8.9 | 8.8 | 8.1 | 8.9 | 7.1 | 10.1 | 9.6 | 7.1 | 3.6 |
| % Return on Equity | 22.2 | 23.2 | 21.5 | 17.7 | 18.4 | 13.2 | 17.3 | 17.9 | 16.4 | 12.0 |

Data as orig reptd.; bef. results of disc opers/spec. items. Per share data adj. for stk. divs.; EPS diluted. E-Estimated. NA-Not Available. NM-Not Meaningful. NR-Not Ranked. UR-Under Review.

**Office:** 28161 North Keith Drive, Lake Forest, IL 60045.
**Telephone:** 847-367-5910.
**Email:** investor@stericycle.com
**Website:** http://www.stericycle.com

**Chrmn, Pres & CEO:** M.C. Miller
**COO & EVP:** R. Kogler
**EVP, CFO & Chief Acctg Officer:** F.J. ten Brink

**Board Members:** T. D. Brown, R. Dammeyer, W. W. Hall, J. T. Lord, M. C. Miller, J. Patience, J. W. Reid-Anderson, J. W. Schuler, R. G. Spaeth

**Founded:** 1989
**Domicile:** Delaware
**Employees:** 9,715

*The McGraw·Hill Companies*

# Stryker Corp

**STANDARD &POOR'S**

| S&P Recommendation **BUY** ★★★★☆ | Price $45.52 (as of Nov 25, 2011) | 12-Mo. Target Price $60.00 | Investment Style Large-Cap Growth |
|---|---|---|---|

**GICS Sector** Health Care
**Sub-Industry** Health Care Equipment

**Summary** This company makes specialty surgical and medical products such as orthopedic implants, endoscopic items and hospital beds.

## Key Stock Statistics (Source S&P, Vickers, company reports)

| | | | | | | | | |
|---|---|---|---|---|---|---|---|---|
| 52-Wk Range | $65.21– 43.73 | S&P Oper. EPS 2011**E** | 3.73 | Market Capitalization(B) | $17.419 | Beta | 0.93 |
| Trailing 12-Month EPS | $3.15 | S&P Oper. EPS 2012**E** | 4.15 | Yield (%) | 1.58 | S&P 3-Yr. Proj. EPS CAGR(%) | 11 |
| Trailing 12-Month P/E | 14.5 | P/E on S&P Oper. EPS 2011**E** | 12.2 | Dividend Rate/Share | $0.72 | S&P Credit Rating | A+ |
| $10K Invested 5 Yrs Ago | $9,122 | Common Shares Outstg. (M) | 382.7 | Institutional Ownership (%) | 65 | | |

## Price Performance

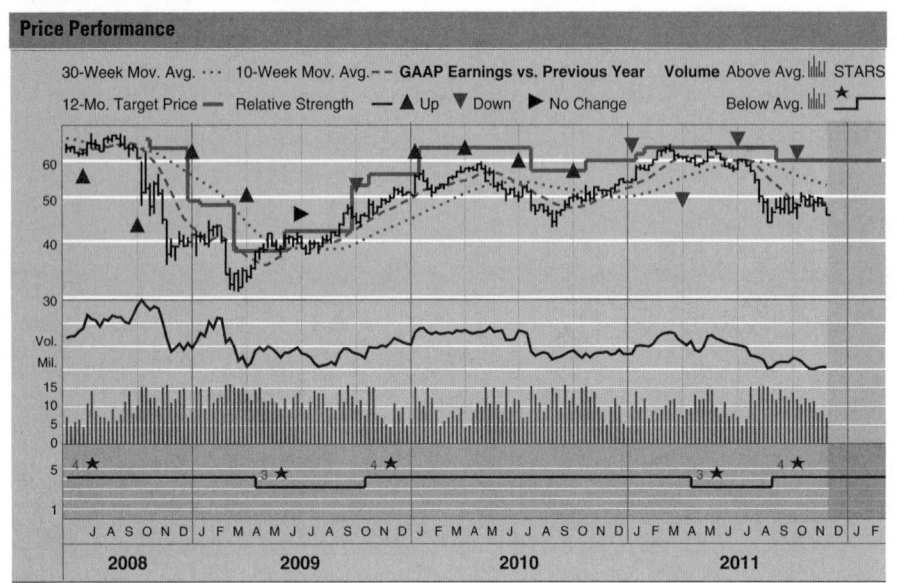

30-Week Mov. Avg. ··· 10-Week Mov. Avg. – – GAAP Earnings vs. Previous Year  Volume Above Avg. STARS
12-Mo. Target Price — Relative Strength — ▲ Up ▼ Down ► No Change  Below Avg. ★

Options: ASE, CBOE, Ph

Analysis prepared by Equity Analyst **Phillip Seligman** on Oct 25, 2011, when the stock traded at **$49.29**.

## Qualitative Risk Assessment

| LOW | MEDIUM | HIGH |
|---|---|---|

Stryker operates in very competitive areas of the global medical device industry, characterized by rapid technological innovation and market share volatility. We believe the medical/surgical supplies unit may be vulnerable to reductions in hospital capital equipment spending, while we think demand for most of its orthopedic products has become less immune to economic cycles.

## Quantitative Evaluations

**S&P Quality Ranking**  A+

| D | C | B- | B | B+ | A- | A | A+ |
|---|---|---|---|---|---|---|---|

**Relative Strength Rank**  MODERATE
45
LOWEST = 1  HIGHEST = 99

## Revenue/Earnings Data

**Revenue (Million $)**

| | 1Q | 2Q | 3Q | 4Q | Year |
|---|---|---|---|---|---|
| 2011 | 2,015 | 2,046 | 2,031 | -- | -- |
| 2010 | 1,799 | 1,758 | 1,768 | 1,995 | 7,320 |
| 2009 | 1,601 | 1,634 | 1,653 | 1,834 | 6,723 |
| 2008 | 1,634 | 1,713 | 1,653 | 1,718 | 6,718 |
| 2007 | 1,426 | 1,464 | 1,453 | 1,658 | 6,001 |
| 2006 | 1,321 | 1,328 | 1,294 | 1,463 | 5,406 |

**Earnings Per Share ($)**

| | | | | | |
|---|---|---|---|---|---|
| 2011 | 0.78 | 0.79 | 0.84 | E1.02 | E3.73 |
| 2010 | 0.80 | 0.80 | 0.85 | 0.74 | 3.19 |
| 2009 | 0.71 | 0.73 | 0.57 | 0.76 | 2.77 |
| 2008 | 0.70 | 0.73 | 0.66 | 0.69 | 2.78 |
| 2007 | 0.58 | 0.58 | 0.55 | 0.66 | 2.37 |
| 2006 | 0.36 | 0.52 | 0.46 | 0.55 | 1.89 |

Fiscal year ended Dec. 31. Next earnings report expected: NA. EPS Estimates based on S&P Operating Earnings; historical GAAP earnings are as reported.

## Highlights

➤ We expect sales to rise by almost 14% in 2011, led by the acquisition of Boston Scientific's (BSX 5.40, Hold) neurovascular business, other acquisitions, new products, and favorable foreign exchange, before slowing in 2012 on the lapping of the acquisitions. While we see industrywide orthopedic sales growth still being tempered by pricing pressures and procedure deferrals, SYK's MDM hip implant line has been making gains. Elsewhere, we expect its hip and knee implant sales to remain soft in Europe amid austerity measures, but to continue to perform well in emerging markets. We also see strong med-surg equipment sales growth continuing, aided by an improved hospital replacement and upgrade market.

➤ We think gross margins will narrow in 2011, on foreign exchange and the relative strength of the med-surg business, before recovering in 2012 on an improving sales mix and manufacturing efficiencies. We expect operating costs to rise as a percentage of sales in 2011, on internal investments, but decline afterward on revenue leverage.

➤ We look for operating EPS of $3.73 in 2011, versus $3.33 in 2010, and we see $4.15 in 2012.

## Investment Rationale/Risk

➤ Despite U.S. hospital spending constraints, SYK appears to be realizing a strong recovery in the med-surg market, and we are encouraged by its moves to diversify. Looking ahead, we still see long-term growth opportunities for SYK's orthopedic (hip, knee, trauma and spine) products segment given active R&D, demographic trends, and assuming procedure trends pick up over time. We see continued momentum for the MDM hip line, and while we expect prosthetic knee sales to remain soft in 2011 and 2012, we believe the market has stabilized and SYK should realize some improvement with a new instrument system to customize knee implants. We view SYK's cash position and cash flow as healthy, providing financial flexibility.

➤ Risks to our recommendation and target price include Medicare reimbursement rate reductions, intensified competition, and rejection of a promising product by the FDA.

➤ Our 12-month target price of $60 reflects a multiple of 14.5X our 2012 EPS estimate. In our view, Stryker's superior projected growth rate relative to peers warrants a premium valuation.

## Dividend Data (Dates: mm/dd Payment Date: mm/dd/yy)

| Amount ($) | Date Decl. | Ex-Div. Date | Stk. of Record | Payment Date |
|---|---|---|---|---|
| 0.180 | 12/08 | 12/29 | 12/31 | 01/31/11 |
| 0.180 | 02/09 | 03/29 | 03/31 | 04/29/11 |
| 0.180 | 06/09 | 06/28 | 06/30 | 07/29/11 |
| 0.180 | 08/19 | 09/28 | 09/30 | 10/31/11 |

Dividends have been paid since 1992. Source: Company reports.

---

**Please read the Required Disclosures and Analyst Certification on the last page of this report.**

The McGraw-Hill Companies

# Stryker Corp

STANDARD
&POOR'S

## Business Summary October 25, 2011

Stryker Corp. traces its origins to a business founded in 1941 by Dr. Homer H. Stryker, a leading orthopedic surgeon and the inventor of several orthopedic products. The company has significant exposure to the artificial hip, prosthetic knee and trauma product areas. International sales accounted for 35% of the total in 2010.

Orthopedic implants (59% of 2010 sales) consist of products such as hip, knee, shoulder and spinal implants, associated implant instrumentation, trauma-related products, and bone cement. Artificial joints are made of cobalt chromium, titanium alloys, ceramics, or ultra-high molecular weight polyethylene, and are implanted in patients whose natural joints have been damaged by arthritis, osteoporosis, other diseases, or injury. SYK also sells trauma-related products, used primarily in the fixation of fractures resulting from sudden injury, including internal fixation devices such as nails, plates and screws, and external fixation devices such as pins, wires and connection bars. In addition, the division sells Simplex bone cement, a material used to secure cemented implants to bone, and the OP-1 Bone Growth Device. Composed of recombinant human osteogenic protein-1 and a bioresorbable collagen matrix, the product induces the formation of new bone when implanted into existing bone, and is approved to treat long bone fractures in patients in whom use of autograft treatments has failed or is not a feasible option. In March 2009, an

FDA panel voted not to recommend the company receive broad-based marketing approval for its OP-1 putty, a new formulation of OP-1. In February 2011, Stryker sold its OP-1 product family for orthopedic bone applications for $60 million.

The medical and surgical equipment unit (41%) comprises four businesses. Stryker Instruments sells powered surgical drills, saws, fixation and reaming equipment, as well as other instruments used for drilling, burring, rasping or cutting bone, wiring or pinning bone fractures, and preparing hip or knee surfaces for the placement of artificial hip or knee joints. Stryker Endoscopy offers medical video cameras, light sources, arthroscopes, laparascopes, powered surgical instruments, and disposable suction/irrigation devices. Stryker Medical produces a wide variety of specialty stretchers customized for acute care and specialty surgical facilities. Stryker Leibinger makes plate and screw systems for craniomaxillofacial surgery to repair small bones in the hands, face and head, and sells a proprietary bone substitute material, BoneSource.

## Company Financials Fiscal Year Ended Dec. 31

| Per Share Data ($) | 2010 | 2009 | 2008 | 2007 | 2006 | 2005 | 2004 | 2003 | 2002 | 2001 |
|---|---|---|---|---|---|---|---|---|---|---|
| Tangible Book Value | 13.80 | 12.58 | 11.28 | 10.84 | 7.98 | 5.75 | 4.44 | 2.98 | 1.42 | 0.65 |
| Cash Flow | 4.21 | 3.74 | 3.25 | 2.79 | 2.69 | 2.34 | 1.78 | 1.71 | 1.30 | 1.09 |
| Earnings | 3.19 | 2.77 | 2.78 | 2.37 | 1.89 | 1.64 | 1.14 | 1.12 | 0.85 | 0.67 |
| S&P Core Earnings | 3.18 | 2.69 | 2.76 | 2.37 | 1.89 | 1.57 | 1.08 | 1.08 | 0.80 | 0.63 |
| Dividends | 0.63 | 0.15 | 0.40 | 0.33 | 0.22 | 0.11 | 0.09 | 0.07 | 0.06 | 0.05 |
| Payout Ratio | 20% | 5% | 14% | 14% | 12% | 7% | 8% | 6% | 7% | 7% |
| Prices:High | 59.72 | 52.66 | 74.94 | 76.89 | 55.92 | 56.32 | 57.66 | 42.68 | 33.74 | 31.60 |
| Prices:Low | 42.74 | 30.82 | 35.38 | 54.89 | 39.77 | 39.74 | 40.30 | 29.83 | 21.93 | 21.65 |
| P/E Ratio:High | 19 | 19 | 27 | 32 | 30 | 34 | 51 | 38 | 40 | 47 |
| P/E Ratio:Low | 13 | 11 | 13 | 23 | 21 | 24 | 35 | 27 | 26 | 32 |

| Income Statement Analysis (Million $) | 2010 | 2009 | 2008 | 2007 | 2006 | 2005 | 2004 | 2003 | 2002 | 2001 |
|---|---|---|---|---|---|---|---|---|---|---|
| Revenue | 7,320 | 6,723 | 6,718 | 6,001 | 5,406 | 4,872 | 4,262 | 3,625 | 3,012 | 2,602 |
| Operating Income | 2,285 | 2,109 | 1,749 | 1,506 | 1,459 | 1,305 | 1,092 | 901 | 751 | 645 |
| Depreciation | 410 | 385 | 195 | 179 | 332 | 290 | 251 | 230 | 186 | 172 |
| Interest Expense | 77.5 | 22.4 | 30.5 | 22.2 | Nil | 7.70 | 6.80 | 22.6 | 40.3 | 67.9 |
| Pretax Income | 1,730 | 1,624 | 1,580 | 1,370 | 1,104 | 1,003 | 717 | 652 | 507 | 406 |
| Effective Tax Rate | NA | 31.8% | 27.4% | 28.0% | 29.5% | 32.7% | 35.0% | 30.5% | 31.8% | 33.0% |
| Net Income | 1,273 | 1,107 | 1,148 | 987 | 778 | 675 | 466 | 454 | 346 | 272 |
| S&P Core Earnings | 1,269 | 1,075 | 1,141 | 987 | 779 | 645 | 441 | 436 | 324 | 257 |

| Balance Sheet & Other Financial Data (Million $) | 2010 | 2009 | 2008 | 2007 | 2006 | 2005 | 2004 | 2003 | 2002 | 2001 |
|---|---|---|---|---|---|---|---|---|---|---|
| Cash | 4,380 | 2,955 | 2,196 | 2,411 | 1,415 | 1,057 | 349 | 65.9 | 37.8 | 50.1 |
| Current Assets | 7,596 | 5,851 | 4,979 | 4,905 | 3,534 | 2,870 | 2,143 | 1,398 | 1,151 | 993 |
| Total Assets | 10,895 | 9,071 | 7,603 | 7,354 | 5,874 | 4,944 | 4,084 | 3,159 | 2,816 | 2,424 |
| Current Liabilities | 1,605 | 1,441 | 1,462 | 1,333 | 1,352 | 1,249 | 1,114 | 850 | 708 | 533 |
| Long Term Debt | 996 | Nil | Nil | Nil | Nil | 184 | 0.70 | 18.8 | 491 | 721 |
| Common Equity | 7,174 | 6,595 | 5,407 | 5,379 | 4,191 | 3,252 | 2,752 | 2,155 | 1,498 | 1,056 |
| Total Capital | 8,170 | 6,595 | 5,568 | 5,524 | 4,191 | 3,436 | 2,753 | 2,174 | 1,989 | 1,777 |
| Capital Expenditures | 182 | 131 | 155 | 188 | 218 | 272 | 188 | 145 | 139 | 162 |
| Cash Flow | 1,684 | 1,493 | 1,343 | 1,165 | 1,110 | 965 | 717 | 683 | 532 | 444 |
| Current Ratio | 4.7 | 4.1 | 3.4 | 3.7 | 2.6 | 2.3 | 1.9 | 1.6 | 1.6 | 1.9 |
| % Long Term Debt of Capitalization | 12.2 | Nil | Nil | Nil | Nil | 5.4 | 0.0 | 0.9 | 24.7 | 40.6 |
| % Net Income of Revenue | 17.4 | 16.5 | 17.1 | 16.4 | 14.4 | 13.9 | 10.9 | 12.5 | 11.5 | 10.4 |
| % Return on Assets | 12.8 | 13.3 | 15.4 | 14.9 | 14.3 | 15.0 | 12.9 | 15.2 | 13.2 | 11.2 |
| % Return on Equity | 18.5 | 18.5 | 21.3 | 20.6 | 20.8 | 22.5 | 19.0 | 24.8 | 27.1 | 28.4 |

Data as orig reptd.; bef. results of disc opers/spec. items. Per share data adj. for stk. divs.; EPS diluted. E-Estimated. NA-Not Available. NM-Not Meaningful. NR-Not Ranked. UR-Under Review.

**Office:** 2825 Airview Blvd, Portage, MI 49002-1802.
**Telephone:** 269-385-2600.
**Website:** http://www.stryker.com
**Chrmn, Pres & CEO:** S.P. MacMillan

**COO:** L.J. Carpenter
**CFO:** C.R. Hartman
**Chief Acctg Officer:** T.M. McKinney
**Treas:** J. Blondia

**Investor Contact:** K.A. Owen (269-385-2600)
**Board Members:** H. E. Cox, Jr., S. M. Datar, R. Doliveux, L. L. Francesconi, A. C. Golston, H. L. Lance, S. P. MacMillan, W. U. Parfet, R. E. Stryker

**Founded:** 1946
**Domicile:** Michigan
**Employees:** 20,036

# Sunoco Inc.

STANDARD
&POOR'S

| S&P Recommendation | HOLD ★★★☆☆ | Price $37.97 (as of Nov 28, 2011) | 12-Mo. Target Price $39.00 | Investment Style Large-Cap Blend |
|---|---|---|---|---|

**GICS Sector** Energy
**Sub-Industry** Oil & Gas Refining & Marketing

**Summary** This leading retailer of transportation fuels and operator of convenience stores in the U.S. East Coast and Midwest also has other interests, including logistics and cokemaking. It plans to exit the refining business.

## Key Stock Statistics (Source S&P, Vickers, company reports)

| | | | | | | | |
|---|---|---|---|---|---|---|---|
| 52-Wk Range | $46.98– 27.36 | S&P Oper. EPS 2011**E** | -1.00 | Market Capitalization(B) | $4.054 | Beta | 0.69 |
| Trailing 12-Month EPS | $-10.37 | S&P Oper. EPS 2012**E** | 3.57 | Yield (%) | 1.58 | S&P 3-Yr. Proj. EPS CAGR(%) | 35 |
| Trailing 12-Month P/E | NM | P/E on S&P Oper. EPS 2011**E** | NM | Dividend Rate/Share | $0.60 | S&P Credit Rating | BB+ |
| $10K Invested 5 Yrs Ago | $6,389 | Common Shares Outstg. (M) | 106.8 | Institutional Ownership (%) | 93 | | |

## Price Performance

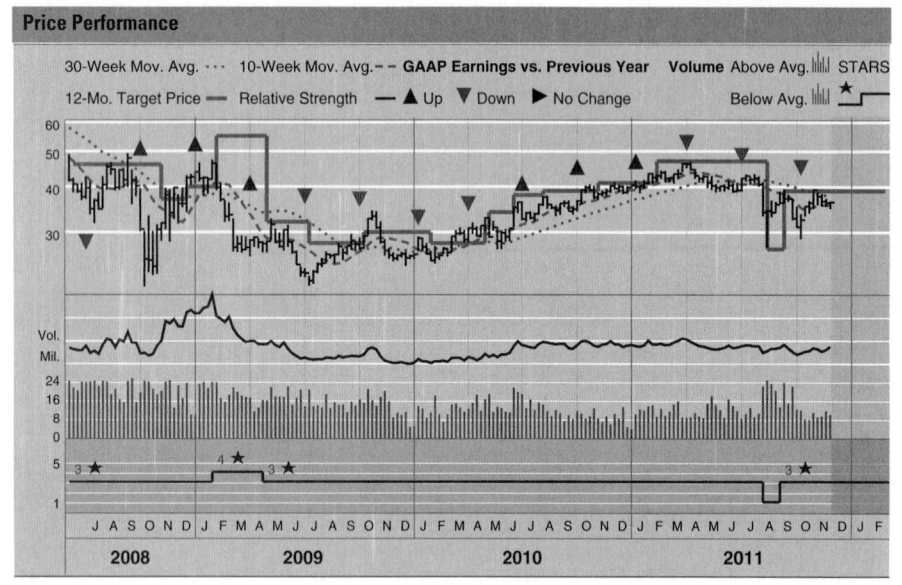

30-Week Mov. Avg. · · · 10-Week Mov. Avg. – – GAAP Earnings vs. Previous Year   Volume Above Avg. STARS
12-Mo. Target Price — Relative Strength — ▲ Up ▼ Down ► No Change   Below Avg.

Options: CBOE, Ph

Analysis prepared by Equity Analyst **Tanjila Shafi** on Nov 28, 2011, when the stock traded at **$36.26**.

## Highlights

➤ Refining throughputs increased 6.6% sequentially to 453,000 b/d in the third quarter of 2011. We believe that SUN's refining segment will be challenged by higher crude prices putting pressure on margins. SUN's refineries mostly process light sweet crude oil, which is tied to the more expensive Brent index versus the WTI index. The company is allocating $135 million to $145 million in capital expenditures for its Refining and Supply segment.

➤ We expect the Logistics segment to produce steady income growth in 2012, based on the July 2010 purchase of Texon, which offers state-of-the-art blending capabilities, pipelines transporting West Texas crude, and terminal facilities. We are encouraged with the logistics segment's initiatives to pursue opportunities at the Marcellus and Utica shales.

➤ We see the company targeting its Logistics and Retail businesses for growth opportunities. Our 2011 forecast is for a loss of $1.00 per share, compared to operating EPS of $1.95 in 2010.

## Investment Rationale/Risk

➤ On September 6, 2011, SUN announced plans to sell or shut down its two remaining refineries and to conduct a comprehensive review of its business. A sale is likely to generate $2 billion, and SUN intends to record a related pretax non-cash charge of $1.9 billion to $2.2 billion in the 2011 third quarter. We view SUN's decision to exit the refining business favorably, as it should enable greater focus on its retail and logistics businesses. SUN completed the sale of its Toledo refinery in the first quarter of 2011. We expect the Logistics segment to produce steady income growth in 2012, reflecting its expanded asset base and the July 2010 purchase of Texon.

➤ Risks to our recommendation and target price include unfavorable changes in economic, industry and operating conditions that would lead to a narrowing of margins.

➤ Our DCF model, assuming a WACC of 7.5% and a terminal growth rate of 3%, and relative valuations lead to our 12-month target price of $39. This represents an expected enterprise value of about 3.5X our 2011 EBITDA estimate, in line with peers.

## Qualitative Risk Assessment

| LOW | MEDIUM | HIGH |
|---|---|---|

Our risk assessment reflects the company's weakened business profile in the volatile and competitive refining industry, and diversification into retail marketing, chemicals, logistics, and cokemaking.

## Quantitative Evaluations

**S&P Quality Ranking**          B+

| D | C | B- | B | B+ | A- | A | A+ |
|---|---|---|---|---|---|---|---|

**Relative Strength Rank**          STRONG
91
LOWEST = 1          HIGHEST = 99

## Revenue/Earnings Data

**Revenue (Million $)**

| | 1Q | 2Q | 3Q | 4Q | Year |
|---|---|---|---|---|---|
| 2011 | 10,061 | 11,445 | 11,562 | -- | -- |
| 2010 | 8,192 | 8,964 | 9,479 | 9,613 | 34,915 |
| 2009 | 6,128 | 7,482 | 8,634 | 8,947 | 31,312 |
| 2008 | 12,813 | 15,426 | 15,447 | 8,479 | 51,558 |
| 2007 | 9,305 | 10,764 | 11,497 | 13,162 | 44,728 |
| 2006 | 8,593 | 10,590 | 10,496 | 9,036 | 38,715 |

**Earnings Per Share ($)**

| | | | | | |
|---|---|---|---|---|---|
| 2011 | -0.84 | -1.03 | -9.80 | E0.30 | E-1.00 |
| 2010 | -0.34 | 1.20 | 0.54 | 0.72 | 2.14 |
| 2009 | 0.05 | -0.59 | -2.67 | -0.04 | -3.16 |
| 2008 | -0.50 | 0.70 | 4.70 | 1.74 | 6.63 |
| 2007 | 1.44 | 4.20 | 1.81 | -0.08 | 7.43 |
| 2006 | 0.59 | 3.22 | 2.76 | 1.00 | 7.59 |

Fiscal year ended Dec. 31. Next earnings report expected: Early February. EPS Estimates based on S&P Operating Earnings; historical GAAP earnings are as reported.

## Dividend Data (Dates: mm/dd Payment Date: mm/dd/yy)

| Amount ($) | Date Decl. | Ex-Div. Date | Stk. of Record | Payment Date |
|---|---|---|---|---|
| 0.150 | 02/03 | 02/14 | 02/16 | 03/10/11 |
| 0.150 | 05/05 | 05/17 | 05/19 | 06/10/11 |
| 0.150 | 07/07 | 08/09 | 08/11 | 09/09/11 |
| 0.150 | 09/01 | 11/08 | 11/10 | 12/09/11 |

Dividends have been paid since 1904. Source: Company reports.

# Sunoco Inc.

**STANDARD &POOR'S**

## Business Summary November 28, 2011

CORPORATE OVERVIEW. Sunoco Inc. (SUN) has been active in the petroleum industry since 1886, and conducts its business through five operating segments: Refining and Supply (segment loss of $8 million in 2010); Retail Marketing (income of $110 million); Chemicals (income of $15 million); Logistics (income of $86 million); and Coke (income of $132 million).

Refining and Supply manufactures refined petroleum products and commodity petrochemicals. As of March 1, 2011, SUN owned and operated two refineries with a crude unit capacity of about 505,000 barrels per day (b/d), located in the Northeast (Marcus Hook, PA, and Philadelphia, PA). In June 2009, SUN sold its Tulsa refinery to Holly Corp. (HOC) for $65 million. In the 2009 fourth quarter, SUN permanently shut down all process units at its Eagle Point refinery in Westville, NJ, in response to weak demand and increased global refining capacity; SUN is exploring options for the site, including use for biofuels production. SUN sold its Toledo, Ohio refinery to PBF Holding Company LLC for approximately $400 million; this transaction closed March 1, 2011. Production available for sale declined 6.8%, to 642,800 b/d, in 2010 (gasoline 52%, middle distillates 36%, residual fuels 5%, petrochemicals 4%, and other 3%).

SUN meets all of its crude oil requirements through purchases from third parties. Approximately 66% of SUN's 2010 crude oil supply came from West Africa, 13% from the U.S., 11% from Canada, 8% from Central Asia, 1% from the North Sea, 0.7% from South and Central America, and 0.4% from lubes extracted from gasoil/naphtha intermediate feedstock. In the 2004 second half, the company began processing limited amounts of lower value high acid sweet crude oils in some of its Northeast refineries; during 2010, about 44,000 b/d of high acid crude oil was processed.

The Chemicals segment manufactures, distributes and markets commodity and intermediate petrochemicals, consisting of aromatic derivatives (cumene, phenol, acetone and bispenol-A) and polypropylene. On March 31, 2010, SUN sold its subsidiary Sunoco Chemicals, Inc. (comprised of its propylene business) to Braskern S.A. for about $350 million.

## Company Financials Fiscal Year Ended Dec. 31

| Per Share Data ($) | 2010 | 2009 | 2008 | 2007 | 2006 | 2005 | 2004 | 2003 | 2002 | 2001 |
|---|---|---|---|---|---|---|---|---|---|---|
| Tangible Book Value | 23.13 | 19.92 | 22.30 | 19.12 | 17.01 | 15.42 | 11.65 | 10.23 | 9.05 | 10.88 |
| Cash Flow | 7.88 | 1.29 | 11.03 | 11.43 | 11.15 | 10.20 | 9.50 | 4.35 | 1.85 | 4.38 |
| Earnings | 2.14 | -3.16 | 6.63 | 7.43 | 7.59 | 7.08 | 4.04 | 2.02 | -0.31 | 2.43 |
| S&P Core Earnings | 1.26 | -2.83 | 6.23 | 6.74 | 7.63 | 7.56 | 4.19 | 2.13 | -0.70 | 1.88 |
| Dividends | 0.60 | 1.20 | 1.17 | 1.08 | 0.95 | 0.75 | 0.58 | 0.51 | 0.50 | 0.50 |
| Payout Ratio | 28% | NM | 18% | 14% | 13% | 11% | 14% | 25% | NM | 21% |
| Prices:High | 41.23 | 47.40 | 73.68 | 86.40 | 97.25 | 85.29 | 42.26 | 26.30 | 21.13 | 21.37 |
| Prices:Low | 24.64 | 21.45 | 21.30 | 56.68 | 57.50 | 38.10 | 25.26 | 14.84 | 13.51 | 14.56 |
| P/E Ratio:High | 19 | NM | 11 | 12 | 13 | 12 | 10 | 13 | NM | 9 |
| P/E Ratio:Low | 12 | NM | 3 | 8 | 8 | 5 | 6 | 7 | NM | 6 |

| Income Statement Analysis (Million $) | 2010 | 2009 | 2008 | 2007 | 2006 | 2005 | 2004 | 2003 | 2002 | 2001 |
|---|---|---|---|---|---|---|---|---|---|---|
| Revenue | 34,915 | 31,312 | 51,558 | 44,728 | 38,715 | 33,764 | 25,508 | 17,929 | 14,384 | 14,063 |
| Operating Income | NA | NA | 1,988 | 1,835 | 2,049 | 2,078 | 1,501 | 934 | 313 | 954 |
| Depreciation, Depletion and Amortization | 497 | 502 | 515 | 480 | 459 | 429 | 818 | 363 | 329 | 321 |
| Interest Expense | 149 | 106 | 72.0 | 127 | 89.0 | 69.0 | 97.0 | 111 | 108 | 103 |
| Pretax Income | 586 | -601 | 1,173 | 1,476 | 1,580 | 1,580 | 995 | 495 | -73.0 | 587 |
| Effective Tax Rate | NA | NM | 33.8% | 35.1% | 38.0% | 38.4% | 39.2% | 37.0% | NM | 32.2% |
| Net Income | 451 | -370 | 776 | 891 | 979 | 974 | 605 | 312 | -47.0 | 398 |
| S&P Core Earnings | 150 | -332 | 729 | 808 | 984 | 1,040 | 626 | 330 | -106 | 307 |

| Balance Sheet & Other Financial Data (Million $) | 2010 | 2009 | 2008 | 2007 | 2006 | 2005 | 2004 | 2003 | 2002 | 2001 |
|---|---|---|---|---|---|---|---|---|---|---|
| Cash | 1,485 | 377 | 240 | 648 | 263 | 919 | 405 | 431 | 390 | 42.0 |
| Current Assets | 5,793 | 3,764 | 2,835 | 4,638 | 4,015 | 3,687 | 2,551 | 2,068 | 1,898 | 1,510 |
| Total Assets | 13,364 | 11,895 | 11,150 | 12,426 | 10,982 | 9,931 | 8,079 | 6,922 | 6,441 | 5,932 |
| Current Liabilities | 4,946 | 4,418 | 3,937 | 5,640 | 4,755 | 4,210 | 3,022 | 2,170 | 1,776 | 1,778 |
| Long Term Debt | 2,136 | 2,061 | 1,705 | 1,724 | 1,705 | 1,234 | 1,379 | 1,350 | 1,453 | 1,142 |
| Common Equity | 3,046 | 2,557 | 2,842 | 2,533 | 2,075 | 2,051 | 1,607 | 1,556 | 1,394 | 1,642 |
| Total Capital | 6,866 | 5,186 | 5,844 | 5,723 | 5,227 | 4,749 | 4,271 | 3,940 | 3,816 | 3,335 |
| Capital Expenditures | 772 | 899 | 1,286 | 1,179 | 1,019 | 970 | 832 | 425 | 385 | 331 |
| Cash Flow | 948 | 151 | 1,291 | 1,371 | 1,438 | 1,403 | 1,423 | 675 | 282 | 719 |
| Current Ratio | 1.2 | 0.9 | 0.7 | 0.8 | 0.8 | 0.9 | 0.8 | 1.0 | 1.1 | 0.8 |
| % Long Term Debt of Capitalization | 31.1 | 44.6 | 29.2 | 30.1 | 32.6 | 26.0 | 32.3 | 34.3 | 38.1 | 34.2 |
| % Return on Assets | 3.6 | NM | 6.6 | 7.6 | 9.4 | 10.8 | 8.0 | 4.7 | NM | 7.0 |
| % Return on Equity | 16.1 | NM | 28.9 | 38.7 | 47.5 | 53.3 | 38.3 | 21.2 | NM | 23.8 |

Data as orig reptd.; bef. results of disc opers/spec. items. Per share data adj. for stk. divs.; EPS diluted. E-Estimated. NA-Not Available. NM-Not Meaningful. NR-Not Ranked. UR-Under Review.

**Office:** 1735 Market St Ste LL, Philadelphia, PA 19103-7583.
**Telephone:** 215-977-3000.
**Email:** sunocoonline@sunocoinc.com
**Website:** http://www.sunocoinc.com

**Chrmn, Pres & CEO:** L.L. Elsenhans
**SVP & CFO:** B.P. MacDonald
**SVP, Secy & General Counsel:** S.L. Fox
**Chief Acctg Officer & Cntlr:** J.P. Krott

**Treas:** C. Uy
**Investor Contact:** T. Harr (215-977-6764)
**Investor Contact:** T.P. Delaney
**Board Members:** C. C. Casciato, G. W. Edwards, L. L. Elsenhans, U. O. Fairbairn, J. P. Jones, III, J. G. Kaiser, J. W. Rowe, J. K. Wulff

**Auditor:** ERNST & YOUNG
**Founded:** 1886
**Domicile:** Pennsylvania
**Employees:** 10,200

*The McGraw-Hill Companies*

# SunTrust Banks Inc.

**STANDARD &POOR'S**

| S&P Recommendation | HOLD ★★★☆☆ | Price $16.53 (as of Nov 25, 2011) | 12-Mo. Target Price $21.00 | Investment Style Large-Cap Blend |
|---|---|---|---|---|

**GICS Sector** Financials
**Sub-Industry** Regional Banks

**Summary** STI is one of the largest regional banks in the U.S., concentrated primarily in Florida, Georgia, Maryland, North Carolina, South Carolina, Virginia, Tennessee, and the District of Columbia.

## Key Stock Statistics (Source S&P, Vickers, company reports)

| | | | | | | | | |
|---|---|---|---|---|---|---|---|---|
| 52-Wk Range | $33.14– 16.41 | S&P Oper. EPS 2011**E** | 1.31 | Market Capitalization(B) | $8.793 | Beta | | 1.43 |
| Trailing 12-Month EPS | $1.05 | S&P Oper. EPS 2012**E** | 1.79 | Yield (%) | 1.21 | S&P 3-Yr. Proj. EPS CAGR(%) | | NM |
| Trailing 12-Month P/E | 15.7 | P/E on S&P Oper. EPS 2011**E** | 12.6 | Dividend Rate/Share | $0.20 | S&P Credit Rating | | BBB |
| $10K Invested 5 Yrs Ago | $2,261 | Common Shares Outstg. (M) | 531.9 | Institutional Ownership (%) | 79 | | | |

## Price Performance

30-Week Mov. Avg. ···· 10-Week Mov. Avg. - - GAAP Earnings vs. Previous Year · Volume Above Avg. STARS
12-Mo. Target Price — Relative Strength — ▲ Up ▼ Down ▶ No Change · Below Avg. ★

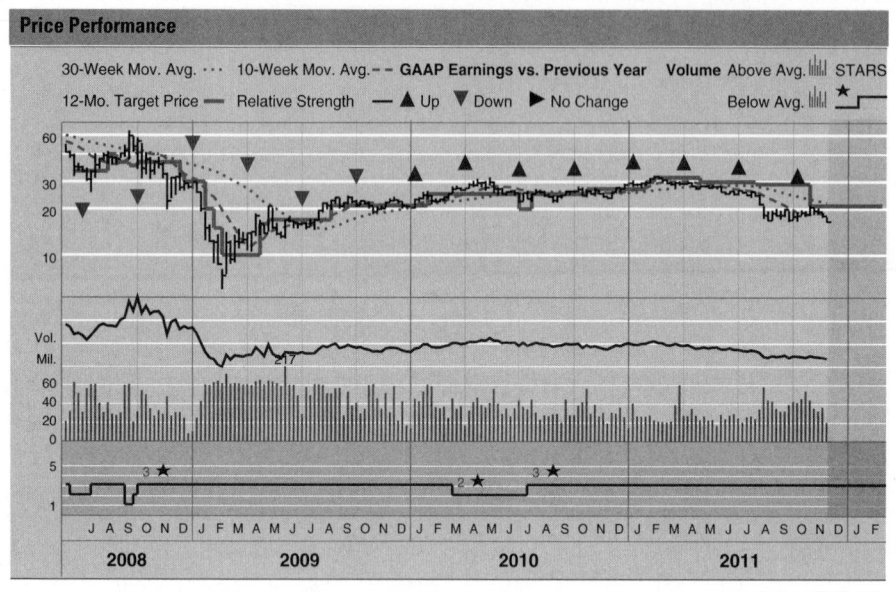

Options: CBOE, P, Ph

Analysis prepared by Equity Analyst **Erik Oja** on Nov 21, 2011, when the stock traded at **$17.59**.

## Highlights

► We see STI's net interest income rising 3.4% in 2011, on a 1.75% increase in loan growth, both higher than peers. However, for 2012, we expect a 1.1% decline, on our expectations for shrinkage in the net interest margin. We look for Regulation E to reduce service charges on deposits to $685 million in 2011, from $760 million in 2010, for core fee income to decline 3.2% in 2011, and for total revenues to fall 0.1%. For 2012, we expect core fee income to rise 2.1%, but total revenues to fall 0.9%.

► STI's third-quarter 2011 nonperforming loans fell for the ninth quarter in a row, to $3.24 billion, or 2.76% of total loans. We think further improvements will come more slowly. Net charge-offs fell to $492 million in the third quarter, from a peak of $1.0 billion in the third quarter of 2009. In the third quarter, STI's allowance for loan losses dropped to $2.60 billion from the peak level of $3.18 billion reached in the first quarter of 2010. We see 2011 loan loss provisions of $1.47 billion and 2012 provisions of $1.20 billion, down from 2010's $2.65 billion.

► We see EPS of $1.31 in 2011 and $1.79 in 2012.

## Investment Rationale/Risk

► STI has been profitable, after preferred dividends, for five quarters now, but we calculate that 75% of EPS in this time period has been generated by releases of reserves for nonperforming loans, a worse than peers result, in our view. We note that STI has made good improvements to credit quality and capital levels, but we see fundamentals, such as noninterest expense controls, and amount of return of capital to shareholders, such as dividends, as well below peers. At the same time, we see STI's current valuation, at 0.80X price to September 30 tangible book value, and 10.0X our forward four quarters EPS estimate of $1.84, at the median of peers.

► Risks to our opinion and target price include slower-than-expected credit quality improvement and a large equity capital raise.

► We base our 12-month target price of $21 on a below peers 0.85X our $24.10 estimate for year-end 2011 tangible book value per share. Our target price equates to a roughly peer equivalent 11.4X our forward four quarters EPS estimate of $1.84.

## Qualitative Risk Assessment

| LOW | MEDIUM | HIGH |
|---|---|---|

Our risk assessment reflects SunTrust's large-cap valuation and history of profitability, offset by exposure to possible further declines in residential and commercial lending credit quality.

## Quantitative Evaluations

**S&P Quality Ranking** · B

| D | C | B- | B | B+ | A- | A | A+ |
|---|---|---|---|---|---|---|---|

**Relative Strength Rank** · WEAK

22

LOWEST = 1 · HIGHEST = 99

## Revenue/Earnings Data

### Revenue (Million $)

| | 1Q | 2Q | 3Q | 4Q | Year |
|---|---|---|---|---|---|
| 2011 | 2,437 | 2,458 | 2,441 | -- | -- |
| 2010 | 2,272 | 2,522 | 2,650 | 2,627 | 10,072 |
| 2009 | 2,851 | 2,765 | 2,433 | 2,372 | 10,420 |
| 2008 | 3,316 | 3,479 | 3,303 | 2,683 | 12,801 |
| 2007 | 3,407 | 3,698 | 3,334 | 3,025 | 13,313 |
| 2006 | 3,130 | 3,299 | 3,384 | 3,447 | 13,260 |

### Earnings Per Share ($)

| | | | | | |
|---|---|---|---|---|---|
| 2011 | 0.08 | 0.33 | 0.39 | E0.51 | E1.31 |
| 2010 | -0.46 | -0.11 | 0.17 | 0.23 | -0.18 |
| 2009 | -2.49 | -0.41 | -0.76 | -0.64 | -3.98 |
| 2008 | 0.82 | 1.53 | 0.88 | -1.08 | 2.13 |
| 2007 | 1.44 | 1.89 | 1.18 | 0.01 | 4.55 |
| 2006 | 1.46 | 1.49 | 1.47 | 1.39 | 5.82 |

Fiscal year ended Dec. 31. Next earnings report expected: NA. EPS Estimates based on S&P Operating Earnings; historical GAAP earnings are as reported.

## Dividend Data (Dates: mm/dd Payment Date: mm/dd/yy)

| Amount ($) | Date Decl. | Ex-Div. Date | Stk. of Record | Payment Date |
|---|---|---|---|---|
| 0.010 | 02/08 | 02/24 | 02/28 | 03/15/11 |
| 0.010 | 04/26 | 05/27 | 06/01 | 06/15/11 |
| 0.050 | 08/09 | 08/30 | 09/01 | 09/15/11 |
| 0.050 | 11/08 | 11/29 | 12/01 | 12/15/11 |

Dividends have been paid since 1985. Source: Company reports.

# SunTrust Banks Inc.

STANDARD
&POOR'S

## Business Summary November 21, 2011

CORPORATE OVERVIEW. SunTrust Banks Inc. has four lines of business: Retail and Commercial Banking, Corporate and Investment Banking, Household Lending, and Wealth and Investment Management.

Retail Banking provides lending and deposit gathering as well as other banking-related products and services to consumers and small businesses with sales up to $10 million. Commercial Banking offers financial products and services, including commercial lending, treasury management, financial risk management, and corporate bankcard services, to enterprises with sales up to $250 million.

The Corporate and Investment Banking segment houses the company's corporate banking, investment banking, capital markets, commercial leasing and merchant banking activities. This segment focuses on companies with sales in excess of $250 million, and concentrates on small-cap and mid-cap growth

companies, raising public and private equity, and providing merger and acquisition advisory services for investment banking.

The Household Lending segment offers residential mortgage products nationally through its retail, broker and correspondent channels.

The Wealth and Investment Management segment provides wealth management products and professional services to individual and institutional clients. The remaining segment revenues are allocated to corporate, other, treasury, and reconciling items.

## Company Financials Fiscal Year Ended Dec. 31

| Per Share Data ($) | 2010 | 2009 | 2008 | 2007 | 2006 | 2005 | 2004 | 2003 | 2002 | 2001 |
|---|---|---|---|---|---|---|---|---|---|---|
| Tangible Book Value | 23.40 | 22.28 | 33.72 | 28.41 | 26.04 | 24.67 | 23.13 | 29.73 | 25.46 | 26.67 |
| Earnings | -0.18 | -3.98 | 2.13 | 4.55 | 5.82 | 5.47 | 5.19 | 4.73 | 4.66 | 4.70 |
| S&P Core Earnings | -0.18 | -2.19 | 1.32 | 4.37 | 5.64 | 5.39 | 5.17 | 4.80 | 4.38 | 4.50 |
| Dividends | 0.04 | 0.22 | 2.85 | 2.92 | 2.44 | 2.20 | 2.00 | 1.80 | 1.72 | 1.60 |
| Payout Ratio | NM | NM | 134% | 64% | 42% | 40% | 39% | 38% | 37% | 34% |
| Prices:High | 32.02 | 30.18 | 70.00 | 94.18 | 85.64 | 75.77 | 76.65 | 71.73 | 70.20 | 72.35 |
| Prices:Low | 20.16 | 6.00 | 19.75 | 60.02 | 69.68 | 65.32 | 61.27 | 51.44 | 51.48 | 57.29 |
| P/E Ratio:High | NM | NM | 33 | 21 | 15 | 14 | 15 | 15 | 15 | 15 |
| P/E Ratio:Low | NM | NM | 7 | 13 | 12 | 12 | 12 | 11 | 11 | 12 |

| Income Statement Analysis (Million $) | | | | | | | | | | |
|---|---|---|---|---|---|---|---|---|---|---|
| Net Interest Income | 4,854 | 4,466 | 4,620 | 4,720 | 4,660 | 4,579 | 3,685 | 3,320 | 3,244 | 3,253 |
| Tax Equivalent Adjustment | 116 | 123 | 118 | 103 | 87.9 | 75.5 | NA | 45.0 | 39.5 | 40.8 |
| Non Interest Income | 4,137 | 3,511 | 4,010 | 3,186 | 3,519 | 3,162 | 2,646 | 2,179 | 2,187 | 2,003 |
| Loan Loss Provision | 2,651 | 4,064 | 2,552 | 683 | 263 | 177 | 136 | 314 | 470 | 275 |
| % Expense/Operating Revenue | 65.7% | 82.3% | 62.6% | 66.2% | 59.0% | 60.6% | 67.3% | 68.4% | 61.5% | 59.2% |
| Pretax Income | 21.0 | -2,327 | 728 | 2,250 | 2,986 | 2,866 | 2,257 | 1,909 | 1,823 | 2,020 |
| Effective Tax Rate | NM | NM | NM | 27.4% | 29.1% | 30.7% | 30.3% | 30.2% | 27.0% | 32.2% |
| Net Income | 189 | -1,564 | 796 | 1,634 | 2,117 | 1,987 | 1,573 | 1,332 | 1,332 | 1,369 |
| % Net Interest Margin | 3.38 | 3.04 | 3.10 | 3.11 | 3.00 | 3.16 | 3.15 | 3.08 | 3.41 | 3.58 |
| S&P Core Earnings | -87.0 | -950 | 463 | 1,542 | 2,045 | 1,957 | 1,570 | 1,351 | 1,253 | 1,310 |

| Balance Sheet & Other Financial Data (Million $) | | | | | | | | | | |
|---|---|---|---|---|---|---|---|---|---|---|
| Money Market Assets | 7,257 | 5,521 | 11,411 | 11,890 | 3,849 | 4,457 | 3,796 | 3,243 | 2,820 | 3,025 |
| Investment Securities | 26,895 | 28,477 | 19,697 | 16,264 | 25,102 | 26,526 | 28,941 | 25,607 | 23,445 | 19,656 |
| Commercial Loans | 34,064 | 32,494 | 27,926 | 48,539 | 47,182 | 33,764 | 31,824 | 30,682 | 28,694 | 28,946 |
| Other Loans | 78,937 | 78,061 | 96,721 | 73,780 | 74,273 | 80,791 | 69,602 | 50,050 | 44,474 | 40,013 |
| Total Assets | 172,874 | 174,165 | 189,289 | 179,574 | 182,162 | 179,714 | 158,870 | 125,393 | 117,323 | 104,741 |
| Demand Deposits | 27,290 | 24,244 | 21,522 | 21,083 | 22,887 | 41,973 | 30,979 | 24,185 | 21,250 | 19,200 |
| Time Deposits | 92,735 | 92,059 | 83,754 | 80,787 | 101,134 | 80,081 | 72,382 | 57,004 | 58,456 | 48,337 |
| Long Term Debt | 13,648 | 17,490 | 26,812 | 22,957 | 18,993 | 20,779 | 22,127 | 15,314 | 11,880 | 12,661 |
| Common Equity | 18,188 | 17,614 | 19,502 | 17,553 | 17,314 | 16,887 | 15,987 | 9,731 | 16,030 | 15,064 |
| % Return on Assets | 0.1 | NM | 0.4 | 0.9 | 1.2 | 1.2 | 1.1 | 1.1 | 1.2 | 1.3 |
| % Return on Equity | 1.1 | NM | 4.6 | 9.2 | 12.3 | 12.1 | 12.2 | 14.4 | 8.6 | 9.3 |
| % Loan Loss Reserve | 2.6 | 2.7 | 1.9 | 1.0 | 0.8 | 0.5 | 1.0 | 1.1 | 1.1 | 1.2 |
| % Loans/Deposits | 94.3 | 93.3 | 112.0 | 100.4 | 107.4 | 171.3 | 104.5 | 106.3 | 101.5 | 108.5 |
| % Equity to Assets | 10.3 | 10.2 | 9.4 | 9.6 | 9.5 | 9.7 | 9.1 | 7.6 | 14.0 | 14.2 |

Data as orig reptd.; bef. results of disc opers/spec. items. Per share data adj. for stk. divs.; EPS diluted. E-Estimated. NA-Not Available. NM-Not Meaningful. NR-Not Ranked. UR-Under Review.

**Office:** 303 Peachtree St NE, Atlanta, GA 30308-3201.
**Telephone:** 404-588-7711.
**Website:** http://www.suntrust.com
**Chrmn:** J.M. Wells, III

**Pres & CEO:** W.H. Rogers, Jr.
**EVP & Chief Admin Officer:** D.F. Dierker
**EVP, Secy & General Counsel:** R.D. Fortin
**EVP & CIO:** T.E. Sullivan

**Investor Contact:** M.A. Chancy (800-568-3476)
**Board Members:** R. Beall, II, A. D. Correll, J. C. Crowe, B. P. Garrett, Jr., D. H. Hughes, M. D. Ivester, J. H. Lanier, K. P. Legg, W. A. Linnenbringer, G. G. Minor, III, D. M. Ratcliffe, W. H. Rogers, Jr., F. S. Royal, T. Watjen, J. M. Wells, III, P. Wynn, Jr.

**Founded:** 1891
**Domicile:** Georgia
**Employees:** 29,056

# SUPERVALU INC.

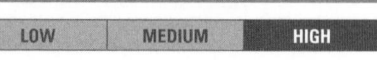

| S&P Recommendation | HOLD ★★★★★ | Price | 12-Mo. Target Price | Investment Style |
|---|---|---|---|---|
| | | $7.03 (as of Nov 25, 2011) | $9.00 | Large-Cap Blend |

**GICS Sector** Consumer Staples
**Sub-Industry** Food Retail

**Summary** This company, one of the largest U.S. food wholesalers, is also one of the biggest supermarket retailers in the U.S.

## Key Stock Statistics (Source S&P, Vickers, company reports)

| | | | | | | | | |
|---|---|---|---|---|---|---|---|---|
| 52-Wk Range | $11.77– 6.26 | S&P Oper. EPS 2012**E** | 1.37 | Market Capitalization(B) | $1.492 | Beta | 1.21 |
| Trailing 12-Month EPS | $0.13 | S&P Oper. EPS 2013**E** | 1.45 | Yield (%) | 4.98 | S&P 3-Yr. Proj. EPS CAGR(%) | 6 |
| Trailing 12-Month P/E | 54.1 | P/E on S&P Oper. EPS 2012**E** | 5.1 | Dividend Rate/Share | $0.35 | S&P Credit Rating | B+ |
| $10K Invested 5 Yrs Ago | $2,425 | Common Shares Outstg. (M) | 212.2 | Institutional Ownership (%) | 93 | | |

## Price Performance

- 30-Week Mov. Avg. · · · ·   10-Week Mov. Avg. – –   **GAAP Earnings vs. Previous Year**   Volume Above Avg. STARS
- 12-Mo. Target Price —   Relative Strength —   ▲ Up   ▼ Down   ► No Change   Below Avg.

Options: CBOE, P, Ph

Analysis prepared by Equity Analyst **Joseph Agnese** on Oct 20, 2011, when the stock traded at **$7.84**.

## Highlights

- We see FY 12 (Feb.) revenues declining 3.0%, reflecting a 3.0% decline in same-store sales (excluding fuel), partially offset by 1% to 2% new store square footage growth. We look for the company to experience store closures associated with the exiting of non-core markets as it accelerates hard-discount store openings and plans to remodel stores in core markets.

- We project that margins will be about flat, as negative sales leverage and aggressive product pricing offset benefits from more efficient promotional spending, reduced administrative costs, savings related to store closures, and a reduction in stock-keeping units in stores resulting in labor and shrink savings. We expect interest expense to decline due to lower interest rates and lower debt levels, which rose significantly as a result of the Albertson's acquisition in June 2006.

- We look for FY 12 operating EPS of $1.37 (excluding $0.13 of charges related to market exits and the impact of a labor dispute), down 2.1% from operating EPS of $1.40 in FY 11 (excluding goodwill and asset impairment charges, store closure and strike-related costs).

## Investment Rationale/Risk

- The company continued to experience same-store sales growth below its closest peers through the first half of FY 12, despite what we consider its strong regional market share positions. We remain cautious on the shares, with sales pressures intensifying as SVU reduces everyday pricing and consumer pressures remaining high as the unemployment rate likely stays at elevated levels through FY 12.

- Risks to our recommendation and target price include worse-than-expected same-store sales growth due to decreased demand or food price deflation, and increased pricing competition.

- The stock recently traded at an enterprise value of 4.1X estimated FY 12 EBITDA of $1.9 billion. Due to what we view as its weak balance sheet and high risks associated with the turnaround of its underperforming stores, we believe the shares should trade below the peer average of 5.5X. Applying an enterprise value to EBITDA multiple of 4.1X, representing a 25% discount to peers -- above the 10-year average discount range to peers of 11% -- to our FY 13 EBITDA estimate of $1.8 billion, we arrive at our 12-month target price of $9.

## Qualitative Risk Assessment

| LOW | MEDIUM | HIGH |
|---|---|---|

Our risk assessment reflects the intensely competitive environment in which the company operates, and threats of new entrants into its markets, partially offset by SVU's strong market share positions.

## Quantitative Evaluations

**S&P Quality Ranking**    B

| D | C | B- | B | B+ | A- | A | A+ |
|---|---|---|---|---|---|---|---|

**Relative Strength Rank**    MODERATE

33

LOWEST = 1    HIGHEST = 99

## Revenue/Earnings Data

**Revenue (Million $)**

| | 1Q | 2Q | 3Q | 4Q | Year |
|---|---|---|---|---|---|
| 2012 | 11,113 | 8,429 | -- | -- | -- |
| 2011 | 11,545 | 8,656 | 8,673 | 8,660 | 37,534 |
| 2010 | 12,715 | 9,461 | 9,216 | 9,205 | 40,597 |
| 2009 | 13,347 | 10,226 | 10,171 | 10,820 | 44,564 |
| 2008 | 13,292 | 10,159 | 10,211 | 10,386 | 44,048 |
| 2007 | 5,783 | 10,666 | 10,657 | 10,301 | 37,406 |

**Earnings Per Share ($)**

| | | | | | |
|---|---|---|---|---|---|
| 2012 | 0.35 | 0.28 | E0.27 | E0.39 | E1.37 |
| 2011 | 0.31 | -6.94 | -0.95 | 0.44 | -7.13 |
| 2010 | 0.53 | 0.35 | 0.51 | 0.46 | 1.85 |
| 2009 | 0.76 | 0.60 | -13.95 | -0.95 | -13.51 |
| 2008 | 0.69 | 0.69 | 0.66 | 0.73 | 2.76 |
| 2007 | 0.57 | 0.61 | 0.54 | 0.57 | 2.32 |

Fiscal year ended Feb. 28. Next earnings report expected: Mid January. EPS Estimates based on S&P Operating Earnings; historical GAAP earnings are as reported.

## Dividend Data (Dates: mm/dd Payment Date: mm/dd/yy)

| Amount ($) | Date Decl. | Ex-Div. Date | Stk. of Record | Payment Date |
|---|---|---|---|---|
| 0.088 | 02/04 | 02/25 | 03/01 | 03/15/11 |
| 0.088 | 04/13 | 05/27 | 06/01 | 06/15/11 |
| 0.088 | 07/25 | 08/30 | 09/01 | 09/15/11 |
| 0.088 | 10/18 | 11/29 | 12/01 | 12/15/11 |

Dividends have been paid since 1936. Source: Company reports.

**Please read the Required Disclosures and Analyst Certification on the last page of this report.**

The McGraw-Hill Companies

# SUPERVALU INC.

## Business Summary October 20, 2011

CORPORATE OVERVIEW. SUPERVALU, organized in 1925 as the successor to two wholesale grocery concerns established in the 1870s, has grown into the largest U.S. food distributor to supermarkets, and the second largest conventional food retailer in the U.S. Retail operations are conducted through limited-assortment stores, food stores, and combination food and drug stores. As of February 2011, the company operated about 2,400 multi-format retail food stores and was the primary grocery supplier to approximately 1,900 stores in addition to its own retail operations.

CORPORATE STRATEGY. The company aims to leverage its retail food and supply chain services by benefiting from economies of scale and its low-cost supply chain network. The company operated 1,114 traditional food stores and 381 hard discount food stores as of February 2011. Traditional food store banners (Acme, Albertson's, Cub Foods, Farm Fresh, Hornbacher's, Jewel-Osco, Shaw's, Shop 'n Save, Shoppers Food & Pharmacy and Star Market) typically

carry 40,000 to 50,000 items and average 40,000 to 60,000 square feet in size.

Hard discount food stores include Save-A-Lot stores. The company licenses 899 Save-A-Lot stores to independent operators. Save-A-Lot food stores are typically 15,000 square feet and stock 1,400 high volume food items as well as a limited number of general merchandise items. The majority of food products offered for sale are private label products. The company positions itself to offer low prices by carrying a limited selection of the most frequently purchased goods. The majority of Save-A-Lot stores are found in small town/rural communities as opposed to urban and suburban locations.

## Company Financials Fiscal Year Ended Feb. 28

| Per Share Data ($) | 2011 | 2010 | 2009 | 2008 | 2007 | 2006 | 2005 | 2004 | 2003 | 2002 |
|---|---|---|---|---|---|---|---|---|---|---|
| Tangible Book Value | NM | NM | NM | NM | NM | 7.37 | 6.52 | 4.84 | 3.24 | 2.54 |
| Cash Flow | -2.76 | 6.34 | -8.43 | 7.55 | 6.79 | 3.55 | 4.75 | 4.34 | 4.14 | 4.08 |
| Earnings | -7.13 | 1.85 | -13.51 | 2.76 | 2.32 | 1.46 | 2.71 | 2.07 | 1.91 | 1.53 |
| S&P Core Earnings | -1.45 | 1.96 | 1.85 | 2.42 | 2.45 | 1.90 | 2.21 | 2.03 | 1.61 | 1.24 |
| Dividends | NA | 0.61 | 0.69 | 0.66 | 0.64 | 0.60 | 0.58 | 0.57 | 0.56 | 0.55 |
| Payout Ratio | NA | 33% | NM | 24% | 28% | 41% | 21% | 27% | 29% | 36% |
| Calendar Year | 2010 | 2009 | 2008 | 2007 | 2006 | 2005 | 2004 | 2003 | 2002 | 2001 |
| Prices:High | 17.89 | 20.38 | 37.46 | 49.78 | 36.59 | 35.88 | 35.15 | 28.84 | 30.81 | 24.10 |
| Prices:Low | 8.33 | 12.13 | 8.59 | 34.46 | 26.14 | 29.55 | 25.70 | 12.60 | 14.75 | 12.60 |
| P/E Ratio:High | NM | 11 | NM | 18 | 16 | 25 | 13 | 14 | 16 | 16 |
| P/E Ratio:Low | NM | 7 | NM | 12 | 11 | 20 | 9 | 6 | 8 | 8 |

| Income Statement Analysis (Million $) | | | | | | | | | | |
|---|---|---|---|---|---|---|---|---|---|---|
| Revenue | 37,534 | 40,597 | 44,564 | 44,048 | 37,406 | 19,864 | 19,543 | 20,210 | 19,160 | 20,909 |
| Operating Income | 1,819 | 2,243 | 2,682 | 2,788 | 2,058 | 750 | 936 | 919 | 870 | 904 |
| Depreciation | 925 | 957 | 1,077 | 1,030 | 879 | 311 | 303 | 302 | 297 | 341 |
| Interest Expense | 547 | 569 | 647 | 733 | 600 | 139 | 138 | 166 | 182 | 194 |
| Pretax Income | -1,523 | 632 | -2,779 | 977 | 747 | 329 | 601 | 455 | 408 | 344 |
| Effective Tax Rate | NA | 37.8% | NM | 39.3% | 39.5% | 37.4% | 35.8% | 38.4% | 37.0% | 40.1% |
| Net Income | -1,510 | 393 | -2,855 | 593 | 452 | 206 | 386 | 280 | 257 | 206 |
| S&P Core Earnings | -305 | 417 | 396 | 518 | 477 | 269 | 313 | 276 | 217 | 166 |

| Balance Sheet & Other Financial Data (Million $) | | | | | | | | | | |
|---|---|---|---|---|---|---|---|---|---|---|
| Cash | 172 | 211 | 240 | 243 | 285 | 686 | 464 | 292 | 29.2 | 12.0 |
| Current Assets | 3,420 | 3,711 | 4,105 | 4,147 | 4,460 | 2,168 | 2,127 | 2,037 | 1,647 | 1,604 |
| Total Assets | 13,758 | 16,436 | 17,604 | 21,062 | 21,702 | 6,038 | 6,278 | 6,153 | 5,896 | 5,825 |
| Current Liabilities | 3,786 | 4,167 | 4,472 | 4,607 | 4,705 | 1,507 | 1,632 | 1,872 | 1,525 | 1,701 |
| Long Term Debt | 6,348 | 7,022 | 7,968 | 8,502 | 9,192 | 1,406 | 1,579 | 1,634 | 2,020 | 1,875 |
| Common Equity | 1,340 | 2,887 | 2,581 | 5,953 | 5,306 | 2,619 | 2,511 | 2,210 | 2,009 | 1,918 |
| Total Capital | 8,091 | 10,522 | 10,549 | 14,455 | 15,006 | 4,079 | 4,240 | 3,986 | 4,146 | 3,873 |
| Capital Expenditures | 597 | 681 | 1,186 | 1,191 | 837 | 308 | 233 | 328 | 383 | 293 |
| Cash Flow | -585 | 1,350 | -1,778 | 1,623 | 1,331 | 517 | 689 | 582 | 554 | 547 |
| Current Ratio | 0.9 | 0.9 | 0.9 | 0.9 | 0.9 | 1.4 | 1.3 | 1.1 | 1.1 | 0.9 |
| % Long Term Debt of Capitalization | 78.5 | 66.7 | 75.5 | 58.8 | 61.3 | 34.5 | 37.2 | 41.0 | 48.7 | 48.4 |
| % Net Income of Revenue | NM | 1.0 | NM | 1.4 | 1.2 | 1.0 | 2.0 | 1.4 | 1.3 | 1.0 |
| % Return on Assets | NM | 2.3 | NM | 2.8 | 3.2 | 3.3 | 6.2 | 4.6 | 4.4 | 3.4 |
| % Return on Equity | NM | 14.4 | NM | 10.5 | 11.4 | 8.0 | 16.3 | 13.3 | 13.2 | 11.1 |

Data as orig reptd.; bef. results of disc opers/spec. items. Per share data adj. for stk. divs.; EPS diluted. E-Estimated. NA-Not Available. NM-Not Meaningful. NR-Not Ranked. UR-Under Review.

**Office:** 7075 Flying Cloud Drive, Eden Prairie, MN 55344.
**Telephone:** 952-828-4000.
**Website:** http://www.supervalu.com
**Chrmn:** W.C. Sales

**Pres & CEO:** C.R. Herkert
**EVP, CFO & Chief Acctg Officer:** S.M. Smith
**EVP & CIO:** W.R. Shurts
**SVP & General Counsel:** T.N. Sheldon

**Investor Contact:** K. Levy (952-828-4540)
**Auditor:** KPMG
**Board Members:** D. R. Chappel, I. S. Cohen, R. E. Daly, S. E. Engel, P. L. Francis, E. C. Gage, C. R. Herkert, S. S. Rogers, M. E. Rubel, W. C. Sales, K. P. Seifert

**Founded:** 1871
**Domicile:** Delaware
**Employees:** 142,000

# Symantec Corp

**STANDARD &POOR'S**

| S&P Recommendation | HOLD ★★★☆☆ | Price<br>$15.33 (as of Nov 25, 2011) | 12-Mo. Target Price<br>$21.00 | Investment Style<br>Large-Cap Blend |
|---|---|---|---|---|

**GICS Sector** Information Technology
**Sub-Industry** Systems Software

**Summary** This company provides software solutions that enable customers to protect their network infrastructure from potential threats and to store their data.

## Key Stock Statistics (Source S&P, Vickers, company reports)

| | | | | | | | | |
|---|---|---|---|---|---|---|---|---|
| 52-Wk Range | $20.50– 15.31 | S&P Oper. EPS 2012**E** | 1.35 | Market Capitalization(B) | $11.301 | Beta | | 0.86 |
| Trailing 12-Month EPS | $0.88 | S&P Oper. EPS 2013**E** | 1.55 | Yield (%) | Nil | S&P 3-Yr. Proj. EPS CAGR(%) | | 12 |
| Trailing 12-Month P/E | 17.4 | P/E on S&P Oper. EPS 2012**E** | 11.4 | Dividend Rate/Share | Nil | S&P Credit Rating | | BBB |
| $10K Invested 5 Yrs Ago | $7,324 | Common Shares Outstg. (M) | 737.2 | Institutional Ownership (%) | 93 | | | |

## Price Performance

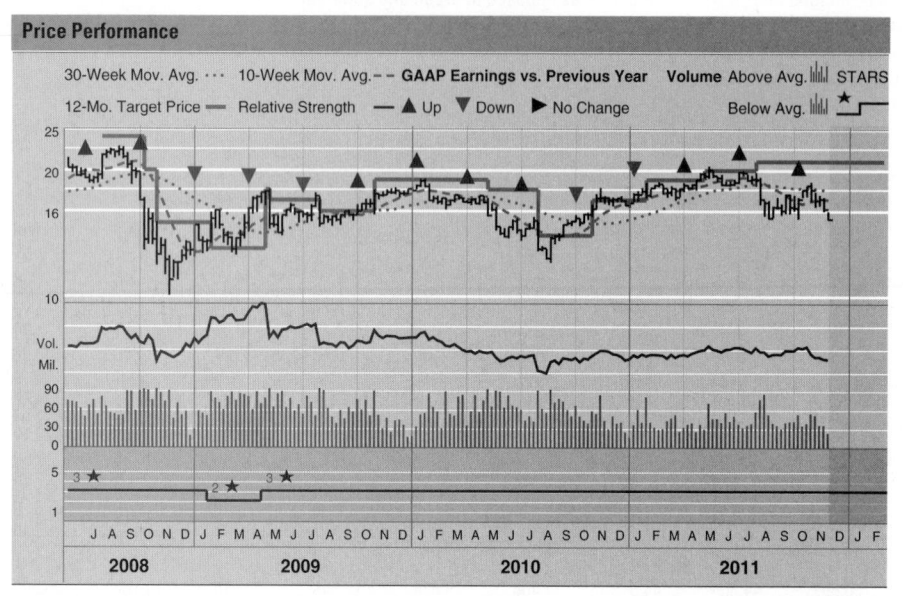

30-Week Mov. Avg. ··· · · 10-Week Mov. Avg. – – **GAAP Earnings vs. Previous Year** **Volume** Above Avg. ⅲ STARS
12-Mo. Target Price — Relative Strength — ▲ Up ▼ Down ► No Change Below Avg. ⅲ ★

Options: ASE, CBOE, P, Ph

Analysis prepared by Equity Analyst **Thomas Smith, CFA** on Aug 08, 2011, when the stock traded at **$16.59**.

## Highlights

► We project revenue growth of 9.3% in FY 12 (Mar.), and 4% in FY 13, following a 3.4% rise in FY 11. Our revenue projection includes the acquisition of VeriSign's (VRSN 28, Hold) security business. Excluding contributions from this acquisition, we think SYMC will grow at a slower pace than the industry average because we believe most of the industry's growth will be in hardware, not software. We anticipate that this will be partially offset by stronger growth in endpoint management, given the proliferation of mobile devices. We also see stronger demand for data storage software due to increased interest in cloud computing.

► We expect gross margins of 84% for FY 12 and FY 13, up from 83% in FY 11. We look for operating expenses to comprise 66% of revenues in FY 12 and 65% in FY 13, down from 67% in FY 11, due to economies of scale. We forecast FY 12 GAAP operating margins of 18%, up from 14% in FY 11.

► We estimate operating EPS of $1.43 for FY 12 and $1.60 for FY 13, compared to $1.24 in FY 11. Our estimates exclude amortization of intangibles and other one-time charges.

## Investment Rationale/Risk

► Our hold recommendation reflects our concern about SYMC's sluggish revenue growth. We believe SYMC will grow slower than the industry average due to loss in market share and its reliance on large contracts, which we think will remain difficult to close. However, we believe the company is making inroads in the consumer market segment with a renewed focus on improving relationships with its channel partners. We are also positive on SYMC's cost-savings efforts, which we think will partially offset the weakness in revenue growth.

► Risks to our recommendation and target price include a weaker-than-expected recovery in the global economy, lower enterprise IT spending, and integration problems associated with recent acquisitions.

► Our 12-month target price of $21 is based on a weighted blend of our discounted cash flow (DCF) and P/E analyses. Our DCF model assumes an 11% WACC and 3% terminal growth, yielding an intrinsic value of $19. From our P/E analysis, we derive a value of $22 based on an industry P/E-to-growth ratio of 1.7X, or 15X our FY 12 operating EPS estimate of $1.43.

## Qualitative Risk Assessment

| LOW | MEDIUM | HIGH |
|---|---|---|

Our risk assessment for Symantec reflects the highly competitive market in which the company operates and integration risks from recent acquisitions.

## Quantitative Evaluations

**S&P Quality Ranking** B

| D | C | B- | B | B+ | A- | A | A+ |
|---|---|---|---|---|---|---|---|

**Relative Strength Rank** MODERATE

32

LOWEST = 1 HIGHEST = 99

## Revenue/Earnings Data

**Revenue (Million $)**

| | 1Q | 2Q | 3Q | 4Q | Year |
|---|---|---|---|---|---|
| 2012 | 1,653 | 1,681 | -- | -- | -- |
| 2011 | 1,433 | 1,480 | 1,604 | 1,673 | 6,190 |
| 2010 | 1,432 | 1,474 | 1,548 | 1,531 | 5,985 |
| 2009 | 1,650 | 1,518 | 1,514 | 1,468 | 6,150 |
| 2008 | 1,400 | 1,419 | 1,515 | 1,540 | 5,874 |
| 2007 | 1,259 | 1,262 | 1,313 | 1,357 | 5,199 |

**Earnings Per Share ($)**

| | | | | | |
|---|---|---|---|---|---|
| 2012 | 0.25 | 0.24 | E0.34 | E0.36 | E1.35 |
| 2011 | 0.20 | 0.17 | 0.17 | 0.22 | 0.76 |
| 2010 | 0.09 | 0.19 | 0.37 | 0.19 | 0.87 |
| 2009 | 0.22 | 0.16 | -8.23 | -0.30 | -8.10 |
| 2008 | 0.10 | 0.06 | 0.15 | 0.22 | 0.52 |
| 2007 | 0.09 | 0.12 | 0.12 | 0.07 | 0.41 |

Fiscal year ended Mar. 31. Next earnings report expected: Late January. EPS Estimates based on S&P Operating Earnings; historical GAAP earnings are as reported.

## Dividend Data

No cash dividends have been paid.

---

**Please read the Required Disclosures and Analyst Certification on the last page of this report.**

The *McGraw·Hill* Companies

# Symantec Corp

**STANDARD &POOR'S**

## Business Summary August 08, 2011

CORPORATE OVERVIEW. Symantec Corp. (SYMC) is a provider of security, storage and systems management solutions that enable enterprises and consumers to protect their network infrastructure from potential threats and to archive and recover their data. Its products include virus protection, firewall, virtual private network, data protection, compliance, vulnerability management, intrusion detection, remote management technologies, and security services.

The company is organized into five operating segments:

Consumer Products -- focuses on Internet security. Key products include Norton 360 and Norton Internet Security, which protect against viruses, worms and other security risks; Norton AntiVirus, which removes viruses, Trojan horses and worms; and Norton SystemWorks, which enables users to maintain and optimize their computers. The Consumer Products segment accounted for 31% and 32% of total revenue in FY 10 (Mar.) and FY 11, respectively.

Security and Compliance -- provides security throughout the network, including behind the gateway and at the client level including servers, desktop PCs, laptops and other mobile devices. Its Information Risk Management solutions enforce data security policies on email, storage systems and archiving. The

company's enterprise security solutions address the following areas: Antivirus, Antispam, Compliance, and Managed Security Services. The Security and Compliance segment accounted for 24% and 25% of total revenue in FY 10 and FY 11, respectively.

Storage and Server Management -- provides software solutions designed to protect, back up, archive and restore data across the enterprise. It also helps customers manage heterogeneous storage and server environments. This segment accounted for 38% and 37% of total revenue in FY 10 and FY 11, respectively.

Services -- assists SYMC's customers in implementing, supporting and maintaining their security, storage and infrastructure software solutions. Services accounted for 7% and 6% of total revenues in FY 10 and FY 11, respectively.

The Other segment is comprised of products nearing the end of their life cycle. Revenues were insignificant during both FY 10 and FY 11.

## Company Financials Fiscal Year Ended Mar. 31

| Per Share Data ($) | 2011 | 2010 | 2009 | 2008 | 2007 | 2006 | 2005 | 2004 | 2003 | 2002 |
|---|---|---|---|---|---|---|---|---|---|---|
| Tangible Book Value | NM | NM | NM | NM | NM | 0.63 | 3.07 | 1.97 | 2.89 | 1.26 |
| Cash Flow | 1.58 | 1.77 | -7.09 | 1.46 | 1.24 | 0.48 | 0.86 | 0.62 | 0.45 | 0.37 |
| Earnings | 0.76 | 0.87 | -8.10 | 0.52 | 0.41 | 0.15 | 0.74 | 0.54 | 0.38 | -0.05 |
| S&P Core Earnings | 0.78 | 0.83 | NA | 0.55 | 0.40 | -0.06 | 0.59 | 0.43 | 0.26 | -0.19 |
| Dividends | NA | Nil | Nil | Nil | Nil | Nil | Nil | Nil | Nil | Nil |
| Payout Ratio | NA | Nil | Nil | Nil | Nil | Nil | Nil | Nil | Nil | Nil |
| Calendar Year | 2010 | 2009 | 2008 | 2007 | 2006 | 2005 | 2004 | 2003 | 2002 | 2001 |
| Prices:High | 19.16 | 18.28 | 22.80 | 21.86 | 22.19 | 26.60 | 34.05 | 17.50 | 11.55 | 9.19 |
| Prices:Low | 12.04 | 12.54 | 10.05 | 15.97 | 14.78 | 16.32 | 17.27 | 9.09 | 6.80 | 3.90 |
| P/E Ratio:High | 25 | 21 | NM | 42 | 54 | NM | 46 | 33 | 30 | 78 |
| P/E Ratio:Low | 16 | 14 | NM | 31 | 36 | NM | 23 | 17 | 18 | 33 |

**Income Statement Analysis** (Million $)

| | 2011 | 2010 | 2009 | 2008 | 2007 | 2006 | 2005 | 2004 | 2003 | 2002 |
|---|---|---|---|---|---|---|---|---|---|---|
| Revenue | 6,190 | 5,985 | 6,150 | 5,874 | 5,199 | 4,143 | 2,583 | 1,870 | 1,407 | 1,071 |
| Operating Income | 1,648 | 1,790 | 1,918 | 1,597 | 1,402 | 942 | 926 | 611 | 417 | 269 |
| Depreciation | 647 | 733 | 837 | 824 | 811 | 340 | 96.3 | 78.8 | 59.6 | 238 |
| Interest Expense | 143 | 129 | 29.7 | 29.5 | 27.2 | 18.0 | 12.3 | 21.2 | 21.2 | 9.17 |
| Pretax Income | 698 | 826 | -6,507 | 713 | 632 | 363 | 858 | 542 | 364 | 45.5 |
| Effective Tax Rate | 15.0% | 13.6% | NM | 34.9% | 36.0% | 56.8% | 37.5% | 31.6% | 31.7% | NM |
| Net Income | 597 | 714 | -6,729 | 464 | 404 | 157 | 536 | 371 | 248 | -28.2 |
| S&P Core Earnings | 611 | 683 | NA | 488 | 393 | -51.0 | 423 | 284 | 157 | -106 |

**Balance Sheet & Other Financial Data** (Million $)

| | 2011 | 2010 | 2009 | 2008 | 2007 | 2006 | 2005 | 2004 | 2003 | 2002 |
|---|---|---|---|---|---|---|---|---|---|---|
| Cash | 2,958 | 3,044 | 1,991 | 2,427 | 2,559 | 2,316 | 1,091 | 2,410 | 1,706 | 1,375 |
| Current Assets | 4,486 | 4,351 | 3,300 | 3,730 | 4,071 | 3,908 | 3,688 | 2,842 | 1,988 | 1,563 |
| Total Assets | 12,719 | 11,232 | 10,645 | 18,092 | 17,751 | 17,913 | 5,614 | 4,456 | 3,266 | 2,503 |
| Current Liabilities | 4,893 | 3,771 | 3,514 | 3,800 | 3,318 | 3,478 | 1,701 | 1,287 | 895 | 579 |
| Long Term Debt | 1,987 | 1,871 | 2,100 | 2,100 | 2,100 | 24.9 | 4.41 | 606 | 607 | 604 |
| Common Equity | 4,528 | 4,548 | 3,948 | 10,973 | 11,602 | 13,668 | 3,705 | 2,426 | 1,764 | 1,320 |
| Total Capital | 7,188 | 6,419 | 6,100 | 13,293 | 14,045 | 14,187 | 3,798 | 3,077 | 2,371 | 1,924 |
| Capital Expenditures | 268 | 248 | 272 | 274 | 420 | 267 | 91.5 | 111 | 192 | 141 |
| Cash Flow | 1,240 | 1,447 | -5,892 | 1,288 | 1,216 | 497 | 633 | 453 | 308 | 210 |
| Current Ratio | 0.9 | 1.2 | 0.9 | 1.0 | 1.2 | 1.1 | 2.2 | 2.2 | 2.2 | 31.3 |
| % Long Term Debt of Capitalization | 27.6 | 29.2 | 34.4 | 15.8 | 15.0 | 0.2 | 0.1 | 19.7 | 25.6 | 0.3 |
| % Net Income of Revenue | 9.6 | 11.9 | NM | 7.9 | 7.8 | 3.8 | 20.8 | 19.8 | 17.7 | NM |
| % Return on Assets | 5.0 | 6.5 | NM | 2.6 | 2.3 | 1.3 | 10.6 | 9.6 | 8.6 | NM |
| % Return on Equity | 13.2 | 16.8 | NM | 4.1 | 3.2 | 1.8 | 17.5 | 17.7 | 16.1 | NM |

Data as orig reptd.; bef. results of disc opers/spec. items. Per share data adj. for stk. divs.; EPS diluted. E-Estimated. NA-Not Available. NM-Not Meaningful. NR-Not Ranked. UR-Under Review.

**Office:** 350 Ellis Street, Mountain View, CA 94043.
**Telephone:** 650-527-8000.
**Email:** investor-relations@symantec.com
**Website:** http://www.symantec.com

**Chrmn:** S.M. Bennett
**Pres & CEO:** E.T. Salem
**EVP & CFO:** J. Beer
**EVP, Secy & General Counsel:** S.C. Taylor

**SVP & Chief Acctg Officer:** P.A. Bullock
**Investor Contact:** H. Corcos (408-517-8324)
**Board Members:** S. M. Bennett, M. A. Brown, F. E. Dangeard, G. B. Laybourne, D. L. Mahoney, R. S. Miller, Jr., E. T. Salem, D. H. Schulman, V. P. Unruh

**Founded:** 1983
**Domicile:** Delaware
**Employees:** 18,600

*The McGraw-Hill Companies*

# Sysco Corp

**STANDARD &POOR'S**

| | | | |
|---|---|---|---|
| **S&P Recommendation** HOLD ★★★☆☆ | **Price**<br>$27.07 (as of Nov 25, 2011) | **12-Mo. Target Price**<br>$30.00 | **Investment Style**<br>Large-Cap Blend |

**GICS Sector** Consumer Staples
**Sub-Industry** Food Distributors

**Summary** Sysco is a large distributor of food and related products, primarily to the foodservice or food-away-from-home industry.

## Key Stock Statistics (Source S&P, Vickers, company reports)

| | | | | | | | | |
|---|---|---|---|---|---|---|---|---|
| 52-Wk Range | $32.76– 25.09 | S&P Oper. EPS 2012**E** | 2.09 | Market Capitalization(B) | $15.864 | Beta | | 0.72 |
| Trailing 12-Month EPS | $1.96 | S&P Oper. EPS 2013**E** | 2.17 | Yield (%) | 3.99 | S&P 3-Yr. Proj. EPS CAGR(%) | | 8 |
| Trailing 12-Month P/E | 13.8 | P/E on S&P Oper. EPS 2012**E** | 13.0 | Dividend Rate/Share | $1.08 | S&P Credit Rating | | A+ |
| $10K Invested 5 Yrs Ago | $8,975 | Common Shares Outstg. (M) | 586.0 | Institutional Ownership (%) | 74 | | | |

## Price Performance

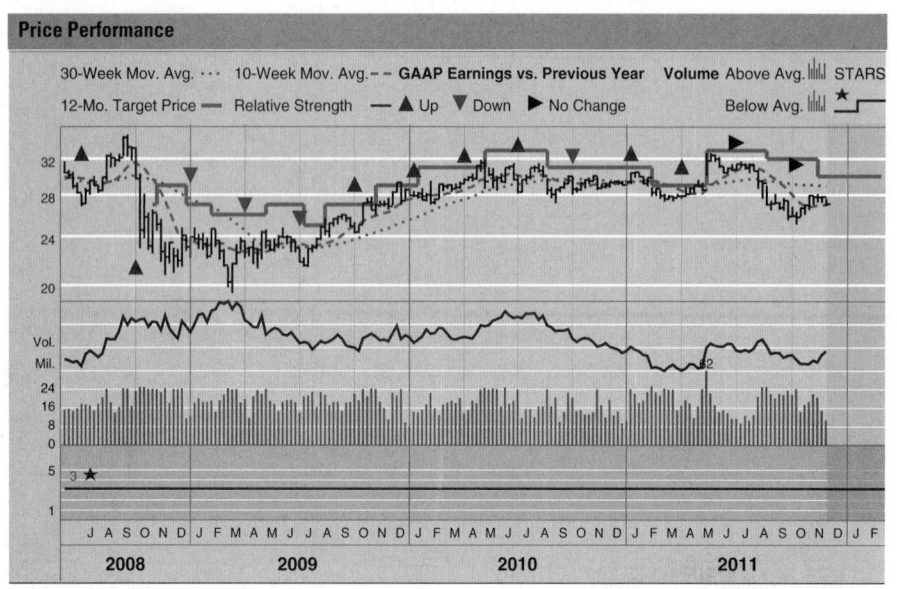

30-Week Mov. Avg. ···· 10-Week Mov. Avg. - - **GAAP Earnings vs. Previous Year** Volume Above Avg. STARS
12-Mo. Target Price — Relative Strength ▲ Up ▼ Down ▶ No Change Below Avg.

Options: ASE, CBOE, P

Analysis prepared by Equity Analyst **Joseph Agnese** on Nov 08, 2011, when the stock traded at **$28.12**.

## Highlights

► Our FY 12 (Jun.) sales growth projection is 6.8%. We remain cautious on underlying demand due to weakness in the U.S. economy. In 52-week FY 11 versus 53-week FY 10, SYY's revenues increased 5.6%, largely reflecting improved case volume and food cost inflation. There was also a modest contribution from acquisitions and foreign currency.

► We look for some operating margin recovery in FY 12. There was margin pressure in FY 11 from food cost inflation, strategic pricing initiatives, changes in sales mix, and fuel costs, partly offset by productivity gains. We also forecast that there will be a negative impact in FY 12 following some effect in FY 11 from costs related to a multi-year program in which SYY is expected to adopt an integrated software system to support the majority of its business processes.

► For FY 12, we estimate EPS of $2.09. FY 11 EPS was $1.96, compared to FY 10's $1.99. FY 11 EPS included a $0.04 charge from a withdrawal from a multi-employer pension plan and an unrelated $0.02 tax benefit.

## Investment Rationale/Risk

► Much of SYY's sales are for restaurants, and we think relatively high levels of unemployment in the U.S. are likely to limit year-ahead growth in what consumers spend at restaurants. Over time, we look for SYY's profitability to benefit from more consolidated purchasing, the addition of regional distribution centers, and management of freight costs and inventory.

► Risks to our recommendation and target price include a slowing of growth rates given SYY's significant size and reach, sharp increases in gasoline prices, and a potential prolonged slowdown in restaurant sales.

► Our 12-month target price of $30 is a blend of our historical and relative analyses. Our historical analysis applies a P/E multiple of 15.7X, below the 10-year historical average, to our calendar 2012 EPS estimate of $2.13 for a value of $33. This valuation reflects some caution related to consumer spending and food price inflation. Our peer analysis applies a 12.1X P/E multiple, in line with the average from a small group of other food distributor stocks, for a $26 value. SYY shares recently had an indicated yield of 3.7%.

## Qualitative Risk Assessment

| LOW | MEDIUM | HIGH |
|---|---|---|

Our risk assessment reflects SYY's operations in a relatively stable industry, in which we believe it has the largest market share.

## Quantitative Evaluations

**S&P Quality Ranking** A+

| D | C | B- | B | B+ | A- | A | A+ |
|---|---|---|---|---|---|---|---|

**Relative Strength Rank** STRONG

72

LOWEST = 1 HIGHEST = 99

## Revenue/Earnings Data

**Revenue (Million $)**

| | 1Q | 2Q | 3Q | 4Q | Year |
|---|---|---|---|---|---|
| 2012 | 10,586 | -- | -- | -- | -- |
| 2011 | 9,751 | 9,385 | 9,762 | 10,426 | 39,323 |
| 2010 | 9,081 | 8,869 | 8,945 | 10,348 | 37,244 |
| 2009 | 9,877 | 9,150 | 8,739 | 9,087 | 36,853 |
| 2008 | 9,406 | 9,240 | 9,147 | 9,730 | 37,522 |
| 2007 | 8,672 | 8,569 | 8,573 | 9,228 | 35,042 |

**Earnings Per Share ($)**

| | | | | | |
|---|---|---|---|---|---|
| 2012 | 0.51 | E0.47 | E0.49 | E0.59 | E2.09 |
| 2011 | 0.51 | 0.44 | 0.44 | 0.57 | 1.96 |
| 2010 | 0.55 | 0.41 | 0.42 | 0.57 | 1.99 |
| 2009 | 0.46 | 0.40 | 0.38 | 0.53 | 1.77 |
| 2008 | 0.43 | 0.43 | 0.40 | 0.55 | 1.81 |
| 2007 | 0.37 | 0.39 | 0.35 | 0.49 | 1.60 |

Fiscal year ended Jun. 30. Next earnings report expected: Early February. EPS Estimates based on S&P Operating Earnings; historical GAAP earnings are as reported.

## Dividend Data (Dates: mm/dd Payment Date: mm/dd/yy)

| Amount ($) | Date Decl. | Ex-Div. Date | Stk. of Record | Payment Date |
|---|---|---|---|---|
| 0.260 | 02/25 | 03/30 | 04/01 | 04/21/11 |
| 0.260 | 05/20 | 06/29 | 07/01 | 07/22/11 |
| 0.260 | 08/26 | 10/05 | 10/07 | 10/28/11 |
| 0.270 | 11/16 | 01/04 | 01/06 | 01/27/12 |

Dividends have been paid since 1970. Source: Company reports.

# Sysco Corp

STANDARD &POOR'S

## Business Summary November 08, 2011

CORPORATE OVERVIEW. Sysco Corp. is a large distributor of food and related products, primarily to the foodservice or food-away-from-home industry. As of July 2011, SYY operated 177 distribution facilities serving about 400,000 customers, including restaurants (62% of FY 11 (Jun.) sales), hospitals and nursing homes (11%), hotel and motels (6%), schools and colleges (5%), and others (16%). In FY 11, U.S. sales represented 89% of SYY's total, and Canada sales represented 9.8%.

Sysco distributes food products, including frozen foods such as meats, fully prepared entrees, fruits, vegetables and desserts; canned and dry foods; fresh meats; dairy and beverage products; imported specialties; and fresh produce. The company also distributes non-food products. These include paper products, tableware such as china and silverware, cookware, restaurant and kitchen equipment and supplies, and cleaning supplies. The company stresses prompt and accurate delivery of orders, and close contact with customers, and also provides customers with ancillary services, such as providing product usage reports, menu-planning advice, food safety training, and assistance in inventory control. No single customer accounted for 10% or more of sales in FY 11. The company owns about 90% of its 8,700 delivery vehicle operating fleet.

CORPORATE STRATEGY. SYY seeks to expand its business by garnering an in-

creased share of products purchased by existing customers, the development of new customers, the use of foldouts (new facilities built in established markets), and an acquisition program. SYY distributes nationally branded merchandise, as well as products packaged under SYY private brands. We believe that Sysco-branded products typically carry wider profit margins than other branded products distributed by the company. From its inception through the end of FY 11, the company had acquired roughly 150 companies or divisions of companies. At July 2, 2011, SYY's balance sheet included $1.205 billion of goodwill.

Over time, we look for SYY's profitability to benefit from an increased amount of consolidated purchasing, the addition of regional distribution centers, and management of freight costs and inventory. Among SYY's supply chain initiatives are (1) the construction of regional distribution centers (RDCs), with two operational as of July 2011 and one planned for construction during FY 12; and (2) improving the capability to view and manage all of SYY's inbound freight, both to RDCs and the operating companies, as a network and not as individual locations.

## Company Financials Fiscal Year Ended Jun. 30

| Per Share Data ($) | 2011 | 2010 | 2009 | 2008 | 2007 | 2006 | 2005 | 2004 | 2003 | 2002 |
|---|---|---|---|---|---|---|---|---|---|---|
| Tangible Book Value | 5.01 | 3.69 | 3.08 | 3.17 | 2.99 | 2.67 | 2.35 | 2.11 | 1.68 | 1.85 |
| Cash Flow | 2.64 | 2.64 | 2.41 | 2.41 | 2.23 | 1.89 | 1.96 | 1.80 | 1.59 | 1.47 |
| Earnings | 1.96 | 1.99 | 1.77 | 1.81 | 1.60 | 1.35 | 1.47 | 1.37 | 1.18 | 1.01 |
| S&P Core Earnings | 2.06 | 2.06 | 1.65 | 1.68 | 1.59 | 1.38 | 1.39 | 1.31 | 1.08 | 0.92 |
| Dividends | 1.03 | 0.99 | 1.16 | 0.82 | 0.72 | 0.64 | 0.56 | 0.48 | 0.40 | 0.32 |
| Payout Ratio | 53% | 50% | 66% | 45% | 45% | 47% | 38% | 35% | 34% | 32% |
| Prices:High | 32.76 | 31.99 | 29.48 | 35.00 | 36.74 | 37.04 | 38.04 | 41.27 | 37.57 | 32.58 |
| Prices:Low | 25.09 | 26.99 | 19.39 | 20.74 | 29.90 | 26.50 | 29.98 | 29.48 | 22.90 | 21.25 |
| P/E Ratio:High | 17 | 16 | 17 | 19 | 23 | 27 | 26 | 30 | 32 | 32 |
| P/E Ratio:Low | 13 | 14 | 11 | 11 | 19 | 20 | 20 | 22 | 19 | 21 |

| Income Statement Analysis (Million $) | 2011 | 2010 | 2009 | 2008 | 2007 | 2006 | 2005 | 2004 | 2003 | 2002 |
|---|---|---|---|---|---|---|---|---|---|---|
| Revenue | 39,323 | 37,244 | 36,853 | 37,522 | 35,042 | 32,628 | 30,282 | 29,335 | 26,140 | 23,351 |
| Operating Income | 2,334 | 2,366 | 2,255 | 2,246 | 2,071 | 1,840 | 1,906 | 1,816 | 1,597 | 1,439 |
| Depreciation | 403 | 390 | 382 | 366 | 363 | 345 | 317 | 284 | 273 | 278 |
| Interest Expense | 118 | 125 | 116 | 118 | 105 | 109 | 75.0 | 69.9 | 72.2 | 62.9 |
| Pretax Income | 1,827 | 1,850 | 1,771 | 1,791 | 1,621 | 1,395 | 1,525 | 1,475 | 1,260 | 1,101 |
| Effective Tax Rate | NA | NA | 40.4% | 38.3% | 38.3% | 39.3% | 37.0% | 38.5% | 38.3% | 38.3% |
| Net Income | 1,152 | 1,180 | 1,056 | 1,106 | 1,001 | 846 | 961 | 907 | 778 | 680 |
| S&P Core Earnings | 1,209 | 1,219 | 987 | 1,022 | 995 | 866 | 890 | 868 | 710 | 618 |

| Balance Sheet & Other Financial Data (Million $) | 2011 | 2010 | 2009 | 2008 | 2007 | 2006 | 2005 | 2004 | 2003 | 2002 |
|---|---|---|---|---|---|---|---|---|---|---|
| Cash | 640 | 609 | 1,087 | 552 | 208 | 202 | 192 | 200 | 421 | 230 |
| Current Assets | 5,733 | 5,076 | 5,271 | 5,175 | 4,676 | 4,400 | 4,002 | 3,851 | 3,630 | 3,185 |
| Total Assets | 11,386 | 10,314 | 10,322 | 10,082 | 9,519 | 8,992 | 8,268 | 7,848 | 6,937 | 5,990 |
| Current Liabilities | 3,575 | 3,009 | 3,150 | 3,499 | 3,415 | 3,226 | 3,458 | 3,127 | 2,701 | 2,239 |
| Long Term Debt | 2,280 | 2,473 | 2,467 | 1,975 | 1,758 | 1,627 | 956 | 1,231 | 1,249 | 1,176 |
| Common Equity | 4,705 | 3,828 | 3,450 | 3,409 | 3,278 | 3,052 | 2,759 | 2,565 | 2,198 | 2,133 |
| Total Capital | 7,192 | 6,308 | 6,444 | 5,925 | 5,037 | 5,403 | 4,440 | 4,483 | 3,945 | 3,750 |
| Capital Expenditures | 636 | 595 | 465 | 516 | 603 | 515 | 390 | 530 | 436 | 416 |
| Cash Flow | 1,555 | 1,570 | 1,438 | 1,473 | 1,364 | 1,191 | 1,278 | 1,191 | 1,051 | 958 |
| Current Ratio | 1.6 | 1.7 | 1.7 | 1.5 | 1.4 | 1.4 | 1.2 | 1.2 | 1.3 | 1.4 |
| % Long Term Debt of Capitalization | 31.7 | 39.2 | 38.3 | 33.3 | 34.9 | 30.1 | 21.5 | 27.4 | 31.7 | 31.4 |
| % Net Income of Revenue | 2.9 | 3.2 | 2.9 | 3.0 | 2.9 | 2.6 | 3.2 | 3.1 | 3.0 | 2.9 |
| % Return on Assets | 10.6 | 11.5 | 10.4 | 11.3 | 10.8 | 9.8 | 11.9 | 12.3 | 12.0 | 12.0 |
| % Return on Equity | 27.0 | 32.4 | 30.8 | 33.1 | 31.6 | 29.1 | 36.1 | 38.1 | 35.9 | 32.1 |

Data as orig reptd.; bef. results of disc opers/spec. items. Per share data adj. for stk. divs.; EPS diluted. E-Estimated. NA-Not Available. NM-Not Meaningful. NR-Not Ranked. UR-Under Review.

**Office:** 1390 Enclave Parkway, Houston, TX, USA 77077-2099.
**Telephone:** 281-584-1390.
**Website:** http://www.sysco.com
**Chrmn:** M.A. Fernandez

**Pres & CEO:** W.J. DeLaney, III
**EVP & CFO:** R.C. Kreidler
**SVP, Chief Acctg Officer & Cntlr:** G.M. Elmer
**SVP, Secy & General Counsel:** R.T. Libby

**Board Members:** J. M. Cassaday, J. B. Craven, W. J. DeLaney, III, M. A. Fernandez, L. C. Glasscock, J. Golden, J. A. Hafner, Jr., H. Koerber, N. S. Newcomb, P. S. Sewell, R. G. Tilghman, J. M. Ward

**Founded:** 1969
**Domicile:** Delaware
**Employees:** 46,000

# Target Corp

**STANDARD &POOR'S**

| S&P Recommendation | **BUY** ★★★★☆ | Price $51.21 (as of Nov 25, 2011) | 12-Mo. Target Price $60.00 | Investment Style Large-Cap Growth |

**GICS Sector** Consumer Discretionary
**Sub-Industry** General Merchandise Stores

**Summary** This company operates about 1,500 Target and 250 SuperTarget general merchandise stores across the U.S.

## Key Stock Statistics (Source S&P, Vickers, company reports)

| | | | | | | | |
|---|---|---|---|---|---|---|---|
| 52-Wk Range | $60.97–45.28 | S&P Oper. EPS 2012**E** | 4.32 | Market Capitalization(B) | $34.578 | Beta | 0.89 |
| Trailing 12-Month EPS | $4.30 | S&P Oper. EPS 2013**E** | 4.64 | Yield (%) | 2.34 | S&P 3-Yr. Proj. EPS CAGR(%) | 7 |
| Trailing 12-Month P/E | 11.9 | P/E on S&P Oper. EPS 2012**E** | 11.9 | Dividend Rate/Share | $1.20 | S&P Credit Rating | A+ |
| $10K Invested 5 Yrs Ago | $9,578 | Common Shares Outstg. (M) | 675.2 | Institutional Ownership (%) | 85 | | |

## Price Performance

30-Week Mov. Avg. · · · 10-Week Mov. Avg. – – GAAP Earnings vs. Previous Year   Volume Above Avg. STARS
12-Mo. Target Price — Relative Strength   ▲ Up ▼ Down ► No Change   Below Avg.

Options: ASE, CBOE, Ph

Analysis prepared by Equity Analyst **Joseph Agnese** on Nov 21, 2011, when the stock traded at **$53.00**.

## Highlights

➤ We look for same-store sales to increase about 3.9% in FY 12 (Jan.) and 4.0% in FY 13, supported by the remodeling of Target stores to the PFresh format, which adds fresh foods; what we see as TGT's success in improving its value proposition to consumers; steps the company is taking to better align store assortments with customer preferences and in matching competitors' pricing; and increased customer penetration of REDcards. Also factoring in our expectations of incremental sales from new stores and lower credit revenues, we see revenues reaching $72.2 billion in FY 13, up from our estimate of $68.8 billion in FY 12.

➤ We look for increased margin pressure in both FY 12 and FY 13 due to higher product costs, new REDcard rewards program costs, and incremental expenses in support of new stores, a relaunch of target.com, store remodels, and TGT's growth infrastructure in Canada. We see these factors partly offset by increased operating leverage, disciplined inventory management, and an expected reduction in bad debt expense.

➤ Assuming share repurchases, we see FY 13 EPS of $4.64, up from our $4.32 FY 12 estimate.

## Investment Rationale/Risk

➤ Our buy recommendation is based on valuation. While we anticipate a slow and uneven economic recovery, we look for TGT to accelerate same-store sales growth through the end of FY 12, supported by higher traffic and cross-shopping of categories the company is seeing in new and remodeled PFresh stores; what we view as improving apparel and beauty assortments; and attractiveness of the REDcard rewards program to cost-conscious shoppers. We also see the Canadian market providing an attractive incremental growth opportunity for the company.

➤ Risks to our recommendation and target price include a loss of business due to changes in consumer confidence, spending habits and buying preferences, as well as increased promotional activity by competitors.

➤ Our 12-month target price of $60 is based on a blend of our historical and relative analyses. Our historical analysis suggests a value of $63, using a forward P/E multiple of 13.6X, the five-year median, applied to our FY 13 EPS estimate. Our peer analysis applies the group median of 12.3X, implying a value of $57.

## Qualitative Risk Assessment

| LOW | MEDIUM | HIGH |

Our risk assessment reflects our view of TGT's fairly consistent earnings track record, and its healthy balance sheet and cash flow, offset by our concerns over potential loss of market share as a result of lackluster merchandising and aggressive pricing by competitors.

## Quantitative Evaluations

**S&P Quality Ranking**   A+

| D | C | B- | B | B+ | A- | A | **A+** |

**Relative Strength Rank**   STRONG

71

LOWEST = 1   HIGHEST = 99

## Revenue/Earnings Data

**Revenue (Million $)**

| | 1Q | 2Q | 3Q | 4Q | Year |
|---|---|---|---|---|---|---|
| 2012 | 15,935 | 16,240 | 16,402 | -- | -- |
| 2011 | 15,593 | 15,532 | 15,605 | 20,661 | 67,390 |
| 2010 | 14,833 | 15,067 | 15,276 | 20,181 | 65,357 |
| 2009 | 14,302 | 15,472 | 15,114 | 19,560 | 64,948 |
| 2008 | 14,041 | 14,620 | 14,835 | 19,872 | 63,367 |
| 2007 | 12,863 | 13,347 | 13,570 | 19,710 | 59,490 |

**Earnings Per Share ($)**

| | 1Q | 2Q | 3Q | 4Q | Year |
|---|---|---|---|---|---|---|
| 2012 | 0.99 | 1.03 | 0.82 | E1.49 | E4.32 |
| 2011 | 0.90 | 0.92 | 0.74 | 1.45 | 4.00 |
| 2010 | 0.69 | 0.79 | 0.58 | 1.24 | 3.30 |
| 2009 | 0.74 | 0.82 | 0.49 | 0.81 | 2.86 |
| 2008 | 0.75 | 0.82 | 0.56 | 1.23 | 3.33 |
| 2007 | 0.63 | 0.70 | 0.59 | 1.29 | 3.21 |

Fiscal year ended Jan. 31. Next earnings report expected: NA. EPS Estimates based on S&P Operating Earnings; historical GAAP earnings are as reported.

## Dividend Data (Dates: mm/dd Payment Date: mm/dd/yy)

| Amount ($) | Date Decl. | Ex-Div. Date | Stk. of Record | Payment Date |
|---|---|---|---|---|
| 0.250 | 01/13 | 02/14 | 02/16 | 03/10/11 |
| 0.250 | 03/10 | 05/16 | 05/18 | 06/10/11 |
| 0.300 | 06/08 | 08/16 | 08/18 | 09/10/11 |
| 0.300 | 09/14 | 11/14 | 11/16 | 12/10/11 |

Dividends have been paid since 1965. Source: Company reports.

**Please read the Required Disclosures and Analyst Certification on the last page of this report.**

The McGraw-Hill Companies

# Target Corp

## Business Summary November 21, 2011

CORPORATE OVERVIEW. In FY 05 (Jan.), Target Corp. (TGT) shed its non-core legacy department store operations, retaining only its eponymous chain of up-scale general merchandise stores that cater to middle- and upper-income consumers. As of April 30, 2011, the company operated 1,503 Target locations and 252 SuperTarget stores. SuperTarget stores combine a full line of groceries with fashion apparel, electronics, home furnishings and other general merchandise found in Target stores. TGT's website serves as both a sales driver and a marketing vehicle. Target.com offers a more extensive selection of merchandise than the company's physical stores, including exclusive online products. To support sales and earnings growth, TGT offers credit to qualified customers. In FY 11, its credit card operations contributed $1.6 billion of revenues.

PRIMARY BUSINESS DYNAMICS. TGT's primary growth drivers are new store openings and same-store sales (sales results for stores open for over one year). From FY 06 through FY 11, the company increased its retail square footage at a compound annual growth rate (CAGR) of 5.6%, as its store count rose from 1,395 to 1,750. Having added a net of 12 Target locations to its store base and remodeled 341 stores in FY 11, TGT plans to add 21 new stores and to remodel 384 stores in FY 12.

From FY 03 through FY 08, same-store sales trended positive, averaging about a 4.5% increase annually. Same-store sales fell 2.9% in FY 09 and 2.5% in FY 10, as consumers' appetite to spend weakened in response to a challenging and uncertain macroeconomic environment. To drive same-store sales, TGT seeks to appeal to customers that are interested in sophisticated styles and quality by offering fashion newness, trusted brands, and exclusive designer labels such as Maternity by Liz Lange. Under the "Expect More. Pay Less." brand promise, the company believes it satisfies customer demand for value by matching Wal-Mart prices on identical and similar items in local markets, and by pricing its differentiated products at deep discounts. This is important for TGT, as it has historically drawn far less traffic from food than main competitor Wal-Mart, in our view. However, the company has also been steadily expanding food assortments in its Target stores as a means of driving shopping frequency and improving convenience for shoppers.

## Company Financials Fiscal Year Ended Jan. 31

| Per Share Data ($) | 2011 | 2010 | 2009 | 2008 | 2007 | 2006 | 2005 | 2004 | 2003 | 2002 |
|---|---|---|---|---|---|---|---|---|---|---|
| Tangible Book Value | 21.85 | 20.47 | 18.10 | 18.44 | 18.17 | 16.25 | 14.63 | 12.14 | 10.38 | 8.68 |
| Cash Flow | 6.86 | 5.98 | 5.22 | 5.30 | 4.93 | 4.29 | 3.45 | 3.45 | 3.14 | 2.70 |
| Earnings | 4.00 | 3.30 | 2.86 | 3.33 | 3.21 | 2.71 | 2.07 | 2.01 | 1.81 | 1.51 |
| S&P Core Earnings | 3.97 | 3.27 | 2.73 | 3.32 | 3.21 | 2.68 | 2.06 | 1.95 | 1.70 | 1.42 |
| Dividends | NA | 0.66 | 0.60 | 0.44 | 0.36 | 0.30 | 0.26 | 0.26 | 0.24 | 0.21 |
| Payout Ratio | NA | 20% | 21% | 13% | 11% | 11% | 13% | 13% | 13% | 14% |
| Calendar Year | 2010 | 2009 | 2008 | 2007 | 2006 | 2005 | 2004 | 2003 | 2002 | 2001 |
| Prices:High | 60.65 | 51.77 | 59.55 | 70.75 | 60.34 | 60.00 | 54.14 | 41.80 | 46.15 | 41.74 |
| Prices:Low | 48.23 | 25.00 | 25.60 | 48.85 | 44.70 | 45.55 | 36.63 | 25.60 | 24.90 | 26.00 |
| P/E Ratio:High | 15 | 16 | 21 | 21 | 19 | 22 | 26 | 21 | 25 | 28 |
| P/E Ratio:Low | 12 | 8 | 9 | 15 | 14 | 17 | 18 | 13 | 14 | 17 |

### Income Statement Analysis (Million $)

| | | | | | | | | | | |
|---|---|---|---|---|---|---|---|---|---|---|
| Revenue | 67,390 | 65,357 | 64,948 | 63,367 | 59,490 | 52,620 | 46,839 | 48,163 | 43,917 | 39,888 |
| Operating Income | 7,336 | 6,696 | 6,228 | 6,931 | 6,565 | 5,732 | 4,860 | 4,839 | 4,476 | 3,759 |
| Depreciation | 2,084 | 2,023 | 1,826 | 1,659 | 1,496 | 1,409 | 1,259 | 1,320 | 1,212 | 1,079 |
| Interest Expense | 760 | 804 | 894 | 747 | 597 | 532 | 674 | 559 | 588 | 464 |
| Pretax Income | 4,495 | 3,872 | 3,536 | 4,625 | 4,497 | 3,860 | 3,031 | 2,960 | 2,676 | 2,216 |
| Effective Tax Rate | NA | 35.7% | 37.4% | 38.4% | 38.0% | 37.6% | 37.8% | 37.8% | 38.2% | 38.0% |
| Net Income | 2,920 | 2,488 | 2,214 | 2,849 | 2,787 | 2,408 | 1,885 | 1,841 | 1,654 | 1,374 |
| S&P Core Earnings | 2,902 | 2,469 | 2,117 | 2,841 | 2,784 | 2,383 | 1,876 | 1,791 | 1,553 | 1,289 |

### Balance Sheet & Other Financial Data (Million $)

| | | | | | | | | | | |
|---|---|---|---|---|---|---|---|---|---|---|
| Cash | 1,712 | 2,200 | 864 | 2,450 | 813 | 1,648 | 2,245 | 716 | 758 | 499 |
| Current Assets | 17,213 | 18,424 | 17,488 | 18,906 | 14,706 | 14,405 | 13,922 | 12,928 | 11,935 | 9,648 |
| Total Assets | 43,705 | 44,533 | 44,106 | 44,560 | 37,349 | 34,995 | 32,293 | 31,392 | 28,603 | 24,154 |
| Current Liabilities | 10,070 | 11,327 | 10,512 | 11,782 | 11,117 | 9,588 | 8,220 | 8,314 | 7,523 | 7,054 |
| Long Term Debt | 15,607 | 15,118 | 17,371 | 15,126 | 8,675 | 9,119 | 9,034 | 10,217 | 10,186 | 8,088 |
| Common Equity | 15,487 | 15,347 | 13,712 | 15,307 | 15,633 | 14,205 | 13,029 | 11,065 | 9,443 | 7,860 |
| Total Capital | 31,213 | 32,161 | 31,538 | 30,903 | 24,885 | 24,175 | 23,036 | 21,282 | 21,080 | 15,948 |
| Capital Expenditures | 2,129 | 1,729 | 3,547 | 4,369 | 3,928 | 3,388 | 3,068 | 3,004 | 3,221 | 3,163 |
| Cash Flow | 5,004 | 4,511 | 4,040 | 4,508 | 4,283 | 3,817 | 3,144 | 3,161 | 2,866 | 2,453 |
| Current Ratio | 1.7 | 1.6 | 1.7 | 1.6 | 1.3 | 1.5 | 1.7 | 1.6 | 1.6 | 1.4 |
| % Long Term Debt of Capitalization | 50.0 | 47.0 | 55.1 | 49.0 | 34.9 | 37.7 | 39.2 | 48.0 | 48.3 | 50.7 |
| % Net Income of Revenue | 4.3 | 3.8 | 3.4 | 4.5 | 4.7 | 4.5 | 4.0 | 3.8 | 3.8 | 3.4 |
| % Return on Assets | 6.6 | 5.6 | 5.0 | 7.0 | 7.7 | 7.1 | 5.9 | 6.1 | 6.3 | 6.3 |
| % Return on Equity | 18.9 | 17.1 | 15.3 | 18.4 | 18.7 | 17.6 | 15.6 | 18.0 | 19.1 | 19.1 |

Data as orig reptd.; bef. results of disc opers/spec. items. Per share data adj. for stk. divs.; EPS diluted. E-Estimated. NA-Not Available. NM-Not Meaningful. NR-Not Ranked. UR-Under Review.

**Office:** 1000 Nicollet Mall, Minneapolis, MN 55403-2467.
**Telephone:** 612-304-6073.
**Website:** http://www.target.com
**Chrmn, Pres & CEO:** G.W. Steinhafel

**Investor Contact:** D.A. Scovanner
**EVP, CFO & Chief Acctg Officer:** D.A. Scovanner
**Treas:** C.L. Haaland
**Secy & General Counsel:** T.R. Baer

**Board Members:** R. S. Austin, C. Darden, M. N. Dillon, J. A. Johnson, M. E. Minnick, A. M. Mulcahy, D. W. Rice, S. W. Sanger, G. W. Steinhafel, J. G. Stumpf, S. Trujillo

**Founded:** 1902
**Domicile:** Minnesota
**Employees:** 355,000

# TECO Energy Inc.

STANDARD &POOR'S

| S&P Recommendation HOLD ★★★★★ | Price $17.51 (as of Nov 25, 2011) | 12-Mo. Target Price $19.00 | Investment Style Large-Cap Value |
|---|---|---|---|

**GICS Sector** Utilities
**Sub-Industry** Multi-Utilities

**Summary** This company owns Tampa Electric Co., which serves the Tampa Bay region in west central Florida and has significant diversified operations related to its core business.

## Key Stock Statistics (Source S&P, Vickers, company reports)

| | | | | | | | |
|---|---|---|---|---|---|---|---|
| 52-Wk Range | $19.66–15.82 | S&P Oper. EPS 2011E | 1.33 | Market Capitalization(B) | $3.778 | Beta | 0.83 |
| Trailing 12-Month EPS | $1.28 | S&P Oper. EPS 2012E | 1.49 | Yield (%) | 4.91 | S&P 3-Yr. Proj. EPS CAGR(%) | 9 |
| Trailing 12-Month P/E | 13.7 | P/E on S&P Oper. EPS 2011E | 13.2 | Dividend Rate/Share | $0.86 | S&P Credit Rating | BBB+ |
| $10K Invested 5 Yrs Ago | $13,395 | Common Shares Outstg. (M) | 215.8 | Institutional Ownership (%) | 56 | | |

## Price Performance

30-Week Mov. Avg. · · · 10-Week Mov. Avg. - - GAAP Earnings vs. Previous Year    Volume Above Avg. STARS
12-Mo. Target Price — Relative Strength — ▲ Up ▼ Down ► No Change    Below Avg.

Options: Ph

Analysis prepared by Equity Analyst **Justin McCann** on Aug 29, 2011, when the stock traded at **$17.75**.

## Qualitative Risk Assessment

| LOW | MEDIUM | HIGH |
|---|---|---|

Our risk assessment reflects the steady cash flow we expect from the regulated electric and gas utilities, which operate within a generally supportive regulatory environment, offset by our view of the much less predictable earnings and cash flow from the unregulated coal and transport operations, particularly given uncertainties concerning tax credits related to the synthetic fuel operations.

## Quantitative Evaluations

**S&P Quality Ranking** B

| D | C | B- | B | B+ | A- | A | A+ |
|---|---|---|---|---|---|---|---|

**Relative Strength Rank** MODERATE

63

LOWEST = 1    HIGHEST = 99

## Highlights

➤ We expect operating EPS in 2011 to increase about 2% from 2010's $1.28, which grew nearly 19% from 2009's $1.08. In the first half of 2011, earnings at Tampa Electric and Peoples Gas were hurt by the much milder weather in the first quarter, while earnings at TECO Coal were down due to higher operating costs and the absence of a tax benefit in the year-earlier period.

➤ For full-year 2011, we expect operating EPS to benefit from a modest recovery in the Florida economy, higher selling prices and continuing strong demand at TECO Coal, and lower interest expense. However, we believe this will be partially offset by lower energy sales at Tampa Electric due to the milder weather. For 2012, we expect operating EPS to increase nearly 14% from anticipated results in 2011, aided by an assumed return to more normal weather.

➤ We expect the TECO Coal subsidiary to have sales of between 8.2 and 8.5 million tons in 2011, with 100% of its sales having already been contracted at an average selling price of $88 a ton, compared to 8.8 million tons at more than $76 per ton in 2010. The cost of production per ton is expected to increase from $69 in 2010 to between $76 and $78 in 2011.

## Investment Rationale/Risk

➤ With TE recently trading at a premium-to-peers P/E of 14.5X our operating EPS estimate for 2011, we believe the shares will realize a relatively modest level of total return in 2011. After a 9.7% increase in 2010, the shares were up about 7.3% in the first 34 weeks of 2011. Despite the weather-related weakness at the utilities, we believe the shares have benefited from strong international demand for coal. For the next 12 months, we expect the stock to reflect the ongoing strength of TECO Coal and, despite a projected customer growth of less than 1%, an expected increase in earnings at the utilities due to an assumed return to normal weather.

➤ Risks to our recommendation and target price include prolonged weakness in the housing market, a sharp decrease in the average P/E of the electric utility group as a whole, and much lower than anticipated earnings from the non-regulated coal operations.

➤ TE's dividend, recently yielding around 4.8%, represents an above-peers payout ratio of 66% of its operating EPS for 2010 and a 65% payout of our EPS estimate for 2011. Our 12-month target price is $19, reflecting a premium-to-peers P/E of 14.5X our 2011 estimate.

## Revenue/Earnings Data

### Revenue (Million $)

| | 1Q | 2Q | 3Q | 4Q | Year |
|---|---|---|---|---|---|
| 2011 | 796.1 | 885.7 | 911.4 | -- | -- |
| 2010 | 912.3 | 898.8 | 901.8 | 775.0 | 3,488 |
| 2009 | 824.0 | 825.2 | 896.3 | 765.0 | 3,311 |
| 2008 | 791.7 | 887.2 | 926.1 | 770.3 | 3,375 |
| 2007 | 821.3 | 866.5 | 990.0 | 858.3 | 3,536 |
| 2006 | 836.4 | 862.6 | 922.9 | 826.2 | 3,448 |

### Earnings Per Share ($)

| | | | | | |
|---|---|---|---|---|---|
| 2011 | 0.24 | 0.36 | 0.42 | E0.31 | E1.33 |
| 2010 | 0.26 | 0.35 | 0.24 | 0.26 | 1.11 |
| 2009 | 0.16 | 0.29 | 0.30 | 0.25 | 1.00 |
| 2008 | 0.15 | 0.24 | 0.27 | 0.10 | 0.77 |
| 2007 | 0.35 | 0.28 | 0.44 | 0.83 | 1.90 |
| 2006 | 0.26 | 0.29 | 0.38 | 0.23 | 1.17 |

Fiscal year ended Dec. 31. Next earnings report expected: Early February. EPS Estimates based on S&P Operating Earnings; historical GAAP earnings are as reported.

## Dividend Data (Dates: mm/dd Payment Date: mm/dd/yy)

| Amount ($) | Date Decl. | Ex-Div. Date | Stk. of Record | Payment Date |
|---|---|---|---|---|
| 0.205 | 02/02 | 02/10 | 02/14 | 02/28/11 |
| 0.215 | 05/04 | 05/12 | 05/16 | 05/27/11 |
| 0.215 | 08/03 | 08/11 | 08/15 | 08/26/11 |
| 0.215 | 11/02 | 11/09 | 11/14 | 11/28/11 |

Dividends have been paid since 1900. Source: Company reports.

---

**Please read the Required Disclosures and Analyst Certification on the last page of this report.**

The McGraw·Hill Companies

# TECO Energy Inc.

**STANDARD &POOR'S**

## Business Summary August 29, 2011

CORPORATE OVERVIEW. TECO Energy (TE) is a holding company for a diverse set of energy companies including the regulated utility subsidiary Tampa Electric Company, which provides retail electric service in west central Florida. TE's other regulated utility is Peoples Gas System, which distributes natural gas in Florida's metropolitan areas. TE's unregulated businesses include TECO Coal, which has coal-mining operations, and TECO Guatemala, which participates in independent power projects and electric distribution in Guatemala. In December 2007, TE completed the sale of TECO Transport, which provided shipping and storage services for coal and other dry-bulk commodities. In 2010, Tampa Electric accounted for 61.7% of TE's consolidated revenues; TECO Coal 19.7%; Peoples Gas System 15.1%; and TECO Guatemala 3.5%.

CORPORATE STRATEGY. Despite the challenges and uncertainties related to

the current state of the economy and housing market in Florida, TECO Energy plans to continue its strategy of investment in Tampa Electric. The company intends to remain focused on the reduction of its debt and to improve its already investment-grade status so as to ensure access to the credit markets and to meet its growing level of necessary capital investment. TE expects to continue its investment in the Peoples Gas infrastructure to serve more customers and to maintain its compliance with federal pipeline standards. The company believes the most significant factors affecting the results of TECO Coal in 2011 will be the cost of its coal production and the ability of the railroads to deliver the contracted volumes.

## Company Financials Fiscal Year Ended Dec. 31

| Per Share Data ($) | 2010 | 2009 | 2008 | 2007 | 2006 | 2005 | 2004 | 2003 | 2002 | 2001 |
|---|---|---|---|---|---|---|---|---|---|---|
| Tangible Book Value | 9.84 | 9.47 | 9.15 | 9.28 | 7.97 | 7.36 | 6.13 | 8.55 | 13.75 | 12.94 |
| Earnings | 1.11 | 1.00 | 0.77 | 1.90 | 1.17 | 1.00 | -2.10 | -0.08 | 1.95 | 2.24 |
| S&P Core Earnings | 1.05 | 0.98 | 0.67 | 1.25 | 1.19 | 1.00 | -1.58 | 0.24 | 1.75 | 2.04 |
| Dividends | 0.82 | 0.80 | 0.80 | 0.78 | 0.76 | 0.76 | 0.76 | 0.93 | 1.41 | 1.37 |
| Payout Ratio | 73% | 80% | 103% | 41% | 65% | 76% | NM | NM | 72% | 61% |
| Prices:High | 18.11 | 16.71 | 21.99 | 18.58 | 17.73 | 19.30 | 15.49 | 17.00 | 29.05 | 32.97 |
| Prices:Low | 14.46 | 8.41 | 10.50 | 14.84 | 14.40 | 14.87 | 11.30 | 9.47 | 10.02 | 24.75 |
| P/E Ratio:High | 16 | 17 | 29 | 10 | 15 | 19 | NM | NM | 15 | 15 |
| P/E Ratio:Low | 13 | 8 | 14 | 8 | 12 | 15 | NM | NM | 5 | 11 |

| Income Statement Analysis (Million $) | 2010 | 2009 | 2008 | 2007 | 2006 | 2005 | 2004 | 2003 | 2002 | 2001 |
|---|---|---|---|---|---|---|---|---|---|---|
| Revenue | 3,488 | 3,311 | 3,375 | 3,536 | 3,448 | 3,010 | 2,669 | 2,740 | 2,676 | 2,649 |
| Depreciation | 313 | 288 | 266 | 264 | 282 | 282 | 282 | 326 | 303 | 298 |
| Maintenance | 185 | 188 | 174 | 184 | 183 | 168 | 141 | 152 | 162 | 151 |
| Fixed Charges Coverage | 2.97 | 2.17 | 1.80 | 2.06 | 1.42 | 1.25 | 1.26 | 2.30 | 2.43 | 2.51 |
| Construction Credits | 3.00 | 13.8 | 8.70 | 6.20 | 3.80 | Nil | 1.00 | 27.4 | 9.60 | 2.60 |
| Effective Tax Rate | 41.5% | 31.6% | 36.8% | 40.4% | 40.2% | 45.1% | NM | NM | NM | NM |
| Net Income | 239 | 214 | 162 | 399 | 246 | 211 | -404 | -14.7 | 298 | 304 |
| S&P Core Earnings | 227 | 210 | 143 | 260 | 248 | 212 | -306 | 44.4 | 267 | 277 |

| Balance Sheet & Other Financial Data (Million $) | 2010 | 2009 | 2008 | 2007 | 2006 | 2005 | 2004 | 2003 | 2002 | 2001 |
|---|---|---|---|---|---|---|---|---|---|---|
| Gross Property | 8,285 | 7,778 | 7,311 | 6,894 | 7,084 | 6,755 | 6,723 | 8,040 | 8,215 | 7,544 |
| Capital Expenditures | 488 | 630 | 583 | 494 | 456 | 295 | 273 | 591 | 1,065 | 966 |
| Net Property | 5,841 | 5,544 | 5,221 | 4,888 | 4,767 | 4,567 | 4,658 | 5,679 | 5,464 | 4,838 |
| Capitalization:Long Term Debt | 3,148 | 3,202 | 3,207 | 3,158 | 3,213 | 3,709 | 3,880 | 4,393 | 3,973 | 2,043 |
| Capitalization:% Long Term Debt | 59.2 | 60.6 | 61.5 | 61.0 | 65.0 | 70.0 | 75.1 | 73.0 | 43.2 | 50.9 |
| Capitalization:Preferred | Nil | Nil | Nil | Nil | Nil | Nil | Nil | Nil | Nil | Nil |
| Capitalization:% Preferred | Nil | Nil | Nil | Nil | Nil | Nil | Nil | Nil | Nil | Nil |
| Capitalization:Common | 2,170 | 2,085 | 2,008 | 2,017 | 1,729 | 1,592 | 1,284 | 1,622 | 5,223 | 1,972 |
| Capitalization:% Common | 40.8 | 39.4 | 38.5 | 39.0 | 35.0 | 30.0 | 24.9 | 27.0 | 56.8 | 49.1 |
| Total Capital | 5,397 | 5,395 | 5,226 | 5,188 | 4,957 | 5,318 | 5,691 | 6,537 | 9,719 | 4,545 |
| % Operating Ratio | 86.9 | 88.3 | 91.4 | 94.3 | 91.9 | 91.4 | 80.2 | 83.7 | 84.0 | 83.7 |
| % Earned on Net Property | 11.0 | 9.0 | 7.6 | 8.6 | 9.0 | 7.7 | NA | 0.3 | 7.6 | 9.6 |
| % Return on Revenue | 6.9 | 6.5 | 4.8 | 11.3 | 7.1 | 7.0 | NM | NM | 11.1 | 11.5 |
| % Return on Invested Capital | 9.6 | 7.4 | 6.1 | 6.3 | 8.5 | 9.3 | 14.2 | 9.6 | 6.4 | 11.9 |
| % Return on Common Equity | 11.3 | 10.5 | 8.1 | 21.3 | 14.8 | 14.7 | NM | NM | 6.5 | 17.5 |

Data as orig reptd.; bef. results of disc opers/spec. items. Per share data adj. for stk. divs.; EPS diluted. E-Estimated. NA-Not Available. NM-Not Meaningful. NR-Not Ranked. UR-Under Review.

**Office:** TECO Plaza, 702 North Franklin Street, Tampa, FL 33602.
**Telephone:** 813-228-1111.
**Website:** http://www.tecoenergy.com
**Chrmn:** S.W. Hudson

**Pres & CEO:** J. Ramil
**SVP, CFO & Chief Acctg Officer:** S.W. Callahan
**Chief Admin Officer:** B. Meece
**Treas:** K.M. Caruso

**Investor Contact:** M.M. Kane (813-228-1772)
**Board Members:** D. Ausley, J. L. Ferman, Jr., S. W. Hudson, J. P. Lacher, L. A. Penn, J. Ramil, T. L. Rankin, W. Rockford, P. L. Whiting

**Founded:** 1899
**Domicile:** Florida
**Employees:** 4,233

The McGraw-Hill Companies

# Tellabs Inc

STANDARD &POOR'S

| **S&P Recommendation** HOLD ★★★★★ | **Price** $3.93 (as of Nov 29, 2011) | **12-Mo. Target Price** $4.00 |
|---|---|---|

**GICS Sector** Information Technology
**Sub-Industry** Communications Equipment

**Summary** This company manufactures voice and data equipment used in public and private communications networks worldwide.

## Key Stock Statistics (Source S&P, Vickers, company reports)

| | | | | | | | |
|---|---|---|---|---|---|---|---|
| 52-Wk Range | $7.31– 3.67 | S&P Oper. EPS 2011**E** | -0.13 | Market Capitalization(B) | $1.434 | Beta | 0.60 |
| Trailing 12-Month EPS | $-0.52 | S&P Oper. EPS 2012**E** | -0.09 | Yield (%) | 2.04 | S&P 3-Yr. Proj. EPS CAGR(%) | 5 |
| Trailing 12-Month P/E | NM | P/E on S&P Oper. EPS 2011**E** | NM | Dividend Rate/Share | $0.08 | S&P Credit Rating | NA |
| $10K Invested 5 Yrs Ago | $3,554 | Common Shares Outstg. (M) | 364.9 | Institutional Ownership (%) | 73 | | |

## Price Performance

30-Week Mov. Avg. · · · · 10-Week Mov. Avg. - - GAAP Earnings vs. Previous Year    Volume Above Avg. STARS
12-Mo. Target Price — Relative Strength — ▲ Up ▼ Down ► No Change    Below Avg.

Options: ASE, CBOE, P, Ph

Analysis prepared by Equity Analyst **Todd Rosenbluth** on Nov 29, 2011, when the stock traded at **$3.94**.

## Qualitative Risk Assessment

| LOW | MEDIUM | **HIGH** |
|---|---|---|

Our risk assessment reflects the competitive pressures the company faces, and its dependence on a consolidating telecom industry.

## Quantitative Evaluations

**S&P Quality Ranking**      B

| D | C | B- | **B** | B+ | A- | A | A+ |
|---|---|---|---|---|---|---|---|

**Relative Strength Rank**      MODERATE

36

LOWEST = 1          HIGHEST = 99

## Highlights

➤ We see sales declining 22% in 2011 and 1.5% in 2012, reflecting a drop in demand for legacy products, particularly the mature core 5500 cross-connect solution, partly offset by higher sales of new products, such as the 7100 optical transport systems. We believe the company is facing increased competition for business at large customer AT&T. We foresee international revenue becoming a larger portion of the overall business mix in 2012.

➤ After an expected narrowing of 2011 gross margins by 900 basis points from 2010 to 39%, largely on an unfavorable product mix shift away from higher-margin digital cross connects, as well as a higher proportion of lower-margin international sales, we look for 40% margins in 2012. In July, TLAB announced a cost reduction program, including a 10% workforce elimination, aimed at stripping $50 million from its annual operating expense rate.

➤ We expect TLAB's loss per share to narrow to $0.09 in 2012, from a projected $0.13 in 2011, including stock compensation expense of $0.08 in 2012.

## Investment Rationale/Risk

➤ We view TLAB's near-term growth prospects and visibility as limited, given that its legacy cross-connect products are in a state of secular decline and our belief that its market position at important customer AT&T is weakening. With a crucial need for higher R&D investment to improve its product portfolio, we expect TLAB to continue to lose money in 2012. However, based on our view of its cash cushion and improving prospects internationally, and the recent decline in the shares, we think the shares are fairly valued.

➤ Risks to our recommendation and target price include reduced spending from major customers, a greater cash burn rate, and slower-than-expected growth product traction.

➤ Our 12-month target price of $4.00 equates to roughly 1X our 2012 sales forecast and 0.9X book value, multiples that are below peers, reflecting our view of TLAB's below industry average sales growth profile. While the company is launching several new products to improve its growth prospects, we think it will face a difficult road toward an operational turnaround.

## Revenue/Earnings Data

### Revenue (Million $)

| | 1Q | 2Q | 3Q | 4Q | Year |
|---|---|---|---|---|---|
| 2011 | 322.4 | 334.2 | 313.8 | -- | -- |
| 2010 | 379.7 | 422.7 | 429.2 | 410.5 | 1,642 |
| 2009 | 361.7 | 385.4 | 389.3 | 389.3 | 1,526 |
| 2008 | 464.1 | 432.5 | 424.1 | 408.3 | 1,729 |
| 2007 | 451.9 | 534.5 | 457.9 | 469.1 | 1,913 |
| 2006 | 514.7 | 549.3 | 522.5 | 454.7 | 2,041 |

### Earnings Per Share ($)

| | 1Q | 2Q | 3Q | 4Q | Year |
|---|---|---|---|---|---|
| 2011 | -0.07 | -0.06 | -0.38 | E-0.03 | E-0.13 |
| 2010 | 0.12 | 0.16 | 0.15 | -0.03 | 0.41 |
| 2009 | 0.02 | 0.04 | 0.07 | 0.16 | 0.29 |
| 2008 | 0.04 | -0.10 | -2.51 | 0.03 | -2.32 |
| 2007 | 0.06 | 0.07 | 0.01 | 0.02 | 0.15 |
| 2006 | 0.11 | 0.12 | 0.13 | 0.07 | 0.43 |

Fiscal year ended Dec. 31. Next earnings report expected: Late January. EPS Estimates based on S&P Operating Earnings; historical GAAP earnings are as reported.

## Dividend Data (Dates: mm/dd Payment Date: mm/dd/yy)

| Amount ($) | Date Decl. | Ex-Div. Date | Stk. of Record | Payment Date |
|---|---|---|---|---|
| 0.020 | 01/28 | 02/09 | 02/11 | 02/25/11 |
| 0.020 | 05/04 | 05/11 | 05/13 | 05/27/11 |
| 0.020 | 07/28 | 08/10 | 08/12 | 08/26/11 |
| 0.020 | 10/27 | 11/02 | 11/04 | 11/18/11 |

Dividends have been paid since 2010. Source: Company reports.

---

**Please read the Required Disclosures and Analyst Certification on the last page of this report.**

The McGraw-Hill Companies

# Tellabs Inc

## Business Summary November 29, 2011

CORPORATE OVERVIEW. Tellabs designs, manufactures, markets and services optical networking, next-generation switching and broadband access solutions. The company's products enable the delivery of wireline and wireless voice, data and video services. Solutions are primarily focused on the last mile of the communications network, the part of the network that is closest to homes and businesses. International sales are an area of focus for TLAB, representing 52% of total sales during the third quarter of 2011. Results are reported in three business segments: broadband, transport and services.

The broadband segment, which accounts for 54% of total sales, enables service providers to deliver bundled voice, video and high-speed Internet data services over copper or fiber networks. Broadband access products include digital loop carriers, digital subscriber line access multiplexers, fiber-to-the-premise (FTTP) optical line terminals for broadband passive optical networks, and voice gateways for voice over Internet protocol (VoIP). Managed access products include aggregation and transport products that deliver wireless and business services outside of the United States. Data products include next-generation packet-switched products that enable wireline and wireless carriers to deliver business services and next-generation wireless services to their customers.

The transport segment, which represents 27% of total sales, enables service providers to transport services and manage bandwidth by adding capacity when and where it is needed. Wireline and wireless providers use these to support wireless services, business services for enterprises, and triple-play voice, video and data services for consumers. Products include the company's core digital cross-connect systems, voice-quality enhancement products, and optical transport systems.

The services segment (18%) delivers deployment, training, support services and professional consulting to customers. Services in the planning phase include network architecture and design, network and applications planning, network management design, migration planning and others. Building services include applications integration, program and project management, installation, testing, network integration, third-party systems integration and others.

## Company Financials Fiscal Year Ended Dec. 31

| Per Share Data ($) | 2010 | 2009 | 2008 | 2007 | 2006 | 2005 | 2004 | 2003 | 2002 | 2001 |
|---|---|---|---|---|---|---|---|---|---|---|
| Tangible Book Value | 4.36 | 4.18 | 4.25 | 4.14 | 3.97 | 3.53 | 3.34 | 3.76 | 4.45 | 5.55 |
| Cash Flow | 0.61 | 0.48 | -2.11 | 0.35 | 0.66 | 0.66 | 0.12 | -0.32 | -0.41 | -0.06 |
| Earnings | 0.41 | 0.29 | -2.32 | 0.15 | 0.43 | 0.39 | -0.07 | -0.58 | -0.76 | -0.44 |
| S&P Core Earnings | 0.40 | 0.28 | -0.69 | 0.16 | 0.44 | 0.38 | -0.14 | -0.71 | -1.03 | -0.68 |
| Dividends | 0.08 | Nil | Nil | Nil | Nil | Nil | Nil | Nil | Nil | Nil |
| Payout Ratio | 20% | Nil | Nil | Nil | Nil | Nil | Nil | Nil | Nil | Nil |
| Prices:High | 9.45 | 7.70 | 7.21 | 13.67 | 17.28 | 11.49 | 11.37 | 9.73 | 17.47 | 67.13 |
| Prices:Low | 5.68 | 3.52 | 3.10 | 6.52 | 8.84 | 6.56 | 7.40 | 5.07 | 4.00 | 8.98 |
| P/E Ratio:High | 23 | 27 | NM | 91 | 40 | 29 | NM | NM | NM | NM |
| P/E Ratio:Low | 14 | 12 | NM | 43 | 21 | 17 | NM | NM | NM | NM |

| Income Statement Analysis (Million $) | | | | | | | | | | |
|---|---|---|---|---|---|---|---|---|---|---|
| Revenue | 1,642 | 1,526 | 1,729 | 1,913 | 2,041 | 1,883 | 1,232 | 980 | 1,317 | 2,200 |
| Operating Income | 261 | 202 | 147 | 124 | 358 | 330 | 152 | -77.1 | -12.7 | 70.9 |
| Depreciation | 77.3 | 75.3 | 87.4 | 90.7 | 104 | 126 | 82.3 | 110 | 143 | 158 |
| Interest Expense | NA | NA | Nil | Nil | Nil | Nil | Nil | 0.70 | 0.90 | 0.51 |
| Pretax Income | 192 | 113 | -952 | 70.2 | 285 | 213 | -10.2 | -245 | -328 | -245 |
| Effective Tax Rate | NA | NM | NM | 7.41% | 31.8% | 17.5% | NM | NM | NM | NM |
| Net Income | 156 | 114 | -930 | 65.0 | 194 | 176 | -29.8 | -242 | -313 | -182 |
| S&P Core Earnings | 151 | 110 | -279 | 68.7 | 198 | 171 | -58.9 | -295 | -427 | -277 |

| Balance Sheet & Other Financial Data (Million $) | | | | | | | | | | |
|---|---|---|---|---|---|---|---|---|---|---|
| Cash | 1,348 | 1,358 | 1,331 | 1,510 | 154 | 1,371 | 293 | 246 | 1,019 | 1,102 |
| Current Assets | 1,913 | 1,898 | 1,936 | 2,112 | 2,233 | 1,873 | 1,819 | 1,499 | 1,534 | 1,945 |
| Total Assets | 2,603 | 2,623 | 2,508 | 3,747 | 3,922 | 3,515 | 3,523 | 2,608 | 2,623 | 2,866 |
| Current Liabilities | 663 | 609 | 541 | 673 | 762 | 525 | 524 | 208 | 257 | 320 |
| Long Term Debt | NA | NA | Nil | Nil | Nil | Nil | Nil | Nil | Nil | 3.39 |
| Common Equity | 1,862 | 1,915 | 1,847 | 2,913 | 2,938 | 2,815 | 2,797 | 2,219 | 2,290 | 2,466 |
| Total Capital | 1,862 | 1,915 | 1,847 | 2,992 | 2,938 | 2,815 | 2,797 | 2,319 | 2,290 | 2,490 |
| Capital Expenditures | 55.6 | 45.9 | 50.1 | 57.7 | 67.2 | 61.8 | 41.4 | 9.50 | 34.1 | 208 |
| Cash Flow | 233 | 189 | -843 | 156 | 298 | 302 | 52.5 | -131 | -171 | -24.5 |
| Current Ratio | 2.9 | 3.1 | 3.6 | 3.1 | 2.9 | 3.6 | 3.5 | 7.2 | 6.0 | 6.1 |
| % Long Term Debt of Capitalization | Nil | Nil | Nil | Nil | Nil | Nil | Nil | Nil | Nil | 0.1 |
| % Net Income of Revenue | 9.5 | 7.5 | NM | 3.4 | 9.5 | 9.3 | NM | NM | NM | NM |
| % Return on Assets | 6.0 | 4.4 | NM | 1.7 | 5.2 | 5.0 | NM | NM | NM | NM |
| % Return on Equity | 8.2 | 6.0 | NM | 2.2 | 6.7 | 6.3 | NM | NM | NM | NM |

Data as orig reptd.; bef. results of disc opers/spec. items. Per share data adj. for stk. divs.; EPS diluted. E-Estimated. NA-Not Available. NM-Not Meaningful. NR-Not Ranked. UR-Under Review.

**Office:** 1415 W Diehl Rd, Naperville, IL 60563-2349.
**Telephone:** 630-798-8800.
**Website:** http://www.tellabs.com
**Chrmn:** M.J. Birck

**Pres & CEO:** R.W. Pullen
**COO:** J.M. Brots
**EVP & CFO:** T.J. Wiggins
**EVP, Chief Admin Officer, Secy & General Counsel:** J.M. Sheehan

**Investor Contact:** T. Scottino (630-798-3602)
**Board Members:** M. J. Birck, B. C. C. Hedfors, F. Ianna, L. W. Kahangi, M. E. Lavin, S. P. Marshall, R. W. Pullen, W. F. Souders, J. H. Suwinski, V. H. Tobkin

**Founded:** 1974
**Domicile:** Delaware
**Employees:** 3,413

# Tenet Healthcare Corp

STANDARD
&POOR'S

| S&P Recommendation | HOLD ★★★★★ | Price $4.17 (as of Nov 25, 2011) | 12-Mo. Target Price $6.00 | Investment Style Large-Cap Value |
|---|---|---|---|---|

**GICS Sector** Health Care
**Sub-Industry** Health Care Facilities

**Summary** This company is among the largest U.S. for-profit hospital managers.

## Key Stock Statistics (Source S&P, Vickers, company reports)

| | | | | | | | |
|---|---|---|---|---|---|---|---|
| 52-Wk Range | $7.70–3.46 | S&P Oper. EPS 2011**E** | 0.42 | Market Capitalization(B) | $1.811 | Beta | 2.29 |
| Trailing 12-Month EPS | $0.42 | S&P Oper. EPS 2012**E** | 0.48 | Yield (%) | Nil | S&P 3-Yr. Proj. EPS CAGR(%) | 13 |
| Trailing 12-Month P/E | 9.9 | P/E on S&P Oper. EPS 2011**E** | 9.9 | Dividend Rate/Share | Nil | S&P Credit Rating | B |
| $10K Invested 5 Yrs Ago | $5,882 | Common Shares Outstg. (M) | 434.3 | Institutional Ownership (%) | NM | | |

## Price Performance

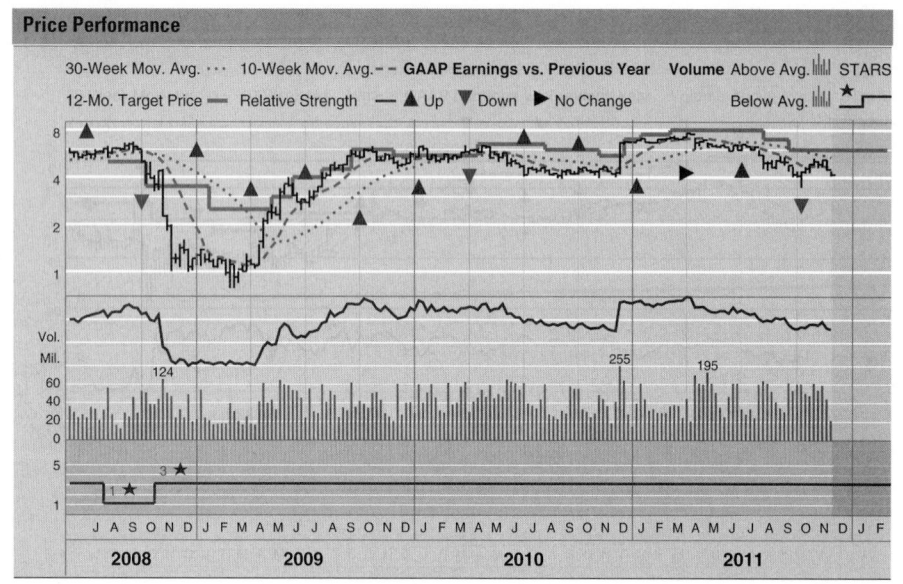

30-Week Mov. Avg. ···  10-Week Mov. Avg. - -  **GAAP Earnings vs. Previous Year**  Volume Above Avg. STARS
12-Mo. Target Price —  Relative Strength —  ▲ Up  ▼ Down  ▶ No Change  Below Avg.

Options: ASE, CBOE, P

Analysis prepared by Equity Analyst **Steven Silver** on Nov 09, 2011, when the stock traded at **$5.16**.

## Qualitative Risk Assessment

| LOW | MEDIUM | HIGH |
|---|---|---|

Our risk assessment reflects our view of Tenet's high debt level and protracted weakness in commercially insured admissions. In addition, we are concerned about the company's strong dependence on third-party reimbursements, including Medicare and Medicaid, which can be unpredictable.

## Quantitative Evaluations

**S&P Quality Ranking**    B-

| D | C | B- | B | B+ | A- | A | A+ |
|---|---|---|---|---|---|---|---|

**Relative Strength Rank**    WEAK

| 24 |
|---|

LOWEST = 1    HIGHEST = 99

## Revenue/Earnings Data

**Revenue (Million $)**

| | 1Q | 2Q | 3Q | 4Q | Year |
|---|---|---|---|---|---|
| 2011 | 2,506 | 2,374 | 2,342 | -- | -- |
| 2010 | 2,339 | 2,303 | 2,262 | 2,301 | 9,205 |
| 2009 | 2,262 | 2,229 | 2,262 | 2,261 | 9,014 |
| 2008 | 2,178 | 2,132 | 2,158 | 2,195 | 8,663 |
| 2007 | 2,218 | 2,171 | 2,212 | 2,251 | 8,852 |
| 2006 | 2,414 | 2,195 | 2,117 | 2,179 | 8,701 |

**Earnings Per Share ($)**

| | 1Q | 2Q | 3Q | 4Q | Year |
|---|---|---|---|---|---|
| 2011 | 0.16 | 0.08 | 0.02 | E0.14 | E0.42 |
| 2010 | 0.16 | 0.07 | 1.68 | 0.10 | 2.01 |
| 2009 | 0.39 | Nil | Nil | 0.04 | 0.43 |
| 2008 | -0.02 | -0.04 | -0.24 | -0.07 | -0.13 |
| 2007 | 0.20 | -0.06 | -0.07 | -0.18 | -0.10 |
| 2006 | -0.03 | -0.95 | -0.06 | -0.83 | -1.85 |

Fiscal year ended Dec. 31. Next earnings report expected: Late February. EPS Estimates based on S&P Operating Earnings; historical GAAP earnings are as reported.

## Dividend Data

Dividends, initiated in 1973, were omitted beginning in 1993. A special dividend of $0.01 a share was paid in March 2000.

## Highlights

➤ We expect revenues to rise 5% in 2011, to $9.67 billion, and 3% in 2012, to $10 billion. We see THC operating in a difficult climate amid elevated unemployment in key markets, which has eroded its commercially insured patient base. In September 2011, THC cited a slowing in such declines. In our view, shifts in THC's patient mix towards the less profitable Medicare and Medicaid populations and lower patient acuity in these segments are likely to weigh on near-term results, but we see solid managed care pricing trends mitigating some of this impact.

➤ We look for EBITDA margins around 12% in 2011 and 2012, up from 11.5% in 2010. We are encouraged by THC's EBITDA margin expansion in recent years on solid cost containment, and by the narrowing of the gap between THC and its peers. We also like the firming of bad debt trends during 2010, and we expect bad debt charges to be around 7.5% of revenues in 2011 and 2012, down from 8% in 2010.

➤ We estimate adjusted EPS of $0.42 in 2011 and $0.48 in 2012, excluding one-time items. We assume about 521 million shares outstanding in 2011 and 470 million in 2012 due to share repurchases.

## Investment Rationale/Risk

➤ Our hold recommendation reflects our outlook for THC shares to remain volatile, given what we view as long-term uncertainty over Medicare reimbursement rates and weaker patient acuity trends. We expect the shares to trade more on fundamentals than M&A speculation, after Community Health Systems (CYH 21, Hold) withdrew its $7.25 per share bid to acquire THC in May 2011. We see potential for THC's complaint against CYH's admission and Medicare reimbursement practices to spark long-term regulatory scrutiny of the hospital industry. Operationally, we see admissions growth remaining volatile in an uneven economic recovery, although we are encouraged by a positive trend that began in early 2011.

➤ Risks to our recommendation and target price include a less favorable government or third-party reimbursement environment, continuing declines in the commercial payer mix, and slower physician recruitment than expected.

➤ Our 12-month target price of $6.00 assumes an EV/EBITDA multiple of about 5.9X our 2012 EBITDA estimate of $1.19 billion, a modest discount to THC's three-year forward historical average.

# Tenet Healthcare Corp

STANDARD
&POOR'S

## Business Summary November 09, 2011

CORPORATE OVERVIEW. Tenet Healthcare ranks as the second largest U.S. for-profit hospital manager. At December 31, 2010, it owned or operated 49 hospitals (classified under continuing operations), with 13,428 licensed beds. The company's coverage area consists of 11 states, with its largest concentrations of hospital beds in Florida (25.9%), Texas (19.5%) and California 17.3%). THC also owns and operates rehabilitation hospitals, a specialty hospital, skilled nursing facilities, and medical office buildings located on or near the general hospital properties. General hospitals accounted for 97% of net revenues in recent years.

CORPORATE STRATEGY. THC seeks to increase revenues at its facilities by improving the quality of care through the implementation of best practices while simultaneously reducing operating costs. It aims to attract and retain nurses, physicians, and other workers to support its ongoing improvement efforts. The company is also focused on reducing the allowance for doubtful accounts and increasing cash flow. THC intends to acquire or divest facilities as market conditions and operational goals warrant.

In March 2003, the company announced its intention to divest or consolidate 14 hospitals, which was completed in February 2004. In January 2004, the company said it intended to divest an additional 27 hospitals, including 19 in California and eight in Louisiana, Massachusetts, Missouri and Texas. These

sales were completed in the second quarter of 2006. In June 2006, the company announced plans to divest another 11 facilities to fund a portion of its settlement with Medicare. At that time, THC said it intended to focus its financial and management resources on its remaining core group of U.S. hospitals.

In January 2003, THC was sued by the U.S. Justice Department for allegedly submitting false claims to Medicare. In October 2003, the Justice Department served THC with a subpoena related to its investigation of Medicare outlier payments. In September 2003, the U.S. Senate launched an investigation into the company's corporate governance practices with respect to federal health care programs. To conclude the investigations, in June 2006, the company entered into a corporate integrity agreement (CIA) with the U.S. Department of Justice, under which THC is subject to annual training and compliance reviews. In conjunction with the agreement, THC agreed to pay $725 million over a period of four years, plus interest, and to waive its right to collect $175 million in Medicare payments for past services. In order to fund the settlement, at that time THC announced it would sell 11 hospitals.

## Company Financials Fiscal Year Ended Dec. 31

| Per Share Data ($) | 2010 | 2009 | 2008 | 2007 | 2006 | 2005 | 2004 | 2003 | 2002 | 2001 |
|---|---|---|---|---|---|---|---|---|---|---|
| Tangible Book Value | 0.84 | NM | NM | NM | NM | NM | 1.63 | 4.85 | 4.40 | 4.40 |
| Cash Flow | 2.68 | 0.01 | 0.83 | 0.59 | -1.12 | -0.51 | -3.02 | -2.00 | 1.54 | 3.24 |
| Earnings | 2.01 | 0.43 | -0.13 | -0.10 | -1.85 | -1.32 | -3.85 | -3.01 | 0.93 | 2.04 |
| S&P Core Earnings | 2.02 | 0.46 | NA | -0.11 | -0.34 | -1.14 | -2.28 | 0.27 | 1.54 | 1.24 |
| Dividends | Nil | Nil | Nil | Nil | Nil | Nil | Nil | Nil | Nil | Nil |
| Payout Ratio | Nil | Nil | Nil | Nil | Nil | Nil | Nil | Nil | Nil | Nil |
| Prices:High | 6.86 | 6.39 | 6.88 | 7.80 | 9.27 | 13.06 | 18.73 | 19.25 | 52.50 | 41.85 |
| Prices:Low | 3.92 | 0.78 | 0.99 | 3.06 | 5.77 | 7.27 | 9.15 | 11.32 | 13.70 | 24.67 |
| P/E Ratio:High | 3 | 15 | NM | NM | NM | NM | NM | NM | 56 | 21 |
| P/E Ratio:Low | 2 | 2 | NM | NM | NM | NM | NM | NM | 15 | 12 |

| Income Statement Analysis (Million $) | | | | | | | | | | |
|---|---|---|---|---|---|---|---|---|---|---|
| Revenue | 9,205 | 9,014 | 8,663 | 8,852 | 8,701 | 9,614 | 9,919 | 13,212 | 8,743 | 13,913 |
| Operating Income | 1,050 | 982 | 694 | 669 | 687 | 571 | 434 | 1,072 | 1,676 | 2,797 |
| Depreciation | 394 | 386 | 335 | 330 | 342 | 382 | 388 | 471 | 302 | 604 |
| Interest Expense | 424 | 445 | 428 | 430 | 409 | 405 | 333 | 296 | 147 | 327 |
| Pretax Income | 158 | 205 | 43.0 | -103 | -1,129 | -701 | -1,616 | -1,829 | 777 | 1,799 |
| Effective Tax Rate | NA | NM | NM | 56.3% | NM | NM | NM | NM | 38.5% | 40.9% |
| Net Income | 1,135 | 218 | 62.0 | -49.0 | -871 | -621 | -1,797 | -1,404 | 459 | 1,025 |
| S&P Core Earnings | 1,110 | 228 | -1.05 | -52.3 | -159 | -561 | -1,061 | 123 | 760 | 607 |

| Balance Sheet & Other Financial Data (Million $) | | | | | | | | | | |
|---|---|---|---|---|---|---|---|---|---|---|
| Cash | 406 | 703 | 523 | 592 | 784 | 1,373 | 654 | 619 | 210 | 38.0 |
| Current Assets | 2,311 | 2,472 | 2,709 | 2,560 | 3,025 | 3,508 | 3,992 | 4,248 | 3,792 | 3,394 |
| Total Assets | 8,500 | 7,953 | 8,174 | 8,393 | 8,539 | 9,812 | 10,078 | 12,298 | 13,780 | 13,814 |
| Current Liabilities | 1,725 | 1,783 | 1,949 | 2,048 | 1,925 | 2,292 | 2,130 | 2,394 | 2,381 | 2,584 |
| Long Term Debt | 3,997 | 4,272 | 4,778 | 4,771 | 4,760 | 4,784 | 4,395 | 4,039 | 3,872 | 3,919 |
| Common Equity | 1,432 | 312 | 103 | 54.0 | 995 | 1,760 | 2,460 | 4,361 | 5,723 | 5,619 |
| Total Capital | 5,936 | 4,971 | 4,982 | 4,944 | 5,862 | 6,756 | 7,166 | 8,404 | 10,121 | 10,227 |
| Capital Expenditures | 463 | 455 | 527 | 729 | 631 | 568 | 454 | 753 | 490 | 889 |
| Cash Flow | 1,505 | 598 | 397 | 281 | -529 | -239 | -1,409 | -933 | 761 | 1,629 |
| Current Ratio | 1.3 | 1.4 | 1.4 | 1.3 | 1.6 | 1.5 | 1.9 | 1.8 | 1.6 | 1.3 |
| % Long Term Debt of Capitalization | 67.3 | 85.9 | 95.9 | 96.5 | 81.2 | 70.8 | 61.3 | 48.1 | 38.3 | 38.3 |
| % Net Income of Revenue | 12.3 | 2.4 | 0.7 | NM | NM | NM | NM | NM | 5.2 | 7.4 |
| % Return on Assets | 13.8 | 2.7 | 0.8 | NM | NM | NM | NM | NM | NM | 7.6 |
| % Return on Equity | 130.2 | 105.1 | 79.0 | NM | NM | NM | NM | NM | NM | 19.2 |

Data as orig reptd.; bef. results of disc opers/spec. items. Per share data adj. for stk. divs.; EPS diluted. E-Estimated. NA-Not Available. NM-Not Meaningful. NR-Not Ranked. UR-Under Review.

**Office:** 1445 Ross Avenue, Suite 1400, Dallas, TX 75202.
**Telephone:** 469-893-2200.
**Email:** feedback@tenethealth.com
**Website:** http://www.tenethealth.com

**Chrmn:** E.A. Kangas
**Pres:** T. Fetter
**COO:** S.L. Newman
**EVP & CIO:** S.F. Brown

**SVP, Secy & General Counsel:** G. Ruff
**Investor Contact:** T. Rice (469-893-2522)
**Board Members:** J. E. Bush, T. Fetter, B. J. Gaines, K. M. Garrison, E. A. Kangas, J. R. Kerrey, F. D. Loop, R. R. Pettingill, R. A. Rittenmeyer, J. A. Unruh

**Founded:** 1967
**Domicile:** Nevada
**Employees:** 56,605

The McGraw-Hill Companies

# TE Connectivity Ltd

**STANDARD &POOR'S**

**S&P Recommendation** HOLD ★★★☆☆

| Price | 12-Mo. Target Price | Investment Style |
|---|---|---|
| $31.71 (as of Nov 30, 2011) | $39.00 | Large-Cap Blend |

**GICS Sector** Information Technology
**Sub-Industry** Electronic Manufacturing Services

**Summary** This company designs, manufactures and markets engineered electronic components and network solutions for the automotive, appliances, aerospace and defense, telecommunications, computers and consumer electronics industries.

## Key Stock Statistics (Source S&P, Vickers, company reports)

| | | | | | | |
|---|---|---|---|---|---|---|
| 52-Wk Range | $38.59– 26.58 | S&P Oper. EPS 2012**E** | 3.20 | Market Capitalization(B) | $13.459 | Beta | 1.97 |
| Trailing 12-Month EPS | $2.81 | S&P Oper. EPS 2013**E** | 3.54 | Yield (%) | 2.27 | S&P 3-Yr. Proj. EPS CAGR(%) | 9 |
| Trailing 12-Month P/E | 11.3 | P/E on S&P Oper. EPS 2012**E** | 9.9 | Dividend Rate/Share | $0.72 | S&P Credit Rating | NA |
| $10K Invested 5 Yrs Ago | NA | Common Shares Outstg. (M) | 424.5 | Institutional Ownership (%) | 90 | | |

## Price Performance

30-Week Mov. Avg. ··· 10-Week Mov. Avg. - - GAAP Earnings vs. Previous Year Volume Above Avg. STARS
12-Mo. Target Price — Relative Strength — ▲ Up ▼ Down ► No Change Below Avg. ★

Options: ASE, CBOE, P

Analysis prepared by Equity Analyst **J. Moorman, CFA** on Nov 08, 2011, when the stock traded at **$35.78**.

## Qualitative Risk Assessment

| LOW | MEDIUM | HIGH |
|---|---|---|

Our risk assessment is based on our view of the company's reliance on cyclical businesses, especially auto components, that are affected by the macroeconomic environment. We see TEL's major electronic component business continuing to affect overall mix and profitability. These factors are only partly offset by our view of TEL's efforts to reorganize its operations and target greater profitability.

## Quantitative Evaluations

**S&P Quality Ranking** NR

| D | C | B- | B | B+ | A- | A | A+ |
|---|---|---|---|---|---|---|---|

**Relative Strength Rank** MODERATE

42

LOWEST = 1     HIGHEST = 99

## Highlights

➤ Following a 19% sales increase in FY 11 (Sep.), benefiting from roughly $1 billion of additional revenue from the December 2010 ADC Telecommunications acquisition, we forecast a 4.8% advance for FY 12 and 5.2% for FY 13. We see the transportation solutions business rebounding strongly from the effects of an auto production slowdown in FY 11 related to the earthquake in Japan. We also expect a solid showing from network solutions, given positive demand trends we see for fiber and data center investment.

➤ Aided by the higher sales volume and a more favorable pricing environment, we see FY 12 gross margins widening modestly, to the 31.0% level. We expect a leaner overall cost structure, primarily from cost synergies associated with ADC Telecommunications, to aid FY 12 operating margins.

➤ After taxes at 28% and factoring in continued share repurchase activity, we estimate FY 12 operating EPS of $3.20 in FY 12 and $3.54 in FY 13, following $3.14 in FY 11. Our estimates exclude restructuring charges and acquisition costs.

## Investment Rationale/Risk

➤ We have a positive long-term view of the auto market's demand for electronic components. We expect to see good results from the data communications and telecom and enterprise network areas going forward. Nevertheless, we are cautious on TEL, given the near-term hurdles of integrating ADCT and the current disruption in Japan, and believe the stock is appropriately valued. We think moving to low-cost regions and exiting low-margin businesses, along with restructuring initiatives, will be beneficial in the long run.

➤ Risks to our recommendation and target price include lower-than-expected benefits from the divestitures of non-strategic businesses, a significant decrease in auto market demand, and a longer-than-expected time to achieve restructuring benefits.

➤ Our 12-month target price of $39 is based on a slight peer-discount P/E of 11X our FY 13 EPS projection of $3.54. We think TEL warrants a peer discount due to what we see as poor earnings quality over the last two fiscal years, along with modest deterioration of the balance sheet since the ADCT acquisition closed.

## Revenue/Earnings Data

### Revenue (Million $)

| | 1Q | 2Q | 3Q | 4Q | Year |
|---|---|---|---|---|---|
| 2011 | 3,200 | 3,472 | 3,729 | 3,911 | 14,312 |
| 2010 | 2,892 | 2,957 | 3,084 | 3,137 | 12,070 |
| 2009 | 2,713 | 2,337 | 2,508 | 2,698 | 10,256 |
| 2008 | 3,558 | 3,662 | 3,908 | 3,706 | 14,834 |
| 2007 | 3,094 | 3,335 | 3,412 | 3,619 | 13,460 |
| 2006 | 2,939 | 3,043 | 3,363 | 3,363 | 12,812 |

### Earnings Per Share ($)

| | | | | | |
|---|---|---|---|---|---|
| 2011 | 0.60 | 0.67 | 0.80 | 0.75 | 2.82 |
| 2010 | 0.37 | 0.66 | 0.72 | 0.56 | 2.32 |
| 2009 | 0.07 | -7.07 | 0.06 | 0.18 | -6.75 |
| 2008 | 1.74 | 0.62 | 0.66 | 0.23 | 3.28 |
| 2007 | 0.48 | 0.15 | -0.17 | 0.16 | -0.29 |
| 2006 | -- | -- | 0.61 | 0.65 | 2.24 |

Fiscal year ended Sep. 30. Next earnings report expected: NA. EPS Estimates based on S&P Operating Earnings; historical GAAP earnings are as reported.

## Dividend Data (Dates: mm/dd Payment Date: mm/dd/yy)

| Amount ($) | Date Decl. | Ex-Div. Date | Stk. of Record | Payment Date |
|---|---|---|---|---|
| 0.160 | 03/10 | 03/04 | 03/08 | 03/16/11 |
| 0.180 | 05/16 | 05/27 | 06/01 | 06/15/11 |
| 0.180 | 08/10 | 08/30 | 09/01 | 09/15/11 |
| 0.180 | 11/18 | 11/29 | 12/01 | 12/15/11 |

Dividends have been paid since 2007. Source: Company reports.

**Please read the Required Disclosures and Analyst Certification on the last page of this report.**

*The McGraw·Hill Companies*

# TE Connectivity Ltd

STANDARD &POOR'S

## Business Summary November 08, 2011

CORPORATE OVERVIEW. Tyco Electronics (TEL) came into existence as a standalone entity following the January 13, 2006, decision by the company's former parent, Tyco International, to separate into three companies: Tyco Electronics, Tyco Healthcare, and Tyco International. Subsequently, Tyco Electronics separated from Tyco International on June 29, 2007, and began trading on the NYSE on July 2, 2007.

Tyco Electronics Ltd. designs, manufactures and markets engineered electronic components, network solutions and undersea telecommunications systems for customers in the automotive, appliances, aerospace and defense, telecommunications, computers, consumer electronics, energy, medical, industrial and communication service provider industries. TEL operates through three reporting segments: Electronic Components, Network Solutions, and Undersea Telecommunications.

Electronic Components supplies passive electronic components, including connectors and interconnect systems, relays, switches, circuit protection de-

vices, touch screens, sensors, and wires and cable, primarily to the automotive, computer, consumer electronics, communication equipment, appliance, aerospace and defense, industrial machinery and instrumentation markets.

Network Solutions is a global supplier of infrastructure components for the telecommunications and energy markets. Its products include connectors, above- and below-ground enclosures, heat shrink tubing, cable accessories, surge arrestors, fiber optic cabling, copper cabling, and racks for copper and fiber networks.

Undersea Telecommunications Systems designs, builds and manages fiber optic networks for the communications and energy markets.

## Company Financials Fiscal Year Ended Sep. 30

| Per Share Data ($) | 2011 | 2010 | 2009 | 2008 | 2007 | 2006 | 2005 | 2004 | 2003 | 2002 |
|---|---|---|---|---|---|---|---|---|---|---|
| Tangible Book Value | NA | 7.77 | 7.52 | 7.59 | 7.33 | NM | NA | NA | NA | NA |
| Cash Flow | 4.12 | 3.46 | -5.63 | 4.43 | 0.79 | 3.29 | NA | NA | NA | NA |
| Earnings | 2.82 | 2.32 | -6.75 | 3.28 | -0.29 | 2.24 | NA | NA | NA | NA |
| Dividends | 0.52 | 0.48 | 0.64 | 0.42 | 0.14 | NA | NA | NA | NA | NA |
| Payout Ratio | 18% | 21% | NM | 13% | NM | NA | NA | NA | NA | NA |
| Prices:High | 38.59 | 35.74 | 24.96 | 40.34 | 41.28 | NA | NA | NA | NA | NA |
| Prices:Low | 26.58 | 23.85 | 7.40 | 12.85 | 31.31 | NA | NA | NA | NA | NA |
| P/E Ratio:High | 14 | 15 | NM | 12 | NM | NA | NA | NA | NA | NA |
| P/E Ratio:Low | 9 | 10 | NM | 4 | NM | NA | NA | NA | NA | NA |

| Income Statement Analysis (Million $) | 2011 | 2010 | 2009 | 2008 | 2007 | 2006 | 2005 | 2004 | 2003 | 2002 |
|---|---|---|---|---|---|---|---|---|---|---|
| Revenue | 14,312 | 12,070 | 10,256 | 14,834 | 13,460 | 12,812 | 11,890 | 11,099 | NA | NA |
| Operating Income | 2,606 | 2,171 | 1,107 | 2,630 | 2,319 | 2,269 | 2,201 | 2,098 | NA | NA |
| Depreciation | 574 | 520 | 515 | 559 | 535 | 531 | 542 | 513 | NA | NA |
| Interest Expense | NA | NA | 165 | 188 | 231 | 256 | NA | NA | NA | NA |
| Pretax Income | 1,629 | 1,558 | -3,670 | 2,157 | 356 | 1,201 | 1,355 | 1,206 | NA | NA |
| Effective Tax Rate | NA | NA | NM | 25.9% | NM | 2.66% | 26.6% | 33.6% | NA | NA |
| Net Income | 1,253 | 1,059 | -3,100 | 1,594 | -144 | 1,163 | 990 | 791 | NA | NA |

| Balance Sheet & Other Financial Data (Million $) | 2011 | 2010 | 2009 | 2008 | 2007 | 2006 | 2005 | 2004 | 2003 | 2002 |
|---|---|---|---|---|---|---|---|---|---|---|
| Cash | 1,219 | 1,990 | 1,521 | 1,086 | 936 | 470 | 284 | NA | NA | NA |
| Current Assets | NA | NA | 5,579 | 7,095 | 9,873 | 6,040 | NA | NA | NA | NA |
| Total Assets | 17,723 | 16,992 | 16,220 | 21,600 | 23,688 | 19,091 | 18,473 | NA | NA | NA |
| Current Liabilities | NA | NA | 2,615 | 3,332 | 6,185 | 9,142 | NA | NA | NA | NA |
| Long Term Debt | 2,668 | 2,319 | 2,316 | 3,161 | 3,373 | 3,371 | 3,816 | NA | NA | NA |
| Common Equity | 7,474 | 7,048 | 7,016 | 11,073 | 11,377 | 11,160 | 9,842 | NA | NA | NA |
| Total Capital | 10,163 | 9,481 | 9,530 | 14,533 | 15,427 | 14,927 | 14,379 | NA | NA | NA |
| Capital Expenditures | 581 | 385 | 328 | 619 | 892 | 560 | 481 | 410 | NA | NA |
| Cash Flow | 1,827 | 1,579 | -2,585 | 2,153 | 391 | 1,694 | 1,532 | 1,304 | NA | NA |
| Current Ratio | 2.0 | 2.0 | 2.1 | 2.1 | 1.6 | 1.0 | 1.7 | NA | NA | NA |
| % Long Term Debt of Capitalization | 26.3 | 24.5 | 24.3 | 21.8 | 21.8 | 22.6 | 26.5 | Nil | NA | NA |
| % Net Income of Revenue | 8.8 | 8.8 | NM | 10.8 | NM | 9.1 | 8.3 | 7.1 | NA | NA |
| % Return on Assets | 7.2 | 6.4 | NM | 7.0 | NM | 6.2 | NA | NA | NA | NA |
| % Return on Equity | 17.3 | 15.1 | NM | 14.2 | NM | 11.1 | NA | NA | NA | NA |

Data as orig reptd.; bef. results of disc opers/spec. items. Per share data adj. for stk. divs.; EPS diluted. E-Estimated. NA-Not Available. NM-Not Meaningful. NR-Not Ranked. UR-Under Review.

**Office:** Rheinstrasse 20, Schaffhausen, Switzerland 8200.
**Telephone:** 41 52 633 66 61.
**Website:** http://www.te.com
**Chrmn:** F.M. Poses

**CEO:** T. Lynch
**COO:** J.B. Donahue
**EVP & CFO:** T.R. Curtin
**EVP & General Counsel:** R.A. Scott

**Investor Contact:** K. Kolstrom (610-893-9551)
**Investor Contact:** J. Roselli (610-893-9559)
**Board Members:** P. R. Brondeau, J. W. Gromer, R. M. Hernandez, T. Lynch, D. J. Phelan, F. M. Poses, L. S. Smith, P. A. Sneed, D. P. Steiner, J. Van Scoter

**Founded:** 2009
**Domicile:** Switzerland
**Employees:** 95,000

# Teradata Corp

**STANDARD &POOR'S**

| S&P Recommendation **BUY** ★★★★☆ | Price<br>$49.48 (as of Nov 25, 2011) | 12-Mo. Target Price<br>$65.00 | Investment Style<br>Large-Cap Blend |
| --- | --- | --- | --- |

**GICS Sector** Information Technology
**Sub-Industry** IT Consulting & Other Services

**Summary** This Ohio-based company, spun off from NCR Corp. in 2007, has global operations focused on data warehousing and enterprise analytics.

## Key Stock Statistics (Source S&P, Vickers, company reports)

| | | | | | |
| --- | --- | --- | --- | --- | --- |
| 52-Wk Range | $62.71– 40.45 | S&P Oper. EPS 2011**E** | 2.17 | Market Capitalization(B) | $8.283 |
| Trailing 12-Month EPS | $1.98 | S&P Oper. EPS 2012**E** | 2.50 | Yield (%) | Nil |
| Trailing 12-Month P/E | 25.0 | P/E on S&P Oper. EPS 2011**E** | 22.8 | Dividend Rate/Share | Nil |
| $10K Invested 5 Yrs Ago | NA | Common Shares Outstg. (M) | 167.4 | Institutional Ownership (%) | 90 |

| | |
| --- | --- |
| Beta | 0.92 |
| S&P 3-Yr. Proj. EPS CAGR(%) | 17 |
| S&P Credit Rating | NA |

## Price Performance

30-Week Mov. Avg. ···· 10-Week Mov. Avg. −− **GAAP Earnings vs. Previous Year** Volume Above Avg. |||| **STARS**
12-Mo. Target Price — Relative Strength — ▲ Up ▼ Down ► No Change Below Avg. |||| ★

Options: CBOE, Ph

Analysis prepared by Equity Analyst **Dylan Cathers** on Nov 07, 2011, when the stock traded at **$56.40**.

## Highlights

➤ We see revenue growth of 19% in 2011, aided by a contribution from the acquisition of Aprimo in January 2011, and 12% in 2012. We think a more restrictive regulatory environment and continuing demand for business intelligence solutions will drive sales. Specifically, we look for strong gains from the Consulting Services segment. TDC reported weak sales in Japan in the September period, but the pipeline remains solid, in our view. We believe TDC will benefit from recent and ongoing investments it has made in expanding its sales territories.

➤ Despite the expected higher revenues, we think gross margins will narrow slightly in 2011 before widening in 2012 as TDC gradually adds to its professional services head count. A higher portion of consulting sales should also be a headwind. We see product gross margins impacted by the amortization of software development costs. We think operating margins will also narrow a bit in 2011 from the 21.4% of 2010, due to ongoing investments in R&D and sales. We expect a modest widening of operating margins.

➤ We estimate operating EPS of $2.17 in 2011 and $2.50 in 2012, aided by share repurchases.

## Investment Rationale/Risk

➤ We view rising interest among enterprises in using their transactional data to improve operations as a primary sales driver for TDC. The company aims to expand by entering new sales territories, and we believe it has the potential to do well based on its one-stop shopping approach to offering business intelligence hardware, software and consulting. We consider the shares to be attractively valued.

➤ Risks to our recommendation and target price include slowdowns in the pace of enterprise spending on information technology, any failure to keep up with rapidly evolving technology, competition on price and quality of products and services, and acquisition integration risks.

➤ Our 12-month target price of $65 is derived from our discounted cash flow analysis blended with our P/E analysis. We incorporate assumptions for an 8.1% weighted average cost of capital and 3% terminal growth in our DCF model, yielding a $70 value. Applying a target P/E multiple of 24X, toward the high end of a historical range for TDC, to our 2012 EPS estimate, we see a $60 value for TDC shares.

## Qualitative Risk Assessment

| LOW | MEDIUM | HIGH |
| --- | --- | --- |

Teradata participates in a large and growing global market we see for storing, retrieving and analyzing data produced by businesses. While competition is heavy for technology and pricing, we believe a stream of revenue from services, and a clean balance sheet, lend some stability.

## Quantitative Evaluations

**S&P Quality Ranking** NR

| D | C | B- | B | B+ | A- | A | A+ |
| --- | --- | --- | --- | --- | --- | --- | --- |

**Relative Strength Rank** MODERATE

34

LOWEST = 1 HIGHEST = 99

## Revenue/Earnings Data

**Revenue (Million $)**

| | 1Q | 2Q | 3Q | 4Q | Year |
| --- | --- | --- | --- | --- | --- |
| 2011 | 506.0 | 581.0 | 602.0 | -- | -- |
| 2010 | 429.0 | 470.0 | 489.0 | 548.0 | 1,936 |
| 2009 | 367.0 | 421.0 | 425.0 | 496.0 | 1,709 |
| 2008 | 375.0 | 455.0 | 439.0 | 493.0 | 1,762 |
| 2007 | 367.0 | 430.0 | 439.0 | 466.0 | 1,702 |
| 2006 | 323.0 | 396.0 | 375.0 | 466.0 | 1,560 |

**Earnings Per Share ($)**

| | | | | | |
| --- | --- | --- | --- | --- | --- |
| 2011 | 0.38 | 0.60 | 0.51 | E0.57 | E2.17 |
| 2010 | 0.39 | 0.44 | 0.44 | 0.50 | 1.77 |
| 2009 | 0.26 | 0.36 | 0.36 | 0.49 | 1.46 |
| 2008 | 0.23 | 0.38 | 0.33 | 0.45 | 1.39 |
| 2007 | 0.24 | 0.27 | 0.16 | 0.46 | 1.10 |
| 2006 | 0.20 | 0.28 | 0.31 | 0.31 | 1.09 |

Fiscal year ended Dec. 31. Next earnings report expected: Mid February. EPS Estimates based on S&P Operating Earnings; historical GAAP earnings are as reported.

## Dividend Data

No cash dividends have been paid.

---

**Please read the Required Disclosures and Analyst Certification on the last page of this report.**

**The McGraw·Hill Companies**

# Teradata Corp

## Business Summary November 07, 2011

CORPORATE OVERVIEW. Teradata Corporation aims to help its enterprise customers make smarter and faster use of their stored data to improve decision-making. It views itself as a global leader in data warehousing and enterprise analytic technologies. The company offers hardware and software, as well as services including consulting, customer support and training. In 2010, 48% of revenues were derived from products (45% for 2009), and 52% (55%) came from services.

Headquartered in Dayton, Ohio, the company has offices throughout the Americas and operates in 60 countries worldwide. It earned 49% of its revenues outside the U.S. in 2009 and 2008. Teradata has a broad customer base, in our view, with the top 10 customers in 2009 representing only about 16% of sales, down from 20% in 2008. In 2009, revenue came 57% from the Americas, 25% from EMEA (Europe, Middle East, Africa), and 18% from APJ (Asia Pacific/Japan), similar to the 2008 breakout. Gross margins have typically been widest for the Americas region, near 58% compared to a company average of 55% in 2008.

Data warehousing is the process of capturing, storing and analyzing data to

gain insight, according to the company. This activity can be a significant source of intelligence for the enterprise and become a competitive advantage. Beyond mere storage of data, modern solutions allow for near real-time information access and analysis. Predictive analytics on customer or business activity may be run. Both long-term strategic and short-term tactical inquiries may be pursued.

In one example of active data warehousing, a business's call center could produce raw data on call attributes (e.g., number of calls, duration, agent, customer, dropped calls, results), which could be a starting point for mapping and analyzing overall interactions with customers, including Internet communications, which could then become the basis for a plan to improve customer satisfaction. The company serves many large clients in the communications industry, as well as in media and entertainment, financial services, government, health care, manufacturing, retail, and transportation.

## Company Financials Fiscal Year Ended Dec. 31

| Per Share Data ($) | 2010 | 2009 | 2008 | 2007 | 2006 | 2005 | 2004 | 2003 | 2002 | 2001 |
|---|---|---|---|---|---|---|---|---|---|---|
| Tangible Book Value | 5.50 | 4.14 | 3.30 | 2.91 | 2.15 | NA | NA | NA | NA | NA |
| Cash Flow | 2.12 | 1.61 | 1.72 | 1.48 | 1.40 | 1.44 | 1.03 | NA | NA | NA |
| Earnings | 1.77 | 1.46 | 1.39 | 1.10 | 1.09 | 1.14 | 0.76 | NA | NA | NA |
| S&P Core Earnings | 1.77 | 1.48 | 1.40 | 1.18 | 1.09 | 1.10 | NA | NA | NA | NA |
| Dividends | Nil | Nil | Nil | Nil | NA | NA | NA | NA | NA | NA |
| Payout Ratio | Nil | Nil | Nil | Nil | NA | NA | NA | NA | NA | NA |
| Prices:High | 43.83 | 32.24 | 27.90 | 30.08 | NA | NA | NA | NA | NA | NA |
| Prices:Low | 26.80 | 12.75 | 11.11 | 22.35 | NA | NA | NA | NA | NA | NA |
| P/E Ratio:High | 25 | 22 | 20 | 27 | NA | NA | NA | NA | NA | NA |
| P/E Ratio:Low | 15 | 9 | 8 | 20 | NA | NA | NA | NA | NA | NA |

| Income Statement Analysis (Million $) | 2010 | 2009 | 2008 | 2007 | 2006 | 2005 | 2004 | 2003 | 2002 | 2001 |
|---|---|---|---|---|---|---|---|---|---|---|
| Revenue | 1,936 | 1,709 | 1,762 | 1,702 | 1,560 | 1,467 | 1,349 | NA | NA | NA |
| Operating Income | 475 | 364 | 393 | 405 | 367 | 339 | 247 | NA | NA | NA |
| Depreciation | 60.0 | 63.0 | 60.0 | 68.0 | 55.0 | 55.0 | 48.0 | NA | NA | NA |
| Interest Expense | NA | NA | Nil | Nil | Nil | Nil | Nil | NA | NA | NA |
| Pretax Income | 414 | 334 | 338 | 322 | 312 | 284 | 199 | NA | NA | NA |
| Effective Tax Rate | NA | 24.0% | 26.0% | 37.9% | 36.5% | 27.5% | 30.7% | NA | NA | NA |
| Net Income | 301 | 254 | 250 | 200 | 198 | 206 | 138 | NA | NA | NA |
| S&P Core Earnings | 300 | 256 | 252 | 213 | 198 | 200 | NA | NA | NA | NA |

| Balance Sheet & Other Financial Data (Million $) | 2010 | 2009 | 2008 | 2007 | 2006 | 2005 | 2004 | 2003 | 2002 | 2001 |
|---|---|---|---|---|---|---|---|---|---|---|
| Cash | 883 | 661 | 442 | 270 | 200 | NA | NA | NA | NA | NA |
| Current Assets | 1,406 | 1,152 | 1,015 | 873 | 645 | 444 | NA | NA | NA | NA |
| Total Assets | 1,883 | 1,569 | 1,445 | 1,295 | 983 | 911 | NA | NA | NA | NA |
| Current Liabilities | 569 | 543 | 540 | 572 | 428 | 370 | NA | NA | NA | NA |
| Long Term Debt | NA | NA | Nil | Nil | Nil | NA | NA | NA | NA | NA |
| Common Equity | 1,189 | 910 | 782 | 631 | 477 | 517 | NA | NA | NA | NA |
| Total Capital | 1,189 | 910 | 777 | 631 | 477 | 517 | NA | NA | NA | NA |
| Capital Expenditures | 34.0 | 29.0 | 19.0 | 50.0 | 20.0 | 18.0 | 14.0 | NA | NA | NA |
| Cash Flow | 361 | 280 | 310 | 268 | 253 | 261 | 186 | NA | NA | NA |
| Current Ratio | 2.5 | 2.1 | 1.9 | 1.5 | 1.5 | 1.2 | NA | NA | NA | NA |
| % Long Term Debt of Capitalization | Nil | Nil | Nil | Nil | Nil | Nil | 10.2 | NA | NA | NA |
| % Net Income of Revenue | 15.6 | 14.9 | 14.2 | 11.8 | 12.7 | 14.0 | 10.2 | NA | NA | NA |
| % Return on Assets | 17.4 | 16.9 | 18.3 | 17.4 | NM | NM | NA | NA | NA | NA |
| % Return on Equity | 28.7 | 30.1 | 35.4 | 32.6 | NM | NM | NA | NA | NA | NA |

Data as orig reptd.; bef. results of disc opers/spec. items. Per share data adj. for stk. divs.; EPS diluted. E-Estimated. NA-Not Available. NM-Not Meaningful. NR-Not Ranked. UR-Under Review.

**Office:** 10000 Innovation Drive, Dayton, OH 45342.
**Telephone:** 937-242-4030.
**Website:** http://www.teradata.com
**Chrmn:** J.M. Ringler

**Pres & CEO:** M.F. Koehler
**COO:** B.A. Langos
**EVP, CFO & Chief Acctg Officer:** S.M. Scheppmann
**CTO:** S.A. Brobst

**Investor Contact:** G. Swearingen (937-242-4600)
**Board Members:** E. P. Boykin, N. E. Cooper, C. T. Fu, D. E. Kepler, II, M. F. Koehler, V. L. Lund, J. M. Ringler, J. G. Schwarz, W. S. Stavropoulos

**Founded:** 1979
**Domicile:** Delaware
**Employees:** 7,400

# Teradyne Inc.

STANDARD &POOR'S

| S&P Recommendation | HOLD ★★★☆☆ | Price | 12-Mo. Target Price | Investment Style |
|---|---|---|---|---|
| | | $11.68 (as of Nov 25, 2011) | $16.00 | Large-Cap Blend |

**GICS Sector** Information Technology
**Sub-Industry** Semiconductor Equipment

**Summary** This company makes automatic test equipment used primarily by the semiconductor and telecommunications industries.

## Key Stock Statistics (Source S&P, Vickers, company reports)

| | | | | | | | | |
|---|---|---|---|---|---|---|---|---|
| 52-Wk Range | $19.19–10.37 | S&P Oper. EPS 2011**E** | 1.32 | Market Capitalization(B) | $2.150 | Beta | 1.77 |
| Trailing 12-Month EPS | $1.32 | S&P Oper. EPS 2012**E** | 1.26 | Yield (%) | Nil | S&P 3-Yr. Proj. EPS CAGR(%) | -5 |
| Trailing 12-Month P/E | 8.9 | P/E on S&P Oper. EPS 2011**E** | 8.8 | Dividend Rate/Share | Nil | S&P Credit Rating | NR |
| $10K Invested 5 Yrs Ago | $7,903 | Common Shares Outstg. (M) | 184.1 | Institutional Ownership (%) | NM | | |

## Price Performance

30-Week Mov. Avg. ···· 10-Week Mov. Avg. - - GAAP Earnings vs. Previous Year   Volume Above Avg. ▌▌▌ STARS
12-Mo. Target Price — Relative Strength — ▲ Up ▼ Down ► No Change   Below Avg. ▌▌▌ ★

Options: ASE, CBOE, P, Ph

Analysis prepared by Equity Analyst **Angelo Zino, CFA** on Oct 28, 2011, when the stock traded at **$14.68**.

## Highlights

➤ We project that revenues will fall 1% in 2012, following our projection for an 11% decline in 2011. We think system-on-chip (SOC) orders should begin to improve sequentially in the first half of 2012, as customers resume test equipment purchases. We expect sales to power management and microcontroller manufacturers to drive revenue. In addition, we believe the SOC test buy rate remains at fairly low levels relative to historical averages. We see the potential for new customer wins in the memory and hard disk drive tester segment.

➤ We forecast an annual gross margin of 50% in 2012, below our 51% margin outlook for 2011. While we think TER has a much improved business model, we expect margins to be pressured by a higher mix of sales from its lower-margin systems test business. We see research and development expenses absorbing 14%-15% of sales in 2011 and 2012. We think previous cost cuts will provide considerable earnings leverage for TER in the future.

➤ We project operating EPS of $1.32 in 2011, excluding $0.21 of non-operating expenses, and $1.26 in 2012. We model an effective tax rate of 11% for 2012.

## Investment Rationale/Risk

➤ Our hold recommendation primarily reflects valuation, our intermediate-term outlook for orders, and our belief that TER will benefit from industry consolidation. We see benefits from higher memory test spending in 2012 and TER's commanding market share position in the test equipment SOC market. Also, we anticipate market share gains in flash memory and hard disk drive test. TER's leadership position in the business and what we view as its strong cash position, offset in part by the competitive and low-growth environment for testers, are incorporated into our opinion. We view positively the recent LitePoint deal by the company, which should expand TER's total available market by about $1 billion.

➤ Risks to our recommendation and target price include narrower-than-anticipated margins, lower-than-projected customer capital spending plans, a weakening global economy, greater-than-anticipated pricing declines, and more competitive pressure.

➤ We derive our 12-month target price of $16 by applying a multiple of 13X to our 2012 EPS forecast of $1.26, near comparable semiconductor equipment peers.

## Qualitative Risk Assessment

| LOW | MEDIUM | **HIGH** |
|---|---|---|

Our risk assessment reflects the historical cyclicality of the semiconductor equipment industry, the lack of visibility in the medium term, and intense competition, which we think are only partially offset by Teradyne's market position and financial strength.

## Quantitative Evaluations

**S&P Quality Ranking**   C

| D | **C** | B- | B | B+ | A- | A | A+ |
|---|---|---|---|---|---|---|---|

**Relative Strength Rank**   **WEAK**

29

LOWEST = 1                    HIGHEST = 99

## Revenue/Earnings Data

**Revenue (Million $)**

| | 1Q | 2Q | 3Q | 4Q | Year |
|---|---|---|---|---|---|
| 2011 | 377.2 | 410.5 | 344.4 | -- | -- |
| 2010 | 329.6 | 454.8 | 502.1 | 322.2 | 1,609 |
| 2009 | 120.6 | 169.6 | 262.2 | 267.1 | 819.4 |
| 2008 | 297.3 | 317.7 | 297.3 | 194.8 | 1,107 |
| 2007 | 258.1 | 288.7 | 299.5 | 260.4 | 1,102 |
| 2006 | 362.9 | 391.6 | 359.1 | 263.2 | 1,377 |

**Earnings Per Share ($)**

| | | | | | |
|---|---|---|---|---|---|
| 2011 | 0.29 | 0.39 | 0.25 | E0.12 | E1.32 |
| 2010 | 0.24 | 0.55 | 0.66 | 0.27 | 1.73 |
| 2009 | -0.53 | -0.39 | 0.04 | 0.09 | -0.77 |
| 2008 | 0.01 | 0.06 | -0.14 | -0.33 | -0.38 |
| 2007 | -0.04 | 0.14 | 0.19 | 0.10 | 0.39 |
| 2006 | 0.23 | 0.40 | 0.33 | 0.06 | 1.03 |

Fiscal year ended Dec. 31. Next earnings report expected: Late January. EPS Estimates based on S&P Operating Earnings; historical GAAP earnings are as reported.

## Dividend Data

No cash dividends have been paid.

---

**Please read the Required Disclosures and Analyst Certification on the last page of this report.**

The **McGraw·Hill** Companies

# Teradyne Inc.

**STANDARD &POOR'S**

## Business Summary October 28, 2011

CORPORATE OVERVIEW. Founded in 1960, Teradyne is a leading global supplier of automatic test equipment (ATE) for the electronics industry. As electronic systems have become more complex, the need for products to test the systems has grown dramatically. TER's product segments include Semiconductor Test (88% of 2010 revenue, 67% in 2009) and Systems Test Group (12%, 33%).

Semiconductor Test products test system on a chip (SOC) semiconductor devices during the manufacturing process. These systems are used for wafer level and device packaging testing and span a broad range of end users and functionality. TER's systems help customers improve and control quality, reduce time to market, increase production yields, and improve product performance. TER's FLEX Test platform is designed for scalability and allows for simultaneous parallel testing, reducing costs. The J750 platform is designed to address the highest volume semiconductor devices such as microcontrollers, with a single circuit board providing up to 64 digital input/output channels. The J750 platform technology has been extended to create the IP 750 Image Sensor test system, which focuses on testing image sensor devices used in digital cameras and other imaging products. The J750 platform has been expanded to include critical new devices that include high-end microcontroller, LCD drivers, and the latest generation of cameras.

TER's acquisition of Nextest expanded its product base to include the Magnum test platform. The Magnum platform offers memory test products for the flash memory and dynamic random access memory (DRAM) markets. TER's Eagle Test acquisition expanded its product offerings to include the ETS platform. The ETS platform is used by chipmakers and assembly and test subcontractors, primarily in the low pin count analog/mixed signal discrete markets that cover more cost-sensitive applications. Its SmartPin technology enables multiple semiconductor devices to be tested simultaneously, or in parallel, on an individual test system, permitting greater test throughput.

## Company Financials Fiscal Year Ended Dec. 31

| Per Share Data ($) | 2010 | 2009 | 2008 | 2007 | 2006 | 2005 | 2004 | 2003 | 2002 | 2001 |
|---|---|---|---|---|---|---|---|---|---|---|
| Tangible Book Value | 5.49 | 2.93 | 3.16 | 6.70 | 6.84 | 5.75 | 5.00 | 4.33 | 4.97 | 8.69 |
| Cash Flow | 2.11 | -0.16 | -1.92 | 0.71 | 1.35 | 0.16 | 1.47 | -0.22 | -3.06 | -0.36 |
| Earnings | 1.73 | -0.77 | -0.38 | 0.39 | 1.03 | -0.31 | 0.84 | -1.03 | -3.93 | -1.15 |
| S&P Core Earnings | 1.71 | -0.76 | -1.21 | 0.37 | 0.92 | -0.80 | 0.37 | -1.44 | -4.25 | -1.65 |
| Dividends | Nil | Nil | Nil | Nil | Nil | Nil | Nil | Nil | Nil | Nil |
| Payout Ratio | Nil | Nil | Nil | Nil | Nil | Nil | Nil | Nil | Nil | Nil |
| Prices:High | 14.44 | 10.96 | 14.50 | 18.53 | 18.08 | 17.33 | 30.70 | 26.31 | 40.20 | 47.21 |
| Prices:Low | 8.84 | 3.24 | 2.80 | 10.02 | 11.50 | 10.80 | 12.53 | 8.75 | 7.10 | 18.43 |
| P/E Ratio:High | 8 | NM | NM | 48 | 18 | NM | 37 | NM | NM | NM |
| P/E Ratio:Low | 5 | NM | NM | 26 | 11 | NM | 15 | NM | NM | NM |

| Income Statement Analysis (Million $) | 2010 | 2009 | 2008 | 2007 | 2006 | 2005 | 2004 | 2003 | 2002 | 2001 |
|---|---|---|---|---|---|---|---|---|---|---|
| Revenue | 1,609 | 819 | 1,107 | 1,102 | 1,377 | 1,075 | 1,792 | 1,353 | 1,222 | 1,441 |
| Operating Income | 516 | 35.7 | 89.6 | 117 | 236 | 27.1 | 318 | 47.3 | -192 | -1.54 |
| Depreciation | 99.8 | 106 | 71.3 | 59.4 | 73.5 | 91.2 | 124 | 152 | 160 | 139 |
| Interest Expense | 19.0 | 16.4 | NA | 0.69 | 11.1 | 16.2 | 18.8 | 20.9 | 21.8 | 4.09 |
| Pretax Income | 395 | -143 | -52.7 | 79.2 | 230 | -80.1 | 188 | -186 | -561 | -326 |
| Effective Tax Rate | NA | 6.17% | NM | 9.29% | 12.0% | NM | 12.1% | NM | NM | NM |
| Net Income | 380 | -134 | -65.3 | 71.9 | 203 | -60.5 | 165 | -194 | -718 | -202 |
| S&P Core Earnings | 375 | -132 | -206 | 68.3 | 179 | -161 | 73.3 | -270 | -777 | -290 |

| Balance Sheet & Other Financial Data (Million $) | 2010 | 2009 | 2008 | 2007 | 2006 | 2005 | 2004 | 2003 | 2002 | 2001 |
|---|---|---|---|---|---|---|---|---|---|---|
| Cash | 807 | 464 | 323 | 638 | 945 | 695 | 285 | 586 | 541 | 586 |
| Current Assets | 1,177 | 762 | 679 | 945 | 889 | 1,095 | 806 | 769 | 809 | 1,207 |
| Total Assets | 1,810 | 1,235 | 1,560 | 1,555 | 1,721 | 1,860 | 1,923 | 1,785 | 1,895 | 2,542 |
| Current Liabilities | 364 | 283 | 367 | 223 | 260 | 515 | 277 | 281 | 279 | 296 |
| Long Term Debt | 150 | 141 | Nil | Nil | Nil | 1.82 | 399 | 408 | 451 | 452 |
| Common Equity | 1,122 | 665 | 1,039 | 1,229 | 1,361 | 1,243 | 1,134 | 950 | 1,028 | 1,764 |
| Total Capital | 1,275 | 808 | 706 | 1,229 | 1,361 | 1,244 | 1,532 | 1,357 | 1,479 | 2,216 |
| Capital Expenditures | 76.0 | 41.9 | 87.2 | 86.1 | 110 | 113 | 165 | 30.8 | 46.4 | 198 |
| Cash Flow | 479 | -27.8 | -327 | 131 | 276 | 30.7 | 290 | -41.5 | -559 | -63.5 |
| Current Ratio | 3.2 | 2.7 | 1.9 | 4.2 | 3.4 | 2.1 | 2.9 | 2.7 | 2.9 | 4.1 |
| % Long Term Debt of Capitalization | 11.8 | 17.5 | Nil | Nil | Nil | 0.1 | 26.0 | 30.0 | 30.5 | 20.4 |
| % Net Income of Revenue | 23.6 | NM | NM | 6.5 | 14.7 | NM | 9.2 | NM | NM | NM |
| % Return on Assets | 24.9 | NM | NM | 4.4 | 11.3 | NM | 8.9 | NM | NM | NM |
| % Return on Equity | 42.5 | NM | NM | 5.6 | 15.6 | NM | 15.9 | NM | NM | NM |

Data as orig reptd.; bef. results of disc opers/spec. items. Per share data adj. for stk. divs.; EPS diluted. E-Estimated. NA-Not Available. NM-Not Meaningful. NR-Not Ranked. UR-Under Review.

**Office:** 600 Riverpark Dr, North Reading, MA 01864-2634.
**Telephone:** 978-370-2700.
**Email:** investorrelations@teradyne.com
**Website:** http://www.teradyne.com

**Chrmn:** A. Carnesale
**Pres & CEO:** M.A. Bradley
**CFO & Chief Acctg Officer:** G.R. Beecher
**Secy & General Counsel:** C.J. Gray

**Investor Contact:** A. Blanchard (978-370-2425)
**Board Members:** J. W. Bagley, M. A. Bradley, A. Carnesale, D. W. Christman, E. J. Gillis, T. E. Guertin, P. J. Tufano, R. A. Vallee

**Founded:** 1960
**Domicile:** Massachusetts
**Employees:** 3,000

**The McGraw·Hill Companies**

# Tesoro Corp

**STANDARD &POOR'S**

| S&P Recommendation **HOLD** ★★★☆☆ | Price $22.37 (as of Nov 25, 2011) | 12-Mo. Target Price $31.00 | Investment Style Large-Cap Blend |
|---|---|---|---|

**GICS Sector** Energy
**Sub-Industry** Oil & Gas Refining & Marketing

**Summary** Tesoro is one of the largest independent refiners and marketers of petroleum products in the U.S., with operations focused on the West Coast.

## Key Stock Statistics (Source S&P, Vickers, company reports)

| | | | | | | | |
|---|---|---|---|---|---|---|---|
| 52-Wk Range | $29.61– 16.01 | S&P Oper. EPS 2011**E** | 5.97 | Market Capitalization(B) | $3.119 | Beta | 1.41 |
| Trailing 12-Month EPS | $4.69 | S&P Oper. EPS 2012**E** | 4.30 | Yield (%) | Nil | S&P 3-Yr. Proj. EPS CAGR(%) | NM |
| Trailing 12-Month P/E | 4.8 | P/E on S&P Oper. EPS 2011**E** | 3.7 | Dividend Rate/Share | Nil | S&P Credit Rating | BB+ |
| $10K Invested 5 Yrs Ago | $6,933 | Common Shares Outstg. (M) | 139.4 | Institutional Ownership (%) | NM | | |

## Price Performance

30-Week Mov. Avg. · · · 10-Week Mov. Avg. - - GAAP Earnings vs. Previous Year   Volume Above Avg. ▮▮▮ STARS
12-Mo. Target Price — Relative Strength — ▲ Up ▼ Down ▶ No Change   Below Avg. ▮▮▮ ★

Options: ASE, CBOE, Ph

Analysis prepared by Equity Analyst **Tanjila Shafi** on Nov 18, 2011, when the stock traded at **$23.82**.

## Highlights

➤ Refining throughputs rose 5.4% sequentially in the third quarter, to 609,000 b/d. For the fourth quarter, we expect throughputs to decline 2% to 3% from the third quarter, due to a decline in throughputs at the Pacific Northwest segment, reflecting seasonally lower rates in Alaska and maintenance at the Anacortes refinery. For all of 2011, we see a double digit increase in throughput volumes, based on higher fuel demand. In 2012, we believe earnings will benefit from the company's ability to source discounted crudes at its Anacortes, Mandan and Salt Lake refineries.

➤ Capital expenditures in 2010 were $287 million, while turnaround spending was $140 million. The company has earmarked $320 million for capital spending in 2011, including regulatory, maintenance and income projects, and an additional $110 million for turnaround spending.

➤ TSO incurred a loss per share of $0.21 in 2010, reflecting low refining margins and a curtailment of operations at the Anacortes refinery. However, income reached positive ground in the second quarter of 2010 on improved fundamentals and cost initiatives, and we expect this trend to continue through 2012.

## Investment Rationale/Risk

➤ We view favorably TSO's initiatives to focus on the western United States, integrate its refining/marketing businesses, form a logistics MLP, and reduce costs. However, with about 58% of its refining capacity concentrated in three refineries, we view TSO as exposed to significant operational risk. While a sizable portion of its refining capacity is of lower complexity, we believe its facilities are strategically sited to benefit from local markets, particularly in above-average-margined California, and we expect TSO to achieve enhanced operational efficiencies from recent refining upgrades. In April 2011, TSO executed the initial public offering of Tesoro Logistics LP, its logistics MLP.

➤ Risks to our recommendation and target price include worse than expected economic, industry and operating conditions that lead to narrower refining margins or decreased sales.

➤ A blend of our discounted cash flow ($31 per share, assuming a WACC of 10.4% and terminal growth of 3%) and relative market valuations leads to our 12-month target price of $31. This represents an expected enterprise value of about 3.0X our 2012 EBITDA estimate, a discount to the peer average.

## Qualitative Risk Assessment

| LOW | MEDIUM | HIGH |
|---|---|---|

Our risk assessment reflects our view of TSO's satisfactory business profile in a competitive and volatile refining industry. While we think the company's asset quality is good, we believe it has moved into a cash conservation mode given difficult refining conditions.

## Quantitative Evaluations

**S&P Quality Ranking** B

| D | C | B- | B | B+ | A- | A | A+ |
|---|---|---|---|---|---|---|---|

**Relative Strength Rank** MODERATE

| 38 |
|---|

LOWEST = 1   HIGHEST = 99

## Revenue/Earnings Data

**Revenue (Million $)**

| | 1Q | 2Q | 3Q | 4Q | Year |
|---|---|---|---|---|---|
| 2011 | 6,435 | 7,963 | 8,101 | -- | -- |
| 2010 | 4,607 | 5,072 | 5,320 | 5,513 | 20,583 |
| 2009 | 3,280 | 4,181 | 4,742 | 4,669 | 16,872 |
| 2008 | 6,531 | 8,754 | 8,698 | 4,326 | 28,309 |
| 2007 | 3,876 | 5,604 | 5,902 | 6,533 | 21,915 |
| 2006 | 3,877 | 4,929 | 5,278 | 4,020 | 18,104 |

**Earnings Per Share ($)**

| | | | | | |
|---|---|---|---|---|---|
| 2011 | 0.74 | 1.52 | 2.39 | E1.32 | E5.97 |
| 2010 | -1.11 | 0.47 | 0.39 | 0.02 | -0.21 |
| 2009 | 0.37 | -0.33 | -0.24 | -1.30 | -1.01 |
| 2008 | -0.60 | -0.03 | 1.86 | 0.70 | 2.00 |
| 2007 | 0.84 | 3.17 | 0.34 | -0.29 | 4.06 |
| 2006 | 0.31 | 2.33 | 1.96 | 1.14 | 5.73 |

Fiscal year ended Dec. 31. Next earnings report expected: Early February. EPS Estimates based on S&P Operating Earnings; historical GAAP earnings are as reported.

## Dividend Data

No cash dividends have been paid since December 2009.

# Tesoro Corp

STANDARD
&POOR'S

## Business Summary November 18, 2011

CORPORATE OVERVIEW. Tesoro Corp. (TSO; formerly Tesoro Petroleum Corp.) is one of the largest independent refiners and marketers of petroleum products in the U.S. The company operates in two business segments: Refining (72.4% of operating income in 2010) and Retail (27.6%).

The Refining segment refines crude oil and other feedstocks at its seven refineries (total refining capacity 664,500 b/d as of December 31, 2010) in the U.S. West and Mid-Continent: California (Wilmington in Los Angeles, CA, 97,000 b/d; Golden Eagle in Martinez, CA, 166,000 b/d), the Pacific Northwest (Anacortes, WA, 120,000 b/d; and Kenai, AK, 72,000 b/d), the Mid-Pacific (Kapolei, HI, 93,500 b/d) and the Mid-Continent (Mandan, ND, 58,000 b/d; and Salt Lake City, UT, 58,000 b/d). Refining yields declined 12.2% to 509,000 b/d in 2010, and included gasoline 45.7%, jet fuel 13.4%, diesel fuel 20.3%, and heavy oils, residual products and other 20.7%.

The company purchases its crude oil and other feedstocks for its refineries from various domestic (about 65% of its 2010 crude oil, with a significant amount from Alaska's North Slope) and foreign (around 35%, with a significant amount from Canada) sources through term agreements (63%), which are mainly short term, and in the spot market. TSO charters tankers to ship crude

oil from foreign and domestic sources to its California, Mid-Pacific and Pacific Northwest refineries. About 38% of its total refining throughput was heavy oil (API specific gravity of 24 or less) in 2010, compared to 32% in 2009.

TSO's crude pipeline system in North Dakota and in Alaska are common carriers subject to regulation by various federal, state and local agencies, including the FERC under the Interstate Commerce Act.

MARKET PROFILE. TSO is one of the largest independent refiners in the U.S. The company operates the largest refineries in Hawaii and Utah, and the second largest in northern California and Alaska. Through its network of retail stations, TSO sells gasoline and diesel fuel in the western and mid-continental U.S. As of December 31, 2010, TSO's retail segment included 880 branded retail stations (under the Tesoro, Mirastar, Shell and USA Gasoline brands), comprising 381 company-operated retail gasoline stations and 499 jobber/dealer stations. Retail fuel sales rose 0.6%, to 1.336 billion gallons, in 2010.

## Company Financials Fiscal Year Ended Dec. 31

| Per Share Data ($) | 2010 | 2009 | 2008 | 2007 | 2006 | 2005 | 2004 | 2003 | 2002 | 2001 |
|---|---|---|---|---|---|---|---|---|---|---|
| Tangible Book Value | 20.74 | 19.84 | 20.78 | 19.48 | 17.09 | 12.12 | 8.31 | 5.70 | 5.00 | 6.75 |
| Cash Flow | 1.81 | 1.14 | 3.97 | 5.82 | 7.50 | 4.92 | 3.50 | 1.72 | 0.11 | 2.07 |
| Earnings | -0.21 | -1.01 | 2.00 | 4.06 | 5.73 | 3.60 | 2.38 | 0.58 | -0.97 | 1.05 |
| S&P Core Earnings | -0.31 | -0.57 | 1.73 | 4.12 | 5.73 | 3.65 | 2.42 | 0.78 | -0.97 | 1.00 |
| Dividends | Nil | 0.35 | 0.40 | 0.35 | 0.20 | 0.10 | Nil | Nil | Nil | Nil |
| Payout Ratio | Nil | NM | 20% | 9% | 3% | 3% | Nil | Nil | Nil | Nil |
| Prices:High | 18.94 | 19.16 | 48.35 | 65.98 | 38.40 | 35.91 | 17.33 | 7.56 | 7.65 | 8.25 |
| Prices:Low | 10.40 | 10.62 | 6.71 | 31.47 | 26.48 | 14.13 | 7.00 | 1.69 | 0.62 | 4.85 |
| P/E Ratio:High | NM | NM | 24 | 16 | 7 | 10 | 7 | 13 | NM | 8 |
| P/E Ratio:Low | NM | NM | 3 | 8 | 5 | 4 | 3 | 3 | NM | 5 |

### Income Statement Analysis (Million $)

| | 2010 | 2009 | 2008 | 2007 | 2006 | 2005 | 2004 | 2003 | 2002 | 2001 |
|---|---|---|---|---|---|---|---|---|---|---|
| Revenue | 20,583 | 16,872 | 28,309 | 21,915 | 18,104 | 16,581 | 12,262 | 8,846 | 7,119 | 5,218 |
| Operating Income | NA | NA | 787 | 1,473 | 1,614 | 1,232 | 881 | 638 | 120 | 290 |
| Depreciation, Depletion and Amortization | 284 | 297 | 274 | 246 | 247 | 186 | 154 | 148 | 131 | 91.2 |
| Interest Expense | 157 | 130 | 111 | 125 | 77.0 | 211 | 167 | 212 | 166 | 52.8 |
| Pretax Income | -25.0 | -188 | 429 | 905 | 1,286 | 831 | 547 | 123 | -181 | 147 |
| Effective Tax Rate | NA | 25.5% | 35.2% | 37.5% | 37.7% | 39.0% | 40.0% | 38.2% | NM | 40.1% |
| Net Income | -29.0 | -140 | 278 | 566 | 801 | 507 | 328 | 76.1 | -117 | 88.0 |
| S&P Core Earnings | -43.5 | -79.6 | 241 | 574 | 800 | 514 | 333 | 101 | -117 | 77.2 |

### Balance Sheet & Other Financial Data (Million $)

| | 2010 | 2009 | 2008 | 2007 | 2006 | 2005 | 2004 | 2003 | 2002 | 2001 |
|---|---|---|---|---|---|---|---|---|---|---|
| Cash | 648 | 413 | 20.0 | 23.0 | 986 | 440 | 185 | 77.2 | 110 | 51.9 |
| Current Assets | 2,928 | 2,223 | 1,646 | 2,600 | 2,811 | 2,215 | 1,393 | 1,024 | 1,054 | 878 |
| Total Assets | 8,732 | 8,070 | 7,433 | 8,128 | 5,904 | 5,097 | 4,075 | 3,661 | 3,759 | 2,662 |
| Current Liabilities | 2,496 | 1,889 | 1,441 | 2,494 | 1,672 | 1,502 | 993 | 687 | 608 | 538 |
| Long Term Debt | 1,822 | 1,810 | 1,609 | 1,657 | 1,029 | 1,044 | 1,215 | 1,605 | 1,907 | 1,113 |
| Common Equity | 3,215 | 3,087 | 3,218 | 3,052 | 2,502 | 1,887 | 1,327 | 965 | 888 | 757 |
| Total Capital | 5,189 | 4,906 | 5,243 | 5,097 | 3,908 | 3,320 | 2,835 | 2,750 | 2,923 | 2,006 |
| Capital Expenditures | 297 | 437 | 650 | 747 | 436 | 258 | 179 | 101 | 204 | 210 |
| Cash Flow | 255 | 157 | 552 | 812 | 1,048 | 693 | 482 | 224 | 13.7 | 173 |
| Current Ratio | 1.2 | 1.2 | 1.1 | 1.0 | 1.7 | 1.5 | 1.4 | 1.5 | 1.7 | 1.6 |
| % Long Term Debt of Capitalization | 35.1 | Nil | 30.7 | 32.5 | 26.3 | 31.4 | 42.9 | 58.4 | 65.2 | 55.4 |
| % Return on Assets | NA | NM | 3.6 | 8.1 | 14.6 | 11.1 | 8.5 | 2.1 | NM | 4.2 |
| % Return on Equity | NA | NA | 16.5 | 20.4 | 36.5 | 31.5 | 28.6 | 8.2 | NM | 13.0 |

Data as orig reptd.; bef. results of disc opers/spec. items. Per share data adj. for stk. divs.; EPS diluted. E-Estimated. NA-Not Available. NM-Not Meaningful. NR-Not Ranked. UR-Under Review.

**Office:** 19100 Ridgewood Parkway, San Antonio, TX 78259.
**Telephone:** 210-626-6000.
**Email:** investor_relations@tesoropetroleum.com
**Website:** http://www.tsocorp.com

**Chrmn:** S.H. Grapstein
**Pres & CEO:** G.J. Goff
**COO:** D.R. Romasko
**CFO:** G.S. Spendlove

**Treas:** T.D. Jackson
**Investor Contact:** S. Phipps (210-283-2882)
**Board Members:** R. F. Chase, G. J. Goff, R. W. Goldman, S. H. Grapstein, J. W. Nokes, S. Tomasky, M. E. Wiley, P. Y. Yang

**Founded:** 1939
**Domicile:** Delaware
**Employees:** 5,300

# Texas Instruments Inc

**STANDARD &POOR'S**

| S&P Recommendation HOLD ★★★★★ | Price $27.79 (as of Nov 25, 2011) | 12-Mo. Target Price $32.00 | Investment Style Large-Cap Growth |
|---|---|---|---|

**GICS Sector** Information Technology
**Sub-Industry** Semiconductors

**Summary** One of the world's largest manufacturers of semiconductors, this company also produces scientific calculator products and DLP products for TVs and video projectors.

## Key Stock Statistics (Source S&P, Vickers, company reports)

| | | | | | | | |
|---|---|---|---|---|---|---|---|
| 52-Wk Range | $36.71– 24.34 | S&P Oper. EPS 2011E | 1.93 | Market Capitalization(B) | $31.754 | Beta | 1.10 |
| Trailing 12-Month EPS | $2.39 | S&P Oper. EPS 2012E | 2.12 | Yield (%) | 2.45 | S&P 3-Yr. Proj. EPS CAGR(%) | 2 |
| Trailing 12-Month P/E | 11.6 | P/E on S&P Oper. EPS 2011E | 14.4 | Dividend Rate/Share | $0.68 | S&P Credit Rating | A+ |
| $10K Invested 5 Yrs Ago | $10,077 | Common Shares Outstg. (M) | 1,142.7 | Institutional Ownership (%) | 82 | | |

## Price Performance

30-Week Mov. Avg. ··· 10-Week Mov. Avg. -- GAAP Earnings vs. Previous Year   Volume Above Avg. STARS
12-Mo. Target Price — Relative Strength — ▲ Up ▼ Down ▶ No Change   Below Avg. ★

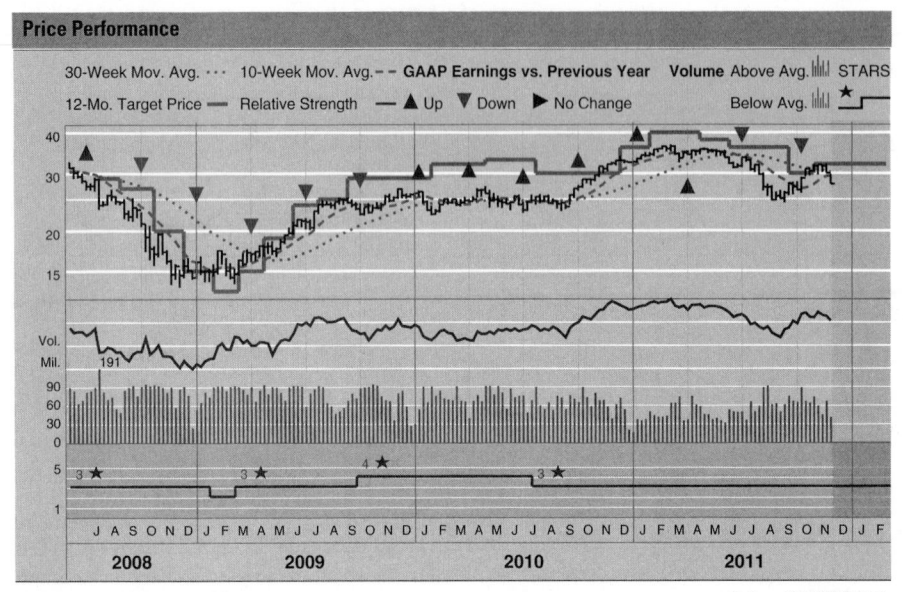

Options: ASE, CBOE, P, Ph

Analysis prepared by Equity Analyst **Angelo Zino, CFA** on Oct 26, 2011, when the stock traded at **$30.95**.

## Qualitative Risk Assessment

| LOW | **MEDIUM** | HIGH |
|---|---|---|

Our risk assessment reflects the cyclicality of the industry in which TXN operates, offset by the large number of company operations, TXN's diverse line of semiconductor products with exposure to many end markets and customers, our view of its low debt levels, and its long corporate history.

## Quantitative Evaluations

**S&P Quality Ranking**                  B+

| D | C | B- | B | **B+** | A- | A | A+ |
|---|---|---|---|---|---|---|---|

**Relative Strength Rank**            MODERATE

48

LOWEST = 1                         HIGHEST = 99

## Revenue/Earnings Data

**Revenue (Million $)**

| | 1Q | 2Q | 3Q | 4Q | Year |
|---|---|---|---|---|---|
| 2011 | 3,392 | 3,458 | 3,466 | -- | -- |
| 2010 | 3,205 | 3,496 | 3,740 | 3,525 | 13,966 |
| 2009 | 2,086 | 2,457 | 2,880 | 3,005 | 10,427 |
| 2008 | 3,272 | 3,351 | 3,387 | 2,491 | 12,501 |
| 2007 | 3,191 | 3,424 | 3,663 | 3,556 | 13,835 |
| 2006 | 3,334 | 3,697 | 3,761 | 3,463 | 14,255 |

**Earnings Per Share ($)**

| | | | | | |
|---|---|---|---|---|---|
| 2011 | 0.55 | 0.56 | 0.51 | E0.31 | E1.93 |
| 2010 | 0.52 | 0.63 | 0.71 | 0.78 | 2.62 |
| 2009 | 0.01 | 0.20 | 0.42 | 0.52 | 1.15 |
| 2008 | 0.49 | 0.44 | 0.43 | 0.08 | 1.45 |
| 2007 | 0.35 | 0.42 | 0.52 | 0.54 | 1.83 |
| 2006 | 0.33 | 0.47 | 0.45 | 0.45 | 1.69 |

Fiscal year ended Dec. 31. Next earnings report expected: Late January. EPS Estimates based on S&P Operating Earnings; historical GAAP earnings are as reported.

## Highlights

➤ We forecast that sales will increase 11% in 2012, aided by the acquisition of National Semiconductor, after a projected decline of 1.9% in 2011. We think near-term results will be limited by uncertain baseband revenues and cautious customer orders due to soft economic conditions. Next year, we see improving demand from the communication infrastructure, smartphone, and automotive markets, and anticipate PC and LCD TV orders rebounding. We also believe TXN will be more aggressive in seeking market share in its higher-margin analog and embedded businesses.

➤ We forecast an annual gross margin of 50% in 2012, similar to our 2011 forecast. We think the completion of the National Semiconductor deal should aid product mix and gross margins longer term. Also, we expect that expenses will rise as TXN expands product offerings and more aggressively pursues share gains. We forecast an operating margin of 23% for both 2011 and 2012.

➤ Our 2012 EPS estimate assumes a 28% effective tax rate and modest decline in the diluted share count.

## Investment Rationale/Risk

➤ Our hold opinion reflects our view of fair valuation and potential share gain, and our belief that fundamentals are nearing trough levels. Despite near term challenges, we believe shorter lead times and tighter customer inventories will result in sequential revenue growth through next year. We believe that TXN's dedication to the analog and embedded markets, coupled with its acquisition of National Semiconductor, will provide healthy long-term growth through market share gains as well as wider margins given a more favorable mix.

➤ Risks to our recommendation and target price include slower-than-peer growth in the analog market, faster-than-anticipated declines in its baseband business, and higher-than-expected costs and expenses related to capacity additions.

➤ Our 12-month target price of $32 is based on our price-to-earnings (P/E) analysis. We apply a P/E multiple of 15X, above the industry average, to our 2012 EPS estimate. We note, however, that excluding amortization and acquisition related charges to our 2012 estimate brings its P/E closer to the industry average assuming this target price.

## Dividend Data (Dates: mm/dd Payment Date: mm/dd/yy)

| Amount ($) | Date Decl. | Ex-Div. Date | Stk. of Record | Payment Date |
|---|---|---|---|---|
| 0.130 | 01/20 | 01/27 | 01/31 | 02/14/11 |
| 0.130 | 04/20 | 04/28 | 05/02 | 05/23/11 |
| 0.130 | 07/21 | 07/28 | 08/01 | 08/22/11 |
| 0.170 | 09/15 | 10/27 | 10/31 | 11/21/11 |

Dividends have been paid since 1962. Source: Company reports.

---

**Please read the Required Disclosures and Analyst Certification on the last page of this report.**

**The McGraw·Hill Companies**

# Texas Instruments Inc

STANDARD &POOR'S

## Business Summary October 26, 2011

CORPORATE OVERVIEW. Texas Instruments is the world's fourth largest semiconductor company, based on revenues. The company's semiconductors are used for various functions including: converting and amplifying signals, interfacing with other devices, managing and distributing power, processing data, canceling noise and improving signal resolution. TXN's product portfolio includes the types of products that are integral to almost all electronic equipment. It offers either custom or standard products. A custom product is designed for a specific customer for a specific application, is sold only to that customer, and is typically sold directly to the customer. A standard product is designed for use by many customers and/or many applications and is generally sold through both distribution and direct channels. Standard products include both proprietary and commodity products. TXN's product segments are analog (43% of sales in 2010), embedded processing (15%), wireless (21%), and other (21%).

Analog semiconductors change real-world signals - such as sound, temperature, pressure or images - by conditioning them, amplifying them, and often converting them to a stream of digital data so the signals can be processed by other semiconductors. Analog products can be further divided by high performance and high volume. High-performance analog products include standard analog semiconductors, such as amplifiers, data converters, low-power radio frequency devices, and interface and power management semiconductors. High-performance analog products generally have long life cycles, often 10 to 20 years. The high-volume products include two product types. The first, high-volume analog, includes products for specific applications, including custom products for specific customers. The life cycles of TXN's high-volume analog products are generally shorter than those of its high-performance analog products. The second product type, standard linear and logic, includes commodity products marketed to many different customers for many different applications.

Embedded processing include digital signal processors (DSPs) and microcontrollers. DSPs perform mathematical computations almost instantaneously to process and improve digital data. Microcontrollers are microprocessors that are designed to control a set of specific tasks for electronic equipment.

## Company Financials Fiscal Year Ended Dec. 31

| Per Share Data ($) | 2010 | 2009 | 2008 | 2007 | 2006 | 2005 | 2004 | 2003 | 2002 | 2001 |
|---|---|---|---|---|---|---|---|---|---|---|
| Tangible Book Value | 7.91 | 6.90 | 6.43 | 6.72 | 7.08 | 6.99 | 7.13 | 6.35 | 5.73 | 6.42 |
| Cash Flow | 3.41 | 1.89 | 2.25 | 2.57 | 2.37 | 2.32 | 1.93 | 1.54 | 0.78 | 0.94 |
| Earnings | 2.62 | 1.15 | 1.45 | 1.83 | 1.69 | 1.39 | 1.05 | 0.68 | -0.20 | -0.12 |
| S&P Core Earnings | 2.59 | 1.19 | 1.40 | 1.81 | 1.68 | 1.26 | 0.86 | 0.40 | -0.16 | -0.34 |
| Dividends | 0.49 | 0.45 | 0.41 | 0.30 | 0.13 | 0.11 | 0.09 | 0.09 | 0.09 | 0.09 |
| Payout Ratio | 19% | 39% | 28% | 16% | 8% | 8% | 9% | 13% | NM | NM |
| Prices:High | 33.93 | 27.00 | 33.24 | 39.63 | 36.40 | 34.68 | 33.98 | 31.67 | 35.94 | 54.69 |
| Prices:Low | 22.28 | 13.70 | 13.38 | 28.24 | 26.77 | 20.70 | 18.06 | 13.90 | 13.10 | 20.10 |
| P/E Ratio:High | 13 | 23 | 23 | 22 | 22 | 25 | 32 | 47 | NM | NM |
| P/E Ratio:Low | 9 | 12 | 9 | 15 | 16 | 15 | 17 | 20 | NM | NM |

| Income Statement Analysis (Million $) | 2010 | 2009 | 2008 | 2007 | 2006 | 2005 | 2004 | 2003 | 2002 | 2001 |
|---|---|---|---|---|---|---|---|---|---|---|
| Revenue | 13,966 | 10,427 | 12,501 | 13,835 | 14,255 | 13,392 | 12,580 | 9,834 | 8,383 | 8,201 |
| Operating Income | 5,316 | 3,128 | 3,794 | 4,580 | 4,419 | 4,222 | 3,756 | 2,493 | 1,977 | 1,246 |
| Depreciation | 913 | 925 | 1,059 | 1,070 | 1,052 | 1,431 | 1,549 | 1,528 | 1,689 | 1,828 |
| Interest Expense | NA | NA | Nil | 1.00 | 7.00 | 9.00 | 21.0 | 39.0 | 57.0 | 61.0 |
| Pretax Income | 4,551 | 2,017 | 2,481 | 3,692 | 3,625 | 2,988 | 2,421 | 1,250 | -346 | -426 |
| Effective Tax Rate | NA | 27.1% | 22.6% | 28.5% | 27.2% | 22.2% | 23.1% | 4.16% | NM | NM |
| Net Income | 3,228 | 1,470 | 1,920 | 2,641 | 2,638 | 2,324 | 1,861 | 1,198 | -344 | -201 |
| S&P Core Earnings | 3,148 | 1,507 | 1,855 | 2,609 | 2,614 | 2,110 | 1,516 | 701 | -275 | -587 |

| Balance Sheet & Other Financial Data (Million $) | 2010 | 2009 | 2008 | 2007 | 2006 | 2005 | 2004 | 2003 | 2002 | 2001 |
|---|---|---|---|---|---|---|---|---|---|---|
| Cash | 3,072 | 2,925 | 2,540 | 2,924 | 1,183 | 1,219 | 2,668 | 1,818 | 949 | 431 |
| Current Assets | 7,060 | 6,114 | 5,790 | 6,918 | 7,854 | 9,185 | 10,190 | 7,709 | 6,126 | 5,775 |
| Total Assets | 13,401 | 12,119 | 11,923 | 12,667 | 13,930 | 15,063 | 16,299 | 15,510 | 14,679 | 15,779 |
| Current Liabilities | 1,981 | 1,587 | 1,532 | 2,025 | 2,078 | 2,346 | 1,925 | 2,200 | 1,934 | 1,580 |
| Long Term Debt | NA | NA | Nil | Nil | Nil | 360 | 368 | 395 | 833 | 1,211 |
| Common Equity | 10,437 | 9,722 | 9,326 | 9,975 | 11,711 | 11,937 | 13,063 | 11,864 | 10,734 | 11,879 |
| Total Capital | 10,437 | 9,722 | 9,385 | 10,024 | 11,734 | 12,320 | 13,471 | 12,318 | 11,696 | 13,421 |
| Capital Expenditures | 1,199 | 753 | 763 | 686 | 1,272 | 1,330 | 1,298 | 800 | 802 | 1,790 |
| Cash Flow | 4,141 | 2,395 | 2,979 | 3,711 | 3,690 | 3,882 | 3,410 | 2,726 | 1,345 | 1,627 |
| Current Ratio | 3.6 | 3.9 | 3.8 | 3.4 | 3.8 | 3.9 | 5.3 | 3.5 | 3.2 | 3.7 |
| % Long Term Debt of Capitalization | Nil | Nil | Nil | Nil | Nil | 2.9 | 2.7 | 3.2 | 7.1 | 9.0 |
| % Net Income of Revenue | 23.1 | 14.1 | 15.4 | 19.1 | 18.5 | 17.4 | 14.8 | 12.2 | NM | NM |
| % Return on Assets | 25.3 | 12.2 | 15.6 | 19.9 | 18.2 | 14.8 | 11.7 | 7.9 | NM | NM |
| % Return on Equity | 32.0 | 15.4 | 19.9 | 24.8 | 22.2 | 18.6 | 14.9 | 10.6 | NM | NM |

Data as orig reptd.; bef. results of disc opers/spec. items. Per share data adj. for stk. divs.; EPS diluted. E-Estimated. NA-Not Available. NM-Not Meaningful. NR-Not Ranked. UR-Under Review.

**Office:** PO Box 660199, Dallas, TX 75266-0199.
**Telephone:** 972-995-3773.
**Website:** http://www.ti.com
**Chrmn, Pres & CEO:** R.K. Templeton

**SVP, CFO & Chief Acctg Officer:** K.P. March
**Treas:** B. Bull
**Secy & General Counsel:** J.F. Hubach
**Investor Contact:** R. Slaymaker (972-995-3773)

**Board Members:** R. W. Babb, Jr., D. A. Carp, C. S. Cox, S. P. MacMillan, P. H. Patsley, R. E. Sanchez, W. R. Sanders, R. J. Simmons, R. K. Templeton, C. T. Whitman
**Founded:** 1930
**Domicile:** Delaware
**Employees:** 28,412

# Textron Inc.

STANDARD &POOR'S

| S&P Recommendation | HOLD ★★★★★ | Price $17.33 (as of Nov 25, 2011) | 12-Mo. Target Price $21.00 | Investment Style Large-Cap Value |
|---|---|---|---|---|

**GICS Sector** Industrials
**Sub-Industry** Aerospace & Defense

**Summary** This aerospace and industrial conglomerate makes Cessna business jets, Bell helicopters, and industrial and military equipment and components. It also operates a diversified commercial finance company.

## Key Stock Statistics (Source S&P, Vickers, company reports)

| | | | | | | | |
|---|---|---|---|---|---|---|---|
| 52-Wk Range | $28.87– 14.66 | S&P Oper. EPS 2011E | 1.15 | Market Capitalization(B) | $4.821 | Beta | 2.69 |
| Trailing 12-Month EPS | $1.02 | S&P Oper. EPS 2012E | 1.65 | Yield (%) | 0.46 | S&P 3-Yr. Proj. EPS CAGR(%) | NM |
| Trailing 12-Month P/E | 17.0 | P/E on S&P Oper. EPS 2011E | 15.1 | Dividend Rate/Share | $0.08 | S&P Credit Rating | BBB- |
| $10K Invested 5 Yrs Ago | $3,889 | Common Shares Outstg. (M) | 278.2 | Institutional Ownership (%) | 83 | | |

## Price Performance

- 30-Week Mov. Avg. ····
- 10-Week Mov. Avg. ---
- GAAP Earnings vs. Previous Year
- Volume Above Avg. ⊔⊔⊔
- STARS
- 12-Mo. Target Price —
- Relative Strength —
- ▲ Up ▼ Down ► No Change
- Below Avg. ⊔⊔⊔ ★

Options: ASE, CBOE, P, Ph

Analysis prepared by Equity Analyst **R. Tortoriello** on Nov 18, 2011, when the stock traded at **$18.52**.

### Highlights

➤ We estimate a 7% rise in sales in 2011, driven by 15% growth at Cessna and 9% growth at Bell Helicopter. Growth at Cessna was aided by easy comparisons, as Cessna revenue declined 23% in 2010. For 2012, we project 1% revenue growth. We expect modest improvement in business jets and slow growth at Cessna and Bell, on improved demand for civil helicopters. We project a 3% decline at Textron Systems on declining defense demand, and modest Industrial improvement on auto demand.

➤ We estimate operating margins of 7.1% in 2011, up from 5.3% in 2010 and 3.0% in 2009. For 2012, we project further improvement, to 9.1%, primarily driven by improvement we expect at Cessna on increased volume and efficiency improvements.

➤ We estimate EPS of $1.15 in 2011, and project growth to $1.65 in 2012. TXT is scaling back its Finance unit to a captive unit serving Bell, Cessna, and E-Z-GO, and we note that it has reduced total receivables from $12.5 billion as of the end of 2007 to $3.5 billion as of September 30, 2011.

### Investment Rationale/Risk

➤ We see TXT making progress toward working out bad debt/liquidity issues, significantly reducing risk of the shares, in our view. At the same time, we see signs that the business jet market is slowly improving, including rising flight hours and declining used aircraft availability. The company saw order improvement in the commercial helicopter side of Bell in the first nine months of 2011, and we expect military helicopter demand (V-22 and H-1) to remain relatively stable through 2012. However, given puts and takes we see in TXT's business, we view the shares as fairly valued.

➤ Risks to our opinion and target price include the higher-than-anticipated loan losses at Textron Financial, and worse-than-anticipated performance at Bell, Cessna, or Industrial.

➤ Our 12-month target price of $21 is based on a 6.5X multiple of our 2012 EBITDA estimate. Over the past 20 years, TXT has recorded an average enterprise value to EBITDA multiple of 9.3X. We assign a lower-than-average multiple to the shares due to our view of lingering financial risk and a slow business jet recovery.

## Qualitative Risk Assessment

| LOW | MEDIUM | HIGH |
|---|---|---|

Our risk assessment reflects our view of TXT's history of highly cyclical earnings, as reflected in its Quality Ranking of B, as well as its significant debt burden and exposure to bad loans through its Finance subsidiary.

## Quantitative Evaluations

### S&P Quality Ranking                                    B

| D | C | B- | B | B+ | A- | A | A+ |
|---|---|---|---|---|---|---|---|

### Relative Strength Rank                    MODERATE

48

LOWEST = 1                                    HIGHEST = 99

## Revenue/Earnings Data

### Revenue (Million $)

| | 1Q | 2Q | 3Q | 4Q | Year |
|---|---|---|---|---|---|
| 2011 | 2,479 | 2,728 | 2,814 | -- | -- |
| 2010 | 2,210 | 2,709 | 2,479 | 3,127 | 10,525 |
| 2009 | 2,526 | 2,612 | 2,549 | 2,813 | 10,500 |
| 2008 | 3,518 | 3,919 | 3,533 | 3,606 | 14,246 |
| 2007 | 2,964 | 3,235 | 3,263 | 3,763 | 13,225 |
| 2006 | 2,632 | 2,820 | 2,837 | 3,201 | 11,490 |

### Earnings Per Share ($)

| | | | | | |
|---|---|---|---|---|---|
| 2011 | 0.10 | 0.29 | 0.45 | E0.32 | E1.15 |
| 2010 | -0.01 | 0.27 | -0.17 | 0.20 | 0.30 |
| 2009 | 0.18 | -0.23 | 0.02 | -0.22 | -0.28 |
| 2008 | 0.93 | 1.03 | 0.85 | -1.44 | 1.38 |
| 2007 | 0.78 | 0.85 | 0.95 | 1.02 | 3.59 |
| 2006 | 0.60 | 0.67 | 0.68 | 0.77 | 2.72 |

Fiscal year ended Dec. 31. Next earnings report expected: Late January. EPS Estimates based on S&P Operating Earnings; historical GAAP earnings are as reported.

## Dividend Data (Dates: mm/dd Payment Date: mm/dd/yy)

| Amount ($) | Date Decl. | Ex-Div. Date | Stk. of Record | Payment Date |
|---|---|---|---|---|
| 0.020 | 02/23 | 03/09 | 03/11 | 04/01/11 |
| 0.020 | 04/27 | 06/08 | 06/10 | 07/01/11 |
| 0.020 | 07/26 | 09/07 | 09/09 | 10/01/11 |
| 0.020 | 10/26 | 12/07 | 12/09 | 01/01/12 |

Dividends have been paid since 1942. Source: Company reports.

---

**Please read the Required Disclosures and Analyst Certification on the last page of this report.**

The McGraw-Hill Companies

# Textron Inc.

## Business Summary November 18, 2011

CORPORATE OVERVIEW. Textron, an $11 billion in estimated 2011 revenue aerospace and industrial conglomerate, conducts business through five operating segments.

The Cessna segment (24% of sales and -5% of operating profits in 2010) primarily makes the Cessna Citation business jets. Product lines include Citation business jets, Caravan single-engine turboprops, Cessna single-engine piston aircraft, and aftermarket services. Based on revenues, Cessna is the world's third largest corporate jet maker, behind Canada's Bombardier and General Dynamics' Gulfstream division; however, it is the world's largest business jet maker in unit volume. The family of business jets currently produced by Cessna includes the Mustang, the Citation CJ1+, CJ2+, CJ3, and CJ4, the Citation XLS+, the Citation Sovereign, and Citation X. The Citation X is the world's fastest business jet, with a maximum speed of Mach 0.92. First delivery of the CJ4 took place in April 2010. The Cessna Caravan (four models) is the world's best-selling utility turboprop. Cessna also offers nine models in its single-engine piston product line. Cessna's private jet business, CitationAir, offers a variety of private jet for hire solutions.

Bell Helicopter (31%; 77%) is the world's third largest rotary-wing aircraft

maker, behind United Technologies' Sikorsky Unit and EADS's Eurocopter unit. Bell makes helicopters and tiltrotor aircraft (the V-22 Osprey) for both military and commercial applications, and provides spare parts and service. Bell supplies advanced military helicopters and support (including spare parts, support equipment, technical data, trainers, etc.) to the U.S. government and military customers outside the U.S. Bell is also a leading supplier of commercially certified helicopters to corporate, offshore petroleum exploration and development, utility, charter, police, fire, rescue, and emergency medical helicopter operators. The V-22 Osprey is a military tiltrotor aircraft built in conjunction with Boeing. Bell also makes the Marine Corps. H-1 helicopter (AH-1Z and UH-1Z), with a program of record that calls for 349 production units. Bell's commercial offerings include the 206L-4, 407, 412EP, 429, and Huey II. Military helicopters accounted for 62% of segment revenue in 2010, with the V-22 alone accounting for 36%.

## Company Financials Fiscal Year Ended Dec. 31

| Per Share Data ($) | 2010 | 2009 | 2008 | 2007 | 2006 | 2005 | 2004 | 2003 | 2002 | 2001 |
|---|---|---|---|---|---|---|---|---|---|---|
| Tangible Book Value | 4.86 | 4.42 | 2.06 | 2.77 | 4.86 | 8.02 | 7.35 | 8.09 | 6.46 | 6.20 |
| Cash Flow | 1.60 | 1.28 | 2.81 | 4.91 | 3.95 | 3.15 | 2.69 | 2.32 | 2.61 | 2.38 |
| Earnings | 0.30 | -0.28 | 1.38 | 3.59 | 2.72 | 1.89 | 1.33 | 1.03 | 1.30 | 0.58 |
| S&P Core Earnings | 0.31 | -0.23 | 1.11 | 3.51 | 2.66 | 2.06 | 1.01 | 0.59 | 0.14 | -0.70 |
| Dividends | 0.08 | 0.08 | 0.92 | 0.85 | 0.78 | 0.70 | 0.66 | 0.65 | 0.65 | 0.65 |
| Payout Ratio | 27% | NM | 67% | 24% | 29% | 37% | 50% | 63% | 50% | NM |
| Prices:High | 25.30 | 21.00 | 70.14 | 74.40 | 49.48 | 40.36 | 37.46 | 29.00 | 26.80 | 30.24 |
| Prices:Low | 15.88 | 3.57 | 10.09 | 43.60 | 37.76 | 32.60 | 25.30 | 13.00 | 16.10 | 15.65 |
| P/E Ratio:High | 84 | NM | 51 | 21 | 18 | 21 | 28 | 28 | 21 | 52 |
| P/E Ratio:Low | 53 | NM | 7 | 12 | 14 | 17 | 19 | 13 | 12 | 27 |

| Income Statement Analysis (Million $) | 2010 | 2009 | 2008 | 2007 | 2006 | 2005 | 2004 | 2003 | 2002 | 2001 |
|---|---|---|---|---|---|---|---|---|---|---|
| Revenue | 10,525 | 10,500 | 14,246 | 13,225 | 11,490 | 10,043 | 10,242 | 9,859 | 10,658 | 12,321 |
| Operating Income | 809 | 830 | 1,974 | 2,120 | 1,703 | 1,450 | 1,260 | 1,171 | 1,285 | 1,461 |
| Depreciation | 393 | 409 | 358 | 336 | 290 | 303 | 353 | 356 | 368 | 514 |
| Interest Expense | 140 | 309 | 432 | 484 | 438 | 290 | 248 | 283 | 330 | 459 |
| Pretax Income | 86.0 | -149 | 658 | 1,300 | 437 | 739 | 528 | 388 | 464 | 393 |
| Effective Tax Rate | NA | 51.0% | 47.7% | 29.6% | NM | 30.2% | 29.4% | 27.6% | 21.6% | 57.8% |
| Net Income | 92.0 | -73.0 | 344 | 915 | 706 | 516 | 373 | 281 | 364 | 166 |
| S&P Core Earnings | 95.9 | -63.9 | 272 | 895 | 690 | 565 | 282 | 161 | 38.6 | -202 |

| Balance Sheet & Other Financial Data (Million $) | 2010 | 2009 | 2008 | 2007 | 2006 | 2005 | 2004 | 2003 | 2002 | 2001 |
|---|---|---|---|---|---|---|---|---|---|---|
| Cash | 898 | 1,748 | 531 | 531 | 780 | 796 | 732 | 843 | 307 | 260 |
| Current Assets | 5,047 | 12,761 | 4,766 | 4,846 | 4,287 | 4,975 | 4,168 | 3,592 | 3,887 | 4,017 |
| Total Assets | 15,282 | 18,940 | 20,020 | 19,956 | 17,550 | 16,499 | 15,875 | 15,090 | 15,505 | 16,052 |
| Current Liabilities | 2,657 | 4,905 | 7,406 | 7,248 | 2,994 | 3,147 | 2,975 | 2,256 | 2,239 | 3,075 |
| Long Term Debt | 2,283 | 3,450 | 6,779 | 6,384 | 6,150 | 7,079 | 6,141 | 6,144 | 7,038 | 5,962 |
| Common Equity | 2,972 | 2,826 | 2,366 | 3,505 | 2,639 | 3,266 | 3,642 | 3,680 | 3,395 | 3,923 |
| Total Capital | 5,274 | 6,410 | 3,924 | 10,363 | 8,799 | 10,816 | 10,246 | 10,224 | 10,842 | 10,253 |
| Capital Expenditures | 270 | 238 | 550 | 401 | 431 | 365 | 302 | 301 | 296 | 532 |
| Cash Flow | 485 | 336 | 702 | 1,251 | 996 | 819 | 726 | 637 | 732 | 680 |
| Current Ratio | 1.9 | 2.1 | 1.8 | 1.2 | 1.4 | 1.6 | 1.4 | 1.6 | 1.7 | 1.3 |
| % Long Term Debt of Capitalization | 43.3 | 53.8 | 172.7 | 61.6 | 69.9 | 65.4 | 59.9 | 60.1 | 64.9 | 58.1 |
| % Net Income of Revenue | 0.9 | NM | 2.4 | 6.9 | 6.1 | 5.1 | 3.6 | 2.9 | 3.4 | 1.3 |
| % Return on Assets | 0.5 | NM | 1.7 | 4.9 | 4.1 | 3.2 | 2.4 | 1.8 | 2.3 | 1.0 |
| % Return on Equity | 3.2 | NM | 11.7 | 29.8 | 23.9 | 14.9 | 10.2 | 7.9 | 9.9 | 4.2 |

Data as orig reptd.; bef. results of disc opers/spec. items. Per share data adj. for stk. divs.; EPS diluted. E-Estimated. NA-Not Available. NM-Not Meaningful. NR-Not Ranked. UR-Under Review.

**Office:** 40 Westminster Street, Providence, RI 02903.
**Telephone:** 401-421-2800.
**Website:** http://www.textron.com
**Chrmn, Pres & CEO:** S.C. Donnelly

**COO:** N.R. Mohanty
**EVP & CFO:** F.T. Connor
**EVP, Secy & General Counsel:** T. O'Donnell
**Chief Admin Officer:** J.D. Butler

**Investor Contact:** D.R. Wilburne (401-457-2353)
**Board Members:** K. M. Bader, R. K. Clark, J. T. Conway, S. C. Donnelly, I. J. Evans, L. K. Fish, J. T. Ford, P. E. Gagne, D. M. Hancock, C. D. Powell, L. G. Trotter, J. L. Ziemer

**Founded:** 1928
**Domicile:** Delaware
**Employees:** 32,000

# Thermo Fisher Scientific Inc

**STANDARD &POOR'S**

| S&P Recommendation | **STRONG BUY** ★★★★★ | Price $44.42 (as of Nov 25, 2011) | 12-Mo. Target Price $70.00 | Investment Style Large-Cap Growth |
|---|---|---|---|---|

**GICS Sector** Health Care
**Sub-Industry** Life Sciences Tools & Services

**Summary** Formed through the November 2006 merger of Thermo Electron and Fisher Scientific, TMO is a leading manufacturer and developer of analytical and laboratory instruments and supplies for life science, drug discovery and industrial applications.

## Key Stock Statistics (Source S&P, Vickers, company reports)

| | | | | | | | |
|---|---|---|---|---|---|---|---|
| 52-Wk Range | $65.86– 44.29 | S&P Oper. EPS 2011**E** | 4.15 | Market Capitalization(B) | $16.803 | Beta | 0.85 |
| Trailing 12-Month EPS | $3.43 | S&P Oper. EPS 2012**E** | 4.85 | Yield (%) | Nil | S&P 3-Yr. Proj. EPS CAGR(%) | 14 |
| Trailing 12-Month P/E | 13.0 | P/E on S&P Oper. EPS 2011**E** | 10.7 | Dividend Rate/Share | Nil | S&P Credit Rating | A |
| $10K Invested 5 Yrs Ago | $9,989 | Common Shares Outstg. (M) | 378.3 | Institutional Ownership (%) | 93 | | |

## Price Performance

30-Week Mov. Avg. · · · 10-Week Mov. Avg. - - GAAP Earnings vs. Previous Year   Volume Above Avg. ▮▮ STARS
12-Mo. Target Price — Relative Strength — ▲ Up ▼ Down ► No Change   Below Avg. ▮▮ ★

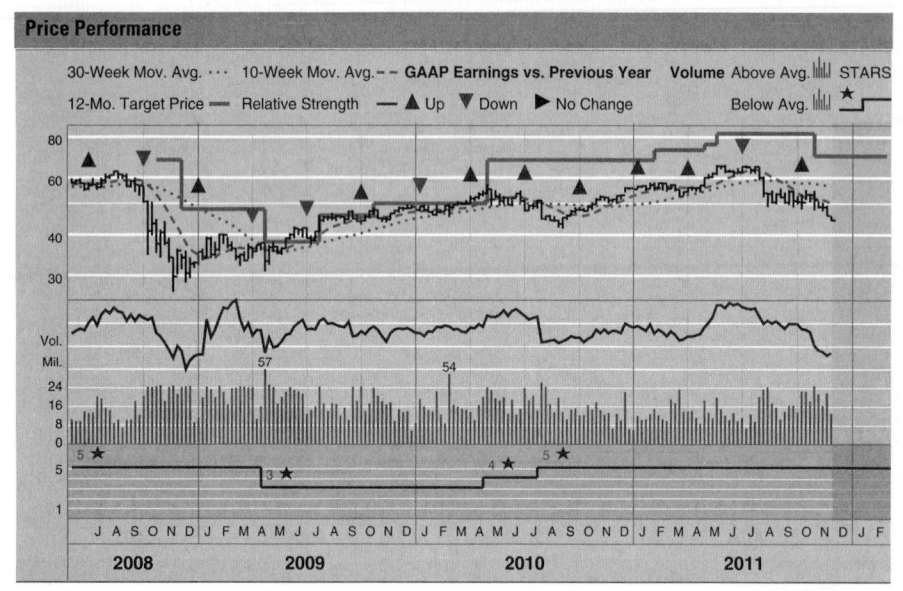

Options: ASE, CBOE, Ph

Analysis prepared by Equity Analyst **Jeffrey Loo, CFA** on Oct 27, 2011, when the stock traded at **$50.65**.

## Highlights

➤ We expect 2011 sales, including the acquisitions of Phadia AB and Dionex, to rise 11%, to $11.67 billion. In 2012, we see sales growing 11% to $12.96 billion. Following the Phadia deal, TMO established a third reporting segment, Specialty Diagnostics, in addition to Analytical Technologies and Laboratory Products. We look for mid-single organic growth in Specialty Diagnostics and Laboratory Products but see only flat growth in Analytical Technologies due to uncertainty over government funding in the U.S. and Europe. We see gross margins improving 30 basis points (bps) and operating margins rising 60 bps in 2011 on leverage.

➤ In August, TMO acquired Sweden-based Phadia AB for $3.5 billion. This deal follows the May acquisition of Dionex, a leading provider of chromatography instruments, for $2.1 billion. Phadia is the global leader in in-vitro allergy diagnostics. We see growth opportunities in the U.S. but see challenges transitioning physicians to in-vitro allergy tests from skin-prick tests, which account for over 80% of the U.S. market.

➤ We estimate EPS of $4.15 and $4.85 in 2011 and 2012, before amortization of intangible assets.

## Investment Rationale/Risk

➤ We view TMO as undervalued at a recent 10.4X our 2012 EPS estimate and a P/E-to-growth ratio of 0.7X, below peers and well below historical levels. While we expect uncertainty over government funding in the U.S. and Europe to continue into 2012, we think TMO's comprehensive product offering, broad geographic coverage and rapid expansion in emerging markets will enable it to capture market share and grow faster than the market. The government end-market accounts for 24% of TMO's sales, but we believe other end-markets are stable and growing. We are encouraged by TMO's capital deployment efforts including acquisitions and extensive stock repurchase programs. Since 2010, TMO has spent $1.99 billion to repurchase 38.1 million shares. As of September 30, $250 million remained in its buyback program.

➤ Risks to our opinion and target price include a slower-than-expected recovery in TMO's end-markets, and loss of market share.

➤ Our 12-month target price of $70 assumes a PEG ratio of 1.0X, slightly below peers, based on our 2012 EPS estimate of $4.85 and a projected three-year EPS growth rate of 14%.

## Qualitative Risk Assessment

| LOW | **MEDIUM** | HIGH |
|---|---|---|

Our risk assessment reflects TMO's broad product lines and geographic coverage, spread across the life sciences, health care and industrial markets, which we believe reduces risk. However, TMO has a proactive acquisition strategy that we believe raises its risk profile.

## Quantitative Evaluations

**S&P Quality Ranking**　　　　　　　　**B**

| D | C | B- | **B** | B+ | A- | A | A+ |
|---|---|---|---|---|---|---|---|

**Relative Strength Rank**　　　　　　**WEAK**

|　　　25　　　| |
|---|---|
LOWEST = 1　　　　　　　　　　　　HIGHEST = 99

## Revenue/Earnings Data

**Revenue (Million $)**

| | 1Q | 2Q | 3Q | 4Q | Year |
|---|---|---|---|---|---|
| 2011 | 2,721 | 2,897 | 2,974 | -- | -- |
| 2010 | 2,675 | 2,649 | 2,684 | 2,781 | 10,789 |
| 2009 | 2,255 | 2,484 | 2,531 | 2,839 | 10,110 |
| 2008 | 2,554 | 2,710 | 2,588 | 2,646 | 10,498 |
| 2007 | 2,338 | 2,386 | 2,401 | 2,621 | 9,746 |
| 2006 | 684.3 | 713.5 | 725.0 | 1,669 | 3,792 |

**Earnings Per Share ($)**

| | 1Q | 2Q | 3Q | 4Q | Year |
|---|---|---|---|---|---|
| 2011 | 0.63 | 0.56 | 0.69 | E1.17 | E4.15 |
| 2010 | 0.55 | 0.57 | 0.66 | 0.75 | 2.52 |
| 2009 | 0.35 | 0.49 | 0.53 | 0.65 | 2.01 |
| 2008 | 0.54 | 0.56 | 0.50 | 0.68 | 2.27 |
| 2007 | 0.31 | 0.42 | 0.51 | 0.53 | 1.76 |
| 2006 | 0.26 | 0.30 | 0.30 | 0.08 | 0.82 |

Fiscal year ended Dec. 31. Next earnings report expected: Early February. EPS Estimates based on S&P Operating Earnings; historical GAAP earnings are as reported.

## Dividend Data

No cash dividends have been paid.

# Thermo Fisher Scientific Inc

STANDARD &POOR'S

## Business Summary October 27, 2011

CORPORATE OVERVIEW. In November 2006, Thermo Electron Corp. and Fisher Scientific completed a stock-for-stock merger. The combined company was renamed Thermo Fisher Scientific (TMO) and is a leading provider of life science and laboratory analytical instruments, equipment, reagents and consumables, software and services for research, analysis, discovery and diagnosis. Following the merger, the company had annual revenues in excess of $9 billion, with over 30,000 employees in 38 countries providing services and sales in over 150 countries. Major end-markets served include drug discovery, proteomics research, biopharma services, molecular diagnostics, immunohistochemistry, cell screening, environmental regulatory compliance, and food safety. TMO believes these markets represent a combined $70 billion to $80 billion annual marketplace. We believe TMO is the largest company within its marketplace, with the broadest product offering and geographic coverage. Since this merger, TMO has completed numerous additional acquisitions.

The Thermo Electron business focuses primarily on the development and manufacture of analytical systems, instruments and components and provides solutions to monitor, collect and analyze data. These instruments are used primarily in life science, drug discovery, clinical, environmental and industrial laboratory applications. The Fisher Scientific business focuses on providing a broad range of over 600,000 scientific research, health care and safety-related products and services. Customers include pharmaceutical and biotechnology companies, colleges and universities, medical research institutions, hospitals and reference labs, and research and development labs.

The company now reports through three business segments: Analytical Technologies, Specialty Diagnostics, and Laboratory Products and Services. Analytical Technologies should account for about 30% of sales and focuses on scientific instruments, bioscience reagents, lab informatics and automation, environmental monitoring instruments and industrial process instruments. Analytical Technologies is comprised primarily of the legacy Thermo Electron business. Specialty Diagnostics should account for 20% of sales and will focus on diagnostic instruments and assays. Laboratory Products and Services, comprised primarily of legacy Fisher Scientific business, should account for about 50% of sales and focuses on lab equipment and consumables and biopharma outsourcing services.

## Company Financials Fiscal Year Ended Dec. 31

| Per Share Data ($) | 2010 | 2009 | 2008 | 2007 | 2006 | 2005 | 2004 | 2003 | 2002 | 2001 |
|---|---|---|---|---|---|---|---|---|---|---|
| Tangible Book Value | 0.14 | 0.27 | NM | NM | NM | 2.32 | 6.19 | 5.00 | 3.79 | 1.33 |
| Cash Flow | 4.40 | 3.88 | 4.10 | 3.46 | 2.00 | 1.95 | 1.70 | 1.35 | 1.35 | 0.81 |
| Earnings | 2.52 | 2.01 | 2.27 | 1.76 | 0.82 | 1.21 | 1.31 | 1.04 | 1.12 | 0.27 |
| S&P Core Earnings | 2.49 | 1.99 | 2.16 | 1.78 | 0.83 | 1.01 | 1.18 | 0.79 | 0.50 | 0.02 |
| Dividends | Nil | Nil | Nil | Nil | Nil | Nil | Nil | Nil | Nil | Nil |
| Payout Ratio | Nil | Nil | Nil | Nil | Nil | Nil | Nil | Nil | Nil | Nil |
| Prices:High | 57.40 | 49.70 | 62.77 | 62.02 | 46.34 | 31.87 | 31.40 | 25.40 | 24.60 | 30.62 |
| Prices:Low | 41.74 | 30.83 | 26.65 | 43.60 | 29.95 | 23.94 | 24.00 | 16.89 | 14.33 | 16.55 |
| P/E Ratio:High | 23 | 25 | 28 | 35 | 57 | 26 | 24 | 24 | 22 | NM |
| P/E Ratio:Low | 17 | 15 | 12 | 25 | 37 | 20 | 18 | 16 | 13 | NM |

| Income Statement Analysis (Million $) | 2010 | 2009 | 2008 | 2007 | 2006 | 2005 | 2004 | 2003 | 2002 | 2001 |
|---|---|---|---|---|---|---|---|---|---|---|
| Revenue | 10,789 | 10,110 | 10,498 | 9,746 | 3,792 | 2,633 | 2,206 | 2,097 | 2,086 | 2,188 |
| Operating Income | 2,114 | 1,905 | 2,059 | 1,823 | 528 | 404 | 319 | 292 | 264 | 265 |
| Depreciation | 770 | 787 | 793 | 757 | 241 | 123 | 66.1 | 58.5 | 56.4 | 98.5 |
| Interest Expense | 84.7 | 118 | 130 | 140 | 51.9 | 26.7 | 11.0 | 18.7 | Nil | 71.8 |
| Pretax Income | 1,165 | 927 | 1,150 | 881 | 209 | 286 | 259 | 219 | 288 | 70.7 |
| Effective Tax Rate | NA | 8.18% | 14.0% | 11.5% | 20.6% | 30.6% | 15.8% | 21.0% | 32.3% | 38.1% |
| Net Income | 1,033 | 851 | 989 | 780 | 166 | 198 | 218 | 173 | 195 | 49.6 |
| S&P Core Earnings | 1,022 | 847 | 941 | 785 | 169 | 164 | 196 | 131 | 79.3 | 5.63 |

| Balance Sheet & Other Financial Data (Million $) | 2010 | 2009 | 2008 | 2007 | 2006 | 2005 | 2004 | 2003 | 2002 | 2001 |
|---|---|---|---|---|---|---|---|---|---|---|
| Cash | 926 | 1,571 | 1,288 | 639 | 667 | 214 | 327 | 304 | 339 | 298 |
| Current Assets | 4,137 | 4,531 | 4,346 | 3,665 | 3,660 | 1,354 | 1,470 | 1,395 | 1,772 | 1,965 |
| Total Assets | 21,387 | 21,601 | 21,090 | 21,207 | 21,262 | 4,252 | 3,577 | 3,389 | 3,647 | 3,825 |
| Current Liabilities | 1,742 | 1,639 | 1,540 | 1,902 | 2,152 | 792 | 579 | 685 | 1,104 | 1,142 |
| Long Term Debt | 2,031 | 2,066 | 2,044 | 2,046 | 2,181 | 469 | 226 | 230 | 451 | 728 |
| Common Equity | 15,361 | 15,431 | 14,927 | 14,488 | 13,912 | 2,793 | 2,666 | 2,383 | 2,033 | 1,908 |
| Total Capital | 17,392 | 17,497 | 16,979 | 18,814 | 18,650 | 3,327 | 2,907 | 2,624 | 2,495 | 2,650 |
| Capital Expenditures | 266 | 208 | 264 | 176 | 76.8 | 43.5 | 50.0 | 46.1 | 51.2 | 84.8 |
| Cash Flow | 1,803 | 1,639 | 1,781 | 1,536 | 407 | 322 | 285 | 231 | 252 | 148 |
| Current Ratio | 2.4 | 2.8 | 2.8 | 1.9 | 1.7 | 1.7 | 2.5 | 2.0 | 1.6 | 1.7 |
| % Long Term Debt of Capitalization | 11.7 | 11.8 | 12.0 | 10.9 | 11.7 | 14.1 | 7.8 | 8.7 | 18.1 | 27.4 |
| % Net Income of Revenue | 9.6 | 8.4 | 9.4 | 8.0 | 4.4 | 7.5 | 9.9 | 8.2 | 9.4 | 2.3 |
| % Return on Assets | 4.8 | 4.0 | 4.7 | 3.7 | 1.3 | 5.1 | 6.3 | 4.9 | 5.2 | 1.1 |
| % Return on Equity | 6.7 | 5.6 | 6.7 | 5.5 | 2.0 | 7.3 | 8.7 | 7.8 | 9.9 | 2.2 |

Data as orig reptd.; bef. results of disc opers/spec. items. Per share data adj. for stk. divs.; EPS diluted. E-Estimated. NA-Not Available. NM-Not Meaningful. NR-Not Ranked. UR-Under Review.

Office: 81 Wyman St PO Box 9046, Waltham, MA 02254-9046.
Telephone: 781-622-1000.
Website: http://www.fishersci.com
Chrmn: J.P. Manzi

Pres & CEO: M.N. Casper
SVP & CFO: P.M. Wilver
SVP, Secy & General Counsel: S.H. Hoogasian
Chief Acctg Officer: P.E. Hornstra

Investor Contact: K.J. Apicerno (781-622-1111)
Board Members: M. N. Casper, N. J. Chai, T. Jacks, J. C. Lewent, T. Lynch, P. J. Manning, J. P. Manzi, W. G. Parrett, M. E. Porter, L. R. Sorensen, S. M. Sperling, E. S. Ullian

Founded: 1956
Domicile: Delaware
Employees: 37,200

# 3M Co

**STANDARD &POOR'S**

| S&P Recommendation | HOLD ★★★★☆ | Price | 12-Mo. Target Price | Investment Style |
|---|---|---|---|---|
| | | $76.13 (as of Nov 25, 2011) | $88.00 | Large-Cap Growth |

**GICS Sector** Industrials
**Sub-Industry** Industrial Conglomerates

**Summary** This diversified global company provides enhanced product functionality in electronics, health care, industrial, consumer, office, telecommunications, safety & security and other markets via coatings, sealants, adhesives, and other chemical additives.

## Key Stock Statistics (Source S&P, Vickers, company reports)

| | | | | | | | |
|---|---|---|---|---|---|---|---|
| 52-Wk Range | $98.19– 68.63 | S&P Oper. EPS 2011**E** | 6.00 | Market Capitalization(B) | $53.355 | Beta | 0.87 |
| Trailing 12-Month EPS | $5.88 | S&P Oper. EPS 2012**E** | 6.45 | Yield (%) | 2.89 | S&P 3-Yr. Proj. EPS CAGR(%) | 7 |
| Trailing 12-Month P/E | 13.0 | P/E on S&P Oper. EPS 2011**E** | 12.7 | Dividend Rate/Share | $2.20 | S&P Credit Rating | AA- |
| $10K Invested 5 Yrs Ago | $10,743 | Common Shares Outstg. (M) | 700.8 | Institutional Ownership (%) | 70 | | |

## Price Performance

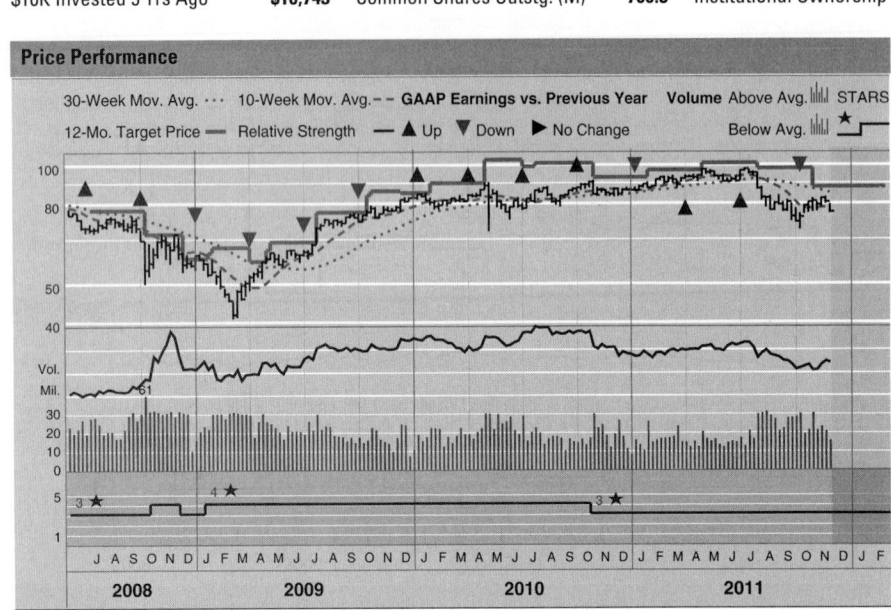

30-Week Mov. Avg. · · · 10-Week Mov. Avg. - - GAAP Earnings vs. Previous Year   Volume Above Avg. STARS
12-Mo. Target Price — Relative Strength — ▲ Up ▼ Down ▶ No Change   Below Avg.

Options: ASE, CBOE, P, Ph

Analysis prepared by Equity Analyst **R. Tortoriello** on Oct 26, 2011, when the stock traded at **$76.78**.

## Highlights

➤ We estimate a sales increase of 12% in 2011, with organic growth of about 4%, on strong emerging market growth and slowing developed market growth. We particularly see growth slowing in Europe, due to political and financial market turmoil. For 2012, we project sales will grow about 3% (excluding potential acquisitions) on continued strength in Health Care, driven by emerging markets, and good Industrial & Transportation growth, with slower growth in the remaining segments.

➤ We estimate operating margins of 20.9% in 2011, down from 22.2% in 2010, on higher pension expense and cost pressure from higher commodity prices. For 2012, we project that margins will remain flat, as we expect some pension headwind to continue and see the potential that volume declines in some businesses will cause inefficiencies.

➤ We estimate EPS of $6.00 in 2011, with growth to $6.45 in 2012, aided by our expectation of a 2% share count reduction due to continued share repurchases.

## Investment Rationale/Risk

➤ We view 3M's ability to generate strong returns on capital and free cash flows positively. In addition, we like the company's innovative, consumable-product business mix, and believe its strategy of marketing new and innovative products to capture global market share and increase operating margins will continue to drive results. That said, we see risk in potential continued economic slowing, particularly in Europe, and a further decline in the LCD businesses and slowing electronics businesses.

➤ Risks to our recommendation and target price include slower global economic growth, execution risk associated with acquisitions, failure to market new and innovative products, and inability to promote growth in developing markets.

➤ Our 12-month target price of $88 is based on an 8.5X enterprise value multiple of our 2012 EBITDA estimate of $7.5 billion. This is below MMM's 10-year historical average EV/EBITDA multiple of 10.5X, due to our view of risks associated with slowing global economic growth.

## Qualitative Risk Assessment

| LOW | MEDIUM | HIGH |
|---|---|---|

Our risk assessment reflects our view of the company's strong historical earnings and dividend growth, as reflected by its A+ Quality Ranking, its leading position in many of the markets it serves, and our view of its strong balance sheet and relatively low debt levels.

## Quantitative Evaluations

**S&P Quality Ranking**   **A+**

| D | C | B- | B | B+ | A- | A | A+ |
|---|---|---|---|---|---|---|---|

**Relative Strength Rank**   **MODERATE**

57

LOWEST = 1                HIGHEST = 99

## Revenue/Earnings Data

**Revenue (Million $)**

| | 1Q | 2Q | 3Q | 4Q | Year |
|---|---|---|---|---|---|
| 2011 | 7,311 | 7,680 | 7,531 | -- | -- |
| 2010 | 6,348 | 6,731 | 6,874 | 6,709 | 26,662 |
| 2009 | 5,089 | 5,719 | 6,193 | 6,122 | 23,123 |
| 2008 | 6,463 | 6,739 | 6,558 | 5,509 | 25,269 |
| 2007 | 5,937 | 6,142 | 6,177 | 6,206 | 24,462 |
| 2006 | 5,595 | 5,688 | 5,858 | 5,782 | 22,923 |

**Earnings Per Share ($)**

| | | | | | |
|---|---|---|---|---|---|
| 2011 | 1.49 | 1.60 | 1.52 | E1.37 | E6.00 |
| 2010 | 1.29 | 1.54 | 1.53 | 1.28 | 5.63 |
| 2009 | 0.74 | 1.12 | 1.35 | 1.30 | 4.52 |
| 2008 | 1.38 | 1.33 | 1.41 | 0.77 | 4.89 |
| 2007 | 1.85 | 1.25 | 1.32 | 1.17 | 5.60 |
| 2006 | 1.17 | 1.15 | 1.18 | 1.57 | 5.06 |

Fiscal year ended Dec. 31. Next earnings report expected: Late January. EPS Estimates based on S&P Operating Earnings; historical GAAP earnings are as reported.

## Dividend Data (Dates: mm/dd Payment Date: mm/dd/yy)

| Amount ($) | Date Decl. | Ex-Div. Date | Stk. of Record | Payment Date |
|---|---|---|---|---|
| 0.550 | 02/08 | 02/16 | 02/18 | 03/12/11 |
| 0.550 | 05/10 | 05/18 | 05/20 | 06/12/11 |
| 0.550 | 08/08 | 08/17 | 08/19 | 09/12/11 |
| 0.550 | 11/14 | 11/22 | 11/25 | 12/12/11 |

Dividends have been paid since 1916. Source: Company reports.

---

**Please read the Required Disclosures and Analyst Certification on the last page of this report.**

**The McGraw-Hill Companies**

## Business Summary October 26, 2011

CORPORATE OVERVIEW. 3M Co. is a global manufacturer operating a broadly diversified business. The company classifies its business into six reportable segments -- Industrial & Transportation, Health Care, Display & Graphics, Consumer & Office, Electro & Communications, and Safety, Security and Protection. Most 3M products involve expertise in product development, manufacturing and marketing, with many of the company's products involving some form of coating, sealant, adhesive, film, or chemical additive that increases the product's overall functionality and useability for consumers. As of the end of 2010, the company employed about 80,000 people globally.

The Industrial & Transportation segment (31.7% of 2010 revenues, 28.5% of operating profits, with a 21% operating margin) serves a broad range of markets, from appliances and electronics to paper and packaging, food and beverages, automotive, automotive aftermarket, aerospace and marine, and other transportation-related industries. Products include pressure-sensitive tapes, abrasives, adhesives, specialty materials, supply chain management software and solutions, insulation components, films, masking tapes, fasteners and ad-

hesives, to name a few.

The Health Care segment (16.7%, 21.6% and 30.2%) serves markets worldwide, including medical and surgical, pharmaceutical, dental, health information systems and personal care, with a variety of medical and surgical, infection prevention, pharmaceutical, drug delivery, dental, personal care and other products and systems.

The Display & Graphics segment (14.3%, 14.3% and 23.1%) serves markets that include electronic display, touch screen, commercial graphics and traffic control materials. Optical products include Vikkuiti display enhancement films for electronic displays, lens systems for projection televisions, and 3M Micro-Touch touch screens and touch monitors.

## Company Financials Fiscal Year Ended Dec. 31

| Per Share Data ($) | 2010 | 2009 | 2008 | 2007 | 2006 | 2005 | 2004 | 2003 | 2002 | 2001 |
|---|---|---|---|---|---|---|---|---|---|---|
| Tangible Book Value | 9.86 | 7.87 | 3.93 | 13.40 | 7.04 | 8.13 | 9.62 | 6.62 | 4.91 | 6.23 |
| Cash Flow | 7.28 | 6.16 | 6.52 | 7.06 | 6.48 | 5.43 | 5.01 | 4.23 | 3.70 | 3.15 |
| Earnings | 5.63 | 4.52 | 4.89 | 5.60 | 5.06 | 4.16 | 3.75 | 3.02 | 2.49 | 1.79 |
| S&P Core Earnings | 5.60 | 4.40 | 3.77 | 4.68 | 4.26 | 4.13 | 3.66 | 2.91 | 1.71 | 0.94 |
| Dividends | 2.10 | 2.04 | 2.00 | 1.92 | 1.84 | 1.68 | 1.44 | 1.32 | 1.24 | 1.20 |
| Payout Ratio | 37% | 45% | 41% | 34% | 36% | 40% | 38% | 44% | 50% | 67% |
| Prices:High | 91.49 | 84.32 | 84.76 | 97.00 | 88.35 | 87.45 | 90.29 | 85.40 | 65.78 | 63.50 |
| Prices:Low | 67.98 | 40.87 | 50.10 | 72.90 | 67.05 | 69.71 | 73.31 | 59.73 | 50.00 | 42.93 |
| P/E Ratio:High | 16 | 19 | 17 | 17 | 17 | 21 | 24 | 28 | 26 | 35 |
| P/E Ratio:Low | 12 | 9 | 10 | 13 | 13 | 17 | 20 | 20 | 20 | 24 |

| Income Statement Analysis (Million $) | 2010 | 2009 | 2008 | 2007 | 2006 | 2005 | 2004 | 2003 | 2002 | 2001 |
|---|---|---|---|---|---|---|---|---|---|---|
| Revenue | 26,662 | 23,123 | 25,269 | 24,462 | 22,923 | 21,167 | 20,011 | 18,232 | 16,332 | 16,079 |
| Operating Income | 7,034 | 6,180 | 6,640 | 6,584 | 6,252 | 5,995 | 5,577 | 4,677 | 4,000 | 3,274 |
| Depreciation | 1,120 | 1,157 | 1,153 | 1,072 | 1,079 | 986 | 999 | 964 | 954 | 1,089 |
| Interest Expense | 201 | 219 | 215 | 210 | 122 | 82.0 | 69.0 | 84.0 | 80.0 | 124 |
| Pretax Income | 5,755 | 4,632 | 5,108 | 6,115 | 5,625 | 4,983 | 4,555 | 3,657 | 3,005 | 2,186 |
| Effective Tax Rate | 27.7% | 30.0% | 31.1% | 32.1% | 30.6% | 34.0% | 33.0% | 32.9% | 32.1% | 32.1% |
| Net Income | 4,085 | 3,193 | 3,460 | 4,096 | 3,851 | 3,234 | 2,990 | 2,403 | 1,974 | 1,430 |
| S&P Core Earnings | 4,060 | 3,110 | 2,672 | 3,418 | 3,242 | 3,227 | 2,918 | 2,319 | 1,356 | 750 |

| Balance Sheet & Other Financial Data (Million $) | 2010 | 2009 | 2008 | 2007 | 2006 | 2005 | 2004 | 2003 | 2002 | 2001 |
|---|---|---|---|---|---|---|---|---|---|---|
| Cash | 4,478 | 3,784 | 2,222 | 2,475 | 1,918 | 1,072 | 2,757 | 1,836 | 618 | 616 |
| Current Assets | 12,215 | 10,795 | 9,598 | 9,838 | 8,946 | 7,115 | 8,720 | 7,720 | 6,059 | 6,296 |
| Total Assets | 30,156 | 27,250 | 25,646 | 24,694 | 21,294 | 20,513 | 20,708 | 17,600 | 15,329 | 14,606 |
| Current Liabilities | 6,089 | 4,897 | 5,839 | 5,362 | 7,323 | 5,238 | 6,071 | 5,082 | 4,457 | 4,509 |
| Long Term Debt | 4,183 | 5,097 | 5,224 | 4,088 | 1,047 | 1,309 | 727 | 1,735 | 2,140 | 1,520 |
| Common Equity | 16,017 | 13,302 | 9,879 | 11,747 | 10,097 | 10,100 | 10,378 | 7,885 | 5,993 | 6,086 |
| Total Capital | 20,200 | 18,399 | 15,548 | 16,515 | 11,433 | 11,409 | 11,105 | 9,620 | 8,133 | 7,606 |
| Capital Expenditures | 1,091 | 903 | 1,471 | 1,422 | 1,168 | 943 | 937 | 677 | 763 | 980 |
| Cash Flow | 5,283 | 4,350 | 4,613 | 5,168 | 4,930 | 4,220 | 3,989 | 3,367 | 2,928 | 2,519 |
| Current Ratio | 2.0 | 2.2 | 1.6 | 1.8 | 1.2 | 1.4 | 1.4 | 1.5 | 1.4 | 1.4 |
| % Long Term Debt of Capitalization | 20.7 | 27.7 | 33.6 | 24.8 | 9.4 | 11.5 | 6.5 | 18.0 | 26.3 | 20.0 |
| % Net Income of Revenue | 15.3 | 13.8 | 13.7 | 16.7 | 16.8 | 15.3 | 14.9 | 13.2 | 12.1 | 8.9 |
| % Return on Assets | 14.2 | 12.1 | 13.8 | 17.8 | 18.4 | 15.7 | 15.6 | 14.6 | 13.2 | 9.8 |
| % Return on Equity | 28.4 | 27.6 | 32.0 | 37.7 | 37.3 | 31.6 | 32.7 | 34.6 | 32.7 | 22.7 |

Data as orig reptd.; bef. results of disc opers/spec. items. Per share data adj. for stk. divs.; EPS diluted. E-Estimated. NA-Not Available. NM-Not Meaningful. NR-Not Ranked. UR-Under Review.

**Office:** 3-M Center, St Paul, MN 55144-1000.
**Telephone:** 651-733-1110.
**Email:** innovation@mmm.com
**Website:** http://www.3m.com

**Chrmn, Pres & CEO:** G.W. Buckley
**COO & EVP:** I.G. Thulin
**SVP & General Counsel:** M.I. Smith
**CFO:** D.W. Meline

**CTO:** F.J. Palensky
**Investor Contact:** M. Colin (651-733-8206)
**Board Members:** L. G. Alvarado, G. W. Buckley, V. D. Coffman, M. L. Eskew, W. J. Farrell, H. L. Henkel, E. M. Liddy, R. S. Morrison, A. L. Peters, R. J. Ulrich

**Founded:** 1902
**Domicile:** Delaware
**Employees:** 80,057

# Tiffany & Co.

**STANDARD
&POOR'S**

| S&P Recommendation **STRONG BUY** ★★★★★ | Price $67.22 (as of Nov 29, 2011) | 12-Mo. Target Price $90.00 | Investment Style Large-Cap Growth |

**GICS Sector** Consumer Discretionary
**Sub-Industry** Specialty Stores

**Summary** Tiffany is a leading international retailer, designer, manufacturer, and distributor of fine jewelry and gift items.

## Key Stock Statistics (Source S&P, Vickers, company reports)

| | | | | | | |
|---|---|---|---|---|---|---|
| 52-Wk Range | $84.49– 54.58 | S&P Oper. EPS 2012E | 3.80 | Market Capitalization(B) | $8.555 | Beta | 1.76 |
| Trailing 12-Month EPS | $3.16 | S&P Oper. EPS 2013E | 4.20 | Yield (%) | 1.73 | S&P 3-Yr. Proj. EPS CAGR(%) | 17 |
| Trailing 12-Month P/E | 21.3 | P/E on S&P Oper. EPS 2012E | 17.7 | Dividend Rate/Share | $1.16 | S&P Credit Rating | NR |
| $10K Invested 5 Yrs Ago | $20,316 | Common Shares Outstg. (M) | 127.3 | Institutional Ownership (%) | 93 | | |

## Price Performance

30-Week Mov. Avg. ··· 10-Week Mov. Avg. - - 12-Mo. Target Price — Relative Strength — GAAP Earnings vs. Previous Year ▲ Up ▼ Down ► No Change Volume Above Avg. Below Avg. STARS

Options: CBOE, P, Ph

Analysis prepared by Equity Analyst **Jason N. Asaeda** on Oct 31, 2011, when the stock traded at **$78.90**.

## Highlights

► Globally, we believe the Tiffany & Co. brand is under-penetrated, presenting TIF with ample growth opportunities. Through selective retail and e-commerce expansion in the Americas, Europe and the Asia-Pacific, and new product introductions, we see net sales reaching $3.67 billion in FY 12 (Jan.) and $4.11 billion in FY 13.

► Excluding nonrecurring charges related to the company's consolidation and relocation of its New York headquarters staff into a single location, we expect gross margins to widen to 59.6% in FY 12 and 59.8% in FY 13, from 59.1% in FY 11, as TIF is taking price increases to offset higher diamond and precious metal prices. Factoring in new store expenses and a planned increase in marketing spending to enhance brand awareness in existing and new markets, we expect the company to leverage SG&A expenses on projected sales growth. This should result in EBIT margins widening to 21.2% in FY 12 and 21.4% in FY 13, from 19.8% in FY 11.

► Assuming modest share buybacks under TIF's $400 repurchase authorization, we see EPS of $3.70 (before $0.20 in charges) in FY 12 and $4.15 in FY 13, versus $2.93 (before $0.08 in charges and $0.02 in tax benefits) in FY 10.

## Investment Rationale/Risk

► Economic growth remains tepid, but with the return of the luxury shopper in the U.S. and many overseas markets, TIF reported a 20% increases in worldwide same-store sales (on a constant-currency basis) in the first half of FY 12. By region, same-store sales rose 21% in the Americas, 38% in Asia-Pacific, 18% in Europe, and 2% in Japan (earthquake-related store closures impacted first-quarter sales). We also believe the company is benefiting from increased consumer demand for brands with established reputations for quality, style and value. These factors, coupled with TIF's international expansion opportunities, improving operating efficiencies, and what we consider a compelling valuation, support our strong buy recommendation.

► Risks to our recommendation and target price include weaker-than-expected global demand for luxury goods, and inability to lease sufficient space for new retail stores in prime locations, particularly in emerging markets.

► We arrive at our 12-month target price of $90 by applying a forward P/E multiple of 21.6X, which is TIF's luxury brand peer group average, to our FY 13 EPS estimate.

## Qualitative Risk Assessment

| LOW | MEDIUM | HIGH |

Our risk assessment reflects our view of TIF's favorable market position as a premier global luxury brand, offset by a cautious outlook for a recovery in U.S. consumer discretionary spending.

## Quantitative Evaluations

**S&P Quality Ranking** A-

| D | C | B- | B | B+ | A- | A | A+ |

**Relative Strength Rank** MODERATE

31

LOWEST = 1     HIGHEST = 99

## Revenue/Earnings Data

**Revenue (Million $)**

| | 1Q | 2Q | 3Q | 4Q | Year |
|---|---|---|---|---|---|
| 2012 | 761.0 | 872.7 | -- | -- | -- |
| 2011 | 633.6 | 668.8 | 681.7 | 1,101 | 3,085 |
| 2010 | 517.6 | 612.5 | 598.2 | 981.4 | 2,710 |
| 2009 | 668.2 | 732.4 | 618.2 | 841.2 | 2,860 |
| 2008 | 595.7 | 662.6 | 627.3 | 1,053 | 2,939 |
| 2007 | 539.2 | 574.9 | 547.8 | 986.4 | 2,648 |

**Earnings Per Share ($)**

| | | | | | |
|---|---|---|---|---|---|
| 2012 | 0.63 | 0.69 | E0.58 | E1.58 | E3.80 |
| 2011 | 0.50 | 0.53 | 0.43 | 1.41 | 2.87 |
| 2010 | 0.22 | 0.46 | 0.34 | 1.09 | 2.12 |
| 2009 | 0.50 | 0.63 | 0.35 | 0.25 | 1.74 |
| 2008 | 0.36 | 0.63 | 0.73 | 0.89 | 2.40 |
| 2007 | 0.30 | 0.29 | 0.21 | 1.02 | 1.80 |

Fiscal year ended Jan. 31. Next earnings report expected: NA. EPS Estimates based on S&P Operating Earnings; historical GAAP earnings are as reported.

## Dividend Data (Dates: mm/dd Payment Date: mm/dd/yy)

| Amount ($) | Date Decl. | Ex-Div. Date | Stk. of Record | Payment Date |
|---|---|---|---|---|
| 0.250 | 02/17 | 03/17 | 03/21 | 04/11/11 |
| 0.290 | 05/19 | 06/16 | 06/20 | 07/11/11 |
| 0.290 | 08/18 | 09/16 | 09/20 | 10/11/11 |
| 0.290 | 11/17 | 12/16 | 12/20 | 01/10/12 |

Dividends have been paid since 1988. Source: Company reports.

**Please read the Required Disclosures and Analyst Certification on the last page of this report.**

*The McGraw-Hill Companies*

# Tiffany & Co.

**STANDARD &POOR'S**

## Business Summary October 31, 2011

**CORPORATE OVERVIEW.** Charles Lewis Tiffany founded Tiffany & Co. in 1837. The Tiffany & Co. brand encompasses jewelry, watches, sterling silver merchandise, china, crystal, stationery, fragrances, and leather accessories. Diamonds are at the heart of the company's jewelry offering, which also includes colored gemstones and silver and gold fashion jewelry. To drive sales, TIF introduces new products annually; however, we believe jewelry bearing the designer names Elsa Peretti, Paloma Picasso, Frank Gehry or Jean Schlumberger are important differentiators. In FY 11 (Jan.), TIF internally produced 60% of what it sold and 60% of its supply of polished diamonds.

TIF has four reportable segments: Americas (51% of FY 11 net sales), Asia-Pacific (18%), Japan (18%), and Europe (12%). Revenues in each segment include sales from Tiffany & Co. stores and boutiques as well as sales in select markets through business-to-business, Internet, catalog and/or wholesale operations. The company's non-reportable segments (1%) consist of wholesale distribution in certain emerging markets such as the Middle East and Russia, wholesale sales of diamonds purchased by the company, and earnings and fees received from a licensing agreement with Luxottica and The Swatch

Group, respectively, for sales transacted under Tiffany & Co. trademarks. At the end of FY 11, TIF had e-commerce-enabled websites in 13 countries, 233 stores in 22 countries, and third-party distribution in over 30 additional countries.

**MARKET PROFILE.** According to global management consulting firm Bain & Company, 2009 was the worst year on record for the luxury market, with sales declining 8% worldwide, to 153 billion euros. That year, sales of jewelry and watches (the "hard luxury" category) plummeted an even steeper 17%. In 2010, however, sales rebounded, as renewed optimism among wealthier consumers led to increased luxury spending, albeit with an increased focus on quality and service (the value equation). Coupled with growing demand in emerging markets, total luxury sales rose 13% to 173 billion euros in 2010, with hard luxury sales increasing an even better 23%.

## Company Financials Fiscal Year Ended Jan. 31

| Per Share Data ($) | 2011 | 2010 | 2009 | 2008 | 2007 | 2006 | 2005 | 2004 | 2003 | 2002 |
|---|---|---|---|---|---|---|---|---|---|---|
| Tangible Book Value | 17.03 | 14.79 | 12.70 | 12.92 | 13.28 | 12.85 | 11.77 | 10.01 | 8.34 | 7.15 |
| Cash Flow | 4.02 | 3.23 | 2.83 | 3.28 | 2.64 | 2.50 | 2.79 | 2.06 | 1.80 | 1.58 |
| Earnings | 2.87 | 2.12 | 1.74 | 2.40 | 1.80 | 1.75 | 2.05 | 1.45 | 1.28 | 1.15 |
| S&P Core Earnings | 2.92 | 2.17 | 1.99 | 1.95 | 1.84 | 1.80 | 1.22 | 1.37 | 1.16 | 1.09 |
| Dividends | 0.95 | 0.68 | 0.66 | 0.38 | 0.38 | 0.30 | 0.23 | 0.19 | 0.16 | 0.16 |
| Payout Ratio | 33% | 32% | 31% | 16% | 16% | 17% | 11% | 13% | 13% | 14% |
| Calendar Year | 2010 | 2009 | 2008 | 2007 | 2006 | 2005 | 2004 | 2003 | 2002 | 2001 |
| Prices:High | 65.76 | 44.49 | 49.98 | 57.34 | 41.29 | 43.80 | 45.22 | 49.45 | 41.00 | 38.25 |
| Prices:Low | 35.81 | 16.70 | 16.75 | 38.17 | 29.63 | 28.60 | 27.00 | 21.60 | 19.40 | 19.90 |
| P/E Ratio:High | 23 | 21 | 29 | 24 | 23 | 25 | 22 | 34 | 32 | 33 |
| P/E Ratio:Low | 12 | 8 | 10 | 16 | 16 | 16 | 13 | 15 | 15 | 17 |

**Income Statement Analysis (Million $)**

| | 2011 | 2010 | 2009 | 2008 | 2007 | 2006 | 2005 | 2004 | 2003 | 2002 |
|---|---|---|---|---|---|---|---|---|---|---|
| Revenue | 3,085 | 2,710 | 2,860 | 2,939 | 2,648 | 2,395 | 2,205 | 2,000 | 1,707 | 1,607 |
| Operating Income | 758 | 579 | 633 | 640 | 533 | 492 | 403 | 446 | 397 | 375 |
| Depreciation | 148 | 139 | 138 | 122 | 118 | 109 | 108 | 90.4 | 78.0 | 64.6 |
| Interest Expense | 47.4 | 50.5 | 29.0 | 16.2 | 26.1 | 23.1 | 22.0 | 14.9 | 15.1 | 19.8 |
| Pretax Income | 547 | 390 | 346 | 522 | 404 | 368 | 472 | 343 | 300 | 289 |
| Effective Tax Rate | NA | 31.9% | 36.4% | 36.6% | 37.2% | 30.8% | 35.6% | 37.1% | 36.6% | 40.0% |
| Net Income | 368 | 266 | 220 | 331 | 254 | 255 | 304 | 216 | 190 | 174 |
| S&P Core Earnings | 375 | 271 | 252 | 269 | 260 | 261 | 181 | 204 | 173 | 164 |

**Balance Sheet & Other Financial Data (Million $)**

| | 2011 | 2010 | 2009 | 2008 | 2007 | 2006 | 2005 | 2004 | 2003 | 2002 |
|---|---|---|---|---|---|---|---|---|---|---|
| Cash | 741 | 786 | 160 | 247 | 177 | 394 | 188 | 276 | 156 | 174 |
| Current Assets | 2,685 | 2,446 | 2,049 | 1,844 | 1,707 | 1,699 | 1,608 | 1,348 | 1,070 | 954 |
| Total Assets | 3,736 | 3,488 | 3,102 | 2,922 | 2,846 | 2,777 | 2,666 | 2,391 | 1,924 | 1,630 |
| Current Liabilities | 480 | 600 | 602 | 585 | 453 | 365 | 400 | 395 | 300 | 341 |
| Long Term Debt | 588 | 520 | 425 | 343 | 406 | 427 | 398 | 393 | 297 | 179 |
| Common Equity | 2,177 | 1,883 | 1,588 | 1,637 | 1,805 | 1,831 | 1,701 | 1,468 | 1,208 | 1,037 |
| Total Capital | 2,827 | 2,610 | 2,014 | 2,046 | 2,211 | 2,257 | 2,132 | 1,884 | 1,505 | 1,216 |
| Capital Expenditures | 127 | 75.4 | 154 | 186 | 182 | 157 | 142 | 273 | 220 | 171 |
| Cash Flow | 516 | 405 | 358 | 453 | 372 | 364 | 412 | 306 | 268 | 238 |
| Current Ratio | 5.6 | 4.1 | 3.4 | 3.2 | 3.8 | 4.7 | 4.0 | 3.4 | 3.6 | 2.8 |
| % Long Term Debt of Capitalization | 20.8 | 19.9 | 21.1 | 16.8 | 18.4 | 18.9 | 18.7 | 20.9 | 19.7 | 14.7 |
| % Net Income of Revenue | 11.9 | 9.8 | 7.7 | 11.3 | 9.6 | 10.6 | 13.8 | 10.8 | 11.1 | 10.8 |
| % Return on Assets | 10.2 | 8.1 | 7.3 | 11.5 | 9.0 | 9.4 | 12.0 | 10.0 | 10.7 | 10.9 |
| % Return on Equity | 18.1 | 15.3 | 13.6 | 19.3 | 14.0 | 14.4 | 19.2 | 16.1 | 16.9 | 17.7 |

Data as orig reptd.; bef. results of disc opers/spec. items. Per share data adj. for stk. divs.; EPS diluted. E-Estimated. NA-Not Available. NM-Not Meaningful. NR-Not Ranked. UR-Under Review.

**Office:** 727 Fifth Avenue, New York, NY 10022.
**Telephone:** 212-755-8000.
**Website:** http://www.tiffany.com
**Chrmn & CEO:** M.J. Kowalski

**Pres:** J.E. Quinn
**COO:** J.S. Petterson
**COO & EVP:** J.N. Fernandez
**SVP & CFO:** P.F. McGuiness

**Investor Contact:** M.L. Aaron (212-230-5301)
**Board Members:** R. M. Bravo, G. E. Costley, L. K. Fish, A. F. Kohnstamm, M. J. Kowalski, C. K. Marquis, P. W. May, J. T. Presby, W. A. Shutzer

**Founded:** 1837
**Domicile:** Delaware
**Employees:** 9,200

# Time Warner Cable Inc

STANDARD
&POOR'S

| S&P Recommendation **BUY** ★★★★☆ | Price $57.64 (as of Nov 25, 2011) | 12-Mo. Target Price $75.00 | Investment Style Large-Cap Growth |
|---|---|---|---|

**GICS Sector** Consumer Discretionary
**Sub-Industry** Cable & Satellite

**Summary** This company is the second largest U.S. cable multiple system operator (MSO), recently serving about 12.1 million video subscribers -- and including high-speed data and voice services -- 26.9 million primary service units that comprise (primarily) residential and business customers.

## Key Stock Statistics (Source S&P, Vickers, company reports)

| | | | | | | | |
|---|---|---|---|---|---|---|---|
| 52-Wk Range | $80.86– 57.40 | S&P Oper. EPS 2011E | 4.47 | Market Capitalization(B) | $18.394 | Beta | 0.73 |
| Trailing 12-Month EPS | $4.33 | S&P Oper. EPS 2012E | 5.57 | Yield (%) | 3.33 | S&P 3-Yr. Proj. EPS CAGR(%) | 15 |
| Trailing 12-Month P/E | 13.3 | P/E on S&P Oper. EPS 2011E | 12.9 | Dividend Rate/Share | $1.92 | S&P Credit Rating | BBB |
| $10K Invested 5 Yrs Ago | NA | Common Shares Outstg. (M) | 319.1 | Institutional Ownership (%) | 89 | | |

## Price Performance

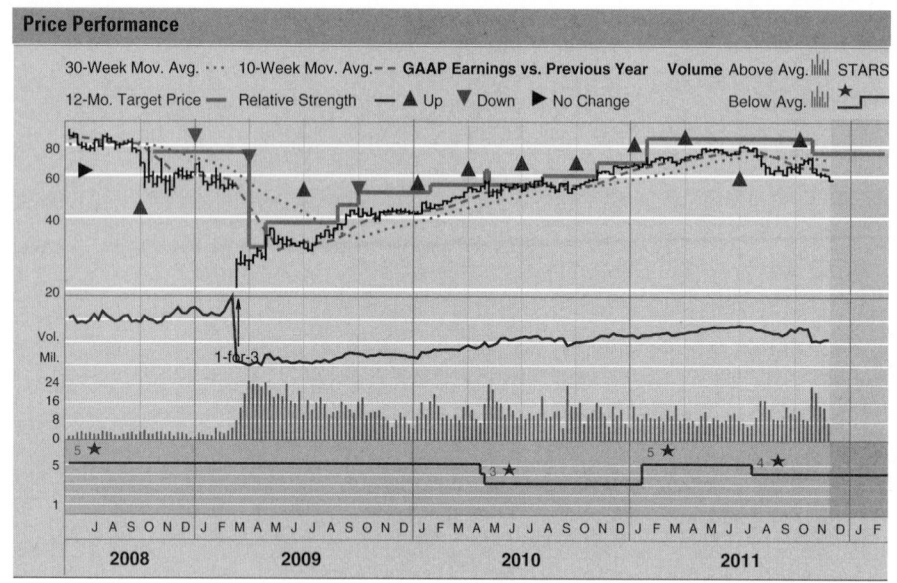

30-Week Mov. Avg. ···  10-Week Mov. Avg. - -  ▬ GAAP Earnings vs. Previous Year   Volume Above Avg. ▙▎▎ STARS
12-Mo. Target Price ▬ Relative Strength ▬ ▲ Up ▼ Down ► No Change    Below Avg. ▙▎▎ ★

Analysis prepared by Equity Analyst **T. Amobi, CFA CPA** on Oct 28, 2011, when the stock traded at **$62.86**.

## Highlights

► We expect total revenues to rise about 4.3% in 2011, to $19.68 billion (including the Navisite acquisition), and 5.0% in 2012, to $20.66 billion, on further penetration of bundled (and single-play) high-speed data and voice services to residential and, increasingly, business customers. We project relatively modest gains in video revenues, aided by rate increases and higher ARPU on advanced video offerings (HD and DVR), versus further subscriber losses. We also expect a strong rebound in local advertising revenues over the next two years.

► We see some margin pressure from programming and marketing expenses, as well as from investments in wireless and home security initiatives, partly offset by lower voice costs (on continued transition from a Sprint contract), some efficiency gains, and other cost savings.

► We see 2011 and 2012 adjusted EBITDA up 3.6% and 4.7%, to about $7.11 billion and $7.45 billion, respectively. After D&A, interest expense and taxes, we forecast 2011 and 2012 operating EPS of $4.47 and $5.57, respectively, with some share buybacks under a $4 billion plan.

## Investment Rationale/Risk

► While TWC's core residential business reflected difficult economic and competitive conditions during the first nine months of 2011, we see significant upside for the nascent business services offerings (including Navisite). We expect potentially sizable synergies (and scale economies) from the pending acquisition of Insight Communications for a relatively attractive valuation. We note TWC's strong balance sheet for sustainable dividends and share buybacks.

► Risks to our recommendation and target price include intensifying competition from satellite TV and telcos; persistent macroeconomic and housing weakness; increased "cord-cutting"; uncertainties related to wireless broadband strategy; potentially dilutive acquisitions; and some regulatory overhang.

► Our 12-month target price of $75 reflects a blend of 5.8X 2012E EV/EBITDA and approximately $3,400 EV/subscriber, which we see as attractively discounted to recent private market transactions. We see declining capital intensity helping sustain continued double-digit FCF growth in the next few years.

## Qualitative Risk Assessment

| LOW | MEDIUM | HIGH |
|---|---|---|

Our risk assessment reflects our expectations for a capable management team to further enhance the company's strong market and competitive position through potential economies of scale from pending acquisitions, counterbalanced against increased competition from traditional and new entrants, as well as exposure to rising programming costs and regulatory risk factors.

## Quantitative Evaluations

**S&P Quality Ranking**      NR

| D | C | B- | B | B+ | A- | A | A+ |
|---|---|---|---|---|---|---|---|

**Relative Strength Rank**      MODERATE

30

LOWEST = 1                        HIGHEST = 99

## Revenue/Earnings Data

**Revenue (Million $)**

| | 1Q | 2Q | 3Q | 4Q | Year |
|---|---|---|---|---|---|
| 2011 | 4,827 | 4,944 | 4,911 | -- | -- |
| 2010 | 4,599 | 4,734 | 4,734 | 4,801 | 18,868 |
| 2009 | 4,364 | 4,474 | 4,498 | 4,532 | 17,868 |
| 2008 | 4,160 | 4,298 | 4,340 | 4,402 | 17,200 |
| 2007 | 3,851 | 4,014 | 4,001 | 4,089 | 15,955 |
| 2006 | 2,385 | 2,721 | 3,209 | 3,651 | 11,767 |

**Earnings Per Share ($)**

| | | | | | |
|---|---|---|---|---|---|
| 2011 | 0.93 | 1.24 | 1.08 | E1.23 | E4.47 |
| 2010 | 0.60 | 0.94 | 1.00 | 1.09 | 3.64 |
| 2009 | 0.48 | 0.89 | 0.76 | 0.91 | 3.05 |
| 2008 | 0.75 | 0.84 | 0.93 | -25.08 | -22.56 |
| 2007 | 0.84 | 0.84 | 0.75 | 0.99 | 3.45 |
| 2006 | 0.60 | 0.60 | 0.87 | 0.69 | 0.75 | 2.85 |

Fiscal year ended Dec. 31. Next earnings report expected: Late January. EPS Estimates based on S&P Operating Earnings; historical GAAP earnings are as reported.

## Dividend Data (Dates: mm/dd Payment Date: mm/dd/yy)

| Amount ($) | Date Decl. | Ex-Div. Date | Stk. of Record | Payment Date |
|---|---|---|---|---|
| 0.480 | 01/27 | 02/24 | 02/28 | 03/15/11 |
| 0.480 | 05/19 | 05/26 | 05/31 | 06/15/11 |
| 0.480 | 07/21 | 08/29 | 08/31 | 09/15/11 |
| 0.480 | 10/20 | 11/28 | 11/30 | 12/15/11 |

Dividends have been paid since 2010. Source: Company reports.

---

**Please read the Required Disclosures and Analyst Certification on the last page of this report.**

The McGraw-Hill Companies

# Time Warner Cable Inc

STANDARD
&POOR'S

## Business Summary October 28, 2011

CORPORATE OVERVIEW. Time Warner Cable Inc. (TWC) is the second largest cable operator in the U.S., with more than 12.3 million video subscribers as of December 31, 2010. After its July 2006 acquisition of Adelphia Communications (for about $8.9 billion in cash plus 16% of its common stock) -- which added a net 3.2 million subscribers -- TWC became a public company on February 13, 2007 (effective date of Adelphia's reorganization plan), and its Class A shares began trading as of March 1, 2007 (the non-trading Class B shares are held by its parent). In March 2009, TWC was spun off from its former 84% equity owner Time Warner (TWX 36, Buy).

As of December 31, 2010, TWC's cable systems passed over 27 million U.S. homes (including the distribution on January 1, 2007, of the Texas/Kansas City JV), nearly 85% of which were located in New York, the Carolinas, Ohio, Southern California and Texas. More than 9.8 million (34.2% penetration) of TWC's homes passed subscribed to a high-speed data service such as Road Runner, with nearly 4.5 million (or 15.8%) to its digital phone service -- both mainly offered to residential, and increasingly commercial, customers. Nearly all of the homes passed were served by a system with at least 750 MHz of capacity.

CORPORATE STRATEGY. The company has embarked on some M&A activity since its March 2009 spin-off as an independent company. In August 2011, TWC agreed to acquire Insight Communications, the 13th largest U.S. cable operator, serving more than 750,000 customers in the Western U.S., for $3 billion in cash, in a deal that is expected to close in the 2012 first half (subject to approvals). Earlier, in June 2011, TWC agreed to acquire New Wave Communications, a smaller cable operator serving about 70,000 customers in Kentucky and Tennessee, for about $260 million in cash, in a deal expected to close in the 2011 fourth quarter.

In April 2011, TWC acquired Navisite, a provider of enterprise-class, cloud-enabled hosting, managed applications and services, for $230 million. In February 2011, TWC and The Los Angeles Lakers reached a deal to launch two regional sports TV networks that will carry all locally available Lakers games -- ahead of the 2012-13 season.

## Company Financials Fiscal Year Ended Dec. 31

| Per Share Data ($) | 2010 | 2009 | 2008 | 2007 | 2006 | 2005 | 2004 | 2003 | 2002 | 2001 |
|---|---|---|---|---|---|---|---|---|---|---|
| Tangible Book Value | NM | NM | NM | NM | NM | NA | NA | NA | NA | NA |
| Cash Flow | 12.34 | 11.84 | -2.32 | 12.60 | 9.05 | 8.75 | 6.72 | 6.29 | NA | NA |
| Earnings | 3.64 | 3.05 | -22.56 | 3.45 | 2.85 | 3.75 | 2.19 | 1.71 | NA | NA |
| S&P Core Earnings | 3.64 | 3.14 | 7.68 | 3.12 | 2.88 | NA | NA | NA | NA | NA |
| Dividends | 1.60 | Nil | Nil | Nil | NA | NA | NA | NA | NA | NA |
| Payout Ratio | 44% | Nil | Nil | Nil | NA | NA | NA | NA | NA | NA |
| Prices:High | 66.77 | 68.23 | 94.68 | 126.34 | NA | NA | NA | NA | NA | NA |
| Prices:Low | 41.00 | 20.19 | 48.90 | 70.81 | NA | NA | NA | NA | NA | NA |
| P/E Ratio:High | 18 | 22 | NM | 37 | NA | NA | NA | NA | NA | NA |
| P/E Ratio:Low | 11 | 7 | NM | 21 | NA | NA | NA | NA | NA | NA |

| Income Statement Analysis (Million $) | 2010 | 2009 | 2008 | 2007 | 2006 | 2005 | 2004 | 2003 | 2002 | 2001 |
|---|---|---|---|---|---|---|---|---|---|---|
| Revenue | 18,868 | 17,868 | 17,200 | 15,955 | 11,767 | 9,498 | 8,484 | 7,699 | NA | NA |
| Operating Income | NA | NA | 76.0 | 5,765 | 4,285 | NA | NA | NA | NA | NA |
| Depreciation | NA | NA | 33.5 | 2,976 | 2,050 | 1,664 | 1,514 | 1,461 | NA | NA |
| Interest Expense | 1,394 | 1,324 | 25.8 | 907 | 646 | 501 | 491 | 514 | NA | NA |
| Pretax Income | 2,196 | 1,912 | -13,072 | 2,028 | 1,664 | 1,535 | 1,305 | 987 | NA | NA |
| Effective Tax Rate | NA | 42.9% | NM | 36.5% | 37.3% | 13.8% | 39.6% | 38.9% | NA | NA |
| Net Income | 1,308 | 1,070 | -7,344 | 1,123 | 936 | 1,253 | 726 | 541 | NA | NA |
| S&P Core Earnings | 1,300 | 1,104 | 2,511 | 1,019 | 945 | NA | NA | NA | NA | NA |

| Balance Sheet & Other Financial Data (Million $) | 2010 | 2009 | 2008 | 2007 | 2006 | 2005 | 2004 | 2003 | 2002 | 2001 |
|---|---|---|---|---|---|---|---|---|---|---|
| Cash | 3,047 | 1,048 | 5,552 | 232 | 51.0 | 12.0 | 102 | NA | NA | NA |
| Current Assets | NA | NA | 57.1 | 1,163 | 910 | NA | NA | NA | NA | NA |
| Total Assets | 45,822 | 43,694 | 47,889 | 56,600 | 55,743 | 43,677 | 43,138 | NA | NA | NA |
| Current Liabilities | NA | NA | 387 | 2,536 | 2,490 | NA | NA | NA | NA | NA |
| Long Term Debt | 23,421 | 22,631 | 17,727 | 13,877 | 300 | 4,455 | 4,898 | NA | NA | NA |
| Common Equity | 9,210 | 8,685 | 17,164 | 24,706 | 23,564 | 21,331 | 20,039 | NA | NA | NA |
| Total Capital | NA | NA | 36,301 | 53,598 | 38,390 | 29,193 | 28,304 | NA | NA | NA |
| Capital Expenditures | NA | NA | 3,522 | 3,433 | 2,718 | 1,975 | 1,712 | 1,637 | NA | NA |
| Cash Flow | 4,437 | 4,155 | -59.1 | 4,099 | 2,986 | 2,917 | 2,240 | 2,002 | NA | NA |
| Current Ratio | 1.4 | 0.7 | 2.3 | 0.5 | 0.4 | 0.3 | 0.3 | NA | NA | NA |
| % Long Term Debt of Capitalization | 71.8 | 72.3 | 48.8 | 25.9 | 0.8 | 17.3 | 19.6 | Nil | NA | NA |
| % Net Income of Revenue | 6.9 | 6.0 | NM | 7.0 | 8.0 | 13.2 | 8.6 | 7.0 | NA | NA |
| % Return on Assets | 2.9 | 2.3 | NM | 2.0 | 1.9 | 2.9 | NA | NA | NA | NA |
| % Return on Equity | 14.6 | 8.3 | NM | 4.7 | 4.2 | 6.1 | NA | NA | NA | NA |

Data as orig reptd.; bef. results of disc opers/spec. items. Per share data adj. for stk. divs.; EPS diluted. E-Estimated. NA-Not Available. NM-Not Meaningful. NR-Not Ranked. UR-Under Review.

**Office:** 60 Columbus Circle, New York, NY 10023.
**Telephone:** 212-364-8200.
**Website:** http://www.timewarnercable.com
**Chrmn & CEO:** G.A. Britt

**Pres & COO:** R.D. Marcus
**EVP & CFO:** I.M. Esteves
**EVP & CTO:** M. LaJoie
**EVP, Secy & General Counsel:** M. Lawrence-Apfelbaum

**Investor Contact:** W. Osbourn, Jr. (203-351-2015)
**Board Members:** C. Black, G. A. Britt, T. H. Castro, D. C. Chang, J. E. Copeland, Jr., P. R. Haje, D. A. James, D. Logan, N. J. Nicholas, Jr., W. H. Pace, E. D. Shirley, J. E. Sununu

**Founded:** 2003
**Domicile:** Delaware
**Employees:** 47,500

# Time Warner Inc.

**STANDARD &POOR'S**

**S&P Recommendation** BUY ★★★★☆

| Price | 12-Mo. Target Price | Investment Style |
|---|---|---|
| $34.82 (as of Nov 30, 2011) | $42.00 | Large-Cap Blend |

**GICS Sector** Consumer Discretionary
**Sub-Industry** Movies & Entertainment

**Summary** This company owns some of the world's leading media and entertainment brands, including Warner Bros. (film/TV studio), Turner cable networks (TNT, TBS, CNN), HBO/Cinemax premium channels, as well as several magazine brands through its Time Inc. publishing businesses.

## Key Stock Statistics (Source S&P, Vickers, company reports)

| | | | | | | | |
|---|---|---|---|---|---|---|---|
| 52-Wk Range | $38.62– 27.62 | S&P Oper. EPS 2011E | 2.87 | Market Capitalization(B) | $34.851 | Beta | 1.13 |
| Trailing 12-Month EPS | $2.63 | S&P Oper. EPS 2012E | 3.21 | Yield (%) | 2.70 | S&P 3-Yr. Proj. EPS CAGR(%) | 13 |
| Trailing 12-Month P/E | 13.2 | P/E on S&P Oper. EPS 2011E | 12.1 | Dividend Rate/Share | $0.94 | S&P Credit Rating | BBB |
| $10K Invested 5 Yrs Ago | NA | Common Shares Outstg. (M) | 1,000.9 | Institutional Ownership (%) | 91 | | |

## Price Performance

30-Week Mov. Avg. ···· 10-Week Mov. Avg. – – GAAP Earnings vs. Previous Year Volume Above Avg. STARS
12-Mo. Target Price — Relative Strength — ▲ Up ▼ Down ▶ No Change Below Avg.

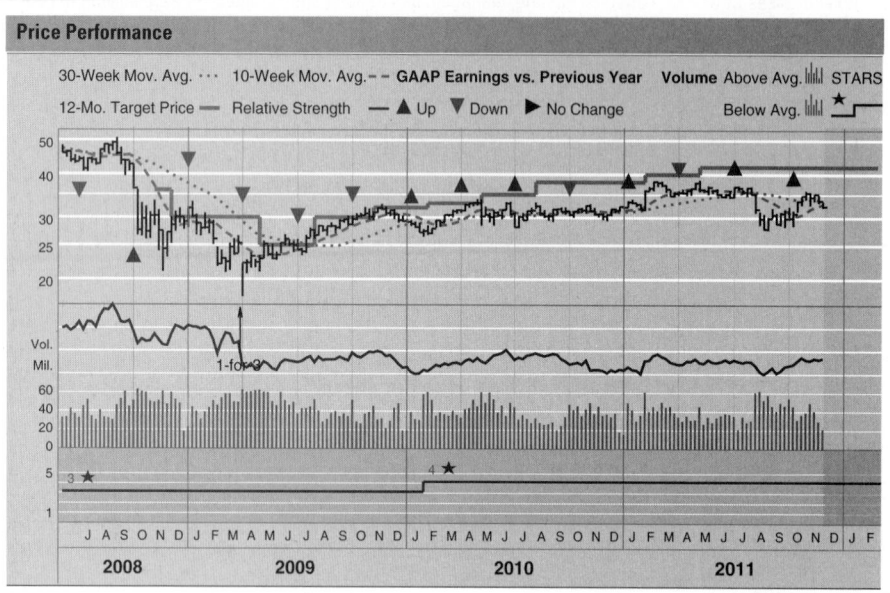

Analysis prepared by Equity Analyst **T. Amobi, CFA CPA** on Nov 03, 2011, when the stock traded at **$33.57.**

Options: ASE, CBOE, P, Ph

## Qualitative Risk Assessment

| LOW | MEDIUM | HIGH |
|---|---|---|

Our risk assessment reflects our view of the company's leading content-oriented businesses, ample financial flexibility, and what we view as an adequate governance framework, offset by cyclical and secular pressures and a relatively volatile earnings stream.

## Quantitative Evaluations

**S&P Quality Ranking** B-

| D | C | B- | B | B+ | A- | A | A+ |
|---|---|---|---|---|---|---|---|

**Relative Strength Rank** STRONG

84

LOWEST = 1 HIGHEST = 99

## Revenue/Earnings Data

**Revenue (Million $)**

| | 1Q | 2Q | 3Q | 4Q | Year |
|---|---|---|---|---|---|
| 2011 | 6,683 | 7,030 | 7,068 | -- | -- |
| 2010 | 6,322 | 6,377 | 6,377 | 7,812 | 26,888 |
| 2009 | 6,086 | 6,013 | 6,366 | 7,320 | 25,785 |
| 2008 | 11,417 | 11,555 | 11,706 | 12,306 | 46,984 |
| 2007 | 11,184 | 10,980 | 11,676 | 12,642 | 46,482 |
| 2006 | 10,327 | 10,519 | 10,912 | 12,466 | 44,224 |

**Earnings Per Share ($)**

| | | | | | |
|---|---|---|---|---|---|
| 2011 | 0.59 | 0.59 | 0.78 | E0.90 | E2.87 |
| 2010 | 0.62 | 0.48 | 0.46 | 0.68 | 2.25 |
| 2009 | 0.39 | 0.35 | 0.49 | 0.51 | 1.74 |
| 2008 | 0.63 | 0.66 | 0.90 | -13.41 | -11.22 |
| 2007 | 0.90 | 0.75 | 0.72 | 0.84 | 3.24 |
| 2006 | 0.78 | 0.60 | 0.99 | 1.29 | 3.63 |

Fiscal year ended Dec. 31. Next earnings report expected: NA. EPS Estimates based on S&P Operating Earnings; historical GAAP earnings are as reported.

## Highlights

➤ We see consolidated revenues up about 9% in 2011 (including the new NCAA pact) and 3% in 2012, to almost $29.3 billion and $30.2 billion, with a solid ad rebound and steady affiliate fee growth at the Turner networks (TNT, TBS, CNN), modestly higher HBO subscriptions, record film/DVD revenues in 2011, and syndication pipeline (e.g., Big Bang Theory). Conversely, we assume stagnant print ads and subscriptions (after some international divestitures), versus growing online and e-book revenues.

➤ Despite record film profits versus higher programming costs in 2011, we see further margin expansion in 2012, helped by higher-margin digital revenues such as a new CW network licensing pact with Netflix (NFLX 82, Hold), plus merchandising and ancillary businesses, against persistent NCAA cost pressures.

➤ We project 2011 and 2012 total adjusted EBIT of $5.9 billion and $6.4 billion, respectively. After D&A and reduced interest expense, we estimate 2011 operating EPS of $2.87 (with a current $5 billion share buybacks plan likely exhausted by year-end), and $3.21 in 2012.

## Investment Rationale/Risk

➤ After TWX's recently lifted full year earnings outlook on relatively encouraging 2011 third quarter results, we think improved near-term visibility also reflects solid ad commitments from the 2011-12 cable TV upfront market and a strong film lineup featuring several major franchise sequels in both 3D and 2D formats (including Harry Potter 7 - Part 2, The Hangover 2, Sherlock Holmes 2, Happy Feet 2, The Dark Knight 2, The Hobbit 1). We note various pioneering multi-platform digital initiatives (premium VOD, HBO GO, TV Everywhere, Ultra-Violet) that could provide longer-term upside.

➤ Risks to our recommendation and target price include weaker consumer spending; a sharp decline in Turner networks ratings; digital disintermediation for HBO ("cord-cutting"); and severe secular challenges for publishing.

➤ Our 12-month target price is $42, blending relatively ample 9.0X 2012E EV/EBITDA and sum-of-the-parts valuation. We project FCF of about $2.1 billion in 2011, and over $3.2 billion in 2012, with ample financial flexibility for share buybacks and dividends (2.9% yield).

## Dividend Data (Dates: mm/dd Payment Date: mm/dd/yy)

| Amount ($) | Date Decl. | Ex-Div. Date | Stk. of Record | Payment Date |
|---|---|---|---|---|
| 0.213 | 10/28 | 11/26 | 11/30 | 12/15/10 |
| 0.235 | 02/02 | 11/28 | 11/30 | 12/15/11 |

Dividends have been paid since 2005. Source: Company reports.

---

**Please read the Required Disclosures and Analyst Certification on the last page of this report.**

*The McGraw·Hill Companies*

# Time Warner Inc.

**STANDARD &POOR'S**

## Business Summary November 03, 2011

CORPORATE OVERVIEW. Time Warner is one of the major media conglomerates -- creating and providing entertainment and information content across its key film, television and publishing divisions. The company's revenues are derived from three primary sources: content (43% of 2010 revenues), subscriptions (33%), advertising (21%), and other (3%).

In March 2009, the company completed a full spin-off of its cable systems businesses owned by Time Warner Cable (TWC 69, Buy). In December 2009, the company also spun off its online subscription and advertising businesses owned by AOL (AOL 15, NR).

The Filmed Entertainment segment (42% of 2010 revenues) includes the Warner Bros. and New Line Cinema studios, and home entertainment businesses, with key franchises such as Harry Potter, Lord of the Rings and Batman. In 2008, the company closed its two specialty film labels -- Warner Independent Films and Picturehouse. In May 2011, TWX acquired Flixster, a cloud-based movie service.

The Networks segment (45%) includes cable networks CNN, HBO/Cinemax and Turner (TNT, TBS). In September 2006, TWX's WB broadcast network merged with CBS's UPN to create the CW network. The Publishing segment (13%) includes Time Inc., with 117 magazine titles worldwide (22 in the U.S., 95 outside the U.S.) -- including Time, People, Sports Illustrated and Fortune.

CORPORATE STRATEGY. CEO Jeffrey Bewkes recently articulated several key priorities, including continued delivery of quality content, improved operating efficiency, international expansion, and exploiting advances in digital technology. Over the next few years, TWX plans up to 20 3-D films in the Imax format. It provides its titles to Netflix and Redbox after a 28-day DVD window. TWX aims to balance the dynamics of emerging distribution windows and platforms, while protecting the economics of its core DVD business.

In May 2009, TWX invested $241.5 million in Central European Media Enterprises for about a 31% equity stake in the European broadcaster.

## Company Financials Fiscal Year Ended Dec. 31

| Per Share Data ($) | 2010 | 2009 | 2008 | 2007 | 2006 | 2005 | 2004 | 2003 | 2002 | 2001 |
|---|---|---|---|---|---|---|---|---|---|---|
| Tangible Book Value | NM | NM | NM | NM | NM | NM | NM | NM | NM | NM |
| Cash Flow | 3.06 | 2.54 | -2.46 | 11.58 | 8.57 | 6.18 | 6.39 | 6.00 | -27.96 | 2.90 |
| Earnings | 2.25 | 1.74 | -11.22 | 3.24 | 3.63 | 1.86 | 2.07 | 2.04 | -28.29 | -3.60 |
| S&P Core Earnings | 2.17 | 1.86 | -6.72 | 2.85 | 3.21 | 2.49 | 1.86 | 1.26 | -10.32 | -3.24 |
| Dividends | 0.85 | 0.75 | 0.75 | 0.71 | 0.63 | 0.30 | Nil | Nil | Nil | Nil |
| Payout Ratio | 38% | 43% | NM | 22% | 17% | 16% | Nil | Nil | Nil | Nil |
| Prices:High | 34.07 | 33.45 | 50.70 | 69.46 | 66.76 | 58.93 | 59.71 | 54.97 | 98.77 | 175.55 |
| Prices:Low | 26.43 | 17.81 | 21.00 | 48.51 | 47.10 | 48.30 | 46.23 | 29.70 | 26.10 | 82.21 |
| P/E Ratio:High | 15 | 19 | NM | 21 | 18 | 32 | 29 | 27 | NM | NM |
| P/E Ratio:Low | 12 | 10 | NM | 15 | 13 | 26 | 22 | 15 | NM | NM |

| Income Statement Analysis (Million $) | 2010 | 2009 | 2008 | 2007 | 2006 | 2005 | 2004 | 2003 | 2002 | 2001 |
|---|---|---|---|---|---|---|---|---|---|---|
| Revenue | 26,888 | 25,785 | 46,984 | 46,482 | 44,224 | 43,652 | 42,081 | 39,496 | 36,955 | 33,765 |
| Operating Income | 6,413 | 6,092 | 19,229 | 19,217 | 14,837 | 14,312 | 13,535 | 11,839 | NA | NA |
| Depreciation | 938 | 998 | 10,481 | 10,488 | 6,953 | 6,781 | 6,743 | 6,086 | NA | NA |
| Interest Expense | 1,178 | 1,293 | 2,275 | 2,509 | 1,971 | 1,622 | 1,754 | 1,926 | 1,900 | 1,576 |
| Pretax Income | 3,919 | 3,283 | -18,623 | 6,795 | 6,826 | 4,007 | 5,206 | 4,763 | -44,156 | -4,465 |
| Effective Tax Rate | NA | 36.4% | NM | 34.4% | 19.6% | 27.2% | 33.0% | 29.0% | NM | NM |
| Net Income | 2,578 | 2,040 | -13,402 | 4,051 | 5,114 | 2,921 | 3,239 | 3,164 | -42,003 | -5,313 |
| S&P Core Earnings | 2,475 | 2,212 | -7,981 | 3,579 | 4,551 | 3,929 | 2,938 | 1,999 | -15,240 | -4,771 |

| Balance Sheet & Other Financial Data (Million $) | 2010 | 2009 | 2008 | 2007 | 2006 | 2005 | 2004 | 2003 | 2002 | 2001 |
|---|---|---|---|---|---|---|---|---|---|---|
| Cash | 3,663 | 4,800 | 6,682 | 1,516 | 1,549 | 4,220 | 6,139 | 3,040 | 1,730 | 771 |
| Current Assets | 13,138 | 13,007 | 16,602 | 12,451 | 10,851 | 13,463 | 14,639 | 12,268 | 11,155 | 10,274 |
| Total Assets | 66,524 | 65,730 | 113,896 | 133,830 | 131,669 | 122,745 | 123,149 | 121,748 | 115,508 | 209,429 |
| Current Liabilities | 8,643 | 8,765 | 13,976 | 12,193 | 12,780 | 12,608 | 14,673 | 15,518 | 13,395 | 12,972 |
| Long Term Debt | 16,523 | 15,357 | 37,916 | 37,304 | 35,233 | 20,238 | 20,703 | 23,458 | 27,354 | 22,792 |
| Common Equity | 32,940 | 33,383 | 42,288 | 58,536 | 60,389 | 62,679 | 60,719 | 56,131 | 52,891 | 150,667 |
| Total Capital | 49,499 | 49,142 | 92,379 | 113,898 | 112,857 | 103,760 | 103,285 | NA | NA | NA |
| Capital Expenditures | 631 | 561 | 4,377 | 4,430 | 4,085 | 3,246 | 3,024 | 2,761 | 3,023 | 3,634 |
| Cash Flow | 3,509 | 3,038 | -2,921 | 14,539 | 12,067 | 9,702 | 9,982 | 9,250 | -41,515 | 4,282 |
| Current Ratio | 1.5 | 1.5 | 1.2 | 1.0 | 0.8 | 1.1 | 1.0 | 0.8 | 0.8 | 0.8 |
| % Long Term Debt of Capitalization | 33.4 | 31.3 | 41.0 | 32.8 | 31.2 | 19.5 | 20.0 | NA | NA | NA |
| % Net Income of Revenue | 9.6 | 7.9 | NM | 8.7 | 11.6 | 6.7 | 7.7 | 8.0 | NM | NM |
| % Return on Assets | 3.9 | 2.3 | NM | 3.1 | 4.0 | 2.4 | 2.6 | 2.7 | NM | NM |
| % Return on Equity | 7.8 | 5.4 | NM | 6.8 | 8.2 | 4.7 | 5.5 | 5.8 | NM | NM |

Data as orig reptd.; bef. results of disc opers/spec. items. Per share data adj. for stk. divs.; EPS diluted. E-Estimated. NA-Not Available. NM-Not Meaningful. NR-Not Ranked. UR-Under Review.

**Office:** 1 Time Warner Ctr, New York, NY 10019-6038.
**Telephone:** 212-484-8000.
**Email:** aoltwir@aoltw.com
**Website:** http://www.timewarner.com

**Chrmn & CEO:** J.L. Bewkes
**EVP, CFO & Chief Admin Officer:** J.K. Martin, Jr.
**EVP & General Counsel:** P.T. Cappuccio
**SVP, Chief Acctg Officer & Cntlr:** P. Desroches

**SVP & Treas:** E.B. Ruggiero
**Investor Contact:** J.E. Burtson
**Board Members:** J. L. Barksdale, W. P. Barr, J. L. Bewkes, S. F. Bollenbach, F. J. Caufield, R. C. Clark, M. Dopfner, J. P. Einhorn, F. Hassan, M. A. Miles, K. J. Novack, P. D. Wachter, D. C. Wright

**Founded:** 1985
**Domicile:** Delaware
**Employees:** 31,000

The McGraw-Hill Companies

# Titanium Metals Corp

**STANDARD &POOR'S**

| S&P Recommendation **BUY** ★★★★☆ | Price $14.13 (as of Nov 25, 2011) | 12-Mo. Target Price $21.00 | Investment Style Large-Cap Blend |
|---|---|---|---|

**GICS Sector** Materials
**Sub-Industry** Diversified Metals & Mining

**Summary** This company is a worldwide integrated producer of titanium metal products.

## Key Stock Statistics (Source S&P, Vickers, company reports)

| | | | | | | | | |
|---|---|---|---|---|---|---|---|---|
| 52-Wk Range | $20.69–13.28 | S&P Oper. EPS 2011E | 0.61 | Market Capitalization(B) | $2.475 | Beta | 1.57 |
| Trailing 12-Month EPS | $0.61 | S&P Oper. EPS 2012E | 0.95 | Yield (%) | 2.12 | S&P 3-Yr. Proj. EPS CAGR(%) | 41 |
| Trailing 12-Month P/E | 23.2 | P/E on S&P Oper. EPS 2011E | 23.2 | Dividend Rate/Share | $0.30 | S&P Credit Rating | NR |
| $10K Invested 5 Yrs Ago | $5,007 | Common Shares Outstg. (M) | 175.2 | Institutional Ownership (%) | 30 | | |

## Price Performance

30-Week Mov. Avg. ···· 10-Week Mov. Avg. ▬ **GAAP Earnings vs. Previous Year** Volume Above Avg. ▥▥ STARS
12-Mo. Target Price ▬ Relative Strength ▬ ▲ Up ▼ Down ► No Change Below Avg. ▥▥ ★

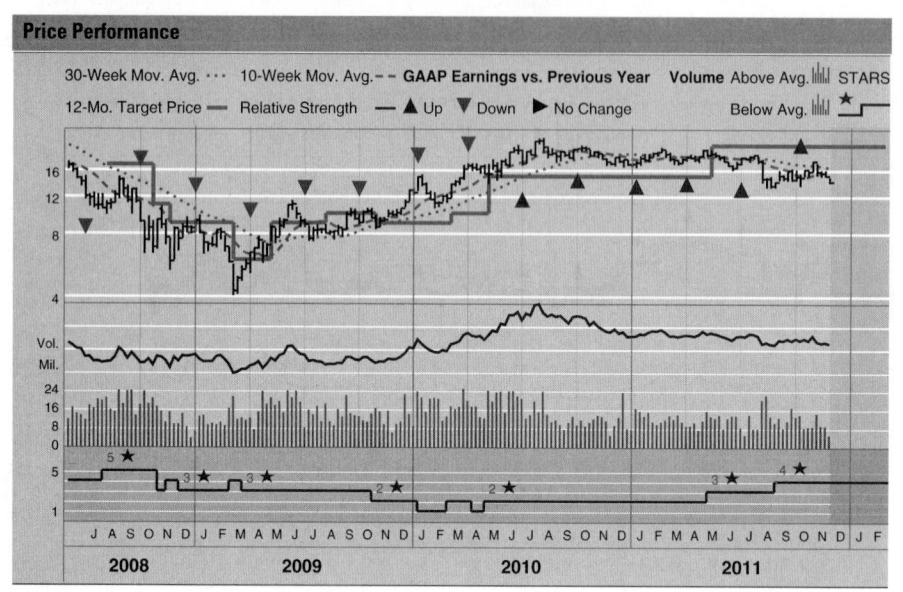

Options: ASE, CBOE, Ph

Analysis prepared by Equity Analyst **Leo J. Larkin** on Sep 01, 2011, when the stock traded at **$15.83**.

## Highlights

▸ Following 2010's sales rise of 11%, we look for a sales advance of 34% in 2011, with projected increases in the volume of shipments and the average realized selling prices for melted and mill products. Our sales outlook assumes GDP growth of 1.7% in 2011, after 2010's rise of 3.0%, which we see boosting demand for durable goods again in the current year. We expect demand to be aided by further rebuilding of inventories in the aerospace supply chain and increased demand for titanium, reflecting greater commercial aircraft manufacturing.

▸ We look for margin expansion and another sizable increase in operating profit in 2011, on a greater volume of shipments and higher average selling prices for the two main segments. After interest expense and taxes, we project operating EPS of $0.76 in 2011, versus 2010's EPS of $0.45.

▸ Longer term, we forecast higher sales and earnings on an upturn in the commercial aerospace industry, growing use of titanium in other industrial applications, and a secular rise in titanium consumption in Asia.

## Investment Rationale/Risk

▸ We view TIE as a beneficiary of an upturn in commercial aerospace, growing acceptance of titanium in other industrial markets, and a secular rise in Asian demand for titanium. We believe these favorable developments, combined with its low debt levels, should enable TIE to capitalize on a cyclical upturn in titanium demand. Following a very sharp decline in the stock price through late August 2011, we think the shares are oversold and attractively valued, recently trading at 15.5X our EPS estimate for 2012, with a dividend yield of nearly 2.0%. Also, we think that reinstatement of the dividend and implementation of the share repurchase program in 2011 should be positive catalysts for the stock.

▸ Risks to our recommendation and target price include lower volume and pricing for both segments in 2012 instead of the gains we project.

▸ Our 12-month target price of $21 is 20.6X our 2012 EPS estimate, which is the mid-point of the company's 10-year historical range. Based on our target multiple, TIE would trade at a premium to the specialty metals peer average of 19.4X.

## Qualitative Risk Assessment

| LOW | MEDIUM | HIGH |
|---|---|---|

Our risk assessment reflects the company's low debt levels and its large share of the markets it serves. Partly offsetting this is its heavy reliance on aerospace industry demand and the volatility of raw material costs.

## Quantitative Evaluations

**S&P Quality Ranking**     B-

| D | C | B- | B | B+ | A- | A | A+ |
|---|---|---|---|---|---|---|---|

**Relative Strength Rank**     MODERATE

33

LOWEST = 1     HIGHEST = 99

## Revenue/Earnings Data

**Revenue (Million $)**

| | 1Q | 2Q | 3Q | 4Q | Year |
|---|---|---|---|---|---|
| 2011 | 252.0 | 272.0 | 262.5 | -- | -- |
| 2010 | 217.5 | 212.0 | 210.3 | 217.3 | 857.2 |
| 2009 | 203.4 | 205.7 | 181.4 | 183.5 | 774.0 |
| 2008 | 293.7 | 297.3 | 295.4 | 265.2 | 1,152 |
| 2007 | 341.7 | 341.2 | 297.3 | 298.6 | 1,279 |
| 2006 | 286.9 | 300.9 | 271.8 | 323.5 | 1,183 |

**Earnings Per Share ($)**

| | 1Q | 2Q | 3Q | 4Q | Year |
|---|---|---|---|---|---|
| 2011 | 0.16 | 0.18 | 0.14 | E0.17 | E0.61 |
| 2010 | 0.09 | 0.11 | 0.12 | 0.13 | 0.45 |
| 2009 | 0.11 | 0.05 | 0.01 | 0.03 | 0.19 |
| 2008 | 0.22 | 0.26 | 0.22 | 0.19 | 0.89 |
| 2007 | 0.41 | 0.42 | 0.29 | 0.61 | 1.46 |
| 2006 | 0.32 | 0.31 | 0.29 | 0.61 | 1.53 |

Fiscal year ended Dec. 31. Next earnings report expected: Early March. EPS Estimates based on S&P Operating Earnings; historical GAAP earnings are as reported.

## Dividend Data (Dates: mm/dd Payment Date: mm/dd/yy)

| Amount ($) | Date Decl. | Ex-Div. Date | Stk. of Record | Payment Date |
|---|---|---|---|---|
| 0.075 | 05/17 | 06/08 | 06/10 | 06/21/11 |
| 0.075 | 08/01 | 09/07 | 09/09 | 09/20/11 |
| 0.075 | 10/27 | 12/07 | 12/09 | 12/20/11 |

Dividends have been paid since 2011. Source: Company reports.

**Please read the Required Disclosures and Analyst Certification on the last page of this report.**

**The McGraw·Hill Companies**

# Titanium Metals Corp

STANDARD &POOR'S

## Business Summary September 01, 2011

CORPORATE OVERVIEW. Titanium Metals Corp. is the one of the world's largest producers of titanium melted and mill products and the largest U.S. producer of titanium sponge (the raw material for titanium). TIE estimates that it accounted for some 15% of global industry shipments of titanium mill products in 2010 and 5% of worldwide sponge production. Melted and mill products and sponge are sold principally to the commercial aerospace industry. Other sources of product demand include the military, industrial and emerging markets. As of December 31, 2010, 28.1% of TIE's common shares were held by Contran Corporation and its subsidiaries, and an additional 8.6% were held by a trust sponsored by Contran.

Products include titanium sponge; melted products (ingot, electrodes and slab); mill products, including billet and bar, plate, strip and pipe; and fabricated products such as spools, pipe fittings, manifolds and vessels. In 2010, mill products accounted for 80% of sales, melted products 12%, and other prod-

ucts (titanium fabrications, titanium scrap and titanium tetrachloride), 8%.

Sales by market sector in 2010 were: commercial aerospace, 62%; military, 18%; industrial and emerging markets, 13%; and other, 7%.

In 2010, North America accounted for 64% of sales, Europe for 27% and other regions for 9%.

CORPORATE STRATEGY. The company's long-term strategy is to maximize the value of its core aerospace business while expanding its presence in non-aerospace markets. Additionally, the company seeks to develop new applications for its products.

## Company Financials Fiscal Year Ended Dec. 31

| Per Share Data ($) | 2010 | 2009 | 2008 | 2007 | 2006 | 2005 | 2004 | 2003 | 2002 | 2001 |
|---|---|---|---|---|---|---|---|---|---|---|
| Tangible Book Value | 6.71 | 6.15 | 5.94 | 6.16 | 4.92 | 2.91 | 1.41 | 1.20 | 1.18 | 1.92 |
| Cash Flow | 0.75 | 0.47 | 1.15 | 1.65 | 1.68 | 0.96 | 0.47 | 0.19 | -0.24 | -0.01 |
| Earnings | 0.45 | 0.19 | 0.89 | 1.46 | 1.53 | 0.86 | 0.28 | -0.11 | -0.53 | -0.33 |
| S&P Core Earnings | 0.50 | 0.23 | 0.80 | 1.35 | 1.29 | 0.82 | 0.29 | -0.08 | -0.37 | -0.41 |
| Dividends | Nil | Nil | 0.30 | 0.08 | Nil | Nil | Nil | Nil | Nil | Nil |
| Payout Ratio | Nil | Nil | 34% | 5% | Nil | Nil | Nil | Nil | Nil | Nil |
| Prices:High | 22.93 | 13.18 | 26.79 | 39.80 | 47.63 | 19.86 | 3.33 | 1.51 | 1.35 | 3.60 |
| Prices:Low | 10.54 | 4.04 | 5.31 | 25.26 | 15.96 | 2.91 | 1.06 | 0.39 | 0.23 | 0.59 |
| P/E Ratio:High | 51 | 69 | 30 | 27 | 31 | 23 | 12 | NM | NM | NM |
| P/E Ratio:Low | 23 | 21 | 6 | 17 | 10 | 3 | 4 | NM | NM | NM |

### Income Statement Analysis (Million $)

| | 2010 | 2009 | 2008 | 2007 | 2006 | 2005 | 2004 | 2003 | 2002 | 2001 |
|---|---|---|---|---|---|---|---|---|---|---|
| Revenue | 857 | 774 | 1,152 | 1,279 | 1,183 | 750 | 502 | 385 | 367 | 487 |
| Operating Income | 173 | 106 | 269 | 420 | 403 | 177 | 43.8 | 17.2 | -9.02 | 28.2 |
| Depreciation | 52.5 | 51.5 | 47.7 | 41.1 | 34.1 | 31.5 | 32.8 | 36.6 | 37.1 | 40.1 |
| Interest Expense | NA | 0.80 | 1.80 | 2.60 | 3.43 | 3.96 | 12.5 | 16.4 | 3.38 | 4.06 |
| Pretax Income | 126 | 56.5 | 237 | 394 | 418 | 185 | 39.0 | -11.3 | -54.5 | 4.47 |
| Effective Tax Rate | NA | 36.6% | 29.1% | 29.7% | 30.7% | 13.2% | NM | NM | NM | NM |
| Net Income | 82.9 | 34.5 | 163 | 268 | 281 | 156 | 39.9 | -12.9 | -67.2 | -41.8 |
| S&P Core Earnings | 89.6 | 42.5 | 145 | 243 | 230 | 136 | 37.9 | -9.92 | -46.4 | -51.7 |

### Balance Sheet & Other Financial Data (Million $)

| | 2010 | 2009 | 2008 | 2007 | 2006 | 2005 | 2004 | 2003 | 2002 | 2001 |
|---|---|---|---|---|---|---|---|---|---|---|
| Cash | 283 | 169 | 45.0 | 90.0 | 86.2 | 17.6 | 54.4 | 35.0 | 6.21 | 24.5 |
| Current Assets | 941 | 807 | 789 | 898 | 758 | 550 | 344 | 276 | 263 | 309 |
| Total Assets | 1,498 | 1,379 | 1,368 | 1,420 | 1,217 | 907 | 666 | 567 | 564 | 699 |
| Current Liabilities | 123 | 105 | 152 | 178 | 211 | 167 | 162 | 78.5 | 92.6 | 122 |
| Long Term Debt | NA | NA | 0.20 | 0.50 | Nil | 57.2 | 12.2 | 9.77 | 217 | 221 |
| Common Equity | 1,209 | 1,104 | 1,076 | 1,129 | 804 | 430 | 206 | 159 | 159 | 298 |
| Total Capital | 1,242 | 1,124 | 1,101 | 1,168 | 918 | 660 | 404 | 180 | 388 | 533 |
| Capital Expenditures | 23.6 | 33.0 | 121 | 101 | 101 | 61.1 | 23.6 | 12.5 | 7.77 | 16.1 |
| Cash Flow | 135 | 85.8 | 210 | 304 | 309 | 175 | 68.4 | 23.7 | -30.1 | -1.63 |
| Current Ratio | 7.7 | 7.7 | 5.2 | 5.1 | 3.6 | 3.3 | 2.1 | 3.5 | 2.8 | 2.5 |
| % Long Term Debt of Capitalization | Nil | Nil | Nil | Nil | Nil | 8.7 | 3.0 | 5.4 | 56.0 | 41.4 |
| % Net Income of Revenue | 9.7 | 4.5 | 14.1 | 21.0 | 23.8 | 20.8 | 8.0 | NM | NM | NM |
| % Return on Assets | NA | NA | 11.7 | 20.3 | 26.5 | 19.4 | 6.5 | NM | NM | NM |
| % Return on Equity | NA | NA | 14.7 | 27.2 | 44.5 | 43.4 | 19.5 | NM | NM | NM |

Data as orig reptd.; bef. results of disc opers/spec. items. Per share data adj. for stk. divs.; EPS diluted. E-Estimated. NA-Not Available. NM-Not Meaningful. NR-Not Ranked. UR-Under Review.

**Office:** 5430 LBJ Freeway, Suite 1700, Dallas, TX 75240-2697.
**Telephone:** 972-233-1700.
**Website:** http://www.timet.com
**Chrmn:** H.C. Simmons

**Pres & CEO:** B.D. O'Brien
**Vice Chrmn:** S.L. Watson
**CFO:** J.W. Brown
**CTO:** M.W. Kearns

**Board Members:** K. R. Coogan, G. R. Simmons, H. C. Simmons, T. P. Stafford, S. L. Watson, T. N. Worrell, P. J. Zucconi

**Founded:** 1950
**Domicile:** Delaware
**Employees:** 2,385

# TJX Companies Inc (The)

**STANDARD &POOR'S**

| **S&P Recommendation** HOLD ★★★☆☆ | **Price** $58.75 (as of Nov 25, 2011) | **12-Mo. Target Price** $66.00 | **Investment Style** Large-Cap Growth |
|---|---|---|---|

**GICS Sector** Consumer Discretionary
**Sub-Industry** Apparel Retail

**Summary** TJX operates seven chains of off-price apparel and home fashion specialty stores in the U.S., Canada, Germany, Poland, Ireland and the U.K.

## Key Stock Statistics (Source S&P, Vickers, company reports)

| | | | | | | | |
|---|---|---|---|---|---|---|---|
| 52-Wk Range | $61.71– 42.55 | S&P Oper. EPS 2012**E** | 3.97 | Market Capitalization(B) | $22.383 | Beta | 0.56 |
| Trailing 12-Month EPS | $3.48 | S&P Oper. EPS 2013**E** | 4.40 | Yield (%) | 1.29 | S&P 3-Yr. Proj. EPS CAGR(%) | 12 |
| Trailing 12-Month P/E | 16.9 | P/E on S&P Oper. EPS 2012**E** | 14.8 | Dividend Rate/Share | $0.76 | S&P Credit Rating | A |
| $10K Invested 5 Yrs Ago | $22,297 | Common Shares Outstg. (M) | 381.0 | Institutional Ownership (%) | 92 | | |

## Price Performance

30-Week Mov. Avg. ···· 10-Week Mov. Avg. – – GAAP Earnings vs. Previous Year   Volume Above Avg. ▐▌▌ STARS
12-Mo. Target Price — Relative Strength   — ▲ Up ▼ Down ► No Change   Below Avg. ▐▌▌ ★

Options: ASE, CBOE

Analysis prepared by Equity Analyst **Jason N. Asaeda** on Nov 17, 2011, when the stock traded at **$59.11**.

### Highlights

➤ We look for consolidated same-store sales to increase in the low single digits in FY 12 (Jan.) and in FY 13, on modest gains in average transaction value and customer traffic. We think TJX's strong value proposition across brands and its ability to respond quickly to changes in customer buying preferences position the company well for market share gains. Coupled with planned expansion, we see net sales reaching $23.0 billion in FY 12 and $24.8 billion in FY 13.

➤ Excluding A.J. Wright consolidation costs in FY 12, we see operating margins widening annually on an increase in off-price buys (purchases made opportunistically and closer to need during a season), which carry higher mark-ups than upfront buys (purchases made before or early in a season), and effective inventory management, partially offsetting new store expenses and higher marketing spend.

➤ We see EPS of $3.97 in FY 12 (before $0.11 of A.J. Wright consolidation costs) and $4.40 in FY 13, versus FY 11's $3.49 (excluding a $0.02 benefit from a reduction in the company's provision for computer intrusion-related costs and $0.21 of A.J. Wright consolidation costs).

### Investment Rationale/Risk

➤ Our hold recommendation is based on valuation. We think the conversion of former A.J. Wright stores to the T.J. Maxx and Marshalls banners has widened the demographic reach of TJX's core Marmaxx division. We also see Marmaxx generating ample operating cash flow to fund various growth initiatives such as the opening of 54 net stores in FY 12 (including six Marshalls locations in Canada) and an additional 130 to 145 stores in FY 13, as well as the planned repurchase of approximately $1.2 billion of company stock in FY 12. In addition, we are encouraged by improving results in Europe, and we look for turnaround initiatives to take effect in Canada over the next quarter or two.

➤ Risks to our recommendation and target price include sales shortfalls due to changes in consumer spending habits and buying preferences; merchandise availability; increased promotional activity by competitors; and fluctuations in foreign currency exchange rates.

➤ Our 12-month target price of $66 is based on a forward EV/EBITDA multiple of 7.7X, TJX's 10-year historical average, applied to our FY 13 EBITDA estimate of $3.23 billion.

### Qualitative Risk Assessment

| LOW | MEDIUM | HIGH |
|---|---|---|

Our risk assessment reflects our view of TJX's leadership position in off-price retail and promising new merchandising and productivity initiatives that could boost sales and profit margins. This is offset by what we see as an inconsistent earnings track record and an uncertain outlook for consumer discretionary spending.

### Quantitative Evaluations

**S&P Quality Ranking**  **A+**

| D | C | B- | B | B+ | A- | A | A+ |
|---|---|---|---|---|---|---|---|

**Relative Strength Rank**  **STRONG**

86

LOWEST = 1                    HIGHEST = 99

### Revenue/Earnings Data

**Revenue (Million $)**

| | 1Q | 2Q | 3Q | 4Q | Year |
|---|---|---|---|---|---|
| 2012 | 5,220 | 5,468 | 5,793 | -- | -- |
| 2011 | 5,017 | 5,068 | 5,526 | 6,332 | 21,942 |
| 2010 | 4,354 | 4,748 | 5,245 | 5,942 | 20,288 |
| 2009 | 4,364 | 4,621 | 4,762 | 5,380 | 19,000 |
| 2008 | 4,108 | 4,313 | 4,737 | 5,488 | 18,647 |
| 2007 | 3,871 | 3,964 | 4,473 | 5,097 | 17,405 |

**Earnings Per Share ($)**

| | | | | | |
|---|---|---|---|---|---|
| 2012 | 0.67 | 0.90 | 1.06 | E1.23 | E3.97 |
| 2011 | 0.80 | 0.74 | 0.92 | 0.85 | 3.30 |
| 2010 | 0.49 | 0.61 | 0.81 | 0.94 | 2.84 |
| 2009 | 0.43 | 0.45 | 0.58 | 0.58 | 2.07 |
| 2008 | 0.34 | 0.45 | 0.54 | 0.66 | 1.66 |
| 2007 | 0.34 | 0.29 | 0.48 | 0.51 | 1.63 |

Fiscal year ended Jan. 31. Next earnings report expected: NA. EPS Estimates based on S&P Operating Earnings; historical GAAP earnings are as reported.

### Dividend Data (Dates: mm/dd Payment Date: mm/dd/yy)

| Amount ($) | Date Decl. | Ex-Div. Date | Stk. of Record | Payment Date |
|---|---|---|---|---|
| 0.150 | 11/30 | 02/08 | 02/10 | 03/03/11 |
| 0.190 | 04/05 | 05/10 | 05/12 | 06/02/11 |
| 0.190 | 06/14 | 08/09 | 08/11 | 09/01/11 |
| 0.190 | 09/08 | 11/08 | 11/10 | 12/01/11 |

Dividends have been paid since 1980. Source: Company reports.

---

**Please read the Required Disclosures and Analyst Certification on the last page of this report.**

*The McGraw·Hill Companies*

# TJX Companies Inc (The)

**STANDARD &POOR'S**

## Business Summary November 17, 2011

COMPANY PROFILE. With over $20 billion in annual revenues, TJX Companies is the largest U.S. off-price family apparel and home fashion retailer. As of October 29, 2011, the company's core Marmaxx Group division operated 980 T.J. Maxx and 884 Marshalls stores. TJX also operated 375 HomeGoods stores in the U.S.; 24 HomeSense and 333 T.K. Maxx stores in Europe; and 85 HomeSense, 218 Winners, six Marshalls, and three StyleSense (a new family footwear and accessories test concept) stores in Canada. The company closed its A.J. Wright business in February 2011.

TJX believes it derives a competitive advantage by offering rapidly changing assortments of quality brand name and designer merchandise at prices usually 20% to 60% below department and specialty store regular prices. With over 2,800 stores, the company has substantial buying power with more than 14,000 vendors worldwide. TJX purchases later in the buying cycle than department and specialty stores. Generally, purchases are for current selling seasons, with a limited quantity of packaway inventory intended for a future selling season. A combination of opportunistic buying, an expansive distribution infrastructure, and a low expense structure enable the company to offer everyday savings to its customers.

PRIMARY BUSINESS DYNAMICS. TJX's primary growth drivers are new store openings and same-store sales (sales results for stores open for all or a portion of two consecutive fiscal years). The company is targeting 5% to 6% annual retail square footage growth from FY 11 through FY 13. In FY 11, retail square footage increased by about 4% with the net addition of 116 stores.

The treasure hunt nature of the off-price shopping experience requires the company to continuously replenish its stores with exciting merchandise to drive same-store sales. By maintaining a liquid inventory position, TJX's buyers can buy close to need and into current market trends. However, this approach subjects the company to risks on the timing, quantity and nature of inventory flowing to the stores. In FY 11, same-store sales rose 4% on a constant currency basis, reflecting higher customer traffic but lower average transaction value.

## Company Financials Fiscal Year Ended Jan. 31

| Per Share Data ($) | 2011 | 2010 | 2009 | 2008 | 2007 | 2006 | 2005 | 2004 | 2003 | 2002 |
|---|---|---|---|---|---|---|---|---|---|---|
| Tangible Book Value | 7.49 | 6.62 | 4.74 | 4.55 | 4.65 | 3.71 | 3.06 | 2.74 | 2.36 | 2.14 |
| Cash Flow | 4.42 | 3.86 | 2.97 | 2.43 | 2.35 | 2.23 | 1.86 | 1.75 | 1.46 | 1.34 |
| Earnings | 3.30 | 2.84 | 2.07 | 1.66 | 1.63 | 1.41 | 1.30 | 1.28 | 1.08 | 0.97 |
| S&P Core Earnings | 3.31 | 2.88 | 2.03 | 1.63 | 1.64 | 1.40 | 1.22 | 1.21 | 1.01 | 0.91 |
| Dividends | NA | 0.47 | 0.42 | 0.27 | 0.23 | 0.17 | 0.14 | 0.13 | 0.12 | 0.11 |
| Payout Ratio | NA | 17% | 15% | 16% | 14% | 12% | 10% | 10% | 11% | 11% |
| Calendar Year | 2010 | 2009 | 2008 | 2007 | 2006 | 2005 | 2004 | 2003 | 2002 | 2001 |
| Prices:High | 48.50 | 40.64 | 37.52 | 32.46 | 29.84 | 25.96 | 26.82 | 23.70 | 22.45 | 20.30 |
| Prices:Low | 35.75 | 19.16 | 17.80 | 25.74 | 22.16 | 19.95 | 20.64 | 15.54 | 15.30 | 13.56 |
| P/E Ratio:High | 15 | 14 | 18 | 20 | 18 | 18 | 21 | 19 | 21 | 21 |
| P/E Ratio:Low | 11 | 7 | 9 | 16 | 14 | 14 | 16 | 12 | 14 | 14 |

| Income Statement Analysis (Million $) | | | | | | | | | | |
|---|---|---|---|---|---|---|---|---|---|---|
| Revenue | 21,942 | 20,288 | 19,000 | 18,647 | 17,405 | 16,058 | 14,913 | 13,328 | 11,981 | 10,709 |
| Operating Income | 2,661 | 2,426 | 1,833 | 1,811 | 1,616 | 1,444 | 1,394 | 1,334 | 1,171 | 1,104 |
| Depreciation | 458 | 435 | 398 | 365 | 353 | 405 | 288 | 238 | 208 | 204 |
| Interest Expense | 39.1 | 39.5 | 38.1 | 39.9 | 39.2 | 39.0 | 33.5 | 27.3 | 25.4 | 25.6 |
| Pretax Income | 2,164 | 1,952 | 1,451 | 1,243 | 1,247 | 1,009 | 1,080 | 1,068 | 938 | 874 |
| Effective Tax Rate | NA | 37.8% | 37.0% | 37.9% | 37.7% | 31.6% | 38.5% | 38.4% | 38.3% | 38.2% |
| Net Income | 1,340 | 1,214 | 915 | 772 | 777 | 690 | 664 | 658 | 578 | 540 |
| S&P Core Earnings | 1,346 | 1,229 | 893 | 756 | 778 | 687 | 615 | 619 | 546 | 506 |

| Balance Sheet & Other Financial Data (Million $) | | | | | | | | | | |
|---|---|---|---|---|---|---|---|---|---|---|
| Cash | 1,818 | 1,745 | 454 | 733 | 857 | 466 | 307 | 246 | 492 | 493 |
| Current Assets | 5,100 | 4,804 | 3,626 | 3,992 | 3,749 | 3,140 | 2,905 | 2,452 | 2,241 | 2,116 |
| Total Assets | 7,972 | 7,464 | 6,178 | 6,600 | 6,086 | 5,496 | 5,075 | 4,397 | 3,940 | 3,596 |
| Current Liabilities | 3,133 | 2,895 | 2,768 | 2,761 | 2,383 | 2,252 | 2,204 | 1,691 | 1,566 | 1,315 |
| Long Term Debt | 774 | 774 | 384 | 853 | 808 | 807 | 599 | 692 | 694 | 702 |
| Common Equity | 3,100 | 2,889 | 2,135 | 2,131 | 2,290 | 1,893 | 1,653 | 1,552 | 1,409 | 1,341 |
| Total Capital | 3,874 | 3,664 | 2,646 | 3,028 | 3,120 | 2,700 | 2,405 | 2,369 | 2,145 | 2,043 |
| Capital Expenditures | 707 | 429 | 583 | 527 | 378 | 496 | 429 | 409 | 397 | 449 |
| Cash Flow | 1,798 | 1,649 | 1,313 | 1,137 | 1,130 | 1,096 | 953 | 897 | 786 | 744 |
| Current Ratio | 1.6 | 1.7 | 1.3 | 1.5 | 1.6 | 1.4 | 1.3 | 1.5 | 1.4 | 1.6 |
| % Long Term Debt of Capitalization | 20.0 | 21.1 | 14.5 | 28.2 | 25.9 | 29.9 | 24.9 | 29.2 | 32.3 | 34.4 |
| % Net Income of Revenue | 6.1 | 6.0 | 4.8 | 4.1 | 4.5 | 4.3 | 4.5 | 4.9 | 4.8 | 5.0 |
| % Return on Assets | 17.4 | 17.8 | 14.3 | 12.2 | 13.4 | 13.1 | 14.0 | 15.8 | 15.3 | 16.6 |
| % Return on Equity | 44.7 | 48.3 | 42.9 | 34.9 | 37.1 | 37.9 | 41.4 | 44.5 | 42.1 | 42.2 |

Data as orig reptd.; bef. results of disc opers/spec. items. Per share data adj. for stk. divs.; EPS diluted. E-Estimated. NA-Not Available. NM-Not Meaningful. NR-Not Ranked. UR-Under Review.

**Office:** 770 Cochituate Road, Framingham, MA 01701.
**Telephone:** 508-390-1000.
**Website:** http://www.tjx.com
**Chrmn:** B. Cammarata

**Pres:** E. Herrman
**CEO:** C.M. Meyrowitz
**EVP, Secy & General Counsel:** A. McCauley
**Chief Admin Officer & Chief Acctg Officer:** J. Naylor

**Investor Contact:** S. Lang (508-390-2323)
**Board Members:** J. B. Alvarez, A. M. Bennett, B. Cammarata, D. T. Ching, M. F. Hines, A. B. Lane, C. M. Meyrowitz, J. F. O'Brien, W. B. Shire

**Founded:** 1956
**Domicile:** Delaware
**Employees:** 166,000

**The McGraw-Hill Companies**

# Torchmark Corp

**STANDARD &POOR'S**

| S&P Recommendation HOLD ★★★☆☆ | Price $39.68 (as of Nov 25, 2011) | 12-Mo. Target Price $43.00 | Investment Style Large-Cap Blend |
|---|---|---|---|

**GICS Sector** Financials
**Sub-Industry** Life & Health Insurance

**Summary** This financial services company derives most of its earnings from its life and health insurance operations.

## Key Stock Statistics (Source S&P, Vickers, company reports)

| | | | | | | | |
|---|---|---|---|---|---|---|---|
| 52-Wk Range | $45.37– 32.77 | S&P Oper. EPS 2011**E** | 4.70 | Market Capitalization(B) | $4.045 | Beta | 1.60 |
| Trailing 12-Month EPS | $4.76 | S&P Oper. EPS 2012**E** | 4.86 | Yield (%) | 1.21 | S&P 3-Yr. Proj. EPS CAGR(%) | 6 |
| Trailing 12-Month P/E | 8.3 | P/E on S&P Oper. EPS 2011**E** | 8.4 | Dividend Rate/Share | $0.48 | S&P Credit Rating | A |
| $10K Invested 5 Yrs Ago | $9,942 | Common Shares Outstg. (M) | 101.9 | Institutional Ownership (%) | 78 | | |

## Price Performance

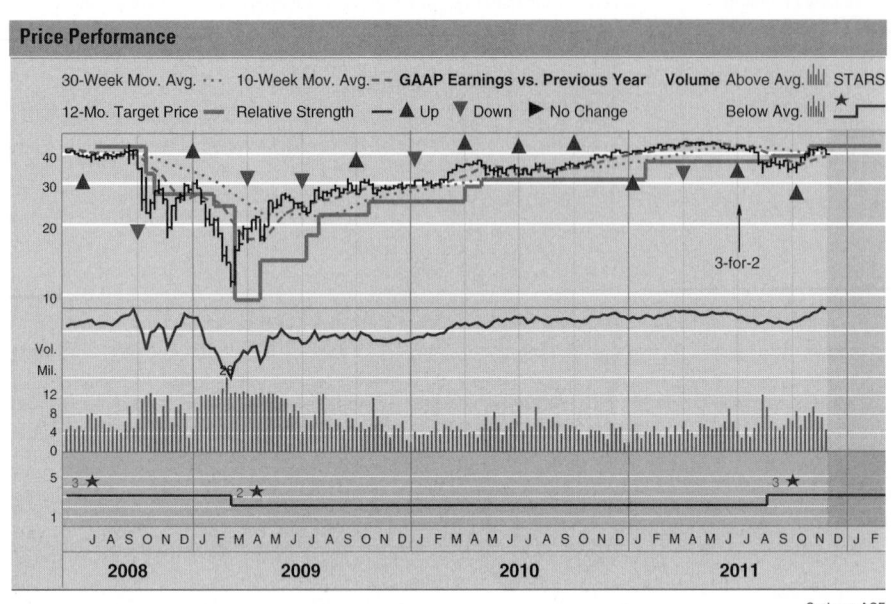

30-Week Mov. Avg. · · · · 10-Week Mov. Avg. - - **GAAP Earnings vs. Previous Year** Volume Above Avg. STARS
12-Mo. Target Price — Relative Strength — ▲ Up ▼ Down ► No Change Below Avg.

3-for-2

Options: ASE

Analysis prepared by Equity Analyst **Cathy Seifert** on Nov 23, 2011, when the stock traded at **$41.28**.

## Qualitative Risk Assessment

| LOW | **MEDIUM** | HIGH |
|---|---|---|

Our risk assessment reflects the company's sizable holdings of below investment grade bonds, and the potential for adverse credit migration in its fixed income portfolio. This is offset by TMK's low leverage, varied product lineup and limited exposure to structured investments. Also, TMK generates what we consider strong cash flow and statutory earnings and uses excess cash flow to pay its dividend and repurchase shares.

## Quantitative Evaluations

**S&P Quality Ranking**                                      **A**

| D | C | B- | B | B+ | A- | **A** | A+ |
|---|---|---|---|---|---|---|---|

**Relative Strength Rank**                          **STRONG**

LOWEST = 1                     81                     HIGHEST = 99

## Highlights

➤ We forecast that life premiums will be up slightly in 2011 and 2012, although growth should be hindered by agent recruitment and retention challenges, lower insert media response rates, and tough comps. We expect sales at American Income to increase on higher producing agent counts. However, we expect sales at Liberty National to decline meaningfully due to distribution-related issues and higher product pricing. We see life underwriting margins improving in coming periods on premium growth, favorable mortality, and improved pricing. We forecast modest sales growth for Direct Response.

➤ We see health segment premiums declining more than 10%, as TMK de-emphasizes that business and reflecting the impact of health care reform. However, we forecast strong sales of medical supplemental products as that business captures disenrollment from Medicare Advantage plans. We believe new health business written will improve margins, and we expect a modest increase in the underwriting margin.

➤ We forecast operating EPS of $4.70 for 2011 and $4.86 for 2012.

## Investment Rationale/Risk

➤ At current levels, we believe the shares are fairly valued on a price/earnings basis, though they trade at a premium to the group on a price-to-book value basis. TMK's ability to generate solid cash flow, produce consistent earnings and repurchase its shares is partly offset by growth prospects that are relatively weak versus the group. In addition, we believe fundamentals in the health business are poor, and we expect lower health premiums to be a drag on top-line growth. We also think lower new money yields will adversely affect investment income as interest rates are likely to remain low. However, we view positively TMK's low leverage in this environment, and we believe concerns about its below investment grade investment portfolio have abated.

➤ Risks to our recommendation and target price include higher than expected investment losses, higher than expected loss ratios for the Medicare Part D business, adverse mortality trends, and a material increase in interest rates.

➤ Our 12-month target price of $43 assumes the shares trade at 8.8X our 2012 operating EPS estimate, at the low end of historical ranges.

## Revenue/Earnings Data

**Revenue (Million $)**

| | 1Q | 2Q | 3Q | 4Q | Year |
|---|---|---|---|---|---|
| 2011 | 829.3 | 877.3 | 837.2 | -- | -- |
| 2010 | 845.7 | 835.9 | 838.9 | 847.2 | 3,368 |
| 2009 | 809.6 | 819.7 | 784.9 | 808.2 | 2,687 |
| 2008 | 872.4 | 860.5 | 753.4 | 840.6 | 2,758 |
| 2007 | 906.0 | 876.6 | 863.6 | 840.5 | 3,487 |
| 2006 | 857.0 | 869.1 | 837.9 | 857.1 | 3,421 |

**Earnings Per Share ($)**

| | | | | | |
|---|---|---|---|---|---|
| 2011 | 0.89 | 1.32 | 1.30 | E1.25 | E4.70 |
| 2010 | 0.93 | 0.97 | 1.13 | 1.23 | 4.24 |
| 2009 | 0.61 | 0.92 | 0.81 | 0.91 | 3.25 |
| 2008 | 0.86 | 0.98 | 0.48 | 1.07 | 3.41 |
| 2007 | 0.91 | 0.88 | 0.94 | 0.94 | 3.67 |
| 2006 | 0.77 | 0.84 | 0.85 | 0.95 | 3.42 |

Fiscal year ended Dec. 31. Next earnings report expected: Early February. EPS Estimates based on S&P Operating Earnings; historical GAAP earnings are as reported.

## Dividend Data (Dates: mm/dd Payment Date: mm/dd/yy)

| Amount ($) | Date Decl. | Ex-Div. Date | Stk. of Record | Payment Date |
|---|---|---|---|---|
| 0.110 | 05/02 | 05/27 | 06/01 | 08/01/11 |
| 3-for-2 | 05/02 | 07/05 | 06/01 | 07/01/11 |
| 0.120 | 08/12 | 10/05 | 10/07 | 11/01/11 |
| 0.120 | 11/11 | 01/04 | 01/06 | 02/01/12 |

Dividends have been paid since 1933. Source: Company reports.

---

**Please read the Required Disclosures and Analyst Certification on the last page of this report.**

**The McGraw·Hill Companies**

# Torchmark Corp

**STANDARD &POOR'S**

## Business Summary November 23, 2011

CORPORATE OVERVIEW. TMK's subsidiaries offer a full line of nonparticipating ordinary individual life products and health insurance, as well as fixed annuities. Traditional whole life insurance constituted 64% of life insurance in force at the end of 2010 as measured by annualized premiums, interest-sensitive whole life 4.3%, term life 29%, and other life products 3.5%. Medicare supplemental insurance accounted for 47% of supplemental health insurance in force at the end of 2010, as measured by annualized premiums, limited-benefit plans 35%, and Medicare Part D 19%. The number of individual health policies in force (excluding Medicare Part D) was 1.57 million at December 31, 2010, versus 1.66 million at prior year end. Medicare Part D enrollees to begin the 2011 plan year were 144,000 at December 31, 2010. We do not expect enrollees to increase in 2011 since TMK intends to continue to de-emphasize its health business. Separate accounts were previously established in relation to TMK's variable life and annuity business. However, TMK exited the variable annuity business in 2010 when it sold its subsidiary United Investors Life Insurance.

Life segment premium revenue accounted for 63% of total premium revenue in 2010 (62% in 2009), and the health segment 38% (38%).

CORPORATE STRATEGY. A key corporate strategy for TMK is to improve its

distribution system. Distribution is through direct solicitation, independent agents, and exclusive agents. The Liberty National exclusive agency markets products to middle-income families in the U.S. Southeast through full-time sales representatives. In 2009, TMK combined its United American agency with its Liberty National exclusive agency and focused the combined sales force on writing life and supplemental health products in middle-income markets. The United American branch office agency focused on health insurance to over-age-50 individuals through exclusive producing agents. The American Income exclusive agency focuses on members of labor unions, credit unions, and other associations in the U.S., Canada and New Zealand. The United Investors agency markets to middle-income Americans through independent agents. The Military Agency consists of a nationwide independent agency comprised of former commissioned and noncommissioned military officers who sell exclusively to military officers and their families. The United American independent agency focuses primarily on health insurance in the U.S. and Canada to individuals over the age of 50.

## Company Financials Fiscal Year Ended Dec. 31

| Per Share Data ($) | 2010 | 2009 | 2008 | 2007 | 2006 | 2005 | 2004 | 2003 | 2002 | 2001 |
|---|---|---|---|---|---|---|---|---|---|---|
| Tangible Book Value | 30.45 | 51.70 | 13.01 | 21.16 | 20.93 | 19.66 | 18.77 | 16.93 | 13.94 | 11.49 |
| Operating Earnings | NA | NA | NA | NA | NA | NA | NA | 2.58 | 2.34 | 2.08 |
| Earnings | 4.24 | 3.25 | 3.41 | 3.67 | 3.42 | 3.12 | 2.83 | 2.49 | 2.12 | 2.07 |
| S&P Core Earnings | 4.09 | 4.05 | 3.87 | 3.57 | 3.38 | 2.86 | 2.69 | 2.45 | 2.26 | 1.82 |
| Dividends | 0.41 | 0.28 | 0.46 | 0.35 | 0.32 | 0.29 | 0.29 | 0.25 | 0.24 | 0.24 |
| Payout Ratio | 10% | 9% | 14% | 9% | 9% | 9% | 10% | 10% | 11% | 12% |
| Prices:High | 41.90 | 31.50 | 44.00 | 47.03 | 43.06 | 38.33 | 38.38 | 30.50 | 28.11 | 28.83 |
| Prices:Low | 28.45 | 10.77 | 17.51 | 39.00 | 35.94 | 33.37 | 29.74 | 22.00 | 20.01 | 21.71 |
| P/E Ratio:High | 10 | 10 | 13 | 13 | 13 | 12 | 14 | 12 | 13 | 14 |
| P/E Ratio:Low | 7 | 3 | 5 | 11 | 11 | 11 | 10 | 9 | 9 | 10 |

| Income Statement Analysis (Million $) | | | | | | | | | | |
|---|---|---|---|---|---|---|---|---|---|---|
| Life Insurance in Force | 145,397 | 152,525 | 147,780 | 145,349 | 141,134 | 139,233 | 134,640 | 126,737 | 118,660 | 113,055 |
| Premium Income:Life | 1,664 | 1,660 | 1,617 | 1,570 | 1,524 | 1,468 | 1,396 | 1,246 | 1,221 | 1,144 |
| Premium Income:A & H | 987 | 1,018 | 1,127 | 1,237 | 1,238 | 1,015 | 1,049 | 1,034 | 1,019 | 1,011 |
| Net Investment Income | 676 | 675 | 671 | 649 | 629 | 603 | 577 | 557 | 519 | 492 |
| Total Revenue | 3,368 | 3,222 | 3,327 | 3,487 | 3,421 | 3,126 | 3,072 | 2,931 | 2,738 | 2,707 |
| Pretax Income | 779 | 660 | 715 | 797 | 774 | 732 | 721 | 655 | 580 | 597 |
| Net Operating Income | NA | NA | NA | NA | NA | NA | NA | 446 | 424 | 393 |
| Net Income | 522 | 405 | 452 | 528 | 519 | 495 | 476 | 430 | 383 | 391 |
| S&P Core Earnings | 504 | 505 | 514 | 514 | 512 | 455 | 452 | 424 | 408 | 343 |

| Balance Sheet & Other Financial Data (Million $) | | | | | | | | | | |
|---|---|---|---|---|---|---|---|---|---|---|
| Cash & Equivalent | 550 | 411 | 223 | 193 | 185 | 178 | 164 | 155 | 140 | 129 |
| Premiums Due | 230 | 197 | 152 | 96.8 | 78.8 | 67.3 | 73.4 | 80.7 | 70.4 | 67.5 |
| Investment Assets:Bonds | 10,543 | 9,696 | 7,817 | 9,226 | 9,127 | 8,837 | 8,715 | 8,103 | 7,194 | 6,526 |
| Investment Assets:Stocks | 17.2 | 16.7 | 16.3 | 21.3 | 41.2 | 48.0 | 36.9 | 57.4 | 24.5 | 0.57 |
| Investment Assets:Loans | 378 | 384 | 360 | 344 | 329 | 317 | 338 | 704 | 401 | 393 |
| Investment Assets:Total | 11,198 | 10,507 | 8,489 | 9,772 | 9,703 | 9,649 | 9,405 | 8,795 | 7,784 | 7,154 |
| Deferred Policy Costs | 3,406 | 3,457 | 3,395 | 3,159 | 2,956 | 2,768 | 2,506 | 2,330 | 2,184 | 2,066 |
| Total Assets | 16,160 | 16,024 | 13,529 | 15,241 | 14,980 | 14,769 | 14,252 | 13,461 | 12,361 | 12,428 |
| Debt | 790 | 796 | 499 | 598 | 598 | 353 | 540 | 693 | 552 | 681 |
| Common Equity | 4,016 | 3,399 | 2,223 | 3,325 | 3,459 | 3,433 | 6,840 | 3,240 | 2,851 | 2,497 |
| % Return on Revenue | 15.5 | 12.6 | 13.6 | 15.1 | 15.2 | 15.8 | 15.5 | 14.7 | 14.0 | 14.4 |
| % Return on Assets | 3.2 | 2.7 | 3.1 | 3.5 | 3.5 | 3.4 | 3.4 | 3.3 | 3.1 | 3.1 |
| % Return on Equity | 14.1 | 14.4 | 16.2 | 15.6 | 15.1 | 14.5 | 7.1 | 14.1 | 14.3 | 16.6 |
| % Investment Yield | 6.4 | 7.1 | 7.3 | 6.7 | 6.5 | 6.3 | 6.4 | 6.7 | 7.0 | 7.2 |

Data as orig reptd.; bef. results of disc opers/spec. items. Per share data adj. for stk. divs.; EPS diluted. E-Estimated. NA-Not Available. NM-Not Meaningful. NR-Not Ranked. UR-Under Review.

**Office:** 3700 S Stonebridge Dr, McKinney, TX 75070-5934.
**Telephone:** 972-569-4000.
**Website:** http://www.torchmarkcorp.com
**Chrmn & CEO:** M.S. McAndrew

**EVP & CFO:** G.L. Coleman
**EVP & General Counsel:** L.M. Hutchison
**Chief Admin Officer:** V.D. Herbel
**Chief Acctg Officer:** D.H. Almond

**Investor Contact:** J.L. Lane (972-569-3627)
**Board Members:** C. E. Adair, D. L. Boren, J. M. Buchan, R. W. Ingram, M. S. McAndrew, L. W. Newton, S. R. Perry, D. M. Rebelez, L. C. Smith, P. J. Zucconi

**Founded:** 1900
**Domicile:** Delaware
**Employees:** 3,291

# Total System Services Inc.

STANDARD &POOR'S

| S&P Recommendation **HOLD** ★★★★★ | Price $18.73 (as of Nov 25, 2011) | 12-Mo. Target Price $20.00 | Investment Style Large-Cap Growth |
|---|---|---|---|

**GICS Sector** Information Technology
**Sub-Industry** Data Processing & Outsourced Services

**Summary** This company processes data, transactions, and payments for domestic and international issuers of credit, debit, commercial, and private-label cards.

## Key Stock Statistics (Source S&P, Vickers, company reports)

| | | | | | |
|---|---|---|---|---|---|
| 52-Wk Range | $20.50– 14.99 | S&P Oper. EPS 2011**E** | 1.12 | Market Capitalization(B) | $3.771 | Beta | 0.95 |
| Trailing 12-Month EPS | $1.07 | S&P Oper. EPS 2012**E** | 1.21 | Yield (%) | 2.14 | S&P 3-Yr. Proj. EPS CAGR(%) | 10 |
| Trailing 12-Month P/E | 17.5 | P/E on S&P Oper. EPS 2011**E** | 16.7 | Dividend Rate/Share | $0.40 | S&P Credit Rating | NA |
| $10K Invested 5 Yrs Ago | $8,906 | Common Shares Outstg. (M) | 201.4 | Institutional Ownership (%) | 63 | | |

## Price Performance

30-Week Mov. Avg. · · · 10-Week Mov. Avg. – – GAAP Earnings vs. Previous Year Volume Above Avg. STARS
12-Mo. Target Price — Relative Strength ▲ Up ▼ Down ► No Change Below Avg.

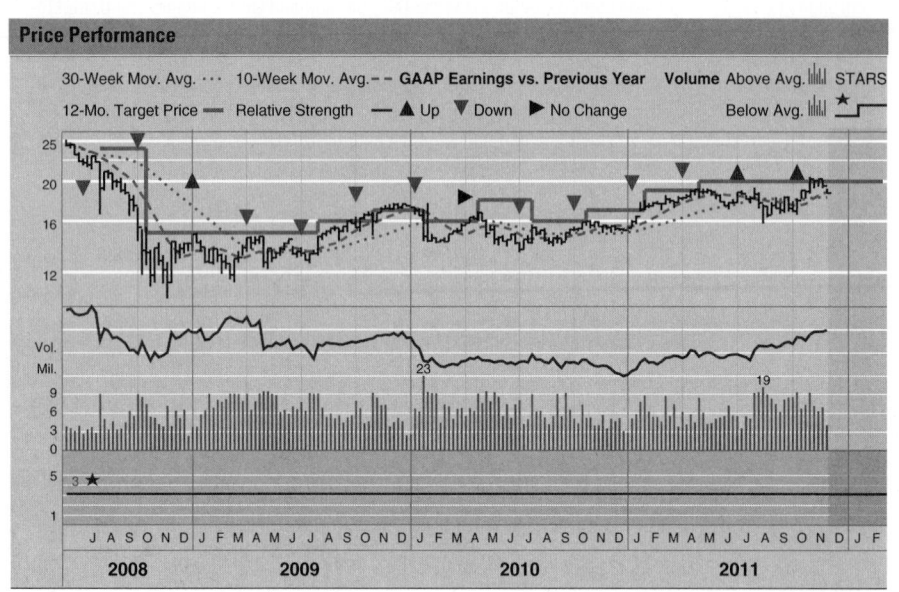

Options: CBOE, Ph

Analysis prepared by Equity Analyst **Dylan Cathers** on Nov 01, 2011, when the stock traded at **$19.43**.

### Highlights

➤ We look for operating revenues (before reimbursable items) to increase about 6.0% in 2011 and 5.5% next year, aided by strong growth in accounts on file, particularly within the Commercial and Government Services areas. We expect business loss and price compression to taper off somewhat and see new client wins adding to internal growth. We also believe that international growth will be a benefit in the coming quarters. The company recently signed an important contract with Capital One Financial (COF 44, Buy).

➤ We anticipate a slight narrowing of operating margins in 2011 due to lower termination fees (which carry wide margins) versus 2010. We expect a modest widening in 2012, reflecting an improved revenue growth outlook and some benefit from headcount cuts and other expense reduction measures taken amid past business losses. We look for ongoing investment in international operations to partly offset these benefits. Despite this, we anticipate rising international profitability in future periods.

➤ We see EPS of $1.12 in 2011 and $1.21 in 2012.

### Investment Rationale/Risk

➤ TSS continues to navigate through a difficult period for its financial institution clients, some of whom experienced considerable financial losses in the recent recession. The environment is improving gradually after recent credit card regulation and a period of declining card issuance. We expect a recent rise in credit card marketing to benefit TSS over time. Business has also been lost due to client consolidation. TSS has continued to add new customers during this period and we expect the revenue hole created by losses to be replaced slowly. We see TSS continuing to manage costs as the economy firms up, but as it expands overseas, we expect investment.

➤ Risks to our recommendation and target price include greater competition from other processors, and increased potential for business disruptions due to industry consolidation. We expect the pace of economic recovery and the prevailing regulatory environment to impact growth.

➤ We apply a 16.5X P/E to our 2012 estimate, near the mean forward P/E of 17.4X for data processing and outsourced services peers, to derive our 12-month target price of $20.

### Qualitative Risk Assessment

| LOW | MEDIUM | HIGH |
|---|---|---|

Our risk assessment reflects our view that the company is navigating past a difficult period with sizable customer losses. We continue to view TSS as a leading provider of card processing services, but we expect the environment to improve gradually as organic growth remains modest.

### Quantitative Evaluations

**S&P Quality Ranking** B+

| D | C | B- | B | B+ | A- | A | A+ |
|---|---|---|---|---|---|---|---|

**Relative Strength Rank** STRONG

75

LOWEST = 1 HIGHEST = 99

### Revenue/Earnings Data

**Revenue (Million $)**

| | 1Q | 2Q | 3Q | 4Q | Year |
|---|---|---|---|---|---|
| 2011 | 429.4 | 447.6 | 459.8 | -- | -- |
| 2010 | 415.4 | 433.8 | 433.2 | 440.0 | 1,718 |
| 2009 | 408.9 | 412.0 | 432.3 | 434.8 | 1,688 |
| 2008 | 461.7 | 483.1 | 500.4 | 493.4 | 1,939 |
| 2007 | 429.6 | 460.2 | 457.6 | 458.5 | 1,806 |
| 2006 | 412.3 | 429.2 | 441.8 | 503.9 | 1,787 |

**Earnings Per Share ($)**

| | | | | | |
|---|---|---|---|---|---|
| 2011 | 0.25 | 0.28 | 0.30 | E0.29 | E1.12 |
| 2010 | 0.26 | 0.25 | 0.25 | 0.24 | 1.00 |
| 2009 | 0.26 | 0.27 | 0.29 | 0.31 | 1.12 |
| 2008 | 0.29 | 0.32 | 0.33 | 0.34 | 1.27 |
| 2007 | 0.29 | 0.33 | 0.35 | 0.23 | 1.20 |
| 2006 | 0.26 | 0.29 | 0.28 | 0.44 | 1.26 |

Fiscal year ended Dec. 31. Next earnings report expected: Late January. EPS Estimates based on S&P Operating Earnings; historical GAAP earnings are as reported.

### Dividend Data (Dates: mm/dd Payment Date: mm/dd/yy)

| Amount ($) | Date Decl. | Ex-Div. Date | Stk. of Record | Payment Date |
|---|---|---|---|---|
| 0.070 | 03/01 | 03/15 | 03/17 | 04/01/11 |
| 0.070 | 05/31 | 06/14 | 06/16 | 07/01/11 |
| 0.070 | 09/06 | 09/14 | 09/16 | 10/03/11 |
| 0.100 | 10/25 | 12/13 | 12/15 | 01/03/12 |

Dividends have been paid since 1990. Source: Company reports.

---

**Please read the Required Disclosures and Analyst Certification on the last page of this report.**

The McGraw-Hill Companies

# Total System Services Inc.

**STANDARD &POOR'S**

## Business Summary November 01, 2011

CORPORATE PROFILE. Total System Services (TSS) provides electronic payment processing, merchant processing and associated services to financial and non-financial institutions, globally. Electronic payment processing services are generated primarily from charges based on the number of accounts on file, transactions and authorizations processed, statements mailed, and other processing services for cardholder accounts on file. These services are provided to issuers of consumer credit, debit, retail, stored value cards as well as government services and commercial card accounts. As of December 2010, TSS had 342.9 million accounts on file, compared to 344.8 million in 2009, 352.5 million in 2008 and 375.5 million in 2007. TSYS derives 49% of processing revenues from transaction volumes arising from accounts on file while 51% are derived from production and what TSS considers to be value-added products and services. The company divides its services into three operating segments: North America Services (54% of 2010 revenue), International Services (19%), and Merchant Services (27%).

PRIMARY BUSINESS DYNAMICS. TSS serves large financial institutions under long-term contracts. This results in revenue concentration that we view as a risk, since these large customers can be acquired, move to a competitor, or in some case, move processing of transactions in-house. In 2008, 2007 and 2006, the company's three largest customers contributed 32.4%, 32.4% and 39.2%, respectively, of total revenues. In 2006, Bank of America moved processing on its consumer card portfolio of about 46 million accounts in-house. In 2007, customer JPMorgan Chase ended its outsourcing agreement with TSS and moved its processing in-house, using a system licensed from TSS. Recent consolidation among financial institutions involving TSS clients include JPMorgan's acquisition of Washington Mutual Bank and Wells Fargo's acquisition of TSS client Wachovia. In 2010, Bank of America accounted for 12.9% of TSS's total revenues. In June 2009, Bank of America notified TSS that it had formed a joint venture to provide merchant services and while TSS still provided merchant services to Bank of America in 2010, we see this portion of its revenue (6% of 2010 revenue) at risk.

## Company Financials Fiscal Year Ended Dec. 31

| Per Share Data ($) | 2010 | 2009 | 2008 | 2007 | 2006 | 2005 | 2004 | 2003 | 2002 | 2001 |
|---|---|---|---|---|---|---|---|---|---|---|
| Tangible Book Value | 3.04 | 4.04 | 3.07 | 3.51 | 5.40 | 4.49 | 4.01 | 3.57 | 3.06 | 2.57 |
| Cash Flow | 1.84 | 1.83 | 1.53 | 1.44 | 2.20 | 1.75 | 1.31 | 1.21 | 1.01 | 0.82 |
| Earnings | 1.00 | 1.12 | 1.27 | 1.20 | 1.26 | 0.99 | 0.76 | 0.71 | 0.64 | 0.53 |
| S&P Core Earnings | 1.00 | 1.12 | 1.27 | 1.20 | 1.26 | 0.95 | 0.74 | 0.69 | 0.60 | 0.51 |
| Dividends | 0.28 | 0.28 | 0.28 | 3.31 | 0.27 | 0.22 | 0.14 | 0.08 | 0.07 | 0.06 |
| Payout Ratio | 28% | 25% | 22% | NM | 21% | 22% | 18% | 11% | 11% | 11% |
| Prices:High | 17.75 | 17.71 | 28.19 | 35.05 | 26.61 | 25.88 | 31.27 | 31.50 | 29.44 | 35.84 |
| Prices:Low | 13.41 | 11.33 | 10.36 | 24.35 | 17.87 | 17.76 | 19.47 | 13.25 | 11.01 | 18.91 |
| P/E Ratio:High | 18 | 16 | 22 | 29 | 21 | 26 | 41 | 44 | 46 | 68 |
| P/E Ratio:Low | 13 | 10 | 8 | 20 | 14 | 18 | 26 | 19 | 17 | 36 |

| Income Statement Analysis (Million $) | 2010 | 2009 | 2008 | 2007 | 2006 | 2005 | 2004 | 2003 | 2002 | 2001 |
|---|---|---|---|---|---|---|---|---|---|---|
| Revenue | 1,718 | 1,688 | 1,939 | 1,806 | 1,787 | 1,603 | 1,187 | 1,053 | 955 | 650 |
| Operating Income | 473 | 481 | 433 | 415 | 542 | 438 | 311 | 289 | 232 | 193 |
| Depreciation | 163 | 156 | 50.5 | 47.1 | 185 | 151 | 109 | 98.4 | 74.5 | 57.4 |
| Interest Expense | 2.90 | 4.10 | 11.3 | 3.13 | 0.57 | 0.37 | 0.94 | Nil | 1.10 | Nil |
| Pretax Income | 315 | 346 | 383 | 383 | 376 | 298 | 228 | 212 | 184 | 156 |
| Effective Tax Rate | NA | 35.1% | 34.4% | 37.5% | 33.6% | 34.7% | 33.9% | 33.4% | 31.5% | 33.9% |
| Net Income | 197 | 220 | 250 | 237 | 249 | 195 | 151 | 141 | 126 | 103 |
| S&P Core Earnings | 196 | 219 | 250 | 237 | 249 | 188 | 145 | 136 | 119 | 99.5 |

| Balance Sheet & Other Financial Data (Million $) | 2010 | 2009 | 2008 | 2007 | 2006 | 2005 | 2004 | 2003 | 2002 | 2001 |
|---|---|---|---|---|---|---|---|---|---|---|
| Cash | 395 | 450 | 220 | 240 | 389 | 238 | 232 | 123 | 113 | 56.0 |
| Current Assets | 737 | 811 | 625 | 587 | 745 | 512 | 448 | 274 | 266 | 206 |
| Total Assets | 1,968 | 1,711 | 1,539 | 1,479 | 1,634 | 1,411 | 1,282 | 1,001 | 783 | 652 |
| Current Liabilities | 200 | 221 | 249 | 274 | 296 | 277 | 278 | 147 | 114 | 103 |
| Long Term Debt | 219 | 192 | 210 | 257 | 3.63 | 3.56 | 4.51 | 29.7 | 0.07 | Nil |
| Common Equity | 1,241 | 1,176 | 989 | 844 | 1,217 | 1,013 | 865 | 733 | 602 | 501 |
| Total Capital | 1,638 | 1,389 | 1,260 | 1,177 | 1,296 | 1,106 | 1,004 | 854 | 668 | 550 |
| Capital Expenditures | 46.6 | 34.0 | 48.0 | 55.3 | 26.5 | 40.9 | 53.9 | 125 | 14.8 | 30.8 |
| Cash Flow | 360 | 359 | 301 | 285 | 434 | 346 | 259 | 239 | 200 | 160 |
| Current Ratio | 3.7 | 3.7 | 2.5 | 2.1 | 2.5 | 1.8 | 1.6 | 1.9 | 2.3 | 2.0 |
| % Long Term Debt of Capitalization | 13.4 | 13.9 | 16.7 | 21.8 | 0.3 | 0.3 | 0.4 | 3.5 | 0.0 | Nil |
| % Net Income of Revenue | 11.5 | 13.1 | 12.9 | 13.2 | 13.9 | 12.1 | 12.7 | 13.4 | 13.2 | 15.8 |
| % Return on Assets | 10.7 | 13.5 | 16.6 | 15.3 | 16.4 | 14.4 | 13.2 | 15.8 | 17.5 | 16.4 |
| % Return on Equity | 16.3 | 20.3 | 27.3 | 23.0 | 22.3 | 20.7 | 18.9 | 21.1 | 22.7 | 22.6 |

Data as orig reptd.; bef. results of disc opers/spec. items. Per share data adj. for stk. divs.; EPS diluted. E-Estimated. NA-Not Available. NM-Not Meaningful. NR-Not Ranked. UR-Under Review.

**Office:** One TSYS Way, Post Office Box 2567, Columbus, GA 31902.
**Telephone:** 706-649-2310.
**Email:** ir@tsys.com
**Website:** http://www.tsys.com

**Chrmn & CEO:** P.W. Tomlinson
**Pres & COO:** M.T. Woods
**EVP & CFO:** J.B. Lipham
**EVP & CTO:** S.W. Humber

**EVP, Chief Acctg Officer & Cntlr:** D.K. Weaver
**Investor Contact:** S. Roberts (706-644-6081)
**Board Members:** J. H. Blanchard, R. Y. Bradley, K. Cloninger, III, W. W. Driver, Jr., G. W. Garrard, Jr., S. E. Harris, M. H. Lampton, W. W. Miller, Jr., H. L. Page, P. W. Tomlinson, J. T. Turner, R. W. Ussery, M. T. Woods, J. D. Yancey, R. K. Yarbrough

**Founded:** 1982
**Domicile:** Georgia
**Employees:** 7,788

# Travelers Companies Inc (The)

**STANDARD
&POOR'S**

| S&P Recommendation | **STRONG BUY** ★★★★★ | Price $53.41 (as of Nov 25, 2011) | 12-Mo. Target Price $72.00 | Investment Style Large-Cap Value |
|---|---|---|---|---|

**GICS Sector** Financials
**Sub-Industry** Property & Casualty Insurance

**Summary** TRV, formed via the 2004 merger of Travelers Property Casualty Corp. and Saint Paul Cos., is a leading provider of commercial property-liability and homeowners and auto insurance.

## Key Stock Statistics (Source S&P, Vickers, company reports)

| | | | | | | | |
|---|---|---|---|---|---|---|---|
| 52-Wk Range | $64.17– 45.97 | S&P Oper. EPS 2011**E** | 3.41 | Market Capitalization(B) | $22.046 | Beta | 0.63 |
| Trailing 12-Month EPS | $3.91 | S&P Oper. EPS 2012**E** | 6.44 | Yield (%) | 3.07 | S&P 3-Yr. Proj. EPS CAGR(%) | 4 |
| Trailing 12-Month P/E | 13.7 | P/E on S&P Oper. EPS 2011**E** | 15.7 | Dividend Rate/Share | $1.64 | S&P Credit Rating | A |
| $10K Invested 5 Yrs Ago | $11,761 | Common Shares Outstg. (M) | 412.8 | Institutional Ownership (%) | 85 | | |

## Price Performance

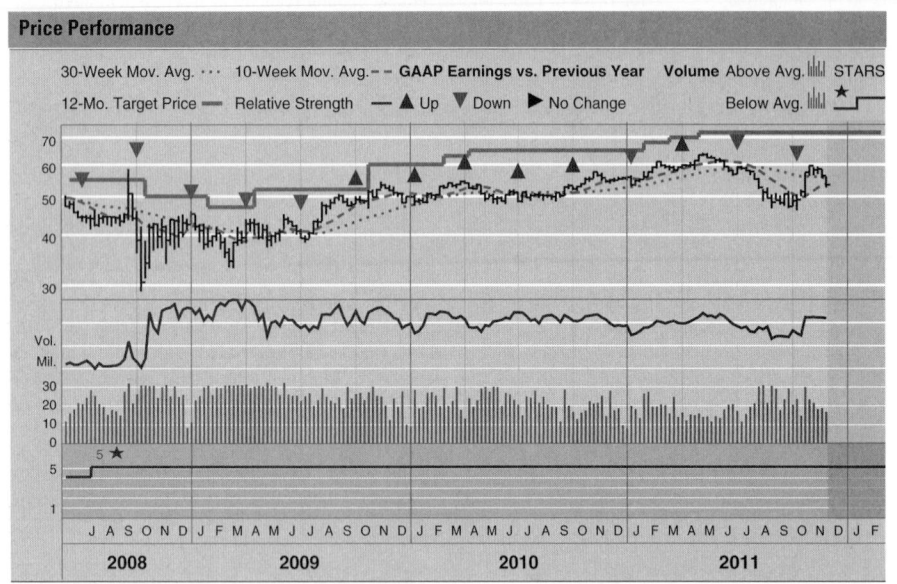

30-Week Mov. Avg. ···  10-Week Mov. Avg. - -  **GAAP Earnings vs. Previous Year**  Volume Above Avg. ▐▐▌ STARS
12-Mo. Target Price —  Relative Strength —  ▲ Up  ▼ Down  ► No Change  Below Avg. ▐▐▌ ★

Options: ASE, CBOE, Ph

Analysis prepared by Equity Analyst **Cathy Seifert** on Oct 31, 2011, when the stock traded at **$58.69**.

## Highlights

➤ We expect earned premium growth of 3% to 6% in 2011, versus the fractional rise reported for 2010. Looking ahead to 2012, earned premium growth should accelerate if an economic recovery gains traction. Our forecast of modestly higher premiums in coming periods is predicated on an increase in demand for commercial insurance products and coverage amid an economic recovery, coupled with TRV's ability to retain its existing client base and leverage new business opportunities.

➤ We believe net investment income trends will be mixed in coming periods, as a recovery in the non-fixed-income portfolio is offset by pressure on the fixed-income portfolio from lower reinvestment rates.

➤ The rebound in operating EPS expected for 2012, to $6.44 a share, from $3.41 a share forecasted for 2011, is skewed by higher catastrophe claims TRV has incurred so far in 2011. TRV reported operating EPS of $6.26 in 2010. Per share results have been helped by share repurchases, which totaled 95.7 million shares in 2010 Amid the higher catastrophe claims, TRV is reducing its share repurchase activity.

## Investment Rationale/Risk

➤ While we think the underwriting and investment environments will remain challenging in the near term, we believe TRV's shares do not appropriately reflect the actions the company has taken in recent years to improve its underwriting results and to better capitalize on what we see as a flight to quality within the property-casualty insurance market. We also view TRV as a prudent underwriter with an above-average quality balance sheet.

➤ Risks to our recommendation and target price include deterioration in asbestos and environmental claims and reserve development, erosion in underwriting trends, a surge in catastrophe losses, and erosion in the credit quality of TRV's investment portfolio.

➤ Our 12-month target price of $72 assumes a multiple of 11.2X our 2012 operating EPS estimate. Our target multiple reflects our assumption that TRV shares will trade at the midpoint of their historical valuation range, but at a slight premium to the peer group average.

## Qualitative Risk Assessment

| LOW | **MEDIUM** | HIGH |
|---|---|---|

Our risk assessment reflects our view of TRV as a leading property-casualty underwriter with a diversified mix of business and sound capital management practices. Offsetting this is our view that TRV may have to add to loss reserves for certain "long tail" liability lines of coverage, and could see impairments to its fixed-income investment portfolio.

## Quantitative Evaluations

**S&P Quality Ranking**  A-

| D | C | B- | B | B+ | **A-** | A | A+ |
|---|---|---|---|---|---|---|---|

**Relative Strength Rank**  MODERATE

70

LOWEST = 1          HIGHEST = 99

## Revenue/Earnings Data

**Revenue (Million $)**

| | 1Q | 2Q | 3Q | 4Q | Year |
|---|---|---|---|---|---|
| 2011 | 6,278 | 6,388 | 6,407 | -- | -- |
| 2010 | 6,119 | 6,179 | 6,482 | 6,332 | 25,112 |
| 2009 | 5,735 | 6,162 | 6,327 | 6,456 | 24,680 |
| 2008 | 6,232 | 6,295 | 6,145 | 5,805 | 24,477 |
| 2007 | 6,427 | 6,612 | 6,526 | 6,491 | 26,017 |
| 2006 | 6,050 | 6,255 | 6,316 | 6,469 | 25,090 |

**Earnings Per Share ($)**

| | | | | | |
|---|---|---|---|---|---|
| 2011 | 1.92 | -0.88 | 0.79 | E1.64 | E3.41 |
| 2010 | 1.25 | 1.35 | 2.11 | 1.95 | 6.62 |
| 2009 | 1.11 | 1.27 | 1.65 | 2.36 | 6.33 |
| 2008 | 1.54 | 1.54 | 0.36 | 1.35 | 4.82 |
| 2007 | 1.56 | 1.86 | 1.81 | 1.64 | 6.86 |
| 2006 | 1.41 | 1.36 | 1.47 | 1.68 | 5.91 |

Fiscal year ended Dec. 31. Next earnings report expected: NA. EPS Estimates based on S&P Operating Earnings; historical GAAP earnings are as reported.

## Dividend Data (Dates: mm/dd Payment Date: mm/dd/yy)

| Amount ($) | Date Decl. | Ex-Div. Date | Stk. of Record | Payment Date |
|---|---|---|---|---|
| 0.360 | 02/02 | 03/08 | 03/10 | 03/31/11 |
| 0.410 | 04/21 | 06/08 | 06/10 | 06/30/11 |
| 0.410 | 08/02 | 09/07 | 09/09 | 09/30/11 |
| 0.410 | 10/19 | 12/07 | 12/09 | 12/30/11 |

Dividends have been paid since 2003. Source: Company reports.

---

**Please read the Required Disclosures and Analyst Certification on the last page of this report.**

*The McGraw-Hill Companies*

# Travelers Companies Inc (The)

**STANDARD &POOR'S**

## Business Summary October 31, 2011

CORPORATE OVERVIEW. The Travelers Companies (TRV) is a leading property-casualty underwriter. Net written premiums of $21.6 billion in 2010 (versus $21.3 billion in 2009) were divided as follows: business insurance 50%; personal lines 35%; and financial, professional and international lines 15% (all of which were not significantly different from the business mix in 2009).

The business insurance lines segment offers a broad array of coverages distributed through a broad network of independent brokers and agencies in the U.S. Business insurance net written premiums of $10.9 billion in 2010 were divided as follows: commercial multi-peril 28%, workers' compensation 24%, commercial automobile 18%, commercial property 15%, and general liability and other 15%. This segment's underwriting results in 2010 deteriorated largely due to a sharp increase in catastrophe losses. The combined loss and expense ratio increased to 91.3% in 2010 (consisting of a loss ratio of 59.1% and an expense ratio of 32.2%), from 86.1% in 2009 (consisting of a loss ratio of 53.9% and an expense ratio of 32.2%).

The financial, professional and international lines segment underwrites a number of specialized lines of business, including lines of coverage related to the surety bond business, the construction industry, and certain types of professional and managerial liability. This unit operates throughout the U.S. and

in the U.K., Canada and Ireland. Net written premiums of $3.2 billion in 2010 (versus $3.3 billion in 2009) were divided as follows: general liability 26%, fidelity and surety 31%, international 38%, and other 5%. Underwriting results in this segment improved slightly in 2010. As a result, the combined (loss and expense) ratio equaled 87.7% in 2010, versus 88.1% in 2009.

The personal lines segment underwrites an array of coverage for personal risks (primarily personal automobile and homeowners' coverage) via a network of independent agencies. Net premiums written of $7.6 billion in 2010 (versus $7.1 billion in 2009) were divided as follows: personal auto 49%, and homeowners' and other 51%. At year-end 2010, the personal lines segment had approximately 7.7 million policies in force (consisting primarily of personal auto and homeowners' insurance policies). Underwriting results in 2010 deteriorated slightly amid higher catastrophe losses and a rise in underwriting expenses. Consequently, the combined ratio in 2010 was 98.3%, versus 94.6% in 2009.

## Company Financials Fiscal Year Ended Dec. 31

| Per Share Data ($) | 2010 | 2009 | 2008 | 2007 | 2006 | 2005 | 2004 | 2003 | 2002 | 2001 |
|---|---|---|---|---|---|---|---|---|---|---|
| Tangible Book Value | 49.56 | 48.03 | 36.08 | 35.56 | 31.85 | 25.66 | 20.93 | 9.52 | 10.29 | 6.66 |
| Operating Earnings | NA | NA | NA | NA | NA | NA | NA | NA | NA | NA |
| Earnings | 6.62 | 6.33 | 4.82 | 6.86 | 5.91 | 2.95 | 1.53 | 1.68 | 0.23 | 1.06 |
| S&P Core Earnings | 6.26 | 6.25 | 5.10 | 6.67 | 5.87 | 2.87 | 1.50 | 3.71 | 0.14 | 2.42 |
| Dividends | 1.41 | 1.23 | 1.19 | 1.13 | 1.01 | 0.91 | 0.74 | 0.28 | Nil | NA |
| Payout Ratio | 21% | 19% | 25% | 16% | 17% | 31% | 48% | 17% | Nil | NA |
| Prices:High | 57.55 | 54.47 | 58.57 | 56.99 | 55.00 | 46.97 | 43.31 | 17.42 | 19.50 | NA |
| Prices:Low | 47.35 | 33.07 | 28.91 | 47.26 | 40.23 | 33.70 | 16.55 | 12.98 | 12.09 | NA |
| P/E Ratio:High | 9 | 9 | 12 | 8 | 9 | 16 | 28 | 10 | 85 | NA |
| P/E Ratio:Low | 7 | 5 | 6 | 7 | 7 | 11 | 11 | 8 | 53 | NA |

| Income Statement Analysis (Million $) | | | | | | | | | | |
|---|---|---|---|---|---|---|---|---|---|---|
| Premium Income | 21,432 | 21,418 | 21,579 | 21,470 | 20,760 | 20,341 | 19,038 | 12,545 | 11,155 | 9,411 |
| Net Investment Income | 3,059 | 2,776 | 2,792 | 3,761 | 3,517 | 3,165 | 2,663 | 1,869 | 1,881 | 2,034 |
| Other Revenue | 621 | 486 | 106 | 825 | 813 | 859 | 20,271 | 725 | 1,234 | 786 |
| Total Revenue | 25,112 | 24,680 | 24,477 | 26,017 | 25,090 | 24,365 | 22,934 | 15,139 | 14,270 | 12,231 |
| Pretax Income | 4,306 | 4,711 | 3,716 | 6,216 | 5,725 | 2,671 | 1,128 | 2,229 | -260 | 1,389 |
| Net Operating Income | NA | NA | NA | NA | NA | NA | NA | NA | NA | NA |
| Net Income | 3,216 | 3,622 | 2,924 | 4,601 | 4,208 | 2,061 | 955 | 1,696 | 216 | 1,062 |
| S&P Core Earnings | 3,015 | 3,548 | 3,087 | 4,464 | 4,171 | 2,001 | 937 | 1,615 | 41.1 | 803 |

| Balance Sheet & Other Financial Data (Million $) | | | | | | | | | | |
|---|---|---|---|---|---|---|---|---|---|---|
| Cash & Equivalent | 991 | 1,080 | 1,173 | 1,132 | 1,286 | 1,098 | 933 | 714 | 432 | 865 |
| Premiums Due | 5,497 | 5,471 | 5,954 | 6,142 | 6,181 | 6,124 | 6,201 | 4,090 | 3,861 | NA |
| Investment Assets:Bonds | 62,820 | 65,847 | 61,275 | 64,920 | 62,666 | 58,983 | 54,256 | 33,046 | 30,003 | NA |
| Investment Assets:Stocks | 519 | 451 | 379 | 488 | 476 | 579 | 791 | 733 | 852 | NA |
| Investment Assets:Loans | Nil | Nil | Nil | Nil | Nil | 145 | 191 | 211 | 258 | 32,843 |
| Investment Assets:Total | 72,024 | 74,403 | 70,199 | 74,818 | 72,268 | 68,287 | 64,710 | 38,652 | 38,425 | 32,619 |
| Deferred Policy Costs | 1,782 | 1,758 | 1,774 | 1,809 | 1,615 | 1,527 | 1,559 | 925 | 873 | NA |
| Total Assets | 105,181 | 109,824 | 109,751 | 115,224 | 113,761 | 113,187 | 111,815 | 64,872 | 64,138 | 57,599 |
| Debt | 6,611 | 6,527 | 6,181 | 6,242 | 4,588 | 5,850 | 5,709 | 2,675 | 2,744 | 3,755 |
| Common Equity | 25,407 | 27,336 | 25,230 | 26,504 | 25,006 | 33,077 | 32,323 | 11,987 | 10,137 | 9,729 |
| Property & Casualty:Loss Ratio | 61.0 | 57.3 | 59.4 | 56.6 | 57.5 | 71.9 | NA | NA | NA | 80.7 |
| Property & Casualty:Expense Ratio | 32.2 | 31.9 | 32.5 | 30.8 | 30.6 | 29.4 | NA | NA | NA | 27.3 |
| Property & Casualty Combined Ratio | 93.2 | 89.2 | 91.9 | 87.4 | 88.1 | 101.3 | 107.7 | 96.9 | 117.4 | 108.0 |
| % Return on Revenue | 12.8 | 14.7 | 12.0 | 17.8 | 20.3 | 8.5 | 4.2 | 11.2 | 1.6 | 8.7 |
| % Return on Equity | 12.2 | 13.8 | 11.3 | 17.9 | 17.8 | 6.3 | 3.7 | 15.3 | NA | 10.7 |

Data as orig reptd.; bef. results of disc opers/spec. items. Per share data adj. for stk. divs.; EPS diluted. E-Estimated. NA-Not Available. NM-Not Meaningful. NR-Not Ranked. UR-Under Review.

**Office:** 385 Washington Street, Saint Paul, MN 55102.
**Telephone:** 651-310-7911.
**Website:** http://www.stpaultravelers.com
**Chrmn & CEO:** J.S. Fishman

**Pres & COO:** B.W. MacLean
**EVP & Chief Admin Officer:** A. Bessette
**EVP & CIO:** M. Lankton
**SVP & Chief Acctg Officer:** D.K. Russell

**Investor Contact:** M. Parr (860-277-0779)
**Board Members:** A. L. Beller, J. H. Dasburg, J. M. Dolan, K. M. Duberstein, J. S. Fishman, L. G. Graev, P. L. Higgins, T. R. Hodgson, C. L. Killingsworth, Jr., D. J. Shepard, L. J. Thomsen

**Founded:** 1853
**Domicile:** Minnesota
**Employees:** 32,000

*The McGraw-Hill Companies*

# T. Rowe Price Group Inc

**STANDARD &POOR'S**

| S&P Recommendation | HOLD ★★★★★ | Price $49.61 (as of Nov 25, 2011) | 12-Mo. Target Price $57.00 | Investment Style Large-Cap Growth |
|---|---|---|---|---|

**GICS Sector** Financials
**Sub-Industry** Asset Management & Custody Banks

**Summary** This company (formerly T. Rowe Price Associates) operates one of the largest no-load mutual fund complexes in the United States.

## Key Stock Statistics (Source S&P, Vickers, company reports)

| | | | | | | | |
|---|---|---|---|---|---|---|---|
| 52-Wk Range | $71.29– 44.68 | S&P Oper. EPS 2011**E** | 2.89 | Market Capitalization(B) | $12.533 | Beta | 1.64 |
| Trailing 12-Month EPS | $2.92 | S&P Oper. EPS 2012**E** | 3.15 | Yield (%) | 2.50 | S&P 3-Yr. Proj. EPS CAGR(%) | 30 |
| Trailing 12-Month P/E | 17.0 | P/E on S&P Oper. EPS 2011**E** | 17.2 | Dividend Rate/Share | $1.24 | S&P Credit Rating | NA |
| $10K Invested 5 Yrs Ago | $12,456 | Common Shares Outstg. (M) | 252.6 | Institutional Ownership (%) | 70 | | |

## Price Performance

- 30-Week Mov. Avg. · · · 10-Week Mov. Avg. - - **GAAP Earnings vs. Previous Year** Volume Above Avg. STARS
- 12-Mo. Target Price — Relative Strength — ▲ Up ▼ Down ► No Change Below Avg. ★

Options: ASE, CBOE, P, Ph

Analysis prepared by Equity Analyst **R. Shepard, CFA** on Oct 26, 2011, when the stock traded at **$51.02**.

## Highlights

➤ Third quarter results showed a net outflow from sponsored mutual funds along with a 13% year-over-year decline in investment advisory fees. We attribute most of the revenue decline to market volatility, and expect inflows to resume as financial markets stabilize. In particular, we look for a steady 2012 increase in flows into TROW's target-date retirement (fixed income) and equity funds, as baby boomers approach retirement. We expect total 2012 revenue growth of about 5%.

➤ We think increased revenues in 2012 will be partially offset by our expectation for TROW to boost advertising spending and capital expenditures. If low interest rates persist, the company may also waive money market fees, as it did in the third quarter of 2011. We see pretax margins widening in 2012 to 45.8%, from 45.4% in 2011, on an increased revenue base. We expect future compensation expenses to approach historical norms in light of TROW's strong investment performance.

➤ We see EPS of $2.89 in 2011 and $3.15 in 2012.

## Investment Rationale/Risk

➤ We think the strong relative performance of TROW's mutual funds will continue to drive asset growth. For the three-year period through September 30, 2011, 80% of the firm's funds outperformed their comparable Lipper average. Despite a healthy capital position and strong fund performance, however, we expect only modest improvement in operating margins given recent market trends favoring fixed income funds (only about 29% of TROW's total assets under management). In addition, recent market volatility may keep some retail clients on the sidelines until the investment environment stabilizes. All told, we view the shares as appropriately valued.

➤ Risks to our recommendation and target price include stock and bond market depreciation, heightened regulatory scrutiny, and increased competition.

➤ Our 12-month target price of $57 assumes a multiple of about 18X our 2012 EPS forecast of $3.15, a premium to peers based on TROW's strong fund performance and low debt levels.

## Qualitative Risk Assessment

| LOW | MEDIUM | HIGH |
|---|---|---|

Our risk assessment reflects the company's strong market share and our view of its consistent net client inflows and impressive relative investment performance, offset by industry cyclicality.

## Quantitative Evaluations

**S&P Quality Ranking** A-

| D | C | B- | B | B+ | A- | A | A+ |
|---|---|---|---|---|---|---|---|

**Relative Strength Rank** MODERATE

52

LOWEST = 1 HIGHEST = 99

## Revenue/Earnings Data

**Revenue (Million $)**

| | 1Q | 2Q | 3Q | 4Q | Year |
|---|---|---|---|---|---|
| 2011 | 682.4 | 713.7 | 679.4 | -- | -- |
| 2010 | 556.2 | 577.4 | 586.1 | 647.5 | 2,371 |
| 2009 | 384.5 | 442.2 | 498.1 | 542.6 | 1,872 |
| 2008 | 560.4 | 587.7 | 555.9 | 417.3 | 2,121 |
| 2007 | 508.4 | 551.1 | 571.0 | 597.8 | 2,233 |
| 2006 | 429.3 | 446.0 | 450.6 | 489.1 | 1,819 |

**Earnings Per Share ($)**

| | | | | | |
|---|---|---|---|---|---|
| 2011 | 0.72 | 0.76 | 0.71 | E0.70 | E2.89 |
| 2010 | 0.57 | 0.59 | 0.64 | 0.72 | 2.53 |
| 2009 | 0.19 | 0.38 | 0.50 | 0.57 | 1.65 |
| 2008 | 0.55 | 0.60 | 0.56 | 0.09 | 1.82 |
| 2007 | 0.51 | 0.58 | 0.63 | 0.68 | 2.40 |
| 2006 | 0.42 | 0.49 | 0.46 | 0.53 | 1.90 |

Fiscal year ended Dec. 31. Next earnings report expected: Late January. EPS Estimates based on S&P Operating Earnings; historical GAAP earnings are as reported.

## Dividend Data (Dates: mm/dd Payment Date: mm/dd/yy)

| Amount ($) | Date Decl. | Ex-Div. Date | Stk. of Record | Payment Date |
|---|---|---|---|---|
| 0.310 | 02/17 | 03/11 | 03/15 | 03/29/11 |
| 0.310 | 06/03 | 06/10 | 06/14 | 06/28/11 |
| 0.310 | 09/02 | 09/12 | 09/14 | 09/28/11 |
| 0.310 | 10/17 | 12/12 | 12/14 | 12/28/11 |

Dividends have been paid since 1986. Source: Company reports.

---

**Please read the Required Disclosures and Analyst Certification on the last page of this report.**

The **McGraw·Hill** Companies

# T. Rowe Price Group Inc

STANDARD
&POOR'S

## Business Summary October 26, 2011

CORPORATE OVERVIEW. T. Rowe Price Group (TROW) is the successor to an investment counseling business formed by the late Thomas Rowe Price, Jr. in 1937. It is now the investment adviser to the T. Rowe Price family of no-load mutual funds, and is one of the largest publicly held U.S. mutual fund complexes. At the end of September 2011, TROW had $453.5 billion in assets under management, down from $482 billion at the end of 2010. Prior to 2010, TROW's assets under management hit a record $400 billion in 2007. As of September 30, 2011, 71% of assets under management were invested in stock and blended asset portfolios, and 29% were invested in bond and money market portfolios.

T. Rowe Price offers mutual funds and separate accounts that employ a broad range of investment styles, including growth, value, sector-focused, tax-efficient, and quantitative index-oriented approaches. The company's investment approach is based upon a strong commitment to proprietary research, sophisticated risk-management processes, and a strict adherence to stated investment objectives. The company employs both fundamental and quantitative methods in performing security analyses, using internal equity and fixed income investment research capabilities. We believe T. Rowe Price's broad

line of no-load mutual funds makes it easy for investors to reallocate assets among funds (which is not the case at some smaller fund companies), contributing to increased client retention.

All of the company's Investor class funds are sold without a sales commission, known as no-load funds. Its Advisors and R class funds, distributed through third-party financial intermediaries, carry 12b-1 fees to cover distribution costs. TROW also manages private accounts for individuals and institutions. Revenues primarily come from investment advisory fees for managing portfolios, which depend largely on the total value and composition of assets under management. At December 31, 2010, the six largest Price funds -- Growth Stock, Equity Income, Mid-Cap Growth, Blue Chip Growth, Value, and Capital Appreciation -- accounted for 25% of investment advisory revenues in 2010 and 21% of assets under management.

## Company Financials Fiscal Year Ended Dec. 31

| Per Share Data ($) | 2010 | 2009 | 2008 | 2007 | 2006 | 2005 | 2004 | 2003 | 2002 | 2001 |
|---|---|---|---|---|---|---|---|---|---|---|
| Tangible Book Value | 10.16 | 8.57 | 7.09 | 7.97 | 6.63 | 5.21 | 3.98 | 2.66 | 1.91 | 1.68 |
| Cash Flow | 2.77 | 1.90 | 2.05 | 2.60 | 2.07 | 1.80 | 1.48 | 1.11 | 0.96 | 20.71 |
| Earnings | 2.53 | 1.65 | 1.82 | 2.40 | 1.90 | 1.58 | 1.26 | 0.89 | 0.76 | 0.76 |
| S&P Core Earnings | 2.53 | 1.72 | 2.03 | 2.40 | 1.90 | 1.43 | 1.16 | 0.78 | 0.67 | 0.65 |
| Dividends | 1.08 | 1.00 | 0.96 | 0.75 | 0.59 | 0.49 | 0.40 | 0.35 | 0.33 | 0.31 |
| Payout Ratio | 43% | 61% | 53% | 31% | 31% | 31% | 32% | 40% | 43% | 40% |
| Prices:High | 65.38 | 55.48 | 70.20 | 65.46 | 48.50 | 37.70 | 31.70 | 23.80 | 21.35 | 21.97 |
| Prices:Low | 42.81 | 20.09 | 24.26 | 44.59 | 34.87 | 27.10 | 21.92 | 19.19 | 10.63 | 11.72 |
| P/E Ratio:High | 26 | 34 | 39 | 27 | 26 | 24 | 25 | 27 | 28 | 29 |
| P/E Ratio:Low | 17 | 12 | 13 | 19 | 18 | 17 | 17 | 22 | 14 | 15 |

| Income Statement Analysis (Million $) | 2010 | 2009 | 2008 | 2007 | 2006 | 2005 | 2004 | 2003 | 2002 | 2001 |
|---|---|---|---|---|---|---|---|---|---|---|
| Income Interest | 6.40 | 7.00 | 6.40 | 5.90 | 5.40 | 4.28 | 3.78 | 3.91 | 3.06 | 32.8 |
| Income Other | 2,364 | 1,865 | 2,115 | 2,227 | 1,814 | 1,512 | 1,277 | 995 | 923 | 995 |
| Total Income | 2,371 | 1,872 | 2,121 | 2,233 | 1,819 | 1,516 | 1,280 | 999 | 926 | 1,028 |
| General Expenses | 1,268 | 1,101 | 1,206 | 1,179 | 982 | 814 | 638 | 585 | 552 | 603 |
| Interest Expense | 3.50 | 4.50 | 5.00 | 4.80 | 4.30 | 4.03 | 3.30 | 3.29 | 4.96 | 12.7 |
| Depreciation | 62.6 | 65.2 | 61.7 | 54.0 | 47.0 | 42.0 | 40.0 | 45.3 | 50.6 | 80.5 |
| Net Income | 672 | 434 | 491 | 671 | 530 | 431 | 337 | 227 | 194 | 196 |
| S&P Core Earnings | 669 | 451 | 548 | 671 | 530 | 391 | 309 | 198 | 169 | 167 |

| Balance Sheet & Other Financial Data (Million $) | 2010 | 2009 | 2008 | 2007 | 2006 | 2005 | 2004 | 2003 | 2002 | 2001 |
|---|---|---|---|---|---|---|---|---|---|---|
| Cash | 813 | 743 | 619 | 785 | 773 | 804 | 500 | 237 | 111 | 79.7 |
| Receivables | 308 | 246 | 177 | 265 | 224 | 175 | 158 | 121 | 96.8 | 104 |
| Cost of Investments | 1,142 | 906 | 721 | 1,002 | 762 | 378 | 329 | 273 | 216 | 154 |
| Total Assets | 3,642 | 3,210 | 2,819 | 3,177 | 2,765 | 2,311 | 1,929 | 1,547 | 1,370 | 1,313 |
| Loss Reserve | Nil | Nil | Nil | Nil | Nil | Nil | Nil | Nil | Nil | Nil |
| Short Term Debt | Nil | Nil | Nil | Nil | Nil | Nil | Nil | Nil | Nil | Nil |
| Capitalization:Debt | Nil | Nil | Nil | Nil | Nil | Nil | Nil | Nil | Nil | 104 |
| Capitalization:Equity | 3,297 | 2,882 | 2,489 | 2,777 | 2,427 | 2,036 | 1,697 | 1,329 | 1,189 | 1,078 |
| Capitalization:Total | 3,297 | 2,882 | 2,489 | 2,777 | 2,427 | 2,036 | 1,697 | 1,329 | 1,189 | 1,181 |
| Price Times Book Value:High | 6.4 | 6.5 | 9.0 | 8.2 | 7.3 | 7.2 | 7.9 | 9.0 | 11.2 | 13.1 |
| Price Times Book Value:Low | 4.2 | 2.3 | 3.4 | 5.6 | 5.3 | 5.2 | 5.5 | 7.2 | 5.6 | 7.0 |
| Cash Flow | 735 | 499 | 553 | 725 | 577 | 473 | 377 | 273 | 245 | 276 |
| % Expense/Operating Revenue | 56.3 | 62.5 | 56.8 | 55.4 | 52.3 | 56.7 | 63.8 | 65.8 | 65.7 | 67.8 |
| % Earnings & Depreciation/Assets | 21.4 | 16.5 | 18.4 | 24.4 | 22.7 | 22.3 | 21.7 | 18.7 | 18.3 | 19.9 |

Data as orig reptd.; bef. results of disc opers/spec. items. Per share data adj. for stk. divs.; EPS diluted. E-Estimated. NA-Not Available. NM-Not Meaningful. NR-Not Ranked. UR-Under Review.

**Office:** 100 East Pratt Street, Baltimore, MD 21202.
**Telephone:** 410-345-2000.
**Email:** info@troweprice.com
**Website:** http://www.troweprice.com

**Chrmn:** B.C. Rogers
**Pres & CEO:** J.A. Kennedy
**Vice Chrmn:** E.C. Bernard
**CFO:** K.V. Moreland

**Chief Acctg Officer & Treas:** J.M. Hiebler
**Board Members:** E. C. Bernard, J. T. Brady, J. A. Broaddus, Jr., D. B. Hebb, Jr., J. A. Kennedy, R. F. MacLellan, B. C. Rogers, A. Sommer, D. S. Taylor, A. M. Whittemore

**Founded:** 1937
**Domicile:** Maryland
**Employees:** 5,052

# Tyco International Ltd

STANDARD
&POOR'S

| | | |
|---|---|---|
| **S&P Recommendation** HOLD ★★★★★ | **Price** $44.33 (as of Nov 25, 2011) | **12-Mo. Target Price** $52.00 |

**Investment Style** Large-Cap Blend

**GICS Sector** Industrials
**Sub-Industry** Industrial Conglomerates

**Summary** Tyco split into three separate publicly traded companies in June 2007, and in September 2011, announced plans to divide its current operations into three other publicly-traded companies.

## Key Stock Statistics (Source S&P, Vickers, company reports)

| | | | | | | | |
|---|---|---|---|---|---|---|---|
| 52-Wk Range | $53.38–37.11 | S&P Oper. EPS 2012E | 3.60 | Market Capitalization(B) | $20.480 | Beta | 1.23 |
| Trailing 12-Month EPS | $3.62 | S&P Oper. EPS 2013E | 4.10 | Yield (%) | 2.26 | S&P 3-Yr. Proj. EPS CAGR(%) | 13 |
| Trailing 12-Month P/E | 12.3 | P/E on S&P Oper. EPS 2012E | 12.3 | Dividend Rate/Share | $1.00 | S&P Credit Rating | BBB |
| $10K Invested 5 Yrs Ago | NA | Common Shares Outstg. (M) | 462.0 | Institutional Ownership (%) | 85 | | |

## Price Performance

- 30-Week Mov. Avg. · · ·
- 10-Week Mov. Avg. – –
- **GAAP Earnings vs. Previous Year**
- Volume Above Avg. STARS
- 12-Mo. Target Price — Relative Strength — ▲ Up ▼ Down ► No Change
- Below Avg. ★

Options: ASE, CBOE, P, Ph

Analysis prepared by Equity Analyst **Michael Jaffe** on Oct 10, 2011, when the stock traded at **$42.92**.

### Highlights

➤ In September 2011, TYC announced plans to split up into three independent publicly traded companies. Under its current structure, we project a 5% rise in revenues in FY 12 (Sep.). Our outlook stems largely from the modest growth being seen in global economies, and our expectation of stabilization of U.S. housing markets. We expect the largest gains in the Security Solutions segment, which we see aided by higher average revenue per user, the continued addition of customers, and lower attrition rates. We also see better overall trends in client markets driving increased demand for TYC's products and services in its Fire Protection and Flow Control segments.

➤ We forecast improved margins in FY 12, aided largely by the ongoing revival in demand that we see for TYC's products and services. We also see profitability being aided by cost controls, a better revenue mix, and further incremental savings related to TYC's restructuring actions.

➤ Our FY 12 EPS forecast of $3.55 compares with our $3.15 FY 11 estimate that excludes $0.11 a share of credits in the first nine months. Operating EPS was $2.68 in FY 10.

### Investment Rationale/Risk

➤ We think that TYC's plans to divide its businesses into three separately traded public companies makes sense, as we believe it derives only limited synergies from its varied businesses and a separation should also allow each unit to become more focused and efficient. Based on these factors and our sum-of-the-parts valuation, we view TYC shares as appropriately valued at current levels.

➤ Risks to our opinion and target price include the inability of Tyco to undertake its planned separation, and a downturn in global economies.

➤ Under our sum-of-the-parts valuation, our calendar 2012 EPS estimate of $3.65 for Tyco is divided with Commercial Fire & Security accounting for $2.34 a share of earnings, Residential Security accounting for $0.71, and Flow Control representing the remaining $0.60. Because of what we view as enhanced operating opportunities for these companies as a result of the planned separation, we apply modest premium-to-peer multiples of these divisions to arrive at our target price of $52, or 14.2X our calendar 2012 forecast.

## Qualitative Risk Assessment

| LOW | MEDIUM | HIGH |
|---|---|---|

Our risk assessment reflects what we see as strong cash flow characteristics and high levels of recurring revenues in a number of Tyco's businesses. However, at the same time, many of Tyco's business segments are highly cyclical in nature.

## Quantitative Evaluations

**S&P Quality Ranking** NR

| D | C | B- | B | B+ | A- | A | A+ |
|---|---|---|---|---|---|---|---|

**Relative Strength Rank** STRONG

76

LOWEST = 1     HIGHEST = 99

## Revenue/Earnings Data

**Revenue (Million $)**

| | 1Q | 2Q | 3Q | 4Q | Year |
|---|---|---|---|---|---|
| 2011 | 4,379 | 3,992 | 4,293 | 4,691 | 17,355 |
| 2010 | 4,246 | 4,169 | 4,274 | 4,493 | 17,016 |
| 2009 | 4,426 | 4,150 | 4,240 | 4,421 | 17,237 |
| 2008 | 4,870 | 4,866 | 5,215 | 5,284 | 20,199 |
| 2007 | 10,329 | 10,838 | 5,085 | 5,028 | 18,781 |
| 2006 | 9,603 | 10,093 | 10,504 | 10,760 | 40,960 |

**Earnings Per Share ($)**

| | | | | | |
|---|---|---|---|---|---|
| 2011 | 1.00 | 0.67 | 0.76 | 0.83 | 3.27 |
| 2010 | 0.63 | 0.65 | 0.50 | 0.55 | 2.31 |
| 2009 | 0.57 | -5.40 | 0.51 | 0.44 | -3.87 |
| 2008 | 0.74 | 0.56 | 0.41 | 0.55 | 2.25 |
| 2007 | 1.48 | 1.68 | -6.13 | 0.42 | -5.09 |
| 2006 | 1.56 | 2.08 | 1.72 | 2.52 | 7.88 |

Fiscal year ended Sep. 30. Next earnings report expected: Late January. EPS Estimates based on S&P Operating Earnings; historical GAAP earnings are as reported.

## Dividend Data (Dates: mm/dd Payment Date: mm/dd/yy)

| Amount ($) | Date Decl. | Ex-Div. Date | Stk. of Record | Payment Date |
|---|---|---|---|---|
| 0.231 | 09/09 | 10/27 | 10/29 | 11/23/10 |
| 0.250 | 03/09 | 10/26 | 10/28 | 11/17/11 |

Dividends have been paid since 1975. Source: Company reports.

---

**Please read the Required Disclosures and Analyst Certification on the last page of this report.**

The McGraw-Hill Companies

# Tyco International Ltd

STANDARD
&POOR'S

## Business Summary October 10, 2011

CORPORATE OVERVIEW. In September 2011, Tyco International announced that it planned to separate into three independent, publicly traded companies. The units will be North American Residential Security; Flow Control; and Commercial Fire and Security. The North American Residential Security business will consist of its ADT unit's residential business, which serves more than six million homes and businesses. The unit will have annualized revenue of about $3 billion, and about 16,000 employees. The Flow Control unit will consist of TYC's current unit of that name, which makes pipes and valves and other products, and is expected to have annual revenues of $4 billion, and 15,000 employees. The Commercial Fire and Security unit will combine TYC's non-residential security business with the current Fire Protection segment, which will have about $10 billion of annual revenues, and 69,000 employees. Consummation of the plan was subject to final approval by TYC directors and shareholders, and the effectiveness of certain regulatory documents.

Prior to the current split-up plan, Tyco International divided its portfolio of businesses into three separate publicly traded companies on June 29, 2007. TYC maintained the units that had been part of its Fire & Security and Engineered Products & Services divisions, and spun off its Healthcare (now Covidien; COV) and Electronics (trading as Tyco Electronics; TEL) units. Subsequently, in FY 11's (Sep.) first quarter, TYC sold a 51% stake in its Electrical & Metal Products business (now operating as Atkore International Group) to

Clayton Dubilier & Rice, LLC, for $713 million in cash (recording a gain of $259 million); and realigned its other businesses into three separate segments (previously operating as four), including two new ones. Tyco's businesses are currently Tyco Security Solutions, Tyco Fire Protection and Flow Control. Tyco derived 51% of its revenues outside the U.S. in FY 10 (including contributions from the former Electrical & Metal Products segment), with the Europe, Middle East and Africa region accounting for 23% of total revenues, Asia/Pacific 18% and Other Americas 10%.

The company's Flow Control division manufactures and services valves, pipes, fittings, valve automation and heat tracing products for the general process, energy, mining, and water and wastewater industries. The company also continues to hold a 49% equity stake in Atkore International, which makes steel tubing and pipe products, pre-wired armored electrical cables, electrical support systems and metal framing systems, which are used primarily by trade contractors in the construction and modernization of non-residential structures.

## Company Financials Fiscal Year Ended Sep. 30

| Per Share Data ($) | 2011 | 2010 | 2009 | 2008 | 2007 | 2006 | 2005 | 2004 | 2003 | 2002 |
|---|---|---|---|---|---|---|---|---|---|---|
| Tangible Book Value | NA | 2.17 | 3.17 | 2.84 | 2.49 | 10.92 | 5.56 | NM | NM | NM |
| Cash Flow | 6.02 | 4.77 | -1.48 | 4.61 | -2.76 | 11.79 | 9.78 | 9.35 | 5.01 | -2.09 |
| Earnings | 3.27 | 2.31 | -3.87 | 2.25 | -5.09 | 7.88 | 6.04 | 5.64 | 2.08 | -6.16 |
| Dividends | 0.23 | 0.66 | 0.61 | 0.35 | 1.90 | 1.20 | 1.60 | 0.20 | 0.20 | 0.20 |
| Payout Ratio | 7% | 29% | NM | 16% | NM | 15% | 26% | 4% | 10% | NM |
| Prices:High | 53.38 | 42.65 | 37.33 | 47.95 | 137.92 | 127.44 | 146.32 | 145.68 | 108.72 | 235.24 |
| Prices:Low | 37.39 | 33.84 | 17.25 | 15.17 | 37.46 | 98.60 | 102.64 | 104.04 | 44.80 | 27.92 |
| P/E Ratio:High | 16 | 18 | NM | 21 | NM | 16 | 24 | 26 | 52 | NM |
| P/E Ratio:Low | 11 | 15 | NM | 7 | NM | 13 | 17 | 18 | 22 | NM |

| Income Statement Analysis (Million $) | | | | | | | | | | |
|---|---|---|---|---|---|---|---|---|---|---|
| Revenue | 17,355 | 17,016 | 17,237 | 20,199 | 18,781 | 40,960 | 39,727 | 40,153 | 36,801 | 35,644 |
| Operating Income | 3,335 | 2,897 | 2,570 | 3,324 | 1,720 | 7,754 | 7,637 | 7,957 | 5,568 | 6,509 |
| Depreciation | 1,318 | 1,203 | 1,133 | 1,154 | 1,151 | 2,065 | 2,100 | 2,176 | 1,472 | 2,033 |
| Interest Expense | NA | NA | 301 | 396 | 313 | 713 | 815 | 963 | 1,148 | 1,077 |
| Pretax Income | 1,893 | 1,270 | -1,751 | 1,431 | -2,181 | 4,884 | 4,192 | 4,159 | 1,803 | -2,811 |
| Effective Tax Rate | NA | NA | NM | 23.4% | NM | 16.4% | 23.5% | 27.4% | 42.4% | NM |
| Net Income | 1,567 | 1,125 | -1,833 | 1,095 | -2,519 | 4,075 | 3,199 | 3,005 | 1,035 | -3,070 |

| Balance Sheet & Other Financial Data (Million $) | | | | | | | | | | |
|---|---|---|---|---|---|---|---|---|---|---|
| Cash | 1,450 | 1,775 | 2,354 | 1,519 | 1,894 | 2,926 | 3,196 | 4,467 | 4,329 | 6,383 |
| Current Assets | NA | NA | 7,967 | 8,541 | 12,345 | 18,785 | 18,537 | 18,545 | 17,240 | 19,765 |
| Total Assets | 26,777 | 27,128 | 25,553 | 28,804 | 32,815 | 63,722 | 62,621 | 63,667 | 63,545 | 66,414 |
| Current Liabilities | NA | NA | 4,716 | 5,657 | 9,101 | 11,066 | 11,835 | 11,152 | 10,572 | 19,632 |
| Long Term Debt | 4,092 | 3,652 | 4,029 | 3,709 | 4,076 | 9,365 | 10,600 | 14,617 | 18,251 | 16,487 |
| Common Equity | 14,182 | 14,084 | 12,941 | 15,494 | 15,624 | 35,419 | 32,450 | 30,292 | 26,369 | 24,791 |
| Total Capital | 18,470 | 17,753 | 16,983 | 19,217 | 19,767 | 44,838 | 43,111 | 44,977 | 44,733 | 41,320 |
| Capital Expenditures | 788 | 718 | 709 | 734 | 669 | 1,569 | 1,272 | 1,015 | 1,170 | 1,709 |
| Cash Flow | 2,885 | 2,328 | -700 | 2,249 | -1,368 | 6,140 | 5,299 | 5,181 | 2,507 | -1,037 |
| Current Ratio | 1.5 | 1.4 | 1.7 | 1.5 | 1.4 | 1.7 | 1.6 | 1.7 | 1.6 | 1.0 |
| % Long Term Debt of Capitalization | 22.2 | 20.6 | 23.7 | 19.3 | 20.6 | 20.9 | 24.6 | 32.5 | 40.8 | 39.9 |
| % Net Income of Revenue | 9.0 | 6.6 | NM | 5.4 | NM | 9.9 | 8.1 | 7.5 | 2.8 | NM |
| % Return on Assets | 5.8 | 4.3 | NM | 3.6 | NM | 6.4 | 5.1 | 4.7 | 1.6 | NM |
| % Return on Equity | 11.1 | 8.3 | NM | 7.0 | NM | 12.0 | 10.2 | 10.6 | 4.1 | NM |

Data as orig reptd.; bef. results of disc opers/spec. items. Per share data adj. for stk. divs.; EPS diluted. E-Estimated. NA-Not Available. NM-Not Meaningful. NR-Not Ranked. UR-Under Review.

**Office:** Freier Platz 10, Schaffhausen, Switzerland 8200.
**Telephone:** 41 52 633 02 44.
**Email:** info@tyco.com
**Website:** http://www.tyco.com

**Chrmn & CEO:** E.D. Breen
**EVP & CFO:** F.S. Sklarsky
**EVP & General Counsel:** J.A. Reinsdorf
**SVP, Chief Acctg Officer & Cntlr:** C.A. Davidson

**Treas:** A. Nayar
**Investor Contact:** A. Franzen (609-720-4665)
**Board Members:** E. D. Breen, M. E. Daniels, T. M. Donahue, B. Duperreault, B. S. Gordon, R. L. Gupta, R. L. Gupta, J. A. Krol, B. R. O'Neill, D. C. Paliwal, W. S. Stavropoulos, S. S. Wijnberg, R. D. Yost

**Founded:** 1960
**Domicile:** Switzerland
**Employees:** 102,000

# Tyson Foods Inc.

**STANDARD &POOR'S**

| S&P Recommendation **HOLD** ★★★☆☆ | Price<br>$19.25 (as of Nov 25, 2011) | 12-Mo. Target Price<br>$20.00 | Investment Style<br>Large-Cap Blend |
|---|---|---|---|

**GICS Sector** Consumer Staples
**Sub-Industry** Packaged Foods & Meats

**Summary** Tyson is one of the world's largest suppliers of beef, chicken and pork products.

## Key Stock Statistics (Source S&P, Vickers, company reports)

| | | | | | | | |
|---|---|---|---|---|---|---|---|
| 52-Wk Range | $20.12– 15.60 | S&P Oper. EPS 2012**E** | 2.06 | Market Capitalization(B) | $5.771 | Beta | 1.12 |
| Trailing 12-Month EPS | $1.97 | S&P Oper. EPS 2013**E** | NA | Yield (%) | 0.83 | S&P 3-Yr. Proj. EPS CAGR(%) | 5 |
| Trailing 12-Month P/E | 9.8 | P/E on S&P Oper. EPS 2012**E** | 9.3 | Dividend Rate/Share | $0.16 | S&P Credit Rating | BBB- |
| $10K Invested 5 Yrs Ago | $13,030 | Common Shares Outstg. (M) | 369.8 | Institutional Ownership (%) | 88 | | |

## Price Performance

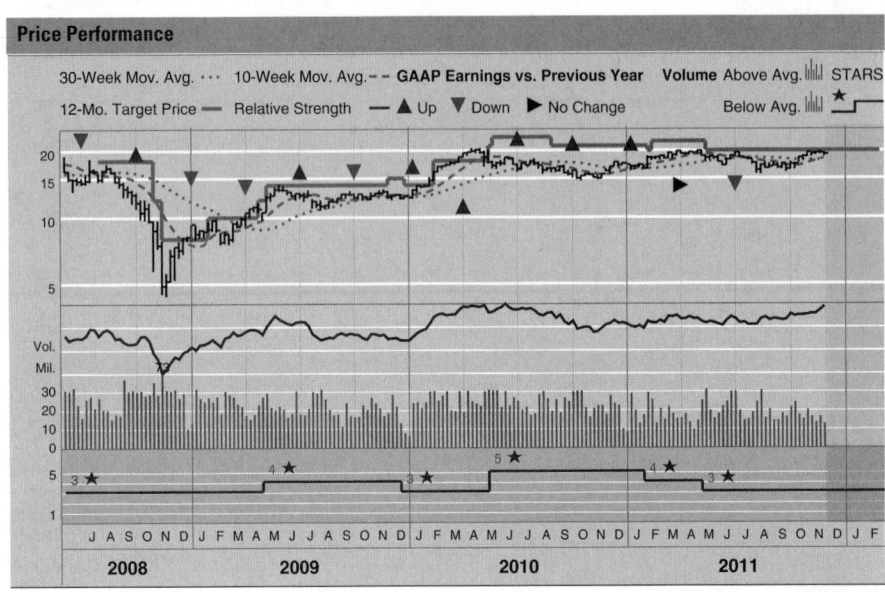

30-Week Mov. Avg. ···· 10-Week Mov. Avg. -- **GAAP Earnings vs. Previous Year**   **Volume** Above Avg. ▊▊ STARS
12-Mo. Target Price — Relative Strength — ▲ Up ▼ Down ▶ No Change   Below Avg. ▊▊ ★

Options: ASE, CBOE, P

Analysis prepared by Equity Analyst **Tom Graves, CFA** on Oct 14, 2011, when the stock traded at **$18.22**.

## Highlights

▶ In FY 12 (Sep.), we look for sales to increase about 5% from the $32.2 billion we project for FY 11, largely due to higher prices. We think chicken prices are likely to benefit if industry production declines. In both fiscal years, we look for beef and chicken to be the largest business segments, based on sales, but for pork to provide the highest segment operating profit margin.

▶ We look for overall profit margin pressure on TSN to ease if prices for corn and wheat used in feed grain remain sharply below the peak levels reached earlier in 2011. Also, we anticipate that TSN's chicken segment will benefit from operating efficiencies.

▶ For FY 12, we project EPS of $2.00, including the prospect of some pressure from higher feed costs in at least the first quarter of the fiscal year. For FY 11, we estimate operating EPS of $1.95, which excludes a benefit of about $0.08 a share from special items in FY 11's first nine months. In FY 10, reported diluted EPS of $2.06 includes a net adverse impact of about $0.13 from special items.

## Investment Rationale/Risk

▶ Over time, we think TSN, as a major diversified protein supplier, is positioned to benefit from improving economic conditions, including rising incomes, and changing diets in developing international markets. We expect TSN's strategy to include a focus on expansion in value-added food products. Meanwhile, in FY 11, we look for capital expenditures to have been about $650 million, up from $550 million in FY 10. We expect that at least a portion of TSN's capital expenditures will result in operational cost savings or improvements.

▶ Risks to our recommendation and target price include weaker-than-expected demand and prices, industry production that is higher than anticipated, higher-than-expected feed costs, and an adverse impact from currency exchange rate fluctuations.

▶ Our 12-month target price of $20 is based on a multiple of 12.6X our calendar 2011 EPS estimate of $1.59, which is similar to a recent average P/E for a small peer group. We think the valuation of TSN shares will be limited by some concern about the extent to which TSN could be vulnerable if grain feed prices move significantly higher.

## Qualitative Risk Assessment

| LOW | MEDIUM | **HIGH** |
|---|---|---|

Our risk assessment reflects the company's cyclical operations, which can be significantly affected by exposure to commodity crop and meat markets, and regulations related to international trade.

## Quantitative Evaluations

**S&P Quality Ranking**   B-

| D | C | **B-** | B | B+ | A- | A | A+ |
|---|---|---|---|---|---|---|---|

**Relative Strength Rank**   **STRONG**

91

LOWEST = 1   HIGHEST = 99

## Revenue/Earnings Data

**Revenue (Million $)**

| | 1Q | 2Q | 3Q | 4Q | Year |
|---|---|---|---|---|---|
| 2011 | 7,615 | 8,000 | 8,247 | -- | 32,266 |
| 2010 | 6,635 | 6,916 | 7,438 | 7,441 | 28,430 |
| 2009 | 6,521 | 6,307 | 66,620 | 7,214 | 26,704 |
| 2008 | 6,766 | 6,612 | 6,849 | 7,201 | 26,862 |
| 2007 | 6,558 | 6,501 | 6,958 | 6,883 | 26,900 |
| 2006 | 6,454 | 6,251 | 6,383 | 6,471 | 25,559 |

**Earnings Per Share ($)**

| | | | | | |
|---|---|---|---|---|---|
| 2011 | 0.78 | 0.42 | 0.51 | E0.32 | 2.04 |
| 2010 | 0.44 | 0.42 | 0.68 | 0.55 | 2.06 |
| 2009 | -0.30 | -0.24 | -0.37 | -1.22 | -1.47 |
| 2008 | 0.10 | 0.20 | -0.01 | 0.13 | 0.24 |
| 2007 | 0.16 | 0.20 | 0.31 | 0.09 | 0.75 |
| 2006 | 0.11 | -0.37 | -0.15 | -0.15 | -0.56 |

Fiscal year ended Sep. 30. Next earnings report expected: Early February. EPS Estimates based on S&P Operating Earnings; historical GAAP earnings are as reported.

## Dividend Data (Dates: mm/dd Payment Date: mm/dd/yy)

| Amount ($) | Date Decl. | Ex-Div. Date | Stk. of Record | Payment Date |
|---|---|---|---|---|
| 0.040 | 02/03 | 05/27 | 06/01 | 06/15/11 |
| 0.040 | 05/05 | 08/30 | 09/01 | 09/15/11 |
| 0.040 | 08/05 | 11/29 | 12/01 | 12/15/11 |
| 0.040 | 11/17 | 02/28 | 03/01 | 03/15/12 |

Dividends have been paid since 1976. Source: Company reports.

---

**Please read the Required Disclosures and Analyst Certification on the last page of this report.**

**The McGraw-Hill Companies**

# Tyson Foods Inc.

STANDARD
&POOR'S

## Business Summary October 14, 2011

CORPORATE OVERVIEW. Tyson Foods is one of the world's largest suppliers of beef, chicken and pork products. It produces a wide variety of brand name protein-based and prepared food products, marketed in the U.S. and some 90 countries around the world.

Most of TSN's operations are in the U.S., and about 96% of FY 10 (Sep.) sales to external customers were sourced from the U.S. TSN's export sales totaled $3.2 billion in FY 10, up from $2.7 billion in FY 09. Export markets include Canada, Central America, China, the European Union, Japan, Mexico, the Middle East, Russia, South Korea, Taiwan and Vietnam. In FY 10, TSN's largest customer, Wal-Mart Stores, Inc., accounted for 13.4% of consolidated sales

CORPORATE STRATEGY. TSN seeks to identify target markets for value-added products; concentrate production, sales and marketing efforts to enhance product demand; and utilize national distribution systems and customer support services. We think the company's scale and diversified product mix is a competitive advantage.

The beef segment (40% of FY 10 segment sales) includes the slaughter of live cattle and fabrication into primal and sub-primal meat cuts and case-ready products. Operations include sales from allied products such as hides and va-

riety meats. The company's products are marketed to various channels, including food retailers, foodservice distributors, restaurant operators and others. The company does not have facilities of its own to raise cattle, but has cattle buyers located in cattle producing areas who visit independent feed yards and buy live cattle on the open spot market.

The chicken segment (34%) includes fresh, frozen and value-added chicken products sold domestically through various channels, including retailers, foodservice distributors, restaurant operators and foodservice establishments such as schools, hotel chains, health care facilities and the military; and also to international markets. Included in this segment are sales from allied products and TSN's chicken breeding stock subsidiary. The segment's raw material includes live chickens that are raised primarily by independent contractors. Corn and soybean meal are also major production costs, and in FY 10 represented roughly 42% of TSN's cost of growing a live chicken.

## Company Financials Fiscal Year Ended Sep. 30

| Per Share Data ($) | 2011 | 2010 | 2009 | 2008 | 2007 | 2006 | 2005 | 2004 | 2003 | 2002 |
|---|---|---|---|---|---|---|---|---|---|---|
| Tangible Book Value | NA | 8.24 | 5.98 | 6.30 | 5.96 | 5.05 | 5.66 | 4.49 | 3.17 | 2.92 |
| Cash Flow | NA | 3.37 | -0.22 | 1.57 | 2.20 | 1.31 | 2.39 | 2.50 | 2.26 | 2.39 |
| Earnings | 2.04 | 2.06 | -1.47 | 0.24 | 0.75 | -0.56 | 0.99 | 1.13 | 0.96 | 1.08 |
| S&P Core Earnings | 1.94 | 2.05 | 0.05 | 0.20 | 0.64 | -0.56 | 1.06 | 1.10 | 0.64 | 1.02 |
| Dividends | 0.20 | 0.16 | 0.16 | 0.16 | 0.16 | 0.16 | 0.16 | 0.16 | 0.16 | 0.16 |
| Payout Ratio | 10% | 8% | NM | 67% | 21% | NM | 16% | 14% | 17% | 15% |
| Prices:High | 20.12 | 20.57 | 14.25 | 67.00 | 24.32 | 17.33 | 19.91 | 21.28 | 15.10 | 15.71 |
| Prices:Low | 15.60 | 12.15 | 7.51 | 4.40 | 13.50 | 12.57 | 12.50 | 12.97 | 7.25 | 9.27 |
| P/E Ratio:High | 10 | 10 | NM | 81 | 32 | NM | 20 | 19 | 16 | 15 |
| P/E Ratio:Low | 8 | 6 | NM | 18 | 18 | NM | 13 | 11 | 8 | 9 |

| Income Statement Analysis (Million $) | | | | | | | | | | |
|---|---|---|---|---|---|---|---|---|---|---|
| Revenue | NA | 28,430 | 26,704 | 26,862 | 26,900 | 25,559 | 26,014 | 26,441 | 24,549 | 23,367 |
| Operating Income | NA | 2,082 | 817 | 878 | 1,130 | 510 | 1,266 | 1,415 | 837 | 1,407 |
| Depreciation | NA | 497 | 455 | 471 | 514 | 517 | 501 | 490 | 458 | 467 |
| Interest Expense | NA | 347 | 313 | 218 | 232 | 268 | 227 | 275 | 592 | 305 |
| Pretax Income | NA | 1,203 | -526 | 154 | 410 | -293 | 528 | 635 | 523 | 593 |
| Effective Tax Rate | NA | NA | NM | 44.2% | 34.6% | NM | 33.1% | 36.5% | 35.6% | 35.4% |
| Net Income | NA | 780 | -536 | 86.0 | 268 | -191 | 353 | 403 | 337 | 383 |
| S&P Core Earnings | 738 | 776 | 21.4 | 71.1 | 228 | -190 | 379 | 392 | 224 | 365 |

| Balance Sheet & Other Financial Data (Million $) | | | | | | | | | | |
|---|---|---|---|---|---|---|---|---|---|---|
| Cash | NA | 978 | 1,004 | 250 | 42.0 | 28.0 | 40.0 | 33.0 | 25.0 | 51.0 |
| Current Assets | NA | 4,618 | 4,375 | 4,361 | 3,596 | 4,187 | 3,485 | 3,532 | 3,371 | 3,144 |
| Total Assets | NA | 10,752 | 10,595 | 10,850 | 10,227 | 11,121 | 10,504 | 10,464 | 10,486 | 10,372 |
| Current Liabilities | NA | 2,545 | 1,993 | 2,103 | 2,115 | 2,846 | 2,157 | 2,293 | 2,475 | 2,093 |
| Long Term Debt | NA | 2,135 | 3,333 | 2,888 | 2,642 | 2,987 | 2,869 | 3,024 | 3,114 | 3,733 |
| Common Equity | NA | 5,166 | 4,352 | 5,014 | 4,731 | 4,900 | 4,615 | 4,912 | 3,954 | 3,662 |
| Total Capital | NA | 7,801 | 8,002 | 8,193 | 7,740 | 8,382 | 8,141 | 8,631 | 7,790 | 8,038 |
| Capital Expenditures | NA | 550 | 368 | 425 | 285 | 531 | 571 | 486 | 402 | 433 |
| Cash Flow | NA | 1,277 | -81.0 | 557 | 782 | 326 | 854 | 893 | 795 | 850 |
| Current Ratio | NA | 1.8 | 2.2 | 2.1 | 1.7 | 1.5 | 1.6 | 1.5 | 1.4 | 1.5 |
| % Long Term Debt of Capitalization | NA | 27.4 | 41.7 | 35.3 | 34.1 | 35.6 | 35.2 | 35.0 | 40.0 | 46.4 |
| % Net Income of Revenue | NA | 2.7 | NM | 0.3 | 1.0 | NM | 1.4 | 1.5 | 1.4 | 1.6 |
| % Return on Assets | NA | 7.3 | NM | 0.8 | 2.5 | NM | 3.4 | 3.8 | 3.2 | 3.6 |
| % Return on Equity | NA | 16.4 | NM | 1.8 | 5.6 | NM | 7.9 | 8.5 | 8.8 | 10.9 |

Data as orig reptd.; bef. results of disc opers/spec. items. Per share data adj. for stk. divs.; EPS diluted. E-Estimated. NA-Not Available. NM-Not Meaningful. NR-Not Ranked. UR-Under Review.

**Office:** 2200 Don Tyson Parkway, Springdale, AR 72762-6999.
**Telephone:** 479-290-4000.
**Email:** tysonir@tyson.com
**Website:** http://www.tyson.com

**Chrmn:** J.H. Tyson
**Pres & CEO:** D. Smith
**COO:** J.V. Lochner
**EVP & CFO:** D. Leatherby

**EVP & General Counsel:** D.L. Van Bebber
**Investor Contact:** J. Kathol
**Board Members:** K. M. Bader, G. E. Banister, Jr., J. D. Kever, K. M. McNamara, B. T. Sauer, R. C. Thurber, B. A. Tyson, J. H. Tyson, A. C. Zapanta

**Founded:** 1935
**Domicile:** Delaware
**Employees:** 115,000

# Union Pacific Corp

**STANDARD &POOR'S**

| S&P Recommendation **HOLD** ★★★☆☆ | Price $95.16 (as of Nov 25, 2011) | 12-Mo. Target Price $107.00 | Investment Style Large-Cap Blend |
| --- | --- | --- | --- |

**GICS Sector** Industrials
**Sub-Industry** Railroads

**Summary** Union Pacific operates the largest U.S. railroad, with over 32,000 miles of rail serving the western two-thirds of the country.

## Key Stock Statistics (Source S&P, Vickers, company reports)

| | | | | | | | |
| --- | --- | --- | --- | --- | --- | --- | --- |
| 52-Wk Range | $107.89– 77.73 | S&P Oper. EPS 2011**E** | 6.49 | Market Capitalization(B) | $45.970 | Beta | 1.17 |
| Trailing 12-Month EPS | $6.29 | S&P Oper. EPS 2012**E** | 7.46 | Yield (%) | 2.52 | S&P 3-Yr. Proj. EPS CAGR(%) | 15 |
| Trailing 12-Month P/E | 15.1 | P/E on S&P Oper. EPS 2011**E** | 14.7 | Dividend Rate/Share | $2.40 | S&P Credit Rating | BBB+ |
| $10K Invested 5 Yrs Ago | $22,643 | Common Shares Outstg. (M) | 483.1 | Institutional Ownership (%) | 85 | | |

## Price Performance

30-Week Mov. Avg. · · · 10-Week Mov. Avg. - - GAAP Earnings vs. Previous Year   Volume Above Avg. STARS
12-Mo. Target Price — Relative Strength  — ▲ Up  ▼ Down  ► No Change   Below Avg.

Options: CBOE, Ph

Analysis prepared by Equity Analyst **Kevin Kirkeby** on Oct 27, 2011, when the stock traded at **$103.50**.

### Highlights

➤ Following an expected 15% increase in 2011, we look for revenues to grow 6.5% in 2012. This reflects projected 3.0% growth in volume and a 3.5% improvement in yield. UNP will continue to benefit from contract renewals, in our view, as several come due either in the fourth quarter of this year or during 2012. We expect fuel surcharge revenues to be largely unchanged next year from 2011 levels. Energy-related carloads and domestic intermodal will be the strongest shipment categories, in our view, while grain should lag due to reduced supplies.

➤ We expect operating expenses to rise as volumes increase in 2012, due to higher wages and incentive compensation. However, we still anticipate a widening of margins during the year due to improved pricing and fuel surcharge coverage in contract renewals. We also anticipate greater asset utilization, visible in both cars per train and ton-miles per employee.

➤ Our EPS estimate for 2011 of $6.49 incorporates a 2.6% reduction in average share count following the anticipated buyback of 10.1 million shares.

### Investment Rationale/Risk

➤ We think a valuation above the midpoint of the historical range is warranted, as we balance the potential for favorable pricing on contract renewals and ongoing volume gains with our expectation that operating costs will start to rise as certain volume thresholds are reached, and what we see as UNP's above peer average investment requirements, including positive train control (PTC) requirements.

➤ Risks to our recommendation and target price include a slower-than-expected recovery in the economy, reduced coal consumption by utilities as a result of government efforts to control carbon dioxide emissions, labor unrest and a faster rate of growth in wages, as well as more regulatory oversight of railroad pricing.

➤ Our relative valuation model suggests an enterprise value-to-EBITDA multiple, using our four-quarter forward estimate, of 8.0X, above the midpoint of the 10-year range but not top quartile, and yields a value of $109. Our discounted cash flow model, which assumes a 10.5% cost of equity, annual free cash flow growth of 11% for five years, and a 3.5% terminal growth rate, estimates an intrinsic value of $105. Blending, we arrive at our 12-month target price of $107.

## Qualitative Risk Assessment

| LOW | **MEDIUM** | HIGH |
| --- | --- | --- |

Our risk assessment reflects UNP's exposure to economic cycles, regulations, and labor and fuel costs, coupled with significant capital expenditure requirements, offset by our view of the company's historically positive cash flow generation and moderate financial leverage.

## Quantitative Evaluations

**S&P Quality Ranking**   A

| D | C | B- | B | B+ | A- | **A** | A+ |
| --- | --- | --- | --- | --- | --- | --- | --- |

**Relative Strength Rank**   STRONG

75

LOWEST = 1        HIGHEST = 99

## Revenue/Earnings Data

**Revenue (Million $)**

| | 1Q | 2Q | 3Q | 4Q | Year |
| --- | --- | --- | --- | --- | --- |
| 2011 | 4,490 | 4,858 | 5,101 | -- | -- |
| 2010 | 3,965 | 4,182 | 4,408 | 4,410 | 16,965 |
| 2009 | 3,415 | 3,303 | 3,671 | 3,754 | 14,143 |
| 2008 | 4,270 | 4,568 | 4,846 | 4,286 | 17,970 |
| 2007 | 3,849 | 4,046 | 4,191 | 4,197 | 16,283 |
| 2006 | 3,710 | 3,923 | 3,983 | 3,962 | 15,578 |

**Earnings Per Share ($)**

| | 1Q | 2Q | 3Q | 4Q | Year |
| --- | --- | --- | --- | --- | --- |
| 2011 | 1.29 | 1.59 | 1.85 | E1.75 | E6.49 |
| 2010 | 1.01 | 1.40 | 1.56 | 1.56 | 5.53 |
| 2009 | 0.72 | 0.92 | 1.02 | 1.08 | 3.75 |
| 2008 | 0.85 | 1.02 | 1.38 | 1.31 | 4.54 |
| 2007 | 0.71 | 0.83 | 1.00 | 0.93 | 3.46 |
| 2006 | 0.58 | 0.72 | 0.77 | 0.89 | 2.96 |

Fiscal year ended Dec. 31. Next earnings report expected: Late January. EPS Estimates based on S&P Operating Earnings; historical GAAP earnings are as reported.

## Dividend Data (Dates: mm/dd Payment Date: mm/dd/yy)

| Amount ($) | Date Decl. | Ex-Div. Date | Stk. of Record | Payment Date |
| --- | --- | --- | --- | --- |
| 0.380 | 02/03 | 02/24 | 02/28 | 04/01/11 |
| 0.475 | 05/05 | 05/26 | 05/31 | 07/01/11 |
| 0.475 | 07/28 | 08/29 | 08/31 | 10/03/11 |
| 0.600 | 11/17 | 11/28 | 11/30 | 01/02/12 |

Dividends have been paid since 1900. Source: Company reports.

**Please read the Required Disclosures and Analyst Certification on the last page of this report.**

The McGraw·Hill Companies

# Union Pacific Corp

**STANDARD &POOR'S**

## Business Summary October 27, 2011

CORPORATE OVERVIEW. Union Pacific operates the largest U.S. railroad, with a network that spans about 32,200 miles, linking Pacific Coast and Gulf Coast ports to midwestern and eastern gateways. The rail lines touch 23 states, as well as the Mexican and Canadian borders. Energy accounted for 22% of freight revenues and 23% of carloadings in 2010. UNP is a major transporter of low-sulfur coal, with about 67% of its energy traffic consisting of coal originating in the Powder River Basin of Wyoming and Montana, primarily delivered to power utilities. In 2010, UNP's intermodal business represented 20% of freight revenue, and accounted for a much larger 38% of total carloads. The industrial products category represented another 16% of freight revenues, while chemicals, agricultural products and automotive contributed 15%, 19% and 8%, respectively, of 2010 freight revenues.

COMPETITIVE LANDSCAPE. The U.S. rail industry has an oligopoly-like structure, with over 80% of revenues generated by the four largest railroads: UNP and Burlington Northern Santa Fe Corp. operating on the West Coast, and CSX Corp. and Norfolk Southern Corp. operating on the East Coast. Railroads simultaneously compete for customers while cooperating by sharing assets, interfacing systems, and completing customer movements. Railroads also compete with trucking, shipping, and pipeline transportation. Rail rates are generally lower than trucking rates, as service is slower and less flexible, in our view, than trucking, which provides most U.S. transportation. We believe the rising price of fuel increases the cost attractiveness of railroads over less fuel-efficient trucking, which should help support industry volumes over the next five years. While large freight integrators, coal and utility companies may exert more pricing power than smaller customers, there has been an increase in shippers across the rail industry filing complaints with the Surface Transportation Board (STB) alleging excessive pricing. In a July 2009 ruling, the STB determined that UNP was seeking rate increases from Oklahoma Gas & Electric that exceeded permissible levels. The STB ordered UNP to reimburse the shipper for amounts already collected, and effectively capped the rate on those particular moves through 2018. We note that UNP has legacy contracts that underly approximately $2 billion in annual revenues that come up for renewal between 2011 and 2015. About 70% of these legacy contracts, ones that have not been repriced since 2004, are in the energy (coal) category, with another 20% in intermodal.

## Company Financials Fiscal Year Ended Dec. 31

| Per Share Data ($) | 2010 | 2009 | 2008 | 2007 | 2006 | 2005 | 2004 | 2003 | 2002 | 2001 |
|---|---|---|---|---|---|---|---|---|---|---|
| Tangible Book Value | 35.48 | 33.00 | 30.70 | 31.73 | 28.34 | 25.58 | 24.25 | 23.93 | 21.00 | 19.15 |
| Cash Flow | 8.48 | 6.61 | 7.23 | 5.92 | 5.23 | 4.13 | 3.27 | 3.96 | 4.60 | 3.93 |
| Earnings | 5.53 | 3.75 | 4.54 | 3.46 | 2.96 | 1.93 | 1.15 | 2.04 | 2.53 | 1.89 |
| S&P Core Earnings | 5.48 | 3.52 | 4.29 | 3.37 | 2.86 | 1.66 | 1.05 | 1.88 | 1.92 | 1.41 |
| Dividends | 1.31 | 1.08 | 0.98 | 0.75 | 0.60 | 0.60 | 0.60 | 0.50 | 0.42 | 0.40 |
| Payout Ratio | 24% | 29% | 22% | 22% | 20% | 31% | 52% | 24% | 16% | 21% |
| Prices:High | 95.78 | 66.73 | 85.80 | 68.78 | 48.75 | 40.63 | 34.78 | 34.75 | 32.58 | 30.35 |
| Prices:Low | 60.41 | 33.28 | 41.84 | 44.79 | 38.81 | 29.09 | 27.40 | 25.45 | 26.50 | 21.88 |
| P/E Ratio:High | 17 | 18 | 19 | 20 | 16 | 21 | 30 | 17 | 13 | 16 |
| P/E Ratio:Low | 11 | 9 | 9 | 13 | 13 | 15 | 24 | 13 | 10 | 12 |

| Income Statement Analysis (Million $) | | | | | | | | | | |
|---|---|---|---|---|---|---|---|---|---|---|
| Revenue | 16,965 | 14,143 | 17,970 | 16,283 | 15,578 | 13,578 | 12,215 | 11,551 | 12,491 | 11,973 |
| Operating Income | 6,468 | 4,836 | 5,462 | 4,696 | 4,121 | 2,970 | 2,406 | 3,200 | 3,530 | 2,072 |
| Depreciation | 1,487 | 1,444 | 1,387 | 1,321 | 1,237 | 1,175 | 1,111 | 1,067 | 1,206 | 1,174 |
| Interest Expense | 602 | 600 | 511 | 482 | 477 | 504 | 527 | 574 | 633 | 701 |
| Pretax Income | 4,433 | 2,987 | 3,656 | 3,009 | 2,525 | 1,436 | 856 | 1,637 | 2,016 | 1,533 |
| Effective Tax Rate | NA | 36.5% | 36.1% | 38.4% | 36.4% | 28.6% | 29.4% | 35.5% | 33.5% | 37.0% |
| Net Income | 2,780 | 1,898 | 2,338 | 1,855 | 1,606 | 1,026 | 604 | 1,056 | 1,341 | 966 |
| S&P Core Earnings | 2,754 | 1,782 | 2,209 | 1,808 | 1,553 | 886 | 551 | 972 | 1,003 | 708 |

| Balance Sheet & Other Financial Data (Million $) | | | | | | | | | | |
|---|---|---|---|---|---|---|---|---|---|---|
| Cash | 1,086 | 1,850 | 1,249 | 878 | 827 | 773 | 977 | 527 | 369 | 113 |
| Current Assets | 3,432 | 3,680 | 2,813 | 2,594 | 2,411 | 2,325 | 2,290 | 2,089 | 2,152 | 1,542 |
| Total Assets | 43,088 | 42,410 | 39,722 | 38,033 | 36,515 | 35,620 | 34,589 | 33,460 | 32,764 | 31,551 |
| Current Liabilities | 2,952 | 2,682 | 2,880 | 3,041 | 3,539 | 3,384 | 2,516 | 2,456 | 2,701 | 2,692 |
| Long Term Debt | 9,003 | 9,636 | 8,607 | 7,543 | 6,000 | 6,760 | 7,981 | 7,822 | 8,928 | 9,386 |
| Common Equity | 17,763 | 16,941 | 15,447 | 15,585 | 15,312 | 13,707 | 12,655 | 12,354 | 10,651 | 9,575 |
| Total Capital | 27,005 | 26,789 | 34,336 | 33,178 | 31,008 | 29,949 | 29,816 | 29,345 | 28,057 | 26,843 |
| Capital Expenditures | 2,482 | 2,384 | 2,780 | 2,496 | 2,242 | 2,169 | 1,876 | 1,752 | 1,887 | 1,736 |
| Cash Flow | 4,267 | 3,342 | 3,725 | 3,176 | 2,843 | 2,201 | 1,715 | 2,123 | 2,547 | 2,140 |
| Current Ratio | 1.2 | 1.4 | 1.0 | 0.9 | 0.7 | 0.7 | 0.9 | 0.9 | 0.8 | 0.6 |
| % Long Term Debt of Capitalization | 33.3 | 36.0 | 25.1 | 22.7 | 19.3 | 22.6 | 26.8 | 26.7 | 31.8 | 35.0 |
| % Net Income of Revenue | 16.4 | 13.4 | 13.0 | 11.4 | 10.3 | 7.6 | 4.9 | 9.1 | 10.7 | 8.1 |
| % Return on Assets | 6.5 | 4.6 | 6.0 | 5.0 | 4.5 | 2.9 | 1.8 | 3.2 | 4.2 | 3.1 |
| % Return on Equity | 16.0 | 11.7 | 15.1 | 12.0 | 11.1 | 7.8 | 4.8 | 9.2 | 13.3 | 10.6 |

Data as orig reptd.; bef. results of disc opers/spec. items. Per share data adj. for stk. divs.; EPS diluted. E-Estimated. NA-Not Available. NM-Not Meaningful. NR-Not Ranked. UR-Under Review.

**Office:** 1400 Douglas Street, Omaha, NE 68179.
**Telephone:** 402-544-5000.
**Website:** http://www.up.com
**Chrmn, Pres, CEO & COO:** J.R. Young

**EVP & CFO:** R.M. Knight, Jr.
**SVP & Chief Admin Officer:** C.R. Eisele
**SVP & Secy:** B.W. Schaefer
**SVP & General Counsel:** J.M. Hemmer

**Investor Contact:** J. Hamann (402-544-4227)
**Board Members:** A. H. Card, Jr., E. B. Davis, Jr., T. J. Donohue, A. W. Dunham, J. R. Hope, C. C. Krulak, M. R. McCarthy, M. W. McConnell, T. F. McLarty, III, S. Rogel, J. H. Villarreal, J. R. Young

**Founded:** 1862
**Domicile:** Utah
**Employees:** 42,884

*The McGraw·Hill Companies*

# UnitedHealth Group Inc

**STANDARD &POOR'S**

| S&P Recommendation BUY ★★★★☆ | Price $48.77 (as of Nov 30, 2011) | 12-Mo. Target Price $57.00 | Investment Style Large-Cap Growth |
|---|---|---|---|

**GICS Sector** Health Care
**Sub-Industry** Managed Health Care

**Summary** This leading health care services company provides health benefit services to over 32 million individuals across the U.S.

## Key Stock Statistics (Source S&P, Vickers, company reports)

| | | | | | | |
|---|---|---|---|---|---|---|
| 52-Wk Range | $53.50– 34.94 | S&P Oper. EPS 2011E | 4.55 | Market Capitalization(B) | $51.990 | Beta | 0.93 |
| Trailing 12-Month EPS | $4.51 | S&P Oper. EPS 2012E | 4.75 | Yield (%) | 1.33 | S&P 3-Yr. Proj. EPS CAGR(%) | 10 |
| Trailing 12-Month P/E | 10.8 | P/E on S&P Oper. EPS 2011E | 10.7 | Dividend Rate/Share | $0.65 | S&P Credit Rating | A- |
| $10K Invested 5 Yrs Ago | $9,581 | Common Shares Outstg. (M) | 1,066.0 | Institutional Ownership (%) | 88 | |

## Price Performance

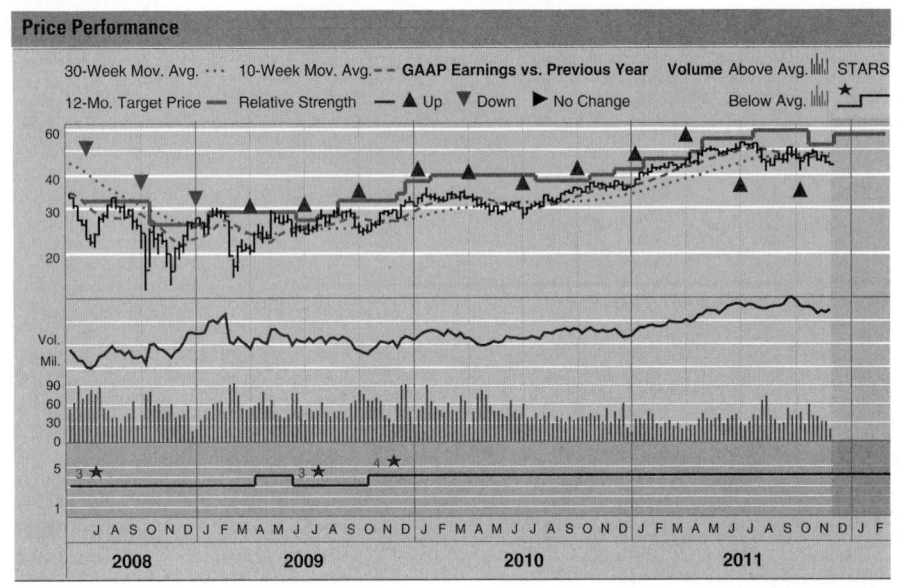

30-Week Mov. Avg. · · · 10-Week Mov. Avg. - - GAAP Earnings vs. Previous Year    Volume Above Avg. STARS
12-Mo. Target Price — Relative Strength — ▲ Up ▼ Down ► No Change    Below Avg. ★

Options: ASE, CBOE, P

## Highlights

► The 12-month target price for UNH has recently been changed to $57.00 from $52.00. The Highlights section of this Stock Report will be updated accordingly.

## Investment Rationale/Risk

► The Investment Rationale/Risk section of this Stock Report will be updated shortly. For the latest News story on UNH from MarketScope, see below.

► 11/30/11 09:24 am ET ... S&P REITERATES BUY OPINION ON SHARES OF UNITEDHEALTH GROUP (UNH 45.88****): At its investor meeting, UNH highlighted its expanding array of services and programs to help lower health care costs for its customers and improve patient outcomes. We believe its capabilities, competitive offerings, and healthy cash flow should enable UNH continue to gain market share in enrollment, and with admin cost control and share buybacks, we view its long-term goal of 13%-16% annual EPS growth as doable. By applying an above-peer 12X P/E to our '12 EPS estimate of $4.75, which we raised by $0.10 on less-conservative cost assumptions, we up our target price $5 to $57. /P.Seligman

## Qualitative Risk Assessment

| LOW | MEDIUM | HIGH |
|---|---|---|

Our risk assessment reflects UNH's leadership in the highly fragmented managed care market, its wide geographic market, and its product diversity, which we believe permits stable operational performance even during periods of economic downturn. However, we see commercial enrollment growth slowing from an expanding base amid intensifying competition.

## Quantitative Evaluations

**S&P Quality Ranking**   A+

| D | C | B- | B | B+ | A- | A | A+ |
|---|---|---|---|---|---|---|---|

**Relative Strength Rank**   STRONG

84

LOWEST = 1          HIGHEST = 99

## Revenue/Earnings Data

**Revenue (Million $)**

| | 1Q | 2Q | 3Q | 4Q | Year |
|---|---|---|---|---|---|
| 2011 | 25,432 | 25,234 | 25,280 | -- | -- |
| 2010 | 23,193 | 23,264 | 23,668 | 24,030 | 94,155 |
| 2009 | 22,004 | 21,655 | 21,695 | 21,784 | 87,138 |
| 2008 | 20,304 | 20,272 | 20,156 | 20,454 | 81,186 |
| 2007 | 19,047 | 18,926 | 18,679 | 18,705 | 75,431 |
| 2006 | 17,581 | 17,863 | 17,970 | 18,128 | 71,542 |

**Earnings Per Share ($)**

| | | | | | |
|---|---|---|---|---|---|
| 2011 | 1.22 | 1.16 | 1.17 | E1.00 | E4.55 |
| 2010 | 1.03 | 0.99 | 1.14 | 0.94 | 4.10 |
| 2009 | 0.81 | 0.73 | 0.89 | 0.81 | 3.24 |
| 2008 | 0.78 | 0.27 | 0.75 | 0.60 | 2.40 |
| 2007 | 0.66 | 0.87 | 0.95 | 0.92 | 3.42 |
| 2006 | 0.63 | 0.70 | 0.80 | 0.84 | 2.97 |

Fiscal year ended Dec. 31. Next earnings report expected: Late January. EPS Estimates based on S&P Operating Earnings; historical GAAP earnings are as reported.

## Dividend Data (Dates: mm/dd Payment Date: mm/dd/yy)

| Amount ($) | Date Decl. | Ex-Div. Date | Stk. of Record | Payment Date |
|---|---|---|---|---|
| 0.125 | 02/10 | 03/03 | 03/07 | 03/21/11 |
| 0.163 | 05/25 | 06/03 | 06/07 | 06/21/11 |
| 0.163 | 08/03 | 09/02 | 09/07 | 09/21/11 |
| 0.163 | 11/04 | 12/05 | 12/07 | 12/21/11 |

Dividends have been paid since 1990. Source: Company reports.

---

**Please read the Required Disclosures and Analyst Certification on the last page of this report.**

The **McGraw·Hill** Companies

# UnitedHealth Group Inc

STANDARD
&POOR'S

## Business Summary October 24, 2011

CORPORATE OVERVIEW. UnitedHealth Group, a U.S. leader in health care management, provides a broad range of health care products and services, including health maintenance organizations (HMOs), point of service (POS) plans, preferred provider organizations (PPOs), and managed fee for service programs.

The company reports results in two business segments, organized by product basis:

The UnitedHealthcare segment (78% of 2010 revenues before eliminations and 82% of operating earnings before one-time costs) consists of the following business units: UnitedHealthcare Employer & Individual coordinates network-based health and well-being services on behalf of multistate mid-sized and local employers and for individuals. The Uniprise unit, which provides these services to large, self-insured accounts in return for administrative fee, was merged into the Employer & individual business. UnitedHealthcare Community & State (formerly AmeriChoice) facilitates and manages health care services for state Medicaid programs and their beneficiaries. UnitedHealthcare Medicare & Retirement (formerly Ovations) delivers health and well-being services to Americans over the age of 50. At September 30, 2011, risk and fee-based Health Care Services enrollment totaled 34,395,000, versus 32,970,000 at December 31, 2010, including commercial risk-based (9,545,000 versus

9,405,000), commercial fee-based (16,255,000 versus 15,405,000), Medicare Advantage (2,215,000 versus 2,070,000), Medicaid (3,485,000 versus 3,320,000), and Standardized Medicare Supplement (2,895,000 versus 2,770,000). In addition, there were 4,830,000 Medicare Part D Stand-alone Prescription Drug Plan members, versus 4,530,000.

The Optum segment consists of the three services businesses: (1) OptumHealth (5% and 7%) provides specialized benefits such as behavioral, dental and vision offerings, and financial services. (2) OptumInsight (formerly Ingenix; 2% and 4%) is a leader in the field of health care data, analysis and application, serving pharmaceutical companies, health insurers and other payors, physicians and other health care providers, large employers and governments. We view OptumInsight as key to the other segments' competitive strengths. (3) OptumRx (formerly Prescription Solutions; 15% and 7%) offers pharmacy benefit management and specialty pharmacy management services to employer groups, union trusts and seniors -- through Medicare prescription drug plans and commercial health plans.

## Company Financials Fiscal Year Ended Dec. 31

| Per Share Data ($) | 2010 | 2009 | 2008 | 2007 | 2006 | 2005 | 2004 | 2003 | 2002 | 2001 |
|---|---|---|---|---|---|---|---|---|---|---|
| Tangible Book Value | NM | NM | NM | 1.18 | 1.55 | NM | 0.04 | 1.24 | 0.79 | 0.88 |
| Cash Flow | NA | NA | 3.19 | 4.00 | 3.44 | 2.82 | 2.26 | 1.72 | 1.26 | 0.90 |
| Earnings | 4.10 | 3.24 | 2.40 | 3.42 | 2.97 | 2.48 | 1.97 | 1.48 | 1.07 | 0.70 |
| S&P Core Earnings | 4.16 | 3.23 | 2.95 | 3.40 | 2.94 | 2.36 | 1.86 | 1.37 | 0.99 | 0.62 |
| Dividends | 0.41 | 0.03 | 0.03 | 0.03 | 0.03 | 0.02 | 0.02 | 0.01 | 0.01 | 0.01 |
| Payout Ratio | 10% | 1% | 1% | 1% | 1% | 1% | 1% | 1% | 1% | 1% |
| Prices:High | 38.06 | 33.25 | 57.86 | 59.46 | 62.93 | 64.61 | 44.38 | 29.34 | 25.25 | 18.20 |
| Prices:Low | 27.13 | 16.18 | 14.51 | 45.82 | 41.44 | 42.63 | 27.73 | 19.60 | 16.96 | 12.63 |
| P/E Ratio:High | 9 | 10 | 24 | 17 | 21 | 26 | 23 | 20 | 24 | 26 |
| P/E Ratio:Low | 7 | 5 | 6 | 13 | 14 | 17 | 14 | 13 | 16 | 18 |

**Income Statement Analysis** (Million $)

| | 2010 | 2009 | 2008 | 2007 | 2006 | 2005 | 2004 | 2003 | 2002 | 2001 |
|---|---|---|---|---|---|---|---|---|---|---|
| Revenue | 94,155 | 87,138 | 81,186 | 75,431 | 71,542 | 45,365 | 37,218 | 28,823 | 25,020 | 23,454 |
| Operating Income | NA | NA | 7,281 | 8,821 | 6,783 | 5,826 | 4,475 | 3,234 | 2,441 | 1,831 |
| Depreciation | NA | NA | 981 | 796 | 670 | 453 | 374 | 299 | 255 | 265 |
| Interest Expense | 481 | 551 | 639 | 544 | 456 | 241 | 128 | 95.0 | 90.0 | 94.0 |
| Pretax Income | 7,383 | 5,808 | 4,624 | 7,305 | 6,528 | 5,132 | 3,973 | 2,840 | 2,096 | 1,472 |
| Effective Tax Rate | NA | 34.2% | 35.6% | 36.3% | 36.3% | 35.7% | 34.9% | 35.7% | 35.5% | 38.0% |
| Net Income | 4,634 | 3,822 | 2,977 | 4,654 | 4,159 | 3,300 | 2,587 | 1,825 | 1,352 | 913 |
| S&P Core Earnings | 4,700 | 3,815 | 3,655 | 4,629 | 4,108 | 3,137 | 2,443 | 1,689 | 1,260 | 812 |

**Balance Sheet & Other Financial Data** (Million $)

| | 2010 | 2009 | 2008 | 2007 | 2006 | 2005 | 2004 | 2003 | 2002 | 2001 |
|---|---|---|---|---|---|---|---|---|---|---|
| Cash | 9,123 | 9,800 | 7,426 | 9,619 | 10,940 | 5,421 | 3,991 | 2,262 | 1,130 | 1,540 |
| Current Assets | NA | NA | 14,990 | 15,544 | 16,044 | 10,640 | 8,241 | 6,120 | 5,174 | 4,946 |
| Total Assets | 63,063 | 59,045 | 55,815 | 50,899 | 48,320 | 41,374 | 27,879 | 17,634 | 14,164 | 12,486 |
| Current Liabilities | NA | NA | 19,761 | 18,492 | 18,497 | 16,644 | 11,329 | 8,768 | 8,379 | 7,491 |
| Long Term Debt | 8,662 | 9,858 | 11,338 | 9,063 | 5,973 | 3,850 | 3,350 | 1,750 | 950 | 900 |
| Common Equity | 25,825 | 23,606 | 20,780 | 20,063 | 20,810 | 17,733 | 10,717 | 5,128 | 4,428 | 3,891 |
| Total Capital | NA | NA | 33,473 | 29,126 | 26,783 | 21,583 | 14,067 | 6,878 | 5,378 | 4,791 |
| Capital Expenditures | NA | NA | 791 | 871 | 728 | 5,876 | 350 | 352 | 419 | 425 |
| Cash Flow | NA | NA | 3,958 | 5,450 | 4,829 | 3,753 | 2,961 | 2,124 | 1,607 | 1,178 |
| Current Ratio | 0.8 | 0.9 | 0.8 | 0.8 | 0.9 | 0.6 | 0.7 | 0.7 | 0.6 | 0.7 |
| % Long Term Debt of Capitalization | 23.4 | 29.5 | 33.9 | 31.1 | 22.3 | 17.8 | 23.8 | 25.4 | 17.7 | 18.8 |
| % Net Income of Revenue | 4.9 | 4.4 | 3.7 | 6.2 | 5.9 | 7.3 | 7.0 | 6.3 | 5.4 | 3.9 |
| % Return on Assets | 7.6 | 6.7 | 5.6 | 9.4 | 9.3 | 9.5 | 11.4 | 11.5 | 10.1 | 7.8 |
| % Return on Equity | 18.8 | 17.2 | 14.6 | 22.8 | 21.5 | 23.2 | 32.7 | 38.2 | 32.5 | 24.1 |

Data as orig reptd.; bef. results of disc opers/spec. items. Per share data adj. for stk. divs.; EPS diluted. E-Estimated. NA-Not Available. NM-Not Meaningful. NR-Not Ranked. UR-Under Review.

**Office:** 9900 Bren Rd E, Minnetonka, MN 55343.
**Telephone:** 952-936-1300.
**Website:** http://www.unitedhealthgroup.com
**Chrmn:** R.T. Burke

**Pres:** W. Guptail
**CEO:** S.J. Hemsley
**COO:** D. Herndon
**EVP & CFO:** D.S. Wichmann

**Investor Contact:** F. Jacobs (800-328-5979)
**Board Members:** W. C. Ballard, Jr., R. T. Burke, R. J. Darretta, S. J. Hemsley, M. J. Hooper, R. A. Lawson, D. W. Leatherdale, G. M. Renwick, K. I. Shine, G. R. Wilensky

**Founded:** 1974
**Domicile:** Minnesota
**Employees:** 87,000

# United Parcel Service Inc

**STANDARD &POOR'S**

| | | | |
|---|---|---|---|
| **S&P Recommendation** BUY ★★★★☆ | **Price** $66.46 (as of Nov 25, 2011) | **12-Mo. Target Price** $95.00 | **Investment Style** Large-Cap Growth |

**GICS Sector** Industrials
**Sub-Industry** Air Freight & Logistics

**Summary** UPS is the world's largest express delivery company, and has established itself as a facilitator of e-commerce.

## Key Stock Statistics (Source S&P, Vickers, company reports)

| | | | | | | | |
|---|---|---|---|---|---|---|---|
| 52-Wk Range | $77.00– 60.74 | S&P Oper. EPS 2011E | 4.30 | Market Capitalization(B) | $48.092 | Beta | 0.83 |
| Trailing 12-Month EPS | $4.12 | S&P Oper. EPS 2012E | 4.90 | Yield (%) | 3.13 | S&P 3-Yr. Proj. EPS CAGR(%) | 14 |
| Trailing 12-Month P/E | 16.1 | P/E on S&P Oper. EPS 2011E | 15.5 | Dividend Rate/Share | $2.08 | S&P Credit Rating | AA- |
| $10K Invested 5 Yrs Ago | $9,748 | Common Shares Outstg. (M) | 965.0 | Institutional Ownership (%) | 69 | | |

## Price Performance

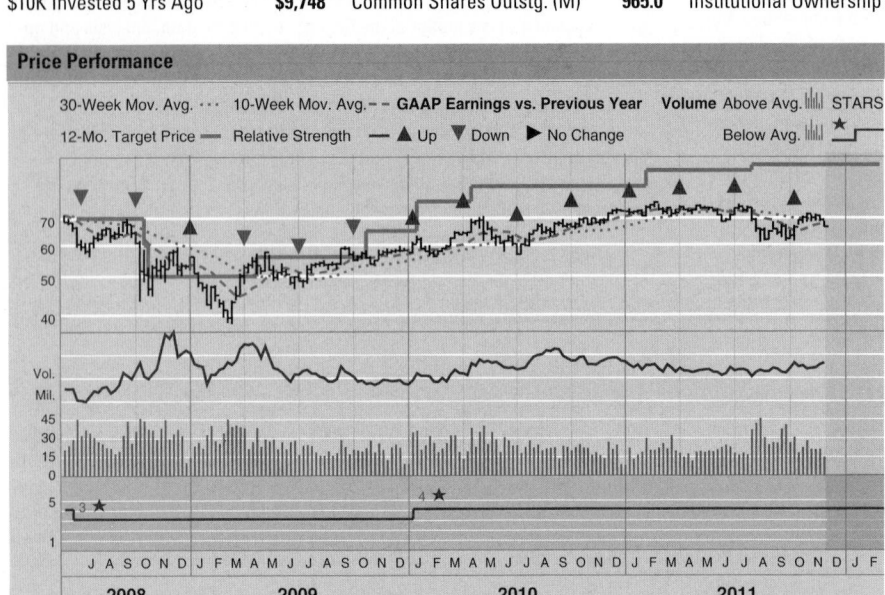

30-Week Mov. Avg. · · · 10-Week Mov. Avg. – – GAAP Earnings vs. Previous Year   Volume Above Avg. STARS
12-Mo. Target Price — Relative Strength — ▲ Up ▼ Down ► No Change   Below Avg.

Options: ASE, CBOE, P, Ph

Analysis prepared by Equity Analyst **Jim Corridore** on Nov 01, 2011, when the stock traded at **$68.97**.

## Highlights

➤ We expect 2011 revenues to rise 8%, followed by 9% growth in 2012. We see gains in U.S. domestic as well as international shipping, driven by strengthening in the U.S. and global economies. We look for international volumes to outpace domestic. We see an 8.5% rise in supply chain and freight revenues in 2010, and 11% in 2012. Fuel surcharges are likely to add to revenues. We expect UPS to be successful in getting customers to absorb rate increases, as we forecast that shipping demand will improve.

➤ We see operating margins improving, mainly from fixed cost leverage on a higher number of package deliveries. UPS should also benefit from an improved package mix, as we think consumers will shift to faster delivery methods as the economy strengthens. We also look for productivity gains from new technology and reduced costs from restructuring actions. The resumption of management pay increases and 401(k) matching is likely to drive increased compensation costs in 2011.

➤ We estimate 2011 EPS of $4.30, up 21% from 2010 operating EPS of $3.56. For 2012, we see EPS rising 14%, to $4.90.

## Investment Rationale/Risk

➤ We think UPS will likely see increased international and domestic volumes and higher pricing as the economy continues to show improvement. We think the company is a strong generator of cash, and we favor its historical use of its funds to pay dividends and repurchase stock. In our view, these positives support our buy opinion on the stock, despite a valuation above that of the S&P 500 on a P/E basis. UPS has temporarily slowed its share repurchase program, but we expect it to eventually resume buybacks, which should provide support for the stock.

➤ Risks to our recommendation and target price include slower economic recovery than we expect, and a possible price war with competitors. Regarding corporate governance, we are concerned that Class A shareholders have 10 votes per share on many matters.

➤ Our 12-month target price of $95 values the stock at about 19X our 2012 EPS estimate, in the middle of UPS's five-year historical P/E range. We view positively the company's return on assets and cash flow from operations.

## Qualitative Risk Assessment

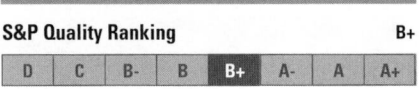

| LOW | MEDIUM | HIGH |
|---|---|---|

Our risk assessment reflects what we see as UPS's geographically diversified and increasing revenue base, a strong balance sheet with ample cash and low debt relative to total capitalization, and a track record of earnings and cash flow growth.

## Quantitative Evaluations

**S&P Quality Ranking**   B+

| D | C | B- | B | B+ | A- | A | A+ |
|---|---|---|---|---|---|---|---|

**Relative Strength Rank**   MODERATE

66

LOWEST = 1   HIGHEST = 99

## Revenue/Earnings Data

**Revenue (Million $)**

| | 1Q | 2Q | 3Q | 4Q | Year |
|---|---|---|---|---|---|
| 2011 | 12,582 | 13,191 | 13,166 | -- | -- |
| 2010 | 11,728 | 12,204 | 12,192 | 13,421 | 49,545 |
| 2009 | 10,938 | 10,829 | 11,153 | 12,377 | 45,297 |
| 2008 | 12,675 | 13,001 | 13,113 | 12,697 | 51,486 |
| 2007 | 11,906 | 12,189 | 12,205 | 13,392 | 49,692 |
| 2006 | 11,521 | 11,736 | 11,662 | 12,628 | 47,547 |

**Earnings Per Share ($)**

| | | | | | |
|---|---|---|---|---|---|
| 2011 | 0.88 | 1.07 | 1.06 | E1.29 | E4.30 |
| 2010 | 0.53 | 0.84 | 0.99 | 1.11 | 3.48 |
| 2009 | 0.40 | 0.44 | 0.55 | 0.75 | 2.14 |
| 2008 | 0.87 | 0.85 | 0.96 | 0.25 | 2.94 |
| 2007 | 0.78 | 1.04 | 1.02 | -2.52 | 0.36 |
| 2006 | 0.89 | 0.97 | 0.96 | 1.04 | 3.86 |

Fiscal year ended Dec. 31. Next earnings report expected: Early February. EPS Estimates based on S&P Operating Earnings; historical GAAP earnings are as reported.

## Dividend Data (Dates: mm/dd Payment Date: mm/dd/yy)

| Amount ($) | Date Decl. | Ex-Div. Date | Stk. of Record | Payment Date |
|---|---|---|---|---|
| 0.520 | 02/03 | 02/10 | 02/14 | 03/02/11 |
| 0.520 | 05/05 | 05/12 | 05/16 | 06/01/11 |
| 0.520 | 08/11 | 08/18 | 08/22 | 09/07/11 |
| 0.520 | 11/03 | 11/09 | 11/14 | 11/30/11 |

Dividends have been paid since 2000. Source: Company reports.

---

**Please read the Required Disclosures and Analyst Certification on the last page of this report.**

*The McGraw·Hill Companies*

# United Parcel Service Inc

**STANDARD &POOR'S**

## Business Summary November 01, 2011

CORPORATE OVERVIEW. United Parcel Service is the world's largest express and package delivery company. It is also a leading commerce facilitator, offering various logistics and financial services. The company, which was privately held since its founding in 1907, had its IPO of Class B stock in November 1999.

CORPORATE STRATEGY. The company seeks to position itself as the primary coordinator of the flow of goods, information and funds throughout the entire supply chain (the movement from the raw materials and parts stage through final consumption of the finished product).

Domestic package delivery services accounted for 60% of revenues in 2010, down from 62% in 2010. About 85% of the 15.5 million daily domestic shipments handled by the company in 2010 were moved by its ground delivery service, which is available to every address in the 48 contiguous states in the U.S. Domestic air delivery is provided throughout the U.S., including next-day air, which is guaranteed by 10:30 a.m. to more than 75% of the U.S. population, and by noon to an additional 15% of the population.

UPS entered the international arena in 1975. In 2010, it handled 2.3 million international shipments per day. S&P believes the international package delivery service (22% of total revenues in 2010) is likely to grow faster than its domestic business over the next several years; it grew revenues 15% in 2010. UPS delivers international shipments to more than 200 countries and territories worldwide and provides delivery within one to two business days to the world's major business centers. Services include export (packages that cross national borders) and domestic (packages that stay within a single country's boundaries). UPS has a portfolio of domestic services in 20 major countries. Transborder services within the European Union are expected to continue to be a growth engine for the company. Asia continues to be an area in which UPS is investing in infrastructure and technology.

## Company Financials Fiscal Year Ended Dec. 31

| Per Share Data ($) | 2010 | 2009 | 2008 | 2007 | 2006 | 2005 | 2004 | 2003 | 2002 | 2001 |
|---|---|---|---|---|---|---|---|---|---|---|
| Tangible Book Value | 5.34 | 4.96 | 4.29 | 9.04 | 11.46 | 12.44 | 12.84 | 12.03 | 11.09 | 9.14 |
| Cash Flow | 5.26 | 3.88 | 4.71 | 2.00 | 5.46 | 4.94 | 4.33 | 3.91 | 4.20 | 3.41 |
| Earnings | 3.48 | 2.14 | 2.94 | 0.36 | 3.86 | 3.47 | 2.93 | 2.55 | 2.87 | 2.12 |
| S&P Core Earnings | 3.35 | 2.09 | 2.61 | 0.20 | 3.78 | 3.40 | 2.87 | 2.46 | 2.48 | 1.70 |
| Dividends | 1.88 | 1.80 | 1.80 | 1.68 | 1.52 | 1.32 | 1.12 | 0.92 | 0.76 | 0.76 |
| Payout Ratio | 54% | 84% | 61% | NM | 39% | 38% | 38% | 36% | 26% | 36% |
| Prices:High | 73.94 | 59.75 | 75.08 | 78.99 | 83.99 | 85.84 | 89.11 | 74.87 | 67.10 | 62.50 |
| Prices:Low | 55.77 | 37.99 | 43.32 | 68.66 | 65.50 | 66.10 | 67.51 | 53.00 | 54.25 | 46.15 |
| P/E Ratio:High | 21 | 28 | 26 | NM | 22 | 25 | 30 | 29 | 23 | 29 |
| P/E Ratio:Low | 16 | 18 | 15 | NM | 17 | 19 | 23 | 21 | 19 | 22 |

| Income Statement Analysis (Million $) | | | | | | | | | | |
|---|---|---|---|---|---|---|---|---|---|---|
| Revenue | 49,545 | 45,297 | 51,486 | 49,692 | 47,547 | 42,581 | 36,582 | 33,485 | 31,272 | 30,646 |
| Operating Income | 7,671 | 5,789 | 7,771 | 8,758 | 8,383 | 7,787 | 6,532 | 5,994 | 5,560 | 5,358 |
| Depreciation | 1,792 | 1,747 | 1,814 | 1,745 | 1,748 | 1,644 | 1,543 | 1,549 | 1,464 | 1,396 |
| Interest Expense | 354 | 445 | 490 | 313 | 211 | 172 | 149 | 121 | 173 | 184 |
| Pretax Income | 5,523 | 3,366 | 5,015 | 431 | 6,510 | 6,075 | 4,922 | 4,370 | 5,009 | 3,937 |
| Effective Tax Rate | 36.8% | 36.1% | 40.1% | 11.4% | 35.5% | 36.3% | 32.3% | 33.7% | 35.0% | 38.4% |
| Net Income | 3,488 | 2,152 | 3,003 | 382 | 4,202 | 3,870 | 3,333 | 2,898 | 3,254 | 2,425 |
| S&P Core Earnings | 3,353 | 2,107 | 2,664 | 212 | 4,109 | 3,784 | 3,261 | 2,790 | 2,820 | 1,948 |

| Balance Sheet & Other Financial Data (Million $) | | | | | | | | | | |
|---|---|---|---|---|---|---|---|---|---|---|
| Cash | 4,081 | 2,100 | 1,049 | 2,604 | 794 | 1,369 | 5,197 | 2,951 | 2,211 | 1,616 |
| Current Assets | 11,569 | 9,275 | 8,845 | 11,760 | 9,377 | 11,003 | 12,605 | 9,853 | 8,738 | 7,597 |
| Total Assets | 33,597 | 31,883 | 31,879 | 39,042 | 33,210 | 35,222 | 33,026 | 28,909 | 26,357 | 24,636 |
| Current Liabilities | 5,902 | 6,239 | 7,817 | 9,840 | 6,719 | 6,793 | 6,483 | 5,518 | 5,555 | 4,629 |
| Long Term Debt | 10,371 | 8,420 | 7,797 | 7,506 | 3,133 | 3,159 | 3,261 | 3,149 | 3,495 | 4,648 |
| Common Equity | 7,979 | 7,630 | 6,780 | 12,183 | 15,482 | 16,884 | 16,384 | 14,852 | 12,455 | 10,248 |
| Total Capital | 18,831 | 16,863 | 16,231 | 22,309 | 21,144 | 20,043 | 25,027 | 18,001 | 15,950 | 14,896 |
| Capital Expenditures | 1,389 | 1,602 | 2,636 | 2,820 | 3,085 | 2,187 | 2,127 | 1,947 | 1,658 | 2,372 |
| Cash Flow | 5,280 | 3,899 | 4,817 | 2,127 | 5,950 | 5,514 | 4,876 | 4,447 | 4,718 | 3,821 |
| Current Ratio | 2.0 | 1.5 | 1.1 | 1.2 | 1.4 | 1.6 | 1.9 | 1.8 | 1.6 | 1.6 |
| % Long Term Debt of Capitalization | 55.1 | 49.9 | 48.0 | 33.7 | 14.8 | 15.8 | 13.0 | 17.5 | 21.9 | 31.2 |
| % Net Income of Revenue | 7.0 | 4.8 | 5.8 | 0.8 | 8.8 | 9.1 | 9.1 | 8.7 | 10.4 | 7.9 |
| % Return on Assets | 10.7 | 6.8 | 8.5 | 1.1 | 12.3 | 11.3 | 10.6 | 10.5 | 12.8 | 10.5 |
| % Return on Equity | 44.7 | 29.9 | 31.7 | 2.8 | 26.0 | 23.3 | 21.3 | 21.2 | 28.7 | 24.3 |

Data as orig reptd.; bef. results of disc opers/spec. items. Per share data adj. for stk. divs.; EPS diluted. E-Estimated. NA-Not Available. NM-Not Meaningful. NR-Not Ranked. UR-Under Review.

**Office:** 55 Glenlake Parkway NE, Atlanta, GA 30328.
**Telephone:** 404-828-6000.
**Website:** http://www.ups.com
**Chrmn & CEO:** D.S. Davis

**COO & SVP:** D.P. Abney
**SVP, CFO, Chief Acctg Officer & Treas:** K. Kuehn
**SVP & CIO:** D. Barnes
**Secy & General Counsel:** T.P. McClure

**Investor Contact:** M. Vale (404-828-6703)
**Board Members:** F. D. Ackerman, M. J. Burns, D. S. Davis, S. E. Eizenstat, M. L. Eskew, W. R. Johnson, C. Kendle, A. M. Livermore, R. H. Markham, C. T. Randt, Jr., J. W. Thompson, C. B. Tome

**Founded:** 1907
**Domicile:** Delaware
**Employees:** 400,600

**The McGraw-Hill Companies**

# U.S. Bancorp

**STANDARD &POOR'S**

| **S&P Recommendation** STRONG BUY ★★★★★ | **Price** $24.61 (as of Nov 29, 2011) | **12-Mo. Target Price** $30.00 | **Investment Style** Large-Cap Blend |
|---|---|---|---|

**GICS Sector** Financials
**Sub-Industry** Diversified Banks

**Summary** Minneapolis-based U.S. Bancorp is the fifth largest bank, by assets, in the United States, with assets of about $330 billion.

## Key Stock Statistics (Source S&P, Vickers, company reports)

| | | | | | | |
|---|---|---|---|---|---|---|
| 52-Wk Range | $28.94–20.10 | S&P Oper. EPS 2011**E** | 2.42 | Market Capitalization(B) | $46.966 | Beta | 1.00 |
| Trailing 12-Month EPS | $2.26 | S&P Oper. EPS 2012**E** | 2.84 | Yield (%) | 2.03 | S&P 3-Yr. Proj. EPS CAGR(%) | 21 |
| Trailing 12-Month P/E | 10.9 | P/E on S&P Oper. EPS 2011**E** | 10.2 | Dividend Rate/Share | $0.50 | S&P Credit Rating | A+ |
| $10K Invested 5 Yrs Ago | $8,284 | Common Shares Outstg. (M) | 1,908.4 | Institutional Ownership (%) | 70 | | |

## Price Performance

30-Week Mov. Avg. ··· 10-Week Mov. Avg. - - GAAP Earnings vs. Previous Year   Volume Above Avg. STARS
12-Mo. Target Price — Relative Strength — ▲ Up ▼ Down ▶ No Change   Below Avg.

Options: ASE, CBOE, Ph

Analysis prepared by Equity Analyst **Erik Oja** on Nov 29, 2011, when the stock traded at **$24.72**.

## Highlights

➤ We expect net interest income to climb 4.9% in 2011, well above peers, driven by loan growth of the same amount, and a stable net interest margin. For 2012, we look for a 2.2% rise in net interest income, with loan growth of 4.1%. We anticipate a 1.0% increase in total noninterest income in 2011, and a 2.0% advance in 2012. We expect total revenues to rise 3.1% in 2011 and 2.1% in 2012.

➤ USB's credit quality is high relative to peers, with a large allowance for loan losses. As of September 30, nonperforming loans totaled $3.58 billion, a lower than peers 1.75% of total loans of $204.8 billion. Nonperforming loans fell 5.8% from the second quarter, better than peers. At September 30, the allowance stood at $4.95 billion, equal to 2.42% of total loans, and 138% of nonperforming loans, also better than peers. For 2011, we expect a provision of $2.30 billion, or 0.83X our net chargeoff forecast of $2.78 billion. In 2012, we see provisions falling to $1.33 billion, or 0.91X our net chargeoff forecast of $1.46 billion. We think the decline of the loan loss provision will be the major driver of earnings growth in 2011, but not in 2012.

➤ We see EPS of $2.42 in 2011 and $2.84 in 2012.

## Investment Rationale/Risk

➤ USB's third-quarter results demonstrated good loan and fee income growth, in our opinion. We also view the quality of third-quarter EPS as relatively high, with a very low reliance on reserve releases and gains. We estimate a $0.05 contribution to third-quarter EPS of $0.64 from the $147 million reserve release (provisions minus net chargeoffs), a far lower contribution than at many peers. For the rest of 2011 and for 2012, we expect above-peers loan growth and total revenue growth, combined with lower loan loss provisioning expenses, and good noninterest expense management.

➤ Risks to our recommendation and target price include further turmoil in Europe, deterioration in the U.S. economy, lower consumer spending, credit quality declines, an equity capital raise, and a dividend cut.

➤ Our 12-month target price of $30 is 10.9X our forward four quarters EPS estimate of $2.74, in line with the median multiple of USB's peers. Our target price equals a higher-than-peers 2.75X multiple on our $10.90 year-end 2011 estimate of tangible book value per share.

## Qualitative Risk Assessment

| LOW | MEDIUM | HIGH |
|---|---|---|

Our risk assessment for U.S. Bancorp reflects our view of the company's solid fundamentals and prudent underwriting practices, along with good geographic and product diversification.

## Quantitative Evaluations

**S&P Quality Ranking**   B+

| D | C | B- | B | B+ | A- | A | A+ |
|---|---|---|---|---|---|---|---|

**Relative Strength Rank**   **STRONG**

73

LOWEST = 1   HIGHEST = 99

## Revenue/Earnings Data

**Revenue (Million $)**

| | 1Q | 2Q | 3Q | 4Q | Year |
|---|---|---|---|---|---|
| 2011 | 5,112 | 5,265 | 5,371 | -- | -- |
| 2010 | 4,911 | 5,105 | 5,187 | 5,315 | 20,518 |
| 2009 | 4,655 | 4,895 | 4,950 | 4,990 | 19,490 |
| 2008 | 5,249 | 4,907 | 4,469 | 4,604 | 19,229 |
| 2007 | 4,883 | 5,091 | 5,178 | 5,156 | 20,308 |
| 2006 | 4,505 | 4,773 | 4,897 | 4,934 | 19,109 |

**Earnings Per Share ($)**

| | | | | | |
|---|---|---|---|---|---|
| 2011 | 0.52 | 0.60 | 0.64 | E0.65 | E2.42 |
| 2010 | 0.34 | 0.45 | 0.45 | 0.49 | 1.73 |
| 2009 | 0.24 | 0.12 | 0.30 | 0.30 | 0.97 |
| 2008 | 0.62 | 0.53 | 0.32 | 0.15 | 1.61 |
| 2007 | 0.63 | 0.65 | 0.62 | 0.53 | 2.43 |
| 2006 | 0.63 | 0.66 | 0.66 | 0.66 | 2.61 |

Fiscal year ended Dec. 31. Next earnings report expected: Late January. EPS Estimates based on S&P Operating Earnings; historical GAAP earnings are as reported.

## Dividend Data (Dates: mm/dd Payment Date: mm/dd/yy)

| Amount ($) | Date Decl. | Ex-Div. Date | Stk. of Record | Payment Date |
|---|---|---|---|---|
| 0.050 | 12/14 | 12/29 | 12/31 | 01/18/11 |
| 0.125 | 03/18 | 03/29 | 03/31 | 04/15/11 |
| 0.125 | 06/21 | 06/28 | 06/30 | 07/15/11 |
| 0.125 | 09/20 | 09/28 | 09/30 | 10/17/11 |

Dividends have been paid since 1863. Source: Company reports.

---

**Please read the Required Disclosures and Analyst Certification on the last page of this report.**

*The McGraw·Hill Companies*

# U.S. Bancorp

**STANDARD
&POOR'S**

## Business Summary November 29, 2011

CORPORATE OVERVIEW. U.S. Bancorp (USB) consists of several major lines of business, which include wholesale banking, consumer banking, wealth management & securities services, payment services, and treasury and corporate support. Wholesale banking offers lending, equipment finance and small ticket leasing, depository, treasury management, capital markets, foreign exchange, international trade services and other financial services to middle-market, large corporate and public sector clients. Consumer banking delivers products and services through banking offices, telephone servicing and sales, online services, direct mail and ATMs. It encompasses community banking, metropolitan banking, in-store banking, small business banking, including lending guaranteed by the Small Business Administration, consumer lending, mortgage banking, consumer finance, workplace banking, student banking, and 24-hour banking.

Wealth management & securities services provides trust, custody, private banking, financial advisory, investment management, retail brokerage services, insurance, custody and mutual fund servicing through five businesses: wealth management, corporate trust, FAF Advisors, institutional trust and cus-

tody, and fund services. Payment services includes consumer and business credit cards, stored-value cards, debit cards, corporate and purchasing card services, consumer lines of credit, and merchant processing.

CORPORATE STRATEGY. In the current economic environment, the company intends to continue focusing on managing credit losses and operating costs, while also utilizing its financial strength to grow market share. It believes it is well positioned for long-term growth in earnings per common share and industry-leading return on common equity. It intends to achieve its financial objectives by providing high-quality customer service, carefully managing costs and, where appropriate, strategically investing in businesses that diversify its operations, generate fee-based revenues, enhance its distribution network or expand its product offerings.

## Company Financials Fiscal Year Ended Dec. 31

| Per Share Data ($) | 2010 | 2009 | 2008 | 2007 | 2006 | 2005 | 2004 | 2003 | 2002 | 2001 |
|---|---|---|---|---|---|---|---|---|---|---|
| Tangible Book Value | 8.98 | 7.21 | 3.97 | 6.31 | 5.34 | 5.62 | 5.87 | 5.77 | 4.93 | 4.64 |
| Earnings | 1.73 | 0.97 | 1.61 | 2.43 | 2.61 | 2.42 | 2.18 | 1.92 | 1.73 | 0.88 |
| S&P Core Earnings | 1.73 | 0.96 | 1.49 | 2.54 | 2.59 | 2.41 | 2.16 | 1.89 | 1.59 | 0.66 |
| Dividends | 0.20 | 0.20 | 1.70 | 1.63 | 1.39 | 1.23 | 1.02 | 0.86 | 0.78 | 0.75 |
| Payout Ratio | 12% | 21% | 106% | 67% | 53% | 51% | 47% | 45% | 45% | 85% |
| Prices:High | 28.43 | 25.59 | 42.23 | 36.84 | 36.85 | 31.36 | 31.65 | 30.00 | 24.50 | 26.06 |
| Prices:Low | 20.44 | 8.06 | 20.22 | 29.09 | 28.99 | 26.80 | 24.89 | 18.56 | 16.05 | 16.50 |
| P/E Ratio:High | 16 | 26 | 26 | 15 | 14 | 13 | 15 | 16 | 14 | 30 |
| P/E Ratio:Low | 12 | 8 | 13 | 12 | 11 | 11 | 11 | 10 | 9 | 19 |

| Income Statement Analysis (Million $) | 2010 | 2009 | 2008 | 2007 | 2006 | 2005 | 2004 | 2003 | 2002 | 2001 |
|---|---|---|---|---|---|---|---|---|---|---|
| Net Interest Income | 9,579 | 8,518 | 7,732 | 6,689 | 6,741 | 7,055 | 7,111 | 7,189 | 6,840 | 6,409 |
| Tax Equivalent Adjustment | 209 | 198 | 134 | 75.0 | 49.0 | 33.0 | 28.6 | 28.2 | 36.6 | 55.9 |
| Non Interest Income | 8,360 | 7,952 | 6,811 | 7,157 | 6,832 | 6,151 | 5,624 | 5,068 | 5,569 | 5,030 |
| Loan Loss Provision | 4,356 | 5,557 | 3,096 | 792 | 544 | 666 | 670 | 1,254 | 1,349 | 2,529 |
| % Expense/Operating Revenue | 52.3% | 50.3% | 47.4% | 49.6% | 45.4% | 44.3% | 45.3% | 45.7% | 83.7% | 57.5% |
| Pretax Income | 4,200 | 2,632 | 4,033 | 6,207 | 6,863 | 6,571 | 6,176 | 5,651 | 5,103 | 2,634 |
| Effective Tax Rate | 22.3% | 15.0% | 27.0% | 30.3% | 30.8% | 31.7% | 32.5% | 34.4% | 34.8% | 35.2% |
| Net Income | 3,317 | 2,205 | 2,946 | 4,324 | 4,751 | 4,489 | 4,167 | 3,710 | 3,326 | 1,707 |
| % Net Interest Margin | 3.88 | 3.67 | 3.66 | 3.47 | 3.65 | 3.97 | 4.25 | 4.49 | 4.61 | 4.45 |
| S&P Core Earnings | 3,320 | 1,783 | 2,606 | 4,470 | 4,674 | 4,470 | 4,135 | 3,655 | 3,062 | 1,280 |

| Balance Sheet & Other Financial Data (Million $) | 2010 | 2009 | 2008 | 2007 | 2006 | 2005 | 2004 | 2003 | 2002 | 2001 |
|---|---|---|---|---|---|---|---|---|---|---|
| Money Market Assets | Nil | Nil | Nil | Nil | Nil | Nil | Nil | Nil | 1,332 | 1,607 |
| Investment Securities | 52,978 | 44,768 | 39,521 | 43,116 | 40,117 | 39,768 | 41,481 | 43,334 | 28,488 | 26,608 |
| Commercial Loans | 83,093 | 82,885 | 89,831 | 80,281 | 74,835 | 71,405 | 67,758 | 65,768 | 68,811 | 71,703 |
| Other Loans | 113,968 | 112,523 | 95,398 | 73,546 | 68,762 | 66,401 | 58,557 | 52,467 | 47,440 | 42,702 |
| Total Assets | 307,786 | 281,176 | 265,912 | 237,615 | 219,232 | 209,465 | 195,104 | 189,286 | 180,027 | 171,390 |
| Demand Deposits | 45,314 | 38,186 | 37,494 | 33,334 | 32,128 | 32,214 | 30,756 | 32,470 | 35,106 | 31,212 |
| Time Deposits | 45,314 | 145,056 | 121,856 | 98,111 | 92,754 | 92,495 | 89,985 | 86,582 | 80,428 | 74,007 |
| Long Term Debt | 158,938 | 32,580 | 38,359 | 43,440 | 37,602 | 37,069 | 22,807 | 33,816 | 31,582 | 28,542 |
| Common Equity | 27,589 | 24,463 | 18,369 | 20,046 | 20,197 | 20,086 | 19,539 | 19,242 | 18,101 | 16,461 |
| % Return on Assets | 1.1 | 0.8 | 1.2 | 1.9 | 2.2 | 2.2 | 2.2 | 2.0 | 1.9 | 1.0 |
| % Return on Equity | 12.7 | 10.3 | 15.3 | 21.2 | 23.6 | 22.7 | 21.5 | 19.7 | 19.2 | 10.8 |
| % Loan Loss Reserve | 2.7 | 2.6 | 1.9 | 1.3 | 1.4 | 1.5 | 1.6 | 2.0 | 2.0 | 2.1 |
| % Loans/Deposits | 96.5 | 106.6 | 116.2 | 118.1 | 117.6 | 111.9 | 105.8 | 100.5 | 100.6 | 111.4 |
| % Equity to Assets | 8.8 | 7.8 | 7.6 | 8.8 | 9.4 | 9.8 | 10.1 | 10.2 | 9.8 | 9.4 |

Data as orig reptd.; bef. results of disc opers/spec. items. Per share data adj. for stk. divs.; EPS diluted. E-Estimated. NA-Not Available. NM-Not Meaningful. NR-Not Ranked. UR-Under Review.

**Office:** US Bancorp Center, 800 Nicollet Mall, Minneapolis, MN 55402.
**Telephone:** 651-466-3000.
**Website:** http://www.usbank.com
**Chrmn, Pres & CEO:** R.K. Davis

**COO & CTO:** J. von Gillern
**EVP, Chief Acctg Officer & Cntlr:** C.E. Gifford
**EVP & Treas:** K.D. Nelson
**EVP, Secy & General Counsel:** L.R. Mitau

**Investor Contact:** J.T. Murphy (612-303-0783)
**Board Members:** D. M. Baker, Jr., Y. M. Belton, A. D. Collins, Jr., R. K. Davis, V. B. Gluckman, J. W. Johnson, O. F. Kirtley, J. W. Levin, D. B. O'Maley, O. M. Owens, R. G. Reiten, C. D. Schnuck, P. T. Stokes

**Founded:** 1929
**Domicile:** Delaware
**Employees:** 60,584

The **McGraw·Hill** Companies

# United States Steel Corp

**STANDARD &POOR'S**

| S&P Recommendation BUY ★★★★☆ | Price $22.27 (as of Nov 25, 2011) | 12-Mo. Target Price $32.00 | Investment Style Large-Cap Value |
|---|---|---|---|

**GICS Sector** Materials
**Sub-Industry** Steel

**Summary** This company manufactures and sells a wide variety of steel sheet, plate, tubular and tin products, coke, and taconite pellets.

## Key Stock Statistics (Source S&P, Vickers, company reports)

| | | | | | | | |
|---|---|---|---|---|---|---|---|
| 52-Wk Range | $64.03– 18.85 | S&P Oper. EPS 2011**E** | 0.69 | Market Capitalization(B) | $3.207 | Beta | 2.43 |
| Trailing 12-Month EPS | $-0.53 | S&P Oper. EPS 2012**E** | 2.93 | Yield (%) | 0.90 | S&P 3-Yr. Proj. EPS CAGR(%) | NM |
| Trailing 12-Month P/E | NM | P/E on S&P Oper. EPS 2011**E** | 32.3 | Dividend Rate/Share | $0.20 | S&P Credit Rating | BB |
| $10K Invested 5 Yrs Ago | $3,098 | Common Shares Outstg. (M) | 144.0 | Institutional Ownership (%) | 79 | | |

## Price Performance

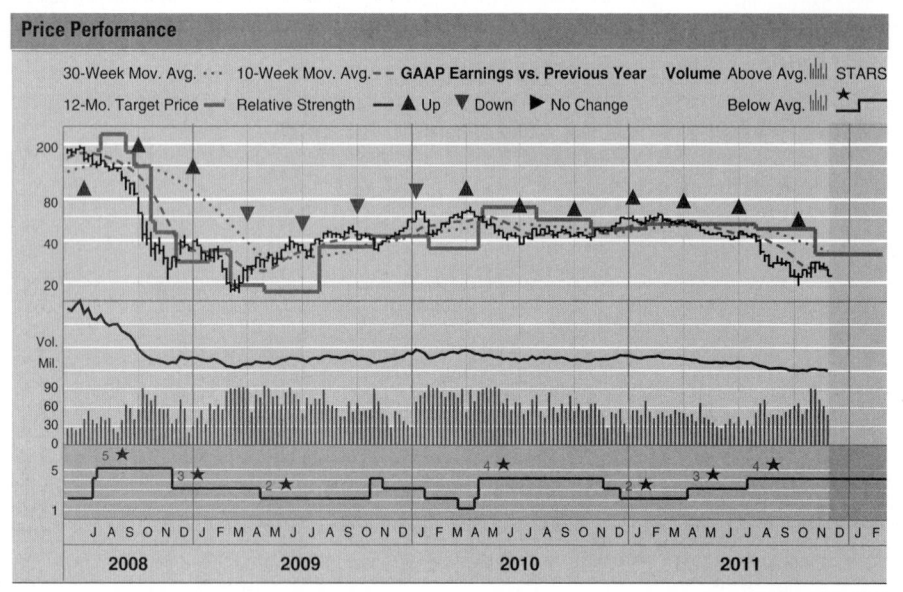

30-Week Mov. Avg. ···  10-Week Mov. Avg.- -  **GAAP Earnings vs. Previous Year**   Volume Above Avg.▐▐▌ STARS
12-Mo. Target Price —  Relative Strength  — ▲ Up ▼ Down ► No Change     Below Avg. ▐▐▌ ★

Options: ASE, CBOE

Analysis prepared by Equity Analyst **Leo J. Larkin** on Nov 09, 2011, when the stock traded at **$25.42**.

## Highlights

➤ Following a projected revenue advance of 13.6% in 2011, we look for a 5.7% gain in 2012, on further increases in tons shipped and steel prices. Our forecast rests on several assumptions. First, S&P forecasts real GDP growth of 1.5% in 2012, versus real GDP growth of 1.7% estimated for 2011. We see further gains in GDP leading to rising demand for durable goods. Second, we think demand for oil country tubular goods will rise again in 2012, as drilling activity picks up for both oil and gas. Third, we see distributors adding more to inventory in 2012 after just modest increases in 2011. Finally, we project more vibrant sales in European operations, following a slight gain in 2011.

➤ Aided by higher volume and revenue per ton, along with less rapidly rising raw material costs, we look for a sizable increase in operating profit in 2012. After interest expense and taxes, we project EPS of $2.93 for 2012, versus operating EPS of $0.69 estimated for 2011.

➤ We think earnings over the long term will increase on industry consolidation, rising demand for oil country tubular goods, and a gradual decline in costs for employee pensions and health care.

## Investment Rationale/Risk

➤ Long term, we see X's earnings rising on a gradual decline in pension and health care costs, well controlled raw material costs in domestic operations, consolidation of the global steel industry, and a secular increase in demand for oil country tubular goods. In particular, we believe the concentration of steel output in the hands of fewer companies will result in greater pricing and production discipline. In turn, we think this will lead to less volatile swings in pricing and profits over the course of the business cycle. Following a recent sharp decline in the stock price, we think X is attractively valued, currently trading at about 8.7X our 2012 EPS estimate.

➤ Risks to our recommendation and target price include declines in steel prices and shipments in 2012 instead of the increases we project.

➤ Our 12-month target price of $32 is based on our view that the shares should trade at a multiple of 11X our 2012 EPS estimate. On this projected multiple, X's valuation would be just above the mid-point of its historical range of the past 10 years.

## Qualitative Risk Assessment

| LOW | MEDIUM | HIGH |
|---|---|---|

Our risk assessment reflects the company's exposure to highly cyclical industries such as autos and construction, along with what we view as its high ratio of liabilities to assets and its unfunded pension and health care liabilities of $4.9 billion at the end of 2010.

## Quantitative Evaluations

**S&P Quality Ranking**                    B-

| D | C | B- | B | B+ | A- | A | A+ |
|---|---|---|---|---|---|---|---|

**Relative Strength Rank**                WEAK

17

LOWEST = 1                          HIGHEST = 99

## Revenue/Earnings Data

**Revenue (Million $)**

| | 1Q | 2Q | 3Q | 4Q | Year |
|---|---|---|---|---|---|
| 2011 | 4,864 | 5,120 | 5,081 | -- | -- |
| 2010 | 3,896 | 4,681 | 4,497 | 4,300 | 17,374 |
| 2009 | 2,750 | 2,127 | 2,817 | 3,354 | 11,048 |
| 2008 | 5,196 | 6,744 | 7,312 | 4,502 | 23,754 |
| 2007 | 3,756 | 4,228 | 4,354 | 4,535 | 16,873 |
| 2006 | 3,728 | 4,107 | 4,106 | 3,774 | 15,715 |

**Earnings Per Share ($)**

| | | | | | |
|---|---|---|---|---|---|
| 2011 | -0.60 | 1.33 | 0.15 | E-0.55 | E0.69 |
| 2010 | -1.10 | -0.17 | -0.35 | -1.74 | -3.36 |
| 2009 | -3.78 | -2.92 | -2.11 | -1.86 | -10.42 |
| 2008 | 1.98 | 5.65 | 7.79 | 2.50 | 17.96 |
| 2007 | 2.30 | 2.54 | 2.27 | 0.30 | 7.40 |
| 2006 | 2.04 | 3.22 | 3.42 | 2.50 | 11.18 |

Fiscal year ended Dec. 31. Next earnings report expected: NA. EPS Estimates based on S&P Operating Earnings; historical GAAP earnings are as reported.

## Dividend Data (Dates: mm/dd Payment Date: mm/dd/yy)

| Amount ($) | Date Decl. | Ex-Div. Date | Stk. of Record | Payment Date |
|---|---|---|---|---|
| 0.050 | 01/25 | 02/07 | 02/09 | 03/10/11 |
| 0.050 | 04/26 | 05/09 | 05/11 | 06/10/11 |
| 0.050 | 07/26 | 08/08 | 08/10 | 09/10/11 |
| 0.050 | 10/25 | 11/07 | 11/09 | 12/10/11 |

Dividends have been paid since 1991. Source: Company reports.

---

**Please read the Required Disclosures and Analyst Certification on the last page of this report.**

*The McGraw-Hill Companies*

# United States Steel Corp

STANDARD
&POOR'S

## Business Summary November 09, 2011

CORPORATE OVERVIEW. Following its acquisition of Stelco Inc. and Lone Star Technologies in 2007, U.S. Steel is the fifth largest steel producer in the world, the largest integrated steel producer headquartered in North America, and one of the largest integrated flat-rolled producers in Central Europe. In 2010, X produced 18.4 million tons of steel in North America and 6.1 million tons of steel in Europe. By way of comparison, X produced 11.7 million tons of steel in North America and 5.1 million tons of steel in Europe in 2009.

The company's other business activities include the production of coke in North America and Central Europe; and the production of iron ore pellets from taconite, transportation services (railroad and barge operations), real estate operations, and engineering and consulting services in North America.

CORPORATE STRATEGY. The company seeks to boost its revenues and earnings by expanding its value-added product mix, becoming a prime supplier of steel to growing European markets, strengthening its balance sheet, and becoming more cost competitive.

MARKET PROFILE. The primary factor affecting demand for steel products is economic growth in general, and growth in demand for durable goods in par-

ticular. The two largest end markets for steel products in the U.S. are autos and construction, which together accounted for 32% of shipments in 2010. Other end markets include appliances, containers, machinery, and oil and gas. Distributors, also known as service centers, accounted for 26% of industry shipments in the U.S. in 2010. Distributors are the largest single market for the steel industry in the U.S. Because distributors sell to a wide variety of OEMs, it is very difficult to trace the final destination of much of the industry's shipments. Consequently, consumption of steel by the auto, construction, and other industries may be higher than the shipment data would suggest. U.S. production was 88.7 million tons in 2010. X's largest end markets in 2010 were distributors (19.4% of tons shipped), appliances (4.6%), converters (30.3%), construction (11.8%), automotive (12.4%), containers (8.9%), oil and gas (6.5%), and other (6.1%). U.S. consumption decreased at a compound annual rate of 2.8% from 2001 through 2010. Global steel production totaled 1.41 billion metric tons in 2010, versus 1.23 billion metric tons in 2009.

## Company Financials Fiscal Year Ended Dec. 31

| Per Share Data ($) | 2010 | 2009 | 2008 | 2007 | 2006 | 2005 | 2004 | 2003 | 2002 | 2001 |
|---|---|---|---|---|---|---|---|---|---|---|
| Tangible Book Value | 12.64 | 18.62 | 25.85 | 28.81 | 36.82 | 25.63 | 32.30 | 7.98 | 15.81 | 28.16 |
| Cash Flow | 1.23 | -5.50 | 23.26 | 11.66 | 14.69 | 11.54 | 11.17 | -0.57 | 4.24 | 1.42 |
| Earnings | -3.36 | -10.42 | 17.96 | 7.40 | 11.18 | 7.00 | 8.37 | -4.09 | 0.62 | -2.45 |
| S&P Core Earnings | -2.29 | -9.64 | 14.34 | 7.42 | 11.76 | 6.64 | 8.74 | -1.06 | -4.10 | -8.47 |
| Dividends | 0.20 | 0.45 | 1.10 | 0.60 | 0.25 | 0.28 | 0.20 | 0.20 | 0.20 | 0.55 |
| Payout Ratio | NM | NM | 6% | 8% | 2% | 4% | 2% | NM | 32% | NM |
| Prices:High | 70.95 | 58.19 | 196.00 | 127.26 | 79.01 | 63.90 | 54.06 | 37.05 | 22.00 | 22.00 |
| Prices:Low | 36.93 | 16.66 | 20.71 | 68.83 | 48.05 | 33.59 | 25.22 | 9.61 | 10.66 | 13.00 |
| P/E Ratio:High | NM | NM | 11 | 17 | 7 | 9 | 6 | NM | 35 | NM |
| P/E Ratio:Low | NM | NM | 1 | 9 | 4 | 5 | 3 | NM | 17 | NM |

| Income Statement Analysis (Million $) | | | | | | | | | | |
|---|---|---|---|---|---|---|---|---|---|---|
| Revenue | 17,374 | 11,048 | 23,754 | 16,873 | 15,715 | 14,039 | 14,108 | 9,458 | 7,054 | 6,375 |
| Operating Income | 520 | -1,056 | 3,406 | 1,804 | 2,143 | 1,740 | 1,964 | 316 | 478 | -61.0 |
| Depreciation | 658 | 661 | 605 | 506 | 441 | 366 | 382 | 363 | 350 | 344 |
| Interest Expense | 274 | 159 | 176 | 163 | 117 | 107 | 138 | 148 | 136 | 153 |
| Pretax Income | -385 | -1,845 | 3,007 | 1,108 | 1,723 | 1,312 | 1,461 | -860 | 13.0 | -546 |
| Effective Tax Rate | NA | 23.8% | 28.4% | 19.7% | 18.8% | 27.8% | 24.0% | NM | NM | NM |
| Net Income | -482 | -1,401 | 2,112 | 879 | 1,374 | 910 | 1,077 | -406 | 61.0 | -218 |
| S&P Core Earnings | -329 | -1,296 | 1,686 | 882 | 1,438 | 847 | 1,104 | -109 | -398 | -755 |

| Balance Sheet & Other Financial Data (Million $) | | | | | | | | | | |
|---|---|---|---|---|---|---|---|---|---|---|
| Cash | 578 | 1,218 | 724 | 401 | 1,422 | 1,479 | 1,037 | 316 | 243 | 147 |
| Current Assets | 5,375 | 5,015 | 5,732 | 4,959 | 5,196 | 4,831 | 4,243 | 3,107 | 2,440 | 2,073 |
| Total Assets | 15,350 | 15,422 | 16,087 | 15,632 | 10,586 | 9,822 | 10,956 | 7,838 | 7,977 | 8,337 |
| Current Liabilities | 3,147 | 2,474 | 2,778 | 3,003 | 2,702 | 2,749 | 2,531 | 2,130 | 1,372 | 1,259 |
| Long Term Debt | 3,517 | 3,345 | 3,064 | 3,147 | 943 | 1,363 | 1,363 | 1,890 | 1,408 | 1,434 |
| Common Equity | 3,851 | 4,676 | 4,895 | 5,531 | 4,365 | 3,108 | 3,754 | 867 | 2,027 | 2,506 |
| Total Capital | 7,585 | 8,343 | 8,132 | 8,736 | 5,346 | 4,719 | 5,959 | 2,989 | 3,658 | 4,672 |
| Capital Expenditures | 676 | 619 | 896 | 692 | 612 | 741 | 579 | 316 | 258 | 287 |
| Cash Flow | 176 | -740 | 2,735 | 1,385 | 1,807 | 1,258 | 1,441 | -59.0 | 411 | 126 |
| Current Ratio | 1.7 | 2.1 | 2.1 | 1.7 | 1.9 | 1.8 | 1.7 | 1.5 | 1.8 | 1.6 |
| % Long Term Debt of Capitalization | 46.4 | 40.1 | 37.7 | 36.0 | 17.6 | 28.9 | 22.9 | 63.2 | 38.5 | 30.7 |
| % Net Income of Revenue | NM | NM | 8.9 | 5.2 | 8.7 | 6.5 | 7.8 | NM | 0.9 | NM |
| % Return on Assets | NM | NM | 13.3 | 6.7 | 13.5 | 8.7 | 11.5 | NM | 0.7 | NM |
| % Return on Equity | NM | NM | 40.5 | 17.8 | 36.6 | 25.6 | 45.8 | NM | 2.7 | NM |

Data as orig reptd.; bef. results of disc opers/spec. items. Per share data adj. for stk. divs.; EPS diluted. E-Estimated. NA-Not Available. NM-Not Meaningful. NR-Not Ranked. UR-Under Review.

**Office:** 600 Grant Street, Pittsburgh, PA 15219-2702.
**Telephone:** 412-433-1121.
**Email:** shareholderservices@uss.com
**Website:** http://www.ussteel.com

**Chrmn & CEO:** J.P. Surma, Jr.
**COO:** G.F. Babcoke
**EVP & CFO:** G.R. Haggerty
**Chief Admin Officer:** D.H. Lohr

**CTO:** A.R. Bridge
**Investor Contact:** N. Harper (412-433-1184)
**Board Members:** D. O. Dinges, J. G. Drosdick, J. J. Engel, R. A. Gephardt, C. R. Lee, F. J. Lucchino, G. G. McNeal, S. E. Schofield, J. P. Surma, Jr., D. S. Sutherland, P. A. Tracey

**Founded:** 2001
**Domicile:** Delaware
**Employees:** 42,000

# United Technologies Corp

**STANDARD &POOR'S**

**S&P Recommendation** BUY ★★★★☆

| Price | 12-Mo. Target Price | Investment Style |
|---|---|---|
| $71.04 (as of Nov 25, 2011) | $92.00 | Large-Cap Growth |

**GICS Sector** Industrials
**Sub-Industry** Aerospace & Defense

**Summary** This aerospace-industrial conglomerate's portfolio includes Pratt & Whitney jet engines, Sikorsky helicopters, Otis elevators, and Carrier air conditioners, among other products.

## Key Stock Statistics (Source S&P, Vickers, company reports)

| | | | | | | | |
|---|---|---|---|---|---|---|---|
| 52-Wk Range | $91.83– 66.87 | S&P Oper. EPS 2011**E** | 5.50 | Market Capitalization(B) | $64.368 | Beta | 1.03 |
| Trailing 12-Month EPS | $5.33 | S&P Oper. EPS 2012**E** | 6.00 | Yield (%) | 2.70 | S&P 3-Yr. Proj. EPS CAGR(%) | 10 |
| Trailing 12-Month P/E | 13.3 | P/E on S&P Oper. EPS 2011**E** | 12.9 | Dividend Rate/Share | $1.92 | S&P Credit Rating | A |
| $10K Invested 5 Yrs Ago | $12,059 | Common Shares Outstg. (M) | 906.1 | Institutional Ownership (%) | 84 | | |

## Price Performance

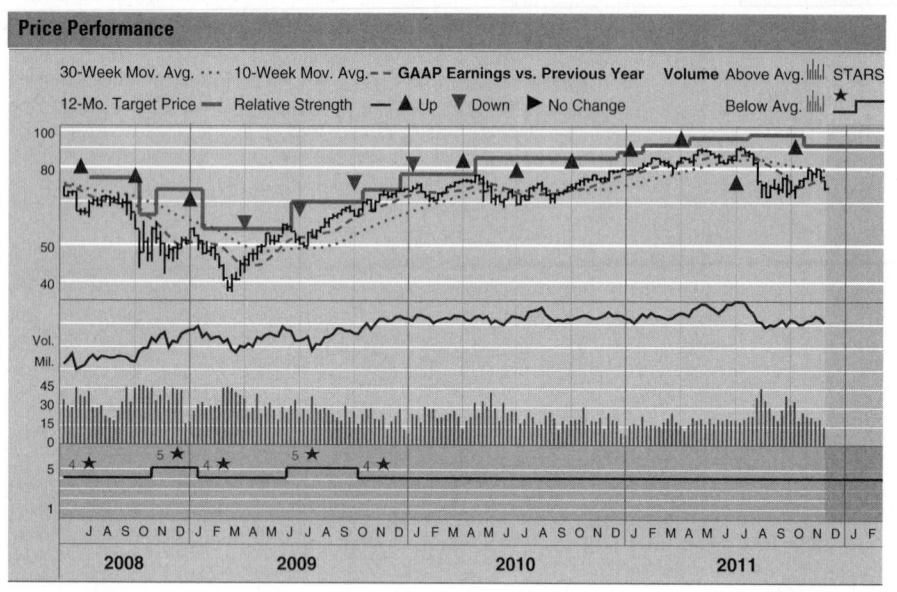

- 30-Week Mov. Avg. · · · 10-Week Mov. Avg. - - GAAP Earnings vs. Previous Year   Volume Above Avg. STARS
- 12-Mo. Target Price — Relative Strength — ▲ Up ▼ Down ► No Change   Below Avg. ★

Options: ASE, CBOE, P, Ph

Analysis prepared by Equity Analyst **R. Tortoriello** on Oct 21, 2011, when the stock traded at **$75.39**.

### Highlights

► In September 2011, UTX agreed to acquire Goodrich Corp. (GR 122 Hold) for $127.50 per share in cash, or $18.4 billion, including $1.9 billion in assumed debt, subject to approvals. Although the purchase price of 11X EBITDA is toward the high end of our view of GR's enterprise value, we believe the planned acquisition would expand UTX's ability to create high-value systems for commercial aircraft makers. We estimate a 7% sales rise in 2011, on global economic improvement. For 2012, we project a 4% rise in sales, as we see some slowing in global economic growth.

► We estimate operating margins of 14.2% in 2011, up from 13.2% in 2010. We project further improvement to 14.8% in 2012, on efficiency improvements, as UTX plans to spend $300 million on restructuring, partially offset by potential pension headwinds.

► We estimate EPS of $5.50 in 2011, rising to $6.00 in 2012. We expect free cash flow (operating cash flow less capital expenditures) in excess of net income in both periods.

### Investment Rationale/Risk

► We see the following trends positively affecting UTX's business: large backlogs of commercial aircraft at both Airbus and Boeing, which we view as providing good production levels through 2013; the expected service entry of the 787; a significant rise in commercial aerospace aftermarket spending; continued strong growth in emerging economies; eventual improvement in the U.S. residential housing market; and modest signs of improvement in commercial construction. We expect headwinds of commodity price inflation and increased pension expense to be offset by what we view as UTX's strong operating leverage.

► Risks to our opinion and target price include the possibility that the global economy slows down, operational issues in UTX's business segments, and a sustained rise in the dollar.

► Our 12-month target price of $92 is based on an enterprise value-to-estimated 2012 EBITDA multiple of about 8.5X, largely in line with the 20-year historical average multiple of 8X, reflecting our view of UTX's strong performance offset by some slowing in the global economy and pension headwinds.

### Qualitative Risk Assessment

| LOW | MEDIUM | HIGH |
|---|---|---|

Our risk assessment is based on our view of UTX's history of steady growth in both earnings and dividends over the past 10 years, as reflected in its S&P Quality Ranking of A+. We also consider UTX's balance sheet to be strong, with long-term debt at 29% of total capital and cash at 9% of assets as of September 2011.

### Quantitative Evaluations

**S&P Quality Ranking**   A+

| D | C | B- | B | B+ | A- | A | A+ |
|---|---|---|---|---|---|---|---|

**Relative Strength Rank**   MODERATE

49

LOWEST = 1   HIGHEST = 99

### Revenue/Earnings Data

**Revenue (Million $)**

| | 1Q | 2Q | 3Q | 4Q | Year |
|---|---|---|---|---|---|
| 2011 | 13,344 | 15,076 | 14,804 | -- | -- |
| 2010 | 12,040 | 13,802 | 13,620 | 14,864 | 54,326 |
| 2009 | 12,199 | 13,060 | 13,187 | 13,979 | 52,920 |
| 2008 | 13,577 | 15,535 | 14,702 | 14,299 | 58,681 |
| 2007 | 12,278 | 13,904 | 13,863 | 14,714 | 54,759 |
| 2006 | 10,446 | 12,046 | 11,972 | 12,654 | 47,829 |

**Earnings Per Share ($)**

| | | | | | |
|---|---|---|---|---|---|
| 2011 | 1.11 | 1.45 | 1.47 | E1.47 | E5.50 |
| 2010 | 0.93 | 1.20 | 1.30 | 1.31 | 4.74 |
| 2009 | 0.78 | 1.05 | 1.14 | 1.15 | 4.12 |
| 2008 | 1.03 | 1.32 | 1.33 | 1.23 | 4.90 |
| 2007 | 0.82 | 1.16 | 1.21 | 1.08 | 4.27 |
| 2006 | 0.76 | 1.09 | 0.99 | 0.87 | 3.71 |

Fiscal year ended Dec. 31. Next earnings report expected: Late January. EPS Estimates based on S&P Operating Earnings; historical GAAP earnings are as reported.

### Dividend Data (Dates: mm/dd Payment Date: mm/dd/yy)

| Amount ($) | Date Decl. | Ex-Div. Date | Stk. of Record | Payment Date |
|---|---|---|---|---|
| 0.425 | 02/07 | 02/16 | 02/18 | 03/10/11 |
| 0.480 | 04/13 | 05/18 | 05/20 | 06/10/11 |
| 0.480 | 06/08 | 08/17 | 08/19 | 09/10/11 |
| 0.480 | 10/12 | 11/16 | 11/18 | 12/10/11 |

Dividends have been paid since 1936. Source: Company reports.

---

**Please read the Required Disclosures and Analyst Certification on the last page of this report.**

The McGraw·Hill Companies

# United Technologies Corp

**STANDARD &POOR'S**

## Business Summary October 21, 2011

CORPORATE OVERVIEW. United Technologies is a multi-industry holding company that conducts business through six business segments: Carrier, Otis, Pratt & Whitney, UTC Fire & Security, Hamilton Sundstrand, and Sikorsky.

Carrier (21% of sales and 13% of operating profits in 2010) is the world's largest maker of heating, ventilating and air-conditioning (HVAC) and refrigeration systems. It offers HVAC, refrigeration systems and food service equipment, and refrigeration-related controls for residential, commercial, industrial and transportation applications. In addition, Carrier provides installation, retrofit, and parts and services for its products, as well as those of other HVAC and refrigeration makers. International sales, including U.S. export sales, accounted for 56% of segment sales in 2010.

Otis (21% of sales and 32% of operating profits) is the world's largest maker of elevators and escalators. Otis designs, manufactures, sells, installs, maintains and modernizes a wide range of passenger and freight elevators for low-, medium- and high-speed applications, as well as a broad line of escalators and moving walkways. International revenues were 82% of total segment revenues in 2010.

Pratt & Whitney (24% and 25%) is a major supplier of jet engines for commercial, business & general aviation, and military aircraft. P&W also sells indus-

trial gas turbines (for industrial power generation) and space propulsion systems. P&W Canada is a leading provider of business, regional, military and light jet engines. P&W's Global Services provides maintenance, repair and overhaul services, and fleet management services for large commercial engines. Key development programs include the F135 engine, for the F-35 Joint Strike Fighter, and the PW1000G geared turbofan engine, which will be used on the Airbus A320neo, among other aircraft. Airbus accounted for 12% of segment sales in 2010, and the U.S. government accounted for 32%. International revenues were 52% of total segment revenues in 2010.

UTC Fire & Security (12% and 9%) is a global provider of security and fire safety products and services, including intruder alarms, access control systems and video surveillance systems, specialty hazard detection and fixed supression products, portable fire extinguishers, fire detection and life safety systems, and other firefighting equipment. In March 2010, UTX purchased GE Security, from General Electric, for $1.8 billion. International sales accounted for 84% of total segment sales in 2010.

## Company Financials Fiscal Year Ended Dec. 31

| Per Share Data ($) | 2010 | 2009 | 2008 | 2007 | 2006 | 2005 | 2004 | 2003 | 2002 | 2001 |
|---|---|---|---|---|---|---|---|---|---|---|
| Tangible Book Value | NM | 0.25 | NM | 2.45 | NM | 0.91 | 1.84 | 2.32 | 1.46 | 1.66 |
| Cash Flow | 6.21 | 5.48 | 6.19 | 5.38 | 4.74 | 4.09 | 3.73 | 3.14 | 2.93 | 2.81 |
| Earnings | 4.74 | 4.12 | 4.90 | 4.27 | 3.71 | 3.12 | 2.76 | 2.35 | 2.21 | 1.92 |
| S&P Core Earnings | 4.67 | 4.05 | 3.81 | 4.17 | 3.64 | 3.05 | 2.59 | 2.16 | 1.32 | 1.14 |
| Dividends | 1.70 | 1.54 | 1.35 | 1.17 | 1.02 | 0.88 | 0.70 | 0.57 | 0.49 | 0.45 |
| Payout Ratio | 36% | 37% | 27% | 27% | 27% | 28% | 25% | 24% | 22% | 23% |
| Prices:High | 79.70 | 70.89 | 77.14 | 82.50 | 67.47 | 58.89 | 53.14 | 48.38 | 38.88 | 43.75 |
| Prices:Low | 62.88 | 37.40 | 41.76 | 61.85 | 54.20 | 48.43 | 40.34 | 26.76 | 24.42 | 20.05 |
| P/E Ratio:High | 17 | 17 | 16 | 19 | 18 | 19 | 19 | 21 | 18 | 23 |
| P/E Ratio:Low | 13 | 9 | 9 | 14 | 15 | 16 | 15 | 11 | 11 | 10 |

| Income Statement Analysis (Million $) | | | | | | | | | | |
|---|---|---|---|---|---|---|---|---|---|---|
| Revenue | 54,326 | 52,920 | 58,681 | 54,759 | 47,829 | 42,725 | 37,445 | 31,034 | 28,212 | 27,897 |
| Operating Income | 8,542 | 8,488 | 9,031 | 8,223 | 7,131 | 6,166 | 5,448 | 4,644 | 4,384 | 4,138 |
| Depreciation | 1,356 | 1,258 | 1,228 | 1,173 | 1,033 | 984 | 978 | 799 | 727 | 905 |
| Interest Expense | 648 | 705 | 689 | 666 | 606 | 498 | 363 | 375 | 381 | 426 |
| Pretax Income | 6,538 | 5,760 | 6,936 | 6,384 | 5,492 | 4,684 | 4,107 | 3,470 | 3,276 | 2,807 |
| Effective Tax Rate | NA | 27.5% | 27.2% | 28.8% | 27.2% | 26.8% | 26.4% | 27.1% | 27.1% | 26.9% |
| Net Income | 4,373 | 3,829 | 4,689 | 4,224 | 3,732 | 3,164 | 2,788 | 2,361 | 2,236 | 1,938 |
| S&P Core Earnings | 4,310 | 3,756 | 3,648 | 4,125 | 3,653 | 3,089 | 2,619 | 2,147 | 1,298 | 1,113 |

| Balance Sheet & Other Financial Data (Million $) | | | | | | | | | | |
|---|---|---|---|---|---|---|---|---|---|---|
| Cash | 4,083 | 4,449 | 4,327 | 2,904 | 2,546 | 2,247 | 2,265 | 1,623 | 2,080 | 1,558 |
| Current Assets | 23,510 | 23,194 | 24,099 | 22,071 | 18,844 | 17,206 | 15,522 | 12,364 | 11,751 | 11,263 |
| Total Assets | 58,493 | 55,762 | 56,469 | 54,575 | 47,141 | 45,925 | 40,035 | 34,648 | 29,090 | 26,969 |
| Current Liabilities | 17,732 | 17,913 | 19,434 | 17,469 | 15,208 | 15,345 | 12,947 | 10,295 | 7,903 | 8,371 |
| Long Term Debt | 10,010 | 8,257 | 9,337 | 8,015 | 7,037 | 5,935 | 4,231 | 4,257 | 4,632 | 4,237 |
| Common Equity | 21,385 | 20,066 | 15,917 | 21,355 | 17,297 | 16,991 | 14,008 | 11,707 | 10,506 | 8,369 |
| Total Capital | 32,659 | 29,645 | 27,379 | 30,282 | 25,170 | 23,704 | 19,149 | 16,673 | 16,445 | 13,899 |
| Capital Expenditures | 865 | 826 | 1,216 | 1,153 | 954 | 929 | 795 | 530 | 586 | 793 |
| Cash Flow | 5,729 | 5,087 | 5,917 | 5,319 | 4,765 | 4,148 | 3,766 | 3,160 | 2,963 | 2,843 |
| Current Ratio | 1.3 | 1.3 | 1.2 | 1.3 | 1.2 | 1.1 | 1.2 | 1.2 | 1.5 | 1.3 |
| % Long Term Debt of Capitalization | 30.7 | 27.9 | 35.6 | 26.5 | 28.0 | 25.0 | 22.1 | 25.5 | 28.2 | 30.5 |
| % Net Income of Revenue | 8.1 | 7.2 | 8.0 | 7.7 | 7.8 | 7.4 | 7.4 | 7.6 | 7.9 | 6.9 |
| % Return on Assets | 7.7 | 6.8 | 8.5 | 8.3 | 8.0 | 7.3 | 7.4 | 7.4 | 8.0 | 7.4 |
| % Return on Equity | 21.1 | 21.3 | 25.2 | 21.9 | 21.8 | 20.2 | 21.7 | 23.9 | 23.0 | 24.2 |

Data as orig reptd.; bef. results of disc opers/spec. items. Per share data adj. for stk. divs.; EPS diluted. E-Estimated. NA-Not Available. NM-Not Meaningful. NR-Not Ranked. UR-Under Review.

**Office:** 1 Financial Plz, Hartford, CT 06103.
**Telephone:** 860-728-7000.
**Email:** invrelations@corphq.utc.com
**Website:** http://www.utc.com

**Chrmn, Pres & CEO:** L.R. Chenevert
**SVP & General Counsel:** C.D. Gill, Jr.
**CFO:** G.J. Hayes
**CTO:** J.M. McQuade

**Chief Acctg Officer & Cntlr:** P.F. Longo
**Investor Contact:** J. Moran (860-728-7062)
**Board Members:** L. R. Chenevert, J. V. Faraci, J. Garnier, J. S. Gorelick, E. A. Kangas, E. Kullman, C. R. Lee, R. D. McCormick, H. McGraw, III, R. B. Myers, H. P. Swygert, A. Villeneuve, C. T. Whitman

**Founded:** 1934
**Domicile:** Delaware
**Employees:** 208,200

*The McGraw·Hill Companies*

# Unum Group

**STANDARD &POOR'S**

| S&P Recommendation | **HOLD** ★★★☆☆ | Price $20.70 (as of Nov 25, 2011) | 12-Mo. Target Price $24.00 | Investment Style Large-Cap Value |
| --- | --- | --- | --- | --- |

**GICS Sector** Financials
**Sub-Industry** Life & Health Insurance

**Summary** The largest provider of individual and group disability insurance products in the U.S. and the U.K., Unum provides other products and services as well.

## Key Stock Statistics (Source S&P, Vickers, company reports)

| | | | | | | | |
| --- | --- | --- | --- | --- | --- | --- | --- |
| 52-Wk Range | $27.16– 19.72 | S&P Oper. EPS 2011E | 2.95 | Market Capitalization(B) | $6.052 | Beta | 1.66 |
| Trailing 12-Month EPS | $2.86 | S&P Oper. EPS 2012E | 3.25 | Yield (%) | 2.03 | S&P 3-Yr. Proj. EPS CAGR(%) | 3 |
| Trailing 12-Month P/E | 7.2 | P/E on S&P Oper. EPS 2011E | 7.0 | Dividend Rate/Share | $0.42 | S&P Credit Rating | BBB- |
| $10K Invested 5 Yrs Ago | $10,926 | Common Shares Outstg. (M) | 292.4 | Institutional Ownership (%) | 97 | | |

## Price Performance

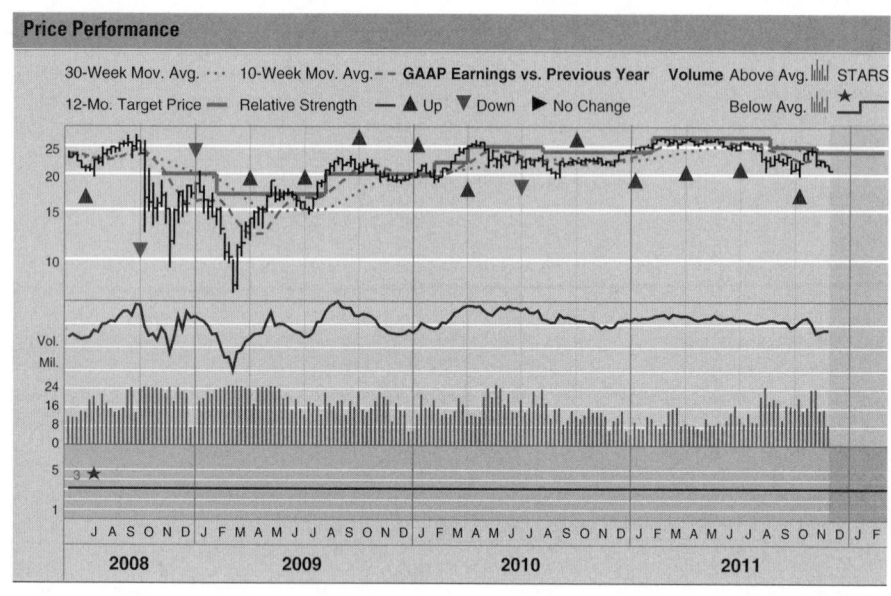

30-Week Mov. Avg. ···· 10-Week Mov. Avg. — **GAAP Earnings vs. Previous Year**   Volume Above Avg. ▮▮▮ STARS
12-Mo. Target Price — Relative Strength — ▲ Up ▼ Down ► No Change   Below Avg. ▮▮▮ ★

Options: ASE, CBOE, P

Analysis prepared by Equity Analyst **Cathy Seifert** on Nov 22, 2011, when the stock traded at **$21.30**.

## Qualitative Risk Assessment

| LOW | **MEDIUM** | HIGH |
| --- | --- | --- |

Our risk assessment reflects regulatory scrutiny surrounding certain claims practices. Although the largest lawsuits have been settled, UNM faces the possibility of additional suits and increased reserving for benefit costs in its claims reassessment. Our risk assessment also reflects the poor macro environment and the possibility of a higher benefit ratio going forward. However, we believe UNM maintains a strong financial position, and we believe it will be more active with capital management than peers.

## Quantitative Evaluations

**S&P Quality Ranking**   B

| D | C | B- | **B** | B+ | A- | A | A+ |
| --- | --- | --- | --- | --- | --- | --- | --- |

**Relative Strength Rank**   MODERATE

39

LOWEST = 1   HIGHEST = 99

## Highlights

➤ We expect premiums to be about flat at Unum US in coming periods as strong sales growth in the supplemental and voluntary lines are offset by a decline in group disability premiums and by lower investment income due to reduced new money yields. We think high unemployment and the lack of wage inflation will adversely affect pricing in Unum US's disability and group life businesses, though we see this trend reversing gradually this year. We expect persistency to drop slightly, and see the benefit ratio elevated due to higher claims due to the poor economy. We believe sales will be challenged in the core market by the weak labor market and the reluctance of employers to add new benefits to existing accounts.

➤ We look for earnings to rise in the mid-single digits at Colonial, as improving sales and lower expenses should more than offset pricing pressure and an increase in the benefit ratio. We expect earnings at Unum UK to be volatile on fluctuating disability claims incidence, foreign currency shifts, and declining persistency.

➤ We forecast operating EPS of $2.95 in 2011 and $3.25 in 2012, excluding realized investment gains or losses.

## Investment Rationale/Risk

➤ While UNM's underwriting results have fared better than many peers in the current environment, we think tempered sales growth, increased claims and restricted disability margins and enrollment levels will crimp results in coming periods. We believe UNM will continue to experience a decline in sales and poor risk results in the large case market. However, it maintains a conservative investment portfolio, and we think its strong capital position will be a competitive advantage that should enable the company to gain market share in some businesses. We expect UNM to use its excess capital and liquidity to continue to repurchase its shares in 2011.

➤ Risks to our recommendation and target price include worse-than-expected client retention and sales following income protection product price increases, unfavorable claims handling in the group income protection area, higher-than-forecast costs for reassessed claims, and investment losses.

➤ Our 12-month target price of $24 assumes that the shares trade at less than 1X estimated 2012 book value, below UNM's historical price/book multiple.

## Revenue/Earnings Data

**Revenue (Million $)**

| | 1Q | 2Q | 3Q | 4Q | Year |
| --- | --- | --- | --- | --- | --- |
| 2011 | 2,563 | 2,565 | 2,546 | -- | -- |
| 2010 | 2,562 | 2,511 | 2,528 | 2,593 | 10,193 |
| 2009 | 2,449 | 2,628 | 2,518 | 2,497 | 10,091 |
| 2008 | 2,541 | 2,675 | 2,443 | 2,324 | 9,982 |
| 2007 | 2,601 | 2,666 | 2,610 | 2,644 | 10,520 |
| 2006 | 2,600 | 2,622 | 2,617 | 2,696 | 10,535 |

**Earnings Per Share ($)**

| | 1Q | 2Q | 3Q | 4Q | Year |
| --- | --- | --- | --- | --- | --- |
| 2011 | 0.72 | 0.75 | 0.69 | E0.77 | E2.95 |
| 2010 | 0.69 | 0.63 | 0.68 | 0.71 | 2.71 |
| 2009 | 0.50 | 0.80 | 0.67 | 0.60 | 2.57 |
| 2008 | 0.46 | 0.69 | 0.32 | 0.13 | 1.62 |
| 2007 | 0.49 | 0.43 | 0.52 | 0.45 | 1.89 |
| 2006 | 0.23 | 0.37 | -0.19 | 0.79 | 1.21 |

Fiscal year ended Dec. 31. Next earnings report expected: Early February. EPS Estimates based on S&P Operating Earnings; historical GAAP earnings are as reported.

## Dividend Data (Dates: mm/dd Payment Date: mm/dd/yy)

| Amount ($) | Date Decl. | Ex-Div. Date | Stk. of Record | Payment Date |
| --- | --- | --- | --- | --- |
| 0.093 | 01/13 | 01/27 | 01/31 | 02/18/11 |
| 0.093 | 04/11 | 04/20 | 04/25 | 05/20/11 |
| 0.105 | 07/15 | 07/27 | 07/29 | 08/19/11 |
| 0.105 | 10/05 | 10/27 | 10/31 | 11/18/11 |

Dividends have been paid since 1925. Source: Company reports.

**Please read the Required Disclosures and Analyst Certification on the last page of this report.**

*The McGraw-Hill Companies*

# Unum Group

## Business Summary November 22, 2011

CORPORATE OVERVIEW. UNM is the largest provider of disability insurance products in the United States and the U.K. through its subsidiaries. The company offers other products, including long-term care insurance, life insurance, group benefits, and related services.

The company has five operating segments: Unum US, Unum UK, Colonial, Individual Disability - Closed Block, and Corporate and Other. Unum US accounted for 61% of operating revenue in 2010, Unum UK 8.1%, Colonial 12%, Individual Disability - Closed Block 17%, and Corporate and Other 2.2%. In 2010, premium income for Unum US declined 3.1%, Unum UK premium income declined roughly 5.2%, and Colonial premium income increased 6.0%.

The Unum US segment includes group income protection insurance, group life and accidental death and dismemberment products, and supplemental and voluntary lines of business. The Unum UK segment includes group long-term income protection insurance, group life products, and individual income protection products issued by Unum Limited and sold primarily in the U.K. through field sales personnel and independent brokers and consultants. The Colonial segment includes a broad line of products sold mainly to employees at their

workplaces, including income protection, life, and cancer and critical illness products. The Corporate and Other segment includes investment income on unallocated corporate assets, interest expense, and certain unallocated corporate income and expense items. In addition, the segment includes products that are no longer actively marketed, with the exception of the closed block business, including individual life and corporate-owned life insurance, reinsurance pools and management operations, group pension, health insurance, and individual annuities.

The Individual Disability Closed Block segment mainly includes individual income protection insurance written on a non cancelable basis with a fixed annual premium. Generally, the policies are individual disability insurance policies designed to be distributed to individuals in a non-workplace setting and written prior to UNM's restructuring of its individual disability business, where the focus was changed to workplace distribution.

## Company Financials Fiscal Year Ended Dec. 31

| Per Share Data ($) | 2010 | 2009 | 2008 | 2007 | 2006 | 2005 | 2004 | 2003 | 2002 | 2001 |
|---|---|---|---|---|---|---|---|---|---|---|
| Tangible Book Value | 27.62 | 32.48 | 18.34 | 21.72 | 21.93 | 23.76 | 23.45 | 22.94 | 25.58 | 21.74 |
| Operating Earnings | NA | NA | NA | NA | NA | NA | NA | NA | 2.52 | 2.44 |
| Earnings | 2.71 | 2.57 | 1.62 | 1.89 | 1.21 | 1.64 | -0.65 | -0.96 | 1.68 | 2.39 |
| S&P Core Earnings | 2.72 | 2.64 | 2.43 | 2.10 | 1.29 | 1.81 | -0.26 | -0.54 | 2.35 | 2.30 |
| Dividends | 0.35 | 0.31 | 0.30 | 0.30 | 0.30 | 0.30 | 0.30 | 0.37 | 0.59 | 0.59 |
| Payout Ratio | 13% | 12% | 19% | 16% | 25% | 18% | NM | NM | 35% | 25% |
| Prices:High | 26.42 | 23.25 | 27.50 | 28.20 | 24.44 | 22.90 | 18.25 | 19.54 | 29.70 | 33.75 |
| Prices:Low | 18.56 | 7.61 | 9.33 | 19.79 | 16.15 | 15.50 | 11.41 | 5.91 | 16.30 | 22.25 |
| P/E Ratio:High | 10 | 9 | 17 | 15 | 20 | 14 | NM | NM | 18 | 14 |
| P/E Ratio:Low | 7 | 3 | 6 | 10 | 13 | 9 | NM | NM | 10 | 9 |

| Income Statement Analysis (Million $) | | | | | | | | | | |
|---|---|---|---|---|---|---|---|---|---|---|
| Life Insurance in Force | 742,630 | 677,278 | 629,069 | 692,012 | 773,070 | 833,363 | 908,034 | 787,199 | 712,826 | 642,988 |
| Premium Income:Life | 1,664 | 1,603 | 1,620 | 1,641 | 1,761 | 7,816 | 5,985 | 1,800 | 1,683 | 1,554 |
| Premium Income:A & H | 5,767 | 5,873 | 6,163 | 6,261 | 6,187 | 1,787 | 1,855 | 5,816 | 5,770 | 5,524 |
| Net Investment Income | 2,496 | 2,347 | 2,389 | 2,410 | 2,321 | 2,188 | 2,159 | 2,158 | 2,086 | 2,003 |
| Total Revenue | 10,193 | 10,091 | 9,982 | 10,520 | 10,535 | 10,437 | 10,465 | 9,992 | 9,613 | 9,395 |
| Pretax Income | 1,331 | 1,292 | 824 | 997 | 465 | 710 | -260 | -435 | 1,019 | 825 |
| Net Operating Income | NA | NA | NA | NA | NA | NA | NA | NA | 614 | 593 |
| Net Income | 886 | 853 | 553 | 672 | 404 | 514 | -192 | -265 | 817 | 582 |
| S&P Core Earnings | 889 | 878 | 824 | 748 | 428 | 570 | -77.1 | -150 | 568 | 564 |

| Balance Sheet & Other Financial Data (Million $) | | | | | | | | | | |
|---|---|---|---|---|---|---|---|---|---|---|
| Cash & Equivalent | 723 | 714 | 656 | 791 | 768 | 688 | 719 | 663 | 734 | 2,515 |
| Premiums Due | 1,666 | 1,732 | 1,785 | 1,915 | 2,057 | NA | NA | NA | NA | NA |
| Investment Assets:Bonds | 40,036 | 37,914 | 31,926 | 35,655 | 35,002 | 34,857 | 32,488 | 31,187 | 27,486 | 24,393 |
| Investment Assets:Stocks | Nil | Nil | 208 | Nil | Nil | 13.6 | 12.9 | 39.1 | 27.9 | 10.9 |
| Investment Assets:Loans | 4,513 | 4,282 | 4,029 | 3,705 | 944 | 3,941 | 3,572 | 3,353 | 3,344 | 3,510 |
| Investment Assets:Total | 46,241 | 43,295 | 37,866 | 40,951 | 40,163 | 39,357 | 36,588 | 35,028 | 31,152 | 28,324 |
| Deferred Policy Costs | 2,521 | 2,483 | 2,472 | 2,381 | 2,983 | 2,913 | 2,883 | 3,052 | 2,982 | 2,675 |
| Total Assets | 57,308 | 54,506 | 49,417 | 52,433 | 52,823 | 51,867 | 50,832 | 49,718 | 45,260 | 42,443 |
| Debt | 2,631 | 2,550 | 2,259 | 2,515 | 2,660 | 3,262 | 2,862 | 2,789 | 1,914 | 2,304 |
| Common Equity | 8,944 | 8,500 | 6,398 | 8,040 | 7,719 | 7,364 | 7,224 | 7,271 | 9,398 | 5,940 |
| % Return on Revenue | 8.7 | 8.5 | 5.5 | 6.4 | 3.9 | 4.9 | NM | NM | 8.5 | 6.2 |
| % Return on Assets | 1.6 | 1.6 | 1.1 | 1.3 | 0.8 | 1.0 | NM | NM | 1.9 | 1.4 |
| % Return on Equity | 10.2 | 11.5 | 7.7 | 8.5 | 5.4 | 7.0 | NM | NM | 9.1 | 10.1 |
| % Investment Yield | 5.6 | 5.8 | 6.1 | 5.9 | 5.8 | 5.8 | 6.0 | 6.5 | 7.0 | 7.3 |

Data as orig reptd.; bef. results of disc opers/spec. items. Per share data adj. for stk. divs.; EPS diluted. E-Estimated. NA-Not Available. NM-Not Meaningful. NR-Not Ranked. UR-Under Review.

**Office:** 1 Fountain Square, Chattanooga, TN 37402.
**Telephone:** 423-294-1011.
**Website:** http://www.unum.com
**Chrmn:** W.J. Ryan

**Pres & CEO:** T. Watjen
**EVP, CFO & Chief Acctg Officer:** R. McKenney
**EVP & General Counsel:** E.L. Bishop, III
**SVP & Treas:** K.A. McMahon

**Investor Contact:** T.A. White (423-294-8996)
**Board Members:** E. M. Caulfield, P. H. Godwin, R. E. Goldsberry, K. T. Kabat, T. A. Kinser, G. C. Larson, A. MacMillan, Jr., E. J. Muhl, M. J. Passarella, W. J. Ryan, T. Watjen

**Founded:** 1887
**Domicile:** Delaware
**Employees:** 9,500

# Urban Outfitters Inc

**STANDARD &POOR'S**

**S&P Recommendation** HOLD ★★★★☆

| | |
|---|---|
| **Price** $25.19 (as of Nov 25, 2011) | **12-Mo. Target Price** $28.00 |

**Investment Style** Large-Cap Growth

**GICS Sector** Consumer Discretionary
**Sub-Industry** Apparel Retail

**Summary** This company primarily operates three specialty retail brands -- Urban Outfitters, Anthropologie, and Free People -- in multi-channel settings.

## Key Stock Statistics (Source S&P, Vickers, company reports)

| | | | | | | | |
|---|---|---|---|---|---|---|---|
| 52-Wk Range | $39.26– 21.47 | S&P Oper. EPS 2012**E** | 1.30 | Market Capitalization(B) | $3.877 | Beta | 0.98 |
| Trailing 12-Month EPS | $1.36 | S&P Oper. EPS 2013**E** | 1.60 | Yield (%) | Nil | S&P 3-Yr. Proj. EPS CAGR(%) | 8 |
| Trailing 12-Month P/E | 18.5 | P/E on S&P Oper. EPS 2012**E** | 19.4 | Dividend Rate/Share | Nil | S&P Credit Rating | NA |
| $10K Invested 5 Yrs Ago | $11,337 | Common Shares Outstg. (M) | 153.9 | Institutional Ownership (%) | 81 | | |

## Price Performance

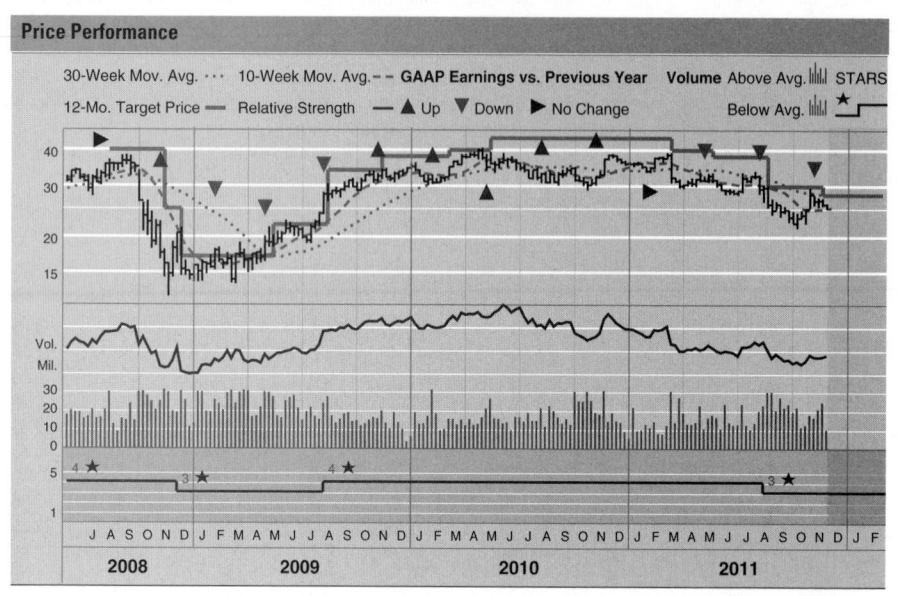

30-Week Mov. Avg. · · · · 10-Week Mov. Avg. – – **GAAP Earnings vs. Previous Year** Volume Above Avg. STARS
12-Mo. Target Price — Relative Strength — ▲ Up ▼ Down ► No Change Below Avg. ★

Options: ASE, CBOE, P, Ph

Analysis prepared by Equity Analyst **Jason N. Asaeda** on Nov 16, 2011, when the stock traded at **$26.85**.

## Highlights

➤ We look for 8% net sales growth in FY 12 (Jan.), to $2.45 billion, followed by a 12% increase in FY 13, to $2.74 billion. URBN's broad and shallow merchandise strategy of frequent inventory flows delivers newness to stores, while creating exclusivity and a sense of urgency that supports full-price sales. Unfortunately, fashion misses in the all important women's apparel category at Anthropologie and Urban Outfitters have hurt results in recent quarters. We think sharper merchandising and a heightened accessories strategy should improve results in FY 13. We see the company doubling its retail brand portfolio over the next five years.

➤ We see increased markdowns to drive sell-through and deleveraging of expenses off a projected mid-single digit comp decline leading to 540 basis points (bps) of EBIT margin contraction in FY 12, to 12.8%. We look for URBN to regain about 100 bps of EBIT margin in FY 13, supported by higher sales and controlled store level inventories.

➤ Factoring in planned share repurchases, we estimate EPS of $1.30 for FY 12 and $1.60 for FY 13.

## Investment Rationale/Risk

➤ Our hold recommendation is based on valuation. We see URBN benefiting from growing consumer demand for differentiated product and an engaging shopping experience. The company's relatively small base of 406 stores across three main retail brands should provide ample opportunity for store expansion globally. URBN has communicated a 1,000-store goal, which we think is appropriate and conservative. We also look for the company to leverage new merchant talent to improve women's apparel sales. However, we see merchandising risk on new assortments for fall/winter.

➤ Risks to our recommendation and target price include the possibility that URBN will fail to continue to source brand-appropriate merchandise while executing an aggressive growth strategy.

➤ Our 12-month target price of $28 is based on a blend of our historical and relative analyses. Our historical analysis suggests a value of $35, using a 10-year historical average forward P/E multiple of 21.7X applied to our FY 13 EPS estimate. Our peer analysis applies the group average of 12.9X, implying a value of $21.

## Qualitative Risk Assessment

| LOW | MEDIUM | HIGH |
|---|---|---|

Our risk assessment reflects what we view as URBN's strong balance sheet and rising cash flow, offset by fashion risk.

## Quantitative Evaluations

**S&P Quality Ranking** B+

| D | C | B- | B | B+ | A- | A | A+ |
|---|---|---|---|---|---|---|---|

**Relative Strength Rank** MODERATE

63

LOWEST = 1 HIGHEST = 99

## Revenue/Earnings Data

**Revenue (Million $)**

| | 1Q | 2Q | 3Q | 4Q | Year |
|---|---|---|---|---|---|
| 2012 | 524.0 | 609.2 | 610.0 | -- | -- |
| 2011 | 480.0 | 552.2 | 573.6 | 668.4 | 2,274 |
| 2010 | 384.8 | 458.6 | 505.9 | 588.5 | 1,938 |
| 2009 | 394.3 | 454.3 | 478.0 | 508.1 | 1,835 |
| 2008 | 314.5 | 348.5 | 379.3 | 465.4 | 1,508 |
| 2007 | 270.0 | 285.6 | 308.4 | 360.8 | 1,225 |

**Earnings Per Share ($)**

| | | | | | |
|---|---|---|---|---|---|
| 2012 | 0.23 | 0.35 | 0.33 | E0.39 | E1.30 |
| 2011 | 0.31 | 0.42 | 0.43 | 0.45 | 1.60 |
| 2010 | 0.18 | 0.29 | 0.36 | 0.45 | 1.28 |
| 2009 | 0.25 | 0.33 | 0.35 | 0.24 | 1.17 |
| 2008 | 0.17 | 0.33 | 0.27 | 0.32 | 0.95 |
| 2007 | 0.12 | 0.15 | 0.21 | 0.21 | 0.69 |

Fiscal year ended Jan. 31. Next earnings report expected: Early March. EPS Estimates based on S&P Operating Earnings; historical GAAP earnings are as reported.

## Dividend Data

No cash dividends have been paid.

---

**Please read the Required Disclosures and Analyst Certification on the last page of this report.**

The **McGraw-Hill** Companies

# Urban Outfitters Inc

**STANDARD &POOR'S**

## Business Summary November 16, 2011

CORPORATE OVERVIEW. Urban Outfitters operates specialty retail stores under the Urban Outfitters, Anthropologie and Free People brands, as well as a wholesale division. The company opened its first store in Philadelphia in 1970, near the University of Pennsylvania. URBN's strategy is to provide unified store environments that establish emotional bonds with the customer. The company also offers products directly to the consumer through its e-commerce websites (www.urbn.com, www.anthropologie.com and www.freepeople.com) and the Urban Outfitters, Anthropologie and Free People catalogs.

MARKET PROFILE. The U.S. apparel market generated $192.7 billion in sales at retail in 2010, up 2%, according to NPD Fashionworld consumer estimated data. Sales of women's apparel represented 56%, men's 27%, and kids' the remaining 17%. While the U.S. apparel market is mature, it is fragmented, with national brands marketed by 20 companies accounting for about 30% of total apparel sales. Private label (or store) brands account for an estimated 40% of apparel sales. With 19 Urban Outfitters and two Anthropologie stores in Europe and its direct-to-consumer catalogs and websites, URBN's breadth is international. In addition to URBN's apparel and accessories product offerings, its merchandise mix includes furniture and home ware and apartment ware, a more fragmented, faster-growing market that S&P estimates at $120 billion at retail.

COMPETITIVE LANDSCAPE. The retail landscape is consolidating, with share accruing to mass merchants and specialty chains as traditional department stores lose ground. Specialty chains, we believe, compete on customer knowledge garnered in daily interactions, focus groups and market intelligence, with this knowledge combined with high customer service levels resulting in an attractive price/value equation for consumers, in our view. By channel, specialty stores account for the largest share of apparel sales (about 32% in 2010). This penetration varies by age for a high of 42% for teenagers (13-19 year olds), to less than 20% for those 45 years and older. Upheaval in the department store and specialty retail channels creates a window of opportunity over the coming 18-24 months for adept retailers and apparel brands to capture increased share. In the past few years, a number of new concepts targeting the 25+ age group launched to questionable success. We believe URBN's distinct market positioning is an ample barrier to new competition, and its design and merchandising competency is not easily replicated.

## Company Financials Fiscal Year Ended Jan. 31

| Per Share Data ($) | 2011 | 2010 | 2009 | 2008 | 2007 | 2006 | 2005 | 2004 | 2003 | 2002 |
|---|---|---|---|---|---|---|---|---|---|---|
| Tangible Book Value | 8.59 | 7.69 | 6.28 | 5.14 | 4.09 | 3.40 | 2.47 | 1.82 | 1.45 | 1.05 |
| Cash Flow | 2.14 | 1.79 | 1.63 | 1.35 | 1.02 | 1.00 | 0.73 | 0.44 | 0.29 | 0.22 |
| Earnings | 1.60 | 1.28 | 1.17 | 0.95 | 0.94 | 0.77 | 0.54 | 0.30 | 0.18 | 0.11 |
| S&P Core Earnings | 1.60 | 1.28 | 1.19 | 0.94 | 0.69 | 0.42 | 0.40 | 0.27 | 0.17 | 0.10 |
| Dividends | Nil | Nil | Nil | Nil | Nil | Nil | Nil | Nil | Nil | Nil |
| Payout Ratio | Nil | Nil | Nil | Nil | Nil | Nil | Nil | Nil | Nil | Nil |
| Calendar Year | 2010 | 2009 | 2008 | 2007 | 2006 | 2005 | 2004 | 2003 | 2002 | 2001 |
| Prices:High | 40.84 | 35.84 | 38.40 | 29.40 | 29.89 | 33.77 | 24.24 | 10.32 | 4.65 | 3.11 |
| Prices:Low | 29.03 | 13.63 | 12.33 | 19.20 | 13.65 | 18.93 | 9.17 | 2.09 | 2.21 | 0.95 |
| P/E Ratio:High | 26 | 28 | 33 | 31 | 43 | 44 | 43 | 34 | 13 | 29 |
| P/E Ratio:Low | 18 | 11 | 11 | 20 | 20 | 25 | 16 | 7 | NA | 9 |

| Income Statement Analysis (Million $) | | | | | | | | | | |
|---|---|---|---|---|---|---|---|---|---|---|
| Revenue | 2,274 | 1,938 | 1,835 | 1,508 | 1,225 | 1,092 | 828 | 548 | 423 | 349 |
| Operating Income | 514 | 425 | 379 | 294 | 220 | 247 | 180 | 103 | 63.6 | 41.0 |
| Depreciation | 92.4 | 86.2 | 79.5 | 68.7 | 55.7 | 39.3 | 31.9 | 22.4 | 18.2 | 15.5 |
| Interest Expense | NA | NA | Nil | Nil | Nil | Nil | Nil | Nil | Nil | Nil |
| Pretax Income | 417 | 344 | 309 | 234 | 170 | 212 | 150 | 81.3 | 46.1 | 25.2 |
| Effective Tax Rate | NA | 36.2% | 35.6% | 31.6% | 31.7% | 38.4% | 39.8% | 40.5% | 40.5% | 40.5% |
| Net Income | 273 | 220 | 199 | 160 | 116 | 131 | 90.5 | 48.4 | 27.4 | 15.0 |
| S&P Core Earnings | 273 | 219 | 203 | 160 | 116 | 71.0 | 65.9 | 43.7 | 25.8 | 13.6 |

| Balance Sheet & Other Financial Data (Million $) | | | | | | | | | | |
|---|---|---|---|---|---|---|---|---|---|---|
| Cash | 457 | 502 | 366 | 185 | 222 | 257 | 219 | 139 | 95.1 | 28.3 |
| Current Assets | 802 | 806 | 624 | 434 | 366 | 385 | 288 | 176 | 145 | 82.1 |
| Total Assets | 1,792 | 1,636 | 1,323 | 1,143 | 899 | 769 | 557 | 360 | 278 | 195 |
| Current Liabilities | 209 | 189 | 141 | 167 | 135 | 134 | 98.3 | 57.8 | 43.1 | 40.8 |
| Long Term Debt | NA | NA | Nil | Nil | Nil | Nil | Nil | Nil | Nil | Nil |
| Common Equity | 1,411 | 1,297 | 1,054 | 853 | 675 | 561 | 402 | 290 | 224 | 146 |
| Total Capital | 1,411 | 1,297 | 1,054 | 853 | 675 | 561 | 402 | 290 | 224 | 146 |
| Capital Expenditures | 144 | 109 | 113 | 115 | 212 | 128 | 75.1 | 33.1 | 22.2 | 22.3 |
| Cash Flow | 365 | 306 | 279 | 229 | 172 | 170 | 122 | 70.8 | 45.6 | 30.5 |
| Current Ratio | 3.8 | 4.3 | 4.4 | 2.6 | 2.7 | 2.9 | 2.9 | 3.0 | 3.4 | 2.0 |
| % Long Term Debt of Capitalization | Nil | Nil | Nil | Nil | Nil | Nil | Nil | Nil | Nil | Nil |
| % Net Income of Revenue | 12.0 | 11.4 | 10.9 | 10.6 | 9.5 | 12.0 | 10.9 | 8.8 | 6.5 | 4.3 |
| % Return on Assets | 15.9 | 14.8 | 16.2 | 15.7 | 13.9 | 19.7 | 19.2 | 15.1 | 11.6 | 8.2 |
| % Return on Equity | 20.2 | 18.7 | 20.9 | 21.0 | 18.8 | 27.2 | 26.1 | 18.8 | 14.8 | 10.9 |

Data as orig reptd.; bef. results of disc opers/spec. items. Per share data adj. for stk. divs.; EPS diluted. E-Estimated. NA-Not Available. NM-Not Meaningful. NR-Not Ranked. UR-Under Review.

**Office:** 5000 S Broad St, Philadelphia, PA 19112-1495.
**Telephone:** 215-454-5500.
**Website:** http://www.urbanoutfitters.com
**Chrmn & Pres:** R.A. Hayne

**CEO:** G.T. Senk
**COO:** F. Zausner
**CFO:** E. Artz
**Chief Acctg Officer & Cntlr:** F.J. Conforti

**Investor Contact:** J.E. Kyees
**Board Members:** E. N. Antoian, S. A. Belair, H. S. Cherken, Jr., R. A. Hayne, J. S. Lawson, III, G. T. Senk, R. H. Strouse

**Founded:** 1976
**Domicile:** Pennsylvania
**Employees:** 16,000

*The McGraw-Hill Companies*

# Valero Energy Corp

**STANDARD &POOR'S**

| | | | |
|---|---|---|---|
| **S&P Recommendation** BUY ★★★★☆ | **Price**<br>$22.27 (as of Nov 30, 2011) | **12-Mo. Target Price**<br>$28.00 | **Investment Style**<br>Large-Cap Blend |

**GICS Sector** Energy
**Sub-Industry** Oil & Gas Refining & Marketing

**Summary** This company, North America's largest oil refiner and one of the largest independent U.S. refined petroleum products retailers, operates refineries that can process sour and acidic crudes.

## Key Stock Statistics (Source S&P, Vickers, company reports)

| | | | | | | | | |
|---|---|---|---|---|---|---|---|---|
| 52-Wk Range | $31.12– 16.40 | S&P Oper. EPS 2011**E** | 4.49 | Market Capitalization(B) | $12.465 | Beta | | 1.41 |
| Trailing 12-Month EPS | $2.81 | S&P Oper. EPS 2012**E** | 4.47 | Yield (%) | 2.69 | S&P 3-Yr. Proj. EPS CAGR(%) | | 36 |
| Trailing 12-Month P/E | 7.9 | P/E on S&P Oper. EPS 2011**E** | 5.0 | Dividend Rate/Share | $0.60 | S&P Credit Rating | | BBB |
| $10K Invested 5 Yrs Ago | $4,182 | Common Shares Outstg. (M) | 559.7 | Institutional Ownership (%) | 82 | | | |

## Price Performance

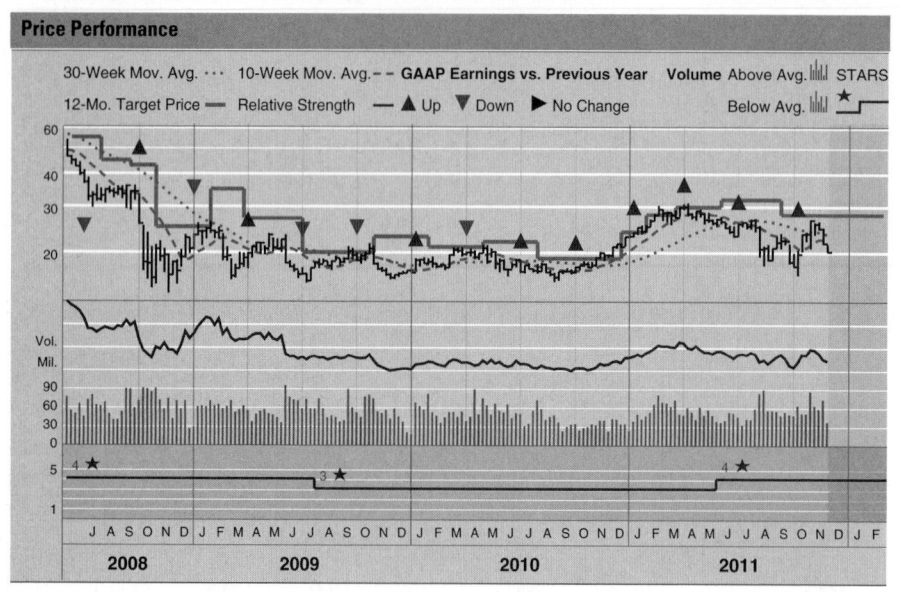

30-Week Mov. Avg. · · · 10-Week Mov. Avg. - - GAAP Earnings vs. Previous Year   Volume Above Avg. STARS
12-Mo. Target Price — Relative Strength  ▲ Up ▼ Down ► No Change   Below Avg. ★

Options: ASE, CBOE, P, Ph

Analysis prepared by Equity Analyst **Tanjila Shafi** on Nov 22, 2011, when the stock traded at **$20.88**.

## Highlights

► The company's 2011 third-quarter refinery throughput volume averaged 2.59 million barrels per day, increasing 18% versus the 2010 third quarter. In the 2011 fourth quarter, we expect refinery throughput volumes of 1.52 million to 1.56 million barrels per day in VLO's Gulf Coast segment; 430,000 to 440,000 barrels per day in its Mid-Continent segment; 440,000 to 460,000 barrels per day in its Northeast segment; and 270,000 to 280,000 barrels per day in its West Coast segment.

► In 2011 and 2012, we believe the company will benefit from increasing distillate demand, leading to higher exports. In 2010, VLO spent $2.3 billion on capital investments. Valero's budget for capital expenditures is $3.2 billion for 2011 and $3.4 billion in 2012. It plans to accelerate its hydrocracker projects at Port Arthur and St. Charles.

► We expect continued improvement through 2012 on a better economic outlook and strategic actions. Our EPS estimates are $4.49 for 2011 and $4.47 for 2012.

## Investment Rationale/Risk

► We believe that the company will benefit from increasing distillate demand and its ability to process heavy and sour crudes. With fuel demand strengthening, we expect refining throughputs to rise (which should permit lower operating expenses per barrel), and we see retail marketing contributing to solid earnings in 2011 and 2012. For the long term, we believe VLO's size and ability to refine lower-cost and quality crude oils are strategic advantages.

► Risks to our recommendation and target price include weaker economic conditions, excess industry refining capacity, and changes in operating conditions that lead to a narrowing of margins or reduced throughput rates.

► A blend of our discounted cash flow ($28 per share, assuming a WACC of 10.2% and terminal growth of 3%) and relative market valuations leads to our 12-month target price of $28. This represents an expected enterprise value of about 4.0X our per-share 2012 EBITDA estimate, slightly higher than the peer average, reflecting its size and the complexity of its refineries.

## Qualitative Risk Assessment

| LOW | MEDIUM | HIGH |
|---|---|---|

Our risk assessment reflects our view of VLO's solid business profile in the volatile and competitive oil refining industry. The company possesses above-average refining complexity, which allows it to process a large amount of lower-cost heavy and sour crudes.

## Quantitative Evaluations

**S&P Quality Ranking** B

| D | C | B- | B | B+ | A- | A | A+ |
|---|---|---|---|---|---|---|---|

**Relative Strength Rank** MODERATE

45

LOWEST = 1                HIGHEST = 99

## Revenue/Earnings Data

**Revenue (Million $)**

| | 1Q | 2Q | 3Q | 4Q | Year |
|---|---|---|---|---|---|
| 2011 | 26,094 | 31,066 | 33,484 | -- | -- |
| 2010 | 19,435 | 21,550 | 22,210 | 21,940 | 81,342 |
| 2009 | 13,329 | 17,375 | 18,523 | 18,867 | 67,271 |
| 2008 | 27,945 | 36,436 | 35,753 | 18,358 | 118,298 |
| 2007 | 18,755 | 24,202 | 23,699 | 28,671 | 95,327 |
| 2006 | 20,941 | 26,781 | 24,319 | 19,792 | 91,833 |

**Earnings Per Share ($)**

| | | | | | |
|---|---|---|---|---|---|
| 2011 | 0.18 | 1.30 | 2.11 | E0.91 | E4.49 |
| 2010 | -0.18 | 0.94 | 0.51 | 0.32 | 1.62 |
| 2009 | 0.59 | -0.48 | -1.12 | -0.32 | -0.65 |
| 2008 | 0.48 | 1.38 | 2.18 | -6.36 | -2.16 |
| 2007 | 1.86 | 3.57 | 1.34 | 1.02 | 7.72 |
| 2006 | 1.32 | 2.98 | 2.55 | 1.80 | 8.64 |

Fiscal year ended Dec. 31. Next earnings report expected: Late January. EPS Estimates based on S&P Operating Earnings; historical GAAP earnings are as reported.

## Dividend Data (Dates: mm/dd Payment Date: mm/dd/yy)

| Amount ($) | Date Decl. | Ex-Div. Date | Stk. of Record | Payment Date |
|---|---|---|---|---|
| 0.050 | 01/25 | 02/14 | 02/16 | 03/16/11 |
| 0.050 | 04/28 | 05/16 | 05/18 | 06/15/11 |
| 0.050 | 07/28 | 08/15 | 08/17 | 09/14/11 |
| 0.150 | 10/27 | 11/14 | 11/16 | 12/14/11 |

Dividends have been paid since 1997. Source: Company reports.

# Valero Energy Corp

STANDARD &POOR'S

## Business Summary November 22, 2011

CORPORATE OVERVIEW. Incorporated in 1981 under the name Valero Refining and Marketing Co., the company changed its name to Valero Energy Co. (VLO) in 1997. In 2001, VLO merged with Ultramar Diamond Shamrock, and in 2005 with Premcor Inc., creating the largest refiner in North America, based on distillation capacity.

The company operates in three business segments: Refining (77% of 2010 operating income, 35% of 2009 operating income), Ethanol (9%; 23%), and Retail (14%, 42%). VLO serves customers in the U.S. (82% of 2010 revenues), Canada (8%), and other countries (10%); no single customer accounted for over 10% of consolidated operating revenues.

The Refining segment includes refining operations, wholesale marketing, product supply and distribution, and transportation operations. As of year-end 2010, the company owned and operated 14 refineries in the U.S., Canada, and Aruba, with a combined throughput capacity of 2.6 million barrels per day (b/d). These capacities by region include: Gulf Coast (seven refineries, 62% of 2010 throughput capacity), the Mid-Continent (three, 17%), the West Coast (two, 12%), and the Northeast (one, 9%).

During 2010, sour crude oils, acidic sweet crude oils and residuals represent-

ed 52% of VLO's throughput volumes; sweet crude oil 31%; and blendstocks and other feedstocks 17%. About 58% of VLO's current crude oil feedstock requirements were purchased through term contracts, with the remainder generally purchased on the spot market. About 78% of 2010 crude oil feedstocks were imported from foreign sources.

The Ethanol segment includes sales of internally produced ethanol and distillers grains. As of December 2010, VLO owned 10 ethanol plants with production capacity of about 1.1 billion gallons per year; three of these facilities were acquired in the 2010 first quarter. Operations are located in the central plains region of the U.S.

VLO is one of the largest independent retailers of refined products in the central and southwest U.S. and eastern Canada. Its retail operations are segregated geographically into two groups: Retail-U.S. System (994 company-operated sites - 80% owned, 20% leased - in 2010) and Retail-Canada (475 retail stores or cardlocks, owned or leased).

## Company Financials Fiscal Year Ended Dec. 31

| Per Share Data ($) | 2010 | 2009 | 2008 | 2007 | 2006 | 2005 | 2004 | 2003 | 2002 | 2001 |
|---|---|---|---|---|---|---|---|---|---|---|
| Tangible Book Value | 26.04 | 25.67 | 29.82 | 31.75 | 23.33 | 15.82 | 9.55 | 5.86 | 3.24 | 3.90 |
| Cash Flow | 4.22 | 2.17 | 0.18 | 9.55 | 10.47 | 7.57 | 3.24 | 2.31 | 1.23 | 2.75 |
| Earnings | 1.62 | -0.65 | -2.16 | 7.72 | 8.64 | 6.10 | 3.27 | 1.27 | 0.21 | 2.21 |
| S&P Core Earnings | 1.45 | -0.67 | 2.32 | 7.73 | 8.32 | 6.02 | 3.25 | 1.25 | 0.14 | 2.14 |
| Dividends | 0.20 | 0.60 | 0.57 | 0.48 | 0.30 | 0.19 | 0.15 | 0.15 | 0.10 | 0.09 |
| Payout Ratio | 12% | NM | NM | 6% | 3% | 3% | 4% | 11% | 48% | 4% |
| Prices:High | 23.70 | 26.20 | 71.12 | 78.68 | 70.75 | 58.63 | 23.91 | 11.77 | 12.49 | 13.15 |
| Prices:Low | 15.49 | 15.29 | 13.94 | 47.66 | 46.84 | 21.01 | 11.43 | 8.05 | 5.79 | 7.88 |
| P/E Ratio:High | 15 | NM | NM | 10 | 8 | 10 | 7 | 9 | 60 | 6 |
| P/E Ratio:Low | 10 | NM | NM | 6 | 5 | 3 | 3 | 6 | 28 | 4 |

| Income Statement Analysis (Million $) | | | | | | | | | | |
|---|---|---|---|---|---|---|---|---|---|---|
| Revenue | 81,342 | 67,271 | 118,298 | 95,327 | 91,833 | 82,162 | 54,619 | 37,969 | 26,976 | 14,988 |
| Operating Income | NA | NA | 20.4 | 8,278 | 9,165 | 6,334 | 2,979 | 1,733 | 920 | 1,139 |
| Depreciation, Depletion and Amortization | 1,473 | 1,527 | 1,038 | 1,360 | 1,155 | 875 | 618 | 511 | 449 | 138 |
| Interest Expense | 484 | 408 | 340 | 466 | 210 | 266 | 260 | 278 | 256 | 102 |
| Pretax Income | 1,498 | -449 | 336 | 6,726 | 8,196 | 5,287 | 2,710 | 989 | 164 | 895 |
| Effective Tax Rate | NA | 21.6% | NM | 32.1% | 33.3% | 32.1% | 33.4% | 36.9% | 35.5% | 37.0% |
| Net Income | 923 | -352 | -1,131 | 4,565 | 5,463 | 3,590 | 1,804 | 622 | 91.5 | 564 |
| S&P Core Earnings | 826 | -366 | 1,212 | 4,572 | 5,258 | 3,534 | 1,785 | 604 | 60.0 | 547 |

| Balance Sheet & Other Financial Data (Million $) | | | | | | | | | | |
|---|---|---|---|---|---|---|---|---|---|---|
| Cash | 3,334 | 825 | 940 | 2,495 | 1,590 | 436 | 864 | 369 | 409 | 346 |
| Current Assets | 13,518 | 10,923 | 9,450 | 14,792 | 10,760 | 8,276 | 5,264 | 3,817 | 3,536 | 4,113 |
| Total Assets | 37,621 | 35,629 | 34,417 | 42,722 | 37,753 | 32,728 | 19,392 | 15,664 | 14,465 | 14,337 |
| Current Liabilities | 8,784 | 7,798 | 6,209 | 11,914 | 8,822 | 7,305 | 4,534 | 3,064 | 3,007 | 4,730 |
| Long Term Debt | 7,515 | 7,163 | 6,264 | 6,470 | 4,657 | 5,156 | 3,901 | 4,245 | 4,867 | 2,805 |
| Common Equity | 15,025 | 14,725 | 15,620 | 18,507 | 18,605 | 14,982 | 7,590 | 5,535 | 4,308 | 4,203 |
| Total Capital | 23,362 | 22,125 | 26,047 | 28,998 | 27,309 | 20,206 | 13,710 | 11,585 | 10,592 | 8,884 |
| Capital Expenditures | 1,730 | 2,327 | 2,790 | 2,260 | 3,187 | 2,133 | 1,292 | 976 | 628 | 394 |
| Cash Flow | 2,396 | 1,175 | 93.0 | 5,529 | 6,616 | 4,452 | 1,791 | 1,128 | 541 | 701 |
| Current Ratio | 1.5 | 1.4 | 1.5 | 1.2 | 1.2 | 1.1 | 1.2 | 1.2 | 1.2 | 0.9 |
| % Long Term Debt of Capitalization | 32.2 | Nil | 24.0 | 22.3 | 17.1 | 25.5 | 28.5 | 36.6 | 45.9 | 31.6 |
| % Return on Assets | NA | NM | NM | 11.4 | 15.5 | 13.8 | 10.3 | 4.1 | 0.6 | 6.0 |
| % Return on Equity | NA | NA | NM | 24.6 | 32.5 | 31.7 | 27.3 | 12.5 | 2.2 | 19.7 |

Data as orig reptd.; bef. results of disc opers/spec. items. Per share data adj. for stk. divs.; EPS diluted. E-Estimated. NA-Not Available. NM-Not Meaningful. NR-Not Ranked. UR-Under Review.

**Office:** One Valero Way, San Antonio, TX 78249-1616.
**Telephone:** 210-345-2000.
**Email:** investorrelations@valero.com
**Website:** http://www.valero.com

**Chrmn, Pres & CEO:** W.R. Klesse
**Investor Contact:** M.S. Ciskowski (210-345-2000)
**EVP, CFO & Chief Acctg Officer:** M.S. Ciskowski
**SVP & Secy:** J.D. Browning

**SVP & Cntlr:** C. Killinger
**Board Members:** E. G. Biggs, R. K. Calgaard, D. M. Carlton, J. D. Choate, W. H. Clark, Jr., R. M. Escobedo, W. R. Klesse, B. Marbut, D. L. Nickles, R. Profusek, S. K. Purcell, W. B. Richardson, S. M. Waters, R. J. Weisenburger, R. Wilkins, Jr.

**Founded:** 1955
**Domicile:** Delaware
**Employees:** 20,313

# Varian Medical Systems Inc

## STANDARD &POOR'S

**S&P Recommendation** HOLD ★★★★★

| Price | 12-Mo. Target Price | Investment Style |
|---|---|---|
| $56.87 (as of Nov 25, 2011) | $68.00 | Large-Cap Growth |

**GICS Sector** Health Care
**Sub-Industry** Health Care Equipment

**Summary** This leading maker of radiotherapy cancer systems also supplies X-ray tubes and flat-panel digital subsystems for imaging in medical, scientific and industrial applications.

### Key Stock Statistics (Source S&P, Vickers, company reports)

| | | | | | | | |
|---|---|---|---|---|---|---|---|
| 52-Wk Range | $72.19– 48.72 | S&P Oper. EPS 2012E | 4.00 | Market Capitalization(B) | $6.664 | Beta | 0.78 |
| Trailing 12-Month EPS | $3.36 | S&P Oper. EPS 2013E | 4.50 | Yield (%) | Nil | S&P 3-Yr. Proj. EPS CAGR(%) | 13 |
| Trailing 12-Month P/E | 16.9 | P/E on S&P Oper. EPS 2012E | 14.2 | Dividend Rate/Share | Nil | S&P Credit Rating | NA |
| $10K Invested 5 Yrs Ago | $11,436 | Common Shares Outstg. (M) | 117.2 | Institutional Ownership (%) | 93 | | |

## Price Performance

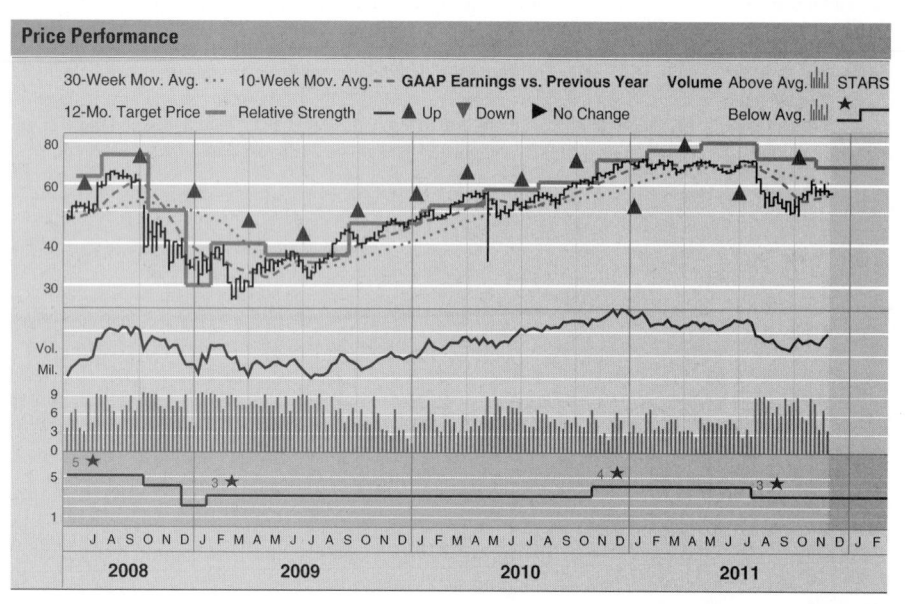

30-Week Mov. Avg. · · · 10-Week Mov. Avg. - - **GAAP Earnings vs. Previous Year** Volume Above Avg. STARS
12-Mo. Target Price — Relative Strength — ▲ Up ▼ Down ▶ No Change Below Avg.

Options: ASE

Analysis prepared by Equity Analyst **Phillip Seligman** on Nov 04, 2011, when the stock traded at **$57.98**.

## Qualitative Risk Assessment

| LOW | MEDIUM | HIGH |
|---|---|---|

Our risk assessment reflects that while Varian offers some of the more technologically advanced products in the oncology equipment industry, it operates in a competitive industry characterized by technological innovation and new product entrants. In addition, although we believe radiation therapy will continue to be an integral component of global cancer treatment protocols, the continued development of drug-based oncology treatments represents a substantial threat to the company's radiation therapy equipment business. In our view, tight credit market conditions globally could also negatively affect capital expenditure decisions by Varian's customers.

## Quantitative Evaluations

**S&P Quality Ranking** B+

| D | C | B- | B | B+ | A- | A | A+ |
|---|---|---|---|---|---|---|---|

**Relative Strength Rank** STRONG

75

LOWEST = 1    HIGHEST = 99

## Highlights

▶ We look for total sales in FY 12 (Sep.) to rise by over 10%, aided by new brachytherapy products and the Calypso acquisition, which complements VAR's motion management technology. Other drivers we see include continued strong demand for RapidArc, led by demand for the new TrueBeam platform, and continued strength in lower-end radiation oncology systems, particularly outside the U.S. We expect strong demand for VAR's X-ray segment products to continue, assuming the diagnostic imaging market recovery is sustainable. We project "other" segment revenues to benefit from security product orders that were delayed in FY 11 and fulfillment of an order from the Scripps Proton Therapy Center. Lastly, we assume currency exchange will still be favorable in FY 12, but to a lesser extent than in FY 11.

▶ We forecast gross margins to widen slightly, on a more favorable sales mix. We expect the R&D cost ratio to remain stable, while the SG&A cost ratio declines slightly, as revenue leverage outweighs internal investment.

▶ We look for FY 12 EPS of $4.00, versus $3.43 in FY 11, and see $4.50 in FY 13.

## Investment Rationale/Risk

▶ Order rates for VAR's oncology products recently declined in North America, and we expect tough comparisons through the first half of FY 12. Elsewhere, VAR is seeing order strength in Northern Europe, the Far East, including Japan, and the rest of the world. Looking ahead, we are encouraged by the promising products VAR has launched in each of its segments. These include advanced x-ray tubes, flat-panel detectors for mammography, smaller security and inspection devices, and radiosurgery products to treat different types of cancers. VAR targets organic growth to over $4.5 billion in sales by 2016; we believe that is doable, assuming demand that the company is realizing for all of its product lines is sustainable.

▶ Risks to our recommendation and target price include unfavorable changes in Medicare reimbursements, competitive pricing, and hospital spending.

▶ Our 12-month target price of $68 is a peer-level 16.5X our calendar 2012 EPS estimate of $4.14. On a comparative P/E basis, we view the multiple as appropriate for the 13% 3-year EPS CAGR we project for a medical device company.

## Revenue/Earnings Data

### Revenue (Million $)

| | 1Q | 2Q | 3Q | 4Q | Year |
|---|---|---|---|---|---|
| 2011 | 579.9 | 648.5 | 649.4 | 719.0 | 2,597 |
| 2010 | 540.9 | 585.6 | 578.0 | 652.1 | 2,357 |
| 2009 | 508.7 | 553.6 | 509.8 | 642.0 | 2,214 |
| 2008 | 451.2 | 518.4 | 507.4 | 592.7 | 2,070 |
| 2007 | 387.9 | 442.6 | 423.7 | 522.4 | 1,777 |
| 2006 | 334.2 | 413.9 | 395.7 | 454.0 | 1,598 |

### Earnings Per Share ($)

| | | | | | |
|---|---|---|---|---|---|
| 2011 | 0.80 | 0.86 | 0.83 | 0.95 | 3.44 |
| 2010 | 0.63 | 0.73 | 0.74 | 0.87 | 2.96 |
| 2009 | 0.56 | 0.64 | 0.68 | 0.78 | 2.65 |
| 2008 | 0.46 | 0.57 | 0.61 | 0.68 | 2.31 |
| 2007 | 0.37 | 0.46 | 0.39 | 0.61 | 1.83 |
| 2006 | 0.30 | 0.41 | 0.49 | 0.61 | 1.80 |

Fiscal year ended Sep. 30. Next earnings report expected: Late January. EPS Estimates based on S&P Operating Earnings; historical GAAP earnings are as reported.

## Dividend Data

Cash dividends were last paid in 1999.

The McGraw-Hill Companies

# Varian Medical Systems Inc

STANDARD
&POOR'S

## Business Summary November 04, 2011

CORPORATE OVERVIEW. Varian is one of the largest manufacturers of oncology diagnostic products, X-ray tubes, and imaging subsystems. The company is focused primarily on capturing share in the global oncology radiation therapy markets. Cancer rates are expected to increase 50% by calendar 2020.

MARKET PROFILE. Driven by an aging global population and improved diagnostic methods, the number of newly diagnosed cancer cases continues to increase. According to estimates published in February 2005 by the Annals of Oncology, nearly 2.9 million new cancer cases were diagnosed during 2004, and the U.S. National Cancer Institute estimates that cancer diagnoses will rise 1.6 million per year by 2010, a 23% increase from the 1.3 million cancers per year seen in 2000. Radiation therapy is commonly used in the treatment of cancer, alone or in combination with surgery or chemotherapy. The most common type of radiotherapy uses X-rays delivered by external beams, and is administered using linear accelerators. In addition to external radiation, radioactive seeds, wires or ribbons are sometimes inserted into a tumor or into a body cavity (brachytherapy), a modality that does not require radiation to pass through healthy tissues.

Varian's oncology systems group (78% of FY 11 (Sep.) revenues) designs, mar-

kets and services hardware and software products for cancer radiation treatment, including linear accelerators, treatment simulators and verification products, and software systems for planning cancer treatment and managing information and images for radiation oncology. Products focus on enabling a new therapy that delivers high doses of radiation to tumors while reducing risk to surrounding tissues. This three-dimensional conformal radiation therapy, called Intensity Modulation Radiation Therapy (IMRT), links treatment planning, information management and driver software to the treatment delivery device, the linear accelerator. This is designed to allow clinicians to determine and deliver a clinically optimized plan of radiation for each patient. IMRT is used to treat head and neck, breast, prostate, pancreatic, lung, liver, gynecological and central nervous system cancers. VAR has also developed image-guided radiation therapy (IGRT), which improves radiation therapy precision by using technologies that compensate for tumor changes and movements during and between treatments.

## Company Financials Fiscal Year Ended Sep. 30

| Per Share Data ($) | 2011 | 2010 | 2009 | 2008 | 2007 | 2006 | 2005 | 2004 | 2003 | 2002 |
|---|---|---|---|---|---|---|---|---|---|---|
| Tangible Book Value | NA | 8.96 | 8.72 | 6.43 | 4.92 | 5.21 | 4.11 | 3.74 | 3.71 | 3.05 |
| Cash Flow | NA | 3.35 | 3.01 | 2.60 | 2.08 | 2.02 | 1.70 | 1.32 | 1.06 | 0.81 |
| Earnings | 3.44 | 2.96 | 2.65 | 2.31 | 1.83 | 1.80 | 1.50 | 1.18 | 0.92 | 0.66 |
| S&P Core Earnings | NA | 2.97 | 2.63 | 2.28 | 1.83 | 1.80 | 1.34 | 1.04 | 0.78 | 0.54 |
| Dividends | NA | Nil | Nil | Nil | Nil | Nil | Nil | Nil | Nil | Nil |
| Payout Ratio | Nil | Nil | Nil | Nil | Nil | Nil | Nil | Nil | Nil | Nil |
| Prices:High | 72.19 | 70.97 | 47.78 | 65.84 | 53.22 | 61.70 | 52.92 | 46.49 | 35.65 | 25.66 |
| Prices:Low | 48.72 | 35.50 | 27.10 | 33.12 | 37.30 | 41.10 | 31.65 | 29.63 | 23.70 | 15.80 |
| P/E Ratio:High | 21 | 24 | 18 | 29 | 29 | 34 | 35 | 39 | 39 | 39 |
| P/E Ratio:Low | 14 | 12 | 10 | 14 | 20 | 23 | 21 | 25 | 26 | 24 |

| Income Statement Analysis (Million $) | 2011 | 2010 | 2009 | 2008 | 2007 | 2006 | 2005 | 2004 | 2003 | 2002 |
|---|---|---|---|---|---|---|---|---|---|---|
| Revenue | 2,597 | 2,357 | 2,214 | 2,070 | 1,777 | 1,598 | 1,383 | 1,236 | 1,042 | 873 |
| Operating Income | 640 | 582 | 519 | 456 | 367 | 339 | 332 | 277 | 219 | 165 |
| Depreciation | NA | 48.3 | 44.6 | 36.7 | 32.2 | 29.6 | 27.1 | 20.8 | 20.3 | 20.4 |
| Interest Expense | NA | 1.30 | 4.10 | 4.88 | 4.79 | 4.65 | 4.70 | 4.67 | 4.38 | 4.49 |
| Pretax Income | 589 | 533 | 475 | 426 | 343 | 319 | 308 | 257 | 201 | 146 |
| Effective Tax Rate | NA | NA | 30.2% | 30.7% | 30.1% | 23.6% | 33.0% | 35.0% | 35.0% | 36.0% |
| Net Income | 409 | 368 | 332 | 295 | 239 | 244 | 207 | 167 | 131 | 93.6 |
| S&P Core Earnings | NA | 369 | 329 | 292 | 240 | 245 | 184 | 148 | 111 | 75.9 |

| Balance Sheet & Other Financial Data (Million $) | 2011 | 2010 | 2009 | 2008 | 2007 | 2006 | 2005 | 2004 | 2003 | 2002 |
|---|---|---|---|---|---|---|---|---|---|---|
| Cash | 584 | 520 | 554 | 397 | 263 | 366 | 378 | 352 | 323 | 299 |
| Current Assets | 1,855 | 1,681 | 1,672 | 1,394 | 1,160 | 1,156 | 1,017 | 885 | 806 | 651 |
| Total Assets | 2,499 | 2,324 | 2,308 | 1,976 | 1,684 | 1,512 | 1,317 | 1,170 | 1,053 | 910 |
| Current Liabilities | 1,126 | 904 | 842 | 782 | 782 | 644 | 544 | 461 | 409 | 358 |
| Long Term Debt | 6.25 | 17.9 | 23.4 | 32.4 | 40.4 | 49.4 | 57.3 | 53.3 | 58.5 | 58.5 |
| Common Equity | 1,244 | 1,275 | 1,312 | 1,027 | 821 | 797 | 659 | 614 | 564 | 504 |
| Total Capital | 1,260 | 1,299 | 1,344 | 1,060 | 862 | 847 | 716 | 667 | 622 | 562 |
| Capital Expenditures | NA | 67.5 | 62.6 | 81.4 | 64.1 | 41.4 | 43.9 | 24.2 | 18.9 | 25.9 |
| Cash Flow | NA | 416 | 376 | 332 | 272 | 273 | 234 | 188 | 151 | 114 |
| Current Ratio | 1.7 | 1.9 | 2.0 | 1.8 | 1.5 | 1.8 | 1.9 | 1.9 | 2.0 | 1.8 |
| % Long Term Debt of Capitalization | 0.5 | 1.4 | 1.7 | 3.1 | 4.7 | 5.8 | 8.0 | 8.0 | 9.4 | 10.4 |
| % Net Income of Revenue | 15.7 | 15.6 | 15.0 | 14.3 | 13.5 | 15.2 | 14.9 | 13.5 | 12.6 | 10.7 |
| % Return on Assets | 16.9 | 15.9 | 15.5 | 16.1 | 15.0 | 17.2 | 16.5 | 15.0 | 13.3 | 11.2 |
| % Return on Equity | 32.4 | 28.4 | 28.4 | 32.0 | 29.6 | 33.4 | 32.2 | 28.4 | 25.3 | 20.3 |

Data as orig reptd.; bef. results of disc opers/spec. items. Per share data adj. for stk. divs.; EPS diluted. E-Estimated. NA-Not Available. NM-Not Meaningful. NR-Not Ranked. UR-Under Review.

**Office:** 3100 Hansen Way, Palo Alto, CA 94304-1030.
**Telephone:** 650-493-4000.
**Website:** http://www.varian.com
**Chrmn:** R.M. Levy

**Pres & CEO:** T.E. Guertin
**COO:** D.R. Wilson
**SVP & CFO:** E.W. Finney
**CTO:** G.A. Zdasiuk

# Ventas Inc.

STANDARD
&POOR'S

| S&P Recommendation | HOLD ★★★☆☆ | Price $49.57 (as of Nov 25, 2011) | 12-Mo. Target Price $56.00 | Investment Style Large-Cap Blend |
|---|---|---|---|---|

**GICS Sector** Financials
**Sub-Industry** Specialized REITS

**Summary** This real estate investment trust invests in health care facilities, including seniors housing, specialty care facilities, hospitals, and medical office buildings.

## Key Stock Statistics (Source S&P, Vickers, company reports)

| | | | | | | | |
|---|---|---|---|---|---|---|---|
| 52-Wk Range | $57.45–43.25 | S&P FFO/Sh. 2011E | 3.30 | Market Capitalization(B) | $14.272 | Beta | 1.31 |
| Trailing 12-Month FFO/Share | $2.63 | S&P FFO/Sh. 2012E | 3.57 | Yield (%) | 4.64 | S&P 3-Yr. FFO/Sh. Proj. CAGR(%) | 9 |
| Trailing 12-Month P/FFO | NA | P/FFO on S&P FFO/Sh. 2011E | 15.0 | Dividend Rate/Share | $2.30 | S&P Credit Rating | BBB |
| $10K Invested 5 Yrs Ago | $16,087 | Common Shares Outstg. (M) | 287.9 | Institutional Ownership (%) | 99 | | |

## Price Performance

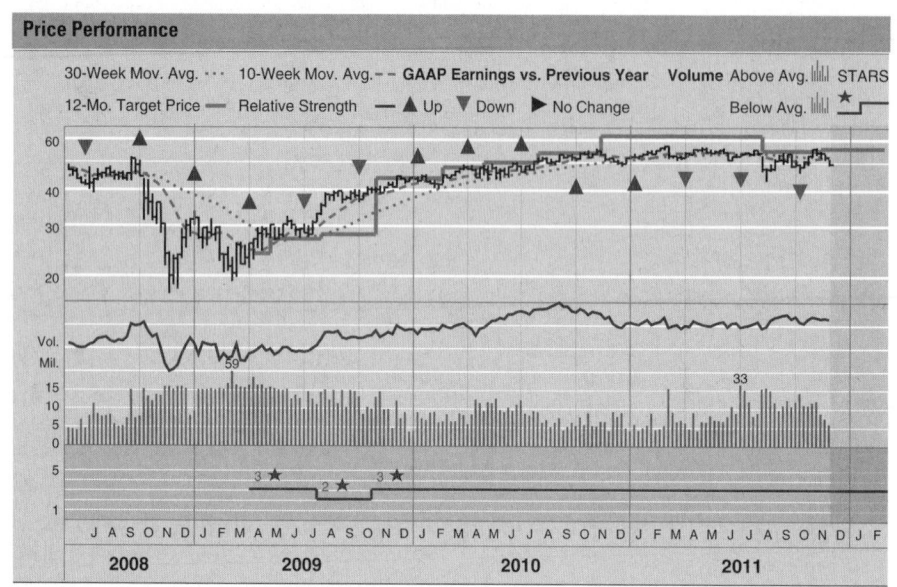

Analysis prepared by Equity Analyst **R. Shepard, CFA** on Nov 08, 2011, when the stock traded at **$54.66.**

### Highlights

► We forecast 2012 revenues will increase 35%, aided by recent acquisitions. Effective July 1, 2011, the trust completed the $7.4 billion acquisition of Nationwide Health Properties. We believe this purchase will enhance VTR's focus on senior housing assets less dependent on revenues from Medicaid and Medicare. For 2012, we estimate that VTR's tenants will generate about 70% of operating income from private pay sources.

► We think VTR's skilled nursing facilities are well protected from recent cuts in Medicare funding for 2012. Its triple net leases place the burden of shifting revenues and related costs onto the operating tenants. In our estimation, current cash flow covers rent payments by about 1.9X, a level we consider adequate. In addition, the trust doesn't face any lease expirations on its skilled nursing assets until 2013.

► We estimate per-share funds from operations (FFO) of $3.30 for 2011, expanding to $3.57 in 2012. Our outlook assumes modest operating synergies from the recent purchase of Nationwide Health and 117 senior living communities from Atria Senior Living Group.

### Investment Rationale/Risk

► We believe VTR has assembled a portfolio of health care properties that is well diversified in terms of asset type, geography, and tenant base. We like the predictable nature of VTR's long-term triple net lease revenue stream, and we believe the stock correlates less with macroeconomic trends than most other REITs. Longer term, we think the trust should benefit from an aging population and an ongoing shift in the delivery of health care services to lower cost settings, such as senior housing and nursing facilities. In the current environment, we favor what we see as VTR's stable revenue stream, solid balance sheet, and relatively secure dividend payout.

► Risks to our recommendation and target price include a severe economic slowdown that reduces demand for private pay seniors housing facilities, and a significant decrease in government reimbursement rates for hospital and nursing facilities.

► Our 12-month target price of $56 is based on a multiple of 15.6X our 2012 FFO per share estimate of $3.57, a moderate premium to less diversified health care REITs with less access to financial capital.

### Qualitative Risk Assessment

| LOW | MEDIUM | HIGH |
|---|---|---|

Our risk assessment reflects VTR's position as the owner of a large and diversified portfolio of health care-related properties that provide what we see as a steady and predictable stream of income.

### Quantitative Evaluations

**S&P Quality Ranking**     B+

| D | C | B- | B | B+ | A- | A | A+ |
|---|---|---|---|---|---|---|---|

**Relative Strength Rank**     MODERATE

56

LOWEST = 1        HIGHEST = 99

### Revenue/FFO Data

**Revenue (Million $)**

| | 1Q | 2Q | 3Q | 4Q | Year |
|---|---|---|---|---|---|
| 2011 | 270.2 | 364.5 | 565.8 | -- | -- |
| 2010 | 241.6 | 244.0 | 264.2 | 267.7 | 1,016 |
| 2009 | 229.4 | 231.9 | 235.8 | 239.0 | 936.1 |
| 2008 | 231.8 | 233.5 | 238.6 | 234.0 | 929.8 |
| 2007 | 119.2 | 193.8 | 226.3 | 232.6 | 771.8 |
| 2006 | 97.81 | 100.3 | 109.7 | 120.6 | 428.4 |

**FFO Per Share ($)**

| | | | | | |
|---|---|---|---|---|---|
| 2011 | 0.62 | 0.57 | 0.91 | E0.87 | E3.30 |
| 2010 | 0.66 | 0.64 | 0.69 | 0.68 | 2.67 |
| 2009 | 0.66 | 0.68 | 0.66 | 0.66 | 2.58 |
| 2008 | 0.75 | 0.73 | 0.81 | 0.69 | 2.74 |
| 2007 | 0.68 | 0.70 | 0.66 | 0.66 | 2.69 |
| 2006 | 0.55 | 0.57 | 0.64 | 0.69 | 2.44 |

Fiscal year ended Dec. 31. Next earnings report expected: NA. FFO Estimates based on S&P Funds From Operations Est..

### Dividend Data (Dates: mm/dd Payment Date: mm/dd/yy)

| Amount ($) | Date Decl. | Ex-Div. Date | Stk. of Record | Payment Date |
|---|---|---|---|---|
| 0.575 | 02/16 | 03/09 | 03/11 | 03/31/11 |
| 0.575 | 05/16 | 06/08 | 06/10 | 06/30/11 |
| 0.126 | 06/20 | 07/05 | 06/30 | 07/01/11 |
| 0.449 | 08/19 | 09/09 | 09/13 | 09/30/11 |

Dividends have been paid since 1999. Source: Company reports.

---

**Please read the Required Disclosures and Analyst Certification on the last page of this report.**

The McGraw-Hill Companies

# Ventas Inc.

## Business Summary November 08, 2011

Ventas Inc. is a health care REIT (real estate investment trust) that specializes in acquiring, financing and owning seniors housing and health care properties and leasing those properties to third parties or operating them through independent third-party managers. At the end of 2010, its portfolio consisted of interests in 602 properties in the United States and Canada, including 240 seniors housing communities, 187 skilled nursing facilities, 40 hospitals and 135 medical office buildings (MOBs) and other properties in 43 states, the District of Columbia and two Canadian provinces. With the exception of its seniors housing communities, which are managed by Sunrise Medical Systems pursuant to long-term management agreements, and the majority of its MOBs, VTR leases its properties to health care operating companies under triple-net or absolute-net leases, which require the tenants to pay all property-related expenses. The trust also had real estate loan investments relating to senior housing and health care companies or properties at the end of 2010.

VTR's seniors housing communities (62.8% of 2010 total revenues) include independent and assisted living communities, and communities providing care for individuals with Alzheimer's disease and other forms of dementia or memory loss. These communities offer residential units on a month-to-month basis

primarily to elderly individuals requiring various levels of assistance. Basic services for residents of these communities include housekeeping, meals in a central dining area and group activities organized by the staff with input from the residents. More extensive care and personal supervision, at additional fees, are also available for such needs as eating, bathing, grooming, transportation, limited therapeutic programs and medication administration, all of which encourage the residents to live as independently as possible according to their abilities. These needs are often met by home health providers in close coordination with the resident's physician and skilled nursing facilities. The skilled nursing facilities (17.8%) typically provide nursing care services to the elderly and rehabilitation and restoration services, including physical, occupational and speech therapies, and other medical treatment for patients and residents who do not require the high technology, care-intensive setting of an acute care or rehabilitation hospital.

## Company Financials Fiscal Year Ended Dec. 31

| Per Share Data ($) | 2010 | 2009 | 2008 | 2007 | 2006 | 2005 | 2004 | 2003 | 2002 | 2001 |
|---|---|---|---|---|---|---|---|---|---|---|
| Tangible Book Value | 15.18 | 15.74 | 14.99 | 13.65 | 6.51 | 6.28 | 1.73 | 0.53 | NM | NM |
| Earnings | 1.38 | 1.27 | 1.30 | 1.15 | 1.25 | 1.31 | 1.19 | 1.21 | 0.75 | 0.75 |
| S&P Core Earnings | 1.38 | 1.27 | 1.30 | 1.15 | 1.25 | 1.14 | 1.18 | 1.08 | 0.70 | 0.56 |
| Dividends | 2.14 | 2.05 | 2.05 | 2.05 | 1.58 | 1.44 | 1.30 | 1.07 | 0.95 | 0.92 |
| Payout Ratio | 155% | 161% | 158% | 105% | 126% | 110% | 109% | 88% | 127% | 123% |
| Prices:High | 56.20 | 44.91 | 52.00 | 47.97 | 42.40 | 32.71 | 29.48 | 22.98 | 13.76 | 12.85 |
| Prices:Low | 40.36 | 19.13 | 17.31 | 23.98 | 29.54 | 24.43 | 20.56 | 11.08 | 10.06 | 5.56 |
| P/E Ratio:High | 41 | 35 | 40 | 42 | 34 | 25 | 25 | 19 | 18 | 17 |
| P/E Ratio:Low | 29 | 15 | 13 | 21 | 24 | 19 | 17 | 9 | 13 | 7 |

| Income Statement Analysis (Million $) | | | | | | | | | | |
|---|---|---|---|---|---|---|---|---|---|---|
| Rental Income | 540 | 501 | 487 | 484 | 418 | NA | NA | 191 | 190 | 185 |
| Mortgage Income | Nil | Nil | Nil | Nil | Nil | NA | NA | Nil | Nil | Nil |
| Total Income | 1,016 | 936 | 930 | 772 | 428 | 333 | 237 | 205 | 197 | 205 |
| General Expenses | 375 | 342 | 348 | 234 | 36.7 | 115 | 18.3 | 15.2 | 54.9 | 16.6 |
| Interest Expense | 179 | 179 | 203 | 204 | 141 | 106 | 66.8 | 66.7 | 82.0 | 91.6 |
| Provision for Losses | Nil | Nil | Nil | Nil | Nil | NA | NA | Nil | Nil | Nil |
| Depreciation | 221 | 201 | 232 | 234 | 120 | 91.9 | 49.0 | 81.7 | 42.1 | 42.0 |
| Net Income | 218 | 195 | 182 | 147 | 131 | 125 | 100 | 96.7 | 53.0 | 51.9 |
| S&P Core Earnings | 218 | 195 | 182 | 141 | 131 | 108 | 99.3 | 87.4 | 49.1 | 38.6 |

| Balance Sheet & Other Financial Data (Million $) | | | | | | | | | | |
|---|---|---|---|---|---|---|---|---|---|---|
| Cash | 21.8 | 107 | 177 | 82.4 | 1.25 | 2,528 | 3.37 | 82.1 | 39.1 | 880 |
| Total Assets | 5,758 | 5,616 | 5,770 | 5,717 | 3,254 | 2,639 | 1,127 | 813 | 896 | 942 |
| Real Estate Investment | 6,748 | 6,293 | NA | 6,290 | 6,161 | NA | NA | 1,090 | 1,221 | 1,231 |
| Loss Reserve | Nil | Nil | Nil | Nil | Nil | NA | NA | Nil | Nil | Nil |
| Net Investment | 5,280 | 5,115 | 5,173 | 5,494 | 3,084 | 2,526 | 1,058 | 681 | 829 | 861 |
| Short Term Debt | 283 | 203 | 118 | Nil | Nil | NA | NA | Nil | Nil | Nil |
| Capitalization:Debt | 2,617 | 2,467 | 3,030 | 3,360 | 2,199 | 1,803 | 843 | 641 | 708 | 848 |
| Capitalization:Equity | 2,387 | 2,466 | 2,148 | 1,824 | 710 | 667 | 160 | 56.3 | 78.3 | -91.1 |
| Capitalization:Total | 5,007 | 4,951 | 5,456 | 5,320 | 2,939 | 2,470 | 1,034 | 56.3 | 816 | 788 |
| % Earnings & Depreciation/Assets | 7.7 | 6.9 | 7.2 | 8.4 | 8.5 | NA | NA | 20.9 | 10.4 | 9.8 |
| Price Times Book Value:High | 3.7 | 2.9 | 3.5 | 3.5 | 6.5 | NA | NA | 43.3 | NM | NM |
| Price Times Book Value:Low | 2.7 | 1.2 | 1.2 | 1.8 | 4.5 | NA | NA | 20.9 | NM | NM |

Data as orig reptd.; bef. results of disc opers/spec. items. Per share data adj. for stk. divs.; EPS diluted. E-Estimated. NA-Not Available. NM-Not Meaningful. NR-Not Ranked. UR-Under Review.

**Office:** 111 South Wacker Drive, Suite 4800, Chicago, IL 60606.
**Telephone:** 312-660-3800.
**Email:** info@ventasreit.com
**Website:** http://www.ventasreit.com

**Pres:** R.J. Lewis
**CEO:** D.A. Cafaro
**EVP & CFO:** R.A. Schweinhart
**EVP, Chief Admin Officer, Secy & General Counsel:** T.R. Riney

**Chief Acctg Officer & Cntlr:** R.J. Brehl
**Investor Contact:** L. Weiner (312-765-0390)
**Board Members:** D. A. Cafaro, D. Crocker, II, R. G. Geary, J. M. Gellert, R. I. Gilchrist, M. J. Lustig, D. M. Pasquale, R. D. Paulson, R. D. Reed, S. Z. Rosenberg, G. J. Rufrano, J. D. Shelton, T. C. Theobald

**Founded:** 1983
**Domicile:** Delaware
**Employees:** 263

# VeriSign Inc

STANDARD &POOR'S

| S&P Recommendation | HOLD ★★★☆☆ | Price | 12-Mo. Target Price | Investment Style |
|---|---|---|---|---|
| | | $31.48 (as of Nov 25, 2011) | $34.00 | Large-Cap Blend |

**GICS Sector** Information Technology
**Sub-Industry** Internet Software & Services

**Summary** This leading provider of Internet domain name registry services and infrastructure assurance services recently sold many of its businesses to focus on core operations.

## Key Stock Statistics (Source S&P, Vickers, company reports)

| | | | | | |
|---|---|---|---|---|---|
| 52-Wk Range | $37.73–27.00 | S&P Oper. EPS 2011**E** 1.30 | Market Capitalization(B) $5.007 | Beta | 0.77 |
| Trailing 12-Month EPS | $0.30 | S&P Oper. EPS 2012**E** 1.70 | Yield (%) Nil | S&P 3-Yr. Proj. EPS CAGR(%) | 16 |
| Trailing 12-Month P/E | NM | P/E on S&P Oper. EPS 2011**E** 24.2 | Dividend Rate/Share Nil | S&P Credit Rating | NA |
| $10K Invested 5 Yrs Ago | $15,403 | Common Shares Outstg. (M) 159.1 | Institutional Ownership (%) NM | | |

## Price Performance

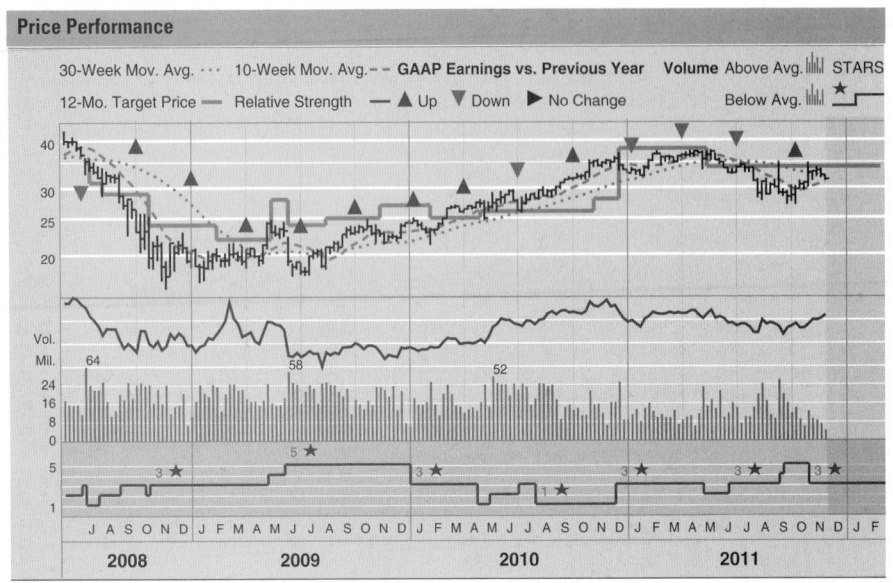

30-Week Mov. Avg. · · · 10-Week Mov. Avg. - - GAAP Earnings vs. Previous Year · Volume Above Avg. STARS
12-Mo. Target Price — Relative Strength — ▲ Up ▼ Down ► No Change · Below Avg.

Options: ASE, CBOE, P, Ph

Analysis prepared by Equity Analyst **Scott Kessler** on Nov 02, 2011, when the stock traded at **$32.08**.

## Highlights

▶ Revenues from continuing operations rose 6% in 2009 and 10% in 2010, despite the adverse effects of the global recession. We project growth of around 13% for 2011 and 12% in 2012.

▶ We believe annual margins bottomed in 2009, reflecting a challenging economic backdrop and expenses related to notable divestiture activity. We think a more focused VRSN will be able to more effectively pursue sales opportunities and efficiencies, and we project higher margins through 2012.

▶ In August 2010, VRSN sold its authentication security business for $1.3 billion. In less than a year, from December 2010 to May 2011, VRSN announced and paid special dividends of $3 per share and $2.75 per share, respectively. Associated obligations amounted to some $1.2 billion, or nearly the value the company received for the authentication business it sold. VRSN continues to focus on stock repurchases, with an additional authorization of $1.1 billion in July 2010. The company's total share repurchase authorization recently stood at around $1 billion.

## Investment Rationale/Risk

▶ We view VRSN as a focused and profitable market leader. We see benefits associated with potential further buyback and dividend activity, and see VRSN as having strong franchises, cash flows and balance sheet metrics. Mark McLaughlin, a former VRSN executive who rejoined VRSN as president and COO in early 2009 and was named CEO in August 2009, was announced as resigning from the company in July 2011.

▶ Risks to our opinion and target price include unexpected weakness in VRSN's core business, less successful efforts to generate shareholder value than we foresee, and the potential for external financing that is not perceived positively by third parties.

▶ Comparing VRSN's P/E and P/E-to-growth multiples with those of the S&P 500 Internet Software & Services sub-industry results in a value of between $21 and $25. Accounting for a premium reflecting VRSN's market position and competitive advantage, and adding the company's recent cash and investments of around $8 a share, results in our 12-month target price of $34.

## Qualitative Risk Assessment

| LOW | MEDIUM | HIGH |
|---|---|---|

Our risk assessment reflects uncertainties related to various aspects of domain name-related businesses, including notable government oversight and related regulations and technological developments and changes.

## Quantitative Evaluations

**S&P Quality Ranking** B-

| D | C | B- | B | B+ | A- | A | A+ |
|---|---|---|---|---|---|---|---|

**Relative Strength Rank** STRONG
79
LOWEST = 1 · HIGHEST = 99

## Revenue/Earnings Data

**Revenue (Million $)**

| | 1Q | 2Q | 3Q | 4Q | Year |
|---|---|---|---|---|---|
| 2011 | 181.5 | 189.8 | 197.0 | -- | -- |
| 2010 | 264.4 | 168.7 | 172.7 | 178.8 | 680.6 |
| 2009 | 255.0 | 256.6 | 258.0 | 262.7 | 1,031 |
| 2008 | 232.5 | 239.2 | 243.0 | 247.0 | 961.7 |
| 2007 | 373.1 | 363.2 | 373.6 | 386.4 | 1,496 |
| 2006 | 372.8 | 390.7 | 399.5 | 412.2 | 1,575 |

**Earnings Per Share ($)**

| | 1Q | 2Q | 3Q | 4Q | Year |
|---|---|---|---|---|---|
| 2011 | 0.25 | -0.05 | 0.36 | E0.38 | E1.30 |
| 2010 | 0.29 | 0.14 | 0.26 | -0.18 | 0.39 |
| 2009 | 0.24 | 0.22 | 0.25 | 0.33 | 1.03 |
| 2008 | 0.08 | -0.07 | 0.21 | 0.24 | 0.46 |
| 2007 | 0.24 | -0.02 | 0.07 | -0.88 | -0.61 |
| 2006 | 0.06 | 1.52 | 0.06 | -0.12 | 1.53 |

Fiscal year ended Dec. 31. Next earnings report expected: Late January. EPS Estimates based on S&P Operating Earnings; historical GAAP earnings are as reported.

## Dividend Data (Dates: mm/dd Payment Date: mm/dd/yy)

| Amount ($) | Date Decl. | Ex-Div. Date | Stk. of Record | Payment Date |
|---|---|---|---|---|
| 3.0 Spl. | 12/10 | 12/16 | 12/20 | 12/28/10 |
| 2.75 Spl. | 04/28 | 05/05 | 05/09 | 05/18/11 |

Dividends have been paid since 2010. Source: Company reports.

**Please read the Required Disclosures and Analyst Certification on the last page of this report.**

The McGraw·Hill Companies

# VeriSign Inc

**STANDARD &POOR'S**

## Business Summary November 02, 2011

CORPORATE OVERVIEW. VeriSign, Inc. provides Internet domain name registry services and infrastructure assurance services.

In August 2010, VRSN sold its Authentication Services business, including outstanding shares of VeriSign Japan, for some $1.3 billion. In November 2010, VRSN discontinued the operations of the Content Portal Services business. The company has completed the process of divesting businesses and discontinuing operations that began in 2007. On a related note, from year-ends 2008 to 2010, VRSN reduced its workforce by about a third (from 3,297 employees to 1,048).

Registry Services operates the authoritative directories for all .com, .net, .cc., .tv and .name domain names, and back-end systems for all .jobs and .edu domain names. In February 2011, VRSN was selected to operate the domain name registry for .gov.

In December 2009, VRSN announced registry increases, effective July 1, 2010, for the fees for .com domains to $7.34 from $6.86, and .net domains to $4.65

from $4.23, consistent with the company's agreements with ICANN (Internet Corporation for Assigned Names and Numbers), the related oversight authority. In July 2011, VRSN announced that as of January 15, 2012, the registry fee for .com domains will increase from $7.34 to $7.85 and for .net domains will increase from $4.65 to $5.11.

The Network Intelligence and Availability Services unit provides infrastructure assurance to organizations, and consists of iDefense (provides cyber-intelligence related to vulnerabilities, malicious code and global threats), Managed DNS (improves the availability of Internet systems through Domain Name System-focused technologies and solutions) and DDoS mitigation (supports online business continuity by providing monitoring and mitigation services related to distributed denial of service attacks).

## Company Financials Fiscal Year Ended Dec. 31

| Per Share Data ($) | 2010 | 2009 | 2008 | 2007 | 2006 | 2005 | 2004 | 2003 | 2002 | 2001 |
|---|---|---|---|---|---|---|---|---|---|---|
| Tangible Book Value | 3.60 | 1.29 | NM | 2.17 | 2.44 | 2.98 | 2.92 | 3.16 | 1.89 | 3.50 |
| Cash Flow | 0.77 | 1.47 | 1.10 | 0.36 | 2.47 | 1.25 | 1.05 | -0.61 | 0.16 | 1.63 |
| Earnings | 0.39 | 1.03 | 0.46 | -0.61 | 1.53 | 0.53 | 0.72 | -1.08 | -20.97 | -65.64 |
| S&P Core Earnings | 0.37 | 1.02 | 0.73 | -0.30 | 1.45 | NA | 0.01 | -1.75 | -8.79 | -35.05 |
| Dividends | 3.00 | Nil | Nil | Nil | Nil | Nil | Nil | Nil | Nil | Nil |
| Payout Ratio | NM | Nil | Nil | Nil | Nil | Nil | Nil | Nil | Nil | Nil |
| Prices:High | 37.18 | 24.99 | 42.50 | 41.96 | 26.77 | 33.67 | 36.09 | 17.55 | 39.23 | 97.75 |
| Prices:Low | 21.21 | 16.89 | 16.23 | 22.92 | 15.95 | 19.01 | 14.94 | 6.55 | 3.92 | 26.25 |
| P/E Ratio:High | 95 | 24 | 92 | NM | 17 | 64 | 50 | NM | NM | NM |
| P/E Ratio:Low | 54 | 16 | 35 | NM | 10 | 36 | 21 | NM | NM | NM |

| Income Statement Analysis (Million $) | 2010 | 2009 | 2008 | 2007 | 2006 | 2005 | 2004 | 2003 | 2002 | 2001 |
|---|---|---|---|---|---|---|---|---|---|---|
| Revenue | 681 | 1,031 | 962 | 1,496 | 1,575 | 1,609 | 1,166 | 1,055 | 1,222 | 984 |
| Operating Income | 317 | 416 | 387 | 309 | 340 | 416 | 242 | 304 | 287 | 277 |
| Depreciation | 67.7 | 86.3 | 128 | 231 | 232 | 191 | 85.6 | 114 | 5,000 | 13,687 |
| Interest Expense | 158 | 47.4 | 41.1 | 18.3 | Nil | Nil | Nil | Nil | 149 | 20.7 |
| Pretax Income | 95.4 | 281 | 119 | -130 | 140 | 248 | 214 | -237 | -4,951 | -13,433 |
| Effective Tax Rate | NA | 28.5% | 39.5% | NM | NM | 42.2% | 12.9% | NM | NM | NM |
| Net Income | 70.0 | 198 | 88.3 | -145 | 378 | 139 | 186 | -260 | -4,961 | -13,356 |
| S&P Core Earnings | 67.2 | 195 | 146 | -72.0 | 359 | -1.39 | 2.76 | -421 | -2,080 | -7,134 |

| Balance Sheet & Other Financial Data (Million $) | 2010 | 2009 | 2008 | 2007 | 2006 | 2005 | 2004 | 2003 | 2002 | 2001 |
|---|---|---|---|---|---|---|---|---|---|---|
| Cash | 2,061 | 1,477 | 789 | 1,378 | 501 | 477 | 331 | 394 | 282 | 306 |
| Current Assets | 2,178 | 1,709 | 1,625 | 1,750 | 1,332 | 1,228 | 1,006 | 880 | 604 | 1,091 |
| Total Assets | 2,444 | 2,470 | 2,726 | 4,023 | 3,974 | 3,173 | 2,593 | 2,100 | 2,391 | 7,538 |
| Current Liabilities | 653 | 886 | 977 | 946 | 1,359 | 938 | 700 | 555 | 665 | 834 |
| Long Term Debt | 582 | 574 | 1,262 | 1,265 | Nil | Nil | Nil | Nil | Nil | Nil |
| Common Equity | 676 | 550 | 169 | 1,528 | 2,377 | 2,032 | 1,692 | 1,414 | 1,579 | 6,506 |
| Total Capital | 1,258 | 1,173 | 1,362 | 2,851 | 2,449 | 2,092 | 1,728 | 1,443 | 1,579 | 6,533 |
| Capital Expenditures | 80.5 | 117 | 104 | 152 | 182 | 140 | 92.5 | 108 | 176 | 380 |
| Cash Flow | 138 | 284 | 221 | 85.9 | 609 | 330 | 272 | -145 | 38.9 | 331 |
| Current Ratio | 3.3 | 1.9 | 1.7 | 1.9 | 1.0 | 1.3 | 1.4 | 1.6 | 0.9 | 1.3 |
| % Long Term Debt of Capitalization | 46.2 | 49.0 | 92.6 | 44.4 | Nil | Nil | Nil | Nil | Nil | Nil |
| % Net Income of Revenue | 10.3 | 19.2 | 9.2 | NM | 24.0 | 8.6 | 16.0 | NM | NM | NM |
| % Return on Assets | 2.9 | 7.8 | 2.6 | NM | 10.6 | 4.8 | 7.9 | NM | NM | NM |
| % Return on Equity | 11.4 | 65.8 | 10.4 | NM | 17.1 | 7.4 | 12.1 | NM | NM | NM |

Data as orig reptd.; bef. results of disc opers/spec. items. Per share data adj. for stk. divs.; EPS diluted. E-Estimated. NA-Not Available. NM-Not Meaningful. NR-Not Ranked. UR-Under Review.

**Office:** 21355 Ridgetop Circle, Dulles, VA 20166.
**Telephone:** 703-948-3200.
**Website:** http://www.verisigninc.com
**Chrmn, Pres & CEO:** D.J. Bidzos

**SVP, Secy & General Counsel:** R.H. Goshorn
**CFO & Cntlr:** J. Calys
**Treas:** D. Atchley
**Investor Contact:** D. Atchley (703-948-4643)

**Board Members:** D. J. Bidzos, W. L. Chenevich, K. A. Cote, R. H. Moore, J. D. Roach, L. A. Simpson, T. Tomlinson

**Founded:** 1995
**Domicile:** Delaware
**Employees:** 1,048

*The McGraw-Hill Companies*

# Verizon Communications Inc

**STANDARD &POOR'S**

| S&P Recommendation HOLD ★★★☆☆ | Price $35.35 (as of Nov 25, 2011) | 12-Mo. Target Price $36.00 | Investment Style Large-Cap Value |
|---|---|---|---|

**GICS Sector** Telecommunication Services
**Sub-Industry** Integrated Telecommunication Services

**Summary** VZ offers wireline, wireless and broadband services primarily in the northeastern United States. It acquired MCI in 2006 and has since sold or spun off non-core assets. Alltel was acquired in early 2009.

## Key Stock Statistics (Source S&P, Vickers, company reports)

| | | | | | | | |
|---|---|---|---|---|---|---|---|
| 52-Wk Range | $38.95–31.60 | S&P Oper. EPS 2011**E** | 2.23 | Market Capitalization(B) | $100.079 | Beta | 0.55 |
| Trailing 12-Month EPS | $2.49 | S&P Oper. EPS 2012**E** | 2.50 | Yield (%) | 5.66 | S&P 3-Yr. Proj. EPS CAGR(%) | 7 |
| Trailing 12-Month P/E | 14.2 | P/E on S&P Oper. EPS 2011**E** | 15.9 | Dividend Rate/Share | $2.00 | S&P Credit Rating | A- |
| $10K Invested 5 Yrs Ago | NA | Common Shares Outstg. (M) | 2,831.1 | Institutional Ownership (%) | 53 | | |

## Price Performance

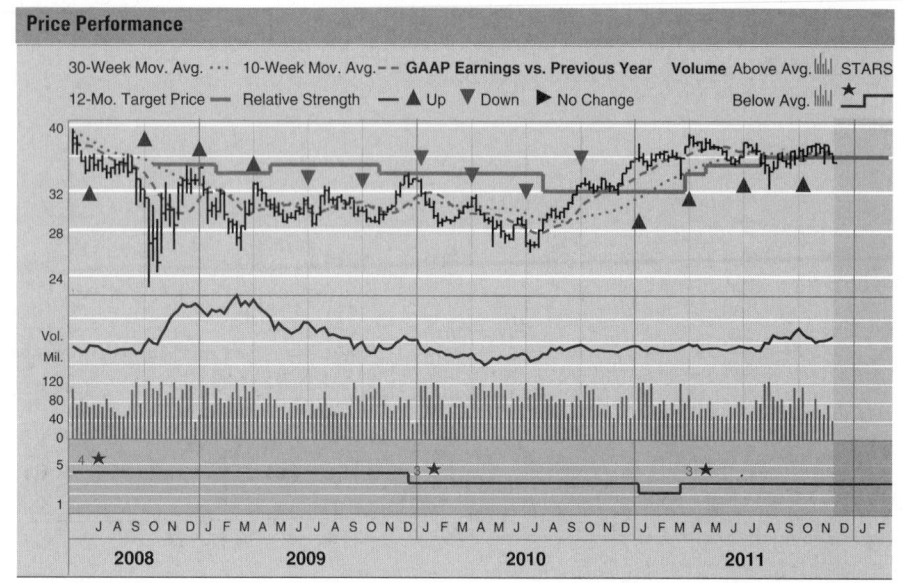

30-Week Mov. Avg. · · · 10-Week Mov. Avg. - - GAAP Earnings vs. Previous Year  Volume Above Avg. ▮▮▮ STARS
12-Mo. Target Price — Relative Strength — ▲ Up ▼ Down ▶ No Change  Below Avg. ▮▮▮ ★

Options: ASE, CBOE, P, Ph

Analysis prepared by Equity Analyst **Todd Rosenbluth** on Oct 25, 2011, when the stock traded at **$36.19**.

## Highlights

➤ We expect revenue growth to $110 billion in 2011 and $115 billion in 2012, driven by increases in wireless data services from new handsets such as the iPhone. On the wireline side, we think the penetration of FiOS services will offset pressure in the mass markets consumer group, but overall segment revenues will likely be hurt by weakness in wholesale. Meanwhile, we expect the enterprise segment to be stable, even as unemployment remains high.

➤ We estimate that the EBITDA margin will narrow to an average of 32% in 2011 before rebounding to 33% in 2012. We see handset subsidies and wireless marketing costs in 2011 and early 2012 offsetting the impact of cost synergies in wireless and workforce reduction benefits. Third-quarter 2011 margins were hurt by storm-related costs and a FiOS backlog.

➤ We expect operating EPS of $2.23 for 2011 and $2.50 in 2012, with higher interest costs in 2011 than in 2010, but excluding the impact of one-time items related to pension accounting. During the first half of 2010, VZ generated $0.12 of EPS from assets that have since been spun off or sold.

## Investment Rationale/Risk

➤ In our view, with its strong operating margin and perception of network quality, the company's wireless segment should be a driver for VZ in 2011 and 2012, even as we see higher subsidies for smartphones launched on 3G and 4G networks. We are encouraged by the relative stability in VZ's wireline segment over the last six months, helped by FiOS gains, and by the company's dividend. We believe wireless industry consolidation should help VZ defend and possibly grow its market share. But we think this is reflected in the stock's valuation.

➤ Risks to recommendation and target price include weaker-than-expected wireless growth, pressure to the macroeconomy that supports demand in the wireline enterprise segment, and an increase in debt leverage.

➤ Our blended 12-month target price of $36 is based on a forward P/E multiple of about 14X our 2012 forecast, a premium to the broader market but near peers to reflect our view of VZ's relatively strong cash flow prospects and the stability of its dividend.

## Qualitative Risk Assessment

| LOW | MEDIUM | HIGH |
|---|---|---|

Our risk assessment reflects our view of VZ's strong cash flow generation and the pricing power it has over its suppliers, offset by the competitive conditions it faces offering telecom services.

## Quantitative Evaluations

**S&P Quality Ranking** B

| D | C | B- | B | B+ | A- | A | A+ |
|---|---|---|---|---|---|---|---|

**Relative Strength Rank** MODERATE

63

LOWEST = 1                    HIGHEST = 99

## Revenue/Earnings Data

**Revenue (Million $)**

| | 1Q | 2Q | 3Q | 4Q | Year |
|---|---|---|---|---|---|
| 2011 | 26,990 | 27,536 | 27,913 | -- | -- |
| 2010 | 26,913 | 26,773 | 26,484 | 26,395 | 106,565 |
| 2009 | 26,591 | 26,861 | 27,265 | 27,091 | 107,808 |
| 2008 | 23,833 | 24,124 | 24,752 | 24,645 | 97,354 |
| 2007 | 22,584 | 23,273 | 23,772 | 23,840 | 93,469 |
| 2006 | 21,221 | 21,876 | 22,449 | 22,598 | 88,144 |

**Earnings Per Share ($)**

| | | | | | |
|---|---|---|---|---|---|
| 2011 | 0.51 | 0.57 | 0.49 | E0.58 | E2.23 |
| 2010 | 0.16 | -0.42 | 0.23 | 0.93 | 0.90 |
| 2009 | 0.58 | 0.52 | 0.41 | -0.23 | 1.29 |
| 2008 | 0.57 | 0.65 | 0.59 | 0.43 | 2.26 |
| 2007 | 0.51 | 0.58 | 0.44 | 0.37 | 1.90 |
| 2006 | 0.57 | 0.43 | 0.53 | 0.48 | 1.87 |

Fiscal year ended Dec. 31. Next earnings report expected: NA. EPS Estimates based on S&P Operating Earnings; historical GAAP earnings are as reported.

## Dividend Data (Dates: mm/dd Payment Date: mm/dd/yy)

| Amount ($) | Date Decl. | Ex-Div. Date | Stk. of Record | Payment Date |
|---|---|---|---|---|
| 0.488 | 12/02 | 01/06 | 01/10 | 02/01/11 |
| 0.488 | 03/04 | 04/06 | 04/08 | 05/02/11 |
| 0.488 | 06/02 | 07/06 | 07/08 | 08/01/11 |
| 0.500 | 09/01 | 10/05 | 10/07 | 11/01/11 |

Dividends have been paid since 1984. Source: Company reports.

---

**Please read the Required Disclosures and Analyst Certification on the last page of this report.**

**The McGraw-Hill Companies**

# Verizon Communications Inc

**STANDARD &POOR'S**

## Business Summary October 25, 2011

CORPORATE OVERVIEW. As of September 2011, Verizon Communications (VZ) provided wireline service to 24.5 million voice connections (down 8% from a year earlier, excluding those sold), and, through its joint venture with Vodafone Group, had 90.7 million wireless customers plus approximately 17 million additional wholesale and other connected devices on its network. We think the relationship with Vodafone remains strong and is unlikely to change.

MARKET PROFILE. Verizon Wireless added a strong 3 million retail post-paid subscribers in the first nine months of 2011 and, together with peer AT&T, has a dominant share of the wireless market. Strong wireless rivalry has raised the level of competition, in our view, with new unlimited service plans and data-equipped devices gaining significant appeal in a highly penetrated market. As of September 2011, Verizon Wireless had a 0.9% monthly post-paid churn rate, and its retail post-paid monthly service revenue per user was $55, up 2.4% from a year earlier. Wireless data average revenue per user rose 16% in the third quarter of 2011 and comprised 41% of service revenues. The segment's EBITDA service margin of 47.8% was the best in the industry, even with handset subsidies. As of September 2011, 39% of Verizon Wireless's retail post-paid customers had a smartphone, and as this percentage grows, particularly helped by Android devices and the new iPhone 4 that came out in

February 2011 on its CDMA network and the iPhone 4GS that launched in October 2011, we expect data revenues to increase; VZ expects to hit 50% smartphone penetration in early 2012.

Verizon also serves the Internet market through its wireline broadband offerings (8.6 million connections) and has increased the speed of its connectivity in what we view as an effort to upgrade DSL subscribers. However, the traditional DSL customer base began to decline in 2010, hurt by the effects of the economy and new, faster fiber offerings gaining traction.

In the third quarter of 2011, revenues at VZ's global enterprise segment rose 2.1%, which was encouraging to us, even though much of the growth was due to an acquisition, given weakness at peers and declines in recent periods. In April 2011, VZ completed its acquisition of Terremark Worldwide, which it expects will help the company support managed IT infrastructure and the cloud service market.

## Company Financials Fiscal Year Ended Dec. 31

| Per Share Data ($) | 2010 | 2009 | 2008 | 2007 | 2006 | 2005 | 2004 | 2003 | 2002 | 2001 |
|---|---|---|---|---|---|---|---|---|---|---|
| Tangible Book Value | NM | NM | NM | NM | NM | NM | NM | NM | NM | NM |
| Cash Flow | 6.69 | 7.10 | 7.37 | 6.85 | 1.87 | 7.61 | 7.67 | 6.14 | 6.56 | 5.22 |
| Earnings | 0.90 | 1.29 | 2.26 | 1.90 | 1.87 | 2.65 | 2.59 | 1.27 | 1.67 | 0.22 |
| S&P Core Earnings | 1.36 | 2.03 | 1.72 | 1.85 | 1.87 | 2.42 | 2.76 | 1.76 | 1.91 | 0.58 |
| Dividends | 1.91 | 1.85 | 1.75 | 1.65 | 1.62 | 1.60 | 1.54 | 1.54 | 1.54 | 1.54 |
| Payout Ratio | NM | 144% | 77% | 88% | 86% | 60% | 60% | 121% | 92% | NM |
| Prices:High | 36.00 | 34.76 | 44.32 | 46.24 | 38.95 | 41.06 | 42.27 | 44.31 | 51.09 | 57.40 |
| Prices:Low | 25.99 | 26.10 | 23.07 | 35.60 | 30.04 | 29.13 | 34.13 | 31.10 | 26.01 | 43.80 |
| P/E Ratio:High | 40 | 27 | 20 | 25 | 21 | 15 | 16 | 35 | 31 | NM |
| P/E Ratio:Low | 29 | 20 | 10 | 19 | 16 | 11 | 13 | 24 | 16 | NM |

| Income Statement Analysis (Million $) | | | | | | | | | | |
|---|---|---|---|---|---|---|---|---|---|---|
| Revenue | 106,565 | 107,808 | 97,354 | 93,469 | 88,144 | 75,112 | 71,283 | 67,752 | 67,625 | 67,190 |
| Depreciation | 16,405 | 16,532 | 14,565 | 14,377 | 14,545 | 14,047 | 13,910 | 13,617 | 13,423 | 13,657 |
| Maintenance | NA | NA | NA | NA | NA | NA | NA | NA | NA | NA |
| Construction Credits | NA | NA | NA | NA | NA | NA | NA | NA | NA | NA |
| Effective Tax Rate | 19.4% | 10.5% | 20.9% | 27.4% | 21.9% | 23.5% | 22.8% | 19.7% | 21.7% | 64.2% |
| Net Income | 2,549 | 3,651 | 6,428 | 5,510 | 5,480 | 7,397 | 7,261 | 3,509 | 4,584 | 590 |
| S&P Core Earnings | 3,856 | 5,778 | 4,893 | 5,370 | 5,467 | 6,774 | 7,724 | 4,859 | 5,250 | 1,557 |

| Balance Sheet & Other Financial Data (Million $) | | | | | | | | | | |
|---|---|---|---|---|---|---|---|---|---|---|
| Gross Property | 211,655 | 228,518 | 215,605 | 213,994 | 204,109 | 193,610 | 185,522 | 180,975 | 178,028 | 169,586 |
| Net Property | 87,711 | 91,466 | 86,546 | 85,294 | 82,356 | 75,305 | 74,124 | 75,316 | 74,496 | 74,419 |
| Capital Expenditures | 16,458 | 17,047 | 17,238 | 17,538 | 17,101 | 15,324 | 13,259 | 11,884 | 11,984 | 17,371 |
| Total Capital | 139,706 | 145,523 | 137,633 | 125,856 | 121,788 | 120,714 | 120,819 | 118,935 | 122,120 | 116,888 |
| Fixed Charges Coverage | 5.8 | 4.6 | 9.4 | 8.6 | 5.9 | 6.7 | 5.1 | 2.5 | 5.5 | 3.6 |
| Capitalization:Long Term Debt | 45,252 | 55,051 | 46,959 | 28,203 | 28,646 | 31,869 | 35,674 | 39,413 | 44,791 | 45,657 |
| Capitalization:Preferred | Nil | Nil | Nil | Nil | Nil | Nil | Nil | Nil | Nil | Nil |
| Capitalization:Common | 38,569 | 41,606 | 41,706 | 50,581 | 48,535 | 39,680 | 37,560 | 33,466 | 33,720 | 32,539 |
| % Return on Revenue | 2.4 | 3.4 | 6.6 | 5.9 | 6.2 | 9.8 | 10.2 | 5.2 | 6.8 | 0.9 |
| % Return on Invested Capital | 8.6 | 9.4 | 10.5 | 9.5 | 9.8 | 10.5 | 8.6 | 5.1 | 7.6 | 4.0 |
| % Return on Common Equity | 6.4 | 8.8 | 13.9 | 11.1 | 12.4 | 19.2 | 20.4 | 10.6 | 13.5 | 1.8 |
| % Earned on Net Property | 16.3 | 15.8 | 19.7 | 18.6 | 17.2 | 37.9 | 36.2 | 28.1 | 34.5 | 50.5 |
| % Long Term Debt of Capitalization | 54.0 | 57.0 | 53.0 | 35.8 | 37.1 | 44.5 | 48.7 | 54.1 | 36.6 | 58.4 |
| Capital % Preferred | Nil | Nil | Nil | Nil | Nil | Nil | Nil | Nil | Nil | Nil |
| Capitalization:% Common | 46.0 | 43.0 | 47.0 | 64.2 | 62.9 | 55.5 | 51.3 | 45.9 | 42.9 | 41.6 |

Data as orig reptd.; bef. results of disc opers/spec. items. Per share data adj. for stk. divs.; EPS diluted. E-Estimated. NA-Not Available. NM-Not Meaningful. NR-Not Ranked. UR-Under Review.

**Office:** 140 West Street, New York, NY 10007.
**Telephone:** 212-395-1000.
**Website:** http://www.verizon.com
**Chrmn:** I.G. Seidenberg

**Pres & CEO:** L.C. McAdam
**EVP & CFO:** F.J. Shammo
**EVP & CTO:** A.J. Melone
**EVP & General Counsel:** R.S. Milch

**Investor Contact:** K. Tarrant (908-559-6029)
**Board Members:** R. L. Carrion, M. F. Keeth, R. W. Lane, L. C. McAdam, S. O. Moose, J. Neubauer, D. T. Nicolaisen, C. Otis, Jr., H. B. Price, I. G. Seidenberg, R. E. Slater, J. W. Snow

**Founded:** 1983
**Domicile:** Delaware
**Employees:** 194,400

The McGraw-Hill Companies

# V.F. Corp

**STANDARD &POOR'S**

## S&P Recommendation  BUY ★★★★☆

**Price** $126.24 (as of Nov 25, 2011)

**12-Mo. Target Price** $150.00

**Investment Style** Large-Cap Blend

**GICS Sector** Consumer Discretionary
**Sub-Industry** Apparel, Accessories & Luxury Goods

**Summary** This global apparel company, with leading shares in denim and daypacks, is transforming itself into a designer and marketer of lifestyle apparel brands.

### Key Stock Statistics (Source S&P, Vickers, company reports)

| | | | | | | | |
|---|---|---|---|---|---|---|---|
| 52-Wk Range | $142.50–80.40 | S&P Oper. EPS 2011E | 8.10 | Market Capitalization(B) | $13.932 | Beta | 0.91 |
| Trailing 12-Month EPS | $6.20 | S&P Oper. EPS 2012E | 9.10 | Yield (%) | 2.28 | S&P 3-Yr. Proj. EPS CAGR(%) | 16 |
| Trailing 12-Month P/E | 20.4 | P/E on S&P Oper. EPS 2011E | 15.6 | Dividend Rate/Share | $2.88 | S&P Credit Rating | A- |
| $10K Invested 5 Yrs Ago | $19,329 | Common Shares Outstg. (M) | 110.4 | Institutional Ownership (%) | 88 | | |

## Price Performance

30-Week Mov. Avg. · · · ·    10-Week Mov. Avg. – – –    **GAAP Earnings vs. Previous Year**    Volume Above Avg. STARS
12-Mo. Target Price ——    Relative Strength —    ▲ Up  ▼ Down  ▶ No Change    Below Avg. ★

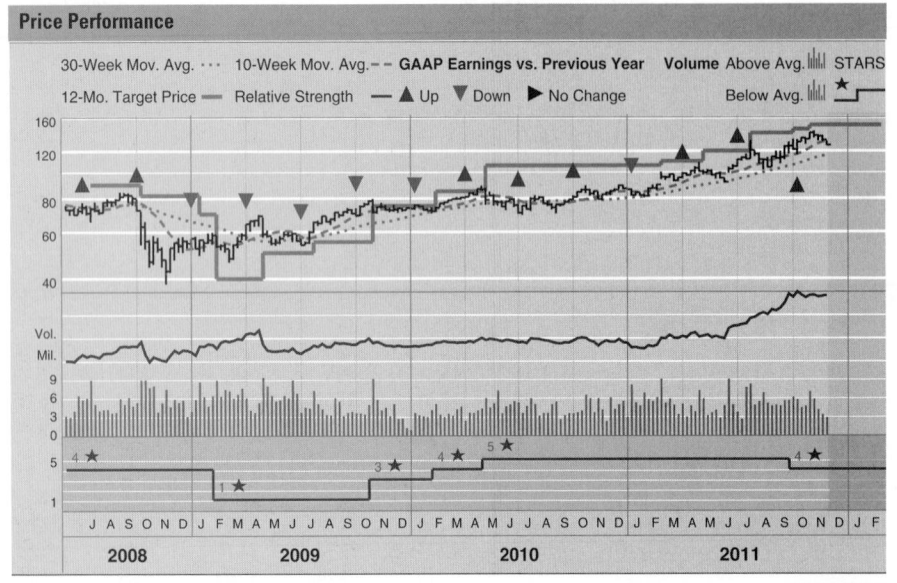

Options: CBOE

Analysis prepared by Equity Analyst **Jason N. Asaeda** on Nov 04, 2011, when the stock traded at **$137.19**.

## Highlights

➤ We see revenues increasing 23% in 2011, to $9.47 billion. We see revenue gains across all coalitions (business segments), led by Outdoor & Action Sports at 42%, including a $700 million revenue contribution from the newly acquired Timberland and SmartWool brands, followed by Imagewear at 13%, Contemporary Brands and Sportswear both at 10%, and Jeanswear at 9%.

➤ We expect EBIT margin pressure in 2011 from product cost inflation, mostly in the domestic mass denim business, to be largely offset by an improving mix of businesses (Outdoor & Action Sports, international and retail) and operating expense leverage. We look for revenues to increase 17% in 2012 and for EBIT margins to expand on lower cotton prices and full-year contribution from the Timberland business. VFC also so expects to realize about $35 million in annual cost synergies.

➤ Factoring in incremental interest expense on acquisition financing, we see 2011 EPS of $8.10, including $0.18 in one-time gains recorded in the first half of the year and $0.20 in estimated full-year acquisition costs. For 2012, we estimate EPS of $9.10.

## Investment Rationale/Risk

➤ We expect strong brand dynamics to enable VFC to gain market share in an uncertain environment. With 70% of its 2010 revenues coming from the U.S. market, we also see exceptional growth opportunities for the company in Europe, Latin America, Mexico, and Asia. In addition, we believe the Timberland acquisition has strengthened VFC's competitive positioning in the global footwear market. We perceive limited integration challenges and expect the company to leverage its core competencies to grow the Timberland's apparel business.

➤ Risks to our recommendation and target price include a severe economic slowdown domestically and a greater-than-expected moderation in consumer spending. International risks include economic weakness and unfavorable currency fluctuations.

➤ Over the past five years, VFC has traded in a forward P/E range of 11.6X-18.6X earnings. Given our positive company outlook, we believe the stock should trade at a premium to the five-year historical average multiple of 14.6X. Our 12-month target price of $150 is based on a peer-average forward P/E multiple of 16.5X applied to our 2012 EPS estimate.

## Qualitative Risk Assessment

| LOW | MEDIUM | HIGH |
|---|---|---|

Our risk assessment reflects our view of VFC's strong cash flow, offset by integration risk as VFC pursues growth via acquisitions.

## Quantitative Evaluations

**S&P Quality Ranking** A

| D | C | B- | B | B+ | A- | A | A+ |
|---|---|---|---|---|---|---|---|

**Relative Strength Rank** STRONG

72

LOWEST = 1                    HIGHEST = 99

## Revenue/Earnings Data

**Revenue (Million $)**

| | 1Q | 2Q | 3Q | 4Q | Year |
|---|---|---|---|---|---|
| 2011 | 1,959 | 1,840 | 2,750 | -- | -- |
| 2010 | 1,750 | 1,594 | 2,232 | 2,126 | 7,703 |
| 2009 | 1,725 | 1,486 | 2,094 | 1,915 | 7,220 |
| 2008 | 1,846 | 1,677 | 2,207 | 1,912 | 7,643 |
| 2007 | 1,674 | 1,517 | 2,073 | 1,955 | 7,219 |
| 2006 | 1,456 | 1,351 | 1,810 | 1,599 | 6,216 |

**Earnings Per Share ($)**

| | | | | | |
|---|---|---|---|---|---|
| 2011 | 1.82 | 1.17 | 2.69 | E2.29 | E8.10 |
| 2010 | 1.47 | 1.00 | 2.22 | 0.49 | 5.18 |
| 2009 | 0.91 | 0.68 | 1.94 | 0.60 | 4.13 |
| 2008 | 1.33 | 0.94 | 2.10 | 1.05 | 5.42 |
| 2007 | 1.17 | 0.93 | 1.86 | 1.46 | 5.41 |
| 2006 | 1.05 | 0.80 | 1.64 | 1.24 | 4.73 |

Fiscal year ended Dec. 31. Next earnings report expected: NA. EPS Estimates based on S&P Operating Earnings; historical GAAP earnings are as reported.

## Dividend Data (Dates: mm/dd Payment Date: mm/dd/yy)

| Amount ($) | Date Decl. | Ex-Div. Date | Stk. of Record | Payment Date |
|---|---|---|---|---|
| 0.630 | 02/22 | 03/09 | 03/11 | 03/21/11 |
| 0.630 | 04/29 | 06/08 | 06/10 | 06/20/11 |
| 0.630 | 07/21 | 09/07 | 09/09 | 09/19/11 |
| 0.720 | 10/24 | 12/07 | 12/09 | 12/19/11 |

Dividends have been paid since 1941. Source: Company reports.

---

**Please read the Required Disclosures and Analyst Certification on the last page of this report.**

**The McGraw-Hill Companies**

# V.F. Corp

**STANDARD &POOR'S**

## Business Summary November 04, 2011

CORPORATE OVERVIEW. VF Corp. is the world's largest apparel manufacturer, and holds the leading position in several market categories, including jeanswear, workwear and daypacks. In early 2011, VFC articulated its strategic plan to add $5 billion in sales by 2015, or a 10% CAGR (compound annual growth rate), driven by a $3 billion increment in its Outdoors & Action Sports coalition, $1 billion in Jeanswear and another $1 billion from other brands. International expansion and a doubling of doors to 1,500 company stores will drive the bulk of the planned $5 billion increment. This plan increases revenue growth from the previous 8%-10% annual target. A 15% operating margin goal was re-affirmed and a $6 billion cumulative cash generation goal was presented. Growing lifestyle brands remains the lynchpin of VFC's growth strategy, with an emphasis on outdoors and action sports brands.

MARKET PROFILE. VFC participates in the broad apparel market, spanning product categories from women's activewear to denim, as well as the outdoor market for apparel and accessories via its lifestyle brands. Apparel is a mature market, with demand mirroring population growth and a modicum related to fashion; it is fragmented, with national brands marketed by 20 companies accounting for about 30% of total apparel sales and the remaining 70% comprised of smaller and/or private label "store" brands. While deflationary pricing pressure has been an industry constant for decades, higher raw material and labor costs are likely to drive price increases in 2011 and could squeeze profit margins for many industry participants, dependent on brand positioning and strength. S&P estimates a 3% increase for 2011 apparel sales, following a 2% gain in 2010, a 5% decrease in 2009, a 4% decline in 2008, and 4% gains in 2007 and 2006.

According to the SGMA (Sporting Goods Manufacturers Association), wholesale sales of sporting goods and fitness equipment (excluding recreational transport such as bikes, boats and snowmobiles), sports apparel, athletic footwear and licensed merchandise in the U.S. increased 3.5%, to $74.2 billion, in 2010. Apparel represents about 40% of the mix, footwear 17%, sporting goods and fitness equipment 33%, and licensed merchandise 10%. Sports apparel and footwear brands more frequently serve a fashion market than a true athletic or active sports market; generally only a third of sports apparel and footwear is purchased with the intent that it will be used in an active sport, according to the NPD Group. The SGMA projects another strong year in 2011 and notes that 60% of its members need more manufacturing capacity and will increase production by nearly 25%, and 88% expect international sales growth this year.

## Company Financials Fiscal Year Ended Dec. 31

| Per Share Data ($) | 2010 | 2009 | 2008 | 2007 | 2006 | 2005 | 2004 | 2003 | 2002 | 2001 |
|---|---|---|---|---|---|---|---|---|---|---|
| Tangible Book Value | 10.75 | 7.90 | 7.54 | 7.86 | 13.18 | 8.78 | 7.56 | 8.61 | 10.91 | 9.97 |
| Cash Flow | 6.77 | 5.66 | 6.72 | 6.48 | 5.74 | 5.56 | 5.53 | 4.64 | 4.35 | 0.00 |
| Earnings | 5.18 | 4.13 | 5.42 | 5.41 | 4.73 | 4.54 | 4.21 | 3.61 | 3.24 | 1.19 |
| S&P Core Earnings | 6.73 | 5.20 | 4.98 | 5.31 | 4.82 | 4.67 | 4.36 | 3.70 | 2.75 | 0.77 |
| Dividends | 2.43 | 2.37 | 2.33 | 2.23 | 1.94 | 1.10 | 1.05 | 1.01 | 0.97 | 0.93 |
| Payout Ratio | 47% | 57% | 43% | 41% | 41% | 24% | 25% | 28% | 30% | 78% |
| Prices:High | 89.74 | 79.79 | 84.60 | 96.20 | 83.10 | 61.61 | 55.61 | 44.08 | 45.64 | 42.70 |
| Prices:Low | 69.24 | 46.06 | 38.22 | 68.15 | 53.25 | 50.44 | 42.06 | 32.62 | 31.50 | 28.15 |
| P/E Ratio:High | 17 | 19 | 16 | 18 | 18 | 14 | 13 | 12 | 14 | 36 |
| P/E Ratio:Low | 13 | 11 | 7 | 13 | 11 | 11 | 10 | 9 | 10 | 24 |

| Income Statement Analysis (Million $) | 2010 | 2009 | 2008 | 2007 | 2006 | 2005 | 2004 | 2003 | 2002 | 2001 |
|---|---|---|---|---|---|---|---|---|---|---|
| Revenue | 7,703 | 7,220 | 7,643 | 7,219 | 6,216 | 6,502 | 6,055 | 5,207 | 5,084 | 5,519 |
| Operating Income | 1,196 | 1,029 | 1,124 | 1,081 | 935 | 944 | 874 | 718 | 729 | 516 |
| Depreciation | 173 | 170 | 144 | 122 | 108 | 116 | 141 | 104 | 107 | 169 |
| Interest Expense | 77.7 | 85.9 | 94.1 | 72.1 | 57.3 | 70.6 | 76.1 | 61.4 | 71.3 | 93.4 |
| Pretax Income | 750 | 655 | 848 | 906 | 777 | 771 | 712 | 599 | 562 | 263 |
| Effective Tax Rate | NA | 30.0% | 28.9% | 32.3% | 31.2% | 32.7% | 33.3% | 33.5% | 35.1% | 47.6% |
| Net Income | 574 | 461 | 603 | 613 | 535 | 519 | 475 | 398 | 364 | 138 |
| S&P Core Earnings | 742 | 581 | 554 | 602 | 544 | 532 | 490 | 406 | 303 | 84.6 |

| Balance Sheet & Other Financial Data (Million $) | 2010 | 2009 | 2008 | 2007 | 2006 | 2005 | 2004 | 2003 | 2002 | 2001 |
|---|---|---|---|---|---|---|---|---|---|---|
| Cash | 792 | 732 | 382 | 322 | 343 | 297 | 486 | 515 | 496 | 332 |
| Current Assets | 2,826 | 2,629 | 2,653 | 2,645 | 2,578 | 2,365 | 2,379 | 2,209 | 2,075 | 2,031 |
| Total Assets | 6,458 | 6,488 | 6,434 | 6,447 | 5,466 | 5,171 | 5,004 | 4,246 | 3,503 | 4,103 |
| Current Liabilities | 1,109 | 1,093 | 1,012 | 1,134 | 1,015 | 1,152 | 1,372 | 872 | 875 | 814 |
| Long Term Debt | 936 | 938 | 1,104 | 1,145 | 635 | 648 | 557 | 956 | 602 | 904 |
| Common Equity | 3,861 | 3,832 | 3,556 | 3,577 | 3,265 | 2,808 | 2,513 | 1,951 | 1,658 | 2,113 |
| Total Capital | 4,800 | 4,971 | 4,662 | 4,722 | 3,901 | 3,479 | 3,096 | 2,938 | 2,297 | 3,062 |
| Capital Expenditures | 112 | 85.9 | 124 | 114 | 127 | 110 | 81.4 | 86.6 | 64.5 | 81.6 |
| Cash Flow | 747 | 632 | 747 | 735 | 643 | 635 | 615 | 502 | 472 | 304 |
| Current Ratio | 2.6 | 2.4 | 2.6 | 2.3 | 2.5 | 2.1 | 1.7 | 2.5 | 2.4 | 2.5 |
| % Long Term Debt of Capitalization | 19.5 | 18.9 | 24.3 | 24.2 | 16.3 | 18.6 | 18.0 | 32.6 | 26.2 | 29.5 |
| % Net Income of Revenue | 7.5 | 6.4 | 7.9 | 8.5 | 8.6 | 8.0 | 7.9 | 7.8 | 7.2 | 2.5 |
| % Return on Assets | 8.9 | 7.1 | 9.4 | 10.3 | 10.1 | 10.2 | 10.3 | 10.3 | 9.6 | 3.3 |
| % Return on Equity | 14.9 | 12.5 | 16.9 | 17.9 | 17.6 | 19.5 | 21.3 | 22.1 | 19.3 | 6.3 |

Data as orig reptd.; bef. results of disc opers/spec. items. Per share data adj. for stk. divs.; EPS diluted. E-Estimated. NA-Not Available. NM-Not Meaningful. NR-Not Ranked. UR-Under Review.

**Office:** 105 Corporate Center Boulevard, Greensboro, NC 27408.
**Telephone:** 336-424-6000.
**Email:** irrequest@vfc.com
**Website:** http://www.vfc.com

**Chrmn, Pres & CEO:** E.C. Wiseman
**CFO:** R.K. Shearer
**Chief Admin Officer, Secy & General Counsel:** C.S. Cummings
**Chief Acctg Officer & Cntlr:** B.W. Batten

**Investor Contact:** C. Knoebel (336-424-6189)
**Board Members:** R. T. Carucci, J. L. Chugg, J. E. De Bedout, U. O. Fairbairn, G. Fellows, R. J. Hurst, L. W. Lang, W. A. McCollough, C. Otis, Jr., E. C. Wiseman

**Founded:** 1899
**Domicile:** Pennsylvania
**Employees:** 47,000

*The McGraw-Hill Companies*

# Viacom Inc

**STANDARD &POOR'S**

| | | | |
|---|---|---|---|
| **S&P Recommendation** STRONG BUY ★★★★★ | **Price** $41.61 (as of Nov 25, 2011) | **12-Mo. Target Price** $60.00 | **Investment Style** Large-Cap Blend |

**GICS Sector** Consumer Discretionary
**Sub-Industry** Movies & Entertainment

**Summary** This pure-play entertainment content provider operates several well known cable networks such as MTV, Nickelodeon, BET and VH1, as well as the Paramount film studio -- with such franchises as Star Trek, Transformers, Mission Impossible and Indiana Jones.

## Key Stock Statistics (Source S&P, Vickers, company reports)

| | | | | | | | |
|---|---|---|---|---|---|---|---|
| 52-Wk Range | $52.67– 35.13 | S&P Oper. EPS 2012**E** | 4.79 | Market Capitalization(B) | $20.838 | Beta | 1.29 |
| Trailing 12-Month EPS | $3.59 | S&P Oper. EPS 2013**E** | 5.61 | Yield (%) | 2.40 | S&P 3-Yr. Proj. EPS CAGR(%) | 15 |
| Trailing 12-Month P/E | 11.6 | P/E on S&P Oper. EPS 2012**E** | 8.7 | Dividend Rate/Share | $1.00 | S&P Credit Rating | BBB+ |
| $10K Invested 5 Yrs Ago | $10,954 | Common Shares Outstg. (M) | 552.2 | Institutional Ownership (%) | 95 | | |

## Price Performance

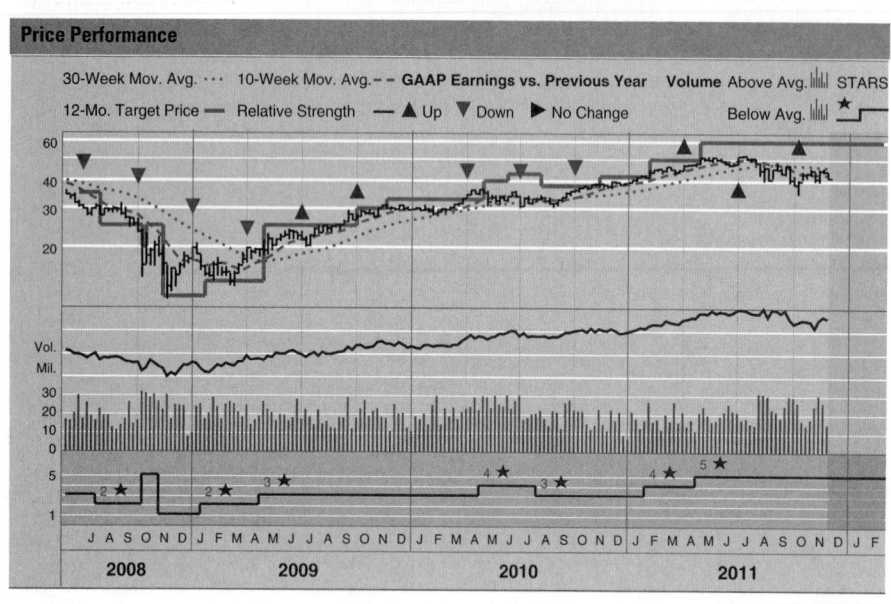

30-Week Mov. Avg. · · · 10-Week Mov. Avg. - - GAAP Earnings vs. Previous Year Volume Above Avg. STARS
12-Mo. Target Price — Relative Strength — ▲ Up ▼ Down ▶ No Change Below Avg. ★

Options: ASE, CBOE, P, Ph

Analysis prepared by Equity Analyst **T. Amobi, CFA CPA** on Nov 14, 2011, when the stock traded at **$45.00**.

### Qualitative Risk Assessment

| LOW | MEDIUM | HIGH |
|---|---|---|

Our risk assessment reflects the company's leading demographically targeted brands, as well as our view of relatively encouraging but recently decelerating growth prospects and ample financial flexibility, offset by exposure to cyclical advertising, a volatile, hit-driven filmed entertainment business, and some governance issues.

### Quantitative Evaluations

**S&P Quality Ranking** NR

| D | C | B- | B | B+ | A- | A | A+ |
|---|---|---|---|---|---|---|---|

**Relative Strength Rank** MODERATE

56

LOWEST = 1 HIGHEST = 99

## Highlights

➤ We expect FY 12 (Sep.) consolidated revenues to edge up 0.5%, to $15.0 billion, assuming that continued healthy growth in worldwide advertising and affiliate revenues will be significantly offset by very difficult comparisons for the film studio, coming off a year of solid growth in theatrical and ancillary revenues, as well as TV license fees, with lower home entertainment revenues. In FY 13, however, we expect a strong 7% rebound in consolidated revenues, to more than $16.0 billion.

➤ Over the next two years, we see overall margins being significantly enhanced by increased operating leverage from several restructuring measures at the international networks and studio operations, combined with growing contributions from high-margin streaming deals, after continued investments in programming.

➤ We estimate FY 12 and FY 13 adjusted consolidated EBIT (after equity compensation) of nearly $4.4 billion and $4.8 billion, respectively, and after interest and taxes, operating EPS of $4.79 and $5.61, with sustained share buybacks under a $10 billion plan (of which $7.2 billion remained as of early November).

## Investment Rationale/Risk

➤ After ending FY 11 on a resounding note, VIA.B offered some encouraging FY 12 guidance, with further visibility on solid domestic ad commitments for the core networks (MTV, BET, Nick), a blockbuster-laden franchise slate of upcoming film releases (Mission Impossible 4, GI Joe 2), and further out, some key follow-on franchise installments (Star Trek, Paranormal Activity). Also, we see potentially sizable upside from increasingly compelling streaming deals with Netflix, Hulu and others. We note VIA.B's ample financial flexibility for recently ramped-up share buybacks.

➤ Risks to our recommendation and target price include a severe macroeconomic slowdown; severe ratings declines for any of the core networks; inherent volatility of film results; foreign currency exposure; and potential issues with corporate governance arising from dual class shares and a controlling shareholder.

➤ Our 12-month target price is $60, blending 9.0X FY 12E EV/EBITDA and 0.8X P/E-to-growth (on 15% long-term growth) -- which we view as attractive relative to peers and the S&P 500 -- noting the recent dividend yield of 2.2%.

## Revenue/Earnings Data

**Revenue (Million $)**

| | 1Q | 2Q | 3Q | 4Q | Year |
|---|---|---|---|---|---|
| 2011 | 3,828 | 3,267 | 3,766 | 4,053 | 14,914 |
| 2010 | -- | 2,732 | 3,275 | 3,330 | 9,337 |
| 2009 | 2,905 | 3,299 | 3,317 | 4,098 | 13,619 |
| 2008 | 3,117 | 3,857 | 3,408 | 4,243 | 14,625 |
| 2007 | 2,746 | 3,186 | 3,271 | 4,248 | 13,423 |
| 2006 | 2,368 | 2,847 | 2,660 | 3,593 | 11,467 |

**Earnings Per Share ($)**

| | | | | | |
|---|---|---|---|---|---|
| 2011 | 1.02 | 0.63 | 0.97 | 0.99 | 3.61 |
| 2010 | -- | 0.42 | 0.71 | 0.80 | 1.92 |
| 2009 | 0.29 | 0.46 | 0.73 | 1.14 | 2.62 |
| 2008 | 0.42 | 0.64 | 0.62 | 0.28 | 1.97 |
| 2007 | 0.29 | 0.63 | 0.67 | 0.84 | 2.41 |
| 2006 | 0.43 | 0.58 | 0.50 | 0.69 | 2.19 |

Fiscal year ended Sep. 30. Next earnings report expected: Early February. EPS Estimates based on S&P Operating Earnings; historical GAAP earnings are as reported.

## Dividend Data (Dates: mm/dd Payment Date: mm/dd/yy)

| Amount ($) | Date Decl. | Ex-Div. Date | Stk. of Record | Payment Date |
|---|---|---|---|---|
| 0.250 | 05/25 | 06/13 | 06/15 | 07/01/11 |
| 0.250 | 05/25 | 06/13 | 06/15 | 07/01/11 |
| 0.250 | 07/26 | 09/13 | 09/15 | 10/03/11 |
| 0.250 | 11/09 | 12/13 | 12/15 | 01/02/12 |

Dividends have been paid since 2010. Source: Company reports.

# Viacom Inc

STANDARD &POOR'S

## Business Summary November 14, 2011

CORPORATE OVERVIEW. Viacom is one of the two public companies created after the January 2006 separation of the "old" Viacom into two independent public entities (the "old" Viacom was renamed CBS Corp.). Each Class A and B shareholder of the "old" Viacom received 0.5 of a share of the corresponding A or B stock of each of the new entities. We believe that the company is the faster growing of the two companies resulting from the separation, and is specifically targeted to growth-oriented investors.

The company's media networks segment (61% of FY 11 (Sep.) revenues) is mainly comprised of MTV Networks (including MTV, Nickelodeon, VH1, Comedy Central, Country Music Television, Spike TV, TV Land, Logo, Neopets, Xfire and VIVA) and BET Networks. In October 2009, as part of a joint venture with Lionsgate and MGM studios, Paramount launched EPIX -- a 50%-owned premium cable channel.

The entertainment segment (39%) mainly comprises Paramount Pictures film studio (and home entertainment). About 33% of FY 11 revenues were derived from ad sales, 27% from feature films (theatrical and home video), 23% from affiliate fees, 10% from TV licensing, and 7% from other ancillary sources

(including merchandise licensing). In 2010, the company divested Harmonix (which developed the Rock Band music video games franchise).

CORPORATE STRATEGY. In February 2011, VIA.B announced a content partnership with online video site Hulu -- followed in March 2011 by a multi-year licensing deal between Paramount and Netflix Canada. In August 2010, EPIX signed a five-year streaming deal with Netflix believed to be worth about $200 million per year. The company has more than 2,500 web sites, and has entered into distribution partnerships with various Internet and technology companies. Over the past few years, the company has made a number of selective digital acquisitions (e.g., online gaming and social media) including Xfire, Y2M, Atom Entertainment, Quizilla, Teenage Mutant Ninja Turtles and Social Express. The company's global footprint traverses Europe and emerging markets (India and China) -- with about 160 channels across 159 countries in 34 languages.

## Company Financials Fiscal Year Ended Sep. 30

| Per Share Data ($) | 2011 | 2010 | 2009 | 2008 | 2007 | 2006 | 2005 | 2004 | 2003 | 2002 |
|---|---|---|---|---|---|---|---|---|---|---|
| Tangible Book Value | NM | NM | NM | NM | NM | NM | NM | NM | NA | NA |
| Cash Flow | 4.13 | 2.30 | 3.16 | 2.55 | 2.99 | 2.70 | 2.08 | 1.78 | NA | NA |
| Earnings | 3.61 | 1.92 | 2.62 | 1.97 | 2.41 | 2.19 | 1.73 | 1.48 | NA | NA |
| S&P Core Earnings | 3.59 | 1.93 | 2.65 | 2.01 | 2.34 | 2.22 | 1.46 | 1.47 | NA | NA |
| Dividends | 1.05 | 0.30 | Nil | Nil | Nil | Nil | Nil | NA | NA | NA |
| Payout Ratio | 29% | 16% | Nil | Nil | Nil | Nil | Nil | NA | NA | NA |
| Prices:High | 52.67 | 40.25 | 31.56 | 44.19 | 45.40 | 43.90 | 44.95 | NA | NA | NA |
| Prices:Low | 35.13 | 27.89 | 13.25 | 11.60 | 33.74 | 32.42 | 39.78 | NA | NA | NA |
| P/E Ratio:High | 15 | 21 | 12 | 22 | 19 | 20 | 26 | NA | NA | NA |
| P/E Ratio:Low | 10 | 15 | 5 | 6 | 14 | 15 | 23 | NA | NA | NA |

| Income Statement Analysis (Million $) | | | | | | | | | | |
|---|---|---|---|---|---|---|---|---|---|---|
| Revenue | 14,914 | 9,337 | 13,619 | 14,625 | 13,423 | 11,467 | 9,610 | 8,132 | 7,304 | 6,051 |
| Operating Income | 4,125 | 2,429 | 3,295 | 3,341 | 3,404 | 3,137 | 2,625 | 2,534 | 2,218 | 1,932 |
| Depreciation | 271 | 222 | 331 | 364 | 393 | 366 | 259 | 2,522 | 198 | 195 |
| Interest Expense | 419 | 326 | 440 | 514 | 487 | 472 | 23.0 | 20.0 | 23.2 | 40.9 |
| Pretax Income | 3,245 | 1,812 | 2,276 | 1,855 | 2,579 | 2,322 | 2,328 | 2,017 | 1,938 | 1,641 |
| Effective Tax Rate | NA | 34.6% | 31.1% | 32.6% | 36.0% | 31.8% | 43.8% | 36.4% | 40.6% | 39.3% |
| Net Income | 2,183 | 1,185 | 1,591 | 1,233 | 1,630 | 1,570 | 1,304 | 1,281 | 1,147 | 994 |
| S&P Core Earnings | 2,132 | 1,183 | 1,607 | 1,257 | 1,588 | 1,592 | 1,165 | 1,282 | NA | NA |

| Balance Sheet & Other Financial Data (Million $) | | | | | | | | | | |
|---|---|---|---|---|---|---|---|---|---|---|
| Cash | 1,021 | 837 | 298 | 792 | 920 | 706 | 361 | 99.2 | 58.3 | NA |
| Current Assets | 5,261 | 4,549 | 4,430 | 4,502 | 4,833 | 4,211 | 3,513 | 2,384 | 3,213 | NA |
| Total Assets | 22,801 | 22,096 | 21,900 | 22,487 | 22,904 | 21,797 | 19,116 | 18,400 | 22,304 | NA |
| Current Liabilities | 3,942 | 3,498 | 3,751 | 4,842 | 5,273 | 4,617 | 3,269 | 2,617 | 3,766 | NA |
| Long Term Debt | 7,187 | 6,721 | 6,650 | 7,897 | 8,060 | 7,584 | 5,702 | 3,718 | NA | NA |
| Common Equity | 8,644 | 9,283 | 8,704 | 7,033 | 7,111 | 7,166 | 7,788 | 9,905 | 15,816 | NA |
| Total Capital | 16,113 | 16,011 | 15,450 | 14,980 | 15,312 | 14,932 | 13,534 | 13,623 | 16,441 | NA |
| Capital Expenditures | 155 | 105 | 141 | 288 | 237 | 210 | 193 | NA | 114 | 122 |
| Cash Flow | 2,454 | 1,407 | 1,922 | 1,597 | 2,023 | 1,936 | 1,563 | 1,533 | 1,345 | 1,189 |
| Current Ratio | 1.3 | 1.3 | 1.2 | 0.9 | 0.9 | 0.9 | 1.1 | 0.9 | 0.9 | NA |
| % Long Term Debt of Capitalization | 44.6 | 42.0 | 43.0 | 52.7 | 52.6 | 50.8 | 42.1 | 27.3 | Nil | Nil |
| % Net Income of Revenue | 14.6 | 12.7 | 11.7 | 8.4 | 12.2 | 13.7 | 13.6 | 15.8 | 15.7 | 16.4 |
| % Return on Assets | 9.7 | NM | 7.2 | 5.4 | 7.3 | 7.7 | 6.9 | NA | NA | NA |
| % Return on Equity | 24.4 | NM | 20.2 | 17.4 | 22.8 | 21.0 | 12.3 | NA | NA | NA |

Data as orig reptd.; bef. results of disc opers/spec. items. Per share data adj. for stk. divs.; EPS diluted. E-Estimated. NA-Not Available. NM-Not Meaningful. NR-Not Ranked. UR-Under Review.

**Office:** 1515 Broadway, New York, NY 10036.
**Telephone:** 212-258-6000.
**Website:** http://www.viacom.com
**Chrmn:** S.M. Redstone

**Pres & CEO:** P.P. Dauman
**Vice Chrmn:** S.E. Redstone
**COO & EVP:** T.E. Dooley
**EVP, Secy & General Counsel:** M.D. Fricklas

**Investor Contact:** J. Bombassei (212-258-6700)
**Board Members:** G. S. Abrams, P. P. Dauman, T. E. Dooley, A. C. Greenberg, R. Kraft, B. J. McGarvie, C. E. Phillips, Jr., S. E. Redstone, S. M. Redstone, F. V. Salerno, W. Schwartz

**Founded:** 2005
**Domicile:** Delaware
**Employees:** 10,580

# Visa Inc

**STANDARD &POOR'S**

| **S&P Recommendation** HOLD ★★★☆☆ | **Price** $89.02 (as of Nov 25, 2011) | **12-Mo. Target Price** $100.00 | **Investment Style** Large-Cap Growth |
|---|---|---|---|

**GICS Sector** Information Technology
**Sub-Industry** Data Processing & Outsourced Services

**Summary** Visa is the world's largest retail electronics payment network and leading payments brand, providing services to consumers, businesses and governments globally.

## Key Stock Statistics (Source S&P, Vickers, company reports)

| | | | | | | | |
|---|---|---|---|---|---|---|---|
| 52-Wk Range | $95.87– 66.50 | S&P Oper. EPS 2012**E** | 6.00 | Market Capitalization(B) | $46.427 | Beta | 0.75 |
| Trailing 12-Month EPS | $4.50 | S&P Oper. EPS 2013**E** | NA | Yield (%) | 0.99 | S&P 3-Yr. Proj. EPS CAGR(%) | 14 |
| Trailing 12-Month P/E | 19.8 | P/E on S&P Oper. EPS 2012**E** | 14.8 | Dividend Rate/Share | $0.88 | S&P Credit Rating | NA |
| $10K Invested 5 Yrs Ago | NA | Common Shares Outstg. (M) | 812.9 | Institutional Ownership (%) | 83 | | |

## Price Performance

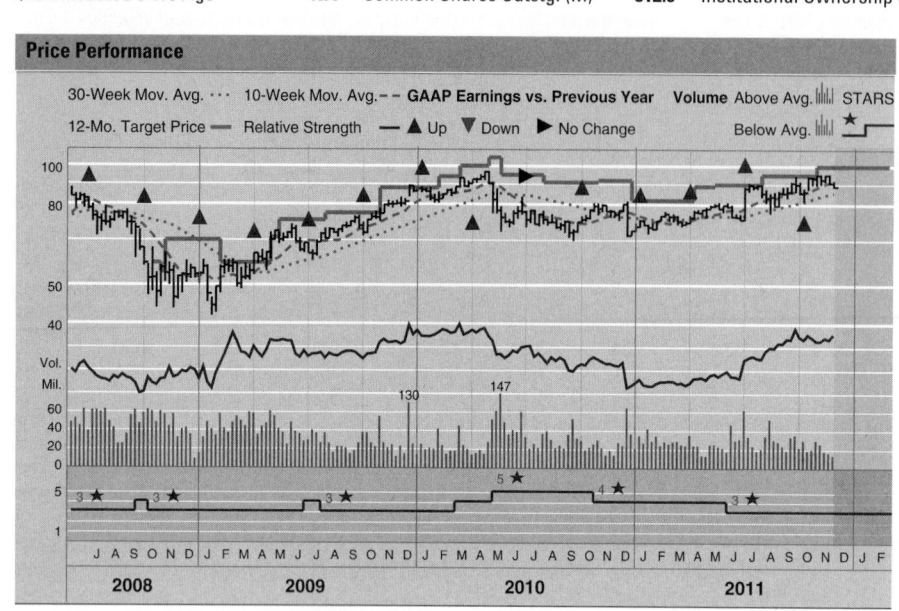

30-Week Mov. Avg. · · · 10-Week Mov. Avg. - - GAAP Earnings vs. Previous Year Volume Above Avg. STARS
12-Mo. Target Price — Relative Strength — ▲ Up ▼ Down ► No Change Below Avg. ★

Options: ASE, CBOE, Ph

## Qualitative Risk Assessment

| LOW | **MEDIUM** | HIGH |
|---|---|---|

Our risk assessment reflects what we view as a dynamic market environment, tempered somewhat by pending litigation risks, an evolving competitive and regulatory environment, and prospects for a slow recovery in domestic consumer spending.

## Quantitative Evaluations

**S&P Quality Ranking** NR

| D | C | B- | B | B+ | A- | A | A+ |
|---|---|---|---|---|---|---|---|

**Relative Strength Rank** STRONG

72

LOWEST = 1    HIGHEST = 99

## Revenue/Earnings Data

**Revenue (Million $)**

| | 1Q | 2Q | 3Q | 4Q | Year |
|---|---|---|---|---|---|
| 2011 | 2,238 | 2,245 | 2,322 | 2,383 | 9,188 |
| 2010 | 1,960 | 1,959 | 2,029 | 2,117 | 8,065 |
| 2009 | 1,739 | 1,647 | 1,646 | 1,879 | 6,911 |
| 2008 | 1,488 | 1,453 | 1,613 | 1,709 | 6,263 |
| 2007 | 845.0 | 813.0 | 1,363 | 1,466 | 5,193 |
| 2006 | -- | -- | -- | -- | 3,899 |

**Earnings Per Share ($)**

| | | | | | |
|---|---|---|---|---|---|
| 2011 | 1.23 | 1.23 | 1.43 | 1.27 | 5.16 |
| 2010 | 1.02 | 0.96 | 0.97 | 1.06 | 4.01 |
| 2009 | 0.74 | 0.71 | 0.97 | 0.69 | 3.10 |
| 2008 | 0.55 | 0.39 | 0.51 | -0.45 | 0.96 |
| 2007 | -- | 0.23 | 0.42 | -2.25 | -1.15 |
| 2006 | -- | -- | -- | -- | 0.60 |

Fiscal year ended Sep. 30. Next earnings report expected: NA. EPS Estimates based on S&P Operating Earnings; historical GAAP earnings are as reported.

## Highlights

➤ The 12-month target price for V has recently been changed to $100.00 from $95.00. The Highlights section of this Stock Report will be updated accordingly.

## Investment Rationale/Risk

➤ The Investment Rationale/Risk section of this Stock Report will be updated shortly. For the latest News story on V from MarketScope, see below.

➤ 11/15/11 02:50 pm ET ... S&P COMMENTS ON PROMINENT INVESTOR'S INTEREST IN IT STOCKS (IBM 189.24*****): Warren Buffet's Berkshire Hathaway (BRK.B 76, Hold) made notable investments in IT bellwethers IBM, Intel (INTC 25, Hold), and Visa (V 96, Hold) in Q3. BRK.B also had a stake in in MasterCard (MA 372, Hold), and thus BRK.B holds interests in 4 of the 12 largest U.S. tech companies by market cap. Interestingly, 3 of these companies are categorized within the GICS IT Services industry. All of them have global franchises and pay dividends, and the 3 IT Services companies have what we view as strong earnings visibility. Equity Strategy has an Overweight opinion on the sector. /S. Kessler

## Dividend Data (Dates: mm/dd Payment Date: mm/dd/yy)

| Amount ($) | Date Decl. | Ex-Div. Date | Stk. of Record | Payment Date |
|---|---|---|---|---|
| 0.150 | 04/25 | 05/18 | 05/20 | 06/07/11 |
| 0.150 | 07/22 | 08/17 | 08/19 | 09/07/11 |
| 0.220 | 10/19 | 11/16 | 11/18 | 12/06/11 |
| 0.220 | 10/19 | 11/16 | 11/18 | 12/06/11 |

Dividends have been paid since 2008. Source: Company reports.

---

**Please read the Required Disclosures and Analyst Certification on the last page of this report.**

The **McGraw·Hill** Companies

# Visa Inc

**STANDARD &POOR'S**

## Business Summary August 11, 2011

**CORPORATE OVERVIEW.** Visa Inc. (V) operates the world's largest retail electronic payments network, providing financial institutions with a broad range of platforms for consumer credit, debit, prepaid and commercial payments. In October 2007, V completed a reorganization via which Visa U.S.A., Visa International, Visa Canada and Inovant, which operated the VisaNet transaction processing system and other related processing systems, became subsidiaries of V.

V derives revenues primarily from card service fees, data processing fees, and international transaction fees. Service fees (over 36% of FY 10 (Sep.) gross operating revenue) reflect payments by customers for their participation in card programs carrying Visa brands. They also include acceptance fees, which are used to support merchant acceptance and ongoing volume growth initiatives. Data processing fees (more than 32%) consist of fees charged to customers for providing transaction processing and other payment services, including processing services provided under V's bilateral services agreement with Visa Europe. International transaction fees (24%) are charged to customers on transactions where the issuer and the merchant are located in different countries. Its other revenues (7%) consist primarily of optional service or product enhancements, such as extended cardholder protection and concierge services, cardholder services and fees for licensing and certification, as well as licensing and other service-related fees from Visa Europe.

Payments volume, the basis for card service fee revenue, and transactions, which drive data processing revenue, are key drivers of V's business. Payments volume increased 17.2% to $3.3 trillion in FY 10, driven by 15% growth in transactions processed, to 47 billion. V's operating revenues from its five largest customers represented approximately 30% (32% in FY 09) of its total operating revenues in FY 10. In addition, operating revenues from its largest customer, JPMorgan Chase, accounted for 10% in FY 09, but was less than 10% in FY 10.

**CORPORATE STRATEGY.** V seeks to grow by expanding its core payments business in new and established geographies and market segments, as well as by broadening its processing capabilities and value-added service offerings for payments and related opportunities. The company intends to continue to expand the size of its payments network to drive the issuance, acceptance and usage of its products globally. V believes that there is a significant opportunity for expanding the usage of its products and services in high-growth geographies in which it currently operates.

## Company Financials Fiscal Year Ended Sep. 30

| Per Share Data ($) | 2011 | 2010 | 2009 | 2008 | 2007 | 2006 | 2005 | 2004 | 2003 | 2002 |
|---|---|---|---|---|---|---|---|---|---|---|
| Tangible Book Value | NA | 2.45 | 2.48 | NM | NM | NA | NA | NA | NA | NA |
| Cash Flow | 5.73 | 4.52 | 3.40 | 0.95 | NA | NA | NA | NA | NA | NA |
| Earnings | 5.32 | 4.01 | 3.10 | 0.96 | -1.15 | 0.60 | NA | NA | NA | NA |
| S&P Core Earnings | 5.06 | 3.95 | 2.67 | 1.95 | 1.87 | 0.57 | NA | NA | NA | NA |
| Dividends | 0.60 | 0.50 | 0.42 | 0.11 | NA | NA | NA | NA | NA | NA |
| Payout Ratio | 11% | 12% | 14% | 11% | NA | NA | NA | NA | NA | NA |
| Prices:High | 95.87 | 97.19 | 89.69 | 89.84 | NA | NA | NA | NA | NA | NA |
| Prices:Low | 67.51 | 64.90 | 41.78 | 43.54 | NA | NA | NA | NA | NA | NA |
| P/E Ratio:High | 18 | 24 | 29 | 94 | NA | NA | NA | NA | NA | NA |
| P/E Ratio:Low | 13 | 16 | 13 | 45 | NA | NA | NA | NA | NA | NA |

| Income Statement Analysis (Million $) | | | | | | | | | | |
|---|---|---|---|---|---|---|---|---|---|---|
| Revenue | 9,188 | 8,065 | 6,911 | 6,263 | 5,193 | 3,899 | NA | NA | NA | NA |
| Operating Income | 5,751 | 4,809 | 3,766 | 3,106 | NA | NA | NA | NA | NA | NA |
| Depreciation | 288 | 265 | 226 | 237 | NA | NA | NA | NA | NA | NA |
| Interest Expense | 32.0 | 72.0 | 115 | 143 | NA | 104 | NA | NA | NA | NA |
| Pretax Income | 5,656 | 4,638 | 4,000 | 1,336 | -1,007 | 738 | NA | NA | NA | NA |
| Effective Tax Rate | NA | NA | 41.2% | 39.8% | NM | 37.0% | NA | NA | NA | NA |
| Net Income | 3,646 | 2,966 | 2,353 | 804 | -892 | 465 | NA | NA | NA | NA |
| S&P Core Earnings | 3,559 | 2,909 | 2,033 | 1,787 | 1,574 | 476 | NA | NA | NA | NA |

| Balance Sheet & Other Financial Data (Million $) | | | | | | | | | | |
|---|---|---|---|---|---|---|---|---|---|---|
| Cash | 3,398 | 4,051 | 4,732 | 6,287 | 7,935 | NA | NA | NA | NA | NA |
| Current Assets | 9,190 | 8,734 | 9,241 | 11,174 | 11,321 | NA | NA | NA | NA | NA |
| Total Assets | 34,760 | 33,408 | 32,281 | 34,981 | 33,250 | NA | NA | NA | NA | NA |
| Current Liabilities | 3,451 | 3,498 | 4,442 | 7,165 | 6,541 | NA | NA | NA | NA | NA |
| Long Term Debt | NA | 32.0 | 44.0 | 55.0 | 40.0 | NA | NA | NA | NA | NA |
| Common Equity | 26,437 | 25,011 | 23,189 | 21,141 | 19,747 | NA | NA | NA | NA | NA |
| Total Capital | 26,437 | 25,058 | 23,249 | 26,143 | 24,560 | NA | NA | NA | NA | NA |
| Capital Expenditures | 353 | 241 | 306 | 415 | NA | NA | NA | NA | NA | NA |
| Cash Flow | 3,934 | 3,231 | 2,579 | 1,041 | NA | NA | NA | NA | NA | NA |
| Current Ratio | 2.7 | 2.5 | 2.1 | 1.6 | 1.7 | NA | NA | NA | NA | NA |
| % Long Term Debt of Capitalization | Nil | 0.1 | 0.2 | 0.2 | 0.2 | Nil | NA | NA | NA | NA |
| % Net Income of Revenue | 39.7 | 36.8 | 34.1 | 12.8 | NM | 11.9 | NA | NA | NA | NA |
| % Return on Assets | 10.7 | 9.0 | 7.0 | 2.4 | NA | NA | NA | NA | NA | NA |
| % Return on Equity | 14.2 | 12.3 | 10.6 | 3.9 | NA | NA | NA | NA | NA | NA |

Data as orig reptd.; bef. results of disc opers/spec. items. Per share data adj. for stk. divs.; EPS diluted. 2007 pro forma bal. sheet (as of Dec. 31, 2007) and income statement; per share data based on Class A and Class C common stock. E-Estimated. NA-Not Available. NM-Not Meaningful. NR-Not Ranked. UR-Under Review.

**Office:** P.O. Box 8999, San Francisco, CA 94128-8999.
**Telephone:** 415-932-2100.
**Website:** http://www.visa.com
**Chrmn & CEO:** J.W. Saunders

**Pres:** J. Partridge
**CFO & Chief Acctg Officer:** B.H. Pollitt, Jr.
**CTO:** M.L. Dreyer
**Secy:** A.S. Pierre

**Investor Contact:** B.H. Pollitt (415-932-2213)
**Board Members:** G. P. Coughlan, M. B. Cranston, J. F. Fernandez-Carbajal, S. N. Johnson, R. W. Matschullat, C. E. Minehan, D. J. Pang, J. W. Saunders, W. S. Shanahan, J. A. Swainson

**Founded:** 2007
**Domicile:** Delaware
**Employees:** 7,500

# Vornado Realty Trust

STANDARD &POOR'S

| S&P Recommendation HOLD ★★★☆☆ | Price $70.73 (as of Nov 25, 2011) | 12-Mo. Target Price $88.00 | Investment Style Large-Cap Blend |
| --- | --- | --- | --- |

**GICS Sector** Financials
**Sub-Industry** Diversified REITS

**Summary** This real estate investment trust owns a diverse group of properties, including Northeast retail properties, New York City office buildings, and other interests.

## Key Stock Statistics (Source S&P, Vickers, company reports)

| | | | | | | | |
| --- | --- | --- | --- | --- | --- | --- | --- |
| 52-Wk Range | $98.77– 68.39 | S&P FFO/Sh. 2011E | 5.38 | Market Capitalization(B) | $13.049 | Beta | 1.62 |
| Trailing 12-Month FFO/Share | $5.04 | S&P FFO/Sh. 2012E | 5.70 | Yield (%) | 3.90 | S&P 3-Yr. FFO/Sh. Proj. CAGR(%) | 3 |
| Trailing 12-Month P/FFO | NA | P/FFO on S&P FFO/Sh. 2011E | 13.1 | Dividend Rate/Share | $2.76 | S&P Credit Rating | BBB+ |
| $10K Invested 5 Yrs Ago | $6,877 | Common Shares Outstg. (M) | 184.5 | Institutional Ownership (%) | 95 | | |

## Price Performance

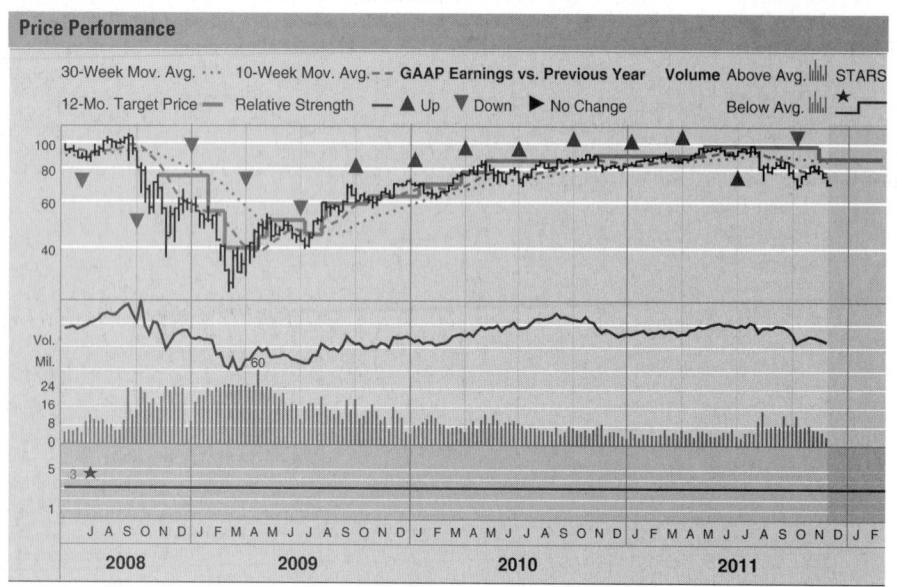

- 30-Week Mov. Avg. · · · 10-Week Mov. Avg. - - GAAP Earnings vs. Previous Year   Volume Above Avg. STARS
- 12-Mo. Target Price — Relative Strength — ▲ Up ▼ Down ► No Change   Below Avg.

Analysis prepared by Equity Analyst **R. Shepard, CFA** on Nov 08, 2011, when the stock traded at **$81.39**.

## Qualitative Risk Assessment

| LOW | MEDIUM | HIGH |
| --- | --- | --- |

Our risk assessment reflects VNO's large market capitalization, and what we see as its financial strength and diversified asset portfolio.

## Quantitative Evaluations

**S&P Quality Ranking**   B

| D | C | B- | B | B+ | A- | A | A+ |
| --- | --- | --- | --- | --- | --- | --- | --- |

**Relative Strength Rank**   MODERATE

30

LOWEST = 1   HIGHEST = 99

## Revenue/FFO Data

**Revenue (Million $)**

| | 1Q | 2Q | 3Q | 4Q | Year |
| --- | --- | --- | --- | --- | --- |
| 2011 | 737.1 | 730.2 | 727.3 | -- | -- |
| 2010 | 685.3 | 684.0 | 697.5 | 713.0 | 2,780 |
| 2009 | 678.6 | 673.8 | 671.2 | 719.0 | 2,743 |
| 2008 | 649.3 | 674.4 | 677.2 | 696.3 | 2,697 |
| 2007 | 736.3 | 792.8 | 853.0 | 888.5 | 3,271 |
| 2006 | 647.3 | 663.0 | 678.5 | 723.3 | 2,712 |

**FFO Per Share ($)**

| | | | | | |
| --- | --- | --- | --- | --- | --- |
| 2011 | 2.61 | 1.27 | 1.05 | E1.18 | E5.38 |
| 2010 | 1.89 | 1.11 | 1.32 | E1.15 | 6.10 |
| 2009 | 1.63 | 0.54 | 1.25 | -- | 3.36 |
| 2008 | 3.27 | 1.27 | 1.06 | -0.50 | 5.16 |
| 2007 | 1.65 | 1.72 | 1.35 | 1.18 | 5.89 |
| 2006 | 1.37 | 1.49 | 1.31 | 1.34 | 5.51 |

Fiscal year ended Dec. 31. Next earnings report expected: Late February. FFO Estimates based on S&P Funds From Operations Est..

### Highlights

➤ We think rental growth will slow for VNO in 2012, reflecting a challenging economic environment. During the third quarter of 2011, rents on new leases fell 1.9% in New York City while gaining 10.0% in the Washington DC market. However, we think VNO is likely to begin facing cutbacks in government leases cutbacks in its large Crystal City development in Washington. In our view, the trust may take some buildings out of service for facility upgrades.

➤ We think VNO is recognizing uneven results from its investment portfolio. During the third quarter, the trust took a $37.5 million markdown on its equity investment in J.C. Penney. In addition, it is restructuring its struggling merchandise showroom operation. In our view other investments may pay more positive returns in 2012, including a 26.2% interest in LNR Property LLC, a special servicer of distressed mortgage debt.

➤ Our FFO estimate is $5.38 for 2011, expanding to $5.70 in 2012. We expect overall office rents to remain steady and estimate a higher earnings contribution from equity investments, including a new real estate investment fund.

### Investment Rationale/Risk

➤ We think VNO has the financial resources to expand a strong portfolio of office and retail assets in supply-limited markets. The trust has begun to put excess cash balances to work buying select assets from distressed sellers. We are less enthusiastic about VNO's direct equity positions in other public companies. In the near term, though, we think a well-diversified operating platform will produce a steady stream of cash flow. With the shares recently trading at a premium to diversified peers based on price to estimated 2011 FFO, we think they appropriately reflect VNO's long-term growth prospects.

➤ Risks to our opinion and target price include rising interest rates, and economic declines in New York and/or Washington, DC. We also have corporate governance concerns related to anti-takeover defenses, including a classified board and blank check preferred stock.

➤ Our 12-month target price of $88 represents a multiple of 15.4X our 2012 FFO per share forecast of $5.70, a premium to other REITs with diversified holdings. We consider the premium warranted by VNO's portfolio of high-quality assets earning relatively consistent investment returns.

## Dividend Data (Dates: mm/dd Payment Date: mm/dd/yy)

| Amount ($) | Date Decl. | Ex-Div. Date | Stk. of Record | Payment Date |
| --- | --- | --- | --- | --- |
| 0.690 | 01/12 | 01/26 | 01/28 | 02/22/11 |
| 0.690 | 04/28 | 05/05 | 05/09 | 05/23/11 |
| 0.690 | 07/28 | 08/08 | 08/10 | 08/22/11 |
| 0.690 | 11/01 | 11/09 | 11/14 | 11/23/11 |

Dividends have been paid since 1990. Source: Company reports.

---

**Please read the Required Disclosures and Analyst Certification on the last page of this report.**

The McGraw-Hill Companies

# Vornado Realty Trust

STANDARD
&POOR'S

## Business Summary November 08, 2011

CORPORATE OVERVIEW. Vornado Realty Trust is a diversified REIT that has interests in a wide range of properties, including office buildings, retail properties, refrigerated warehouses, a hotel, and dry warehouses, among others, primarily in the Northeast. The company conducts its business through, was the sole general partner of, and, as of December 31, 2010, owned 93.2% of the limited partnership interests in, Vornado Realty L.P.

MARKET PROFILE. During 2010, VNO derived 50% of operating segment EBITDA from office properties. The market for office leases is inherently cyclical. The U.S. office market tends to track the overall economy on a lagged basis. At year-end 2010, we believe the national vacancy rate was about 18.0%, reflecting deterioration since its cyclical low of about 12.5% at the end of 2007.

Local economic conditions, particularly the employment level, play an important role in determining competitive dynamics. In our opinion, VNO's principal target markets, the New York City metropolitan area and Washington DC, have vacancy rates below the average nationwide. In addition, unlike many markets, rates on new or renewed leases in these markets are often at higher rates than those previously in place. At December 31, 2010, VNO owned or had an interest in 113 office properties totaling 40.3 million sq. ft. The New

York portfolio was 95.6% occupied at December 31, 2010; the Washington, DC, portfolio was 94.3% occupied.

In 2010, VNO derived about 19% of EBITDA from its retail segment. As of December 31, 2010, the retail portfolio included about 25.6 million sq. ft. in northeast U.S. states, Washington DC, and Puerto Rico. For VNO, as well as other retail-oriented REITs, location and the financial health and growth of its retail tenants are among the most important factors affecting the success of its portfolio. Further, the companies in this industry enjoy relatively high barriers to entry, since developing new shopping centers requires large amounts of capital as well as time-consuming regulatory approvals which have been difficult to obtain in the recent past amid concerns about traffic and pollution. We expect VNO to focus on the re-development of acquired properties, including the Manhattan Mall, in New York City, and shopping centers acquired in Northern New Jersey and Long Island, New York.

## Company Financials Fiscal Year Ended Dec. 31

| Per Share Data ($) | 2010 | 2009 | 2008 | 2007 | 2006 | 2005 | 2004 | 2003 | 2002 | 2001 |
|---|---|---|---|---|---|---|---|---|---|---|
| Tangible Book Value | 28.23 | 27.46 | 27.79 | 34.57 | 35.22 | 31.38 | 26.86 | 24.15 | 21.68 | 21.15 |
| Earnings | 3.35 | Nil | 1.16 | 2.86 | 3.13 | 3.27 | 3.75 | 2.29 | 2.18 | 2.50 |
| S&P Core Earnings | 3.10 | -0.01 | 1.13 | 2.69 | 2.62 | 3.09 | 3.62 | 3.63 | 2.15 | 2.58 |
| Dividends | 2.60 | 3.20 | 3.65 | 3.45 | 3.25 | 3.85 | 2.89 | 2.91 | 2.97 | 2.31 |
| Payout Ratio | 78% | NM | NM | 107% | 104% | 118% | 77% | 127% | 136% | 92% |
| Prices:High | 91.67 | 73.96 | 108.15 | 136.55 | 131.35 | 89.70 | 76.99 | 55.84 | 47.20 | 42.03 |
| Prices:Low | 61.25 | 27.01 | 36.66 | 82.82 | 83.28 | 68.25 | 47.00 | 33.25 | 33.20 | 34.47 |
| P/E Ratio:High | 27 | NM | 93 | 42 | 42 | 27 | 21 | 24 | 22 | 17 |
| P/E Ratio:Low | 18 | NM | 32 | 26 | 27 | 21 | 13 | 15 | 15 | 14 |

| Income Statement Analysis (Million $) | | | | | | | | | | |
|---|---|---|---|---|---|---|---|---|---|---|
| Rental Income | 2,271 | 2,222 | 2,211 | 1,989 | 1,568 | 1,397 | 1,345 | 1,261 | 1,249 | 842 |
| Mortgage Income | Nil | Nil | Nil | Nil | Nil | Nil | Nil | Nil | Nil | Nil |
| Total Income | 2,779 | 2,743 | 2,697 | 3,271 | 2,712 | 2,548 | 1,707 | 1,503 | 1,435 | 986 |
| General Expenses | 1,314 | 1,320 | 1,264 | 2,935 | 1,588 | 1,488 | 825 | 706 | 668 | 472 |
| Interest Expense | 560 | 634 | 608 | 635 | 478 | 341 | 242 | 230 | 240 | 173 |
| Provision for Losses | Nil | Nil | Nil | Nil | Nil | Nil | Nil | Nil | Nil | Nil |
| Depreciation | 472 | 540 | 537 | 530 | 397 | 335 | 243 | 215 | 206 | 124 |
| Net Income | 724 | 54.3 | 241 | 510 | 607 | 507 | 514 | 285 | 263 | 267 |
| S&P Core Earnings | 571 | -1.06 | 178 | 426 | 393 | 435 | 476 | 421 | 236 | 238 |

| Balance Sheet & Other Financial Data (Million $) | | | | | | | | | | |
|---|---|---|---|---|---|---|---|---|---|---|
| Cash | 691 | 535 | 1,527 | 1,858 | 2,690 | 763 | NA | NA | NA | NA |
| Total Assets | 20,517 | 20,185 | 21,418 | 22,479 | 17,954 | 13,637 | 11,581 | 9,519 | 9,018 | 6,777 |
| Real Estate Investment | 17,675 | 17,950 | 17,870 | 18,972 | 13,553 | 11,449 | 9,757 | 7,748 | 7,560 | 4,690 |
| Loss Reserve | Nil | Nil | Nil | Nil | Nil | Nil | Nil | Nil | Nil | Nil |
| Net Investment | 14,911 | 15,455 | 15,709 | 16,565 | 11,585 | 9,776 | 8,349 | 6,879 | 6,822 | 4,184 |
| Short Term Debt | 874 | 852 | 357 | 527 | 778 | 398 | Nil | Nil | Nil | Nil |
| Capitalization:Debt | 10,020 | 10,088 | 12,292 | 12,426 | 9,056 | 5,857 | 4,937 | 3,768 | 3,622 | 1,643 |
| Capitalization:Equity | 5,533 | 5,419 | 4,841 | 5,293 | 5,322 | 4,260 | 3,301 | 2,827 | 2,362 | 2,101 |
| Capitalization:Total | 18,178 | 17,989 | 19,567 | 20,038 | 16,335 | 12,208 | 8,238 | 8,767 | 8,287 | 5,693 |
| % Earnings & Depreciation/Assets | 5.9 | 2.9 | 3.5 | 5.1 | 6.3 | 6.6 | 7.1 | 5.4 | 5.9 | 5.9 |
| Price Times Book Value:High | 3.2 | 2.7 | 3.9 | 3.9 | 3.7 | 2.9 | 2.9 | 2.3 | 2.2 | 2.0 |
| Price Times Book Value:Low | 2.2 | 1.0 | 1.3 | 2.4 | 2.4 | 2.2 | 1.7 | 1.4 | 1.5 | 1.6 |

Data as orig reptd.; bef. results of disc opers/spec. items. Per share data adj. for stk. divs.; EPS diluted. E-Estimated. NA-Not Available. NM-Not Meaningful. NR-Not Ranked. UR-Under Review.

# Vulcan Materials Co

STANDARD
&POOR'S

**S&P Recommendation** SELL ★ ★ ★ ★ ★

| | |
|---|---|
| **Price** $29.42 (as of Nov 25, 2011) | **12-Mo. Target Price** $27.00 |
| **Investment Style** Large-Cap Growth | |

**GICS Sector** Materials
**Sub-Industry** Construction Materials

**Summary** This company is the nation's largest producer of aggregates in the United States, and is also a major supplier of asphalt and concrete used in road construction and the building of commercial, residential and public buildings and infrastructure.

## Key Stock Statistics (Source S&P, Vickers, company reports)

| | | | | | | | |
|---|---|---|---|---|---|---|---|
| 52-Wk Range | $48.26– 25.06 | S&P Oper. EPS 2011E | -0.85 | Market Capitalization(B) | $3.802 | Beta | 1.29 |
| Trailing 12-Month EPS | $-0.69 | S&P Oper. EPS 2012E | -0.25 | Yield (%) | 0.14 | S&P 3-Yr. Proj. EPS CAGR(%) | NM |
| Trailing 12-Month P/E | NM | P/E on S&P Oper. EPS 2011E | NM | Dividend Rate/Share | $0.04 | S&P Credit Rating | BB |
| $10K Invested 5 Yrs Ago | $3,762 | Common Shares Outstg. (M) | 129.2 | Institutional Ownership (%) | 94 | | |

## Price Performance

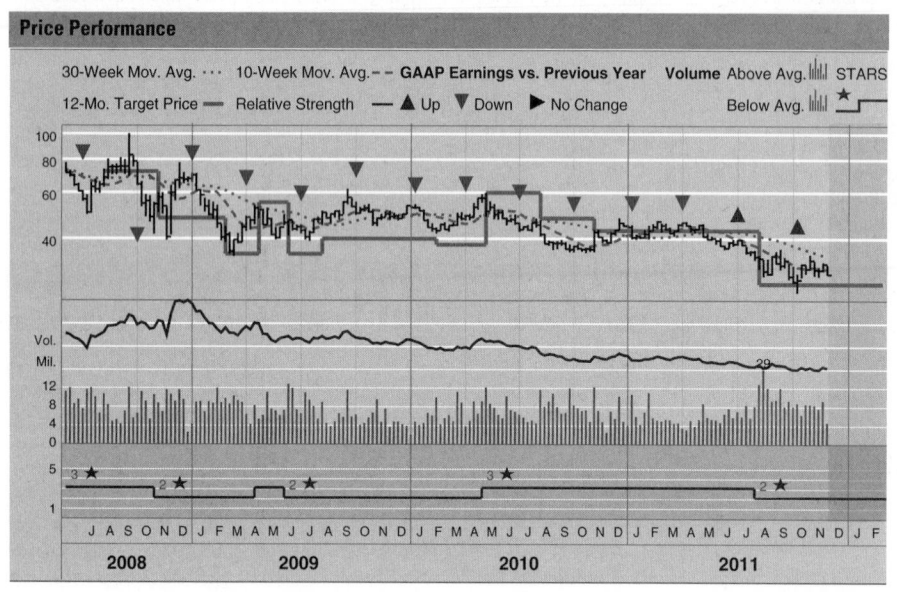

30-Week Mov. Avg. · · · 10-Week Mov. Avg. - - **GAAP Earnings vs. Previous Year** Volume Above Avg. ||||| STARS
12-Mo. Target Price — Relative Strength — ▲ Up ▼ Down ▶ No Change Below Avg. ||||| ★

Analysis prepared by Equity Analyst **S. Benway, CFA** on Nov 15, 2011, when the stock traded at **$30.56**.

Options: P

## Qualitative Risk Assessment

| LOW | **MEDIUM** | HIGH |
|---|---|---|

Our risk assessment reflects that VMC's earnings are exposed to the construction industry, which is cyclical and in an extended downturn. However, about half of its aggregates volume comes from more stable public construction, and free cash flow generation at VMC has historically been strong.

## Quantitative Evaluations

**S&P Quality Ranking**                                    B

| D | C | B- | **B** | B+ | A- | A | A+ |
|---|---|---|---|---|---|---|---|

**Relative Strength Rank**                       **MODERATE**

46

LOWEST = 1                                          HIGHEST = 99

## Revenue/Earnings Data

**Revenue (Million $)**

| | 1Q | 2Q | 3Q | 4Q | Year |
|---|---|---|---|---|---|
| 2011 | 487.2 | 702.0 | 760.8 | -- | -- |
| 2010 | 493.3 | 736.2 | 743.2 | 586.2 | 2,559 |
| 2009 | 600.3 | 721.9 | 778.2 | 590.1 | 2,690 |
| 2008 | 817.3 | 1,022 | 1,013 | 799.2 | 3,651 |
| 2007 | 687.2 | 878.8 | 904.9 | 856.9 | 3,328 |
| 2006 | 708.7 | 888.2 | 929.3 | 816.3 | 3,342 |

**Earnings Per Share ($)**

| | | | | | |
|---|---|---|---|---|---|
| 2011 | -0.50 | -0.05 | 0.17 | E-0.38 | E-0.85 |
| 2010 | -0.35 | -0.18 | 0.08 | -0.36 | -0.80 |
| 2009 | -0.29 | 0.14 | 0.38 | -0.10 | 0.16 |
| 2008 | 0.13 | 1.27 | 0.54 | 0.14 | 2.08 |
| 2007 | 0.91 | 1.46 | 1.47 | 0.83 | 4.66 |
| 2006 | 0.70 | 1.47 | 1.45 | 1.19 | 4.79 |

Fiscal year ended Dec. 31. Next earnings report expected: Early February. EPS Estimates based on S&P Operating Earnings; historical GAAP earnings are as reported.

### Highlights

➤ After the nearly one-third drop in revenues over the past two years, we see little change in 2011. Demand for construction aggregates is expected to remain depressed due to continued weakness in housing and commercial construction. However, some improvement in demand is expected as public construction should benefit from stimulus spending. Pricing for aggregates is also forecast to increase 1%-3% due to more stable demand. We expect sales to rebound 3%-5% in 2012.

➤ Operating margins are forecast to worsen slightly in 2011 from the minimal levels of 2010. Vulcan has reduced administrative costs during this downturn and has a relatively flexible cost structure, in our view. However, excess capacity still exists at the company, and facilities are likely to be under utilized this year. Higher volume should help margins in 2012.

➤ We project a loss of $0.85 per share in 2011 and a loss of $0.25 in 2012. The solid growth trends that Vulcan has historically exhibited have been disrupted over the past three years, although we believe the worst is over. Nevertheless, recovery is likely to be slow.

### Investment Rationale/Risk

➤ We expect conditions in most of Vulcan's markets to remain weak in 2011. Our forecast is for little improvement in home starts, and infrastructure activity is likely to remain below historical levels. We project that commercial construction will hit bottom in 2011. Industrial markets should provide some stability as they are more long term in nature. We look for an increase in housing starts in 2012 to moderately boost demand for construction aggregates. In our view, the shares are overvalued at current levels.

➤ Risks to our recommendation and target price include demand being stronger than we project due to a faster recovery in residential construction activity than we currently expect, and public infrastructure spending being helped by new funding by the federal government.

➤ Our discounted cash flow model, which assumes a 9.7% weighted average cost of capital, low capital spending again in 2011 and 2012, and 3% cash flow growth in perpetuity, indicates intrinsic value of $27, which is our 12-month target price.

## Dividend Data (Dates: mm/dd Payment Date: mm/dd/yy)

| Amount ($) | Date Decl. | Ex-Div. Date | Stk. of Record | Payment Date |
|---|---|---|---|---|
| 0.250 | 02/11 | 02/23 | 02/25 | 03/10/11 |
| 0.250 | 05/13 | 05/25 | 05/27 | 06/10/11 |
| 0.250 | 07/08 | 08/24 | 08/26 | 09/09/11 |
| 0.010 | 10/14 | 11/21 | 11/23 | 12/09/11 |

Dividends have been paid since 1934. Source: Company reports.

---

**Please read the Required Disclosures and Analyst Certification on the last page of this report.**

*The McGraw-Hill Companies*

# Vulcan Materials Co

## Business Summary November 15, 2011

CORPORATE OVERVIEW. Vulcan Materials is the largest U.S. producer of construction aggregates, primarily crushed stone, sand, and gravel. It is also a major producer of asphalt and ready-mix concrete and a leading producer of cement in Florida. Proven and probable reserves of aggregates were estimated at 14.7 billion tons at the end of 2010. Vulcan shipped 148 million tons of aggregates in 2010. It principally serves markets in 21 states, the District of Columbia, and the local markets surrounding its operations in Mexico and the Bahamas from its 319 aggregates facilities. Construction aggregates were 67% of sales in 2010, asphalt mix and concrete 31%, and cement was 2%. VMC estimates that 55% of its aggregates shipments in 2010 went to publicly funded construction projects, nearly half of which was for highway construction projects, and 45% was used for privately funded residential and nonresidential construction.

PRIMARY BUSINESS DYNAMICS. Public sector construction spending is generally more stable than in the private sector, in part because public sector spending is less sensitive to interest rates and is often supported by multi-year legislation and programs. Public construction is typically funded through a combination of federal state and local sources. The federal transportation bill is the principal source of federal funding for public infrastructure and transportation projects. For over two decades, the federal funding component

of these projects has been provided through a series of six-year bills. The multi-year aspect of these bills is critically important because it provides state departments of transportation with the ability to plan and execute long-term and complex highway projects. Federal highway spending is primarily determined by this six-year authorization bill and annual budget appropriations using funds largely taken from the Federal Highway Trust Fund, which receives taxes on gasoline and other levies. State highway and bridge projects supplement federal funding with state fuel taxes and vehicle registration fees. Private nonresidential construction includes a wide array of project types and generally is more aggregates intensive than residential construction but less so than public construction. Demand in private nonresidential construction is driven by job growth, vacancy rates, private infrastructure needs, and demographic trends. The majority of residential construction activity is for single-family houses with the remainder consisting of multi-family construction. Household formation is a primary driver of housing demand along with mortgage rates.

## Company Financials Fiscal Year Ended Dec. 31

| Per Share Data ($) | 2010 | 2009 | 2008 | 2007 | 2006 | 2005 | 2004 | 2003 | 2002 | 2001 |
|---|---|---|---|---|---|---|---|---|---|---|
| Tangible Book Value | 1.37 | 2.19 | NM | NM | 14.60 | 15.05 | 13.77 | 12.01 | 11.04 | 10.02 |
| Cash Flow | 2.18 | 3.46 | 3.53 | 7.33 | 7.04 | 5.43 | 4.88 | 4.87 | 4.47 | 4.89 |
| Earnings | -0.80 | 0.16 | 2.08 | 4.66 | 4.79 | 3.30 | 2.52 | 2.18 | 1.86 | 2.17 |
| S&P Core Earnings | -0.89 | NA | 1.20 | 4.22 | 4.53 | 3.17 | 2.29 | 1.89 | 1.51 | 1.81 |
| Dividends | 1.00 | 1.48 | 1.96 | 1.84 | 1.48 | 1.16 | 1.04 | 0.97 | 0.94 | 0.90 |
| Payout Ratio | NM | NM | 94% | 39% | 31% | 35% | 41% | 44% | 51% | 41% |
| Prices:High | 59.90 | 71.26 | 100.25 | 128.62 | 93.85 | 76.31 | 55.53 | 48.60 | 49.95 | 55.30 |
| Prices:Low | 35.40 | 34.30 | 39.52 | 77.04 | 65.85 | 52.36 | 41.94 | 28.75 | 32.35 | 37.50 |
| P/E Ratio:High | NM | NM | 48 | 28 | 20 | 23 | 22 | 22 | 27 | 25 |
| P/E Ratio:Low | NM | NM | 19 | 17 | 14 | 16 | 17 | 13 | 17 | 17 |

| Income Statement Analysis (Million $) | | | | | | | | | | |
|---|---|---|---|---|---|---|---|---|---|---|
| Revenue | 2,559 | 2,690 | 3,651 | 3,328 | 3,342 | 2,895 | 2,454 | 2,892 | 2,797 | 3,020 |
| Operating Income | 348 | 516 | 814 | 954 | 914 | 690 | 623 | 618 | 560 | 649 |
| Depreciation | 382 | 395 | 389 | 266 | 225 | 221 | 245 | 277 | 268 | 278 |
| Interest Expense | 181 | 175 | 187 | 53.4 | 26.3 | 37.1 | 40.3 | 54.1 | 55.0 | 61.3 |
| Pretax Income | -192 | -19.2 | 327 | 668 | 703 | 480 | 376 | 311 | 260 | 324 |
| Effective Tax Rate | NA | 197.0% | 29.5% | 30.6% | 32.1% | 28.4% | 30.4% | 28.3% | 25.8% | 31.3% |
| Net Income | -103 | 18.7 | 231 | 463 | 477 | 344 | 261 | 223 | 190 | 223 |
| S&P Core Earnings | -115 | -0.71 | 132 | 419 | 452 | 328 | 236 | 194 | 155 | 186 |

| Balance Sheet & Other Financial Data (Million $) | | | | | | | | | | |
|---|---|---|---|---|---|---|---|---|---|---|
| Cash | 47.5 | 26.4 | 46.9 | 34.9 | 55.2 | 275 | 271 | 417 | 171 | 101 |
| Current Assets | 772 | 743 | 894 | 1,157 | 731 | 1,165 | 1,418 | 1,050 | 790 | 730 |
| Total Assets | 8,338 | 8,534 | 9,176 | 8,936 | 3,424 | 3,589 | 3,665 | 3,637 | 3,448 | 3,398 |
| Current Liabilities | 566 | 857 | 1,663 | 2,528 | 494 | 579 | 427 | 543 | 298 | 344 |
| Long Term Debt | 2,428 | 2,116 | 2,154 | 1,530 | 322 | 323 | 605 | 339 | 858 | 906 |
| Common Equity | 3,965 | 4,052 | 3,784 | 3,760 | 2,001 | 2,127 | 2,014 | 1,803 | 1,697 | 1,604 |
| Total Capital | 6,398 | 6,554 | 6,626 | 5,961 | 2,611 | 2,725 | 2,967 | 2,573 | 2,993 | 2,829 |
| Capital Expenditures | 86.3 | 110 | 401 | 483 | 435 | 216 | 204 | 194 | 249 | 287 |
| Cash Flow | 280 | 413 | 387 | 729 | 702 | 565 | 506 | 501 | 458 | 501 |
| Current Ratio | 1.4 | 0.9 | 0.5 | 0.5 | 1.5 | 2.0 | 3.3 | 1.9 | 2.7 | 2.1 |
| % Long Term Debt of Capitalization | 37.9 | 32.3 | 32.5 | 25.7 | 12.3 | 11.9 | 20.4 | 13.2 | 28.7 | 32.0 |
| % Net Income of Revenue | NM | 0.7 | 6.3 | 13.9 | 14.3 | 11.9 | 10.6 | 7.7 | 6.8 | 7.4 |
| % Return on Assets | NM | 0.2 | 2.6 | 7.5 | 13.6 | 9.5 | 7.2 | 6.3 | 5.6 | 6.7 |
| % Return on Equity | NM | 0.5 | 6.1 | 16.1 | 23.1 | 16.6 | 13.7 | 12.8 | 11.5 | 14.5 |

Data as orig reptd.; bef. results of disc opers/spec. items. Per share data adj. for stk. divs.; EPS diluted. E-Estimated. NA-Not Available. NM-Not Meaningful. NR-Not Ranked. UR-Under Review.

**Office:** 1200 Urban Center Drive, Birmingham, AL 35242.
**Telephone:** 205-298-3000.
**Email:** ir@vmcmail.com
**Website:** http://www.vulcanmaterials.com

**Chrmn & CEO:** D.M. James
**EVP & CFO:** D. Sansone
**SVP & General Counsel:** R.A. Wason, IV
**Chief Acctg Officer, Cntlr & CIO:** E.A. Khan

**Treas:** C.W. Burton, Jr.
**Investor Contact:** M. Warren (205-298-3220)
**Board Members:** P. W. Farmer, H. A. Franklin, D. M. James, A. M. Korologos, D. J. McGregor, R. T. O'Brien, J. T. Prokopanko, D. B. Rice, V. J. Trosino, K. Wilson-Thompson

**Founded:** 1910
**Domicile:** New Jersey
**Employees:** 7,994

# Walgreen Co

**STANDARD &POOR'S**

| **S&P Recommendation** BUY ★★★★☆ | **Price** $32.47 (as of Nov 25, 2011) | **12-Mo. Target Price** $40.00 | **Investment Style** Large-Cap Growth |
|---|---|---|---|

**GICS Sector** Consumer Staples
**Sub-Industry** Drug Retail

**Summary** The largest U.S. retail drug chain in terms of revenues, this company operates more than 8,000 drug stores throughout the U.S. and Puerto Rico.

## Key Stock Statistics (Source S&P, Vickers, company reports)

| | | | | | | | |
|---|---|---|---|---|---|---|---|
| 52-Wk Range | $47.11– 30.34 | S&P Oper. EPS 2012E | 3.04 | Market Capitalization(B) | $28.875 | Beta | 0.97 |
| Trailing 12-Month EPS | $2.94 | S&P Oper. EPS 2013E | 3.47 | Yield (%) | 2.77 | S&P 3-Yr. Proj. EPS CAGR(%) | 14 |
| Trailing 12-Month P/E | 11.0 | P/E on S&P Oper. EPS 2012E | 10.7 | Dividend Rate/Share | $0.90 | S&P Credit Rating | A |
| $10K Invested 5 Yrs Ago | $8,627 | Common Shares Outstg. (M) | 889.3 | Institutional Ownership (%) | 67 | | |

## Price Performance

- 30-Week Mov. Avg.
- 10-Week Mov. Avg.
- 12-Mo. Target Price
- Relative Strength
- GAAP Earnings vs. Previous Year
- ▲ Up ▼ Down ► No Change
- Volume Above Avg. STARS Below Avg.

Options: ASE, CBOE, P

Analysis prepared by Equity Analyst **Joseph Agnese** on Oct 10, 2011, when the stock traded at **$33.63**.

## Qualitative Risk Assessment

| LOW | MEDIUM | HIGH |
|---|---|---|

Our risk assessment reflects the company's strong market share positions in the relatively stable U.S. retail drug industry, partly offset by growth of non-traditional competitors and potential adverse legislation.

## Quantitative Evaluations

**S&P Quality Ranking** A+

| D | C | B- | B | B+ | A- | A | A+ |
|---|---|---|---|---|---|---|---|

**Relative Strength Rank** MODERATE

57

LOWEST = 1          HIGHEST = 99

## Revenue/Earnings Data

**Revenue (Million $)**

| | 1Q | 2Q | 3Q | 4Q | Year |
|---|---|---|---|---|---|
| 2011 | 17,344 | 18,502 | 18,371 | 17,967 | 72,184 |
| 2010 | 16,364 | 16,987 | 17,199 | 16,870 | 67,420 |
| 2009 | 14,947 | 16,475 | 16,210 | 15,703 | 63,335 |
| 2008 | 14,028 | 15,394 | 15,016 | 14,597 | 59,034 |
| 2007 | 12,709 | 13,934 | 13,698 | 13,422 | 53,762 |
| 2006 | 10,900 | 12,163 | 12,175 | 12,170 | 47,409 |

**Earnings Per Share ($)**

| | | | | | |
|---|---|---|---|---|---|
| 2011 | 0.62 | 0.80 | 0.65 | 0.87 | 2.94 |
| 2010 | 0.49 | 0.68 | 0.47 | 0.49 | 2.12 |
| 2009 | 0.41 | 0.65 | 0.53 | 0.44 | 2.02 |
| 2008 | 0.46 | 0.69 | 0.58 | 0.45 | 2.17 |
| 2007 | 0.43 | 0.65 | 0.56 | 0.40 | 2.03 |
| 2006 | 0.34 | 0.51 | 0.46 | 0.41 | 1.72 |

Fiscal year ended Aug. 31. Next earnings report expected: NA. EPS Estimates based on S&P Operating Earnings; historical GAAP earnings are as reported.

## Highlights

➤ We see sales advancing 6.1% in FY 12 (Aug.), to roughly $76.6 billion, from $72.2 billion in FY 11, fueled by about 250 net new store openings, acquisitions, and a 3% increase in comparable-store sales. We see front-end growth benefiting from the completed rollout of store remodelings across a majority of stores in FY 11, including new merchandising initiatives that we expect to help boost non-pharmacy sales.

➤ We expect margins to expand in FY 12 on an improved product mix, lower labor costs, reduced inventory markdowns and increased sales of wider-margin generic drugs, partially offset by increased drug reimbursement pressures. We see sales of lower-priced, but wider-margin, generic drugs accelerating in FY 12, reflecting the loss of patent protection on a number of significant branded drugs. We expect the company's investment in health clinics to be accretive to earnings in FY 12. We project interest expense to decline slightly, reflecting lower interest rates.

➤ Following a significant reduction in share count due to an active share repurchase program, we look for EPS to increase 15% in FY 12, to $3.04, from $2.64 in FY 11.

## Investment Rationale/Risk

➤ The company sold its pharmacy benefit management company, Walgreens Health Initiatives Inc., to Catalyst Health Solution Inc. for $525 million in cash in June 2011. We believe this transaction will help the company better differentiate itself from its closest peer while allowing it to focus on its core drug store operations and fast-growing specialty pharmacy and mail order services.

➤ Risks to our recommendation and target price include a weaker-than-expected economy, increased competition from peers and other retail formats, and legislative changes that may affect drug reimbursements.

➤ We believe the shares should trade at a premium to the S&P 500 as the company's progress on initiatives to improve merchandising and efforts to remodel existing stores should lead to an acceleration of earnings growth. Applying a multiple of 13.3X to our FY 12 EPS estimate of $3.04, representing a 6.0% premium to the P/E multiple on the S&P 500, results in a value of $40, which is our 12-month target price.

## Dividend Data (Dates: mm/dd Payment Date: mm/dd/yy)

| Amount ($) | Date Decl. | Ex-Div. Date | Stk. of Record | Payment Date |
|---|---|---|---|---|
| 0.175 | 01/13 | 02/16 | 02/18 | 03/12/11 |
| 0.175 | 04/11 | 05/18 | 05/20 | 06/11/11 |
| 0.225 | 07/13 | 08/17 | 08/19 | 09/12/11 |
| 0.225 | 10/12 | 11/09 | 11/14 | 12/12/11 |

Dividends have been paid since 1933. Source: Company reports.

---

**Please read the Required Disclosures and Analyst Certification on the last page of this report.**

*The McGraw-Hill Companies*

# Walgreen Co

**STANDARD &POOR'S**

## Business Summary October 10, 2011

CORPORATE OVERVIEW. Walgreen Co. is one of the largest drug store chains in the U.S., based on sales and store count. In 1909, the company's founder, Charles Rudolph Walgreen Sr., purchased one of the busiest drug stores on Chicago's South Side, and transformed it by constructing an ice cream fountain that featured his own brand of ice cream. The ice cream fountain was the forerunner of the famous Walgreen's soda fountain, which became the main attraction for customers from the 1920s through the 1950s. People lined up to buy a product that WAG invented in the early 1920s: the milkshake. The company continued to be innovative by pioneering computerized pharmacies connected by satellite in 1981, completing chain wide point-of-sale scanning in 1991, and introducing freestanding stores with drive-thru pharmacies in 1992.

MARKET PROFILE. Walgreen operates one of the largest U.S. drug store chain based on sales, generating $72.2 billion in sales in FY 11 (Aug.). The company

filled about 819 million prescriptions in FY 11, accounting for about 20% of the U.S. retail prescription drug market. The company experienced a 7.6% growth rate in prescription volume (after adjusting 90-day prescriptions for 30-day equivalents) in FY 10, outpacing our estimate of a low single digit growth rate for the industry. WAG pharmacy sales rose 6.3% in FY 10, to about $42 billion, versus our estimate of a low single digit growth rate for the total industry, on comparable prescription sales growth of 2.3%. Sales of non-pharmacy items outperformed competitors, with the company increasing market share in most of its core categories versus drug store, grocery and mass merchant competition.

## Company Financials Fiscal Year Ended Aug. 31

| Per Share Data ($) | 2011 | 2010 | 2009 | 2008 | 2007 | 2006 | 2005 | 2004 | 2003 | 2002 |
|---|---|---|---|---|---|---|---|---|---|---|
| Tangible Book Value | 13.06 | 12.14 | 13.06 | 11.56 | 10.13 | 9.61 | 8.69 | 8.04 | 7.02 | 6.08 |
| Cash Flow | 4.11 | 3.16 | 3.01 | 3.01 | 2.70 | 2.28 | 1.99 | 1.71 | 1.47 | 1.29 |
| Earnings | 2.94 | 2.12 | 2.02 | 2.17 | 2.03 | 1.72 | 1.52 | 1.32 | 1.14 | 0.99 |
| S&P Core Earnings | 2.64 | 2.12 | 2.01 | 2.17 | 2.03 | 1.71 | 1.44 | 1.27 | 1.07 | 0.93 |
| Dividends | 0.75 | 0.59 | 0.48 | 0.40 | 0.33 | 0.27 | 0.22 | 0.18 | 0.16 | 0.15 |
| Payout Ratio | 26% | 28% | 24% | 18% | 16% | 16% | 15% | 14% | 14% | 15% |
| Prices:High | 47.11 | 40.20 | 40.69 | 39.00 | 49.10 | 51.60 | 49.01 | 39.51 | 37.42 | 40.70 |
| Prices:Low | 30.34 | 26.26 | 21.39 | 21.28 | 35.80 | 39.55 | 39.66 | 32.00 | 26.90 | 27.70 |
| P/E Ratio:High | 16 | 19 | 20 | 18 | 24 | 30 | 32 | 30 | 33 | 41 |
| P/E Ratio:Low | 10 | 12 | 11 | 10 | 18 | 23 | 26 | 24 | 24 | 28 |

| Income Statement Analysis (Million $) | 2011 | 2010 | 2009 | 2008 | 2007 | 2006 | 2005 | 2004 | 2003 | 2002 |
|---|---|---|---|---|---|---|---|---|---|---|
| Revenue | 72,184 | 67,420 | 63,335 | 59,034 | 53,762 | 47,409 | 42,202 | 37,508 | 32,505 | 28,681 |
| Operating Income | 5,017 | 4,488 | 4,442 | 4,202 | 3,827 | 3,274 | 2,906 | 2,546 | 2,194 | 1,932 |
| Depreciation | 1,086 | 1,030 | 975 | 840 | 676 | 572 | 482 | 403 | 346 | 307 |
| Interest Expense | 71.0 | 85.0 | 99.0 | 30.0 | Nil | Nil | Nil | Nil | Nil | Nil |
| Pretax Income | 4,294 | 3,373 | 3,164 | 3,430 | 3,189 | 2,754 | 2,456 | 2,176 | 1,889 | 1,637 |
| Effective Tax Rate | NA | NA | 36.6% | 37.1% | 36.0% | 36.4% | 36.5% | 37.5% | 37.8% | 37.8% |
| Net Income | 2,714 | 2,091 | 2,006 | 2,157 | 2,041 | 1,751 | 1,560 | 1,360 | 1,176 | 1,019 |
| S&P Core Earnings | 2,444 | 2,089 | 1,997 | 2,158 | 2,042 | 1,754 | 1,478 | 1,302 | 1,104 | 955 |

| Balance Sheet & Other Financial Data (Million $) | 2011 | 2010 | 2009 | 2008 | 2007 | 2006 | 2005 | 2004 | 2003 | 2002 |
|---|---|---|---|---|---|---|---|---|---|---|
| Cash | 1,556 | 1,880 | 2,587 | 443 | 255 | 920 | 577 | 1,696 | 1,017 | 450 |
| Current Assets | 12,322 | 11,922 | 12,049 | 10,433 | 9,511 | 9,705 | 8,317 | 7,764 | 6,358 | 5,167 |
| Total Assets | 27,454 | 26,275 | 25,142 | 22,410 | 19,314 | 17,131 | 14,609 | 13,342 | 11,406 | 9,879 |
| Current Liabilities | 8,083 | 7,433 | 6,769 | 6,644 | 6,744 | 5,755 | 4,481 | 4,078 | 3,421 | 2,955 |
| Long Term Debt | 2,396 | 2,389 | 2,336 | 1,377 | Nil | Nil | Nil | Nil | Nil | Nil |
| Common Equity | 14,847 | 14,400 | 14,376 | 12,869 | 11,104 | 10,116 | 8,890 | 8,228 | 7,196 | 6,230 |
| Total Capital | 17,243 | 16,789 | 16,712 | 14,396 | 11,263 | 10,257 | 9,130 | 8,556 | 7,424 | 6,407 |
| Capital Expenditures | 1,213 | 1,014 | 1,927 | 2,225 | 1,785 | 1,338 | 1,238 | 940 | 795 | 934 |
| Cash Flow | 3,800 | 3,121 | 2,981 | 2,997 | 2,717 | 2,323 | 2,042 | 1,763 | 1,522 | 1,327 |
| Current Ratio | 1.5 | 1.6 | 1.8 | 1.6 | 1.4 | 1.7 | 1.9 | 1.9 | 1.9 | 1.7 |
| % Long Term Debt of Capitalization | 13.9 | 14.2 | 14.0 | 9.6 | Nil | Nil | Nil | Nil | Nil | Nil |
| % Net Income of Revenue | 3.8 | 3.1 | 3.2 | 3.7 | 3.8 | 3.7 | 3.7 | 3.6 | 3.6 | 3.6 |
| % Return on Assets | 10.1 | 8.1 | 8.4 | 10.3 | 11.2 | 11.0 | 11.2 | 10.9 | 11.0 | 10.9 |
| % Return on Equity | 18.6 | 14.5 | 14.7 | 18.0 | 19.2 | 18.4 | 18.3 | 17.6 | 17.5 | 17.8 |

Data as orig reptd.; bef. results of disc opers/spec. items. Per share data adj. for stk. divs.; EPS diluted. E-Estimated. NA-Not Available. NM-Not Meaningful. NR-Not Ranked. UR-Under Review.

**Office:** 108 Wilmot Road, Deerfield, IL 60015.
**Telephone:** 847-315-2500.
**Email:** investor.relations@walgreens.com
**Website:** http://www.walgreens.com

**Chrmn:** A.G. McNally
**Pres & CEO:** G.D. Wasson
**EVP, Secy & General Counsel:** T.J. Sabatino, Jr.
**SVP, Chief Acctg Officer & Cntlr:** M.M. Scholz

**SVP & CIO:** T.J. Theriault
**Investor Contact:** R.J. Hans (847-940-2500)
**Board Members:** D. J. Brailer, S. A. Davis, W. C. Foote, M. P. Frissora, G. L. Graham, A. G. McNally, N. M. Schlichting, D. Y. Schwartz, A. Silva, J. A. Skinner, G. D. Wasson

**Founded:** 1901
**Domicile:** Illinois
**Employees:** 247,000

*The McGraw-Hill Companies*

# Wal-Mart Stores Inc

**STANDARD & POOR'S**

| S&P Recommendation | STRONG BUY ★★★★★ | Price<br>$56.89 (as of Nov 25, 2011) | 12-Mo. Target Price<br>$67.00 | Investment Style<br>Large-Cap Blend |
|---|---|---|---|---|

**GICS Sector** Consumer Staples
**Sub-Industry** Hypermarkets & Super Centers

**Summary** The largest retailer in North America, Wal-Mart operates a chain of discount department stores, wholesale clubs, and combination discount stores and supermarkets.

## Key Stock Statistics (Source S&P, Vickers, company reports)

| | | | | | | | |
|---|---|---|---|---|---|---|---|
| 52-Wk Range | $59.40– 48.31 | S&P Oper. EPS 2012E | 4.54 | Market Capitalization(B) | $196.079 | Beta | 0.31 |
| Trailing 12-Month EPS | $4.73 | S&P Oper. EPS 2013E | 4.91 | Yield (%) | 2.57 | S&P 3-Yr. Proj. EPS CAGR(%) | 9 |
| Trailing 12-Month P/E | 12.0 | P/E on S&P Oper. EPS 2012E | 12.5 | Dividend Rate/Share | $1.46 | S&P Credit Rating | AA |
| $10K Invested 5 Yrs Ago | $13,197 | Common Shares Outstg. (M) | 3,446.6 | Institutional Ownership (%) | 31 | | |

## Price Performance

30-Week Mov. Avg. · · · 10-Week Mov. Avg. - - GAAP Earnings vs. Previous Year   Volume Above Avg. | STARS
12-Mo. Target Price — Relative Strength — ▲ Up ▼ Down ► No Change   Below Avg. | ★

Options: ASE, CBOE, P, Ph

Analysis prepared by Equity Analyst **Joseph Agnese** on Nov 15, 2011, when the stock traded at **$57.41**.

## Highlights

➤ We expect net revenues to rise 5.7% in FY 13 (Jan.), to $474.5 billion, from our estimate of $449.1 billion in FY 12, driven by 13% growth in international sales and the addition of about 4% new retail square footage, with square footage growth (excluding acquisitions) shifting toward international markets from domestic, partially offset by store closures. We look for U.S. comparable-store sales, excluding fuel, to rise 2.5%, on benefits from an expanded merchandise assortment.

➤ We estimate that EBIT margins will narrow slightly as an aggressive pricing strategy, increased product cost inflation, and a shift in mix due to higher sales within the international segment offsets benefits from improved sales leveraging on productivity improvements.

➤ Due to an active share repurchase program, we see shares outstanding declining 3.0% in FY 12, following an estimated 5.5% reduction in shares in FY 12. Overall, we project operating EPS of $4.91 for FY 13, up 8.1% from our estimate of operating EPS of $4.54 in FY 12 (excluding $0.03 in one-time acquisition related costs).

## Investment Rationale/Risk

➤ We believe the company is well positioned to benefit from both increased demand due to merchandise improvements in domestic stores and a focus on consolidating its international markets. We see limited downside risk due to a weakening economic environment, reflecting its offerings of staples and basic discretionary items.

➤ Risks to our recommendation and target price include economic pressures such as rising unemployment or lower consumer confidence, which we think would negatively affect WMT's core customers and the company's results, and unfavorable foreign currency exchange rates.

➤ We expect an improvement in both domestic and international earnings results in FY 13. As a result, we believe the stock should trade at a premium to the P/E multiple of the S&P 500 and in line with its historical average P/E. Applying a multiple of 13.6X, an 8% premium to the P/E of the S&P 500 but in line with WMT's five-year median forward P/E, to our FY 13 EPS estimate of $4.91 implies a value of $67, which is our 12-month target price.

## Qualitative Risk Assessment

| LOW | MEDIUM | HIGH |
|---|---|---|

Our risk assessment of Wal-Mart reflects our view of the company's high-quality earnings, as reflected in its top S&P Quality Ranking of A+, its dominant market share positions, continued price leadership, and strong cash flow generation.

## Quantitative Evaluations

**S&P Quality Ranking**     A+

| D | C | B- | B | B+ | A- | A | A+ |
|---|---|---|---|---|---|---|---|

**Relative Strength Rank**     STRONG

89

LOWEST = 1      HIGHEST = 99

## Revenue/Earnings Data

**Revenue (Million $)**

| | 1Q | 2Q | 3Q | 4Q | Year |
|---|---|---|---|---|---|
| 2012 | 104,189 | 109,366 | 110,226 | -- | -- |
| 2011 | 99,097 | 103,016 | 101,239 | 115,600 | 421,849 |
| 2010 | 94,242 | 100,910 | 99,411 | 113,651 | 408,214 |
| 2009 | 94,070 | 101,544 | 97,634 | 107,996 | 405,607 |
| 2008 | 85,387 | 91,990 | 90,880 | 106,269 | 378,799 |
| 2007 | 79,613 | 85,430 | 84,467 | 99,078 | 348,650 |

**Earnings Per Share ($)**

| | 1Q | 2Q | 3Q | 4Q | Year |
|---|---|---|---|---|---|
| 2012 | 0.98 | 1.09 | 0.97 | E1.48 | E4.54 |
| 2011 | 0.88 | 0.97 | 0.95 | 1.41 | 4.18 |
| 2010 | 0.77 | 0.88 | 0.84 | 1.23 | 3.72 |
| 2009 | 0.76 | 0.86 | 0.77 | 0.96 | 3.35 |
| 2008 | 0.68 | 0.86 | 0.70 | 1.03 | 3.16 |
| 2007 | 0.64 | 0.72 | 0.62 | 0.95 | 2.92 |

Fiscal year ended Jan. 31. Next earnings report expected: Late February. EPS Estimates based on S&P Operating Earnings; historical GAAP earnings are as reported.

## Dividend Data (Dates: mm/dd Payment Date: mm/dd/yy)

| Amount ($) | Date Decl. | Ex-Div. Date | Stk. of Record | Payment Date |
|---|---|---|---|---|
| 0.365 | 03/03 | 03/09 | 03/11 | 04/04/11 |
| 0.365 | 03/03 | 05/11 | 05/13 | 06/06/11 |
| 0.365 | 03/03 | 08/10 | 08/12 | 09/06/11 |
| 0.365 | 03/03 | 12/07 | 12/09 | 01/03/12 |

Dividends have been paid since 1973. Source: Company reports.

# Wal-Mart Stores Inc

**STANDARD &POOR'S**

## Business Summary November 15, 2011

CORPORATE OVERVIEW. Walmart, the largest retailer in North America, has set its sights on other parts of the world. The company's operations are divided into three divisions: Walmart U.S. (FY 11(Jan.) sales $260.3 billion), Sam's Club ($493.5 billion), and Walmart International ($109.2 billion). Internationally, WMT recently operated 63 units in Argentina, 479 in Brazil, 325 in Canada, 549 in Central America, 279 in Chile, 328 in China (through joint ventures), 414 in Japan, 1,730 in Mexico, 385 in the U.K, and five in India (through joint ventures).

MARKET PROFILE. With over 100 million people walking into Walmart stores every week, the company is a dominant player in many of the markets in which it competes. With FY 11 sales of about $140 billion within supermarket-related categories (grocery), the Walmart U.S. division is the largest supermarket operator in the U.S., commanding about 25% market share of the $500+ billion supermarket industry. Other major product categories within the Walmart division include entertainment ($31 billion in estimated sales in FY 11), hardlines ($28 billion), health and wellness ($28 billion), apparel ($18 billion), and home ($13 billion). Sam's Club is the second largest warehouse club in the U.S., with sales of $49.5 billion in FY 11. About 60% of Sam's Club sales were generated from food, beverage, health and wellness categories.

## Company Financials Fiscal Year Ended Jan. 31

| Per Share Data ($) | 2011 | 2010 | 2009 | 2008 | 2007 | 2006 | 2005 | 2004 | 2003 | 2002 |
|---|---|---|---|---|---|---|---|---|---|---|
| Tangible Book Value | 14.73 | 14.43 | 12.75 | 12.22 | 11.57 | 9.84 | 9.12 | 7.83 | 6.78 | 5.95 |
| Cash Flow | 6.43 | 5.56 | 5.06 | 4.72 | 4.23 | 3.81 | 3.44 | 2.91 | 2.58 | 2.22 |
| Earnings | 4.18 | 3.72 | 3.35 | 3.16 | 2.92 | 2.68 | 2.41 | 2.03 | 1.81 | 1.50 |
| S&P Core Earnings | 4.18 | 3.72 | 3.42 | 3.16 | 2.92 | 2.66 | 2.41 | 2.03 | 1.79 | 1.47 |
| Dividends | NA | 1.09 | 0.95 | 0.67 | 0.67 | 0.60 | 0.52 | 0.36 | 0.30 | 0.28 |
| Payout Ratio | NA | 29% | 28% | 21% | 23% | 22% | 22% | 18% | 17% | 19% |
| Calendar Year | 2010 | 2009 | 2008 | 2007 | 2006 | 2005 | 2004 | 2003 | 2002 | 2001 |
| Prices:High | 56.27 | 57.51 | 63.85 | 51.44 | 52.15 | 54.60 | 61.31 | 60.20 | 63.94 | 58.75 |
| Prices:Low | 47.77 | 46.25 | 43.11 | 42.09 | 42.31 | 42.31 | 51.08 | 46.25 | 43.72 | 42.00 |
| P/E Ratio:High | 13 | 15 | 19 | 16 | 18 | 20 | 25 | 30 | 35 | 39 |
| P/E Ratio:Low | 11 | 12 | 13 | 13 | 14 | 16 | 21 | 23 | 24 | 28 |

### Income Statement Analysis (Million $)

| | 2011 | 2010 | 2009 | 2008 | 2007 | 2006 | 2005 | 2004 | 2003 | 2002 |
|---|---|---|---|---|---|---|---|---|---|---|
| Revenue | 421,849 | 408,214 | 405,607 | 378,799 | 348,650 | 312,427 | 285,222 | 256,329 | 244,524 | 217,799 |
| Operating Income | 33,183 | 31,663 | 26,580 | 24,784 | 22,298 | 23,247 | 18,729 | 16,525 | 15,075 | 15,367 |
| Depreciation | 7,641 | 7,157 | 6,739 | 6,317 | 5,459 | 4,717 | 4,405 | 3,852 | 3,432 | 3,290 |
| Interest Expense | 2,205 | 2,065 | 2,272 | 1,467 | 1,809 | 1,420 | 1,187 | 996 | 1,063 | 1,326 |
| Pretax Income | 23,538 | 22,066 | 20,898 | 20,198 | 18,968 | 17,358 | 16,105 | 14,193 | 12,719 | 10,751 |
| Effective Tax Rate | 32.2% | 32.4% | 34.2% | 34.2% | 33.6% | 33.4% | 34.7% | 36.1% | 35.3% | 36.2% |
| Net Income | 15,355 | 14,414 | 13,254 | 12,884 | 12,178 | 11,231 | 10,267 | 8,861 | 8,039 | 6,671 |
| S&P Core Earnings | 15,355 | 14,414 | 13,505 | 12,880 | 12,178 | 11,134 | 10,267 | 8,861 | 7,955 | 6,592 |

### Balance Sheet & Other Financial Data (Million $)

| | 2011 | 2010 | 2009 | 2008 | 2007 | 2006 | 2005 | 2004 | 2003 | 2002 |
|---|---|---|---|---|---|---|---|---|---|---|
| Cash | 7,395 | 7,907 | 7,275 | 5,569 | 7,373 | 6,414 | 5,488 | 5,199 | 2,758 | 2,161 |
| Current Assets | 51,893 | 48,331 | 48,949 | 47,585 | 46,588 | 43,824 | 38,491 | 34,421 | 30,483 | 28,246 |
| Total Assets | 180,663 | 170,706 | 163,429 | 163,514 | 151,193 | 138,187 | 120,223 | 104,912 | 94,685 | 83,451 |
| Current Liabilities | 58,484 | 55,561 | 55,390 | 58,454 | 51,754 | 48,826 | 42,888 | 37,418 | 32,617 | 27,282 |
| Long Term Debt | 40,692 | 33,231 | 31,349 | 29,799 | 30,735 | 30,171 | 23,669 | 20,099 | 19,608 | 18,732 |
| Common Equity | 68,542 | 70,749 | 65,285 | 64,608 | 61,573 | 53,171 | 49,396 | 43,623 | 39,337 | 35,102 |
| Total Capital | 120,115 | 110,517 | 104,673 | 102,259 | 94,468 | 84,809 | 74,388 | 65,206 | 60,307 | 55,041 |
| Capital Expenditures | 12,699 | 12,184 | 11,499 | 14,937 | 15,666 | 14,563 | 12,893 | 10,308 | 9,355 | 8,383 |
| Cash Flow | 23,600 | 21,571 | 19,993 | 19,201 | 17,637 | 15,948 | 14,672 | 12,713 | 11,471 | 9,961 |
| Current Ratio | 0.9 | 0.9 | 0.9 | 0.8 | 0.9 | 0.9 | 0.9 | 0.9 | 0.9 | 1.0 |
| % Long Term Debt of Capitalization | 33.9 | 30.1 | 30.0 | 29.1 | 32.5 | 35.6 | 31.8 | 30.8 | 32.5 | 34.0 |
| % Net Income of Revenue | 3.6 | 3.5 | 3.3 | 3.4 | 3.5 | 3.5 | 3.6 | 3.5 | 3.3 | 3.1 |
| % Return on Assets | 8.7 | 8.6 | 8.1 | 8.2 | 8.4 | 8.7 | 9.1 | 8.9 | 9.0 | 8.3 |
| % Return on Equity | 22.1 | 21.2 | 20.4 | 20.4 | 21.2 | 21.9 | 22.1 | 21.3 | 21.6 | 20.1 |

Data as orig reptd.; bef. results of disc opers/spec. items. Per share data adj. for stk. divs.; EPS diluted. E-Estimated. NA-Not Available. NM-Not Meaningful. NR-Not Ranked. UR-Under Review.

**Office:** 702 S.W. 8th Street, Bentonville, AR 72716.
**Telephone:** 479-273-4000.
**Website:** http://www.walmartstores.com
**Chrmn:** S.R. Walton

**Pres & CEO:** M. Duke
**COO:** D. Sloneker
**EVP, Secy & General Counsel:** J.J. Gearhart
**SVP & CTO:** N. Stewart

**Investor Contact:** M. Beckstead (479-277-9558)
**Board Members:** A. M. Alvarez, J. W. Breyer, M. M. Burns, J. I. Cash, Jr., R. C. Corbett, D. N. Daft, M. Duke, G. B. Penner, S. S. Reinemund, H. L. Scott, Jr., A. M. Sorenson, J. Walton, S. R. Walton, C. J. Williams, L. S. Wolf

**Founded:** 1945
**Domicile:** Delaware
**Employees:** 2,100,000

*The McGraw-Hill Companies*

# Washington Post Co (The)

**STANDARD &POOR'S**

**S&P Recommendation** HOLD ★★★★★

| Price | 12-Mo. Target Price | Investment Style |
|---|---|---|
| $343.76 (as of Nov 25, 2011) | $350.00 | Large-Cap Growth |

**GICS Sector** Consumer Discretionary
**Sub-Industry** Publishing

**Summary** WPO publishes The Washington Post newspaper, operates TV stations and cable systems, and provides education and database services.

## Key Stock Statistics (Source S&P, Vickers, company reports)

| | | | | | | | |
|---|---|---|---|---|---|---|---|
| 52-Wk Range | $455.69–308.50 | S&P Oper. EPS 2011E | 18.27 | Market Capitalization(B) | $2.231 | Beta | 0.95 |
| Trailing 12-Month EPS | $16.52 | S&P Oper. EPS 2012E | 18.57 | Yield (%) | 2.73 | S&P 3-Yr. Proj. EPS CAGR(%) | -3 |
| Trailing 12-Month P/E | 20.8 | P/E on S&P Oper. EPS 2011E | 18.8 | Dividend Rate/Share | $9.40 | S&P Credit Rating | A- |
| $10K Invested 5 Yrs Ago | $5,119 | Common Shares Outstg. (M) | 7.7 | Institutional Ownership (%) | 100 | | |

## Price Performance

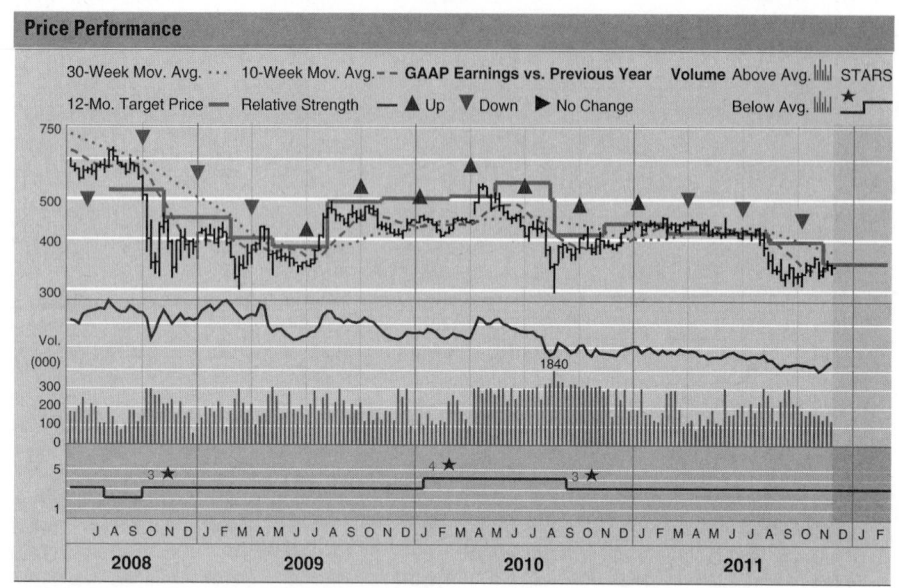

30-Week Mov. Avg. ··· 10-Week Mov. Avg. - - GAAP Earnings vs. Previous Year  Volume Above Avg. STARS
12-Mo. Target Price — Relative Strength — ▲ Up ▼ Down ▶ No Change  Below Avg.

Analysis prepared by Equity Analyst **Joseph Agnese** on Nov 08, 2011, when the stock traded at **$340.88**.

## Highlights

➤ We look for revenues to decline 2.2% in 2012, to $4.143 billion, from our estimate of $4.235 billion in 2011. The company's education segment is implementing a new program in 2011 under which students may withdraw during a risk-free period and not have to pay for coursework. We believe early withdrawals will more than offset benefits we see from new students attracted to the program. We expect television segment revenues to benefit in 2012 due to the Olympics and increased political advertising due to a presidential election. We believe newspaper segment revenues will decline about 5.0% as advertising dollars continue to shift online.

➤ We expect operating margins to narrow in 2012 as decreased sales leverage and increasing regulatory related operating costs in the education segment offset improved sales leverage from broadcasting and continued cost cutting and lower newsprint pricing within the publishing segment.

➤ After a significant reduction in share count due to an active share repurchase program, we see EPS rising to $18.57 in 2012, from our estimate of $18.27 in 2011.

## Investment Rationale/Risk

➤ We believe recently enacted government regulations will negatively impact the education segment in 2011 and 2012 as the company rolls out a new enrollment program to help it and students better gauge future successful graduation. While the publishing segment remains exposed to significant secular pressures, we believe broadcasting is well positioned to benefit from increased advertising spending in 2012 due to the Olympics and a presidential election.

➤ Risks to our recommendation and target price include the potential for federal rule changes to result in a reduction in Title IV funding and enrollments for Kaplan schools. Regarding corporate governance, holders of non-publicly traded Class A shares (as of March 23, 2011) have the right to elect a majority of the directors, which we believe may not be in the best interests of common (Class B) stockholders.

➤ We think WPO should trade in line with peers' median EV/EBITDA multiple due to its diverse operations. Applying an EV/EBITDA multiple of 5.7X, in line with a weighted average of peers, to our 2012 EBITDA estimate of $538.9 million results in our 12-month target price of $350.

## Qualitative Risk Assessment

| LOW | MEDIUM | HIGH |
|---|---|---|

Our risk assessment incorporates our view of a highly competitive environment for advertising among publishers and other media, and a significant negative trend in print advertising and circulation, partially offset by the recurring nature of a significant portion of company revenues.

## Quantitative Evaluations

**S&P Quality Ranking** B+

| D | C | B- | B | B+ | A- | A | A+ |
|---|---|---|---|---|---|---|---|

**Relative Strength Rank** STRONG

74

LOWEST = 1    HIGHEST = 99

## Revenue/Earnings Data

### Revenue (Million $)

| | 1Q | 2Q | 3Q | 4Q | Year |
|---|---|---|---|---|---|
| 2011 | 1,064 | 1,073 | 1,033 | -- | -- |
| 2010 | 1,171 | 1,202 | 1,190 | 1,190 | 4,724 |
| 2009 | 1,054 | 1,128 | 1,149 | 1,238 | 4,570 |
| 2008 | 1,063 | 1,106 | 1,129 | 1,164 | 4,462 |
| 2007 | 985.6 | 1,047 | 1,023 | 1,126 | 4,180 |
| 2006 | 948.3 | 969.0 | 946.9 | 1,041 | 3,905 |

### Earnings Per Share ($)

| | | | | | |
|---|---|---|---|---|---|
| 2011 | 1.87 | 5.92 | -0.50 | E6.32 | E18.27 |
| 2010 | 4.91 | 10.25 | 9.12 | 9.42 | 34.26 |
| 2009 | -2.04 | 1.30 | 1.81 | 8.71 | 9.78 |
| 2008 | 4.08 | -0.31 | 1.08 | 2.01 | 6.87 |
| 2007 | 6.70 | 7.19 | 7.60 | 8.72 | 30.19 |
| 2006 | 8.48 | 8.17 | 7.60 | 9.97 | 34.21 |

Fiscal year ended Dec. 31. Next earnings report expected: Late February. EPS Estimates based on S&P Operating Earnings; historical GAAP earnings are as reported.

## Dividend Data (Dates: mm/dd Payment Date: mm/dd/yy)

| Amount ($) | Date Decl. | Ex-Div. Date | Stk. of Record | Payment Date |
|---|---|---|---|---|
| 2.350 | 01/20 | 01/27 | 01/31 | 02/11/11 |
| 2.350 | 02/22 | 04/20 | 04/25 | 05/06/11 |
| 2.350 | 06/09 | 07/21 | 07/25 | 08/05/11 |
| 2.350 | 09/08 | 10/20 | 10/24 | 11/04/11 |

Dividends have been paid since 1956. Source: Company reports.

---

**Please read the Required Disclosures and Analyst Certification on the last page of this report.**

# Washington Post Co (The)

**STANDARD &POOR'S**

## Business Summary November 08, 2011

CORPORATE OVERVIEW. The Washington Post operates principally in three areas of the media business: newspaper publishing, television broadcasting, and cable television. Through its subsidiary Kaplan, Inc., the company also provides educational services for individuals, schools and businesses.

The company divides Kaplan's various educational businesses (61% of 2010 revenues) into four categories: higher education (62% of segment revenues in 2010), test preparation (14%), international (20%),and Kaplan ventures (3.9%). Higher education includes Kaplan's domestic post-secondary education businesses, including fixed facility colleges and online post-secondary and career programs. We note that approximately 82% of Kaplan's higher education revenues (50% of total Kaplan revenues) came from Title IV (federal financial aid) programs in 2010, and thus we believe the segment is vulnerable to budget cuts for education spending. Test preparation includes standardized test prep for college, graduate school and professional licensing and advanced designation exams and includes live tutoring services. International includes U.K., Ireland, Singapore, Australia, Hong Kong and China businesses. Kaplan ventures division manages and develops business lines in markets adjacent to

Kaplan's core educational businesses such as compliance training in the pharmaceutical and medical technology industries and assistance in licensure and registration filings for insurance carriers, agencies and brokers/dealers. Part of the company's strategy in the education business is to grow through acquisition; along those lines, Kaplan made two acquisitions in 2009, following nine in both 2008 and 2007.

The Newspaper division (14%) includes The Washington Post, Express (a free weekly tabloid), Post-Newsweek Media, the Slate group, and other publications. WPNI holds an interest in Classified Ventures, a company that provides online classified advertising databases for cars, apartment rentals and residential real estate. In 2010, advertising represented 66% of The Washington Post's revenue, with subscription fees contributing 32%.

## Company Financials Fiscal Year Ended Dec. 31

| Per Share Data ($) | 2010 | 2009 | 2008 | 2007 | 2006 | 2005 | 2004 | 2003 | 2002 | 2001 |
|---|---|---|---|---|---|---|---|---|---|---|
| Tangible Book Value | 103.24 | 97.63 | 89.89 | NM | 143.64 | 103.66 | 92.76 | 64.70 | 59.82 | 50.31 |
| Cash Flow | 65.56 | 44.12 | 37.42 | 55.26 | 57.76 | 53.26 | 54.04 | 43.38 | 40.93 | 38.62 |
| Earnings | 34.26 | 9.78 | 6.87 | 30.19 | 34.21 | 32.59 | 34.59 | 25.12 | 22.61 | 24.06 |
| S&P Core Earnings | 33.64 | 14.33 | 12.62 | 25.02 | 30.53 | 26.50 | 29.88 | 15.68 | 12.98 | -1.24 |
| Dividends | 9.00 | 8.60 | 8.60 | 8.20 | 7.80 | 7.40 | 7.00 | 5.80 | 5.60 | 5.60 |
| Payout Ratio | 26% | 88% | 125% | 27% | 23% | 23% | 20% | 23% | 25% | 23% |
| Prices:High | 547.58 | 495.60 | 823.25 | 885.23 | 815.00 | 982.03 | 999.50 | 819.50 | 743.00 | 651.50 |
| Prices:Low | 295.56 | 300.16 | 320.00 | 726.93 | 690.00 | 716.00 | 790.21 | 650.03 | 516.00 | 470.00 |
| P/E Ratio:High | 16 | 51 | NM | 29 | 24 | 30 | 29 | 33 | 33 | 27 |
| P/E Ratio:Low | 9 | 31 | NM | 24 | 20 | 22 | 23 | 26 | 23 | 20 |

| Income Statement Analysis (Million $) | 2010 | 2009 | 2008 | 2007 | 2006 | 2005 | 2004 | 2003 | 2002 | 2001 |
|---|---|---|---|---|---|---|---|---|---|---|
| Revenue | 4,724 | 4,570 | 4,462 | 4,180 | 3,905 | 3,554 | 3,300 | 2,839 | 2,584 | 2,417 |
| Operating Income | 853 | 542 | 598 | 716 | 682 | 713 | 748 | 497 | 549 | 358 |
| Depreciation | 280 | 323 | 288 | 239 | 222 | 198 | 185 | 174 | 172 | 138 |
| Interest Expense | 30.5 | 31.6 | 24.7 | 24.1 | 25.3 | 26.8 | 28.0 | 27.8 | 33.8 | 49.6 |
| Pretax Income | 523 | 149 | 145 | 481 | 519 | 500 | 542 | 383 | 354 | 388 |
| Effective Tax Rate | NA | 38.7% | 54.7% | 40.0% | 36.5% | 37.1% | 38.7% | 37.0% | 38.8% | 40.7% |
| Net Income | 307 | 92.8 | 65.7 | 289 | 330 | 314 | 333 | 241 | 216 | 230 |
| S&P Core Earnings | 299 | 134 | 119 | 238 | 293 | 255 | 287 | 150 | 124 | -13.4 |

| Balance Sheet & Other Financial Data (Million $) | 2010 | 2009 | 2008 | 2007 | 2006 | 2005 | 2004 | 2003 | 2002 | 2001 |
|---|---|---|---|---|---|---|---|---|---|---|
| Cash | 811 | 863 | 748 | 373 | 348 | 216 | 119 | 87.4 | 28.8 | 31.5 |
| Current Assets | 1,362 | 1,388 | 1,352 | 995 | 935 | 818 | 754 | 496 | 383 | 397 |
| Total Assets | 5,158 | 5,186 | 5,158 | 6,005 | 5,381 | 4,585 | 4,317 | 3,902 | 3,584 | 3,559 |
| Current Liabilities | 1,008 | 990 | 1,094 | 1,013 | 803 | 695 | 688 | 712 | 736 | 434 |
| Long Term Debt | 397 | 396 | 400 | 401 | 402 | 404 | 426 | 422 | 406 | 1,862 |
| Common Equity | 2,814 | 2,940 | 2,858 | 3,461 | 3,160 | 2,638 | 2,412 | 2,075 | 1,837 | 1,683 |
| Total Capital | 3,239 | 3,358 | 3,630 | 4,583 | 4,173 | 3,477 | 3,254 | 2,814 | 2,517 | 3,781 |
| Capital Expenditures | 244 | 258 | 289 | 290 | 284 | 238 | 205 | 126 | 153 | 224 |
| Cash Flow | 586 | 414 | 353 | 526 | 551 | 511 | 518 | 414 | 387 | 367 |
| Current Ratio | 1.4 | 1.4 | 1.2 | 1.0 | 1.2 | 1.2 | 1.1 | 0.7 | 0.5 | 0.9 |
| % Long Term Debt of Capitalization | 12.3 | Nil | 11.0 | 8.7 | 9.6 | 11.6 | 13.1 | 15.0 | 16.1 | 49.3 |
| % Net Income of Revenue | 6.5 | 2.0 | 1.5 | 6.9 | 8.4 | 8.8 | 10.1 | 8.5 | 8.4 | 9.5 |
| % Return on Assets | NA | NA | 1.2 | 5.1 | 6.6 | 7.1 | 8.0 | 6.4 | 6.1 | 6.8 |
| % Return on Equity | NA | NA | 2.1 | 8.7 | 11.3 | 12.4 | 14.9 | 12.3 | 12.2 | 14.4 |

Data as orig reptd.; bef. results of disc opers/spec. items. Per share data adj. for stk. divs.; EPS diluted. E-Estimated. NA-Not Available. NM-Not Meaningful. NR-Not Ranked. UR-Under Review.

**Office:** 1150 15th Street NW, Washington, DC 20071.
**Telephone:** 202-334-6000.
**Website:** http://www.washpostco.com
**Chrmn & CEO:** D. Graham

**SVP & CFO:** H. Jones
**CTO:** Y. Kochar
**Chief Acctg Officer:** W.R. Cooney
**Treas:** D.J. Lynch

**Investor Contact:** J.B. Morse, Jr. (202-334-6662)
**Board Members:** L. C. Bollinger, C. C. Davis, B. Diller, J. L. Dotson, Jr., T. S. Gaynor, D. Graham, A. M. Mulcahy, R. L. Olson, L. D. Thompson, G. R. Wagoner, Jr., K. Weymouth

**Founded:** 1947
**Domicile:** Delaware
**Employees:** 20,000

# Waste Management Inc.

STANDARD
&POOR'S

| S&P Recommendation | HOLD ★★★★★ | Price | 12-Mo. Target Price | Investment Style |
|---|---|---|---|---|
| | | $30.31 (as of Nov 25, 2011) | $37.00 | Large-Cap Blend |

**GICS Sector** Industrials
**Sub-Industry** Environmental & Facilities Services

**Summary** This Houston-based company is the largest U.S. trash hauling/disposal concern.

## Key Stock Statistics (Source S&P, Vickers, company reports)

| | | | | | | | |
|---|---|---|---|---|---|---|---|
| 52-Wk Range | $39.69–27.75 | S&P Oper. EPS 2011**E** | 2.15 | Market Capitalization(B) | $13.953 | Beta | 0.59 |
| Trailing 12-Month EPS | $2.05 | S&P Oper. EPS 2012**E** | 2.35 | Yield (%) | 4.49 | S&P 3-Yr. Proj. EPS CAGR(%) | 9 |
| Trailing 12-Month P/E | 14.8 | P/E on S&P Oper. EPS 2011**E** | 14.1 | Dividend Rate/Share | $1.36 | S&P Credit Rating | BBB |
| $10K Invested 5 Yrs Ago | $9,548 | Common Shares Outstg. (M) | 460.3 | Institutional Ownership (%) | 81 | | |

## Price Performance

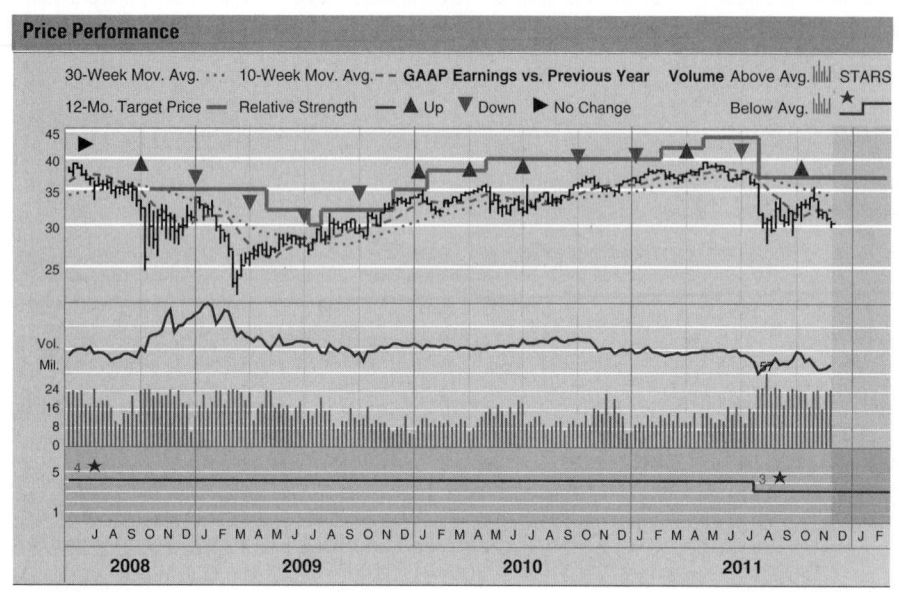

30-Week Mov. Avg. ···· 10-Week Mov. Avg. -- **GAAP Earnings vs. Previous Year**   **Volume** Above Avg. STARS
12-Mo. Target Price — Relative Strength — ▲ Up ▼ Down ► No Change   Below Avg.

Options: ASE, CBOE, P, Ph

Analysis prepared by Equity Analyst **Stewart Scharf** on Nov 03, 2011, when the stock traded at **$31.35**.

### Highlights

➤ We expect low single digit organic revenue growth to continue through 2012, driven primarily by close to 2% higher core collection and disposal pricing, and favorable, albeit more stable, commodity recycling prices, while C&D (construction and demolition) volume remains soft. Although more competitive pricing will likely lead to WM selectively deciding which customers to try to retain, we believe the company will be able to maintain market share within its historical range. In our view, the "churn" rate should improve in 2012 to the high end of its historical 9% to 10% range.

➤ In our view, gross margins (before D&A) will narrow somewhat in 2011, from 37.5% in 2010, with some improvement in 2012 as pricing pressures and mix issues subside. We see EBITDA margins gradually expanding from our 25.7% forecast for 2011 (25.8% in 2010), as improved productivity and cost controls offset higher technology and waste-to-energy upgrade costs.

➤ We project an effective tax rate above 35% for 2011, with operating EPS of $2.15, followed by 9% growth to $2.35 in 2012.

### Investment Rationale/Risk

➤ Our hold opinion is based on adverse market conditions that continue to affect volume, as well as pricing levels. We expect WM to continue with its expansion strategy while generating strong cash targeted for niche acquisitions, alternative energy projects, share buybacks and dividends.

➤ Risks to our opinion and target price include a significant rise in fuel costs, a prolonged downturn in the U.S. economy, a sharp drop in recycling prices and demand, a lower customer retention rate due to competitive pricing, and an inability to raise prices enough to meet return on invested capital (ROIC) goals.

➤ Correlating various relative metrics, including the stock's historical five-year average P/E multiple, we believe the shares should trade at a modest discount-to-peers P/E of 16X our operating EPS estimate for 2012, valuing the stock at $38. Based on our discounted cash flow model, assuming a 7.5% weighted average cost of capital and a 3% terminal growth rate, our intrinsic value estimate is $36. Blending these metrics, we derive our 12-month target price of $37.

### Qualitative Risk Assessment

| LOW | MEDIUM | HIGH |
|---|---|---|

Our risk assessment reflects soft volume due to weak economic conditions, offset by our view of a solid balance sheet, with strong cash generation for dividends, share buybacks, debt paydowns, and niche acquisitions. In addition, we view corporate governance practices as sound.

### Quantitative Evaluations

**S&P Quality Ranking**  B+

| D | C | B- | B | B+ | A- | A | A+ |
|---|---|---|---|---|---|---|---|

**Relative Strength Rank**  MODERATE

51

LOWEST = 1    HIGHEST = 99

### Revenue/Earnings Data

**Revenue (Million $)**

| | 1Q | 2Q | 3Q | 4Q | Year |
|---|---|---|---|---|---|
| 2011 | 3,103 | 3,347 | 3,522 | -- | -- |
| 2010 | 2,935 | 3,158 | 3,235 | 3,187 | 12,515 |
| 2009 | 2,810 | 2,952 | 3,023 | 3,006 | 11,791 |
| 2008 | 3,266 | 3,489 | 3,525 | 3,108 | 13,388 |
| 2007 | 3,188 | 3,358 | 3,403 | 3,361 | 13,310 |
| 2006 | 3,229 | 3,410 | 3,441 | 3,283 | 13,363 |

**Earnings Per Share ($)**

| | 1Q | 2Q | 3Q | 4Q | Year |
|---|---|---|---|---|---|
| 2011 | 0.39 | 0.50 | 0.58 | E0.63 | E2.15 |
| 2010 | 0.37 | 0.51 | 0.51 | 0.59 | 1.98 |
| 2009 | 0.31 | 0.50 | 0.56 | 0.64 | 2.01 |
| 2008 | 0.48 | 0.64 | 0.63 | 0.44 | 2.19 |
| 2007 | 0.42 | 0.64 | 0.54 | 0.61 | 2.23 |
| 2006 | 0.34 | 0.76 | 0.55 | 0.46 | 2.10 |

Fiscal year ended Dec. 31. Next earnings report expected: NA. EPS Estimates based on S&P Operating Earnings; historical GAAP earnings are as reported.

### Dividend Data (Dates: mm/dd Payment Date: mm/dd/yy)

| Amount ($) | Date Decl. | Ex-Div. Date | Stk. of Record | Payment Date |
|---|---|---|---|---|
| 0.340 | 03/01 | 03/09 | 03/11 | 03/25/11 |
| 0.340 | 05/13 | 05/31 | 06/02 | 06/17/11 |
| 0.340 | 08/23 | 09/01 | 09/06 | 09/23/11 |
| 0.340 | 11/08 | 11/28 | 11/30 | 12/16/11 |

Dividends have been paid since 1998. Source: Company reports.

# Waste Management Inc.

**STANDARD &POOR'S**

## Business Summary November 03, 2011

CORPORATE OVERVIEW. Waste Management, the largest waste disposal company in North America, provides collection, transfer, recycling and resource recovery, as well as disposal services. It also owns U.S. waste-to-energy facilities. As of December 31, 2010, it served nearly 20 million customers through 294 transfer stations and 271 owned or operated landfills (including five hazardous waste landfills), 17 waste-to-energy plants and five independent power production plants, 98 recycling plants and 127 beneficial-use landfill gas projects. In 2010, revenues from the North American solid waste (NASW) business were: 57% collection; 18% landfill; 6.1% waste-to-energy (Wheelabrator Technologies unit); 9.1% transfer; 8.1% recycling; and 2.2% other. WM's average remaining landfill life at December 31, 2010, was 40 years, and 45 years when considering remaining permitted capacity and projected annual disposal volume. The company's average fleet age is about 7.5 years. WM's internalization rate at September 30, 2011, was 67.8%, down slightly from 67.9% a year ago. WM believes that for every 1% reduction in its customer "churn" ratio (about 10% at 2010 year end; WM target range below 10%), it adds $25 million to EBIT (earnings before interest and taxes). The company has hedges in place on 30% of its merchant energy stream (more than 65% of its total annual energy stream for 60-day to nine-month periods), as its waste-to-energy electricity sales on a merchant basis had increased to 53% at the end of 2010, from 33% at the start of 2009. WM's long-term goal is for an energy portfolio 80% contracted or hedged and 20% floating. About 40% of WM's collection business has annual pricing adjustments based on the CPI (Consumer Price Index), with most contracts renewing July 1.

CORPORATE STRATEGY. In our view, WM will use its strong cash generation primarily for acquisitions, dividends and share buybacks, with more favorable acquisition multiples leading to a rise in acquired revenues. In October 2007, the company announced an environmental initiative under which it planned to invest in waste-based energy production, recycling and new waste technologies, including up to $500 million a year for 10 years to increase the fuel efficiency of its fleet. We view this as a positive long-term environmental strategy as more methane in landfills is converted into energy. In March 2010, WM acquired a 40% interest in Shanghai Environment Group (SEG), a leading waste-to-energy company in China, for $142 million. In April 2010, it bought a waste-to-energy plant in Virginia for $150 million.

## Company Financials Fiscal Year Ended Dec. 31

| Per Share Data ($) | 2010 | 2009 | 2008 | 2007 | 2006 | 2005 | 2004 | 2003 | 2002 | 2001 |
|---|---|---|---|---|---|---|---|---|---|---|
| Tangible Book Value | 0.50 | 0.85 | 0.57 | 0.52 | 1.52 | 1.10 | 0.91 | 0.24 | 0.21 | 0.43 |
| Cash Flow | 4.55 | 4.38 | 4.87 | 4.64 | 4.66 | 4.50 | 3.90 | 3.44 | 5.29 | 2.97 |
| Earnings | 1.98 | 2.01 | 2.19 | 2.23 | 2.10 | 2.09 | 1.60 | 1.21 | 1.33 | 0.80 |
| S&P Core Earnings | 1.92 | 2.01 | 2.15 | 2.18 | 2.08 | 1.90 | 1.48 | 1.09 | 1.17 | 1.04 |
| Dividends | 1.26 | 1.16 | 1.08 | 0.96 | 0.88 | 0.80 | 0.75 | 0.01 | 0.01 | 0.01 |
| Payout Ratio | 64% | 58% | 49% | 43% | 42% | 38% | 47% | 1% | 1% | 1% |
| Prices:High | 37.25 | 34.18 | 39.25 | 41.19 | 38.64 | 31.03 | 31.42 | 29.72 | 31.25 | 32.50 |
| Prices:Low | 31.11 | 22.10 | 24.51 | 32.40 | 30.08 | 26.80 | 25.67 | 19.39 | 20.20 | 22.51 |
| P/E Ratio:High | 19 | 17 | 18 | 18 | 18 | 15 | 20 | 25 | 23 | 41 |
| P/E Ratio:Low | 16 | 11 | 11 | 15 | 14 | 13 | 16 | 16 | 15 | 28 |

| Income Statement Analysis (Million $) | | | | | | | | | | |
|---|---|---|---|---|---|---|---|---|---|---|
| Revenue | 12,515 | 11,791 | 13,388 | 13,310 | 13,363 | 13,074 | 12,516 | 11,574 | 11,142 | 11,322 |
| Operating Income | 3,242 | 3,186 | 3,577 | 3,746 | 3,388 | 3,167 | 3,021 | 2,841 | 2,870 | 3,034 |
| Depreciation | 1,194 | 1,166 | 1,323 | 1,259 | 1,334 | 1,361 | 1,336 | 1,265 | 2,444 | 1,371 |
| Interest Expense | 473 | 426 | 472 | 521 | 545 | 496 | 455 | 439 | 462 | 541 |
| Pretax Income | 1,631 | 1,473 | 1,797 | 1,784 | 1,518 | 1,140 | 1,214 | 1,129 | 1,240 | 792 |
| Effective Tax Rate | NA | 28.0% | 37.2% | 30.2% | 21.4% | NM | 20.3% | 35.8% | 34.2% | 35.9% |
| Net Income | 1,002 | 994 | 1,087 | 1,163 | 1,149 | 1,182 | 931 | 719 | 823 | 503 |
| S&P Core Earnings | 924 | 994 | 1,066 | 1,133 | 1,139 | 1,072 | 864 | 643 | 725 | 653 |

| Balance Sheet & Other Financial Data (Million $) | | | | | | | | | | |
|---|---|---|---|---|---|---|---|---|---|---|
| Cash | 540 | 1,153 | 480 | 348 | 614 | 666 | 443 | 135 | 264 | 730 |
| Current Assets | 2,482 | 3,010 | 2,335 | 2,480 | 3,182 | 3,451 | 2,819 | 2,588 | 2,700 | 3,124 |
| Total Assets | 21,476 | 21,154 | 20,227 | 20,175 | 20,600 | 21,135 | 20,905 | 20,656 | 19,631 | 19,490 |
| Current Liabilities | 2,485 | 2,901 | 3,036 | 2,598 | 3,268 | 3,257 | 3,205 | 3,332 | 3,173 | 3,721 |
| Long Term Debt | 8,687 | 8,124 | 7,491 | 8,008 | 7,495 | 8,165 | 8,182 | 7,997 | 8,062 | 7,709 |
| Common Equity | 6,260 | 6,285 | 5,902 | 5,902 | 6,222 | 6,222 | 5,971 | 5,563 | 5,308 | 5,392 |
| Total Capital | 15,842 | 15,464 | 15,160 | 15,521 | 15,357 | 15,931 | 14,435 | 15,473 | 13,389 | 14,241 |
| Capital Expenditures | 1,104 | 1,179 | 1,221 | 1,211 | 1,329 | 1,180 | 1,258 | 1,200 | 1,287 | 1,328 |
| Cash Flow | 2,196 | 2,160 | 2,410 | 2,422 | 2,483 | 2,543 | 2,267 | 1,984 | 3,267 | 1,874 |
| Current Ratio | 1.0 | 1.0 | 0.8 | 1.0 | 1.0 | 1.1 | 0.9 | 0.8 | 0.9 | 0.8 |
| % Long Term Debt of Capitalization | 54.8 | 52.5 | 49.4 | 51.5 | 48.8 | 51.3 | 56.7 | 51.7 | 60.2 | 54.1 |
| % Net Income of Revenue | 8.0 | 8.4 | 8.1 | 8.7 | 8.6 | 9.0 | 7.4 | 6.2 | 7.4 | 4.4 |
| % Return on Assets | 4.7 | 4.8 | 5.4 | 5.7 | 5.5 | 5.6 | 4.5 | 3.5 | 4.2 | 2.6 |
| % Return on Equity | 16.0 | 16.3 | 18.6 | 19.3 | 18.6 | 19.6 | 16.1 | 13.2 | 15.4 | 9.9 |

Data as orig reptd.; bef. results of disc opers/spec. items. Per share data adj. for stk. divs.; EPS diluted. E-Estimated. NA-Not Available. NM-Not Meaningful. NR-Not Ranked. UR-Under Review.

**Office:** 1001 Fannin Street, Suite 4000, Houston, TX 77002.
**Telephone:** 713-512-6200.
**Website:** http://www.wm.com
**Chrmn:** J.C. Pope

**Pres & CEO:** D.P. Steiner
**EVP & CFO:** S. Preston
**SVP & General Counsel:** R.L. Wittenbraker
**SVP & CIO:** P. Bhasin

**Investor Contact:** J. Alderson (713-394-2281)
**Board Members:** B. H. Anderson, P. S. Cafferty, F. M. Clark, Jr., P. W. Gross, J. C. Pope, W. R. Reum, S. G. Rothmeier, D. P. Steiner, T. H. Weidemeyer

**Founded:** 1894
**Domicile:** Delaware
**Employees:** 42,800

The McGraw-Hill Companies

# Waters Corp

**STANDARD &POOR'S**

| S&P Recommendation **BUY** ★★★★☆ | Price $72.55 (as of Nov 25, 2011) | 12-Mo. Target Price $107.00 | Investment Style Large-Cap Growth |
|---|---|---|---|

**GICS Sector** Health Care
**Sub-Industry** Life Sciences Tools & Services

**Summary** This company manufactures scientific and industrial analytical equipment such as liquid chromatography, thermal analysis and mass spectrometry products.

## Key Stock Statistics (Source S&P, Vickers, company reports)

| | | | | | | | |
|---|---|---|---|---|---|---|---|
| 52-Wk Range | $100.00– 71.12 | S&P Oper. EPS 2011E | 4.80 | Market Capitalization(B) | $6.501 | Beta | 1.07 |
| Trailing 12-Month EPS | $4.53 | S&P Oper. EPS 2012E | 5.34 | Yield (%) | Nil | S&P 3-Yr. Proj. EPS CAGR(%) | 15 |
| Trailing 12-Month P/E | 16.0 | P/E on S&P Oper. EPS 2011E | 15.1 | Dividend Rate/Share | Nil | S&P Credit Rating | NA |
| $10K Invested 5 Yrs Ago | $14,375 | Common Shares Outstg. (M) | 89.6 | Institutional Ownership (%) | 95 | | |

## Price Performance

30-Week Mov. Avg. ···· 10-Week Mov. Avg. --- GAAP Earnings vs. Previous Year   Volume Above Avg. STARS
12-Mo. Target Price — Relative Strength — ▲ Up ▼ Down ► No Change   Below Avg. ★

Options: ASE, CBOE, Ph

Analysis prepared by Equity Analyst **Jeffrey Loo, CFA** on Nov 21, 2011, when the stock traded at **$72.91**.

## Highlights

➤ We see sales growing 12% in 2011 to $1.85 billion, and 8% in 2012 to $2.0 billion, on steady improvement across WAT's end-markets and broad-based geographic improvement, particularly in emerging markets, including China and Eastern Europe. However, worldwide government funding for government and academic facilities, outside of China and Latin America, remain challenging, particularly in the U.S. and Europe. Japan, which accounts for about 10% of WAT's sales, appears to be rebounding following the recent tragic events in early 2011. We also see improvement in the industrial end-markets and believe heightened global food safety concerns, along with new regulations in various countries, will drive revenues.

➤ We expect gross margins to improve 50 basis points (bps) in 2011 on manufacturing cost reductions, partially offset by margin pressure from new product introductions. We look for operating margins to rise 100 bps on leverage and a lower cost structure.

➤ We see EPS of $4.80 in 2011 and $5.34 in 2012, aided by stock buybacks and continued lower effective tax rates of about 16.5%.

## Investment Rationale/Risk

➤ We believe the shares, recently trading at a 1.1X PEG ratio, slightly below peers, are attractively valued. WAT maintains a leading market share in the chromatography segment, and we believe recent product introductions will enable it to potentially expand its market share. We think the robust acceptance of newly introduced instruments including the Acquity UPLC H-Class and WAT's new high-end mass spectrometry system, the Xevo TQ-S, should continue throughout the year, as labs upgrade their instruments. The new Acquity UPLC I-Class started shipping in the third quarter and we anticipate solid sales. However, we note that tight worldwide government funding could continue through 2011 and into early 2012.

➤ Risks to our recommendation and target price include weaker-than-expected equipment sales to the life sciences and pharmaceutical end-markets and slower-than-expected recovery in industrial end-markets.

➤ Based on our P/E-to-growth (PEG) analysis, using our forward 12 months EPS forecast, a PEG ratio of 1.4X, in line with peers, and a 15% projected three-year growth rate, our 12-month target price is $107.

## Qualitative Risk Assessment

| LOW | MEDIUM | HIGH |
|---|---|---|

Our risk assessment reflects WAT's strong market share in the liquid chromatography and mass spectrometry markets, offset by a highly competitive marketplace and reliance on customer demand for expensive instruments.

## Quantitative Evaluations

**S&P Quality Ranking** B+

| D | C | B- | B | B+ | A- | A | A+ |
|---|---|---|---|---|---|---|---|

**Relative Strength Rank** MODERATE

41

LOWEST = 1   HIGHEST = 99

## Revenue/Earnings Data

**Revenue (Million $)**

| | 1Q | 2Q | 3Q | 4Q | Year |
|---|---|---|---|---|---|
| 2011 | 427.6 | 447.6 | 454.5 | -- | -- |
| 2010 | 367.7 | 391.1 | 401.0 | 483.6 | 1,643 |
| 2009 | 333.1 | 362.8 | 374.0 | 428.9 | 1,499 |
| 2008 | 371.7 | 398.8 | 386.3 | 418.3 | 1,575 |
| 2007 | 330.8 | 352.6 | 352.6 | 437.0 | 1,473 |
| 2006 | 290.2 | 301.9 | 301.2 | 386.9 | 1,280 |

**Earnings Per Share ($)**

| | | | | | |
|---|---|---|---|---|---|
| 2011 | 1.01 | 1.07 | 1.10 | E1.52 | E4.80 |
| 2010 | 0.79 | 0.90 | 1.02 | 1.36 | 4.06 |
| 2009 | 0.75 | 0.72 | 0.79 | 1.08 | 3.34 |
| 2008 | 0.67 | 0.82 | 0.71 | 1.01 | 3.21 |
| 2007 | 0.54 | 0.59 | 0.52 | 0.96 | 2.62 |
| 2006 | 0.42 | 0.46 | 0.49 | 0.78 | 2.13 |

Fiscal year ended Dec. 31. Next earnings report expected: NA. EPS Estimates based on S&P Operating Earnings; historical GAAP earnings are as reported.

## Dividend Data

No cash dividends have been paid.

# Waters Corp

## Business Summary November 21, 2011

CORPORATE OVERVIEW. Waters manufactures, distributes, and services analytical instruments to the pharmaceutical, life sciences, biochemical, industrial, academic, and government end-markets. Analytical instruments and components manufactured include high-performance liquid chromatography (HPLC) instruments, columns and other consumables, mass spectrometry (MS) instruments that can be integrated with other analytical instruments, and thermal analysis (TA) and rheology instruments. HPLC is the standard technique to identify and analyze constituent components of various chemicals and materials. Its unique performance capabilities let it separate and identify 80% of known chemicals and materials. HPLC is used to analyze substances in a variety of industries for R&D, quality control, and process engineering applications. Pharmaceutical and life science industries use HPLC primarily to identify new drugs.

In March 2004, WAT introduced a novel technology that it describes as Ultra Performance Chromatography, the Acquity UPLC. WAT believes the Acquity UPLC provides more comprehensive chemical separation and faster analysis times compared to the HPLC. MS is an analytical technique used to identify unknown compounds, quantify known materials, and elucidate the structural and chemical properties of molecules by measuring the masses of individual molecules that have been converted into ions. These products serve diverse markets, including pharmaceutical and environmental industries. The TA In-

struments division makes and services thermal analysis and rheology instruments used for the physical characterization of polymers and related materials. Thermal analysis measures physical characteristics of materials as a function of temperature. Changes in temperature affect several characteristics of materials, such as their physical state, weight, dimension and mechanical and electrical properties, which may be measured using thermal analysis techniques. As a result, thermal analysis is widely used to develop, produce and characterize materials in industries such as plastics, chemicals and pharmaceuticals.

WAT has supplemented its internal growth with various strategic acquisitions. In March 2004, it acquired NuGenesis Technologies Corp. for about $43 million. NuGenesis and Creon Lab formed the company's new Lab Informatics market segment. In March 2006, WAT acquired VICAM, a provider of bioseparation and rapid detection instruments for food safety. In August 2006, WAT acquired Thermometric AB, and in November 2006, it acquired Environmental Resource Associates, a provider of environmental testing and services. In 2007 WAT acquired Calorimetry Sciences Corporation.

## Company Financials Fiscal Year Ended Dec. 31

| Per Share Data ($) | 2010 | 2009 | 2008 | 2007 | 2006 | 2005 | 2004 | 2003 | 2002 | 2001 |
|---|---|---|---|---|---|---|---|---|---|---|
| Tangible Book Value | 6.49 | 3.97 | 2.48 | 5.71 | NM | NM | 3.05 | 2.67 | NM | 3.19 |
| Cash Flow | 4.72 | 3.93 | 3.50 | 2.88 | 2.57 | 2.12 | 2.16 | 1.60 | 1.40 | 1.08 |
| Earnings | 4.06 | 3.34 | 3.21 | 2.62 | 2.13 | 1.74 | 1.82 | 1.34 | 1.12 | 0.84 |
| S&P Core Earnings | 4.09 | 3.34 | 3.21 | 2.62 | 2.18 | 1.57 | 1.45 | 1.18 | 0.99 | 1.07 |
| Dividends | Nil | Nil | Nil | Nil | Nil | Nil | Nil | Nil | Nil | Nil |
| Payout Ratio | Nil | Nil | Nil | Nil | Nil | Nil | Nil | Nil | Nil | Nil |
| Prices:High | 81.00 | 63.09 | 81.84 | 81.53 | 51.64 | 51.57 | 49.80 | 33.42 | 39.25 | 85.38 |
| Prices:Low | 55.97 | 30.00 | 32.21 | 48.55 | 37.06 | 33.99 | 33.10 | 19.79 | 17.86 | 22.33 |
| P/E Ratio:High | 20 | 19 | 25 | 31 | 24 | 30 | 27 | 25 | 35 | NM |
| P/E Ratio:Low | 14 | 9 | 10 | 19 | 17 | 20 | 18 | 15 | 16 | NM |

| Income Statement Analysis (Million $) | | | | | | | | | | |
|---|---|---|---|---|---|---|---|---|---|---|
| Revenue | 1,643 | 1,499 | 1,575 | 1,473 | 1,280 | 1,158 | 1,105 | 958 | 890 | 859 |
| Operating Income | 511 | 452 | 436 | 389 | 355 | 330 | 321 | 271 | 251 | 258 |
| Depreciation | 62.6 | 57.3 | 29.1 | 27.5 | 46.2 | 43.7 | 41.9 | 33.8 | 37.2 | 34.0 |
| Interest Expense | 12.1 | 11.0 | 38.5 | 56.5 | 51.7 | 24.7 | 10.1 | 2.37 | 2.48 | 1.26 |
| Pretax Income | 438 | 387 | 372 | 323 | 263 | 275 | 286 | 224 | 195 | 147 |
| Effective Tax Rate | NA | 16.4% | 13.4% | 17.1% | 15.5% | 26.4% | 21.6% | 23.6% | 22.1% | 22.3% |
| Net Income | 382 | 323 | 322 | 268 | 222 | 202 | 224 | 171 | 152 | 115 |
| S&P Core Earnings | 385 | 324 | 322 | 268 | 227 | 183 | 179 | 150 | 134 | 147 |

| Balance Sheet & Other Financial Data (Million $) | | | | | | | | | | |
|---|---|---|---|---|---|---|---|---|---|---|
| Cash | 946 | 630 | 429 | 693 | 514 | 494 | 539 | 357 | 313 | 227 |
| Current Assets | 1,581 | 1,172 | 956 | 1,237 | 1,000 | 913 | 974 | 715 | 636 | 523 |
| Total Assets | 2,328 | 1,916 | 1,623 | 1,881 | 1,617 | 1,429 | 1,460 | 1,131 | 1,011 | 887 |
| Current Liabilities | 386 | 395 | 290 | 658 | 686 | 604 | 493 | 379 | 320 | 281 |
| Long Term Debt | 700 | 500 | 500 | 500 | 500 | 500 | 250 | 125 | Nil | Nil |
| Common Equity | 1,069 | 848 | 661 | 586 | 362 | 284 | 679 | 590 | 665 | 582 |
| Total Capital | 1,769 | 1,348 | 1,161 | 1,086 | 862 | 784 | 929 | 715 | 665 | 582 |
| Capital Expenditures | 62.7 | 93.8 | 69.1 | 60.3 | 51.4 | 51.0 | 66.2 | 34.6 | 37.9 | 42.4 |
| Cash Flow | 444 | 381 | 352 | 296 | 268 | 246 | 266 | 205 | 189 | 148 |
| Current Ratio | 4.1 | 2.9 | 3.3 | 1.9 | 1.5 | 1.5 | 2.0 | 1.9 | 2.0 | 1.9 |
| % Long Term Debt of Capitalization | 39.6 | 37.1 | 43.1 | 46.0 | 58.0 | 63.8 | 26.9 | 17.5 | Nil | Nil |
| % Net Income of Revenue | 23.2 | 21.6 | 20.5 | 18.2 | 17.4 | 17.4 | 20.3 | 17.8 | 17.1 | 13.3 |
| % Return on Assets | 18.0 | 18.3 | 18.4 | 15.3 | 14.6 | 14.0 | 17.3 | 15.9 | 16.0 | 14.5 |
| % Return on Equity | 39.8 | 42.9 | 51.7 | 56.5 | 68.8 | 42.0 | 35.3 | 27.2 | 24.3 | 22.2 |

Data as orig reptd.; bef. results of disc opers/spec. items. Per share data adj. for stk. divs.; EPS diluted. E-Estimated. NA-Not Available. NM-Not Meaningful. NR-Not Ranked. UR-Under Review.

**Office:** 34 Maple Street, Milford, MA 01757-3696.
**Telephone:** 508-478-2000.
**Email:** info@waters.com
**Website:** http://www.waters.com

**Chrmn, Pres & CEO:** D.A. Berthiaume
**CFO & Chief Admin Officer:** J.A. Ornell
**Chief Acctg Officer & Cntlr:** W.J. Curry
**Secy & General Counsel:** M.T. Beaudouin

**Board Members:** J. Bekenstein, M. J. Berendt, D. A. Berthiaume, E. W. Conard, L. H. Glimcher, C. A. Kuebler, W. J. Miller, J. A. Reed, T. P. Salice

**Founded:** 1991
**Domicile:** Delaware
**Employees:** 5,381

# STANDARD &POOR'S

## armaceuticals Inc.

| | Price | 12-Mo. Target Price | Investment Style |
|---|---|---|---|
| ion **BUY** ★★★★☆ | $65.83 (as of Nov 28, 2011) | $80.00 | Large-Cap Blend |

ealth Care
Pharmaceuticals

**Summary** This company produces generic and branded drugs. In December 2009, Watson acquired international generic drugmaker Arrow Group for about $1.8 billion in cash and stock.

## Key Stock Statistics (Source S&P, Vickers, company reports)

| | | | | | | | | |
|---|---|---|---|---|---|---|---|---|
| 52-Wk Range | $73.35– 48.20 | S&P Oper. EPS 2011E | 4.60 | Market Capitalization(B) | $8.371 | Beta | | 0.43 |
| Trailing 12-Month EPS | $1.45 | S&P Oper. EPS 2012E | 5.70 | Yield (%) | Nil | S&P 3-Yr. Proj. EPS CAGR(%) | | 15 |
| Trailing 12-Month P/E | 45.4 | P/E on S&P Oper. EPS 2011E | 14.3 | Dividend Rate/Share | Nil | S&P Credit Rating | | BBB |
| $10K Invested 5 Yrs Ago | $25,297 | Common Shares Outstg. (M) | 127.2 | Institutional Ownership (%) | 91 | | | |

## Price Performance

30-Week Mov. Avg. — 10-Week Mov. Avg. - - GAAP Earnings vs. Previous Year   Volume Above Avg. STARS
12-Mo. Target Price — Relative Strength — ▲ Up ▼ Down ► No Change   Below Avg.

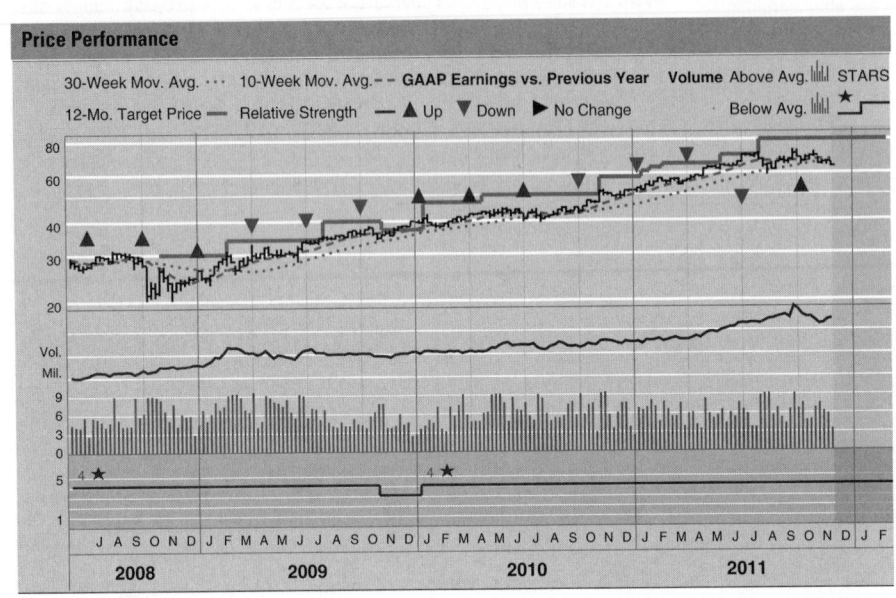

Options: ASE, CBOE, Ph

Analysis prepared by Equity Analyst **Herman Saftlas** on Nov 28, 2011, when the stock traded at **$65.75**.

## Highlights

► We project 2012 revenue growth of about 20% from the $4.5 billion that we forecast for 2011. The gain should largely reflect a sharp rise in generics sales, boosted by shared exclusivity generic sales of Lipitor, and contributions from generic versions of Toprol XL, Lovenox and Lidoderm. The recent acquisition of Greek generic drugmaker Specifar should boost foreign sales. We also project robust growth for branded drugs, supported by gains in Rapaflo, Gelnique and Trelstar, and Prochieve (subject to FDA clearance). We also see a sharp rise in distribution revenues in 2012.

► In our opinion, adjusted gross margins in 2012 will probably be comparable with the 44% that we estimate for 2011, with higher volume and manufacturing efficiencies offsetting a less profitable sales mix. We also think net margins should benefit from reduced SG&A and R&D expense ratios, while net non-operating expenses are also likely to decline.

► After an estimated adjusted effective tax rate similar to the 36% indicated for 2011, we project cash EPS of $5.70 for 2012, up from an estimated $4.60 in 2011.

## Investment Rationale/Risk

► We believe that WPI's diversified business platform, which comprises growing positions in generics, branded drugs and drug distribution, coupled with cost-streamlining measures, will provide the underpinnings for above-average EPS growth in the years ahead. We credit WPI with efforts to expand its overseas footprint through the acquisitions of Specifar, a generic drugmaker in Greece, and the Arrow Group, a British generics firm that brought valuable marketing rights to generic Lipitor. WPI has about 130 ANDAs under review at the FDA, as well as a large number of filings in foreign countries. We also see long-term opportunities for the branded business.

► Risks to our recommendation and target price include intensified competitive pressures in key generic and branded product lines, as well as possible R&D pipeline disappointments.

► Our 12-month target price of $80 applies a peer-parity P/E of 14X to our 2012 cash EPS estimate. Our target price is also supported by our DCF model, which assumes decelerating cash flow growth over the next 10 years, a WACC of 9.1%, and perpetuity growth of 2%.

## Qualitative Risk Assessment

| LOW | MEDIUM | HIGH |
|---|---|---|

Our risk assessment reflects risks common to the generic pharmaceutical business, which include the need to successfully develop generic products, obtain regulatory approvals and legally challenge branded patents. However, we believe these risks are offset by the company's wide and diverse generic portfolio and the balance afforded by WPI's branded drug business.

## Quantitative Evaluations

**S&P Quality Ranking**  B-

| D | C | B- | B | B+ | A- | A | A+ |
|---|---|---|---|---|---|---|---|

**Relative Strength Rank**  MODERATE

68

LOWEST = 1                    HIGHEST = 99

## Revenue/Earnings Data

### Revenue (Million $)

| | 1Q | 2Q | 3Q | 4Q | Year |
|---|---|---|---|---|---|
| 2011 | 876.5 | 1,082 | 1,082 | -- | -- |
| 2010 | 856.5 | 875.3 | 882.4 | 952.7 | 3,567 |
| 2009 | 667.4 | 677.8 | 662.1 | 785.7 | 2,793 |
| 2008 | 627.0 | 622.6 | 640.7 | 645.2 | 2,536 |
| 2007 | 671.6 | 603.0 | 594.7 | 627.3 | 2,497 |
| 2006 | 407.2 | 510.4 | 440.5 | 621.2 | 1,979 |

### Earnings Per Share ($)

| | 1Q | 2Q | 3Q | 4Q | Year |
|---|---|---|---|---|---|
| 2011 | 0.36 | 0.42 | 0.54 | E1.61 | E4.60 |
| 2010 | 0.57 | 0.57 | 0.21 | 0.15 | 1.48 |
| 2009 | 0.43 | 0.46 | 0.55 | 0.51 | 1.96 |
| 2008 | 0.45 | 0.53 | 0.62 | 0.50 | 2.09 |
| 2007 | 0.29 | 0.33 | 0.31 | 0.34 | 1.27 |
| 2006 | 0.23 | -0.15 | 0.31 | -4.80 | -4.37 |

Fiscal year ended Dec. 31. Next earnings report expected: Mid February. EPS Estimates based on S&P Operating Earnings; historical GAAP earnings are as reported.

## Dividend Data

No cash dividends have been paid.

---

**Please read the Required Disclosures and Analyst Certification on the last page of this report.**

The *McGraw-Hill* Companies

# Watson Pharmaceuticals Inc.

**STANDARD &POOR'S**

## Business Summary November 28, 2011

CORPORATE PROFILE. Watson Pharmaceuticals is a leading maker of generic pharmaceuticals that targets difficult to produce niche off-patent drugs. WPI significantly expanded its U.S. generic business with the acquisitions of Andrx Corp. in 2006, and U.K.-based Arrow Group in late 2009. WPI also offers a line of specialty branded pharmaceuticals, largely in the areas of urology, cancer and women's health.

Many WPI pharmaceuticals incorporate the company's novel proprietary drug delivery systems, such as transmucosal, vaginal and transdermal systems that allow for defined rates of drug release. Generic drugs accounted for about 65% of revenues and 88% of operating income in 2010, branded drugs for 11% and 7%, and distribution operations for 24% and 5%. Third-party manufactured products accounted for about 57% of Watson's revenues in 2010.

WPI markets some 160 generic drug products in the U.S. and 54 in Canada, comprising a broad cross section of therapeutic categories. Key segments include oral contraceptives, analgesics, antihypertensives, diuretics, antiulcers, antipsychotics, anti-inflammatories, analgesics, hormone replacements, antispasmodics and antidiarrheals. Arrow Group markets some 50 generic products in Europe, Asia, South Africa and Australia.

During 2010, WPI filed 34 Abbreviated New Drug Applications (ANDAs) with the FDA, and a total of 145 applications globally. As of July 2011, WPI had over 130 ANDAs pending before the FDA, of which some 34% comprised either first to file or shared exclusive opportunities. An additional 600 applications are on file outside of the U.S.

Branded pharmaceuticals comprise treatments for incontinence, cancer, pain management and other conditions. Key products include Trelstar, a treatment for prostate cancer; Oxytrol oxybutynin transdermal patch and Gelnique oxytrol gel to treat urinary incontinence; Androderm, a testosterone transdermal patch; Rapaflo, a treatment for enlarged prostates; ella, a novel oral emergency contraceptive; Prochieve, a drug to prevent pre-term birth; and Crinone, a treatment for infertility. WPI's branded rights to Ferrlecit, a nephrology product used to treat iron deficiency anemia, ended at the end of 2009.

The company sells its products primarily through distributors and chain drug stores, such as McKesson Corp. (11% of net revenues in 2010) and Walgreen (14%).

## Company Financials Fiscal Year Ended Dec. 31

| Per Share Data ($) | 2010 | 2009 | 2008 | 2007 | 2006 | 2005 | 2004 | 2003 | 2002 | 2001 |
|---|---|---|---|---|---|---|---|---|---|---|
| Tangible Book Value | 5.86 | 3.06 | 6.51 | 3.56 | 0.09 | 8.81 | 7.97 | 5.54 | 4.33 | 3.79 |
| Cash Flow | 3.75 | 3.53 | 3.48 | 3.37 | -2.23 | 2.87 | 2.07 | 2.78 | 2.45 | 2.01 |
| Earnings | 1.48 | 1.96 | 2.09 | 1.27 | -4.37 | 1.21 | 1.27 | 1.86 | 1.64 | 1.07 |
| S&P Core Earnings | 2.02 | 2.12 | 1.96 | 1.24 | -4.32 | 1.09 | 1.16 | 1.64 | 1.36 | 0.52 |
| Dividends | Nil | Nil | Nil | Nil | Nil | Nil | Nil | Nil | Nil | Nil |
| Payout Ratio | Nil | Nil | Nil | Nil | Nil | Nil | Nil | Nil | Nil | Nil |
| Prices:High | 52.20 | 40.25 | 32.70 | 33.91 | 35.27 | 36.93 | 49.19 | 50.12 | 33.25 | 66.39 |
| Prices:Low | 37.26 | 23.05 | 20.17 | 25.02 | 21.35 | 27.99 | 24.50 | 26.90 | 17.95 | 26.50 |
| P/E Ratio:High | 35 | 21 | 16 | 27 | NM | 31 | 39 | 27 | 20 | 62 |
| P/E Ratio:Low | 25 | 12 | 10 | 20 | NM | 23 | 19 | 14 | 11 | 25 |

### Income Statement Analysis (Million $)

| | 2010 | 2009 | 2008 | 2007 | 2006 | 2005 | 2004 | 2003 | 2002 | 2001 |
|---|---|---|---|---|---|---|---|---|---|---|
| Revenue | 3,567 | 2,793 | 2,536 | 2,497 | 1,979 | 1,646 | 1,641 | 1,458 | 1,223 | 1,161 |
| Operating Income | 716 | 638 | 539 | 515 | 364 | 450 | 419 | 439 | 386 | 404 |
| Depreciation | 282 | 189 | 171 | 254 | 218 | 207 | 107 | 100 | 86.6 | 101 |
| Interest Expense | 84.1 | 34.2 | 28.2 | 44.5 | 22.1 | 14.5 | 13.3 | 25.8 | 22.1 | 27.8 |
| Pretax Income | 251 | 363 | 358 | 224 | -411 | 219 | 237 | 318 | 279 | 199 |
| Effective Tax Rate | NA | 38.8% | 33.5% | 37.1% | NM | 37.0% | 36.1% | 36.2% | 37.0% | 41.5% |
| Net Income | 183 | 222 | 238 | 141 | -445 | 138 | 151 | 203 | 176 | 116 |
| S&P Core Earnings | 251 | 240 | 222 | 138 | -441 | 123 | 137 | 178 | 146 | 56.3 |

### Balance Sheet & Other Financial Data (Million $)

| | 2010 | 2009 | 2008 | 2007 | 2006 | 2005 | 2004 | 2003 | 2002 | 2001 |
|---|---|---|---|---|---|---|---|---|---|---|
| Cash | 294 | 215 | 521 | 216 | 161 | 630 | 680 | 574 | 273 | 329 |
| Current Assets | 1,799 | 1,771 | 1,458 | 1,174 | 1,262 | 1,360 | 1,370 | 1,323 | 921 | 890 |
| Total Assets | 5,827 | 5,992 | 3,678 | 3,472 | 3,761 | 3,080 | 3,244 | 3,283 | 2,663 | 2,528 |
| Current Liabilities | 821 | 1,052 | 482 | 445 | 690 | 246 | 256 | 339 | 375 | 245 |
| Long Term Debt | 1,016 | 1,150 | 825 | 899 | 1,124 | 588 | 588 | 723 | 332 | 416 |
| Common Equity | 3,283 | 3,023 | 2,109 | 1,849 | 1,680 | 2,104 | 2,243 | 2,057 | 1,798 | 1,672 |
| Total Capital | 4,299 | 4,481 | 3,108 | 2,928 | 3,008 | 2,692 | 2,831 | 2,924 | 2,282 | 2,274 |
| Capital Expenditures | 67.5 | 71.9 | 100 | 75.1 | 44.4 | 78.8 | 69.2 | 151 | 87.5 | 62.0 |
| Cash Flow | 465 | 411 | 409 | 395 | -227 | 345 | 258 | 303 | 262 | 218 |
| Current Ratio | 2.2 | 1.7 | 3.0 | 2.6 | 1.8 | 5.5 | 5.4 | 3.9 | 2.5 | 3.6 |
| % Long Term Debt of Capitalization | 23.6 | 25.7 | 26.5 | 30.7 | 37.4 | 21.8 | 20.8 | 24.7 | 14.5 | 18.3 |
| % Net Income of Revenue | 5.1 | 8.0 | 9.4 | 5.7 | NM | 8.4 | 9.2 | 13.9 | 14.4 | 10.0 |
| % Return on Assets | 3.1 | 4.6 | 6.7 | 3.9 | NM | 4.4 | 4.6 | 6.8 | 6.8 | 4.6 |
| % Return on Equity | 5.8 | 8.7 | 12.1 | 8.0 | NM | 6.4 | 7.0 | 10.5 | 10.1 | 7.2 |

Data as orig reptd.; bef. results of disc opers/spec. items. Per share data adj. for stk. divs.; EPS diluted. E-Estimated. NA-Not Available. NM-Not Meaningful. NR-Not Ranked. UR-Under Review.

**Office:** Morris Corporate Center III, 400 Interpace Parkway, Parsippany, NJ 07054.
**Telephone:** 862-261-7000.
**Website:** http://www.watson.com
**Chrmn:** A.L. Turner

**Pres & CEO:** P.M. Bisaro
**EVP, CFO, Chief Acctg Officer & Treas:** R.T. Joyce
**Secy & General Counsel:** D.A. Buchen
**Investor Contact:** P. Eisenhaur (862-261-7488)

**Board Members:** P. M. Bisaro, C. W. Bodine, M. J. Fedida, M. J. Feldman, A. F. Hummel, C. M. Klema, J. Michelson, A. S. Tabatznik, R. R. Taylor, A. L. Turner, F. G. Weiss

**Founded:** 1983
**Domicile:** Nevada
**Employees:** 6,030

*The McGraw-Hill Companies*

# WellPoint Inc

**STANDARD &POOR'S**

| S&P Recommendation | BUY ★★★★☆ | Price $63.70 (as of Nov 25, 2011) | 12-Mo. Target Price $78.00 | Investment Style Large-Cap Growth |

**GICS Sector** Health Care
**Sub-Industry** Managed Health Care

**Summary** This managed health organization is the largest in the U.S., serving 34.2 million members mainly under the Blue Cross and/or Blue Shield license in 14 states.

## Key Stock Statistics (Source S&P, Vickers, company reports)

| | | | | | | |
|---|---|---|---|---|---|---|
| 52-Wk Range | $81.92–55.56 | S&P Oper. EPS 2011**E** | 7.10 | Market Capitalization(B) | $22.159 | Beta | 0.99 |
| Trailing 12-Month EPS | $7.61 | S&P Oper. EPS 2012**E** | 7.60 | Yield (%) | 1.57 | S&P 3-Yr. Proj. EPS CAGR(%) | 7 |
| Trailing 12-Month P/E | 8.4 | P/E on S&P Oper. EPS 2011**E** | 9.0 | Dividend Rate/Share | $1.00 | S&P Credit Rating | A- |
| $10K Invested 5 Yrs Ago | $8,894 | Common Shares Outstg. (M) | 347.9 | Institutional Ownership (%) | 88 | | |

## Price Performance

30-Week Mov. Avg. · · · 10-Week Mov. Avg. - - GAAP Earnings vs. Previous Year   Volume Above Avg. STARS
12-Mo. Target Price — Relative Strength ▲ Up ▼ Down ▶ No Change   Below Avg.

Options: ASE, CBOE, Ph

Analysis prepared by Equity Analyst **Phillip Seligman** on Nov 01, 2011, when the stock traded at **$67.16**.

## Highlights

➤ We look for operating revenues to rise by 4% to $61.1 billion in 2011, and by 4.6% to $62.8 billion in 2012. Drivers we see include continued gains in National Accounts enrollment; higher Medicare Advantage (MA) enrollment, aided by age-ins and a recent acquisition; and higher Medicaid enrollment. But we see these gains partly offset by attrition within National Accounts as each year progresses and fully insured membership declines.

➤ We expect benefit expenses to rise 190 basis points (bps) as a percentage of premiums (medical loss ratio, or MLR) in 2011 and another 50 bps in 2012. We attribute this trend mainly to health care reform, lower favorable claims reserve development in 2011 and none in 2012, the assumption of more normalized medical cost trends, and rate pressures in the Medicaid business. We expect the SG&A expense ratio to decline on cost controls.

➤ We estimate 2011 operating EPS of $7.10, versus 2010's $6.74, as the lower net income we forecast is outweighed by share buybacks. We look for $7.60 in 2012, aided by SG&A leverage and a lower average share count.

## Investment Rationale/Risk

➤ We think WLP has been executing well in a soft economy, and we believe it has the scale, well-diversified membership and strong cash flow to manage better than most insurers amid health care reform. WLP has initiatives under way to improve operating efficiencies, and launched programs to improve the quality of, and lower costs for, medical care. One program we view as promising is its plan to expand the senior-oriented neighborhood care center model of its recent CareMore Health Group acquisition into its other markets. The only significant weakness we see is its large exposure to individual and small group markets with MLRs below the health care reform's mandated floors, requiring rebates in 2012. Separately, we believe the initiation in 2011 of a $0.25 per quarter cash dividend enhances the stock's attractiveness.

➤ Risks to our recommendation and target price include enrollment losses above our expectations, higher medical cost trends, and unfavorable regulatory changes.

➤ Our 12-month target price of $78 reflects a near peer-level multiple of 10.2X our 2012 EPS estimate.

## Qualitative Risk Assessment

| LOW | MEDIUM | HIGH |

Our risk assessment reflects WLP's leadership in the highly fragmented managed care market. We believe that its geographic, market, and product diversity and Blue Cross/Blue Shield tie are competitive strengths. However, we think its commercial enrollment growth going forward will be limited by heightened competition amid the difficult economic environment, but it should see meaningful Medicare and Medicaid enrollment growth.

## Quantitative Evaluations

**S&P Quality Ranking** B+

| D | C | B- | B | B+ | A- | A | A+ |

**Relative Strength Rank** MODERATE
54
LOWEST = 1   HIGHEST = 99

## Revenue/Earnings Data

**Revenue (Million $)**

| | 1Q | 2Q | 3Q | 4Q | Year |
|---|---|---|---|---|---|
| 2011 | 14,894 | 15,101 | 15,398 | -- | -- |
| 2010 | 15,099 | 14,457 | 14,598 | 14,648 | 58,802 |
| 2009 | 15,143 | 15,413 | 15,425 | 19,047 | 65,028 |
| 2008 | 15,554 | 15,667 | 14,961 | 15,070 | 61,251 |
| 2007 | 15,079 | 15,260 | 15,234 | 15,561 | 61,134 |
| 2006 | 13,820 | 14,152 | 14,426 | 14,556 | 56,953 |

**Earnings Per Share ($)**

| | 1Q | 2Q | 3Q | 4Q | Year |
|---|---|---|---|---|---|
| 2011 | 2.44 | 1.89 | 1.90 | E1.11 | E7.10 |
| 2010 | 1.96 | 1.71 | 1.84 | 1.40 | 6.94 |
| 2009 | 1.16 | 1.43 | 1.53 | 5.95 | 9.88 |
| 2008 | 1.07 | 1.44 | 1.60 | 0.65 | 4.76 |
| 2007 | 1.26 | 1.35 | 1.45 | 1.51 | 5.56 |
| 2006 | 1.09 | 1.17 | 1.29 | 1.28 | 4.82 |

Fiscal year ended Dec. 31. Next earnings report expected: Late January. EPS Estimates based on S&P Operating Earnings; historical GAAP earnings are as reported.

## Dividend Data (Dates: mm/dd Payment Date: mm/dd/yy)

| Amount ($) | Date Decl. | Ex-Div. Date | Stk. of Record | Payment Date |
|---|---|---|---|---|
| 0.250 | 02/23 | 03/08 | 03/10 | 03/25/11 |
| 0.250 | 07/27 | 09/07 | 09/09 | 09/23/11 |
| 0.250 | 10/26 | 12/07 | 12/09 | 12/23/11 |

Dividends have been paid since 2011. Source: Company reports.

# WellPoint Inc

STANDARD
&POOR'S

## Business Summary November 01, 2011

CORPORATE OVERVIEW. WellPoint, Inc. was formed by the merger consummated on November 30, 2004, between publicly traded managed care giants Anthem, Inc. and WellPoint Health Networks Inc. (WHN). All prior historical data in this report are for Anthem. WLP is the largest publicly traded commercial health benefits company in the U.S., serving 34.4 million members as of September 30, 2011 (versus 33.3 million at December 31, 2010), and an independent licensee of the Blue Cross and Blue Shield Association. It serves members as the Blue Cross licensee for California and the Blue Cross or Blue Cross and Blue Shield (BCBS) licensee in all or parts of 13 other states. WLP also serves members in various parts of the U.S. as UniCare and conducts insurance operations in all 50 states and Puerto Rico through an affiliate.

WLP's network-based managed care plans include preferred provider organizations (PPOs), health maintenance organizations (HMOs), point-of-service plans (POS), traditional indemnity plans and other hybrid plans, including consumer-driven health plans (CDHPs), hospital only, and limited benefit products. It also provides managed care services to self-funded customers. In addition, WLP provides specialty and other products and services, including

pharmacy benefit management, group life and disability insurance, dental, vision, behavioral health, workers compensation and long-term care insurance. Approximately 93% of 2010 operating revenue was derived from premium income and 6% from administrative services and other revenues.

The customer base includes local groups (15,296,000 members as of September 30, 2011, versus 15,216,000 as of December 31, 2010); individuals under age 65 (1,855,000 versus 1,905,000); National Accounts (multi-state employers primarily headquartered in WLP's service area with 1,000 or more eligible employees, with 5% or more located outside headquarters state -- 7,435,000 versus 7,029,000); BlueCard (enrollees of non-owned BCBS plans who receive benefits in WLP's BCBS markets -- 4,961,000 versus 4,711,000); Seniors (1,442,000 versus 1,215,000); State Sponsored (1,849,000 versus 1,756,000); and Federal Employee Program (1,517,000 versus 1,447,000).

## Company Financials Fiscal Year Ended Dec. 31

| Per Share Data ($) | 2010 | 2009 | 2008 | 2007 | 2006 | 2005 | 2004 | 2003 | 2002 | 2001 |
|---|---|---|---|---|---|---|---|---|---|---|
| Tangible Book Value | 6.75 | 7.42 | NM | 0.60 | 2.92 | 2.78 | 2.03 | 8.44 | 5.76 | 7.71 |
| Cash Flow | NA | NA | 5.84 | 6.24 | 4.82 | 3.94 | 2.05 | 3.59 | 2.90 | 2.23 |
| Earnings | 6.94 | 9.88 | 4.76 | 5.56 | 4.82 | 3.94 | 3.05 | 2.73 | 2.26 | 1.65 |
| S&P Core Earnings | 6.70 | 5.82 | 6.00 | 5.50 | 4.79 | 3.82 | 2.69 | 2.49 | 1.93 | 1.16 |
| Dividends | Nil | Nil | Nil | Nil | Nil | Nil | Nil | Nil | Nil | Nil |
| Payout Ratio | Nil | Nil | Nil | Nil | Nil | Nil | Nil | Nil | Nil | Nil |
| Prices:High | 70.00 | 60.89 | 90.00 | 89.95 | 80.37 | 80.40 | 58.88 | 41.45 | 37.75 | 25.95 |
| Prices:Low | 46.52 | 29.32 | 27.50 | 72.90 | 65.50 | 54.58 | 36.10 | 26.50 | 23.20 | 18.00 |
| P/E Ratio:High | 10 | 6 | 19 | 16 | 17 | 20 | 19 | 15 | 17 | 16 |
| P/E Ratio:Low | 7 | 3 | 6 | 13 | 14 | 14 | 12 | 10 | 10 | 11 |

| Income Statement Analysis (Million $) | | | | | | | | | | |
|---|---|---|---|---|---|---|---|---|---|---|
| Revenue | 58,802 | 65,028 | 61,251 | 61,134 | 56,953 | 45,136 | 20,815 | 16,771 | 13,282 | 10,445 |
| Operating Income | NA | NA | 4,297 | 6,117 | 5,748 | 4,750 | 2,072 | 1,595 | 1,093 | 733 |
| Depreciation | NA | NA | 564 | 411 | 430 | 634 | 279 | 245 | 157 | 121 |
| Interest Expense | 419 | 447 | 470 | 448 | 404 | 226 | 142 | 131 | 98.5 | 60.2 |
| Pretax Income | 4,354 | 7,403 | 3,122 | 5,258 | 4,914 | 3,890 | 1,443 | 1,219 | 808 | 525 |
| Effective Tax Rate | NA | 35.9% | 20.2% | 36.4% | 37.0% | 36.7% | 33.5% | 36.1% | 31.6% | 35.0% |
| Net Income | 2,887 | 4,746 | 2,491 | 3,345 | 3,095 | 2,464 | 960 | 774 | 549 | 342 |
| S&P Core Earnings | 2,785 | 2,797 | 3,143 | 3,308 | 3,077 | 2,402 | 842 | 708 | 467 | 240 |

| Balance Sheet & Other Financial Data (Million $) | | | | | | | | | | |
|---|---|---|---|---|---|---|---|---|---|---|
| Cash | 1,789 | 4,816 | 2,208 | 6,535 | 2,602 | 2,897 | 1,457 | 523 | 744 | 406 |
| Current Assets | NA | NA | 12,130 | 13,032 | 11,807 | 25,945 | 19,358 | 8,865 | 7,877 | 5,300 |
| Total Assets | 50,167 | 52,125 | 48,403 | 52,060 | 51,760 | 51,405 | 39,738 | 13,439 | 12,293 | 6,277 |
| Current Liabilities | NA | NA | 15,020 | 14,388 | 15,323 | 14,857 | 11,571 | 4,772 | 4,449 | 2,963 |
| Long Term Debt | 8,148 | 8,338 | 7,834 | 9,024 | 6,493 | 6,325 | 4,277 | 1,663 | 1,659 | 818 |
| Common Equity | 23,813 | 24,863 | 21,432 | 22,990 | 25,299 | 25,755 | 20,331 | 6,000 | 5,362 | 2,060 |
| Total Capital | NA | NA | 31,365 | 35,018 | 35,142 | 35,386 | 27,204 | 8,188 | 7,412 | 2,878 |
| Capital Expenditures | NA | NA | 346 | 322 | 194 | 162 | 137 | 111 | 123 | 70.4 |
| Cash Flow | NA | NA | 3,054 | 3,756 | 3,095 | 2,464 | 1,239 | 1,019 | 706 | 463 |
| Current Ratio | 1.9 | 1.9 | 0.8 | 0.9 | 0.8 | 1.7 | 1.7 | 1.9 | 1.8 | 1.8 |
| % Long Term Debt of Capitalization | 24.9 | 25.1 | 25.0 | 25.8 | 18.5 | 17.9 | 15.7 | 20.3 | 22.4 | 28.4 |
| % Net Income of Revenue | 4.9 | 7.3 | 4.1 | 5.5 | 62.1 | 5.5 | 4.7 | 4.6 | 50.8 | 35.6 |
| % Return on Assets | 5.6 | 9.4 | 5.0 | 6.5 | 6.0 | 5.4 | 3.6 | 6.0 | 5.9 | 5.7 |
| % Return on Equity | 11.9 | 20.5 | 11.2 | 14.1 | 12.1 | 10.7 | 7.2 | 13.6 | 14.8 | 17.2 |

Data as orig reptd.; bef. results of disc opers/spec. items. Per share data adj. for stk. divs.; EPS diluted. E-Estimated. NA-Not Available. NM-Not Meaningful. NR-Not Ranked. UR-Under Review.

**Office:** 120 Monument Circle, Indianapolis, IN 46204-4903.
**Telephone:** 317-488-6000.
**Email:**
anthem.corporate.communications@anthem.com
**Website:** http://www.wellpoint.com

**Chrmn, Pres & CEO:** A.F. Braly
**Investor Contact:** W.S. Deveydt (317-488-6390)
**EVP & CFO:** W.S. Deveydt
**SVP & Treas:** D. Kretschmer

**Chief Acctg Officer & Cntlr:** J.E. Gallina
**Board Members:** L. D. Baker, Jr., S. B. Bayh, A. F. Braly, S. P. Burke, R. Dixon, Jr., J. A. Hill, W. Y. Jobe, W. G. Mays, R. G. Peru, W. J. Ryan, G. A. Schaefer, Jr., J. M. Ward

**Founded:** 1944
**Domicile:** Indiana
**Employees:** 37,500

# Wells Fargo & Co

**STANDARD &POOR'S**

| S&P Recommendation **BUY** ★★★★☆ | Price<br>$23.51 (as of Nov 25, 2011) | 12-Mo. Target Price<br>$30.00 | Investment Style<br>Large-Cap Blend |
|---|---|---|---|

**GICS Sector** Financials
**Sub-Industry** Diversified Banks

**Summary** This bank holding company provides banking, insurance, investment, mortgage and consumer finance services throughout North America.

## Key Stock Statistics (Source S&P, Vickers, company reports)

| | | | | | | | | |
|---|---|---|---|---|---|---|---|---|
| 52-Wk Range | $34.25–22.58 | S&P Oper. EPS 2011**E** | 2.83 | Market Capitalization(B) | $123.981 | Beta | 1.31 |
| Trailing 12-Month EPS | $2.70 | S&P Oper. EPS 2012**E** | 2.97 | Yield (%) | 2.04 | S&P 3-Yr. Proj. EPS CAGR(%) | 10 |
| Trailing 12-Month P/E | 8.7 | P/E on S&P Oper. EPS 2011**E** | 8.3 | Dividend Rate/Share | $0.48 | S&P Credit Rating | AA- |
| $10K Invested 5 Yrs Ago | $7,494 | Common Shares Outstg. (M) | 5,273.5 | Institutional Ownership (%) | 80 | | |

## Price Performance

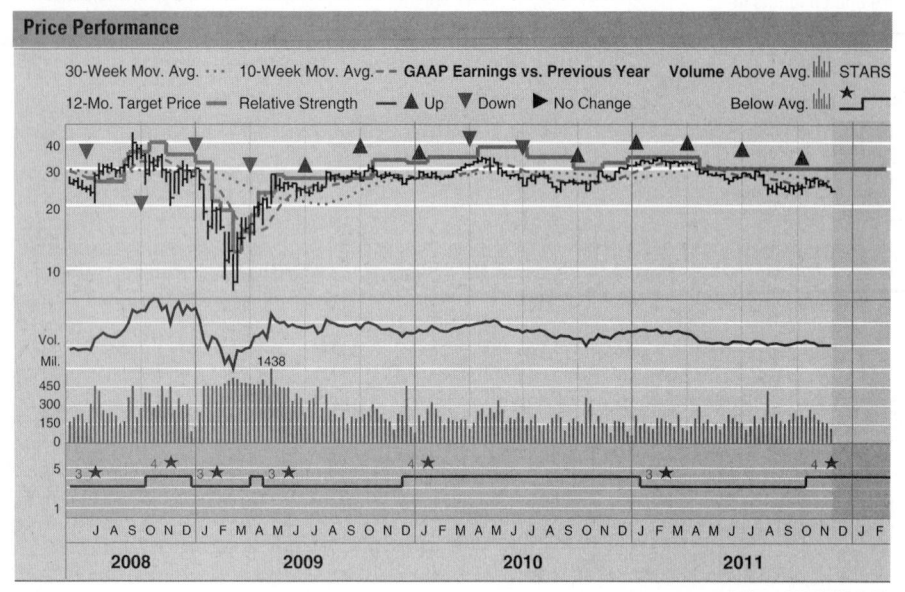

30-Week Mov. Avg. · · · 10-Week Mov. Avg. - - GAAP Earnings vs. Previous Year   Volume Above Avg. |ılıl STARS
12-Mo. Target Price — Relative Strength — ▲ Up ▼ Down ► No Change   Below Avg. |ılıl ★

Options: ASE, CBOE, P, Ph

Analysis prepared by Equity Analyst **Erik Oja** on Oct 31, 2011, when the stock traded at **$26.42**.

## Qualitative Risk Assessment

| LOW | **MEDIUM** | HIGH |
|---|---|---|

Our risk assessment reflects what we see as solid business fundamentals and a strong customer base, offset by increased risk stemming from the Wachovia acquisition combined with declining tangible capital levels.

## Quantitative Evaluations

**S&P Quality Ranking**                    A-

| D | C | B- | B | B+ | **A-** | A | A+ |
|---|---|---|---|---|---|---|---|

**Relative Strength Rank**                    MODERATE

45

LOWEST = 1                                    HIGHEST = 99

## Revenue/Earnings Data

**Revenue (Million $)**

| | 1Q | 2Q | 3Q | 4Q | Year |
|---|---|---|---|---|---|
| 2011 | 22,150 | 22,092 | 21,264 | -- | -- |
| 2010 | 23,526 | 23,417 | 22,906 | 22,474 | 93,249 |
| 2009 | 23,954 | 25,044 | 24,750 | 24,888 | 98,636 |
| 2008 | 13,652 | 13,728 | 12,772 | 11,828 | 51,980 |
| 2007 | 12,570 | 13,268 | 13,796 | 13,959 | 53,596 |
| 2006 | 11,217 | 11,882 | 12,286 | 12,594 | 47,979 |

**Earnings Per Share ($)**

| | | | | | |
|---|---|---|---|---|---|
| 2011 | 0.67 | 0.70 | 0.72 | E0.72 | E2.83 |
| 2010 | 0.45 | 0.55 | 0.60 | 0.61 | 2.21 |
| 2009 | 0.56 | 0.57 | 0.56 | 0.08 | 1.75 |
| 2008 | 0.60 | 0.53 | 0.49 | -0.79 | 0.75 |
| 2007 | 0.66 | 0.67 | 0.68 | 0.37 | 2.38 |
| 2006 | 0.60 | 0.61 | 0.64 | 0.64 | 2.49 |

Fiscal year ended Dec. 31. Next earnings report expected: Late January. EPS Estimates based on S&P Operating Earnings; historical GAAP earnings are as reported.

## Dividend Data (Dates: mm/dd Payment Date: mm/dd/yy)

| Amount ($) | Date Decl. | Ex-Div. Date | Stk. of Record | Payment Date |
|---|---|---|---|---|
| .07 Spl. | 03/18 | 03/24 | 03/28 | 03/31/11 |
| 0.120 | 04/20 | 05/04 | 05/06 | 06/01/11 |
| 0.120 | 07/26 | 08/03 | 08/05 | 09/01/11 |
| 0.120 | 10/25 | 11/02 | 11/04 | 12/01/11 |

Dividends have been paid since 1939. Source: Company reports.

## Highlights

➤ For 2011, due to a continuing run-off of legacy loans, we expect net interest income to fall 4.3%, following a 3.4% decline in 2010. While WFC's funding costs are among the lowest in the industry, they have little room to fall further. Our 2011 core fee income estimate is for a decline of 7.8%, due to the impact of regulatory reform and reduced mortgage banking activity, and we expect total revenues to be down 5.7% in 2011. However, for 2012, we see net interest income rising 2.1% and core revenues increasing 1.0%.

➤ In the 2011 third quarter, WFC reduced its loan loss provision by 1.5%, to $1.811 billion, and its allowance by 4.1%, to $20.04 billion. The allowance is now equal to 91.5% of nonaccrual loans of $21.9 billion, an adequate level, in our view. Nonaccrual loans fell 5.0% from June 30, as $2.61 billion of net chargeoffs offset a $1.47 million increase in new nonperforming loans. Taking all of this and our 2011 net chargeoff forecast of $11.1 billion into account, we expect loan loss provisions of $7.7 billion in 2011, down from $15.8 billion in 2010.

➤ We see EPS of $2.83 in 2011 and $2.97 in 2012.

## Investment Rationale/Risk

➤ WFC's third-quarter results hit record highs for net income and EPS, but were disappointing to many investors, who focused on the poor trading results and a significant drop in the net interest margin. Net interest income fell 1.3% from the prior quarter, on a 17 basis point drop in the net interest margin, which offset a 1.0% increase in the loan portfolio. However, core fee income, excluding volatile trading results and gains/losses, grew 2.3%. Core revenues rose 0.3%, but total revenues, including trading, fell 3.7%. Noninterest expenses fell to 61.2% of net revenues from first-quarter levels, well below peers, despite elevated legal and personnel costs from mortgage modifications and foreclosures. We think trading results will bounce back, and we also see WFC's interest-earning asset growth as tops among peers.

➤ Risks to our recommendation and target price include higher FDIC fees, debit card interchange caps, credit card regulation, higher costs of U.S. financial regulatory reform, and foreclosure and mortgage putbacks.

➤ Our 12-month target price of $30 is based on a slight premium-to-peers multiple of 10.2X our forward four quarters EPS estimate of $2.95.

Stock Report | November 26, 2011 | NYS Symbol: **WFC**

# Wells Fargo & Co

## Business Summary October 31, 2011

CORPORATE OVERVIEW. WFC is a diversified financial services company with operations around the world. WFC offers a range of financial services in over 80 different business lines. WFC delineates three different business segments when reporting results: Community Banking, Wholesale Banking, and Wealth, Brokerage and Retirement.

WFC is the successor to the banking portion of the business founded by Henry Wells and William G. Fargo in 1852. WFC's California banking business was separated from the express business in 1905, and was merged in 1960 with American Trust Company, another of the oldest banks in the Western United States, and became Wells Fargo Bank, N.A., a national banking association, in 1968.

In 1967, WFC, together with three other California banks, introduced the Master Charge credit card to its customers as part of its plan to challenge Bank of America (BAC 7 Buy) in the consumer lending business. Later, Master Charge become MasterCard Inc. (MA 349 Hold), an independent company. In 1986, WFC acquired Crocker National Bank, making WFC the 10th largest U.S. bank. In 1996, WFC acquired First Interstate Bancorp, with assets of $55 billion, and became the ninth largest U.S. bank.

The Riegle-Neal Interstate Banking and Branching Act of 1995 allowed banks to merge across state lines beginning June 1997, thereby creating interstate branches. In 1998, Wells Fargo was acquired by Minneapolis-based Norwest Corporation, the 11th largest bank in the U.S., with 1997 assets of $88.5 billion. The new company became the seventh largest U.S. bank, and assumed the name Wells Fargo, capitalizing on the nearly 150-year history of that nationally recognized name. Following the acquisition, the company transferred its headquarters to WFC's headquarters in San Francisco and merged its operating subsidiary with WFC's operating subsidiary in Sioux Falls.

Most recently, in 2008, WFC purchased Wachovia Corp, at the height of the U.S. financial crisis. When the merger closed on January 1, 2009, WFC became the fourth largest bank in the U.S.

## Company Financials Fiscal Year Ended Dec. 31

| Per Share Data ($) | 2010 | 2009 | 2008 | 2007 | 2006 | 2005 | 2004 | 2003 | 2002 | 2001 |
|---|---|---|---|---|---|---|---|---|---|---|
| Tangible Book Value | 15.75 | 12.74 | 3.31 | 5.55 | 10.13 | 8.76 | 7.95 | 7.04 | 6.11 | 4.90 |
| Earnings | 2.21 | 1.75 | 0.75 | 2.38 | 2.49 | 2.25 | 2.05 | 1.83 | 1.66 | 0.99 |
| S&P Core Earnings | 2.21 | 1.77 | 0.57 | 2.39 | 2.47 | 2.18 | 1.96 | 1.78 | 1.57 | 0.84 |
| Dividends | 0.20 | 0.49 | 1.30 | 1.18 | 1.08 | 1.00 | 0.93 | 0.75 | 0.55 | 0.50 |
| Payout Ratio | 9% | 28% | 173% | 50% | 43% | 44% | 45% | 41% | 33% | 51% |
| Prices:High | 34.25 | 31.53 | 44.69 | 37.99 | 36.99 | 32.35 | 32.02 | 29.59 | 26.72 | 27.41 |
| Prices:Low | 23.02 | 7.80 | 19.89 | 29.29 | 30.31 | 28.81 | 27.16 | 21.64 | 21.65 | 19.13 |
| P/E Ratio:High | 16 | 18 | 63 | 16 | 15 | 14 | 16 | 16 | 16 | 28 |
| P/E Ratio:Low | 10 | 4 | 27 | 12 | 12 | 13 | 13 | 12 | 13 | 19 |

| Income Statement Analysis (Million $) | | | | | | | | | | |
|---|---|---|---|---|---|---|---|---|---|---|
| Net Interest Income | 44,757 | 46,324 | 25,143 | 20,974 | 19,951 | 18,504 | 17,150 | 16,007 | 14,855 | 12,460 |
| Tax Equivalent Adjustment | 629 | 706 | 321 | 146 | 116 | 110 | 104 | NA | NA | NA |
| Non Interest Income | 40,453 | 42,362 | 16,776 | 17,473 | 15,021 | 14,054 | 12,530 | 12,323 | 9,348 | 7,227 |
| Loan Loss Provision | 15,752 | 21,668 | 15,979 | 4,939 | 2,204 | 2,383 | 1,717 | 1,722 | 1,733 | 1,780 |
| % Expense/Operating Revenue | 59.2% | 55.3% | 54.1% | 59.4% | 59.3% | 58.2% | 64.8% | 60.7% | 52.2% | 65.5% |
| Pretax Income | 19,001 | 17,998 | 3,585 | 11,627 | 12,745 | 11,548 | 10,769 | 9,477 | 8,854 | 5,479 |
| Effective Tax Rate | 33.4% | 29.6% | 20.7% | 30.7% | 33.4% | 33.6% | 34.9% | 34.6% | 35.5% | 37.5% |
| Net Income | 12,362 | 12,275 | 2,842 | 8,057 | 8,482 | 7,671 | 7,014 | 6,202 | 5,710 | 3,423 |
| % Net Interest Margin | 4.26 | 4.28 | 4.83 | 4.74 | 4.83 | 4.86 | 4.89 | 5.08 | 5.57 | 5.36 |
| S&P Core Earnings | 11,620 | 8,084 | 1,937 | 8,099 | 8,401 | 7,423 | 6,722 | 6,055 | 5,374 | 2,894 |

| Balance Sheet & Other Financial Data (Million $) | | | | | | | | | | |
|---|---|---|---|---|---|---|---|---|---|---|
| Money Market Assets | 132,053 | 83,924 | 104,317 | 10,481 | 11,685 | 16,211 | 14,020 | 2,745 | 3,174 | 2,530 |
| Investment Securities | 172,654 | 172,710 | 151,569 | 72,951 | 42,629 | 41,834 | 33,717 | 32,953 | 27,947 | 40,308 |
| Commercial Loans | 164,378 | 172,562 | 218,298 | 152,841 | 122,065 | 108,903 | 98,515 | 48,729 | 47,292 | 47,547 |
| Other Loans | 592,889 | 610,208 | 625,519 | 229,354 | 273,069 | 201,934 | 189,071 | 204,344 | 149,342 | 124,952 |
| Total Assets | 1,258,128 | 1,243,646 | 1,309,639 | 575,442 | 481,996 | 481,741 | 427,849 | 387,798 | 349,259 | 307,569 |
| Demand Deposits | 191,256 | 181,356 | 150,837 | 84,348 | 89,119 | 87,712 | 81,082 | 74,387 | 74,094 | 65,362 |
| Time Deposits | 656,686 | 642,662 | 630,565 | 260,112 | 221,124 | 226,738 | 193,776 | 173,140 | 142,822 | 121,904 |
| Long Term Debt | 156,893 | 203,861 | 267,158 | 99,393 | 72,404 | 79,668 | 73,580 | 63,642 | 50,205 | 38,530 |
| Common Equity | 118,382 | 103,743 | 68,307 | 47,660 | 45,492 | 40,335 | 37,596 | 34,255 | 30,107 | 26,996 |
| % Return on Assets | 1.0 | 1.0 | 0.3 | 1.5 | 1.8 | 1.7 | 1.7 | 1.7 | 1.7 | 1.2 |
| % Return on Equity | 11.1 | 14.3 | 4.9 | 17.2 | 19.8 | 19.7 | 19.5 | 19.3 | 20.0 | 12.8 |
| % Loan Loss Reserve | 3.0 | 3.1 | 2.4 | 1.4 | 1.1 | 1.1 | 1.2 | 1.3 | 1.5 | 1.8 |
| % Loans/Deposits | 89.3 | 95.0 | 110.7 | 107.1 | 113.8 | 111.9 | 118.6 | 117.0 | 117.3 | 110.9 |
| % Equity to Assets | 8.8 | 6.7 | 6.2 | 8.9 | 8.9 | 8.6 | 8.8 | 8.7 | 8.7 | 9.2 |

Data as orig reptd.; bef. results of disc opers/spec. items. Per share data adj. for stk. divs.; EPS diluted. E-Estimated. NA-Not Available. NM-Not Meaningful. NR-Not Ranked. UR-Under Review.

**Office:** 420 Montgomery Street, San Francisco, CA 94104.
**Telephone:** 866-878-5865.
**Website:** http://www.wellsfargo.com
**Chrmn, Pres & CEO:** J.G. Stumpf

**COO & CTO:** C.W. Edwards
**EVP & CFO:** T.J. Sloan
**EVP & Chief Admin Officer:** P.R. Callahan
**EVP, Chief Acctg Officer & Cntlr:** R.D. Levy

**Board Members:** J. D. Baker, II, E. L. Chao, J. S. Chen, L. H. Dean, S. E. Engel, E. Hernandez, Jr., D. M. James, M. J. McDonald, C. H. Milligan, N. G. Moore, P. J. Quigley, J. M. Runstad, S. W. Sanger, J. G. Stumpf, S. G. Swenson

**Founded:** 1929
**Domicile:** Delaware
**Employees:** 272,200

Redistribution or reproduction is prohibited without written permission. Copyright ©2011 The McGraw-Hill Companies, Inc.

The McGraw·Hill Companies

# Western Digital Corp

**STANDARD &POOR'S**

| S&P Recommendation **HOLD** ★★★★★ | Price $25.00 (as of Nov 25, 2011) | 12-Mo. Target Price $27.00 | Investment Style Large-Cap Blend |

**GICS Sector** Information Technology
**Sub-Industry** Computer Storage & Peripherals

**Summary** This company designs and manufactures hard disk drives for personal computing.

## Key Stock Statistics (Source S&P, Vickers, company reports)

| | | | | | | | | |
|---|---|---|---|---|---|---|---|---|
| 52-Wk Range | $41.87– 22.64 | S&P Oper. EPS 2012**E** | -1.59 | Market Capitalization(B) | $5.845 | Beta | 1.38 |
| Trailing 12-Month EPS | $3.26 | S&P Oper. EPS 2013**E** | 3.84 | Yield (%) | Nil | S&P 3-Yr. Proj. EPS CAGR(%) | NM |
| Trailing 12-Month P/E | 7.7 | P/E on S&P Oper. EPS 2012**E** | NM | Dividend Rate/Share | Nil | S&P Credit Rating | NA |
| $10K Invested 5 Yrs Ago | $11,715 | Common Shares Outstg. (M) | 233.8 | Institutional Ownership (%) | 90 | | |

## Price Performance

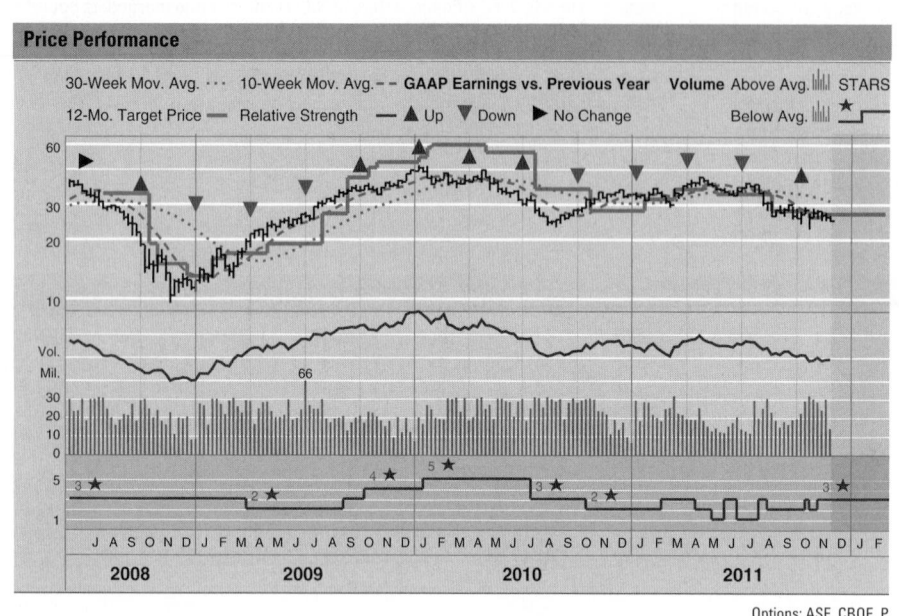

30-Week Mov. Avg. · · · 10-Week Mov. Avg. – – GAAP Earnings vs. Previous Year   Volume Above Avg. STARS
12-Mo. Target Price — Relative Strength — ▲ Up ▼ Down ► No Change   Below Avg. ★

Options: ASE, CBOE, P

Analysis prepared by Equity Analyst **Jim Yin, CFA** on Nov 15, 2011, when the stock traded at **$25.05**.

## Highlights

► We expect revenues to decrease 21% in FY 12 (Jun.), after falling 3.3% in FY 11, reflecting the recent flood in Thailand, which caused WDC to shut down its two main production facilities there. The two facilities accounted for about 60% of the company's production capacity. Additionally, we believe unit shipments of hard disk drives will be constrained by the availability of key components, as the flood has also damaged part suppliers' facilities. However, we think the reduced unit shipments will be partially offset by higher hard disk drive prices.

► We project gross margins of 12% in FY 12, compared to 19% in FY 11. We think gross margins will be hurt by low utilization rates with WDC's two main facilities in Thailand closed. We forecast operating margins of -4.4% in FY 12, compared to 8.2% in FY 11.

► We estimate a loss per share of $1.59 in FY 12, compared to EPS of $3.09 in FY 11. Our forecast for a loss in FY 12 reflects lost production and potential charges related to the flood. We estimate EPS of $3.84 in FY 13, assuming both Thailand facilities are back in production by the middle of 2012.

## Investment Rationale/Risk

► We recently raised our recommendation to hold, from sell, on valuation. The flood in Thailand has shut down WDC's two main production facilities there. Although we expect extensive damages to the equipment and the buildings, we believe WDC will recover, given its strong balance sheet. We also think WDC's long-term profitability will improve due to further industry consolidation.

► Risks to our recommendation and target price include a slow recovery from the Thailand flood, a weaker global economy, lower PC unit growth, and faster adoption of solid-state drives.

► Our 12-month target price of $27 is based on a blend of price to sales (P/S) and P/E analyses. We apply a peer-discount P/S ratio of 0.3X to our FY 13 revenue per share estimate to derive a $25 valuation. We think WDC warrants a peer discount as a result of the higher volatility due to increased risks following the Thailand flood. Our P/E analysis derives a value of $29, based on 7.5X our FY 13 EPS estimate of $3.84, a multiple within the range of 5.3X-12.2X of the past five years.

## Qualitative Risk Assessment

| LOW | MEDIUM | **HIGH** |

Our risk assessment reflects the volatility of the disk drive industry, including significant exposure to the PC sector and ongoing erosion of average selling prices.

## Quantitative Evaluations

**S&P Quality Ranking** B

| D | C | B- | **B** | B+ | A- | A | A+ |

**Relative Strength Rank** MODERATE

34

LOWEST = 1     HIGHEST = 99

## Revenue/Earnings Data

**Revenue (Million $)**

| | 1Q | 2Q | 3Q | 4Q | Year |
|---|---|---|---|---|---|
| 2012 | 2,694 | -- | -- | -- | -- |
| 2011 | 2,396 | 2,475 | 2,252 | 2,403 | 9,526 |
| 2010 | 2,208 | 2,619 | 2,641 | 2,382 | 9,850 |
| 2009 | 2,109 | 1,823 | 1,592 | 1,928 | 7,453 |
| 2008 | 1,766 | 2,204 | 2,111 | 1,993 | 8,074 |
| 2007 | 1,264 | 1,428 | 1,410 | 1,367 | 5,468 |

**Earnings Per Share ($)**

| | | | | | |
|---|---|---|---|---|---|
| 2012 | 1.01 | E-1.34 | E-0.84 | E-0.41 | E-1.59 |
| 2011 | 0.84 | 0.96 | 0.62 | 0.67 | 3.09 |
| 2010 | 1.25 | 1.85 | 1.71 | 1.13 | 5.93 |
| 2009 | 0.93 | 0.06 | 0.22 | 0.86 | 2.08 |
| 2008 | 0.31 | 1.39 | 1.23 | 0.94 | 3.84 |
| 2007 | 0.46 | 0.57 | 0.53 | 0.94 | 2.50 |

Fiscal year ended Jun. 30. Next earnings report expected: NA. EPS Estimates based on S&P Operating Earnings; historical GAAP earnings are as reported.

## Dividend Data

No cash dividends have been paid.

# Western Digital Corp

**STANDARD &POOR'S**

## Business Summary November 15, 2011

CORPORATE OVERVIEW. Western Digital designs, develops, manufactures and markets hard disk drives. The company's hard drives are used in desktop PC, notebook computers, enterprise servers, network attached storage devices, and consumer electronics products such as personal/digital video recorders, and satellite and cable set-top boxes. WDC's hard drive products include 3.5- and 2.5-inch form factor drives with capacities ranging from 40 gigabytes to 2 terabyte and rotation speeds up to 10,000 revolutions per minute. The company believes that these form factors represent its major growth areas, with 3.5-inch form factor hard drives used in the desktop, enterprise, consumer electronic and external storage markets, and 2.5-inch form factor hard drives serving the mobile PC/laptop, consumer electronic and external storage markets.

WDC entered the solid-state drive market by acquiring SiliconSystems in the first quarter of 2009. A solid-state drive is a storage device that uses semiconductor rather than magnetic disks and heads to store data and is more commonly used in notebooks because of its lighter weight and higher durability. We expect the solid-state drive market segment to grow faster than the rest of the industry given the rapid growth of netbooks. However, we think solid-

state drives represented a small percentage of WDC's FY 11 (Jun.) total sales.

Drives are sold globally to OEMs, distributors and retailers. Sales to OEMs accounted for 49% of revenues in FY 11, down from 51% in FY 10. Distributors made up 32% (31%) and retailers 19% (18%).

Historically, WDC believes that sales of PCs and hard disk drives were similar in volume. However, over the past five years, the company's research indicates that growth in hard drives has outpaced the PC market. This shifting dynamic is based on a number of factors, including the growth of alternative products such as consumer electronics devices, the expansion of the external hard drive market, which allows for a more convenient way to store music and photos, and the increased use of multiple hard drives to deal with capacity constraints and safety issues.

## Company Financials Fiscal Year Ended Jun. 30

| Per Share Data ($) | 2011 | 2010 | 2009 | 2008 | 2007 | 2006 | 2005 | 2004 | 2003 | 2002 |
|---|---|---|---|---|---|---|---|---|---|---|
| Tangible Book Value | 22.60 | 19.37 | 13.17 | 11.16 | 7.73 | 5.24 | 3.29 | 2.36 | 1.61 | 0.54 |
| Cash Flow | 5.65 | 8.12 | 4.20 | 5.66 | 3.42 | 2.48 | 1.54 | 1.17 | 1.13 | 0.51 |
| Earnings | 3.09 | 5.93 | 2.08 | 3.84 | 2.50 | 1.76 | 0.91 | 0.70 | 0.88 | 0.28 |
| S&P Core Earnings | 3.20 | 6.01 | 2.01 | 3.88 | 2.50 | 1.82 | 0.87 | 0.58 | 0.81 | 0.14 |
| Dividends | NA | Nil | Nil | Nil | Nil | Nil | Nil | Nil | Nil | Nil |
| Payout Ratio | Nil | Nil | Nil | Nil | Nil | Nil | Nil | Nil | Nil | Nil |
| Prices:High | 41.87 | 47.44 | 44.96 | 40.00 | 31.70 | 24.70 | 19.15 | 13.55 | 14.95 | 8.96 |
| Prices:Low | 22.64 | 23.06 | 11.49 | 9.48 | 16.21 | 15.90 | 9.84 | 6.39 | 6.44 | 2.98 |
| P/E Ratio:High | 14 | 8 | 22 | 10 | 13 | 14 | 21 | 19 | 17 | 32 |
| P/E Ratio:Low | 7 | 4 | 6 | 2 | 6 | 9 | 11 | 9 | 7 | 11 |

| Income Statement Analysis (Million $) | | | | | | | | | | |
|---|---|---|---|---|---|---|---|---|---|---|
| Revenue | 9,526 | 9,850 | 7,453 | 8,074 | 5,468 | 4,341 | 3,639 | 3,047 | 2,719 | 2,151 |
| Operating Income | 1,383 | 2,035 | 1,106 | 1,468 | 625 | 526 | 332 | 257 | 237 | 96.5 |
| Depreciation | 602 | 510 | 479 | 413 | 210 | 160 | 135 | 102 | 50.4 | 45.8 |
| Interest Expense | 1.00 | 5.00 | 17.0 | 52.0 | 4.00 | 3.70 | Nil | Nil | Nil | 8.13 |
| Pretax Income | 780 | 1,520 | 501 | 981 | 443 | 382 | 202 | 155 | 188 | 52.1 |
| Effective Tax Rate | NA | NA | 6.19% | 11.6% | NM | NM | 1.93% | 2.51% | 4.03% | NM |
| Net Income | 726 | 1,382 | 470 | 867 | 564 | 395 | 198 | 151 | 181 | 53.2 |
| S&P Core Earnings | 751 | 1,400 | 454 | 875 | 564 | 407 | 186 | 125 | 166 | 27.0 |

| Balance Sheet & Other Financial Data (Million $) | | | | | | | | | | |
|---|---|---|---|---|---|---|---|---|---|---|
| Cash | 3,490 | 2,734 | 1,794 | 1,107 | 700 | 551 | 485 | 378 | 393 | 224 |
| Current Assets | 5,487 | 4,720 | 3,230 | 2,731 | 2,029 | 1,492 | 1,181 | 857 | 744 | 528 |
| Total Assets | 8,118 | 7,328 | 5,291 | 4,871 | 2,901 | 2,073 | 1,589 | 1,159 | 866 | 637 |
| Current Liabilities | 2,170 | 2,023 | 1,525 | 1,564 | 1,130 | 859 | 818 | 587 | 506 | 493 |
| Long Term Debt | 150 | 294 | 400 | 482 | 10.0 | 19.4 | 32.6 | 52.7 | Nil | Nil |
| Common Equity | 5,488 | 4,709 | 3,192 | 2,696 | 1,716 | 1,157 | 702 | 488 | 327 | 103 |
| Total Capital | 5,782 | 5,109 | 3,592 | 3,205 | 1,726 | 1,177 | 735 | 540 | 327 | 103 |
| Capital Expenditures | 778 | 737 | 519 | 615 | 324 | 302 | 233 | 132 | 61.9 | 47.7 |
| Cash Flow | 1,328 | 1,892 | 949 | 1,280 | 774 | 554 | 333 | 253 | 231 | 99.0 |
| Current Ratio | 2.5 | 2.3 | 2.1 | 1.8 | 1.8 | 1.7 | 1.4 | 1.5 | 1.5 | 1.1 |
| % Long Term Debt of Capitalization | 2.6 | 5.8 | 11.1 | 15.0 | 0.6 | 1.6 | 4.4 | 9.8 | Nil | Nil |
| % Net Income of Revenue | 7.6 | 14.0 | 6.3 | 10.7 | 10.3 | 9.1 | 5.5 | 5.0 | 6.7 | 2.5 |
| % Return on Assets | 9.4 | 21.9 | 9.3 | 22.3 | 22.6 | 21.6 | 14.4 | 14.9 | 24.1 | 9.3 |
| % Return on Equity | 14.2 | 35.0 | 16.0 | 39.3 | 39.3 | 42.5 | 33.4 | 37.1 | 84.0 | 97.1 |

Data as orig reptd.; bef. results of disc opers/spec. items. Per share data adj. for stk. divs.; EPS diluted. E-Estimated. NA-Not Available. NM-Not Meaningful. NR-Not Ranked. UR-Under Review.

**Office:** 3355 Michelson Drive, Suite 100, Irvine, CA 92612.
**Telephone:** 949-672-7000.
**Website:** http://www.westerndigital.com
**Chrmn:** T.E. Pardun

**Pres & CEO:** J.F. Coyne
**COO:** T.M. Leyden
**SVP & CFO:** W.U. Nickl
**SVP, Secy & General Counsel:** M.C. Ray

**Investor Contact:** R. Blair
**Board Members:** K. A. Cote, J. F. Coyne, H. T. DeNero, W. L. Kimsey, M. D. Lambert, L. J. Lauer, M. E. Massengill, R. H. Moore, T. E. Pardun, A. Shakeel

**Founded:** 1970
**Domicile:** Delaware
**Employees:** 65,431

*The McGraw-Hill Companies*

# Western Union Co

**STANDARD &POOR'S**

| **S&P Recommendation** HOLD ★★★★★ | **Price**<br>$16.30 (as of Nov 25, 2011) | **12-Mo. Target Price**<br>$21.00 | **Investment Style**<br>Large-Cap Blend |
|---|---|---|---|

**GICS Sector** Information Technology
**Sub-Industry** Data Processing & Outsourced Services

**Summary** Spun off from First Data Corp. in September 2006, Western Union is a leading independent provider of consumer money transfer services.

## Key Stock Statistics (Source S&P, Vickers, company reports)

| | | | | | | | |
|---|---|---|---|---|---|---|---|
| 52-Wk Range | $22.03– 14.55 | S&P Oper. EPS 2011E | 1.55 | Market Capitalization(B) | $10.092 | Beta | 1.45 |
| Trailing 12-Month EPS | $1.49 | S&P Oper. EPS 2012E | 1.75 | Yield (%) | 1.96 | S&P 3-Yr. Proj. EPS CAGR(%) | 10 |
| Trailing 12-Month P/E | 10.9 | P/E on S&P Oper. EPS 2011E | 10.5 | Dividend Rate/Share | $0.32 | S&P Credit Rating | A- |
| $10K Invested 5 Yrs Ago | $7,552 | Common Shares Outstg. (M) | 619.1 | Institutional Ownership (%) | 92 | | |

## Price Performance

30-Week Mov. Avg. · · ·   10-Week Mov. Avg. – –   **GAAP Earnings vs. Previous Year**   **Volume** Above Avg. ▎▌▎ STARS
12-Mo. Target Price —   Relative Strength —   ▲ Up ▼ Down ▶ No Change   Below Avg. ▎▌▎ ★

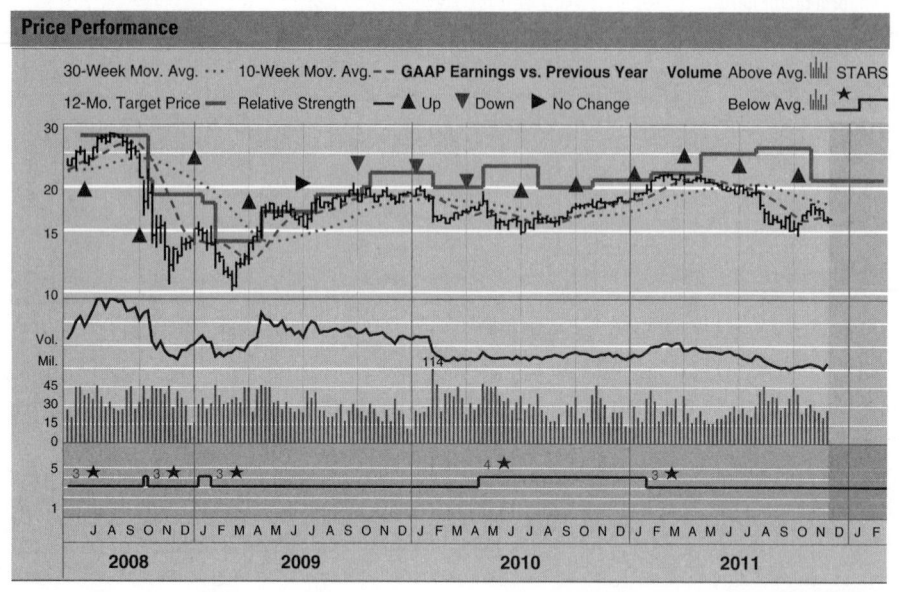

Options: ASE, CBOE, P, Ph

## Qualitative Risk Assessment

| LOW | MEDIUM | HIGH |
|---|---|---|

Our risk assessment reflects the sluggish global macroeconomy, which we expect will impact transaction volumes, offset by what we see as relatively high barriers to entry in WU's businesses.

## Quantitative Evaluations

**S&P Quality Ranking**   NR

| D | C | B- | B | B+ | A- | A | A+ |
|---|---|---|---|---|---|---|---|

**Relative Strength Rank**   MODERATE

62

LOWEST = 1   HIGHEST = 99

## Highlights

➤ The 12-month target price for WU has recently been changed to $21.00 from $26.00. The Highlights section of this Stock Report will be updated accordingly.

## Investment Rationale/Risk

➤ The Investment Rationale/Risk section of this Stock Report will be updated shortly. For the latest News story on WU from MarketScope, see below.

➤ 10/26/11 12:00 pm ET ... S&P REITERATES HOLD OPINION ON SHARES OF WESTERN UNION (WU 16.96***): WU posts adjusted Q3 EPS of $0.40 vs. $0.37, $0.02 above our forecast and $0.01 better than the consensus estimate from Capital IQ. Revenues rose 6%, above our projection, with outperformance across all major revenue segments. We note C2C growth in Asia Pacific of 11% and WU Business Solutions gains of 30%. We are raising our EPS estimates to $1.55 from $1.52 for '11 and to $1.75 from $1.73 for '12, reflecting trends we view as intact. However, based on revised P/E and P/E-to-growth analyses, we are lowering our 12-month target to $21 from $26. WU's indicated yield is 1.8%. /S. Kessler

## Revenue/Earnings Data

**Revenue (Million $)**

| | 1Q | 2Q | 3Q | 4Q | Year |
|---|---|---|---|---|---|
| 2011 | 1,283 | 1,366 | 1,411 | -- | -- |
| 2010 | 1,233 | 1,273 | 1,330 | 1,357 | 5,193 |
| 2009 | 1,201 | 1,254 | 1,314 | 1,314 | 5,084 |
| 2008 | 1,266 | 1,347 | 1,377 | 1,292 | 5,282 |
| 2007 | 1,131 | 1,203 | 1,257 | 1,309 | 4,900 |
| 2006 | 1,043 | 1,114 | 1,140 | 1,173 | 4,470 |

**Earnings Per Share ($)**

| | | | | | |
|---|---|---|---|---|---|
| 2011 | 0.32 | 0.41 | 0.38 | E0.38 | E1.55 |
| 2010 | 0.30 | 0.33 | 0.36 | 0.37 | 1.36 |
| 2009 | 0.32 | 0.31 | 0.26 | 0.32 | 1.21 |
| 2008 | 0.27 | 0.31 | 0.33 | 0.34 | 1.24 |
| 2007 | 0.25 | 0.26 | 0.28 | 0.32 | 1.11 |
| 2006 | 0.29 | 0.29 | 0.34 | 0.28 | 1.19 |

Fiscal year ended Dec. 31. Next earnings report expected: Early February. EPS Estimates based on S&P Operating Earnings; historical GAAP earnings are as reported.

## Dividend Data (Dates: mm/dd Payment Date: mm/dd/yy)

| Amount<br>($) | Date<br>Decl. | Ex-Div.<br>Date | Stk. of<br>Record | Payment<br>Date |
|---|---|---|---|---|
| 0.070 | 12/08 | 12/16 | 12/20 | 12/31/10 |
| 0.070 | 02/25 | 03/16 | 03/18 | 03/31/11 |
| 0.080 | 09/15 | 09/22 | 09/26 | 10/07/11 |

Dividends have been paid since 2006. Source: Company reports.

---

**Please read the Required Disclosures and Analyst Certification on the last page of this report.**

The McGraw·Hill Companies

# Western Union Co

## Business Summary July 27, 2011

CORPORATE OVERVIEW. Western Union is a leading independent provider of consumer money transfer services. WU offers its services through a network of about 445,000 agent locations (at December 31, 2010) spanning more than 200 countries and territories. The company provides its services globally, mainly under the Western Union brand name and also under the Orlandi Valuta and Vigo brands. WU derives the majority of revenues from fees that consumers pay when they send money. The company's main segments include consumer-to-consumer (C2C; 84% of 2010 revenues) and Global Business Payments (formerly consumer-to-business or C2B; 14%).

WU's core C2C services allow customers to transfer money to other individuals. The majority of these transfers are originated in cash at Western Union agent locations, although consumers can also send money via the Internet, telephone, credit or debit card and, in some cases, through bank debits. In 2010, C2C transactions increased 9%, to approximately 214 million, while C2C transaction fees grew about 2%.

Through its Global Business Payments segment, consumers or businesses can make payments to businesses electronically, over the telephone, via the Internet, or at one of WU's agent locations. The company has long-standing relationships with billers such as utilities, auto finance companies, mortgage servicers, financial service providers and government agencies that accept such payments. In 2010, WU's Global Business Payment transactions increased fell 2%, to 405 million, while transaction fees fell 7%.

CORPORATE STRATEGY. The pursuit of growth through international expansion is a key tenet of Western Union's growth strategy. The company believes that a majority of its C2C transactions involve at least one non-U.S. location. Outside the United states, WU's revenue base is well-diversified geographically, in our view. Building on and maintaining its well-recognized consumer brand is another key element to the company's strategy. WU spent between 4%-6% of revenues on marketing, advertising and developing customer loyalty programs from 2007 through 2010. The company also invested about 3% of annual revenues in selective price reductions on its C2C services in individual markets depending on the dynamics within those markets in 2006 and 2007; such reductions accounted for 1% of revenues in 2008, 2% in 2009 and 4% in 2010. We think the difference in growth between transaction fees and transaction volumes is evidence of this strategy.

## Company Financials Fiscal Year Ended Dec. 31

| Per Share Data ($) | 2010 | 2009 | 2008 | 2007 | 2006 | 2005 | 2004 | 2003 | 2002 | 2001 |
|---|---|---|---|---|---|---|---|---|---|---|
| Tangible Book Value | NM | NM | NM | NM | NM | NM | NA | NA | NA | NA |
| Cash Flow | 1.62 | 1.43 | 1.33 | 1.17 | 1.32 | NA | NA | NA | NA | NA |
| Earnings | 1.36 | 1.21 | 1.24 | 1.11 | 1.19 | 0.96 | NA | NA | NA | NA |
| S&P Core Earnings | 1.37 | 1.29 | 1.22 | 1.11 | 1.18 | 1.10 | 0.95 | NA | NA | NA |
| Dividends | 0.25 | 0.06 | 0.04 | 0.04 | 0.01 | NA | NA | NA | NA | NA |
| Payout Ratio | 18% | 5% | 3% | 4% | 1% | NA | NA | NA | NA | NA |
| Prices:High | 20.26 | 20.64 | 28.62 | 24.83 | 24.14 | NA | NA | NA | NA | NA |
| Prices:Low | 14.65 | 10.05 | 10.48 | 15.00 | 16.85 | NA | NA | NA | NA | NA |
| P/E Ratio:High | 15 | 17 | 23 | 22 | 20 | NA | NA | NA | NA | NA |
| P/E Ratio:Low | 11 | 8 | 8 | 14 | 14 | NA | NA | NA | NA | NA |

| Income Statement Analysis (Million $) | | | | | | | | | | |
|---|---|---|---|---|---|---|---|---|---|---|
| Revenue | 5,193 | 5,084 | 5,282 | 4,900 | 4,470 | 3,988 | 3,524 | 3,121 | NA | NA |
| Operating Income | 1,536 | 1,437 | 1,500 | 1,393 | 1,415 | NA | 1,168 | 1,051 | NA | NA |
| Depreciation | 176 | 154 | 61.7 | 49.1 | 104 | NA | 79.2 | 78.4 | NA | NA |
| Interest Expense | 170 | 158 | 171 | 189 | 53.0 | 202 | 6.40 | NA | NA | NA |
| Pretax Income | 1,145 | 1,132 | 1,239 | 1,222 | 1,335 | 1,063 | 1,098 | 970 | NA | NA |
| Effective Tax Rate | NA | 25.0% | 25.8% | 29.9% | 31.5% | 29.5% | 31.5% | 34.1% | NA | NA |
| Net Income | 910 | 849 | 919 | 857 | 914 | 749 | 752 | 639 | NA | NA |
| S&P Core Earnings | 914 | 904 | 908 | 857 | 913 | 859 | 734 | NA | NA | NA |

| Balance Sheet & Other Financial Data (Million $) | | | | | | | | | | |
|---|---|---|---|---|---|---|---|---|---|---|
| Cash | 2,157 | 1,685 | 1,296 | 2,030 | 1,422 | 1,186 | 470 | NA | NA | NA |
| Current Assets | 2,157 | 1,985 | 1,850 | 1,959 | 1,631 | NA | 1,520 | NA | NA | NA |
| Total Assets | 7,929 | 7,353 | 5,578 | 5,784 | 5,321 | 4,659 | 3,307 | NA | NA | NA |
| Current Liabilities | 877 | 1,020 | 1,350 | 1,468 | 882 | NA | 218 | NA | NA | NA |
| Long Term Debt | 3,290 | 3,049 | 2,561 | 2,500 | 2,996 | 3,500 | 9.90 | NA | NA | NA |
| Common Equity | 583 | 354 | -8.10 | 50.7 | -315 | -687 | 1,909 | NA | NA | NA |
| Total Capital | 3,873 | 3,402 | 2,823 | 2,814 | 2,681 | 2,183 | 1,919 | NA | NA | NA |
| Capital Expenditures | 53.3 | 59.7 | 53.9 | 83.5 | 64.0 | NA | 26.5 | 23.6 | NA | NA |
| Cash Flow | 1,086 | 1,003 | 981 | 906 | 1,018 | NA | 831 | 717 | NA | NA |
| Current Ratio | 2.5 | 1.7 | 2.1 | 1.3 | 1.9 | NA | 7.0 | NA | NA | NA |
| % Long Term Debt of Capitalization | 85.0 | 89.6 | 90.7 | 88.8 | 112.0 | 160.3 | 0.5 | Nil | NA | NA |
| % Net Income of Revenue | 17.5 | 16.7 | 17.4 | 17.5 | 20.4 | 18.8 | 21.3 | 20.5 | NA | NA |
| % Return on Assets | 11.9 | 13.1 | 16.2 | 15.4 | 18.3 | NA | NA | NA | NA | NA |
| % Return on Equity | 194.4 | NM | NM | NM | NM | NA | NA | NA | NA | NA |

Data as orig reptd.; bef. results of disc opers/spec. items. Per share data adj. for stk. divs.; EPS diluted. Pro forma data in 2005; balance sheet and book value as of Jun. 30, 2006. E-Estimated. NA-Not Available. NM-Not Meaningful. NR-Not Ranked. UR-Under Review.

**Office:** 12500 East Belford Avenue, Englewood, CO 80112.
**Telephone:** 866-405-5012.
**Website:** http://www.westernunion.com
**Chrmn:** J.M. Greenberg

**Pres & CEO:** H. Ersek
**COO & CTO:** R. Heller
**EVP & CFO:** S.T. Scheirman
**EVP, Secy & General Counsel:** D.L. Schlapbach

**Investor Contact:** G. Kohn (720-332-8276)
**Board Members:** D. S. Devitre, H. Ersek, J. M. Greenberg, B. D. Holden, R. Mendoza, M. A. Miles, Jr., D. Stevenson, L. F. levinson, W. von Schimmelmann

**Founded:** 1851
**Domicile:** Delaware
**Employees:** 7,000

# Weyerhaeuser Co

**STANDARD &POOR'S**

| S&P Recommendation | HOLD ★★★☆☆ | Price $15.48 (as of Nov 25, 2011) | 12-Mo. Target Price $19.00 | Investment Style Large-Cap Blend |
|---|---|---|---|---|

**GICS Sector** Financials
**Sub-Industry** Specialized REITS

**Summary** One of the world's largest integrated forest products companies, WY grows timber; makes and sells forest products and pulp; and engages in real estate construction and development.

## Key Stock Statistics (Source S&P, Vickers, company reports)

| | | | | | | | |
|---|---|---|---|---|---|---|---|
| 52-Wk Range | $25.33–14.82 | S&P Oper. EPS 2011E | 0.35 | Market Capitalization(B) | $8.304 | Beta | 1.18 |
| Trailing 12-Month EPS | $0.81 | S&P Oper. EPS 2012E | 0.60 | Yield (%) | 3.88 | S&P 3-Yr. Proj. EPS CAGR(%) | 25 |
| Trailing 12-Month P/E | 19.1 | P/E on S&P Oper. EPS 2011E | 44.2 | Dividend Rate/Share | $0.60 | S&P Credit Rating | BBB- |
| $10K Invested 5 Yrs Ago | $7,528 | Common Shares Outstg. (M) | 536.4 | Institutional Ownership (%) | 84 | | |

## Price Performance

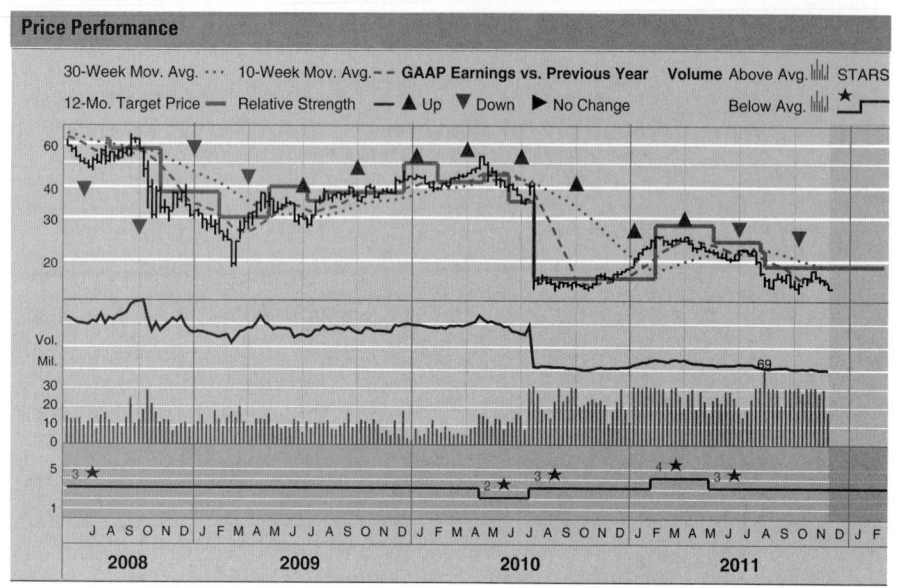

30-Week Mov. Avg. · · · 10-Week Mov. Avg. - - - **GAAP Earnings vs. Previous Year** Volume Above Avg. STARS
12-Mo. Target Price — Relative Strength ▲ Up ▼ Down ▶ No Change Below Avg.

Options: CBOE, P

Analysis prepared by Equity Analyst **S. Benway, CFA** on Nov 10, 2011, when the stock traded at **$16.65**.

### Highlights

➤ We see sales rising 1%-3% from continuing operations in 2011. S&P expects residential construction to show only slight recovery in 2011 before a more significant improvement begins in 2012. This should lead to somewhat lower prices for lumber and panels on average in 2011. However, log sales to Asia are likely to rise and demand and pricing for fibers is also expected to be higher. In 2012, we project a sales increase of 6%-10%.

➤ We look for conditions in housing-related business to remain difficult in coming quarters. Although timberland margins (excluding land sale gains) are likely to remain below normal due to deferred harvests, they are expected to rise on higher prices. Margins in the fibers business are expected to remain quite strong due to robust demand and pricing in that sector. Our estimate is for operating margins of 9.3% in 2011 and 11.4% in 2012, up from 8.8% in 2010.

➤ For 2011, we see an operating profit of $0.35 per share, excluding unusual items but including land sales gains, compared to operating earnings of $0.49 in 2010. For 2012, we forecast EPS of $0.60.

### Investment Rationale/Risk

➤ WY has divested assets to focus on its timber, wood products, real estate and fiber businesses. Although the steep downturn in the residential construction sector has hurt many of these businesses, the sector has likely bottomed and WY should see strong margins once volume recovers. The company recently adopted the REIT form of corporate structure, which will likely result in greater cash flows and higher dividend payouts in the future. However, we see the shares as fairly valued.

➤ Risks to our recommendation and target price include the lack of a housing recovery, a significant decline in wood product and pulp prices, and decreased values for timberland.

➤ Our discounted cash flow model, which assumes a 9.0% weighted average cost of capital, strong cash flow growth in 2012, and 3% growth in perpetuity, derives an intrinsic value of $23. Our dividend discount metric assumes a $0.60 payout in 2012, a required rate of return of 8.0%, and constant dividend growth of 4%, and values the shares at $15. Our 12-month target of $19 is an equally weighted blend of these two measures.

## Qualitative Risk Assessment

| LOW | MEDIUM | HIGH |
|---|---|---|

Our risk assessment reflects that Weyerhaeuser operates in a cyclical industry, with large capital requirements and significant variability in both costs and prices. However, the company is one of the largest in the industry, and we believe it has a major base of assets and modest debt levels.

## Quantitative Evaluations

**S&P Quality Ranking** B-

| D | C | B- | B | B+ | A- | A | A+ |
|---|---|---|---|---|---|---|---|

**Relative Strength Rank** MODERATE

36

LOWEST = 1     HIGHEST = 99

## Revenue/Earnings Data

**Revenue (Million $)**

| | 1Q | 2Q | 3Q | 4Q | Year |
|---|---|---|---|---|---|
| 2011 | 1,578 | 1,610 | 1,569 | -- | -- |
| 2010 | 1,419 | 1,805 | 1,664 | 1,664 | 6,552 |
| 2009 | 1,275 | 1,391 | 1,407 | 1,455 | 5,528 |
| 2008 | 2,096 | 2,174 | 2,107 | 1,760 | 8,018 |
| 2007 | 3,891 | 4,334 | 4,146 | 3,937 | 16,308 |
| 2006 | 5,256 | 5,657 | 5,328 | 5,655 | 21,896 |

**Earnings Per Share ($)**

| | 1Q | 2Q | 3Q | 4Q | Year |
|---|---|---|---|---|---|
| 2011 | 0.18 | 0.04 | 0.25 | E-0.01 | E0.35 |
| 2010 | -0.09 | 0.07 | 3.51 | 0.32 | 3.99 |
| 2009 | -1.25 | -0.50 | Nil | -0.83 | -2.58 |
| 2008 | -1.08 | -0.98 | -0.95 | -5.67 | -8.61 |
| 2007 | -0.07 | 0.17 | 0.34 | -0.21 | 0.23 |
| 2006 | -2.36 | 1.20 | 0.75 | 1.67 | 1.44 |

Fiscal year ended Dec. 31. Next earnings report expected: Early February. EPS Estimates based on S&P Operating Earnings; historical GAAP earnings are as reported.

## Dividend Data (Dates: mm/dd Payment Date: mm/dd/yy)

| Amount ($) | Date Decl. | Ex-Div. Date | Stk. of Record | Payment Date |
|---|---|---|---|---|
| 0.150 | 02/10 | 02/25 | 03/01 | 03/15/11 |
| 0.150 | 04/14 | 05/11 | 05/13 | 06/01/11 |
| 0.150 | 08/11 | 08/30 | 09/01 | 09/15/11 |
| 0.150 | 10/13 | 11/08 | 11/11 | 12/01/11 |

Dividends have been paid since 1933. Source: Company reports.

**Please read the Required Disclosures and Analyst Certification on the last page of this report.**

The **McGraw-Hill** Companies

# Weyerhaeuser Co

## Business Summary November 10, 2011

CORPORATE OVERVIEW. Weyerhaeuser, one of the world's largest integrated forest products companies, is primarily engaged in growing and harvesting timber; the production, distribution and sale of wood and paper products; and real estate development. Through its timberlands segment (14% of 2010 sales), WY manages 20.5 million acres of forestland through company-owned or leased property in eight states and Canada. It owns 5.8 million acres of these lands. This division grows and harvests trees for use as lumber, other wood and building products, and pulp and paper. It also exports logs to other countries, mostly in Asia, and sells mineral and oil and gas rights on its lands. The wood products business (41%) produces and sell softwood and hardwood lumber, plywood and veneer, composite panels, oriented strand board, and engineered lumber. About 70% of these products are used in new residential construction for floor and roof joists, structural framing, sheathing, and sub-flooring. Other lumber products are used in furniture, cabinets, decking, and pallets. The cellulose fibers unit (30%) is one of the world's largest producers of absorbent pulp used in products such as diapers and feminine hygiene products. It also makes liquid packaging board used in containers for milk, juice, and tea, paper grade pulp, and specialty pulp used in textiles, absorbent products and specialty packaging. Through Weyerhaeuser Real Estate Com-

pany (15%), the company is involved in the development of single-family housing and residential lots, including the development of master-planned communities.

MARKET PROFILE. Weyerhaeuser operates in a highly cyclical and capital-intensive industry. Demand for the company's products is dependent on a number of factors including consumer spending, white collar employment levels, domestic and Japanese new home construction and repair and remodeling activity, and movements in currency exchange rates. Historical prices for pulp and wood products have been volatile, and, despite its size, Weyerhaeuser has had only a limited direct influence over the timing and extent of price changes for its products. Pricing is significantly affected by the relationship between supply and demand, and supply is influenced primarily by fluctuations in available manufacturing capacity.

## Company Financials Fiscal Year Ended Dec. 31

| Per Share Data ($) | 2010 | 2009 | 2008 | 2007 | 2006 | 2005 | 2004 | 2003 | 2002 | 2001 |
|---|---|---|---|---|---|---|---|---|---|---|
| Tangible Book Value | NA | 19.00 | 22.58 | 27.35 | 28.92 | 27.81 | 24.84 | 17.44 | 15.80 | 25.45 |
| Cash Flow | NA | -0.18 | -5.80 | 4.43 | 6.88 | 7.80 | 10.76 | 7.23 | 6.63 | 5.94 |
| Earnings | 3.99 | -2.58 | -8.61 | 0.23 | 1.44 | 2.36 | 5.43 | 1.30 | 1.09 | 1.61 |
| S&P Core Earnings | 3.58 | -3.55 | -7.30 | -0.25 | 2.97 | 1.79 | 4.37 | 0.70 | -0.75 | NA |
| Dividends | 26.56 | 0.60 | 2.40 | 2.40 | 2.20 | 1.90 | 1.60 | 1.60 | 1.60 | 1.60 |
| Payout Ratio | NM | NM | NM | NM | 182% | 81% | 29% | 123% | 147% | 99% |
| Prices:High | 53.69 | 46.80 | 73.75 | 87.09 | 75.50 | 71.85 | 68.59 | 64.70 | 68.09 | 63.50 |
| Prices:Low | 17.18 | 18.67 | 28.68 | 59.67 | 54.25 | 60.62 | 55.06 | 45.40 | 37.35 | 42.77 |
| P/E Ratio:High | 14 | NM | NM | NM | 62 | 30 | 13 | 50 | 62 | 39 |
| P/E Ratio:Low | 4 | NM | NM | NM | 45 | 26 | 10 | 35 | 34 | 27 |

| Income Statement Analysis (Million $) | | | | | | | | | | |
|---|---|---|---|---|---|---|---|---|---|---|
| Revenue | 6,552 | 5,528 | 8,018 | 16,308 | 21,896 | 22,629 | 22,665 | 19,873 | 18,521 | 14,545 |
| Operating Income | NA | 158 | 38.0 | 1,628 | 2,914 | 3,443 | 4,028 | 2,716 | 2,455 | 1,689 |
| Depreciation | 503 | 508 | 593 | 925 | 1,283 | 1,337 | 1,322 | 1,318 | 1,225 | 876 |
| Interest Expense | 452 | 434 | 550 | 586 | 531 | 730 | 829 | 796 | 771 | 344 |
| Pretax Income | 96.0 | -842 | -2,707 | 59.0 | 826 | 906 | 1,945 | 436 | 371 | 516 |
| Effective Tax Rate | NA | 32.5% | NM | 13.6% | 57.0% | 35.8% | 34.0% | 33.9% | 35.0% | 31.4% |
| Net Income | 1,283 | -545 | -1,819 | 51.0 | 355 | 582 | 1,283 | 288 | 241 | 354 |
| S&P Core Earnings | 1,146 | -762 | -1,542 | -53.0 | 728 | 444 | 1,029 | 156 | -168 | 2.35 |

| Balance Sheet & Other Financial Data (Million $) | | | | | | | | | | |
|---|---|---|---|---|---|---|---|---|---|---|
| Cash | 1,467 | 1,918 | 2,432 | 114 | 243 | 1,104 | 1,197 | 202 | 122 | 204 |
| Current Assets | NA | 5,221 | 6,085 | 5,990 | 4,121 | 4,876 | 5,293 | 4,021 | 3,888 | 3,061 |
| Total Assets | 13,429 | 15,250 | 16,735 | 23,806 | 26,862 | 28,229 | 29,954 | 28,109 | 28,219 | 18,293 |
| Current Liabilities | NA | 995 | 1,864 | 2,921 | 3,129 | 3,255 | 3,149 | 2,525 | 2,994 | 1,863 |
| Long Term Debt | 5,060 | 5,683 | 5,557 | 6,522 | 7,675 | 8,262 | 10,144 | 12,397 | 12,721 | 5,715 |
| Common Equity | 4,612 | 4,044 | 4,814 | 7,981 | 9,095 | 9,800 | 9,255 | 7,109 | 6,623 | 6,695 |
| Total Capital | NA | 9,740 | 12,228 | 17,830 | 20,461 | 22,097 | 23,932 | 23,800 | 23,400 | 14,787 |
| Capital Expenditures | NA | 239 | 608 | 880 | 837 | 861 | 492 | 608 | 930 | 660 |
| Cash Flow | NA | -37.0 | -1,226 | 976 | 1,638 | 1,919 | 2,605 | 1,606 | 1,466 | 1,230 |
| Current Ratio | 3.9 | 5.5 | 3.4 | 2.1 | 1.3 | 1.5 | 1.7 | 1.6 | 1.3 | 1.6 |
| % Long Term Debt of Capitalization | 52.3 | 58.4 | 45.4 | 36.6 | 37.5 | 37.4 | 42.4 | 52.1 | 54.4 | 38.6 |
| % Net Income of Revenue | 19.6 | NM | NM | 0.3 | 1.6 | 2.6 | 5.7 | 1.4 | 1.3 | 2.4 |
| % Return on Assets | 9.0 | NM | NM | 0.2 | 1.3 | 2.0 | 4.4 | 1.0 | 1.0 | 1.9 |
| % Return on Equity | 29.6 | NM | NM | 0.6 | 3.8 | 6.1 | 15.7 | 4.2 | 3.6 | 5.2 |

Data as orig reptd.; bef. results of disc opers/spec. items. Per share data adj. for stk. divs.; EPS diluted. E-Estimated. NA-Not Available. NM-Not Meaningful. NR-Not Ranked. UR-Under Review.

**Office:** 33663 Weyerhaeuser Way South, Federal Way, WA 98063-9777.
**Telephone:** 253-924-2345.
**Email:** invrelations@weyerhaeuser.com
**Website:** http://www.weyerhaeuser.com

**Chrmn:** C.R. Williamson
**Pres & CEO:** D.S. Fulton
**COO:** J.M. Hillman
**SVP & CTO:** M.P. Drake

**CFO:** P. Bedient
**Investor Contact:** K.F. McAuley (253-924-2058)
**Board Members:** D. A. Cafaro, M. A. Emmert, D. S. Fulton, J. I. Kieckhefer, W. Murdy, N. Piasecki, R. H. Sinkfield, D. M. Steuert, K. Williams, C. R. Williamson

**Founded:** 1900
**Domicile:** Washington
**Employees:** 14,250

# Whirlpool Corp

**STANDARD &POOR'S**

**S&P Recommendation** HOLD ★★★★★

| Price | 12-Mo. Target Price | Investment Style |
|---|---|---|
| $46.05 (as of Nov 25, 2011) | $58.00 | Large-Cap Blend |

**GICS Sector** Consumer Discretionary
**Sub-Industry** Household Appliances

**Summary** Whirlpool, which acquired Maytag in 2006, is the world's largest manufacturer of home appliances. Sears, Roebuck is its biggest customer.

## Key Stock Statistics (Source S&P, Vickers, company reports)

| | | | | | | |
|---|---|---|---|---|---|---|
| 52-Wk Range | $92.28– 46.02 | S&P Oper. EPS 2011E | 9.77 | Market Capitalization(B) | $3.520 | Beta | 1.87 |
| Trailing 12-Month EPS | $4.55 | S&P Oper. EPS 2012E | 5.31 | Yield (%) | 4.34 | S&P 3-Yr. Proj. EPS CAGR(%) | 5 |
| Trailing 12-Month P/E | 10.1 | P/E on S&P Oper. EPS 2011E | 4.7 | Dividend Rate/Share | $2.00 | S&P Credit Rating | BBB- |
| $10K Invested 5 Yrs Ago | $6,160 | Common Shares Outstg. (M) | 76.4 | Institutional Ownership (%) | NM | | |

## Price Performance

30-Week Mov. Avg. · · · 10-Week Mov. Avg. - - GAAP Earnings vs. Previous Year   Volume Above Avg. STARS
12-Mo. Target Price — Relative Strength   ▲ Up ▼ Down ► No Change   Below Avg.   ★

Options: CBOE, P

Analysis prepared by Equity Analyst **Jim Yin, CFA** on Nov 03, 2011, when the stock traded at **$51.22**.

## Highlights

➤ We expect sales to rise 3.0% in 2012, following an increase of 2.9% projected for 2011. Our outlook for weak growth in both 2011 and 2012 reflects the sluggish economic recovery in the U.S. and uncertainty about sovereign debt issues in Europe. In addition to weak demand, we see increased competition in Latin America, which had been one of WHR's fastest growing regions. We think these headwinds will be partially offset by continued strength in Asia.

➤ We look for gross margins of 13.4% and 14.0% in 2011 and 2012, respectively, down from 14.8% in 2010 due to higher raw material costs. We think rising commodity prices are somewhat mitigated by gains in manufacturing efficiency. Excluding one-time charges, we see a non-GAAP operating margin of 3.7% and 4.3% in 2011 and 2012, respectively, down from 5.5% in 2010.

➤ Reflecting material federal energy tax credits, we estimate operating EPS of $9.77 for 2011, compared to $9.65 in 2010, excluding one-time charges of $1.68 and $4.75 in the respective years. For 2012, we estimate operating EPS of $5.31, assuming a 28% tax rate.

## Investment Rationale/Risk

➤ Our hold recommendation reflects our concern about a slower global economic recovery. Although we see strong demand for appliances in Asia and Latin America, economic growth has slowed recently in Europe and the U.S. In addition to weaker demand, we think operating margins will be hurt by higher material costs, as WHR should have difficulty in raising its prices in the current environment. We remain cautious on WHR shares despite a significant price decline.

➤ Risks to our opinion and target price include another economic recession that further weakens business conditions or growth prospects in WHR's major markets, particularly in the Americas and Europe; more competition and/or market share losses; and narrower margins resulting from higher raw material costs.

➤ Our 12-month target price of $58 is based on a target P/E of 10.9X, slightly below the midpoint of the historical range for WHR and peers, applied to our 2012 EPS projection, reflecting a more-normal tax environment than in 2011 and our cautious near-term macroeconomic outlook.

## Qualitative Risk Assessment

| LOW | MEDIUM | HIGH |
|---|---|---|

Our risk assessment reflects WHR's leading market share across many brands, offset by intense industry rivalry and heightened competition from foreign companies. We view home appliances to be cyclical, but less so than other large-ticket items, like home furnishings or automobiles.

## Quantitative Evaluations

**S&P Quality Ranking** B+

| D | C | B- | B | B+ | A- | A | A+ |
|---|---|---|---|---|---|---|---|

**Relative Strength Rank** WEAK

18

LOWEST = 1    HIGHEST = 99

## Revenue/Earnings Data

**Revenue (Million $)**

| | 1Q | 2Q | 3Q | 4Q | Year |
|---|---|---|---|---|---|
| 2011 | 4,401 | 4,730 | 4,625 | -- | -- |
| 2010 | 4,272 | 4,534 | 4,519 | 5,041 | 18,366 |
| 2009 | 3,569 | 4,169 | 4,497 | 4,864 | 17,099 |
| 2008 | 4,614 | 5,076 | 4,902 | 4,315 | 18,907 |
| 2007 | 4,389 | 4,854 | 4,840 | 5,325 | 19,408 |
| 2006 | 3,536 | 4,747 | 4,843 | 4,954 | 18,080 |

**Earnings Per Share ($)**

| | 1Q | 2Q | 3Q | 4Q | Year |
|---|---|---|---|---|---|
| 2011 | 2.17 | -2.10 | 2.27 | E2.63 | E9.77 |
| 2010 | 2.13 | 2.64 | 1.02 | 2.19 | 7.97 |
| 2009 | -0.91 | 1.04 | 1.15 | 1.24 | 4.34 |
| 2008 | 1.22 | 1.53 | 2.15 | 0.60 | 5.50 |
| 2007 | 1.55 | 2.00 | 2.20 | 2.39 | 8.10 |
| 2006 | 1.70 | 1.26 | 1.68 | 1.67 | 6.35 |

Fiscal year ended Dec. 31. Next earnings report expected: Early February. EPS Estimates based on S&P Operating Earnings; historical GAAP earnings are as reported.

## Dividend Data (Dates: mm/dd Payment Date: mm/dd/yy)

| Amount ($) | Date Decl. | Ex-Div. Date | Stk. of Record | Payment Date |
|---|---|---|---|---|
| 0.430 | 02/15 | 02/23 | 02/25 | 03/15/11 |
| 0.500 | 04/18 | 05/18 | 05/20 | 06/15/11 |
| 0.500 | 08/16 | 08/24 | 08/26 | 09/15/11 |
| 0.500 | 10/17 | 11/16 | 11/18 | 12/15/11 |

Dividends have been paid since 1929. Source: Company reports.

# Whirlpool Corp

**STANDARD &POOR'S**

## Business Summary November 03, 2011

CORPORATE OVERVIEW. Whirlpool Corp. (WHR) manufactures and markets a full line of major appliances and related products, primarily for home use. Products are manufactured in 12 countries and marketed worldwide under 13 main brand names. The company's growth strategy over the past several years has been to introduce innovative new products, strengthen customer loyalty, expand its global footprint, enhance distribution channels, and make strategic acquisitions where appropriate.

MARKET PROFILE. Of WHR's total sales in 2009, 56% were from North America. As the market leader, WHR's major product brands in the U.S. include Whirlpool, Maytag, KitchenAid, Jenn-Air, Roper, Estate, Admiral, Magic Chef, Amana, and Inglis. In Europe, which generated 19% of sales, products are marketed under the Whirlpool, Maytag, Amana, Bauknecht, Ignis, Laden, Polar and KitchenAid brand names. Markets also include Latin America and Asia.

About 22% of total sales in 2009 were from Latin America which is its fastest-growing market. In this region, WHR markets and distributes its major home appliances under the Whirlpool, Maytag, KitchenAid, Brastemp, Consul, and Eslabon de Lujo brand names. It manages appliance sales and distribution in Brazil, Argentina, Chile, and Peru through a Brazilian subsidiary, and in Bolivia, Paraguay, and Uruguay through outside distributors. Also, WHR manages appliance sales and distribution in Central American countries, the Caribbean, Venezuela, Colombia, Guatemala, and Ecuador through its Brazilian subsidiary and through distributors. In Latin America, Whirlpool has manufacturing facilities only in Brazil.

COMPETITIVE LANDSCAPE. The company has been able to retain a number one position in brand and market share in most global regions. Combined with high reliability, WHR has developed strong customer loyalty. Competitors in the appliance industry include long-time incumbents Electrolux and General Electric, as well as expanding foreign operations such as LG Electronics, Bosch Siemens, Samsung, Fisher & Paykel, and Haier from China.

## Company Financials Fiscal Year Ended Dec. 31

| Per Share Data ($) | 2010 | 2009 | 2008 | 2007 | 2006 | 2005 | 2004 | 2003 | 2002 | 2001 |
|---|---|---|---|---|---|---|---|---|---|---|
| Tangible Book Value | 9.29 | 1.86 | NM | 6.06 | NM | 21.49 | 19.85 | 15.23 | 5.82 | 11.10 |
| Cash Flow | 15.53 | 11.28 | 13.36 | 15.52 | 13.54 | 12.65 | 12.35 | 12.00 | 9.62 | 6.32 |
| Earnings | 7.97 | 4.34 | 5.50 | 8.10 | 6.35 | 6.19 | 5.90 | 5.91 | 3.78 | 0.50 |
| S&P Core Earnings | 9.19 | 4.34 | 3.17 | 7.33 | 6.33 | 5.99 | 5.58 | 5.71 | 2.12 | -1.91 |
| Dividends | 1.72 | 1.72 | 1.72 | 1.72 | 2.15 | 1.72 | 1.72 | 1.36 | 1.36 | 1.02 |
| Payout Ratio | 22% | 40% | 31% | 21% | 34% | 28% | 29% | 23% | 36% | NM |
| Prices:High | 118.44 | 85.01 | 98.00 | 118.00 | 96.00 | 86.52 | 80.00 | 73.35 | 79.80 | 74.20 |
| Prices:Low | 71.00 | 19.19 | 30.19 | 72.10 | 74.07 | 60.78 | 54.53 | 42.80 | 39.23 | 45.88 |
| P/E Ratio:High | 15 | 20 | 18 | 15 | 15 | 14 | 14 | 12 | 21 | NM |
| P/E Ratio:Low | 9 | 4 | 5 | 9 | 12 | 10 | 9 | 7 | 10 | NM |

| Income Statement Analysis (Million $) | 2010 | 2009 | 2008 | 2007 | 2006 | 2005 | 2004 | 2003 | 2002 | 2001 |
|---|---|---|---|---|---|---|---|---|---|---|
| Revenue | 18,366 | 17,099 | 18,907 | 19,408 | 18,080 | 14,317 | 13,220 | 12,176 | 11,016 | 10,343 |
| Operating Income | 1,637 | 1,257 | 1,347 | 1,717 | 1,428 | 1,291 | 1,218 | 1,219 | 1,207 | 1,147 |
| Depreciation | 555 | 525 | 597 | 593 | 550 | 442 | 445 | 427 | 405 | 396 |
| Interest Expense | 225 | 219 | 203 | 203 | 202 | 130 | 128 | 137 | 143 | 162 |
| Pretax Income | 586 | 293 | 246 | 786 | 620 | 598 | 615 | 652 | 468 | 89.0 |
| Effective Tax Rate | NA | NM | NM | 14.9% | 20.3% | 28.6% | 34.0% | 35.0% | 41.2% | 48.3% |
| Net Income | 650 | 328 | 418 | 647 | 486 | 422 | 406 | 414 | 262 | 34.0 |
| S&P Core Earnings | 714 | 327 | 241 | 587 | 484 | 408 | 384 | 401 | 147 | -130 |

| Balance Sheet & Other Financial Data (Million $) | 2010 | 2009 | 2008 | 2007 | 2006 | 2005 | 2004 | 2003 | 2002 | 2001 |
|---|---|---|---|---|---|---|---|---|---|---|
| Cash | 1,368 | 1,380 | 146 | 201 | 262 | 524 | 243 | 249 | 192 | 316 |
| Current Assets | 7,315 | 7,025 | 6,044 | 6,555 | 6,476 | 4,710 | 4,514 | 3,865 | 3,327 | 3,311 |
| Total Assets | 15,584 | 15,094 | 13,532 | 14,009 | 13,878 | 8,248 | 8,181 | 7,361 | 6,631 | 6,967 |
| Current Liabilities | 6,149 | 5,941 | 5,563 | 5,893 | 6,002 | 4,301 | 3,985 | 3,589 | 3,505 | 3,082 |
| Long Term Debt | 2,195 | 2,502 | 2,002 | 1,668 | 1,798 | 745 | 1,160 | 1,134 | 1,092 | 1,295 |
| Common Equity | 4,226 | 3,664 | 3,006 | 3,911 | 3,283 | 1,745 | 1,606 | 1,301 | 796 | 2,126 |
| Total Capital | 6,921 | 6,640 | 5,277 | 5,648 | 5,481 | 2,749 | 3,074 | 2,734 | 2,083 | 3,725 |
| Capital Expenditures | 593 | 541 | 547 | 536 | 576 | 484 | 511 | 423 | 430 | 378 |
| Cash Flow | 1,205 | 853 | 1,015 | 1,240 | 1,036 | 864 | 851 | 841 | 667 | 430 |
| Current Ratio | 1.2 | 1.2 | 1.1 | 1.1 | 1.1 | 1.1 | 1.1 | 1.1 | 0.9 | 1.1 |
| % Long Term Debt of Capitalization | 31.7 | 37.7 | 37.9 | 29.5 | 32.8 | 27.1 | 37.8 | 41.5 | 52.4 | 34.8 |
| % Net Income of Revenue | 3.5 | 1.9 | 2.2 | 3.3 | 2.7 | 2.9 | 3.1 | 3.4 | 2.4 | 0.3 |
| % Return on Assets | 4.2 | 2.3 | 3.0 | 4.6 | 4.4 | 5.1 | 5.2 | 5.9 | 3.9 | 0.5 |
| % Return on Equity | 16.5 | 9.8 | 12.1 | 18.0 | 19.3 | 25.2 | 27.9 | 40.6 | 22.8 | 1.5 |

Data as orig reptd.; bef. results of disc opers/spec. items. Per share data adj. for stk. divs.; EPS diluted. E-Estimated. NA-Not Available. NM-Not Meaningful. NR-Not Ranked. UR-Under Review.

**Office:** 2000 North M-63, Benton Harbor, MI 49022-2692.
**Telephone:** 269-923-5000.
**Email:** info@whirlpool.com
**Website:** http://www.whirlpoolcorp.com

**Chrmn & CEO:** J.M. Fettig
**EVP & CFO:** R. Templin
**SVP & General Counsel:** K. Hewitt
**CTO:** S. Sarraf

**Chief Acctg Officer & Cntlr:** L.M. Venturelli
**Investor Contact:** G. Fritz (269-923-2641)
**Board Members:** S. R. Allen, G. T. DiCamillo, J. M. Fettig, K. J. Hempel, M. F. Johnston, W. T. Kerr, J. D. Liu, H. Manwani, M. L. Marsh, W. D. Perez, M. A. Todman, M. White

**Founded:** 1906
**Domicile:** Delaware
**Employees:** 70,758

*The McGraw-Hill Companies*

# Whole Foods Market Inc

**STANDARD &POOR'S**

| S&P Recommendation **BUY** ★★★★☆ | Price $63.55 (as of Nov 25, 2011) | 12-Mo. Target Price $75.00 | Investment Style Large-Cap Blend |
|---|---|---|---|

**GICS Sector** Consumer Staples
**Sub-Industry** Food Retail

**Summary** This company owns and operates the largest U.S. chain of natural and organic foods supermarkets.

## Key Stock Statistics (Source S&P, Vickers, company reports)

| | | | | | | | |
|---|---|---|---|---|---|---|---|
| 52-Wk Range | $74.45– 46.13 | S&P Oper. EPS 2012E | 2.27 | Market Capitalization(B) | $11.260 | Beta | 1.05 |
| Trailing 12-Month EPS | $1.93 | S&P Oper. EPS 2013E | 2.60 | Yield (%) | 0.88 | S&P 3-Yr. Proj. EPS CAGR(%) | 16 |
| Trailing 12-Month P/E | 32.9 | P/E on S&P Oper. EPS 2012E | 28.0 | Dividend Rate/Share | $0.56 | S&P Credit Rating | BB+ |
| $10K Invested 5 Yrs Ago | $13,499 | Common Shares Outstg. (M) | 177.2 | Institutional Ownership (%) | 87 | | |

## Price Performance

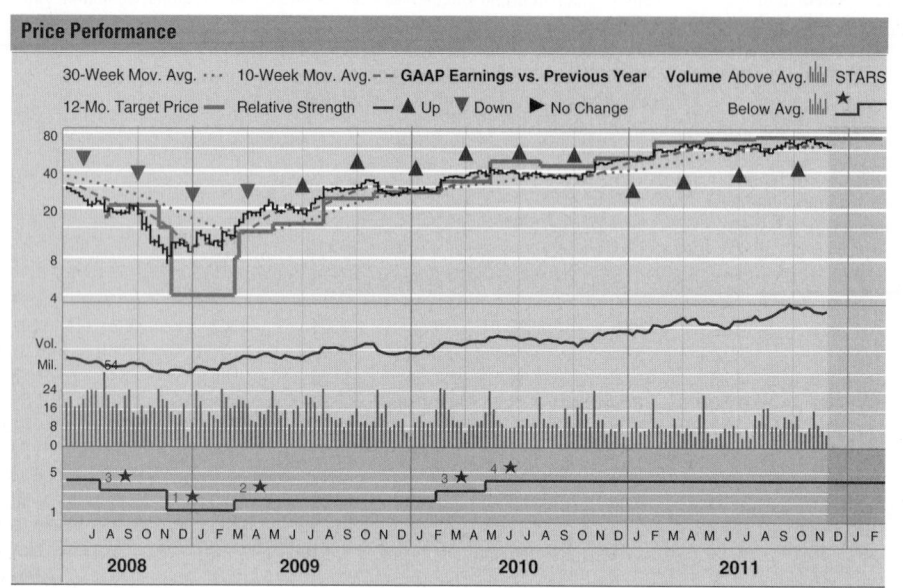

30-Week Mov. Avg. · · · · 10-Week Mov. Avg. – – ■ GAAP Earnings vs. Previous Year   Volume Above Avg. STARS
12-Mo. Target Price — Relative Strength — ▲ Up ▼ Down ► No Change   Below Avg.

Options: ASE

Analysis prepared by Equity Analyst **Joseph Agnese** on Nov 08, 2011, when the stock traded at **$68.51**.

## Highlights

➤ We expect FY 12 (Sep.) sales to increase 15%, to $11.6 billion, from $10.1 billion in FY 11, reflecting square footage growth of 7.5% from the opening of up to 25 net new stores, and as an increased selection of low-priced products and food inflation result in a comparable-store sales advance of about 8.5%. We look for comparable-store sales to continue to be driven primarily by greater traffic due to favorable industry demand for natural and organic foods and as increased value offerings lure lower-income shoppers to stores.

➤ We believe margins will expand in FY 12, reflecting increased operating leverage and distribution efficiencies, despite our projection for a rise in new store opening costs as the company re-accelerates new store expansion. We see improved inventory management leading to lower shrink expense and contributing to increased labor productivity. We expect net interest income to rise in FY 12 due to the elimination of long-term debt and increased investment income.

➤ We project that FY 12 EPS will increase 18%, to $2.27, from $1.93 in FY 11.

## Investment Rationale/Risk

➤ We believe the adoption of a new pricing strategy, increased lower-priced (value) product offerings, and the re-acceleration of square footage expansion will lead to above-average industry sales growth levels in FY 12 and beyond. In addition to funding an acceleration in square footage growth, we expect the company to utilize free cash flow by increasing its dividend and repurchasing shares.

➤ Risks to our recommendation and target price include lower-than-expected comparable-store sales growth on weaker-than-expected consumer demand and a slowdown in economic growth, with particular weakness for high-income individuals.

➤ Due to a stronger-than-expected rebound in comparable-store sales results in FY 11, we believe the stock should trade about in line with its seven-year historical P/E multiple of 33.5X. This P/E multiple is 2.4X the P/E multiple we project for the S&P 500, representing a 15% premium to its seven-year average premium of 2.1X. Applying a 33X multiple to our FY 12 EPS estimate of $2.27 results in a share value of $75, which is our 12-month target price.

## Qualitative Risk Assessment

| LOW | MEDIUM | HIGH |
|---|---|---|

Our risk assessment reflects our view of WFM's strong balance sheet and growing natural and organic food industry sales momentum, partly offset by the intensely competitive environment in the retail food industry.

## Quantitative Evaluations

**S&P Quality Ranking** B

| D | C | B- | B | B+ | A- | A | A+ |
|---|---|---|---|---|---|---|---|

**Relative Strength Rank** MODERATE

53

LOWEST = 1     HIGHEST = 99

## Revenue/Earnings Data

**Revenue (Million $)**

| | 1Q | 2Q | 3Q | 4Q | Year |
|---|---|---|---|---|---|
| 2011 | 3,004 | 2,351 | 2,400 | 2,354 | 10,108 |
| 2010 | 2,639 | 2,106 | 2,163 | 2,097 | 9,006 |
| 2009 | 2,467 | 1,858 | 1,878 | 1,829 | 8,032 |
| 2008 | 2,457 | 1,866 | 1,841 | 1,789 | 7,954 |
| 2007 | 1,871 | 1,463 | 1,514 | 1,743 | 6,592 |
| 2006 | 1,667 | 1,312 | 1,338 | 1,291 | 5,607 |

**Earnings Per Share ($)**

| | | | | | |
|---|---|---|---|---|---|
| 2011 | 0.51 | 0.51 | 0.50 | 0.42 | 1.93 |
| 2010 | 0.32 | 0.39 | 0.38 | 0.33 | 1.43 |
| 2009 | 0.20 | 0.19 | 0.25 | 0.20 | 0.85 |
| 2008 | 0.28 | 0.29 | 0.24 | 0.01 | 0.82 |
| 2007 | 0.38 | 0.32 | 0.35 | 0.24 | 1.29 |
| 2006 | 0.40 | 0.36 | 0.37 | 0.28 | 1.41 |

Fiscal year ended Sep. 30. Next earnings report expected: Early February. EPS Estimates based on S&P Operating Earnings; historical GAAP earnings are as reported.

## Dividend Data (Dates: mm/dd Payment Date: mm/dd/yy)

| Amount ($) | Date Decl. | Ex-Div. Date | Stk. of Record | Payment Date |
|---|---|---|---|---|
| 0.100 | 02/28 | 04/08 | 04/12 | 04/22/11 |
| 0.100 | 06/07 | 06/22 | 06/24 | 07/05/11 |
| 0.100 | 09/08 | 09/15 | 09/19 | 09/29/11 |
| 0.140 | 11/02 | 01/11 | 01/13 | 01/24/12 |

Dividends have been paid since 2011. Source: Company reports.

# Whole Foods Market Inc

STANDARD
&POOR'S

## Business Summary November 08, 2011

CORPORATE OVERVIEW. Whole Foods Market, established in 1980, has grown into the largest U.S. retailer of natural and organic foods, with $10.1 billion in sales in FY 11 (Sep.). Reflecting a series of store openings and acquisitions, the company has expanded from a single Austin, TX, store in 1980 to a chain of over 300 stores in 37 states plus Washington, DC, Canada, and the United Kingdom. The company strives to differentiate its stores from those of its competitors by tailoring its product mix, customer service attitude and store environment to appeal to health conscious and gourmet customers.

CORPORATE STRATEGY. The company opens or acquires stores in existing regions, and in metropolitan areas in which it believes it can become the leading natural foods supermarket retailer. In developing new stores, WFM seeks to open large format units of about 35,000 sq. ft., located on premium sites, often in urban, highly populated areas. Although approximately 30% of its store base consists of acquired stores, the company expects more of its future growth to come from developing new stores. As of November 2011, WFM's had signed leases for 62 stores averaging approximately 35,300 square feet in size, which is about 7.2% smaller than its existing store base average. It oper-

ated about 11.8 million square feet of retail space, and had about 2.2 million square feet (18.5% of existing sq. ft.) of retail space under development as of November 2011.

Stores average about 38,000 sq. ft., and offer a selection of some 30,000 food and non-food products. Each store contributes an average of over $33 million in annual sales and averages about 8.3 years old. Products sold include natural and organic foods and beverages; dietary supplements; natural personal care products; natural household goods; and educational products. Natural foods can be defined as foods that are minimally processed, largely or completely free of artificial ingredients, preservatives and other non-naturally occurring chemicals, and as near as possible to their whole, natural state. Organic foods are based on the minimal use of off-farm inputs and on management practices that restore, maintain and enhance the ecology.

## Company Financials Fiscal Year Ended Sep. 30

| Per Share Data ($) | 2011 | 2010 | 2009 | 2008 | 2007 | 2006 | 2005 | 2004 | 2003 | 2002 |
|---|---|---|---|---|---|---|---|---|---|---|
| Tangible Book Value | NA | 9.53 | 6.38 | 5.47 | 4.97 | 9.00 | 9.06 | 6.82 | 5.57 | 4.21 |
| Cash Flow | 3.55 | 3.00 | 2.66 | 2.49 | 2.60 | 2.48 | 1.93 | 1.84 | 1.54 | 1.34 |
| Earnings | 1.93 | 1.43 | 0.85 | 0.82 | 1.29 | 1.41 | 0.99 | 1.05 | 0.83 | 0.70 |
| S&P Core Earnings | NA | 1.44 | 0.92 | 0.82 | 1.29 | 1.40 | -0.21 | 0.85 | 0.70 | 0.58 |
| Dividends | 0.40 | Nil | Nil | 0.78 | 0.69 | 0.88 | 0.42 | 0.23 | Nil | Nil |
| Payout Ratio | 21% | Nil | Nil | 95% | 53% | 62% | 42% | 22% | Nil | Nil |
| Prices:High | 74.45 | 51.75 | 34.40 | 42.48 | 53.65 | 78.27 | 79.90 | 48.74 | 33.81 | 27.30 |
| Prices:Low | 47.83 | 26.88 | 9.06 | 7.04 | 36.00 | 45.56 | 44.14 | 32.96 | 22.39 | 17.74 |
| P/E Ratio:High | 39 | 36 | 40 | 52 | 42 | 56 | 81 | 47 | 41 | 39 |
| P/E Ratio:Low | 25 | 19 | 11 | 9 | 28 | 32 | 45 | 32 | 27 | 25 |

| Income Statement Analysis (Million $) | | | | | | | | | | |
|---|---|---|---|---|---|---|---|---|---|---|
| Revenue | 10,108 | 9,006 | 8,032 | 7,954 | 6,592 | 5,607 | 4,701 | 3,865 | 3,149 | 2,690 |
| Operating Income | 843 | 725 | 559 | 470 | 484 | 475 | 363 | 341 | 285 | 248 |
| Depreciation | 287 | 276 | 255 | 234 | 186 | 156 | 134 | 112 | 98.0 | 85.9 |
| Interest Expense | 3.88 | 33.1 | 42.1 | 42.4 | 4.21 | 0.03 | 2.22 | 7.25 | 8.11 | 10.4 |
| Pretax Income | 552 | 412 | 251 | 207 | 305 | 340 | 237 | 229 | 173 | 141 |
| Effective Tax Rate | NA | NA | 41.5% | 44.6% | 40.0% | 40.0% | 42.5% | 40.0% | 40.0% | 40.0% |
| Net Income | 343 | 246 | 147 | 115 | 183 | 204 | 136 | 137 | 104 | 84.5 |
| S&P Core Earnings | NA | 242 | 128 | 115 | 183 | 202 | -28.0 | 109 | 85.0 | 70.4 |

| Balance Sheet & Other Financial Data (Million $) | | | | | | | | | | |
|---|---|---|---|---|---|---|---|---|---|---|
| Cash | 654 | 462 | 430 | 30.5 | Nil | 2.25 | 309 | 198 | 166 | 12.6 |
| Current Assets | 1,453 | 1,162 | 1,055 | 623 | 668 | 624 | 673 | 485 | 364 | 172 |
| Total Assets | 4,292 | 3,987 | 3,783 | 3,381 | 3,213 | 2,043 | 1,889 | 1,520 | 1,197 | 943 |
| Current Liabilities | 879 | 748 | 684 | 666 | 785 | 510 | 418 | 331 | 240 | 176 |
| Long Term Debt | 17.4 | 508 | 739 | 929 | 736 | 8.61 | 12.9 | 165 | 163 | 162 |
| Common Equity | 2,991 | 2,373 | 1,628 | 1,506 | 1,459 | 1,404 | 1,366 | 988 | 776 | 589 |
| Total Capital | 3,009 | 2,882 | 2,780 | 2,435 | 2,195 | 1,413 | 1,379 | 1,173 | 942 | 751 |
| Capital Expenditures | 365 | 257 | 315 | 522 | 140 | 132 | 116 | 110 | 84.1 | 61.4 |
| Cash Flow | 630 | 516 | 374 | 348 | 369 | 360 | 270 | 249 | 202 | 170 |
| Current Ratio | 1.7 | 1.6 | 1.5 | 0.9 | 0.9 | 1.2 | 1.6 | 1.5 | 1.5 | 1.0 |
| % Long Term Debt of Capitalization | 0.6 | 17.6 | 26.6 | 38.2 | 33.5 | 0.6 | 0.9 | 14.0 | 17.3 | 21.6 |
| % Net Income of Revenue | 3.4 | 2.7 | 1.8 | 1.4 | 2.8 | 3.6 | 2.9 | 3.5 | 3.3 | 3.1 |
| % Return on Assets | 8.3 | 6.3 | 4.1 | 3.5 | 7.0 | 10.4 | 8.0 | 10.1 | 9.7 | 9.5 |
| % Return on Equity | 12.8 | 12.3 | 9.4 | 7.7 | 12.8 | 14.7 | 11.8 | 15.5 | 15.2 | 16.9 |

Data as orig reptd.; bef. results of disc opers/spec. items. Per share data adj. for stk. divs.; EPS diluted. E-Estimated. NA-Not Available. NM-Not Meaningful. NR-Not Ranked. UR-Under Review.

**Office:** 550 Bowie Street, Austin, TX 78703-4644.
**Telephone:** 512-477-4455.
**Website:** http://www.wholefoodsmarket.com
**Chrmn:** J.B. Elstrott, Jr.

**Pres & COO:** A.C. Gallo
**Co-CEO:** J.P. Mackey
**Co-CEO:** W. Robb
**EVP, CFO, Chief Acctg Officer & Secy:** G.J. Chamberlain

**Investor Contact:** C. McCann (512-477-4455)
**Board Members:** J. B. Elstrott, Jr., G. E. Greene, S. M. Hassan, S. Kugelman, J. P. Mackey, B. W. Nordstrom, W. Robb, J. A. Seiffer, M. Siegel, J. D. Sokoloff, R. Sorenson, W. A. Tindell, III

**Founded:** 1978
**Domicile:** Texas
**Employees:** 58,300

The McGraw-Hill Companies

# Williams Cos Inc. (The)

**STANDARD &POOR'S**

| **S&P Recommendation** HOLD ★★★★★ | **Price** $29.70 (as of Nov 25, 2011) | **12-Mo. Target Price** $33.00 | **Investment Style** Large-Cap Blend |
|---|---|---|---|

**GICS Sector** Energy
**Sub-Industry** Oil & Gas Storage & Transportation

**Summary** This integrated natural gas company plans to separate its midstream and exploration businesses into two publicly traded companies.

## Key Stock Statistics (Source S&P, Vickers, company reports)

| | | | | | | | |
|---|---|---|---|---|---|---|---|
| 52-Wk Range | $33.47– 21.90 | S&P Oper. EPS 2011E | 1.76 | Market Capitalization(B) | $17.506 | Beta | 1.27 |
| Trailing 12-Month EPS | $1.67 | S&P Oper. EPS 2012E | 1.75 | Yield (%) | 3.37 | S&P 3-Yr. Proj. EPS CAGR(%) | 33 |
| Trailing 12-Month P/E | 17.8 | P/E on S&P Oper. EPS 2011E | 16.9 | Dividend Rate/Share | $1.00 | S&P Credit Rating | BBB- |
| $10K Invested 5 Yrs Ago | $12,373 | Common Shares Outstg. (M) | 589.4 | Institutional Ownership (%) | 81 | | |

## Price Performance

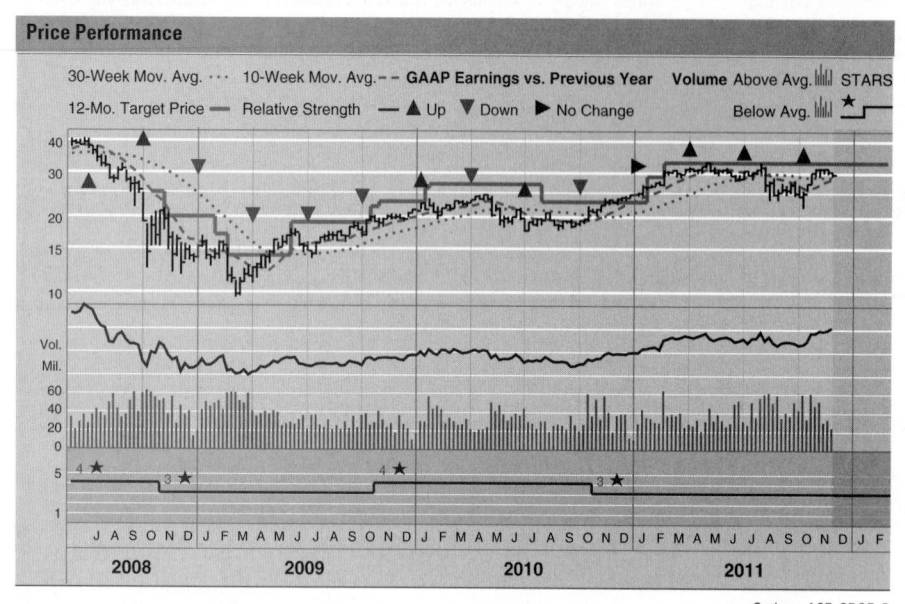

30-Week Mov. Avg. ··· 10-Week Mov. Avg. - - GAAP Earnings vs. Previous Year  Volume Above Avg. STARS
12-Mo. Target Price — Relative Strength — ▲ Up ▼ Down ▶ No Change  Below Avg. ★

Options: ASE, CBOE, P

Analysis prepared by Equity Analyst **Tanjila Shafi** on Nov 23, 2011, when the stock traded at **$29.47**.

## Qualitative Risk Assessment

| LOW | MEDIUM | HIGH |
|---|---|---|

Our risk assessment reflects the volatility of WMB's E&P segment, offset by a business portfolio focused on regulated industries with largely fixed returns.

## Quantitative Evaluations

**S&P Quality Ranking** B

| D | C | B- | B | B+ | A- | A | A+ |
|---|---|---|---|---|---|---|---|

**Relative Strength Rank** STRONG

89

LOWEST = 1         HIGHEST = 99

## Revenue/Earnings Data

**Revenue (Million $)**

| | 1Q | 2Q | 3Q | 4Q | Year |
|---|---|---|---|---|---|
| 2011 | 2,575 | 26,669 | 2,703 | -- | -- |
| 2010 | 2,596 | 2,292 | 2,304 | 2,424 | 9,616 |
| 2009 | 1,922 | 1,909 | 2,098 | 2,326 | 8,255 |
| 2008 | 3,204 | 3,701 | 3,245 | 2,202 | 12,352 |
| 2007 | 2,368 | 2,824 | 2,860 | 2,506 | 10,558 |
| 2006 | 3,028 | 2,715 | 3,300 | 2,770 | 11,813 |

**Earnings Per Share ($)**

| | | | | | |
|---|---|---|---|---|---|
| 2011 | 0.55 | 0.38 | 0.47 | E0.38 | E1.76 |
| 2010 | -0.33 | 0.32 | -2.15 | 0.29 | -1.87 |
| 2009 | -0.29 | 0.21 | 0.24 | 0.29 | 0.75 |
| 2008 | 0.70 | 0.70 | 0.62 | 0.23 | 2.26 |
| 2007 | 0.28 | 0.40 | 0.38 | 0.34 | 1.39 |
| 2006 | 0.22 | -0.11 | 0.19 | 0.25 | 0.55 |

Fiscal year ended Dec. 31. Next earnings report expected: Mid February. EPS Estimates based on S&P Operating Earnings; historical GAAP earnings are as reported.

## Highlights

➤ In 2011, we believe that profits for the company's midstream and gas pipeline segment will be $1.8 billion to $1.9 billion, compared to an adjusted segment profit of $1.54 billion in 2010. We see the company's midstream unit benefiting from higher per-unit NGL margins and NGL equity volumes. We expect projects placed into service from its Transco system to expand earnings in 2011. The company has earmarked $1.5 billion to $1.9 billion for capital expenditures in 2011.

➤ The company has guided for profits at its midstream and gas pipeline business of $1.7 billion to $2.2 billion in 2012. We expect its midstream Canada & olefins segment to benefit from the expansion of ethylene capacity at its Geismer facility.

➤ The company posted a loss per share of $1.87 in 2010. We estimate 2011 and 2012 EPS of $1.76 and $1.75, respectively, on improved pricing and lower operating costs.

## Investment Rationale/Risk

➤ WMB plans to separate its midstream and exploration businesses into two publicly traded companies via a tax-free spin-off to Williams' shareholders by year-end 2011. The company plans to use the IPO proceeds to reduce its corporate debt. We view the potential separation positively, as it should allow WMB to focus on its midstream business. In addition, WMB increased its quarterly dividend by 25%, to $0.25 per share in November, and plans to boost payments by 10% to 15% annually.

➤ Risks to our recommendation and target price include sharply higher interest rates, slower-than-projected economic growth, a sustained decline in natural gas prices, and lower rates for FERC regulated pipelines.

➤ Our 12-month target price of $33 is based on 19X our 2012 EPS estimate, in line with historical multiples.

## Dividend Data (Dates: mm/dd Payment Date: mm/dd/yy)

| Amount ($) | Date Decl. | Ex-Div. Date | Stk. of Record | Payment Date |
|---|---|---|---|---|
| 0.125 | 01/20 | 03/09 | 03/11 | 03/28/11 |
| 0.200 | 04/26 | 06/08 | 06/10 | 06/27/11 |
| 0.200 | 07/20 | 08/24 | 08/26 | 09/12/11 |
| 0.250 | 11/17 | 12/07 | 12/09 | 12/27/11 |

Dividends have been paid since 1974. Source: Company reports.

---

**Please read the Required Disclosures and Analyst Certification on the last page of this report.**

**The McGraw·Hill Companies**

# Williams Cos Inc. (The)

**STANDARD &POOR'S**

## Business Summary November 23, 2011

CORPORATE OVERVIEW. The Williams Companies (WMB) primarily finds, produces, gathers, processes and transports natural gas. Operations are concentrated in the Pacific Northwest, Rocky Mountains, Gulf Coast, Southern California and Eastern Seaboard.

In February 2009, WMB announced a business strategy focused on migrating to an integrated natural gas business comprised of a smaller portfolio of natural gas businesses, reducing debt and increasing liquidity via asset sales, strategic levels of financing, and reductions in operating costs. Beginning with the first quarter of 2010, WMB's business segments are Exploration & Production, Williams Partners and Other.

CORPORATE STRATEGY. WMB has transitioned toward aggressively focusing on the market in which it perceives a sustainable competitive advantage, primarily its E&P segment and its midstream segment. WMB has about 4.5 Tcfe of proved reserves (97% natural gas, 58% proved developed), with natural gas

produced from tight sands formations and coal bed methane.

Reduced drilling activity in 2009 due to the global recession led to a 4% decline in production in 2010. In the Piceance Basin, which represents about 57% of total WMB volumes, production fell 3%. In the Powder River Basin, WMB was producing about 230 million cubic feet per day, down 6% in 2010. In July 2010, WMB purchased 42,000 net acres from Alta Resources LLC and its partners and a 5% overriding royalty interest on 48,500 gross acres associated with the acquisition for $599 million. In December 2010, WMB purchased 85,800 net acres in the Bakken Shale for $949 million. WMB expected $1.3 billion-$1.6 billion of E&P capex in 2011.

## Company Financials Fiscal Year Ended Dec. 31

| Per Share Data ($) | 2010 | 2009 | 2008 | 2007 | 2006 | 2005 | 2004 | 2003 | 2002 | 2001 |
|---|---|---|---|---|---|---|---|---|---|---|
| Tangible Book Value | 12.44 | 12.75 | 12.85 | 9.51 | 8.48 | 7.70 | 7.06 | 5.96 | 7.15 | 9.43 |
| Cash Flow | 2.17 | 3.35 | 4.46 | 3.16 | 1.97 | 1.75 | 1.37 | 1.27 | 0.53 | 3.17 |
| Earnings | -1.87 | 0.75 | 2.26 | 1.39 | 0.55 | 0.53 | 0.18 | -0.03 | -1.14 | 1.67 |
| S&P Core Earnings | -0.02 | 0.80 | 2.14 | 1.41 | 0.84 | 0.66 | 0.05 | -0.29 | -1.34 | 1.40 |
| Dividends | 0.49 | 0.44 | 0.43 | 0.39 | 0.35 | 0.25 | 0.08 | 0.04 | 0.42 | 0.68 |
| Payout Ratio | NM | 59% | 19% | 28% | 63% | 47% | 44% | NM | NM | 41% |
| Prices:High | 24.89 | 21.54 | 40.75 | 37.74 | 28.32 | 25.72 | 17.18 | 10.73 | 26.35 | 46.44 |
| Prices:Low | 17.53 | 9.52 | 11.69 | 25.17 | 19.35 | 15.18 | 8.49 | 2.51 | 0.78 | 20.80 |
| P/E Ratio:High | NM | 29 | 18 | 27 | 51 | 49 | 95 | NM | NM | 28 |
| P/E Ratio:Low | NM | 13 | 5 | 18 | 35 | 29 | 47 | NM | NM | 12 |

| Income Statement Analysis (Million $) | | | | | | | | | | |
|---|---|---|---|---|---|---|---|---|---|---|
| Revenue | 9,616 | 8,255 | 12,352 | 10,558 | 11,813 | 12,584 | 12,461 | 16,834 | 5,608 | 11,035 |
| Operating Income | NA | NA | 3,853 | 2,938 | 2,124 | 1,972 | 1,903 | 1,849 | 1,566 | 3,389 |
| Depreciation | 2,185 | 1,469 | 1,310 | 1,082 | 866 | 740 | 668 | 671 | 775 | 798 |
| Interest Expense | 581 | 585 | 594 | 685 | 659 | 664 | 833 | 1,241 | 1,325 | 747 |
| Pretax Income | -946 | 943 | 2,221 | 1,461 | 579 | 557 | 246 | 71.0 | -617 | 1,533 |
| Effective Tax Rate | NA | 38.1% | 32.1% | 35.9% | 35.6% | 38.4% | 53.4% | 51.3% | NM | 41.1% |
| Net Income | -916 | 508 | 1,334 | 847 | 333 | 317 | 93.2 | 15.2 | -502 | 835 |
| S&P Core Earnings | -10.7 | 471 | 1,266 | 854 | 516 | 388 | 45.9 | -158 | -699 | 703 |

| Balance Sheet & Other Financial Data (Million $) | | | | | | | | | | |
|---|---|---|---|---|---|---|---|---|---|---|
| Cash | 252 | 1,188 | 800 | 1,699 | 2,269 | 1,597 | 930 | 2,316 | 2,019 | 1,301 |
| Current Assets | 2,530 | 3,793 | 4,411 | 5,538 | 6,322 | 9,697 | 6,044 | 8,795 | 12,886 | 12,938 |
| Total Assets | 24,972 | 25,280 | 26,006 | 25,061 | 25,402 | 29,443 | 23,993 | 27,022 | 34,989 | 38,906 |
| Current Liabilities | 2,574 | 2,477 | 3,519 | 4,431 | 4,694 | 8,450 | 5,146 | 6,270 | 11,309 | 13,495 |
| Long Term Debt | 8,597 | 8,258 | 7,683 | 7,757 | 7,622 | 7,591 | 7,712 | 11,040 | 11,896 | 10,621 |
| Common Equity | 7,288 | 8,447 | 8,440 | 6,375 | 6,073 | 5,428 | 4,956 | 4,102 | 4,778 | 6,044 |
| Total Capital | 19,054 | 17,292 | 20,127 | 18,558 | 17,656 | 15,741 | 15,238 | 17,595 | 20,723 | 21,532 |
| Capital Expenditures | 2,755 | 2,314 | 3,475 | 2,816 | -2,509 | 1,299 | 787 | 957 | 1,824 | 1,922 |
| Cash Flow | 1,269 | 1,977 | 2,644 | 1,929 | 1,198 | 1,057 | 762 | 657 | 274 | 1,633 |
| Current Ratio | 1.0 | 1.5 | 1.3 | 1.3 | 1.3 | 1.1 | 1.2 | 1.4 | 1.1 | 1.0 |
| % Long Term Debt of Capitalization | 45.1 | Nil | 38.2 | 41.8 | 43.2 | 48.2 | 50.6 | 62.7 | 57.4 | 49.3 |
| % Net Income of Revenue | NM | 6.2 | 10.8 | 8.0 | 2.8 | 2.5 | 0.7 | 0.1 | NM | 7.6 |
| % Return on Assets | NA | 2.0 | 5.2 | 3.4 | 1.2 | 1.2 | 0.4 | 0.0 | NM | 2.3 |
| % Return on Equity | NA | NA | 18.0 | 13.6 | 5.8 | 6.1 | 2.1 | 0.0 | NM | 14.0 |

Data as orig reptd.; bef. results of disc opers/spec. items. Per share data adj. for stk. divs.; EPS diluted. E-Estimated. NA-Not Available. NM-Not Meaningful. NR-Not Ranked. UR-Under Review.

**Office:** 1 Williams Ctr, Tulsa, OK 74172-0140.
**Telephone:** 918-573-2000.
**Website:** http://www.williams.com
**Chrmn:** F. MacInnis

**Pres & CEO:** A.S. Armstrong
**SVP & CFO:** D.R. Chappel
**SVP & Chief Admin Officer:** R.L. Ewing
**SVP & General Counsel:** J.J. Bender

**Investor Contact:** T.N. Campbell (918-573-2944)
**Board Members:** A. S. Armstrong, J. R. Cleveland, K. B. Cooper, I. F. Engelhardt, W. R. Granberry, W. E. Green, J. H. Hinshaw, W. R. Howell, W. G. Lowrie, F. MacInnis, J. D. Stoney, L. A. Sugg

**Founded:** 1908
**Domicile:** Delaware
**Employees:** 5,022

The **McGraw-Hill** Companies

# Windstream Corp

STANDARD &POOR'S

| **S&P Recommendation** | STRONG BUY ★★★★★ | **Price** $11.13 (as of Nov 25, 2011) | **12-Mo. Target Price** $14.00 | **Investment Style** Large-Cap Value |
|---|---|---|---|---|

**GICS Sector** Telecommunication Services
**Sub-Industry** Integrated Telecommunication Services

**Summary** This company was formed through the July 2006 combination of former Alltel wireline assets and Valor Communications and continues to grow via acquisitions. It provides telephone service to 3 million lines in rural markets.

## Key Stock Statistics (Source S&P, Vickers, company reports)

| | | | | | | | |
|---|---|---|---|---|---|---|---|
| 52-Wk Range | $14.40–10.76 | S&P Oper. EPS 2011E | 0.77 | Market Capitalization(B) | $5.741 | Beta | 0.87 |
| Trailing 12-Month EPS | $0.51 | S&P Oper. EPS 2012E | 0.87 | Yield (%) | 8.98 | S&P 3-Yr. Proj. EPS CAGR(%) | 5 |
| Trailing 12-Month P/E | 21.8 | P/E on S&P Oper. EPS 2011E | 14.5 | Dividend Rate/Share | $1.00 | S&P Credit Rating | BB- |
| $10K Invested 5 Yrs Ago | $12,308 | Common Shares Outstg. (M) | 515.8 | Institutional Ownership (%) | 54 | | |

## Price Performance

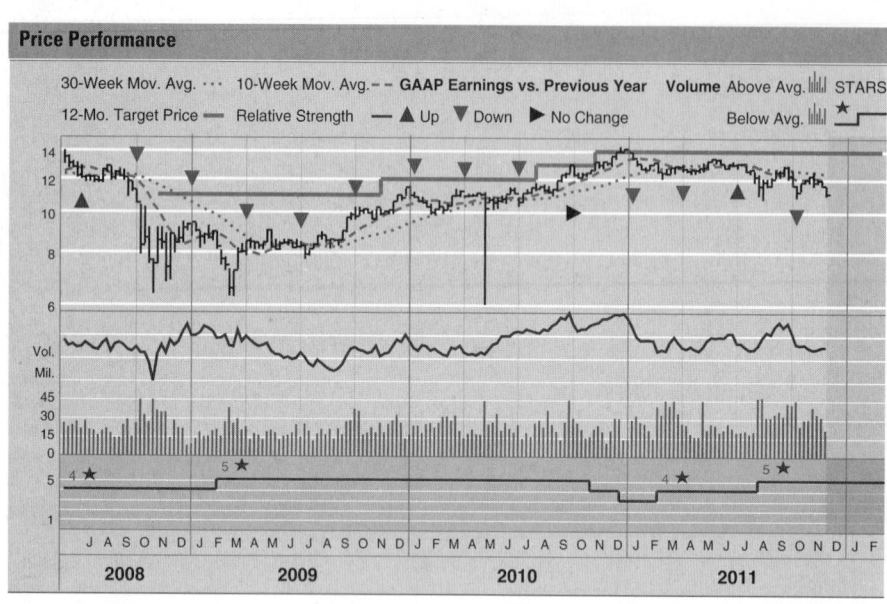

Options: CBOE, Ph

Analysis prepared by Equity Analyst **Todd Rosenbluth** on Nov 10, 2011, when the stock traded at **$11.88**.

### Highlights

➤ We project revenues of $4.10 billion in 2011, including contributions from recently closed acquisitions, down fractionally on a pro forma basis from 2010. In 2012, we expect fractional improvement to $4.13 billion, driven by gains in the business segment. Within consumer, we see broadband customer additions nearly offsetting the impact of access line losses, but growth will likely slow given an above-average penetration rate. Recent acquisitions have expanded the revenue stream, which should help as the economy improves.

➤ We expect WIN to generate EBITDA of $1.98 billion in 2011 and $2.03 billion in 2012, helped by acquisitions as well as cost synergies from consolidated billing systems. We forecast that EBITDA margins will average 49% in 2012, down from the low 50% area in prior years, due to the addition of recently acquired lower-margin operations.

➤ We forecast operating EPS of $0.77 in 2011 and $0.87 in 2012. Unlike in the past, we do not expect any share repurchases, as stock has been issued to support mergers.

### Investment Rationale/Risk

➤ Even with increased capital spending to support broadband and other initiatives, we view WIN's dividend, recently yielding an above-average 8.4%, as secure. WIN's access line base has been more stable than that of peers, and business demand has been strong despite a sluggish economy. We believe recent acquisitions are being integrated smoothly, although there are risks as WIN aims to close one more by early 2012. With our view of WIN's stronger fundamentals than many peers, we see the shares as undervalued.

➤ Risks to our recommendation and target price include increased cable telephony competition, federal or state regulatory changes that pressure cash flow, and inability to support the dividend.

➤ Using a projected enterprise value/EBITDA multiple of 7X, a slight premium to rural telecom peers with similar operating structures, we arrive at our 12-month target price of $14. At our target price, WIN's dividend yield would still be an above-average 7%, but its P/E multiple would be higher than peers.

### Qualitative Risk Assessment

| LOW | MEDIUM | HIGH |
|---|---|---|

Our risk assessment reflects the stable rural markets that WIN serves and our view of its lower-than-peer debt leverage, offset by potential risks in integrating acquisitions.

### Quantitative Evaluations

**S&P Quality Ranking** NR

| D | C | B- | B | B+ | A- | A | A+ |
|---|---|---|---|---|---|---|---|

**Relative Strength Rank** MODERATE
46
LOWEST = 1        HIGHEST = 99

### Revenue/Earnings Data

**Revenue (Million $)**

| | 1Q | 2Q | 3Q | 4Q | Year |
|---|---|---|---|---|---|
| 2011 | 1,023 | 1,030 | 1,023 | -- | -- |
| 2010 | 847.9 | 917.3 | 965.8 | 981.0 | 3,712 |
| 2009 | 755.0 | 752.9 | 734.3 | 754.4 | 2,997 |
| 2008 | 811.7 | 799.9 | 794.1 | 777.5 | 3,172 |
| 2007 | 783.7 | 826.7 | 822.6 | 827.8 | 3,261 |
| 2006 | 703.0 | 125.5 | 771.4 | 827.6 | 3,033 |

**Earnings Per Share ($)**

| | | | | | |
|---|---|---|---|---|---|
| 2011 | 0.05 | 0.18 | 0.14 | E0.20 | E0.77 |
| 2010 | 0.17 | 0.17 | 0.18 | 0.15 | 0.66 |
| 2009 | 0.20 | 0.21 | 0.18 | 0.18 | 0.77 |
| 2008 | 0.28 | 0.27 | 0.24 | 0.21 | 0.98 |
| 2007 | 0.21 | 0.24 | 0.25 | 1.25 | 1.94 |
| 2006 | -- | 0.22 | 0.21 | 0.25 | 1.02 |

Fiscal year ended Dec. 31. Next earnings report expected: NA. EPS Estimates based on S&P Operating Earnings; historical GAAP earnings are as reported.

### Dividend Data (Dates: mm/dd Payment Date: mm/dd/yy)

| Amount ($) | Date Decl. | Ex-Div. Date | Stk. of Record | Payment Date |
|---|---|---|---|---|
| 0.250 | 02/09 | 03/29 | 03/31 | 04/15/11 |
| 0.250 | 05/04 | 06/28 | 06/30 | 07/15/11 |
| 0.250 | 08/03 | 09/28 | 09/30 | 10/17/11 |
| 0.250 | 11/02 | 12/28 | 12/30 | 01/17/12 |

Dividends have been paid since 2006. Source: Company reports.

# Windstream Corp

**STANDARD &POOR'S**

## Business Summary November 10, 2011

**CORPORATE OVERVIEW.** In July 2006, Alltel Corp. spun off its wireline operations into a separate entity. Immediately after the consummation of the tax free spin-off, the entity merged with Valor Communications, and the resulting company was renamed Windstream Corporation. As of September 2011, WIN had 3.2 million access lines. The company also had 1.35 million broadband customers (with 60% of residential voice access lines), with a 4% increase in residential additions on a pro forma basis. WIN operates primarily in rural markets in the southern U.S., such as Lexington, KY, and Lincoln, NE, with an average of about 20 access lines per square mile.

**CORPORATE STRATEGY.** Since becoming a public company, WIN has looked to make small acquisitions and benefit from expense savings (consolidating call centers and IT systems) and expanding service bundles via broadband and digital TV. Combined, four deals made in 2009 and 2010 provided $55 million in synergies in 2010, according to the company. In December 2010, two additional deals were completed that have provided added synergies in 2011. Meanwhile, WIN announced plans in August 2011 to acquire PAETEC Holding, pending necessary approvals, valued at $2.3 billion.

WIN provides a wholesale satellite TV product from EchoStar with 449,000 customers (up 16% from a year ago), to retain its wireline customers and improve revenue per customer; 22% of residential customers have such service.

During 2010, WIN had success in upgrading existing DSL customers with higher-speed offerings and expected by the end of 2011 to be offering 12 Mbps of broadband service to 40% of its customers, 10 times the speed of traditional DSL service, in certain markets. WIN has also targeted its broadband product to customers without a wireline phone.

In the first nine months of 2011, WIN made investments to support fiber-to-the-cell opportunities, in an effort to benefit from wireless backhaul demand. The company expects to see increased business revenues in 2012 from these and future initiatives.

**COMPETITIVE LANDSCAPE.** We believe that WIN's access line count, which fell 3.8% in the 12 months ended September 2011, has been hurt by wireless and cable competition. Wireless coverage in rural markets has improved in recent years, and we think that many customers have dropped their landlines. However, the line loss percentage has improved from 5% in mid-2009 and is less severe than at peers.

## Company Financials Fiscal Year Ended Dec. 31

| Per Share Data ($) | 2010 | 2009 | 2008 | 2007 | 2006 | 2005 | 2004 | 2003 | 2002 | 2001 |
|---|---|---|---|---|---|---|---|---|---|---|
| Tangible Book Value | NM | NM | NM | NM | NM | NM | NA | NA | NA | NA |
| Cash Flow | 2.15 | 2.02 | 2.10 | 3.08 | 1.88 | 2.08 | 2.22 | NA | NA | NA |
| Earnings | 0.66 | 0.77 | 0.98 | 1.94 | 1.02 | 0.83 | 0.96 | NA | NA | NA |
| S&P Core Earnings | 0.71 | 0.88 | 0.87 | 0.98 | 0.95 | 0.80 | 0.80 | NA | NA | NA |
| Dividends | 1.00 | 1.00 | 1.00 | 1.00 | 0.38 | NA | NA | NA | NA | NA |
| Payout Ratio | 152% | 130% | 102% | 52% | 37% | NA | NA | NA | NA | NA |
| Prices:High | 14.40 | 11.65 | 14.05 | 15.63 | 14.43 | NA | NA | NA | NA | NA |
| Prices:Low | 6.02 | 6.28 | 6.37 | 12.38 | 11.13 | NA | NA | NA | NA | NA |
| P/E Ratio:High | 22 | 15 | 14 | 8 | 14 | NA | NA | NA | NA | NA |
| P/E Ratio:Low | 9 | 8 | 7 | 6 | 11 | NA | NA | NA | NA | NA |

| Income Statement Analysis (Million $) | | | | | | | | | | |
|---|---|---|---|---|---|---|---|---|---|---|
| Revenue | 3,712 | 2,997 | 3,172 | 3,261 | 3,033 | 3,414 | 2,934 | NA | NA | NA |
| Operating Income | NA | NA | 1,646 | 1,705 | 1,398 | 1,617 | NA | NA | NA | NA |
| Depreciation | 694 | 538 | 493 | 540 | 450 | 593 | 509 | NA | NA | NA |
| Interest Expense | 522 | 410 | 416 | 443 | 210 | 391 | 35.6 | NA | NA | NA |
| Pretax Income | 505 | 546 | 718 | 1,169 | 722 | 662 | 646 | NA | NA | NA |
| Effective Tax Rate | NA | 38.7% | 39.4% | 21.6% | 38.3% | 40.5% | 40.2% | NA | NA | NA |
| Net Income | 311 | 335 | 435 | 917 | 446 | 394 | 386 | NA | NA | NA |
| S&P Core Earnings | 332 | 379 | 385 | 462 | 451 | 382 | 382 | NA | NA | NA |

| Balance Sheet & Other Financial Data (Million $) | | | | | | | | | | |
|---|---|---|---|---|---|---|---|---|---|---|
| Cash | 42.3 | 1,063 | 297 | 72.0 | 387 | 119 | NA | NA | NA | NA |
| Current Assets | 688 | 1,456 | 709 | 498 | 877 | 533 | NA | NA | NA | NA |
| Total Assets | 11,354 | 9,145 | 8,009 | 8,211 | 8,031 | 7,751 | NA | NA | NA | NA |
| Current Liabilities | 986 | 709 | 665 | 641 | 685 | 459 | NA | NA | NA | NA |
| Long Term Debt | 7,187 | 6,271 | 5,358 | 5,331 | 5,456 | 5,525 | NA | NA | NA | NA |
| Common Equity | 831 | 261 | 252 | 700 | 470 | 533 | NA | NA | NA | NA |
| Total Capital | 8,156 | 6,556 | 6,681 | 7,137 | 6,917 | 7,064 | NA | NA | NA | NA |
| Capital Expenditures | 415 | 298 | 318 | 366 | 374 | NA | 338 | NA | NA | NA |
| Cash Flow | 1,004 | 872 | 928 | 1,457 | 895 | 987 | 895 | NA | NA | NA |
| Current Ratio | 0.7 | 2.1 | 1.1 | 0.8 | 1.3 | 1.2 | NA | NA | NA | NA |
| % Long Term Debt of Capitalization | 88.1 | 95.7 | 80.2 | 74.7 | 78.9 | 78.2 | Nil | NA | NA | NA |
| % Net Income of Revenue | 8.4 | 11.2 | 13.7 | 28.1 | 14.7 | 11.5 | 13.2 | NA | NA | NA |
| % Return on Assets | 3.0 | 3.9 | 5.4 | 11.3 | 6.9 | NA | NA | NA | NA | NA |
| % Return on Equity | 56.9 | 130.4 | 91.4 | 156.8 | 22.5 | NA | NA | NA | NA | NA |

Data as orig reptd.; bef. results of disc opers/spec. items. Per share data adj. for stk. divs.; EPS diluted. E-Estimated. NA-Not Available. NM-Not Meaningful. NR-Not Ranked. UR-Under Review.

**Office:** 4001 Rodney Parham Road, Little Rock, AR 72212.
**Telephone:** 501-748-7000.
**Website:** http://www.windstream.com
**Chrmn:** D.E. Foster

**Pres & CEO:** J. Gardner
**COO:** B.K. Whittington
**EVP, Secy & General Counsel:** J.P. Fletcher
**CFO:** A.W. Thomas

**Investor Contact:** M. Michaels (501-748-7578)
**Board Members:** C. Armitage, S. E. Beall, III, D. E. Foster, F. X. Frantz, J. Gardner, J. T. Hinson, J. K. Jones, W. A. Montgomery, A. L. Wells

**Founded:** 2000
**Domicile:** Delaware
**Employees:** 10,086

*The McGraw-Hill Companies*

# Wisconsin Energy Corp

STANDARD &POOR'S

| S&P Recommendation | **HOLD** ★★★☆☆ | | | |
|---|---|---|---|---|

**Price** $31.91 (as of Nov 25, 2011)  **12-Mo. Target Price** $34.00  **Investment Style** Large-Cap Blend

**GICS Sector** Utilities
**Sub-Industry** Multi-Utilities

**Summary** WEC serves more than 1.1 million electric customers in Wisconsin and Michigan's Upper Peninsula, and more than 1 million natural gas customers in Wisconsin.

## Key Stock Statistics (Source S&P, Vickers, company reports)

| | | | | | | | |
|---|---|---|---|---|---|---|---|
| 52-Wk Range | $33.63–27.00 | S&P Oper. EPS 2011E | 2.18 | Market Capitalization(B) | $7.380 | Beta | 0.34 |
| Trailing 12-Month EPS | $2.27 | S&P Oper. EPS 2012E | 2.29 | Yield (%) | 3.26 | S&P 3-Yr. Proj. EPS CAGR(%) | 13 |
| Trailing 12-Month P/E | 14.1 | P/E on S&P Oper. EPS 2011E | 14.6 | Dividend Rate/Share | $1.04 | S&P Credit Rating | A- |
| $10K Invested 5 Yrs Ago | $15,748 | Common Shares Outstg. (M) | 231.3 | Institutional Ownership (%) | 69 | | |

## Price Performance

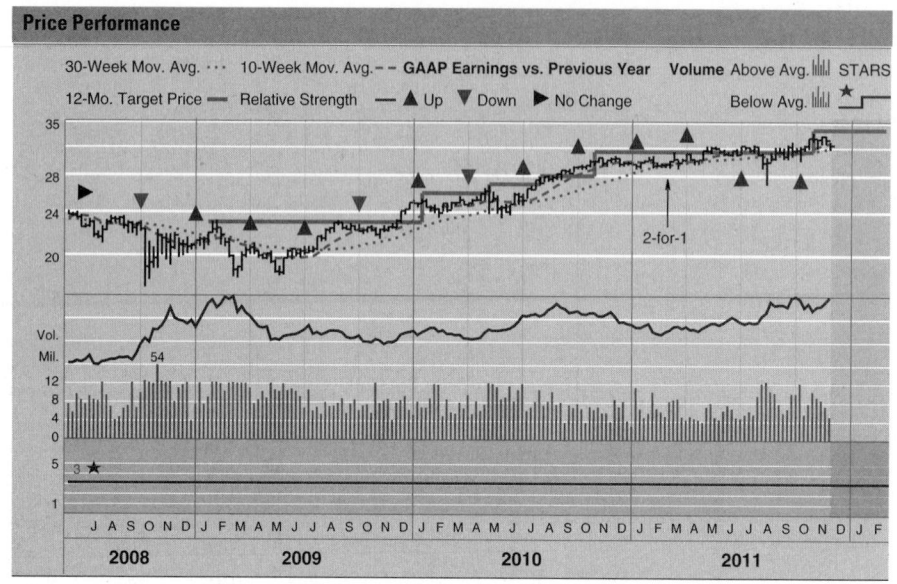

Analysis prepared by Equity Analyst **Justin McCann** on Oct 31, 2011, when the stock traded at **$32.65**.

### Qualitative Risk Assessment

| LOW | MEDIUM | HIGH |
|---|---|---|

Our risk assessment reflects our view of the company's strong and steady cash flow from the regulated utility operations, and a regulatory environment that has historically been supportive. We believe this is only partially offset by the higher risk profile of the company's non-regulated power generating subsidiary and the high level of capital expenditures the company expects to incur over the next five years.

### Quantitative Evaluations

**S&P Quality Ranking** A

| D | C | B- | B | B+ | A- | A | A+ |
|---|---|---|---|---|---|---|---|

**Relative Strength Rank** STRONG

78

LOWEST = 1    HIGHEST = 99

## Highlights

➤ We expect operating EPS in 2011 to grow about 13% from 2010's $1.92, which had grown 20% from 2009's $1.60. The growth should reflect the coming on line of the new Oak Creek Unit 2 power plant, the largely favorable weather, and a modest improvement in certain sectors of the company's service territory economy.

➤ In the first nine months of 2011, operating EPS of $1.69 was $0.30 above the year-earlier level, driven by the strong customer demand for natural gas in the first quarter due to the colder winter weather, and the new Oak Creek Unit 2 power plant, which commenced operations in January 2011 and more than offset the milder weather in the second quarter. Although the weather in the third quarter was not as favorable as in the exceptionally hot summer in 2010, it was still much warmer than normal.

➤ For 2012, we expect operating EPS to increase about 5% from anticipated results in 2011, aided by share repurchases and WEC's rate base investments in a 26%-owned transmission company. We would expect, however, these positives to be partially offset by the assumed return to more normal summer weather.

## Investment Rationale/Risk

➤ With the stock up more than 11% in the first 43 weeks of 2011, we believe the shares have become fairly valued at their recent level. The increase followed strong gains of 18% in 2010 and nearly 20% in 2009, which substantially outperformed WEC's electric and gas utility peers. With the 30% increase in the payout (effective with the March 1 payment), the recent yield from the dividend rose from 2.4% to 3.2%, and the payout ratio from 41% to 54% of WEC's operating EPS for 2010. While the yield is still well below peers (4.2%), we believe that the company's policy will result in additional dividend increases over the next couple of years.

➤ Risks to our recommendation and target price include unfavorable regulatory rulings, a downturn in the service territory economy, unscheduled power generation outages, and an investor shift out of the utilities sector.

➤ Beginning in 2012, we expect WEC to raise its dividend by about 13% in 2012 and then at an annual rate of 8% to 9% through 2015, which would make it more competitive with peers. Our 12-month target price is $34, reflecting a premium-to-peers P/E multiple of 14.8X our operating EPS estimate for 2012.

### Revenue/Earnings Data

**Revenue (Million $)**

| | 1Q | 2Q | 3Q | 4Q | Year |
|---|---|---|---|---|---|
| 2011 | 1,329 | 991.7 | 1,053 | -- | -- |
| 2010 | 1,256 | 890.9 | 973.2 | 1,090 | 4,203 |
| 2009 | 1,396 | 842.5 | 821.9 | 1,067 | 4,128 |
| 2008 | 1,432 | 946.1 | 852.5 | 1,201 | 4,431 |
| 2007 | 1,301 | 906.5 | 881.5 | 1,149 | 4,238 |
| 2006 | 1,247 | 814.4 | 839.8 | 1,095 | 3,996 |

**Earnings Per Share ($)**

| | | | | | |
|---|---|---|---|---|---|
| 2011 | 0.72 | 0.41 | 0.55 | E0.50 | E2.18 |
| 2010 | 0.55 | 0.37 | 0.48 | 0.53 | 1.92 |
| 2009 | 0.60 | 0.27 | 0.25 | 0.48 | 1.60 |
| 2008 | 0.52 | 0.25 | 0.33 | 0.43 | 1.52 |
| 2007 | 0.43 | 0.25 | 0.35 | 0.40 | 1.42 |
| 2006 | 0.44 | 0.25 | 0.30 | 0.33 | 1.32 |

Fiscal year ended Dec. 31. Next earnings report expected: Early February. EPS Estimates based on S&P Operating Earnings; historical GAAP earnings are as reported.

### Dividend Data (Dates: mm/dd Payment Date: mm/dd/yy)

| Amount ($) | Date Decl. | Ex-Div. Date | Stk. of Record | Payment Date |
|---|---|---|---|---|
| 0.260 | 01/20 | 02/10 | 02/14 | 03/01/11 |
| 0.260 | 04/21 | 05/11 | 05/13 | 06/01/11 |
| 0.260 | 07/21 | 08/10 | 08/12 | 09/01/11 |
| 0.260 | 10/20 | 11/09 | 11/14 | 12/01/11 |

Dividends have been paid since 1939. Source: Company reports.

# Wisconsin Energy Corp

**STANDARD &POOR'S**

## Business Summary October 31, 2011

CORPORATE OVERVIEW. Wisconsin Energy Corporation (WEC) is a holding company that primarily operates in two segments: utility energy and non-utility energy. The principal utilities (under the trade name We Energies) are Wisconsin Electric Power Company and Wisconsin Gas LLC). WEC's real estate business, Wispark LLC, had holdings of $46.3 million as of December 31, 2010. On May 4, 2010, WEC completed the sale of the Edison Sault Electric Company for about $63 million. In April 2009, WEC sold its water utility for $14.5 million. WEC's non-regulated segment consists primarily of We Power, which was formed to design, construct, own and lease to Wisconsin Electric the new generating capacity included in WEC's "Power the Future" strategy. In 2010, utility operations contributed 99.1% of total operating revenues.

CORPORATE STRATEGY. WEC's goal has been to strengthen its utility business through the development of a reliable power supply and through the upgrading of its infrastructure, and the divestiture of its non-energy operations. WEC has completed the implementation of its "Power the Future" strategy, which has significantly expanded its rate base and is expected to greatly improve the supply and reliability of power in its service territory. The company had invested in four new electric generation facilities (the final two of which were placed into service in January 2011 and February 2010) and has also upgraded its existing facilities. The strategy also included an upgrade of the company's existing distribution facilities. WEC is also working to further enhance its operational synergies through its integration of the businesses of

Wisconsin Electric and Wisconsin Gas, which it believes will result in improved customer satisfaction.

MARKET PROFILE. In 2010, We Energies served more than 1.12 million electric customers in Wisconsin and (through its Edison Sault unit) the Upper Peninsula of Michigan, more than 1.06 million gas customers in Wisconsin, and about 460 steam customers in Milwaukee. Over the next five years, WEC estimates that the utility energy segment in the service territories will grow at an annual rate of 0.5% to 1.0%; annual peak electric demand is also projected to grow at a rate of 0.5% to 1.0%. In 2010, residential customers accounted for 37.9% of electric utility revenues from ongoing operations (36.4% in 2009); small commercial/industrial customers 31.4% (32.0%); large commercial and industrial users 23.1% (22.3%); other retail 0.7% (0.8%); other wholesale 4.6% (4.3%); resale-utilities 1.4% (1.8%); and other 0.9% (2.3%). Residential customers accounted for 63.4% of gas utility revenues in 2010 (62.6% in 2009); commercial/industrial customers 31.3% (32.4%); transported gas 4.0% (3.2%); and other 1.3% (1.8%). In 2010, coal accounted for 53.9% of WEC's total fuel sources; purchased power 35.4%; natural gas 8.7%; hydroelectric 1.0%; and wind 1.0%.

## Company Financials Fiscal Year Ended Dec. 31

| Per Share Data ($) | 2010 | 2009 | 2008 | 2007 | 2006 | 2005 | 2004 | 2003 | 2002 | 2001 |
|---|---|---|---|---|---|---|---|---|---|---|
| Tangible Book Value | 14.37 | 13.37 | 12.38 | 11.36 | 10.46 | 0.36 | 8.77 | 6.43 | 5.63 | 5.31 |
| Earnings | 1.92 | 1.60 | 1.52 | 1.42 | 1.32 | 1.28 | 0.52 | 1.03 | 0.72 | 0.89 |
| S&P Core Earnings | 1.44 | 1.93 | -0.16 | 2.70 | 2.70 | 2.55 | 0.84 | 1.97 | 0.93 | 1.19 |
| Dividends | 0.80 | 0.68 | 0.54 | 0.50 | 0.46 | 0.44 | 0.42 | 0.40 | 0.40 | 0.40 |
| Payout Ratio | 42% | 42% | 36% | 35% | 35% | 34% | 81% | 39% | 56% | 45% |
| Prices:High | 30.51 | 25.31 | 24.81 | 25.24 | 24.35 | 20.42 | 17.30 | 16.84 | 13.24 | 12.31 |
| Prices:Low | 23.42 | 18.16 | 17.45 | 20.53 | 19.08 | 16.67 | 14.75 | 11.28 | 10.09 | 9.56 |
| P/E Ratio:High | 16 | 16 | 16 | 18 | 18 | 16 | 34 | 16 | 18 | 14 |
| P/E Ratio:Low | 12 | 11 | 12 | 14 | 14 | 13 | 29 | 11 | 14 | 11 |

| Income Statement Analysis (Million $) | 2010 | 2009 | 2008 | 2007 | 2006 | 2005 | 2004 | 2003 | 2002 | 2001 |
|---|---|---|---|---|---|---|---|---|---|---|
| Revenue | 4,203 | 4,128 | 4,431 | 4,238 | 3,996 | 3,816 | 3,431 | 4,054 | 3,736 | 3,929 |
| Depreciation | 317 | 349 | 332 | 328 | 326 | 332 | 327 | 332 | 321 | 342 |
| Maintenance | NA | NA | NA | NA | NA | NA | NA | NA | NA | NA |
| Fixed Charges Coverage | 4.12 | 4.42 | 4.41 | 4.00 | 3.60 | 3.61 | 2.64 | 2.68 | 2.03 | 2.17 |
| Construction Credits | NA | NA | NA | NA | NA | NA | 2.80 | 18.6 | 11.2 | 15.2 |
| Effective Tax Rate | 35.5% | 36.6% | 37.7% | 39.1% | 35.9% | 33.0% | 39.7% | 35.6% | 38.8% | 41.9% |
| Net Income | 454 | 377 | 359 | 337 | 313 | 304 | 122 | 244 | 167 | 209 |
| S&P Core Earnings | 339 | 227 | -18.7 | 320 | 319 | 302 | 98.5 | 233 | 108 | 142 |

| Balance Sheet & Other Financial Data (Million $) | 2010 | 2009 | 2008 | 2007 | 2006 | 2005 | 2004 | 2003 | 2002 | 2001 |
|---|---|---|---|---|---|---|---|---|---|---|
| Gross Property | 13,226 | 12,543 | 11,832 | 10,805 | 10,476 | 9,651 | 9,025 | 9,017 | 8,406 | 8,014 |
| Capital Expenditures | 798 | 818 | 1,137 | 1,212 | 929 | 745 | 637 | 659 | 557 | 672 |
| Net Property | 9,602 | 9,071 | 8,517 | 7,681 | 7,053 | 6,363 | 5,903 | 5,926 | 4,399 | 4,188 |
| Capitalization:Long Term Debt | 3,962 | 3,906 | 4,105 | 3,203 | 3,104 | 3,061 | 3,270 | 3,605 | 3,261 | 3,468 |
| Capitalization:% Long Term Debt | 51.0 | 52.3 | 55.2 | 50.8 | 51.8 | 50.9 | 55.3 | 60.1 | 60.4 | 62.8 |
| Capitalization:Preferred | Nil | Nil | Nil | Nil | Nil | Nil | Nil | Nil | Nil | Nil |
| Capitalization:% Preferred | Nil | Nil | Nil | Nil | Nil | Nil | Nil | Nil | Nil | Nil |
| Capitalization:Common | 3,802 | 3,567 | 3,337 | 3,099 | 2,889 | 2,955 | 2,645 | 2,393 | 2,139 | 2,056 |
| Capitalization:% Common | 49.0 | 47.7 | 44.8 | 49.2 | 48.2 | 49.1 | 44.7 | 39.9 | 39.6 | 37.2 |
| Total Capital | 8,238 | 7,769 | 8,298 | 6,902 | 6,618 | 6,666 | 6,507 | 6,712 | 6,039 | 6,147 |
| % Operating Ratio | 86.7 | 89.2 | 90.0 | 90.4 | 90.2 | 89.2 | 86.9 | 88.6 | 86.8 | 88.4 |
| % Earned on Net Property | 8.7 | 7.6 | 8.2 | 8.4 | 8.5 | 9.2 | 6.5 | 9.6 | 10.7 | 14.5 |
| % Return on Revenue | 10.8 | 9.1 | 8.1 | 7.9 | 7.8 | 8.0 | 3.6 | 6.0 | 4.5 | 5.3 |
| % Return on Invested Capital | 7.5 | 6.2 | 6.1 | 6.8 | 7.5 | 7.2 | 7.1 | 8.1 | 13.6 | 8.0 |
| % Return on Common Equity | 12.3 | 10.9 | 11.1 | 11.2 | 11.2 | 10.8 | 4.9 | 10.5 | 8.0 | 10.2 |

Data as orig reptd.; bef. results of disc opers/spec. items. Per share data adj. for stk. divs.; EPS diluted. E-Estimated. NA-Not Available. NM-Not Meaningful. NR-Not Ranked. UR-Under Review.

**Office:** 231 West Michigan Street, Milwaukee, WI 53201.
**Telephone:** 414-221-2345.
**Website:** http://www.wisconsinenergy.com
**Chrmn, Pres & CEO:** G.E. Klappa

**CFO:** F.D. Kuester
**Chief Admin Officer:** K.A. Rappe
**Treas:** J.P. Keyes
**Secy:** S.H. Martin

**Investor Contact:** C.F. Henderson (414-221-2592)
**Board Members:** J. F. Bergstrom, B. L. Bowles, P. W. Chadwick, R. A. Cornog, C. S. Culver, T. J. Fischer, G. E. Klappa, U. Payne, Jr., F. P. Stratton, Jr.

**Founded:** 1981
**Domicile:** Wisconsin
**Employees:** 4,596

The *McGraw-Hill* Companies

# Wyndham Worldwide Corp

**STANDARD &POOR'S**

| S&P Recommendation | HOLD ★★★☆☆ | Price $32.90 (as of Nov 25, 2011) | 12-Mo. Target Price $36.00 | Investment Style Large-Cap Blend |

**GICS Sector** Consumer Discretionary
**Sub-Industry** Hotels, Resorts & Cruise Lines

**Summary** This company sells interests in vacation ownership resorts, facilitates the exchange and rental of access to vacation properties, and franchises hotels.

## Key Stock Statistics (Source S&P, Vickers, company reports)

| | | | | | | | |
|---|---|---|---|---|---|---|---|
| 52-Wk Range | $36.00– 24.76 | S&P Oper. EPS 2011E | 2.50 | Market Capitalization(B) | $5.067 | Beta | 2.96 |
| Trailing 12-Month EPS | $2.53 | S&P Oper. EPS 2012E | 2.75 | Yield (%) | 1.82 | S&P 3-Yr. Proj. EPS CAGR(%) | 8 |
| Trailing 12-Month P/E | 13.0 | P/E on S&P Oper. EPS 2011E | 13.2 | Dividend Rate/Share | $0.60 | S&P Credit Rating | BBB- |
| $10K Invested 5 Yrs Ago | $11,229 | Common Shares Outstg. (M) | 154.0 | Institutional Ownership (%) | 98 | | |

## Price Performance

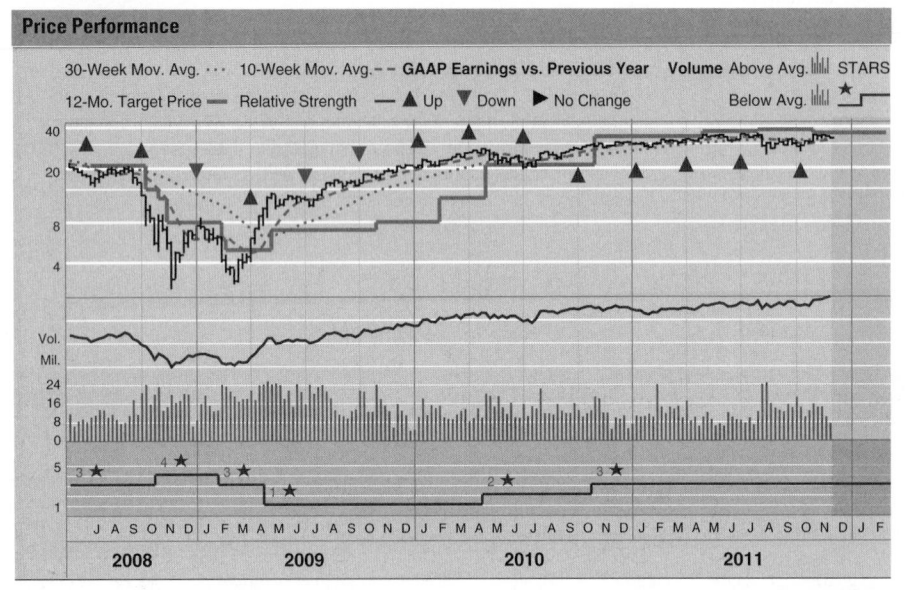

Analysis prepared by Equity Analyst **Esther Kwon, CFA** on Oct 27, 2011, when the stock traded at **$35.18**.

Options: CBOE, Ph

## Qualitative Risk Assessment

| LOW | MEDIUM | HIGH |

Our risk assessment reflects our view that the company's business is sensitive to changes in consumer confidence and hotel room demand, as well as the receptivity of credit markets to its securitized vacation ownership receivables.

## Quantitative Evaluations

**S&P Quality Ranking** NR

| D | C | B- | B | B+ | A- | A | A+ |

**Relative Strength Rank** STRONG

87

LOWEST = 1      HIGHEST = 99

## Highlights

▸ For 2011, we project about a 10% revenue increase, led by lodging RevPAR growth in the mid-single digits, with a room count increase in the low single digits, after adjusted revenue growth of 8% in 2010 (excluding $187 million of vacation ownership revenue associated with percentage of completion accounting in 2009). We forecast a strong double-digit rate rise in vacation exchange and rentals revenue, and we expect vacation ownership tours and volume per guest to rise modestly in 2011. For 2012, we forecast a 4.4% rise in revenue.

▸ We see expenses a bit higher in 2011 versus 2010, primarily from the effects of cost cuts enacted in 2009 being somewhat outweighed by modest cost inflation, but lower as a percentage of revenue. On a significantly higher effective tax rate of 38.6%, compared to approximately 34% in 2010, but fewer shares outstanding, we estimate EPS of $2.50, up from operating EPS of $2.00 in 2010. For 2012, we project EPS of $2.75.

▸ We estimate adjusted EBITDA in 2011 of approximately $980 million, up from an adjusted $861 million in 2010. For 2012, we forecast adjusted EBITDA of over $1 billion.

## Investment Rationale/Risk

▸ We believe lodging industry fundamentals will likely improve this year, and we see cost reductions improving the EBITDA margin. While we remain somewhat cautious on timeshare segment results and more limited exposure to stronger international lodging trends, we believe WYN's significant valuation discount to peers and to its historical average adequately incorporates these potential risks.

▸ Risks to our recommendation and target price include a dramatic decline in consumer confidence and a related reduction in travel spending. Also, a tighter market for financing would likely hamper growth.

▸ We believe the stock should have a lower enterprise value/EBITDA multiple than some lodging industry peers in our coverage universe, given the company's higher revenue mix of vacation exchange, ownership sales and financing, as well as legacy tax liabilities. Our 12-month target price of $36 reflects an enterprise value/EBITDA multiple of approximately 7X applied to our 2012 EBITDA estimate, a significant discount to the lodging peer average of approximately 13X and below its historical forward average of 8.8X.

## Revenue/Earnings Data

**Revenue (Million $)**

| | 1Q | 2Q | 3Q | 4Q | Year |
|---|---|---|---|---|---|
| 2011 | 952.0 | 1,090 | 1,212 | -- | -- |
| 2010 | 886.0 | 963.0 | 1,065 | 937.0 | 3,851 |
| 2009 | 901.0 | 920.0 | 1,016 | 913.0 | 3,750 |
| 2008 | 1,012 | 1,132 | 1,226 | 911.0 | 4,281 |
| 2007 | 1,012 | 1,100 | 1,216 | 1,032 | 4,360 |
| 2006 | 870.0 | 955.0 | 1,047 | 970.0 | 3,842 |

**Earnings Per Share ($)**

| | | | | | |
|---|---|---|---|---|---|
| 2011 | 0.41 | 0.67 | 1.08 | E0.49 | E2.50 |
| 2010 | 0.27 | 0.51 | 0.84 | 0.43 | 2.05 |
| 2009 | 0.25 | 0.39 | 0.57 | 0.40 | 1.61 |
| 2008 | 0.24 | 0.55 | 0.80 | -7.62 | -6.03 |
| 2007 | 0.45 | 0.52 | 0.65 | 0.59 | 2.20 |
| 2006 | 0.46 | 0.37 | 0.45 | 0.48 | 1.77 |

Fiscal year ended Dec. 31. Next earnings report expected: NA. EPS Estimates based on S&P Operating Earnings; historical GAAP earnings are as reported.

## Dividend Data (Dates: mm/dd Payment Date: mm/dd/yy)

| Amount ($) | Date Decl. | Ex-Div. Date | Stk. of Record | Payment Date |
|---|---|---|---|---|
| 0.150 | 02/25 | 03/08 | 03/10 | 03/25/11 |
| 0.150 | 05/12 | 05/24 | 05/26 | 06/10/11 |
| 0.150 | 08/11 | 08/23 | 08/25 | 09/09/11 |
| 0.150 | 11/10 | 11/21 | 11/23 | 12/09/11 |

Dividends have been paid since 2007. Source: Company reports.

---

**Please read the Required Disclosures and Analyst Certification on the last page of this report.**

The McGraw-Hill Companies

# Wyndham Worldwide Corp

## Business Summary October 27, 2011

Wyndham Worldwide Corp. provides hospitality products and services to individual consumers and business customers in the United States and internationally. The company offers its products under the following brands: Wyndham Hotels and Resorts, Ramada, Days Inn, Super 8, Howard Johnson, Wyndham Rewards, Wingate by Wyndham, Microtel, RCI, The Registry Collection, ResortQuest, Landal GreenParks, Novasol, Hoseasons, cottages4you, James Villa Holidays, Wyndham Vacation Resorts, and WorldMark by Wyndham.

The Lodging segment franchises hotels in the upscale, midscale, economy and extended stay segments of the lodging industry and provides hotel management services for full-service hotels globally. As of December 31, 2010, the company's lodging business, Wyndham Hotel Group, comprised 15 brands, with approximately 7,210 hotels representing approximately 612,700 rooms on six continents and approximately 900 hotels representing approximately 102,700 rooms in the development pipeline.

The company's management business offers hotel owners the benefits of a global brand and a range of management, marketing and reservation services. In addition to the standard franchise services, its hotel management business provides hotel owners with professional oversight and operations support services, such as hiring, training and supervising the managers and employees that operate the hotels, as well as annual budget preparation, financial analysis, and food and beverage services.

The Vacation Exchange and Rentals segment provides vacation exchange products and services and access to distribution systems and networks to resort developers and owners of intervals of vacation ownership interests (VOIs), and it markets vacation rental properties primarily on behalf of independent owners, vacation ownership developers, and other hospitality providers.

The company's vacation exchange and rentals business has access for specified periods, in a majority of cases on an exclusive basis, to approximately 97,000 vacation properties, which comprise approximately 4,000 vacation ownership resorts around the world through its vacation exchange business, and approximately 93,000 vacation rental properties with approximately 87,000 properties located principally in Europe and approximately 6,000 located in the U.S. The properties available to leisure travelers through its vacation exchange and rentals business include vacation ownership condominiums, homes, villas, cottages, bungalows, campgrounds, hotel rooms and suites, city apartments, fractional private residences, luxury destination clubs, and yachts.

## Company Financials Fiscal Year Ended Dec. 31

| Per Share Data ($) | 2010 | 2009 | 2008 | 2007 | 2006 | 2005 | 2004 | 2003 | 2002 | 2001 |
|---|---|---|---|---|---|---|---|---|---|---|
| Tangible Book Value | 1.53 | 1.41 | NM | NM | NM | NM | NA | NA | NA | NA |
| Cash Flow | 2.98 | 2.59 | -5.00 | 2.96 | 2.63 | 2.37 | NA | NA | NA | NA |
| Earnings | 2.05 | 1.61 | -6.03 | 2.20 | 1.77 | 1.73 | NA | NA | NA | NA |
| S&P Core Earnings | 2.05 | 1.61 | 1.47 | 2.20 | 1.75 | 1.97 | NA | NA | NA | NA |
| Dividends | 0.48 | 0.16 | 0.16 | 0.08 | Nil | Nil | NA | NA | NA | NA |
| Payout Ratio | 23% | 10% | NM | 4% | Nil | Nil | NA | NA | NA | NA |
| Prices:High | 31.41 | 21.45 | 25.00 | 39.40 | 34.87 | NA | NA | NA | NA | NA |
| Prices:Low | 19.44 | 2.77 | 2.55 | 23.28 | 25.48 | NA | NA | NA | NA | NA |
| P/E Ratio:High | 15 | 13 | NM | 18 | 20 | NA | NA | NA | NA | NA |
| P/E Ratio:Low | 10 | 2 | NM | 11 | 14 | NA | NA | NA | NA | NA |

| Income Statement Analysis (Million $) | | | | | | | | | | |
|---|---|---|---|---|---|---|---|---|---|---|
| Revenue | 3,851 | 3,750 | 4,281 | 4,360 | 3,842 | 3,471 | 3,014 | 2,652 | NA | NA |
| Operating Income | 909 | 834 | 865 | 821 | 824 | 699 | 719 | 602 | NA | NA |
| Depreciation | 173 | 178 | 184 | 139 | 148 | 135 | 119 | 107 | NA | NA |
| Interest Expense | 167 | 114 | 99.0 | 96.0 | 67.0 | 41.0 | 34.0 | 6.00 | NA | NA |
| Pretax Income | 563 | 493 | -887 | 655 | 542 | 523 | 587 | 500 | NA | NA |
| Effective Tax Rate | NA | 40.6% | NM | 38.5% | 35.1% | 29.8% | 39.9% | 37.2% | NA | NA |
| Net Income | 379 | 293 | -1,074 | 403 | 352 | 367 | 349 | 299 | NA | NA |
| S&P Core Earnings | 379 | 293 | 261 | 404 | 352 | 419 | NA | NA | NA | NA |

| Balance Sheet & Other Financial Data (Million $) | | | | | | | | | | |
|---|---|---|---|---|---|---|---|---|---|---|
| Cash | 156 | 155 | 136 | 276 | 269 | 106 | 94.0 | NA | NA | NA |
| Current Assets | 1,752 | 1,740 | 1,914 | 2,056 | 2,052 | 1,874 | 2,075 | NA | NA | NA |
| Total Assets | 9,416 | 9,352 | 9,573 | 10,459 | 9,520 | 8,590 | 8,343 | NA | NA | NA |
| Current Liabilities | 1,575 | 1,885 | 2,169 | 2,180 | 1,977 | 2,212 | 1,179 | NA | NA | NA |
| Long Term Debt | 3,537 | 3,183 | 3,331 | 3,195 | 1,322 | 1,733 | 1,478 | NA | NA | NA |
| Common Equity | 2,917 | 2,688 | 2,342 | 3,516 | 3,559 | 3,464 | 4,679 | NA | NA | NA |
| Total Capital | 6,688 | 6,255 | 6,136 | 7,638 | 5,663 | 5,987 | 6,447 | NA | NA | NA |
| Capital Expenditures | 167 | 135 | 187 | 194 | 191 | 134 | 116 | 102 | NA | NA |
| Cash Flow | 552 | 471 | -890 | 542 | 500 | 502 | 468 | 406 | NA | NA |
| Current Ratio | 1.1 | 0.9 | 0.9 | 0.9 | 1.0 | 0.9 | 1.8 | NA | NA | NA |
| % Long Term Debt of Capitalization | 52.9 | Nil | 54.3 | 41.8 | 23.3 | 28.9 | 22.9 | Nil | NA | NA |
| % Net Income of Revenue | 9.8 | 7.8 | NM | 9.2 | 9.2 | 10.5 | 11.6 | 11.3 | NA | NA |
| % Return on Assets | NA | NA | NM | 4.0 | 3.8 | NA | NA | NA | NA | NA |
| % Return on Equity | NA | NA | NM | 11.4 | 8.2 | NA | NA | NA | NA | NA |

Data as orig reptd.; bef. results of disc opers/spec. items. Per share data adj. for stk. divs.; EPS diluted. E-Estimated. NA-Not Available. NM-Not Meaningful. NR-Not Ranked. UR-Under Review.

**Office:** 22 Sylvan Wy, Parsippany, NJ 07054.
**Telephone:** 973-753-6000.
**Website:** http://www.wyndhamworldwide.com
**Chrmn & CEO:** S.P. Holmes

**EVP & CFO:** T.G. Conforti
**EVP, Secy & General Counsel:** S.G. McLester
**SVP & Chief Acctg Officer:** N. Rossi
**SVP & CIO:** D. Kornick

**Investor Contact:** M. Happer (973-753-5500)
**Board Members:** M. J. Biblowit, J. E. Buckman, G. Herrera, S. P. Holmes, M. B. Mulroney, P. Richards, M. H. Wargotz

**Founded:** 2003
**Domicile:** Delaware
**Employees:** 26,400

# STANDARD & POOR'S

# Wynn Resorts Ltd

| | | | |
|---|---|---|---|
| **S&P Recommendation** BUY ★★★★☆ | **Price** $107.02 (as of Nov 25, 2011) | **12-Mo. Target Price** $154.00 | **Investment Style** Large-Cap Growth |

**GICS Sector** Consumer Discretionary
**Sub-Industry** Casinos & Gaming

**Summary** This company is involved in the design, development, financing and construction of gaming projects in Las Vegas and Macau.

## Key Stock Statistics (Source S&P, Vickers, company reports)

| | | | | | | | | |
|---|---|---|---|---|---|---|---|---|
| 52-Wk Range | $172.58–99.21 | S&P Oper. EPS 2011E | 5.42 | Market Capitalization(B) | $13.289 | Beta | 2.45 |
| Trailing 12-Month EPS | $4.28 | S&P Oper. EPS 2012E | 6.27 | Yield (%) | 1.87 | S&P 3-Yr. Proj. EPS CAGR(%) | 25 |
| Trailing 12-Month P/E | 25.0 | P/E on S&P Oper. EPS 2011E | 19.7 | Dividend Rate/Share | $2.00 | S&P Credit Rating | BB+ |
| $10K Invested 5 Yrs Ago | $15,067 | Common Shares Outstg. (M) | 124.2 | Institutional Ownership (%) | 62 | | |

## Price Performance

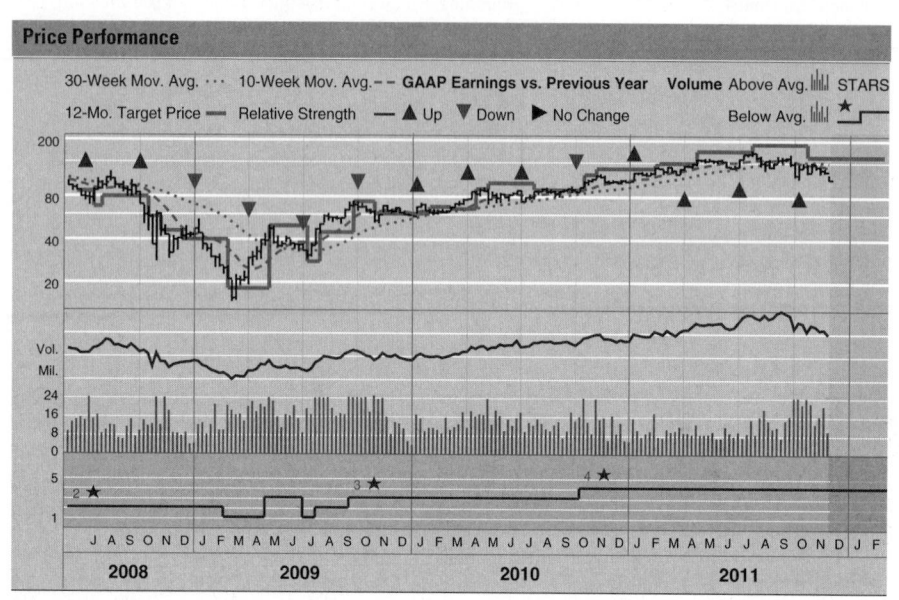

30-Week Mov. Avg. · · · · 10-Week Mov. Avg. – – **GAAP Earnings vs. Previous Year** Volume Above Avg. STARS
12-Mo. Target Price — Relative Strength — ▲ Up ▼ Down ► No Change Below Avg.

Options: ASE, CBOE, P, Ph

Analysis prepared by Equity Analyst **Esther Kwon, CFA** on Oct 21, 2011, when the stock traded at **$120.40**.

## Highlights

► We estimate that net revenue for 2011 will rise over 25% from the $4.2 billion reported for 2010, bolstered by a full year's results from the Encore at Wynn Macau, which opened in April 2010, including approximately 410 luxury suites and four villas, in addition to retail and gaming space. In the U.S., we forecast revenues will continue to improve this year, as higher-priced convention and group business returns and room rates at Wynn Las Vegas benefit from its recent refurbishment program. In Macau, we estimate that WYNN's revenues will rise at a double-digit rate after jumping nearly 60% in 2010. We forecast 9% revenue growth in 2012.

► For 2011, we see EBITDA property margins rising, driven by improvement in efficiencies at the Encore in Macau and increased leverage on higher volumes at both properties. In Las Vegas, we project accelerating improvement on higher convention and group rates, and completion of the remodeling of rooms at Wynn Las Vegas in the second quarter of 2011.

► With our projection for slightly more shares outstanding, we estimate EPS of $5.42 for 2011, up significantly from 2010's operating EPS of $2.11. For 2012, we forecast EPS of $6.27.

## Investment Rationale/Risk

► We see WYNN's results benefiting from strength in its Macau operations, which we estimate will account for approximately 70% of 2011 total property EBITDA. We also expect improving Las Vegas Strip fundamentals as higher-margin convention visitation likely accelerates, its relatively affluent customer base continues to spend, and hotel room supply growth slows markedly in 2011 and 2012, after large increases in 2008 and 2009. Longer term, we see the development of a project on the Cotai Strip in Macau as a driver for further growth.

► Risks to our recommendation and target price include the possibility that profit from Macau will be lower than we expect, or that Las Vegas properties will experience an accelerated decline in room revenue or gaming handle.

► Our 12-month target price of $154 is based on an EV/EBITDA multiple of 12X our 2012 EBITDA estimate, a premium to gaming peers but below the historical average. We believe a higher-than-peers multiple is warranted given WYNN's exposure to the Macau market, which we see as having better prospects over the long term, and our view of its solid balance sheet compared to many peers.

## Qualitative Risk Assessment

| LOW | MEDIUM | HIGH |
|---|---|---|

In our view, there is likely to be an opportunity for additional expansion by WYNN in Macau. However, we see uncertainty surrounding the regulatory environment.

## Quantitative Evaluations

**S&P Quality Ranking** NR

| D | C | B- | B | B+ | A- | A | A+ |
|---|---|---|---|---|---|---|---|

**Relative Strength Rank** WEAK

15

LOWEST = 1     HIGHEST = 99

## Revenue/Earnings Data

**Revenue (Million $)**

| | 1Q | 2Q | 3Q | 4Q | Year |
|---|---|---|---|---|---|
| 2011 | 1,260 | 1,367 | 1,298 | -- | -- |
| 2010 | 908.9 | 1,033 | 1,006 | 1,237 | 4,185 |
| 2009 | 740.0 | 723.3 | 773.1 | 809.3 | 3,046 |
| 2008 | 778.7 | 825.2 | 769.2 | 614.3 | 2,987 |
| 2007 | 635.3 | 687.5 | 653.4 | 711.3 | 2,688 |
| 2006 | 277.2 | 273.4 | 318.1 | 563.6 | 1,432 |

**Earnings Per Share ($)**

| | 1Q | 2Q | 3Q | 4Q | Year |
|---|---|---|---|---|---|
| 2011 | 1.39 | 0.97 | 1.01 | E1.39 | E5.42 |
| 2010 | 0.22 | 0.42 | -0.27 | 0.91 | 1.29 |
| 2009 | -0.30 | 0.21 | 0.28 | -0.04 | 0.17 |
| 2008 | 0.41 | 2.42 | 0.49 | -1.49 | 1.92 |
| 2007 | 0.54 | 0.82 | 0.41 | 0.57 | 2.34 |
| 2006 | -0.12 | -0.20 | 6.43 | -0.51 | 6.24 |

Fiscal year ended Dec. 31. Next earnings report expected: Mid February. EPS Estimates based on S&P Operating Earnings; historical GAAP earnings are as reported.

## Dividend Data (Dates: mm/dd Payment Date: mm/dd/yy)

| Amount ($) | Date Decl. | Ex-Div. Date | Stk. of Record | Payment Date |
|---|---|---|---|---|
| 0.500 | 04/19 | 04/29 | 05/03 | 05/17/11 |
| 0.500 | 07/18 | 07/26 | 07/28 | 08/11/11 |
| 0.500 | 10/19 | 10/31 | 11/02 | 11/16/11 |
| 5.0 Spl. | 11/02 | 11/21 | 11/23 | 12/21/11 |

Dividends have been paid since 2009. Source: Company reports.

---

**Please read the Required Disclosures and Analyst Certification on the last page of this report.**

The **McGraw·Hill** Companies

# Wynn Resorts Ltd

STANDARD &POOR'S

## Business Summary October 21, 2011

CORPORATE OVERVIEW. Wynn Resorts is involved in the design, development, financing and construction of gaming projects in Las Vegas and Macau. The company's first such project, Wynn Las Vegas, opened in April 2005. We believe that the cost of this project was about $2.7 billion.

Wynn Las Vegas, which occupies about 215 acres of land, includes 2,716 guest rooms and suites, an approximate 110,000 sq. ft. casino with 147 table games, 1,842 slot machines, 22 food and beverage outlets, an 18-hole golf course, about 223,000 sq. ft. of meeting space, a Ferrari and Maserati dealership, and about 74,000 sq. ft. of retail space.

The company also operates the Encore at Wynn Las Vegas, which includes about 2,034 guest suites, plus an approximately 76,000 square foot casino with 95 table games, 778 slot machines, entertainment and other facilities. This facility opened in December 2008.

In China, the company is operating Wynn Macau under a 20-year concession agreement with the government of Macau. The initial stage of Wynn Macau opened in September 2006, and included about 600 hotel rooms or suites, about 100,000 sq. ft. of gaming space, seven restaurants, and additional facili-

ties. A second phase included additional casino space and other facilities. We believe that Wynn Macau, including the second phase, had a project budget of about $1.2 billion.

The Encore at Wynn Macau, which opened in April 2010, includes approximately 410 luxury suites and villas in addition to restaurants, retail and gaming space.

Also, the company has submitted an application for a land concession on 52 acres in Macau's Cotai Strip area, where we expect additional WYNN-related development could occur. There are a limited number of companies with casino operating rights in Macau.

Stephen Wynn, Elaine Wynn and Aruze USA together own 35.6% of the total shares outstanding.

## Company Financials Fiscal Year Ended Dec. 31

| Per Share Data ($) | 2010 | 2009 | 2008 | 2007 | 2006 | 2005 | 2004 | 2003 | 2002 | 2001 |
|---|---|---|---|---|---|---|---|---|---|---|
| Tangible Book Value | 17.76 | 24.39 | 13.75 | 16.79 | 14.75 | 14.16 | 15.64 | 11.38 | 11.70 | 12.92 |
| Cash Flow | 5.83 | 3.59 | 4.32 | 4.24 | 7.20 | 0.13 | -2.29 | -0.54 | -0.49 | -0.25 |
| Earnings | 1.29 | 0.17 | 1.92 | 2.34 | 6.24 | -0.92 | -2.37 | -0.62 | -0.68 | -0.45 |
| S&P Core Earnings | 1.29 | 0.17 | 1.92 | 2.29 | 1.00 | -1.00 | -2.41 | -0.64 | -0.69 | -84.35 |
| Dividends | 8.50 | 4.00 | Nil | 6.00 | 6.00 | Nil | Nil | Nil | Nil | NA |
| Payout Ratio | NM | NM | Nil | 256% | 96% | Nil | Nil | Nil | Nil | NA |
| Prices:High | 117.50 | 74.90 | 124.77 | 176.14 | 98.45 | 76.45 | 72.99 | 28.61 | 14.39 | NA |
| Prices:Low | 59.70 | 14.50 | 28.06 | 85.53 | 52.44 | 42.06 | 27.50 | 12.76 | 10.76 | NA |
| P/E Ratio:High | 91 | NM | 65 | 75 | 16 | NM | NM | NM | NM | NA |
| P/E Ratio:Low | 46 | NM | 15 | 37 | 8 | NM | NM | NM | NM | NA |

| Income Statement Analysis (Million $) | | | | | | | | | | |
|---|---|---|---|---|---|---|---|---|---|---|
| Revenue | 4,185 | 3,046 | 2,987 | 2,688 | 1,432 | 722 | 0.20 | 1.02 | 1.16 | 1.16 |
| Operating Income | 1,032 | 674 | 608 | 708 | 249 | 77.5 | -81.5 | -46.9 | -24.8 | 0.73 |
| Depreciation | 406 | 411 | 263 | 220 | 175 | 103 | 6.98 | 5.74 | 8.93 | 8.16 |
| Interest Expense | 223 | 211 | 260 | 188 | 206 | 103 | 2.69 | 9.03 | 1.90 | NA |
| Pretax Income | 337 | 42.1 | 149 | 327 | 799 | -90.8 | -207 | -45.8 | -30.8 | -17.7 |
| Effective Tax Rate | NA | 7.12% | NM | 21.1% | 21.3% | NM | NM | NM | NM | NM |
| Net Income | 160 | 20.7 | 210 | 258 | 629 | -90.8 | -206 | -48.9 | -31.7 | -17.7 |
| S&P Core Earnings | 160 | 20.7 | 210 | 252 | 44.1 | -98.6 | -210 | -50.9 | -32.0 | -17.3 |

| Balance Sheet & Other Financial Data (Million $) | | | | | | | | | | |
|---|---|---|---|---|---|---|---|---|---|---|
| Cash | 1,259 | 1,992 | 1,134 | 1,275 | 789 | 434 | 330 | 342 | 110 | 39.3 |
| Current Assets | 1,561 | 2,283 | 1,411 | 1,582 | 1,096 | 685 | 451 | 402 | 112 | 41.6 |
| Total Assets | 6,675 | 7,582 | 6,743 | 6,299 | 4,660 | 3,945 | 3,464 | 1,733 | 1,399 | 389 |
| Current Liabilities | 888 | 726 | 724 | 585 | 511 | 270 | 170 | 71.2 | 20.7 | 4.02 |
| Long Term Debt | 3,280 | 3,587 | 4,290 | 3,539 | 2,381 | 2,091 | 1,628 | 730 | 382 | 1,501 |
| Common Equity | 2,238 | 3,034 | 1,593 | 1,948 | 1,646 | 1,563 | 1,644 | 1,002 | 992 | 972 |
| Total Capital | 5,806 | 6,750 | 5,886 | 5,640 | 4,123 | 3,654 | 3,272 | 1,733 | 1,378 | 2,473 |
| Capital Expenditures | 284 | 541 | 1,333 | 1,007 | 643 | 877 | 1,008 | 415 | 66.3 | 29.1 |
| Cash Flow | 722 | 431 | 473 | 478 | 804 | 12.5 | -199 | -43.1 | -22.8 | -9.56 |
| Current Ratio | 1.8 | 3.2 | 2.0 | 2.7 | 2.1 | 2.5 | 2.7 | 5.7 | 5.4 | 10.4 |
| % Long Term Debt of Capitalization | 56.5 | Nil | 72.9 | 62.8 | 57.7 | 57.2 | 49.8 | 42.1 | 27.7 | 0.1 |
| % Net Income of Revenue | 3.8 | 0.7 | 7.0 | 9.6 | 43.9 | NM | NM | NM | NM | NM |
| % Return on Assets | NA | NA | 3.2 | 4.7 | 14.6 | NM | NM | NM | NM | NM |
| % Return on Equity | NA | NA | 11.9 | 14.4 | 39.2 | NM | NM | NM | NM | NM |

Data as orig reptd.; bef. results of disc opers/spec. items. Per share data adj. for stk. divs.; EPS diluted. E-Estimated. NA-Not Available. NM-Not Meaningful. NR-Not Ranked. UR-Under Review.

**Office:** 3131 Las Vegas Blvd S, Las Vegas, NV 89109.
**Telephone:** 702-733-4444.
**Email:** investorrelations@wynnresorts.com
**Website:** http://www.wynnresorts.com

**Chrmn & CEO:** S.A. Wynn
**Vice Chrmn:** K. Okada
**COO:** M.D. Schorr
**SVP, Secy & General Counsel:** K. Sinatra

**CFO, Chief Acctg Officer & Treas:** M. Maddox
**Investor Contact:** J. Strzemp (702-770-7555)
**Board Members:** L. Chen, R. Goldsmith, R. R. Irani, R. J. Miller, J. A. Moran, K. Okada, M. D. Schorr, A. V. Shoemaker, D. B. Wayson, E. P. Wynn, S. A. Wynn, A. Zeman

**Founded:** 2002
**Domicile:** Nevada
**Employees:** 16,405

# Xcel Energy Inc.

**STANDARD &POOR'S**

| S&P Recommendation HOLD ★★★☆☆ | Price $25.20 (as of Nov 25, 2011) | 12-Mo. Target Price $26.00 | Investment Style Large-Cap Value |
|---|---|---|---|

**GICS Sector** Utilities
**Sub-Industry** Multi-Utilities

**Summary** This company offers energy-related products and services to 3.4 million electricity customers and 1.9 million natural gas customers in eight western and midwestern states.

## Key Stock Statistics (Source S&P, Vickers, company reports)

| | | | | | | |
|---|---|---|---|---|---|---|
| 52-Wk Range | $26.36–21.20 | S&P Oper. EPS 2011E | 1.75 | Market Capitalization(B) | $12.221 | Beta | 0.40 |
| Trailing 12-Month EPS | $1.72 | S&P Oper. EPS 2012E | 1.84 | Yield (%) | 4.13 | S&P 3-Yr. Proj. EPS CAGR(%) | 7 |
| Trailing 12-Month P/E | 14.7 | P/E on S&P Oper. EPS 2011E | 14.4 | Dividend Rate/Share | $1.04 | S&P Credit Rating | A- |
| $10K Invested 5 Yrs Ago | $13,920 | Common Shares Outstg. (M) | 485.0 | Institutional Ownership (%) | 62 | | |

## Price Performance

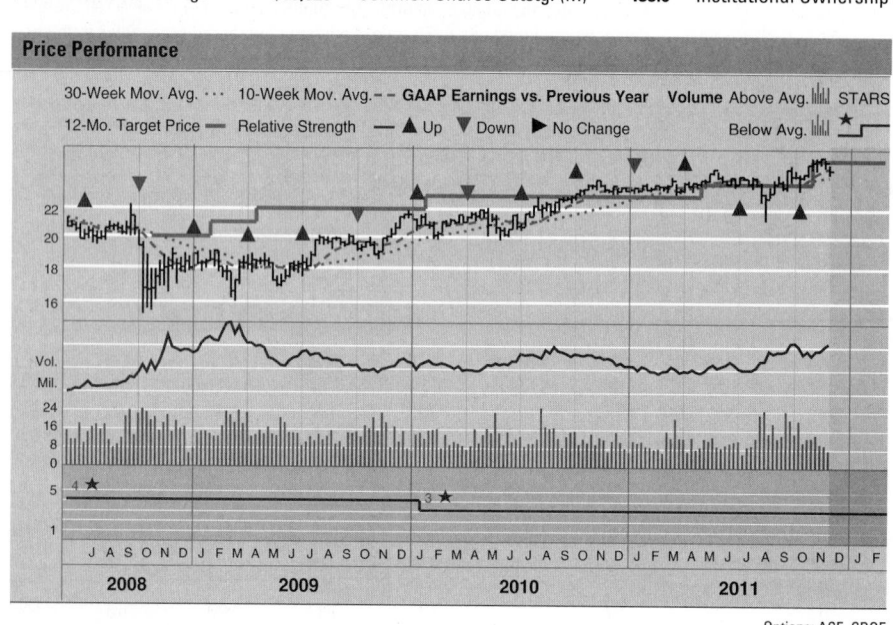

30-Week Mov. Avg. ···· 10-Week Mov. Avg. - - GAAP Earnings vs. Previous Year Volume Above Avg. STARS
12-Mo. Target Price — Relative Strength — ▲ Up ▼ Down ▶ No Change Below Avg.

Analysis prepared by Equity Analyst **Justin McCann** on Oct 31, 2011, when the stock traded at **$25.97**.

## Highlights

▸ We expect operating EPS in 2011 to increase approximately 8% from 2010's $1.62. The projected growth in earnings should reflect electric rate increases in Texas and Wisconsin, approved interim electric rate hikes in Minnesota and North Dakota, and a gas rate increase in Colorado. Earnings have also benefited from the two natural gas power plants the company acquired in December 2010.

▸ Operating EPS of $1.43 in the first nine months of 2011 was $0.10 above the year-earlier level, as the benefit of rate increases more than offset the impact of the cooler than normal first quarter, the implementation of lower seasonal rates in Colorado, higher operation and maintenance costs and depreciation and amortization expenses, and 5.3% more shares outstanding.

▸ For 2012, we expect operating EPS to increase approximately 5% from projected results in 2011, aided by anticipated rate hikes in Colorado, New Mexico, North and South Dakota and Wisconsin. We expect only modest growth in electric and gas sales. Although the company does not plan to issue any new equity in 2012, it has said it would remain open should an opportunistic financial option emerge.

## Investment Rationale/Risk

▸ We believe the stock is appropriately valued at its recent level. The shares were up more than 11% in the first 43 weeks of 2011. This followed an 11% gain in 2010, which reflected, in our view, the recovery in the utility sector, a solid earnings outlook, and the expectation for a gradual recovery in the economy. As of October 25, 2011, XEL had available credit lines of $2.364 billion and cash of $55.2 million. We believe this $2.419 billion of total liquidity is more than adequate for XEL's near-term requirements.

▸ Risks to our recommendation and target price include the possibility of a severe economic downturn in the company's service territory, unfavorable legislative or regulatory decisions, and/or a sharp decline in the average P/E of XEL's electric and gas utility peers.

▸ We expect the shares to be partially supported by the yield from the dividend (recently 4.0%), although it is below the recent electric and gas utility peer average (4.2%). We expect the company to increase its dividend at a rate of 2% to 4% a year. Our 12-month target price of $26 reflects a premium-to-peers P/E of 14X our operating EPS estimate for 2012.

## Qualitative Risk Assessment

| LOW | MEDIUM | HIGH |
|---|---|---|

Our risk assessment reflects the steady cash flow that we expect from the regulated electric and gas utility operations, which have a relatively low-cost power supply, our view of a relatively healthy economy in most of the company's service territory, and a generally supportive regulatory environment.

## Quantitative Evaluations

**S&P Quality Ranking** B

| D | C | B- | B | B+ | A- | A | A+ |
|---|---|---|---|---|---|---|---|

**Relative Strength Rank** STRONG

79

LOWEST = 1 HIGHEST = 99

## Revenue/Earnings Data

**Revenue (Million $)**

| | 1Q | 2Q | 3Q | 4Q | Year |
|---|---|---|---|---|---|
| 2011 | 2,817 | 2,438 | 2,832 | -- | -- |
| 2010 | 2,807 | 2,308 | 2,629 | 2,567 | 10,311 |
| 2009 | 2,696 | 2,016 | 2,315 | 2,618 | 9,644 |
| 2008 | 3,028 | 2,616 | 2,852 | 2,708 | 11,203 |
| 2007 | 2,764 | 2,267 | 2,400 | 2,603 | 10,034 |
| 2006 | 2,888 | 2,074 | 2,412 | 2,467 | 9,840 |

**Earnings Per Share ($)**

| | | | | | |
|---|---|---|---|---|---|
| 2011 | 0.42 | 0.33 | 0.69 | E0.31 | E1.75 |
| 2010 | 0.36 | 0.29 | 0.67 | 0.29 | 1.61 |
| 2009 | 0.38 | 0.25 | 0.48 | 0.37 | 1.49 |
| 2008 | 0.35 | 0.24 | 0.51 | 0.36 | 1.46 |
| 2007 | 0.28 | 0.16 | 0.59 | 0.31 | 1.34 |
| 2006 | 0.36 | 0.24 | 0.53 | 0.23 | 1.35 |

Fiscal year ended Dec. 31. Next earnings report expected: Late January. EPS Estimates based on S&P Operating Earnings; historical GAAP earnings are as reported.

## Dividend Data (Dates: mm/dd Payment Date: mm/dd/yy)

| Amount ($) | Date Decl. | Ex-Div. Date | Stk. of Record | Payment Date |
|---|---|---|---|---|
| 0.253 | 12/15 | 12/21 | 12/23 | 01/20/11 |
| 0.253 | 02/23 | 03/22 | 03/24 | 04/20/11 |
| 0.260 | 05/18 | 06/21 | 06/23 | 07/20/11 |
| 0.260 | 08/24 | 09/20 | 09/22 | 10/20/11 |

Dividends have been paid since 1910. Source: Company reports.

Options: ASE, CBOE

# Xcel Energy Inc.

**STANDARD &POOR'S**

## Business Summary October 31, 2011

CORPORATE OVERVIEW. Xcel Energy Inc. (XEL) is a holding company with a diverse portfolio of regulated and nonregulated subsidiaries. The company's utility subsidiaries are Northern States Power Company of Minnesota and Wisconsin (NSPM and NSPW, respectively), Public Service Company of Colorado (PSCo), and Southwestern Public Service Co. (SPS), which provide electric and gas services in eight western and midwestern states, and West-Gas Interstate Inc. (WGI), an interstate natural gas pipeline. XEL's nonregulated subsidiaries include Eloigne Co., which operates rental housing projects. The electric utility operations accounted for 81.9% of operating revenues in 2010; the natural gas utility operations for 17.3%; and non-regulated and other for 0.8%.

CORPORATE STRATEGY. XEL plans to continue investing in the core utility business and to earn the authorized returns. The company has a strong focus

on system reliability and continues to invest in transmission and distribution systems. To recover the cost without the delay caused by the filing of rate cases, XEL gets regulatory approval for rate riders. This ensures fair returns on the company's investment. The company is also working to apply intelligence technology to its electric grid, creating a "smart grid" that will provide customers with more reliability, choice and control over their energy use. Given the current economic environment, XEL remains committed to maintaining a strong balance sheet to provide it with the financial flexibility to respond appropriately to the challenges and opportunities it will face.

## Company Financials Fiscal Year Ended Dec. 31

| Per Share Data ($) | 2010 | 2009 | 2008 | 2007 | 2006 | 2005 | 2004 | 2003 | 2002 | 2001 |
|---|---|---|---|---|---|---|---|---|---|---|
| Tangible Book Value | 16.76 | 15.92 | 15.35 | 14.70 | 14.28 | 13.11 | 12.99 | 12.95 | 11.44 | 17.91 |
| Earnings | 1.61 | 1.49 | 1.46 | 1.34 | 1.35 | 1.20 | 1.27 | 1.23 | -4.36 | 2.27 |
| S&P Core Earnings | 1.58 | 1.51 | 1.11 | 1.31 | 1.35 | 1.15 | 1.21 | 1.03 | -4.57 | 1.68 |
| Dividends | 1.00 | 0.97 | 0.94 | 0.91 | 0.88 | 0.85 | 0.81 | 0.75 | 1.13 | 1.50 |
| Payout Ratio | 62% | 65% | 65% | 68% | 65% | 71% | 64% | 61% | NM | 66% |
| Prices:High | 24.36 | 21.94 | 22.90 | 25.03 | 23.63 | 20.19 | 18.78 | 17.40 | 28.49 | 31.85 |
| Prices:Low | 19.81 | 16.01 | 15.32 | 19.59 | 17.80 | 16.50 | 15.48 | 10.40 | 5.12 | 24.19 |
| P/E Ratio:High | 15 | 15 | 16 | 19 | 18 | 17 | 15 | 14 | NM | 14 |
| P/E Ratio:Low | 12 | 11 | 10 | 15 | 13 | 14 | 12 | 8 | NM | 11 |

| Income Statement Analysis (Million $) | 2010 | 2009 | 2008 | 2007 | 2006 | 2005 | 2004 | 2003 | 2002 | 2001 |
|---|---|---|---|---|---|---|---|---|---|---|
| Revenue | 10,311 | 9,644 | 11,203 | 10,034 | 9,840 | 9,625 | 8,345 | 7,938 | 9,524 | 15,028 |
| Depreciation | 978 | 916 | 948 | 827 | 822 | 782 | 708 | 756 | 1,037 | 949 |
| Maintenance | NA | NA | NA | NA | NA | NA | NA | NA | NA | NA |
| Fixed Charges Coverage | 3.09 | 2.95 | 2.92 | 2.62 | 2.43 | 2.43 | 2.36 | 2.50 | 1.54 | 2.37 |
| Construction Credits | 84.8 | 116 | 103 | 71.8 | 56.0 | 0.88 | 33.6 | NA | NA | NA |
| Effective Tax Rate | 36.7% | 35.1% | 34.4% | 33.8% | 24.2% | 25.8% | 23.2% | 23.7% | NM | 28.2% |
| Net Income | 752 | 686 | 646 | 576 | 569 | 499 | 527 | 510 | -1,661 | 785 |
| S&P Core Earnings | 732 | 688 | 487 | 554 | 566 | 472 | 498 | 417 | -1,745 | 579 |

| Balance Sheet & Other Financial Data (Million $) | 2010 | 2009 | 2008 | 2007 | 2006 | 2005 | 2004 | 2003 | 2002 | 2001 |
|---|---|---|---|---|---|---|---|---|---|---|
| Gross Property | 33,273 | 30,858 | 29,546 | 26,726 | 25,219 | 24,054 | 23,160 | 22,371 | 29,119 | 31,770 |
| Capital Expenditures | 2,161 | 1,711 | 2,050 | 2,096 | 1,626 | 1,304 | 1,274 | 951 | 1,503 | 5,366 |
| Net Property | 20,663 | 18,508 | 17,689 | 16,676 | 15,549 | 14,696 | 14,096 | 13,667 | 18,816 | 21,165 |
| Capitalization:Long Term Debt | 9,263 | 7,889 | 7,732 | 6,342 | 6,450 | 5,898 | 6,493 | 6,519 | 7,044 | 12,612 |
| Capitalization:% Long Term Debt | 53.1 | 51.6 | 52.2 | 49.8 | 52.1 | 51.3 | 55.0 | 55.0 | 59.6 | 66.7 |
| Capitalization:Preferred | 105 | 105 | 105 | 105 | 105 | 105 | 105 | 105 | 105 | 105 |
| Capitalization:% Preferred | 0.60 | 0.70 | 0.70 | 0.80 | 0.85 | 0.91 | 0.89 | 0.89 | 0.89 | 0.56 |
| Capitalization:Common | 8,084 | 7,283 | 6,964 | 6,301 | 5,817 | 5,484 | 5,203 | 5,222 | 4,665 | 6,194 |
| Capitalization:% Common | 46.3 | 47.7 | 47.1 | 49.4 | 47.0 | 47.7 | 44.1 | 44.1 | 39.5 | 32.8 |
| Total Capital | 17,507 | 15,821 | 17,699 | 15,415 | 14,751 | 13,813 | 14,019 | 14,017 | 13,303 | 22,040 |
| % Operating Ratio | 88.5 | 88.6 | 90.6 | 89.5 | 89.9 | 98.6 | 88.8 | 88.1 | 78.0 | 87.1 |
| % Earned on Net Property | 8.3 | 8.1 | 8.1 | 8.4 | 7.8 | 13.0 | 7.8 | 8.0 | 13.0 | 10.7 |
| % Return on Revenue | 7.3 | 7.1 | 5.8 | 5.7 | 5.8 | 5.2 | 6.3 | 6.4 | NM | 5.2 |
| % Return on Invested Capital | 7.6 | 7.6 | 7.0 | 7.4 | 7.4 | 6.9 | 7.0 | 7.3 | 12.4 | 10.9 |
| % Return on Common Equity | 9.8 | 9.6 | 9.7 | 9.4 | 10.1 | 9.2 | 10.1 | 10.1 | NM | 13.5 |

Data as orig reptd.; bef. results of disc opers/spec. items. Per share data adj. for stk. divs.; EPS diluted. E-Estimated. NA-Not Available. NM-Not Meaningful. NR-Not Ranked. UR-Under Review.

**Office:** 414 Nicollet Mall, Minneapolis, MN 55401.
**Telephone:** 612-330-5500.
**Website:** http://www.xcelenergy.com
**Chrmn, Pres & CEO:** B.G. Fowke, III

**COO:** K.T. Larson
**SVP & CFO:** T.S. Madden
**SVP & Chief Admin Officer:** M.E. McDaniel, Jr.
**SVP & General Counsel:** S.M. Wilensky

**Investor Contact:** P. Johnson (612-215-4535)
**Board Members:** F. W. Corrigan, R. K. Davis, B. G. Fowke, III, A. F. Moreno, C. J. Policinski, A. P. Sampson, J. J. Sheppard, D. A. Westerlund, K. Williams, T. V. Wolf

**Founded:** 1909
**Domicile:** Minnesota
**Employees:** 11,290

*The McGraw-Hill Companies*

# Xerox Corp

**STANDARD &POOR'S**

| S&P Recommendation | **STRONG BUY** ★★★★★ | Price $7.57 (as of Nov 25, 2011) | 12-Mo. Target Price $10.00 | Investment Style Large-Cap Blend |
|---|---|---|---|---|

**GICS Sector** Information Technology
**Sub-Industry** Office Electronics

**Summary** This company serves the worldwide document processing market, offering a complete line of copiers, printers and other office equipment, as well as business process outsourcing services.

## Key Stock Statistics (Source S&P, Vickers, company reports)

| | | | | | | | |
|---|---|---|---|---|---|---|---|
| 52-Wk Range | $12.08– 6.55 | S&P Oper. EPS 2011**E** | 1.10 | Market Capitalization(B) | $10.500 | Beta | 1.60 |
| Trailing 12-Month EPS | $0.74 | S&P Oper. EPS 2012**E** | 1.22 | Yield (%) | 2.25 | S&P 3-Yr. Proj. EPS CAGR(%) | 18 |
| Trailing 12-Month P/E | 10.2 | P/E on S&P Oper. EPS 2011**E** | 6.9 | Dividend Rate/Share | $0.17 | S&P Credit Rating | BBB- |
| $10K Invested 5 Yrs Ago | $4,904 | Common Shares Outstg. (M) | 1,387.1 | Institutional Ownership (%) | 84 | | |

## Price Performance

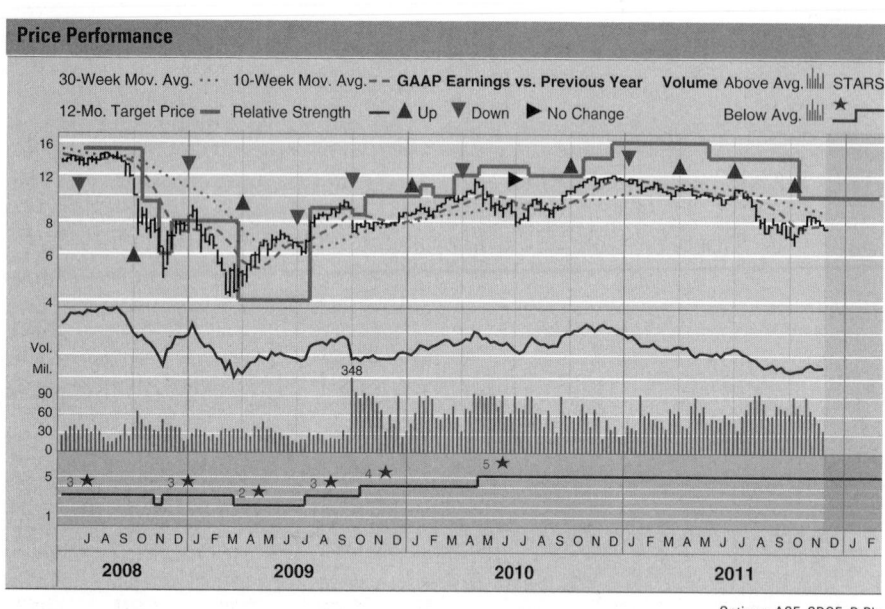

30-Week Mov. Avg. · · · 10-Week Mov. Avg. – – GAAP Earnings vs. Previous Year   Volume Above Avg. STARS
12-Mo. Target Price — Relative Strength   ▲ Up ▼ Down ► No Change   Below Avg.

Options: ASE, CBOE, P, Ph

Analysis prepared by Equity Analyst **Dylan Cathers** on Oct 31, 2011, when the stock traded at **$8.18**.

## Highlights

➤ We expect revenues to rise 6% in 2011 and 1% in 2012. The rebound in demand for printers may not be as strong as we originally expected, given the uncertain economic backdrop. We have some concerns about IT spending budgets for next year, both for the enterprise market and for the U.S. federal government, as XRX is affected by elongated contract signing times. Still, we expect sales of printers to be solid, and we look for growth in the services segment, particularly in business process and document outsourcing.

➤ We expect net margins, excluding acquisition and restructuring-related charges, to widen in 2011 and 2012, as unit volumes rise, cost control initiatives continue, and higher-margin services are added to the sales mix. We see these positives as being somewhat offset by start-up costs for new contracts and investments in the business.

➤ We estimate operating EPS of $1.10 in 2011 and $1.22 in 2012, excluding acquisition and restructuring charges. We assume a modest pace of share buyback activity.

## Investment Rationale/Risk

➤ We believe XRX is recovering from a cyclical slowdown in demand for printers, although we are cautious regarding the coming quarters, and it is benefiting from having more service offerings as a result of the 2010 Affiliated Computer Services acquisition. We foresee more stability in overall results, as well as opportunities for new sales to an expanded customer base. We think XRX is realizing some of the potential savings from several rounds of restructuring and from sales of new color printing products.

➤ Risks to our recommendation and target price include integration risks arising from the ACS acquisition, an aggressive pricing environment, and challenges in deploying new products and services effectively. Also, the company might not recover from supply chain effects from the Japan earthquake as rapidly as we project.

➤ We apply a target multiple of 8.2X, below the level for Information Technology sector peers in the S&P 500 Index, to our 2012 EPS estimate of $1.22 to arrive at our 12-month target price of $10. We see a compelling valuation based on our view of rising earnings amid steadier revenue patterns.

## Qualitative Risk Assessment

| LOW | MEDIUM | HIGH |
|---|---|---|

Xerox operates in the cyclical office electronics industry, marked by lively price and marketing competition for often commoditized printer, copier, scanner and multifunction products. It also operates in the usually steadier and faster-growing business process management industry.

## Quantitative Evaluations

**S&P Quality Ranking**   B

| D | C | B- | B | B+ | A- | A | A+ |
|---|---|---|---|---|---|---|---|

**Relative Strength Rank**   MODERATE
51
LOWEST = 1   HIGHEST = 99

## Revenue/Earnings Data

**Revenue (Million $)**

| | 1Q | 2Q | 3Q | 4Q | Year |
|---|---|---|---|---|---|
| 2011 | 5,465 | 5,614 | 5,583 | -- | -- |
| 2010 | 4,721 | 5,508 | 5,428 | 5,976 | 21,633 |
| 2009 | 3,554 | 3,731 | 3,675 | 4,219 | 15,179 |
| 2008 | 4,335 | 4,533 | 4,370 | 4,370 | 17,608 |
| 2007 | 3,836 | 4,208 | 4,302 | 4,882 | 17,228 |
| 2006 | 3,695 | 3,977 | 3,844 | 4,379 | 15,895 |

**Earnings Per Share ($)**

| | | | | | |
|---|---|---|---|---|---|
| 2011 | 0.19 | 0.22 | 0.22 | E0.34 | E1.10 |
| 2010 | -0.04 | 0.16 | 0.17 | 0.12 | 0.43 |
| 2009 | 0.05 | 0.16 | 0.14 | 0.20 | 0.55 |
| 2008 | -0.27 | 0.24 | 0.29 | Nil | 0.26 |
| 2007 | 0.24 | 0.28 | 0.27 | 0.41 | 1.19 |
| 2006 | 0.20 | 0.26 | 0.54 | 0.22 | 1.22 |

Fiscal year ended Dec. 31. Next earnings report expected: Late January. EPS Estimates based on S&P Operating Earnings; historical GAAP earnings are as reported.

## Dividend Data (Dates: mm/dd Payment Date: mm/dd/yy)

| Amount ($) | Date Decl. | Ex-Div. Date | Stk. of Record | Payment Date |
|---|---|---|---|---|
| 0.043 | 02/22 | 03/29 | 03/31 | 04/29/11 |
| 0.043 | 05/26 | 06/28 | 06/30 | 07/29/11 |
| 0.043 | 07/14 | 09/28 | 09/30 | 10/31/11 |
| 0.043 | 10/13 | 12/28 | 12/30 | 01/31/12 |

Dividends have been paid since 2008. Source: Company reports.

# Xerox Corp

STANDARD
&POOR'S

## Business Summary October 31, 2011

CORPORATE OVERVIEW. Xerox is a large operator in the global document markets, providing document equipment such as printing and publishing systems; digital copiers; laser and solid ink printers; fax machines; and digital multifunctional devices, which can print, copy, scan and fax. Increasingly, the company has also aimed at related service markets, including traditional supplies and printer support, and newer areas, such as document management and business processes. The latter range from claims reimbursement and electronic toll transactions to customer call centers and HR benefits management. By improving client document systems through managed print services, the company claims it can save an enterprise up to 30% on its printing costs.

The company operates in over 160 countries and derived about 64% of revenues in 2010 from the U.S., 11% from Europe, and 25% from other areas. The company has manufacturing plants in the U.S. and Europe, and also outsources manufacturing via a multi-year master supply agreement with Flextronics. The company owns 25% of Fuji Xerox, an unconsolidated subsidiary.

In 2010, Technology segment sales represented 48% (66% of sales in 2009) of total revenue, Services segment 44% (23%), and Other 8% (11%). The Technology segment includes sales of products and supplies, and associated technical service and financing. In 2010, most of the Technology revenue came from mid-range business (56%), including multifunction printers, copiers, digital printing presses and light production printers and copiers sold to enterprises of all sizes. Other Technology sub-categories include Entry business (22%) that focuses on products for small and mid-size business customers, and High-End business (22%) that focuses on high-end digital monochrome and color systems in the graphics communications industry and for large enterprises.

Services segment revenue is mainly business process outsourcing (BPO) (53% of Services segment revenue in 2010), document outsourcing (34%), and information technology outsourcing (13%).

## Company Financials Fiscal Year Ended Dec. 31

| Per Share Data ($) | 2010 | 2009 | 2008 | 2007 | 2006 | 2005 | 2004 | 2003 | 2002 | 2001 |
|---|---|---|---|---|---|---|---|---|---|---|
| Tangible Book Value | NM | 3.08 | 2.50 | 4.93 | 5.04 | 4.68 | 4.29 | 1.57 | NM | 0.52 |
| Cash Flow | 1.25 | 0.91 | 0.94 | 1.88 | 1.95 | 1.62 | 1.45 | 1.25 | 1.38 | 1.72 |
| Earnings | 0.43 | 0.55 | 0.26 | 1.19 | 1.22 | 0.90 | 0.78 | 0.36 | 0.10 | -0.17 |
| S&P Core Earnings | 0.47 | 0.52 | 0.73 | 1.16 | 1.27 | 0.88 | 0.75 | 0.53 | -0.17 | -1.33 |
| Dividends | 0.17 | 0.17 | 0.17 | 0.04 | Nil | Nil | Nil | Nil | Nil | 0.05 |
| Payout Ratio | 39% | 31% | 65% | 3% | Nil | Nil | Nil | Nil | Nil | NM |
| Prices:High | 12.08 | 9.75 | 16.43 | 20.18 | 17.31 | 17.02 | 17.24 | 13.89 | 11.45 | 11.35 |
| Prices:Low | 7.67 | 4.12 | 4.83 | 15.26 | 13.16 | 12.40 | 12.55 | 7.90 | 4.20 | 4.69 |
| P/E Ratio:High | 28 | 18 | 63 | 17 | 14 | 19 | 22 | 39 | NM | NM |
| P/E Ratio:Low | 18 | 7 | 19 | 13 | 11 | 14 | 16 | 22 | NM | NM |

| Income Statement Analysis (Million $) | 2010 | 2009 | 2008 | 2007 | 2006 | 2005 | 2004 | 2003 | 2002 | 2001 |
|---|---|---|---|---|---|---|---|---|---|---|
| Revenue | 21,633 | 15,179 | 17,608 | 17,228 | 15,895 | 15,701 | 15,722 | 15,701 | 15,849 | 17,008 |
| Operating Income | 2,861 | 1,347 | 2,340 | 2,699 | 2,165 | 2,159 | 2,451 | 2,585 | 2,803 | 3,011 |
| Depreciation | 1,097 | 698 | 613 | 656 | 636 | 637 | 686 | 748 | 1,035 | 1,332 |
| Interest Expense | 346 | 256 | 567 | 316 | 305 | 231 | 708 | 362 | 401 | 457 |
| Pretax Income | 893 | 668 | -1.00 | 1,535 | 922 | 928 | 1,116 | 494 | 306 | 418 |
| Effective Tax Rate | NA | 22.8% | NM | 26.0% | NM | NM | 30.5% | 27.1% | 19.6% | NM |
| Net Income | 606 | 485 | 230 | 1,135 | 1,210 | 933 | 776 | 360 | 154 | -109 |
| S&P Core Earnings | 645 | 457 | 670 | 1,101 | 1,235 | 862 | 666 | 434 | -128 | -931 |

| Balance Sheet & Other Financial Data (Million $) | 2010 | 2009 | 2008 | 2007 | 2006 | 2005 | 2004 | 2003 | 2002 | 2001 |
|---|---|---|---|---|---|---|---|---|---|---|
| Cash | 1,211 | 3,799 | 1,229 | 1,099 | 1,399 | 1,322 | 3,218 | 2,477 | 2,887 | 3,990 |
| Current Assets | 8,639 | 9,731 | 8,150 | 8,540 | 8,754 | 8,736 | 10,928 | 10,335 | 11,019 | 12,600 |
| Total Assets | 30,600 | 24,032 | 22,447 | 23,543 | 21,709 | 21,953 | 24,884 | 24,591 | 25,458 | 27,689 |
| Current Liabilities | 6,417 | 4,461 | 5,450 | 4,077 | 4,698 | 4,346 | 6,300 | 7,569 | 7,787 | 10,260 |
| Long Term Debt | 7,887 | 8,925 | 7,422 | 7,571 | 6,284 | 6,765 | 7,767 | 8,739 | 11,485 | 11,815 |
| Common Equity | 12,006 | 7,050 | 6,238 | 8,588 | 7,080 | 6,319 | 6,244 | 3,291 | 1,893 | 1,820 |
| Total Capital | 21,765 | 17,104 | 15,329 | 16,159 | 13,364 | 13,973 | 14,900 | 13,418 | 14,001 | 14,313 |
| Capital Expenditures | 355 | 95.0 | 206 | 236 | 215 | 181 | 204 | 197 | 146 | 219 |
| Cash Flow | 1,682 | 796 | 843 | 1,791 | 1,846 | 1,512 | 1,389 | 1,037 | 1,116 | 1,209 |
| Current Ratio | 1.4 | 2.2 | 1.5 | 2.1 | 1.9 | 2.0 | 1.7 | 1.4 | 1.4 | 1.2 |
| % Long Term Debt of Capitalization | 36.2 | 52.2 | 48.4 | 46.8 | 47.0 | 48.4 | 52.1 | 65.1 | 82.0 | 82.5 |
| % Net Income of Revenue | 2.8 | 3.2 | 1.3 | 6.5 | 7.6 | 5.9 | 4.9 | 2.3 | 1.0 | NM |
| % Return on Assets | 2.2 | 2.1 | 1.0 | 5.0 | 5.5 | 4.0 | 3.1 | 1.4 | 0.6 | NM |
| % Return on Equity | 6.4 | 7.3 | 3.1 | 14.4 | 18.1 | 13.9 | 14.7 | 11.1 | 4.4 | NM |

Data as orig reptd.; bef. results of disc opers/spec. items. Per share data adj. for stk. divs.; EPS diluted. E-Estimated. NA-Not Available. NM-Not Meaningful. NR-Not Ranked. UR-Under Review.

**Office:** 45 Glover Ave, Norwalk, CT 06856-4505.
**Telephone:** 203-968-3000.
**Website:** http://www.xerox.com
**Chrmn & CEO:** U.M. Burns

**COO:** J.A. Firestone
**EVP & CFO:** L. Maestri
**SVP, Secy & General Counsel:** D.H. Liu
**CTO:** S.V. Vandebroek

**Investor Contact:** J.H. Lesko (800-828-6396)
**Board Members:** G. A. Britt, U. M. Burns, R. J. Harrington, W. C. Hunter, R. J. Keegan, R. A. McDonald, N. J. Nicholas, Jr., C. Prince, III, A. N. Reese, M. A. Wilderotter

**Founded:** 1906
**Domicile:** New York
**Employees:** 136,500

# Xilinx Inc

**STANDARD &POOR'S**

**S&P Recommendation** HOLD ★★★☆☆

| Price | 12-Mo. Target Price | Investment Style |
|---|---|---|
| $30.07 (as of Nov 25, 2011) | $32.00 | Large-Cap Growth |

**GICS Sector** Information Technology
**Sub-Industry** Semiconductors

**Summary** This company is the world's largest supplier of programmable logic chips and related development system software.

## Key Stock Statistics (Source S&P, Vickers, company reports)

| | | | | | | | | |
|---|---|---|---|---|---|---|---|---|
| 52-Wk Range | $37.37– 26.55 | S&P Oper. EPS 2012**E** | 1.88 | Market Capitalization(B) | $7.892 | Beta | | 1.00 |
| Trailing 12-Month EPS | $2.20 | S&P Oper. EPS 2013**E** | 2.22 | Yield (%) | 2.53 | S&P 3-Yr. Proj. EPS CAGR(%) | | -2 |
| Trailing 12-Month P/E | 13.7 | P/E on S&P Oper. EPS 2012**E** | 16.0 | Dividend Rate/Share | $0.76 | S&P Credit Rating | | BBB |
| $10K Invested 5 Yrs Ago | $12,253 | Common Shares Outstg. (M) | 262.5 | Institutional Ownership (%) | NM | | | |

## Price Performance

30-Week Mov. Avg. · · · 10-Week Mov. Avg. – – GAAP Earnings vs. Previous Year    Volume Above Avg. ▫▫▫ STARS

12-Mo. Target Price — Relative Strength — ▲ Up ▼ Down ► No Change    Below Avg. ▫▫▫ ★

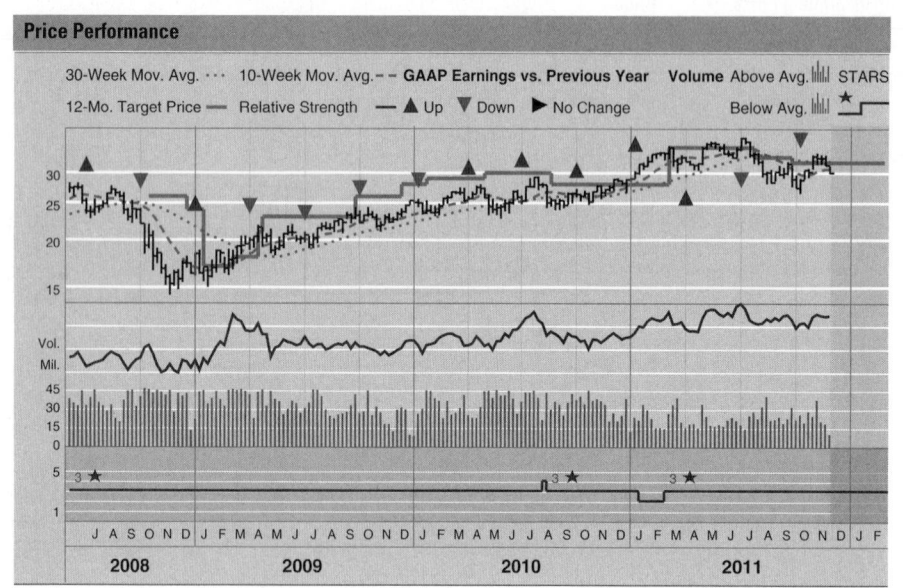

Options: ASE, CBOE, P

Analysis prepared by Equity Analyst **Angelo Zino, CFA** on Oct 20, 2011, when the stock traded at **$29.98**.

## Highlights

➤ We project that revenues will fall 5.9% in FY 12 (Mar.), but rebound 6.8% in FY 13. We believe long-term growth will be supported by the roll-out of LTE and FPGAs replacing ASICs. We are positive about the proprietary nature of XLNX's products, their long product cycles, and its next generation products, which should provide a reliable sales base. Near term, we anticipate lower orders as customers digest inventories in the Communications and Industrial markets. XLNX recently generated 44% and 33% of its sales from the communications and Industrials related markets.

➤ We think XLNX will be able to maintain fairly steady gross margins in the mid-60% area due to what we view as its cost-effective manufacturing partnerships with chip foundries and its product portfolio of higher-margin programmable devices. We see minor fluctuations based on varying customer and product mixes and yields. However, we expect rising R&D expenses to support new products and related sales. We look for operating margins to widen to 31% in FY 13 from our 28% estimate in FY 12.

➤ Our FY 12 EPS estimate of $1.88 and FY 13 view of $2.22 assume an effective tax rate of 14%.

## Investment Rationale/Risk

➤ Our hold recommendation reflects valuation as well as our view of the uncertain end-market environment over the next several quarters. Having improved its cost structure, XLNX boasts above-industry profitability and returns, and also has what we see as a strong balance sheet and cash flows. However, we are concerned about new offerings from its main rival Altera (ALTR 34, Hold). Despite this, we think orders are likely to rebound in the first half of calendar year 2012, at which point we believe inventories and end-demand will be better aligned. Based on all of these factors, we view the shares as fairly valued at current levels.

➤ Risks to our recommendation and target price include weaker-than-expected economic conditions, greater-than-anticipated market-share loss, higher costs from its foundry partners, and weak development and execution on the 28nm node.

➤ Our 12-month target price of $32 is based on a price-to-earnings multiple of 14.7X, above the peer average but below historical levels to account for our view of relative growth, return on equity, and risk, applied to our calendar 2012 EPS estimate.

## Qualitative Risk Assessment

| LOW | MEDIUM | HIGH |
|---|---|---|

Our risk assessment reflects the cyclicality of the semiconductor industry, offset by the company's position as the largest competitor in a fast-growing niche, its diverse end markets, and its sharing of factory operations risk with chip foundry partners.

## Quantitative Evaluations

**S&P Quality Ranking**      B

| D | C | B- | B | B+ | A- | A | A+ |
|---|---|---|---|---|---|---|---|

**Relative Strength Rank**      MODERATE

60

LOWEST = 1          HIGHEST = 99

## Revenue/Earnings Data

**Revenue (Million $)**

| | 1Q | 2Q | 3Q | 4Q | Year |
|---|---|---|---|---|---|
| 2012 | 615.5 | 555.2 | -- | -- | -- |
| 2011 | 594.7 | 619.7 | 567.2 | 587.9 | 2,369 |
| 2010 | 376.2 | 415.0 | 513.4 | 529.0 | 1,834 |
| 2009 | 488.3 | 483.5 | 458.4 | 395.0 | 1,825 |
| 2008 | 445.9 | 444.9 | 474.8 | 475.8 | 1,841 |
| 2007 | 481.4 | 467.2 | 450.7 | 443.5 | 1,843 |

**Earnings Per Share ($)**

| | | | | | |
|---|---|---|---|---|---|
| 2012 | 0.56 | 0.47 | E0.39 | E0.46 | E1.88 |
| 2011 | 0.58 | 0.65 | 0.58 | 0.59 | 2.39 |
| 2010 | 0.14 | 0.23 | 0.38 | 0.54 | 1.29 |
| 2009 | 0.30 | 0.29 | 0.51 | 0.26 | 1.36 |
| 2008 | 0.28 | 0.30 | 0.35 | 0.34 | 1.25 |
| 2007 | 0.24 | 0.27 | 0.26 | 0.27 | 1.02 |

Fiscal year ended Mar. 31. Next earnings report expected: NA. EPS Estimates based on S&P Operating Earnings; historical GAAP earnings are as reported.

## Dividend Data (Dates: mm/dd Payment Date: mm/dd/yy)

| Amount ($) | Date Decl. | Ex-Div. Date | Stk. of Record | Payment Date |
|---|---|---|---|---|
| 0.160 | 01/19 | 02/07 | 02/09 | 03/02/11 |
| 0.190 | 03/14 | 05/14 | 05/18 | 06/08/11 |
| 0.190 | 07/20 | 08/08 | 08/10 | 08/31/11 |
| 0.190 | 10/19 | 11/07 | 11/09 | 11/30/11 |

Dividends have been paid since 2004. Source: Company reports.

---

**Please read the Required Disclosures and Analyst Certification on the last page of this report.**

*The McGraw-Hill Companies*

# Xilinx Inc

**STANDARD &POOR'S**

## Business Summary October 20, 2011

CORPORATE OVERVIEW. Founded in 1984, Xilinx is the world's leading supplier of programmable logic devices (PLDs) based on market share. These devices include field programmable gate arrays (FPGAs) and complex programmable logic devices (CPLDs). They are standard integrated circuits (ICs) that are programmed by customers to perform desired logic operations. The company believes it provides high levels of integration and creates significant time and cost savings for electronic equipment manufacturers in the telecommunications, networking, computing and industrial markets.

Products are classified as new, mainstream, base and support. New Products accounted for 43% of FY 11 (Mar.) sales, Mainstream Products 28%, Base Products 25%, and Support Products 4%. Revenue by end market in FY 11 broke down as follows: 47% Communications, 32% Industrial and Other, 15% Consumer and Automotive, and 6% Data Processing.

MARKET PROFILE. There are three primary types of integrated circuits used in most digital devices: processors, which are used for control and computing

tasks; memory products, which are used to store information; and logic devices, which manage the interchange and manipulation of digital signals within a system, according to Xilinx. Logic devices can be further split into two categories, fixed and programmable. Fixed logic devices, such as application specific integrated circuits (ASIC) and application specific standard products (ASSP), define the group of logic devices that are manufactured with a permanent set of instructions or functions. Conversely, programmable logic devices, such as field programmable gate arrays (FPGA) and complex programmable devices (CPLD) are not permanent, and the instructions can be more easily reprogrammed. Since both fixed and programmable logic devices can be used in the same devices, there is a natural competition between the technologies.

## Company Financials Fiscal Year Ended Mar. 31

| Per Share Data ($) | 2011 | 2010 | 2009 | 2008 | 2007 | 2006 | 2005 | 2004 | 2003 | 2002 |
|---|---|---|---|---|---|---|---|---|---|---|
| Tangible Book Value | 8.46 | 7.26 | 5.74 | 5.45 | 5.54 | 7.53 | 7.24 | 6.79 | 5.44 | 5.26 |
| Cash Flow | 2.61 | 1.53 | 1.58 | 1.46 | 1.24 | 1.19 | 1.05 | 1.05 | 0.57 | -0.02 |
| Earnings | 2.39 | 1.29 | 1.36 | 1.25 | 1.02 | 1.00 | 0.87 | 0.85 | 0.36 | -0.34 |
| S&P Core Earnings | 2.40 | 1.30 | 1.48 | 1.28 | 1.01 | 0.78 | 0.58 | 0.57 | 0.05 | -0.31 |
| Dividends | 0.64 | 0.60 | 0.56 | 0.36 | 0.36 | 0.28 | 0.20 | Nil | Nil | Nil |
| Payout Ratio | 27% | 47% | 41% | 29% | 35% | 28% | 23% | Nil | Nil | Nil |
| Calendar Year | 2010 | 2009 | 2008 | 2007 | 2006 | 2005 | 2004 | 2003 | 2002 | 2001 |
| Prices:High | 29.40 | 25.45 | 28.21 | 30.50 | 29.98 | 32.30 | 45.40 | 39.20 | 47.15 | 59.25 |
| Prices:Low | 22.75 | 15.00 | 14.28 | 21.14 | 18.35 | 21.25 | 25.21 | 18.50 | 13.50 | 19.52 |
| P/E Ratio:High | 12 | 20 | 21 | 24 | 29 | 32 | 47 | 46 | NM | NM |
| P/E Ratio:Low | 10 | 12 | 10 | 17 | 18 | 21 | 26 | 22 | NM | NM |

### Income Statement Analysis (Million $)

| | 2011 | 2010 | 2009 | 2008 | 2007 | 2006 | 2005 | 2004 | 2003 | 2002 |
|---|---|---|---|---|---|---|---|---|---|---|
| Revenue | 2,369 | 1,834 | 1,825 | 1,841 | 1,843 | 1,726 | 1,573 | 1,398 | 1,156 | 1,016 |
| Operating Income | 863 | 527 | 513 | 485 | 424 | 489 | 442 | 412 | 283 | 87.3 |
| Depreciation | 58.9 | 65.2 | 61.0 | 61.0 | 73.9 | 69.5 | 63.1 | 67.9 | 72.5 | 106 |
| Interest Expense | 18.4 | 6.58 | 29.0 | 0.17 | Nil | Nil | Nil | Nil | Nil | 0.06 |
| Pretax Income | 771 | 422 | 498 | 474 | 431 | 457 | 401 | 351 | 170 | -193 |
| Effective Tax Rate | NA | 15.2% | 24.6% | 21.1% | 18.7% | 22.4% | 21.9% | 13.6% | 26.0% | NM |
| Net Income | 642 | 357 | 376 | 374 | 351 | 354 | 313 | 303 | 126 | -114 |
| S&P Core Earnings | 643 | 360 | 409 | 382 | 348 | 277 | 205 | 204 | 18.1 | -103 |

### Balance Sheet & Other Financial Data (Million $)

| | 2011 | 2010 | 2009 | 2008 | 2007 | 2006 | 2005 | 2004 | 2003 | 2002 |
|---|---|---|---|---|---|---|---|---|---|---|
| Cash | 1,926 | 1,387 | 1,325 | 1,296 | 636 | 783 | 449 | 337 | 214 | 230 |
| Current Assets | 2,623 | 1,907 | 1,752 | 1,820 | 1,700 | 1,648 | 1,466 | 1,302 | 1,175 | 999 |
| Total Assets | 4,141 | 3,184 | 2,826 | 3,137 | 3,179 | 3,174 | 3,039 | 2,937 | 2,422 | 2,335 |
| Current Liabilities | 368 | 357 | 233 | 341 | 303 | 345 | 298 | 381 | 314 | 196 |
| Long Term Debt | 891 | 355 | 690 | 1,000 | 1,000 | Nil | Nil | Nil | Nil | Nil |
| Common Equity | 2,415 | 2,120 | 1,738 | 1,672 | 1,773 | 2,729 | 2,674 | 2,483 | 1,951 | 1,904 |
| Total Capital | 3,306 | 2,475 | 2,511 | 2,756 | 2,875 | 2,821 | 2,741 | 2,556 | 2,108 | 2,140 |
| Capital Expenditures | 65.0 | 28.2 | 39.1 | 45.6 | 111 | 67.0 | 61.4 | 41.0 | 46.0 | 94.9 |
| Cash Flow | 701 | 423 | 437 | 435 | 425 | 424 | 376 | 371 | 198 | -7.51 |
| Current Ratio | 7.1 | 5.3 | 7.5 | 5.3 | 5.6 | 4.8 | 4.9 | 3.4 | 3.7 | 5.1 |
| % Long Term Debt of Capitalization | 27.0 | 14.3 | 27.5 | 36.3 | 34.8 | Nil | Nil | Nil | Nil | Nil |
| % Net Income of Revenue | 27.1 | 19.5 | 20.6 | 20.3 | 19.0 | 20.5 | 19.8 | 21.7 | 10.9 | NM |
| % Return on Assets | 17.5 | 11.9 | 12.6 | 11.8 | 11.0 | 11.4 | 10.5 | 11.3 | 5.3 | NM |
| % Return on Equity | 28.3 | 18.5 | 22.0 | 21.7 | 15.6 | 13.1 | 12.1 | 13.7 | 6.5 | NM |

Data as orig reptd.; bef. results of disc opers/spec. items. Per share data adj. for stk. divs.; EPS diluted. E-Estimated. NA-Not Available. NM-Not Meaningful. NR-Not Ranked. UR-Under Review.

**Office:** 2100 Logic Drive, San Jose, CA 95124-3400.
**Telephone:** 408-559-7778.
**Email:** ir@xilinx.com
**Website:** http://www.xilinx.com

**Chrmn:** P.T. Gianos
**Pres & CEO:** M.N. Gavrielov
**COO:** R.G. Petrakian
**Investor Contact:** J.A. Olson

**SVP, CFO & Chief Acctg Officer:** J.A. Olson
**Board Members:** J. L. Doyle, J. G. Fishman, M. N. Gavrielov, P. T. Gianos, W. G. Howard, Jr., J. M. Patterson, A. A. Pimentel, M. C. Turner, Jr., E. W. Vanderslice

**Founded:** 1984
**Domicile:** Delaware
**Employees:** 3,099

# XL Group Plc

**STANDARD &POOR'S**

| S&P Recommendation **BUY** ★★★★☆ | Price $18.92 (as of Nov 25, 2011) | 12-Mo. Target Price $25.00 | Investment Style Large-Cap Blend |
|---|---|---|---|

**GICS Sector** Financials
**Sub-Industry** Property & Casualty Insurance

**Summary** Bermuda-based XL, which originally provided excess liability coverage, has expanded into providing a broad array of commercial lines insurance, reinsurance, and other risk management services.

## Key Stock Statistics (Source S&P, Vickers, company reports)

| | | | | | | | |
|---|---|---|---|---|---|---|---|
| 52-Wk Range | $25.43– 17.69 | S&P Oper. EPS 2011E | 1.18 | Market Capitalization(B) | $6.064 | Beta | 2.54 |
| Trailing 12-Month EPS | $0.72 | S&P Oper. EPS 2012E | 2.64 | Yield (%) | 2.33 | S&P 3-Yr. Proj. EPS CAGR(%) | 1 |
| Trailing 12-Month P/E | 26.3 | P/E on S&P Oper. EPS 2011E | 16.0 | Dividend Rate/Share | $0.44 | S&P Credit Rating | NA |
| $10K Invested 5 Yrs Ago | $3,150 | Common Shares Outstg. (M) | 320.5 | Institutional Ownership (%) | 99 | | |

## Price Performance

30-Week Mov. Avg. · · · 10-Week Mov. Avg. - - GAAP Earnings vs. Previous Year  Volume Above Avg. STARS
12-Mo. Target Price — Relative Strength — ▲ Up ▼ Down ► No Change  Below Avg.

Options: CBOE, P, Ph

Analysis prepared by Equity Analyst **Cathy Seifert** on Nov 18, 2011, when the stock traded at **$19.73**.

### Highlights

➤ We expect property-casualty earned premiums to rise 5% to 7% in 2011, and by a greater amount in 2012 if recent written premium trends continue. These expected rates of growth contrast with a decline of 2.3% reported for 2010. Our forecast reflects our view of improved stability of the XL franchise, contributions from expansion efforts, and an easing of competitive pricing pressures.

➤ We expect net investment income to rise modestly in coming periods, versus declines of 9.2% in 2010 and 21% in 2009. The rather sharp drop experienced in 2009 reflected steps XL took to lower the risk profile of its investment portfolio. The rebound in profitability we are forecasting for 2012 is skewed by heavy catastrophe claims experienced so far in 2011.

➤ We estimate operating EPS of $1.18 for 2011 and $2.64 for 2012, versus $2.40 of operating EPS reported for 2010 and $2.69 of operating EPS reported for 2009. XL reported a 2008 net loss of $11.02 a share, due mainly to a $1.4 billion charge taken to (among other things) terminate a reinsurance agreement with Syncora Holdings (formerly Security Capital Assurance).

### Investment Rationale/Risk

➤ We view favorably steps XL has taken to strengthen its underwriting and investment standards. At current levels, the shares are trading at less than 8X our 2012 operating EPS estimate and less than September 30, 2011, tangible common equity. These multiples represent discounts to the peer group averages that we believe are not entirely warranted. Although we think a degree of execution risk remains, XL is making progress in rebuilding its franchise and de-risking its balance sheet.

➤ Risks to our recommendation and target price include a greater-than-anticipated decline in premium rates and underwriting margins; more significant deterioration in the credit quality of XL's investment portfolio; and not fully executing on its balance sheet restructuring.

➤ Our 12-month target price of $25 assumes that the shares will trade at less than 1X estimated 2012 tangible book value. This still represents a discount to most of XL's peers.

## Qualitative Risk Assessment

| LOW | MEDIUM | **HIGH** |
|---|---|---|

Our risk assessment reflects our concerns about XL's exposure to catastrophe losses and the adequacy of its loss reserves in certain liability lines of business, and our view that it could face writedowns of its fixed income investment portfolio and certain other investments.

## Quantitative Evaluations

**S&P Quality Ranking** NR

| D | C | B- | B | B+ | A- | A | A+ |
|---|---|---|---|---|---|---|---|

**Relative Strength Rank** MODERATE

45

LOWEST = 1                                    HIGHEST = 99

## Revenue/Earnings Data

**Revenue (Million $)**

| | 1Q | 2Q | 3Q | 4Q | Year |
|---|---|---|---|---|---|
| 2011 | 1,615 | 1,695 | 1,658 | -- | -- |
| 2010 | 1,637 | 1,553 | 1,620 | 1,589 | 6,399 |
| 2009 | 1,555 | 1,725 | 1,486 | 1,448 | 6,194 |
| 2008 | 2,174 | 2,125 | 1,744 | 1,106 | 7,148 |
| 2007 | 2,483 | 2,597 | 2,153 | 1,902 | 9,136 |
| 2006 | 2,473 | 2,499 | 2,364 | 2,496 | 9,833 |

**Earnings Per Share ($)**

| | | | | | |
|---|---|---|---|---|---|
| 2011 | -0.73 | 0.70 | 0.14 | E0.67 | E1.18 |
| 2010 | 0.37 | 0.56 | 0.23 | 0.57 | 1.73 |
| 2009 | 0.53 | 0.23 | -0.03 | -0.12 | 0.61 |
| 2008 | 1.20 | 1.34 | -6.09 | -4.36 | -11.02 |
| 2007 | 3.06 | 3.00 | 1.82 | -6.88 | 1.15 |
| 2006 | 2.56 | 2.10 | 2.32 | 2.62 | 9.60 |

Fiscal year ended Dec. 31. Next earnings report expected: Early February. EPS Estimates based on S&P Operating Earnings; historical GAAP earnings are as reported.

## Dividend Data (Dates: mm/dd Payment Date: mm/dd/yy)

| Amount ($) | Date Decl. | Ex-Div. Date | Stk. of Record | Payment Date |
|---|---|---|---|---|
| 0.110 | 11/02 | 12/13 | 12/15 | 12/30/11 |

Dividends have been paid since 1992. Source: Company reports.

---

**Please read the Required Disclosures and Analyst Certification on the last page of this report.**

The McGraw·Hill Companies

# XL Group Plc

**STANDARD &POOR'S**

## Business Summary November 18, 2011

CORPORATE OVERVIEW. Bermuda-based XL Capital was formed in 1986 by a consortium of Fortune 500 companies to provide excess liability coverage. Since then, XL has expanded (mostly via acquisitions) to include insurance, reinsurance, and other financial services. In January 2010, XL re domesticated its holding company to Ireland from the Cayman Islands. Gross written premiums of nearly $6.67 billion in 2010 (down from $6.69 billion in 2009) were divided: insurance 66%, reinsurance 28%, and life operations 6%.

Insurance business written includes general liability, as well as other specialized types of liability coverage, such as directors' and officers' liability and professional and employment practices liability coverage. An array of property coverage, as well as marine and aviation coverage, is also offered. Insurance net written premiums of $3.46 billion in 2010 were divided: professional liability 38%, casualty 19%, property 12%, marine/energy/aviation/satellite 16%, and other specialty lines 15%.

Reinsurance business written includes treaty and facultative reinsurance to primary insurers of casualty risk. Reinsurance net written premiums totaled $1.54 billion in 2010 and were divided: property 37%, casualty 14%, property catastrophe 21%, professional lines 14%, marine, energy aviation and satellite 7%, and other lines (including political risk, surety and structured indemnity)

6%.

Life operations include reinsurance written from other life insurers, principally to help in managing mortality, morbidity, survivorship, investment and lapse risks. Net written premiums totaled $382.1 million in 2010 and were divided: annuity risks 33%, life insurance 67%. In December 2008, XL completed a strategic review of its life reinsurance business, which is now in runoff mode.

In July 2001, the company acquired Winterthur International, for about $330.2 million in cash (as adjusted). As part of the transaction, XL received certain post-closing arrangements protecting it against (among other things) certain types of adverse loss development. XL valued the post-closing payment at $1.45 billion, and Winterthur Swiss Insurance Co. (the seller) believed the post-closing payment was $541 million. In December 2005, an independent actuarial review concluded that Winterthur's estimate was closer than the estimate submitted by XL. As a result of this difference, XL recorded a fourth-quarter 2005 after-tax charge of $834.2 million.

## Company Financials Fiscal Year Ended Dec. 31

| Per Share Data ($) | 2010 | 2009 | 2008 | 2007 | 2006 | 2005 | 2004 | 2003 | 2002 | 2001 |
|---|---|---|---|---|---|---|---|---|---|---|
| Tangible Book Value | 30.88 | 25.09 | 16.74 | 41.31 | 45.93 | 37.08 | 42.55 | 37.07 | 36.13 | 28.35 |
| Operating Earnings | NA | NA | NA | NA | NA | NA | NA | NA | 5.10 | -3.67 |
| Earnings | 1.73 | 0.61 | -11.02 | 1.15 | 9.60 | -9.14 | 8.13 | 2.69 | 2.88 | -4.55 |
| Dividends | 0.40 | 0.40 | 1.14 | 1.52 | 1.52 | 2.00 | 1.96 | 1.92 | 1.88 | 1.84 |
| Payout Ratio | 23% | 66% | NM | 76% | 16% | NM | 24% | 71% | 65% | NM |
| Prices:High | 22.52 | 19.03 | 52.26 | 85.67 | 72.90 | 79.80 | 82.00 | 88.87 | 98.48 | 96.50 |
| Prices:Low | 15.59 | 2.56 | 2.65 | 48.16 | 59.82 | 60.03 | 66.70 | 63.49 | 58.45 | 61.50 |
| P/E Ratio:High | 13 | 31 | NM | 43 | 8 | NM | 10 | 33 | 34 | NM |
| P/E Ratio:Low | 9 | 4 | NM | 24 | 6 | NM | 8 | 24 | 20 | NM |

| Income Statement Analysis (Million $) | 2010 | 2009 | 2008 | 2007 | 2006 | 2005 | 2004 | 2003 | 2002 | 2001 |
|---|---|---|---|---|---|---|---|---|---|---|
| Premium Income | 5,414 | 5,707 | 6,640 | 7,205 | 7,570 | 2,238 | 1,406 | 6,969 | 5,990 | 3,476 |
| Net Investment Income | 1,198 | 1,320 | 1,769 | 2,249 | 1,978 | 1,475 | 995 | 780 | 735 | 563 |
| Other Revenue | -213 | -833 | -1,261 | -318 | 8,904 | 8,864 | 7,426 | 268 | -147 | 18.0 |
| Total Revenue | 6,399 | 6,194 | 7,148 | 9,136 | 9,833 | 11,285 | 10,028 | 8,017 | 6,578 | 4,057 |
| Pretax Income | 806 | 195 | -2,331 | 534 | 2,007 | -1,194 | 1,260 | 451 | 442 | -764 |
| Net Operating Income | NA | NA | NA | NA | NA | NA | NA | NA | 701 | -465 |
| Net Income | 643 | 75.0 | -2,554 | 276 | 1,763 | -1,252 | 1,167 | 412 | 406 | -576 |

| Balance Sheet & Other Financial Data (Million $) | 2010 | 2009 | 2008 | 2007 | 2006 | 2005 | 2004 | 2003 | 2002 | 2001 |
|---|---|---|---|---|---|---|---|---|---|---|
| Cash & Equivalent | 3,373 | 3,994 | 4,717 | 4,328 | 2,656 | 4,085 | 2,631 | 2,698 | 3,785 | 2,044 |
| Premiums Due | 2,415 | 2,598 | 4,273 | 4,610 | 4,698 | 4,842 | 4,934 | 4,847 | 4,833 | 2,182 |
| Investment Assets:Bonds | 28,173 | 28,058 | 25,636 | 33,608 | 36,121 | 32,310 | 25,100 | 19,494 | 14,483 | 10,832 |
| Investment Assets:Stocks | 84.8 | 17.8 | 361 | 855 | 891 | 869 | 963 | 583 | 575 | 548 |
| Investment Assets:Loans | Nil | Nil | Nil | Nil | Nil | Nil | Nil | Nil | Nil | Nil |
| Investment Assets:Total | 32,427 | 31,822 | 29,477 | 39,585 | 42,137 | 38,171 | 30,066 | 22,821 | 17,956 | 13,741 |
| Deferred Policy Costs | 633 | 654 | 714 | 755 | 870 | 866 | 845 | 778 | 688 | 394 |
| Total Assets | 45,023 | 45,580 | 45,682 | 57,762 | 59,309 | 58,455 | 49,015 | 40,764 | 35,647 | 27,963 |
| Debt | 2,464 | 2,451 | 3,190 | 2,869 | 3,368 | 3,413 | 2,721 | 1,905 | 1,878 | 1,605 |
| Common Equity | 10,539 | 9,432 | 6,615 | 9,948 | 16,422 | 14,078 | 12,286 | 10,171 | 6,569 | 5,437 |
| Property & Casualty:Loss Ratio | 63.8 | 61.5 | 66.1 | 59.8 | 60.7 | 107.1 | 68.6 | 75.3 | 68.0 | 105.0 |
| Property & Casualty:Expense Ratio | 31.0 | 32.1 | 29.6 | 29.0 | 27.8 | 25.8 | 27.4 | 27.3 | 29.0 | 34.9 |
| Property & Casualty Combined Ratio | 98.4 | 93.6 | 95.7 | 88.8 | 88.5 | 132.9 | 96.0 | 102.6 | 97.0 | 139.9 |
| % Return on Revenue | 10.0 | 1.2 | NM | 3.0 | 18.6 | NM | 11.9 | 5.2 | 6.0 | NM |
| % Return on Equity | 5.9 | 1.0 | NM | 2.1 | 11.3 | NM | 10.0 | 3.9 | 6.6 | NM |

Data as orig reptd.; bef. results of disc opers/spec. items. Per share data adj. for stk. divs.; EPS diluted. E-Estimated. NA-Not Available. NM-Not Meaningful. NR-Not Ranked. UR-Under Review.

**Office:** 1 Hatch Street Upper, Dublin, Ireland 2.
**Telephone:** 353 (1) 405-2033.
**Website:** http://www.xlgroup.com
**Chrmn:** R.R. Glauber

**Pres:** P. Rochaix
**CEO:** M.S. McGavick
**EVP & CFO:** P.R. Porrino
**EVP, Secy & General Counsel:** K.R. Gould

**Investor Contact:** D.R. Radulski (441-294-7460)
**Board Members:** R. Ayer, D. R. Comey, R. R. Glauber, H.
N. Haag, S. B. Labarge, J. Mauriello, M. S. McGavick, E.
M. McQuade, S. Rich, C. S. Rose, E. E. Thrower, J. M.
Vereker
**Founded:** 1986
**Domicile:** Cayman Islands
**Employees:** 3,576

**The McGraw·Hill Companies**

# Xylem Inc

**STANDARD &POOR'S**

| S&P Recommendation | HOLD ★ ★ ★ ☆ ☆ | Price $23.88 (as of Dec 8, 2011) | 12-Mo. Target Price $27.00 | Investment Style Large-Cap Blend |

**GICS Sector** Industrials
**Sub-Industry** Industrial Machinery

**Summary** This company, spun off from ITT Corp. on October 31, 2011, is a world leader in the design, manufacture and application of highly engineered technologies for the water industry.

## Key Stock Statistics (Source S&P, Vickers, company reports)

| | | | | | | | |
|---|---|---|---|---|---|---|---|
| 52-Wk Range | $28.28–22.67 | S&P Oper. EPS 2012E | 2.00 | Market Capitalization(B) | $4.408 | Beta | NA |
| Trailing 12-Month EPS | $1.76 | S&P Oper. EPS 2013E | 2.15 | Yield (%) | 1.70 | S&P 3-Yr. Proj. EPS CAGR(%) | 7 |
| Trailing 12-Month P/E | 13.6 | P/E on S&P Oper. EPS 2012E | 11.9 | Dividend Rate/Share | $0.40 | S&P Credit Rating | BBB |
| $10K Invested 5 Yrs Ago | NA | Common Shares Outstg. (M) | 184.6 | Institutional Ownership (%) | NA | | |

## Price Performance

30-Week Mov. Avg. ···   10-Week Mov. Avg. - -   **GAAP Earnings vs. Previous Year**   Volume Above Avg. STARS
12-Mo. Target Price —   Relative Strength —   ▲ Up  ▼ Down  ▶ No Change   Below Avg.

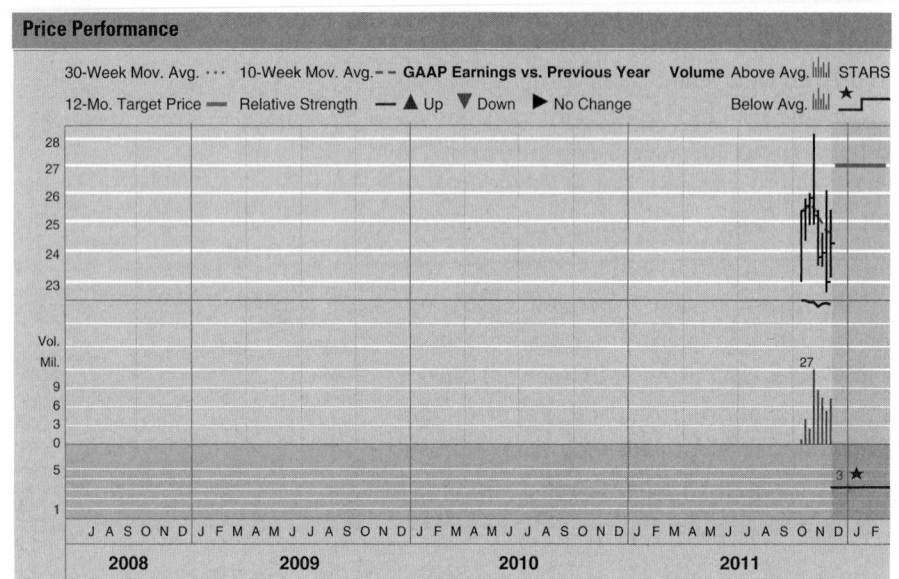

Analysis prepared by Equity Analyst **Stewart Scharf** on Dec 08, 2011, when the stock traded at **$24.27**.

### Highlights

➤ We expect organic revenue growth to continue at a mid-single digits pace in 2012, driven by demand for industrial water and irrigation products and, to a lesser extent, building services, due in part to new energy efficient solutions and increased volume of dewatering equipment. Acquisitions should add 1% to 2% to revenue growth annually long term.

➤ Gross margins are likely to expand to above 39% in 2012, from our projection of 38.6% in 2011 (37.9% in 2010), as volume leverage, pricing initiatives, improved productivity and relatively stable commodity costs offset higher labor and overhead costs. We see EBITDA margins widening in 2012 by about 30 basis points, to 16.3%, as improved operating efficiencies outweigh acquisition-related costs and higher selling and marketing and R&D expenses.

➤ We forecast a higher effective tax rate in 2012 of near 27%, and we see operating EPS of $2.00, up from our pro forma projection of $1.95 (before at least $0.29 of separation costs and a $0.01 restructuring charge) in 2011.

### Investment Rationale/Risk

➤ We recently initiated coverage on XYL with a hold opinion, based on our view that demand for water infrastructure products and services will continue to pick up gradually, especially in emerging regions, while the company expands via acquisitions. However, we think uncertain market conditions in Europe could limit growth in the near term. Our valuation metrics also indicate that the shares are fairly valued.

➤ Risks to our recommendation and target price include higher debt levels and costs as an independent company following the recent spin-off, a prolonged economic downturn, geopolitical issues, negative foreign exchange, inability to integrate acquisitions or find suitable new candidates, and adverse weather conditions.

➤ Our 12-month target price of $27 is based on a blend of our relative and discounted cash flow (DCF) metrics. Applying forward P/E and enterprise value-to-EBITDA multiples in line with XYL's closest peers leads to a $25 value, while our DCF model derives intrinsic value of $29, assuming a 3% terminal growth rate and a weighted average cost of capital (WACC) of 8.6%.

## Qualitative Risk Assessment

| LOW | MEDIUM | HIGH |

Our risk assessment reflects our view of stable cash generation and potential market share expansion as the company focuses on emerging regions where water treatment is needed. However, uncertain global economies and sovereign debt issues, volatile commodity costs and government budget shortfalls remain a concern to us.

## Quantitative Evaluations

**S&P Quality Ranking**                                          NR

| D | C | B- | B | B+ | A- | A | A+ |

**Relative Strength Rank**                                      NA

## Revenue/Earnings Data

**Revenue (Million $)**

| | 1Q | 2Q | 3Q | 4Q | Year |
|---|---|---|---|---|---|
| 2011 | 890.0 | 971.0 | 939.0 | -- | -- |
| 2010 | 686.0 | 775.0 | 870.5 | 870.5 | 3,202 |
| 2009 | -- | -- | -- | -- | 2,849 |
| 2008 | -- | -- | -- | -- | 3,291 |
| 2007 | -- | -- | -- | -- | -- |
| 2006 | -- | -- | -- | -- | -- |

**Earnings Per Share ($)**

| | 1Q | 2Q | 3Q | 4Q | Year |
|---|---|---|---|---|---|
| 2011 | -- | -- | 0.42 | E0.42 | E1.95 |
| 2010 | -- | -- | -- | -- | -- |
| 2009 | -- | -- | -- | -- | -- |
| 2008 | -- | -- | -- | -- | -- |
| 2007 | -- | -- | -- | -- | -- |
| 2006 | -- | -- | -- | -- | -- |

Fiscal year ended Dec. 31. Next earnings report expected: NA. EPS Estimates based on S&P Operating Earnings; historical GAAP earnings are as reported.

## Dividend Data (Dates: mm/dd Payment Date: mm/dd/yy)

| Amount ($) | Date Decl. | Ex-Div. Date | Stk. of Record | Payment Date |
|---|---|---|---|---|
| 0.101 | 11/02 | 11/14 | 11/16 | 12/31/11 |

Dividends have been paid since 2011. Source: Company reports.

---

**Please read the Required Disclosures and Analyst Certification on the last page of this report.**

The McGraw-Hill Companies

# Xylem Inc

## Business Summary December 08, 2011

CORPORATE OVERVIEW. Xylem Inc., which was spun off from ITT Corp. (ITT 20, Buy) on October 31, 2011, designs, manufactures and applies highly engineered technologies for the water industry. The company, which was called ITT WCO until July 2011, is a leading equipment and service provider for water and wastewater applications, with a broad portfolio of products and services addressing the full cycle of water, from collection, distribution and use to the return of water to the environment. XYL has leading market positions in core areas of the water equipment industry: transport, treatment, test, building services, industrial processing, and irrigation. XYL operates in two segments: Water Infrastructure (59% of 2010 revenues) and Applied Water (41%). In both segments, XYL benefits from a large and growing installed base of products driving growth in aftermarket sales (40% of total revenues) for replacement parts and services.

The Water Infrastructure segment focuses on the transportation (74% of segment revenues), treatment (20%) and testing (6%) of water, offering a range of products including water and wastewater pumps, treatment and testing equipment, and controls and systems. Key brands include Flygt, Wedeco, Godwin Pumps, WTW, Sanitaire, AADI and Leopold.

The Applied Water segment encompasses all the uses of water and focuses

on the residential, commercial, industrial and agricultural markets. Building services accounted for 55% of segment revenues in 2010, while industrial water made up 38%, and irrigation 7%. The segment's major products include pumps, valves, heat exchangers, controls and dispensing equipment. Key brands in this segment include Goulds, Bell & Gossett, AC Fire, Standard, Flojet, Lowara, Jabsco and Flowtronex.

The company's global manufacturing footprint enables it to optimize sourcing, lower production costs and localize products. XYL serves a global customer base across diverse end markets, selling its products in more than 140 countries through a balanced distribution network consisting of a direct sales force and independent channel partners. In 2010, approximately 65% of XYL's revenues were generated outside the United States, with 18% of that from emerging markets. Total revenues were: 35% from the U.S., 39% from Europe, 11% from Asia Pacific, and 15% Other. The end market mix was 40% public utility, 35% industrial, 13% commercial, 9% residential, and 3% agricultural.

## Company Financials Fiscal Year Ended Dec. 31

| Per Share Data ($) | 2011 | 2010 | 2009 | 2008 | 2007 | 2006 | 2005 | 2004 | 2003 | 2002 |
|---|---|---|---|---|---|---|---|---|---|---|
| Tangible Book Value | NA | NA | NA | NA | NA | NA | NA | NA | NA | NA |
| Cash Flow | NA | NA | NA | NA | NA | NA | NA | NA | NA | NA |
| Earnings | NA | NA | NA | NA | NA | NA | NA | NA | NA | NA |
| S&P Core Earnings | NA | 1.82 | 1.47 | NA | NA | NA | NA | NA | NA | NA |
| Dividends | NA | NA | NA | NA | NA | NA | NA | NA | NA | NA |
| Payout Ratio | NA | NA | NA | NA | NA | NA | NA | NA | NA | NA |
| Prices:High | NA | NA | NA | NA | NA | NA | NA | NA | NA | NA |
| Prices:Low | NA | NA | NA | NA | NA | NA | NA | NA | NA | NA |
| P/E Ratio:High | NA | NA | NA | NA | NA | NA | NA | NA | NA | NA |
| P/E Ratio:Low | NA | NA | NA | NA | NA | NA | NA | NA | NA | NA |

### Income Statement Analysis (Million $)

| | 2011 | 2010 | 2009 | 2008 | 2007 | 2006 | 2005 | 2004 | 2003 | 2002 |
|---|---|---|---|---|---|---|---|---|---|---|
| Revenue | NA | 3,202 | 2,849 | 3,291 | NA | NA | NA | NA | NA | NA |
| Operating Income | NA | 495 | 377 | 418 | NA | NA | NA | NA | NA | NA |
| Depreciation | NA | 92.0 | 70.0 | 62.0 | NA | NA | NA | NA | NA | NA |
| Interest Expense | NA | NA | NA | NA | NA | NA | NA | NA | NA | NA |
| Pretax Income | NA | 388 | 277 | 312 | NA | NA | NA | NA | NA | NA |
| Effective Tax Rate | NA | NA | NA | NA | NA | NA | NA | NA | NA | NA |
| Net Income | NA | 329 | 263 | 224 | NA | NA | NA | NA | NA | NA |
| S&P Core Earnings | NA | 334 | 268 | NA | NA | NA | NA | NA | NA | NA |

### Balance Sheet & Other Financial Data (Million $)

| | 2011 | 2010 | 2009 | 2008 | 2007 | 2006 | 2005 | 2004 | 2003 | 2002 |
|---|---|---|---|---|---|---|---|---|---|---|
| Cash | NA | 131 | 81.0 | NA | NA | NA | NA | NA | NA | NA |
| Current Assets | NA | 1,336 | 1,088 | NA | NA | NA | NA | NA | NA | NA |
| Total Assets | NA | 3,735 | 2,535 | NA | NA | NA | NA | NA | NA | NA |
| Current Liabilities | NA | 649 | 571 | NA | NA | NA | NA | NA | NA | NA |
| Long Term Debt | NA | NA | NA | NA | NA | NA | NA | NA | NA | NA |
| Common Equity | NA | 2,719 | 1,687 | NA | NA | NA | NA | NA | NA | NA |
| Total Capital | NA | 2,719 | 1,687 | NA | NA | NA | NA | NA | NA | NA |
| Capital Expenditures | NA | 94.0 | 62.0 | 67.0 | NA | NA | NA | NA | NA | NA |
| Cash Flow | NA | 421 | 333 | 286 | NA | NA | NA | NA | NA | NA |
| Current Ratio | NA | 2.1 | 1.9 | NA | NA | NA | NA | NA | NA | NA |
| % Long Term Debt of Capitalization | NA | Nil | Nil | NA | NA | NA | NA | NA | NA | NA |
| % Net Income of Revenue | NA | 10.3 | 9.2 | 6.8 | NA | NA | NA | NA | NA | NA |
| % Return on Assets | NA | 10.5 | NA | NA | NA | NA | NA | NA | NA | NA |
| % Return on Equity | NA | 14.9 | NA | NA | NA | NA | NA | NA | NA | NA |

Data as orig reptd.; bef. results of disc opers/spec. items. Per share data adj. for stk. divs.; EPS diluted. E-Estimated. NA-Not Available. NM-Not Meaningful. NR-Not Ranked. UR-Under Review.

**Office:** 1133 Westchester Avenue, Suite N200, White Plains, NY 10604.
**Telephone:** 914-323-5700.
**Website:** http://www.xyleminc.com
**Chrmn:** M.I. Tambakeras

**Pres & CEO:** G.W. McClain
**SVP & CFO:** M.T. Speetzen
**SVP, Secy & General Counsel:** F.R. Jimenez
**Chief Acctg Officer:** J. Connolly

**Board Members:** C. J. Crawford, J. J. Hamre, V. D. Harker, S. R. Loranger, G. W. McClain, S. N. Mohapatra, M. I. Tambakeras

**Employees:** 0

# Yahoo! Inc

**STANDARD &POOR'S**

| **S&P Recommendation** STRONG BUY ★★★★★ | **Price** $15.70 (as of Nov 29, 2011) | **12-Mo. Target Price** $20.00 | **Investment Style** Large-Cap Growth |

**GICS Sector** Information Technology
**Sub-Industry** Internet Software & Services

**Summary** This company is one of the world's largest providers of online content and services.

## Key Stock Statistics (Source S&P, Vickers, company reports)

| | | | | | | | |
|---|---|---|---|---|---|---|---|
| 52-Wk Range | $18.84–11.09 | S&P Oper. EPS 2011E | 0.85 | Market Capitalization(B) | $19.473 | Beta | 0.87 |
| Trailing 12-Month EPS | $0.82 | S&P Oper. EPS 2012E | 0.95 | Yield (%) | Nil | S&P 3-Yr. Proj. EPS CAGR(%) | 10 |
| Trailing 12-Month P/E | 19.2 | P/E on S&P Oper. EPS 2011E | 18.5 | Dividend Rate/Share | Nil | S&P Credit Rating | NR |
| $10K Invested 5 Yrs Ago | $5,387 | Common Shares Outstg. (M) | 1,240.3 | Institutional Ownership (%) | 74 | | |

## Price Performance

30-Week Mov. Avg. ···· 10-Week Mov. Avg. -- **GAAP Earnings vs. Previous Year** Volume Above Avg. STARS
12-Mo. Target Price — Relative Strength — ▲ Up ▼ Down ► No Change Below Avg. ★

Options: ASE, CBOE, P, Ph

Analysis prepared by Equity Analyst **Scott Kessler** on Oct 21, 2011, when the stock traded at **$16.18**.

## Highlights

➤ We project that adjusted revenues excluding traffic acquisition costs will increase around 3% to 5% in 2011 and 2012, reflecting solid demand for display advertising, benefits of a search/advertising deal with Microsoft (MSFT 27, Buy), and challenges in terms of execution and monetization.

➤ We believe revenues will continue to benefit from secular growth in online advertising. We think annual operating margins bottomed in 2008, due to changed broadband alliances and aggressive investments in new initiatives, and we see improvements through 2012. EPS should benefit from a $3 billion share repurchase program announced in June 2010.

➤ YHOO announced a search/advertising pact with MSFT in 2009. MSFT powers YHOO's search results and non-premium-related advertising, and YHOO sells premium search inventory. Although the deal was initially perceived by some as disappointing, we think it will enable YHOO to better focus and invest in its core operations, and we see financial benefits, despite some top-line issues. MSFT has guaranteed certain related revenues into 2013.

## Investment Rationale/Risk

➤ Following the departure of former CEO Carol Bartz and an announcement that YHOO is pursuing strategic alternatives, we think there is significant interest in some/all of the company. We not only see considerable value in YHOO's major investments in Asia-based businesses, but note stabilization in the display business, benefits from the MSFT deal, and potential associated with proprietary content/video.

➤ Risks to our opinion and target price include the potential for strategic alternatives to not be successfully explored or pursued, digital users spending more time with non-YHOO offerings, and sales execution challenges.

➤ Without the value of YHOO's Asia-based equity holdings, our relative P/E and P/E-to-growth analyses yield a value of $11. Our DCF analysis, with assumptions including a WACC of 12.7%, projected annual FCF growth of 5% from 2011 to 2015, and a perpetuity growth rate of 3%, results in an intrinsic value of $6. Adding the value of YHOO's Asia-based investments (which we estimate at $10/share, with a 30% tax rate) and cash/investments (about $2/share) results in our 12-month target price of $20.

## Qualitative Risk Assessment

| LOW | MEDIUM | HIGH |
|---|---|---|

The company is a large leader in a number of areas related to Internet content and services. However, in our view, many of the markets in which it participates change rapidly and have relatively low barriers to entry.

## Quantitative Evaluations

**S&P Quality Ranking** B

| D | C | B- | **B** | B+ | A- | A | A+ |

**Relative Strength Rank** STRONG

87

LOWEST = 1   HIGHEST = 99

## Revenue/Earnings Data

**Revenue (Million $)**

| | 1Q | 2Q | 3Q | 4Q | Year |
|---|---|---|---|---|---|
| 2011 | 1,214 | 1,229 | 1,217 | -- | -- |
| 2010 | 1,597 | 1,601 | 1,601 | 1,525 | 6,325 |
| 2009 | 1,580 | 1,573 | 1,575 | 1,732 | 6,460 |
| 2008 | 1,818 | 1,798 | 1,786 | 1,806 | 7,209 |
| 2007 | 1,672 | 1,698 | 1,768 | 1,832 | 6,969 |
| 2006 | 1,567 | 1,576 | 1,580 | 1,702 | 6,426 |

**Earnings Per Share ($)**

| | | | | | |
|---|---|---|---|---|---|
| 2011 | 0.17 | 0.18 | 0.23 | E0.27 | E0.85 |
| 2010 | 0.22 | 0.15 | 0.30 | 0.24 | 0.90 |
| 2009 | 0.08 | 0.10 | 0.13 | 0.11 | 0.42 |
| 2008 | 0.37 | 0.09 | 0.04 | -0.22 | 0.29 |
| 2007 | 0.10 | 0.11 | 0.11 | 0.15 | 0.47 |
| 2006 | 0.11 | 0.11 | 0.11 | 0.19 | 0.52 |

Fiscal year ended Dec. 31. Next earnings report expected: NA. EPS Estimates based on S&P Operating Earnings; historical GAAP earnings are as reported.

## Dividend Data

No cash dividends have been paid.

# Yahoo! Inc

STANDARD
&POOR'S

## Business Summary October 21, 2011

CORPORATE OVERVIEW. Yahoo! is one of the world's largest Internet companies. It classifies properties in three categories: Communications and Communities (including mail and messaging offerings, as well as Yahoo Groups and Flickr), Search and Marketplaces (including search offerings, Yahoo Shopping, Yahoo Travel, Yahoo Real Estate, Yahoo Autos and Yahoo Small Business) and Media (including the Yahoo homepage and My Yahoo, as well as information/entertainment offerings related to news, sports, finance, entertainment and lifestyles). These offerings are available on PCs, mobile devices, tablets and TVs.

Hundreds of millions of users every month visit the online properties of YHOO and its unconsolidated subsidiaries (not including the 35% stake in Yahoo Japan and a 43% interest in privately held Chinese Internet conglomerate Alibaba Group as of December 2010), making it one of the world's most popular Internet destinations.

Blake Jorgensen became CFO in 2007. Soon thereafter, co-founder Jerry Yang replaced Terry Semel as CEO, and long-time CFO Sue Decker became president and COO. Many other important executives have also left YHOO since early 2007, with the pace and magnitude of these departures peaking around mid-2008. Carol Bartz replaced Jerry Yang as CEO and Sue Decker left in 2009, and Tim Morse replaced Jorgensen as CFO in 2009. In 2010, YHOO hired key executives Blake Irving (chief product officer) and Ross Levinsohn (head of the company's Americas businesses). Bartz left the company in 2011 and Morse is the interim CEO.

## Company Financials Fiscal Year Ended Dec. 31

| Per Share Data ($) | 2010 | 2009 | 2008 | 2007 | 2006 | 2005 | 2004 | 2003 | 2002 | 2001 |
|---|---|---|---|---|---|---|---|---|---|---|
| Tangible Book Value | 6.59 | 6.18 | 5.26 | 3.70 | 4.25 | 3.59 | 2.94 | 1.64 | 1.47 | 1.52 |
| Cash Flow | 1.40 | 0.94 | 0.87 | 0.94 | 0.89 | 1.54 | 0.79 | 0.31 | 0.18 | 0.03 |
| Earnings | 0.90 | 0.42 | 0.29 | 0.47 | 0.52 | 1.28 | 0.58 | 0.19 | 0.09 | -0.08 |
| S&P Core Earnings | 0.78 | 0.33 | 0.33 | 0.46 | 0.51 | 0.56 | 0.24 | 0.03 | -0.32 | -0.85 |
| Dividends | Nil | Nil | Nil | Nil | Nil | Nil | Nil | Nil | Nil | Nil |
| Payout Ratio | Nil | Nil | Nil | Nil | Nil | Nil | Nil | Nil | Nil | Nil |
| Prices:High | 19.12 | 18.02 | 30.25 | 34.08 | 43.66 | 43.45 | 39.79 | 22.74 | 10.68 | 21.69 |
| Prices:Low | 12.94 | 10.81 | 8.94 | 22.27 | 22.65 | 30.30 | 20.57 | 8.25 | 4.47 | 4.01 |
| P/E Ratio:High | 21 | 43 | NM | 73 | 84 | 34 | 69 | NM | NM | NM |
| P/E Ratio:Low | 14 | 26 | NM | 47 | 44 | 24 | 35 | NM | NM | NM |

| Income Statement Analysis (Million $) | | | | | | | | | | |
|---|---|---|---|---|---|---|---|---|---|---|
| Revenue | 6,325 | 6,460 | 7,209 | 6,969 | 6,426 | 5,258 | 3,575 | 1,625 | 953 | 717 |
| Operating Income | 1,513 | 1,252 | 1,477 | 1,355 | 1,481 | 1,505 | 1,000 | 455 | 198 | 34.5 |
| Depreciation | 683 | 739 | 790 | 659 | 540 | 397 | 311 | 160 | 109 | 131 |
| Interest Expense | NA | NA | NA | Nil | Nil | Nil | Nil | Nil | Nil | Nil |
| Pretax Income | 1,466 | 825 | 693 | 1,000 | 293 | 2,672 | 1,280 | 391 | 180 | -81.1 |
| Effective Tax Rate | NA | 26.6% | 37.9% | 33.7% | NM | 28.7% | 34.2% | 37.6% | 39.7% | NM |
| Net Income | 1,232 | 598 | 424 | 660 | 751 | 1,896 | 840 | 238 | 107 | -92.8 |
| S&P Core Earnings | 1,065 | 470 | 464 | 651 | 744 | 840 | 353 | 35.5 | -377 | -966 |

| Balance Sheet & Other Financial Data (Million $) | | | | | | | | | | |
|---|---|---|---|---|---|---|---|---|---|---|
| Cash | 2,884 | 3,291 | 3,452 | 2,001 | 2,601 | 2,561 | 3,512 | 1,310 | 774 | 926 |
| Current Assets | 4,346 | 4,595 | 4,746 | 3,238 | 3,750 | 3,450 | 4,090 | 1,722 | 970 | 1,052 |
| Total Assets | 14,928 | 14,936 | 13,690 | 12,230 | 11,514 | 10,832 | 9,178 | 5,932 | 2,790 | 2,379 |
| Current Liabilities | 1,626 | 1,718 | 1,705 | 2,300 | 1,474 | 1,204 | 1,181 | 708 | 412 | 359 |
| Long Term Debt | NA | NA | 43.0 | Nil | 750 | 750 | 750 | 750 | Nil | Nil |
| Common Equity | 12,558 | 12,493 | 11,242 | 9,533 | 9,161 | 8,566 | 7,101 | 4,363 | 2,262 | 1,967 |
| Total Capital | 12,596 | 12,519 | 11,269 | 9,545 | 9,919 | 9,316 | 7,896 | 5,151 | 2,294 | 1,997 |
| Capital Expenditures | 714 | 434 | 675 | 602 | 689 | 409 | 246 | 117 | 51.6 | 86.2 |
| Cash Flow | 1,914 | 1,337 | 1,214 | 1,319 | 1,291 | 2,293 | 1,151 | 398 | 216 | 37.8 |
| Current Ratio | 2.7 | 2.7 | 2.8 | 1.4 | 2.5 | 2.9 | 3.5 | 2.4 | 2.4 | 2.9 |
| % Long Term Debt of Capitalization | Nil | Nil | 0.4 | Nil | 7.6 | 8.0 | 9.5 | 14.6 | Nil | Nil |
| % Net Income of Revenue | 19.5 | 9.3 | 5.9 | 9.5 | 11.7 | 36.0 | 23.5 | 14.6 | 11.2 | NM |
| % Return on Assets | 8.3 | 4.2 | 3.3 | 5.6 | 6.7 | 18.9 | 11.1 | 5.5 | 4.1 | NM |
| % Return on Equity | 9.8 | 5.0 | 4.1 | 7.1 | 8.5 | 24.2 | 14.6 | 7.2 | 5.1 | NM |

Data as orig reptd.; bef. results of disc opers/spec. items. Per share data adj. for stk. divs.; EPS diluted. E-Estimated. NA-Not Available. NM-Not Meaningful. NR-Not Ranked. UR-Under Review.

**Office:** 701 First Avenue, Sunnyvale, CA 94089.
**Telephone:** 408-349-3300.
**Email:** investor_relations@yahoo-inc.com
**Website:** http://www.yahoo.com

**Chrmn:** R.J. Bostock
**CEO & CFO:** T.R. Morse
**SVP & CIO:** L. Rabbe
**CSO:** P. Raghavan

**CTO:** R. Stata
**Board Members:** R. J. Bostock, P. S. Hart, S. M. James, V. I. Joshi, D. W. Kenny, A. Kern, B. D. Smith, G. L. Wilson, J. Yang

**Founded:** 1995
**Domicile:** Delaware
**Employees:** 13,600

# YUM! Brands Inc.

**STANDARD &POOR'S**

| **S&P Recommendation** HOLD ★★★☆☆ | **Price** $52.72 (as of Nov 25, 2011) | **12-Mo. Target Price** $56.00 | **Investment Style** Large-Cap Growth |
|---|---|---|---|

**GICS Sector** Consumer Discretionary
**Sub-Industry** Restaurants

**Summary** This company operates, franchises, has interests in or licenses the largest number of fast food restaurants in the world, with more than 37,000 units in over 110 countries, including the KFC, Pizza Hut and Taco Bell chains.

## Key Stock Statistics (Source S&P, Vickers, company reports)

| | | | | | | | |
|---|---|---|---|---|---|---|---|
| 52-Wk Range | $57.75– 46.27 | S&P Oper. EPS 2011E | 2.77 | Market Capitalization(B) | $24.277 | Beta | 0.94 |
| Trailing 12-Month EPS | $2.55 | S&P Oper. EPS 2012E | 3.12 | Yield (%) | 2.16 | S&P 3-Yr. Proj. EPS CAGR(%) | 11 |
| Trailing 12-Month P/E | 20.7 | P/E on S&P Oper. EPS 2011E | 19.0 | Dividend Rate/Share | $1.14 | S&P Credit Rating | BBB- |
| $10K Invested 5 Yrs Ago | $18,509 | Common Shares Outstg. (M) | 460.5 | Institutional Ownership (%) | 78 | | |

## Price Performance

30-Week Mov. Avg. · · · 10-Week Mov. Avg. – – GAAP Earnings vs. Previous Year  Volume Above Avg. ▐▌▐ STARS
12-Mo. Target Price —  Relative Strength —  ▲ Up ▼ Down ► No Change  Below Avg. ▐▌▐ ★

Options: ASE, CBOE, Ph

Analysis prepared by Equity Analyst **Jim Yin, CFA** on Oct 10, 2011, when the stock traded at **$50.74**.

## Highlights

▶ We expect revenues to rise 5.6% in 2012, following a 9.8% advance projected for 2011. We believe most of the growth will come as a result of new store openings internationally. YUM plans to open about 1,500 new international units in 2011, including about 600 in China and 900 at the Yum Restaurants International division (YRI). Additionally, we see same-store sales in China increasing at a low-teens rate, reflecting the rise in that country's wealth. However, we forecast a 3% decline in U.S. restaurant sales, given weakness in consumer confidence.

▶ We look for restaurant margins in 2012 of 16.6%, a 40 basis point improvement over the 16.2% projected for 2011. Although food and other commodity cost inflation will likely hurt overall results, we think price pressure will abate in 2012. We see operating margins widening to 16.1% in 2012, from 14.8% in 2011, on improved profitability in international markets and lower general and administrative expenses due to economies of scale.

▶ We project 2011 and 2012 EPS of $2.77 and $3.12, respectively, compared to $2.38 in 2010.

## Investment Rationale/Risk

▶ We believe YUM is making steady progress expanding internationally, especially in China and other emerging countries. We think strong economic growth and the rise of the middle class in these geographical regions should represent significant growth opportunities. However, we believe additional efforts are needed to reinvigorate results at U.S. including upgrading the brand images and broadening the menu offerings. We are also concerned about a slower global economy and margin pressure from higher food input costs.

▶ Risks to our recommendation and target price include slower economic growth, in particular in international markets, less favorable energy, food and labor costs, and a material strengthening of the dollar (making foreign profits worth less in dollars).

▶ Our 12-month target price of $56 is based on our relative P/E analysis, in which we apply a 18X multiple to our 2012 EPS estimates. Although this multiple is slightly above peers, we think this is warranted given our view of YUM's attractive international growth prospects.

## Qualitative Risk Assessment

| LOW | MEDIUM | HIGH |
|---|---|---|

YUM competes primarily in the fast food industry, in which its concepts possess a very strong brand name presence domestically and in certain foreign markets. However, operating margins can vary widely due to fluctuations in food costs. Furthermore, YUM's profits can be affected by changing currency exchange rates given its large and fast-growing international business.

## Quantitative Evaluations

**S&P Quality Ranking** A

| D | C | B- | B | B+ | A- | A | A+ |
|---|---|---|---|---|---|---|---|

**Relative Strength Rank** STRONG

74

LOWEST = 1    HIGHEST = 99

## Revenue/Earnings Data

### Revenue (Million $)

| | 1Q | 2Q | 3Q | 4Q | Year |
|---|---|---|---|---|---|
| 2011 | 2,425 | 2,816 | 3,274 | -- | -- |
| 2010 | 2,345 | 2,574 | 2,862 | 3,562 | 11,343 |
| 2009 | 2,217 | 2,476 | 2,778 | 3,365 | 10,836 |
| 2008 | 2,408 | 2,653 | 2,835 | 3,383 | 11,279 |
| 2007 | 2,223 | 2,367 | 2,564 | 3,262 | 10,416 |
| 2006 | 2,085 | 2,182 | 2,278 | 3,016 | 9,561 |

### Earnings Per Share ($)

| | | | | | |
|---|---|---|---|---|---|
| 2011 | 0.54 | 0.65 | 0.80 | E0.78 | E2.77 |
| 2010 | 0.50 | 0.59 | 0.74 | 0.56 | 2.38 |
| 2009 | 0.46 | 0.63 | 0.69 | 0.45 | 2.22 |
| 2008 | 0.50 | 0.45 | 0.58 | 0.43 | 1.96 |
| 2007 | 0.35 | 0.39 | 0.50 | 0.44 | 1.68 |
| 2006 | 0.29 | 0.34 | 0.42 | 0.42 | 1.46 |

Fiscal year ended Dec. 31. Next earnings report expected: Early February. EPS Estimates based on S&P Operating Earnings; historical GAAP earnings are as reported.

## Dividend Data (Dates: mm/dd Payment Date: mm/dd/yy)

| Amount ($) | Date Decl. | Ex-Div. Date | Stk. of Record | Payment Date |
|---|---|---|---|---|
| 0.250 | 03/25 | 04/13 | 04/15 | 05/06/11 |
| 0.250 | 05/19 | 07/13 | 07/15 | 08/05/11 |
| 0.285 | 09/14 | 10/12 | 10/14 | 11/04/11 |
| 0.285 | 11/18 | 01/11 | 01/13 | 02/03/12 |

Dividends have been paid since 2004. Source: Company reports.

**Please read the Required Disclosures and Analyst Certification on the last page of this report.**

The **McGraw-Hill** Companies

# YUM! Brands Inc.

STANDARD
&POOR'S

## Business Summary October 10, 2011

CORPORATE PROFILE. Yum! Brands has the world's largest quick service restaurant (QSR) system, with over 37,000 restaurants, including licensee units, in more than 110 countries and territories. The company operates and franchises restaurants under the KFC, Pizza Hut, Taco Bell, Long John Silver's and A&W All American Food concepts. In 2010, the company's brands generated $11.3 billion in worldwide revenues, up 4.7% from 2009.

KFC (originally Kentucky Fried Chicken) is the leader in the U.S. chicken QSR segment, with about a 40% market share at year-end 2010 (42% in 2009), according to NPD Group CREST. At the end of 2010, there were 5,055 units in the U.S. and 11,798 units internationally, of which 15% in the U.S. and 29% internationally were operated by the company.

Pizza Hut is the world's largest restaurant chain specializing in ready-to-eat pizza products. At December 31, 2010, it led the U.S. pizza QSR segment with about a 14% market share (14%). As of December 2010, there were 7,542 units in the U.S. and 5,890 units internationally, of which 6% in the U.S. and 22% of the non-U.S. units were operated by the company.

Taco Bell is the leader in the U.S. Mexican food QSR segment, with about a 52% market share (52%). At the end of 2010, it had 5,634 units in the U.S. and 262 units internationally. About 22% of U.S. and 1% of international locations were operated by YUM.

Long John Silver's is the leader in the U.S. seafood QSR segment, with a 37% market share. At the end of 2010, it had 964 units in the U.S. and 31 units internationally. There were also 86 multi-brand locations that include LJS.

A&W services A&W draft root beer, floats, as well as hot dogs and hamburgers in nine countries. At the end of 2010, it had 322 units in the U.S. and 317 units internationally. All the units are operated by franchisees.

## Company Financials Fiscal Year Ended Dec. 31

| Per Share Data ($) | 2010 | 2009 | 2008 | 2007 | 2006 | 2005 | 2004 | 2003 | 2002 | 2001 |
|---|---|---|---|---|---|---|---|---|---|---|
| Tangible Book Value | 0.94 | NM | NM | 0.27 | 0.81 | 1.04 | 1.20 | 0.42 | NM | NM |
| Cash Flow | 3.64 | 3.42 | 3.10 | 2.67 | 2.46 | 2.07 | 1.95 | 1.67 | 1.54 | 1.39 |
| Earnings | 2.38 | 2.22 | 1.96 | 1.68 | 1.46 | 1.28 | 1.21 | 1.01 | 0.94 | 0.81 |
| S&P Core Earnings | 2.40 | 2.16 | 1.76 | 1.69 | 1.51 | 1.26 | 1.15 | 1.04 | 0.80 | 0.68 |
| Dividends | 0.88 | 0.78 | 0.68 | 0.52 | 0.26 | 0.22 | 0.10 | Nil | Nil | Nil |
| Payout Ratio | 37% | 35% | 35% | 31% | 18% | 17% | 8% | Nil | Nil | Nil |
| Prices:High | 52.47 | 36.96 | 41.73 | 40.60 | 31.84 | 26.90 | 23.74 | 17.71 | 16.58 | 13.33 |
| Prices:Low | 32.49 | 23.37 | 21.50 | 27.51 | 22.11 | 22.37 | 16.07 | 10.77 | 10.18 | 7.89 |
| P/E Ratio:High | 22 | 17 | 21 | 24 | 22 | 21 | 20 | 18 | 18 | 16 |
| P/E Ratio:Low | 14 | 11 | 11 | 16 | 15 | 18 | 13 | 11 | 11 | 10 |

| Income Statement Analysis (Million $) | 2010 | 2009 | 2008 | 2007 | 2006 | 2005 | 2004 | 2003 | 2002 | 2001 |
|---|---|---|---|---|---|---|---|---|---|---|
| Revenue | 11,343 | 10,836 | 11,279 | 10,416 | 9,561 | 9,349 | 9,011 | 8,380 | 7,757 | 6,953 |
| Operating Income | 2,435 | 2,185 | 1,971 | 1,808 | 1,724 | 1,538 | 1,518 | 1,471 | 1,375 | 1,220 |
| Depreciation | 589 | 580 | 560 | 533 | 479 | 469 | 448 | 401 | 370 | 354 |
| Interest Expense | 175 | 212 | 253 | 199 | 154 | 127 | 129 | 173 | 172 | 158 |
| Pretax Income | 1,594 | 1,396 | 1,280 | 1,191 | 1,108 | 1,026 | 1,026 | 886 | 858 | 733 |
| Effective Tax Rate | NA | 22.4% | 24.7% | 23.7% | 25.6% | 25.7% | 27.9% | 30.2% | 32.1% | 32.9% |
| Net Income | 1,178 | 1,071 | 964 | 909 | 824 | 762 | 740 | 618 | 583 | 492 |
| S&P Core Earnings | 1,170 | 1,041 | 863 | 913 | 849 | 754 | 704 | 635 | 494 | 416 |

| Balance Sheet & Other Financial Data (Million $) | 2010 | 2009 | 2008 | 2007 | 2006 | 2005 | 2004 | 2003 | 2002 | 2001 |
|---|---|---|---|---|---|---|---|---|---|---|
| Cash | 1,426 | 353 | 164 | 789 | 319 | 158 | 62.0 | 192 | 130 | 110 |
| Current Assets | 2,313 | 1,208 | 951 | 1,481 | 901 | 837 | 747 | 806 | 730 | 547 |
| Total Assets | 8,316 | 7,148 | 6,506 | 7,242 | 6,353 | 5,698 | 5,696 | 5,620 | 5,400 | 4,388 |
| Current Liabilities | 2,448 | 1,653 | 1,722 | 2,062 | 1,724 | 1,605 | 1,376 | 1,461 | 1,520 | 1,805 |
| Long Term Debt | 2,915 | 3,207 | 3,564 | 2,924 | 2,045 | 1,649 | 1,731 | 2,056 | 2,299 | 1,552 |
| Common Equity | 1,576 | 1,025 | -112 | 1,139 | 1,437 | 1,449 | 1,595 | 1,120 | 594 | 104 |
| Total Capital | 4,677 | 4,321 | 3,509 | 4,063 | 3,482 | 3,098 | 3,326 | 3,176 | 2,893 | 1,656 |
| Capital Expenditures | 796 | 797 | 935 | 742 | 614 | 609 | 645 | 663 | 760 | 636 |
| Cash Flow | 1,767 | 1,651 | 1,524 | 1,442 | 1,303 | 1,231 | 1,188 | 1,019 | 953 | 846 |
| Current Ratio | 0.9 | 0.7 | 0.6 | 0.7 | 0.5 | 0.5 | 0.5 | 0.6 | 0.5 | 0.3 |
| % Long Term Debt of Capitalization | 62.3 | 74.2 | 101.6 | 71.9 | 58.7 | 53.2 | 52.0 | 64.7 | 79.5 | 93.7 |
| % Net Income of Revenue | 10.4 | 9.9 | 8.6 | 8.7 | 8.6 | 8.2 | 8.2 | 7.4 | 7.5 | 7.1 |
| % Return on Assets | 15.2 | 15.7 | 14.0 | 13.4 | 13.6 | 13.4 | 13.1 | 11.2 | 11.9 | 11.5 |
| % Return on Equity | 90.6 | NM | NM | 70.6 | 57.1 | 50.1 | 54.5 | 72.1 | 167.0 | NM |

Data as orig reptd.; bef. results of disc opers/spec. items. Per share data adj. for stk. divs.; EPS diluted. E-Estimated. NA-Not Available. NM-Not Meaningful. NR-Not Ranked. UR-Under Review.

**Office:** 1441 Gardiner Lane, Louisville, KY 40213.
**Telephone:** 502-874-8300.
**Email:** yum.investors@yum.com
**Website:** http://www.yum.com

**Chrmn, Pres & CEO:** D.C. Novak
**Vice Chrmn:** J.S. Su
**SVP & Chief Acctg Officer:** T.F. Knopf
**SVP, Secy & General Counsel:** C.L. Campbell

**CFO:** R.T. Carucci
**Investor Contact:** S. Schmitt (502-874-8785)
**Board Members:** D. W. Dorman, M. Ferragamo, J. D. Grissom, B. Hill, R. Holland, Jr., K. G. Langone, J. S. Linen, T. C. Nelson, D. C. Novak, T. M. Ryan, J. S. Su, R. D. Walter

**Founded:** 1997
**Domicile:** North Carolina
**Employees:** 378,000

The *McGraw-Hill* Companies

# Zimmer Holdings Inc.

**STANDARD &POOR'S**

| S&P Recommendation **BUY** ★★★★☆ | Price $47.41 (as of Nov 25, 2011) | 12-Mo. Target Price $66.00 | Investment Style Large-Cap Growth |
|---|---|---|---|

**GICS Sector** Health Care
**Sub-Industry** Health Care Equipment

**Summary** This company, spun off by Bristol-Myers Squibb in August 2001, manufactures orthopedic reconstructive implants, fracture management products, and dental implants.

## Key Stock Statistics (Source S&P, Vickers, company reports)

| | | | | | | | |
|---|---|---|---|---|---|---|---|
| 52-Wk Range | $69.93– 47.25 | S&P Oper. EPS 2011**E** | 4.79 | Market Capitalization(B) | $8.495 | Beta | 1.08 |
| Trailing 12-Month EPS | $3.34 | S&P Oper. EPS 2012**E** | 5.25 | Yield (%) | Nil | S&P 3-Yr. Proj. EPS CAGR(%) | 9 |
| Trailing 12-Month P/E | 14.2 | P/E on S&P Oper. EPS 2011**E** | 9.9 | Dividend Rate/Share | Nil | S&P Credit Rating | A- |
| $10K Invested 5 Yrs Ago | $6,521 | Common Shares Outstg. (M) | 179.2 | Institutional Ownership (%) | 90 | | |

## Price Performance

30-Week Mov. Avg. · · · 10-Week Mov. Avg. - - GAAP Earnings vs. Previous Year   Volume Above Avg. ▋▋▍ STARS
12-Mo. Target Price — Relative Strength — ▲ Up ▼ Down ► No Change   Below Avg. ▋▋▍ ★

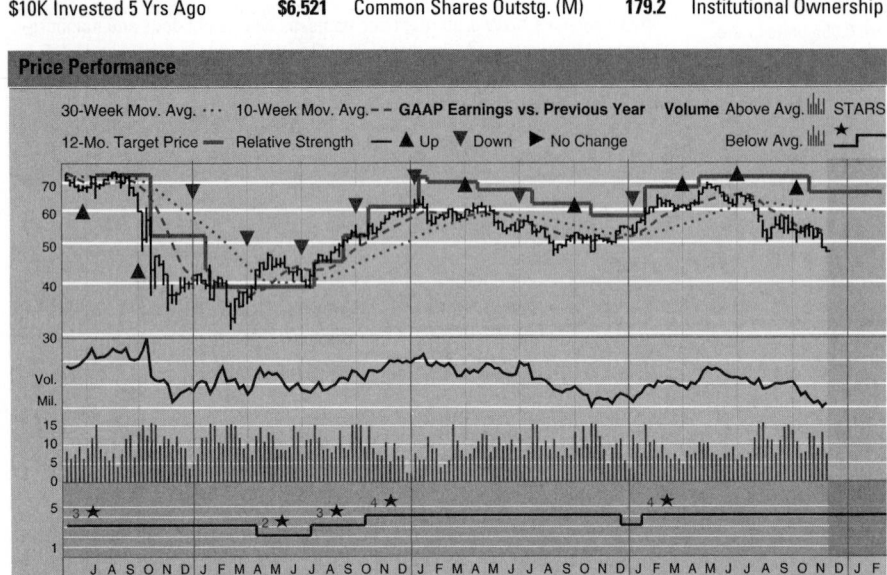

Options: ASE, CBOE, P, Ph

Analysis prepared by Equity Analyst **Phillip Seligman** on Nov 02, 2011, when the stock traded at **$51.52**.

## Qualitative Risk Assessment

| LOW | MEDIUM | HIGH |
|---|---|---|

Our risk assessment reflects Zimmer's operations in a highly competitive industry characterized by relatively short product life cycles, requiring a significant number of new product introductions to maintain market share and gross profit margins. Many of the company's customers are reimbursed by the federal government through Medicare, and a more restrictive budgetary environment could result in lower prices paid to medical device suppliers such as Zimmer. However, this is offset by the company's position as one of the dominant manufacturers in the orthopedic device industry, with substantial global sales force capabilities and an expansive product line.

## Quantitative Evaluations

**S&P Quality Ranking** B+

| D | C | B- | B | B+ | A- | A | A+ |
|---|---|---|---|---|---|---|---|

**Relative Strength Rank** MODERATE

30

LOWEST = 1          HIGHEST = 99

## Highlights

► We project revenues to climb 5.2% in 2011, to over $4.4 billion, and another 4.4% in 2012, to more than $4.6 billion. We project reconstruction sales growth to accelerate in 2011, on new products, including new extremities products, hip cup systems, and patient-specific instruments for knee implants. We also see ZMH's hip sales benefiting from its avoidance of the shrinking metal-on-metal hip category. Elsewhere, we look for spine implant and U.S. knee sales to remain weak, while trauma, dental and surgical products sales remain relatively strong. We also see favorable foreign exchange adding 260 basis points (bps) to 2011 sales growth and to a lesser extent in 2012, while pricing pressure should be a 100 bps drag in both years, by our analysis.

► We expect gross margins will narrow in 2011 and some more in 2012, on currency hedging losses in 2011 and continued pricing pressures in 2012. We expect R&D spending to be essentially flat as a percentage of sales, while the SG&A cost ratio declines on cost control initiatives.

► We estimate adjusted EPS of $4.79 for 2011, versus $4.33 in 2010. We look for $5.25 in 2012.

## Investment Rationale/Risk

► We think ZMH will gain market share in hips, trauma and surgical products on new products, while its new instrumentation helps close its gap in the knee market. Moreover, we think the long-term global demand drivers for ZMH's orthopedic implants remain intact, given aging populations and the rise of obesity levels. Although the hip, knee and spine markets have slowed in the U.S. amid challenging economic conditions, we expect procedure volumes in the U.S. to exhibit modestly improved comparisons in 2012, assuming the lapping of the cyclical downturn associated with increased unemployment levels. Meanwhile, we expect ZMH sales to remain strong in the Asia-Pacific region.

► Risks to our recommendation and target price include lower Medicare reimbursement and significant device reimbursement cuts in key overseas markets.

► Our 12-month target price is $66, or 12.5X our 2012 EPS estimate. This multiple represents a discount to ZMH's historical levels to reflect our view of the soft orthopedic markets.

## Revenue/Earnings Data

**Revenue (Million $)**

| | 1Q | 2Q | 3Q | 4Q | Year |
|---|---|---|---|---|---|
| 2011 | 1,116 | 1,137 | 1,032 | -- | -- |
| 2010 | 1,063 | 1,058 | 965.0 | 1,135 | 4,220 |
| 2009 | 992.6 | 1,020 | 975.6 | 1,107 | 4,095 |
| 2008 | 1,059 | 1,080 | 952.2 | 1,030 | 4,121 |
| 2007 | 950.2 | 970.6 | 903.2 | 1,074 | 3,898 |
| 2006 | 860.4 | 881.6 | 819.8 | 933.6 | 3,495 |

**Earnings Per Share ($)**

| | 1Q | 2Q | 3Q | 4Q | Year |
|---|---|---|---|---|---|
| 2011 | 1.08 | 1.06 | 1.01 | E1.35 | E4.79 |
| 2010 | 1.01 | 0.82 | 0.96 | 0.18 | 2.97 |
| 2009 | 0.91 | 0.98 | 0.70 | 0.74 | 3.32 |
| 2008 | 1.02 | 0.99 | 0.95 | 0.75 | 3.72 |
| 2007 | 0.98 | 0.97 | 0.19 | 1.12 | 3.26 |
| 2006 | 0.82 | 0.81 | 0.76 | 1.02 | 3.40 |

Fiscal year ended Dec. 31. Next earnings report expected: Late January. EPS Estimates based on S&P Operating Earnings; historical GAAP earnings are as reported.

## Dividend Data

No cash dividends have been paid.

# Zimmer Holdings Inc.

STANDARD &POOR'S

## Business Summary November 02, 2011

CORPORATE OVERVIEW. Zimmer Holdings primarily designs, develops, manufactures and markets orthopedic reconstructive implants and fracture management products. The former division of Bristol-Myers Squibb (BMY) was spun off to BMY shareholders in August 2001.

Zimmer's reconstructive implants (76% of 2010 sales) are used to restore function lost due to disease or trauma in joints such as knees, hips, shoulders and elbows. The company offers a wide range of products for specialized knee procedures, including The NexGen Complete Knee Solution, NexGen Legacy, NexGen Revision Knee, Innex Total Knee System, M/G Unicompartmental Knee System, and Prolong Highly Crosslinked Polyethylene Articular Surface material. Hip replacement products include the VerSys Hip System, the ZMR Hip System, the Trilogy Acetabular System and a line of specialty hip products. The company also continues to develop a portfolio of minimally invasive hip replacement procedures. ZMH sells the Coonrad/Morrey product line of elbow replacement implant products, along with a line of restorative dental products.

In the spine (5%) and trauma (6%) areas, the company sells devices used to

reattach or stabilize damaged bone and tissue to support the body's natural healing process. The most common stabilization of bone fractures concerns the internal fixation of bone fragments, which can involve the use of an assortment of plates, screws, rods, wires and pins. ZMH offers a line of products designed for use in fracture fixation. In October 2008, the company acquired the spinal business of Abbott Labs for $360 million in cash.

ZMH makes and markets other orthopedic surgical products (8%) used by surgeons for orthopedic as well as non-orthopedic procedures. Products include tourniquets, blood management systems, wound debridgement products, powered surgical instruments, pain management devices, and orthopedic soft goods that provide support and/or heat retention and compression for trauma of the knee, ankle, back and upper extremities, including the shoulder, elbow, neck and wrist.

## Company Financials Fiscal Year Ended Dec. 31

| Per Share Data ($) | 2010 | 2009 | 2008 | 2007 | 2006 | 2005 | 2004 | 2003 | 2002 | 2001 |
|---|---|---|---|---|---|---|---|---|---|---|
| Tangible Book Value | 12.08 | 9.78 | 8.96 | 9.76 | 7.15 | 7.94 | 2.52 | 0.38 | 1.88 | 0.41 |
| Cash Flow | 4.66 | 4.89 | 4.92 | 4.22 | 4.21 | 3.68 | 2.92 | 1.87 | 1.43 | 0.89 |
| Earnings | 2.97 | 3.32 | 3.72 | 3.26 | 3.40 | 2.93 | 2.19 | 1.38 | 1.31 | 0.77 |
| S&P Core Earnings | 3.85 | 3.67 | 3.56 | 3.94 | 3.36 | 2.73 | 2.08 | 1.31 | 1.24 | 0.70 |
| Dividends | Nil | Nil | Nil | Nil | Nil | Nil | Nil | Nil | Nil | Nil |
| Payout Ratio | Nil | Nil | Nil | Nil | Nil | Nil | Nil | Nil | Nil | Nil |
| Prices:High | 64.77 | 60.64 | 80.92 | 94.38 | 79.11 | 89.10 | 89.44 | 71.85 | 43.00 | 33.30 |
| Prices:Low | 46.27 | 30.67 | 34.10 | 63.00 | 52.20 | 60.19 | 64.40 | 38.02 | 28.00 | 24.70 |
| P/E Ratio:High | 22 | 18 | 22 | 29 | 23 | 30 | 41 | 52 | 33 | 43 |
| P/E Ratio:Low | 16 | 9 | 9 | 19 | 15 | 21 | 29 | 28 | 21 | 32 |

| Income Statement Analysis (Million $) | 2010 | 2009 | 2008 | 2007 | 2006 | 2005 | 2004 | 2003 | 2002 | 2001 |
|---|---|---|---|---|---|---|---|---|---|---|
| Revenue | 4,220 | 4,095 | 4,121 | 3,898 | 3,495 | 3,286 | 2,981 | 1,901 | 1,372 | 1,179 |
| Operating Income | 1,496 | 1,480 | 1,510 | 1,553 | 1,369 | 1,297 | 1,026 | 633 | 426 | 272 |
| Depreciation | 340 | 337 | 275 | 230 | 197 | 186 | 181 | 103 | 25.0 | 23.4 |
| Interest Expense | 56.5 | 20.6 | 7.00 | NA | 4.00 | 14.0 | 32.0 | 13.0 | 12.0 | 7.40 |
| Pretax Income | 860 | 998 | 1,122 | 1,132 | 1,169 | 1,040 | 732 | 438 | 389 | 241 |
| Effective Tax Rate | NA | 28.1% | 24.3% | 31.6% | 28.5% | 29.5% | 25.9% | 33.6% | 33.7% | 37.8% |
| Net Income | 597 | 717 | 849 | 773 | 835 | 733 | 542 | 291 | 258 | 150 |
| S&P Core Earnings | 775 | 789 | 812 | 936 | 823 | 682 | 515 | 277 | 244 | 137 |

| Balance Sheet & Other Financial Data (Million $) | 2010 | 2009 | 2008 | 2007 | 2006 | 2005 | 2004 | 2003 | 2002 | 2001 |
|---|---|---|---|---|---|---|---|---|---|---|
| Cash | 934 | 758 | 213 | 466 | 266 | 233 | 155 | 78.0 | 16.0 | 18.4 |
| Current Assets | 3,008 | 2,738 | 2,179 | 2,083 | 1,746 | 1,576 | 1,561 | 1,339 | 612 | 509 |
| Total Assets | 7,998 | 7,786 | 7,239 | 6,634 | 5,974 | 5,722 | 5,696 | 5,156 | 859 | 745 |
| Current Liabilities | 702 | 691 | 771 | 749 | 628 | 607 | 701 | 645 | 401 | 373 |
| Long Term Debt | 1,142 | 1,128 | 460 | 104 | 100 | 82.0 | 624 | 1,008 | Nil | 214 |
| Common Equity | 5,771 | 5,639 | 5,650 | 5,450 | 4,921 | 4,683 | 3,943 | 3,143 | 366 | 78.7 |
| Total Capital | 6,913 | 6,766 | 6,114 | 5,554 | 5,024 | 4,767 | 4,574 | 4,158 | 366 | 293 |
| Capital Expenditures | 272 | 229 | 488 | 331 | 142 | 105 | 101 | 45.0 | 34.0 | 54.7 |
| Cash Flow | 937 | 1,055 | 1,124 | 1,003 | 1,032 | 919 | 723 | 394 | 283 | 173 |
| Current Ratio | 4.3 | 4.0 | 2.8 | 2.8 | 2.8 | 2.6 | 2.2 | 2.1 | 1.5 | 1.4 |
| % Long Term Debt of Capitalization | 16.5 | 16.7 | 7.5 | 1.8 | 1.9 | 1.7 | 13.6 | 24.2 | Nil | 73.0 |
| % Net Income of Revenue | 14.1 | 17.5 | 20.6 | 19.8 | 23.8 | 22.3 | 18.1 | 15.3 | 18.9 | 12.7 |
| % Return on Assets | 7.6 | 9.6 | 12.2 | 12.3 | 14.2 | 12.8 | 9.9 | 9.7 | 32.1 | 22.4 |
| % Return on Equity | 10.5 | 12.7 | 15.3 | 14.9 | 17.3 | 16.9 | 15.2 | 10.6 | 115.0 | NM |

Data as orig reptd.; bef. results of disc opers/spec. items. Per share data adj. for stk. divs.; EPS diluted. E-Estimated. NA-Not Available. NM-Not Meaningful. NR-Not Ranked. UR-Under Review.

**Office:** 345 East Main Street, Warsaw, IN 46580.
**Telephone:** 574-267-6131.
**Email:** zimmer.infoperson@zimmer.com
**Website:** http://www.zimmer.com

**Chrmn:** J.L. McGoldrick
**Pres & CEO:** D. Dvorak
**COO:** R.C. Stair
**CFO:** J.T. Crines

**CSO:** C.R. Blanchard
**Investor Contact:** P. Blair (574-371-8042)
**Board Members:** B. J. Bernard, M. N. Casper, D. Dvorak, L. C. Glasscock, R. A. Hagemann, A. J. Higgins, J. L. McGoldrick, C. B. Pickett

**Founded:** 1927
**Domicile:** Delaware
**Employees:** 8,800

# Zions BanCorp

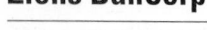
**STANDARD &POOR'S**

| S&P Recommendation **HOLD** ★★★☆☆ | Price $14.74 (as of Nov 25, 2011) | 12-Mo. Target Price $20.00 | Investment Style Large-Cap Blend |
|---|---|---|---|

**GICS Sector** Financials
**Sub-Industry** Regional Banks

**Summary** ZION has almost 500 full-service banking offices in Utah, California, Texas, Nevada, Arizona, and five other western states.

## Key Stock Statistics (Source S&P, Vickers, company reports)

| | | | | | | | |
|---|---|---|---|---|---|---|---|
| 52-Wk Range | $25.60–13.18 | S&P Oper. EPS 2011E | 0.91 | Market Capitalization(B) | $2.716 | Beta | 1.28 |
| Trailing 12-Month EPS | $-0.01 | S&P Oper. EPS 2012E | 0.93 | Yield (%) | 0.27 | S&P 3-Yr. Proj. EPS CAGR(%) | NM |
| Trailing 12-Month P/E | NM | P/E on S&P Oper. EPS 2011E | 16.2 | Dividend Rate/Share | $0.04 | S&P Credit Rating | BBB- |
| $10K Invested 5 Yrs Ago | $2,000 | Common Shares Outstg. (M) | 184.3 | Institutional Ownership (%) | 90 | | |

## Price Performance

- 30-Week Mov. Avg. · · · 10-Week Mov. Avg. – – GAAP Earnings vs. Previous Year   Volume Above Avg. STARS
- 12-Mo. Target Price — Relative Strength — ▲ Up ▼ Down ► No Change   Below Avg.

Options: CBOE, Ph

Analysis prepared by Equity Analyst **Erik Oja** on Nov 02, 2011, when the stock traded at **$17.09**.

## Highlights

➤ We expect net interest income to rise 1.8% in 2011, on our forecast for 0.1% loan shrinkage, a 0.6% increase in interest-earning assets, and a decrease in the net interest margin. We project a 6.0% rise in net interest income in 2012, on our expectation that the loan portfolio will grow 1.5%. We forecast that core revenue (excluding gains and losses) will increase 2.1% in 2011 and 5.2% in 2012.

➤ We see credit quality improving rapidly in 2011, and expect nonperforming loans to be only 2.53% of total leans by the end of the year. We estimate 2011 net chargeoffs of $455 million, down from $974 million in 2010, and 2011 loan loss provisions of just $95 million, down from $852 million in 2010. We look for ZION's 2011 loan loss provision to be only 0.20X net charge-offs, signifying large reserve releases, which, if they happen as we expect, should be a strong boost to earnings. We see ZION's September 30 allowance for loan losses of $1.15 billion, equal to an above-peers 112.5% of nonperforming loans, as sufficiently high to allow this amount of reserve releases.

➤ We see EPS of $0.91 in 2011 and $0.93 in 2012.

## Investment Rationale/Risk

➤ ZION returned to profitability (to common shares, after TARP dividends) in the first quarter of 2011, due to rapid improvement in credit quality, which allowed for a large drop-off in loan loss provisioning expenses. ZION expects profitability to common to be sustained in all of 2011, and we agree with this assessment. We believe the main drivers for ZION will be how well the economy and the housing market recovers, thus helping vacancy rates, rental income, and cap rates on properties, and potentially boosting ZION's credit quality and loan growth. Also, ZION's capital structure, which is more complex than peers', is evolving towards a greater degree of simplicity and lower cost, a positive, in our view.

➤ Risks to our recommendation and target price include declining housing industry indicators, and worsening employment trends.

➤ Our 12-month target price of $20 is based on an in line with peers multiple of 1.0X our year-end estimate of tangible book value per share of $19.40. This equals an above-peers 19.2X our forward four quarters EPS estimate of $1.04, a reflection of recovering earnings.

## Qualitative Risk Assessment

| LOW | MEDIUM | HIGH |
|---|---|---|

Our risk assessment reflects the company's credit exposure to housing and commercial real estate in California, Arizona, and Nevada, offset by its sizable capital levels and recent progress toward resolution of nonperforming assets.

## Quantitative Evaluations

**S&P Quality Ranking**   B

| D | C | B- | **B** | B+ | A- | A | A+ |
|---|---|---|---|---|---|---|---|

**Relative Strength Rank**   WEAK

25

LOWEST = 1   HIGHEST = 99

## Revenue/Earnings Data

**Revenue (Million $)**

| | 1Q | 2Q | 3Q | 4Q | Year |
|---|---|---|---|---|---|
| 2011 | 686.5 | 687.0 | 675.4 | -- | -- |
| 2010 | 673.3 | 693.2 | 692.1 | 687.3 | 2,746 |
| 2009 | 494.4 | 1,250 | 902.5 | 672.0 | 3,319 |
| 2008 | 901.1 | 795.3 | 825.3 | 642.9 | 3,165 |
| 2007 | 915.9 | 931.0 | 963.6 | 807.3 | 3,776 |
| 2006 | 767.1 | 824.1 | 876.9 | 901.2 | 3,369 |

**Earnings Per Share ($)**

| | | | | | |
|---|---|---|---|---|---|
| 2011 | 0.08 | 0.16 | 0.35 | E0.31 | E0.91 |
| 2010 | -0.57 | -0.84 | -0.47 | -0.62 | -2.48 |
| 2009 | -7.47 | -0.21 | -1.43 | -1.26 | -9.92 |
| 2008 | 0.98 | 0.65 | 0.31 | -4.37 | -2.66 |
| 2007 | 1.36 | 1.43 | 1.22 | 0.40 | 4.42 |
| 2006 | 1.28 | 1.35 | 1.42 | 1.32 | 5.36 |

Fiscal year ended Dec. 31. Next earnings report expected: Late January. EPS Estimates based on S&P Operating Earnings; historical GAAP earnings are as reported.

## Dividend Data (Dates: mm/dd Payment Date: mm/dd/yy)

| Amount ($) | Date Decl. | Ex-Div. Date | Stk. of Record | Payment Date |
|---|---|---|---|---|
| 0.010 | 02/08 | 02/17 | 02/22 | 02/28/11 |
| 0.010 | 05/12 | 05/19 | 05/23 | 05/27/11 |
| 0.010 | 08/10 | 08/23 | 08/25 | 08/31/11 |
| 0.010 | 11/09 | 11/17 | 11/21 | 11/30/11 |

Dividends have been paid since 1966. Source: Company reports.

---

**Please read the Required Disclosures and Analyst Certification on the last page of this report.**

The **McGraw-Hill** Companies

# Zions BanCorp

STANDARD
&POOR'S

## Business Summary November 02, 2011

**CORPORATE OVERVIEW.** ZION provides a full range of banking and related services through banking subsidiaries in ten western and southwestern states as follows: Zions First National Bank in Utah and Idaho; California Bank & Trust, Amegy Corporation and its subsidiary, Amegy Bank, in Texas, National Bank of Arizona, Nevada State Bank, Vectra Bank Colorado, in Colorado and New Mexico, The Commerce Bank of Washington, and The Commerce Bank of Oregon. ZION's parent company also owns and operates certain nonbank subsidiaries that engage in the development and sale of financial technologies and related services, and in wealth management services.

**MARKET PROFILE.** As of June 30, 2010 (latest available FDIC branch-level data), ZION had 496 branches, and about $40.4 billion in deposits. About 50.5% of deposits were concentrated in Utah and California. In Utah, ZION had 107 branches, $11.1 billion in deposits, and a deposit market share of about 4.1%,

up from 4.0% a year earlier, ranking eighth. In California, ZION had 107 branches, $9.3 billion in deposits, and a deposit market share of 1.1%, ranking 13th. In Texas, ZION had 84 branches, $9.2 billion in deposits, and a market share of 1.9%, ranking seventh. In Arizona, ZION had 76 branches, $3.7 billion of deposits, and a deposit market share of about 4.3%, ranking fourth. In Nevada, ZION had 55 branches and $3.4 billion in deposits, with a market share of 1.8%, ranking fifth. In addition, ZION had a total of 64 branches and $3.6 billion in deposits in Colorado, Idaho, Washington State, New Mexico and Oregon.

## Company Financials Fiscal Year Ended Dec. 31

| Per Share Data ($) | 2010 | 2009 | 2008 | 2007 | 2006 | 2005 | 2004 | 2003 | 2002 | 2001 |
|---|---|---|---|---|---|---|---|---|---|---|
| Tangible Book Value | 19.09 | 20.35 | 27.24 | 27.02 | 25.15 | 20.45 | 23.29 | 20.96 | 17.21 | 15.19 |
| Earnings | -2.48 | -9.92 | -2.67 | 4.42 | 5.36 | 5.16 | 4.47 | 3.74 | 3.44 | 3.15 |
| S&P Core Earnings | -2.45 | -5.65 | -0.67 | 4.46 | 5.36 | 5.04 | 4.33 | 4.42 | 3.17 | 2.42 |
| Dividends | 0.04 | 0.10 | 1.61 | 1.68 | 1.47 | 1.44 | 1.26 | 1.02 | 0.80 | 0.80 |
| Payout Ratio | NM | NM | NM | 38% | 27% | 28% | 28% | 27% | 23% | 25% |
| Prices:High | 30.29 | 25.52 | 57.05 | 88.56 | 85.25 | 77.67 | 69.29 | 63.86 | 59.65 | 64.00 |
| Prices:Low | 12.88 | 5.90 | 21.07 | 45.70 | 75.13 | 63.33 | 54.08 | 39.31 | 34.14 | 42.30 |
| P/E Ratio:High | NM | NM | NM | 20 | 16 | 15 | 16 | 17 | 17 | 20 |
| P/E Ratio:Low | NM | NM | NM | 10 | 14 | 12 | 12 | 11 | 10 | 13 |

| Income Statement Analysis (Million $) | | | | | | | | | | |
|---|---|---|---|---|---|---|---|---|---|---|
| Net Interest Income | 1,727 | 1,898 | 1,972 | 1,882 | 1,765 | 1,361 | 1,174 | 1,095 | 1,035 | 950 |
| Tax Equivalent Adjustment | 22.0 | 22.8 | 23.7 | 26.1 | 24.3 | 21.1 | NA | NA | NA | NA |
| Non Interest Income | 426 | 126 | 191 | 395 | 527 | 439 | 425 | 426 | 402 | 388 |
| Loan Loss Provision | 852 | 2,017 | 650 | 152 | 72.6 | 43.0 | 44.1 | 69.9 | 71.9 | 73.2 |
| % Expense/Operating Revenue | NA | NA | 58.9% | 61.7% | 57.4% | 56.4% | 57.8% | 63.7% | 59.8% | 63.9% |
| Pretax Income | -403 | -1,623 | -315 | 738 | 913 | 742 | 624 | 546 | 481 | 440 |
| Effective Tax Rate | NM | NM | NM | 32.0% | 34.8% | 35.5% | 35.3% | 39.1% | 34.9% | 35.8% |
| Net Income | -296 | -1,216 | -266 | 494 | 583 | 480 | 406 | 340 | 317 | 290 |
| % Net Interest Margin | 3.73 | 3.94 | 4.18 | 4.43 | 4.63 | 4.58 | 4.32 | 4.45 | 4.56 | 4.64 |
| S&P Core Earnings | -408 | -703 | -73.1 | 483 | 579 | 469 | 394 | 402 | 292 | 223 |

| Balance Sheet & Other Financial Data (Million $) | | | | | | | | | | |
|---|---|---|---|---|---|---|---|---|---|---|
| Money Market Assets | 4,706 | 732 | 2,703 | 1,500 | 369 | 667 | 593 | 569 | 543 | 280 |
| Investment Securities | 5,095 | 4,548 | 4,509 | 6,895 | 6,790 | 6,996 | 5,786 | 5,402 | 4,238 | 3,463 |
| Commercial Loans | 18,234 | 19,139 | 34,333 | 31,508 | 27,559 | 23,122 | 16,337 | 10,404 | 13,648 | 4,110 |
| Other Loans | NA | NA | 7,659 | 7,744 | 7,260 | 7,131 | 6,395 | 9,613 | 5,195 | 13,304 |
| Total Assets | 51,035 | 51,123 | 55,093 | 52,947 | 46,970 | 42,780 | 31,470 | 28,558 | 26,566 | 24,304 |
| Demand Deposits | 13,654 | 12,324 | 9,683 | 9,618 | 25,869 | 9,954 | 6,822 | 5,883 | 5,117 | 4,481 |
| Time Deposits | 27,281 | 29,517 | 31,633 | 27,305 | 9,113 | 22,689 | 16,471 | 15,014 | 15,015 | 13,361 |
| Long Term Debt | 1,943 | 2,033 | 2,657 | 2,815 | 2,495 | 2,746 | 1,919 | 1,843 | 1,310 | 781 |
| Common Equity | 4,592 | 4,190 | 4,920 | 5,053 | 4,747 | 4,237 | 2,790 | 2,540 | 2,374 | 2,281 |
| % Return on Assets | NM | NM | NM | 1.0 | 1.3 | 1.3 | 2.0 | 1.2 | 1.2 | 1.3 |
| % Return on Equity | NM | NM | NM | 9.8 | 12.9 | 13.7 | 15.2 | 13.8 | 13.6 | 14.3 |
| % Loan Loss Reserve | 3.9 | 3.8 | 1.6 | 1.2 | 1.1 | 1.1 | 1.2 | 0.9 | 1.4 | 1.5 |
| % Loans/Deposits | 90.1 | 96.4 | 101.2 | 103.1 | 99.1 | 92.3 | 97.1 | 142.6 | 96.0 | 97.0 |
| % Equity to Assets | 8.6 | 8.6 | 9.2 | 9.8 | 10.0 | 9.5 | 13.3 | 8.9 | 9.2 | 8.8 |

Data as orig reptd.; bef. results of disc opers/spec. items. Per share data adj. for stk. divs.; EPS diluted. E-Estimated. NA-Not Available. NM-Not Meaningful. NR-Not Ranked. UR-Under Review.

**Office:** One South Main Street, 15th Floor, Salt Lake City, UT 84133-1109.
**Telephone:** 801-524-4787.
**Website:** http://www.zionsbancorporation.com
**Chrmn, Pres & CEO:** H.H. Simmons

**EVP, Secy & General Counsel:** T.E. Laursen
**SVP, Chief Acctg Officer & Cntlr:** A.J. Hume
**CFO:** D.L. Arnold
**Investor Contact:** C.B. Hinckley (801-524-4787)

**Board Members:** J. C. Atkin, R. D. Cash, P. Frobes, J. D. Heaney, R. B. Porter, S. D. Quinn, H. H. Simmons, L. E. Simmons, S. Wheelwright, S. T. Williams

**Founded:** 1961
**Domicile:** Utah
**Employees:** 10,524